Research Guide/Index   Volume 22

The World Book Encyclopedia

WORLD
BOOK
a Scott Fetzer company
Chicago
www.worldbook.com

The World Book Encyclopedia

For information on other World Book publications, visit our website at **www.worldbook.com** or call **1-800-WORLDBK (967-5325)**. For information about sales to schools and libraries, call **1-800-975-3250 (United States); 1-800-837-5365 (Canada)**.

World Book, Inc.
233 North Michigan Avenue
Chicago, IL 60601
U.S.A.

Beyond the Page
Use your smartphone or tablet to scan this QR code and see a chronology of events, activities, and other special material prepared by World Book editors. (You will need to download a QR code reader to your device if you have not already done so.) If you do not have a mobile device, simply type this URL into your browser: http://www.worldbook.com/current

About the SPINESCAPE®

The encyclopedia is available in both traditional and SPINESCAPE bindings. The SPINESCAPE design for the 2013 edition—*Giving Wings to Knowledge*—represents the power of curiosity and the beauty of knowledge through the image of a dazzling macaw soaring through a tropical rain forest. The flight of birds has long symbolized aspiration. *The World Book Encyclopedia* invites readers to engage their curiosity and fuel their aspiration for knowledge, exploring its pages confident that what they find in them is accurate, authoritative, and understandable.

Library of Congress Cataloging-in-Publication Data

The World Book encyclopedia.
    p. cm.
    Includes index.
    Summary: "A 22-volume, highly illustrated, A-Z general encyclopedia for all ages, featuring sections on how to use World Book, other research aids, pronunciation key, a student guide to better writing, speaking, and research skills, and comprehensive index"--Provided by publisher.
    ISBN 978-0-7166-0113-5
    1. Encyclopedias and dictionaries. I. World Book, Inc.
    AE5.W55 2013
    031--dc23
                        2012024690

Printed in the United States of America by RR Donnelley, Willard, Ohio
1st printing November 2012

About this volume

This volume consists of two basic parts:

A comprehensive index to *World Book*

An instructional section, A Student Guide to Better Writing, Speaking, and Research Skills

The index includes more than 175,000 entries that direct you to information in *World Book*. The index, together with *World Book*'s extensive system of cross-references, its single alphabetical arrangement, and its other ease-of-use features, helps you find what you want to know quickly and easily. For general instructions on how to find a fact or an article in *World Book*, see the section "How to use *World Book*" in Volume A. To learn how to use the Index, see page 2 of this volume. The index itself begins on page 37.

The section "A Student Guide to Better Writing, Speaking, and Research Skills" begins on page 4. It includes practical advice on such topics as improving your writing skills and preparing a short report, a book review, and a term paper; preparing, rehearsing, and delivering a speech; and using a library's resources and tapping other sources of information. Related information on conducting research follows on page 35. Included are a *Glossary* of terms and abbreviations encountered in research and information on two systems for arranging materials in a library—*Dewey Decimal Classification* and *Library of Congress Classification*.

This volume was prepared with the advice of the *World Book* Advisory Board, other leading educators, practicing teachers, and skilled librarians.

How to use the index

The index is designed to help you find information in *World Book*. It tells you what articles have information on the subject you are looking up. To make it even easier for you to find what you seek, the index refers you to the specific volume and page where the information appears. If it sends you to a fairly long article, it tells you which section or sections of that article to look for.

The references to *World Book* appear under *index headings* that are printed in heavy type. These headings are arranged in alphabetical order. To find where *World Book* contains information on your subject, simply look for an index heading that seems to match the subject you are seeking. For example, if you are looking for information on employment, look for the index heading

Employment

and you have found the references you want.

If the index heading you find is also the title of an article in *World Book,* the volume and page number are shown immediately after the heading. In the case of

Mythology M: 973

the index heading and article title are the same, and the article begins on page 973 of the M volume. Page numbers in the two C volumes are indicated with *C* and *Ci*, and those in the two S volumes are indicated with *S* and *So*. Page numbers for the volumes that contain more than one letter indicate the letter you seek, rather than the first letter of the volume. For example, the reference to "Yankee Doodle" sends you to Y: 552, page 552 of the W-X-Y-Z volume.

If the heading you find is not the title of an article, you will find the titles of *World Book* articles listed as *index entries* in light type under the heading:

Air mass
Air turbulence **A: 201**

If the article referred to is divided into sections, you will find the appropriate subheadings in parentheses between the article title and the page number, pinpointing the place where the information may be found:

Aksum [ancient country] **A: 255** *with map*
Africa (Early civilizations) **A: 130**
Eritrea (History) **E: 353-354**

Sometimes you will find two page numbers after a title and subheading. They indicate that the section referred to covers more than one page and begins on the first page listed, but the information you seek appears on the second:

Chinatown
New York City (Manhattan) **N: 323-324**

The index entries listed under an index heading normally appear in alphabetical order. But if one entry is much more important as a source of the information you seek, it appears first:

College
Universities and colleges **U: 206**
Adolescent (Education) **A: 64**

Some headings have only a few entries under them. Others, such as the Africa heading, have many. In many long lists, you will find the entries divided into smaller groups under such subjects as Agriculture, Art and architecture, and Education.

Identifiers, words or phrases in brackets, indicate which of several similar headings is the one you seek:

Core [botany]
Core [electrical device]
Core [geology]
Core [nuclear device]
CORE [organization]
Core [sun]

Some identifiers are not complete in themselves, but the article titles that follow them complete the identification.

Lincoln, William Wallace [son of]
Lincoln, Abraham (Lincoln's family) **L: 315**

Cross-references guide you in using the index. A *see* reference means that the information you seek appears under another heading, rather than the one you have chosen:

Feisal
See Faisal *in this index*

A *see also* reference indicates that another heading in the index has entries you may want to look up.

Accident
    See also First aid *in this index*

Many cross-references send you to lists of Related articles in another article:

    See also the list of Related articles in the American literature *article*

You can thus find the long lists of articles in *World Book,* such as this list of American authors, but these lists do not take up space in the index.

References to illustrations appear along with other references in this index, not separately. The wording shows whether you will find both pictures and text information or only pictures on the pages listed. If the entry says *with picture, with portrait, with diagram, with map,* or a similar phrase, it indicates that text material appears on the page named and that a related illustration appears on the same page or the page facing it. In the case of

Airplane propeller
    Airplane (General aviation planes) **A: 211**
      with picture

the text information appears on A: 211 and is accompanied by a picture showing a propeller plane.

If the entry says *picture on, diagram on,* or *map on* a given page, it indicates that the illustration listed is related to the subject of the index heading you found, even though no significant text information on that subject appears on the same page. In the case of

Revere, Paul
    Boston Massacre *picture on* **B: 505**

the picture illustrates Revere's handiwork but the Boston Massacre article does not go into detail about Revere.

The order of headings in this index is alphabetical, with the items arranged word by word, not letter by letter, just as they are in *World Book*:

    Consumer Price Index
    Consumer protection
    Consumers League, National

Letters are usually regarded as separate words unless they normally form parts of a larger word or an acronym:

    E [letter]
    E Pluribus Unum
    Eakins, Thomas
    EAM [organization]

Numbers at the beginnings of headings are treated as though they were spelled out, even when they appear as figures:

    Fifth Republic
    50° July isotherm
    Fifty-Four Forty or Fight

A Student Guide to Better

Writing, Speaking, and Research Skills

Do you panic when faced with a writing assignment? Are you nervous about getting up to speak before a group? Do you sometimes find it difficult to find the right research materials? You're not alone. Many students have the same problems. That's why we developed this section—to help you improve your skills in these important areas.

A Student Guide to Better Writing, Speaking, and Research Skills consists of three parts. Part one, A Guide to Writing Skills, includes practical tips to help you become a better

writer. It also provides how-to advice on preparing a short report and on preparing a book report.

In addition, Part one takes you through the various steps involved in preparing a research paper: from making a schedule and choosing a topic, through background reading and making an outline, to writing a first draft, making the final copy, and preparing citations and a list of sources.

Part two, A Guide to Speaking Skills, covers the six basic steps in

preparing a speech. It also provides useful information on the different kinds of speeches and easy-to-follow tips on rehearsing and delivering a speech. The section concludes with helpful hints on the effective use of audio-visual aids.

A Guide to Research Skills, part three, helps you get the most of the resources from the library or media center. It includes detailed information about library catalog systems and reference sources. It tells how to evaluate reference sources and how to prepare source cards and take notes.

The section provides guidance for tapping sources of information outside the library, such as conducting an interview or using television or the Internet as a source.

A Student Guide to Better Writing, Speaking, and Research Skills concludes with a Glossary of terms and abbreviations often encountered in research. The guide also provides information on two library classification systems—Dewey Decimal Classification and Library of Congress Classification.

Contents

A Guide to Writing Skills 6
Writing Tips 6
Preparing a Short Report 10
Preparing a Book Report 12
Preparing a Research
  Paper 14
A Guide to Speaking Skills 20
Preparing a Speech 20
Rehearsing and Delivering
  a Speech 23
A Guide to Research Skills 26
Getting to Know
  the Library 26

Reference and Source
  Materials 28
Preparing Source Cards 32
Taking Notes 32
Using Other Sources 33
Documenting Sources 34
Related Information
Glossary 35
Dewey Decimal Classification
  and Library of Congress
  Classification 36

The illustrations in the feature were prepared for WORLD BOOK by Mike Eagle and Lyle Miller, Kirchoff-Wohlberg, Inc.

A Guide to

WRITING SKILLS

Learning to be an effective writer is an important part of education. Schoolwork involves a steady stream of writing assignments, and many jobs require the writing of effective letters, memos, and reports. Writing also plays a role in personal life, when people fill in forms or write e-mails or letters to friends and relatives.

Good writing gets its message across so clearly that the reader knows exactly what the writer meant to say. It also holds the reader's attention so completely that the entire message—not just a fragment of it—is received.

For most people, writing well is not an easy task. People who have no trouble expressing themselves out loud may freeze when they pick up a pencil. Like any other skill, writing requires practice. The more you do it, the better you become.

Writing Tips

Practice helps. Every time you write, you practice a skill and get better at it. Practice is good because it gets you into the habit of using written words to express yourself. Your practice writing does not have to be perfect.

You can get into the writing habit in many ways. Keep a journal or diary to record your experiences, thoughts, and feelings. Write letters or e-mails to a pen pal, friends, or relatives. Try writing a fan letter to your favorite author, TV personality, or rock star. And remember to send post cards when you travel. Also, consider writing your own invitations and greeting cards instead of buying commercially produced ones.

This article contains information designed to help students improve writing skills in general. It also provides specific guidelines for preparing school assignments or projects, and research papers.

Preliminary steps for success. Some of your school writing assignments, such as themes, essays, and stories, are based on your own opinions, ideas, or imagination. Other writing assignments, such as book reports and research papers, are based on facts gained from reading and research. Whatever the assignment may be, your work will proceed more smoothly if you follow these suggestions before you begin putting words on paper:

1. Be sure you understand the specifics of the assignment, such as its length and whether the topic is your choice or assigned.

2. Plan ahead and organize your time to help assure that you have enough time to do a good job.

3. If the topic is your choice, select one that interests you, one that you already know something about, or one that you're eager to learn more about.

4. Jot down ideas whenever and wherever they occur to you. Simply talking about your assignment with friends can trigger ideas that you might be able to use in your paper.

5. Develop an outline to organize your thoughts and to guide your writing so you do not forget a point you intended to include. A simple list of the main ideas may be adequate for a short assignment. Major assignments may require a more formal outline.

The three-part plan. Many writing projects can be organized into three parts: (1) the introduction, (2) the body, and (3) the conclusion. In the introduction, you briefly introduce your topic, giving the reader a preview of what is to come. The body of the paper—the longest part by far—provides the facts, examples, and details that support the main idea expressed in the introduction. The conclusion summarizes and restates the main idea.

The three parts of your paper should work together to make an effective whole. Strive for an attention-getting introduction—one that will arouse interest and encourage your reader to read on. In the body, make sure each point relates to the subject you are discussing. Do not stray into unrelated material or get caught up in trivial details that do not support your main idea. Your conclusion is your last chance to impress the reader. Try to make it as strong and effective as you can.

As you get ready to start writing, think of the three parts of your paper in terms of this simple formula.

1. Tell the reader what you are going to say.

2. Say it.

3. Tell the reader what you said.

Writing the first draft. When the time comes for you to write a first draft, do not just wait for the perfect sentence to come to mind. At this stage, you simply need to put down the information and ideas you have gathered. Do not feel you have to use complete sentences. You can go back later to change and improve your work. Do not feel you have to begin with the introduction, especially if you are having difficulty with it. In many cases, you will think of an effective introduction after you have written the body of your paper.

Always write or type your first draft on one side of the paper only, with wide margins to allow plenty of room for revisions. If you write the draft, use every other line of the paper. If you type it, use double- or triple-spacing.

Revising your work. Think of writing as a building process, with words, sentences, and paragraphs as building blocks. Your goal is to choose the best words; to put them together into clear, grammatical sentences; to form the sentences into logical, coherent paragraphs; and to link the paragraphs into a well-organized paper.

Do not expect to reach your goal the first time around. In most cases, writing involves a lot of rewriting—turning out as many drafts as necessary to produce the best results.

After you have completed your first draft, the best thing to do is forget about your paper for a while. Leave it alone for an hour, a day, or several days if time permits. Then look at it again with a fresh, critical eye.

Editing your own work is one of the hardest and most important tasks in turning out a well-written paper. Reading your work aloud will help you catch parts that need revision. Parts that sound unnatural or do not make sense require reworking. Look for weak spots in content, organization, and writing style, as well as for errors in grammar, spelling, capitalization, and punctuation. Keep a dictionary, thesaurus, and grammar book nearby. If you work on a computer, use such built-in aids as the dictionary or spell checker.

> **"Like any other skill, writing requires practice. The more you do it, the better you become."**

enclosures that resemble sleeping bags. These **enclosures,** ~~enclosures~~ enable astronauts to sleep ~~unstrapped~~ **without being,** ~~without~~ floating **down to keep from,** **about.**

Eating and drinking. Eating aboard the space shuttle **also requires** **astronauts to,** ~~involves~~ adjust~~ing~~ to the conditions of weightlessness. ~~Astronauts~~ **They** eat their meals with their feet strapped down ~~to keep~~ ~~them from floating about.~~ **Their,** Food must be nutritious, easy to eat, and convenient **to,** ~~so~~ store. Foods include frozen or chilled soups, vegetables, and meats. The shuttle has ~~ways to heat~~ **facilities for heating** food. The astronauts **use** ~~eat with~~ dishes and silverware.

"Editing your own work is one of the... most important tasks in turning out a well-written paper... Look for weak spots in content, organization, and writing style, as well as for errors in grammar, spelling, capitalization, and punctuation."

Use a colored pencil and make your corrections right on the paper. If you add one or more sentences, write them in the margin and use an arrow to show where the additions should go. If you want to take out material, do not erase it or black it out completely. Instead, draw a neat line through the material or draw a circle around it. That way, if you later decide to restore the material or move it somewhere else, it will still be readable. If you are using a computer, save the revised file under a name different from the original.

Judging the content. To judge the content of your paper, keep in mind your reader and your purpose. Ask yourself these questions: Is the introduction as effective as I can make it? Will it arouse the reader's interest? Does the body of the paper include all the points I wanted to cover? Will the reader understand what I am trying to say? Are there enough examples or details to support my main idea? Does the paper have gaps that need to be filled? Are there parts that do not really fit and so should be eliminated? Does my conclusion leave a strong impression?

Checking the organization. Be sure each paragraph has a *topic sentence*. A topic sentence expresses the central idea of the paragraph. All other sentences in the paragraph should relate to the topic sentence. If you have a sentence that doesn't seem to fit in the paragraph, move it to another paragraph or eliminate it. Do not make it a paragraph by itself. Every paragraph should consist of at least two sentences. Make sure your paragraphs flow smoothly from one to the next in logical order.

Style pointers. Style—the way you express yourself—can make a big difference in the effectiveness of your writing. A paper that has all the necessary information but is boring to read may leave the reader disappointed and unimpressed. To make your writing as interesting and effective as it can be, keep in mind these points:

1. Use specific, vivid words, including action verbs. If you are writing a report on the Pueblo Indians, for example, tell how the Indians *dug* irrigation ditches, *wove* cloth, and *carved* dolls, not how they *made* ditches, cloth, and dolls.

2. Vary your sentence structure. Do not write a paper that consists entirely of short, simple sentences. Avoid beginning too many sentences with the same word.

3. Use interesting comparisons to bring statistics to life. For example, a figure for the population of India is more interesting if you add the fact that more people live in India than in all the countries of North and South America combined.

4. Avoid wordiness, unnecessary "big words," and overused expressions. Do not use excess words that only take up space. For example, write *today* or *now* rather than *at the present time,* and *if* rather than *in the event that.* Do not use words that you yourself do

not understand or that are intended merely to impress your reader. For example, write *end* rather than *termination,* and *best* rather than *optimum.* Replace overused expressions, called *clichés,* with fresher expressions. *Hungry as a bear, the last straw,* and *last but not least* are examples of clichés.

5. Avoid overly formal writing. Think of writing as a kind of conversation with yourself or a friend. For certain assignments, your writing style may be more formal than your everyday conversation. However, try to make your writing sound natural.

Common grammatical errors. Mistakes in grammar can confuse the reader and even change the meaning of what you write. Here are some of the most common grammatical problems you should look for as you revise your work.

1. *Run-on sentences* consist of two or more independent clauses written together without a proper connection. A comma alone cannot be used to link such clauses.

Example: It stopped raining, we played the rest of the game.
There are several ways to correct the error.
Make two separate sentences:
It stopped raining. We played the rest of the game.
Use a semicolon to link the independent clauses:
It stopped raining; we played the rest of the game.
Use a conjunction, such as *and* or *but*, to link the clauses:
It stopped raining, and we played the rest of the game.
Make one of the clauses a phrase or dependent clause:
After it stopped raining, we played the rest of the game.

2. *Sentence fragments* are incomplete sentences. Phrases and depend-

ent clauses cannot stand alone as sentences. To correct a fragment, you can join it to a sentence or add words to make it a sentence.
Fragment: known for their skill as hunters.
Correction: Known for their skill as hunters, lions have little trouble finding food.
or
Lions are known for their skill as hunters.

3. *Subject-verb agreement.* A subject and verb must agree in number and person.
Number: The *star appears* at dusk. [singular]
The *stars appear* at dusk. [plural]
Person: *I am* careful. [First person singular]
You are careful. [Second person singular]
She is careful. [Third person singular]
We are careful. [First person plural]
You are careful. [Second person plural]
They are careful. [Third person plural]

4. *Pronoun agreement.* As shown above, a pronoun used as a subject must agree with its verb. A pronoun must also agree with its *antecedent*—that is, the particular noun to which it refers.
Bill rode *his* bike to school.
The women announced *their* decision.

5. *Unclear pronoun references.* Pronouns can cause confusion if their antecedents are not clear.
Confusing: When Karen told Ann the story, she looked surprised.
Clear: When Karen told Ann the story, Ann looked surprised.
or

Ann looked surprised when Karen told her the story.

6. *A dangling modifier* is an element in a sentence that seems to modify a word that it does not logically modify.
Dangling: Running at record-breaking speed, the race was the highlight of the day.
Correct: Running at record-breaking speed, Kelly made the race the highlight of the day.

7. *A misplaced modifier* is a phrase or clause too far from the word it modifies. As a result, it may seem to modify another word.
Misplaced: Jack ran to his mother *waving the letter.*
Correct: *Waving the letter,* Jack ran to his mother.

8. *Shifts in verb tense.* Generally, you should use one verb tense throughout your paper. If your paper describes past events, you should use the past tense. For many other papers, you will use the present tense. Be consistent in whichever tense you choose.

After you have completed all your revisions, your work should be the best it can be. You are then ready to produce the final copy. The next sections provide specific suggestions on how to prepare a short report, book report, and research paper as well as general guidelines for producing the final copy.

"A short report demands a narrow topic... Topics that could be... handled in a short report might be 'How white blood cells fight disease,' 'Tools used by colonial farmers,' or 'Life aboard the space station.' "

Preparing a Short Report

During a school year, you will probably be asked to write short reports on various subjects. The typical short report runs from 300 to 500 words and involves gathering information from one or more sources. This research provides you with "raw material"—the information you need for your report. As writer, your job is to produce a finished product—a report that presents the research information in your own words in a clear, interesting manner.

Before you write. The section *Writing Tips* included a list of preliminary steps to follow before you begin a writing task. Here are some additional suggestions that apply specifically to short reports.

Understanding the assignment. Be sure you know how long the report should be. Your teacher may give you a specific figure, such as 400

words, or a range, such as 300 to 500 words. It probably will not matter if you go a bit over or under the number of words assigned, but stay close to the target.

You need to know if your teacher expects a *summary report* or a *critical report.* In a summary report, you present the information you have found without expressing any opinions or judgments. For example, a paper describing the founding of the United Nations could be presented as a summary report. In a critical report, on the other hand, you are expected to present your own reactions to the information you have found. You need to evaluate the information, take a stand, and justify your stand with supporting points. In a critical report on the United Nations, you might take a position for or against continued United States membership in the organization.

If your teacher lets you choose between a summary report and a critical report, wait and see how you react to the research material before you decide. If you find yourself strongly agreeing or disagreeing with what you read, a critical report might be in order. On the other hand, if the information seems straightforward and noncontroversial, a summary report would be appropriate.

Choosing a topic. A short report demands a narrow topic. You simply will not have enough space to cover a lot of territory. For example, if you tried to write a paper on "The circulatory system," "Life in colonial America," or "Space travel," you would find yourself swamped with information. Topics that could be more easily handled in a short report might be "How white blood cells fight disease," "Tools used by colonial farmers," or "Life aboard a space station."

One way to get ideas on how to limit your topic is to check an encyclopedia. Using the index or the search feature, look for the general subject heading you are interested in, such as *Circulatory system*. The article titles listed under the heading will give you a starting point for narrowing your topic. Then check the individual articles to see what they cover and how they are organized. A subheading in one of the articles might give you the idea you need for a suitable topic. Other sources of ideas include the table of contents of a book covering your topic or the articles listed under your topic in a periodical index.

Background reading will help you become familiar with your topic. Encyclopedia articles on your topic are good sources for background reading. As you read, you can decide what kinds of information you would like to include in your report and what can be left out. It is a good idea to jot down a list of points to serve as a sort of preliminary outline and a guide to your research. Your list might take the form of a series of questions you hope to answer in your report. If your topic is "Life aboard a space station," for example, your questions might include: What does the inside of a station look like? How big are the crew's quarters? How do the astronauts eat? How do they spend most of their time?

Researching the topic involves finding sources, reading them, and taking notes on what you have read. The encyclopedia articles you used for your background reading may have included *additional resources*—lists of books or websites that provide additional information about your subject. You can also look through the catalog at your school or public library and check such basic reference works as *Readers' Guide to Periodical Literature* and *The World*

Almanac and Book of Facts.

After you have found good source material, you need to read it carefully and take accurate notes. For a short report that requires only a few sources, you may find it easiest to take notes on lined paper or a notepad. Many people prefer using index cards, however, because they can easily be arranged and organized. If you are using electronic reference materials, you can print out the information you need or save it on a flash drive.

Preparing an outline is the last step you need to do before writing your report. Prepare an outline even if your teacher does not ask for one. An outline will help you organize your notes and make writing your first draft easier.

Begin preparing the outline by gathering all your notes and reviewing them. Then decide how the information can be organized into major topics and subtopics. Assign a heading to each topic and subtopic. Next, arrange the headings in logical order. For a short report, your outline can be simple, with only a few main headings and subheadings. In the next column, see an example of an outline for the report on "Life aboard a space station."

This kind of outline is a *topic outline*. It uses words or phrases for headings. A *sentence outline* uses complete sentences for headings. You should be consistent in using one form or the other. Do not mix phrases and sentences in the same outline. For more detailed information about outline format, see page 15.

Writing a short report. After you have completed your outline, stop and think about the information you have gathered. What is the main idea you have discovered? Summarize

I. The crew's quarters
   A. Size
   B. Arrangement
II. Basic needs
   A. Breathing
   B. Sleeping
   C. Eating and drinking
   D. Eliminating wastes
III. Daily tasks
   A. Operating the
      space station
   B. Communicating with
      Earth
   C. Performing scientific
      experiments

your main idea and make it your thesis sentence. Put the thesis sentence at or near the beginning of your paper. It should tell the reader what your paper is about and should guide you as you write. All the points you make in your report should relate in some way to the thesis sentence. Here is an example of a thesis sentence for the report on "Life aboard a space station":

A look inside a space station shows how people can adapt to living under unusual circumstances.

When you are ready to write your first draft, keep your notes and outline nearby. Focus on your thesis sentence and begin. Your notes should provide you with the specific details and examples you need to support your thesis statement. Follow the suggestions given in the section *Writing Tips* as you write and revise your work.

Preparing the final copy.
After making your last revision, you are ready to prepare a clean, fresh copy of your report. If your teacher has given you instructions on how to submit the report, follow them exactly. Otherwise, you can use these guidelines.

If you can, type your report. Be sure to double-space it. Make your margins 1 to 1 ½ inches (2 ½ to 4 centimeters) wide on the left and 1 inch (2 ½ centimeters) on the right, and on the top and bottom.

If you cannot type, write your report in ink on white, lined paper, using one side only. Try to write as neatly as possible.

Before you submit your paper, reread it carefully to make sure you have copied everything correctly from your final version. Check, too, for last-minute mistakes in spelling or punctuation and for typing errors. Correct the errors neatly.

"Begin preparing the outline by gathering all your notes and reviewing them. Then decide how the information can be organized into major topics..."

Preparing a Book Report

As a student, you will probably write many short papers about books. A written report about a book may be only a brief summary, or it may be a lengthy analysis.

Before you write. See the section *Writing Tips* for a list of preliminary steps that apply to various writing assignments. Also, here are some specific suggestions to help you prepare for writing a good paper about a book.

Understanding the assignment. It is important that you understand exactly what you are expected to cover in a book report. Does your teacher simply want a summary of the book? If the book is a novel, for example, does your teacher want only a brief retelling of the story? Or are you expected to write a critique, in which you state your reactions and give your opinions about the book? Be sure you

understand the assignment before you start reading. That way, you will know what factors to pay particular attention to as you read the book.

Choosing a book. If you are allowed to choose the book for your report, you should pick one you think you will enjoy reading, whether it is fiction or nonfiction. Also consider how much time you have available. Select a book you can finish well within your time for the assignment.

Consider the reading level of the book. Do not pick a book that is too easy to read just so you can finish it quickly. But do not choose a book in which the content, vocabulary, or writing style is too difficult. Select a book that seems to be at or slightly above your reading level. The booklists at the end of many *World Book* articles are divided into categories for younger and older readers. If you

have trouble selecting an appropriate book, ask your teacher or librarian for suggestions.

Hints for effective reading. If the book you are to report on has a preface or introduction, be sure to read it. It may contain information that will help you understand the author's purpose, the period in which the book was written, and other factors that can help you judge the book fairly. You can also gain background information by checking other sources, such as *World Book,* for a biography of the author or articles on other related subjects.

If the teacher has specified the topic you are to report on, pay particular attention to the parts of the book that pertain to that topic. Take notes as you go along, and record page numbers of passages you want to remember. If the book is your own copy, you

may underline or otherwise highlight important parts and make notes in the margins.

Choosing an appropriate topic. If the topic of your book report is your choice, take time after you finish the book to think about what you have read. Ask yourself questions to help decide on a topic. What impressed you particularly about the book? In the case of a novel, for example, did the story keep you interested to the very end? Did you sympathize with the characters? In the case of a biography, did you feel you really got to know the subject? Did the author present an unbiased view of the subject? Did

you learn anything especially interesting about human nature, a historical period, or another country?

You may decide there were more things you did not like about the book than you liked. Whatever your overall impression was, it is best to select one or two aspects of the book as the topic of your book report.

Preparing an outline. After you have decided what your topic will be, it is helpful to make an outline to guide your writing. The outline may consist of a simple list of points you want to cover. Or it may be a traditional outline, as described in the

section *Preparing a Short Report*.

Writing a book report. Follow the suggestions given in the section *Writing Tips* on pages 6-9 as you write the first draft and revisions. Remember the need for a strong introduction, a supportive body, and an effective conclusion.

In the body of your book report, back up your thesis sentence with direct references to the book. Interweave your personal comments with summaries of specific parts of the book or direct quotations. If you quote directly, be sure to copy accurately, use quotation marks, and in-

"Ask yourself questions to help decide on a topic. What impressed you particularly about the book?... In the case of a biography, did you feel you really got to know the subject?"

clude the page number in parentheses after the quotation. If you quote from a source other than the book you are reporting on, you will need to use a citation. See page 17 for information on how to prepare citations.

When you are ready to prepare your final copy, follow your teacher's instructions precisely. If you have no instructions, use the guidelines on page 19. Double-check quoted material to ensure you have copied the material exactly.

Preparing a Research Paper

"Research paper." The very words make some students quake with fear. Preparing a research paper is a big job. But if you go about it the right way, it is a manageable task. It helps to start out with a confident attitude.

Think of your research paper assignment as a chance to learn a lot more about something that interests you. It is an opportunity to develop skills in information gathering, organization, and writing. These skills will make you better equipped to handle many other school assignments and perhaps job duties later in life.

Like a short report, a research paper, or *term paper,* is based on research. But a research paper is longer—generally eight or more pages—and it requires checking more sources. It also has more parts, including a title page, an outline, citations, and a list of sources. The following sections give specific guidelines you will need to prepare a research paper.

Before you write. You may be surprised to learn that actually *writing* your research paper is one of the last steps you will do after receiving the assignment. Many tasks need to be completed before you can even begin writing.

Making a schedule. Planning ahead is a good idea for any writing assignment. For a research paper, it is a must. You might have several weeks, or even months, to prepare a research paper. Whatever you do, do not let yourself be lulled into thinking you can relax until a week or two before the deadline. As soon as you get your research paper assignment, make a schedule.

Consider other assignments and commitments you have. Plan to spend a certain number of hours a day—perhaps two or three—working on your paper. Then mark the due date for the paper on your calendar. Count backward to plan blocks of time for finishing the final draft, revising the first draft, writing the first draft, organizing your note cards, and preparing a final outline.

Follow these guidelines to plan a realistic schedule:

1. Give yourself at least an hour per page to write the first draft.

2. Plan to spend at least two hours per page revising the first draft. (Do not include the final outline and the list of sources in this estimate.)

3. Allow about an hour per page to type the final copy, including all text pages, the final outline, and the list of sources. That hour or so includes time for proofreading, making corrections, and placing citations correctly.

4. Allow one day to organize your notes and one day to prepare your final outline.

The time left will be used to choose your topic, read, gather information, and take notes.

Choosing a topic. In most cases, your instructor will allow you to choose the topic for your research paper. Remember that you will be spending much time on your research paper, so be sure you choose a topic you are really interested in. Even if you do not particularly like the subject, you can probably find a specific topic within the subject area that appeals to you. For example, perhaps you do not care much for United States history, but you love music. A U.S. history research paper on songs of the American Civil War could be more fun to prepare than you thought.

Be sure to narrow the topic of your research paper to manageable size. Do not be fooled into thinking you will have plenty of time and space to cover a broad topic. It is far better to cover a narrow topic in depth than to skim over a broad topic. See the section *Preparing a Short Report* for how to narrow your topic.

Another important point to consider in selecting a research paper topic is the availability of research materials. Go to the library or media center and check the library catalog and *Readers' Guide to Periodical Literature* to be sure enough books or articles have been written on your topic. If no such books or articles are available, your topic may be too recent or too specialized.

Background reading. After you have chosen your research paper topic, do some background reading. A good, up-to-date encyclopedia like

"Planning ahead is a good idea for any writing assignment. For a research paper, it's a must... Consider other assignments and commitments you may have..."

World Book is an excellent place to begin. An encyclopedia will not give you all the information you need, but it will provide an overview of the topic. Search for your topic and read the various articles that deal with it. Most likely, your background reading will turn up aspects of your topic you had not thought of. You may find yourself reshaping your topic according to something that strikes your interest. As you read, jot down ideas that occur to you about what you would like to cover in your paper. Note charts, tables, photographs, maps, and bibliographies that could be helpful.

The preliminary outline. With your background reading behind you, you are ready to prepare a preliminary outline for your research paper. The outline will help you organize your thoughts and guide you as you do your research.

Begin your preliminary outline by figuring out what the main idea, or purpose, of your research paper is. This purpose is called the *thesis*. As you are determining your thesis, also decide what kind of *approach* your paper will take. If your subject inspires strong opinions, you may want to take a *pro* or *con* approach, in which you take a stand for or against a certain proposition. Some papers use a *descriptive* approach or an *explanatory* approach. Others try to *prove* or *disprove* a theory or idea. You may choose to *compare* or *contrast* two or more things or show the *cause and effect* of something. A *chronological* approach, which traces the order in which events occurred, suits some topics. Others lend themselves to an *analytical* approach, in which a topic is thoroughly examined.

After you have decided on your thesis and approach, ask yourself what points you want to cover to support your thesis. Write down each point as the basis of your preliminary outline. At this stage, you need not be too concerned about the order or completeness of your outline. Remember it is a *preliminary* outline; so keep it simple. You are likely to change it as you explore your topic in greater depth. The important thing is that you give yourself a clear direction before you begin to conduct your research.

Preparing a list of sources. The next step you need to perform is preparing a list of sources to consult in your research. To begin with, go back to the encyclopedia articles you read earlier to see if they include lists of sources to check for additional information. Many *World Book* articles, for example, include *bibliographies*—lists of books for further reading.

In addition, many of the sources you consult for your paper will include additional source lists or bibliographies. You will find additional sources when you check the catalog, magazine and newspaper indexes, and online sources in your library.

For each source you locate—book, article, pamphlet, DVD, compact disc

(CD), website, and so on—make a note. If you are using a computer, you can add each source you find to one list. If you are writing your source list, use one index card for each source. These cards will be easy to organize and alphabetize when you later prepare your final list of sources. If a source does not have usable information, make a note on your list, or draw a line through its card. But keep the note so that you will have a record of every source you checked in doing your research.

Doing research. The quality of your research paper depends greatly on the information in it. It is important to find reliable, interesting information and record it in accurate notes.

You may need to examine various kinds of sources before you find the best possible ones. Books and articles are traditional sources. But you may discover that your best information comes from a survey or interview, the Internet, or a museum or historical society in your community. Valuable information may turn up in places you least expect to find it. The notes on a record jacket, for example, could provide interesting details for a report on the origins of rock music. View your research as an investigation. You are out to track down leads and find the facts you will need to write the best paper you can.

See "A Guide to Research Skills" beginning on page 26 for detailed suggestions on how to use the library or media center and on how to get information from various sources. The guide also gives specific instructions on taking notes.

The final outline. When you feel you have all the information you need, it is time to review and organize your notes. Go back and read your notes carefully. Then look at your thesis statement. Does it still make

sense? Should it be changed somewhat on the basis of what you learned from your research? Remember, the thesis statement should summarize the purpose of your paper. Be sure you have it right before you go any further.

Next, arrange your information according to your preliminary outline. Does the outline still work? Is your approach still appropriate? Should you change or rearrange any of the main headings? Are there information gaps that need additional research? Can any of your notes be set aside because they do not further the purpose of your paper?

All these questions will help you get ready to prepare your final outline. The final outline will direct your writing. It should be an accurate guide to what you plan to include in your paper.

After you have arranged your information in logical order, group it into large, obvious divisions. These divisions will be your main topics. Three to five main topics are generally enough for a research paper. Next, see how your main topics can be subdivided. These subtopics must relate to the main topic. You must have at least two subtopics under a main topic—or none at all.

The final outline may be either a topic outline or a sentence outline, but not a combination of them. In either outline form, all the headings must be expressed in parallel phrasing. All topics of equal importance must be equally indented. Topics and subtopics are identified by Roman numerals, capital letters, Arabic numerals, and lower-case letters, in that order, followed by periods. The bottom of this page shows an example of a final outline for a research paper, preceded by the thesis sentence.

Writing your research paper. At this stage, most of the work is behind you. Writing should go smoothly if you have done a good job on all the preceding steps.

Writing the first draft. With your final outline before you and your notes arranged in proper order, you are ready to begin writing your first draft. Write or type the draft on one side of the paper only. Use double- or triple-spacing and wide margins to make later revisions easier.

As you write your first draft, concentrate on putting your ideas down in a clear and orderly fashion, with smooth transitions from one point to the next. Your thesis sentence should appear in the introduction and guide you as you write. The details you include in the body of your report

---

THESIS SENTENCE: Computers are learning tools that can significantly improve the writing skills of students, and they should be made available to everyone.

   I.   Current availability
  II.   Uses in the classroom
        A. Encyclopedia and Internet research
        B. Interactive learning programs
        C. Testing spelling and other skills
        D. Word processing
 III.   Benefits to users
        A. Individualized instruction
        B. Immediate feedback
        C. High student interest and motivation
  IV.   Sources of funding
        A. Government programs
           1. Federal
           2. State
           3. Local
        B. Private foundations
        C. Local organizations

should relate to the thesis sentence. Your conclusion should restate your thesis in an effective way.

If you use a quotation, copy it exactly and enclose it in quotation marks. A quotation that is more than five lines long should be indented and single-spaced, with no quotation marks. If you omit part of a quotation, use an ellipsis (. . .) in place of the part left out. If you need to add words of your own to make the meaning of the quotation clear, enclose those words in brackets ([ ]).

Preparing citations. Quotations and certain other material in your research paper require citations. The main purpose for citations in a research paper is to *document sources*—that is, to give credit to the author whose words or ideas you are using. Even if you restate someone else's idea or opinion in your own words, you must credit that person. Otherwise you may be guilty of *plagiarism*—stealing someone else's words or ideas and passing them off as your own. You should also use citations for facts or figures that a reader might have cause to question.

There are several standard citation styles that vary slightly from one another. The MLA style, published by the Modern Language Association, is the standard style for works in the arts and the humanities. It is also the most widely used style for writers of research papers.

In MLA style, you acknowledge your sources by inserting brief parenthetical citations within the text of the paper. The citations appear in more detailed form in an alphabetical list—often called a *works-cited list*—at the end of the paper.

The parenthetical citation in the following sentence is an example of MLA citation style:

More than 80 percent of South Korea's population attends college (Connor 339).

The citation tells readers that the information in the sentence came from a book edited by someone named Connor and appears on page 339 in the book. Readers can get more detailed information from the list of works cited at the end of the paper:

Connor, Mary E., ed. *The Koreas: Asia in Focus.* Santa Barbara: ABC-CLIO, 2009.

The works-cited list contains all the sources—books, articles, pamphlets, websites, and so on—that you used to prepare your research paper. Do not include sources that you consulted but did not use. The works-cited list tells the reader both where you found your information and where further information on the topic can be obtained.

Common titles for the list of sources include *Works Cited, Bibliography, Literature Cited,* and *Sources Cited.* But the word *bibliography,* strictly speaking, refers only to print sources, such as books and articles. MLA style favors the broader title *Works Cited* because many research papers draw on nonprint sources, such as films, recordings, and websites. Follow your teacher's instructions when choosing a title and style for your list of sources.

The following examples show the MLA style for citing websites, books, magazines, television programs, and other types of sources in a list of works cited.

How to cite a page or an article from a website (including an online encyclopedia):

Format: Author's name, last name first [if given]. "Article or web page title." [enclosed in double quotation marks] *Website title.* [in italics] Publisher's name [if not available, use N.p.], date of publication. [day, month, and year; if no date is available, use n.d.] Publication medium. Access date [day, month, year].

Example: Maney, Patrick J. "Roosevelt, Eleanor." *World Book Student.* World Book, 2011. Web. 11 Jan. 2011.

How to cite an article from a DVD encyclopedia:

Format: Author's name, last name first [if given]. "Article title." [enclosed in double quotation marks] *Publication title.* [in italics] Name of editor preceded by Ed. [if given]. Edition [if stated]. City of publication: Publisher's name, year of publication. Medium of publication.

Example: Garrison, David L. "Marine biology." *World Book Multimedia Encyclopedia.* 2012 edition. Chicago: World Book, 2012. DVD.

How to cite an article from a print encyclopedia:

Format: Author's name, last name first [if given]. "Article title." [enclosed in double quotation marks] *Publication title.* [in italics] Edition [if stated]. Year of publication [do not include if stated in edition information]. Publication medium.

Example: Beller, Steven. "Vienna." *The World Book Encyclopedia.* 2012 ed. Print.

How to cite a book with one author:

Format: Author's name, last name first. *Full book title.* [in italics] Edition [if stated]. Number of volumes [if a multivolume work]. City of publication: Publisher's name, year of publication. Publication medium.

Example: Stiles, T. J. *The First Tycoon: The Epic Life of Cornelius Vanderbilt.* New York: Knopf, 2009. Print.

How to cite a book with two or more authors:

Format: Author's name, last name first, next listed author's name(s) in normal form. *Full book title.* [in italics] Edition [if stated]. Number of volumes [if a multivolume work]. City of publication: Publisher's name, year of publication. Publication medium.

Example: Gates, Henry L., Jr., and Evelyn B. Higginbotham, eds. *African American National Biography.* 8 vols. New York: Oxford University Press, 2008. Print.

How to cite an article from a magazine published every week or every two weeks:

Format: Author's name, last name first. "Article title." [enclosed in double quotation marks] *Publication title* [in italics] date of publication: page numbers. Publication medium.

Example: Zakaria, Fareed. "A New Afghanistan Strategy." *Newsweek* 9 Feb. 2009: 36-37. Print.

How to cite a magazine article published monthly or bimonthly:

Format: Author's name, last name first. "Article title." [enclosed in double quotation marks] *Publication title* [in italics] date of publication: page numbers. Publication medium.

Example: Gropnik, Alison. "How Babies Think." *Scientific American* July 2010: 76-81. Print.

How to cite a radio or TV program:

Format: "Episode or segment title." [enclosed in double quotation marks] *Program title.* [in italics] Name of the network. Call letters, city of local station [if any], broadcast date. Medium of reception (Radio or Television).

Example: "The Big Gamble." *60 Minutes.* CBS. WBBM, Chicago, 9 Jan. 2011. Television.

How to cite a newspaper article:

Format: Author's name, last name first. "Article title." [enclosed in double quotation marks] *Publication title* [in italics] complete date of publication, edition [if given], section letter or number [if applicable]: page numbers. Publication medium.

Example: Petrie, Kari. "Let There Be Light—and Data Streaming." *USA Today* 10 Jan. 2011, sec. B: 5. Print.

How to cite a pamphlet:

Format: Author's name, last name first. *Pamphlet title.* [in italics]. City of publication: Publisher's name, year of publication. Publication medium.

Example: Modern Language Association. *Language Study in the Age of Globalization: The College-Level Experience.* New York: MLA, n.d. Print.

How to cite a program on a videocassette or videodisc:

Format: *Program title.* [in italics] Director [if given]. Producer. Original release date [if relevant]. Medium. Distributor, year of release.

Example: *The Incredible Human Body.* Dir. Alexander Grasshoff. National Geographic Video. Videocassette. National Geographic Society, 2002.

How to cite a government publication:

Format: Government name. Issuing agency name. *Publication title.* [in italics] City of publication: Publisher, year of publication.

Example: United States. Census Bureau. *Statistical Abstract of the United States: 2011.* Alexandria, VA: National Technical Information Service, 2010.

How to cite a personal interview:

Format: Interviewed person's name, last name first. Kind of interview. Date of interview.

Example: Kwon, Hayden. Personal interview. 15 Oct. 2012.

For further guidance on MLA style, refer to the most current edition of the *MLA Handbook for Writers of Research Papers.*

Some other citation styles use endnotes or footnotes rather than parenthetical citations. Endnotes appear at the end of the paper, and footnotes appear at the bottom of each page that has one or more citations. Use the style that your teacher prefers.

Preparing an appendix. You may decide to include tables, charts, graphs, diagrams, lists, or other material with your research paper. If so, place the material at the end of the paper and label each item Appendix A, Appendix B, and so on. Each item should also be given a title. In the appropriate place in your text, you can refer to the material with a cross-reference to the specific appendix. You can write, for example, "For a graph showing the nation's population growth, see Appendix A."

Revising your first draft. If time

"Prepare a title page...Fasten your paper in the upper left-hand corner, or put it in a folder or binder...Then congratulate yourself. You're finished, and the paper is ready to turn in."

permits, set aside the first draft of your research paper for at least a day before you begin to revise it. Then cast a critical eye on it and judge it for content, organization, and style, as well as for such mechanical details as grammar, spelling, and punctuation. See the section *Revising your work* for detailed guidelines on revising your paper.

Revising a research paper involves a few more steps than are needed for most other written work. First, see that your parenthetical citations have the required information and are in the proper style. Second, check any direct quotations to be sure they are worded accurately. Finally, check the list of sources (Works Cited) to see that it is alphabetized properly and that each entry has all the required information with correct punctuation.

The final copy. If your teacher has given you a style sheet, follow it precisely as you prepare your final copy. If there is no style sheet, follow these guidelines:

1. Type or print out your report on high-quality white paper, using one side only. (If you must prepare a handwritten report, write in ink on standard ruled paper.)

2. Leave a margin of 1 to 1 ½ inches (2 ½ to 4 centimeters) on the left and 1 inch (2 ½ centimeters) on the right, top, and bottom of the paper. But start the outline page 2 inches (5 centimeters) from the top.

3. Double-space the text.

4. Indent paragraphs five spaces.

5. Single-space the outline, but double-space between the main headings.

6. Begin each item on the list of sources at the left margin and indent the second and following lines five spaces. Single-space within each entry, but double-space between entries.

7. Single-space quotations that are indented rather than run-in with the text.

8. Number all pages except the title page. Use lower-case Roman numerals (i, ii, iii, ...) for the outline pages and Arabic numerals (1, 2, 3, ...) for all other pages. Center the number at the bottom of the first page of the outline, the text, and the list of sources. Center the number at the top of all other pages.

9. Prepare a title page, which contains the title, your name, and the date. You may also include the name of the teacher and class.

After you have finished typing or writing all the parts of your paper, assemble them in this order:

1. The title page.

2. The final outline, including the title of the paper and the thesis sentence.

3. The text of the paper, with the title of the paper repeated in all capital letters on the first page.

4. The list of sources.

5. The appendix, if included.

Fasten your paper in the upper left-hand corner, or put it in a folder or binder. You may want to make an extra copy. Then congratulate yourself. You're finished, and the paper is ready to turn in.

A Guide to

SPEAKING SKILLS

If you're like most people, you spend a lot of time talking. Yet the thought of making a speech before an audience may fill you with dread. If so, you're not alone. Many people are terrified if they have to make a public speech.

The guidelines given here for preparing and delivering a speech can help you become a confident speaker. You may never have to address a huge audience. But as a student, you'll give a variety of oral presentations. And chances are that sometime during your life you will be asked to give a committee report at a club meeting, ask for donations for a charity, or make a presentation to your boss. Learning how to handle speaking situations with ease is a skill well worth developing. Speaking skills will help you communicate more effectively in a wide variety of everyday situations.

Preparing a Speech

There are six basic steps to follow in preparing a speech. They are (1) analyzing the audience, (2) choosing a topic, (3) determining the purpose of the speech, (4) gathering information, (5) organizing the content, and (6) choosing a format.

Analyzing the audience. To speak effectively before a group of people, you need to know something about them. You need to know such factors as their age and educational level and their attitudes regarding various subjects. You also must know the size of your audience.

Age and educational level. People of different ages and educational levels have different vocabularies and different abilities to understand ideas. Be sure your audience can understand what you're talking about and adjust your vocabulary to their abilities. Also consider how much knowledge about the topic your audience already has. For example, a speech about African folk crafts presented to

a group of 8-year-olds would be far different from a speech on the same topic presented to a group of high school students. The language you use and the number and kinds of facts you present would differ.

Attitudes. If you are presenting a controversial topic, try to find what attitude your audience already holds toward the topic. Are most of the members inclined to agree or disagree with the position you will present? Or are they indifferent? If they're indifferent or likely to disagree, you may have to gather more facts and present them more forcefully to be effective.

Size. A large group may require a more formal speech presentation than a small group. If the group is large, you may be speaking behind a podium or on a stage. If the group is small, you simply may be seated at a table with the other members of the group. These factors may influence your choice of speech format and your delivery techniques.

Choosing a topic. There are several points to consider in choosing a topic. First, choose a topic that interests you or that you already know something about. You're more likely to enjoy preparing and delivering a speech on a topic you like than on one you don't particularly care about. You're also more likely to get a good response from your audience. Second, consider the probable interests of your audience. A speech on how to improve scores on video games might win an enthusiastic response from a group of 11-year-olds. But such a speech would probably be of little interest to a group of senior citizens. Third, make sure the topic and tone of your speech fit the occasion. You would not make the same kind of speech at a graduation ceremony that you would at a pep rally. Fourth, if your topic requires research, see that

the necessary information is readily available. Finally, make sure you can cover your topic adequately within the time allowed. Limit your topic so you can present your main idea and support it with meaningful details.

Determining the purpose. Almost every speech has at least one of three main purposes: (1) to inform, (2) to persuade, or (3) to entertain. An *informative speech* provides information and consists largely of facts presented in a straightforward manner. A *persuasive speech* tries to convince an audience to do something or adopt a particular point of view. Persuasive speeches may rely on emotional appeals as well as facts to achieve their purpose. An *entertaining speech* provides a pleasant experience for the audience and may have a more informal tone than the other two kinds of speeches.

Many speeches have two or three main purposes. For example, you may try to entertain the members of your audience in order to win them over—or persuade them—to accept your point of view.

Gathering information. If your speech requires information you don't already have, you'll need to do research. Here are three ways to go about it:

1. *Observe the subject matter itself.* If your speech is about how newspapers are recycled, for example, you could visit a recycling plant to ob-

serve the process.

2. *Use the library.* The books, magazines, newspapers, pamphlets, online databases, websites, and other materials you'll find will provide information on almost any topic.

3. *Interview an expert or others who have firsthand knowledge.* If you're preparing a speech on the effects of budget cutbacks on elementary schools, for example, you might interview the principal and some of the teachers at a local elementary school.

For pointers on how to do research, see "A Guide to Research Skills" on pages 26-34.

Organizing the content. Like a written report, a good speech needs good organization. Most speeches are organized in three parts: (1) the introduction, (2) the body, and (3) the conclusion.

As you develop the content of your speech, always keep in mind the importance of attracting your audience's interest in the beginning and holding it to the end. The introduction to your speech needs to tell the members of your audience what your speech is about—but in a way that will make them want to listen. Don't begin by saying, "This speech is about...." Instead, try using a personal anecdote or lead in with a dramatic statement.

In the body of the speech, present

> **"Be sure your audience can understand what you're talking about and adjust your vocabulary to their abilities."**

your main points and supporting details. Make sure the details are closely related to your topic and interesting to your audience. You can present your main points in several ways, depending on your topic. You can arrange them in order of importance, putting the most important points first. You can use chronological order, describing events in the order in which they occurred. In some speeches, you might discuss a topic that is new to your audience or difficult to understand. In such cases, begin with the simplest facts and work your way up to the more difficult ones. Or think of something that the members of your audience already know about that could help them understand the new or more difficult topic.

The conclusion of your speech is your last opportunity to impress the members of your audience. Try to leave them with something to think about. In many cases, a quotation from a famous person could provide a memorable conclusion to your topic.

An outline can help you organize the ideas and facts that make up each part of your speech. The phrases or sentences of the outline briefly state the points to be presented. You may use a formal outline format like the one on page 11 in "A Guide to Writing Skills." Or your outline may consist of a simple list of points to be covered—in proper order, of course. You can use the outline as a guide when you deliver your speech.

Choosing a method. You need to decide what method to use in delivering your speech. You have four choices: (1) reading the speech, (2) memorizing the speech, (3) speaking impromptu, and (4) speaking extemporaneously. In choosing a speech method, make sure it is one you are comfortable with and one that suits the occasion. Each method has advantages and disadvantages.

Reading the speech may seem like the safest method. You don't have to worry about forgetting anything, and you can make sure your speech precisely fits the allotted time. But reading your speech also has disadvantages. You may become so engrossed in your manuscript that you forget to look up at the audience. You may begin speaking in a monotone, causing your listeners to lose interest. Once they've lost interest, the point of your speech may never get across. Reading your speech also makes it difficult to adjust the content in response to audience reactions.

If you choose to read your speech, type it double-spaced or write it out neatly so that you can read it easily. Some people write their speeches on large note cards and make an effort to look up at the audience at least at the end of each card.

Memorizing the speech requires that you first write it out and then memorize it word for word. Depending on the length of the speech, this type of delivery could mean hours or days of extra preparation time and effort. This method also has several other disadvantages. You might skip an important point or forget what comes next. You might concentrate so hard on remembering the speech that your voice sounds unnatural. And you'll be unlikely to add remarks or otherwise adjust your speech to suit the mood of the audience. If you decide to memorize your speech, keep in mind the need to make your delivery natural and relaxed.

Speaking impromptu requires little or no preparation. As a result, it is rarely used for a formal speech. Comments offered at a committee meeting or club gathering are examples of impromptu speaking. This method can succeed only if you are well informed about the subject. An impromptu speech enables you to give a lively, spontaneous delivery. What you say can be suited specifically to the mood of the audience. But an impromptu speech risks being unorganized. Without adequate preparation, you may ramble and never get your point across effectively. If you know ahead of time that you'd like to say something at a meeting or other occasion, take at least a few minutes to organize your thoughts and perhaps jot down your main ideas to serve as a checklist.

Speaking extemporaneously is the most commonly used type of delivery in public speaking. You organize your ideas in a written outline and use it as a guide when you give your speech. An extemporaneous speech has the advantage of being both organized and spontaneous. Although you don't write down the complete speech, you can refer to the key words or sentences of the outline to keep yourself "on track." You can easily add or omit details on the basis of audience reaction. And it's not as difficult to maintain eye contact with your audience when you speak extemporaneously as it is when you read from a manuscript.

To take full advantage of the flexibility of the extemporaneous speech, learn about your topic in depth. Gather more details than you'll actually need. That way, you'll have a full stock of material to draw upon to keep your speech interesting. You can also vary the content, depending on the audience's reaction.

A speaker's check list.

There are many steps involved in the preparation of an effective speech. It is easy to forget a step or two along the way. And yet this would be the kind of mistake that could ruin a presentation. If you are about to begin the preparation of a speech, use the following questions to make sure you "cover all the bases."

	YES	NO
1. Have I carefully studied and analyzed the audience?	_____	_____
2. Have I chosen a topic for my speech that not only interests me, but is also adaptable to the likes and dislikes of my audience?	_____	_____
3. Have I set the purpose of my speech?	_____	_____
4. Have I carefully gathered all of the information and materials I will need to document my speech?	_____	_____
5. Have I developed a well-organized and logical outline for my speech?	_____	_____
6. Have I rehearsed my presentation to the point that I am sure I can deliver the speech confidently and without hesitation?	_____	_____

Rehearsing and Delivering a Speech

After you've completed all the steps in preparing your speech, you're ready to begin rehearsing unless you're going to give an impromptu speech. Rehearsing is obviously necessary for a memorized speech, but it is also vital to a good extemporaneous speech or to a speech you plan to read. The more you rehearse your speech, the more confident you'll be when the time comes to deliver it.

As you rehearse, remember that you want to convey more than information. You also want to convey enthusiasm for your topic. If *you* sound interested, your *audience* will be more likely to listen to, and enjoy, your speech.

How to rehearse. Begin rehearsing by using your outline or reading aloud from your manuscript. As you repeat the speech many times, you'll come to depend less and less on your written words. If possible, make a recording of your speech and listen to it critically. You may find that you're not pronouncing all your words clearly or that you're going too fast or too slow.

Next, practice in front of a mirror, paying attention to your posture and gestures. Then, ask someone to listen to your speech and give an honest reaction to both content and delivery. Your listener may be able to spot distracting mannerisms that you should correct, such as clenching your fists at your sides or shuffling your feet. You can also make a video recording of yourself to observe your strengths and weaknesses. Finally, if you will be delivering your speech in an unfamiliar place, try to practice it there at least once. That way, you can practice with a podium and microphone if they are to be provided.

Your voice. The way you use your voice can add greatly to the impression you make when delivering your speech. As you speak, pay special attention to the *volume, speed,* and *pitch* of your voice and to the *clarity*

of your pronunciation.

Volume. Obviously, you'll want to speak loudly enough so that the audience can easily hear you. You'll have to consider such factors as the size of the room, whether you'll be using a microphone, and whether there are outside noises you must speak over. Try to vary your volume to make your voice sound more interesting. At times, you might speak more loudly to emphasize an important point. At other times, you might gain attention by speaking more softly, making the audience listen more carefully.

Speed. Don't speak so fast that you slur your words or become difficult to understand. If you have a time limit, pace yourself so that you can finish your speech without having to hurry at the end. Varying your speed from time to time can make your speech more effective. You can slow down to emphasize a point. And a dramatic pause at the end of a particularly important statement can be an effective technique.

Pitch is how high or low your voice sounds. You vary your pitch automatically during normal conversation. Your voice sounds higher when you are excited and lower when you are serious. During a speech, your voice should follow this natural pattern of pitch variation. Try to avoid speaking in a monotone.

Clarity of pronunciation. Speak as distinctly as you can without sounding unnatural. Avoid saying "er" or "uh" between words or phrases. Enunciate word endings, such as *ing,* clearly.

Your appearance and the way you use your body can be almost as important as your voice when you give a speech. Dress neatly in comfortable clothing that is appropriate

to your audience. Avoid wearing unusual clothes or jewelry that might distract the audience or get in your way as you speak. Stand up straight, but in a relaxed manner. Don't slouch or lean on the podium if you're using one. Try to keep a pleasant expression on your face.

As you speak, keep eye contact with your audience. Don't look up at the ceiling or down at the floor. If you're reading from a manuscript, hold it up slightly so that you can easily glance at the audience from time to time.

Gestures can help emphasize important parts of your speech. But don't overdo them. If you gesture constantly, you'll lessen the effect and make the audience more aware of your gestures than your words. And make sure your gestures look natural and blend smoothly with what you're saying.

Audio-visual aids can enliven your presentation. Such aids include drawings, photographs, maps, charts, graphs, diagrams, chalkboards, models, slides, computer graphics, DVD's, and compact discs (CD's). Audio-visual aids can add welcome variety to your speech and help hold the audience's attention. They can enable the audience to understand exactly what you mean. Audio-visual aids can also make your speech more memorable by leaving the audience with a more vivid impression of your topic than words alone can convey.

Whichever kind of audio-visual aid you choose, be sure it serves a definite purpose. An effective aid should clarify, illustrate, or dramatize a fact or idea. For example, a speech explaining how the human ear works would benefit from a drawing, model, or computer animation of an ear. A discussion of dialects might be greatly enhanced by an audio recording.

Be sure your audio-visual aid fits your needs precisely. If you want to show where major battles of the American Civil War occurred, for example, don't use a map of the entire Western Hemisphere. In graphs and charts, the use of different colors can make statistical comparisons much easier to understand. You also need to be sure that your visual aid is big enough to be seen by the entire audience and that it is clearly labeled. Take into consideration the size of the room and the size of the audience as you choose and prepare your audio-visual aids.

Rehearse with your audio-visual aids so you can incorporate them smoothly into your speech. Here's a list of points to remember when using audio-visual aids:

1. Have them set up and ready to use before your speech. If an aid is particularly interesting or unusual, it may be a good idea to have the aid handy, but hidden, until the appropriate time in your speech. Otherwise, your audience may be too distracted to pay close attention to the earlier parts of your speech.

2. Mount illustrations and set them up on an easel, rather than trying to hold them while speaking.

"The more you rehearse your speech, the more confident you'll be when the time comes to deliver it... Begin rehearsing by using your outline... Practice in front of a mirror, paying attention to your posture and gestures."

"Audio-visual aids can add welcome variety to your speech... They can also make your speech more memorable by leaving the audience with a more vivid impression of your topic than words alone can convey."

3. If you're going to write on a chalkboard or paper, remember to keep turning back to your listeners to keep your eye contact with them.

4. If you'll be using such equipment as a film, a tape, a DVD player, or a computer, check it out before you speak. Be sure it's in good working order and that an electrical outlet is nearby.

5. Don't pass a visual aid around during your speech. It's too distracting. If you have material to pass out,

do it before or after your speech.

6. Don't stand in front of a visual aid or block the view of part of the audience.

7. Remember to talk to the audience, not to the aid.

Stage fright. When the time finally comes to deliver your speech, you may suffer from that common ailment—stage fright. To keep your nervousness from working against you, concentrate on what the person

speaking before you is saying, rather than worry about your own presentation.

When your turn comes, take a deep breath or two to help stay calm. *Act* confident, even if you don't *feel* confident. Remember that your audience is rooting for you to do well. Walk briskly to your place and look directly at the audience to gain its attention. Once you begin speaking, your nervousness will decrease.

A Guide to

RESEARCH SKILLS

Questions. Life is full of them. Most of us spend time each day asking questions and finding the answers to them. What's the quickest way to get to the museum? How much will a new computer cost? Who can fix that flat tire? Some questions are easily answered. But others are more difficult, and you may need help in finding the answers.

Research involves locating and retrieving information—answers to questions. Once you have the information, you can then work with it or communicate it to others. You may use the results of your research to help make a decision. Or you may communicate your research results in some schoolwork.

Once you learn where to go or whom to ask to get answers to your

questions, you have developed skills that you can use all your life. Research skills are useful in school, in a career, and in many everyday situations. Developing good research skills can help you find information more quickly and efficiently.

Getting to Know the Library

What the library provides. For many people doing research, the library is the first place that comes to mind. Libraries—or *media centers* in many schools—contain more information than any one person could learn in a lifetime. That information comes in many forms. Books, e-books, *periodicals* (magazines and journals), and sources on the Internet make up the major part of most school and public libraries. Many

This section will help you become familiar with sources of information. You can learn how to find information in a library and elsewhere. You can also learn how to take notes and put your information to good use.

libraries also have audiotapes and videotapes, brochures and pamphlets, compact discs (CD's), DVD's, maps, and photographs and prints. In addition, a library may have audiotape and videotape recorders, CD players, copiers, projectors, satellite dishes, and other equipment.

Whether you are using a small school library or the main branch of a major city library system, it is a good idea to find out what materials

and services the library provides. Some libraries offer online orientations to familiarize you with their services. Many libraries have brochures that describe what they offer. Browse in the library and become familiar with the various sections.

Sections of the library. Most libraries have two major sections—the general circulation section and the reference section. The general circulation section contains books and other materials that may be checked out of the library. In that section, you're likely to find all the fiction and most of the nonfiction books your library owns. The reference section has materials that, in most instances, cannot be checked out of the library. Most books in the reference section are not the kinds you would read from cover to cover. They include encyclopedias, dictionaries, atlases, and other reference works that play an important role in research. In some libraries, the reference section may consist of a few shelves. In other libraries, it may be a separate room or a series of rooms.

Librarians themselves are an excellent resource when doing research. They can help you find an answer to a specific question, such as "When was Babe Ruth born?" Or they can direct you to sources that contain information on a broader topic, such as the history of baseball. Some libraries have several librarians who specialize in different kinds of information and services. For example, a reference librarian would be more familiar with the library's reference section than a children's librarian would be. For more information about librarians, see **Library** (Assisting patrons; Communicating information).

Exploring the library catalog. The library catalog is your guide to locating the resources of the library. It has information about every book the library contains and gives its location. Catalogs may also include entries for CD's, DVD's, e-books, and other nonprint items. If your library does not include entries for nonprint items in its catalog, ask where such material is indexed.

Library catalogs take various forms, from traditional card catalogs to computer or online catalogs. It is important to learn how to use whatever type of catalog your library has. If you go directly to the shelves without checking the catalog, you may never know about books that have been checked out or are waiting to be reshelved. If you know your library has a particular book, but cannot find it on the shelves, the librarian may be able to see if it is waiting to be shelved. Most online catalogs show if an item is on the shelf or checked out. If the book has been checked out, you can ask that a "reserve" be put on it. You will then be notified when the book is returned.

Understanding call numbers. Call numbers are used to *classify* (group) nonfiction books and other materials according to subject area. Then the books are arranged on the shelves based on their classification. The call number of a book appears in the book's catalog entry and on the spine of the book itself. The call number is important because it acts as the book's "address." It tells you exactly where to find the book on the shelves.

Most public and school libraries use the Dewey Decimal Classification System to classify nonfiction books. Some large libraries use the Library of Congress Classification System (LC). A letter and number code based on the main entry name appears below the Dewey or LC number. See page 38 for a guide to the Dewey and LC systems.

Online catalog records contain helpful information about books and other items in the library. This information includes the title, subject, author, publisher and copyright date, number of pages, illustration information, and call number.

Item Information	Catalog Record

Encyclopedia of insects and spiders
Preston–Mafham, Rod.

Personal Author: Preston–Mafham, Rod.

Title: Encyclopedia of insects and spiders / Rod and Ken Preston–Mafham.

Publication info: San Diego, CA : Thunder Bay Press, 2005.

Physical descrip: 288 p. : col. ill. ; 25cm.

Subject term: Insects.

Subject term: Spiders.

Added author: Preston–Mafham, Ken.

ISBN: 1592234283 (trade)

Call number: 595.7 PRE 2005

If a call number has the letters R or REF in front of it, the book is in the reference section. Most libraries shelve biographies together, separate from other nonfiction. Biographies are arranged in alphabetical order according to the last name of the person the book is about. If only letters or the letter F appears instead of a call number, the book is fiction. Such books are shelved in alphabetical order by the author's last name.

When you find an entry in the catalog for a book you want to use, copy down the call number, title, and author. Go to the appropriate section of the library. The call number should guide you to the book.

Online library catalogs allow users to search for information on books and other media through a computer system. Online catalogs in some libraries only store information about materials available on site. Other catalogs are *networked,* or connected, to other libraries and collections. You may be able to obtain materials from these collections through interlibrary loan.

You can access information in computer catalogs by using the *keyword search technique.* For example, to find information about Siamese cats, you can type the keyword *Siamese*. The computer then searches the database for all "matches" or "hits" of that word. The keyword may appear anywhere in the title, subject, or description of the topic.

Using a specific keyword, such as *Siamese,* helps you find information quickly. Your search would be slower if a general word was used, such as *cat*. If your search turns up nothing, you then can try using a broader keyword. Likewise, starting any search with a general word, such as *war, history, geography,* or *science,* will probably yield too much material.

Words such as *or, and,* and *not,* called *Boolean operators,* connect keywords. Use *or* if you need to expand a topic or are unsure about how a topic is listed. For example, you can search under "Britain or United Kingdom" if you are uncertain about the proper word. *And* narrows the scope of your search. For information on the history of the United Kingdom, you would search under "United Kingdom and History." Using *not* helps limit your search. For example, if you want information on the Reformation leader Martin Luther but not on the civil rights leader Martin Luther King, your search terms might be "Martin *and* Luther *not* King."

Online catalogs also allow searches by author, by subject, and by title. Many also allow you to limit your search to materials published before or after a certain date or to certain types of materials. Most online catalogs indicate if material is in the library or checked out. With many online catalogs, you can print out information you need.

Paper card catalogs are the traditional form of library catalog. The card catalog consists of one or more cabinets with drawers of file cards arranged alphabetically. For most books, there is one card under the author's name, one under the book title, and one or more under the general subject. Some books may have additional cards for a joint au-

thor, editor, translator, or illustrator.

The author card is called the *main entry.* The other cards are *added entries.* They look like the main entry, but they have an additional line at the top, giving the title, the subject, or some other heading above the author's name. The cards are arranged in alphabetical order, according to the words on the top line. Each drawer has author cards, title cards, and subject cards, all interfiled alphabetically.

The subject cards are the best place to begin library research if you don't have a specific title or author in mind. To find books on your topic, you first need to think of an appropriate subject heading. Try to think in specific terms, rather than broad generalities. For example, look under HIMALAYA, rather than MOUNTAINS; DICKINSON, EMILY, rather than POETS. If you have trouble finding books on your topic, ask the librarian to suggest subject headings.

Other kinds of catalogs. Some libraries have catalogs in book form, with separate volumes for listings by author, subject, and title. Other libraries store catalog information on microfilm. In microfilm catalogs, printed material is photographed and greatly reduced in size, so that many lines fit onto a small piece of film. Special equipment enables the user to enlarge the film image so it can be read on a screen.

Reference and Source Materials

Kinds of reference materials. You can find many answers to your research questions in reference materials. Some reference works, such as almanacs and encyclopedias, provide information directly. Other works, such as indexes and bibliographies, tell you where to find in-

formation. *General* reference works cover a variety of subjects. *World Book* is an example of a general reference work. *Special* or *subject* reference works, such as *The New Grove Dictionary of Music and Musicians* and *The Encyclopedia of the American Revolution,* provide information

on only one subject. Such reference works cover a subject in greater detail than general reference works.

Many reference books and indexes are available online via the Internet. Many of these sources are in multimedia format. They supply photographs, graphics, sound, and video; information originally published in other sources, such as newspapers or magazines; or articles in books. These sources are discussed more fully on pages 30-31.

Like the rest of the nonfiction collection, the reference section is arranged according to subject. Familiarize yourself with the part of the reference collection that contains materials for your research. Then you will be able to refer to them quickly when you need information.

Frequently used reference works. Most libraries have hundreds or thousands of reference materials. You will not use all of them. But some works will become reliable sources of information that you turn to again and again. The most frequently used reference works include encyclopedias, yearbooks, almanacs, dictionaries, and periodical and newspaper indexes.

Encyclopedias can be a good place to begin research. They contain thousands of articles on a variety of topics. Thus, the subject you are interested in is likely to be covered in some form. Reading an encyclopedia article can give you a good introduction to your topic. It can provide you with many of the facts you will need. The encyclopedia will also list related information, both encyclopedia articles and other sources.

Yearbooks are annual supplements to encyclopedias. Together with yearly almanacs, they provide up-to-date statistics and other facts on

many topics, including business, politics, sports, entertainment, foreign countries, and population. These sources can be useful for information about current events. Archives, or collections of yearbook articles, can also be a good source of information on recent history. *World Book Student* and *World Book Advanced* include such articles covering nearly a century in their *Back in Time* feature.

Dictionaries. Most people think of a dictionary as a source to use when they want to know how to spell or pronounce a word or learn what it means. But if you take time to become familiar with a good dictionary, you may be surprised at the other

kinds of information you find. For example, it may contain information about grammar, writing style, and *etymology* (how words originated). Many dictionaries list foreign alphabets and words, common signs and symbols, and place names. Some print dictionaries show how to proofread a manuscript.

Periodical and newspaper indexes. Magazines and newspapers are valuable sources of information, especially for topics of current interest that may not be covered adequately in books. They can also give you present-day views of events, issues, and people of the past. Periodical and newspaper indexes are the reference

Dewey Decimal Classification

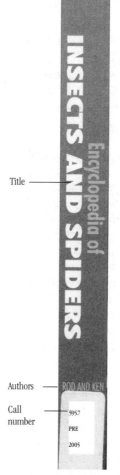

Title

Authors — ROD AND KEN

Call number

595.7

PRE

2005

This numbering system, devised by Melvil Dewey in 1876, is a method for classifying books by subject so that books on related materials are shelved together. There are 10 main classes, 000 to 900, each of which is divided into 10 subclasses or divisions (*e.g.*, 590). These are further divided into 10 sections (*e.g.*, 595). Continued decimal notation (*e.g.*, 595.7) permits ever-finer subdivisions. In this case, the last subdivision is Insecta (Insects). A number appears on each library book and determines the way books are arranged in the library. By getting the number from the library catalog, you can quickly locate any book on the shelves.

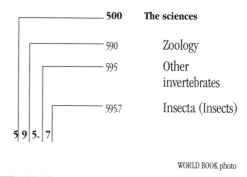

500	**The sciences**
590	Zoology
595	Other invertebrates
595.7	Insecta (Insects)

5 9 5. 7

tools that can tell you where to find articles on your topic in such sources. Some online sources provide methods of searching newspapers and magazines, and enable the user to select and read articles of interest. Others, such as *World Book Student* and *World Book Advanced,* contain links to relevant magazine articles.

Readers' Guide to Periodical Literature is the most widely used guide to magazine articles. It indexes articles from over 400 leading nontechnical magazines. *Readers' Guide* is issued several times a year in paperback. Each year's issues are then reissued in a bound volume. The periodicals included may vary from volume to volume, so be sure to check the list that appears in the volume you're using. You will also need to find out which periodicals your library has in its collection. *Readers' Guide* is also available online.

The entries in *Readers' Guide* appear in alphabetical order by subject and author and, sometimes, by title. Abbreviations are used for many parts of the entry, including the name of the magazine, the date of the issue, the volume and number of the issue, and the page number where the article can be found. An explanation of the abbreviations appears in the front of each volume of the guide. Be sure to read it so that you can understand the entry. Here's a sample entry for an article on employee health insurance:

Employee health insurance
Broken Promises [Retiree medical benefits] M. Andrews. graph il. *Money* v34 no5 p49-50 My 2005.

The entry tells you that an article titled "Broken Promises," by M. Andrews, begins on page 49 of the May 2005 issue of *Money Magazine.* It discusses retiree medical benefits. The article is illustrated and has a graph.

In addition to *Readers' Guide,* there are some specialized guides to

periodicals, such as the *Art Index* and the *Business Periodicals Index.* These works may lead you to articles not indexed in *Readers' Guide.*

The New York Times Index is an index to the articles in *The New York Times.* Many libraries subscribe to this newspaper because it offers wide coverage of national and international news. Entries in the index are listed alphabetically, mainly by subject.

Online reference materials
are carried by many libraries. Online sources provide information quickly. Some online sources provide video, sound, and motion in addition to text.

Keyword searching is used to find information in most online sources. Some sources also have a site map, menu, or table of contents.

Many online reference works have information similar to that in a print version. Such works include dictionaries, the Bible, William Shakespeare's plays, ZIP Codes and addresses, and Bartlett's *Familiar Quotations.*

Online encyclopedias store all the information found in a multivolume set of encyclopedias. *World Book Student* and *World Book Advanced* are online versions of *The World Book Encyclopedia.* They contain such encyclopedic information as text, maps, and pictures; additional features from annuals covering recent events or history; and audio, video, animations, and other multimedia information. Such encyclopedias as *The McGraw-Hill Encyclopedia of Science and Technology* are also available online.

Online periodical indexes, such as *InfoTrac,* index hundreds of magazines and journals. In addition to bibliographic information, online indexes may include a summary of

the article or the full text. Most online periodical indexes are searched by using keywords.

The Internet has become a popular information source. Government agencies, businesses, nonprofit organizations, and individuals provide free or fee-based access to their websites. Each is a collection of information taken from other publications or produced specifically for online delivery.

Search features on the Internet allow keyword searching to find new websites or specific information. The Internet is especially useful when you are looking for information that changes often. For example, you might go to a newspaper's website to search on a developing news story.

Before using the Internet, you should think about your information needs and your search strategy. There is generally a wealth of information on the Internet, but some of it is unreliable or of poor quality.

Getting what you need. In most school and public libraries, you can go to the shelves directly to find the item you want. But in some large libraries, you'll need to fill out a *call slip* and request the item from someone who works at the library.

Most libraries keep current issues of newspapers and magazines on shelves for easy access. Past issues may be kept as bound volumes or on microfilm. Bound volumes consist of all the issues for a particular period bound together in one volume. The volumes are put on the shelves by order of their date. On microfilm, pages are photographed and greatly reduced in size. The images appear on a reel or on a sheet called *microfiche.* A viewing machine enlarges the images and projects them on a screen so you can read the pages. Microfilm of newspapers and magazines is gener-

ally stored in file cabinets. You may be able to get bound volumes and microfilm yourself, or you may need to fill out a call slip. Libraries also subscribe to such databases as Lexis-Nexis. These databases provide access to magazine and newspaper articles not freely available on the Internet.

Judging the value of reference and source materials. After you have the references and sources you want, how can you judge if they are really useful? There are several factors to consider:

Scope of coverage. Turn to a book's index to see how much it covers your topic. If your topic appears on several pages, the work is worth checking carefully. A website may have an index or a search feature. You can use either to see how much there is on your topic.

Publication date. If you're doing research in a rapidly developing field, such as computers, you will want the latest material available. But if you're dealing with a historical topic, such as the Korean War, the publication date may not be as important. In a book, the publication date often appears on the back of the title page.

On a website, if the publication date is not available, spot check the website by searching on it for a recent event, such as the death of a famous person. If the site contains the current information, it is more likely that the rest of the site is kept up to date.

Authoritativeness. Is the author well known in the field? Has the author written other works on this subject? The book jacket or introduction can help you find out.

Are there citations, appendixes, or other indications of careful scholarship? If you are consulting periodicals, it may be wise to avoid articles in popular magazines not recognized

as authoritative. If you have doubts about a particular magazine article, check with your teacher or a librarian to see if it would be acceptable.

If you use a newspaper as a source, keep in mind that the information presented is perishable. Ongoing events are covered in newspapers on a day-to-day basis as more information comes to light. As a result, comprehensive coverage on a topic is seldom available in one newspaper article.

If you are using the Internet to find sources, one way to ensure authoritativeness is to use websites with a ".org," ".gov," or ".edu" extension. They indicate the official sites of organizations, government agencies, and educational institutions.

Websites with ".com" extensions are generally owned by companies or individuals and are often less authoritative. For example, if you wanted to find reliable information about Glacier National Park, it would be best to go to the U.S. National Park Service government website, rather than a personal web page entitled, "My trip to Glacier National Park." Although the latter website may have interesting information, it is likely to be narrower in focus, to be opinion-based, or to omit important information.

Bias. Does the author have an apparent bias that could hamper the objectivity of the book or article? For example, if you are doing research on the 1967 Arab-Israeli war, a book, article, or website on the subject by either an Arab or an Israeli author might be biased. Although it could be an interesting source to include among others, it would be unwise to use it as your main source.

Edition. Check the title page or copyright page to see if the book is a first edition or a revised edition. If there have been several editions, it could mean that the book has been

well received and is considered reliable. Try to use the latest edition.

Reading level. Skimming a few pages will tell you if a book, article, or website is easy to understand or if it is chiefly for scholars in the field. Does it use technical language? Are unfamiliar words defined?

Special features. Check to see if the book, article, or website has illustrations, maps, charts, a glossary, a list of sources, or other helpful features. Some websites provide animations, simulations, and video and audio files. Such features may suggest that the source is a useful one.

Overall quality. Judging the quality of a book is relatively easy. If it is in a library, it will have been carefully chosen. However, there are thousands of websites, and judging their quality can be more difficult.

The presentation of information on a website does not necessarily determine the reliability of that information. However, to minimize the time spent researching your topic, you should avoid sites that are poorly organized or slow to use because of advertising or irrelevant graphics.

There are certain things to look for in a website. Some questions to ask are: Is the layout of the website logical and easy to understand? Is it easy to find your way around the site? Is biographical information provided about authors who publish articles on the site? Is background and contact information available about the organization that controls the site?

Getting the most out of a reference work. To make full use of a reference work, take time to familiarize yourself with its organization before you plunge in to search for information. See if the book or website has an introductory section

on how to use it, a key to abbreviations, or similar helpful information.

Consult the table of contents to get an idea of what the reference work covers and how the material is organized. The table of contents lists chapter titles and such features as illustrations and maps. Do not neglect to check material in the front and back of the book. An introduction and author's foreword can have valuable information. Appendixes may include charts, tables, the text of documents, and author's notes. Lists of sources can provide you with titles of additional books or websites to check.

When you are ready to find specific information, turn to the index or search feature. The index or search feature offers quicker access to information in the book or website than the table of contents offers. Most reference books have one general index, which lists proper names, titles, and topics together. Some works have several indexes—for example, an author index, a title index, and a subject index. Some websites offer more than one method of searching. Always check the index or search feature to find the information you want.

To use an index, think of the word that most clearly identifies your topic. For information on the Nile River, for example, look under "Nile," not "River." For information on the presidency of Nelson Mandela, look under "Mandela," not "presidency."

After you have located the proper pages, skim the text quickly to see if it has the information you need. Look at headings; the first, or *topic,* sentence of each paragraph; and concluding summaries. This method should help you spot main ideas. If the source has useful information, fill out a source card, read the text carefully, and take notes.

Preparing Source Cards

You should prepare a source card for every source you consult—books, magazine and newspaper articles, pamphlets, DVD's, CD's, and so on. Source cards are simply file cards that contain all the information you'll need later when you prepare a list of sources for your report.

To prepare source cards, use standard-sized cards, ruled or unruled, and write in ink on one side only. Use one card for each source you consult. That way, it will be easy to arrange the cards in alphabetical order later. Use the same format for your source cards that you'll use for the final list of sources. (See pages 17-18 for samples of the list of sources format.) If you number each source record at the top, you can use this number in your notes to identify the source of the note. It is also a good idea to include in the source record the call number of the book and the library where you found it. Then if you need to check the source again, you will know exactly where to find it.

Taking Notes

Good research depends on good notes. The information you find in reference works must be clearly and accurately recorded in your notes. Only then can the information become part of a well-organized and well-written report. There are various ways to go about taking notes. It is important to find a system that works well for you.

One of the best systems uses note cards. Take notes in ink, on one side of the card only. Put only one item—fact, quotation, or idea—on each card. This method will make it easier to arrange and combine your notes in any order you want. Write the source number (taken from your source card) in the upper right-hand corner of the note card. Include the page number of the source in case you need that information for a footnote later. Write a short heading—called a *slug*—at the top of the card to identify the topic or subtopic the note refers to. If you've prepared an outline, the slug should correspond to a heading in your outline.

Before you write or type a note, evaluate the material you have read to make sure the information is worth recording. If it is, do not just copy it word for word. Paraphrase or summarize the information. You may also wish to add personal reactions or other comments on your notes. If so, circle them, write them in a different color, or use some other method to distinguish them.

Generally, make notes in your own words because they reflect *your* thinking, not somebody else's. You should use direct quotes only when the author's words are particularly striking, when you want to refer to an expert's knowledge or opinion, or when you want to hold an author accountable for a particular idea or statement.

The library and the Internet are by no means the only sources for research material. People and places near and far can provide information that will make your research more complete and more interesting.

Number each source card.

5

Preston-Mafham, Ron and Ken.
Encyclopedia of Insects and Spiders.
San Diego, CA. Thunder Bay Press, 2005.

When citing a book, include the authors' last names, first names, the title and publisher of the book, the city of publication, and the year the book was published.

QL463 .P714 2005   Carnegie Library of Pittsburgh

This is the Library of Congress call number for the book. Libraries using the Dewey Decimal system would list the item as 595.7 P939 2005 or 595.7 PRE.

Note the name of the library where you found the book.

WORLD BOOK illustration

Using Other Sources

Writing or e-mailing for information. Government agencies and business and professional associations can be important sources of information. By contacting such organizations, you may be able to get reliable statistics and other facts that would be difficult to track down elsewhere. For example, if you were writing a report about literacy in Canada, it might be helpful to e-mail or write to Canada's provincial departments of education for the most recent statistics on literacy. Furthermore, these sources publish a variety of pamphlets and other materials that you can use for research. Many of these materials are free or inexpensive.

Your library has directories with addresses of government, business, and other organizations. The Internet is another source of addresses.

When you write for information, keep in mind that some groups are better equipped than others to handle requests. Make your request specific and reasonable. If you are requesting information by mail, include a self-addressed, stamped envelope for the reply. Most important, do not assume that the reply will arrive by the time you need it. It might not. Be prepared to use information from other sources if necessary.

Conducting an interview can be an effective way to get facts and

Arachnid characteristics   5

Arachnids are often confused with insects, although they are built differently. Arachnids have two body regions, whereas insects have three. Arachnids normally have eight legs instead of the insect's six.
Note: Follow this with the different types of spiders.

Preston-Mafham, Ron and Ken.   p.248

The slug goes here. If you already made an outline, use the main topics as slugs.

This number should correspond to the related source card.

Limit each card to one idea and use your own words.

Write notes to yourself in a different color or circle them.

Authors' names   Page number

WORLD BOOK illustration

personal viewpoints that add special interest to your report. Begin with a courteous phone call or letter identifying yourself and requesting an interview. Specify the sort of information you need. Make yourself available at a time that is convenient for the person you are contacting.

Before the interview, read background material about the topic. That way, you will be better able to ask intelligent questions and follow-ups. Prepare a list of questions ahead of time.

Listen carefully during the interview. Take notes on important points and be careful to write direct quotations exactly as they are said. Be sure to ask permission to use a direct quote. Ask for clarification of points you don't understand and the spelling of unfamiliar terms or names.

A tape recorder or digital voice recorder can eliminate the need for taking lengthy notes by hand. But again ask permission beforehand. Some people object to being recorded or "freeze" when you begin recording.

Before you leave the interview, be sure to write down accurately the subject's name, position or title, and place of business. You will need this information for your list of sources. Do not forget to thank your subject at the end of the interview. Also follow up with a thank-you note.

Conducting a survey is another way to get unique material. You can ask people questions in person or develop a questionnaire. In either case, phrase your questions carefully so that people can respond easily and clearly. Surveys that use a "yes or no" or "for or against" format are the easiest to evaluate. You may want to include a "no opinion" category. Or you may prefer a format that allows for a range of opinion. Whatever method you choose, take care to record the results accurately.

Using television as a source. Television documentaries, news programs, and interview shows can give you access to expert opinions and valuable information. If you watch a television program as part of your research, be prepared to take careful notes. Be sure to note the name of the program, the network, and the date of broadcast for your list of sources.

Museums, art galleries, and historical societies may enable you to explore your subject firsthand. For example, a report on the painter Vincent van Gogh could be enhanced by a visit to an art museum that exhibits some of his works. Many museums and other cultural centers have libraries or other research facilities open to the public. See what your community has to offer that can help you understand your topic better.

Documenting Sources

When preparing a report or research paper, it is important that you *document* (give credit to) the person whom you are quoting or whose ideas you are using. Presenting another person's work or ideas as one's own is called *plagiarism.* Plagiarism is *unethical* (morally wrong).

Citations tell readers where you found your information and where further information on the topic can be obtained. There are several different styles for citing research. Most styles involve notes—such as parenthetical citations or footnotes—within the text and a complete list of sources at the end of the document. The list of sources should contain all the books, articles, interviews, websites, and other sources that you used for your report or research paper.

Glossary

A selected list of terms and abbreviations commonly encountered in research.

Abr. Abridged; abridgment

added entry The heading above the author line on a catalog card. The card is filed by this entry.

annotation A brief description of the content of a book.

anon. Anonymous (author unknown)

appendix A section that follows the text, containing material relative to but not essential to the subject.

bibliography A list of books or other sources. May be general, selective, on a particular subject, or have a common theme, often annotated.

bk., bks. Book(s)

c. or *ca. circa,* about. Refers to an approximate date (*e.g., c.* 1340).

call number The classification number used to request a book.

CD-ROM *Compact Disc Read-Only Memory.* A small disc used to hold text, graphics, video, and sound for catalogs and reference works.

cf. Confer; compare one source with another.

ch., chap., chaps. Chapter(s)

class number The number by which a book is identified in a classification system (*e.g.,* the Dewey Decimal Classification System or the Library of Congress Classification System). It indicates the subject matter of the book.

col., cols. Column(s)

continuation A work (*e.g., The World Almanac)* issued at regular intervals.

copr.; © **Copyright** The copyright notice usually consists of the symbol © (with or without the word copyright) and the year in which the book was copyrighted. May apply to the entire work or only a part. It generally appears on the *verso* (back side) of the title page.

cross-reference A reference to another entry. A *see* reference is to the preferred entry, the one under which the material appears; a *see also* reference is to related material.

cumulate The contents of several volumes arranged into one volume.

database Information stored in a computer.

DVD-ROM *Digital Video* (or *Versatile) Disc Read-Only Memory.* A compact disc that can hold between 8 and 20 times as much information as a CD-ROM.

documentation Support for a statement, as in a footnote or bibliography.

e.g. exempli gratia, for example

ed., eds. Editor(s); edition(s)

ellipsis Three spaced periods used to indicate an omission. At the beginning of a sentence, may or may not be followed by a capital letter; at the end of a sentence, is preceded by a period.

et al. *et alii,* and others

et seq. *et sequens,* and following

etc. *et cetera,* and so forth

f., ff. And the following (*e.g.,* pp. 65 f.: pp. 64 ff.)

fig., figs. Figure(s)

front. *Frontispiece* (picture facing the title page of a book or of a section of a book)

hot link In an online document, a text or illustrative link that, when activated, leads to another document.

hypertext In an online document, highlighted text that, when activated, leads to another document.

i.e. id est, that is

ibid. ibidem, the same. In a footnote, refers to the book cited in immediately preceding reference. Ibid. takes the place of the author's name, the title, and any identical material in the preceding footnote. The page number may differ.

id. idem, the same. Used in place of the author's name in additional references within a single footnote.

il., illus. Illustrations, illustrator, illustrated

infra See below; to be mentioned later.

Internet A global computer network that links smaller networks, including government facilities, universities, corporations, and individuals.

l., ll Line(s)

LC Library of Congress

loc. cit. loco citato, in the place cited. In a footnote, refers to a passage already identified when there are intervening references to other sources.

main entry The catalog card that has full information about a book (the author card).

MS., MSS. Manuscript(s)

n., nn. Note(s)

N.B. *Nota bene,* note well; take notice

n.d. No date of publication or copyright given.

n.p. No publisher given.

network An information system that links several pieces of computer equipment and computer databases together for sharing information among many users and stations.

no., nos. Number(s)

op. cit. opere citato, in the work cited. In a footnote, refers to a previously identified work when a different part is cited and there are intervening references. Pages are included in the citation.

OPAC (Online Public Access Catalog) The official name for the online card catalog.

p., pp. Page(s)

paraphrase A restatement conveying the general meaning of the original.

pass. passim, here and there; throughout the work (*e.g.,* pp. 60, 81, *et pass.)*

periodical Primarily a magazine, published at regular or irregular intervals.

printing date The year the book is printed (usually appears on the title page). Not always the same as the copyright date.

pseud. Pseudonym, a name other than an author's real name; a pen name.

pub. Published, publication

q.v. quod vide, which see

recto Right-hand page of a book; the back of a verso page

rev. Revised, revision

scope Extent of treatment, coverage

series title The collective title for a group of books.

sic So, thus, in this way. Used within brackets in a quotation to show that an error is in the original: "It was to [sic] late."

sup., supp., suppl. Supplement

supra See above; previously mentioned

thesis The statement of purpose, the proposition to be explained or proved.

tr., trans. Translator, translation

v., vol., vols. Volume(s)

v. vide, see

verso Left-hand page of a book; the back of a recto page

viz. videlicet, namely. Introduces examples or lists.

vs. Versus, against

website A site location on the World Wide Web. Each website contains a home page, and may also contain additional documents and files. Each site is owned and managed by an individual, company, or organization.

World Wide Web A system of Internet servers that support specially formatted documents, which can be easily accessed using a web browser. Not all Internet servers are part of the web.

Dewey Decimal Classification

000	**Computer science, information & general works**		**500**	**Science**
010	Bibliographies		510	Mathematics
020	Library & information sciences		520	Astronomy
030	Encyclopedias & books of facts		530	Physics
040			540	Chemistry
050	Magazines, journals & serials		550	Earth sciences & geology
060	Associations, organizations & museums		560	Fossils & prehistoric life
070	News media, journalism & publishing		570	Life sciences; biology
080	Quotations		580	Plants (Botany)
090	Manuscripts & rare books		590	Animals (Zoology)
100	**Philosophy**		**600**	**Technology**
110	Metaphysics		610	Medicine & health
120	Epistemology		620	Engineering
130	Parapsychology & occultism		630	Agriculture
140	Philosophical schools of thought		640	Home & family management
150	Psychology		650	Management & public relations
160	Logic		660	Chemical engineering
170	Ethics		670	Manufacturing
180	Ancient, medieval, & eastern philosophy		680	Manufacture for specific uses
190	Modern western philosophy		690	Building & construction
200	**Religion**		**700**	**Arts**
210	Philosophy & theory of religion		710	Landscaping & area planning
220	The Bible		720	Architecture
230	Christianity & Christian theology		730	Sculpture, ceramics & metalwork
240	Christian practice & observance		740	Drawing & decorative arts
250	Christian pastoral practice & religious orders		750	Painting
260	Christian organization, social work & worship		760	Graphic arts
270	History of Christianity		770	Photography & computer art
280	Christian denominations		780	Music
290	Other religions		790	Sports, games & entertainment
300	**Social sciences, sociology & anthropology**		**800**	**Literature, rhetoric & criticism**
310	Statistics		810	American literature in English
320	Political science		820	English & Old English literatures
330	Economics		830	German & related literatures
340	Law		840	French & related literatures
350	Public administration & military science		850	Italian, Romanian & related literatures
360	Social problems & social services		860	Spanish & Portuguese literatures
370	Education		870	Latin & Italic literatures
380	Commerce, communications & transportation		880	Classical & modern Greek literatures
390	Customs, etiquette & folklore		890	Other literatures
400	**Language**		**900**	**History**
410	Linguistics		910	Geography & travel
420	English & Old English languages		920	Biography & genealogy
430	German & related languages		930	History of ancient world (to ca. 499)
440	French & related languages		940	History of Europe
450	Italian, Romanian & related languages		950	History of Asia
460	Spanish & Portuguese languages		960	History of Africa
470	Latin & Italic languages		970	History of North America
480	Classical & modern Greek languages		980	History of South America
490	Other languages		990	History of other areas

Library of Congress Classification

The system of classification devised by the Library of Congress uses 21 letters of the alphabet to represent the principal branches of knowledge. Subdivision is achieved by adding second letters and Arabic numerals through 9999.

A	General works	J	Political science	R	Medicine
B	Philosophy, psychology, religion	K	Law	S	Agriculture
C	Auxiliary sciences of history	L	Education	T	Technology
D	World history	M	Music and books on music	U	Military science
E-F	History of the Americas	N	Fine arts	V	Naval science
G	Geography, anthropology, recreation	P	Language and literature	Z	Bibliography, library science, information resources
H	Social sciences	Q	Mathematics and science		

The Index to World Book

A

A [letter] A: 1 *with pictures*
Å [symbol]
 Angstrom A: 467
A-10 Thunderbolt [airplane]
 Air Force, United States *picture on* A: 191
A & P [company] *See* Great Atlantic and Pacific Tea Company *in this index*
À Becket, Thomas [English religious leader] *See* Becket, Saint Thomas *in this index*
A cappella [music]
 Barbershop quartet singing B: 107
 Singing S: 472
A-frame tent
 Tent (Kinds of tents) T: 168
A horizon [geology]
 See also Topsoil *in this index*
À Kempis, Thomas [German author]
 Thomas à Kempis T: 262
A. Philip Randolph Institute
 Rustin, Bayard R: 567
A posteriori knowledge
 Philosophy (Epistemology) P: 384
A priori knowledge
 Philosophy (Epistemology) P: 384; (Rationalism) P: 388
"A-Tisket, A-Tasket" [song]
 Fitzgerald, Ella F: 190
A. Ya. Vaganova Russian Ballet Academy [Saint Petersburg]
 Saint Petersburg [Russia] (Education and cultural life) S: 55
Aa [geology]
 Volcano (Lava) V: 439
A.A. [organization] *See* Alcoholics Anonymous *in this index*
AAA [agency] *See* Agricultural Adjustment Administration *in this index*
AAAS [organization]
 American Association for the Advancement of Science A: 468
Aachen [Germany] A: 2
 Architecture *picture on* A: 618
 Charlemagne (Administration and influence) C: 379
Aachen Cathedral
 Aachen A: 2
Aachen situla [sculpture]
 Sculpture (Early medieval sculpture) S: 248-249 *with picture*
AAES [organization] *See* American Association of Engineering Societies *in this index*
AAF [military unit] *See* Army Air Forces *in this index*
Aaiun, El [Western Sahara] *See* El Aaiun *in this index*
AALS [organization]
 Law (Law education) L: 138
Aalsmeer flower auction
 Flower *picture on* F: 273
Aalto, Alvar [Finnish architect] A: 2
 Architecture *picture on* A: 607
 Furniture *picture on* F: 583
Aalto Theater
 Aalto, Alvar A: 2
AAM [weapon] *See* Air-to-air missile *in this index*
Aandahl, Fred G. [American political leader]
 North Dakota (table) N: 513
Aardema, Verna [American author]
 Literature for children *picture on* L: 373
Aardman Animations [film studio]
 Animation (New diversity) A: 514c
Aardvark [animal] A: 2 *with picture*
 Animal *picture on* A: 476
 Anteater A: 541
 Mammal (table) M: 129 *with picture*
Aardwolf [animal] A: 2 *with picture*
Aarhus [Denmark]
 Århus A: 661
Aaron [Biblical figure] A: 3
 Birthstone B: 380
Aaron, Hank [American baseball player] A: 3 *with portrait*
 Baseball (table: Hall of Fame) B: 134; (Recent developments) B: 137; (table: Modern major league records) B: 138 *with picture*
Aaron, Henry [American baseball player] *See*

Aaron, Hank *in this index*
Aaron Manby [ship]
 Ship (Ships of iron) S: 424-425
Aaronic order
 Mormons (Church organization) M: 807
AARP [organization] A: 3
 Retirement R: 266
AAU [organization] *See* Amateur Athletic Union *in this index*
ABA [organization] *See* American Baptist Association; American Bar Association *in this index*
Ababemba [language and culture]
 Bemba B: 246
Abacá [plant] A: 3
 Philippines (Agriculture) P: 378 *with picture*
 Rope (Natural-fiber rope) R: 473
Abacha, Sani [Nigerian political leader]
 Nigeria (Changes in government) N: 418
Abaco Islands [Atlantic]
 Bahamas (Land and climate) B: 29 *with map*
Abacus [architecture]
 Column (The Greek orders) Ci: 865
Abacus [calculator] A: 3
Abacus, Book of the [book by Fibonacci]
 Fibonacci, Leonardo F: 89
Abadan [Iran] A: 3
Abaft
 Ship (Nautical terms) S: 405
Abajo Mountains [Utah]
 Utah (Land regions) U: 240-242 *with map*
Abalone [sea animal] A: 3
Abalone pearl
 Pearl (Shape) P: 217
Abalone steak [food]
 Abalone A: 4
Abandonment A: 4
 See also Desertion *in this index*
Abaya [clothing]
 Clothing (International fashion) Ci: 696; (Clothing under Islam) Ci: 697-698
 Saudi Arabia (Clothing) S: 157-158
ABBA [pop group]
 Sweden (Music) So: 1027-1028
Abbado, Claudio [Italian conductor] A: 4
Abbai River [Ethiopia]
 Lake Tana L: 46
Abbas I [shah of Iran] A: 4
 Iran (The Safavid dynasty) I: 405
 Isfahan I: 462
 Safavid dynasty S: 8
Abbas, Mahmoud [Palestinian political leader] A: 4
 Fatah F: 54
 Gaza Strip G: 74
 Hamas H: 28
 Israel (The early 2000's) I: 489-490
 Palestine (The continuing conflict and peace efforts) P: 106
 Palestine Liberation Organization (History) P: 106-107
 Palestinian Authority (History) P: 107
Abbas the Great *See* Abbas I *in this index*
Abbāsids [ancient people]
 Arabs (The rise and spread of Islam) A: 589-590
 Baghdad (History) B: 26
 Egypt (Muslim rule) E: 130
 Harūn al-Rashid H: 79
 Iraq (Arab rule) I: 413
 Islamic Empire I: 470
 Mamluks M: 115
 Middle East (The spread of Islam) M: 533
 Muslims (The Muslim Empire) M: 964c
 World, History of the (The Islamic world) W: 434-435
`Abbāyah [clothing]
 Arabs (Clothing) A: 588
Abbe, Cleveland [American meteorologist]
 Ohio (Interesting facts) O: 681
Abbess [religious title]
 Abbot A: 4
 Convent Ci: 1024
Abbett, Leon [American political leader]
 New Jersey (table) N: 249
Abbey [monastery]
 Abbot A: 4
Abbey Theatre [Ireland]
 Gregory, Lady G: 388

 Irish literature (The Irish literary revival) I: 431; (Drama) I: 432
 Yeats, William Butler Y: 555
Abbisit Vejjajiva [Thai political leader]
 Thailand (Recent developments) T: 228
Abbot [religious title] A: 4
Abbotsford [estate]
 Scott, Sir Walter S: 222
Abbott [American social workers] A: 4
Abbott, Berenice [American photographer]
 Atget, Eugène A: 852
Abbott, Edith [American social worker]
 Abbot A: 4
Abbott, Edward "Teddy Blue" [American cowboy]
 Western frontier life in America (The cattle drive) W: 237
Abbott, Grace [American social worker]
 Abbot A: 4
Abbott, Sir John Joseph Caldwell [Canadian political leader] A: 5 *with portrait*
 Thompson, Sir John Sparrow David (Prime minister) T: 264
Abbott, Robert Sengstacke [American journalist] A: 6 *with portrait*
 Coleman, Bessie Ci: 771
Abbottabad [Pakistan]
 Afghanistan War M: 94
 Bin Laden, Osama B: 307
 Pakistan (Recent developments) P: 100
Abboud, Ibrahim [Sudanese general]
 Sudan (Independence) So: 953
Abbreviation A: 7
 See also the articles on specific letters of the alphabet
 Capitalization (Many abbreviations) C: 197
 Postal Service, United States (table) P: 700
ABC [television network] A: 7
 Television (The national networks) T: 113; (History of U.S. television broadcasting) T: 117-118
 Walt Disney Company W: 21
ABC, Inc. [company]
 Walt Disney Company W: 21
Abd al-Malik ibn Marwān [Muslim ruler]
 Islamic Empire I: 470
 Muslims (The Muslim Empire) M: 964c
Abd-al-Mumin [Berber leader]
 Rabat R: 46
Abd al-Rahmān [Arab ruler]
 Muslims (The fall of the Abbāsids) M: 964c
'Abd al-Sabur, Salah [Egyptian author]
 Arabic literature (Poetry) A: 583
Abd al-Wahhab, Muhammad ibn [Arab religious leader]
 Saudi Arabia (The Saud dynasty) S: 160-161
Abdallahi, Sidi Ould Cheikh [Mauritanian political leader]
 Mauritania (History) M: 315-316
Abdel Rahman, Sheik Omar [Egyptian cleric]
 New York City (Problems) N: 342-343
Abdomen [anatomy] A: 8 *with diagram*
 See also the list of Related articles in the Abdomen article
 Insect *diagram on* I: 286; (Abdomen) I: 288
 Peritonitis P: 288
 Spider (The spider's body) So: 783-784 *with picture*
Abdominal hernia [disorder]
 Hernia H: 212
Abdominal muscles [anatomy]
 Physical fitness (Abdominal strength) P: 434
Abdominal oblique muscle [anatomy]
 Human body (table) H: 422 *with diagram*
Abduh, Muhammad [Egyptian lawyer] A: 9
 Muslims (Reform and renewal) M: 964d
Ábdu'l-Bahá [religious author]
 Bahá'u'lláh B: 28
Abdul Ilah [prince of Iraq]
 Iraq (Independence) I: 413
Abdul-Jabbar, Kareem [American basketball player] A: 9 *with picture*
 Basketball *picture on* B: 153
 Chamberlain, Wilt *picture on* C: 371
Abdul Rahman, Tunku [Malaysian political leader]
 Malaysia (Building national unity) M: 102
Abdülhamit II [sultan of the Ottoman Empire]
 Armenia (History) A: 718b

Ottoman Empire (The empire ends) O: 878
Turkey (The Ottoman decline) T: 510; (The Young
Turks) T: 510
Abdullah [king of Saudi Arabia] A: 9
Fahd F: 6
Abdullah II [king of Jordan] A: 9
Jordan (Recent developments) J: 165
Abdullah, Rania al- [queen of Jordan]
Abdullah II A: 9
Jordan (Recent developments) J: 165
Abdullah ibn Hussein [emir of Jordan]
Jordan (History) J: 164
Abdur Rahman Khan [emir of Afghanistan]
Afghanistan (The Anglo-Afghan wars) A: 95
Abdurrahman Wahid [Indonesian political leader]
Indonesia (Recent developments) I: 239
Abe, Kobo [Japanese author]
Japanese literature (The modern period) J: 62
Abe, Shinzo [Japanese political leader]
Japan (Recent developments) J: 59
Abe Lincoln in Illinois [play by Sherwood]
Sherwood, Robert Emmet S: 398
Abednego [Biblical figure]
Daniel, Book of D: 33
Abegweit [island]
Prince Edward Island P: 783
Abel [Biblical figure] A: 9
Cain C: 15
Jehovah's Witnesses J: 89
Abel, John Jacob [American chemist]
Drug (The drug revolution) D: 359
Abelard, Peter [French philosopher] A: 9
Abella, Rosalie Silberman [Canadian jurist]
Supreme Court of Canada (table) So: 997 with
portrait
Abelson, P. H. [American physicist]
Neptunium N: 130
Abenaki Indians
Indian, American (Indians of the Northeast)
I: 154-155
Maine (Early days) M: 89
Abercrombie, Neil [American political leader]
Hawaii (table) H: 105
Aberdeen [Scotland] A: 10
Aberdeen, Earl of [British political leader]
United Kingdom (table: British prime ministers)
U: 72
Aberdeen and Temair, Marquess of [British
statesman] A: 10
Aberdeen-Angus [breed]
Cattle (Aberdeen-Angus) C: 308 with picture;
(table) C: 312
Aberhart, William [Canadian political leader]
Alberta (table) A: 328
Abernathy, Ralph David [American social
reformer] A: 10 with portrait
Aberration [optics] A: 10 with diagrams
Telescope (Optical telescopes) T: 103-104
ABET, Inc.
Engineering (Professional organizations and
standards) E: 289
Abgeordnetenhaus [legislature]
Berlin (Government) B: 263
Abhisit Vejjajiva [Thai political leader]
Thailand (Recent developments) T: 228
Abidjan [Côte d'Ivoire] A: 11
Africa picture on A: 110
Côte d'Ivoire Ci: 1084a, picture on Ci: 1084b
Yamoussoukro Y: 550
Abilene [Kansas] A: 11
Westward movement in America (Cattle frontiers)
W: 251
Ability
Careers (Aptitudes) C: 215
Intelligence I: 319
Testing (Tests of learning ability) T: 182a
Ability to pay principle
Income tax (Current issues) I: 102
AbioCor artificial heart
Artificial heart A: 760 with picture
Abiotic environment
Ecology (Ecosystems) E: 54
Environment (Abiotic environment) E: 329
Abkhaz [language]
Abkhazia A: 11
Abkhazia [region] A: 11
Georgia (History) G: 111
Ablative case [grammar]
Case (Cases in Latin) C: 271-272
Able-bodied seaman
Ship (Officers and crew) S: 410
ABM [weapon] See Antiballistic missile in this index
ABM Treaty [1972]
Arms control (Arms control in the mid-1900's)
A: 721-722

Bush, George Walker (Arms control) B: 722h
Abnormal psychology A: 11
Psychology (Major fields of psychology) P: 848
ABO blood groups
Blood (The ABO blood groups) B: 412
Abolition movement [social reform] A: 12
See also the list of Related articles in the Abolition
movement article
African Americans (The antislavery movement)
A: 136h
Amistad Rebellion A: 433
Civil War, American (The Compromise of 1850)
Ci: 616
Emancipation Proclamation (Early views on
emancipation) E: 253
Garrison, William Lloyd G: 45
Grimké G: 393
Liberty Party L: 233
Lundy, Benjamin L: 523
Massachusetts (Progress as a state) M: 292
Ohio picture on O: 701
Philadelphia (Industrial beginnings) P: 366
Slavery (The decline of slavery) S: 504
Still, William So: 900
United States, History of the (The abolition
movement) U: 173
Women's movement (The beginnings of women's
movements) W: 384-385
Abolitionist Union Humane Society
Lundy, Benjamin L: 523
Abomasum [zoology]
Cattle (Stomach) C: 307 with diagram
Ruminant R: 519 with diagram
Abominable Snowman [legendary creature] See
Yeti in this index
Aboriginal Development Commission
Aborigines, Australian (Aboriginal life today)
A: 14
Aboriginal English [dialect]
Aborigines, Australian A: 13
Aboriginal Land Rights (Northern Territory) Act
[1976]
Aborigines, Australian (Aboriginal life today)
A: 14
Aborigines, Australian [people] A: 13 with pictures
Australia A: 894; (People) A: 900; (Painting)
A: 905 with picture; (History) A: 919
Boomerang B: 475
Bora ground B: 481
Exploration (Exploring Australia's interior) E: 448
National park (Australia) N: 42b-42c; (The rights
of original inhabitants) N: 42i
Outback O: 879
Races, Human (Climatic adaptations) R: 58
Rain forest (Australia and the Pacific Islands)
R: 126c
Stolen Generation So: 907
Tasmania (History) T: 49
Uluru U: 17
Abortion A: 14
Birth control (Methods of birth control) B: 378-
379; (In other countries) B: 379
Medical ethics M: 361
Miscarriage M: 617
National Right to Life Committee N: 60
Planned Parenthood Federation of America
P: 515
Roe v. Wade R: 399
Supreme Court of the United States (Civil rights)
So: 1001; (table) So: 1002
Terrorism (Terrorist groups and movements)
T: 178-179
Women's movement (In Western societies)
W: 386
Above the line cost
Motion picture (Preparing the final budget)
M: 851
Abraham [Biblical figure] A: 16
Hittites (History) H: 269-270
`Īd al-Ad-hā I: 25
Isaac I: 461
Ishmael I: 462
Islam (Prophets) I: 463; (The Five Pillars of Islam)
I: 463-464
Jews (Beginnings) J: 120
Judaism (The covenant with God) J: 179
Kaaba K: 208
Muslims (Before Muhammad) M: 964
Old Testament (Origins) O: 740
Qur'ān Q: 44
Religion (Judaism) R: 219
Sodom and Gomorrah So: 569
Abraham, F. Murray [American actor]
Motion picture (Best performance by an actor:
1984) M: 862a
Abraham, Spencer [American political leader]
Bush, George Walker (table) B: 722h

Energy, Department of (table) E: 276
Abraham and Isaac [woodcut by Van Leyden]
Van Leyden, Lucas picture on V: 283
Abraham and the Three Angels [painting]
Painting (Gothic painting) P: 50 with picture
Abraham Lincoln [book by Sandburg]
Sandburg, Carl S: 108; (His prose) S: 108
Abraham Lincoln [ship]
Aircraft carrier (The United States carrier fleet)
A: 206
Navy, United States picture on N: 82
Abraham Lincoln Bicentennial Commission
Lincoln's Birthday L: 329
**Abraham Lincoln Birthplace National Historical
Park** [Kentucky]
National Park System (table: National historical
parks) N: 56
**Abraham Lincoln Presidential Library and
Museum** [Springfield]
Illinois (Places to visit) I: 62
Lincoln, Abraham (Presidential library) L: 326
Abrahamson, Laura Iversen [American farmer]
Western frontier life in America (Farming) W: 238
Abram See Abraham in this index
Abramovich, Shalom Jacob [Yiddish author]
Hebrew literature (Modern Hebrew literature)
H: 162-163
Yiddish literature Y: 566
Abrams, Creighton W. [American general]
Vietnam War (The opposing forces) V: 375
Abrasive
Ceramics (Kinds of ceramic products) C: 359
Machine tool M: 18
Abrasive wheel cutting
Grinding and polishing (Grinding methods)
G: 395
Abreva [drug]
Cold sore Ci: 761
Abrikosov, Alexei A. [Russian-American physicist]
Nobel Prizes (Physics: 2003) N: 442
Abrupt appearance [belief]
Creationism (Recent developments) Ci: 1124
Abrupt climate change
Ice age (Evidence from modern galciers and from
caves) I: 7
Abruzzo, Ben [American balloonist]
Balloon (Long-distance balloon flights) B: 62
ABS [chemical]
Detergent and soap (The development of
detergents) D: 165
ABS [plastic]
Plastics (table) P: 556
Absalom [Biblical figure]
David (King of Israel) D: 45
Absalom, Absalom! [book by Faulkner]
Faulkner, William F: 55
Absalom and Achitophel [book by Dryden]
Dryden, John D: 370
English literature (John Dryden) E: 318
Absaroka Range [mountains]
Montana (Land regions) M: 752
Wyoming (Land regions) W: 526
Abscess [disorder] A: 17
Teeth (Performing root canal therapy) T: 83
Abscisic acid
Hormone (Other growth regulators) H: 337
Abscissa [mathematics]
Geometry (Analytic geometry) G: 105 with
diagrams
Abscission zone [botany]
Leaf (The leaf becomes fully grown) L: 152
Absecon Island [New Jersey]
Atlantic City A: 862
Absent without leave [military law] See AWOL in
this index
Absentee voting
Voting (Methods of voting) V: 449-450
Absolute advantage [economics]
International trade (Why nations trade) I: 348
Absolute dating [archaeology]
Archaeology (Dating) A: 598
Absolute dictatorship [government]
Absolutism A: 17
Absolute magnitude [astronomy]
Magnitude M: 62
Star diagrams on So: 844, So: 849; (Magnitude
and luminosity) So: 842
Absolute monarchy
Absolutism A: 17
French Revolution (Background) F: 524-525
Government (Monarchy) G: 286
Monarchy M: 700
Absolute monarchy [government]
Absolutism A: 17
Absolute property interest [law]
Property P: 827
Absolute temperature scale

Gas [physics] (Gas laws) **G:** 48
Absolute value
  Algebra (Positive and negative numbers)
    A: 352-353
Absolute veto
  Veto **V:** 346
Absolute zero [temperature] **A:** 17
  Heat (Refrigeration) **H:** 154; (The third law of
    thermodynamics) **H:** 154
  Matter (States of matter) **M:** 311
  Metric system (Heat) **M:** 440
  Superconductivity **So:** 992
  Temperature **T:** 130
  Thermodynamics **T:** 253
Absolutely True Diary of a Part-Time Indian, The
  [book by Alexie]
  Alexie, Sherman **A:** 345
Absolutism [political science] **A:** 17
  Political science (Constitutionalism) **P:** 639
Absorber [device]
  Refrigeration (The gas refigerator) **R:** 202 *with*
    diagram
Absorber cleaner [device]
  Air cleaner (Other types of air cleaners) **A:** 176
Absorption and adsorption [physics] **A:** 17 *with*
  diagrams
  Air cleaner (Other types of air cleaners) **A:** 176
  Charcoal (Uses of charcoal) **C:** 377
  Chromatography **C:** 537
  Ink (Printing inks) **I:** 273
  Laser (Producing laser light) **L:** 84
  Light (Reflection and absorption) **L:** 287
  Natural gas liquids **N:** 64
  Silica gel **S:** 457
Absorption hygrometer [measuring device]
  Hygrometer (Other hygrometers) **H:** 474
Absorption line [physics]
  Astronomy (Spectroscopy) **A:** 840
  Star (Color and temperature) **So:** 843-844
  Telescope (Analyzing spectra) **T:** 105
Abstinence-only program
  Sex education (How sex education is taught)
    S: 336
Abstract art A: 18
  Kandinsky, Wassily **K:** 213 *with picture*
  Modernism **M:** 685
  Painting (Abstract painting) **P:** 34; (The 1900's in
    Europe) **P:** 77 *with pictures*; (Abstract artists)
    P: 88 *with picture*
Abstract Expressionism [art] **A:** 18 *with picture*
  De Kooning, Willem **D:** 94 *with picture*
  Gorky, Arshile **G:** 277 *with picture*
  Krasner, Lee **K:** 386
  Mitchell, Joan **M:** 677
  Newman, Barnett **N:** 378
  Painting (Abstract Expressionism) **P:** 84 *with*
    picture
  Pollock, Jackson **P:** 646
  Rothko, Mark **R:** 487 *with picture*
  Stella, Frank **So:** 886
  Still, Clyfford **So:** 900
  Tomlin, Bradley Walker **T:** 326 *with picture*
  United States *picture on* **U:** 116
Abstract noun [grammar]
  Noun (Abstract and concrete nouns) **N:** 552
Abstract of title [law]
  Deed **D:** 81
Abstract reasoning aptitude
  Careers (Aptitudes) **C:** 215
Abstract surrealism [art]
  Painting (Surrealism) **P:** 81
Abstraction [philosophy]
  Child (The preteen-age years) **C:** 450
  Piaget, Jean **P:** 445
Absurd, Theater of the *See* Theater of the absurd
  in this index
Abū Bakr [Muslim caliph]
  Muhammad (His religious life) **M:** 910-911
  Muslims (The early caliphs) **M:** 964a
  Religion (Islam) **R:** 223
  Shi'ites **S:** 400
  Sunnis **So:** 991
Abu Dhabi [state, United Arab Emirates]
  United Arab Emirates **U:** 43
Abu Dhabi [city, United Arab Emirates] **A:** 19
  United Arab Emirates **U:** 43, *picture on* **U:** 44
Abu Ghraib [prison]
  Bush, George Walker (Iraq) **B:** 722i
  Iraq War (Disagreements over the war) **I:** 414f
  Prisoner of war **P:** 808
  War crime (Wars in Iraq) **W:** 27
Abu Mazen [Palestinian political leader] *See* Abbas,
  Mahmoud *in this index*
Abu Nuwas [Arab poet]
  Arabic literature (Poetry) **A:** 583
Abu Sayyaf Group
  Philippines (Recovering democracy) **P:** 381;

  (Recent developments) **P:** 381
Abu Simbel, Temples of [Egypt] **A:** 19
  Ramses II **R:** 134 *with picture*
Abū Tālib Manāf ibn Abd al-Muttalib [uncle of]
  Muhammad (Early life) **M:** 910
Abu Tammam [Arab poet]
  Arabic literature (Poetry) **A:** 583
Abu Zaby [United Arab Emirates] *See* Abu Dhabi
  in this index
Abubakar, Abdulsalami [Nigerian political leader]
  Nigeria (Changes in government) **N:** 418
Abuja [Nigeria] **A:** 19
  Lagos **L:** 31
  Nigeria **N:** 410 *with picture*
Abul Fazl [Indian author]
  Biography (The Renaissance) **B:** 313
Aby [cat] *See* Abyssinian cat *in this index*
Abyssal plain [oceanography]
  Atlantic Ocean (The Mid-Atlantic Ridge) **A:** 864
  Deep sea (The deep-sea floor) **D:** 82a
  Ocean (Deep-sea peaks, valleys, and plains)
    O: 662
Abyssinia [former African region]
  Bruce, James **B:** 647
  Ethiopia **E:** 368
Abyssinian cat
  Cat *picture on* **C:** 288; (Short-haired breeds)
    C: 290
Abzug, Bella Savitzky [American political leader]
  A: 19
AC [electricity] *See* Alternating current *in this index*
Ac [symbol]
  Actinium **A:** 30
Acacia [plant] **A:** 19 *with picture*
  Australia *picture on* **A:** 915; (Native plants) **A:** 911
  Catechu **C:** 299
  Plant (How plants protect themselves) **P:** 540-
    541 *with picture*
Academic American Encyclopedia [books]
  Encyclopedia (Encyclopedias of the 1800's and
    1900's) **E:** 268b
Academic aptitude test
  Testing (Tests of learning ability) **T:** 182a
Academic art
  Painting (The 1800's) **P:** 67
Academic debate
  Debate (Academic debate) **D:** 64
Academic Festival Overture [music by Brahms]
  Brahms, Johannes (His music) **B:** 549
Academic freedom A: 20
Academic Skepticism [philosophy]
  Skepticism **S:** 481
Academic World Book [encyclopedia]
  Encyclopedia (Today's encyclopedias)
    E: 268b-269
Academica [book by Cicero]
  Skepticism **S:** 481
Académie Française, L' [organization] *See* French
  Academy *in this index*
Academy [ancient Greece]
  Aristotle (Aristotle's life) **A:** 663
  Plato (Plato's life) **P:** 567
Academy [organization] **A:** 20
Academy [school]
  Colonial life in America (Education) **Ci:** 803
  Education (Development of U.S. education)
    E: 102
  Virginia (Schools) **V:** 402
Academy Awards [motion pictures]
  Motion picture (Festivals and awards) **M:** 861
    with picture; (table) **M:** 861 *with picture*
Academy of Arts and Letters, American
  American Academy of Arts and Letters **A:** 407
Academy of Arts and Sciences, American
  American Academy of Arts and Sciences **A:** 407
Academy of Ethical and Political Science
  Institute of France **I:** 305
Academy of Fine Arts [France]
  Institute of France **I:** 305
Academy of Inscriptions and Belles Lettres
  Institute of France **I:** 305
Academy of Model Aeronautics
  Airplane, Model **A:** 240
Academy of Motion Picture Arts and Sciences
  A: 20
  Motion picture (Festivals and awards) **M:** 861
    with picture
Academy of Music
  Philadelphia (The arts) **P:** 363
Academy of Natural Sciences
  Philadelphia (Libraries and museums) **P:** 363-364
Academy of Sciences [France]
  Institute of France **I:** 305
Academy of Television Arts and Sciences
  Television (Television awards) **T:** 116
Acadia [Canadian history] **A:** 21 *with map*
  Cajuns **C:** 19

  Grand Pré **G:** 309
  New Brunswick *pictures on* **N:** 184; (French rivals)
    N: 196
  Nova Scotia (Exploration and settlement) **N:** 567-
    568; (The struggle in Acadia) **N:** 568
Acadia National Park [Maine] **A:** 21
  Camping *picture on* **C:** 92
  Maine (Places to visit) **M:** 78 *with picture*
  National Park System (table: National parks) **N:** 48
Acadian flycatcher [bird]
  Flycatcher **F:** 311 *with picture*
Acadian Geology [book by Dawson]
  Dawson, Sir John William **D:** 51
Acadian Museum [New Brunswick]
  New Brunswick (Museums) **N:** 185
Acadiana [Louisiana]
  Louisiana *picture on* **L:** 499; (Places to visit) **L:** 488
Acallam na Senórach [story]
  Irish literature (Heroic tales, romances, and sagas)
    I: 430
Acamprosate [drug]
  Alcoholism (Treatment) **A:** 338
Acanthocephala [zoology]
  Animal (A classification of the animal kingdom)
    A: 506 *with picture*
Acanthodes [fish]
  Prehistoric animal *picture on* **P:** 738
Acanthodian [zoology]
  Fish (The first fish) **F:** 171
Acanthus [shrub] **A:** 21
Acapulco [Mexico] **A:** 21 *with picture*
ACBL [organization]
  Bridge (Regulation of tournaments) **B:** 605
Accelerando
  Music (table) **M:** 954
Acceleration [physics]
  Motion (Describing motion) **M:** 844
  Calculus (Differential calculus) **C:** 22-23
  Falling bodies, Law of **F:** 17
  Force (Acceleration) **F:** 369
  G **G:** 2
  Gravitation **G:** 331
  Inertia **I:** 262
  Mass **M:** 268
  Metric system (Space and time) **M:** 437
  Relativity (Inertial frames) **R:** 210-211; (Principle
    of equivalence) **R:** 211-212
  Velocity (Acceleration) **V:** 297
Accelerator [chemistry]
  Rubber (Compounding and mixing) **R:** 505
Accelerator [device]
  Automobile *diagram on* **A:** 952
  Rocket (Ion rockets) **R:** 389
Accelerator, Particle *See* Particle accelerator *in*
  this index
Accelerator mass spectrometry [technique]
  Archaeology (Dating) **A:** 598
Accelerometer [measuring device]
  Acoustics **A:** 29
  Automatic flight control system (How an AFCS
    works) **A:** 944
  Inertial guidance **I:** 263
Accent [language] **A:** 22
Accent [music]
  Music (Rhythm) **M:** 951
Accent light
  Lighting (In the home) **L:** 296
Acceptable Time, An [book by L'Engle]
  L'Engle, Madeleine **L:** 191
Acceptance [economics]
  Draft **D:** 318
Acceptance speech
  Political convention (Making nominations)
    P: 629-630
Access point [computing]
  Wireless communication (Wireless networking)
    W: 345
Accessory [decoration]
  Interior design (Selecting accessories) **I:** 333 *with*
    pictures
Accessory [heraldry]
  Heraldry (Elements of a coat of arms) **H:** 196 *with*
    pictures
Accessory molecule [biochemistry]
  Immune system (The cell-mediated immune
    response) **I:** 88
Accident
  See also First aid; Safety *in this index*
  Fire department (Emergency rescue operations)
    F: 124; (Special fire vehicles) **F:** 127
  Safety **S:** 9
  Trauma center **T:** 405
Accident, The [book by Wiesel]
  Wiesel, Elie **W:** 299
Accident insurance
  No-fault insurance **N:** 438
Accidental [music]

Music (Indicating pitch) **M:** 952-953
Accidental death rider
  Insurance (Riders) **I:** 311
Accidental infanticide [crime]
  Infanticide **I:** 264
Accidental President [term for]
  Vice president of the United States **V:** 348
Accipiter [bird]
  Bird of prey **B:** 374a
  Hawk **H:** 111
Accius, Lucius [Roman poet]
  Latin literature (Early Latin literature) **L:** 115-116
Acclimatization [biology]
  Adaptation **A:** 46
Accolade [ceremony]
  Knights and knighthood (Knighting) **K:** 348
Accommodation [physiology]
  Eye (Focusing) **E:** 462-463 *with picture*
  Farsightedness **F:** 48
Accommodations of Desire [painting by Dalí]
  Dalí, Salvador *picture on* **D:** 10
Accordion [musical instrument] **A:** 22 *with pictures*
Account executive [occupation]
  Advertising (Creating advertisements) **A:** 76a
Account manager [occupation]
  Advertising (Creating advertisements) **A:** 76a
"Account of a Visit from St. Nicholas, An" [poem
  by Moore] *See* "'Twas the Night Before Christmas"
  in this index
Account take-over [crime]
  Identity theft **I:** 46
Accountability [education]
  Curriculum (Curriculum changes) **Ci:** 1197
  Education (Accountability testing) **E:** 106
  Teaching (The effectiveness of teaching) **T:** 69
Accountancy *See* Accounting *in this index*
Accounting A: 22
  Bookkeeping **B:** 472 *with pictures*
  Careers (Technical and mathematical
    occupations) **C:** 232
  Computer (Spreadsheet programs) **Ci:** 917
Accra [Ghana] **A:** 24
  Ghana *picture on* **G:** 180
Accreditation [education]
  Community college (Accrediting) **Ci:** 898
  Universities and colleges (Accrediting) **U:** 207
Accretion [geology]
  Growth (In nonliving things) **G:** 404
  Jupiter (Formation of Jupiter) **J:** 200b
  Life (Growth) **L:** 275
  Satellite (Formation) **S:** 150
Accretion disk [astronomy]
  Neutron star **N:** 155
Acculturation [anthropology]
  Culture (Contact with other cultures) **Ci:** 1189
Accumulator [device]
  Hybrid car **H:** 461
ACCUS [organization]
  Automobile racing (Racing organizations)
    A: 976-977
Accusative case [grammar]
  Case (Cases in Latin) **C:** 271-272
Accutane [drug]
  Acne **A:** 28
Ace [aviation] **A:** 24
  Air force (World War I) **A:** 185
  Air Force, United States (World War I) **A:** 194
  World War I (The war in the air) **W:** 460-461
Ace [tennis]
  Tennis (The serve) **T:** 163
ACE inhibitor [drug]
  Blood pressure **B:** 416
Ace Ventura: Pet Detective [film]
  Carrey, Jim **C:** 247
Aceh [province, Indonesia]
  Indonesia (Recent developments) **I:** 239
  Sumatra **So:** 972
Acehnese [people]
  Sumatra **So:** 971
ACEI [organization] *See* Childhood Education
  International, Association for *in this index*
Acela Express [train]
  Railroad (Intercity trains) **R:** 105-106
  Transportation *picture on* **T:** 391
Acellular microorganism
  Microbiology (Microorganisms) **M:** 513
Acerola [tree] **A:** 24 *with picture*
Acesulfame-K [synthetic food]
  Artificial sweetener **A:** 761
Acetabulum [anatomy]
  Hip **H:** 238
Acetal [plastic]
  Plastics (table) **P:** 556
Acetaminophen [drug] **A:** 24
  Analgesic **A:** 448
  Pain (Treatment) **P:** 22
Acetate [fiber] **A:** 25

Cellulose (Industrial uses) **C:** 341
  Fiber (Regenerated fibers) **F:** 87
  Textile (Manufactured fibers) **T:** 213
Acetic acid [chemical] **A:** 25
  Acid (The strength of an acid) **A:** 27
  Cider **Ci:** 552
  Vinegar (Making vinegar) **V:** 386
Acetification [industrial process]
  Vinegar (Making vinegar) **V:** 386
Acetobacter [bacteria]
  Vinegar (Making vinegar) **V:** 386
Acetone [chemical] **A:** 25
Acetyl-coenzyme A [compound]
  Krebs cycle **K:** 387
  Metabolism (Catabolism) **M:** 424
Acetylation [process]
  Acetate **A:** 25
Acetylcholine [biochemistry]
  Alzheimer's disease (Treatment) **A:** 399
  Atropine **A:** 878
  Myasthenia gravis **M:** 970e
Acetylene [gas] **A:** 25
  Gas [fuel] (How gas is manufactured) **G:** 55
  Hydrocarbon (Aliphatic hydrocarbons) **H:** 465
  Welding (Gas welding) **W:** 189
Acetylsalicylic acid [drug] *See* Aspirin *in this index*
Acevedo Vilá, Aníbal [Puerto Rican political leader]
  Puerto Rico (Puerto Rico today) **P:** 884
Achaean League [ancient Greece]
  Achaeans **A:** 25
Achaeans [people] **A:** 25
Achaemenid Empire
  Aryans **A:** 764
  Persia, Ancient (The Achaemenid Empire) **P:** 298
    picture and *with map*
  Sculpture (Middle Eastern) **S:** 233 *with picture*
Acheampong, I. K. [Ghanaian political leader]
  Ghana (History) **G:** 179-180
Achebe, Chinua [Nigerian author] **A:** 25
Achene [botany]
  Sycamore **So:** 1062
Achernar [star]
  Star (table: The 10 brightest stars as seen from
    Earth) **So:** 842
Acheron [legendary river]
  Hades **H:** 4
Acheson, Dean Gooderham [American statesman]
  A: 26
  Truman, Harry S. (table) **T:** 469
Acheson, Edward [American inventor]
  Graphite **G:** 323
Acheson-Lilienthal Report [U.S. history]
  Acheson, Dean Gooderham **A:** 26
Achieved status [sociology]
  Clothing (Identity) **Ci:** 687-688
Achievement test
  Testing (Tests of learning achievement) **T:** 182
Achille Lauro [ship]
  Reagan, Ronald Wilson (Terrorism) **R:** 170
Achilles [legendary figure] **A:** 26
  Alexander the Great (His youth) **A:** 342
  Hector **H:** 164
  Iliad **I:** 51
  Priam **P:** 774
  Trojan War (The siege of Troy) **T:** 449
  Ulysses (The Trojan War) **U:** 17-18
Achilles and Ajax Playing Checkers [painting by
  Exekias]
  Painting (Greek painting) **P:** 42 *with picture*
Achilles tendon [anatomy] **A:** 26
  Leg (The leg) **L:** 182
Achondrite
  Meteor (Meteorites) **M:** 432
Achondroplasia [disorder]
  Dwarfism (Causes) **D:** 394-395
Acid [chemistry] **A:** 26
  See also the list of Related articles in the Acid *article*
  Acid reflux **A:** 27
  Antacid **A:** 529
  Etching **E:** 364
  First aid (Eye injury) **F:** 140
  Food additive (Kinds of additives) **F:** 339-340
  Gardening (Analyzing the soil) **G:** 31-32
  Hydrogen (Compounds) **H:** 469
  Litmus **L:** 391
  Neutralization **N:** 154
  pH **P:** 353
  Soil (Chemical conditions) **So:** 575
Acid dye
  Dye (Synthetic dyes) **D:** 395-396
Acid rain **A:** 27
  Amphibian (Amphibians and people) **A:** 442
  Appalachian Mountains (Recreation and wildlife)
    A: 568
  Conservation (Energy conservation) **Ci:** 983-984;
    (Canada) **Ci:** 988
  Energy supply (Environmental effects) **E:** 281

Environmental pollution *picture on* **E:** 333; (Air
    pollution) **E:** 331
  Global warming (Geoengineering) **G:** 232c
  Petroleum (Air pollution) **P:** 345
  Rain (Characteristics of rain) **R:** 122-123
  Water pollution (Industrial wastes) **W:** 136
Acid reflux [disorder] **A:** 27
Acid rock [music] *See* Psychedelic rock *in this index*
Acid test [geology]
  Mineral (Other identification tests) **M:** 567
Acidimeter [measuring device]
  Hydrometer **H:** 471
Acidophile [biology]
  Extremophile **E:** 458
Acidophilus milk [food]
  Milk (At a processing plant) **M:** 547
Acini [anatomy]
  Breast **B:** 590
Acklins Island [Bahamas]
  Bahamas (Land and climate) **B:** 29 *with map*
ACL [anatomy] *See* Anterior cruciate ligament *in
  this index*
ACLU [organization] *See* American Civil Liberties
  Union *in this index*
Acmeists [literature]
  Russian literature (Post-symbolism) **R:** 563
Acne [disorder] **A:** 27 *with diagrams*
  Dermatology **D:** 153
  Pimple **P:** 466
  Pore **P:** 678
Aco, Michel [French explorer]
  Iowa (Exploration and early settlement) **I:** 393
Acoelomate [biology]
  Coelom **Ci:** 753
Acoma [hill, New Mexico]
  New Mexico (Land regions) **N:** 266
Acoma Indians
  United States, History of the *picture on* **U:** 151
Aconcagua [mountain, Argentina] **A:** 28
  Andes Mountains (Physical features) **A:** 452 *with
    map*
  Argentina (The Andean Region) **A:** 653
  Mountain (table) **M:** 896 *with diagram*
  South America (The Andes Mountains) **So:** 626
    with picture
  Volcano (table) **V:** 442b
Aconite [plant] **A:** 28 *with picture*
Aconitine [chemical]
  Aconite **A:** 28
Acorn [nut] **A:** 28
  Indian, American (Before European contact)
    I: 163-164
  Oak **O:** 635 *with pictures*
  Plant (How plants protect themselves) **P:** 540-541
Acorn squash [vegetable]
  Squash (Winter squashes) **So:** 813 *with picture*
Acorn woodpecker [bird]
  Woodpecker (Kinds) **W:** 394
Acoustic fan [device]
  Hearing aid (History) **H:** 131
Acoustic-homing torpedo
  Torpedo (How a torpedo works) **T:** 340d-341
Acoustic mine
  Mine warfare (Naval mines) **M:** 565
Acoustic neuroma [disorder]
  Ear (Diseases) **E:** 12
Acoustic spectrum [physics]
  Acoustics **A:** 28
Acoustical engineering
  Engineering (Other specialized fields) **E:** 287
Acoustical guitar
  Guitar **G:** 435 *with pictures*
Acoustician [scientist]
  Acoustics **A:** 29
Acoustics [physics] **A:** 28
  Physics (Sound) **P:** 437
  Sound (table) **So:** 599; (Controlling sound)
    So: 604
Acquired blindness
  Blindness **B:** 401
Acquired immunity [physiology]
  Immune system **I:** 87
Acquired immunodeficiency syndrome [disorder]
  See AIDS *in this index*
Acquired immunological tolerance
  Burnet, Sir Macfarlane **B:** 708
Acquired land
  Public lands **P:** 857
Acquisition [business]
  Merger **M:** 417
Acquisition editor [occupation]
  Publishing (Editors and fact checkers) **P:** 867
Acquisitions librarian
  Library (Careers for librarians) **L:** 255
Acquittal [law]
  Jury (Petit juries) **J:** 202
  Trial (Reaching a verdict) **T:** 436

Acre [former name, Akko]
Crusades (Other Crusades) Ci: 1161
Acre [measurement] A: 29
Acreage allotment [agriculture]
Farm and farming (Federal farm programs) F: 44
Acrisius [Greek mythology]
Perseus P: 295
Acrobatic skiing
Skiing (Freestyle skiing) S: 483
Acrobatics
Circus *picture on* Ci: 565; (At the circus) Ci: 562 *with picture*
Gymnastics G: 447 *with pictures*
Acrocorinth [ruins, Greece]
Citadel Ci: 567
Corinth Ci: 1053
Acromegaly [disorder]
Giant G: 183
Human growth hormone H: 427
Acromion [anatomy]
Collarbone Ci: 773 *with diagram*
Acronym [abbreviation]
Abbreviation A: 7
Memory (Mnemonic devices) M: 393
Slang (Acronyms) S: 500
Acrophobia [psychology]
Phobia P: 392
Acropolis [hill] A: 29 *with picture*
Architecture (Classical Greek architecture) A: 615-616
Athens (Landmarks) A: 854-855 *with picture and map*; (The Acropolis and its buildings) A: 856
Greece, Ancient (The land) G: 366; (The arts) G: 369
Parthenon P: 183
Across the River and Into the Trees [book by Hemingway]
Hemingway, Ernest (Later years) H: 180
Acrylic [material] A: 29
Fiber (Synthetic fibers) F: 87
Interior design (Choosing patterns and textures) I: 332
Plastics (table) P: 556; (Growth of the plastics industry) P: 560
Rugs and carpets (Materials used in rugs and carpets) R: 514
Acrylic paint
Paint (Household paints) P: 23
Painting (Synthetic resins) P: 40
Acrylonitrile [chemical]
Cyanide Ci: 1202
ACT [territory] *See* Australian Capital Territory *in this index*
ACT [test]
College entrance examination (In the United States) Ci: 775
Act of ...
Laws that begin Act of *or* Act for *appear under their key words, as in* Union, Act of
Act of God [law]
Common carrier Ci: 874
Acta Apostolicae Sedis [newspaper]
Vatican City (Communications) V: 288
Acta Diurna [journalism]
Communication (During ancient times) Ci: 879
Journalism (The first newspapers) J: 174
Rome, Ancient (Transportation and communication) R: 443-444
ACTH [hormone]
Adrenal gland A: 67
Endorphin E: 272
Hormone (Endocrine control hormones) H: 336
Steroid (The adrenal steroids) So: 894-895
Acting
Careers (Sports and entertainment) C: 230-231
Hispanic Americans (Entertainment and arts) H: 249-250
Method acting M: 434
Motion picture (How motion pictures are made) M: 848 *with pictures*; (table: Academy Award winners) M: 862
Opera (The singers) O: 792
Shakespeare, William (Acting companies) S: 352
Television (Planning and preparation) T: 110c-110d
Theater T: 232; (Casting) T: 236; (The performers) T: 237 *with pictures*
Actinide [chemistry] A: 30
Element, Chemistry *diagram on* E: 221
Lanthanide L: 69
Actinium [element] A: 30
Radiation (Naturally radioactive substances) R: 77
Actinoid [chemistry] *See* Actinide *in this index*
Actinomyces [bacteria]
Actinomycosis A: 30
Actinomycosis [disease] A: 30
Actinopterygian [zoology]

Fish (The Age of Fishes) F: 171
Action [gun]
Handgun (Parts of a handgun) H: 43
Rifle (The parts of a rifle) R: 338
Action [piano]
Piano (The action) P: 446 *with picture*
ACTION [U.S.]
Peace Corps P: 207
Action at a distance [physics]
Relativity (General relativity) R: 211
Action figure [toy]
Doll (The 1960's) D: 293
Action for Cities [program]
United Kingdom (City life) U: 55
Action painting [art]
Abstract Expressionism A: 19
Painting (Abstract Expressionism) P: 84-85
Action potential [physiology]
Brain (Action potentials) B: 557
Myelin M: 970f
Nervous system (Conduction along the axon) N: 135
Actium, Battle of [31 B.C.] A: 30
Agrippa, Marcus A: 162
Cleopatra (Cleopatra and Mark Antony) Ci: 662a-662b
Rome, Ancient (The later years of the republic) R: 445-446
Activated carbon
Water (Purifying and treating water) W: 126
Activated charcoal
Charcoal C: 377; (Uses of charcoal) C: 377
Activated sludge process
Sewage (Secondary treatment) S: 330 *with diagram*
Activation energy [chemistry]
Chemical reaction C: 397 *with diagram*
Activation product [physics]
Radiation (Artificial radioactive substances) R: 77-78
Active autofocus [photography]
Camera (Automatic focusing) C: 82
Photography (Types of lenses) P: 411
Active euthanasia
Death (The right to die) D: 61
Euthanasia (Active euthanasia) E: 421
Active galactic nucleus [astronomy]
Quasar Q: 9
Active galaxy [astronomy]
Galaxy (Other types of galaxies) G: 8b
Active imagination [psychology]
Jung, Carl Gustav (His theories) J: 195
Active immunity
Immune response (How the body develops immunity) I: 88a
Active immunization *See* Vaccine *in this index*
Active layer [geology]
Arctic (Soil conditions) A: 636
Permafrost P: 289
Active medium [electronics]
Laser L: 81; (Parts of a laser) L: 83 *with diagram*
Active noise cancellation [sound]
Sound (Modern acoustics) So: 606
Active prominence [astronomy]
Sun (Prominences) So: 981 *with picture*
Active religious order [group]
Religious life R: 226
Active sonar system
Sonar (How sonar works) So: 591
Active structural-acoustic control [sound]
Sound (Modern acoustics) So: 606
Active voice [grammar]
Conjugation Ci: 951
Voice V: 437
Active volcano
Volcano (Predicting eruptions) V: 442a-442b
Activity badge
Boy Scouts *pictures on* B: 536
Activity center
Preschool (Preschool instruction) P: 756b
Activity series [chemistry] *See* Electromotive series *in this index*
Acton, Lord [British historian] A: 30
Actor and actress *See* Acting *in this index*
Actors Studio
Method acting M: 434
Actress *See* Acting *in this index*
Acts of the Apostles [New Testament] A: 31
Bible (table) B: 281; (The Acts of the Apostles) B: 284
Jesus Christ (The New Testament Gospels) J: 104-105
New Testament (The Acts of the Apostles) N: 287
Acts of the Apostles [tapestry]
Tapestry (History) T: 39-40
Actual cash value
Insurance (Property and liability insurance) I: 312

Actual fraud [law]
Fraud F: 496
Actual malice [law]
Libel L: 226
Actual tide [geology]
Tide (The actual tide) T: 282
Actuary [career]
Insurance I: 309; (Careers in the industry) I: 315
Actuator [machine]
Materials M: 300b
Acuff, Roy [American musician] A: 31
Country music (Emergence of the country music industry) Ci: 1098b-1098c
Popular music *picture on* P: 670
Acupuncture [treatment] A: 31 *with picture*
Alternative medicine A: 388
Asian Americans (Asian influences on American culture) A: 812c-812d
Cancer (Alternative medicine) C: 173
China (Health care) C: 485
Medicine (China and India) M: 372
Acushnet [ship]
Melville, Herman (His early life) M: 390
Acute angle [mathematics]
Angle A: 462 *with diagram*
Acute epiglottis [disorder]
Croup Ci: 1157
Acute glaucoma [disorder]
Eye (Glaucoma) E: 466
Acute glomerulonephritis [disorder]
Scarlet fever (Complications) S: 173
Acute hemolytic transfusion reaction [disorder]
Blood transfusion (Risks of transfusion) B: 417
Acute infection [medicine]
Virus (Infection) V: 428-428a
Acute mountain sickness
Altitude sickness A: 390
Acute otitis media [disorder]
Ear (Diseases) E: 12
Acute pain
Pain P: 21
Acute retroviral syndrome [disorder]
AIDS (Stages of HIV infection) A: 164a
Acute triangle [geometry]
Triangle (Kinds of triangles) T: 437 *with diagram*
Acutely psychotic infanticide [homicide]
Infanticide I: 264
ACV [insurance]
Insurance (Property and liability insurance) I: 312
ACV [vehicle] *See* Air cushion vehicle *in this index*
Acyclovir [drug]
Antiviral drug A: 560
Cold sore Ci: 761
Elion, Gertrude Belle E: 236
Herpes, Genital H: 214
A.D. [calendar] A: 31
Calendar (Some calendars today) C: 29
Christian Era C: 522e
Ad [communications] *See* Advertising *in this index*
AD [disease] *See* Alzheimer's disease *in this index*
Ad [sports]
Tennis (Scoring) T: 162-163
Ad Dawhah *See* Doha *in this index*
Ad interim committee
State government (Organization) So: 863-864
Ad-lib
Radio (Putting a show on the air) R: 86
Ad libitum
Music (table) M: 954
Ad valorem tariff [economics]
Tariff (Main kinds of tariffs) T: 43
ADA [enzyme] *See* Adenosine deaminase *in this index*
ADA [law] *See* Americans with Disabilities Act *in this index*
ADA [organization]
Americans for Democratic Action A: 431
Adagio [dance]
Ballet (A ballet class) B: 46-47
Adagio [music]
Music (table) M: 954
Adagio for Strings [music by Barber]
Barber, Samuel B: 16
Adalat [drug]
Calcium channel blocker C: 21
Adam [Scottish architects] A: 31 *with picture*
Adam, James [Scottish architect]
Adam (family) A: 31
Adam, Robert [Scottish architect]
Adam (family) A: 31 *with picture*
Architecture (Neoclassical architecture) A: 623-624 *with picture*
Furniture (English neoclassical furniture) F: 579 *with picture*
Museum *picture on* M: 937
Adam and Eve [Biblical figures] A: 32
Byzantine art *picture on* B: 750

Eden E: 76
Islam (Prophets) I: 463
Roman Catholic Church (Sin, the Incarnation, and salvation) R: 403
Adam Bede [book by Eliot]
Eliot, George E: 237
Adams, Abigail Smith [wife of John Adams] A: 32
Adams, John *picture on* A: 36; (Adams's family) A: 34; (Life in the White House) A: 39
First ladies of the United States F: 142
Washington, George (Life in the Executive Mansion) W: 101-102
Adams, Alva [American political leader]
Colorado (Interesting facts) Ci: 829; (table) Ci: 844
Adams, Ansel [American photographer] A: 32 *with picture*
Adams, Brock [American government official]
Carter, Jimmy (table) C: 257
Transportation (table) T: 400
Adams, Brooks [American historian] A: 33
Adams, Charles [son of]
Adams, John (Adams's family) A: 34-35
Adams, Charles Francis [1807-1886, American statesman] A: 33
Adams, John Quincy (Adams's family) A: 41
Civil War, American (Relations with Europe) Ci: 623
Adams, Charles Francis [1866-1954, American government official]
Hoover, Herbert Clark (table) H: 330
Adams, George Washington [son of]
Adams, John Quincy (Adams's family) A: 41
Adams, Gerry [Irish political leader] A: 33
Adams, Sir Grantley Herbert [West Indian political leader]
Barbados (History) B: 104
Adams, Henry [American colonist]
Adams, John (Childhood) A: 34
Adams, Henry [American historian] A: 33
American literature (Nonfiction writers) A: 420
Biography (The 1800's) B: 420
Adams, J. M. G. [Barbadian political leader]
Barbados (History) B: 104
Adams, Jewett W. [American political leader]
Nevada (table) N: 173
Adams, John [American composer]
Classical music (Classical music today) Ci: 651 *with picture*
Opera (American opera) O: 800
Adams, John [British adventurer]
Pitcairn Island P: 498
Adams, John [father of]
Adams, John (Childhood) A: 34
Adams, John [son of]
Adams, John Quincy (Adams's family) A: 41
Adams, John [U.S. president] A: 34 *with pictures*
Adams, Abigail Smith A: 32
Constitution of the United States (The background of the Constitution) Ci: 1000
Declaration of Independence *picture on* D: 77
First ladies of the United States F: 142
Hamilton, Alexander (Political disputes) H: 33
Jefferson, Thomas (The Declaration of Independence) J: 79 *with picture*; (Vice president) J: 82; (The sage of Monticello) J: 87
Logan Act L: 423
Marshall, John (Political career) M: 230
Revolution, American *picture on* R: 278; (The Treaty of Paris) R: 286
United States, History of the (Problems in foreign affairs) U: 163
Vice president of the United States (President of the Senate) V: 352; (Early days) V: 352-353
Washington, George (table) W: 102; (Farewell Address) W: 106
Adams, John C. [British astronomer]
Astronomy (Finding new objects) A: 848
Neptune (Discovery) N: 129
Adams, John Quincy [U.S. president] A: 40 *with pictures*
Adams, Charles Francis A: 33
Amistad Rebellion A: 433
Calhoun, John Caldwell (Early career) C: 35
Electoral College (History) E: 164
Public opinion poll (History) P: 863
United States, History of the (The election of 1824) U: 170
Adams, Louisa Johnson [wife of John Q. Adams]
Adams, John Quincy *picture on* A: 42; (Diplomat) A: 41
First ladies of the United States (table) F: 142
Adams, Mount [New Hampshire]
New Hampshire (Mountains) N: 220 *with map*
Adams, Samuel [American patriot] A: 44 *with portrait*
Boston Tea Party B: 506

Massachusetts (table) M: 288
Revere, Paul R: 267
Revolution, American (The Tea Act) R: 273-274
Adams, Samuel Hopkins [American author] A: 44
Adams, Scott [American cartoonist] A: 44 *with picture*
Adams, Sherman [American government official] A: 44
Eisenhower, Dwight David (Midterm elections) E: 154
New Hampshire (table) N: 223
Adams, Susanna [daughter of]
Adams, John (Adams's family) A: 34-35
Adams, Susanna Boylston [mother of]
Adams, John (Childhood) A: 34
Adams, Thomas [American druggist]
Chewing gum (History) C: 416-417
Chicle C: 446
Adams, Thomas [American lawyer]
Adams, John (Adams's family) A: 34-35
Adams, Victoria [British singer]
Beckham, David B: 197
Adams, William H. [American political leader]
Colorado (table) Ci: 844
"Adams and Liberty" [song]
"Star-Spangled Banner" (How the song became famous) So: 854
Adam's apple [anatomy]
Larynx L: 79
Adams Museum and House [Deadwood]
South Dakota (Museums) So: 668
Adams National Historic Site [Quincy, Massachusetts]
Adams, John *picture on* A: 35
Adams, John Quincy *picture on* A: 41
Adams National Historical Park [Massachusetts]
National Park System (table: National historical parks) N: 56
Adam's needle [tree]
Yucca Y: 575
Adams-Onís Treaty [1819]
Florida (The second Spanish period) F: 262
Louisiana Purchase (Boundary disputes) L: 503
Adams ring [astronomy]
Neptune (Satellites and rings) N: 129
Planetary ring P: 5145
Adamson, George [British conservationist]
Adamson, Joy A: 45
Adamson, Joy [British conservationist] A: 45
Adamson Act [1916]
Goethals, George Washington (Engineer and supply officer) G: 246
Wilson, Woodrow (Legislative program) W: 322-323
Adán Buenosayres [book by Marechal]
Latin American literature (The mid-1900's) L: 114
Adapid [animal]
Primate (The evolution of primates) P: 778b
Adaptation [biology] A: 45 *with picture*
See also Natural selection *in this index*
Animal (Animals of the polar regions) A: 484; (The bodies of animals) A: 488 *with picture*
Fish (Bony fish) F: 147-148
Human (Human body) H: 413
Island (How life develops on islands) I: 473
Life (Adaptation) L: 275
Plant (The evolution of plants) P: 544
Races, Human (Evolutionary theory) R: 53-54; (The population approach) R: 57; (Climatic adaptations) R: 58
Adapter [electronic device]
Telephone (VoIP phone calls) T: 97-98
Adaptive immune system [biology]
Virus (Immune response) V: 428a
Adaptive immunity [physiology] *See* Acquired immunity *in this index*
Adaptive optics
Astronomy (Adaptive optics) A: 842
Light (Light in medicine) L: 292
Telescope (Producing detailed images) T: 103; (Adaptive optics systems) T: 106
ADB [organization] *See* Asian Development Bank *in this index*
ADD [disorder] *See* Attention deficit disorder *in this index*
Adda River [Italy]
Lake Como L: 37 *with map*
Addams, Charles [American cartoonist] A: 46
Cartoon (Single panel cartoons) C: 265-266 *with picture*
Addams, Jane [American social reformer] A: 46 *with portrait*
American literature (Nonfiction writers) A: 420
Hull House H: 412
King, William Lyon Mackenzie (Education) K: 325
Nobel Prizes *picture on* N: 448; (Peace: 1931) N: 448a *with picture*

Addams family [fictional characters]
Addams, Charles A: 46
Addax [animal] A: 46 *with picture*
Animal *picture on* A: 483
Addend [mathematics]
Addition (Writing addition) A: 49
Adder [electronics]
Electronics (Digital circuits) E: 213-214
Adder [snake] A: 46 *with picture*
Viper V: 391
Adderley, Cannonball [American saxophonist]
Davis, Miles *picture on* D: 49
Adder's-tongue [plant] *See* Dogtooth violet *in this index*
Addiction
See also Drug abuse *in this index*
Electronic game (Controversy) E: 205
Smoking S: 520
Adding machine
See also Calculator *in this index*
Abacus A: 3
Burroughs, William B: 711
Adding Machine, The [play by Rice]
Drama *picture on* D: 339
Rice, Elmer R: 328
Addington, Henry [British political leader]
United Kingdom (table: British prime ministers) U: 72
Addis Ababa [Ethiopia] A: 47 *with picture*
Ethiopia E: 368 *with picture*; (Transportation and communication) E: 371
Menelik II M: 400
Addison, Joseph [English author] A: 47
English literature (Addison and Steele) E: 318
Essay (Personal essays) E: 359
Steele, Sir Richard So: 882
Addison, Thomas [British doctor] A: 48
Addison's disease A: 48
Addison, Thomas A: 48
Addition [mathematics] A: 48 *with pictures*
Algebra (Addition) A: 354
Arithmetic (Addition) A: 665 *with pictures*; (Subtraction) A: 666; (Arithmetic of negative numbers) A: 668-669
Binary number (In arithmetic) B: 307
Decimal system (Addition and subtraction) D: 71 *with diagrams*
Fraction (Calculations using fractions) F: 446
Additive [industry]
See also Food additive *in this index*
Gasoline (Gasoline additives) G: 61
Livestock (Feed) L: 397
Plastics (Making synthetic resins) P: 556
Additive color mixture
Color (Mixing colored lights) Ci: 821-822 *with diagram*
Addonizio, Hugh [American political leader]
Newark (History) N: 357-358
Address [correspondence]
Letter writing (The inside address) L: 210 *with picture*; (The envelope address) L: 211 *with pictures*
Address, Forms of [language] A: 53
Capitalization (Titles) C: 196
Letter writing (The salutation) L: 210
Addresses to the German Nation [book by Fichte]
Fichte, Johann Gottlieb F: 90
Adductor muscle [zoology]
Hand *diagrams on* H: 40
Human body (table) H: 422 *with diagram*
Mollusk (Bivalves) M: 695
Oyster (Shell) O: 890 *with diagram*
Scallop S: 170 *with picture*
Shell *diagram on* S: 385; (Bivalves) S: 388
Ade, George [American author] A: 54
Adelaide [Australia] A: 55
Exploration (Exploring Australia's interior) E: 448
South Australia So: 639 *with picture and map*
Adelaide Festival Centre [Adelaide]
South Australia *picture on* So: 639
Adelchi [play by Manzoni]
Italian literature (Romanticism) I: 495
Adélie penguin [bird] A: 55 *with picture*
Antarctica (Living things) A: 534-535 *with picture*
Penguin *pictures on* P: 239
Adelman, Leonard [American computer scientist]
Codes and ciphers (Public-key systems) Ci: 750
Adelphean [literary society]
Sorority So: 597
Adelphi [buildings, London]
Adam [family] A: 32
Adelson e Salvini [opera by Bellini]
Bellini, Vincenzo B: 244
Aden [city, Yemen] A: 55
Yemen Y: 561; (Economy) Y: 563 *with picture*
Aden Protectorates [former region]
Yemen (Formation of South Yemen) Y: 563

Adena Indians
Mound builders (Woodland Period) **M: 882**
Adena State Memorial [Chillicothe]
Ohio (Places to visit) **O: 690**
Adenauer, Konrad [German statesman] **A: 55** *with portrait*
De Gaulle, Charles André Joseph Marie (The Fifth Republic) **D: 91**
Germany (West Germany) **G: 170**
Adenauer Allee [street, Bonn]
Bonn (The city) **B: 460**
Adenine [biochemistry]
DNA **D: 258**
Heredity (The structure of DNA) **H: 205**
RNA **R: 357**
Adenoids [anatomy]
Lymphatic system (Lymphoid tissue) **L: 534**
Tonsil **T: 329**
Adenosine deaminase [enzyme]
Gene therapy **G: 82**
Heredity (The era of genetic engineering) **H: 209**
Adenosine triphosphate *See* ATP *in this index*
Adeodatus I [pope]
Pope (table) **P: 666**
Adeodatus II [pope]
Pope (table) **P: 666**
Ader, Clément [French engineer]
Airplane (Powered flight) **A: 230**
Áder, János [Hungarian political leader]
Hungary (Recent developments) **H: 448**
ADH [hormone] *See* Antidiuretic hormone *in this index*
ADHD [disorder] *See* Attention deficit disorder *in this index*
Adhesion [physics] **A: 56**
Adhesion [physiology] **A: 56**
Adhesive A: 56
Gum **G: 440**
Woodworking (Fastening) **W: 398**
Adi Granth [book]
Sikhism (Beliefs and practices) **S: 455**
Adirondack Cottage Sanitarium [New York]
Trudeau, Edward Livingston **T: 460**
Adirondack Mountains [New York] **A: 56**
New York (Land regions) **N: 304** *with map*; (Mountains) **N: 306**; (Lakes) **N: 306-307**
Adirondack Park [New York]
Adirondack Mountains **A: 56**
New York (Places to visit) **N: 302**
Adit [passage]
Mining (Mining terms) **M: 577**
Adja [people]
Benin (People) **B: 249**
Adjacent side [geometry]
Polygon **P: 650** *with diagram*
Adjectival [grammar]
Adjective (Classifying adjectives) **A: 57**
Adjective [grammar] **A: 56**
Adverb (Simple adverbs) **A: 70**; (Adverb-adjective confusion) **A: 71**
Capitalization (Adjectives taken from proper nouns) **C: 196**
Comparison **Ci: 902b**
Grammar **G: 303**
Participle **P: 184**
Adjudication
Debate (Adjudication) **D: 64**
Adjustable gastric banding [surgery]
Bariatric surgery **B: 109**
Adjustable-rate mortgage
Mortgage **M: 820**
Adjusted gross income
Income tax (Figuring the individual income tax) **I: 104**
Adjustment [treatment]
Chiropractic **C: 514**
Adjutant [bird] **A: 58** *with picture*
Adjuvant drug therapy [medicine]
Cancer (Multimodality therapy) **C: 172**
Adkins, Homer Martin [American political leader]
Arkansas (table) **A: 712**
Adler, Alfred [Austrian psychiatrist] **A: 58**
Freud, Sigmund (His life) **F: 530**
Adler, Dankmar [American architect] **A: 58**
Architecture (Early modern architecture in America) **A: 629**
Sullivan, Louis Henri **So: 970**
Wright, Frank Lloyd (Early career) **W: 507**
Adler Planetarium & Astronomy Museum [Chicago]
Chicago (Museums) **C: 428-429**
Illinois (Museums) **I: 56**
Adlerian psychology
Adler, Alfred **A: 58**
Administration
Political science (Public administration) **P: 638**
Administration, Office of [U.S.]

President of the United States (The executive branch) **P: 764**
Administration for Children and Families [U.S. government] *See* Children and Families, Administration for *in this index*
Administration of Justice Act [1774]
Intolerable Acts **I: 353**
Administration on Aging [U.S.]
Health and Human Services, Department of (Organization) **H: 128**
Administrative agency
Law (Public law) **L: 130-131**
Administrative law
Law (Public law) **L: 130-131**
Administrative ruling
Law (Public law) **L: 130-131**; (How laws are changed) **L: 132**
Administrative support
Careers (Administrative support) **C: 219** *with picture*
Administrator [law] **A: 58**
Will (Administration) **W: 307**
Admirable Crichton, The [play by Barrie]
Barrie, J. M. **B: 118**
Admiral [butterfly]
Butterfly *picture on* **B: 735**
Admiral [rank] **A: 58**
Navy, United States *pictures on* **N: 86**
Rank, Military (table) **R: 140**
Admiral David Farragut [sculpture by Saint-Gaudens]
Saint-Gaudens, Augustus **S: 33**
Admiral Nakhimov [ship]
Shipwreck (table: Major shipwrecks) **S: 428**
Admiral of the Ocean Sea [title]
Columbus, Christopher *picture on* **Ci: 861**
Admiralty [government] **A: 59**
Admiralty Board [Britain]
Admiralty **A: 59**
Admiralty Islands [Papua New Guinea] **A: 59** *with picture*
Bismarck Archipelago **B: 382**
Admiralty law *See* Maritime law *in this index*
Admission [law]
Confession **Ci: 936**
Admixture
Cement and concrete (Materials) **C: 343**
Admonitions of the Instructress to the Court Ladies [painting by Gu Kaizhi]
Gu Kaizhi **G: 407**
Painting (Chinese painting) **P: 44-45** *with picture*
Adobe [building material] **A: 59** *with picture*
Indian, American (Shelter) **I: 136d-141**; (Before European contact) **I: 166-167**
Pueblo Indians (Early history and way of life) **P: 871** *with picture*
Adobo [food]
Philippines (Way of life) **P: 374-375**
Adoian, Vosdanig Manoog [American painter] *See* Gorky, Arshile *in this index*
Adolescent A: 60 *with pictures*
See also Teenager *in this index*
Acne **A: 27**
Anorexia nervosa **A: 519**
Drug abuse (Causes and effects of drug abuse) **D: 364**
Erikson, Erik Homburger **E: 352**
Growth (Growth rate) **G: 405**
Optimist International **O: 813**
Pimple **P: 466**
Psychoanalysis (Psychoanalytic theory) **P: 846**
Sexuality (Biological factors) **S: 337-338**
Adolescent, The [play by Fonvizin]
Russian literature (The classical movement) **R: 559-560**
Adolescent egocentrism [psychology]
Adolescent (Intellectual development) **A: 61-62**
Adolescent medicine
Medicine (table) **M: 369**
Adolphus, Gustavus *See* Gustavus Adolphus *in this index*
Adonai [name for God]
God **G: 243**
Jehovah **J: 89**
Adonais [poem by Shelley]
Shelley, Percy Bysshe (His life) **S: 391**
Adonis [legendary figure] **A: 65** *with picture*
Aphrodite **A: 565**
Phoenicia (Religion) **P: 393-394**
Adonis [plant] **A: 65** *with picture*
Adonis blue [butterfly]
Butterfly *picture on* **B: 734**
Adoption [law] **A: 65**
See also Foster person *in this index*
Family (Family relationships) **F: 21**
Adoption Assistance [program]
Children's Bureau **C: 457**

Adoration of the Kings [painting by Leonardo]
Leonardo da Vinci (Leonardo's life) **L: 199** *with picture*; (Paintings) **L: 200b**
Adoration of the Shepherds, The [painting by Giorgione]
Jesus Christ *picture on* **J: 104**
Adoula, Cyrille [Congolese political leader]
Congo, Democratic Republic of the (Civil disorder) **Ci: 940c**
ADPKD [disease]
Polycystic kidney disease **P: 649**
Adrastea [satellite]
Jupiter (Inner satellites) **J: 200a** *with picture*
Planetary ring **P: 514d**
Adrenal body [zoology]
Frog *picture on* **F: 537**
Adrenal cortex [anatomy]
Adrenal gland **A: 67** *with diagram*
Cortisone **C: 1073**
Hormone (Metabolic hormones) **H: 335-336**; (Blood composition hormones) **H: 336**
Stress (How stress affects the body) **So: 926-927**
Adrenal gland [anatomy] **A: 67** *with diagram*
Addison's disease **A: 48**
Cortisone **C: 1073**
Epinephrine **E: 343**
Gland (Endocrine glands) **G: 207** *with diagram*; (table) **G: 208**
Human body (table) **H: 422** *with diagram*
Steroid (The adrenal steroids) **So: 894**
Stress (How stress affects the body) **So: 926-927**
Adrenalin [hormone]
See also Epinephrine *in this index*
Adrenal gland **A: 67**
Drug (The drug revolution) **D: 359**
Hormone (Stress hormones) **H: 336**
Adria [Italy]
Adriatic Sea **A: 68**
Adrian [Roman emperor] *See* Hadrian *in this index*
Adrian I [pope]
Pope (table) **P: 666**
Adrian II [pope]
Pope (table) **P: 666**
Adrian III, Saint [pope]
Pope (table) **P: 666**
Adrian IV [pope] **A: 67**
Pope (table) **P: 666**
Adrian V [pope]
Pope (table) **P: 666**
Adrian VI [pope]
Pope (table) **P: 666**
Adrian, Edgar Douglas [British physiologist]
Nobel Prizes (Physiology or medicine: 1932) **N: 445**
Adrianople [Turkey]
Edirne **E: 77**
Adrianople, Battle of [378]
Edirne **E: 77**
Adrianople, Treaty of [1829]
Turkey (The Ottoman decline) **T: 510**
Adriatic Sea [Mediterranean] **A: 68** *with map*
Adsorption *See* Absorption and adsorption *in this index*
Adsorption cleaner
Air cleaner (Other types of air cleaners) **A: 176**
Adulis [ancient city]
Aksum **A: 255** *with map*
Adult education A: 68 *with pictures*
Careers (Teaching) **C: 231**
Correspondence school **Ci: 1071**
Education (Kinds of education) **E: 87-88**
Library (Services for adults) **L: 241**
Literacy (Illiteracy in the United States) **L: 351-352**
United States (Schools) **U: 113** *with picture*
Adult stage [entomology]
Ant (Reproduction) **A: 524** *with picture*
Adultery
Marriage (Marriage problems) **M: 221**
Adulthood
Adolescent (The "invention" of adolescence) **A: 60**
Adult education **A: 68**
Growth (When people stop growing) **G: 406**
Indian, American (Children) **I: 136c**
Minor **M: 607**
Sleep (Human sleep patterns) **S: 506**
Voting (Who may vote) **V: 449**
Adunis [Lebanese poet]
Arabic literature (Poetry) **A: 583**
Advance [publishing]
Publishing (Contracts and advances) **P: 866**
Advance directive [document]
Death (The right to die) **D: 61**
Euthanasia (Termination of life-sustaining treatment) **E: 421**
Living will **L: 399**
Advanced Camera for Surveys

Hubble Space Telescope (History) H: 404
Advanced Cruise Missile
   Guided missile (Air-to-surface missiles) G: 426
Advanced Encryption Standard [cryptology]
   Codes and ciphers (Later developments) Ci: 751-752
Advanced Light Source [physics]
   Lawrence Berkeley National Laboratory L: 146
Advanced light water reactor [machine]
   Nuclear energy (Advanced fission reactors) N: 594
Advanced Medium Range Air-to-Air Missile
   Guided missile (Air-to-air missiles) G: 426
Advanced Photon Source [machine]
   X rays *picture on* X: 542
Advanced Placement Program
   College entrance examination (In the United States) Ci: 775
Advanced Research Projects Agency [U.S.]
   Internet (The early Internet) I: 350g
Advanced train control system
   Railroad (Other train controls) R: 112
Advancement of Learning, The [book by Bacon]
   Bacon, Francis B: 18
   Philosophy (Modern philosophy) P: 388
Advantage [tennis]
   Tennis (Scoring) T: 162-163
Advection fog
   Fog F: 314 *with diagram*
Advent [religion] A: 70
   Christianity (Forms of worship) C: 522h-523
   Christmas (Religious practices) C: 533 *with picture*
Advent wreath
   Christmas (Religious practices) C: 533 *with picture*
Adventists [religious groups] A: 70
   Seventh-day Adventists S: 328
Adventitious bud [botany]
   Bud B: 666
Adventitious root [botany]
   Root (Kinds of roots) R: 469-470 *with diagram*
Adventure [organization]
   Camp Fire USA *picture on* C: 90; (Small group programs) C: 88 *with picture*
Adventure [ship]
   Cook, James (Second Pacific voyage) Ci: 1026
Adventure Aquarium [Camden]
   New Jersey (Places to visit) N: 240
Adventure Galley [ship]
   Kidd, William K: 311
Adventure Science Center [Nashville]
   Tennessee (Museums) T: 139 *with picture*
Adventure story
   Literature for children (Adventure and survival stories) L: 359
Adventurer [English history]
   London Company L: 445
Adventures of Augie March, The [book by Bellow]
   Bellow, Saul B: 244
   Novel (After World War II) N: 574
Adventures of Huckleberry Finn [book by Twain]
   See Huckleberry Finn *in this index*
Adventures of Master F. J., The [book by Gascoigne]
   Gascoigne, George G: 60
Adventures of Pinocchio, The [book by Collodi]
   Collodi, Carlo Ci: 776
   Fairy (Fairy tales) F: 11
Adventures of Prince Achmed [film]
   Animation (Animation in Europe) A: 514b
Adventures of Tom Sawyer, The [book by Twain]
   See Tom Sawyer *in this index*
Adventures of Uncle Sam, The [book]
   Uncle Sam U: 19
Adverb [grammar] A: 70
   Adjective (Usage) A: 57
   Comparison Ci: 902b
   Grammar G: 303
   Verb (Multiple-word verbs) V: 315
Adverbial [grammar]
   Adverb A: 70
Advergame
   Internet (Advertising) I: 350b
Adverse possession [law]
   Occupancy O: 647
   Title T: 302
Advertising A: 72 *with pictures*
   Careers (Sales) C: 229-230
   Cartoon (Advertising) C: 266; (Developing the idea) C: 266-267
   Cigarette T: 553
   Colonial life in America (Why the colonists came to America) Ci: 788
   Commercial art Ci: 872
   Consumer protection (The right to information) Ci: 1018
   E-mail E: 3
   Internet (Advertising) I: 350b

Journalism (Criticism of the press) J: 173
Magazine (Scheduling the advertising) M: 43; (How magazines earn income) M: 44
Marketing (Promotion) M: 214
Modeling (A model's work) M: 685
Motion picture (Distribution) M: 860
Neon *picture on* N: 124
Newspaper (The business department) N: 382; (Preparing advertisements) N: 383; (Advertising) N: 385
Propaganda (Businesses) P: 824
Public relations (Methods) P: 863-864
Radio (Stations and networks) R: 90
Sales S: 62
Television (Commercial television) T: 110a; (The national networks) T: 113; (Commercial stations) T: 114
Tobacco (History) T: 307-308
Advertising agency
   Advertising (Creating advertisements) A: 76a; (Advertising agencies) A: 77; (The development of advertising agencies) A: 79
Advertising art *See* Commercial art *in this index*
Advertising campaign
   Advertising (Creating advertisements) A: 76a
Advertising Council [organization]
   Advertising (Advertising associations) A: 77
Advertising Review Board, National
   Advertising (Advertising associations) A: 77
Advertising service and supply house
   Advertising (Production) A: 76b
Advertising song [biology]
   Bird (Calls and songs) B: 354
Advertising Standards Canada [organization]
   Consumer protection (The right to information) Ci: 1018
Advice and consent [government]
   Constitution of the United States (Article II, Section 2) Ci: 1009
"Advice to My Country" [Madison]
   Madison, James (Later years) M: 36
Advocacy journalism
   Journalism (Influencing public opinion) J: 173
Advocates' Library
   Edinburgh E: 77
Adwa, Battle of [1896]
   Ethiopia (Menelik II) E: 371
Adz [tool]
   Indian, American *picture on* I: 139
AE [pen name]
   Russell, George William R: 524
Aeacus [Greek mythology]
   Hades H: 4
AEC *See* Atomic Energy Commission *in this index*
Aëdes aegypti [mosquito]
   Yellow fever Y: 556
A.E.F. [organization] A: 81
   American Legion (History) A: 413
   Pershing, John Joseph P: 295
   World War I (American troops in Europe) W: 463 *with picture*
AEG Turbine Factory [Berlin]
   Architecture (Early modern architecture in Europe) A: 627-629 *with picture*
   Behrens, Peter B: 221
Aegean Bronze Age
   Aegean civilization A: 82
Aegean civilization A: 82 *with picture and map*
   Painting (Aegean painting) P: 41 *with picture*
   Sculpture (Aegean) S: 234 *with pictures*
Aegean Islands [Mediterranean]
   Greece (The Aegean Islands) G: 358 *with map*
Aegean Sea [Mediterranean] A: 83 *with map*
   Dardanelles D: 35
Aegeus [Greek mythology]
   Medea M: 360
   Theseus T: 257
Aegis [Roman mythology] A: 84
   Minerva M: 572
Aegisthus [legendary figure]
   Cassandra C: 275
   Clytemnestra Ci: 715
   Electra E: 165
Aegospotami, Battle of [405 B.C.]
   Lysander L: 538
AEI [organization] *See* American Enterprise Institute for Public Policy Research *in this index*
Aelfric [English author]
   English literature (Old English prose) E: 315
Aelia Capitolina [former city]
   Jerusalem (Roman rule) J: 101
Aemilianus [Roman emperor]
   Rome, Ancient (table) R: 447
Aeneas [Greek mythology] A: 84
   See also Aeneid *in this index*
   Aeolus A: 84
   Mythology *picture on* M: 988; (The *Aeneid*) M: 983

Aeneid [book by Virgil] A: 84
   Dido D: 195
   Juno J: 197
   Laocoön L: 70
   Latin literature (The Augustan Age) L: 116
   Mythology (The *Aeneid*) M: 983
   Neptune N: 128
   Poetry (Ancient poetry) P: 595-596
   Trojan War (The fall of Troy) T: 449
   Virgil (His works) V: 391-392
Aeolian harp [musical instrument] A: 84
Aeolians [ancient people] A: 84
Aeolus [Greek mythology] A: 84
Aepycamelus [animal]
   Prehistoric animal *picture on* P: 740
Aerated water
   Mineral water M: 572
Aeration [process]
   Sewage (Secondary treatment) S: 330 *with diagram*
   Water (Purifying and treating water) W: 126
Aerenchyma [botany]
   Wetland (Plant life) W: 252a
Aerial [device] *See* Antenna *in this index*
Aerial ballet [circus act]
   Circus *picture on* Ci: 565
Aerial Experiment Association
   Bell, Alexander Graham (His later life) B: 241
Aerial-ladder truck
   Fire department (Ladder trucks) F: 126 *with picture*
Aerial perspective [art]
   Leonardo da Vinci (Paintings) L: 200b
   Perspective P: 304 *with picture*
Aerial photogrammetry [cartography]
   Photogrammetry P: 405
Aerial photography
   Archaeology (Locating sites) A: 595-596 *with picture*
   City planning *picture on* Ci: 600
   Fairchild, Sherman Mills F: 9
   Map (How maps are made) M: 180; (Mapmaking and modern technology) M: 185
   Photogrammetry P: 405 *with pictures*
Aerial root [botany]
   Root (Kinds of roots) R: 469-470 *with diagram*
Aerial skiing [sport]
   Skiing (Freestyle skiing) S: 483
Aerial spraying [process]
   Airplane (Special-purpose planes) A: 212 *with picture*
Aerial stem [botany]
   Plant (Stems) P: 529
Aerial survey
   See also Photogrammetry *in this index*
   Surveying (Types of surveys) So: 1011
Aerial yellow jacket [insect]
   Hornet H: 340
Aerialist [performer]
   Circus (At the circus) Ci: 562 *with picture*
Aerie [chapter]
   Eagles, Fraternal Order of E: 6
Aerie [nest]
   Eagle (Nests) E: 4
Aero Club of America
   Aviation (The first flying regulations) A: 987
Aerobatics
   Airplane (Special-purpose planes) A: 212-213 *with picture*
Aerobe [bacteriology]
   Bacteria (Where bacteria live) B: 21
   Environmental pollution (Water pollution) E: 334
   Water pollution *diagram on* W: 137; (Disruption of natural processes) W: 138
Aerobee
   Rocket (High-altitude rockets) R: 390
Aerobic power
   Physical fitness (Performance-related fitness) P: 433-434; (Health-related fitness) P: 434
Aerobics [exercise] A: 84
   Hydrotherapy *picture on* H: 473
   Physical fitness (Developing physical fitness) P: 435
   Running R: 520
Aerodonetics [study]
   Glider (After World War I) G: 230
Aerodrome [aircraft]
   Airplane (Powered flight) A: 230-231
   Langley, Samuel Pierpont L: 61
Aerodynamics [physics] A: 85 *with pictures*
   See also the list of Related articles in the Aerodynamics *article*
   Airplane A: 208; (First human flights) A: 230
   Fluid mechanics (External fluid mechanics) F: 304
   Parachute (Parts of a parachute) P: 142
   Sailing (Why a boat sails) S: 25
Aeroflot [airline]

Russia (Transportation and communication)
R: 546
Aerogel [insulating material] A: 88 *with picture*
Materials *picture on* M: 301
Aeronautic Association, National
National Aeronautic Association N: 27
Aeronautical chart
Airplane (Pilotage) A: 226
Map (Navigation maps) M: 178
Aeronautical Division [U.S. Army]
Air Force, United States (Early years) A: 194
Aeronautics *See* Airplane; Aviation *in this index*
**Aeronautics and Space Administration,
National** *See* National Aeronautics and Space
Administration *in this index*
Aeroplane *See* Airplane *in this index*
Aerosol [chemistry] A: 89 *with diagram*
Air (Particles in the air) A: 170
Colloid Ci: 777
Dust D: 390
Global warming (Causes of global warming)
G: 232; (Geoengineering) G: 232c
Ozone hole O: 894
Aerosol can
Aerosol A: 89 *with picture*
Aerospace engineering
Engineering (Aerospace engineering) E: 284
Aerospace industry
Aviation A: 983; (Industry mergers) A: 991
Aerospace medicine A: 89
**Aerospace Workers, International Association of
Machinists and** *See* Machinists and Aerospace
Workers, International Association of *in this index*
Aerotowing [aviation]
Hang gliding H: 51
Aeschylus [Greek dramatist] A: 90
Drama (Tragedy) D: 326
Furies F: 566 *with picture*
Greek literature (Drama) G: 377
Sophocles So: 595
Aesculapius [Roman mythology] *See* Asclepius *in
this index*
Aesir [Norse mythology]
Mythology (The construction of the world)
M: 986
Aeson [Greek mythology]
Jason J: 64
Aesop [Greek storyteller]
Aesop's fables A: 90
Aesop's fables [stories] A: 90
Allegory A: 371
Fable F: 3
La Fontaine, Jean de L: 29
Literature for children (Fables) L: 359 *with picture*
Aesthetic Education of Mankind [book by Schiller]
Schiller, Johann Christoph Friedrich von S: 175
Aesthetic experience
Philosophy (Aesthetics) P: 385
Aesthetics [philosophy] A: 90
Art and the arts (The aesthetic experience)
A: 745; (Enjoying the arts) A: 748; (Studying
the arts) A: 748
Philosophy (Aesthetics) P: 385
Aestivation *See* Estivation *in this index*
Aeta [people]
Philippines (Early days) P: 379
Aethra [Greek mythology]
Theseus T: 257
Aëtius, Flavius [Roman military leader]
Valentinian III V: 264
Aetna, Mount *See* Mount Etna *in this index*
AFA [organization]
Arts, American Federation of A: 763
Afaan Oromo [language]
Ethiopia (People) E: 368
Afars [people]
Djibouti (People) D: 256
Ethiopia (People) E: 368
Afars and Issas [former territory]
Djibouti D: 256
AFB [organization] *See* American Foundation for
the Blind *in this index*
AFC [electronics] *See* Automatic frequency control
in this index
AFCS [aviation] *See* Automatic flight control system
in this index
AFDC [program] *See* Aid to Families with
Dependent Children *in this index*
Afer, Publius Terentius *See* Terence *in this index*
Afewerk, Issaias [Eritrean political leader]
Eritrea (History) E: 353-354
Affective disorder [psychology] *See* Mood disorder
in this index
Affel, Herman A. [American engineer]
Cable (Telephone cables) C: 6
Coaxial cable (History) Ci: 740
Affenpinscher [dog] A: 91

Dog *picture on* D: 274
Affidavit [law] A: 91
Affiliate [communications]
Radio (Stations and networks) R: 90
Television (The U.S. television industry) T: 113
Affinity [sociology]
Family (Family relationships) F: 21
Affirmation [law]
Oath (Affirmation) O: 639
Affirmative action [employment] A: 91
African Americans (Economic and social
progress) A: 136p-136q; (Developments since
1970) A: 136r
Civil rights (Major changes in the field of civil
rights) Ci: 609
Conservatism (Features of political conservatism)
Ci: 991
Liberalism (Features of liberalism) L: 228
Stevens, John Paul So: 896
Affirmative defense [law]
Sexual harassment (Sexual harassment law)
S: 337
Affluent Society, The [book by Galbraith]
Galbraith, John Kenneth G: 9
Affordability
Housing (Affordable housing) H: 391
Afforestation [process]
Forestry (Planting) F: 405
AFGE [organization] *See* American Federation of
Government Employees *in this index*
Afghan hound [dog] A: 91
Dog *picture on* D: 271
Afghan wars *See* Afghanistan War; Anglo-Afghan
wars *in this index*
Afghānī, Jamāl al-Din al- [Iranian political leader]
Abduh, Muhammad A: 9
Muslims (Reform and renewal) M: 964d
Afghanistan A: 92 *with pictures and maps*
*See also the list of Related articles in the
Afghanistan article*
Asia (The decline of Communism) A: 808
Bin Laden, Osama B: 307
Brezhnev, Leonid Ilyich (Policies) B: 596
Bush, George Walker (Bush's first administration
[2000-2003]) B: 722g; (Afghanistan) B: 723
Carter, Jimmy (Foreign affairs) C: 257-258
Clinton, Bill (International affairs) Ci: 682f
Cold War Ci: 763
Communism (Communist influence in other
areas) Ci: 894
Gorbachev, Mikhail Sergeyevich (International
policies) G: 272
Guerrilla warfare (History) G: 420 *with picture*
Immigration (Asia) I: 85
International relations (The war against
terrorism) I: 346
Karzai, Hamid K: 247
Khyber Pass K: 309 *with map*
Middle East M: 530; (The 1970's and 1980's)
M: 534a
Pashtuns P: 190
Qa`ida, Al- Q: 2
September 11 terrorist attacks S: 310
Taliban T: 19
Turkestan (Afghan Turkestan) T: 501
Union of Soviet Socialist Republics (The collapse
of détente) U: 40
United States, History of the (September 11
terrorist attacks) U: 196d
Afghanistan War [2001-] A: 97
Afghanistan (Recent developments) A: 96
Air Force, United States (The war in Afghanistan)
A: 196
Bush, George Walker (Terrorist attacks and
military action) B: 722f; (Afghanistan) B: 722h
Improvised explosive device I: 95
Karzai, Hamid K: 247
Navy, United States (Wars in Iraq and
Afghanistan) N: 89
North Atlantic Treaty Organization (History)
N: 471
Obama, Barack (Foreign affairs) O: 641
Pakistan (Musharraf) P: 100
September 11 terrorist attacks (Global war on
terrorism) S: 310a
Taliban T: 19
World, History of the (The war on terrorism)
W: 448b
AFL [organization] *See* American Federation of
Labor *in this index*
AFL-CIO [organization] *See* American Federation of
Labor and Congress of Industrial Organizations
in this index
Aflatoxin [botany]
Mycotoxin M: 970f
AFM [device] *See* Atomic force microscope *in this*

index
Afonso I [king of Kongo]
Kongo K: 364
Afonso I [king of Portugal]
Lisbon (History) L: 348
Portugal (Founding the Portuguese nation)
P: 693
Afonso Henriques [king of Portugal] *See* Afonso I
in this index
Africa A: 98 *with pictures and maps*
Bird (Birds of Africa) B: 344h *with pictures*
Library (Africa) L: 252
Arts
Africa (The arts) A: 115 *with pictures*
Bell *picture on* B: 239
Doll (Traditional dolls) D: 287 *with picture*
Music (African music) M: 956
Pottery *picture on* P: 717
Sculpture (African sculpture) S: 239 *with
pictures*
Business and industry
Africa (Communication) A: 129
Bank (Banks throughout the world) B: 91
Newspaper (In Africa and the Middle East)
N: 386
Railroad (In Africa) R: 114
Television (In Africa) T: 116
Textile (In Africa) T: 218
Health and welfare
AIDS (AIDS around the world) A: 166; (History)
A: 166
Medicine (Unequal distribution of medical
care) M: 377
Sleeping sickness S: 507
History
Africa (History) A: 129 *with pictures*
Amistad Rebellion A: 433
Berlin Conference B: 266
Cold War (Africa) Ci: 768
Colonialism (Later colonialism) Ci: 813-814;
(Effects of colonialism) Ci: 815
Columbus, Christopher (The plan to sail
westward) Ci: 858
Exploration (The first explorers) E: 439;
(Reaching the tip of Africa) E: 443 *with map*;
(The exploration of Africa) E: 448 *with map*
Henry the Navigator H: 191
Hispanic Americans (Cultural backgrounds)
H: 247 *with picture*
Human being (Human physical development)
H: 414
Immigration (Africa) I: 85
Kingsley, Mary Henrietta K: 331
Magic (Africa and the Americas) M: 50
Nubia N: 578
Patriotism (Foundations of patriotism) P: 198
Prehistoric people (The earliest hominids)
P: 744; (The first human beings) P: 746;
(Migration from Africa) P: 747; (The origin of
Homo sapiens) P: 748-749
Roman Catholic Church (In Africa) R: 411
Slavery (The Middle Ages) S: 501-502; (Modern
times) S: 502
Stanley and Livingstone So: 837 *with map*
Union of Soviet Socialist Republics (Brezhnev
comes to power) U: 39
United Nations *picture on* U: 90
World, History of the (African civilizations)
W: 437 *with picture*; (Imperialism) W: 445;
(The birth of new nations) W: 448 *with
picture*
Language
Africa (Languages) A: 105
Language (Other language families) L: 66
Natural resources
Conservation (Africa) Ci: 990
Diamond (Where natural diamonds are found)
D: 181
National park (table) N: 42f
Rain forest (Africa) R: 126b *with map*
People
Africa (People) A: 104 *with pictures*
African Americans (The African background)
A: 136c *with pictures and maps*
Arabs A: 584
Clothing *pictures on* Ci: 687, Ci: 692; (Clothing
of Africa) Ci: 698 *with picture*
Family (Non-Western families) F: 24 *with picture*
Population (World population) P: 672
Races, Human R: 52; (Susceptibility to genetic
diseases) R: 58
Vodou V: 436
Physical features
Africa (The land) A: 116b *with pictures and
maps*
Continent Ci: 1021
Continental divide Ci: 1022

Great Rift Valley **G: 347**
Monsoon **M: 740**
Plate tectonics (The rifting of continents) **P: 562** *with diagrams*
Africa, Star of *See* Star of Africa *in this index*
Africa Nova [Roman province]
Libya (Early days) **L: 267**
Africaine, L' [opera by Meyerbeer]
Meyerbeer, Giacomo **M: 479**
African American English
African Americans (Developments since 1970) **A: 136r**
African American History, Museum of [Detroit]
See Museum of African American History *in this index*
African American literature A: 136
American literature (Nonfiction writers) **A: 420**; (The Harlem Renaissance) **A: 422**; (The African American experience) **A: 424**; (Works by minority writers) **A: 425**; (Drama) **A: 426**
Harlem Renaissance **H: 61**
Novel (After World War II) **N: 574**; (The novel today) **N: 575**
African-American Struggle for Freedom, The [book by Myers]
Myers, Walter Dean **M: 970f**
African Americans A: 136b *with pictures*
See also the list of *Related articles in the* African Americans *article*
Arts
See also African American literature *in this index*
Ballet (Ballet in the United States) **B: 53-54**
Country music (The roots of country music) **Ci: 1098a**
Dance (Modern dance) **D: 30-31**
Folk art *picture on* **F: 320**
Folk music (American folk music) **F: 321-322**
Folklore *picture on* **F: 325**
Gospel music **G: 277**
Popular music (Popular music before recording) **P: 669**; (The recording era) **P: 671**
Rap music **R: 141**
Rhythm and blues **R: 320**
Rock music (Beginnings of rock music) **R: 376**; (Rock 'n' roll gains popularity) **R: 377**; (Soul music) **R: 380a**; (Rap) **R: 380d**
Spiritual **So: 796**
United States *picture on* **U: 111**
Health
African Americans (Health issues) **A: 136s**
Prostate cancer **P: 829**
Sickle cell anemia **S: 447**
History
Amistad Rebellion **A: 433**
Atlanta (History) **A: 861**
Buffalo Soldiers **B: 680**
Civil War, American (Blacks and the war) **Ci: 621** *with picture*
Colonial life in America (The lower class) **Ci: 794**
Family (Early Western families in America) **F: 22-23**
Freedom (The 1900's) **F: 503**
Freedom riders **F: 508**
Gay Nineties (Social developments) **G: 72**
Great Depression (Human suffering) **G: 340-341**
Illinois (The early 1900's) **I: 75**
Latin America (Ancestry) **L: 92-94**
Liberia **L: 229**
Lynching **L: 535**
March on Washington **M: 196**
Mississippi (The mid-1900's) **M: 644**
New Deal (Helping industry and labor) **N: 201**
North America (People) **N: 458-459**
Pioneer life in America (Why the pioneers headed west) **P: 476-477**
Pittsburgh (People) **P: 500b**
Reconstruction **R: 176** *with picture*
Revolution, American (The fighting forces) **R: 278-279**
Scalawags **S: 169**
Scottsboro case **S: 223**
Selma marches **S: 290**
Slavery (Slavery in the United States) **S: 502** *with picture*
Tuskegee Airmen **T: 525**
United States, History of the (The South and white supremacy) **U: 183-185**; (Poverty and discrimination) **U: 195** *with picture*; (Protests and progress [1960-1999]) **U: 196** *with picture*
Voting (Who may vote) **V: 449**
Voting Rights Act of 1965 **V: 451**
Washington, D.C. (The issue of slavery) **W: 86**
Western frontier life in America (Newcomers) **W: 234** *with picture*

World War II (Producing for the war) **W: 495**
Organizations
Association for the Study of African American Life and History **A: 819**
Black Caucus, Congressional **B: 386**
Black Muslims **B: 389**
Black Panther Party **B: 390**
Congress of Racial Equality **Ci: 941**
Freedmen's Bureau **F: 500**
Knights of Peter Claver **K: 352**
Masonry (History) **M: 267-268**
Nation of Islam **N: 26**
National Association for the Advancement of Colored People **N: 29**
National Medical Association **N: 40**
Southern Christian Leadership Conference **So: 688**
Student Nonviolent Coordinating Committee **So: 932**
United Negro College Fund **U: 97**
Urban League **U: 219**
Recreation and sports
Baseball (Postwar baseball) **B: 136** *with pictures*
Boxing (Bare knuckles to gloves) **B: 532**
Cowboy (The early cowboys) **Ci: 1112**
Slavery See Slavery *in this index*
Social issues
Chicago (Ethnic groups) **C: 426**; (Social problems) **C: 427**
Civil rights (The struggle for the rights of African Americans) **Ci: 609**
Economics *picture on* **E: 62**
Education (Education for whom?) **E: 107**
Ghetto (Ghettos today) **G: 181**
Local government (Population changes) **L: 407**
Minority group (African Americans) **M: 610**
Name (Black names) **N: 5**
New Orleans (Ethnic groups) **N: 280**
Racial profiling **R: 61**
Riot (Expressive riots) **R: 348**
Segregation **S: 284**; (Racial segregation in the United States) **S: 285**
Washington, D.C. (People) **W: 81**
African Art, National Museum of [Washington, D.C.] *See* National Museum of African Art *in this index*
African Association
Park, Mungo **P: 168**
African ball python [snake]
Snake *picture on* **S: 526**; (Protection against predators) **S: 531**
African Burial Ground National Monument [New York]
National Park System (table: National monuments) **N: 50**
African civet [animal]
Civet **Ci: 604** *with picture*
African Democratic Rally Party [political party]
Burkina Faso (History) **B: 706-707**
African Development Bank
Foreign aid (Regional development programs) **F: 385**
African elephant
Animal *pictures on* **A: 469, A: 477**
Ear (The ears of animals) **E: 12-E:13** *with picture*
Elephant **E: 226** *with pictures*
Ivory **I: 521**
African fish-eagle [bird]
Bird (Birds of Africa) **B: 344h** *with picture*
Eagle (Other kinds of eagles) **E: 5**
African Freedom Day
May **M: 321**
African Gaboon viper [snake]
Snake *picture on* **S: 526**; (Vipers) **S: 535**
Viper **V: 391**
African giant swallowtail [butterfly]
Butterfly (Swallowtails) **B: 738**
African goose [bird]
Goose (Kinds of geese) **G: 270**
African hunting dog [animal]
Mammal *picture on* **M: 124**
African independent church
South Africa (Religion) **So: 613**
African jacana [bird]
Bird (Birds of Africa) **B: 344h** *with picture*
African Lakes Corporation
Malawi (History) **M: 97-98**
African lion
Animal *picture on* **A: 477**
Lion **L: 340** *with pictures*
African lion hound
Rhodesian ridgeback **R: 318**
African Methodist Episcopal Church [religious group] **A: 137**
Allen, Richard **A: 372**
African Methodist Episcopal Zion Church [religious group] **A: 137**

African National Congress [political organization] **A: 137**
Inkatha Freedom Party **I: 273**
Luthuli, Albert John **L: 529**
Mandela, Nelson **M: 136**
Mbeki, Thabo **M: 331**
South Africa (Political parties) **So: 609**; (The Union of South Africa) **So: 618-619**
Xhosa **X: 544**
African oak [tree]
Teak **T: 71**
African ostrich [bird]
Bird *picture on* **B: 329**
African Party for the Independence of Cape Verde [political party]
Cape Verde (Government) **C: 189-190**; (History) **C: 190-191**
African Party for the Independence of Guinea and Cape Verde [political party]
Guinea-Bissau (Government) **G: 432**; (History) **G: 434**
African race [theory]
Races, Human (The geographical-race theory) **R: 53-54**
African rock python [snake]
Python **P: 922**
African secretary-bird [bird]
Bird of prey **B: 374a**
African sleeping sickness [disease]
Sleeping sickness **S: 507**
Tsetse fly **T: 474**
African slender-snouted crocodile
Crocodile (Kinds of crocodiles) **Ci: 1149-1150**
African snail
Shell (Gastropods) **S: 385**
African Squadron [U.S. history]
Perry, Matthew Calbraith **P: 294**
African teak [tree]
Teak **T: 71**
African traditional religion
Magic (Africa and the Americas) **M: 50**
African Union [organization] **A: 137**
Africa (Africa since independence) **A: 135**
Comoros (History) **So: 900-901**
Darfur **D: 36**
Flag *picture on* **F: 216**
Somalia (History) **So: 589-590**
African Unity, Organization of *See* Organization of African Unity *in this index*
African violet [plant] **A: 138** *with picture*
Flower *picture on* **F: 292**
Gardening *picture on* **G: 37**
African vulture
Animal *picture on* **A: 477**
Africans [people]
See also Blacks *in this index*
South Africa (People) **So: 609**
Africanus [Roman general] *See* Scipio Africanus, Publius Cornelius *in this index*
Afrifa, Akwasi Amankwa [Ghanaian political leader]
Ghana (History) **G: 179-180**
Afrikaans language
Afrikaners **A: 138**
South Africa (Languages) **So: 609**; (Arrival of Europeans) **So: 617-618**
Afrikakorps [World War II]
Rommel, Erwin **R: 450**
World War II (The Western Desert Campaign) **W: 476-477**
Afrikaners [people] **A: 138**
Africa (European colonization in Africa) **A: 133-134**
Anglo-Boer Wars **A: 463**
Cape Colony **C: 188**
Concentration camp (Other concentration camps) **Ci: 927**
Hertzog, James Barry Munnik **H: 217**
Smuts, Jan Christiaan **S: 522**
South Africa (People) **So: 609**; (History) **So: 617**
Swaziland (History) **So: 1019**
Afro [hair style]
Hairdressing (The 1900's) **H: 12-13** *with picture*
Afro-American Symphony [music by Still]
Still, William Grant **So: 901**
Afro-Americans *See* African Americans *in this index*
Afro-Asian languages
Africa (Languages) **A: 105**
Language *map on* **L: 65**; (Other language families) **L: 66**
Afrocentrism [education]
African Americans (Developments since 1970) **A: 136r**
Segregation (De facto segregation) **S: 285-286**
Afrosocorid [mammal]
Mammal (table) **M: 128** *with picture*
AFS Intercultural Programs [organization] **A: 138**

AFSC [organization] *See* American Friends Service Committee *in this index*

AFSCME [organization] *See* American Federation of State, County, and Municipal Employees *in this index*

AFT [organization] *See* American Federation of Teachers *in this index*

Aft [ship]
Sailing (Hull) **S: 23**
Ship (Nautical terms) **S: 405**

After Henry [book by Didion]
Didion, Joan **D: 195**

After the Fall [play by Miller]
Miller, Arthur **M: 553**

After the Hunt [painting by Harnett]
Harnett, William Michael *picture on* **H: 64**

Afterbirth
Baby (Birth) **B: 6**
Childbirth (The birth process) **C: 456**
Placenta **P: 505**
Reproduction, Human (The stages of labor) **R: 249**

Afterburner [engine]
Jet propulsion (Turbojet) **J: 111-114**

Afterdamp [gas]
Damp **D: 22**

Afterimage
Color (Surprising color-vision effects) **Ci: 819** *with picture*

Afterlife *See* Life after death *in this index*

Afternoon of a Faun, The [ballet]
Nijinsky, Vaslav *picture on* **N: 421**

"**Afternoon of a Faun, The**" [poem by Mallarmé]
Mallarmé, Stéphane **M: 110**

Aftershock [geology]
San Francisco earthquake of 1906 **S: 99**

Ag [symbol]
Silver (Properties of silver) **S: 463**

Aga Khan IV [Ismaili religious leader]
Islam (Divisions of Islam) **I: 466**

Agadez [Niger]
Niger (History) **N: 409**

Against Heresies [book by Irenaeus]
Irenaeus, Saint **I: 429**

Against Interpretation [book by Sontag]
Sontag, Susan **So: 594**

Agamemnon [legendary figure] **A: 138**
Achilles **A: 26**
Iliad **I: 51**
Iphigenia **I: 397**
Lesbos **L: 206**
Trojan War (The beginning of the war) **T: 449**

Agamemnon [ship, 1700's]
Nelson, Horatio (Wounded at Calvi) **N: 121**

Agapetus I, Saint [pope]
Pope (table) **P: 666**

Agapetus II [pope]
Pope (table) **P: 666**

Agar [extract]
Algae (Kinds of algae) **A: 349**
Bacteriology (Studying bacteria) **B: 22**
Seaweed (Uses) **S: 277**

Agaric [fungus]
Mushroom (Kinds of mushrooms) **M: 943** *with pictures*

Agassi, Andre [American tennis player] **A: 139** *with portrait*

Agassiz, Lake
Lake Agassiz **L: 35**

Agassiz, Louis [American naturalist] **A: 139**
Geology (Experimental geology) **G: 99**

Agate [mineral] **A: 139** *with picture*
Chalcedony **C: 369**
Gem *picture on* **G: 78**

Agate Fossil Beds National Monument [Nebraska] **A: 139**
National Park System (Areas preserved for natural features) **N: 45-46**; (table: National monuments) **N: 50**

Agatho, Saint [pope]
Pope (table) **P: 666**

Agave *See* Century plant; Maguey; Sisal *in this index*

Agave weevil [insect]
Beetle *picture on* **B: 218**

Agawa Canyon [Ontario]
Ontario (Places to visit) **O: 774** *with picture*

AGB star
Star (Intermediate-mass stars) **So: 848**

Agbade [clothing]
Benin (People) **B: 249**

Agbar Tower
Barcelona *picture on* **B: 108**

Agca, Mehmet Ali [Turkish public figure]
John Paul II **J: 134**

Age [demographics]
See also Aging
Population (Age) **P: 673**

Age discrimination [sociology] *See* Ageism *in this index*

Age Discrimination in Employment Act [1967]
Ageism **A: 140**

Age of Anxiety, The [book by Auden]
Auden, W. H. **A: 881**

Age of consent [law]
Rape [crime] **R: 141**

Age of Dinosaurs *See* Mesozoic Era *in this index*

Age of Fable, The [book by Bulfinch]
Bulfinch, Thomas **B: 687**

Age of Fishes *See* Devonian Period *in this index*

Age of Innocence, The [book by Wharton]
Wharton, Edith **W: 265**

Age of Innocence, The [painting by Reynolds]
Reynolds, Sir Joshua *picture on* **R: 289**

Age of Jackson [U.S. history]
Jackson, Andrew **J: 6**

Age of Jackson, The [book by Schlesinger]
Schlesinger, Arthur Meier, Jr. **S: 177**

Age of Liberty [Swedish history]
Sweden (The Age of Liberty) **So: 1034**

Age of majority
Minor **M: 607**

Age of Mammals *See* Cenozoic Era *in this index*

Age of Pericles *See* Golden Age of Athens *in this index*

Age of print
McLuhan, Marshall **M: 343**

Age of Rationalism *See* Enlightenment *in this index*

Age of Reason *See* Enlightenment *in this index*

Age of Reason [book by Paine]
Paine, Thomas (French revolutionary) **P: 22-23**

Age of Roosevelt, The [book by Schlesinger]
Schlesinger, Arthur Meier, Jr. **S: 177**

Age of Uncertainty, The [book by Galbraith]
Galbraith, John Kenneth **G: 10**

Age-related macular degeneration [disorder]
Macular degeneration **M: 26**

Age-specific birth rate [statistics]
Birth and death rates **B: 377**

Age spots
Skin (Skin color) **S: 490**

Age Unlimited [boat]
Raft **R: 102**

Aged *See* Geriatrics; Old age *in this index*

Agee, James [American author] **A: 139**

Ageism [sociology] **A: 140**
Gray Panthers **G: 335**
Old age (Attitudes toward old age) **O: 738-739**

Agency, Advertising *See* Advertising agency *in this index*

Agency, Independent [government] *See* Independent agency *in this index*

Agency for Healthcare Research and Quality [U.S.]
Health and Human Services, Department of (Organization) **H: 128**

Agency for International Development [U.S.] **A: 140**
Alliance for Progress **A: 375**
Food for Peace **F: 340**
Foreign aid (Economic development and mutual security) **F: 383-384**
Library (International library programs) **L: 254**
State, Department of **So: 860**; (Since World War II) **So: 862**

Agency for Toxic Substances and Disease Registry
Health and Human Services, Department of (Organization) **H: 128**

Agenda
Parliamentary procedure (table) **P: 176**

Agenda 21 [program]
Environmental impact statement **E: 329**

Agenor [Greek mythology]
Cadmus **C: 12**
Europa **E: 379**

Agent [biology]
Flower (Cross-pollination) **F: 295**

Agent [law] **A: 140**
Partnership (Rights and responsibilities of partners) **P: 188**

Agent, Insurance *See* Insurance agent *in this index*

Agent, Literary *See* Literary agent *in this index*

Agent, Theatrical
Motion picture (Developing the story) **M: 848-849**

Agent Orange [herbicide] **A: 140** *with picture*
Dioxin **D: 215**
Herbicide (Hazards of herbicides) **H: 198**
Vietnam War (Growing protest) **V: 376**

Ageratum [plant] **A: 141** *with picture*

Aggregate [geology]
Cement and concrete (Materials) **C: 343**
Rock **R: 371**

Aggregate culture

Hydroponics (Methods of hydroponics) **H: 472** *with diagram*

Aggregate demand [economics]
Money (Monetary policy) **M: 717**

Aggregate fruit
Fruit (Types of fruits in botany) **F: 546** *with pictures*
Plant (Seeds) **P: 531**

Aggregation [zoology]
Squirrel (Territories and groups) **So: 815**

Aggregation, Signs of
Algebra (Symbols in algebra) **A: 354**

Aggression [behavior] **A: 141**
Adler, Alfred **A: 58**
Bullying **B: 698**
Child (Aggressive behavior) **C: 453**
Dominance **D: 301**

Aggression [international relations]
Nonaggression pact **N: 452**

Aggressive house spider
House spider **H: 388**

Agile wallaby [mammal]
Wallaby (Kinds of wallabies) **W: 15**

Agility trial
Dog (Dog competitions) **D: 280-281**

Agincourt, Battle of [1415] **A: 141**
Archery (History) **A: 603-604**
England (The Hundred Years' War) **E: 306**
Feudalism (The decline of feudalism) **F: 83**
Henry V [of England] **H: 187**
War (Technological advancements) **W: 25**

Aging [biology] **A: 141**
See also Geriatrics; Old age *in this index*
Deafness (Aging) **D: 57**
Disease **D: 226**; (Diseases associated with aging) **D: 230**
Middle age **M: 521**
Progeria **P: 811**
Skin (Skin color) **S: 490**

Aging [industrial process]
See also Ripening *in this index*
Tobacco (Aging) **T: 307**
Wine (How wine is made) **W: 337-338** *with picture*

Agitato
Music (table) **M: 954**

Agitator [device]
Vacuum cleaner **V: 258** *with diagram*
Washing machine (Types) **W: 45** *with diagrams*

Agitprop
Propaganda (History) **P: 824-825**

Aglaia [Greek mythology]
Graces **G: 296** *with picture*

AGM [missile] *See* Air-to-ground missile *in this index*

Agnatha
Fish (A classification of fish) **F: 172**

Agnes Grey [book by Brontë]
Brontë sisters (Their works) **B: 637**

Agnew, Spiro Theodore [American political leader] **A: 142** *with portrait*
Ford, Gerald Rudolph (The resignation of Agnew) **F: 375**
Maryland (table) **M: 255**; (The mid-1900's) **M: 259**
Nixon, Richard Milhous (The 1968 election) **N: 432** *with picture*; (Events at home) **N: 435-436**
Republican Party (The Watergate scandal) **R: 257**
United States, History of the (Political scandals) **U: 196b**
Vice president of the United States (Growth of the vice presidency) **V: 353**

Agnon, Shmuel Yosef [Israeli author] **A: 143**
Hebrew literature (Modern Hebrew literature) **H: 162-163**

Agnosticism [belief] **A: 143**
See also Atheism *in this index*
God (Ideas about God) **G: 244**
Huxley, Thomas Henry **H: 459**
Ingersoll, Robert Green **I: 270**

Agony [painting by Gorky]
Gorky, Arshile *picture on* **G: 277**

Agony and the Ecstasy The [film]
Heston, Charlton **H: 220**

Agony in the Garden, The [painting by Mantegna]
Jesus Christ *picture on* **J: 108a**

Agora [ancient Athens]
Athens (Other buildings) **A: 857**
Greece, Ancient (The land) **G: 366** *with picture*

Agoraphobia [psychology]
Mental illness (Anxiety disorders) **M: 405-406**
Panic disorder **P: 130**
Phobia **P: 392**

Agouti [animal] **A: 143** *with picture*

Agouti coat
Cat (Short-haired breeds) **C: 290**

Agra [India] **A: 143**
Ramadan *picture on* **R: 132**

Agraphia [disorder]

Aphasia **A: 565**
Agrarian Democratic Party
  Moldova (History) **M: 690a-690b**
Agrarian law
  Land reform **L: 57**
Agre, Peter [American chemist]
  Nobel Prizes (Chemistry: 2003) **N: 444**
Agreement [grammar]
  Pronoun **P: 819**
Agreement [law]
  Contract **Ci: 1023**
Agreements of the People [pamphlets]
  Levellers **L: 217**
Agri Dagi [mountain, Turkey] *See* Mount Ararat *in this index*
Agribusiness A: 143
  Agriculture (Industrialized agriculture) **A: 150**
  Farm Credit System **F: 45**
  FFA **F: 84**
Agricola [book by Tacitus]
  Biography (Early biographies) **B: 312-313**
AGRICOLA [database]
  Library (United States government libraries)
  L: 248
Agricola, Georgius [German geologist]
  Geology (The Renaissance) **G: 98**
Agricola, Gnaeus Julius [Roman general] **A: 144**
  Scotland (The Roman invasion) **S: 219**
Agricultural Adjustment Administration
  Great Depression (The New Deal) **G: 341**
  New Deal (Helping the farmers) **N: 201**
Agricultural College of Colorado
  Colorado State University **Ci: 849**
Agricultural cooperative
  Farm Credit System **F: 45**
Agricultural Credit Act [1987]
  Farm Credit System (History) **F: 46**
Agricultural Credit Association
  Farm Credit System (Organization) **F: 45**
Agricultural economics
  Economics *picture on* **E: 63**; (Fields of economics)
  E: 64
Agricultural education A: 144 *with picture*
  FFA **F: 84**
  4-H **F: 433**
Agricultural engineering
  Engineering (Other specialized fields) **E: 287**
Agricultural experiment station A: 145
Agricultural fair
  Fair (Agricultural fairs) **F: 7**
Agricultural inspector
  Careers (Farming, fishing, and forestry) **C: 222**
Agricultural Labor Relations Act [1974]
  Huerta, Dolores Fernandez **H: 408**
Agricultural Library, National
  Library (United States government libraries)
  L: 248 *with picture*
Agricultural Marketing Act [1929]
  Hoover, Herbert Clark (Champion of prosperity)
  H: 329
Agricultural research
  Agricultural experiment station **A: 145**
Agricultural scientist
  Careers (Life, physical, and social sciences) **C: 225**
Agricultural spray plane
  Airplane (Special-purpose planes) **A: 212** *with picture*
Agricultural Stabilization and Conservation Service [U.S.] **A: 145**
Agriculture A: 146 *with pictures and maps*
  See also Farm and farming *in this index, the list of Related articles in the* Agriculture *article, and the* Economy *section of the various country articles, such as* Argentina (Economy).
  Agricultural education **A: 144**
  Agriculture, Department of **A: 161**
  Air pollution (Agriculture) **A: 199**
  Civilization (Development) **Ci: 635**
  Clay **Ci: 658**
  Deforestation (Agriculture) **D: 90**
  Environmental pollution (Agriculture) **E: 337**
  Famine (Causes of famine) **F: 26**; (Effects of famine) **F: 26a**
  Food supply (Limited agricultural resources) **F: 348**
  Human being (Hunting and gathering societies) **H: 415**
  Incubator (Agricultural incubators) **I: 106**
  Industry (Industry in developing countries) **I:I: 261** *with picture*
  Invention (Prehistoric times) **I: 358**; (The early and middle 1900's) **I: 363**
  Phenology **P: 356**
  Physiocrats **P: 444**
  Prehistoric people (The rise of agriculture) **P: 752**; (The end of prehistoric times) **P: 753-754a**
  Rome, Ancient (Agriculture) **R: 443**

  State government (Agriculture) **So: 865**
  Technology (Agriculture and civilization) **T: 74**
  Truck (Agricultural uses) **T: 457**
  Water pollution (Nonpoint sources) **W: 138**
Agriculture, Census of
  Census (Kinds of censuses) **C: 346-347**
Agriculture, Department of [U.S.] **A: 161** *with picture*
  Agricultural education (History) **A: 145**
  Cooperative Extension System **Ci: 1037**
  Farm and farming (Obtaining management assistance) **F: 43-44**
  4-H (Government organization) **F: 434**
  Library (United States government libraries) **L: 248**
  Livestock (Marketing livestock) **L: 398**
  Meat (How to select meat) **M: 347**
  Obesity (Prevention of obesity) **O: 642b**
  Soil (How soils are classified) **So: 576**
  Washington, D.C. *map on* **W: 76**
  Wheat (Commercial classes of wheat) **W: 269**
Agriculture, Secretary of [office]
  Agriculture, Department of **A: 161**
  Flag *picture on* **F: 211**
Agriculture and Agri-Foods Canada [education program]
  Agricultural education (In other countries) **A: 145**
Agrimony [botany] **A: 162**
Agrippa, Marcus [Roman general] **A: 162**
  Actium, Battle of **A: 30**
  Aqueduct (Ancient aqueducts) **A: 580**
  Augustus (Rise to power) **A: 889**
Agrippina the Younger [mother of Nero] **A: 162**
  Claudius **C: 657**
  Nero **N: 130**
Agrobacterium tumefaciens [bacteria]
  Gall **G: 13**
Agroforestry [study]
  Forestry (Community forestry) **F: 406**
Agronomy [agriculture] **A: 162**
  Botany (Uses of plants) **B: 508**
  Farm and farming (Modern crop production) **F: 33** *with pictures*
Agua Caliente Indians
  Palm Springs **P: 110**
Agua de panela [drink]
  Colombia (Food and drink) **Ci: 781**
Aguardiente [drink]
  Latin America (Food and drink) **L: 97-98**
Aguas Calientes [Peru]
  Peru *picture on* **P: 310**
Aguascalientes [state, Mexico] **A: 163**
Ague [disease]
  Colonial life in America (Health and medicine) **Ci: 809**
Aguilera, Christina [American singer] **A: 163**
  Rock music (Teen pop) **R: 380d-381** *with picture*
Aguinaldo, Emilio [Filipino patriot] **A: 163**
  Philippines (Revolt against the Spaniards) **P: 379-380**; (The Spanish-American War) **P: 380**
Aguirre, Emiliano [Spanish anthropologist]
  Prehistoric people (table) **P: 754**
Aguirre Cerda, Pedro [Chilean political leader]
  Chile (Years of progress) **C: 469**
Aguiyi-Ironsi, Johnson [Nigerian general]
  Nigeria (Civil war) **N: 418**
Agustín I [emperor of Mexico]
  Iturbide, Agustín de **I: 520**
Agustini, Delmira [Uruguayan poet]
  Latin American literature (The early 1900's) **L: 113**
Ah, Wilderness! [play by O'Neill]
  O'Neill, Eugene (His life) **O: 762**
Ahab [king of ancient Israel]
  Elijah **E: 236**
  Moabite stone **M: 681**
Ahab [literary figure]
  Melville, Herman (His literary career) **M: 390**
Ahad Ha-am [Hebrew poet]
  Hebrew literature (Modern Hebrew literature) **H: 162-163**
Ahaggar Mountains [Algeria]
  Algeria (The Sahara) **A: 363**
  Sahara (Land and climate) **S: 20**
Ahasuerus [king of Persia]
  Esther, Book of **E: 360**
  Purim **P: 909**
Ahasuerus [legendary figure]
  Wandering Jew **W: 22**
Ahern, Bertie [Irish political leader]
  Ireland (table) **I: 428**
Ahern, James [American dramatist]
  Herne, James A. **H: 212**
Ahidjo, Ahmadou [Cameroon political leader]
  Cameroon (History) **C: 86**
Ahimsa [religion]
  India (Hinduism) **I: 116**
Ahmad, Muhammad [Sudanese political leader]

  Omdurman **O: 760**
  Sudan (Egyptian and British control) **So: 953**
Ahmad Ibn Mājid [Arab sailor]
  Exploration (The voyage around Africa) **E: 444**
Ahmad Shah I [sultan of Gujarat]
  Ahmadabad **A: 163**
Ahmadabad [India] **A: 163**
Ahmadinejad, Mahmoud [Iranian political leader] **A: 163**
  Iran (Recent developments) **I: 406b**
  Journalism (Journalism today) **J: 175**
  Middle East (The 2000's) **M: 534b**
Ahmadu Bello University
  Nigeria (Education) **N: 413-414**
Ahmed, Iajuddin [Bangladeshi political leader]
  Bangladesh (Recent developments) **B: 86**
Ahmed, Sharif Sheik [Somali political leader]
  Somalia (History) **So: 589-590**
Ahmed Al-Fateh Moqsue [Bahrain]
  Manama **M: 132**
Ahmed Ibn Tulun mosque [Cairo, Egypt]
  Cairo (The city) **C: 16**
Ahmes [Egyptian mathematician]
  Algebra (History) **A: 359**
Ahounta, Djimdoumalbaye [Chadian anthropologist]
  Prehistoric people (table) **P: 754**
Ahriman [spirit]
  Zoroastrianism (Beliefs) **Z: 607**
Ahtisaari, Martti [Finnish political leader]
  Finland (The late 1900's) **F: 118**
  Nobel Prizes (Peace: 2008) **N: 449**
Ahu [archaeology]
  Easter Island **E: 45**
Ahura Mazda [Persian god]
  Persia, Ancient *picture on* **P: 298**; (Religion) **P: 297**
  Zoroastrianism (Beliefs) **Z: 607** *with picture*; (History) **Z: 607**
Ai [animal]
  Sloth **S: 508b**
AI [science] *See* Artificial intelligence *in this index*
AIA [organization]
  Architecture (Education and training) **A: 634**
AIAA [organization] *See* American Institute of Aeronautics and Astronautics *in this index*
AID [organization] *See* Agency for International Development *in this index*
Aid [riding]
  Horse (To control a horse) **H: 353**
Aid to Families with Dependent Children [program] **A: 163**
  Welfare (National welfare systems) **W: 191**
Aida [opera by Verdi]
  Opera *picture on* **O: 790**; (Giuseppe Verdi) **O: 798**; *(Aida)* **O: 801**
Aidid, Mohammed Farah [Somali political leader]
  Somalia (History) **So: 589**
AIDS [disease] **A: 164** *with pictures and map*
  Adolescent (Risk taking) **A: 64**
  Africa (Africa since independence) **A: 135** *with picture*
  Blood (Infections) **B: 414**
  Blood transfusion (Risks of transfusion) **B: 417**
  Chimpanzee (Chimpanzees and people) **C: 473**
  Condom **Ci: 929**
  Disease *picture on* **D: 225**; (table) **D: 226**; (Viral diseases) **D: 227**
  Epidemic **E: 343**
  Evolution (Direct observation of evolution) **E: 431**
  Fungal disease (In people) **F: 558**
  Hemophilia (Treatment) **H: 182-183**
  Herpes, Genital **H: 214**
  Homosexuality (Attitudes toward homosexuality) **H: 307**
  Immune system (Other disorders of the immune system) **I: 88c**; (Further breakthroughs) **I: 88d**
  Medical ethics **M: 361**
  Medicine (Unequal distribution of medical care) **M: 377**
  Pneumonia **P: 586**
  Prostitution **P: 830**
  Sexually transmitted disease **S: 338b**
  South Africa (Recent developments) **So: 621** *with picture*
  Tanzania (People) **T: 31**
AIDS quilt [memorial]
  AIDS (Public awareness) **A: 165**
Aiga [family]
  Pacific Islands (Food) **P: 6**
  Samoa (People) **S: 80a**
Aigrette [feather]
  Egret **E: 119**
Aiguille du Midi [mountain, Europe]
  Mont Blanc **M: 741**
Aiken, Conrad Potter [American poet] **A: 167**
Aiken, George David [American political leader]
  Vermont (table) **V: 333**

Aiken, George L. [American dramatist]
Stowe, Harriet Beecher **So:** 916
Aiken, Howard [American educator]
Computer (The first electronic computers)
Ci: 924b
Aikido [martial art] **A:** 167 *with picture*
Martial arts **M:** 234
Aikman, Troy [American football player] **A:** 168
Ailanthus [tree] **A:** 168
Tree *pictures on* **T:** 420
Aileron [airplane]
Airplane (The wing) **A:** 213 *with picture*; (Basic
movements and controls) **A:** 222-223 *with
diagrams*
Glider (The wings) **G:** 228
Ailey, Alvin [American choreographer] **A:** 168 *with
picture*
Dance (Modern dance) **D:** 30-31
Ailurophobia [psychology]
Phobia **P:** 392
AIM [organization] *See* American Indian Movement
in this index
AIM [weapon] *See* Air interceptor missile *in this
index*
Aimag [political province]
Mongolia (Government) **M:** 721-722
Aimar, Pablo [Argentine soccer player] **A:** 168
Ainslie, Lake [Nova Scotia]
Nova Scotia (Rivers and lakes) **N:** 562-564 *with
map*
Ainsworth, William [British author]
Turpin, Dick **T:** 519
Aintree Race Course [Liverpool]
Grand National **G:** 308
Ainu [people, Japan] **A:** 168
Japan (Ancestry) **J:** 35-38 *with picture*
Kuril Islands **K:** 393
Sakhalin **S:** 58
Air A: 169 *with pictures*
See also Climate; Wind *in this index*
Aerodynamics **A:** 85
Air pollution **A:** 197 *with pictures*
Anaximenes **A:** 449
Empedocles **E:** 261
Jet stream **J:** 115
Waves **W:** 150
Air, Liquid *See* Liquid air *in this index*
Air and Space Museum, National *See* National Air
and Space Museum *in this index*
Air attaché [military officer]
Attaché **A:** 878
Air bag [safety device] *See* Airbag *in this index*
Air battery [device]
Battery (Types and uses of batteries) **B:** 171
Air bladder [zoology]
Fish (Special organs) **F:** 163 *with diagram*
Air-blast circuit breaker [device]
Circuit breaker **Ci:** 558
Air-blast freezing [process]
Food, Frozen (Commercial methods of quick
freezing) **F:** 338
Food preservation (Freezing) **F:** 342-343
Air brake [device]
Brake (Air brakes) **B:** 562
Locomotive (Diesel locomotives) **L:** 414-415
Railroad (Rolling stock) **R:** 107
Westinghouse, George **W:** 242
Air Canada [airline]
Canada (Air travel) **C:** 126
Air carrier airport *See* Commercial service airport
in this index
Air circulation
Air conditioning (Circulating the air) **A:** 179
Air cleaner [device] **A:** 175
Air conditioning (Cleaning the air) **A:** 177
Deodorizer **D:** 148
Gasoline engine (The fuel system) **G:** 65
Air Combat Command
Air Force, United States (Combat commands)
A: 193
Langley Air Force Base **L:** 61
Strategic Air Command **So:** 919
Air Commerce, Bureau of [U.S.]
Aviation (Aviation progress) **A:** 988-989
Air Commerce Act [1926]
Aviation (Aviation progress) **A:** 988-989
Air compressor [device] **A:** 176
Brake (Air brakes) **B:** 562
Jet propulsion (Turbojet) **J:** 111
Pneumatic tool **P:** 586
Turbine (Gas turbine systems) **T:** 497
Air-Conditioned Nightmare, The [book by Miller]
Miller, Henry **M:** 554
Air conditioning A: 176 *with diagrams*
Air cleaner (Uses) **A:** 175
Filter **F:** 103
Heat pipe **H:** 156

House (Heating and air conditioning) **H:** 383
Skyscraper (Service areas) **S:** 497
Air-cooled engine
Gasoline engine (Cooling) **G:** 63-64
Air-core transformer [device]
Transformer **T:** 372
Air curing [process]
Tobacco (Kinds of tobacco) **T:** 305 *with picture*;
(Curing tobacco) **T:** 307
Air current *See* Current, Air *in this index*
Air cushion vehicle A: 181 *with pictures*
Amphibious warfare (History of amphibious
warfare) **A:** 442-443
Ducted propeller **D:** 377
Transportation *picture on* **T:** 391; (Water
transportation) **T:** 384
Air-data system [aviation]
Automatic flight control system (How an AFCS
works) **A:** 944
Air defense
Radar (In the military) **R:** 65
Air drying [industrial process]
Lumber (Seasoning) **L:** 519
Air embolism [disorder]
Diving, Underwater (Dangers of underwater
diving) **D:** 246
Air-entrained concrete
Cement and concrete (Air-entrained concrete)
C: 343
Air express [mail]
Airmail **A:** 207
Air force A: 182 *with pictures*
See also the list of Related articles in the Air force
article
Flag (Military flags) **F:** 195-208 *with picture*
Air Force, Canadian *See* Royal Canadian Air Force
in this index
Air Force, Department of the [U.S.] **A:** 187
Air Force, United States (The Department of the
Air Force) **A:** 193
Air Force, United States A: 188 *with pictures*
Air force (The United States Air Force) **A:** 184
Area 51 **A:** 645
Army, United States (The early 1900's) **A:** 738
Civil Air Patrol **Ci:** 604
Defense, Department of **D:** 87
Flag *picture on* **F:** 211
Lawrence, Robert Henry Jr. **L:** 146
Medals, decorations, and orders (Military awards)
M: 355 *with pictures*
National Guard **N:** 37
NORAD **N:** 453
RAND Corporation **R:** 136
Rank, Military **R:** 139
Reserve Officers Training Corps (Air Force ROTC)
R: 258
United States Air Force Academy **U:** 197 *with
pictures*
Air Force Academy, United States *See* United
States Air Force Academy *in this index*
Air Force Cross
Medals, decorations, and orders (table) **M:** 357
with picture
Air Force Global Strike Command
Air Force, United States (Combat commands)
A: 193
Air Force Materiel Command
Air Force, United States (Support commands)
A: 193
Air Force One [airplane] **A:** 196
Air Force Reserve [U.S.]
Air Force, United States (Air Force reserves)
A: 194
Air Force Reserve Command
Air Force, United States (Support commands)
A: 193
Air Force Reserve Officers Training Corps
Reserve Officers Training Corps (Air Force ROTC)
R: 258
Air Force Space Command
Air Force, United States (Combat commands)
A: 193
Air Force Special Operations Command
Air Force, United States (Combat commands)
A: 193
Air France-KLM [airline]
France (Transportation) **F:** 470
Air interceptor missile [weapon]
Air Force, United States (Missiles) **A:** 191
Guided missile (Air-to-air missiles) **G:** 426
Air-Launched AntiRadar Missile
Guided missile (Air-to-surface missiles) **G:** 426
Air-launched missile
Air force (Missiles) **A:** 183
Air Force, United States (Missiles) **A:** 191
Air letter
Postal Service, United States (Stamps and other

mailing materials) **P:** 699
Air Line Pilots Association A: 197
Air lock A: 197 *with diagram*
Caisson **C:** 19
Space exploration (Leaving the spacecraft)
So: 704
Air mail *See* Airmail *in this index*
Air mass
Air turbulence **A:** 201
Weather (table: Weather terms) **W:** 157;
(Synoptic-scale systems) **W:** 159 *with diagram*
Air mass thunderstorm
Thunderstorm **T:** 272
Air Medal
Medals, decorations, and orders (table) **M:** 357
Air Mobility Command
Air Force, United States (Support commands)
A: 193
Aïr Mountains [Niger]
Niger (Land and climate) **N:** 408
Air National Guard
Air Force, United States (Air Force reserves)
A: 194
National Guard **N:** 37
Air Patrol, Civil [U.S.] *See* Civil Air Patrol *in this index*
Air piracy *See* Hijacking *in this index*
Air plant *See* Epiphyte *in this index*
Air pollution A: 197 *with pictures*
See also Environmental pollution *in this index*
Air cleaner **A:** 175
Asbestos (Hazards of asbestos) **A:** 765
Automobile (Air pollution) **A:** 964
Catalytic converter **C:** 298
City (City life) **C:** 574; (Physical problems) **Ci:** 591
Coal (Coal as a fuel) **Ci:** 718; (Coal research)
Ci: 730
Disease (Environmental and occupational
diseases) **D:** 230
Dust (Influence on human health) **D:** 390
Electric car **E:** 165
Environmental pollution (Types of pollution)
E: 331 *with picture*
Gas [fuel] (Gas and the environment) **G:** 56
Gasoline (Pollution control) **G:** 62
Gasoline engine (Air pollution controls) **G:** 66
Incinerator **I:** 100
Lawn (Lawns and the environment) **L:** 144
Los Angeles (Recent developments) **L:** 470
Mexico (City life) **M:** 454
Mexico City (Environmental problems) **M:** 477
Minnesota (The late 1900's) **M:** 606
National park (Changes in the environment)
N: 42h
Ozone **O:** 893
Persian Gulf War of 1991 *picture on* **P:** 300d
Smoke **S:** 520
Transportation (Environmental problems) **T:** 398
United Kingdom (Climate) **U:** 61-62
Virginia (Pollution problems) **V:** 422
Weather (How people affect the weather) **W:** 170
World *picture on* **W:** 418
Air pressure
See also Atmospheric pressure *in this index*
Tire (History) **T:** 297-298
Air pump *See* Pump *in this index*
Air Quality Act [1967]
Air pollution (In the United States) **A:** 199
Air quality standards
Air pollution (Control of air pollution) **A:** 199
Air resistance
Air (Air resistance) **A:** 172 *with diagrams*
Motion (Motion in everyday life) **M:** 844
Air route
Aviation (Aviation agencies) **A:** 985-986
Air sac [anatomy]
See also Alveolus *in this index*
Human body (Air passages) **H:** 420-421
Air speed
Airplane (Measuring flying speed) **A:** 225
Air-speed indicator [instrument]
Airplane (Measuring flying speed) **A:** 225
Air staff [military]
Air Force, United States (Organization of the Air
Force) **A:** 193
Air taxi
Airplane (General aviation planes) **A:** 211
Aviation (General aviation activities) **A:** 984 *with
picture*
Air terminal *See* Airport *in this index*
Air thermometer
Thermometer (Thermal expansion
thermometers) **T:** 254
Air-to-air missile [weapon]
Guided missile *picture on* **G:** 425; (Air-to-air
missiles) **G:** 426
Air-to-ground missile [weapon]
Air Force, United States (Missiles) **A:** 191

Air-to-surface missile [weapon]
Guided missile (Air-to-surface missiles) **G: 426**
Air traffic control
Airplane (Safety) **A: 227**
Airport *picture on* **A: 243**; (The control tower) **A: 245**; (Air traffic control) **A: 246**
Careers (Transportation) **C: 235**
Navigation *picture on* **N: 71**
Radar (In aviation) **R: 64** *with picture*
Air traffic control center
Airport (The control tower) **A: 245**
Aviation (Aviation agencies) **A: 985-986**
Air train
Air cushion vehicle (History) **A: 181**
Air Training Command
Air Force, United States (Support commands) **A: 193**
Air Transport Association, International *See* International Air Transport Association *in this index*
Air Transport Association of America A: 200
Air travel *See* Aircraft; Airplane *in this index*
Air turbulence A: 200
Air University
Air Force, United States (Support commands) **A: 193**
Air washer [device]
Air conditioning (Cleaning the air) **A: 177-178**
Airbag [safety device] **A: 200** *with picture*
Automobile (The passenger compartment) **A: 950-951**
Electronics (Automation) **E: 207-208**
Nader, Ralph **N: 2**
Airborne troops A: 201 *with picture*
Army (Armies in the two world wars) **A: 728**
Parachute (Uses of parachutes) **P: 142**
Airborne Warning and Control System
Air Force, United States *picture on* **A: 192**; (Defense and deterrence) **A: 190**
Airbrush [painting] **A: 201** *with picture*
Airbus [company]
Aviation (Aircraft manufacturing) **A: 984**; (Internationalization) **A: 991**
Airco D.H.4 [airplane]
World War I *picture on* **W: 457**
Aircraft
See also Airplane *in this index*
Aircraft carrier **A: 206**
Airship **A: 250** *with pictures*
Autogiro **A: 942** *with picture*
Automatic flight control system **A: 944**
Aviation (Aircraft manufacturing) **A: 984**
Balloon **B: 57** *with pictures*
Blimp **B: 400**
Engineering (Aerospace engineering) **E: 284**
Glider **G: 228** *with picture*
Guided missile **G: 423** *with pictures*
Helicopter **H: 169** *with pictures*
Ornithopter **O: 858**
Renaissance *picture on* **R: 236**
Seattle (Economic expansion) **S: 276**
Test pilot **T: 182**
V/STOL **V: 452**
Aircraft, Military A: 201 *with pictures*
Air force **A: 182** *with picture*
Air Force, United States (Planes and weapons of the Air Force) **A: 190** *with pictures*
Airplane *picture on* **A: 211**; (Military planes) **A: 212**
Airport (Military airfields) **A: 243**
Area 51 **A: 645**
Automation (Uses of automation) **A: 944**
Aviation (Aircraft manufacturing) **A: 984**; (History of the aviation industry) **A: 986-987**
Bomber **B: 453** *with pictures*
Guided missile **G: 423** *with pictures*
Helicopter (For military missions) **H: 170** *with pictures*
Jet propulsion (Turbojet) **J: 111-114** *with pictures*
Korean War (The air war) **K: 382**
Marine Corps, United States (Marine aviation) **M: 208**
Mitchell, Billy **M: 677**
Navy (Ships and aircraft) **N: 77**
Navy, United States (Naval aviation) **N: 84**
Unmanned aerial vehicle **U: 212**
World War I *picture on* **W: 457**; (The war in the air) **W: 460** *with picture*
World War II (The air war) **W: 482**
Aircraft carrier [ship] **A: 206** *with pictures*
Navy (Aircraft carriers) **N: 78**
Navy, United States (Combat ships) **N: 84**
Warship *picture on* **W: 43**; (Aircraft carriers) **W: 39**
World War II *picture on* **W: 485**
Aircraft instrument
Airplane (The controls and instruments) **A: 217** *with picture*; (Basic movements and controls)

A: 222-223 *with picture*
Aircraft model
Airplane, Model **A: 240** *with pictures*
Aire, River [England]
Leeds **L: 180**
Airedale terrier [dog] **A: 207**
Dog *picture on* **D: 272**
Airfoil [device]
Aerodynamics (Lift) **A: 85**
Airframe [device]
Airplane (The parts of an airplane) **A: 213**
Airlift [mission]
Air force (Transport missions) **A: 183**
Airline
Airport (Commercial service airports) **A: 243**
Aviation (Airline operations) **A: 984**; (The first airlines) **A: 988**; (Aviation progress) **A: 988**; (The industry comes of age) **A: 989**; (A new age of flight) **A: 990**; (Jobs with airlines and airports) **A: 992**
National Mediation Board **N: 40**
Railway Labor Act **R: 122**
Transportation (Intercity public transportation) **T: 393-394**
Airline Deregulation Act [1978]
Aviation (Deregulation and mergers) **A: 991**
Public utility (History) **P: 867**
Airline hijacking *See* Hijacking *in this index*
Airline stewardess *See* Flight attendant *in this index*
Airline transport pilot license
Aviation (Jobs with airlines and airports) **A: 992**
Airliner
Airplane *picture on* **A: 208**; (Commercial transport planes) **A: 210** *with picture*
Transportation *pictures on* **T: 390**
Airmail A: 207
Airplane (The golden age) **A: 235**
Aviation (Aviation progress) **A: 988** *with picture*
Postal Service, United States (Technological advancements) **P: 701** *with picture*
Airman [rank]
Rank, Military (table) **R: 140**
Airman's Medal
Medals, decorations, and orders (table) **M: 357**
Airplane A: 208 *with pictures*
See also the list of Related articles in the Airplane *article*
Aerodynamics **A: 85**
Air (Air resistance) **A: 172**
Air conditioning (Air conditioners for vehicles) **A: 179**
Air turbulence **A: 200**
Aircraft carrier **A: 206**
Airport **A: 242** *with pictures*
Army (Armies in the two world wars) **A: 728**
Aviation **A: 983** *with pictures*
Bomber **B: 453** *with pictures*
Computer *picture on* **Ci: 920**
Fourth dimension **F: 438**
Inertial guidance **I: 263**
Invention (The inventive process) **I: 355-357**
Map (Navigation maps) **M: 177-178**; (Mapmaking and modern technology) **M: 185**
Propeller (Airplane propellers) **P: 826** *with picture*
Radar (In aviation) **R: 64**
Rocket (Atmospheric research) **R: 386**; (Rocket-powered airplanes) **R: 391**
Ship (Passenger vessels) **S: 426**
Shoran **S: 434**
Signaling (Aircraft signaling) **S: 454**
Sikorsky, Igor Ivanovich **S: 456** *with picture*
Starter (Airplane starters) **So: 859**
Television *picture on* **T: 127**
Terrorism (Hijackings) **T: 176**; (Security measures) **T: 177**; (The September 11 terrorist attacks) **T: 179**
Transportation (Air transportation) **T: 384**; (The beginnings of modern transportation) **T: 390** *with pictures*
United States *picture on* **U: 132**
Weather (Weather balloons, airplanes, and ships) **W: 163**
Wind shear **W: 332**
Wind tunnel **W: 333**
Wright brothers **W: 508** *with picture*
Airplane, Model A: 240 *with pictures*
Remote control (Applications of remote control) **R: 230**
Airplane pilot
Airplane (Learning to fly) **A: 226**; (Air navigation) **A: 226**
Aviation (Careers in aviation) **A: 992**
Airplane propeller
Airplane (General aviation planes) **A: 211** *with picture*; (Propellers) **A: 217** *with pictures*; (Drag and thrust) **A: 221** *with diagram*

Propeller (Airplane propellers) **P: 826** *with picture*
Airport A: 242 *with pictures*
See also the Transportation sections in specific city, country, state, and province articles
Aviation (Airport operations) **A: 985** *with picture*; (Jobs with airlines and airports) **A: 992**
Beacon **B: 179**
Fire department (Special fire vehicles) **F: 127**
Airport crash truck
Fire department (Special fire vehicles) **F: 127**
Airport master plan
Airport (Airport development) **A: 248**
Airport security
Airport *picture on* **A: 248**; (Airport security) **A: 247**
September 11 terrorist attacks (Weakened economy) **S: 310b**
Terrorism (Security measures) **T: 177** *with picture*
Airport Surveillance Radar
Airport (Air traffic control) **A: 246-247**
Airpower [military]
Mitchell, Billy **M: 677**
Airscrew *See* Airplane propeller *in this index*
Airship A: 250 *with pictures*
Air Force, United States (World War I) **A: 194**
Airplane (First human flights) **A: 230**
Balloon **B: 57**
Blimp **B: 400**
Airsickness
Motion sickness **M: 874**
Airways
Aviation (Aviation agencies) **A: 985-986**
Airy, Sir George B. [British astronomer]
Neptune (Discovery) **N: 129**
Ã'ishah [wife of Muhammad]
Muslims (The early caliphs) **M: 964a**; (Ali) **M: 964b**
Ã'ishah [organization]
Muslims (Reform and renewal) **M: 964d-965**
Aisling [poem]
Irish literature (Modern works in Gaelic) **I: 431**
Aisling Oenguso [story]
Irish literature (Heroic tales, romances, and sagas) **I: 430**
Aisne River [France] **A: 253**
Aites [legendary figure]
Medea **M: 360**
Aitken, William Maxwell [British publisher] *See* Beaverbrook, Lord *in this index*
Aitutaki [island, Pacific]
Cook Islands **Ci: 1026**
Aiun, El [West Sahara] *See* El Aaiun *in this index*
Aix-la-Chapelle [Germany] *See* Aachen *in this index*
Aix-la-Chapelle, Congress of [1818] **A: 253**
Ambassador **A: 404**
Aix-la-Chapelle, Treaty of [1748]
French and Indian wars (King George's War) **F: 512**
Louisbourg **L: 477**
Maria Theresa **M: 199**
Nova Scotia (The struggle in Acadia) **N: 568**
Succession wars (The War of the Austrian Succession) **So: 950**
Ajaccio [Corsica]
Corsica (Size and description) **Ci: 1072** *with map*
Ajanta [India]
India (Architecture and sculpture) **I: 119**; (The golden age) **I: 129**
Painting (Indian painting) **P: 44**
Ajax the Greater [legendary figure] **A: 253**
Ajax the Lesser [legendary figure] **A: 253**
Ajegaq [game]
Inuit (Recreation) **I: 354f**
Ajiaco [food]
Colombia (Food and drink) **Ci: 781**
Ajman [state]
United Arab Emirates **U: 43**
Ak-Sar-Ben, Knights of [organization] *See* Knights of Ak-Sar-Ben *in this index*
Aka [people]
Africa (Peoples of Africa) **A: 104**
Akaka Falls [Hawaii]
Hawaii (Places to visit) **H: 98**
Akan [people]
Côte d'Ivoire (People) **Ci: 1084a**
Akanyaru River [Burundi-Rwanda]
Rwanda (Land) **R: 571** *with map*
AKARI [satellite]
Telescope (Infrared telescopes) **T: 108**
Akashi Kaikyo Bridge [Japan]
Bridge (table: Suspension) **B: 603**
Akayev, Askar [Kyrgyz political leader]
Kyrgyzstan (Independence) **K: 400**
Akbar [Mughal emperor] **A: 253**
India (The Mughal Empire) **I: 129**
Mughal Empire **M: 910**
Muslims (The Mughal Empire) **M: 964d**
Akbarnama [book by Abul Fazl]
Biography (The Renaissance) **B: 313**

AKC [organization] *See* American Kennel Club *in this index*
Akela [rank]
  Boy Scouts (Cub Scouting) **B:** 537
Akerlof, George Arthur [American economist]
  Nobel Prizes (Economics: 2001) **N:** 449
Akerman, Amos T. [American government official]
  Grant, Ulysses S. (table) **G:** 316
  Justice, Department of (table) **J:** 203
Akhenaten [king of ancient Egypt] **A:** 253 *with picture*
  Egypt, Ancient (The New Kingdom) **E:** 143 *with picture*
  Mythology (The influence of Egyptian mythology) **M:** 980
  Nefertiti **N:** 119
  Sun worship *picture on* **So:** 988
  Tutankhamun **T:** 526
Akhetaten [ancient city]
  Akhenaten **A:** 253
  Egypt, Ancient (The New Kingdom) **E:** 143
Akhmatova, Anna [Soviet author]
  Russian literature (World War II) **R:** 564
Akhnaten [opera by Glass]
  Glass, Philip **G:** 224
Akialoa [bird]
  Hawaiian honeycreeper *picture on* **H:** 110
Akihito [emperor of Japan] **A:** 253 *with portrait*
  Government *picture on* **G:** 288
  Hirohito (After the war) **H:** 242
  Japan (Postwar boom) **J:** 58-59
Akimiski [island, Hudson Bay]
  James Bay **J:** 28
Akita [dog] **A:** 253 *with picture*
Akiva ben Joseph [Jewish scholar] **A:** 254
  Jews (Roman rule) **J:** 122
Akkad [ancient city]
  Sargon of Akkad **S:** 126
Akkadian [language]
  Babylonia (Language and literature) **B:** 13
  Hittites (Way of life) **H:** 269
Akkadians [ancient people]
  Babylonia (The Akkadian and Neo-Sumerian periods) **B:** 14
  Mesopotamia **M:** 422
  World, History of the (The Tigris-Euphrates Valley) **W:** 422-424
Aklavik [Northwest Territories]
  Inuvik **I:** 354j
Akmola [Kazakhstan] *See* Astana *in this index*
Akmolinsk [Kazakhstan] *See* Astana *in this index*
Ako ombe [tree]
  Plant *picture on* **P:** 527
Akosombo Dam [Volta River]
  Lake Volta **L:** 48 *with map*
Akron [Ohio] **A:** 254
Akron [airship]
  Airship (Between world wars) **A:** 252
Aksakov, Sergey [Russian author]
  Russian literature (Early realism) **R:** 562
Aksum [ancient city]
  Aksum **A:** 255
Aksum [ancient country] **A:** 255 *with map*
  Africa (Early civilizations) **A:** 130
  Eritrea (History) **E:** 353-354
  Ethiopia (History) **E:** 371
Aku-Aku [book by Heyerdahl]
  Heyerdahl, Thor **H:** 221
Akuffo, Frederick William Kwasi [Ghanaian political leader]
  Ghana (History) **G:** 179-180
Akvavit [drink] *See* Aquavit *in this index*
Al [symbol]
  Aluminum **A:** 391
Al ...
  Names beginning Al *are alphabetized as single words:* Al-Azhar University *appears after* Alaska
ALA [organization] *See* American Library Association *in this index*
Alabama [ship] **A:** 255 *with picture*
  Grant, Ulysses S. (Foreign relations) **G:** 316
  Neutrality (Rights and duties) **N:** 153
  Washington, Treaty of **W:** 109
Alabama [state] **A:** 256 *with pictures and maps*
  See also the list of Related articles in the Alabama *article*
  Scottsboro case **S:** 223
  Selma marches **S:** 290 *with picture*
Alabama, University of **A:** 279
  Wallace, George Corley W: 16
Alabama **Claims** [U.S. history]
  Grant, Ulysses S. (Foreign relations) **G:** 316
  Washington, Treaty of **W:** 109
Alabama Indians
  Creek Indians **Ci:** 1125
Alabama Platform [U.S. history]
  Alabama (Early statehood) **A:** 275-276

Alabama River [Alabama] **A:** 279
Alabama secession convention [U.S. history]
  Alabama (The Civil War and Reconstruction) **A:** 276
Alabaster [mineral] **A:** 280 *with pictures*
Aladdin [literary figure] **A:** 280
  Arabian Nights **A:** 582b
Aladdin's turban [plant]
  Gourd *picture on* **G:** 281
Alagnak Wild River [Alaska]
  National Park System (table: National parkways and other national parklands) **N:** 55
Alais, Peace of [1629]
  Richelieu, Cardinal (Strengthening the monarchy) **R:** 331
Alamance, Battle of [1771]
  North Carolina (Places to visit) **N:** 482; (Revolution and independence) **N:** 492
  Westward movement in America (Regional conflict) **W:** 245-246
Alameda [park]
  Mexico City (Downtown) **M:** 476-476a
Alamein, El *See* El Alamein *in this index*
Alamo [San Antonio, Texas] **A:** 280 *with picture*
  San Antonio (The city) **S:** 84
  Texas (Places to visit) **T:** 194 *with picture*
Alamo, Battle of the [1836]
  Alamo (The siege) **A:** 280 *with picture*
  Crockett, Davy (The Alamo) **Ci:** 1148d *with picture*
  Mexico (Difficulties of the early republic) **M:** 471
  San Antonio (History) **S:** 86-87
  Santa Anna, Antonio López de (War with Texas) **S:** 113
Alamo chain [U.S. history]
  Mission life in America (Western missions) **M:** 618-619
Alamo City
  San Antonio **S:** 84
Alanbrooke, Lord [British general] **A:** 281
Al-Anon [organization] **A:** 281
Al Aqabah [Jordan]
  Jordan (Transportation and communications) **J:** 164
Al Aqsa [mosque]
  Jerusalem (Islamic sites) **J:** 96 *with map*
Alarcón, Fabián [Ecuadorean political leader]
  Ecuador (The 1900's) **E:** 73-74
Alarcón, Pedro Antonio de [Spanish author] **A:** 281
  Spanish literature (The 1800's) **So:** 761-762
Alaric [king of the Visigoths] **A:** 281
  Goths **G:** 280
ALARM [missile]
  Guided missile (Air-to-surface missiles) **G:** 426
Alarm, Burglar
  Burglar alarm **B:** 704
Alarm reaction [physiology]
  Stress (How stress affects the body) **So:** 926
Alas, Leopoldo *See* Clarín *in this index*
Alaska **A:** 282 *with pictures and maps*
  See also the list of Related articles in the Alaska *article*
  Exploration (The Russians in Siberia) **E:** 447
  Exxon Valdez oil spill **E:** 459
  Flag *picture on* **F:** 209
  Glacier *picture on* **G:** 203
  Iditarod **I:** 6
  Indian, American (Indians of the Subarctic) **I:** 153
  Inuit **I:** 354 *with map*; (History) **I:** 354g; (The Inuit today) **I:** 354h
  Roosevelt, Theodore (Foreign policy) **R:** 465
  Russia (Expansion in Asia) **R:** 551
  State, Department of *picture on* **So:** 862
  United States (Climate) **U:** 126 *with picture*
  United States, History of the *map on* **U:** 184
Alaska, University of **A:** 305
  Alaska *picture on* **A:** 286
Alaska blackfish [fish]
  Blackfish **B:** 393
Alaska-cedar [tree]
  Cedar (Scale-leaved cedars) **C:** 324
Alaska Highway **A:** 305
  Alaska (Places to visit) **A:** 290; (Transportation) **A:** 299; (World War II) **A:** 301-303
  Yukon (Economy) **Y:** 579
Alaska Marine Highway *See* Inside Passage *in this index*
Alaska National Interest Lands Conservation Act [1980]
  Alaska (Land-use issues) **A:** 304
Alaska Native Brotherhood
  Alaska (The early 1900's) **A:** 301
Alaska Native Claims Settlement Act [1971]
  Alaska (Land-use issues) **A:** 304
  Aleuts **A:** 340
  Indian, American (In the United States) **I:** 179
  Tlingit Indians **T:** 303

Alaska Native Sisterhood
  Alaska (The early 1900's) **A:** 301
Alaska Panhandle
  Alaska (Land regions) **A:** 292
Alaska Permanent Fund
  Alaska (The discovery of oil) **A:** 304
Alaska pipeline *See* Trans-Alaska Pipeline System *in this index*
Alaska pollock [fish]
  Pollock **P:** 646
Alaska Purchase [U.S. history]
  United States, History of the *map on* **U:** 184
Alaska Railroad
  Railroad (Railroad systems) **R:** 112
Alaska Range [mountains, Alaska]
  Alaska (Land regions) **A:** 292
Alaska SeaLife Center [Seward]
  Alaska (Recent developments) **A:** 304
Alaska State Library [Juneau]
  Alaska (Libraries and museums) **A:** 286
Alaska State Museum [Juneau]
  Alaska (Libraries and museums) **A:** 286
Alaska Time Zone
  Time (Time zones in the United States and Canada) **T:** 289-292 *with maps*
Alaskan brown bear
  Bear **B:** 182, *picture on* **B:** 186; (Brown bears) **B:** 184
Alaskan fur seal
  Mammal *picture on* **M:** 116
Alaskan malamute [dog] **A:** 305
  Dog *picture on* **D:** 267
  Sled dog **S:** 505
Al-Askari shrine [Iraq]
  Iraq War (Resistance to the coalition) **I:** 414e-414f *with picture*
  Terrorism (The Iraq War [2003-2011]) **T:** 180
Alateen [organization]
  Al-Anon **A:** 281
Alaungpaya [king of Myanmar]
  Myanmar (British conquest and rule) **M:** 970d
  Yangon **Y:** 551
Alawi [ruling family]
  Morocco (Corsairs and sharifs) **M:** 814
Al-Azhar mosque [Cairo, Egypt]
  Cairo (The city) **C:** 16
Al-Azhar University [Cairo] **A:** 305
  Arabs (Education) **A:** 587
  Cairo (Education and cultural life) **C:** 16; (History) **C:** 17
  Fāṭimid dynasty **F:** 55
  Universities and colleges (European universities) **U:** 210
Al-Aziz, Abd [sultan of Morocco]
  Morocco (French and Spanish control) **M:** 814
Alba [kingdom]
  Scotland (Beginning of the Scottish kingdom) **S:** 219
Alba, Duke of [Spanish general] **A:** 305
  Belgium (Habsburg rule) **B:** 233
Alba Longa [ancient city]
  Romulus and Remus **R:** 450a
Alba Madonna, The [painting by Raphael]
  Madonna and Child *picture on* **M:** 37
Albacore [fish]
  Tuna **T:** 485
Albania **A:** 306 *with pictures and map*
  Cold War (The Iron Curtain descends) **Ci:** 763-764; (The great blocs split) **Ci:** 769
  Communism (In Eastern Europe) **Ci:** 896-897
  Flag *picture on* **F:** 205
  Hoxha, Enver **H:** 402
  Warsaw Pact **W:** 39
Albanian language
  Language (Indo-European) **L:** 65-66
Albanians [people]
  Kosovo (People) **K:** 384a; (History) **K:** 384b
  Macedonia (People) **M:** 12; (History) **M:** 12a-12b
Al-Bannā, Hasan [Egyptian teacher]
  Muslim Brotherhood **M:** 964
  Muslims (Reform and renewal) **M:** 964d-965
Albano, Lake [Italy]
  Lake Albano **L:** 35
Albans [people]
  Mythology (The seven kings) **M:** 983
Albany [New York] **A:** 309
  New York *picture on* **N:** 291
Albany Congress [1754] **A:** 310
  Franklin, Benjamin (The Plan of Union) **F:** 489
  French and Indian wars (The French and Indian War) **F:** 512-513
Albany Plan of Union [U.S. history]
  Albany Congress **A:** 310
  Franklin, Benjamin (The Plan of Union) **F:** 489
Al-Basra [Iraq] *See* Basra *in this index*
Al Batinah [region]
  Oman (Land and climate) **O:** 758

Albatross [bird] A: 310 *with picture*
Animal *picture on* A: 498
Antarctica (Living things) A: 534-535 *with picture*
Al-Baydh, Ali Salim [Yemeni political leader]
Yemen (Unification) Y: 564
Albedo [botany]
Orange (The fruit and the tree) O: 814
Albee, Edward [American dramatist] A: 310
American literature (Drama) A: 426 *with portrait*
Theater *picture on* T: 246
Albee, Fred H. [American doctor]
Surgery (History) So: 1007
Albemarle, Duke of [1608-1670] *See* Monck, George *in this index*
Albemarle, Duke of [1653-1688]
Boxing (The revival of boxing) B: 532
Albemarle County
North Carolina (Exploration and settlement) N: 490-492; (Colonial days) N: 492
Albemarle Island
Galapagos Islands G: 7 *with map*
Albéniz, Isaac [Spanish composer] A: 311
Alberich [opera character]
Opera: *(Ring of the Nibelung, The)* O: 806-807
Albers, Josef [German-American painter] A: 311 *with picture*
Albert [antipope]
Pope (table) P: 666
Albert [prince of Monaco]
Rainier III R: 129
Albert I [king of Belgium] A: 311
Belgium (The world wars) B: 234
Albert I [prince of Monaco]
Monaco (History) M: 700
Albert II [king of Belgium]
Belgium (Recent developments) B: 235
Albert II [prince of Monaco]
Monaco (History) M: 700
Albert, Carl Bert [American political leader] A: 311
Albert, Lake [Africa] *See* Lake Albert *in this index*
Albert, Prince [husband of Queen Victoria] A: 311
Victoria (Personal life) V: 356
Albert Canal [waterway, Belgium]
Canal (table) C: 164
Albert Edward Nyanza [lake, Africa] *See* Lake Albert *in this index*
Albert Memorial Chapel [England]
Windsor Castle W: 335
Albert Nile [river, Uganda]
Lake Albert L: 35
Albert Nyanza [lake, Africa] *See* Lake Albert *in this index*
Albert of Hohenzollern [German crusader]
Teutonic Knights T: 183
Alberta A: 312 *with pictures and maps*
See also the list of Related articles in the Alberta *article*
Canada, Government of *picture on* C: 131
Prairie Provinces P: 733
Alberta, University of A: 331
Edmonton (Education) E: 84
Alberta Agenda [document]
Harper, Stephen Joseph (Member of Parliament) H: 66a
Alberta Five [Canadian history] *See* Famous Fve *in this index*
Alberta Plain
Alberta (Land regions) A: 322
Alberti, Leon Battista [Italian architect] A: 331
Architecture (Early Renaissance architecture) A: 620-621 *with picture*
Italy (Architecture) I: 504
Perspective P: 305
Alberto Lleras Dam [Colombia]
Dam (table) D: 18
Albertosaurus [dinosaur] A: 232
Albertson, Jack [American actor]
Motion picture (Best performance by an actor in a supporting role: 1968) M: 862b
Albertus Magnus, Saint [German philosopher] A: 332
Arsenic A: 744
Physics (The Middle Ages) P: 438
Albigenses [religious group] A: 332
Innocent III (Crusades) I: 275
Paris, Treaties of (The treaty of 1229) P: 167
Albinism [disorder] *See* Albino *in this index*
Albino [biology] A: 332
Evolution (How mutations change a species) E: 428
Eye (The uveal tract) E: 460-461
Horse (Color types) H: 345-346 *with picture*
Albion [English history]
Chalk C: 370
Al Borak [legendary animal]
Horse (table: Famous horses in history and legend) H: 361

Albright, Madeleine Korbel [American diplomat] A: 332
Clinton, Bill (Domestic events) Ci: 682f
United Nations (table) U: 86
Al Bu Said [ruling family]
Oman (History) O: 759
Album quilt
Quilt Q: 41
Albumen [egg]
See also Albumin *in this index*
Bird (The reproductive system) B: 366
Egg (Shell membranes) E: 117 *with picture*
Albumin [protein] A: 333
Blood (Transporting nutrients and wastes) B: 408; (Regulating the volume of blood components) B: 410
Liver (Other functions) L: 394
Plasma (Functions of plasma) P: 551
Protein (How the body uses proteins) P: 832
Albuquerque [New Mexico] A: 333
New Mexico *picture on* N: 257; (table: Average monthly weather) N: 268
Albuterol [drug]
Bronchodilator B: 637
Alcalá Zamora, Niceto [Spanish political leader]
Spain (The Spanish republic) So: 750
Alcan Highway *See* Alaska Highway *in this index*
Alcan Inc. A: 333
Aluminum (In Canada) A: 396-397; (Growth of the aluminum industry) A: 397
Kitimat K: 341
Alcatraz [former prison, San Francisco] A: 333
Alcatraz Island
Alcatraz A: 333
Alcayaga, Lucila Godoy *See* Mistral, Gabriela *in this index*
Alcazar [architecture] A: 334
Castle *picture on* C: 281
Santo Domingo S: 117
Alchemist, The [play by Jonson]
Jonson, Ben J: 160
Alchemy [study] A: 334
Alcoholic beverage (History) A: 337
Chemistry (Alchemy) C: 400 *with picture*
Magic (Europe) M: 50
Alcibiades [Greek general] A: 334
Peloponnesian War P: 232
Alcid [bird] *See* Auk *in this index*
Alcindor, Lew [basketball player] *See* Abdul-Jabbar, Kareem *in this index*
Alcmaeonid clan [Greek history]
Cleisthenes Ci: 661
Alcmene [Greek mythology]
Hercules (Early life) H: 198
Alcoa Inc. [company] A: 334
Alcan Inc. A: 333
Aluminum (Growth of the aluminum industry) A: 397
Alcock, Sir John William [British aviator]
Alcock and Brown A: 335
Alcock and Brown [British aviators] A: 335
Alcohol [chemistry] A: 335
Corn (Industrial uses) Ci: 1057; (The fermentation and distilling industry) Ci: 1062
Disinfectant D: 235
Distillation (Simple distillation) D: 238 *with diagram*
Ethanol E: 364
Methanol M: 434
Nutrition (Beware of alcohol) N: 628
Thermometer (Thermal expansion thermometers) T: 254
Alcohol abuse
Alcoholism A: 337
Alcohol dependence *See* Alcoholism *in this index*
Alcohol, Tobacco, Firearms and Explosives, Bureau of [U.S.] A: 336
Alcoholic *See* Alcoholism *in this index*
Alcoholic beverage A: 336
Adolescent (Alcohol and drug abuse) A: 63
Brewing B: 595
Depressant D: 150
Distillation (Simple distillation) D: 238-239
Distilling D: 239
Driving while intoxicated D: 348
Drug (Antianxiety and hypnotic drugs) D: 352
Drug abuse (Abuse of legal drugs) D: 361
Fetal alcohol syndrome F: 80
Grain (Other uses) G: 301
Mind (Alterations of the mind) M: 563
Nutrition (Beware of alcohol) N: 628
Prohibition P: 814
Alcoholics Anonymous [organization] A: 337
Al-Anon A: 281
Drug abuse (Treatment of substance use disorders) D: 364
Overeaters Anonymous O: 881

Alcoholism [disease] A: 337
Al-Anon A: 281
Alcoholics Anonymous A: 337
Benzodiazepine B: 255
Breath testing B: 591
City (Social problems) Ci: 591
Delirium tremens D: 116
Disulfiram D: 240
Health (Tobacco, alcohol, and drug abuse) H: 126-127
Mental illness (Substance use disorders) M: 406
Alcoholometer [measuring device]
Hydrometer H: 471
Alcools [poem by Apollinaire]
Apollinaire, Guillaume A: 566
Alcor [star]
Big and Little Dippers (The Big Dipper) B: 296
Alcorn, James L. [American political leader]
Mississippi (table) M: 640
Alcott, Bronson [American social reformer] A: 338
Alcott, Louisa May A: 338
American literature (Nonfiction prose) A: 418
Alcott, Louisa May [American author] A: 338
American literature (The sentimental novel) A: 415-418
Literature for children (Masterpieces of fiction) L: 363
Alcyone [poems by Lampman]
Lampman, Archibald L: 54
Aldabra Islands
British Indian Ocean Territory B: 632
Alden, John and Priscilla [American colonists] A: 338
Longfellow, Henry Wadsworth (Narrative poems) L: 450
Alder [tree] A: 339
Tree *pictures on* T: 420
Alder, Kurt [German chemist]
Nobel Prizes (Chemistry: 1950) N: 443
Alder Gulch
Montana (Interesting facts) M: 743
Alderdice, Frederick C. [Canadian political leader]
Newfoundland and Labrador (Ruin and recovery) N: 377
Alderman [office]
City government Ci: 595
Ward W: 35
Aldermen, Board of *See* City council *in this index*
Alderney [island, English Channel]
Channel Islands C: 376 *with map*
Aldhelm, Saint [English religious leader]
Literature for children (Early children's literature) L: 361
Aldobrandini, Ippolito [pope] *See* Clement VIII *in this index*
Aldosterone [hormone]
Adrenal gland A: 67
Hormone (Blood composition hormones) H: 336
Hypertension (Causes) H: 476
Steroid (The adrenal steroids) So: 894-895
Aldrich, Chester H. [American political leader]
Nebraska (table) N: 110
Aldrich, Nelson Wilmarth [American political leader]
Taft, William Howard (Legislative defeats) T: 10-11
Aldridge, Ira [American actor] A: 339 *with portrait*
Aldrin, Buzz [American astronaut] A: 339
Armstrong, Neil Alden A: 723
Astronaut (Achievements in space) A: 829-830 *with picture*; (table) A: 830
Exploration (Human space travel) E: 452
Space exploration (Landing on the moon) So: 717 *with pictures*
Television *picture on* T: 110
Aldrin, Edwin Eugene, Jr. [American astronaut] *See* Aldrin, Buzz *in this index*
Aldus Manutius *See* Manutius, Aldus *in this index*
Ale [drink]
Alcoholic beverage (Beer) A: 336
Beer B: 211
Aleatory music A: 339
Cage, John C: 14
Classical music (Experimental music) Ci: 650
Alecto [Greek mythology]
Furies F: 566
Alegría, Ciro [Peruvian author]
Latin American literature (The mid-1900's) L: 114
Aleichem, Sholem [Jewish author] *See* Sholem Aleichem *in this index*
Aleixandre, Vicente [Spanish poet] A: 339
Alekhine, Alexander [Russian chess player]
Chess (World chess champions) C: 414
Alemán, Mateo [Spanish author]
Spanish literature (The 1600's) So: 759
Alemán Lacayo, José Arnoldo [Nicaraguan political leader]

Nicaragua (The late1900's) **N**: 400-401
Alemanni [people]
 Valentinian I **V**: 264
Alemannians [people]
 Switzerland (Early days) **So**: 1058-1059
Alemannic [language]
 Liechtenstein **L**: 272
Alencar, José de [Brazilian author]
 Brazil (The arts) **B**: 576-577
 Latin American literature (Romanticism) **L**: 112-113
Aleph, The [stories by Borges]
 Borges, Jorge Luis **B**: 487
Aleppo [Syria] **A**: 340
 Syria *picture on* **So**: 1074
Aleppo pine [tree]
 Pine (Other pines) **P**: 470
Alessandri Palma, Arturo [Chilean political leader]
 Chile (Era of changes) **C**: 469; (Years of progress) **C**: 469
Alessandri Rodríguez, Jorge [Chilean political leader]
 Chile (Years of progress) **C**: 469
Aletsch Glacier [Switzerland]
 Alps (How the Alps were formed) **A**: 384-385
 Glacier (Famous glaciers) **G**: 204
Aleutian Islands [Alaska] **A**: 340 *with map*
 Alaska (Interesting facts) **A**: 283; (Land regions) **A**: 292; (World War II) **A**: 301
 Aleuts **A**: 340
Aleutian Range [mountains, Alaska]
 Alaska (Land regions) **A**: 292
Aleuts [people] **A**: 340
 Alaska (Population) **A**: 286
 Indian, American (Peoples of the Arctic) **I**: 152
 Indian reservation **I**: 188
 Inuit (Alaska) **I**: 354h-354i
 Mask *picture on* **M**: 265
Alewife [fish] **A**: 340 *with picture*
Alexander [American Indian chief]
 Massasoit **M**: 296
Alexander [king of Macedonia] *See* Alexander the Great *in this index*
Alexander [king of Serbia]
 Peter I **P**: 323
Alexander I [czar of Russia] **A**: 341
 Aix-la-Chapelle, Congress of **A**: 253
 Helsinki **H**: 179
 Napoleon I (Disaster in Russia) **N**: 16
 Russia (Alexander I) **R**: 550
Alexander I [king of Greece]
 Constantine I **Ci**: 993
 Greece (World War I) **G**: 363
Alexander I [king of Yugoslavia] **A**: 341
 Croatia (History) **Ci**: 1148a-1148b
 Peter I **P**: 323
 Serbia (A new country) **S**: 314-315
 Yugoslavia (A new country) **Y**: 576
Alexander II [czar of Russia] **A**: 341
 Anarchism **A**: 448
 Russia (Alexander II) **R**: 551
Alexander III [pope] **A**: 341
Alexander III [czar of Russia] **A**: 341
 Russia (Alexander III) **R**: 551
Alexander III [king of Scotland]
 Scotland (Struggles with England) **S**: 219
Alexander IV [king of Macedonia]
 Alexander the Great (His death) **A**: 344
Alexander V [antipope]
 Pope (table) **P**: 666
Alexander VI [pope] **A**: 341
 Borgia, Cesare **B**: 488
 Borgia, Lucrezia **B**: 488
 Columbus, Christopher (Return to Spain) **Ci**: 861
 Line of Demarcation **L**: 333
 Savonarola, Girolamo **S**: 166
Alexander VII [pope]
 Sculpture (European sculpture) **S**: 253 *with picture*
Alexander VIII [pope]
 Pope (table) **P**: 666
Alexander, Grover Cleveland [American baseball player] **A**: 342
 Baseball (table: Hall of Fame) **B**: 134; (The early 1900's) **B**: 135; (table: Modern major league records) **B**: 138
Alexander, Harold Rupert Leofric George [British statesman] *See* Alexander of Tunis, Earl *in this index*
Alexander, Joshua W. [American government official]
 Commerce, Department of (table) **Ci**: 871
 Wilson, Woodrow (table) **W**: 323
Alexander, Lamar [American political leader]
 Education, Department of (table) **E**: 110
 Tennessee (table) **T**: 152
Alexander, Lloyd [American author] **A**: 342

Newbery Medal (table) **N**: 359
 Regina Medal (table: 1986) **R**: 206
Alexander, Moses [American political leader]
 Idaho (table) **I**: 42
Alexander, Nathaniel [American political leader]
 North Carolina (table) **N**: 490
Alexander, William [American artist]
 Mission life in America *picture on* **M**: 619
Alexander, Sir William [British settler]
 Nova Scotia (The struggle in Acadia) **N**: 568
Alexander Archipelago [islands, Alaska]
 Alaska (Coastline) **A**: 294
 Coast Ranges **Ci**: 739
Alexander Graham Bell Association for the Deaf and Hard of Hearing
 Bell, Alexander Graham (His later life) **B**: 241
 Deafness (Education) **D**: 59
Alexander Graham Bell National Historic Site
 Canada (table: National historic sites) **C**: 114
 Nova Scotia (Places to visit) **N**: 560
Alexander Helios [son of]
 Cleopatra (Cleopatra and Mark Antony) **Ci**: 662a-662b
Alexander Nevsky [music by Prokofiev]
 Prokofiev, Sergei Sergeyevich **P**: 817
Alexander of Battenberg [prince of Bulgaria]
 Battenberg **B**: 167
Alexander of Tunis, Earl [British statesman] **A**: 342
Alexander Sarcophagus
 Sculpture (Classical sculpture) **S**: 245-246 *with picture*
Alexander the Great [king of Macedonia] **A**: 342 *with picture and map*
 Darius III **D**: 36
 Diogenes **D**: 214
 Europe (Ancient Greece) **E**: 407 *with map*
 Exploration (The Greeks) **E**: 441 *with map*
 Greece, Ancient (The Hellenistic Age) **G**: 374 *with picture*
 India (Persian and Greek invasions) **I**: 128
 Macedonia **M**: 11
 Memphis **M**: 394
 Olympias **O**: 746
Alexander's dark band
 Rainbow (How to find a rainbow) **R**: 127-128
"Alexander's Feast" [poem by Dryden]
 Dryden, John **D**: 370
"Alexander's Ragtime Band" [song by Berlin]
 Berlin, Irving **B**: 266
Alexandra [wife of Edward VII]
 Edward VII **E**: 113
Alexandra Falls [waterfall, Northwest Territories]
 Northwest Territories *picture on* **N**: 531
Alexandra Feodorovna [wife of Nicholas II]
 Nicholas II [czar] **N**: 402 *with picture*
 Rasputin, Grigori Efimovich **R**: 145
Alexandra Land [island, Arctic]
 Franz Josef Land **F**: 494
Alexandria [Egypt] **A**: 344
 Alexander the Great (Invasion of Asia) **A**: 342-343
 Greek literature (The Hellenistic Age) **G**: 378
 Middle East *picture on* **M**: 531
 Seven Wonders of the Ancient World *picture on* **S**: 327; (The Lighthouse of Alexandria) **S**: 325
Alexandria [Virginia] **A**: 345
 Washington, D.C. (Choosing the capital) **W**: 85
 Washington, George (Professional surveyor) **W**: 93
Alexandria Quartet, The [books by Durrell]
 Durrell, Lawrence **D**: 389
Alexandrian Library [Egypt]
 Information retrieval (History) **I**: 269
 Library (Ancient libraries of papyrus) **L**: 257-258 *with picture*
Alexandrine [poetry]
 Drama (Neoclassical playwrights) **D**: 333-334
 French literature (Classical drama) **F**: 520
 Poetry (Stress meters) **P**: 593-594; (table) **P**: 594; (Renaissance poetry) **P**: 596
Alexandrite [gem] **A**: 345
 Gem *pictures on* **G**: 78
Alexandroupolis [Greece]
 Greece (table: Average monthly weather) **G**: 359
Alexeieff, Alexander [Russian-born artist]
 Animation (Animation in Europe) **A**: 514a
Alexeyev, Rostislav [Soviet scientist]
 Hydrofoil (Modern hydrofoil development) **H**: 468
Alexia [disorder]
 Aphasia **A**: 565
Alexie, Sherman [American author] **A**: 345
 American literature (Works by minority writers) **A**: 425
Alexis [son of Nicholas II]
 Nicholas II [czar] *picture on* **N**: 403
 Rasputin, Grigori Efimovich **R**: 145
Alexis I [czar of Russia]

Romanov **R**: 426
 Russia (table: Czars and empresses) **R**: 549
Alexis, Jacques-Edouard [Haitian political leader]
 Haiti (History) **H**: 15-17
Alexius I Comnenus [Byzantine emperor]
 Byzantine Empire (The middle period) **B**: 754
 Crusades (How the Crusades began) **Ci**: 1159-1160
Alfalfa [plant] **A**: 345 *with pictures*
Alfalfa weevil [insect]
 Weevil **W**: 180
Alfano, Franco [Italian composer]
 Puccini, Giacomo **P**: 870
Alfaro, Eloy [Ecuadorean general]
 Ecuador (Independence) **E**: 73
Al-Fateh University [Tripoli]
 Libya (Education) **L**: 266
Alferov, Zhores Ivanovich [Russian physicist]
 Nobel Prizes (Physics: 2000) **N**: 442
Alfieri, Vittorio [Italian author] **A**: 348
 Italian literature (The Baroque period and the Enlightenment) **I**: 494-495
Alfilaria [plant]
 Geranium **G**: 136
Alfio [opera character]
 Opera: (*Cavalleria Rusticana*) **O**: 803
Alfisol [soil]
 Indiana (Natural resources) **I**: 211
 Soil *map on* **So**: 575; (How soils are classified) **So**: 576
Alfonsín, Raúl [Argentine political leader]
 Argentina (The "dirty war") **A**: 658
Alfonso I d'Este [duke of Ferrara]
 Borgia, Lucrezia **B**: 488
Alfonso II d'Este [duke of Ferrara]
 Tasso, Torquato **T**: 50
Alfonso VI [king of León and Castile]
 Cid, The **Ci**: 552
 Madrid (History) **M**: 40
 Portugal (Founding the Portuguese nation) **P**: 693
Alfonso X [king of Castile]
 Cádiz **C**: 12
 Spanish literature (Early medieval literature) **So**: 757-758
Alfonso XII [king of Spain]
 Spain (The reign of Isabella II) **So**: 748-749
Alfonso XIII [king of Spain] **A**: 348
 Franco, Francisco (As dictator) **F**: 483
 Spain (The reign of Alfonso XIII) **So**: 749
 Spanish Civil War (Background to the war) **So**: 756
Alfonso, Pedro [Spanish author]
 Spanish literature (Early medieval literature) **So**: 757-758
"Alfred Hitchcock Presents" [television program]
 Hitchcock, Alfred **H**: 263
Alfred P. Murrah Federal Building
 Oklahoma City bombing **O**: 737 *with picture*
Alfred the Great [king of the West Saxons] **A**: 348
 Anglo-Saxons **A**: 464
 England (The Anglo-Saxon period) **E**: 304-305
 English literature (Old English prose) **E**: 315
 Navy (Navies in the Middle Ages) **N**: 79
Al Fujayrah [state]
 United Arab Emirates **U**: 43
Al-Fustat [Egyptian history]
 Cairo (History) **C**: 17
Alfvén, Hannes Olof Gösta [Swedish physicist]
 Nobel Prizes (Physics: 1970) **N**: 441
Alga [biology] *See* Algae *in this index*
Algae [biology] **A**: 349 *with picture*
 See also Seaweed *in this index*
 Coral reef (How coral reefs form) **Ci**: 1048b-1049
 Diatom **D**: 185
 Earth (Earth's early development) **E**: 26-27
 Environmental pollution (Water pollution) **E**: 334
 Eutrophication (How eutrophication occurs) **E**: 421
 Lichen **L**: 269 *with pictures*
 Nummulite **N**: 608
 Photosynthesis **P**: 430
 Spore (Algal and fungal spores) **So**: 802 *with diagram*
 Water plant **W**: 136
 Water pollution (Disruption of natural processes) **W**: 138
Algal bloom [biology]
 Agriculture (Pollution) **A**: 153
 Algae **A**: 349
 Eutrophication (How eutrophication occurs) **E**: 421
Algebra [mathematics] **A**: 350 *with pictures*
 Al-Khwārizmī **A**: 370
 Factor (Algebraic factors) **F**: 5
 Gauss, Carl Friedrich **G**: 70
 Geometry (Analytic geometry) **G**: 105

Mathematics (Branches of mathematics) **M: 303;** (Arab mathematics) **M: 306**
Algebraic geometry
Geometry (Rise of non-Euclidean geometry) **G: 106**
Algebraic notation
Chess (Chess notation) **C: 413**
Algebraic topology [mathematics]
Topology (Algebraic topology) **T: 332** *with picture*
Alger, Horatio [American author] **A: 359**
Alger, Russell A. [American political leader]
McKinley, William (table) **M: 342**
Michigan (table) **M: 507**
Algeria A: 360 *with pictures and maps*
Barbary States **B: 105** *with map*
De Gaulle, Charles André Joseph Marie (The Fifth Republic) **D: 91**
Flag *picture on* **F: 198**
Foreign Legion (History) **F: 386**
France (History) **F: 471-476**
Middle East **M: 530**
World, History of the *picture on* **W: 448**
Algerian ivy [plant]
Ivy *picture on* **I: 522**
Algerian Revolution [1954]
Algeria (The Algerian Revolution) **A: 365**
Algiers [Algeria] **A: 365**
Africa *picture on* **A: 108**
Algeria **A: 360** *with picture*
World, History of the *picture on* **W: 448**
Algiers [district]
New Orleans (The city) **N: 278**
Algiers, University of
Algeria (Education) **A: 362**
Algin [extract]
Algae (Kinds of algae) **A: 349**
Ocean (The importance of the ocean) **O: 653-654**
Algol [star]
Perseus **P: 295**
Algoma, November [painting by Jackson]
Jackson, Alexander Young *picture on* **J: 5**
Algonkin Indians *See* Algonquin Indians *in this index*
Algonquian [language group]
Algonquin Indians **A: 366**
Indian, American (Indians of the Northeast) **I: 154-155**
Massachusetts (Early days) **M: 289**
Rhode Island (Early days) **R: 312**
United States, History of the (The first Americans) **U: 149**
Vermont (Indian days) **V: 334**
Wampum **W: 22**
Wigwam **W: 300**
Algonquian Town of Pomeioc [painting by White]
Indian, American *picture on* **I: 156**
Algonquin Indians A: 366
Champlain, Samuel de (The founding of Quebec) **C: 373**
Algonquin Peak [mountain, New York]
New York (Mountains) **N: 306**
Algonquin Round Table [literary group]
Parker, Dorothy **P: 170**
Algorithm [mathematics] **A: 366**
Codes and ciphers **Ci: 749**
Information retrieval (How information retrieval works) **I: 268b**
Algren, Nelson [American author] **A: 366**
Alguaciles [horsemen]
Bullfighting (The order of the bullfight) **B: 696**
Alhacen [Arab scientist] *See* Alhazen *in this index*
Al-Hafidh, Abd [sultan of Morocco]
Morocco (French and Spanish control) **M: 814-815**
Al Hajar [mountains]
Oman (Land and climate) **O: 758**
Al-Hakim [caliph of Egypt]
Druses **D: 368**
Al-Hakim, Tawfiq [Egyptian author]
Arabic literature (Drama) **A: 584**
Al-Hallaj [Muslim religious leader]
Sufism **So: 959**
Alhambra [Granada, Spain] **A: 366** *with picture*
Islamic art (Other buildings) **I: 468;** (Carved and molded plaster) **I: 470**
Spain (Architecture) **So: 738** *with picture*
Alharizi, Judah [Hebrew author]
Hebrew literature (Medieval works) **H: 162**
Alhazen [Arab scientist] **A: 366**
Color (Early theories of color vision) **Ci: 825-826**
Light (Early ideas) **L: 285**
Mathematics (Arab mathematics) **M: 306**
Optics (History) **O: 813**
Photography (Early developments) **P: 422**
Al Hillah [Iraq]
Babylon **B: 11**
Al-Huss, Salim [Lebanese political leader]

Lebanon (Political struggle) **L: 174**
Ali [Muslim leader] *See* Ali ibn Abī Tālib *in this index*
Ali, Laila [American boxer]
Boxing (Women's boxing) **B: 532b-533** *with picture*
Ali, Muhammad [American boxer] **A: 367** *with portrait*
Boxing *picture on* **B: 533;** (The Ali era) **B: 532a** *with picture;* (Women's boxing) **B: 532b-533**
Olympic Games (The postwar games) **O: 751-752**
Ali Ahmad Said [Lebanese poet]
Arabic literature (Poetry) **A: 583**
Ali Baba [literary figure]
Arabian Nights **A: 582b**
Ali ibn Abī Tālib [Muslim leader]
Muhammad (Early life) **M: 910**
Muslims (Muhammad) **M: 964a;** (The early caliphs) **M: 964a**
Shi`ites **S: 400**
Alí Muhammad [Iranian religious leader]
Bahá'ís **B: 27**
Ali Reza [Muslim leader]
Meshad **M: 421**
Alia, Ramiz [Albanian government official]
Albania (Communist control) **A: 308**
Alianza Federal de Mercedes [organization]
Hispanic Americans (The Chicano movement) **H: 256**
Alianza País [political party]
Ecuador (Recent developments) **E: 74**
Alianza Popular Revolucionaria Americana [political party]
Peru (The rise of APRA) **P: 316;** (Return to civilian government) **P: 316**
Alibates Flint Quarries National Monument [Texas]
National Park System (table: National monuments) **N: 50**
Alice [fictional character]
Naylor, Phyllis Reynolds **N: 91**
Alice [literary figure]
See also Alice in Wonderland *in this index*
Carroll, Lewis (The *Alice* books) **C: 249**
Alice in Wonderland [book by Carroll] **A: 367**
Carroll, Lewis **C: 248** *with picture*
Literature for children (Fantasies) **L: 359;** (Masterpieces of fiction) **L: 363**
Tenniel, Sir John **T: 160** *with picture*
Alice's Adventures in Wonderland [book by Carroll]
See Alice in Wonderland *in this index*
Alice's Adventures under Ground [story by Carroll]
Alice in Wonderland **A: 367**
Alicyclic [chemistry]
Hydrocarbon (Alicyclics) **H: 465**
Alidade [instrument]
Surveying (Early tools) **So: 1011-1012**
Al-Idrīsī [Arab explorer]
Exploration (Muslim exploration) **E: 442**
Map (Maps in the Middle Ages) **M: 183-184**
`Ālids [Arab history]
Arabs (The rise and spread of Islam) **A: 589-590**
Alien [extraterrestrial]
Extraterrestrial intelligence **E: 458**
Unidentified flying object **U: 27**
Alien [person] **A: 367**
Citizenship **Ci: 569;** (What it means to be a citizen) **Ci: 569**
Deportation **D: 149**
Illegal alien **I: 51**
Immigration and Naturalization Service **I: 86**
Alien and Sedition Acts [1798] **A: 368**
Adams, John (The Alien and Sedition Acts) **A: 38**
Jefferson, Thomas (Vice president) **J: 82**
Kentucky (Statehood) **K: 291**
Kentucky and Virginia Resolutions **K: 295**
United States, History of the (The Alien and Sedition Acts) **U: 163**
Alien Enemies Act [1798]
Alien **A: 368**
Alien and Sedition Acts **A: 368**
Alien Friends Act [1798]
Alien and Sedition Acts **A: 368**
Alien Registration Act of 1940 *See* Smith Act *in this index*
Alienation [psychology] **A: 368**
Alighieri, Dante *See* Dante Alighieri *in this index*
Alignment [archaeology]
Megalithic monuments **M: 383**
Al-Ikhwān al-Muslimūn [organization] *See* Muslim Brotherhood *in this index*
Aliki [American author]
Literature for children *picture on* **L: 381**
Alimentary canal [anatomy] **A: 368** *with diagram*
Digestive system **D: 202** *with diagram*
Human body (The digestive system) **H: 419**
Stomach **So: 907**
Alimony [law] **A: 369**

Divorce (Financial arrangements) **D: 254**
Sex discrimination (Changes in laws) **S: 335**
Alinghi [boat]
America's Cup **A: 431**
Alinsky, Saul David [American social reformer] **A: 369**
Aliphatic hydrocarbon [chemistry]
Hydrocarbon (Aliphatic hydrocarbons) **H: 465**
Alison's House [play by Glaspell]
Glaspell, Susan **G: 210**
Aliteracy
Reading (Reading problems) **R: 161**
Alito, Samuel Anthony, Jr. [American jurist] **A: 369**
Supreme Court of the United States *picture on* **So: 999**
Aliyev, Heydar [Azerbaijani political leader]
Azerbaijan (History) **A: 997-998**
Aliyev, Ilham [Azerbaijani political leader]
Azerbaijan (Recent developments) **A: 998**
Alizarin [dye]
Mordant **M: 801**
Al-Jazeera [news service]
Television (In the Middle East) **T: 116**
Al Jazirah [region, Sudan] *See* Gezira, El *in this index*
Al Jizah *See* Giza *in this index*
Alkali [chemistry]
See also Base *in this index*
Base **B: 123**
Detergent and soap (How soap is made) **D: 164**
First aid (Eye injury) **F: 140**
Food additive (Kinds of additives) **F: 339-340**
Gardening (Analyzing the soil) **G: 31-32**
Turmeric **T: 515**
Alkali feldspar [mineral]
Feldspar **F: 68**
Granite **G: 311**
Alkali metal [chemistry] **A: 369**
Element, Chemical *diagram on* **E: 221**
Alkali metal halide [chemistry]
Alkali metal **A: 369**
Alkali metal hydroxide [chemistry]
Alkali metal **A: 369**
Alkaline earth metal [chemistry]
Element, Chemical *diagram on* **E: 221**
Magnesium (Properties) **M: 54**
Alkaline primary battery [device]
Battery (Primary batteries) **B: 169;** (Types and uses of batteries) **B: 171**
Alkaloid [chemistry] **A: 369**
Nightshade **N: 421**
Alkane [chemistry]
Hydrocarbon (Aliphatic hydrocarbons) **H: 465**
Alkatiri, Mari [Timorese political leader]
East Timor (History) **E: 41-42**
Alkene [chemistry]
Hydrocarbon (Aliphatic hydrocarbons) **H: 465**
Al-Khalifa, Hamad bin Isa [king of Bahrain]
Bahrain (History) **B: 30-31**
Al Khalifah Arabs
Bahrain (History) **B: 30**
Alkhanov, Alu [Chechen political leader]
Chechnya **C: 390**
Al-Khuwarizmi [Persian scholar]
Encyclopedia (The first reference works) **E: 268a**
Al-Khwārizmī [Arab mathematician] **A: 370**
Algebra (History) **A: 359**
Mathematics (Arab mathematics) **M: 306**
Number (The Hindu-Arabic numeral system) **N: 607**
Al-Krim, Abd [Moroccan political leader]
Morocco (French and Spanish control) **M: 814-815**
Al-Kuwatly, Shukri [Syrian political leader]
United Arab Republic **U: 46**
Alkylation [industrial process]
Petroleum (Conversion) **P: 344-345**
Alkylbenzene sulfonate [chemical]
Detergent and soap (The development of detergents) **D: 165**
Alkyne [chemistry]
Hydrocarbon (Aliphatic hydrocarbons) **H: 465**
All About Eve [film]
Motion picture (Best picture: 1950) **M: 861**
All About My Mother [film]
Almodóvar, Pedro **A: 380**
All-America Football Conference
Football (The rise of professional football) **F: 367**
National Football League **N: 35**
All-American Canal [canal, Arizona-California]
Canal (Major canals in the United States and Canada) **C: 164**
Imperial Valley **I: 92**
All-American Girls Professional Baseball League
Baseball (Depression and war) **B: 136**
All-American Soap Box Derby [Akron, Ohio]
Soap Box Derby **So: 543**
All-around competition [event]

Gymnastics (Men's events) **G:** 448-449; (Women's events) **G:** 449
All Basotho Convention [political party]
 Lesotho (History) **L:** 208
All-Burma Students' Union [political movement]
 Myanmar (British conquest and rule) **M:** 970d
All Creatures Great and Small [book by Herriot]
 Herriot, James **H:** 216
All-England Championship
 Tennis (table) **T:** 166b
All England Women's Hockey Association
 Field hockey (History) **F:** 93
All for Love [play by Dryden]
 Dryden, John **D:** 369
All Green Shall Perish [book by Mallea]
 Latin American literature (The mid-1900's) **L:** 114
All Hallow Summer [weather]
 Indian summer **I:** 189
All Hallow's Eve [holiday]
 All Saints' Day **A:** 370
 Halloween **H:** 24a
"All in the Family" [television series]
 Television (The 1970's) **T:** 119 *with picture*
All-India Muslim League
 Muslim League **M:** 964
All My Sons [play by Miller]
 Miller, Arthur **M:** 553
All-or-nothing phenomenon
 Nervous system (The beginning of an impulse) **N:** 135
All-purpose flour
 Flour (Types of flour) **F:** 268
All Quiet on the Western Front [book by Remarque]
 Remarque, Erich Maria **R:** 228
All Quiet on the Western Front [film]
 Motion picture (Best picture: 1929-30) **M:** 861
All Saints' Church, Margaret Street [London]
 Architecture (The Gothic Revival) **A:** 626
All Saints' Day A: 370
 Día de los muertos **D:** 178
 Halloween **H:** 24a; (All Saints' and All Souls' Day) **H:** 25
 New Orleans (Ethnic groups) **N:** 280-281
"All She Wants to Do is Rock" [song]
 Rock music (Musical roots) **R:** 376
All Souls College
 Oxford, University of **O:** 887
All Souls' Day
 Día de los muertos **D:** 178
 Halloween (All Saints' and All Souls' Day) **H:** 25
 Latin America (Recreation) **L:** 98
All-Star Baseball Game
 Baseball (All-Star Game) **B:** 130; (Depression and war) **B:** 136
All-Star Hockey Game
 Hockey (Famous players and All-Star teams) **H:** 281
All-suite hotel
 Hotel (History) **H:** 376-377
All-terrain vehicle A: 370
All the Best: My Life in Letters and Other Writings [book by Bush]
 Bush, George Herbert Walker (Later years) **B:** 722a
"All the Girls I've Loved Before" [song]
 Nelson, Willie **N:** 123
All the King's Men [book by Warren]
 Warren, Robert Penn **W:** 37
All the King's Men [film]
 Motion picture (Best picture: 1949) **M:** 861
All Things Bright and Beautiful [book by Herriot]
 Herriot, James **H:** 216
All Things Wise and Wonderful [book by Herriot]
 Herriot, James **H:** 216
All-wheel drive
 Transmission (Transmissions and drives) **T:** 375
Alla prima [painting]
 Painting (Baroque) **P:** 58
Allagash Falls [Maine]
 Maine *picture on* **M:** 82
Allah [religion] **A:** 370
 God **G:** 243
 Islam **I:** 463
 Islamic art (Characteristics) **I:** 467
 Muslims (The Arabs before Islam) **M:** 964a
 Qur'ān (Teachings) **Q:** 44
 Religion (Islam) **R:** 223
Allahabad [India] **A:** 370
Allain, William A. [American political leader]
 Mississippi (table) **M:** 640
Allais, Maurice [French economist]
 Nobel Prizes (Economics: 1988) **N:** 449
Allan, Sir Hugh [Canadian businessman]
 Abbott, Sir John Joseph Caldwell (Early political career) **A:** 5-6; (The Pacific Scandal) **A:** 6
 Macdonald, Sir John Alexander (The Pacific

Scandal) **M:** 9
 Mackenzie, Alexander (Leader of the opposition) **M:** 22
Allan, John [foster father of]
 Poe, Edgar Allan (Poe's life) **P:** 589
Allawi, Iyad [Iraqi political leader]
 Iraq (The Iraq War) **I:** 414a-414b; (A new government) **I:** 414b
Allegheny Front
 West Virginia (Land regions) **W:** 218
Allegheny Mountains [U.S.] **A:** 371 *with map*
 Pennsylvania (Land regions) **P:** 256 *with picture*
 West Virginia *picture on* **W:** 206; (Land regions) **W:** 218
Allegheny Plateau [region, U.S.] *See* Appalachian Plateau *in this index*
Allegheny Portage Railroad National Historic Site [Pennsylvania]
 National Park System (table: National historic sites) **N:** 52
Allegheny River [New York-Pennsylvania] **A:** 371
 Pittsburgh (The city) **P:** 500a *with picture*
Allegiance, Oath of *See* Oath of allegiance *in this index*
Allegiance, Pledge of *See* Pledge of Allegiance *in this index*
Allegory A: 371
 Mythology (The study of myths) **M:** 988
Allegory of Love, The [book by Lewis]
 Lewis, C. S. **L:** 220
Allegri, Antonio [Italian artist] *See* Correggio *in this index*
Allegro [dance]
 Ballet (table) **B:** 45
Allegro [music]
 Music (table) **M:** 954
"Allegro, L'" [poem by Milton]
 Milton, John (His early life and works) **M:** 557
Allele [genetics]
 Genetic testing (How genes carry information) **G:** 84d
 Heredity (Patterns of heredity) **H:** 202
 Races, Human **R:** 57 *with map*
Allele frequency [genetics]
 Heredity (Gene pools and allele frequency) **H:** 203-204
Allen, Augustus C. [American settler]
 Houston **H:** 394
Allen, Ebenezer [American settler]
 Rochester (Government and history) **R:** 370
Allen, Ethan [American soldier] **A:** 371
 Arnold, Benedict (A courageous soldier) **A:** 741
 Fort Ticonderoga **F:** 416
 Green Mountain Boys **G:** 380
 Vermont *picture on* **V:** 335
Allen, Forrest C. [American basketball coach]
 Rupp, Adolph **R:** 521
Allen, Frank G. [American political leader]
 Massachusetts (table) **M:** 288
Allen, George Felix [American political leader]
 Virginia (table) **V:** 417
Allen, Gracie [American entertainer]
 Burns, George **B:** 709
 Radio (The Golden Age of Broadcasting) **R:** 92 *with picture*
Allen, Henry J. [American political leader]
 Kansas (table) **K:** 234; (Spirit of reform) **K:** 237-238
Allen, Henry W. [American political leader]
 Louisiana (table) **L:** 496
Allen, John K. [American settler]
 Houston **H:** 394
Allen, Marcus [American football player]
 Football (table) **F:** 363
Allen, Oscar K. [American political leader]
 Louisiana (table) **L:** 496
Allen, Paul [American businessman]
 Computer (The personal computer) **Ci:** 924c-924d
 Gates, Bill **G:** 67
 Microsoft Corporation **M:** 519
Allen, Philip [American political leader]
 Rhode Island (table) **R:** 311
Allen, Phog [American basketball coach]
 Rupp, Adolph **R:** 521
Allen, Richard [American religious leader] **A:** 372
 African Methodist Episcopal Church **A:** 137
 Jones, Absalom **J:** 157
Allen, William [American jurist]
 Allentown **A:** 373
Allen, William [American political leader] **A:** 371
 Ohio (table) **O:** 699
Allen, William Francis [American publisher]
 Spiritual **So:** 796
Allen, Woody [American director] **A:** 372
 Motion picture (Best achievement in directing: 1977) **M:** 862; (A new generation of

filmmakers) **M:** 871-872
Allen-Bradley Clock Tower
 Milwaukee (Annual events and places of interest) **M:** 560
Allen Telescope Array
 Extraterrestrial intelligence **E:** 458
 SETI Institute **S:** 323
Allenby, Lord [British general] **A:** 372
 World War I (The fighting ends) **W:** 463
Allende, Isabel [Chilean author] **A:** 372
 Latin American literature (The post-Boom) **L:** 114
Allende Gossens, Salvador [Chilean political leader] **A:** 373
 Allende, Isabel **A:** 372
 Chile (Marxism and military rule) **C:** 470
 Pinochet Ugarte, Augusto **P:** 474
Allentown [area]
 Buffalo (Other interesting places to visit) **B:** 678
Allentown [Pennsylvania] **A:** 373
Allergen [biochemistry]
 Allergy **A:** 373
 Anaphylactic shock **A:** 448
 Dust mite **D:** 392
 Immune system (Allergies) **I:** 88c
Allergic conjunctivitis [disorder]
 Allergy **A:** 373
Allergic rhinitis [disorder]
 Hay fever (Treatment) **H:** 116
 Immune system (The humoral immune response) **I:** 88
 Rhinitis **R:** 293
Allergy [disease] **A:** 373
 Anaphylactic shock **A:** 448
 Antibiotic (Allergic reactions) **A:** 551
 Asthma (Causes) **A:** 824-825
 Croup **Ci:** 1157
 Disease (Disorders of the immune system) **D:** 229-230
 Drug (Effect on the body) **D:** 354
 Dust mite **D:** 392
 Eczema **E:** 74
 Hay fever **H:** 116
 Herbal medicine **H:** 197
 Hives **H:** 270
 Immune system (Allergies) **I:** 88c
 MedicAlert **M:** 361
 Medicine (table) **M:** 369
 Milk (Milk in the human diet) **M:** 546
 Peanut **P:** 213
 Poisonous plant **P:** 602
AllerMax [drug]
 Antihistamine **A:** 556
Alley cat
 Cat (Breeds of cats) **C:** 290
Alley Theatre
 Theater *picture on* **T:** 246
Alleyn, Roderick [fictional character]
 Marsh, Ngaio **M:** 228
Alliance [Malaysian history]
 Malaysia (Building national unity) **M:** 102
Alliance [political science]
 See also Allies; Central Powers *in this index*
 Balance of power **B:** 36
 Foreign policy (Influences on foreign policy) **F:** 387
 International relations (Treaties) **I:** 344
Alliance for Austria's Future [political party]
 Austria (Recent developments) **A:** 940
Alliance for Children and Families
 Social work (Family and child welfare) **So:** 558
Alliance for Progress [program] **A:** 374
 Foreign aid (Economic development and mutual security) **F:** 383-384
 Kennedy, John Fitzgerald (Other developments) **K:** 266
 Pan-American conferences (Stronger ties) **P:** 113
Alliance of Free Democrats [political party]
 Hungary (Politics) **H:** 439; (Multiparty elections) **H:** 448
Allied Command Operations [military]
 North Atlantic Treaty Organization (Organization) **N:** 471
Allied Command Transformation [military]
 North Atlantic Treaty Organization (Organization) **N:** 471
Allied High Commission [German history]
 Germany (West Germany) **G:** 170
Allied Invasion *See* Normandy Invasion *in this index*
Allies [World Wars I and II]
 United States, History of the (World War I and postwar growth [1917-1929]) **U:** 188; (World War II) **U:** 193
 World War I **W:** 452 *with pictures and maps*; (table: The Allies) **W:** 453
 World War II **W:** 468 *with pictures and maps*; (table: The Allies) **W:** 471

Alligator A: 375 *with pictures*
Crocodile Ci: 1149
Reptile (Crocodilians) R: 251
Alligator gar [fish]
Gar G: 28
Alligator Reef Light Station [Florida]
Lighthouse *picture on* L: 295
Alligator snapping turtle
Snapping turtle S: 537
Turtle (Snapping turtles) T: 523
Allin, Roger [American political leader]
North Dakota (table) N: 513
Al Lisan [Jordan]
Dead Sea D: 56
Allison, Abraham K. [American political leader]
Florida (table) F: 260
Allison, Bobby [American race driver]
Automobile racing (table: NASCAR Sprint Cup champions) A: 981
Alliteration [poetry] A: 376
Poetry (table) P: 594; (Sounds) P: 594-595
Allocation [economics] *See* Distribution *in this index*
Allopolyploidy [biology]
Evolution (Evolution of new species) E: 429-430
Allopurinol [drug]
Gout G: 281
Allosaurus [dinosaur] A: 376
Dinosaur *pictures on* D: 206c, D: 207
Allotrope [chemistry]
Allotropy A: 377
Manganese (Properties) M: 139
Phosphorus P: 403
Sulfur (Properties) So: 966
Allotropy [chemistry] A: 377
Allouez, Claude Jean [French religious leader]
Wisconsin (European exploration and settlement) W: 365
Allowance [tax law]
Income tax (Defining taxable income) I: 102
Allowance race
Horse racing (Allowance races) H: 365
Alloy [metal] A: 377 *with picture*
Aluminum A: 391
Bismuth B: 383
Cobalt (Uses) Ci: 741
Gold (Gold alloys) G: 251
Iron and steel I: 436
Materials (Metals and alloys) M: 300d
Metallurgy (Physical metallurgy) M: 427
Money (Modern U.S. currency) M: 713-714
Solution (Solid solutions) So: 587
Zinc Z: 594
Alloy, Polymeric
Plastics (The chemistry of plastics) P: 556
Alloy steel
Alloy (Alloys of iron) A: 377-378
Iron and steel (Kinds of iron and steel) I: 436-437
Allred, James V. [American political leader]
Texas (table) T: 203
All's Well That Ends Well [play by Shakespeare]
Shakespeare, William: (*All's Well That Ends Well*) S: 362
Allspice [spice]
Pimento P: 465
Alluvial diamond
Diamond (Where natural diamonds are found) D: 181
Alluvial fan [geology]
River (Alluvial fans and deltas) R: 353 *with diagram*
Allylic
Plastics (table) P: 556
Alma-Ata [Kazakhstan] *See* Almaty *in this index*
Alma mater A: 379
Alma-Tadema, Sir Lawrence [British artist]
Painting (Later neoclassicism) P: 67-68; (The art world, 1850-1900) P: 73
al-Ma'arri [Arabic poet]
Arabic literature (Poetry) A: 583
Almagest [book by Ptolemy]
Mathematics (The Greeks) M: 306
Ptolemy P: 854
Almagro, Diego de [Spanish explorer]
Chile (Spanish conquest) C: 468
Exploration (Spain's conquests in the New World) E: 445
Latin America *map on* L: 105
Pizarro, Francisco (First expeditions) P: 504; (Later life) P: 504
Al-Mahdi, Muhammad [Islamic religious leader]
Islam (Divisions of Islam) I: 466
Al Mahdi, Sadiq [Sudanese political leader]
Sudan (Civil war) So: 953
Almanac [book] A: 379 *with picture*
Calendar *picture on* C: 29
Navigation (Keeping time) N: 71

Almandine [gem]
Garnet G: 45
Mineral *picture on* M: 569
Al-Mansūr, Abū Jʿafar [caliph of Abbāsid empire]
Baghdad (History) B: 26
Almaty [Kazakhstan] A: 379
Kazakhstan K: 250a
Almaviva, Count [literary figure]
Opera: (*Barber of Seville, The*) O: 801 *with picture*; (*Marriage of Figaro, The*) O: 805-806
Almayer's Folly [book by Conrad]
Conrad, Joseph Ci: 973
Al-Megrahi, Abdel Basset Ali [Libyan public figure]
Libya (United Nations sanctions) L: 268
Almeida, Francisco de [Portuguese government official]
Magellan, Ferdinand (Early life) M: 45-46
Almodóvar, Pedro [Spanish director] A: 380
Spain (Motion pictures) So: 739
Almohad Empire
Berbers B: 256
Almond [nut] A: 380 *with picture*
Nut (Kinds of nuts) N: 621 *with picture*
Plant *picture on* P: 535
Almond, Edward M. [American general]
Korean War (The Inchon landing) K: 381
Almond, J. Lindsay, Jr. [American political leader]
Virginia (table) V: 417
Almond, Lincoln C. [American political leader]
Rhode Island (table) R: 311
Almoravid Dynasty
Berbers B: 256
Almoravids [people]
Ghana Empire G: 181 *with map*
Almquist, Carl Jonas Love [Swedish author]
Scandinavian literature (The Golden Age) S: 171
Almsgiving
Islam (The Five Pillars of Islam) I: 463-464
Al Muharraq [island, Bahrain]
Bahrain (Land and climate) B: 30 *with map*
Al-Mutanabbi [Arab poet]
Arabic literature (Poetry) A: 583
Almy & Brown [textile firm]
Slater, Samuel S: 501
Al-Nahyan [family]
Abu Dhabi A: 19
Alnico alloy [metal]
Alloy (Other alloys) A: 378
Magnetism (Permanent magnets) M: 60
Alnilam [novel by Dickey]
Dickey, James D: 190
Aloe [plant] A: 380 *with picture*
Aloe vera [plant]
Aloe A: 380
Aloha Festivals
Hawaii (Visitor's guide) H: 98 *with picture*
"Aloha Oe" [song]
Liliuokalani, Lydia Kamekeha L: 303
Aloha shirt
Hawaii (Clothing) H: 94
Pacific Islands (Clothing) P: 7
Aloha State [name for]
Hawaii H: 88
Aloha Tower [Honolulu]
Hawaii (Places to visit) H: 98
Alois [Lichtensteiner ruler]
Liechtenstein (History) L: 273
Alomar, Roberto [American baseball player]
Baseball (table: Hall of Fame) B: 134
Along This Way [book by Johnson]
Johnson, James Weldon Ji: 143
Alonso, Fernando [Spanish-born race driver]
Automobile racing (table: Formula One World Drivers' Championship) A: 980
Alonso, Yonder [American baseball player]
Hispanic Americans *picture on* H: 245
Alouettes, Montreal
Football (Canadian Football League) F: 364
Montreal (Sports) M: 775
Alp [letter]
A A: 1 *with picture*
Alpaca [animal] A: 380 *with picture*
Mammal *picture on* M: 119
Alpenhorn [musical instrument] *See* Alphorn *in this index*
Alpha [letter]
A A: 1 *with picture*
Alphabet (The Greeks) A: 383
Alpha cells
Pancreas P: 128
Alpha Centauri [star] A: 381
Star (Brightness of stars) So: 840; (table: The 10 brightest stars as seen from Earth) So: 842; (table: The 10 known stars nearest Earth) So: 843
Alpha decay [physics]

Transmutation of elements T: 378
Alpha fetoprotein [chemical]
Testicular cancer T: 182
Alpha-hemolytic streptococcus [bacterium]
Streptococcus So: 926
Alpha interferon [drug]
Interferon I: 324
Alpha Lyrae [star] *See* Vega *in this index*
Alpha Orionis [star] *See* Betelgeuse *in this index*
Alpha particle [radiation] A: 381
See also Alpha ray *in this index*
Atom (Radioactivity) A: 873
Helium H: 175
Nuclear energy (The beginning of nuclear physics) N: 590
Radiation *picture on* R: 78; (Particle radiation) R: 76; (Dose) R: 79-80; (Discovery of radioactivity) R: 81
Radium R: 100
Radon (Radon decay) R: 100
Star (Destruction of light nuclei) So: 846
Transmutation of elements T: 379
Alpha ray [radiation]
See also Alpha particle *in this index*
Nuclear energy (The beginning of nuclear physics) N: 590
Alpha Ridge [geography]
Arctic Ocean (The deep basin) A: 643 *with map*
Alpha wave [physiology]
Electroencephalograph E: 200
Alphabet A: 381 *with pictures*
See also the articles on specific letters, such as A, and the list of Related articles in the Alphabet *article*
Braille B: 550 *with pictures*
Communication (Early writing systems) Ci: 879
Flag *pictures on* F: 196
Greek language (Alphabet) G: 376 *with pictures*
Handwriting (Early forms of writing) H: 49-50
Hebrew language H: 161 *with pictures*
Latin language (Alphabet) L: 114
Morse code *pictures on* M: 819
Phoenicia (Language) P: 393
Phonetics (An international phonetic alphabet) P: 400
Rune R: 520
Russian language (Alphabet) R: 557 *with pictures*
Shorthand S: 435 *with pictures*
Alphabet, Cipher
Codes and ciphers (Substitution) Ci: 750
Alphabetical arrangement
Dictionary D: 192
Encyclopedia (Arrangement of content) E: 266
Alphadon [animal]
Prehistoric animal *picture on* P: 739
Alpher, Ralph A. [American physicist]
Big bang B: 297
Alphonsus Liguori, Saint [Italian religious leader] A: 384
Alphorn [musical instrument] A: 384 *with picture*
Alpine avens
Flower *picture on* F: 289
Alpine fir [tree]
Plant *picture on* P: 524
Alpine forget-me-not [plant]
Flower *picture on* F: 289
Plant *picture on* P: 524
Alpine ibex [animal]
Goat (Domestic goats) G: 239
Ibex I: 3
Alpine lewisia [plant]
Flower *picture on* F: 289
Alpine Mountain System [Europe]
Europe (The Alpine Mountain System) E: 393 *with picture*
Alpine phacelia [flower]
Flower *picture on* F: 289
Alpine pond
Pond (Kinds of ponds) P: 656
Alpine skiing
Olympic Games (Winter Olympic Games) O: 746d
Skiing *diagrams on* S: 484; (Alpine skiing) S: 482 *with picture*; (Ski equipment and clothing) S: 483; (Alpine competitions) S: 486
Alpine style climbing
Mountain climbing (Styles of mountain climbing) M: 897
Alpine tundra
Flower (Flowers of alpine tundras) F: 289 *with pictures*
Tundra T: 485
Alpinism *See* Mountain climbing *in this index*
Alprazolam [drug]
Benzodiazepine B: 256
Alps [mountains, Europe] A: 384 *with pictures and map*
See also the list of Related articles in the Alps *article*

Austria A: 928 *with picture, pictures on* A: 932, A: 937; (Land and climate) A: 933
Europe *picture on* E: 381; (The Alpine Mountain System) E: 393 *with picture*
Germany (The Bavarian Alps) G: 157 *with picture and map*
Glacier (Famous glaciers) G: 204
Ice age (Evidence of ice ages and their climates) I: 6-7
Italy I: 496 *with picture*; (The Alpine Slope) I: 506 *with picture*
Mountain (Fold-thrust mountains) M: 893
Switzerland (The Swiss Alps) So: 1055 *with map*
Tyrol T: 542 *with map*
Al Qahirah
Cairo (History) C: 17
Al-Qaʿida [organization] *See* Qaʿida, Al- *in this index*
Al Qayrawan [Tunisia]
Fātimid dynasty F: 55
Al-Qays, Imru [Arab poet]
Arabic literature (Poetry) A: 583
ALS [disease] *See* Amyotrophic lateral sclerosis *in this index*
Al-Sabah, Sheik al-Salim [Kuwaiti ruler]
Kuwait (History) K: 396
Al-Sabah, Sheik Jabir al-Ahmad [Kuwaiti ruler]
Kuwait (History) K: 396
Al-Sabah, Sheik Saad al-Abdullah al-Salim [Kuwaiti ruler]
Kuwait (History) K: 396-397
Al-Sabah, Sheik Sabah al-Ahmad al-Jabir [Kuwaiti ruler]
Kuwait (History) K: 396
Al-Sabah [ruling family]
Kuwait (Government) K: 395; (History) K: 396
al-Sabur, Salah ʿAbd [Egyptian author]
Arabic literature (Poetry) A: 583
Alsace-Lorraine [region, France] A: 387 *with map*
France *picture on* F: 466
Rhine River (The Rhine in history) R: 293
Ruhr (History) R: 518
Al Salam Boccaccio 98 [ship]
Shipwreck (table: Major shipwrecks) S: 428
Al-Sayyab, Badr Shakir [Iraqi author]
Arabic literature (Poetry) A: 583
Al-Shuqayri, Ahmad [Palestinian political leader]
Palestine Liberation Organization (History) P: 106
Alsop, Mary O'Hara [American author]
O'Hara, Mary O: 679
Alsted, Johann Heinrich [German theologian]
Encyclopedia (From the 1200's to the 1600's) E: 268a
Alston, Walter [American baseball manager]
Baseball (table: Hall of Fame) B: 134
Alta River dam
Norway *picture on* N: 544
Sami (History) S: 80
Altai Mountains [Asia] A: 387
Kazakhstan (Land and climate) K: 250b *with map*
Altai wapiti [animal]
Elk (The European elk) E: 242
Altaic language
Language *map on* L: 65; (Other language families) L: 66
Altamont [California]
Rock music (Outdoor rock festivals) R: 380b
Altar [religion] A: 388
Riemenschneider, Tilman *picture on* R: 337
Sculpture (Roman sculpture) S: 247-248 *with picture*
Altar of Peace [sculpture]
Rome, Ancient (Sculpture, painting, and mosaics) R: 442
Alternate host [biology]
Rust R: 567
Alternating current [electricity]
Capacitor C: 186
Edison, Thomas Alva (Personal life) E: 81
Electric current (Direct and alternating current) E: 168
Electric generator E: 170
Electric motor E: 178
Electricity (Direct and alternating current) E: 193-194
Electronics (Diodes) E: 210-212
Inductance I: 240
Induction coil I: 240
Technology (The use of electricity) T: 75
Tesla, Nikola T: 181
Transformer T: 371
Vacuum tube (Kinds of vacuum tubes) V: 258-259
Westinghouse Electric Corporation W: 242
Alternating-current generator
Electric generator E: 170; (Alternating-current generators) E: 171 *with diagrams*
Alternating-current motor

Electric motor E: 178; (AC motors) E: 181 *with diagram*
Alternation of generations [genetics] A: 388
Fern (Life cycle of a fern) F: 75 *with picture*
Hornwort H: 341
Kelp K: 257
Moss (How mosses live) M: 834-835
Plant (Sexual reproduction) P: 532 *with diagram*
Spore (Plant spores) So: 801
Alternativa [ceremony]
Bullfighting (Types of bullfights) B: 695
Alternative assessment [education]
Testing (Current issues in testing) T: 182a
Alternative medicine A: 388
Cancer (Alternative medicine) C: 173
Alternative minimum tax
Income tax (Figuring the individual income tax) I: 104
Alternative rock
Rock music (Alternative rock) R: 381; (Rock music today) R: 381
Alternative school [education] A: 388
Education (What should be taught?) E: 105
School (Growth and reform) S: 184
Alternator *See* Alternating-current generator *in this index*
Altgeld, John Peter [American political leader] A: 389
Cleveland, Grover (Labor unrest) Ci: 672-673
Illinois (table) I: 71; (Industrial development) I: 74-75
Al-Thani, Hamad bin Khalifa [ruler of Qatar]
Qatar (History) Q: 3
Al-Thani, Khalifa bin Hamad [ruler of Qatar]
Qatar (History) Q: 3
Al-Thani family [rulers of Qatar]
Qatar (Government) Q: 3
Althing [government]
Iceland (National government) I: 20; (Early days) I: 23; (Great disasters) I: 23
Parliament (Parliaments in other countries) P: 174-175
Althusius, Johannes [German political scientist]
Political science (Secularism) P: 639
Altimeter [instrument] A: 389
Barometer (Uses) B: 116
Mountain (Measuring mountains) M: 896b
Altiplano [region, South America]
Andes Mountains (Physical features) A: 452
Bolivia (The Andean Highlands) B: 444 *with picture and map*; (Climate) B: 446
South America *picture on* So: 623; (The Andes Mountains) So: 626-628
Altis [ancient region]
Olympia O: 745
Altitude [astronomy]
Altitude A: 390
Altitude [aviation]
Airplane (Changing altitude) A: 221
Altitude [geography] A: 390
Altimeter A: 389
Climate (Why climates vary) Ci: 676
Mountain (Measuring mountains) M: 896b
Weather (Air temperature) W: 157
Altitude [geometry]
Triangle (Perimeter and area) T: 437
Altitude record
Glider (table) G: 230
Altitude sickness A: 390
Altitudinal migration
Migration (Types of migration) M: 538
Altman, Robert [American film director] A: 390
Altman, Sidney [American chemist]
Nobel Prizes (Chemistry: 1989) N: 444
Alto [music] *See* Contralto *in this index*
Alto flute [musical instrument]
Flute F: 307
Alto-rilievo [art]
Relief (High relief) R: 212 *with picture*
Altocumulus cloud
Cloud *pictures on* Ci: 709; (Kinds of clouds) Ci: 707 *with picture*
Alton Locke [book by Kingsley]
Kingsley, Charles K: 331
Alton Observer [newspaper]
Lovejoy, Elijah Parish L: 508
Altostratus cloud
Cloud (Middle clouds) Ci: 707
Altricial bird
Bird (Caring for the young) B: 359
Altruism
Golden rule G: 256
Social psychology So: 552
Altruistic infanticide [homicide]
Infanticide I: 264
Al-Tusi, Nasir al-Din [Persian mathematician]
Mathematics (Arab mathematics) M: 306

ALU [electronics] *See* Digital logic unit *in this index*
Alum [chemistry] A: 390
Water (Purifying and treating water) W: 126
Alumina [mineral] A: 390
Aluminum (Corrosion resistance) A: 392; (Sources of aluminum) A: 392-393; (How aluminum is produced) A: 393 *with diagram*
Bauxite B: 174
Ceramics (Kinds of ceramic products) C: 359-360
Aluminium *See* Aluminum *in this index*
Aluminum [element] A: 391 *with pictures*
Alloy (Alloys for strength and lightness) A: 378
Bauxite B: 174
Electrolysis (Uses of electrolysis) E: 200
Wire (Uses of wire) W: 344
Aluminum bronze [metal]
Bronze (Silicon and aluminum bronze) B: 638
Aluminum Company of America *See* Alcoa Inc. *in this index*
Aluminum Company of Canada, Ltd.
Kitimat K: 341
Aluminum hydroxide [compound]
Antacid A: 529
Aluminum oxide *See* Alumina *in this index*
Aluminum sulfate [chemical]
Water (Purifying and treating water) W: 126
Alva, Duke of [Spanish general] *See* Alba, Duke of *in this index*
Alvarado, Pedro de [Spanish conqueror] A: 398
El Salvador (Colonial period) E: 252
Guatemala (Colonial period) G: 416
Latin America *map on* L: 105; (The conquest of the American Indians) L: 103
San Pedro Sula S: 105
Alvarado, Salvador [Mexican political leader]
Yucatán Peninsula Y: 575
Alvarez, Carlos [American political leader]
Miami (History) M: 480-481
Alvarez Armelino, Gregorio [Uruguayan political leader]
Uruguay (Military government) U: 228
Alvarez de Toledo, Fernando [Spanish general] *See* Alba, Duke of *in this index*
Álvaro Obregón Dam [Mexico]
Dam (table) D: 18
Alveolar macrophage
Tuberculosis (Primary infection) T: 477-478
Alveoli [anatomy] *See* Alveolus *in this index*
Alveolus [lung structure]
Blood (Carrying oxygen and carbon dioxide) B: 408 *with diagram*
Emphysema (How emphysema affects breathing) E: 262 *with diagrams*
Hemoglobin H: 182
Human body (The air passages) H: 420-421; (The exchange of carbon dioxide and oxygen) H: 421 *with picture*
Lung (Parts of the lungs) L: 523; (Gas exchange in the lungs) L: 523-524 *with diagram*
Respiration (Structures of breathing) R: 260
Tuberculosis (How tuberculosis affects the body) T: 477
Alveolus [tooth structure]
Teeth (Periodontal ligament) T: 81 *with diagram*
Alvin [submersible]
Marine biology (Biological oceanographers) M: 205
Ocean (Submersibles) O: 663 *with picture*
Pacific Ocean (Scientific research) P: 15
Alvin Ailey American Dance Theater
Ailey, Alvin A: 168 *with picture*
Alward, David [Canadian political leader]
New Brunswick (table) N: 195
Always the Young Strangers [book by Sandburg]
Sandburg, Carl S: 108
ALWR [nuclear reactor] *See* Advanced light water reactor *in this index*
Alyattes [king of Lydia]
Croesus Ci: 1150
Alyssum, Sweet [plant]
Sweet alyssum So: 1036 *with picture*
Alzheimer, Alois [German psychiatrist]
Alzheimer's disease A: 398
Alzheimer's disease A: 398
Brain B: 550a; (Memory and imagination) B: 553 *with diagram*; (Genetic disorders) B: 558
Disease (Diseases associated with aging) D: 230-231
Hormone replacement therapy H: 338
Mental illness (Dementia) M: 405
Senility S: 300
Am [symbol]
Americium A: 431
A.M. [time]
Hour H: 379
AM screening
Printing (Preparing illustrations for reproduction)

P: 797
AMA [organization] *See* American Medical Association *in this index*
Amadeus [film]
Motion picture (Best picture: 1984) M: 861
Amadeus [play by Shaffer]
Shaffer, Peter S: 342
Amadís of Gaul [book] A: 399
Spanish literature (The 1400's) So: 758
Amado, Jorge [Brazilian author] A: 399
Brazil (The arts) B: 576-577
Latin American literature (The early 1900's) L: 113
Amager [island, Denmark]
Copenhagen Ci: 1038
Amago salmon [fish]
Salmon (Kinds of salmon) S: 70
Amahl and the Night Visitors [opera by Menotti]
Menotti, Gian Carlo M: 403
Amalekites [ancient people] A: 400
Amalgam [metal]
Metallurgy (Amalgamation) M: 427
Silver (Uses of silver) S: 463
Teeth (Dental decay) T: 82-83
Amalgamated Association of Iron and Steel
Homestead Strike H: 305
Amalgamated Association of Iron, Steel, and Tin Workers [labor union]
United Steelworkers U: 204
Amalgamated Clothing and Textile Workers Union
Hillman, Sidney H: 232
UNITE HERE U: 43
Amalgamated Meat Cutters and Butcher Workmen of North America
United Food and Commercial Workers International Union U: 47
Amalgamated Transit Union
Labor movement (table) L: 8
Amalgamated Wood Workers of America
Carpenters and Joiners of America, United Brotherhood of C: 246
Amalgamation [process] *See* Amalgam *in this index*
Amalienburg Pavilion [Germany]
Architecture *picture on* A: 623
Amalthea [satellite]
Jupiter (Inner satellites) J: 200a *with picture*
Planetary ring P: 514d
Amana Church Society [religious group]
Amanites A: 400
Amana Colonies [Iowa]
Iowa (Places to visit) I: 384 *with picture*
Amanita [fungus]
Mushroom (Poisonous mushrooms) M: 945 *with pictures*
Amanites [religious group] A: 400
Brethren B: 593
Amanullah Khan [emir of Afghanistan]
Afghanistan (Independence) A: 95
Amaranth [plant] A: 400 *with picture*
Amarcord [film]
Fellini, Federico F: 68
Amargosa Range [mountains, California]
Death Valley D: 62
Amarillo [Texas] A: 400
Amarna Revolution [ancient Egyptian history]
Egypt, Ancient (The New Kingdom) E: 143
Nefertiti N: 119
Amaryllis [plant] A: 400 *with picture*
Flower (table) F: 301 *with picture*
Amaterasu-Omikami [Shinto goddess]
Religion (Shinto) R: 221
Amateur astronomy
Astronomy (Learning about astronomy) A: 846
Amateur Athletic Union A: 401
Amateur Baseball Congress, American
Baseball (Amateur leagues) B: 131
Amateur Boxing Association of England
Boxing (Amateur boxing) B: 531
Amateur Hockey Association of the United States
Hockey (Amateur development) H: 281
Amateur league
Baseball (Amateur leagues) B: 131
Amateur radio *See* Radio, Amateur *in this index*
Amateur Softball Association [U.S.]
Softball (History) So: 572
Amati, Andrea [Italian violin maker]
Amati family A: 401
Amati, Antonio [Italian violin maker]
Amati family A: 401
Amati, Girolamo [Italian violin maker]
Amati family A: 401
Amati, Nicolo [Italian violin maker]
Amati family A: 401
Amati family [Italian violin makers] A: 401
Amauta [teacher]
Inca (Communication and learning) I: 97

Amazing Stories [magazine]
Science fiction (The early 1900's) S: 205
Amazon ant
Ant (Slave-making ants) A: 526
Amazon.com [company]
Book (Modern books) B: 468
E-book E: 2
Internet (Commerce) I: 350b; (The Web forms) I: 350g
Retailing (Nonstore retailing) R: 265
Amazon molly [fish]
Molly M: 696
Amazon parrot [bird]
Parrot (Kinds of parrots) P: 179
Amazon rain forest [South America] A: 401 *with pictures and map*
Deforestation *picture on* D: 89
Rain forest (The Americas) R: 126b
Amazon River [South America] A: 402 *with picture and map*
Brazil (Land and climate) B: 577 *with picture*
Exploration (Exploring the New World) E: 444-445
Inland waterway I: 274
Orellana, Francisco de O: 851
Rain forest (The Americas) R: 126b
River (table) R: 352
South America (Rivers) So: 628; (Animal and plant life) So: 631
Amazon River dolphin
Mammal *picture on* M: 117
River dolphin R: 354
Amazon stone [rock]
Feldspar F: 68
Amazonia National Park [Brazil]
National park (table) N: 42g
Amazonian manatee [animal]
Manatee M: 132
Amazonian Period
Mars (Periods of evolution) M: 226b-226c
Amazons [Greek mythology] A: 404
Amazon River (History) A: 404
Ambassador [diplomat] A: 404
Address, Forms of (Officials of the United States) A: 53; (Foreign officials in the United States) A: 54
Diplomacy (Diplomatic representatives) D: 216
Government (Foreign affairs) G: 283
International law I: 340
Ambassador extraordinary and plenipotentiary [diplomat]
Ambassador A: 404
Diplomacy (Diplomatic representatives) D: 216
Ambassadors, Girl Scout
Girl Scouts (Girls Scouts of the USA) G: 196
Ambassadors, The [book by James]
James, Henry (His works) J: 26
Ambedkar, B. R. [Indian political leader]
Buddhism (The sangha) B: 668
Amber A: 404 *with picture*
Electricity (Early discoveries) E: 196
Fossil (Other processes) F: 425
Gem *picture on* G: 78
Amber Spyglass, The [book by Pullman]
Pullman, Philip P: 900
Ambergris [industrial product] A: 405
Whale (American whaling) W: 262-263
Amberina glass
Glass (Types of art glass) G: 220
Amberjack [fish] A: 405 *with picture*
Ambient diving
Diving, Underwater (Ambient diving) D: 245 *with picture*
Ambler, Eric [British author] A: 405
Amblyopia [disease]
Blindness (Diseases) B: 401
Ambon [Indonesia]
Indonesia (The Molucca Islands) I: 234
Amboseli National Park [Kenya]
Bird *picture on* B: 328
National park (Kenya) N: 42d; (table) N: 42f
Ambrones [ancient people]
Teutons T: 183
Ambrose, Saint [Italian religious leader] A: 405
Augustine, Saint (His life) A: 888
Ambrosia [mythology] A: 405
Ambrosian Library [Milan]
Library (Italy) L: 261
Ambrozic, Aloysius Matthew [Canadian religious leader] A: 405
Ambulance A: 405 *with picture*
Emergency Medical Services E: 258
Fire department (Emergency medical operations) F: 124
Paramedic (Duties) P: 153
Radio (In public safety) R: 84
Society for the Prevention of Cruelty to Animals

picture on So: 563
Ambulatory [structure]
Architecture *picture on* A: 618; (table) A: 608 *with picture*
Cathedral (The plan of a cathedral) C: 301 *with diagram*
Ambulatory dialysis [medicine]
Kidney (Kidney diseases) K: 312
Ambulatory surgery
Surgery (A typical operation) So: 1006
Ambushing hawk [bird]
Hawk H: 111
AMD [disorder] *See* Age-related macular degeneration *in this index*
A.M.E. [organization] *See* African Methodist Episcopal Church *in this index*
A.M.E. Zion [organization] *See* African Methodist Episcopal Zion Church *in this index*
Ameba [microorganism] A: 406 *with picture*
Protozoan (Sarcodines) P: 837-838
Amebelodon [animal]
Prehistoric animal *picture on* P: 740
Amebic colitis [disease]
Colitis Ci: 772
Amebic dysentery [disease]
Ameba A: 406
Dysentery D: 383
Ameboid cell [biology]
Ameba A: 406
Ameche, Alan [American football player]
Football (table) F: 363
Ameche, Don [American actor]
Motion picture (Best performance by an actor in a supporting role: 1985) M: 862b
Amelia [book by Fielding]
Fielding, Henry (His novels) F: 94
Amelia Goes to the Ball [opera by Menotti]
Menotti, Gian Carlo M: 402
Amelung glass
Glass (Types of art glass) G: 220
Amen Corner, The [book by Baldwin]
Baldwin, James B: 39
Amendment [legislation] A: 406
See also specific amendments, such as First Amendment, *in this index*
Congress of the United States (Proposing constitutional amendments) Ci: 946
Constitution Ci: 995
Constitution of the United States (Amendments) Ci: 1002; (Article V) Ci: 1010; (Amendments to the Constitution) Ci: 1011-1016
Parliamentary procedure (Motions) P: 176
Amenemhet [king of ancient Egypt]
Egypt, Ancient (The Middle Kingdom) E: 143
Amenhotep IV [pharaoh of Egypt] *See* Akhenaten
Ament [botany] *See* Catkin *in this index*
America [continents] A: 407
See also Central America; North America; South America *in this index*
Central America C: 354 *with map*
Columbus, Christopher (Third voyage westward) Ci: 862
Exploration (The age of European exploration) E: 443 *with map*; (Linking the globe) E: 446
Map (Advances in European cartography) M: 184; (Mapping the Americas) M: 184
North America N: 458 *with pictures and maps*
Rain forest (The Americas) R: 126b *with map*
South America So: 622 *with pictures and maps*
America [country] *See* United States *in this index*
America [hymn] A: 407
America [ocean liner]
Virginia (Interesting facts) V: 399
America [sailboat]
America's Cup A: 431
Sailing (America's Cup) S: 27
*America*³ [sailboat]
America's Cup A: 431
America First Committee [U.S. history] A: 407
America Online, Inc. *See* AOL *in this index*
"America the Beautiful" [song] A: 407
Bates, Katharine Lee B: 162
America the Beautiful quarter [coin]
Money (Quarters) M: 714
America Today [painting by Benton]
Benton, Thomas Hart B: 254
American Academy of Arts and Letters A: 407
American Academy of Arts and Sciences A: 407
American Advertising Federation
Advertising (Advertising associations) A: 77
American aloe [plant] *See* Century plant *in this index*
American Amateur Baseball Congress
Baseball (Amateur leagues) B: 131
American Anti-Slavery Society [U.S. history]
Abolition movement A: 12
Garrison, William Lloyd G: 45

Philadelphia (Industrial beginnings) **P:** 366-367
Phillips, Wendell **P:** 382
American arborvitae [tree]
Tree *pictures on* **T:** 424
American Arctic Paleosiberian [language group]
Indian, American (Language groups) **I:** 149-150
American art
Colonial life in America (Painting) **Ci:** 807 *with picture*
Indian, American (Painting) **I:** 146
Painting (Painting outside France) **P:** 72; (The 1900's in North America) **P:** 82 *with pictures*
Sand painting **S:** 107
Sculpture (Early sculpture) **S:** 242 *with pictures*; (American sculpture) **S:** 255 *with pictures*
Western frontier life in America (Art) **W:** 239
American Art Portrait Gallery Building [Washington, D.C.]
Washington, D.C. *map on* **W:** 76
American Association for the Advancement of Science A: 408
American Association for the Relief of Misery on the Battlefields
Red Cross (In the United States) **R:** 187
American Association of Advertising Agencies
Advertising (Advertising associations) **A:** 77
American Association of Classified School Employees
Labor movement (table) **L:** 8
American Association of Family and Consumer Sciences
Family and consumer sciences (Career requirements) **F:** 26
American Association of Retired Persons *See* AARP *in this index*
American Association of Variable Star Observers
Astronomy (Learning about astronomy) **A:** 846
American Astronomical Society
Astronomy (Astronomy associations) **A:** 849
American avocet [bird]
Avocet **A:** 993 *with picture*
National Wildlife Refuge System *picture on* **N:** 62
American Ballet, School of
Balanchine, George **B:** 37
Lincoln Center for the Performing Arts **L:** 327
American Ballet Theatre
Ballet (Ballet in the United States) **B:** 53-54
American Baptist Association A: 408
American Baptist Churches in the U.S.A. A: 408
Baptists (Baptists in America) **B:** 101
American Bar Association A: 408
Law (Law education) **L:** 138
Law Day, U.S.A. **L:** 141
Rose, Uriah Milton **R:** 477
American Baseball League *See* American League *in this index*
American Basketball Association
Basketball (The history of professional basketball) **B:** 154a-155
National Basketball Association **N:** 30
American Battle Monuments Commission [U.S.] **A:** 408
National cemetery **N:** 31
American Beauty [film]
Motion picture (Best picture: 1999) **M:** 861
American beech [tree]
Tree *pictures on* **T:** 420
American Bell Telephone Company
Telephone (The Bell System) **T:** 100-101
American Bible Society
Bible (Modern English translations) **B:** 286
American Bicentennial Celebration *See* Bicentennial Celebration, American *in this index*
American bittern [bird]
Bird *picture on* **B:** 355
American black oystercatcher [bird]
Oystercatcher **O:** 893
American Board of Pathology
Forensic pathology **F:** 389a
American Board of Plastic Surgery
Plastic surgery (Qualifications for a plastic surgeon) **P:** 553
American bond [construction]
Brick (Bonds) **B:** 599 *with picture*
American Book Trade Directory [publication]
Book collecting (Collecting books) **B:** 469
American Bowling Congress
Bowling (The 1900's) **B:** 524b
American Broadcasting Company *See* ABC *in this index*
American Buffalo [play by Mamet]
Mamet, David **M:** 115
American butterfish [fish]
Butterfish **B:** 731 *with picture*
American Cancer Society A: 408
American Capitalism [book by Galbraith]
Galbraith, John Kenneth **G:** 9

American chameleon *See* Anole *in this index*
American Chemical Society A: 408
Science *picture on* **S:** 195
American chestnut [tree]
Chestnut **C:** 415 *with pictures*
American Circus Corporation
Circus (The Golden Age) **Ci:** 564
American Civil Liberties Union A: 408
Creationism (The 1900's) **Ci:** 1123
Ginsburg, Ruth Bader **G:** 192
American Claimant, The [book by Twain]
Twain, Mark (Later works) **T:** 530
American class [breeds]
Chicken (Kinds of chickens) **C:** 441 *with picture*
American cocker [dog]
Cocker spaniel **Ci:** 744
American College of Cardiology [organization]
Medicine (Medical organizations) **M:** 370
American College Testing Program
College entrance examination **Ci:** 775
American Colonies *See* Colonial life in America *in this index*
American Colonization Society
African Americans (Free blacks) **A:** 136g
Liberia (The Liberian settlement) **L:** 231
Monrovia **M:** 740
American Commonwealth, The [book by Bryce]
Bryce, James **B:** 656
American Contract Bridge League
Bridge (Regulation of tournaments) **B:** 605
American Cookery [book by Simmons]
Connecticut (Interesting facts) **Ci:** 953
American copper [butterfly] *picture on* **B:** 734
Insect *picture on* **I:** 282
American Council on Education A: 409
American cowslip [plant]
Cowslip **Ci:** 1113
American cream [horse]
Horse (table: Some types and breeds of horses) **H:** 343; (Draft horses) **H:** 346-347
American Crisis, The [book by Paine]
American literature (The revolutionary period [1765-1787]) **A:** 415
Bradford, William, III **B:** 544
Paine, Thomas (American revolutionary) **P:** 22
American crocodile
Crocodile (Kinds of crocodiles) **Ci:** 1149-1150 *with picture*
Endangered species *picture on* **E:** 271; (table) **E:** 270
American crossbill [bird]
Crossbill **Ci:** 1155 *with picture*
American crow [bird]
Crow (Kinds of crows) **Ci:** 1157 *with picture*
American curl [cat]
Cat (Long-haired breeds) **C:** 292
American dagger moth
Moth *picture on* **M:** 841
American Dam [Mexico-U.S.]
Rio Grande (Upper course) **R:** 346-347
American darter [bird]
Anhinga **A:** 467
American Dental Association A: 409
Dentistry (Organizations) **D:** 145
American Dental Hygienists' Association
Dental hygiene (Career) **D:** 143
American Dictionary of the English Language, An [book by Webster]
Webster, Noah **W:** 178
American Dilemma: The Negro Problem and Modern Democracy, An [book by Mydral]
Myrdal, Gunnar **M:** 971
American dipper [bird]
Dipper **D:** 217 *with picture*
American dog tick [animal]
Rocky Mountain spotted fever **R:** 394
Tick **T:** 279
American dogwood [plant]
Dogwood **D:** 284 *with picture*
American Dream, An [book by Mailer]
Mailer, Norman **M:** 67
American eagle [bird]
Great Seal of the United States (The face) **G:** 348
American Eagle [coin]
Eagle **E:** 6
American Education Week
American Legion (Activities) **A:** 412
Education Week, American **E:** 111
American eel
Eel **E:** 114
Fish *picture on* **F:** 159
Sargasso Sea (Origin of the seaweed) **S:** 125-126
American-Egyptian cotton *See* Pima cotton *in this index*
American Elasmobranch Society
Shark (Sharks and people) **S:** 376
American elk

Elk **E:** 241 *with picture*
American elm
Elm (Kinds) **E:** 245 *with picture*
Plant *picture on* **P:** 525
Tree *pictures on* **T:** 421
American Enterprise Institute for Public Policy Research A: 409
American Eskimo dog A: 409 *with picture*
American Exodus: A Record of Human Erosion, An [book by Lange]
Lange, Dorothea **L:** 61
American Expeditionary Forces *See* A.E.F. *in this index*
American Falls [waterfall, New York]
Niagara Falls **N:** 391 *with picture*; (Description) **N:** 391-392 *with picture*; (History) **N:** 392-393
American Farm Bureau Federation
Farm and farming (Farm organizations) **F:** 44
American Federation of Arts
Arts, American Federation of **A:** 763
American Federation of Government Employees A: 409
Labor movement (table) **L:** 8
American Federation of Labor
Labor movement (The first nationwide labor organizations) **L:** 9-10
American Federation of Labor and Congress of Industrial Organizations (History) **A:** 410
Gompers, Samuel **G:** 268
Green, William **G:** 380
Industrial Workers of the World **I:** 255
Lewis, John L. **L:** 221
United Automobile Workers **U:** 46
United States, History of the (Early reform efforts) **U:** 185
American Federation of Labor and Congress of Industrial Organizations A: 409
See also the separate entries American Federation of Labor *and* Congress of Industrial Organizations
Carpenters and Joiners of America, United Brotherhood of **C:** 246
Labor movement (The levels of union organization) **L:** 8
Meany, George **M:** 345
United Automobile Workers **U:** 46
American Federation of Musicians *See* Musicians, American Federation of *in this index*
American Federation of State, County, and Municipal Employees A: 410
Labor movement (table) **L:** 8
American Federation of Teachers A: 410
Labor movement (table) **L:** 8
Teaching (Teachers organizations) **T:** 69
American FFA degree
FFA (Degrees) **F:** 85-86
American Field Service [organization]
AFS Intercultural Programs **A:** 138
American flag *See* United States flag *in this index*
American flamingo [bird]
Flamingo **F:** 226
American Football Conference
Football (Professional competition) **F:** 364
National Football League **N:** 35
American Football League
Football (table: U.S. professional football champions) **F:** 365; (The rise of professional football) **F:** 367
National Football League **N:** 35
American Foundation for the Blind
Blindness (Education and training) **B:** 403
Disability (The 1900's) **D:** 221
American foxhound [dog] **A:** 411 *with picture*
Dog *picture on* **D:** 270
American Friends Service Committee A: 411
Nobel Prizes (Peace: 1947) **N:** 448a
Peace Corps (History) **P:** 208
American Fur Company [U.S. history]
Missouri (Statehood and expansion) **M:** 669
Nebraska (American exploration and settlement) **N:** 111-112
American GI Forum of the United States A: 411
Hispanic Americans (Effects of World War II) **H:** 253
American Girl doll
Doll (The 1980's) **D:** 293 *with picture*
American gooseberry [fruit]
Gooseberry **G:** 271
American Gothic [painting by Wood]
Painting (Regionalism) **P:** 82-83 *with picture*
Wood, Grant **W:** 390
American Graffiti [film]
Lucas, George **L:** 513
American Heart Association A: 411
American Historical Association
Historical Association, American **H:** 260
American history *See* United States, History of the

American History, National Museum of See
National Museum of American History *in this index*

American holly [tree]
Tree *pictures on* T: 422

American Home Economics Association
Family and consumer sciences (History) F: 26

American Humane Association
Humane society H: 430
Rodeo R: 397

"American Idol" [television program]
Fox F: 441
Television *picture on* T: 110; (The early 2000's)
T: 120

American Immigrant Wall of Honor
Ellis Island E: 244

American in Paris, An [film]
Motion picture (Best picture: 1951) M: 861

American in Paris, An [music by Gershwin]
Gershwin, George G: 174

American Independent Party See American Party
in this index

American Indian See Indian, American *in this index*

American Indian Movement [organization] A: 411
Indian, American (In the United States) I: 179
South Dakota (The mid-1900's) So: 684
Wounded Knee W: 502

**American Indian Movement Grand Governing
Council**
American Indian Movement A: 412

American Indian Religious Freedom Act [1978]
Indian, American (Political gains) I: 182

American Indians, National Congress of See
National Congress of American Indians *in this index*

**American Institute of Aeronautics and
Astronautics** A: 412

American Institute of Architects
Architecture (Education and training) A: 634

American Institute of Public Opinion
Gallup, George Horace G: 16

American International Group [company]
Bank (Crisis in finance) B: 95

American Iron and Steel Institute
Iron and Steel Institute, American I: 453

American ivy [plant]
Virginia creeper V: 424 *with picture*

American Kennel Club [organization] A: 412
Dog (Kinds of dogs) D: 265-266; (Dog
competitions) D: 280
United Kennel Club U: 47

American kestrel [bird]
Bird (Birds of grasslands) B: 336 *with picture*
Bird of prey *picture on* B: 374a
Falcon (The American kestrel) F: 14 *with picture*
Kestrel K: 307

American Landrace [hog]
Hog (American breeds) H: 285 *with picture*;
(table) H: 286

American Language, The [book by Mencken]
Mencken, H. L. M: 398

American Law Schools, Association of
Law (Law education) L: 138

American League
Baseball (Players) B: 125; (Major leagues) B: 130;
(table) B: 130; (Professional baseball) B: 133-
134b

American Legion [organization] A: 412 *with picture*
Boys State B: 541
Roosevelt, Theodore, Jr. R: 469
Veterans' organizations (In the United States)
V: 344-345

American Legion Auxiliary [organization] A: 413
with picture
Girls State G: 200

American Liberty League
Liberty League L: 233

American Library Association A: 413
Dewey, Melvil D: 177
Library (International library programs) L: 254;
(Professional associations) L: 256
Literature for children (Awards) L: 367

American linden [tree]
Linden L: 331
Tree *pictures on* T: 422

American literature A: 414 *with pictures*
See also the list of Related articles in the American
literature *article*
Colonial life in America (Literature) Ci: 806
Lost Generation L: 472
Novel (The United States) N: 573; (After World
War II) N: 574
Pulitzer Prizes (Prizes in literature, drama, and
music) P: 886b; (table) P: 894
Realism (In fiction) R: 171-172
United States, History of the (The Lost Generation

and Flaming Youth) U: 190
Western frontier life in America (Literature)
W: 239 *with picture*

American lobster [sea animal]
Lobster L: 405 *with pictures*

American Lung Association A: 428

American Lutheran Church, The [religious group]
Evangelical Lutheran Church in America E: 421

American Magazine, The
Magazine (History) M: 44
Pennsylvania (Interesting facts) P: 245;
(Communication) P: 262

American manual alphabet
Sign language S: 453 *with picture*

American Medical Association A: 428
Chiropractic C: 515
Hypnosis (Enhancing memory) H: 479; (Dangers
of hypnosis) H: 479
Medicine (Medical organizations) M: 370;
(Professional organizations and medical
reform) M: 376

American Mercury [magazine]
Mencken, H. L. M: 398
Roaring Twenties (Cultural trends) R: 364

American Morse Code
Morse code M: 819

American Motors Corporation
Automobile (Challenges to the Big Three) A: 972
Nash, Charles William N: 22

American mountain ash [tree]
Tree *pictures on* T: 422

American mulberry [plant]
Mulberry M: 913

American Municipal Association
National League of Cities N: 40

American Museum [New York City]
Barnum, P. T. B: 115

American Museum of Immigration
Liberty Island L: 233

American Museum of Natural History [New York
City] A: 428
Andrews, Roy Chapman A: 456

American Museum of Science and Energy
Tennessee (Places to visit) T: 144

American National Game of Baseball, The
[lithograph by Currier and Ives]
Baseball *picture on* B: 133

American Normal School Association
National Education Association N: 34

American Nursery and Landscape Association
Nursery N: 614

American Nurses' Association
Nursing (History) N: 619

American Occupational Therapy Association
Occupational therapy (Careers) O: 649

American Osteopathic Association
Osteopathic medicine (Careers in osteopathic
medicine) O: 867

American oystercatcher [bird]
Bird (Birds of the seacoasts) B: 342 *with picture*
Oystercatcher O: 893

American Party [political party] A: 428
LeMay, Curtis Emerson L: 187
Wallace, George Corley W: 16

American Party [U.S. history] See Know-Nothings
in this index

American pasqueflower [plant] See Eastern
pasqueflower *in this index*

American Pharmaceutical Association
Pharmacy (Training and careers in pharmacy)
P: 354-355

American Philosophical Society
Colonial life in America (Science) Ci: 808-809
Franklin, Benjamin (Civic leader) F: 487-488
Philadelphia (Libraries and museums) P: 363-364

American Physical Therapy Association
Physical therapy (Careers in physical therapy)
P: 435

American pipit [bird]
Pipit P: 492 *with picture*

American pit bull terrier [dog]
Dogfighting D: 282
Pit bull P: 497

American plan [travel]
Hotel (Resort hotels) H: 376

American plum
Plum (Kinds of plums) P: 577 *with picture*

American Podiatric Medical Association
Podiatry P: 589

American Point System [printing]
Type (Sizes of type) T: 537

American Postal Workers Union
Labor movement (table) L: 8

American process
Olive (Harvesting and preparation for market)
O: 743

American Professional Football Association

Football (The rise of professional football) F: 367
National Football League N: 35

American Psychological Association
Psychology (Careers in psychology) P: 850-851

American Psychological Society
Psychology (Careers in psychology) P: 850-851

American Public Health Association
Public health (History) P: 857

American quarter horse [breed]
Horse (table: Some types and breeds of horses)
H: 343

American Railway Express Company
Airmail A: 207
Wells, Fargo & Company W: 195

American Railway Union [labor union]
Debs, Eugene Victor D: 65
Labor movement (Opposition to unions) L: 10-11
Pullman Strike P: 900

American Recovery and Reinvestment Act [2008]
Obama, Barack (Domestic issues) O: 640g
Vocational education (The 1900's and early
2000's) V: 435

American Red Cross [organization]
Red Cross (The American Red Cross) R: 185

American redstart [bird]
Bird (Birds of forests and woodlands) B: 334 *with
picture*
Redstart R: 192
Warbler W: 35

American Revolution See Revolution, American
in this index

American Revolution, Daughters of the
[organization] See Daughters of the American
Revolution *in this index*

American Revolution, Sons of the [organization]
Sons of the American Revolution So: 594

**American Revolution Bicentennial
Administration** [U.S.]
Bicentennial Celebration, American B: 289

American rhythm style
Ballroom dancing B: 63

American robin [bird]
Bird *picture on* B: 333
Robin R: 366 *with picture*

American Rocket Society
Space exploration (The first space rockets)
So: 706-707

American sable [animal] See Pine marten *in this
index*

American Samoa [islands, Pacific] A: 429 *with
picture and map*
Clothing *picture on* Ci: 690
Flag *picture on* F: 213
Mead, Margaret M: 344
Territory (Territories in the United States) T: 174

American Samoa, National Park of [American
Samoa] A: 430
National Park System (table: National parks) N: 48

"American Scholar, The" [speech by Emerson]
Emerson, Ralph Waldo (His prose works) E: 259

American shorthair [cat]
Cat (Short-haired breeds) C: 290

American Sign Language
Deafness (Special language techniques) D: 58;
(Deaf community and culture) D: 59-60
Language (Signed languages) L: 63 *with diagram*
Sign language S: 453 *with diagram*

American smooth style [dancing]
Ballroom dancing B: 63

**American Society for Information Science and
Technology**
Library (Information science) L: 251

**American Society for the Prevention of Cruelty
to Animals**
Society for the Prevention of Cruelty to Animals
So: 563

**American Society of Composers, Authors and
Publishers** A: 430

American Society of Interior Designers
Interior design (Training) I: 334

American sole [fish]
Sole So: 582 *with picture*

American Spanish [dialect]
Spanish language So: 756b

American Speech and Hearing Association
Speech therapy (History) So: 774

**American Speech-Language-Hearing
Association**
Speech therapy (History) So: 774

American Staffordshire terrier [dog] A: 430
Dog *picture on* D: 273
Dogfighting D: 282
Pit bull P: 497

**American Standard Code for Information
Interchange** [computing]
Computer (Computer code) Ci: 911

American States, Organization of See

Organization of American States *in this index*
American Stock Exchange [stock exchange]
A: 430
New York City (Finance) N: 334
Stock exchange (History) So: 904
American sycamore [tree]
Tree *pictures on* T: 423
American System [U.S. history]
Clay, Henry (National leader) Ci: 658
Monroe, James ("The American System") M: 736
Tariff (United States tariffs) T: 44
United States, History of the (The American System) U: 165
Whig Party (The first program) W: 280
American system of manufacturing
Whitney, Eli (Arms manufacturer) W: 295
American Tail, An [film]
Animation (The animation revival) A: 514c
American Teaching Method
Skiing (Ski instruction) S: 486
American Telephone and Telegraph Company
AT&T Inc. A: 851
Telephone (The Bell System) T: 100
Videophone V: 360
American Tragedy, An [book by Dreiser]
Dreiser, Theodore D: 346
Naturalism (Naturalism in fiction) N: 65
American Tree Farm System [program]
Tree farming T: 432
American trotter [horse] *See* Standardbred *in this index*
American-type locomotive
Railroad (Developments in the United States) R: 115
American Unitarian Association [religious group]
Unitarian Universalist Association U: 42
Unitarians (Organization) U: 43
American Veterans Committee
Veterans' organizations (In the United States) V: 344-345
American Veterans of World War II, Korea, and Vietnam *See* AMVETS *in this index*
American Veterinary Medical Association
Veterinary medicine (Careers in veterinary medicine) V: 346
American water spaniel [dog] A: 430
Dog *picture on* D: 269
American Weekly Mercury [newspaper]
Pennsylvania (Communication) P: 262
American white pelican [bird]
Pelican (Kinds) P: 231
American wigeon [bird]
Bird (Birds of inland waters and marshes) B: 340 *with picture*
Wigeon W: 299
American windmill
Windmill W: 334
American Wire Gauge
Wire (Sizes of wire) W: 344
American wirehair cat
Cat (Short-haired breeds) C: 290
American Woman Suffrage Association
Woman suffrage (Growth of the movement) W: 380
Women's movement (The right to vote) W: 385
American Zoo and Aquarium Association
Zoo (Wildlife conservation) Z: 600
Americanism [beliefs]
Leo XIII L: 198
Roman Catholic Church (During the 1800's) R: 412
American's Creed A: 431
Americans for Democratic Action [organization] A: 431
Bus (Bus regulations) B: 715
Civil rights (Major changes in the field of civil rights) Ci: 609-610
Disability (The 1900's) D: 221-222
Dwarfism (Living with dwarfism) D: 395
Education (Education for children with disabilities) E: 107
America's Cup [award] A: 431
Sailing (America's Cup) S: 27 *with picture*
America's Dairyland [name for]
Wisconsin W: 346
America's Main Street [name for]
Pennsylvania Avenue National Historic Site P: 270
Americium [element] A: 431
Transuranium element T: 401
Americo-Liberians [people]
Liberia (People) L: 229
AmeriCorps [organization]
USA Freedom Corps U: 229
Amerigo Vespucci [Italian explorer] *See* Vespucci, Amerigo *in this index*
Amerinds [people]

Indian, American (American Indians or Native Americans?) I: 136c
Ames, Adelbert [American political leader]
Mississippi (table) M: 640
Ames, Benjamin [American political leader]
Maine (table) M: 87
Ames, Fisher [American political leader]
Adams, John Quincy (U.S. senator) A: 41
Ames, Oakes [American businessman]
Credit Mobilier of America Ci: 1125
Ames, Oliver [American political leader]
Massachusetts (table) M: 288
Amethyst [gem] A: 432
Gem *picture on* G: 78
Amex [stock exchange] *See* American Stock Exchange *in this index*
Amhara [people]
Ethiopia (People) E: 368
Amharic [language]
Ethiopia (People) E: 368
Amherst [New York]
Buffalo (The city) B: 677
Amherst, Lord Jeffery [British general] A: 432
Amherst College
Folger Shakespeare Library F: 315
Amide [compound]
Aramid A: 591
Amidships [term]
Ship (Nautical terms) S: 405 *with diagram*
Amiens [France] A: 432
Amiens, Treaty of [1802]
Napoleon I (Peacemaking) N: 15
Napoleonic Wars (A brief peace) N: 18
Amiens Cathedral [France]
Architecture *picture on* A: 619
Gothic art (High Gothic architecture) G: 279 *with picture*
Amillennialism [religion]
Millennium M: 553
Amin Dada, Idi [Ugandan political leader] A: 432
Tanzania (The united republic and socialism) T: 35
Uganda (History) U: 3-4
Amino acid [biochemistry] A: 432
Acid (Organic acids) A: 27
Cell (Producing energy) C: 332-333 *with diagram*
Dietary supplement D: 200
Food (Building and repairing tissues) F: 331
Food supply (Protein) F: 346
Heredity (The flow of genetic information) H: 205
Hormone (How hormones work) H: 337
Life *diagram on* L: 277; (Proteins) L: 278
Metabolism (Catabolism) M: 424
Nutrition (Proteins) N: 625
Pauling, Linus Carl P: 202
Protein (The structure of proteins) P: 832; (How the body uses proteins) P: 832
Vitamin (Vitamin B$_6$, pantothenic acid, and biotin) V: 431-432
Aminoglycoside [antibiotic]
Streptomycin So: 926
Amir [title] *See* Emir *in this index*
Amis, Kingsley [British author] A: 432
Amis, Martin [British author]
Amis, Kingsley A: 433
English literature (Recent English fiction) E: 323
Novel (The novel today) N: 575
Amish [religious group] A: 433 *with picture*
Evolution (Genetic drift) E: 429
Minority group M: 608
Pennsylvania *picture on* P: 248
Pennsylvania Dutch P: 270
Amish Acres [Nappannee]
Indiana (Places to visit) I: 206
Amistad, La [ship]
African Americans (The growth of slavery) A: 136f-136g
Amistad Rebellion A: 433
New Haven (The city) N: 229
Amistad Dam [Mexico-U.S.]
Rio Grande (Middle course) R: 347
Amistad National Recreation Area [Texas]
National Park System (table: National recreation areas) N: 49
Amistad Rebellion [U.S. history] A: 433
Adams, John Quincy (The Amistad Rebellion) A: 43
Amitriptyline [drug]
Antidepressant A: 553
Amman [Jordan] A: 433
Jordan J: 160 *with picture*
Ammann, Jacob [Swiss religious leader]
Amish A: 433
Ammeter [instrument]
Electric meter E: 176
Ammocoete [animal]
Lamprey (Habits) L: 55

Ammonia [chemical] A: 433
Anhydrous ammonia A: 467
Coal (Coal as a raw material) Ci: 719-720
Fertilizer (Inorganic fertilizers) F: 79
Haber process H: 2
Hydrogen (Uses) H: 469
Liver (Purification of the blood) L: 394
Molecule (Individual molecules) M: 692-693 *with diagram*
Ammonia gelatin [chemical]
Dynamite (Kinds of dynamite) D: 397
Ammonia maser [electronics]
Maser M: 263
Ammonite [animal]
Devonian Period D: 175
Ammonium [chemical]
Cyanobacteria Ci: 1202
Ammonium hydroxide [chemical]
Ammonia (Properties of ammonia) A: 434
Ammonium nitrate [chemical]
Ammonia (Uses) A: 434
Nitric acid N: 425
Ammons, A. R. [American poet] A: 434
Ammons, Elias M. [American political leader]
Colorado (table) Ci: 844
Ammons, Teller [American political leader]
Colorado (table) Ci: 844
Ammunition [A: 434 *with pictures*
Cartridge C: 268
Handgun (Types of handguns) H: 43
Magazine M: 46
Amnesia [disorder] A: 437
Brain (Memory and imagination) B: 554
Hypnosis (Hypnotic phenomena) H: 478
Memory (Memory disorders) M: 394
Mental illness (Dissociative disorders) M: 406
Amnesty [law] A: 437
Ford, Gerald Rudolph (The amnesty program) F: 377
Immigration (The fourth wave) I: 83
Truth commission T: 474
Amnesty and Reconstruction, Proclamation of [1865]
Lee, Robert E. (Last years) L: 179
Amnesty International [organization] A: 438
Human rights (Independent organizations) H: 428a
Nobel Prizes (Peace: 1977) N: 448b
Political prisoner P: 638
Amniocentesis [medicine] A: 438
Genetic counseling (Reasons for seeking genetic counseling) G: 84a
Pregnancy (Medical care) P: 734-735
Reproduction, Human (Checking the fetus) R: 248
Amniote [animal]
Amphibian (The history of amphibians) A: 441
Carboniferous Period C: 208
Earth (The Paleozoic Era) E: 27
Mammal (The ancestors of mammals) M: 126
Prehistoric animal (The move onto land) P: 737
Reptile (The evolution of reptiles) R: 252
Tetrapod (Modern tetrapods) T: 183 *with diagram*
Amniotic fluid [physiology]
Amniocentesis A: 438
Reproduction, Human (Nourishing the embryo) R: 247
Amniotic sac [physiology]
Baby (The developing baby) B: 4-5 *with diagram*
Childbirth (The birth process) C: 456
Amoco Corporation
BP B: 541
Amoeba *See* Ameba *in this index*
Amoebic dysentery *See* Amebic dysentery *in this index*
Amon [Egyptian god] *See* Amun *in this index*
Amon-Re [Egyptian god] *See* Amun-Re *in this index*
Among the Millet [poems by Lampman]
Lampman, Archibald L: 54
Amonute [name for]
Pocahontas P: 588
Amor [Roman god] *See* Cupid *in this index*
Amor asteroid
Asteroid (Orbital groups) A: 824a
Amoretti [poems by Spenser]
Spenser, Edmund (Spenser's other poems) So: 778
Amorphous carbon [chemistry]
Carbon (Forms of carbon) C: 204
Charcoal C: 377
Amorphous silica [mineral]
Silica S: 457
Amorsolo, Fernando [Filipino artist]
Philippines (The arts) P: 375
Amortized mortgage loan
Housing (The United States) H: 391
Amos [Biblical figure]

Amos, Book of **A:** 438
Amos, Book of [Bible] **A:** 438
Amos Fortune, Free Man [book by Yates]
  Yates, Elizabeth **Y:** 553
"Amos 'n' Andy" [radio program]
  Radio (The Golden Age of Broadcasting) **R:** 92
Amosite [material]
  Asbestos (Types of asbestos) **A:** 765
Amount of substance [chemistry]
  Metric system (Chemistry) **M:** 440
Amoxicillin [medication]
  Ampicillin **A:** 443
  Penicillin (Early history) **P:** 240-241
Amoy [China] *See* Xiamen *in this index*
Amp [measurement] *See* Ampere *in this index*
Ampere [measurement] **A:** 438
  Electric current (Conductors and insulators)
    E: 168
  Metric system (Structure of the metric system)
    M: 437; (Electricity) **M:** 440
Ampère, André Marie [French physicist] **A:** 438
  Electricity (Electricity and magnetism) **E:** 197
  Electromagnetism **E:** 203
  Magnetism (Electricity and magnetism) **M:** 60d
  Physics (Developments in the 1800's) **P:** 440
Amphetamine [drug] **A:** 438
  Drug (Stimulants) **D:** 352; (The drug revolution)
    D: 359
  Drug abuse (table: Some commonly abused
    drugs) **D:** 363
  Methamphetamine **M:** 433
  Stimulant **So:** 901
Amphib [ship] *See* Amphibious ship *in this index*
Amphibian [airplane]
  Airplane (Seaplanes) **A:** 212 *with picture*
Amphibian [zoology] **A:** 439 *with pictures*
  Animal (table: Length of life of animals) **A:** 473; (A
    table of animal intelligence) **A:** 493
  Brain (Among vertebrates) **B:** 560
  Evolution (Geographic distribution of species)
    E: 430-431
  Heart (Amphibians and reptiles) **H:** 146 *with
    diagram*
  Prehistoric animal (The move onto land) **P:** 737;
    (Amphibians) **P:** 738 *with picture*
  Reproduction (Amphibians) **R:** 243
  Tetrapod **T:** 182b *with diagram*
Amphibious assault [warfare]
  Navy (Wartime roles) **N:** 77
Amphibious ship A: 442 *with picture*
  Navy (Amphibious ships) **N:** 78
  Navy, United States (Combat ships) **N:** 84
  Warship (Amphibious warfare ships) **W:** 40;
    (Warships in the two world wars) **W:** 41-42
    with picture
Amphibious warfare A: 442
  Amphibious ship **A:** 442
  Marine **M:** 203
  Navy (Wartime roles) **N:** 77
  Warship (Amphibious warfare ships) **W:** 40
Amphibole [mineral] **A:** 443
  Asbestos (Types of asbestos) **A:** 765
  Hornblende **H:** 339
Amphibolite [rock]
  Rock (table) **R:** 373 *with picture*
Amphictyonic League [ancient Greece]
  Peace (Ancient Greece and Rome) **P:** 206
Amphion [Greek mythology]
  Niobe **N:** 424
Amphioxus [sea animal] **A:** 443 *with picture*
  Animal (Invertebrates and vertebrates) **A:** 488
    with diagram
Amphisbaenian [animal] **A:** 443 *with picture*
  Reptile (Lizards, amphisbaenians, and snakes)
    R: 250
Amphitheater [structure]
  Drama *picture on* **D:** 326
  Rome, Ancient (Recreation) **R:** 440
Amphitrite [Greek mythology]
  Neptune **N:** 128
  Nereids **N:** 130
  Poseidon **P:** 697
Amphitruo [play by Plautus]
  Plautus **P:** 570
Amphotericin [drug]
  Antibiotic (Other kinds of antibiotics) **A:** 550
Amphotericin B [drug]
  Antibiotic (Disruption of the cell membrane)
    A: 550
  Fungal disease (In people) **F:** 558
Ampicillin [medication] **A:** 443
  Antibiotic (table) **A:** 551
  Penicillin (Forms of penicillin) **P:** 240; (Early
    history) **P:** 240-241
Amplification [physics]
  Electronics *diagram on* **E:** 211; (Transistors) **E:** 212
  Laser (Producing laser light) **L:** 84

Transistor (What transistors do) **T:** 372
Amplifier [electronics]
  Electric guitar **E:** 173
  Electronics *diagram on* **E:** 211; (Transistors) **E:** 212
  Hearing aid **H:** 130 *with diagram*
  Phonograph (Parts of a phonograph) **P:** 400-401
    with diagram
  Radio (How radio programs are received) **R:** 88-
    89 *with diagram*
  Stereophonic sound system (Parts of a stereo
    system) **So:** 892
  Tape recorder (Erasing and recording) **T:** 38
  Television (Receiving television signals) **T:** 124
    with diagrams
  Transistor (The bipolar transistor as an amplifier)
    T: 373
  Vacuum tube (Triodes) **V:** 259
Amplitude [physics]
  Electronics (Digital-analog conversion) **E:** 214
  Light (The properties of waves) **L:** 285-286 *with
    diagram*
  Radio (Transmitting radio waves) **R:** 86
  Richter magnitude **R:** 334
  Sound (Intensity and loudness) **So:** 600 *with
    diagram*
  Vibration **V:** 347
  Waves *diagram on* **W:** 150; (Measuring waves)
    W: 152
Amplitude modulation [electronics]
  Antenna **A:** 543
  Frequency modulation **F:** 528
  Radio (Transmitting radio waves) **R:** 86 *with
    diagram*
  Wireless communication (How wireless
    communication works) **W:** 344
Ampulla [anatomy]
  Ear (The inner ear) **E:** 8
  Reproduction, Human (Fertilization) **R:** 246
Ampullae of Lorenzini [zoology]
  Shark (Senses) **S:** 375
Amputation [surgery] **A:** 443
  Artificial limb (Preparation of an artificial limb)
    A: 760
  Surgery (Some common surgical operations)
    So: 1006
AMRAAM [missile]
  Guided missile (Air-to-air missiles) **G:** 426
Amritsar [India] **A:** 444
  India (India under Indira Gandhi) **I:** 133-134
  Sikhism *picture on* **S:** 455
Amritsar Massacre [1919]
  Gandhi, Mohandas Karamchand (Gandhi's
    independence campaigns) **G:** 25
  India (Rise of Indian nationalism) **I:** 131
AMS [illness]
  Altitude sickness **A:** 390
Amsterdam [book by McEwan]
  McEwan, Ian **M:** 333
Amsterdam [Netherlands] **A:** 444 *with picture*
  Netherlands *picture on* **N:** 141; (National
    government) **N:** 139 *with picture*
Amsterdam, University of
  Netherlands (Education) **N:** 142
Amsterdam-Rhine Canal [Netherlands]
  Canal (table) **C:** 164
Amsterdam Stock Exchange
  Architecture (Early modern architecture in
    Europe) **A:** 627-628 *with picture*
AMT [tax]
  Income tax (Figuring the individual income tax)
    I: 104
Amtrak [corporation] **A:** 445
  Interstate Commerce Commission **I:** 352
  Railroad *map on* **R:** 106, *picture on* **R:** 108;
    (Railroad systems) **R:** 112
Amtrak's Hudson River Tunnel [New Jersey-New
  York]
  Hudson River tunnels (Amtrak's Hudson River
    Tunnel) **H:** 407
Amu Darya [river, Asia]
  Uzbekistan (Land and climate) **U:** 254
Amulet A: 445
  Clothing (Protection) **Ci:** 687
  Magic (Magical objects) **M:** 49
Amulius [legendary figure]
  Romulus and Remus **R:** 450a
Amun [Egyptian god] **A:** 445
  Akhenaten **A:** 253
  Egypt, Ancient (Religion) **E:** 137
  Hatshepsut **H:** 86
  Mythology (Other Egyptian divinities) **M:** 980
Amun-Re [Egyptian god]
  Egypt, Ancient *picture on* **E:** 140; (Religion) **E:** 137;
    (The New Kingdom) **E:** 143
  Mythology *picture on* **M:** 977; (Other Egyptian
    divinities) **M:** 980
  Thebes **T:** 250

Amun-Re, Temple of *See* Karnak, Temple of *in this
  index*
Amundsen, Roald [Norwegian explorer] **A:** 445
    with picture and map
  Antarctica *picture on* **A:** 531, *map on* **A:** 538;
    (Exploration) **A:** 535-536 *with picture*
  Exploration *picture on* **E:** 439; (Arctic exploration)
    E: 449 *with map*
  Northwest Passage **N:** 529 *with picture*
Amundsen Basin [geography]
  Arctic Ocean (The deep basin) **A:** 643 *with map*
Amundsen-Scott South Pole Station
  Antarctica (Scientific research) **A:** 540
Amur River [Siberia] **A:** 446
Amusement park A: 446
    See also Theme park *in this index*
  Denmark (Recreation) **D:** 136-137 *with picture*
  Ferris wheel **F:** 77 *with picture*
  Merry-go-round **M:** 419
  Roller coaster **R:** 402
Amusements *See* Recreation *in this index*
AMVETS [organization] **A:** 446
  Veterans' organizations (In the United States)
    V: 344-345
Amygdala [anatomy]
  Brain (Regulating emotions) **B:** 554
  Dream (The biology of dreams) **D:** 344-345
Amylase [enzyme]
  Digestive system (In the small intestine) **D:** 202;
    (From mouth to stomach) **D:** 202
  Malt **M:** 112
Amyloid [protein]
  Alzheimer's disease (Diagnosis) **A:** 398
Amyloid-beta peptide [physiology]
  Alzheimer's disease (Causes) **A:** 399
Amyloid precursor protein [physiology]
  Alzheimer's disease (Causes) **A:** 399
Amylose [botany]
  Rice (Kinds of rice) **R:** 323-324
Amyotrophic lateral sclerosis [disease] **A:** 446
  Gehrig, Lou **G:** 75
  Gulf War syndrome **G:** 438
  Hawking, Stephen William **H:** 113
Amytal [drug]
  Barbiturate (Medical uses) **B:** 107
An [mythology]
  Mythology (Sumerian mythology) **M:** 976-977
An Duong [Vietnamese ruler]
  Vietnam (Nam Viet) **V:** 369
An Lushan [Manchurian military leader]
  Tang dynasty (The middle years) **T:** 26
Anabaptists [religious group] **A:** 447
  Christianity (Protestant churches) **C:** 522g; (The
    Radical Reformation) **C:** 525
  Hutterites **H:** 459
  Mennonites **M:** 401
  Protestantism (The radical reform movements)
    P: 835
  Reformation (Zwingli and the Anabaptists)
    R: 197-198
Anabasis [book by Xenophon]
  Xenophon **X:** 543
Anableps [fish] **A:** 447 *with picture*
  Fish *picture on* **F:** 145
Anabolic steroid [drug]
  Baseball (Recent developments) **B:** 137-139
  Bonds, Barry **B:** 456
  Doping **D:** 309
  Drug abuse (Steroids) **D:** 362
  Olympic Games (Charges of steroid use) **O:** 753
  Steroid (The sex steroids) **So:** 894
  Testosterone **T:** 182a
Anabolism [physiology]
  Metabolism (Anabolism) **M:** 424
Anacapa Island [California]
  Channel Islands National Park **C:** 375
Anacletus, Saint [pope]
  Pope (table) **P:** 666
Anacletus II [antipope]
  Pope (table) **P:** 666
Anaconda [snake] **A:** 447 *with picture*
  Boa **B:** 426
  Snake *picture on* **S:** 526
Anaconda Company
  Montana (Statehood) **M:** 760; (The mid-1900's)
    M: 760
Anacostia Community Museum [Washington,
  D.C.]
  Washington, D.C. (Smithsonian museums)
    W: 71-73
Anacostia River
  Washington, D.C. (The city) **W:** 78-79
Anacreon [Greek poet] **A:** 447
Anacreontics [poetry]
  Anacreon **A:** 447
Anacrusis [poetry]
  Poetry (table) **P:** 594

Anadromous fish [zoology]
Fish (Fish migrations) F: 151
Fishing (Fishing tips) F: 179
Anaemia [disorder] *See* Anemia *in this index*
Anaerobe [bacteria]
Bacteria (Where bacteria live) B: 21
Anaerobic capacity
Physical fitness (Performance-related fitness)
P: 433-434
Anaerobic power
Physical fitness (Performance-related fitness)
P: 433-434
Anaesthesia *See* Anesthesia *in this index*
Anagen [anatomy]
Hair (Cycles of hair growth) H: 10
Anagenesis [biology]
Evolution (Main ideas of evolutionary theory)
E: 426; (Direct observation of evolution) E: 431
Anaheim [California] A: 447
Anaheim Ducks [team]
Hockey (table: National Hockey League) H: 281
Anahoe Island Refuge
Nevada (Plant and animal life) N: 168
Anal clasper [zoology]
Butterfly (The larva) B: 741 *with diagram*
Anal fin [zoology]
Fish (Fins) F: 160-161 *with picture*
Anal phase [psychology]
Libido L: 233
Psychoanalysis (Psychoanalytic theory) P: 846
Anal proleg [zoology]
Butterfly (The larva) B: 741 *with diagram*
Anal sac [zoology]
Dog (Behavior) D: 277
Analgesic [drug] A: 448
Drug (Drugs that affect the nervous system)
D: 352
Narcotic N: 21
Opiate O: 810
Pain (Treatment) P: 22
Analog [magazine]
Science fiction (The Golden Age) S: 205
Analog circuit [electronics]
Electronics (Analog circuits) E: 214
Analog computer A: 448
Computer Ci: 908
Analog meter
Electric meter (Analog meters) E: 176
Analog oscilloscope [instrument]
Oscilloscope O: 862
Analog signal [electronics]
Cellular telephone C: 340
Digital technology D: 203
Digital video recorder D: 203
Electronics (How electronic circuits process
information) E: 213
Hearing aid (History) H: 131
Phonograph (How phonographs work) P: 400
Tape recorder T: 37 *with diagrams*
Telecommunications T: 89
Telephone (Traditional phone calls) T: 96
Television (Broadcasting) T: 123
Videotape recorder (How videotape recorders
work) V: 360
Analog telephone adapter [electronic device]
Telephone (VoIP phone calls) T: 97-98
Analog-to-digital converter [device]
Compact disc (Recording) Ci: 901
Electric meter (Digital meters) E: 177
Photography (Capturing digital images) P: 420
Analog watch
Watch (How watches work) W: 114
Analog xerography
Copying machine (Electrostatic copying) Ci: 1045
Analogous trait [biology]
Homology H: 307
Analogue [compound]
Prostaglandin P: 829
Analysis
Criticism Ci: 1146
Psychoanalysis P: 846
Statistics (Analyzing the data) So: 868
Analysis of Beauty, The [book by Hogarth]
Hogarth, William H: 288
Analysts [literature]
Homer (Analysts and unitarians) H: 304
Analytic Cubism [art]
Cubism Ci: 1181 *with picture*
Painting (Cubism) P: 77-78
Picasso, Pablo (Cubism) P: 448b
Analytic geometry
Geometry (Types of geometry) G: 103; (Analytic
geometry) G: 105; (Beginnings of modern
geometry) G: 106
Mathematics (Branches of mathematics) M: 303;
(Mathematics and the scientific revolution)
M: 306-307

Analytic Philosophy
Philosophy (Philosophy in the 1900's) P: 390
Wittgenstein, Ludwig W: 374
Analytic phonics
Reading (Phonics instruction) R: 159
Analytic process [industry]
Manufacturing (Making products) M: 170
Analytical balance [device]
Balance B: 34
Analytical engine [machine]
Babbage, Charles B: 2
Computer (Punched-card devices) Ci: 924a-924b
Analytical index [reference]
Index I: 107
Analytical Mechanics [book by Lagrange]
Lagrange, Joseph-Louis L: 31
Analytical psychology
Jung, Carl Gustav J: 194
Anamorphosis [art]
Lascaux Cave L: 80
Anand, Viswanathan [Indian chess player]
Chess (World chess champions) C: 414
Anangu [people]
Uluru U: 17
Ananke [satellite]
Jupiter (Outer satellites) J: 200a
Anansi [folk character]
Folklore F: 322
Anapest [poetry]
Poetry (table) P: 594
Anaphase [biology]
Cell (Mitosis) C: 330-331
Anaphora [language]
Shakespeare, William (Rhetoric) S: 368
Anaphylactic shock [disorder] A: 448
Allergy (Allergic reactions) A: 373-374
Anarchism [political science]
Government (Anarchism) G: 288
Haymarket Riot H: 122
Proudhon, Pierre Joseph (Ideas) P: 838
Russia (Alexander II) R: 551
Sacco-Vanzetti case S: 4
Anarchy, The [English history]
Stephen [English king] So: 890
Anasazi [people] A: 448a *with picture*
Archaeology *picture on* A: 597
Architecture (Pre-Columbian architecture) A: 614
Arizona (Early days) A: 688
Canyon de Chelly National Monument C: 185
Chaco Culture National Historical Park C: 365
Indian, American *picture on* I: 152; (Indians of the
Southwest) I: 166
Mesa Verde National Park M: 420
New Mexico (Indian peoples) N: 272 *with picture*
Pueblo Indians (Early history and way of life)
P: 871
Utah (Indian days) U: 246 *with picture*
Anastasia, Grand Duchess [daughter of Czar
Nicholas II]
Nicholas II [czar] *picture on* N: 403
Anastasia Krupnik [book by Lowry]
Lowry, Lois L: 511
Anastasis, The [fresco]
Byzantine art *picture on* B: 750
Anatolia [region, Turkey]
Asia Minor A: 812a *with map*
Ottoman Empire (The beginning of the empire)
O: 878
Turkey T: 502 *with maps*; (The land) T: 507
Anatolian culture [Greek history]
Aegean civilization A: 82
Anatolian shepherd [dog] A: 448b *with picture*
Anatomic pathology [medicine]
Forensic pathology F: 389a
Anatomical Procedures [book by Galen]
Galen G: 10
*Anatomical Study on the Motion of the Heart and
Blood in Animals, An* [book by Harvey]
Harvey, William H: 81
Anatomy A: 448b
See also Comparative anatomy *in this index*
Biology (table) B: 317
Human body (table) *diagrams on* H: 422
Leonardo da Vinci (Leonardo's works) L: 200-200a
Physiology P: 445
Science (The life sciences) S: 193
Anatomy Lesson, The [book by Roth]
Roth, Philip R: 487
Anatomy Lesson of Professor Tulp [painting by
Rembrandt]
Rembrandt (Early Amsterdam years) R: 229
World, History of the *picture on* W: 440
Anatomy of Criticism [book by Frye]
Frye, Northrop F: 549
Mythology (Literary approaches) M: 990-991
Anawrahta [Burmese ruler]
Myanmar (Early days) M: 970d

Anaxagoras [Greek philosopher] A: 448b
Pre-Socratic philosophy (The teachings of
Parmenides) P: 772-773
Anaximander [Greek philosopher] A: 448b
Pre-Socratic philosophy (The first pre-Socratics)
P: 772
Anaximenes [Greek philosopher] A: 449
Pre-Socratic philosophy (The first pre-Socratics)
P: 772
Anaya, Toney [American political leader]
New Mexico (table) N: 272
Anaza [people]
Kuwait (History) K: 396
ANC [organization] *See* African National Congress
in this index
ANC [sound] *See* Active noise cancellation *in this
index*
Ancash region [Peru]
Earthquake (Landslides or avalanches) E: 34
Ancel, Michel [French game designer]
Electronic game *picture on* E: 204c
Ancestor worship [religion] A: 449
Ancestral being [religion]
Aborigines, Australian (Aboriginal life) A: 14
Ancestral Pueblo [American Indians] *See* Anasazi
in this index
Ancestry
Genealogy G: 82
Name (Ancestors) N: 6
Anchises [Greek mythology]
Mythology *picture on* M: 988
Anchor A: 449 *with pictures*
Anchor arm [architecture]
Bridge (Cantilever bridges) B: 601 *with diagram*
Anchorage [Alaska] A: 449 *with picture*
Alaska *picture on* A: 283; (Population) A: 286;
(table; Average monthly weather) A: 295;
(Statehood) A: 303 *with picture*
Anchorage [construction]
Bridge (Suspension bridges) B: 601-602 *with
diagram*
"Anchors Aweigh" [song]
Navy, United States N: 83
Anchovy [fish] A: 450 *with picture*
Ancient civilization A: 450
See also the list of Related articles in the Ancient
civilization *article*
Alchemy A: 334
Calendar (History) C: 30
Civilization (Development) Ci: 635
Clothing (Clothing of the ancient world) Ci: 696
with pictures
Food (Ancient times) F: 336
Law (The development of law) L: 133
Medicine (History) M: 371-372 *with pictures*
Painting (Early painting) P: 40
Seven Wonders of the Ancient World S: 325,
pictures on S: 326-327
World, History of the (Early centers of civilization)
W: 422 *with pictures and map*
Ancient Egypt *See* Egypt, Ancient *in this index*
**Ancient Egyptian Arabic Order of Nobles of the
Mystic Shrine** *See* Shriners International *in this
index*
Ancient Greece *See* Greece, Ancient *in this index*
Ancient Macmillan plaid
Tartan *picture on* T: 47
Ancient Mystical Order Rosae Crucis
[organization] *See* Rosicrucian Order *in this index*
Ancient Persia *See* Persia, Ancient *in this index*
Ancient Rome *See* Rome, Ancient *in this index*
Ancient Voices of Children [music by Crumb]
Crumb, George Ci: 1159
Ancon [ship]
Panama Canal (The oceans united) P: 126
Ancón, Treaty of [1883]
Peru (The War of the Pacific) P: 315
Ancona [breed]
Chicken (Mediterranean class chickens) C: 441;
(table) C: 443
Anconeus [anatomy]
Arm A: 717
Ancus Marcius [legendary figure]
Mythology (The seven kings) M: 983
Ancyluris formossissima [butterfly]
Butterfly *picture on* B: 735
Ancyra [ancient city]
Galatia G: 8
AND-gate [computer]
Electronics (Digital circuits) E: 213-214
And the Migrants Kept Coming [painting by
Lawrence]
African Americans *picture on* A: 136b
Andalusian Scenes [works by Estébanez Calderón]
Spanish literature (The 1800's) So: 761-762
Andaman and Nicobar Islands [India]
Bay of Bengal B: 175

Tsunami of 2004 **T: 476**
Andante [music]
  Music (table) **M: 954**
Andean cock-of-the-rock [bird]
  Bird (Birds of Central and South America) **B: 344a** *with picture*
Andean Community [organization] **A: 450**
  South America (International trade) **So: 637**
Andean condor [bird]
  Bird of prey *picture on* **B: 374b**; (Physical appearance) **B: 374a**
  Condor **Ci: 929** *with picture*
  Vulture (New World vultures) **V: 454**
Andean deer *See* Huemul *in this index*
Andean-Equatorial [language group]
  Indian, American (Language groups) **I: 149-150**
Andean Indians
  Cocaine (History) **Ci: 743**
  Indian, American (Indians of the Andes) **I: 173** *with pictures and map*
Anders, William Alison [American astronaut]
  Astronaut (Achievements in space) **A: 829**
  Space exploration (Orbiting the moon) **So: 715**
Andersen, Arthur [accounting firm]
  Enron Corporation **E: 327**
Andersen, Elmer L. [American political leader]
  Minnesota (table) **M: 602**
Andersen, Hans Christian [Danish author] **A: 451**
  Fairy (Fairy tales) **F: 11**
  Literature for children (Traditional literature) **L: 357-358**
  Storytelling (The 1800's) **So: 915**
Anderson, Bronco Billy [American actor]
  Great Train Robbery, The **G: 349**
Anderson, C. Elmer [American political leader]
  Minnesota (table) **M: 602**
Anderson, Carl David [American physicist] **A: 451**
  Antimatter **A: 556**
  Muon **M: 928**
Anderson, Charles [American political leader]
  Ohio (table) **O: 699**
Anderson, Clinton Presba [American political leader]
  Agriculture, Department of (table) **A: 161**
Anderson, Eugenie [American diplomat]
  Owen, Ruth Bryan **O: 883**
Anderson, Forrest H. [American political leader]
  Montana (table) **M: 757**
Anderson, Hugh J. [American political leader]
  Maine (table) **M: 87**
Anderson, John, Jr. [American political leader]
  Kansas (table) **K: 234**
Anderson, Judith [Australian actress] **A: 451**
Anderson, Marian [American singer] **A: 451** *with portrait*
  African Americans *picture on* **A: 136m**; (The Great Depression) **A: 136n**
Anderson, Maxie [American balloonist]
  Balloon (Long-distance balloon flights) **B: 62**
Anderson, Maxwell [American dramatist] **A: 452**
Anderson, Michael P. [American astronaut]
  Columbia disaster **Ci: 852**
  Space exploration (The Columbia disaster) **So: 725**
Anderson, Philip Warren [American physicist]
  Nobel Prizes (Physics: 1977) **N: 441**
Anderson, Robert [Union military leader]
  Fort Sumter **F: 416**
  Lincoln, Abraham (Fort Sumter and war) **L: 321**
Anderson, Robert B. [American government official]
  Eisenhower, Dwight David (table) **E: 152**
Anderson, Sherwood [American author] **A: 452** *with portrait*
  American literature (Realist fiction) **A: 422**
Anderson, Sigurd [American political leader]
  South Dakota (table) **So: 680**
Anderson, Sparky [American baseball manager]
  Baseball (table: Hall of Fame) **B: 134**
Anderson, Victor E. [American political leader]
  Nebraska (table) **N: 110**
Anderson, Wendell R. [American political leader]
  Minnesota (table) **M: 602**
Andersonville National Historic Site [Georgia]
  National Park System (table: National historic sites) **N: 52**
Andersonville prison [U.S. history]
  Civil War, American (Prisons) **Ci: 630-631**
Andes, Crown of the
  Crown *picture on* **Ci: 1158**
Andes Mountains [South America] **A: 452** *with picture and map*
  Argentina (The Andean Region) **A: 653** *with picture*
  Bolivia (The Andean Highlands) **B: 444** *with map*
  Chile (The Central Valley) **C: 464-465** *with picture*
  Colombia (The Andes Mountains) **Ci: 782**

Ecuador **E: 67**
Indian, American (Indians of the Andes) **I: 173**
Mountain *picture on* **M: 891**; (The Andes Mountains) **M: 895**
Peru **P: 306** *with picture*; (The highlands) **P: 311** *with map*
South America (Land regions) **So: 626** *with picture*
Andesine [mineral]
  Feldspar **F: 68**
Andesite [rock]
  Mars (Crust) **M: 225**
  Rock (Extrusive rock) **R: 371**
Andhra Pradesh [state, India]
  India (Languages) **I: 114**; (India in the 1950's and early 1960's) **I: 133**
Andhras dynasty
  India (Southern India) **I: 129**
Andisol [soil]
  Soil *map on* **So: 575**; (How soils are classified) **So: 576**
Andorra A: 454 *with picture and map*
  Flag *picture on* **F: 205**
Andorra la Vella [Andorra] **A: 455** *with picture*
  Andorra **A: 454** *with picture*
Andrada e Silva, José Bonifácio de [Brazilian government official] **A: 455**
Andrade, Mario de [Brazilian author]
  Latin American literature (The early 1900's) **L: 113**
Andradite [gem]
  Garnet **G: 45**
Andre, Daniel [American aviator]
  Aviation (table: Aviation speed records) **A: 990**
André, John [British spy] **A: 456**
  Arnold, Benedict (Turns traitor) **A: 742**
  Lafayette, Marquis de (Service to the United States) **L: 28**
André, Louis [French religious leader]
  Wisconsin (European exploration and settlement) **W: 365-366**
"Andrea del Sarto" [poem by Browning]
  Browning, Robert (Browning's poems) **B: 646-647**
Andrea Doria [ship]
  Shipwreck (table: Major shipwrecks) **S: 428**
Andreanof Islands [Alaska]
  Alaska *picture on* **A: 287**
Andretti, Mario [American race driver] **A: 456**
  Automobile racing (table: Formula One World Drivers' Championship) **A: 980**; (table: Indianapolis 500 winners) **A: 980**
Andrew, John A. [American political leader]
  Massachusetts (table) **M: 288**
Andrew, Prince [British prince]
  Elizabeth II (The royal family) **E: 240**
Andrew, Saint [apostle] **A: 456**
  Peter, Saint (Early life) **P: 324**
Andrew Johnson National Historic Site [Tennessee]
  National Park System (table: National historic sites) **N: 52**
Andrew W. Mellon Foundation *See* Mellon Foundation *in this index*
Andrews, Charles B. [American political leader]
  Connecticut (table) **Ci: 967**
Andrews, James J. [Union spy]
  Civil War, American (Raids) **Ci: 629**
Andrews, Julie [British actress] **A: 456** *with portrait*
  Motion picture (Best performance by an actress: 1964) **M: 862**
Andrews, Roy Chapman [American explorer] **A: 456**
Andrews's Raid [U.S. history]
  Civil War, American (Raids) **Ci: 629**
Andreyev, Leonid [Russian author]
  Russian literature (Symbolism) **R: 563**
Andrić, Ivo [Yugoslav author]
  Nobel Prizes (Literature: 1961) **N: 447**
Androconia [zoology]
  Butterfly (The life cycle of butterflies) **B: 739-740**
Androgen [hormone]
  Adrenal gland **A: 67**
  Hormone (Growth and sex hormones) **H: 336**
  Steroid (The sex steroids) **So: 894**
Androgyny [trait]
  Sexuality (Androgyny) **S: 338a**
Android [smartphone]
  Cellular telephone (History) **C: 341**
Andromaque [play by Racine]
  French literature (Classical drama) **F: 520**
Andromeda [constellation] **A: 457**
Andromeda [Greek mythology] **A: 457**
Andromeda Galaxy [astronomy] **A: 457** *with picture*
  Andromeda **A: 457**
  Galaxy (Galaxy groups, clusters, and beyond) **G: 9**
  Hubble, Edwin Powell **H: 403**
  Local Group **L: 409**

Triangulum Galaxy **T: 439**
Universe **U: 205**
Andronicus, Livius [Greek author]
  Latin literature (Early Latin literature) **L: 115**
Andronicus of Rhodes [Greek editor]
  Aristotle (Aristotle's place in Western thought) **A: 664**
Andropov, Yuri Vladimirovich [Soviet political leader]
  Gorbachev, Mikhail Sergeyevich (Early life and political rise) **G: 272**
  Union of Soviet Socialist Republics (The rise of Gorbachev) **U: 40**
Andros, Sir Edmund [English colonial official]
  Connecticut (Defending the colony) **Ci: 970**
  Massachusetts (Troubles with England) **M: 291**
Andros Island [Caribbean Sea]
  Bahamas (Land and climate) **B: 29** *with map*
Androscoggin River [U.S.]
  Maine (Rivers and lakes) **M: 82**
  New Hampshire (Rivers and lakes) **N: 220** *with map*
Androsterone [hormone]
  Hormone (Growth and sex hormones) **H: 336**
Andrus, Cecil D. [American political leader]
  Carter, Jimmy (table) **C: 257**
  Idaho (table) **I: 42**
  Interior, Department of the (table) **I: 325**
Andrus, Ethel Percy [American educator]
  AARP **A: 3**
Andrus, Leonard [American businessman]
  Deere, John **D: 87**
Anegada [island]
  Virgin Islands, British **V: 393**
Aneirin [Welsh poet]
  Wales (The arts) **W: 9**
Anemia [disorder] **A: 457**
  See also Pernicious anemia; Sickle cell anemia *in this index*
  Blood (Diagnostic tests) **B: 413**; (Anemia) **B: 414**
  Cancer (Erythropoietin) **C: 173**
  Cell (Metabolic diseases) **C: 336-337**
  Chloramphenicol **C: 516**
  Iron (How iron is used in medicine) **I: 435**
  Leukemia **L: 215**
  Nutrition (Deficiency diseases) **N: 630-631**
  Thalassemia **T: 228**
Anemic anoxia [disorder]
  Anoxia **A: 519**
Anemometer [instrument] **A: 458**
  Weather (Land-based observation stations) **W: 162**
Anemone [botany] **A: 458**
Anemone, Sea [sea animal] *See* Sea anemone *in this index*
Anemonefish
  Clownfish **Ci: 714** *with picture*
  Fish *picture on* **F: 155**
Aneroid barometer [instrument]
  Altimeter **A: 389**
  Barometer (Kinds of barometers) **B: 115** *with diagram*
Anesidemus [Greek philosopher]
  Skepticism **S: 481**
Anesthesia [medicine] **A: 458**
  Acupuncture **A: 31**
  Barbiturate (Medical uses) **B: 107**
  Benzocaine **B: 255**
  Childbirth (Methods of childbirth) **C: 456-457**
  Coca **Ci: 742**
  Cocaine **Ci: 742**
  Dentistry **D: 143**; (Modern dentistry) **D: 144**
  Drug (Anesthetics) **D: 352**; (The drug revolution) **D: 359**
  Halothane **H: 27**
  Hypnosis (Enhancing health care) **H: 479**; (Scientific studies) **H: 480**
  Lidocaine **L: 270**
  Long, Crawford Williamson **L: 446**
  Medicine (The first anesthetic) **M: 375** *with picture*
  Menthol **M: 410**
  Morton, William Thomas Green **M: 821**
  Nitrous oxide **N: 427**
  Surgery (Anesthesia) **So: 1004**
Anesthesin [drug]
  Benzocaine **B: 255**
Anesthesiologist [career]
  Anesthesiology **A: 459**
  Surgery (A typical operation) **So: 1006**
Anesthesiology [medicine] **A: 459**
  Medicine (Medicine) **M: 369**
Anesthetic *See* Anesthesia *in this index*
Anethole [chemical]
  Licorice **L: 270**
Aneto, Pico de [mountain, Spain]
  Pyrenees **P: 920**

Aneurysm [disorder] **A:** 459
  DeBakey, Michael Ellis **D:** 63
Anfinsen, Christian Boehmer [American chemist]
  Nobel Prizes (Chemistry: 1972) **N:** 444
ANFO [explosive]
  Dynamite (History) **D:** 397
Ang Lee [Chinese-born director]
  Motion picture (Best achievement in directing:
    2005) **M:** 862
Angekok [shaman]
  Inuit (Religion) **I:** 354e
Angel [religion] **A:** 459
  Michael, Saint **M:** 482
Angel, Jimmy [American pilot]
  Angel Falls **A:** 460
Angel Falls [waterfall, Venezuela] **A:** 459
  South America (Waterfalls) **So:** 628 *with picture*
  Venezuela (The Guiana Highlands) **V:** 302
  Waterfall (table: Famous waterfalls of the world)
    W: 143 *with picture*
Angel food cake
  Cake **C:** 19
Angel of Death and the Sculptor, The [sculpture
  by French]
  French, Daniel Chester **F:** 511
Angela Merici, Saint [Italian religious leader]
  Religious life (Religious life in the 1500's and
    1600's) **R:** 227
Angelfish [fish] **A:** 460 *with picture*
  Fish *picture on* **F:** 155
Angelico, Fra [Italian painter] **A:** 460 *with picture*
  Painting (The 1400's) **P:** 52-53 *with picture*
Angéline de Montbrun [book by Conan]
  Canadian literature (Fiction: 1850-1918) **C:** 157
Angell, Sir Norman [British economist]
  Nobel Prizes (Peace: 1933) **N:** 448a
Angelo [literary figure]
  Shakespeare, William: *(Measure for Measure)*
    S: 362
Angelotti, Cesare [opera character]
  Opera: *(Tosca)* **O:** 807
Angelou, Maya [American author] **A:** 460
  Arkansas *picture on* **A:** 714
Angels Fall [play by Wilson]
  Wilson, Lanford **W:** 317
Angels in America [play by Kushner]
  American literature (Drama) **A:** 426
  Drama (Later United States drama) **D:** 340-341
Angels of Anaheim, Los Angeles [team] *See* Los
  Angeles Angels of Anaheim *in this index*
Angel's-trumpet [plant]
  Datura **D:** 43
Angelus [prayer]
  Annunciation **A:** 518
Anger
  Emotion (The basic emotion approach) **E:** 261
Ångerman River [Sweden]
  Sweden *picture on* **So:** 1029
Angevin [English history]
  Plantagenet **P:** 550
Angina pectoris [disorder] **A:** 461
  Beta-blocker **B:** 274
  Calcium channel blocker **C:** 21
  Heart (Symptoms and diagnosis) **H:** 137
Angiogenesis [biology] **A:** 461
  Angina pectoris **A:** 461
  Cancer (Molecular medicine) **C:** 173-174
  Thalidomide **T:** 229
Angiogenesis inhibitor [medicine]
  Angiogenesis **A:** 461
  Cancer (Molecular medicine) **C:** 173-174
Angiogenesis-stimulating growth factor
  [biology]
  Angiogenesis **A:** 461
Angiogram [medicine]
  Heart (Symptoms and diagnosis) **H:** 137-138
    with picture
Angiography [medicine] *See* Coronary
  angiography *in this index*
Angioplasty [medicine] **A:** 461 *with diagrams*
  Angina pectoris **A:** 461
  Arteriosclerosis (Prevention and treatment)
    A: 750
  Disease (Medical treatment) **D:** 232-233
  Heart (Treatment) **H:** 138; (Progress in treatment
    and prevention) **H:** 145
Angiosperm [botany] **A:** 462 *with picture*
  Earth (The Mesozoic Era) **E:** 27-28
  Flower **F:** 271; (The evolution of flowering plants)
    F: 299
  Fruit (Types of fruits in botany) **F:** 544
  Paleobotany **P:** 102
  Plant (Angiosperms) **P:** 520 *with pictures*; (Parts
    of plants) **P:** 528; (Sexual reproduction) **P:** 532-
    533 *with picture*; (The evolution of plants)
    P: 544-545; (Classification of plants) **P:** 546-547
    with pictures

  Seed **S:** 280 *with diagrams*
  Tree *pictures on* **T:** 417; (Broadleaf trees) **T:** 414
Angiotensin [chemical]
  Hypertension (Causes) **H:** 476
Angiotensin converting enzyme inhibitor [drug]
  Heart (Valve disease) **H:** 141-142
Angiotensin receptor blocker [drug]
  Blood pressure **B:** 416
Angkor [ancient city] **A:** 462
  Cambodia (History) **C:** 72
Angkor National Park [Cambodia]
  National park (table) **N:** 42f
Angkor Thom [ancient city] *See* Angkor *in this index*
Angkor Wat, Temple of [Cambodia]
  Angkor **A:** 462
  Architecture (Indian architecture) **A:** 613 *with
    picture*
Angle [ancient people] *See* Angles *in this index*
Angle [geometry] **A:** 462 *with diagrams*
  Geometry (The study of geometry) **G:** 101 *with
    diagram*; (Congruence) **G:** 102 *with diagram*;
    (Bisecting an angle) **G:** 103 *with diagrams*
  Radian **R:** 73
  Triangle **T:** 437 *with diagrams*
Angle of attack [engineering]
  Aerodynamics (Lift) **A:** 85 *with diagram*
  Airplane *diagrams on* **A:** 224; (Changing altitude)
    A: 221
  Helicopter (Lift) **H:** 171 *with diagram*
  Hydrofoil (Fully submerged hydrofoils) **H:** 467
Angle of incidence [physics]
  Light (Reflection and absorption) **L:** 287
  Mirror (Plane mirrors) **M:** 616 *with diagrams*
  Reflection **R:** 194
  Refraction **R:** 199 *with diagram*
  Waves (Refraction and reflection) **W:** 152-153
Angle of reflection [physics]
  Mirror (Plane mirrors) **M:** 616 *with diagrams*
  Reflection **R:** 194
Angle of Repose [book by Stegner]
  Stegner, Wallace **So:** 883
Angle of view [optics]
  Photography (Lenses and focusing) **P:** 410
Angler [sports]
  Fishing **F:** 175
Anglerfish A: 463
  Animal *picture on* **A:** 487
  Deep sea (Fish) **D:** 82b-82c *with picture*
  Fish *pictures on* **F:** 156, **F:** 167
Angler's knot
  Knots, hitches, and splices *diagram on* **K:** 356
Angles [ancient people] **A:** 463
  Anglo-Saxons **A:** 464 *with map*
  England (The Germanic invasions) **E:** 304; (The
    Anglo-Saxon period) **E:** 304
  Saxons **S:** 168
Anglesey [island, United Kingdom]
  Wales (Rivers and coastline) **W:** 11 *with map*
Angleworm *See* Earthworm *in this index*
Anglia [English history]
  England (The Anglo-Saxon period) **E:** 304
Anglican Communion [religious group] **A:** 463
  See also Church of England *in this index*
  Archbishop of Canterbury **A:** 601
  Christianity (Organization) **C:** 522g
  Episcopal Church **E:** 344
  Jefferson, Thomas (Virginia lawmaker) **J:** 80
  Protestantism (The conservative reform
    movements) **P:** 834
  Reformation (In England) **R:** 198
  Roman Catholic Church (The church today)
    R: 412-413
  Thirty-Nine Articles **T:** 259
  Tutu, Desmond **T:** 527
Anglican Consultative Council
  Anglican Communion (Organization) **A:** 463
Anglicanorum Coetibus [document]
  Roman Catholic Church (The church today)
    R: 412-413
Anglicans *See* Anglican Communion *in this index*
Angling *See* Fishing *in this index*
Anglo-Afghan wars
  Afghanistan (The Anglo-Afghan wars) **A:** 95 *with
    picture*; (Independence) **A:** 95
  India (British India) **I:** 130-131
  Khyber Pass **K:** 309
Anglo-America [region]
  North America **N:** 458
Anglo-Boer Wars [South African history] **A:** 463
  Canada, History of (Foreign relations) **C:** 146
  Cape Colony **C:** 188
  Churchill, Sir Winston Leonard Spencer (Soldier
    and reporter) **C:** 546 *with picture*
  Kimberley **K:** 317
  Kitchener, Horatio Herbert **K:** 338
  Laurier, Sir Wilfrid (Relations with the United
    Kingdom) **L:** 126

  Quebec (Early years as a province) **Q:** 30
  South Africa (Discovery of diamonds and gold)
    So: 618
  United Kingdom (Gladstone and Disraeli) **U:** 69
Anglo-Catholic [religion]
  Wilberforce, Samuel **W:** 300
Anglo-Chinese War, First [1839-1842]
  China (Clash with the Western powers) **C:** 502
  Hong Kong (British control) **H:** 319
  Shanghai (History) **S:** 372
Anglo-Chinese War, Second [1850-1860]
  China (Clash with the Western powers) **C:** 502
Anglo-Irish Agreement [1985]
  Ireland (The Republic of Ireland) **I:** 427-428
  Northern Ireland (The Troubles) **N:** 525
  United Kingdom (Thatcher) **U:** 73
Anglo-Irish Treaty [1921]
  Irish Republican Army (Beginnings) **I:** 433
  Ulster Unionist Party **U:** 15
Anglo-Japanese Alliance [1902]
  Meighen, Arthur (First term) **M:** 386
Anglo-Nepalese War [1814-1816]
  Gurkhas **G:** 443
Anglo-Nubian goat
  Goat *picture on* **G:** 241; (Domestic goats) **G:** 239
Anglo-Persian Oil Company
  Iran (The Qajar dynasty) **I:** 406
Anglo-Saxon [language]
  English language (The development of English)
    E: 313
  English literature (Old English literature) **E:** 314
Anglo-Saxon Attitudes [book by Wilson]
  Wilson, Angus **W:** 316
Anglo-Saxon Chronicle [literature] **A:** 464
  Alfred the Great **A:** 349
  English literature (Old English prose) **E:** 315
Anglo-Saxons [people] **A:** 464 *with maps*
  Alfred the Great **A:** 348
  Angles **A:** 463
  Egbert **E:** 116
  England (The Anglo-Saxon period) **E:** 304
  English literature (Old English literature) **E:** 314
  Humberside **H:** 431
  Jutes **J:** 204
  Saxons **S:** 168
  Wales (Struggles against the Anglo-Saxons)
    W: 12
Anglo-Transvaal War [1880-1881]
  Anglo-Boer Wars **A:** 463
Angola A: 464 *with pictures and map*
  Cuba (Foreign relations) **Ci:** 1178
  Flag *picture on* **F:** 198
  Portuguese language **P:** 695
Angora [hair] **A:** 467
Angora cat
  Cat *picture on* **C:** 289; (Long-haired breeds) **C:** 292
Angora goat
  Goat *picture on* **G:** 241; (Domestic goats) **G:** 239
  Mohair **M:** 687
Angora rabbit
  Rabbit (Domestic rabbits) **R:** 46 *with picture*
Angostura [Venezuelan history]
  Bolívar, Simón (Fight for freedom) **B:** 441
  Ciudad Bolívar **Ci:** 604
Angry Young Men [literature]
  Amis, Kingsley **A:** 432
  English literature (Literature after World War II)
    E: 322-323
Angstrom [measurement] **A:** 467
  Weights and measures (Miscellaneous weights
    and measures) **W:** 184
  X rays (Wavelength) **X:** 541
Ångström, Anders Jonas [Swedish physicist]
  Angstrom **A:** 467
Anguilla [island, Caribbean Sea] **A:** 467
  West Indies (Abolition and independence
    movements) **W:** 205
Angular momentum [physics]
  Pauli, Wolfgang **P:** 201
  Satellite (Satellites of the terrestrial planets)
    S: 150
Angus, Rita [New Zealand painter]
  New Zealand (The arts) **N:** 349
Angus cattle
  Cattle (Aberdeen-Angus) **C:** 308 *with picture*
Anhedral crystal
  Crystal (Crystallization) **Ci:** 1166
Anhinga [bird] **A:** 467
  Bird *picture on* **B:** 351
Anhydration [chemistry]
  Hydrate **H:** 462
Anhydride [chemical] **A:** 467
Anhydrous ammonia [chemical] **A:** 467
Ani [bird] **A:** 467
Aniakchak National Monument [Alaska]
  National Park System (table: National
    monuments) **N:** 50

Aniakchak National Preserve [Alaska]
  National Park System (table: National preserves)
    N: 58
Anicetus, Saint [pope]
  Pope (table) P: 666
Aniline [chemical] A: 467
  Indigo I: 223
Animal A: 468 *with pictures and maps*
  See also the lists of Related articles in the Animal
    and Zoology articles
  Carbon cycle C: 206
  Classification, Scientific (Groups in classification)
    Ci: 655 *with pictures*
  Life L: 274 *with pictures*
  Plant P: 516; (The reproduction of plants) P: 532-
    533 *with picture*
  Soil (Effects of living things) So: 573
  Anatomy and physiology
    Brain (The brain in other animals) B: 559 *with*
      pictures
    Cell (Inside a living cell) C: 328 *with diagram*
    Ear (The ears of animals) E: 12 *with pictures*
    Embryo E: 257
    Eye (Eyes of animals) E: 469 *with pictures*
    Fur F: 561
    Heart (Hearts of animals) H: 146 *with diagrams*
    Homology H: 306
    Magnetism *picture on* M: 60c; (Magnets in
      living things) M: 61
    Metamorphosis M: 428
    Mind (Parts of the mind) M: 562-563
    Muscle M: 933
    Nervous system (The nervous system in other
      animals) N: 136
    Nitrogen (Nitrogen and life) N: 425
    Nitrogen cycle N: 426
    Protective coloration P: 831 *with picture*
    Respiration R: 260
    Skeleton S: 479 *with diagrams*
    Ultrasound (Animal uses of ultrasound) U: 16
    Venom V: 308
  Behavior
    Culture Ci: 1186
    Frisch, Karl von F: 534
    Hibernation H: 222
    Instinct I: 305
    Language (Other species and language) L: 64
    Lorenz, Konrad Zacharias L: 454
    Migration M: 538
    Photoperiodism P: 430
    Play P: 570
    Psychology *picture on* P: 849
    Reproduction R: 242
    Sleep (Sleep in animals) S: 506
    Sociobiology So: 563
    Territoriality T: 174
    Tinbergen, Nikolaas T: 294
  Change over time
    Adaptation A: 45
    Balance of nature B: 34
    Evolution E: 426
    Extinction E: 456 *with picture*
    Fossil F: 422 *with picture*
    Global warming (Impact of global warming)
      G: 232a
  Habitats
    Deep sea (Deep-sea life) D: 82a *with pictures*
    Desert (Desert animals) D: 156
    Ecology E: 53
    Forest (The life of the forest) F: 396
    Habitat H: 3
    Mountain (As a home for plants and animals)
      M: 892
    Ocean (Life in the ocean) O: 655 *with pictures*
    Rain forest R: 126 *with pictures*
    Seashore (Life on rocky shores) S: 270 *with*
      pictures
    Wetland W: 252a *with picture*
  Humans and animals
    Agriculture (Agricultural products) A: 147 *with*
      picture
    Animal (Animals and people) A: 471 *with*
      pictures; (The future of animals) A: 504
    Animal experimentation A: 509
    Biodiversity (Kinds of biodiversity) B: 310
    Breeding (Animal breeding) B: 592
    Circus Ci: 562 *with pictures*
    Cloning Ci: 682l *with pictures*
    Comparative psychology Ci: 902a
    Conservation (Biodiversity conservation)
      Ci: 976
    Disease (Spread of infectious diseases) D: 228
    Drug (Animals) D: 355
    Endangered species E: 269 *with pictures*
    First aid (Animal bites or stings) F: 138
    Game G: 21
    Genetic engineering (Uses of genetic

      engineering) G: 84b
    Hunting H: 450
    Invasive species I: 354j
    Livestock L: 396
    Materials (Animal fibers) M: 300d
    Mummy (Egyptian mummies) M: 925-926
    Mythology (Other Egyptian divinities) M: 980
    Oil spill (Effects) O: 707
    Pet P: 319 *with pictures*
    Transplant (Sources of donor organs) T: 380
    Vegetarianism V: 294
    Veterinary medicine V: 345 *with pictures*
    Wildlife conservation W: 303
    Zoo Z: 599 *with pictures*
Animal, Prehistoric *See* Prehistoric animal *in this*
  index
Animal breeding
  Breeding (Animal breeding) B: 592
  Careers (Farming, fishing, and forestry) C: 222
  Cattle (Breeding) C: 311
  Hybrid H: 460
  Livestock (Breeding livestock) L: 398
  Pedigree P: 228
Animal communities *See* Community [biology] *in*
  this index
Animal Crackers [film]
  Marx Brothers M: 238
Animal dye
  Dye (Natural dyes) D: 396
Animal experimentation A: 509
  Animal rights movement A: 510
Animal Farm [book by Orwell]
  Orwell, George O: 860
Animal geography [biology]
  Wallace, Alfred Russel W: 15
Animal husbandry [agriculture] *See* Livestock *in*
  this index
Animal Kingdom [theme park]
  Walt Disney Company W: 21
Animal magnetism
  Hypnosis (Mesmerism) H: 479
  Mesmer, Franz Anton M: 421
Animal protection movement
  Animal rights movement A: 510
Animal protein
  Food supply (Protein) F: 346
Animal quarantine [law]
  Quarantine Q: 7
Animal rights activist
  Animal rights movement A: 510
Animal rights movement A: 510
  Fox hunting F: 442
  Fur (Controversy over fur) F: 563
  People for the Ethical Treatment of Animals
    P: 277
  Terrorism (Terrorist groups and movements)
    T: 178-179
Animal science
  Livestock L: 396
Animal starch
  Carbohydrate (Kinds of carbohydrates) C: 203
Animal story
  Literature for children (Animal stories) L: 359
Animal tracks
  Bear *picture on* B: 185
  Beaver *picture on* B: 193
  Deer *picture on* D: 83
  Giraffe *pictures on* G: 195
  Lion *picture on* L: 341
  Raccoon *picture on* R: 50
  Rat *picture on* R: 146
  Squirrel *picture on* Sq: 816
  Tiger *picture on* T: 285
Animal training
  Animal (A table of animal intelligence) A: 493
  Dog (Training a dog) D: 280 *with pictures*
  Dolphin (Dolphin training and research) D: 299
  Homing pigeon H: 305
  Horse (Training horses) H: 359 *with picture*
  Lion (Training lions) L: 343
  Mouse *picture on* M: 902
Animal Welfare Act [1966]
  Animal experimentation (Laws and regulations)
    A: 510
Animal worship [religion] A: 510
Animalcule [biology]
  Leeuwenhoek, Anton van L: 181
Animales Mexicanos [book by del Campo]
  Literature for children *picture on* L: 355
Animalia [biology]
  Animal (The scientific classification of animals)
    A: 472
  Kingdom K: 328
Animation [motion pictures] A: 511 *with pictures*
  Advertising (Production) A: 76b
  Computer graphics (In entertainment and the
    arts) Ci: 924g *with picture*

  Disney, Walt D: 235 *with pictures*
  Motion picture (The computer revolution) M: 872
Animation [religion]
  Abortion (Abortion history) A: 15
Animato [music]
  Music (table) M: 954
Animator [artist]
  Animation (Traditional animation) A: 512 *with*
    picture
Anime [animation]
  Animation (New diversity) A: 514c
Animism [religion] A: 514d
  Animal worship A: 510
  Asia (Religions) A: 784
  Mythology (Anthropological approaches) M: 989
  Religion (Earlier theories) R: 218
  Sami (Religion) S: 79
Anion [chemistry]
  Electrolyte E: 201
  Ion (Behavior of ions) I: 371-372
Anise [plant] A: 515
Anise swallowtail [butterfly]
  Butterfly *picture on* B: 736
Anishinabe Indians *See* Chippewa Indians *in this*
  index
Anjou, Philip of *See* Philip V [king of Spain] *in this*
  index
Anjou dynasty [European history]
  See also Plantagenet *in this index*
  Hungary (The Kingdom of Hungary) H: 445
Anjou pear
  Pear (Varieties) P: 215
Anjouan [island, Comoros]
  Comoros Ci: 899
Ankara [Turkey] A: 515
  Galatia G: 8
  Turkey *picture on* T: 505
Ankle [anatomy] A: 515 *with diagram*
  Ligament L: 281
Ankylosaur [dinosaur]
  Dinosaur (True dinosaurs) D: 206b-206c
Ankylosaurus [dinosaur] A: 515
  Dinosaur *picture on* D: 207
Ankylosing spondylitis [disease]
  Arthritis (Other forms of arthritis) A: 752
Ann Arbor [Michigan] A: 516
Anna [Indian coin]
  Coin collecting *picture on* Ci: 758
Anna, Antonio López de Santa *See* Santa Anna,
  Antonio López de *in this index*
Anna, Donna [opera character]
  Opera: *(Don Giovanni)* O: 803
Anna Bolena [opera by Donizetti]
  Donizetti, Gaetano D: 307
Anna Christie [play by O'Neill]
  O'Neill, Eugene O: 762
Anna in the Tropics [play by Cruz]
  Hispanic Americans *picture on* H: 248
Anna Karenina [book by Tolstoy]
  Russian literature (The 1860's and 1870's) R: 562
  Tolstoy, Leo (His masterpieces) T: 322
"Annabel Lee" [poem by Poe]
  American literature (Poetry) A: 418-419
Annal [narrative]
  Rome, Ancient (Literature) R: 443
Annals [book by Tacitus]
  History (The ancient Greeks and Romans)
    H: 261-262
  Tacitus, Cornelius T: 4
Annals [poem by Ennius]
  Latin literature (Early Latin literature) L: 115-116
Annam [region, Vietnam]
  Indochina (The Khmer) I: 225; (French influence)
    I: 225
  Vietnam (French rule) V: 370
Annamite Range [mountains, Vietnam]
  Vietnam (Central Vietnam) V: 368
Annan, Kofi Atta [Ghanaian diplomat] A: 516 *with*
  portrait
  Cyprus (History) Ci: 1207
  Iraq War (Disagreements over the war) I: 414f-
    415
  United Nations (The secretary-general) U: 83 *with*
    portrait; (Policy disagreements) U: 96
Annand, William [Canadian political leader]
  Nova Scotia (table) N: 567
Annapolis [Maryland] A: 516
  Maryland *picture on* M: 249
  United States capitals U: 199
  United States Naval Academy U: 202
Annapolis Convention [U.S. history] A: 516
  Articles of Confederation A: 759
  Constitution of the United States (The need for
    the Constitution) Ci: 998-999
Annapolis River
  Nova Scotia (Rivers and lakes) N: 562 *with map*
Annapolis Royal [Nova Scotia] A: 516

Nova Scotia (The struggle in Acadia) **N: 568**
Annapolis Valley [region, Nova Scotia]
Nova Scotia (Economy) **N: 565**
Annapurna [mountain range, Nepal] **A: 516**
Annapurna I [mountain, Nepal]
Annapurna **A: 516**
Mountain (table) **M: 896** with diagram
Anna's Art Adventure [book by Sortland]
Literature for children picture on **L: 354**
Anne [empress of Russia]
Russia (table: Czars and empresses) **R: 549**
Anne [queen of Britain] **A: 517** with portrait
England (War with France) **E: 309**; (The Augustan
Age) **E: 309**
Marlborough, Duke of **M: 215**
Stuart, House of **So: 931**
United Kingdom (History) **U: 67**; (table: British
monarchs) **U: 72**
Anne, Princess [British princess]
Elizabeth II (The royal family) **E: 240**
Anne, Saint [mother of Mary] **A: 517**
Anne Boleyn See Boleyn, Anne in this index
Anne of Austria [wife of Louis XIII] **A: 517**
Buckingham, Duke of **B: 664**
Fronde **F: 541**
Louis XIV **L: 475**
Mazarin, Jules **M: 331**
Anne of Brittany [wife of Louis XII]
Scotland (The House of Stuart) **S: 219**
Anne of Cleves [wife of Henry VIII]
Henry VIII [of England] **H: 188**
Anne of Green Gables [book by Montgomery]
Canadian literature (Fiction: 1850-1918) **C: 157-
158**
Montgomery, Lucy Maud **M: 766**
Prince Edward Island (Visitor's guide) **P: 788**
Annealing [industrial process]
Glass (Annealing) **G: 216**
Iron and steel (Finishing) **I: 447**
Annelida [zoology] See Segmented worm in this
index
Annenberg Foundation
Foundation (table) **F: 430**
Annenberg School for Communications
Pennsylvania, University of **P: 270**
Annexation [political science] **A: 517**
Local government (Conflicts in authority) **L: 408**
Metropolitan area (Annexation) **M: 443**
Minority group (The creation of minority groups)
M: 609
Annie Get Your Gun [musical]
Merman, Ethel **M: 418**
Oakley, Annie **O: 638**
Annie Hall [film]
Allen, Woody **A: 372**
Motion picture (Best picture: 1977) **M: 861**
Annihilation [physics]
Antimatter **A: 556**
Gamma rays **G: 24**
Anning, Mary [British scientist] **A: 517**
Anniversary, Wedding
Wedding anniversary **W: 178**
Anno Domini [calendar] See A.D. in this index
Annobón [island, Equatorial Guinea]
Equatorial Guinea **E: 346** with map
Annual [botany] **A: 518**
Flower (Garden flowers) **F: 274**; (Garden annuals)
F: 276 with pictures
Fruit **F: 544**
Gardening (Planning an informal flower garden)
G: 32-34
Grass (The grass plant) **G: 324**
Plant (Germination) **P: 535-537**
Vegetable **V: 292**
Weed (How weeds grow) **W: 179**
Annual baby's-breath [plant]
Baby's-breath **B: 14**
Annual ring [botany]
Climate (Growth rings) **Ci: 679**
Sequoia (Age) **S: 310d**
Stem (Woody stems) **So: 887**
Tree (How trunks and branches grow thicker)
T: 418-419 with diagram
Annuit coeptis [motto]
Great Seal of the United States (The reverse side)
G: 348
Annuitant [insurance]
Insurance (Annuities) **I: 311**
Annuity [insurance] **A: 518**
Insurance (Annuities) **I: 311** with diagram
Pension (Private pension plans) **P: 273**
Annular eclipse [astronomy]
Eclipse (Solar eclipses) **E: 51**
Annulet [symbol]
Heraldry picture on **H: 195**
Annuli [zoology]
Earthworm **E: 39**

Annulment [law] **A: 518**
Divorce **D: 253**
Marriage (Laws concerning marriage) **M: 219**
Annulus [botany]
Mushroom (Parts of a mushroom) **M: 942**
Annunciation [painting by Fra Angelico]
Angelico, Fra picture on **A: 460**
Annunciation [religion] **A: 518**
Jesus Christ (Early life) **J: 105-106**
Annunciation, The [painting by Campin]
Campin, Robert **C: 91** with picture
Annunciation, The [painting by Fra Angelico]
Painting (The 1400's) **P: 52-53** with picture
Annunciation, The [painting by van Eyck]
Painting (The northern Renaissance) **P: 57** with
picture
Annunciation device [electronics]
Burglar alarm **B: 704**
Annunzio, Gabriele d' [Italian author] See
D'Annunzio, Gabriele in this index
Anoa [animal]
Buffalo **B: 674**
Anode [electricity]
Battery (How batteries work) **B: 168** with diagram
Crookes tube **Ci: 1153** with diagram
Electricity (Sources of current) **E: 194**
Electrolysis (How electrolysis works) **E: 200** with
diagram
Fuel cell (How a fuel cell works) **F: 551** with
diagram
Silver (Extracting and refining silver) **S: 464-465**
Vacuum tube (How a vacuum tube works) **V: 258**
with diagram
X rays diagram on **X: 541**
Anodizing [electrolysis] **A: 518**
Aluminum (Electrochemical finishes) **A: 396**
Anointing of the sick [religion] **A: 518**
Christianity (Sacraments) **C: 522h**
Eastern Orthodox Churches (Sacraments)
E: 46-47
Roman Catholic Church (Worship) **R: 403-404**
Anole [animal] **A: 518** with picture
Chameleon **C: 372**
Evolution (Directional selection) **E: 428**
Anomalistic month [time]
Month **M: 767**
Anomalous component cosmic rays
Cosmic rays (Anomalous component cosmic
rays) **Ci: 1076**
Anomalous sunflower [plant]
Evolution (Direct observation of evolution)
E: 431-432 with picture
Anopheles mosquito [insect]
Malaria **M: 95** with picture
Mosquito pictures on **M: 831, M: 833**
Anoplura [entomology]
Insect (table) **I: 300**
Anorexia nervosa [disorder] **A: 519**
Adolescent (Eating disorders) **A: 63-64**
Eating disorder **E: 48**
Mental illness (Eating disorders) **M: 406**
Another Country [book by Baldwin]
Baldwin, James **B: 39**
Another Part of the Forest [play by Hellman]
Hellman, Lillian **H: 178**
Anouilh, Jean [French dramatist] **A: 519**
Anovulation [disorder]
Infertility (Causes) **I: 265**
Anoxia [disorder] **A: 519**
Anoxic anoxia [disorder]
Anoxia **A: 519**
Anschluss [European history]
Austria (After World War I) **A: 939**
World War II (Aggression on the march) **W: 470-
472**
Anschütz-Kämpfe, Hermann [German scientist]
Gyrocompass **G: 453**
Gyroscope (History) **G: 454**
Anse aux Meadows National Historic Park, L'
[Newfoundland and Labrador]
Canada, History of (Early European exploration)
C: 138-139
Newfoundland and Labrador (Places to visit)
N: 368 with picture
Anselm, Saint [English religious leader] **A: 519**
William II **W: 308**
Ansgar, Saint [Frankish monk]
Sweden (The early kingdom) **So: 1032**
Anson, Cap [American baseball player]
Baseball (table: Hall of Fame) **B: 134**; (Early
strategy and stars) **B: 134b**
Answer [law]
Court (How civil courts work) **Ci: 1102**
Answer [music]
Classical music (Fugue) **Ci: 645**
Fugue **F: 553**
Answer print [filmmaking]

Motion picture (The answer print) **M: 856**
Ant [insect] **A: 520** with pictures
Animal pictures on **A: 480**
Aphid **A: 565**
Bird (Feather care) **B: 354-355**
Fire ant **F: 122**
Formic acid **F: 410**
Hamilton, William Donald **H: 33**
Insect picture on **I: 283**; (Abdomen) **I: 288**; (Smell)
I: 291; (Family life) **I: 294-295** with picture
Life cycle on **L: 276**
Parasite (Life cycle) **P: 154** with diagram;
(Influence on behavior) **P: 155**
Plant (How plants protect themselves) **P: 540-
541** with picture
Wilson, Edward Osborne **W: 316**
"Ant and the Grasshopper, The" [fable]
Aesop's fables **A: 90**
Ant bread
Ant (Harvester ants) **A: 526**
Ant farm
Ant (Keeping an ant farm) **A: 528**
Ant lion [insect larva] **A: 529** with picture
Ant-loving cricket [insect]
Cricket **Ci: 1130**
Antabuse [drug]
Alcoholism (Treatment) **A: 338**
Disulfiram **D: 240**
Antacid [drug] **A: 529**
Antaeus [Greek mythology]
Hercules (Other adventures) **H: 199**
Antagonist [chemistry]
Prostaglandin **P: 829**
Antakya [Turkey]
Antioch **A: 557**
Antananarivo [Madagascar] **A: 529**
Madagascar **M: 27** with picture
Antarctic Bottom Water
Atlantic Ocean (Subsurface currents) **A: 866**
Antarctic Circle [geography] **A: 529**
Climate (The role of latitude) **Ci: 676**
Midnight sun **M: 536**
Antarctic Circumpolar Current
Antarctica (Ocean) **A: 532**
Ocean (Circulation) **O: 658**
Antarctic Convergence [geography]
Antarctica (Ocean) **A: 532**
Southern Ocean (Boundaries) **So: 688**
Antarctic fur seal
Antarctica (Living things) **A: 534-535** with picture
Antarctic intermediate water
Pacific Ocean (Water masses) **P: 15**
Southern Ocean (Water masses) **So: 688b**
Antarctic Ocean See Southern Ocean in this index
Antarctic Peninsula
Antarctica (Land) **A: 531** with map
Antarctic Treaty [1959]
Antarctica **A: 531**; (International agreements)
A: 538
Southern Ocean (Boundaries) **So: 688**
Antarctica A: 530 with pictures and maps
Animal (Animals of the polar regions) **A: 484** with
picture and map
Antarctic Circle **A: 529**
Bird (Birds of the ocean and the Antarctic) **B: 344**
with pictures
Byrd, Richard Evelyn **B: 746**
Continent **Ci: 1021**
Cook, James (Second Pacific voyage) **Ci: 1026**
Enderby Land **E: 272**
Exploration (The exploration of Antarctica) **E: 450**
with picture and map
Ice age (Evidence from modern glaciers and from
caves) **I: 7**
Ice formation **I: 9**
Iceberg (Antarctic icebergs) **I: 17**
Icecap **I: 19**
Ozone **O: 893**
Ozone hole **O: 894** with pictures
South Pole **So: 685**
Southern Ocean **So: 688**
Antares [star]
Star picture on **So: 847**
Anteater [animal] **A: 540** with picture
Animal picture on **A: 481**
Mammal (table) **M: 129** with picture
Pangolin **P: 130**
Anteater, Spiny [animal] See Echidna in this index
Antebellum Trail
Georgia (Places to visit) **G: 122**
Antecedent [grammar] **A: 541**
Pronoun **P: 819**
Antelope A: 541 with pictures
Addax **A: 46**
Animal picture on **A: 501**
Gazelle **G: 74** with picture
Steenbok **So: 883**

Antelope Island [Utah]
Great Salt Lake **G:** 347
Antelope jack rabbit
Jack rabbit **J:** 3
Ante-mortem inspection
Meat packing (Inspection and stunning) **M:** 351
Antenna [communications] **A:** 543 *with pictures*
Communications satellite (How communications
satellites work) **Ci:** 888b *with picture*
Radar *picture on* **R:** 66; (The antenna) **R:** 71 *with
diagram*
Radio (Transmitting radio waves) **R:** 86 *with
diagram*; (The antenna) **R:** 88
Television (Broadcasting) **T:** 123; (Receiving
television signals) **T:** 124 *with diagram*
Antenna cleaner [entomology]
Bee (Legs) **B:** 201
Antennae [entomology] **A:** 544 *with pictures*
Ant (Sense organs) **A:** 522 *with picture*
Beetle (The bodies of beetles) **B:** 215-216 *with
diagram*
Butterfly (The head) **B:** 738 *with diagram*
Fly (Head) **F:** 309 *with diagrams*
Insect (Eyes and antennae) **I:** 287 *with diagrams*;
(Smell) **I:** 291 *with picture*
Moth (The head) **M:** 837-838 *with diagram*
Anterior cruciate ligament [anatomy] **A:** 544
Anterograde amnesia [psychology]
Brain (Memory and imagination) **B:** 554
Memory (Memory disorders) **M:** 394
Anterus, Saint [pope]
Pope (table) **P:** 666
Anthem [book by Rand]
Rand, Ayn **R:** 136
Anthem [music]
Classical music (The Reformation) **Ci:** 646-647
Anthemius [Roman emperor]
Rome, Ancient (table) **R:** 447
Anthemius of Tralles [Byzantine architect]
Architecture (Byzantine architecture) **A:** 617
Anther [botany]
Flower (The stamens) **F:** 293
Plant (Flowers) **P:** 531 *with picture*; (Sexual
reproduction) **P:** 532-533 *with picture*
Seed (Seed development in angiosperms) **S:** 281
Antheridium [botany]
Fern (Life cycle of a fern) **F:** 75
Liverwort **L:** 396
Moss (How mosses live) **M:** 834-835
Anthocyanin [pigment]
Leaf (The leaf changes color) **L:** 152
Anthony, Earl [American bowler]
Bowling *picture on* **B:** 524
Anthony, George T. [American political leader]
Kansas (table) **K:** 234
Anthony, Henry B. [American political leader]
Rhode Island (table) **R:** 311
Anthony, Marc [American singer]
Lopez, Jennifer **L:** 453
Anthony, Susan Brownell [American social
reformer] **A:** 544 *with portrait*
Dollar (The United States dollar) **D:** 295
Woman suffrage (Growth of the movement)
W: 380
Women's movement (The right to vote) **W:** 385
Anthony Dollar
Dollar (The United States dollar) **D:** 295
Money (Dollar coins) **M:** 714
Anthony of Padua, Saint [Italian religious leader]
A: 545
Anthony of Thebes, Saint [Christian monk] **A:** 545
Monasticism (Christian monasticism) **M:** 701
Religious life (Religious life in early Christianity)
R: 226
Anthophyta [botany]
Flower (The classifying of flowers) **F:** 298
Anthracene [chemical]
Hydrocarbon (Aromatics) **H:** 465
Anthracite [coal]
Coal (Coal rank) **Ci:** 718; (How coal was formed)
Ci: 720-721; (Where coal is found) **Ci:** 721
Fuel (Solid fuels) **F:** 550
Heating (Coal) **H:** 160
Pennsylvania (Mining) **P:** 261-262
Anthracnose [plant disease]
Alfalfa (Diseases and pests) **A:** 347
Bean (Pests and diseases) **B:** 182
Raspberry (Diseases and pests) **R:** 145
Anthrax [disease] **A:** 545
Bacteria (Harmful bacteria) **B:** 20
Cattle (Diseases) **C:** 312-313
Koch, Robert **K:** 360
Medicine (Scientific study of the effects of
disease) **M:** 375 *with picture*
Pasteur, Louis (His work in medicine) **P:** 193
September 11 terrorist attacks (Anthrax attacks)
S: 310b

Anthropoid [zoology]
Ape **A:** 563 *with pictures*
Primate **P:** 777; (Anthropoids) **P:** 778 *with pictures*
Anthropology A: 545 *with pictures*
*See also the list of Related articles in the
Anthropology article*
Archaeology **A:** 594
Blood (The significance of blood groups) **B:** 412
Careers (Life, physical, and social sciences)
C: 225-226 *with picture*
Culture (How people study culture) **Ci:** 1189
Ethnography **E:** 373
Mythology (Anthropological approaches) **M:** 989
Prehistoric people **P:** 744; (Studying prehistoric
people) **P:** 754a *with picture*
Psychology (Psychology and other sciences)
P: 847
Races, Human **R:** 52
Science (The social sciences) **S:** 194
Anthropology, Museum of [Vancouver]
British Columbia *picture on* **B:** 616
Anthropomorphic divinity
Mythology (Mythical beings) **M:** 975
Anthroposophy [spiritual movement]
Steiner, Rudolf **So:** 886
Anthurium [plant] **A:** 550
Anti-...
*Headings beginning Anti- are alphabetized as
single words:* Anti-Masonic Party *appears after*
Antihistamine
Anti-A antibody
Blood (The ABO blood groups) **B:** 412
Antiaircraft defense [warfare]
Artillery (Antiaircraft artillery) **A:** 763 *with pictures*
Machine gun (Antiaircraft weapons) **M:** 16
Radar (In the military) **R:** 65
Antianxiety and hypnotic drug
Depressant **D:** 149
Mental illness (Somatic therapy) **M:** 407
Tranquilizer **T:** 369
Antianxiety drug
Benzodiazepine **B:** 255
Drug (Drugs that affect the nervous system)
D: 352
Mental illness (Somatic therapy) **M:** 407
Tranquilizer **T:** 369
Antiapoptotic gene [biology]
Apoptosis **A:** 566
Antiarrhythmic [drug]
Drug (Antiarrhythmics) **D:** 351
Anti Atlas Mountains [Africa]
Atlas Mountains **A:** 869
Antiatom [physics]
Antimatter **A:** 556
Anti-B antibody
Blood (The ABO blood groups) **B:** 412
Antiballistic missile
Guided missile *diagram on* **G:** 425; (Surface-to-air
missiles) **G:** 426
Nixon, Richard Milhous (The national scene)
N: 433-434
Antibaryon [physics]
Hadron **H:** 5
Antibiotic [medication] **A:** 550 *with pictures*
See also the list of Related articles in the Antibiotic
article
Agriculture (Reforming agricultural practices)
A: 151
Bacteria (Protection against harmful bacteria)
B: 20
Disease **D:** 226; (Medical treatment) **D:** 232
Drug (Drugs that fight infection) **D:** 351; (The
drug revolution) **D:** 359
Dubos, René Jules **D:** 372
Farm and farming (Livestock care) **F:** 39
Fermentation **F:** 73
Fungi (The importance of fungi) **F:** 559-560
Gonorrhea **G:** 268
Pneumonia (Treatment and prevention) **P:** 587
Sexually transmitted disease (Diagnosis and
treatment) **S:** 339
Typhoid fever (Treatment and prevention) **T:** 539
Antibody [physiology]
AIDS (Diagnosis) **A:** 164b
Allergy (Allergic reactions) **A:** 373
Antitoxin **A:** 559
Bacteria (Protection against harmful bacteria)
B: 20
Blood (White blood cells) **B:** 408; (The ABO blood
groups) **B:** 412
Cancer (Monoclonal antibodies) **C:** 173
Disease (Immune responses) **D:** 231-232 *with
picture*
Drug (Vaccines) **D:** 351
Food (Regulating body processes) **F:** 331
Gamma globulin **G:** 23
Immune system (Parts of the immune system)

I: 87
Immunization **I:** 89
Influenza (How influenza spreads) **I:** 268b
Kidney (Kidney diseases) **K:** 312
Lymphatic system (Lymphocytes) **L:** 534
Measles (Cause and effects) **M:** 346
Monoclonal antibody **M:** 731
Plasma (Functions of plasma) **P:** 551
Protein (How the body uses proteins) **P:** 832
Rh factor **R:** 289
Serum **S:** 319
Virus (Infection) **V:** 429
Anticholinergic drug
Parkinson disease (Treatment with drugs) **P:** 170
Anticholinesterase [medication]
Myasthenia gravis **M:** 970f
Antichrist [religion] **A:** 553
Anticleia [legendary figure]
Ulysses (The Trojan War) **U:** 17
Anticline [geology]
Petroleum *diagram on* **P:** 337; (Migration)
P: 333-334
Anticoagulant [medication] **A:** 553
Ocean (Medicines) **O:** 654
Stroke (Prevention) **So:** 930
Anticodon [genetics]
Heredity (Translation) **H:** 208
Anticonvulsant [drug] **A:** 553
Anti-Corn Law League [British history]
Cobden, Richard **Ci:** 741
Corn Laws **Ci:** 1064
Anticosti [island, Quebec] **A:** 553
Anticruelty society *See* Humane society *in this
index*
Anticyclone [weather]
Air (Air movement) **A:** 171-172
Calms, Regions of (The horse latitudes) **C:** 69
Jupiter (Ovals) **J:** 199-200
Weather (Synoptic-scale systems) **W:** 159-161
Antidepressant [drug] **A:** 553
Depression **D:** 151
Fibromyalgia **F:** 90
Psychiatry (Somatic therapy) **P:** 845
Antidiuretic hormone
Diabetes (Diabetes insipidus) **D:** 180
Hormone (Blood composition hormones) **H:** 336
Antidote [medication] **A:** 554
Poison **P:** 600
Antidraft riot [1863]
Riot (During the 1800's) **R:** 348-349
Anti-Dreyfusards [French history]
Dreyfus affair (Efforts to clear Dreyfus's name)
D: 347-348
Anti-Drug Abuse Acts [1986, 1988]
Drug abuse (Reducing demand) **D:** 365
Antietam, Battle of [1862]
Civil War, American (table) **Ci:** 624; (Battle of
Antietam) **Ci:** 627 *with picture*
Lee, Robert E. (Opening campaigns) **L:** 178
Lincoln, Abraham (Building the army) **L:** 321-322
Maryland (The Civil War) **M:** 258-259 *with picture*
McClellan, George Brinton (Military career)
M: 332c-**M:** 332d
President of the United States *picture on* **P:** 764
Antietam National Battlefield [Maryland]
National Park System (table: National battlefields)
N: 55
Anti-Fascist People's Freedom League [Myanmar]
Myanmar (World War II) **M:** 970d
Anti-Federalists [U.S. history] **A:** 554
Constitution of the United States (Ratifying the
Constitution) **Ci:** 1001
Antifermion [subatomic particle]
Fermion **F:** 74
Antiferromagnetic material [physics]
Magnetism (In materials) **M:** 60c *with diagram*
Antifreeze [chemical] **A:** 554
Freezing point **F:** 510
Glycol **G:** 237
Antigelling agent [chemical]
Glue (How glue is made) **G:** 236
Antigen [protein]
Blood (Blood groups) **B:** 412
Cancer (Monoclonal antibodies) **C:** 173
Immune system **I:** 87
Monoclonal antibody **M:** 731
Transplant (Preventing rejection) **T:** 380-381
Antigen presentation [physiology]
Immune system (Antigen-presenting cells) **I:** 88
Antigen-presenting cell [physiology]
Immune system (Antigen-presenting cells) **I:** 88
Antiglobalization [political science]
Globalization (The debate over globalization)
G: 233
Antigone [literary figure] **A:** 554 *with picture*
Antigone [play by Anouilh]
Anouilh, Jean **A:** 519

Antigonid dynasty [Greek history] **A:** 554
Antigonish [Nova Scotia]
　Nova Scotia (Visitor's guide) **N:** 560
Antigonus I [king of Macedonia]
　Antigonid dynasty **A:** 555
Antigonus II [king of Macedonia]
　Antigonid dynasty **A:** 555
Antigorite [mineral]
　Serpentine **S:** 318
Antigravity [physics] **A:** 555
Antigua [Guatemala] **A:** 555
　Guatemala (Colonial period) **G:** 416
Antigua and Barbuda A: 555 *with picture and map*
　Flag *picture on* **F:** 200
Antihistamine [medication] **A:** 556
　Allergy (Treatment) **A:** 374
　Hay fever (Treatment) **H:** 116
Antihypertensive [drug]
　Drug (Antihypertensives) **D:** 352
Anti-icer [additive]
　Gasoline (Gasoline blends and additives)
　　G: 61-62
Antiknock gasoline
　Gasoline (Engine requirements) **G:** 61
Anti-Lebanon Mountains [mountains, Asia]
　Lebanon (Land and climate) **L:** 172
　Syria (The mountains) **So:** 1073
Antilepton [atomic particle]
　Lepton **L:** 206
Anti-litter law
　Oregon (Interesting facts) **O:** 827
Antilles [Caribbean Sea] *See* Greater Antilles; Lesser
　Antilles; Netherlands Antilles *in this index*
Antilles Current [Atlantic]
　Caribbean Sea (Currents) **C:** 237
Antilock-braking system
　Automobile (The brake system) **A:** 950
　Brake (Hydraulic brakes) **B:** 560-562 *with diagram*
Antimacassar [cloth]
　Hairdressing (The 1800's) **H:** 12
Anti-Masonic Party [U.S. history] **A:** 556
　Political convention (The history of national
　　conventions) **P:** 630
Antimasque [literature]
　Masque **M:** 268
Antimatter [physics] **A:** 556
　Antigravity **A:** 555
　Astronomy (Gamma-ray astronomy) **A:** 845
　Matter (Unusual forms of matter) **M:** 311
　Meson **M:** 421
　Neutrino **N:** 154
　Radiation (Beta particles) **R:** 76
　Subatomic particle **So:** 936
　Van Allen belts **V:** 269
Antimicrobial [medicine]
　Drug (Drugs that fight infection) **D:** 351
Antimicrobial agent [nutrition]
　Food additive (Kinds of additives) **F:** 339
Antimissile missile
　Guided missile (Surface-to-air missiles) **G:** 426
Antimolecule [chemistry]
　Antimatter **A:** 556
Anti-Monopoly Party [U.S. history] **A:** 557
Antimony [element] **A:** 557
　Metalloid **M:** 426
Antimony chloride [chemical]
　Hydrolysis **H:** 471
Antineutrino [physics]
　Neutrino **N:** 154
　Radiation (Beta particles) **R:** 76
Anting [behavior]
　Bird (Feather care) **B:** 354-355
Antinomians [religious group]
　Hutchinson, Anne Marbury **H:** 458
Antioch [Turkey] **A:** 557
Antiochus III [Seleucid king]
　Hannibal (After the war) **H:** 52-53
Antiochus IV [Seleucid king]
　Daniel, Book of **D:** 33
　Jerusalem (Ancient times) **J:** 100
　Jews (The Hellenistic period) **J:** 121
　Judah Maccabee **J:** 179
Antiope [Greek mythology]
　Farnese Bull **F:** 46
Antioxidant [chemical] **A:** 557
　Flavonoid **F:** 230
　Food additive (Kinds of additives) **F:** 339
　Food preservation (Additives) **F:** 343
　Gasoline (Gasoline blends and additives)
　　G: 61-62
　Rubber (General-purpose synthetic rubbers)
　　R: 504
　Tea (Tea and health) **T:** 63
　Vegetarianism **V:** 295
Antiparticle [physics]
　Antimatter **A:** 556
　Astronomy (Gamma-ray astronomy) **A:** 845

　Electron **E:** 203
　Gamma rays **G:** 24
　Subatomic particle **So:** 936
Antipersonnel mine [weapon]
　Mine warfare (Land mines) **M:** 564
Antiperspirant
　Deodorant **D:** 148
Antipholus [literary figure]
　Shakespeare, William: *(The Comedy of Errors)*
　　S: 355
Antiphonaire, L' [book by Aquin]
　Canadian literature (Modern literature: 1945 to
　　the present) **C:** 159-160
Antipope [religion]
　Pope (Early days) **P:** 662
Antipoverty program *See* Poverty *in this index*
Antiproton [physics]
　Antimatter **A:** 556
　Particle accelerator (How accelerators work)
　　P: 184-186
　Physics (Advances in the mid-1900's) **P:** 442
　Subatomic particle **So:** 936
　Van Allen belts **V:** 269
Antipsychotic drug [medication]
　Mental illness (Somatic therapy) **M:** 407
　Psychiatry (Somatic therapy) **P:** 845
　Tranquilizer **T:** 369
Antiquarian-book store
　Book collecting (Collecting books) **B:** 469
Antiquarianism
　Archaeology (Beginnings) **A:** 599
　History (Antiquarian research and the
　　philosophes) **H:** 262
Antiquark [physics]
　Gluon **G:** 237
　Hadron **H:** 5
　Meson **M:** 421
　Psi particle **P:** 844
　Quark **Q:** 7
Antique A: 557 *with pictures*
　Button *pictures on* **B:** 745
　Doll (Doll collecting) **D:** 294
　Enamel *picture on* **E:** 264
　Watch *pictures on* **W:** 114
Antique and Modern Poems [work by Vigny]
　French literature (Romantic poetry) **F:** 521
Antiquities Act [1906]
　National Park System (History) **N:** 58
Antiquity [artwork]
　Antique **A:** 557
Antirenters [U.S. history] **A:** 558
　New York (Growing prosperity) **N:** 316-318
Anti-retroviral drug
　Retrovirus **R:** 266
Anti-Rh [physiology]
　Rh factor **R:** 289
Antirust agent [additive]
　Gasoline (Gasoline blends and additives)
　　G: 61-62
Anti-Semitism A: 559
　Arab-Israeli conflict (Historical background)
　　A: 582
　B'nai B'rith **B:** 426
　Dreyfus, Alfred (Efforts to clear Dreyfus's name)
　　D: 347-348
　Herzl, Theodor **H:** 217
　Hitler, Adolf (Mein Kampf) **H:** 266; (World War
　　II) **H:** 268
　Hitler Youth **H:** 269
　Holocaust (Before the Holocaust) **H:** 296
　Jews (Jews in Christian Europe) **J:** 122; (The
　　growth of anti-Semitism) **J:** 123
　Kristallnacht **K:** 388
　Nazism (The birth of Nazism) **N:** 92
　Nuremberg **N:** 613
　Prejudice **P:** 754b
　Semites **S:** 293
　Wagner, Richard (Wagner's philosophy) **W:** 4
　Zionism (Movement to Palestine) **Z:** 595
Antiseptic [medication] **A:** 559
　Bacteria (Protection against harmful bacteria)
　　B: 20
　Disinfectant **D:** 235
　Hospital (The 1800's) **H:** 373
　Iodine (Uses of iodine) **I:** 370
　Lister, Sir Joseph **L:** 349
　Medicine *picture on* **M:** 374; (Antiseptic surgery)
　　M: 375
　Surgery (Antiseptics and asepsis) **So:** 1004
Antiserum [medication]
　Drug (Antiserums and globulins) **D:** 351
　Immune system (Passive immunity) **I:** 88b
　Serum **S:** 319
Anti-Slavery Convention of American Women
　[1837]
　Mott, Lucretia Coffin **M:** 880
Antislavery movement *See* Abolition movement

in this index
Antisocial behavior [psychology]
　Mental illness (Personality disorders) **M:** 406
Antisolar point [physics]
　Rainbow (How to find a rainbow) **R:** 127 *with
　　diagram*
Antisthenes [Greek philosopher]
　Cynic philosophy **Ci:** 1205
Antistrophe [poetry]
　Ode **O:** 673
　Poetry (Lyric poetry) **P:** 591
Antisubmarine helicopter
　Helicopter *picture on* **H:** 170
Antisubmarine missile
　Submarine (Attack submarines) **So:** 939-940
　Torpedo (How a torpedo works) **T:** 340d-341
Anti-Tampering Act, Federal [1983]
　Drug (U.S. drug laws) **D:** 357-358
Antitank mine
　Mine warfare (Land mines) **M:** 564 *with diagrams*
Antithesis [literature]
　Shakespeare, William (Rhetoric) **S:** 368
Antithesis [philosophy]
　Hegel, G. W. F. (Hegel's dialectic) **H:** 165
Antitoxin [physiology] **A:** 559
　Bacteria (Protection against harmful bacteria)
　　B: 20
　Diphtheria (Treatment) **D:** 215
　Immune system (The study of the immune
　　system) **I:** 88d
　Serum **S:** 319
　Tetanus **T:** 182b
Antitrust laws A: 560
　Business (Antitrust laws) **B:** 727
　Business ethics **B:** 728
　Capitalism (Ensuring competition) **C:** 195
　Telephone (Competition in the U.S. telephone
　　industry) **T:** 101
Antitumor drug
　Drug (Antitumor drugs) **D:** 353
Antivenin [drug]
　Snake (Snakes and people) **S:** 532
Antiviral drug A: 560
　AIDS (Treatment) **A:** 164b; (Providing medical
　　care) **A:** 166
　Virus (Antiviral drugs) **V:** 428a
Antivirus software
　Computer security **Ci:** 925
　Computer virus **Ci:** 925
Antivivisection
　Animal experimentation **A:** 509
Antiwar movement
　Fonda, Jane **F:** 326
　Iraq War (Disagreements over the war) **I:** 414f
　New Left **N:** 255
　Pacifism **P:** 18
　Vietnam War (Reactions in the United States)
　　V: 375 *with picture*; (Vietnamization) **V:** 376
Antler [zoology]
　Caribou *picture on* **C:** 237
　Deer **D:** 82d *with picture*; (Antlers) **D:** 83 *with
　　pictures*
　Horn **H:** 338 *with picture*
　Moose (The body of a moose) **M:** 798 *with picture*
　Reindeer **R:** 208 *with picture*
Antofagasta [Chile]
　Chile (Climate) **C:** 465
Antoine, André [French producer]
　Drama (Early realism) **D:** 338
Antoinette, Marie [queen of France] *See* Marie
　Antoinette *in this index*
Antoinette de Mirecourt [book by Leprohon]
　Canadian literature (Fiction: 1850-1918) **C:** 157
Antonescu, Ion [Romanian political leader]
　Romania (World War II) **R:** 424
Antonine emperors
　Rome, Ancient (The Roman Empire) **R:** 446-447
Antonine Wall
　Antoninus Pius **A:** 561
　Roman walls **R:** 414
Antoninus Pius [Roman emperor] **A:** 561
　Hadrian **H:** 5
　Marcus Aurelius **M:** 197
Antonio [literary figure]
　Shakespeare, William: *(The Merchant of Venice)*
　　S: 358
Antonioni, Michelangelo [Italian director] **A:** 561
Antonov An-124 [aircraft]
　Aircraft, Military (Transports) **A:** 203
Antony, Mark [literary figure]
　Shakespeare, William: *(Julius Caesar)* **S:** 360;
　　(Antony and Cleopatra) **S:** 364
Antony, Mark [Roman military leader] **A:** 561
　Actium, Battle of **A:** 30
　Augustus **A:** 889
　Caesar, Julius (Last victories) **C:** 13-14
　Cicero, Marcus Tullius (His life) **Ci:** 552

Cleopatra **Ci: 662a**
Egypt, Ancient (Roman rule) **E: 144**
Navy (Ancient navies) **N: 79**
Octavia **O: 669**
Rome, Ancient (The later years of the republic)
R: 445-446
Triumvirate **T: 448**
Antony and Cleopatra [play by Shakespeare]
Dryden, John **D: 370**
Shakespeare, William (Dramatic conventions)
S: 354; (*Antony and Cleopatra*) **S: 364**
Antrim, Mountains of
Northern Ireland (Surface features) **N: 522-523**
with map
Antshrike [bird]
Bird (Birds of Central and South America) **B: 344a**
with picture
Antwerp [Belgium] **A: 561**
Belgium (City life) **B: 226**
Anubis [Egyptian god] **A: 562**
Mythology pictures on **M: 973, M: 977, M: 978**;
(Mythical beings) **M: 975**; (Other Egyptian
divinities) **M: 980**
Anura [zoology]
Frog (Kinds of frogs) **F: 539**
Anurognathus [extinct animal]
Pterosaur **P: 854**
Anus [anatomy]
Colostomy **Ci: 850**
Inflammatory bowel disease **I: 266**
Insect (Abdomen) **I: 288**; (Digestive system) **I: 289**
with diagram
Intestine **I: 352** with diagram
Anvers [Belgium] *See* Antwerp in this index
Anvil [anatomy]
Ear (The middle ear) **E: 7-8** with diagram
Anvil [tool]
Forging **F: 409**
"Anvil Chorus" [music by Verdi]
Opera: (*Trovatore, Il*) **O: 808**
Anwal, Battle of [1921]
Alfonso XIII **A: 348**
Anxiety [emotion]
Anxiety disorder **A: 562**
Existentialism (What is existentialism?) **E: 437**
Personality (Personality traits) **P: 301**; (Freud's
psychoanalytic theory) **P: 302**; (Emotional
reactions) **P: 302**
Tranquilizer **T: 369**
Anxiety disorder [psychology] **A: 562**
Benzodiazepine **B: 255**
Mental illness (Anxiety disorders) **M: 405**
Phobia **P: 392**
Anyang [ancient city]
Jade **J: 20**
Shang dynasty **S: 371**
Anza, Juan Bautista de [Mexican explorer]
San Francisco (Settlement by Europeans) **S: 97**
Tucson **T: 481**
Anza-Borrego Desert State Park [California]
San Diego (Recreation) **S: 90a**
Anzaldúa, Gloria [American poet]
American literature (Diverse voices) **A: 424**
Anzio [Italy]
World War II (The invasion of Italy) **W: 483**
ANZUS [alliance]
Cold War (The West rearms) **Ci: 764**
New Zealand (International tensions) **N: 355-356**
Ao dai [clothing]
Vietnam (Clothing) **V: 366**
AOL [company]
Time Warner Inc. **T: 292d**
Aoraki/Mount Cook [mountain, New Zealand]
Mountain (table) **M: 896** with diagram
New Zealand (The South Island) **N: 351** with
picture
Aoraki/Mount Cook National Park [New Zealand]
National park (table) **N: 42f**
Aorangi *See* Aoraki/Mount Cook in this index
Aorta [anatomy] **A: 562**
Abdomen **A: 8**
Aneurysm **A: 459**
Artery (Principal arteries) **A: 751**
Frog picture on **F: 537**
Heart (Blood vessels) **H: 135** with picture;
(Blockage of blood flow) **H: 141**
Human body (table) **H: 422** with diagram
Insect (Circulatory system) **I: 288** with diagram
Marfan syndrome **M: 198**
Pulse **P: 900a**
Aortic valve [anatomy]
Heart (Chambers, valves, and inner lining)
H: 133-135 with pictures; (Blockage of blood
flow) **H: 141**
Aoun, Michel [Lebanese political leader]
Lebanon (Political struggle) **L: 174**
Aozou Strip [Chad]

Chad (History) **C: 367**
AP *See* Associated Press in this index
Apache Indians A: 562
Cochise **Ci: 743**
Geronimo **G: 173**
Indian, American (Shelter) **I: 136d**; (Indians of the
Southwest) **I: 166-168**
Indian wars (Apache warfare) **I: 195**
Apache Trail
Arizona (Places to visit) **A: 678**
Apalachee Indians
Appalachian Mountains **A: 568**
Apapane [bird]
Hawaiian honeycreeper picture on **H: 110**
Aparajito [film]
Ray, Satyajit **R: 152**
Aparicio, Luis [American baseball player]
Baseball (table: Hall of Fame) **B: 134**
Apartheid [law] **A: 562**
Africa (Struggles for independence) **A: 134-135**
African National Congress **A: 137**
Biko, Steve **B: 299**
Botha, P. W. **B: 510**
Coetzee, J. M. **Ci: 753**
De Klerk, Frederik Willem **D: 94**
Hertzog, James Barry Munnik **H: 217**
Human rights (Trade and diplomatic measures)
H: 428a
Malan, Daniel François **M: 95**
Mandela, Nelson **M: 136**
Minority group (Minority groups in other
countries) **M: 610**
Oligarchy **O: 742**
Olympic Games (Boycotts) **O: 753**
Racism (History) **R: 62**
South Africa **So: 608**; (People) **So: 609**; (History)
So: 617-619
Soweto **So: 689**
Sullivan, Leon Howard **So: 969**
Tutu, Desmond **T: 527**
Verwoerd, Hendrik **V: 341**
Vorster, Balthazar Johannes **V: 449**
Apartment
Housing (Kinds of housing) **H: 389** with picture
Rome, Ancient (City life) **R: 438** with picture
Shelter picture on **S: 393**
Apartment, The [film]
Motion picture (Best picture: 1960) **M: 861**
Apatite [mineral]
Crystal (Classifying crystals) **Ci: 1166-1167** with
picture
Fertilizer (Inorganic fertilizers) **F: 79**
Apatosaurus [dinosaur] **A: 563**
Dinosaur **D: 206**; (True dinosaurs) **D: 206b-209**
with picture
APBA [organization]
Motorboat racing **M: 876**
Ape [animal] **A: 563** with pictures
Animal (A table of animal intelligence) **A: 493**
Brain diagram on **B: 559**
Human being picture on **H: 414**; (Physical
characteristics) **H: 413**
Prehistoric people (Prehuman ancestors) **P: 744**
Primate diagram on **P: 778b**; (Anthropoids)
P: 778; (Conservation) **P: 778c**
Yerkes, Robert Mearns **Y: 564**
APEC [organization] *See* Asia-Pacific Economic
Cooperation in this index
Apelles [Greek artist] **A: 564**
Apene [race]
Olympic Games (The ancient games) **O: 750**
Apennine Tunnel [Italy] **A: 564**
Tunnel (table) **T: 491**
Apennines [mountains, Italy] **A: 564**
Genoa **G: 89** with picture
Italy (The Apennines) **I: 508**
Aperture [photography]
Camera (How a camera works) **C: 80** with diagram
Motion picture diagram on **M: 858**; (The camera)
M: 856
Photography (How a camera works) **P: 407** with
diagram; (Aperture size) **P: 412** with diagram
Aperture [zoology]
Shell diagram on **S: 385**
Whelk **W: 279**
Aperture antenna [device]
Antenna (Types of antennas) **A: 543**
Aperture-priority mode [photography]
Camera (Automatic exposure control) **C: 82**
Apex [botany]
Plant (Stems) **P: 529**
Apex [zoology]
Shell diagram on **S: 385**
Apgar, Virginia [American physician] **A: 564**
Apgar score **A: 565**
Apgar score [medicine] **A: 565**
Apgar, Virginia **A: 564**

Aphasia [disorder] **A: 565**
Speech therapy (Types of disorders) **So: 773**
Aphelion [astronomy]
Orbit **O: 819**
Aphid [insect] **A: 565** with picture
Alfalfa (Diseases and pests) **A: 347-348**
Ant (Dairying ants) **A: 526** with picture
Insect pictures on **I: 281, I: 285**; (Family life) **I: 294-
295** with picture
Pea (Diseases and pests) **P: 205**
Aphid lion [insect] *See* Lacewing in this index
Aphrodite [Greek mythology] **A: 565**
See also Venus [Roman mythology] in this index
Adonis **A: 65**
Ares **A: 645**
Mythology (table) **M: 981**
Pygmalion **P: 914**
Trojan War (The beginning of the war) **T: 449**
Troy (The legendary Troy) **T: 454**
Uranus **U: 217**
Aphthous stomatitis [disorder]
Canker sore **C: 177**
Aphthous ulcer [disorder]
Canker sore **C: 177**
API [shipping company]
Ship picture on **S: 426**
Apia [Samoa] **A: 566**
Samoa **S: 80** with picture
Apiary
Bee (As an industry) **B: 206-207**
Apical meristem [botany]
Bud **B: 665** with diagram
Plant (Stems) **P: 529**
Root (The root tip) **R: 470** with diagram
Apicomplexan [zoology]
Protozoan (Apicomplexans) **P: 838** with picture
Apiculture
Bee (As an industry) **B: 206**
Apis [mythology]
Serapis **S: 312**
APL [shipping company]
Ship picture on **S: 426**
Aplacophora [sea animal]
Mollusk (Aplacophora) **M: 696**
Aplastic anemia [disorder]
Anemia (Insufficient production of red blood
cells) **A: 457**
Aplomado falcon [bird]
Falcon picture on **F: 13**; (Other North American
falcons) **F: 14**
Apnea [disorder]
Sleep apnea **S: 507**
Apocalypse [New Testament] *See* Revelation, Book
of in this index
Apocalypse Now [motion picture]
Coppola, Francis Ford **Ci: 1044**
Apocrine gland
Skin (Hair, nails, and glands) **S: 489**
Apocrypha [religion]
Bible (The Christian Old Testament) **B: 282**
Esther, Book of **E: 361**
Gospels **G: 278**
New Testament (Other early Christian writings)
N: 287
Old Testament (Contents) **O: 741**
Apocryphal play
Shakespeare, William (Shakespeare's plays)
S: 354; (Folios) **S: 369**
Apodaca, Jerry [American political leader]
New Mexico (table) **N: 272**
ApoE [protein] *See* Apolipoprotein E in this index
Apogee [astronomy]
Moon (Rotation and orbit) **M: 783**
Orbit **O: 819**
Space exploration (Kinds of earth orbits) diagram
on **So: 697**
Apolipoprotein E [protein]
Alzheimer's disease (Causes) **A: 399**
Apollinaire, Guillaume [French poet] **A: 565**
Picasso, Pablo (The Rose Period) **P: 448a**
Apollo [Greek mythology] **A: 566**
Cassandra **C: 275**
Daphne **D: 35**
Delphi **D: 117**
Greece, Ancient picture on **G: 371**
Iphigenia **I: 397**
Midas **M: 521**
Muses **M: 937**
Mythology (table) **M: 981**
Orion **O: 856**
World, History of the picture on **W: 428**
Apollo asteroid
Asteroid (Orbital groups) **A: 824a**
Apollo Belvedere [sculpture]
Vatican City (Vatican Palace) **V: 287**
Apollo butterfly
Endangered species picture on **E: 271**

Apollo program [space exploration]
Space exploration (Apollo: Mission to the moon) **So: 714** *with pictures*
Aldrin, Buzz **A: 339**
Armstrong, Neil Alden **A: 723**
Astronaut (Achievements in space) **A: 829** *with picture*; (Advanced mission training) **A: 832**
Borman, Frank **B: 488**
Conrad, Charles, Jr. **Ci: 973**
Florida *picture on* **F: 263**
Grissom, Virgil Ivan **G: 396**
Haise, Fred Wallace, Jr. **H: 13**
Lovell, James Arthur, Jr. **L: 509**
Moon *picture on* **M: 791**; (Apollo missions) **M: 795**
National Aeronautics and Space Administration **N: 28**
Nixon, Richard Milhous (The national scene) **N: 433-434**
Schirra, Walter Marty, Jr. **S: 176**
Schmitt, Harrison Hagan **S: 177**
Science *picture on* **S: 204**
Swigert, John Leonard, Jr. **So: 1041**
Young, John Watts **Y: 572**
Apollo-Soyuz Test Project
Astronaut (Achievements in space) **A: 829-830**
Space exploration (The Apollo-Soyuz Test Project) **So: 721** *with picture*
Apollonian drive [philosophy]
Nietzsche, Friedrich (Classical scholarship) **N: 406**
Apollonios of Tralles [Greek sculptor]
Farnese Bull **F: 46**
Apollonius of Rhodes [Greek poet]
Greek literature (The Hellenistic Age) **G: 378**
Apologia pro Vita Sua [book by Newman]
Kingsley, Charles **K: 331**
Newman, John Henry **N: 378**
Apologies [book by Justin the Martyr]
Justin the Martyr, Saint **J: 204**
Apologue [literature]
Spanish literature (Early medieval literature) **So: 757-758**
Apology, The [book by Plato]
Plato (The dialogues) **P: 567**
Socrates (The Socratic problem) **So: 567**
Apology for Actors, An [pamphlet by Heywood]
Heywood, Thomas **H: 221**
Apology for the Life of Mrs. Shamela Andrews, An [book by Fielding]
English literature (The rise of the novel) **E: 318-319**
Fielding, Henry (His novels) **F: 94-95**
Apomixis [botany]
Plant (Asexual reproduction) **P: 535**
Aponte, José Antonio [Cuban revolutionary]
Cuba (Early years) **Ci: 1175-1176**
Aponte Martínez, Luis [Puerto Rican religious leader] **A: 566**
Apoptosis [biology] **A: 566**
Cancer (Molecular medicine) **C: 173**
Death (Medical aspects of death) **D: 61**
Apoptotic body [biology]
Apoptosis **A: 566**
Apostate, The [name for]
Julian **J: 186**
Apostle bird *See* Apostlebird *in this index*
Apostle Islands [Wisconsin]
Lake Superior (Description) **L: 45** *with map*
Wisconsin (Places to visit) **W: 356**
Apostle Islands National Lakeshore [Wisconsin]
National Park System (table: National lakeshores) **N: 58**
Apostle of Germany [name for]
Boniface, Saint **B: 459**
Apostle of Mexican Democracy [name for]
Madero, Francisco Indalecio **M: 30**
Apostlebird **A: 566**
Apostles [religious group] **A: 566**
Bible (The New Testament) **B: 282**
Christianity (The early church) **C: 523**
Jesus Christ (Followers) **J: 106-107**
Apostles, The [literary group]
Tennyson, Lord (His life) **T: 166f**
Apostles' Creed [religion] **A: 567**
Christianity (Creeds and catechisms) **C: 522h**
Apostolic delegate [diplomat]
Vatican City (Diplomatic corps) **V: 288**
Apostolic See [religion]
Pope **P: 660**
Apostolic succession [religion]
Bishop **B: 381**
Apostrophe [punctuation]
Punctuation (The apostrophe) **P: 903**
Apothecaries' weight [measurement] **A: 567**
Avoirdupois **A: 994**
Apothecary [career]
Pharmacy **P: 354**
Apothem [geometry]
Hexagon **H: 220** *with diagram*
Octagon **O: 669**
App [electronics] *See* Application software *in this index*
Appalachian dulcimer [musical instrument]
Dulcimer **D: 380** *with picture*
Appalachian Mountains [North America] **A: 567** *with map*
Canada (The Appalachian Region) **C: 118** *with picture*
Coal (Where coal is found) **Ci: 721**
Forest (Deciduous forests) **F: 394**
Mountain (The Appalachian Mountains) **M: 895**
North America (Land regions) **N: 462-464**
North Carolina (Land regions) **N: 484**
Pioneer life in America **P: 476**; (Crossing the Appalachians) **P: 477**; (Pioneers and Indians) **P: 485**
United States *map on* **U: 123**; (The Appalachian Highlands) **U: 120** *with picture*
Appalachian National Scenic Trail **A: 568**
National Park System (table: National parkways and other national parklands) **N: 55**
Appalachian Plateau [region, U.S.]
See also Cumberland Plateau *in this index*
Alabama (Land regions) **A: 268**
Georgia (Land regions) **G: 124**
Kentucky (Land regions) **K: 285** *with picture*
Ohio (Land regions) **O: 692**
Pennsylvania (Land regions) **P: 256**
United States (The Appalachian Highlands) **U: 120-121**
Virginia (Land regions) **V: 410**
West Virginia (Land regions) **W: 218**
Appalachian Region
Quebec (Land regions) **Q: 22** *with map*
Appalachian Ridge and Valley Region
Georgia (Land regions) **G: 124**
Appalachian Spring [ballet]
Copland, Aaron **Ci: 1040**
United States *picture on* **U: 119**
Appalachian State University [North Carolina]
North Carolina, University of **N: 495**
Appalachian Trail *See* Appalachian National Scenic Trail *in this index*
Appaloosa [breed]
Horse (table: Some types and breeds of horses) **H: 343**; (Color types) **H: 344-345** *with picture*
Apparel *See* Clothing *in this index*
Apparent magnitude [astronomy]
Magnitude **M: 62**
Star (Magnitude and luminosity) **So: 842**
Apparent wind [physics]
Aerodynamics (Lift and drag in a sailboat) **A: 86-87** *with diagram*
Appassionato [music]
Music (table) **M: 954**
Appeal [advertising]
Advertising (Advertising techniques) **A: 76** *with picture*
Appeal [law] **A: 568**
Parliamentary procedure (table) **P: 176**
Supreme Court of the United States (Authority of the Supreme Court) **So: 998**
Trial (The criminal defendant's rights) **T: 436-437**
Appeal bond [law]
Bonding **B: 455**
Appeal to the Christian Women of the South [pamphlet by Grimké]
Grimké (Angelina Emily Grimké) **G: 394**
Appeal to the Colored Citizens of the World, An [pamphlet by Walker]
Walker, David **W: 13**
Appeal to the Great Spirit [sculpture by Dallin]
Dallin, Cyrus Edwin **D: 16** *with picture*
Appeals, Court of *See* Court of Appeals *in this index*
Appeals, Lord of [office]
Parliament (The House of Lords) **P: 173-174**
Appearance and Reality [book by Bradley]
Bradley, Francis Herbert **B: 544**
Appeasement policy
Chamberlain, Neville **C: 371**
Munich Agreement (Consequences) **M: 928**
World War II (The failure of appeasement) **W: 472**
Appellant [law]
Appeal **A: 568**
Appellate court
Court (Types of courts) **Ci: 1101**; (Federal courts) **Ci: 1102**
Supreme Court of the United States (Original and appellate jurisdiction) **So: 998**
Trial (The criminal defendant's rights) **T: 436-437**
United States, Government of the (Lower court system) **U: 144**
Appellate judge [office]
Judge **J: 183**
Appellate jurisdiction [law]
Supreme Court of the United States (Original and appellate jurisdiction) **So: 998**
Appendectomy [surgery]
Appendicitis (Treatment) **A: 569**
Surgery (A typical operation) **So: 1005**
Appendicitis [disease] **A: 569**
Appendicular skeleton [anatomy]
Mammal (Skeleton) **M: 118-119**
Skeleton (The appendicular skeleton) **S: 480** *with diagrams*
Appendix [anatomy] **A: 569** *with diagrams*
Appendicitis **A: 569**
Human body (table) **H: 422** *with diagram*
Appendix [balloon]
Balloon (Gas balloons) **B: 58**
Appendix [reference]
Book (Inside a book) **B: 464-465**
A Guide to Writing Skills **Research Guide: 18**
Apperson, Edgar and Elmer [American mechanics]
Haynes, Elwood **H: 122**
Appert, Nicolas [French inventor]
Food preservation (Modern food preservation) **F: 344**
Appetite [philosophy]
Plato (Psychology and politics) **P: 568**
Appetite [physiology]
Weight control (How body weight is determined) **W: 181**
Appian Way [ancient Rome] **A: 569** *with picture and map*
Apple [fruit] **A: 570** *with pictures*
Bud *picture on* **B: 665**
Codling moth **Ci: 752**
Fruit (Simple fruits) **F: 544** *with picture*
Halloween (Fortunetelling) **H: 24b**
Maine (Agriculture) **M: 86**
Plant *picture on* **P: 530**
Tree *pictures on* **T: 420**
United States *picture on* **U: 132**
Washington (Agriculture) **W: 62**
Apple banana
Banana **B: 72**
Apple butter [food] **A: 573**
Apple Inc. **A: 573**
Computer (Personal computers) **Ci: 909-910**; (The personal computer) **Ci: 924c**
Desktop publishing **D: 158**
Jobs, Steve **J: 129**
Apple juice [drink]
Cider **Ci: 552**
Apple maggot [insect] **A: 573**
Apple (Pests and diseases) **A: 572**
Fly (table) **F: 310**
Apple of Discord [Greek mythology]
Paris **P: 159**
Apple scab [plant disease]
Apple (Pests and diseases) **A: 572**
Applebee, Constance M. K. [British sportswoman]
Field hockey (History) **F: 93**
Applegate, Jesse [American pioneer]
Pioneer life in America (Life on the trail) **P: 486-487**
Apples of the Hesperides [Greek mythology]
Hercules (The twelve labors) **H: 198-199**
Hesperides **H: 218**
Appleseed, Johnny [American frontiersman] **A: 573** *with picture*
Appleton, Frances [wife of Henry Wadsworth Longfellow] *See* Longfellow, Frances Appleton *in this index*
Appleton, Jane Means [wife of Franklin Pierce] *See* Pierce, Jane Appleton *in this index*
Application, Letter of
Careers (Contacting employers) **C: 218**
Letter writing (Letters of application) **L: 211** *with picture*
Application form
Careers (Completing job applications) **C: 218**
Application fraud [crime]
Identity theft **I: 46**
Application software [electronics]
Cellular telephone **C: 340**
Computer (Computer software) **Ci: 917**
Software (Application software) **So: 572**
Applied anthropology
Anthropology (Careers in anthropology) **A: 549**
Applied arts
Decorative arts **D: 80**
Fine arts **F: 104**
Applied entomology [science]
Entomology (What entomologists study) **E: 328**
Applied mathematics
Mathematics (The importance of mathematics) **M: 302**
Applied physics
Physics (Employment) **P: 443**

Applied science
Science (The importance of science) **S:** 191
Appling, Luke [American baseball player]
Baseball (table: Hall of Fame) **B:** 134
Appliqué [handicraft] **A:** 574 *with picture*
Quilt **Q:** 41 *with picture*
Appliqué lace
Lace **L:** 20 *with picture*
Appointment [politics]
Constitution of the United States (Article II, Section 2) **Ci:** 1009
Patronage **P:** 198
Appointment, The [book by Müller]
German literature (Recent German literature) **G:** 142
Appold, John G. [British inventor]
Pump (History) **P:** 901
Appomattox [opera by Glass]
Glass, Philip **G:** 224
Appomattox Court House [Virginia] **A:** 574 *with picture*
Civil War, American (The South surrenders) **Ci:** 633 *with picture*
Grant, Ulysses S. (Grant in command) **G:** 315
Lee, Robert E. (Final engagements) **L:** 179
National Park System (table: National historical parks) **N:** 56
Virginia *picture on* **V:** 419
Apportionment [political science] **A:** 574
House of Representatives (Size) **H:** 385
Senate (Membership of the U.S. Senate) **S:** 294
Supreme Court of the United States (Election issues) **So:** 1001
Apposition [grammar] **A:** 575
Appositive [grammar] *See* Apposition *in this index*
Appraisal [economics] **A:** 575
Eminent domain **E:** 260
Appraisal approach [psychology]
Emotion (The appraisal approach) **E:** 261
Apprentice [labor] **A:** 575
Careers (Apprenticeships) **C:** 217
Colonial life in America (Education) **Ci:** 803
Education (History) **E:** 97
Guild (Craft guilds) **G:** 428
Labor movement (Conducting apprenticeship programs) **L:** 7; (Craft guilds) **L:** 9
Vocational education (Other sources) **V:** 434
Apprenticeship of Duddy Kravitz, The [book by Richler]
Richler, Mordecai **R:** 331
Approach [movement]
Diving **D:** 243 *with diagram*
Approaching Chimney Rock [painting by Jackson]
Pioneer life in America *picture on* **P:** 476
Appropriation bill [government]
Budget (Preparation of the U.S. budget) **B:** 671
National budget (Creating a budget) **N:** 30
Approximation [mathematics]
Calculus (Finding areas) **C:** 24
Cube root **Ci:** 1180
APRA [political party] *See* Alianza Popular Revolucionaria Americana *in this index*
Apraxia [disorder]
Aphasia **A:** 565
Rett syndrome **R:** 266
Speech therapy (Types of disorders) **So:** 773
"Après-midi d'un faune, L" [poem by Mallarmé]
Mallarmé, Stéphane **M:** 110
Apricot [fruit] **A:** 575 *with picture*
April [month] **A:** 576 *with pictures*
April fish
April Fools' Day **A:** 578
April Fools' Day [custom] **A:** 577
Aprilis [month]
Calendar (The Romans) **C:** 31
Apron [structure]
Airport (Loading aprons and taxiways) **A:** 245
Apse [architecture]
Architecture (table) **A:** 608 *with picture*; (Medieval architecture) **A:** 617
Byzantine art (Early Byzantine churches) **B:** 749-750
Cathedral (The plan of a cathedral) **C:** 301 *with diagram*
Apsyrtos [legendary figure]
Medea **M:** 360
Aptitude [psychology]
Careers (Aptitudes) **C:** 215
Aptitude test
Testing (Tests of learning ability) **T:** 182a; (Tests of aptitude and interest) **T:** 182a
Apu Trilogy [film series]
India (Motion pictures) **I:** 121
Ray, Satyajit **R:** 152
Apuleius, Lucius [Roman author]
Latin literature (The Imperial Period) **L:** 116-117
Novel (Ancient Greek and Roman narratives)

N: 572
Apulia [region, Italy]
Italy (Apulia and the Southeastern Plains) **I:** 508
Apulian Aqueduct [Italy]
Aqueduct (Present-day aqueducts) **A:** 580
Apurímac River [Peru]
Amazon River (The course of the Amazon) **A:** 403
Aqaba, Gulf of *See* Gulf of Aqaba *in this index*
Aqmola [former name] *See* Astana *in this index*
Aqua [satellite]
Satellite, Artificial *picture on* **S:** 150f
Aqua regia [chemistry]
Nitric acid **N:** 425
Platinum **P:** 566
Aquaculture [farming] **A:** 578
Aquarium, Public (Research) **A:** 578b
Fish (Food and game fish) **F:** 146
Fishing industry (Fish farms) **F:** 182 *with picture*
Hawaii (Economic changes) **H:** 109
Ocean (The importance of the ocean) **O:** 653-654
Panama (Fishing) **P:** 119
Seafood **S:** 265
Aqualung [device]
Cousteau, Jacques-Yves **Ci:** 1106
Diving, Underwater (History) **D:** 247
Exploration (Deep-sea exploration) **E:** 450-451
Skin diving (History) **S:** 494
Aquamarine [gem] **A:** 579
Gem *picture on* **G:** 78
Aquarena Springs [San Marcos]
Texas (Places to visit) **T:** 194
Aquarist [person]
Aquarium, Home **A:** 578
Aquarium, Home A: 578 *with pictures*
Pet (Pets for the home) **P:** 319-320
Tropical fish **T:** 450
Aquarium, Public A: 578b *with pictures*
Aquarius [astrology] **A:** 579 *with picture*
Astrology (History) **A:** 827
Zodiac (The zodiac in astrology) **Z:** 597 *with picture*
Aquatic animal
Animal (Kinds of animals) **A:** 472
Aquatic bed [area]
Wetland **W:** 252a; (Aquatic beds) **W:** 252b
Aquatic plant *See* Water plant *in this index*
Aquatic region [geography]
Plant (Aquatic regions) **P:** 528
Aquavit [drink]
Alcoholic beverage (Other distilled drinks) **A:** 337
Aqueduct [water system] **A:** 580
Agriculture (Rome) **A:** 156
City *picture on* **Ci:** 580
Rome, Ancient (Architecture and engineering) **R:** 442 *with picture*
World, History of the *picture on* **W:** 429
Aqueous geochemistry
Geochemistry **G:** 91
Aqueous humor [physiology]
Eye (The uveal tract) **E:** 460-462; (Glaucoma) **E:** 466
Aquidneck Island
Rhode Island **R:** 296; (Islands) **R:** 306; (Settlement) **R:** 312
Aquifer [geology]
Artesian well **A:** 751 *with diagram*
Geothermal energy **G:** 136
Ground water **G:** 401
Irrigation (Ground water) **I:** 456
Water (Sources of supply) **W:** 124
Aquin, Hubert [Canadian author]
Canadian literature (Modern literature: 1945 to the present) **C:** 159-160
Aquinas, Saint Thomas [Christian theologian] **A:** 580
Angel **A:** 459
Christianity (Other Christian writings) **C:** 522h
Civil disobedience (History of civil disobedience) **Ci:** 607
Dominicans **D:** 306
Maritain, Jacques **M:** 212
Philosophy (Medieval philosophy) **P:** 388
Physics (The Middle Ages) **P:** 438
Political science (Scholasticism) **P:** 639
Scholasticism (History) **S:** 179
Aquincum [Hungarian history]
Budapest (History) **B:** 666
Aquino, Benigno [Philippine political leader]
Aquino, Corazon **A:** 580a
Aquino, Benigno, Jr. [Philippine political leader]
Aquino, Benigno Simeon Cojuangco, III **A:** 580a
Philippines (The Marcos era) **P:** 380-381
Aquino, Benigno Simeon Cojuangco, III [Philippine political leader] **A:** 580a
Phillipines (Recent developments) **P:** 381
Aquino, Corazon [Philippine political leader] **A:** 580a

Philippines (The Marcos era) **P:** 380-381
Aquino, Noynoy *See* Aquino, Benigno Simeon Cojuangco, III *in this index*
Aquitaine [France]
Charlemagne *map on* **C:** 379
Eleanor of Aquitaine **E:** 157
Gascony **G:** 60
Aquitaine, Duke of *See* Henry II [of England] *in this index*
Aquitani [people]
Gaul **G:** 70
Aquitanian Lowlands [region]
France (The land) **F:** 464
Ar [symbol]
Argon **A:** 660
Ar-Rifai Mosque
Cairo *picture on* **C:** 16
Ara Pacis [sculpture]
Rome, Ancient (Sculpture, painting, and mosaics) **R:** 442
Arab *See* Arabs *in this index*
Arab Americans A: 580a *with pictures and map*
Minority group (Arab Americans) **M:** 610
Racial profiling **R:** 61
Arab Emirates, United *See* United Arab Emirates *in this index*
Arab Emirates of the South, Federation of the
Yemen (Formation of South Yemen) **Y:** 563
Arab Empire *See* Islamic Empire *in this index*
Arab-Israeli conflict A: 582 *with picture and map*
Air force (Wars in the Middle East) **A:** 187
Arabs (Arabs today) **A:** 590
Arafat, Yasir **A:** 591
Army (Armies in the nuclear age) **A:** 728
Asia (Arab-Israeli conflicts) **A:** 810 *with picture*
Begin, Menachem **B:** 219
Gaza Strip **G:** 73
International relations (The Arab-Israeli conflict) **I:** 346
Intifada **I:** 353
Israel (The early 2000's) **I:** 489
Jews (The rebirth of Israel) **J:** 124
Meir, Golda **M:** 387
Middle East (History) **M:** 533-534 *with picture*
Palestine Liberation Organization (History) **P:** 106
Palestinians **P:** 107
Rabin, Yitzhak **R:** 50
Sadat, Anwar el- **S:** 7
Saudi Arabia (Continued progress) **S:** 161-162
Suez Canal (History) **So:** 958
1948-1949
Arab-Israeli conflict (The 1948 war) **A:** 582
Jerusalem (History) **J:** 100-101
Palestine (World War II and the division of Palestine) **P:** 105
1956
Arab-Israeli conflict (The Suez crisis of 1956) **A:** 582
Egypt (Republic) **E:** 132
1967 (The Six-Day War)
Arab-Israeli conflict (The 1967 war) **A:** 582a *with picture*
Cold War (The great blocs split) **Ci:** 769
Egypt (Progress and conflict) **E:** 133
Hussein I **H:** 457
Israel (The Six-Day War) **I:** 488
Jordan (History) **J:** 164-165
Nasser, Gamal Abdel **N:** 24
Palestine (The continuing conflict and peace efforts) **P:** 106
Syria (The continuing Arab-Israeli conflict) **So:** 1075
West Bank (History and government) **W:** 200
1973
Arab-Israeli conflict (The 1973 war) **A:** 582a
Egypt (Renewed warfare and peace) **E:** 133
Kuwait (History) **K:** 396
Organization of the Petroleum Exporting Countries **O:** 855
United Nations (Peacekeeping operations) **U:** 90-91
Arab League [alliance] **A:** 582b
Arabs **A:** 584; (The search for unity) **A:** 590-590a
Egypt (The 1940's) **E:** 132
Flag *picture on* **F:** 216
Arab Maghreb Union [organization]
Africa (Africa since independence) **A:** 135
Arab Spring [Middle Eastern history]
Middle East (2011 protests) **M:** 534b
Arab world [region]
Arab Americans **A:** 580a
Arabs **A:** 584 *with map*
Arabesque [ballet]
Ballet (table) **B:** 45 *with picture*
Arabesque [decoration]
Islamic art (Design motifs) **I:** 467-468
Arabia [region] *See* Arabian Peninsula *in this index*

Arabian American Oil Company See Aramco *in this index*
Arabian camel [animal] See Dromedary *in this index*
Arabian Desert [region, Arabia] A: 582b
Arabian Desert [region, Egypt]
  Egypt (The Eastern Desert) E: 126 *with map*
  Sahara S: 20
Arabian Gulf [name for]
  Persian Gulf P: 300
Arabian horse
  Horse (table: Some types and breeds of horses)
    H: 343 *with picture*; (Light horses) H: 343-345
    with picture
  Horse racing (Thoroughbred horses) H: 363
Arabian Nights [stories] A: 582b
  Aladdin A: 280
  Arabic literature (Fiction) A: 583-584
  Burton, Sir Richard Francis B: 712
  Hārūn al-Rashīd H: 80
  Literature for children (Traditional literature)
    L: 357-358
Arabian Peninsula A: 583
  Arabs (Land of the Arabs) A: 585; (History) A: 589
  Asia (Way of life in Southwest Asia) A: 774
Arabian Sea [Indian Ocean] A: 583
Arabic alphabet
  Alphabet (Aramaic, Hebrew, and Arabic) A: 383
  Arabic language A: 583
Arabic language A: 583
  Africa (Languages) A: 105
  Alphabet (Aramaic, Hebrew, and Arabic) A: 383
  Arabs A: 584; (Language) A: 586
  Egypt (Language) E: 123
  Middle East (Identity and language) M: 530
  Qur'ān Q: 44
Arabic literature A: 583
  Arabs (Literature and the arts) A: 587
Arabic numerals A: 584
  Al-Khwārizmī A: 370
  Decimal system D: 70
  Fibonacci, Leonardo F: 89
  Number (History) N: 606
Arabica coffee See Coffea arabica *in this index*
Arabs [people] A: 584 *with pictures and map*
  See also Arab Americans *in this index; and the list*
  of Related articles in the Arabs *article*
  Africa (Peoples of Africa) A: 104-105; (Ways of life
    in northern Africa) A: 107
  Alchemy A: 334
  Arithmetic (Written arithmetic methods) A: 669
  Asia (The people) A: 778 *with picture*; (Country
    life) A: 779
  Bedouins B: 199
  Middle East (People) M: 530
  Morocco (People) M: 811
  Music (Arab music) M: 956
  Palestine Liberation Organization P: 106
  United Arab Emirates (People) U: 44
  West Bank W: 199
  Arab countries
    Algeria A: 360
    Bahrain (History) B: 30
    Egypt E: 120
    Iraq (People) I: 409
    Kuwait (People) K: 395
    Lebanon (Ethnic groups and religion) L: 171
    Libya L: 264
    Qatar (People) Q: 3
    Saudi Arabia (People) S: 156 *with picture*
    Sudan (People) So: 952
    Syria (People) So: 1071
    Tunisia T: 487
  History
    Abraham A: 16
    Arab-Israeli conflict A: 582
    Biology (Beginnings) B: 317-318 *with picture*
    Crusades (How the Crusades began) Ci: 1159
    Horse (Horses and people) H: 360-361
    Israel (Arabs) I: 480
    Jerusalem (The people of Jerusalem) J: 96
    Jews (The Zionist movement) J: 123
    Lawrence, T. E. L: 146
    Map (Maps in the Middle Ages) M: 183
    Mathematics (Arab mathematics) M: 306
    Muslims M: 964
    Number (The Hindu-Arabic numeral system)
      N: 607
    Palestine (Arab control) P: 104; (World War I
      and the Balfour Declaration) P: 105; (World
      War II and the division of Palestine) P: 105
    Science (The Middle Ages) S: 197 *with picture*
    Ship (Sailing ships in the 1900's) S: 423 *with*
      picture
    Tanzania (The development of trade) T: 34-35
    United Arab Emirates U: 43
    World, History of the (The Islamic world)

    W: 434-435
    Yemen (People) Y: 562
    Zionism (The Balfour Declaration) Z: 595-596
ARABSAT [satellites]
  Arab League A: 582b
Aracari [bird]
  Toucan T: 347 *with picture*
Arachne [Greek mythology] A: 590b
Arachnid [zoology] A: 590b
  Arthropod A: 752 *with picture*
  Eye (Eyes of animals) E: 469
  Spider So: 782
  Tick T: 279
Arachnophobia [psychology]
  Phobia P: 392
  Spider (Spiders in the home) So: 790
Arad, Michael [American architect]
  National September 11 Memorial and Museum
    N: 61
  September 11 terrorist attacks (Moving forward)
    S: 310b-310c
Arad, Ron [Israeli designer]
  Furniture *picture on* F: 587
Arafat [plain, Saudi Arabia]
  Islam (The Five Pillars of Islam) I: 463-464
Arafat, Yasir [Palestinian political leader] A: 590b
  with portrait
  Fatah F: 54
  Israel (The early 1990's) I: 489; (The early 2000's)
    I: 489
  Middle East (History) M: 533-534a
  Palestine Liberation Organization (History) P: 106
  Palestinian Authority (History) P: 107
  United Nations *picture on* U: 93
Aragats, Mount [Armenia] See Mount Aragats *in this index*
Arago, François [French physicist]
  Photogrammetry P: 405
Aragon [region, Spain]
  Castile and Aragon C: 279
Aragon, Louis [French poet]
  Dadaism D: 2
  French literature (Surrealism) F: 522-523
Aragonite [mineral]
  Pearl (Characteristics of pearls) P: 217
Arakan Yoma [mountains, Myanmar]
  Myanmar (Land regions) M: 970c *with map*
Aral Sea [lake, Kazakhstan-Uzbekistan] A: 591
  with map
  Conservation (Water conservation) Ci: 977-978
  Lake (table) L: 34
Aramaic language A: 591
  Alphabet (Aramaic, Hebrew, and Arabic) A: 383;
    (Scripts of Asia) A: 383
  Assyria (Language and literature) A: 821
  Bible B: 279; (Translations of the Bible) B: 284
  Old Testament (Ancient translations) O: 741
  Persia, Ancient (Language and literature) P: 297
Aramco [company]
  Saudi Arabia (The new kingdom) S: 161;
    (Continued progress) S: 161-162
Aramid [fiber] A: 591
  Composite materials (Hybrid composites)
    Ci: 904-905
  Rope (Synthetic-fiber rope) R: 473
Aran Islands [Ireland]
  Ireland (Surface features) I: 422
Araneomorph [spider]
  Spider So: 782
Arango, Doroteo [birth name of]
  Villa, Pancho V: 384
Aranjuez, Treaty of [1777]
  Dominican Republic (History) D: 304-305
Aransas National Wildlife Refuge [Texas]
  Bird (Bird refuges) B: 368
Arantes do Nascimento, Edson [birth name of]
  Pelé P: 231
Aranyakas [religious writings]
  Hinduism (The Vedas) H: 235
Arapaho Indians A: 591
  Indian, American *picture on* I: 161; (Indians of the
    Plains) I: 158-159
Arapaima [fish]
  Fish *picture on* F: 157
Ararat [ancient country] A: 592
  Noah N: 439
Ararat, Mount [volcano, Turkey] See Mount Ararat
  in this index
Aras River [river, Asia]
  Armenia (Land and climate) A: 718a *with map*
Arau, Alfonso [Mexican director]
  Latin America (Motion pictures) L: 101
Araucana, La [poem by Ercilla y Zúñiga]
  Chile (The arts) C: 463
  Latin American literature (Colonial literature)
    L: 112
  Spanish literature (The 1500's) So: 758-759

Araucanian Indians See Mapuche *in this index*
Araucaria [botany]
  Tree (Needleleaf trees) T: 414-415
Arawak Indians A: 592
  Barbados (History) B: 104
  Columbus, Christopher (The first landing) Ci: 860
  Dominica (History) D: 302
  Grenada (History and government) G: 389
  Haiti (History) H: 15
  Hispanic Americans (In Puerto Rico and Cuba)
    H: 247
  Indian, American (Indians of the Caribbean)
    I: 172
  Jamaica (History) J: 24
  Puerto Rico (Spanish rule) P: 883
  West Indies (Early days) W: 205
Arbat [district, Moscow]
  Moscow (Entertainment and recreation) M: 825
    with picture
ARBED [company]
  Luxembourg (Economy) L: 531
Arbela, Battle of [331 B.C.]
  Alexander the Great (Victory over Darius) A: 343
  Darius III D: 36
  Persia, Ancient (The Achaemenid Empire) P: 298
Arbenz Guzmán, Jacobo [Guatemalan political
  leader]
  Central America (Developments since the mid-
    1900's) C: 356
  Guatemala (The mid-1900's) G: 417
  Latin America (Political circumstances in the early
    to middle 1900's) L: 109-110
Arber, Werner [Swiss physiologist]
  Nobel Prizes (Physiology or medicine: 1978)
    N: 446
Arbitration [law] A: 592
  International law (Courts and arbitration) I: 341
  Labor movement (Handling labor disputes) L: 6
  National Mediation Board N: 40
  Railway Labor Act R: 122
  Strike (Strike settlements) So: 928
Arbor Day [custom] A: 592
  Nebraska (Statehood) N: 112
Arbor Day [painting by Wood]
  Wood, Grant W: 390
Arbor Lodge [Nebraska City]
  Nebraska (Places to visit) N: 102
Arboreal animal
  Mammal (In trees) M: 122 *with diagram*
Arboretum [park] A: 592
Arborist [occupation]
  Tree surgery T: 433
Arborvitae [tree]
  Cedar (Scale-leaved cedars) C: 324
  Tree *pictures on* T: 424
Arbuckle Mountains
  Oklahoma *picture on* O: 726; (Land regions)
    O: 724 *with map*
Arbuckle Wilderness [Davis]
  Oklahoma (Places to visit) O: 722
Arbus, Diane [American photographer] A: 592
  Photography (A diversity of styles) P: 426-427
Arbusto Energy Incorporated
  Bush, George Walker (Business career) B: 722e
Arbuthnot, John [Scottish author]
  John Bull J: 133
Arbuthnot, May Hill [American author]
  Regina Medal (table: 1964) R: 206
Arbutus [plant]
  Trailing arbutus T: 368 *with picture*
Arc [geometry]
  Circle (Parts of a circle) Ci: 558 *with diagram*
  Geometry (Some basic geometric constructions)
    G: 103 *with diagrams*
  Pendulum P: 236 *with diagram*
  Rainbow (How to find a rainbow) R: 127 *with*
    diagram
Arc, Joan of See Joan of Arc, Saint *in this index*
Arc de Triomphe [Paris] A: 593
  France *picture on* F: 452
  Paris (Gardens, squares, and parks) P: 162 *with*
    picture and map
  Unknown soldier U: 211
Arc light
  Electric light (Gaseous-discharge lamps) E: 174
    with picture
  Electric power (Early developments) E: 186
Arc welding [industrial process]
  Helium (Uses) H: 176 *with picture*
  Noble gas N: 451
  Welding (Arc welding) W: 189 *with diagram*
Arcade [architecture]
  Architecture (table) A: 608 *with picture*; (Islamic
    architecture) A: 613
Arcade game
  Electronic game E: 204a; (Other platforms)
    E: 204d; (Arcade games) E: 204d

Nintendo N: 423
Arcadia [region, Greece] A: 593
Arcadia [book by Sidney]
Sidney, Sir Philip S: 449
Arcadia [literary style]
Italian literature (The Baroque period and the Enlightenment) I: 494-495
Arcadian League [Greek history]
Arcadia A: 593
Arcadian stag [Greek mythology]
Hercules (The twelve labors) H: 198-199
Arcadius [Byzantine emperor]
Theodosius I T: 252
Arcaro, Eddie [American jockey] A: 593
Arcas [Greek mythology]
Big and Little Dippers (The Little Dipper) B: 296
Arcelor Mittal [company]
Iron and steel (Recent developments) I: 452
Manufacturing (table) M: 170
Arcesilaus [Greek philosopher]
Skepticism S: 481
Arch [anatomy]
Foot (The arches) F: 352 *with diagram*
Arch [architecture] A: 593 *with diagram*
Architecture (table) A: 608 *with picture;* (Roman architecture) A: 616
Bridge (Arch bridges) B: 601 *with diagrams*
Building construction (Beams, girders, and columns) B: 682-683
Rome, Ancient (Architecture and engineering) R: 442 *with picture*
Arch bridge
Bridge (Arch bridges) B: 601 *with diagrams*
Arch dam
Dam (Masonry dams) D: 17
Arch of Constantine [ruins]
Constantine the Great Ci: 993
Rome (Other remains) R: 433 *with picture*
Arch of Septimius Severus [ruins]
Forum, Roman F: 421 *with picture*
Arch of the aorta [anatomy]
Aorta A: 562
Arch of Triumph *See* Arc de Triomphe *in this index*
Archaea [organisms] A: 593
Animal A: 468
Classification, Scientific (Groups in classification) Ci: 655
Domain D: 300
Flagellum F: 224
Kingdom K: 328
Ocean (The food cycle) O: 655-658
Prokaryote P: 817
Archaebacteria [organisms] *See* Archaea *in this index*
Archaefructus [plant]
Flower (The evolution of flowering plants) F: 299 *with picture*
Archaeocyte [reproduction]
Sponge (Asexual reproduction) So: 800
Archaeology A: 594 *with pictures*
See also the list of Related articles in the Archaeology *article*
Anthropology (Archaeology) A: 546
Culture (How people study culture) Ci: 1189 *with picture*
Prehistoric people P: 744; (Examining prehistoric sites) P: 754a
Science *picture on* S: 191
Archaeology of Knowledge, The [book by Foucault]
Foucault, Michel F: 429
Archaeometry [science]
Archaeology (Dating) A: 598
Archaeopteryx [extinct bird] A: 601
Bird (The first known birds) B: 369
Fossil *picture on* F: 425
Prehistoric animal (Birds) P: 738
Archaic Period
Mound builders (Archaic Period) M: 881
Paleo-Indians P: 102
Archaic triad [mythology]
Mythology (Roman divinities) M: 982
Archangel [Russia] *See* Arkhangelsk *in this index*
Archangel [religion]
Angel A: 459
Archangel Michael, Cathedral of
Kremlin K: 387
Moscow (Famous landmarks) M: 823-824
Archbald, Robert W. [American jurist]
Impeachment (History) I: 91
Archbishop [title] A: 601
Address, Forms of (Members of the clergy) A: 54
Archbishop of Canterbury [title] A: 601
Augustine of Canterbury, Saint A: 888
England (Religion) E: 298
Archduke [title]
Duke D: 380

Archean Eon [geology]
Earth (Age of Earth) E: 26
Archegonium [botany]
Fern (Life cycle of a fern) F: 75
Liverwort L: 396
Moss (How mosses live) M: 834-835
Archelaos [Greek sculptor]
Greece, Ancient *picture on* G: 373
Archelon [turtle]
Turtle T: 520
Archer, Frederick Scott [British photographer]
Photography (Technical improvements) P: 423
Archer, The [constellation] *See* Sagittarius *in this index*
Archer-Daniels-Midland [company]
Manufacturing (table) M: 170
Archerfish [fish] A: 601 *with picture*
Fish *picture on* F: 145
Archery [sport] A: 601 *with picture*
See also Bow and arrow *in this index*
Olympic Games (Summer Olympic Games) O: 746e
Archery Association, National
Archery (Target archery) A: 602-603
Archery Federation, International
Archery (Target archery) A: 602-603
Arches National Park [Utah] A: 604
National Park System (table: National parks) N: 48
Archetype [psychology]
Jung, Carl Gustav (His theories) J: 195
Mythology (Psychological approaches) M: 990
Archibald, Adams George [Canadian political leader]
Confederation of Canada (Fathers of Confederation) Ci: 935 *with picture*
Archidamian War [431-421 B.C.]
Peloponnesian War P: 232
Archidamus [king of Sparta]
Peloponnesian War P: 232
Archimedean screw [device] A: 604 *with diagram*
Invention (Ancient Greece) I: 359
Archimedean solid [geometry] A: 604 *with diagram*
Archimedes [Greek mathematician] A: 604
See also Archimedes's principle *in this index*
Airplane (Early experiments and ideas) A: 229
Calculus (History) C: 25
Elevator (History) E: 235
Physics *picture on* P: 440
Archimedes [crater]
Moon (Craters) M: 789
Archimedes's principle [physics]
Archimedes (His discoveries) A: 605
Fluid mechanics (Fluid statics) F: 304
Hydraulics (Laws of hydrostatics) H: 463-464
Mathematics (The Greeks) M: 306
Archipelago [geography] A: 605
Archipenko, Alexander [Russian-American sculptor] A: 605
Architect [career]
Architecture (Careers) A: 634 *with pictures*
Careers (Technical and mathematical occupations) C: 232 *with picture*
House (Building a house) H: 380
Ship (Building a ship) S: 413
Architects, American Institute of
Architecture (Education and training) A: 634
Architects Collaborative, The [organization]
Architecture (Walter Gropius) A: 630
Gropius, Walter G: 397
Architectural acoustics
Acoustics A: 29
Architecture A: 606 *with pictures*
See also the list of Related articles in the Architecture *article*
Arabs (Architecture) A: 588 *with picture*
Baroque (Baroque architecture) B: 117
China (Architecture) C: 490
Furniture (Recent developments) F: 584
Greece, Ancient (The arts) G: 369
Interior design I: 326
Mechanical drawing M: 353
Postmodernism P: 709
Renaissance *pictures on* R: 235; (The fine arts) R: 236
Rome, Ancient (Architecture and engineering) R: 442 *with picture*
School (Improvements in school design) S: 184 *with picture*
Sculpture (As part of architecture) S: 229; (The peak of architectural sculpture) S: 249 *with picture*
Architrave [structure]
Architecture (table) A: 608 *with picture;* (Minoan architecture) A: 615
Archival fingerprint identification
Fingerprinting (Fingerprint identification)

F: 106-107
Archival research
History (History in the universities) H: 262
Archon [title]
Areopagus A: 645
Athens (Earliest times) A: 857
Archosaur [extinct animal]
Bird (The evolution of birds) B: 369
Dinosaur D: 206a
Archy [fictional character]
Marquis, Don M: 218
Archytas [300's B.C., Greek inventor]
Airplane (Early experiments and ideas) A: 229
Screw (History) S: 226
Archytas [Greek scholar]
Sound (Early ideas about sound) So: 605
Arcite [literary figure]
Shakespeare, William: (*The Two Noble Kinsmen*) S: 366
Arco [Idaho]
Idaho (Postwar changes) I: 44
Arcology [experimental city]
Soleri, Paolo So: 583 *with picture*
Arcosanti [experimental city, Arizona]
Soleri, Paolo So: 583 *with picture*
Arctic A: 635 *with pictures and map*
See also the list of Related articles in the Arctic *article*
Animal (Animals of the polar regions) A: 484 *with pictures and map*
Bernier, Joseph Elzéar B: 271
Bird (Birds of the Arctic) B: 343 *with pictures*
Canada (Arctic life) C: 107; (The Arctic Basin) C: 120
Exploration (Arctic exploration) E: 449 *with map*
Flower (Flowers of the Arctic tundra) F: 283 *with pictures*
Global warming (Rapid change in the Arctic) G: 232a
Indian, American (Peoples of the Arctic) I: 152 *with picture and map*
Inuit I: 354
Lichen (The importance of lichens) L: 269 *with picture*
MacMillan, Donald Baxter M: 25
Ozone hole O: 894
Peary, Robert Edwin P: 224
Tundra T: 485
Arctic air mass [meteorology]
Weather (Synoptic-scale systems) W: 159 *with diagram*
Arctic Archipelago [region, Nunavut]
Nunavut (Land and resources) N: 609 *with map*
Arctic bottom water
Arctic Ocean (Water masses) A: 643-644
Arctic Circle [geography] A: 640
Climate (The role of latitude) Ci: 676
Midnight sun M: 536
Nunavut (Land and resources) N: 609
Arctic Coastal Plain [Alaska]
Alaska (Land regions) A: 292-294
Arctic desert [region]
Tundra T: 485
Arctic fox A: 640
Animal *picture on* A: 485
Fox (Arctic foxes) F: 440 *with picture*
Arctic gentian [plant]
Flower *picture on* F: 289
Arctic ground squirrel
Animal (Animals of the polar regions) A: 484
Arctic hare [animal]
Animal *picture on* A: 484
Arctic haze [meteorology]
Arctic Ocean (Threats) A: 644
Arctic hurricane
Arctic Ocean (Climate) A: 641
Storm (Polar lows) So: 913
Arctic Islands
Canada (The Arctic Islands) C: 117 *with map*
Arctic loon [bird]
Animal *picture on* A: 485
Arctic lupine [plant]
Flower *picture on* F: 283
Arctic National Wildlife Refuge [Alaska]
Alaska (Federally protected lands) A: 294
Bush, George Walker (Environmental issues) B: 722g
Arctic Ocean A: 640 *with pictures and maps*
See also Arctic *in this index*
Arctic A: 635; (Climate change) A: 640
Atlantic Ocean (Boundaries and size) A: 864
Maelstrom M: 40
Ocean (The world ocean) O: 651
Arctic poppy [plant]
Flower *picture on* F: 283
Arctic redpoll [bird]
Redpoll R: 191

Arctic tern [bird] **A: 644** *with picture*
Animal *picture on* **A: 468**
Bird *picture on* **B: 329**; (Birds of the Arctic) **B: 343** *with picture*; (Bird migration) **B: 360**
Tern **T: 172**
Arctic wolf [animal]
Wolf **W: 375**
Arcturus [star]
Boötes **B: 480**
Star (table: The 10 brightest stars as seen from Earth) **So: 842**
Árd-rí [title]
Ireland (History) **I: 425**
Ardabil rug
Islamic art *picture on* **I: 469**
Ardashir I [king of Persia]
Iran (The Sassanian dynasty) **I: 405**
Parthia **P: 183**
Persia, Ancient *picture on* **P: 299**; (The Sasanian dynasty) **P: 299**
Arden, Mary [mother of]
Shakespeare, William (His life in Stratford) **S: 345-346**
Ardennes Mountains and Forest [Europe] **A: 644**
Belgium (The Ardennes) **B: 231** *with picture*
Bulge, Battle of the **B: 694**
Luxembourg (Land) **L: 531**
Ardgowan National Historic Site [Prince Edward Island]
Canada (table: National historic sites) **C: 114**
Ardil [fiber]
Peanut (In industry) **P: 214**
Ardipithecus [hominid] **A: 644**
Ardipithecus kadabba [hominid]
Ardipithecus **A: 644**
Human being (Prehuman ancestors) **H: 414**
Prehistoric people (The earliest hominids) **P: 744**
Ardipithecus ramidus [hominid]
Ardipithecus **A: 644**
Human being (Prehuman ancestors) **H: 414**
Prehistoric people (The earliest hominids) **P: 744**; (table) **P: 754** *with map*
Arduenna [forest] *See* Ardennes Mountains and Forest *in this index*
Are You There God? It's Me, Margaret [book by Blume]
Blume, Judy **B: 425**
Area [mathematics] **A: 644**
Calculus (Finding areas) **C: 24** *with diagrams*
Cylinder **Ci: 1204**
Fraction (Calculations using fractions) **F: 446-448** *with diagram*
Metric system (Space and time) **M: 437**; (The metric system at a glance) **M: 438** *with pictures*; (Metric conversion table) **M: 439** *with pictures*
Rhombus **R: 318**
Square measure **So: 811**
Triangle (Perimeter and area) **T: 437**
Weights and measures (table: Surface or area) **W: 185**
Area 51 [military base, Nevada] **A: 645**
Area bombing
World War II (The air war) **W: 482**
Area mining
Mining (Area mining) **M: 575** *with diagram*
Area rug
Interior design (Planning on paper) **I: 330-331**; (Choosing patterns and textures) **I: 332**
Arecibo [Puerto Rico]
Puerto Rico *picture on* **P: 878**
Arecibo Observatory [Puerto Rico] **A: 645**
Telescope (Types of radio telescopes) **T: 106-107** *with picture*
ARENA [political party] *See* Nationalist Republican Alliance *in this index*
Arena Chapel [Padua]
Mural *picture on* **M: 929**
Arena Football League
Football (New professional leagues) **F: 368**
Arena polo [sport]
Polo (Indoor polo) **P: 647**
Arena Stage [Washington, D.C.]
Theater *picture on* **T: 244**
Arenal National Park [Costa Rica]
Costa Rica *picture on* **Ci: 1080**
Arendt, Hannah [American philosopher] **A: 645**
Areole [botany]
Cactus (Parts of the cactus) **C: 10**
Saguaro **S: 19**
Areopagitica [book by Milton]
Freedom of the press (History) **F: 508**
Milton, John (Middle years) **M: 557**
Areopagus [ancient Athens] **A: 645**
Solon **So: 586**
Arepa [food]
Venezuela (Food) **V: 301**
Arequipa [Peru] **A: 645**

Ares [Greek mythology] **A: 645**
See also Mars *in this index*
Mythology (table) **M: 981**
Ares, Hill of [ancient Athens]
Areopagus **A: 645**
Aresø, Lake [Denmark]
Denmark (Lakes and rivers) **D: 138**
Arévalo, Juan José [Guatemalan political leader]
Guatemala (The mid-1900's) **G: 417**
ARF [organization]
Association of Southeast Asian Nations **A: 820**
Arfvedson, Johann August [Swedish chemist]
Lithium **L: 386**
Argali [breed]
Sheep (Wild sheep) **S: 380**
Argall, Samuel [English sea captain]
Delaware (Exploration and early settlement) **D: 110**
Nova Scotia (The struggle in Acadia) **N: 568**
Argand, Aimé [Swiss chemist]
Lamp (Fat or oil lamps) **L: 52-53**
Lighthouse (Development of the lighthouse) **L: 294**
Argand lamp
Lamp (Fat or oil lamps) **L: 52-53** *with picture*; (Gas lamps) **L: 53** *with picture*
Lighthouse (Development of the lighthouse) **L: 294**
Argent [color]
Heraldry (Expansion) **H: 194** *with picture*
Argentina **A: 646** *with pictures and maps*
See also the list of Related articles in the Argentina article
Clothing *picture on* **Ci: 695**
Falkland Islands **F: 15**
Flag *picture on* **F: 200**
Human rights (Independent organizations) **H: 428a**
Immigration (Latin America) **I: 85**
Indian, American (Indians of the Andes) **I: 173**
Latin America (Early years of independence) **L: 107-108**
National park (Argentina) **N: 42b** *with picture*
Pampas **P: 113**
Patagonia **P: 194**
United Kingdom (Thatcher) **U: 73**
Vice president **V: 347**
Argentite [mineral]
Silver (Sources of silver) **S: 464**
Argersinger v. Hamlin [U.S. history]
Gideon v. Wainwright **G: 188**
Supreme Court of the United States (table) **So: 1002**
Arges [legendary figure]
Cyclops **Ci: 1204**
Argo [diving vessel]
Ocean (Submersibles) **O: 663**
Argo [Greek mythology]
Argonauts **A: 660**
Argus **A: 661**
Argo-Jason [diving vessel]
Ballard, Robert Duane **B: 43**
Argon [element] **A: 660**
Argonaut [sea animal] **A: 660** *with picture*
Mollusk (Octopuses and squids) **M: 695**
Shell (Octopuses and squids) **S: 388**
Argonautica [poem by Apollonius of Rhodes]
Greek literature (The Hellenistic Age) **G: 378**
Argonauts [Greek mythology] **A: 660** *with map*
Golden Fleece **G: 255**
Hercules (Other adventures) **H: 199**
Jason **J: 64**
Argonauts, Toronto [team] *See* Toronto Argonauts *in this index*
Argonauts of the Western Pacific [book by Malinowski]
Ethnography **E: 373**
Argonia [Kansas]
Salter, Susanna Madora **S: 76a**
Argonne National Laboratory [Illinois] **A: 660**
Chicago (Industry) **C: 431-432**
Illinois (The mid-1900's) **I: 75-76**
X rays *picture on* **X: 542**
Argos [Greek mythology] *See* Argus *in this index*
Arguedas, José María [Peruvian author]
Latin American literature (The early 1900's) **L: 113**
Argument
Logic **L: 425**
Philosophy (Logic) **P: 384**
Argus [Greek mythology] **A: 660**
Hera **H: 194**
Io **I: 369** *with picture*
Argus [ship]
Aircraft carrier (History) **A: 207**
Argyll, Duke of [Canadian statesman]
Lorne, Marquess of **L: 455**
Arhat [religion]

Buddhism (The Theravada) **B: 669**
Århus [Denmark] **A: 661**
Aria [music]
Opera (Recitative and arias) **O: 792**; (Early Baroque opera) **O: 797**
Aria da Capo [play by Millay]
Millay, Edna St. Vincent **M: 552**
Ariadne [legendary figure]
Dionysus **D: 215**
Theseus **T: 257**
Ariane [rocket]
International Space Station **I: 346b**
Rocket (Liquid-propellant rockets) **R: 388**
Space exploration *picture on* **So: 699**; (European nations) **So: 726** *with picture*
Arianespace [organization]
European Space Agency **E: 418**
Arianism [religion] **A: 661**
Ambrose, Saint **A: 405**
Arius **A: 669**
Constantine the Great **Ci: 993**
Nicene Councils **N: 402**
Theodoric **T: 252**
Arias de Ávila, Pedro [Spanish explorer]
Panama City **P: 128**
Arias Peace Initiative
Arias Sánchez, Oscar **A: 661**
Arias Sánchez, Oscar [Costa Rican political leader] **A: 661**
Costa Rica (The late 1900's) **Ci: 1084**
Arica [province, Chile]
Rain (Some rainfall records) **R: 124** *with map*
Aridisol [soil]
Soil *map on* **So: 575**; (How soils are classified) **So: 576**
Ariel [essay by Rodó]
Latin American literature (Modernism) **L: 113**
Rodó, José Enrique **R: 399**
Uruguay (The arts) **U: 225**
Ariel [satellite]
Satellite (The middle-sized icy satellites of Saturn and Uranus) **S: 150c**
Uranus *picture on* **U: 219**
Ariel glass
Glass (Types of art glass) **G: 220-221**
Aries [astrology] **A: 661** *with picture*
Zodiac (The zodiac in astrology) **Z: 597** *with picture*
Arif, Abdul Rahman [Iraqi political leader]
Iraq (The republic) **I: 414**
Arif, Abdul Salam [Iraqi political leader]
Iraq (The republic) **I: 414** *with picture*
Arikara Indians **A: 661**
Mandan Indians **M: 135**
South Dakota (Early days) **So: 681**
Arimaspian [Greek mythology]
Griffin **G: 393**
Ariosto, Ludovico [Italian poet] **A: 662**
Drama (Italian Renaissance drama) **D: 330**
Italian literature (Humanism and the Renaissance) **I: 494**
Aristarchus [Greek astronomer] **A: 662**
Copernicus, Nicolaus (Theories of heavenly motion) **Ci: 1039**
Physics (The Greeks) **P: 438**
Aristida grass [plant]
Desert *picture on* **D: 155**
Aristide, Jean-Bertrand [Haitian political leader] **A: 662**
Clinton, Bill (International affairs) **Ci: 682e**
Haiti (History) **H: 15-17**
Aristides [Greek statesman] **A: 662**
Themistocles **T: 251**
Aristides [horse]
Horse (table: Famous horses in history and legend) **H: 361**
Kentucky Derby (table) **K: 296**
Aristocracy [government] **A: 662**
Aristophanes [Greek dramatist] **A: 662**
Drama (Old Comedy) **D: 327**
Euripides **E: 378**
Greek literature (Drama) **G: 377**
Aristotle [Greek philosopher] **A: 663** *with portrait*
Boethius, Anicius Manlius Severinus **B: 436**
Economics (Early theories) **E: 63**
Encyclopedia (The first reference works) **E: 268a**
Government (Ancient Greece) **G: 289**
Interest (History) **I: 323**
Middle Ages (Learning and the arts) **M: 527**
Plato (Plato's life) **P: 567** *with picture*
Psychology (Beginnings) **P: 849**
Sophocles **So: 595**
Thales **T: 228**
Arts
Criticism (History of literary criticism) **Ci: 1146**
Drama (Tragedy) **D: 325**; (The structure of drama) **D: 325**

Greek literature (Philosophical literature)
G: 377-378
Italian literature (Humanism and the
Renaissance) I: 494
Oratory (Classical orators) O: 819
Education
Alexander the Great (His youth) A: 342
Library (Greece) L: 258
Lyceum L: 532
Philosophy
Aristotle (Aristotle's writings) A: 663
Democracy (Famous quotations about
democracy) D: 120
Ethics (Ancient ethics) E: 366
Greece, Ancient (Philosophy, science, and the
arts) G: 368-369
Peripatetic philosophy P: 288
Philosophy (Aristotle) P: 387; (Medieval
philosophy) P: 388
Political science (The development of political
science) P: 639
Scholasticism (History) S: 179
Science
Aristotle (Philosophy of nature) A: 664
Air (The study of air) A: 175
Astronomy (Earth-centered theories) A: 835;
(History) A: 846-847
Botany (The history of botany) B: 509
Chemistry (Beginnings) C: 400
Classification, Scientific (Development of
classification) Ci: 656
Galileo (Mature scientific career) G: 11
Geology (The ancient Greeks) G: 97
Gravitation G: 331
Heredity (Early ideas about heredity) H: 208
Meteorology M: 432
Photography (Early developments) P: 422
Physics (The Greeks) P: 438
Science (Ancient Greece) S: 196
Sound (Early ideas about sound) So: 605
Zoology (History) Z: 606
Aristotle Contemplating the Bust of Homer
[painting by Rembrandt]
Aristotle *picture on* A: 663
Arita porcelain
Porcelain (Oriental porcelain) P: 676-677
Arithmetic A: 665 *with pictures*
See also the list of Related articles in the Arithmetic
article
Mathematics (Branches of mathematics) M: 303
Arithmetic, Fundamental theorem of *See*
Fundamental theorem of arithmetic *in this index*
Arithmetic average *See* Mean *in this index*
Arithmetic/logic unit *See* Digital logic unit *in this
index*
Arithmetic mean [mathematics] *See* Mean *in this
index*
Arithmetic progression [mathematics]
Progression (Arithmetic progressions) P: 812
Series S: 316b
Arithmetic series [mathematics]
Series S: 316b; (Working with finite series)
S: 316b
Arius [early Christian] A: 669
See also Arianism *in this index*
Ariyoshi, George R. [American political leader]
Asian Americans (Notable Asian American "firsts")
A: 812f
Hawaii (table) H: 105
Arizona A: 670 *with pictures and maps*
See also the list of Related articles in the Arizona
article
Mission life in America (Western missions)
M: 618-619
Arizona [ship]
Hawaii *picture on* H: 107
Pearl Harbor (The war memorials) P: 219 *with
picture*
Arizona, University of A: 693 *with picture*
Light (Studying light) L: 292-293
Telescope *picture on* T: 108
Arizona Cardinals [team]
Football (National Football League) F: 364
Arizona City [former name]
Yuma Y: 582
Arizona Diamondbacks [team]
Baseball (table) B: 130
Arizona poppy [plant]
Flower *picture on* F: 291
Arizona-Sonora Desert Museum
Arizona (Places to visit) A: 678
Arizona State University A: 693
Arjuna [legendary figure]
Bhagavad-Gita B: 276
Hinduism (The Ramayana and the Mahabharata)
H: 236
Krishna K: 388

Ark [religion] A: 693
Judaism (The synagogue) J: 181
Mount Ararat M: 883
Noah N: 439
Ark [ship]
Maryland (Exploration and settlement) M: 256
Ark of the Covenant [religion] A: 693 *with picture*
David (King of Israel) D: 45
Tabernacle T: 2
Arkansas A: 694 *with pictures and maps*
See also the list of Related articles in the Arkansas
article
Clinton, Bill Ci: 682
Clinton, Hillary Rodham Ci: 682h
Creationism (The 1900's) Ci: 1123-1124
Evolution (Acceptance of evolution) E: 433-434
Arkansas, University of A: 715
Arkansas *picture on* A: 699
Arkansas Democrat-Gazette [newspaper]
Arkansas (Communication) A: 711
Arkansas Gazette [newspaper]
Arkansas (Communication) A: 711
Arkansas Post National Memorial
Arkansas (Places to visit) A: 704
National Park System (table: National memorials)
N: 54
Arkansas River [U.S.] A: 715 *with map*
Arkansas (Rivers and lakes) A: 706
Oklahoma (Rivers and lakes) O: 727
Arkansas River Development Program [U.S.]
Arkansas (The late 1900's) A: 715
Arkansaw Territory
Arkansas (Territorial years) A: 712
Arkham House [publishing firm]
Derleth, August D: 152
Arkhangelsk [Russia] A: 716
Arkin, Alan [American actor]
Motion picture (Best performance by an actor in
a supporting role: 2006) M: 862b
Arktos [constellation]
Arctic Ocean A: 641
Arkwright, Sir Richard [British inventor] A: 716
Industrial Revolution (Spinning machines)
I: 248-249
Slater, Samuel S: 501
Spinning (The water frame) So: 794
Arlandes, Marquis d' [French balloonist]
Airplane (First human flights) A: 230
Balloon (History) B: 60-61
Arlberg technique
Skiing (The development of modern skiing)
S: 487
Arlberg Tunnels [Austria]
Tunnel (table) T: 491
Arlen, Harold [American lyricist]
Wizard of Oz, The W: 374
Arles [France]
France *picture on* F: 461
Arlésienne Suites, L' [music by Bizet]
Bizet, Georges B: 385
Arlington [Virginia] A: 716
Arlington House [estate]
Arlington National Cemetery A: 716
Lee, Robert E. *picture on* L: 179
National Park System (table: National memorials)
N: 54
Arlington National Cemetery [Virginia] A: 716
with picture
Unknown soldier U: 12
Washington, D.C. (Arlington National Cemetery)
W: 78 *with picture*
Arliss, George [British actor]
Motion picture (Best performance by an actor:
1929-30) M: 862a
Arm [anatomy] A: 717 *with diagram*
Human body (Anatomy of the human body)
H: 422 *with diagram*
Skeleton (The appendicular skeleton) S: 480 *with
diagrams*
Armada, Spanish *See* Spanish Armada *in this index*
Armadillo [animal] A: 717 *with picture*
Animal *picture on* A: 494
Mammal *picture on* M: 127; (table) M: 128 *with
picture*
Pangolin P: 130
Shell *picture on* S: 384
Armageddon [hill, Israel] A: 717
Armaments *See* Weapon *in this index*
Armaments, Limitation of *See* Arms control *in
this index*
Armani, Giorgio [Italian fashion designer] A: 718
Armas, Plaza de [Peru]
Lima (The city) L: 305 *with picture*
Armature [device]
Electric generator (Parts of a generator) E: 170
with diagrams; (How AC generators work)
E: 171

Electric motor (Parts of an electric motor) E: 179
Starter (Automobile starters) So: 858 *with
diagram*
Telegraph (The Morse telegraph) T: 90
Armbruster, William [designer]
Furniture (Recent developments) F: 584
ARMD [disorder] *See* Age-related macular
degeneration *in this index*
Armed forces
Address, Forms of (Other forms) A: 54
African Americans (World War II [1939-1945])
A: 136n-136o
Air force A: 182 *with pictures*
Air Force, United States A: 188
Aircraft, Military A: 201 *with pictures*
Arms control A: 721
Army A: 724 *with pictures*
Army, United States A: 730
Canadian Armed Forces C: 154
Careers (Armed forces schools) C: 217;
(Community and social services) C: 221
Censorship (Military censorship) C: 346
Defense, Department of D: 87
Draft, Military D: 318
Foreign policy (Military strength) F: 387
Government (Defense) G: 283
Helmet H: 179 *with pictures*
Marine M: 203 *with picture*
Marine Corps, United States M: 206 *with pictures*
Military training M: 544
Militia M: 544
Navy N: 76 *with pictures*
Navy, United States N: 82 *with pictures*
Oath (Military oaths) O: 639
Radio (In defense) R: 84 *with picture*
Rank, Military R: 139
Red Cross (Services to military personnel) R: 185
Signaling (Military signaling) S: 454
Uniform Code of Military Justice U: 27
War (Organization and control) W: 24
Armed Forces Movement [Portuguese history]
Portugal (The 1974 revolution) P: 694
Armenia A: 718 *with pictures and map*
Armenian Genocide A: 719
Azerbaijan (History) A: 997-998
Caucasus C: 317
Flag *picture on* F: 202
Union of Soviet Socialist Republics (History) U: 35
Armenian Church [religious group]
Armenia (People) A: 718-718a
Armenian Genocide [European history] A: 719
Armenian language
Alphabet (Other alphabets) A: 383
Armenia (People) A: 718-718a
Language (Indo-European) L: 65-66
Armenian Plateau [region, Asia]
Armenia (Land and climate) A: 718a *with picture*
Azerbaijan (Land and climate) A: 996-997
Armenian Rhapsody No. 1 [music by Hovhaness]
Hovhaness, Alan H: 399
Armenians [people]
Armenia (People) A: 718
Union of Soviet Socialist Republics (People) U: 31
Armer, Laura Adams [American author]
Newbery Medal (table) N: 359
Armey, Dick [American political leader] A: 719
Armies of the Night, The [book by Mailer]
Mailer, Norman M: 67
Armijo, Manuel [Mexican military leader]
New Mexico (Mexican rule) N: 273-275
Armill [symbol]
Coronation (The British coronation) Ci: 1068
Armin, Robert [English actor]
Shakespeare, William (Acting companies)
S: 352-353
Armistead, W. H. [American chemist]
Glass (table) G: 218
Armistice [1918] *See* Versailles, Treaty of *in this
index*
Armistice [warfare]
Truce T: 456
Armistice Day [custom]
Veterans Day V: 344
Armor A: 719 *with pictures*
Army, United States (Weapons and equipment of
the Army) A: 734
Heraldry (The development of heraldry) H: 194
Indian, American *pictures on* I: 139
Knights and knighthood (Armor) K: 350 *with
picture*
Shield S: 400 *with pictures*
Vikings (Weapons and armor) V: 382 *with picture*
Armor [zoology]
Animal *picture on* A: 494; (Armor) A: 496
Armor-piercing bomb
Bomb (Armor-piercing bombs) B: 450 *with
diagram*

Armor-piercing bullet
Ammunition (How shells explode) A: 436
Bullet B: 695
Armored catfish
Catfish picture on C: 300
Armored personnel carrier
Army, United States picture on A: 736
Armored reconnaissance vehicle
Tank T: 27
Armored-vehicle ammunition
Ammunition (Armored-vehicle ammunition)
A: 436 with picture
Armorer [occupation]
Armor (During the Middle Ages) A: 719-720
Armorial [book]
Heraldry (Expansion) H: 194
Armory Show [1913]
Davis, Stuart D: 50
Duchamp, Marcel D: 373
Armour, Jean [wife of]
Burns, Robert (Burns's life) B: 710
Armour, Philip Danforth [American businessman]
A: 721
Cudahy, Michael Ci: 1184
Armour and Company
Armour, Philip Danforth A: 721
Arms, Coat of See Coat of arms in this index
Arms, College of
Heraldry (Heraldry today) H: 196
Arms control A: 721
Bush, George Herbert Walker (International
affairs) B: 721
Bush, George Walker (Arms control) B: 722h
Gorbachev, Mikhail Sergeyevich (International
policies) G: 272
Guided missile (Postwar developments) G: 427
International relations (Treaties) I: 344; (The Cold
War ends) I: 346
Kennedy, John Fitzgerald (Arms control) K: 266
Nuclear Nonproliferation Treaty N: 595
Nuclear weapon (Controlling nuclear weapons)
N: 600
Peace (Arms control) P: 207
Pugwash Conferences on Science and World
Affairs P: 886
Strategic Arms Limitation Talks So: 919
Strategic Arms Reduction Treaty So: 919
Union of Soviet Socialist Republics (Détente)
U: 39
United Nations (Arms control) U: 92
Washington Conference W: 109
Arms limitation See Arms control in this index
Arms of assumption
Heraldry (Heraldry today) H: 196
Arms race
Cold War (The West rearms) Ci: 764; (To the brink
and back) Ci: 765
International relations (The Cold War begins)
I: 345
Arms reduction See Arms control in this index
Armstrong, Edwin Howard [American engineer]
A: 722
Armstrong, Ernest H. [Canadian political leader]
Nova Scotia (table) N: 567
Armstrong, Henry Jackson, Jr. [American boxer]
Boxing (Boxing's Golden Age) B: 532-532a
Armstrong, John [American government official]
Jackson, Andrew (Jackson the soldier) J: 8-9
Madison, James (table) M: 35
Monroe, James (Secretary of state) M: 736
Armstrong, Lance [American cyclist] A: 722
Bicycle racing (Road races) B: 292-293
Armstrong, Louis [American musician] A: 723 with
portrait
Hines, Earl H: 237
Jazz picture on J: 72; (The 1920's) J: 70
United States picture on U: 118
Armstrong, Neil Alden [American astronaut]
A: 723 with portrait
Astronaut (Achievements in space) A: 829-830;
(table) A: 830
Exploration (Human space travel) E: 452
Space exploration (Landing on the moon)
So: 715-717 with pictures
United States, History of the (The space race)
U: 196
Armstrong, Samuel [American political leader]
Massachusetts (table) M: 288
Armstrong, William Howard [American author]
Newbery Medal (table) N: 359
Army A: 724 with pictures
See also Army, United States, in this index and the
list of Related articles in the Army article
Cavalry C: 318
Flag (Military flags) F: 195-196 with pictures
Army, Canadian See Canadian Army in this index
Army, Department of the [U.S.] A: 729

Army, United States A: 730 with pictures
See also the list of Related articles in the Army,
United States article
Air Force, United States (History) A: 194
Army, Department of the A: 729
Asian Americans (World War II and Japanese
Americans) A: 812f
Buffalo Soldiers B: 680
Defense, Department of D: 87
Division D: 247
Flag picture on F: 211; (Military flags) F: 195-196
Infantry (Divisions) I: 264
Medals, decorations, and orders (Military awards)
M: 355 with pictures
National Guard N: 37
Rank, Military R: 139
Reserve Officers Training Corps (Army ROTC)
R: 258
United States Army War College U: 198
United States Military Academy U: 201
Army Air Corps
Air Force, United States (Between world wars)
A: 195
Tuskegee Airmen T: 525
Army Air Forces
Air Force, United States (World War II) A: 195
Roswell R: 484
Army ant
Ant (Army ants) A: 525 with picture
Insect (Family life) I: 294-296
Army Command and General Staff College
Army, United States (Training an officer) A: 733-
734
Army General Staff [U.S.]
Army, Department of the A: 729
Army group
Army (The organization of armies) A: 725
Army Materiel Command
Army, United States (Army commands) A: 736
Army-McCarthy hearings [U.S. history]
McCarthy, Joseph Raymond M: 332b
Television (Early programs) T: 118 with picture
Army Museum [Paris]
Paris (Museums and art galleries) P: 164-165
Army, Navy, and Air Force Veterans [organization]
Veterans' organizations (In Canada) V: 345
Army of Italy [French history]
Napoleonic Wars (The Army of Italy) N: 17
Army of Northern Virginia
Lee, Robert E. (Opening campaigns) L: 178
Army of the Andes [Latin American history]
Flag picture on F: 217
Army of the Cumberland [U.S. history]
Rosecrans, William Starke R: 478
Army of the Future, The [book by De Gaulle]
De Gaulle, Charles André Joseph Marie (Early life)
D: 90-91
Army Reserve [U.S.]
Army, United States (Organization of the Army)
A: 735
Army Reserve Officers Training Corps
Reserve Officers Training Corps (Army ROTC)
R: 258
Army secretariat
Army, United States (Army Department
headquarters) A: 736
**Army Special Operations Command, United
States**
Army, United States (Army commands) A: 736
Army staff
Army, United States (Army Department
headquarters) A: 736
Army War College See United States Army War
College in this index
Armyworm [insect] A: 740
Arn, Edward F. [American political leader]
Kansas (table) K: 234
Arnall, Ellis [American political leader]
Georgia (table) G: 130
Arnaud, Émile [French statesman]
Pacifism P: 17
Arnauld, Antoine [French philosopher]
Pascal, Blaise P: 190
Arnaz, Desi [American actor] A: 741
Ball, Lucille B: 43
Arnaz, Desi, Jr. [American actor/musician]
Arnaz, Desi A: 741
Arnaz, Lucie [American actress]
Arnaz, Desi A: 741
Arnica [medication]
Arnica A: 741
Arnica [plant] A: 741 with picture
Arno, Peter [American cartoonist]
Cartoon (Single panel cartoons) C: 265-266
Arno River [Italy] A: 741
Arno Valley [region, Italy]
Arno River A: 741

Arnold, Benedict [American traitor] A: 741 with
portrait
André, John A: 456
Petersburg P: 325
Revolution, American (The evacuation of Boston)
R: 275; (The invasion of Canada) R: 275-276;
(The campaign in New York) R: 281-282;
(Victory at Saratoga) R: 282; (Camden) R: 285;
(The end of the war) R: 286
Richmond (History) R: 333
Arnold, Billy [American race car driver]
Automobile racing (table: Indianapolis 500
winners) A: 980
Arnold, Eddy [American singer] A: 742
Arnold, Henry Harley [American general] A: 742
Air Force, United States (World War II) A: 195
Arnold, Kenneth [American pilot]
Unidentified flying object U: 27
Arnold, Lemuel H. [American political leader]
Rhode Island (table) R: 311
Arnold, Magda [American psychologist]
Emotion (The appraisal approach) E: 261
Arnold, Margaret Shippen [wife of]
Arnold, Benedict (A disappointed officer)
A: 741-742
Arnold, Matthew [British poet] A: 742
English literature (Later Victorian literature)
E: 321
Arnold, Richard Edward [birth name of]
Arnold, Eddy A: 742
Arnold, Ripley A. [American military leader]
Fort Worth (History) F: 418
Arnold, Thomas [British educator]
Arnold, Matthew A: 743
Rugby School R: 513
Arnoldson, Klas Pontus [Swedish statesman]
Nobel Prizes (Peace: 1908) N: 448
Arnolfini Wedding, The [painting by Van Eyck]
Van Eyck, Jan V: 282
Arnot, Adolphus [pseudonym]
Burr, Aaron (Tried for treason) B: 711
Aromatase inhibitor [drug]
Breast cancer B: 591
Aromatic hydrocarbon [chemistry]
Aramid A: 591
Hydrocarbon (Aromatics) H: 465
Kerosene (Properties) K: 306
Petrochemicals P: 329
Aronson, J. Hugo [American political leader]
Montana (table) M: 757
Aroostook Plateau [region, Maine]
Maine (Land regions) M: 80
Aroostook War [1839]
Maine (Statehood) M: 89
New Brunswick (The Aroostook War) N: 198
Arosa [Switzerland]
Switzerland picture on So: 1050
Arosemena Gómez, Otto [Ecuadorean political
leader]
Ecuador (The 1900's) E: 73
Arosemena Monroy, Carlos Julio [Ecuadorean
political leader]
Ecuador (The 1900's) E: 73
Arouet, François Marie [real name of]
Voltaire V: 346
Around the World in Eighty Days [book by Verne]
Verne, Jules V: 338
Around the World in 80 Days [film]
Motion picture (Best picture: 1956) M: 861
Arp, Jean [French artist] A: 743
Painting (Dadaism) P: 80
Árpád [Magyar chief]
Hungary (History) H: 445
Árpád dynasty [Hungarian history]
Hungary (The Kingdom of Hungary) H: 445
ARPAnet [computer network]
Computer (The Internet) Ci: 920
Internet (The early Internet) I: 350g
Arpeggio
Music (table) M: 954
Arpino, Gerald [American choreographer] A: 743
ARPKD [disease]
Polycystic kidney disease P: 649
Arquebus [gun]
Harquebus H: 67 with picture
Arrack [drink]
Date palm (Uses) D: 42
Arraignment [law]
Court (How courts work) Ci: 1101
Criminal justice system (Pretrial procedures)
Ci: 1143
Law enforcement (Trial) L: 141
Arrangement in Gray and Black [painting by
Whistler]
Whistler, James Abbott McNeill W: 282 with
picture
Array [engineering]

Solar energy (Using photovoltaic cells) **So: 578**
Array [mathematics]
  Determinant **D: 166**
Array antenna [electronics]
  Antenna (Types of antennas) **A: 543**
Arrector pili [anatomy]
  Hair *diagram on* **H: 9**; (Glands and muscles) **H: 10**
Arrest [law] **A: 743**
  Miranda v. Arizona **M: 616**
  Police (Police activities) **P: 620-621**
Arrested Development [musical group]
  Rock music *picture on* **R: 380d**
Arresting gear [ship]
  Aircraft carrier (Flight operations) **A: 206** *with picture*
Arrhenius, Svante August [Swedish chemist]
  Chemistry (Development of physical chemistry) **C: 404**
  Nobel Prizes (Chemistry: 1903) **N: 442**
Arrhythmia [disorder] **A: 743**
  Defibrillator **D: 88**
  Electrocardiograph **E: 199**
  Heart (Diagnosis and treatment) **H: 139**; (Abnormal heart rhythms) **H: 142**
Arrington, Richard, Jr. [American political leader]
  Birmingham (History) **B: 376**
Arriola, Don Andres d' [Spanish military leader]
  Pensacola **P: 272**
Arrival and Departure [book by Koestler]
  Koestler, Arthur **K: 361**
Arrow [weapon]
  Archery (Arrows) **A: 602** *with picture*
  Arrowhead **A: 743** *with pictures*
  Indian, American *picture on* **I: 144**; (Hunting, gathering, and fishing) **I: 141**
Arrow, Kenneth Joseph [American economist] **A: 743**
  Economics (Modern economics) **E: 64-65**
Arrow keys [computer]
  Keyboard **K: 308** *with picture*
Arrow of time [physics]
  Time (Arrows of time) **T: 292b**
Arrow poison frog [amphibian]
  Color *picture on* **Ci: 816**
  Frog *picture on* **F: 536**
Arrow to the Sun [book by McDermott]
  McDermott, Gerald **M: 332h**
Arrow worm *See* Chaetognatha *in this index*
Arrowhead [weapon] **A: 743** *with pictures*
Arrowroot [plant] **A: 744**
  Tapioca **T: 41**
Arrowsmith [book by Lewis]
  Lewis, Sinclair **L: 221**
Arroyo [geography]
  Desert (Desert climate and land) **D: 155-156**
Arroyo Seco Parkway
  California (Transportation) **C: 58**
  Road (Modern roads) **R: 362**
Ars Nova [music]
  Classical music (Secular music) **Ci: 646**
Arsenal of democracy [policy]
  World War II (The arsenal of democracy) **W: 478**
Arsenault, Aubin E. [Canadian political leader]
  Prince Edward Island (table) **P: 791**
Arsenic [element] **A: 744**
  Arsenical **A: 745**
  Metalloid **M: 426**
  Poison (Kinds of poisons) **P: 600**
Arsenic trioxide [chemical]
  Arsenic **A: 744**
Arsenical [medication] **A: 745**
Arson [crime] **A: 745**
  Crime scene investigation (At the laboratory) **Ci: 1141**
  Fire department (Fire cause and arson investigation) **F: 124**
  Pyromania **P: 920**
Arson dog
  Police dog **P: 626**
Arsphenamine [medication]
  Ehrlich, Paul **E: 145**
Art *See* Art and the arts; Commercial art; Prehistoric art *in this index*
ART [medicine] *See* Assisted reproductive technology *in this index*
"Art" [poem by Gautier]
  Gautier, Théophile **G: 70**
Art, Commercial *See* Commercial art *in this index*
Art, Philosophy of *See* Aesthetics *in this index*
Art and Architecture Building [Connecticut]
  Rudolph, Paul **R: 509** *with picture*
Art and the arts **A: 745** *with pictures*
  See also the list of Related articles in the Art and the arts *article and the Arts sections in specific country articles, such as* Mexico (Arts)
  Avant-garde **A: 982**
  Careers (Art, design, and communications) **C: 220**

with picture
  Criticism **Ci: 1146**
  Dance (Artistic reasons) **D: 24**
  Foundation (Arts and humanities) **F: 431**
  Hobby (The arts) **H: 272**
  Humanism (Humanism and the arts) **H: 431**
  Indian, American (Arts and crafts) **I: 145** *with pictures*
  Philosophy (Aesthetics) **P: 385**
  Plato (Art) **P: 569**
  Publishing (Art and design) **P: 867**; (Books as art) **P: 869**
  Works Progress Administration **W: 405**
Art appreciation
  Art and the arts (Enjoying the arts) **A: 748**
Art as Experience [book by Dewey]
  Dewey, John **D: 177**
Art Deco [design] **A: 749** *with picture*
  Fashion **F: 50**
  Furniture *picture on* **F: 584**; (Art Deco) **F: 583**
Art director [occupation]
  Encyclopedia *picture on* **E: 268**
  Motion picture (Assembling the production team) **M: 850**
  Newspaper (The editorial department) **N: 381-382**
Art Ensemble of Chicago [music]
  Jazz (Recent developments) **J: 73-74**
Art for art's sake [slogan]
  Avant-garde **A: 982**
  French literature (Gautier and Nerval) **F: 521**
  Gautier, Théophile **G: 70**
  George, Stefan **G: 109**
Art Gallery of Ontario [Toronto]
  Ontario (Places to visit) **On:**
  Toronto (The arts) **T: 340a**; (Recent developments) **T: 340c**
Art Institute of Chicago **A: 749**
  Chicago (Museums) **C: 428-429** *with picture*
  Illinois *picture on* **I: 63**
Art museum
  Museum (Art museums) **M: 938**
Art music *See* Classical music *in this index*
Art Nouveau [design] **A: 749** *with picture*
  Beardsley, Aubrey Vincent **B: 188** *with picture*
  Furniture *picture on* **F: 581**; (Art Nouveau) **F: 582**
  Tiffany, Louis Comfort **T: 283**
Art of Fugue, The [music by Bach]
  Bach, Johann Sebastian (His works) **B: 16-17**
Art of Love [book by Ovid]
  Ovid **O: 882**
Art of Loving, The [book by Fromm]
  Fromm, Erich **F: 541**
Art of Poetry [book by Horace]
  Criticism (History of literary criticism) **Ci: 1146**
  Latin literature (The Augustan Age) **L: 116**
Art of Poetry, The [book by Boileau-Despréaux]
  Boileau-Despréaux, Nicolas **B: 439**
  French literature (Classical poetry) **F: 520**
Art rock
  Rock music (Progressive rock) **R: 380b**
Art Ross Trophy
  Hockey (Professional leagues) **H: 278-279**
Artamanovs' Business, The [book by Gorki]
  Russian literature (Late realism) **R: 562-563**
Artaphernes [Persian soldier]
  Marathon, Battle of (The battle) **M: 191**
Artaud, Antonin [French dramatist]
  Drama (Experimental theater) **D: 340**
Artaxerxes V [king of Persia]
  Alexander the Great (Victory over Darius) **A: 343**
Arte popular [handicrafts]
  Latin America (Handicrafts) **L: 102**
Artemesinin [drug]
  Malaria (Treatment and prevention) **M: 96**
Artemis [Greek mythology] **A: 750**
  See also Diana *in this index*
  Iphigenia **I: 397**
  Mythology (table) **M: 981**; (Greek divinities) **M: 982**
  Orion **O: 856**
  Selene **S: 289**
Artemis, Temple of [Turkey]
  Ephesus **E: 341**
  Seven Wonders of the Ancient World *picture on* **S: 326**; (The Temple of Artemis at Ephesus) **S: 325**
Arteriolar sclerosis [disease]
  Arteriosclerosis **A: 750**
Arteriosclerosis [disease] **A: 750**
  Angina pectoris **A: 461**
  Artery (The walls of arteries) **A: 751**
  Cerebral hemorrhage **C: 361**
  Chelation therapy **C: 396**
  Circulatory system (Disorders of the circulatory system) **Ci: 561**
  Stroke (Causes) **So: 930**

Artery [anatomy] **A: 750** *with diagram*
  Aneurysm **A: 459**
  Angioplasty **A: 461** *with diagram*
  Blood (What blood does in the body) **B: 408**
  Circulatory system (The blood vessels) **Ci: 559** *with picture*
  First aid (Pressure on arteries) **F: 137**
  Heart **H: 132** *with diagram*; (Blood vessels) **H: 135** *with diagram*
  Human body (The blood vessels) **H: 421**; (table) **H: 422** *with diagram*
  Pulse **P: 900a**
  Vein **V: 295**
Artesian basin
  Artesian well **A: 751**
Artesian Basin, Great
  Australia (Underground water) **A: 910**
Artesian well [geology] **A: 751** *with diagram*
  Australia (Underground water) **A: 910**
  Queensland (Land and climate) **Q: 39**
  Well (Water wells) **W: 193**
Artha [Hinduism]
  Manu **M: 168**
Arthritis [disorder] **A: 751** *with diagrams*
  Disability **D: 218**
  Disease (Diseases associated with aging) **D: 230**
  Psoriasis **P: 844**
  Rheumatism **R: 291**
  Rheumatology **R: 291**
  Spine **So: 793**
Arthropod [zoology] **A: 752**
  Animal (A classification of the animal kingdom) **A: 506-507** *with picture*
  Invertebrate **I: 366**
  Prehistoric animal (The earliest animals) **P: 736**
Arthroscope [instrument]
  Arthroscopy **A: 753** *with picture*
  Endoscope **E: 273**
  Fiber optics (Uses of optical fibers) **F: 88-89**
Arthroscopy [medicine] **A: 753** *with picture*
  Surgery (Some common surgical operations) **So: 1006**
Arthur [grandson of Henry II]
  John **J: 132**
Arthur [prince of Wales]
  Catherine of Aragon **C: 303**
  Henry VII [of England] **H: 188**
Arthur, Chester Alan [U.S. president] **A: 754** *with pictures*
  Garfield, James Abram (Election of 1880) **G: 42**; (table) **G: 42**
  Hayes, Rutherford Birchard (Civil service reform) **H: 121**
  Republican Party (Political inactivity) **R: 255**
  Vice president of the United States (Tyler takes over) **V: 353**
Arthur, Ellen Lewis Herndon [wife of]
  Arthur, Chester Alan *picture on* **A: 756**; (Arthur's family) **A: 755**
Arthur, Gabriel [English explorer]
  Tennessee (Exploration) **T: 153**
Arthur, Harold J. [American political leader]
  Vermont (table) **V: 333**
Arthur, King [legendary figure] **A: 757**
  Camelot **C: 79**
  Excalibur **E: 435**
  Gawain, Sir **G: 71**
  Geoffrey of Monmouth **G: 91**
  Hartmann von Aue **H: 79**
  Holy Grail (The search for the Grail) **H: 299** *with picture*
  Knights and knighthood (Knighthood in literature) **K: 351**
  Lancelot, Sir **L: 56**
  Literature for children (Epics) **L: 358**
  Malory, Sir Thomas **M: 111**
  Merlin **M: 417**
  Mythology (Welsh myths) **M: 985**
  Round Table **R: 491**
  Tennyson, Lord (His poems) **T: 166f-167**
Arthur, Owen [Barbadian political leader]
  Barbados (History) **B: 104**
Arthur Andersen [accounting firm]
  Accounting (The history of accounting) **A: 23**
  Enron Corporation **E: 327**
Arthur Kill [waterway]
  New York City (The city) **N: 323**
Arthur M. Sackler Gallery
  Washington, D.C. *map on* **W: 76**; (Smithsonian museums) **W: 71-72**
Artibonite Valley [Haiti]
  Haiti *picture on* **H: 14**
Artichoke [plant] **A: 758** *with picture*
Article [grammar] **A: 758**
Articles of Confederation [1781] **A: 758**
  Annapolis Convention **A: 516**
  Interstate commerce (The commerce clause)

I: 351
Maryland (Statehood) M: 258
President of the United States (The founding of the presidency) P: 767
Revolution, American (Patriot governments) R: 280
United States, Government of the (Growth of the federal government) U: 145
United States, History of the (Establishing a government) U: 161
Virginia (Independence and statehood) V: 420
Articles of incorporation See Incorporation, Articles of in this index
Articles of Union
Constitution Ci: 994
Articles of War [U.S. history] A: 759
Articulated armor
Diving, Underwater (Diving in vehicles) D: 246
Articulation [anatomy]
Joint J: 155 with pictures
Articulation [music]
Music (Indicating expression) M: 955
Articulation [speech]
Speech So: 773
Speech therapy (Types of disorders) So: 773
Artifact [archaeology]
Archaeology (What archaeologists study) A: 595 with picture; (Surveying sites) A: 596-597 with picture; (Evaluation) A: 598
Artificial bait
Fishing pictures on F: 177; (Bait) F: 178
Artificial eye A: 759
Artificial fur
Fur (Artificial fur) F: 561
Artificial heart A: 759 with picture
Heart (The first heart transplants and artificial hearts) H: 145
Artificial insemination [reproduction]
Breeding (Animal breeding) B: 592
Dairying (Improvements in dairy farming) D: 7-8
Fertilization F: 78
Infertility (Treatment) I: 265
Reproduction, Human (Fertilization) R: 246
Surrogate birth So: 1010
Artificial intelligence A: 760
Computer (Artificial intelligence [AI] software) Ci: 920
Artificial lake
Lake (How lakes are formed) L: 32 with picture
Artificial light
See also Lighting in this index
Light (Sources of light) L: 283
Photography (Light) P: 414; (Artificial lighting devices) P: 416
Artificial limb A: 760 with picture
Biomedical engineering picture on B: 325
Disability picture on D: 218
Prosthetics P: 830 with picture
Artificial materials See Synthetics in this index
Artificial organ
See also Artificial heart in this index
Biomedical engineering (Biomechanics) B: 324 with picture
Iron lung I: 453 with picture
Artificial regeneration
Forestry picture on F: 406; (Planting) F: 405
Artificial respiration
Asphyxiation A: 816
Drowning (Giving first aid) D: 349
First aid (Restoring breathing) F: 138 with pictures
Respirator R: 261
Artificial satellite See Satellite, Artificial in this index
Artificial selection [biology]
Breeding B: 592
Evolution (Artificial selection) E: 432 with picture
Artificial silk See Rayon in this index
Artificial snow
Snow (Artificial snow) S: 539
Artificial sweetener A: 761
Saccharin S: 4
Soft drink (How soft drinks are made) So: 570
Artificial turf A: 761
Artificial valve [medicine]
Heart (Valve disease) H: 141-142 with picture
Artigas, José Gervasio [Uruguayan patriot] A: 762
Uruguay (Independence) U: 227
Artillery [weapons] A: 762 with pictures
See also the Related articles in the Artillery article
Ammunition A: 435; (Artillery ammunition) A: 435 with pictures
Army A: 724
Army, United States (Artillery) A: 734
Firearm F: 132 with picture
Weapon (Artillery) W: 154b
World War I (Trench warfare) W: 457-458 with picture

Artiodactyla [zoology]
Mammal (table) M: 128 with picture
Artist
See also the list of Related articles in the Painting and Sculpture articles
Careers (Art, design, and communications) C: 220
Commercial art Ci: 872
Encyclopedia (Basic steps in the preparation of a World Book article) E: 268 with picture
Painting P: 28
Artist, The [film]
Motion picture (Best picture: 2011) M: 861
Artist and repertoire executive [occupation]
Recording industry (Before recording) R: 180-181
Artistic director [occupation]
Ballet B: 44
Artistic skating
Roller skating (Artistic skating) R: 402a
Artist's model
Modeling (Kinds of models) M: 684
Arts See Art and the arts in this index
Arts, American Federation of A: 763
Arts, Bachelor of See Bachelor's degree in this index
Arts, Master of See Master's degree in this index
Arts and crafts See Handicraft in this index
Arts and Crafts Movement
Architecture (Early modern architecture in Europe) A: 627
Arts & Culture Centre [St. John's]
Newfoundland and Labrador (Libraries and museums) N: 364
Arts and Industries Building [Washington, D.C.]
Washington, D.C. (Smithsonian museums) W: 71-72
Arts and Letters, American Academy of
American Academy of Arts and Letters A: 407
Arts and Letters, National Institute of
American Academy of Arts and Letters A: 407
Arts and Sciences, American Academy of
American Academy of Arts and Sciences A: 407
Arts Centre, National
Ottawa (The National Arts Centre) O: 872 with picture
ARU [labor union] See American Railway Union in this index
Aru Islands [Indonesia]
Indonesia (The Molucca Islands) I: 234
Aruba [island, Caribbean Sea] A: 764
Netherlands (The Kingdom of the Netherlands) N: 139
Netherlands Antilles N: 151
North America picture on N: 464
Arum [plant] A: 764 with picture
Flower picture on F: 272
Arusha [Tanzania]
Africa picture on A: 99
Aryan Nation [political group]
Nazism (Neo-Nazism) N: 92-93
Aryans [people] A: 764
Afghanistan (Early invasions) A: 95
Asia (The people) A: 781; (The Indus Valley) A: 805
India (The Aryans) I: 128
Iran (Early days) I: 405
Mythology (Genetic relationships) M: 976
Persia, Ancient P: 296
Sanskrit literature (The Vedic period) S: 112
World, History of the (The Mauryan Empire in India) W: 430
Aryans [racial concept]
Aryans A: 764
Nazism N: 92
Races, Human (Race and discrimination) R: 59
Arzew [Algeria]
Algeria (Manufacturing and construction) A: 363-364 with picture
Arzú Irigoyen, Alvaro Enrique [Guatemalan political leader]
Guatemala (Political developments) G: 417
As [symbol]
Arsenic A: 745
As for Me and My House [book by Ross]
Canadian literature (Literature between the world wars) C: 158-159
As Good As It Gets [film]
Nicholson, Jack N: 404
As I Lay Dying [book by Faulkner]
American literature (Modernist fiction) A: 421-422
Faulkner, William F: 55
As Long As We're Together [book by Blume]
Blume, Judy B: 425
As You Like It [play by Shakespeare]
Shakespeare, William: (As You Like It) S: 359; (Rhetoric) S: 368
ASAC [sound] See Active structural-acoustic control

in this index
Asado [food]
Argentina (Food and drink) A: 650
Asafetida [medication]
Pioneer life in America (Health) P: 483
Asahi Shimbun
Newspaper (In Asia) N: 386
Asamblea Nacional [legislature]
Ecuador (Government) E: 68
Asanga [sculpture]
Sculpture (Japan) S: 239 with picture
Asante [people] See Ashanti in this index
Asante-hene [ruler]
Ashanti A: 767
Asare, Meshack [Ghanaian illustrator]
Literature for children picture on L: 355
Asbaje y Ramirez, Juana Inés See Juana Inés de la Cruz in this index
Asbestos [Quebec]
Trudeau, Pierre Elliott (Entry into public life) T: 462
Asbestos [fiber] A: 764 with picture
Disease (Environmental and occupational diseases) D: 230
Quebec (Postwar Quebec) Q: 32
Asbestosis [disorder]
Asbestos (Hazards of asbestos) A: 765
Asbjørnsen, Peter Christen [Norwegian author] A: 766
Storytelling (The 1800's) So: 915
Asbury, Francis [American religious leader] A: 766
Methodists (Early history) M: 435
Ascanius [legendary figure]
Mythology (The Aeneid) M: 983
ASCAP [organization]
American Society of Composers, Authors and Publishers A: 430
Ascari, Alberto [Italian race car driver]
Automobile racing (table: Formula One World Drivers' Championship) A: 980
Ascariasis [disease]
Roundworm R: 492
Ascaris lumbricoides [animal]
Roundworm R: 491
Ascending aorta [anatomy]
Aorta A: 562
Ascending colon [anatomy]
Colon [anatomy] Ci: 786
Intestine (The large intestine) I: 353 with diagram
Ascension [island, Atlantic] A: 766
Animal (Animal travelers) A: 502-503
Ascension [religion]
Jesus Christ (The Resurrection) J: 108b
Ascension Day [custom]
Easter (The end of the Easter season) E: 43
Asceticism [philosophy] A: 766
Asch, Sholem [Israeli author] A: 766
Ascham, Roger [English author]
Archery (History) A: 603-604
Ascidian [sea animal]
Sea squirt S: 262b
ASCII [computing] See American Standard Code for Information Interchange in this index
Ascites [disease]
Cirrhosis Ci: 566
Asclepius [Greek mythology] A: 767
Epidaurus E: 342
Greece, Ancient picture on G: 371; (Religion) G: 367
Imhotep I: 79
Medusa M: 383
Mythology (Symbols) M: 975
Ascorbic acid See Vitamin C in this index
Ascribed status [sociology]
Clothing (Identity) Ci: 687
ASCS [organization]
Agricultural Stabilization and Conservation Service A: 145
ASEAN [organization] See Association of Southeast Asian Nations in this index
ASEAN Regional Forum
Association of Southeast Asian Nations A: 820
Aseptic packaging
Food preservation (Aseptic packaging) F: 343
Packaging P: 18
Aseptic surgery [medicine]
Medicine (Antiseptic surgery) M: 375 with picture
Surgery (Antiseptics and asepsis) So: 1004
Asexual reproduction
See also Budding; Spore in this index
Reproduction (Through asexual reproduction) R: 242 with picture
Animal (How animals reproduce) A: 496 with diagrams
Cloning (Clones in nature) Ci: 684
Heredity (Sex cells and reproduction) H: 201
Life (Reproduction) L: 275

Plant (The reproduction of plants) P: 532 *with pictures*
Asfaw, Berhane [Ethiopian anthropologist]
 Prehistoric people (table) P: 754
Asgard [Scandinavian mythology]
 Mythology (The construction of the world) M: 986
 Vikings (Religion) V: 380
Ash [mineral] A: 767
 Fire (What fire produces) F: 121
Ash [tree] A: 767
 Emerald ash borer B: 258
 Tree *pictures on* T: 420, T: 422, T: 426
Ash borer [beetle]
 Emerald ash borer B: 258
Ash Lawn [estate]
 Monroe, James (Monroe's family) M: 735-736
Ash Shariqah [state]
 United Arab Emirates U: 43; (History) U: 45
"Ash Wednesday" [poem by Eliot]
 Eliot, T. S. (His works) E: 237-238
Ash Wednesday [religion] A: 767
 Easter (The beginning of Lent) E: 42
Ashanti [people] A: 767
 Africa *picture on* A: 116, *picture on* A: 116b
 Doll (Dolls in festivals and customs) D: 287-288 *with picture*
 Ghana (People) G: 178; (History) G: 179
Ashanti to Zulu [book by Musgrove]
 Dillon, Leo and Diane D: 204
Ashbery, John [American poet] A: 767
 American literature (Poetry) A: 423
 Postmodernism P: 709
Ashburn, Richie [American baseball player]
 Baseball (Hall of Fame) B: 134
Ashburton, Lord [British statesman]
 Webster-Ashburton Treaty W: 178
Ashcan School [art] A: 768 *with picture*
 Henri, Robert H: 185
 Lawson, Ernest L: 147
 Prendergast, Maurice Brazil P: 756
 Realism (In painting) R: 172
Ashcroft, John David [American government official] A: 768
 Bush, George Walker (table) B: 722h
 Justice, Department of (table) J: 203
 Missouri (table) M: 668
Ashcroft, Peggy [British actress]
 Motion picture (Best performance by an actress in a supporting role: 1984) M: 862b
 Shakespeare, William *picture on* S: 363
Ashe, Arthur [American tennis player] A: 768 *with portrait*
Ashe, Samuel [American political leader]
 North Carolina (table) N: 490
Ashes [remains]
 Cremation Ci: 1126
Ashes, The [award]
 Cricket (History) Ci: 1134-1135
Ashes to Ashes [play by Pinter]
 Pinter, Harold P: 475
Asheville [North Carolina] A: 768
 North Carolina (table: Monthly average weather) N: 486
Ashgabat [Turkmenistan] A: 769
Ashikaga [Japanese history]
 Japan (Rise of the shogun) J: 54
 Shogun S: 433
Ashkenazic [language]
 Hebrew language H: 162
Ashkenazim [people] A: 769
 Israel (Jews) I: 480
 Jews J: 120
 Sephardim S: 307
 Yiddish language Y: 565
Ashkenazy, Vladimir [Russian-born Icelandic musician] A: 769
Ashkhabad [Turkmenistan] *See* Ashgabat *in this index*
Ashland [estate]
 Clay, Henry (The Compromise of 1850) Ci: 659
Ashleaf maple [tree]
 Maple (Boxelder) M: 187
 Tree *pictures on* T: 420
Ashley, William Henry [American explorer]
 Fur trade (The 1800's) F: 565
 South Dakota (Exploration and fur trade) So: 681
 Wyoming (Exploration) W: 533
Ashmolean Museum [England]
 Museum (Early museums) M: 939
Ashmun Institute
 Lincoln University L: 329
Ashoka [emperor of India] A: 769
 Asia (The Indus Valley) A: 805
 Buddhism (The sangha) B: 668
 India (The Mauryan Empire) I: 128
 Mauryan Empire M: 318

World, History of the (The Mauryan Empire in India) W: 430
Ashrama [Hinduism]
 Manu M: 168
Ashton, Enrico [opera character]
 Opera: (*Lucia di Lammermoor*) O: 804
Ashton, Sir Frederick [British choreographer] A: 769
 Ballet (Ballet in England) B: 53
 Fonteyn, Margot F: 327
Ashton, Lucia [opera character]
 Opera: (*Lucia di Lammermoor*) O: 804
Ashton-Warner, Sylvia [New Zealand author]
 New Zealand (The arts) N: 349
Ashur [Assyrian god]
 Assyria (Religion) A: 821; (Government) A: 822
Ashūrā [celebration]
 Islam (Holidays and celebrations) I: 465
Ashurbanipal [king of Assyria] A: 769
 Assyria (Language and literature) A: 821
 Gilgamesh, Epic of G: 190
 Library (Ancient libraries of clay) L: 257
 Nineveh N: 423
 World, History of the *picture on* W: 428
Asi-Yaholo [name for]
 Osceola O: 862
Asia A: 770 *with pictures and maps*
 See also the list of Related articles in the Asia *article*
 Bird (Birds of Asia) B: 344f *with pictures*
 Boxing (Boxing in Asia) B: 531
 Conservation (Asia) Ci: 989 *with picture*
 Library (Libraries of the world) L: 252-253
 Magic (Asia) M: 50
 Monsoon M: 740
 National park (table) N: 42f
 Roman Catholic Church (In Asia) R: 411
 Arts
  Dance *picture on* D: 23; (Dances to watch) D: 28 *with pictures*
  Drama (Asian drama) D: 336 *with pictures*
  Music (Asian music) M: 955 *with pictures*
  Painting (Asian painting) P: 44 *with pictures*
  Sculpture (Asian sculpture) S: 236 *with pictures*
  Television (In Asia) T: 116
 Business and industry
  Bank (Banks throughout the world) B: 91
  Newspaper (In Asia) N: 386
  Railroad (In Asia) R: 114
  Textile (In Asia) T: 218
  Wheat (Asia) W: 272 *with map*
 History
  Colombo Plan Ci: 785
  Colonialism (Later colonialism) Ci: 813-814
  Columbus, Christopher (The plan to sail westward) C: 858
  Communication (The rise of printing) Ci: 879
  Exploration (Medieval European exploration) E: 442
  Immigration (The fourth wave) I: 83; (Asia) I: 85
  Indian, American (The first Americans) I: 151
  Prehistoric people (Migration from Africa) P: 747; (The origin of *Homo sapiens*) P: 748-749
  Russia (Expansion in Asia) R: 551
  World, History of the (Imperialism) W: 445; (The birth of new nations) W: 448
 People
  Arabs A: 584
  Clothing *pictures on* Ci: 693; (Clothing of Asia) Ci: 698 *with picture*
  Language (Other language families) L: 66
  Name (Asian names) N: 5
  Population (World population) P: 672
 Physical features
  Continent Ci: 1021
  Continental divide Ci: 1022
  Himalaya H: 233
  Rain forest (Asia) R: 126b *with map*
Asia Foundation
 Library (International library programs) L: 254
Asia Minor [region, Asia] A: 812a *with map*
 Alexander the Great (Invasion of Asia) A: 342-343
 Turkey T: 502 *with maps*
Asia-Pacific Economic Cooperation [organization] A: 812a
Asiago [cheese]
 Cheese (Very hard, or grating, cheese) C: 392 *with picture*
Asian Americans [people] A: 812b *with pictures and map*
 Education (Bilingual education) E: 107
 Immigration *picture on* I: 83
 Los Angeles (Ethnic groups) L: 463
 Minority group (Asian Americans) M: 610
Asian clam [mollusk]
 Clam (Types of clams) Ci: 637 *with picture*
Asian cockroach

Cockroach Ci: 745
Asian coral snake
 Coral snake Ci: 1050
Asian Development Bank A: 814
 Foreign aid (Regional development programs) F: 385
Asian Drama: An Inquiry into the Poverty of Nations [book by Myrdal]
 Myrdal, Gunnar M: 971
Asian elephant
 Elephant E: 226 *with pictures*
 Endangered species (table) E: 270
Asian fairy-bluebird
 Bird (Birds of Asia) B: 344f *with picture*
Asian flu [disease]
 Influenza (Flu epidemics) I: 268b
Asian fruit pigeon [bird]
 Pigeon (The body of a pigeon) P: 458-459; (Wild pigeons) P: 460
Asian long-horned beetle [insect]
 Invasive species (Managing invasive species) I: 354k
Asian Pacific American Heritage Month
 May M: 321
Asian pear
 Pear (Varieties) P: 215
Asian pipe snake
 Snake (Other snake families) S: 535
Asian race [theory]
 Races, Human (The geographical-race theory) R: 54
Asian rice
 Rice (Kinds of rice) R: 323
Asian tiger [country]
 Asia (A new era) A: 812
Asian whip snake
 Snake *picture on* S: 524
Asians [people]
 See also Asia; Asian Americans *in this index*
 Africa (Peoples of Africa) A: 104-105
 Races, Human (The clinal approach) R: 55-56
 South Africa (People) So: 609; (Ways of life) So: 611
Asiatic Barred Zone [U.S. history]
 Asian Americans (Asian immigration halted) A: 812e
 Immigration (The third wave) I: 82-83
Asiatic black bear [animal]
 Bear *picture on* B: 186; (Asiatic black bears) B: 185
Asiatic class [breeds]
 Chicken (Kinds of chickens) C: 441; (table) C: 443
Asiatic cotton *See* Old World cotton *in this index*
Asiatic Exclusion League [U.S. history]
 Asian Americans (The second wave) A: 812e
Aside [drama]
 Shakespeare, William (Dramatic conventions) S: 354
Asimov, Isaac [American author] A: 814
Asir [region]
 Saudi Arabia (The Western Highlands) S: 158 *with picture and map*
ASIS&T [organization]
 Library (Information science and technology) L: 251
Askaniya Nova National Park [Ukraine]
 National park (table) N: 42f
Askew, Reubin O'D. [American political leader]
 Florida (table) F: 260
Askia I, the Great *See* Askia Muhammad *in this index*
Askia Muhammad [king of the Songhai] A: 814
 African Americans (The cultural heritage) A: 136c
 Mali (History) M: 108-109
 Songhai Empire So: 593
ASL *See* American Sign Language *in this index*
ASM [weapon] *See* Air-to-surface missile *in this index*
Asmara [Eritrea] A: 814
 Eritrea E: 352 *with picture*
ASMP [missile]
 Guided missile (Air-to-surface missiles) G: 426
ASN Canada FIA [organization]
 Automobile racing (Racing organizations) A: 976
Aso [rock]
 Abuja A: 19
Asoka [emperor of India] *See* Ashoka *in this index*
Asp [snake] A: 814 *with picture*
 Cleopatra (Cleopatra and Mark Antony) Ci: 662a-662b
Asp viper [snake]
 Snake *picture on* S: 534
Asparagus [plant] A: 814 *with pictures*
 Vegetable (Stems) V: 292 *with picture*
Asparagus bean [plant]
 Cowpea Ci: 1113
Asparagus beetle [insect]
 Beetle *picture on* B: 218

Asparagus fern [plant]
Asparagus **A:** 815 *with picture*
Aspartame [chemical]
Artificial sweetener **A:** 761
Phenylketonuria **P:** 357
Aspdin, Joseph [British inventor]
Cement and concrete (History) **C:** 345
Aspect [astrology]
Horoscope (Parts of a horoscope) **H:** 341
Aspen [Colorado] **A:** 815
Colorado *picture on* **Ci:** 828
Aspen [tree] **A:** 815
Tree *pictures on* **T:** 420
Aspen Institute for Humanistic Studies
Aspen **A:** 815
Aspen Music Festival
Aspen **A:** 815
Asperger syndrome [disorder]
Autism **A:** 941
Aspern-Essling, Battle of [1809]
Napoleonic Wars (The Austrian War) **N:** 18-19
with map
Asphalt [mineral] **A:** 815
Gravel **G:** 330
Asphyxiation [disorder] **A:** 816
Aspidistra [plant] **A:** 816
Aspinall Storage Unit [water system]
Colorado (The mid-1900's) **Ci:** 847
Aspinwall [former name]
Colón **C:** 786
Aspirant [pronunciation]
Consonant **Ci:** 992
Aspirin [medication] **A:** 816
Analgesic **A:** 448
Heart (Treatment) **H:** 138
Salicylic acid **S:** 66
Asquith, Herbert Henry [British political leader]
A: 816
Churchill, Sir Winston Leonard Spencer (World
War I) **C:** 547
Liberal Democrats (A major party) **L:** 227
ASROC [weapon] *See* Antisubmarine missile *in
this index*
Ass [animal]
Donkey **D:** 307
Assad, Bashar al- [Syrian political leader] **A:** 816
Obama, Barack (Syria and Iran) **O:** 642
Syria (The early 2000's) **So:** 1076
Assad, Hafez al- [Syrian political leader] **A:** 817
Assad, Bashar al- **A:** 816
Syria (Independence) **So:** 1075
Assam [state, India]
India (Religious and ethnic unrest) **I:** 134
Assam tea
Tea (Processing tea) **T:** 62
Assassin, The [book by O'Flaherty]
O'Flaherty, Liam **O:** 678
Assassination [crime] **A:** 817
Terrorism (Assassinations and kidnappings)
T: 175
Assassins [Asian history] *See* Hashshashins *in this
index*
Assateague Island National Seashore [Maryland-
Virginia]
Maryland (Places to visit) **M:** 248
National Park System (table: National seashores)
N: 57
Virginia (Visitor's guide) **V:** 408
Assault [crime]
Assault and battery **A:** 817
Crime (table) **Ci:** 1137
Assault [horse]
Kentucky Derby (table) **K:** 296
Assault and battery [crime] **A:** 817
Assault weapon
Clinton, Bill (National affairs) **Ci:** 682d
Gun control (Approaches to gun control)
G: 440-441
Assay office [laboratory]
Assaying (Wet assaying) **A:** 817
Assaying [metallurgy] **A:** 817
Assemblage [art]
Nevelson, Louise **N:** 178 *with picture*
Painting (The revival of subject matter) **P:** 86
Rauschenberg, Robert **R:** 150
Sculpture (The sculptor at work) **S:** 232;
(Assemblages) **S:** 257 *with picture*
Assembler [occupation]
Careers (Production) **C:** 229
Assembler [program]
Computer (Compiling or assembling a program)
Ci: 923
Computer language (Assembly languages)
Ci: 924h
Assemblies of Aesopic Tales [book]
Aesop's fables **A:** 90
Assemblies of God [religious group] **A:** 817

Pentecostal churches (Major Pentecostal
churches) **P:** 275-276
Assembly [government]
Colonial life in America (Colonial government)
Ci: 795
League of Nations (Powers and organization)
L: 159
Assembly [religion]
Presbyterians **P:** 756a
Assembly, Freedom of *See* Freedom of assembly
in this index
Assembly language
Computer (Using programming languages)
Ci: 923
Computer language (Assembly languages)
Ci: 924h
Assembly line [industry] **A:** 818
Airplane (Mass production) **A:** 229
Automobile **A:** 946, *diagram on* **A:** 957, *picture
on* **A:** 965; (Manufacturing) **A:** 958 *with picture*;
(The birth of the automobile industry) **A:** 966
Aviation (World War I [1914-1918]) **A:** 987
Conveyor belt (Uses) **Ci:** 1024 *with picture*
Edison, Thomas Alva (Ore milling and cement)
E: 81
Factory (Kinds of factories) **F:** 5
Ford, Henry **F:** 380 *with picture*
Ford Motor Company **F:** 382
France *picture on* **F:** 469
Kaiser, Henry John **K:** 210
Manufacturing (How science helps
manufacturing) **M:** 171
Mass production **M:** 269
Assembly of First Nations
Indian, American (In Canada) **I:** 178b
Assembly of the Republic
Portugal (National government) **P:** 687
Assembly plant
Airplane (Mass production) **A:** 229 *with picture*
Asser, Tobias Michael Carel [Dutch statesman]
Nobel Prizes (Peace: 1911) **N:** 448
Assessment [taxation] **A:** 818
Property tax **P:** 827
Asset [bookkeeping]
Bookkeeping (Double-entry bookkeeping) **B:** 472
Asset [economics]
Economics (table) **E:** 60
Assets account
Bookkeeping (Accounts) **B:** 472 *with picture*
Assigned frequency [electronics]
Radio (Broadcasting power and frequency)
R: 87-88
Assignee [law]
Assignment **A:** 818
Bankruptcy (Features of bankruptcy) **B:** 97
Receiver **R:** 174
Assignment [law] **A:** 818
Assignment [policy]
Australia (Macquarie's administration) **A:** 921
Assignor [law]
Assignment **A:** 818
Assimilation [physiology] **A:** 818
Assimilation [sociology] **A:** 818
Culture (Culture and society) **Ci:** 1188
Immigration (Effects of immigration) **I:** 81
Indian, American (In Canada) **I:** 178
Jews (The Jews today) **J:** 124
Minority group (Relationships between groups)
M: 609
Assiniboia [Canadian history] **A:** 818 *with map*
Assiniboine Indians A: 818-819
Indian, American *picture on* **I:** 141
Assiniboine River [Saskatchewan]
Saskatchewan (Rivers and lakes) **S:** 138 *with map*
Assis, Joaquim Maria Machado de [Brazilian
author] *See* Machado de Assis, Joaquim Maria *in
this index*
Assisi, Francis of *See* Francis of Assisi, Saint *in this
index*
Assist [sports]
Hockey (Hockey terms) **H:** 275
Assistant, The [book by Malamud]
Malamud, Bernard **M:** 95
Novel (After World War II) **N:** 574
Assistant professor
Universities and colleges (Faculty) **U:** 208
Assisted migration [policy]
Australia (Expansion) **A:** 922
Assisted reproductive technology
Infertility (Treatment) **I:** 265
Assisted suicide *See* Physician-assisted suicide *in
this index*
Assisting heart [medicine]
DeBakey, Michael Ellis **D:** 63
Heart (Development of heart surgery) **H:** 144-145
Assistive technology
Blindness *picture on* **B:** 402

Disability **D:** 218 *with picture*; (Health care and
assistive devices) **D:** 221
Assman psychrometer [instrument]
Hygrometer (The psychrometer) **H:** 474
Associate [fraternity]
Fraternity (Membership) **F:** 495-496
Associate professor
Universities and colleges (Faculty) **U:** 208
Associated Fraternities of America [organization]
Fraternal organization (History) **F:** 495
Associated Press [news service] **A:** 819
Journalism (The growth of U.S. newspapers)
J: 174
Newspaper (News services) **N:** 383
Associated State of Vietnam [Vietnamese history]
Vietnam (The First Indochina War) **V:** 371
Associate's degree [education]
Degree, College (The associate's degree) **D:** 91
Education (Higher education) **E:** 92
Association [psychology] **A:** 819
Association [social unit]
Indian, American (Family groups) **I:** 136c
Association Croquet [game]
Croquet **Ci:** 1154 *with diagram*
Association football [sport] *See* Soccer *in this index*
**Association for Childhood Education
International** *See* Childhood Education
International, Association for *in this index*
Association for Library Service to Children
Literature for children (Awards) **L:** 367
**Association for Supervision and Curriculum
Development**
Teaching (Teachers organizations) **T:** 69
**Association for the Study of African American
Life and History A:** 819
Black History Month **B:** 388
Woodson, Carter Godwin **W:** 395
Association magazine
Magazine (Other magazines) **M:** 42
Association neuron [anatomy]
Nervous system (How the nervous system works)
N: 132 *with diagram*; (Complex pathways)
N: 134 *with diagram*
Association of American Law Schools
Law (Law education) **L:** 138
Association of Boxing Commissions
Boxing (Amateur boxing) **B:** 530
Association of Christian Schools International
Parochial school **P:** 178
Association of Evangelical Lutheran Churches
Evangelical Lutheran Church in America **E:** 422
Association of Junior Leagues International Inc.
Junior Leagues **J:** 196
**Association of Letter Carriers of the United
States of America, National**
Labor movement (table) **L:** 8
Association of National Advertisers
Advertising (Advertising associations) **A:** 77
Association of Public Radio Stations
National Public Radio **N:** 59
Association of Research Libraries
Library (Research libraries) **L:** 247
Association of Southeast Asian Nations A: 820
Common market **Ci:** 875
Vietnam (Recent developments) **V:** 372
Association of Teacher Educators
Teaching (Teachers organizations) **T:** 69
Association of Zoos and Aquariums
Zoo (How zoos operate) **Z:** 603
Associative Law of Addition
Algebra (Basic algebra) **A:** 354
Associative Law of Multiplication
Algebra (Basic algebra) **A:** 354
Assonance [poetry]
Poetry (table) **P:** 594; (Sounds) **P:** 594-595
Assumption [religion] **A:** 820
August **A:** 886
Pius XII **P:** 503
Assumption, Arms of [emblem]
Heraldry (Heraldry today) **H:** 196
Assumption of state debts [U.S. history]
Washington, George (Finances) **W:** 103
**Assumption of the Blessed Virgin Mary, Basilica
of the**
Baltimore (The people) **B:** 68
Latrobe, Benjamin Henry **L:** 118
Assumption of the Virgin [painting by El Greco]
Art and the arts *picture on* **A:** 746
Assur [Assyrian god] *See* Ashur *in this index*
Assurbanipal *See* Ashurbanipal *in this index*
Assyria [ancient country] **A:** 820 *with picture and
map*
See also the list of Related articles in the Assyria
article
Architecture (Mesopotamian architecture) **A:** 611
Army (Ancient armies) **A:** 726
Asia (The Tigris-Euphrates Valley) **A:** 804

Babylon (The Old Babylonian period) B: 11
Clothing *picture on* Ci: 696
Palestine (Invasions and conquests) P: 104
Samaritans S: 78
Sculpture (Middle Eastern) S: 233
World, History of the (Civilizations of southwest Asia) W: 426
Assyrian language
Assyria (Language and literature) A: 821
Astaire, Adele [American entertainer]
Astaire, Fred A: 822
Astaire, Fred [American entertainer] A: 822 *with picture*
Rogers, Ginger R: 400
Astana [Kazakhstan] A: 823
Kazakhstan K: 250a, *picture on* K: 250b; (History) K: 251-252
Astarte [Semitic goddess] A: 823
Astatine [element] A: 823
Halogen H: 26
Astell, Mary [British author]
Feminism F: 69
Astemizole [drug]
Antihistamine A: 556
Aster [plant] A: 823
Flower (Garden perennials) F: 278 *with picture*
Asterisk [reference]
Footnote F: 369
Asterius [legendary figure]
Europa E: 379
Asteroid [astronomy] A: 823 *with pictures*
Crater Ci: 1121 *with diagrams*
Dinosaur (Why dinosaurs died out) D: 213
Eros E: 354
Extinction (Mass extinction) E: 456
Moon (Origin and evolution of the moon) M: 788
Planet P: 507
Prehistoric animal (The Age of Mammals) P: 740
Satellite S: 149
Solar system (Asteroids) So: 581
Space exploration (Probes to asteroids) So: 711
Asteroid belt [astronomy]
Asteroid A: 823
Ceres C: 362
Asthenosphere [geology]
Hot spot H: 374a
Mantle M: 168
Mountain (Forces that shape mountains) M: 894 *with diagram*
Plate tectonics (Structure of tectonic plates) P: 561
Asthma [disorder] A: 824b
African Americans (Health issues) A: 136s
Allergy A: 373
Bronchodilator B: 637
Dust mite D: 392
Hay fever (Symptoms) H: 116
Helium (Uses) H: 176
Astigmatism [disorder] A: 825 *with diagrams*
Eye (Astigmatism) E: 464 *with pictures*
Glasses (Prescription glasses) G: 224-225
Astigmatism [optics]
Aberration (Point aberration) A: 10
Astley, Philip [British performer]
Circus (The birth of the circus) Ci: 562b *with picture*
Astley, Thea [Australian writer]
Australia (Literature) A: 904-905
Aston, Francis William [British physicist]
Nobel Prizes (Chemistry: 1922) N: 443
Thomson, Sir Joseph John T: 265
Astor, John Jacob [American businessman] A: 825
Chouteau, Pierre, Jr. C: 522
Missouri (Statehood and expansion) M: 669
North West Company N: 519
Oregon (Exploration and settlement) O: 846
Washington (Settlement) W: 66
Astor, Lady [British political leader] A: 826
Astor, Lady A: 826
Astoria [Oregon] A: 826
Astor, John Jacob A: 825
Astoria Bridge [Oregon]
Bridge (table: Continuous truss) B: 603
Astounding Science Fiction [magazine]
Science fiction (The Golden Age) S: 205
Astraea [pen name] *See* Behn, Aphra *in this index*
Astrakhan [fur]
Karakul K: 245
Astrobiology [science] A: 826
Life (The search for life on other worlds) L: 280
SETI Institute S: 323
Astrodome [Houston]
Houston (Landmarks) H: 395

Astrogeology [science]
Moon (Describing lunar evolution) M: 794
Shoemaker, Eugene Merle S: 433
Astrolabe [instrument] A: 826
Exploration (The age of European exploration) E: 443 *with picture*
Navigation (Early instruments) N: 74
Astrologer
Astrology A: 826
Astrology A: 826 *with picture*
Horoscope H: 341
House H: 384
Zodiac (The zodiac in astrology) Z: 597
Astronaut A: 828 *with pictures*
See also Space exploration *in this index*
Aerospace medicine A: 89
Careers (Life, physical, and social sciences) C: 225-226 *with picture*
World, History of the *picture on* W: 448b
Astronautics A: 833
Astronomer [occupation]
Astronomy A: 834; (Careers) A: 849
Careers (Life, physical, and social sciences) C: 225-226
Science *picture on* S: 191
Astronomer royal [title]
Greenwich Observatory, Royal G: 387
"Astronomical Advantages of an Extra-Terrestrial Observatory" [paper by Spitzer]
Spitzer, Lyman, Jr. So: 797
Astronomical Almanac, The
Almanac A: 379
Astronomical horizon
Horizon H: 335
Astronomical Society of the Pacific
Astronomy (Astronomy associations) A: 849
Astronomical unit [measurement]
Astronomy (Units of distance) A: 837-838
Planet (The planets of our solar system) P: 511
Transit T: 374
Weights and measures (Miscellaneous weights and measures) W: 184
Astronomical zenith [astronomy]
Zenith Z: 589
Astronomy A: 834 *with pictures*
See also the list of Related articles in the Astronomy article
Computer (Scientific visualization software) Ci: 919
Radar (In scientific research) R: 67-68 *with picture*
Science (The physical sciences) S: 193; (Ancient Greece) S: 196; (Achievements of the mid-1900's) S: 202
Telescope T: 102 *with pictures*
X rays (In astronomy) X: 541
Astronomy Capital of the World [nickname]
Arizona (Interesting facts about Arizona) A: 671
Astrophel and Stella [poems by Sidney]
Sidney, Sir Philip S: 449
Astrophysicist [career]
Astrophysics A: 850
Astrophysics [astronomy] A: 850
Astronomy (Advances in astrophysics) A: 848
Astros, Houston [team] *See* Houston Astros *in this index*
Asturias, Miguel Angel [Guatemalan author] A: 850
Latin American literature (The mid-1900's) L: 114
Astyages [king of Media]
Cyrus the Great Ci: 1208
Media M: 360
Asunción [Paraguay] A: 850
Paraguay P: 144 *with pictures*
Aswan [Egypt] A: 851
Egypt (Climate) E: 127
Aswan High Dam [Nile River, Egypt] A: 851
Cold War (The Suez crisis) Ci: 766
Egypt (The Nile Valley and Delta) E: 125; (Agriculture) E: 128-129; (Energy sources) E: 129 *with picture*; (Republic) E: 132; (Progress and conflict) E: 133
Lake Nasser L: 41 *with map*
Nile River N: 422
Suez Canal (History) So: 958
Suez crisis So: 959
Asylum [international law] A: 851
Illegal alien I: 51
Political prisoner P: 638
Refugee (The rights of refugees) R: 203
Asymmetrical system [cryptology] *See* Public-key system *in this index*
Asymptotic giant branch [astronomy]
Star (Intermediate-mass stars) So: 848-849
Asynchronous communication
Internet (Communication without limits) I: 350e
At [symbol]
Astatine A: 823

AT&T Broadband [company]
AT&T Inc. A: 852
AT&T Corp.
AT&T Inc. A: 851
AT&T Inc. A: 851
Public utility (History) P: 867
Telegraph (Decline) T: 92
Telephone (In the United States) T: 99; (The Bell System) T: 100; (Competition in the U.S. telephone industry) T: 101
AT&T Wireless [company]
AT&T Inc. A: 852
At-large election
House of Representatives (Size) H: 385
At the Moulin Rouge [painting by Toulouse-Lautrec]
Painting (Postimpressionism) P: 75
Toulouse-Lautrec, Henri de T: 348 *with picture*
ATA [organization]
Air Transport Association of America A: 200
Atabalipa [Inca emperor] *See* Atahualpa *in this index*
Atacama Desert [region] A: 852
Chile (The Northern Desert) C: 464 *with picture*
Atacama Indians
Chile (Early days) C: 467
Atahualpa [Inca emperor] A: 852
De Soto, Hernando (Early expeditions) D: 160
Inca (The empire) I: 98-99
Indian, American *picture on* I: 143; (After European contact) I: 175
Latin America (The conquest of the American Indians) L: 103-104
Pizarro, Francisco (Conquest of Peru) P: 504 *with picture*
Ataíde, Mestre [Brazilian painter]
Brazil (The arts) B: 576
Atala [book by Chateaubriand]
Chateaubriand, François-René de C: 387
Atambaev, Almazbek [Kyrgyz political leader]
Kyrgyzstan (Independence) K: 400
Atanasoff, John V. [American physicist]
Computer (The first electronic computers) Ci: 924b
Atari [company]
Electronic game (The rise and fall of Atari) E: 204d
Atatürk, Kemal [Turkish political leader] A: 852
Ankara A: 515
Istanbul (History) I: 491-492
Ottoman Empire (The empire ends) O: 878
Sèvres, Treaty of S: 329
Turkey (After World War I) T: 511 *with picture*
Ataxia [disorder] A: 852
Cerebral palsy (Types) C: 361
ATC [safety device]
Railroad (Automatic train controls) R: 112
Atchafalaya River
Louisiana (Rivers, bayous, and lakes) L: 490
Atchison, David Rice [American political leader] A: 853
Taylor, Zachary (Taylor's administration) T: 60
Atchison, Topeka and Santa Fe Railway
Los Angeles (Development and growth) L: 470
Topeka T: 332
Atemiwaza [technique]
Judo (Judo techniques) J: 185
Aten [Egyptian god]
Akhenaten A: 253
Egypt, Ancient (The New Kingdom) E: 143 *with picture*
Mythology (The influence of Egyptian mythology) M: 980
Tutankhamun T: 526
Aten asteroid
Asteroid (Orbital groups) A: 824a
ATF [agency] *See* Alcohol, Tobacco, Firearms and Explosives, Bureau of *in this index*
Atget, Eugène [French photographer] A: 852 *with picture*
Athabasca, Lake [Canada] *See* Lake Athabasca *in this index*
Athabasca Glacier [Alberta]
Alberta (Places to visit) A: 320 *with picture*
Athabasca River [Canada] A: 853
Athabasca tar sands [region, Alberta]
Bituminous sands B: 384
Athabaskan Indians
British Columbia (Early days) B: 628
Athamas [legendary figure]
Golden Fleece G: 255
Athanasius, Saint [early Christian] A: 853
Bible (Formation of the New Testament) B: 284
Religious life (Religious life in early Christianity) R: 226
Atharvaveda [religious book]
Vedas V: 291

Atheism A: 853
  Dawkins, Richard D: 51
  God (Ideas about God) G: 244
Athena [Greek mythology] A: 853
  See also Minerva *in this index*
  Arachne A: 590b
  Greece, Ancient *pictures on* G: 370
  Medusa M: 383
  Mythology *pictures on* M: 973, M: 979; (table)
    M: 981; (Greek divinities) M: 982
  Pegasus P: 229
  Perseus P: 295
  Ulysses (Return to Ithaca) U: 18
Athena Nike, Temple of [Athens]
  Acropolis A: 29
Athena Parthenos [sculpture by Phidias]
  Phidias P: 357
Athenaeum, Boston *See* Boston Athenaeum *in this index*
Athenaeus of Naucratis [Greek author]
  Greek literature (The Greco-Roman Age) G: 378
Athenagoras I [Greek religious leader]
  Eastern Orthodox Churches (History) E: 45-46
Atheneum [Indiana]
  Meier, Richard M: 384
Athens [Greece] A: 854 *with pictures and map*
  Ancient Athens
  Acropolis A: 29 *with picture*
  Areopagus A: 645
  Aristides A: 662
  Athena A: 853
  Athens (The ancient city) A: 856
  Ballot (Older customs) B: 63
  Boxing (Ancient history) B: 531
  City (Government) Ci: 581
  City-state Ci: 603
  Democracy (Origins of democracy) D: 122
  Education (Ancient Greek education) E: 98
  Greece, Ancient *picture on* G: 366; (Education)
    G: 367; (Government) G: 372 *with map*;
    (History) G: 372-373
  Law (The influence of ancient Greece) L: 133
  Oratory (Beginnings) O: 818
  Painting (Greek painting) P: 42
  Peloponnesian War P: 232
  Pericles P: 287
  Pisistratus P: 496
  Plato (Plato's life) P: 567
  Socrates (Socrates's life) So: 567
  Solon So: 586
  Themistocles T: 251
  Thirty Tyrants T: 259
  Women's movement (In ancient societies)
    W: 384
  World, History of the (The Greeks) W: 428-429
  Modern Athens
  Athens (The modern city) A: 854
  Europe *picture on* E: 391
  Greece So: 352 *with picture*; (table: Average
    monthly weather) G: 359
  Olympic Games (The recent games)
    O: 753-754
Athens of America [nickname]
  Boston B: 495
Athens of the South [name for]
  Nashville N: 23
Atherosclerosis [disease]
  Aneurysm A: 459
  Arteriosclerosis A: 750
  Cholesterol (Cholesterol and heart disease)
    C: 520
  Disease (Diseases associated with aging) D: 230
  Heart (Causes) H: 137
  Stroke (Causes) So: 930
Athetoid cerebral palsy [disorder]
  Cerebral palsy (Types) C: 361
Athi River [Africa]
  Kenya (Rivers and lakes) K: 301 *with map*
Athlete [occupation]
  Blood doping B: 415
  Careers (Sports and entertainment) C: 230 *with picture*
Athlete's foot [disease] A: 858
  Fungicide F: 560
  Ringworm R: 344
  Skin (Infections) S: 490
Athletics, Oakland [team] *See* Oakland Athletics *in this index*
Athlone, Earl of [British military leader] A: 858
Athos, Mount [religious community] *See* Mount Athos *in this index*
Atitlán, Lake [Guatemala] *See* Lake Atitlán *in this index*
Atiu [island, Pacific]
  Cook Islands Ci: 1026
Ativan [drug]
  Benzodiazepine B: 256

Atiyeh, Victor G. [American political leader]
  Oregon (table) O: 845
Atka [Alaska]
  Alaska *picture on* A: 287
Atkins, Chet [American guitarist] A: 858
Atkinson, George W. [American political leader]
  West Virginia (table) W: 225
Atkinson, William Y. [American political leader]
  Georgia (table) G: 130
Atlanta [Georgia] A: 859 *with pictures and map*
  Georgia G: 112, *picture on* G: 113; (Population)
    G: 116; (Transportation) G: 129
  Olympic Games (The recent games) O: 753
  United States *picture on* U: 115
Atlanta Braves [team]
  Baseball (table) B: 130
Atlanta Compromise [U.S. history]
  Washington, Booker T. (Racial leader) W: 89
Atlanta Falcons [team]
  Football (National Football League) F: 364
Atlanta Hawks [team]
  Basketball (table) B: 150
Atlanta History Center
  Georgia (Places to visit) G: 122
Atlanta Project
  Atlanta (Social problems) A: 860a
Atlantic [potato]
  Potato *picture on* P: 711, P: 712
Atlantic [ship]
  Shipwreck (table: Major shipwrecks) S: 428
Atlantic, Battle of the [1941-1945]
  World War II *pictures on* W: 476; (The Battle of the
    Atlantic) W: 478
Atlantic bonito [fish]
  Bonito B: 460
Atlantic cable
  Cable (Telegraph cables) C: 5-6
  Field, Cyrus West F: 91
Atlantic Canada *See* Atlantic Provinces *in this index*
Atlantic Charter [1941] A: 862 *with picture*
  Churchill, Sir Winston Leonard Spencer (Meetings
    with Roosevelt) C: 548
  Roosevelt, Franklin Delano (Roosevelt's third
    administration [1941-1945]) R: 456
  United Nations (The Atlantic Charter) U: 94
  World War II (The strategy) W: 480-481
Atlantic City [New Jersey] A: 862 *with picture*
  New Jersey N: 230 *with picture*; (table: Average
    monthly weather) N: 244
Atlantic Coastal Plain [region]
  Georgia (Land regions) G: 124
  South Carolina (Land regions) So: 652 *with map*
  United States (The Coastal Lowlands) U: 121
Atlantic cod [fish]
  Cod (Appearance and habits) Ci: 748
  Fish *picture on* F: 153
Atlantic croaker [fish]
  Drum D: 367 *with picture*
Atlantic Division
  Hockey (table: National Hockey League) H: 281
Atlantic Fleet
  Navy, United States (The Operating Forces) N: 85
Atlantic Flyway [route]
  Bird (Where birds migrate) B: 360-361
Atlantic halibut [fish]
  Halibut H: 20
Atlantic herring [fish]
  Herring H: 215
Atlantic Intracoastal Waterway [U.S.] A: 863 *with
    picture and map*
Atlantic mackerel [fish]
  Fish *picture on* F: 153
  Mackerel M: 23
Atlantic menhaden [fish]
  Menhaden M: 400
Atlantic meridional overturning circulation
  [oceanography]
  Atlantic Ocean (Subsurface currents) A: 866
Atlantic Monthly [magazine]
  Holmes, Oliver Wendell (His life) H: 294
  Howells, William Dean H: 401
Atlantic Ocean A: 864 *with map*
  Arctic Ocean (Waters) A: 643
  Caribbean Sea C: 236
  Deep sea (The deep-sea floor) D: 82a
  Erie Canal E: 351 *with map*
  Exploration (The age of European exploration)
    E: 442 *with map*
  Fishing industry (Where fish are caught) F: 181-
    182
  Hurricane H: 452
  Ocean (The world ocean) O: 651 *with picture*
  Plate tectonics (Plate movement) P: 563
Atlantic Philanthropies [foundation]
  Foundation (table) F: 430
Atlantic Provinces [Canada] A: 867
  Canada (Atlantic Canada) C: 101

Atlantic puffin [bird]
  Puffin P: 885
Atlantic Records [company]
  Rock music (Soul music) R: 380a
Atlantic ridley sea turtle *See* Kemp's ridley sea
  turtle *in this index*
Atlantic salmon
  Maine (Plant and animal life) M: 82-83
  Salmon S: 69 *with pictures*; (Kinds of salmon)
    S: 70
Atlantic Salmon Museum
  New Brunswick (Places to visit) N: 188
Atlantic spotted dolphin [sea animal]
  Dolphin (Other species) D: 297
Atlantic States [U.S.] A: 868
Atlantic sturgeon [fish]
  Sturgeon So: 933
Atlantic Telegraph Company
  Cable (Telegraph cables) C: 5-6
Atlantic Time Zone
  Standard time (Time zones) So: 835
Atlantic Wall
  World War II (D-Day) W: 483-484
Atlantic white-cedar [tree]
  Cedar (Scale-leaved cedars) C: 324
Atlantic white-sided dolphin [sea animal]
  Dolphin *picture on* D: 298
Atlantic wolffish
  Fish *picture on* F: 153
Atlantica [book by Rudbeck]
  Sweden (Literature) So: 1026
Atlantis [legendary island] A: 868
Atlantis [space shuttle]
  International Space Station (History) I: 346b-347
  Space exploration *picture on* So: 722; (Docking
    with Mir) So: 725
Atlas [book by Mercator]
  Mercator, Gerardus M: 411
Atlas [book] A: 868 *with picture*
Atlas [Greek mythology] A: 868 *with picture*
  Hesperides H: 218
Atlas 5 [rocket]
  Rocket *picture on* R: 387
  Space exploration *picture on* So: 699
Atlas cedar [tree]
  Cedar (Needle-leaved cedars) C: 324
Atlas Mountains [Africa] A: 869
  Africa (Mountains) A: 119
  Atlantic Ocean A: 864
  Morocco (Land regions) M: 813 *with picture*
  Tunisia (Land regions) T: 488 *with map*
Atlas Shrugged [book by Rand]
  Rand, Ayn R: 136
Atlasov, Vladimir V. [Russian soldier]
  Exploration (The Russians in Siberia) E: 447
Atlatl [weapon]
  Anasazi (Way of life) A: 448a
  Aztec (Warfare) A: 1002
  Indian, American (Early days) I: 151
  Paleo-Indians P: 102
  Weapon (Prehistoric weapons) W: 154a
ATM [machine] *See* Automated teller machine *in
  this index*
Atman [religion]
  Brahman B: 548
  Religion (A doctrine of salvation) R: 215-216
Atmosphere [measurement] A: 869
Atmosphere [gas] A: 869
  Air A: 169; (Origin of the atmosphere) A: 174
  Carbon cycle C: 206
  Climate (Atmospheric circulation) Ci: 676a
  Dust (Influence on climate) D: 390
  Earth (The atmosphere) E: 18 *with picture*;
    (Atmospheric circulation) E: 22; (Earth's early
    development) E: 26-27
  Environmental pollution (Air pollution) E: 331
  Greenhouse effect G: 382
  Hydrosphere H: 472
  Ionosphere I: 373
  Jupiter (Atmosphere) J: 199
  Mars (Atmosphere) M: 226a
  Meteorology M: 432
  Moon (The exosphere of the moon) M: 788
  Ozone O: 893
  Sky S: 496
  Space exploration (The beginning of space)
    So: 696; (Returning to the earth) So: 701
  Star (Twinkling of stars) So: 840
  Stratosphere So: 921
  Telescope (Adaptive optics systems) T: 106
  Titan T: 299
  Troposphere T: 451
  Uranus (Structure and composition) U: 218
  Weather (What causes weather) W: 157;
    (Mathematical models) W: 166
Atmospheric aerosol
  Aerosol A: 89

Dust D: 390
Atmospheric perspective [art]
Painting (Roman painting) P: 42-43
Atmospheric pressure
Air *diagrams on* A: 170; (Weight and pressure)
A: 171 *with diagrams*
Atmosphere A: 869
Barometer B: 115
Boiling point B: 439
Cyclone Ci: 1203
Hurricane (How a hurricane forms) H: 453
Isobar I: 474 *with map*
Mars (Atmosphere) M: 226a
Melting point M: 390
Pressure P: 773
Tornado (Air pressure) T: 335
Vacuum V: 256
Weather (Air pressure) W: 157; (Planetary-scale
systems) W: 158
Atole [food]
Mexico (Food and drink) M: 456
Atoll [geology] A: 869 *with pictures*
Coral reef (Kinds of coral reefs) Ci: 1048b
Island (Coral islands) I: 472
Pacific Islands (The low islands) P: 8
Atom [physics] A: 870 *with pictures*
See also Atomic... *and* Nuclear... *in this index*
Atomism A: 877
Bohr, Niels B: 438
Bond B: 454
Chemical reaction C: 397
Chemistry (Fundamental ideas of chemistry)
C: 398-399
Computer graphics *picture on* Ci: 924h
Democritus D: 129
Electricity (Electric charge) E: 191 *with diagram*
Electron E: 203
Electron microscope *picture on* E: 204
Element, Chemical (The periodic table of the
elements) E: 219
Force (Kinds of force) F: 370
Ion I: 371 *with diagrams*
Laser (Producing laser light) L: 84 *with diagrams*
Leucippus L: 214
Light *diagram on* L: 287; (How light is produced)
L: 283
Magnetic resonance imaging M: 56
Magnetism (How magnetism works) M: 60b
Materials (The role of bonds) M: 301
Matter (Structure of matter) M: 310
Mechanist philosophy M: 355
Molecule (Individual molecules) M: 692
Nanotechnology N: 10
Nuclear energy (Atoms and nuclei) N: 581 *with
diagram*
Pauling, Linus Carl P: 202
Physics (Atomic, molecular, and electron physics)
P: 437; (Uncovering the secrets of the atom)
P: 442
Quantum mechanics (Quanta of energy) Q: 6
Quasicrystal Q: 9
Radiation (Radiation and radioactivity) R: 75
Relativity (General relativity) R: 211
Rutherford, Ernest R: 569
Science (Science in the early 1900's) S: 201
Spectrum So: 772
Star (Fusion in stars) So: 846
Transmutation of elements T: 378
Atom smasher *See* Particle accelerator *in this index*
Atomic bomb
See also Nuclear weapon *in this index*
Air force (Air forces in the nuclear age) A: 186
Army (Armies in the nuclear age) A: 728
Bomb *diagrams on* B: 451, B: 452
Cold War (The West rearms) Ci: 764
Einstein, Albert (Letter to President Roosevelt)
E: 147
Hiroshima H: 242
Manhattan Project M: 141
Nagasaki N: 3
New Mexico (World War II) N: 275 *with picture*
Nuclear energy (The development of nuclear
weapons) N: 590
Nuclear weapon N: 596
Oppenheimer, J. Robert O: 812
Potsdam Conference P: 715
Radiation (Artificial radioactive substances) R: 77
United States, History of the (World War II) U: 193
with picture
Washington (The mid-1900's) W: 68
World, History of the *picture on* W: 446
World War II (The atomic bomb) W: 493 *with
picture*; (The nuclear age) W: 497
Atomic Bomb Dome
Hiroshima H: 243
Atomic clock A: 877
Atom (Recent discoveries) A: 876

Clock (Kinds of clocks) Ci: 682i
Time (Clocks that count repeated actions) T: 289-
292; (Time in today's world) T: 292
Atomic dipole [physics]
Magnetism (How magnetism works) M: 60b-60c
with diagrams
Atomic energy *See* Nuclear energy *in this index*
Atomic Energy Agency, International *See*
International Atomic Energy Agency *in this index*
Atomic Energy Commission [U.S.] A: 877
Nevada (The mid-1900's) N: 176
Nuclear energy (The first peaceful uses) N: 591;
(The spread of nuclear capability) N: 591
Oppenheimer, J. Robert O: 812
South Carolina (The mid-1900's) So: 662
Atomic Energy of Canada Limited
Nuclear energy (Organization of the industry)
N: 589
Atomic fission *See* Fission *in this index*
Atomic force microscope
Microscope (Scanning probe microscopes)
M: 519
Scanning probe microscope S: 172 *with picture*
Atomic fusion *See* Fusion *in this index*
Atomic mass number [physics]
See also Relative atomic mass *in this index*
Atom (The atomic mass number) A: 871
Element, Chemical (The periodic table of the
elements) E: 219
Isotope I: 476
Molecule (Individual molecules) M: 692-693
Nuclear energy (Isotopes) N: 581
Atomic number [physics]
Atom (The atomic number) A: 871
Element, Chemical (The periodic table of the
elements) E: 219; (table) E: 220
Isotope I: 476
Moseley, Henry Gwyn-Jeffreys M: 828
X rays (Penetrating power) X: 541
Atomic particle *See* Subatomic particle *in this index*
Atomic physics
Physics (Atomic, molecular, and electron physics)
P: 437
Atomic power *See* Nuclear energy *in this index*
Atomic submarine *See* Nuclear submarine *in this
index*
Atomic theory
Atom (Development of the atomic theory) A: 874
Bohr, Niels B: 438
Chemistry (Beginnings) C: 400; (Dalton's atomic
theory) C: 402
Dalton, John D: 16
Pauli, Wolfgang P: 201
Rutherford, Ernest R: 569
Science (Scientific advances of the 1800's)
S: 200-201
Atomic vapor laser isotope separation
Uranium (Separating uranium isotopes) U: 215-
216
Atomic weapon *See* Nuclear weapon *in this index*
Atomic weight *See* Relative atomic mass *in this
index*
Atomism [philosophy] A: 877
Atom (Development of the atomic theory) A: 874
Democritus D: 129
Leucippus L: 214
Pre-Socratic philosophy (The teachings of
Parmenides) P: 772-773
Atoms for Peace [program]
Eisenhower, Dwight David (Foreign affairs)
E: 152-153
Atonal music
Classical music (Atonal music) Ci: 649
Modernism M: 685
Music (Tone) M: 950-951
Atonement [book by McEwan]
McEwan, Ian M: 334
Atonement, Day of *See* Yom Kippur *in this index*
Atopic eczema [disease]
Asthma (Causes) A: 825
Eczema E: 74
Atopy [physiology]
Allergy (The development of allergies) A: 374
ATP [biochemistry]
Aerobics A: 85
Biosynthesis B: 326
Cell (Producing energy) C: 332 *with diagrams*;
(Producing proteins) C: 333-334
Mitochondria M: 679
Muscle (How muscles work) M: 935
Phosphorus P: 403
Respiration (Cellular respiration) R: 261
Atreus, Treasury of [Mycenae]
Architecture (Mycenaean architecture) A: 615
Atrial fibrillation [disorder] *See* Fibrillation *in this
index*
Atrial natriuretic factor [hormone]

Hypertension (Causes) H: 476
Atrial septal defect [anatomy]
Heart (Abnormal openings in the heart) H: 141
Atrioventricular node [anatomy]
Heart (Regulating the heart rate) H: 135-136
Atrioventricular valve [anatomy]
Heart *diagram on* H: 136; (Chambers, valves, and
inner lining) H: 133-135
Atrium [anatomy]
Heart *diagram on* H: 136; (Chambers, valves, and
inner lining) H: 133 *with pictures*; (The work
of the heart) H: 135; (Abnormal openings in
the heart) H: 141; (Abnormal heart rhythms)
H: 142; (Hearts of animals) H: 146
Atrium [architecture] A: 877 *with picture*
Architecture (Medieval architecture) A: 617
Rome, Ancient (City life) R: 438 *with picture*
Atrocity [crime]
War crime W: 27
Atrophic macular degeneration [disorder]
Macular degeneration M: 26
Atrophy [disease] A: 877
Muscle (Disorders of the muscles) M: 935-936
Atropine [drug] A: 877
Belladonna B: 242
Atropos [mythology]
Fates F: 54
ATS [safety device]
Railroad (Other train controls) R: 112
Atsina Indians
Gros Ventre Indians G: 398
Attaché [diplomat] A: 878
Attachment [law] A: 878
Attachment disk [zoology]
Spider (How spiders use silk) So: 786
Attack aircraft
Air force (Aircraft and missiles) A: 183
Attack at Dawn [painting by Schreyvogel]
Indian wars *picture on* I: 194
Attack helicopter
Helicopter *picture on* H: 169; (For military
missions) H: 170
Attack on St. Charles [painting by Hartnell]
Canada, History of *picture on* C: 144
Attack plane
Air Force, United States (Other aircraft) A: 191
with picture
Aircraft, Military (Bombers) A: 202 *with picture*
Attack submarine
Submarine (Attack submarines) So: 939 *with
pictures*
Warship *picture on* W: 43; (Submarines) W: 41
Attainder [law] A: 878
Civil rights (Due process) Ci: 608
Attalus I [king of Pergamum]
Galatia G: 8
Attalus III [king of Pergamum]
Rome, Ancient (The Roman Republic) R: 444-445
Attan [dance]
Afghanistan (The arts) A: 94
Attar [perfume] A: 878
Rose R: 474
Attenborough, Richard [British actor/director]
Motion picture (Best achievement in directing:
1982) M: 862
Attention [psychology]
Brain (Attention and consciousness) B: 554
Hypnosis H: 478
Attention deficit disorder A: 878
Child (Obstacles to learning) C: 453
Learning disabilities (Types) L: 165
Attenuated virus vaccine [medicine]
Virus (Vaccines) V: 428a
Attic [construction]
House (table) H: 380
Attic [language]
Greek language (Development of ancient Greek)
G: 376
Attic Greek
Greek language (Development of ancient Greek)
G: 376
Attic Nights [book by Gellius]
Latin literature (The Imperial Period) L: 116-117
Attica [region, Greece]
Athens A: 854
Attica Correctional Facility [New York]
Prison (Current problems) P: 808
Riot (During the 1900's) R: 349
Attila [king of the Huns] A: 879 *with map*
Goths G: 280
Huns H: 449
Nibelungenlied: (The background) N: 395
Attire *See* Clothing *in this index*
Attitude [ballet]
Ballet (table) B: 45 *with picture*
Attlee, Clement Richard [British political leader]
A: 879

Cold War (The alliance breaks up) **Ci:** 763
Labour Party (History) **L:** 16
United Kingdom (The welfare state) **U:** 71
Atto [prefix]
Metric system (Metric prefixes) **M:** 439
Attorney *See* Lawyer *in this index*
Attorney, District [office]
District attorney **D:** 240
Attorney, Power of [law] *See* Power of attorney *in this index*
Attorney general [U.S. office] **A:** 879
Address, Forms of (Officials of the United States) **A:** 53
Deportation **D:** 149
Flag *picture on* **F:** 211
Independent counsel **I:** 107
Justice, Department of **J:** 202
State government (Other officers) **So:** 863
Attu Island [Alaska]
Alaska (Interesting facts) **A:** 283; (World War II) **A:** 301
Attucks, Crispus [American colonial figure] **A:** 880
African Americans (Colonial times) **A:** 136d-136f *with picture*
Revolution, American (The Townshend Acts) **R:** 273
Atum [Egyptian god]
Mythology (The Great Ennead) **M:** 979
ATV [vehicle] *See* All-terrain vehicle *in this index*
Atwater's prairie-chicken [bird]
Prairie chicken **P:** 732
Atwood, Margaret [Canadian author] **A:** 880
Canadian literature (Characteristics of Canadian literature) **C:** 156; (Modern English-Canadian fiction) **C:** 160 *with portrait*
Atzerodt, George [American public figure]
Lincoln, Abraham (The trial of the conspirators) **L:** 326
AU [organization] *See* African Union *in this index*
Au [symbol]
Gold (Physical properties) **G:** 249
Au Lac [kingdom]
Vietnam (Nam Viet) **V:** 369
Aubagne [France]
Foreign Legion (Service in the Legion) **F:** 386
Aubrey, John [English author]
Biography (The 1600's) **B:** 313
Auburn Automobile Company
Sports car (History) **So:** 803
Auburn Cord Duesenberg Automobile Museum
Indiana (Places to visit) **I:** 206
Auburn System
Prison (During the 1800's) **P:** 807
Auburn University A: 880
Alabama *picture on* **A:** 260
AUC [organization] *See* United Self-Defense Forces of Colombia *in this index*
Auchincloss, Louis [American author] **A:** 880
Auckland [New Zealand] **A:** 880 *with picture*
New Zealand **N:** 346 *with picture*
Auction [sale] **A:** 881
E-commerce (Business-to-consumer transactions) **E:** 2
Flower *picture on* **F:** 273
Auction bridge [game]
Bridge (History) **B:** 605-606
Auction market
Farm and farming (Marketing farm products) **F:** 42
Food (Marketing) **F:** 335
Livestock (Marketing livestock) **L:** 398
Meat packing (Marketing livestock and meat) **M:** 350
Auction pinochle [game]
Pinochle **P:** 474
Auctioneer [career]
Auction **A:** 881
Audacity of Hope, The [book by Obama]
Obama, Barack (A second autobiography) **O:** 640d
Auden, W. H. [British poet] **A:** 881
English literature (Poetry between the wars) **E:** 322
Audhumla [Norse mythology]
Mythology *picture on* **M:** 975; (The creation of life) **M:** 985-986
Audi [automobile]
Automobile *picture on* **A:** 969
Sports car (History) **So:** 803
Audience
Public speaking (Approach to a speech) **P:** 864
A Guide to Speaking Skills **Research Guide:** 20
Audience research [media]
Television (Choosing new programs) **T:** 113
Audiencia of Guatemala [Latin American history]
Central America (The colonial period) **C:** 355; (Independence) **C:** 355

Guatemala (Colonial period) **G:** 416
Nicaragua (The colonial period) **N:** 398
Audio book [recording] *See* Audiobook *in this index*
Audio compact disc [recording]
Compact disc **Ci:** 901
Audio console [instrument]
Television (The control room) **T:** 112
Audio engineer [career]
Television (The control room) **T:** 112 *with picture*
Audio file [computing]
Computer file **Ci:** 924g
Audio-frequency wave [physics]
Radio (From sound waves to electric waves) **R:** 86 *with diagram*; (The intermediate-frequency amplifier and detector) **R:** 89
Audio materials
Audio-visual materials (Audio materials) **A:** 883
Blindness (Aids for blind people) **B:** 402
Audio surveillance [electronics] *See* Wiretapping *in this index*
Audio-visual materials [education] **A:** 882 *with picture*
Filmstrip **F:** 103
Library (Variety of information) **L:** 235 *with picture*; (School libraries) **L:** 244
Teaching (Guiding and assisting student learning) **T:** 66
A Guide to Speaking Skills **Research Guide:** 24
Audiobook [recording] **A:** 881
Book (Modern books) **B:** 468
Publishing (Books) **B:** 468
Audiology [health care] **A:** 882
Deafness (Detection of hearing problems) **D:** 58 *with picture*
Audiometer [instrument]
Deafness (Detection of hearing problems) **D:** 58 *with picture*
Audion tube [device]
De Forest, Lee **D:** 89
Vacuum tube (History) **V:** 259
Audit [business] **A:** 884
Accounting (Auditing) **A:** 23
Internal Revenue Service **I:** 337
Audition [drama]
Motion picture (Assembling the cast) **M:** 851
Television (Talent) **T:** 110d
Auditor [career]
Audit **A:** 884
Auditorium [room]
Opera **O:** 790
Theater (The auditorium) **T:** 233
Auditorium Building [Chicago]
Adler, Dankmar **A:** 58
Sullivan, Louis Henri **So:** 970
Auditory arts
Fine arts **F:** 104
Auditory canal [anatomy]
Ear *diagrams on* **E:** 8, **E:** 10, *picture on* **E:** 13; (The outer ear) **E:** 7
Auditory nerve [anatomy]
Deafness (Sensorineural hearing loss) **D:** 57
Ear (The inner ear) **E:** 8-9; (Diseases) **E:** 12
Tinnitus **T:** 294
Auditory ossicle [anatomy]
Ear (The middle ear) **E:** 7-8 *with diagram*; (Diseases) **E:** 12
Audubon, Jean [father of]
Audubon, John James (His life) **A:** 884
Audubon, John James [American naturalist] **A:** 884 *with picture*
Audubon Society, National **A:** 885
Conservation (Early conservation problems) **Ci:** 985
Louisiana (Places to visit) **L:** 488
Audubon Park
Zoo *picture on* **Z:** 600
Audubon Society, National [organization] **A:** 885
Bird (Bird study and protection) **B:** 367
Audumla [Norse mythology]
Mythology (Teutonic mythology) **M:** 985-986
Auer, Carl [Austrian chemist] *See* Welsbach, Baron von *in this index*
Auerbach, Red [American basketball coach] **A:** 885
Basketball *picture on* **B:** 154
Auerstädt, Battle of [1806]
Napoleonic Wars (The alliance of Prussia and Russia) **N:** 18 *with map*
Augean stables [Greek mythology]
Hercules (The twelve labors) **H:** 198-199
Augeas [Greek mythology]
Hercules (The twelve labors) **H:** 198-199
Auger [machine]
Coal (Auger mining) **Ci:** 722
Auger [tool]
Drill (Wood drills) **D:** 348
Auger, Pierre V. [French physicist]
Cosmic rays (Cosmic ray research) **Ci:** 1077

Auger mining
Coal (Auger mining) **Ci:** 722
Augier, Émile [French dramatist]
French literature (Realism) **F:** 522
Augmented interval [music]
Music (Harmony) **M:** 951
Augrabies Falls [South Africa]
Orange River **O:** 817
Augsburg [Germany] **A:** 885
Augsburg, Diet of [1530]
Augsburg Confession **A:** 885
Augsburg, Peace of [1555]
Germany (The Reformation) **G:** 164
Reformation (Martin Luther) **R:** 197
Schmalkaldic League **S:** 177
Thirty Years' War (Causes of the war) **T:** 259
Augsburg, War of the League of [1689-1697]
French and Indian wars (King William's War) **F:** 512
Grand Alliance **G:** 305
Augsburg Cathedral [Germany]
Stained glass (Early stained-glass windows) **So:** 822
Augsburg Confession [religion] **A:** 885
Luther, Martin (Building and defending the church) **L:** 528
Lutherans (Doctrine) **L:** 529
Melanchthon, Philipp **M:** 388
Reformation (Martin Luther) **R:** 197 *with picture*
Augur [ancient Rome] **A:** 885
Rome, Ancient (Religion) **R:** 441
August [month] **A:** 886 *with pictures*
Julian calendar **J:** 187
August, John [pen name]
De Voto, Bernard Augustine **D:** 176
August: Osage County [play]
Theater *picture on* **T:** 245
August 1914 [book by Solzhenitsyn]
Solzhenitsyn, Alexander **So:** 587
August Revolution [Vietnamese history]
Vietnam (The August Revolution of 1945) **V:** 370
Augusta [Georgia] **A:** 888
Augusta [Maine] **A:** 888
Maine **M:** 68
Augusta National Golf Course
Georgia (Visitor's guide) **G:** 122
Augustan Age [English history]
Anne **A:** 517
England (The Augustan Age) **E:** 309
English literature (The Augustan Age) **E:** 318
Poetry (Neoclassical poetry) **P:** 596
Augustan Age [Roman Empire]
Augustus (Other achievements) **A:** 890
Classicism (Rome) **Ci:** 653
Latin literature (The Augustan Age) **L:** 116
Auguste clown
Clown **Ci:** 713
Augustine, Mildred Wirt [American author]
Keene, Carolyn **K:** 254
Augustine, Saint [Christian theologian] **A:** 888
Ambrose, Saint **A:** 405
Autobiography **A:** 942
Christianity (Other Christian writings) **C:** 522h
Neoplatonism **N:** 124
Philosophy (Medieval philosophy) **P:** 388 *with picture*
Predestination **P:** 734
Augustine of Canterbury, Saint [Italian missionary] **A:** 888
Archbishop of Canterbury **A:** 601
England (The Germanic invasions) **E:** 304
Augustinians [religious group]
Friar **F:** 532
Augustinus [book by Jansen]
Jansen, Cornelius **J:** 29
Augustus [Roman emperor] **A:** 889 *with picture and map*
Actium, Battle of **A:** 30
Aeneid **A:** 84
Agrippa, Marcus **A:** 162
August **A:** 886
Caesar **C:** 12
Cleopatra (Cleopatra and Mark Antony) **Ci:** 662a
February **F:** 60
Galatia **G:** 8
Latin literature (The Augustan Age) **L:** 116
Navy (Ancient navies) **N:** 79
Ovid **O:** 791
Postal services (Ancient times) **P:** 703
Praetorian Guard **P:** 729
Rome (Other remains) **R:** 433
Rome, Ancient (The later years of the republic) **R:** 445-446; (The Roman Empire) **R:** 446
Tiberius **T:** 275
Urban renewal (History) **U:** 220
Virgil (His life) **V:** 391
Augustus II, the Strong [king of Poland]

Succession wars (The War of the Polish Succession) **So: 950**
Augustus, Mausoleum of [building]
Rome (Other remains) **R: 433**
Auk [bird] **A: 890** *with pictures*
Bird (Extinct birds) **B: 369-370** *with picture*
Auklet [bird]
Bird *picture on* **B: 368**; (Other means of communication) **B: 354**
Aulaire, D' [American authors] *See* D'Aulaire *in this index*
Aulavik National Park [Northwest Territories]
Canada (table: National parks and national park reserves) **C: 113**
"Auld Lang Syne" [song] **A: 890**
Burns, Robert **B: 710**
Aulos [musical instrument]
Classical music (Early music) **Ci: 645**
Greece, Ancient (Education) **G: 367**
Aumann, Robert John [Israeli-American economist]
Nobel Prizes (Economics: 2005) **N: 449**
Aung San [Burmese political leader]
Myanmar (History) **M: 970d**
Aung San Suu Kyi [Burmese political leader] **A: 890** *with portrait*
Myanmar (Military rule) **M: 970e**; (Recent developments) **M: 970e**
Aunt
Family (Family relationships) **F: 21**
Aura [musical instrument]
Harmonica **H: 62**
Aura [photography]
Kirlian photography **K: 336**
Aura [physiology]
Migraine **M: 537**
Aura River [Finland]
Finland *picture on* **F: 111**
Aurangzeb [Mughal emperor] **A: 891**
India (The Mughal Empire) **I: 129-130**
Mughal Empire **M: 910**
Aurélia [poems by Nerval]
French literature (Gautier and Nerval) **F: 521-522**
Nerval, Gérard de **N: 131**
Aurelian [Roman emperor] **A: 891**
Aurelian Wall [ruins]
Rome (Other remains) **R: 433**
Aurelius, Marcus [Roman emperor] *See* Marcus Aurelius *in this index*
Aurelius Augustinus [name for]
Augustine, Saint (His life) **A: 888**
Auricle [anatomy]
Ear *diagram on* **E: 8**, *pictures on* **E: 13**; (The outer ear) **E: 7** *with diagram*
Aurochs [animal] **A: 891**
Cattle (Early cattle) **C: 315**
Lascaux Cave **L: 80** *with picture*
Aurora [meteorology] **A: 891** *with picture*
Air (The thermosphere) **A: 174**
Celsius, Anders **C: 342**
Jupiter (Magnetic field) **J: 198-199**
Light *picture on* **L: 284**; (How light is produced) **L: 283**
Magnetism (Earth) **M: 60d**
Northwest Territories (Tourism) **N: 532**
Seven natural wonders of the world (The aurora borealis) **S: 324b** *with picture*
Aurora [Nevada]
Nevada (Interesting facts about Nevada) **N: 157**
Aurora [Roman mythology] **A: 891** *with picture*
Aurora 7 [spacecraft]
Carpenter, M. Scott **C: 246**
Aurora australis *See* Aurora *in this index*
Aurora borealis *See* Aurora *in this index*
Aurora Leigh [book by Browning]
Browning, Elizabeth Barrett **B: 646**
Auschwitz [concentration camp] **A: 892**
Concentration camp (Nazi concentration camps) **Ci: 926-927**
Holocaust (The camps) **H: 296a-296b** *with map*
Mengele, Josef **M: 400**
Ausonius [Roman poet]
Latin literature (Later periods) **L: 117**
Aussie [dog] *See* Australian shepherd *in this index*
Austen, Jane [British author] **A: 892**
English literature (Romantic prose) **E: 320**
Gothic novel **G: 279**
Literature (Judging literature) **L: 352-353**
Novel (Britain) **N: 573**
Auster, Paul [American author]
American literature (Experimental styles) **A: 425**
Austerlitz, Battle of [1805] **A: 892**
Napoleon I (Dominates Europe) **N: 15**
Austerlitz, Frederick [birth name of]
Astaire, Fred **A: 822**
Austin [Nevada]
Nevada (Places to visit) **N: 164**

Austin [Texas] **A: 892** *with picture*
Austin, Alfred [British poet]
Poet laureate (table: Poets laureate of the United Kingdom) **P: 590**
Austin, Horace [American political leader]
Minnesota (table) **M: 602**
Austin, Moses [Texas pioneer]
Texas (American settlement) **T: 206**
Austin, Stephen Fuller [Texas political leader] **A: 893**
Texas (American settlement) **T: 206**
Texas Rangers (Early days) **T: 210**
Austin, Warren R. [American diplomat]
United Nations (table) **U: 86**
Austin High School [Chicago, Illinois]
Jazz (The 1920's) **J: 70**
Austral Islands [Pacific]
French Polynesia **F: 524**
Australasia A: 893
Australia A: 894 *with pictures and maps*
Business and industry
Australia (Manufacturing) **A: 914**; (Agriculture) **A: 916**
Aluminum (Leading aluminum-producing countries) **A: 396**
Bank (Australia and New Zealand) **B: 92**
Dollar (The dollar in other countries) **D: 295** *with pictures*
International trade (Why nations trade) **I: 348**
Money (History of the pound) **M: 709-710**
Newspaper (In Australia and New Zealand) **N: 386**
Prickly pear **P: 776**
Television (In Australia and New Zealand) **T: 117**
Textile (In Australia and New Zealand) **T: 218**
Wheat (Australia) **W: 273** *with map*
Education
Australia (Education) **A: 903**
Library (Australia and East Asia) **L: 253**
School (In other countries) **S: 183**
Government
Australia (Government) **A: 894**
Colombo Plan **Ci: 785**
Impeachment (Canada and Australia) **I: 92**
Parliament (Parliaments in other countries) **P: 174**
Police (In other countries) **P: 623**
Territory **T: 174**
Health and welfare
Aviation (General aviation activities) **A: 984**
Disability (The 1900's) **D: 221-222**
Managed care plans (In other countries) **M: 131**
Pension (Pensions in other countries) **P: 273**
Social security (Social security in other countries) **So: 556**
Welfare (Welfare throughout the world) **W: 190**
History
Australia (History) **A: 919** *with pictures and maps*
Camel **C: 77**
Dampier, William **D: 22**
Exploration (Exploring the Pacific) **E: 447** *with map*; (Exploring Australia's interior) **E: 448** *with map*
Great Depression (Effects in Australia) **G: 342**
Labor Day **L: 2**
Pacific Islands (Pacific alliances and independence movements) **P: 12**
Papua New Guinea (History) **P: 141**
Penal colony **P: 235**
Stolen Generation **So: 907**
Tasman, Abel Janszoon **T: 48**
Transportation of convicts **T: 400**
Victoria **T: 356**
Woman suffrage (Australia) **W: 381**
Natural resources
Australia (Animals and plants) **A: 911** *with map*
Bird (Birds of Australia and New Zealand) **B: 346** *with pictures*
Conservation (Australia) **Ci: 989**
Diamond (Where natural diamonds are found) **D: 181-182**
Dingo **D: 205**
Gold rush (Gold rushes in other countries) **G: 254**
Marsupial (History of marsupials) **M: 233**
National park (Australia) **N: 42b** *with picture*; (table) **N: 42f**; (The rights of original inhabitants) **N: 42i**
Prehistoric animal (The distribution of mammals) **P: 741**
Rain forest (Australia and the Pacific Islands) **R: 126c** *with map*
People
Australia (Population and ancestry) **A: 900** *with pictures*

Aborigines, Australian **A: 13**
Immigration (Australia and New Zealand) **I: 85**
Installment plan **I: 304**
Prehistoric people (The spread of settlement) **P: 752**
Races, Human (Climatic adaptations) **R: 58**
Physical features
Australia (The land) **A: 907** *with pictures*
Australian Desert **A: 927**
Continent **Ci: 1021**
Great Barrier Reef **G: 336**
Outback **O: 879**
Recreation and sports
Australia (Recreation) **A: 903** *with pictures*
Baseball (Baseball around the world) **B: 132**
Boomerang **B: 475**
Boxing (Boxing in Australia and New Zealand) **B: 531**
Cricket (History) **Ci: 1134-1135**
Social and cultural life
Circus (The circus goes international) **Ci: 563**
Girl Scouts (Australia) **G: 199**
Remembrance Day **R: 229**
Transportation
Railroad (In Australia and New Zealand) **R: 114**; (Railroads today) **R: 118-119**
Transcontinental railroad (Around the world) **T: 371**
Australia, Order of
Medals, decorations, and orders (table) **M: 359**
Australia-New Zealand Closer Economic Relations Trade Agreement
Common market **Ci: 875**
Australia II [boat]
America's Cup **A: 431**
Australian Aborigines [people] *See* Aborigines, Australian *in this index*
Australian Alps [mountain range]
Australia *picture on* **A: 912**; (Mountains) **A: 908** *with map*
Australian Association of the Deaf
Deafness (Education) **D: 59**
Australian ballot
Ballot (In the United States) **B: 63**
Australian beak [butterfly]
Butterfly *picture on* **B: 737**
Australian bonito [fish]
Bonito **B: 460**
Australian Broadcasting Corporation
Australia (Communication) **A: 919**
Australian Bureau of Statistics
Unemployment (Measuring unemployment) **U: 22-23**
Australian Capital Territory [region, Australia] **A: 926**
Canberra **C: 166**
Australian cattle dog A: 926
Dog *picture on* **D: 276**
Australian Consumers Association
Consumer protection (The right to information) **Ci: 1018**
Australian Country Party [political party]
Australia (Between the wars) **A: 924**
Australian Defence Force
Australia (The armed forces) **A: 900**
Australian Desert [region, Australia] **A: 927**
Desert *picture on* **D: 154**
Australian heeler [dog]
Australian cattle dog **A: 927**
Australian Labor Party [political party]
Australia (Political parties) **A: 897**; (Building a nation) **A: 923**
Gillard, Julia **G: 190**
Rudd, Kevin Michael **R: 508**
Australian National Boxing Federation
Boxing (Boxing in Australia and New Zealand) **B: 531**
Australian nut *See* Macadamia nut *in this index*
Australian Open [tournament]
Tennis (table: Australian Open) **T: 166**
Australian pelican [bird]
Pelican (Kinds) **P: 231**
Australian pine [tree] *See* Beefwood *in this index*
Australian race [theory]
Races, Human (The geographical-race theory) **R: 54**
Australian Rules football
Australia (Recreation) **A: 903** *with picture*
Australian Securities and Investments Commission
Interest (Regulation of interest rates) **I: 323**
Australian shepherd [dog] **A: 927** *with picture*
Australian terrier [dog] **A: 927**
Dog *picture on* **D: 272**
Australopithecus [hominid] **A: 927**
Broom, Robert **B: 641**
Human being (Prehuman ancestors) **H: 414-415**

Prehistoric people *pictures on* **P:** 748; (Prehuman ancestors) **P:** 444-445 *with picture*; (table) **P:** 754 *with map*
Australopithecus aethiopicus [hominid]
Australopithecus **A:** 927
Prehistoric people (Types of australopithecines) **P:** 745
Australopithecus afarensis [hominid]
Australopithecus **A:** 927
Johanson, Donald Carl **J:** 131
Laetoli fossil site **L:** 26
Prehistoric people *picture on* **P:** 748; (Types of australopithecines) **P:** 745; (table) **P:** 754
Australopithecus africanus [hominid]
Australopithecus **A:** 927
Prehistoric people *picture on* **P:** 748; (Types of australopithecines) **P:** 745 *with picture*
Australopithecus anamensis [hominid]
Australopithecus **A:** 927
Leakey, Meave Gillian **L:** 161
Prehistoric people (Types of australopithecines) **P:** 745; (table) **P:** 754
Australopithecus boisei [hominid]
Australopithecus **A:** 927
Leakey, Mary Douglas **L:** 161
Leakey, Richard Erskine Frere **L:** 161
Prehistoric people *pictures on* **P:** 743; (Types of australopithecines) **P:** 745 *with picture*
Australopithecus garhi [hominid]
Australopithecus **A:** 927
Prehistoric people (Types of australopithecines) **P:** 745
Australopithecus robustus [hominid]
Australopithecus **A:** 927
Prehistoric people *picture on* **P:** 748; (Types of australopithecines) **P:** 745
Australopithecus sediba [hominid]
Australopithecus **A:** 927
Prehistoric people (Types of australopithecines) **P:** 745-746
Australorp [breed]
Chicken (table) **C:** 443
Austrasia [former region]
Charlemagne *map on* **C:** 379
Austria A: 928 *with pictures and maps*
See also the list of Related articles in the Austria *article*
Air force (History) **A:** 184-185
Austerlitz, Battle of **A:** 892
Bomb (History) **B:** 452 *with picture*
Christmas *picture on* **C:** 530
Clothing *picture on* **Ci:** 694
Euro **E:** 378
Flag **F:** 194, *picture on* **F:** 205
German language **G:** 137
German literature **G:** 138
Germany (The Revolution of 1848) **G:** 165; (East Germany) **G:** 170
Great Depression *picture on* **G:** 339
Habsburg, House of **H:** 3
Poland (The partitions) **P:** 612 *with maps*
Revolution of 1848 **R:** 288
Russo-Turkish wars **R:** 566b
Saint-Germain, Treaty of **S:** 34
Seven Weeks' War **S:** 324b
Seven Years' War **S:** 328
Succession wars (The War of the Austrian Succession) **So:** 950
Thirty Years' War (The Swedish-French period) **T:** 260
Tyrol **T:** 542 *with map*
Ukraine (Russian rule) **U:** 12
Austria [ship]
Shipwreck (table: Major shipwrecks) **S:** 428
Austria-Hungary [European history] **A:** 940
Austria (Austria-Hungary) **A:** 939 *with map*
Bosnia-Herzegovina (History) **B:** 492-493
Croatia (History) **Ci:** 1148a-1148b
Czech Republic (Habsburg rule) **Ci:** 1213
Flag *picture on* **F:** 217
Franz Joseph **F:** 494
Germany (The unification of Germany) **G:** 165 *with map*
Hungary (Austria-Hungary) **H:** 446
Serbia (A new country) **S:** 314-315
Slovakia (History) **S:** 508d-509
Vienna **V:** 361
World War I **W:** 452
Yugoslavia (Land of the South Slavs) **Y:** 576
Austrian Crescent [potato]
Potato *picture on* **P:** 711
Austrian People's Party [political party]
Austria (Political parties) **A:** 930-931
Austrian pine [tree]
Pine (Other pines) **P:** 470
Austrian State Treaty [1955]
Austria (After World War II) **A:** 939-940

Austrian Succession, War of the *See* Succession wars *in this index*
Austrian Tyrol [region, Austria]
Tyrol **T:** 542 *with map*
Austro-Hungarian Monarchy *See* Austria-Hungary *in this index*
Austro-Prussian War *See* Seven Weeks' War *in this index*
Austro-Sardinian War [1859]
Italy (Italy united) **I:** 515
Austronesian language *See* Malayo-Polynesian language *in this index*
Authentic cadence [music]
Music (Harmony) **M:** 951-952 *with diagram*
Authentication [security]
Biometrics **B:** 325
Author
American Society of Composers, Authors and Publishers **A:** 430
Copyright **Ci:** 1046
Publishing (Preparing content for publication) **P:** 866; (Marketing) **P:** 867
Writing **W:** 511
Authoritarianism [political science] **A:** 941
Government **G:** 282
World (Forms of government) **W:** 407-412b
Authority
Power (Forms of power) **P:** 727
Religion (Chief characteristics of religion) **R:** 215
Authorized strike
Strike (Kinds of strikes) **So:** 928
Authorized Version [Bible] *See* King James Version *in this index*
Autism [disorder] **A:** 941
Fragile X syndrome **F:** 451
Rett syndrome (Symptoms) **R:** 266
Autism spectrum disorder
Autism **A:** 941
Auto *See* Automobile *in this index*
Auto-hypnosis
Hypnosis (Modifying thoughts and behaviors) **H:** 479
Autoantibody [physiology]
Anemia (Excessive destruction of red blood cells) **A:** 458
Immune system (Autoimmune disorders) **I:** 88c
Autobahn [road, Germany]
Germany (Transportation) **G:** 162
Road (Modern roads) **R:** 362
Autobiography [book by Cellini]
Cellini, Benvenuto **C:** 339
Autobiography [book by Wright]
Wright, Frank Lloyd **W:** 507
Autobiography [literature] **A:** 942
See also Biography *in this index*
Pulitzer Prizes (table) **P:** 896
Autobiography of Alice B. Toklas, The [book by Stein]
Stein, Gertrude **So:** 884
Autobiography of an Ex-Colored Man, The [book by Johnson]
Johnson, James Weldon **J:** 143
Autobiography of Benjamin Franklin, The [book by Franklin]
American literature (Philadelphia) **A:** 415
Autobiography **A:** 942
Franklin, Benjamin **F:** 487
Autobiography of Malcolm X, The [book by Malcolm X]
Malcolm X **M:** 103
Autobiography of Values [book of Lindbergh's writings]
Lindbergh, Charles Augustus (After the war) **L:** 330-331
Autocephalous Orthodox Church [religion]
Ukraine (Religion) **U:** 8-9
Autochrome plate [photography]
Lumière brothers **L:** 522
Photography (Dramatic changes) **P:** 425
Autoclave [machine]
Nylon (How nylon is made) **N:** 633
Autocracy [political science]
Autocrat of the Breakfast-Table, The [book by Holmes]
Holmes, Oliver Wendell (His writings) **H:** 294-295
Autocue [machine]
Television (Talent) **T:** 110d
Autoexposure [photography] *See* Automatic exposure control *in this index*
Autofocus [photography] *See* Automatic focusing *in this index*
Autofrettage [industrial process]
Artillery (The monoblock process) **A:** 763
Autogiro [aircraft] **A:** 942 *with picture*
Autograft [medicine]
Skin grafting **S:** 494
Autograph A: 943 *with picture*

Autoignition [engineering]
Gasoline (Engine requirements) **G:** 61
Autoimmune response [physiology]
Celiac disease **C:** 325
Disease (Disorders of the immune system) **D:** 229-230
Immune system **I:** 87c; (Autoimmune disorders) **I:** 88c
Autoimmunity [physiology] *See* Autoimmune response *in this index*
Automated clearinghouse [banking]
Bank (Electronic banking) **B:** 89-90
Automated external defibrillator [device]
Defibrillator **D:** 88
Automated teller machine A: 944
Bank (Electronic banking) **B:** 89 *with picture*
Smart card **S:** 513
Automatic [gun]
Handgun (Types of handguns) **H:** 43 *with picture*
Rifle (Kinds of rifles) **R:** 338 *with picture*
Automatic block signal system [device]
Railroad (Automatic block signal systems) **R:** 111 *with pictures*
Automatic caller identification [service]
Telephone (Residential services) **T:** 98
Automatic color balance [photography] *See* Automatic white balance *in this index*
Automatic deduction
Bank (Providing a means of payment) **B:** 89
Automatic exposure control
Camera (Automatic controls) **C:** 80
Automatic flight control system [aviation] **A:** 944
Airplane (The controls and instruments) **A:** 217; (Engineering improvements) **A:** 237
Gyroscope **G:** 453
Servomechanism **S:** 320
Sperry, Elmer Ambrose **So:** 779
Automatic focusing
Camera (Automatic controls) **C:** 80
Photography (Types of lenses) **P:** 411
Automatic frequency control
Radio (table) **R:** 84
Automatic gearshift *See* Automatic transmission *in this index*
Automatic mode [photography]
Camera (Automatic exposure control) **C:** 82
Automatic nailer [tool]
Nail **N:** 3
Automatic pilot [navigation]
See also Automatic flight control system *in this index*
Ship (Navigation) **S:** 410-411
Automatic stay [law]
Bankruptcy (In the United States) **B:** 97
Automatic teller machine *See* Automated teller machine *in this index*
Automatic train control [safety device]
Railroad (Other train controls) **R:** 112
Automatic train stop [safety device]
Railroad (Other train controls) **R:** 112
Automatic transmission
Automobile (The transmission) **A:** 948-949
Transmission (How an automatic transmission works) **T:** 376 *with diagrams*
Automatic typewriter
Typewriter (History) **T:** 539
Automatic white balance [photography]
Camera (Automatic controls) **C:** 80-81
Automation [industry] **A:** 944 *with diagram*
See also the list of Related articles in the Automation *article*
Electronics (Automation) **E:** 207
Farm and farming *pictures on* **F:** 37, **F:** 38
Meat packing (Trends and changes in meat packing) **M:** 352
Robot **R:** 369
Ship (Nuclear power and automation) **S:** 426
Automatism [art]
Masson, André **M:** 296
Painting (Surrealism) **P:** 81
Automobile A: 946 *with pictures*
See also Automobile racing; Electric car; Hybrid car; Sports car *in this index; and the list of Related articles in the* Automobile *article*
Environment and safety
Air pollution (Control of air pollution) **A:** 199
Airbag **A:** 200 *with picture*
Carbon footprint **C:** 207
Driving while intoxicated **D:** 348
Electric car **E:** 165 *with picture*
Global warming (Ways to limit global warming) **G:** 232b
Safety (Safety in transportation) **S:** 14
Traffic (Traffic problems) **T:** 365
History
Assembly line **A:** 818
Bush, George Walker (Economy) **B:** 722j-723

City (Metropolitan cities) Ci: 588-589
Detroit (The mid-1900's) D: 171 with picture
Duryea brothers D: 390
Flint F: 235
Ford, Henry F: 380
Horse (Horses and people) H: 360-362 with picture
Indiana (Progress as a state) I: 216 with picture
Invention (The early and middle 1900's) I: 363
Mass production M: 269
Roaring Twenties (Rising prosperity) R: 363 with picture
Transportation (Land transportation) T: 383; (The beginnings of modern transportation) T: 390 with picture; (Private transportation) T: 392
United States, History of the (New products) U: 180; (The economy--boom and bust) U: 191 with picture; (Suburban growth) U: 195
Parts and maintenance
Air conditioning (Air conditioners for vehicles) A: 179
Battery (Lead-acid batteries) B: 170 with diagram
Brake (Mechanical brakes) B: 560; (Hydraulic brakes) B: 560-561
Lacquer L: 22
Machine (Efficiency) M: 14
Microelectromechanical systems M: 513
Paint picture on P: 23; (Industrial paints) P: 24
Plastics (To replace metals) P: 554; (Growth of the plastics industry) P: 560
Radio (Radio since the 1950's) R: 94
Starter So: 858 with diagram
Torsion bar suspension T: 343 with diagram
Transmission T: 375 with diagrams
Production
Asia picture on A: 787
Europe (Manufacturing) E: 401
Industry (Expansion) I: 260
Japan picture on J: 50
Michigan picture on M: 503; (Manufacturing) M: 505
Ontario (Manufacturing) O: 780
Automobile, Model [hobby] A: 974 with pictures
Automobile Club de France
Automobile racing (Growth of organized automobile racing) A: 979
Automobile Competition Committee for the United States
Automobile racing (Racing organizations) A: 976
Automobile insurance
Insurance (Automobile insurance) I: 313
No-fault insurance N: 438
Automobile mechanic [career]
Industrial arts (Industrial arts courses) I: 242
Automobile model See Automobile, Model in this index
Automobile racing [sport] A: 975 with pictures
Hot rod H: 374a
Le Mans L: 187
NASCAR N: 21
Tire (Low profile tires) T: 297
Automobile Workers, United See United Automobile Workers in this index
Automotive Engineers, Society of
Horsepower (S.A.E. horsepower) H: 367
Autonomic nervous system
Brain (Regulating body processes) B: 553
Heart H: 132; (Regulating the heart rate) H: 135-136
Human body (The autonomic nervous system) H: 426
Hypothalamus H: 481
Muscle (Smooth muscles) M: 934-935
Nervous system (The autonomic nervous system) N: 133 with diagram
Autonomous community
Spain (Local government) So: 733
Autonomous region
China (Political divisions) C: 477
Xinjiang X: 545
Autonomous underwater vehicle
Ocean (Submersibles) O: 663
Autonomy [government]
Government (table) G: 284
Autopilot See Automatic flight control system in this index
Autopsy [medicine] A: 981
Forensic pathology F: 389a
Medical examiner M: 361
Pathology P: 196
Autos sacramentales [plays by Calderón de la Barca]
Calderón de la Barca, Pedro C: 27
Drama (Religious plays) D: 333

Spanish literature (The 1600's) So: 759-760
Autosomal dominant polycystic kidney disease
Polycystic kidney disease P: 649
Autosomal recessive polycystic kidney disease
Polycystic kidney disease P: 649
Autosome [genetics]
Down syndrome D: 316
Autotomy [biology]
Starfish (The life of a starfish) So: 856-857
Autotroph [botany]
Plant (Photosynthesis) P: 537
Autotrophic bacteria
Bacteria (How bacteria obtain food) B: 21
Autry, Gene [American singer] A: 981
Western frontier life in America (Entertainment) W: 240
Autumn [season] A: 981
Indian summer I: 189
Season (The four seasons) S: 270 with diagram
Autumn adonis [plant]
Adonis A: 65 with picture
Autumn crocus [flower]
Colchicum Ci: 760 with picture
Autumn Sonata [book by Valle-Inclán]
Spanish literature (The Generation of 1898) So: 762
Autumnal equinox [astronomy]
Equinox E: 348 with diagram
Harvest moon H: 81
AUV [vehicle]
Ocean (Submersibles) O: 663
Auxiliary [soldier]
Rome, Ancient (The army) R: 438
Auxiliary ship
Navy (Auxiliary ships) N: 78
Navy, United States (Auxiliary ships) N: 84
Auxiliary verb [grammar]
Grammar (Function words) G: 303
Tense T: 168
Verb (Auxiliary verbs) V: 314
Auxin [hormone] A: 981
Hormone (Plant hormones) H: 337
Plant (Hereditary factors) P: 538
Tropism T: 451
Auyuittuq National Park [Nunavut]
Canada (table: National parks and national park reserves) C: 110-113
Nunavut (Economy) N: 610
AV-8B Harrier II [airplane]
Bomber picture on B: 453
A-V materials See Audio-visual materials in this index
A-V node [anatomy]
Heart (Regulating the heart rate) H: 135-136
AV valve [anatomy] See Atrioventricular valve in this index
Ava [shrub] See Kava in this index
Available light [photography] See Natural light in this index
Avalanche A: 982
Earthquake (Landslides or avalanches) E: 34
Landslide L: 60
Volcano (Avalanches and landslides) V: 440
Avalée des avalés, L' [book by Aquin]
Canadian literature (Modern literature: 1945 to the present) C: 159-160
Avalokitesvara [religion]
Bodhisattva B: 434
Avalon Peninsula [region, Newfoundland and Labrador]
Newfoundland and Labrador (Population) N: 364; (Land regions) N: 370 with map
St. John's (Description) S: 36
Avant-garde [arts] A: 982
Modernism M: 685
Performance art P: 285
Avars [people]
Russia (Early days) R: 547
Avarua [Cook Islands]
Cook Islands Ci: 1026
Avastin [drug]
Angiogenesis A: 461
Avatar [computing]
Internet (Identity and privacy) I: 350f
Avatar [film]
Cameron, James C: 84
Motion picture (Motion pictures today) M: 872-873
Avatar [Hinduism]
Vishnu V: 429
AVC [organization]
Veterans' organizations (In the United States) V: 344-345
Ave Maria Grotto [Alabama]
Alabama (Places to visit) A: 266
Avenida 9 de Julio [road]
Buenos Aires (The city) B: 672

Avens [plant]
See also Mountain avens in this index
Flower picture on F: 289
Aventine Hill
Rome R: 429
Avenue of Flags [Columbus, Ohio]
Columbus (The city) Ci: 854
Avenue of the Americas [New York City]
New York picture on N: 291
Avenue of the Arts
Philadelphia (Downtown Philadelphia) P: 359
Avenue Q [musical]
Musical comedy (Musical comedy today) M: 961
Average [statistics] A: 982
Mean M: 345
Median M: 361
Mode M: 684
Statistics (Probability) So: 868-869
Averill, Earl [American baseball player]
Baseball (table: Hall of Fame) B: 134
Avery, Oswald T. [American geneticist]
Cell (The 1900's) C: 337-338
Avery, Waightstill [American lawyer]
Jackson, Andrew (Lawyer) J: 8
Avery, William H. [American political leader]
Kansas (table) K: 234
Avery Fisher Hall
Lincoln Center for the Performing Arts L: 327
Avery Island [Louisiana]
Louisiana (Places to visit) L: 488 with picture
Aves [zoology]
Bird (A classification of birds) B: 371
Avesta [religious book]
Persia, Ancient (Religion) P: 297
Zoroastrianism (Beliefs) Z: 607
Avi [American author] A: 982
Newbery Medal (table) N: 359
Avian influenza [disease] A: 982
Poultry (Raising poultry) P: 720-721
Swine flu So: 1048
Aviation A: 983 with pictures and maps
See also Aircraft, Military; Airline; Airplane in this index; and the list of Related articles in the Aviation article
Air force A: 182
Air Force, United States A: 188
Air turbulence A: 200
Army, United States (Army aviation) A: 734
Fourth dimension F: 438
Great-circle route G: 338
Jet stream J: 116
Radar (In aviation) R: 64
September 11 terrorist attacks (Weakened economy) S: 310b
Aviation and Transportation Security Act [2001]
Transportation Security Administration T: 400
Aviation medicine
Aerospace medicine A: 89
Aviator, The [film]
Motion picture (The computer revolution) M: 872
Avicenna [Arab philosopher] A: 992
Geology (The Romans) G: 98
Medicine (During the Middle Ages) M: 373
Science (The Middle Ages) S: 197
Avignon [France] A: 992 with picture
France (Growth of royal power) F: 472-473
Avignon Papacy
Pope (The troubles of the papacy) P: 664
Roman Catholic Church (The Avignon papacy) R: 407
Ávila Camacho, Manuel [Mexican political leader] A: 993
Mexico (During and after World War II) M: 473
Avildsen, John [American director]
Motion picture (Best achievement in directing: 1976) M: 862
Avionics [electronics]
Automatic flight control system (How an AFCS works) A: 944
Avison, Margaret [Canadian poet]
Canadian literature (Modern Canadian poets) C: 161
Avitus [Roman emperor]
Rome, Ancient (table) R: 447
Aviz, House of [Portuguese history]
Portugal (Founding the Portuguese nation) P: 693
AVLIS [industrial method] See Atomic vapor laser isotope separation in this index
Avocado [fruit] A: 993 with picture
Fruit (Subtropical fruits) F: 546 with picture
Rain forest (Economic value) R: 126c
Avocet [bird] A: 993 with picture
Bird picture on B: 344e
National Wildlife Refuge System picture on N: 62
Avogadro, Amedeo [Italian physicist] A: 994
Chemistry (Development of physical chemistry)

C: 404
Gas [physics] (Gas laws) **G:** 48-49
Avogadro constant [physics]
Gas [physics] (Avogadro's law) **G:** 49
Mole **M:** 691
Avogadro's law [physics]
Avogadro, Amedeo **A:** 994
Chemistry (Development of physical chemistry) **C:** 404
Gas [physics] (Gas laws) **G:** 48-49
Avoirdupois [measurement] **A:** 994
Weights and measures (table: Weight and mass) **W:** 187
Avoirdupois pound [measurement]
Pound **P:** 721
Avon, Earl of [British political leader] *See* Eden, Sir Anthony *in this index*
Avon, River [England] **A:** 994
Avondale Shipyard [Louisiana]
New Orleans (Industry) **N:** 282-283 *with picture*
Avril, Prosper [Haitian political leader]
Haiti (History) **H:** 15-17
Avro Vulcan bomber
Aircraft, Military *picture on* **A:** 205
Avtalyon [Israel]
Israel (Rural life) *picture on* **I:** 481
Avvakum [Russian author]
Russian literature (Western influences) **R:** 559
Avventura, L' [film]
Antonioni, Michelangelo **A:** 561
AWACS [defense] *See* Airborne Warning and Control System *in this index*
Awake and Sing! [play by Odets]
Odets, Clifford **O:** 674
Awakening, The [novel by Chopin]
American literature (Women writers) **A:** 420
Chopin, Kate **C:** 521
Awakening Land, The [trilogy by Richter]
Richter, Conrad **R:** 333
Awami League [political party]
Bangladesh (East Pakistan) **B:** 85-86
Mujibur Rahman **M:** 912
Award [labor]
Arbitration **A:** 592
Awards and prizes
Caldecott Medal **C:** 26
FFA (Awards) **F:** 86
Literature for children (Awards) **L:** 367
Medals, decorations, and orders **M:** 355 *with pictures*
Motion picture (Festivals and awards) **M:** 861
Newbery Medal **N:** 358
Nobel Prizes **N:** 439
Pulitzer Prizes **P:** 886a
Regina Medal **R:** 206
Spingarn Medal **So:** 793
Television (Television awards) **T:** 116; (International television awards) **T:** 117
Awn [botany] *See* Beard *in this index*
AWOL [military law]
Amnesty (Since the early 1900's) **A:** 437
Desertion **D:** 157
Ax [tool] **A:** 994
Fire department (Trucks and vehicles) **F:** 126-127 *with picture*
Tomahawk **T:** 324
Ax [weapon]
Vikings (Weapons and armor) **V:** 382
Axel [skating]
Ice skating *diagram on* **I:** 12
Axel, Richard [American physiologist]
Nobel Prizes (Physiology or medicine: 2004) **N:** 447
Axelrod, Julius [American physiologist]
Nobel Prizes (Physiology or medicine: 1970) **N:** 446
Axel's Castle [book by Wilson]
Wilson, Edmund **W:** 316
Axial-flow compressor [machine]
Jet propulsion (Turbojet) **J:** 111
Axial-flow pump [machine]
Pump (Axial-flow pumps) **P:** 900b
Axial rib [zoology]
Shell *diagram on* **S:** 385
Axial skeleton [anatomy]
Mammal (Skeleton) **M:** 118
Skeleton (The axial skeleton) **S:** 479 *with diagrams*
Axillary artery [anatomy]
Human body **H:** 422 *with diagram*
Axiom [geometry] **A:** 994
Geometry (Axiomatic system) **G:** 102
Axion [physics]
Dark matter **D:** 37
Axis [alliance] **A:** 994
Germany (Nazi Germany) **G:** 167-168
World War II **W:** 468

Axis [botany]
Germination **G:** 173
Axis [mathematics]
Geometry (Analytic geometry) **G:** 105 *with diagrams*
Parabola **P:** 141 *with diagram*
Axis [mechanics]
Gyroscope (Gyroscopic inertia) **G:** 453 *with diagram*
Moon (The movements of the moon) **M:** 783
Planet *diagram on* **P:** 509; (Rotation) **P:** 510
Axis, of Earth
Climate (Changes in the earth's orbit) **Ci:** 677 *with diagram*
Earth (How Earth moves) **E:** 17 *with diagram*
Season (The four seasons) **S:** 271 *with diagram*
Axis deer *See* Chital *in this index*
Axis of symmetry [physics]
Symmetry (An axis of symmetry) **So:** 1066 *with diagram*
Axis Sally [American public figure]
World War II (Propaganda) **W:** 494-495
Axle [mechanism] *See* Wheel and axle *in this index*
Axminster [floor covering]
Rugs and carpets (Weaving) **R:** 515-516; (History) **R:** 517
Axon [anatomy]
Brain (The cerebrum) **B:** 550a-550b; (How neurons work) **B:** 557 *with diagram*
Myelin **M:** 970f
Nervous system *diagrams on* **N:** 134; (Parts of a neuron) **N:** 133
Axson, Ellen Louise [wife of Woodrow Wilson] *See* Wilson, Ellen Axson *in this index*
Axum [ancient history] *See* Aksum *in this index*
Ayacucho, Battle of [1824]
Sucre, Antonio José de **So:** 951
Ayatollah [title]
Khomeini, Ruhollah **K:** 308b
Ayckbourn, Alan [British playwright] **A:** 994 *with portrait*
Aycock, Charles Brantley [American educator] **A:** 995
North Carolina (Schools) **N:** 476-477; (table) **N:** 490; (The early 1900's) **N:** 493
Aye-aye [animal] **A:** 995 *with picture*
Primate (Aye-ayes) **P:** 778 *with picture*
Ayer & Son, N. W. [agency]
Advertising (The development of advertising agencies) **A:** 79
Ayers, Jake, Sr. [American public figure]
Mississippi (The early 2000's) **M:** 645
Ayers, Roy E. [American political leader]
Montana (table) **M:** 757
Ayers Rock [Australia] *See* Uluru *in this index*
Ayllón, Lucas Vásquez de [Spanish settler] **A:** 995
Hispanic Americans (Exploration and settlement) **H:** 250
North Carolina (Exploration and settlement) **N:** 490
South Carolina (Exploration and settlement) **So:** 659
Ayllu [family group]
Inca (Family and social life) **I:** 96
Aylwin Azócar, Patricio [Chilean political leader]
Chile (Crisis and democracy) **C:** 470
Aymara Indians
Bolivia (History) **B:** 446
La Paz **L:** 72 *with picture*
Peru (Languages) **P:** 309
'Ayn [letter]
O **O:** 634 *with picture*
Ayodhya [India]
India (Religious and ethnic unrest) **I:** 134
Ayodhya [kingdom]
Rama **R:** 131
Ramayana **R:** 132
Ayrault, Jean-Marc [French political leader]
France (Recent developments) **F:** 478
Ayrshire [cattle]
Cattle (Ayrshire) **C:** 310 *with picture*; (table) **C:** 313
Dairying (Dairy products) **D:** 5-6
Ayub Khan, Mohammad [Pakistani political leader]
India (India under Indira Gandhi) **I:** 133
Pakistan (Independence) **P:** 99
Ayudhya [Thailand] *See* Ayutthaya *in this index*
Ayuntamiento [building]
Manila (History) **M:** 143
Ayurvedic medicine [India]
India (The golden age) **I:** 129
Medicine (China and India) **M:** 372
Ayutthaya [ancient city]
Thailand (Early kingdoms) **T:** 226
Ayutthaya [kingdom]
Thailand (History) **T:** 226
Ayyubid dynasty [Egyptian history]

Cairo (History) **C:** 17-18
Egypt (Muslim rule) **E:** 130
Azadirachtin [compound]
Neem tree **N:** 119
Azalea [plant] **A:** 995
Flower (Flowering shrubs) **F:** 281 *with picture*
Poisonous plant (Some poisonous plants) **P:** 602
Azali Assoumani [Comoran political leader]
Comoros (History) **C:** 900-901
Azande [people]
Magic (Magical actions) **M:** 49
Azarian, Mary [American illustrator]
Caldecott Medal (table: 1999) **C:** 26
Azathioprine [drug]
Transplant (Preventing rejection) **T:** 380-381
Azerbaijan **A:** 996, **A:** 996 *with picture and map*
Armenia (History) **A:** 718b
Caucasus **C:** 317
Azerbaijani [language]
Azerbaijan (People) **A:** 996
Azerbaijanis [people]
Armenia (History) **A:** 718b
Azerbaijan (People) **A:** 996
Union of Soviet Socialist Republics (People) **U:** 31
Azimuth [navigation] **A:** 998
Azimuthal mount [astronomy]
Telescope (Controlling a telescope) **T:** 105
Azinger, Paul [American golfer]
Golf (U.S. PGA Championship) **G:** 265
Azithromycin [drug]
Antibiotic (table) **A:** 551
Aziz, Mohamed Ould Abdel [Mauritanian military leader]
Mauritania (History) **M:** 315-316
Azores [islands, Atlantic] **A:** 998 *with maps*
Portugal **P:** 686
Azorín [Spanish author]
Spanish literature (The Generation of 1898) **So:** 762
Azov, Port of [Black Sea]
Peter I, the Great (Foreign policy) **P:** 324
Azov, Sea of [Russia] **A:** 998
Black Sea **B:** 390 *with map*
AZT [drug]
AIDS (Treatment) **A:** 164b; (Prevention) **A:** 165
Aztec [people] **A:** 999 *with pictures and maps*
Agriculture (In the Americas) **A:** 157
Architecture (Pre-Columbian architecture) **A:** 614
Chocolate (History) **C:** 519
Clothing (Maya and Aztec) **Ci:** 700
Cortés, Hernán (Arrival in Mexico) **Ci:** 1072-1073 *with map*
Exploration (Spain's conquests in the New World) **E:** 445 *with diagram*
Hieroglyphics (Other hieroglyphic writing) **H:** 227
Hispanic Americans (In Mexico) **H:** 247
Indian, American **I:** 136 *with picture, pictures on* **I:** 140, **I:** 178a; (Empires and states) **I:** 144; (Why the Indians fought) **I:** 144-145; (Weapons) **I:** 144; (Religion) **I:** 146-147 *with picture*; (Trading centers) **I:** 149 *with picture*; (Writing) **I:** 150; (Indians of Middle America) **I:** 169 *with pictures*
Latin America *pictures on* **L:** 103, **L:** 106 ; (Early inhabitants) **L:** 102; (The conquest of the American Indians) **L:** 103
Manuscript *picture on* **M:** 173
Mexico (The Toltec and the Aztec) **M:** 468 *with map*; (The Spanish conquest) **M:** 469
Mexico City (City of the Aztec) **M:** 478
Mixtec Indians **M:** 680
Montezuma II **M:** 764b *with picture*
Mythology *picture on* **M:** 973; (Aztec mythology) **M:** 987 *with picture*
Tenochtitlan **T:** 167
Teotihuacán **T:** 169
Tlaxcala **T:** 303
Toltec Indians **T:** 323
World, History of the (Civilizations in the Americas) **W:** 437
Aztec Calendar Stone [sculpture]
Aztec (Arts and crafts) **A:** 1001 *with picture*
Aztec Eagle, Order of the
Medals, decorations, and orders (table) **M:** 359 *with picture*
Aztec Ruins National Monument [New Mexico] **A:** 1004
National Park System (table: National monuments) **N:** 50
Aztec-Tanoan [language group]
Aztec (Language) **A:** 1002
Indian, American (Language groups) **I:** 149-150
Aztlan [Aztec region]
Aztec (The Aztec migration) **A:** 1003
Aztreonam [drug]
Antibiotic (Antibacterial antibiotics) **A:** 550
Azucena [opera character]

Opera: (Trovatore, Il) O: 808
Azuela, Mariano [Mexican author]
Latin American literature (The early 1900's) **L:** 113
Azul... [book by Darío]
Darío, Rubén **D:** 36
Latin American literature (Modernism) **L:** 113
Azure [color]
Heraldry (Expansion) **H:** 194 *with picture*
Azurite [mineral] **A:** 1004
Mineral *picture on* **M:** 569
Azusa Street Apostolic Faith Mission
Pentecostal churches (Major Pentecostal churches) **P:** 275

B

B [letter] **B:** 1 *with pictures*
B [symbol]
Boron **B:** 490
B-1 [airplane]
Air Force, United States (Bombers) **A:** 191
Carter, Jimmy (Early programs) **C:** 257
B-1B [airplane]
Aircraft, Military (Bombers) **A:** 202 *with picture*
B-2 bomber [airplane]
Air Force, United States *picture on* **A:** 192; (Bombers) **A:** 191
Aircraft, Military (Bombers) **A:** 202
Bomber **B:** 454
B2B transaction *See* Business-to-business transaction *in this index*
B-15 [iceberg]
Iceberg (Antarctic icebergs) **I:** 17
B-17 [airplane]
Airplane *picture on* **A:** 234
Bomber (History) **B:** 453
World War II *pictures on* **W:** 481, **W:** 485; (The air war) **W:** 482
B-29 [airplane]
Bomber (History) **B:** 453
B-52 [airplane]
Air Force, United States (Bombers) **A:** 191
Vietnam War (The opposing forces) **V:** 375 *with picture*
B-52's [rock group]
Rock music (New wave and mainstream rock) **R:** 380c
B-58 Hustler [airplane]
Airplane *picture on* **A:** 237; (Supersonic airplanes) **A:** 238
B cell [physiology]
Blood (Protecting against disease) **B:** 410; (Formation of new blood components) **B:** 411
Disease (Immune responses) **D:** 231-232
Epstein-Barr virus **E:** 345
Immune system *diagram on* **I:** 88b; (Parts of the immune system) **I:** 87; (The immune response) **I:** 88 *with diagram*
Monoclonal antibody **M:** 731
Thymus **T:** 274
Virus (Immune response) **V:** 428a
B complex *See* Vitamin B complex *in this index*
B. F. Goodrich Company *See* Goodrich Company, B. F. *in this index*
B lymphocyte [physiology] *See* B cell *in this index*
B quark [physics] *See* Bottom quark *in this index*
Ba [symbol]
Barium **B:** 110
Baal [Canaanite god] **B:** 2
Phoenicia (Religion) **P:** 393
Ba'al Shem Tov [Jewish religious leader] **B:** 2
Jews (Eastern European religious movements) **J:** 123
Baalbek [Lebanon]
Lebanon (Ancient times) **L:** 172
Baalzebub [name for]
Beelzebub **B:** 211
Baath Party [political party]
Hussein, Saddam **H:** 457
Iraq (The republic) **I:** 414
Syria (National government) **So:** 1070
Báb [Iranian religious leader]
Bahá'ís **B:** 214
Bahá'u'lláh **B:** 28
Bab Ballads [poems by Gilbert]
Gilbert, Sir William Schwenck **G:** 189
Gilbert and Sullivan **G:** 190
Babangida, Ibrahim Badamosi [Nigerian political leader]
Nigeria (Changes in government) **N:** 418
Babar [Mughal emperor] *See* Babur *in this index*
Babb, Belle Aurelia [American educator]
Mansfield, Arabella Babb **M:** 166
Babbage, Charles [British mathematician] **B:** 2
Computer (Punched-card devices) **Ci:** 924a-924b
Mathematics (In the 1800's) **M:** 307
Babbine Chief [painting by Kane]
Indian, American *picture on* **I:** 162

Babbitt [book by Lewis]
American literature (Satirists) **A:** 422
Lewis, Sinclair **L:** 221
Babbitt, Bruce E. [American political leader]
Arizona (table) **A:** 687
Clinton, Bill (table) **Ci:** 682d
Interior, Department of the (table) **I:** 325
Babbitt, George F. [literary figure]
Lewis, Sinclair **L:** 221
Babbitt, Isaac [American inventor]
Babbitt metals **B:** 2
Babbitt, Milton [American composer]
Classical music (Atonal music) **Ci:** 649-650
Babbitt metals B: 2
Bearing (Plain bearings) **B:** 188
Lead (Uses) **L:** 149
Babbler [bird] **B:** 2 *with picture*
Babcock, Alpheus [American inventor]
Piano (History) **P:** 447-448
Babcock, Orville [American government official]
Grant, Ulysses S. (Foreign relations) **G:** 316; (Government frauds) **G:** 317
Babcock, Stephen Moulton [American chemist]
Milk (History of the milk industry) **M:** 549
Babcock, Tim M. [American political leader]
Montana (table) **M:** 757
Babcock State Park [West Virginia]
United States *picture on* **U:** 120
Babe [fictional animal]
Bunyan, Paul **B:** 701
Minnesota (Places to visit) **M:** 594
Babe Ruth League
Baseball (Amateur leagues) **B:** 131-132
Babel, Isaak Emanuilovich [Russian author]
Russian literature (The period of rebirth) **R:** 564
Babel, Tower of [Babylon] *See* Tower of Babel *in this index*
Babelthuap [island, Palau]
Melekeok **M:** 389
Babenberg [European history]
Austria (Early years) **A:** 936
Babes in Toyland [operetta by Herbert]
Herbert, Victor **H:** 197
"Babi Yar" [poem by Yevtushenko]
Yevtushenko, Yevgeny **Y:** 565
Babi Yar [Soviet Union] **B:** 3
Babies'-breath [plant] *See* Baby's-breath *in this index*
Babies'-slippers [plant] *See* Bird's-foot trefoil *in this index*
Babine Lake [British Columbia]
British Columbia (Rivers, waterfalls, and lakes) **B:** 624
Babirusa [animal] **B:** 3 *with picture*
Baboon [animal] **B:** 3 *with picture*
Monkey *picture on* **M:** 726; (Group life) **M:** 728-729; (Communication) **M:** 729
Primate (Old World monkeys) **P:** 778a
Babouche [clothing]
Shoe *picture on* **S:** 432
Baboushka and the Three Kings [book by Sidjakov and Robbins]
Sidjakov, Nicolas **S:** 448 *with picture*
Babur [Mughal emperor] **B:** 3
Akbar **A:** 253
India (History) **I:** 131; (The Mughal Empire) **I:** 129
Mongol Empire (Breakup) **M:** 721
Mughal Empire **M:** 910
Muslims *picture on* **M:** 965; (The Mughal Empire) **M:** 964d
Punjab (History) **P:** 903-904
Baby B: 4 *with pictures*
See also Child *in this index*
Apgar, Virginia **A:** 564
Apgar score **A:** 565
Blue baby **B:** 419
Cerebral palsy **C:** 361
Colic **Ci:** 772
Fairy (Fairies and people) **F:** 11
Gonorrhea **G:** 268
Heart (Birth defects) **H:** 140
Herpes, Genital **H:** 214
Incubator (Incubators for babies) **I:** 106
Infant mortality **I:** 264
Infanticide **I:** 264
Neonatology **N:** 124
Pregnancy (Prenatal care) **P:** 734b
Reproduction, Human **R:** 244 *with picture*; (The newborn infant) **R:** 249 *with picture*
Sexuality (Before birth) **S:** 338
Shaken baby syndrome **S:** 343
Sleep (Human sleep patterns) **S:** 506
Sudden infant death syndrome **So:** 956
Thalidomide **T:** 229
Toy (Toys for infants) **T:** 353
"Baby, It's Cold Outside" [song by Loesser]
Loesser, Frank **L:** 420

Baby and Child Care [book by Spock]
Spock, Benjamin McLane **So:** 797
Baby Bells [companies]
Telephone (Competition in the U.S. telephone industry) **T:** 101
Baby blues [disorder]
Postpartum depression **P:** 709
Baby boom generation [demography] **B:** 11
Family (Changes) **F:** 23-24
Generation X **G:** 84
Local government (Population changes) **L:** 407-408
National debt (Economic growth and rising national debt) **N:** 34
Population (United States population) **P:** 673
Social security (Funding issues) **So:** 555
Teaching (Job opportunities) **T:** 68
United States (Population) **U:** 108-109
Baby box [psychology]
Skinner, B. F. **S:** 495
Baby doll [toy]
Doll (Wax dolls) **D:** 290; (Porcelain dolls) **D:** 290-291
Baby house
Dollhouse **D:** 296
Baby One More Time [recording]
Spears, Britney **S:** 769
Baby Snooks [stage role]
Brice, Fanny **B:** 597
Baby teeth
Teeth (Deciduous teeth) **T:** 79 *with picture*
Babylon [ancient city] **B:** 11 *with picture*
Alexander the Great (Return westward) **A:** 343-344
Communication *picture on* **Ci:** 880
Employment agency **E:** 263
Mythology *picture on* **M:** 976; (Babylonian mythology) **M:** 978
Babylon, Hanging Gardens of *See* Hanging Gardens of Babylon *in this index*
Babylonia [ancient civilization] **B:** 13 *with map*
See also the list of Related articles in the Babylonia *article*
Architecture (Mesopotamian architecture) **A:** 611
Army (Ancient armies) **A:** 726
Asia (The Tigris-Euphrates Valley) **A:** 804
Astrology (History) **A:** 827
Astronomy (History) **A:** 846-847
Book (Early books) **B:** 465
Calendar (History) **C:** 30
Chaldeans **C:** 369 *with map*
Fraction (History) **F:** 449
Geometry (History) **G:** 106
Hammurabi **H:** 35
Jerusalem (Ancient times) **J:** 100
Law (Early developments in the East) **L:** 133
Map (Ancient maps) **M:** 182
Mathematics (Early civilization) **M:** 303
Mythology *pictures on* **M:** 976, **M:** 990; (Babylonian mythology) **M:** 978
Number (The Babylonians) **N:** 606
Palestine (Invasions and conquests) **P:** 104
Phoenicia (Foreign control) **P:** 394
Pythagorean theorem (Origins) **P:** 921
Science (Early civilizations) **S:** 196
Babylonian Captivity [papal history]
Pope (The troubles of the papacy) **P:** 664
Reformation (Religious causes) **R:** 196
Babylonian Captivity of the Church, The [book by Luther]
Luther, Martin (The break with the Roman Catholic Church) **L:** 528
Babylonian Exile [Jewish history]
Ezekiel, Book of **E:** 470
Ezra, Book of **E:** 470
Isaiah, Book of **I:** 462
Jews (Foreign domination) **J:** 121
Joel, Book of **J:** 130
Kings, Books of **K:** 330
Nebuchadnezzar II **N:** 116
Old Testament (Origins) **O:** 740-741
Baby's Bouquet, The [book]
Crane, Walter **Ci:** 1120
Literature for children (The rise of illustration) **L:** 364
Baby's-breath [plant] **B:** 14 *with picture*
Baby's Opera [book]
Literature for children (The rise of illustration) **L:** 364
BAC [measure] *See* Blood alcohol concentration *in this index*
Baca, Elfego [Mexican-American frontiersman] **B:** 14 *with portrait*
Baca, Jimmy Santiago [American poet]
American literature (Diverse voices) **A:** 424
Bacar, Mohamed [Comoran political leader]
Comoros (History) **C:** 900-901
Baccalauréat [test]

France (Education) F: 460-461
Baccalaureate [education]
Graduation G: 297
Baccarat [gambling]
Gambling (Baccarat) G: 21
Baccarat glass
Glass (Types of art glass) G: 220
Bacchanalia [custom]
Bacchus B: 15
Bacchus [Roman mythology] **B: 15**
See also Dionysus *in this index*
Faun F: 56
Mythology (table) M: 981
Bach, Anna Magdalena [wife of]
Bach, Johann Sebastian (His life) B: 15-16
Bach, Carl Philipp Emanuel [German composer]
B: 15
Bach, Johann Christian [German composer] B: 15
Bach, Johann Sebastian [German composer] B: 15
with portrait
Buxtehude, Dietrich B: 745
Canon C: 182
Cantata C: 183
Classical music *picture on* Ci: 648; (The Baroque
period) Ci: 647
Couperin, François Ci: 1100
Mendelssohn, Felix M: 399
Passion music P: 191
Vivaldi, Antonio V: 433
Bach, Maria Barbara [wife of]
Bach, Johann Sebastian (His life) B: 15
Bach, Wilhelm Friedemann [son of]
Bach, Johann Sebastian (His life) B: 15
Bache, Sarah Franklin [daughter of]
Franklin, Benjamin (Printer) F: 487
Bachelet, Michelle [Chilean political leader] B: 17
with portrait
Chile (Recent developments) C: 470
Latin America (In the early 2000's) L: 111
Bachelor herd [zoology]
Impala I: 90
Bachelor's-button [flower] B: 17
Flower *picture on* F: 276
Bachelor's degree
Degree, College (The bachelor's degree) D: 92
Education (Higher education) E: 92
Universities and colleges (Degrees) U: 209
Bachianas Brasileiras [music by Villa-Lobos]
Brazil (The arts) B: 576-577
Bachman, John [American naturalist]
Audubon, John James (His works) A: 885
Bacillary dysentery [disease] *See* Shigellosis *in
this index*
Bacilli [bacteriology]
Bacteria (The structure of bacteria) B: 20-21 *with
picture*
Bacillus anthracis [bacteria]
Anthrax A: 545
Bacteriology (History) B: 22
Bacillus thuringiensis [bacteria]
Genetically modified food G: 85
Mosquito (Mosquitoes and people) M: 834
Back [anatomy] **B: 17**
Back Bay [district, Boston]
Boston (Back Bay) B: 497 *with picture*
Back bench [politics]
Parliament (How the House of Commons works)
P: 173
Back crawl
Swimming *pictures on* So: 1044; (The basic
strokes) So: 1043
Back-formation [language]
Slang (Shortened or lengthened words) S: 499
Back Home [book by Pinkney]
Literature for children *picture on* L: 370
Back Home, April 1865 [painting by Lea]
Reconstruction *picture on* R: 176
Back judge
Football (The officials) F: 362
Back-lift
Cricket (The batting side) Ci: 1133
Back lighting
Photography (Direction) P: 415 *with picture*
Back lot
Motion picture (Filming on location) M: 852
Back stroke [cricket]
Cricket (The batting side) Ci: 1133-1134 *with
picture*
Back swamp
River (Flood plains) R: 353
Back-to-Africa movement [U.S. history]
Garvey, Marcus G: 47
Back to basics [education]
Curriculum (Curriculum changes) Ci: 1197
"Back to Normalcy" [slogan]
Harding, Warren Gamaliel H: 56
Backache B: 17

Back B: 17
Backband [harness]
Harness *diagram on* H: 63
Backboard [basketball]
Basketball (The court) B: 143 *with diagrams*
Backbone [anatomy] *See* Spine *in this index*
Backbone Mountain [Maryland]
Maryland (Land regions) M: 250
Backcombing
Hairdressing (The 1900's) H: 12
Backcourt [basketball]
Basketball (Basketball terms) B: 145
Backfield [football]
Football (The offensive team) F: 356 *with
diagrams*
Backfire
Forestry (Fire and forests) F: 407
Backflow prevention device
Plumbing (The water supply system) P: 577
Backgammon [game] **B: 17** *with picture*
Background
Reading (Comprehending what is perceived)
R: 157
Background artist
Animation (Traditional animation) A: 512 *with
picture*
Background extinction [biology]
Extinction (Background extinction) E: 456
Prehistoric animal (Evolution and extinction)
P: 742
Backhand drive [tennis]
Tennis *pictures on* T: 164; (The ball in play) T: 163
Backing [material]
Rugs and carpets (Materials used in rugs and
carpets) R: 514; (Tufting) R: 515
Backing fabric
Embroidery (Materials) E: 256
Backlight [electronics]
Computer (Monitors) Ci: 916
Backpack [equipment]
Camping *picture on* C: 93
Backpacking [sport]
Hiking H: 230
BackRub [search engine]
Google Inc. G: 270
Backsaw [tool]
Saw (Handsaws) S: 166 *with picture*
Woodworking (Cutting) W: 397 *with picture*
Backstroke [swimming]
Swimming *pictures on* So: 1044; (The basic
strokes) So: 1043
Backswimmer [insect]
Insect *picture on* I: 281
Water bug W: 133
Backwoods brag
Crockett, Davy (The legends) Ci: 1148d
Backwoods preacher
Circuit rider C: 559
Backyard croquet [game]
Croquet Ci: 1154
Bacon [food] **B: 18**
Bacon, Francis [English philosopher] **B: 18** *with
portrait*
Enlightenment (Influence of the Enlightenment)
E: 326b
Essay (Formal essays) E: 359
Philosophy (Modern philosophy) P: 388
Prose P: 828
Science (The scientific revolution) S: 198
Bacon, Francis [British painter] **B: 18**
Bacon, Henry [American architect]
Lincoln Memorial L: 328 *with picture*
Bacon, Nathaniel [American colonial leader] **B: 19**
Bacon's Rebellion B: 19
Virginia *picture on* V: 420; (Westward expansion)
V: 418
Bacon, Robert [American government official]
Roosevelt, Theodore (table) R: 466
Bacon, Roger [English philosopher] **B: 19**
Airplane (Early experiments and ideas) A: 229-
230
Ornithopter O: 858
Physics (The Middle Ages) P: 438
Bacon, Roger S. [Canadian political leader]
Nova Scotia (table) N: 567
Bacon, Walter W. [American political leader]
Delaware (table) D: 109
Bacon's Rebellion [U.S. history] **B: 19**
Bacon, Nathaniel B: 19
Berkeley, Sir William B: 259
House of Burgesses H: 384
Jamestown J: 29
Virginia *picture on* V: 420
Bacteria [biology] **B: 19** *with pictures*
Animal A: 468
Archaea A: 593
Bacteriology B: 22

Biofilm B: 311
Campylobacter C: 97
Cell (Shapes of cells) C: 328; (Bacteria) C: 330
Chlamydia C: 516
Classification, Scientific (Groups in classification)
Ci: 655
Deep sea (Deep-sea life) D: 82a
Domain D: 300
E. coli E: 2
Environmental pollution (Water pollution) E: 334
Eutrophication (How eutrophication occurs)
E: 421
Flagellum F: 224 *with picture*
Food preservation (How food spoils) F: 341
Kingdom K: 328
Life *picture on* L: 274
Microbiology M: 513
Ocean (The food cycle) O: 655-658
Photosynthesis P: 430
Prokaryote P: 817
Saprophyte S: 122
Spore (Bacterial spores) So: 802 *with diagram*
Streptococcus So: 926
Toxin T: 353
Virus V: 427
Diseases and pathology
Antibiotic A: 550
Blood (Protecting against disease) B: 410 *with
pictures*
Brucellosis B: 648
Cephalosporin C: 359
Disease *picture on* D: 229; (Bacterial diseases)
D: 227; (Fighting disease) D: 231; (Medical
treatment) D: 232
Food poisoning F: 340
Gonorrhea G: 268
Heart (Inflammatory heart disease) H: 142
Human body *picture on* H: 417
Immune system I: 87
Legionnaires' disease L: 184
Leprosy (Causes) L: 204
Listeria L: 349
Lyme disease L: 533
Meningitis M: 400
Parasite P: 153
Pneumonia (How pneumonia develops) P: 586
Sexually transmitted disease S: 338b
Stomach (Peptic ulcers) So: 908
Strep throat So: 925
Tuberculosis T: 477 *with pictures*
Divisions
Ampicillin A: 443
Penicillin P: 240
Sterilization So: 894
Streptomycin So: 926
History
Lederberg, Joshua L: 175
Lister, Sir Joseph L: 349
Pasteur, Louis P: 193
Uses
Cheese (Separating the curd) C: 392
Decay D: 67
Drug (Genes and bacteria) D: 355
Fermentation F: 73
Genetic engineering (Uses of genetic
engineering) G: 84b-84c
Legume L: 185
Bacterial blight [disease]
Soybean (Diseases and pests) So: 692
Bacterial endocarditis [disorder]
Heart (Inflammatory heart disease) H: 142
Bacterial meningitis [disease]
Meningitis M: 400
Bacterial pustule [disease]
Soybean (Diseases and pests) So: 692
Bacterial spore [biology]
Bacteria (Where bacteria live) B: 21
Bacterial vaginosis [disease]
Pelvic inflammatory disease P: 233
Bacteriological warfare *See* Chemical-biological-
radiological warfare *in this index*
Bacteriology [science] **B: 22**
Biology (table) B: 317
Koch, Robert K: 360
Bacteriophage [biology]
Virus (Structure) V: 427-428 *with picture*
Bactria [ancient region]
Afghanistan (Early invasions) A: 95
Bactrian camel [animal]
Camel C: 76; (Camels and people) C: 77 *with
picture*
Camel's-hair cloth C: 79
Bad Aachen [resort]
Aachen A: 2
Bad Beginning, The [book by Snicket]
Snicket, Lemony S: 538
Bad Child's Book of Beasts, The [book by Belloc]

Belloc, Hilaire **B:** 244
Bad conduct discharge
Military discharge **M:** 543
Bad Godesberg [district, Germany]
Bonn (The city) **B:** 460
Bad Seed, The [play by Anderson]
Anderson, Maxwell **A:** 452
Badawi, Abdullah bin Ahmad [Malaysian political leader]
Malaysia (Recent developments) **M:** 102-103
Baddeleyite [mineral]
Zirconium **Z:** 596
Baden-Baden [Germany] **B:** 23
Baden-Powell, Agnes [British social reformer]
Baden-Powell, Lord **B:** 23
Girl Guides **G:** 195
Baden-Powell, Lord [British social reformer] **B:** 23
Boy Scouts **B:** 534
Girl Guides **G:** 195
Girl Scouts (History) **G:** 200
Baden-Powell, Olave [British social worker]
Girl Scouts (History) **G:** 200
Baden-Powell, Robert Stephenson Smyth *See* Baden-Powell, Lord *in this index*
Badge [emblem]
Air Force, United States *pictures on* **A:** 189
Boy Scouts *pictures on* **B:** 536
Flag (table) **F:** 193
Girl Scouts *pictures on* **G:** 198
Knighthood, Orders of (Honorary orders) **K:** 347 *with pictures*
Badge of Military Merit *See* Purple Heart *in this index*
Badger [animal] **B:** 23 *with picture*
Badger, George Edmund [American government official]
Harrison, William Henry (table) **H:** 76
Tyler, John (table) **T:** 534
Badger, William [American political leader]
New Hampshire (table) **N:** 223
Badger State [nickname]
Wisconsin **W:** 347
Badi II Abu Daqn [sultan of Funj]
Funj Sultanate **F:** 560
Badlands [geology] **B:** 24
Alberta (Places to visit) **A:** 320 *with picture*
North Dakota *picture on* **N:** 508
South Dakota (The Great Plains) **So:** 674 *with map*
Badlands [book by Kroetsch]
Canadian literature (Modern English-Canadian fiction) **C:** 160
Badlands National Park [South Dakota] **B:** 24
National Park System (table: National parks) **N:** 48
South Dakota *picture on* **So:** 673
Badminton [game] **B:** 24 *with pictures*
Olympic Games (Summer Olympic Games) **O:** 746e
Badoglio, Pietro [Italian political leader]
Italo-Ethiopian War **I:** 495
World War II (The invasion of Italy) **W:** 483
Badwater [region, California]
Death Valley **D:** 62 *with picture*
BAE Systems [company]
Aviation (Aircraft manufacturing) **A:** 984
United Kingdom (Manufacturing) **U:** 63-64
Baeda [English historian] *See* Bede, Saint *in this index*
Baekeland, Leo Hendrik [American chemist] **B:** 25
Phenolic **P:** 356
Plastics (The invention of Bakelite) **P:** 559
Baer, Karl Ernst von [German scientist] **B:** 25
Baer, Max [American boxer]
Braddock, James J. **B:** 543 *with picture*
Baer, Ralph [German-born engineer]
Electronic game (History) **E:** 204d
Baeyer, Adolf von [German chemist]
Indigo **I:** 223
Nobel Prizes (Chemistry: 1905) **N:** 442
Baez, Joan [American singer] **B:** 25
Baez, Mimi [American musician]
Baez, Joan **B:** 25
Baffin, William [English explorer] **B:** 25
Baffin Island [Nunavut] **B:** 25 *with map*
Nunavut (Land and resources) **N:** 609 *with picture and map*
Bag [packaging]
Packaging **P:** 18
Paper bag **P:** 138
Bag ammunition
Ammunition (Artillery ammunition) **A:** 435-436
Bag wig
Hairdressing (The 1700's) **H:** 12
Baganda [people] *See* Ganda *in this index*
Bagasse [fiber]
Grass (Sugar cane) **G:** 326
Bagaza, Jean-Baptiste [Burundi political leader]

Burundi (History) **B:** 713-714
Bagby, Arthur P. [American political leader]
Alabama (table) **A:** 274
Baggage
Airplane *picture on* **A:** 218
Airport (Airline passenger services) **A:** 246
Baggage handler [occupation]
Airport (Airline passenger services) **A:** 246
Baghdad [Iraq] **B:** 26 *with picture*
Iraq **I:** 408 *with picture;* (The Iraq War) **I:** 414a
Iraq War (Military action) **I:** 414d *with picture*
Muslims (The Abbāsids) **M:** 964c
Persian Gulf War of 1991 (The air war) **P:** 300c *with picture*
World, History of the (The Islamic world) **W:** 434-435
Baghdad Battery [artifact]
Battery (History) **B:** 170
Baghdad Pact [1955]
Cold War (To the brink and back) **Ci:** 765
Iraq (The 1950's) **I:** 413-414
Baghouse [device]
Incinerator **I:** 100
Bagley, John J. [American political leader]
Michigan (table) **M:** 507
Bagnell Dam [Osage River, Missouri]
Lake of the Ozarks **L:** 42 *with map*
Missouri (Progress as a state) **M:** 671
Bagpipe [musical instrument] **B:** 26 *with pictures*
Scotland *picture on* **S:** 214; (The arts) **S:** 215-217
Bagrat III [king of Abkhazia]
Abkhazia **A:** 11
Baguio City [Philippines] **B:** 27
Baguirmi [former kingdom]
Chad (History) **C:** 367
Bagzane, Mount [Niger]
Niger (Land and climate) **N:** 408
Bahadur, Jung [Nepalese political leader]
Nepal (History) **N:** 126
Bahá'í House of Worship [Wilmette, Illinois]
Bahá'ís *picture on* **B:** 27
Bahá'ís [religious group] **B:** 27 *with picture*
Bahá'u'lláh **B:** 27
Iran (Religion) **I:** 401
Bahamas [islands] **B:** 28 *with picture and map*
Columbus, Christopher (The first landing) **Ci:** 860
Flag *picture on* **F:** 200
West Indies **W:** 201
Bahamonde, Francisco Franco [Spanish political leader]
Franco, Francisco (His early life) **F:** 483
Bahasa Indonesia [language]
Indonesia **I:** 226; (People) **I:** 227
Malay language **M:** 98
Bahasa Malaysia [language]
Malay language **M:** 98
Malaysia (People) **M:** 98b-98c
Bahá'u'lláh [Persian religious leader] **B:** 27
Bahá'ís **B:** 27
Bahia [Brazil] *See* Salvador *in this index*
Bahia grass
Lawn (Types of lawns) **L:** 142
Bahia wood [tree]
Brazilwood **B:** 587
Bahr al Jabal [river, Africa] *See* White Nile *in this index*
Bahrain **B:** 29 *with picture and map*
Flag *picture on* **F:** 202
Middle East **M:** 530
Bahram Gur Hunting the Wild Ass [painting]
Painting (Islamic painting) **P:** 48 *with picture*
Bahutu [people] *See* Hutu *in this index*
Baidu [company]
Viacom Inc. **V:** 347
Baiji [animal]
River dolphin **R:** 354
Baikal, Lake [Siberia] *See* Lake Baikal *in this index*
Baikal-Amur Mainline [railroad]
Siberia (History) **S:** 446
Baikal Mountains
Russia (The Central Siberian Plateau) **R:** 541 *with picture*
Bail [cricket]
Cricket **Ci:** 1131
Bail [law] **B:** 31
Arrest **A:** 743
Criminal justice system (Pretrial procedures) **Ci:** 1143
Bail bond [insurance]
Bail **B:** 31
Bonding **B:** 455
Insurance (Surety bonds) **I:** 314
Bailey [courtyard]
Castle (Structure) **C:** 280 *with picture*
Bailey, Carl E. [American political leader]
Arkansas (table) **A:** 712
Bailey, Carolyn Sherwin [American author]

Newbery Medal (table) **N:** 359
Bailey, Frederick Augustus Washington [birth name of]
Douglass, Frederick **D:** 313
Bailey, James A. [American businessman]
Barnum, P. T. **B:** 115
Circus (The circus goes international) **Ci:** 563-564
Bailey, Nathan [English publisher]
Dictionary (Early English dictionaries) **D:** 194
Bailey, Thomas L. [American political leader]
Mississippi (table) **M:** 640
Bailey, Willis Joshua [American political leader]
Kansas (table) **K:** 234
Bailiff [office]
Affidavit **A:** 91
Bailout plan
Bank (Crisis in finance) **B:** 95
Bush, George Walker (Economy) **B:** 722j-723
Obama, Barack (Domestic issues) **O:** 640g
Bain, Alexander [Scottish physicist]
Fax machine (History) **F:** 58
Bain Capital [company]
Romney, Mitt (Business career) **R:** 450
Bainimarama, Frank [Fijian political leader]
Fiji (History) **F:** 98-99
Bainter, Fay [American actress]
Motion picture (Best performance by an actress in a supporting role: 1938) **M:** 862b
Baird, John Logie [Scottish engineer] **B:** 31
Television (Early development) **T:** 127
Baird, Spencer F. [American naturalist]
National Museum of Natural History **N:** 41
Baird's beaked whale
Whale *picture on* **W:** 257
Bairro Alto [district, Portugal]
Lisbon *picture on* **L:** 348
Bait [fishing]
Fishing *pictures on* **F:** 177; (Bait) **F:** 178
Bait [tool]
Glass (Glass terms) **G:** 222
Bait-casting reel
Fishing (Reels) **F:** 176-177 *with picture*
Bait fishing
Fishing industry (Hooks) **F:** 185
Baixa [district, Portugal]
Lisbon (The city) **L:** 348
Baja California [state, Mexico] **B:** 31
Mexicali **M:** 444
Baja California Sur [state, Mexico] **B:** 32
Bajer, Fredrik [Danish statesman]
Nobel Prizes (Peace: 1908) **N:** 448
Bajío [region]
Mexico (The Mesa Central) **M:** 462
Bajnai, Gordon [Hungarian political leader]
Hungary (Recent developments) **H:** 448
Bake kettle [container]
Colonial life in America (Food and drink) **Ci:** 802
Bakelite [plastic]
Baekeland, Leo Hendrik **B:** 25
Phenolic **P:** 356
Plastics (The invention of Bakelite) **P:** 559
Baker [occupation]
Careers *picture on* **C:** 229
Baker, Augusta [American editor]
Regina Medal (table: 1981) **R:** 206
Baker, Buck [American race car driver]
Automobile racing (table: NASCAR Sprint Cup champions) **A:** 981
Baker, Conrad [American political leader]
Indiana (table) **I:** 214
Baker, Florence [British explorer]
Exploration (The exploration of Africa) **E:** 448-449
Baker, George [American religious leader]
Divine, Father **D:** 241
Baker, Ginger [British drummer]
Clapton, Eric **Ci:** 638
Baker, Sir Herbert [English architect]
New Dehli (History) **N:** 203
Baker, Home Run [American baseball player]
Baseball (table: Hall of Fame) **B:** 134
Baker, Howard Henry, Jr. [American political leader] **B:** 32
Baker, James Addison, III [American government official]
Reagan, Ronald Wilson (table) **R:** 169
Baker, Jean Rio [American pioneer]
Western frontier life in America (Newcomers) **W:** 234
Baker, Josephine [American entertainer] **B:** 32 *with portrait*
Baker, Joshua [American political leader]
Louisiana (table) **L:** 496
Baker, Nathaniel B. [American political leader]
New Hampshire (table) **N:** 223
Baker, Newton Diehl [American statesman]
Wilson, Woodrow (table) **W:** 323
Baker, Norma Jean [birth name of]

Monroe, Marilyn M: 739
Baker, Ray Stannard [American social reformer]
Muckrakers M: 908
Baker, Sam A. [American political leader]
Missouri M: 668
Baker, Sir Samuel White [British explorer]
Exploration (The exploration of Africa) E: 448-449
Baker, Terry [American football player]
Football (table) F: 363
Baker-Berry Library
Dartmouth College D: 39
Baker v. Carr [U.S. history]
Apportionment A: 574
Supreme Court of the United States (Election issues) So: 1001; (table) So: 1002
Tennessee (The mid-1900's) T: 156
Baker's yeast
Fungi (The importance of fungi) F: 559-560
Yeast (How yeast is used) Y: 554; (How yeast is made) Y: 555
Bakersfield sound [music]
Country music (The Bakersfield sound) Ci: 1098a
Bakery
Bread (How yeast bread is made) B: 588 *with picture*
Conveyor belt (Uses) Ci: 1024-1025
Bakery, Confectionery and Tobacco Workers' International Union
Labor movement (table) L: 8
Bakewell, Robert [British farmer]
Cattle (Beginning of breeding) C: 315
Bakiev, Kurmanbek [Kyrgyz political leader]
Kyrgyzstan (Independence) K: 400
Baking B: 32 *with picture*
Bread B: 588
Cooking (Baking) Ci: 1028
Pie (Baking a pie) P: 452
Baking chocolate
Chocolate (Chocolate products) C: 518
Baking powder B: 33
Baking soda *See* Bicarbonate of soda *in this index*
Bakke, Allan [American public figure]
Bakke case B: 33
Bakke case [U.S. history] B: 33
Supreme Court of the United States (table) So: 1002
Bakr, Ahmed Hasan al- [Iraqi political leader]
Iraq (The republic) I: 414
Baku [Azerbaijan] B: 34
Azerbaijan A: 996 *with picture*
Bakufu [Japanese history]
Kamakura period K: 212
Shogun S: 433
Bakunin, Mikhail [Russian author]
Anarchism A: 448
Baky [Azerbaijan] *See* Baku *in this index*
Balaguer, Joaqín [Dominican political leader]
Dominican Republic (History) D: 304-305
Balak [king of Moab]
Mount Pisgah M: 886
Balaklava, Battle of [1854] B: 34
Nightingale, Florence (Service in Crimea) N: 420
Balalaika [musical instrument] B: 34 *with picture*
Balance [design]
Design (Harmony) D: 157 *with pictures*
Balance [instrument] B: 34 *with picture*
Scale, Weighing (Balances) S: 169
Balance [physiology]
Audiology A: 882
Dizziness D: 256
Ear (The sense of balance) E: 11
Gravity, Center of G: 333
Lever L: 217
Posture P: 710
Balance beam [sports]
Gymnastics *picture on* G: 450; (Women's events) G: 449
Balance of nature [biology] B: 34
Ant (The importance of ants) A: 528
Bird (In nature) B: 330
Carnivore C: 243
Ecology (Changes in ecosystems) E: 56
Endangered species E: 269
Eutrophication (How eutrophication occurs) E: 421
Fish (Fish in the balance of nature) F: 147 *with diagram*
Mammal (Mammals in the balance of nature) M: 118
Plant (In ecosystems) P: 518
Snake (Snakes and the environment) S: 532
Balance of payments [economics] B: 36
Devaluation D: 173
Balance of power [diplomacy] B: 36
International relations (History) I: 345
Peace (From the 1400's to the 1700's) P: 206
Balance of trade [economics]

Balance of payments B: 36
Japan (International trade) J: 50-51
Mercantilism M: 411
Balance sheet
Accounting (Financial reports) A: 22-23
Bookkeeping (Bookkeeping and financial statements) B: 473
Balance spring [device]
Watch (Mechanical watches) W: 114
Balance wheel [device]
Clock (Mechanical clocks) Ci: 682j
Watch (Mechanical watches) W: 114 *with picture*
Balanced aquarium
Pet (Pets for the home) P: 319-320
Balanced diet
Diet (Normal diet) D: 199
Nutrition (Eat a balanced diet) N: 626
Balanced fund [investment]
Mutual fund M: 969
Balanced Rock [Colorado]
Garden of the Gods G: 29
Rock (table) R: 374
Balanchine, George [American choreographer] B: 37
Ballet (Ballet in the United States) B: 53
Kirstein, Lincoln Edward K: 337
Tallchief, Maria T: 20
Balancing Agriculture With Industry [government program]
Mississippi (The early 1900's) M: 642-644
Balancing selection [biology]
Evolution (Balancing or diversifying selection) E: 429
Bâlănești, Mount [Moldova]
Moldova (Land and climate) M: 690-690a
Balarama [Hindu deity]
Juggernaut J: 186
Balard, Antoine J. [French chemist]
Bromine B: 636
Balaton, Lake [Hungary]
Hungary *picture on* H: 442
Balbinus [Roman emperor]
Rome, Ancient (table) R: 447
Balboa, Vasco Núñez de [Spanish explorer] B: 37 *with picture and map*
Exploration *map on* E: 443; (Exploring the New World) E: 444-445
Latin America *map on* L: 105 ; (European discovery and exploration) L: 103
Pacific Islands (European explorers) P: 12
Pacific Ocean P: 14
Panama (The Spanish colonial period) P: 120
Panama Canal (Early efforts) P: 125
Balboa Park
San Diego (Cultural life) S: 90 *with picture*
Balch, Emily Greene [American economist]
Nobel Prizes (Peace: 1946) N: 448a
Balch Institute
Philadelphia (Libraries and museums) P: 363-364
Balchen, Bernt [Norwegian-American aviator]
Airplane (Fliers of the golden age) A: 237
Exploration (The exploration of Antarctica) E: 450
Bald eagle
Alaska (Interesting facts) A: 283 *with picture*
Bird (Endangered species) B: 370
Eagle E: 3 *with picture*; (Food) E: 5; (Kinds of eagles) E: 5
Bald face [marking]
Horse (Coat and skin) H: 348-349
Bald Soprano, The [play by Ionesco]
Ionesco, Eugène I: 372
Baldacci, John [American political leader]
Maine (table) M: 87
Baldcypress [tree] B: 38
Cypress Ci: 1205
Tree (table) on T: 424
United States *picture on* U: 121
Wetland *picture on* W: 253
Balder [Norse mythology] B: 38
Loki L: 426
Mythology (The construction of the world) M: 986; (The end of the world) M: 987
Baldfaced hornet
Hornet H: 340
Insect *picture on* I: 283
Baldness B: 38
Hair (Disorders of the hair and scalp) H: 10
Baldpate [bird] *See* Wigeon *in this index*
Baldridge, H. C. [American political leader]
Idaho (table) I: 42
Baldrige, Malcolm, Jr. [American government official]
Commerce, Department of (table) Ci: 871
Reagan, Ronald Wilson (table) R: 169
Baldwin, Abraham [American political leader] B: 39
Baldwin, Anna [American inventor]

Milking machine M: 550
Baldwin, Henry [American jurist]
Supreme Court of the United States (table) So: 1000
Baldwin, Henry P. [American political leader]
Michigan (table) M: 507
Baldwin, James [American author] B: 39
African American literature (The 1900's) A: 136a
African Americans (The growing movement) A: 136o-136p *with picture*
American literature (Fiction and other prose) A: 424
Novel (After World War II) N: 574
Baldwin, Matthias William [American inventor] B: 39 *with picture*
Baldwin, Ralph B. [American astronomer]
Moon (Describing lunar evolution) M: 794
Baldwin, Raymond E. [American political leader]
Connecticut (table) Ci: 967
Baldwin, Robert [Canadian political leader] B: 40
Baldwin, Roger S. [American political leader]
Connecticut (table) Ci: 967
Baldwin, Simeon E. [American political leader]
Connecticut (table) Ci: 967
Baldwin, Stanley [British political leader] B: 40
United Kingdom (The rise of the Labour Party) U: 70
Baldwin Locomotive Works
Baldwin, Matthias William B: 40
Baldwin of Flanders [Byzantine emperor]
Crusades (The Fourth Crusade) Ci: 1161
Bale [industry]
Cotton (Ginning and baling) Ci: 1091
Hay H: 115 *with picture*
Rubber (Manufacturing rubber products) R: 504
Bale, Christian [British actor]
Motion picture (Best performance by an actor in a supporting role: 2010) M: 862b
Balearic Islands [province, Spain] B: 40
Spain (The Balearic Islands) So: 740 *with map*
Baleen [zoology]
Animal (Filtering mechanisms) A: 490-491 *with picture*
Blue whale B: 421
Bowhead whale B: 520
Bryde's whale B: 656
Fin whale F: 103
Gray whale G: 335
Humpback whale H: 436
Whale (Kinds of baleen whales) W: 255 *with picture*
Baleen whale
Animal (Filtering mechanisms) A: 490-491 *with picture*
Humpback whale H: 436
Whale (Kinds of baleen whales) W: 255 *with pictures*; (Group life) W: 261
Baler [machine]
Hay H: 115 *with picture*
Balewa, Sir Abubakar Tafawa [Nigerian statesman]
Nigeria (Independence) N: 417
Balfour, Arthur James [British statesman] B: 40
Balfour Declaration B: 40
Balfour, Earl of *See* Balfour, Arthur James *in this index*
Balfour Declaration [1917] B: 40
Arab-Israeli conflict (Historical background) A: 582
Balfour, Arthur James B: 40
Israel (Beginnings of a new state) I: 486
Jerusalem (British rule) J: 101
Jews (The Zionist movement) J: 123
Jordan (The Palestinian conflict) J: 164
Palestine (World War I and the Balfour Declaration) P: 105
Weizmann, Chaim W: 188
Zionism (The Balfour Declaration) Z: 595
Balfour Report [1926]
Balfour, Arthur James B: 40
King, William Lyon Mackenzie *picture on* K: 326
Bali [island, Indonesia] B: 41
Asia (The arts) A: 785
Dance (Asian theatrical dance) D: 28-29 *with picture*
Family *picture on* F: 22
Indonesia (The arts) I: 232 *with picture*; (The Lesser Sunda Islands) I: 234; (Recent developments) I: 237
Terrorism (Recent developments) T: 180
Bali-Hinduism [religion]
Indonesia (Religion) I: 232
Baliles, Gerald L. [American political leader]
Virginia (table) V: 417
Baline, Israel [real name of]
Berlin, Irving B: 266
Balinese cat

Cat *picture on* **C: 289**; (Long-haired breeds) **C: 292**
Baling machine [farming]
  Cotton (Ginning and baling) **Ci: 1091**
Balintawak [clothing]
  Philippines (Way of life) **P: 374-375**
Balkan Mountains [Europe]
  Balkans (Location, size, and description) **B: 41-42**
  Bulgaria (The land) **B: 691** *with map*
Balkan Peninsula
  Greece **G: 352**
Balkan wars [European history]
  Bulgaria (The Balkan wars) **B: 692**
  Macedonia [historic region] **M: 12**
  World War I (Beginning of the war) **W: 455**
  The First Balkan War (1912-1913)
    Albania (Independence) **A: 307**
    Balkans (The First Balkan War) **B: 42**
    Greece (George I) **G: 362**
  The Second Balkan War (1913)
    Balkans (The Second Balkan War) **B: 42**
    Greece (George I) **G: 362**
    London, Treaties of (The Treaty of 1913) **L: 444**
Balkans [region, Europe] **B: 41** *with map*
  Berlin, Congress of **B: 265**
  Bulgaria **B: 688** *with map*
  United States, History of the (The Balkan
    conflicts) **U: 196d**
  World War I (The rise of nationalism) **W: 452-453**;
    (Beginning of the war) **W: 455**
  World War II (Fighting in the Balkans) **W: 477**
Balkenende, Jan Peter [Dutch political leader]
  Netherlands (Recent developments) **N: 150**
Balkhash, Lake [Kazakhstan] *See* Lake Balkhash
  in this index
Ball, George [American diplomat]
  United Nations (table) **U: 86**
Ball, Hugo [German poet]
  Dadaism **D: 2**
Ball, Lucille [American actress] **B: 43** *with portrait*
  Arnaz, Desi **A: 741**
Ball-and-socket joint [anatomy]
  Hip **H: 238** *with diagram*
  Joint **J: 155** *with diagram*
  Shoulder **S: 437** *with picture*
Ball bearing
  Bearing (Rolling element bearings) **B: 189** *with
    diagram*
Ball bullet
  Bullet **B: 695**
Ball for Daisy, A [book by Raschka]
  Raschka, Chris **R: 144**
Ball-jointed doll
  Doll (The 2000's) **D: 295**
Ball lightning
  Lightning (Appearance) **L: 300**
Ball mill [industry]
  Cement and concrete (Crushing and grinding)
    C: 344
  Copper *picture on* **Ci: 1041**; (Milling) **Ci: 1042**
  Gold (Exposing the gold) **G: 253**
  Paint (Grinding) **P: 24-25**
Ball of the foot [anatomy]
  Foot (The bones) **F: 352**
Ball peen hammer [tool]
  Hammer **H: 34** *with picture*
Ball python, African [snake]
  Snake *picture on* **S: 526**; (Protection against
    predators) **S: 526**
Balla, Giacomo [Italian painter]
  Futurism **F: 589**
Ballad [poetry] **B: 43**
  Country music (The roots of country music)
    Ci: 1098a
  Folk music (Kinds of folk music) **F: 321**
  Literature for children (Ballads) **L: 358**
  Poetry (Narrative poetry) **P: 591**
  Spanish literature (The 1400's) **So: 758**
Ballad of Baby Doe, The [opera by Moore]
  Moore, Douglas Stuart **M: 796**
Ballad of Reading Gaol, The [poem by Wilde]
  Wilde, Oscar **W: 302**
Ballad of the Sad Café, The [book by McCullers]
  McCullers, Carson **M: 332g**
Ballad opera
  Drama (England) **D: 335**
Ballade [art form] **B: 43**
  French literature (Lyric poetry) **F: 518**
"Ballade of Dead Ladies" [poem by Villon]
  Ballade **B: 43**
Balladur, Edouard [French political leader]
  France (Socialists win power) **F: 478**
Ballard, Robert Duane [American oceanographer]
  B: 43
  Exploration (Deep-sea exploration) **E: 450-451**
Ballast [construction]
  Railroad (The roadbed and route) **R: 109** *with
    picture*

Ballast [electricity]
  Fluorescent lamp **F: 305** *with diagram*
Ballast [weight]
  Airship (Control) **A: 251**
  Balloon (Zero-pressure balloons) **B: 59**;
    (Operation of a gas balloon) **B: 60**
  Great Lakes (Invasive species) **G: 345**
  Ruffe **R: 509**
  Ship (Basic structure) **S: 403-404**
Balled and burlapped plant
  Nursery **N: 614**
Ballerina [dancer]
  Ballet (table) **B: 45**
Ballet [dance] **B: 44** *with pictures*
  See also the list of Related articles in the Ballet
    article
  Art and the arts *picture on* **A: 748**
  Dance (European and American theatrical dance)
    D: 29-30 *with picture*
  Diaghilev, Sergei Pavlovich **D: 180**
  Russia *picture on* **R: 526**; (Ballet) **R: 537**
  United States *picture on* **U: 119**
Ballet Comique de la Reine
  Ballet *picture on* **B: 52**; (The birth of ballet)
    B: 50-51
Ballet d'action [style]
  Ballet *picture on* **B: 52**; (History) **B: 50-51**
Ballet Folklórico of Mexico [dance company]
  Dance *picture on* **D: 26**
  Latin America (Dance) **L: 101**
  Mexico City (Cultural life and recreation) **M: 476b**
Ballet shoe
  Ballet *picture on* **B: 47**
Ballets Russes [dance company] **B: 55**
  Ballet (Ballet in Russia) **B: 52**
  Diaghilev, Sergei Pavlovich **D: 180**
  Picasso, Pablo (Picasso as a designer) **P: 448b**
Balli, Nicolás [Spanish settler]
  Padre Island **P: 20**
Balli Kombetar [political group]
  Albania (World War II) **A: 307-308**
Ballinger, Richard A. [American government
  official]
  Interior, Department of the (table) **I: 325**
  Taft, William Howard (Legislative defeats) **T: 10-
    11**; (table) **T: 11**
Ballinger-Pinchot controversy [U.S. history]
  Taft, William Howard (Legislative defeats)
    T: 10-11
Balliol, John [king of Scotland]
  Bruce, Robert **B: 648**
  Edward I **E: 112**
  Scotland (Fight for independence) **S: 219**
Balliol College
  Oxford, University of **O: 887**
Ballista [weapon]
  Weapon (Siege weapons) **W: 154b**
Ballistic missile
  Guided missile (Ballistic missiles) **G: 425** *with
    pictures*
Ballistic Missile Early Warning System
  Air Force, United States (Defense and deterrence)
    A: 190
  Radar *map on* **R: 66**; (In the military) **R: 65**
Ballistic missile submarine
  Submarine (Ballistic missile submarines) **So: 941**
    with diagram
  Warship (Submarines) **W: 41**; (Warships in the
    nuclear age) **W: 42-43**
Ballistics [engineering] **B: 56** *with picture*
Ballonet [aerodynamics]
  Airship (Ballonets) **A: 251** *with diagram*
Balloon [aircraft] **B: 57** *with pictures*
  Air force (History) **A: 184-185** *with picture*
  Aircraft, Military (The first military aircraft) **A: 204**
    with picture
  Airplane **A: 209**, *picture on* **A: 229**; (First human
    flights) **A: 230**
  Bomb (History) **B: 452** *with picture*
  Franklin, Benjamin (Other studies) **F: 489**
  Helium (Uses) **H: 176**
  Montgolfier brothers **M: 765**
  Piccard, Auguste **P: 450**
  Piccard, Jean **P: 450**
  Radiosonde **R: 99**
  Weather *picture on* **W: 164**; (Weather balloons,
    airplanes, and ships) **W: 163**
Balloon angioplasty [surgery]
  Angioplasty **A: 462** *with diagram*
  Disease (Medical treatment) **D: 232-233**
Balloon barrage
  Balloon (Balloons in war) **B: 61** *with picture*
Balloon flower
  Flower *picture on* **F: 279**
Balloon-payment mortgage
  Mortgage **M: 820**
Balloon tire

Tire (History) **T: 297-298**
Ballooning [zoology]
  Spider *picture on* **So: 787**; (Spiderlings) **So: 788**
Ballot [voting] **B: 63**
  Voting (Methods of voting) **V: 449**
Ballpoint pen
  Ink (Writing inks) **I: 273**
  Pen **P: 233** *with picture*
Ballroom dancing B: 63
  Dance (Social dances) **D: 26-28** *with pictures*
Bally Manufacturing Company
  Slot machine **S: 508a**
Balm [plant] **B: 63** *with picture*
Balm in Gilead [play by Wilson]
  Wilson, Lanford **W: 317**
Balm of Gilead [tree] **B: 64**
  Poplar **P: 668**
Balmaceda, José Manuel [Chilean political leader]
  Chile (Era of changes) **C: 469**
Balmat, Jacques [French mountain climber]
  Alps (Climbing the Alps) **A: 386**
  Mont Blanc **M: 741**
Balochi [people]
  Oman (People) **O: 757-758**
  Pakistan (Cultural groups and languages) **P: 93**
Balochistan [province, Pakistan]
  Pakistan (Provincial and local government) **P: 93**;
    (Land and climate) **P: 96** *with map*; (History)
    P: 98
Balsa [wood] **B: 64** *with pictures*
  Airplane, Model (Indoor models) **A: 241**
Balsam [plant]
  Flower (Garden annuals) **F: 276** *with picture*;
    (table) **B: 300** *with picture*
  Impatiens **I: 90**
Balsam, Martin [American actor]
  Motion picture (Best performance by an actor in
    a supporting role: 1965) **M: 862b**
Balsam fir [tree] **B: 64** *with pictures*
  Fir **F: 119**
  Tree *pictures on* **T: 424**
Balsam Mecca [fragrance] *See* Balm of Gilead *in
  this index*
Balsam poplar [tree]
  Poplar **P: 668** *with picture*
Balthasar [Biblical figure]
  Magi **M: 48**
Balthazar [book by Durrell]
  Durrell, Lawrence **D: 389**
Balthus [French artist] **B: 64** *with picture*
Baltic Sea [Europe] **B: 65** *with map*
Baltic States B: 65
  See also Estonia; Latvia; Lithuania *in this index*
  Bush, George Herbert Walker (International
    affairs) **B: 721-722**
  Union of Soviet Socialist Republics (World War II)
    U: 37; (Threats to unity) **U: 40-41**
Baltimore [Maryland] **B: 66** *with pictures and maps*
  Maryland (table: Average monthly weather)
    M: 252
  United States, History of the *picture on* **U: 155**
  United States capitals **U: 199**
Baltimore, David [American physiologist]
  Nobel Prizes (Physiology or medicine: 1975)
    N: 446
Baltimore, Lord
  See Calvert, Cecilius; Calvert, Charles; Calvert,
    George *in this index*
Baltimore and Ohio Railroad
  Locomotive (History) **L: 417**
  Railroad (Developments in the United States)
    R: 115; (Expansion in the United States) **R: 115**
Baltimore clipper [ship]
  Clipper ship **Ci: 682h**
Baltimore College of Dental Surgery
  Dentistry (Early dentistry) **D: 144-145**
Baltimore Colts [team]
  Shula, Don **S: 442**
Baltimore Harbor
  Baltimore **B: 66** *with picture*
  Maryland *picture on* **M: 253**
Baltimore Museum of Art
  Maryland (Museums) **M: 244**
Baltimore oriole [bird] **B: 70**
  Bird *picture on* **B: 358**; (Birds of forests and
    woodlands) **B: 334** *with picture*
Baltimore Orioles [team]
  Baseball (table) **B: 130**
Baltimore Ravens [team]
  Football (National Football League) **F: 364**
Baltimore Sun [newspaper]
  Mencken, H. L. **M: 397**
**Baltimore-Washington International Thurgood
  Marshall Airport** [Maryland]
  Washington, D.C. (Transportation) **W: 84-85**
Balto-Slavic [language]
  Language (Indo-European) **L: 65-66**

Baltoscandia [region, Europe]
  Scandinavia **S:** 170
Balzac, Honoré de [French author] **B:** 71 *with portrait*
  French literature (Romantic fiction) **F:** 521
  Novel (France) **N:** 573
Balzar, Fred B. [American political leader]
  Nevada (table) **N:** 173
Bam [Iran]
  Iran (Recent developments) **I:** 406b
Bam [tile]
  Mah-jongg **M:** 64 *with picture*
Bam i Dunya [region, Asia]
  Pamirs **P:** 112
Bamako [Mali] **B:** 71
  Mali **M:** 106 *with map*
Bambara [people]
  Mali (People) **M:** 106
Bambara, Toni Cade [American author]
  Novel (The novel today) **N:** 575
Bamberger, Simon [American political leader]
  Utah (table) **U:** 245
Bambi [film]
  Disney, Walt (Full-length movies) **D:** 236
Bamboo [plant] **B:** 71 *with pictures*
  Grass (Woody grasses) **G:** 326
  Panda **P:** 128
Bamboula [music by Gottschalk]
  Gottschalk, Louis Moreau **G:** 280
Bamiléké [people]
  Cameroon (People) **C:** 85
Ban Ki-moon [South Korean diplomat] **B:** 72 *with portrait*
  United Nations (The secretary-general) **U:** 83 *with portrait*
Banaba [island, Pacific Ocean]
  Kiribati **K:** 335
Banana **B:** 72 *with pictures*
  Costa Rica *picture on* **Ci:** 1083
  Ecuador *picture on* **E:** 72
  Fruit (Tropical fruit) **F:** 546 *with picture*
  Plantain **P:** 550
Banana bird
  Oriole **O:** 856
Banana poka [plant]
  Conservation (Biodiversity conservation) **Ci:** 976-977
Banana republic
  Honduras (Independence) **H:** 312-313
Bananier, Le [music by Gottschalk]
  Gottschalk, Louis Moreau **G:** 280
Banaras [India] *See Varanasi in this index*
Banat [region]
  Romania (Land regions) **R:** 419-420 *with map;* (World War I) **R:** 424
Banbury machine
  Tire (Preliminary operations) **T:** 295-296
Bancroft, Anne [American actress]
  Motion picture (Best performance by an actress: 1962) **M:** 862
Bancroft, Dave [American baseball player]
  Baseball (table: Hall of Fame) **B:** 134
Bancroft, George [American historian] **B:** 74
  Polk, James Knox **P:** 640; (Election of 1844) **P:** 642
  United States Naval Academy (History) **U:** 204
Band [music] **B:** 74 *with picture*
  Country music (The instruments) **Ci:** 1098
  Drum corps **D:** 368
Band [radio]
  Radio (How radio programs are received) **R:** 88
Band [sociology]
  Indian, American (Bands) **I:** 143
  Nomad **N:** 452
Band clutch [engine]
  Transmission (Clutches) **T:** 377
Band saw [tool]
  Lumber *picture on* **L:** 520
  Saw (Power saws) **S:** 167 *with picture*
Band-tailed pigeon
  Pigeon (Wild pigeons) **P:** 460
Banda, Hastings Kamuzu [Malawi political leader] **B:** 75
  Malawi (History) **M:** 97-98
Banda, Joyce [Malawi political leader]
  Malawi (History) **M:** 97-98
Banda, Rupiah [Zambian political leader]
  Zambia (History) **Z:** 585-586
Bandage **B:** 75
  First aid (Burns) **F:** 138-139; (Frostbite) **F:** 141
Bandama River [Côte d'Ivoire]
  Côte d'Ivoire (The land) **Ci:** 1084a *with map*
Bandanna [clothing]
  Cowboy (His clothing) **Ci:** 1108-1109
Bandar Seri Begawan [Brunei]
  Brunei **B:** 650 *with map*
Bandaranaike, S. W. R. D. [Sri Lankan political leader]

Bandaranaike, Sirimavo **B:** 75
  Sri Lanka (History) **So:** 819
Bandaranaike, Sirimavo [Sri Lankan political leader] **B:** 75 *with portrait*
Banded gecko [reptile]
  Gecko *picture on* **G:** 75
Banded iguana
  Iguana **I:** 50
Banded iron formation [geology]
  Taconite **T:** 5
Banded krait [snake]
  Snake *picture on* **S:** 534
Banded sea snake
  Snake *picture on* **S:** 529
Banded woollybear [insect]
  Insect *picture on* **I:** 282
  Woollybear **W:** 402
Bandeirantes [South American history]
  São Paulo (History) **S:** 119
Bandelier National Monument [New Mexico]
  National Park System (table: National monuments) **N:** 50
  New Mexico *picture on* **N:** 273
Banderilla [bullfighting]
  Bullfighting (The order of the bullfight) **B:** 696-697 *with picture*
Banderillero [bullfighting]
  Bullfighting (The order of the bullfight) **B:** 696 *with picture*
Bandicoot [animal] **B:** 76 *with picture*
  Animal (Introduction of new species) **A:** 505
  Mammal *picture on* **M:** 128
  Marsupial (Kinds of marsupials) **M:** 232-233
Bandilor top [toy]
  Top (History of tops) **T:** 331
Banding [conservation] *See Birdbanding in this index*
Bandipur National Park [India]
  National park (table) **N:** 42f
Bandit **B:** 76
  See also the list of Related articles in the Bandit article
Bandjarmasin [Indonesia] *See Banjarmasin in this index*
Bandung [Indonesia] **B:** 76
Bandura [musical instrument]
  Ukraine (The arts) **U:** 9
Bandura, Albert [Canadian psychologist]
  Developmental psychology (Learning theory) **D:** 174
Bandwidth [electronics]
  Telephone (Cellular phone calls) **T:** 97
Bandy [sport]
  Norway (Recreation) **N:** 540
Banff [Alberta] **B:** 76
  Lake Louise **L:** 39
  Rocky Mountains *picture on* **R:** 396
Banff National Park [Alberta] **B:** 76 *with picture*
  Canada (table: National parks and national park reserves) **C:** 113
  Lake Louise **L:** 39
  National park *picture on* **N:** 42a; (Canada) **N:** 42c
Banff Park Museum National Historic Site [Alberta]
  Canada (table: National historic sites) **C:** 114
Bang [people]
  Bangladesh (Early history) **B:** 85
Bangalore [India] *See Bengaluru in this index*
Bangers and mash [food]
  England (Food and drink) **E:** 295-296
Bangerter, Norman H. [American political leader]
  Utah (table) **U:** 245
Banghāzī [Libya] *See Benghāzī in this index*
Bangkok [Thailand] **B:** 77 *with picture*
  Asia *picture on* **A:** 803
  Thailand **T:** 221 *with picture*
Bangladesh **B:** 78 *with pictures and maps*
  Asia (Other struggles) **A:** 810-811
  Bengal **B:** 248
  Dhaka **D:** 178
  Flood (Seacoast floods) **F:** 237
  India (India under Indira Gandhi) **I:** 133-134
  Pakistan **P:** 92; (Civil war) **P:** 99-100
Bangladesh Nationalist Party
  Bangladesh (Political parties) **B:** 79; (The new nation) **B:** 86
Bangladeshis [people]
  Bangladesh **B:** 78; (Population and ancestry) **B:** 79-80 *with pictures*
Bangor [Maine] **B:** 87
Bangui [Central African Republic] **B:** 87
  Central African Republic **C:** 352 *with picture*
  Ubangi River **U:** 2
Bangweulu, Lake [Zambia]
  Lake Bangweulu **L:** 36
Bani Yas [family]
  Abu Dhabi **A:** 19

Banian [tree] *See Banyan tree in this index*
Banishment
  Deportation **D:** 149
  Exile **E:** 437
Banjarmasin [Indonesia] **B:** 87
  Indonesia (Borneo) **I:** 233
Banjo [musical instrument] **B:** 87 *with pictures*
  Jazz (The guitar) **J:** 69
  Popular music (1840's to the Civil War) **P:** 669
  West Virginia *picture on* **W:** 210
Banjo Lesson, The [painting by Tanner]
  Tanner, Henry Ossawa **T:** 29 *with picture*
Banjul [Gambia] **B:** 87
  Gambia **G:** 18
Bank **B:** 88 *with pictures*
  See also the list of Related articles in the Bank article
  Automated teller machine **A:** 944
  Clearinghouse **Ci:** 659
  Federal Deposit Insurance Corporation **F:** 63
  Federal Reserve System **F:** 65
  Great Depression (The farm depression and bank failures) **G:** 339; (Economic breakdown) **G:** 340 *with picture*
  Industrial Revolution (The role of capital) **I:** 251
  Investment **I:** 366
  New Deal (Helping savers and investors) **N:** 200
  Roosevelt, Franklin Delano (The banking crisis) **R:** 452
  Switzerland (Banking) **So:** 1058
  Treasury, Department of the (Department functions) **T:** 407
  United States, History of the (Investment and banking) **U:** 181
Bank [formation]
  Grand Banks **G:** 305
Bank [river]
  River (Channels) **R:** 352
Bank balance
  Check (How the checking system works) **C:** 390391
Bank charter
  Bank (Regulation of U.S. banks) **B:** 92
Bank holding company
  Bank (Regulation of U.S. banks) **B:** 92
Bank Holding Company Act [1956]
  Bank (Diversification and mergers) **B:** 94-95
Bank holiday [U.S. history] **B:** 96
  Bank (The crisis of 1933) **B:** 93-94
  New Deal (Helping savers and investors) **N:** 200
  Roosevelt, Franklin Delano (The banking crisis) **R:** 452
Bank note [money]
  Bank (The First Bank of the United States) **B:** 92 *with picture*
  Money *pictures on* **M:** 708, **M:** 709; (Privately issued bank notes) **M:** 713
Bank of America **B:** 96
Bank of America Plaza
  Dallas (Landmarks) **D:** 11 *with picture*
Bank of Canada **B:** 96
  Canada, Government of (Money and taxation) **C:** 136
Bank of China [Hong Kong]
  Hong Kong (The metropolis) **H:** 316
Bank of Credit and Commerce International SA
  Clifford, Clark McAdams **Ci:** 674
Bank of England **B:** 96
  Bank (Central banks) **B:** 91
Bank of Japan
  Tokyo (Finance) **T:** 317
Bank of the South
  Latin America (In the early 2000's) **L:** 111
Bank of the United States [U.S. history] **B:** 96
  First Bank of the United States
    Bank of the United States (The First Bank of the United States) **B:** 92
    Bank (The First Bank of the United States) **B:** 92
    Jefferson, Thomas (Secretary of state) **J:** 81-82
    United States, History of the (Financial problems) **U:** 162-163
  Second Bank of the United States
    Bank of the United States (The Second Bank of the United States) **B:** 96
    Bank (The Second Bank of the United States) **B:** 93
    Biddle, Nicholas **B:** 294
    Jackson, Andrew (The Bank of the United States) **J:** 11
    Taney, Roger Brooke **T:** 25
    United States, History of the (Jackson as president) **U:** 171
    Washington, George (Constitutional debate) **W:** 103
  Wildcat bank **W:** 301
Bank Secrecy Act [1970]
  Money laundering **M:** 718

Bank statement
Check (How the checking system works)
C: 390-391
Bank swallow [bird]
Swallow So: 1015 *with picture*
BankAmerica Corporation
Bank of America B: 96
Bankhead Tunnel [Alabama]
Mobile (History) M: 681-682
Banking [aviation]
Airplane (The wing) A: 213; (Changing direction)
A: 222
Banking Act [1933]
Bank (The crisis of 1933) B: 93-94
Bank holiday B: 96
Federal Reserve System (History) F: 66
Bankruptcy [law] B: 97
Receiver R: 174
Bankruptcy code [1978]
Bankruptcy (In the United States) B: 97
Bankruptcy Reform Act [1978]
Bankruptcy (In the United States) B: 97
Banks, Dennis [American activist]
American Indian Movement A: 411
Banks, Ernie [American baseball player]
Baseball (table: Hall of Fame) B: 134
Banks, Nathaniel P. [Union general]
Massachusetts (table) M: 288
Bann [river, Ireland]
Lough Neagh L: 474
Northern Ireland (Lakes, rivers, and bays) N: 523
with map
Banneker, Benjamin [American mathematician]
B: 98 *with portrait*
Washington, D.C. (Building the city) W: 85-86
Banner [flag]
Flag (Interesting facts about flags) F: 193
Banner [journalism]
Newspaper (table) N: 383
Banner ad
Advertising (The Internet) A: 74
Internet (Advertising) I: 350b
Bannister, Sir Roger [British athlete] B: 98 *with picture*
Track and field (Track and field today) T: 360
Bannock [Montana]
Montana (Places to visit) M: 750 *with picture*
Bannock Indians B: 98
Idaho (Indian fighting) I: 44
Bannock War [1878]
Bannock Indians B: 98
Bannockburn, Battle of [1314] B: 99
Bruce, Robert B: 648
England (The beginnings of Parliament) E: 306
Scotland *picture on* S: 220; (Fight for
independence) S: 219
Banny, Charles Konan [Ivorian political leader]
Côte d'Ivoire (History) Ci: 1084b-1085
Banquet, The [poems by Dante]
Dante Alighieri (His works) D: 34
*Banquet of Officers of the Civic Guard of Saint
George at Haarlem, 1616* [painting by Hals]
Painting (The Dutch masters) P: 62 *with picture*
Banqueting House [London]
Architecture (Later Renaissance architecture)
A: 621-622
Jones, Inigo J: 158 *with picture*
London (Palaces) L: 435
Banquo [literary figure]
Shakespeare, William: (*Macbeth*) S: 363
Banshee [Irish legend] B: 99
Fairy (Solitary fairies) F: 10
Bantam [bird] B: 99
Bantamweight [category]
Boxing (table) B: 355
Banting, Sir Frederick Grant [Canadian doctor]
B: 99
Drug (The drug revolution) D: 359
Insulin (History) I: 308
Nobel Prizes (Physiology or medicine: 1923)
N: 445
Banto faro [geography]
Gambia (Land) G: 19
Bantu [people] B: 99 *with picture*
Africa (Languages) A: 105
Bemba B: 246
Cameroon (History) C: 86
Pygmies P: 914
South Africa (Languages) So: 609-611; (History)
So: 617
Banū Hāshim [clan]
Muslims (Muhammad) M: 964a
Banū Umayyā [clan]
Muslims (Muhammad) M: 964a
Bañuelos, Romana Acosta [American government
official] B: 100 *with portrait*
Banville, John [Irish author]

Irish literature (Fiction) I: 432
Banyan tree [tree] B: 100 *with picture*
Banzai attack [warfare]
World War II (The South Pacific) W: 489
Bao Dai [emperor of Vietnam]
Indochina (World War II) I: 225
Vietnam (The First Indochina War) V: 371
Bao Ninh [Vietnamese author]
Vietnam (The arts) V: 366-368
Baobab [tree] B: 100 *with pictures*
Africa *picture on* A: 125
Tree *picture on* T: 426; (Interesting facts about
trees) T: 411 *with picture*
Baphaeon, Battle of [1310]
Osman I O: 865
Baptism [religion] B: 101 *with picture*
Baptists B: 101
Bath (Religious bathing) B: 163-164
Christianity (Sacraments) C: 522h *with picture*
Eastern Orthodox Churches (Sacraments)
E: 46-47
Luther, Martin (The break with the Roman
Catholic Church) L: 528
Lutherans (Doctrine) L: 529
Mormons (Church doctrines and ordinances)
M: 806-807
Pentecostal churches (Beliefs and practices)
P: 275
Protestantism (Celebration of the sacraments)
P: 834
Religion *picture on* R: 214
Roman Catholic Church (Worship) R: 403
Baptism of Christ [painting by Piero della
Francesca]
Jesus Christ *picture on* J: 106
Baptism of Christ, The [painting by Verrocchio and
Leonardo da Vinci]
Leonardo da Vinci (Paintings) L: 200b
Verrocchio, Andrea del V: 339 *with picture*
Baptist Federation of Canada [religious group]
Baptists (Baptists in America) B: 101
Baptist World Alliance
Baptists B: 101
Baptistery [Florence]
Ghiberti, Lorenzo G: 181
Baptists [religious group] B: 101
American Baptist Association A: 408
American Baptist Churches in the U.S.A. A: 408
Protestantism (The radical reform and free
church movements) P: 835
Southern Baptist Convention So: 687
Bar [law] B: 102
Inns of Court I: 275
Law (Licensing of lawyers) L: 139
Bar [measurement]
Barometer B: 115
Isobar I: 474
Pascal P: 189
Bar [music]
Music (Indicating time values) M: 953-954
Bar Association, American See American Bar
Association *in this index*
Bar at the Folies Bergère [painting by Manet]
Manet, Édouard M: 139 *with picture*
Bar coding B: 102
Laser *picture on* L: 81; (Scanning) L: 82
Postal services *picture on* P: 704; (Sorting) P: 703
Bar graph
Graph (Bar graphs) G: 321 *with pictures*
Bar-headed goose
Bird *picture on* B: 329
Bar Kokhba [Jewish warrior]
Akiva ben Joseph A: 254
Jerusalem (Roman rule) J: 101
Bar magnet
Magnetism *diagram on* M: 59
Bar mill [factory]
Iron and steel (Rolling) I: 445-447
Bar mitzvah [religion] B: 102
Judaism *picture on* J: 179; (Special occasions)
J: 182
Bar soap
Detergent and soap (Bar soaps) D: 164 *with
picture*
Bar steel
Iron and steel (Rolling) I: 445-447 *with diagram*
Bar-tailed godwit [bird]
Bird *pictures on* B: 361
Godwit G: 246
Barabbas [Biblical figure] B: 102
Jesus Christ (The trial) J: 108-108b
Barak [Israelite leader]
Deborah D: 65
Barak, Ehud [Israeli political leader] B: 102
Israel (The 1990's) I: 489; (The 2000's) I: 489
Sharon, Ariel S: 377
Baraka, Amiri [American author] B: 103 *with*

portrait
American literature (The African American
experience) A: 424; (Drama) A: 426
Barangay [village]
Philippines (Local government) P: 373
Baranof, Alexander [Russian businessman]
Alaska (The Russian era) A: 301
Baranof Island [Alaska]
Sitka S: 477
Bárány, Robert [Austrian physiologist]
Nobel Prizes (Physiology or medicine: 1914)
N: 445
Barasti [house]
Bahrain (People) B: 30
Baratynsky, Yevgeny [Russian poet]
Russian literature (Early Romanticism) R: 560-561
Barb [entomology]
Bee (Sting) B: 202
Barb [feather]
Bird (Feathers) B: 362
Barbados B: 103 *with picture and map*
Flag *picture on* F: 200
West Indies *picture on* W: 201
Barbados aloe [plant]
Aloe A: 380 *with picture*
Barbados cherry [fruit]
Acerola A: 24 *with picture*
Barbados thread snake
Snake S: 524, *picture on* S: 526
Barbara, Saint [early Christian]
Madonna and Child (Painters of the Madonna)
M: 37-38
"Barbara Allen" [song]
Folk music (Kinds of folk music) F: 321
"Barbara Frietchie" [poem by Whittier]
Frietchie, Barbara F: 533
Barbara Fritchie House and Museum
Maryland *picture on* M: 248
Barbarian B: 104
Greece, Ancient G: 366
Middle Ages (The Germanic invasions) M: 523;
(The Germanic kingdoms) M: 523
Vandals V: 279
World, History of the (Medieval Europe) W: 432
Barbarians, The [opera by Glass]
Glass, Philip G: 224
Barbarossa [Barbary pirate] B: 105
Algeria (Ottoman rule) A: 364
Barbarossa [Holy Roman emperor] See Frederick I
[Holy Roman emperor] *in this index*
Barbary ape [animal] B: 105 *with picture*
Macaque M: 2
Barbary pirates
Barbary States B: 105
Libya (Early days) L: 267
Tripoli T: 448
Barbary States [North African history] B: 105 *with
map*
Jefferson, Thomas (War with Tripoli) J: 84
Barbasco [drug]
Jívaro Indians J: 128
Barbé-Marbois, François de [French government
official]
Louisiana Purchase (Napoleon's decision) L: 503
Barbeau, Mount [Nunavut]
Nunavut (Land and resources) N: 609 *with map*
Barbecue [cooking] B: 106
Barbed wire B: 106
Cowboy (On the ranch) Ci: 1110
Barbel [zoology]
Bullhead B: 697 *with picture*
Catfish C: 300 *with pictures*
Loach L: 403
Nurse shark N: 614
Barbell [weight]
Weightlifting W: 183 *with picture*
Barbeque [cooking] See Barbecue *in this index*
Barber B: 106
See also Hairdressing *in this index*
Careers (Personal services) C: 228
Surgery (History) So: 1007
Barber, Amos W. [American political leader]
Wyoming (table) W: 532
Barber, John [British engineer]
Turbine (History) T: 498-500
Barber, Samuel [American composer] B: 106
Barber of Seville, The [opera by Rossini]
Opera (*Barber of Seville, The*) O: 801 *with picture*;
(*Marriage of Figaro, The*) O: 805-806;
Rossini, Gioacchino Antonio R: 484
Barber of Seville, The [play by Beaumarchais]
French literature (The Enlightenment) F: 520-521
Opera (*Marriage of Figaro, The*) O: 805-806
Barber Vintage Motorsports Museum and Park
[Birmingham]
Alabama (Places to visit) A: 266
Barbera, Joseph [American animator]

Animation (Animation in the mid-1900's) **A: 514b**
Barberry [shrub] **B: 106** *with picture*
 Rust **R: 567**
Barbershop harmony [music]
 Barbershop quartet singing **B: 107**
Barbershop Harmony Society
 Barbershop quartet singing **B: 107**
Barbershop quartet singing B: 107
Barbet [bird]
 Bird (Birds of Asia) **B: 344f** *with picture*
Barbican Centre [London]
 London (The arts) **L: 433** *with picture*
Barbie doll
 Doll (Modern dolls) **D: 292** *with picture*
Barbier, Charles [French military leader]
 Braille **B: 550**
Barbier, Jules [French librettist]
 Opera: *(Faust)* **O: 804**
Barbirolli, Sir John [British conductor] **B: 107**
Barbital [drug]
 Barbiturate **B: 107**
Barbiturate [drug] **B: 107**
 Depressant **D: 150**
 Drug (Antianxiety and hypnotic drugs) **D: 352**;
  (The drug revolution) **D: 359**
 Drug abuse (table: Some commonly abused
  drugs) **D: 363**
 Thiopental **T: 258**
Barbizon [France]
 Barbizon School **B: 107**
Barbizon School [art] **B: 107** *with picture*
 Corot, Camille **Ci: 1069**
 Inness, George **I: 274**
 Millet, Jean François **M: 555**
 Painting (Romanticism) **P: 68**
Barbon, Nicholas [English businessman]
 Insurance (The growth of insurance) **I: 315**
Barbour, Haley [American political leader]
 Mississippi (table) **M: 640**
Barbour, James [American political leader]
 Adams, John Quincy (table) **A: 43**
 Virginia (table) **V: 417**
Barbour, Philip P. [American jurist]
 Supreme Court of the United States (table)
  So: 1000
Barbs [drug] *See* Barbiturate *in this index*
Barbuda [island, Caribbean Sea]
 Antigua and Barbuda **A: 555** *with map*
Barbule [zoology]
 Bird (Feathers) **B: 362**
 Feather (Kinds and parts of feathers) **F: 59** *with
  diagram*
Barcarole [music] **B: 108**
Barcelona [Spain] **B: 108** *with picture*
 International trade *picture on* **I: 348**
 Olympic Games (The recent games) **O: 753**
Barcelona chair
 Bauhaus *picture on* **B: 173**
 Furniture (The Bauhaus) **F: 582-583** *with picture*
Barchan [geology]
 Desert (Desert climate and land) **D: 155-156**
Barchester Towers [book by Trollope]
 Trollope, Anthony **T: 449**
Bard [minstrel] **B: 109**
 Homer (Homer's poems) **H: 303**; (The Homeric
  question today) **H: 304**
 Irish literature (Early Irish literature) **I: 430**
 Minstrel **M: 611**
"Bard, The" [poem by Gray]
 Gray, Thomas **G: 335**
Bardeen, John [American physicist] **B: 109**
 Electricity (The electronic age) **E: 198**
 Electronics (The solid-state revolution) **E: 215**
  with picture
 Superconductivity **So: 992**
 Transistor **T: 372**
Bardem, Javier [Spanish actor]
 Motion picture (Best performance by an actor in
  a supporting role: 2007) **M: 862b**
Bardiya [king of Persia]
 Darius I **D: 36**
Bare-knuckle boxing [sports]
 Boxing *picture on* **B: 531**; (The revival of boxing)
  B: 532 *with picture*
Bare-root plant
 Nursery **N: 614**
Bareback riding [sport]
 Rodeo **R: 397**
Barenboim, Daniel [Israeli musician] **B: 109**
 Du Pré, Jacqueline **D: 387**
Barents, Willem [Dutch navigator] **B: 109**
 Arctic (Search for the Northwest Passage)
  A: 638-639
 Exploration (The search for a northern passage)
  E: 446
Barents Island [Arctic]
 Svalbard **So: 1014**

Barents Sea [Arctic] **B: 109**
Baret, Jeanne [French explorer]
 Exploration (Exploring the Pacific) **E: 447-448**
Bargate [wall]
 Southampton **So: 686** *with picture*
Barge [boat] **B: 109**
 Inland waterway **I: 273**
 Ship (Egyptian ships) **S: 415**
 Transportation (Freight transportation) **T: 395**
  with picture
Barge dog *See* Schipperke *in this index*
Bargello [stitch]
 Needlepoint **N: 118**
Barges on the Thames [painting by Derain]
 Derain, André *picture on* **D: 152**
Bari throne [sculpture]
 Sculpture (The 1000's) **S: 249** *with picture*
Bariatric surgery **B: 109** *with diagram*
 Obesity (Surgery) **O: 642b**; (Treatment for
  children) **O: 642b-643**
Barisan Mountains [volcanoes]
 Indonesia (Sumatra) **I: 233**
Barite [mineral]
 Barium **B: 110**
 Crystal (Classifying crystals) **Ci: 1166-1167** *with
  picture*
Barito River [Borneo]
 Borneo (The land and its resources) **B: 489** *with
  map*
Baritone [music]
 Opera (The singers) **O: 792**
 Singing (Voice classification) **S: 472**
Baritone horn [musical instrument]
 Music *picture on* **M: 949**; (Wind instruments)
  M: 949-950
Barium [element] **B: 110**
Barium carbonate [chemical]
 Barium **B: 110**
Barium ferrite [chemical]
 Barium **B: 110**
Barium nitrate [chemical]
 Barium **B: 110**
 Saltpeter **S: 76a**
Barium oxide [chemical]
 Barium **B: 110**
 Saltpeter **S: 76a**
Barium sulfate [chemical]
 Barium **B: 110**
Barium test [medicine]
 Barium **B: 110**
Bark [botany] **B: 110** *with diagram*
 Birch **B: 327** *with pictures*
 Cork (The tree) **Ci: 1054**
 Lenticel **L: 196b**
 Tree (Trunk and branches) **T: 416** *with diagram*
Bark beetle
 Arctic (Climate change) **A: 640**
 Dutch elm disease **D: 392**
 Elm (Diseases) **E: 245**
Bark grafting
 Grafting (Kinds of grafting) **G: 298** *with picture*
Bark painting [art]
 Australia (Painting) **A: 905** *with picture*
Barker, Pat [British author]
 English literature (Recent English fiction) **E: 323**
Barking
 Dog (Behavior) **D: 277**
Barking deer [animal] *See* Muntjac *in this index*
Barking frog [animal]
 Frog (Other frogs) **F: 540**
Barking Sands [Hawaii]
 Hawaii (Places to visit) **H: 98**
Barkla, Charles Glover [British physicist]
 Nobel Prizes (Physics: 1917) **N: 440**
Barkley, Alben William [American political leader]
 B: 111 *with portrait*
 Truman, Harry S. (Election of 1948) **T: 470**
Barkley, Charles [American basketball player]
 B: 112 *with portrait*
Barlach, Ernst Heinrich [German sculptor] **B: 112**
Barley [plant] **B: 112** *with pictures*
 Alcoholic beverage (Beer) **A: 336**
 Brewing (Malting) **B: 595**
 Malt **M: 112**
Barley malt [grain]
 Beer **B: 211**
Barlick, Al [American baseball player]
 Baseball (table: Hall of Fame) **B: 134**
Barlow's disease
 Scurvy **S: 261**
Barm [yeast]
 Yeast (How yeast is made) **Y: 555**
Barn **B: 113** *with picture*
 Cattle *picture on* **C: 307**
 Dairying (Housing) **D: 7**
Barn cleaner [machine]
 Dairying (Housing) **D: 7**

"Barn Dance" [radio program]
 Country music (Early commercial success)
  Ci: 1098b
Barn-door skate [sea animal]
 Skate **S: 478**
Barn owl
 Bird of prey **B: 374a**
 Owl (Important owls) **O: 884** *with picture*
Barn swallow [bird]
 Bird *picture on* **B: 344d**
 Swallow **So: 1014** *with picture*
Barnabas [Biblical figure] **B: 113**
 Mark, Saint **M: 213**
 Paul, Saint (Missionary career) **P: 200**
Barnaby Rudge [book by Dickens]
 Dickens, Charles (The first phase) **D: 188**
Barnacle [sea animal] **B: 113** *with pictures*
 Crustacean *picture on* **Ci: 1163**
 Larva **L: 78**
 Ocean *picture on* **O: 656**
Barnard, Christiaan Neethling [South African
  doctor] **B: 114**
 Heart (The first heart transplants and artificial
  hearts) **H: 145**
 Surgery (History) **So: 1007-1008**
Barnard, Edward Emerson [American astronomer]
 B: 114
Barnard, Frederick Augustus Porter [American
  educator] **B: 114**
Barnard College [New York]
 Barnard, Frederick Augustus Porter **B: 114**
 Columbia University (Affiliated institutions)
  Ci: 853
Barnard's Star [star]
 Star (table: The 10 known stars nearest Earth)
  So: 843
Barnburners [U.S. history] **B: 114**
 Free Soil Party **F: 499**
Barnegat Lighthouse
 New Jersey (Places to visit) **N: 240** *with picture*
Barnes, Julian [British author]
 Novel (The novel today) **N: 575**
Barnes, Roy [American political leader]
 Georgia (table) **G: 130**
Barnes Foundation
 Philadelphia (Libraries and museums) **P: 363-364**
Barnes icecap
 Icecap **I: 19**
Barnet, Battle of [1471]
 Henry VI [of England] **H: 187**
Barnett, Ross R. [American political leader]
 Mississippi (table) **M: 640**
Barnett, William [British inventor]
 Gasoline engine (Development of the gasoline
  engine) **G: 66**
Barnette, E. T. [American businessman]
 Fairbanks **F: 9**
Barney's Version [book by Richler]
 Richler, Mordecai **R: 331**
Barnstorming [aviation]
 Airplane (The golden age) **A: 235**
Barnum, P. T. [American businessman] **B: 115** *with
  portrait*
 Bridgeport **B: 606**
 Circus (The Greatest Show on Earth) **Ci: 563**
 Lind, Jenny **L: 329** *with picture*
 United States, History of the (Cultural changes)
  U: 173
Barnum & Bailey Circus
 Barnum, P. T. **B: 115**
 Circus (The circus goes international) **Ci: 563-564**
 Ringling brothers **R: 343**
Barnum Museum [Connecticut]
 Circus (Places to visit and annual events) **Ci: 566**
Barograph [measuring device]
 Barometer (Kinds of barometers) **B: 115-116**
Baroja, Pío [Spanish author]
 Spanish literature (The Generation of 1898)
  So: 762
Barometer [measuring device] **B: 115** *with
  diagrams*
 Air (Weight and pressure) **A: 171**
 Hydraulics (Use of hydrostatic principles) **H: 463**
 Weather (Land-based observation stations)
  W: 162
Barometer Rising [book by MacLennan]
 MacLennan, Hugh **M: 25**
Baron [title] **B: 116**
 Henry III **H: 186**
 Magna Carta (Reasons for the charter) **M: 52-53**
 Nobility (In the United Kingdom) **N: 450**
Baron Munchausen's Narrative [book]
 Munchausen, Baron **M: 927**
Baron Scarpia [opera character]
 Opera: *(Tosca)* **O: 807**
Baroness [title]
 Baron **B: 116**

Lady **L:** 25
Nobility (In the United Kingdom) **N:** 450
Baronet [title]
    Baron **B:** 116
Barong tagalog [clothing]
    Philippines (Way of life) **P:** 374-375
Barophile [biology]
    Extremophile **E:** 458
Baroque [arts] **B:** 116
    Architecture (Baroque architecture) **A:** 622
    Austria (Architecture) **A:** 932
    Bach, Johann Sebastian **B:** 15
    Bernini, Gian Lorenzo **B:** 271
    Borromini, Francesco **B:** 491
    Classical music (The Baroque period) **Ci:** 647
    Europe (From 1600 to 1900) **E:** 392
    German literature (Baroque literature) **G:** 139
    Italian literature (The Baroque period and the
        Enlightenment) **I:** 494
    Italy (Arts) **I:** 504 *with picture*
    Latin America (Architecture) **L:** 99 *with picture*
    Latin American literature (Colonial literature)
        L: 112
    Opera (Baroque opera) **O:** 797
    Painting (The 1600's and 1700's) **P:** 58 *with
        pictures*
    Rococo **R:** 396
    Sculpture (European sculpture) **S:** 253 *with
        picture*
    Spanish literature (The 1600's) **So:** 759
Baroque pearl
    Pearl (Shape) **P:** 217
Barossa Valley [region, Australia] **B:** 117
Barotrauma [disorder]
    Diving, Underwater (Dangers of underwater
        diving) **D:** 246
Barquisimeto [Venezuela] **B:** 117
Barr, William P. [American government official]
    Justice, Department of (table) **J:** 203
Barrack-Room Ballads [book by Kipling]
    Kipling, Rudyard (Early literary success) **K:** 334
Barracuda [fish] **B:** 117 *with picture*
    Fish *picture on* **F:** 153
Barragán, Luis [Mexican architect]
    Latin America (Architecture) **L:** 99
Barranca del Cobre [canyon, Mexico]
    Mexico (The Plateau of Mexico) **M:** 461-462 *with
        map*
Barras, Vicomte de [French political leader]
    Josephine **J:** 168
    Napoleon I (The "whiff of grapeshot") **N:** 14
Barratt's Chapel
    Delaware (Places to visit) **D:** 102 *with picture*
Barrault, Jean-Louis [French actor] **B:** 118
Barre [ballet]
    Ballet (The ballet studio) **B:** 46 *with picture*
Barre, Mohamed Siad [Somalian military leader]
    Somalia (History) **So:** 589
Barré-Sinoussi, Françoise [French biologist]
    Nobel Prizes (Physiology or medicine: 2008)
        N: 447
Barred antshrike [bird]
    Bird *picture on* **B:** 344a
Barred feather
    Chicken (Kinds of chickens) **C:** 441
Barred owl
    Owl (Important owls) **O:** 884
Barred spiral galaxy [astronomy]
    Galaxy (Spiral galaxies) **G:** 8a *with picture*
    Milky Way (Shape of the galaxy) **M:** 550
Barrel [container] **B:** 118 *with diagrams*
Barrel [gun]
    Firearm (Mechanism) **F:** 132 *with diagrams*
    Handgun (Parts of a handgun) **H:** 43 *with pictures*
    Rifle (The parts of a rifle) **R:** 338 *with diagram*
Barrel [measurement]
    Barrel **B:** 118
    Petroleum (table) **P:** 332
    Weights and measures (Miscellaneous weights
        and measures) **W:** 184
Barrel burnishing [industrial process]
    Aluminum (Mechanical finishes) **A:** 396
Barrel cactus [plant]
    Cactus (Kinds of cactuses) **C:** 11 *with picture*
    Plant *picture on* **P:** 526
Barrel organ [musical instrument]
    Hand organ **H:** 41
Barrel racing
    Rodeo *picture on* **R:** 398; (Barrel racing) **R:** 397
Barrel sponge [animal]
    Deep sea (Invertebrates) **D:** 82a-82b *with picture*
Barrel vault [architecture]
    Vault **V:** 291
Barren ground caribou [animal]
    Caribou **C:** 238
    Mammal *picture on* **M:** 125
Barren grounds [region]

Northwest Territories (Barren grounds) **N:** 531
Barren Lives [book by Ramos]
    Latin American literature (The early 1900's) **L:** 113
Barrera [bullfighting]
    Bullfighting (The bullring) **B:** 695
Barrett, David [Canadian political leader]
    British Columbia (table) **B:** 628; (The late 1900's)
        B: 630-631
Barrett, Elizabeth [British poet] *See* Browning,
    Elizabeth Barrett *in this index*
Barrett, Frank A. [American political leader]
    Wyoming (table) **W:** 532
Barrette, Antonio [Canadian political leader]
    Quebec (table) **Q:** 29
Barrie, J. M. [Scottish author] **B:** 118
    Peter Pan **P:** 325
Barrier beach
    Beach **B:** 178
Barrier island
    Island *diagram on* **I:** 471; (Barrier islands) **I:** 473
    Lagoon **L:** 30
Barrier Reef [Australia] *See* Great Barrier Reef *in
    this index*
Barrier reef [geology]
    Coral reef (Kinds of coral reefs) **Ci:** 1048b
Barringer, Daniel M. [American engineer]
    Meteor Crater **M:** 432
Barringer Crater *See* Meteor Crater *in this index*
Barrio [district]
    Buenos Aires (The city) **B:** 672
    Hispanic Americans (Conflict) **H:** 252
    Los Angeles (East Los Angeles) **L:** 461-462 *with
        picture*
Barrios, Justo Rufino [Guatemalan political leader]
    B: 118
Barrister [law]
    Lawyer **L:** 147
Barron, James [American military leader] **B:** 119
    Decatur, Stephen **D:** 67
    War of 1812 (Impressment of seamen) **W:** 29
Barron, William Wallace [American political
    leader]
    West Virginia (table) **W:** 225
Barroso, José Manuel [Portuguese political leader]
    Bono *picture on* **B:** 462
Barrow [Alaska]
    Alaska (table; Average monthly weather) **A:** 295
    United States (Climate) **U:** 126 *with picture*
Barrow [animal]
    Hog (table) **H:** 284
Barrow, Dean [Belize political leader]
    Belize (History) **B:** 238
Barrow, Edward G. [American sportsman]
    Baseball (table: Hall of Fame) **B:** 134
Barrow, Errol W. [Barbadian political leader]
    Barbados (History) **B:** 104
Barrow, Joe Louis [birth name of]
    Louis, Joe **L:** 477
Barrows, Lewis O. [American political leader]
    Maine (table) **M:** 87
Barry [design]
    Heraldry *picture on* **H:** 195
Barry, Sir Charles [British architect]
    Architecture (The Gothic Revival) **A:** 626
Barry, John [American military leader] **B:** 119
Barry, John S. [American political leader]
    Michigan (table) **M:** 507
Barry, Marion S., Jr. [American political leader]
    Kelly, Sharon Pratt **K:** 257
Barry, Philip [American dramatist] **B:** 119
Barry, William T. [American government official]
    Jackson, Andrew (table) **J:** 11
Barrymore [family] **B:** 119 *with picture*
Barrymore, Diana [American actress]
    Barrymore **B:** 119
Barrymore, Drew [American actress]
    Barrymore **B:** 119
Barrymore, Ethel [American actress]
    Barrymore **B:** 119 *with picture*
    Motion picture (Best performance by an actress
        in a supporting role: 1944) **M:** 862b
Barrymore, John [American actor]
    Barrymore **B:** 119 *with picture*
Barrymore, Lionel [American actor]
    Barrymore **B:** 119 *with picture*
    Motion picture (Best performance by an actor:
        1930-31) **M:** 862a
Barrymore, Maurice [American actor]
    Barrymore **B:** 119
"Bars Fight" [poem by Terry]
    African American literature (Early works) **A:** 136-
        136a
"Barsetshire Novels" [books by Trollope]
    Trollope, Anthony **T:** 449
Barstow, John L. [American political leader]
    Vermont (table) **V:** 333
Barstow, William A. [American political leader]

Wisconsin (table) **W:** 365
BART [transit system] *See* Bay Area Rapid Transit
    System *in this index*
Barter [economics] **B:** 120
    Colonial life in America (Money) **Ci:** 811
    Egypt, Ancient (Work of the people) **E:** 138
    Trade (The use of money) **T:** 362
    Trading post **T:** 365
Barter sale [transaction]
    Television (Syndicated programming) **T:** 114
Barth, John [American author] **B:** 120
    American literature (Experimental styles) **A:** 425
Barth, Karl [Swiss theologian] **B:** 120
    Christianity (Neo-Orthodoxy) **C:** 526
Bartholdi, Auguste-Charlotte [French model]
    Statue of Liberty *picture on* **So:** 874
Bartholdi, Frédéric Auguste [French sculptor]
    B: 120
    Statue of Liberty **So:** 872, *picture on* **So:** 874;
        (History) **So:** 876
Bartholomew, Saint [apostle] **B:** 120
Bartholomew Fair [English history]
    Doll (The Middle Ages) **D:** 288
Bartholomew's Day Massacre *See* Saint
    Bartholomew's Day, Massacre of *in this index*
Bartle Frere, Mount [Australia]
    Queensland (Land and climate) **Q:** 39
Bartleson, John [American pioneer]
    California (American settlement) **C:** 60
Bartlett, Dewey F. [American political leader]
    Oklahoma (table) **O:** 730
Bartlett, Edward Lewis [American political leader]
    B: 120
Bartlett, Jennifer [American artist]
    Painting (New image painting) **P:** 87
Bartlett, John [American publisher] **B:** 120
Bartlett, John H. [American political leader]
    New Hampshire (table) **N:** 223
Bartlett, Josiah [American patriot] **B:** 121
    New Hampshire (table) **N:** 223
Bartlett, Robert Abram [Canadian-American
    explorer] **B:** 121
Bartlett, Washington [American political leader]
    California (table) **C:** 59
Bartlett pear
    Pear (Varieties) **P:** 215
Bartley, Mordecai [American political leader]
    Ohio (table) **O:** 699
Bartley, Thomas W. [American political leader]
    Ohio (table) **O:** 699
Bartók, Béla [Hungarian composer] **B:** 121
    Classical music (The 1900's) **Ci:** 649
    Hungary (The arts) **H:** 442
Bartoletti, Bruno [Italian conductor]
    Opera *picture on* **O:** 793
Bartolo, Doctor [literary figure]
    Opera (Barber of Seville, The) **O:** 801 *with picture*
Barton, Andrew [American composer]
    Yankee Doodle **Y:** 552
Barton, Bruce [American author]
    Roaring Twenties (Rising prosperity) **R:** 363
Barton, Clara [American nurse] **B:** 121 *with portrait*
    Civil War, American (Hospitals) **Ci:** 630
    Red Cross (In the United States) **R:** 187
Barton, Sir Derek [British chemist]
    Nobel Prizes (Chemistry: 1969) **N:** 443
Barton, Edmund [Australian political leader]
    Australia (table) **A:** 923
Barton, George E. [American architect]
    Occupational therapy (History) **O:** 649
Barton, Otis [American diver]
    Exploration (Deep-sea exploration) **E:** 450-451
Barton, William [American heraldist]
    Great Seal of the United States **G:** 348
Barton, William H. [Canadian statesman]
    United Nations (table) **U:** 86
Bartram, John [American botanist]
    Colonial life in America (Science) **Ci:** 808-809
Barú, Volcán [mountain, Panama]
    Panama (The Central Highland) **P:** 119
Baruch [Bible]
    Bible (The Christian Old Testament) **B:** 282
Baruch, Bernard Mannes [American government
    official] **B:** 122
    World War I (The United States enters the war)
        W: 462
Barya saltpeter [chemical] *See* Barium nitrate *in
    this index*
Barycenter [astronomy]
    Earth (Earth and its moon) **E:** 18
Barye, Antoine Louis [French artist] **B:** 122
    Minotaur *picture on* **M:** 611
Baryon [physics] **B:** 122
    Hadron **H:** 5
    Quark **Q:** 7
    Subatomic particle (Composite particles) **So:** 937
Baryonyx [dinosaur] **B:** 122

Baryshnikov, Mikhail [Soviet-born dancer] **B: 122**
with picture
Ballet *picture on* **B: 55**; (Ballet in Russia) **B: 52-53**
Barzun, Jacques [American educator] **B: 123**
Baseball (The 1900's) **B: 134-135**
Bas-relief [art]
Assyria *picture on* **A: 821**
Cameo **C: 80**
Drama *picture on* **D: 327**
Relief **R: 213**
Basal cell [anatomy]
Skin (Epidermis) **S: 489** *with picture*
Basal cell cancer [disease]
Skin cancer (Nonmelanoma skin cancer) **S: 492**
Basal ganglia [anatomy]
Lesch-Nyhan syndrome **L: 206**
Basal metabolic rate [physiology]
Metabolism (Control of metabolism) **M: 424**
Basal reader [textbook]
Reading (The developmental method) **R: 157**
Basalt [china]
Wedgwood ware **W: 179**
Basalt [geology] **B: 123**
Earth (The lithosphere) **E: 20**
Giant's Causeway *picture on* **G: 184**
Global warming (Carbon sequestration) **G: 232c**
Igneous rock **I: 49**
Mars (Crust) **M: 225**
Moon *picture on* **M: 790**; (Origin and evolution of the moon) **M: 788**
Ocean (How the sea floor was formed) **O: 662**
Rock (Extrusive rock) **R: 371**; (table) **R: 373** *with picture*
Volcano (Flood basalts) **V: 442a**
Basaltic magma [material]
Moon (Mantle) **M: 791**
Basaseachic Falls [waterfall, Mexico]
Waterfall (table: Famous waterfalls of North America) **W: 142**
Bascarsija [area]
Bosnia-Herzegovina *picture on* **B: 494**
Basch, Samuel Siegfried von [Austrian physician]
Heart (Invention of new medical instruments) **H: 144**
Bascio, Matteo da [Italian religious leader]
Capuchins **C: 199**
Bascom Hall
Wisconsin, University of *picture on* **W: 370**
Bascule bridge [construction]
Bridge (Moveable bridges) **B: 602** *with diagram*
Base [baseball]
Baseball (The infield) **B: 126** *with diagrams*
Base [chemistry] **B: 123**
See also Alkali *in this index*
Heredity (The flow of genetic information) **H: 205**
Hydroxide **H: 474**
Litmus **L: 391**
Molecular biology (The beginning of molecular biology) **M: 691-692**
Neutralization **N: 154**
pH **P: 353**
Soil (Chemical conditions) **So: 575**
Base [electronics]
Transistor (How transistors work) **T: 372-373** *with diagram*
Base [genetics]
DNA **D: 258**
Genetic engineering (How genes are reintroduced into cells) **G: 84b**
Genetic testing (How genes carry information) **G: 84d**
Human Genome Project (The structure and importance of genomes) **H: 427**
Base [geometry]
Cylinder **Ci: 1204** *with picture*
Base [mathematics]
Logarithms **L: 424**
Number (The decimal system) **N: 605**
Power **P: 728**
Base ball [name for]
Baseball (From rounders to baseball) **B: 132**
Base-burner shell
Ammunition (Artillery ammunition) **A: 435**
Base charge [explosives]
Detonator **D: 167**
Base community [religion]
Liberation theology **L: 228**
Base data [cartography]
Map (Observation and measurement) **M: 180**
Base exchange [store]
Post exchange **P: 699**
Base hit [baseball]
Baseball (Reaching base) **B: 129**; (table: Modern major league records) **B: 138**
Base isolation [building construction]
Earthquake (Building design) **E: 34** *with diagram*
Base line [surveying]

Public lands (Management of public lands) **P: 858**
Base metal
Alloy **A: 377**
Money (Chinese coins) **M: 707**
Base on balls [baseball]
Baseball (Reaching base) **B: 129**
Base pair [genetics]
DNA **D: 258**
Genetic engineering (How genes are reintroduced into cells) **G: 84b** *with diagram*
Heredity (The structure of DNA) **H: 205-206**
Molecular medicine **M: 692**
Watson, James Dewey **W: 147**
Base period [economics]
Inflation (Measuring inflation) **I: 267**
Base quantity [measurement]
Metric system (Structure of the metric system) **M: 437**
Base running [baseball]
Baseball (Base running) **B: 128**; (Base runners—advancing and outs) **B: 129** *with picture*
Base station
Cellular telephone **C: 340**
Telephone (Cellular phone calls) **T: 97**
Base station controller [electronic device]
Telephone (Cellular phone calls) **T: 97**
Base ten system [mathematics] *See* Decimal system *in this index*
Base two system [mathematics] *See* Binary number *in this index*
Base unit [measurement]
Metric system (Kinds of metric units) **M: 436**
Base word [language]
Spelling (Base words) **So: 776**
Base year [economics]
Gross domestic product (Real GDP) **G: 399**
Baseball [ball]
Baseball (Equipment) **B: 125** *with picture*
Baseball [sport] **B: 124** *with pictures*
See also the list of Related articles in the Baseball *article*
Cuba *picture on* **Ci: 1172**
Doubleday, Abner **D: 312**
Glove *picture on* **G: 235**
Indiana (Interesting facts) **I: 197**
Little League Baseball **L: 391**
Softball **So: 571**
United States *picture on* **U: 115**
Baseball Congress, National
Baseball (Amateur leagues) **B: 131-132**
Baseball Hall of Fame [New York]
Baseball (table: Hall of Fame) **B: 134**
Cooperstown **Ci: 1037**
Hall of fame *picture on* **H: 24**; (Sports halls of fame) **H: 23**
New York *picture on* **N: 296**; (Places to visit) **N: 302**
Baseball Players Association, Major League
Labor movement (table) **L: 8**
Baseburner [range]
Heating (History) **H: 160-161**
Basel [Switzerland] **B: 140**
Basel, Council of [1433]
Hussites **H: 458**
Baselitz, Georg [German artist]
Painting (Neoexpressionism) **P: 87**
Basement [architecture]
House *diagram on* **H: 383**; (The foundation) **H: 380**
Insulation (In buildings) **I: 306** *with diagram*
Basenji [dog] **B: 140**
Dog *picture on* **D: 271**
Basescu, Traian [Romanian political leader]
Romania (Recent developments) **R: 426**
BASF [company]
Manufacturing (table) **M: 170**
Bashford, Coles [American political leader]
Wisconsin (table) **W: 365**; (Statehood) **W: 366**
Bashir, Umar Hassan Ahmad al- [Sudanese political leader]
Sudan (Civil war) **So: 953**; (Violence in Darfur) **So: 954**
Basho [tournament]
Sumo **So: 973**
Basho, Matsuo [Japanese poet]
Haiku **H: 8**
BASIC [computer language]
Computer (Using programming languages) **Ci: 923**
Microsoft Corporation **M: 519**
Basic chemical [industry]
Chemistry (The chemical industry) **C: 405**
Basic emotion approach [psychology]
Emotion (The basic emotion approach) **E: 261**
Basic exemption [economics]
Flat tax **F: 228**
Basic Law [1997]
Hong Kong (Government) **H: 319**; (The return to

Chinese rule) **H: 320**
Basic oxygen process [manufacturing]
Iron and steel (The basic oxygen process [BOP]) **I: 441** *with diagrams*
Oxygen (Other uses of oxygen) **O: 889**
Basic state pension
Pension (Pensions in other countries) **P: 273**
Basic training [military]
Air Force, United States (Recruit training) **A: 188**
Army, United States (Training a soldier) **A: 730** *with pictures*
Coast Guard, United States (Training a recruit) **Ci: 736**
Marine Corps, United States (Training a Marine) **M: 206**
Navy, United States (Training a sailor) **N: 83**
Basic transport airport
Airport (General aviation airports) **A: 243**
Basic utility airport
Airport (General aviation airports) **A: 243**
Basidium [botany]
Mushroom (Parts of a mushroom) **M: 942** *with picture*
Basie, Count [American bandleader] **B: 140**
Basij [militia]
Iran (National government) **I: 399**
Basil [plant] **B: 140**
Basil I [Byzantine emperor]
Byzantine Empire (The middle period) **B: 754**
Basil II [Byzantine emperor]
Bulgaria (The first Bulgarian kingdom) **B: 692**
Byzantine Empire (The middle period) **B: 754**
Basil, Saint [early Christian] **B: 140**
Christianity (The medieval church) **C: 524**
Monasticism (Christian monasticism) **M: 701**
Religious life (Religious life in early Christianity) **R: 226**
Basilar membrane [anatomy]
Ear *diagram on* **E: 10**; (The inner ear) **E: 8-9** *with diagram*
Basilica [architecture] **B: 140**
Architecture (Medieval architecture) **A: 617** *with picture*
Church **C: 541**
Basilica Aemilia [ruins]
Forum, Roman **F: 421** *with picture*
Basilica Julia [ruins]
Forum, Roman **F: 421** *with picture*
Basilica of ...
Basilicas appear under their key words, as in Constantine, Basilica of
Basilique Notre-Dame [basilica]
Montreal *picture on* **M: 775**
Quebec (Churches) **Q: 36**
Basin [geography] **B: 141**
Moon (Basins) **M: 789**; (Determining the origin of craters) **M: 793-794**
River **R: 351**
Basin Head Fisheries Museum [Prince Edward Island]
Prince Edward Island (Places to visit) **P: 788**
Basin irrigation [agriculture]
Egypt (Agriculture) **E: 128**
Basin Park Hotel [Eureka Springs]
Arkansas (Interesting facts about Arkansas) **A: 695**
Basinger, Kim [American actress]
Motion picture (Best performance by an actress in a supporting role: 1997) **M: 862b**
Basis of Union [document]
United Church of Canada (Doctrine and organization) **U: 46**
Baskerville [type face]
Baskerville, John **B: 141**
Type *pictures on* **T: 536**
Baskerville, John [British printer] **B: 141**
Book (The 1600's and 1700's) **B: 467**
Basket *See* Basket making *in this index*
Basket [sports]
Basketball (The court) **B: 143** *with picture*
Basket Makers [people]
Nevada (Indian days) **N: 173**
Basket making [art] **B: 141** *with pictures*
Indian, American *pictures on* **I: 138, I: 139, I: 140**; (Basketry) **I: 145** *with picture*; (Before European contact) **I: 163-164**
Weaving (The plain weave) **W: 173**
Willow **W: 314**
Basket of Discipline [religion]
Buddhism (The dharma) **B: 668**
Basket of Discourses [religion]
Buddhism (The dharma) **B: 668**
Basket of the Higher Dharma [religion]
Buddhism (The dharma) **B: 668**
Basket stitch
Knitting *picture on* **K: 354**
Basket willow [plant]

Osier O: 863
Basketball [sport] B: 143 *with pictures*
　China *picture on* C: 485
　Indian, American (Recreation) I: 142
　Indiana *picture on* I: 200
　Luisetti, Hank L: 516
　Naismith, James N: 4
　National Basketball Association N: 30
　Olympic Games (The recent games) O: 753
Basketball Association of America
　National Basketball Association N: 30
Basketball Hall of Fame *See* Naismith Memorial
　Basketball Hall of Fame *in this index*
Basketry *See* Basket making *in this index*
Basketweave stitch
　Needlepoint N: 118
Baskin, Leonard [American artist] B: 155
Basking shark [fish] B: 155 *with picture*
　Shark (Kinds of sharks) S: 375
Basophil [cell]
　Blood (Protecting against disease) B: 410
　Immune system (Allergies) I: 88c
Basotho [people]
　Lesotho (People) L: 206
Basotho Congress Party
　Lesotho (History) L: 208
Basov, Nikolai Gennadievich [Russian physicist]
　Laser (History) L: 86
　Nobel Prizes (Physics: 1964) N: 441
　Prokhorov, Alexander Mikhailovich P: 817
Basque Homeland and Freedom [political group]
　See ETA *in this index*
Basque Nationalist Action party
　Basques B: 156
Basques [people] B: 156
　Bilbao B: 299
　Boise B: 440
　Charlemagne (Military conquests) C: 379
　Gascony G: 60
　Spain (Language) So: 733; (Growth and
　　discontent) So: 751; (Political changes) So: 751
　Terrorism (Terrorist groups and movements)
　　T: 178
　Whale (The Basque people) W: 262
Basquiat, Jean-Michel [American artist]
　Painting (Recent painting) P: 87 *with picture*
Basra [ancient province]
　Persian Gulf War of 1991 (Disputes between Iraq
　　and Kuwait) P: 300b
Basra [Iraq] B: 156
Bass [fish] B: 156 *with pictures*
　Fish F: 153
Bass [musical instrument] B: 157 *with picture*
　Jazz (The bass) J: 69
　Music (Stringed instruments) M: 948 *with picture*
Bass [singing]
　Opera (The singers) O: 792
　Singing (Voice classification) S: 472
Bass, George [British explorer]
　Australia *map on* A: 921; (Mapping the continent)
　　A: 922
　Victoria (History) V: 357
Bass, Robert P. [American political leader]
　New Hampshire (table) N: 223
Bass, Sam [American bandit]
　Texas (Conquering the frontier) T: 207
Bass-bar [music]
　Violin (Parts of the violin) V: 389
Bass clef [music]
　Music (Indicating pitch) M: 952-953 *with picture*
Bass drum [musical instrument]
　Drum D: 367
Bass flute [musical instrument]
　Flute F: 307
Bass Strait [Australia-Tasmania]
　Tasmania (Land and climate) T: 48
Bass trombone [musical instrument]
　Trombone T: 450
Bass viol [musical instrument] *See* Bass *in this index*
Bassa [people]
　Liberia (People) L: 229
Basse-taille [art]
　Enamel (Techniques) E: 264
Basse-Terre [island, Caribbean Sea]
　Guadeloupe G: 408
Basset hound [dog] B: 158
　Dog *picture on* D: 271
Basseterre [Caribbean Sea]
　Saint Kitts and Nevis S: 38 *with picture*
Bassett, Richard [American political leader] B: 158
　Delaware (table) D: 109
Basso buffo [music]
　Opera (The singers) O: 792
Basso cantante [music]
　Opera (The singers) O: 792
Basso continuo [music]
　Bach, Johann Sebastian (His works) B: 16

Classical music (The Baroque period) Ci: 647
　Orchestra (Beginnings) O: 822
Basso Narok [former name]
　Lake Turkana L: 47
Bassoon [musical instrument] B: 158 *with pictures*
　Music (Wind instruments) M: 949 *with picture*
Basswood [tree] *See* Linden *in this index*
Bast [Egyptian mythology]
　Cat (History) C: 296
Bastarache, Michel [Canadian jurist]
　Supreme Court of Canada (table) So: 997 *with
　　portrait*
Bastet [Egyptian mythology]
　Cat (History) C: 296
Bastia [Corsica]
　Corsica (Size and description) Ci: 1072 *with map*
Bastian, Adolf [German anthropologist]
　Anthropology (Development of field research)
　　A: 548
Bastidas, Rodrigo de [Spanish explorer]
　Panama (The Spanish colonial period) P: 120
　Santa Marta S: 115
Bastille [French history] B: 158 *with picture*
　France (The French Revolution) F: 474 *with
　　picture*
　French Revolution (The revolution begins) F: 525
　World, History of the *picture on* W: 443
Bastille Day [holiday] B: 158
　France (Holidays) F: 460 *with picture*
Basting [stitch]
　Sewing (Hand stitches) S: 332
Basuto [people]
　Lesotho (People) L: 207
Basutoland [former protectorate]
　Lesotho (History) L: 208
Basutoland National Party [political party]
　Lesotho (History) L: 208
Bat [animal] B: 158 *with pictures*
　Animal *pictures on* A: 483, A: 492
　Ear (The ears of animals) E: 12 *with picture*
　Hand (Animal hands) H: 40
　Mammal *picture on* M: 117; (In the air) M: 122
　　with diagram; (table) M: 128 *with picture*
　Vampire bat V: 268 *with picture*
Bat [sports]
　Baseball (Equipment) B: 125
　Cricket (Equipment) Ci: 1131-1132 *with picture*
Bat-eared fox [animal]
　Fox (Bat-eared foxes) F: 440
Bat mitzvah [religion] B: 162
　Bible *picture on* B: 279
　Judaism (Special occasions) J: 182
Bataan Death March [World War II] B: 162 *with
　map*
　World War II (Early Japanese victories) W: 487-
　　488 *with picture*
Bataan Peninsula [region, Philippines]
　Bataan Death March B: 162 *with map*
　MacArthur, Douglas (World War II) M: 3
　World War II (Early Japanese victories) W: 487-
　　488
Batak [people]
　Indonesia (Rural life) I: 229
　Sumatra So: 971
Batalha [Portugal]
　Portugal *picture on* P: 690
Batasuna [political group]
　Basques B: 156
Batavia [former name]
　Jakarta (History) J: 22
Batavian Republic [Dutch history]
　Netherlands (The 1700's) N: 149
Batch freezer [machine]
　Ice cream (How ice cream is made) I: 8-9
Batch furnace [machine]
　Furnace (Heating the charge) F: 567
Batchelder, Nahum J. [American political leader]
　New Hampshire (table) N: 223
Bate, William B. [American political leader]
　Tennessee (table) T: 152
"Bateau ivre, Le" [poem by Rimbaud]
　Rimbaud, Arthur R: 341
Bateau Lavoir [building]
　Picasso, Pablo (The Blue Period) P: 448a
Batéké [people]
　Congo, Republic of the (People) Ci: 940d
Batéké Plateau [region]
　Congo, Republic of the (Land) Ci: 940d-940e
　　with map
Bates, Edward [American government official]
　Emancipation Proclamation *picture on* E: 254
　Justice, Department of (table) J: 203
　Lincoln, Abraham (table) L: 323
Bates, Frederick [American political leader]
　Missouri (table) M: 668
Bates, Henry Walter [British naturalist]
　Animal (Camouflage) A: 493-496

Bates, John L. [American political leader]
　Massachusetts (table) M: 288
Bates, Katharine Lee [American poet] B: 162
　America the Beautiful A: 407
Bates, Kathy [American actress]
　Motion picture (Best performance by an actress:
　　1990) M: 862a
Batesian mimicry [zoology]
　Animal (Camouflage) A: 493-496
　Snake (Protection against predators) S: 531
Bath [England] B: 163
　Georgian architecture G: 136
Bath [North Carolina]
　North Carolina (Colonial days) N: 492
Bath [hygiene] B: 163 *with pictures*
　Baby (Bathing the baby) B: 10 *with picture*
　Dog (Grooming) D: 278
　Hydrotherapy H: 472 *with picture*
　Indus Valley civilization *picture on* I: 241
　Pet *picture on* P: 319; (Cleanliness) P: 322
　Rome (Baths) R: 433
　Rome, Ancient (Recreation) R: 440
　Sauna S: 163
　Space exploration (Meeting basic needs in space)
　　So: 703
　Turkish bath T: 514
Bath, Order of the [award] B: 165
　Knighthood, Orders of (Honorary orders) K: 347
　　with pictures
Bath, The [painting by Cassatt]
　Cassatt, Mary *picture on* C: 275
　Painting (New visual sources) P: 72
Bath Iron Works [Maine]
　Maine (Transportation) M: 86-87 *with picture*
Bath sponge
　Sponge (Skeleton) So: 799
Bathers [painting by Fragonard]
　Painting (Rococo painting) P: 65-66 *with picture*
Bathing *See* Bath *in this index*
Batholith [geology]
　Rock (Intrusive rocks) R: 371-372
Bathroom
　Interior design *picture on* I: 331
　Safety (In the bathroom) S: 10 *with picture*
Baths of Caracalla [ruins]
　Architecture (Roman architecture) A: 616
　Rome *picture on* R: 430; (Baths) R: 433
Baths of Diocletian [ruins]
　Rome (Baths) R: 433
Bathsheba [Biblical figure] B: 165
　David (King of Israel) D: 45
　Solomon So: 584
Bathtub
　Bath (History) B: 164 *with pictures*
Bathurst [Gambia]
　Banjul B: 87
Bathyscaph [diving vessel]
　Diving, Underwater (Diving in vehicles) D: 246
　Exploration (Deep-sea exploration) E: 450-451
　Pacific Ocean (Scientific research) P: 15
　Piccard, Auguste P: 450
　Piccard, Jacques P: 450
Bathysphere [diving vessel]
　Diving, Underwater (Diving in vehicles) D: 246
　Exploration (Deep-sea exploration) E: 450-451
Batik [craft] B: 165
　Indonesia (The arts) I: 232-233
　Malaysia (Clothing) M: 98d
Bating [industrial process]
　Leather (Preparing the hides) L: 167
Batista y Zaldívar, Fulgencio [Cuban political
　leader] B: 165
　Castro, Fidel C: 283
　Castro, Raúl C: 283
　Cuba (History) Ci: 1175-1177 *with picture*
　Latin America (Political circumstances in the early
　　to middle 1900's) L: 109-110
Batlle Ibáñez, Jorge [Uruguayan political leader]
　Uruguay (The late 1900's) U: 228
Batlle y Ordóñez, José [Uruguayan political
　leader]
　Uruguay (Reforms in the early 1900's) U: 227
Batman [fictional character] B: 165 *with picture*
Batman [film]
　Batman B: 166
　Burton, Tim B: 712
Batman, John [Australian pioneer]
　Melbourne (History) M: 389
Batoche National Historic Site [Saskatchewan]
　Canada (table: National historic sites) C: 114
Baton [sports]
　Baton twirling B: 167
Baton Rouge [Louisiana] B: 166 *with picture*
　Louisiana L: 478, *picture on* L: 479
Baton twirling B: 167 *with picture*
Batsman [cricket]
　Cricket Ci: 1131; (The batting side) Ci: 1133-1134

with picture

Batt, Phil [American political leader]
Idaho (table) I: 42

Batt insulation
Insulation (In buildings) I: 306 *with picture*

Battalion [military unit]
Army (The organization of armies) A: 725
Army, United States (table) A: 737
Infantry (Divisions) I: 264

Battelle Memorial Institute [Ohio] B: 167
Columbus (Economy) Ci: 855

Batten [scenery]
Theater (Kinds of scenery) T: 239-240

Battenberg [German history] B: 167

Batter [baking]
Baking (Baking ingredients) B: 33

Batter [sports]
Baseball (Batting) B: 128 *with pictures*

Battered child syndrome
Child abuse C: 455

Battering ram [munitions] B: 167 *with picture*

Batter's box [baseball]
Baseball (The infield) B: 126 *with diagram*

Battersea Park [London]
London (Parks) L: 435-436

Battery [baseball]
Baseball (Player positions) B: 127

Battery [device] B: 168 *with pictures*
See also Solar cell *in this index*
Automobile *diagram on* A: 952; (Power systems)
A: 947-948 *with diagram*; (Providing electric
power) A: 951; (Powering electric and hybrid
cars) A: 954 *with diagram*; (The electric car)
A: 965
Clock (Electric clocks) Ci: 682k
Edison, Thomas Alva (Batteries) E: 81
Electric car E: 165
Electricity (Sources of current) E: 194 *with
diagram*
Electrode E: 200
Fuel cell F: 551
Hearing aid H: 130 *with diagram*
Hydrometer H: 471
Ignition (Parts of an ignition system) I: 49
Lead L: 148 *with picture*

Battery [law]
Assault and battery A: 817

Battery [military]
Army (The organization of armies) A: 725
Army, United States (table) A: 737

Battery ignition [engine]
Ignition (Parts of an ignition system) I: 49

Batting [cricket]
Cricket (The batting side) Ci: 1133 *with picture*

Batting average [baseball]
Baseball (Baseball terms) B: 124; (table: Modern
major league records) B: 138

Batting helmet
Baseball (Equipment) B: 125

Batting order
Baseball (The game) B: 128

Battle
*Historical battles appear under their key words, as
in Blenheim, Battle of. See also War and the list
of Related articles in the Army and Navy articles*

Battle, John S. [American political leader]
Virginia (table) V: 419

Battle Above the Clouds See Chattanooga, Battle
of *in this index*

"Battle Beyond the Don, The" [poem]
Russian literature (The literature of Tatar
captivity) R: 559

Battle Born State [nickname]
Nevada N: 157

Battle Creek [Michigan] B: 172
Michigan (Interesting facts) M: 489;
(Manufacturing) M: 505

Battle Creek Sanitarium
Michigan (Interesting facts) M: 489

Battle efficiency pennant [U.S.]
Flag *picture on* F: 194

Battle fatigue [psychology] *See* Post-traumatic
stress disorder *in this index*

Battle flag
Flag (Military flags) F: 195-196

Battle group [military unit]
Navy (The organization of navies) N: 77

"Battle Hymn of the Republic" [hymn] B: 172
Civil War, American (The home front) Ci: 622
Howe, Julia Ward H: 400

Battle Monument [Maryland]
Baltimore (Other interesting places to visit) B: 69

Battle Monument [New Jersey]
Trenton (Description) T: 434

Battle of ...
*Historical battles appear under their key words, as
in Bulge, Battle of the*

Battle of Anghiari [painting by Leonardo]
Leonardo da Vinci (Return to Florence) L: 199

Battle of Flowers Parade
Flower *picture on* F: 274

Battle of Lepanto, The [painting by Vicentino]
Navy *picture on* N: 80

Battle of San Romano, The [painting by Uccello]
Uccello, Paolo U: 3 *with picture*

Battle of the Amazons [painting by Rubens]
Painting (Baroque) P: 58-61 *with picture*

Battle of the Books, The [book by Swift]
Swift, Jonathan (Swift's other works) So: 1040-
1041 *with picture*

Battle of the Châteauguay National Historic Site
[Quebec]
Canada (table: National historic sites) C: 114

Battle of the Gods and Giants [sculpture]
Sculpture (Archaic sculpture) S: 245 *with picture*

Battle of the Restigouche National Historic Site
[Quebec]
Canada (table: National historic sites) C: 114

Battle of the sexes [tennis]
Tennis (Tennis today) T: 166d-166e

Battle royal [contest]
Luchas libre L: 514

Battle streamer
Flag (Military flags) F: 195-196

Battlement [architecture]
Castle (Structure) C: 280

Battleship B: 172 *with picture*
Navy (The history of navies) N: 79
Navy, United States (Combat ships) N: 84
Warship *pictures on* W: 43; (The birth of the
modern battleship) W: 41
Washington Conference W: 109
World War I (A build-up of military might)
W: 453-454

Battleship North Carolina Memorial [Wilmington]
North Carolina (Places to visit) N: 482

Battleship Potemkin, The [film] *See* Potemkin *in
this index*

Battling Bob [nickname]
La Follette (Robert Marion La Follette, Sr.) L: 29

Batu [Mongol warrior]
Russia (Mongol rule) R: 548

Batutsi [people] *See* Tutsi *in this index*

Batyushkov, Konstantin [Russian poet]
Russian literature (Preromanticism) R: 560

Baudelaire, Charles [French poet] B: 173
French literature (Symbolism) F: 522
Poetry (Beginnings of modern poetry) P: 597
Symbolism So: 1066

Baudelaire children [fictional characters]
Snicket, Lemony S: 538

Baudouin [king of Belgium]
Belgium (After World War II) B: 235

Bauhaus [art] B: 173
Architecture (Walter Gropius) A: 630 *with picture*
Breuer, Marcel Lajos B: 595
Feininger, Lyonel F: 68
Furniture (The Bauhaus) F: 582
Germany *picture on* G: 155
Gropius, Walter G: 397

Baum, L. Frank [American author] B: 174

Baum, William Wakefield [American religious
leader]
Cardinal (table: American cardinals) C: 211

Baumgartner, Felix [Austrian skydiver]
Balloon (Balloon explorations) B: 62

Bausch & Lomb [company]
Light (Studying light) L: 292

Bauxite [mineral] B: 174
Alumina A: 390
Aluminum (Sources of aluminum) A: 392-393
with map; (How aluminum is produced) A: 393
with diagram
Guinea (Economy) G: 430-431 *with picture*
Jamaica J: 23

Bavadra, Timoci [Fijian political leader]
Fiji (History) F: 98-99

Bavaria [state, Germany] B: 174 *with map*
Germany *picture on* G: 145; (The breakup of
Charlemagne's empire) G: 162

Bavarian Alps [mountains, Germany]
Germany (The Bavarian Alps) G: 157 *with picture
and map*

Bavarian Folk Costume Day [festival]
Folk dancing *picture on* F: 320

Bavarian Succession, War of the *See* Succession
wars *in this index*

BAWI [government program]
Mississippi (The early 1900's) M: 643-644

Baxter, Anne [American actress]
Motion picture (Best performance by an actress
in a supporting role: 1946) M: 862b

Baxter, Elisha [American political leader]
Arkansas (table) A: 712; (Reconstruction) A: 714

Baxter, John B. M. [Canadian political leader]
New Brunswick (table) N: 195

Baxter, Percival P. [American political leader]
Maine (table) M: 87

Baxter, Warner [American actor]
Motion picture (Best performance by an actor:
1928-29) M: 862a

Bay [color]
Horse (Coat and skin) H: 348-349

Bay [geography] B: 175
Ocean (The world ocean) O: 651
Seashore (Life on muddy shores) S: 270

Bay Area Rapid Transit system [San Francisco]
Oakland (Economy) O: 637
San Francisco (Transportation and
communication) S: 97

Bay Area style [architecture]
Morgan, Julia M: 804

Bay Bridge *See* San Francisco-Oakland Bay Bridge
in this index

Bay Colony *See* Massachusetts Bay Colony *in this
index*

Bay leaves [cooking herb]
Laurel L: 121 *with picture*

Bay of Bengal [Indian Ocean] B: 175 *with map*

Bay of Biscay [Atlantic Ocean] B: 175 *with map*

Bay of Fundy [Atlantic Ocean] B: 175 *with map*
Atlantic Ocean (Tides) A: 866
Moncton M: 702
New Brunswick (Interesting facts) N: 181;
(Coastline) N: 190-192 *with picture*

Bay of Naples [Italy]
Naples (The city) N: 12 *with picture*

Bay of Pigs invasion [U.S. history] B: 175
Cold War (The Bay of Pigs) Ci: 768
Cuba (The Bay of Pigs invasion) Ci: 1178
Kennedy, John Fitzgerald (Cuba) K: 265

Bay of Silence, The [book by Mallea]
Latin American literature (The mid-1900's) L: 114

Bay Psalm Book [book] B: 176
Book (The 1600's and 1700's) B: 467 *with picture*
Daye, Stephen D: 54
Massachusetts (Communication) M: 287

Bay Settlement
Belize (History) B: 238

Bay shilling [money]
Pine-tree shilling P: 471 *with pictures*

Bay State [name for]
Massachusetts M: 271

Bay window
Window W: 334

Baya weaver [bird]
Weaver W: 172

Bayar, Celâl [Turkish political leader]
Turkey (The 1950's and 1960's) T: 511

Bayard, Thomas Francis [American political
leader]
Cleveland, Grover (table) Ci: 671

Bayberry [tree] B: 176 *with pictures*

Bayberry wax [tree product]
Bayberry B: 176

Baye St. Laurens [bay]
Gulf of Saint Lawrence G: 437

Bayer, Karl Joseph [Austrian chemist]
Aluminum (Refining the bauxite) A: 393; (Growth
of the aluminum industry) A: 397

Bayer filter mosaic [electronics]
Photography (Capturing digital images) P: 420-
421 *with picture*

Bayer process [industry]
Aluminum (Refining the bauxite) A: 393; (Growth
of the aluminum industry) A: 397

Bayerischer Wald National Park [Germany]
National park (table) N: 42f

Bayern [Germany] *See* Bavaria *in this index*

Bayeux Tapestry [artwork] B: 176 *with picture*
England *picture on* E: 305
Norman Conquest *picture on* N: 456

Bayezit II [sultan of the Ottoman Empire]
Turkey (The rise of the Ottoman Empire) T: 510

Bayh, Birch Evans, Jr. [American political leader]
B: 177

Bayh, Evan [American political leader]
Bayh, Birch Evans, Jr. B: 177
Indiana (table) I: 214

Baykal, Lake [Siberia] *See* Lake Baikal *in this index*

Baykonur Cosmodrome [Kazakhstan]
Kazakhstan (Economy) K: 250b-251

Bayley, Elizabeth Ann [birth name of]
Seton, Saint Elizabeth Ann S: 323

Baylor, Elgin [American basketball player] B: 177
Basketball *picture on* B: 153; (The history of
professional basketball) B: 154a-155

Baylor College of Medicine
Menninger Clinic M: 401

Bayon [temple]
Angkor A: 462

Bayonet [weapon] B: 177 *with picture*
Army (The rise of modern armies) A: 727
Revolution, American (Weapons and tactics)
R: 279-280 *with picture*
Bayonne [New Jersey]
New Jersey *picture on* N: 247
Bayonne Bridge [New Jersey]
Bridge (table: Steel arch) B: 603
New York City (Transportation) N: 334
Bayou [waterway] B: 177
Louisiana (Rivers, bayous, and lakes) L: 490
Bayou Folk [book by Chopin]
Chopin, Kate C: 521
Bayou Goula Indians
Baton Rouge (Government and history) B: 166
Bayou State [name for]
Louisiana L: 478
Bayreuth [Germany] B: 177
Bayreuth Festival
Bayreuth B: 177
Germany G: 154
Bayt [letter]
B B: 1 *with picture*
Bayta Llahm [name for Bethlehem]
Bethlehem B: 274
Bazaar [market] B: 177
Asia (City life) A: 780
Iran (City life) I: 401 *with picture*
Bazardyuzyu [mountain, Azerbaijan]
Azerbaijan (Land and climate) A: 996-997 *with map*
Baze, Russell [Canadian-born jockey]
Horse racing (History) H: 366
Bazooka [weapon] B: 177 *with picture*
Rocket (Military use) R: 386 *with picture*
BBB [organization] *See* Better Business Bureau *in this index*
BBC [company] *See* British Broadcasting Corporation *in this index*
BBC Trust
British Broadcasting Corporation B: 611
B.C. [calendar] B: 178
Calendar (Some calendars today) C: 29
"B.C." [comic strip]
Cartoon *pictures on* C: 267
BC Medical Services Foundation
Vancouver Foundation V: 278
B.C.C.I. [organization] *See* Bank of Credit and Commerce International SA *in this index*
B.C.E. [calendar]
B.C. B: 178
BCG [medication]
Tuberculosis (Prevention of tuberculosis) T: 479
BCS theory [physics]
Superconductivity So: 992
Be [symbol]
Beryllium B: 273
Beach B: 178
Los Angeles (Recreation) L: 467 *with picture*
Ocean (Waves) O: 659
Beach, Amy [American composer] B: 178
Beach Boys [musical group] B: 178 *with picture*
Rock music (Independent producers) R: 379; (Fresh directions) R: 380
Beach hopper [animal]
Crustacean (Growth and development) Ci: 1163-1164 *with picture*
Beach of Falesá, The [book by Stevenson]
Stevenson, Robert Louis (Novels) So: 898
Beach plum [shrub] B: 179
Beach volleyball [sport] B: 179 *with picture*
Olympic Games (Summer Olympic Games) O: 746e-746f
Beachey, Lincoln [American aviator]
Aviation *picture on* A: 988
Beachhead [military]
Amphibious warfare (Steps in amphibious operations) A: 442
Beaching
Whale (Life span) W: 261-262 *with picture*
Beacon B: 179
Beacon Hill [Boston]
Boston (Beacon Hill) B: 497 *with picture*
Beaconsfield, Earl of *See* Disraeli, Benjamin *in this index*
Bead
Beadwork B: 179 *with pictures*
Rosary R: 473
Wampum W: 22
Bead [tire]
Tire (Assembling a tire) T: 296 *with diagram*
Bead lightning
Lightning (Appearance) L: 300
Bead mill [machine]
Paint (Grinding) P: 24-25
Beaded lizard
Lizard (Defenses) L: 400

Beadle, George Wells [American geneticist] B: 179
Cell (The 1900's) C: 337-338
Beadwork [handicraft] B: 179 *with pictures*
Beagle [dog] B: 180 *with picture*
Dog *picture on* D: 271
Beagle [ship]
Darwin, Charles Robert (Darwin's life) D: 40
Evolution (Darwin's theory) E: 432
Beagle 2 [spacecraft]
Mars (Observation by spacecraft) M: 226c-226d
Beak [zoology]
See also Bill [zoology] *in this index*
Evolution (Geographic distribution of species) E: 430-431 *with picture*
Beaked whale
Whale *picture on* W: 257; (Beaked whales) W: 258
Beaker folk [ancient people]
Scotland (History) S: 218
"Beale Street Blues" [song]
Memphis (The city) M: 394
Beam [construction]
Building construction (Beams, girders, and columns) B: 682-683
House (The frame) H: 382 *with diagram*
Skyscraper (Building skyscrapers) S: 497
Beam [measurement]
Ship (Nautical terms) S: 405
Beam cutting [manufacturing]
Machine tool (Beam cutting) M: 19
Beam pump
Petroleum (Primary recovery) P: 341-342
Beam-riding guidance
Guided missile (Beam-riding guidance) G: 426 *with diagram*
Beam scale [instrument]
Scale, Weighing (Mechanical scales) S: 169
Beam system [communications]
Marconi, Guglielmo (Short-wave radio) M: 197
Beamon, Bob [American athlete]
Olympic Games (The 1968 games) O: 752
Bean [plant] B: 180 *with pictures*
Nutrition (Carbohydrates) N: 625
Bean, Judge Roy [American frontiersman] B: 182 *with picture*
Bean, The [sculpture]
Chicago (Places to visit) C: 430-431
Bean beetle [insect] B: 182 *with picture*
Bean curd [food]
Tofu T: 308
Bean of history *See* Broad bean *in this index*
Beanbag chair
Furniture (Radical modern design) F: 585 *with picture*
Beanes, William [American public figure]
Key, Francis Scott K: 308
"Star-Spangled Banner" (How the song came to be written) So: 854
Beantown [nickname]
Boston (Early settlement) B: 503
Bear [animal] B: 182 *with pictures*
Animal *pictures on* A: 478, A: 484, A: 485, A: 507
Hibernation (Warm-blooded hibernators) H: 222 *with picture*
Panda K: 128
Bear [economics] *See* Bear market *in this index*
Bear [rank]
Boy Scouts (Cub Scouting) B: 535
Bear Dance, Preparing for a Bear Hunt [painting by Catlin]
Dance *picture on* D: 24
Bear Driver [constellation]
Boötes B: 480
Bear Flag [U.S. history]
Flag *picture on* F: 210
Bear Flag Revolt [1846]
California (The Mexican War) C: 60-62
Mexican War (The occupation of New Mexico and California) M: 446
Bear Lake [Utah-Idaho]
Utah (Rivers and lakes) U: 242 *with map*
Bear market [economics]
Bears and bulls B: 189
Bear Mountain Bridge [Hudson River]
New York *picture on* N: 290
Bear River [river, U.S.]
Wyoming (Rivers and lakes) W: 528
Bear River, Battle of [1863]
Bannock Indians B: 98
Bear Stearns & Co. [bank]
Bank (Crisis in finance) B: 95
Bearbaiting [sport]
Bear (Brown bears) B: 184
Beard [botany]
Wheat *pictures on* W: 269; (Structure) W: 267-268 *with diagram*
Beard [hair] B: 186
Burnside, Ambrose Everett B: 710 *with picture*

Beard, Daniel Carter [American naturalist] B: 187
Bearded bellbird
Bellbird B: 243
Bearded collie [dog] B: 187 *with picture*
Bearded dragon [lizard] B: 187 *with picture*
Bearded Mille Fleur [chicken]
Chicken *picture on* C: 442
Bearden, Romare [American artist] B: 187 *with pictures*
Beardsley, Aubrey Vincent [British artist] B: 188 *with picture*
Art Nouveau A: 750
Beardsley, William S. [American political leader]
Iowa (table) I: 391
Bearing [industry] B: 188 *with diagrams*
Bearing [navigation]
Navigation (Piloting) N: 70-71
Bearing-wall construction
Building construction (Types of construction) B: 683 *with picture*
House (The frame) H: 382
Bears, Chicago [team] *See* Chicago Bears *in this index*
Bears and bulls [economics] B: 189
Stock exchange (Stock prices and indexes) So: 904
Bears Paw Mountains [Montana]
Indian wars (The Nez Perce War [1877]) I: 194
Montana (Land regions) M: 752 *with map*
Bearskin Neck [Rockport]
Massachusetts (Places to visit) M: 280 *with picture*
Beartooth Highway
Montana (Places to visit) M: 750
Beartooth Mountains
Montana (Land regions) M: 752
Beast Butler [nickname]
Butler, Benjamin Franklin B: 729
Beast of burden
Transportation (Land transportation) T: 383
Beat [journalism]
Newspaper (Gathering information) N: 382
Beat [physics]
Acoustics A: 29
Sound (Beats) So: 604 *with diagram*
Beat [police]
Police (Police activities) P: 620
Beat movement [cultural history] B: 189
American literature (Variations on Modernist poetry) A: 423
Ferlinghetti, Lawrence F: 73
Ginsberg, Allen G: 192
Kerouac, Jack K: 306
Poetry (Poetry of the 1900's) P: 597
Beater [tool]
Weaving (How a loom works) W: 173-174 *with picture*
Beatification [religion]
Saint (Roman Catholic saints) S: 30
Beating to windward
Sailing (Basic sailing maneuvers) S: 26 *with diagram*
Beatitudes [New Testament] B: 189
Beatlemania
Rock music *picture on* R: 380
Beatles [musical group] B: 189 *with picture*
Hairdressing (The 1900's) H: 12-13
Lennon, John L: 195
McCartney, Paul M: 332c
Rock music (The British invasion) R: 379; (Fresh directions) R: 380 *with picture*
Beatnik
Beat movement B: 189
Beaton, David [Scottish religious leader]
Knox, John (Early years) K: 358
Beatrice [literary figure]
Dante Alighieri (His life) D: 33
Divine Comedy D: 242
Shakespeare, William (*Much Ado About Nothing*) S: 360
Beatrix [queen of the Netherlands] B: 190 *with portrait*
Netherlands (Political changes) N: 150
Beatty, Paul [American author]
African American literature (Recent developments) A: 136a
Beatty, Warren [American actor] B: 190 *with portrait*
Motion picture (Best achievement in directing: 1981) M: 862
Beau Brummell [British public figure] *See* Brummell, George Bryan *in this index*
Beaubear's Island Shipbuilding National Historic Site [New Brunswick]
Canada (table: National historic sites) C: 114
Beauchamp, Kathleen Mansfield [British author] *See* Mansfield, Katherine *in this index*
Beauchamps, Pierre [French dance teacher]

Ballet (The rise of professional ballet) B: 51
Beaufort, Duke of [British nobleman]
  Badminton B: 24
Beaufort, Sir Francis [British admiral]
  Wind (The Beaufort wind scale) W: 330
Beaufort, Margaret [mother of Henry VII]
  Tudor, House of T: 481
Beaufort Gyre [current]
  Arctic Ocean (Sea ice) A: 641
Beaufort scale [meteorology]
  Wind (The Beaufort wind scale) W: 330
Beauharnais, Eugène de [son of]
  Josephine J: 168
Beauharnais, Hortense de [daughter of]
  Josephine J: 168
Beauharnais, Josephine de See Josephine in this index
Beauharnais, Vicomte Alexandre de [French nobleman]
  Josephine J: 168
Beaujoyeulx, Balthasar de [Italian musician]
  Ballet (The birth of ballet) B: 50-51
Beaulieu, Edict of [1576]
  Henry III [king of France] H: 186
Beaulieu, Priscilla [wife of]
  Presley, Elvis P: 772
Beaulieu, Victor-Lévy [Canadian author]
  Canadian literature (Modern literature: 1945 to the present) C: 159-160
Beaulne, Yvon [Canadian diplomat]
  United Nations (table) U: 86
Beaumarchais, Pierre Augustin Caron de [French dramatist] B: 191
  French literature (The Enlightenment) F: 520-521
  Opera: (Marriage of Figaro, The) O: 805-806
Beaumont [Texas] B: 191
Beaumont, Francis [English dramatist] B: 191
  English literature (Jacobean drama) E: 317
  Fletcher, John F: 234
Beaumont, John [English nobleman]
  Viscount V: 429
Beaumont, William [American doctor] B: 191
  Michigan (Interesting facts) M: 489
Beauport [Quebec]
  Quebec, Battle of (Bombardment of Quebec) Q: 37
Beauregard, Pierre Gustave Toutant [Confederate general] B: 191
  Civil War, American (The commanding officers) Ci: 618; (Fort Sumter) Ci: 624
  Lincoln, Abraham (Fort Sumter and war) L: 321
Beautician [career]
  Hairdressing H: 11
Beautiful Mind, A [film]
  Crowe, Russell Ci: 1158
  Motion picture (Best picture: 2001) M: 861
Beauty
  Aesthetics A: 90
  Art and the arts (Beauty) A: 746-747
  Philosophy (Aesthetics) P: 385
Beauty and the Beast [film]
  Dion, Céline D: 214
"Beauty is truth, truth beauty" [quotation]
  Keats, John (His work) K: 253-254
Beauvais, Armand [American political leader]
  Louisiana (table) L: 496
Beauvoir [estate]
  Davis, Jefferson (His last years) D: 48
Beauvoir, Simone de [French author] B: 191 with portrait
  French literature (Existentialism) F: 523; (The middle and late 1900's) F: 523
  Philosophy picture on P: 389
Beaux-Arts, École des [school, Paris] See École des Beaux-Arts in this index
Beaux' Stratagem, The [play by Farquhar]
  Farquhar, George F: 47
Beaven, Robert [Canadian political leader]
  British Columbia (table) B: 628
Beaver [animal] B: 192 with pictures
  Animal picture on A: 478
  Fur picture on F: 562; (table) F: 561
  Fur trade F: 564
  Mammal diagram on M: 121
Beaver, James Addams [American political leader]
  Pennsylvania (table) P: 263
Beaver Dam, Battle of [1813]
  Secord, Laura Ingersoll S: 278
Beaver Island [Lake Michigan]
  Michigan (Islands) M: 500
Beaver Scout [rank]
  Scouts Canada (Age groups) S: 224
Beaver State [name for]
  Oregon O: 826
Beaver-tail cactus
  Flower picture on F: 291
Beaverbrook, Lord [British publisher] B: 195

Beaverhead Mountains
  Montana (Land regions) M: 752
Beavers Bend State Park
  Oklahoma picture on O: 713
Beban, Gary [American football player]
  Football (table) F: 363
Bebb, William [American political leader]
  Ohio (table) O: 699
Bébé [doll]
  Doll (Porcelain dolls) D: 290-291
Bebel, August [German political leader] B: 196
Bebop [music]
  Davis, Miles D: 49
  Gillespie, Dizzy G: 190
  Jazz (Bebop) J: 72 with picture
  Monk, Thelonious M: 725
  Parker, Charlie P: 169
BEC [physics] See Bose-Einstein condensate in this index
"Because I Could Not Stop for Death" [poem by Dickinson]
  Dickinson, Emily (Her poems) D: 190-191
Because of Winn-Dixie [book by DiCamillo]
  DiCamillo, Kate D: 186
Beccaria, Cesare [Italian criminologist] See Beccaria, Marchese di in this index
Beccaria, Marchese di [Italian criminologist]
  Criminology (History) C: 1145
  Italian literature (The Baroque period and the Enlightenment) I: 494-495
Bêche-de-mer [food]
  Trepang T: 435
Bechet, Sidney [American musician] B: 196
Bechuanaland Protectorate
  Botswana (History) B: 512
  Rhodes, Cecil John (Gains Rhodesia) R: 317
Becker, Boris [German tennis player] B: 196
Becker, Gary Stanley [American economist]
  Economics (Modern economics) E: 64-65
  Nobel Prizes (Economics: 1992) N: 449
Becker muscular dystrophy [disease]
  Muscular dystrophy (Other muscular dystrophies) M: 937
Becket [play by Anouilh]
  Anouilh, Jean A: 519
Becket, Saint Thomas [English religious leader] B: 196
  England (Struggles for power) E: 305-306
  Henry II [of England] H: 185
Beckett, Samuel [Irish-French author] B: 196
  Drama (Theater of the Absurd) D: 340 with picture
  French literature (Developments in drama) F: 523
  Irish literature (Drama) I: 432
  Novel (After World War II) N: 574
Beckham, David [British soccer player] B: 197
Beckham, J. C. W. [American political leader]
  Kentucky (The early 1900's) K: 293-294
Beckley, Jake [American baseball player]
  Baseball (table: Hall of Fame) B: 134
Beckley Exhibition Coal Mine [Beckley]
  West Virginia (Places to visit) W: 216
Beckmann, Max [German painter] B: 197 with picture
  Germany (Painting and sculpture) G: 155
Becknell, William [American frontiersman]
  New Mexico (Mexican rule) N: 273-275
  Santa Fe Trail S: 115
  Westward movement in America (The Santa Fe Trail) W: 249
Beckwourth, James Pierson [American frontiersman] B: 197
  Bannock Indians B: 98
Beckwourth Pass [Sierra Nevada Mountains]
  Beckwourth, James Pierson B: 197
Becque, Henri François [French dramatist]
  French literature (Naturalism) F: 522
Bécquer, Gustavo Adolfo [Spanish poet]
  Spanish literature (The 1800's) So: 761
Becquerel [measurement]
  Curie Ci: 1194
Becquerel, Alexandre Edmond [French physicist]
  Becquerel, Antoine César B: 197
  Solar energy (The development of photovoltaic cells) So: 577
Becquerel, Antoine César [French physicist] B: 197
Becquerel, Antoine Henri [French physicist] B: 197
  Curie, Marie Skłodowska Ci: 1194
  Nuclear energy (Early developments) N: 589
  Physics (The beginning of modern physics) P: 440-441
  Radiation (Discovery of radioactivity) R: 81
  Uranium (History of the use of uranium) U: 216
Becquerel, Louis Alfred [French physicist]
  Becquerel, Antoine César B: 197
Bed [agriculture]
  Cotton (Planting) Ci: 1090

BED [disorder] See Binge eating in this index
Bed [furniture] B: 197 with pictures
  Colonial life in America (Furnishings) Ci: 797
  Furniture F: 568; (Ancient Egypt) F: 570
  Pioneer life in America (Furniture and household utensils) P: 481
Bed [geology]
  Coal (How coal was formed) Ci: 720-721
  Ore B: 825
  Sedimentary rock S: 280
Bed [painting by Rauschenberg]
  Painting picture on P: 85; (The revival of subject matter) P: 86
Bed [printing]
  Printing (Letterpress printing) P: 799-800
Bed [river]
  River (Channels) R: 352
Bed [zoology]
  Oyster (Young) O: 891
Bed bug [insect] B: 198
  Insect picture on I: 281
Bed trick [theater]
  Shakespeare, William (Dramatic conventions) S: 354
Bedbug [insect] See Bed bug in this index
Bedchamber, Lady of the [title]
  Royal Household of the United Kingdom R: 498
Beddington Zero [housing project]
  Housing (Sustainable housing) H: 392-393 with picture
Bede, Saint [English historian] B: 199
  English literature (Old English prose) E: 315
Bedford, Gunning, Sr. [American political leader]
  Delaware (table) D: 109
Bedford, Gunning, Jr. [American political leader] B: 199
Bedford Flag [U.S. history]
  Flag picture on F: 210
Bedford-Stuyvesant [district, New York City]
  New York City (Brooklyn) N: 326-328
Bédié, Henri Konan [Ivorian political leader]
  Côte d'Ivoire (History) Ci: 1084b-1085
Bedlam [place]
  Mental illness (Early attitudes) M: 408
Bedle, Joseph D. [American political leader]
  New Jersey (table) N: 249
Bedlington terrier [dog] B: 199
  Dog picture on D: 273
Bedloe, Isaac [American landowner]
  Statue of Liberty (Description) So: 873
Bedloe's Island [New York City]
  Liberty Island L: 233
  Statue of Liberty (Description) So: 873
Bednorz, Johannes Georg [German physicist]
  Nobel Prizes (Physics: 1987) N: 442
Bedouins [people] B: 199
  Africa (Rural life) A: 107
  Arabs (Life in the Arab world) A: 586
  Egypt (People) E: 123
  Jordan (Way of life) J: 162
  Saudi Arabia (Rural life) S: 157
  Syria (People) So: 1071
Bedrock [geology]
  Glacier (How glaciers shape the land) G: 203-204 with diagrams
Bedroom
  Interior design pictures on I: 328, I: 332
Bedsore [disorder] B: 199
  Ulcer U: 15
Bedstead [furniture]
  Bed (Types of beds) B: 198
Bedstraw [plant] B: 199
Bee [insect] B: 200 with pictures
  See also Bumble bee; Honey bee in this index
  First aid (Injected poisons) F: 137-138
  Flower (Other uses) F: 273-274; (Cross-pollination) F: 295 with picture
  Frisch, Karl von F: 534
  Insect pictures on I: 283-284; (Wings) I: 288; (Family life) I: 294-295 with picture
  Mimicry M: 562
  Plant (Sexual reproduction) P: 532-533 with picture
  Pollen (Cross-pollination) P: 645 with pictures
Bee, Barnard E. [Confederate general]
  Jackson, Stonewall J: 16
Bee assassin [insect]
  Bee (Enemies) B: 205
Bee-eater [bird] B: 208
  Bird (Birds of Europe) B: 344c with picture
Bee fly [insect] B: 208 with picture
Bee Gees [rock group]
  Rock music (Disco) R: 380c
Bee hummingbird [bird]
  Animal picture on A: 469
  Bird picture on B: 329
  Hummingbird picture on H: 434; (Size) H: 433

Bee martin [bird] *See* Kingbird *in this index*
Bee orchid
  Flower *picture on* F: 272
Bee purple [color]
  Butterfly (The head) B: 738 *with picture*
Bee tree *See* Linden *in this index*
Beebe, Mike [American political leader]
  Arkansas (table) A: 712
Beebe, William [American naturalist] B: 208 *with portrait*
  Exploration (Deep-sea exploration) E: 450-451
Beebread [biology]
  Bee (From egg to adult) B: 202-203
Beech [tree] B: 208 *with pictures*
  Tree *pictures on* T: 420
Beech marten [animal]
  Marten M: 233
Beecham, Sir Thomas [British conductor] B: 209
Beecher, Catharine Esther [American educator] B: 209
  Family and consumer sciences (History) F: 26
  Stowe, Harriet Beecher (Her life) So: 916
Beecher, Henry Ward [American religious leader] B: 209
  Stowe, Harriet Beecher (Her life) So: 916
Beecher, Lyman [American religious leader] B: 209
  Stowe, Harriet Beecher (Her life) So: 916
Beeches, The [estate]
  Coolidge, Calvin (Later years) Ci: 1033
Beechnut
  Beech B: 208 *with picture*
Beechwood
  Beech B: 209
  Wood *picture on* W: 389
Beeckman, R. Livingston [American political leader]
  Rhode Island (table) R: 311
Beef [food] B: 209 *with diagrams*
  Cattle C: 306; (Beef cattle) C: 308; (Dual-purpose cattle) C: 311
  Creutzfeldt-Jakob disease Ci: 1129
  Meat *pictures on* M: 349; (Kinds of meat) M: 347
  Meat packing M: 350
  Veal V: 291
Beefalo [animal]
  Buffalo (Protection of bison) B: 675
Beefeater [nickname]
  Yeoman Y: 564
Beefmaster [cattle]
  Cattle (Beefmaster) C: 308 *with picture*; (table) C: 312
Beefmaster [tomato]
  Tomato (The tomato plant) T: 324-325
Beefwood [tree] B: 211 *with picture*
Beehive [nest] *See* Hive *in this index*
Beehive House [Salt Lake City]
  Utah (Places to visit) U: 238
Beehive State [name for]
  Utah U: 231
Beehive tomb
  Architecture (Mycenaean architecture) A: 615
Beekeeping
  Bee (Beekeeping) B: 206 *with diagram*
Beelzebub [Biblical figure] B: 211
Beeper [machine] *See* Pager *in this index*
Beer B: 211
  Alcoholic beverage (Beer) A: 336
  Brewing B: 595
  Coal (Developments in England) Ci: 731
  England (Food and drink) E: 295-296
  Germany (Food and drink) G: 150
  Hop H: 332
  Indian, American (Food) I: 136d
  Oktoberfest O: 738
  Yeast Y: 554
Beer Hall Putsch [German history]
  Hitler, Adolf (The Beer Hall Putsch) H: 266
  Ludendorff, Erich Friedrich Wilhelm L: 515
  Munich (History) M: 927
Beerbohm, Max [British author] B: 211
Beernaert, Auguste Marie François [Belgian statesman]
  Nobel Prizes (Peace: 1909) N: 448
Beers, Clifford Whittingham [American social reformer] B: 212
Beers, George [Canadian lacrosse player]
  Lacrosse (History) L: 24
Beersheba [Israel] B: 212
Beery, Wallace [American actor]
  Motion picture (Best performance by an actor: 1931-1932) M: 862a
Beeswax B: 212
  Bee (Making wax) B: 204
  Candle C: 175
Beet [plant] B: 212 *with picture*
  Sugar beet So: 962
Beet sugar

Sugar (Sugar from sugar beets) So: 961-962
  Sugar beet So: 962
Beet yellows [disease]
  Sugar beet (Raising sugar beets) So: 962
Beethoven, Johann van [brother of]
  Beethoven, Ludwig van (Beethoven's life) B: 213
Beethoven, Johann van [father of]
  Beethoven, Ludwig van (Beethoven's life) B: 213
Beethoven, Karl van [brother of]
  Beethoven, Ludwig van (Beethoven's life) B: 213
Beethoven, Ludwig van [German composer]
  B: 213 *with portrait*
  Austria (Music) A: 932
  Autograph *picture on* A: 943
  Classical music (The Classical period) Ci: 647-648 *with picture*; (The Romantic era) Ci: 648
  Germany G: 153
  Liszt, Franz (His works) L: 350
  Music (Melody) M: 951
  Symphony So: 1067
Beethoven-House
  Bonn (Education and cultural life) B: 461
Beetle [automobile]
  Automobile *picture on* A: 969
  Volkswagen AG V: 444
Beetle [insect] B: 214 *with pictures*
  Animal *picture on* A: 507
  Flower (Beetles and flies) F: 295
  Insect *pictures on* I: 283, I: 285; (Wings) I: 288
Beetleweed [plant]
  Coltsfoot Ci: 851
Beezus and Ramona [book by Cleary]
  Cleary, Beverly C: 660
Befana, La [legendary figure]
  Christmas (In Italy) C: 531; (Gift giving) C: 534
  Folklore (Holidays) F: 325
Begay, Harrison [American painter]
  Indian, American *picture on* I: 168
Beggar on Horseback [play by Connelly and Kaufman]
  Connelly, Marc Ci: 972
Beggar-ticks [plants] B: 219 *with picture*
Beggar's-button [plant] *See* Burdock *in this index*
Beggar's Opera, The [opera by Gay]
  Gay, John G: 71
  Hogarth, William H: 288
Beggarweed [plant] B: 219
Bégin, Louis N. [Canadian religious leader]
  Cardinal (table: Canadian cardinals) C: 211
Begin, Menachem [Israeli political leader] B: 219 *with portrait*
  Arab-Israeli conflict (The Camp David Accords) A: 582a
  Carter, Jimmy (Foreign affairs) C: 257-258 *with picture*
  Egypt (Renewed warfare and peace) E: 133 *with picture*
  Israel (The Camp David Accords) I: 488
  Sadat, Anwar el- S: 2
"Begin the Beguine" [song by Porter]
  Porter, Cole P: 682
Beginning reader book
  Literature for children (Picture books) L: 356 ; (The middle and late 1900's) L: 365
Begley, Ed [American actor]
  Motion picture (Best performance by an actor in a supporting role: 1962) M: 862b
Begole, Josiah W. [American political leader]
  Michigan (table) M: 507
Begonia [plant] B: 219 *with picture*
  Flower *picture on* F: 292; (Garden perennials grown from bulbs) F: 280 *with picture*; (table) F: 300 *with picture*
  Gardening *picture on* G: 37
Behaim, Martin [German navigator]
  Globe G: 233
  Map (Advances in European cartography) M: 184
Behan, Brendan [Irish author] B: 220 *with portrait*
  Irish literature (Drama) I: 432
Behavior B: 220
  Animal behavior
  Animal (How animals protect themselves) A: 493; (Courtship behavior) A: 497 *with pictures*; (How animals raise their young) A: 498 *with pictures*; (Animal migration) A: 502
  Bird (How birds live) B: 350 *with pictures*
  Comparative psychology Ci: 902a
  Dog (Why dogs do the things they do) D: 263 *with pictures*; (Behavior) D: 277
  Dominance D: 301
  Estivation E: 361
  Ethology E: 373
  Hibernation H: 222
  Instinct I: 304
  Migration M: 538
  Pheromone P: 357

  Play P: 570
  Sociobiology So: 563
  Territoriality T: 174
  Human behavior
  Abnormal psychology A: 11
  Aggression A: 141
  Child (The preschool years) C: 449; (Motivating the child's behavior) C: 451; (Special challenges and concerns) C: 452
  Collective behavior Ci: 774
  Culture Ci: 1186
  Displacement behavior D: 237
  Enlightenment (The orderliness of nature) E: 326a-326b
  Ergonomics E: 350
  Etiquette E: 374
  Freud, Sigmund (On behavior) F: 530
  Fromm, Erich F: 541
  Habit (How we learn habits) H: 2
  Hull, Clark Leonard H: 412
  Learning L: 162
  Merton, Robert King M: 419
  Morale M: 800
  Personality (Personality and environment) P: 302
  Psychoanalysis P: 846
  Psychology P: 847
  Social psychology So: 552
  Socialization So: 562
  Sociology So: 564
Behavior modification [psychology]
  Attention deficit disorder A: 879
  Education (How people learn) E: 89-90
  Learning (Theories of learning) L: 163-164
  Weight control (Behavior modification) W: 182
Behavioral genetics
  Psychology (Modern psychology) P: 850
Behavioral intervention
  See also Behavioral psychotherapy *in this index*
  Autism (Treatment) A: 942
Behavioral psychotherapy
  Anxiety disorder A: 562
  Chronic fatigue syndrome C: 539
  Mental illness (Psychotherapy) M: 407
  Psychiatry (Psychotherapy) P: 845
  Psychotherapy (Cognitive-behavioral psychotherapy) P: 852
Behavioral sciences *See* Anthropology; Behavior; Psychology; Sociology *in this index*
Behavioral test
  Audiology A: 882
Behaviorism [psychology]
  Abnormal psychology (Cognitive-behavioral theories) A: 12; (History) A: 12
  Gestalt psychology G: 175
  Psychology (Behaviorism) P: 849; (Modern psychology) P: 850
  Skinner, B. F. S: 495
  Watson, John Broadus W: 147
Beheading [execution]
  Guillotine G: 429 *with picture*
Behind-the-ear hearing aid
  Hearing aid (Styles) H: 130 *with picture*
Behistun Rock [Iran]
  Cuneiform Ci: 1192
Behn, Aphra [English author] B: 221
Behrens, Peter [German architect] B: 221
  Architecture (Early modern architecture in Europe) A: 627-629 *with picture*
Behring, Emil von [German bacteriologist]
  Immune system (The study of the immune system) I: 88d
  Nobel Prizes (Physiology or medicine: 1901) N: 444
Behrman, S. N. [American dramatist] B: 221
Beiderbecke, Bix [American musician] B: 222
  Jazz (The 1920's) J: 70 *with picture*
BeiDou navigation system
  Navigation (Satellite navigation) N: 73
Beijerinck, Martinus [Dutch botanist]
  Virus (Discovery) V: 427
Beijing [China] B: 222 *with pictures and maps*
  Architecture *picture on* A: 612
  China C: 474 *with picture, picture on* C: 477
  Olympic Games (The recent games) O: 753-755
Beijing Capital International Airport
  Airport (table) A: 245
Beijing duck [food]
  China (Food) C: 484
Beijing opera
  China (Theater) C: 490 *with picture*
  Dance (Asian theatrical dance) D: 28-29
  Drama (China) D: 336 *with picture*
  Music (Chinese music) M: 956
Beinecke Rare Book and Manuscript Library
  Library *picture on* L: 246
  Yale University (The Yale campus) Y: 548-549

Being [philosophy]
Existentialism E: 437
Heidegger, Martin H: 165
Idealism I: 46
Philosophy P: 383
Santayana, George S: 115
Sartre, Jean-Paul S: 127
Being and Having [book by Marcel]
Marcel, Gabriel M: 193
Being and Nothingness [book by Sartre]
Sartre, Jean-Paul S: 127
Beirut [Lebanon] B: 224
Lebanon L: 170 *with picture*; (War and terrorism)
L: 173 *with picture*
Beja [people]
Sudan (People) So: 951
Bejart, Maurice [French-born choreographer]
Ballet (Ballet in Europe) B: 54
Bekaa [valley, Lebanon]
Lebanon (Land and climate) L: 172
Békésy, Georg von [American physiologist]
Nobel Prizes (Physiology or medicine: 1961)
N: 446
Bel [measurement]
Decibel D: 70
Bel-Ami [book by De Maupassant]
De Maupassant, Guy D: 118
Bel canto [music]
Horne, Marilyn H: 340
Opera (table) O: 791; (Opera seria and opera buffa) O: 797
Belafonte, Harry [American entertainer] B: 224
with portrait
Belaney, Archibald Stansfeld [Canadian naturalist]
Grey Owl G: 392
Belarus B: 224a *with pictures and map*
Flag *picture on* F: 205
Russia (The new nation) R: 555
Strategic Arms Reduction Treaty So: 919
Belarusian [language]
Belarus (People) B: 224a
Belarusians [people]
Belarus (People) B: 224a
Union of Soviet Socialist Republics (People) U: 31
Belasco, David [American dramatist] B: 224d
Belau [Pacific] *See* Palau *in this index*
Belaúnde Terry, Fernando [Peruvian political leader]
Peru (The rise of APRA) P: 316; (Socialist reforms)
P: 316
Belay device [tool]
Climbing (Technical climbing) Ci: 680
Belaying [technique]
Climbing (Technical climbing) Ci: 680 *with picture*
Mountain climbing (Basic mountaineering equipment and methods) M: 897
Belch, Sir Toby [literary figure]
Shakespeare, William: (*Twelfth Night*) S: 360-361
Belding's yellowthroat [bird]
Yellowthroat Y: 560
Belém [Brazil] B: 224d *with picture*
Bélep Islands [Pacific]
New Caledonia N: 200
Belfast [Northern Ireland] B: 224d *with picture*
Northern Ireland *picture on* N: 521
United Kingdom *picture on* U: 48
Belfast Agreement [1998] *See* Good Friday
Agreement *in this index*
Belfry of Bruges and Other Poems, The [poems by Longfellow]
Longfellow, Henry Wadsworth (Author and world celebrity) L: 450
Belgae [people]
Belgium (History) B: 232
Gaul G: 70
Belgian Congo [African history]
Belgium (Independence) B: 233-234
Congo, Democratic Republic of the (Belgian rule)
Ci: 940b
Belgian hare
Rabbit R: 46 *with picture*
Belgian horse
Horse (table: Some types and breeds of horses)
H: 343; (Draft horses) H: 346 *with picture*
Belgian Malinois [dog] B: 225 *with picture*
Belgian sheepdog B: 225 *with picture*
Belgian Tervuren [dog] B: 225 *with picture*
Belgica [ship]
Amundsen, Roald (Other achievements) A: 446
Belgium B: 226 *with pictures and maps*
See also the list of Related articles in the Belgium *article*
Benelux B: 248
Christmas (In The Netherlands, Belgium, and Luxembourg) C: 531
Colonialism (Later colonialism) Ci: 813-814

Congo, Democratic Republic of the (Belgian rule)
Ci: 940b
Euro E: 379
Flanders F: 227 *with map*
Industrial Revolution (Belgium) I: 253
London, Treaties of (The Treaty of 1839) L: 444
Mercier, Désiré Joseph M: 413
New Year's Day (Modern customs) N: 289
Rwanda (History) R: 571
Wallonia W: 18 *with maps*
Walloons W: 18
World War I W: 452
World War II (The invasion of the Low Countries)
W: 474
Belgium, Commission for Relief in [Belgian history]
Hoover, Herbert Clark (Food administrator)
H: 328
Belgrade [Serbia] B: 236 *with picture*
Serbia S: 312 *with picture*
Belief
Clothing (Cultural beliefs and values) Ci: 691
Culture Ci: 1186
Hume, David (Hume's thought) H: 432
Pragmatism P: 729
Religion (Belief in a deity) R: 215
"Believe It or Not" [cartoon]
Ripley, Robert LeRoy R: 350
Belinsky, Vissarion [Russian author]
Russian literature (The age of realism) R: 562
Belize B: 236 *with pictures and map*
Flag *picture on* F: 200
Belize City B: 238
Belize B: 236 *with picture*
Belknap, William Worth [American government official]
Grant, Ulysses S. (table) G: 316; (Government frauds) G: 317
Impeachment (History) I: 91
Bell B: 238 *with pictures*
See also the list of Related articles in the Bell *article*
Carillon C: 238
Electric bell E: 165 *with diagram*
Jazz (The brass) J: 69
Lightning L: 299
Orchestra bells O: 823
Bell [zoology]
Moose (The body of a moose) M: 798 *with picture*
Bell, Acton *See* Brontë, Anne *in this index*
Bell, Alexander [British actor]
Bell, Alexander Graham (His early life) B: 240
Bell, Alexander Graham [Scottish-born American inventor] B: 240 *with picture*
Autograph *picture on* A: 943
Communication (The telephone) Ci: 882 *with picture*; (Famous first words) Ci: 884
Dolbear, Amos E. D: 284
Gray, Elisha G: 334
Hydrofoil (History) H: 468 *with picture*
Kite (History) K: 340-341
Speech therapy (History) So: 774
Telephone (History) T: 99
Bell, Alexander Melville [Scottish educator]
Bell, Alexander Graham (His early life) B: 240
Speech therapy (History) So: 774
Bell, Allen [American inventor]
Lie detector L: 271
Bell, Andrew [British educator]
School (The development of British schools)
S: 185
Bell, Sir Charles [British physician]
Bell's palsy B: 245
Bell, Charles H. [American political leader]
New Hampshire (table) N: 223
Bell, Charles J. [American political leader]
Vermont (table) V: 333
Bell, Cool Papa [American baseball player]
Baseball (table: Hall of Fame) B: 134; (Postwar baseball) B: 136
Bell, Currer *See* Brontë, Charlotte *in this index*
Bell, Elisa Symonds [Scottish artist]
Bell, Alexander Graham (His early life) B: 240
Bell, Ellis *See* Brontë, Emily *in this index*
Bell, Frank [American political leader]
Nevada (table) N: 173
Bell, Griffin Boyette [American government official]
Justice, Department of (table) J: 203
Bell, John [American political leader] B: 241
Lincoln, Abraham (Election of 1860) L: 318
New Hampshire (table) N: 223
Bell, John C., Jr. [American political leader]
Pennsylvania (table) P: 263
Bell, John H. [Canadian political leader]
Prince Edward Island (table) P: 791
Bell, Joseph [Scottish doctor]
Holmes, Sherlock H: 296

Bell, Julia [British geneticist]
Fragile X syndrome F: 450
Bell, Mabel Hubbard [wife of]
Bell, Alexander Graham (The Boston teacher)
B: 240
Bell, P. Hansborough [American political leader]
Texas (table) T: 203
Bell, Samuel [American political leader]
New Hampshire (table) N: 223
Bell, Susan Jocelyn [British astronomer] *See* Bell
Burnell, Jocelyn *in this index*
Bell, Terrel H. [American government official]
Education, Department of (table) E: 110
Reagan, Ronald Wilson (table) R: 169
Bell, The [book by Murdoch]
Murdoch, Iris M: 930
Bell Aircraft Company
Airplane (During World War II [1939-1945]) A: 238
Bell Burnell, Jocelyn [British astronomer] B: 242
Astronomy (Finding pulsars) A: 849
Pulsar P: 900a
Bell Canada Enterprises [company]
Canada (Telephone and Internet service) C: 127
Bell curve [graph]
Statistics (Probability) So: 868-869 *with diagram*
Bell for Adano, A [book by Hersey]
Hersey, John H: 216
Bell Jar, The [book by Plath]
Plath, Sylvia P: 566
Bell Laboratories *See* Bell Telephone Laboratories
in this index
Bell-lyra [musical instrument]
Glockenspiel G: 234
Bell metal
Bell (How bells are made) B: 238
Bell miner [bird]
Bird (Birds of Australia and New Zealand) B: 346
with picture
Bell of Saint Patrick's Will [Belfast]
Bell (History) B: 239
Bell pepper [plant]
Pepper P: 278 *with picture*
Bell ringer
Bell (Uses of bells) B: 239
Bell Rock [reef, Scotland]
Inchcape Rock I: 99
Bell Rock Lighthouse
Inchcape Rock I: 99
Bell Rock Lighthouse [North Sea]
Stevenson, Robert So: 897
"Bell Song" [music by Delibes]
Delibes, Léo D: 116
Bell System
AT&T Inc. A: 851
Telephone (The Bell System) T: 100
Bell Telephone Company
Bell, Alexander Graham (The telephone) B: 241
Telephone (The Bell System) T: 100
Bell Telephone Laboratories
Invention (Research laboratories) I: 357
Bell tower *See* Campanile *in this index*
Bell X-1 [aircraft]
Airplane *picture on* A: 235; (Supersonic airplanes)
A: 238
Jet propulsion (Development of jet propulsion)
J: 114-115
Sonic boom So: 593
Yeager, Charles Elwood Y: 554
Bell X-1A [aircraft]
Yeager, Charles Elwood Y: 554
Bella Coola Indians B: 242
Belladonna [plant] B: 242
Atropine A: 878
Nightshade N: 421 *with picture*
Poison (Kinds of poisons) P: 600
Belladonna lily [plant]
Amaryllis A: 401 *with picture*
Bellamy, Edward [American author] B: 242
Bellamy, Francis [American editor]
Pledge of Allegiance P: 572
Bellarmine, Saint Robert Francis Romulus [Italian religious leader] B: 242
Bellas Artes, Palacio de
Mexico City (Cultural life and recreation) M: 476b
with picture
Bellay, Joachim du [French poet] *See* Du Bellay,
Joachim *in this index*
Bellbird B: 243 *with picture*
Bird *picture on* B: 348
Belle Boyd in Camp and Prison [book by Boyd]
Boyd, Belle B: 539
Belle Isle [park]
Detroit (Parks) D: 170
Belle Isle, Strait of [Labrador-Newfoundland]
Gulf of Saint Lawrence G: 437
Belleau Wood, Battle of [1918]
World War I (The last campaigns) W: 463

Bellecourt, Clyde H. [American activist]
American Indian Movement **A:** 411
Bellecourt, Vernon [American activist]
American Indian Movement **A:** 412
Bellefontaine, Evangeline [literary figure]
Longfellow, Henry Wadsworth (Narrative poems)
L: 450
Bellerive, Jean-Max [Haitian political leader]
Haiti (History) **H:** 15-17
Bellerophon [Greek mythology]
Chimera **C:** 471
Pegasus **P:** 229
Bellevue [Nebraska]
Nebraska (Places to visit) **N:** 102
Bellevue House [Ontario]
Canada (table: National historic sites) **C:** 114
Bellflower [plant] **B:** 243
Flower (table) **F:** 300 with picture
Plant picture on **P:** 524
Belligerent [warfare]
Neutrality **N:** 153
Bellingrath Gardens and Home
Alabama (Places to visit) **A:** 266 with picture
Bellingshausen, Fabian von [Russian explorer]
Antarctica map on **A:** 538; (Early exploration)
A: 536
Exploration (The exploration of Antarctica) **E:** 450
with map
Bellini, Gentile [Italian painter] **B:** 243
Bellini, Giovanni [Italian painter] **B:** 243 with
picture
Francis of Assisi, Saint picture on **F:** 481
Bellini, Jacopo [Italian artist] **B:** 243
Bellini, Vincenzo [Italian composer] **B:** 244
Bellino, Joe [American football player]
Football (table) **F:** 363
Bellman, Carl Michael [Swedish author]
Scandinavian literature (The 1700's) **S:** 171
Bellmon, Henry [American political leader]
Oklahoma (table) **O:** 730; (The mid-1900's) **O:** 734
Bello, Andrés [Venezuelan poet]
Latin American literature (Romanticism) **L:** 112-
113
Belloc, Hilaire [British author] **B:** 244
Belloni, José [Uruguayan sculptor]
Uruguay picture on **U:** 228
Bellot Strait [Canada]
Northwest Passage **N:** 529
Bellow, Saul [American author] **B:** 244
American literature (Fiction and other prose)
A: 424 with portrait
Novel (After World War II) **N:** 574
Bellows [device] **B:** 244
Camera (View cameras) **C:** 83 with picture
Iron and steel (The Iron Age) **I:** 449-450
Bellows, George Wesley [American artist] **B:** 244
with picture
Bells, Orchestra [musical instrument] See
Orchestra bells in this index
Bells, The [music by Rachmaninoff]
Rachmaninoff, Sergei Vassilievich **R:** 61
Bells and Grass [poems by De la Mare]
Regina Medal **R:** 206
Bell's palsy [disease] **B:** 244
BellSouth Building [Nashville]
Nashville (The city) **N:** 23
BellSouth Corporation
AT&T Inc. **A:** 852
Bellwort [plant]
Plant picture on **P:** 525
Belly of Paris, The [book by Zola]
Zola, Émile **Z:** 598
Belmondo, Jean-Paul [French actor]
Motion picture picture on **M:** 871
Belmont Stakes [horse racing]
Horse racing (Types of horse races) **H:** 364-365
Kentucky Derby **K:** 295
Belmopan [Belize] **B:** 245
Belo, Carlos Felipe Ximenes [Timorese political
leader]
East Timor (History) **E:** 41
Nobel Prizes (Peace: 1996) **N:** 448b
Belo Horizonte [Brazil] **B:** 245
Belorussia See Belarus in this index
Beloved [book by Morrison]
Morrison, Toni **M:** 817
Belovezha Forest [Belarus-Poland]
Belarus (Land) **B:** 224b with picture
Below
Ship (Nautical terms) **S:** 405
Beloye More [Russia]
White Sea **W:** 292
Belsen [concentration camp] See Bergen-Belsen
in this index
Belshazzar [Babylonian leader]
Handwriting on the wall **H:** 50
Belshazzar's Feast [music by Walton]

Walton, Sir William **W:** 22
Belt [astronomy]
Jupiter (Zones and belts) **J:** 199
Saturn (Atmosphere) **S:** 150j
Belt [garment]
Judo (Learning judo) **J:** 184-185
Karate (Karate training) **K:** 245-246
Belt cities
Washington, D.C. (Metropolitan area) **W:** 80-81
Belt conveyor See Conveyor belt in this index
Beltane [festival]
May Day **M:** 322
Witchcraft (Witchcraft as a religion) **W:** 371-372
Belted kingfisher [bird]
Bird (Birds of inland waters and marshes) **B:** 340
with picture
Kingfisher **K:** 329 with picture
Beltsville [Maryland]
Washington, D.C. (Metropolitan area) **W:** 80-81
Beltway [road]
Road (Bypasses) **R:** 358
Beluga sturgeon [fish]
Caviar **C:** 322
Sturgeon **So:** 934
Beluga whale [fish] **B:** 245 with picture
Aquarium, Public picture on **A:** 579
Whale picture on **W:** 257; (Belugas and narwhals)
W: 258
Belukha [mountain, Russia]
Altai Mountains **A:** 388
Belváros [district]
Budapest (City) **B:** 666
Belvedere Courtyard [Vatican City]
Bramante, Donato **B:** 562
Belvedere Palace
Vienna (The city) **V:** 361-362
Bely, Andrey [Russian author]
Russian literature (Symbolism) **R:** 563
Belyayev, Pavel I. [Soviet cosmonaut]
Space exploration (Voskhod and Gemini: The first
multiperson space flights) **So:** 714 with picture
Belzec [concentration camp]
Concentration camp (Nazi concentration camps)
Ci: 926-927
Bemba [language and culture] **B:** 246
Bemba, Jean-Pierre [Congolese political leader]
Congo, Democratic Republic of the (New
government) **Ci:** 940d
Bembo, Pietro [Italian author]
Italian literature (Humanism and the
Renaissance) **I:** 494
Bemelmans, Ludwig [American author] **B:** 246
Bémont, Gustave [French physicist]
Curie, Pierre **Ci:** 1194
Radiation (Discovery of radioactivity) **R:** 81
Radium **R:** 100
Ben Ali, Zine El-Abidine [Tunisian political leader]
Middle East (2011 protests) **M:** 534b
Tunisia (History) **T:** 489-490
Ben and Me [book by Lawson]
Lawson, Robert **L:** 147
Ben Bella, Ahmed [Algerian political leader] **B:** 246
Algeria (Independence) **A:** 365
Ben-Gurion, David [Israeli political leader] **B:** 246
Israel (Independence and conflict) **I:** 487
Jews picture on **J:** 124
Ben-Hur [book by Wallace]
Wallace, Lew **W:** 16
Ben-Hur [film]
Heston, Charlton **H:** 220
Motion picture (Best picture: 1959) **M:** 861
Ben Matthias, Joseph [Jewish historian]
Josephus, Flavius **J:** 169
Ben Nevis [mountain] **B:** 246
Scotland (Recreation) **S:** 214-215; (Land regions)
S: 217 with picture
Ben-Yehuda Street
Jerusalem picture on **J:** 97
Benacerraf, Baruj [American physician]
Nobel Prizes (Physiology or medicine: 1980)
N: 446
Benadryl [drug]
Antihistamine **A:** 556
Benares [India] See Varanasi in this index
Benavente, Jacinto [Spanish dramatist]
Nobel Prizes (Literature: 1922) **N:** 447
Spanish literature (Drama) **So:** 763
Bench [mining]
Mining (Open-pit mining) **M:** 575
Bench, Johnny [American baseball player]
Baseball (table: Hall of Fame) **B:** 134
Bench press [weightlifting]
Weightlifting **W:** 183
Bench show
Dog (Dog competitions) **D:** 280
Bench trial [law]
Court (How courts work) **Ci:** 1101-1102

Bench warrant [law]
Warrant **W:** 37
Benchmark crude
Petroleum (How prices are set) **P:** 346
Bend [knot]
Knots, hitches, and splices **K:** 355
Bend on [flag]
Flag (table) **F:** 193
Benday dot [art]
Painting (Pop Art) **P:** 86 with picture
Bender, Chief [American baseball player]
Baseball (table: Hall of Fame) **B:** 134
Bending magnet
Magnetism (In science and medicine) **M:** 60b
Bending the Bow [poems by Duncan]
Duncan, Robert **D:** 384
Bendix, Vincent [American inventor] **B:** 246
Bendjedid, Chadli [Algerian political leader]
Algeria (Recent developments) **A:** 365
Bends [disorder] **B:** 246
Caisson **C:** 19
Diving, Underwater (Dangers of underwater
diving) **D:** 246
Hyperbaric oxygen chamber **H:** 475
Bendy [heraldry]
Heraldry picture on **H:** 195
Benedick [literary figure]
Shakespeare, William: (Much Ado About Nothing)
S: 360 with picture
Benedict X [antipope]
Pope (table) **P:** 666
Benedict XI [pope]
Pope (table) **P:** 666
Benedict XII [antipope]
Pope (table) **P:** 666
Benedict XIII [pope]
Pope (table) **P:** 666
Benedict XIV [pope]
Pope (The 1700's and 1800's) **P:** 665
Benedict XV [pope] **B:** 247
Benedict XVI [pope] **B:** 247
Pope pictures on **P:** 660, **P:** 661; (The 1900's and
2000's) **P:** 665-667 with picture; (table) **P:** 666
Roman Catholic Church (The church today)
R: 412
Benedict, Ruth Fulton [American anthropologist]
B: 247
Benedict, Saint See Benedict of Nursia, Saint in
this index
Benedict, Zadoc [American businessman]
Hat (History) **H:** 84-85
Benedict of Nursia, Saint [Italian religious leader]
B: 247
Benedictines **B:** 248
Christianity (The medieval church) **C:** 524
Monasticism (Christian monasticism) **M:** 701
Monte Cassino **M:** 762
Religious life (Religious life in the Middle Ages)
R: 226
Roman Catholic Church (The early Middle Ages)
R: 406
Benedictine oblate [person]
Benedictines **B:** 248
Benedictines [religious group] **B:** 248
Benedict XVI **B:** 247
Monasticism picture on **M:** 700
Monte Cassino **M:** 762
Pope (The early Middle Ages) **P:** 663
Religious life (Religious life in the Middle Ages)
R: 226
Benedictus, Edouard [French chemist]
Glass (table) **G:** 218
Benedum Center for the Performing Arts
Pittsburgh (The arts) **P:** 500c
Beneficiary
Insurance (Life insurance) **I:** 309
Trust fund (How a trust fund works) **T:** 473
Beneficiation [process]
Coal (Cleaning coal) **Ci:** 726
Benefit [payment]
See also Fringe benefit in this index
Insurance **I:** 309
Pension **P:** 272
Sex discrimination (Changes in laws) **S:** 335
Social security (Social Security in the United
States) **So:** 553
Benefit [philosophy]
Ethics (Modern ethics) **E:** 366
Benefit-cost analysis See Cost-benefit analysis in
this index
Benefit society
Fraternal organization **F:** 495
Benelux [alliance] **B:** 248
Luxembourg (History) **L:** 531
Benelux Treaty [1958]
Benelux **B:** 248
Beneš, Eduard [Czech political leader] **B:** 248

Czech Republic (The creation of Czechoslovakia)
   Ci: 1213
Czechoslovakia (The formation of
   Czechoslovakia) Ci: 1215; (The Munich
   Agreement) Ci: 1215
Benét, Stephen Vincent [American author] B: 248
Benét, William Rose [American author]
   Wylie, Elinor W: 515
Bénévent, Prince de See Talleyrand in this index
Benevolent and Protective Order of Elks See Elks,
   Benevolent and Protective Order of in this index
Benga [people]
   Equatorial Guinea (History) E: 347
Bengal [region, Asia] B: 248
   Bangladesh B: 78
   India (Rise of Indian nationalism) I: 131; (World
      War II [1939-1945]) I: 132
Bengal, Bay of
   Bay of Bengal B: 175 with map
Bengali [language]
   India (Languages) I: 114
Bengali literature
   Bangladesh (The arts) B: 82
   Tagore, Rabindranath T: 13
Bengalis [people]
   Bangladesh (Population and ancestry) B: 79-80
Bengals, Cincinnati [team] See Cincinnati Bengals
   in this index
Bengaluru [India] B: 248
   Automobile picture on A: 963
   India pictures on I: 108, I: 109, I: 116
Benghāzī [Libya] B: 249
   Libya (Strained relations with the United States)
      L: 268
Benguela Current
   Atlantic Ocean (Moving ocean waters) A: 866
Benign prostatic hyperplasia [disorder]
   Prostate gland P: 830
Benign tumor
   Biopsy B: 326
   Cancer (Conclusive diagnosis) C: 171
   Skin (Tumors) S: 491
   Tumor T: 484
Benigni, Roberto [Italian actor/director]
   Motion picture (Best performance by an actor:
      1998) M: 862a
Benin [country] B: 249 with picture and map
   Flag picture on F: 198
   French West Africa F: 527 with map
Benin [former kingdom] B: 250 with map
   Nigeria (Early kingdoms) N: 417
   Pottery (Early pottery) P: 718
Benjamin [Biblical figure] B: 251
   Joseph (The prime minister) J: 1168
Benjamin, Judah Philip [Confederate statesman]
   B: 251
Benjamin, Tribe of [Bible]
   Benjamin B: 251
Benjamin Franklin [book by Van Doren]
   Van Doren, Carl V: 280
Benjamites [ancient people]
   Benjamin B: 251
Bennett, Arnold [British author] B: 251
   English literature (Literature before World War
      I) E: 322
Bennett, Caleb P. [American political leader]
   Delaware (table) D: 109
Bennett, Floyd [American aviator]
   Airplane (Fliers of the golden age) A: 237
   Exploration (The North Pole) E: 450
Bennett, James Gordon [American editor] B: 251
   Journalism (The growth of U.S. newspapers)
      J: 174
Bennett, James Gordon, Jr. [American journalist]
   B: 251
   Mackay, John William M: 20
Bennett, John O. [American political leader]
   New Jersey (table) N: 249
Bennett, Michael [American choreographer]
   Musical comedy (The modern musical emerges)
      M: 960
Bennett, Richard Bedford [Canadian statesman]
   B: 252 with pictures
   Canada, History of (The Great Depression) C: 148
   Great Depression (Effects in Canada) G: 341-342
   King, William Lyon Mackenzie (Second term as
      prime minister) K: 327
   New Brunswick N: 180
   Progressive Conservative Party P: 812
Bennett, Robert Foster [American political leader]
   Kansas (table) K: 234
Bennett, Viscount See Bennett, Richard Bedford
   in this index
Bennett, William Andrew Cecil [Canadian political
   leader]
   British Columbia (table) B: 628; (The mid-1900's)
      B: 630
Bennett, William John [American government
   official]
   Education, Department of (table) E: 110
   Reagan, Ronald Wilson (table) R: 169
Bennett, William R. [American physicist]
   Laser (History) L: 86
Bennett, William R. [Canadian political leader]
   British Columbia (table) B: 628
   Campbell, Kim (Provincial legislator) C: 90c
Bennington, Battle of [1777]
   Revolution, American (table) R: 276; (Victory at
      Saratoga) R: 282-283
   Vermont picture on V: 336; (The Revolutionary
      War in America) V: 334
Bennington Battle Monument
   Vermont (Places to visit) V: 326 with picture
Bennington Museum
   Vermont (Museums) V: 322
Bennu [mythology]
   Phoenix P: 399
Benny, Jack [American entertainer] B: 254
Benso, Camillo [Italian political leader] See Cavour,
   Count di in this index
Benson, Craig [American political leader]
   New Hampshire (table) N: 223
Benson, Elmer A. [American political leader]
   Minnesota (table) M: 602
Benson, Ezra Taft [American political leader]
   Agriculture, Department of (table) A: 161
   Eisenhower, Dwight David (table) E: 152
Benson, Frank W. [American political leader]
   Oregon (table) O: 845
Benson, William S. [American admiral]
   Navy, United States ("The Great White Fleet")
      N: 88
Bent [grass] See Bentgrass in this index
Bent, Charles [American political leader]
   Taos T: 36
Bent, William [American pioneer]
   Colorado (Exploration and settlement) Ci: 845
Benteen, Frederick W. [American soldier]
   Custer, George Armstrong (The battle) Ci: 1200
   Little Bighorn, Battle of the L: 391
Bentgrass [grass] B: 254
   Lawn (Types of lawns) L: 142
Bentham, Jeremy [British philosopher] B: 254
   Dickens, Charles (The second phase) D: 188-189
   Ethics (Bentham and Mill) E: 367
   Mill, James M: 552
   Philosophy (Philosophy in the 1800's) P: 390
   Political science (Liberalism) P: 639
   Radicalism (In Europe) R: 82
   Utilitarianism U: 251
Benthic fish
   Fishing (Fishing tips) F: 179
Benthos [biology]
   Ocean pictures on O: 656, O: 657; (The benthos)
      O: 655
Benthoscope [diving vessel]
   Diving, Underwater (Diving in vehicles) D: 246
Bentley, Robert [American political leader]
   Alabama (table) A: 274
Benton, Robert [American director]
   Motion picture (Best achievement in directing:
      1979) M: 862
Benton, Thomas Hart [American political leader]
   B: 254
Benton, Thomas Hart [American painter] B: 254
   Painting picture on P: 38; (Regionalism) P: 83
   Pollock, Jackson P: 646
Benton, William Burnett [American businessman]
   Encyclopedia (Encyclopedias of the 1800's and
      1900's) E: 268b
Benton Lake National Wildlife Refuge
   Montana (Interesting facts) M: 743
Bentonite [earth]
   Clay Ci: 658
Bentonville [North Carolina]
   North Carolina (The Civil War and
      Reconstruction) N: 493
Bentonville Battlefield
   North Carolina (Places to visit) N: 482
Bent's Fort
   Colorado picture on Ci: 846; (Exploration and
      settlement) Ci: 845
Bent's Old Fort National Historic Site [Colorado]
   Colorado (Places to visit) Ci: 836
   National Park System (table: National historic
      sites) N: 52
Bentsen, Lloyd Millard, Jr. [American political
   leader] B: 254 with portrait
   Dukakis, Michael Stanley (Political career) D: 380
Benz, Karl [German engineer] B: 255
   Automobile picture on A: 963; (The gasoline car)
      A: 965-966
   Gasoline engine (Development of the gasoline
      engine) G: 66
Invention (The late 1800's) I: 362
Benz & Company
   Daimler AG D: 5
Benzedrine [medication]
   Amphetamine A: 439
   Drug abuse (table: Some commonly abused
      drugs) D: 363
Benzene [chemical] B: 255 with diagram
Benzene ring [chemistry]
   Benzene B: 255 with diagram
   Toluene T: 323
Benzocaine [drug] B: 255
Benzodiazepine [drug] B: 255
   Alcoholism (Treatment) A: 338
   Delirium tremens D: 116
Benzoic acid [chemical]
   Toluene T: 323
Benzol [chemical] See Benzene in this index
Beograd [Serbia] See Belgrade in this index
Beothuk Indians B: 256
   Newfoundland and Labrador (Early European
      exploration) N: 375
Beowulf [poem] B: 256
   English literature picture on E: 316; (Old English
      poetry) E: 314-315
Bequest [law]
   Will W: 306
Berber [language]
   Egypt (Language) E: 123
Berbera [city]
   Somaliland So: 590
Berbers [people] B: 256
   Africa (Peoples of Africa) A: 104-105
   Algeria (Ancestry) A: 361; (History) A: 364
   Barbary States B: 105
   Ghana Empire G: 181 with map
   Libya (People) L: 265; (Early days) L: 267
   Morocco (Arab conquest) M: 814
   Sahara (History) S: 22
Berbice [river, Guyana]
   Guyana (Land) G: 446 with map
Berbick, Trevor [Jamaican-born boxer]
   Boxing (The late 1900's) B: 532b
Berceo, Gonzalo de [Spanish poet]
   Spanish literature (Early medieval literature)
      So: 757-758
Berck, Judith [American author]
   Literature for children (Information books) L: 361
Berdimuhammedov, Gurbanguly [Turkmen
   political leader]
   Turkmenistan (History) T: 514b
Berdyaev, Nicolas [Russian philosopher] B: 256
Bérégovoy, Pierre [French political leader]
   France (Socialists win power) F: 478
Bérenger, Paul [Mauritian political leader]
   Mauritius (History) M: 317
Beresford, Tommy and Tuppence [literary figures]
   Christie, Agatha C: 527
Beret
   Hat picture on H: 84
Beretta [firearm]
   Handgun (Double-action semiautomatic pistols)
      H: 44
Berezhnaya, Elena [Russian athlete]
   Olympic Games (The recent games) O: 753-754
Berg, Alban [Austrian composer] B: 256
   Classical music (Atonal music) Ci: 649-650 with
      picture
   Opera (The search for new forms) O: 799-800;
      (Wozzeck) O: 808
Berg, Otto [German chemist]
   Rhenium R: 290
Berg, Patty [American golfer]
   Golf (Women's golf) G: 266 with picture
Berg, Paul [American chemist]
   Nobel Prizes (Chemistry: 1980) N: 444
   Sanger, Frederick S: 110
Bergamot [plant] B: 257
Bergamot orange [tree]
   Bergamot B: 257
Bergelson, David [Russian author]
   Yiddish literature Y: 566
Bergen [Norway] B: 257
Bergen [U.S. history]
   New Jersey picture on N: 252; (Settlement) N: 250
Bergen, Edgar [American ventriloquist]
   Ventriloquism picture on V: 309
Bergen-Belsen [concentration camp] B: 257
Berger, Oscar [British cartoonist]
   Caricature picture on C: 238
Berger, Oscar [Guatemalan political leader]
   Guatemala (Political developments) G: 417
Berger, Victor L. [American political leader] B: 257
Berger v. New York [U.S. history]
   Wiretapping (Laws concerning wiretapping)
      W: 345
Bergerac, Cyrano de See Cyrano de Bergerac,

Savinien de *in this index*
Bergeson, Ole [American settler]
Saint Cloud **S:** 32
Bergh, Henry [American philanthropist]
Humane society **H:** 430
Bergius, Friedrich [German chemist]
Nobel Prizes (Chemistry: 1931) **N:** 443
Bergland, Robert S. [American government
official]
Agriculture, Department of (table) **A:** 161
Carter, Jimmy (table) **C:** 257
Bergman, Ingmar [Swedish director] **B:** 257
Motion picture (The art film revival) **M:** 870 *with
picture*
Sweden *picture on* **So:** 1028; (Motion pictures)
So: 1028
Bergman, Ingrid [Swedish actress] **B:** 257 *with
portrait*
Motion picture (Best performance by an actress:
1944, 1956) **M:** 862; (Best performance by an
actress in a supporting role: 1974) **M:** 862b
Bergson, Henri [French philosopher] **B:** 258
Bergström, Sune Karl [Swedish chemist]
Nobel Prizes (Physiology or medicine: 1982)
N: 446
Beria, Lavrenti Pavlovitch [Soviet political leader]
Stalin, Joseph (Rule by terror) **So:** 826-827
Beriberi [disease] **B:** 258
Bread (History) **B:** 589
Vitamin (History) **V:** 432
Berimbau [musical instrument]
Capoeira **C:** 197
Bering, Vitus [Danish navigator] **B:** 258
Alaska *picture on* **A:** 302; (European exploration)
A: 300-301
Arctic (Search for the Northwest Passage)
A: 638-639
Exploration *map on* **E:** 451; (The Russians in
Siberia) **E:** 447
Bering Island [Bering Sea]
Bering, Vitus **B:** 258
Bering Land Bridge National Preserve [Alaska]
National Park System (table: National preserves)
N: 58
Bering Sea [North Pacific] **B:** 258 *with map*
Bering, Vitus **B:** 258
Bering Sea Arbitration [1893]
Thompson, Sir John Sparrow David (Prime
minister) **T:** 264
Bering Sea controversy [Britain-U.S.] **B:** 258
Harrison, Benjamin (International affairs) **H:** 73
Bering Strait [Alaska-Siberia]
Arctic (Search for the Northwest Passage)
A: 638-639
Bering, Vitus **B:** 258
Exploration (Exploring the Pacific) **E:** 447-448
Indian, American (Early days) **I:** 151
Prehistoric people (The spread of settlement)
P: 752
Berio, Luciano [Italian composer] **B:** 259
Berisha, Sali [Albanian political leader]
Albania (End of Communist rule) **A:** 308-309
Berkeley [California] **B:** 259
Berkeley [estate]
Harrison, William Henry *picture on* **H:** 75
Virginia (Places to visit) **V:** 408
Berkeley, Busby [American director/
choreographer]
Motion picture (Movies in the 1930's) **M:** 867
with picture
Berkeley, George [Irish philosopher] **B:** 259
Idealism **I:** 46
Philosophy (Empiricism) **P:** 389
Psychology (Beginnings) **P:** 849
Berkeley, Lord John [English colonial official]
New Jersey (English control) **N:** 250
Berkeley, Sir William [English colonial official]
B: 259
Bacon, Nathaniel **B:** 19
Bacon's Rebellion **B:** 19
House of Burgesses **H:** 384
Virginia *picture on* **V:** 420; (Royal governors and
Cromwell) **V:** 418 *with picture*
Berkelium [element] **B:** 259
Element, Chemical (Names and symbols of
elements) **E:** 219
Transuranium element **T:** 401
Berkman, Alexander [Russian-American social
reformer]
Goldman, Emma **G:** 258
Berkshire [hog]
Hog (Kinds of hogs) **H:** 285 *with pictures*; (table)
H: 286
Berkshire Hathaway Inc. [company]
Buffett, Warren Edward **B:** 680
Nebraska (Service industries) **N:** 107
Berkshire Hills [Massachusetts]

Green Mountains **G:** 381
Massachusetts *picture on* **M:** 284; (Land regions)
M: 282
Berkshire Valley
Massachusetts (Land regions) **M:** 282
Berlage, Hendrik Petrus [Dutch architect]
Architecture *picture on* **A:** 627; (Early modern
architecture in Europe) **A:** 627-628
Berle, Milton [American comedian]
Television (Early programs) **T:** 118 *with picture*
Berlin [Germany] **B:** 260 *with pictures and maps*
Berlin Airlift **B:** 266
Berlin Wall **B:** 266
Bonn (History) **B:** 461
Cold War (The Berlin blockade) **Ci:** 764; (The
Berlin Wall) **Ci:** 768; (The Cold War in the
1970's) **Ci:** 770
Germany *pictures on* **G:** 145, **G:** 152, **G:** 171; (East
Germany) **G:** 170; (The unification of East and
West Germany) **G:** 171
Kennedy, John Fitzgerald (Berlin) **K:** 265
Olympic Games (Between the wars) **O:** 751
Union of Soviet Socialist Republics (History)
U: 35-37
World War II (Peace with Germany) **W:** 498
Berlin, Congress of [1878] **B:** 265
Bulgaria (Ottoman rule) **B:** 692
Congress **Ci:** 941
Montenegro (History) **M:** 763
Berlin, Irving [American composer] **B:** 266
"God Bless America" **G:** 244
Berlin, University of *See* Humboldt University *in
this index*
Berlin Airlift [1948-1949] **B:** 266
Air Force, United States (Peacetime emergencies)
A: 190; (The Berlin airlift) **A:** 195
Berlin (The Soviet blockade) **B:** 264
Clay, Lucius Dubignon **Ci:** 659
Cold War (The Berlin blockade) **Ci:** 764 *with
picture*
Germany (The division of Germany) **G:** 169-170
Berlin Conference [1884-1885] **B:** 266
Africa (Colonial rule) **A:** 134
Berlin Decree [French history]
Continental System **Ci:** 1022
Milan Decree **M:** 541
Napoleon I (Fall from power) **N:** 15
Berlin Exhibition [1879]
Electric railroad *picture on* **E:** 188
Berlin Wall B: 266
Berlin **B:** 260; (Economy) **B:** 262; (The Berlin Wall)
B: 264; (A united Berlin) **B:** 265 *with picture*
Cold War (The Berlin Wall) **Ci:** 768 *with picture*
Europe *picture on* **E:** 414
Germany **G:** 145; (People) **G:** 147-150; (East
Germany) **G:** 170
Berlin Zoo [Germany]
Zoo (History) **Z:** 604
Berliner, Emile [German-American inventor] **B:** 267
Phonograph (History) **P:** 401
Telephone (The Bell System) **T:** 100
Berliner Zeitung [newspapers]
Berlin (Transportation and communication)
B: 263
Berlioz, Hector [French composer] **B:** 267
Classical music *picture on* **Ci:** 650; (The Romantic
era) **Ci:** 648
Liszt, Franz (His life) **L:** 349-350
Berlusconi, Silvio [Italian political leader] **B:** 267
Italy (Recent developments) **I:** 519
Bermuda [British dependency] **B:** 267 *with picture
and map*
Bermuda grass
Grass (The grass plant) **G:** 324 *with pictures*
Lawn (Types of lawns) **L:** 142
Bermuda onion
Onion (Cultivation) **O:** 763 *with picture*
Bermuda Triangle [Atlantic Ocean] **B:** 269
Bermúdez, Juan de [Spanish explorer]
Bermuda (History) **B:** 268
Bern [Switzerland] **B:** 269 *with picture*
Postal Union, Universal **P:** 708
Switzerland **So:** 1050; (table: Average monthly
weather) **So:** 1056
Bernadette, Saint [French religious leader] **B:** 269
Lourdes **L:** 507
Bernadotte, Folke [Swedish diplomat]
Bunche, Ralph Johnson **B:** 699
Bernadotte, Jean Baptiste Jules [French general]
B: 269
Sweden (The Napoleonic Wars) **So:** 1034
Bernard, Claude [French physiologist] **B:** 270
Biology (Materialistic physiology and the cell
theory) **B:** 319
Curare **Ci:** 1193
Bernard, Henriette-Rosine [birth name of]
Bernhardt, Sarah **B:** 270

Bernard, Réseau Jean [cave, France]
Cave (table) **C:** 320
Bernard of Clairvaux, Saint [French religious
leader] **B:** 270
Crusades (The Second Crusade) **Ci:** 1160
Knights Templars **K:** 353
Bernardin, Joseph Louis [American religious
leader] **B:** 270
Berne [Switzerland] *See* Bern *in this index*
Berne Convention [1989]
Copyright (International agreements) **Ci:** 1048
Berners-Lee, Tim [British computer scientist]
B: 270
HyperText Markup Language **H:** 477
Internet (The Web forms) **I:** 350g *with picture*
World Wide Web **W:** 500
Bernese Alps [mountains]
Switzerland (The Swiss Alps) **So:** 1055-1056
Bernese mountain dog B: 270
Dog *picture on* **D:** 267
Bernese Oberland [area]
Bern (The Bernese Oberland) **B:** 269
Bernhard [prince of Netherlands]
Juliana **J:** 187
Bernhard, Thomas [Austrian author]
German literature (Postwar German literature
[1945-1990]) **G:** 142
Bernhardt, Sarah [French actress] **B:** 270
Bernheim, Hippolyte [French doctor]
Hypnosis (Scientific studies) **H:** 480
Bernier, Joseph Elzéar [Canadian explorer] **B:** 271
Bernini, Gian Lorenzo [Italian sculptor] **B:** 271
Architecture *picture on* **A:** 620; (Baroque
architecture) **A:** 622
Baroque (Baroque sculpture) **B:** 117
Borromini, Francesco **B:** 491
Italy *picture on* **I:** 505
Saint Peter's Basilica (The exterior) **S:** 53; (The
interior) **S:** 53
Sculpture (European sculpture) **S:** 253 *with
picture*
Bernoulli, Daniel [Swiss mathematician]
Aerodynamics (Lift) **A:** 85
Bernoulli's principle **B:** 271
Hydraulics (Laws of hydrodynamics) **H:** 464
Mathematics (Developments in the 1700's)
M: 307
Bernoulli, Jakob [Swiss mathematician]
Mathematics (Developments in the 1700's)
M: 307
Bernoulli, Johann [Swiss mathematician]
Mathematics (Developments in the 1700's)
M: 307
Bernoulli's principle [physics] **B:** 271
Aerodynamics (Lift) **A:** 85
Hydraulics (Laws of hydrodynamics) **H:** 464 *with
diagrams*
Bernstein, Carl [American journalist]
Watergate (The break-in and cover-up) **W:** 144
Bernstein, Eduard [German political leader]
Socialism (Moderate socialism) **So:** 561
Bernstein, Leonard [American musician] **B:** 271
Musical comedy (The modern musical emerges)
M: 960
Berossus [Babylonian author]
Seven Wonders of the Ancient World (The
Hanging Gardens of Babylon) **S:** 325
Berra, Yogi [American baseball player]
Baseball (table: Hall of Fame) **B:** 134
Berrien, John M. [American government official]
Jackson, Andrew (table) **J:** 11; (Split with
Calhoun) **J:** 11
Justice, Department of (table) **J:** 203
Berrill, Roland [Australian lawyer]
Mensa International **M:** 403
Berry [fruit] **B:** 271
See also the list of Related articles in the Berry
article
Coffee (From bean to cup) **Ci:** 753-754 *with
pictures*
Fruit (Simple fruits) **F:** 544 *with pictures*
Berry, Chuck [American singer] **B:** 271
Rock music (The first generation) **R:** 377 *with
picture*; (Setbacks) **R:** 379
Berry, Duc de [French nobleman]
Middle Ages *picture on* **M:** 522
Painting (Gothic painting) **P:** 50-51
Berry, Halle [American actress] **B:** 272 *with portrait*
African Americans *picture on* **A:** 136s
Motion picture (Best performance by an actress:
2001) **M:** 862a
Berry, James Henderson [American political
leader]
Arkansas (table) **A:** 712
Berry, Martha McChesney [American educator]
B: 272
Berry, Nathaniel S. [American political leader]

New Hampshire (table) **N:** 223
Berry, Thomas [American political leader]
South Dakota (table) **So:** 680
Berry, William F. [American businessman]
Lincoln, Abraham (Search for a career) **L:** 314
Berry College
Berry, Martha McChesney **B:** 272
Berrybender [fictional characters]
McMurtry, Larry **M:** 343
Berryman, John [American poet] **B:** 272
American literature ("Confessional" poetry)
A: 423
Berserker [warrior]
Vikings (Warfare) **V:** 381-382
Bersianik, Louky [Canadian poet]
Canadian literature (Modern Canadian poets)
C: 161
Bertelli, Angelo [American football player]
Football (table) **F:** 363
Bertelsmann Foundation
Foundation (table) **F:** 430
Bertha, Queen [queen of France]
Mother Goose (Who was Mother Goose?) **M:** 842
Berthelot, Marcelin [French chemist]
Acetylene **A:** 25
Berthollet, Claude L. [French chemist]
Proust, Joseph Louis **P:** 838
Bertin, Jean [French inventor]
Air cushion vehicle (History) **A:** 181
Bertoia, Harry [American sculptor]
Furniture *picture on* **F:** 583; (The retro style) **F:** 584
Bertolucci, Bernardo [Italian director]
Motion picture (Best achievement in directing:
1987) **M:** 862
Berton, Pierre [Canadian author] **B:** 272
Bertram [literary figure]
Shakespeare, William: (All's Well That Ends Well)
S: 362
Bertrand, Jean-Jacques [Canadian political leader]
Quebec (table) **Q:** 29
Bertrandite [mineral]
Beryllium **B:** 272
Berwanger, Jay [American football player]
Football (table) **F:** 363
Beryl [mineral] **B:** 272
Beryllium **B:** 272
Emerald **E:** 257
Gem (Color) **G:** 77
Berylliosis [disease]
Beryllium **B:** 273
Beryllium [element] **B:** 272
X rays (Penetrating power) **X:** 541
Berzelius, Jöns Jakob [Swedish chemist] **B:** 273
Chemistry (Dalton's atomic theory) **C:** 402
Selenium **S:** 289
Zirconium **Z:** 597
Besançon, Diet of
Adrian IV **A:** 67
Besant, Annie Wood [British social reformer]
B: 273
Beshear, Steve [American political leader]
Kentucky (table) **K:** 290
Besht *See* Ba'al Shem Tov *in this index*
Beside the Sea [paintings by Motherwell]
Motherwell, Robert **M:** 843
Beslan [Russia]
Terrorism (Recent developments) **T:** 180
Bess [opera character]
Opera: *(Porgy and Bess)* **O:** 806
Bessarabia [region, Europe] **B:** 273
Moldova (History) **M:** 690a
Union of Soviet Socialist Republics (World War
II) **U:** 37
Bessborough, Earl of [British statesman] **B:** 273
Bessemer, Sir Henry [British inventor] **B:** 273
Iron and steel (The birth of modern steelmaking)
I: 450
Bessemer process [steelmaking]
Bessemer, Sir Henry **B:** 273
Iron and steel (The birth of modern steelmaking)
I: 450 *with picture*
Best, Charles Herbert [Canadian physiologist]
B: 273
Banting, Sir Frederick Grant **B:** 99
Insulin (History) **I:** 308
"Best Books for Young Adults" [booklist]
Literature for children (Booklists) **L:** 368
Best Friend of Charleston, The [locomotive]
Charleston (Government and history) **C:** 383-384
Locomotive (History) **L:** 417
Railroad (Developments in the United States)
R: 115
South Carolina (Interesting facts about South
Carolina) **So:** 641 *with picture*
Best Man, The [play by Vidal]
Vidal, Gore **V:** 359
Best Management Practices [guidelines]

Water pollution (Nonpoint control) **W:** 138
Best Years of Our Lives, The [film]
Motion picture (Best picture: 1946) **M:** 861
Bestiary [literature]
Manuscript (European manuscripts of the Middle
Ages) **M:** 173-174
Bestla [Norse mythology]
Mythology (The creation of life) **M:** 985-986
Beta [letter]
Alphabet (The Greeks) **A:** 383
B **B:** 1 *with picture*
Beta [recording system]
Videotape recorder (History) **V:** 361
Beta-blocker [drug] **B:** 274
Angina pectoris **A:** 461
Blood pressure **B:** 416
Heart (Treatment) **H:** 138; (Progress in treatment
and prevention) **H:** 145
Migraine **M:** 538
Beta-carotene [chemical]
Antioxidant **A:** 557
Beta cell
Diabetes (Type 1 diabetes) **D:** 179
Pancreas **P:** 86
Beta decay [physics]
Force (The weak force) **F:** 371
Transmutation of elements **T:** 378
Beta-endorphin [physiology]
Endorphin **E:** 272
Beta-hemolytic streptococcus [bacteria]
Strep throat **So:** 925
Streptococcus **So:** 926
Beta interferon [drug]
Interferon **I:** 324
Beta particle [physics] **B:** 274
Atom (Radioactivity) **A:** 873
Nuclear energy (The beginning of nuclear
physics) **N:** 590
Radiation *picture on* **R:** 78; (Particle radiation)
R: 76; (Discovery of radioactivity) **R:** 81
Transmutation of elements **T:** 379
Wu, Chien-shiung **W:** 513
Beta ray [physics]
Nuclear energy (The beginning of nuclear
physics) **N:** 590
Beta waves [physiology]
Electroencephalograph **E:** 200
Betancourt, Rómulo [Venezuelan political leader]
Venezuela (The road to democracy) **V:** 305
Betatron [machine]
Illinois, University of (History) **I:** 77
Betel [stimulant] **B:** 274
Pacific Islands (Food) **P:** 6
Betelgeuse [star] **B:** 274
Orion **O:** 856
Star *picture on* **So:** 842
Bethe, Hans Albrecht [American physicist]
Astronomy (Advances in astrophysics) **A:** 848
Nobel Prizes (Physics: 1967) **N:** 441
Bethel African Methodist Episcopal Church
[religious group]
Allen, Richard **A:** 372
Bethel Bible College
Pentecostal churches (Major Pentecostal
churches) **P:** 275
Bethesda [Maryland]
Washington, D.C. *picture on* **W:** 81
Bethlehem [Jordan] **B:** 274 *with picture*
Bethlehem [Pennsylvania]
Easter (Other customs) **E:** 44
Bethune, Mary McLeod [American educator]
B: 275 *with portrait*
African Americans (The Great Depression)
A: 136a
Béthune, Maximilien de [French government
official]
France (The age of absolutism) **F:** 473
Bethune, Norman [Canadian surgeon] **B:** 275
Bethune-Cookman College
Bethune, Mary McLeod **B:** 275
Bethune Memorial House National Historic Site
[Ontario]
Canada (table: National historic sites) **C:** 114
Betjeman, John [British poet] **B:** 275
Betrayal of Christ, The
Stained glass *picture on* **So:** 822
Betrayed by Rita Hayworth [book by Puig]
Latin American literature (The "Boom") **L:** 114
Betrothed, The [book by Manzoni]
Italian literature (Romanticism) **I:** 495
Manzoni, Alessandro **M:** 174
Betsy Ross House
Philadelphia (Downtown Philadelphia) **P:** 359
Betta [fish]
Fightingfish **F:** 96 *with picture*
Bette Peak [mountain]
Libya (Land and climate) **L:** 266

Better Boy Hybrid [tomato]
Tomato (The tomato plant) **T:** 324-325
Better Business Bureau B: 275
Consumer protection **Ci:** 1018; (The right to be
heard) **Ci:** 1018-1019
Betti, Ugo [Italian dramatist]
Drama (Italian drama) **D:** 339
Betting
England (Recreation) **E:** 296-297
Gambling **G:** 20
Horse racing (Betting) **H:** 365
Betts v. Brady [U.S. history]
Gideon v. Wainwright **G:** 188
Betty lamp
Lamp (Fat or oil lamps) **L:** 52
Between Rounds [painting by Eakins]
Eakins, Thomas *picture on* **E:** 6
Between Scylla and Charybdis [expression]
Scylla **S:** 261
Beuel [district]
Bonn (The city) **B:** 460
Beutler, Bruce A. [American physiologist]
Nobel Prizes (Physiology or medicine: 2011)
N: 447
Bevel gear
Gear **G:** 75
Beverage
See specific beverages, such as Alcoholic beverage;
Coffee; Soft drink *in this index*
Beverage Container Act [1971]
Oregon (The late 1900's) **O:** 849
Beverage truck [vehicle]
Truck (Kinds of trucks) **T:** 457
Beveridge, John L. [American political leader]
Illinois (table) **I:** 71
Beverley, Robert [American historian]
American literature (Virginia) **A:** 414
Beverly Hills [California] **B:** 276
California *picture on* **C:** 37
Los Angeles *picture on* **L:** 460; (Metropolitan
area) **L:** 462
Beverwyck [former village]
Albany (Government and history) **A:** 309-310
Bevilacqua, Anthony Joseph [American religious
leader]
Cardinal (table: American cardinals) **C:** 211
Bewick, Thomas [British naturalist] **B:** 276
Bewick's wren [bird]
Wren *picture on* **W:** 503; **W:** 504
Bey [title]
Egypt (Ottoman and French control) **E:** 130
Tunisia (History) **T:** 489
Beyle, Marie Henri [birth name of]
Stendhal **So:** 889
Beyoncé [American singer/actress] **B:** 276
Beyond Good and Evil [book by Nietzsche]
Nietzsche, Friedrich (Nietzsche and religion)
N: 406-407
Beyond the Horizon [play by O'Neill]
O'Neill, Eugene **O:** 762
Realism (In drama) **R:** 172
Bezalel [Israelite craftworker]
Ark of the Covenant **A:** 693
Bezer [ancient city]
Cities of refuge **Ci:** 568
Bezoar goat
Goat *picture on* **G:** 240; (Wild goats) **G:** 239
Bhagavad-Gita [religious book] **B:** 276
Hinduism (The Ramayana and the Mahabharata)
H: 236
India (Literature) **I:** 120
Krishna **K:** 388
Mahabharata **M:** 64
Vishnu **V:** 429
Bhagavad-Purana [religious book]
Krishna **K:** 388
Bhakti cults [Buddhism]
India (Literature) **I:** 120
Bhangra [dance]
India (Music and dance) **I:** 120-121
Bharal [sheep]
Sheep (Wild sheep) **S:** 380
Bharat Scouts and Guides
Girl Scouts (India) **G:** 199
Bharata [Indian author]
Drama (India) **D:** 336
Bharata [legendary figure]
Mahabharata **M:** 64
Bharata natyam [dance]
Dance (Asian theatrical dance) **D:** 28-29
India (Music and dance) **I:** 120-121
Bharatiya Janata Party [political party]
India (Politics) **I:** 111; (Religious and ethnic
unrest) **I:** 134
Bhopal disaster [Indian history] **B:** 276
Environmental pollution (Hazardous waste)
E: 334-335

Bhumibol Adulyadej [king of Thailand]
Thailand (In World War II [1939-1945]) T: 227
Bhut Jolokia [plant]
Chili pepper C: 471
Bhutan B: 276 *with picture and map*
Asia *picture on* A: 783
Flag *picture on* F: 202
Bhutias [people]
Sikkim (People) S: 456
Bhutto, Benazir [Pakistani political leader] B: 278
with portrait
Pakistan (Struggle for democracy) P: 100;
(Musharraf) P: 100
Terrorism (Recent developments) T: 180
Bhutto, Zulfikar Ali [Pakistani political leader]
Pakistan (Civil war) P: 99-100; (Struggle for
democracy) P: 100
Bi [art]
China *picture on* C: 489
Bi [symbol]
Bismuth B: 383
Bi Sheng [Chinese printer]
Invention (China) I: 359
Printing (The invention of movable type) P: 803
Type (History) T: 537
BIA [organization] *See* Indian Affairs, Bureau of *in*
this index
Bia, Mount [Laos]
Laos (Land and climate) L: 71 *with map*
Biafra [people]
Igbo I: 48
Biafra [region]
Famine (Other causes) F: 26-26a
Nigeria (Civil war) N: 418
Biafran War [1967-1970]
Nigeria (Civil war) N: 418
Bialik, Chaim Nachman [Hebrew author] B: 278
Hebrew literature (Modern Hebrew literature)
H: 162-163
Białowieża Forest [Belarus-Poland]
Belarus (Land) B: 224b *with picture*
Białowieża National Park [Poland]
National park (table) N: 42f
Bianca e Gernando [opera by Bellini]
Bellini, Vincenzo B: 244
Bianchi, Pietro [Italian architect]
Architecture (Neoclassical architecture) A: 623-
624
Bias [electronics]
Electronics (Diodes) E: 210 *with diagram*
Bias [point of view]
See also Prejudice *in this index*
History (The interpretation) H: 261
Bias [sewing]
Sewing (Laying out the pattern) S: 332
Bias belted tire
Tire (Types of tires and tread patterns) T: 297
Bias tire
Tire (Types of tires and tread patterns) T: 297
Biathlon [sport] B: 278
Olympic Games (Winter Olympic Games) O: 746d
Skiing (Nordic competitions) S: 487
Bibb, George M. [American government official]
Tyler, John (table) T: 534
Bibb, Thomas [American political leader]
Alabama (table) A: 274
Bibb, William Wyatt [American political leader]
Alabama (table) A: 274
Bibb lettuce [plant]
Lettuce (Kinds of lettuce) L: 214 *with picture*
Bible B: 279 *with pictures*
See also Hebrew Bible; New Testament; Old
Testament, *and the list of Related articles in the*
Bible *article*
Anglican Communion (Beliefs and worship)
A: 463
Antichrist A: 553
Ark of the Covenant A: 693
Biography (Early biographies) B: 312
Book (The development of printed books) B: 466
Christianity (Writings) C: 522g
Creationism Ci: 1123
Dead Sea Scrolls D: 56
Eastern Orthodox Churches (Doctrines) E: 46
Education (The Reformation) E: 100
Eliot, John E: 237
English literature (Prose writings) E: 317
Evangelicalism E: 422
Evolution (Acceptance of evolution) E: 433
Fundamentalism (Development of Protestant
fundamentalism) F: 556
Genesis G: 84
German literature (The Reformation) G: 139
Hampton Court Conference H: 36
History (The Bible and post-Roman history)
H: 262
Illuminated manuscript I: 78

Literacy (The spread of literacy in the West)
L: 351
Mormons (Church doctrines and ordinances)
M: 806
Mythology (Babylonian mythology) M: 978
New Testament N: 287
Old Testament O: 740
Parable P: 141
Protestantism (Authority of the Bible) P: 834
Rashi R: 144
Red Sea R: 190
Spinoza, Baruch So: 795
Talmud T: 21
Tyndale, William T: 535
Vatican Council II (The Constitution of Divine
Revelation) V: 289
Vulgate V: 453
Wales (The arts) W: 9-10
Wycliffe, John W: 515
Yiddish literature Y: 566
Biblica [organization]
Bible (Modern English translations) B: 286
Bibliography [reference] B: 288
Book (Inside a book) B: 464-465
Literature for children (Booklists) L: 368
A Guide to Research Skills **Research Guide:** 32
A Guide to Writing Skills **Research Guide:** 16
Bibliometrics [library science]
Information science I: 269
Bibliotheca Alexandrina [library]
Library (Africa) L: 252-253
Bibliothèque Nationale de France [Paris] B: 288
France (Museums and libraries) F: 461
Library (France) L: 260
Bibliotherapy [psychology]
Language arts L: 67
Bicameral legislature
Apportionment A: 574
Government (Branches of government) G: 284
Legislature L: 184
Bicarbonate [chemistry]
Carbonate C: 208
Bicarbonate ion
Respiration (Gas transport between the lungs
and tissues) R: 261
Bicarbonate of soda B: 288
Baking powder B: 33
Soda So: 568
Sodium (Uses) So: 569
Bicentennial Celebration, American B: 288
Ford, Gerald Rudolph (Life in the White House)
F: 378
Biceps [anatomy]
Arm A: 717 *with diagram*
Human body (table) H: 422 *with diagram*
Muscle (Skeletal muscles) M: 933
Bichat, Marie François Xavier [French doctor]
B: 289
Bichir [fish]
Fish *picture on* F: 149
Bichon frise [dog] B: 289 *with picture*
Bickerdyke, Mary Ann Ball [American social
worker] B: 289
Bickerstaff Papers [book by Swift]
Swift, Jonathan (Swift's other works) So: 1040-
1041
Bickett, Thomas W. [American political leader]
North Carolina (table) N: 490
Bicolor gourd
Gourd *picture on* G: 281
Bicuspid
Teeth (Permanent teeth) T: 79-80 *with pictures*
Bicuspid aortic valve [disorder]
Heart (Blockage of blood flow) H: 141
Bicycle B: 289 *with pictures*
See also Unicycle *in this index*
Bicycle racing B: 292 *with pictures*
China *picture on* C: 499
Netherlands (Holidays and recreation) N: 141
with picture; (Transportation) N: 147
Safety (Safety in transportation) S: 14
Tire (History) T: 297
Transportation *picture on* T: 393; (The beginnings
of modern transportation) T: 390
Weight control (table) W: 182
Bicycle motocross [sport]
Bicycle (Juvenile bikes) B: 290 *with picture*
Bicycle racing (Bicycle motocross races) B: 293
Bicycle racing [sport] B: 292 *with pictures*
France (Recreation) F: 460 *with picture*
Olympic Games (Summer Olympic Games)
O: 746e-746f
Tour de France T: 348
Bicycle Thieves, The [film]
De Sica, Vittorio D: 157
Motion picture (Postwar Realism) M: 869 *with*
picture

Bicycle tire pump
Pump (Bicycle tire pumps) P: 901 *with diagrams*
Bicycle Wheel [sculpture by Duchamp]
Sculpture (Assemblages) S: 257-258 *with picture*
Bid [economics]
Building trade (The contracting system) B: 685
Bid [fraternity]
Fraternity (Membership) F: 495
Bidayuh [people]
Dayaks D: 53
Bidding [cards]
Bridge B: 604; (Bidding) B: 604
Biddle, Francis [American government official]
Justice, Department of (table) J: 203
Roosevelt, Franklin Delano (table) R: 454
Truman, Harry S. (table) T: 469
Biddle, John [English religious leader]
Unitarians (History) U: 42
Biddle, Nicholas [American businessman] B: 294
Bank of the United States (The Second Bank of
the United States) B: 96
Jackson, Andrew (The Bank of the United States)
J: 11-12
Biden, Joe [American political leader] B: 294 *with*
portrait
Obama, Barack *picture on* O: 641; (The 2008
election) O: 640f *with picture*
Biden, Neilia Hunter [wife of]
Biden, Joe (Early life and family) B: 294
Bidet [bath fixture]
Bath (Bathing for cleanliness) B: 163
Bidirectional microphone
Microphone M: 516
Bidonville [slum]
Morocco (Way of life) M: 811
Bidwell, John [American pioneer]
California (American settlement) C: 60
B.I.E. [organization]
World's fair W: 500
Bieber, Justin [Canadian singer]
Canada *picture on* C: 112
Bieber, Owen Frederick [American labor leader]
B: 295
Biedermeier [art]
Furniture (The Biedermeier and Restauration
styles) F: 580 *with picture*
Biela's comet [astronomy]
Comet (table) Ci: 868
Bielski, Asael [Polish resistance fighter]
Bielski partisans B: 295
Bielski, Tuvia [Polish resistance fighter]
Bielski partisans B: 295
Bielski, Zus [Polish resistance fighter]
Bielski partisans B: 295
Bielski partisans [European history] B: 295
Biencourt de Poutrincourt, Jean de [French
colonist] *See* Poutrincourt, Jean de Biencourt de
in this index
Biennial [botany] B: 295
Flower (Garden flowers) F: 274; (Garden
biennials) F: 277 *with pictures*
Gardening (Planning an informal flower garden)
G: 32-34
Plant (Germination) P: 535-537
Vegetable V: 292
Weed (How weeds grow) W: 179
Bienvenu [French inventor]
Helicopter (Early designs and experiments)
H: 173
Bienville, Sieur de *See* Le Moyne, Jean Baptiste,
Sieur de Bienville *in this index*
Bierce, Ambrose [American author] B: 295
Bierstadt, Albert [American painter] B: 295 *with*
picture
Painting (Light and shade) P: 35
Pioneer life in America *picture on* P: 486
Bifilar pendulum
Pendulum (Other pendulums) P: 238
Bifocals [lens]
Franklin, Benjamin *picture on* F: 490; (Other
studies) F: 489
Glasses (Prescription glasses) G: 224-225 *with*
diagrams
Bifurcation [fingerprinting]
Fingerprinting *picture on* F: 106
Big and Little Dippers [constellations] B: 296
Big Apple [nickname]
New York City N: 322
Big Apple Circus
Circus (The circus today) Ci: 564-565
Big band jazz
Jazz (The sound of jazz) J: 68 *with picture*
Popular music (Other new styles of popular
music) P: 671
Big bang [cosmology] B: 296
Antimatter A: 557
Cosmic microwave background (CMB) radiation

Ci: 1075
Cosmology (Microwave radiation) Ci: 1078
Dark energy D: 37
Dark matter D: 37
Fusion F: 589
Gravitation (Expansion of the universe) G: 332
Hoyle, Fred H: 402
Inflation theory I: 268a
Redshift (Cosmological redshift) R: 192
Universe (Changing views of the universe)
U: 205-206
Big Belt Mountains
Montana (Land regions) M: 752
Big Ben [London] B: 297 *with picture*
London (The Houses of Parliament) L: 435
Big Bend National Park [Texas] B: 297
National Park System (table: National parks) N: 48
Texas *picture on* T: 184
Big Bend Tunnel [West Virginia]
Henry, John H: 189
Big Bertha [gun]
Krupp K: 389
Big bluestem [plant]
Plant *picture on* P: 526
Big Bonanza [U.S. history]
Comstock Lode Ci: 926
Western frontier life in America (Mining) W: 234-235
Big Bonanza Mine [Nevada]
Mackay, John William M: 20
Big Boy [locomotive]
Locomotive (History) L: 417 *with picture*
Big brother [fraternity]
Fraternity (Membership) F: 495-496
Big Brothers Big Sisters of America [organization]
B: 297
Big-character poster
China (Communication) C: 498-499
Big crunch [astronomy]
Universe (The future of the universe) U: 206
Big Cypress National Preserve [Florida]
National Park System (table: National preserves)
N: 58
Big Cypress Swamp [Florida]
Everglades National Park E: 424
Florida (Land regions) F: 254
Big D [nickname]
Dallas D: 11
Big Dig [project]
Boston (Building boom) B: 504
Big Diomede Island [Alaska]
Alaska (Coastline) A: 294
Big Dipper [constellation]
Astronomy *picture on* A: 834
Big and Little Dippers (The Big Dipper) B: 296
North Star *picture on* N: 519
Big dipper firefly [insect]
Firefly F: 134 *with picture*
Big-eared fox See Bat-eared fox *in this index*
Big Foot [American Indian chief]
Indian wars (Wounded Knee) I: 194
South Dakota (Territorial days) So: 681-683
Big Foot [legendary creature] See Bigfoot *in this index*
Big Four [California history]
California (Early statehood) C: 62
Big Four [world history]
Germany (Occupied Germany) G: 169
Versailles, Treaty of V: 339
World War I (The Paris Peace Conference) W: 465
Big game [hunting]
Game G: 21
Hunting (Kinds of hunting) H: 450
Big-headed turtle
Turtle (Other kinds of turtles) T: 524
Big Hole, Battle of
Montana (Indian fighting) M: 758-760
Big Hole National Battlefield [Montana]
National Park System (table: National battlefields)
N: 55
Big Island, The
Hawaii (Hawaii) H: 100
Big Knives [U.S. history]
Illinois (Early national period) I: 72
Big-leaf magnolia [tree]
Magnolia M: 63 *with picture*
Big League
Little League Baseball L: 391
Big-leaved hydrangea [plant]
Flower *picture on* F: 281
Big Lick [former name]
Roanoke R: 362
Big man system [sociology]
Pacific Islands (Melanesians) P: 4-5
Big Manitou Falls
Wisconsin (Rivers, waterfalls, and lakes) W: 358-360

Big Money, The [book by Dos Passos]
Dos Passos, John D: 311
Big Muddy [name for]
Missouri River M: 674
Big Ole [legendary figure]
Bunyan, Paul B: 701
Big Room
Carlsbad Caverns National Park C: 239
Big Sandy River [Kentucky-West Virginia]
Ohio River O: 705
Big Self-Portrait [painting by Close]
Painting (People) P: 31-32 *with picture*
Big Sioux River
South Dakota *picture on* So: 676
Big Sisters of America [organization]
Big Brothers Big Sisters of America B: 297
Big skate [sea animal]
Skate S: 478
Big Sky Country [nickname]
Montana M: 742
Big Sleep, The [film]
Hawks, Howard H: 114
Big Snowy Mountains
Montana (Land regions) M: 752
Big South Fork National River and Recreation Area [Kentucky-Tennessee]
National Park System (table: National parkways and other national parklands) N: 55
Big Spring [Michigan]
Michigan (Places to visit) M: 498
Big stick [U.S. history]
Monroe Doctrine (The Roosevelt Corollary)
M: 739-740
Roosevelt, Theodore (Governor of New York)
R: 463; (Friction with Japan) R: 467
Big Thicket National Preserve [Texas]
National Park System (table: National preserves)
N: 58
Texas *picture on* T: 198
Big Thompson River
Colorado (The mid-1900's) Ci: 847; (The late 1900's) Ci: 847
Big Three [manufacturers]
Automobile (Economic impact) A: 959; (The rise of the Big Three) A: 968; (Challenges to the Big Three) A: 972
Big Three [World War II]
Churchill, Sir Winston Leonard Spencer (The Big Three) C: 549 *with picture*
Cold War (The alliance breaks up) Ci: 763
Roosevelt, Franklin Delano *picture on* R: 458; (The Big Three) R: 457
Stalin, Joseph (World War II) So: 827
United Nations (The San Francisco Conference)
U: 95
World War II *picture on* W: 479; (The war in Europe and North Africa) W: 480
Big top See Circus *in this index*
Big tree [name for]
Sequoia S: 310d
Big Unit [nickname]
Johnson, Randy J: 153
Big Whack [theory]
Moon (Origin and evolution of the moon) M: 788 *with picture*
Big Wood River
Idaho (Interesting facts about Idaho) I: 27
Bigamy [law] B: 298
Bigelow, Erastus B. [American inventor]
Rugs and carpets (History) R: 517
Bigelow, Hobart B. [American political leader]
Connecticut (table) Ci: 967
Bigelow, Kathryn [American film director]
Motion picture (Best achievement in directing: 2009) M: 862
Bigeye tuna [fish]
Tuna T: 485
Bigfoot [legendary creature] B: 298
See also Yeti *in this index*
Bigge, John Thomas [Australian government official]
Australia (Macquarie's administration) A: 921
Bigger, Samuel [American political leader]
Indiana (table) I: 214
Bigger Splash, A [painting by Hockney]
Hockney, David *picture on* H: 282
Biggest Bear, The [book by Ward]
Ward, Lynd Kendall W: 36
Biggs, Benjamin T. [American political leader]
Delaware (table) D: 109
Bighorn [animal] B: 298 *with picture*
Animal *picture on* A: 474
Bighorn Canyon National Recreation Area
[Montana-Wyoming]
National Park System (table: National recreation areas) N: 49
Bighorn Crags [mountains]

Idaho (Mountains) I: 36
Bighorn Mountains
Wyoming (Land regions) W: 526
Bighorn sheep
Nevada (Plant and animal life) N: 168 *with picture*
Bight [knot]
Knots, hitches, and splices (The language of knots) K: 356
Bigleaf maple [tree]
Maple (Bigleaf maple) M: 187
Bigler, John [American political leader]
California (table) C: 59
Bigler, William [American political leader]
Pennsylvania (table) P: 263
Biglow Papers, The [book by Lowell]
Lowell, James Russell (Literary success) L: 510
Bigmouth buffalo fish
Buffalo B: 676 *with picture*
Bigordi, Domenico di Tommaso [Italian painter]
Ghirlandajo, Domenico G: 182
Bigtooth aspen [tree]
Aspen A: 815
Biha, Leopold [Burundi political leader]
Burundi (History) B: 713-714
Bihor Mountains
Romania (Surface features) R: 419
Bihzad, Kamal ad-Din [Persian painter] B: 299
with picture
Islamic art (Books) I: 470
Bijagós Islands
Guinea-Bissau G: 432
Bike See Bicycle; Motorcycle *in this index*
Bikini Atoll [islands, Pacific] B: 299
Biko, Steve [South African political leader] B: 299
Bilandic, Michael A. [American political leader]
Byrne, Jane Margaret B: 747
Bilateral acoustic neurofibromatosis [disorder]
Neurofibromatosis N: 152
Bilateral aid
Foreign aid (Kinds of foreign aid) F: 383
Bilateral kinship [sociology]
Family (Non-Western families) F: 24
Bilateral symmetry [form]
Flower (The parts of a flower) F: 293
Bilateral trade agreement
Reciprocal trade agreement R: 175
Bilateral treaty
Fishing industry (International commissions and treaties) F: 187-188
International relations (Treaties) I: 344
Bilbao [Spain] B: 299
Gehry, Frank G: 76 *with picture*
Bilbo, Theodore Gilmore [American political leader]
Mississippi (table) M: 640
Bild [newspaper]
Germany (Communication) G: 162
Bilderdijk, Willem [Dutch author]
Netherlands (Arts) N: 142-144
Bildungsroman [literature]
German literature (German Classicism) G: 139; (Realism) G: 141
Bile [physiology] B: 300
Digestive system (In the small intestine) D: 202
Gallbladder G: 14
Human body (The small intestine and large intestine) H: 420
Jaundice J: 65
Liver L: 393
Nutrition (How the body uses food) N: 624
Bile duct [anatomy]
Liver *picture on* L: 394; (Structure of the liver)
L: 393
Bile salts [physiology]
Bile B: 300
Bilge board [boat]
Sailing (Hull) S: 23; (Controlling direction) S: 25
Bilharziasis [disease]
Schistosomiasis S: 176
Bilingual education B: 300
Bill of rights (Canada's Constitution) B: 301
Education (Education for whom?) E: 107 *with picture*
Hispanic Americans (Education) H: 256 *with picture*
Reading (Causes of reading difficulties) R: 161-162
Sánchez, George Isidore S: 106
Bilingual Education Act [1968]
Hispanic Americans (Education) H: 256
Bilirubin [pigment]
Hepatitis H: 192
Jaundice J: 65
Liver (Purification of the blood) L: 394; (Diseases of the liver) L: 394
Bill [document] B: 300
Amendment A: 406

Canada, Government of (How a bill becomes law in Canada) C: 132 *with diagrams*
Congress of the United States (How Congress makes laws) Ci: 944
Constitution of the United States (Article I, Section 7) Ci: 1006
Senate (Considering legislation) S: 295
United States, Government of the (How a bill becomes law in the United States) U: 141 *with diagrams*
Bill [zoology]
Bird (Bills) B: 362 *with pictures*
Duck (The features of a duck) D: 374 *with pictures*
Bill 170 [law]
Montreal (Recent developments) M: 779
Bill and Melinda Gates Foundation See Gates Foundation *in this index*
Bill of attainder [law] *See Attainder in this index*
Bill of credit
Money (Bills of credit) M: 710
Bill of exchange [banking]
Bill (In bookkeeping) B: 300
Money (Bills of credit) M: 710
Bill of goods [commerce]
Bill (In commerce) B: 300
Bill of indictment [law]
Bill (In law) B: 301
Bill of lading [commerce]
Bill (In transportation) B: 300
Negotiable instrument (Forms) N: 119
Bill of rights B: 301
Civil rights B: 607
Democracy (Constitutional government) D: 121
Freedom (During the Enlightenment) F: 503
Human rights (The development of human rights) H: 428
Bill of Rights [Canada]
See also Rights and Freedoms, Canadian Charter of *in this index*
Civil rights (Civil rights in other countries) Ci: 610
Diefenbaker, John George (Member of Parliament) D: 197
Bill of Rights [England]
Bill of rights (English Bill of Rights) B: 301
England (The Restoration) E: 309
Glorious Revolution G: 234
Parliament (Parliament gains strength) P: 174
Petition of Right P: 327
William III W: 309
Bill of Rights [France]
Bill of rights (French Bill of Rights) B: 301
Bill of Rights [U.S.]
See also specific amendments, such as First Amendment, *in this index*
Bill of rights (The Constitution of the United States) B: 301
Civil rights (Civil rights in the United States) Ci: 606
Constitution of the United States (The Bill of Rights) Ci: 1001; (Amendments to the Constitution) Ci: 1011
Henry, Patrick (Career as governor) H: 190
Jefferson, Thomas (National statesman) J: 81
Mason, George (His constitutional views) M: 265-266
United States, History of the (The Bill of Rights) U: 162
Bill of Rights Day [custom] B: 304
Bill of rights (The Constitution of the United States) B: 301
Billboard
Advertising (Outdoor signs) A: 75
Poster P: 708
Billbug [insect] *See Weevil in this index*
Billet [metal]
Aluminum (Casting the molten aluminum) A: 394 *with picture*
Brass (Making brass) B: 565
Extrusion E: 459 *with diagram*
Iron and steel (Ingot casting) I: 445 *with diagram*
Wire (How wire is made) W: 343-344
Billfish [fish]
Gar G: 28 *with picture*
Billiards [game] B: 304 *with pictures*
Chaos C: 376
Billiards at Half-Past Nine [book by Böll]
Böll, Heinrich B: 448
Billings [Montana] B: 306
Montana *picture on* M: 743; (table: Average monthly weather) M: 754
Billings, Franklin S. [American political leader]
Vermont (table) V: 333
Billings, William [American composer] B: 306
Popular music (Popular music before recording) P: 669
Schuman, William S: 188
Billion [number] B: 306

Bills, Buffalo [team]
Football (National Football League) F: 364
Billy Budd [book by Melville]
Melville, Herman (His later life) M: 391
Billy goat
Goat G: 239
Billy the Kid [American bandit] B: 306
Garrett, Pat G: 45
New Mexico (Territorial days) N: 275
Biloxi [Mississippi] B: 307
Biloxi Shrimp Festival
Mississippi (Visitor's guide) M: 632 *with picture*
Biltmore Estate
North Carolina (Places to visit) N: 482 *with picture*
Biltong [food]
Pemmican P: 233
Bimetallic standard [economics]
Money (Money in the new United States) M: 712
Bimetallic strip
Thermostat (How thermostats work) T: 256
Bimetallic thermometer
Thermometer (Thermal expansion thermometers) T: 254 *with diagram*
Bimini [legendary island]
Ponce de León, Juan (Florida expeditions) P: 655
Bin Laden, Osama [Saudi-born Muslim leader]
B: 307 *with portrait*
Afghanistan War M: 94
Clinton, Bill (International affairs) Ci: 682f
Navy SEALs, United States (History) N: 91
Obama, Barack (Death of bin Laden) O: 641 *with picture*
Pakistan (Recent developments) P: 100
Qa'ida, Al- Q: 2
September 11 terrorist attacks S: 310
Taliban T: 19
Terrorism (The changing face of terrorism) T: 179; (The September 11 terrorist attacks) T: 179
United States, History of the (Death of bin Laden) U: 196f
World, History of the (The war on terrorism) W: 448b
Binary code [electronics]
Binary number (History) B: 308
Computer (Computer code) Ci: 911
Digital technology D: 203
Electronics (Digital circuits) E: 213
Photography (Digital photography) P: 420
Telephone (Traditional phone calls) T: 96
Binary fission [reproduction]
Bacteria (How bacteria reproduce) B: 21 *with picture*
Reproduction (Through asexual reproduction) R: 242-243 *with picture*
Binary form [music]
Classical music (Sectional form) Ci: 644
Binary number B: 307
See also Binary code *in this index*
Arithmetic A: 665
Number (The binary system) N: 605; (Binary numbers) N: 607
Binary operation code [electronics]
Computer (Microprocessors) Ci: 912
Binary opposition
Mythology (Structuralist approaches) M: 991
Binary pulsar [astronomy]
Arecibo Observatory A: 645
Gravitation (Gravitational waves) G: 332
Binary star B: 308
Black hole (Galactic black holes) B: 388
Lyra L: 537
Nova N: 553 *with picture*
Star (Binary stars) So: 852 *with picture*
Supernova (Thermonuclear supernovae) So: 994
Telescope (X-ray telescopes) T: 109
Binary system [astronomy]
Satellite (Nonplanetary satellites) S: 150c
Binaural hearing
Ear (How sounds reach the brain) E: 10-11
Binder [machine]
Reaper R: 173
Binder [material]
Painting (Materials and techniques) P: 36 *with picture*; (Pastel) P: 39; (Synthetic resins) P: 40
Binding [device]
Skiing (Ski bindings) S: 485 *with diagram*
Binding [process] *See Bookbinding in this index*
Binding arbitration [labor]
Strike (Strike settlements) So: 928
Binding of the Years [ceremony]
Aztec (Religion) A: 1000-1001
Binding out [custom]
Colonial life in America (Education) Ci: 803
Bindusara [emperor of India]
Mauryan Empire M: 318
Bindweed [plant] B: 308
Binet, Alfred [French psychologist] B: 308

Intelligence (Theories of intelligence) I: 319
Binet-Simon intelligence test
Binet, Alfred B: 308
Bing, Dave [American political leader]
Detroit (The early 2000's) D: 171
Binge eating B: 308
Bulimia B: 694
Eating disorder E: 48
Mental illness (Eating disorders) M: 406
Bingen [Germany]
Mouse Tower M: 902
Bingham, George Caleb [American painter] B: 308 *with picture*
United States, History of the *picture on* U: 174
Bingham, Hiram [American explorer]
Connecticut (table) Ci: 967
Bingham, Kinsley S. [American political leader]
Michigan (table) M: 507
Bingham, Tom [American pioneer]
Wind Cave National Park W: 331
Binnacle [device]
Compass (Deviation) Ci: 903
Ship (Nautical terms) S: 405
Binnig, Gerd Karl [German physicist]
Nobel Prizes (Physics: 1986) N: 442
Binns, Patrick G. [Canadian political leader]
Prince Edward Island (table) P: 791; (The late 1900's) P: 793
Binoche, Juliette [French actress]
Motion picture (Best performance by an actress in a supporting role: 1996) M: 862b
Binocular vision
Bird (Sight) B: 364-365 *with diagram*
Bird of prey (Senses) B: 374a
Eye (Depth perception) E: 463-464
Binoculars B: 309 *with diagram*
Bird (Bird watching) B: 367
Binomial [mathematics]
Algebra (Other definitions) A: 354
Binomial theorem B: 309
Binomial [name]
Flower (Scientific names) F: 298
Binomial nomenclature [biology]
Botany (The development of modern botany) B: 509
Classification, Scientific (The language of classification) Ci: 655
Binomial theorem [mathematics] B: 309
Bioacoustics
Acoustics A: 29
Bioanthropology
Anthropology (Physical anthropology) A: 546 *with picture*
Biochemistry B: 310
Biology (table) B: 317
Careers (Life, physical, and social sciences) C: 225
Chemistry (Current research) C: 405
Bioclip [process]
Wool (Processing of wool) W: 400
Bioconversion [chemical process]
Energy supply (Solid and liquid wastes) E: 279
Biodegradable materials
Packaging (The packaging industry) P: 18
Plastics (Plastics and the environment) P: 560-561
Biodiesel [fuel]
Biofuel B: 312
Biodiversity [ecology] B: 310
Agriculture (Threats to biodiversity) A: 153; (Preserving genetic diversity) A: 160
Animal (Destruction of habitat) A: 504
Conservation (To maintain the quality of life) Ci: 976; (Biodiversity conservation) Ci: 976 *with picture*
Coral reef (Coral reefs and the environment) Ci: 1049
Deforestation D: 89
National park N: 42a
Oyster (Oyster reefs and biodiversity) O: 892
Plant (Loss of biodiversity) P: 543
Biodiversity conservation
Conservation (Biodiversity conservation) Ci: 976 *with picture*
Biodiversity International [organization]
Banana (The banana industry) B: 73-74
Bioecological model [psychology]
Child (The influence of the child's environment) C: 452
Bioelectrochemistry
Electrochemistry E: 200
Bioethics [study] B: 310
See also Medical ethics *in this index*
Biofeedback
Motion sickness M: 874
Biofilm [biology] B: 311
Bioflavonoid [enzyme] *See Flavonoid in this index*
Biofuel B: 312

Agriculture (Fuel and raw materials) **A:** 148;
(Alternative sources of energy) **A:** 160
Automobile (Power systems) **A:** 947-948
Biomass **B:** 322
Global warming (Increased fuel efficiency)
G: 232b
Plant (As raw materials) **P:** 517
Switchgrass **So:** 1049
Biogenesis [biology] **B:** 312
Huxley, Thomas Henry **H:** 459
Biogenetic theory [biology]
Biogenesis **B:** 312
Biogenic rock [geology]
Earth (Sedimentary rocks) **E:** 21
Biogeography
Evolution (Geographic distribution of species)
E: 430
Geography (Physical geography) **G:** 94 *with
picture*
Wilson, Edward Osborne **W:** 316
Biographer [author]
Biography **B:** 312
Biographia Literaria [book by Coleridge]
Coleridge, Samuel Taylor (His writing) **Ci:** 772
Biographical dictionary
Dictionary (Specialized dictionaries) **D:** 192
Biography [literature] **B:** 312
See also Autobiography *in this index*
Literature for children (Biographies) **L:** 361 *with
picture;* (The early 2000's) **L:** 366
Pulitzer Prizes (table) **P:** 896
"Biography of the Life of Manuel" [books by
Cabell]
Cabell, James Branch **C:** 3
Bioinformatics [science]
Biomedical engineering (Developing) **B:** 325
Molecular biology (Molecular biology today)
M: 692
Bioinstrumentation
Biomedical engineering (Specialty areas of
biomedical engineering) **B:** 324
Bioko [island, Equatorial Guinea]
Equatorial Guinea **E:** 346 *with map*
Biological agent *See* Biological weapon *in this
index*
Biological anthropology
Anthropology (Physical anthropology) **A:** 546
with picture
Biological child
Family (Family relationships) **F:** 21
Biological clock [biology] **B:** 314
Biological diversity *See* Biodiversity *in this index*
Biological drug
Pure food and drug laws (Biological drugs) **P:** 908
Biological environment
Life (The biological environment) **L:** 276
Biological materials
Materials (Biological materials) **M:** 300d
Biological oceanography
Marine biology (Biological oceanographers)
M: 205
Ocean (Careers in oceanography) **O:** 666
Oceanography **O:** 667
Biological parent
Parent **P:** 156
Biological psychology
Psychology (Major fields of psychology) **P:** 848
Biological resource
Natural resources (Uses and importance) **N:** 64
Biological response modifier [medicine]
Cancer (Biological response modifiers) **C:** 172
Biological rhythm
Biological clock (Importance of biological clocks)
B: 315
Biological science
Science (The life sciences) **S:** 193
Biological theory [psychiatry]
Abnormal psychology (Theories of abnormal
psychology) **A:** 12
Biological weapon
Anthrax **A:** 545
Biological Weapons Convention **B:** 315
Chemical-biological-radiological-warfare
(Biological) **C:** 396
Civil defense (Focus on terrorism) **Ci:** 606
Peace (Arms control) **P:** 207
Smallpox **S:** 513
Technology (Challenges of technology) **T:** 77
Terrorism (Biological attacks) **T:** 176
Biological Weapons Convention [1972] **B:** 315
Arms control (Arms control in the mid-1900's)
A: 721-722
Biologist
Biology **B:** 316 *with pictures*
Biology B: 316 *with pictures*
See also Botany; Zoology *in this index; and the list
of Related articles in the* Biology *article*

Classification, Scientific **Ci:** 653
Developmental biology **D:** 173
Ecology **E:** 53
Life **L:** 274
Molecular biology **M:** 691
Psychology (Psychology and other sciences)
P: 847
Science (The life sciences) **S:** 193; (The
Enlightenment) **S:** 199
Sociobiology **So:** 563
Biology, Marine *See* Marine biology *in this index*
Bioluminescence [biochemistry] **B:** 322
Beetle (Fireflies) **B:** 217
Deep sea (Invertebrates) **D:** 82a-82b
Firefly (Body) **F:** 134
Lanternfish **L:** 68
Light *picture on* **L:** 284; (Luminescence and
fluorescence) **L:** 283
Luminescence **L:** 522
Phosphorescence **P:** 402
Biomass B: 322
Fuel **F:** 550
Synthetic fuel **So:** 1068
Biomass, Pyramid of
Ecology (Energy flow) **E:** 54-55
Biomaterials
Biomedical engineering (Specialty areas of
biomedical engineering) **B:** 324
Biome [biology] **B:** 322 *with map*
See also the list of Related articles in the Biome
article
Ecology (Communities) **E:** 54
Plant (Where plants live) **P:** 520 *with map;* (The
evolution of plants) **P:** 544-545
Taiga **T:** 14
Tundra **T:** 485
Biomechanics
Biomedical engineering (Specialty areas of
biomedical engineering) **B:** 324
Biomedical engineering B: 324 *with pictures*
Engineering (Biomedical engineering) **E:** 284
with picture
Medicine (The medical revolution) **M:** 376-377
Biomedical ethics
Medical ethics **M:** 361
Biometrics [measurement] **B:** 325
Lock (Electric locks) **L:** 412
Biomimetic carbon-monoxide detector
[instrument]
Carbon-monoxide detector **C:** 207
Bionics [biology] **B:** 326
Biophysics B: 326
Biology (table) **B:** 317
Bioplasma
Kirlian photography **K:** 336
Biopsy [medicine] **B:** 326
Cancer (Conclusive diagnosis) **C:** 171-172
Lung cancer **L:** 525
Oncology **O:** 761
Ovarian cancer **O:** 881
Pap test **P:** 132
Bioremediation [waste disposal]
Hazardous wastes (Disposal of hazardous wastes)
H: 122
Oil spill (Responses) **O:** 707
Biorhythm B: 326
Biosignature [signal]
Astrobiology **A:** 826
Biosphere [geography]
Earth (Earth's spheres) **E:** 18-20 *with picture*
Life (Living things and their environment) **L:** 275
Biosynthesis [biochemistry] **B:** 326
Biotechnology B: 326
Biomedical engineering (Developing) **B:** 325
Technology (Emerging technologies) **T:** 76
Bioterrorism *See* Germ warfare *in this index*
Biotic environment
Environment (Biotic environment) **E:** 329
Biotin [vitamin]
Vitamin (Vitamin B_6, pantothenic acid, and biotin)
V: 431; (table) **V:** 431
Nutrition (Vitamins) **N:** 626
Biotite [mineral]
Glauconite **G:** 226
Mica **M:** 482
Biotransformation
Drug (Action in the body) **D:** 353-354
Bip [clown]
Marceau, Marcel **M:** 193
Biped [zoology]
Dinosaur **D:** 206
Skeleton (Animal skeletons) **S:** 480
Bipedal locomotion
Laetoli fossil site **L:** 26
Prehistoric people (Prehuman ancestors) **P:** 744
Biplane
Aircraft, Military (The first military aircraft) **A:** 204

with pictures
Airplane (The Wright brothers) **A:** 231 *with
pictures*
BIPM [organization] *See* Weights and Measures,
International Bureau of *in this index*
Bipolar disorder [psychiatry] **B:** 327
Depression **D:** 151
Lithium **L:** 386
Mental illness (Mood disorders) **M:** 405
Psychiatry (Somatic therapy) **P:** 845
Bipolar junction transistor [electronic
component]
Electronics *diagram on* **E:** 211; (Transistors) **E:** 212
Bipolar system [political science]
Balance of power **B:** 37
Bipolar transistor [electronics]
Transistor (How transistors work) **T:** 372 *with
diagram*
Bir Hakeim, Battle of [1942]
Foreign Legion (History) **F:** 386
Birch [tree] **B:** 327 *with pictures*
Tree *pictures on* **T:** 420, **T:** 426
Wood *picture on* **W:** 389
Birchbark
Birch (Paper birch) **B:** 327 *with pictures*
"Birches" [poem by Frost]
Blank verse **B:** 398
Bird B: 328 *with pictures*
See also the list of Related articles in the Bird *article*
Animal (table: Length of life of animals) **A:** 473;
(A table of animal intelligence) **A:** 493;
(Incubation) **A:** 498 *with picture*
Archaeopteryx **A:** 601
Avian influenza **A:** 982
Brain (Among vertebrates) **B:** 560 *with diagram*
Dinosaur *picture on* **D:** 206a
Earth (The Mesozoic Era) **E:** 27
Egg (Birds' eggs) **E:** 116; (How embryos develop)
E: 117
Flower (Other agents) **F:** 295
Gizzard **G:** 202 *with diagram*
Hand (Animal hands) **H:** 40
Hawaii (Land and climate) **H:** 100
Heart (Birds and mammals) **H:** 146
Instinct **I:** 304
Molting **M:** 697
Pet **P:** 319 *with picture*
Prehistoric animals (Birds) **P:** 738; (The study of
prehistoric animals) **P:** 741-742
Reproduction (How reproduction has evolved)
R: 243
Skin (Animal skin) **S:** 491
Tetrapod **T:** 182b *with diagram*
Velociraptor **V:** 297
West Nile virus **W:** 205
Bird, Larry [American basketball player] **B:** 373
Basketball *picture on* **B:** 154b
Johnson, Magic **J:** 152
Bird cage
Pet (Housing) **P:** 322
Bird dog
Dog (Sporting dogs) **D:** 268 *with pictures*
Bird flu [disease] *See* Avian influenza *in this index*
Bird in Space [sculpture by Brancusi]
Sculpture (Cubism and futurism) **S:** 257 *with
picture*
Bird louse [insect]
Louse **L:** 507
Bird migration
Bird (Bird migration) **B:** 360 *with pictures*
Bird-of-paradise [bird] **B:** 373 *with pictures*
Animal (Courtship behavior) **A:** 497
Bird-of-paradise flower [plant] **B:** 374
Flower *picture on* **F:** 292
Bird of prey B: 374 *with pictures*
Bird (Kinds of food) **B:** 350 *with picture*
Bird refuge
Bird (Bird refuges) **B:** 368
Miner, Jack **M:** 565
Bird sanctuary *See* Bird refuge *in this index*
Bird shot [ammunition]
Shotgun **S:** 436
Bird Singing in the Moonlight [painting by Graves]
Graves, Morris *picture on* **G:** 330
Bird snare
Indian, American *picture on* **I:** 140
Bird watching
Bird (Bird watching) **B:** 367
Bird Week
May **M:** 321
Bird Woman [American Indian] *See* Sacagawea *in
this index*
Birdbanding
Bird (Birdbanding) **B:** 368 *with picture*
Birdcage evening primrose [plant]
Flower *picture on* **F:** 291
Birdhouse

Bird (Bird watching) B: 367 *with diagrams*
Birdie
Golf (table) G: 261
Birdlime [tree product]
Banyan tree B: 100
Holly H: 293
Birds [play by Aristophanes]
Aristophanes A: 663
Birds Directive [law]
Bird (Protective laws and treaties) B: 368
Bird's eye maple [tree]
Maple (Sugar maple) M: 186
Bird's-foot trefoil [plant] B: 374b
Trefoil T: 434
Bird's-foot violet [plant]
Violet V: 388 *with picture*
Bird's-nest soup [food] B: 375
Food (Why diets differ around the world) F: 331
Birds of America [book by Audubon]
Audubon, John James (His works) A: 885
Birdseye, Clarence [American inventor] B: 375
Food, Frozen F: 338
Food preservation (Modern food preservation)
F: 344
Birdseye, Debbie Holsclaw [American author]
Literature for children (Information books) L: 361
Birdseye, Tom [American author]
Literature for children (Information books) L: 361
Birdstone [sculpture]
Sculpture (Early sculpture) S: 242-243
Birdwhistell, Ray L. [American anthropologist]
Communication (The study of communication)
Ci: 887
Kinesics K: 319
Birdwing [butterfly]
Butterfly B: 732 *with picture*
Bireme [ship]
Galley G: 15
Ship *picture on* S: 417
Birendra [king of Nepal]
Nepal (History) N: 126-127
Birgitta, Saint *See* Bridget, Saint *in this index*
Birkenau [concentration camp]
Auschwitz A: 892
Birkenhead [ship]
Shipwreck (table: Major shipwrecks) S: 428
Birkhoff, George D. [American mathematician]
Geometry (Axioms) G: 102
Birling [sport] B: 375
Birman cat
Cat *picture on* C: 289; (Long-haired breeds) C: 292
Birmingham [Alabama] B: 375 *with picture*
Alabama *picture on* A: 257; (Average monthly
weather) A: 270
King, Martin Luther, Jr. (The growing movement)
K: 321
Birmingham [England] B: 376 *with picture*
Birmingham [ship]
Navy, United States ("The Great White Fleet")
N: 88
Birmingham, Peter de [English settler]
Birmingham (History) B: 377
Birnbaum, Nathan [birth name of]
Burns, George B: 709
Birney, Alice Josephine McLellan [American social
reformer] B: 377
Birney, James G. [American political leader]
Abolition movement A: 13
Liberty Party L: 233
Birth
See also Childbirth; Reproduction, Human *in
this index*
Sex ratio S: 336
Whale *picture on* W: 261
Birth and death rates B: 377 *with diagram*
Baby boom generation B: 11
Birth control (The birth control movement)
B: 378
Infant mortality I: 264
Population P: 672
Sex ratio S: 336
Teaching (Job opportunities) T: 68
Vital statistics (Using vital statistics) V: 429
Birth canal [anatomy]
Childbirth C: 456
Vagina V: 259
Birth certificate B: 377
Footprinting *picture on* F: 369
Pennsylvania Dutch *picture on* P: 270
Vital statistics (Collecting and publishing vital
statistics) V: 429
Birth chart [astrology] *See* Horoscope *in this index*
Birth control B: 378
Abortion (In other countries) A: 16
Condom C: 929
Famine (Fighting famine) F: 26a-26b
Parent (Changes in parenthood) P: 156

Pet (Birth control) P: 322
Planned Parenthood Federation of America
P: 515
Population (Population control) P: 674
Sanger, Margaret S: 110
Vasectomy V: 287
Women's movement (Birth control) W: 385
Birth control pill
Birth control (Methods of birth control) B: 378
Estrogen E: 363
Hormone (Medical uses) H: 337
Birth defect B: 380
See also Hereditary disease; *and the list of Related
articles in the* Birth defect *article*
Apgar, Virginia A: 565
Deafness (Birth defects) D: 57
Genetic engineering (Uses of genetic
engineering) G: 84b-84c
Heart (Birth defects) H: 140
Rh factor R: 290
Rubella R: 506
Syphilis So: 1069
Thalidomide T: 229
Toxoplasmosis T: 353
Birth number
Numerology N: 608
Birth of a Nation, The [film]
Gish, Lillian G: 201
Griffith, D. W. G: 393
Motion picture (D. W. Griffith) M: 864-865 *with
picture*
Birth of God [recording]
Jazz (Cool jazz) J: 72
Birth of Tragedy, The [book by Nietzsche]
Nietzsche, Friedrich (Classical scholarship) N: 406
Birth of Venus [painting by Botticelli]
Botticelli, Sandro B: 513
Painting (The 1400's) P: 52-53 *with picture*
Birth parent
Adoption A: 66; (Rights of adoptive parents and
adoptees) A: 66-67
Birth Project, The [art]
Chicago, Judy C: 437
Birth rate *See* Birth and death rates *in this index*
Birthday Party, The [play by Pinter]
Pinter, Harold P: 475
Birthdays of famous people
*See the tables of events in the articles on specific
months of the year*
Birthing room
Childbirth (Methods of childbirth) C: 456-457
Birthmark B: 380
Mole M: 691
"Birthmark, The" [story by Hawthorne]
Hawthorne, Nathaniel (His stories and sketches)
H: 115
Birthplace of Canada [Charlottetown]
Prince Edward Island (Places to visit) P: 788
Birthstone [gem] B: 380
Biscay, Bay of *See* Bay of Biscay *in this index*
Biscayne National Park [Florida] B: 381
National Park System (table: National parks) N: 48
Biscoe, John [British navigator]
Antarctica (Early exploration) A: 536
Enderby Land E: 272
Biscuit doll *See* Bisque doll *in this index*
Bisection [mathematics]
Geometry (Some basic geometric constructions)
G: 103 *with diagrams*
Bisexuality
Gay rights movement G: 73
Homosexuality H: 307
Sexuality (Sexual orientation) S: 338b
Bishkek [Kyrgyzstan] B: 381
Bishop [chess]
Chess (The board and the men) C: 411-412 *with
diagram*; (The moves) C: 412
Bishop [title] B: 381
Address, Forms of (Members of the clergy) A: 54
Christianity (The early church) C: 523
Eastern Orthodox Churches (Clergy) E: 46
Hat *picture on* H: 85
Vatican Council II (The Dogmatic Constitution on
the Church) V: 289
Bishop, Billy [Canadian flier] B: 381
Ace A: 24
Bishop, Elizabeth [American poet] B: 381
American literature (Poetry) A: 423
Bishop, Henry [American composer]
Popular music (Revolutionary War to 1840) P: 669
Bishop, J. Michael [American physiologist]
Nobel Prizes (Physiology or medicine: 1989)
N: 446
Bishop, Joey [American entertainer]
Sinatra, Frank S: 468
Bishop, Maurice [Grenada political leader]
Grenada (History and government) G: 389

Bishop, Richard M. [American political leader]
Ohio (table) O: 699
Bishop, William Avery [Canadian flyer] *See* Bishop,
Billy *in this index*
Bishop Hill [former town]
Illinois (Places to visit) I: 62
Bishop Museum
Hawaii (Museums) H: 95 *with picture*
Honolulu (Cultural life) H: 321
Bishop of Rome [title]
Pope P: 660
**"Bishop Orders His Tomb at Saint Praxed's
Church, The"** [poem by Browning]
Browning, Robert (Browning's poems) B: 647
Bislama [language]
Vanuatu (People) V: 284
Bismarck [North Dakota] B: 382
Exploration (Crossing North America) E: 447
Bismarck [ship] B: 382
World War II (The Battle of the Atlantic) W: 478
Bismarck, Otto von [Prussian statesman] B: 382
with portrait
Christianity (The 1800's) C: 526
Franco-Prussian War (Background to the war)
F: 483
Germany (The unification of Germany) G: 165;
(The German Empire) G: 166; (Foreign policy)
G: 166
Napoleon III (His defeat) N: 17
Prussia (German empire) P: 843
Seven Weeks' War S: 324b
World War I (The Triple Alliance) W: 455
Bismarck Archipelago [islands, Pacific] B: 382
Bismarck-Schönhausen, Prince *See* Bismarck,
Otto von *in this index*
Bismuth [element] B: 383
Bismuth chloride [chemical]
Salt, Chemical S: 75
Bison [animal]
Buffalo B: 674 *with pictures*
Conservation (Conservation in the United States)
Ci: 985 *with picture*
Indian, American *picture on* I: 136a; (Indians of
the Plains) I: 158
Bison, European [animal] *See* Wisent *in this index*
Bison with turned head, A [prehistoric art]
Sculpture (Prehistoric sculpture) S: 233 *with
picture*
Bisque doll
Doll (Porcelain dolls) D: 290; (The early 1900's)
D: 291
Bissagos Islands
Guinea-Bissau G: 432
Bissau [Guinea-Bissau] B: 383
Guinea-Bissau G: 432 *with picture*
Bissell, Clark [American political leader]
Connecticut (table) Ci: 967
Bissell, Emily P. [American artist]
Delaware (Interesting facts about Delaware)
D: 97
Bissell, M. R. [American businessman]
Michigan (Interesting facts) M: 489
Bissell, William H. [American political leader]
Illinois (table) I: 71
Bissell, Wilson S. [American government official]
Cleveland, Grover (table) Ci: 672
Bisson, Auguste and Louis [French
photographers]
Photography (Artistic advances) P: 424-425
Bister [pigment]
Soot So: 595
Bit [computing]
Computer (Computer code) Ci: 911
Computer chip (Word length) Ci: 924f
Electronics (Digital circuits) E: 213
Bit [money]
Money *picture on* M: 708; (History of United
States currency) M: 710
Piece of eight P: 452
Bit [riding equipment]
Horse (table: Riding equipment) H: 351; (The
bridle) H: 352 *with pictures*
Bit [tool]
Drill (Metal drills) D: 348
Petroleum (A rotary drilling rig) P: 338-339 *with
picture*
Woodworking (Drilling) W: 398 *with pictures*
Bitch [dog]
Dog (table: Dog terms) D: 263
Bite [injury]
First aid (Animal bites or stings) F: 138;
(Snakebite) F: 141
Biting midge [insect]
Midge M: 535
Bitmap [electronics]
Type T: 536
Bits per second [computing]

Modem M: 685
Bitter beer
England (Food and drink) E: 295-296
Bitter Bierce [nickname]
Bierce, Ambrose B: 295
Bitter cassava [plant]
Cassava C: 276
Bitter orange [tree]
Orange (Sour or bitter oranges) O: 815
Petitgrain oil P: 327
Bitter root [plant] B: 383
Bitter rot [plant disease]
Rot R: 485
Bitter Sweet [operetta by Coward]
Coward, Noël Ci: 1107
Bittern [bird] B: 383 *with picture*
Bird *picture on* B: 355; (Birds of Central and South America) B: 344a *with picture*
Bitternut hickory [tree] B: 384 *with picture*
Hickory H: 224
Bitterroot Range [mountains]
Bitter root B: 383
Coeur d'Alene Mountains Ci: 753
Idaho (Mountains) I: 36
Lewis and Clark expedition (West to the Rockies) L: 222b-222c *with picture*
Montana (Land regions) M: 752
Bittersweet [plant] B: 384 *with picture*
Bittersweet chocolate
Chocolate (Dark chocolate) C: 519
Bitterweed [plant]
Ragweed R: 103
Bitumen [mineral] B: 384
Bituminous sands B: 384
Road (Paving) R: 359 *with picture*
Bituminous coal
Bitumen B: 384
Coal (Coal rank) Ci: 718; (The uses of coal) Ci: 718-719; (How coal was formed) Ci: 720-721; (Where coal is found) Ci: 721
Fuel (Solid fuels) F: 550
Heating (Coal) H: 160
Illinois (Natural resources) I: 67
Indiana (Natural resources) I: 211
Bituminous macadam [building material]
Road (Paving) R: 359
Bituminous sands B: 384
Alberta (Natural resources) A: 325
Energy supply (Fossil fuels) E: 277-278
Fuel (Synthetic liquid fuels) F: 550
Bivalve [zoology]
Mollusk (Bivalves) M: 695 *with picture*
Shell *diagrams on* S: 385, *pictures on* S: 387; (Kinds of mollusk shells) S: 385-388 *with diagram*
Starfish (The life of a starfish) So: 856
Bivouac [entomology]
Ant (Army ants) A: 525-526
Bixby, Horace [American riverboat captain]
Twain, Mark (Travels) T: 528-529
Biya, Paul [Cameroon political leader]
Cameroon (History) C: 86-87
Bizet, Georges [French composer] B: 385
Opera *picture on* O: 793; *(Carmen)* O: 802 *with picture*
Bizimungu, Pasteur [Rwandan political leader]
Rwanda (History) R: 571-572
Bizzozero, Giulio [Italian biologist]
Blood (History of blood research) B: 414
Bjerknes, Vilhelm [Norwegian physicist] B: 385
Meteorology (History) M: 433
Björling, Jussi [Swedish singer] B: 385
Bk [symbol]
Berkelium B: 259
Black [people] *See* African Americans; Blacks *in this index*
Black, Charles A. [husband of]
Temple, Shirley T: 131
Black, Clint [American musician]
Country music (Modern country music) Ci: 1098c-1099 *with picture*
Black, Davidson [Canadian anthropologist] B: 385
Peking fossils P: 230
Prehistoric people (table) P: 754
Black, Frank Sweet [American political leader]
New York (table) N: 313
Black, G. V. [American dentist]
Dentistry (Modern dentistry) D: 144-145
Black, Hugo Lafayette [American jurist] B: 385
Black, James [American blacksmith]
Bowie knife B: 520
Black, Sir James [British pharmacologist]
Nobel Prizes (Physiology or medicine: 1988) N: 446
Black, Jeremiah S. [American government official]
Buchanan, James (table) B: 661
Justice, Department of (table) J: 203

Black, Joseph [Scottish chemist] B: 385
Chemistry (The phlogiston theory) C: 401
Black, Shirley Temple [American actress] *See* Temple, Shirley *in this index*
Black Americans *See* African Americans *in this index*
Black and tan coonhound [dog] B: 385
Dog *picture on* D: 271
Black and Tans [Irish history]
Ireland (The Irish Free State) I: 427
United Kingdom (Postwar problems) U: 70
Black and White [book by Macaulay]
Macaulay, David M: 4
Black-and-white negative film
Photography (Film photography) P: 416 *with pictures;* (Developing the film) P: 419
Black-and-white warbler [bird]
Warbler W: 35 *with picture*
Black Angus cattle *See* Aberdeen-Angus *in this index*
Black Arts Movement
African American literature (The 1900's) A: 136a
American literature (The African American experience) A: 424
Black ash [tree]
Ash A: 767
Black Ball Line
Ship (Packet ships) S: 421
Black bass [fish]
Bass (Black bass) B: 156 *with pictures*
Black bear
Bear (Kinds of bears) B: 184 *with picture*
Black Beauty [book by Sewell]
Literature for children (Masterpieces of fiction) L: 363
Black-bellied plover [bird]
Plover P: 574
Black Belt [region]
Alabama (Land regions) A: 268
Mississippi *picture on* M: 623; (Land regions) M: 634
Black Bess [horse]
Turpin, Dick T: 519
Black-billed cuckoo [bird]
Cuckoo Ci: 1182 *with picture*
Black-billed gull [bird]
Gull (Kinds of gulls) G: 439
Black birch [tree]
Birch (Sweet birch) B: 327
Black blizzard [weather]
Dust Bowl D: 391
South Dakota (Boom-and-bust economy) So: 684
Black body [physics]
Light (Photons) L: 286
Planck, Max Karl Ernst Ludwig P: 507
Black Book, The [book by Durrell]
Durrell, Lawrence D: 389
Black Box [book by Oz]
Hebrew literature (A new generation of Hebrew writers) H: 163
Black box [electronic device] *See* Flight recorder *in this index*
Black Boy [book by Wright]
Wright, Richard W: 508
Black brant [bird]
Brant B: 564 *with picture*
Black bread mold
Fungi (Parts of a fungus) F: 558-559 *with picture*
Mold M: 689
Black buck *See* Blackbuck *in this index*
Black bullhead [fish]
Bullhead B: 697
Black Cabinet [U.S. history]
African Americans (The Great Depression) A: 136n
Black Canyon of the Gunnison National Park [Colorado] B: 385
National Park System (table: National parks) N: 48
Black-capped capuchin [monkey]
Capuchin C: 199
Black-capped chickadee [bird]
Bird *picture on* B: 358
Chickadee C: 439 *with picture*
Black Caribs [people]
Honduras (Ancestry) H: 309
Black Caucus, Congressional [organization] B: 386
Mfume, Kweisi M: 479
Rangel, Charles Bernard R: 139
Black codes [U.S. history] B: 386
African Americans (The first years of freedom) A: 136j
Reconstruction (The black codes) R: 177
Black cohosh [plant]
Snakeroot S: 537
Black Consciousness Movement [South African history]
Biko, Steve B: 299

Black Corinth Raisin
Raisin (Varieties) R: 129
Black cottonwood [tree]
Cottonwood Ci: 1095
Black crappie [fish]
Fish *picture on* F: 159
Black-crested gibbon [animal]
Gibbon G: 185
Black cricket [insect]
Cricket Ci: 1130 *with picture*
Black Crook, The [musical]
Musical comedy (The first musicals) M: 959 *with picture*
Black crowned-crane [bird]
Bird (Birds of Africa) B: 344h *with picture*
Black cutch [tree product] *See* Catechu *in this index*
Black Death [disease] B: 386
Cat (History) C: 296
Middle Ages (A halt in progress) M: 528
Painting (The 1300's) P: 51-52
Plague (History of plague) P: 506
Black Dragon Society [Japanese history]
Assassination A: 817
Black drum [fish]
Drum D: 367 *with picture*
Black dwarf star [astronomy]
Star (Black-dwarf phase) So: 849
Sun So: 975; (Evolution of the sun) So: 982
White dwarf W: 285
Black Eagle [award]
Knighthood, Orders of (Honorary orders) K: 347
Black Earth Belt [region]
Russia (Agriculture) R: 544-545
Black English
African Americans (Developments since 1970) A: 136r
Black-eyed pea [plant]
Cowpea C: 1113
Black-eyed Susan [plant] B: 386 *with picture*
Black fever [disease]
Kala-azar K: 210
Black-figure style
Painting (Greek painting) P: 42 *with picture*
Black fly [insect]
Gnat G: 238
Black-footed ferret [animal]
Endangered species (table) E: 270
Ferret F: 76 *with picture*
Black Forest [region, Germany] B: 386
Europe *picture on* E: 401
Germany (The Black Forest) G: 156 *with picture*
Black fox
Fox (Kinds of foxes) F: 440
Black friars [religious group]
Friar F: 532
Black Friday [U.S. history] B: 387
Fisk, James F: 189
Gould, Jay G: 280
Grant, Ulysses S. (Political corruption) G: 315-316
Black George [nickname] *See* Petrović, Djordje *in this index*
Black ground beetle
Beetle *picture on* B: 218
Black Hand [organization]
World War I (The assassination of an archduke) W: 455
Black Hawk [Sauk Indian chief] B: 387 *with picture*
Indian wars (Black Hawk) I: 192
Sauk Indians S: 163
Wisconsin (Territorial days) W: 366
Black Hawk [Ute Indian chief]
Utah (Indian relations) U: 246
Black Hawk [helicopter]
Army, United States *picture on* A: 730
Black Hawk [sculpture by Taft]
Illinois (Places to visit) I: 62
Black Hawk Purchase [U.S. history]
Iowa I: 374; (Territorial days) I: 393
Black Hawk War [1832]
Black Hawk B: 387
Indian wars (Black Hawk) I: 192
Iowa I: 374, *picture on* I: 394; (Territorial days) I: 393
Lincoln, Abraham (The Black Hawk War) L: 314
Sauk Indians S: 163
Wisconsin (Territorial days) W: 366 *with picture*
Black Hawk War [1865-1867]
Utah (Indian relations) U: 246
Black Heritage Trail
Massachusetts (Places to visit) M: 280
Black Hills [mountains, South Dakota-Wyoming] B: 387
Indian wars (Little Bighorn) I: 193
South Dakota So: 664; (Land regions) So: 674 *with picture and map*
Western frontier life in America (Mining) W: 234-235

Wyoming (Land regions) W: 526; (Indian and settler conflicts) W: 534
Black Hills National Forest
  South Dakota (Places to visit) So: 672
Black Hills Passion Play [South Dakota]
  Passion play *picture on* P: 191
Black History Month B: 388
Black hole [astronomy] B: 388
  Andromeda Galaxy A: 457
  Astronomy *picture on* A: 841
  Binary star B: 308
  Einstein, Albert (The general theory of relativity) E: 146b
  Galaxy (Galaxy evolution) G: 9
  Gravitation (Black holes) G: 332
  Hawking, Stephen William H: 113
  Milky Way (The center of the galaxy) M: 551
  Quasar Q: 8
  Relativity (Gravitational waves) R: 212
  Star (Black holes) So: 851
  Supernova (Results of supernovae) So: 994
  Telescope (X-ray telescopes) T: 109
  Universe (Size of the universe) U: 205
  X rays (In astronomy) X: 541
Black Hole of Calcutta [history of India] B: 389
Black Horse [New Testament]
  Horse (table: Famous horses in history and legend) H: 361
Black huckleberry [shrub]
  Huckleberry H: 404
Black humor [literature] B: 389
  Novel (The middle and late 1900's) N: 575
  Satire S: 150h
Black imported fire ant [insect]
  Fire ant F: 122
Black Iris [painting by O'Keeffe]
  Painting (Georgia O'Keeffe) P: 83 *with picture*
Black Jack [nickname]
  Logan, John Alexander L: 423
  Pershing, John Joseph (Mexican campaign) P: 296
Black Kettle [American Indian chief] B: 389
  Indian wars (Sand Creek) I: 192; (Washita River) I: 193
Black Lamb and Grey Falcon [book by West]
  West, Rebecca W: 199
Black-legged kittiwake [bird]
  Kittiwake K: 341 *with picture*
Black letter type [printing]
  Type (Classes of type) T: 537
Black-letter writing
  Handwriting (Later writing styles) H: 50
  Paleography P: 103
Black Lines [painting by Kandinsky]
  Painting (Expressionism) P: 78-79 *with picture*
Black locust [plant]
  Locust L: 418 *with pictures*
Black lung [disease] B: 389
  Coal (Mine safety) Ci: 729
  Dust (Influence on human health) D: 390
Black Madonna and Child [painting]
  Bearden, Romare *picture on* B: 188
Black Magic [boat]
  America's Cup A: 431
Black mamba [snake]
  Snake *picture on* S: 526; (How snakes move) S: 529
Black market [crime] B: 389
  Rationing R: 148
Black market adoption
  Adoption (Black market adoptions) A: 66
Black marlin [fish]
  Marlin M: 215
Black Mask [magazine]
  Detective story (History) D: 163
Black Mass
  Devil worship D: 175
Black medic [plant]
  Shamrock S: 371
Black Mesa [Oklahoma]
  Oklahoma (Land regions) O: 724-727
Black Monday [English history]
  Monday M: 702
Black Mountain College [North Carolina]
  Olson, Charles O: 745
Black Mountain poets
  American literature (Poetry) A: 423
  Creeley, Robert Ci: 1126
  Duncan, Robert D: 384
Black mulberry [plant]
  Mulberry M: 913 *with picture*
Black Muslims [organization] B: 389
  See also Nation of Islam *in this index*
  African Americans *picture on* A: 136o; (Black militancy) A: 136q
  Farrakhan, Louis F: 47
  Malcolm X M: 103

Muhammad, Elijah M: 911
  Name (Black names) N: 5-6
Black nationalism
  Minority group (African Americans) M: 610
  Nation of Islam N: 26
Black nightshade [plant]
  Belladonna B: 242
Black oak [tree]
  Oak (Red oaks) O: 635
  Plant *picture on* P: 525
Black olive [fruit]
  Olive (Harvesting and preparation for market) O: 743
Black opal [gem]
  Opal O: 788
Black Paintings [paintings by Stella]
  Stella, Frank So: 886
Black Panther Party [organization] B: 390
  African Americans (Black militancy) A: 136q
  Carmichael, Stokely C: 241
Black Panther Party for Self-Defense
  Black Panther Party B: 390
Black pearl
  Pearl (Color) P: 217
Black pepper [spice]
  Pepper P: 277 *with picture*
Black phosphorus [mineral]
  Phosphorus P: 403
Black pine [tree]
  Pine (Other pines) P: 470
Black plate
  Printing (Process color printing) P: 802 *with picture*
Black powder [ammunition]
  Gunpowder (Kinds of gunpowder) G: 441
  Rocket (History) R: 390
Black Power
  African Americans (Black militancy) A: 136q
  Carmichael, Stokely C: 241
  Cleaver, Eldridge Ci: 660
  King, Martin Luther, Jr. (Later years) K: 322
  Minority group (African Americans) M: 610
  Student Nonviolent Coordinating Committee So: 932
Black Prince [English history] *See* Edward [the Black Prince] *in this index*
Black racer [snake]
  Racer R: 51
Black rat [animal]
  Rat R: 146 *with picture*; (The body of a rat) R: 146 *with picture*
Black rhinoceros [animal]
  Endangered species (table) E: 270
  Poaching *picture on* P: 587
  Rhinoceros (Kinds of rhinoceroses) R: 294-295 *with picture*
Black Riders and Other Lines, The [poems by Crane]
  Crane, Stephen Ci: 1120
Black right whale
  Whale *picture on* W: 256; (Right whales) W: 255
Black rot [plant disease]
  Rot R: 485
Black sage [plant]
  Plant *picture on* P: 525
Black Sea B: 390 *with map*
  Dardanelles D: 35
  Romania (Recreation) R: 418 *with picture*; (Land and climate) R: 419 *with map*
  Russia (Early days) R: 547
Black sea bass [fish]
  Blackfish B: 393 *with picture*
  Fish *picture on* F: 153
Black Seminole [U.S. history] B: 391 *with picture*
Black Shirt [fascism]
  Mussolini, Benito (Fascist dictator) M: 967
Black skimmer [bird]
  Bird *picture on* B: 351; (Birds of the seacoasts) B: 342 *with picture*
  Skimmer S: 488
Black Skin, White Masks [book by Fanon]
  Fanon, Frantz Omar F: 27
Black smoker [oceanography]
  Hydrothermal vent H: 473 *with picture*
  Ocean (Discoveries) O: 664
Black snakeroot
  Snakeroot S: 537
Black Soul, The [book by O'Flaherty]
  O'Flaherty, Liam O: 678
Black Sox Scandal
  Baseball (The Black Sox Scandal) B: 135
Black spruce [tree]
  Tree *pictures on* T: 425
Black Stallion, The [book by Farley]
  Farley, Walter F: 28
Black Stallion series [books by Farley]
  Farley, Walter F: 28

Black stem rust [plant disease]
  Barberry B: 107
  Plant *picture on* P: 540
  Rust R: 567
Black Stone [religion]
  Islam (The Five Pillars of Islam) I: 463-464
  Kaaba K: 208
  Mecca (The city) M: 352
  Muslims (Before Muhammad) M: 964-964a
Black stork [bird]
  Stork So: 913 *with picture*
Black studies movement
  African Americans (Developments since 1970) A: 136r
Black swallower [fish]
  Fish *picture on* F: 145
Black swallowtail butterfly
  Insect *picture on* I: 282
Black swan [bird]
  Swan (Kinds) So: 1016 *with picture*
Black-tailed deer *See* Mule deer *in this index*
Black-tailed godwit [bird]
  Godwit G: 246 *with picture*
Black-tailed jack rabbit
  Jack rabbit J: 3 *with picture*
Black-tailed prairie dog
  Prairie dog P: 732 *with picture*
Black tea
  Tea (Processing tea) T: 62
Black-thighed falconet [bird]
  Bird of prey (Physical appearance) B: 374a
Black-throated blue warbler [bird]
  Warbler W: 35
Black-throated green warbler [bird]
  Warbler W: 35
Black Thunder [book by Bontemps]
  Bontemps, Arna Wendell B: 463
Black tupelo [tree]
  Tree *pictures on* T: 424
  Tupelo T: 492
Black Virgin [sculpture]
  Montserrat M: 780
Black Volta [river, Burkina Faso]
  Burkina Faso (Land) B: 706
Black vulture [bird]
  Vulture (New World vultures) V: 454 *with picture*
Black walnut [tree]
  Leaf *picture on* L: 154
  Tree *pictures on* T: 424
  Walnut W: 19
Black Warrior River
  Tombigbee River T: 326
Black Warrior-Tombigbee-Mobile river system [waterway, U.S.]
  Alabama (Transportation) A: 273
Black widow [spider] B: 391 *with picture*
Black wildebeest [animal]
  Wildebeest W: 302
Black willow [tree]
  Tree *pictures on* T: 424
  Willow W: 315
Black-winged damselfly
  Insect *picture on* I: 280
Blackback [fish] *See* Winter flounder *in this index*
Blackball [voting]
  Ballot (Older customs) B: 63
Blackbeard [English pirate] B: 391
  Pirate (Other regions) P: 495 *with picture*
  South Carolina *picture on* So: 659
Blackberry [plant] B: 392 *with picture*
  Dewberry D: 176
  Fruit (Types of fruits in botany) F: 544-546 *with picture*
BlackBerry [smartphone]
  Cellular telephone (History) C: 341
Blackbird B: 392 *with picture*
  Bird *picture on* B: 358
  Wetland *picture on* W: 253
Blackbirder [slavery]
  Pacific Islands (Missionaries, traders, and settlers) P: 12
Blackboard
  Chalkboard C: 370
Blackboard Jungle, The [book by McBain]
  McBain, Ed M: 332
Blackbuck [animal] B: 392 *with picture*
  Animal *picture on* A: 476
  Antelope (Habits and appearance) A: 542
Blackburn, Elizabeth H. [American biologist]
  Nobel Prizes (Physiology or medicine: 2009) N: 447
Blackburnian warbler [bird]
  Bird (Birds of forests and woodlands) B: 334 *with picture*
  Warbler W: 35 *with picture*
Blackdamp [gas]
  Damp D: 22

Blackdevil deep-sea angler
Fish *picture on* F: 156
Blackett, Patrick Maynard Stuart [British physicist]
Nobel Prizes (Physics: 1948) N: 441
Blackfeet Indians B: 392
Alberta (History) A: 329
Crowfoot Ci: 1158
Indian, American (Indians of the Plains) I: 158-159
Blackfish [fish] B: 393 *with picture*
Blackfish [sea animal]
Dolphin (Other species) D: 297
Pilot whale P: 464
Blackfish, Chief [American Indian leader]
Boone, Daniel (Indian captivity) B: 478; (Escape and battle) B: 478
Blackfoot Confederacy
Blackfeet Indians B: 392
Blackfoot Indians *See* Blackfeet Indians *in this index*
Blackfriars Theatre [English history]
Shakespeare, William (The King's Men) S: 348; (The Elizabethan theater) S: 351
Blackgum [tree]
Tree *pictures on* T: 424
Tupelo T: 492
Blackhawk UH-60 helicopter
Aircraft, Military *picture on* A: 202
Blackhawks, Chicago [team]
Hockey (table: National Hockey League) H: 281
Blackhead [disorder]
Acne A: 27
Pimple P: 466
Pore P: 678
Blackjack [game]
Gambling (Blackjack) G: 21
Blackjack oak [tree]
Oak (Red oaks) O: 635-636
Blackleg [disease]
Cattle (Diseases) C: 313
Blacklegged tick [animal]
Deer tick D: 87 *with picture*
Blacklist B: 393
Blockade B: 406
Labor movement (Opposition to unions) L: 10
McCarthyism M: 332c
Un-American Activities Committee U: 19
Blackmail [crime] B: 394
Extortion E: 457
Blackmail [film]
Hitchcock, Alfred H: 263
Blackmouth salmon *See* Chinook salmon *in this index*
Blackmun, Harry Andrew [American jurist] B: 394
Nixon, Richard Milhous (The national scene) N: 433-434
Roe v. Wade R: 399
Blackout [electricity]
California (The beginning of the 2000's) C: 64
Electric power (Providing reliable service) E: 185; (Electric power today) E: 186-187
Blackpoll warbler [bird]
Bird (Bird migration) B: 360
Blacks [people]
See also African Americans *in this index*
Africa (Peoples of Africa) A: 104
African National Congress A: 137
Races, Human (The three-race theory) R: 53; (The social significance of race) R: 59
Racism (History) R: 62
Segregation (Segregation in other countries) S: 286
Slavery (The Middle Ages) S: 501-502
South Africa So: 608; (People) So: 609; (Ways of life) So: 611; (History) So: 617
Blacksmith [occupation]
Forging (Hand forging) F: 409 *with picture*
Pioneer life in America *picture on* P: 481
Blackstone, Harry [American magician]
Magician (Illusions) M: 51-52
Blackstone, William [American settler]
Boston (Early settlement) B: 503
Blackstone, Sir William [British jurist] B: 394
Magna Carta (The charter after 1215) M: 53
Blackstone Canal [Massachusetts]
Worcester W: 403
Blackstone School of Law
Correspondence school Ci: 1071
Blackstrap molasses [food]
Molasses M: 689
Blacktail [animal]
Mule deer M: 914
Blackton, J. Stuart [American artist]
Animation (Early animation) A: 514a
Blacktop [building material]
Asphalt (Paving with asphalt) A: 815

Road *picture on* R: 361; (Paving) R: 359
Blackwell, Antoinette Brown [American religious leader] B: 394 *with portrait*
Blackwell, Elizabeth [American doctor] B: 394
Blackwell, Emily [American physician]
Blackwell, Elizabeth B: 395
Blackwell, Henry [American social reformer]
Woman suffrage (Growth of the movement) W: 380
Blackwood [tree product]
Rosewood R: 480
Blackwood, Frederick Temple [British statesman]
Dufferin and Ava, Marquess of D: 378
Mackenzie, Alexander (The Pacific Railway dispute) M: 22
Bladder [anatomy] B: 395 *with diagram*
Cancer (Classification by primary body site) C: 167-168
Frog *picture on* F: 537
Human body (table) H: 422 *with diagram*
Incontinence I: 106
Kidney (How the kidneys produce urine) K: 311-312 *with diagram*
Prostate cancer P: 829
Saccharin S: 4
Bladder, Gall *See* Gallbladder *in this index*
Bladderwort [plant] B: 395 *with picture*
Blade [botany]
Grass (The grass plant) G: 324 *with picture*
Leaf (The blade) L: 129 *with pictures*
Plant (Leaves) P: 529-531 *with picture*
Blade [tool]
Knife K: 345 *with pictures*
Razor R: 153
Scissors S: 208
Sword So: 1061 *with pictures*
Bladensburg, Battle of [1814]
Maryland (The War of 1812 and industrial development) M: 258
War of 1812 (Campaigns of 1814) W: 31
Blagojevich, Rod [American political leader]
Illinois (table) I: 71; (The death penalty) I: 76; (Corruption cases) I: 76
Impeachment (In the United States) I: 90-91
Blaine, James Gillespie [American statesman] B: 396
Cleveland, Grover (Election of 1884) Ci: 670
Garfield, James Abram (table) G: 42
Grant, Ulysses S. (Government frauds) G: 317
Harrison, Benjamin (Election of 1888) H: 71; (table) H: 71
Hayes, Rutherford Birchard (Campaign of 1876) H: 120
Mugwumps M: 910
Blaine, John J. [American political leader]
Wisconsin (table) W: 365
Blair, Andrew G. [Canadian political leader]
New Brunswick (table) N: 195
Blair, Anthony Charles Lynton [full name of]
Blair, Tony B: 397
Blair, Austin [American political leader]
Michigan (table) M: 507
Blair, Bonnie [American skater] B: 396
Olympic Games (The recent games) O: 753
Blair, Eric Arthur [birth name of]
Orwell, George O: 860
Blair, Francis Preston, Sr. [American editor]
Kitchen Cabinet K: 337
Blair, Francis Preston, Jr. [American political leader] B: 396
Grant, Ulysses S. (Election of 1868) G: 315
Blair, James T., Jr. [American political leader]
Missouri (table) M: 668
Blair, John [American jurist] B: 396
Blair, Montgomery [American political leader]
Emancipation Proclamation *picture on* E: 254
Lincoln, Abraham (table) L: 323
Blair, Tony [British political leader] B: 396 *with portrait*
Brown, Gordon B: 642
Iraq War (Disagreements over the war) I: 414f-415
Labour Party (Recent developments) L: 17
United Kingdom (Political changes) U: 74 *with picture*
Blair House [Washington, D.C.]
Washington, D.C. *map on* W: 76; (White House) W: 74-75
Blake [book by Delany]
African American literature (The 1800's) A: 136a
Blake, Edward [Canadian political leader]
Laurier, Sir Wilfrid (The execution of Louis Riel) L: 124-125
Ontario (table) O: 783
Blake, Nicholas [pen name]
Day-Lewis, Cecil D: 53
Blake, W. S. [American glassmaker]

Glass (Types of art glass) G: 220
Blake, William [British poet] B: 397
English literature (The Preromantics) E: 319-320
Blakelock, Ralph Albert [American painter] B: 397 *with picture*
Blakely Mountain Dam [Ouachita River, Arkansas]
Lake Ouachita L: 44 *with map*
Blakeney, Allan E. [Canadian political leader]
Saskatchewan (table) S: 144
Blakey, Art [American musician] B: 397
Blalock, Alfred [American doctor]
Taussig, Helen Brooke T: 52
Blanc, Louis [French political leder]
Socialism (Early socialist ideas) So: 560
Blanc, Mont *See* Mont Blanc *in this index*
Blanc de noir [wine]
Wine (Types of wine) W: 336
Blanchard, Doc [American football player]
Football (table) F: 363
Blanchard, Hiram [Canadian political leader]
Nova Scotia (table) N: 567
Blanchard, James [American political leader]
Michigan (table) M: 507
Blanchard, Jean-Pierre [French balloonist] B: 398
Balloon (The growth of ballooning) B: 61
Blanchard, Newton C. [American political leader]
Louisiana (table) L: 496
Blanchard Springs Caverns
Arkansas (Places to visit) A: 704 *with picture*
Blanche of Castile [queen of France]
Louis IX L: 474
Blanche of Lancaster [wife of]
John of Gaunt J: 134
Lancaster L: 55
Blanchett, Cate [Australian actress]
Motion picture (Best performance by an actress in a supporting role: 2004) M: 862b
Blanching [food]
Dehydrated food D: 93
Food, Frozen (Freezing food at home) F: 338-339
Food preservation (Freezing) F: 342
Blanco, Kathleen B. [American political leader]
Louisiana (table) L: 496; (The early 2000's) L: 501
Blanco, Salvador Jorge [Dominican political leader]
Dominican Republic (History) D: 304-305
Blanco Party [political party]
Uruguay (Politics) U: 223; (Civil war) U: 227; (Struggles for power) U: 227
Blancs, Les [play by Hansberry]
Hansberry, Lorraine H: 53
Bland, James A. [American composer] B: 398
Bland-Allison Act [1878]
Cleveland, Grover (The currency and the tariff) Ci: 671
Hayes, Rutherford Birchard (Money problems) H: 121
Blanes, Juan Manuel [Uruguayan artist]
Uruguay (The arts) U: 225
Blank [disk]
Money *picture on* M: 711; (Minting coins) M: 714-715
Blank, Maria Aleksandrovna [mother of]
Lenin, V. I. (Boyhood) L: 191
Blank cartridge [ammunition]
Cartridge C: 268
Blank verse [poetry] B: 398
Drama (Elizabethan playwrights) D: 331
Poetry (table: Forms) P: 594; (Forms) P: 595
Shakespeare, William (Verse form) S: 368
Blankers-Koen, Fanny [Dutch athlete]
Olympic Games (The postwar games) O: 751
Blanket, Indian *See* Indian blanket *in this index*
Blanket bond
Insurance (Crime insurance) I: 314
Blanket cylinder [printing]
Newspaper (Printing the newspaper) N: 385 *with picture*
Printing (Offset lithography) P: 798 *with diagram*
Blanket fidelity bond [economics]
Bonding B: 455
Blanket insulation
Insulation (In buildings) I: 306 *with picture*; (In industry) I: 306 *with picture*
Blanket-to-blanket press
Printing (Offset presses) P: 798-799 *with diagram*
Blanket toss [game]
Inuit (Recreation) I: 354f
Blanketflower [plant]
Gaillardia G: 6 *with picture*
Blanton, Leonard Ray [American political leader]
Tennessee (table) T: 152
Blarney Castle [Ireland]
Blarney Stone B: 398
Blarney Stone [Ireland] B: 398
Blasco Ibáñez, Vicente [Spanish author] B: 398
Spanish literature (The 1800's) So: 761-762

Blasdel, Henry Goode [American political leader]
Nevada (table) N: 173; (Statehood) N: 174-176
Blasis, Carlo [Italian ballet teacher]
Ballet (Romantic ballet) B: 51
Blasko, Bela Ferenc [birth name of]
Lugosi, Bela L: 515
Blassie, Michael [American serviceman]
Unknown soldier U: 212
Blast furnace
Colonial life in America (Ironmaking) Ci: 811
Iron and steel (How iron is made) I: 439 with
diagram; (The Iron Age) I: 449-450
Lead (Production) L: 149-150
Metallurgy (Smelting) M: 426
Blast wave
Bomb B: 450
Nuclear weapon (Blast wave) N: 599
Blasting
Dynamite D: 397 with picture
Explosive E: 453
Blasting agent [chemical]
Explosive (Blasting agents) E: 454
Blasting cap [explosive]
Detonator D: 167
Dynamite D: 397
Fuse F: 588
Blastocoele [embryology]
Coelom Ci: 753
Blastocyst [physiology] See Blastula in this index
Blastomycosis [disease]
Fungal disease (In people) F: 558
Blastula [biology]
Coelom Ci: 753
Stem cell So: 889
Blatch, Harriot Eaton Stanton [American social
reformer] B: 398 with portrait
Woman suffrage (Growth of the movement)
W: 380-381
Blatchford, Samuel [American jurist]
Supreme Court of the United States (table)
So: 1000
Blattaria [entomology]
Insect (table) I: 299
Blau, Eugene Ormandy [birth name of]
Ormandy, Eugene O: 857
Blaue Reiter, Der [art]
Expressionism (Expressionist painting) E: 455
Germany picture on G: 155
Kandinsky, Wassily K: 213
Painting (Expressionism) P: 78 with picture
Blavatsky, Elena Petrovna [American philosopher]
Theosophy T: 252
Blaxland, Gregory [Australian pioneer]
Australia map on A: 921
Blazar [astronomy]
Quasar Q: 9
Blaze [marking]
Horse (Coat and skin) H: 348-349
Blaze [trail]
Road (The first roads) R: 361
Blazing star [plant] B: 398
Flower (Flowers of prairies and dry plains) F: 286
with picture
Blazonry
Heraldry (Expansion) H: 194 with pictures
Bleach B: 399
Chlorine (Uses of chlorine) C: 516-517
Hydrogen peroxide H: 470
Hypochlorous acid H: 480
Bleachers [book by Grisham]
Grisham, John G: 396
Bleaching
Coral reef (Coral reefs and people) Ci: 1049
Cotton (Finishing) Ci: 1091
Global warming (Harm to ocean life) G: 232a
Great Barrier Reef G: 336
Bleak House [book by Dickens]
Dickens, Charles (The second phase) D: 188
English literature (Early Victorian literature) E: 321
Blechynden, Richard [British businessman]
Tea (History) T: 63-64
Bleda [brother of]
Attila A: 879
Bleeding B: 399
See also Bloodletting in this index
Anemia (Loss of blood) A: 458
Artery A: 750
Blood picture on B: 412; (Controlling bleeding)
B: 411; (Bleeding disorders) B: 414
First aid (First aid for bleeding) F: 136 with
pictures; (Nosebleed) F: 141
Hemophilia H: 182
Hemorrhage H: 183
Laser (Heating) L: 82-83
Menstruation M: 404 with diagrams
Nosebleed N: 549
Tourniquet T: 350

Bleeding heart [plant] B: 399 with picture
Flower F: 279 with picture
Bleeding-heart pigeon
Pigeon (The body of a pigeon) P: 458-459 with
picture
Bleeding Kansas [U.S. history]
African Americans (The deepening division over
slavery) A: 136h-136i with picture
Kansas K: 216; ("Bleeding Kansas") K: 235
Blegen, Carl [American archaeologist]
Messenia M: 423
Troy (The archaeological Troy) T: 455
Blemish
Pimple P: 466
Blend [language]
Slang (Blends) S: 500
Blend [plastics]
Plastics (The chemistry of plastics) P: 556
Blended family [sociology]
Family (Varieties of families) F: 20
Blended whiskey
Whiskey W: 282
Blending [industrial process]
Cotton (Cleaning and blending) Ci: 1091
Blending inheritance [theory]
Evolution (Acceptance of evolution) E: 433
Blenheim, Battle of [1704] B: 400
Blenheim Palace [estate, England]
Architecture (Baroque architecture) A: 622
Churchill, Sir Winston Leonard Spencer (Boyhood
and education) C: 545 with picture
Vanbrugh, Sir John V: 269
Blennerhassett Island
West Virginia (Places to visit) W: 216
Blenny [fish]
Fish picture on F: 144
Blériot, Louis [French aviator] B: 400
Airplane picture on A: 232; (Other pioneer planes
and fliers) A: 233-234
Blériot XI [airplane]
Airplane picture on A: 232; (Other pioneer planes
and fliers) A: 233-234
Blessed Virgin Mary [mother of Jesus] See Mary
[mother of Jesus] in this index
Blessing of the fleet [ceremony]
Connecticut picture on Ci: 960
Blessing Way, The [book by Hillerman]
Hillerman, Tony H: 232
Bligh, William [British sea captain] B: 400
Australia (The New South Wales Corps) A: 920-
921
Tonga T: 327
Blight [plant disease] B: 400
Apple (Pests and diseases) A: 572
Cotton (Diseases) Ci: 1090
Fungicide F: 560
Great Irish Famine G: 343
Lily L: 304
Pea (Diseases and pests) P: 205
Pear (Diseases and pests) P: 216
Potato (Potato pests) P: 713
Soybean (Diseases and pests) So: 692
Blimp [airship] B: 400
Advertising picture on A: 73
Airship (Nonrigid airships) A: 250 with picture
Blind, American Foundation for the See American
Foundation for the Blind in this index
Blind, The [play by Maeterlinck]
Maeterlinck, Maurice M: 41
Blind Assassin, The [book by Atwood]
Atwood, Margaret A: 880
Blind baked bread [food]
Pie (Baking a pie) P: 452
Blind mole-rat [animal]
Mole-rat M: 691
Blind snake
Snake (Classification of snakes) S: 535
Blind spot [driving]
Automobile (Operating a car) A: 954-955
Blind spot [vision] B: 400
Eye (The retina) E: 462
Blind Woman [photograph by Strand]
Photography picture on P: 425
Blindfish See Cavefish in this index
Blinding of Samson [painting by Rembrandt]
Rembrandt (Early Amsterdam years) R: 229
Blindness B: 401 with pictures
Braille B: 550
Disability (Visual disabilities) D: 219
Glaucoma G: 226
Guide dog G: 422 with picture
Keller, Helen K: 255
Trachoma T: 355
Blindness Information Center, National
Blindness (Education and training) B: 403
Blindstitch
Sewing (Hand stitches) S: 332

Blindworm [animal] B: 403 with picture
Bliss, Aaron T. [American political leader]
Michigan (table) M: 507
Bliss, Cornelius N. [American government official]
Interior, Department of the (table) I: 325
McKinley, William (table) M: 342
Bliss, Mary Elizabeth [daughter of]
Taylor, Zachary (Life in the White House) T: 60
with portrait
White House hostesses W: 291
Bliss, William W. S. [American government official]
Taylor, Zachary (Life in the White House) T: 60
Blister [disorder] B: 403
Blister [glass]
Glass (Glass terms) G: 222
Blister copper
Copper (Smelting) Ci: 1043
Blister gas
Chemical-biological-radiological warfare
(Chemical) C: 396
Blithe Spirit [play by Coward]
Coward, Noël Ci: 1107
Blithedale Romance, The [book by Hawthorne]
Hawthorne, Nathaniel (His novels) H: 115
Blithewold Mansion, Gardens and Arboretum
[Bristol]
Rhode Island (Places to visit) R: 304 with picture
Blitz [football]
Football (table) F: 356
Blitz, The [World War II]
London (The Blitz) L: 442 with picture
World War II pictures on W: 475; (The Battle of
Britain) W: 476
Blitzkrieg [World War II] B: 403
Army (Armies in the two world wars) A: 728
Germany (World War II) G: 168
World War II (The invasion of Poland) W: 472-473
with picture
Blitzstein, Marc [American composer] B: 403
Blixen-Finecke, Karen [Danish author] See
Dinesen, Isak in this index
Blizzard [weather] B: 404
Bloat [disease]
Cattle (Diseases) C: 313
Blobel, Günter [German-born biologist]
Nobel Prizes (Physiology or medicine: 1999)
N: 446
Bloc Québécois [political party] B: 404
Bouchard, Lucien B: 515
Campbell, Kim (The 1993 election) C: 90d
Canada, Government of (Political parties) C: 136
Canada, History of (The 1993 national election)
C: 151
Chrétien, Jean (The 1993 election) C: 522c
Political party (Other parties) P: 636-637
Bloch, Ernest [Swiss-American composer] B: 404
Sessions, Roger S: 320
Bloch, Felix [Swiss-American physicist]
Magnetism (Magnetic resonance) M: 61
Bloch, Konrad Emil [American chemist] B: 404
Block [mechanism]
Block and tackle B: 404 with diagrams
Block [track]
Railroad (Traffic control) R: 110-111
Block, Adriaen [Dutch explorer]
Connecticut (Dutch exploration) Ci: 968
New York City (Settlement) N: 341
Rhode Island (Exploration) R: 312
Block, Harlon H. [American soldier]
Iwo Jima, Battle of picture on I: 523
Block, Herbert Lawrence [American cartoonist]
B: 404 with picture
Block, John R. [American government official]
Agriculture, Department of (table) A: 161
Reagan, Ronald Wilson (table) R: 169
Block and tackle [machine] B: 404 with diagrams
Crane (table) C: 1119 with pictures
Block caving [mining]
Mining (Caving) M: 576
Block excavation
Archaeology (Excavating sites) A: 597
Block form
Letter writing (The form) L: 211 with picture
Block grant
City government (Sources of revenue) Ci: 597
Urban renewal (History) U: 220
Block Island
Rhode Island (Places to visit) R: 304 with picture;
(Islands) R: 306 with map; (table: Average
monthly weather) R: 308
Block printing [printing method] B: 405 with
pictures
Book (The development of printed books) B: 466
Communication (The rise of printing) Ci: 879
Printing (History) P: 802; (The invention of
movable type) P: 803
Woodcut W: 392 with pictures

World, History of the (China) **W:** 435 *with picture*
Block signal
Railroad (Traffic control) **R:** 110
Block train
Railroad (At classification yards) **R:** 110
Blockade [warfare] **B:** 405
Civil War, American (Battle of Mobile Bay) **Ci:** 632
Neutrality (Rights and duties) **N:** 153
World War I (The war at sea) **W:** 460; (The fighting ends) **W:** 463
Blockhouse [fortification]
Pioneer life in America (Defending a settlement) **P:** 485
Blocking [industrial process]
Fur (Cutting and sewing) **F:** 563
Blocking [sports]
Boxing *picture on* **B:** 529
Blocking [staging]
Motion picture (Shooting the movie) **M:** 852-853
Theater (Rehearsing) **T:** 236-237 *with picture*
Bloembergen, Nicolaas [American physicist]
Nobel Prizes (Physics: 1981) **N:** 441
Bloemfontein [South Africa] **B:** 406
Blog [computing] **B:** 406
Internet (Communication) **I:** 350b; (The evolving Internet) **I:** 350g-350h
Publishing (Blogs and websites) **P:** 869
Blogger [person]
Blog **B:** 406
Blogger [software]
Blog **B:** 406
Blogosphere [community]
Blog **B:** 406
Blogring [group]
Blog **B:** 406
Blok, Alexander [Russian poet]
Russian literature (Symbolism) **R:** 563
Blomdahl, Karl-Birger [Swedish composer]
Opera (Opera today) **O:** 800
Blomidon Provincial Park [Nova Scotia]
Nova Scotia *picture on* **N:** 564
Blood B: 407 *with pictures*
See also Bleeding; Blood clot; Circulatory system *in this index; and the list of Related articles in the* Blood *article*
Blood transfusion **B:** 416
Bone marrow transplant **B:** 457
Crime scene investigation (Collecting evidence) **Ci:** 1140-1141
Death (Medical aspects of death) **D:** 61
Forensic science (What a forensic scientist analyzes) **F:** 389
Galen **G:** 10
Disorders
Blood (Blood disorders) **B:** 414
Anemia **A:** 457
Cancer (table) **C:** 170
Hypoglycemia **H:** 480
Leukemia **L:** 215
Nutrition (Heart disease) **N:** 630
Sickle cell anemia **S:** 447 *with picture*
Von Willebrand's disease **V:** 448
Physiology
Cell *picture on* **C:** 328
Cholesterol **C:** 520
Circulatory system (The blood) **Ci:** 559
Gamma globulin **G:** 23
Heart **H:** 132; (The work of the heart) **H:** 135
Hemoglobin **H:** 182
Human body (The circulatory system) **H:** 421 *with picture;* (The blood) **H:** 421 *with picture*
Iron (How bodies use iron) **I:** 435
Kidney (How the kidneys produce urine) **K:** 311
Liver (Purification of the blood) **L:** 394
Plasma **P:** 551 *with picture*
Respiration (Gas transport between the lungs and tissues) **R:** 261
Serum **S:** 319
Spleen **So:** 797
Triglyceride **T:** 442
Blood, Council of [Spanish history]
Alba, Duke of **A:** 305
Blood, Henry H. [American political leader]
Utah (table) **U:** 245
Blood, Robert O. [American political leader]
New Hampshire (table) **N:** 223
"Blood, toil, tears, and sweat" [quotation]
Churchill, Sir Winston Leonard Spencer (World War II begins) **C:** 547
Blood alcohol concentration
Breath testing **B:** 591
Driving while intoxicated **D:** 348
Blood and Belonging [book by Ignatieff]
Ignatieff, Michael **I:** 48
Blood and Sand [book by Blasco Ibáñez]
Blasco Ibáñez, Vicente **B:** 398
Blood bank

Blood (Blood transfusions) **B:** 413
Blood transfusion **B:** 416
Drew, Charles Richard **D:** 347
Blood blister [disorder]
Blister **B:** 403
Blood-brain barrier
Brain (From harmful substances) **B:** 551
Blood cell separator [machine]
Blood transfusion (How blood is collected) **B:** 416-417
Blood clot [disorder]
Blood *pictures on* **B:** 412; (Controlling bleeding) **B:** 411
C-reactive protein **C:** 2
Circulatory system (Disorders of the circulatory system) **Ci:** 561
Embolism **E:** 256
Fibrin **F:** 90
Heart (Causes) **H:** 137; (Heart attack) **H:** 138 *with diagrams*
Stroke **So:** 929
Blood count [medicine] **B:** 415
Blood (Blood tests) **B:** 413
Blood diamond [gem]
Africa (Mining) **A:** 127
Northwest Territories (The late 1900's) **N:** 534
Blood donor
Blood (Blood groups) **B:** 412
Blood transfusion **B:** 416
Blood doping [crime] **B:** 415
Doping **D:** 309
Blood feud [quarrel]
Feud **F:** 81
Blood fluke
Flatworm **F:** 229 *with diagram*
Blood group
Blood (Blood groups) **B:** 412
Blood transfusion (How blood is collected) **B:** 416-417
Races, Human (The clinal approach) **R:** 55-56
Rh factor **R:** 289
Blood Indians
Blackfeet Indians **B:** 393
Blood Knot, The [book by Fugard]
Fugard, Athol **F:** 553
Blood libel [Jewish history]
Jews (Jews in Christian Europe) **J:** 122
Blood on the Fields [music by Marsalis]
Marsalis, Wynton **M:** 227
Blood orange [tree]
Orange (Sweet oranges) **O:** 815
Blood plasma *See* Plasma *in this index*
Blood platelet *See* Platelet *in this index*
Blood poisoning B: 416
Blood pressure B: 416
See also Hypertension *in this index*
Heart (Regulating blood pressure) **H:** 136
Blood purge [German history]
Himmler, Heinrich **H:** 234
Blood sugar [physiology]
Carbohydrate (Kinds of carbohydrates) **C:** 203
Diabetes **D:** 179
Glucose **G:** 236
Blood test
AIDS (Diagnosis) **A:** 164b
Allergy (Diagnosis) **A:** 374
Blood (Blood tests) **B:** 413
Blood count **B:** 415
Marriage (Laws concerning marriage) **M:** 219
Blood transfusion B: 416
AIDS (How HIV is transmitted) **A:** 164b; (Prevention) **A:** 165
Blood (Blood groups) **B:** 412; (Blood transfusions) **B:** 413 *with picture*
Blood doping **B:** 415
Hepatitis (Hepatitis B) **H:** 192
Intravenous injection **I:** 354
Red Cross (Biomedical services) **R:** 185
Rh factor **R:** 290
Blood Transfusion Service, National
Red Cross (Health services) **R:** 186
Blood type *See* Blood group *in this index*
Blood vessel [anatomy]
Aneurysm **A:** 459
Angiogenesis **A:** 461
Artery **A:** 750
Blood (What blood does in the body) **B:** 408
Calcium channel blocker **C:** 21
Capillary **C:** 192
Circulatory system (The blood vessels) **Ci:** 559 *with pictures*
First aid (First aid for bleeding) **F:** 136-137 *with picture*
Heart (Blood vessels) **H:** 135 *with picture*
Human body (The blood vessels) **H:** 421; (Anatomy of the human body) **H:** 422 *with diagram*

Vein **V:** 295
Bloodhound B: 417
Dog *picture on* **D:** 271
Hound **H:** 379 *with picture*
Bloodless Revolution [political movement]
Rhode Island (Political reform) **R:** 315
Bloodletting [history of medicine] **B:** 417
Blood *picture on* **B:** 407; (History of blood research) **B:** 414
Pioneer life in America (Health) **P:** 483
Surgery (History) **So:** 1007
Bloodroot [plant] **B:** 417 *with picture*
Flower (Flowers of woodlands and forests) **F:** 284 *with picture*
Plant *picture on* **P:** 525
Bloodsmoor Romance, A [book by Oates]
Oates, Joyce Carol **O:** 639
Bloodstone [gem]
Gem *picture on* **G:** 78
Bloodsucker [animal] *See* Leech *in this index*
Bloodworm [insect]
Midge **M:** 535
Bloody Bill [1833]
Force bill **F:** 371
Bloody Flag
Pirate (A pirate's life) **P:** 494-495
Bloody Marsh, Battle of [1742]
Georgia (English colony) **G:** 131-132
Oglethorpe, James Edward **O:** 679
Bloody Mary [queen of England] *See* Mary I *in this index*
Bloody nose *See* Nosebleed *in this index*
Bloody Sunday B: 418
Northern Ireland
Bloody Sunday **B:** 418
Russia
Bloody Sunday **B:** 418
Lenin, V. I. (Revolt) **L:** 192
Russia (The Revolution of 1905) **R:** 552
Russian Revolution of 1917 (The 1905 Revolution) **R:** 566
United States
Bloody Sunday **B:** 418
Selma marches **S:** 291
Voting Rights Act of 1965 **V:** 451
Bloom [industry]
Iron and steel (Making iron products) **I:** 441; (Ingot casting) **I:** 445 *with diagram*
Bloom [oceanography]
Atlantic Ocean (Pollution) **A:** 867
Pacific Ocean (Offshore pollution) **P:** 17
Bloom, Leopold [literary figure]
Joyce, James **J:** 177
Bloomer, Amelia Jenks [American social reformer]
B: 418 *with picture*
Bloomer, Dexter C. [husband of]
Bloomer, Amelia Jenks **B:** 418
Bloomer, Elizabeth "Betty" [wife of Gerald Ford]
See Ford, Betty *in this index*
Bloomers [clothing]
Bloomer, Amelia Jenks **B:** 418 *with picture*
Bloomfield, Joseph [American political leader]
New Jersey (table) **N:** 249
Bloomfield, Leonard [American linguist]
Linguistics (Structuralism) **L:** 337
Bloomsbury Group [British history] **B:** 419
English literature (Literature before World War I) **E:** 322
Strachey, Lytton **So:** 917
Woolf, Virginia **W:** 401
Blos, Joan [American author]
Newbery Medal (table) **N:** 359
Blossom
Flower **F:** 270
Blossom family [fictional characters]
Byars, Betsy **B:** 746
Blossom Time [operetta by Romberg]
Romberg, Sigmund **R:** 427
Bloudy Tenent of Persecution, The [pamphlet by Williams]
Williams, Roger (In Rhode Island) **W:** 311
Blount, Edward [English publisher]
Shakespeare, William (Shakespeare's plays) **S:** 354; (Folios) **S:** 369
Blount, William [1749-1800, American political leader] **B:** 419
Impeachment (History) **I:** 91
Blount, Willie [1768-1835, American political leader]
Tennessee (table) **T:** 152
Blount, Winton M. [American government official]
Nixon, Richard Milhous (table) **N:** 433
Blount House
Knoxville (Description) **K:** 359
Blow [zoology]
Whale (Respiratory system) **W:** 259-260 *with picture*

Blow, Kurtis [American rapper]
Rap music **R: 141**

Blow chair
Furniture (Radical modern design) **F: 585** *with picture*

Blow fly [insect]
Larva *picture on* **L: 78**

Blow molding
Antique (Glass) **A: 558**
Doll (The doll industry today) **D: 294**
Plastics *picture on* **P: 558**; (Making plastic products) **P: 557**
Polystyrene **P: 651**

Blow-over
Glass (Glass terms) **G: 222**

Blow-Up [film]
Antonioni, Michelangelo **A: 561**

Blowback system
Machine gun (Operation) **M: 15**

Blowfish [fish] *See* Porcupinefish *in this index*

Blowgun [weapon] **B: 419**
Indian, American *picture on* **I: 140**
Jívaro Indians *picture on* **J: 128**

Blowhole [zoology]
Blue whale **B: 421**
Dolphin (The bodies of dolphins) **D: 297-298**
Mammal (Internal organ systems) **M: 119-120**
Whale (Respiratory system) **W: 259-260** *with picture*

"Blowin' in the Wind" [song]
Dylan, Bob **D: 397**

Blowing [industrial process]
Bottle **B: 513**

Blowout [geology]
Nebraska (Land regions) **N: 104**

Blowpipe [musical instrument]
Bagpipe **B: 26** *with picture*

Blowpipe [tool]
Glass *picture on* **G: 216**; (Blowing) **G: 215**; (Early times) **G: 217-218**

Blowpipe [weapon] *See* Blowgun *in this index*

Bloxham, William D. [American political leader]
Florida (table) **F: 260**

BLS [agency] *See* Labor Statistics, Bureau of *in this index*

BLU-82B [bomb]
Bomb (General-purpose [GP] bombs) **B: 450**

Blu-ray player [electronics]
Stereophonic sound system (Parts of a stereo system) **So: 892**

Blubber [fat] **B: 419**
Bowhead whale **B: 520**
Cetacean **C: 364**
Dolphin (The bodies of dolphins) **D: 297**
Seal (The body of a seal) **S: 266**
Whale (Skin and blubber) **W: 259**; (The Basque people) **W: 262**; (Processing whale products) **W: 263**

Blücher [locomotive]
Stephenson, George **So: 890**

Blücher, Gebhard Leberecht von [Prussian general] **B: 419**
Napoleon I (The Hundred Days and Waterloo) **N: 16**
Prussia (Napoleonic period) **P: 843**
Waterloo, Battle of (The battle) **W: 145**

Blue [butterfly]
Butterfly *pictures on* **B: 732, B: 733**; (Blues, coppers, and hairstreaks) **B: 734** *with pictures*

Blue [color]
Color *diagrams on* **Ci: 821**
Indigo **I: 223**

Blue, Robert D. [American political leader]
Iowa (table) **I: 391**

Blue Angel, The [film]
Dietrich, Marlene **D: 200**
Von Sternberg, Josef **V: 448**

Blue Angels [aviators]
Airplane *picture on* **A: 212**

Blue baby **B: 419**
Cyanosis **Ci: 1203**
Heart (Blockage of blood flow) **H: 141**
Taussig, Helen Brooke **T: 52**

Blue bear [animal]
Bear (American black bears) **B: 184**

Blue beech [tree]
Ironwood **I: 454**
Leaf *picture on* **L: 153**

Blue belly [bird] *See* Swift *in this index*

Blue Bird, The [play by Maeterlinck]
Maeterlinck, Maurice **M: 41**

Blue Black [painting by Kelly]
Painting (Abstract artists) **P: 88-89** *with picture*

Blue Bombers, Winnipeg [team] *See* Winnipeg Blue Bombers *in this index*

Blue Book, Project
Unidentified flying object **U: 27**

Blue Boy, The [painting by Gainsborough]
Gainsborough, Thomas **G: 7** *with picture*

Blue-breasted quail [bird]
Quail **Q: 4**

Blue cedar [tree]
Tree *picture on* **T: 426**

Blue cheese
Cheese (Semisoft cheese) **C: 392**

Blue chip stock [investment]
Dow Jones average **D: 316**

Blue chromis [fish]
Fish *picture on* **F: 155**

Blue crab [sea animal] **B: 419** *with picture*
Crab **Ci: 1115** *with diagram*
Crustacean *picture on* **Ci: 1164**

Blue crew
Submarine (Life aboard a submarine) **So: 941**

Blue Cross and Blue Shield [organization] **B: 420**
Hospital (The 1900's) **H: 374**

Blue-diademed motmot [bird]
Bird *picture on* **B: 344b**

Blue earth [soil]
Amber **A: 404**

Blue-faced parrotfinch [bird]
Bird (Birds of the Pacific Islands) **B: 349** *with picture*

Blue flag [plant]
Plant *picture on* **P: 547**
Wetland *picture on* **W: 253**

"Blue flu" [boycott]
Labor movement (Handling labor disputes) **L: 6**

Blue-footed booby [bird]
Booby **B: 464** *with picture*

Blue grama [plant]
Grass *picture on* **G: 325**

Blue Grass Boys [band]
Country music (Bluegrass music) **Ci: 1098a** *with picture*
Monroe, Bill **M: 733**

Blue-green algae *See* Cyanobacteria *in this index*

Blue Grotto [Capri, Italy]
Capri **C: 198**
Cave (table) **C: 320**

Blue gum [tree]
Eucalyptus **E: 376**

Blue heeler [dog]
Australian cattle dog **A: 927**

Blue Hen [chicken] **B: 420**

Blue Hen's Chickens [military company]
Blue Hen **B: 420**

"Blue Hotel, The" [story by Crane]
Crane, Stephen **Ci: 1120**

Blue huckleberry [shrub]
Huckleberry **H: 404**

Blue Jackets, Columbus [team]
Hockey (table: National Hockey League) **H: 281**

Blue jay [bird] **B: 420** *with picture*
Bird *picture on* **B: 358**; (Birds of urban areas) **B: 333** *with picture*
Jay **J: 66**

Blue Jays, Toronto [team] *See* Toronto Blue Jays *in this index*

Blue jeans [clothing] *See* Jeans *in this index*

Blue jet [meteorology]
Lightning (Jets, sprites, and elves) **L: 301**

Blue Lake [New Mexico]
Pueblo Indians (Contact with other peoples) **P: 871**

Blue laws [U.S. history] **B: 420**
Colonial life in America (Religion) **Ci: 804-805**
Sunday **So: 989**

Blue Lodge
Masonry (Organization) **M: 267**; (The lodges and degrees of Masonry) **M: 267**

Blue lorikeet [bird]
Bird (Birds of the Pacific Islands) **B: 349** *with picture*

Blue marlin [fish]
Marlin **M: 215**

Blue Men [name for]
Tuareg **T: 476**

Blue mold
Mold **M: 689**

Blue Monday
Monday **M: 702**

Blue moon **B: 420**

Blue Mosque [Istanbul, Turkey]
Istanbul (The city) **I: 490-491**

Blue Mountains [Australia]
Jamaica (Land and climate) **J: 24**

Blue Mountains National Park [Australia]
National park (table) **N: 42f**

Blue Nile [river, Africa]
Lake Tana **L: 46**
Nile River (The course of the Nile) **N: 422** *with picture and map*
Sudan (Way of life) **So: 951**; (Land and climate)

So: 951 *with map*

Blue Period
Picasso, Pablo (The Blue Period) **P: 448a**

Blue peter
Flag (Flags that talk) **F: 208**

Blue Rider [art] *See* Blaue Reiter, Der *in this index*

Blue Ridge [region, U.S.]
See also Blue Ridge Mountains *in this index*
Appalachian Mountains (Physical features) **A: 568**
Georgia (Land regions) **G: 124**
South Carolina (Land regions) **So: 652** *with map*

Blue Ridge Mountains [U.S.] **B: 421** *with picture*
Luray Caverns **L: 526**
Maryland (Land regions) **M: 250**
North Carolina *picture on* **N: 472**
South Carolina (Land regions) **So: 652** *with picture and map*; (Rivers, waterfalls, and lakes) **So: 652-654**
Tennessee *picture on* **T: 134**; (Land regions) **T: 146**
United States (The Appalachian Highlands) **U: 120**
Virginia *picture on* **V: 398**; (Land regions) **V: 410**
West Virginia (Land regions) **W: 218**

Blue Ridge Parkway [road]
Blue Ridge Mountains **B: 421** *with picture*
National Park System (table: National parkways and other national parklands) **N: 55**; (History) **N: 58-59**
Virginia (Visitor's guide) **V: 408**

Blue-ringed octopus
Octopus (Octopuses and people) **O: 673**

Blue Room
White House *picture on* **W: 289**; (Public rooms) **W: 286** *with picture*

Blue screen [cinematography]
Animation (Lighting and rendering) **A: 513-514a** *with picture*

Blue shark [fish] **B: 421**

Blue Shield [insurance] *See* Blue Cross and Blue Shield *in this index*

Blue shift [astronomy] *See* Blueshift *in this index*

Blue spruce [tree]
Spruce (Kinds) **So: 809** *with picture*

Blue Sword, The [book by McKinley]
McKinley, Robin **M: 337**

Blue tang surgeonfish
Fish *picture on* **F: 154**

Blue thistle [plant]
Viper's bugloss **V: 391**

Blue tit [bird]
Bird *picture on* **B: 344d**; (Birds of Europe) **B: 344c**

Blue vitriol [chemical]
Hydrate **H: 462**

Blue whale **B: 421**
Animal *picture on* **A: 469**; (Animal travelers) **A: 502**
Antarctica (Living things) **A: 534** *with picture*
Endangered species (table) **E: 270**
Mammal *picture on* **M: 117**
Whale (Rorquals) **W: 255** *with picture*

Blue wildebeest [animal]
Wildebeest **W: 302** *with picture*

Blue-winged teal [bird]
Bird (Birds of inland waters and marshes) **B: 340** *with picture*

Blue-yellow defect [disorder]
Color blindness **Ci: 827**

Blue yodel [music]
Country music (The roots of country music) **Ci: 1098a-1098b**
Rodgers, Jimmie **R: 398**

Blueback *See* Sockeye salmon *in this index*

Bluebell [plant] **B: 422** *with picture*
Flower *picture on* **F: 291**
Lungwort **L: 525**

Blueberry [shrub] **B: 422** *with picture*
Fruit (Temperate fruits) **F: 546** *with picture*
Michigan *picture on* **M: 505**
Plant *picture on* **P: 531**

Bluebird [bird] **B: 422** *with picture*
Bird *pictures on* **B: 358, B: 367**; (Birds of Asia) **B: 344f** *with picture*

Bluebonnet [plant] **B: 423**

Bluebottle [plant]
Bachelor's-button **B: 17**

Bluebottle fly [insect]
Fly (The body of a fly) **F: 309**
Insect *picture on* **I: 285**

Bluebuck [animal]
Antelope (Habits and appearance) **A: 542**

Bluefin tuna [fish]
Fish *picture on* **F: 153**
Tuna **T: 485**

Bluefish [fish] **B: 423** *with picture*
Fish *picture on* **F: 152**

Bluegill [fish]
Fish *picture on* **F: 158**

Sunfish So: 990
Bluegrass [music]
Country music (Bluegrass music) **Ci: 1098a** *with picture*
Bluegrass [plant] **B: 424**
Grass *picture on* **G: 325**
Lawn (Types of lawns) **L: 142**
Bluegrass Louisville American Music Fest
Kentucky *picture on* **K: 283**
Bluegrass Region
Kentucky (Land regions) **K: 285**; (Natural resources) **K: 287**
Ohio (Land regions) **O: 692**
Bluegrass State [name for]
Kentucky **K: 272**
Bluehead wrasse [fish]
Fish *picture on* **F: 155**
Bluejacket [sailor]
Navy, United States (A typical day) **N: 83**
Bluenose [boat] **B: 424** *with picture*
Bluenose II [boat]
Bluenose **B: 424**
Nova Scotia (Places to visit) **N: 560**
Bluenosers [people]
Nova Scotia **N: 555**
Blueprint [construction] **B: 424**
Blues [music] **B: 424**
Country music (The roots of country music) **Ci: 1098a-1098b**
Gaye, Marvin **G: 73**
Handy, W. C. **H: 50**
Jazz (The roots of jazz) **J: 70**
Johnson, Robert **J: 153**
King, B. B. **K: 320**
Mississippi *picture on* **M: 626**
Popular music (Ragtime, jazz, and blues) **P: 670**; (The recording era) **P: 671**
Rhythm and blues **R: 320**
Rock music (Musical roots) **R: 376**
Blues, Father of the [name for]
Handy, W. C. **H: 50**
Blues, Saint Louis [team]
Hockey (table: National Hockey League) **H: 281**
Blues for Mister Charlie [play by Baldwin]
Baldwin, James **B: 39**
Bluesbreakers [rock group]
Rock music (Fresh directions) **R: 380**
Blueshift [physics]
Astronomy (Spectroscopy) **A: 840-841-**; (Radio and microwave astronomy) **A: 843** *with picture*
Redshift (The Doppler redshift) **R: 192**
Bluest Eye, The [book by Morrison]
Morrison, Toni **M: 817**
Bluestem grass [plant]
Grass *picture on* **G: 325**
Plant *picture on* **P: 526**
Bluestone [rock]
Stonehenge **So: 911**
Bluestone Scenic River National Parkway [West Virginia]
National Park System (table: National parkways and other national parklands) **N: 55**
Bluestriped grunt [fish]
Fish *picture on* **F: 155**
Bluethroat [bird]
Bird (Birds of Europe) **B: 344c** *with picture*
Bluford, Guion Stewart, Jr. [American astronaut] **B: 425** *with portrait*
African Americans *picture on* **A: 136p**
Astronaut (table) **A: 830**
Blumberg, Baruch Samuel [American physiologist]
Nobel Prizes (Physiology or medicine: 1976) **N: 446**
Blume, Judy [American author] **B: 425**
Blumenthal, W. Michael [American government official]
Carter, Jimmy (table) **C: 257**
Blundell, James [British physician]
Blood transfusion (History) **B: 417**
Blunderbuss [gun] **B: 425** *with picture*
Blunt, Matt [American political leader]
Missouri (table) **M: 668**
Blunt, Roy [American political leader] **B: 426**
Blunt point nail
Nail (The parts of a nail) **N: 3**
Bluntnose stingray [animal]
Animal *picture on* **A: 487**
Blurb [text]
Publishing (Marketing) **P: 867**
Blush [wine] *See* Rosé *in this index*
Bly, Nellie [American journalist] **B: 426** *with portrait*
Blyleven, Bert [American baseball player]
Baseball (table: Hall of Fame) **B: 134**
Blyth [surname]
Barrymore **B: 119**
Blythe, Virginia Cassidy [mother of]

Clinton, Bill (Early life) **Ci: 682a**
Blythe, William Jefferson, III [father of]
Clinton, Bill (Early life) **Ci: 682a**
Blythe, William Jefferson, IV [birth name of]
Clinton, Bill (Boyhood) **Ci: 682a**
BMEWS *See* Ballistic Missile Early Warning System *in this index*
BMI [measurement]
Obesity **O: 642** *with diagram*
BMI-for-age [measurement]
Obesity **O: 642**
BMR [medicine] *See* Basal metabolic rate *in this index*
BMT [subway]
New York City (Transportation) **N: 334-335**
BMW [company]
Manufacturing (table) **M: 170**
BMX [sport] *See* Bicycle motocross *in this index*
B'nai B'rith [organization] **B: 426** *with picture*
Bo Juyi [Chinese poet]
Chinese literature (Poetry) **C: 511**
Boa [snake] **B: 426**
Snake (Boas) **S: 535**
Boa constrictor [snake] **B: 427**
Animal *picture on* **A: 480**
Boa **B: 426**
Snake *picture on* **S: 533**
Boa Vista [island]
Cape Verde **C: 189** *with map*
Boabdil [king of Granada] **B: 427**
Boadicea [queen of the Iceni] *See* Boudicca *in this index*
Boar [animal]
Hog (table) **H: 284**
Boar, Wild [animal] **B: 427** *with picture*
Animal *picture on* **A: 479**
Hog (Wild hogs) **H: 286**
Board book
Literature for children (Infant and toddler books) **L: 356**; (Books for beginning readers) **L: 365**
Board foot [measurement]
Lumber (table) **L: 518**
Board game
Artificial intelligence (Planning and problem solving) **A: 760**
Game (Board games) **G: 22**
Board of chosen freeholders
New Jersey (Local government) **N: 249**
Board of commissioners [government]
County (Forms of county governments) **Ci: 1099**
Board of directors
Corporation (Business corporations) **Ci: 1069-1070**
Board of education *See* Education, Board of *in this index*
Board of Estimate
New York City (Government) **N: 339-340**
Board of governors
Federal Reserve System (Organization) **F: 65**
Board of health [U.S.]
Health, Board of **H: 127**
Board of Public Works [Washington, D.C.]
Washington, D.C. (Territorial government abolished) **W: 86**
Board of regents
Universities and colleges (Governing boards) **U: 208L**
Board of supervisors [government]
County (Forms of county governments) **Ci: 1099**
Board of Tax Appeals [U.S. history]
Tax Court, United States **T: 52**
Board of trade [economics] *See* Commodity exchange *in this index*
Board of trustees
Universities and colleges (Governing boards) **U: 208L**
Board of War and Ordnance [U.S. history]
Army, United States (The Continental Army) **A: 737-738**
Boarding around [custom]
Pioneer life in America (Education) **P: 484**
Boarding bridge
Airport (The passenger terminal) **A: 244**
Boarding school [education]
Education (Education in other countries) **E: 96**
Boards [hockey]
Hockey (The rink) **H: 274**
Boardwalk
Atlantic City **A: 862** *with picture*
Boardwalk Hall
Atlantic City **A: 863**
Boas, Franz [American anthropologist] **B: 427**
Anthropology (Development of field research) **A: 548**
Boat *See* Boating; Ship *in this index*
Boat-Building near Flatford Mill [painting by Constable]

Painting (Romanticism) **P: 68** *with picture*
Boat burial [ceremony]
Vikings (Daily life) **V: 379**
Boat orchid [plant]
Orchid *picture on* **O: 824**
Boat people
Vietnam (Postwar Vietnam) **V: 371-372**
Boat racing
See also Rowing; Yacht *in this index*
America's Cup **A: 431**
Bluenose **B: 424** *with picture*
Iceboating (Iceboat races) **I: 19** *with pictures*
Motorboat racing **M: 876** *with pictures*
Sailing (Sailboat racing) **S: 27** *with pictures*
Boat song [music]
Barcarole **B: 108**
Boat-tailed grackle [bird]
Grackle **G: 296**
Boating **B: 428** *with pictures*
See also Ship *in this index and the list of Related articles in the* Boating *article*
Canoeing **C: 180** *with pictures*
Iceboating **I: 18** *with pictures*
Pacific Islands *picture on* **P: 7**
Plastics *picture on* **P: 554**
Rowing **R: 493**
Safety (In water sports) **S: 13**
Sailing **S: 23** *with pictures*
Boaz [Biblical figure]
Ruth, Book of **R: 568**
Bob [hair style]
Hairdressing (The 1900's) **H: 12**
Bob [weight]
Pendulum (Clock pendulums) **P: 237**
Bob Bullock Texas State History Museum [Austin]
Texas (Places to visit) **T: 194**
Bob Jones University **B: 432**
Bobadilla, Francisco de [Spanish government official]
Columbus, Christopher (Columbus in disgrace) **Ci: 862-863**
Bobber
Fishing (Floats) **F: 178** *with picture*
Bobbin [device]
Sewing machine *pictures on* **S: 334**
Weaving (How a loom works) **W: 173-174**
Bobbin lace
Lace *picture on* **L: 22**
Bobbin lace [fabric]
Lace **L: 20** *with pictures*
Bobbsey Twins [literary figures]
Stratemeyer, Edward **So: 920**
Bobby [police]
Peel, Sir Robert **P: 228**
Police (Early law enforcement in England) **P: 624** *with picture*
Bobcat [rank]
Boy Scouts (Cub Scouting) **B: 535**
Bobcat [wildcat] **B: 432** *with picture*
Animal *picture on* **A: 483**
Lynx **L: 536**
Wildcat **W: 301**
Bobo [people]
Burkina Faso (People) **B: 706**
Bobolink [bird] **B: 433**
Bird *pictures on* **B: 358, B: 361**
Bobsledding [sport] **B: 433** *with picture*
Olympic Games (Winter Olympic Games) **O: 746d**
Sled **S: 505**
Tobogganing **T: 308**
Bobwhite [bird]
Bird (In nature) **B: 330** *with picture*; (Birds of brushy areas) **B: 338** *with picture*
Partridge **P: 188**
Quail **Q: 4**
Boca, La [district, Buenos Aires]
Buenos Aires (The city) **B: 672** *with picture*
Boccaccio, Giovanni [Italian author] **B: 433**
French literature (The Renaissance) **F: 519**
Italian literature (Humanism and the Renaissance) **I: 494**
Renaissance (Petrarch and Giovanni Boccaccio) **R: 233-234**
Boccherini, Luigi [Italian composer] **B: 434**
Boccie [game]
Bowling (Other kinds of bowling) **B: 524b**
Boccioni, Umberto [Italian sculptor] **B: 434**
Futurism **F: 589** *with pictures*
Sculpture (Form and treatment) **S: 230-231** *with picture*
Bock, Jerry [American composer]
Musical comedy (The modern musical emerges) **M: 960**
Bock lager [drink]
Beer **B: 211**
Bodark [tree] *See* Osage orange *in this index*
Bode, Johann E. [German astronomer]

Asteroid (History of study) **A: 824b**
Bode's law **B: 434**
Uranus **U: 217**
Bodega y Quadra, Juan Francisco de la [Spanish explorer]
Washington (Discovery and exploration) **W: 66**
Bodegone [art]
Painting (The Spanish masters) **P: 64**
Bodensee [lake, Europe]
Lake Constance **L: 37**
Bode's law [astronomy] **B: 434**
Asteroid (History of study) **A: 824b**
Bodhidharma [Chinese religious leader]
Zen **Z: 589**
Bodhisattva [religion] **B: 434**
Buddhism (The Mahayana) **B: 669**
God (Personal Gods) **G: 243**
Korea, History of *picture on* **K: 367**
Sculpture (China) **S: 238** *with picture*
Bodleian Library [University of Oxford] **B: 434**
Bodley, Sir Thomas [English diplomat]
Bodleian Library **B: 434**
Bodman, Samuel [American government official]
Bush, George Walker (table) **B: 722h**
Energy, Department of (table) **E: 276**
Bodmer, Karl [Swiss artist]
Buffalo *picture on* **B: 675**
Indian, American *pictures on* **I: 158, I: 159, I: 161**
Bodo [people]
India (Religious and ethnic unrest) **I: 134**
Bodoni, Giambattista [Italian printer] **B: 434**
Book (The 1600's and 1700's) **B: 467**
Bodwell, Joseph R. [American political leader]
Maine (table) **M: 87**
Body [computing]
HyperText Markup Language **H: 477**
Body, Human *See* Human body *in this index*
"Body and Soul" [song]
Hawkins, Coleman **H: 114**
Body art B: 434 *with picture*
Africa *picture on* **A: 116a**; (Fine arts) **A: 115** *with picture*
Clothing (Clothing of Africa) **Ci: 698**
Tattooing **T: 51**
Body cavity [anatomy]
Hernia **H: 212**
Body cell [biology] *See* Somatic cell *in this index*
Body check [sports]
Lacrosse (Men's lacrosse) **L: 23**
Body Count [recording]
Rock music (Rap) **R: 380d**
Body gripper [trap] *See* Conibear *in this index*
Body language B: 435
Communication (The study of communication) **Ci: 887**
Dog (Behavior) **D: 277**
Kinesics **K: 319**
Body louse [insect]
Louse **L: 507** *with picture*
Body mass index [measurement]
Obesity **O: 642** *with diagram*
Body odor
Skin (Hair, nails, and glands) **S: 489-490**
Body of Liberties [document]
Colonial life in America (table) **Ci: 794**
Body stalk [anatomy]
Reproduction, Human (Development of the embryo) **R: 247** *with diagram*
Body temperature *See* Temperature, Body *in this index*
Body wave [geology]
Earthquake (How an earthquake spreads) **E: 37**
Bodybuilders, International Federation of
Bodybuilding **B: 435**
Bodybuilding [sport] **B: 435**
Weightlifting **W: 183**
Bodysurfing [sport]
Surfing **So: 1004**
Boe, Nils [American political leader]
South Dakota (table) **So: 680**
Boehmite [mineral]
Bauxite (How bauxite forms) **B: 174**
Boehner, John Andrew [American political leader] **B: 435**
Boeing, William Edward [American businessman] **B: 435**
Aviation (World War I [1914-1918]) **A: 987-988**
Boeing 314 Clipper [airplane]
Airplane (Engineering improvements) **A: 237**
Boeing 707 [airplane]
Airplane *picture on* **A: 236**; (The jet age) **A: 238**
Boeing 747 [airplane]
Airplane *pictures on* **A: 216, A: 237**; (Commercial transport planes) **A: 210** *with picture*; (The jet age) **A: 238**
Aviation (A new age of flight) **A: 990-991**
Jet propulsion (Power in a jet engine) **J: 111**

Boeing 777 [airplane]
Airplane *pictures on* **A: 208, A: 218**; (Commercial transport planes) **A: 210**
Boeing Air Transport
Boeing, William Edward **B: 435**
Boeing Company [manufacturer]
Aviation (Aircraft manufacturing) **A: 984**; (World War I [1914-1918]) **A: 987-988**
Seattle (Manufacturing) **S: 275**; (Economic expansion) **S: 276**
Washington (Interesting facts about Washington) **W: 47**
Boelcke, Oswald [German aviator]
Richthofen, Baron Manfred von **R: 334**
Boeotia [district, ancient Greece] **B: 436**
Boeotian League [ancient Greece]
Boeotia **B: 436**
Pelopidas **P: 232**
Thebes **T: 251**
Boer War [1880-1881]
Smuts, Jan Christiaan **S: 522**
South Africa (Discovery of diamonds and gold) **So: 618**
Boer War [1899-1902] *See* Anglo-Boer Wars *in this index*
Boers [people] *See* Afrikaners *in this index*
Boesman and Lena [book by Fugard]
Fugard, Athol **F: 553**
Boethius, Anicius Manlius Severinus [Roman philosopher] **B: 436**
BOF [furnace]
Iron and steel (The basic oxygen process [BOP]) **I: 441** *with diagrams*
Bog [area] **B: 436** *with diagram*
Cranberry **C: 1116**
Ice age (Evidence of ice ages and their climates) **I: 6-7**
Peat **P: 225**
Pond (Kinds of ponds) **P: 656**
Wetland **W: 252a**; (Bogs and fens) **W: 252b**
Bog body [human remains]
Bog **B: 436**
Mummy (Other mummies) **M: 926**
Bog cranberry [fruit]
Lingonberry **L: 335** *with picture*
Bog iron ore
Limonite **L: 308**
Bog onion *See* Jack-in-the-pulpit *in this index*
Bog spavin [disease]
Spavin **So: 767**
Bog turtle
Wetland *picture on* **W: 253**
Boganda, Barthelemy [Central African political leader]
Central African Republic (History) **C: 353**
Bogart, Humphrey [American actor] **B: 436** *with portrait*
Huston, John **H: 458**
Motion picture (Best performance by an actor: 1951) **M: 862a**
Bogey [golf]
Golf (table) **G: 261**
Bogeyman
Fairy **F: 10**
Boggs, J. Caleb [American political leader]
Delaware (table) **D: 109**
Boggs, Lilburn W. [American political leader]
Missouri (table) **M: 668**
Boggs, T. Hale [American political leader]
Warren Report **W: 37**
Boggs, Wade [American baseball player]
Baseball (Hall of Fame) **B: 134**
Bogong moth B: 437
Moth (Migration) **M: 839**
Bogotá [Colombia] **B: 437** *with picture*
Colombia *picture on* **Ci: 778**
Bohème, La [opera by Puccini]
Opera *picture on* **O: 802**; *(Bohème, La)* **O: 801**
Puccini, Giacomo **P: 869**
Bohemia [region, Czech Republic] **B: 437** *with map*
Czech Republic (History) **Ci: 1209**; (History) **Ci: 1213**
Czechoslovakia **Ci: 1215** *with maps*
Moravia **M: 801**
Sudetenland **So: 957**
Bohemian Basin [Czech Republic]
Czech Republic (Land and climate) **Ci: 1211** *with map*
Bohemian Forest [Czech Republic]
Czech Republic (Land and climate) **Ci: 1211** *with map*
Bohemian glass
Glass (Types of art glass) **G: 220**
Bohemian Lights [book by Valle-Inclán]
Spanish literature (The Generation of 1898) **So: 762**
Bohemian-Moravian Highlands [region, Czech Republic]

Czech Republic (Land and climate) **Ci: 1211** *with map*
Bohemian Mountains [Czech Republic]
Czech Republic (Land and climate) **Ci: 1211** *with map*
Bohemian waxwing [bird]
Bird *picture on* **B: 351**
Waxwing **W: 154**
Bohemond of Taranto [French crusader]
Crusades (The First Crusade) **Ci: 1160** *with map*
Bohío [dwelling]
Cuba (Way of life) **Ci: 1170**
Böhl de Faber, Cecilia *See* Caballero, Fernán *in this index*
Böhm, Theobald [German flutist]
Flute **F: 307**
Bohnenberger, G. C. [German inventor]
Gyroscope (History) **G: 454**
Bohol [island, Philippines]
Philippines (The main islands) **P: 376-378** *with map*
Bohr, Aage Niels [Danish physicist]
Nobel Prizes (Physics: 1975) **N: 441**
Bohr, Niels [Danish physicist] **B: 438**
Atom *diagram on* **A: 875**; (The first descriptions of atomic structure) **A: 875-876**
Chemistry (Development of physical chemistry) **C: 404-405**
Heisenberg, Werner **H: 167**
Light (Photons) **L: 286-287**
Physics (Quantum theory) **P: 441**; (Uncovering the secrets of the atom) **P: 442**
Quantum mechanics (Quantized orbits) **Q: 6**
Radiation (The quantum theory) **R: 81**
Science (Science in the early 1900's) **S: 201**
Spectrum **So: 772**
Bohrium [element] **B: 438**
Transuranium element **T: 401**
Boiardo, Matteo Maria [Italian poet]
Italian literature (Humanism and the Renaissance) **I: 494**
Boies, Horace [American political leader]
Iowa (table) **I: 391**
Boii [people]
Bohemia **B: 437**
Boil [disorder] **B: 438** *with diagrams*
Pore **P: 678**
Skin (Infections) **S: 490**
Boileau-Despréaux, Nicolas [French poet] **B: 439**
French literature (Classical poetry) **F: 520**
Boiler [device] **B: 439**
Bismuth **B: 383**
Distillation **D: 238**
Heating (Steam and hot-water heating systems) **H: 159**
Locomotive (Steam locomotives) **L: 417**
Steam engine (How steam engines work) **So: 880**
Boiling
Cooking (Boiling) **Ci: 1029**
Boiling off [process]
Silk (Boiling off and weighting) **S: 460**
Boiling point B: 439
Evaporation (How evaporation occurs) **E: 422-423**
Gas [physics] (How gases behave) **G: 48**
Heat (Changes in state) **H: 153** *with diagram*
Pressure **P: 773**
Steam **So: 880**
Boiling Spring Lake [California]
Lassen Volcanic National Park **L: 87**
Boiling water reactor
Idaho National Laboratory **I: 46**
Nuclear energy *picture on* **N: 584**; (Steam production) **N: 587**
Bois Blanc Island Lighthouse and Blockhouse [Ontario]
Canada (table: National historic sites) **C: 114**
Bois d'arc [tree] *See* Osage orange *in this index*
Bois de Boulogne [park]
Paris (Gardens, squares, and parks) **P: 162-163** *with map*
Bois de Vincennes [park]
Paris (Gardens, squares, and parks) **P: 162-163**
Boise [Idaho] **B: 440**
Idaho **I: 26** *with pictures*; (Places to visit) **I: 34**; (table: Average monthly weather) **I: 39**
Boito, Arrigo [Italian composer] **B: 440**
Verdi, Giuseppe **V: 316**
Bojangles [nickname]
Robinson, Bill **R: 367**
Bojaxhiu, Agnes Gonxha [birth name of]
Teresa, Mother **T: 169**
Bok, Edward William [American editor]
Bell (Uses of bells) **B: 239**
Magazine (Magazines in the 1800's) **M: 45**
Bok choy [vegetable]
Chinese cabbage **C: 509**

BOK Tower [Tulsa]
Tulsa (History) **T:** 483-484
Bokassa, Jean-Bedel [Central African political leader]
Central African Republic (History) **C:** 353
Bokmål [language]
Norway (Language) **N:** 539
Bokor [priest]
Zombie **Z:** 598
Bola [weapon]
Indian, American *picture on* **I:** 140; (Before European contact) **I:** 177 *with picture*
Sling **S:** 508a
Bolack, Tom [American political leader]
New Mexico (table) **N:** 272
Bolaños Geyer, Enrique [Nicaraguan political leader]
Nicaragua (Recent developments) **N:** 401
Bolas spider
Spider *picture on* **So:** 783; (Orb weavers) **So:** 789-790
Bold Forbes [horse]
Kentucky Derby (table) **K:** 296
Boldface [printing]
Proofreading (Proofreaders' marks) **P:** 822
Boldrewood, Rolf [Australian author]
Australia (Literature) **A:** 904-905
Bolero [dance] **B:** 440
Ballroom dancing **B:** 63
Bolesław I [king of Poland]
Poland (The early Polish state) **P:** 611
Bolesław II [king of Poland]
Stanislas, Saint **So:** 836
Bolete [fungus]
Mushroom (Kinds of mushrooms) **M:** 943 *with pictures*
Boleyn, Anne [wife of Henry VIII] **B:** 440 *with portrait*
Catherine of Aragon **C:** 303
Henry VIII [of England] **H:** 188
Wolsey, Thomas **W:** 379
Bolger, Jim [New Zealand political leader] **B:** 441
Bolger, Ray [American actor]
Garland, Judy *picture on* **G:** 44
Bolide [astronomy]
Fireball **F:** 133
Meteor **M:** 430
Bolin, Wesley [American political leader]
Arizona (table) **A:** 687
Bolingbroke [literary figure]
Shakespeare, William: *(Richard II)* **S:** 357
Bolingbroke, Henry [king of England] *See* Henry IV *in this index*
Bolingbroke, Lord [British philosopher]
Freethinker **F:** 509
Bolívar, Simón [Venezuelan general] **B:** 441 *with portrait*
Bolivia (Independence) **B:** 447
Colombia (Independence) **Ci:** 783
Flag *picture on* **F:** 217
Latin America *picture on* **L:** 108; (The movement toward independence) **L:** 106-107
Pan-American conferences (The original Pan-Americanism) **P:** 113
Peru (The war of independence) **P:** 315
San Martín, José de **S:** 105
Sucre, Antonio José de **So:** 951
Venezuela (The struggle for independence) **V:** 304
Bolívar City *See* Ciudad Bolívar *in this index*
Bolivia B: 442 *with pictures and maps*
See also the list of Related articles in the Bolivia *article*
Andean Community **A:** 450
Bolívar, Simón **B:** 441
Clothing *picture on* **Ci:** 695
Flag *picture on* **F:** 200
Food *picture on* **F:** 329
Indian, American (Indians of the Andes) **I:** 173; (Indians of the Tropical Forest) **I:** 175
Latin America (Early years of independence) **L:** 107-108
Peru (The War of the Pacific) **P:** 315
Bolivian Alternative for the Americas [organization]
Latin America (In the early 2000's) **L:** 111
Bolivian coca [plant]
Coca **Ci:** 742
Bolkiah, Sultan Haji Hassanal [Brunei political leader]
Brunei (Government) **B:** 650
Boll [plant part]
Boll weevil **B:** 448 *with picture*
Cotton *picture on* **Ci:** 1088; (Uses of cotton) **Ci:** 1086 *with pictures*; (The cotton plant) **Ci:** 1086-1087
Böll, Heinrich [German author] **B:** 448

German literature (Postwar German literature [1945-1990]) **G:** 142
Boll weevil [insect] **B:** 448 *with picture*
Alabama (Interesting facts) **A:** 257
Cotton (Insect pests) **Ci:** 1090; (The boll weevil) **Ci:** 1093
Insect *picture on* **I:** 285
Weevil **W:** 180
Bolling, Edith [wife of Woodrow Wilson] *See* Wilson, Edith Bolling *in this index*
Bollworm [insect]
See also Corn earworm *in this index*
Cotton (Insect pests) **Ci:** 1090 *with picture*
Bologna [Italy] **B:** 448
Bologna, University of [Italy] **B:** 448
Education (The rise of the universities) **E:** 99-100
Italy (Education) **I:** 504
Law (The Middle Ages) **L:** 134-135
Universities and colleges (European universities) **U:** 210
Bolometer [instrument] **B:** 448
Bolsheviks [Russian history] **B:** 449
Communism (Before 1917) **Ci:** 892
Cossacks **Ci:** 1079
Kerensky, Alexander Feodorovich **K:** 305
Krupskaya, Nadezhda Konstantinovna **K:** 389
Lenin, V. I. (Beginnings of revolution) **L:** 192
Russia (Nicholas II) **R:** 551-552
Russian Revolution of 1917 **R:** 565
Stalin, Joseph (Young revolutionist) **So:** 825; (Rise to power) **So:** 826
Union of Soviet Socialist Republics (History) **U:** 35
Bolshoi Ballet [Moscow] **B:** 449
Ballet (Ballet in Russia) **B:** 52-53
Moscow **M:** 825 *with picture*
Russia (Ballet) **R:** 537
Bolt [firearms]
Firearm (Mechanism) **F:** 132-133
Bolt [hardware] **B:** 449 *with pictures*
Bolt [lock]
Lock (Types of locks) **L:** 410 *with pictures*
Bolt, Usain [Jamaican runner]
Olympic Games *picture on* **O:** 749; (The recent games) **O:** 753-755
Bolt-action rifle [gun]
Rifle (Kinds of rifles) **R:** 338 *with pictures*
Bolt cutters [tool]
Fire department *picture on* **F:** 127
Bolting [agriculture]
Gibberellin **G:** 185
Bolton, Guy [British author]
Kern, Jerome **K:** 305
Bolton, John R. [American diplomat]
United Nations (table) **U:** 86
Boltzmann, Ludwig [Austrian physicist] **B:** 449
Boltzmann distribution [physics]
Boltzmann, Ludwig **B:** 449
Bolyai, János [Hungarian mathematician]
Geometry (Rise of non-Euclidean geometry) **G:** 106
Lobachevsky, Nikolai **L:** 404
Mathematics (In the 1800's) **M:** 307
Bomarc missile [weapon]
Canada, History of (The return of the Liberals) **C:** 149
Bomarzo [opera by Ginastera]
Opera (Opera today) **O:** 800 *with picture*
Bomb [weapon] **B:** 450 *with pictures*
See also Atomic bomb; Hydrogen bomb *in this index*
Ballistics **B:** 56
Computer *pictures on* **Ci:** 918
Fragmentation **F:** 451
Improvised explosive device **I:** 95
Terrorism (Bombings) **T:** 175
Bomb bay
Bomber **B:** 453
Bomb squad
Police (Other activities) **P:** 621-622 *with picture*
Bombachas [clothing]
Brazil (Clothing) **B:** 574
Bombardier beetle
Beetle *picture on* **B:** 215; (Ground beetles) **B:** 217
Bombarding particle
Nuclear energy (Nuclear fission) **N:** 582
Bombay [India] *See* Mumbai *in this index*
Bombay cat
Cat (Short-haired breeds) **C:** 290
Bombay Hook National Wildlife Refuge [Delaware]
Delaware *picture on* **D:** 96
Bomber [airplane] **B:** 453 *with pictures*
Air force (Aircraft and missiles) **A:** 183
Air Force, United States (Bombers) **A:** 191 *with picture*; (World War I) **A:** 194
Aircraft, Military (Bombers) **A:** 202 *with pictures*
Airplane (Military planes) **A:** 212; (World War

I [1914-1918]) **A:** 234; (During World War II [1939-1945]) **A:** 238
Vietnam War (The opposing forces) **V:** 375
World War II (The air war) **W:** 482
Bombing system
Bomber **B:** 453
Bomblet [weapon]
Bomb (Kinds of bombs) **B:** 450
Bombyx mori [moth]
Cocoon **Ci:** 747
Moth (The importance of moths) **M:** 839-840 *with picture*
Silk (Cultivated silk) **S:** 459
Bomi Hills
Liberia (Land and climate) **L:** 230
Bomoh [healer]
Magic (Asia) **M:** 50
Bomoseen Lake
Vermont (Rivers and lakes) **V:** 328-330 *with map*
Bon Homme
South Dakota (Schools) **So:** 668
Bon Jovi [rock group]
Rock music (New wave and mainstream rock) **R:** 380c-380d
Bon Marché [Paris]
Department store **D:** 148
Bon Pays [region]
Luxembourg (Land) **L:** 531
Bonaire [island, Caribbean Sea]
Netherlands Antilles **N:** 151
Bonampak [Mayan site]
Maya *picture on* **M:** 323; (The Maya heritage) **M:** 326
Bonanza Creek [Yukon]
Klondike **K:** 344
Bonanzaville, USA [West Fargo]
North Dakota (Places to visit) **N:** 504 *with picture*
Bonaparte, Carlo [Corsican lawyer]
Napoleon I (Boyhood) **N:** 14
Bonaparte, Charles Joseph [American political leader]
Federal Bureau of Investigation (History) **F:** 62
Roosevelt, Theodore (table) **R:** 466
Bonaparte, Louis [king of The Netherlands]
Napoleon III (Early life) **N:** 17
Bonaparte, Napoleon *See* Napoleon I *in this index*
Bonaventure, Saint [Italian religious leader] **B:** 454
Bonaventure Island
Quebec (Places to visit) **Q:** 20
Bond [bricklaying]
Brick (Bonds) **B:** 599
Bond [economics] **B:** 454
Commodity exchange (Forward and futures contracts) **Ci:** 873
Interest **I:** 321
Investment (Bonds) **I:** 368
Investment banking **I:** 369
Money (Monetary policy) **M:** 717
Savings bond **S:** 166
Stock exchange **So:** 903
Bond [chemistry] **B:** 454
Cell (Producing energy) **C:** 332-333
Materials **M:** 300b; (The role of bonds) **M:** 301
Matter (Structure of matter) **M:** 310-311
Mineral (Chemical bonds) **M:** 570 *with diagram*
Molecule (Individual molecules) **M:** 692-693
Spectroscopy **So:** 772
Valence **V:** 260
Water (How water is held together) **W:** 131
Bond [law]
Bail **B:** 31
Bond, Carrie Jacobs [American composer] **B:** 454
Bond, Christopher Samuel [American political leader]
Missouri (table) **M:** 668
Bond, Edward [British dramatist]
English literature (Recent English drama) **E:** 323
Bond, James [fictional character]
Connery, Sean **Ci:** 973
Fleming, Ian **F:** 232
Bond, Julian [American political leader] **B:** 455
Georgia (The mid-1900's) **G:** 134
Spingarn Medal (table: 2009) **So:** 794
Bond, Laura [wife of]
Borden, Sir Robert Laird (Early life) **B:** 483
Bond, Shadrach [American political leader]
Illinois (table) **I:** 71; (Early statehood) **I:** 74
Bond trader [finance]
Bank (Careers in banking) **B:** 95
Bondage of the Will, The [book by Luther]
Luther, Martin (Reformation leader) **L:** 528
Bondar, Roberta [Canadian astronaut] **B:** 455 *with portrait*
Astronaut (table) **A:** 830
Bondarenko, Valentin V. [Soviet cosmonaut]
Astronaut (Accidents in space) **A:** 830
Space exploration (Vostok and Mercury: The first

human beings in space) So: 712-713
Bonded fabric
Textile (Other textiles) T: 215
Bondfield, Margaret Grace [British political leader]
B: 455
Bonding [insurance] B: 455
Bondman See Peasant; Serf in this index
Bonds, Barry [American baseball player] B: 455
with portrait
Baseball picture on B: 139; (Recent
developments) B: 137; (table: Modern major
league records) B: 138
Bondsman [law]
Bail B: 31
Bone [anatomy] B: 456 with diagrams
See also Skeleton and the names of specific bones
such as Collarbone in this index
Bone bank B: 457
Cartilage C: 263
Collagen Ci: 773
First aid (Fractures and dislocations) F: 140
Forensic science picture on F: 389
Fracture F: 450 with diagrams
Human body (The skeletal system) H: 418;
(Anatomy of the human body) H: 422 with
diagrams
Nutrition (Other diseases) N: 631
Orthopedics O: 860
Osteomyelitis O: 866
Osteoporosis O: 867 with pictures
Osteosclerosis O: 868
Rheumatology R: 291
Rickets R: 334 with picture
Space exploration (Living in space) So: 701-703
Tendon T: 132
Transplant (Tissue transplants) T: 379
Bone, Henry [English artist]
England picture on E: 308
Bone ash
Porcelain (Bone china) P: 676
Bone bank [medicine] B: 457
Bone bruise [injury]
Bruise B: 650
Bone china
Porcelain (Bone china) P: 676
Bone conduction
Ear (How sounds travel to the inner ear) E: 9-10
Bone gelatin
Gelatin G: 76
Bone glue
Glue (Types of glue) G: 236
Bone marrow [anatomy]
Anemia (Insufficient production of red blood
cells) A: 457
Antibiotic (Damage to organs and tissues) A: 551
Biopsy B: 326
Blood (Formation of new blood components)
B: 411; (Blood transfusions) B: 413
Bone (Structure of the bones) B: 456
Bone marrow transplant B: 457
Cancer (Classification by primary body site)
C: 167-168
Human body (The skeletal system) H: 418
Immune system diagrams on I: 88a, I:88b; (Parts
of the immune system) I: 87
Iron (How bodies use iron) I: 435
Leukemia L: 215
Osteomyelitis O: 866
Osteosclerosis O: 868
Radiation sickness R: 81
Stem cell So: 889
Bone marrow transplant [medicine] B: 457 with
picture
Sickle cell anemia S: 448
Thalassemia T: 228
Transplant (Tissue transplants) T: 379
Bone spavin [disease]
Spavin So: 767
Bone turnover See Remodeling in this index
Boneblack [pigment]
Ivory black I: 521
Bonefish [fish] B: 458 with picture
Bones, Helen Woodrow [cousin of Woodrow
Wilson]
White House hostesses W: 291
Bonesana, Cesare [Italian criminologist]
Criminology (History) Ci: 1145
Boneset [plant] B: 458
Boneyard
Dominoes D: 306
Bonfils, Frederick Gilmer [American editor] B: 458
Bonfire [custom]
Halloween (Halloween symbols) H: 24b
Bonfire of the Vanities, The [book by Wolfe]
American literature (Essays) A: 426
Bong, Richard I. [American aviator]
Ace A: 24

Bong Range [mountains, Liberia]
Liberia (Land and climate) L: 230
Bongo [animal]
Animal picture on A: 481
Antelope A: 541
Bongo, Ali Ben [Gabonese political leader]
Gabon (History) G: 3-4
Bongo, El Hadj Omar [Gabonese political leader]
Gabon (History) G: 3-4
Bongo drums B: 458 with picture
Bonham, John [British drummer]
Led Zeppelin L: 175
Bonheur, Rosa [French painter] B: 458 with picture
Buffalo Bill picture on B: 679
Painting (Women artists) P: 73-74
Bonheur d'occasion [book by Roy]
Canadian literature (Modern literature: 1945 to
the present) C: 159
Roy, Gabrielle R: 494
Bonhoeffer, Dietrich [German theologian] B: 459
Bonhomme Richard [ship]
Jones, John Paul (Defeat of the *Serapis*) J: 158
Navy, United States picture on N: 90
Revolution, American picture on R: 280
Boni, Yayi [Benin political leader]
Benin (History) B: 250
Boniface IV, Saint [pope]
All Saints' Day A: 370
Boniface VII [antipope]
Pope (table) P: 666
Boniface VIII [pope] B: 459
Church and state (History) C: 542
Philip IV P: 370
Pope (The peak of papal power) P: 663-664
Roman Catholic Church (Boniface VIII) R: 407
Rome, University of R: 449
Boniface, Saint [English-born religious leader]
B: 459
Charles Martel C: 383
Bonifacio, Andrés [Filipino patriot]
Philippines (Revolt against the Spaniards)
P: 379-380
Bonifácio, José [Brazilian government official] See
Andrada e Silva, José Bonifácio de in this index
Bonifacio, Strait of
Sardinia S: 124
Bonin Islands [Japan] B: 460
Japan (The Ryukyu and Bonin islands) J: 48
Tokyo (The Tokyo Metropolitan Prefecture)
T: 313-314
Boning knife
Knife (Types of knives) K: 345-346 with picture
Bonito [fish] B: 460 with picture
Bonn [Germany] B: 460 with picture
Bonn, University of [Germany]
Bonn (The city) B: 460
Bonn Convention [agreement]
Bird (Protective laws and treaties) B: 368
Bonnard, Pierre [French painter] B: 461
France picture on F: 463
Bonne Chanson, La [music by Fauré]
Fauré, Gabriel Urbain F: 56
Bonnefoy, Yves [French poet]
French literature (Recent French literature) F: 523
Bonner, John W. [American political leader]
Montana (table) M: 757
Bonner, Yelena [Soviet activist]
Sakharov, Andrei Dmitriyevich S: 59
Bonnet, Stede [British pirate] B: 462
Bonnet Carré Spillway [waterway]
Louisiana (Rivers, bayous, and lakes) L: 490
New Orleans (Civic improvements) N: 284
Bonnet doll
Doll (Porcelain dolls) D: 290-291
Bonnethead [fish]
Hammerhead shark H: 35
Bonneville, Benjamin de [American explorer]
B: 461
Bonneville Dam B: 462
Oregon Trail O: 850
Wyoming (Exploration) W: 533
Bonneville, Lake [former lake] See Lake Bonneville
in this index
Bonneville Dam [Columbia River, Oregon-
Washington] B: 462
Oregon (Places to visit) O: 836; (The early 1900's)
O: 849 with picture
Bonneville Salt Flats
Utah (Interesting facts) U: 231; (Places to visit)
U: 238 with picture
Bonney, William H. [name for]
Billy the Kid B: 306
Bonnie and Clyde [film]
Beatty, Warren B: 190
Bonnie Prince Charlie [Scottish pretender] See
Stuart, Charles Edward in this index
Bonny, Anne [English pirate]

Pirate (Other regions) P: 495
Bono [Irish singer] B: 462 with picture
U2 U: 2
Bonobo [animal] B: 462 with picture
Ape A: 563
Chimpanzee C: 471
Primate (Great apes) P: 778a
Bonsack, James A. [American inventor]
Cigarette Ci: 553
Tobacco (History) T: 307-308
Bonsai [gardening] B: 463 with picture
Bonspiel [contest]
Curling (The rink) Ci: 1196
Bontebok [animal]
Antelope (Antelope and people) A: 542-543
Bontemps, Arna Wendell [American author]
B: 463
Cullen, Countee Ci: 1184
Harlem Renaissance H: 61
Bonus Army March [U.S. history]
Hoover, Herbert Clark (The "Bonus Army") H: 330
Bonus bill [1932]
Hoover, Herbert Clark (The "Bonus Army") H: 330
Bony fish [zoology]
Fish pictures on F: 149; (Kinds of fish) F: 147
Bony labyrinth
Ear (The inner ear) E: 8
Booby [bird] B: 463 with picture
Bird (Birds of the ocean and the Antarctic) B: 344
with picture
Booby trap
Mine warfare (Land mines) M: 564
Boogie-woogie [music]
Blues B: 425
Gospel music G: 277
Jazz (The swing era) J: 71
Book B: 464 with pictures
Audiobook A: 881
Book collecting B: 468
Bookbinding B: 470 with picture
Braille B: 550 with picture
Communication (The rise of printing) Ci: 879
E-book E: 2
Encyclopedia (Preparing an encyclopedia in book
form) E: 266 with pictures
Hornbook H: 339 with picture
Illuminated manuscript I: 78 with picture
Indian, American picture on I: 172
International standard book number I: 347
Islamic art (Books) I: 470
Library L: 234 with pictures
Mildew M: 542
Publishing (Scheduling, printing, and posting)
P: 867; (Books) P: 868
Scroll S: 227 with picture
Writing W: 511
Book [Bible]
Bible B: 279
New Testament N: 287
Old Testament O: 740
Book [cards]
Bridge (Scoring) B: 605
Book [libretto]
Musical comedy (The book) M: 959
Book [measurement]
Silk (Reeling) S: 460
Book account [finance]
Colonial life in America (Money) Ci: 811
Book club
Publishing (Marketing) P: 867-868-
Book collecting B: 468
Book lung [zoology]
Arachnid A: 590b
Spider (Respiratory system) So: 785 with diagram
Book match
Match (Safety matches) M: 299; (The invention of
book matches) M: 300a with pictures
Ohio (Interesting facts) O: 681
Book of Changes
I Ching I: 2
Book of Common Prayer
Anglican Communion (Beliefs and worship)
A: 463
Church of England (Doctrines) C: 542
Ridley, Nicholas R: 336
Book of Concord [religious book]
Lutheran Church-Missouri Synod L: 529
Book of Daniel, The [book by Doctorow]
Doctorow, E. L. D: 260
Book of Delight [book by Zabara]
Hebrew literature (Medieval works) H: 162
Book of Documents [speeches]
Chinese literature (Beginnings) C: 511
Book of Good Love [book by Ruiz]
Ruiz, Juan R: 519
Spanish literature (Early medieval literature)
So: 757-758

Book of Hours [prayer book]
Illuminated manuscript I: 78
Book of Kells [manuscript] B: 469 *with picture*
Book (The Middle Ages) B: 466
Painting (Early medieval painting in the West)
P: 49
Book of Kings [Bible] *See* Kings, Books of *in this index*
Book of Margery Kempe, The
Early English drama (Middle English prose) E: 316
Book of Martyrs, The [book by Foxe]
Biography (The Renaissance) B: 313
Book of Mormon [religious book]
Mormons M: 806; (Revelations) M: 808
Smith, Joseph (Early life) S: 517
Book of Nonsense, A [book by Lear]
Limerick L: 307
Book of Optics [book by Alhazen]
Alhazen A: 366
Book of Psalms [Bible] *See* Psalms, Book of *in this index*
Book of Roger, The [geography]
Exploration (Muslim exploration) E: 442
Book of sentences [philosophy]
Scholasticism (The Scholastic method) S: 179
Book of Songs [poems]
Chinese literature (Beginnings) C: 511
Book of Songs [poems by Heine]
Heine, Heinrich H: 166
Book of Songs [poems by Petrarch] *See* Canzoniere *in this index*
Book of Splendor [religious book]
Hebrew literature (Medieval works) H: 162
Book of the Courtier, The [book by Castiglione]
Castiglione, Baldassare C: 279
Italian literature (Humanism and the Renaissance) I: 494
Renaissance (The ideal courtier) R: 235
Book of the Covenant [Bible]
Exodus E: 438
Book of the Dead [religious book]
Egypt, Ancient (The afterlife) E: 137-138
Manuscript (Illustrated manuscripts) M: 174
Book of the Duchess, The [poem by Chaucer]
Chaucer, Geoffrey (Poetry) C: 388
Book of the Twelve [Bible]
Bible (The Prophets) B: 280-281
Book of the Year for Children Award
Literature for children (Awards) L: 367
Book report B: 469
A Guide to Writing Skills **Research Guide: 12**
Book review B: 470
Literature for children (Book reviews) L: 367
Book Week B: 470 *with picture*
Bookbinding B: 470 *with picture*
Islamic art (Books) I: 470
Booker T. and the MG's [band]
Rock music (Soul music) R: 380a
Booker T. Washington commemorative half dollar
Coin collecting *picture on* Ci: 758
Booker T. Washington National Monument [Virginia] B: 472
National Park System (table: National monuments) N: 50
Booking
Modeling (Model agencies) M: 685
Bookkeeping [economics] B: 472 *with pictures*
Accounting A: 23
Booklist [publication]
Literature for children (Booklists) L: 368
Booklist [magazine]
American Library Association A: 413
Booklouse [insect] B: 474
Bookmaker [occupation]
Horse racing (Betting) H: 365
Bookmaking [betting]
Horse racing (Betting) H: 365
Bookmobile [library] B: 474
Library (Active community service) L: 236-237;
(Spreading the service) L: 241 *with picture*
Bookplate [label] B: 474 *with picture*
Books of Chronicles *See* Chronicles, Books of *in this index*
Books on tape
Book (Modern books) B: 468
Boole, George [British mathematician]
Boolean algebra B: 474
Computer (History) Ci: 924a
Information theory I: 269
Logic (Modern logic) L: 425
Set theory (History) S: 322
Boolean algebra [mathematics] B: 474 *with diagrams*
Computer (History) Ci: 924a
Boolean logic
Computer (History) Ci: 924a

Boolean operator [research]
Information retrieval (How information retrieval works) I: 268b
Search engine S: 269
A Guide to Research Skills **Research Guide: 27**
Boom [barrier]
Oil spill (Responses) O: 707 *with picture*
Boom [economics]
Economics (table) E: 60
South Dakota (Boom-and-bust economy) So: 684
Boom [machine]
Crane Ci: 1119 *with picture*
Fire department (Ladder trucks) F: 126 *with picture*
Mining (Surface mining methods) M: 575
Boom [microphone]
Microphone M: 516 *with picture*
Television (Microphones) T: 111
Boom [ship]
Sailing (Spars) S: 23-24 *with diagram*
Boom [zoology]
Taiga T: 14
Boom town [U.S. history] B: 475
Boomer [animal]
Mountain beaver M: 897
Boomer [demography] *See* Baby boom generation *in this index*
Boomer [U.S. history]
Oklahoma (Great land rushes) O: 732
Boomer state [nickname]
Oklahoma O: 712
Boomerang [weapon] B: 475 *with pictures*
Indian, American *picture on* I: 139; (Hunting, gathering, and fishing) I: 141
Boomslang [snake]
Snake *picture on* S: 534
Boon, Ratliff [American political leader]
Indiana (table) I: 214
Boone, Daniel [American pioneer] B: 476 *with picture and map*
Charleston (Government and history) C: 384
Frankfort F: 484
Kentucky (Early settlement) K: 292
Missouri (Settlement) M: 669
Tennessee (Early settlement) T: 153
Westward movement in America (Crossing the Appalachians) W: 246
Boone, Jemima [daughter of]
Boone, Daniel (The Wilderness Road) B: 477-478
Boone, Pat [American singer]
Rock music (A variety of styles) R: 378-379
Boone, Rebecca [wife of]
Boone, Daniel (Marriage) B: 477
Frankfort F: 484
Boone & Scenic Valley Railroad and Museum
Iowa (Places to visit) I: 384
Boone's Lick [book by McMurtry]
McMurtry, Larry M: 343
Boonesborough [Kentucky]
Boone, Daniel (The Wilderness Road) B: 477-478;
(Indian captivity) B: 478; (Escape and battle) B: 478
Kentucky (Exploration and early settlement) K: 291
Boosaaso [Puntland]
Puntland P: 904
Boosalis, Helen [American political leader]
Nebraska (The late 1900's) N: 115
Booster rocket
Rocket *diagram on* R: 385
Space exploration *picture on* So: 700; (Getting into space and back) So: 698; (Space shuttles) So: 723
Booster shot [medicine]
Immunization (Active immunization) I: 89
Boot
Shoe S: 430 *with picture*
Skiing (Ski boots) S: 485 *with diagram*
Boot camp
Coast Guard, United States (Training a recruit) Ci: 736
Marine Corps, United States (Training a Marine) M: 206
Navy, United States (Training a sailor) N: 83
Boot Hill
Dodge City D: 261
Kansas (Places to visit) K: 226
Boot sector virus [computing]
Computer virus Ci: 925
Boötes [constellation] B: 480
Booth, Edwin Thomas [American actor] B: 480 *with portrait*
Booth, Evangeline Cory [British social reformer] B: 480
Booth, Sir Felix [British merchant]
Boothia Peninsula B: 481
Booth, John Wilkes [American assassin] B: 480

with portrait
Lincoln, Abraham (End of the war) L: 325-326;
(Assassination) L: 326
Mudd, Samuel Alexander M: 909
Booth, Junius Brutus [British-American actor] B: 480
Booth, Newton [American political leader]
California (table) C: 59
Booth, Shirley [American actress]
Motion picture (Best performance by an actress: 1952) M: 862
Booth, William [British social reformer] B: 480
Salvation Army (History) S: 76b
Boothia Peninsula [region, Canada] B: 481
Bootlace worm
Animal *picture on* A: 506
Worm *picture on* W: 501
Bootleg record
Recording industry (Releasing the recording) R: 182
Bootlegging [crime]
Prohibition (Life during prohibition) P: 815
United States, History of the (Prohibition) U: 189-190
BOP *See* Basic oxygen process *in this index*
Bop [music]
Gillespie, Dizzy G: 190
Herman, Woody H: 211
Jazz (Bebop) J: 72 *with picture*
Bopp, Franz [German linguist]
Language (The science of language) L: 66-67
Bopple nut *See* Macadamia nut *in this index*
Bor [Norse mythology]
Mythology (The creation of life) M: 985-986
Bora [wind]
Croatia (Land and climate) Ci: 1148a
Bora, Katherina von [wife of Martin Luther]
Luther, Martin (Reformation leader) L: 528
Bora Bora [island, Pacific]
Pacific Islands *picture on* P: 8
Bora ground [structure] B: 481
Borach, Fannie [birth name of]
Brice, Fanny B: 597 *with portrait*
Borage family [botany]
Flower (table) F: 300 *with picture*
Borah, William Edgar [American political leader] B: 481
Idaho *picture on* I: 43; (Early statehood) I: 44
Borah Peak [mountain, Idaho]
Idaho (Mountains) I: 36
Rocky Mountains (Chief ranges of the Rockies) R: 394-395 *with map*
Borax [chemical] B: 481 *with picture*
Death Valley D: 62
Sodium (Uses) So: 569
BORAX III [reactor]
Idaho National Laboratory I: 46
Borazon [crystal] B: 482
Borbeck Castle
Essen E: 359
Borchardt [gun]
Handgun (Rapid-fire handguns) H: 45
Bordaberry, Juan Maria [Uruguayan political leader]
Uruguay (Military government) U: 228
Bordeaux [region, France] B: 482 *with picture*
Wine (Wines from France) W: 337
Borden, Andrew [father of]
Borden, Sir Robert Laird (Early life) B: 483
Borden, Eunice Jane Laird [mother of]
Borden, Sir Robert Laird (Early life) B: 483
Borden, Gail [American inventor]
Milk (History of the milk industry) M: 549
Borden, Laura Bond [wife of]
Borden, Sir Robert Laird (Early life) B: 483
Borden, Lizzie [American public figure] B: 482 *with portrait*
Borden, Sir Robert Laird [Canadian statesman] B: 483 *with pictures*
Canada, History of (Foreign relations) C: 146;
(World War I and independence [1914-1931]) C: 146-147
Laurier, Sir Wilfrid (The conscription crisis) L: 126
Progressive Conservative Party P: 812
Border
Theater (Kinds of scenery) T: 239
Border collie [dog] B: 486 *with picture*
Border decoration [art]
Illuminated manuscript I: 78 *with picture*
Border forsythia [plant]
Flower *picture on* F: 281
Border Patrol, United States
Immigration (The fourth wave) I: 83
Immigration and Naturalization Service I: 86
Border state [U.S. history]
Civil War, American (How the states lined up) Ci: 617

Confederate States of America (The border states) Ci: 932
Border terrier [dog] B: 487 *with picture*
Borderlight
Theater (Lighting methods) T: 240-241
Borderline personality disorder [psychiatry] B: 487
Bordet, Jules-Jean-Baptiste-Vincent [Belgian physiologist]
Nobel Prizes (Physiology or medicine: 1919) N: 445
Borduas, Paul-Émile [Canadian poet]
Canadian literature (Modern Canadian poets) C: 161
Bore [gun]
Artillery (Parts of an artillery weapon) A: 762
Shotgun S: 436
Bore [tide]
Amazon River (The course of the Amazon) A: 403
Moncton M: 702
New Brunswick (Rivers and lakes) N: 192
Reversing Falls of Saint John R: 269
Bore [tool] *See* Drill *in this index*
Boré, Étienne de [American inventor]
Louisiana (Spanish Louisiana) L: 498
Boreal chickadee [bird]
Chickadee C: 439
Boreal forest *See* Taiga *in this index*
Borecole *See* Kale *in this index*
Borel, Jean [Swiss immunologist]
Cyclosporine Ci: 1204
Borelli, Giovanni A. [Italian mathematician]
Airplane (Early experiments and ideas) A: 229-230
Boreman, Arthur I. [American political leader]
Pierpont, Francis Harrison P: 457
West Virginia (table) W: 225
Boren, David L. [American political leader]
Oklahoma (table) O: 730
Borer [insect]
See also Corn borer *in this index*
Beetle *picture on* B: 218
Borg, Björn [Swedish tennis player] B: 487
Tennis (Tennis today) T: 166d-166e *with picture*
Borges, Jorge Luis [Argentine author] B: 487
Argentina (The arts) A: 651-652
Fiction (History) F: 90-91
Latin American literature (The mid-1900's) L: 114
Novel (The novel today) N: 575
Borgia, Cesare [Italian political leader] B: 487
Borgia, Lucrezia B: 488
Borgia, Lucrezia [Italian public figure] B: 488
Borgia, Rodrigo [birth name of]
Alexander VI A: 341
Borglum, Gutzon [American sculptor] B: 488
Mount Rushmore National Memorial M: 887
Stone Mountain So: 910
Borglum, Lincoln [American sculptor]
Mount Rushmore National Memorial M: 887
Borglum, Solon [American sculptor]
Borglum, Gutzon B: 488
Borgnine, Ernest [American actor]
Motion picture (Best performance by an actor: 1955) M: 862a
Borie, Adolph E. [American government official]
Grant, Ulysses S. (table) G: 316
Boring [excavation]
See also Drilling *in this index*
Coal (Auger mining) Ci: 722
Machine tool (Hole machining) M: 17-18
Tunnel (How tunnels are built) T: 490 *with diagram*
Boring machine
Industrial Revolution (The steam engine) I: 249
Boring sponge [animal]
sponge (Kinds of sponges) So: 800
Boriquas [people]
Hispanic Americans H: 244
Boris Godunov [ruler of Russia] *See* Godunov, Boris *in this index*
Boris Godunov [opera by Mussorgsky]
Mussorgsky, Modest M: 967
Opera: (Boris Godunov) O: 801-802 *with picture*
Boris Godunov [play by Pushkin]
Pushkin, Alexander (His works) P: 911-912
Russian literature (Early Romanticism) R: 560-561
Bork, Robert H. [American government official]
Watergate (The tape controversy) W: 144
Borlaug, Norman Ernest [American biologist] B: 488
Wheat (Breeding new varieties of wheat) W: 277 *with picture*
Borman, Frank [American astronaut] B: 488
Astronaut (Achievements in space) A: 829
Space exploration (Voskhod and Gemini: The first multiperson space flights) So: 714; (Orbiting the moon) So: 715

Bormann, Martin [Nazi leader] B: 488
Born, Bertrand de [French troubadour]
Knights and knighthood (Knighthood in literature) K: 351
Born, Max [German physicist] B: 489
"Born again" [religion]
Pentecostal churches (Major Pentecostal churches) P: 275
Born Free [book by Adamson]
Adamson, Joy A: 45
Born Guilty [book by Rojas]
Latin American literature (The mid-1900's) L: 114
Born in the U.S.A. [recording by Springsteen]
Rock music (Rock videos and MTV) R: 380c
Springsteen, Bruce So: 809
Born on the Fourth of July [film]
Stone, Oliver So: 909
Borneo [island, East Indies] B: 489 *with pictures and map*
Brunei B: 650
Indonesia (The Greater Sunda Islands) I: 233 *with map*; (Climate) I: 234
Malaysia M: 98a
Rain forest (Asia) R: 126b; (Scientific value) R: 126c
Bornholm [island]
Denmark (Land regions) D: 137-138
Bornite [ore]
Copper (Copper ores) Ci: 1042
Mineral *picture on* M: 568
Bornu [African history]
Kanem K: 213
Borobudur [monument]
Indonesia *picture on* I: 237; (The arts) I: 232-233
Sculpture (The Indian influence) S: 237 *with picture*
Borodin, Alexander [Russian composer] B: 490
Rimsky-Korsakov, Nikolai R: 342
Borodino, Battle of [1812]
Napoleon I (Disaster in Russia) N: 16
Boron [element] B: 490
California (Mining) C: 57
Gay-Lussac, Joseph Louis G: 71
Metalloid M: 426
Semiconductor (Doped crystals) S: 291-292
Tourmaline T: 349
Boron, Robert de [French poet]
Excalibur E: 435
Bororo Indians
Brazil *picture on* B: 572
Mythology (Structuralist approaches) M: 991
Borosilicate glass
Glass (Borosilicate glass) G: 213
Borough [political unit] B: 490
Alaska (Local government) A: 300
County (Importance) Ci: 1099
Local government (Units of local government) L: 407
London (Residential areas and housing) L: 432; (Borough governments) L: 439
Metropolitan area M: 442
New York City (The city) N: 323; (Government) N: 339-340
Borrelia burgdorferi [bacteria]
Lyme disease L: 533
Borrelly, Comet
Comet (table) Ci: 868; (Studying comets) Ci: 868
Borromini, Francesco [Italian architect] B: 491
Architecture (Baroque architecture) A: 622
Italy (Architecture) I: 504 *with picture*
Borrowing *See* Loan *in this index*
Borrowing [mathematics]
Subtraction (How to borrow) So: 946
Bors [legendary figure]
Holy Grail (The search for the Grail) H: 299
Borsch [food]
Ukraine (Food and drink) U: 8
Borzage, Frank [American director]
Motion picture (Best achievement in directing: 1927-28, 1931-32) M: 862
Borzoi [dog] B: 491
Dog *picture on* D: 270
Wolfhound W: 378
Bosc pear
Pear (Varieties) P: 215
Boscán, Juan [Spanish poet]
Spanish literature (The 1500's) So: 758
Bosch, Carl [German chemist]
Haber process H: 2
Nobel Prizes (Chemistry: 1931) N: 443
Bosch, Hieronymus [Dutch painter] B: 491 *with picture*
Bosch, Juan [Dominican political leader]
Dominican Republic (History) D: 304-305
Bosch Foundation, Robert
Foundation (table) F: 430
Boscovich, Rudjer Josip [Croatian mathematician]

Atom (The birth of the modern atomic theory) A: 875
Bose, Nandlal [Indian painter]
India (Painting) I: 119-120
Bose, Satyendra Nath [Indian physicist]
Boson B: 494
Bose-Einstein condensate [physics]
Absolute zero A: 17
Matter (States of matter) M: 311
Bosnia and Hercegovina *See* Bosnia-Herzegovina *in this index*
Bosnia-Herzegovina B: 491 *with pictures and map*
Air Force, United States (The Balkans) A: 196
Austria-Hungary A: 941
Berlin, Congress of B: 265
Clinton, Bill (International affairs) Ci: 682e
Concentration camp (Other concentration camps) Ci: 927
Croatia (History) Ci: 1148a-1148b
Culture (Culture and society) Ci: 1188
Flag *picture on* F: 205
International relations (The Balkan conflicts) I: 346
North Atlantic Treaty Organization (History) N: 471
Serbia (History) S: 314-316
Srebrenica massacre So: 816
United States, History of the (The Balkan conflicts) U: 196d
War crime (The United Nations and war crimes) W: 27
Yugoslavia Y: 576
Bosniaks [people]
Air Force, United States (The Balkans) A: 196
Bosnia-Herzegovina (People) B: 492; (History) B: 492-493
Serbia (The breakup of Yugoslavia) S: 316
Srebrenica massacre So: 816
United States, History of the (The Balkan conflicts) U: 196d
Yugoslavia (The breakup of Yugoslavia) Y: 577
Boson [physics] B: 494
Fermion F: 74
Supersymmetry So: 995
Bosporus [strait, Turkey] B: 494 *with map*
Dardanelles D: 35
Istanbul (The city) I: 490
Bosporus Bridge [Turkey]
Bridge (table: Suspension) B: 603
Bosque Redondo [reservation]
Indian wars (Navajo conflicts) I: 195
Boss, The [nickname]
Springsteen, Bruce So: 808
Bossa nova [music]
Getz, Stan G: 177
Boston [Massachusetts] B: 495 *with pictures and maps*
Architecture *picture on* A: 624
Colonial life in America *picture on* Ci: 791; (Commercial expansion) Ci: 792
Massachusetts (table: Average monthly weather) M: 284; (The early 1900's) M: 293; (The mid-1900's) M: 293
Money (Tree shillings) M: 710
Old North Church *picture on* O: 740
Revolution, American (Background and causes of the revolution) R: 271; (The beginning of the war) R: 274
Boston Academy of Music
Mason, Lowell M: 266
Boston Adventure [book by Stafford]
Stafford, Jean So: 820
Boston African American National Historic Site [Massachusetts]
National Park System (table: National historic sites) N: 52
Boston Athenaeum
Boston (Libraries and museums) B: 502
Massachusetts (Libraries) M: 274 *with picture*
Boston Brahmins [literature]
Boston (People) B: 500
Boston Bruins [team]
Hockey (table: National Hockey League) H: 281; (Professional hockey) H: 281
Orr, Bobby O: 859
Boston Celtics [team]
Auerbach, Red A: 885
Basketball (table) B: 150
McHale, Kevin M: 336
Boston Common [park]
Boston *picture on* B: 500; (Downtown Boston) B: 496-497
Park (History) P: 168
Boston English High School
Massachusetts M: 270
Boston Harbor
Massachusetts *picture on* M: 292

Boston Harbor Islands National Recreation Area
National Park System (table: National recreation areas) N: 49
Boston ivy [plant]
Ivy I: 522
Boston Latin School
Boston (Education) B: 501
Massachusetts M: 270; (Schools) M: 274
Boston lettuce [plant]
Lettuce (Kinds of lettuce) L: 214 *with picture*
Boston Lighthouse
Lighthouse (The lighthouse keeper) L: 295
Boston Marathon [race]
Boston (Recreation) B: 502
United States *picture on* U: 115
Boston Marriage [play by Mamet]
Mamet, David M: 115
Boston Massacre [U.S. history] B: 505 *with picture*
Adams, John (In New England) A: 35-36
Adams, Samuel (The patriot) A: 44
African Americans (Colonial times) A: 136d-136f *with picture*
Attucks, Crispus A: 880
Boston (Resistance and revolution) B: 503
Revolution, American (The Townshend Acts) R: 273 *with picture*
United States, History of the (Renewed conflict) U: 158
Boston Mountains
Arkansas (Land regions) A: 706
Boston Museum of Science [Massachusetts]
Boston (Libraries and museums) B: 502
Boston National Historical Park [Massachusetts]
National Park System (table: National historical parks) N: 56
Boston News-Letter [newspaper]
Advertising (The impact of printing) A: 79
Colonial life in America (Communication) Ci: 806
Journalism (Early American journalism) J: 174
Massachusetts (Communication) M: 287
Boston Pilgrims [team]
Massachusetts (Interesting facts) M: 271
Boston Pops Orchestra
Boston (The arts) B: 501 *with picture*
Fiedler, Arthur F: 91
Boston Port Act [1774] B: 505
Intolerable Acts I: 353
Maryland (The Revolutionary War) M: 258
Boston Post Road [New York-Boston] B: 505
Boston Public Library
Boston (Libraries and museums) B: 502
Boston Red Sox [team]
Baseball (table) B: 130
Boston shilling [money]
Pine-tree shilling P: 471 *with pictures*
Boston Tea Party [U.S. history] B: 506 *with picture*
Adams, John (In New England) A: 35-36
Adams, Samuel (The patriot) A: 44
Boston (Resistance and revolution) B: 503
Boston Port Act B: 505
Franklin, Benjamin (A delegate in London) F: 490
Massachusetts (Pre-Revolutionary days) M: 291
New Jersey (The American Revolution) N: 250
United States, History of the (Renewed conflict) U: 158
Boston terrier [dog] B: 506
Dog *picture on* D: 275
Boswell, James [Scottish author] B: 506 *with portrait*
Biography (The 1700's) B: 313-314
English literature (The Johnson circle) E: 319 *with picture*
Johnson, Samuel J: 153
Bosworth Field [English history]
England (The Wars of the Roses) E: 306-307
Henry VII [of England] H: 187
Bot [parasite]
Bot fly B: 507
Bot fly [insect] B: 507 *with picture*
Insect (Family life) I: 294-295
Botanic Garden, United States [Washington, D.C.] B: 507
Washington, D.C. *map on* W: 76; (United States Botanic Garden) W: 71
Botanical garden B: 507 *with picture*
Arboretum A: 592
Flower *picture on* F: 275
Gardening G: 30
Kingstown K: 332
Botanical Garden [Montreal] See Jardin Botanique *in this index*
Botanical insecticide
Insecticide (Botanical insecticides) I: 302
Botany B: 508 *with pictures*
See also Plant *in this index and the list of Related articles in the* Botany *article*
Arboretum A: 592

Biology (table) B: 317
Botanical garden B: 507
Fruit (Types of fruits in botany) F: 544
Life L: 274
Plant (Kinds of plants) P: 518
Prehistoric people P: 744
Botany Bay [Australia] B: 510
Botany Bay kino [tree product]
Eucalyptus E: 376
Botero, Fernando [Colombian painter]
Colombia (The arts) Ci: 781
Botetourt, Lord [British colonial official]
Washington, George (The coming revolution) W: 96
Botev, Khristo [Bulgarian poet]
Bulgaria (The arts) B: 690-691
Botev Peak [Bulgaria]
Bulgaria (The land) B: 691 *with map*
Both Members of This Club [painting by Bellows]
Bellows, George Wesley B: 244
Botha, Louis [South African political leader] B: 510
South Africa (The Union of South Africa) So: 618-619
Botha, P. W. [South African political leader] B: 510
De Klerk, Frederik Willem D: 94
South Africa (The dismantling of apartheid) So: 620
Bothe, Walther [German physicist]
Nobel Prizes (Physics: 1954) N: 441
Bothnia, Gulf of See Gulf of Bothnia *in this index*
Bothwell, Earl of [Scottish nobleman] B: 510
Mary, Queen of Scots (Her reign) M: 239
Botnet [computing]
Internet (Internet crime) I: 350f
Boto [animal] See Amazon River dolphin *in this index*
Botrange Mountain
Belgium (The Ardennes) B: 231
Botrytis blight [plant disease]
Lily L: 304
Botswana B: 510 *with pictures and maps*
Africa *picture on* A: 127
Flag *picture on* F: 198
Rhodes, Cecil John (Gains Rhodesia) R: 317
Böttger, Johann Friedrich [German chemist] B: 512
Dresden china D: 346
Porcelain (German porcelain) P: 677
Pottery (Pottery of the 1700's and 1800's) P: 718
Botticelli, Sandro [Italian painter] B: 512 *with picture*
Graces G: 296 *with picture*
Leonardo da Vinci (Return to Florence) L: 199
Painting (The 1400's) P: 52-53 *with picture*
Bottle B: 513 *with diagram*
Glass *diagram on* G: 214; (Glass containers) G: 212
Packaging P: 18
Bottle gourd [plant] See Calabash *in this index*
Bottle Houses [Cape Egmont]
Prince Edward Island (Interesting facts) P: 783 *with picture*
Bottle-nosed dolphin [sea animal] See Bottlenose dolphin *in this index*
Bottle of Banyuls, The [painting by Gris]
Cubism (The arts) Ci: 1181
Painting (Still-life paintings) P: 33; (Cubism) P: 77-78
Bottle tree [tree] B: 514 *with picture*
Tree *picture on* T: 426
Bottlebrush [tree]
Flower *picture on* F: 294
Bottled gas See Liquefied petroleum gas *in this index*
Bottlenose dolphin [sea animal]
Dolphin *picture on* D: 298; (Bottlenose dolphins) D: 297
Whale *picture on* W: 261
Bottlenose whale
Antarctica (Living things) A: 534-535 *with picture*
Bottler truck
Truck *picture on* T: 459; (Kinds of trucks) T: 457
Bottolfsen, C. A. [American political leader]
Idaho (table) I: 42
Bottom [literary figure]
Shakespeare, William: (A Midsummer Night's Dream) S: 357
Bottom [tool]
Plow (The tractor plow) P: 575 *with pictures*
Bottom line [business]
Accounting (Financial reports) A: 22-23
Bottom quark [physics]
Quark Q: 7
Subatomic particle (Elementary particles) So: 937; (Theoretical research) So: 938
Bottomless Lakes [New Mexico]
New Mexico (Land regions) N: 266-268

Bottomley, Jim [American baseball player]
Baseball (table: Hall of Fame) B: 134
Botulism [disease] B: 514
Bacteria (Harmful bacteria) B: 20
Food poisoning F: 340
Food preservation (How food spoils) F: 341
Botvinnik, Mikhail [Soviet chess player]
Chess (World chess champions) C: 414
Bou Regreg [river, Morocco]
Rabat R: 46
Boubou [clothing]
Senegal (People) S: 297-298
Bouchard, Lucien [Canadian political leader] B: 515
Bloc Québécois B: 404
Campbell, Kim (The 1993 election) C: 90d
Chrétien, Jean (The 1993 election) C: 522c
Quebec (The late 1900's) Q: 32-33
Bouchard, Michel Marc [Canadian playwright]
Canadian literature (Modern Canadian drama) C: 161
Bouchard, Thomas J. [American psychologist]
Intelligence (The roles of heredity and environment) I: 319
Boucher, François [French painter] B: 515 *with picture*
Fragonard, Jean Honoré F: 451
Painting (Rococo painting) P: 65
Rococo R: 396
Boucherville, C.-B. de [Canadian political leader]
Quebec (table) Q: 29
Boucicault, Dion [Irish-American dramatist] B: 515
Irish literature (Early works in English) I: 431
Boucicaut, Aristide [French merchant]
Department store D: 148
Bouck, William C. [American political leader]
New York (table) N: 313
Bouctouche [New Brunswick]
New Brunswick *picture on* N: 184
Boudicca [queen of the Iceni] B: 515
Boudreau, Lou [American baseball player]
Baseball (table: Hall of Fame) B: 134
Bouffant [hairstyle]
Hairdressing (The 1900's) H: 12
Bougainville [island, Solomon Islands] B: 515
Papua New Guinea (History) P: 141
Bougainville, Louis-Antoine, Comte de [French explorer]
Exploration (Exploring the Pacific) E: 447 *with map*
Society Islands So: 563
Tahiti T: 14
Bougainvillea [plant] B: 516 *with picture*
Boughton, George H. [British painter]
Pilgrims *picture on* P: 463
Bouguereau, William [French painter]
Painting (The art world, 1850-1900) P: 73
Bouillabaisse [food]
France (Food and drink) F: 459-460
Boulder Canyon Project [conservation]
Hoover Dam H: 332
Boulder Dam See Hoover Dam *in this index*
Bouldering [sport]
Climbing Ci: 679
Boulding, Kenneth Ewart [American economist] B: 516
Boulez, Pierre [French composer/conductor] B: 516
Boulle, André Charles [French cabinetmaker]
Furniture (Louis XIV furniture) F: 575; (The Régence style) F: 576 *with picture*
Boulton, Matthew [British businessman]
Watt, James W: 148
Boumedienne, Houari [Algerian political leader]
Algeria (Independence) A: 365
Bound East for Cardiff [play by O'Neill]
O'Neill, Eugene (His life) O: 762
Bound morpheme [linguistics]
Language (Words and morphemes) L: 62
Boundary [sports]
Cricket (Scoring) Ci: 1132
Boundary layer
Aerodynamics (Friction drag) A: 86
Boundary Peak [mountain]
Nevada (Land regions) N: 166 *with map*
Boundary Waters Canoe Area Wilderness [Minnesota]
Minnesota (Places to visit) M: 594
Boundary Waters Treaty [1909]
Great Lakes G: 343
International Joint Commission I: 340
Bounty [reward]
Civil War, American (Building the armed forces) Ci: 618
Bounty [ship]
Bligh, William B: 400
Pitcairn Island P: 498

Tonga **T:** 327
Bounty jumper [U.S. history]
Civil War, American (Building the armed forces)
Ci: 618
Bouquet garden
Gardening (Production gardens) **G:** 31
Bourassa, Henri [Canadian political leader] **B:** 516
Laurier, Sir Wilfrid (Relations with the United
Kingdom) **L:** 126; (The conscription crisis)
L: 126
Bourassa, Robert [Canadian political leader]
Quebec (table) **Q:** 29; (The late 1900's) **Q:** 32-33
Bourbaki, Nicolas [pen name]
Mathematics (Philosophies of mathematics)
M: 307
Bourbon [drink]
Alcoholic beverage (Whiskey) **A:** 337; (History)
A: 337
Whiskey **W:** 282
Bourbon [French history] **B:** 516
France (Religious wars) **F:** 473
Spain (Bourbon reforms) **So:** 748
Bourbon Democrat [U.S. history]
South Carolina (Industrial growth) **So:** 660-662
Bourbon Red turkey
Turkey (Domestic turkeys) **T:** 513 with picture
Bourbon Reforms [French history]
Charles III **C:** 381
Bourbon Street
New Orleans (Downtown New Orleans) **N:** 278-
279 with picture
Bourdon tube
Gauge (Pressure gauges) **G:** 69
Bourgeois, Léon Victor-Auguste [French
statesman]
Nobel Prizes (Peace: 1920) **N:** 448a
Bourgeois Poet, The [book by Shapiro]
Shapiro, Karl Jay **S:** 372
Bourgeoisie [sociology]
Communism (The ideas of Marx) **Ci:** 890
Marx, Karl: (Das Kapital) **M:** 237
Middle class **M:** 529
Social class (How people are categorized) **So:** 550
Bourges Cathedral [France]
Architecture picture on **A:** 619
Bourgmont, Étienne Veniard de [French explorer]
Nebraska (Exploration) **N:** 111
Bourguiba, Habib [Tunisian political leader] **B:** 517
Tunisia (History) **T:** 489
Bourke, Mary Terese Winifred [Irish political
leader] See Robinson, Mary in this index
Bourke-White, Margaret [American
photographer] **B:** 517
Economics picture on **E:** 62
Photography (Dramatic changes) **P:** 425-426
Bourn, Augustus O. [American political leader]
Rhode Island (table) **R:** 311
Bournonville, August [Danish choreographer]
Ballet (Romantic ballet) **B:** 51-52
Denmark (Arts) **D:** 136
Boussance [people]
Burkina Faso (People) **B:** 706
Boustrophedon [writing]
Greek language (Alphabet) **G:** 376
Bout [zoology]
Hibernation (Warm-blooded hibernators) **H:** 222
Bouteflika, Abdelaziz [Algerian political leader]
Algeria (Recent developments) **A:** 365
Bouthillier de Rancé, Armand-Jean le [French
monk]
Trappists **T:** 404
Boutros-Ghali, Boutros [Egyptian diplomat]
B: 517
United Nations (The secretary-general) **U:** 83
with portrait
Boutwell, George S. [American political leader]
Grant, Ulysses S. (Political corruption) **G:** 315-316;
(table) **G:** 316
Johnson, Andrew (Impeachment) **J:** 140
Massachusetts (table) **M:** 288
Bouvier, Jacqueline Lee [American public figure]
See Onassis, Jacqueline Kennedy in this index
Bouvier des Flandres [dog] **B:** 517
Dog picture on **D:** 276
Bouzouki [musical instrument]
Greece (Arts) **G:** 356
Bovay, Alvan E. [American political leader]
Republican Party (Origin) **R:** 253
Bovet, Daniel [Swiss chemist]
Nobel Prizes (Physiology or medicine: 1957)
N: 446
Bovine growth hormone See Bovine somatotropin
in this index
Bovine somatotropin [hormone]
Hormone (Agricultural uses) **H:** 337-338
Milk (History of the milk industry) **M:** 549
Bovine spongiform encephalopathy See Mad

cow disease in this index
Bovine tuberculosis [disease]
Veterinary medicine (On farms and ranches)
V: 345
Bow [musical instrument]
Bass **B:** 157 with picture
Cello **C:** 339 with picture
Violin (The bow) **V:** 389 with pictures
Bow [ship]
Sailing (Hull) **S:** 23 with diagram
Ship diagram on **S:** 405; (Basic structure) **S:** 403
Bow and arrow
See also Archery in this index
Archery **A:** 601
Arrowhead **A:** 743 with pictures
Crossbow **Ci:** 1156 with picture
Indian, American pictures on **I:** 138, **I:** 140, **I:** 160;
(Weapons) **I:** 144 with picture
Weapon (Ancient and medieval weapons)
W: 154a with picture
Bow echo [meteorology]
Derecho **D:** 152
Bow hunting
Archery **A:** 601
Bow Lake [Alberta]
Banff National Park **B:** 77
Bow saw [tool]
Saw picture on **S:** 167
Bow shock [physics]
Heliosphere (Shock waves) **H:** 175
Bow Street runners [English history]
Fielding, Henry (His life) **F:** 94
Police (Early law enforcement in England) **P:** 624
Bow stroke [canoeing]
Canoeing (Paddling and steering) **C:** 181
Bow thruster [propeller]
Ship (Engine-driven ships) **S:** 406
Bow tie
Necktie **N:** 117
Bow window
Window **W:** 334
Bowditch, Nathaniel [American astronomer]
B: 517
Bowdoin, James [American political leader]
Massachusetts (table) **M:** 288
Bowed kite
Kite (Types of kites) **K:** 339 with picture
Bowel [anatomy] See Intestine in this index
Bowell, Sir Mackenzie [Canadian political leader]
B: 518 with pictures
Tupper, Sir Charles (Prime minister) **T:** 494
Bowen, Elizabeth [Anglo-Irish author] **B:** 519
Irish literature (Drama) **I:** 432
Bowen, Otis R. [American political leader]
Health and Human Services, Department of
(table) **H:** 128
Indiana (table) **I:** 214
Bowen's Wharf [Newport]
Rhode Island picture on **R:** 297
Bower [nest]
Bowerbird **B:** 519 with picture
Bowerbird [bird] **B:** 519 with picture
Animal (Courtship behavior) **A:** 497
Bird (Courtship and mating) **B:** 356
Bowere, A. D. O. [American artist]
Westward movement in America picture on
W: 250
Bowering, George [Canadian author]
Canadian literature (Modern English-Canadian
fiction) **C:** 160
Bowerman, Jay [American political leader]
Oregon (table) **O:** 845
Bowers Mansion
Nevada (Places to visit) **N:** 164
Bowers v. Hardwick [U.S. history]
Homosexuality (Attitudes toward homosexuality)
H: 307
Bowery [district, New York City]
Stuyvesant, Peter **So:** 935
Bowes-Lyon, Elizabeth Angela Marguerite See
Elizabeth, the Queen Mother in this index
Bowfin [fish] **B:** 520 with picture
Dogfish **D:** 283
Fish (Bony fish) **F:** 147-148
Bowhead whale [whale] **B:** 520
Whale picture on **W:** 257; (Right whales) **W:** 255
Bowie, David [British singer]
Rock music (The early 1970's) **R:** 380b
Bowie, James [American frontiersman] **B:** 520 with
picture
Alamo (Early days) **A:** 280
Texas (The Texas revolution) **T:** 206
Bowie, Oden [American political leader]
Maryland (table) **M:** 255
Bowie, Robert [American political leader]
Maryland (table) **M:** 255
Bowie knife B: 520 with picture

Bowing ectoproct [animal]
Animal picture on **A:** 507
Bowl [container]
Lapis lazuli picture on **L:** 73
Sculpture picture on **S:** 243
Bowl-and-doily spider
Spider picture on **So:** 788
Bowl game [football]
Football (College competition) **F:** 364
Bowl refill tube
Plumbing (How toilets work) **P:** 579 with diagram
Bowler, James M. [Australian anthropologist]
Prehistoric people (table) **P:** 754
Bowles, Camilla Parker [wife of Prince Charles] See
Parker Bowles, Camilla in this index
Bowles, Chester [American government official]
Connecticut (table) **Ci:** 967
Bowline knot
Knots, hitches, and splices (Useful knots) **K:** 356
with diagram
Bowling [skill]
Cricket (The fielding side) **Ci:** 1134 with pictures
Bowling [sport] **B:** 521 with pictures
Bowling ball
Bowling (The ball) **B:** 523
Lawn bowling **L:** 144 with picture
Bowling Congress, American
Bowling (The 1900's) **B:** 524b
Bowling crease
Cricket (The field) **Ci:** 1131
Bowling Federation, International
Bowling (The 1900's) **B:** 524b
Bowling green
Lawn bowling **L:** 144
Bowling pin
Bowling (The pins) **B:** 523 with pictures
Bowls [lawn bowling]
England (Recreation) **E:** 296-297
Lawn bowling **L:** 144 with picture
Bowman's capsule [anatomy]
Kidney (How the kidneys produce urine) **K:** 311
with diagram
Bowser, William J. [Canadian political leader]
British Columbia (table) **B:** 628
Bowsight [device]
Archery (Other equipment) **A:** 602 with diagrams
Bowwood [tree] See Osage orange in this index
Box [container]
Packaging **P:** 18
Box [tree] **B:** 524b
Box: Tales from the Darkroom, The [book by Grass]
Grass, Günter **G:** 326
Box girder bridge
Bridge (Girder bridges) **B:** 600-601
Box jellyfish [zoology] See Sea wasp in this index
Box kite
Kite (Types of kites) **K:** 339 with picture; (History)
K: 340-341
Box seat
Opera **O:** 791
Box set [theater]
Drama (Early realism) **D:** 338
Box turtle
Turtle (Pond, box, and water turtles) **T:** 522
Boxelder [tree] **B:** 525 with pictures
Elder **E:** 157
Maple (Boxelder) **M:** 187
Tree pictures on **T:** 420
Boxelder bug [insect] **B:** 525 with picture
Boxer [dog] **B:** 525
Dog picture on **D:** 267
Boxer Protocol [1901]
Boxer Rebellion **B:** 525
Boxer Rebellion [1900] **B:** 525
Beijing (History) **B:** 223-224
China (The Boxer Rebellion) **C:** 503 with picture
Hay, John Milton **H:** 116
Hoover, Herbert Clark (Engineer and
businessman) **H:** 328
McKinley, William (America becomes a world
power) **M:** 341
Boxing [sport] **B:** 526 with pictures
See also Kickboxing in this index
Mixed martial arts **M:** 680
Olympic Games (Summer Olympic Games)
O: 746e-746f
Sculpture picture on **S:** 247
Boxing Australia Inc.
Boxing (Boxing in Australia and New Zealand)
B: 531
Boxing Canada [organization]
Boxing (Boxing in Canada) **B:** 530
Boxing Day [custom] **B:** 533
Boxing gloves
Boxing (Equipment) **B:** 526-527
Boxing New Zealand Inc.
Boxing (Boxing in Australia and New Zealand)

B: 531
Boxter [car]
Porsche AG P: 679
Boxwood [tree] See Box in this index
Boy
See also Male in this index
Adolescent (Physical development) A: 60-61
Baby B: 4
Child C: 448
Sexuality (Biological factors) S: 337
Boy actress
Shakespeare, William (Acting companies) S: 352;
(Dramatic conventions) S: 354
Boy of the Three-Year Nap, The [book by Snyder]
Literature for children picture on L: 378
Boy Pioneers [organization]
Beard, Daniel Carter B: 187
Boy Scout Handbook
Boy Scouts (Boys Scouts of America) B: 534
Boy Scout knife
Knife (Types of knives) K: 345-346 with picture
Boy Scouts B: 534 with pictures
Baden-Powell, Lord B: 23
Beard, Daniel Carter B: 187
Seton, Ernest Thompson S: 323
Boy with a Squirrel [painting by Copley]
Copley, John Singleton Ci: 1040
Boyar [Russian history]
Russia (The rise of Moscow) R: 548
Boyce, William D. [American businessman]
Boy Scouts B: 534
Boycott B: 539
Chavez, Cesar Estrada C: 389
Hanseatic League H: 54
International relations (Nonmilitary sanctions)
I: 345
Labor movement (Handling labor disputes) L: 6
Montgomery bus boycott M: 767
Olympic Games (The postwar games) O: 751-
752; (Boycotts) O: 753
Parks, Rosa Louise P: 171
Sanctions, Economic S: 106
Boycott, Charles C. [English businessman]
Boycott B: 539
Boyd, Alan Stephenson [American government
official]
Johnson, Lyndon Baines (table) J: 151
Transportation, Department of (table) T: 400
Boyd, Alfred [Canadian political leader]
Manitoba (table) M: 159; (The Red River
Rebellion) M: 160-162
Boyd, Belle [Confederate spy] B: 539
Boyd, James E. [American political leader]
Nebraska (table) N: 110
Boyd Orr, Lord [British nutritionist]
Nobel Prizes (Peace: 1949) N: 448a
Boyden, Seth [American inventor]
Newark (History) N: 357-358
Boyé, Jean [French aviator]
Airplane (Notable airplane flights) A: 236
Boyer, Jean-Pierre [Haitian political leader]
Haiti (History) H: 15-16
Boyer, Joe [American race driver]
Automobile racing (table: Indianapolis 500
winners) A: 980
Boyer, Paul Delos [American chemist]
Nobel Prizes (Chemistry: 1997) N: 444
Boyle, Danny [British film director] B: 539
Motion picture (Best achievement in directing:
2008) M: 862
Boyle, Emmet D. [American political leader]
Nevada (table) N: 173
Boyle, Robert [Irish chemist] B: 539
Chemistry (Alchemy) C: 400-401
Gas [physics] (Gas laws) G: 48
Pressure P: 773
Science (The scientific revolution) S: 198
Boyle, Willard S. [American physicist]
Nobel Prizes (Physics: 2009) N: 442
Boyle's law [chemistry]
Boyle, Robert B: 539
Gas [physics] (Gas laws) G: 48 with pictures
Pressure P: 773
Boymans-Van Beuningen Museum
Rotterdam R: 489
Boyne, Battle of the [1690] B: 539
Ireland (Religious persecution) I: 426
Northern Ireland (Protestant settlement) N: 524
Georgia (table) G: 130
Boys & Girls Clubs of America [organization]
B: 540 with picture
Boys' Brigade [organization] B: 540
Boys' Day
Doll (Dolls in festivals) D: 287
Boys Nation [meeting]
Boys State B: 541

Boys State [meeting] B: 541
American Legion (Activities) A: 412
Boys Town [film]
Tracy, Spencer T: 362
Boys Town [Nebraska] B: 541
Flanagan, Edward Joseph F: 227
Boysenberry [plant] B: 541 with picture
Dewberry D: 176
Bozeman, John M. [American frontiersman]
Bozeman Trail B: 541
Bozeman Trail [U.S. history] B: 541
Bridger, Jim B: 607
Red Cloud R: 185
Wyoming (Indian and settler conflicts) W: 534
Bozizé, François [Central African political leader]
Central African Republic (Government) C: 352;
(History) C: 353
BP [company] B: 541
Gulf oil spill of 2010 G: 437
Manufacturing (table) M: 170
BP Amoco [company] See BP in this index
BPD [disorder] See Borderline personality disorder
in this index
Bps [computing] See Bits per second in this index
Brabançon [dog]
Brussels griffon B: 653
Brabant, Duke of [Belgian nobleman]
Belgium (The Middle Ages) B: 232-233
Brabant Revolution [Belgian history]
Belgium (The Brabant Revolution) B: 233
Brabham, Jack [Australian race driver]
Automobile racing (table: Formula One World
Drivers' Championship) A: 980
Brace, Charles Loring [American social reformer]
B: 542
Brace root [botany]
Corn (How the plant develops) Ci: 1057-1058
with picture
Bracebridge Hall [book by Irving]
Irving, Washington (Years in Europe) I: 460
Bracelet
Jewelry J: 117 with picture
Bracero [U.S. history]
Hispanic Americans (Effects of World War II)
H: 253
Braces [dentistry]
Dentistry (Orthodontics) D: 143-144 with picture
Orthodontics O: 860
Teeth (Malocclusion) T: 84-85
Brachial artery [anatomy]
Human body (table) H: 422 with diagram
Brachial vein [anatomy]
Human body (table) H: 422 with diagram
Brachialis [anatomy]
Arm A: 717
Brachionus calyciflorus [animal]
Animal picture on A: 506
Brachiopoda [zoology]
Animal (A classification of the animal kingdom)
A: 506-507 with picture
Prehistoric animal (The earliest animals) P: 736
Brachioradialis [anatomy]
Human body (table) H: 422 with diagram
Brachiosaurus [dinosaur] B: 542
Dinosaur pictures on D: 206d, D: 210; (True
dinosaurs) D: 206b-209
Brachytherapy [medicine]
Cancer (Radiation therapy) C: 172
Bracing
Tree surgery T: 433
Brack, Kenny [American race driver]
Automobile racing (table: Indianapolis 500
winners) A: 980
Bracken [plant]
Fern (Kinds of ferns) F: 75 with picture
Bracken, John [Canadian political leader]
Manitoba (table) M: 159; (Political developments)
M: 162
Bracket, Tax See Tax bracket in this index
Bracket creep [economics]
Income tax (Effects of inflation) I: 103
Bracket fungi
Mushroom (Mushroomlike fungi) M: 945
Brackets
Punctuation (Brackets) P: 903
Brackett, John Q. A. [American political leader]
Massachusetts (table) M: 288
Brackins, Monroe [American rancher]
Western frontier life in America (Ranching)
W: 236
Braconid wasp [insect]
Ichneumon wasp I: 24
Bract [botany]
Banana (How bananas grow) B: 73
Bunchberry B: 699
Flower (Variations in flower structure) F: 294
with picture

Inflorescence I: 268a
Leaf (Bracts) L: 157 with picture
Pineapple (The pineapple plant) P: 472
Raceme R: 51
Bradbury, Ray [American author] B: 542
Bradbury Science Museum [Los Alamos]
New Mexico (Places to visit) N: 264 with picture
Braddock, Edward [English general] B: 542 with
picture
Boone, Daniel (Tales of a hunter's paradise)
B: 477
Braddock's Road B: 543
Franklin, Benjamin (The Plan of Union) F: 489-
490
French and Indian wars (The French and Indian
War) F: 512-513
Washington, George (Braddock's defeat) W: 94
with picture
Braddock, James J. [American boxer] B: 543 with
picture
Louis, Joe L: 477
Braddock's Defeat [painting by Deming]
Braddock, Edward picture on B: 543
Braddock's Road [U.S. history] B: 543
Bradford [England] B: 543
Bradford, Andrew [American editor]
Pennsylvania (Interesting facts) P: 245
Bradford, Augustus W. [American political leader]
Maryland (table) M: 255
Bradford, John [American journalist]
Kentucky (Communication) K: 289
Bradford, Roark [American author] B: 544
Bradford, Robert F. [American political leader]
Massachusetts (table) M: 288
Bradford, Sam [American football player]
Football (table) F: 363
Bradford, William [1590-1657, American colonial
official] B: 544
Mayflower Compact M: 328
Pilgrims P: 463
Plymouth Colony (The first year) P: 583
Thanksgiving Day (Plymouth Colony) T: 230
Bradford, William [1663-1752, American printer]
B: 544
Bradford, William [1755-1795, American
government official]
Justice, Department of (table) J: 203
Washington, George (table) W: 102
Bradford, William, III [1722-1791, American
publisher] B: 544
Bradham, Caleb [American pharmacist]
PepsiCo, Inc. P: 279
Bradley, Bill [American political leader] B: 544 with
portrait
Bradley, Francis Herbert [British philosopher]
B: 544
Bradley, James [English astronomer] B: 545
Bradley, John H. [American soldier]
Iwo Jima, Battle of picture on I: 523
Bradley, Joseph P. [American jurist]
Supreme Court of the United States (table)
So: 1000
Bradley, Lewis R. [American political leader]
Nevada (table) N: 173
Bradley, Omar Nelson [American general] B: 545
Bradley, Owen [American record producer]
Country music picture on Ci: 1098c
Bradley, Tom [American political leader] B: 545
with portrait
African Americans picture on A: 136p; (Politics)
A: 136s
Los Angeles (Recent developments) L: 470
Bradley, W. C. [American businessman]
Columbus G: 854
Bradley Center
Milwaukee (The city) M: 558-559
Bradshaw, Terry [American football player] B: 545
with picture
Bradstreet, Anne [American poet] B: 546
American literature (New England) A: 414
Bradwell v. State [U.S. history]
Supreme Court of the United States (Civil rights)
So: 1001
Brady, Alice [American actress]
Motion picture (Best performance by an actress
in a supporting role: 1937) M: 862b
Brady, Diamond Jim [American businessman]
B: 546
Brady, James Buchanan [birth name of]
Brady, Diamond Jim B: 546
Brady, James H. [American political leader]
Idaho (table) I: 42
Brady, Mathew B. [American photographer] B: 546
with picture
Barton, Clara picture on B: 121
Civil War, American (The home front) Ci: 622
Davis, Jefferson picture on D: 48

Douglas, Stephen Arnold *picture on* D: 313
Johnson, Andrew *picture on* J: 136
Lincoln, Abraham *pictures on* L: 322, L: 325
Photography (Artistic advances) P: 424-425 *with picture*
White House *picture on* W: 290
Brady, Nicholas Frederick [American government official] B: 546
Reagan, Ronald Wilson (table) R: 169
Brady, Tom [American football player] B: 547 *with picture*
Brady bill [1994]
Clinton, Bill (National affairs) Ci: 682d
Gun control (Approaches to gun control) G: 440-441
Brady Commission
Brady, Nicholas Frederick B: 546
Bradycardia [disorder]
Heart (Abnormal heart rhythms) H: 142
Braemar [Scotland]
Scotland (Recreation) S: 214
Braga [Portugal] B: 547
Braganza, House of [Portuguese history]
Portugal (Spanish conquest) P: 694
Bragg, Braxton [Confederate general] B: 547
Civil War, American (The commanding officers) Ci: 618; (Battle of Perryville) Ci: 629; (Battle of Chickamauga) Ci: 629
Bragg, Thomas [American political leader]
North Carolina (table) N: 490
Bragg, Sir William Henry [British physicist] B: 547
Bragg, Sir William Lawrence B: 547
Bragg, Sir William Lawrence [British physicist] B: 547
Bragg, Sir William Henry B: 547
Nobel Prizes (Physics: 1915) N: 440
Bragi [Norse mythology]
Mythology (The construction of the world) M: 986
Brahe, Tycho [Danish astronomer] B: 548
Astronomy (Sun-centered theories) A: 835-836; (Developing the modern view) A: 847
Kepler, Johannes (His life) K: 305
Brahma [breed]
Chicken (Asiatic class chickens) C: 441; (table) C: 443
Brahma [Hindu god]
Brahman B: 548
Brahman [animal]
Cattle (Other beef cattle) C: 309
Brahman [Hindu god] B: 548
Hinduism (Deities) H: 236
Polytheism P: 652
Religion (A doctrine of salvation) R: 215-216
Brahmanas [religious books]
Hinduism (The Vedas) H: 235
Sanskrit literature (The Vedic period) S: 112
Vedas V: 291
Brahmans [sociology]
Aryans A: 764
Caste C: 279
Dravidians D: 342
Hinduism (Caste) H: 236
Priest P: 776
Brahmaputra River [Asia] B: 548
Bangladesh B: 78; (Rivers and streams) B: 83
Ganges River G: 27
India (The Northern Plains) I: 121
Brahmi number system
Decimal system (Invention of the decimal system) D: 73
Brahmi script
Alphabet (Scripts of Asia) A: 383
Brahmo Samaj [organization]
Rammohun Roy R: 133
Brahms, Johannes [German composer] B: 548 *with portrait*
Dvořák, Antonín D: 394
Schumann, Clara S: 188
Braid, James [British doctor]
Hypnosis (Scientific studies) H: 480
Braided rug
Rugs and carpets (Other methods) R: 516; (History) R: 517
Braiding [handicraft] B: 549 *with pictures*
Braille [alphabet] B: 550 *with pictures*
Blindness (Aids for blind people) B: 402
Braille, Louis B: 550
Disability *picture on* D: 220; (Visual disabilities) D: 219
Library (Services for special groups) L: 241
Braille, Louis [French inventor] B: 550
Braille B: 550
Braillewriter [machine]
Braille B: 550
Brain [anatomy] B: 550a *with pictures*
See also the list of Related articles in the Brain

article
Anticonvulsant A: 553
Attention deficit disorder A: 878
Autism (Causes) A: 942
Bird (The nervous system) B: 366 *with diagram*
Cancer (Radiation therapy) C: 172
Cerebrospinal fluid C: 362
Color (The roles of the eyes and brain) Ci: 818-819
Death (Medical aspects of death) D: 61
Depression D: 151
Disease (Diseases associated with aging) D: 230-231
Dopamine D: 309
Dream D: 344
Ear (The sense of balance) E: 11
Ecstasy E: 66
Electroencephalograph E: 200
Emotion (Emotion and the brain) E: 261
Endorphin E: 272
Eye (Depth perception) E: 463
Human being H: 413
Human body *picture on* H: 417; (table) H: 422 *with diagram*
Language (Signed languages) L: 63-64
Learning (Theories of learning) L: 163-164
Lobotomy L: 405
Magnetic resonance imaging M: 56 *with picture*
Mammal M: 117
Mind (Parts of the mind) M: 562
Myelin M: 970f
Nervous system N: 132 *with diagrams*
Pain (How the body feels pain) P: 21-22
Perception (Factors affecting perception) P: 283
Phrenology P: 430
Positron emission tomography P: 697 *with picture*
Prehuman people P: 743; (Prehuman ancestors) P: 744; (The first human beings) P: 746; (The multiple origins theory) P: 749-750
Prion P: 804
Reading (How we read) R: 156-157; (Physical disabilities) R: 162
Reproduction, Human (Development of organs and organ systems) R: 248
Ritalin R: 350
Schizophrenia S: 176
Senility S: 300
Sleep (The need for sleep) S: 507
Stroke So: 929
Taste T: 50
Weight control (How body weight is determined) W: 181
Brain bank
Brain *picture on* B: 556
Brain damage
Brain (From injury) B: 550d; (Sensing the environment) B: 552; (Disorders of the brain) B: 557
Language (The sounds of language) L: 63-64
Causes
Cerebral hemorrhage C: 361
Concussion Ci: 929
Inhalant I: 271
Intellectual disability (Causes) I: 318
Learning disabilities (Causes) L: 165
Mental illness (Physical changes in the brain) M: 406
Disorders
Alzheimer's disease A: 398
Aphasia A: 565
Cerebral palsy C: 361
Epilepsy E: 343
Fetal alcohol syndrome F: 80
Paralysis (Paralysis of central nervous system origin) P: 152
Persistent vegetative state P: 300f
Shaken baby syndrome S: 343
Spastic paralysis So: 767
Tay-Sachs disease T: 56
Brain death
Death (Defining death) D: 61
Organ donation O: 852
Transplant (Sources of donor organs) T: 380
Brain Games Network [company]
Chess (History) C: 414
Brain hemisphere See Cerebral hemisphere in this index
Brain pacemaker [medicine]
Spastic paralysis So: 767
Brain stem [anatomy]
Brain (The parts of the brain) B: 550a *with diagram*; (From injury) B: 550d; (Controlling movement) B: 553; (Attention and consciousness) B: 554-555
Dream (The biology of dreams) D: 344-345
Nervous system (The central nervous system) N: 132-133 *with diagram*

Serotonin S: 318
Taste T: 51
Brain Trust [U.S. history]
New Deal (The Hundred Days) N: 200
Roosevelt, Franklin Delano (The Hundred Days) R: 453
Brain wave [physiology]
Sleep (The structure of sleep) S: 506; (Sleep in animals) S: 506
Braine, John [British author]
English literature (Literature after World War II) E: 322-323
Brainwashing [psychology] B: 560
Prisoner of war P: 808
Propaganda P: 823
Brake [mechanism] B: 560 *with diagram*
Automobile *diagram on* A: 948; (The brake system) A: 950; (Operating a car) A: 954; (Batteries and braking) A: 954 *with diagram*
Bicycle (Steering and stopping) B: 290 *with diagrams*
Brake fluid
Brake (Hydraulic brakes) B: 560
Brake horsepower [measurement]
Horsepower (Brake horsepower) H: 367
Brake pad
Brake (Mechanical brake) B: 560 *with diagram*
Brake shoe [mechanism]
Brake (Mechanical brakes) B: 560 *with diagram*
Brakeman
Railroad (Railroad workers) R: 113
Bramah, Joseph [British cabinetmaker]
Plumbing (History) P: 580
Bramante, Donato [Italian architect] B: 562 *with picture*
Architecture (Later Renaissance architecture) A: 621
Saint Peter's Basilica (History) S: 54
Bramble [botany] B: 562
Brampton stock [plant]
Stock So: 903
Bran [food] B: 562
Flour (How white flour is milled) F: 269
Oats O: 640
Wheat (Structure) W: 267-268 *with diagram*
Bran layer [botany]
Rice (Structure) R: 323 *with diagram*; (Removing the bran layers) R: 326
Branca, Giovanni [Italian engineer]
Turbine (History) T: 498-499
Branch [botany]
Pruning P: 841 *with picture*
Tree (Trunk and branches) T: 416 *with diagram*
Branch, Emmett Forest [American political leader]
Indiana (table) I: 214
Branch, John [American political leader]
Jackson, Andrew (table) J: 11; (Split with Calhoun) J: 11
North Carolina (table) N: 490
Branch collar [botany]
Tree surgery T: 433
Branch Davidians [cult]
Cult (Modern cults) Ci: 1185
Reno, Janet R: 240
Branch library
Library (Kinds of public libraries) L: 240
Branch line
Railroad (Tracks) R: 108
Branchial heart [zoology]
Octopus (The body of an octopus) O: 672
Brancusi, Constantin [Romanian sculptor] B: 563
Modigliani, Amedeo M: 686
Romania (The arts) R: 419
Sculpture (Cubism and futurism) S: 257 *with picture*
Brand [mark] See Branding in this index
Brand [play by Ibsen]
Ibsen, Henrik (His plays) I: 4
Brand, Hennig [German alchemist]
Phosphorus P: 403
Brand, Vance D. [American astronaut]
Astronaut (Achievements in space) A: 829-830
Brand manager [occupation]
Advertising (Advertising departments) A: 77
Brand name See Trademark in this index
Brandeis, Louis Dembitz [American jurist] B: 563
Brandenberger, Jacques Edwin [Swiss chemist]
Cellophane (History) C: 340
Brandenburg [German history] B: 563
Berlin (History) B: 264
Prussia (Early history) P: 843
Brandenburg [region, Germany]
Germany (The rise of Prussia) G: 164
Brandenburg Concertos [music by Bach]
Bach, Johann Sebastian (His works) B: 16
Brandenburg Gate [Berlin]
Berlin (Downtown Berlin) B: 260-261 *with picture*

Germany *picture on* **G: 171**
Brandenburg v. Ohio [U.S. history]
  Schenck v. United States **S: 174**
  Supreme Court of the United States (Freedom of speech) **So: 1001**; (table) **So: 1002**
Brandenburger Tor [gate] *See* Brandenburg Gate *in this index*
Branding [burning]
  Body art **B: 435**
  Cowboy (The roundup) **Ci: 1111** *with picture*
  Ranching (Life on a cattle ranch) **R: 134-135** *with picture*
Brando, Marlon [American actor] **B: 563** *with portrait*
  Motion picture *picture on* **M: 872**; (Best performance by an actor: 1954, 1972) **M: 862a**
Brandon [Manitoba] **B: 563**
Brandon, Gerard C. [American political leader]
  Mississippi (table) **M: 640**
Brandon, William W. [American political leader]
  Alabama (table) **A: 274**
Brandt, Georg [Swedish chemist]
  Cobalt **Ci: 740**
Brandt, Willy [German political leader] **B: 563**
  Germany (West Germany) **G: 170**
Brandy [drink]
  Alcoholic beverage (Brandy) **A: 336**; (History) **A: 337**
Brandywine, Battle of [1777]
  Maryland (The Revolutionary War) **M: 258**
  Revolution, American (table) **R: 276**; (Brandywine and Germantown) **R: 282**
Brangus [cattle]
  Cattle (Other beef cattle) **C: 309**
Branigin, Roger D. [American political leader]
  Indiana (table) **I: 214**
Brann, Louis J. [American political leader]
  Maine (table) **M: 87**
Brannan, Charles F. [American government official]
  Agriculture, Department of (table) **A: 161**
  Truman, Harry S. (table) **T: 469**
Branner, John [American educator]
  Hoover, Herbert Clark (Education) **H: 326-327**
Bransfield, Edward [British explorer]
  Antarctica (Early exploration) **A: 536**
  Exploration (The exploration of Antarctica) **E: 450**
Branson [Missouri] [B:]
  Missouri (Places to visit) **M: 660** *with picture*; (The early 2000's) **M: 672**
Branstad, Terry E. [American political leader]
  Iowa (table) **I: 391**
Brant [bird] **B: 564** *with picture*
  Goose (Kinds of geese) **G: 270** *with picture*
Brant, Isabella [wife of]
  Rubens, Peter Paul (His life) **R: 506**
Brant, Joseph [American Indian chief] **B: 564**
  Iroquois Indians **I: 455**
Branting, Karl Hjalmar [Swedish statesman]
  Nobel Prizes (Peace: 1921) **N: 448a**
Braque, Georges [French painter] **B: 564**
  Cubism **Ci: 1181** *with picture*
  Painting (Cubism) **P: 77** *with picture*
  Picasso, Pablo (Cubism) **P: 448b**
Bras d'Or Lake [lagoon, Nova Scotia]
  Cape Breton Island **C: 187**
  Nova Scotia (Rivers and lakes) **N: 562** *with map*
Brasher doubloon [coin]
  Coin collecting *picture on* **Ci: 758**
Brasileiro [language]
  Portuguese language **P: 695**
Brasília [Brazil] **B: 564** *with picture*
  Brazil **B: 567**, *picture on* **B: 569**
  City (Future cities) **Ci: 593**
  City planning (Building new communities) **Ci: 601**
  Niemeyer, Oscar **N: 406** *with picture*
Brass [metal] **B: 565** *with pictures*
  Alloy (Other alloys) **A: 378**
Brass Center of the World [name for]
  Waterbury **W: 141**
Brass instrument [music]
  Jazz (The brass) **J: 69**
  Music (Wind instruments) **M: 949** *with pictures*
  Orchestra **O: 820** *with pictures*
Brass quintet [ensemble]
  Chamber music **C: 371**
Brass section [music]
  Orchestra (The musicians) **O: 820**
Bratislava [Slovakia] **B: 566**
Brattain, Walter Houser [American physicist] **B: 566**
  Electricity (The electronic age) **E: 198**
  Electronics (The solid-state revolution) **E: 215** *with picture*
  Transistor **T: 372**
Brattle organ [pipe organ]

New Hampshire (Interesting facts) **N: 209** *with picture*
Bratz doll
  Doll (The 2000's) **D: 295**
Braulio Carrillo National Park [Costa Rica]
  National park (Costa Rica) **N: 42c**
Braun, Carol Moseley [American political leader]
  See Moseley Braun, Carol *in this index*
Braun, Eva [mistress of Hitler] **B: 566** *with portrait*
  Hitler, Adolf (Death) **H: 268**
Braun, Karl Ferdinand [German physicist]
  Marconi, Guglielmo **M: 197**
  Nobel Prizes (Physics: 1909) **N: 440**
Braun, Wernher von [German-American engineer]
  See Von Braun, Wernher *in this index*
Braunschweig [Germany]
  Brunswick **B: 652**
Brava [island]
  Cape Verde **C: 189** *with map*
Brave Little Tailor, The [book by Dugin]
  Literature for children *picture on* **L: 355**
Brave New World [book by Huxley]
  English literature (Fiction between the wars) **E: 322**
  Huxley, Aldous Leonard **H: 459**
Braveheart [film]
  Gibson, Mel **G: 187**
  Motion picture (Best picture: 1995) **M: 861**
Braves, Atlanta [team] *See* Atlanta Braves *in this index*
Bravura [dancing]
  Baryshnikov, Mikhail **B: 123**
Brawne, Fanny [British public figure]
  Keats, John (His life) **K: 253**
Braxton, Carter [American patriot] **B: 566**
Bray, John Randolph [American cartoonist]
  Animation (Pioneers of American animation) **A: 514a-514b**
Bray, Thomas [English missionary]
  Library (Libraries in the United States) **L: 261**
  Maryland (Libraries) **M: 244**
  North Carolina (Libraries) **N: 477**
  Rhode Island (Libraries) **R: 300**
Brayer [tool]
  Block printing **B: 405** *with picture*
Brazel, Wayne [American public figure]
  Garrett, Pat **G: 45**
Brazel, William W. (Mac) [American public figure]
  Roswell **R: 484**
Brazil **B: 567** *with pictures and maps*
  See also the list of Related articles in the Brazil *article*
  Cabral, Pedro Álvares **C: 8**
  Capoeira **C: 197**
  Clothing *picture on* **Ci: 695**
  Ethanol **E: 365**
  Exploration (Exploring the New World) **E: 444-445**
  Flag *picture on* **F: 200**
  Immigration (Latin America) **I: 85**
  International Space Station **I: 346b**
  Latin America (Early settlers in Brazil) **L: 106**; (The movement toward independence) **L: 106-107**; (Early years of independence) **L: 107-108**
  Line of Demarcation **L: 333**
  Palmares **P: 110**
  Portugal (Empire and wealth) **P: 693-694** *with map*; (A weakening monarchy) **P: 694**
  Portuguese language **P: 695**
  Rio de Janeiro (History) **R: 346**
  Television (In Latin America) **T: 117**
  Yanomami Indians **Y: 552**
Brazil [coffee]
  Coffee (Kinds of coffee) **Ci: 755**
Brazil Current
  Atlantic Ocean (Currents) **A: 866**
Brazil nut **B: 587** *with picture*
  Nut (Kinds of nuts) **N: 621**
Brazilian Democratic Movement Party
  Brazil (Politics) **B: 569**
Brazilian free-tailed bat [animal]
  Bat (Brazilian free-tailed bats) **B: 161**
Brazilian Highlands [mountains, Brazil]
  South America (The Eastern Highlands) **So: 628**
Brazilian jiu-jitsu [martial art]
  Martial arts (Mixed martial arts [MMA]) **M: 234a**
  Mixed martial arts **M: 680**
Brazilian literature
  Latin American literature (Colonial literature) **L: 112**
Brazilian Social Democracy Party
  Brazil (Politics) **B: 569**
Brazilwood [tree] **B: 587**
  Violin (The bow) **V: 389**
Brazos River [Texas]
  Waco **W: 2**
Brazza, Pierre Savorgnan de [French explorer]

Brazzaville **B: 587**
  Congo, Republic of the (History) **Ci: 940e**
Brazzaville [Congo, Republic of the] **B: 587**
  Congo, Republic of the **Ci: 940d** *with picture*
BRCA1 gene
  Breast cancer **B: 591**
  Genetic testing (Disorders involving more than one gene) **G: 85**
BRCA2 gene
  Breast cancer **B: 591**
Breach of contract [law]
  Contract **Ci: 1023**
Breach of promise [law] **B: 587**
Breach of the peace [law] **B: 587**
Breach of warranty [law]
  Product liability suit **P: 810**
Breaching [zoology]
  Whale *picture on* **W: 260**
Bread **B: 588** *with pictures*
  Air conditioning (In business and industry) **A: 176-177**
  Baking **B: 32**
  Colonial life in America (Food and drink) **Ci: 802**
  Flour **F: 268** *with diagram and picture*
  Food (Food from plants) **F: 329**
  Nutrition (Carbohydrates) **N: 625**
  Passover **P: 192**
  Rye (Uses) **R: 573**
  Yeast **Y: 554** *with diagrams*
Bread flour
  Flour (Types of flour) **F: 268**
Bread mold
  Mold **M: 689**
Bread wheat [plant]
  Wheat (Species of wheat) **W: 269** *with picture*
Breadbasket of America [nickname]
  Kansas **K: 216**; (The nation's breadbasket) **K: 237**
Breadbasket of Europe [nickname]
  Ukraine (Agriculture) **U: 11**
Breadfruit [food] **B: 589**
Breadth [measurement]
  Flag (Manufacturing flags) **F: 222**
"Break, Break, Break" [poem by Tennyson]
  Poetry **P: 591**
Break-away roping
  Rodeo (All-women's rodeos) **R: 398**
Break dancing
  Hip-hop **H: 238**
Break of Noon [play by Claudel]
  French literature (The early years) **F: 522**
Breakaway
  Hockey (Hockey terms) **H: 275**
Breakbone fever *See* Dengue *in this index*
Breaker cam [device]
  Ignition (Development of ignition systems) **I: 50**
Breaker points [electricity]
  Ignition (Development of ignition systems) **I: 50**
Breakers, The [estate]
  Hunt, Richard Morris **H: 450** *with picture*
  Rhode Island *picture on* **R: 296**
Breakeven level [physics]
  Nuclear energy (Experimental fusion devices) **N: 592-593**
Breakfast at Tiffany's [book by Capote]
  Capote, Truman **C: 198**
Breakfast cereal [food]
  Cereal **C: 360**
  Kellogg, W. K. **K: 256**
  Oatmeal **O: 640**
  Wheat (Food for people) **W: 266-267** *with picture*
Breakfast of Champions [book by Vonnegut]
  Vonnegut, Kurt **V: 448**
Breakfast piece [art]
  Painting (Still-life paintings) **P: 33**; (The Dutch masters) **P: 62-63** *with picture*
Breakfast Table [painting by Heda]
  Painting (Still-life paintings) **P: 33**; (The Dutch masters) **P: 62-63** *with picture*
Breaking the flag
  Flag (Raising and lowering the flag) **F: 219**
"Breaks, The" [song]
  Rap music **R: 141**
Breakspear, Nicholas [pope] *See* Adrian IV *in this index*
Breakwater [harbor] **B: 589** *with picture*
  Harbor **H: 55**
Bream [fish] **B: 590**
Brearley, David [American jurist] **B: 590**
Breast [anatomy] **B: 590** *with diagram*
  Amazons **A: 404**
  Mammography **M: 129**
  Mastectomy **M: 296**
  Pregnancy (Changes in breasts) **P: 734b**
  Prosthetics **P: 830**
  Sexuality (Biological factors) **S: 337-338**
Breast cancer [disorder] **B: 591**
  Breast **B: 590**

Cancer *picture on* C: 167; (Classification by primary body site) C: 167-168; (table) C: 170; (Surgery) C: 172
Hormone replacement therapy H: 338
Mammography M: 129
Mastectomy M: 296
Menopause M: 402
Tamoxifen T: 23
Taxol T: 56
Thermography T: 254
Breast-feeding
Baby (The first month) B: 6; (Feeding procedures) B: 9
Hormone (Other hormones) H: 336
Kwashiorkor K: 398
La Leche League International L: 49
Breastbone *See* Sternum *in this index*
Breasted, James Henry [American archaeologist] B: 591
Breastplate [armor]
Armor *picture on* A: 720
Breaststroke
Swimming *pictures on* So: 1044; (The basic kicks) So: 1043; (The basic strokes) So: 1043
Breath control [music]
Singing (Training the voice) S: 472
Breath-hold diving [sport]
Diving, Underwater (Ambient diving) D: 245
Skin diving S: 492 *with pictures*
Breath testing [law enforcement] B: 591
Driving while intoxicated D: 348
Breathalyzer [machine]
Breath testing B: 591
Breathing [physiology]
See also Respiration *in this index*
Allergy A: 373
Animal (Adaptations for breathing) A: 491 *with pictures*
Diaphragm D: 184
Diving, Underwater (Dangers of underwater diving) D: 246
Dolphin (The bodies of dolphins) D: 297-298
First aid (Restoring breathing) F: 138
Hyperventilation H: 477
Iron lung I: 453
Lung L: 523
Nose *diagram on* N: 549
Respiration (External respiration) R: 260 *with diagrams*
Sleep apnea S: 507
Space exploration (Meeting basic needs in space) So: 703
Whale (Respiratory system) W: 259 *with pictures*
Breathless [film]
Godard, Jean-Luc G: 244
Motion picture (The New Wave in France) M: 870 *with picture*
Brébeuf, Saint Jean de [French missionary] B: 591
Breccia [rock]
Moon (Basins) M: 789
Rock (Clastic sediments) R: 372; (table) R: 373 *with picture*
Brecht, Bertolt [German dramatist] B: 591
Drama (Epic theater) D: 339
German literature (Expressionism) G: 141-142
Weill, Kurt W: 188
Breckinridge, John [American government official]
Jefferson, Thomas (table) J: 83
Justice, Department of (table) J: 203
Breckinridge, John Cabell [Confederate general] B: 592
Lincoln, Abraham (Election of 1860) L: 318
Republican Party *picture on* R: 256
Breckinridge, Sophonisba [American social reformer] B: 592
Chicago, University of (Research program) C: 438
Breda [Netherlands] B: 592
Breda, Treaty of [1667]
Breda B: 592
French Guiana (History) F: 515
New Brunswick (French rivals) N: 196
New York (Under English rule) N: 314-315
Bredesen, Phil [American political leader]
Tennessee (table) T: 152
Breech [gun]
Firearm (Mechanism) F: 132 *with diagrams*
Breech birth
Childbirth (The birth process) C: 456
Breechblock [gun]
Artillery (Parts of an artillery weapon) A: 762
Breechcloth [clothing]
Colonial life in America (Clothing) Ci: 799-802
Indian, American (Clothing) I: 136d
Breeches
Clothing (The 1600's) Ci: 701 *with picture*
Breed [biology] *See* Breeding *in this index*
Breed standard

Dog (Dog competitions) D: 280
Breeder reactor [machine]
Energy supply (Nuclear energy) E: 278
Nuclear energy (Nuclear fission) N: 582-583; (Advanced fission reactors) N: 594
Breeders' Cup [race]
Horse racing (Stakes races) H: 364-365
Breeding [genetics] B: 592
See also Captive breeding *in this index*
Agriculture (Industrialized agriculture) A: 150; (Agricultural genetics) A: 158
Cat (Breeds of cats) C: 290
Cattle (Breeding) C: 311
Estrous cycle E: 363
Eugenics E: 377
Evolution (Artificial selection) E: 432
Farm and farming (Livestock breeding) F: 39
Flower (Flower breeding) F: 297
Frog (Mating) F: 538
Fruit (Developing new fruit cultivars) F: 548
Grafting (Uses of grafting) G: 298
Horse (Breeding horses) H: 358
Horticulture (Research in horticulture) H: 370
Hybrid H: 460
Lawn (Types of lawns) L: 142
Livestock (Breeding livestock) L: 398
Mammal (Mating) M: 122
Mutation M: 968
Pedigree P: 228
Plant (Breeding and genetics) P: 542
Breeding competition
Horse (Horse shows) H: 356
Breeding cycle *See* Estrous cycle *in this index*
Breeding season [biology]
Estrous cycle E: 363
Breedlove, Craig [American race driver] B: 593
Breedlove, Sarah [American businesswoman] *See* Walker, Madam C. J. *in this index*
Breed's Hill
Bunker Hill, Battle of B: 700
Breeze
Wind (table) W: 330
Breezing Up [painting by Homer]
United States *picture on* U: 117
Bréguet, Louis [French inventor]
Helicopter (Development of the helicopter) H: 173 *with picture*
Breit, Gregory [American physicist]
Radar (The first uses of radar) R: 71
Breitenfeld, Battle of [1631]
Thirty Years' War (The Swedish period) T: 260
Breitling Orbiter 3 [balloon]
Balloon *picture on* B: 62
Bremen [Germany] B: 593
Bremer, Arthur H. [American public figure]
Wallace, George Corley W: 16
Bremsstrahlung [physics]
Radiation (Causes of radiation) R: 78-79
X rays (How X rays are produced) X: 542
Brennan, Francis J. [American religious leader]
Cardinal (table: American cardinals) C: 211
Brennan, Joseph E. [American political leader]
Maine (table) M: 87
Brennan, Peter J. [American government official]
Ford, Gerald Rudolph (table) F: 378
Labor, Department of (table) L: 2
Brennan, Walter [American actor]
Motion picture (Best performance by an actor in a supporting role: 1936, 1938, 1940) M: 862a
Brennan, William Joseph, Jr. [American jurist] B: 593
Brenner, Sydney [South African-born biologist]
Nobel Prizes (Physiology or medicine: 2002) N: 447
Brenner Pass [Austria-Italy] B: 593
Alps *picture on* A: 385; (Alpine travel) A: 386
Brenston, Jackie [American musician]
Rock music (Sun Records) R: 376
Brent goose *See* Brant *in this index*
Brentano, Clemens [German author]
Lorelei L: 454
Brer Rabbit [literary figure]
Harris, Joel Chandler H: 68
Breslau [Germany] *See* Wrocław *in this index*
Bresnahan, Roger [American baseball player]
Baseball (table: Hall of Fame) B: 134
Brest [France] B: 593
Brest-Litovsk, Treaty of [1918]
Lenin, V. I. (Lenin the dictator) L: 194
Russian Revolution of 1917 (The October Revolution) R: 566
Union of Soviet Socialist Republics (The October Revolution) U: 35
World War I (The Russian Revolution) W: 461-462
Brethren [religious group] B: 593
Moravian Church M: 801
Brethren, Church of the [religious group] B: 594

Brethren of Purity [group]
Encyclopedia (The first reference works) E: 268a
Brétigny, Treaty of [1360]
Hundred Years' War H: 437
Breton [language]
Brittany (Culture) B: 633
Breton, André [French poet] B: 594
French literature (Surrealism) F: 522-523
Painting (Surrealism) P: 81; (Europeans in America) P: 84
Surrealism So: 1010
Breton, Jules Adolphe [French painter] B: 594 *with picture*
Bretón de los Herreros, Manuel [Spanish author]
Spanish literature (The 1800's) So: 761
Bretons [people]
Brittany B: 633
Brett, George [American baseball player]
Baseball (table: Hall of Fame) B: 134
Brett, Jacob [British engineer]
Cable (Telegraph cables) C: 5
Brett, John [British engineer]
Cable (Telegraph cables) C: 5
Bretton Woods [conference] B: 594
Morgenthau, Henry, Jr. M: 805
New Hampshire (The mid-1900's) N: 226-227
Breuckelen [former spelling]
Brooklyn B: 640
Breuer, Marcel Lajos [Hungarian architect] B: 594
Furniture (The Bauhaus) F: 582-583 *with picture*; (Recent developments) F: 584
Meier, Richard M: 384
Brevet [rank]
Rank, Military R: 139
Brewer, Albert P. [American political leader]
Alabama (table) A: 274
Brewer, David J. [American jurist]
Supreme Court of the United States (table) So: 1000
Brewer, Earl L. [American political leader]
Mississippi (table) M: 640
Brewer, Jan [American political leader]
Arizona (table) A: 687; (The early 2000's) A: 692
Brewers, Milwaukee [team] *See* Milwaukee Brewers *in this index*
Brewer's yeast
Yeast (How yeast is used) Y: 554-555
Brewery and Soft Drink Conference of the International Brotherhood of Teamsters
Labor movement L: 8
Brewery and Soft Drink Workers' Conference--U.S.A. and Canada [labor union]
Labor movement (table) L: 8
Brewing [industrial process] B: 595 *with pictures*
Africa *picture on* A: 127
Brewster, Benjamin H. [American government official]
Arthur, Chester Alan (table) A: 756
Justice, Department of (table) J: 203
Brewster, Sir David [Scottish physicist]
Kaleidoscope K: 211
Brewster, Harlan C. [Canadian political leader]
British Columbia (table) B: 628
Brewster, Ralph Owen [American political leader]
Maine (table) M: 87
Brewster, William [American colonial leader] B: 596
Pilgrims P: 462
Breyer, Stephen Gerald [American jurist] B: 596
Supreme Court of the United States *picture on* So: 999
Brezhnev, Leonid Ilyich [Soviet political leader] B: 596
Cold War (The Cold War in the 1970's) Ci: 770
Communism (Under Stalin's successors) Ci: 893
Kosygin, Aleksei Nikolaevich K: 385
Russia (The Cold War) R: 554 *with picture*
Union of Soviet Socialist Republics (History) U: 35-39 *with picture*
United States, History of the (The end of the Cold War) U: 196d
Brian [fictional character]
Paulsen, Gary P: 202
Brian Boru [Irish king] B: 596
Ireland (The Viking raiders) I: 425
Briand, Aristide [French statesman] B: 596
Kellogg-Briand Pact K: 256
Briard [dog] B: 597
Dog *picture on* D: 276
Briarwood [shrub]
Heath H: 156
Bribery [crime] B: 597
Extortion E: 457
Brice, Fanny [American actress] B: 597 *with portrait*
Brice, James [American political leader]
Maryland (table) M: 255
Brice's Cross Roads, Battle of [1864]

Forrest, Nathan Bedford **F:** 410
Brices Cross Roads National Battlefield Site [Mississippi]
    National Park System (table: National battlefields) **N:** 55
Brick B: 597 *with pictures*
    Adobe **A:** 59 *with picture*
    Ceramics (Kinds of ceramic products) **C:** 359
    House (Building materials) **H:** 380
Brick cutter
    Brick (Forming bricks) **B:** 597-598 *with picture*
Brick masonry
    Brick (Bricklaying) **B:** 598-599
Bricker, John William [American political leader] **B:** 599
    Eisenhower, Dwight David (Challenges from the Old Guard) **E:** 152
    Ohio (table) **O:** 699
Bricklayer [career]
    Building trade (Career opportunities) **B:** 686
Bricklayers and Allied Craftsmen, International Union of
    Labor movement (table) **L:** 8
Bricklayer's hammer
    Hammer *picture on* **H:** 34
Bricklaying
    Brick (Bricklaying) **B:** 598
Bricktown District [Oklahoma City]
    Oklahoma (Places to visit) **O:** 722
Brickwork
    Brick (Bricklaying) **B:** 598-599
Bridal veil
    Marriage (Wedding ceremonies) **M:** 220
Bridal wreath [shrub] **B:** 599
    Flower *picture on* **F:** 281
Bridalveil Fall [waterfall, Yosemite National Park] **B:** 599
    Waterfall (table: Famous waterfalls of North America) **W:** 142
    Yosemite National Park (Waterfalls) **Y:** 570
Bride
    Marriage (Wedding ceremonies) **M:** 220
Bride, Saint [Irish nun]
    Brigid, Saint **B:** 609
Bride of Lammermoor, The [book by Scott]
    Opera: *(Lucia di Lammermoor)* **O:** 804
Bride price
    Africa (Marriage and the family) **A:** 113
    Marriage (Other marriage laws and practices) **M:** 220-221
Brideshead Revisited [book by Waugh]
    Waugh, Evelyn **W:** 149
Bridesmaid
    Marriage (Wedding ceremonies) **M:** 220
Bridewealth [gift]
    Africa (Marriage and the family) **A:** 113
Bridge [engineering] **B:** 600 *with pictures*
    See also the list of Related articles in the Bridge [engineering] *article*
    Brooklyn Bridge *picture on* **B:** 640
    Minneapolis (Recent developments) **M:** 583
    Telford, Thomas **T:** 129
Bridge [game] **B:** 604 *with pictures*
Bridge [musical instrument]
    Guitar **G:** 435 *with diagram*
    Violin (Parts of the violin) **V:** 389 *with diagram*
Bridge [platform]
    Ship **S:** 405 *with diagram;* (Basic structure) **S:** 403-404
Bridge [zoology]
    Turtle (Shell) **T:** 521
Bridge, Dental
    Dentistry **D:** 143
    Teeth (Dental decay) **T:** 82-84
Bridge, The [art] *See* Brücke, Die *in this index*
Bridge, The [poem by Crane]
    Crane, Hart **Ci:** 1120
Bridge clothing
    Clothing (Marketing categories of fashion) **Ci:** 705
Bridge dialect
    Pidgin English **P:** 452
Bridge grafting [horticulture]
    Grafting (Other kinds of grafting) **G:** 299
Bridge of San Luis Rey, The [book by Wilder]
    Wilder, Thornton **W:** 303
Bridge of Sighs [Venice, Italy] **B:** 606 *with picture*
Bridge of the Americas [Panama Canal]
    Pan American Highway (Development) **P:** 114
    Panama *picture on* **P:** 115
    Panama Canal *map on* **P:** 123
Bridge on the River Kwai, The [film]
    Lean, David **L:** 162
    Motion picture (Best picture: 1957) **M:** 861
Bridge, Structural, Ornamental, and Reinforcing Iron Workers, International Association of
    Labor movement (table) **L:** 8

Bridge to Terabithia [book by Paterson]
    Paterson, Katherine **P:** 195
Bridgeport [Connecticut] **B:** 606 *with picture*
    Connecticut: table: Average monthly weather **Ci:** 964
Bridgeport [neighborhood]
    Chicago (The South Side) **C:** 424-425
Bridger, Jim [American frontiersman] **B:** 606 *with portrait*
    Bannock Indians **B:** 98
    Glass, Hugh **G:** 224
    Salt Lake City (History) **S:** 76a
    Utah (Early exploration) **U:** 246
    Wyoming (Exploration) **W:** 533
Bridger Mountains
    Montana (Land regions) **M:** 752
Bridges, Alfred Renton
    Bridges, Harry **B:** 607
Bridges, Calvin B. [American biologist]
    Heredity (The birth of genetics) **H:** 208
Bridges, Harry [American labor leader] **B:** 607
Bridges, Jeff [American actor]
    Motion picture (Best performance by an actor: 2009) **M:** 862a
Bridges, Robert Seymour [British poet]
    Poet laureate (table: Poets laureate of the United Kingdom) **P:** 590
Bridges, Ruby [American civil rights leader] **B:** 607
    Segregation *picture on* **S:** 284
Bridges, Styles [American political leader]
    New Hampshire (table) **N:** 223
Bridget, Saint [Swedish saint]
    Bridget, Saint **B:** 607
Bridgetown [Barbados] **B:** 607
    Barbados **B:** 103 *with picture*
    West Indies *picture on* **W:** 202
Bridging [scouting]
    Girl Scouts (Girl Scouts of the USA) **G:** 196
Bridgman, Laura Dewey [American public figure] **B:** 607
Bridgman, Percy Williams [American physicist]
    Nobel Prizes (Physics: 1946) **N:** 440
Bridle [kite]
    Kite (How kites fly) **K:** 339 *with diagram*
Bridle [riding equipment]
    Harness **H:** 63 *with diagram*
    Horse (table: Riding equipment) **H:** 351; (The bridle) **H:** 352 *with pictures*
Bridled titmouse [bird]
    Titmouse **T:** 302
Brie [cheese]
    Cheese (Soft cheese) **C:** 392 *with picture*
Brief [law] **B:** 608
    Trial (The criminal defendant's rights) **T:** 436-437
Brief History of Time, A [book by Hawking]
    Hawking, Stephen William **H:** 113
Brief Lives [book by Aubrey]
    Biography (The 1600's) **B:** 313
Brief Moment [play by Behrman]
    Behrman, S. N. **B:** 222
Briefing room
    Airport (The passenger terminal) **A:** 244
Brier [plant] **B:** 608 *with picture*
    Pipe **P:** 489 *with picture*
Brieux, Eugène [French dramatist] **B:** 608
    French literature (Realism) **F:** 522
Brig [prison]
    Brig **B:** 608
Brig [ship] **B:** 608 *with picture*
Brigade [firefighting]
    Fire department (Firefighting) **F:** 123
Brigade [military] **B:** 608
Brigade 2506 [Cuban history]
    Bay of Pigs invasion **B:** 176
Brigadier general
    General **G:** 82
    Rank, Military (table) **R:** 140
Briggs, Ansel [American political leader]
    Iowa (table) **I:** 391; (Statehood) **I:** 395
Briggs, Frank A. [American political leader]
    North Dakota (table) **N:** 513
Briggs, George N. [American political leader]
    Massachusetts (table) **M:** 288
Briggs, Henry [English mathematician]
    Logarithms (History) **L:** 424
Briggs-Vlacq tables [mathematics]
    Logarithms (History) **L:** 424
Brigham, Paul [American political leader]
    Vermont (table) **V:** 333
Brigham City [Utah] **B:** 608
Brigham Young University B: 608
    Mormons (Church organization) **M:** 807-808
    Provo **P:** 840 *with picture*
Bright, Richard [British doctor] **B:** 609
Bright tobacco
    Tobacco (Flue-cured tobacco) **T:** 306
Brightness
    Color (Lightness) **Ci:** 824

Light (Energy and brightness) **L:** 290 *with diagram*
Light meter **L:** 293
Brightness measurement *See* Magnitude *in this index*
Brighton-Allston [district, Boston]
    Boston (Brighton-Allston) **B:** 500
Brighton and Hove [England] **B:** 609
Bright's disease
    Bright, Richard **B:** 609
    Kidney (Kidney diseases) **K:** 312
    Nephritis **N:** 127
Brigid, Saint [Irish saint] **B:** 609
Brigitta, Saint [Swedish saint]
    Bridget, Saint **B:** 607
Brill-Zinsser disease
    Typhus (Epidemic typhus) **T:** 540
Brilliance [physical property]
    Gem (Index of refraction) **G:** 77; (Value of gems) **G:** 79
BRIMC nations [economics]
    Developing country **D:** 173
    Third World (The economic Third World) **T:** 258-259
Brimstone missile
    Guided missile (Air-to-surface missiles) **G:** 426
Brin, Sergey [Russian-American businessman]
    Google Inc. **G:** 270
Brine [salt water]
    See also Seawater *in this index*
    Mining (Pumping methods) **M:** 577
    Olive (Harvesting and preparation for market) **O:** 743
    Salt **S:** 72
Brine shrimp
    Crustacean *picture on* **Ci:** 1164
Brinegar, Claude S. [American government official]
    Ford, Gerald Rudolph (table) **F:** 378
    Transportation, Department of (table) **T:** 400
Bringing Them Home [report]
    Stolen Generation **So:** 907
Bringing Up Baby [film]
    Motion picture (Movies in the 1930's) **M:** 867-868 *with picture*
Brink, Carol Ryrie [American author] **B:** 609
    Newbery Medal (table) **N:** 359
Briosco, Andrea [Italian sculptor]
    Sculpture (Early Renaissance) **S:** 252
Brisbane [Australia] **B:** 609 *with picture*
Brisbane, Arthur [American editor] **B:** 610
Brisbane, Sir Thomas [Australian political leader]
    Brisbane **B:** 610
Briscoe, Dolph [American political leader]
    Texas (table) **T:** 203
Brisingr [book by Paolini]
    Paolini, Christopher **P:** 132
Brisket
    Meat *picture on* **M:** 349
Brissot de Warville, Jacques-Pierre [French political leader]
    Girondists **G:** 201
Bristle [hair] **B:** 610
    Hair **H:** 9
Bristlecone pine [tree] **B:** 610 *with pictures*
    California (Natural resources) **C:** 54
    Pine *picture on* **P:** 470; (Western pines) **P:** 469
    Plant *picture on* **P:** 524; (Interesting facts about plants) **P:** 519 *with picture*
    Wildlife conservation (Lower-risk species) **W:** 304
Bristlemouth [fish]
    Fish *picture on* **F:** 156; (Saltwater environments) **F:** 150
Bristol [England] **B:** 610
Bristol board
    Cardboard **C:** 209
Bristol Channel [England-Wales] **B:** 611
Bristow, Benjamin Helm [American government official]
    Grant, Ulysses S. (Government frauds) **G:** 317
    Treasury, Department of the (table) **T:** 407
    Whiskey Ring **W:** 282
Britain *See* United Kingdom *in this index*
Britain, Battle of [1940]
    Air force (World War II) **A:** 185
    Churchill, Sir Winston Leonard Spencer (The Battle of Britain) **C:** 548 *with picture*
    World War II (The Battle of Britain) **W:** 476
Britannia [English history]
    England (The Roman conquest) **E:** 303
Britannia [ship]
    Nova Scotia (Interesting facts) **N:** 555 *with picture*
Britannia metal [metal] **B:** 611
    Pewter **P:** 352
British America B: 611
British and Foreign Unitarian Association
    Unitarians (History) **U:** 42

British Antarctic Territory [region, Antarctica]
Falkland Islands F: 15
British Art Center [Yale University]
Architecture picture on A: 633
British Association for the Advancement of Science
Metric system (Evolution of the metric system) M: 441
British Boxing Board of Control [organization]
Boxing (Professional boxing) B: 531
British Broadcasting Corporation B: 611 with picture
Baird, John Logie B: 31
Communication picture on Ci: 885
London (Communication) L: 438
Radio (Government regulation of radio) R: 90-91
United Kingdom (Communication) U: 66
World War II (Propaganda) W: 494-495
British Cameroons [former colony] B: 611
Cameroon (History) C: 86
British Civil Service Department
Civil service (Civil service in other lands) Ci: 613
British Columbia B: 612 with pictures and maps
See also the list of Related articles in the British Columbia article
Canada (British Columbia) C: 104
Canada, Government of picture on C: 131
Mackenzie, Alexander (The Pacific Railway dispute) M: 22
Queen Charlotte Islands Q: 39
British Columbia, University of B: 631
British Columbia Liberal Party
British Columbia (Politics) B: 628
British Columbia Lions [team]
Football (Canadian Football League) F: 364
Vancouver (Sports) V: 276
British Columbia Railway Company
British Columbia (The mid-1900's) B: 630
British Commonwealth of Nations See Commonwealth of Nations in this index
British Commonwealth Trans-Antarctic Expedition [1957-1958]
Fuchs, Sir Vivian Ernest F: 549
British Deaf Association
Deafness (Education) D: 59
British East Africa [former name]
Kenya (British rule) K: 303
British East India Company [European history]
Bangladesh (The East India Company) B: 85
East India Company E: 40
India (The rise of the East India Company) I: 130
Indonesia (The coming of the Europeans) I: 237
Kolkata (History) K: 363
Raffles, Sir Stamford R: 101
Singapore (History) S: 471
Straits Settlements So: 918
United States, History of the (Renewed conflict) U: 158
British Empire
See also Commonwealth of Nations in this index
United Kingdom (History) U: 67; (Decline of the empire) U: 71 with map
Kipling, Rudyard K: 333
Rhodes, Cecil John R: 317
Victoria (Events of her reign) V: 355 with map
British Empire, Order of the [title]
Knighthood, Orders of (Honorary orders) K: 347
British Guiana [former name]
Guyana G: 445; (History) G: 446
British Honduras [former name] See Belize in this index
British India [history of India]
Bangladesh (British India) B: 85
India map on I: 132; (British India) I: 130; (Rise of Indian nationalism) I: 131
Muslim League M: 964
Pakistan (Colonialism) P: 99
British Indian Ocean Territory [colony] B: 632
British invasion [music]
Rock music (The British invasion) R: 379
British-Irish Council B: 632
Northern Ireland (Government) N: 521-522
United Kingdom (Regional government) U: 50
British Isles B: 632
United Kingdom (The land) U: 58 with map
British Library [London] B: 632
Library picture on L: 235
London (Museums and libraries) L: 434
British Medical Association
Medicine (Medical organizations) M: 370
British Museum [London] B: 632
Architecture (The Greek Revival) A: 625-626
London picture on L: 433; (Museums and libraries) L: 434
Museum (Museums of the 1700's) M: 939
British North America Act [1867] B: 632
Canada, Government of (The constitution) C: 129

Canada, History of (Confederation) C: 144; (Constitutional changes) C: 151
Confederation of Canada (Approval of confederation) Ci: 934-935
Education (Development of Canadian education) E: 102
Famous Five F: 26b
Law (The development of Canadian law) L: 136
Macdonald, Sir John Alexander (Forming the Dominion) M: 7
Ontario (Confederation) O: 786
Privy Council P: 808b
Quebec (Early years as a province) Q: 30
School (The development of Canadian schools) S: 184
British Open [tournament]
Golf (British Open) G: 264
British Overseas Airways Corporation
Aviation (A new age of flight) A: 990
British Petroleum Company See BP in this index
British Raj [government] See British India in this index
British shorthair
Cat (Short-haired breeds) C: 290
British Sign Language
Deafness (Special language techniques) D: 58
British Somaliland [Somali history]
Somalia (History) So: 589
Somaliland So: 590
British South Africa Company
Rhodes, Cecil John (Gains Rhodesia) R: 317
Zambia (History) Z: 585
British thermal unit [measurement] B: 632
Air conditioning (Capacity of air conditioners) A: 179-180
Calorie C: 70
Coal (How composition affects value) Ci: 717
Heat (Temperature and heat) H: 150
British Togoland [former colony]
Togo (History) T: 310-311
British Virgin Islands See Virgin Islands, British in this index
British West Indies [islands, Atlantic] B: 633
Britons [people]
England (The Germanic invasions) E: 304
Brittany [region, France] B: 633 with picture and map
France (The land) F: 464 with picture and map
Brittany [dog] B: 633 with picture
Brittany spaniel See Brittany in this index
Britten, Benjamin [British composer] B: 634
Brittle star [sea animal] B: 634 with picture
Deep sea picture on D: 82
Brittlebush [plant]
Flower (Flowers of the desert) F: 290 with picture
Plant picture on P: 526
Brixham [England]
United Kingdom picture on U: 61
Brno [Czech Republic] B: 634
Broaching [industrial process]
Machine tool (Planing, shaping, and broaching) M: 18 with picture
Broad and Alien Is the World [book by Alegría]
Latin American literature (The mid-1900's) L: 114
Broad axe [weapon]
Vikings (Weapons and armor) V: 382
Broad bean [plant] B: 634
Vetch V: 343
Broad-Breasted White [turkey]
Turkey (Domestic turkeys) T: 513
Broad jump [sport]
Track and field (Jumping events) T: 357 with picture
Broad-leaved India rubber plant
Gardening picture on G: 37
Broad-spectrum antibiotic
Antibiotic (Antibacterial antibiotics) A: 550
Broad spectrum penicillin [drug]
Penicillin (Forms of penicillin) P: 240
Broad-winged hawk [bird]
Buzzard B: 745
Broadband communications B: 634
Computer (Internet service providers) Ci: 921
Internet (Hardware) I: 350c
Telephone (VoIP phone calls) T: 97; (Improvements in telephone technology) T: 100-101
Broadbent, Jim [British actor]
Motion picture (Best performance by an actor in a supporting role: 2001) M: 862b
Broadbill [bird]
Bird picture on B: 344g
Broadcast band [electronics]
Radio (How radio programs are received) R: 88
Television (Broadcasting) T: 123
Broadcast frequency
Radio (From electric waves to radio waves) R: 86

with diagram
Broadcast meteorologist
Weather (Careers in weather) W: 170
Broadcasting
Frequency modulation F: 528
Radio (Broadcasting) R: 83 with picture; (How radio programs are broadcast) R: 86 with diagrams; (History) R: 91
Television T: 110; (Broadcasting) T: 123
Broadcasting, Bureau of See International Broadcasting Bureau in this index
Broadcasting Board of Governors
Voice of America V: 437
Broadcloth [fabric] B: 635
Broadleaf tree
Flower (Flowers of woodlands and forests) F: 284 with pictures
Leaf L: 151 with pictures
Plant (Temperate deciduous forests) P: 523
Tree pictures on T: 413, T: 420; (Broadleaf trees) T: 414; (Trees around the world) T: 428; (Broadleaf forests) T: 428 with picture
Broadloom carpet
Rugs and carpets R: 513
Broadside [music]
Popular music (Popular music before recording) P: 669
Broadtail [fur]
Karakul K: 245
Broadway [New York City] B: 635
New York City (Manhattan) N: 323-324; (The arts) N: 336
Theater (The producer) T: 235; (New York City) T: 244 with picture
Broadway Melody, The [film]
Motion picture (Best picture: 1928-29) M: 861
Broadwood, John [British businessman]
Piano (History) P: 447-448
Brobdingnag [fictional place]
Gulliver's Travels G: 440
Swift, Jonathan: (Gulliver's Travels) So: 1040
Broca, Pierre Paul [French surgeon]
Brain (Language) B: 556
Brocade [fabric]
Textile (table: Textile terms) T: 213
Broca's area [anatomy]
Brain (Language) B: 556
Broccoli [plant] B: 635 with picture
Evolution (Artificial selection) E: 432 with picture
Vegetable (Flower buds) V: 292 with picture
Brock, Sir Isaac [British general] B: 635
War of 1812 (Land campaign of 1812) W: 31; (Queenston Heights) W: 33
Brock, Lou [American baseball player]
Baseball (table: Hall of Fame) B: 134; (Recent developments) B: 137
Brock, William E., III [American government official]
Labor, Department of (table) L: 2
Brocket deer
Deer (table) D: 85 with picture; (Central and South American deer) D: 85-86
Brockhaus, Friedrich Arnold [German publisher]
Encyclopedia (Encyclopedias of the 1800's and 1900's) E: 268b
Brockhouse, Bertram Neville [Canadian physicist]
Nobel Prizes (Physics: 1994) N: 442
Brod, Max [Hungarian author]
Kafka, Franz K: 209
Brodsky, Joseph [Soviet-born poet] B: 636
Nobel Prizes (Literature: 1987) N: 448
Poet laureate (table: Poets laureate of the United States) P: 590
Brody, Adrien [American actor]
Motion picture (Best performance by an actor: 2002) M: 862a
Brog, Ehud [Israeli political leader] See Barak, Ehud in this index
Brogden, C. H. [American political leader]
North Carolina (table) N: 490
Broglie, Louis Victor de [French physicist] See De Broglie, Louis Victor in this index
Brogue [language]
Ireland (Language) I: 418
Brogue [shoe]
Tartan T: 47
Broiler [food]
Chicken (Producing meat) C: 445 with pictures
Poultry (Raising poultry) P: 720
Broiling
Cooking (Grilling and broiling) Ci: 1028
Broken Blossoms [film]
Griffith, D. W. G: 393
Broken grades
Tea (Grades of tea) T: 63
Broken Heart, The [play by Ford]
Ford, John F: 381

Broken Top [mountain, Oregon]
National forest *picture on* N: 35
Broken wind [disease]
Heaves H: 161
Broker [commerce]
Bank *picture on* B: 94
Commodity exchange Ci: 873
Cotton (Selling) Ci: 1091
Insurance (How insurance is sold) I: 315
Investment (How investors buy stocks) I: 369
Real estate R: 171
Stock exchange So: 903
Brokerage company
Stock exchange (Trading) So: 904
Brokerage house
Stock exchange (Trading) So: 904
Brolga [bird]
Bird (Birds of Australia and New Zealand) B: 346
with picture
Brome [grass]
Grass *picture on* G: 325
Bromeliad [plant] B: 636
Bromfield, Louis [American author] B: 636
Bromide [chemistry]
Anticonvulsant A: 553
Bromine [element] B: 636
Element, Chemical (Names and symbols of elements) E: 219
Halogen H: 26
Bronc *See* Bronco *in this index*
Bronc riding
Rodeo R: 397
Bronchial circulation [physiology]
Lung (Parts of the lungs) L: 523
Bronchial pneumonia [disorder]
Pneumonia (How pneumonia develops) P: 586
Bronchial tube [anatomy]
Bronchitis B: 636
Lung *diagram on* L: 524; (Parts of the lungs) L: 523
Bronchiole [anatomy]
Bronchodilator B: 637
Emphysema *diagram on* E: 262
Human body (The air passages) H: 420-421
Lung *diagram on* L: 524; (Parts of the lungs) L: 523
Bronchitis [disease] B: 636
Bronchodilator B: 637
Chronic obstructive pulmonary disease C: 539
Emphysema E: 262
Poultry (Raising poultry) P: 720-721
Bronchodilator [drug] B: 637
Asthma (Treatment) A: 825
Bronchoscope [instrument] B: 637
Lung cancer L: 525
Surgery (Instruments) So: 1005
Bronchus [anatomy]
Asthma A: 824b
Cancer *diagram on* C: 168
Disease (Natural barriers) D: 231
Human body (table) H: 422 *with diagram*
Lung (Parts of the lungs) L: 523
Lung cancer L: 525
Bronck, Jonas [New York settler]
New York City (Settlement) N: 341
Bronco [animal] B: 637
Cowboy (His horse) Ci: 1109
Horse (table: Horse terms) H: 343
Bronco Buster [sculpture by Remington]
Remington, Frederic *picture on* R: 230
Broncos, Denver [team] *See* Denver Broncos *in this index*
Bronfenbrenner, Urie [American psychologist]
Child (The influence of the child's environment) C: 452
Bronstein, Lev Davidovich [birth name of]
Trotsky, Leon T: 452
Brontë, Anne [British author]
Brontë sisters B: 637
Brontë, Charlotte [British author]
Brontë sisters B: 637
English literature (Early Victorian literature) E: 321
Novel (Britain) N: 573
Brontë, Emily [British author]
Brontë sisters B: 637
English literature (Early Victorian literature) E: 321
Novel (Britain) N: 573
Brontë, Patrick [father of]
Brontë sisters (Their lives) B: 637
Brontë sisters [British authors] B: 637
Brontes [legendary figure]
Cyclops Ci: 1204
Brontosaurus [dinosaur] *See* Apatosaurus *in this index*
Bronx [borough, New York City]
New York City (The city) N: 323; (The Bronx) N: 328 *with picture*

Bronx Zoo
New York City (The Bronx) N: 328; (Parks) N: 338
Bronze [metal] B: 637 *with pictures*
Alloy (The first alloys) A: 377
Bronze Age B: 638
China (Bronze and jade) C: 488 *with pictures*
Copper (Early civilizations) Ci: 1044
Bronze Age [anthropology] B: 638
Aegean civilization A: 82
Bronze (History) B: 638
Iron Age I: 435
Prehistoric people (The end of prehistoric times) P: 753-754a
Tool (History of tools) T: 330
Bronze Bow, The [book by Speare]
Speare, Elizabeth George So: 768
"Bronze Horseman, The" [poem by Pushkin]
Russian literature (Early Romanticism) R: 560-561
Bronze Star Medal
Medals, decorations, and orders (table) M: 357
Bronze turkey
Turkey (Domestic turkeys) T: 513 *with picture*
Bronzeville [former district, Chicago]
Illinois (The early 1900's) I: 75
Brooch
Pin P: 466 *with pictures*
Brood [biology]
Duck (Ducklings) D: 375 *with picture*
Brood ball [entomology]
Dung beetle D: 385 *with picture*
Brood nest [entomology]
Bee (The honey bee colony) B: 201
Brood parasite [bird]
Bird (Brood parasites) B: 359
Brooder
Chicken *picture on* C: 444
Brook
River *diagram on* R: 353; (Tributaries) R: 351-352
Brook Farm [commune] B: 639
Hawthorne, Nathaniel (Life) H: 114
Brook lamprey [animal]
Lamprey (Body) L: 54 *with picture*
Brook stickleback [fish]
Stickleback So: 899
Brook trout [fish]
Fish *picture on* F: 159
Trout (Other trout) T: 454
Brooke, Alan Francis [British general] *See* Alanbrooke, Lord *in this index*
Brooke, Edward William [American political leader] B: 639
Brooke, Frances [Canadian author] B: 639
Canadian literature (Early English-Canadian literature) C: 157
Brooke, Sir James [rajah of Sarawak]
Borneo (History) B: 490
Malaysia (Coming of the Europeans) M: 101
Brooke, John [husband of]
Brooke, Frances B: 639
Brooke, Leonard Leslie [British painter] B: 639
Brooke, Robert [American political leader]
Virginia (table) V: 417
Brooke, Rupert [British poet] B: 639
English literature (Literature before World War I) E: 322
Brookfield [Vermont]
Vermont (Libraries) V: 322
Brookfield Zoo
Chicago (Places to visit) C: 430
Illinois (Places to visit) I: 62 *with picture*
Brookgreen Gardens [Georgetown]
South Carolina (Places to visit) So: 650
Brookhaven National Laboratory [Long Island] B: 639
Brookings, Robert S. [American businessman]
Brookings Institution B: 640
Brookings Institution [Washington, D.C.] B: 640
Brookley Industrial Complex [Mobile]
Mobile (History) M: 681-682
Brooklyn [borough, New York City] B: 640 *with picture*
New York City (The city) N: 323; (Brooklyn) N: 326 *with picture*
Brooklyn [bowling]
Bowling (table) B: 521
Brooklyn Bridge [New York City] B: 640 *with picture*
Arthur, Chester Alan *picture on* A: 755
Bridge (Suspension) B: 603
New York City (Brooklyn) N: 326
Brooklyn Dodgers [team]
Brooklyn B: 640
Robinson, Jackie R: 368
Brooklyn Heights [district]
New York City (Brooklyn) N: 326-328
Brooks, Bryant B. [American political leader]
Wyoming (table) W: 532
Brooks, Garth [American singer] B: 641

Country music *picture on* Ci: 1098; (Modern country music) Ci: 1098c
Brooks, Gwendolyn [American poet] B: 641
African American literature (The 1900's) A: 136a
American literature (The African American experience) A: 424 *with portrait*
Brooks, James [American political leader]
Credit Mobilier of America Ci: 1125
Brooks, James L. [American director]
Motion picture (Best achievement in directing: 1983) M: 862
Brooks, John [American political leader]
Massachusetts (table) M: 288
Brooks, Joseph [American political leader]
Arkansas (Reconstruction) A: 714
Brooks, Mark [American golfer]
Golf (U.S. PGA Championship) G: 265
Brooks, Preston Smith [American political leader]
Civil War, American (The Kansas-Nebraska Act) Ci: 616
Sumner, Charles So: 973
Brooks, Ralph G. [American political leader]
Nebraska (table) N: 110
Brooks, Van Wyck [American author] B: 641
Brooks Range [mountains, Alaska]
Alaska (The Rocky Mountain System) A: 294
Rocky Mountains (Chief ranges of the Rockies) R: 394
Broom [shrub] B: 641
Broom [tool]
Curling (The rink) Ci: 1196 *with diagrams*
Broom, Jacob [American political leader] B: 641
Broom, Robert [Scottish-born paleontologist] B: 641
Broomcorn [plant]
Sorghum (Broomcorn) So: 596
Broome, James E. [American political leader]
Florida (table) F: 260
Brossard, Nicole [Canadian poet]
Canadian literature (Modern Canadian poets) C: 161
Broth [food]
Bread (How yeast bread is made) B: 588-589
Brothel
Prostitution P: 830
Brother-in-law
Family (Family relationships) F: 21
Brother Jonathan [U.S. history] B: 641
Connecticut (The Revolutionary War) Ci: 970
Brotherhood of ...
Brotherhoods appear under their key words, as in Locomotive Engineers, Brotherhood of
Brothers, The [play by Terence]
Terence T: 169
Brothers Karamazov, The [book by Dostoevsky]
Dostoevsky, Fyodor D: 311
Nihilism N: 421
Russian literature (The 1860's and 1870's) R: 562
Brothers of the Christian School, Institute of the [religious order]
Jean Baptiste de la Salle, Saint J: 75
Brotulid fish
Fish *picture on* F: 156
Brough, Charles Hillman [American political leader]
Arkansas (table) A: 712
Brough, John [American political leader]
Ohio (table) O: 699
Broughton, J. Melville [American political leader]
North Carolina (table) N: 490
Broughton, Jack [British boxer]
Boxing (The revival of boxing) B: 532
Broughton, William [English explorer]
Mount Hood M: 885
Oregon (Exploration and settlement) O: 846
Brout, Robert [Belgian physicist]
Higgs, Peter Ware H: 227
Brouthers, Dan [American baseball player]
Baseball (table: Hall of Fame) B: 134
Brouwer, Luitzen [Dutch mathematician]
Mathematics (Philosophies of mathematics) M: 307
Broward, Napoleon B. [American political leader]
Florida (table) F: 260
Brower, Edna May [wife of]
Diefenbaker, John George (Young lawyer) D: 197
Brown, A. R. Radcliffe-
Radcliffe-Brown, A. R. R: 73
Brown, Aaron V. [American government official]
Tennessee (table) T: 152
Brown, Albert G. [American political leader]
Mississippi (table) M: 640
Brown, Albert O. [American political leader]
New Hampshire (table) N: 223
Brown, Sir Arthur Whitten [British aviator]
Alcock and Brown A: 335
Brown, Benjamin Gratz [American political leader]

B: 642
Missouri (table) M: 668
Brown, Charles Brockden [American author]
B: 642
Novel (The United States) N: 573
Brown, Charlie [cartoon character]
Schulz, Charles Monroe S: 187 *with picture*
Brown, Claude [American author]
American literature (Works by minority writers)
A: 425
Brown, D. Russell [American political leader]
Rhode Island (table) R: 311
Brown, David M. [American astronaut]
Columbia disaster Ci: 852
Space exploration (The Columbia disaster)
So: 725
Brown, Denise Scott [American author]
Venturi, Robert V: 310
Brown, Edmund Gerald [American political leader]
California (table) C: 59
Nixon, Richard Milhous (Defeat in California)
N: 432
Brown, Edmund Gerald, Jr. [American political
leader]
California (table) C: 59; (The beginning of the
2000's) C: 64
Clinton, Bill (The Democratic nomination)
Ci: 682c
Brown, Ethan Allen [American political leader]
Ohio (table) O: 699
Brown, Father [literary figure]
Detective story (The pattern) D: 162
Brown, Frank [American political leader]
Maryland (table) M: 255
Brown, Fred H. [American political leader]
New Hampshire (table) N: 223
Brown, George [Canadian patriot] B: 642
Confederation of Canada (Moves toward
confederation) Ci: 933; (Fathers of
Confederation) Ci: 935 *with picture*
Macdonald, Sir John Alexander (Forming the
Dominion) M: 7
Macdonald, John Sandfield M: 10
Mackenzie, Alexander (Member of the Reformers)
M: 21
Brown, George S. [American military leader]
Joint Chiefs of Staff (table) J: 156
Brown, Gordon [British political leader] B: 642
with portrait
Brown, Gratz [American political leader] *See*
Brown, Benjamin Gratz *in this index*
Brown, H. Rap [American social reformer]
African Americans (Black militancy) A: 136q-136r
Student Nonviolent Coordinating Committee
So: 932
Brown, Henry B. [American jurist]
Supreme Court of the United States (table)
So: 1000
Brown, Herbert Charles [American chemist]
Nobel Prizes (Chemistry: 1979) N: 444
Brown, Jacob Jennings [American general]
War of 1812 (Campaigns of 1814) W: 31; (Lundy's
Lane) W: 32-33
Brown, James [American singer] B: 642
Rock music (Soul music) R: 380a
Brown, Jesse [American government official]
B: 643
Veterans Affairs, Department of (table) V: 343
Brown, Jim [American football player] B: 643
Payton, Walter P: 204
Brown, John [American social reformer] B: 643
with portrait
Abolition movement A: 13
African Americans (The deepening division over
slavery) A: 136h-136i
Civil War, American (Raid at Harpers Ferry) Ci: 616
Harpers Ferry H: 66b
Kansas *picture on* K: 236; ("Bleeding Kansas")
K: 235
Lee, Robert E. (Other duties) L: 178
Marine Corps, United States (The 1800's) M: 208-
209
United States, History of the (The "irrepressible
conflict") U: 176
West Virginia (The Civil war and statehood)
W: 226 *with picture*
Brown, John C. [American political leader]
Tennessee (table) T: 152
Brown, John W. [American political leader]
Ohio (table) O: 699
Brown, Joseph E. [American political leader]
Georgia (table) G: 130
Brown, Joseph M. [American political leader]
Georgia (table) G: 130
Brown, Joshuah Purdy [American performer]
Circus (The circus grows) Ci: 562b
Brown, Lee P. [American political leader]

Houston (Population growth) H: 398
Brown, Linda [American public figure]
African Americans (The civil rights movement)
A: 136o *with picture*
Brown v. Board of Education of Topeka B: 645
Brown, Marcia Joan [American artist] B: 643
Regina Medal (table: 1977) R: 206
Brown, Margaret Wise [American author] B: 643
Brown, Mather [American painter]
Adams, John *picture on* A: 36
Brown, Michael [American government official]
Hurricane Katrina (The aftermath) H: 456
Brown, Michael E. [American astronomer]
Astronomy (Finding new objects) A: 848
Eris E: 352
Planet (Haumea) P: 512
Brown, Michael Stuart [American physiologist]
Nobel Prizes (Physiology or medicine: 1985)
N: 446
Brown, Mordecai [American baseball player]
Baseball (table: Hall of Fame) B: 134
Brown, Moses [American businessman]
Rhode Island (Industrial expansion) R: 313
Brown, Mount [British publisher]
Stamp collecting (Origins) So: 829-830
Brown, Neill S. [American political leader]
Tennessee (table) T: 152
Brown, Oliver [American public figure]
Brown v. Board of Education of Topeka B: 645
Brown, Ray [American baseball player]
Baseball (table: Hall of Fame) B: 134
Brown, Robert [Scottish biologist] B: 644
Brown, Ronald Harmon [American government
official] B: 644
Brown, Roy [American singer]
Rock music (Musical roots) R: 376
Brown, Sterling A. [American author]
American literature (The Harlem Renaissance)
A: 422
Brown, Thomas [American political leader]
Florida (table) F: 260
Brown, Tim [American football player]
Football (table) F: 363
Brown, Walter F. [American government official]
Hoover, Herbert Clark (table) H: 330
Brown, Willard [American baseball player]
Baseball (table: Hall of Fame) B: 134
Brown, William [British sea captain]
Honolulu (History) H: 322
Brown, William Wells [American author]
African American literature (The 1800's) A: 136a
Brown, Willie [American political leader]
San Francisco (Recent developments) S: 99
Brown algae
Algae (Kinds of algae) A: 349
Seaweed (Kinds) S: 276 *with picture*
Brown and Sharpe gauge [measurement]
Wire (Sizes of wire) W: 344
Brown bat [animal]
Bat (Some kinds of bats) B: 161
Brown bear
Animal *picture on* A: 478
Bear *picture on* B: 183; (Brown bears) B: 184
Grizzly bear G: 397 *with picture*
Mammal *picture on* M: 124
Brown bullhead [fish]
Bullhead B: 697
Brown coal *See* Lignite *in this index*
Brown County craft shops [Indiana]
Indiana (Places to visit) I: 206
Brown creeper [bird]
Bird *picture on* B: 363
Creeper Ci: 1126
Brown dwarf [astronomy] B: 644 *with picture*
Planet (The first discoveries) P: 513-514
Brown fat [anatomy]
Warm-blooded animal W: 36
Brown-headed cowbird
Bird *picture on* B: 336; (Brood parasites) B: 359
Brown-headed nuthatch [bird]
Nuthatch N: 623
Brown hyena [animal]
Hyena H: 474
Brown lung [disease] B: 644
Dust (Influence on human health) D: 390
Brown mustard
Mustard M: 968
Brown pelican [bird]
Bird (Birds of the seacoasts) B: 342 *with picture*
Pelican (Kinds) P: 231 *with picture*
Brown rat [animal]
Rat R: 146
Brown recluse [spider] B: 645 *with picture*
Brown rice [food]
Rice (Food) R: 323
Brown rot [fungus]
Peach (Diseases) P: 211

Rot R: 485
Brown shirts [German history]
Hitler, Adolf (Birth of the Nazi Party) H: 265-266
Brown sugar
Sugar (Uses of sugar) So: 959-960
Brown Swiss [cattle]
Cattle (Brown Swiss) C: 311 *with picture*; (table)
C: 313
Dairying (Dairy cattle) D: 6
Brown thrasher [bird] B: 645
Bird *pictures on* B: 338, B: 358
Thrasher T: 268 *with picture*
Brown tree snake
Invasive species (How invasive species affect
habitats) I: 354j
Snake (Snakes as invasive species) S: 532
Brown trout [fish]
Trout *picture on* T: 453
Brown University B: 645
Rhode Island (Libraries) R: 300 *with picture*
**Brown v. Board of Education National Historic
Site** [Kansas]
National Park System (table: National historic
sites) N: 52
Brown v. Board of Education of Topeka [U.S.
history] B: 645
African Americans (The civil rights movement)
A: 136o
Education (The federal government and
education) E: 94; (School desegregation)
E: 104; (Education for whom?) E: 107
Fourteenth Amendment F: 438
Marshall, Thurgood M: 231
National Association for the Advancement of
Colored People N: 29
Supreme Court of the United States (table)
So: 1002
United States, Government of the (The Supreme
Court) U: 145
Brownback, Sam [American political leader]
Kansas (table) K: 234
Browne, Anthony [British author]
Literature for children *picture on* L: 354
Browne, Charles Farrar [American humorist]
Ward, Artemus W: 35
Browne, Hablot Knight [British artist]
Dickens, Charles *picture on* D: 189
Browne, Sir Thomas [English physician]
English literature (Prose writings) E: 317
Prose P: 828
Browne, Thomas Alexander [Australian author]
Australia (Literature) A: 904-905
Brownell, Herbert, Jr. [American government
official]
Eisenhower, Dwight David (table) E: 152
Justice, Department of (table) J: 203
Brownian motion [physics]
Brown, Robert B: 644
Einstein, Albert (Famous theories) E: 146-146a
Fractal F: 443
Ion (Behavior of ions) I: 371
Suspension So: 1012
Brownie [fairy]
Fairy F: 9
Brownies, Girl Scout
Girl Scouts (Girl Scouts of the USA) G: 196;
(Brownies) G: 198
Browning [cooking]
Cooking (Methods) Ci: 1029
Browning, Elizabeth Barrett [British poet] B: 646
with portrait
Browning, Robert (Browning's life) B: 646
Sonnet So: 593
Browning, Gordon [American political leader]
Tennessee (table) T: 152
Browning, John Moses [American inventor] B: 646
Handgun (Rapid-fire handguns) H: 45
Browning, Orville H. [American government
official]
Interior, Department of the (table) I: 325
Browning, Robert [British poet] B: 646
Browning, Elizabeth Barrett B: 646
English literature (Later Victorian literature)
E: 321
Pied Piper of Hamelin P: 453
Browning automatic [gun]
Handgun (Rapid-fire handguns) H: 45
Brownlee, John E. [Canadian political leader]
Alberta (table) A: 328
Brownlow, William G. [American political leader]
Tennessee (table) T: 152
Brownout [electricity]
Electric power (Providing reliable service) E: 185
Brownrigg, William [English physician]
Platinum (History) P: 567
Browns, Cleveland
Football (National Football League) F: 364

Brownson, Nathan [American political leader]
Georgia (table) G: 130
Brownstone [rock]
Sandstone S: 110
Brownsville [district]
New York City (Brooklyn) N: 326-328
Brownsville [Texas]
Rio Grande (Lower course) R: 347
Browntail moth [insect] B: 647
Tussock moth T: 526
Browridge [anatomy]
Gorilla *diagram on* G: 276
Prehistoric people (The first human beings)
P: 746 *with picture;* (The multiple origins
theory) P: 749-750
Browser [computing] *See* Web browser *in this index*
Broz, Josip [Yugoslav political leader] *See* Tito,
Josip Broz *in this index*
Brubeck, Dave [American musician] B: 647
Jazz *picture on* J: 73
Bruce, Ailsa Mellon [American philanthropist]
Mellon Foundation M: 389
Bruce, Blanche Kelso [American political leader]
B: 647 *with portrait*
Bruce, Sir David [British doctor] B: 647
Bruce, James [British statesman] *See* Elgin, Earl of
in this index
Bruce, James [Scottish explorer] B: 647
Exploration (The exploration of Africa) E: 448
with map
Bruce, Robert [king of Scotland] B: 648
Bannockburn, Battle of B: 99
Edward I E: 112
Scotland *picture on* S: 220; (Fight for
independence) S: 219
Bruce, Stanley [Australian political leader]
Australia (table) A: 923
Bruce Peninsula National Park [Ontario]
Canada (table: National parks and national park
reserves) C: 113
Brucella [bacteria]
Brucellosis B: 648
Brucellosis [disease] B: 648
Bruce, Sir David B: 647
Cattle (Diseases) C: 313
Veterinary medicine V: 345
Bruch, Max [German composer] B: 648
Bruchac, Joseph [American author]
Literature for children *picture on* L: 360
Brücke, Die [art]
Expressionism (Expressionist painting) E: 455
Painting (Expressionism) P: 78
Brucker, Wilber M. [American political leader]
Michigan (table) M: 507
Bruckner, Anton [Austrian composer] B: 648
Bruderhof [sociology]
Hutterites H: 459
Bruegel, Jan, the Elder [Flemish painter]
Bruegel, Pieter, the Elder B: 649
Bruegel, Pieter, the Elder [Flemish painter] B: 648
with picture
Painting (The northern Renaissance) P: 57 *with
picture*
Tower of Babel *picture on* T: 351
Bruegel, Pieter, the Younger [Flemish painter]
Bruegel, Pieter, the Elder B: 649
Bruges [Belgium] B: 649
City *picture on* Ci: 583
Bruhn, Erik [Danish dancer] B: 649
Ballet (Ballet in Canada) B: 54
Bruin [animal]
Bear (Brown bears) B: 184
Bruins, Boston [team] *See* Boston Bruins *in this
index*
Bruise [injury] B: 650
Arnica A: 741
Brulé, Étienne [French explorer] B: 650
Michigan (French exploration and settlement)
M: 508
Ontario (European exploration) O: 784
Brumbaugh, Martin Grove [American political
leader]
Pennsylvania (table) P: 263
Brumidi, Constantino [Italian artist]
Capitol, United States C: 197
Brummell, Beau *See* Brummell, George Bryan *in
this index*
Brummell, George Bryan [British public figure]
B: 650
Clothing (The 1800's) Ci: 704-705
Brundtland, Gro Harlem [Norwegian political
leader]
Norway (Political changes) N: 547
Bruneau River
Nevada (Rivers and lakes) N: 166 *with map*
Brunei B: 650 *with picture and map*
Borneo B: 489 *with map*

Flag *picture on* F: 202
Brunel, Isambard Kingdom [English engineer]
B: 651
Ship (Ships of iron) S: 424-425
Brunelleschi, Filippo [Italian architect] B: 651 *with
picture*
Architecture (Early Renaissance architecture)
A: 620 *with picture*
Italy (Architecture) I: 504
Perspective P: 305
Renaissance *picture on* R: 235; (Arts of the 1300's
and early 1400's) R: 236
Brunet, Michel [French anthropologist]
Prehistoric people (table) P: 754
Brunhild [legendary figure] B: 652
Nibelungenlied N: 395
Brünn [Czech Republic] *See* Brno *in this index*
Brünnhilde [literary figure]
Brunhild B: 652
Bruno, Giordano [Renaissance philosopher] B: 652
Bruno of Cologne, Saint [German religious leader]
Carthusians C: 261
Brunsdale, C. Norman [American political leader]
North Dakota (table) N: 513
Brunswick [German history] B: 652
Brunswick B: 652
Brunswick-Lüneburg [German history]
Brunswick B: 652
Brunswick-Wolfenbüttel [German history]
Brunswick B: 652
Bruny Island [Australia]
Tasmania (Land and climate) T: 48
Brush [electrical device]
Electric motor (The commutator) E: 180 *with
diagram*
Brush [tool] B: 652
See also Paint brush *in this index*
Teasel T: 73
Brush company
Fire department (Additional operations) F: 124
Brush foot [entomology]
Butterfly (Brush-footed butterflies) B: 736
Insect (Legs) *picture on* I: 287
Brush-footed butterfly
Butterfly *pictures on* B: 735; (Brush-footed
butterflies) B: 736
Brush-tailed possum
Possum P: 698
Brush wolf
Coyote Ci: 1114 *with picture*
Brusilov, Alexei [Russian general]
World War I (Eastern Europe) W: 459-460
Brussels [Belgium] B: 652 *with picture*
Belgium B: 226 *with picture, picture on* B: 229;
(Regions and language communities) B: 227
with picture
Brussels griffon [dog] B: 653
Dog *picture on* D: 274
Brussels lace [fabric]
Lace *picture on* L: 21
Brussels Satellite Convention [1985]
Copyright (International agreements) Ci: 1048
Brussels sprouts [plant] B: 653
Evolution (Artificial selection) E: 432
Brut [legendary figure] B: 654
Brut [wine]
Champagne C: 373
Brut, The [poem by Layamon]
Round Table (Origin) R: 491
Brutalists [architecture]
Architecture (Architecture today) A: 632
Brute-force attack [cryptology]
Codes and ciphers (Unbreakable ciphers) Ci: 751
Bruton, John [Irish political leader]
Ireland (table) I: 428
Bruton Parish Church [Williamsburg]
Virginia (Places to visit) V: 408
Brutus [book by Cicero]
Cicero, Marcus Tullius (His works) Ci: 552
Brutus [literary figure]
Shakespeare, William: (*Julius Caesar*) S: 360
Brutus, Marcus Junius [Roman general] B: 654
Caesar, Julius (Assassination) C: 14
Cassius Longinus, Gaius C: 277
Bruxelles [Belgium] *See* Brussels *in this index*
Bruyère, Jean de la [French author] *See* La Bruyère,
Jean de, *in this index*
Bryan, Ashley [American author]
Laura Ingalls Wilder Award (table) L: 121
Literature for children *picture on* L: 356
Regina Medal (table: 2011) R: 206
Bryan, Charles Wayland [American political
leader] B: 654
Nebraska (table) N: 110
Bryan, George [American political leader]
Pennsylvania (table) P: 263
Bryan, Jimmy [American race driver]
Automobile racing (table: Indianapolis 500

winners) A: 980
Bryan, John Neely [American trader]
Dallas (History) D: 15
Bryan, Rebecca [wife of]
Boone, Daniel B: 477
Bryan, Richard Hudson [American political leader]
Nevada (table) N: 173
Bryan, William Jennings [American statesman]
B: 654 *with portrait*
Cleveland, Grover (Saving the gold standard)
Ci: 673
Democratic Party (After the Civil War) D: 125
McKinley, William (Crisis and triumph) M: 340
Populism (The People's Party) P: 675
Scopes trial S: 209 *with picture*
Tennessee (The early 1900's) T: 154-156
Wilson, Woodrow (Presidential candidate) W: 322
Bryant, C. Farris [American political leader]
Florida (table) F: 260
Bryant, Carolyn [American public figure]
Emmett Till case E: 260
Bryant, Gyude [Liberian political leader]
Liberia (Recent developments) L: 232
Bryant, Kobe [American basketball player] B: 655
Bryant, Louise [American journalist]
Reed, John R: 194
Bryant, Paul [American football coach] B: 655
Bryant, Phil [American political leader]
Mississippi (table) M: 640
Bryant, Roy [American public figure]
Emmett Till case E: 260
Bryant, William Cullen [American poet] B: 655
American literature (Literature of a young nation
[1788-1830]) A: 415; (Poetry) A: 418
February (Quotations) F: 61
March (Quotations) M: 195
Bryaxis [Greek sculptor]
Seven Wonders of the Ancient World (The
Mausoleum at Halicarnassus) S: 325
Bryce, Ebenezer [American public figure]
Bryce Canyon National Park B: 656
Bryce, James [British historian] B: 656
Bryce Canyon National Park [Utah] B: 656
National Park System (table: National parks) N: 48
Utah *picture on* U: 238
Bryde's whale B: 656
Whale (Rorquals) W: 255-258
Bryn Mawr College
Philadelphia (Education) P: 362-363
Thomas, Martha Carey T: 261
Brynhild [legendary figure] *See* Brunhild *in this
index*
Brynner, Yul [American actor]
Motion picture (Best performance by an actor:
1956) M: 862a
Bryophyte [botany] B: 656
Plant (Nonvascular plants) P: 518; (Classification
of plants) P: 546 *with pictures*
Bryozoan [animal] B: 656
Animal (A classification of the animal kingdom)
A: 506-507 *with picture*
Bryson, John [American government official]
Commerce, Department of (table) Ci: 871
Obama, Barack (table) O: 640h
Brzezinski, Zbigniew Kazimierz [American
government official] B: 657
BST [synthetic hormone] *See* Bovine somatotropin
in this index
BT Tower
London (Rebuilding) L: 442
BTE hearing aid
Hearing aid (Styles) H: 130 *with picture*
Btu [measurement] *See* British thermal unit *in this
index*
Buade, Louis de *See* Frontenac, Comte de *in this
index*
Bubble chamber [physics]
Particle detector (Bubble chambers) P: 186
Bubble eye [fish]
Goldfish *picture on* G: 258
Bubble gum B: 657
Chewing gum (Ingredients) C: 416
Bubblegum music
Rock music (Bubblegum music) R: 380a
Buber, Martin [German-Israeli philosopher] B: 657
Religion (Earlier theories) R: 218-219
Bubi [people]
Equatorial Guinea (People) E: 346; (History)
E: 347
Buboes [disorder]
Plague (Forms of plague) P: 506
Bubonic plague [disease]
Black Death B: 386
London (War, plague, and fire) L: 441
Plague (Forms of plague) P: 506
Races, Human (The clinal approach) R: 55-56
Bucaram Ortiz, Abdalá [Ecuadorean political

leader]
Ecuador (The 1900's) **E:** 73-74
Buccaneer [pirate]
Haiti (History) **H:** 15-16
Pirate **P:** 494; (The Caribbean) **P:** 495
Buccaneers, Tampa Bay [team] See Tampa Bay
Buccaneers in this index
Bucephala [ancient city]
Alexander the Great (His youth) **A:** 342
Bucephalus [horse]
Alexander the Great (His youth) **A:** 342
Horse (table: Famous horses in history and
legend) **H:** 361
Bucer, Martin [German theologian]
Calvin, John (His life) **C:** 70-71
Buch, Leopold von [German geologist]
Geology (The rock dispute) **G:** 98-99
Buchan, John [British statesman] **B:** 657
Governor General's Literary Awards **G:** 294
Buchanan, James [U.S. president] **B:** 658 with
pictures
Civil War, American (Developments in the
political party system) **Ci:** 616
Frémont, John Charles **F:** 511
Ostend Manifesto **O:** 866
Young, Brigham (Settles in Utah) **Y:** 571
Buchanan, James, Sr. [father of]
Buchanan, James (Early life) **B:** 658
Buchanan, James McGill [American economist]
Nobel Prizes (Economics: 1986) **N:** 449
Buchanan, James P. [American political leader]
Johnson, Lyndon Baines (Election to the House)
J: 146
Buchanan, John [Canadian political leader]
Nova Scotia (table) **N:** 567
Buchanan, John P. [American political leader]
Tennessee (table) **T:** 152
Buchanan plaid
Tartan picture on **T:** 47
Bucharest [Romania] **B:** 662 with picture
Europe at night **E:** 389
Bucharest, Treaty of [1913]
Balkans (The Second Balkan War) **B:** 42
Bûche de Noël [food]
Christmas (Christmas feasting) **C:** 534-535
Buchenwald [concentration camp] **B:** 663
Holocaust picture on **H:** 296a
Buchner, Eduard [German chemist]
Nobel Prizes (Chemistry: 1907) **N:** 442
Büchner, Georg [German author] **B:** 663
German literature (Other writers) **G:** 140
Opera: (Wozzeck) **O:** 808
Buchtel, Henry A. [American political leader]
Colorado (table) **Ci:** 844
Buchwald, Art [American journalist] **B:** 663
Buck [animal]
Deer **D:** 82d with picture
Goat **G:** 239
Buck, C. Douglass [American political leader]
Delaware (table) **D:** 109
Buck, Frank [American hunter] **B:** 663
Buck, Linda B. [American physiologist]
Nobel Prizes (Physiology or medicine: 2004)
N: 447
Buck, Pearl S. [American author] **B:** 663
Buck Island Reef National Monument [Virgin
Islands] **B:** 663
National Park System (table: National
monuments) **N:** 50
Buck teeth [disorder]
Teeth (Malocclusion) **T:** 84 with picture
Buckboard [vehicle]
Carriage **C:** 248
Bucker [career]
Lumber (Cutting down trees) **L:** 518
Bucket [tool]
Mining (Surface mining methods) **M:** 575
Bucket brigade
Fire department (Fire protection in Europe)
F: 127-128
Buckeye [bird]
Chicken (table) **C:** 443
Buckeye [tree]
Horsechestnut **H:** 366
Buckeye State [nickname]
Ohio **O:** 680
Buckhorn [weed]
Lawn picture on **L:** 143
Bucking [logging]
Lumber picture on **L:** 520
Bucking bronco See Bronco in this index
Buckingham, Duke of [English general] **B:** 663
Buckingham, Duke of [English nobleman]
Buckingham Palace **B:** 664
Buckingham, William A. [American political
leader]
Connecticut (table) **Ci:** 967

Buckingham Memorial Fountain [Chicago]
Chicago (Places to visit) **C:** 430 with picture
Buckingham Palace [London] **B:** 664 with picture
London (Palaces) **L:** 435; (Ceremonies) **L:** 437
with picture
United Kingdom picture on **U:** 63
Buckland, William [British scholar]
Dinosaur (Dinosaur discoveries) **D:** 213
Buckland Abbey [estate]
Drake, Sir Francis (Voyage around the world)
D: 322
Buckler [armor]
Gladiator **G:** 206
Shield **S:** 400
Buckley, James L. [American political leader]
Buckley, William F., Jr. **B:** 664
Buckley, William F., Jr. [American journalist] **B:** 664
Buckminsterfullerene [molecule]
Carbon (Fullerenes) **C:** 205 with diagram
Buckner, Simon Bolivar [Confederate general]
B: 664
Civil War, American (Battles of Fort Henry and
Fort Donelson) **Ci:** 628-629
Bucks, Milwaukee [team]
Basketball (table) **B:** 150
Buckshot [ammunition]
Musket **M:** 962
Shotgun **S:** 436
Buckskin [leather] **B:** 664
Indian, American (Clothing) **I:** 136d
Buckson, David P. [American political leader]
Delaware (table) **D:** 109
Bucktails [U.S. history] **B:** 664
Buckthorn [shrub] **B:** 664 with picture
Buckwheat [plant] **B:** 665 with picture
Plant picture on **P:** 525
Buckyball [molecule] See Buckminsterfullerene in
this index
Buckytube [molecule] See Carbon nanotube in
this index
Bucolics [poems by Virgil]
Virgil (His works) **V:** 391
Bucur [Romanian legendary figure]
Bucharest **B:** 663
Bud [botany] **B:** 665 with pictures
See also Budding in this index
Bulb **B:** 686
Leaf (A leaf begins its life) **L:** 152 with pictures
Plant (Stems) **P:** 529 with pictures; (Germination)
P: 535-537 with diagram
Tree (How trees grow taller) **T:** 418
Bud grafting
Grafting (Other kinds of grafting) **G:** 299
Bud scale [botany]
Leaf (A leaf begins its life) **L:** 152; (Protective
leaves) **L:** 156
Plant (Stems) **P:** 529 with picture
Tree (How trees grow taller) **T:** 418
Buda [former city, Hungary]
Budapest **B:** 666
Budapest [Hungary] **B:** 666 with picture
Hungary **H:** 438 with pictures
Budd, James H. [American political leader]
California (table) **C:** 59
Buddenbrooks [book by Mann]
German literature (Impressionism,
Neoromanticism, and Symbolism) **G:** 141
Mann, Thomas **M:** 164
Buddha [Indian religious leader] **B:** 667
Buddhism **B:** 667 with picture
China pictures on **C:** 489
Dharma **D:** 178
India (The Aryans) **I:** 128
Monasticism (Non-Christian monasticism) **M:** 701
Nepal (People) **N:** 125
Religion (Buddhism) **R:** 220 with picture
Sculpture (India) **S:** 236-237 with picture
Buddha Amitabha with the Eight Great
Bodhisattvas [scroll]
Korea, History of picture on **K:** 367
Buddhism [religion] **B:** 667 with pictures
Asia picture on **A:** 771; (Religions) **A:** 773; (Way of
life in Southeast Asia) **A:** 783-784 with pictures
Bodhisattva **B:** 434
Buddha **B:** 667
China picture on **C:** 475; (Religion) **C:** 485;
(Sculpture and pottery) **C:** 488 with pictures
Dalai Lama **D:** 9
Dance (Asian theatrical dance) **D:** 28
Dharma **D:** 178
Education (Early Chinese and Indian education)
E: 99
Exploration (Chinese exploration) **E:** 442
Feasts and festivals (In Buddhism) **F:** 58
Funeral customs (Preparation of the body) **F:** 557
God **G:** 243
Heaven **H:** 161

India (Buddhism) **I:** 117
Japan picture on **J:** 42; (Religion) **J:** 40
Korea, History of (Early years) **K:** 366 with pictures
Korea, South picture on **K:** 376
Kushan Empire **K:** 394
Lamaism **L:** 49
Laos (People) picture on **L:** 70
Marriage (Wedding ceremonies) **M:** 220
Meditation **M:** 380
Missionary **M:** 620
Monasticism (Non-Christian monasticism) **M:** 701
New Age movement **N:** 178
Painting (Indian painting) **P:** 44; (Japanese
painting) **P:** 47
Religion **R:** 215; (Buddhism) **R:** 220; (Taoism)
R: 221
Saint (Non-Christian saints) **S:** 29
Sculpture (India) **S:** 236 with pictures
Thailand (Religion) **T:** 224
Tokyo (Ethnic groups and religion) **T:** 314
Vietnam (Religion) **V:** 366
World, History of the (The Mauryan Empire in
India) **W:** 430
Zen **Z:** 588
Buddhist Temple Amid Clearing Mountain Peaks
[painting]
China picture on **C:** 488
Budding [grafting]
Grafting (Other kinds of grafting) **G:** 299
Budding [reproduction]
See also Bud in this index
Animal (Asexual reproduction) **A:** 496 with
diagram
Coral (Stony corals) **Ci:** 1048a
Fungi (How a fungus lives) **F:** 559
Hydra **H:** 462 with picture
Jellyfish **J:** 90
Reproduction (Through asexual reproduction)
R: 242
Sea anemone **S:** 262
Sponge (Asexual reproduction) **So:** 800
Virus diagram on **V:** 427; (Infection) **V:** 428
Buddy list [communication]
Instant messaging **I:** 304
Budge, Don [American tennis player] **B:** 669
Tennis (Tennis tournaments) **T:** 165
Budgerigar [bird]
Bird (As pets) **B:** 331 with picture
Parakeet **P:** 151 with pictures
Parrot (Kinds of parrots) **P:** 179
Budget [economics] **B:** 669
City government (City finances) **Ci:** 597
School (Public schools) **S:** 182
Budget, Bureau of the [U.S. history] **B:** 672
Budget, Household
Budget (Personal and family budgets) **B:** 669
Income diagram on **I:** 101
Budget, National See National budget in this index
Budget deficit [economics] See Deficit in this index
Budget motel
Motel **M:** 836
Budgie [bird] See Budgerigar in this index
Budi Utomo [organization]
Indonesia (The rise of nationalism) **I:** 237
Budo [sport]
Martial arts (Japanese martial arts) **M:** 234
Buell, Don Carlos [Union general]
Civil War, American (The war in the West--1862-
1864) **Ci:** 628
Buena Vista, Battle of [1847]
Davis, Jefferson (His political career) **D:** 47-48
Mexican War (Principal battles) **M:** 447
Mexico (Difficulties of the early republic) **M:** 471
Taylor, Zachary (Mexican War) **T:** 58-59 with
picture
Buenos Aires [Argentina] **B:** 672 with pictures
Argentina **A:** 646 with pictures; (City life) **A:** 648;
(Settlement and colonial life) **A:** 655-656
Buenos Aires, University of
Argentina (Education) **A:** 650
Buffalo [animal] **B:** 674 with picture
See also Bison; Carabao; Water buffalo; Wisent in
this index
Buffalo [fish] **B:** 676 with picture
Buffalo [New York] **B:** 676 with picture
New York (table: Average monthly weather)
N: 307
Buffalo, Port of [New York]
Buffalo (Economy) **B:** 677
Buffalo and Erie County Botanical Gardens
[Buffalo]
Buffalo (Other interesting places to visit) **B:** 678
Buffalo Bayou [river, Texas]
Houston (Commercial city) **H:** 398
Buffalo Bill [American frontiersman] **B:** 679 with
picture
Nebraska picture on **N:** 113; (Places to visit)

N: 102 *with picture*
Western frontier life in America (Entertainment) W: 240
Buffalo Bill Historical Center [Cody, Wyoming]
Wyoming (Libraries and museums) W: 520-521
Buffalo Bill Museum and Grave
Colorado (Places to visit) Ci: 836
Buffalo Bill State Historical Park [Nebraska]
Nebraska (Places to visit) N: 102
Buffalo Bills [team]
Football (National Football League) F: 364
Buffalo Bill's Wild West Show
Oakley, Annie O: 638
Buffalo ceremonials B: 679
Buffalo chip [fuel]
Western frontier life in America (Fuel) W: 238
Buffalo dance
Indian, American (Ceremonies) I: 148
North Dakota *picture on* N: 514
Buffalo Germans [team]
Basketball (The history of professional basketball) B: 154a
Buffalo grass [plant]
Grass *picture on* G: 325
Buffalo Horn [American Indian chief]
Idaho (Indian fighting) I: 44
Buffalo National River [Arkansas]
Arkansas *picture on* A: 694
National Park System (table: National parkways and other national parklands) N: 55
Buffalo rifle [gun]
Rifle *picture on* R: 339
Buffalo Sabres [team]
Hockey (table: National Hockey League) H: 281
Buffalo Soldiers [U.S. history] B: 680
Pershing, John Joseph (Teacher-soldier) P: 296
Buffalo treehopper [insect]
Insect *picture on* I: 281
Buffaloberry [shrub] B: 680 *with picture*
Buffet dinner
Restaurant (Kinds of restaurants) R: 262
Buffett, Warren Edward [American businessman] B: 680
Buffett Partnership [company]
Buffett, Warren Edward B: 680
Buffing
Grinding and polishing (Polishing) G: 395
Buffon, Georges-Louis Leclerc, Comte de [French naturalist]
Evolution (Early theories) E: 432
Buffoonery
Humor (The types of humor) H: 435-436
Bug [automobile] *See* Beetle *in this index*
Bug [computer]
Computer (Compiling or assembling a program) Ci: 923
Bug [electronic device]
Radio (Special uses) R: 85
Bug [entomology] B: 680
See also Insect *in this index*
Buganda [area]
Ganda G: 24
Buganda [former kingdom]
Uganda (History) U: 3-4
Bugbane [plant] B: 680 *with picture*
Snakeroot S: 537
Bugging [electronics] *See* Wiretapping *in this index*
Buggy [vehicle]
Carriage C: 248
Bugle [musical instrument] B: 681 *with picture*
Drum corps D: 368
Bugmouth [fish]
Menhaden M: 400
Bugs Bunny [cartoon character]
Animation *picture on* A: 514c
Buhaina, Abdullah ibn [real name of]
Blakey, Art B: 397
Bui Xuan Phai [Vietnamese artist]
Vietnam (The arts) V: 366
Buick, David Dunbar [American businessman] B: 681
Buick Motor Company
Buick, David Dunbar B: 681
Durant, William Crapo D: 388
Flint F: 235
Nash, Charles William N: 22
Build [acting]
Theater (Conservation and build) T: 238
Builder [chemical]
Detergent and soap (The kettle method) D: 164
Builder's level [tool]
Level L: 217
Builder's trials
Ship (Launching and outfitting) S: 413
Building and loan association *See* Savings and Loan Association *in this index*
Building Arts, National Museum of the

Washington, D.C. *map on* W: 76
Building code [law]
Building permit B: 684
Fire department (Fire prevention and fire safety) F: 125
House (Building a house) H: 380
Building construction B: 681 *with pictures*
See also the list of Related articles in the Building construction *article*
Architecture A: 606
Building permit B: 684
Building trade B: 685
Careers (Construction, maintenance, and repair) C: 221 *with picture*
Crane Ci: 1119 *with pictures*
Earthquake (Reducing earthquake damage) E: 34 *with diagram*
Engineering (Civil engineering) E: 285
Helicopter (For transportation and construction work) H: 170
House (Building a house) H: 380
Inca (Arts and architecture) I: 98
Insulation I: 306 *with pictures*
Pyramids P: 916 *with pictures*
United States *picture on* U: 131
Building material
See also the Building materials section of the list of Related articles in the Building construction *article*
Adobe A: 59 *with picture*
Brick B: 597 *with pictures*
Building stone B: 685
Ceramics (Kinds of ceramic products) C: 359
House (Building materials) H: 380
Lumber L: 517 *with pictures*
Plastics (To replace metals) P: 554-555
Shelter (Why shelters differ around the world) S: 392
Building of the Trojan Horse, The [painting by Tiepolo]
Mythology *picture on* M: 980
Building paper [building construction]
House (The frame) H: 382
Building permit [law] B: 684
Building science
Carpentry C: 247
Building society *See* Savings and loan association *in this index*
Building stone B: 685 *with picture*
Marble (Uses) M: 192
Quarrying Q: 7
Building trade B: 685
Buile Shuibhne [story]
Irish literature (Heroic tales, romances, and sagas) I: 430
Buisson, Ferdinand-Édouard [French educator]
Nobel Prizes (Peace: 1927) N: 448a
Bujumbura [Burundi] B: 686
Bujutsu [sport]
Martial arts (Japanese martial arts) M: 234
Bukoba [ship]
Shipwreck (table: Major shipwrecks) S: 428
Bukovina
Romania (Land regions) R: 419-420 *with map*; (World War I) R: 424
Bula shirt
Pacific Islands (Clothing) P: 7
Bulawayo [Zimbabwe] B: 686
Bulb [botany] B: 686 *with diagram*
Flower (Garden perennials grown from bulbs) F: 280 *with pictures*
Gardening (Planting and transplanting) G: 34
Vegetable (Bulbs) V: 292 *with picture*
Bulb [electronics]
Vacuum tube V: 258
Bulb, Light *See* Light bulb *in this index*
Bulb scale [botany]
Leaf (Storage leaves) L: 156 *with picture*
Bulbar paralysis [disease]
Poliomyelitis (Kinds of poliomyelitis) P: 626
Bulbourethral gland
Gland (table) G: 209
Bulbul [bird] B: 687 *with picture*
Bulfinch, Charles [American architect] B: 687
Architecture (Neoclassical architecture) A: 623-624 *with picture*
Bulfinch, Thomas [American historian] B: 687
Bulganin, Nikolai Aleksandrovich [Soviet political leader] B: 687
Malenkov, Georgi Maximilianovich M: 105
Union of Soviet Socialist Republics (The rise of Khrushchev) U: 38
Bulgaria B: 688 *with pictures and maps*
Balkans (The First Balkan War) B: 42; (The Second Balkan War) B: 42
Berlin, Congress of B: 265
Flag *picture on* F: 205

Macedonia [historic region] M: 11 *with map*
Music *picture on* M: 955
Warsaw Pact W: 39
World War I (Eastern Europe) W: 459-460
Bulgarian Orthodox Church
Bulgaria (Religion) B: 691
Bulgarian Socialist Party [political party]
Bulgaria (Government) B: 688
Bulgars [people]
Bulgaria (People) B: 689
Bulge [astronomy]
Galaxy (Spiral galaxies) G: 8a
Bulge, Battle of the [1944] B: 694
Luxembourg (History) L: 531
Ridgway, Matthew Bunker R: 336
World War II (The Battle of the Bulge) W: 484
Bulguksa Temple
Korea, History of *picture on* K: 366
Bulimia [disorder] B: 694
Adolescent (Eating disorders) A: 63-64
Eating disorder E: 48
Mental illness (Eating disorders) M: 406
Bulk blend fertilizer
Fertilizer (Production and sale) F: 80
Bulk carrier [ship] *See* Dry bulk carrier *in this index*
Bulk plant
Herbal medicine H: 196
Bulkeley, Morgan G. [American political leader]
Baseball (table: Hall of Fame) B: 134
Connecticut (table) Ci: 967
Bulkhead [wall]
Ship *diagram on* S: 405; (Basic structure) S: 403
Bull [animal]
Bullfighting B: 695 *with pictures*
Cattle C: 306; (Breeding) C: 311-312
Dolphin (The life of dolphins) D: 298
Elephant (Kinds of elephants) E: 227 *with picture*
Spain *picture on* So: 736-737
Bull [economics] *See* Bull market *in this index*
Bull [religion] B: 694
Bull, Henryk Johan [Norwegian businessman]
Antarctica (Early exploration) A: 536
Bull, John [symbol]
John Bull J: 133 *with picture*
Bull, Peter [British actor]
Motion picture *picture on* M: 871
Bull, William [American engineer]
Savannah S: 165
Bull kelp [plant]
Seaweed *picture on* S: 277
Bull market [economics]
Bears and bulls B: 189
Bull moose [animal]
Moose (The body of a moose) M: 798 *with picture*
Bull Moose Party *See* Progressive Party *in this index*
Bull pen
Baseball (Foul territory) B: 127
Bull riding
Rodeo R: 397
Bull Run, Battle of [1861]
Civil War, American (table) Ci: 624; (First Battle of Bull Run) Ci: 625
Jackson, Stonewall J: 16
Lincoln, Abraham (Building the army) L: 321
McDowell, Irvin M: 333
Bull Run, Battle of [1862]
Civil War, American (table) Ci: 624; (Second Battle of Bull Run) Ci: 627
Lee, Robert E. (Opening campaigns) L: 178
McDowell, Irvin M: 333
Porter, Fitz-John P: 682
Bull shark B: 694 *with picture*
Fish *picture on* F: 152
Shark (Kinds of sharks) S: 375
Bull terrier B: 695
Dog *picture on* D: 272
Miniature bull terrier M: 573
Pit bull P: 497
Bull trout
Trout *picture on* T: 453; (Other trout) T: 454
Bulla [seal]
Bull B: 694
Bullbat [bird] *See* Nighthawk *in this index*
Bullboat [boat]
Indian, American (Transportation) I: 142
Bulldog B: 695
Dog *pictures on* D: 275
French bulldog F: 513
Pit bull P: 497
Bulldog pickerel [fish]
Pickerel P: 450
Pike P: 461
Bulldogging
Rodeo (Steer wrestling) R: 397
Bulldozer [machine] B: 695
Bulle Rock [horse]
Horse (table: Famous horses in history and

legend) **H: 361**
Bullet [ammunition] **B: 695**
　Ammunition (Small-arms ammunition) **A: 435**
　　with pictures
　Ballistics **B: 56** *with picture*
　Forensic science (Firearms) **F: 389**
　Pioneer life in America (Tools) **P: 483**
Bullet-resisting glass
　Glass (Specialty glasses) **G: 212**
Bullet train
　Japan (Industry) **J: 32**
　Railroad (In Asia) **R: 114**
　Tokyo (Transportation) **T: 318**
　Transportation (Intercity public transportation)
　　T: 393-394
Bullet tuna [fish]
　Tuna **T: 485**
Bulletproof vest
　Armor (Later developments) **A: 720-721** *with*
　　picture
Bullfighting [sport] **B: 695** *with pictures*
　Mexico *picture on* **M: 457**; (Recreation) **M: 458**
　Portugal **P: 689** *with picture*
　Spain (Recreation) **So: 733-736**
Bullfinch [bird] **B: 697**
Bullfrog [animal] **B: 697**
　Frog (Adult frogs) **F: 539**; (True frogs) **F: 540**;
　　(Other frogs) **F: 540**
Bullhead [fish] **B: 697** *with picture*
　Catfish **C: 300**
　Fish *picture on* **F: 158**
Bullins, Ed [American playwright]
　African American literature (The 1900's) **A: 136a**
Bullion [metal]
　Gold (Money) **G: 251** *with picture*
Bullion coin
　Coin collecting (Collecting United States coins)
　　Ci: 757
　Money (U.S. coins) **M: 713**
Bullion stitch
　Crochet **Ci: 1148d**
Bullmastiff [dog] **B: 697** *with picture*
Bullock, Alexander H. [American political leader]
　Massachusetts (table) **M: 288**
Bullock, Rufus B. [American political leader]
　Georgia (table) **G: 130**
Bullock, Sandra [American actress]
　Motion picture (Best performance by an actress:
　　2009) **M: 862a**
Bullock, William A. [American inventor]
　Printing (New presses and typecasting machines)
　　P: 803
Bullock's oriole [bird]
　Oriole **O: 856**
Bulls, Chicago [team] *See* Chicago Bulls *in this*
　index
Bull's-eye
　Darts **D: 39** *with picture*
Bullying [psychology] **B: 698**
　Child (Social problems) **C: 453**
Bülow, Cosima von [wife of]
　Wagner, Richard (Later career) **W: 4**
Bulow, W. J. [American political leader]
　South Dakota (table) **So: 680**
Bulrush [plant] **B: 698**
Bulwark
　Ship (Nautical terms) **S: 405**
Bulwer, Sir Henry [British diplomat]
　Clayton-Bulwer Treaty **C: 659**
Bulwer-Lytton, Edward George Earle Lytton
　[British author] **B: 698**
Bumble bee [insect] **B: 698** *with picture*
　Animal *picture on* **A: 484**
　Bee (Social bees) **B: 205**
　Insect *picture on* **I: 283**
Bumblebee bat [animal] *See* Kitti's hog-nosed bat
　in this index
Bumblebee sphinx moth
　Moth *picture on* **M: 837**
Bump skiing *See* Mogul (skiing) *in this index*
Bumpers, Dale Leon [American political leader]
　Arkansas (table) **A: 712**
Bumppo, Natty [literary figure]
　Cooper, James Fenimore **Ci: 1034**
Buna N [synthetic material]
　Rubber (Development of synthetic rubbers)
　　R: 501
Buna S [synthetic material]
　Rubber (Development of synthetic rubbers)
　　R: 501
Bunau-Varilla, Philippe [French businessman]
　Panama Canal (The United States and the canal)
　　P: 125
Bunch plant
　Peanut (The peanut plant) **P: 213-214**
Bunchberry [plant] **B: 699**
　Flower *picture on* **F: 284**

Bunche, Ralph Johnson [American statesman]
　B: 699
Bund [road]
　Shanghai (The city) **S: 371**
Bundesrat [government]
　Austria (The Federal Assembly) **A: 929**
　Germany (Parliament) **G: 147**; (The German
　　Empire) **G: 166**
Bundesrepublik Deutschland *See* Germany *in*
　this index
Bundestag [government]
　Germany (Parliament) **G: 147**; (The German
　　Confederation) **G: 165**
Bundeswehr [armed forces]
　Germany (Armed forces) **G: 147**
Bundschuh [flag]
　Peasants' War **P: 224**
Bung
　Barrel **B: 118** *with picture*
Bunin, Ivan [Russian author] **B: 699**
　Russian literature (Symbolism) **R: 563**
Bunion [disorder] **B: 700**
Bunker [fish]
　Menhaden **M: 400**
Bunker [sports]
　Golf (Hazards) **G: 261**
Bunker Hill, Battle of [1775] **B: 700**
　Gage, Thomas **G: 5**
　Prescott, William **P: 757**
　Revolution, American (Bunker Hill) **R: 275** *with*
　　map; (table) **R: 276**
　Salem, Peter **S: 61**
Bunkhouse
　Ranching (History) **R: 136**
Bunny ears cactus [plant]
　Gardening *picture on* **G: 37**
Bunraku [drama]
　Puppet (Rod puppets) **P: 906** *with picture*
Bunratty Castle
　Ireland *picture on* **I: 420**
Bunsen, Robert Wilhelm [German chemist] **B: 700**
　Cesium **C: 364**
　Optics (History) **O: 813**
　Range (History) **R: 138**
　Rubidium **R: 507**
Bunsen burner **B: 700** *with diagram*
　Bunsen, Robert Wilhelm **B: 700**
Bunt [baseball]
　Baseball (Outs by batters) **B: 128-129** *with*
　　pictures
Bunt [plant disease] *See* Stinking smut *in this index*
Bunting [bird] **B: 700**
　Bird (Birds of grasslands) **B: 336** *with picture*
　Indigo bunting **I: 223** *with picture*
Bunting [fabric]
　Flag (Hanging the flag indoors) **F: 219**;
　　(Manufacturing flags) **F: 222**
Bunting, Eve [author]
　Regina Medal (table: 1997) **R: 206**
Buntline, Ned [American dramatist]
　Western frontier life in America (Entertainment)
　　W: 240
Buñuel, Luis [Spanish director] **B: 700**
　Latin America (Motion pictures) **L: 101**
　Motion picture (Postwar Realism) **M: 869**
　Spain (Motion pictures) **So: 739**
Buñuelos [food]
　Christmas (Christmas feasting) **C: 534-535**
Bunyan, John [English author] **B: 700**
　English literature (Restoration prose) **E: 318**
　Literature for children (The Puritans) **L: 362**
Bunyan, Paul [legendary figure] **B: 700**
　Minnesota (Places to visit) **M: 594**
Buon fresco [art]
　Painting (Fresco painting) **P: 38**
Buonaparte *See under* Bonaparte *in this index*
Buonarroti, Michelangelo [Italian sculptor] *See*
　Michelangelo *in this index*
Buoninsegna, Duccio di [Italian painter]
　Jesus Christ *picture on* **J: 108a**
Buoy [navigation] **B: 701**
　Beacon **B: 179**
　Boating *picture on* **B: 429**; (Buoys and other safety
　　aids) **B: 430**
　Coast Guard, United States *picture on* **Ci: 738**
　Ocean (Research ships) **O: 662-663**
　Weather (Weather balloons, airplanes, and ships)
　　W: 163
Buoy boat
　Whale (Hunting techniques) **W: 263**
Buoyancy [physics]
　Archimedes (His discoveries) **A: 605**
　Fish (Special organs) **F: 163**
　Ship (How ships work) **S: 403**
Buoyancy compensator
　Skin diving (Kinds of skin diving) **S: 493** *with*
　　pictures

Bur [botany]
　Cocklebur **Ci: 744**
　Cotton (Development) **Ci: 1087**
Bur grass [plant]
　Sandbur **S: 107**
Bur oak [tree]
　Oak (White oaks) **O: 635**
Bur sage [plant]
　Plant *picture on* **P: 526**
Bur Said [Egypt]
　Port Said **P: 681**
Burakumin [people]
　Japan (Ancestry) **J: 35-38**
Buran [space shuttle]
　Space exploration (The Soviet space shuttle)
　　So: 723
Burano [Italy]
　Venice (Economy) **V: 307-308**
Buraq [legendary creature]
　Muslims *picture on* **M: 964b**
Burbage, Cuthbert [English actor]
　Globe Theatre **G: 233**
Burbage, James [English producer]
　English literature (Elizabethan drama) **E: 317**
　Shakespeare, William (The Globe Theatre) **S: 348**;
　　(Theater buildings) **S: 351**
Burbage, Richard [English actor]
　Shakespeare, William (The Globe Theatre) **S: 348**
Burbank [California] **B: 701**
Burbank [potato]
　Burbank, Luther (His achievements and methods)
　　B: 702
Burbank, Luther [American horticulturist] **B: 701**
　Prickly pear **P: 776**
Burbidge, Geoffrey [British astronomer]
　Astronomy (Advances in astrophysics) **A: 848**
Burbidge, Margaret [British astronomer]
　Astronomy (Advances in astrophysics) **A: 848**
Burchard, Samuel D. [American religious leader]
　Cleveland, Grover (Election of 1884) **Ci: 670**
Burchfield, Charles Ephraim [American painter]
　B: 702 *with picture*
Burden of proof [law]
　Evidence (Burden of proof) **E: 426**
Burdick, Quentin N. [American political leader]
　North Dakota (Politics) **N: 513**
Burdock [plant] **B: 702** *with picture*
Bureau of ...
　Bureaus appear under their key words, as in
　　Reclamation, Bureau of
Bureaucracy [government] **B: 703**
　Red tape **R: 190**
　Weber, Max **W: 176**
Burford, Anne [American government official]
　Environmental Protection Agency **E: 340**
Burgee [symbol]
　Flag (table) **F: 193**
Burgee, John [American architect]
　Architecture (Architecture today) **A: 632-633**
　Johnson, Philip Cortelyou **J: 152**
Burger, Warren Earl [American jurist] **B: 703** *with*
　portrait
　Ford, Gerald Rudolph *pictures on* **F: 376, F: 377**
Bürgerschaft [government]
　Hamburg **H: 29**
Burgess [U.S. history]
　House of Burgesses **H: 384**
Burgess, Anthony [British author] **B: 703**
Burgess, Ernest W. [American sociologist]
　Collective behavior **C: 774**
Burgess, Thornton Waldo [American author]
　B: 703
Burgesses, House of *See* House of Burgesses *in*
　this index
Burghers [people]
　Sri Lanka (People) **So: 817**
Burghers of Calais, The [play by Kaiser]
　Kaiser, Georg **K: 210**
Burghers of Calais, The [sculpture by Rodin]
　Philadelphia *picture on* **P: 364**
　Rodin, Auguste **R: 399**
Burghley, Lord [English government official]
　B: 703
Bürgi, Jobst [Swiss mathematician]
　Logarithms (History) **L: 424**
Burglar alarm **B: 704**
Burglary [crime] **B: 704**
　Crime (table) **Ci: 1137**
Burgomaster [title]
　Mayor **M: 330**
Burgoyne, John [British general] **B: 704** *with*
　picture
　Revolution, American (Victory at Saratoga) **R: 282**
　　with picture
　Saratoga, Battle of **S: 123**
Burgraves, The [play by Hugo]
　Hugo, Victor (Political activity) **H: 410**

Burgtheater [building]
Vienna *picture on* V: 362
Burgundians [people]
Gaul G: 70
Joan of Arc, Saint (Joan sees the king) J: 128
Nibelungenlied: (The background) N: 395
Switzerland (Early days) So: 1058-1059
Burgundy [region, France] B: 705
Grape *picture on* G: 319
Maximilian I M: 319
Wine (Wines from France) W: 337
Buri [Norse mythology]
Mythology *picture on* M: 975; (The creation of life) M: 985-986
Burial [custom]
Catacombs C: 297
Funeral customs (Burial) F: 557
Indian, American (Current issues) I: 182
Necropolis N: 117
Prehistoric people (How the Neandertals lived) P: 751
Pyramids (Egyptian pyramids) P: 916
Sarcophagus S: 124
Tomb T: 325
Burial at Ornans, A [painting by Courbet]
Courbet, Gustave Ci: 1100 *with picture*
Burial mask
Mask (Burial masks and death masks) M: 265 *with picture*
Burial mound
Mound builders M: 881 *with picture*
Burial of Count Orgaz, The [painting by El Greco]
Greco, El G: 351
Burin [tool]
Engraving *picture on* E: 326; (Engraving the plate) E: 325
Van Leyden, Lucas V: 284
Burin Peninsula
Newfoundland and Labrador (Land regions) N: 370 *with map*
Burj Khalifa [building, Dubai]
Dubai D: 370 *with picture*
Skyscraper (table) S: 498 *with picture*
Burka [clothing] *See* Burqa *in this index*
Burke, Andrew H. [American political leader]
North Dakota (table) N: 513
Burke, Anne M. [American educator]
Special Olympics So: 771
Burke, Edmund [British political leader] B: 705
English literature (The Johnson circle) E: 319
Hastings, Warren H: 83
Burke, John [American political leader] B: 705
North Dakota (table) N: 513
Burke, John [Irish publisher]
Burke's *Peerage* B: 705
Burke, Robert O'Hara [Irish explorer]
Australia *map on* A: 921; (Mapping the continent) A: 922
Exploration (Exploring Australia's interior) E: 448 *with map*
Burke, Thomas [American political leader]
North Carolina (table) N: 490
Burke's *Peerage* [book] B: 705
Burkett, Jesse [American baseball player]
Baseball (table: Hall of Fame) B: 134
Burkina Faso B: 705 *with picture and map*
Flag *picture on* F: 198
Burkitt, Denis P. [British physician]
Health food (History) H: 129
Burkitt's lymphoma [disease]
Epstein-Barr virus E: 345
Burlap [fabric] B: 707
Burleigh, A. Peter [American diplomat]
United Nations (table) U: 86
Burleigh, Edwin C. [American political leader]
Maine (table) M: 87
Burleigh, Harry Thacker [American musician] B: 707
Burleigh, Lord [English government official]
Burghley, Lord B: 703
Burlesque [entertainment] B: 707
Burlesque [literature]
Drama (England) D: 335
Humor (The types of humor) H: 435-436
Burley Griffin, Lake [Australia]
Canberra *picture on* C: 166
Burlingame Treaty [1868]
Oriental Exclusion Acts O: 855
Burlington [Vermont] B: 707
Vermont *picture on* V: 319; (table: Average monthly weather) V: 330
Burlington, Lord [English architect]
Architecture (The Palladian Revival) A: 623 *with picture*
Burlington Northern Santa Fe Corporation
Railroad (Railroad systems) R: 112
Burlington *Zephyr* [train] *See* Zephyr *in this index*

Burma *See* Myanmar *in this index*
Burma Road [Myanmar-China] B: 708
World War II (Early Japanese victories) W: 487; (The China-Burma-India theater) W: 491
Burma Socialist Programme Party
Myanmar (Socialist republic) M: 970d
Burmeister's porpoise
Porpoise P: 679
Burmese cat
Cat *picture on* C: 288; (Short-haired breeds) C: 290
Burmese glass
Glass (Types of art glass) G: 220 *with picture*
Burmese python
Python P: 922
Snake (Snakes as invasive species) S: 532; (Snakes as pets) S: 532
Burmese Way to Socialism, The [document]
Myanmar (Socialist republic) M: 970d
Burn [injury] B: 708
First aid (Burns) F: 138
Skin (Burns) S: 490
Sunburn So: 989
Burn This [play by Wilson]
Wilson, Lanford W: 317
Burne-Jones, Sir Edward [British artist] B: 708
Knights and knighthood *picture on* K: 348
Painting (The Pre-Raphaelite Brotherhood) P: 71
Burnell, Jocelyn Bell [British astronomer] *See* Bell Burnell, Jocelyn *in this index*
Burner
Bunsen burner B: 700 *with diagram*
Heating (Oil) H: 159
Range (Gas ranges) R: 138
Burnet, David G. [American political leader]
Texas (The Texas revolution) T: 206
Burnet, Sir Macfarlane [Australian doctor] B: 708
Burnett, Frances Hodgson [American author] B: 708
Burnett, Ivy Compton- [British author] *See* Compton-Burnett, Ivy *in this index*
Burnett, Peter H. [American political leader]
California (table) C: 59; (Early statehood) C: 62
Burney, Dwight W. [American political leader]
Nebraska (table) N: 110
Burney, Fanny [British author] B: 708
Burney, Frances *See* Burney, Fanny *in this index*
Burnham, Daniel Hudson [American architect] B: 709 *with picture*
Architecture (Early modern architecture in America) A: 629 *with picture*
Baguio City B: 27
Chicago (A city reborn) C: 435
Root, John Wellborn R: 472
Burnham, Forbes [Guyana political leader]
Guyana (History) G: 446-447
Burnham Tavern [Machias]
Maine (Places to visit) M: 78
Burning *See* Combustion *in this index*
Burning, Flag *See* Flag burning *in this index*
Burning [in art]
Painting (Encaustic painting) P: 36-38
Burning Patience [book by Skármeta]
Latin American literature (The post-Boom) L: 114
Burning Water [book by Bowering]
Canadian literature (Modern English-Canadian fiction) C: 160
Burnley, James H. [American government official]
Transportation, Department of (table) T: 400
Burnoose [garment]
Algeria (Clothing) A: 361
Morocco (Way of life) M: 811-812
Burnquist, Joseph A. A. [American political leader]
Minnesota (table) M: 602
Burns, George [American actor] B: 709
Motion picture (Best performance by an actor in a supporting role: 1975) M: 862b
Radio (The Golden Age of Broadcasting) R: 92 *with picture*
Burns, John A. [American political leader]
Hawaii (table) H: 105
Burns, Ken [American filmmaker] B: 709
Burns, Lucy [American social reformer]
Woman suffrage (Growth of the movement) W: 380-381
Burns, Robert [Scottish poet] B: 709 *with portrait*
"Auld Lang Syne" A: 890
Bannockburn, Battle of B: 99
English literature (The Preromantics) E: 319-320
Burns, Tommy [Canadian boxer]
Boxing (Bare knuckles to gloves) B: 532 *with picture*
Burns, W. Haydon [American political leader]
Florida (table) F: 260
Burnside, Ambrose Everett [Union general] B: 710 *with portrait*
Civil War, American (Battle of Fredericksburg)

Ci: 627
Lincoln, Abraham (Building the army) L: 321
Rhode Island (table) R: 311; (The Civil War) R: 313
Burnsides [nickname]
Burnside, Ambrose Everett B: 710 *with picture*
"Burnt Norton" [poem by Eliot]
Eliot, T. S. (His works) E: 237-238
Burqa [clothing]
Afghanistan (Way of life) A: 92a-93 *with picture*
Clothing (Protection) Ci: 687
Pakistan (Clothing) P: 96
Burr [art]
Engraving (Dry point) E: 326
Burr, Aaron [American political leader] B: 710 *with portrait*
Electoral College (History) E: 164
Hamilton, Alexander (Political disputes) H: 33
Jefferson, Thomas (Election of 1800) J: 83; (Election of 1804) J: 86; (The Burr conspiracy) J: 86
Vice president of the United States (Early days) V: 352-353
Burrard Inlet
Vancouver V: 274 *with map*
Burris, Roland [American political leader]
Illinois (Corruption cases) I: 76
Burro *See* Donkey *in this index*
Burroughs, Edgar Rice [American author] B: 711
Burroughs, John [American political leader]
New Mexico (table) N: 272
Burroughs, William [American inventor] B: 711
Burroughs, William S. [American author]
Burroughs, William B: 711
Burroughs Wellcome Company
Elion, Gertrude Belle E: 236
Burrow [animal home]
Chipmunk C: 513 *with picture*
Muskrat M: 964
Prairie dog (Habits) P: 732
Rabbit (Homes) R: 48
Spider (Tarantulas) So: 790
Trap-door spider T: 402
Woodchuck W: 392
Burrowing owl
Bird (Birds of grasslands) B: 336 *with picture*
Owl (Important owls) O: 884-886 *with picture*
Burrows, Abe [American dramatist]
Loesser, Frank L: 420
Burrus [Roman military leader]
Seneca, Lucius Annaeus S: 296
Bursa [anatomy]
Bursitis B: 711
Bursch, Daniel [American astronaut]
Astronaut (table) A: 830
Bursitis [disorder] B: 711
Burst [painting]
Gottlieb, Adolph G: 280 *with picture*
Burstyn, Ellen [American actress]
Motion picture (Best performance by an actress: 1974) M: 862
Burt, Francis [American government official]
Nebraska (Territorial days) N: 112
Burton, H. G. [American political leader]
North Carolina (table) N: 490
Burton, Harold H. [American jurist]
Supreme Court of the United States (table) So: 1000
Burton, Richard [British actor]
Taylor, Elizabeth T: 57 *with picture*
Burton, Sir Richard Francis [British explorer] B: 712
Exploration (The exploration of Africa) E: 448 *with map*
Lake Tanganyika L: 46
Burton, Robert [British author]
English literature (Prose writings) E: 317
Burton, Tim [American film director] B: 712
Animation (New diversity) A: 514c
Depp, Johnny D: 149
Burton, William [American political leader]
Delaware (table) D: 109
Buru [island]
Indonesia (The Molucca Islands) I: 234
Burundi B: 712 *with picture and map*
Flag *picture on* F: 198
Ruanda-Urundi R: 499
Burying beetle [insect] B: 714
Insect *picture on* I: 283
Burying the hatchet
Tomahawk T: 324
Bus [vehicle] B: 714 *with picture*
Air conditioning (Air conditioners for vehicles) A: 179
Careers (Transportation) C: 235
Freedom riders F: 508
Transit T: 374
Transportation *picture on* T: 390, *picture on*

T: 393; (Land transportation) T: 383
Bus boycott [U.S. history] *See* Montgomery bus boycott *in this index*
Bus Stop [play by Inge]
Inge, William I: 270
Busbee, George D. [American political leader]
Georgia (table) G: 130
Busch, Kurt [American race driver]
Automobile racing (table: NASCAR Sprint Cup champions) A: 981
Busch Gardens Tampa Bay [Tampa]
Florida (Places to visit) F: 252 *with picture*
Buschmann, Friedrich [German inventor]
Harmonica H: 62
Bush [botany] B: 715
Shrub S: 441
Bush [region]
Australia (Country life) A: 902
Bush, Barbara [daughter of George W. Bush]
Bush, George Walker (Bush's family) B: 722e *with picture*
Bush, Barbara Pierce [wife of George H. W. Bush]
Bush, George Herbert Walker *pictures on* B: 719, B: 722; (Bush's family) B: 717 *with picture*
Bush, George Walker (Family background) B: 722c *with picture*
First ladies of the United States (table) F: 142
Bush, Dorothy Walker [mother of]
Bush, George Herbert Walker (Early life) B: 716-717
Bush, George Herbert Walker [U.S. president]
B: 716 *with pictures*
Baker, James Addison, III B: 32
Bush, George Walker B: 722b, *picture on* B: 722d; (Family background) B: 722c *with picture*
Cheney, Richard Bruce C: 407
Clinton, Bill (Election as president) Ci: 682c-682d
Cold War (The Cold War after 1980) Ci: 770
Iran-contra affair (Charges and court actions) I: 407
Noriega, Manuel Antonio N: 454
Panama (The Noriega years) P: 120-121
Persian Gulf War of 1991 (The world's reaction) P: 300b-300c
Quayle, Dan Q: 9
Reagan, Ronald Wilson (The Iran-contra affair) R: 170
Republican Party (Victories in the 1980's) R: 257 *with picture*
United Nations (table) U: 86
United States, History of the (The Persian Gulf War) U: 196d
Vice president V: 349 *with portrait*
Vice president of the United States (Growth of the vice presidency) V: 353-354
Bush, George Walker [U.S. president] B: 722b *with pictures*
Bush, George Herbert Walker (Later years) B: 722a *with picture*
Bush v. Gore B: 724
Cheney, Richard Bruce C: 407
Clinton, Bill (Later years) Ci: 682g
Democratic Party (The early 2000's) D: 128
Election of 2000 E: 161
Executive order E: 436
Exploration (Human space travel) E: 452
Gonzales, Alberto R. G: 268
Gore, Al G: 273
Hispanic Americans (Hispanic American immigration today) H: 255
Homeland Security, Department of (History) H: 301
Iraq War I: 414c
Nevada (The early 2000's) N: 177
No Child Left Behind Act N: 438
Obama, Barack O: 640b
Republican Party (The early 2000's) R: 257
Rice, Condoleezza R: 327
September 11 terrorist attacks S: 310
Space exploration (The Columbia disaster) So: 725-726
Stem cell So: 889
Terrorism (The September 11 terrorist attacks) T: 179
Texas (table) T: 203; (Recent developments) T: 209
United Nations (Policy disagreements) U: 96
United States, History of the (The United States in the 2000's [2000-]) U: 196d
Bush, Jeb [American political leader]
Bush, George Herbert Walker (Bush's family) B: 717
Bush, George Walker (Governor of Texas) B: 722e *with picture*
Florida (table) F: 260
Bush, Jenna [daughter of George W. Bush]
Bush, George Walker (Bush's family) B: 722e *with*

picture
Bush, John [American political leader] *See* Bush, Jeb *in this index*
Bush, Jonathan [brother of]
Bush, George Herbert Walker (Early life) B: 716-717
Bush, Laura Welch [wife of George W. Bush]
Bush, George Walker (Bush's family) B: 722e *with picture*
First ladies of the United States (table) F: 142
Bush, Nancy [sister of]
Bush, George Herbert Walker (Early life) B: 716-717
Bush, Prescott, Jr. [brother of]
Bush, George Herbert Walker (Early life) B: 716
Bush, Prescott Sheldon [father of]
Bush, George Herbert Walker (Early life) B: 716-717
Bush, Robin [daughter of George H. W. Bush]
Bush, George Herbert Walker (Bush's family) B: 717
Bush, George Walker (Early life) B: 722c-722d
Bush, William [brother of]
Bush, George Herbert Walker (Early life) B: 716-717
Bush ballad [poetry]
Australia (Literature) A: 904-905
Bush elephant
Elephant (Kinds of elephants) E: 227
Bush Exploration Company
Bush, George Walker (Business career) B: 722e
Bush nut *See* Macadamia nut *in this index*
Bush pilot
Alaska (Transportation) A: 299
Bush v. Gore [2000] B: 724 *with picture*
Election of 2000 E: 161
Supreme Court of the United States (Election issues) So: 1001; (table) So: 1002
Bushbaby [animal] *See* Galago *in this index*
Bushel [measurement] B: 723
Bushell, John [Canadian printer]
Printing (Early printing in North America) P: 803
Bushfield, Harlan J. [American political leader]
South Dakota (table) So: 680
Bushido [military code]
World War II (The South Pacific) W: 489
Bushmaster [snake] B: 723
Snake *picture on* S: 530
Viper V: 391
Bushmen [people] *See* San *in this index*
Bushnell, Asa S. [American political leader]
Ohio (table) O: 699
Bushnell, David [American inventor]
Mine warfare (History) M: 565
Submarine (Early submarines) So: 942
Bushnell, E. W. [American manufacturer]
Ice skating (History) I: 16
Bushnell, Nolan [American programmer]
Electronic game (Arcade games) E: 204d
Bushrangers [Australian history]
Kelly, Ned K: 257
Bushy Run, Battle of [1763]
Pennsylvania (Colonial wars) P: 264-265
Busia, Kofi [Ghanaian political leader]
Ghana (History) G: 179-180
Busiel, Charles A. [American political leader]
New Hampshire (table) N: 223
Business B: 724 *with pictures*
See also Industry *in this index and the list of Related articles in the* Business *article*
Antitrust laws A: 560
Capital C: 192
Cooperative Ci: 1035
Economics (The organization of economies) E: 58
Environmental pollution (Business and industry) E: 336
Inflation (Effects on business) I: 268
Internet (Commerce) I: 350b; (The Internet and society) I: 350e
Investment (Direct investments) I: 367
Law (Private law) L: 130
Marketing M: 214
Mathematics (In business) M: 302
Office work O: 677
Outsourcing O: 880
Pension P: 272
Roaring Twenties (Rising prosperity) R: 363
State government (Business and labor) So: 865
Telephone (Business services) T: 98
Business, National Alliance of [organization]
National Alliance of Business N: 28
Business accounting
Accounting (Fields of accounting) A: 23
Business casual style
Clothing (The 1900's and 2000's) Ci: 705
Business corporation
Corporation Ci: 1070

Business cycle [economics] B: 728
Capitalism (Stabilizing the economy) C: 195
Depression D: 150
Economics (Economic growth) E: 62
Great Depression G: 338
Marx, Karl: (*Das Kapital*) M: 237
National Bureau of Economic Research N: 31
Recession R: 175
Business Cycles [book by Schumpeter]
Schumpeter, Joseph Alois S: 188
Business ethics B: 727
Conflict of interest Ci: 936
Business income insurance
Insurance (Other types of property and liability insurance) I: 313
Business law
Law (Private law) L: 130
Business letter
Letter writing (Business letters) L: 211 *with pictures*
Business plane
Airplane (General aviation planes) A: 211-212
Business section [district]
City (Description) Ci: 589
Business-to-business transaction
E-commerce (Business-to-business transactions) E: 2
Business-to-consumer transaction
E-commerce (Business-to-consumer transactions) E: 2
Busing [U.S. history]
Boston (Conflict over schools) B: 504
Charlotte (Government and history) C: 385
Education (Education for whom?) E: 107
Louisville (Changes during the 1900's) L: 506
Nixon, Richard Milhous (The national scene) N: 433-434
Segregation (The beginning of change) S: 285
Bussy, A. A. [French chemist]
Beryllium B: 273
Bussy D'Ambois [play by Chapman]
Chapman, George C: 377
Bust [zoology]
Taiga T: 14
Bustamante, José Luis [Peruvian political leader]
Peru (The rise of APRA) P: 316
Bustee [slum]
Kolkata (People) K: 363 *with picture*
"Buster Brown" [comic strip]
Outcault, Richard Felton O: 879
Bustle [clothing]
Clothing (The 1700's) Ci: 703-704 *with picture*; (The 1800's) Ci: 704-705
Busy lizzy [plant]
Impatiens I: 90 *with picture*
Butadiene [gas]
Furfural F: 566
Rubber (Development of synthetic rubbers) R: 501; (General-purpose synthetic rubbers) R: 504
Butane [gas]
Gas [fuel] (In the home) G: 51
Isomer I: 475
Molecule (Individual molecules) M: 692-693 *with diagram*
Natural gas liquids N: 64
Butane and propane [gas] B: 728
See also Butane; Propane *in this index*
Butchart Gardens [British Columbia]
British Columbia (Places to visit) B: 620 *with picture*
Flower *picture on* F: 275
Landscape architecture *picture on* L: 59
Butcher, James [American political leader]
Maryland (table) M: 255
Butcherbird [bird]
Bird (Birds of Australia and New Zealand) B: 346 *with picture*
Shrike S: 439
Bute, Earl of [British political leader]
United Kingdom (table: British prime ministers) U: 72
Butenandt, Adolf Friedrich Johann [German chemist]
Nobel Prizes (Chemistry: 1939) N: 443
Buteo [bird]
Buzzard B: 745
Hawk H: 111
Buthelezi, Mangosuthu Gatsha [South African political leader]
Inkatha Freedom Party I: 273
Butler, Andrew P. [American political leader]
Sumner, Charles So: 973
Butler, Benjamin Franklin [American general] B: 729
Anti-Monopoly Party A: 557
Farragut, David Glasgow F: 47

Louisiana (The American Civil War [1861-1865])
  L: 498
Massachusetts (table) M: 288
Butler, Benjamin Franklin [American government official]
  Jackson, Andrew (table) J: 11
  Justice, Department of (table) J: 203
  Van Buren, Martin (table) V: 273
Butler, David [American political leader]
  Nebraska (table) N: 110; (Statehood) N: 112
Butler, Lady Elizabeth [British artist] *See*
  Thompson, Elizabeth *in this index*
Butler, Ezra [American political leader]
  Vermont (table) V: 333
Butler, Frank E. [husband of]
  Oakley, Annie O: 638
Butler, Nicholas Murray [American educator]
  Nobel Prizes (Peace: 1931) N: 448a
Butler, Pierce [1744-1822, American political leader] B: 729
Butler, Pierce [American jurist]
  Supreme Court of the United States (table)
  So: 1000
Butler, R. Paul [American astronomer]
  Planet (The first discoveries) P: 513
Butler, Rhett [literary figure]
  Gone with the Wind G: 268
  Mitchell, Margaret M: 678
Butler, Robert N. [American physician]
  Ageism A: 140
Butler, William Orlando [American political leader]
  B: 729
  Fillmore, Millard (Vice president) F: 101
Butler Library
  Columbia University (Other facilities) Ci: 853
Butley [play by Gray]
  Gray, Simon G: 283
Butor, Michel [French author]
  French literature (The middle and late 1900's)
  F: 523
Butte [geology] B: 729 *with picture*
Butte [Montana] B: 729
Butte County [South Dakota]
  Geographic center of the United States G: 92
Butte Hill [region]
  Montana (Statehood) M: 760
Butter [food] B: 730 *with diagram*
  Cattle (Dairy cattle) C: 309-310
  Churn C: 550
  Margarine M: 198
Butter-and-eggs [plant]
  Toadflax T: 305 *with picture*
Buttercup [plant] B: 731 *with picture*
  Cell *picture on* C: 327
  Flower *picture on* F: 287; (table) F: 300 *with picture*
Buttercup chicken
  Chicken (Mediterranean class chickens) C: 441;
  (table) C: 443
Buttercup comb [biology]
  Chicken (Kinds of chickens) C: 441 *with picture*
Butterfat [food]
  Butter (Composition and food value) B: 731
  Cattle (Dairy cattle) C: 309-310
  Dairying (Dairy cattle) D: 6
Butterfield, William [British architect]
  Architecture (The Gothic Revival) A: 626 *with picture*
Butterfish [fish] B: 731 *with picture*
Butterfly B: 732 *with pictures*
  Animal (Animal travelers) A: 502-503
  Caterpillar C: 299
  Chrysalis C: 539
  Flower (Cross-pollination) F: 295
  Insect *picture on* I: 282; (Legs) I: 287-288; (Wings)
  I: 288
  Metamorphosis M: 428
  Mimicry M: 561
  Pupa P: 904
Butterfly chair
  Furniture *picture on* F: 583; (The retro style) F: 584
Butterfly farm
  Butterfly (Butterfly conservation) B: 743 *with picture*
Butterfly fish *See* Butterflyfish *in this index*
Butterfly garden
  Butterfly (Butterfly conservation) B: 743
Butterfly lily [plant]
  Mariposa lily M: 212 *with picture*
Butterfly roof
  Roof *picture on* R: 450c
Butterfly stroke
  Swimming (The basic strokes) So: 1043-1044
  with pictures
Butterfly weed [plant]
  Milkweed M: 551
Butterflyfish B: 743 *with picture*

Adaptation *picture on* A: 45
Animal *picture on* A: 487
Fish *pictures on* F: 155
Ocean *picture on* O: 656
Butterhead lettuce
  Lettuce (Kinds of lettuce) L: 214 *with pictures*
Buttermilk [food] B: 744
  Butter (Churning) B: 730
Buttermilk snake
  Racer R: 51
Butternut [tree] B: 744
  Tree *pictures on* T: 421
  Walnut W: 19
Butterprint [plant] *See* Velvetleaf *in this index*
Butterwort [plant] B: 744 *with picture*
  Leaf *picture on* L: 157
Button [botany]
  Mushroom (How a mushroom grows) M: 942-
  943 *with picture*
Button [clothing] B: 744 *with pictures*
  Sewing (Fastenings) S: 332
Button, Dick [American skater]
  Ice skating (History) I: 16
  Olympic Games (The postwar games) O: 751
Button, Jensen [British race car driver]
  Automobile racing (table: Formula One World
  Drivers' Championship) A: 980
Button, Sir Thomas [English explorer]
  Manitoba (Newcomers) M: 160 *with picture*
  Prairie Provinces (History) P: 733
Button mushroom *See* Table mushroom *in this index*
Button snakeroot [plant]
  Blazing star B: 398
  Snakeroot S: 537
Button spider
  Spider (Dangerous spiders) So: 790
Buttons, Red [American actor]
  Motion picture (Best performance by an actor in
  a supporting role: 1957) M: 862a
Buttonwood [tree]
  Sycamore So: 1062
Buttonwood Agreement [former name]
  New York Stock Exchange N: 345
Buttress [archery]
  Archery (Target archery) A: 602
Buttress [architecture]
  See also Flying buttress *in this index*
  Architecture (Architectural terms) A: 608 *with pictures*; (Gothic architecture) A: 618-619 *with pictures*
Buttress dam
  Dam (Masonry dams) D: 17
Buttrick, Barbara [British-born boxer]
  Boxing (Women's boxing) B: 532b-533
Butyl rubber
  Rubber (Special-purpose rubbers) R: 504
Butz, Earl Lauer [American government official]
  Agriculture, Department of (table) A: 161
  Nixon, Richard Milhous (table) N: 433
Buurgplatz [mountain]
  Luxembourg (Land) L: 531
Buxtehude, Dietrich [Swedish-German composer]
  B: 745
  Bach, Johann Sebastian (His works) B: 16
Buy-back center
  Recycling (Collecting materials) R: 184
Buy term and invest the difference [strategy]
  Insurance (Buying life insurance) I: 311
Buying *See* Consumption [economics] *in this index*
Buying club [economics]
  Cooperative (History) Ci: 1036-1037
Buying committee [business]
  Sales (Wholesaling) S: 62
Buyoya, Pierre [Burundi political leader]
  Burundi (History) B: 713-714
Buzkashi [game]
  Afghanistan (Recreation) A: 94
Buzz [marketing]
  Advertising (Recent developments) A: 80
  Internet (Spreading ideas) I: 350e-350f
Buzzard [bird] B: 745 *with picture*
  Balance of nature *picture on* B: 35
  Hawk H: 111
Bwindi Impenetrable National Park [Uganda]
  National park (table) N: 42f
By, John [British military leader]
  Ottawa (Bytown) O: 874
By-election [voting]
  House of Commons H: 384
  Parliament (How members are elected) P: 173
By-line [journalism]
  Newspaper (table) N: 383
  Writing (Preparing and submitting a manuscript)
  W: 512
By Love Possessed [book by Cozzens]
  Cozzens, James Gould Ci: 1114

Byars, Betsy [American author] B: 746
  Newbery Medal (table) N: 359
  Regina Medal (table: 1987) R: 206
Byatt, A. S. [British author]
  English literature (Recent English fiction) E: 323
Bycatch
  Conservation (Ocean conservation) Ci: 978-979
  Fishing industry (Fishery conservation) F: 187
Bye [sports]
  Cricket (Scoring) Ci: 1132
Bye-Lo Baby
  Doll (After the war) D: 292 *with picture*
Byelarus *See* Belarus *in this index*
Byelorussia *See* Belarus *in this index*
Byelorussians [people] *See* Belarusians *in this index*
Byerly Turk [horse]
  Horse racing (Thoroughbred horses) H: 363
Bylaws [parliamentary procedure] B: 746
  Parliamentary procedure (Bylaws) P: 175
Byllynge, Edward [American colonial leader]
  New Jersey (English control) N: 250
Bylot, Robert [English explorer]
  Northwest Passage N: 528
Byng, Julian Hedworth George [British statesman] B: 746
  Governor general G: 294
  Meighen, Arthur (Prime minister) M: 386
Bypass [road]
  Road (Bypasses) R: 358
Bypass surgery *See* Coronary artery bypass surgery *in this index*
Byrd, Harry Flood [American political leader]
  Kennedy, John Fitzgerald (The 1960 campaign)
  K: 263-264
  Virginia (table) V: 417; (Progress in government
  and industry) V: 422
Byrd, Richard Evelyn [American explorer] B: 746
  with picture
  Airplane (Fliers of the golden age) A: 237
  Antarctica (Exploration by air) A: 537 *with picture
  and map*
  Exploration (The North Pole) E: 450
Byrd, Robert Carlyle [American political leader]
  B: 747
  West Virginia (Recent developments) W: 229
Byrd, William [English composer] B: 747
  Tallis, Thomas T: 21
Byrd, William, II [American government official]
  B: 747
  American literature (Virginia) A: 414
  Diary D: 184
Byrds, The [rock group]
  Rock music (Fresh directions) R: 380
Byrne, Brendan T. [American political leader]
  New Jersey (table) N: 249
Byrne, David [Scottish-born singer]
  Rock music (World music) R: 380d
Byrne, Frank M. [American political leader]
  South Dakota (table) So: 680
Byrne, Jane Margaret [American political leader]
  B: 747 *with portrait*
  Chicago (Political developments in the late
  1900's) C: 436
Byrne, Joe [Australian outlaw]
  Kelly, Ned K: 257
Byrnes, James Francis [American statesman]
  B: 747
  Truman, Harry S. (table) T: 469
Byron, Anne Isabella Milbanke [wife of]
  Byron, Lord (Byron's life) B: 748
Byron, George Gordon *See* Byron, Lord *in this index*
Byron, Lord [British poet] B: 748 *with portrait*
  English literature (Romantic poetry) E: 320
Byron, Red [American race driver]
  Automobile racing (table: NASCAR Sprint Cup
  champions) A: 981
Byronic hero [literature]
  Byron, Lord (Byron's poetry) B: 748
Byssinosis *See* Brown lung *in this index*
Byte [measurement]
  Computer (Computer code) Ci: 911
Bytown [fomer name]
  Ottawa (Bytown) O: 874
Bytown, College of
  Ottawa, University of O: 875
Byway
  Road (The first roads) R: 361
Byzantine architecture
  Architecture (Byzantine architecture) A: 617
  Byzantine art (Architecture) B: 749 *with picture*
  Italy (Architecture) I: 504
  Russia (Architecture) R: 536 *with picture*
  World, History of the (The Byzantine Empire)
  W: 434 *with picture*
Byzantine art B: 749 *with pictures*
  Byzantine Empire (Religion) B: 753 *with pictures*

Cimabue, Giovanni Ci: 553 *with picture*
Mosaic M: 822
Painting (Early Christian and Byzantine art) P: 49
with picture
World, History of the *picture on* W: 430
Byzantine Empire B: 752 *with pictures and maps*
Bulgaria (The first Bulgarian kingdom) B: 692
Byzantine art (The development of Byzantine
art) B: 749
Christianity (The Roman Empire splits) C: 524
Clothing (The Middle Ages) Ci: 700 *with picture*
Constantine the Great Ci: 993
Crusades (The Fourth Crusade) Ci: 1161
Cyprus (History) Ci: 1207
Europe *map on* E: 406; (The Byzantine Empire)
E: 408
Greece (Ottoman rule) G: 361
Greece, Ancient (Roman rule) G: 374
Greek language (Later developments) G: 376
Istanbul (History) I: 491
Law (The Middle Ages) L: 134
Osman I O: 865
Rome, Ancient R: 436, *map on* R: 447; (The
decline of the empire) R: 447-448
Theodoric T: 252
World, History of the (The Byzantine Empire)
W: 434
Byzantine rite [religion]
Eastern Catholic Churches E: 45
Byzantium
Byzantine Empire B: 752

C

C [letter] C: 1 *with pictures*
G G: 1
C [computer language]
Computer (Using programming languages)
Ci: 923
C [symbol]
Carbon (Chemical properties) C: 203
C. Turner Joy [destroyer]
Vietnam War (The Gulf of Tonkin incident) V: 375
C-5 Galaxy [airplane]
Air Force, United States *picture on* A: 192; (Other
aircraft) A: 191
C-5A Galaxy [airplane]
Airplane *picture on* A: 211; (Military planes)
A: 212
C-14 dating See Radiocarbon dating *in this index*
C-17 Globemaster III [aircraft]
Aircraft, Military *picture on* A: 203
C₆₀ [molecule] See Buckminsterfullerene *in this
index*
C-band [conmmunications]
Communications satellite (How communications
satellites work) Ci: 888b *with picture*
C clef [music]
Music (Indicating pitch) M: 952-953 *with picture*
C++ [computer language]
Computer (Using programming languages)
Ci: 923
C quark [physics] See Charm *in this index*
C-reactive protein [medicine] C: 2
Heart (Risk factors) H: 137
C-type asteroid [astronomy]
Asteroid (Composition) A: 824
Ca [symbol]
Calcium C: 21
CA 125 [protein]
Ovarian cancer O: 881
Cab-over-engine [design]
Truck (Common features of trucks) T: 458
Cabal [conspiracy] C: 2
Washington, George (The army) W: 99
Cabala [religion] See Kabbalah *in this index*
Cabalistic Painting [painting by Schnabel]
Schnabel, Julian *picture on* S: 177
Caballero, Fernán [Spanish author]
Spanish literature (The 1800's) So: 761-762
Caballo Reservoir [New Mexico]
Rio Grande (Upper course) R: 346-347 *with map*
Rio Grande Project R: 347
Cabaret [cafe]
Berlin (The arts) B: 262
Cabbage [plant] C: 2 *with picture*
Chinese cabbage C: 509 *with picture*
Evolution (Artificial selection) E: 432 *with picture*
Flower (table) F: 300 *with picture*
Cabbage butterfly
Butterfly *picture on* B: 737; (Sulphurs and whites)
B: 738
Cabbage palm [tree] See Sabal palmetto *in this
index*
Cabbage Patch doll
Doll (The 1980's) D: 293
Cabbage rose [plant]
Rose (Types of roses) R: 474-475

Cabbage tree palm [tree]
Tree *picture on* T: 426
Cabbageworm [insect]
Insect (Quarantine systems) I: 285 *with picture*
Cabell, James Branch [American author] C: 3
Cabell, William H. [American political leader]
Virginia (table) V: 417
Caber [sports]
Nova Scotia (Visitor's guide) N: 560
Scotland (Recreation) S: 214
Cabet, Étienne [French political leader]
Nauvoo N: 69
Cabeza de Vaca, Álvar Núñez [Spanish explorer]
C: 3
Latin America *map on* L: 105
New Mexico (Exploration, conquest, and
settlement) N: 273
Texas (Spanish exploration) T: 204
Cabildo [museum, Buenos Aires]
Buenos Aires (The city) B: 672
Cabildo [museum, New Orleans]
Louisiana (Museums) L: 483
New Orleans (Downtown New Orleans) N: 278
Cabin
Sailing *picture on* S: 25
Cabin, The [book by Blasco Ibáñez]
Spanish literature (The 1800's) So: 761-762
Cabin in the Cotton [painting by Pippin]
Pippin, Horace *picture on* P: 492
Cabin tent
Tent (Kinds of tents) T: 168
Cabinda [district, Angola] C: 3
Angola A: 464
Cabinet [government] C: 3
Address, Forms of (Officials of the United States)
A: 53
Canada, Government of (The Cabinet) C: 130
Emancipation Proclamation *picture on* E: 254
Government (Parliamentary democracy) G: 286
Ministry M: 578
Parliament P: 172
Presidential assistant P: 770
Prime minister P: 778c
Prime minister of Canada (Roles of the prime
minister) P: 778c-778d; (History) P: 780
South Africa (National government) So: 608
United Kingdom *picture on* U: 50; (National
government) U: 49; (The beginning of cabinet
government) U: 67
United States, Government of the (Executive
departments and agencies) U: 140
Washington, George (Cabinet) W: 102 *with
picture*
Cabinet dollhouse
Dollhouse D: 296
Cabinet-Maker and Upholsterer's Guide, The
[book by Hepplewhite]
Hepplewhite, George H: 193
Cabinet Mountains
Montana (Land regions) M: 752
Cabinet of Dr. Caligari, The [film]
Motion picture (Filmmaking in Europe) M: 866
with picture
Cabinet system [government] See Parliamentary
system *in this index*
Cabinetmaker
Carpentry C: 246
Pioneer life in America *picture on* P: 481
Woodworking W: 396
Cable [communications] C: 4 *with pictures*
Coaxial cable (Coaxial cables) C: 740 *with picture*
Fiber optics *picture on* F: 88
Field, Cyrus West F: 91
Insulator, Electric I: 308 *with picture*
Telegraph (Service expansion and improvement)
T: 91
Telephone (Traditional phone calls) T: 96-97;
(Improvements in telephone technology)
T: 100
Cable [construction]
Bridge (Suspension bridges) B: 601-602 *with
diagram*; (Cable-stayed bridges) B: 602 *with
diagram*
Rope (Wire rope) R: 473
Cable, George Washington [American author] C: 7
American literature (Realists) A: 419
Cable car C: 7
San Francisco (Transportation and
communication) S: 97 *with picture*; (Continued
prosperity) S: 97-98
Cable-laid rope
Rope (How rope is made) R: 473
Cable modem [electronic device]
Computer (A modem or a network interface
card) Ci: 915
Modem M: 685
Telephone (VoIP phone calls) T: 97

Cable News Network [television network] C: 7
Turner, Ted T: 518
Cable-stayed bridge
Bridge (Cable-stayed bridges) B: 602 *with
diagram*
Cable stitch
Knitting *picture on* K: 354; (Knitting the fabric)
K: 354
Cable television
Boxing (Boxing in the United States) B: 530;
(Boxing today) B: 533
Cable (Coaxial cables) C: 4-5
Cable News Network C: 7
Digital video recorder D: 203
Internet (Hrdware) I: 350c
Journalism (Television) J: 172; (Criticism of the
press) J: 173
Television (Cable television) T: 110c; (Cable
and satellite systems) T: 115; (History of U.S.
television broadcasting) T: 117-120; (Tuner)
T: 124
Cable-tool drilling
Gas [fuel] (Producing gas) G: 55
Cabochon cutting
Gem (Cutting and polishing) G: 79 *with pictures*
Lapidary L: 73
Opal O: 789
Ruby R: 508
Caboclos [people]
Brazil (Ancestry) B: 572
Caboet, Lord of [Spanish nobleman]
Andorra (History) A: 455
Caboose
Railroad (Passenger and freight cars) R: 107-108
Cabot, John [Italian explorer] C: 7
Arctic (Search for the Northwest Passage) A: 638
Canada, History of (Early European exploration)
C: 138-139
Exploration (Exploring the New World) E: 444
with map
Flag *picture on* F: 215
Newfoundland and Labrador N: 361; (Early
European exploration) N: 375
Nova Scotia (Exploration and settlement) N: 567
St. John's S: 36
Cabot, Sebastian [Italian explorer] C: 8
Exploration (Spain's conquests in the New World)
E: 445
Río de la Plata R: 346
Cabot Strait [Canada-Newfoundland]
Gulf of Saint Lawrence G: 437
Cabot Trail
Cape Breton Island C: 187
Nova Scotia *picture on* N: 564; (Places to visit)
N: 560 *with picture*
Caboto, Giovanni [Italian explorer] See Cabot,
John, *in this index*
Cabral, Amilcar [Portuguese Guinean political
leader]
Guinea-Bissau (History) G: 434
Cabral, Gonzalo [Portuguese navigator]
Azores A: 998
Latin America *map on* L: 105
Cabral, Luis [Guinea-Bissau political leader]
Guinea-Bissau (History) G: 434
Cabral, Pedro Álvares [Portuguese explorer] C: 8
Brazil (Portuguese rule) B: 583
Dias, Bartolomeu D: 185
Exploration *map on* E: 443; (Exploring the New
World) E: 444-445
Portugal (The age of exploration) P: 693
Cabrera Infante, Guillermo [Cuban author]
Cuba (The arts) Ci: 1171-1172
Cabrillo, Juan Rodríguez [Portuguese explorer]
C: 8
Cabrillo National Monument C: 9
California (Spanish and English exploration) C: 60
Latin America *map on* L: 105
Cabrillo National Monument [California] C: 9
National Park System (table: National
monuments) N: 50
Cabrini, Saint Frances Xavier [American social
worker] C: 9 *with portrait*
Cabrini-Green Homes [Chicago]
Chicago (The North Side) C: 423-424
Cabriole
Furniture (China) F: 571 *with picture*
Cacao [tree] C: 9 *with picture*
Africa *picture on* A: 111
Chocolate (The cacao tree) C: 518; (Harvesting
the cacao beans) C: 518; (History) C: 519
Cacaxtla [city, Mexico]
Tlaxcala T: 303
Cache [computing]
Computer (Microprocessors) Ci: 912
Web browser W: 175
Cachucha [dance]

Ballet (Romantic ballet) **B:** 51
Cacique [American Indians]
Latin America (Colonial rule) **L:** 104-105
Cacomistle [animal]
Animal *picture on* **A:** 482
Ringtail **R:** 344
Cactus [plant] **C:** 9 *with pictures*
Arizona (Plant and animal life) **A:** 683 *with picture*
Flower (Flowers of the desert) **F:** 290 *with picture;*
(table) **F:** 300 *with picture*
Gardening *picture on* **G:** 37
Mexico *picture on* **M:** 449
Plant *pictures on* **P:** 521, **P:** 527, **P:** 530, **P:** 538;
(Deserts) **P:** 523 *with picture;* (Movement of
water) **P:** 537
Saguaro **S:** 19
United States *picture on* **U:** 108
Cactus Jack [nickname]
Garner, John Nance **G:** 45
Cactus wren [bird]
Animal *picture on* **A:** 483
Bird (Birds of the desert) **B:** 339 *with picture*
Wren **W:** 504
CAD [design] *See* Computer-aided design *in this
index*
CAD [medicine] *See* Coronary artery disease *in
this index*
Cadaver
See also Corpse *in this index*
Transplant (Sources of donor organs) **T:** 380
Cadaver dog
Police dog **P:** 626
CADD [design] *See* Computer-aided design and
drafting *in this index*
Caddie Woodlawn [book by Brink]
Brink, Carol Ryrie **B:** 609
Caddisfly [insect] **C:** 11
Caddo Indians **C:** 11
Texas (Indian days) **T:** 204
Cadence [rhythm]
Music (Harmony) **M:** 951-952 *with diagrams*
Cadency, Mark of
Heraldry (Elements of a coat of arms) **H:** 196 *with
pictures*
Cadenza [music]
Concerto **Ci:** 928
Music (table) **M:** 954
Cadet [military]
Coast Guard, United States (Life in the Coast
Guard) **Ci:** 736
United States Air Force Academy **U:** 197 *with
picture*
United States Coast Guard Academy (Entrance
requirements) **U:** 199 *with pictures*
United States Military Academy **U:** 201 *with
picture*
Cadet match [wrestling]
Wrestling (Internaational competition) **W:** 505-
506
Cadettes, Girl Scout
Girl Scouts (Girl Scouts of the USA) **G:** 196
Cadillac [automobile]
Automobile (The birth of the automobile
industry) **A:** 966 *with pictures*
General Motors Company **G:** 83
Cadillac, Antoine de Lamothe [French colonial
official] *See* Lamothe, Antoine Laumet de, Sieur
de Cadillac *in this index*
Cadillac Automobile Company
Automobile (The birth of the automobile
industry) **A:** 966
Cadillac Mountain [Maine]
Acadia National Park **A:** 21
Maine (Mountains) **M:** 82
Cádiz [Spain] **C:** 11
Phoenicia (Language) **P:** 393
Spanish Armada (The two fleets) **So:** 755
Cadmium [element] **C:** 12
Cadmium sulfide photocell [sensor]
Light meter **L:** 294
Cadmus [Greek mythology] **C:** 12
Cadorna, Luigi [Italian general]
World War I (The Italian Front) **W:** 459
Cadre [military]
Army, United States (World War II) **A:** 739
Caduceus [emblem]
Mercury **M:** 416
Cadwalader, Thomas [American colonial leader]
New Jersey (Libraries) **N:** 235
Cady, Hamilton Perkins [American scientist]
Kansas (Interesting facts) **K:** 217
Cady, Raymond Davis [American inventor]
Match (The invention of book matches) **M:** 300a
Caecilian [amphibian] **C:** 12 *with picture*
Amphibian *picture on* **A:** 439; (Kinds of
amphibians) **A:** 440 *with picture*
Caecus, Appius Claudius [Roman government

official]
Appian Way **A:** 569
Caedmon [English poet]
English literature (Old English poetry) **E:** 314
Caelian Hill
Rome **R:** 429
Caenolestid [mammal]
Mammal (table) **M:** 128 *with picture*
Marsupial (Kinds of marsupials) **M:** 232
Caenorhabditis elegans [worm]
Human Genome Project **H:** 427
Caernarfon [Wales]
Wales (Revolts against England) **W:** 12
Caesar [title] **C:** 12
Caesar, Augustus *See* Augustus *in this index*
Caesar, Julius [literary figure]
Shakespeare, William: *(Julius Caesar)* **S:** 360
Caesar, Julius [Roman general] **C:** 13 *with picture*
Antony, Mark **A:** 561
Augustus **A:** 889
Calendar (The Julian calendar) **C:** 31
Cassius Longinus, Gaius **C:** 277
Chartres **C:** 386
Cicero, Marcus Tullius (His life) **Ci:** 552
Cleopatra **Ci:** 662a
England (The Roman conquest) **E:** 303
February **F:** 60
Gaul **G:** 70
History (The ancient Greeks and Romans)
H: 261-262
Julian calendar **J:** 187
July **J:** 188
Latin literature (The age of Cicero) **L:** 116
Library (Rome) **L:** 258
Pompey the Great **P:** 655
Quirinal Hill **Q:** 43
Rome, Ancient (The later years of the republic)
R: 445
Rubicon **R:** 507
Triumvirate **T:** 448
Caesarea Augusta [former name]
Saragossa **S:** 123
Caesarean section [childbirth] *See* Cesarean
section *in this index*
Caesarion [son of]
Cleopatra (Cleopatra and Caesar) **Ci:** 662a
Caesarodunum [former town]
Tours **T:** 350
Caesar's Palace
Nevada *picture on* **N:** 157
Caesura
Poetry (Rhythm and meter) **P:** 591-593; (table)
P: 594
Caetano, Marcello [Portuguese government
official]
Portugal (The Salazar dictatorship) **P:** 694
Salazar, António de Oliveira **S:** 60
Cafe [restaurant]
Greece *picture on* **G:** 356
Paris *picture on* **P:** 161
Café-au-lait spot [disorder]
Neurofibromatosis **N:** 152
Cafeteria
Restaurant (Kinds of restaurants) **R:** 262
Caffeine [chemical] **C:** 14
Coffee (Kinds of coffee) **Ci:** 755
Stimulant **So:** 901
Tea (Tea and health) **T:** 63
CAFTA-DR [agreement] *See* Dominican Republic-
Central America-United States Free Trade
Agreement *in this index*
Caftan [clothing]
Clothing (Clothing under Islam) **Ci:** 697-698
Morocco (Way of life) **M:** 811-812
Cage
Circus *picture on* **Ci:** 562a
Cage, John [American composer] **C:** 14
Aleatory music **A:** 339
Classical music (Experimental music) **Ci:** 650
Cunningham, Merce **Ci:** 1192
Performance art **P:** 285
Piano (History) **P:** 447-448
Postmodernism **P:** 709
Cage, Nicolas [American actor]
Motion picture (Best performance by an actor:
1995) **M:** 862a
Cagliari, Paolo [Italian painter]
Veronese, Paolo **V:** 338
Cagney, James [American actor] **C:** 14 *with picture*
Motion picture (Best performance by an actor:
1942) **M:** 862a
Cahaba
Alabama (Early statehood) **A:** 275
Cahaya Bahari [ship]
Shipwreck (table: Major shipwrecks) **S:** 428
Cahill, Thaddeus [American inventor]
Electronic music **E:** 205

Cahill, William T. [American political leader]
New Jersey (table) **N:** 249
Cahokia [Illinois]
Illinois (French and British control) **I:** 72
Cahokia Mounds [Illinois]
Illinois (Places to visit) **I:** 62
Mound builders (Mississippian Period) **M:** 883
with picture
Cahuchu [tree]
Rubber (First uses) **R:** 500-501
Cahuilla Indians
Palm Springs **P:** 110
Caicos Islands
Turks and Caicos Islands **T:** 514b
Caillebotte, Gustave [French artist]
Painting (Edouard Manet and the Impressionists)
P: 71
Caillié, René [French explorer]
Exploration (The exploration of Africa) **E:** 448
with map
Caiman [animal]
Alligator **A:** 375
Crocodile **Ci:** 1149
Reptile (Crocodilians) **R:** 251
Cain [Biblical figure] **C:** 15
Abel **A:** 9
Cain, James M. [American author] **C:** 15
Caine, Michael [British actor]
Motion picture (Best performance by an actor in
a supporting role: 1986, 1999) **M:** 862b
Caine Mutiny, The [book by Wouk]
Wouk, Herman **W:** 502
Caine Mutiny Court-Martial, The [play by Wouk]
Wouk, Herman **W:** 502
Cairenes [people]
Cairo (People) **C:** 16
Cairn terrier [dog] **C:** 15
Dog *picture on* **D:** 273
Cairo [Egypt] **C:** 15 *with pictures and map*
Africa *picture on* **A:** 99
Egypt **E:** 120 *with picture, picture on* **E:** 124; (City
life) **E:** 123; (Climate) **E:** 127
Fātimid dynasty **F:** 55
Cairo Conference [1943]
Chiang Soong Mei-ling **C:** 419
"Cairo Trilogy" [books by Mahfouz]
Mahfouz, Naguib **M:** 65
Cairo University
Cairo (Education and cultural life) **C:** 16
Egypt (Education) **E:** 124-125
Caisson [construction] **C:** 18 *with diagram*
Air lock **A:** 197 *with diagram*
Building construction (Constructing a skyscraper)
B: 683-684
Caisson [munitions]
Artillery (Field artillery) **A:** 762
Caisson disease *See* Bends *in this index*
Caius, John [English scholar]
Dog (History) **D:** 281
Caius, Saint [pope]
Pope (table) **P:** 666
Cajun music
Country music (Cajun music) **Ci:** 1098a
Cajuns [people] **C:** 19
Acadia **A:** 21
Louisiana **L:** 478; (Population) **L:** 482 *with picture;*
(Spanish Louisiana) **L:** 498
Cake [food] **C:** 19
Cake flour
Flour (Types of flour) **F:** 268
Cakes and Ale [book by Maugham]
Maugham, W. Somerset **M:** 312
Cakewalk [dance]
Popular music (Ragtime, jazz, and blues) **P:** 670
Cakobau [Fiji chief]
Fiji (History) **F:** 98
Calabash [gourd] **C:** 19
Gourd **G:** 281 *with picture*
Calabash [tree]
Calabash **C:** 19
Caladium [plant] **C:** 19 *with picture*
Calais [France] **C:** 20
Hundred Years' War **H:** 437
Calakmul Biosphere Reserve
Campeche **C:** 91
Calamine [mineral]
Zinc **Z:** 594
Calamistrum [zoology]
Spider (How spiders make silk) **So:** 786
Calamity Jane [American frontierswoman] **C:** 20
with portrait
South Dakota (Territorial days) **So:** 681
Calamus *See* Quill *in this index*
"Calamus" [poems by Whitman]
Whitman, Walt (His work) **W:** 294
Calatrava, Santiago [Spanish architect]
September 11 terrorist attacks (Moving forward)

S: 310b-310c

Calceolaria [plant]
Figwort family F: 97
Calciferol [vitamin]
Vitamin (Vitamin D) V: 430
Calcification [medicine]
Mammography M: 130
Calcite [mineral] C: 20
Alabaster A: 280
Dolomite D: 296
Limestone L: 307
Mineral *picture on* M: 569
Polarized light (Polarizing filters) P: 618
Sand S: 106
Stalactite So: 824
Calcitonin [hormone]
Hormone (Blood composition hormones) H: 336
Thyroid gland T: 274
Calcium [element] C: 20
Milk (Minerals) M: 546
Nutrition (Minerals) N: 625-626
Osteoporosis (Prevention and treatment) O: 868
Rickets R: 334
Calcium antagonist [drug] *See* Calcium channel
blocker *in this index*
Calcium blocker [drug] *See* Calcium channel
blocker *in this index*
Calcium carbide [chemical] C: 21
Calcium carbonate [mineral] C: 21
Antacid A: 529
Calcite C: 20
Chalk C: 35
Coral (Stony corals) Ci: 1048a
Coral reef (How coral reefs form) Ci: 1048b-1049
Dolomite D: 296
Limestone L: 307
Salt, Chemical S: 75
Calcium channel blocker [drug] C: 21 *with
diagrams*
Angina pectoris A: 461
Blood pressure B: 416
Heart (Treatment) H: 138; (Progress in treatment
and prevention) H: 145
Migraine M: 538
Calcium cyanamide [chemical]
Calcium carbide C: 21
Calcium hydroxide [chemical]
Lime L: 306
Calcium nitrate [chemical]
Saltpeter S: 76a
Calcium oxide [chemical]
Glass (Soda-lime glass) G: 213
Lime L: 306
Calculator C: 22 *with picture*
Abacus A: 3
Arithmetic A: 665 *with picture*; (Calculation tools)
A: 669
Computer (History) Ci: 924a
Decimal system (Use of decimals smaller than
one) D: 73
Electronics (How an electronic system works)
E: 208 *with picture*
Calculus [dentistry]
Teeth (Dental checkups) T: 82; (Periodontal
diseases) T: 85 *with picture*
Calculus [mathematics] C: 22 *with diagrams*
Archimedes (His mathematics) A: 605
Mathematics (Branches of mathematics) M: 303;
(Mathematics and the scientific revolution)
M: 306-307
Physics (Newton) P: 439
Calcutta [India] *See* Kolkata *in this index*
Caldecott, Randolph [British artist] C: 25
Literature for children *picture on* L: 362; (The rise
of illustration) L: 364
Caldecott Medal [award] C: 26 *with pictures*
Literature for children (Awards) L: 367
Melcher, Frederic Gershom M: 389
Calder, Alexander [American sculptor] C: 26 *with
picture*
Chicago (Places to visit) C: 430-431
Mobile M: 682
Sculpture (Form and treatment) S: 230-231 *with
picture*
Calder Hall [England]
Electric power (Growth of the electric power
industry) E: 186
Caldera [geology]
Crater Ci: 1121
Moon (Determining the origin of craters)
M: 793-794
Volcano (Silicic caldera complexes) V: 442 *with
picture*
Caldera, Rafael [Venezuelan political leader]
Venezuela (The late 1900's) V: 305
Calderón, Rafael [Costa Rican political leader]
Costa Rica (Rebellions and reforms) Ci: 1084

Calderón, Sila María [Puerto Rican political leader]
Puerto Rico (Puerto Rico today) P: 884
Calderón de la Barca, Pedro [Spanish dramatist]
C: 27
Drama (Secular drama) D: 333
Spanish literature (The 1600's) So: 759-760
Calderón Hinojosa, Felipe [Mexican political
leader] C: 27 *with portrait*
Mexico (Recent developments) M: 474
Calderone, Mary Steichen [American doctor] C: 27
Caldwell, Erskine [American author] C: 28
Caldwell, Jonathan [American military leader]
Blue Hen B: 420
Caldwell, Millard F. [American political leader]
Florida (table) F: 260
Caldwell, Sarah [American conductor] C: 28
Caldwell, T. R. [American political leader]
North Carolina (table) N: 490
Calé [people]
Roma R: 402b
Calèche [vehicle]
Quebec (Recreation) Q: 36
Caledonia [Scottish history] C: 28
Scotland (The Roman invasion) S: 219
Caledonia Argus [newspaper]
Harding, Warren Gamaliel (Childhood) H: 56
Caledonian Canal [waterway, Scotland]
Scotland (Rivers and lakes) S: 217 *with map*
Calendar C: 28 *with pictures*
Aztec (Religion) A: 1000 *with picture*
Christian Era C: 522e
Egypt, Ancient (Sciences) E: 139
Indian, American (Writing) I: 150
Julian calendar J: 187
Maya (Communication and learning) M: 324
Month M: 767
Universities and colleges (The academic
calendar) U: 209
Year (The calendar year) Y: 554
Calendar [government]
Congress of the United States (Passing a bill)
Ci: 945
Calendar month
Month M: 767
Calendar Round [cycle]
Calendar (The Maya) C: 31
Calendar Stone [sculpture]
Aztec (Arts and crafts) A: 1001 *with picture*
Calendar year
Leap year L: 162
Calender [machine]
Paper (Sheet formation) P: 135-136
Rubber (Shaping) R: 505
Calendering [industrial process]
Paper (Sheet formation) P: 135-136 *with diagram*;
(Special kinds of paper) P: 136
Plastics (Laminating) P: 558 *with picture*
Polyvinyl chloride P: 652
Rubber (Shaping) R: 505
Textile (Finishing the fabric) T: 217
Tire (Preliminary operations) T: 295-296
Calends [Roman calendar]
Month M: 767
Calendula [plant] C: 32 *with picture*
Calf [anatomy]
Leg (The leg) L: 182 *with diagram*
Calf [animal]
Camel (Young) C: 79 *with picture*
Cattle C: 306; (Breeding) C: 311-312
Dolphin (The life of dolphins) D: 298
Elephant *picture on* E: 231; (Elephant families)
E: 229
Meat (Kinds of meat) M: 347
Veal V: 291
Whale (Reproduction) W: 260 *with picture*
Calf bone [anatomy]
Human body (table) H: 422 *with diagram*
Calf roping
Rodeo R: 397
Calfa, Marián [Czechoslovak political leader]
Czechoslovakia (The Velvet Revolution) Ci: 1216
Calgary [Alberta] C: 32 *with pictures and map*
Alberta *picture on* A: 313; (table: Average
monthly weather) A: 324
Calgary, University of C: 35
Calgary Flames [team]
Hockey (table: National Hockey League) H: 281
Calgary Stampede [rodeo]
Alberta *picture on* A: 321
Calgary (History) C: 34
Calgary Stampeders [team]
Football (Canadian Football League) F: 364
Calgary Tower
Calgary (The city) C: 33 *with picture*
Calgary Zoo
Alberta (Places to visit) A: 320
Calhoun, John Caldwell [American political

leader] C: 35 *with portrait*
Adams, John Quincy (table) A: 43
Compromise of 1850 Ci: 907
Jackson, Andrew (Election of 1828) J: 10; (Split
with Calhoun) J: 11
Nullification N: 603
South Carolina (Nullification) So: 660
United States, History of the (The War of 1812)
U: 165; (Jackson as president) U: 171; (The
nation divided [1850-1869]) U: 174
Cali [Colombia]
Colombia (Civil war) Ci: 784
Caliban [literary figure]
Shakespeare, William: (*The Tempest*) S: 365
Caliber [measurement]
Ammunition (The bullet) A: 435 *with picture*
Bullet B: 695
Gun G: 440
Rifle (Kinds of rifles) R: 338
Calicivirus [viral disease]
Conservation (Australia) Ci: 989-990
Calico [fabric] C: 35
Calico Bush [book by Field]
Field, Rachel F: 92
Calico cat
Cat (Coat) C: 287 *with picture*
Calico ryukin [fish]
Goldfish *picture on* G: 258
Calico salmon *See* Chum salmon *in this index*
Calicut [India]
Exploration (The voyage around Africa) E: 444
Califano, Joseph Anthony, Jr. [American
government official] C: 35
California C: 36 *with pictures and maps*
See also the list of Related articles in the California
article
Asian Americans (History of Asian immigration)
A: 812d
Automobile (Air pollution) A: 964
Divorce (No-fault divorce) D: 251
Earthquake (Predicting earthquakes) E: 38b
Environmental pollution (Government action)
E: 335
Flag *picture on* F: 210
Forty-Niners F: 420
Global warming (Other measures) G: 232d
Gold rush (Gold rushes in the United States)
G: 254
Hispanic Americans (In the Southwest) H: 251
Indian, American (Indians of California) I: 163
with picture and map
Ladybug L: 25
Mission life in America (Western missions)
M: 618-619 *with picture*
Pioneer life in America (Crossing the Plains)
P: 485-486
Plate tectonics (Transform plate boundaries)
P: 563
Polk, James Knox (The Mexican War) P: 643
Raisin R: 129
Same-sex marriage S: 78
United States *picture on* U: 125; (Climate) U: 126
with picture
United States, History of the (The nation divided
[1850-1869]) U: 174-175
Westward movement in America (California)
W: 249
California, Gulf of *See* Gulf of California *in this
index*
California, University of C: 65
California (Schools) C: 40; (Libraries) C: 40; (The
mid-1900's) C: 62-63
Los Alamos National Laboratory L: 455
Los Angeles (Education) L: 463-464 *with picture*
Supreme Court of the United States (table)
So: 1002
California buckwheat [plant]
Plant *picture on* P: 525
California condor [bird]
Animal (Breeding in captivity) A: 505
Bird (Endangered species) B: 370 *with picture*
Condor (The California condor) C: 929 *with picture*
Endangered species *picture on* E: 271; (table)
E: 270
Vulture (New World vultures) V: 454
Wildlife conservation (Endangered species)
W: 304
California Electric Light Company
Electric power (Early developments) E: 186
California flyingfish [fish]
Fish *picture on* F: 152
California gull
Bird (Birds of inland waters and marshes) B: 340
with picture
California Institute of Technology [Pasadena]
C: 65
Jet Propulsion Laboratory J: 115

Palomar Observatory P: 112
California laurel [tree]
Laurel L: 121
California live oak
Oak (Red oaks) O: 635-636
California-Pacific International Exposition
[1935-1936]
California (Progress as a state) C: 62
California Palace of the Legion of Honor
San Francisco (Libraries and museums) S: 96
California poppy [plant]
Flower *picture on* F: 288
Poppy P: 668
California quail [bird]
Quail Q: 4
California rattail [fish]
Fish *picture on* F: 156
California red fir [tree]
Fir F: 120 *with picture*
California redwood [tree]
Redwood R: 192
Sequoia S: 310d
California scrub oak
Oak (Red oaks) O: 635-636
Plant *picture on* P: 525
California sea lion
Seal (Seals and fishing crews) S: 267
California sheepshead [fish]
Redfish R: 191
Wrasse W: 503
California State Colleges
California State University C: 65
California State University C: 65
California (Schools) C: 40
San Bernardino S: 87 *with picture*
California State Water Project
California (Water) C: 54-55
California Trail [U.S. history]
Wyoming W: 517; (The great trails) W: 533
California white oak
Oak (White oaks) O: 635
Tree *pictures on* T: 423
Californian [newspaper]
California (Communication) C: 58
Californios [people]
Hispanic Americans (In the Southwest) H: 251
Californium [element] C: 66
Transuranium element T: 401
Caligula [Roman emperor] C: 66
Agrippina the Younger A: 162
Caligula [play by Camus]
Camus, Albert C: 97
Caliper [measuring device] C: 66 *with pictures*
Divider D: 241
Micrometer M: 514 *with picture*
Vernier V: 338
Caliper brake
Bicycle (Steering and stopping) B: 290 *with
diagram*
Brake (Mechanical brakes) B: 560
Caliph [title]
Arabs (The rise and spread of Islam) A: 589-590
Egypt (Muslim rule) E: 130
Islamic Empire I: 470
Middle East (The spread of Islam) M: 533
Muslims (The early caliphs) M: 964a
Religion (Islam) R: 223
Shi'ites S: 400
World, History of the (The Islamic world) W: 434
Calisthenics C: 66
Calisto [literary figure]
Spanish literature (The 1400's) So: 758
Calistus I, Saint [pope]
Pope (table) P: 666
Calistus II [pope]
Pope (table) P: 666
Calistus III [antipope]
Pope (table) P: 666
Calistus III [pope]
Pope (table) P: 666
Call
Square dancing So: 811
Call and response pattern [music]
Folk music (American folk music) F: 321-322
Gospel music G: 277
Call blocking [service]
Telephone (Residential services) T: 98-99
Call forwarding [service]
Telephone (Residential services) T: 98
Call It Sleep [book by Roth]
Roth, Henry R: 487
Call letters [communications]
Radio (table) R: 84
Call Me Ishmael [book by Olson]
Olson, Charles O: 745
Call Me Madam [musical]
Merman, Ethel M: 418

Call number
Library (Organizing materials) L: 255
A Guide to Research Skills **Research Guide: 28**
Call of the Toad, The [book by Grass]
Novel (The novel today) N: 575
Call of the Wild, The [book by London]
London, Jack L: 444
Call option [investment]
Commodity exchange (Options contracts) Ci: 874
Call service
Prostitution P: 830
Call waiting [service]
Telephone (Residential services) T: 98
Calla [plant] C: 66 *with picture*
Calla lily [plant]
Calla C: 67
Callable bond
Bond (Kinds of bonds) B: 454
Callaghan, James [British political leader] C: 67
United Kingdom (Economic recovery—and
collapse) U: 72-73
Callaghan, Morley [Canadian author] C: 67
Callahan, Harry [American photographer]
Photography (A diversity of styles) P: 426-427
Callaloo [food]
Virgin Islands, United States (Food) V: 394
Callampa [slum]
Chile (City life) C: 460
Callao [Peru] C: 67
Callas, Maria [Greek singer] C: 67 *with portrait*
Callaway Gardens [park, Pine Mountain]
Georgia (Places to visit) G: 122 *with picture*
Callbeck, Catherine [Canadian political leader]
Prince Edward Island (table) P: 791; (The late
1900's) P: 793
Called strike
Baseball (Outs by batters) B: 128; (Rule changes)
B: 133
Caller [dancing]
Square dancing So: 811
Caller I.D. [telephone service] *See* Automatic caller
identification *in this index*
Calles, Plutarco Elías [Mexican political leader]
Ávila Camacho, Manuel A: 993
Mexico (Reforms of the early 1900's) M: 472
Calley, William L., Jr. [American soldier]
My Lai Massacre M: 969
Vietnam War (Growing protest) V: 376
War crime (The Vietnam War) W: 27
Callicrates [Greek architect]
Parthenon P: 183
Calligrammes [poems by Apollinaire]
Apollinaire, Guillaume A: 566
Calligraphy [writing] C: 67 *with pictures*
Arabs (Literature and the arts) A: 587-588
China (Painting) C: 487 *with picture*
Handwriting H: 46
Callimachus [Greek poet]
Greek literature (The Hellenistic Age) G: 378
Information retrieval (History) I: 269
Calling card [electronic device]
Telephone (Other services) T: 98
Calling hare [animal]
Pika P: 461 *with picture*
Calling the Role After an Engagement, Crimea
[painting by Thompson]
Painting (Women artists) P: 73-74 *with picture*
Calliope [Greek mythology]
Muses M: 937
Calliope [musical instrument] C: 68 *with picture*
Calliope hummingbird
Hummingbird (Size) H: 433
Calliopsis [plant]
Coreopsis Ci: 1052
Callisto [Greek mythology]
Artemis A: 750
Big and Little Dippers (The Little Dipper) B: 296
Boötes B: 480
Callisto [satellite] C: 68 *with picture*
Galileo G: 13
Jupiter (Galilean satellites) J: 200a
Callot, Jacques [French artist] C: 69 *with picture*
Callous *See* Callus *in this index*
Callus [disorder] C: 69
Bone (Broken bones) B: 456-457 *with diagram*
Keratin K: 305
Calm [weather]
Wind (table) W: 330
Calm, No. 357 [painting by Kandinsky]
Kandinsky, Wassily *picture on* K: 213
Calms, Regions of [geography] C: 69
Calmy-Rey, Micheline [Swiss political leader]
Switzerland (Recent developments) So: 1061
Calomel [medication]
Mercury (Compounds) M: 414
Caloric restriction
Aging (Overcoming aging) A: 142

Caloric theory
Heat (The study of heat) H: 154
Physics (Developments in the 1800's) P: 440
Calorie [measurement] C: 70
Energy (Units of work and energy) E: 274-275
Food supply (Calories) F: 346 *with picture*
Heat (Temperature and heat) H: 150
Metric system (Non-SI metric units) M: 440
Nutrition (Kinds of nutrients) N: 625; (Deficiency
diseases) N: 630
Obesity (Causes of obesity) O: 642a
Weight control W: 181; (table) W: 182
Calorimeter [instrument]
Calorie C: 70
Particle detector (Sampling calorimeters) P: 187
Caloris Basin [Mercury]
Mercury (Surface and atmosphere) M: 414
Space exploration *picture on* So: 709
Calotype
Communication (The 1800's) Ci: 881-882
Photography (The invention of photography)
P: 422-423
Talbotype T: 19
Calpolli [group]
Aztec (The Aztec empire) A: 999; (Family life)
A: 1001
Caltech [nickname]
California Institute of Technology C: 65
Caltrans District 7 Headquarters [Los Angeles]
Mayne, Thom M: 328 *with picture*
Calumet *See* Peace pipe *in this index*
Calumet region [Indiana]
Gary G: 47
Calusa [people]
Ponce de León, Juan (Florida expeditions)
P: 655-656
Calvary [New Testament] C: 70
Jesus Christ (The Crucifixion) J: 108b
Calvary cross [symbol]
Cross *picture on* Ci: 1155
Calvert, Cecilius [English colonial official] C: 70
Maryland M: 240; (Exploration and settlement)
M: 256
United States, History of the (Virginia and
Maryland) U: 153
Calvert, Charles [English colonial official] C: 70
Calvert, George [English political leader] C: 70
Maryland (Exploration and settlement) M: 256
Newfoundland and Labrador (Colonization)
N: 375
Calvert, Leonard [British colonial official]
Calvert, Cecilius C: 70
Claiborne's Rebellion Ci: 636
Maryland (Colonial days) M: 256
United States, History of the (Virginia and
Maryland) U: 153
Calvert, Lorne A. [Canadian political leader]
Saskatchewan (table) S: 144
Calvin, John [French-Swiss religious leader] C: 70
with portrait
Christianity (The Reformed tradition) C: 525
Classical music (The Reformation) Ci: 646-647
Geneva G: 87
Hymn (History) H: 475
Predestination P: 734
Presbyterians (Teaching and worship) P: 756a
Protestantism (The conservative reform
movements) P: 834-835
Puritans (Puritan beliefs) P: 910
Reformation (John Calvin) R: 198
Switzerland (Religious civil wars) So: 1060
Calvin, Melvin [American chemist]
Chemistry (Development of organic chemistry)
C: 404 *with picture*
Nobel Prizes (Chemistry: 1961) N: 443
Calvin and Hobbes [comic strip]
Comics *picture on* Ci: 870
Calving [geography]
Antarctica (Ice) A: 532
Glacier (How glaciers form) G: 202-203 *with
picture*
Iceberg (Antarctic icebergs) I: 17
Calvinism [religion]
Calvin, John (Calvinism) C: 71
Edwards, Jonathan E: 114
Religious life (Religious life in the 1700's and
1800's) R: 227
Weber, Max W: 176
Calvino, Italo [Italian author]
Novel (The novel today) N: 575
Calypso [Greek mythology]
Odyssey: (The *Odyssey* begins) O: 675
Calypso [music] C: 71
Calypso [satellite]
Saturn (Satellites) S: 151-152
Calypso [ship]
Cousteau, Jacques-Yves Ci: 1106

Calyx [botany]
Flower (The calyx) F: 293 *with picture*
Plant (Flowers) P: 531 *with picture*
Calzabigi, Ranieri di [Italian poet]
Gluck, Christoph Willibald G: 235
Calzone [food]
Pizza P: 504
Cam [lock]
Lock *picture on* L: 410
CAM [manufacturing] *See* Computer-aided machining; Computer-aided manufacturing *in this index*
Camacho, Manuel Ávila *See* Ávila Camacho, Manuel *in this index*
Camara, Moussa Dadis [Guinean political leader]
Guinea (History) G: 432
Camargo, Marie Anne Cupis de [French dancer]
Ballet (The rise of professional ballet) B: 51
Camber [physics]
Aerodynamics (Lift) A: 85
Cambest [horse]
Harness racing (History) H: 64
Cambiale di matrimonio, La [opera by Rossini]
Rossini, Gioacchino Antonio R: 484
Cambium [botany]
Bark (Inner bark) B: 110 *with diagram*
Grafting (Kinds of grafting) G: 298-299 *with picture*
Plant (Germination) P: 535-537 *with picture*
Root (Secondary tissues) R: 471 *with diagram*
Rubber (The rubber tree) R: 502
Stem (Herbaceous stems) So: 887
Tree (Trunk and branches) T: 416 *with diagram*
Cambodia C: 71 *with pictures and map*
Architecture (Indian architecture) A: 613 *with picture*
Cold War (To the brink and back) Ci: 765; (The Vietnam War) Ci: 769
Communism (Expansion in Southeast Asia) Ci: 894
Dance (Asian theatrical dance) D: 28-29
Flag *picture on* F: 202
France (The Fourth Republic) F: 475-476
Geneva Accords G: 87
Immigration *picture on* I: 81
Indochina I: 224 *with map*
Khmer Rouge K: 308b
Nixon, Richard Milhous (Events at home) N: 435
United Nations *picture on* U: 90
Vietnam (Invasion of Cambodia) V: 372
Vietnam War *map on* V: 373; (The invasion of Cambodia) V: 376; (Other effects in Southeast Asia) V: 377
Cambrai, Battle of [1917]
Tank (History) T: 27
Cambrian Explosion [geology]
Cambrian Period C: 74
Cambrian Mountains [Wales]
United Kingdom (Wales) U: 59 *with map*
Wales (Surface features) W: 11 *with map*
Cambrian Period [geology] C: 74
Earth (The Paleozoic Era) E: 27; (table) E: 30
Prehistoric animal (The first animals with backbones) P: 736; (table) P: 738
Cambridge [England] C: 74
England (The beginnings of Parliament) E: 306
Cambridge [Massachusetts] C: 74
Cambridge, University of [England] C: 75
Cambridge C: 74
England (The beginnings of Parliament) E: 306
Cambridge Flag [U.S. history]
Flag (First United States flags) F: 208-210 *with picture*
Cambridge Modern History [book by Acton]
Acton, Lord A: 30
Cambridge Platonists [philosophers]
Plato (Plato's place in Western thought) P: 569
Cambridge Shakespeare [book]
Shakespeare, William (Editions of the 1700's and 1800's) S: 369-370
Cambyses [Persian ruler]
Persia, Ancient (The Achaemenid Empire) P: 298
World, History of the (Civilizations of southwest Asia) W: 426
Camcorder [electronic device] C: 75 *with picture*
Camera *picture on* C: 83; (Motion-picture cameras) C: 84
Motion picture *picture on* M: 857
Television (VCR's and DVR's) T: 110c
Videotape recorder (Types of videotape recorders) V: 360
Camden [New Jersey] C: 76
Camden, Battle of [1780] C: 76
Revolution, American (table) R: 276; (Camden) R: 285
Camden, William [English historian]
History (Antiquarian research and the

philosophes) H: 262
Came [fine arts]
Stained glass (How stained-glass windows are made) So: 821-822
Camel [animal] C: 76 *with pictures*
Asia *picture on* A: 778
Dromedary D: 348
Sahara (People) S: 21 *with picture*
Camel, Battle of the [A.D. 656]
Muslims (Alī) M: 964b
Camel caravan [transportation]
Caravan C: 202
Camel cricket [insect]
Cricket Ci: 1131
Camel of the prairies [nickname]
Conestoga wagon Ci: 931
Camelback [house]
New Orleans (Residential districts) N: 279
Camellia [plant] C: 79 *with picture*
Camelot [legendary castle] C: 79
Arthur, King A: 757
Camel's-hair cloth [fabric] C: 79
Camel (Camels and people) C: 77
Camels Hump [mountain, Vermont]
Vermont *picture on* V: 318
Camembert [cheese]
Cheese (Soft cheese) C: 392 *with picture*
Cameo [gem] C: 80
Camera C: 80 *with pictures*
See also Camcorder; Television camera *in this index*
Charge-coupled device C: 378
Copying machine (Projection copying) Ci: 1045
Journalism (Television journalism) J: 175
Land, Edwin Herbert L: 56
Motion picture (Shooting the movie) M: 852; (The camera) M: 856 *with pictures*
Photography P: 406; (Cameras) P: 417 *with pictures*
Stereoscope So: 893
Videotape recorder V: 360
Camera obscura [device] C: 84 *with diagram*
Photography (Early developments) P: 422
Camera phone
Photography (Other types of cameras) P: 409
Camera rehearsal *See* Dress rehearsal *in this index*
Camerata [group]
Opera (The development of opera) O: 797
Cameron, David [British political leader] C: 84
Cameron, Donald W. [Canadian political leader]
Nova Scotia (table) N: 567
Cameron, James [Canadian-born film director] C: 84
Diving, Underwater (Diving in vehicles) D: 246
Motion picture (Best achievement in directing: 1997) M: 862
Cameron, James D. [American government official]
Grant, Ulysses S. (table) G: 316
Cameron, Julia Margaret [British photographer] C: 84
Photography (Artistic advances) P: 424 *with picture*
Cameron, Simon [American government official]
Lincoln, Abraham (table) L: 323
Cameron, William E. [American political leader]
Virginia (table) V: 417
Cameron plaid
Tartan *picture on* T: 47
Camerone, Battle of [1863]
Foreign Legion (History) F: 386
Cameroon C: 85 *with pictures and map*
British Cameroons B: 611
Flag *picture on* F: 198
Nigeria (Independence) N: 417
Cameroon, Mount *See* Mount Cameroon *in this index*
Cameroon People's Democratic Movement [political party]
Cameroon (History) C: 86-87
Camille [play by Dumas]
Dumas, Alexandre, fils D: 382
Camino Real, El [road] *See* El Camino Real *in this index*
Cammarano, Salvatore [Italian librettist]
Opera: (*Lucia di Lammermoor*) O: 804; (*Trovatore, Il*) O: 808
Camões, Luis de [Portuguese author]
Portugal (The arts) P: 689-690
Camogie [sport]
Ireland (Recreation) I: 420
Camomile [plant] C: 87 *with picture*
Camorra [Italian history]
Mafia M: 41
Camouflage [biology]
See also Protective coloration *in this index*
Animal (How animals protect themselves) A: 493

with picture
Plant *picture on* P: 541
Camouflage [warfare] C: 87 *with picture*
Camp, Walter [American football coach]
Football (The history of football) F: 365
Camp David [Maryland] C: 87
Cold War (The spirit of Camp David) Ci: 767
President of the United States (Recreation) P: 767 *with picture*
Camp David Accords [1978]
Arab-Israeli conflict (The Camp David Accords) A: 582a
Egypt (Renewed warfare and peace) E: 133 *with picture*
Israel (The Camp David Accords) I: 488
Middle East (The 1970's and the 1980's) M: 534a
Camp Dearborn [park]
Dearborn D: 60
Camp Dubois [U.S. history]
Lewis and Clark expedition (Preparation) L: 222a
Camp Fire USA [organization] C: 88 *with pictures*
Camp H. M. Smith [Hawaii] C: 90
Camp Knox [Kentucky]
Fort Knox F: 413
Camp Lejeune [North Carolina] C: 90
Camp McDowell [U.S. history]
Phoenix (History) P: 398-399
Camp meeting [religion] C: 90
Pioneer life in America (Religion) P: 484
Camp Pendleton [California] C: 90
Camp Sebago-Wohelo
Camp Fire USA (History) C: 90
Camp X-Ray
Bush, George Walker (Homeland security) B: 722g
Guantánamo G: 411
Campa Indians
Indian, American *picture on* I: 176
Campaign [advertising]
Advertising (Creating advertisements) A: 76a
Campaign [glassmaking]
Glass (Melting) G: 215
"Campaign, The" [poem by Addison]
Addison, Joseph A: 47
Campaign director
Election campaign (Campaign organizations) E: 160
Campaign funds [politics]
Election campaign (Campaign financing) E: 160
Federal Election Commission F: 63
Political party (Raising funds) P: 633
Taft, William Howard (Legislative achievements) T: 11
Campaign medal
Medals, decorations, and orders (Military awards) M: 355
Campanella, Roy [American baseball player]
Baseball (table: Hall of Fame) B: 134
Campanella, Tommaso [Italian philosopher]
Italian literature (The Baroque period and the Enlightenment) I: 494
Campanile [architecture] C: 90
Bell (Uses of bells) B: 239
Campanile of Saint Mark
Venice (The city) V: 306 *with picture and map*
Campanula [plant] C: 90a *with picture*
Campau, Louis [American pioneer]
Grand Rapids G: 309
Campbell, Alex B. [Canadian political leader]
Prince Edward Island (table) P: 791
Campbell, Alexander [American religious leader]
Disciples of Christ D: 223
Campbell, Alexander [Canadian political leader]
Confederation of Canada (Fathers of Confederation) Ci: 935 *with picture*
Campbell, Andrew J. [American explorer]
Luray Caverns L: 526
Campbell, Avril Phaedra *See* Campbell, Kim *in this index*
Campbell, Ben Nighthorse [American political leader] C: 90a *with portrait*
Campbell, Bennett [Canadian political leader]
Prince Edward Island (table) P: 791
Campbell, Colen [Scottish architect]
Architecture (The Palladian Revival) A: 623
Campbell, David [American political leader]
Virginia (table) V: 417
Campbell, Donald [British boat racer] C: 90a
Campbell, Douglas L. [Canadian political leader]
Manitoba (table) M: 159
Campbell, Earl [American football player]
Football (table) F: 363
Campbell, George T. [father of Campbell, Kim (Early life) C: 90b-90c *with picture*
Campbell, Gordon [Canadian political leader]
British Columbia (table) B: 628
Campbell, Jack M. [American political leader]

New Mexico (table) N: 272
Campbell, James [American government official]
Pierce, Franklin (table) P: 456
Campbell, James E. [American political leader]
Ohio (table) O: 699
Campbell, Jane L. [American political leader]
Cleveland (Recent developments) Ci: 667
Campbell, John [American publisher]
Journalism (Early American journalism) J: 174
Printing (Early printing in North America) P: 803
Campbell, John A. [American government official]
Wyoming (Territorial progress) W: 534
Campbell, John Archibald [American jurist]
Hampton Roads Conference H: 37
Supreme Court of the United States (table)
So: 1000
Campbell, John D. [harness driver]
Harness racing (History) H: 64
Campbell, John Douglas Sutherland [Canadian statesman]
Lorne, Marquess of L: 455
Campbell, John W., Jr. [American editor]
Science fiction (The Golden Age) S: 205
Campbell, Joseph [American scholar] C: 90a
Mythology (Literary approaches) M: 990
Campbell, Kim [Canadian political leader] C: 90b
with pictures
Canada, History of (The 1993 national election)
C: 151
Chrétien, Jean (The 1993 election) C: 522c
Mulroney, Brian (The constitutional crisis) M: 918
Campbell, Sir Malcolm [British boat racer]
Campbell, Donald C: 90a
Campbell, Mrs. Patrick [British actress] C: 91
Campbell, Phyllis Cook [mother of]
Campbell, Kim (Early life) C: 90b-90c
Campbell, Robert [American businessman]
Wyoming (Exploration) W: 533
Campbell, Robert [British explorer]
Yukon (History) Y: 581
Campbell, Thane A. [Canadian political leader]
Prince Edward Island (table) P: 791
Campbell, Thomas [American religious leader]
Disciples of Christ D: 223
Campbell, Thomas E. [American political leader]
Arizona (table) A: 687
Campbell, Thomas M. [American political leader]
Texas (table) T: 203
Campbell, Wilfred [Canadian poet]
Canadian literature (Poetry: 1850-1918) C: 157
Campbell, William B. [American political leader]
Tennessee (table) T: 152
Campbell-Bannerman, Sir Henry [British political leader]
United Kingdom (table: British prime ministers)
U: 72
Campbell plaid
Tartan *picture on* T: 47
Campeachy [former city]
Laffite, Jean L: 29
Campeche [state, Mexico] C: 91
Campeche [city, Mexico]
Campeche C: 91
Campernelle jonquil [plant]
Jonquil J: 159
Campesino [people]
Bolivia (Way of life) B: 443
Colombia (People) Ci: 779
Campfire
Camping (Building a campfire) C: 94 *with picture*
Campground
Forestry (Recreation areas) F: 407 *with picture*
Camphor [chemical] C: 91
Plastics (The invention of Celluloid) P: 559
Camphor [tree]
Camphor C: 91 *with picture*
Campin, Robert [Belgian painter] C: 91 *with picture*
Campine [region, Belgium]
Belgium (The Kempenland) B: 230
Camping C: 92 *with pictures*
Camp Fire USA (Camp Fire USA programs) C: 88
with picture
Canoeing (Canoe camping) C: 182
Hiking H: 230
National Park System (Camping) N: 47
Recreational vehicle R: 183
Tent T: 168
Camping trailer [vehicle]
Recreational vehicle *picture on* R: 183; (Folding camping trailers) R: 184
Trailer (Recreational trailers) T: 367
Campion [plant]
Flower *picture on* F: 289
Plant *picture on* P: 524
Campion, Thomas [English poet]
English literature (Elizabethan poetry) E: 316
Campo, Rafael Martín del [Mexican author]

Literature for children *picture on* L: 355
Campo Formio, Treaty of [1797]
Napoleon I (Victories in Italy) N: 14
Napoleonic Wars (The Army of Italy) N: 18
Campoamor, Ramón de [Spanish poet]
Spanish literature (The 1800's) So: 761
Campobello Island [New Brunswick]
New Brunswick (Places to visit) N: 188 *with picture*
Roosevelt, Franklin Delano (Battle with polio)
R: 451
Roosevelt Campobello International Park R: 469
Cámpora, Héctor José [Argentine political leader]
Argentina (Argentina under Perón) A: 657-658
Camptosaurus [dinosaur] C: 96
Dinosaur *picture on* D: 207
Campus [education]
Universities and colleges (School organization)
U: 208
Campus design prison
Prison (Prison buildings) P: 806
Campus Martius [ancient Rome]
Rome (Other remains) R: 433
Campus Martius [fort, Ohio]
Ohio Company (The second Ohio Company)
O: 704-705
Campus Martius Museum [Marietta]
Ohio (Places to visit) O: 690
Campus school
Laboratory school L: 16
Campylobacter [bacteria] C: 97
Antibiotic (History) A: 552
Food poisoning F: 340
Campylobacteriosis [illness]
Campylobacter C: 97
Camshaft [device]
Gasoline engine *picture on* G: 63; (The camshaft)
G: 64
Camus, Albert [French author] C: 97
French literature (Existentialism) F: 523
Novel (Existentialism) N: 574
Can [container]
Food preservation (Canning) F: 341 *with picture*
Packaging P: 18
Tin can T: 294
Can buoy [navigation]
Buoy B: 701
Can line [manufacturing]
Tin can T: 294
Canaan [ancient region]
See also Canaanites *in this index*
Abraham A: 16
Jews (Beginnings) J: 120-121; (The Exodus) J: 121
Joshua J: 169
Moses (Journey to Canaan) M: 829
Canaan dog C: 97
Dog *picture on* D: 276
Canaanites [ancient people] C: 97
Baal B: 2
Deborah D: 65
Palestine (Early history and settlement) P: 104
with map
Phoenicia (Way of life) P: 392
Canada C: 98 *with pictures and maps*
See also the list of Related articles in the Canada *article*
Agriculture
Canada (Agriculture) C: 124
Cooperative (In Canada) Ci: 1036
Meat packing (Quality grading) M: 351
Nunavut N: 608
Wheat (table) W: 274 *with map*
Art and architecture
Canada (The arts) C: 109 *with pictures*
Group of Seven G: 402
Communications and mass media
Encyclopedia (Encyclopedias of the 1800's and 1900's) E: 268b
Newspaper (In Canada) N: 386
Radio (Government regulation of radio)
R: 90-91
Television (In Canada) T: 117
Theater (Canada) T: 247
Defense
See also Canadian Armed Forces *in this index*
Civil defense (How civil defense is administered) Ci: 605
Education
Canada (Education) C: 107
Community college (Two-year colleges in Canada) Ci: 899
Education (Education in Canada) E: 95; (Development of Canadian education) E: 102; (Education for whom?) E: 107
High school (High schools in other countries)
H: 228
Literacy (Literacy in Canada) L: 352

School (In Canada) S: 183; (The development of Canadian schools) S: 184
Teaching (Becoming a teacher) T: 67
Finance and banking
Bank (Canada) B: 92
Bank of Canada B: 96
Dollar (The dollar in other countries) D: 295
with picture
Money order M: 718 *with picture*
Government See Canada, Government of *in this index*
Health and welfare
Illegal alien I: 51
Managed care plans (In other countries) M: 131
Marijuana (Medical marijuana) M: 202
Medicine (Canada) M: 367; (Financing advanced medical care) M: 377
Pension (Pensions in other countries) P: 273
Pure food and drug laws (Food and drug laws in Canada) P: 909
Red Cross (The Canadian Red Cross) R: 186
Retirement R: 265
Social security (Social security in Canada)
So: 556; (History) So: 556-557
Unemployment insurance (Canadian plan)
U: 24
Welfare (Welfare throughout the world) W: 191
History See Canada, History of *in this index*
Labor
Child labor (Canadian laws) C: 456
Labor movement (In Canada) L: 14
Unemployment (Unemployment levels throughout the world) U: 23
Language and literature See Canadian literature *in this index*
Manufacturing
Canada (Manufacturing) C: 124
Electric power (In Canada) E: 186
Manufacturing (In Canada) M: 169
Textile (In the United States and Canada) T: 218
Mining
Canada (Mining) C: 124
Aluminum (In Canada) A: 396
Copper (Leading producers) Ci: 1042
Gold (World gold production) G: 253
Nickel (Mining nickel) N: 404
Uranium (Sources of uranium) U: 214
Natural resources
Conservation (Canada) Ci: 988
Fishing industry (Inland fisheries) F: 182
Forest products (The forest products industry)
F: 403
Lumber (History) L: 521-522
Parks and monuments
Canada (table: National parks and national park reserves) C: 113
National park (Canada) N: 42c
Park (Kinds of parks) P: 167-168
People
Canada (Population) C: 105
Adoption (The adoption process) A: 66
Bella Coola Indians B: 242
Census (Modern censuses) C: 350
Citizenship (Canadian citizenship) Ci: 571
Civil rights (Civil rights in other countries)
Ci: 610
Housing (Canada) H: 392
Indian, American (Native Americans today)
I: 179
Indian reservation I: 188
Inuit I: 354 *with map*; (History) I: 354g; (The Inuit today) I: 354h-354i
"O Canada" O: 635
Police (In Canada) P: 623 *with picture*
Physical features
Canada (The land) C: 112 *with pictures*
Great Lakes G: 343 *with maps*
Inland waterway I: 274
Klondike K: 344 *with picture and map*
Rocky Mountains R: 394 *with picture and map*
Saint Lawrence River S: 41
Saint Lawrence Seaway S: 42 *with map*
Soo Canals (The Canadian canal) So: 595 *with map*
Recreation and sports
Boxing (Boxing in Canada) B: 530
Football (Canadian football) F: 364
Hockey H: 274; (Beginnings) H: 280
Lacrosse (History) L: 24
Ringette R: 343
Religion
Canada (Religion) C: 108
United Church of Canada U: 46
Social and cultural life
Ballet (Ballet in Canada) B: 54
Flower (table) F: 275
Girl Scouts (Girl Guides of Canada-Guides du

Canada) G: 198
Holiday (In Canada) H: 291
Library (Canadian government libraries) L: 249
Marriage (Laws concerning marriage) M: 219
Museum (Early Canadian museums) M: 940
Remembrance Day R: 229
Thanksgiving Day (Thanksgiving Day in
Canada) T: 230
Tree (table) T: 414
Valentine's Day (In the United States and
Canada) V: 261
Women's movement (In Western societies)
W: 386
Technology and science
Astronaut (A look at the astronauts) A: 831
International Space Station I: 346b
Space exploration (Canada) So: 727
Transportation
Canada (Transportation) C: 126
Aviation (Aviation agencies) A: 985-986
Railroad (Intercity trains) R: 105; (In Canada)
R: 113
Trans-Canada Highway T: 369
Transportation (Passenger and freight carriers)
T: 397
Canada, Armed Forces of *See* Canadian Armed
Forces *in this index*
Canada, Constitution of *See* Constitution of
Canada *in this index*
Canada, Dominion of [Canadian history]
British North America Act B: 632
Canada, History of (Confederation) C: 144;
(Growth of the Dominion [1868-1913]) C: 144
Confederation of Canada Ci: 933; (Approval of
confederation) Ci: 934-935
Macdonald, Sir John Alexander (Forming the
Dominion) M: 7
Manitoba (The Red River Rebellion) M: 160
Prince Edward Island (Self-government) P: 791
Quebec (Early years as a province) Q: 30; (The
1800's) Q: 37
Saskatchewan (North-West Territories) S: 146
Canada, Federal Court of
Canada, Government of (The courts) C: 136
Canada, Government of C: 128 *with pictures*
See also the list of Related articles in the Canada,
Government of, *article*
Abortion (In other countries) A: 16
Bank of Canada B: 96
Bill of rights (Canada's Constitution) B: 301
Canadian Armed Forces C: 154
Civil service (Civil service in other lands) Ci: 613
Fire department (Fire protection in North
America) F: 128
Foreign policy (Historical and social traditions)
F: 387
Governor general G: 294
House of Commons H: 384
Impeachment (Canada and Australia) I: 92
Insurance (Government regulation) I: 315
Liberal Party of Canada L: 227
Naturalization (Naturalization in Canada) N: 67
New Democratic Party N: 203
North American Free Trade Agreement N: 470
Parliament (Parliaments in other countries) P: 174
Political party (Political parties in Canada) P: 636
Postal services (Canadian mail service) P: 707
Prime minister of Canada P: 778c
Progressive Conservative Party P: 812
Senate (Senates in other countries) S: 296
Sexual harassment (Sexual harassment law)
S: 337
Supreme Court of Canada So: 996 *with pictures*
Taxation (Taxation in other countries) T: 55
Territory T: 174
Canada, History of C: 138 *with pictures and maps*
See also the list of Related articles in the Canada,
History of *article*
Civil rights (Civil rights in other countries) Ci: 610
Confederation of Canada Ci: 933
Exploration (The French and English in North
America) E: 446
Flag *pictures on* F: 214; (Flags of the United States
and Canada) F: 208
Franklin, Benjamin (A delegate in London) F: 490
Fur trade F: 564
Governor general G: 294
Great Depression (Effects in Canada) G: 341
Immigration (Canada) I: 84
Indian, American (Peoples of the Arctic) I: 152
with picture; (Indians of the Subarctic) I: 153;
(The destruction of Indian America) I: 177-178;
(Indians in the early and mid-1900's) I: 178b;
(Native Americans today) I: 180
Law (The development of Canadian law) L: 136
Métis M: 435
Money *picture on* M: 706; (History of the pound)

M: 709-710
New France N: 204 *with picture*
Northwest Passage N: 528
Prairie Provinces P: 733
Prime minister of Canada (History) P: 780
Quebec, Battle of Q: 37
Revolution, American (The invasion of Canada)
R: 275
Roman Catholic Church (In Canada) R: 412
Seigneurial system S: 287
Torrens system (In Canada) T: 342
Trading post T: 365
Tupper, Sir Charles T: 493
United Empire Loyalists U: 47
Woman suffrage (Canada) W: 381
World War II (On the home front) W: 495
Canada, Order of [award]
Medals, decorations, and orders (table) M: 359
with picture
Canada, Province of [Canadian history]
Quebec Conference Q: 38
Canada, River of
Saint Lawrence River (History) S: 42
Canada, Supreme Court of
Canada, Government of (The courts) C: 136
Canada balsam [tree product]
Balsam fir B: 64
Canada Basin [geography]
Arctic Ocean (The deep basin) A: 643 *with map*
Canada Council for the Arts
Canada (The arts) C: 109
Governor General's Literary Awards G: 294
Canada Cup [tournament]
Hockey (The late 1900's and early 2000's) H: 282
Canada Day [holiday] C: 153
Canada Elections Act
Prime minister of Canada (How the prime
minister is chosen) P: 778d-779
"Canada First" [Canadian history]
Mair, Charles M: 93
Canada goose [bird] C: 153
Bird *picture on* B: 360; (Birds of the Arctic) B: 343
with picture
Goose (Kinds of geese) G: 270 *with picture*
Canada hemp [plant]
Dogbane D: 282
Canada Mortgage and Housing Corporation
Housing (Canada) H: 392
Canada Pension Plan
Retirement R: 265
Social security (Social security in Canada)
So: 556; (History) So: 556-557
Canada Place [Vancouver]
Vancouver (The middle and late 1900's) V: 277
Canada Post Corporation
Postal services (Canadian mail service) P: 707
Canada Steamship Lines
Martin, Paul (Business career) M: 234c
Canada Temperance Act [1878]
Prohibition (Prohibition in Canada) P: 816
Canada thistle [plant] C: 154
Thistle T: 260
Canada wild rye [plant]
Plant *picture on* P: 526
Canada's Banana Belt [region]
Ontario (Visitor's guide) O: 774
Canada's Breadbasket [name for]
Saskatchewan S: 128
Canada's Sun Parlor [region]
Ontario (Visitor's guide) O: 774
Canadian Alliance [political party]
Canada, Government of (Political parties) C: 136
Canada, History of (Canada under Chrétien)
C: 152
Chrétien, Jean (Prime minister) C: 522c-522d
Conservative Party of Canada Ci: 992
Day, Stockwell D: 52
Harper, Stephen Joseph (Member of Parliament)
H: 66a
Political party (Other parties) P: 636-637
Progressive Conservative Party P: 812
Canadian Armed Forces C: 154 *with pictures*
Air force *picture on* A: 182
Canada, Government of (Armed forces) C: 137
NORAD N: 453
Royal Canadian Legion R: 495
Royal Military College of Canada R: 498
Veterans' organizations (In Canada) V: 345
Canadian Army
Canadian Armed Forces (Organization) C: 154
with pictures; (Weapons and equipment) C: 154
Canadian Association of Rocketry
Rocket, Model (Model rocket clubs and
competition) R: 393
Canadian Association of the Deaf
Deafness (Education) D: 59
"Canadian Authors Meet, The" [poem by Scott]

Canadian literature (Literature between the
world wars) C: 158-159
Canadian bacon [food]
Bacon B: 18
Canadian Badlands [Alberta]
Alberta (Places to visit) A: 320 *with picture*
Canadian Basin [geography]
Arctic Ocean (The deep basin) A: 643
Canadian Blood Services
Red Cross (Health services) R: 186
Canadian Boating Federation
Motorboat racing M: 876
Canadian Broadcasting Corporation C: 156
Canada (Television and radio) C: 127
Clarkson, Adrienne Ci: 642
Radio (Government regulation of radio) R: 90-91
Television (In Canada) T: 117
Canadian Charter of Rights and Freedoms [1982]
See Rights and Freedoms, Canadian Charter of
in this index
Canadian content quota
Canada (Communication) C: 126-127
Canadian Corps [military unit]
Currie, Sir Arthur Ci: 1197
Canadian Currency Act [1871]
Legal tender L: 182
Canadian Dental Association
Dentistry (Organizations) D: 145
Canadian dollar [money]
Coin collecting *picture on* Ci: 758
Dollar (The dollar in other countries) D: 295 *with*
pictures
Canadian Education Association C: 156
Teaching (Teachers organizations) T: 69
Canadian fivepins
Bowling (Canadian fivepins) B: 524
Canadian flag
Canada, History of (The return of the Liberals)
C: 149-150
Flag (Displaying the flag) F: 218
Canadian Food Inspection Agency Act
Pure food and drug laws (Food and drug laws in
Canada) P: 909
Canadian football
Football (Canadian football) F: 364 *with diagram*
Grey Cup G: 391
Canadian Football Hall of Fame and Museum
[Ontario]
Hamilton (The city) H: 30 *with map*
Canadian Football League
Football (Canadian football) F: 364
Grey Cup G: 391
Canadian Forest Service
Forestry (History) F: 408
Canadian 4-H Council
4-H (Canadian groups) F: 434
Canadian 4-H Foundation
4-H (Canadian groups) F: 434
Canadian Group of Painters [art]
Group of Seven G: 402
Canadian hemlock [tree]
Hemlock H: 182
Canadian Hockey Association *See* Hockey Canada
in this index
Canadian Hockey League
Hockey (Professional leagues) H: 278
Canadian Labour Congress [labor union]
Labor movement (In Canada) L: 14
Canadian Legion, Royal [organization]
Veterans' organizations (In Canada) V: 345
Canadian Library Association C: 156
Literature for children (Awards) L: 367
Canadian literature C: 156 *with pictures*
See also the list of Related articles in the Canadian
literature *article*
Canadian lynx [wildcat]
Lynx L: 536
Canadian Medical Association
Medicine (Medical organizations) M: 370
Canadian Mounted Police *See* Royal Canadian
Mounted Police *in this index*
Canadian Museum of Civilization [Gatineau]
Canada *picture on* C: 111
Canadian National Railway Company
British Columbia (Transportation) B: 627
Canada (Transportation) C: 126
Montreal (Transportation) M: 775-776
Railroad (In Canada) R: 113
Canadian Northern Railway
Edmonton (History) E: 85
Canadian Nuclear Safety Commission
Nuclear energy (Government regulation) N: 589
Canadian Pacific Railway Company
Abbott, Sir John Joseph Caldwell (The Pacific
Scandal) A: 6
British Columbia *picture on* B: 629;
(Transportation) B: 627

Calgary (Economy) C: 34
Canada (Transportation) C: 126
Greater Sudbury G: 351
Macdonald, Sir John Alexander *pictures on* M: 9;
   (National prosperity) M: 10
Mackenzie, Alexander (The Pacific Railway
   dispute) M: 22
Railroad (In Canada) R: 113; (The first
   transcontinental rail lines) R: 116
Regina (History) R: 206
Saskatchewan (North-West Territories) S: 146
Canadian Professional Boxing Federation
   Boxing (Boxing in Canada) B: 530
**Canadian Radio-television and
Telecommunications Commission**
   Canada (Television and radio) C: 127
   Radio (Government regulation of radio) R: 90-91
Canadian Rangers
   Canadian Armed Forces (Land Force) C: 154
Canadian Real Estate Association
   Real estate R: 171
Canadian Red Cross
   Red Cross (The Canadian Red Cross) R: 186
Canadian Rockies [mountains, Canada]
   Canada (The Rocky Mountains) C: 116
   North America *picture on* N: 458
   Rocky Mountains R: 394 *with picture and map*;
      (Chief ranges of the Rockies) R: 394
Canadian Security Intelligence Service
   Royal Canadian Mounted Police (History)
      R: 497-498
Canadian Shield [region, Canada-U.S.] C: 162
   Alberta (Land regions) A: 322
   Canada (The Canadian Shield) C: 117 *with map*
   Labrador Peninsula L: 17
   Manitoba *picture on* M: 156; (Land regions)
      M: 154
   Newfoundland and Labrador (Land regions)
      N: 370 *with map*
   North America (Land regions) N: 462-464
   Ontario (Land regions) O: 776 *with map*
   Quebec *picture on* Q: 24; (Land regions) Q: 22
      with map; (Natural resources) Q: 27
   Saskatchewan (Land regions) S: 138
Canadian Soccer Association
   Soccer (Soccer competition) So: 548; (History)
      So: 549
Canadian Space Agency
   Garneau, Marc G: 44
Canadian transcontinental railroad
   Abbott, Sir John Joseph Caldwell (Early political
      career) A: 5-6
Canadian Transportation Agency
   Aviation (Aviation agencies) A: 985-986
   Railroad (In Canada) R: 113
Canadian Union Catalogue
   Library (Canadian government libraries) L: 249
Canadian Warplane Heritage Museum [Mount
   Hope]
   Ontario (Places to visit) O: 774
Canadian Wheat Board
   Wheat (Buying and selling wheat) W: 274
Canadian whisky
   Whiskey W: 282
Canadiana [magazine]
   Library (Canadian government libraries) L: 249
Canadiana Suite [music by Peterson]
   Peterson, Oscar P: 325
Canadiens, Montreal [team]
   Hockey (table: National Hockey League) H: 281
   Montreal (Sports) M: 775 *with picture*
Canaima National Park [Venezuela]
   National park (table) N: 42g
Canal [astronomy]
   Mars (Observation from Earth) M: 226c
Canal [waterway] C: 162 *with pictures*
   Beaver (Building dams and canals) B: 195 *with
      picture*
   Fulton, Robert (The inventor) F: 555
   Irrigation (Bringing irrigation water to farms)
      I: 457 *with picture and map*
   Transportation (Development of inland
      transport) T: 388-389
Canal du Midi [waterway, France]
   Canal (History) C: 164-165
Canal Street
   New Orleans *picture on* N: 282; (Downtown New
      Orleans) N: 278-279
Canal Zone *See* Panama Canal Zone *in this index*
Canalized river
   Canal C: 162
Cananaean [apostle] *See* Simon, Saint *in this index*
Canarian dog *See* Dogo Canario *in this index*
Canarsie Indians
   Brooklyn B: 640
Canary [bird] C: 165 *with picture*
   Bird (As pets) B: 331 *with picture*

Canary, Martha [American frontierswoman] *See*
   Calamity Jane *in this index*
Canary Current
   Ocean (Circulation) O: 656
Canary Islands [islands, Atlantic] C: 165 *with map*
   Columbus, Christopher (Sailing west) Ci: 860
   Pine *picture on* P: 469
   Spain (The Canary Islands) So: 740
Canary Wharf [district]
   London (Dealing with problems) L: 442-443
Canasta [game] C: 166
   Card game C: 209
Canaveral, Cape *See* Cape Canaveral *in this index*
Canaveral National Seashore [Florida]
   National Park System (table: National seashores)
      N: 57
Canberra [Australia] C: 166 *with picture*
   Australia *picture on* A: 897
Canby, E. R. S. [Union general]
   Captain Jack C: 199
   Farragut, David Glasgow F: 47
Canby, William J. [grandson of Betsy Ross]
   Flag (First United States flags) F: 208-210
   Ross, Betsy R: 481
Cancellation [mail]
   Stamp collecting (Cancellations) So: 830
Cancellation [mathematics]
   Fraction (Calculations using fractions) F: 446-448
Cancellation [physics]
   Interference I: 324 *with diagram*
Cancellation [sports]
   Horseshoe pitching (Scoring) H: 368
Cancellous tissue [anatomy]
   Bone (Structure of the bones) B: 456 *with
      diagram*
Cancer [constellation]
   Tropic of Cancer T: 450
Cancer [disease] C: 167 *with pictures*
   See also specific cancers, such as Breast cancer, *in
      this index*
   AIDS (Opportunistic illness) A: 164a
   Angiogenesis A: 461
   Antibiotic (Other kinds of antibiotics) A: 550
   Artificial sweetener A: 761
   Biopsy B: 326
   Bladder B: 395
   Bone marrow transplant B: 457
   Brain (Tumors) B: 558
   Cell (Cancer) C: 336
   Chemotherapy C: 407
   Circumcision Ci: 561
   Cloning (Gene and cell cloning) Ci: 684
   DES D: 153
   Disease (Cancer) D: 229
   Epithelioma E: 345
   Eye (Diseases of the uveal tract) E: 467; (Diseases
      of the retina) E: 467
   Fox, Terry F: 441
   Hormone replacement therapy H: 338
   Immune system *picture on* I: 88c
   Laetrile L: 26
   Malignancy M: 110
   Mastectomy M: 296
   Monoclonal antibody M: 731
   Nutrition (Cancer) N: 630
   Oncology O: 761
   Pap test P: 132
   Platinum (Uses) P: 566-567
   Radiation (Refining the uses of radiation) R: 81
   Radium R: 100
   Radon (How radon affects health) R: 100
   Rous, Francis Peyton R: 492
   Smoking (Why smoking is dangerous) S: 520
   Taxol T: 56
   Teeth (Oral cancer) T: 86
   Thalidomide T: 229
   Tumor T: 484
   X rays X: 540
Cancer [astrology] C: 174 *with picture*
   Zodiac (The zodiac in astrology) Z: 597 *with
      picture*
Cancer, Tropic of [geography] *See* Tropic of Cancer
   in this index
Cancer Control Month
   American Cancer Society A: 408
Cancer Society, American *See* American Cancer
   Society *in this index*
Cancer Ward [book by Solzhenitsyn]
   Solzhenitsyn, Alexander So: 587
Cancha [arena]
   Jai alai J: 21
Cancionero de Baena [poetry]
   Spanish literature (The 1400's) So: 758
Cancionero de Stúñiga [poetry]
   Spanish literature (The 1400's) So: 758
Cancún [Mexico] C: 174
   Mexico *picture on* M: 466

Candela [measurement] C: 175
   Foot-candle F: 353
   Light (Energy and brightness) L: 290
   Metric system (Structure of the metric system)
      M: 437; (Light) M: 440
Candid picture
   Photography (Dramatic changes) P: 425-426
Candida [fungus]
   Fungal disease (In people) F: 558
   Vaginitis V: 260
Candidate [politics]
   Political convention P: 628
   Political party (Selecting candidates) P: 631
   Primary election P: 776
Candidate primary [election]
   Political convention (Delegate selection) P: 628-
      629
Candide [book by Voltaire]
   French literature (The Enlightenment) F: 520
   Voltaire V: 446
Candide [musical]
   Bernstein, Leonard B: 271
Candiru [fish]
   Catfish C: 300
Candle C: 175 *with picture*
   Easter (Easter symbols) E: 43-44
   Invention *picture on* I: 356
   Lamp (Fat or oil lamps) L: 52 *with picture*
   Light *picture on* L: 284
   Time (Clocks that measure change) T: 289
"Candle in the Wind" [song]
   John, Elton J: 133
Candle millet [grain]
   Millet M: 555
Candle power [measurement]
   Candela C: 175
Candlemas Day [custom] C: 175
Candlepins [game]
   Bowling (Other kinds of bowling) B: 524b
Candler, Allen D. [American political leader]
   Georgia (table) G: 130
Candler, Asa G. [American businessman]
   Coca-Cola Company Ci: 742
Candlestick
   Colonial life in America *picture on* Ci: 808
Candlewood [shrub]
   Ocotillo O: 669 *with picture*
Candling
   Chicken (Producing eggs) C: 443-445 *with picture*
   Poultry (Marketing poultry and eggs) P: 721
Candomblé [religion]
   Brazil (Religion) B: 575
   Latin America (Religion) L: 98-99
   Magic (Africa and the Americas) M: 50
CANDU heavy water reactor
   Nuclear energy (Organization of the industry)
      N: 589
Candy C: 175 *with picture*
Candytuft [plant] C: 177 *with picture*
Cane [book by Toomer]
   American literature (The Harlem Renaissance)
      A: 422
   Toomer, Jean T: 330
Cane juice
   Sugar (Making cane sugar) So: 961 *with diagram*
Cane River Creole National Historic Park
   [Louisiana]
   Louisiana (Places to visit) L: 488
   National Park System (table: National historical
      parks) N: 56
Cane sugar
   Sugar (Making cane sugar) So: 961 *with diagram*;
      (Sugar from sugar cane) So: 961
   Sugar cane So: 963
Cane toad C: 177
Canebrake [thicket]
   Bamboo B: 72
Canetti, Elias [Bulgarian-born author]
   Nobel Prizes (Literature: 1981) N: 448
Canfranc Tunnel [France-Spain]
   Pyrenees P: 920
Canine *See* Dog *in this index*
Canine parvovirus [disease] C: 177
Canine teeth [anatomy]
   See also Fang [zoology] *in this index*
   Animal (Teeth and jaws) A: 491 *with picture*
   Dog (Body structure) D: 263-265
   Hippopotamus (The body of a river
      hippopotamus) H: 240 *with picture*
   Lion (The body of a lion) L: 340-341 *with picture*
   Mammal (What mammals eat) M: 121 *with
      diagrams*
   Teeth (Deciduous teeth) T: 79; (Permanent teeth)
      T: 79 *with pictures*
Canio [opera character]
   Opera *picture on* O: 805; *(Pagliacci)* O: 806
Canis Major [constellation]

Sirius **S:** 476
Canisius, Saint Peter [German religious leader]
  C: 177
Canister [medicine]
  Bronchodilator **B:** 637
Canister vacuum cleaner
  Vacuum cleaner **V:** 258 *with diagram*
Canker sore [disorder] **C:** 177
Cankerworm [insect] **C:** 177 *with picture*
  Moth (Measuringworm moths) **M:** 841 *with
    picture*
Canna [plant] **C:** 178 *with picture*
  Flower *picture on* **F:** 279
Cannabis [drug] *See Marijuana in this index*
Cannae [ancient city]
  Hannibal (His military campaigns) **H:** 52
Cannes [France] **C:** 178
Cannes International Film Festival
  Motion picture *picture on* **M:** 863; (Festivals and
    awards) **M:** 861
Cannibal C: 178
  Carib Indians **C:** 236
Canning [food processing]
  Beef (Grades of beef) **B:** 209
  Botulism **B:** 514
  Fishing industry (Methods of processing) **F:** 186
  Food preservation (Canning) **F:** 341 *with pictures*
  Salmon (Salmon fishing) **S:** 70
Canning, George [British diplomat]
  Adams, John Quincy (Secretary of state) **A:** 42
  Castlereagh, Viscount **C:** 282
  Peel, Sir Robert **P:** 229
  United Kingdom (table: British prime ministers)
    U: 72
Cannizzaro, Stanislao [Italian chemist] **C:** 179
Cannon [weapon] **C:** 179 *with picture*
  Army (Armies in the Middle Ages) **A:** 727
  Artillery (How artillery is made) **A:** 763 *with
    picture*
  Civil War, American *picture on* **Ci:** 619
  Revolution, American (Weapons and tactics)
    R: 279-280 *with picture*
  Weapon (Artillery) **W:** 154b
Cannon [zoology]
  Horse (Legs and hoofs) **H:** 349 *with picture*
Cannon, Annie Jump [American astronomer]
  C: 179
Cannon, Billy [American football player]
  Football (table) **F:** 363
Cannon, Joseph Gurney [American political
  leader] **C:** 179
  Speaker (In the United States) **So:** 768
  Taft, William Howard (Legislative defeats) **T:** 10
Cannon, Newton [American political leader]
  Tennessee (table) **T:** 152
Cannon, William [American political leader]
  Delaware (table) **D:** 109
Cannon-ball tree C: 179 *with picture*
Cannon Beach [Oregon]
  Oregon *picture on* **O:** 826
Cannon House Office Building [Washington, D.C.]
  Washington, D.C. *map on* **W:** 76
Cannon Mountain
  New Hampshire (Mountains) **N:** 220
Cannonball Express [train]
  Jones, Casey **J:** 157
Cannonism [U.S. history]
  Taft, William Howard (Legislative defeats) **T:** 10
Cano, Juan Sebastián del [Spanish explorer]
  Exploration *map on* **E:** 443; (Magellan's globe-
    circling expedition) **E:** 445
  Magellan, Ferdinand (The end of the voyage)
    M: 47
Canoe
  Birch (Paper birch) **B:** 327
  Boating (Types of boats) **B:** 428; (Early boats)
    B: 431 *with picture*
  Canoeing (Canoes) **C:** 180 *with picture*
  Frontenac, Comte de *picture on* **F:** 541
  Indian, American *picture on* **I:** 154;
    (Transportation) **I:** 142; (Before European
    contact) **I:** 162-163 *with picture*
  Ohio (Interesting facts) **O:** 681 *with picture*
  Outrigger **O:** 880
  Pacific Islands *picture on* **P:** 3; (Transportation)
    P: 11
  Transportation (Water transportation) **T:** 384
Canoe birch [tree]
  Birch (Paper birch) **B:** 327 *with pictures*
Canoeing [sport] **C:** 180 *with picture*
  Olympic Games (Summer Olympic Games)
    O: 746e-746f
Canola [plant]
  Manitoba (Agriculture) **M:** 157 *with picture*
  Saskatchewan (Agriculture) **S:** 143
Canola oil [vegetable oil] **C:** 182
  Rape [plant] **R:** 142

Vegetable oil **V:** 294
Canon [music] **C:** 182
  Counterpoint (1097)
  Desprez, Josquin **D:** 161
Canon [religion]
  Bible **B:** 279
  Christianity (The early church) **C:** 523
  New Testament (Books) **N:** 287
  Old Testament (Contents) **O:** 740
  Saint (Christian saints) **S:** 29
Cañon [geology] *See Canyon in this index*
Canon and Gigue in D Major [music by Pachelbel]
  Pachelbel, Johann **P:** 2
Canon law [religion]
  Law (The Middle Ages) **L:** 134
Canon of Medicine [book by Avicenna]
  Avicenna **A:** 992
  Medicine (During the Middle Ages) **M:** 373
Canonical hour [religion]
  Hour **H:** 379
Canonization [religion] **C:** 183
  Saint (Christian saints) **S:** 29; (Roman Catholic
    saints) **S:** 30
Canons of Ethics of Engineers
  Engineering (Professional organizations and
    standards) **E:** 289-290
Canopic jar
  Mummy (Egyptian mummies) **M:** 925-926
Canopus [star]
  Star (table: The 10 brightest stars as seen from
    Earth) **So:** 842
Canopus in Argos: Archives [books by Lessing]
  Lessing, Doris **L:** 208
Canopy [botany]
  Amazon rain forest **A:** 401
  Animal (Animals of the tropical forests) **A:** 480
  Forest (The canopy) **F:** 391 *with picture*
  Rain forest (Structure and growth) **R:** 126a
Canopy [device]
  Parachute (Parts of a parachute) **P:** 142 *with
    picture*
Canossa [Italy]
  Gregory VII, Saint **G:** 387
Canova, Antonio [Italian sculptor] **C:** 183 *with
  picture*
Canso Causeway
  Nova Scotia (The early to middle 1900's) **N:** 570
Canso d'amor [poetry]
  Troubadour **T:** 452
Cant [lumber]
  Lumber *picture on* **L:** 520
Cantabile
  Music (table) **M:** 954; (Indicating expression)
    M: 955
Cantabrian Mountains
  Spain (The Northern Mountains) **So:** 740
Cantabrian Sea
  Bay of Biscay **B:** 176
Cantaloupe [fruit]
  Muskmelon **M:** 963 *with picture*
Cantata [music] **C:** 183
  Classical music (Oratorios) **Ci:** 644
Cantell, Kari J. [Finnish biologist]
  Interferon **I:** 324
Canter [gait]
  Horse (Gaits) **H:** 353 *with picture*
Canterbury [England] **C:** 183
  England (The Germanic invasions) **E:** 304
Canterbury, Archbishop of *See Archbishop of
  Canterbury in this index*
Canterbury bell [plant] **C:** 183
  Flower *picture on* **F:** 277
Canterbury Cathedral
  England *picture on* **E:** 298
Canterbury Female Boarding School
  Crandall, Prudence **Ci:** 1117
Canterbury Plains
  New Zealand (The South Island) **N:** 351-352
    with map
Canterbury Tales [stories by Chaucer] **C:** 183 *with
  picture*
  Chaucer, Geoffrey **C:** 388
  English literature (The age of Chaucer) **E:** 316
  Folklore (Folk tales) **F:** 323-324
  Manuscript *picture on* **M:** 173
Canth, Minna [Finnish dramatist]
  Finland (The arts) **F:** 112
"Canticle of the Sun" [poem by Francis of Assisi]
  Francis of Assisi, Saint **F:** 482
  Italian literature (The Middle Ages) **I:** 494
Canticles [Bible]
  Song of Solomon **So:** 592
Cantilever [architecture] **C:** 184
  Architecture (table) **A:** 608 *with picture*
  Bridge (Cantilever bridges) **B:** 601 *with diagram*
Cantilever arm [architecture]
  Bridge (Cantilever bridges) **B:** 601 *with diagram*

Cantilever bridge
  Bridge (Cantilever bridges) **B:** 601 *with diagram*
  Cantilever **C:** 184
Cantilever wing
  Airplane *picture on* **A:** 232; (The wing) **A:** 213;
    (World War I [1914-1918]) **A:** 234-235
Cantinflas [film character]
  Mexico (Motion pictures) **M:** 460
Cantiones sacrae [music by Byrd]
  Tallis, Thomas **T:** 21
Cantle [riding equipment]
  Cowboy (His saddle) **Ci:** 1109
  Saddle **S:** 8 *with pictures*
Canto [poetry]
  Divine Comedy **D:** 242
Canton [China] *See Guangzhou in this index*
Canton [Ohio] **C:** 184
Canton [flag]
  Flag *diagram on* **F:** 194
Canton Tower
  Guangzhou (The city) **G:** 410 *with picture*
Cantonese [dialect]
  Chinese language (Spoken Chinese) **C:** 510
Cantonment [city district]
  India (City life) **I:** 115
Cantor [religion]
  Judaism (The cantor) **J:** 181
Cantor, Georg [German mathematician]
  Fractal **F:** 443
  Mathematics (In the 1800's) **M:** 307
  Set theory (History) **S:** 322
Cantoria [sculpture by Della Robbia]
  Della Robbia, Luca **D:** 116
Cantos [poem by Pound]
  American literature (Modernist poetry) **A:** 421
  Pound, Ezra **P:** 722
Cantril, Hadley [American psychologist]
  Communication (The effects of media) **Ci:** 887
  Public opinion poll (History) **P:** 863
Canuck, Janey [pen name]
  Murphy, Emily Gowan **M:** 931
Canucks, Vancouver [team]
  Hockey (table: National Hockey League) **H:** 281
  Vancouver (Sports) **V:** 276
Canute [king of England] **C:** 184
  England (The Anglo-Saxon period) **E:** 304-305
  Vikings (The Danish Vikings) **V:** 383
Canvas [fabric] **C:** 184
  Needlepoint **N:** 118 *with picture*
  Painting (Supports) **P:** 36
  Tent (Kinds of tents) **T:** 168
Canvasback [bird] **C:** 184 *with picture*
  Bird (Birds of inland waters and marshes) **B:** 340
    with picture
Canvass [voting]
  Election campaign (Getting out the vote) **E:** 160
Canyon [natural feature] **C:** 185
  Atlantic Ocean (The Atlantic seafloor) **A:** 864
  Mars (Canyons) **M:** 226
  Ocean (The continental slope) **O:** 662
  River (Canyons) **R:** 352
  Valley (Kinds of valleys) **V:** 265
Canyon de Chelly National Monument [Arizona]
  C: 185 *with picture*
  Arizona (Places to visit) **A:** 678
  National Park System (table: National
    monuments) **N:** 50
Canyonlands National Park [Utah] **C:** 185
  National Park System (table: National parks) **N:** 48
  Utah *picture on* **U:** 246
Canzona [music]
  Classical music (Instrumental music) **Ci:** 646
Canzoniere [poems by Petrarch]
  Italian literature (Humanism and the
    Renaissance) **I:** 494
  Petrarch **P:** 327
Cão, Diogo [Portuguese navigator]
  Congo River **Ci:** 940f
Cao Dai [religion]
  Vietnam (Religion) **V:** 366
Cao Xueqin [Chinese author]
  Chinese literature (Drama and fiction) **C:** 511-512
Caoilte [legendary character]
  Irish literature (Heroic tales, romances, and sagas)
    I: 430
Caoineadh [poem]
  Irish literature (Modern works in Gaelic) **I:** 431
Caoineadh Airt Ui Laoghaire [poem by O'Leary]
  Irish literature (Modern works in Gaelic) **I:** 431
Caoutchouc
  Rubber (First uses) **R:** 500-501
CAP [aeronautics] *See Civil Air Patrol in this index*
Cap [botany]
  Mushroom (Parts of a mushroom) **M:** 942 *with
    picture*; (How a mushroom grows) **M:** 942-943
    with pictures
Cap [clothing]

Hat **H:** 83
CAP [policy] *See* Common Agricultural Policy *in this index*
Cap and gown [clothing]
Graduation **G:** 297
Cap-and-trade system
Global warming (Types of policies) **G:** 232c
Cap Diamant [Quebec]
Quebec (The city) **Q:** 34
Cap-Français [former name]
Cap-Haïtien **C:** 186
Cap-Haïtien [Haiti] **C:** 185
Columbus, Christopher (The first landing)
Ci: 860-861
Capa, Robert [American photographer]
Photography (Dramatic changes) **P:** 425-426
Capablanca, José R. [Cuban chess player]
Chess (World chess champions) **C:** 414
Capacitance [electricity]
Capacitor (Capacitance) **C:** 186
Capacitor [device] **C:** 186 *with pictures*
Ceramics (Kinds of ceramic products) **C:** 359
Computer chip (Structure) **Ci:** 924e
Electronics (Passive components) **E:** 212
Microphone (Condenser microphones) **M:** 517
Television (Solid-state cameras) **T:** 122
Capacity-building assistance [social work]
National Council of La Raza **N:** 33
Capacity measure
Metric system (The metric system at a glance)
M: 438 *with pictures*; (Metric conversion table)
M: 439 *with pictures*
Weights and measures (table: Volume and
capacity) **W:** 186
Cape [geography] **C:** 186 *with picture*
Cape Breton Development Corporation
Nova Scotia (The early to middle 1900's) **N:** 570
Cape Breton Highlands National Park [Nova
Scotia]
Canada (table: National parks and national park
reserves) **C:** 113
Nova Scotia (Places to visit) **N:** 560
Cape Breton Island [Nova Scotia] **C:** 187 *with maps*
Nova Scotia *pictures on* **N:** 561, **N:** 565; (Rivers
and lakes) **N:** 562 *with map*; (The struggle in
Acadia) **N:** 568; (The early to middle 1900's)
N: 570
Cape buffalo [animal]
Animal *picture on* **A:** 494
Buffalo **B:** 674 *with picture*
National park *picture on* **N:** 42d
Water buffalo **W:** 133
Cape Canaveral [Florida] **C:** 187
Cape **C:** 186
Florida (The mid-1900's) **F:** 264 *with picture*
Kennedy Space Center **K:** 270 *with map*
Cape Coast [Ghana]
City *picture on* **C:** 591
Cape Cod [Massachusetts] **C:** 188 *with map*
Cape **C:** 187
Massachusetts (Places to visit) **M:** 280 *with picture*
Cape Cod Canal [waterway, Massachusetts]
Canal **C:** 164
Cape Cod National Seashore
Massachusetts (Places to visit) **M:** 280
National Park System (table: National seashores)
N: 57
Cape Colony [South African history] **C:** 188
Rhodes, Cecil John (Gains Rhodesia) **R:** 317;
(Conflict with the Boers) **R:** 317;
South Africa (Arrival of Europeans) **So:** 617-618
Cape Columbia [Canada]
Peary, Robert Edwin ("The Pole at last!") **P:** 224
Cape Diamond [region, Quebec]
Quebec (The city) **Q:** 34
Cape Eternity [region, Quebec]
Saguenay River **S:** 20
Cape Fear River
North Carolina (Rivers, waterfalls, and lakes)
N: 484 *with map*
Cape Foulweather [region, Oregon]
Cape **C:** 186
Cape Hatteras [region, North Carolina] **C:** 188
North Carolina **N:** 472-473 *with picture*
Cape Hatteras National Seashore [North Carolina]
National Park System (table: National seashores)
N: 57
Cape Henlopen [region, Delaware]
Delaware Bay **D:** 113
Cape Horn [region, Chile] **C:** 188 *with maps*
Cape jasmine gardenia [plant]
Flower *picture on* **F:** 292
Gardenia **G:** 29
Cape Kennedy *See* Cape Canaveral *in this index*
Cape Krusenstern National Monument [Alaska]
National Park System (table: National
monuments) **N:** 50

Cape leadwort [plant]
Plumbago **P:** 577
Cape Lookout National Seashore [North Carolina]
National Park System (table: National seashores)
N: 57
Cape May [New Jersey]
New Jersey *picture on* **N:** 234
Cape Morris Jesup [region, Greenland]
Greenland **G:** 383 *with map*
Cape Mountains [South Africa]
South Africa (The Cape Mountains Region)
So: 615 *with map*
Cape of Good Hope [region, South Africa] **C:** 188
with maps
Cape Colony **C:** 188
Da Gama, Vasco **D:** 4
Dias, Bartolomeu **D:** 185
Exploration (Reaching the tip of Africa) **E:** 443-
444
Portugal (The age of exploration) **P:** 693
Cape Peninsula [region, South Africa]
Cape of Good Hope **C:** 188
Cape pigeon [bird]
Antarctica *picture on* **A:** 535
Cape Point [region]
Cape of Good Hope **C:** 188
Cape Province [former colony] *See* Cape Colony
in this index
Cape Puget [region, Alaska]
Puget, Peter **P:** 886
Cape Saint Mary's Ecological Reserve
[Newfoundland and Labrador]
Newfoundland and Labrador (Places to visit)
N: 368 *with picture*
Cape Saint Vincent, Battle of [1797]
Nelson, Horatio (Wounded at Calvi) **N:** 121-122
Cape Split [Nova Scotia]
Nova Scotia *picture on* **N:** 561
Cape Town [South Africa] **C:** 189 *with picture*
South Africa (Government) **So:** 608 *with picture*
Cape Town, University of [South Africa]
Africa *picture on* **A:** 115
Cape Trinity [region, Quebec]
Saguenay River **S:** 20
Cape Verde [region, Quebec] **C:** 189 *with pictures and map*
Flag *picture on* **F:** 198
Guinea-Bissau (History) **G:** 434
Portugal (Empire and wealth) **P:** 693-694 *with
map*
Cape Verde Islands *See* Cape Verde *in this index*
Cape York [region, Greenland] **C:** 191
Cape York Peninsula [Australia]
Torres, Luis Vaez de **T:** 342 *with map*
Capecchi, Mario R. [American biologist]
Nobel Prizes (Physiology or medicine: 2007)
N: 447
Čapek, Josef [Czech author]
Čapek, Karel **C:** 191
Čapek, Karel [Czech author] **C:** 191
Capelin [fish] **C:** 191
Capella [star]
Star (table: The 10 brightest stars as seen from
Earth) **So:** 842
Caper [plant] **C:** 191 *with picture*
Caper bush [plant]
Caper **C:** 191 *with picture*
Capernaum [ancient city]
Jesus Christ (Ministry) **J:** 106
Caperton, Gaston [American political leader]
West Virginia (table) **W:** 225
Capet, Hugh [king of France] *See* Hugh Capet *in
this index*
Capet, Widow [name for]
Marie Antoinette (Downfall of the monarchy)
M: 200
Capetian dynasty [French history] **C:** 191
France (The Capetian dynasty) **F:** 471 *with map*;
(Growth of royal power) **F:** 472 *with map*
Capillarity [physics] **C:** 191 *with diagram*
Pen (Fountain pens) **P:** 233
Surface tension **So:** 1003
Water (The properties of water) **W:** 129-130
Capillary [anatomy] **C:** 192
Blood (What blood does in the body) **B:** 408 *with
pictures*
Brain (From harmful substances) **B:** 551
Circulatory system (The blood vessels) **Ci:** 559
with picture
Heart (Discovery of circulation) **H:** 144
Human body (The blood vessels) **H:** 421
Kidney (How the kidneys produce urine) **K:** 311-
312 *with picture*
Lung (Gas exchange in the lungs) **L:** 523-524
with diagram
Lymphatic system **L:** 533, *diagram on* **L:** 534
Respiration (Structures of breathing) **R:** 260
Vein **V:** 295

Capistrano [California]
San Juan Capistrano **S:** 103
Capital [architecture]
Architecture (table) **A:** 608 *with picture*
Column **Ci:** 865 *with pictures*
Capital [economics] **C:** 192
Bank (Banks throughout the world) **B:** 91
Capitalism (How capitalism differs from central
planning) **C:** 194
Economics (Economic growth) **E:** 62
Flat tax **F:** 228
Industrial Revolution (The role of capital) **I:** 251
Industry (Capital) **I:** 258 *with diagram*
Capital account [economics]
Balance of payments (How the balance of
payment is determined) **B:** 36
Capital **C:** 192
Capital asset pricing model
Capital **C:** 192
Capital budget
Budget (A capital budget) **B:** 671
Capital Center Project
Providence (Government and history) **P:** 840
Capital Cities Communications
ABC **A:** 7
Capital EX [fair]
Edmonton (Culture and recreation) **E:** 84-85
Capital gains [economics]
Capital gains tax **C:** 192
Flat tax **F:** 228
Income tax (Defining taxable income) **I:** 102-103
Investment (Stocks) **I:** 368
Capital gains tax C: 192
Taxation (Income taxes) **T:** 53
Capital goods [economics]
Industry (By the way goods are used) **I:** 257;
(Capital) **I:** 258
Investment **I:** 366
Manufacturing (Kinds of manufacturing) **M:** 169
Capital-intensive industry
Industry (Capital goods) **I:** 258
Capital market
Capital **C:** 192
Capital offense [law]
Murder **M:** 930
Capital punishment [law] **C:** 193
Colonial life in America (Crime and punishment)
Ci: 796
Electrocution **E:** 200
Gas chamber **G:** 59
Illinois (The death penalty) **I:** 76
Lethal injection **L:** 209
Murder **M:** 930
Supreme Court of the United States (Criminal
law) **So:** 1001
Capital ship
Warship (The age of sailing ships) **W:** 41
Capital stock *See* Stock *in this index*
Capitalism [economics] **C:** 194
See also Free enterprise system *in this index*
Communism (The ideas of Marx) **Ci:** 890
Economics **E:** 58; (The organization of
economies) **E:** 58; (Distribution of income)
E: 63
Industrial Revolution **I:** 246; (The role of capital)
I: 251
Lenin, V. I. **L:** 191
Marx, Karl **M:** 236
Protestant ethic **P:** 833
Smith, Adam **S:** 515
Syndicalism **So:** 1067
Weber, Max **W:** 176
Welfare state **W:** 192
World (Economic systems) **W:** 412b
World, History of the (The Industrial Revolution)
W: 444-445
Capitalism and Freedom [book by Friedman]
Friedman, Milton **F:** 533
Capitalism, Socialism, and Democracy [book by
Schumpeter]
Schumpeter, Joseph Alois **S:** 188
Capitalist *See* Capitalism *in this index*
Capitalist class [sociology] *See* Bourgeoisie *in this
index*
Capitalization C: 196
Capitals, Washington [team]
Hockey (table: National Hockey League) **H:** 281
Capitals of the states
United States (table: Facts in brief about the
states) **U:** 104
Capitals of the United States *See* United States
capitals *in this index*
Capitan, Louis [French anthropologist]
Prehistoric people (table) **P:** 754
Capitate bone
Hand (Parts of the hand) **H:** 40
Capitation tax *See* Poll tax *in this index*

Capitol [building] **C: 197**
Capitol, United States [Washington, D.C.] **C: 197**
Architecture (Neoclassical architecture) **A: 623-624**
Congress of the United States *picture on* **Ci: 945**
Global warming *picture on* **G: 232b**
Latrobe, Benjamin Henry **L: 118**
Senate *picture on* **S: 294**
Statuary Hall **So: 870** *with picture*
United States, Government of the *picture on* **U: 136**
United States, History of the *picture on* **U: 148**
Walter, Thomas Ustick **W: 21**
Washington, D.C. *map on* **W: 76**; (United States Capitol) **W: 71** *with picture*
Capitol Hill [Washington, D.C.]
Capitol, United States **C: 197**
Washington, D.C. (Capitol Hill) **W: 71**
Capitol Reef National Park [Utah] **C: 197**
National Park System (table: National parks) **N: 48**
Capitoline Hill [Rome]
Mythology (Roman divinities) **M: 982-983**
Rome **R: 429**
Capitoline triad
Mythology (Roman divinities) **M: 982**
Caplock [gun]
Musket **M: 962**
Capodimonte [palace]
Naples (Way of life) **N: 12-13**
Capoeira [martial art] **C: 197**
Martial arts *picture on* **M: 234**
Capone, Al [American gangster] **C: 197** *with portrait*
Illinois (Prohibition and the Great Depression) **I: 75**
Ness, Eliot **N: 136**
Prohibition (Life during prohibition) **P: 815**
Caporetto, Battle of [1917]
World War I (Allied failures) **W: 461**
Capote [bullfighting]
Bullfighting (The order of the bullfight) **B: 696**
Capote, Truman [American author] **C: 198**
American literature (Experimental styles) **A: 425**
Novel (The novel today) **N: 575**
Capp, Al [American cartoonist] **C: 198**
Cappadocia [region, Turkey]
Turkey *picture on* **T: 507**
Cappelletti, John [American football player]
Football (table) **F: 363**
Capper, Arthur [American political leader]
Kansas (table) **K: 234**
Capper-Volstead Act [1922]
Cooperative (History) **Ci: 1036**
Capra, Frank [American director] **C: 198**
Motion picture (Best achievement in directing: 1934, 1936, 1938) **M: 862**
Capri [island, Italy] **C: 198**
Caprices, The [etchings by Goya]
Goya, Francisco **G: 295**
Capricorn [astrology] **C: 198** *with picture*
Zodiac (The zodiac in astrology) **Z: 597** *with picture*
Capricorn [constellation]
Tropic of Capricorn **T: 450**
Capricorn, Tropic of [geography] *See* Tropic of Capricorn *in this index*
Caprifig [fruit]
Fig **F: 96**
Caprine arthritic encephalitis [disease]
Goat (Disease) **G: 241**
Caprivi Strip
Namibia (People) **N: 8**
Caprolactam [chemical]
Nylon (History) **N: 633**
Caproni-Campini CC2 [aircraft]
Jet propulsion (Development of jet propulsion) **J: 113-114**
Capsaicin [compound]
Pepper **P: 278**
Capsaicinoid [compund]
Chili pepper **C: 471**
Capsian culture
Berbers **B: 256**
Capsicum [plant] *See* Pepper [plant] *in this index*
Capstan [device]
Tape recorder (How tape recorders work) **T: 37** *with picture*
Capsule [anatomy]
Sprain **So: 805**
Capsule [biology]
Bacteria (The structure of bacteria) **B: 20** *with diagram*
Moss (How mosses live) **M: 834-835**
Capsule [medication]
Drug *picture on* **D: 350**
Captain [rank]
Rank, Military (table) **R: 140**

Ship (Officers and crew) **S: 410** *with picture*
Captain Hook [literary figure]
Peter Pan **P: 325**
Captain Jack [American Indian leader] **C: 199** *with portrait*
Indian wars (The Modoc War [1872-1873]) **I: 194**
Modoc Indians **M: 686**
Captain Nemo [literary figure]
Verne, Jules **V: 337**
"Captain Underpants" series [books by Pilkey]
Pilkey, Dav **P: 464**
Captains Courageous [book by Kipling]
Kipling, Rudyard (Kipling in America) **K: 334**
Captains Courageous [film]
Tracy, Spencer **T: 362**
Captain's Daughter, The [book by Pushkin]
Russian literature (Early Romanticism) **R: 560-561**
Captains-Regent [office]
San Marino (Government) **S: 103**
Caption, Closed *See* Closed captioning *in this index*
Captive, The [book by Proust]
Proust, Marcel **P: 838**
Captive balloon
Balloon (Captive balloons) **B: 60**; (Balloons in war) **B: 61** *with picture*
Captive breeding [conservation]
Animal (Breeding in captivity) **A: 505** *with picture*
Bird (Endangered species) **B: 370** *with picture*
Condor (Outlook for the California condor) **Ci: 930**
Conservation (Biodiversity conservation) **Ci: 976-977**
Endangered species (Protecting endangered species) **E: 270-271**
Panda (Protecting pandas) **P: 129**
Zoo (Wildlife conservation) **Z: 600**; (The evolution of zoos) **Z: 605**
Captive mine
Coal (Coal producers) **Ci: 728**
CAPTOR [mine]
Mine warfare (Naval mines) **M: 565**
Capture [chess]
Chess (The moves) **C: 412-413**
Capture and Death of Sitting Bull [lithograph by Kurz and Allison]
Westward movement in America *picture on* **W: 251**
Capture of the Hessians at Trenton [painting by Trumbull]
Hessians *picture on* **H: 219**
Capuche [clothing]
Capuchins **C: 199**
Capuchin [animal] **C: 199** *with picture*
Capuchins [religious group] **C: 199**
Capulet [fictional family]
Shakespeare, William: *(Romeo and Juliet)* **S: 357-358**
Capulin Volcano National Monument [New Mexico] **C: 200**
National Park System (table: National monuments) **N: 50**
Capybara [animal] **C: 200** *with picture*
Rodent **R: 397**
Car
See also Automobile *in this index*
Cable car **C: 7**
Elevator **E: 233** *with diagrams*
Car Allowance Rebate System
Automobile (The 2000's) **A: 972-973**
Car bottom furnace
Furnace (Heating the charge) **F: 567**
Carabao [animal]
Buffalo **B: 674**
Water buffalo **W: 133**
Carabiner [tool] *See* Karabiner *in this index*
Caracal [animal] **C: 200** *with picture*
Caracalla [Roman emperor]
Rome, Ancient (table) **R: 447**
Caracara [bird] **C: 201** *with picture*
Bird of prey **B: 374a**
Caracas [Venezuela] **C: 200**
Venezuela **V: 298** *with pictures*; (Education) **V: 301** *with pictures*
Caracul [fur]
Karakul **K: 245**
Carafa, Gian Pietro [pope]
Paul IV **P: 200**
Carajá Indians
Indian, American *picture on* **I: 176**
Caramel [food]
Candy (Chewy candies) **C: 176**
Carapace [zoology]
Crab **Ci: 1115**
Turtle (Shell) **T: 521** *with diagram*
Carat [measurement] **C: 201**
See also Karat *in this index*
Diamond (Where natural diamonds are found)

D: 181-182 *with pictures*
Gem (Some famous gems) **G: 79**
Weights and measures (Miscellaneous weights and measures) **W: 184**
Caravaggio, Michelangelo Merisi da [Italian painter] **C: 201** *with picture*
Baroque (Baroque painting) **B: 117**
Painting (Baroque) **P: 58** *with picture*; (Classicism) **P: 61**; (The Spanish masters) **P: 64**
Caravan [travel] **C: 202**
Caravel [ship] **C: 202** *with picture*
Columbus, Christopher (The plan to sail westward) **Ci: 858**
Exploration (The age of European exploration) **E: 443** *with picture*
Caraway [plant] **C: 202**
Caraway, Hattie Ophelia Wyatt [American political leader] **C: 202**
Arkansas *picture on* **A: 713**; (The early 1900's) **A: 714**
Caraway, Thaddeus [American political leader]
Caraway, Hattie Ophelia Wyatt **C: 202**
Carbamate insecticide
Insecticide (Carbamate insecticides) **I: 302**
Carbamazepine [drug]
Anticonvulsant **A: 553**
Carbamide *See* Urea *in this index*
Carbarsone [medication]
Arsenical **A: 745**
Carbatine
Shoe *picture on* **S: 432**
Carberry, John Joseph [American religious leader]
Cardinal (table: American cardinals) **C: 211**
Carbide [chemical] **C: 202**
Carbine [gun] **C: 202**
Carbohydrate [nutrition] **C: 202** *with diagrams*
Fat substitute **F: 53**
Flour (The chemistry of flour) **F: 268**
Food (Producing energy) **F: 330**
Human body (Chemical elements and molecules) **H: 417**
Life (Carbohydrates) **L: 278**
Milk (Carbohydrates) **M: 546**
Nutrition (Kinds of nutrients) **N: 625**
Starch **So: 855**
Sugar **So: 959**
Carbolic acid [chemical]
Antiseptic (History) **A: 559**
Carbon [element] **C: 203** *with diagrams*
Carbide **C: 202**
Carbon cycle **C: 205** *with diagram*
Charcoal **C: 377**
Chemistry (Development of organic chemistry) **C: 404**
Diamond (What diamonds are) **D: 181**
Fire (Gases) **F: 122**
Graphite **G: 323**
Life (The chemical basis of life) **L: 277** *with diagram*
Metalloid **M: 426**
Organic chemistry **O: 853**
Radiocarbon **R: 97**
Rubber (The chemistry of rubber) **R: 501**
Soil **So: 573**
Star (Hydrogen fusion) **So: 846-847**
Carbon 12 [isotope]
Carbon (Chemical properties) **C: 203**
Carbon 14 *See* Radiocarbon *in this index*
Carbon aerogel
Carbon (Amorphous carbons) **C: 205**
Carbon black
Carbon (Amorphous carbons) **C: 205**
Ink **I: 272**
Petrochemicals (History) **P: 329**
Carbon cycle [biology] **C: 205** *with diagram*
See also Photosynthesis *in this index*
Carbon dating *See* Radiocarbon dating *in this index*
Carbon dioxide [gas] **C: 206** *with diagram*
Air (Changes in the atmosphere) **A: 175**
Air pollution (Atmosphere) **A: 199**
Animal (Pollution) **A: 504**
Baking powder **B: 33**
Blood (What blood does in the body) **B: 408** *with diagram*
Carbon cycle **C: 206** *with diagram*
Climate **Ci: 675**; (Changes in CO_2 concentration) **Ci: 677**; (Human activity) **Ci: 678**
Damp **D: 22**
Dry ice **D: 369**
Fire (Gases) **F: 122**
Global warming (Causes of global warming) **G: 232**; (Ways to limit global warming) **G: 232b**; (Government action on global warming) **G: 232c**; (How scientists study global warming) **G: 232d**
Greenhouse effect (The natural greenhouse effect) **G: 382-383**

Heart (The work of the heart) **H:** 135
Human body (The exchange of carbon dioxide and oxygen) **H:** 421 *with picture*
Leaf (Obtaining the raw materials) **L:** 155 *with diagram*
Lung (Gas exchange in the lungs) **L:** 523
Mars (Atmosphere) **M:** 226a
Molecule (Individual molecules) **M:** 692-693 *with diagram*
Photosynthesis **P:** 430
Plant (In ecosystems) **P:** 518; (Global warming) **P:** 544
Refrigeration (Dry ice) **R:** 201
Respiration **R:** 260
Carbon dioxide cycle [biology] *See* Photosynthesis *in this index*
Carbon dioxide extinguisher
Fire extinguisher (Liquefied gas extinguishers) **F:** 130
Carbon disulfide [chemical]
Sulfide **So:** 966
Carbon footprint [measurement] **C:** 207
Carbon footprint calculator [survey]
Carbon footprint **C:** 207
Carbon-in-pulp [industrial process]
Gold (Leaching) **G:** 253
Carbon microphone
Microphone (Carbon microphones) **M:** 516
Carbon monoxide [gas] **C:** 207
Air pollution (Forms of transportation) **A:** 198
Catalytic converter **C:** 298
Coal (Mine safety) **Ci:** 729
Damp **D:** 22
Parkinson disease (Causes) **P:** 170
Smoking (Why smoking is dangerous) **S:** 520
Carbon-monoxide detector [instrument]
Air pollution *picture on* **A:** 199
Carbon monoxide poisoning
Fire (Gases) **F:** 122
Hyperbaric oxygen therapy **H:** 476
Poison (Kinds of poison) **P:** 601
Safety (Other precautions) **S:** 11
Carbon nanotube [molecule]
Carbon (Fullerenes) **C:** 205 *with diagram*
Carbon-neutral housing *See* Zero carbon housing *in this index*
Carbon-nitrogen-oxygen cycle [physics]
Star (Hydrogen fusion) **So:** 846
Carbon offset [policy]
Global warming (Types of policies) **G:** 232c
Carbon sequestration
Global warming (Ways to limit global warming) **G:** 232b
Carbon steel
Alloy (Alloys of iron) **A:** 377-378
Iron and steel (Kinds of iron and steel) **I:** 436-437
Carbon tax
Global warming (Types of policies) **G:** 232c-232d
Carbon tissue [printing]
Printing (Gravure cylinders) **P:** 800
Carbon-zinc battery [device]
Battery (Primary batteries) **B:** 169 *with diagram*; (Types and uses of batteries) **B:** 171
Carbonaceous chondrite [meteor]
Asteroid (Composition) **A:** 824
Life (Creating simple organic compounds) **L:** 279
Carbonari [Italian history]
Mazzini, Giuseppe **M:** 331
Sicilies, Kingdom of the Two **S:** 446
Carbonate [chemical] **C:** 208
Earth (The lithosphere) **E:** 20
Carbonate-silcate cycle [geology]
Earth (History of Earth) **E:** 25
Carbonated beverage
Brewing (Finishing) **B:** 595
Tartaric acid **T:** 47
Carbonated water
Soft drink (How soft drinks are made) **So:** 570
Carboniferous Period [geology] **C:** 208
Coal (How coal was formed) **Ci:** 720-721
Earth (The Paleozoic Era) **E:** 27; (table) **E:** 30
Forest (The first forests) **F:** 397-398 *with picture*
Plant (The evolution of plants) **P:** 544-545
Prehistoric animal (table) **P:** 738
Carbonization [chemistry]
Coal (Coal as a raw material) **Ci:** 719-720
Fossil (Carbonization) **F:** 425 *with picture*
Carborundum [abrasive]
Gem (Cutting and polishing) **G:** 79
Silicon **S:** 458
Carboxymethyl cellulose [material]
Cellulose (Industrial uses) **C:** 341
Carburetor [engine] **C:** 208
Automobile (The fuel system) **A:** 953
Fuel injection **F:** 552
Gasoline engine (The fuel system) **G:** 65
Carburizing [industrial process]

Metallurgy (Physical metallurgy) **M:** 427
Carcassonne [France] **C:** 208
Citadel **Ci:** 567
Carcieri, Donald [American political leader]
Rhode Island (table) **R:** 311
Carcinogen [medicine]
Cancer **C:** 167; (Genes damaged by substances in the environment) **C:** 170; (Avoiding carcinogens) **C:** 171
Carcinoma [disease]
Cancer (Classification by tissue) **C:** 168
Tumor **T:** 484
Card [boxing]
Boxing (Boxing in the United States) **B:** 530
Card [electronics]
Computer (Parts of computers) **Ci:** 911-912
Card, Andrew H., Jr. [American government official]
Transportation, Department of (table) **T:** 400
Card access system [lock]
Lock (Electric locks) **L:** 412 *with picture*
Card catalog [library]
Index **I:** 107
Library (Technology) **L:** 251
A Guide to Research Skills **Research Guide:** 27-29
Card game **C:** 209 *with pictures*
Gambling **G:** 20
Game (Card games) **G:** 22
Card sliver [yarn]
Cotton *picture on* **Ci:** 1092; (Making cotton into cloth) **Ci:** 1091
Card table
Colonial life in America *picture on* **Ci:** 808
Cardamom [fruit] **C:** 209
Cardan, Jerome [Italian mathematician] *See* Cardano, Girolamo *in this index*
Cardano, Girolamo [Italian mathematician]
Electricity (Early discoveries) **E:** 196
Cardboard **C:** 209
Cardenal, Ernesto [Nicaraguan poet]
Latin American literature (The mid-1900's) **L:** 114
Cárdenas, García López de [Spanish explorer]
Grand Canyon (History) **G:** 307
Cárdenas, Lázaro [Mexican political leader] **C:** 210
Ávila Camacho, Manuel **A:** 993
Mexico (Reforms of the early 1900's) **M:** 472-473
Cardiac assist device [medicine]
Heart (Heart failure) **H:** 143
Cardiac catheterization [surgery]
Heart (Symptoms and diagnosis) **H:** 137-138 *with picture*
Cardiac cycle [medicine]
Heart (Regulating the heart rate) **H:** 135-136
Cardiac muscle [anatomy]
Heart (Outer lining and muscle) **H:** 133
Human body (The cardiac muscle) **H:** 419
Muscle *diagram on* **M:** 933; (Cardiac muscle) **M:** 935
Cardiac pacemaker [medicine]
Electronics (Transistors) **E:** 212
Cardiff [Wales] **C:** 210
United Kingdom *picture on* **U:** 48
Wales *picture on* **W:** 11
Cardigan, Mount *See* Mount Cardigan *in this index*
Cardigan Welsh corgi [dog] **C:** 210 *with picture*
Pembroke Welsh corgi **P:** 233
Cardinal [title] **C:** 210
Address, Forms of (Members of the clergy) **A:** 54
Pope (Early days) **P:** 662; (Present procedures) **P:** 662
Roman Catholic Church (Church organization) **R:** 404
Cardinal [bird] **C:** 211 *with picture*
Bird *picture on* **B:** 358; (Birds of urban areas) **B:** 333 *with picture*
Cardinal, Douglas [Canadian architect]
Canada *picture on* **C:** 111; (Architecture) **C:** 112
Cardinal flower [plant] **C:** 212
Lobelia **L:** 405
Cardinal myzomela [bird]
Bird (Birds of the Pacific Islands) **B:** 349 *with picture*
Cardinal points [navigation]
Compass **Ci:** 902b
Cardinal Secretary of State
Vatican City (Administration) **V:** 288
Cardinals, Arizona [team]
Football (National Football League) **F:** 364
Cardinals, College of *See* Sacred College of Cardinals *in this index*
Cardinals, Saint Louis [team] *See* Saint Louis Cardinals *in this index*
Cardinal's bark [plant product]
Cinchona **Ci:** 553
Carding [manufacturing]
Cotton *picture on* **Ci:** 1092; (Cleaning and blending) **Ci:** 1091

Textile *picture on* **T:** 216
Thread (Making thread from natural fibers) **T:** 269
Wool (Making yarn) **W:** 400 *with picture*
Carding length fiber
Wool (Processing of wool) **W:** 400
Carding machine
Cotton *picture on* **Ci:** 1092; (Cleaning and blending) **Ci:** 1091
Cardini [British magician]
Magician (Sleight of hand) **M:** 51
Cardiogram [medicine] *See* Electrocardiogram *in this index*
Cardiograph *See* Electrocardiograph *in this index*
Cardiology **C:** 212
Heart **H:** 132
Medicine (table) **M:** 369
Cardiomyopathy [disorder]
Heart (Cardiomyopathy) **H:** 142
Cardiopulmonary resuscitation **C:** 212 *with pictures*
Adult education *picture on* **A:** 68
Boy Scouts (First Class Scout) **B:** 537
First aid (Heart attack) **F:** 141
Heart (Symptoms) **H:** 139
Safety (In offices) **S:** 14
Cardiotonic
Drug (Cardiotonics) **D:** 351
Cardiovascular disease
See also Coronary artery disease; Heart disease; Stroke *in this index*
Disease (Diseases associated with aging) **D:** 230
Drug (Drugs that affect the heart and blood vessels) **D:** 351
Carditis [disorder]
Rheumatic fever **R:** 291
Cardizem [drug]
Calcium channel blocker **C:** 21
Cardo [area]
Jerusalem *picture on* **J:** 97
Cardoso, Fernando Henrique [Brazilian political leader]
Brazil (Return to civilian government) **B:** 586
Cardozo, Benjamin Nathan [American jurist] **C:** 213
Cards [game]
Card game **C:** 209
Carducci, Giosuè [Italian poet] **C:** 213
Italian literature (Romanticism) **I:** 495
CARE [organization] **C:** 213
Eagles, Fraternal Order of E: 6
Foreign aid (Kinds of foreign aid) **F:** 383
Career and technical education *See* Vocational education *in this index*
Career education **C:** 213
Careers (Sources of information) **C:** 216
Vocational education **V:** 434
Career exploration
Cooperative education **Ci:** 1037
Career guidance
Guidance (Vocational or career guidance) **G:** 422
Career ladder
Careers (Chances for advancement) **C:** 216
Careers **C:** 214 *with pictures*
See also the list of Related articles in the Careers article.
Adolescent (Career planning) **A:** 64
Career education **C:** 213
Culture (Forming patterns) **Ci:** 1187
Sex discrimination (Persistence of sex discrimination) **S:** 335
Caretaker, The [play by Pinter]
Pinter, Harold **P:** 475
Carew, Rod [American baseball player]
Baseball (table: Hall of Fame) **B:** 134
Carew Tower [building]
Cincinnati (The city) **Ci:** 554 *with map*
Carey, G. R. [American inventor]
Electronics (The vacuum tube era) **E:** 215
Carey, Hugh L. [American political leader]
New York (table) **N:** 313
Carey, Joseph M. [American political leader]
Wyoming (table) **W:** 532; (Territorial progress) **W:** 534-536
Carey, Mariah [American singer] **C:** 236
Carey, Max [American baseball player]
Baseball (table: Hall of Fame) **B:** 134
Carey, Peter [Australian author]
Australia (Literature) **A:** 904-905
Carey, Robert D. [American political leader]
Wyoming (table) **W:** 532
Carey, William [English missionary]
Baptists (Early history) **B:** 101
Cargo [shipping]
Airplane *pictures on* **A:** 209, **A:** 218
Airport (Cargo handling) **A:** 246 *with picture*
Aviation (Airline operations) **A:** 984-985 *with picture*

Net *picture on* N: 137
Ship (Kinds of ships) S: 407 *with pictures*
Transportation (Water transportation) T: 384
Cargo, David F. [American political leader]
New Mexico (table) N: 272
Cargo net
Net *picture on* N: 137
Cargo ship
Greece, Ancient *picture on* G: 369
Ship S: 402 *with picture;* (Kinds of ships) S: 406
with pictures; (A ship at sea) S: 410; (Phoenician
and Greek ships) S: 415 *with pictures;* (Roman
ships) S: 416
Transportation (Ancient Greece) T: 386-387
Carías Andino, Tiburcio [Honduran political
leader]
Honduras (Revolutions and reforms) H: 313
Carib Indians C: 236
Barbados (History) B: 104
Cannibal C: 179
Canoeing (History) C: 182
Dominica (History) D: 302
Honduras (Ancestry) H: 309
Indian, American *pictures on* I: 140
Ponce de León, Juan (Florida expeditions)
P: 655-656
Saint Lucia (History) S: 51
Virgin Islands, United States (Exploration) V: 396
West Indies (Early days) W: 205
Caribbean Community and Common Market
[organization] *See* CARICOM *in this index*
Caribbean Current [Atlantic]
Caribbean Sea (Currents) C: 237
Caribbean Indians
Indian, American *picture on* I: 146; (Indians of the
Caribbean) I: 172 *with pictures and map*
Caribbean Indies [former name]
East Indies E: 40
Caribbean Islands *See* West Indies *in this index*
Caribbean reef squid [animal]
Squid (Kinds of squids) So: 814a *with picture*
Caribbean Sea 236 *with map*
World, History of the *map on* W: 441
Cariboo Mountains
British Columbia (Land regions) B: 622 *with map*
Cariboo Road
British Columbia (Transportation) B: 627
Caribou [city, Maine]
Maine (table: Average monthly weather) M: 83
Caribou [animal] C: 237 *with picture*
Animal *picture on* A: 485
Arctic (Animal life) A: 637 *with picture*
Inuit I: 354; (Clothing) I: 354b-354c; (Hunting and
fishing) I: 354d-354e
Mammal *picture on* M: 125
Nunavut (Land and resources) N: 609
Reindeer R: 208
Caricature C: 238 *with pictures*
Carpetbaggers *picture on* C: 247
Cartoon (Editorial cartoons) C: 263-265
CARICOM [organization]
West Indies (Trade) W: 204
Caries [dentistry]
Teeth (Diseases and defects of the teeth) T: 82
with pictures
Carillo, Felipe [Mexican political leader]
Yucatán Peninsula Y: 575
Carillon [musical instrument] C: 238 *with picture*
Bell (Chimes and carillons) B: 239; (Famous bells)
B: 239-240
Carillon Barracks National Historic Site [Quebec]
Canada (table: National historic sites) C: 114
Carinus [Roman emperor]
Rome, Ancient (table) R: 447
Cariocas [people]
Rio de Janeiro (People) R: 345
Carjacking [crime]
Crime scene investigation Ci: 1140
Carl XVI Gustaf [king of Sweden] C: 239
**Carl D. Perkins Vocational and Technical
Education Act** [2006]
Vocational education (The 1900's and early
2000's) V: 435
Carl D. Perkins Vocational Education Act [1984]
Vocational education (The 1900's and early
2000's) V: 435
Carl Sandburg Home National Historic Site
[North Carolina]
National Park System (table: National historic
sites) N: 52
Carl Vinson [ship]
Aircraft carrier (The United States carrier fleet)
A: 206 *with picture*
Carl Zeiss [firm]
Planetarium (Modern planetariums) P: 514b
Carle, Eric [American author]
Laura Ingalls Wilder Award (table) L: 121

Regina Medal (table: 1999) R: 206
Carleton, Sir Guy [British colonial official] C: 239
Canada, History of (The Quebec Act) C: 141-142
Revolution, American (The invasion of Canada)
R: 275-276; (The campaign in New York)
R: 281-282
Carleton, James H. [American general]
Indian wars (Navajo conflicts) I: 195
Carleton, Mount
New Brunswick (Land regions) N: 190 *with picture
and map*
Carleton Martello Tower National Historic Site
[New Brunswick]
Canada (table: National historic sites) C: 114
New Brunswick *picture on* N: 189
Carlin [Nevada]
Gold (History of gold) G: 253
Carlin, John W. [American political leader]
Kansas (table) K: 234
Carlin, Thomas [American political leader]
Illinois (table) I: 71
Carlisle, John G. [American government official]
Cleveland, Grover (table) Ci: 672
Carlists [Spanish history]
Spain (The reign of Isabella II) So: 748
Carloman [king of the Franks]
Charlemagne (Military conquests) C: 379
Carlos [king of Portugal]
Portugal (The first Portuguese republic) P: 694
Carlos, John [American runner]
Olympic Games *picture on* O: 754; (The 1968
games) O: 752
Carlos, Juan *See* Juan Carlos I *in this index*
Carlota, Empress [wife of]
Maximilian M: 319
Carlsbad Caverns National Park [New Mexico]
C: 239 *with picture*
Cave (table) C: 320
National Park System (table: National parks) N: 48
New Mexico (Places to visit) N: 264 *with picture*
Carlson, Arne H. [American political leader]
Minnesota (table) M: 602
Carlson, Chester F. [American physicist]
Copying machine (Electrostatic copying) Ci: 1045
Xerox Corporation X: 544
Carlson, Frank [American political leader]
Kansas (table) K: 234
Carlson, George A. [American political leader]
Colorado (table) Ci: 844
Carlsson, Arvid [Swedish biologist]
Nobel Prizes (Physiology or medicine: 2000)
N: 447
Carlton, Doyle E. [American political leader]
Florida (table) F: 260
Carlton, Steve [American baseball player]
Baseball (table: Hall of Fame) B: 134
Carlucci, Frank C. [American government official]
Defense, Department of (table) D: 87
Carlyle, Thomas [Scottish author] C: 240 *with
portrait*
Biography (The 1800's) B: 314
English literature (Early Victorian literature) E: 321
Carmack, George W. [American prospector]
Klondike K: 344
Yukon (History) Y: 581
Carman, Bliss [Canadian poet] C: 240
Canadian literature (Poetry: 1850-1918) C: 157
May (Quotations) M: 321
October (Quotations) O: 671
Carme [satellite]
Jupiter (Outer satellites) J: 200a
Carmel [California] C: 240
Carmelites [religious group] C: 241
Friar F: 532
Religious life (table) R: 227; (Religious life in the
1500's and 1600's) R: 227
Teresa, Saint T: 170
Carmen [ballet]
Petit, Roland P: 326
Carmen [opera by Bizet]
Bizet, Georges B: 385
Mérimée, Prosper M: 417
Opera *picture on* O: 793; *(Carmen)* O: 802 *with
picture*
"Carmen" [story by Mérimée]
Mérimée, Prosper M: 417
Opera: *(Carmen)* O: 802
Carmina Burana [music by Orff]
Orff, Carl O: 851

Carmine [dye]
Dye (Natural dyes) D: 396
Lake L: 35
Carnahan, Mel [American political leader]
Missouri (table) M: 668
Carnarvon, Lord [British Egyptologist]
Archaeology *picture on* A: 599
Carnassial teeth
Lion (The body of a lion) L: 340-341 *with picture*
Carnation [plant] C: 241 *with picture*
Flower (table) F: 201 *with picture*
Carnauba palm [tree]
Palm (Products of palms) P: 109
Carnauba wax
Wax (Vegetable wax) W: 153
Carnaval [custom]
France (Holidays) F: 460
Carnavalet Museum
Paris (Museums and art galleries) P: 164-165
Carnegie, Andrew [American philanthropist]
C: 241 *with portrait*
Carnegie Corporation of New York C: 243
Carnegie Foundation for the Advancement of
Teaching C: 243
Foundation (History) F: 431
Iron and steel (Growth of the steel industry)
I: 451
Library (Libraries in the United States) L: 261-262
United States, History of the (Industrialization
and reform [1870-1916]) U: 179-180
Carnegie, Dale [American author] C: 242
Carnegie Corporation of New York [foundation]
C: 243
Foundation (Education) F: 430-431
**Carnegie Foundation for the Advancement of
Teaching** C: 243
Carnegie Hall [New York City]
Carnegie, Andrew (Carnegie's contributions to
society) C: 242
Carnegie Hero Fund Commission
Carnegie, Andrew (Carnegie's contributions to
society) C: 242
Carnegie Institution of Washington
Carnegie, Andrew (Carnegie's contributions to
society) C: 242
Mount Wilson Observatory M: 890
Carnegie libraries
Library (Libraries in the United States) L: 261-262
Carnegie Medal
Medals, decorations, and orders (Civilian awards)
M: 355
Carnegie Mellon University
Carnegie, Andrew (Carnegie's contributions to
society) C: 242
Carnegie Museums of Pittsburgh
Pittsburgh (Museums and libraries) P: 500c
Carnegie Steel Company
Carnegie, Andrew (Rise to wealth) C: 242
Homestead Strike H: 305
Carnelian [gem]
Gem *picture on* G: 78
Carney, Art [American actor]
Motion picture (Best performance by an actor:
1974) M: 862a
Carney, Thomas [American political leader]
Kansas (table) K: 234
Carnival [celebration] C: 243
Brazil (Recreation) B: 575 *with picture*
Easter (Easter customs) E: 44
Rio de Janeiro (People) R: 345-346
Carnival [music by Dvořák]
Dvořák, Antonín D: 394
Carnival of Harlequin [painting by Miró]
Painting (Surrealism) P: 81-82 *with picture*
Carnival of the Animals, The [music by Saint-
Saëns]
Saint-Saëns, Camille S: 56
Carnivore [zoology] C: 243
Animal (A table of animal intelligence) A: 493
Mammal (What mammals eat) M: 121 *with
diagram;* (table) M: 128 *with picture*
Carnivorous bat [animal]
Bat (Carnivorous bats) B: 161
Carnivorous plant [botany] C: 243
Butterwort B: 744 *with picture*
Leaf (Insect-capturing leaves) L: 157 *with picture*
Plant (Environmental factors) P: 538-539 *with
picture*
Venus's-flytrap V: 314
Wetland (Plant life) W: 252a-252b
Carnosaur [dinosaur]
Dinosaur (Saurischians) D: 208-211
Carnot, Lazare Nicolas Marguerite [French
political leader]
French Revolution (Terror and equality) F: 526-
527
Carnutes [people]

Chartres C: 386
"Caro nome" [aria]
  Opera: *(Rigoletto)* O: 806
Carob [tree] C: 244
Carol [song]
  Christmas (Christmas carols) C: 535
Carol I [king of Romania]
  Romania (The origins of modern Romania) R: 423
Carol II [king of Romania]
  Romania (Depression and fascism) R: 424
Carolana, Province of [U.S. history]
  North Carolina (Exploration and settlement)
  N: 490
  South Carolina (Exploration and settlement)
  So: 659
Carolina [U.S. history]
  South Carolina (Exploration and settlement)
  So: 659
  United States, History of the (North Carolina,
  South Carolina, and Georgia) U: 156
Carolina chickadee [bird]
  Chickadee C: 439
Carolina Cup Steeplechase
  South Carolina (Visitor's guide) So: 650
Carolina hemlock [tree]
  Hemlock H: 182
Carolina Hurricanes [team]
  Hockey (table: National Hockey League) H: 281
Carolina jessamine [plant] *See* Yellow jessamine
in this index
Carolina mantid [insect]
  Insect *picture on* I: 280
Carolina Panthers [team]
  Football (National Football League) F: 364
Carolina parakeet [bird]
  Bird (Extinct birds) B: 369-370
  Parakeet P: 151
  Parrot (Kinds of parrots) P: 179
Carolina poplar [tree]
  Poplar P: 668
Carolina silverbell [plant]
  Silverbell S: 465
Carolina wolf spider
  Spider *picture on* So: 789
Carolina wren [bird]
  Bird (Birds of brushy areas) B: 338 *with picture*
  Wren W: 504
Caroline [princess of Monaco]
  Rainier III R: 129
Caroline [ship]
  Harrison, William Henry (The *Caroline* affair) H: 76
Caroline [wife of]
  George II G: 106b
Caroline drama
  Drama (Jacobean and Caroline drama) D: 332
Caroline Islands [Pacific Ocean] C: 244
  Pacific Islands, Trust Territory of the P: 13
  Palau P: 101
  World War II (Island hopping in the Central
  Pacific) W: 489
Caroline minuscule [handwriting] *See* Carolingian
minuscule *in this index*
Carolingian architecture
  Architecture (Carolingian architecture) A: 618
  with picture
Carolingian art C: 244 *with picture*
  Painting (Early medieval painting in the West)
  P: 49-50
  Sculpture (Early medieval sculpture) S: 248
Carolingian Empire
  Belgium (The Middle Ages) B: 232
  France (The Carolingian dynasty) F: 471
  Franks F: 494
  Middle Ages (The Carolingian Empire) M: 524
Carolingian minuscule [handwriting]
  Charlemagne (Administration and influence)
  C: 379
  Paleography P: 103
Carolingian Renaissance [European history]
  Charlemagne (Administration and influence)
  C: 379-380
  Middle Ages (The Carolingian Empire) M: 524
Carolinians [people]
  Micronesia, Federated States of (People) M: 515
  Northern Mariana Islands, Commonwealth of the
  (People) N: 526
Carollo, Joe [American political leader]
  Miami (History) M: 480-481
Carom billiards [game]
  Billiards (Carom billiards) B: 306
Carotene
  Carrot C: 249
  Leaf (The leaf changes color) L: 152
  Milk (Fats) M: 546
  Vitamin (Vitamin A) V: 430
Carotenoid [chemical]
  Antioxidant A: 557

Carothers, Wallace Hume [American chemist]
  Nylon (History) N: 633
Carotid artery [anatomy]
  Artery (Principal arteries) A: 751
  Human body (table) H: 422 *with diagram*
  Pulse P: 900a
  Stroke (Prevention) So: 930
Carotid endarterectomy [surgery]
  Stroke (Prevention) So: 930
Carousel
  Merry-go-round M: 419
Carousel [musical]
  Molnár, Ferenc M: 696
  Rodgers, Richard R: 398
Carow, Edith Kermit [wife of Theodore Roosevelt]
  See Roosevelt, Edith Carow *in this index*
Carp [fish] C: 245 *with picture*
  Fish *picture on* F: 159
  Goldfish G: 257 *with pictures*
Carpaccio, Vittore [Italian painter]
  World, History of the *picture on* W: 438
Carpal bone [anatomy]
  Frog *picture on* F: 537
  Hand (Parts of the hand) H: 40 *with diagram*
  Human body (table) H: 422 *with diagram*
  Wrist W: 510 *with diagram*
Carpal tunnel syndrome [disorder] C: 245 *with
diagram*
Carpathia [ship]
  Titanic T: 300
Carpathian Mountains [Europe] C: 245
  Galicia G: 10
  Poland (The Western Carpathian Mountains)
  P: 609
  Romania (Surface features) R: 419
  Slovakia (Land and climate) S: 508d
  Ukraine (The Eastern Carpathian Mountains) U: 9
  with map
Carpel [botany]
  Angiosperm A: 462 *with picture*
  Flower (The parts of a flower) F: 293 *with picture*
  Plant (Flowers) P: 531 *with picture*; (Sexual
  reproduction) P: 532-533
Carpenter [career]
  Building trade (Career opportunities) B: 686
  Carpentry C: 246
  Woodworking W: 396
Carpenter, C. C. [American settler]
  Oklahoma (Great land rushes) O: 732
Carpenter, Cyrus C. [American political leader]
  Iowa (table) I: 391
Carpenter, Francis [American artist]
  Emancipation Proclamation *picture on* E: 254
Carpenter, M. Scott [American astronaut] C: 246
  Space exploration (Vostok and Mercury: The
  first human beings in space) So: 712-713 *with
  picture*
Carpenter ant
  Ant *pictures on* A: 521; (Life in an ant colony)
  A: 522-523
Carpenter bee
  Bee (Solitary bees) B: 205-206 *with picture*
**Carpenters and Joiners of America, United
Brotherhood of** [labor union] C: 246
  Labor movement (table) L: 8
Carpenter's level [tool]
  Level L: 217 *with picture*
Carpentier, Alejo [Cuban author]
  Cuba (The arts) Ci: 1171-1172
  Latin American literature (The mid-1900's) L: 114
Carpentier, Georges [French boxer]
  Boxing (Boxing's Golden Age) B: 532-532a
Carpentry C: 246
Carper, Tom [American political leader]
  Delaware (table) D: 109
Carpet *See* Rugs and carpets *in this index*
Carpet beetle [insect] C: 246 *with picture*
  Insect *picture on* I: 285
Carpet chameleon [reptile]
  Rain forest *picture on* R: 126c
Carpet grass
  Lawn (Types of lawns) L: 142
Carpet python
  Snake *picture on* S: 533
Carpet sweeper
  Michigan (Interesting facts) M: 489
Carpetbaggers [U.S. history] C: 246 *with picture*
  Reconstruction (The Republicans in the South)
  R: 179
Carpio, Lope Félix de Vega [Spanish dramatist]
  Vega, Lope de V: 292
Carr, Elias [American political leader]
  North Carolina (table) N: 490
Carr, Emily [Canadian painter] C: 247
Carr, Gerald P. [American astronaut]
  Astronaut *picture on* A: 831
Carr, Ralph L. [American political leader]

  Colorado (table) Ci: 844
Carrà, Carlo [Italian painter]
  Futurism F: 589
Carracci, Agostino [Italian artist]
  Painting (Baroque) P: 58-59
Carracci, Annibale [Italian painter]
  Baroque (Baroque painting) B: 117
  Painting (Baroque) P: 58-59
Carracci, Lodovico [Italian artist]
  Painting (Baroque) P: 58-59
Carrack [ship]
  Ship *picture on* S: 420
Carrageen *See* Irish moss *in this index*
Carrageenin [extract]
  Food additive (Kinds of additives) F: 339
  Seaweed (Uses) S: 277
Carranza, Venustiano [Mexican political leader]
  C: 247
  Mexican Revolution of 1910 (The revolution)
  M: 445
  Mexico (The Revolution of 1910) M: 472; (The
  Constitution of 1917) M: 472
  Obregón, Álvaro O: 643
  Villa, Pancho V: 384
  Wilson, Woodrow (Crisis in Mexico) W: 323
Carrasquilla, Tomás [Colombian author]
  Latin American literature (Realism) L: 113
Carrauntoohil [mountain, Ireland]
  Ireland (Surface features) I: 422 *with map*
Carré, Ferdinand [French engineer]
  Refrigeration (Mechanical refrigeration) R: 201
Carré, Michel [French librettist]
  Opera: *(Faust)* O: 804
Carrel, Alexis [French biologist]
  Lindbergh, Charles Augustus (Good-will
  ambassador) L: 330
  Nobel Prizes (Physiology or medicine: 1912)
  N: 445
Carrera, José Miguel [Chilean political leader]
  Chile (Independence) C: 468
Carrera, Rafael [Guatemalan political leader]
  El Salvador (Independence) E: 252
  Guatemala (Independence) G: 417
Carreta, La [monument]
  Uruguay *picture on* U: 228
Carrey, Jim [Canadian American actor] C: 247 *with
portrait*
Carriacou [island, Caribbean Sea]
  Grenada G: 388
  Grenadines G: 390
Carriage [machine]
  Lumber *picture on* L: 517; (Sawing logs) L: 519
Carriage [vehicle] C: 248
Carriage at Louvenciennes [painting by Pissarro]
  Pissarro, Camille *picture on* P: 497
Carriage bolt [hardware]
  Bolt B: 449 *with picture*
Carrick [region, Scotland]
  Bruce, Robert B: 648
Carrick bend
  Knots, hitches, and splices (Useful knots) K: 356
  with diagram
Carrie [book by King]
  King, Stephen K: 323
Carrier [mechanism]
  Transmission (Planetary gears) T: 377 *with
  diagrams*
Carrier [medicine]
  Cystic fibrosis Ci: 1208
  Genetic counseling (Reasons for seeking genetic
  counseling) G: 84a
  Genetic testing (Genes associated with disease)
  G: 84d
  Hemophilia (How hemophilia is inherited) H: 182
  with diagram
  Insect (Harmful insects) I: 284
Carrier [ship]
  Aircraft carrier A: 206 *with pictures*
  Warship *picture on* W: 43; (Aircraft carriers) W: 39
Carrier, Common *See* Common carrier *in this index*
Carrier, Willis H. [American engineer]
  Air conditioning (History) A: 180
Carrier element [physics]
  Radiochemistry R: 98
Carrier frequency [radio]
  Antenna A: 543
Carrier phase GPS [navigation]
  Global Positioning System G: 232
Carrier pigeon [bird] C: 248 *with picture*
Carrier projectile
  Ammunition A: 435
Carrier shell snail [animal]
  Shell *picture on* S: 386
Carrier task force [military]
  Aircraft carrier A: 206
Carrier wave [communications]
  Antenna A: 543

Radio (From electric waves to radio waves) R: 86 *with diagram*
Wireless communication (How wireless communication works) W: 344
Carriers of Ladders, The [book by Merwin]
Merwin, W. S. M: 420
Carrillo, Braulio [Costa Rican political leader]
Costa Rica (Independence) Ci: 1084
Carrion [animals]
Bird (Kinds of food) B: 350
Vulture V: 453
Carrion crow [bird]
Crow (Kinds of crows) Ci: 1157
Carrizo Plains [region, California]
San Andreas Fault *picture on* S: 83
Carroll [American family] CI: 248
Carroll, Beryl F. [American political leader]
Iowa (table) I: 391
Carroll, Charles [American patriot]
Carroll C: 248
Carroll, Daniel [American political leader]
Carroll C: 248
Carroll, John [American religious leader]
Carroll C: 248
Roman Catholic Church (In the United States) R: 412
Carroll, John Lee [American political leader]
Maryland (table) M: 255
Carroll, Lewis [British author] C: 248 *with pictures*
Alice in Wonderland A: 367
Literature for children *picture on* L: 376; (Fantasies) L: 359; (Masterpieces of fiction) L: 363
Tenniel, Sir John T: 160
Carroll, Madeleine [British actress]
Motion picture *picture on* M: 868
Carroll, Thomas King [American political leader]
Maryland (table) M: 255
Carroll, Wayne T. [American journalist]
Feboldson, Febold F: 59
Carroll, William [American political leader]
Tennessee (table) T: 152
Carros [vehicles]
Drama (Religious plays) D: 333 *with picture*
Carrot [plant] C: 249 *with picture*
Flower (table) F: 301 *with picture*
Gardening (Planning a kitchen garden) G: 34
Plant (Roots) P: 528 *with picture*
Vegetable (Roots) V: 292 *with picture*
Wild carrot W: 300 *with picture*
Carrousel
Merry-go-round M: 419
Carruthers, Garrey [American political leader]
New Mexico (table) N: 272
"Carry Me Back to Old Virginia" [song]
Bland, James A. B: 398
Carry-out restaurant
Restaurant (Kinds of restaurants) R: 262
Carrying [mathematics]
Addition (How to carry) A: 50
Multiplication (How to carry in multiplication) M: 922
Carrying capacity
Conservation (Conservation of grazing lands) Ci: 981
Ecology (Populations) E: 53
Carsickness
Motion sickness M: 874
Carso [plateau]
Italy (The Adriatic Plain) I: 508
Carson, Benjamin [American surgeon]
Spingarn Medal (table: 2006) So: 794
Carson, Christopher *See* Carson, Kit *in this index*
Carson, Johnny [American entertainer]
Carson, Kit [American frontiersman] C: 250 *with portrait*
Arizona (Indian fighting) A: 690
Indian wars (Navajo conflicts) I: 195
Navajo Indians N: 70
New Mexico (Territorial days) N: 275
Carson, Rachel [American biologist] C: 250
Conservation (Renewed interest in conservation) Ci: 986
DDT D: 55
Pest control (Effects of pesticide use) P: 318
Carson, William [Scottish doctor]
Newfoundland and Labrador (Representation and independence) N: 377
Carson City [Nevada] C: 251
Carson County
Nevada (Early settlement) N: 174; (The Comstock Lode) N: 174
Carson Pirie Scott and Company Building [Chicago]
Architecture *picture on* A: 630; (Early modern architecture in America) A: 629
Carson River

Nevada (Rivers and lakes) N: 166 *with map*
Carson Sink [region, Nevada]
Great Basin G: 336 *with map*
Carswell, G. Harrold [American jurist]
Nixon, Richard Milhous (The national scene) N: 433-434
Cart [vehicle]
Transportation (Land transportation) T: 383-384; (The first great civilizations) T: 385-386 *with picture*
Cartagena [Colombia]
Drake, Sir Francis (Expeditions against Spain) D: 322
Cartagena [Spain] C: 251
Cartagena Agreement [1969]
Andean Community A: 450
Cartago [Costa Rica]
Costa Rica *picture on* Ci: 1081; (Colonial period) Ci: 1083
Carte, Richard D'Oyly [British producer] *See* D'Oyly Carte, Richard *in this index*
Cartel [business] C: 251
Colombia (Civil war) Ci: 784
Inflation (The cost-push theory) I: 268
Carter, A. P. [American singer]
Carter Family C: 260
Carter, Amy Lynn [daughter of]
Carter, Jimmy *picture on* C: 259; (Carter's family) C: 253
Carter, Anita [American singer]
Carter Family C: 260
Carter, Billy [brother of]
Carter, Jimmy (Boyhood) C: 252
Carter, Don [American bowler] C: 251
Carter, Elliott [American composer] C: 251
Carter, Frederic Bowker Terrington [Canadian political leader]
Confederation of Canada (Fathers of Confederation) Ci: 935
Carter, Gary [American baseball player]
Baseball (table: Hall of Fame) B: 134
Carter, Gerald Emmett [Canadian religious leader]
Cardinal (table: Canadian cardinals) C: 211
Carter, Gloria [sister of]
Carter, Jimmy (Boyhood) C: 252
Carter, Helen [American singer]
Carter Family C: 260
Carter, Howard [British archaeologist] C: 251
Archaeology *picture on* A: 599
Tutankhamun T: 526
Carter, James Earl, Sr. [father of]
Carter, Jimmy (Boyhood) C: 252
Carter, James Earl, Jr. [U.S. president] *See* Carter, Jimmy *in this index*
Carter, Janette [American singer]
Carter Family C: 260
Carter, Jimmy [U.S. president] C: 252 *with pictures*
African Americans (Politics) A: 136s
Arab-Israeli conflict (The Camp David Accords) A: 582a
Brzezinski, Zbigniew Kazimierz B: 657
Clinton, Bill (International affairs) Ci: 682e
Cuba (Recent developments) Ci: 1179
Democratic Party (The late 1900's) D: 127
Egypt (Renewed warfare and peace) E: 133 *with picture*
Federal Emergency Management Agency F: 63
Ford, Gerald Rudolph (The 1976 election) F: 378-379
Georgia (table) G: 130
Iran (Revolution and the Islamic Republic) I: 406a
Maine *picture on* M: 92
Mondale, Walter Frederick M: 702
National Park System (table: National historic sites) N: 52-53
Olympic Games (Boycotts) O: 753
Panama Canal (The canal under Panamanian control) P: 127
Union of Soviet Socialist Republics (The collapse of détente) U: 40
United States, History of the (The end of the Cold War) U: 160d
Carter, Joe [American singer]
Carter Family C: 260
Carter, June [American musician]
Carter Family C: 260
Cash, Johnny C: 273
Carter, Lillian Gordy [mother of]
Carter, Jimmy (Boyhood) C: 252
Carter, Maybelle Addington [American singer]
Carter Family C: 260
Carter, Robert [American publisher]
Lowell, James Russell (Early career) L: 510
Carter, Robert L. [American attorney]
Spingarn Medal (table: 2004) So: 794
Carter, Rosalynn Smith [wife of Jimmy Carter]
Carter, Jimmy *picture on* C: 259; (Carter's family)

C: 253
First ladies of the United States (table) F: 142
Carter, Ruth [sister of]
Carter, Jimmy (Boyhood) C: 252
Carter, Sara Dougherty [American singer]
Carter Family C: 260
Carter, Shawn Corey [real name of]
Jay-Z J: 67
Carter, William Alton, III [brother of]
Carter, Jimmy (Boyhood) C: 252
Carter Family [musical group] C: 260
Country music (Early commercial success) Ci: 1098b
Carter Presidential Center
Atlanta (Museums and libraries) A: 860b
Carteret, Sir George [English colonial official]
New Jersey (English control) N: 250
Carteret, Philip [English colonial leader]
Elizabeth E: 238
Carteret, Philip [English explorer]
Pitcairn Island P: 498
Carter's Grove [estate]
Virginia (Places to visit) V: 408
Williamsburg (Williamsburg today) W: 313
Cartesian system [geometry]
Geometry (Analytic geometry) G: 105 *with diagram*
Cartesianism [philosophy]
Descartes, René D: 154
Carthage [ancient city] C: 260 *with pictures and map*
Cato, Marcus Porcius, the Elder C: 304
Dido D: 195
Dionysius the Elder D: 214
Libya (Early days) L: 267
Mythology (The *Aeneid*) M: 983
Phoenicia (The spread of Phoenician influence) P: 394-395
Punic Wars P: 903
Regulus, Marcus Atilius R: 206
Rome, Ancient (The Roman Republic) R: 444
Tunisia (History) T: 489
Utica U: 251
Carthage [Illinois]
Young, Brigham (Mormon leader) Y: 571
Carthusians [religious group] C: 261
Cartier, Sir George Étienne [Canadian patriot] C: 261
Canada, History of (Confederation) C: 144
Confederation of Canada (Moves toward confederation) Ci: 933; (Fathers of Confederation) Ci: 935 *with picture*
Macdonald, Sir John Alexander (Associate provincial prime minister) M: 7
Cartier, Jacques [French explorer] C: 261 *with picture*
Canada, History of (Early European exploration) C: 138-139
Canadian literature (Beginnings of Canadian literature) C: 156
Exploration *map on* E: 443; (The search for a northern passage) E: 446
Gulf of Saint Lawrence G: 437
Montreal M: 768; (Exploration) M: 777
New Brunswick (Exploration and settlement) N: 196
Northwest Passage N: 528
Prince Edward Island (Exploration and early history) P: 791
Quebec [city] (Early days) Q: 36
Quebec [province] (The beginning of European rule) Q: 30
Roberval, Jean François de La Roque, Sieur de R: 365
Saint Lawrence River (History) S: 42
Cartier-Brébeuf National Historic Site [Quebec]
Canada (table: National historic sites) C: 114
Cartier-Bresson, Henri [French photographer] C: 262 *with picture*
Photography (Dramatic changes) P: 425-426
Cartilage [anatomy] C: 263
Connective tissue C: 972
Dwarfism (Causes) D: 394
Joint J: 155
Rib R: 320 *with diagram*
Cartography
Atlas A: 868
Careers (Technical and mathematical occupations) C: 232
Geography (Mapping) G: 95
Map M: 176
Cartoon [design]
Cartoon C: 263
Fresco F: 529
Painting (Gothic painting) P: 50
Stained glass (How stained-glass windows are made) So: 821

Tapestry (How tapestries are made) T: 39
Cartoon [drawing] C: 263 *with pictures*
See also Animation *and the list of Related articles in the* Cartoon *article*
Addams, Charles A: 46
Advertising (Production) A: 76b
Comics Ci: 869 *with pictures*
Disney, Walt D: 235 *with pictures*
Franklin, Benjamin (Publisher) F: 487
Kennedy, John Fitzgerald *picture on* K: 268
Nast, Thomas N: 24
Public opinion (The press) P: 860
Pulitzer Prizes (table) P: 892
Republican Party *pictures on* R: 254, R: 256
Cartouche [ancient Egypt]
Cartouche C: 267 *with picture*
Hieroglyphics (Deciphering hieroglyphic writing) H: 226-227
Cartouche [architecture] C: 267 *with picture*
Cartouche [cartography]
Cartouche C: 268
Cartouche [heraldry]
Cartouche C: 268
Cartridge [ammunition] C: 268
Ammunition (Small-arms ammunition) A: 435 *with pictures*
Dynamite D: 397
Firearm (Mechanism) F: 132
Handgun (Types of handguns) H: 43 *with picture*
Rifle (Rifle cartridges) R: 339
Cartridge [electronics]
Phonograph (Parts of a phonograph) P: 400-401 *with diagram*
Cartridge fuse
Fuse F: 589 *with diagram*
Cartwright, Alexander [American sportsman]
Baseball (Alexander Cartwright) B: 133; (Rule changes) B: 133; (table: Hall of Fame) B: 134
Cartwright, Edmund [British inventor] C: 268
Industrial Revolution (Weaving machines) I: 249
Invention (Economic needs) I: 355
Rugs and carpets (History) R: 517
Weaving (History) W: 174-175
Cartwright, Peter [American religious leader]
Lincoln, Abraham (Search for advancement) L: 316
Revivalism R: 269
Caruncle [zoology]
Turkey (The body of a turkey) T: 513
Carus [Roman emperor]
Rome, Ancient (table) R: 447
Carus, Titus Lucretius [Roman philosopher] *See* Lucretius *in this index*
Caruso, Enrico [Italian singer] C: 268
Radio (The start of broadcasting) R: 92
Carved parallel turn
Skiing *diagram on* S: 484
Carvel, Elbert N. [American political leader]
Delaware (table) D: 109
Carver, George Washington [American botanist] C: 268 *with picture*
African Americans *picture on* A: 136k; (The Harlem Renaissance and other achievements) A: 136m-136n
Alabama (Interesting facts) A: 257
Autograph *picture on* A: 943
Invention (The early and middle 1900's) I: 363
Peanut (History) P: 215
Tuskegee University T: 525
Carver, John [American colonial leader] C: 269
Massasoit M: 295
Plymouth Colony (The founding of Plymouth Colony) P: 582
Carver, Raymond [American author] C: 269
American literature (Fiction and other prose) A: 424
Carville, Edward P. [American political leader]
Nevada (table) N: 173
Carving [art]
Indian, American (Carving) I: 145 *with picture*
Inuit (Arts and crafts) I: 354f
Islamic art *picture on* I: 468; (Decorative arts) I: 469-470
Ivory (Ivory carving) I: 521 *with pictures*
Leathercraft (Cutting and assembling) L: 169 *with picture*
Maori *picture on* M: 175
Phoenicia *picture on* P: 393
Sculpture (The sculptor at work) S: 232 *with picture*
Woodcarving W: 391 *with diagrams*
Carving, Meat
Meat *pictures on* M: 348
Cary, Joyce [British author] C: 269
Cary, Mary Ann Shadd [American educator] C: 270
Caryatid [sculpture]
Elgin Marbles E: 236

Sculpture (As part of architecture) S: 229-230
CAS [company]
Columbus (Economy) Ci: 855
Casa de las Américas [organization]
Cuba (The arts) Ci: 1171-1172
Casa Grande [building]
Arizona *picture on* A: 671
Casa Grande Ruins National Monument [Arizona] C: 270
National Park System (table: National monuments) N: 50
Casa Guidi [villa, Florence]
Browning, Elizabeth Barrett B: 646
Casa Guidi Windows [book by Browning]
Browning, Elizabeth Barrett B: 646
Casa Loma [castle]
Toronto *picture on* T: 340c; (Landmarks) T: 338-339
Casa Rosada [building]
Argentina *picture on* A: 647
Buenos Aires (The city) B: 672
Casaba [fruit] C: 270 *with picture*
Muskmelon M: 963
Casablanca [Morocco] C: 270
Casablanca [film]
Bogart, Humphrey B: 436
Motion picture (Best picture: 1943) M: 861; (Movies and World War II) M: 869
Casablanca Conference [1943]
World War II (The strategy) W: 480-481
Casals, Pablo [Spanish cellist] C: 270
Casals Festival [music]
Casals, Pablo C: 271
Casamance [region, Senegal]
Senegal S: 297
Casanova, Giacomo [Italian public figure] C: 271 *with portrait*
Casas, Bartolomé de las [Spanish missionary] *See* Las Casas, Bartolomé de *in this index*
Casbah [district]
Algiers A: 365
Cascade [geography]
Waterfall W: 141
Cascade Falls [Minnesota]
Minnesota (Lakes, rivers, and waterfalls) M: 598-599
Cascade Range [mountains, Canada-U.S.] C: 271
California (Land regions) C: 48
Oregon *picture on* O: 840; (Land regions) O: 838 *with map*
United States (The Pacific Ranges and Lowlands) U: 125
Washington (Land regions) W: 58 *with map*
Cascade Tunnel [tunnel, Washington]
Washington (Transportation) W: 64
"Cascadilla Falls" [poem by Ammons]
Ammons, A. R. A: 434
Cascara sagrada [shrub] C: 271 *with pictures*
Case [bookbinding]
Bookbinding (Covering a book) B: 472
Case [debating]
Debate (Types of resolutions) D: 64
Case [grammar] C: 271
Declension D: 79
Noun (Number and case) N: 552
Case, Clarence E. [American political leader]
New Jersey (table) N: 249
Case, Norman S. [American political leader]
Rhode Island (table) R: 311
Case history
Medicine (Diagnosis) M: 364
Psychology (Systematic assessment) P: 848
Case law
Law (Common law systems) L: 132
Case method [education] C: 272
Architecture (Education and training) A: 634
Law (Law education) L: 138
Case of the Velvet Claws, The [book by Gardner]
Gardner, Erle Stanley G: 39
Case study
Abnormal psychology (Studies in abnormal psychology) A: 12
Criminology (Case studies) Ci: 1145
Sociology (Field observation) So: 566
Casearia bridelioides [tree]
Plant *picture on* P: 527
Cased pencil
Pencil (Cased pencils) P: 236 *with picture*
Casein [protein] C: 272
Leather (Final processing) L: 168-169
Milk (Proteins) M: 546
Casement window
Window W: 334
Casework
Adoption (The adoption process) A: 66
Social work (Methods of social work) So: 558 *with picture*

Casey, James [American businessman]
United Parcel Service, Inc. U: 97
Casey, Robert P. [American political leader]
Pennsylvania (table) P: 263
"Casey at the Bat" [poem by Thayer]
Literature for children (Masterpieces of poetry) L: 364
Casey Jones *See* Jones, Casey *in this index*
Casey Jones Home & Railroad Museum [Jackson]
Tennessee (Places to visit) T: 144
Cash [money]
Money (Chinese coins) M: 707
Cash, Johnny [American singer] C: 272
Carter Family C: 260
Country music *picture on* Ci: 1098d
Nelson, Willie N: 123
Cash, Rosanne [American singer]
Cash, Johnny C: 273
Cash aid program
Poverty (Social welfare programs) P: 725
Welfare (Cash aid programs) W: 190
Cash dispenser *See* Automated teller machine *in this index*
Cash flows, Statement of
Accounting (Financial reports) A: 22-23
Bookkeeping (Bookkeeping and financial statements) B: 473
"Cash for Clunkers" program *See* Car Allowance Rebate System *in this index*
Cash fund [economics] *See* Money market fund *in this index*
Cash grain farm
Farm and farming (Specialized crop farms) F: 30
Cash lease [rent]
Plantation (Skilled-labor plantations) P: 551
Tenant farming T: 132
Cash machine *See* Automated teller machine *in this index*
Cash market [economics]
Commodity exchange (Cash market contracts) Ci: 873
Cash order [economics]
Installment plan I: 304
Cash register C: 273 *with picture*
Ritty, James R: 351
Cash value [insurance]
Insurance (Major types of life insurance) I: 309
Investment (Life insurance policies) I: 369
Cashew [nut] C: 273 *with picture*
Nut (Kinds of nuts) N: 621
Cashier's check [banking]
Check (Special checking services) C: 391
Cashmere [fabric] C: 274
Cashmere goat [animal] C: 274 *with picture*
Goat (Domestic goats) G: 239
Casimir I [king of Poland]
Poland (The early Polish state) P: 611
Casimir, Hendrik Brugt Gerhard [Dutch physicist]
Vacuum (In particle physics) V: 256-257
Casimir effect [physics]
Vacuum (In particle physics) V: 256-257
Casimir the Great [king of Poland] *See* Casimir III *in this index*
Casina [play by Plautus]
Plautus P: 570
Casing [container]
Petroleum (Completing the well) P: 340-341 *with diagram*
Casing [food]
Meat packing (Sausage making) M: 352
Sausage S: 163
Casing [munitions]
Ammunition (Small-arms ammunition) A: 435 *with diagram*
Rifle (Rifle cartridges) R: 339
Casinghead gasoline
Gasoline (Gasoline production) G: 61
Casino [game]
Card game C: 209
Casino [place]
Atlantic City A: 862
Gambling (Types of gambling) G: 20; (Modern gambling) G: 21
Indian, American (Social and economic progress) I: 180-181 *with picture*
Las Vegas (History) L: 89
Monaco M: 699
Nevada *picture on* N: 171; (Service industries) N: 169
Casino Royale [book by Fleming]
Fleming, Ian F: 233
"Cask of Amontillado, The" [story by Poe]
Poe, Edgar Allan (Fiction and theory of fiction) P: 590
Casket
Funeral customs (Preparation of the body) F: 557
Caslon, William [English printer]

Book (The 1600's and 1700's) **B:** 467
Caslon, William, IV [English printer]
Type (Classes of type) **T:** 537
Casper [Wyoming] **C:** 274
Wyoming (Population) **W:** 520; (Territorial progress) **W:** 534-536
Caspian Sea [Europe-Asia] **C:** 274 *with map*
Asia (Coastline, bays, seas, and lakes) **A:** 795-796
Azerbaijan (Land and climate) **A:** 996-997 *with picture*
Europe (Lakes) **E:** 395
Iran *picture on* **I:** 404; (Caspian Sea Coast) **I:** 403
Lake (table) **L:** 34
Russia (Rivers and lakes) **R:** 541
Caspian tern [bird]
Tern **T:** 172
Casque [biology]
Guineafowl **G:** 435
Cass [West Virginia]
West Virginia (Places to visit) **W:** 216
Cass, Lewis [American political leader] **C:** 275
Buchanan, James (Prelude to war) **B:** 661
Fillmore, Millard (Vice president) **F:** 101
Polk, James Knox (Election of 1844) **P:** 642
Popular sovereignty **P:** 672
Van Buren, Martin (Later years) **V:** 273
Cassady, Howard [American football player]
Football (table) **F:** 363
Cassai, Tommaso [Italian painter] *See Masaccio in this index*
Cassander [king of Macedonia]
Thessaloniki **T:** 258
Cassandra [legendary figure] **C:** 275
Paris **P:** 159
Cassapanca [furniture]
Furniture (Italy) **F:** 572
Cassaria [play by Ariosto]
Drama (Italian Renaissance drama) **D:** 330
Cassation, Court of [law]
France (Courts) **F:** 455
Cassatt, Mary [American painter] **C:** 275 *with pictures*
Impressionism (American Impressionism) **I:** 94
Painting (Edouard Manet and the Impressionists) **P:** 71; (Women artists) **P:** 73
Cassava [shrub] **C:** 276 *with pictures*
Indian, American (Indians of the Tropical forest) **I:** 175
Tapioca **T:** 41
Cassava mealybug [insect]
Invasive species (Managing invasive species) **I:** 354k
Cassegrain telescope
Telescope (Reflecting telescopes) **T:** 104
Cassette [electronics]
Audio-visual materials (Audio materials) **A:** 883
Recording industry **R:** 180
Tape recorder (Kinds of tape recorders) **T:** 38 *with picture*
Cassette tape recorder [electronics]
Tape recorder (Kinds of tape recorders) **T:** 38 *with picture*
Cassia [plant] **C:** 276
Cinnamon **Ci:** 557
Cassiar Mountains
British Columbia (Land regions) **B:** 622
Cassin, René-Samuel [French jurist]
Nobel Prizes (Peace: 1968) **N:** 448b
Cassini [space probe] **C:** 276 *with picture*
Enceladus **E:** 265
Heliosphere (Probing the heliosphere) **H:** 175
Iapetus **I:** 2
Jupiter (History of Jupiter study) **J:** 200b
Planet (Saturn) **P:** 511
Planetary ring **P:** 514d
Satellite (Phoebe) **S:** 150c; (Exploration by spacecraft) **S:** 150c
Saturn **S:** 150i *with pictures*
Titan **T:** 299
Cassini, Giovanni Domenico [Italian-born French astronomer] **C:** 277
Iapetus **I:** 2
Map (Advances in European cartography) **M:** 184
Saturn (History of study) **S:** 153
Cassini, Jean-Dominique [Italian-born French astronomer] *See Cassini, Giovanni Domenico in this index*
Cassini division [astronomy]
Cassini, Giovanni Domenico **C:** 277
Saturn (Rings) **S:** 150j *with diagram*
Cassino [Italy]
World War II (The invasion of Italy) **W:** 483
Cassin's auklet [bird]
Bird *picture on* **B:** 368
Cassiodorus [Roman nobleman]
Library (Medieval collections) **L:** 259
Cassiopeia [constellation] **C:** 277

Cassiopeia [Greek mythology]
Andromeda **A:** 457
Cassiopeia **C:** 277
Cassiterite [mineral] **C:** 277
Tin (Where tin is found) **T:** 293
Cassius [literary figure]
Shakespeare, William: *(Julius Caesar)* **S:** 360
Cassius Longinus, Gaius [Roman general] **C:** 277
Caesar, Julius (Assassination) **C:** 14
Cassock [vestment]
Pope *picture on* **P:** 661
Casson, Alfred Joseph [Canadian painter]
Group of Seven **G:** 402
Cassone
Furniture (Italy) **F:** 572 *with picture*
Cassoulet [food]
France (Food and drink) **F:** 459-460
Cassowary [bird] **C:** 277 *with picture*
Cast [drama]
Motion picture (Assembling the cast) **M:** 851
Cast [form]
Fossil (How fossils form) **F:** 425 *with picture*
Cast and casting [manufacturing] **C:** 278 *with pictures*
Aluminum (Casting the molten aluminum) **A:** 394; (Casting) **A:** 395
Automobile (Manufacturing) **A:** 958
Bell (How bells are made) **B:** 238
Copper (How copper metal is produced) **Ci:** 1041 *with diagrams*
Die and diemaking **D:** 195
Foundry **F:** 432
Glass (Casting) **G:** 216
Iron and steel (Shaping and finishing steel) **I:** 445 *with diagrams*
Plastics (Casting) **P:** 558 *with picture*
Cast iron **C:** 279
Iron and steel (Kinds of iron and steel) **I:** 436-437; (Making iron products) **I:** 441
Nickel (Industrial uses) **N:** 404
Tin (Uses) **T:** 293
Cast-iron stove
Range *picture on* **R:** 138
Cast the First Stone [book by Himes]
Himes, Chester **H:** 234
Castalian spring [stream, Greece]
Parnassus **P:** 177
Castanets [musical instrument] **C:** 279 *with picture*
Caste [entomology]
Ant (Castes) **A:** 523
Termite (The termite colony) **T:** 171
Caste [sociology] **C:** 279
Asia (The people) **A:** 781-782
Bangladesh (Religion) **B:** 82
Hinduism (Caste) **H:** 236
India (Social structure) **I:** 116; (The Aryans) **I:** 128
Segregation (Segregation in other countries) **S:** 286
Social class (Class structure) **So:** 550
World, History of the (The Mauryan Empire in India) **W:** 430
Caste War [1847]
Quintana Roo **Q:** 43
Castel dell'Ovo [castle]
Naples (The city) **N:** 12
Castel Gandolfo [villa]
Pope (The daily life of the pope) **P:** 662; (The 1700's and 1800's) **P:** 665
Castel Sant'Elmo [castle]
Naples (The city) **N:** 12
Castello, Dan [American performer]
Circus (History) **Ci:** 562b-563
Castelo Branco, Humberto de Alencar [Brazilian political leader]
Brazil (Return to constitutional government) **B:** 585-586; (Under military rule) **B:** 586
Castiglione, Baldassare [Italian author] **C:** 279
Italian literature (Humanism and the Renaissance) **I:** 494
Renaissance (The ideal courtier) **R:** 235-236
Castile and Aragon [Spanish history] **C:** 279
Spain (The Christian kingdoms) **So:** 746
Castilian [dialect]
Spain (Language) **So:** 733
Spanish language (Castilian Spanish) **So:** 756b; (Castilian Spanish) **So:** 757
Castilian Grammar [book by Nebrija]
Spanish literature (The 1400's) **So:** 758
Castilla, Ramón [Peruvian political leader] **C:** 280
Peru (The early republic) **P:** 315
Castillo de San Marcos National Monument [Florida] **C:** 280
Florida *picture on* **F:** 252
National Park System (table: National monuments) **N:** 50
Castilloa [botany]
Rubber (The rubber tree) **R:** 502

Casting [fishing]
Fishing **F:** 175
Casting [manufacturing] *See Cast and casting in this index*
Casting [theater]
Motion picture (Assembling the cast) **M:** 851
Theater (Casting) **T:** 236 *with picture*
Casting Away of Mrs. Lecks and Mrs. Aleshine, The [book by Stockton]
Stockton, Frank Richard **So:** 906
Casting director [career]
Motion picture (Assembling the cast) **M:** 851
Casting on
Knitting (Knitting the fabric) **K:** 354
Castle [building]
Washington, D.C. (Smithsonian museums) **W:** 71-73
Castle [chess]
Chess (How chess is played) **C:** 413
Castle [fortification] **C:** 280 *with pictures*
Citadel *picture on* **C:** 567
Crusades *picture on* **Ci:** 1160
Rhine River *picture on* **R:** 293
Shelter (The Middle Ages) **S:** 393
Windsor Castle **W:** 335 *with picture*
World, History of the *picture on* **W:** 432
Castle [platform]
Ship (The cog) **S:** 417
Castle, Irene Foote [American dancer]
Ballroom dancing **B:** 63
Castle, Michael N. [American political leader]
Delaware (table) **D:** 109
Castle, The [book by Kafka]
Kafka, Franz **K:** 209
Castle, Vernon [American dancer]
Ballroom dancing **B:** 63
Castle, Wendell [American designer]
Furniture (Post-modern design) **F:** 585-586
Castle and Cooke, Inc. [company]
Hawaii (Lanai) **H:** 102
Castle Clinton National Monument [New York] **C:** 282
National Park System (table: National monuments) **N:** 50
New York (Places to visit) **N:** 302
Castle Garden
Castle Clinton National Monument **C:** 282
Castle Hill [Budapest]
Budapest (City) **B:** 666
Castle Hill National Historic Site [Newfoundland]
Canada (table: National historic sites) **C:** 114
Castle of Otranto, The [book by Walpole]
English literature (Romantic prose) **E:** 320
Gothic novel **G:** 279
Romance **R:** 415
Walpole, Horace **W:** 19
Castle of São Jorge
Lisbon (The city) **L:** 348
Castle Rackrent [play by Edgeworth]
Irish literature (Early works in English) **I:** 431
Castle Rock
Edinburgh **E:** 77
Castlereagh, Viscount [British statesman] **C:** 282
Aix-la-Chapelle, Congress of **A:** 253
Castor [star]
Gemini **G:** 80
Castor [substance] *See Castoreum in this index*
Castor [zoology]
Beaver (The life of a beaver) **B:** 193-194
Castor and Pollux [Greek mythology] **C:** 282
Castor oil **C:** 282 *with picture*
Castor tree
Castor oil **C:** 282 *with picture*
Plant (Interesting facts about plants) **P:** 519
Poisonous plant (Some poisonous plants) **P:** 602
Castoreum [substance]
Beaver **B:** 192
Castration
Cat (Birth control) **C:** 295-296
Dog (Social and moral responsibilities) **D:** 279-280
Pet (Birth control) **P:** 322
Castries [Saint Lucia] **C:** 282
Saint Lucia **S:** 50
Castro, Fidel [Cuban political leader] **C:** 283 *with portrait*
Bay of Pigs invasion **B:** 175
Carter, Jimmy (Later years) **C:** 259
Castro, Raúl **C:** 283
Cold War *picture on* **Ci:** 766; (The Bay of Pigs) **Ci:** 768
Communism (The spread of Communism) **Ci:** 893-894
Cuba **Ci:** 1169; (History) **Ci:** 1175-1177 *with picture*
Eisenhower, Dwight David (A break with Cuba) **E:** 154

Guantánamo **G:** 411
Guerrilla warfare (History) **G:** 420
Guevara, Che **G:** 421
Havana **H:** 86
Hispanic Americans (Cuban immigration) **H:** 254
Kennedy, John Fitzgerald (Cuba) **K:** 265
Latin America (Political circumstances in the early to middle 1900's) **L:** 109-110 *with picture*
Union of Soviet Socialist Republics *picture on* **U:** 38
West Indies (Abolition and independence movements) **W:** 205
Castro, Guillén de [Spanish dramatist]
Spanish literature (The 1600's) **So:** 759
Castro, Raúl [Cuban political leader] **C:** 283
Castro, Fidel **C:** 283
Cuba (The Castro revolution) **Ci:** 1177; (Recent developments) **Ci:** 1179 *with picture*
Castro, Raul Hector [American political leader] **C:** 283
Arizona (table) **A:** 687
Castro, Rosalía de [Spanish poet]
Spanish literature (The 1800's) **So:** 761
Castro Alves, Antônio de [Brazilian poet]
Brazil (The arts) **B:** 576-577
Castro Ruz, Fidel [Cuban political leader] *See* Castro, Fidel *in this index*
Castroneves, Helio [race driver]
Automobile racing (table: Indianapolis 500 winners) **A:** 980
Casual game
Electronic game (Personal computers) **E:** 204c-204d
Casual shoe
Shoe (Kinds of shoes) **S:** 431 *with pictures*
Casuarina [tree] *See Beefwood in this index*
Caswell, Richard [American political leader]
North Carolina (table) **N:** 490; (Revolution and independence) **N:** 492
Cat C: 284 *with pictures*
See also the list of Related articles in the Cat article
Animal *pictures on* **A:** 471, **A:** 472
Brain *diagram on* **B:** 559
Cloning *picture on* **Ci:** 684
Eye (Eyes of animals) **E:** 469
Parasite (Influence on behavior) **P:** 155
Pet **P:** 319 *with picture*
Skull **S:** 495 *with picture*
Toxoplasmosis **T:** 353
Cat and Mouse [book by Grass]
German literature (Postwar German literature [1945-1990]) **G:** 142
Cat distemper [disease] *See Panleukopenia in this index*
Cat Fanciers' Association, Incorporated [organization]
Cat (Cat associations and shows) **C:** 296
Cat in the Hat, The [book by Dr. Seuss]
Literature for children *picture on* **L:** 363
Cat Island
Bahamas (Land and climate) **B:** 29 *with map*
Cat on a Hot Tin Roof [play by Williams]
Williams, Tennessee **W:** 312
CAT scan *See Computed tomography in this index*
Cat show
Cat (Cat associations and shows) **C:** 296
Catabolism [physiology]
Metabolism (Catabolism) **M:** 424
Catacombs [burial] **C:** 297
Painting (Early Christian and Byzantine art) **P:** 49
Rome (The catacombs) **R:** 433 *with picture*
Catacombs of San Sebastiano
Rome (The catacombs) **R:** 433
Catadromous fish [zoology]
Fish (Fish migrations) **F:** 151
Catalan [language]
Andorra (People) **A:** 454
Romance language **R:** 415
Spain (Language) **So:** 733
Spanish language (Castilian Spanish) **So:** 757
Catalan forge
Iron and steel (The Iron Age) **I:** 449-450
Catalanas [breed]
Chicken (table) **C:** 443
Cataldo Mission
Idaho (Places to visit) **I:** 34
Catalepsy [disorder] **C:** 297
Catalexis
Poetry (table) **P:** 594
Çatalhöyük [ancient city]
Turkey (History) **T:** 509
Catalina Island [California]
California (Coastline) **C:** 50
Catalog
Mail-order business **M:** 66
Cataloging
Library (The growth of information and technology) **L:** 237-238; (The work of librarians) **L:** 255
Library of Congress **L:** 264
A Guide to Research Skills **Research Guide:** 27-30
Cataloging in Publication [program]
Library of Congress **L:** 264
Catalogue of Nebulae and of Star Clusters [book by Messier]
Messier, Charles **M:** 423
Catalonia [region, Spain]
Spain (Language) **So:** 733; (Political changes) **So:** 751
Catalpa [tree] **C:** 297
Tree *pictures on* **T:** 421
Catalysis [chemistry] **C:** 297
Nickel (Industrial uses) **N:** 404
Catalyst [chemical]
Catalysis **C:** 297
Catalytic converter **C:** 298
Enzyme **E:** 340
Fuel cell (How a fuel cell works) **F:** 551
Hydrogenation **H:** 470
Life (Developing complexity) **L:** 279
Materials (Chemical properties) **M:** 300b-300c
Nanotechnology (Applications of nanotechnology) **N:** 10
Platinum (Uses) **P:** 566
Sodium (Uses) **So:** 569
Vitamin (How vitamins work) **V:** 432
Zeolite **Z:** 589
Catalytic converter C: 298
Air pollution (Control of air pollution) **A:** 199
Automobile (The exhaust system) **A:** 953
Gasoline (Pollution control) **G:** 62
Gasoline engine (Air pollution control) **G:** 66
Platinum (Uses) **P:** 566
Catalytic cracking [industrial process]
Petroleum (Conversion) **P:** 344
Catamaran [boat] **C:** 298
Boating *picture on* **B:** 431; (Sailboats) **B:** 429
Cataplexy [disorder] **C:** 298
Narcolepsy **N:** 20
Catapult [machine] **C:** 298 *with picture*
Aircraft carrier (Flight operations) **A:** 206 *with diagram*
Archimedes (His inventions) **A:** 605
Army (Armies in the Middle Ages) **A:** 727
Weapon (Siege weapons) **W:** 154b
Cataract [disorder] **C:** 299
Blindness (Diseases) **B:** 401
Eye (Cataract) **E:** 466 *with picture*
Cataract [geography]
Waterfall **W:** 141
Cataract Falls [Indiana]
Indiana *picture on* **I:** 196
Catawba Indians
Indian, American (Indians of the Southeast) **I:** 157
Catbird [bird] **C:** 299 *with picture*
Bird *on* **B:** 358; (Birds of brushy areas) **B:** 338 *with picture*
Catboat
Sailing (Catboats and sloops) **S:** 24 *with picture*
Catbrier [plant]
Greenbrier **G:** 381
Catch-22 [book by Heller]
Heller, Joseph **H:** 177
Novel (The middle and late 1900's) **N:** 575
Catcher
Baseball (Equipment) **B:** 125 *with picture*; (Player positions) **B:** 127
Catcher boat
Whale *picture on* **W:** 264; (Hunting techniques) **W:** 263
Catcher in the Rye, The [book by Salinger]
Novel (After World War II) **N:** 574
Salinger, J. D. **S:** 66
Catcher interference
Baseball (Reaching base) **B:** 129
Catcher's box
Baseball (The infield) **B:** 126 *with diagram*
Catcher's mitt
Baseball (Equipment) **B:** 125 *with picture*
Catchstitch
Sewing (Hand stitches) **S:** 332
Catchup *See Ketchup in this index*
Catclaw acacia [plant]
Acacia **A:** 20 *with picture*
Catechism [religion]
Christianity (Creeds and catechisms) **C:** 522h
Catechism of the Catholic Church [religion]
Roman Catholic Church (John Paul II) **R:** 411
Catechu [tree product] **C:** 299
Categorical syllogism
Logic (The categorical syllogism) **L:** 425
Catenary [device]
Electric railroad (Kinds of electric railroads) **E:** 188 *with picture*
Locomotive (Electric locomotives) **L:** 416
Caterpillar [insect] **C:** 299 *with picture*
Armyworm **A:** 740
Butterfly **B:** 733 *with picture*; (The larva) **B:** 741 *with pictures*
Cankerworm **C:** 177
Chrysalis **C:** 539
Gypsy moth **G:** 452 *with picture*
Insect (Muscular system) **I:** 289; (Hearing) **I:** 290; (Complete metamorphosis) **I:** 293
Jumping bean *picture on* **J:** 190
Larva **L:** 78 *with picture*
Metamorphosis (The larva) **M:** 428
Moth **M:** 837 *with picture*; (The larva) **M:** 839 *with pictures*
Spruce budworm *picture on* **So:** 810
Tent caterpillar **T:** 168 *with picture*
Caterpillar Inc. [company]
Peoria **P:** 277
Catesby, Robert [English public figure]
Gunpowder Plot **G:** 442
Catfish [fish] **C:** 300 *with pictures*
Animal *picture on* **A:** 492
Bullhead **B:** 697 *with picture*
Fish *picture on* **F:** 145
Catgut [cord] **C:** 301
Ligature **L:** 281
Cathari [religious sect]
Albigenses **A:** 332
Catharsis [psychology] **C:** 301
Aristotle (Literary criticism) **A:** 664
Cathay [alternate name, China] **C:** 301
Mongol Empire (European contacts) **M:** 720
Polo, Marco **P:** 648 *with map*
Cathedral C: 301 *with pictures*
Architecture (Gothic architecture) **A:** 618-619 *with pictures*
City (Description) **Ci:** 582 *with picture*
Córdoba **Ci:** 1051 *with picture*
Gothic art **G:** 278 *with picture*
Middle Ages (The Christian church) **M:** 523-524 *with picture*
Notre Dame, Cathedral of *picture on* **N:** 551
World, History of the (The Byzantine Empire) **W:** 434 *with picture*
Cathedral [book by Carver]
Carver, Raymond **C:** 269
Cathedral [book by Macaulay]
Literature for children *picture on* **L:** 384
Cathedral: The Story of Its Construction [book by Macaulay]
Macaulay, David **M:** 4
Cathedral Church of Saint Peter and Saint Paul *See Washington National Cathedral in this index*
Cathedral mosque [building]
Mosque **M:** 830
Cathedral of ...
Cathedrals appear under their key words, as in Notre Dame, Cathedral of
Cathedral Spires [rock, Colorado]
Garden of the Gods **G:** 29
Cather, Willa [American author] **C:** 302 *with portrait*
American literature (Realist fiction) **A:** 422
Catherine I [empress of Russia]
Russia (table: Czars and empresses) **R:** 549
Catherine II [empress of Russia] *See Catherine the Great in this index*
Catherine, Duchess of Cambridge [wife of Prince William] **C:** 302 *with portrait*
William, Prince **W:** 309
Catherine, Saint [daughter of]
Bridget, Saint **B:** 607
Catherine de Médicis [wife of Henry II] **C:** 303 *with portrait*
Ballet (The birth of ballet) **B:** 50-51
Charles IX **C:** 381
Henry II [of France] **H:** 186
Henry III [king of France] **H:** 186
Huguenots (The massacre) **H:** 410
Medici **M:** 362
Tuileries **T:** 481
Catherine of Aragon [wife of HenryVIII] **C:** 303
Boleyn, Anne **B:** 440
England (The Wars of the Roses) **E:** 306-307
Henry VII [of England] **H:** 188
Henry VIII [of England] **H:** 188
Catherine of Siena, Saint [Italian religious leader] **C:** 303
Correggio *picture on* **Ci:** 1071
Catherine the Great [empress of Russia] **C:** 303 *with portrait*
Diamond (Famous diamonds) **D:** 182
Jones, John Paul (Russian service) **J:** 159
Russia (Music) **R:** 536; (table: Czars and empresses) **R:** 549; (Catherine the Great) **R:** 550 *with picture*
Russo-Turkish wars **R:** 566b

Catherwood, Frederick [English artist]
Stephens, John Lloyd **So:** 890
Catheter [medicine]
Angioplasty **A:** 461 *with diagram*
Cardiology **C:** 212
Heart (Symptoms and diagnosis) **H:** 137-138
with picture
Radiology **R:** 99
Catheterization [medicine] *See* Catheter *in this index*
Cathode [electricity]
Battery (How batteries work) **B:** 168 *with diagram*
Crookes tube **Ci:** 1153 *with diagram*
Electricity (Sources of current) **E:** 194
Electrolysis (How electrolysis works) **E:** 200 *with diagram*
Fuel cell (How a fuel cell works) **F:** 551 *with diagram*
Silver (Extracting and refining silver) **S:** 464-465
Television (Flat-panel displays) **T:** 126
Vacuum tube (How a vacuum tube works) **V:** 258 *with diagram*
X rays *diagram on* **X:** 541
Cathode-ray tube [electronics]
Ci: 916
Computer (Monitors) **C:** 916
Electronics (Early experiments) **E:** 215 *with picture*
Oscilloscope **O:** 862 *with picture*
Projector (Digital data projectors) **P:** 817
Television (Display devices) **T:** 125
Vacuum tube (Cathode-ray tubes) **V:** 259
Cathode rays [electronics]
Crookes tube **Ci:** 1153 *with diagram*
Thomson, Sir Joseph John **T:** 264
Catholic Advertising Program
Knights of Columbus **K:** 352
Catholic Association [organization]
O'Connell, Daniel **O:** 668
Catholic Church *See* Eastern Catholic Churches;
Roman Catholic Church *in this index*
Catholic Educational Association, National *See*
National Catholic Educational Association *in this index*
Catholic Emancipation Act [1829]
O'Connell, Daniel **O:** 668
Wellington, Duke of (Political career) **W:** 195
Catholic Foreign Mission Society of America [religious group]
Missionary (Organization) **M:** 621
Catholic Library Association C: 304
Regina Medal **R:** 206
Catholic Periodical and Literature Index
Catholic Library Association **C:** 304
Catholic Reformation *See* Counter Reformation *in this index*
Catholic Revival *See* Counter Reformation *in this index*
Catholic Union
Roman Catholic Church (The decline of church influence) **R:** 410
Catholic University of America
Roman Catholic Church (In the United States) **R:** 412
Catholic University of Louvain
Belgium (Education) **B:** 229-230
Catholic Workers [organization]
Day, Dorothy **D:** 52
Catholic Youth Organization C: 304
Catilina, Lucius Sergius *See* Catiline *in this index*
Catiline [Roman political leader] **C:** 304
Caesar, Julius (Alliance with Pompey) **C:** 13
Cicero, Marcus Tullius (His works) **Ci:** 552
Cation [chemistry]
Electrolyte **E:** 201
Ion (Behavior of ions) **I:** 371-372
Pyroxene **P:** 920
Soil (Chemical conditions) **So:** 575-576
Catkin [botany] **C:** 304
Alder **A:** 339
Birch **B:** 327
Flower (Variations in flower structure) **F:** 294
Poplar **P:** 667
Pussy willow **P:** 912 *with picture*
Walnut **W:** 19
Willow **W:** 315
Catlin, George [American painter] **C:** 304
Dance *picture on* **D:** 24
Indian, American *pictures on* **I:** 136a, **I:** 136d, **I:** 143, **I:** 157, **I:** 161
National park (The early national parks) **N:** 42j
Osceola *picture on* **O:** 862
United States, History of the *picture on* **U:** 170
Catmint *See* Catnip *in this index*
Catnip [plant] **C:** 304 *with picture*
Cat (Training) **C:** 294
Cato [play by Addison]
Addison, Joseph **A:** 47
Cato, Marcus Porcius, the Elder [Roman political

leader] **C:** 304
Latin literature (Early Latin literature) **L:** 115-116
Cato, Marcus Porcius, the Younger [Roman political leader] **C:** 304
Cato the Censor *See* Cato, Marcus Porcius, the Elder *in this index*
Catoctin Mountain Park [Maryland]
National Park System (table: National parkways and other national parklands) **N:** 55
Catron, John [American jurist]
Supreme Court of the United States (table) **So:** 1000
Cats [musical]
Lloyd Webber, Andrew **L:** 403
Cat's Cradle [book by Vonnegut]
Vonnegut, Kurt **V:** 448
Cat's cradle [game]
Magic (Homeopathic magic) **M:** 49-50
Cat's-eye [gem] **C:** 305
Gem *picture on* **G:** 78
Cats in Krasinski Square, The [book by Hesse]
Hesse, Karen **H:** 219
Cat's-tail [plant]
Timothy **T:** 292d
Catskill Aqueduct [New York City]
Aqueduct (Present-day aqueducts) **A:** 580
Catskill Mountains [New York] **C:** 305
Plateau **P:** 565
Catsup *See* Ketchup *in this index*
Catt, Carrie Chapman [American social reformer] **C:** 305 *with portrait*
Woman suffrage (Growth of the movement) **W:** 380
Cattail [plant] **C:** 305 *with picture*
Cattail millet [grain]
Millet **M:** 555
Cattalo [animal]
Buffalo (Protection of bison) **B:** 675
Cattle C: 306 *with pictures*
See also Cow [female cattle] *in this index and the list of Related articles in the* Cattle *article*
Africa *picture on* **A:** 110
Amarillo **A:** 400
Argentina (Agriculture) **A:** 654 *with picture*
Aurochs **A:** 891
Australia *picture on* **A:** 919; (Agriculture) **A:** 916
Canada *picture on* **C:** 124
Colorado *picture on* **C:** 829
Cowboy (On the ranch) **Ci:** 1110
Dairying **D:** 6 *with pictures*
Farm and farming (Specialized livestock farms) **F:** 31 *with picture*
India (Hinduism) **I:** 116
Iowa (Agriculture) **I:** 389
Kansas (The great cattle towns) **K:** 237
Livestock **L:** 396 *with picture*
Mad cow disease **M:** 26
Meat (Kinds of meat) **M:** 347
Meat packing **M:** 350
Montana (Agriculture) **M:** 757
Nebraska *picture on* **N:** 95
North Dakota *picture on* **N:** 497
Nuer **N:** 602
Oklahoma (Agriculture) **O:** 729 *with picture*
Ox **O:** 886
Queensland *picture on* **Q:** 39
Ranching (History) **R:** 134 *with picture*
Saskatchewan (Agriculture) **S:** 143
Texas (Agriculture) **T:** 202
Veal **V:** 291
Western frontier life in America (Ranching) **W:** 236 *with picture*
Westward movement in America (Cattle frontiers) **W:** 251
Wyoming (Agriculture) **W:** 531
Cattle brand
Ranching (Life on a cattle ranch) **R:** 134-135 *with picture*
Cattle drive [ranching]
Cowboy *picture on* **Ci:** 1108; (The trail drive) **Ci:** 1111
Kansas *picture on* **K:** 238
Ranching (History) **R:** 136
Western frontier life in America (The cattle drive) **W:** 237
Westward movement in America (Cattle frontiers) **W:** 251
Cattle egret [bird]
Egret (Kinds) **E:** 119
Cattle grub [insect]
Bot fly **B:** 507
Warble fly **W:** 34
Cattle plague [disease]
Rinderpest **R:** 342
Cattle Raid of Cooley, The [poem]
Cuchulainn **Ci:** 1182
Irish literature (Heroic tales, romances, and sagas)

I: 430
Maeve, Queen **M:** 41
Mythology (The Ulster cycle) **M:** 985
Cattle ranch *See* Ranching *in this index*
Cattle show
Cattle (Show cattle) **C:** 315
Cattle tick [animal] **C:** 316 *with picture*
Cattle warble [insect]
Warble fly **W:** 34
Catton, Bruce [American historian] **C:** 316
Catts, Sidney J. [American political leader]
Florida (table) **F:** 260
Catullus, Gaius Valerius [Roman poet] **C:** 316
Latin literature (The age of Cicero) **L:** 116
Cauca River [Colombia]
Colombia (The Andes Mountains) **Ci:** 782
South America (Rivers) **So:** 628
Caucasian rug
Rugs and carpets (Oriental rugs) **R:** 516-517
Caucasians [people]
Turkey (People) **T:** 505
Caucasoid race
Races, Human (The three-race theory) **R:** 53-54 *with picture*
Caucasus [region, Eurasia] **C:** 317
Caucasus Mountains [Europe-Asia] **C:** 317
Azerbaijan (Land and climate) **A:** 996 *with map*
Georgia (Land and climate) **G:** 110 *with map*
Russia (Land regions) **R:** 539 *with map*
Cauchy, Augustin Louis [French mathematician]
Mathematics (In the 1800's) **M:** 307
Caucus [politics] **C:** 317
Election (Nomination of candidates) **E:** 158
Election campaign (Winning the nomination) **E:** 159
House of Representatives (Organization of the U.S. House) **H:** 387
Political convention (Delegate selection) **P:** 628-629
Political party (Selecting candidates) **P:** 631
Primary election (History) **P:** 777
Senate (The leaders of the senate) **S:** 294-295
Caucus-convention system [politics]
Caucus **C:** 317
Political convention (Delegate selection) **P:** 628-629
Caudal fin [zoology]
Fish (Fins) **F:** 160-161 *with picture*
Caudal vertebra [anatomy]
Mammal (Skeleton) **M:** 118-119 *with diagram*
Caudillo [title]
Latin America (The movement toward independence) **L:** 106
Caudillo, El [title]
Franco, Francisco **F:** 483
Caulerpa [seaweed]
Invasive species (How invasive species affect habitats) **I:** 354j-354k
Caulfield, Henry S. [American political leader]
Missouri (table) **M:** 668
Cauliflower [plant] **C:** 317 *with picture*
Evolution (Artificial selection) **E:** 432 *with picture*
Caulking
Palm (Products of palms) **P:** 109
Caunotaucarius [name for]
Washington, George (Messenger to the French) **W:** 93-94
Causality [philosophy]
Aristotle (Philosophy of nature) **A:** 664
Hume, David (Hume's thought) **H:** 432
Metaphysics (Causality) **M:** 429
Spinoza, Baruch **So:** 795
Cause and effect [philosophy] *See* Causality *in this index*
Causey, Peter F. [American political leader]
Delaware (table) **D:** 109
Caustic soda *See* Sodium hydroxide *in this index*
Cautantowwit [Indian god]
Indian summer **I:** 189
Cautery [medicine]
Surgery (History) **So:** 1007
Cauthen, Steve [American jockey]
Horse racing (History) **H:** 366
Cautionary Tales [book by Belloc]
Belloc, Hilaire **B:** 244
Cauto River [Cuba]
Cuba (The land) **Ci:** 1172 *with map*
Cavafy, Constantine [Greek poet]
Greek literature (Modern Greek literature) **G:** 378
Cavalcade [film]
Motion picture (Best picture: 1932-33) **M:** 861
Cavalcanti, Guido [Italian poet]
Italian literature (The Middle Ages) **I:** 494
Cavalier [English history]
England (The Civil War) **E:** 308
Hairdressing (The 1600's) **H:** 12
Hat *picture on* **H:** 84

Cavalier King Charles spaniel [dog] C: 318
Cavalier poets [English literature]
  English literature (Metaphysical and Cavalier poets) E: 317
  Lovelace, Richard L: 509
  Poetry (Renaissance poetry) P: 596
  Suckling, Sir John So: 951
Cavaliers, Cleveland [team] See Cleveland Cavaliers in this index
Cavalleria Rusticana [opera by Mascagni]
  Italy *picture on* I: 505
  Mascagni, Pietro M: 262
  Opera (Verismo opera) O: 799; *(Cavalleria Rusticana)* O: 803
"Cavalleria Rusticana" [story by Verga]
  Verga, Giovanni V: 317
Cavalry C: 318 *with picture*
Cavazos, Lauro Fred [American government official] C: 318
  Hispanic Americans (Political gains) H: 256
CAVE [electronic device]
  Virtual reality V: 427
Cave [geology] C: 319 *with pictures*
  See also the list of Related articles in the Cave article
  Ice age (Evidence from modern galciers and from caves) I: 7
Cave, The [book by Warren]
  Warren, Robert Penn W: 37
Cave dwellers [anthropology] C: 321
  Nevada (Indian days) N: 173
  Prehistoric people (How the Neandertals lived) P: 751
Cave man See Cave dwellers in this index
Cave of Machpelah See Machpelah, Cave of in this index
Cave painting
  Cro-Magnons Ci: 1147
  Horse *picture on* H: 360
  Lascaux Cave L: 80 *with picture*
  Mask M: 263
  Painting (Prehistoric painting) P: 40
  Prehistoric people (The appearance of art) P: 752 *with picture*
Caveat emptor [phrase] C: 321
  Consumer protection (History of consumer protection) Ci: 1019
Cavefish C: 321 *with picture*
  Eye *picture on* E: 468
  Fish *picture on* F: 158
Cavelier, René-Robert [French explorer] See La Salle, René-Robert Cavelier, Sieur de in this index
Cavell, Edith Louisa [British nurse] C: 322
Cavendish, Henry [British physicist] C: 322
  Chemistry (The phlogiston theory) C: 401
  Hydrogen H: 468
Cavendish, Victor Christian William [British colonial official]
  Devonshire, Duke of D: 175
Cavendish, William [British nobleman]
  Hobbes, Thomas (His life) H: 272
Cavern See Cave in this index
Cavernous hemangioma [disorder]
  Birthmark B: 380
Caviar [food] C: 322
  Russia (Fishing industry) R: 546
  Shad S: 341
  Sturgeon So: 933
Caving [hobby]
  Cave (Caving) C: 321
Caving [mining]
  Mining (Underground mining methods) M: 576
Cavitation [mechanism]
  Propeller (Ship propellers) P: 826
Cavity [dentistry]
  Dentistry D: 143
  Teeth (Dental decay) T: 82-83 *with pictures*
Cavour, Camillo Benso See Cavour, Count di in this index
Cavour, Count di [Italian political leader] C: 322
  Italy (Italy united) I: 515
  Napoleon III (Foreign affairs) N: 17
Cavy [animal] C: 322
Cawdrey, Robert [English educator]
  Dictionary (Early English dictionaries) D: 194
Cawnpore [India] See Kanpur in this index
Caxton, William [English printer] C: 322
  Advertising (The impact of printing) A: 79
  Encyclopedia (From the 1200's to the 1600's) E: 268a
  Malory, Sir Thomas M: 112
Caxtons, The [book by Bulwer-Lytton]
  Bulwer-Lytton, Edward George Earle Lytton B: 698
Cayenne [French Guiana] C: 322
  French Guiana F: 514 *with picture*
Cayenne, Smooth [fruit]

Pineapple (The pineapple plant) P: 472
Cayenne pepper [seasoning] C: 323
  Pepper P: 278
Cayetano, Ben [American political leader]
  Hawaii (table) H: 105
Cayley, Sir George [British physicist]
  Airplane (First human flights) A: 230
  Glider (Early days) G: 230
Cayman Brac [island, Caribbean]
  Cayman Islands C: 323
Cayman Islands [Caribbean] C: 323
Cayuga and Seneca Canal [waterway, New York]
  Finger Lakes F: 104
  New York State Canal System N: 345 *with map*
Cayuga Indians C: 323
  Indian, American (Indians of the Northeast) I: 154
  Iroquois Indians I: 455
Cayuga Lake [New York]
  Finger Lakes F: 104
  New York (Lakes) N: 306-307
Cayuse Indians
  Whitman, Marcus W: 293
  Whitman, Narcissa W: 294
Cayuse War [1847-1850]
  Oregon (Indian treaties and conflicts) O: 846
CB [radio] See Citizens band radio in this index
CBC See Canadian Broadcasting Corporation in this index
CBE See Competency-based education in this index
CBO See Congressional Budget Office in this index
CBP [agency] See Customs and Border Protection, United States in this index
CBR warfare See Chemical-biological-radiological warfare in this index
CBS [television network] C: 323
  Television (The national networks) T: 113; (History of U.S. television broadcasting) T: 117
  Viacom Inc. V: 347
CBS Corporation
  Viacom Inc. V: 347
  Westinghouse Electric Corporation W: 242
CCC [corporation] See Commodity Credit Corporation in this index
CCC [U.S. history] See Civilian Conservation Corps in this index
CCD [electronics] See Charge-coupled device in this index
CCF [organization] See Co-operative Commonwealth Federation in this index
CCR5 antagonist [drug]
  AIDS (Treatment) A: 164b-165
CCU [medicine] See Coronary care unit in this index
CD [banking] See Certificate of deposit in this index
CD [electronics] See Compact disc in this index
Cd [symbol]
  Cadmium C: 12
  Candela C: 175
CD changer [machine]
  Compact disc (Playback) Ci: 901
CD4 cell [biology]
  AIDS (How HIV affects the body) A: 164
CD4 receptor [biology]
  AIDS (How HIV affects the body) A: 164
CD player [electronics] See Compact disc player in this index
CD-R [electronics]
  Compact disc (Other formats) Ci: 902
  Computer (CD drives) Ci: 915-916
CD-ROM [electronics]
  Compact disc Ci: 901
  Computer *picture on* Ci: 913; (CD drives) Ci: 915
  Electronic games (Gaming platforms) E: 204c; (The growth of computer gaming) E: 204e
  Electronics (Digital circuits) E: 213-214
  Encyclopedia (Today's encyclopedias) E: 268b
  Library (The growth of information and technology) L: 237-238
  A Guide to Research Skills **Research Guide: 29**
CD-ROM player [machine]
  Compact disc Ci: 901
CD-RW [recording]
  Compact disc (CD-RW) Ci: 902
  Computer (CD drives) Ci: 915-916
CDC [organization] See Centers for Disease Control and Prevention in this index
CDU [German political party] See Christian Democratic Union in this index
C.E. [calendar]
  B.C. B: 178
Ce [symbol]
  Cerium C: 362
Cease and desist order
  Federal Trade Commission F: 66
Ceaușescu, Elena [Romanian public figure]
  Ceaușescu, Nicolae C: 323
  Romania (Protests and political change) R: 425
Ceaușescu, Nicolae [Romanian political leader]

C: 323
  Communism (In Eastern Europe) Ci: 896-897
  Romania (Opposition to the Soviet Union) R: 425; (Protests and political change) R: 425
Cebu City [Philippines] C: 323
Cebu Island [Philippines]
  Philippines (The main islands) P: 376-378 *with map*
Cech, Thomas Robert [American chemist]
  Nobel Prizes (Chemistry: 1989) N: 444
Cecil, Edgar Algernon Robert Gascoyne [British statesman]
  Nobel Prizes (Peace: 1937) N: 448a
Cecil, Robert Arthur Talbot Gascoyne- [British political leader] See Salisbury, Marquess of in this index
Cecil, William [British inventor]
  Gasoline engine (Development of the gasoline engine) G: 66
Cecil, William [English government official]
  Burghley, Lord B: 704
  Elizabeth I (Problems at home and abroad) E: 238
Cecilia [book by Burney]
  Burney, Fanny B: 709
Cecilia, Saint [Christian martyr] C: 324
Cecropia moth [insect]
  Cocoon Ci: 747 *with picture*
  Insect *picture on* I: 292
  Moth *pictures on* M: 838
Cecrops [Greek mythology]
  Athens (Earliest times) A: 857
Cecum [anatomy]
  Colon C: 786
  Intestine (The large intestine) I: 353 *with diagram*
  Spider (Digestive system) So: 785 *with diagram*
CEDA [political party]
  Spain (The Spanish republic) So: 750
Cedar [tree] C: 324 *with pictures*
  Conifer Ci: 950
  Juniper J: 196
  Pencil (Cased pencils) P: 236
  Tree *pictures on* T: 425, T: 426
Cedar Breaks National Monument [Utah]
  National Park System (table: National monuments) N: 50
Cedar Creek and Belle Grove National Historical Park [Virginia]
  National Park System (table: National historical parks) N: 56
Cedar elm
  Elm (Kinds) E: 244-245
Cedar of Lebanon [tree]
  Cedar (Needle-leaved cedars) C: 324 *with picture*
Cedar Rapids [Iowa] C: 324
  Amanites A: 400
Cedar River
  Iowa (Rivers and lakes) I: 386
Cedar waxwing [bird]
  Bird *picture on* B: 358; (Birds of forests and woodlands) B: 334 *with picture*
  Waxwing W: 153 *with picture*
Cedilla [mark]
  Diacritical mark D: 180
Cédras, Raoul [Haitian military leader]
  Clinton, Bill (International affairs) Ci: 682e
Ceftriaxone [medication]
  Antibiotic (Antibacterial antibiotics) A: 550; (table) A: 551
Ceilidh Trail
  Nova Scotia (Places to visit) N: 560
Cel animation
  Animation (Traditional animation) A: 512 *with pictures*; (Pioneers of American animation) A: 514a-514b
Cela, Camilo José [Spanish author]
  Nobel Prizes (Literature: 1989) N: 448
  Spanish literature (Spanish literature today) So: 763
Celadon ware
  Porcelain (Painting) P: 676
Celebes [island, Indonesia] See Sulawesi in this index
"Celebrated Jumping Frog of Calaveras County, The" [story by Twain]
  Twain, Mark (Newspaper work in the West) T: 529
Celebration [Florida]
  Holiday H: 291
  Walt Disney Company W: 21
Celebrex [drug]
  Aspirin A: 816
Celebrezze, Anthony Joseph [American government official]
  Health and Human Services, Department of (table) H: 124
Celera Genomics Corporation [company]
  Biology (Current research and issues) B: 320-321
  Gene mapping G: 81

Heredity (The Human Genome Project) **H:** 210
Human Genome Project (The work of the Human Genome Project) **H:** 427
Medicine (The challenge of genetics) **M:** 378
Celery [plant] **C:** 324 *with picture*
Celery cabbage [plant] *See* Chinese cabbage *in this index*
Celesta [musical instrument] **C:** 325 *with picture*
Celeste, Richard F. [American political leader]
Ohio (table) **O:** 699
"Celeste Aïda" [aria]
Opera: *(Aida)* **O:** 801
Celestial coordinate system [astronomy]
Astronomy *diagrams on* **A:** 842; (Locating objects in space) **A:** 838
Celestial equator
Astronomy (Locating objects in space) **A:** 838
Equator (The celestial equator) **E:** 346
Equinox **E:** 348
Zodiac (The origin of the zodiac) **Z:** 597
Celestial globe
Globe **G:** 233
Celestial Mechanics [book by Laplace]
Bowditch, Nathaniel **B:** 517
Laplace, Marquis de **L:** 73
Celestial navigation
Navigation (Celestial navigation) **N:** 71 *with picture*
Celestial pole
Astronomy (How the stars move) **A:** 835; (Locating objects in space) **A:** 838
Navigation (Keeping time) **N:** 71
Pole **P:** 618
Star (Rising and setting of stars) **So:** 842
Celestial sphere [astronomy]
Astronomy (Locating objects in space) **A:** 838
Celestina, La [play]
Spanish literature (The 1400's) **So:** 758
Celestine I, Saint [pope]
Pope (table) **P:** 666
Celestine II [antipope]
Pope (table) **P:** 666
Celestine II [pope]
Pope (table) **P:** 666
Celestine III [pope]
Pope (table) **P:** 666
Celestine IV [pope]
Pope (table) **P:** 666
Celestine V, Saint [pope]
Pope (table) **P:** 666
Celestite [mineral]
Strontium **So:** 930
Celiac disease C: 325
Gluten **G:** 237
Celiac plexus [anatomy] *See* Solar plexus *in this index*
Celibacy [custom] **C:** 325
Family (Development of the Western family) **F:** 22
Pope (The early Middle Ages) **P:** 663
Religious life (Religious life in early Christianity) **R:** 226
Céline, Louis-Ferdinand [French author] **C:** 325
Novel (New directions in the novel) **N:** 573-574
Cell [biology] **C:** 326 *with pictures*
See also the list of Related articles in the Cell *article*
Aging (How aging occurs) **A:** 141
Apoptosis **A:** 566
Archaea **A:** 593
Bacteria (The structure of bacteria) **B:** 20 *with diagram*
Biosynthesis **B:** 326
Botany (What botanists study) **B:** 508
Brain (Brain cells) **B:** 550c
Cellulose **C:** 341
Cloning **Ci:** 682l; (Gene and cell cloning) **Ci:** 684
DNA **D:** 258
Flagellum **F:** 224
Growth (In living things) **G:** 404
Heredity (Chromosomes and genes) **H:** 201; (The flow of genetic information) **H:** 205
Histology **H:** 260
Human body (Cells and tissues) **H:** 417 *with picture*
Krebs cycle **K:** 386
Life (The structure of living things) **L:** 276 *with diagram*
Mitochondria **M:** 679
Molecular biology (The beginning of molecular biology) **M:** 691-692
Monoclonal antibody **M:** 731
Mutation **M:** 968
Plant (Parts of plants) **P:** 528
Protein (How the body uses proteins) **P:** 832
Protoplasm **P:** 837
Technology (Emerging technologies) **T:** 76
Tissue **T:** 298
Pathology

AIDS (How HIV affects the body) **A:** 163
Cancer **C:** 167 *with picture*
Death (Medical aspects of death) **D:** 61
Sickle cell anemia **S:** 447 *with picture*
Virus *diagram on* **V:** 427; (Infection) **V:** 427
Reproduction
Chromosome **C:** 538
Egg (How embryos develop) **E:** 117
Fertilization **F:** 78
Gene **G:** 81
Stem cell **So:** 889
Cell [communications]
Cellular telephone **C:** 340 *with diagram*
Cell [electricity] *See* Battery *in this index*
Cell [entomology]
Bee (The honey bee colony) **B:** 201 *with picture*
Cell [meteorology]
Thunderstorm **T:** 272
Cell [political science]
Terrorism (Terrorist organizations) **T:** 176
Union of Soviet Socialist Republics (The Communist Party) **U:** 29
Cell [prison]
Prison (Prison cells) **P:** 806 *with picture*
Cell [spreadsheet]
Computer (Spreadsheet programs) **Ci:** 917
Spreadsheet **So:** 805 *with picture*
Cell assembly [anatomy]
Brain (Memory and imagination) **B:** 554
Cell body [anatomy]
Nervous system *diagrams on* **N:** 134; (Parts of a neuron) **N:** 133
Cell culture [biology]
Culture **Ci:** 1190
Cell division [biology]
Baby (The developing baby) **B:** 4-5
Cancer **C:** 167
Cell (Cell division) **C:** 330 *with pictures*
Chromosome **C:** 538
Embryo **E:** 257
Evolution (Mutation) **E:** 427-428
Heredity (Sex cells and reproduction) **H:** 201
Cell-mediated immune response [physiology]
Immune system *diagram on* **I:** 88b; (The immune response) **I:** 88
Virus (Immune response) **V:** 428a
Cell membrane [biology]
Antibiotic (Disruption of the cell membrane) **A:** 550
Bacteria (The structure of bacteria) **B:** 20 *with diagram*
Cell (Inside a living cell) **C:** 328; (The cytoplasm) **C:** 329 *with diagrams*
Life (Cells) **L:** 277
Lipid (Importance of lipids) **L:** 344
Cell phone *See* Cellular telephone *in this index*
Cell sap [botany]
Sap (Cell sap) **S:** 121
Cell suicide [biology] *See* Apoptosis *in this index*
Cell theory [biology]
Biology (Materialistic physiology and the cell theory) **B:** 319
Cell trafficking [physiology]
Allergy (Allergic reactions) **A:** 373-374
Cell wall [biology]
Antibiotic (Antibacterial antibiotics) **A:** 550; (Prevention of cell wall formation) **A:** 550
Bacteria (The structure of bacteria) **B:** 20 *with diagram*
Cell (Inside a living cell) **C:** 328 *with diagram*
Cellar spider
Daddy longlegs **D:** 3
Spider (Tangled-web weavers) **So:** 789
Celler-Kefauver Act [1950]
Antitrust law **A:** 560
Monopoly and competition (History) **M:** 732
Cellini, Benvenuto [Italian sculptor] **C:** 339 *with picture*
Sculpture (Michelangelo) **S:** 252-253 *with picture*
Cello [musical instrument] **C:** 339 *with picture*
China *picture on* **C:** 490
Music (Stringed instruments) **M:** 948 *with picture*
Cellophane [material] **C:** 340
Cellucci, Argeo Paul [American political leader]
Massachusetts (table) **M:** 288
Cellular microorganism
Microbiology (Microorganisms) **M:** 513
Cellular Pathology [book by Virchow]
Virchow, Rudolf **V:** 391
Cellular plastics
Plastics (Foaming) **P:** 558
Cellular telephone C: 340 *with diagram*
Codes and ciphers (Modern applications of cryptography) **Ci:** 752
Etiquette (Telephone etiquette) **E:** 374
Fax machine (How a fax machine works) **F:** 57
Internet *diagram on* **I:** 350c, *picture on* **I:** 350f;

(The World Wide Web) **I:** 350d; (The evolving Internet) **I:** 350g
Photography (Other types of cameras) **P:** 409
Publishing (Newspapers) **P:** 868
Safety (Motor vehicle safety) **S:** 14
Telephone (Types of telephones) **T:** 94-95 *with picture*; (Cellular phone calls) **T:** 97 *with picture*; (Improvements in telephone technology) **T:** 100-101
Text messaging **T:** 211
Cellular vessel [ship]
Containerization **Ci:** 1021
Celluloid [plastic]
Plastics (The invention of Celluloid) **P:** 559
Cellulose C: 341
Carbohydrate (Kinds of carbohydrates) **C:** 203; (How the body uses carbohydrates) **C:** 204
Cellophane **C:** 340
Fiber (Regenerated fibers) **F:** 87
Lacquer **L:** 22
Lignin **L:** 302
Paper **P:** 134
Plastics (The invention of Celluloid) **P:** 559
Rayon (How rayon is made) **R:** 153 *with diagram*
Ruminant **R:** 519
Termite **T:** 171
Tree (How trunks and branches grow thicker) **T:** 418
Wood (The composition of wood) **W:** 390
Cellulose acetate [substance]
Acetate **A:** 25
Cellulose (Industrial uses) **C:** 341
Plastics (table) **P:** 556; (The invention of Celluloid) **P:** 559
Cellulose nitrate [material]
Cellulose (Industrial uses) **C:** 341
Cellulose xanthate [chemical]
Rayon (How rayon is made) **R:** 153
Cellulosics
Fiber (Regenerated fibers) **F:** 87
Celsius, Anders [Swedish astronomer] **C:** 341
Celsius scale **C:** 342
Celsius scale [temperature] **C:** 342
Celsius, Anders **C:** 341
Fahrenheit scale **F:** 6
Metric system (Heat) **M:** 440
Celtic cross [symbol]
Cross *picture on* **Ci:** 1155
Ireland (The arts) **I:** 421-422 *with picture*
Celtic language
Celts **C:** 343
England (History) **E:** 303
Gaelic languages **G:** 5
Gaul **G:** 70
Ireland (Language) **I:** 418
Language (Indo-European) **L:** 65-66
Name (Celtic names) **N:** 5
Celtics, Boston [team]
Basketball (table) **B:** 150
Celtics, Original [team]
Basketball (The history of professional basketball) **B:** 154a
Celts [ancient people] **C:** 342 *with picture*
Austria (Early years) **A:** 936
Druids **D:** 367
England (Ancestry) **E:** 294; (History) **E:** 303
English language (Origins) **E:** 313
Gaels **G:** 5
Gaul **G:** 70
Halloween **H:** 24a; (Samhain) **H:** 25
Ireland (History) **I:** 425
Mythology (Celtic mythology) **M:** 984 *with picture*
New Year's Day (Early customs) **N:** 289
Painting (Early medieval painting in the West) **P:** 49
Scotland (History) **S:** 218-219
Wales (History) **W:** 11
Celtuce [plant]
Lettuce (Kinds of lettuce) **L:** 214 *with picture*
Cement and concrete C: 343
Building construction (Foundations) **B:** 682
Edison, Thomas Alva (Ore milling and cement) **E:** 81
Gravel **G:** 330
Road (Paving) **R:** 359
Cemented steel
Iron and steel (The first steel) **I:** 450
Cementum [anatomy]
Teeth (Cementum) **T:** 81 *with diagram*
Cemetery
National cemetery **N:** 31
Potter's field **P:** 715
Cemetery Hill
Civil War, American (Battle of Gettysburg) **Ci:** 627-628
Cemetery Ridge
Civil War, American (Battle of Gettysburg)

Ci: 627-628
Gettysburg, Battle of **G:** 176
Cenobitic religious life
Religious life (The Eastern Orthodox Churches)
R: 227
Cenotaph [memorial, London]
Lutyens, Sir Edwin Landseer **L:** 530
Cenozoic Era [geology] **C:** 345
Earth (The Cenozoic Era) **E:** 28 *with pictures;*
(table) **E:** 30
Forest (Later forests) **F:** 398
Mammal (The Age of Mammals) **M:** 127
Plant (The evolution of plants) **P:** 544-545
Prehistoric animal (The world of prehistoric
animals) **P:** 736; (The Age of Mammals) **P:** 740
with picture
Censer [incense burner] **C:** 345 *with picture*
Censor [office]
Censorship (Military censorship) **C:** 346
Censorship C: 345
Comstock Law **Ci:** 926
Internet (The Internet and politics) **I:** 350f
Ireland (The arts) **I:** 421
Journalism (Journalism in free societies) **J:** 174;
(Journalism in government-controlled
societies) **J:** 174
Library (Censorship and policy issues) **L:** 239
Motion picture (Censorship and self-regulation)
M: 860
Obscenity and pornography (Legal history for
obscenity) **O:** 644
Plato (Art) **P:** 569
Propaganda (Censorship) **P:** 824
Public opinion (Public opinion and government)
P: 860-861
Radio (Government regulation of radio) **R:** 90-91
Russian literature (Late Romanticism) **R:** 561;
(Soviet literature) **R:** 564
Censure [government]
Congress of the United States (Reviewing its own
members) **Ci:** 946
Census [biology]
Bird (Field trips) **B:** 368
Census [population] **C:** 346 *with pictures and map*
Computer (Foundations of data processing)
Ci: 924b
Demography **D:** 129
Domesday Book **D:** 300
Literacy (Illiteracy in the United States) **L:** 351
Population (Census) **P:** 673
Statistics (Collecting the data) **So:** 868
Census Bureau, United States C: 350
Census (United States censuses) **C:** 346
Commerce, Department of (Functions) **Ci:** 871
Crime (Unreported crime) **Ci:** 1138
Map (Database development) **M:** 180
Unemployment (Measuring unemployment)
U: 22
Census metropolitan area
Metropolitan area (Defining metropolitan areas)
M: 442
Cent [money] **C:** 350 *with pictures*
Money (U.S. coins) **M:** 713-714
Penny **P:** 271
Centaur [Greek mythology] **C:** 350 *with picture*
Hercules (The death of Hercules) **H:** 199
Mythology *picture on* **M:** 981
Centaur asteroid
Asteroid (Orbital groups) **A:** 824a
Centauri A and B [stars]
Alpha Centauri **A:** 381
Centenary Square [Birmingham, England]
Birmingham **B:** 376 *with picture*
Centennial Centre [Manitoba]
Manitoba (Places to visit) **M:** 152
Centennial Exposition [Philadelphia]
Museum (Early United States museums) **M:** 939-
940
Philadelphia (A growing city) **P:** 367
World's fair **W:** 500
Centennial Olympic Park
Georgia *picture on* **G:** 116
Centennial State [name for]
Colorado **Ci:** 829
Centéotl [Aztec god]
Mythology (Aztec mythology) **M:** 987
Center [geometry]
Polygon **P:** 650 *with diagram*
Sphere **So:** 779 *with diagram*
Center [political science]
Conservatism **C:** 991
Center [sports]
Basketball (The players) **B:** 144
Football (The offensive team) **F:** 356 *with
diagrams*
Center, The [Hong Kong, China]
Skyscraper *picture on* **S:** 497

Center-beam car
Railroad *picture on* **R:** 108
Center City [Philadelphia]
Philadelphia (Continued growth) **P:** 367
Center cut [meat]
Ham (Kinds of ham) **H:** 28 *with pictures*
**Center for Cultural and Technical Interchange
Between East and West**
Hawaii (Statehood) **H:** 108-109
Center for Health Statistics, National
Vital statistics (Collecting and publishing vital
statistics) **V:** 429-430
Center for Independent Living [organization]
Disability (The 1900's) **D:** 221-222
Center for Research Libraries, The [Chicago]
Library (Research libraries) **L:** 247
Center for Science in the Public Interest C: 351
Center for State Policy and Leadership
[organization]
Illinois, University of (The Springfield campus)
I: 77
Center for the Book
Library of Congress **L:** 264
Center frequency [electronics] *See* Carrier
frequency *in this index*
Center line
Field hockey (The field and equipment) **F:** 92
with diagram
Center of curvature [optics]
Mirror (Convex mirrors) **M:** 616-617 *with
diagrams*
Center of domestication [agriculture]
Agriculture (Centers of domestication) **A:** 154
Prehistoric people (The rise of agriculture) **P:** 752
Center of gravity *See* Gravity, Center of *in this index*
Center of mass *See* Mass, Center of *in this index*
Center of population [geography]
United States *map on* **U:** 109
Center of symmetry
Crystal (Classifying crystals) **Ci:** 1166
Symmetry (A center of symmetry) **So:** 1067
Center of the United States
Geographic center of the United States **G:** 92
Center pass [sports]
Field hockey (The game) **F:** 93 *with diagram*
Center-pivot irrigation
Farm and farming *picture on* **F:** 33
Center spot
Soccer (Starting the game) **So:** 546
Center work
Ballet (A ballet class) **B:** 46-47 *with picture*
Centerboard [boat]
Sailing (Hull) **S:** 23 *with diagram;* (Controlling
direction) **S:** 25
Centering the puck
Hockey (Hockey terms) **H:** 275
Centerless grinding
Machine tool (Abrasive processes) **M:** 19
Centers for Disease Control and Prevention
[U.S.] **C:** 351
Disease (Governments) **D:** 234
Health and Human Services, Department of
(Organization) **H:** 128
Obesity **O:** 643
Quarantine **Q:** 7
Centers for Medicare and Medicaid Services
[U.S.]
Health and Human Services, Department of
(Organization) **H:** 128
Medicaid **M:** 361
Centi [prefix]
Metric system (Use of standard prefixes) **M:** 437;
(Metric prefixes) **M:** 439; (Selection of Si
prefixes) **M:** 440
Centigrade scale *See* Celsius scale *in this index*
Centimeter [measurement] **C:** 351
Metric system (A center of "family units" per quantity)
M: 437; (The metric system at a glance) **M:** 438
with pictures
Centimeter-gram-second [measurement]
Dyne **D:** 398
Centinel of the North-Western Territory
[newspaper]
Ohio (Communication) **O:** 698
Centipede [animal] **C:** 351 *with picture*
Arthropod **A:** 752 *with picture*
Centipede grass [plant]
Lawn (Types of lawns) **L:** 142
Central [division, Hong Kong]
Hong Kong (The metropolis) **H:** 316
Central African Empire [former name]
Central African Republic (History) **C:** 353
Central African Republic C: 352 *with picture and
map*
Flag *picture on* **F:** 198
French Equatorial Africa **F:** 514
Central air conditioning

Air conditioning (Kinds of air conditioners) **A:** 179
with diagram
Central Alps [mountains, Austria]
Austria (Land regions) **A:** 933-934 *with map*
Central America C: 354 *with map*
See also the list of Related articles in the Central
America *article*
City (Ancient cities) **Ci:** 578
Hispanic Americans (Central American migration)
H: 255
Indian, American (Indians of Middle America)
I: 169 *with pictures and map;* (Indians of the
Caribbean) **I:** 172 *with pictures*
Railroad (In other countries) **R:** 113
Rain forest (The Americas) **R:** 126b *with map*
Central America [ship]
Shipwreck (table: Major shipwrecks) **S:** 428
Central America, United Provinces of [Latin
American history]
Central America (Independence) **C:** 355
Costa Rica (Independence) **Ci:** 1084
Delgado, José Matías **D:** 115
El Salvador (Independence) **E:** 252
Flag *picture on* **F:** 217
Guatemala (Independence) **G:** 417
Honduras (Independence) **H:** 312
Latin America (The movement toward
independence) **L:** 106-107
Nicaragua (Independence) **N:** 398-399
Central America and the Caribbean [region]
North America (Land regions) **N:** 462-464
Central America Federation
Central America (Attempts at unification)
C: 355-356
Central America Free Trade Agreement [2004]
Central America (Developments since the mid-
1900's) **C:** 356
Central American Common Market
Guatemala City **G:** 418
Central American Court of Justice [Latin
American history]
Central America (Attempts at unification)
C: 355-356
Central American river turtle
Turtle (Other kinds of turtles) **T:** 524
Central Arizona Project
Arizona (The late 1900's) **A:** 691
Phoenix (Recent developments) **P:** 399
Central Artery [highway]
Massachusetts (The early 2000's) **M:** 293
Central Asia
Asia (Way of life in Central Asia) **A:** 790 *with
pictures;* (The land) **A:** 792; (Plants) **A:** 799
with map
Martial arts (Central and South Asian martial arts)
M: 234a
Central bank
Bank (Central banks) **B:** 91
Depression (Depressions since World War II)
D: 150
Federal Reserve System **F:** 65
Money (Monetary policy) **M:** 717
Central Canada Exhibition
Ottawa (Annual events) **O:** 873
Central chimpanzee
Chimpanzee **C:** 471
Central City
Colorado (Places to visit) **Ci:** 836
Central city [area]
Metropolitan area **M:** 442
Central College Association
National Education Association **N:** 34
Central Command
Air Force, United States (Combat commands)
A: 193
Central committee
China (The Communist Party) **C:** 477
Communism (Communist party structures)
Ci: 891
Union of Soviet Socialist Republics (The
Communist Party) **U:** 29
Central Conference of American Rabbis
Bible (Modern English translations) **B:** 286
Central dispatch office
Police (Records and communications) **P:** 621
Central Division
Hockey (table: National Hockey League) **H:** 281
Central dogma [biology]
Molecular biology (The beginning of molecular
biology) **M:** 691-692
Central European University Foundation
Foundation (International affairs) **F:** 431
Central Flyway [route]
Bird (Where birds migrate) **B:** 360-361
Central heating
Heating (Central heating systems) **H:** 157
House (Heating and air conditioning) **H:** 383

Central High School [Little Rock]
　African Americans (The civil rights movement)
　　A: 1360 *with picture*
　Arkansas (The mid-1900's) **A:** 714 *with picture*
　Eisenhower, Dwight David (Civil rights) **E:** 153-
　　154
Central Intelligence Agency [U.S.] **C:** 356
　Bush, George Herbert Walker (CIA director) **B:** 718
　Central America (Developments since the mid-
　　1900's) **C:** 356
　Espionage (History) **E:** 358
　Iran-contra affair (Background) **I:** 407
　Propaganda (After World War II) **P:** 825
Central Japan International Airport
　Japan (Transportation) **J:** 51-52
Central limit theorem
　Statistics (Probability) **So:** 868-869
Central nervous system [anatomy]
　See also Brain; Spinal cord *in this index*
　Human body (The central nervous system) **H:** 425
　Myelin **M:** 970f
　Nervous system (Divisions of the nervous system)
　　N: 132 *with diagram*
　Paralysis (Paralysis of central nervous system
　　origin) **P:** 152
　Reproduction, Human (Development of organs
　　and organ systems) **R:** 248
　Reye's syndrome **R:** 288
　Spastic paralysis **So:** 767
Central office
　Telephone (Traditional phone calls) **T:** 96
Central Office of Vigilance
　Vatican City (Armed forces) **V:** 288
Central Pacific Railroad
　Railroad (The first transcontinental rail lines)
　　R: 116 *with picture*
　Sacramento (History) **S:** 6
　Transcontinental railroad (The United States)
　　T: 370-371
　Western frontier life in America (Improvements in
　　transportation) **W:** 233
Central Park [New York City]
　Cleopatra's Needles **Ci:** 662b *with picture*
　New York City *picture on* **N:** 331; (Manhattan)
　　N: 323-325; (Parks) **N:** 338
　Olmsted, Frederick Law **O:** 745
　Park (History) **P:** 168
Central Park [painting by Prendergast]
　Prendergast, Maurice Brazil *picture on* **P:** 755
Central Pine Belt
　Alabama (Land regions) **A:** 268
Central planning [economics] *See* Planned
　economy *in this index*
Central Plateau [region of Mexico]
　Mexico (The Mesa Central) **M:** 462 *with picture*
Central Powers [alliance]
　Germany (World War I) **G:** 166
　United States, History of the (World War I and
　　postwar growth [1917-1929]) **U:** 188
　World War I **W:** 452, *maps on* **W:** 454, **W:** 456,
　　W: 459, **W:** 460, **W:** 464; (table: The Allies)
　　W: 453
Central processing unit [electronics] *See*
　Microprocessor; Processor *in this index*
Central Railway [South America]
　Andes Mountains (Transportation) **A:** 453
　Peru (Transportation) **P:** 314
　Railroad (Worldwide development) **R:** 116-117
Central receiver system
　Solar energy (Central receiver systems) **So:** 579
Central sensitization [physiology]
　Pain (How the body feels pain) **P:** 21-22
Central Treaty Organization [alliance]
　Cold War (To the brink and back) **Ci:** 765
Central University [Caracas]
　Venezuela (Education) **V:** 301
Central Utah Project
　Utah (The early 2000's) **U:** 249
Central vacuum cleaner
　Vacuum cleaner **V:** 258
Central Valley [region, California]
　California (Land regions) **C:** 48
Central Valley Project
　San Joaquin River **S:** 100
Centralized dispatching
　Railroad (Automatic block signal systems) **R:** 111
Centralized Traffic Control [transportation]
　Railroad (Automatic block signal systems) **R:** 111
Centre Block [building]
　Ottawa (The Parliament Buildings) **O:** 872
Centrex service
　Telephone (Business services) **T:** 98
Centrifugal casting [manufacturing]
　Cast and casting (Other types of casting) **C:** 278
Centrifugal-flow compressor
　Jet propulsion (Turbojet) **J:** 111
Centrifugal force [physics] **C:** 357

Centrifugal method
　Uranium (Separating uranium isotopes) **U:** 215
　　with diagram
Centrifugal pump
　Pump (Dynamic pumps) **P:** 900b *with diagram*
Centrifuge [machine] **C:** 357 *with picture*
　Cell (Looking at a cell) **C:** 327
　Coal (Cleaning coal) **Ci:** 726-727
　Plasma (Uses in medicine) **P:** 551 *with picture*
　Sugar (Obtaining raw sugar) **So:** 961 *with
　　diagram*
Centriole [biology]
　Cell (The cytoplasm) **C:** 329 *with diagram*;
　　(Mitosis) **C:** 330
Centripetal acceleration
　Velocity (Acceleration) **V:** 297
Centripetal force [physics] **C:** 358 *with diagram*
　Centrifugal force **C:** 357
Centroid method of factor analysis [psychology]
　Thurstone, Louis Leon **T:** 273
Centrosaurus [dinosaur]
　Dinosaur (True dinosaurs) **D:** 206b-208
Centuries [book by Nostradamus]
　Nostradamus **N:** 549
Centurion [ancient Rome]
　Legion **L:** 183
Century [time] **C:** 358
**Century II Performing Arts and Convention
　Center** [Wichita]
　Kansas *picture on* **K:** 225
　Wichita (The city) **W:** 297
Century 21 [Seattle, Washington]
　Washington *picture on* **W:** 67
Century Aluminum Company
　Aluminum (In the United States) **A:** 396
Century City [California]
　Los Angeles (West Los Angeles) **L:** 461
Century of Dishonor, A [book by Jackson]
　Jackson, Helen Hunt **J:** 14
Century of Louis the Great, The [book by Perrault]
　Perrault, Charles **P:** 293
Century of Progress Exposition [Chicago]
　Chicago (Ending a century of progress) **C:** 436
Century plant [plant] **C:** 358 *with picture*
　Aloe **A:** 380
　Sisal **S:** 476
Century Safe [time capsule]
　Time capsule **T:** 292c
Cepeda, Orlando [American baseball player]
　Baseball (table: Hall of Fame) **B:** 134
Cephalic vein [anatomy]
　Human body (table) **H:** 422 *with diagram*
Cephalonia [island, Greece]
　Ionian Islands **I:** 373 *with map*
Cephalopod [zoology]
　Mollusk (Octopuses and squids) **M:** 695 *with
　　picture*
Cephalosporin [medication] **C:** 359
　Penicillin (How penicillins work) **P:** 240
Cephalothorax [zoology]
　Arachnid **A:** 590b
　Shrimp (The body of a shrimp) **S:** 439
　Spider (The spider's body) **So:** 783-784 *with
　　picture*
Cepheid variable [astronomy]
　Leavitt, Henrietta Swan **L:** 170
Cepheus [Greek mythology]
　Andromeda **A:** 457
Ceram [island, Indonesia]
　Indonesia (The Molucca Islands) **I:** 234
Ceramic insulation
　Insulation (In industry) **I:** 306-307
Ceramic microphone
　Microphone (Crystal microphones and ceramic
　　microphones) **M:** 516 *with picture*
Ceramics [material] **C:** 359 *with pictures*
　See also Pottery *in this index*
　Antique (Ceramic antiques) **A:** 558
　Clay **Ci:** 658
　Composite materials **Ci:** 904
　Materials (Ceramics) **M:** 300d *with picture*
　Plastics (To replace glass and ceramics) **P:** 555
　Porcelain **P:** 675
　Pottery **P:** 716
　Superconductivity **So:** 992
　Tile **T:** 287
Ceratopsian [dinosaur]
　Dinosaur (True dinosaurs) **D:** 206b-206c *with
　　picture*
Ceratosaur [dinosaur]
　Coelophysis **Ci:** 753
Cerberus [Greek mythology]
　Hercules (The twelve labors) **H:** 198-199
Cercopithecine [monkey]
　Primate (Old World monkeys) **P:** 778a
Cercus [entomology]
　Insect *diagram on* **I:** 286; (Abdomen) **I:** 288

Cere [zoology]
　Parakeet **P:** 151 *with picture*
Cereal C: 360
　Agriculture (Food from plants) **A:** 147 *with picture*
　Barley **B:** 112
　Bran **B:** 562
　Corn **Ci:** 1056 *with pictures*
　Food (Food from plants) **F:** 329
　Food supply (Cereal grains) **F:** 347
　Grain **G:** 301
　Grass (Cereals) **G:** 326
　Livestock (Feed) **L:** 397
　Michigan (Interesting facts) **M:** 489;
　　(Manufacturing) **M:** 505
　Millet **M:** 555
　Nutrition (Kinds of nutrients) **N:** 625
　Oatmeal **O:** 640
　Oats **O:** 640
　Rice **R:** 322
　Rye **R:** 573
　Wheat **W:** 266
Cereal Bowl of America [name for]
　Michigan (Interesting facts) **M:** 489;
　　(Manufacturing) **M:** 505
Cerealia [Roman history]
　Ceres **C:** 362
Cerebellum [anatomy]
　Bird (The nervous system) **B:** 366
　Brain (The parts of the brain) **B:** 550a *with
　　diagram*; (Among vertebrates) **B:** 560
　Human body (table) **H:** 422 *with diagram*
　Nervous system (The central nervous system)
　　N: 132-133 *with diagram*
Cerebral aneurysm [disorder]
　Stroke (Causes) **So:** 930
Cerebral arteriosclerosis [disease]
　Senility **S:** 300
Cerebral cortex [anatomy]
　Brain *diagram on* **B:** 553; (The parts of the brain)
　　B: 550a-550b *with diagram*; (From injury)
　　B: 550d; (Language) **B:** 556
　Concussion **Ci:** 929
　Dream (The biology of dreams) **D:** 344-345
　Memory **M:** 392
　Nervous system (In vertebrates) **N:** 136
　Persistent vegetative state **P:** 300f
Cerebral edema [illness]
　Altitude sickness **A:** 390
Cerebral embolism [disorder]
　Stroke (Causes) **So:** 930
Cerebral hemisphere [anatomy]
　Brain (The parts of the brain) **B:** 550a-550b *with
　　diagram*; (Differences in individual brains)
　　B: 550c-550d; (Language) **B:** 556
Cerebral hemorrhage [disorder] **C:** 361
　Stroke (Causes) **So:** 930
Cerebral malaria [disease]
　Malaria (Symptoms) **M:** 95
Cerebral palsy C: 361
　Brain (Cerebral palsy) **B:** 556
　Disability **D:** 218
　Occupational therapy (Helping people with
　　physical disabilities) **O:** 648
Cerebral thrombosis [disorder]
　Stroke (Causes) **So:** 930
Cerebrospinal fluid [physiology] **C:** 362
　Brain (From injury) **B:** 550d
　Meningitis (Symptoms and diagnosis) **M:** 401
　Respiration (Control of breathing) **R:** 261
Cerebrum [anatomy]
　Bird (The nervous system) **B:** 366
　Brain (The parts of the brain) **B:** 550a *with
　　diagram*; (Among vertebrates) **B:** 560
　Human body (table) **H:** 422 *with diagram*
　Nervous system (The central nervous system)
　　N: 132 *with diagram*
Ceremonial march
　March **M:** 193
Ceremonial mask
　Mask (Ceremonial masks) **M:** 264 *with pictures*
Ceremony [book by Silko]
　American literature (Works by minority writers)
　　A: 425
Ceremony [sociology]
　Indian, American *picture on* **I:** 164; (Ceremonies)
　　I: 148 *with picture*
　Marriage (Wedding ceremonies) **M:** 220
　Masonry **M:** 266
　Mythology (Anthropological approaches)
　　M: 989-990
Ceremony of Carols, A [music by Britten]
　Britten, Benjamin **B:** 634
Ceres [goddess] **C:** 361
　See also Demeter *in this index*
　Mythology (table) **M:** 981
Ceres [asteroid] **C:** 362
　Asteroid **A:** 824; (Sizes and shapes) **A:** 824;

(History of study) **A:** 824b
Dwarf planet **D:** 394
Planet (The dwarf planets) **P:** 512
Solar system (Dwarf planets) **So:** 580
Cereus [plant]
Flower *picture on* **F:** 272
Cerezo Arévalo, Marco Vinicio [Guatemalan political leader]
Guatemala (Political developments) **G:** 417
Ceriman [plant]
Monstera **M:** 741
Cerium [element] **C:** 362
Cermak, Anton J. [American political leader]
Roosevelt, Franklin Delano (An uneasy transition) **R:** 452
CERN [organization] **C:** 363
Berners-Lee, Tim **B:** 270
Internet *picture on* **I:** 350d
Particle accelerator (How accelerators work) **P:** 184-186
Physics (Employment) **P:** 443
UNESCO (Science) **U:** 24-25
Cero [fish]
Kingfish **K:** 329
Cerro Gordo, Battle of [1847]
Mexican War (Principal battles) **M:** 447 *with picture*
Cerro Santa Lucia [Santiago]
Chile *picture on* **C:** 459
Cerro Tololo Inter-American Observatory [Chile]
National Optical Astronomy Observatories **N:** 42
Cerros de Celaque [mountains]
Honduras (The Mountainous Interior) **H:** 309
Certificate of deposit [banking] **C:** 363
Bank (Safeguarding deposits) **B:** 88
Investment (Indirect investments) **I:** 367
Certificated airline
Aviation (Airline operations) **A:** 984-985
Certification
Aviation (Careers in aviation) **A:** 992
Organic food (Standards) **O:** 853
Teaching (Certification of teachers) **T:** 68
Certified check [banking]
Check (Special checking services) **C:** 391
Certified mail
Postal Service, United States (Extra protection) **P:** 700
Certified nursing assistant *See* Nurse's aide *in this index*
Certified public accountant
Accounting (Fields of accounting) **A:** 23
Audit **A:** 884
Certiorari, Petition for [law]
Supreme Court of the United States (Writ of certiorari) **So:** 999
Certiorari, Writ of [law] **C:** 363
Appeal **A:** 568
Supreme Court of the United States (Writ of certiorari) **So:** 999
Cervantes, Miguel de [Spanish author] **C:** 363
Don Quixote **D:** 306
Novel (Early novels) **N:** 572
Proverb **P:** 839
Spanish literature (The 1500's) **So:** 758-759; (The 1600's) **So:** 759
Cervera y Topete, Pascual [Spanish admiral]
Sampson, William Thomas **S:** 81
Cervical cancer [disorder] **C:** 364
Cancer (Classification by primary body site) **C:** 167-168
Human papillomavirus **H:** 427
Cervical intraepithelial neoplasia [disorder]
Cervical cancer **C:** 364
Cervical vertebra [anatomy]
Mammal (Skeleton) **M:** 118-119 *with diagram*
Skeleton (The axial skeleton) **S:** 479-480 *with diagrams*
Spine **So:** 792 *with diagram*
Cervix [anatomy]
Cervical cancer **C:** 364
Childbirth (The birth process) **C:** 456
Gonorrhea **G:** 268
Pap test **P:** 132
Reproduction, Human (The stages of labor) **R:** 249
Uterus **U:** 251
Vagina **V:** 259
Césaire, Aimé [West Indian poet and playwright]
Latin America (Painting) **L:** 99-100
Cesalpino, Andrea [Italian anatomist]
Heart (Discovery of circulation) **H:** 144
Cesare Angelotti [opera character]
Opera: *(Tosca)* **O:** 807
Cesarean section [medicine]
Childbirth (The birth process) **C:** 456
Conjoined twins **C:** 950
Reproduction, Human (The stages of labor)

R: 249
Surgery (Obstetrics and gynecology) **So:** 1007
Cesario [literary figure]
Shakespeare, William: *(Twelfth Night)* **S:** 360-361
Cesium [element] **C:** 364
Fallout (The fallout hazard) **F:** 19 *with map*
Radiation (Radiation and radioactivity) **R:** 75; (Artificial radioactive substances) **R:** 77
Céspedes, Augusto [Bolivian author]
Bolivia (The arts) **B:** 444
Céspedes, Carlos Manuel de [Cuban patriot]
Cuba (Struggle against Spain) **Ci:** 1176
Cessna Citation Bravo [airplane]
Airplane *picture on* **A:** 210
Cesspool [pit]
Plumbing (History) **P:** 580
Cesta [equipment]
Jai alai **J:** 21 *with picture*
Cestus [ancient Rome]
Boxing (Ancient history) **B:** 531
Cetacean [zoology] **C:** 364
See also Dolphin; Porpoise; River dolphin; Whale *in this index*
Mammal (table) **M:** 128 *with picture*
Ceuta [Morocco]
Henry the Navigator **H:** 191
Ceviche [food]
Cooking (Other cooking methods) **Ci:** 1028
Ceylon *See* Sri Lanka *in this index*
Cézanne, Paul [French painter] **C:** 364 *with pictures*
Braque, Georges **B:** 564
Derain, André **D:** 152
Painting (Postimpressionism) **P:** 75 *with picture*
Picasso, Pablo (Early sculptures) **P:** 448a-448b
Postimpressionism **P:** 709
Cf. [abbreviation]
Cross-reference **Ci:** 1155
CF [disease] *See* Cystic fibrosis *in this index*
Cf [symbol]
Californium **C:** 66
CF-18 Hornet [aircraft]
Air force *picture on* **A:** 182
CFA [organization]
Consumer Federation of America **Ci:** 1017
CFC [chemical] *See* Chlorofluorocarbon *in this index*
CFL [device] *See* Compact fluorescent lamp *in this index*
CFL [league] *See* Canadian Football League *in this index*
CFS [disorder] *See* Chronic fatigue syndrome *in this index*
CFTR [genetics] *See* Cystic fibrosis transmembrane conductance regulator *in this index*
CG [motion pictures] *See* Computer graphics *in this index*
CGG [genetics]
Fragile X syndrome **F:** 451
CGI [motion pictures] *See* Computer-generated imagery *in this index*
CGPM [organization] *See* Weights and Measures, General Conference on *in this index*
CGS system [measurement]
Dyne **D:** 398
Metric system (Evolution of the metric system) **M:** 441
Cha-cha [dance]
Ballroom dancing **B:** 63
Latin America (Dance) **L:** 101
Chac [Maya god]
Maya (Religion) **M:** 322
Chacma [animal]
Baboon **B:** 3
Chacmool [sculpture]
Maya *picture on* **M:** 324
Chaco [region, South America] *See* Gran Chaco *in this index*
Chaco Canyon [New Mexico]
Anasazi (History) **A:** 448a
Chaco Culture National Historical Park [New Mexico] **C:** 365
National Park System (table: National historical parks) **N:** 56
New Mexico (Places to visit) **N:** 264
Chaco War [1932-1935]
Bolivia (Territorial losses) **B:** 447
Paraguay (Military ruin) **P:** 149
Chacoan peccary [animal]
Peccary **P:** 226
Chaconne [music]
Counterpoint **Ci:** 1097
Chad C: 365 *with picture and map*
Famine *picture on* **F:** 26b
Flag *picture on* **F:** 198
French Equatorial Africa **F:** 514
Chad [paper]
Ballot (In the United States) **B:** 63
Election of 2000 (Court challenges) **E:** 161

Voting machine (Kinds of electoral voting machines) **V:** 450
Chad, Lake [Africa]
Lake Chad **L:** 36
Chador [clothing]
Iran (Clothing) **I:** 402 *with picture*
Chadri [clothing] *See* Burqa *in this index*
Chadwick, Henry [American author]
Baseball (table: Hall of Fame) **B:** 134
Chadwick, Sir James [British physicist] **C:** 368
Nuclear energy (Artificial fission) **N:** 590
Physics (Uncovering the secrets of the atom) **P:** 442
Rotblat, Joseph **R:** 487
Chadwick, Stephen F. [American political leader]
Oregon (table) **O:** 845
Chaeronea, Battle of [338 B.C.]
Alexander the Great (His youth) **A:** 342
Boeotia **B:** 436
Demosthenes **D:** 129
Chaetoceros [zoology]
Diatom *picture on* **D:** 186
Chaetognatha [zoology]
Animal (A classification of the animal kingdom) **A:** 507 *with picture*
Chafee, John Hubbard [American political leader]
Rhode Island (table) **R:** 311
Chaff [warfare]
Ammunition (Artillery ammunition) **A:** 435-436
Radar (Advances during World War II) **R:** 72
Chafee, Lincoln [American political leader]
Rhode Island (table) **R:** 311
Chaffee, Roger B. [American astronaut]
Astronaut (Accidents in space) **A:** 830-831
Space exploration (Making ready) **So:** 715
Chagall, Marc [Russian-born artist] **C:** 368 *with picture*
Chicago (Places to visit) **C:** 430-431
Illinois *picture on* **I:** 53
Opera *picture on* **O:** 805
Stained glass (Decline and revival) **So:** 823 *with picture*
Chagas disease
Trypanosome **T:** 474
Chagga [people]
Tanzania (Population and ancestry) **T:** 31
Chagnon Foundation, Lucie and André
Foundation (table) **F:** 430
Chagos Archipelago [islands, Indian Ocean]
British Indian Ocean Territory **B:** 632
Chagres River [Panama] **C:** 369
Panama Canal (Gatun Lake) **P:** 123 *with map*
Chaikin, Joseph [American dramatist]
Drama (Experimental theater) **D:** 340
Chaikovsky, P. I. [Russian composer] *See* Tchaikovsky, Peter Ilich *in this index*
Chain [weaving]
Rugs and carpets (Weaving) **R:** 515 *with pictures*
Chain, Ernst Boris [British biochemist] **C:** 369
Penicillin (Early history) **P:** 240
Chain broadcasting
Radio (The start of broadcasting) **R:** 92
Chain cent [money]
Cent *pictures on* **C:** 350
Chain gang [prison] **C:** 369
Chain hoist [mechanism]
Block and tackle (An endless chain hoist) **B:** 405 *with diagram*
Chain lightning
Lightning (Appearance) **L:** 300
Chain mail
Armor (During the Middle Ages) **A:** 719
Gauntlet **G:** 70
Chain of custody [criminology]
Crime scene investigation (At the laboratory) **Ci:** 1141
Chain-of-Lakes [California]
Lassen Volcanic National Park **L:** 87
Chain of title [law]
Title **T:** 302
Chain pickerel [fish]
Pickerel **P:** 450 *with picture*
Pike **P:** 461
Chain reaction [nuclear energy]
Nuclear energy (Nuclear fission) **N:** 582-583 *with diagram*; (Chain reactions) **N:** 586; (The development of nuclear energy) **N:** 589; (The development of nuclear weapons) **N:** 591
Nuclear weapon (Fission weapons) **N:** 596-597
Uranium (Fissionability) **U:** 215
Chain restaurant
Restaurant (Chains and franchises) **R:** 262
Chain saw [tool]
Saw (Power saws) **S:** 167 *with picture*
Chain silicate
Silicate **S:** 458
Chain stitch

Crochet **Ci: 1148c** *with diagrams*
Chain store C: 369
Retailing (Chain stores) **R: 265**
Chained stitch
Embroidery (Embroidery stitches) **E: 257** *with picture*
Chainring
Bicycle (Power and speed) **B: 290** *with diagram*
Chair [furniture]
Antique *picture on* **A: 558**
Art and the arts *picture on* **A: 747**
Eames, Charles **E: 6**
Furniture **F: 568** *with pictures*
Jefferson, Thomas *picture on* **J: 78**
Chairs, The [play by Ionesco]
Ionesco, Eugène **I: 372**
Chaise [vehicle]
Carriage **C: 248**
Chaitya
Architecture (Indian architecture) **A: 613**
Chakiris, George [American actor]
Motion picture (Best performance by an actor in a supporting role: 1961) **M: 862b**
Chakri dynasty [Thai history]
Thailand (The Bangkok era) **T: 227**
Chalaza [zoology]
Egg (The white) **E: 117** *with diagram*
Chalazion [disorder]
Eye *picture on* **E: 468**; (Diseases of the outer parts) **E: 468**
Chalcedon, Council of [451]
Roman Catholic Church (The recognition of Christianity) **R: 405-406**; (Conflict with the East) **R: 406**
Chalcedon, Council of [A.D. 451]
Copts **Ci: 1045**
Leo I, Saint **L: 197**
Chalcedony [mineral] **C: 369**
Agate **A: 139**
Cameo **C: 80**
Jasper **J: 64**
Quartz (Types) **Q: 8**
Sardonyx **S: 125**
Chalchiuhtlicue [Aztec goddess]
Mythology (Aztec mythology) **M: 987**
Chalcocite [mineral] **C: 369**
Chalcogenide glass
Glass (Specialty glasses) **G: 212-213**
Chalcolithic Period
Bronze Age **B: 639**
Chalcopyrite [mineral] **C: 369**
Copper (Copper ores) **Ci: 1042**
Mineral *picture on* **M: 568**
Chaldaeans [people] *See* Chaldeans *in this index*
Chaldean Church [religious group]
Eastern Catholic Church **E: 45**
Chaldean Empire *See* Neo-Babylonian Empire *in this index*
Chaldeans [people] **C: 369** *with map*
Chalet [house]
Austria (Way of life) **A: 931**
Chalfie, Martin [American chemist]
Nobel Prizes (Chemistry: 2008) **N: 444**
Chalgrin, Jean François Thérèse [French artist]
Arc de Triomphe **A: 593**
Chalk C: 370
Drawing (Materials and techniques) **D: 342** *with picture*
Chalk River Nuclear Laboratories [Ontario]
Ontario (The mid-1900's) **O: 786-787**
Chalkboard C: 370
Audio-visual materials (Chalkboards, dry-erase boards, and flip charts) **A: 882**
Eraser **E: 349**
Challenge [cryptology]
Codes and ciphers (Modern applications of cryptography) **Ci: 752**
Challenge and response [history]
Civilization (Rise and fall) **Ci: 636**
Challenge to Liberty, The [book by Hoover]
Hoover, Herbert Clark (Elder statesman) **H: 330**
Challenger [ship]
Atlantic Ocean (The beginnings of scientific oceanography) **A: 867**
Exploration (Deep-sea exploration) **E: 450**
Pacific Ocean (Scientific research) **P: 15**
Challenger [space shuttle]
See also Challenger disaster *in this index*
Astronaut (Achievements in space) **A: 829-830**
Garneau, Marc **G: 44**
Ride, Sally Kristen **R: 335**
Challenger Deep [oceanography]
Deep **D: 81**
Pacific Ocean (The ocean floor) **P: 14**
Challenger disaster [U.S. history] **C: 370**
Astronaut (Accidents in space) **A: 830-831**
McAuliffe, Christa **M: 332**

National Aeronautics and Space Administration **N: 28**
Onizuka, Ellison Shoji **O: 763**
Space exploration (The Challenger disaster) **So: 725**
Challis [fabric]
Textile (table: Textile terms) **T: 213**
Challoner, Richard [English religious leader]
Vulgate **V: 453**
Chama Cha Mapinduzi [political party]
Tanzania (Government) **T: 30**; (The united republic and socialism) **T: 35**; (After socialism) **T: 35**
Chambelane [role]
Quinceañera **Q: 42**
Chambellan, René [American sculptor]
Newbery Medal **N: 358** *with picture*
Chamber [anatomy]
Heart (Chambers, valves, and inner lining) **H: 133**; (Hearts of animals) **H: 146** *with diagrams*
Chamber [device]
Firearm (Mechanism) **F: 132** *with diagrams*
Chamber music C: 370
Classical music *picture on* **Ci: 648**; (Chamber music) **Ci: 643** *with picture*
Chamber Music Society of Lincoln Center
Lincoln Center for the Performing Arts **L: 327**
Chamber of commerce [organization] **C: 371**
Chamber of Commerce, United States [organization] **C: 371**
Chamber of Deputies [government]
Italy (Parliament) **I: 499**
Chamber orchestra
Orchestra (The structure of a symphony orchestra) **O: 820**
Chamber tomb *See* Dolmen *in this index*
Chambered nautilus [sea animal]
Nautilus **N: 69** *with picture*
Shell *pictures on* **S: 387**; (Octopuses and squids) **S: 388**
Chamberlain, Abiram [American political leader]
Connecticut (table) **Ci: 967**
Chamberlain, Sir Austen [British statesman]
Chamberlain, Neville **C: 371**
Nobel Prizes (Peace: 1925) **N: 448a**
Chamberlain, George E. [American political leader]
Oregon (table) **O: 845**
Chamberlain, Joseph [British political leader]
Chamberlain, Neville **C: 371**
Laurier, Sir Wilfrid (Relations with the United Kingdom) **L: 126**
Chamberlain, Joshua Lawrence [American political leader]
Maine (table) **M: 87**
Chamberlain, Neville [British statesman] **C: 371**
Churchill, Sir Winston Leonard Spencer (World War II begins) **C: 547**
Macmillan, Harold **M: 25**
Munich Agreement (Agreement) **M: 928**
United Kingdom ("Peace in our time") **U: 70**
World War II (The failure of appeasement) **W: 472**
Chamberlain, Owen [American physicist]
Physics (Advances in the mid-1900's) **P: 442**
Chamberlain, Wilt [American basketball player] **C: 371** *with picture*
Basketball *picture on* **B: 153**; (The history of professional basketball) **B: 154a-155**
Chambers, Ephraim [British author]
Encyclopedia (An age of experiment) **E: 268a**
Chambers, Paul [American bassist]
Davis, Miles *picture on* **D: 49**
Chambers, Whittaker [American public figure] **C: 372**
Hiss, Alger **H: 259** *with picture*
Nixon, Richard Milhous *picture on* **N: 430**
Chambers, Sir William [British architect]
Architecture (Neoclassical architecture) **A: 623**
Chambray [fabric]
Textile (table: Textile terms) **T: 213**
Chameleon [reptile] **C: 372** *with picture*
Animal *picture on* **A: 469**; (Camouflage) **A: 493**
Lizard (Defenses) **L: 400**
Rain forest *picture on* **R: 126c**
Chamfron
Armor *picture on* **A: 720**
Chamise [plant]
Plant *picture on* **P: 525**
Chamizal National Memorial [Texas]
National Park System (table: National memorials) **N: 54**
Chamois [animal] **C: 372** *with picture*
Chamois skin [leather]
Chamois **C: 373**
Leather (Kinds of leather) **L: 167** *with picture*
Chamomile [plant] *See* Camomile *in this index*
Chamorro, Pedro Joaquín [Nicaraguan journalist]

Chamorro, Violeta Barrios de **C: 373**
Chamorro, Violeta Barrios de [Nicaraguan political leader] **C: 373** *with portrait*
Nicaragua (The late1900's) **N: 400-401**
Ortega, Daniel **O: 859**
Chamorros [people]
Guam (People) **G: 408**
Mariana Islands **M: 199**
Northern Mariana Islands, Commonwealth of the (People) **N: 526**
Champ Car [organization]
Automobile racing (Indy and Champ car racing) **A: 977**
Champ de Mars [park, Paris]
Eiffel Tower **E: 146**
Paris *picture on* **P: 161**; (Gardens, squares, and parks) **P: 162-163** *with map*
Champagne [province, France]
Champagne **C: 373**
Middle Ages (Economic recovery) **M: 526-527**
Wine (Wines from France) **W: 337**
Champagne [wine] **C: 373**
Wine (Sparkling wines) **W: 336**; (Wines from France) **W: 337**
Champasak [Laotian history]
Indochina (A new kingdom) **I: 225**; (French influence) **I: 225**
Champions Tour [golf]
Golf (Golf today) **G: 267**
Champlain, Lake [Canada-U.S.]
Lake Champlain **L: 36** *with map*
Vermont (Rivers and lakes) **V: 328-330** *with map*
Champlain, Samuel de [French explorer] **C: 373** *with picture and map*
Brulé, Étienne **B: 650**
Canada, History of *picture on* **C: 138**; (Early settlements) **C: 140**
Du Gua, Pierre, Sieur de Monts **D: 379**
Exploration (The French and English in North America) **E: 446** *with map*
Maine *picture on* **M: 90**
Map (Mapping the Americas) **M: 184-185**
New Brunswick (Exploration and settlement) **N: 196** *with picture*
New York (Exploration and settlement) **N: 314**
Nova Scotia (Exploration and settlement) **N: 567-568**
Ontario (European exploration) **O: 784**
Ottawa River **O: 875**
Poutrincourt, Jean de Biencourt de **P: 723**
Prince Edward Island (Exploration and early history) **P: 791**
Quebec **Q: 34**; (Early days) **Q: 36**
Quebec [province] **Q: 11**
Saint John **S: 35**
Vermont (Exploration and settlement) **V: 334**
Champlain and Saint Lawrence [railroad]
Railroad (Canada's first steam-powered railway) **R: 115**
Champlain Canal [waterway, New York]
New York State Canal System **N: 345** *with map*
Vermont *picture on* **V: 335, V: 336**
Champlain in Huronia [painting by Woods]
Canada, History of *picture on* **C: 138**
Champlevé [art]
Enamel (Techniques) **E: 264**
Champollion, Jean-François [French archaeologist]
Hieroglyphics (Deciphering hieroglyphic writing) **H: 226-227**
Rosetta stone **R: 480**
Champs Élysées [street, Paris]
Paris (Gardens, squares, and parks) **P: 162** *with pictures and map*
World War II *pictures on* **W: 475, W: 484**
Chamuscado, Francisco Sánchez [Spanish explorer]
New Mexico (Exploration, conquest, and settlement) **N: 273**
Chan [religion]
Buddhism (Meditation) **B: 669**
Zen **Z: 589**
Chan Chan [ancient city]
Peru (History) **P: 314**
Chance, Frank [American baseball player]
Baseball (table: Hall of Fame) **B: 134**
Chance composition [choreography]
Cunningham, Merce **Ci: 1192**
Chance music *See* Aleatory music *in this index*
Chancellor [title]
Equity **E: 348**
Germany (Executive) **G: 147**
Prime minister **P: 778c**
Universities and colleges (Administration) **U: 208**
Chancellorsville, Battle of [1863]
Civil War, American (table) **Ci: 624**; (Battle of Chancellorsville) **Ci: 627** *with map*

Hooker, Joseph **H: 324**
Jackson, Stonewall (His death) **J: 16-17**
Lincoln, Abraham (Building the army) **L: 321**
Chancery, Court of [law] *See* Court of chancery *in this index*
Chancre [infection]
Syphilis **So: 1069**
Chandelier
White House *pictures on* **W: 289**
Chandigarh [city, India]
Le Corbusier **L: 175**
Chandigarh [territory, India]
Punjab **P: 903**
Chandler, Edward Barron [Canadian political leader]
Confederation of Canada (Fathers of Confederation) **Ci: 935** *with picture*
Chandler, Happy [American political leader]
Baseball (table: Hall of Fame) **B: 134**
Kentucky (table) **K: 290**
Chandler, Raymond [American author] **C: 374**
American literature (Popular forms) **A: 422-423**
Parker, Robert B. **P: 170**
Chandler, William E. [American government official]
Arthur, Chester Alan (table) **A: 756**
Chandler, Zachariah [American political leader] **C: 374**
Chandler Circle [geography]
North Pole **N: 517**
South Pole **So: 685**
Chandni Chowk [district]
Delhi (The city) **D: 115**
Chandos portrait
Shakespeare, William *picture on* **S: 345**
Chandra X-ray Observatory [spacecraft]
Astronomy (X-ray astronomy) **A: 845**
Observatory (Satellite observatories) **O: 645**
Chandragupta I [emperor of India]
Gupta dynasty (Rise and fall of the dynasty) **G: 442**
Chandragupta II [emperor of India]
Gupta dynasty (Rise and fall of the dynasty) **G: 442**
India (The golden age) **I: 129**
Chandragupta Maurya [emperor of India] **C: 374**
India (The Mauryan Empire) **I: 128**
Mauryan Empire **M: 318**
Chandrasekhar, Subrahmanyan [American astrophysicist] **C: 374**
Chandrasekhar limit [physics]
Chandrasekhar, Subrahmanyan **C: 374**
Chandrayaan-1 [spacecraft]
Moon (Recent exploration) **M: 795**
Space exploration (Lunar probes) **So: 708-710;** (India) **So: 727**
Chanel, Coco [French fashion designer] **C: 374**
Chanel No. 5 [perfume]
Chanel, Coco **C: 375**
Chang [conjoined twin]
Conjoined twins **Ci: 950** *with picture*
Chang Ch'ien [Chinese emperor] *See* Zhang Qian *in this index*
Chang-Diaz, Franklin [American astronaut]
Astronaut (table) **A: 830**
Chang Heng [Chinese astronomer] *See* Zhang Heng *in this index*
Chang Jiang *See* Yangtze River *in this index*
Changa [insect]
Mole cricket **M: 691**
Changamire Empire [African history]
Zimbabwe (History) **Z: 592-593**
Chang'an [former name, Xian]
Han dynasty **H: 38**
Tang dynasty **T: 25**
World, History of the (China) **W: 435**
Changbai Mountains [China]
China (The Eastern Highlands) **C: 492** *with map*
Changdok Palace
Seoul (The city) **S: 304**
Change, Social *See* Social change *in this index*
Chang'e 1 [spacecraft]
Moon (Recent exploration) **M: 795**
Space exploration (Lunar probes) **So: 708-710**
Change of life *See* Menopause *in this index*
Change of Skin [book by Fuentes]
Fuentes, Carlos **F: 553**
Change of venue [law]
Trial (The criminal defendant's rights) **T: 436-437**
Change to Win Coalition
American Federation of Labor and Congress of Industrial Organizations (History) **A: 410**
Carpenters and Joiners of America, United Brotherhood of **C: 246**
Labor movement (Recent developments) **L: 14**
United Food and Commercial Workers International Union **U: 47**

Changeling
Fairy (Fairies and people) **F: 11**
Changing Light at Sandover, The [book by Merrill]
American literature (Variations on Modernist poetry) **A: 423**
Merrill, James **M: 419**
Changing-of-the-guard ceremony
London (Other places of interest) **L: 437** *with picture*
Channel [electronics]
Radio (Broadcasting power and frequency) **R: 87-88;** (Stereophonic receivers) **R: 89**
Television (Broadcasting) **T: 123**
Transistor (Metal oxide semiconductor field effect transistors [MOSFET's]) **T: 374**
Channel [meteorology]
Lightning **L: 299**
Channel [natural feature]
Atlantic Ocean (The Atlantic seafloor) **A: 864**
Mars (Channels, valleys, and gullies) **M: 226** *with picture*
River (Channels) **R: 352** *with diagram*
Strait **So: 917**
Channel [spiritualism] *See* Medium [spiritualism] *in this index*
Channel bass [fish]
Redfish **R: 191**
Channel catfish [fish]
Catfish **C: 300**
Fish *picture on* **F: 158**
Channel Islands [California]
California (Coastline) **C: 50**
Channel Islands [United Kingdom] **C: 375** *with map*
Guernsey **G: 419**
Jersey **J: 93**
Sark **S: 126**
Channel Islands National Park [California] **C: 375**
National Park System (table: National parks) **N: 48**
Channel of distribution
Marketing (Distribution) **M: 214**
Channel rockfish
Fish *picture on* **F: 156**
Channel Tunnel [England-France] **C: 375** *with diagram*
English Channel **E: 311**
Europe (Transportation) **E: 405**
France (Transportation) **F: 470**
Tunnel (table) **T: 491;** (History) **T: 491-492**
United Kingdom *picture on* **U: 73**
Channeling machine
Marble (Properties) **M: 192**
Channing, Chad [American drummer]
Nirvana **N: 424**
Channing, William Ellery [American religious leader]
Unitarians (History) **U: 42**
Chanson [music]
Classical music (Music in other countries) **Ci: 646**
Song **So: 592**
Chanson d'amor [poetry]
Trouvère **T: 454**
Chanson de geste [poetry]
French literature (Narrative poetry) **F: 518**
Knights and knighthood (Knighthood in literature) **K: 351**
Chanson d'Eve, La [music by Fauré]
Fauré, Gabriel Urbain **F: 56**
Chant [music] *See* Gregorian chant *in this index*
Chantal, Saint Jane de [French religious leader]
Francis de Sales, Saint **F: 481**
Chantecler
Chicken (table) **C: 443**
Chanter
Bagpipe **B: 26** *with picture*
Chanterelle [fungus]
Mushroom (Mushroomlike fungi) **M: 945**
Chantey [song]
Folklore (Folk songs) **F: 324**
Music (In work) **M: 947**
Chanukah *See* Hanukkah *in this index*
Chanute, Octave [American engineer]
Airplane (First human flights) **A: 230**
Chao, Elaine L. [American government official]
Asian Americans (Notable Asian American "firsts") **A: 812f**
Bush, George Walker (table) **B: 722h**
Labor, Department of (table) **L: 2**
Chao Phraya River [Thailand]
Thailand (The Central Plain) **T: 225**
Chao Tzu-yang *See* Zhao Ziyang *in this index*
Chaophraya Chakri [king of Thailand]
Thailand (The Bangkok era) **T: 227**
Chaos [Greek mythology]
Mythology (The Greek creation myth) **M: 980**
Chaos [region, California]
Lassen Volcanic National Park **L: 87**

Chaos [science] **C: 376**
Mathematics (Philosophies of mathematics) **M: 307**
Chaos Crags
Lassen Volcanic National Park **L: 87**
Chaos Jumbles
Lassen Volcanic National Park **L: 87**
Chaotianmen [China]
Bridge (table: Steel arch) **B: 603**
Chaotic system [science]
Chaos **C: 376**
Chapais, Jean-Charles [Canadian political leader]
Confederation of Canada (Fathers of Confederation) **Ci: 935**
Chapala, Lake
Mexico (The Plateau of Mexico) **M: 461** *with map*
Chaparajos [clothing]
Cowboy (His clothing) **Ci: 1108-1109**
Chaparral [shrubs] **C: 376**
Biome **B: 324;** (table) **B: 323** *with map*
Flower (Flowers of summer-dry regions) **F: 288** *with pictures*
Plant (Chaparrals) **P: 523** *with map;* (Plants of the chaparral) **P: 525** *with picture*
Chapatti [food]
Bread (Kinds of bread) **B: 588** *with picture*
India (Food and drink) **I: 118** *with picture*
Pakistan (Food and drink) **P: 96**
Chapbook [pamphlet]
Storytelling (The Middle Ages) **So: 915**
Chapel of the Rosary [Venice]
Matisse, Henri **M: 310**
Chaperon [hat]
Clothing *picture on* **Ci: 701**
Chapin, Roy D. [American government official]
Commerce, Department of (table) **Ci: 871**
Hoover, Herbert Clark (table) **H: 330**
Chapleau, J.-Adolphe [Canadian political leader]
Quebec (table) **Q: 29**
Chaplin, Charlie [British actor] **C: 376** *with portrait*
Motion picture *picture on* **M: 847**
Sennett, Mack *picture on* **S: 301**
Chapman, Colin [British engineer]
Automobile racing (Development of racing cars) **A: 979**
Chapman, George [English author] **C: 377**
Chapman, Graham [British actor]
Cleese, John **Ci: 661** *with picture*
"Monty Python's Flying Circus" **M: 780**
Chapman, John [American frontiersman] *See* Appleseed, Johnny *in this index*
Chapman, Mark David [American assassin]
Beatles **B: 190**
Lennon, John **L: 196**
Chapman, Mount [North Carolina-Tennessee]
Great Smoky Mountains **G: 348**
Chapman, Oscar L. [American government official]
Interior, Department of the (table) **I: 325**
Truman, Harry S. (table) **T: 469**
Chapman, Reuben [American political leader]
Alabama (table) **A: 274**
Chappaquiddick Island [Massachusetts]
Kennedy, Edward Moore **K: 259**
Chappe, Claude [French inventor]
Communication (The 1700's) **Ci: 880-881** *with picture*
Chaps [clothing]
Cowboy (His clothing) **Ci: 1108-1109** *with picture*
Horse (Clothes for riding) **H: 351**
Chapter FFA degree
FFA (Degrees) **F: 85**
Chapter 7
Bankruptcy (In the United States) **B: 97**
Chapter 13
Bankruptcy (In the United States) **B: 97**
Chapultepec, Battle of [1847]
Mexican War (Scott's campaign) **M: 446-447;** (Principal battles) **M: 447**
Mexico (Difficulties of the early republic) **M: 471**
Mexico City (Independence) **M: 478**
Chapultepec Park
Mexico City (Residential and commercial centers) **M: 476a** *with picture*
Char
Combustion **Ci: 867**
Char, René [French poet]
French literature (Surrealism) **F: 522-523**
Char Minar [palace, India]
Hyderabad **H: 461**
Characin [fish]
Tetra **T: 182b**
Character [literature]
Comedy **Ci: 867**
Drama (The structure of drama) **D: 325**
Literature (Characters) **L: 353**
Theater (Creating a role) **T: 238**
Character [writing]

China (Languages) C: 481-482
Chinese language (Written Chinese) C: 509-510
  with pictures
Japanese language J: 61
Character borrowing
Chinese language (Written Chinese) C: 509-510
Character doll
Doll (Before World War I) D: 291
Character education [education] C: 377
Character generator [device]
Television (Adding special effects) T: 112
Character reading [pseudoscience]
Graphology G: 323
Characteristic [light pattern]
Lighthouse (Identifying lighthouses) L: 294
Characteristic [mathematics]
Logarithms (Common logarithms) L: 424
Characteristic piece
Classical music (Solo music) Ci: 643
Characteristic X rays
X rays (How X rays are produced) X: 542
Characterization [drama]
Theater (Creating a role) T: 238
Characters of Shakespeare's Plays [book by Hazlitt]
Hazlitt, William H: 123
Characters of Theophrastus, The [book by La Bruyère]
French literature (Classical prose) F: 520
La Bruyère, Jean de L: 19
Charbonneau, Toussaint [Canadian explorer]
Lewis and Clark expedition (Up the Missouri) L: 222a-222b
Sacagawea S: 4
Charcas [colony]
Bolivia (Colonial rule) B: 447
Charcoal C: 377
Barbecue B: 106
Carbon (Amorphous carbons) C: 205
Drawing *picture on* D: 344
Gas mask G: 60
Industrial Revolution (Early ironmaking) I: 249
Charcoal briquette
Charcoal (Uses of charcoal) C: 377
Charcot, Jean Martin [French doctor]
Freud, Sigmund (His life) F: 530
Hypnosis (Scientific studies) H: 480
Unconscious U: 20
Chard [plant]
Swiss chard So: 1049 *with picture*
Chardin, Jean Baptiste Siméon [French painter] C: 377
Chardonnet, Hilaire [French chemist]
Clothing (Clothing materials) Ci: 695
Chares [Greek sculptor]
Seven Wonders of the Ancient World (The Colossus of Rhodes) S: 325
Charest, Jean [Canadian political leader] C: 378
Campbell, Kim (Prime minister) C: 90d
Quebec (table) Q: 29; (Recent developments) Q: 33
Charge [furnace]
Furnace (Sources of heat) F: 567; (Heating the charge) F: 567
Iron and steel (The basic oxygen process [BOP]) I: 441; (The electric furnace process) I: 442-443
Charge [heraldry]
Heraldry (Elements of a coat of arms) H: 196 *with pictures*
Charge [materials]
Iron and steel (The blast furnace process) I: 440
Charge, Cavalry [military tactic]
Cavalry C: 318 *with picture*
Charge, Electric [physics] *See* Electric charge *in this index*
Charge account
Credit (Types of credit) Ci: 1124
Interest I: 320
Charge bargaining [law]
Plea bargaining P: 571
Charge carrier [physics] *See* Free electron *in this index*
Charge-coupled device [electronics] C: 378
Astronomy (Optical astronomy) A: 839-840
Camcorder (How a camcorder works) C: 75
Camera C: 80
Electronics (Light-sensing devices) E: 213
Hubble Space Telescope (How the telescope works) H: 403
Image orthicon I: 79
Photography (Capturing digital images) P: 420 *with picture*
Sun (Studying the sun) So: 982
Telescope T: 102; (Detecting faint objects) T: 103
Television *diagram on* T: 124; (Solid-state cameras) T: 122
Chargé d'affaires [diplomat]

Foreign Service (Beginnings) F: 388-388a
"Charge of the Light Brigade" [poem by Tennyson]
Balaklava, Battle of B: 34
Charge of the Rough Riders at San Juan Hill, The [painting by Remington]
Spanish-American War *picture on* So: 754
Charge to the jury [law]
Jury (Petit juries) J: 202
Trial (Presenting evidence) T: 436
Chargers, San Diego [team] *See* San Diego Chargers *in this index*
Charging [industrial process]
Iron and steel (The blast furnace process) I: 440
Charging grand jury
Grand jury G: 308
Chari River
Chad (Land and climate) C: 366-367 *with map*
Chariot [vehicle] C: 378
Army (Ancient armies) A: 726
Byzantine Empire *picture on* B: 753
Egypt, Ancient (Trade and transportation) E: 139
Hittites (Way of life) H: 269
Rome, Ancient (Recreation) R: 440 *with picture*
Transportation (The first great civilizations) T: 385-386 *with picture*
Charioteer of Delphi [sculpture]
Sculpture (Form and treatment) S: 230 *with picture*
Chariots of Fire [film]
Motion picture (Best picture: 1981) M: 861
Charismatic Christianity
Pentecostal churches (Major Pentecostal churches) P: 275
Religion (Religion today) R: 223
Charitable trust [economics]
Trust fund (Kinds of trusts) T: 474
Charitable Uses, Statute of [1601]
Philanthropy P: 368
Charity
Income tax (Income tax complexity) I: 103-104
Philanthropy P: 368
Charity Organization Society
Colorado (Interesting facts) Ci: 829
Social work (History) So: 559
United Way Worldwide U: 204
Charity School of Philadelphia [former name]
Pennsylvania, University of P: 269
Charivari [custom]
Folklore (Superstitions and customs) F: 324-325
Pioneer life in America (Social activities) P: 485
Charlemagne [Frankish emperor] C: 378 *with picture and map*
Aachen A: 2
Architecture (Carolingian architecture) A: 618
Austria (Early years) A: 936
Belgium (The Middle Ages) B: 232
Carolingian art C: 244
Europe (The Middle Ages) E: 409 *with map*
France (The Carolingian dynasty) F: 471 *with picture*
Franks F: 494
Germany (Kingdom of the Franks) G: 162
Holy Roman Empire H: 299
Italy (The Middle Ages) I: 513
Leo III, Saint L: 197
Middle Ages (The Carolingian Empire) M: 524
Mother Goose (Who was Mother Goose?) M: 842
Painting (Early medieval painting in the West) P: 48-49
Roland R: 401
Roman Catholic Church (Charlemagne) R: 407
Saxons S: 168
Sculpture (Medieval sculpture) S: 248
Tithe T: 301
Charles [prince of Wales] *See* Charles, Prince *in this index*
Charles [Scottish pretender]
Scotland (Union with England) S: 220
Charles I [emperor of Austria] C: 380
Charles I [king of England] C: 380
Buckingham, Duke of B: 663
Cromwell, Oliver (Rise to power) Ci: 1151
Divine right of kings D: 242
England (The first Stuarts) E: 308; (The Civil War) E: 308 *with picture*
James (James I) J: 25
Laud, William L: 121
London (War, plague, and fire) L: 441
Long Parliament L: 448
Maryland (Exploration and settlement) M: 256
Newfoundland and Labrador (Colonization) N: 375
North Carolina (Exploration and settlement) N: 490
Painting (Baroque) P: 58-61 *with picture*
Parliament (Parliament gains strength) P: 174

Petition of Right P: 327
Postal services (The creation of the Penny Post) P: 706
Pym, John P: 915
Rump Parliament R: 519
Scotland (War with the king) S: 220
South Carolina (Exploration and settlement) So: 659
Stuart, House of So: 931
Van Dyck, Sir Anthony V: 281
Whig Party W: 280
Charles I [king of Spain] *See* Charles V (Holy Roman emperor) *in this index*
Charles II [king of England] C: 380
Cabal C: 2
Cavalier King Charles spaniel C: 318
Clothing (The 1600's) Ci: 703
Dryden, John D: 370
England (The Restoration) E: 309
Gwyn, Nell G: 447
Hobbes, Thomas (His life) H: 272
Horse racing (History) H: 366
Long Parliament L: 448
Monck, George M: 701
Monmouth, Duke of M: 730
North Carolina (Exploration and settlement) N: 490
Nunavut (Arrival of the Europeans) N: 612
Penn, William (Founds Pennsylvania) P: 242
Pennsylvania (Exploration and settlement) P: 264
Restoration R: 263
Scotland (War with the king) S: 220
South Carolina (Exploration and settlement) So: 659
United States, History of the (The Middle Colonies) U: 154-155; (North Carolina, South Carolina, and Georgia) U: 156
Virginia (Royal governors and Cromwell) V: 418
Charles II [king of France] C: 380
Germany (The breakup of Charlemagne's empire) G: 162
Verdun, Treaty of V: 316
Charles II [king of Spain]
Succession wars (The War of the Spanish Succession) So: 950
Charles III [king of France] C: 380
Normans N: 456
Charles III [king of Spain] C: 380
Bourbon (In Naples and Sicily) B: 517
Mexico (Spanish rule) M: 469-470
Paraguay (Jesuit missionaries) P: 149
Charles IV [Holy Roman emperor]
Bohemia B: 437
Czech Republic (The rise of Bohemia) Ci: 1213
Luxembourg (History) L: 531
Prague (History) P: 730
Charles V [Holy Roman emperor; also Charles I of Spain] C: 381
Augsburg Confession A: 885
Austria (The Habsburgs) A: 937
Belgium (Habsburg rule) B: 233
Clement VII Ci: 662a
Cortés, Hernán (After the conquest) Ci: 1073
Exploration (Magellan's globe-circling expedition) E: 445
Francis I F: 480
Habsburg, House of H: 3
Holy Roman Empire (The House of Habsburg) H: 300
Italy (Spanish and Austrian rule) I: 514
Latin America (Protecting the Indians) L: 105
Magellan, Ferdinand (Planning the expedition) M: 46
Maximilian I M: 319
Mexico (Spanish rule) M: 469
Netherlands (Spanish control) N: 148
Reformation (Martin Luther) R: 149
Spain (The Spanish Empire) So: 747
William I, Prince of Orange W: 308
Charles V [king of France] C: 381
Bibliothèque Nationale de France B: 288
Charles VI [Holy Roman emperor]
Austria (Wars in the 1700's and 1800's) A: 937-938
Maria Theresa M: 199
Pragmatic sanction P: 729
Succession wars (The War of the Spanish Succession) So: 950; (The War of the Austrian Succession) So: 950
Charles VI [king of France]
Henry V [of England] H: 187
Henry VI [king of England] H: 187
Charles VII [Holy Roman emperor] C: 381
Charles VII [king of France] C: 381
Joan of Arc, Saint (Joan sees the king) J: 128
Louis XI L: 474
Charles VIII [king of France] C: 381

Italy (Rise of the city-states) I: 513-514
Charles IX [king of France] C: 381
  Catherine de Médicis C: 303
  Saint Bartholomew's Day, Massacre of S: 31
Charles X [king of France] C: 382
  France (The revolutions of 1830 and 1848) F: 474
  July Revolution J: 190
Charles X [king of Sweden] C: 382
Charles XI [king of Sweden] C: 382
Charles XII [king of Sweden] C: 382
  Sweden (The age of expansion) So: 1034
Charles XIII [king of Sweden]
  Norway (Union with Sweden) N: 545-546
Charles XIV [king of Sweden and Norway]
  Bernadotte, Jean Baptiste Jules B: 270
  Sweden (The Napoleonic Wars) So: 1034
Charles, Ezzard [American boxer]
  Boxing (Boxing's Golden Age) B: 532-532a
Charles, Jacques Alexandre César [French physicist]
  Airplane (First human flights) A: 230
  Balloon (The hydrogen balloon) B: 61
  Gas [physics] (Gas laws) G: 48-49
Charles, Nick and Nora [literary figures]
  Hammett, Dashiell H: 35
Charles, Prince [prince of Wales] C: 382 *with portrait*
  Diana, Princess of Wales D: 183
  Elizabeth II (The royal family) E: 240
  Prince of Wales P: 794
  William, Prince W: 309
Charles, Ray [American singer] C: 383 *with portrait*
Charles Albert [king of Sardinia]
  Italy (Italy united) I: 515
  Sardinia, Kingdom of S: 125
Charles Bent House
  Taos T: 36
Charles Bridge [Prague]
  Czech Republic *picture on* Ci: 1209
  Prague (The city) P: 730
Charles Center
  Baltimore (The city) B: 67
Charles de Gaulle Airport
  Airport (table) A: 245
Charles E. Merrill & Co.
  Merrill, Charles M: 418
Charles H. Wright Museum of African American History [Detroit] *See* Museum of African American History *in this index*
Charles Island
  Galapagos Islands G: 7 *with map*
Charles Martel [Frankish ruler] C: 383
  France (The Carolingian dynasty) F: 471
Charles Mound
  Illinois (Land regions) I: 64
Charles of Mecklenburg-Strelitz [father of]
  Louise of Mecklenburg-Strelitz L: 477
Charles Pinckney National Historic Site [South Carolina]
  National Park System (table: National historic sites) N: 52
Charles River [Massachusetts]
  Massachusetts *picture on* M: 281
Charles Robert [king of Hungary]
  Hungary (The Kingdom of Hungary) H: 445
Charles Sheldon Antelope Refuge
  Nevada (Plant and animal life) N: 168
Charles Stewart Mott Foundation *See* Mott Foundation *in this index*
Charles the Bald *See* Charles II [king of France] *in this index*
Charles the Bold [duke of Burgundy]
  France (A period of wars) F: 473
  Louis XI L: 474
Charles the Great *See* Charlemagne *in this index*
Charles the Simple *See* Charles III [king of France] *in this index*
Charles the Wise *See* Charles V [king of France] *in this index*
Charles Town [former name]
  Charleston (Government and history) C: 384
  Colonial life in America (Geographic divisions) Ci: 791
Charles Town [West Virginia]
  West Virginia (Places to visit) W: 216
Charles Towne [English settlement]
  Nassau N: 24
Charles Towne Landing [Charleston]
  Colonial life in America (Places to visit) Ci: 800
  South Carolina (Places to visit) So: 650
Charles University
  Czech Republic (Education) Ci: 1211
  Prague (The city) P: 730
Charles Wly Theatre
  Dallas (Cultural life) D: 14
Charlesbank Outdoor Gymnasium [Boston]
  Playground P: 571

Charles's law [chemistry]
  Gas [physics] (Gas laws) G: 48 *with pictures*
  Gay-Lussac, Joseph Louis G: 71
Charleston [former name]
  Lake Charles L: 36
Charleston [South Carolina] C: 383 *with picture*
  Revolution, American (Savannah and Charleston) R: 284
  South Carolina So: 640 *with picture, picture on* So: 661; (Population) So: 644 *with pictures*; (table: Average monthly weather) So: 654; (Exploration and settlement) So: 659
Charleston [West Virginia] C: 384
  West Virginia *picture on* W: 207; (table: Average monthly weather) W: 220
Charleston, College of
  Charleston (The city) C: 383
Charleston, Oscar [American baseball player]
  Baseball (table: Hall of Fame) B: 134
Charleston Library Society [U.S. history]
  Museum (Early United States museums) M: 939
Charleston Museum
  South Carolina (Museums) So: 645
Charlestown [former name]
  Lake Charles L: 36
Charlestown [Massachusetts]
  Boston (Charlestown) B: 500; (Early settlement) B: 503
Charleville, Charles [French explorer]
  Tennessee (Exploration) T: 153
Charley clown
  Clown Ci: 713
Charlie and the Chocolate Factory [book by Dahl]
  Dahl, Roald D: 5
Charlie Brown [cartoon character]
  Schulz, Charles Monroe S: 187 *with picture*
Charlie Brown [sculpture by Serra]
  Serra, Richard S: 318
Charlie Needs a Cloak [book by de Paola]
  DePaola, Tomie D: 148
Charlois, August H. P. [French astronomer]
  Eros E: 355
Charlotte [wife of George III]
  Charlotte C: 384
Charlotte [North Carolina] C: 384
  North Carolina *picture on* N: 473; (table: Monthly average weather) N: 486
Charlotte Amalie [Virgin Islands] C: 385
  Virgin Islands, United States *picture on* V: 396; (Government) V: 393-394 *with picture*; (Islands) V: 395; (Clothing and architecture) V: 395
Charlotte Bobcats [team]
  Basketball (table) B: 150
  Jordan, Micheal (Life and career) J: 166
Charlotte/Douglas International Airport
  Airport (table) A: 245
Charlotte Observer [newspaper]
  North Carolina (Communication) N: 489
Charlotte's Web [book by White]
  Literature for children *picture on* L: 363
  White, E. B. W: 284
Charlottesville [Virginia] C: 385
  Jefferson, Thomas *picture on* J: 78
Charlottetown [Prince Edward Island] C: 385
  Prince Edward Island P: 782 *with picture*; (Visitor's guide) P: 788 *with picture*; (table: Average monthly weather) P: 790a
Charlottetown accord [Canadian history]
  Campbell, Kim (The 1993 election) C: 90d
  Canada, History of (The constitutional crisis) C: 151
  Chrétien, Jean (Election as party leader) C: 522c
  Trudeau, Pierre Elliott (Later years) T: 465
Charlottetown Conference [1864]
  Canada, History of (Confederation) C: 144
  Confederation of Canada (Moves toward confederation) Ci: 933 *with picture*
  Prince Edward Island *picture on* P: 792
Charm [magic]
  Amulet A: 445
  Evil eye E: 426
  Fetish F: 81
  Magic *picture on* M: 50; (Magical objects) M: 49
  Witchcraft (Witchcraft as sorcery) W: 371
Charm [physics]
  Psi particle P: 844
  Quark Q: 7
  Subatomic particle (Elementary particles) So: 937; (Theoretical research) So: 938
Charmides
  Plato (Plato's life) P: 567
Charmides [book by Plato]
  Plato (The early dialogues) P: 568; (The theory of forms) P: 568
Charolais [breed]
  Cattle (Charolais) C: 308 *with picture*; (table) C: 312

Charon [Greek mythology]
  Hades H: 4
Charon [satellite]
  Naval Observatory, United States N: 70
  Planet (Pluto) P: 512
  Pluto P: 581
  Satellite (Physical characteristics) S: 149; (Nonplanetary satellites) S: 150c
Charpak, Georges [French physicist]
  Nobel Prizes (Physics: 1992) N: 442
  Particle detector (Tracking chambers) P: 187
Charro suit
  Mexico (Clothing) M: 456-457
Charrúa Indians
  Uruguay (Early days) U: 227
Chart
  Graph (Circle graphs) G: 322 *with picture*
  Map (Navigation maps) M: 178
  Navigation (Traditional navigation) N: 70
Charter [document] C: 385
  Charter school C: 386
  Colonial life in America (Economic reasons) Ci: 788; (Changes in colonial control) Ci: 790-791
  Constitution Ci: 994
  Magna Carta M: 52
Charter flight
  Aviation (Airline operations) A: 984-985
Charter Oak [U.S. history]
  Connecticut (Defending the colony) Ci: 970
Charter of ...
  Charters appear under their key words, as in Privileges, Charter of
Charter school C: 386
  Alberta (Schools) A: 317
  Education (Control and support of U.S. education) E: 94
  School (Growth and reform) S: 184
  Washington, D.C. (Education) W: 81
Chartered accountant
  Accounting (Fields of accounting) A: 23
Chartered bank
  Bank (Canada) B: 92
Chartered colony
  United States, History of the (The American Colonies [1607-1753]) U: 152-153
Chartered Life Underwriter
  Insurance (Careers in the industry) I: 315
Chartered Property Casualty Underwriter
  Insurance (Careers in the industry) I: 315
Charterhouse [British secondary school]
  School (British secondary school) C: 386
Charterhouse of Parma, The [book by Stendhal]
  Stendhal So: 889
Chartism [British history] C: 386
  Carlyle, Thomas (Later career) C: 240
Chartres [France] C: 386
Chartres Cathedral [France] C: 386 *with picture*
  Chartres C: 386
  Europe *picture on* E: 392
  Stained glass (Technical improvements) So: 823
Chartreuse [drink]
  Carthusians C: 261
Chartreux [cat]
  Cat (Short-haired breeds) C: 290
Chartwell Manor [estate]
  Churchill, Sir Winston Leonard Spencer (Leader of the opposition) C: 549
Charybdis [whirlpool, Mediterranean]
  Scylla S: 261
  Whirlpool W: 281
Chase, Ira Joy [American political leader]
  Indiana (table) I: 214
Chase, Martha [American dollmaker]
  Doll (Cloth dolls) D: 289
Chase, Salmon Portland [American jurist] C: 387
  Emancipation Proclamation *picture on* E: 254
  Free Soil Party F: 499
  Lincoln, Abraham (Election of 1860) L: 318; (First inauguration) L: 320; (table) L: 323
  Ohio (table) O: 699
Chase, Samuel [American jurist] C: 387
  Impeachment (History) I: 91
  Jefferson, Thomas (The courts) J: 84
Chase, William Merritt [American painter] C: 387 *with picture*
Chase Manhattan Bank
  JPMorgan Chase & Co. J: 177
Chase National Bank
  JPMorgan Chase & Co. J: 177
Chasing [engraving]
  Islamic art (Metalware) I: 469
Chasm [geology]
  Canyon C: 185
Chassis
  Automobile *diagrams on* A: 957
Chastisements, The [poems by Hugo]
  Hugo, Victor (Exile and return) H: 410; (His works)

H: 410
Chasuble [vestment]
Pope *picture on* P: 661
Chat [bird]
Thrush T: 271
Chat room [computing]
Computer (The Internet) Ci: 920-921
Chat-thrush [bird]
Thrush T: 271
Château [architecture]
Architecture (Later Renaissance architecture)
A: 621 *with picture*
France (Architecture) F: 463 *with picture*
Chateau De Mores
North Dakota (Places to visit) N: 504
Château Frontenac [hotel, Quebec City]
Quebec Q: 34 *with picture*
Château Queyras [castle]
Castle *picture on* C: 280
Château Ramezay Museum
Montreal (Museums) M: 773
Quebec (Museums) Q: 15
Château-Thierry, Battle of [1918]
World War I (The last campaigns) W: 463
Chateaubriand, François-René de [French author]
C: 387
French literature (The Preromantics) F: 521
Chateaubriand and His Literary Circle [book by
Sainte-Beuve]
Sainte-Beuve, Charles Augustin S: 58
Châtelet, Marquise du [French author] C: 388
Voltaire (Exile and return to France) V: 446
Chatham, Earl of *See* Pitt, William *in this index*
Chatham Island
Galapagos Islands G: 7 *with map*
Chatham Islands
New Zealand (Other islands) N: 352
Chatham Lake [New Brunswick]
New Brunswick (Interesting facts) N: 181 *with
picture*
Chatoyant effect
Cat's-eye C: 305
Chatsky [literary figure]
Russian literature (Early Romanticism) R: 560-561
Chattahoochee River [Alabama-Georgia]
Alabama (Rivers and lakes) A: 270
Chattahoochee River National Recreation Area
[Georgia]
National Park System (table: National recreation
areas) N: 49
Chattanooga [Tennessee] C: 388
Chattanooga, Battle of [1863]
Civil War, American (table) Ci: 624; (Battle of
Chattanooga) Ci: 630
Chattel [law]
Real estate R: 171
Chatterjee, Bankim Chandra [Indian author]
India (Literature) I: 120
Chatterji, Saratchandra [Indian author]
India (Literature) I: 120
Chatterton [play by Musset]
French literature (Romantic drama) F: 521
Chatterton, Fenimore [American political leader]
Wyoming (table) W: 532
Chattopadhyaya, Saratcandra [Indian author]
India (Literature) I: 120
Chaubunagungamaug, Lake [Massachusetts]
Massachusetts (Rivers and lakes) M: 284-285
Chaucer, Geoffrey [English poet] C: 388
Book *picture on* B: 464
Canterbury Tales C: 183
English literature (The age of Chaucer) E: 316
Folklore (Folk tales) F: 323-324
Language (Language change) L: 64
Manuscript *picture on* M: 173
Valentine, Saint V: 260
Chaudhry, Mahendra [Fijian political leader]
Fiji (History) F: 98-99
Chaudière Falls [falls, Canada]
Ottawa River O: 875
Chaudière River [river, Quebec]
Quebec (Rivers, waterfalls, and lakes) Q: 24
Chautauqua [education] C: 389
Adult education (History of adult education in
the United States) A: 69
Lyceum L: 532
Chautauqua Institution, The [education]
Chautauqua (The Chautauqua Institution) C: 389
New York (Lakes) N: 306-307
Chautauqua Lake
New York (Lakes) N: 306-307
Chautauqua Literary and Scientific Circle, The
[education]
Chautauqua (The Chautauqua Literary and
Scientific Circle) C: 389
Chautauqua Sunday School Assembly [1874]
Woman's Christian Temperance Union W: 382

Chauveau, Pierre-J.-O. [Canadian political leader]
Quebec (table) Q: 29; (Early years as a province)
Q: 30
Chauvet Cave [France]
Prehistoric people *picture on* P: 753
Chauvin, Yves [French chemist]
Nobel Prizes (Chemistry: 2005) N: 444
Chauvinism [attitude]
Patriotism (Abuses of patriotism) P: 198
Chaves, Federico [Paraguayan political leader]
Paraguay (Political unrest) P: 150
Chávez, Carlos [Mexican composer] C: 389
Chavez, Cesar Estrada [American labor leader]
C: 389 *with portrait*
Hispanic Americans (The Chicano movement)
H: 256 *with picture*
Huerta, Dolores Fernandez H: 408
Labor movement (New groups become
unionized) L: 14 *with picture*
Migrant labor M: 538
United Farm Workers of America U: 47
Chavez, Dennis [American political leader] C: 390
Chávez, Federico [Paraguayan political leader]
Paraguay (Political unrest) P: 149
Chávez, Julio César [Mexican boxer]
Boxing *picture on* B: 532b
Chávez Frías, Hugo [Venezuelan political leader]
C: 389
Latin America (In the early 2000's) L: 111
Venezuela (The late 1900's) V: 305; (Recent
developments) V: 305
Chavín de Huantar [ancient city, Peru]
Indian, American (Indians of the Andes) I: 173
Chavín Indians
Indian, American (Indians of the Andes) I: 173
Peru (History) P: 314
Sculpture (Early sculpture) S: 242 *with picture*
Chawla, Kalpana [American astronaut]
Columbia disaster Ci: 852
Space exploration (The Columbia disaster)
So: 725
Chayote [plant] C: 390 *with picture*
"Che mi frena" [aria]
Opera: (*Lucia di Lammermoor*) O: 804
Cheaha Mountain
Alabama (Land regions) A: 268
Cheaha Mountain State Park [Anniston]
Alabama *picture on* A: 256
Cheap money [U.S. history]
Hayes, Rutherford Birchard (Money problems)
H: 121
Cheboi, Kiptalam [Kenyan anthropologist]
Prehistoric people (table) P: 754
Chechen-Ingush Autonomous Republic [former
name]
Chechnya C: 390
Chechnya [republic, Russia] C: 390 *with map*
Moscow (Recent developments) M: 827
Putin, Vladimir Vladimirovich P: 912
Russia (The new nation) R: 555; (The rise of Putin)
R: 555; (Recent developments) R: 555
Terrorism (Recent developments) T: 180
Check [banking] C: 390
Bank (Providing a means of payment) B: 89
Forgery F: 408
Money (The money supply) M: 715
Negotiable instrument (Forms) N: 119
Check [chess]
Chess (How chess is played) C: 413
Check [hockey]
Hockey (Hockey skills) H: 276-277
Check [manufacturing]
Glass (Glass terms) G: 222
Check, Traveler's *See* Traveler's check *in this index*
Check digit [number]
International standard book number I: 347
Checkbook
Check (How the checking system works) C: 390
Checkbook money [economics]
Check (Checks and the economy) C: 391
Checker chamber [industry]
Iron and steel (The open-hearth process) I: 443-
444 *with diagram*
Checkerboard
Checkers (The) C: 391
Checkered lily [plant]
Fritillary F: 535
Checkering [decoration]
Rifle (The parts of a rifle) R: 338
Checkers [game] C: 391
"Checkers speech" [U.S. history]
Nixon, Richard Milhous (The 1952 campaign)
N: 430-431
Checkerspot [butterfly]
Butterfly (Brush-footed butterflies) B: 736
Checking account
Bank (Providing a means of payment) B: 89

Check C: 390
Checkmate
Chess C: 411
Checkoff agreement
Labor movement (Arranging contracts) L: 4-5
Checkpoint Charlie [Berlin]
Cold War *picture on* Ci: 767
Checks and balances C: 391
Democracy (Controls on power) D: 121
Freedom (Limits on political freedom) F: 502
Government (Presidential democracy) G: 285
United States, Government of the (Separation of
powers) U: 137
Cheddar cheese
Cheese (Hard cheese) C: 392 *with picture*;
(Treating the curd) C: 393
Cheddaring [process]
Cheese (Treating the curd) C: 393
Chee, Jim [literary figure]
Hillerman, Tony H: 232
Cheekbone [anatomy]
Human body (table) H: 422 *with diagram*
Cheerleading C: 392
Cheese [food] C: 392 *with pictures*
Casein C: 272
Cattle (Brown Swiss) C: 311
Dairying D: 6
Netherlands (Manufacturing) N: 146
Nutrition (Proteins) N: 625
South Dakota *picture on* So: 677
Wisconsin *picture on* W: 363
Cheetah [animal] C: 395 *with picture*
Animal *picture on* A: 472
Endangered species (table) E: 270
Taxidermy *pictures on* T: 55
Cheever, Eddie [American race driver]
Automobile racing (table: Indianapolis 500
winners) A: 980
Cheever, John [American author] C: 395
Chef [occupation]
Careers (Tourism and hospitality) C: 233-234
with picture
Chef's knife
Knife (Types of knives) K: 345 *with picture*
Cheju Island [North Korea]
Korea, South (The land) K: 378-378a *with map*
Chek Lap Kok [island]
Hong Kong (The land) H: 318
Cheka [Russian history]
Communism (Under Lenin) Ci: 892
Lenin, V. I. (Rule by terror) L: 194
Russian Revolution of 1917 (The October
Revolution) R: 566
Stalin, Joseph (Rule by terror) So: 826
Chekhov, Anton [Russian author] C: 395
Drama (Russian drama and Chekhov) D: 338
Moscow Art Theater M: 828
Realism (In drama) R: 172
Russian literature (Late realism) R: 562-563
Short story S: 434
Chela [claw]
Crab Ci: 1115
Fiddler crab F: 91 *with picture*
Chelation therapy [medicine] C: 396
Chelicera [zoology]
Spider (Chelicerae) So: 784 *with pictures*
Chelmno [concentration camp]
Concentration camp (Nazi concentration camps)
Ci: 926-927
Chelsea [district] *See* Kensington and Chelsea *in
this index*
Cheltenham Festival
United Kingdom (The arts) U: 58
Chemical C: 396
Occupational medicine O: 647
Chemical agent *See* Chemical weapon *in this index*
Chemical-biological-radiological warfare C: 396
Anthrax A: 545
Army, United States (Logistic units) A: 735
Biological Weapons Convention B: 315
Chemical Weapons Convention C: 397
World War I (Trench warfare) W: 457-458 *with
picture*
Chemical bomb [weapon]
Bomb (Other bombs) B: 451
Chemical bond *See* Bond *in this index*
Chemical bonding [process]
Textile (Nonwovens) T: 215
Chemical burn
Burn (First-aid care) B: 708
First aid (Burns) F: 138-139
Chemical change
Chemistry C: 398
Electrochemistry E: 199
Oxidation O: 888
Senses (Internal senses) S: 302
Chemical compound

Chemistry (Fundamental ideas of chemistry)
C: 398-399
Chemical culture [agriculture] *See* Hydroponics
in this index
Chemical decomposition
Soil (How soil forms) So: 573
Chemical element *See* Element, Chemical *in this
index*
Chemical energy
Electrochemistry E: 199
Energy supply (Chemical energy) E: 279
Chemical engineering
Engineering (Chemical engineering) E: 285 *with
picture*
Chemical formula
Chemical reaction C: 397
Chemical equilibrium *See* Equilibrium, Chemical
in this index
Chemical evolution
Life (Modern explanations) L: 278-279 *with
diagram*
Chemical formula
Berzelius, Jöns Jakob B: 273
Chemical fuel
Fuel (Chemical fuels) F: 551
Chemical grenade [weapon]
Grenade G: 350
"Chemical History of a Candle, The" [lecture]
Faraday, Michael F: 27
Chemical industry C: 397
Chemistry (The chemical industry) C: 405
Drug (Chemical laboratories) D: 354
Forest products (Chemical products) F: 402 *with
pictures*
Petrochemicals P: 329
Chemical machining
Machine tool (Chemical machining) M: 19
Chemical oceanography
Ocean (Careers in oceanography) O: 666
Oceanography O: 667
Water (Fresh water from the sea) W: 127
Chemical properties
Materials (Chemical properties) M: 300b
Chemical reaction C: 397 *with diagram*
Catalysis C: 297
Cell (Inside a living cell) C: 328
Combustion Ci: 866
Compound C: 906
Electrolysis E: 200
Equilibrium, Chemical E: 347
Heat (Sources of heat) H: 149
Nuclear weapon (How nuclear weapons work)
N: 596
Oxidation O: 888
Photochemistry P: 404
Chemical rocket
Rocket R: 384
Chemical sediment [geology]
Earth (Sedimentary rocks) E: 21
Rock (Chemical sediments) R: 372
Chemical Society, American
American Chemical Society A: 408
Chemical symbol
Berzelius, Jöns Jakob B: 273
Element, Chemical (Names and symbols of
elements) E: 219; (table) E: 219
Chemical weapon
Arms control (History of arms control) A: 721-722
Chemical-biological-radiological warfare
(Chemical) C: 396
Chemical Weapons Convention C: 397
Civil defense (Focus on terrorism) Ci: 606
Gulf War syndrome G: 438
Peace (Arms control) P: 207
Technology (Challenges of technology) T: 77
Terrorism (Chemical attacks) T: 176 *with picture*
Weapon (World War I) W: 154b
Chemical Weapons Convention [1997] C: 397
Chemins du Roi, Les [Canadian history]
Quebec (Transportation) Q: 28
Chemise [garment]
Clothing (The Renaissance) Ci: 702-703
Chemisorption [physics]
Absorption and adsorption (Adsorption) A: 18
Chemistry C: 398 *with pictures*
See also the list of Related articles in the Chemistry
article
Careers (Life, physical, and social sciences)
C: 225-226
Element, Chemical E: 219
Inorganic chemistry I: 276
Metric system (Chemistry) M: 440
Science (The physical sciences) S: 193; (The
Enlightenment) S: 199
Chemnitz [Germany] C: 407
Chemoreceptor [anatomy]
Hunger H: 449

Respiration (Control of breathing) R: 261
Senses (Internal senses) S: 302
Chemosterilant
Insecticide I: 301
Chemosynthesis [biology]
Deep sea (Environment) D: 82-82a
Hydrothermal vent H: 473
Ocean (The food cycle) O: 655-658
Chemotherapy [medicine] C: 407
AIDS (Treatment) A: 164b-165
Breast cancer B: 591
Cancer (Drug therapy) C: 172
Cervical cancer C: 364
Colon cancer Ci: 786
Drug (The drug revolution) D: 359
Immune system (Other problems) I: 88d
Leukemia (Acute leukemias) L: 215
Lung cancer L: 525
Ovarian cancer O: 881
Ch'en Jung *See* Chen Rong *in this index*
Chen Rong [Chinese painter] C: 407
Chen Shui-bian [Taiwanese political leader]
Taiwan (History) T: 17-18
Cheney, Amy Marcy [birth name of]
Beach, Amy B: 178
Cheney, Dick [American political leader] *See*
Cheney, Richard Bruce *in this index*
Cheney, Lynne Ann Vincent [wife of Richard
Cheney]
Cheney, Richard Bruce (Early life) C: 407
Cheney, Person C. [American political leader]
New Hampshire (table) N: 223
Cheney, Richard Bruce [American political leader]
C: 407 *with portrait*
Bush, George Walker (The campaign) B: 722f
with picture
Vice president of the United States (Growth of
the vice presidency) V: 353-354
Wyoming (Recent developments) W: 537
Cheng He [Chinese explorer] *See* Zheng He *in this
index*
Ch'eng-tu [China] *See* Chengdu *in this index*
Chengdu [China] C: 408
China pictures on C: 474, C: 499
Chengtu [China] *See* Chengdu *in this index*
Chénier, André [French poet]
French literature (The Preromantics) F: 521
Chenille [textile] C: 408
Chenla [former kingdom]
Cambodia (History) C: 72
Chennai [India] C: 408
India picture on I: 120
Chennault, Claire Lee [American aviator] C: 408
Flying Tigers F: 312
World War II (China) W: 492
Chenonceaux [France]
France picture on F: 462
Cheops [king of ancient Egypt] *See* Khufu *in this
index*
Cheque *See* Check *in this index*
Chequy [symbol]
Heraldry picture on H: 195
Cher [American actress]
Motion picture (Best performance by an actress:
1987) M: 862a
Cherbourg [France] C: 408
Cherbourg-Octeville [region, France] C: 408
Cherenkov, Pavel Alekseyevich [Russian physicist]
Nobel Prizes (Physics: 1958) N: 441
Cherimoya [tree] C: 408
Chermayeff, Serge [architect]
Mendelsohn, Eric M: 399
Chernobyl disaster C: 408
Belarus (History) B: 224b-224c
Cancer (Radiation) C: 170
Fallout (History) F: 19 *with map*
Nuclear energy (Safety concerns) N: 591-592
with picture
Radiation (Dose) R: 79-80 *with picture*
Ukraine (The Chernobyl disaster) U: 13
Chernomyrdin, Viktor Stepanovich [Russian
political leader]
Yeltsin, Boris Nikolayevich Y: 561
Chernozem [earth]
Prairie (Climate and soil) P: 731
Russia (Land regions) R: 539; (Agriculture)
R: 544-545
Cherokee Advocate [newspaper]
Oklahoma (Communication) O: 730
Cherokee Heritage Center [Oklahoma]
Oklahoma (Places to visit) O: 722
Cherokee Indian Reservation
North Carolina (Places to visit) N: 482
Cherokee Indians C: 409 *with picture*
Georgia (Early statehood) G: 132
Indian, American (Writing) I: 150; (Indians of the
Southeast) I: 157

Indian Territory I: 189 *with map*
Jackson, Andrew (The Indian issue) J: 13
Oklahoma (Schools) O: 716
Ross, John R: 482
Sequoyah S: 312
Trail of Tears T: 367 *with map*
United States, History of the (The Indian removal)
U: 172 *with picture*
Cherokee Mounted Rifles [U.S. history]
Watie, Stand W: 147
Cherokee Nation
Cherokee Indians C: 409
Cherokee Nation v. Georgia [U.S. history]
Jackson, Andrew (The Indian issue) J: 13
Cherokee Trail [Wyoming]
Wyoming (The great trails) W: 533-534
Cherokee Trail of Tears, 1838, The [painting by
Janes]
Cherokee Indians picture on C: 409
Cherry [bowling]
Bowling (table) B: 521
Cherry [fruit] C: 409 *with pictures*
Fruit (Simple fruits) F: 544 *with picture*
Tanager T: 24
Tree pictures on T: 417, T: 421
Wood picture on W: 389
Cherry, Francis [American political leader]
Arkansas (table) A: 712
Cherry, R. Gregg [American political leader]
North Carolina (table) N: 490
Cherry birch [tree]
Birch (Sweet birch) B: 327
Cherry laurel [shrub] C: 410 *with picture*
Laurel L: 121
Cherry Orchard, The [play by Chekhov]
Chekhov, Anton C: 395
Cherry pepper [plant]
Pepper P: 278
Cherry picker [machine]
Cherry picture on C: 410
Cherry salmon
Salmon picture on S: 69; (Kinds of salmon) S: 70
Chersiphron [Greek architect]
Seven Wonders of the Ancient World (The Temple
of Artemis at Ephesus) S: 325
Chert [rock]
Flint F: 236
Quartz (Types) Q: 8
Taconite T: 5
Chertoff, Michael [American government official]
Bush, George Walker (table) B: 722h
Homeland Security, Department of (table) H: 301
Cherubini, Luigi [Italian composer] C: 410
Bell (Uses of bells) B: 239
Chervenkov, Vulko [Bulgarian political leader]
Bulgaria (Communist rule) B: 693
Chesapeake [ship]
Barron, James B: 119
Jefferson, Thomas (The struggle for neutrality)
J: 86-87
Lawrence, James L: 146
War of 1812 (Impressment of seamen) W: 29
Chesapeake and Delaware Canal [waterway]
Canal (table) C: 164
Delaware (Transportation) D: 108
Chesapeake and Ohio Canal [waterway] C: 411
**Chesapeake and Ohio Canal National Historical
Park**
National Park System (table: National historical
parks) N: 56
Chesapeake Bay C: 411 *with map*
Maryland D: 240 *with picture*; (Coastline) M: 252
Virginia (Pollution problems) V: 422
Chesapeake Bay Bridge-Tunnel [Virginia]
Bridge (table: Combination) B: 603
Chesapeake Bay Maritime Museum [Maryland]
Maryland (Places to visit) M: 248
Chesapeake Bay retriever [dog] C: 411 *with
picture*
Dog pictures on D: 268, D: 277
Chesapeake Colonies
Colonial life in America picture on Ci: 792;
(Geographic divisions) Ci: 791 *with map*
Revolution, American (Fighting in the
Chesapeake and Southern colonies) R: 276
Chesbro, Jack [American baseball player]
Baseball (table: Hall of Fame) B: 134; (table:
Modern major league records) B: 138
Cheshire Cat [fictional animal]
Carroll, Lewis (The *Alice* books) C: 249
Chesnutt, Charles Waddell [American author]
C: 411
African American literature (The 1800's) A: 136a
American literature (Realists) A: 419
Chess [game] C: 411 *with pictures*
Chess Records [company]
Rock music (Sun Records) R: 376

Chest [anatomy] C: 414
  Cardiopulmonary resuscitation C: 213
  Diaphragm D: 184
  Lung (Parts of the lungs) L: 523
  Pleura P: 573
Chest [furniture]
  Furniture (The Middle Ages) F: 571 *with picture*
Chest protector
  Baseball (Equipment) B: 125 *with picture*
Chest X ray
  X rays *picture on* X: 540
Chester White [breed]
  Hog (Kinds of hogs) H: 285 *with picture*; (table) H: 286
Chesterfield, Earl of [British author] C: 415
Chesterton, G. K. [British author] C: 415
  Belloc, Hilaire B: 244
  Detective story (The pattern) D: 162
Chestnut [tree] C: 415 *with pictures*
  Fruit (Simple fruits) F: 544 *with picture*
  Nut (Kinds of nuts) N: 621
  Tree *pictures on* T: 421, T: 426
Chestnut, Water [plant]
  Water chestnut W: 134
Chestnut beetle [insect]
  Beetle *picture on* B: 218
Chestnut blight [plant disease]
  Chestnut C: 415
  Fungicide F: 560
  Invasive species (How invasive species affect habitats) I: 354j-354k
Chestnut-collared longspur [bird]
  Bird *picture on* B: 415
Chesuncook Lake [Maine]
  Penobscot River P: 271
Chet [letter]
  H H: 1 *with picture*
Chetniks [soldiers]
  Serbia (World War II) S: 315-316
  Yugoslavia (World War II) Y: 576
Chettle, Henry [English author]
  Shakespeare, William (Early career in London) S: 347
Chetumal [city, Mexico]
  Quintana Roo Q: 43
Cheves, Langdon [American banker]
  Bank of the United States (The Second Bank of the United States) B: 96
Cheviot and Leicester [breed]
  Sheep *picture on* S: 380
Cheviot Hills [United Kingdom]
  United Kingdom (The Southern Uplands) U: 59 *with map*
Chevon [food]
  Goat (Products) G: 239
Chevrolet [automobile]
  Automobile *pictures on* A: 966, A: 967; (The growth of government regulation) A: 971
  Plastics (Growth of the plastics industry) P: 560
  Sports car *picture on* So: 803
Chevrolet, Arthur [American businessman]
  Chevrolet, Louis C: 415
Chevrolet, Gaston [American race driver]
  Automobile racing (table: Indianapolis 500 winners) A: 980
Chevrolet, Louis [American businessman] C: 415
Chevrolet Brothers Aircraft Company
  Chevrolet, Louis C: 415
Chevrolet Motor Company
  Chevrolet, Louis C: 415
  Durant, William Crapo D: 388
Chevron [architecture]
  Chevron C: 416
Chevron [emblem] C: 416
  Heraldry *picture on* H: 195
  Insignia I: 303
Chevron Texaco Corporation [company]
  Manufacturing (table) M: 170
  Standard Oil Company So: 834
Chevrotain [animal]
  Animal *picture on* A: 481
Chevy Volt [car]
  Electric car (History) E: 165-166
Chewing *See* Mastication *in this index*
Chewing gum C: 416 *with diagrams*
  Chicle C: 446
  Gum G: 440
Chewing louse [insect]
  Louse L: 507
Chewing tobacco
  Smoking S: 520
  Tobacco T: 305
Cheyenne [Wyoming] C: 417 *with picture*
  Wyoming W: 517 *with picture*; (Population) W: 520; (Schools) W: 520; (table: Average monthly weather) W: 528
Cheyenne, The [sculpture by Remington]

  Sculpture (American sculpture) S: 255-256 *with picture*
Cheyenne Frontier Days [festival]
  Cheyenne *picture on* C: 418; (Description) C: 417
  Wyoming *picture on* W: 517; (Visitor's guide) W: 524 *with pictures*
Cheyenne Indians C: 417 *with picture*
  Indian, American *pictures on* I: 161; (Indians of the Plains) I: 158-159
  Indian wars (Wars on the Plains) I: 192
  Little Bighorn, Battle of the L: 391
  Poetry (Rhythm and meter) P: 591-592
  South Dakota (Early days) So: 681
Cheyenne River
  South Dakota (Rivers and lakes) So: 676 *with map*
Chhattisgarh [state, India]
  India (Recent developments) I: 134
Chi [force]
  T'ai chi chuan T: 14
Chi [letter]
  X X: 539 *with picture*
Chiang Ch'ing *See* Jiang Qing *in this index*
Chiang Ching-kuo [Chinese government official] C: 418
  Taiwan (History) T: 17-18
Chiang Kai-shek [Chinese political leader] C: 418 *with portrait*
  Acheson, Dean Gooderham A: 26
  Beijing (History) B: 223-224
  Chiang Soong Mei-ling C: 419
  China (History) C: 499-504
  Cold War (Communist expansion in Asia) Ci: 764
  Mao Zedong (His life) M: 174
  Roosevelt, Franklin Delano (The Big Three) R: 457
  Sino-Japanese War of 1937-1945 S: 474
  Sun Yat-sen (His later efforts) So: 989
  Taiwan T: 15; (History) T: 17-18
  World War II (China) W: 492
Chiang Mai [Thailand] C: 419
  Thailand (History) T: 226
Chiang Soong Mei-ling [Chinese public figure] C: 419 *with portrait*
  Chiang Kai-shek (Nationalist victory) C: 418
Chianti [wine]
  Wine (Wines from Italy) W: 337
Chiao [money]
  Yuan Y: 575
Chiao Chih [Vietnamese history]
  Indochina (The Viets) I: 224-225
Chiapas [state, Mexico] C: 419
  Indian, American (Current issues) I: 182-183
  Mexico (Opposition to the PRI) M: 474
Chiaroscuro [painting]
  Gentileschi, Artemisia G: 90
  Leonardo da Vinci (Paintings) L: 200b
  Painting (The 1600's and 1700's) P: 58-59
Chiaroscuro woodcut [art]
  Cranach, Lucas, the Elder Ci: 1116
Chibcha Indians C: 419
  Colombia *picture on* Ci: 781; (Early days) Ci: 783
  El Dorado E: 157
  Indian, American (Indians of the Caribbean) I: 172
Chicago [Illinois] C: 420 *with pictures and maps*
  Architecture (Early modern architecture in America) A: 629 *with picture*
  Burnham, Daniel Hudson B: 709 *with picture*
  Chicago Fire C: 438
  City (The people) Ci: 586
  Daley, Richard Joseph D: 9
  Du Sable, Jean Baptiste Point D: 390
  Geography *map on* G: 93
  Hispanic Americans (Where Hispanic Americans live) H: 246
  Illinois (Visitor's guide) I: 62 *with pictures*; (table: Average monthly weather) I: 66
  King, Martin Luther, Jr. (The Chicago campaign) K: 322
  Thompson, William Hale T: 264
  Water (How Chicago treats its water) W: 124 *with pictures*
Chicago [film]
  Motion picture (Best picture: 2002) M: 861
"Chicago" [poem by Sandburg]
  Sandburg, Carl (His poetry) S: 108
Chicago, Judy [American artist] C: 437
  Sculpture (As a record of history) S: 228-229 *with picture*; (From the mid-1900's to the early 2000's) S: 259-260
Chicago, University of C: 437
  Argonne National Laboratory A: 660
  Illinois *picture on* I: 73
  Nuclear energy (The development of nuclear weapons) N: 590-591 *with picture*
  Yerkes Observatory Y: 565
Chicago Avenue Pumping Station [Chicago]
  Chicago Fire C: 438

Chicago Bears [team]
  Football (National Football League) F: 364
  Halas, George Stanley H: 17
Chicago Blackhawks [team] *See* Blackhawks, Chicago *in this index*
Chicago Board of Trade
  See also CME Group *in this index*
  Chicago (Places to visit) C: 430; (Growth as a city) C: 434-435
  Wheat (Buying and selling wheat) W: 274
Chicago Bulls [team]
  Basketball (table) B: 150
  Jordan, Michael J: 166
  Rose, Derrick R: 476
Chicago Cubs [team]
  Baseball (table) B: 130
Chicago Defender [newspaper]
  Abbott, Robert Sengstacke A: 6
  Chicago (Communications) C: 433
Chicago Drainage Canal *See* Chicago Sanitary and Ship Canal *in this index*
Chicago Fire [1871] C: 438
  Architecture (Early modern architecture in Chicago) A: 629
  Chicago (The Great Chicago Fire) C: 435 *with picture*
  Illinois *picture on* I: 73
Chicago History Museum
  Chicago (Museums) C: 428-429
Chicago Mercantile Exchange *See* CME group *in this index*
Chicago Natural History Museum *See* Field Museum *in this index*
Chicago Picasso, The [sculpture by Picasso]
  Chicago (Places to visit) C: 430-431 *with picture*
Chicago Public Library
  Chicago (Libraries) C: 430
Chicago riots [1968]
  Chicago (The mid-1900's) C: 436
  Riot (During the 1900's) R: 349
Chicago River [Illinois]
  Chicago (The city) C: 420; (Dealing with aging infrastructure) C: 437
  Chicago Sanitary and Ship Canal C: 438
  Great Lakes (Drainage) G: 344
Chicago Sanitary and Ship Canal C: 438
  Canal (Major canals in the United States and Canada) C: 164; (table) C: 164
  Chicago (The city) C: 420; (The West Side) C: 424; (Trade) C: 432
  Great Lakes (Drainage) G: 344; (Water routes to the sea) G: 344
  Illinois (Industrial development) I: 74-75
Chicago School [architecture]
  Architecture *picture on* A: 630; (Early modern architecture in America) A: 629
  Burnham, Daniel Hudson B: 709
  Chicago (Architecture) C: 428
  Root, John Wellborn R: 472
  Sullivan, Louis Henri So: 970
Chicago School [literature]
  Sandburg, Carl S: 108
Chicago Stock Exchange [Chicago]
  Chicago (Finance) C: 433
Chicago Strike *See* Pullman Strike *in this index*
Chicago style [music]
  Jazz (The 1920's) J: 70
  Johnson, Robert J: 153
Chicago style pizza [food]
  Pizza P: 504
Chicago Sun-Times [newspaper]
  Chicago (Communications) C: 433
  Field, Marshall, I (His family) F: 92
Chicago Symphony Orchestra
  Chicago (The arts) C: 428
  Orchestra *picture on* O: 821
Chicago Transit Authority
  Chicago (Transportation) C: 433
Chicago Tribune [newspaper]
  Chicago (Communications) C: 433
  McCormick, Robert Rutherford M: 332f
  Medill, Joseph M: 379
Chicago Union Stock Yards
  Chicago (Industry) C: 431-432; (Growth as a city) C: 434-435
Chicago White Sox [team]
  Baseball (table) B: 130; (The Black Sox Scandal) B: 135
  Jackson, Shoeless Joe J: 16
Chicanos [people]
  Hispanic Americans H: 244; (The Chicano movement) H: 256
  Los Angeles (East Los Angeles) L: 461-462 *with picture*
Chicha [drink]
  Inca (Food, clothing, and shelter) I: 95-96
  Indian, American (Food) I: 136d

Chichén Itzá [ancient city, North America] **C:** 439
　Indian, American *picture on* **I:** 170
　Maya (The Maya heritage) **M:** 326
　Toltec Indians **T:** 323
Chichewa [language]
　Malawi (People) **M:** 96-97
Chichimec Indians
　Aguascalientes **A:** 163
　Mexico (The Classic Period) **M:** 468
Chichishima [island, Japan]
　Bonin Islands **B:** 460
Chick [bird]
　Bird (Laying and hatching eggs) **B:** 357-359 *with pictures*
　Chicken (Raising chicks) **C:** 443
　Penguin (The life of penguins) **P:** 238 *with picture*
Chickadee [bird] **C:** 439 *with picture*
　Bird *picture on* **B:** 358
Chickamauga, Battle of [1863]
　Civil War, American (table) **Ci:** 624; (Battle of Chickamauga) **Ci:** 629
　Georgia *picture on* **G:** 133
Chickamauga and Chattanooga National Military Park
　National Park System (table: National military parks) **N:** 55
Chickamauga Dam [Tennessee River]
　Chattanooga **C:** 388
Chickamauga Indians
　Chattanooga **C:** 388
Chickasaw Indians C: 439
　Indian, American (Indians of the Southeast) **I:** 157
　Indian Territory **I:** 189 *with map*
　Mississippi (Early days) **M:** 641; (Exploration and early settlement) **M:** 641
Chickasaw National Recreation Area [Oklahoma]
　National Park System (table: National recreation areas) **N:** 49
Chickee [dwelling]
　Indian, American *picture on* **I:** 158
　Seminole Indians **S:** 293
Chicken C: 440 *with pictures*
　Agriculture *picture on* **A:** 151
　Bird *picture on* **B:** 358; (As a source of food and raw materials) **B:** 330
　Blue Hen **B:** 420
　Cockfighting **Ci:** 744
　Egg **E:** 116; (Development of the bird's egg) **E:** 117; (How embryos develop) **E:** 117-118; (Uses of eggs) **E:** 118
　Incubator **I:** 106
　Poultry **P:** 720 *with picture*
　Rhode Island Red **R:** 316
　Skeleton *diagram on* **S:** 481
Chicken mite [animal]
　Mite **M:** 678
Chickenpox [disease] **C:** 446
　Disease (table) **D:** 226
Chickpea [plant] **C:** 446 *with picture*
Chicle [tree product] **C:** 446 *with picture*
　Chewing gum (History) **C:** 416
　Gum **G:** 440
　Rain forest (Economic value) **R:** 126c
　Sapodilla **S:** 122
Chiclero [occupation]
　Chicle **C:** 446 *with picture*
Chicomecóatl [Aztec goddess]
　Mythology (Aztec mythology) **M:** 987
Chicomoztoc [Aztec region]
　Aztec (The Aztec migration) **A:** 1003
Chicora [U.S. history]
　Ayllón, Lucas Vásquez de **A:** 995
Chicory [plant] **C:** 446
　Coffee (Kinds of coffee) **Ci:** 755
　Flower *picture on* **F:** 291
Chicxulub Basin [Mexico]
　Asteroid (Impacts on Earth) **A:** 824b *with map*
　Earth (The Mesozoic Era) **E:** 27-28
　Meteor (Impact craters and basins) **M:** 432
Chief [title]
　Indian, American *pictures on* **I:** 160, **I:** 162; (Tribes) **I:** 143 *with picture*; (Indians of the Southeast) **I:** 157-158
　Pacific Islands (Polynesians) **P:** 5
Chief executive [office]
　Government (Executive) **G:** 284
　President of the United States **P:** 758
Chief justice [office] **C:** 447
　Supreme Court of Canada (Organization) **So:** 996 *with portrait*
　Supreme Court of the United States (How the Supreme Court is organized) **So:** 998; (table) **So:** 1000
Chief of naval operations [office]
　Navy, Department of the **N:** 81
　Navy, United States (The Navy Department) **N:** 85
Chief of staff [military officer]

Air Force, United States (The Department of the Air Force) **A:** 193
　Army, Department of the **A:** 729
　Army, United States (Army Department headquarters) **A:** 736
　Defense, Department of (Organization) **D:** 87
　Joint Chiefs of Staff **J:** 156
　Marine Corps, United States (Headquarters) **M:** 208
Chief of state [office]
　Government (Heads of government) **G:** 283
　President of the United States (Chief of state) **P:** 766
Chief of the defence staff
　Canadian Armed Forces (Organization) **C:** 154
Chiefdom [social unit]
　Indian, American (Tribes) **I:** 143
Chiefs, Kansas City [team] *See* Kansas City Chiefs *in this index*
Chiengmai [Thailand] *See* Chiang Mai *in this index*
Chiffon cake
　Cake **C:** 19
Chifley, Ben [Australian political leader]
　Australia (table) **A:** 923
Chigger [animal] **C:** 447 *with picture*
　Mite **M:** 678
Chignecto Bay [Canada]
　Bay of Fundy **B:** 175
Chignon [hairstyle]
　Hairdressing (The Renaissance) **H:** 11-12
Chigoe [insect]
　Chigger **C:** 447
　Flea (Kinds of fleas) **F:** 232
Chihuahua [city, Mexico] **C:** 447
Chihuahua [state, Mexico] **C:** 447
Chihuahua [dog] **C:** 447 *with picture*
　Chihuahua **C:** 447
　Dog *pictures on* **D:** 265, **D:** 274
Chihuahuan raven [bird]
　Raven **R:** 151
Chikamatsu Monzaemon [Japanese dramatist]
　Japanese literature (The Tokugawa period) **J:** 62
Chikyu [research ship]
　Ocean drilling programs **O:** 667
Chilblain [disorder] **C:** 447
Child C: 448 *with pictures*
　See also Child welfare; Literature for children *in this index; and the list of Related articles in the* Child *article*
　Adolescent (The "invention" of adolescence) **A:** 60
　Airbag (Safety concerns) **A:** 201
　Bullying **B:** 698
　Cancer (Cancer in children) **C:** 169
　Child abuse **C:** 454
　Children's home **C:** 457
　Colonial life in America (Colonists at home) **Ci:** 796; (Education and religion) **Ci:** 803
　Culture (Learning) **Ci:** 1187
　Developmental psychology **D:** 174
　Divorce (Child custody arrangements) **D:** 254
　Doll **D:** 286 *with pictures*
　Domestic violence **D:** 301
　Early childhood education **E:** 15
　Family **F:** 20
　Foster care **F:** 428
　Halloween **H:** 24a *with picture*
　Health (Emotional development) **H:** 126
　Home schooling **H:** 301
　Imagination **I:** 79
　Infanticide **I:** 264
　Intellectual disability **I:** 317
　Language **L:** 62
　Library (Services for children) **L:** 240 *with picture*; (Elementary school libraries) **L:** 244
　Minor **M:** 607
　Obesity **O:** 642
　Occupational therapy (Helping people with physical disabilities) **O:** 648
　Parent **P:** 156
　Pediatrics **P:** 227
　Pet **P:** 319
　Playground **P:** 570
　Progeria **P:** 811
　Reading (Developing good readers) **R:** 159
　Safety *picture on* **S:** 14
　Sex education **S:** 336
　Sexuality (In childhood) **S:** 338
　Special education **So:** 770
　Television (Effects on young people) **T:** 121
　Toy **T:** 353
Child, Lydia Maria [American social reformer] **C:** 454
Child abuse C: 454
　Child (Problems in the home) **C:** 453
　Children and Families, Administration for **C:** 457
　Shaken baby syndrome **S:** 343
Child Abuse and Neglect, Office on

Child abuse C: 455
Child care
　Day care (Day care for children) **D:** 52
　Early childhood education (Child-care programs) **E:** 15
　Education (Early childhood education) **E:** 91
　Poverty (Social welfare programs) **P:** 725
　School (Preschools) **S:** 181
　Women's movement (In Western societies) **W:** 386-387 *with picture*
Child-care center
　Day care (Day care for children) **D:** 52
Child City [Mooseheart, Illinois]
　Moose International Inc. **M:** 799
Child custody [law]
　Adoption (The adoption process) **A:** 66
　Divorce (Child custody arrangements) **D:** 254
Child in Time, The [book by McEwan]
　McEwan, Ian **M:** 333
Child labor C: 455
　Fair Labor Standards Act **F:** 8
　Industrial Revolution *picture on* **I:** 252; (The working class) **I:** 251
　Sweatshop **So:** 1019
Child Labor Act [1916]
　Wilson, Woodrow (Legislative program) **W:** 322-323
Child labor amendment [U.S. history]
　Child labor (U.S. federal laws) **C:** 455
Child life worker [career]
　Hospital (Nonmedical services) **H:** 373
Child marriage
　Family (Non-Western families) **F:** 24
Child pornography
　Obscenity and pornography (Regulating pornography) **O:** 644
Child Protection and Toy Safety Act [1969]
　Toy (History) **T:** 354
Child psychoanalysis [psychotherapy]
　Freud, Anna **F:** 530
Child-rearing
　Child (The role of the family) **C:** 451
Child safety seat
　Safety (Motor vehicle safety) **S:** 14 *with picture*
Child support
　Children and Families, Administration for **C:** 457
Child Support Enforcement [program]
　Children and Families, Administration for **C:** 457
Child welfare [social work] **C:** 456
　Child abuse **C:** 455
　Childhood Education International, Association for **C:** 457
　Children and Families, Administration for **C:** 457
　Children's Bureau **C:** 457
　Children's home **C:** 457
　Social work (Family and child welfare) **So:** 558
　UNICEF **U:** 26 *with picture*
　United Nations (Aid to children) **U:** 88 *with picture*
Child Welfare League of America
　Child welfare **C:** 456
Child Welfare League of Canada
　Child welfare **C:** 456
Child Welfare Services
　Children's Bureau **C:** 457
Childbirth C: 456
　See also Birth *in this index*
　Baby (Birth) **B:** 6
　Cerebral palsy (Causes) **C:** 361
　Fairy (Fairies and people) **F:** 11
　Midwife **M:** 536
　Multiple birth **M:** 919
　Obstetrics and gynecology **O:** 646
　Postpartum depression **P:** 209
　Pregnancy **P:** 734a *with picture*
　Premature birth **P:** 755
　Reproduction, Human **R:** 244 *with picture*; (Birth) **R:** 248 *with pictures*
　Sexually transmitted disease (How STD's are transmitted) **S:** 338b
　Surrogate birth **So:** 1010
Childe Harold's Pilgrimage [poem by Byron]
　Byron, Lord (Byron's life) **B:** 748; (Byron's poetry) **B:** 748
Childeric III [king of the Franks]
　Merovingian dynasty **M:** 418
　Pepin the Short **P:** 277
Childhood *See* Child *in this index*
Childhood and Society [book by Erikson]
　Erikson, Erik Homburger **E:** 352
Childhood Education International, Association for C: 457
　Preschool (Preschools in the United States) **P:** 757
Children *See* Child *in this index*
Children and Families, Administration for [U.S.] **C:** 457
　Health and Human Services, Department of (Organization) **H:** 128

"Children of Adam" [poems by Whitman]
Whitman, Walt (His work) **W: 294**
Children of Don [legendary people]
Mythology (Welsh myths) **M: 985**
Children of Llyr [legendary people]
Mythology (Welsh myths) **M: 985**
Children of Violence, The [books by Lessing]
Lessing, Doris **L: 208**
Children's Aid Society
Brace, Charles Loring **B: 542**
Children's Book Council
Book Week **B: 470**
Children's Bureau [U.S.] **C: 457**
Kelley, Florence **K: 255**
Lathrop, Julia Clifford **L: 90**
Parent education (History) **P: 157**
Wald, Lillian D. **W: 7**
Children's court
Juvenile court **J: 205**
Children's Crusade [European history]
Crusades (The Children's Crusade) **Ci: 1161**
Pied Piper of Hamelin **P: 453**
Children's Day
Doll (Dolls in festivals) **D: 287** *with picture*
Children's Defense Fund
Clinton, Hillary Rodham **Ci: 682h**
Children's Fund, United Nations *See* UNICEF *in this index*
Children's Games [painting by Bruegel]
Bruegel, Pieter the Elder **B: 649** *with picture*
Children's home C: 457
Children's Hour, The [play by Hellman]
Hellman, Lillian **H: 178**
Children's librarian
Library (Services for children) **L: 240**
Literature for children (The role of librarians) **L: 366**
Children's literature *See* Literature for children *in this index*
Children's magazine
Magazine (Consumer magazines) **M: 42**
Children's zoo
Zoo (Displaying animals) **Z: 601** *with picture*; (The evolution of zoos) **Z: 605**
Childress, Sarah [wife of James Knox Polk] *See* Polk, Sarah Childress *in this index*
Childs, Richard S. [American businessman]
City government (The council-manager form) **Ci: 596**
Child's Garden of Verses, A [book by Stevenson]
Literature for children (Poetry) **L: 357**
Stevenson, Robert Louis (Other writings) **So: 898-899**
Chile C: 458 *with pictures and maps*
See also the list of Related articles in the Chile *article*
Andean Community **A: 450**
Clothing *picture on* **C: 695**
Indian, American (Indians of the Andes) **I: 173**
Latin America (Early years of independence) **L: 107-108**
Peru (The War of the Pacific) **P: 315**
Chile nut [seed]
Monkey puzzle tree **M: 730**
Chile pepper [plant] *See* Chili pepper *in this index*
Chile pine *See* Monkey puzzle tree *in this index*
Chile saltpeter [chemical]
Saltpeter **S: 76a**
Chilean clover
Alfalfa (History) **A: 348**
Chiles, Lawton [American political leader]
Florida (table) **F: 260**
Chili pepper [plant] **C: 471** *with picture*
Pepper **P: 278**
Chilkat Indians
Indian, American *picture on* **I: 162**
Yukon (History) **Y: 581**
Chilkat River [Alaska]
Alaska (Interesting facts) **A: 283**
Chilkoot Trail [British Columbia]
Canada (table: National historic sites) **C: 114**
Chill, Wind [weather] *See* Wind chill *in this index*
Chillicothe [Ohio]
Ohio (Exploration and settlement) **O: 700**; (Statehood) **O: 700**
Chillingworth, Roger [literary figure]
Hawthorne, Nathaniel (His novels) **H: 115**
Chillon [castle, Switzerland]
Lake Geneva **L: 38** *with map*
Chills and fever
Malaria (Symptoms) **M: 95**
Chilopod [zoology]
Arthropod **A: 752** *with picture*
Chiluba, Frederick [Zambian political leader]
Zambia (History) **Z: 585-586**
Chilwa, Lake [Mozambique]
Stanley and Livingstone (Livingstone's

discoveries) **So: 837** *with map*
Chimaera [fish]
Fish (Sharks, rays, and chimaeras) **F: 148** *with picture*
Chimborazo [volcano, Ecuador] **C: 471**
Mountain (table) **M: 896** *with diagram*
Chimera [art]
Chimera **C: 471**
Chimera [Greek mythology] **C: 471**
Chimères, Les [poems by Nerval]
Nerval, Gérard de **N: 131**
Chimes [musical instrument] **C: 471**
Bell (Chimes and carillons) **B: 239**
Orchestra bells **O: 823**
Chimney [oceanography]
Hydrothermal vent **H: 473**
Chimney [structure]
Heating (Fireplaces) **H: 160**
Chimney, Lamp
Lamp (Fat or oil lamps) **L: 52** *with pictures*
Chimney Rock
North Carolina (Places to visit) **N: 482**
Chimney Rock National Historic Site [Nebraska]
Nebraska (Places to visit) **N: 102** *with picture*
Chimney swift [bird]
Bird *picture on* **B: 353**
Swift **So: 1038**
Chimpanzee C: 471 *with pictures*
AIDS (History) **A: 166**
Ape **A: 563** *with picture*
Bonobo **B: 462**
Comparative psychology *picture on* **Ci: 902a**
Goodall, Jane **G: 269**
Human being (Prehuman ancestors) **H: 414**
Language (Other species and language) **L: 64**
Primate (Great apes) **P: 778a**
Psychology *picture on* **P: 849**
Chimu Indians
Peru (History) **P: 314**
Chin [anatomy]
Face **F: 3**
Chin [people]
Myanmar (Early days) **M: 970d**
Ch'in dynasty *See* Qin dynasty *in this index*
China [ceramics] *See* Porcelain *in this index*
China [country] **C: 474** *with pictures and maps*
See also Taiwan; *the list of Related articles in the* China *article; and headings beginning* Chinese... *in this index*
Agriculture and fishing
Agriculture *picture on* **A: 146**; (China) **A: 156**; (In China and the Middle East) **A: 157**
Cotton (Leading cotton-producing countries) **Ci: 1089** *with map*
Fishing industry **F: 180**
Meat packing **M: 350**
Sheep (table) **S: 382**
Wheat (table) **W: 273** *with map*
Art and architecture
China (The arts) **C: 487** *with pictures*
Archaeology *picture on* **A: 595**
Architecture (Chinese architecture) **A: 612** *with picture*
Asia (The arts) **A: 789**
Bed *picture on* **B: 198**
Calligraphy *picture on* **C: 68**
Dance (Asian theatrical dance) **D: 28-29**
Drama (China) **D: 336** *with picture*
Furniture (China) **F: 571** *with pictures*
Ivory (Ivory carving) **I: 521**
Jade **J: 20**
Lacquerware **L: 22** *with picture*
Mask (Theatrical masks) **M: 265**
Music (Chinese music) **M: 956**
Painting (Landscapes and seascapes) **P: 32-33** *with picture*; (Chinese painting) **P: 44** *with pictures*; (Japanese painting) **P: 47**
Porcelain *picture on* **P: 675**; (Oriental porcelain) **P: 676**
Pottery *picture on* **P: 716**; (Early pottery) **P: 718**
Sculpture (China) **S: 238** *with picture*
Terra-cotta army of Xi'an **T: 172** *with picture*
Communications and mass media
China (Communication) **C: 498**
Newspaper (In Asia) **N: 386**
Television (In Asia) **T: 116**
Defense
China (The armed forces) **C: 481**
Air force (The Chinese Air Force) **A: 184** *with picture*
Army (The Chinese Army) **A: 726**
Navy *picture on* **N: 77**; (Major navies of the world) **N: 78** *with picture*; (Navies in the Middle Ages) **N: 79**
Education
China (Education) **C: 486** *with picture*
Asia (Education) **A: 789**

Education (Early Chinese and Indian education) **E: 99**
Library (Australia and East Asia) **L: 253-254**; (Libraries in the East) **L: 261**
Literacy (Literacy in other countries) **L: 352**
Government
China (Government) **C: 475**
Communism (Communism in practice) **Ci: 890-892**
Economics (The organization of economies) **E: 58-59**
Freedom of assembly (In other countries) **F: 504**
Government (Asia and the Middle East) **G: 289**
Police (In other countries) **P: 623** *with picture*
Health and welfare
Abortion (In other countries) **A: 16**
Acupuncture **A: 31**
Birth control (Birth control today) **B: 379**
Housing (Other countries) **H: 392**
Medicine (China and India) **M: 372**
History
China (History) **C: 499** *with pictures*
Albania (Communist control) **A: 308**
Army (Ancient armies) **A: 726-727**
Asia (Way of life in East Asia) **A: 785**; (The rise of the Japanese Empire) **A: 806**; (The spread of Communism) **A: 807**
Asian Americans (History of Asian immigration) **A: 812d**
Bush, George Herbert Walker (Envoy to China) **B: 718**
Cathay **C: 301**
Chiang Kai-shek **C: 418**
City (Government) **Ci: 585**
Clinton, Bill (International affairs) **Ci: 682f**
Cold War **Ci: 763**; (Communist expansion in Asia) **Ci: 764**; (To the brink and back) **Ci: 765**; (The great blocs split) **Ci: 769**; (The Cold War in the 1970's) **Ci: 770**
Communism (World War II) **Ci: 893-894**; (China after Mao) **Ci: 896**
Cultural Revolution **Ci: 1185**
Exploration (The Chinese) **E: 441** *with picture*; (Chinese exploration) **E: 442**
Famine (Causes of famine) **F: 26** *with picture*
Flag *picture on* **F: 217**
Genghis Khan (History) **G: 88**
Guerrilla warfare (Types of guerrilla movements) **G: 420**
Hong Kong **H: 316**; (History) **H: 319**
Immigration (The second wave) **I: 82**; (Canada) **I: 84**
India (India in the 1950's and early 1960's) **I: 133**
Indochina **I: 224**
International relations (New patterns of international relations) **I: 345**
Japan (Chinese influence) **J: 53**
Kashmir **K: 247**
Korea, History of (Early years) **K: 366**; (The Choson dynasty) **K: 366-367**
Korean War **K: 379**
Manchuria (History) **M: 134**
Mao Zedong **M: 174**
Map (Maps in the Middle Ages) **M: 183**
Mathematics (Chinese mathematics) **M: 306**
Money (How money developed) **M: 705-706** *with pictures*
Mongol Empire (Invasions) **M: 720**
Mummy (Other mummies) **M: 926**
Nanking Massacre **N: 10**
Nixon, Richard Milhous (Foreign policy) **N: 432-433**
Olympic Games (Boycotts) **O: 753**
Opium (History) **O: 811**
Philosophy (Eastern philosophy) **P: 386**
Polo, Marco **P: 647** *with map*
Qin dynasty **Q: 4**
Russia (Expansion in Asia) **R: 551**
Russo-Japanese War (Underlying causes) **R: 566a**
Science (Early civilizations) **S: 196**
Silk Road **S: 461**
Sino-Japanese War of 1894-1895 **S: 473**
Sino-Japanese War of 1937-1945 **S: 473**
Tang dynasty **T: 25** *with picture and map*
Tibet **T: 276**; (History and government) **T: 277**
Treaty port **T: 409**
Union of Soviet Socialist Republics (Khrushchev's policies) **U: 38-39**
United Nations (Membership questions) **U: 95**
United States, History of the (The end of the Cold War) **U: 196d**
Vietnam (Nam Viet) **V: 369**
World, History of the (The Huang He Valley) **W: 425**; (The unification of China) **W: 431**

with picture; (China) W: 435 with picture;
(Developments in China and Japan) W: 442
World War II (Aggression on the march) W: 470;
(Japan attacks) W: 479; (The China-Burma-
India theater) W: 491
Language and literature
See also Chinese language; Chinese literature
in this index
Book (The development of printed books)
B: 466 with picture
Manuscript (Paper manuscripts) M: 173
Manufacturing
Aluminum (The aluminum industry) A: 396
Automobile (Where cars are made) A: 959
Iron and steel (In China) I: 448
Silk (History) S: 460
Natural resources
Conservation (Asia) Ci: 989
Panda (Protecting pandas) P: 129
Three Gorges Dam T: 270
People
China (People) C: 481 with pictures
Asia (The people) A: 786; (Life in China) A: 786
Family (Home life) F: 21 with picture
Hmong H: 270
Recreation and sports
Karate K: 245
Martial arts M: 234
Religion
China (Religion) C: 485
Asia (Religions) A: 786
Confucianism Ci: 936
Religion (Confucianism) R: 220
Taoism T: 36
Social and cultural life
China (Way of life) C: 482
Calendar (The Chinese calendar) C: 30
Circus (History) C: 562b
Clothing picture on Ci: 693; (Clothing of Asia)
Ci: 696
Dragon D: 319
Food (Why diets differ around the world)
F: 331
Technology and science
Coal (History of coal use) Ci: 731
Fishing industry (Inland fisheries) F: 182
Heart (Early beliefs about the heart) H: 143
Invention (China) I: 359
Number (The Chinese) N: 607
Printing (History) P: 802
Railroad (In Asia) R: 114
Rocket (History) R: 390 with picture
Ship pictures on S: 421, S: 423; (Chinese ships)
S: 419
Space exploration (China) So: 727
Trade
Macau M: 4
Tea (History) T: 63
Trade route (Early trade routes) T: 363
Trudeau, Pierre Elliott (Foreign affairs) T: 463-
464
China, Communist See China in this index
China, Nationalist See Taiwan in this index
China, People's Republic of See China in this index
China, Republic of See Taiwan in this index
China aster [plant]
Aster A: 823
China clay See Kaolin in this index
China grass [plant]
Ramie R: 133
China Import and Export Fair
Guangzhou (Economy) G: 410
China Petroleum & Chemical [company]
Manufacturing (table) M: 170
China poblana [clothing]
Mexico (Clothing) M: 456-457
China Sea C: 508 with map
China-wood oil [tree product]
Tung oil T: 486
Chinaberry [tree]
Poisonous plant (Some poisonous plants) P: 602
Chinampa [agriculture]
Aztec (Agriculture) A: 1002
Indian, American (Before European contact)
I: 169-171
Lake Xochimilco L: 48
China's Sorrow See Huang He in this index
Chinatown
Asian Americans picture on A: 812b
California (Population) C: 40
Canada picture on C: 105
Chicago (The South Side) C: 424-425
Minority group (Asian Americans) M: 610
New York City (Manhattan) N: 323-324
San Francisco picture on S: 95; (Downtown San
Francisco) S: 92-93
Vancouver (The city) V: 274 with map

Chinaware See Porcelain in this index
Chinch bug [insect] C: 508 with picture
Insect picture on I: 281
Lawn picture on L: 143
Chincha Indians
Chinchilla C: 509
Chincha Islands [islands, Pacific]
Guano G: 411
Chinchilla [animal] C: 508 with picture
Animal picture on A: 474
Fur picture on F: 562; (table) F: 561
Chinchilla, Laura [Costa Rican political leader]
Costa Rica (The late 1900's) Ci: 1084
Chinchilla cat
Cat (Coat) C: 287
Chincoteague Island [island, Virginia]
Virginia (Visitor's guide) V: 408 with picture
Chindits [World War II commandos] See Wingate's
Raiders in this index
Chinese [people]
China (People) C: 481
Hong Kong (Ancestry) H: 317
Malaysia (People) M: 98b-98c
Chinese alligator
Alligator A: 375
Chinese Americans
Asian Americans A: 812b
California (Early statehood) C: 62
Minority group (Asian Americans) M: 610
Oriental Exclusion Acts O: 855
Riot (During the 1800's) R: 349
Western frontier life in America (Newcomers)
W: 234
Chinese cabbage [plant] C: 509 with picture
Chinese calendar
Calendar (The Chinese calendar) C: 30
Chinese New Year C: 512
Chinese City [district]
Shanghai (The city) S: 371-272
Chinese Communist Party
China C: 475; (Government) C: 475; (Way of life)
C: 482; (The arts) C: 487; (History) C: 499-504
Hu Jintao H: 402
Jiang Zemin J: 125
Mao Zedong (His life) M: 174
Chinese crested [dog] C: 509 with picture
Chinese delphinium [plant]
Flower picture on F: 279
Chinese Eastern Railway
Russo-Japanese War (Underlying causes) R: 566a
Trans-Siberian Railroad T: 401
Chinese elm
Elm (Diseases) E: 245
Chinese Exclusion Act [1882]
Asian Americans (The first wave of Asian
immigration) A: 812d
Oriental Exclusion Acts O: 855
Chinese giant salamander
Amphibian picture on A: 441
Chinese goose [bird]
Goose (Kinds of geese) G: 270 with picture
Chinese gooseberry See Kiwi fruit in this index
Chinese hibiscus [plant]
Hibiscus H: 223 with picture
Chinese jade [mineral]
Jade (Jadeite) J: 20
Chinese-Japanese wars See Sino-Japanese War
of 1894-1895; Sino-Japanese War of 1937-1945
in this index
Chinese juniper [tree]
Juniper J: 196 with picture
Chinese language C: 509 with pictures
Alphabet (Other alphabets) A: 383-384
Asia (The Huang He and Yangtze valleys) A: 805
China (Languages) C: 481
Hong Kong (Languages) H: 317
Lin Yutang L: 309
Name (The history of names) N: 7
Writing system (Phonetization) W: 513
Chinese literature C: 511
Chinese Nationalist Party [political party]
Beijing (History) B: 223-224
Chinese New Year [festival] C: 512
New Year's Day (Modern customs) N: 289 with
picture
Chinese pear
Pear (Varieties) P: 215
Chinese peony [plant]
Peony P: 276
Chinese rug
Rugs and carpets (Oriental rugs) R: 516-517
Chinese shar-pei [dog] C: 512 with picture
Dog D: 262 with picture
Chinese soapberry [plant]
Soapberry So: 543
Chinese State Circus
Circus (The circus today) Ci: 564-565 with picture

Chinese Turkestan
Turkestan (Chinese Turkestan) T: 501
Chinese water chestnut [plant]
Water chestnut W: 134 with picture
Chinese water deer
Deer (Young) D: 84; (table) D: 85
Chinese wisteria [plant]
Wisteria W: 370
Chinese wool-handed crab
Crustacean (Reproduction) Ci: 1163
Chinese zodiac See Eastern zodiac in this index
Chingis Khan See Genghis Khan in this index
Chingo Smith of the Erie Canal [book by Adams]
Adams, Samuel Hopkins A: 44
Chinking [construction]
Log cabin L: 422 with picture
Pioneer life in America (A pioneer settlement)
P: 479-480
Chinlon [sport]
Myanmar (Recreation) M: 970a
Chinnereth, Sea of [name for]
Galilee, Sea of G: 11
Chinoise, La [film]
Godard, Jean-Luc G: 244
Chinoiserie [art]
Furniture (The Rococo style) F: 576-577
Paperwork (Wallpaper) P: 138
Wallpaper W: 19
Chinook [aircraft]
Army, United States picture on A: 736
Chinook [weather] C: 512
Colorado (Climate) Ci: 841
Foehn F: 313
Wind (Local winds) W: 329-330
Chinook Indians C: 513
Indian, American (Language) I: 149-150
Portland [Oregon] (History) P: 684
Chinook salmon [fish]
Salmon picture on S: 69; (Kinds of salmon) S: 70
Chinquapin [tree]
Chestnut C: 415
Chinstrap penguin
Antarctica (Living things) A: 534-535 with picture
Chip [electronics] See Computer chip; Silicon in
this index
Chip log [measuring device]
Log (Logs used in the past) L: 421
Chipa [food]
Paraguay (Food and drink) P: 146
Chipewyan Indians
Manitoba (Precontact era) M: 160
Saskatchewan (Early days) S: 144
Chipmunk [animal] C: 513 with picture
Animal picture on A: 479
Chipp, Don [Australian political leader]
Australia (Political upheavals) A: 925
Chippendale, Thomas [British cabinetmaker]
C: 513
Chippendale furniture
Chippendale, Thomas C: 513
Furniture picture on F: 577; (Chippendale
furniture) F: 579
Chippenham, Battle of [875]
Alfred the Great A: 348
Chipper-canter [machine]
Lumber picture on L: 520
Chippewa, Battle of [1814]
War of 1812 (Campaigns of 1814) W: 31
Chippewa Indians C: 514
Indian, American pictures on I: 156, I: 182;
(Indians of the Northeast) I: 154-155
Minnesota (Early days) M: 603
Ontario (Original inhabitants) O: 784
Potawatomi Indians P: 714
Totem T: 346
Chippewa National Forest [Minnesota]
Minnesota (Places to visit) M: 594
Chipping sparrow [bird]
Sparrow So: 764
CHIPS See Clearing House Interbank Payments
System in this index
Chirac, Jacques René [French political leader]
C: 514
France (Socialists win power) F: 478
Chiral form [geometry]
Symmetry (A plane of symmetry) So: 1066
Chiriaeff, Ludmilla [Latvian-Canadian dancer]
Ballet (Ballet in Canada) B: 54
Chiricahua Indians
Cochise Ci: 743
Geronimo G: 173
Chiricahua National Monument [Arizona]
National Park System (table: National
monuments) N: 50
Chirico, Giorgio de [Italian painter] C: 514 with
picture
Chirikov, Aleksei I. [Russian sailor]

Exploration (The Russians in Siberia) E: 447
Chiromancy See Palmistry *in this index*
Chiron [Greek mythology]
  Centaur C: 351
Chiropractic C: 514
  Alternative medicine A: 388
Chiropractic, Doctor of [degree]
  Chiropractic C: 515
Chiropractor [career]
  Chiropractic C: 514
Chiroptera [zoology]
  Mammal (table) M: 128 *with picture*
Chisel [tool]
  Woodcarving W: 391 *with diagram*
  Woodworking (Cutting) W: 397 *with pictures*
Chisel plow
  Corn (Preparing the soil) Ci: 1060
  Farm and farming (Preparing the soil) F: 35 *with
    pictures*
  Plow (Other types of plow bottoms) P: 576 *with
    picture*
Chishima [islands, Pacific] See Kuril Islands *in this
  index*
Chisholm, Jesse [American frontiersman]
  Chisholm Trail C: 515
Chisholm, Shirley [American political leader]
  C: 515 *with portrait*
Chisholm Trail [U.S. history] C: 515
  Abilene A: 11
  Cowboy (The growth of the cattle industry)
    Ci: 1111-1112
  Oklahoma (After the Civil War) O: 731-732
  Western frontier life in America (The cattle drive)
    W: 237
Chishona [language]
  Zimbabwe (People) Z: 592
Chisinau [capital city, Moldova] C: 515
Chisos Mountains [mountains, Mexico-U.S.]
  Big Bend National Park B: 297
  Texas *picture on* T: 184; (Mountains) T: 198
Chissano, Joaquim [Mozambican political leader]
  Mozambique (History) M: 905-906
Chiswick House [London]
  Architecture (The Palladian Revival) A: 623 *with
    picture*
Chital [animal]
  Animal *picture on* A: 481
  Deer (table) D: 85 *with picture*; (Asian and
    European deer) D: 86
Chitimukulu [chief]
  Bemba B: 246
Chitin [biology]
  Arthropod A: 753
  Insect (Skeleton) I: 286
  Moth (The pupa) M: 839
  Shrimp (The body of a shrimp) S: 439-440
Chiton [clothing]
  Clothing (Greece) Ci: 697 *with picture*
  Tunic T: 487
Chiton [sea animal] C: 515
  Mollusk (table) M: 695; (Chitons) M: 696
  Shell (Kinds of mollusk shells) S: 385-388 *with
    picture*
Chitral Valley
  Pakistan *picture on* P: 92
Chittenden, Thomas [American political leader]
  Vermont (table) V: 333
Chitterlings [food]
  Hog (Food) H: 286
Chitty Chitty Bang Bang [book by Fleming]
  Fleming, Ian F: 233
Chivalry [custom]
  Etiquette (The origins of etiquette) E: 374
  Knights and knighthood K: 348; (The code of
    chivalry) K: 348-350
  Middle Ages (Life of the people) M: 526
  Novel (Medieval narratives) N: 572
Chive [plant] C: 516 *with picture*
Chivington, John M. [American military leader]
  Black Kettle B: 389
  Western frontier life in America (Settlers and
    Native Americans) W: 239
Chlamydia [disease] C: 516
  Disease (table) D: 226
  Koala K: 360
  Sexually transmitted disease S: 338b
Chlamydia pneumoniae [bacteria]
  Chlamydia C: 516
Chlamydia psittaci [bacteria]
  Chlamydia C: 516
Chlamydia trachomatis [bacteria]
  Chlamydia C: 516
  Pelvic inflammatory disease P: 233
Chlamys [clothing]
  Clothing (Greece) Ci: 697
Chloracne [disorder]
  Dioxin D: 215

Chloramphenicol [medication] C: 516
  Antibiotic (table) A: 551
  Typhus (Treatment) T: 541
Chlorate of potash [chemical]
  Match (Safety matches) M: 299
Chlordane [chemical]
  Insecticide (Chlorinated hydrocarbon
    insecticides) I: 302
Chlordiazepoxide [drug]
  Benzodiazepine B: 256
Chloride [chemistry] C: 516
  Salt, Chemical S: 75
Chlorinated hydrocarbon insecticide
  Insecticide (Chlorinated hydrocarbon
    insecticides) I: 302
Chlorinated lime [chemical]
  Disinfectant D: 235
Chlorine [element] C: 516
  See also the list of Related articles in the Chlorine
    article
  Bleach B: 399
  Compound Ci: 906
  Halogen H: 26
  Hypochlorous acid H: 480
  Water (Purifying and treating water) W: 126
Chlorofluorocarbon [chemical compound] C: 517
  Air (Changes in the atmosphere) A: 175
  Air pollution (Industrial processes) A: 198
  Environmental pollution *picture on* E: 333;
    (Air pollution) E: 331; (Government action)
    E: 335-336
  Food, Frozen (Liquid immersion freezing) F: 338
  Ozone hole O: 894
Chloroform [chemical] C: 517
  Water pollution (Human illness) W: 138
Chlorolabe [anatomy]
  Eye (The retina) E: 462
Chlorophyll [botany] C: 517
  Algae (Structure of algae) A: 349
  Leaf (The leaf changes color) L: 152
  Mushroom M: 941
  Photosynthesis P: 430
  Plant (Leaves) P: 529; (Photosynthesis) P: 537
  Saprophyte S: 122
  Tree (Leaves) T: 417
Chloroplast [botany] C: 518
  Algae (Structure of algae) A: 349
  Cell (The cytoplasm) C: 329 *with diagram*
  Chlorophyll C: 517
  Leaf (Photosynthesis) L: 155 *with diagram*
  Photosynthesis P: 430
  Plant (Photosynthesis) P: 537
  Tree (Leaves) T: 417
Chloroquine [medication]
  Malaria (Treatment and prevention) M: 96
  Quinine Q: 42
Chlorpromazine [medication] C: 518
Choanocyte [zoology]
  Sponge (Special cells) So: 799 *with diagram*
Choate, Pat [American economist]
  Perot, Ross P: 292
Chobe National Park [Botswana]
  National park (table) N: 42f
Chocolate [food] C: 518 *with picture*
  Cacao C: 9
  Candy (Chocolate candies) C: 176
  Carob C: 244
  Hershey, Milton Snavely H: 216
  Pennsylvania (Interesting facts) P: 245
Chocolate liquor
  Chocolate (Manufacturing chocolate) C: 518
Chocolate liquor [food product]
  Chocolate (Manufacturing chocolate) C: 518
Choctaw Indians C: 519 *with picture*
  Code talkers Ci: 749
  Indian, American (Indians of the Southeast) I: 157
  Indian Territory I: 189 *with map*
  Mississippi (Territorial days) M: 641; (The late
    1900's) M: 645
Choi Kyu Hah [Korean political leader]
  Korea, South (History) K: 378c
Choice [publication]
  American Library Association A: 413
Choice meat
  Beef (Grades of beef) B: 209
  Meat packing (Quality grading) M: 351
Choke [engine]
  Carburetor C: 208
Choke [gun]
  Shotgun S: 436
Chokecherry [fruit]
  Tree *pictures on* T: 421
Chokedamp [gas]
  Damp D: 22
Choking [disorder]
  First aid (Restoring breathing) F: 138; (Choking)
    F: 139 *with pictures*

Chola Empire [Indian history]
  India (Southern India) I: 129
Cholecalciferol [vitamin]
  Vitamin (Vitamin D) V: 430
Cholecystokinin [hormone]
  Gallbladder G: 14
Cholera [disease] C: 519
  Epidemic E: 343
  Map (Development of thematic and inventory
    mapping) M: 185
  Public health (History) P: 857
Cholesterol [biochemistry] C: 520
  Arteriosclerosis (Causes) A: 750
  Beef (Food value) B: 211
  Bile B: 300
  Bloch, Konrad Emil B: 404
  Butter (Composition and food value) B: 731
  Ester E: 360
  Fat (Fats and disease) F: 53
  Heart (Coronary artery disease) H: 137; (Progress
    in treatment and prevention) H: 145-146
  Lipid (Kinds of lipids) L: 345
  Liver (Other functions) L: 394
  Margarine M: 198
  Meat (Food value of meat) M: 346-347
  Milk (Milk in the human diet) M: 546
  Nutrition (Limit intake of saturated fats, trans fats,
    and cholesterol) N: 628; (Heart disease) N: 630
  Physical fitness (Cholesterol levels) P: 434
  Psyllium P: 853
  Seafood S: 264
  Statin S: 867
  Trans fats T: 369
  Triglyceride T: 442
  Vegetarianism V: 295
Choli [clothing]
  Clothing (India) Ci: 699
Choline [vitamin]
  Vitamin (table) V: 431; (Vitamin B$_{12}$, folic acid, and
    choline) V: 432
Cholinesterase [enzyme]
  Alzheimer's disease (Treatment) A: 399
Cholinesterase inhibitor [drug]
  Alzheimer's disease (Treatment) A: 399
Cholla cactus [plant]
  Cactus (Kinds of cactuses) C: 11
  Flower *picture on* F: 291
  Plant *picture on* P: 526
Cholo [people]
  Bolivia (Way of life) B: 443 *with picture*
Cholon [district]
  Ho Chi Minh City H: 271
Choluteca River
  Honduras (The Southern Coast) H: 310
Chomedey, Paul de [French explorer] See
  Maisonneuve, Sieur de *in this index*
Chomette, René-Lucien [birth name of]
  Clair, René Ci: 636
Chomolungma [mountain] See Mount Everest *in
  this index*
Chomsky, Noam [American linguist] C: 520
  Language (The science of language) L: 66-67
  Linguistics (The generative theory of language)
    L: 337
  Socialism (The New Left) So: 561
Chondrichthyes [zoology]
  Fish (table) F: 172 *with pictures*
Chondrite [geology]
  Earth (Earth's interior) E: 23
  Meteor (Meteorites) M: 432
Chondrodisplasia [disorder]
  Dwarfism (Causes) D: 394-395
Chondrostean [zoology]
  Fish (The Age of Fishes) F: 171
Chongmyo Royal Shrine
  Seoul (The city) S: 304
Chongqing [China] C: 521
Chopin, Frédéric François [Polish composer]
  C: 521 *with portrait*
  Ballade B: 43
  Liszt, Franz (His life) L: 349-350
  Sand, George S: 106
Chopin, Kate [American author] C: 521
  American literature (Women writers) A: 420
Chopiniana [ballet]
  Ballet (Ballet in Russia) B: 52
Chopper [aircraft]
  Helicopter H: 169
Chopsticks [utensil] C: 521
Choquette, Ernest [Canadian author]
  Canadian literature (Fiction: 1850-1918) C: 157
Choral music
  Classical music (Choral music) Ci: 644 *with picture*
Choral ode [poetry]
  Drama (Tragedy) D: 326
  Greek literature (Lyric poetry) G: 377
  Ode O: 673

Poetry (Lyric poetry) **P: 591**
Chorale [music] **C: 522**
Classical music (The Reformation) **Ci: 646**
Chord [geometry]
Circle (Parts of a circle) **Ci: 558** *with diagram*
Geometry (Non-Euclidean geometry) **G: 105**
Sphere **So: 780**
Chord [music]
Harmony **H: 62**
Music (Harmony) **M: 951** *with diagrams*
Chordate [biology] **C: 522**
Animal (A classification of the animal kingdom)
A: 506-507 *with picture*
Invertebrate **I: 366**
Chordotonal organ [entomology]
Ant (Sense organs) **A: 522**
Chorea [disorder] **C: 522**
Huntington's disease **H: 451**
Rheumatic fever **R: 291**
Chorea [veterinary medicine]
Distemper **D: 238**
Choregus [ancient Greece]
Drama (Tragedy) **D: 326**
Choreographer
Ballet **B: 44;** (Choreography) **B: 49** *with picture*
Musical comedy (Dancing) **M: 959**
Choreography
Ballet (table) **B: 45;** (Choreography) **B: 49** *with picture*; (Music) **B: 50**
Ice skating (Singles skating) **I: 12**
Chorion [biology]
Baby *diagrams on* **B: 5**
Placenta **P: 505**
Chorionic cavity [pregnancy]
Reproduction, Human (Nourishing the embryo) **R: 247** *with diagram*
Chorionic villus sampling [medicine]
Genetic counseling (Reasons for seeking genetic counseling) **G: 84a**
Pregnancy (Medical care) **P: 734-735**
Choroid [anatomy]
Eye *picture on* **E: 461;** (The uveal tract) **E: 460-462**
Choroiditis [disease]
Eye (Diseases of the uveal tract) **E: 467**
Chôros [music by Villa-Lobos]
Villa-Lobos, Heitor **V: 384**
Chorus
Classical music (Choral music) **Ci: 644** *with picture*
Drama (Greek drama) **D: 326-327**
Opera (The singers) **O: 792** *with picture*; (The stage director) **O: 794**
Poetry (Ancient poetry) **P: 595-596**
Chorus Line, A [musical]
Musical comedy (The modern musical emerges) **M: 960**
Chosen People [religion]
Judaism (The covenant with God) **J: 179**
Choson [ancient state]
Korea, History of (Early years) **K: 366;** (The Choson dynasty) **K: 366**
October **O: 670**
Seoul **S: 304**
Choson dynasty [Korean history]
Seoul (History) **S: 306**
Chott [geography]
Algeria (The High Plateaus) **A: 363**
Chou dynasty *See* Zhou dynasty *in this index*
Chou En-lai [Chinese leader] *See* Zhou Enlai *in this index*
Chouart, Médard [French explorer] *See* Groseilliers, Médard Chouart, Sieur des *in this index*
Chouteau, François [American businessman]
Kansas City [Missouri] (History) **K: 242**
Chouteau, Jean Pierre [American businessman] **C: 522**
Chouteau, Pierre, Jr. [American financier] **C: 522**
Chouteau, René Auguste [American frontiersman] **C: 522**
Missouri (Settlement) **M: 669**
Saint Louis (Early settlement) **S: 49**
Chouteau's Landing
Kansas City [Missouri] (History) **K: 242-243**
Chow chow [dog] **C: 522**
Dog **D: 262** *with picture*
CHP system *See* Complete heat and power system *in this index*
Chrétien, Aline Chaîné [wife of]
Chrétien, Jean (College years and early career) **C: 522a** *with picture*
Chrétien, Jean [Canadian political leader] **C: 522a** *with pictures*
Campbell, Kim (The 1993 election) **C: 90d**
Canada, History of (The 1993 national election) **C: 151;** (Canada under Chrétien) **C: 152;** (Recent developments) **C: 152**
Liberal Party of Canada **L: 227**
Martin, Paul **M: 234b** *with picture*

Chrétien de Troyes [French poet] **C: 522d**
Hartmann von Aue **H: 79**
Holy Grail **H: 299**
Lancelot, Sir **L: 56**
Chrism [oil]
Coronation (Development) **Ci: 1068**
Roman Catholic Church (Confirmation) **R: 404**
Chrisman, Arthur [American author]
Newbery Medal (table) **N: 359**
Chrismation [religion] *See* Confirmation *in this index*
Christ, Jesus *See* Jesus Christ *in this index*
Christ, Order of [military order]
Henry the Navigator **H: 191**
Christ and Culture [book by Niebuhr]
Niebuhr, H. Richard **N: 405**
Christ and Saint Thomas [sculpture by Verrocchio]
Verrocchio, Andrea del **V: 339**
Christ at Emmaus [painting by Rembrandt]
Rembrandt *picture on* **R: 228**
Christ Before Pilate [tapestry]
Jesus Christ *picture on* **J: 108a**
Christ Church [Alexandria]
Virginia (Places to visit) **V: 408**
Christ Church [Boston]
Old North Church **O: 740** *with picture*
Christ Church [Philadelphia]
Philadelphia (Downtown Philadelphia) **P: 359**
Christ Church Cathedral [Dublin]
Dublin (History) **D: 371**
Christ Disputing with the Elders [fresco by Giotto]
Jesus Christ *picture on* **J: 106**
Christ of the Apocalypse [painting]
Painting (Romanesque painting) **P: 50** *with picture*
Christ on the Road to Calvary [painting by Martini]
Jesus Christ *picture on* **J: 108b**
Christ the Redeemer [sculpture]
Rio de Janeiro (The city) **R: 345**
South America *picture on* **So: 622**
Christ the Savior Cathedral [Moscow]
Moscow (Recent developments) **M: 827**
"Christabel" [poem by Coleridge]
Coleridge, Samuel Taylor (His writing) **Ci: 772**
Christaller, Walter [German geographer]
Geography (The growth of geography) **G: 96**
Christchurch [New Zealand] **C: 522d**
Christening [custom]
Ship (Launching and outfitting) **S: 413**
Christening [religion] *See* Baptism *in this index*
Christian [literary figure]
Bunyan, John **B: 700**
Christian [religion] *See* Christianity *in this index*
Christian III [king of Denmark]
Denmark (A great power) **D: 139-140**
Christian IV [king of Denmark] **C: 522d**
Oslo **O: 864**
Thirty Years' War (The Danish period) **T: 260**
Christian IX [king of Denmark] **C: 522d**
Frederik VIII **F: 498**
Christian X [king of Denmark] **C: 522d**
Denmark (Social and political reforms) **D: 140**
Christian, Charlie [American guitarist] **C: 522d**
Jazz *picture on* **J: 71;** (Cool jazz) **J: 72**
Christian, Fletcher [British seaman]
Pitcairn Island **P: 498**
Christian, Letitia [wife of John Tyler] *See* Tyler, Letitia Christian *in this index*
Christian art *See* Religious art *in this index*
Christian Association, Young Men's *See* Young Men's Christian Association *in this index*
Christian Association, Young Women's *See* Young Women's Christian Association *in this index*
Christian Athletes, Fellowship of
Fellowship of Christian Athletes **F: 69**
Christian Brothers [religious order]
Jean Baptiste de La Salle, Saint **J: 75**
Religious life (table) **R: 227**
Christian Church [religious group]
Disciples of Christ **D: 223**
Christian Coalition of America [organization] **C: 522e**
Christian Democratic Appeal [political party]
Netherlands (Recent developments) **N: 150**
Christian Democratic Party [political party]
Italy (The Italian republic) **I: 517-518**
Christian Democratic People's Party [political party]
Hungary (Multiparty elections) **H: 448**
Christian Democratic Union [political party]
Germany (Politics) **G: 147;** (East Germany) **G: 170-171**
Merkel, Angela **M: 417**
Christian Democratic Union-Czech People's Party [political party]
Czech Republic (Politics) **Ci: 1210**
Christian Endeavor International [ministry]

C: 522e
Christian Era C: 522e
Christian fundamentalism [religious movement]
Fundamentalism (Development of Protestant fundamentalism) **F: 556**
Religion (Religion today) **R: 223**
Christian humanism [philosophy]
Humanism (The spread of humanism) **H: 431**
Renaissance (Christian humanism) **R: 238**
Christian Mission
Salvation Army (History) **S: 76b-77**
Christian name
Name (Given names) **N: 5**
Christian Realism [philosophy]
Niebuhr, Reinhold **N: 406**
Christian Reformed Church [religious group] **C: 522e**
Christian Science Monitor, The [newspaper]
Christian Scientists (Organization) **C: 522e**
Christian Scientists [religious group] **C: 522e**
Eddy, Mary Baker **E: 75**
Christian Social Union [political party]
Germany (Politics) **G: 147**
Merkel, Angela **M: 417**
Christian Socialism [philosophy]
Kingsley, Charles **K: 331**
Christiania [former name]
Oslo **O: 864**
Christianity [religion] **C: 522f** *with pictures*
See also Jesus Christ *in this index*
Angel **A: 459**
Arabs (Religion) **A: 586**
Bible **B: 279;** (The Christian Old Testament) **B: 282;** (The Bible in worship) **B: 286**
Church **C: 541**
Creationism **Ci: 1123**
Cross **Ci: 1155**
Deacon **D: 55**
Devil **D: 174**
Eastern Orthodox Churches **E: 45**
Education (Christian education in the Middle Ages) **E: 99**
Europe (Religions) **E: 386**
Fast **F: 52**
Feasts and festivals (In Christianity) **F: 58**
Gnosticism **G: 238**
Gospels **G: 278**
Grace **G: 295**
Halloween (History) **H: 25**
Heaven **H: 161**
Heresy **H: 210**
History (The Bible and post-Roman history) **H: 262**
Jerusalem **J: 94a**
Latin America (Colonial rule) **L: 104**
Lebanon (Ethnic groups and religion) **L: 171**
Lord's Prayer **L: 454**
Marriage *picture on* **M: 219;** (Wedding ceremonies) **M: 220**
Materialism **M: 300b**
Middle East (Religion) **M: 531**
Missionary **M: 620**
Monasticism (Christian monasticism) **M: 701**
New Testament **N: 287** *with picture*
Old Testament **O: 740**
Patrick, Saint **P: 197**
Paul, Saint **P: 200**
Protestantism **P: 833**
Religion **R: 215** *with picture*; (Christianity) **R: 222;** (Religion today) **R: 223**
Religious life **R: 226**
Resurrection **R: 264**
Saint (Christian saints) **S: 29**
Slavery (The Middle Ages) **S: 501**
Ten Commandments **T: 132**
Trinity **T: 447**
Witchcraft (Witchcraft as a religion) **W: 371-372**
Art and music
Architecture (Medieval architecture) **A: 617**
Byzantine art **B: 749** *with pictures*
Communication (During the Middle Ages) **Ci: 879**
Madonna and Child **M: 37** *with picture*
Painting (Medieval painting) **P: 48** *with pictures*
Renaissance (Christian humanism) **R: 238**
Spiritualism (Spiritualism and religion) **So: 796**
Stained glass (Early stained-glass windows) **So: 822** *with picture*
History
Africa (The rise of Christianity) **A: 130**
Byzantine Empire (Religion) **B: 753**
Church and state (History) **C: 542**
Constantine the Great **Ci: 993**
Crusades **Ci: 1159**
Cult (Kinds of cults) **Ci: 1185**
Education (Religion and early Western education) **E: 98-99**

Family (Development of the Western family) F: 22
Freedom (The Middle Ages) F: 502
Freedom of religion (In the United States) F: 505
Julian J: 186
Justinian I J: 204
Luther, Martin L: 527
Middle Ages (The Christian church) M: 523
Mission life in America M: 618
Mysteries M: 972
Philosophy (Aristotle) P: 387; (Medieval philosophy) P: 388
Pliny the Younger P: 574
Reformation R: 195
Religion (Christianity) R: 222
Rome, Ancient (Religion) R: 441-442; (The decline of the empire) R: 447-448
Theodosius I T: 252
Tithe T: 301
World, History of the (The Romans) W: 429-430; (Medieval Europe) W: 432; (The Byzantine Empire) W: 434 *with pictures*
Christianity or Europe [essay by Novalis]
Novalis N: 571
Christians and Jews, National Conference of See National Conference for Community and Justice *in this index*
Christiansborg Palace [Copenhagen]
Denmark *picture on* D: 133
Christianson, Theodore [American political leader]
Minnesota (table) M: 602
Christiansted [Virgin Islands]
Virgin Islands (Clothing and architecture) V: 395
Virgin Islands, United States (Islands) V: 395
Christiansted National Historic Site [Virgin Islands]
National Park System (table: National historic sites) N: 52
Christie, Agatha [British author] C: 527
Christie, Christopher J. [American political leader]
New Jersey (table) N: 249
Christie, Julie [British actress]
Motion picture (Best performance by an actress: 1965) M: 862
Christina [queen of Sweden]
Charles X [of Sweden] C: 382
Christina River
Delaware *picture on* D: 97
Wilmington (History) W: 315
Christina's World [painting by Wyeth]
Painting (Space) P: 28
Wyeth, Andrew *picture on* W: 515
Christkind [legendary figure]
Christmas (In Germany) C: 530
Christmas [holiday] C: 528 *with pictures*
December D: 68
Folklore (Holidays) F: 325
Twelfth Night T: 531
Christmas Bird Count [conservation]
Audubon Society, National A: 885
Christmas card
Christmas (Christmas cards) C: 536 *with picture*
Greeting card G: 387
Christmas Carol, A [book by Dickens]
Christmas (Other customs) C: 536
Dickens, Charles (The first phase) D: 188
Ghost G: 182
Christmas disease
Hemophilia (Major types of hemophilia) H: 182
Christmas Garland, A [book by Beerbohm]
Beerbohm, Max B: 212
Christmas Island [Kiribati] See Kiritimati Atoll *in this index*
Christmas Oratorio [music by Bach]
Bach, Johann Sebastian (His works) B: 16
Christmas orchid [plant]
Orchid *picture on* O: 824
Christmas rose [plant]
Flower *picture on* F: 279
Hellebore H: 177
Christmas Seal
American Lung Association A: 428
Christmas tree [custom]
Christmas (Christmas decorations) C: 535
Fir F: 119
Tree *picture on* T: 427
Christmas tree [industry]
Petroleum (Completing the well) P: 340-341 *with picture*
Christo [Bulgarian-born sculptor] C: 537
Sculpture (From the mid-1900's to the early 2000's) S: 259-260 *with picture*
Christofias, Demetris [Cypriot political leader]
Cyprus (History) C: 1207-1208
Christophe, Henri [Haitian patriot] C: 537
Haiti (History) H: 15-16

Christophe Colomb [opera by Milhaud]
Milhaud, Darius M: 543
Christopher [antipope]
Pope (table) P: 666
Christopher, Saint [early Christian] C: 537
Christopher, Warren Minor [American government official] C: 537
Christopher Robin [literary figure]
Milne, A. A. M: 556
Christy, E. P. [American singer]
Foster, Stephen Collins F: 428
Minstrel show M: 612
Christy, Howard Chandler [American painter]
Constitution of the United States *picture on* Ci: 996
Westward movement in America *picture on* W: 247
Christy Minstrels
Minstrel show M: 612
Chroma
Color (Characteristics of color) Ci: 824 *with diagrams*
Chromatic aberration [light]
Aberration A: 10 *with diagram*
Telescope (Refracting telescopes) T: 103-104
Chromatic adaptation [vision]
Color (Surprising color-vision effects) Ci: 819
Chromatic harmonica [musical instrument]
Harmonica *picture on* H: 62
Chromatic induction [vision]
Color (Surprising color-vision effects) Ci: 819
Chromatic scale
Music (Tone) M: 950-951 *with diagram*
Chromatin [biology]
Cell (Before 1900) C: 337
Chromatography [chemistry] C: 537
Chromatophore [biology]
Fish (Skin and color) F: 160
Octopus (The life of an octopus) O: 673
Photosynthesis P: 430
Squid (The body of a squid) So: 814
Chrome [metal]
Chromium C: 538
Chrome tanning [industrial process]
Leather (Tanning) L: 167 *with picture*
Chrome yellow [pigment]
Chromium C: 538
Chrominance signal [electronics]
Television (Encoding the color signals) T: 123
Chromis [fish]
Fish *picture on* F: 155
Chromite [mineral]
Chromium C: 538
Chromium [element] C: 538
Stainless steel So: 823
Chromophore [astronomy]
Jupiter (Atmosphere) J: 199
Chromosome [genetics] C: 538 *with picture*
See also Gene *in this index*
Autism (Causes) A: 942
Cell (The nucleus) C: 328 *with diagrams*; (Mitosis) C: 330; (Meiosis) C: 331; (Before 1900) C: 337
Cystic fibrosis Ci: 1208
DNA D: 258
Down syndrome D: 316
Evolution (Mutation) E: 427
Gene G: 81
Gene mapping G: 81
Genetic engineering (How genes are reintroduced into cells) G: 84b
Genetic testing (How genes carry information) G: 84d
Genetics (Molecular genetics) G: 86
Genomics G: 90
Heredity H: 200; (Chromosomes and genes) H: 201; (Patterns of heredity) H: 202; (Sources of genetic variation) H: 203
Human Genome Project (The structure and importance of genomes) H: 427
Huntington's disease H: 451
Intellectual disability (Causes) I: 318
Lesch-Nyhan syndrome L: 206
Life (Cells) L: 277
Mutation M: 968
Plant (Hereditary factors) P: 538
Races, Human (Mutation) R: 58
Reproduction (How genes are transferred) R: 242
Reproduction, Human (How sex is determined) R: 246
Sexuality (Before birth) S: 338
Weismann, August W: 188
Chromosphere [sun]
Sun *picture on* So: 985; (Zones of the sun) So: 979-980 *with picture*
Chronic fatigue syndrome [disorder] C: 538
Chronic obstructive pulmonary disease C: 539
Chronic pain

Pain P: 21
Chronic wasting disease
Deer (Endangered species) D: 86
Elk E: 242
Chronicle [literature]
French literature (Early prose) F: 519
Russian literature (Nonreligious literature) R: 559
Chronicler's Work [Bible]
Bible (The Writings) B: 281-282
Chronicles [book by Froissart]
Froissart, Jean F: 541
Chronicles, Books of [Bible] C: 539
Bible (The Writings) B: 281-282
Chronicles of England, Scotland, and Ireland See Holinshed's Chronicles *in this index*
Chronicles of Japan See Nihongi *in this index*
Chronicles of Narnia, The [book by Lewis]
Lewis, C. S. L: 220
Chronicles of the Giant Gargantua [book]
Rabelais, François R: 49
Chronobiology [science]
Biological clock B: 314
Chronological age [psychology]
Intelligence quotient (Calculating IQ) I: 319
Chronometer [instrument] C: 539
Clock *picture on* Ci: 682j
Exploration (Exploring the Pacific) E: 447
Navigation (Keeping time) N: 71
Chronopathology [medicine]
Biological clock (Biological clocks in people) B: 315
Chronopharmacology [medicine]
Biological clock (Biological clocks in people) B: 315
Chrysalis [entomology] C: 539 *with picture*
Butterfly (The pupa) B: 741 *with picture*
Metamorphosis (The pupa) M: 428 *with picture*
Chrysanthemum [plant] C: 539
Daisy D: 8
Flower (Garden perennials) F: 278 *with picture*
Gardening *picture on* G: 33
Viroid V: 426
Chrysanthemum, Supreme Order of the
Medals, decorations, and orders (table) M: 359
Chryseis [legendary figure]
Agamemnon A: 139
Chryselephantine statue [sculpture]
Ivory (Ivory carving) I: 521
Chrysler, Walter Percy [American businessman] C: 540
Chrysler Corporation See Chrysler Group LLC *in this index*
Chrysler Group LLC [company]
Automobile *picture on* A: 971; (Economic impact) A: 959; (The Great Depression) A: 970; (Challenges to the Big Three) A: 972; (The 2000's) A: 972
Chrysler, Walter Percy C: 540
Daimler AG D: 6
Dodge brothers D: 260
Iacocca, Lee I: 2
Michigan (Depression and recovery) M: 509-511 *with picture*
Sports car (History) So: 803
Chrysler Hall
Norfolk (Description) N: 453-454
Chrysler Museum
Norfolk (Description) N: 453-454
Chrysoberyl [gem]
Alexandrite A: 345
Cat's-eye C: 305
Gem *picture on* G: 78
Chrysostom, Saint John [Christian religious leader] C: 540
Chrysotile [material]
Asbestos (Types of asbestos) A: 765
Serpentine S: 318
Chu, Steven [American physicist]
Asian Americans (Notable Asian American "firsts") A: 812f
Energy, Department of (table) E: 276
Nobel Prizes (Physics: 1997) N: 442
Obama, Barack (table) O: 640h
Chuang-tzu [book] See Zhuangzi *in this index*
Chuang Tzu [Chinese philosopher] See Zhuangzi *in this index*
Chub [fish] C: 540 *with picture*
Chub mackerel [fish]
Mackerel M: 24
Chubb, Lewis W. [American chemist]
Glass (table) G: 218
Chuck wagon C: 540
Cowboy (The trail drive) Ci: 1111
Chuck-will's widow [bird]
Whip-poor-will W: 281
Chuckwalla [reptile] C: 540 *with picture*
Iguana I: 50

Chugach Mountains
Alaska (Land regions) **A: 292** *with picture*
Anchorage *picture on* **A: 450**
Chugach National Forest [Alaska]
Alaska (Places to visit) **A: 290**
Chukar [bird]
Partridge **P: 189**
Chukker
Polo (The game) **P: 646**
Chula [music]
Portugal (The arts) **P: 689-690**
Chulalongkorn [king of Thailand]
October **O: 670**
Thailand (Modernization) **T: 227**
Chum salmon [fish]
Salmon *picture on* **S: 69**; (Kinds of salmon) **S: 70**
Chumash Indians C: 540
Chun Doo Hwan [Korean military leader]
Korea, South (History) **K: 378c**
Ch'ung-ch'ing [China] *See* Chongqing *in this index*
Chungking [China] *See* Chongqing *in this index*
Chunkey [game]
Indian, American (Recreation) **I: 142-143**
Chunnel [nickname] *See* Channel Tunnel *in this index*
Chuño [food]
Bolivia (Food) **B: 443**
Inca (Food, clothing, and shelter) **I: 95-96**
Potato (History) **P: 713**
Chuquicamata [mine, Chile]
Chile (Mining) **C: 466** *with picture*
Church [religion] **C: 541**
Architecture (Medieval architecture) **A: 617-619** *with pictures*; (Renaissance architecture) **A: 620** *with pictures*
Byzantine art (Architecture) **B: 749** *with picture*
City (Description) **Ci: 582** *with picture*
United States *picture on* **U: 114**
Church, Frederic Edwin [American painter] **C: 541** *with picture*
Church and state C: 542
City (Government) **Ci: 581**
Constitution of the United States (Amendment 1) **Ci: 1011**; (Article VI) **Ci: 1011**
Evolution (Acceptance of evolution) **E: 433**
Freedom of religion **F: 505**
Parochial school **P: 178**
Quebec Act **Q: 38**
Reformation (Political causes) **R: 197**
Religious education (Public schools) **R: 225**
School prayer **S: 185**
Supreme Court of the United States (Church and state) **So: 1001**; (table) **So: 1002**
Test Acts **T: 181**
Totalitarianism **T: 346**
Church Dogmatics [book by Barth]
Barth, Karl **B: 120**
Church mode [music]
Classical music (Church music) **Ci: 645**
Church music *See* Sacred music *in this index*
Church of ...
Religious groups whose names begin Church of... *appear below; church buildings appear under their key words, as in* San Lorenzo, Church of
Church of Christ [religious group] *See* Churches of Christ *in this index*
Church of Christ, Scientist [religious group]
Christian Scientists **C: 522e**
Church of England [religious group] **C: 542**
See also Anglican Communion *in this index*
Archbishop of Canterbury **A: 601**
Boleyn, Anne **B: 440**
Christianity (The Reformation) **C: 524**
Elizabeth I (Problems at home and abroad) **E: 238**
England (Religion) **E: 298** *with picture*; (The English Reformation) **E: 307**
Episcopal Church **E: 344**
Hampton Court Conference **H: 36**
Laud, William **L: 121**
Methodists **M: 434**
Puritans (Puritan beliefs) **P: 910**; (History) **P: 910**
Religious life (Religious life in the 1700's and 1800's) **R: 227**
Test Acts **T: 181**
Thirty-Nine Articles **T: 259**
United Kingdom (Religion) **U: 56**
Church of God in Christ, The [religious group] **C: 543**
Pentecostal churches (Major Pentecostal churches) **P: 275-276**
Church of Jesus Christ of Latter-day Saints [religious group] *See* Mormons *in this index*
Church of Jesus Christ of Latter Day Saints, Reorganized *See* Community of Christ *in this index*
Church of Scotland [religious group]
Scotland (Religion) **S: 215**

United Kingdom (Religion) **U: 56**
Church of the Brethren *See* Brethren, Church of the *in this index*
Church of the Gesù [Rome]
Counter Reformation *picture on* **Ci: 1097**
Church of the Nazarene [religious group] **C: 543**
Church school
Parochial school **P: 177**
Religious education **R: 225**
Churches, World Council of
Protestantism (The ecumenical movement) **P: 835**
Churches of Christ [religious group] **C: 543**
Churches of Christ, National Council of the *See* National Council of Churches *in this index*
Churches of God [religious groups] **C: 543**
Churchill [Manitoba]
Hudson Bay **H: 405**
Manitoba (Places to visit) **M: 152**; (table: Average monthly weather) **M: 156**
Churchill, Caryl [British dramatist] **C: 543**
English literature (Recent English drama) **E: 323**
Churchill, Clementine Hozier [wife of]
Churchill, Sir Winston Leonard Spencer (Churchill's family) **C: 547** *with portrait*
Churchill, Diana [daughter of]
Churchill, Sir Winston Leonard Spencer (Churchill's family) **C: 547**
Churchill, Jennie Jerome [mother of]
Churchill, Sir Winston Leonard Spencer (Boyhood and education) **C: 545** *with picture*
Churchill, John [brother of]
Churchill, Sir Winston Leonard Spencer (Boyhood and education) **C: 545-546** *with picture*
Churchill, Marigold [daughter of]
Churchill, Sir Winston Leonard Spencer (Churchill's family) **C: 547**
Churchill, Mary [daughter of]
Churchill, Sir Winston Leonard Spencer (Churchill's family) **C: 547**
Churchill, Randolph [son of]
Churchill, Sir Winston Leonard Spencer (Churchill's family) **C: 547**
Churchill, Lord Randolph [British political leader]
Churchill, Sir Winston Leonard Spencer (Boyhood and education) **C: 545**
Churchill, Sarah [daughter of]
Churchill, Sir Winston Leonard Spencer (Churchill's family) **C: 547**
Churchill, Sarah Jennings [wife of Marlborough]
Anne **A: 517**
Marlborough, Duke of **M: 215**
Churchill, Thomas J. [American political leader]
Arkansas (table) **A: 712**
Churchill, Sir Winston Leonard Spencer [British statesman] **C: 544** *with pictures*
Atlantic Charter **A: 862** *with picture*
Autograph *picture on* **A: 943**
Caricature *picture on* **C: 238**
Cold War (The alliance breaks up) **Ci: 763**; (The Iron Curtain descends) **Ci: 763**
Democracy (Famous quotations about democracy) **D: 120**
Iron Curtain **I: 453**
London *picture on* **L: 442**
Marlborough, Duke of **M: 215**
Potsdam Conference **P: 715**
Quebec (The early 1900's) **Q: 37**
Roosevelt, Franklin Delano (Roosevelt's third administration [1941-1945]) **R: 456**; (The Big Three) **R: 457**; (Yalta Conference) **R: 458** *with picture*
Stalin, Joseph (World War II) **So: 827**
Tehran Conference **T: 88**
Union of Soviet Socialist Republics (Results of the war) **U: 37**
United Kingdom ("Peace in our time") **U: 70**
World War II *picture on* **W: 479**; (The conquest of Denmark and Norway) **W: 473**; (The war in Europe and North Africa) **W: 480**
Yalta Conference **Y: 549**
Churchill Downs [Louisville]
Kentucky Derby **K: 295**
Louisville (History) **L: 506**
Churchill Falls [Newfoundland and Labrador]
Churchill River **C: 550**
Newfoundland and Labrador (The late 1900's) **N: 377**
Churchill Memorial and Library [Fulton]
Missouri (Places to visit) **M: 660**
Churchill River [Manitoba-Saskatchewan] **C: 550**
Churchill River [Newfoundland and Labrador] **C: 550**
Newfoundland and Labrador (Rivers and lakes) **N: 370** *with map*
Churn C: 550
Butter (Churning) **B: 730**

Churrasco
Brazil (Food and drink) **B: 574-575**
Churrigueresque [architecture]
Architecture (Baroque architecture) **A: 622**
Churubusco, Battle of [1847]
Mexican War (Scott's campaign) **M: 446-447**; (Principal battles) **M: 447**
Churyumov-Gerasimenko [comet]
Comet (Studying comets) **Ci: 868-869**
Chuuk Islands [Pacific] **C: 550**
Caroline Islands **C: 244**
Pacific Islands, Trust Territory of the **P: 13, P: 13**
World War II (Island hopping in the Central Pacific) **W: 489-490**
Chuuk state
Chuuk Islands **T: 465**
Micronesia, Federated States of **M: 515**
Chylak, Nestor [American baseball umpire]
Baseball (table: Hall of Fame) **B: 134**
Chyle [physiology]
Intestine (The small intestine) **I: 353**
Lymphatic system (Absorption of fats) **L: 535**
Chyme [physiology]
Alimentary canal **A: 368**
Colon **Ci: 786**
Digestive system (From mouth to stomach) **D: 202**
Human body (The mouth, esophagus, and stomach) **H: 419-420**
Stomach (The stomach's work) **So: 908**
CIA [agency] *See* Central Intelligence Agency *in this index*
Ciardi, John [American poet] **Ci: 551** *with portrait*
Cibao [region, Dominican Republic]
Dominican Republic (Land) **D: 304**
Cibber, Colley [English actor/author]
Poet laureate (table: Poets laureate of the United Kingdom) **P: 590**
Pope, Alexander **P: 667**
Cíbola, Seven Cities of [legend] **Ci: 551**
Coronado, Francisco Vásquez de **Ci: 1067**
Estevanico **E: 360**
Exploration (Spain's conquests in the New World) **E: 445-446**
Indian, American (After European contact) **I: 168**
New Mexico (Exploration, conquest, and settlement) **N: 273**
Texas (Spanish exploration) **T: 204**
Zuni Indians **Z: 609**
Ciboney Indians
Cuba (Early years) **Ci: 1175**
West Indies (Early days) **W: 205**
CIC hearing aid
Hearing aid (Styles) **H: 130** *with picture*
Cicada [insect] **Ci: 551** *with picture*
Insect *pictures on* **I: 281**; **I: 292**; (Hearing) **I: 290-291**
Locust **L: 418**
Ciccone, Madonna Louise Veronica [birth name of]
Madonna **M: 37**
Cicely [herb] *See* Sweet cicely *in this index*
Cicero, Marcus Tullius [Roman orator] **Ci: 551** *with portrait*
Augustus **A: 889**
Catiline **C: 304**
Civil rights (Natural law) **Ci: 610**
Classicism (Rome) **Ci: 653**
Damocles **D: 21**
Democracy (Origins of democracy) **D: 122**
Forum, Roman **F: 421**
Government (Ancient Rome) **G: 289**
Latin literature (The age of Cicero) **L: 116**
Oratory (Classical orators) **O: 819**
Renaissance (Petrarch and Giovanni Boccaccio) **R: 234**
Rome, Ancient *picture on* **R: 444**
Roscius, Quintus **R: 474**
Ciconia, Johannes [Belgian composer]
Wallonia **W: 18**
C.I.D. [police] *See* Scotland Yard *in this index*
Cid, The [play by Corneille]
Corneille, Pierre **Ci: 1065**
Drama (Neoclassical playwrights) **D: 333**
French literature (Classical drama) **F: 520**
Cid, The [Spanish hero] **Ci: 552**
Spain (The Christian kingdoms) **So: 746**
Spanish literature (Early medieval literature) **So: 757-758**
Cider [drink] **Ci: 552**
Cider House Rules, The [book by Irving]
Irving, John **I: 459**
Cider vinegar
Cider **Ci: 552**
Cid's Youth, The [play by Castro]
Spanish literature (The 1600's) **So: 759**
CIE System

Color (The CIE System of Color Specification)
Ci: 824
Ciechanover, Aaron [Israeli chemist]
Nobel Prizes (Chemistry: 2004) N: 444
Cienfuegos, Nicasio Álvarez de [Spanish poet]
Spanish literature (The 1700's) So: 760-761
Cierva, Juan de la [Spanish inventor]
Autogiro A: 943
Cigar Ci: 552
Cuba (Manufacturing) Ci: 1173 *with picture*
Smoking S: 520
Tobacco T: 305; (Cigar leaf tobacco) T: 306
Cigar [horse]
Horse racing (History) H: 366
Cigar-Makers' International Union [labor union]
Gompers, Samuel G: 268
Cigar store Indian [sculpture]
Folk art (Sculpture) F: 317 *with picture*
Cigarette Ci: 552
Filter F: 103
Flax (Growing and processing seed flax) F: 231
Smoking S: 520
Tobacco T: 305
Cigarette [sculpture by Smith]
Sculpture (Varieties of abstraction) S: 258 *with picture*
Cigrand, Bernard J. [American educator]
Flag Day F: 223
Ciguatera [disease]
Barracuda B: 118
Cilia [biology] Ci: 553
Cell (The cytoplasm) C: 329
Clam (The body of a clam) Ci: 637
Disease (Natural barriers) D: 231
Lung (Other jobs of the lungs) L: 524
Nose N: 548
Oyster (Body organs) O: 890
Paramecium P: 152 *with picture*
Protozoan (Ciliates) P: 838 *with picture*
Reproduction, Human (The human reproductive system) R: 244-245
Smoking (Why smoking is dangerous) S: 520
Ciliary body [anatomy]
Eye (The uveal tract) E: 460-461 *with picture*
Ciliate [biology]
Protozoan (Ciliates) P: 838 *with picture*
Ciliated cell [biology]
Fallopian tube F: 18
Çiller, Tansu [Turkish political leader]
Turkey (Political changes) T: 512
Cimabue, Giovanni [Italian painter] Ci: 553 *with picture*
Giotto (His life) G: 193
Madonna and Child (Painters of the Madonna) M: 37-38
Painting (The 1300's) P: 51
Renaissance *picture on* R: 234
Cimarron [film]
Motion picture (Best picture: 1930-31) M: 861
Cimbri [ancient people]
Germany (Ancient times) G: 162
Teutons T: 183
Cimino, Michael [American director]
Motion picture (Best achievement in directing: 1978) M: 862
Cimmerians [ancient people] Ci: 553
Russia (Early days) R: 547
Ukraine (Early days) U: 11-12
Cimon [Greek political leader] Ci: 553
Pericles P: 287; (War with Sparta) P: 287
CIN [disorder] *See* Cervical intraepithelial neoplasia *in this index*
Cinch ring [riding equipment]
Saddle *diagrams on* S: 7
Cinchona [tree] Ci: 553
Plant (As medicines) P: 517-518
Quinine Q: 42
Cincinnati [Ohio] Ci: 554 *with picture and map*
Cincinnati, Society of the Ci: 556
Ohio (table: Average monthly weather) O: 695
Cincinnati [horse]
Horse (table: Famous horses in history and legend) H: 361
Cincinnati, Society of the [organization] Ci: 556
Veterans' organizations (In the United States) V: 344
Cincinnati, University of
Cincinnati (Education) Ci: 555 *with map*
Cincinnati Art Museum
Cincinnati (Museums) Ci: 555 *with map*
Ohio (Museums) O: 685
Cincinnati Bengals [team]
Cincinnati (Sports) Ci: 556
Football (National Football League) F: 364
Cincinnati Observatory
Ohio (Interesting facts) O: 681
Cincinnati Red Stockings [former team]

Baseball (Professional baseball) B: 133
Ohio *picture on* O: 701
Cincinnati Reds [team]
Baseball (table) B: 130
Cincinnati (Sports) Ci: 556
Cincinnati Southern Railway
Cincinnati (The 1800's) Ci: 556
Cincinnatus, Lucius Quinctius [Roman patriot] Ci: 557
Cinco de Mayo [holiday] Ci: 557
Hispanic Americans (Holidays) H: 250
Texas (Annual events) *picture on* T: 195
Cinder cone
Moon (Rilles) M: 790
"Cinderella" [story]
Folklore *picture on* F: 324; (Characteristics of folklore) F: 323
Grimm's Fairy Tales G: 394
Cinderella Man, The [nickname]
Braddock, James J. B: 543
Cinema *See* Motion picture *in this index*
Cinema Novo [movement]
Motion picture (Movies in the 1960's) M: 870
CinemaScope [motion pictures]
Motion picture (Postwar American movies) M: 869
Cinémathèque Française [museum]
Paris (Museums and art galleries) P: 164-165
Cinématographe [machine]
Lumière brothers L: 522
Cinematographer [career]
Motion picture (Assembling the production team) M: 850 *with picture*
Cinerama [motion pictures]
Motion picture (Postwar American movies) M: 869
Cineraria [plant] Ci: 557 *with picture*
Cinereous vulture [bird]
Vulture (Old World vultures) V: 454
Cingular Wireless [company]
AT&T Inc. A: 852
Cingulata [zoology]
Mammal (table) M: 128 *with picture*
Cinna, Lucius Cornelius [Roman political leader]
Caesar, Julius (Early life) C: 13
Cinnabar [mineral] Ci: 557
Mercury (Sources) M: 413 *with picture*
Cinnamon [spice] Ci: 557 *with picture*
Cinnamon bear
Bear (American black bears) B: 184
Cinnamon fern [plant]
Plant *picture on* P: 547
Cinnamon teal [bird]
Teal T: 71 *with picture*
Cinque, Joseph [African slave]
African Americans (The growth of slavery) A: 136f-136g
Amistad Rebellion A: 433
Cinquefoil [plant] Ci: 557
Flower (Flowers of the Arctic tundra) F: 283 *with picture*
CIO [union] *See* Congress of Industrial Organizations *in this index*
Cio-cio-san [opera character]
Opera: (*Madama Butterfly*) O: 804 *with picture*
Cipher
Codes and ciphers Ci: 749
Cipher machine
Codes and ciphers (Cipher machines) Ci: 750
Ciphertext
Codes and ciphers Ci: 749; (Communications security) Ci: 749
Ciprofloxacin [medication]
Antibiotic (table) A: 551
Circadian rhythm [biology]
Biological clock (Daily rhythms) B: 315
Pineal gland P: 471
Circe [Greek mythology] Ci: 557
Odyssey: (Odysseus describes his wanderings) O: 675
Scylla S: 261
Circle [geometry] Ci: 558 *with diagrams*
Degree D: 92
Geometry (Non-Euclidean geometry) G: 105 *with diagram*
Pi P: 445
Circle [organization]
Girl Scouts (Brownies) G: 198
Circle dance
Dance (Ritual ethnic dances) D: 25
Circle Game, The [poems by Atwood]
Atwood, Margaret A: 880
Circle graph
Graph (Circle graphs) G: 322 *with picture*
Circle racing
Motorboat racing (Types of racing) M: 877
Circuit [government]

United States, Government of the (Lower court system) U: 144
Circuit, Electric *See* Electric circuit *in this index*
Circuit, Electronic *See* Electronic circuit *in this index*
Circuit board [electronics]
Computer (Parts of computers) Ci: 911-912
Computer chip (External connections) Ci: 924f
Electronics (Types of electronic circuits) E: 209-210 *with picture*
Telephone (The circuit board) T: 95
Circuit breaker [electricity] Ci: 558
Electric circuit E: 166
Electricity (Controlling electric current) E: 195
Fuse F: 589
House (Electrical wiring) H: 382
Circuit Court of Appeals [law]
Court (Federal courts) Ci: 1102
Court of appeals Ci: 1105
Circuit justice [office]
Court of appeals Ci: 1105
Circuit rider [U.S. history] Ci: 558
Asbury, Francis A: 766
Methodists (Early history) M: 435
Pioneer life in America (Religion) P: 484
Circuit switching [electronics]
Telephone (How a telephone call travels) T: 95
Circular accelerator [machine]
Particle accelerator (How accelerators work) P: 184 *with diagrams*
Circular cylinder [geometry]
Cylinder C: 1204
Circular orbit [physics]
Space exploration (Kinds of earth orbits) *diagram on* So: 697
Circular saw [tool]
Lumber *picture on* L: 520
Saw (Power saws) S: 167 *with picture*
Woodworking (Cutting) W: 397 *with picture*
Circulation [physiology] *See* Circulatory system *in this index*
Circulation [publishing]
Advertising (Magazines) A: 74
Newspaper (Circulation) N: 385
Circulatory disorder
See also Cardiovascular disease *in this index*
Blood (Blood disorders) B: 414
Blood pressure B: 416
Blue baby B: 419
Embolism E: 256
Stroke So: 929
Circulatory shock [disorder]
Shock S: 429
Circulatory system Ci: 559 *with diagrams*
Aorta A: 562
Artery A: 750
Bird (The circulatory system) B: 366
Blood B: 407
Butterfly (The internal organs) B: 739 *with diagram*
Fish (Circulatory system) F: 163
Harvey, William H: 81
Heart H: 132; (Discovery of circulation) H: 144
Human body (The circulatory system) H: 421 *with diagram*; (table) H: 422 *with diagram*
Insect (Circulatory system) I: 288 *with diagram*
Lung (Gas exchange in the lungs) L: 523-524
Lymphatic system L: 533 *with diagram*
Mammal (Internal organ systems) M: 119
Medicine (The beginnings of modern research) M: 374
Reproduction, Human (Development of organs and organ systems) R: 248
Spider (Circulatory system) So: 785 *with diagram*
Vein V: 295
Circumcision [surgery] Ci: 561
AIDS (Prevention) A: 165
Judaism (Special occasions) J: 182
Penis P: 241
Surgery (History) So: 1007
Circumference [geometry]
Circle (Parts of a circle) Ci: 558 *with diagram*
Pi P: 445
Circumference, of Earth
Columbus, Christopher (The plan to sail westward) Ci: 858
Earth (Earth's size and shape) E: 18
Equator E: 346
Eratosthenes E: 349
Hellenistic Age H: 177
Circumferential
Road (Bypasses) R: 358
Circumflex
Diacritical mark D: 180
Circumstantial evidence [law]
Evidence (Kinds of evidence) E: 426
Forensic science (General kinds of evidence) F: 388b

Circus Ci: 562 *with pictures*
  Barnum, P. T. **B:** 115
  Cirque du Soleil Ci: 566
  Clown Ci: 713
  Lion (Training lions) **L:** 343
  Picasso, Pablo (The Rose Period) **P:** 448a
  Ringling brothers **R:** 343
  United States, History of the *picture on* **U:** 183
Circus City Festival [Indiana]
  Circus (Places to visit and annual events) Ci: 566
Circus Flora [Missouri]
  Circus (The circus today) Ci: 564-565
Circus march [music]
  March **M:** 193
Circus Maximus [Roman Empire]
  City *picture on* Ci: 580
  Hippodrome **H:** 240
  Rome, Ancient (Recreation) **R:** 440 *with picture*
Circus Oz [Australia]
  Circus (The circus today) Ci: 564-565
Circus World [Baraboo]
  Circus (Places to visit and annual events) Ci: 566
  Wisconsin (Places to visit) **W:** 356
Cirque [geology]
  Alps (How the Alps were formed) **A:** 384
  Glacier *diagram on* **G:** 204; (Kinds of glaciers)
    G: 202
Cirque du Soleil [circus] Ci: 566
  Canada *picture on* **C:** 111
  Circus (The circus today) Ci: 564-565 *with picture*
  Swimming (Synchronized swimming) **So:** 1047
Cirque glacier [geology]
  Glacier (Kinds of glaciers) **G:** 202
Cirque Médrano [circus]
  Picasso, Pablo (The Rose Period) **P:** 448a
Cirrate octopod [animal]
  Deep sea *picture on* **D:** 82; (Invertebrates)
    D: 82a-82b
Cirrhosis [disorder] Ci: 566
  Alcoholism (Effects of alcoholism) **A:** 338
  Hepatitis **H:** 192
  Liver (Diseases of the liver) **L:** 394-395
Cirri [biology]
  Barnacle **B:** 114 *with picture*
  Deep sea (Invertebrates) **D:** 82a-82b
Cirrocumulus cloud
  Cloud *picture on* Ci: 709; (High clouds) Ci: 707
Cirrostratus cloud
  Cloud *picture on* Ci: 709; (Kinds of clouds) Ci: 707
Cirrus cloud
  Cloud *pictures on* Ci: 709; (Kinds of clouds)
    Ci: 707 *with picture*
Cirrus fibratus cloud
  Cloud *picture on* Ci: 709
Cirrus floccus cloud
  Cloud *picture on* Ci: 709
CIS [confederation] *See* Commonwealth of
  Independent States *in this index*
Cisalpine Gaul [former region]
  Gaul **G:** 70 *with map*
Cisneros, Henry Gabriel [American political
  leader] Ci: 567 *with portrait*
  San Antonio (History) **S:** 86-87
Cistercians [religious group] Ci: 567
  Bernard of Clairvaux, Saint **B:** 270
  Merton, Thomas **M:** 419
  Trappists **T:** 404
Cisterna chyli [anatomy]
  Lymphatic system (Absorption of fats) **L:** 535
    with diagram
Cistertium *See* Cistercians *in this index*
Citadel [Egypt]
  Cairo (The city) **C:** 116
Citadel [fortification] Ci: 567 *with picture*
Citadel, The [book by Cronin]
  Cronin, A. J. Ci: 1152
Citadel, The [Quebec City]
  Quebec [city] (The city) **Q:** 34
  Quebec [province] (Places to visit) **Q:** 20
Citadel, The [the school, South Carolina]
  South Carolina (Schools) *picture on* **So:** 644
Citadel and York Redoubt [Halifax]
  Nova Scotia (Places to visit) **N:** 560
Citadel of King Sargon II [Assyria]
  Architecture (Mesopotamian architecture) **A:** 611
    with picture
Citation [horse]
  Arcaro, Eddie **A:** 593
Citation analysis
  Information science **I:** 269
Citation Star
  Medals, decorations, and orders (table) **M:** 357
Cité Libre [magazine]
  Trudeau, Pierre Elliott (Entry into public life)
    T: 462
Cité Souterrain *See* Underground City *in this index*
Cîteaux, Order of [religious group] *See* Cistercians

in this index
CITES [agreement] *See* Convention on International
  Trade in Endangered Species of Wild Fauna and
  Flora *in this index*
Citibank [bank] Ci: 567
Citicorp [company]
  Citibank Ci: 567
Cities *See* City *in this index*
Cities of refuge [ancient Palestine] Ci: 568
Cities of the Plain [book by Proust]
  Proust, Marcel **P:** 838
Citigroup [company]
  Bank (Diversification and mergers) **B:** 94
  Citibank Ci: 568
Citizen
  Greece, Ancient (The people) **G:** 367
Citizen Action Party [political party]
  Costa Rica (Recent developments) Ci: 1084
Citizen Corps [organization]
  USA Freedom Corps **U:** 229
Citizen Kane [film] Ci: 568
  Motion picture (Movies in the 1930's) **M:** 868
    with picture
  Welles, Orson **W:** 194
Citizen King *See* Louis Philippe *in this index*
Citizen of the World, The [essays by Goldsmith]
  Goldsmith, Oliver **G:** 259
Citizen's arrest
  Arrest **A:** 743
Citizens band radio Ci: 568 *with picture*
  Radio (In private communications) **R:** 84-85
  Walkie-talkie **W:** 14
Citizens United v. Federal Election Commission
  [court case]
  Political action committee **P:** 627
Citizenship Ci: 568 *with pictures*
  Citizenship and Immigration Services, United
    States Ci: 572
  Constitution of the United States (Amendment
    14) Ci: 1013
  Dred Scott Decision **D:** 345
  European Union (Internal affairs) **E:** 418
  Immigration and Naturalization Service **I:** 86
  Indian, American (In the United States) **I:** 179
  Law (Ancient Roman law) **L:** 133-134
  Naturalization **N:** 66
  Rome, Ancient (The people) **R:** 437
Citizenship Act [1977]
  Citizenship (Canadian citizenship) Ci: 571
**Citizenship and Immigration Services, United
  States** [agency] Ci: 572
  Immigration and Naturalization Service **I:** 86
  Naturalization **N:** 67
Citizenship Day *See* Constitution Day and
  Citizenship Day *in this index*
Citizenship education *See* Civics *in this index*
Citlaltépetl [mountain, Mexico] *See* Orizaba, Pico
  de *in this index*
Citrange [plant] Ci: 572 *with picture*
Citrate [chemical]
  Citric acid Ci: 573
Citric acid [chemical] Ci: 573
Citrin [chemical] Ci: 573
Citrine [mineral]
  Quartz (Types) **Q:** 8
Citron [fruit] Ci: 573 *with picture*
Citronella [oil] Ci: 573
Citronellal [chemical]
  Citronella Ci: 573
Citrus [botany] Ci: 573
  Florida (Agriculture) **F:** 259; (The late 1900's)
    F: 264-265
  Fruit (Subtropical fruits) **F:** 546
  Lake (Climate) **L:** 33
Citrus canker [plant disease]
  Orange (Pests and diseases) **O:** 815
City Ci: 574 *with pictures and maps*
  African Americans (The black migration to the
    North) **A:** 136m
  City government Ci: 594
  City planning Ci: 598
  Civilization Ci: 635
  Climate (Human activity) Ci: 678
  Conservation (Urban conservation) Ci: 984
  Culture (Invention) Ci: 1189
  Curfew Ci: 1194
  Environmental pollution (History) **E:** 338
  Europe (City life) **E:** 387
  Latin America (City life) **L:** 95 *with pictures*
  Local government **L:** 406
  Metropolitan area **M:** 442
  Middle East (Ways of life) **M:** 530
  New York City (Housing) **N:** 332; (Social
    problems) **N:** 332
  Police (City police) **P:** 622
  Soleri, Paolo **So:** 583 *with picture*
  Suburb **So:** 949

Transit T: 374
  United States, History of the (Industrialization
    and reform [1870-1916]) **U:** 179-180; (The rich
    and the poor) **U:** 182; (The Roaring Twenties)
    U: 189; (The civil rights movement) **U:** 196a
  Urban renewal **U:** 220
  Water (City water systems) **W:** 124 *with pictures*
  Weather (How people affect the weather) **W:** 170
  World, History of the (The Industrial Revolution)
    W: 444
City, The [district]
  London **L:** 428, *picture on* **L:** 438; (Greater
    London) **L:** 428-429; (Residential areas and
    housing) **L:** 432; (Expansion beyond the walls)
    L: 440-441
City bank
  Bank (Asia and the Middle East) **B:** 91
City Beautiful movement
  City planning (The Industrial Revolution) Ci: 603
City center [business]
  Shopping center **S:** 434
City commission [political science] *See* City council
  in this index
City council [political science]
  City government (Forms of city
    government) Ci: 595; (Forms of city
    government) Ci: 595
  Mayor **M:** 330
City Dionysia [ancient Greece]
  Drama (Greek drama) **D:** 326
City Duma [legislature]
  Moscow (Government) **M:** 826; (Revolution and
    Soviet rule) **M:** 827
City government Ci: 594 *with diagrams*
  City *picture on* Ci: 575; (Governmental problems)
    Ci: 592
  Local government (Units of loval government)
    L: 406
  Mayor **M:** 330
City Hall [Philadelphia]
  Philadelphia (Downtown Philadelphia) **P:** 359
    with picture
City Hall [Stockholm]
  Sweden (Fine arts) **So:** 1027
City Hall [Toronto]
  Toronto *picture on* **T:** 340b; (Landmarks) **T:** 338
City Hall Plaza
  Korea, South *picture on* **K:** 375
City Hotel [New York City]
  Hotel (History) **H:** 376-377
City Island
  New York City (The Bronx) **N:** 328-329
City jail
  Prison (Types of correctional institutions) **P:** 805
City Lights [film]
  Chaplin, Charlie **C:** 376
City manager [government]
  City government (The council-manager form)
    Ci: 596 *with diagram*
City of Brotherly Love [name for]
  Philadelphia **P:** 358
City of Glasgow [ship]
  Shipwreck (table: Major shipwrecks) **S:** 428
City of God, The [book by Augustine]
  Augustine, Saint (His beliefs) **A:** 888
  Millennium **M:** 553
  Philosophy (Medieval philosophy) **P:** 388
City of Light [nickname]
  Paris **P:** 160
City of Oranges [nickname]
  Salto **S:** 76a
City of Rocks National Reserve [Idaho]
  National Park System (table: National parkways
    and other national parklands) **N:** 55
City of Roses [nickname]
  Portland (Oregon) **P:** 683
City of Sails [nickname]
  Auckland **A:** 880
City of Salina [train]
  Railroad (The 1920's and the Great Depression)
    R: 118
City of the Sun, The [book by Campanella]
  Italian literature (The Baroque period and the
    Enlightenment) **I:** 494
City of Washington, The [U.S. history]
  United States capitals **U:** 199
City Park [New Orleans]
  New Orleans (Residential districts) **N:** 279;
    (Recreation) **N:** 282
City planning Ci: 598 *with pictures*
  City *pictures on* Ci: 579, Ci: 580; (Future cities)
    Ci: 593
  Conservation (Careers in conservation) Ci: 990
  Housing (New towns) **H:** 390
  Landscape architecture **L:** 59
  Rome, Ancient (City life) **R:** 438
  Sociology (Careers) **So:** 567
  Soleri, Paolo **So:** 583 *with picture*

Urban renewal U: 220
Zoning Z: 598
City Rises, The [painting by Boccioni]
Futurism *picture on* F: 590
City-state [political unit] Ci: 603
Athens (Earliest times) A: 857
Babylonia (Sumerian city-states) B: 14
Europe (Ancient Greece) E: 407
Free city F: 498
Greece, Ancient G: 366; (Government) G: 372;
(The development of the Greek city-state)
G: 372
Hittites (History) H: 269
Italy (Rise of the city-states) I: 513-514 *with map*
Phoenicia (Government) P: 394
Renaissance *map on* R: 233
War (Ancient times) W: 25
World, History of the (The Tigris-Euphrates Valley)
W: 422-424; (The Greeks) W: 428
City University of New York *See* New York, City
University of *in this index*
CityPlex Tower [Tulsa]
Tulsa (History) T: 483-484
Ciudad Bolívar [Venezuela] Ci: 604
Bolívar, Simón (Fight for freedom) B: 441
Orinoco River O: 856
Ciudad Juárez [Mexico]
Juárez J: 178
Ciudad Trujillo [former name]
Santo Domingo S: 117
Civet [animal] Ci: 604 *with picture*
Civic center [public buildings]
San Francisco (Downtown San Francisco) S: 92-93
Wright, Frank Lloyd *picture on* W: 507
Civic Center of Des Moines
Des Moines *picture on* D: 160
Civic Conservatory [Saskatoon]
Saskatchewan (Places to visit) S: 136
Civic Democratic Party [political party]
Czech Republic (Politics) Ci: 1210; (Recent
developments) Ci: 1214
Civic Forum [political party]
Czechoslovakia (The Velvet Revolution) Ci: 1216
Civic humanism [philosophy]
Humanism (Work of the humanists) H: 431
Civic Platform [political party]
Poland (Politics) P: 605; (Recent developments)
P: 615
Civics Ci: 604
Civil Aeronautics Board [U.S.]
Aviation (Deregulation and mergers) A: 991
Civil Air Patrol [U.S.] Ci: 604
Air Force, United States (Civil Air Patrol [CAP])
A: 194
Civil Aviation Authority
Aviation (Aviation agencies) A: 985-986
Civil Aviation Organization, International *See*
International Civil Aviation Organization *in this
index*
Civil ceremony
Marriage (Wedding ceremonies) M: 220
Civil code *See* Code Napoléon *in this index*
Civil court [law]
Court (Types of courts) Ci: 1101; (How civil courts
work) Ci: 1102
Civil defense Ci: 605 *with picture*
Nuclear weapon (INuclear defense) N: 600
"Civil Disobedience" [essay by Thoreau]
Civil disobedience (History of civil disobedience)
Ci: 607
Thoreau, Henry David (His beliefs and works)
T: 266
Civil disobedience [law] Ci: 606
India (Rise of Indian nationalism) I: 131
Revolution (Features of revolution) R: 269
Civil Disorders, National Advisory Commission
on *See* Kerner Commission Report *in this index*
Civil engineering [career]
Engineering (Civil engineering) E: 285 *with
picture*; (History) E: 288
Civil flag
Flag (Civil and state flags) F: 195
Civil forfeiture [law]
Forfeiture F: 408
Civil heraldry
Heraldry (Heraldry today) H: 196
Civil justice treaty
Treaty (Kinds of treaties) T: 408-409
Civil law Ci: 607
Court (Courts in other countries) Ci: 1102
Crime Ci: 1135
Law (Private law) L: 130; (Civil law systems) L: 132
Law enforcement L: 141
Legal aid L: 182
Tort T: 344
Civil liberties
See also Civil rights *in this index*

Human rights (Types of human rights) H: 428
Civil Liberties Act [1988]
Asian Americans (World War II and Japanese
Americans) A: 812f-813
Japanese American internment J: 60
Mineta, Norman Yoshio M: 572
Civil Liberties Union, American [organization] *See*
American Civil Liberties Union *in this index*
Civil marriage [law]
Civil union Ci: 613
Civil partnership [law]
Civil union Ci: 613
Civil rights Ci: 607
See also Freedom; Human rights *in this index; and
the list of Related articles in the* Civil rights *article*
Alabama (Interesting facts) A: 257
American Civil Liberties Union A: 408
American GI Forum of the United States A: 411
American Indian Movement A: 411
Citizenship (The rights of citizens) Ci: 569
Class action Ci: 642
Democracy (Majority rule and minority rights)
D: 120
Disability (Needs, services, and supports) D: 220
Education (Education for whom?) E: 107
Gay rights movement G: 73
Racial profiling R: 61
Segregation S: 284
Terrorism (Counterterrorism and civil rights)
T: 177
Documents and laws
Attainder A: 878
Bill of rights B: 301
Constitution of the United States (The Bill of
Rights) Ci: 1001; (Amendment 14) Ci: 1013;
(Amendment 15) Ci: 1014
Ex parte Milligan E: 435
Grandfather clause G: 310
Great Society (Legislation) G: 349
Habeas corpus H: 2
Law L: 130
Patriot Act P: 197
Supreme Court of the United States (Civil
rights) So: 1001; (table) So: 1002
Toleration Act T: 321
Wiretapping (Laws concerning wiretapping)
W: 345
History
African Americans (The civil rights movement)
A: 136o *with pictures*
Alabama (The mid-1900's) A: 278
American literature (Works by minority writers)
A: 425
Bloody Sunday (In the United States) B: 418
Emmett Till case E: 260
Housing (Housing since 1900) H: 391-392
Indian, American (Indians in the early and mid-
1900's) I: 178b
Jim Crow J: 126
March on Washington M: 196
Mississippi (The mid-1900's) M: 644
Montgomery bus boycott M: 767
Northern Ireland (The Troubles) N: 525
Reconstruction (The Civil Rights Act) R: 178
Roosevelt, Franklin Delano (The home front)
R: 457-458
Scottsboro case S: 223
Selma marches S: 290
Slavery (Effects of slavery) S: 503-504
United States, History of the (Poverty and
discrimination) U: 195 *with picture*; (Protests
and progress [1960-1999]) U: 196 *with
picture*
Voting Rights Act of 1965 V: 451
Women's movement (In Western societies)
W: 386
Civil Rights, Commission on [U.S.] Ci: 611
Civil Rights Act of 1866 [U.S. history]
Black codes B: 386
Reconstruction (The Civil Rights Act) R: 178
Civil Rights Act of 1957 [U.S. history]
Civil rights (The struggle for the rights of African
Americans) Ci: 609
National Association for the Advancement of
Colored People N: 29
Civil Rights Act of 1960 [U.S. history]
Civil rights (The struggle for the rights of African
Americans) Ci: 609
Civil Rights Act of 1964 [U.S. history] Ci: 611
Bakke case B: 33
Civil rights (The struggle for the rights of African
Americans) Ci: 609; (The struggle for women's
rights) Ci: 609
Equal Employment Opportunity Commission
E: 345
Filibustering F: 99
Great Society (Legislation) G: 349

Johnson, Lyndon Baines (The national scene)
J: 148
King, Martin Luther, Jr. (The growing movement)
K: 321
National Association for the Advancement of
Colored People N: 29
Personnel management (Development of
personnel management) P: 303
Segregation (De facto segregation) S: 285-286
Sex discrimination (Changes in laws) S: 335
Sexual harassment (Sexual harassment law)
S: 337
United States, History of the (The civil rights
movement) U: 196a
Women's movement (Legal gains) W: 386
Civil Rights Act of 1968 [U.S. history]
African Americans (Unrest in the cities) A: 136q
Civil rights (The struggle for the rights of African
Americans) Ci: 609
Johnson, Lyndon Baines (The Great Society)
J: 150
Open housing O: 789
United States, History of the (The civil rights
movement) U: 196a
Civil Rights Division [Department of Justice]
Civil rights (The struggle for the rights of African
Americans) Ci: 609
Civil Rights Memorial Center
Alabama (Places to visit) A: 266
Civil rights movement [U.S. history] *See* Civil rights
in this index
Civil service [government] Ci: 611
Arthur, Chester Alan (Civil service reform) A: 756
Astronaut A: 828
City government (Local government) Ci: 597
Government (Careers in government) G: 291
Grant, Ulysses S. (Political corruption) G: 315
Han dynasty H: 38
Hayes, Rutherford Birchard (Civil service reform)
H: 121
Pension (Federal pension plans) P: 272-273
Republican Party (Political inactivity) R: 255
Song dynasty So: 592
United Kingdom (Gladstone and Disraeli) U: 69
Civil Service Act [1883]
Arthur, Chester Alan (Civil service reform) A: 756
Civil service (History) Ci: 613
United States, History of the (Government and
business reforms) U: 186
Civil Service Act [Canada, 1908]
Civil service (Civil service in other lands) Ci: 613
Civil Service Commission, United States
Civil service (History) Ci: 613
Civil Service Employees Association
Labor movement (table) L: 8
Civil Service Reform Act [1978]
Civil service (History) Ci: 613
Civil Service Retirement System
Pension (Federal pension plans) P: 272-273
Civil suit [law]
Debt D: 65
Jury (Petit juries) J: 202
Law (Private law) L: 130
Civil union [law] Ci: 613
See also Same-sex union *in this index*
Gay rights movement (History of gay rights) G: 73
Marriage (Same-sex unions and marriages)
M: 220
Same-sex marriage S: 78
Vermont (Recent developments) V: 337
Civil war
War W: 23
Civil War, American Ci: 614 *with pictures and maps*
See also the lists of military leaders in the Civil War,
American *article*
Bahamas (History) B: 29
Democratic Party (The slavery issue) D: 124
Douglass, Frederick D: 314
Draft, Military (Military drafts throughout history)
D: 318
Flag *picture on* F: 209
Fort Sumter F: 416
Indian Territory I: 190
Indian wars (Wars on the Plains) I: 192
Lincoln, Abraham (Lincoln's administration [1861-
1865]) L: 320 *with pictures*
Mason-Dixon Line M: 266
Minnesota (Statehood) M: 604
Money (Money in the American Civil War) M: 713
National cemetery N: 31
New York (Growing prosperity) N: 316-318
Railroad (Expansion in the United States) R: 115-
116
Seward, William Henry S: 331
Telegraph (Uses for the telegraph) T: 91
United States, History of the (The American Civil
War) U: 177 *with pictures and map*

Virginia (The Civil War and Reconstruction) V: 421
War correspondent W: 26
Washington, D.C. (The Civil War) W: 86
Aftermath
  Democratic Party (After the Civil War) D: 125
  Income tax (History of U.S. income taxes) I: 105
  Radicalism (In the United States) R: 82
  Reconstruction R: 176
  States' rights (Early history) So: 866
  United States, Government of the (The rise of
    big government) U: 146
  United States, History of the (Reconstruction)
    U: 178 *with picture*
  War (table) W: 25
  Whale (American whaling) W: 262-263
Arts
  American literature (The Age of Realism [1871-
    1913]) A: 419
  Brady, Mathew B. B: 546
  Photography (Artistic advances) P: 424-425
    with picture
  Popular music (The American Civil War [1861-
    1865]) P: 669
Background and causes
  Abolition movement A: 12
  African Americans (The American Civil War)
    A: 136i *with picture*
  Brown, John B: 643
  Buchanan, James (Election of 1856) B: 660;
    (Prelude to war) B: 661
  Compromise of 1850 Ci: 906
  Cotton (In the U.S. South) Ci: 1093
  Crittenden Compromise Ci: 1147
  Douglas, Stephen Arnold D: 312
  Dred Scott Decision D: 345
  Kansas-Nebraska Act K: 243
  Popular sovereignty P: 672
  Proslavery movement P: 828
  Slavery (Effects of slavery) S: 503-504
  Slidell, James S: 508
  Uncle Tom's Cabin U: 20
  United States, History of the (The nation
    divided [1850-1869]) U: 174 *with picture*
Events
  Emancipation Proclamation E: 253
  Gettysburg, Battle of G: 176
  Gettysburg Address G: 176
  Hampton Roads Conference H: 37
  Trent Affair T: 435
Weapons and forces
  Air force (History) A: 184-185
  Army, United States (The Civil War [1861-1865])
    A: 738
  Balloon (Balloons in war) B: 61
  Cavalry C: 318
  Mine warfare (History) M: 565
  Navy, United States (The Civil War [1861-1865])
    N: 88
  Torpedo (History) T: 341
  Warship *pictures on* W: 42
Civil War, Bosnian
  Bosnia-Herzegovina (History) B: 492-493
Civil War, Chinese
  China (Civil war) C: 504
Civil War, Colombian
  Colombia (Political disorder) Ci: 784
Civil War, English
  Charles I [of England] C: 380
  Clarendon, Earl of Ci: 638
  Cromwell, Oliver (Rise to power) Ci: 1151
  England (The Civil War) E: 308
  Hobbes, Thomas H: 272
  James (James I) J: 25
  Laud, William L: 121
  Levellers L: 217
  Long Parliament L: 448
Civil War, Georgian
  Georgia [country] (History) G: 111
  Shevardnadze, Eduard Amvrosiyevich S: 399
Civil War, Irish [1922-1923]
  Ireland (The Irish Free State) I: 427
  Irish literature (Drama) I: 432
Civil War, Lebanese
  Beirut B: 224
  Lebanon (Economy) L: 172; (War and terrorism)
    L: 173 *with picture*
Civil War, Russian *See* Russian Revolution of 1917
  in this index
Civil War, Spanish *See* Spanish Civil War *in this
  index*
Civil War, Sudanese
  Sudan (Civil war) So: 953
Civil War Museum
  Louisiana (Museums) L: 483
*Civil Wars: A Tree Is Best Measured When It's
  Down, The* [opera]
  Glass, Philip G: 224

Civiletti, Benjamin R. [American government
  official]
  Carter, Jimmy (table) C: 257
  Justice, Department of (table) J: 203
Civilian award
  Medals, decorations, and orders (Civilian awards)
    M: 355
Civilian Conservation Corps [U.S. history] Ci: 635
  Adult education (History of adult education in
    the United States) A: 69-70
  Conservation (The rise of the conservation
    movement) Ci: 985-986 *with picture*
  Great Depression (The New Deal) G: 341
  Michigan (Depression and recovery) M: 509 *with
    picture*
  New Deal (Helping the needy) N: 201
  Roosevelt, Franklin Delano (The Hundred Days)
    R: 453
  South Dakota (Boom-and-bust economy) So: 684
Civilian Defense Mobilization, Office of [U.S.]
  Civil defense (History of civil defense in the
    United States) C: 517
Civilian Vocational Rehabilitation Act [1920]
  Vocational rehabilitation V: 436
Civilization Ci: 635
  See also Culture; World, History of the *in this index*
  Ancient civilization A: 450
  Conservation (The rise of civilization) Ci: 984
  Culture Ci: 1186
  World, History of the W: 420
Civilization and Barbarism [book by Sarmiento]
  Latin American literature (Romanticism) L: 112-
    113
Cixous, Hélène [French author]
  French literature (The middle and late 1900's)
    F: 523
CJD [disease] *See* Creutzfeldt-Jakob disease
Cl [symbol]
  Chlorine (Chemical properties) C: 517
CLA [organization] *See* Canadian Library
  Association; Catholic Library Association *in this
  index*
Cladding [physics]
  Cable *diagram on* C: 6; (Fiber-optic cables) C: 5
  Fiber optics F: 88 *with diagram*
  Nuclear energy (Fuel preparation) N: 586
Cladistics [biology]
  Classification, Scientific Ci: 653
Cladogenesis [biology]
  Evolution (Main ideas of evolutionary theory)
    E: 426
Cladogram [biology]
  Classification, Scientific Ci: 653
Claflin, Tennessee [American businesswoman]
  Woodhull, Victoria Claflin W: 393
Claflin, William [American political leader]
  Massachusetts (table) M: 288
Claiborne, Harry E. [American jurist]
  Impeachment (History) I: 91-92
Claiborne, William [American colonial leader]
  Claiborne's Rebellion Ci: 636
  Maryland (Exploration and settlement) M: 256;
    (Colonial days) M: 256
Claiborne, William Charles Cole [American
  political leader]
  Laffite, Jean L: 28
  Louisiana (table) L: 496; (Territorial days) L: 498
Claiborne's Rebellion [U.S. history] Ci: 636
Claim [law]
  Insurance I: 309
Claim association
  Squatter's rights So: 814
Claim-jumper [U.S. history]
  Pre-emption P: 734a
Claiming race
  Horse racing (Claiming races) H: 365
Claims, Court of [law]
  Court of claims Ci: 1105
Claims adjuster [occupation]
  Insurance (Careers in the industry) I: 315
Claims Court, United States
  Court of claims Ci: 1105
Clair, René [French director] Ci: 636
"Clair de Lune" [music by Debussy]
  Debussy, Claude D: 66
Clairvoyance Ci: 636
  Extrasensory perception (What
    parapsychologists study) E: 457
  Fortunetelling F: 419
Clallam Women Weaving a Blanket [painting by
  Kane]
  Indian, American *picture on* I: 162
Clam [animal] Ci: 636 *with pictures*
  Biology *picture on* B: 316
  Cockle Ci: 744
  Deep sea *picture on* D: 82; (Invertebrates)
    D: 82a-82b

Geoduck G: 91 *with picture*
Mollusk (Bivalves) M: 695
Shell S: 384 *with picture*
Claman, Henry N. [American biochemist]
  Immune system (Further breakthroughs) I: 88d
Clamp
  Woodworking (Gluing) W: 398 *with pictures*
Clamp-on skate
  Roller skating (Roller skates) R: 402
Clamshell orchid
  Flower (Flowers of the tropics and subtropics)
    F: 292 *with picture*
Clamworm
  Worm *picture on* W: 501
Clan [sociology] Ci: 638
  Africa (Marriage and the family) A: 113
  Arabs (Family life) A: 587
  Family (Non-Western families) F: 24
  Indian, American (Family groups) I: 136c
  Kyrgyzstan (People) K: 398-399
  Scotland S: 211
  Tartan T: 46
  World, History of the (The rise of Japanese
    civilization) W: 435-436 *with picture*
Clandestine Marriage, The [play by Garrick and
  Colman]
  Garrick, David G: 45
Clanton, Ike [American frontiersman]
  Earp, Wyatt E: 15
Clapboard [construction]
  Lumber (History) L: 521-522
  Pioneer life in America (A pioneer settlement)
    P: 479-480 *with picture*
  Shelter (In early America) S: 393
Clapper [device]
  Carillon C: 239
Clapperton, Hugh [Scottish explorer]
  Exploration *map on* E: 449
Clapskate
  Ice skating (Speed skating) I: 13
Clapstick
  Motion picture *picture on* M: 851; (Shooting the
    movie) M: 852-853 *with picture*
Clapton, Eric [British musician] Ci: 637
  Rock music (Fresh directions) R: 380
Clara [fictional character]
  Nutcracker, The N: 622 *with picture*
Clara Barton National Historic Site [Maryland]
  National Park System (table: National historic
    sites) N: 52
Clara Morison [book by Spence]
  Australia (Literature) A: 904-905
Clare, Saint [Italian religious leader]
  Franciscans F: 482
Clarel [poem by Melville]
  Melville, Herman (His later life) M: 391
Clarendon, Earl of [English political leader] Ci: 638
Claret-cup cactus
  Flower *picture on* F: 290
Clari [opera by Bishop]
  Payne, John Howard P: 204
Clarification [industrial process]
  Cheese (Processing the milk) C: 392
  Wine (Clarifying and aging the wine) W: 338
Clarifier [machine]
  Milk (At a processing plant) M: 547-548
Clarín [Spanish author]
  Spanish literature (The 1800's) So: 761-762
Clarinet [musical instrument] Ci: 638 *with pictures*
  Jazz (The reeds) J: 69 *with picture*
  Music (Wind instruments) M: 949 *with picture*
Clarissa [book by Richardson]
  Richardson, Samuel R: 330
Clarity Act [2000]
  Dion, Stéphane D: 214
Clark [American family] Ci: 638
Clark, Abraham [American patriot] Ci: 638
Clark, Alonzo M. [American political leader]
  Wyoming (table) W: 532
Clark, Ann Nolan [American author]
  Newbery Medal (table) N: 359
  Regina Medal (table: 1963) R: 206
Clark, Barney B. [American patient]
  Artificial heart A: 759
  Heart (The first heart transplants and artificial
    hearts) H: 145
Clark, Barzilla W. [American political leader]
  Idaho (table) I: 42
Clark, Carol Higgins [American author]
  Clark, Mary Higgins Ci: 642
Clark, Champ [American political leader]
  Wilson, Woodrow (Presidential candidate) W: 322
Clark, Charles [American political leader]
  Mississippi (table) M: 640
Clark, Charles Joseph [Canadian political leader]
  See Clark, Joe *in this index*
Clark, Chase A. [American political leader]

Idaho (table) I: 42

Clark, Christy [Canadian political leader]
British Columbia (table) B: 628

Clark, Francis E. [American religious leader]
Christian Endeavor International C: 522e

Clark, George Rogers [American military leader]
Ci: 639
Clark, William Ci: 642
Illinois (Early national period) I: 72
Indiana (Exploration and settlement) I: 215
Northwest Territory (Early history) N: 534
Revolution, American (The Illinois campaign)
R: 284 with picture
Virginia (Independence and statehood) V: 420
Westward movement in America (The
Revolutionary War) W: 246

Clark, Glen [Canadian political leader]
British Columbia (table) B: 628

Clark, Helen Elizabeth [New Zealand political
leader] Ci: 639

Clark, Henry T. [American political leader]
North Carolina (table) N: 490

Clark, Jim [British race driver]
Automobile racing (table: Formula One World
Drivers' Championship) A: 980; (table:
Indianapolis 500 winners) A: 980

Clark, Joe [American political leader]
African Americans (During the late 1800's)
A: 136k-136l

Clark, Joe [Canadian political leader] Ci: 639 with
pictures
Canada, History of (Economic developments)
C: 151
Mulroney, Brian (Election as party leader) M: 917

Clark, John [American political leader]
Delaware (table) D: 109
Georgia (table) G: 130

Clark, Kenneth Bancroft [American psychologist]
Ci: 641
Social psychology So: 552

Clark, Laurel Blair Salton [American astronaut]
Columbia disaster Ci: 852
Space exploration (The Columbia disaster)
So: 725

Clark, M. Lewis [American businessman]
Kentucky Derby K: 297
Louisville (History) L: 506

Clark, Mamie Phipps [American psychologist]
Social psychology So: 552

Clark, Mark Wayne [American general] Ci: 642
Korean War (The truce talks) K: 382-383
World War II (The invasion of Italy) W: 483

Clark, Mary Higgins [American author] Ci: 642

Clark, Myron Holley [American political leader]
New York (table) N: 313

Clark, Ramsey [American lawyer]
Clark (Ramsey Clark) Ci: 638

Clark, Robert G. [American political leader]
Mississippi (The mid-1900's) M: 644-645

Clark, Tom Campbell [American jurist]
Clark (Tom Campbell Clark) Ci: 638
Truman, Harry S. (table) T: 469

Clark, William [American explorer] Ci: 642
Clark, George Rogers Ci: 639
Exploration (Crossing North America) E: 447
with map
Lewis, Meriwether L: 221
Lewis and Clark expedition L: 222 with portrait
Rocky Mountains (History) R: 395-396
South Dakota (Exploration and fur trade) So: 681
Westward movement in America (Exploration)
W: 248

Clark, William A. [American businessman]
Montana (Statehood) M: 760

Clark, William P. [American government official]
Interior, Department of the (table) I: 325

Clark Air Base [Philippines]
Philippines (Independence) P: 380; (Recovering
democracy) P: 381

Clark County [Nevada]
Las Vegas L: 87

Clarke, Arthur C. [British-born author] Ci: 642
Communications satellite (History) Ci: 888b

Clarke, Austin [Irish poet]
Irish literature (Poetry) I: 433

Clarke, Fred [American baseball player]
Baseball (table: Hall of Fame) B: 134

Clarke, George J. [Canadian political leader]
New Brunswick (table) N: 195

Clarke, George W. [American political leader]
Iowa (table) I: 391

Clarke, Henry J. H. [Canadian political leader]
Manitoba (table) M: 159

Clarke, James Paul [American political leader]
Arkansas (table) A: 712

Clarke, John [American colonial leader]
Rhode Island (Settlement) R: 312

Clarke, John H. [American jurist]
Supreme Court of the United States (table)
So: 1000

Clarke, Marcus [Australian author]
Australia (Literature) A: 904-905

Clark's nutcracker [bird]
Nutcracker N: 622 with picture

Clarkson, Adrienne [Canadian political leader]
Ci: 642
Martin, Paul M: 235

Clarkson, John [American baseball player]
Baseball (table: Hall of Fame) B: 134

Clarkson, Thomas [British abolitionist]
Abolition movement A: 12

Clash, The [band]
Punk rock P: 904

Clasper [zoology]
Fish (Reproductive system) F: 163
Shark (The body of a shark) S: 374

Class [biology]
Animal (The scientific classification of animals)
A: 472-473
Classification, Scientific (Groups in classification)
Ci: 655

Class [law]
Class action Ci: 642

Class [religion]
Methodists (Early history) M: 435

Class [sociology] See Social class in this index

Class action [law] Ci: 642
Consumer protection (The right to be heard)
Ci: 1018-1019
Smoking (Smoking regulations) S: 521

Class evidence
Forensic science (Class and individual evidence)
F: 388b

Class I railroad
Railroad (Railroad systems) R: 112-113

Class representative [law]
Class action Ci: 642

Class structure [sociology]
Social class (Class structure) So: 550

Class struggle [political science]
Communism (The ideas of Marx) Ci: 890
Economic determinism E: 57
Marx, Karl: (Das Kapital) M: 237

Classic
Literature (Judging literature) L: 352

Classic modern style
Furniture (Recent developments) F: 584

Classic of the Way and the Virtue, The [book]
Chinese literature (Beginnings) C: 511
Taoism T: 36

Classic rock
Rock music (Rock music today) R: 381

Classic shrub
Rose (Types of roses) R: 474-475

Classical architecture
Architecture (Classical Greek architecture) A: 615

Classical Chinese [language]
Chinese language (Development) C: 510

Classical conditioning [psychology]
Behavior (Learning) B: 220
Education (How people learn) E: 89
Learning (Classical conditioning) L: 163

Classical economics
Economics (The classical economists) E: 64
Laissez faire L: 31
Liberalism (Features of liberalism) L: 228
Marshall, Alfred M: 228
Ricardo, David R: 321

Classical education
Education (The Renaissance) E: 100

Classical hemophilia [disease]
Hemophilia (Major types of hemophilia) H: 182

Classical mechanics [physics]
Quantum mechanics Q: 6

Classical music Ci: 643 with pictures
See also Music in this index and the list of Related
articles in the Classical Music article
Ballet (Music) B: 50
India (Music and dance) I: 120
Jazz (New directions) J: 73
Modernism M: 685
Music (Western music) M: 955
Popular music P: 669
Pulitzer Prizes (Prizes in literature, drama, and
music) P: 886b; (table) P: 899

Classical ode [poetry]
Poetry (Lyric poetry) P: 591

Classical opera
Opera (Classical opera) O: 798

Classical physics
Subatomic particle (Early theories) So: 937
Time (Our understanding of time) T: 292a

Classical prophet [religion]
Prophet P: 827

Classical regular [astronomy]
Satellite (Satellites of the gas giants) S: 150-150a

Classical symphony
Orchestra (History) O: 822
Symphony So: 1067

Classical tutu [costume]
Ballet (Sets and costumes) B: 49-50

Classicism [philosophy] Ci: 653 with picture
Beethoven, Ludwig van (Beethoven's place in
music history) B: 214
Classical music (The Classical period) Ci: 647
French literature (The classical age) F: 520
German literature (German Classicism) G: 139
Painting (Classicism) P: 61 with picture
Realism R: 171
Russian literature (The classical movement)
R: 559

Classification, Scientific Ci: 653 with pictures
Animal (The scientific classification of animals)
A: 472; (A classification of the animal kingdom)
A: 506
Biology (The origins of scientific classification)
B: 318
Bird (A classification of birds) B: 371
Botany (What botanists study) B: 508
Fish (A classification of fish) F: 172 with pictures
Flower (How flowers are named and classified)
F: 298
Fossil (Classifying fossils) F: 427
Linnaeus, Carolus L: 337
Plant (Kinds of plants) P: 518; (Classification of
plants) P: 546

Classification Act [1923]
Civil service (History) Ci: 613

Classification yard [railroad]
Railroad (Freight operations) R: 109 with pictures

Classified ad
Newspaper (Preparing advertisements) N: 383

Classified information
Central Intelligence Agency (Functions) C: 356

**Classified School Employees, American
Association of**
Labor movement (table) L: 8

Classing [grading]
Cotton (Classing) Ci: 1091

Classis [religion]
Reformed Church in America R: 199

Classless society [sociology]
Marx, Karl: (Das Kapital) M: 237
Union of Soviet Socialist Republics (Privileged
classes) U: 32

Clastic sediment [geology]
Rock (Clastic sediments) R: 372

Clathrate hydrate [ice]
Ice (Ice "cages") I: 5

Claude [French artist] Ci: 656
Classicism picture on Ci: 653
Painting (Composition) P: 35; (Classicism) P: 61

Claude, Albert [American physiologist]
Nobel Prizes (Physiology or medicine: 1974)
N: 446

Claude, Georges [French engineer]
Liquid air (Making liquid air) L: 347

Claude process
Liquid air (Making liquid air) L: 347 with diagram

Claudel, Paul [French author] Ci: 656
French literature (The early years) F: 522
Milhaud, Darius M: 543

Claudio [literary figure]
Shakespeare, William: (Much Ado About Nothing)
S: 360 with picture; (Measure for Measure)
S: 362

Claudius [literary figure]
Shakespeare, William: (Hamlet) S: 361; (Rhetoric)
S: 368

Claudius [Roman emperor] Ci: 656
Agrippina the Younger A: 162
England (The Roman conquest) E: 303
Nero N: 130

Claudius II [Roman emperor]
Gallienus G: 15
Rome, Ancient (table) R: 447

Claudius Ptolemaeus [Egyptian astronomer] See
Ptolemy in this index

Claudius the God [book by Graves]
Graves, Robert G: 330

Claus, C.F. [English chemist]
Sulfur (How sulfur is obtained) So: 967

Claus conversion
Sulfur (How sulfur is obtained) So: 967

Clause [grammar] Ci: 657
Sentence (Sentence classifications) S: 303

Clausewitz, Karl von [Prussian author] Ci: 657

Clausius, Rudolf Julius Emmanuel [German
physicist] Ci: 657

Clauson, Clinton [American political leader]
Maine (table) M: 87

Claustrophobia [psychology]
Mental illness (Anxiety disorders) M: 405-406
Phobia P: 392
Claver, Saint Peter [Spanish-born priest]
Knights of Peter Claver K: 352
Clavichord [musical instrument] Ci: 657
Piano (History) P: 447
Clavicle [anatomy]
Bird (Skeleton and muscles) B: 364 *with diagram*
Collarbone Ci: 773
Claw [device]
Motion picture *diagram on* M: 858; (The camera)
M: 856-857
Claw [zoology]
Animal *pictures on* A: 494
Bear (The body of a bear) B: 183
Bird (Legs and feet) B: 364
Cat (Body size and structure) C: 286 *with picture*
Lobster (Body) L: 405-406 *with pictures*
Claw hammer
Hammer H: 34 *with picture*
Clawless otter
Otter (Body) O: 876
Clay [earth] Ci: 657 *with picture*
Ceramics (Properties of ceramics) C: 359
Gravel G: 329
Grinding and polishing (Grinding wheels) G: 395
Kaolin K: 244
Loam L: 403
Pottery P: 715
Rhône River R: 318
Soil (Minerals) So: 573
Clay, Cassius Marcellus [American boxer] *See* Ali,
Muhammad *in this index*
Clay, Cassius Marcellus [American social reformer]
Ci: 658
Clay, Clement Comer [American political leader]
Alabama (table) A: 274
Clay, Henry [American statesman] Ci: 658 *with picture*
Adams, John Quincy (Election of 1824) A: 42;
(table) A: 43
Duel D: 378
Electoral College (History) E: 164
Jackson, Andrew (Election of 1824) J: 9-10
Missouri Compromise M: 674
Monroe, James ("The American System") M: 736
Polk, James Knox (Election of 1844) P: 642
Randolph, John R: 137
Speaker (In the United States) So: 768
Tariff (United States tariffs) T: 44
Tyler, John (Opposition to the Whigs) T: 534; (The
Whigs disown Tyler) T: 534
United States, History of the (The War of 1812)
U: 165; (The nation divided [1850-1869])
U: 174-175 *with picture*
Whig Party (The first program) W: 280
Clay, Lucius Dubignon [American military leader]
Ci: 659
Clay, Mount
New Hampshire (Mountains) N: 220
Clay animation
Animation (Stop-motion animation) A: 514a
Clay disk [target]
Trapshooting T: 404
Clay tablet
Book (Early books) B: 465
Library (Ancient libraries of clay) L: 257 *with
picture*
Mythology (Greek mythology) M: 980
Publishing (Kinds of publishing) P: 868
Claymore [weapon]
Sword So: 1061 *with picture*
Clayton, Adam [Irish musician]
Bono B: 462
U2 U: 2
Clayton, John [English clergyman]
Gas [fuel] (First uses of manufactured gas) G: 57
Clayton, John Middleton [American political
leader] Ci: 659
Clayton-Bulwer Treaty Ci: 659
Clayton, Joshua [American political leader]
Delaware (table) D: 109
Clayton, Powell [American political leader]
Arkansas (table) A: 712
Clayton Antitrust Act [1914]
Antitrust laws A: 560
Capitalism (Ensuring competition) C: 195
Gompers, Samuel G: 268
Monopoly and competition (History) M: 732
Wilson, Woodrow (Legislative program) W: 322-
323
Clayton-Bulwer Treaty [1850] Ci: 659
Buchanan, James (Minister to the United
Kingdom) B: 660
Clayton, John Middleton Ci: 659
Panama Canal (Early efforts) P: 125

Taylor, Zachary (The Nicaragua Canal) T: 60
CLC [labor union]
Labor movement (In Canada) L: 14
Clea [book by Durrell]
Durrell, Lawrence D: 389
Clean Air Act [U.S., 1963]
Gasoline engine (Air pollution controls) G: 66
Clean Air Act [U.S., 1970]
Coal (Coal research) Ci: 730
Environmental pollution (Government action)
E: 335-336
Gasoline (Pollution control) G: 62
Clean Air Act Amendments [U.S., 1990]
Acid rain A: 27
Air pollution (Control of air pollution) A: 199
Bush, George Herbert Walker (National affairs)
B: 720
Gasoline (Pollution control) G: 62
Clean Air Acts [Britain]
London (Dealing with problems) L: 442
Clean and jerk
Weightlifting W: 183
Clean coal technology
Coal (Recent developments) Ci: 732
Clean Monday
Lent L: 196b
Clean plowing
Farm and farming (Preparing the soil) F: 35
Clean room
Air conditioning (In business and industry)
A: 176-177
Clean suit [garment]
Crime scene investigation (Collecting evidence)
Ci: 1140-1141
Clean Water Act [1972]
Environmental pollution (Government action)
E: 335
Cleaning, Dry *See* Dry cleaning *in this index*
Cleaning fluid
Carbon tetrachloride C: 207
Dry cleaning (How clothes are dry cleaned)
D: 368
Cleanliness
Bath B: 163
Health (Cleanliness) H: 126
Cleanout plug
Plumbing (The drain-waste-vent system) P: 578
Cleanser
Detergent and soap D: 163
Clear [sports]
Badminton (Playing) B: 24-25
Clear-air turbulence
Air turbulence A: 200
Clear and present danger test [U.S. history]
Schenck v. United States S: 174
Clear Grits [Canadian history]
Liberal Party of Canada L: 227
Clear Lake
Iowa (Rivers and lakes) I: 386
Clearcutting
Forestry (Harvesting) F: 404 *with picture*
Clearing After Snowfall Along the River [painting]
Wang Wei *picture on* W: 23
Clearing bank
Bank (Europe) B: 92
Clearing House Interbank Payments System
Clearinghouse Ci: 660
Clearing the zone
Hockey (Playing the game) H: 277
Clearinghouse [economics] Ci: 659 *with diagram*
Commodity exchange (Forward and futures
contracts) C: 873
Clearwater Beach [Florida]
Florida *picture on* F: 243
Cleary, Beverly [American author] Ci: 660
Newbery Medal (table) N: 359
Regina Medal (table: 1980) R: 206
Cleavage [physical property]
Gem (Cleavage) G: 77
Mineral (Cleavage) M: 567 *with picture*; (Chemical
bonds) M: 570 *with diagram*
Cleavage plane [mineralogy]
Mineral (Chemical bonds) M: 570 *with diagram*
Cleavage site [genetics]
Gene mapping G: 81
Genetic engineering (How genes are
reintroduced into cells) G: 84b
Genomics G: 90
Cleaveland, Moses [American settler]
Cleveland (Early settlement) Ci: 666
Cleaver, Eldridge [American social reformer]
Ci: 660
American literature (Works by minority writers)
A: 425
Cleaves, Henry B. [American political leader]
Maine (table) M: 87
CLEC [company] *See* Competitive local exchange

carrier *in this index*
Cleese, John [British actor] Ci: 661 *with picture*
"Monty Python's Flying Circus" M: 780
Clef [music]
Music (Indicating pitch) M: 952-953 *with pictures*
Cleft grafting
Grafting (Kinds of grafting) G: 298 *with picture*
Cleft lip [birth defect]
Cleft palate Ci: 661
Cleft palate [birth defect] Ci: 661
Reproduction, Human (Development of organs
and organ systems) R: 248
Clegg, Nick [British political leader]
Liberal Democrats (Coalition government) L: 227
Cleisthenes [Athenian political leader] Ci: 661
Athens (Democracy) A: 857
Greece, Ancient (New forms of government)
G: 372-373
Pericles P: 287
Cleitus [friend of]
Alexander the Great (Central Asia and the Indus)
A: 343
Clematis [plant] Ci: 661 *with picture*
Clemenceau, Georges [French statesman] Ci: 662
with portrait
Foch, Ferdinand F: 313
Versailles, Treaty of V: 339
World War I (The Paris Peace Conference) W: 465
Clemens, Olivia Langdon [wife of]
Twain, Mark (Return to the East) T: 529
Clemens, Orion [brother of]
Twain, Mark (Boyhood) T: 528; (Newspaper work
in the West) T: 529
Clemens, Roger [American baseball player] Ci: 662
Clemens, Samuel Langhorne [American author]
See Twain, Mark *in this index*
Clement I, Saint [pope] Ci: 662
Pope (The early papacy) P: 663
Clement III [antipope]
Pope (table) P: 666
Clement III [pope]
Pope (table) P: 666
Clement V [pope]
Church and state (History) C: 542
France (Growth of royal power) F: 472-473
Knights Templars K: 353
Philip IV P: 370
Clement VII [antipope] Ci: 662
Pope (table) P: 666
Clement VII [pope] Ci: 662
Boleyn, Anne B: 440
Michelangelo (The Last Judgment) M: 486
Clement VIII [pope] Ci: 662a
Clement XIV [pope]
Jesuits (History) J: 103
Pope (table) P: 666
Clement, Frank G. [American political leader]
Tennessee (table) T: 152
Clement, Percival W. [American political leader]
Vermont (table) V: 333
Clemente, Roberto [American baseball player]
Ci: 662a *with portrait*
Baseball (table: Hall of Fame) B: 134
Clementi, Muzio [Italian composer] Ci: 662a
Clementine [space probe]
Moon (Recent exploration) M: 795 *with picture*
Space exploration (Lunar probes) So: 708-709
Clements, Bill [American political leader]
Texas (table) T: 203
Clements, Frederick [American ecologist]
Botany (Later developments) B: 509
Clemm, Maria [aunt of]
Poe, Edgar Allan (Poe's life) P: 589
Clemm, Virginia [wife of]
Poe, Edgar Allan (Poe's life) P: 589
Clemson University
South Carolina *picture on* So: 645
Clendenin, George [American political leader]
Charleston (Government and history) C: 384
Cleomenes [king of Sparta]
Cleisthenes Ci: 661
Cleopatra [literary figure]
Shakespeare, William (Dramatic conventions)
S: 354; (*Antony and Cleopatra*) S: 364
Cleopatra [queen of ancient Egypt] Ci: 662a
Alexandria (History) A: 344
Antony, Mark A: 561
Augustus (Rise to power) A: 889
Caesar, Julius (Civil war) C: 13
Egypt, Ancient *picture on* E: 143; (Roman rule)
E: 144
Octavia O: 669
Cleopatra Selene [daughter of]
Cleopatra (Cleopatra and Mark Antony)
Ci: 662a-662b
Cleopatra's Needles [New York and London]
Ci: 662b *with picture*

Clepsydra [measuring device]
Water clock **W: 134**
Clerestory [architecture] **Ci: 662b**
Architecture (Romanesque architecture) **A: 618**
Clergy
Address, Forms of (Members of the clergy) **A: 54**
Careers (Community and social services) **C: 221**
with picture
Christianity (Church leadership) **C: 522g**
Middle Ages (Life of the people) **M: 526**
Minister **M: 578**
Priest **P: 776**
Rabbi **R: 46**
Religion (How the major religions are organized)
R: 218
Seminary **S: 292**
Vatican Council II (The Dogmatic Constitution on
the Church) **V: 289**
Clergyman's Daughter, A [book by Orwell]
Orwell, George **O: 860**
Clerical work
Careers (Administrative support) **C: 219**
Clerk [religion]
Quakers (Worship) **Q: 5**
Clerk, Sir Dugald [British engineer]
Diesel engine (History) **D: 199**
Clerk of court [office] **Ci: 662b**
Clermont [boat] **Ci: 662b**
Fulton, Robert **F: 555** *with picture*
Livingston, Robert R. **L: 399**
Ship *picture on* **S: 423**; (The first steamboats)
S: 424
Steamboat **So: 882**
Clermont, Council of [1095]
Crusades (How the Crusades began) **Ci: 1159-
1160**
Urban II **U: 219**
Cletus, Saint [pope]
Pope (table) **P: 666**
Cleve, Per Theodor [Swedish chemist]
Helium **H: 176**
Holmium **H: 296**
Thulium **T: 272**
Cleveland [Ohio] **Ci: 663** *with pictures and map*
Ohio *picture on* **O: 681**; (table: Average monthly
weather) **O: 695**
Cleveland, Chauncey F. [American political leader]
Connecticut (table) **Ci: 967**
Cleveland, Frances Folsom [wife of Grover
Cleveland]
Cleveland, Grover (Cleveland's family) **Ci: 671**
with picture
First ladies of the United States (table) **F: 142**
Cleveland, Grover [U.S. president] **Ci: 668** *with
pictures*
Democratic Party (After the Civil War) **D: 125**
Harrison, Benjamin **H: 70**
Hawaii (The Republic of Hawaii) **H: 108**
Labor Day **L: 3**
Monroe Doctrine (The Monroe Doctrine in
action) **M: 739**
Mugwumps **M: 910**
New York (table) **N: 313**
Pullman Strike **P: 900a**
Thurman, Allen Granberry **T: 273**
Cleveland, Mount [Montana]
Glacier National Park (Mountains) **G: 205**
Cleveland: Now [government program]
Cleveland (Social problems) **Ci: 665**
Cleveland, Rose [sister of]
Cleveland, Grover (Life in the White House)
Ci: 671
White House hostesses **W: 291**
Cleveland bay [breed]
Horse (table: Some types and breeds of horses)
H: 343; (Heavy harness horses) **H: 347**
Cleveland Browns [team]
Football (National Football League) **F: 364**
Cleveland Cavaliers [team]
Basketball (table) **B: 150**
James, LeBron **J: 27**
Cleveland Clinic Foundation
Cleveland (Service industries) **Ci: 666**
Cleveland Indians [team]
Baseball (table) **B: 130**
Feller, Bob **F: 68**
Cleveland Museum of Art
Ohio (Museums) **O: 685**
Cleveland Museum of Natural History
Ohio (Interesting facts) **O: 681** *with picture*
Cleveland Orchestra
Cleveland (The arts) **Ci: 665**
Szell, George **So: 1077**
Cleveland Penny Press [newspaper]
Scripps, Edward Wyllis **S: 227**
Cleveland Play House
Cleveland (The arts) **Ci: 665**

Cleveland Public Library [Ohio]
Cleveland (Museums and libraries) **Ci: 666**
Library (Research libraries) **L: 247**
Cleveland Transit System
Cleveland (Economy) **Ci: 666**
Clever Hans [horse]
Horse (table: Famous horses in history and
legend) **H: 361**
CLI [computing] *See* Command line interface *in
this index*
Cliburn, Van [American pianist] **Ci: 674** *with picture*
Cliche Royal Commission
Mulroney, Brian (Young lawyer) **M: 916-917**
Click beetle [insect] **Ci: 674** *with picture*
Beetle *picture on* **B: 218**; (Click beetles) **B: 217**
Click language
Africa (Languages) **A: 105**
Clicking [computing]
Computer (A mouse) **Ci: 912-914**
Client [computer]
Computer network **Ci: 925**
Client [law]
Lawyer **L: 147**
Client, The [book by Grisham]
Grisham, John **G: 396**
Client-centered therapy
Psychotherapy (Humanistic-experiential
psychotherapy) **P: 852**
Client-server network [computing]
Computer (Personal computers) **Ci: 909**
Computer network **Ci: 925**
Cliff [geology] **Ci: 674**
Cliff dwellers [people] *See* Anasazi *in this index*
Cliff frog
Frog (Other frogs) **F: 540**
Cliff Palace
Anasazi *picture on* **A: 448a**
Mesa Verde National Park **M: 420**
Cliff swallow [bird]
Swallow **So: 1014** *with picture*
Cliff Walk [Newport]
Rhode Island *picture on* **R: 296**; (Places to visit)
R: 304
Clifford, Clark McAdams [American government
official] **Ci: 674**
Clifford, John H. [American political leader]
Massachusetts (table) **M: 288**
Clifford, Nathan [American government official]
Justice, Department of (table) **J: 203**
Polk, James Knox (table) **P: 643**
Supreme Court of the United States (table)
So: 1000
Cliffs of Dover [England] *See* Dover, Cliffs of *in
this index*
Cliffside field [region, Texas]
Helium (Production) **H: 176**
Clifty Falls
Indiana (Rivers, lakes, and waterfalls) **I: 208**
Climacteric *See* Menopause *in this index*
Climate [weather] **Ci: 675** *with pictures and map*
See also Global warming *in this index*
Colony **Ci: 815**
Dinosaur (Land and climate) **D: 206a**; (Why
dinosaurs died out) **D: 213**
El Niño **E: 245**
Enlightenment (The orderliness of nature)
E: 326a-326b
Fossil (Recording Earth's changes) **F: 424**
Greenhouse effect **G: 382**
Ice age **I: 6**
Irrigation **I: 456**
Lake (Climate) **L: 33**
Life (The physical environment) **L: 275**
Mountain (In affecting climate) **M: 891**
Nuclear winter **N: 602**
Ocean (As an influence on climate) **O: 654**
Phenology **P: 356**
Plant (Where plants live) **P: 520**
Races, Human (Climatic adaptations) **R: 58**
Rain forest (Environmental value) **R: 126c-126d**
Shelter (Why shelters differ around the world)
S: 392
Soil (Influence of climate) **So: 574**
Weather **W: 157**
Weather satellite **W: 171**
Climate feedback [meteorology]
Greenhouse effect (Increases in greenhouse
gases) **G: 383**
Climate model
Global warming (How scientists study global
warming) **G: 232d**
Climate simulation
Global warming *diagram on* **G: 232c**; (How
scientists study global warming) **G: 232d**
Climatic optimum [geology]
Middle Ages (The High Middle Ages) **M: 526**
Climatology

Climate (Kinds of climates) **Ci: 676a**
Geography (Physical geography) **G: 94**
Global warming (How scientists study global
warming) **G: 232d**
Humboldt, Baron von **H: 432**
Climax [literature]
Literature (Plot) **L: 353**
Climax community
Ecology (Changes in communities) **E: 54**
Climbing [sport] **Ci: 679** *with pictures*
See also Mountain climbing *in this index*
Climbing perch [fish] **Ci: 680** *with picture*
Climbing rose [plant]
Rose (Types of roses) **R: 474** *with picture*; (table)
R: 474
Clinching
Boxing *picture on* **B: 529**
Cline [cartography]
Races, Human (The clinal approach) **R: 55-56**
with map
Cline, Patsy [American singer] **Ci: 681**
Country music *picture on* **Ci: 1098c**
Clines, Thomas G. [American public figure]
Iran-contra affair (Charges and court actions)
I: 407
Clingmans Dome [mountain, Tennessee] **Ci: 681**
Tennessee (Land regions) **T: 146** *with map*
Clingstone peach [fruit]
Peach (Cultivars) **P: 210**
Clinic, Legal
Law (The right to legal assistance) **L: 137-138**
Clinic of Doctor Agnew, The [painting by Eakins]
Eakins, Thomas **E: 6**
Clinic of Doctor Gross, The [painting by Eakins]
Eakins, Thomas **E: 6**
Clinical engineering
Biomedical engineering (Specialty areas of
biomedical engineering) **B: 324-325**
Clinical ethics
Medical ethics **M: 361**
Clinical pathology [medicine]
Forensic pathology **F: 389a**
Pathology **P: 196**
Clinical pharmacology [science]
Pharmacology **P: 354**
Clinical pharmacy
Pharmacy (Training and careers in pharmacy)
P: 354
Clinical psychology **Ci: 681**
Psychology (Major fields of psychology) **P: 848**
Clinical research [medicine]
Medicine (Medical researchers) **M: 369-370**
Clinical training
Medicine (A career as a doctor) **M: 370**
Clinical trial
Cancer (Clinical trials) **C: 174**
Clinker
Cement and concrete (Burning) **C: 344**
Clinker-built vessel
Ship (Viking ships) **S: 416**
Clinopyroxene [mineral]
Pyroxene **P: 920**
Clinton, Bill [U.S. president] **Ci: 682** *with pictures*
African Americans *picture on* **A: 136t**
AIDS *picture on* **A: 164**
Arkansas *picture on* **A: 714**; (table) **A: 712**
Bush, George Herbert Walker (The 1992 election)
B: 722a
Clinton, Hillary Rodham **Ci: 682h**
DeLay, Tom **D: 114**
Democratic Party (The late 1900's) **D: 127** *with
picture*
Edwards, John **E: 114**
Gore, Al (Political career) **G: 274**
Impeachment (History) **I: 91-92**
Iran (After Khomeini) **I: 406a**
Israel *picture on* **I: 489**
President of the United States (Term of office)
P: 758-762; (The impeachment of Bill Clinton)
P: 769
Reno, Janet **R: 240**
Republican Party (Control of Congress) **R: 257**
Starr, Kenneth Winston **So: 857**
United States, History of the (The Clinton
impeachment) **U: 196d**
Clinton, Chelsea [daughter of]
Clinton, Bill (Clinton's family) **Ci: 682b** *with picture*
Clinton, De Witt [American political leader]
Ci: 682g
Castle Clinton National Monument **C: 282**
Erie Canal **E: 351**
New York (table) **N: 313**; (Growing prosperity)
N: 316
Van Buren, Martin (U.S. senator) **V: 271**
Clinton, George [American political leader]
Ci: 682g
New York (table) **N: 313**; (Statehood) **N: 315**

Vice president of the United States **V: 348** *with portrait*
Clinton, Sir Henry [British general] **Ci: 682h**
André, John **A: 456**
Arnold, Benedict (Turns traitor) **A: 742**
Cornwallis, Charles **Ci: 1066**
Revolution, American (Lexington and Concord) **R: 274-275**; (Fighting in the Chesapeake and Southern colonies) **R: 276-278**; (France's entry into the Revolutionary War) **R: 283**; (The end of the war) **R: 286**
Clinton, Hillary Rodham [American government official] **Ci: 682h** *with portrait*
African Americans *picture on* **A: 136t**
Clinton, Bill (Clinton's family) **Ci: 682b** *with picture*; (Later years) **Ci: 682g**
First ladies of the United States **F: 143**
Obama, Barack *picture on* **O: 640f**; (Presidential nomination) **O: 640e**
Clinton, James [American general]
New York (Statehood) **N: 315**
Clinton, Roger [stepfather of]
Clinton, Bill (Early life) **Ci: 682a**
Clinton, William Jefferson [U.S. president] *See* Clinton, Bill *in this index*
Clinton's Ditch
Erie Canal **E: 351**
Clio [Greek mythology]
Muses **M: 937**
Clipper ship Ci: 682h *with picture*
Ship (Clipper ships) **S: 422** *with picture*
Transportation (The age of overseas expansion) **T: 388** *with picture*
Clippers, Los Angeles [team]
Basketball (table) **B: 150**
Clipping [language]
Slang (Shortened or lengthened words) **S: 499**
Clipping [sports]
Football (Violations and penalties) **F: 363**
Clitellum [zoology]
Earthworm **E: 39** *with picture*
Clitoris [anatomy]
Circumcision **Ci: 561**
Vagina **V: 260**
Clive, Robert [British colonial official] **Ci: 682i**
Bangladesh (The East India Company) **B: 85**
India (The rise of the East India Company) **I: 130**
Cloaca [zoology]
Bird (The digestive system) **B: 365-366**
Platypus **P: 570**
Snake (Internal organs) **S: 527** *with diagram*; (Reproduction) **S: 529-530**
Cloche [hat]
Hat (History) **H: 84-85** *with picture*
Clock Ci: 682i *with pictures*
Antique *picture on* **A: 558**
Atomic clock **A: 877**
Chronometer **C: 539**
Colonial life in America (Furnishings) **Ci: 797-798**
Hour **H: 379**
Pendulum (Clock pendulums) **P: 237**
Quartz (Uses) **Q: 8**
Time (Measuring time) **T: 288**
Watch **W: 114** *with pictures*
Water clock **W: 134**
Clock speed [electronics]
Computer chip (Clock speed) **Ci: 924f**
Clockers [film]
Lee, Spike **L: 180**
Clockmaker, The [book by Haliburton]
Canadian literature (Early English-Canadian literature) **C: 157**
Clockwork Orange, A [book by Burgess]
Burgess, Anthony **B: 703**
Clodia [ancient Roman]
Catullus, Gaius Valerius **C: 316**
Clodius parnassian [butterfly]
Butterfly *picture on* **B: 736**
Clofazimine [drug]
Leprosy (Treatment) **L: 205**
Clog [shoe]
Shoe *picture on* **S: 432**
Cloisonné [art]
Enamel (Techniques) **E: 264**
Cloister [architecture] **Ci: 682k** *with picture*
Architecture (Carolingian architecture) **A: 618**
Cloister [religious community]
Convent **C: 1024**
Cloisters [museum, New York City]
Metropolitan Museum of Art (The Cloisters) **M: 444**
Clonazepam [drug]
Anticonvulsant **A: 553**
Clone [biology]
See also Cloning *in this index*
Cloning **Ci: 682l**
Cloned DNA [biology] *See* Recombinant DNA *in this index*

Cloning [biology] **Ci: 682l** *with pictures*
Agriculture (Preserving genetic diversity) **A: 160**
Bioethics **B: 310**
Biology (Current research and issues) **B: 320-321**
Genetic engineering (Uses of genetic engineering) **G: 84b**
Heredity (The era of genetic engineering) **H: 209**
Plant (Asexual reproduction) **P: 535**
Primate (The study of nonhuman primates) **P: 778c**
Clooney, George [American actor/director] **Ci: 684** *with portrait*
Motion picture (Best performance by an actor in a supporting role: 2005) **M: 862b**
Close, Chuck [American artist] **Ci: 684** *with picture*
Painting (People) **P: 31-32** *with picture*
Close binary [astronomy]
Nova **N: 553**
Close of Play [play by Gray]
Gray, Simon **G: 334**
Close-up magic
Magician (Close-up magic) **M: 51**
Closed basin [geography]
Basin **B: 141**
Closed captioning [television] **Ci: 685** *with picture*
Deafness (Assistive technology) **D: 58-59**
Disability (Hearing disabilities) **D: 219**
Shorthand machine **S: 435**
Closed circuit
Electric circuit **E: 166**
Closed-circuit television
Television (Closed-circuit television) **T: 110c** *with picture*
Closed couplet [poetry]
Couplet **Ci: 1100**
Poetry (table) **P: 594**
Closed die forging
Forging (Machine forging) **F: 409-410**
Closed-end investment company
Investment (Other kinds of direct investments) **I: 368**
Mutual fund **M: 969**
Closed fracture [injury]
Fracture **F: 450** *with diagram*
Closed gentian [plant]
Gentian **G: 90**
Closed nutrient cycle [agriculture]
Agriculture (Artificial fertilizers) **A: 158**
Closed primary [voting]
Election (Nomination of candidates) **E: 158**
Primary election (Open and closed) **P: 776-777**
Closed shop [labor] **Ci: 685**
Labor movement (Organizing workers) **L: 4**
Open shop **O: 789**
Right-to-work law **R: 340**
Taft-Hartley Act **T: 13**
Closed-stack system
Library (Other features) **L: 237**
Closed system [physics]
Heat (Thermodynamics) **H: 155**
Closely Watched Trains [film]
Motion picture (Movies in the 1960's) **M: 870-871**
Clostridium botulinum [bacteria]
Botulism **B: 514**
Food poisoning **F: 340**
Food preservation (How food spoils) **F: 341**
Clostridium tetani [bacteria]
Tetanus **T: 182b**
Closure [parliamentary procedure] *See* Cloture *in this index*
Closure [psychology]
Gestalt psychology **G: 175**
Perception (Principles of perception) **P: 284**
Clot *See* Blood clot *in this index*
Clotbur [plant] *See* Burdock *in this index*
Clotel, or The President's Daughter [book by Brown]
African American literature (The 1800's) **A: 136a**
Cloth [fabric]
See also Textile *in this index*
Cotton (Making cotton into cloth) **Ci: 1091**
Doll (Cloth dolls) **D: 289**
Painting (Supports) **P: 36**
Weaving **W: 173** *with pictures*
Cloth beam
Weaving (How a loom works) **W: 173-174**
Cloth-of-gold crocus [plant]
Crocus **Ci: 1150**
Flower *picture on* **F: 280**
Clothes moth [insect]
Cocoon *picture on* **C: 747**
Clothing Ci: 686 *with pictures*
See also Costume *in this index; the list of Related articles in the* Clothing *article; and the* Way of life *or* People *sections of the various country articles, such as* Argentina (Way of life)

Armor **A: 719** *with pictures*
Army *picture on* **A: 725**
Button (Button legends) **B: 745** *with pictures*
Colonial life in America (Clothing) **Ci: 799** *with picture*
Cotton (Cotton fibers) **Ci: 1086**
Easter (Wearing new clothes) **E: 44**
Egypt, Ancient (Food, clothing, and shelter) **E: 137**
Fashion **F: 50**
Fire department (Protective clothing) **F: 127** *with picture*
Fur **F: 561**
Greece, Ancient (Food, clothing, and shelter) **G: 367**
Hat **H: 83**
Inca *picture on* **I: 98**; (Food, clothing, and shelter) **I: 95-96**
Indian, American *pictures on* **I: 138**; (Clothing) **I: 136d**; (Before European contact) **I: 166-167**
Inuit *picture on* **I: 354d**; (Clothing) **I: 354b**
Modeling **M: 684**
Pioneer life in America (Clothing) **P: 482** *with picture*
Prehistoric people (The use of fire) **P: 747**
Rome, Ancient (Clothing) **R: 440**
Sewing **S: 331**
Shoe **S: 430** *with pictures*
Skiing (Ski clothing) **S: 485**
Tartan **T: 46** *with pictures*
United Kingdom (Manufacturing) **U: 63-65**
Western frontier life in America (Life on the farms) **W: 238**
Clothing industry *See* Garment industry *in this index*
Clotho [mythology]
Fates **F: 54**
Clotting *See* Blood clot *in this index*
Clotting factor [blood]
Blood (Controlling bleeding) **B: 411**
Blood transfusion **B: 416**
Hemophilia **H: 182**
Plasma (Functions of plasma) **P: 551**
Von Willebrand's disease **V: 448**
Cloture [parliamentary procedure] **Ci: 707**
Filibustering **F: 99**
Parliamentary procedure (Motions) **P: 176**
Senate (Considering legislation) **S: 295**
Cloud Ci: 707 *with pictures*
Air (Moisture in the air) **A: 170**
Cloud seeding **C: 711**
Dew point **D: 176**
Dust (Influence on climate) **D: 390**
Earth *picture on* **E: 16**
Fog **F: 314**
Hurricane **H: 452**
Lamarck, Chevalier de **L: 50**
Lightning **L: 299** *with pictures*
Mars (Clouds) **M: 226b**
Rain (Characteristics of rain) **R: 122-123**
Thunderstorm **T: 272**
Tornado (How a tornado forms) **T: 334** *with diagram*
Water (Water in the air) **W: 120** *with diagram*
Weather (Humidity) **W: 158** *with picture*; (Synoptic-scale systems) **W: 159-160**; (Weather satellites) **W: 163-164**; (Science project: A cloud in a bottle) **W: 168**
Cloud City [nickname]
Leadville **L: 150**
Cloud computing
Internet (Cloud computing) **I: 350b**
Cloud condensation nucleus
Air (Moisture in the air) **A: 170**
Cloud (How clouds form) **Ci: 708-709**
Rain (Formation of rain) **R: 123** *with diagram*
Cloud Gate [sculpture]
Chicago (Places to visit) **C: 430-431**
Cloud Nine [play by Churchill]
Churchill, Caryl **C: 543**
Cloud radar
Radar (In scientific research) **R: 68**
Cloud seeding [meteorology] **C: 711** *with diagram*
New Hampshire (Interesting facts) **N: 209** *with picture*
Rain (The ice-crystal process) **R: 124**
Weather (How people affect the weather) **W: 170**
Cloud-to-cloud lightning
Lightning (Origin and destination) **L: 300** *with diagram*
Cloud-to-ground lightning
Lightning **L: 299** *with diagram*
Cloudburst [weather] **Ci: 712**
Clouded leopard [animal] **Ci: 712** *with picture*
Clouded sulfur [insect]
Insect *picture on* **I: 282**
Clouds [play by Aristophanes]

Aristophanes A: 663
Cloud's Rest
  Yosemite National Park (Rock masses) Y: 570
Clough, David M. [American political leader]
  Minnesota (table) M: 602
Clove [spice] Ci: 712 *with pictures*
Clove hitch
  Knots, hitches, and splices (Two half hitches)
    K: 357 *with diagram*
Cloven hoof [zoology]
  Goat (The bodies of goats) G: 240
Clover [plant] Ci: 712 *with picture*
  Flower *picture on* F: 287
  Lawn *picture on* L: 143
Clover mite [animal]
  Mite M: 678
Cloverbuds [program]
  4-H F: 433
Cloverleaf [road]
  Road (Intersections) R: 358-359
Clovis I [king of the Franks] Ci: 713
  Belgium (The Middle Ages) B: 232
  Fleur-de-lis F: 234 *with picture*
  France (Victory of the Franks) F: 471
  Franks F: 494
  Gaul G: 70
  Germany (Kingdom of the Franks) G: 162
  Merovingian dynasty M: 418
  Paris (Early years) P: 166
  Salic law S: 66
Clovis culture
  Paleo-Indians P: 102
Clown Ci: 713 *with picture*
  Circus (At the circus) Ci: 562 *with pictures*
Clown, The [book by Böll]
  Böll, Heinrich B: 448
Clown anemonefish
  Fish *picture on* F: 155
Clown loach [fish]
  Fish *picture on* F: 157
  Loach L: 403
Clown triggerfish
  Fish *picture on* F: 154
Clownfish Ci: 714 *with picture*
Club [suit]
  Card game (History) C: 209
Club [weapon]
  Indian, American *pictures on* I: 138, I: 144
Club drug
  Drug abuse (table: Some commonly abused
    drugs) D: 363; (Club drugs) D: 363
Club hair [anatomy]
  Hair (Cycles of hair growth) H: 10
Club moss [botany] Ci: 714 *with pictures*
  Flower *picture on* F: 289
  Plant *picture on* P: 522; (Lycophytes) P: 518;
    (Classification of plants) P: 546 *with picture*
  Tree (Fossil trees) T: 415
Club-moss ivesia [plant]
  Flower *picture on* F: 289
Club wheat [plant]
  Wheat (Species of wheat) W: 269 *with picture*
Clubfoot [disorder] Ci: 715
Cluj-Napoca [Romania]
  Transylvania T: 402
Clumber spaniel [dog] Ci: 715
Clumping [physiology]
  Blood (The significance of blood groups) B: 412
    with picture
Cluniac reform [history of religion]
  Pope (The early Middle Ages) P: 663
  Roman Catholic Church (Cluniac reform) R: 407
Cluny Museum
  Paris (Museums and art galleries) P: 164-165
Cluster [astronomy] *See* Galaxy cluster; Star cluster
  in this index
Cluster bomb
  Bomb (Kinds of bombs) B: 450; (Dangers to
    civilians) B: 452
Clutch [engine]
  Automobile (The transmission) A: 948-949
  Starter (Automobile starters) So: 858 *with
    diagram*
  Transmission (Clutches) T: 377 *with diagram*; (The
    clutch) T: 378 *with diagram*
Clutch [zoology]
  Bird (Laying and hatching eggs) B: 357
  Bird of prey (Reproduction and growth) B: 374a
  Turtle (Reproduction) T: 521
Clutch plate [engine]
  Transmission (The clutch) T: 378
Cluttering [speech defect]
  Speech therapy (Types of disorders) So: 773
Clyde, George D. [American political leader]
  Utah (table) U: 245; (The mid-1900's) U: 249
Clyde, River
  Scotland (Rivers and lakes) S: 217 *with map*

Clydesdale
  Horse (table: Some types and breeds of horses)
    H: 343; (Draft horses) H: 346 *with picture*
Clymer, George [American patriot] Ci: 715
Clytemnestra [ballet]
  Graham, Martha G: 301
Clytemnestra [legendary figure] Ci: 715
  Cassandra C: 275
  Electra E: 165
Cm [symbol]
  Curium (The bodies of goats) C: 1194
CMA [organization] *See* Country Music Association
  in this index
CMB [energy] *See* Cosmic microwave background
  (CMB) radiation *in this index*
CME Group [commodity exchange]
  Chicago (Places to visit) C: 430; (Finance) C: 433
    with picture
  Commodity exchange Ci: 873
  Economics *picture on* E: 58
  Illinois *picture on* I: 69; (Service industries) I: 67
CME Group Index Services LLC [company]
  Dow Jones averages D: 315
CMOS [electronics] *See* Complementary metal-
  oxide semiconductor *in this index*
CN North America [railway system] *See* Canadian
  National Railway Company *in this index*
CN Tower [Toronto]
  Ontario (Places to visit) O: 774
  Toronto (Landmarks) T: 338 *with picture*
Cnicin [poison]
  Spotted knapweed So: 804
Cnidarian [zoology] Ci: 715
  Animal (A classification of the animal kingdom)
    A: 506 *with picture*
  Invertebrate I: 365
  Jellyfish J: 90
CNN [television network] *See* Cable News Network
  in this index
CNO cycle [physics] *See* Carbon-nitrogen-oxygen
  cycle *in this index*
Cnossus [ancient Greece] *See* Knossos *in this index*
CNTU [labor federation]
  Labor movement (In Canada) L: 14
Cnut [king of England] *See* Canute *in this index*
Co [symbol]
  Cobalt Ci: 740
Coach [sports]
  Baseball (Players) B: 125; (Player positions) B: 127
  Basketball (The coach) B: 145 *with picture*
  Careers (Sports and entertainment) C: 230
  Football (The coaches) F: 358
Coach [train]
  Railroad (Passenger service) R: 105; (Passenger
    and freight cars) R: 107 *with picture*
Coach [vehicle]
  Colonial life in America (Transportation) Ci: 805-
    806 *with picture*
  Transportation (Development of land transport)
    T: 388-389 *with picture*
Coach dog
  Dalmatian D: 16
Coach horse
  Horse (table: Some types and breeds of horses)
    H: 343; (Heavy harness horses) H: 347
Coach's box
  Baseball (Foul territory) B: 127 *with diagram*
Coachwhip [shrub]
  Ocotillo O: 669 *with picture*
Coachwhip [snake]
  Snake *picture on* S: 533
Coagulant [physiology]
  Blood (Controlling bleeding) B: 411
  Fibrin F: 90
Coagulation [chemistry]
  Anticoagulant A: 553
  Bleeding (How bleeding is stopped) B: 399
  Colloid Ci: 777
  Rubber (Separating the latex) R: 503
  Water (Purifying and treating water) W: 126
Coahuiltec Indians
  San Antonio (History) S: 86
Coal Ci: 716 *with pictures and map*
  See also the list of Related articles in the Coal *article*
  Carboniferous Period C: 208
  China (Manufacturing and mining) C: 495-496
  Coke Ci: 759
  Energy supply (Fossil fuels) E: 277; (Depletion of
    fuel reserves) E: 281
  England (Mining) E: 302
  Environmental pollution (History) E: 338
  Europe *picture on* E: 403
  Fossil fuel F: 427
  Fuel (Solid fuels) F: 550
  Heating (Coal) H: 160
  Kentucky (Mining) K: 289
  Lignite L: 302

  Mining M: 574
  Montana (Natural resources) M: 755
  North Dakota (Interesting facts) N: 497 *with
    picture*
  Peat P: 225
  Pennsylvania (Mining) P: 261
  Petrochemicals (History) P: 329
  Plant (As raw materials) P: 517
  Poland (Natural resources) P: 610
  Polo, Marco (Later life) P: 648-649
  Rock (Organic sediments) R: 372-373; (table)
    R: 373 *with picture*
  Wales (Economy) W: 11
  West Virginia (Mining) W: 223 *with picture*;
    (History) W: 226-229 *with picture*
Coal and Steel Community, European *See*
  European Coal and Steel Community *in this index*
Coal auger [machine]
  Coal (Auger mining) Ci: 722
Coal ball [geology]
  Coal (The composition of coal) Ci: 717
Coal basin [geology]
  Coal (Where coal is found) Ci: 721
Coal bed [geology]
  Coal (How coal was formed) Ci: 720-721
Coal bed methane [gas]
  Coal (Developments in North America) Ci: 731-
    732
Coal dust
  Coal (Mine safety) Ci: 729
Coal-fueled power plant
  Kentucky *picture on* K: 289
Coal gas *See* Coke oven gas *in this index*
Coal gasifier tar
  Tar T: 41
Coal mining *See* Mining *in this index*
Coal oil *See* Kerosene *in this index*
Coal petrography [process]
  Coal (Analyzing coal composition) Ci: 716
Coal processing
  Coal (Cleaning coal) Ci: 726
Coal tar Ci: 733
  Coal (Coal as a raw material) Ci: 719-720
  Coke Ci: 759
  Tar T: 41
Coal-tar dye
  Dye (History) D: 396
  Lake L: 35
Coal workers' pneumoconiosis [disease] *See* Black
  lung *in this index*
Coalbanks
  Lethbridge L: 209
Coalescence [chemistry]
  Paint (Household paints) P: 23
Coalescence process [meteorology]
  Rain (Formation of rain) R: 123-124 *with diagram*
Coalition [political science] Ci: 733
  Democracy (Political parties) D: 120-121
  Government (Parliamentary democracy) G: 286
  Parliament P: 172
  Political party (Multiparty systems) P: 634
  Prime minister P: 778c
  Union of Soviet Socialist Republics (Beginnings of
    the Cold War) U: 38
Coalition of American Public Employees
  [organization]
  Farmer, James Leonard F: 46
Coalition Provisional Authority
  Iraq (The Iraq War) I: 414a
  Iraq War (After the fall of the Hussein regime)
    I: 414d
Coalition warfare
  Army A: 724
Coanda, Henri-Marie [Romanian inventor] Ci: 733
Coanda effect [aerodynamics]
  Coanda, Henri-Marie Ci: 733
Coarctation of the aorta [disorder]
  Heart (Blockage of blood flow) H: 141
Coarse crystalline quartz
  Quartz (Types) Q: 8
Coarse-wooled sheep
  Sheep (Coarse-wooled sheep) S: 382
  Wool (Sources of wool) W: 399
Coase, Ronald Harry [British-born economist]
  Nobel Prizes (Economics: 1991) N: 449
Coast Guard, United States Ci: 734 *with pictures*
  Boating (Boating regulations) B: 429
  Flag *picture on* F: 211
  Helicopter *picture on* H: 170
  Iceberg (Icebergs and people) I: 18
  Medals, decorations, and orders (Civilian awards)
    M: 355
  Navy, United States (The Coast Guard) N: 85
  Oil spill (Responses) O: 707-708
  Radar (In ship navigation) R: 65
  Ship (A ship at sea) S: 410; (Safety) S: 411-412
    with picture

United States Coast Guard Academy **U:** 199
Coast Guard Academy, United States *See* United
States Coast Guard Academy *in this index*
Coast Guard Auxiliary [organization]
Coast Guard, United States (Safety) **Ci:** 734-735;
(World War II) **Ci:** 737-738
Coast Guard Medal
Medals, decorations, and orders (table) **M:** 357
Coast Mountains
British Columbia (Land regions) **B:** 622 *with map*
Canada (The Pacific Ranges and Lowlands) **C:** 115
Coast Ranges [mountains, North America] **Ci:** 739
California *picture on* **C:** 51; (Land regions) **C:** 48
Oregon (Land regions) **O:** 838 *with map*
United States (The Pacific Ranges and Lowlands)
U: 125-126
Coast redwood [tree]
Redwood **R:** 192
Coast Salish [American Indians]
Salish Indians (The Coast Salish) **S:** 67
Coast Salish [language]
Bella Coola Indians **B:** 242
Coastal Islands
Finland (Land regions) *map on* **F:** 113
Coastal Lowlands [region, Finland]
Finland (Land regions) *map on* **F:** 113
Coastal Lowlands [region, U.S.]
North America (Land regions) **N:** 462-464
United States (Land regions) **U:** 123; (The Coastal
Lowlands) **U:** 121 *with picture*
Coastal plain [geography]
Plain **P:** 506 *with picture*
Coastal Sami [people]
Sami **S:** 79
Coastal wetland
Wetland (Water and soil) **W:** 252a
Coaster brake
Bicycle (Steering and stopping) **B:** 290
Coat [zoology]
Cat (Coat) **C:** 287 *with pictures*
Dog (Coat) **D:** 265; (Grooming) **D:** 278
Horse (Coat and skin) **H:** 348
Coat of arms [heraldry]
Heraldry **H:** 194 *with pictures*
Coati [animal] **Ci:** 739 *with picture*
Animal *picture on* **A:** 480
Coatimundi [animal] *See* Coati *in this index*
Coatlique [Aztec goddess]
Latin America *picture on* **L:** 103
Coatsworth, Elizabeth [American author] **Ci:** 740
Newbery Medal (table) **N:** 359
Coaxial cable [electronics] **Ci:** 740 *with picture*
Cable *diagram on* **C:** 7; (Coaxial cables) **C:** 4 *with
diagram*
Television (Coaxial cable and fiber-optic cable)
T: 123
Coaxial propeller
Airplane (Propellers) **A:** 217
Coaxial-rotor helicopter
Helicopter (Types of helicopters) **H:** 170-171 *with
diagram*
Cob [bird]
Swan **So:** 1016
Cobain, Kurt [American singer]
Nirvana **N:** 424 *with picture*
Rock music (Alternative rock) **R:** 381
Cobalamin *See* Vitamin B$_{12}$ *in this index*
Cobalt [element] **Ci:** 740
Vitamin (Vitamin B$_{12}$, folic acid, and choline)
V: 432
Cobalt 60 [isotope]
Cobalt (Uses) **Ci:** 741
Cobalt blue
Porcelain (Painting) **P:** 676
CoBank
Farm Credit System (Organization) **F:** 45
Cobb, Howell [American government official]
Georgia (table) **G:** 130
Cobb, Rufus W. [American political leader]
Alabama (table) **A:** 274
Cobb, Sue Bell [American jurist]
Alabama (The 2000's) **A:** 279
Cobb, Ty [American baseball player] **Ci:** 741 *with
portrait*
Baseball (table: Hall of Fame) **B:** 134; (The early
1900's) **B:** 135; (table: Modern major league
records) **B:** 138
Cobb, William T. [American political leader]
Maine (table) **M:** 87
Cobble Hill [district]
New York City (Brooklyn) **N:** 326-328
Cobden, Richard [British political leader] **Ci:** 741
Peel, Sir Robert (Prime minister) **P:** 229
Cobequid Mountains
Nova Scotia (Land regions) **N:** 562 *with map*
Cobnut
Filbert **F:** 99 *with pictures*

Hazel **H:** 122
Cobo, Albert E. [American political leader]
Detroit (The city) **D:** 167-168
Cobo Conference/Exhibition Center
Detroit (The city) **D:** 167-168
COBOL [computer language]
Computer (Using programming languages)
Ci: 923
Hopper, Grace Murray **H:** 334
COBRA [law] *See* Consolidated Omnibus Budget
and Reconciliation Act *in this index*
Cobra [snake] **Ci:** 741 *with picture*
Asp **A:** 814 *with picture*
Snake *pictures on* **S:** 526; **S:** 534; (Protection
against predators) **S:** 531
Snake charming **S:** 536
Cobra plant
Pitcher plant **P:** 499
Coburn, Abner [American political leader]
Maine (table) **M:** 87
Coburn, Charles [American actor]
Motion picture (Best performance by an actor in
a supporting role: 1943) **M:** 862a
Coburn, James [American actor]
Motion picture (Best performance by an actor in
a supporting role: 1998) **M:** 862b
Cobweb
Spider (Tangled-web weavers) **So:** 789
Cobweb weaver [spider]
Spider (Tangled-web weavers) **So:** 789
Coca [shrub] **Ci:** 742
Bolivia (Food) **B:** 443-444; (Economy) **B:** 446
Cocaine **Ci:** 742
Colombia *picture on* **Ci:** 784; (Agriculture) **Ci:** 783
Latin America *picture on* **L:** 110 ; (Food and drink)
L: 97-98
Peru (Food) **P:** 310
Coca-Cola [soft drink]
Coca-Cola Company **Ci:** 742
Coca-Cola Company **Ci:** 742
Advertising *pictures on* **A:** 80
Atlanta (Manufacturing) **A:** 860b *with picture*
Fox Quesada, Vicente **F:** 442
Cocaine [drug] **Ci:** 742
African Americans (Social struggles) **A:** 136s-136t
Bolivia (Food) **B:** 443-444
Coca **Ci:** 742
Colombia *picture on* **Ci:** 784
Dentistry (Modern dentistry) **D:** 144-145
Drug abuse (Abuse of illegal drugs) **D:** 362;
(table: Some commonly abused drugs) **D:** 363;
(History) **D:** 365
Latin America *picture on* **L:** 110
Cocci [bacteriology]
Bacteria (The structure of bacteria) **B:** 20 *with
picture*
Coccidioidomycosis [disease]
Fungal disease (In people) **F:** 558
Coccidiosis [disease]
Poultry (Raising poultry) **P:** 720-721
Coccolithophore [sea animal]
Ocean *picture on* **O:** 656; (The plankton) **O:** 655
Coccygeal vertebra [anatomy] *See* Coccyx *in this
index*
Coccyx [anatomy]
Human body (table) **H:** 422 *with diagram*
Skeleton (The axial skeleton) **S:** 479-480 *with
diagram*
Spine **So:** 792 *with diagram*
Cochimí Indians
Baja California Sur **B:** 32
Cochin [chicken]
Chicken (Asiatic class chickens) **C:** 441; (table)
C: 443
Cochin China [region, Vietnam]
Indochina (French influence) **I:** 225
Vietnam (French rule) **V:** 370
Cochise [American Indian chief] **Ci:** 743
Cochlea [anatomy]
Ear (The inner ear) **E:** 8 *with diagram*
Cochlear duct [anatomy]
Ear *diagrams on* **E:** 10; (The inner ear) **E:** 8-9 *with
diagram*
Cochlear fluid [anatomy]
Ear (How sounds travel to the inner ear) **E:** 9-10
Cochlear implant [surgery]
Deafness (Medical treatment) **D:** 58
Cochlear nerve [anatomy]
Ear (The inner ear) **E:** 8-9
Cochran, Eddie [American singer]
Rock music (Setbacks) **R:** 379
Cochran, Elizabeth [birth name of]
Bly, Nellie **B:** 426
Cochran, Jacqueline [American aviator] **Ci:** 743
Cochran, John P. [American political leader]
Delaware (table) **D:** 109
Cochran, Robert Leroy [American political leader]

Nebraska (table) **N:** 110
Cochrane, Mickey [American baseball player]
Baseball (table: Hall of Fame) **B:** 134
Cock [gun]
Flintlock **F:** 236
Harquebus **H:** 67
Cock-of-the-rock [bird] **Ci:** 743 *with picture*
Bird (Birds of Central and South America) **B:** 344a
with picture
Cockade [ornament]
Clothing (The 1700's) **Ci:** 703-704
Cockatiel [bird] **Ci:** 743 *with picture*
Parrot (Kinds of parrots) **P:** 179
Cockatoo [bird] **Ci:** 744 *with pictures*
Parrot *picture on* **P:** 180; (Kinds of parrots) **P:** 179
Cockburn, James [Canadian political leader]
Confederation of Canada (Fathers of
Confederation) **Ci:** 935
Cockcroft, Sir John Douglas [British physicist]
Ci: 744
Particle accelerator (How accelerators work)
P: 184
Cockcroft-Walton accelerator [machine]
Particle accelerator (How accelerators work)
P: 184
Cocked hat
Colonial life in America (Clothing) **Ci:** 799
Cocker spaniel [dog] **Ci:** 744
Dog *pictures on* **D:** 265, **D:** 269
English cocker spaniel **E:** 311
Cockerell, Christopher [British inventor]
Air cushion vehicle (History) **A:** 181
Cockerill, John [British businessman]
Industrial Revolution (Spread of the Industrial
Revolution) **I:** 252-253
Cockerill, William [British businessman]
Industrial Revolution (Spread of the Industrial
Revolution) **I:** 252
Cockfighting [sport] **Ci:** 744
Cockle [sea animal] **Ci:** 744
Cocklebur [plant] **Ci:** 744 *with picture*
Cockney [people] **Ci:** 745
London (Ancestry) **L:** 430
Cockpit [structure]
Airplane (The fuselage) **A:** 214; (The controls and
instruments) **A:** 217 *with picture*
Kayaking **K:** 250 *with picture*
Cockpit of the Revolution [name for]
New Jersey **N:** 231
Cockrel, Kenneth V. [American political leader]
Detroit (The early 2000's) **D:** 171
Cockrell, Kenneth D. [American astronaut]
International Space Station *picture on* **I:** 346b
Cockrell Hill [community]
Dallas (The city) **D:** 11
Cockroach [insect] **Ci:** 745 *with picture*
Antennae *picture on* **A:** 544
Insect (Hearing) **I:** 285; (Hearing) **I:** 290
Cockscomb [plant] **Ci:** 745 *with picture*
Cockspur [plant]
Sandbur **S:** 107
Cockspur [tree]
Hawthorn **H:** 114
Tree *pictures on* **T:** 421
Cocksure [book by Richler]
Richler, Mordecai **R:** 331
Cocktail [drink]
Alcoholic beverage (Distilled drinks) **A:** 336
Cocktail Party, The [play by Eliot]
Eliot, T. S. (His works) **E:** 237-238
Coco-de-mer [tree]
Plant (Interesting facts about plants) **P:** 519 *with
picture*
Seychelles (Land and climate) **S:** 340
Tree (Interesting facts about trees) **T:** 411
Cocoa [food]
Cacao **C:** 9
Chocolate (Chocolate products) **C:** 518
Cocoa bean [food]
Chocolate (The cacao tree) **C:** 518
Cocoa butter
Cacao **C:** 9
Chocolate (Manufacturing chocolate) **C:** 518
Vegetable oil (Uses) **V:** 294
Cocoanuts, The [film]
Marx Brothers **M:** 238
Coconut
Coconut palm (The coconut) **Ci:** 746 *with pictures*
Copra **Ci:** 1045
Nut (Kinds of nuts) **N:** 621
Palm (The fruits) **P:** 109
Plant (Seeds) **P:** 531 *with picture*
Coconut crab
Animal *picture on* **A:** 469
Hermit crab **H:** 212
Coconut milk
Coconut palm (The coconut) **Ci:** 746

Coconut oil
Copra **Ci: 1045**
Vegetable oil (Uses) **V: 294**
Coconut palm [tree] **Ci: 746** *with pictures*
Pacific Islands (Food) **P: 6**
Palm (The fruits) **P: 109**
Coconut-stearin [by-product]
Copra **Ci: 1045**
Cocoon [biology] **Ci: 747** *with pictures*
Estivation **E: 361**
Lungfish **L: 525**
Moth (The pupa) **M: 839** *with pictures*
Pupa **P: 904**
Silk (Spinning the cocoon) **S: 459** *with picture*;
(Discovery of silk) **S: 460** *with pictures*
Wasp (Life cycle) **W: 111**
Cocos Islands [Indian Ocean]
Straits Settlements **So: 918**
Cocteau, Jean [French author] **Ci: 747**
French literature (Developments in drama) **F: 523**
Picasso, Pablo (Picasso as a designer) **P: 448b**
Cod [fish] **Ci: 747** *with picture*
Fish *picture on* **F: 153**
COD service
Postal Service, United States (Other services)
P: 700
Coddington, William [American colonial leader]
Rhode Island (Settlement) **R: 312**
Code
Codes and ciphers **Ci: 749**; (Codes) **Ci: 750**
Code [law] **Ci: 748**
Civil law **C: 607**
Draco **D: 317**
Law (Civil law systems) **L: 132**
Code and answering pennant
Flag (Flags that talk) **F: 208**
Code Civil *See* Code Napoléon *in this index*
Code Napoléon [French law] **Ci: 748**
Civil law **Ci: 607**
Law (The first modern law codes) **L: 135-136**
Napoleon I (Administrator and lawmaker) **N: 15**
Code Noir [legal system]
Louisiana (French Louisiana) **L: 497-498**
Code of Hammurabi *See* Hammurabi, Code of *in
this index*
Code of Justinian *See* Justinian Code *in this index*
Code of Manu [Hinduism]
Manu **M: 168**
Code talkers [American history] **Ci: 749**
Codeine [drug] **Ci: 749**
Analgesic **A: 448**
Drug abuse (Heroin) **D: 362**; (table: Some
commonly abused drugs) **D: 363**
Opiate **O: 810**
Codes and ciphers Ci: 749 *with diagrams*
World War II (The secret war) **W: 493-494**
Codex [book]
Book (Early books) **B: 465-466**
Manuscript (Illustrated manuscripts) **M: 174**
Maya *picture on* **M: 325**
Publishing (Kinds of publishing) **P: 868**
Codex Borbonicus [document]
Aztec *picture on* **A: 1002**
Codex Florentino [document]
Aztec *picture on* **A: 1000**
Codex Sinaiticus [manuscript]
Library (Medieval collections) **L: 259**
Codey, Richard J. [American political leader]
New Jersey (table) **N: 249**
Codfish *See* Cod *in this index*
Codice [manuscript]
Latin America (Painting) **L: 99**
Codicil [law]
Will (Codicil) **W: 307**
Codification movement
Law (The first modern law codes) **L: 135**
Codling moth [insect] **Ci: 752** *with picture*
Apple (Pests and diseases) **A: 572**
Pear (Diseases and pests) **P: 216**
Codon [biology]
Cell (Producing proteins) **C: 333-334**; (The
genetic code) **C: 336**
Heredity (How proteins are made) **H: 206**
Cody, John Patrick [American religious leader]
Cardinal (table: American cardinals) **C: 211**
Cody, William Frederick [American frontiersman]
See Buffalo Bill *in this index*
Coeducation Ci: 752
Coefficient [mathematics]
Algebra (Other definitions) **A: 354**
Coefficient of friction [physics]
Friction (Laws of friction) **F: 532**
Coefficient of linear expansion [physics]
Heat (Changes in size) **H: 152-153**
Coefficient of thermal expansion [physics]
Materials (Thermal properties) **M: 300c**
Coelacanth [fish] **Ci: 752** *with picture*

Animal *picture on* **A: 507**
Fish (Fleshy-finned fish) **F: 148** *with picture*
Coelenterate [animal] *See* Cnidarian *in this index*
Coelho, Gonçalo [Portuguese explorer]
Rio de Janeiro **R: 345**
Vespucci, Amerigo (Life and expeditions) **V: 342**
Coelho, Pedro [Portuguese political leader]
Portugal (The early 2000's) **P: 695**
Coelom [biology] **Ci: 753** *with diagram*
Coelophysis [dinosaur] **Ci: 753**
Dinosaur (True dinosaurs) **D: 206b-211**
Coelurosaur [dinosaur]
Dinosaur (Saurischians) **D: 208-211**
Ornitholestes **O: 857**
Coen, Ethan and Joel [American producers/
directors]
Motion picture (Best achievement in directing:
2007) **M: 862**; (A new generation of
filmmakers) **M: 871-872**
Coenzyme [biochemistry]
Enzyme (Structure) **E: 341**
Vitamin (How vitamins work) **V: 432**
Coenzyme A [biochemistry]
Lipmann, Fritz Albert **L: 345**
Vitamin (Vitamin B$_{12}$, pantothenic acid, and
biotin) **V: 431-432**
Coercion
Power (Forms of power) **P: 727**
Coercive Acts *See* Intolerable Acts *in this index*
Coetzee, J. M. [South African author] **Ci: 753**
Coeur d'Alene Lake
Idaho *picture on* **I: 27**; (Rivers, waterfalls, springs,
and lakes) **I: 38**
Coeur d'Alene Mountains [Idaho-Montana]
Ci: 753
Idaho (Mountains) **I: 36**
Coevolution [biology]
Flower (The evolution of flowering plants) **F: 299**
Plant (The evolution of plants) **P: 544-545**
Coexistence [international relations] *See* Peaceful
coexistence *in this index*
Coffea arabica [plant]
Coffee (The coffee plant) **Ci: 754**
Coffea robusta [plant]
Coffee (The coffee plant) **Ci: 754**; (Kinds of coffee)
Ci: 755
Coffee Ci: 754 *with pictures*
Brazil (Agriculture) **B: 581** *with picture*
Burundi (Economy) **B: 713** *with picture*
Chicory **C: 446**
Colombia (Agriculture) **Ci: 783** *with picture*
El Salvador *picture on* **E: 251**
Guatemala (Agriculture) **G: 416** *with picture*
Panama (Agriculture) **P: 119** *with picture*
Puerto Rico (Agriculture) **P: 882** *with map*
Rwanda (Economy) **R: 571**
São Paulo **S: 117**
Coffee [painting by Portinari]
Brazil *picture on* **B: 576**
Coffee bean
Coffee (Preparation for market) **Ci: 754** *with
picture*
Coffee break
Coffee **Ci: 754**
Coffee Cantata [music by Bach]
Bach, Johann Sebastian (His works) **B: 16**
Coffee house Ci: 755
Coffeetree, Kentucky [tree]
Kentucky coffeetree **K: 295**
Cofferdam [construction]
Dam (Construction) **D: 19**
Coffin [funeral]
Funeral customs (Preparation of the body) **F: 557**
Mummy (Egyptian mummies) **M: 925-926** *with
picture*
Sarcophagus **S: 124**
Coffin, Levi [American social reformer]
Underground railroad **U: 20**
Coffin, Long Tom [literary figure]
Cooper, James Fenimore **Ci: 1035**
Coffin, O. Vincent [American political leader]
Connecticut (table) **Ci: 967**
Coffin, Robert Peter Tristram [American author]
Ci: 756
Cog
Ship *picture on* **S: 420**; (The cog) **S: 417**
Cogito, ergo sum [philosophy]
Descartes, René (His philosophy) **D: 154**
Cognac [drink]
Alcoholic beverage (Brandy) **A: 336**
Cognate [language]
Etymology (Etymons and cognates) **E: 376**
Cognition
Learning (Theories of learning) **L: 163-164**
Cognitive-behavioral theory
Abnormal psychology (Theories of abnormal
psychology) **A: 12**

Cognitive-behavioral therapy
Anxiety disorder **A: 562**
Binge eating **B: 308**
Chronic fatigue syndrome **C: 539**
Hoarding **H: 271**
Pain (Treatment) **P: 22**
Panic disorder **P: 130**
Psychotherapy (Cognitive-behavioral
psychotherapy) **P: 852**
Cognitive development [psychology]
Piaget, Jean **P: 445**
Cognitive disability
Dementia **D: 118**
Disability (Mental illness and cognitive
disabilities) **D: 219**
Cognitive psychology
Psychology (Major fields of psychology) **P: 848**
Cognitive school [psychology]
Psychology (Modern psychology) **P: 850**
Cognitive theory [psychology]
Education (How people learn) **E: 89-90**
Cognitive therapy
Mental illness (Psychotherapy) **M: 407-408**
Cogswell, Alice [American public figure]
Gallaudet **G: 14**
Cogwheel
Wheel and axle **W: 278**
Cohabitation
Marriage (The path to marriage) **M: 219**
Cohan, George M. [American composer] **Ci: 756**
Musical comedy (The first musicals) **M: 959-960**
Cohen, Abner [British anthropologist]
Anthropology (The middle and late 1900's)
A: 549
Cohen, Fred [American computer scientist]
Computer virus **926**
Cohen, Judith Sylvia [birth name of]
Chicago, Judy **C: 437**
Cohen, Leonard [Canadian author] **Ci: 756**
Cohen, Paul [American record producer]
Country music *picture on* **Ci: 1098c**
Cohen, Stanley [American physiologist]
Nobel Prizes (Physiology or medicine: 1986)
N: 446
Cohen, Wilbur J. [American government official]
Health and Human Services, Department of
(table) **H: 128**
Cohen, William Sebastian [American government
official] **Ci: 756**
Cohen-Tannoudji, Claude [Algerian physicist]
Nobel Prizes (Physics: 1997) **N: 442**
Coherence theory [philosophy]
Philosophy (Epistemology) **P: 384**
Coherent light
Laser (Characteristics of laser light) **L: 84** *with
diagram*
Light (Lasers) **L: 291**
Cohesion [physics] **Ci: 756**
Siphon **S: 475**
Cohl, Émile [French artist]
Animation (Early animation) **A: 514a**
Coho [fish]
Fish *picture on* **F: 159**
Salmon (Kinds of salmon) **S: 70**
Cohort [Roman Empire]
Army (Ancient armies) **A: 726**
Legion **L: 183**
Cohosh [plant]
Snakeroot **S: 537**
Coil [electricity]
Induction coil **I: 240**
Coil method [pottery]
Indian, American (Pottery) **I: 145**
Pottery *picture on* **P: 718**; (Shaping the clay)
P: 716
Coiling [weaving]
Basket making (Methods) **B: 141-142** *with
pictures*
Coin [money]
Coin collecting **Ci: 756**, *pictures on* **Ci: 758**
Die and diemaking *diagram on* **D: 195**
Dollar **D: 294** *with pictures*
Eagle **E: 6**
Gresham's law **G: 391**
Mint **M: 612**
Money **M: 704** *with picture, pictures on* **M: 711**;
(How money developed) **M: 705** *with pictures*;
(U.S. coins) **M: 713**; (Minting coins) **M: 714**
Coin collecting [hobby] **Ci: 756** *with pictures*
Gold (Money) **G: 251**
Coinage
Slang (Coinages) **S: 500**
Coinage metal [trade]
Silver (Uses of silver) **S: 463**
Coincidence range finder [instrument]
Rangefinder **R: 139**
Coining press

Money (Modern coins) **M: 707**; (Minting coins) **M: 714-715**
Coir [fiber]
Coconut palm (The coconut) **Ci: 746-747**
Coit, Stanton [American social worker]
Settlement house **S: 324**
Coke [fuel] **Ci: 759** *with diagrams*
Bitumen **B: 384**
Carbon (Graphite) **C: 205**
Coal (Coal as a raw material) **Ci: 719**; (Developments in England) **Ci: 731**
Coal tar **Ci: 733**
Graphite **G: 323**
Industrial Revolution (The revolution in ironmaking) **I: 249**
Iron and steel (The blast furnace process) **I: 440** *with diagram*
Petroleum coke **P: 350**
Coke, Sir Edward [English jurist]
Williams, Roger (Early life) **W: 311**
Coke, Richard [American political leader]
Texas (table) **T: 203**; (The Civil War and Reconstruction) **T: 207**
Coke, Thomas [American religious leader]
Methodists (Early history) **M: 435**
Coke oven
Coke **Ci: 759** *with diagram*
Coke oven gas **Ci: 759**
Coke oven gas [fuel] **Ci: 759**
Coal (Coal as a raw material) **Ci: 719-720**
Coke **Ci: 759** *with diagram*
Gas [fuel] (How gas is manufactured) **G: 55**
Coking coal
Coal (Coal as a raw material) **Ci: 719**
Col [geology]
Alps (How the Alps were formed) **A: 384**
Cola di Rienzo [Italian government official] **Ci: 759**
Rome (Feudal times and the Renaissance) **R: 434**
Cola nut See Kola nut *in this index*
Colbath, Jeremiah Jones [birth name of]
Wilson, Henry [American political leader] **W: 317**
Colbert, Claudette [American actress]
Motion picture (Best performance by an actress: 1934) **M: 862**
Colbert, Jean Baptiste [French government official]
France (The age of absolutism) **F: 473**
Louis XIV **L: 475**
Colbred sheep
Sheep *picture on* **S: 381**
Colburn, I. W. [American chemist]
Glass (table) **G: 218**
Colby, Anthony [American political leader]
New Hampshire (table) **N: 223**
Colchester Zoo [United Kingdom]
Zoo *picture on* **Z: 602**
Colchicine [drug]
Colchicum **Ci: 760**
Gout **G: 281**
Triticale **T: 448**
Colchicum [plant] **Ci: 760** *with picture*
Crocus **Ci: 1150**
Colchis [legendary country]
Golden Fleece **G: 255**
Colcord, Roswell K. [American political leader]
Nevada (table) **N: 173**
Cold, Common [disease] **Ci: 760**
Immune system (Active immunity) **I: 88a**
Nose **N: 549**
Rhinitis **R: 293**
Sneezing **S: 538**
Cold-blooded animal [zoology] **Ci: 761**
Amphibian **A: 439**
Animal (Some common ways of grouping animals) **A: 472**
Dinosaur (How dinosaurs lived) **D: 211**; (Reproduction and growth) **D: 211**
Fish **F: 145**
Hibernation (Cold-blooded hibernators) **H: 222**
Lizard **L: 399**
Reptile **R: 250**
Snake **S: 524**
Cold chain market
Meat packing (Marketing livestock and meat) **M: 350-351**
Cold dark matter [physics]
Dark matter **D: 37**
Cold desert
Desert **D: 155**
Cold frame [gardening] **Ci: 761** *with picture*
Pepper **P: 278**
Cold front [weather]
Weather (Synoptic-scale systems) **W: 159-160** *with diagram*
Cold Harbor, Battle of [1864]
Civil War, American (table) **Ci: 624**; (Battle of Cold Harbor) **Ci: 631**

Cold heading [industrial process]
Riveting **R: 356**
Cold-pack cheese
Cheese (Process cheese) **C: 393-394**
Cold-pressing [industrial process]
Olive oil **O: 744**
Vegetable oil (Production) **V: 294**
Cold rolling [industrial process]
Iron and steel (Rolling) **I: 445-447** *with diagram*
Cold seep [oceanography]
Deep sea (The deep-sea floor) **D: 82a**
Cold sore [disease] **Ci: 761**
Cold storage **Ci: 761**
See also Food, Frozen *in this index*
Food preservation (Cold storage) **F: 342**
Cold type
Printing (Phototypesetting) **P: 797**
Type **T: 536**
Cold War [international relations] **Ci: 762** *with pictures*
See also the list of Related articles in the Cold War *article*
Air force (Air forces in the nuclear age) **A: 186**
Berlin **B: 260**
Berlin Wall **B: 266**
Central America (Developments since the mid-1900's) **C: 356**
Central Intelligence Agency (History) **C: 356**; (Functions) **C: 356-357**
Civil defense (The Cold War) **Ci: 606**
Communism (The Cold War) **Ci: 895**
Cuban missile crisis **Ci: 1179**
Education (What should be taught?) **E: 105**
Europe (The Cold War) **E: 415**
Foreign aid (Economic development and mutual security) **F: 383-384**
France (The Fourth Republic) **F: 475-476**
Franco, Francisco (As dictator) **F: 483**
Germany (The division of Germany) **G: 169**
Guided missile (Postwar developments) **G: 427**
India (India in the 1950's and early 1960's) **I: 133**
International relations (The Cold War begins) **I: 345**
Internet (History) **I: 350g**
Middle East (Cold War alliances) **M: 534**
Navy (Navies during the Cold War) **N: 80**
North Atlantic Treaty Organization **N: 470**
Nuclear weapon (Nuclear strategy) **N: 600**; (The Cold War) **N: 601**
Organization for Security and Co-operation in Europe **O: 854**
Pan-American conferences (Stronger ties) **P: 113**
Propaganda (After World War II) **P: 825**
Radio Free Europe/Radio Liberty **R: 96**
Russia (The Cold War) **R: 554**
Socialism (The Cold War) **So: 561**
Spain (Involvement in the Cold War) **So: 751**
Third World **T: 258**
Truman, Harry S. (The Truman Doctrine) **T: 470**
Union of Soviet Socialist Republics (History) **U: 35-38**
United Nations (The end of the Cold War) **U: 92**
United States, Government of the (Responding to world events) **U: 146**
United States, History of the (The Cold War) **U: 195**; (The end of the Cold War) **U: 196d**
War **W: 23**; (Clashing ideologies) **W: 23**; (The United Nations) **W: 25**; (The Cold War era) **W: 26**
World, History of the (The rise of Communism and the Cold War) **W: 446**; (The end of the Cold War) **W: 448**
Cold wave
Hairdressing (The 1900's) **H: 12**
Cold working [manufacturing]
Artillery (The monoblock process) **A: 763**
Cole [warship]
Yemen (Unification) **Y: 564**
Cole, Henry [British businessman]
Greeting cards **G: 387**
Cole, Nat King [American musician] **Ci: 770** *with portrait*
Cole, Natalie [American singer]
Cole, Nat King **Ci: 771**
Cole, Thomas [American painter] **Ci: 771** *with picture*
Hudson River School **H: 406**
Coleman, Ann [fiancée of]
Buchanan, James (Tragedy) **B: 658-659**
Coleman, Bessie [American aviator] **Ci: 771** *with portrait*
Coleman, James P. [American political leader]
Mississippi (table) **M: 640**
Coleman, Norm [American political leader]
Minnesota (The early 2000's) **M: 606**
Coleman, Ornette [American saxophonist]
Jazz (Recent developments) **J: 73-74**

Coleman, William Thaddeus, Jr. [American government official]
Transportation, Department of (table) **T: 400**
Coleman A. Young Municipal Center
Detroit (The city) **D: 167-168**
Coleoptera [entomology]
Beetle (Kinds of beetles) **B: 216-217**
Insect *pictures on* **I: 283**; (table) **I: 300**
Coleridge, Samuel Taylor [British poet] **Ci: 771**
English literature (Romantic poetry) **E: 320**
Epigram **E: 343**
Lake Poets **L: 44**
Poetry (Romantic poetry) **P: 597**
Southey, Robert **So: 688b**
Wordsworth, William **W: 404**
Coleridge, Sara [British author]
July (Quotations) **J: 189**
Coles, Edward [American political leader]
Illinois (table) **I: 71**
Coles, George [Canadian political leader]
Confederation of Canada (Fathers of Confederation) **Ci: 935** *with picture*
Colette [French author] **Ci: 772**
Coleus [botany] **Ci: 772** *with picture*
Gardening *picture on* **G: 37**
Colewort See Kale *in this index*
Colfax, Schuyler [American political leader] **Ci: 772**
Credit Mobilier of America **Ci: 1125**
Grant, Ulysses S. (Election of 1868) **G: 315**
Vice president of the United States **V: 348** *with portrait*
Colhua-Mexica [people]
Aztec **A: 999**
Colic [disorder] **Ci: 772**
Coligny, Gaspard de [French political leader]
Catherine de Médicis **C: 303**
Huguenots **H: 410**
Saint Bartholomew's Day, Massacre of **S: 31**
Colin Clouts Come Home Againe [poem by Spenser]
Spenser, Edmund (Spenser's other poems) **So: 778**
Colines, Simon de [French printer]
Book (The spread of printed books) **B: 467**
Coliseum See Colosseum *in this index*
Colitis [disease] **Ci: 772**
Crohn's disease **Ci: 1150**
Diarrhea **D: 184**
Inflammatory bowel disease **I: 266**
Collaborating Centre for Research on the Epidemiology of Disasters [organization]
Flood (Reducing flood losses) **F: 238**
Collage [art] **Ci: 773** *with picture*
Braque, Georges **B: 564**
Cubism **Ci: 1181** *with picture*
Dadaism *picture on* **D: 3**
Picasso, Pablo (Cubism) **P: 448b** *with picture*
Schwitters, Kurt **S: 190**
Collagen [protein] **Ci: 773**
Bone (Composition of bone) **B: 456**
Connective tissue **Ci: 972**
Gelatin **G: 76**
Scleroderma **S: 209**
Tannic acid **T: 29**
Collamer, Jacob [American political leader]
Taylor, Zachary (table) **T: 60**
Collar [machine]
Die and diemaking *picture on* **D: 195**
Collar [riding equipment]
Harness **H: 63** *with diagram*
Invention (The Middle Ages) **I: 359**
Collar cell [zoology]
Sponge (Special cells) **So: 799** *with diagram*
Collar mining
Mining (Area mining) **M: 575**
Collarbone [anatomy] **Ci: 773** *with diagram*
Human body (table) **H: 422** *with diagram*
Shoulder **S: 437** *with picture*
Collards [vegetable] **Ci: 774**
Collared anteater [animal]
Anteater **A: 541**
Collared dove [bird]
Pigeon (Pigeons and human beings) **P: 460**
Collared lemming [animal]
Animal *picture on* **A: 485**
Collared lizard [reptile]
Lizard *picture on* **L: 401**
Collared peccary [animal]
Peccary **P: 226** *with picture*
Collateral [economics]
Bank (The crisis of 1933) **B: 93-94**
Credit (Lending institutions) **Ci: 1124**
Collateral trust bond
Bond (Kinds of bonds) **B: 454**
Collected Papers of Charles Sanders Peirce, The [book by Peirce]
Peirce, Charles Sanders **P: 230**

Collected Stories of Jean Stafford, The [book by Stafford]
Stafford, Jean So: 820
Collected Verse [book by Hillyer]
Hillyer, Robert Silliman H: 232
Collectibles Ci: 774
Antique A: 557
Doll (Doll collecting) D: 294
Collecting [hobby]
Doll (Doll collecting) D: 294
Hobby (Collecting) H: 272
Rock (Rocks as a hobby) R: 373 *with picture*
Shell (Collecting shells) S: 388 *with pictures*
Collecting tubule [anatomy]
Kidney (How the kidneys produce urine) K: 311-312 *with diagram*
Collection agency Ci: 774
Collection box [mail] *See* Mailbox *in this index*
Collection development [library]
Library (Providing materials) L: 235-236; (The work of librarians) L: 255
Collection of Hymns [book by Wesley]
Methodists (Early history) M: 435
Collective [group]
China (Rural life) C: 482-483
Collective bargaining [labor]
Civil service (Federal civil service) Ci: 612
Industrial relations (Collective bargaining) I: 245
Labor movement (Arranging contracts) L: 4 *with pictures*
Labor union L: 16
National Labor Relations Act N: 39
Strike (Functions of strikes) So: 928
Wisconsin (A battle over collective bargaining) W: 369
Collective behavior [sociology] Ci: 774
Collective community
Communal society Ci: 877
Inuit (New ways of life) I: 354g-354h
Israel (Rural life) I: 481
Kibbutz K: 310
Collective creation [drama]
Canadian literature (Modern Canadian drama) C: 161
Collective farm [agriculture] Ci: 774
See also State farm *in this index*
Asia (Life in China) A: 786; (Farm organization) A: 800
China (Rural life) C: 482; (Agriculture) C: 497
Communism (Under Stalin) Ci: 892
Cooperative (In other countries) Ci: 1036
Czech Republic (Agriculture) Ci: 1213
Czechoslovakia (Communist rule) Ci: 1216
Germany (Rural life) G: 150
Korea, North (Rural life) K: 370; (Agriculture and fishing) K: 372-373
Russia (Agriculture) R: 544
Stalin, Joseph (The five-year plan) So: 826
Ukraine (Agriculture) U: 11
Union of Soviet Socialist Republics (Agriculture) U: 34; (Stalin's policies) U: 36
Collective noun [grammar]
Noun (Collective nouns) N: 552
Collective ownership
Socialism So: 560
Collective pitch lever
Helicopter (Piloting a helicopter) H: 171
Collective security [international relations]
International relations (Collective security) I: 345
League of Nations L: 159
Peace (Collective security) P: 207
Collective unconscious [psychology]
Jung, Carl Gustav (His theories) J: 195
Mythology (Psychological approaches) M: 990
Collectivism [economics] Ci: 775
Collectivization [political program]
Ukraine (Soviet rule) U: 13
Uzbekistan (History) U: 254
Collector [electronics]
Transistor (How transistors work) T: 372-373 *with diagram*
Vacuum tube (How a vacuum tube works) V: 258
Colleen Bawn, The [play by Boucicault]
Boucicault, Dion B: 515
College
Universities and colleges U: 206
Adolescent (Education) A: 64
College entrance examination Ci: 775
Community college Ci: 898
Physical education (University and college programs) P: 432
School (Colleges and universities) S: 182
Collège [high school]
France (Education) F: 460-461
College, Junior *See* Community college *in this index*
College and Academy of Philadelphia

Pennsylvania, University of P: 270
College and Research Libraries [publication]
American Library Association A: 413
College Basketball Invitational
Basketball (College competition) B: 150-151
College Board [organization]
College entrance examination (In the United States) P: 775
College degree *See* Degree, College *in this index*
Collège d'enseignement général et professionel [school]
Canada (Education) C: 107-108
College entrance examination Ci: 775
Psychology (Systematic assessment) P: 848
College Football Hall of Fame [Indiana]
Hall of fame (Sports halls of fame) H: 23
College of ...
Colleges appear under their key words, as in New Jersey, College of
College of Cardinals *See* Sacred College of Cardinals *in this index*
College preparatory school
Education (Secondary education) E: 92
High school (High schools in the United States) H: 228
College World Series [baseball]
Omaha (Cultural life and recreation) O: 756
Collegiality [religion]
Pope (The 1900's and 2000's) P: 665
Vatican Council II (The Dogmatic Constitution on the Church) V: 289-390
Collegiate Church of Saint Peter [London] *See* Westminster Abbey *in this index*
Collegiate 4-H [program]
4-H F: 433
Collegiate School
Yale, Elihu Y: 548
Yale University (History) Y: 549
Collembola [entomology]
Insect *picture on* I: 280; (table) I: 299
Collie [dog] Ci: 776 *with picture*
Dog *pictures on* D: 265, D: 276
Collier, Henry Watkins [American political leader]
Alabama (table) A: 274
Collimating lens
Spectrometer So: 772 *with diagram*
Collin, Jonas [friend of]
Andersen, Hans Christian A: 451
Colline [opera character]
Opera: (*Bohème, La*) O: 801
Collins, Anthony [English philosopher]
Freethinker F: 509
Collins, Billy [American poet]
Poet laureate (table: Poets laureate of the United States) P: 590
Collins, David [Australian settler]
Hobart H: 272
Collins, Eddie [American baseball player]
Baseball (table: Hall of Fame) B: 134
Collins, Eileen Marie [American astronaut] Ci: 776 *with portrait*
Astronaut (table) A: 830
Collins, Floyd [American explorer]
Mammoth Cave National Park M: 130
Collins, Jimmy [American baseball player]
Baseball (table: Hall of Fame) B: 134
Collins, John [American political leader]
Delaware (table) D: 109
Rhode Island (table) R: 311
Collins, John S. [American businessman]
Miami Beach M: 482
Collins, Julia C. [American author]
African American literature (The 1800's) A: 136a
Collins, LeRoy [American political leader]
Florida (table) F: 260
Collins, Max Allan [American author]
Graphic novel G: 323
Collins, Michael [American astronaut]
Space exploration (Landing on the moon) So: 717
Collins, Michael [Irish political leader]
Irish Republican Army (Division in the IRA) I: 433
Sinn Féin (History) S: 473
Collins, Mount [North Carolina-Tennessee]
Great Smoky Mountains G: 348
Collins, Thomas [American political leader]
Delaware (table) D: 109
Collins, Thomas [Canadian religious leader]
Cardinal (table: Canadian cardinals) C: 211
Collins, Wilkie [British author] Ci: 776
Detective story (The pattern) D: 162
Collins, William Wilkie
Collins, Wilkie Ci: 776
Collins, Zerubbabel [American sculptor]
Sculpture (American sculpture) S: 255 *with picture*
Collip, James Bertram [Canadian biochemist]

Banting, Sir Frederick Grant B: 99
Insulin (History) I: 308
Collision insurance
Insurance (Automobile insurance) I: 313
Collisional shard [astronomy]
Satellite (Satellites of the gas giants) S: 150-150a
Collodi, Carlo [Italian author] Ci: 776
Fairy (Fairy tales) F: 11
Collodion [chemical]
Photography *picture on* P: 424; (Technical improvements) P: 423
Collodion cotton
Guncotton G: 441
Colloid [chemistry] Ci: 777
Suspension So: 1012
Ultramicroscope U: 16
Colloided powder
Gold (Other uses) G: 251
Gunpowder (Kinds of gunpowder) G: 441
Colloquialism
Novel (The United States) N: 573
Slang S: 499
Colloquy of the Old Men, The [story]
Irish literature (Heroic tales, romances, and sagas) I: 430
Collor de Mello, Fernando [Brazilian political leader]
Brazil (Return to civilian government) B: 586
Collotype printing
Printing (Collotype printing) P: 801
Collusion [economics]
Consumer protection (The right to choose) Ci: 1018
Industry (Collusion) I: 260
Colman, George [British author]
Garrick, David G: 45
Colman, Norman J. [American government official]
Agriculture, Department of (table) A: 161
Cleveland, Grover (table) Ci: 671
Colman, Ronald [British actor]
Motion picture (Best performance by an actor: 1947) M: 862a
Colo [gorilla]
Gorilla (Gorillas in captivity) G: 276
Colôane [island, Pacific Ocean]
Macau M: 4
Colobine [monkey]
Primate (Old World monkeys) P: 778a
Colobus [monkey] Ci: 777
Monkey *picture on* M: 728
Primate (Old World monkeys) P: 778a
Cologne [Germany] Ci: 777
Agrippina the Younger A: 162
Housing *picture on* H: 390
Cologne [perfume]
Perfume P: 286
Cologne Cathedral
Cologne Ci: 777
Colom, Álvaro [Guatemalan political leader]
Guatemala (Political developments) G: 417
"Colomba" [story by Mérimée]
Mérimée, Prosper M: 417
Colombia Ci: 778 *with pictures and maps*
See also the list of Related articles in the Colombia *article*
Andean Community A: 450
Bolívar, Simón B: 441
Flag *picture on* F: 200
Herrera, Tomás H: 214
Indian, American (Indians of the Caribbean) I: 172; (Indians of the Andes) I: 173; (Indians of the Tropical Forest) I: 175
Panama (Colombian rule) P: 120
Colombian coca [plant]
Coca Ci: 742
Colombian Conservative Party
Colombia (Politics) Ci: 779
Colombian Liberal Party
Colombia (Politics) Ci: 779
Colombo [Sri Lanka] Ci: 785
Sri Lanka So: 817, *picture on* So: 819
Colombo, Cristoforo [Italian explorer] *See* Columbus, Christopher *in this index*
Colombo, Domenico [father of]
Columbus, Christopher (Early years) Ci: 857
Colombo Plan [economics] Ci: 785
Colón [Panama] Ci: 786
Panama (Way of life) P: 116
Colon [punctuation] Ci: 786
Punctuation (The colon) P: 902
Colon [anatomy] Ci: 786
Colon cancer Ci: 786
Colostomy Ci: 850
Diverticulitis D: 240 *with picture*
Fiber, Dietary F: 88
Inflammatory bowel disease I: 266

Colón, Archipiélago de *See* Galapagos Islands *in this index*
Colón, Cristóbal *See* Columbus, Christopher *in this index*
Colon cancer [disorder] **Ci: 786**
 Cancer (Classification by primary body site) **C: 167-168**; (table) **C: 170**
 Colonoscopy **Ci: 815**
Colón Theater [Buenos Aires]
 Argentina (The arts) **A: 651**
Colonel [rank]
 Army, United States *picture on* **A: 732**
 Marine Corps, United States *pictures on* **M: 207**
 Rank, Military (table) **R: 140**
Colonia [government]
 Mexico City (Residential and commercial centers) **M: 476a**
Colonial architecture
 Architecture (Colonial architecture in America) **A: 624** *with pictures*
 Colonial life in America (Houses) **Ci: 796** *with picture*
 Georgian architecture **G: 136**
Colonial bentgrass [plant]
 Bentgrass **B: 254**
Colonial Dames of America, National Society of the Ci: 786
Colonial life in America [U.S. history] **Ci: 787** *with pictures and map*
 See also Pioneer life in America *in this index and the list of Related articles in the* Colonial Life in America *article*
 African Americans (Colonial times) **A: 136d**
 Agriculture (Colonial agriculture) **A: 157**
 American literature (Colonial literature [1608-1764]) **A: 414**
 Clothing (Clothing of Europe and the Americas) **Ci: 703-704**
 Cotton (American colonists) **Ci: 1092**
 Divorce **D: 253**
 Draft, Military (Military drafts throughout history) **D: 318**
 Fire department (Fire protection in North America) **F: 128**
 Glass (Early American glass) **G: 222**
 Hispanic Americans (Cultural backgrounds) **H: 247**; (Exploration and settlement) **H: 250**
 Immigration (The first wave) **I: 82**
 Indentured servant **I: 106**
 Indian wars (Colonial days) **I: 190**
 Iron and steel (The Iron Age) **I: 449-450**
 Journalism (Early American journalism) **J: 174**
 Law (Beginnings of U.S. law) **L: 136**
 Log cabin **L: 422** *with picture*
 Minutemen **M: 613**
 Money *pictures on* **M: 707**; (Paper money) **M: 708-709** *with pictures*; (History of United States currency) **M: 710**
 Navy, United States (The earliest colonial warships) **N: 85**
 New France (Colonial life) **N: 204**
 New Year's Day (Early customs) **N: 289**
 Pewter (History) **P: 352-353**
 Plymouth Colony **P: 582** *with pictures*
 Popular music (Popular music before recording) **P: 669**
 Postal Service, United States (Colonial times) **P: 700**
 Postal services (Postal service in the United States) **P: 706**
 Revolution, American (Background and causes of the revolution) **R: 271**
 Rice (History) **R: 326-327**
 School (The development of U.S. schools) **S: 183**
 Slavery (Modern times) **S: 502**
 United States, History of the (The American Colonies [1607-1753]) **U: 152** *with pictures and map*
 Wampum **W: 22**
 Williamsburg *pictures on* **W: 313**
Colonial life in Latin America
 Argentina (Settlement and colonial life) **A: 655**
 Chile (Colonial period) **C: 468**
 Honduras (The colonial period) **H: 312**
 Indian, American (Indians of Middle America) **I: 169-171**; (Indians of the Andes) **I: 173-175**; (Indians of the Marginal Regions) **I: 176-177**; (In Latin America) **I: 178**
 Latin America (Colonial rule) **L: 104**; (Colonial discontent) **L: 106**
 Latin American literature (Colonial literature) **L: 112**
 Mexico (Spanish rule) **M: 469**; (Revolt against the Spaniards) **M: 470**
 Paraguay (Jesuit missionaries) **P: 149**
 Venezuela (European exploration and settlement) **V: 304**

Colonial National Historical Park [Virginia]
 Colonial life in America (Places to visit) **Ci: 800** *with picture*
 National Park System (table: National historical parks) **N: 56**
 Williamsburg (Williamsburg today) **W: 313**
 Yorktown **Y: 569**
Colonial organism
 Life (The structure of living things) **L: 276-277**
Colonialism [political science] **Ci: 813**
 See also Imperialism *in this index and the list of Related articles in the* Colonialism *article*
 Africa (European colonization in Africa) **A: 133**
 Arabs (Ottoman and European rule) **A: 590**
 Asia (History) **A: 804-806** *with picture*
 Colony **Ci: 815**
 Europe (Colonial expansion) **E: 413**
 Government (The rise of monarchies and nation-states) **G: 290**
 Imperialism **I: 92**
 Middle East (History) **M: 533-534**
 Minority group (The creation of minority groups) **M: 609**; (Relationships between groups) **M: 609**
 Muslims (Colonialism) **M: 964d**
 Racism (History) **R: 62**
 World, History of the *map on* **W: 439**; (Imperialism) **W: 445**; (The birth of new nations) **W: 448**
 World War I (Competition for colonies) **W: 454**
Colonna, Piazza
 Rome **R: 429**
Colonnade
 Architecture (table) **A: 608** *with picture*; (Islamic architecture) **A: 613**
Colonnade of the Congress [Brussels]
 Unknown soldier **U: 211**
Colonoscope [instrument]
 Colonoscopy **Ci: 815**
Colonoscopy [medicine] **Ci: 815**
Colony [biology]
 See also Community *in this index*
 Ant **A: 520**
 Bee **B: 200**
 Penguin (The life of penguins) **P: 238** *with picture*
 Prairie dog (Habits) **P: 732**
 Termite **T: 171**
Colony [political unit] **Ci: 815**
 Colonialism **Ci: 813**
 Commonwealth of Nations (Dependencies) **Ci: 876**
 Minority group (The creation of minority groups) **M: 609**
 World, History of the (The colonization of America) **W: 441**
Colony [Roman history]
 Rome, Ancient (The army) **R: 438**
Colony, Penal *See* Penal colony *in this index*
Colony collapse disorder
 Bee (As an industry) **B: 206-207**
Colony House
 Newport **N: 379**
Colophon
 Book (Inside a book) **I: 464-465**
Color Ci: 816 *with pictures*
 Culture (Using symbols) **Ci: 1187**
 Flag **F: 194**
 Frog (Skin) **F: 536-537**
 Gem (Qualities of gem minerals) **G: 77**
 Interior design (Elements of design) **I: 327** *with pictures*; (Pattern and texture) **I: 328**; (Using color) **I: 331**
 Light *diagram on* **L: 287**; (Sources of light) **L: 283** *with picture*; (The spectrum of light sources) **L: 284** *with diagram*; (Diffraction) **L: 288**
 Mineral (Other identification tests) **M: 567**
 Newton, Sir Isaac (Light and color) **N: 389**
 Paint (Shading) **P: 25**
 Painting (The elements of painting) **P: 34-35**
 Photography (Taking good photographs) **P: 409-410**; (Light) **P: 414-415**
 Pigment **P: 461**
 Protective coloration **P: 831**
 Rainbow **R: 127**
 Sculpture (Form and treatment) **S: 230-231**
 Sun (Color) **So: 977**
Color [poems by Cullen]
 Cullen, Countee **Ci: 1184**
Color [subatomic physics]
 Subatomic particle (The Standard Model) **So: 938**
Color balance
 Photography (Color balance) **P: 417**
Color blindness [birth defect] **Ci: 827** *with pictures*
 Blindness **B: 401**
 Color (The roles of the eyes and brain) **Ci: 818-819**
 Dalton, John **D: 16**
 Eye (Color blindness) **E: 466**

 Mammal (Senses) **M: 120-121**
Color burst [electronics]
 Television (Encoding the color signals) **T: 123**
Color by addition
 Color *diagram on* **Ci: 822**; (Mixing colored lights) **Ci: 821**
Color by subtraction
 Color (Mixing colorants) **Ci: 819-820** *with diagrams*
Color circle
 Color (Producing color harmony) **Ci: 823** *with diagram*
Color deficiency *See* Color blindness *in this index*
Color-field painting [art]
 Painting (Color-field painting) **P: 85** *with picture*
Color filter
 Photography (Filters) **P: 416**
Color filter array [electronics]
 Photography (Capturing digital images) **P: 420-421** *with picture*
Color guard [marching group]
 Flag (Carrying the flag) **F: 219**
Color harmony
 Color (Producing color harmony) **Ci: 823** *with diagrams*
Color Intervals at Provincetown [drawing by Hofmann]
 Drawing *picture on* **D: 343**
Color negative film
 Photography (Film photography) **P: 416**; (Developing the film) **P: 419** *with diagrams*
Color of Money, The [film]
 Newman, Paul **N: 379**
Color printing
 Printing (Printing in color) **P: 801** *with pictures*
Color Purple, The [book by Walker]
 African American literature (The 1900's) **A: 136a**
 Walker, Alice **W: 13**
Color Purple, The [film]
 Winfrey, Oprah **W: 338**
Color reversal film
 Photography (Film photography) **P: 416**; (Developing the film) **P: 419** *with diagrams*
Color scheme
 Interior design (Using color) **I: 331** *with pictures*
Color sensitivity
 Photography (Color sensitivity) **P: 417**
Color television
 Television (Creating television signals) **T: 121-122**; (Technological advances) **T: 127**
Color triangle
 Color *diagram on* **Ci: 822**
Color vision
 Color (How we *see* color) **Ci: 818-819** *with picture*
 Color blindness **Ci: 827**
Color vision deficiency *See* Color blindness *in this index*
Color wheel
 Color (Producing color harmony) **Ci: 823** *with diagram*
Colorado Ci: 828 *with pictures and maps*
 See also the list of Related articles in the Colorado *article*
 Civil rights (Major changes in the field of civil rights) **Ci: 609-610**
 Gold rush (Gold rushes in the United States) **G: 254**
 Great Sand Dunes National Park **G: 347**
 United States *picture on* **U: 124**
Colorado, University of Ci: 848
Colorado Aqueduct [California]
 Aqueduct (Present-day aqueducts) **A: 580**
Colorado Avalanche [team]
 Hockey (table: National Hockey League) **H: 281**
Colorado-Big Thompson Project [water system]
 Colorado (The mid-1900's) **Ci: 847**
 Colorado River **Ci: 849**
Colorado blue columbine [plant]
 Columbine **Ci: 853**
 Flower *picture on* **F: 284**
Colorado City [former name]
 Yuma **Y: 582**
Colorado Desert [region, California] **Ci: 848**
 California (The Basin and Range Region) **C: 50**
Colorado National Monument [Colorado] **Ci: 848**
 Colorado *picture on* **Ci: 840**
 National Park System (table: National monuments) **N: 50**
Colorado Party [political party]
 Paraguay (Political unrest) **P: 149**; (Stroessner's rule and overthrow) **P: 149-150**
 Uruguay (Politics) **U: 223**; (Civil war) **U: 227**; (Struggles for power) **U: 227**
Colorado Plateau [region, U.S.]
 Colorado (Land regions) **Ci: 838**
 United States (The Western Plateaus, Basins, and Ranges) **U: 125**

Utah (Land regions) **U: 240** *with map*
Colorado potato beetle [insect]
Beetle (Leaf beetles) **B: 217**
Potato beetle **P: 714** *with picture*
Colorado River [U.S.] **Ci: 848** *with map*
Arizona (Rivers, waterfalls, and lakes) **A: 682**
California (Rivers, waterfalls, and lakes) **C: 50-51**
Grand Canyon **G: 306** *with map*
Grand Canyon National Park (Recreational activities) **G: 307-308** *with map*
Irrigation **I: 456**
Powell, John Wesley **P: 726**
River (table) **R: 352**
Seven natural wonders of the world (The Grand Canyon) **S: 324**
Utah (Rivers and lakes) **U: 242** *with map*
Colorado River Storage Project
Colorado (The mid-1900's) **Ci: 847**
Colorado Rockies [team]
Baseball (table) **B: 130**
Colorado Springs [Colorado] **Ci: 849**
Colorado squawfish
Minnow **M: 607**
Colorado State University Ci: 849
Colorant
Color (Mixing colorants) **Ci: 819-821** *with diagrams*
Ink **I: 272**
Coloratura soprano
Opera (table) **O: 791**; (The singers) **O: 792**
Colorbearer
Flag (Carrying the flag) **F: 219**
Colorectal cancer [disease]
Colon cancer **Ci: 786**
Colored [racial category] *See* Coloured *in this index*
Colored glass
Glass (Specialty glasses) **G: 212**; (Colored glass) **G: 214**
Stained glass **So: 821** *with pictures*
Colored pencil
Pencil (Colored pencils) **P: 236**
Colored people *See* African Americans; Blacks *in this index*
Colored People, National Association for the Advancement of *See* National Association for the Advancement of Colored People *in this index*
Colored Women, National Association of
Terrell, Mary Church **T: 173**
Colorfast
Dye (How dyes work) **D: 395**
Coloring, Protective *See* Protective coloration *in this index*
Coloring agent
Food additive (Kinds of additives) **F: 339**
Colorpoint coat
Cat (Coat) **C: 287** *with picture*
Colorpoint shorthair
Cat (Short-haired breeds) **C: 290**
Colors [flag]
Flag (table) **F: 193**; (Military flags) **F: 195-196**; (First United States flags) **F: 208-210**
Colosio, Luis Donaldo [Mexican political leader]
Mexico (Opposition to the PRI) **M: 474**
Zedillo Ponce de León, Ernesto **Z: 588**
Colossal Cave Adventure [electronic game]
Electronic game (Early computer games) **E: 204d**
Colossal scale [art]
Sculpture (Kinds of sculpture) **S: 230**
Colossal squid
Squid (Kinds of squids) **So: 814a**
Colosseum [Rome] **Ci: 849** *with picture*
City *picture on* **Ci: 580**
Italy *picture on* **I: 497**
Rome (The Colosseum) **R: 433** *with picture*
Colossians, Epistle to the [New Testament] **Ci: 850**
Bible (The Letters) **B: 284**
Colossus of Rhodes [sculpture by Chares]
Rhodes **R: 317**
Seven Wonders of the Ancient World *picture on* **S: 327**; (The Colossus of Rhodes) **S: 325**
Colostomy [surgery] **Ci: 850**
Surgery (Some common surgical operations) **So: 1006**
Colour *See* Color *in this index*
Coloured [racial category]
South Africa (People) **So: 609**; (Ways of life) **So: 611**
Zimbabwe (People) **Z: 592**
Colposcope [instrument]
Pap test **P: 132**
Colquitt, Alfred H. [American political leader]
Georgia (table) **G: 130**
Colquitt, Oscar B. [American political leader]
Texas (table) **T: 203**
Colt [horse]
Horse *picture on* **H: 359**; (table: Horse terms) **H: 343**; (Life history) **H: 351**

Horse racing (Thoroughbred horses) **H: 363-364**
Colt, Samuel [American businessman] **Ci: 850** *with portrait*
Arizona (Libraries and museums) **A: 674**
Connecticut (The 1800's) **Ci: 970**
Weapon (Firearms) **W: 154b**
Colt .45 [gun]
Handgun (Types of handguns) **H: 43** *with picture*
Colt Paterson [gun]
Handgun (Rapid-fire handguns) **H: 45**
Colter [tool]
Plow (The tractor plow) **P: 575**
Colter, John [American explorer] **Ci: 850**
Wyoming (Exploration) **W: 533**
Yellowstone National Park (History) **Y: 559-560**
Coltrane, Alice [American musican]
Coltrane, John **Ci: 851**
Coltrane, John [American saxophonist] **Ci: 850**
Colts, Baltimore [team] *See* Baltimore Colts *in this index*
Colts, Indianapolis [team] *See* Indianapolis Colts *in this index*
Coltsfoot [plant] **Ci: 851** *with picture*
Colubrid [zoology] **Ci: 1126**
Snake (Fangs and venom glands) **S: 528**; (The evolution of snakes) **S: 534-535**; (Colubrids) **S: 535**
Colugo [mammal]
Flying lemur **F: 312** *with picture*
Colum, Padraic [Irish dramatist]
Regina Medal (table: 1961) **R: 206**
Columba, Saint [Irish missionary]
Irish literature (Early Irish literature) **I: 430**
Scotland (Beginning of the Scottish kingdom) **S: 219**
Columbarium [burial vault]
Cremation **Ci: 1126**
Columbia [name for U.S.] **Ci: 851**
Columbia [Maryland]
Washington, D.C. (Metropolitan area) **W: 80-81** *with map*
Columbia [Missouri] **Ci: 851**
Columbia [South Carolina] **Ci: 851**
South Carolina *pictures on* **So: 635, So: 649**; (Population) **So: 644**
Columbia [company]
Motion picture (Movies become big business) **M: 865-866**
Columbia [space shuttle]
See also Columbia disaster *in this index*
Astronaut (Achievements in space) **A: 829-830**
Rocket (The space age) **R: 391**
Space exploration (The shuttle era begins) **So: 723** *with picture*
Columbia, Mount
Alberta (The Rocky Mountains and Foothills) **A: 322** *with map*
Columbia Broadcasting System *See* CBS *in this index*
Columbia disaster [U.S. history] **Ci: 852**
Astronaut (Accidents in space) **A: 830-831**
International Space Station (History) **I: 346b-347**
National Aeronautics and Space Administration **N: 28**
Space exploration (The Columbia disaster) **So: 725**
Columbia Glacier
Alaska (Glaciers) **A: 295**
Columbia Icefield [Alberta]
Alberta (Places to visit) **A: 320** *with picture*
Jasper National Park **J: 64**
Columbia Institution for the Instruction of the Deaf and Dumb and the Blind
Disability (Early beliefs) **D: 221**
Columbia Plateau [region, U.S.]
Idaho (Land regions) **I: 36**
Nevada (Land regions) **N: 166**
Oregon (Land regions) **O: 838** *with map*
United States (The Western Plateaus, Basins, and Ranges) **U: 125**
Columbia River [river, Canada-U.S.] **Ci: 852** *with map*
Canada (The Pacific Basin) **C: 120**
Exploration (Crossing North America) **E: 447**
Grand Coulee Dam **G: 308**
Gray, Robert **G: 334**
Inland waterway **I: 274**
Jetty **J: 117** *with picture*
Lewis and Clark expedition **L: 222c-222d** *with picture*
Oregon **O: 826**; (Land and climate) **O: 838-840** *with map*
Washington (Land regions) **W: 58-60** *with map*
Columbia River Gorge [region, Oregon-Washington]
Oregon (Places to visit) **O: 836**
Columbia River Treaty [1964]

British Columbia (The mid-1900's) **B: 630**
Montana (Rivers and lakes) **M: 752-754**
Columbia University Ci: 853
See also Teachers College, Columbia University *in this index*
New York (Libraries) **N: 294**
Pulitzer, Joseph (His bequests) **P: 886a**
Universities and colleges (The oldest U.S. universities and colleges) **U: 210**
Columbian Museum of Chicago [former name]
Field Museum (History) **F: 94**
Columbian Order *See* Tammany, Society of *in this index*
Columbine [literary figure]
Pantomime **P: 131**
Columbine [plant] **Ci: 853**
Colorado *picture on* **Ci: 828**
Flower (Flowers of woodlands and forests) **F: 284** *with picture*
Columbine High School shooting Co: 853
Colorado (The late 1900's) **Ci: 847**
Denver (History) **D: 147-148**
Columbite [mineral]
Tantalum **T: 29**
Columbite [painting by Valcin]
Latin America *picture on* **L: 100**
Columbium [element]
Niobium **N: 424**
Columbus [Georgia] **Ci: 854**
Columbus [New Mexico]
Mexico (The Constitution of 1917) **M: 472**
Columbus [Ohio] **Ci: 854** *with picture and map*
Ohio *pictures on* **O: 681, O: 684**
Columbus [pen name]
Adams, John Quincy (Lawyer and writer) **A: 40-41**
Columbus, Bartholomew [brother of]
Columbus, Christopher (Early years) **Ci: 857**; (Success in Spain) **Ci: 858**; (Trouble, settlement, and exploration) **Ci: 862**
Santo Domingo **S: 117**
Columbus, Christopher [Italian explorer] **Ci: 857** *with pictures and map*
Atlantic Ocean (Exploration) **A: 867**
Canada, History of (Early European exploration) **C: 138-139**
Cannibal **C: 179**
Cattle (American cattle) **C: 315**
Colombia **C: 778**
Corn (European corn production) **Ci: 1062**
Cuba (Early years) **Ci: 1175**
Dominica (History) **D: 302**
Dominican Republic (History) **D: 304** *with picture*
Exploration **E: 439**, *map on* **E: 443**; (Columbus reaches America) **E: 444**; (Exploring the New World) **E: 444**
Flag *picture on* **F: 209**
Food (Foods of the New World) **F: 336**
Indian, American **I: 136**
Isabella I **I: 461**
Latin America *map on* **L: 105**; (European discovery and exploration) **L: 103**
Lemon (History) **L: 188-189**
Map (Advances in European cartography) **M: 184**
Panama (The Spanish colonial period) **P: 120**
Ponce de León, Juan (Early life and career) **P: 655**
Puerto Rico **P: 872**
Renaissance (The heritage of the Renaissance) **R: 238-239**
United States, History of the (America before colonial times) **U: 149**
Venezuela **V: 298**
Virgin Islands, United States **V: 393**; (Exploration) **V: 396**
West Indies **W: 201**; (The colonial period) **W: 205**
Columbus, Diego [brother of]
Columbus, Christopher (Early years) **Ci: 857**; (Trouble, settlement, and exploration) **Ci: 862**
Columbus, Diego [son of]
Columbus, Christopher (Young adulthood) **Ci: 857-858**
Columbus, Ferdinand [son of]
Columbus, Christopher (Years of waiting) **Ci: 858**; (Fourth voyage westward) **Ci: 863**
Columbus, Knights of [organization]
Knights of Columbus **K: 352**
Columbus Blue Jackets [team]
Hockey (table: National Hockey League) **H: 281**
Columbus Day [custom] **Ci: 865**
Columbus Dispatch [newspaper]
Newspaper (Recent trends) **N: 386-387**
Columbus Museum of Art
Columbus (Cultural life and recreation) **Ci: 855**
Column [architecture] **Ci: 865** *with pictures*
Architecture (table) **A: 608** *with picture*
Building construction (Beams, girders, and columns) **B: 682-683**
Sculpture (As part of architecture) **S: 229**

Column [mathematics]
  Addition (Adding 10's and 1's) **A: 50**
Column of July [Paris]
  July Revolution **J: 190** *with picture*
Column of King Sigismund
  Warsaw (The city) **W: 38**
Column of Marcus Aurelius [ruins]
  Rome (Other remains) **R: 433**
Column still
  Distilling **D: 239**
Columnar cell [physiology]
  Epithelium **E: 345**
Columnar snow crystals
  Snow (How snow forms) **S: 539** *with picture*
Columnar transposition
  Codes and ciphers (Transposition) **Ci: 749**
Coma [astronomy]
  Comet **Ci: 867**
  Halley's Comet **H: 24**
Coma [disorder] **Ci: 866**
  Persistent vegetative state **P: 300f**
Coma [optics]
  Aberration (Point aberration) **A: 10**
Coma Cluster [astronomy]
  Dark matter **D: 37**
Comanche [horse]
  Horse (table: Famous horses in history and
    legend) **H: 361**
Comanche Indians **Ci: 866**
  Code talkers **Ci: 749**
  Indian, American *picture on* **I: 136d**; (Indians of
    the Plains) **I: 158-159**
  Quanah **Q: 5**
  Texas Rangers (Early days) **T: 210-211**
Comanche Village, A [painting by Catlin]
  Indian, American *picture on* **I: 136d**
Comaneci, Nadia [Romanian gymnast] **Ci: 866**
  Olympic Games *picture on* **O: 754**; (Boycotts)
    O: 753
Comarca [territory]
  Panama (Local government) **P: 116**
Comayagüela [Honduras]
  Tegucigalpa **T: 87**
Comb [zoology]
  Chicken (The body of a chicken) **C: 440** *with*
    pictures
Comb-footed spider
  Spider (Tangled-web weavers) **So: 789**
Comb jelly [sea animal] *See* Ctenophore *in this*
  index
Comba, Juan [Spanish artist]
  Drama *picture on* **D: 333**
Combat command [military unit]
  Air Force, United States (Combat commands)
    A: 193
Combat correspondent
  War correspondent **W: 26**
Combat engineer
  Engineers, Corps of **E: 291**
Combat fatigue [psychology] *See* Post-traumatic
  stress disorder *in this index*
Combat knife
  Knife (Types of knives) **K: 345-346**
Combat mission [warfare]
  Air force (The role of air forces) **A: 182**
  Air Force, United States (Offense) **A: 190**
Combat of the Kearsarge and the Alabama
  [painting by Manet]
  Alabama picture on **A: 255**
  Manet, Édouard **M: 139**
Combat ritual [zoology]
  Snake (Battles among male snakes) **S: 532**
Combat ship
  Navy, United States (Combat ships) **N: 84**
Combat unit
  Army, United States (Weapons and equipment of
    the Army) **A: 734**
Combination [boxing]
  Boxing (Boxing skills) **B: 529**
Combination carrier [ship]
  Tanker (Kinds of tankers) **T: 28**
Combination padlock
  Lock (Mechanical locks) **L: 411-412**
Combination printing
  Photography (Artistic advances) **P: 424**
Combination truck [vehicle]
  Truck (Kinds of trucks) **T: 457**
Combinations [mathematics]
  Permutations and combinations **P: 290**
Combinatorics [mathematics]
  Permutations and combinations **P: 290**
Combine [machine] **Ci: 866**
  Corn *picture on* **Ci: 1062**; (Harvesting) **Ci: 1061**
  North Dakota *picture on* **N: 511**
  Oats (Harvesting oats) **O: 640a** *with picture*
  Peanut *picture on* **P: 215**
  Potato (Harvesting) **P: 713** *with picture*

Reaper **R: 173**
Rice (Harvesting) **R: 326** *with picture*
Soybean **So: 691** *with picture*
Wheat (Harvesting) **W: 272** *with picture*
Combine painting [art]
  Rauschenberg, Robert **R: 150**
Combined Chiefs of Staff [World War II]
  Joint Chiefs of Staff **J: 156**
Combined competition
  Skiing (Alpine competitions) **S: 486-487**
Combined operations units [military]
  Commando **Ci: 871**
Combined statistical area
  Metropolitan area (Defining metropolitan areas)
    M: 442 *with map*
Combined warfare
  Army **A: 724**
Combing [fiber]
  Thread (Making thread from natural fibers) **T: 269**
  Wool (Making yarn) **W: 400**
Combing length fiber
  Wool (Processing of wool) **W: 400**
Combining volumes, Law of
  Gay-Lussac, Joseph Louis **G: 71**
Combite [custom]
  Haiti (People) **H: 14**
Combo [music]
  Jazz (The sound of jazz) **J: 68** *with picture*
Combs, Earle [American baseball player]
  Baseball (table: Hall of Fame) **B: 134**
Combustible material
  Fire (Kinds of fire) **F: 120**
  Fire extinguisher **F: 130**
Combustion [chemistry] **Ci: 866**
  Air pollution (Chief sources of air pollution)
    A: 198
  Carbon dioxide **C: 206**
  Carbon monoxide **C: 207**
  Chemical reaction **C: 397**
  Environmental pollution (Air pollution) **E: 331**;
    (Solid waste) **E: 334**
  Fire (What is fire?) **F: 120**
  Heat (Chemical reactions) **H: 149**
  Lavoisier, Antoine Laurent **L: 129**
  Oxidation **O: 888** *with picture*
  Science (The Enlightenment) **S: 199**
Combustion chamber
  Electric power (Fossil-fueled steam electric power
    plants) **E: 183** *with diagram*
  Gasoline engine (The cylinder head) **G: 64** *with*
    diagrams
  Guided missile (The engine) **G: 424**
  Jet propulsion (Power in a jet engine) **J: 111** *with*
    diagram
  Rocket (Parts of a rocket) **R: 385**; (Solid-propellant
    rockets) **R: 387** *with diagram*
  Turbine (Gas turbines) **T: 497-498**
Combustion cleaner
  Air cleaner (Other types of air cleaners) **A: 176**
Combustion furnace
  Furnace (Sources of heat) **F: 567** *with diagram*
Comcast Center
  Philadelphia (Recent developments) **P: 367**
Comcast Corporation
  AT&T Inc. **A: 852**
Come Back, Little Sheba [play by Inge]
  Inge, William **I: 270**
Come Hither [book by De la Mare]
  De la Mare, Walter **D: 95**
Comeback City [name for]
  Cleveland (Comeback City) **Ci: 667**
COMECON [economic alliance]
  Cold War (The containment policy) **Ci: 764**
Comedia de Calisto y Melibea [play]
  Spanish literature (The 1400's) **So: 758**
Comédie-Française [theater group]
  Drama (France) **D: 335**
  Paris (Arts) **P: 164**
  Theater (France) **T: 248**
Comédie-Italienne [theater group]
  Drama (France) **D: 335**
Comédie larmoyante
  Drama (France) **D: 335**
Comédiens du Roi, Les [theater group]
  Drama (The French theater) **D: 333**
Comedies, Histories & Tragedies [book by
  Shakespeare] *See* First Folio *in this index*
Comédies et Proverbes [plays by Musset]
  Musset, Alfred de **M: 966**
Comedy [drama] **Ci: 867**
  Drama (Comedy) **D: 325**; (New Comedy) **D: 327**;
    (Roman drama) **D: 328**; (Italian Renaissance
    drama) **D: 330**; (England) **D: 334**
  French literature (Classical drama) **F: 520**
  Greek literature (Drama) **G: 377**
  Plautus **P: 570**
  Shakespeare, William (Shakespeare's plays)

S: 354-355
Comedy of character
  Comedy **Ci: 867**
Comedy of Errors, The [play by Shakespeare]
  Shakespeare, William: (The Comedy of Errors)
    S: 355
Comedy of humours
  Drama (Elizabethan playwrights) **D: 331-332**
Comedy of ideas
  Comedy **Ci: 867**
Comedy of manners
  Comedy **Ci: 867**
  Drama (England) **D: 334**
  English literature (Restoration drama) **E: 318**
Comedy of menace
  Pinter, Harold **P: 475**
Comegys, Cornelius P. [American political leader]
  Delaware (table) **D: 109**
Comenius, John Amos [Czech educator]
  Literature for children (Early children's literature)
    L: 361-362
  Universal language **U: 205**
Comer, Braxton Bragg [American political leader]
  Alabama (table) **A: 274**
Comet [airplane]
  Airplane *picture on* **A: 235**; (The jet age) **A: 238**
  Aviation (A new age of flight) **A: 990**
Comet [astronomy] **Ci: 867** *with pictures*
  Halley, Edmond **H: 24**
  Halley's Comet **H: 24** *with diagram*
  Halo **H: 26**
  Meteor (Meteor showers) **M: 431**
  Moon (Origin and evolution of the moon) **M: 788**
  Oort cloud **O: 788**
  Shoemaker, Eugene Merle **S: 433**
  Solar system (Comets) **So: 581**
  Space exploration (Probes to comets) **So: 711**
Comet [train]
  Railroad (The 1920's and the Great Depression)
    R: 118
Cometary globule
  Star *picture on* **So: 845**
Comets, The [band]
  Rock music *picture on* **R: 378**
Comfort bicycle
  Bicycle (Road bikes) **B: 289**
Comic book
  Cartoon **C: 263**
  Comics **Ci: 870**
  Graphic novel **G: 322** *with picture*
Comic opera [music]
  Gilbert and Sullivan **G: 190**
  Opera (Opera seria and opera buffa) **O: 797**
Comic strip
  Cartoon **C: 263**
  Comics (Comic strips) **Ci: 869**
Comics **Ci: 869** *with pictures*
  See also Comic book; Comic strip *in this index*
  Cartoon **C: 263**; (Developing the idea) **C: 266-267**
    with pictures
Comics Code Authority
  Comics (Comic books) **Ci: 869**
"Comin' Thro' the Rye" [song]
  Burns, Robert **B: 710**
Cominform [organization]
  Cold War (The containment policy) **Ci: 764**
Coming and Going of the Pony Express, The
  [painting by Remington]
  Pony express *picture on* **P: 658**
Coming of Age in Samoa [book by Mead]
  Mead, Margaret **M: 344**
Coming Race, The [book by Bulwer-Lytton]
  Bulwer-Lytton, Edward George Earle Lytton
    B: 698
Comino [island, Mediterranean]
  Malta **M: 113** *with map*
Cominotto [island, Mediterranean]
  Malta **M: 113** *with map*
COMINT [cryptology] *See* Communications
  intelligence *in this index*
Comintern [organization]
  Communism (The spread of Communism) **Ci: 893**
  Lenin, V. I. (Civil war) **L: 194**
Comiskey, Charles A. [American baseball player]
  Baseball (table: Hall of Fame) **B: 134**
Comiskey Park [Chicago]
  Baseball (Depression and war) **B: 136**
Comitia tributa [government]
  Plebeians **P: 572**
Comma [punctuation]
  Punctuation (The comma) **P: 903**
Commager, Henry Steele [American historian]
  Ci: 870
Command [military unit]
  Air force (The organization of air forces) **A: 183**
  Air Force, United States (Organization of the Air
    Force) **A: 193**

Army, United States (Organization of the Army)
A: 735-736; (table) A: 737
Navy, United States (The Operating Forces) N: 85
Command economy See Planned economy in
this index
Command flag
Flag (Military flags) F: 195-208
Command guidance
Guided missile (Command guidance) G: 426 with
diagram
Command line interface [electronics]
Computer (Input devices) Ci: 912; (Operating
system software) Ci: 917
Command of the Army Act [1867]
Reconstruction (The impeachment of Johnson)
R: 178
Command/service module
Space exploration (Apollo: Mission to the moon)
So: 714-715 with pictures
Command ship
Navy, United States (Combat ships) N: 84
Commandant [military officer]
Coast Guard, United States (Organization of the
Coast Guard) Ci: 736
Marine Corps, United States (Headquarters)
M: 208
Commandant of the Marine Corps [military
officer]
Navy, Department of the N: 81
Commander [rank]
Rank, Military (table) R: 140
Commander astronaut
Astronaut A: 828
Commander in chief [rank] Ci: 870
Constitution of the United States (Article II,
Section 2) Ci: 1009
President of the United States (Commander in
chief) P: 765
Rank, Military R: 139
Commandments, Ten See Ten Commandments in
this index
Commando [soldier] Ci: 870
Army (Attack) A: 725
Guerrilla warfare (Guerrilla warfare techniques)
G: 419
Rangers R: 139
Commedia [poem by Dante]
Divine Comedy D: 242
Commedia dell' arte [theater]
Drama (Commedia dell'arte) D: 331 with picture;
(Italy) D: 335
Italian literature (Humanism and the
Renaissance) I: 494
Pantomime P: 131
Commemorative law
United States, Government of the (Functions)
U: 138
Commemorative sculpture
Sculpture (As monuments and memorials) S: 229
Commemorative stamp
Postal Service, United States pictures on P: 701;
(Stamps and other mailing materials) P: 699
Stamp collecting (Special stamps) So: 830 with
pictures
Commencement [education]
Graduation G: 297
Universities and colleges (The academic calndar)
U: 208 with picture
Commendation Medal
Medals, decorations, and orders (table) M: 357
Commensalism [biology]
Symbiosis So: 1065
Commentaries [essays by Story]
Story, Joseph So: 914
Commentaries on American Law [book by Kent]
Kent, James K: 271
Commentaries on the Gallic War [book by Caesar]
Caesar, Julius (Other talents) C: 14
Gaul G: 70
History (The ancient Greeks and Romans)
H: 261-262
Commentaries on the Laws of England [book by
Blackstone]
Blackstone, Sir William B: 394
Magna Carta (The charter after 1215) M: 53
Commentariolus [essay by Copernicus]
Copernicus, Nicolaus (Life) Ci: 1039
Commentary
Journalism (Influencing public opinion) J: 173
Commerce, Chamber of
Chamber of commerce C: 371
Commerce, Department of [U.S.] Ci: 871 with
picture
Balance of payments (How the balance of
payments is determined) B: 36
Washington, D.C. map on W: 76
Commerce, Secretary of [office]

Commerce, Department of Ci: 871
Flag picture on F: 211
Commerce and Labor, Department of [U.S.
history]
Commerce, Department of (History) Ci: 871
Labor, Department of (History) L: 2
Commerce clause
Constitution of the United States (Article I,
Section 8) Ci: 1007
Interstate commerce I: 350h
Commercial [advertising]
Advertising (Television) A: 73; (Radio) A: 74;
(Social effects) A: 78
Radio (Stations and networks) R: 90
Television (The national networks) T: 113; (Effects
of television) T: 120-121
Commercial agent [diplomat]
Consul Ci: 1017
**Commercial and Industrial Development
Corporation**
Ottawa (The 1900's) O: 875
Commercial arbitration
Arbitration (Commercial arbitration) A: 592
Commercial art Ci: 872
Airbrush A: 201 with picture
Careers (Art, design, and communications) C: 220
Copyright (Works protected) Ci: 1046
Pop Art P: 659
Poster P: 708
Commercial attaché [diplomat]
Attaché A: 878
Commercial bank
Bank (Commercial banks) B: 90
Commercial bribery [crime]
Bribery B: 597
Commercial Bureau of the American Republics
Pan-American conferences (The "new" Pan
Americanism) P: 113
Commercial Cable Company
Mackay, John William M: 20
Commercial credit [economics]
Credit (Types of credit) Ci: 1124
Commercial gambling
Gambling (Types of gambling) G: 20
Commercial grade [meat]
Beef (Grades of beef) B: 209
Commercial hotel
Hotel (Kinds of hotels) H: 376 with picture
Commercial law
Law (Private law) L: 130
Commercial model
Modeling (Kinds of models) M: 684
Commercial multiple-peril insurance
Insurance (Other types of property and liability
insurance) I: 313
Commercial paper [economics] Ci: 872
Commercial photography
Photography (Commercial photography) P: 428
Commercial pilot license
Aviation (Jobs in general aviation) A: 992
Commercial service airport
Airport (Kinds of airports) A: 243
Commercial soybean [plant]
Soybean (The soybean plant) So: 689
Commercial television
Television (Commercial television) T: 110a; (The
U.S. television industry) T: 113
Commercial top shell
Shell picture on S: 386
Commercial transport plane
Airplane (Commercial transport planes) A: 210
with pictures
Aviation (Aircraft manufacturing) A: 984
Commercial treaty
Treaty (Kinds of treaties) T: 408-409
Commerzbank building
Frankfurt F: 485
Commines, Philippe de [French author]
French literature (Early prose) F: 519
Comminuted fracture [injury]
Fracture F: 450 with diagram
Commission [income]
Advertising (Advertising agencies) A: 77
Painting P: 28
Percentage (Commissions) P: 281
Commission, Military Ci: 872
Canadian Armed Forces (Recruitment and
training) C: 155
Reserve Officers Training Corps R: 258
Commission firm [selling]
Meat packing (Marketing livestock and meat)
M: 350
Commission form of government [political
science]
City government Ci: 595; (The commission form)
Ci: 596
Commission Internationale de L'Éclairage

Color (The CIE System of Color Specification)
Ci: 824
Commission on ...
*Most commissions are listed under their key words,
as in Civil Rights, Commission on*
Commission pennant
Flag (Military flags) F: 195-208
Commissioned Corps [U.S.]
Surgeon general of the United States So: 1004
Commissioned officer [rank]
Rank, Military R: 139; (table) R: 140
Commissioners, Board of
County (Forms of county governments) Ci: 1099
Committee
Parliamentary procedure (Committees) P: 175
Senate (Senate committees) S: 295 with picture
United States, Government of the (Committee
system) U: 138; (How a bill moves through
Congress) U: 142
Committee for Foreign Affairs [U.S. history]
State, Department of (Establishment) So: 860-
861
Committee for Industrial Organization [labor
union]
American Federation of Labor and Congress of
Industrial Organizations (History) A: 410
Congress of Industrial Organizations (History) A: 941
Labor movement (Formation of the CIO) L: 12
Lewis, John L. L: 221
Committee for State Security See KGB in this index
Committee for the Re-election of the President
[U.S. history]
Watergate (The break-in and cover-up) W: 144
Committee of Public Safety [French history]
Danton, Georges-Jacques D: 34
French Revolution (Terror and equality) F: 526-
527
Reign of Terror R: 207
Robespierre (Revolutionary leader) R: 366
Committee of Secret Correspondence [U.S.
history]
State, Department of (Establishment) So: 860-
861
Committee of the whole [parliamentary
procedure] Ci: 872
Committee on Disarmament [UN]
United Nations (Arms control) U: 92
Committee on Internal Security
Un-American Activities Committee U: 18
Committee on State Security See KGB in this index
**Committee to Defend America by Aiding the
Allies** [U.S. history]
America First Committee A: 407
**Committee to Investigate the National Defense
Program** [U.S. history]
Truman, Harry S. (The Truman Committee) T: 468
Committees of correspondence [U.S. history]
Ci: 872
Adams, Samuel (The patriot) A: 44
Revolution, American (The Townshend Acts)
R: 273; (The Intolerable Acts) R: 274
Committees of safety [U.S. history] Ci: 873
Madison, James (Political and public career)
M: 33
Commode [furniture]
Furniture picture on F: 576
Commodity Credit Corporation [U.S.] Ci: 873
Agricultural Stabilization and Conservation
Service A: 145
Commodity exchange [economics] Ci: 873
Agriculture (Commodity trading) A: 152
Bears and bulls B: 189
Illinois picture on I: 69; (Service industries) I: 67
Petroleum (How prices are set) P: 346
Wheat (Buying and selling wheat) W: 274
Commodity Futures Trading Commission [U.S.]
Commodity exchange Ci: 873
Commodity goods
Industry (Product differentiation) I: 260
Commodity money
Colonial life in America (Money) Ci: 811
Money M: 704
Commodity organization [economics]
Farm and farming (Farm organizations) F: 44
Commodore John Barry Bridge [Pennsylvania]
Bridge (table: Cantilever) B: 603
Commodus [Roman emperor]
Gladiator G: 206
Rome, Ancient (The decline of the empire)
R: 447; (table) R: 447
Common Agricultural Policy
European Union (Internal affairs) E: 418
Milk (Marketing) M: 547
Common ancestry [biology]
Evolution (Main ideas of evolutionary theory)
E: 426
Common Bible

Bible (Modern English translations) **B: 286**
Common bile duct [anatomy]
  Bile **B: 300**
  Gallbladder **G: 14**
  Liver (Structure of the liver) **L: 393**
Common blue violet [plant]
  Violet **V: 388**
Common bream [fish]
  Bream **B: 590**
Common brick
  Brick (Building bricks) **B: 597**
Common buzzard [bird]
  Hawk (Migration) **H: 111**
Common carrier [transportation] **Ci: 874**
  Truck (Industrial uses) **T: 456**
  United Parcel Service, Inc. **U: 97**
Common case [grammar]
  Case (Nouns) **C: 272**
  Declension **D: 80**
  Grammar (Inflection) **G: 303**
Common Cause [organization] **Ci: 874**
  Gardner, John William **G: 39**
Common coleus [plant]
  Gardening *picture on* **G: 37**
Common crow [bird]
  Crow (Kinds of crows) **Ci: 1157** *with picture*
Common crow [butterfly]
  Butterfly *picture on* **B: 735**
Common cuckoo [bird]
  Bird *picture on* **B: 344e**; (Birds of Europe) **B: 344c**
  Cuckoo **Ci: 1182**
Common daffodil [plant]
  Daffodil **D: 3** *with picture*
Common denominator
  Fraction (Comparing fractions) **F: 446**
Common difference [mathematics]
  Progression **P: 812**
Common dolphin [sea animal]
  Dolphin *pictures on* **D: 298, D: 299**; (The common dolphins) **D: 297**
Common factor [mathematics]
  Factor (Common factors) **F: 4**
Common fiddleneck [plant]
  Flower (Flowers of summer-dry regions) **F: 288** *with picture*
Common Foreign and Security Policy
  European Union **E: 418**
Common forget-me-not [plant]
  Forget-me-not *picture on* **F: 409**
Common gallinule [bird]
  Gallinule **G: 16**
Common garden canna [plant]
  Flower *picture on* **F: 279**
Common gender [grammar]
  Gender **G: 80**
Common Glory, The [play by Green]
  Green, Paul Eliot **G: 379**
Common house spider
  House spider **H: 388**
Common ice plant
  Ice plant **I: 9**
Common law Ci: 874
  Civil law **Ci: 607**
  Code **C: 748**
  Court (Courts in other countries) **Ci: 1102**; (Development of civil-law and common-law courts) **Ci: 1104**
  England (Struggles for power) **E: 305-306**
  Henry II [of England] **H: 185**
  Law (Common law systems) **L: 132**; (The Middle Ages) **L: 134-135**; (Beginnings of U.S. law) **L: 136**
  Lien **L: 273**
  Louisiana (Courts) **L: 496**
  Public utility (History) **P: 867**
  Trial (History) **T: 437**
Common-law marriage
  Marriage (Other marriage laws and practices) **M: 220**
Common logarithms
  Logarithms (Common logarithms) **L: 424**
Common loon [bird]
  Bird (Birds of inland waters and marshes) **B: 340** *with picture*
  Loon **L: 452**
Common market [economics] **Ci: 875**
  Association of Southeast Asian Nations **A: 820**
  European Free Trade Association **E: 417**
  European Union **E: 418**
Common measure [poetry]
  Ballad (The ballad style) **B: 43**
  Poetry (Rhythm and meter) **P: 591-592**
Common monkshood [plant]
  Aconite **A: 28** *with picture*
Common moorhen [bird]
  Bird *picture on* **B: 344e**
  Gallinule **G: 16**

Common mullein [plant]
  Mullein **M: 914** *with picture*
Common musk turtle
  Turtle (Mud and musk turtles) **T: 522** *with picture*
Common myna [bird]
  Bird (Birds of Asia) **B: 344f** *with picture*
  Myna **M: 970f** *with picture*
Common nighthawk [bird]
  Nighthawk **N: 419** *with picture*
Common nightingale [bird]
  Bird *picture on* **B: 344d**; (Birds of Europe) **B: 344c**
Common noun [grammar]
  Noun (Proper and common nouns) **N: 552**
Common oakblue [butterfly]
  Butterfly *picture on* **B: 734**
Common opal [gem]
  Opal **O: 788**
Common oystercatcher [bird]
  Oystercatcher **O: 893**
Common pear
  Pear (Varieties) **P: 215**
Common persimmon [plant]
  Persimmon **P: 300e**
Common Prayer, Book of *See* Book of Common Prayer *in this index*
Common quail [bird]
  Quail **Q: 4**
Common ratio [mathematics]
  Progression **P: 812**
  Series **S: 316b**; (Working with infinite series) **S: 317**
Common redpoll [bird]
  Redpoll **R: 191** *with picture*
Common school [education]
  See also Public school *in this index*
  Mann, Horace **M: 164**
Common Sense [pamphlet by Paine]
  Declaration of Independence (The Continental Congress) **D: 74**
  Paine, Thomas (American revolutionary) **P: 22**
  Revolution, American (The Declaration of Independence) **R: 278**
  United States, History of the (The Revolutionary War begins) **U: 159-160**
Common shelduck
  Bird *picture on* **B: 344e**
Common-Slavic [language]
  Russian language (History) **R: 557**
Common snapping turtle
  Turtle (Snapping turtles) **T: 522** *with picture*
Common snipe [bird]
  Snipe **S: 538** *(with picture)*
Common starling [bird]
  Migration (How migrating animals find their way) **M: 539**
  Starling **So: 857** *with picture*
Common stock [economics]
  Investment (Stocks) **I: 368**
  Stock (Kinds of stock) **So: 903**
Common sunflower [plant]
  Flower *picture on* **F: 277**
Common swallowtail [butterfly]
  Butterfly *picture on* **B: 737**
Common tern [bird]
  Bird *picture on* **B: 344e**; (Birds of the seacoasts) **B: 342** *with picture*; (Birds of Europe) **B: 344c**
Common toad [animal]
  Toad *picture on* **T: 303**
Common wart hog
  Wart hog **W: 44** *with picture*
Common wheat [plant]
  Wheat (Species of wheat) **W: 269** *with picture*
Common wombat [animal]
  Wombat **W: 382** *with picture*
Common woolly monkey
  Monkey *picture on* **M: 728**
Common zebra [common zebra]
  Zebra **Z: 587**
Commoner, Barry [American biologist] **Ci: 875**
Commoner, The [newspaper]
  Bryan, Charles Wayland **B: 654**
  Bryan, William Jennings (Democratic Party leader) **B: 654-655**
Commonplaces [book by Melanchthon]
  Melanchthon, Philipp **M: 388**
Commons, House of *See* House of Commons *in this index*
Commons Chamber [London]
  Parliament *picture on* **P: 172**
Commonwealth [political unit] **Ci: 875**
Commonwealth, The [newspaper]
  Howe, Julia Ward **H: 401**
  Howe, Samuel Gridley **H: 401**
Commonwealth Franchise Act of 1902 [Australia]
  Woman suffrage (Australia) **W: 381**
Commonwealth Games Ci: 875
  Edmonton (History) **E: 85**

Commonwealth of Australia *See* Australia *in this index*
Commonwealth of Australia Constitution Act [1901]
  Australian Capital Territory **A: 926**
Commonwealth of England [English history]
  Cromwell, Oliver (Rise to power) **Ci: 1151-1152**
  England (The Civil War) **E: 308-309**
Commonwealth of Independent States [confederation] **Ci: 875**
  Communism (The Soviet Union under Gorbachev) **Ci: 895-896**
  Estonia (Independence regained) **E: 363**
  Minsk **M: 611**
  Russia **R: 526**; (The breakup of the U.S.S.R.) **R: 554**
  Union of Soviet Socialist Republics (The breakup of the Soviet Union) **U: 41**
  Yeltsin, Boris Nikolayevich **Y: 561**
Commonwealth of Nations [alliance] **Ci: 876**
  Canada, History of (Independence) **C: 147**
  United Kingdom (Ancestry) **U: 55**; (Decline of the empire) **U: 71**
Commonwealth of the Northern Mariana Islands *See* Northern Mariana Islands, Commonwealth of the *in this index*
Commonwealth Office [United Kingdom]
  Foreign policy (The executive) **F: 387**
Commonwealth Preference [economics]
  Commonwealth of Nations (History) **Ci: 876-877**
Communal society [anthropology] **Ci: 877**
  Amanites **A: 400**
  Brook Farm **B: 639**
  Collectivism **Ci: 775**
  Cult (Kinds of cults) **Ci: 1185**
  Doukhobors **D: 314**
  Hutterites **H: 459**
  New Harmony **N: 228** *with pictures*
  Oneida Community **O: 761**
  Shakers **S: 343** *with picture*
Commune [agriculture]
  Communal society **Ci: 877**
Commune [political unit]
  Belgium (Regions and language communities) **B: 227**
  China (Rural life) **C: 482**
  France (Local government) **F: 455**
  Italy (Local government) **I: 499**
Commune of Paris [French history] *See* Paris Commune *in this index*
Communicable disease *See* Infectious disease *in this index*
Communication Ci: 878 *with pictures*
  See also the list of Related articles in the Communication article
  Alphabet **A: 381**
  Autism (Symptoms) **A: 941**
  Careers (Art, design, and communications) **C: 220** *with picture*
  Clothing (Clothing as communication) **Ci: 689**
  Colonial life in America (Communication) **Ci: 806** *with picture*
  Comparative psychology **Ci: 902a**
  Handwriting **H: 46**
  Human being (Cultural characteristics) **H: 414**
  Indian, American (Language) **I: 149** *with pictures*
  Kinesics **K: 319**
  Language **L: 62**
  McLuhan, Marshall **M: 343**
  Public relations (Methods) **P: 863**
  Writing system **W: 512**
  Animal communication
    Ant (Communication) **A: 525**
    Bird (How birds communicate) **B: 354**
    Dog (Behavior) **D: 277**
    Dolphin (Social life) **D: 299**
  Technology
    AT&T Inc. **A: 851**
    Cable **C: 4** *with pictures*
    Cellular telephone **C: 340**
    Coaxial cable (Uses) **C: 740**
    Communications satellite **Ci: 888a**
    Electricity (In communication) **E: 191**
    Electronics (Uses of electronics) **E: 207**
    Fiber optics (Uses of optical fibers) **F: 88**
    Internet (Uses) **I: 350**; (Communication) **I: 350b**; (The Internet culture) **I: 350e**
    Laser (How lasers are used) **L: 82**
    Pager **P: 20**
    Radiation (Uses of radiation) **R: 74**
    Space exploration (Communicating with Earth) **So: 704**
    Technology (The use of electricity) **T: 75**; (Benefits of technology) **T: 76**
    Telephone **T: 94** *with picture*
    Television **T: 110**
    United States, History of the (Advances in transportation and communications) **U: 170**

Wireless communication W: 344
Communication device [electronics]
Burglar alarm B: 704
Communications, Office of See Ofcom in this index
Communications center
Police (Records and communications) P: 621
with picture
Communications intelligence
Codes and ciphers Ci: 749; (Communications intelligence) Ci: 750
Communications satellite Ci: 888a with pictures
Antenna (Types of antennas) A: 543
Communication (The development of television) Ci: 885 with picture
Communications Satellite Corporation Ci: 889
Maine picture on M: 91
Radio, Amateur (Uses of amateur radio) R: 95
Satellite, Artificial picture on S: 150d; (table) S: 150e; (Types of artificial satellites) S: 150f
Telecommunications T: 89
Telephone (Traditional phone calls) T: 96-97 with diagram
Television (Satellite television) T: 110c; (Satellites) T: 123
Communications Satellite Corporation Ci: 889
Communications security
Codes and ciphers Ci: 749; (Communications security) Ci: 749
Communications Security Establishment
Canadian Armed Forces (Organization) C: 154
Communications trench [warfare]
World War I (The deadlock on the Western Front) W: 457
Communications Workers of America
Labor movement (table) L: 8
Communion [religion] Ci: 889
Careers picture on C: 221
Christianity (Sacraments) C: 522h
Eastern Orthodox Churches (Services) E: 46; (Sacraments) E: 46-47
Holy Grail (The search for the Grail) H: 299
Jesus Christ (The Last Supper) J: 108
Lutherans (Doctrine) L: 529
Mass M: 269
Protestantism (Celebration of the sacraments) P: 834
Roman Catholic Church (Worship) R: 403-404
Transubstantiation T: 401
Communism Ci: 889 with pictures
See also Communist party in this index and the list of Related articles in the Communism article
Capitalism C: 194; (Capitalism in former Communist nations) C: 196
Christianity (In Communist nations) C: 526
Civil rights (Civil rights in other countries) Ci: 610
Collective farm Ci: 775
Collectivism Ci: 775
Dictatorship D: 191
Economics (Karl Marx and Communism) E: 64 with picture
Freedom of religion (In other countries) F: 505
Government (Communism) G: 286; (Totalitarianism and Communism) G: 291
Local government (Unitary systems) L: 408
Philosophy (Philosophy in the 1800's) P: 390
Social class (Class structure) So: 550
Socialism (Karl Marx) So: 560
Tariff (Modern tariff policies) T: 44
Third World T: 258
World (Economic systems) W: 412b
World War II (Economic problems) W: 469
Asia
Communism (The spread of Communism) Ci: 893-894; (China after Mao) Ci: 896
Asia (The spread of Communism) A: 807 with picture
Balkans (Communist rule) B: 42
Brainwashing B: 560
Cambodia (History) C: 72-73
Chinese literature C: 511; (Modern Chinese literature) C: 512
Khmer Rouge K: 308b
Korea, North K: 368
Mao Zedong M: 174
Thailand (Military rule) T: 227
Tibet (History and government) T: 277
United Nations (Military actions) U: 91
Viet Cong V: 363
Vietnam (History) V: 369-371
Europe
Communism (European reality in the early 1900's) Ci: 890; (In Eastern Europe) Ci: 896
Albania (Communist control) A: 308
Belarus (History) B: 224b-224c
Berlin B: 260
Berlin Wall B: 266
Bulgaria (Communist rule) B: 693

Cold War Ci: 762
Czech Republic Ci: 1209; (The arts) Ci: 1211; (Economy) Ci: 1211; (History) Ci: 1213-1214
Czechoslovakia (Communist rule) Ci: 1216
Engels, Friedrich E: 283
Estonia (History) E: 362-363
Europe (The Industrial Revolution) E: 413; (The Cold War) E: 415; (The collapse of Communism) E: 416
Germany (The division of Germany) G: 169; (East Germany) G: 170
Hungary (History) H: 445-447
Latvia (History) L: 119-120
Lithuania (History) L: 389-390
Luxemburg, Rosa L: 532
Macedonia M: 12
Marx, Karl M: 236
North Atlantic Treaty Organization N: 470
Organization for Security and Co-operation in Europe O: 854
Poland P: 604; (History) P: 611-613
Romania (The arts) R: 419; (Communist control) R: 424
Slovakia S: 508b
Ukraine (Soviet rule) U: 13
United Nations (The end of the Cold War) U: 92
Yugoslavia (World War II) Y: 576; (Communist rule) Y: 576
Latin America
Communism (Communist influence in other areas) Ci: 894
Cuba Ci: 1169
Iran-contra affair (Background) I: 406b
Latin America (Political circumstances in the early to middle 1900's) L: 109-110
Union of Soviet Socialist Republics
Communism (Communism in the Soviet Union) Ci: 892
Cold War Ci: 762
KGB K: 308a
Lenin, V. I. L: 191; (Lenin the dictator) L: 194
Politburo P: 627
Propaganda (History) P: 824-825
Russia (Politics) R: 531; (Civil war and the formation of the U.S.S.R.) R: 553
Russian Revolution of 1917 R: 565
Socialism (The Cold War) So: 561; (The fall of the Soviet Union) So: 562
Stalin, Joseph So: 824
Union of Soviet Socialist Republics U: 28
United States, History of the (The end of the Cold War) U: 196d
World, History of the (The rise of Communism and the Cold War) W: 446; (The end of the Cold War) W: 448
World War II (New power struggles) W: 497
United States
Academic freedom (The 1900's) A: 20
McCarthy, Joseph Raymond M: 332b
McCarthyism M: 332b
Nixon, Richard Milhous (Career in Congress) N: 430
Un-American Activities Committee U: 18
United States, History of the (The Cold War) U: 195
Communist China See China in this index
Communist Manifesto [book by Marx and Engels]
Communism (The ideas of Marx) Ci: 890
Engels, Friedrich E: 283
Marx, Karl (Marriage and move to Paris) M: 236-237; (The Communist Manifesto) M: 237
Socialism (Karl Marx) So: 560
Communist party
See also Chinese Communist Party in this index
Bulgaria (Government) B: 688
Communism (The role of the party) Ci: 891; (Communist party structures) Ci: 891; (The party state) Ci: 891; (In non-Communist countries) Ci: 897
Cuba (Government) Ci: 1169
Flynn, Elizabeth Gurley F: 313
Germany (Politics) G: 147
Gorbachev, Mikhail Sergeyevich (Early life and political rise) G: 272
Honecker, Erich H: 314
Hungary (History) H: 445-447
Indonesia (The fall of Sukarno) I: 238
Italy (Economic problems and political change) I: 518; (Social problems) I: 518
Khrushchev, Nikita Sergeyevich (Soviet dictator) K: 309
Korea, North K: 368
Kosygin, Aleksei Nikolaevich K: 385
Latvia (History) L: 119-120
Lenin, V. I. L: 191; (Lenin the dictator) L: 194
Lithuania (History) L: 389-390
Mao Zedong (His life) M: 174

Medina, Harold Raymond M: 380
Mongolia (History) M: 723
Moscow M: 823
Pol Pot P: 603
Poland P: 604; (History) P: 611-613
Politburo P: 627
Political party P: 631; (One-party systems) P: 633-634; (Third parties) P: 636
Romania (Government) R: 417; (Communist control) R: 424
Russia (Politics) R: 531; (The October Revolution) R: 553; (The new nation) R: 555
Russian Revolution of 1917 (The October Revolution) R: 566
Serbia (History) S: 314-316
Slovakia (Economy) S: 508d; (History) S: 508d-509
Smith Act S: 518
Ukraine (Politics) U: 6
Union of Soviet Socialist Republics (Government) U: 29; (History) U: 35-36
Uzbekistan (Government) U: 253
Women's movement (In Eastern Europe and the former Soviet republics) W: 387
Yugoslavia (World War II) Y: 576; (Communist rule) Y: 576
Communist Party of Vietnam [political party]
Vietnam (Government) V: 365
Community [biology]
Animal (Animal homes and communities) A: 501
Ant (Life in an ant colony) A: 522
Bee B: 200 with pictures
Chimpanzee (The life of a chimpanzee) C: 472
Community Ci: 898
Ecology (Communities) E: 54
Fish (Fish in the balance of nature) F: 147
Habitat H: 3
Insect (Family life) I: 294-295 with picture
Portuguese man-of-war P: 696
Wasp (Group life) W: 112
Community [sociology] Ci: 898
City planning (History) Ci: 598
Law L: 130
Library (Active community service) L: 236
Police (In the United States since the mid-1900's) P: 624
Public health P: 855
Town T: 352
Community Chests
Colorado (Interesting facts) Ci: 829
Community college [education] Ci: 898
Careers (Community colleges) C: 217
Education (Higher education) E: 92
School (Community colleges) S: 182
Vocational education (Community and junior colleges) V: 434
Community correctional center
Prison (Reforms in the 1900's) P: 807-808
Community development
Mott Foundation M: 880
Community Family Club
Camp Fire USA (Community Family Club) C: 89
Community forestry
Forestry (Community forestry) F: 406
Community foundation
Foundation (Kinds of foundations) F: 430
Community health nurse
Nursing (Community health nursing) N: 617
Community hospital
Hospital (Type of ownership) H: 371
Community Mental Health Centers Construction Act [1963]
Mental illness (The mid-1990's) M: 409
Community of Christ [religious group] Ci: 899
Smith, Joseph S: 517
Community organization work
Social work (Methods of social work) So: 558
Community planning See City planning in this index
Community property [law] Ci: 899
Divorce (Financial arrangements) D: 254
Dower D: 316
Community Reinvestment Act [1977]
Bank (Changes in banking laws) B: 94
Open housing O: 789
Community Service Organization
Huerta, Dolores Fernandez H: 408
Community supported agriculture
Agriculture (Local food movements) A: 151
Community theater
Theater (Nonprofessional theater groups) T: 246
Community treatment center
Criminal justice system (Problems in the correctional system) Ci: 1144
Mental illness (Treatment settings) M: 408
Community trust
Foundation (Community foundations) F: 430

Community worker
Careers (Community and social services) **C: 221** *with picture*
Commutative Law of Addition
Algebra (Basic algebra) **A: 354**
Commutative Law of Multiplication
Algebra (Basic algebra) **A: 354**
Commutator [device]
Electric generator *diagrams on* **E: 172**; (Direct-current generators) **E: 173**
Electric motor (The commutator) **E: 180** *with diagram*
Tesla, Nikola (The alternating-current system) **T: 181**
Commutator segment [device]
Electric generator (How DC generators work) **E: 173**
Commuter
Transportation (Urban public transportation) **T: 393**
Commuter airline
Aviation (General aviation activities) **A: 984**
Commuter center
Universities and colleges (Residence) **U: 209**
Commuter college
Community college (Importance to students) **Ci: 899**
Commuter train
Electric railroad **E: 188** *with picture*
Railroad (Commuter trains) **R: 105** *with picture*
Transit **T: 375**
Como, Lake [Italy]
Lake Como **L: 37** *with map*
Comoe National Park [Côte d'Ivoire]
National park (table) **N: 42f**
Comorian language
Comoros (People) **Ci: 900**
Comoros Ci: 899 *with picture and map*
Flag *picture on* **F: 198**
Mayotte **M: 330**
Compact camera
Photography (Compact cameras) **P: 408**
Compact disc [electronics] **Ci: 901** *with pictures*
Audio-visual materials (Audio materials) **A: 883**
Communication (In recording) **Ci: 886**
Computer (CD drives) **Ci: 915**
Copyright (Users' rights) **Ci: 1047**
Dictionary (Modern dictionaries) **D: 194**
Digital technology **D: 203**
Electronics *picture on* **E: 206**; (Digital circuits) **E: 213-214**
Encyclopedia (Today's encyclopedias) **E: 268b**
Invention (Recent developments) **I: 364**
Laser (Recording, storing, and transmitting information) **L: 82**
Popular music (New technologies) **P: 671**
Recording industry **R: 180**; (History) **R: 182**
Tachometer **T: 4**
Compact disc player
Stereophonic sound system (Parts of a stereo system) **So: 892**
Compact disc read-only memory *See* CD-ROM *in this index*
Compact fluorescent lamp
Fluorescent lamp **F: 305**
Interior design (Selecting accessories) **F: 305**
Light bulb **L: 293**
Compact of Free Association [government] *See* Free Association, Compact of *in this index*
Compact tissue [anatomy]
Bone (Structure of the bones) **B: 456** *with diagram*
Compadre [godparent]
Family (Family relationships) **F: 21**
Compagnia di San Paolo [foundation]
Foundation (table) **F: 430**
Companionate family
Family (Changes) **F: 23**
Companionway
Ship (Nautical terms) **S: 405**
Company [ballet]
Ballet **B: 44**
Company [military]
Army (The organization of armies) **A: 725**; (Armies in the Middle Ages) **A: 727**
Army, United States (table) **A: 737**
Company [unit]
Fire department (Firefighting) **F: 123**
Company-sponsored foundation
Foundation (Kinds of foundations) **F: 430**
Compaoré, Blaise [African political leader]
Burkina Faso (History) **B: 706-707**
Comparative advantage [economics]
Free trade (The theory of free trade) **F: 499**
International trade (Why nations trade) **I: 348**
Ricardo, David **R: 321**
Comparative anatomy

Anatomy **A: 448b**
Biology (The origins of scientific classification) **B: 318**
Evolution (Comparative anatomy) **E: 431**
Skeleton *diagram on* **S: 481**
Zoology (What zoologists study) **Z: 606-607**
Comparative degree [grammar]
Adjective (Comparison of adjectives) **A: 57**
Comparison (The three degrees of comparison) **Ci: 902b**
Comparative government
Political science (Comparative government) **P: 638**
Comparative linguistics
Language (The science of language) **L: 66-67**
Linguistics **L: 335**; (Comparative and historical linguistics) **L: 336**; (Comparative and historical research) **L: 337**
Mythology (Comparative approaches) **M: 989**
Comparative pathology
Pathology **P: 196**
Comparative psychology Ci: 902a *with picture*
Comparative reconstruction
Linguistics (Comparative reconstruction) **L: 336**
Comparative systems [economics]
Economics (Fields of economics) **E: 64**
Comparator [device]
Automation (How automation works) **A: 945** *with diagram*
Comparison [grammar] **Ci: 902b**
Adjective (Comparison of adjectives) **A: 57**
Grammar (Inflection) **G: 303**
Inflection **I: 268a**
Comparison [mathematics]
Percentage (Comparisons) **P: 281**
"Comparison between Laughing and Sentimental Comedy, A" [essay by Goldsmith]
Goldsmith, Oliver **G: 259**
Compass [mathematics]
Circle **Ci: 558**
Geometry (Some basic geometric constructions) **G: 103**
Compass [navigation] **Ci: 902b** *with picture*
Automatic flight control system (How an AFCS works) **A: 944**
Exploration (Medieval exploration) **E: 441-442**
Lodestone **L: 419**
Magnetism (Magnetic poles) **M: 59**
Navigation (Traditional navigation) **N: 70**; (Satellite navigation) **N: 73**
Surveying (Early tools) **So: 1011**
Compass card
Compass **Ci: 902b**
Compass plant Ci: 903 *with picture*
Compass rose [cartography]
Navigation *picture on* **N: 75**
Compassionate conservatism
Bush, George Walker **B: 722b**; (The campaign) **B: 722f**
Compendium of Theological Studies [book by Bacon]
Bacon, Roger (His life) **B: 19**
"Compensation" [essay by Emerson]
Emerson, Ralph Waldo (His prose works) **E: 259**
Compensation [income]
Workers' compensation **W: 405**
Compensatory damages [law]
Damages **D: 20**
Competency-based education Ci: 903
Teaching (The effectiveness of teacher training) **T: 70**
Competency test
Curriculum (Curriculum changes) **Ci: 1197**
Competition [biology]
Balance of nature (Competition) **B: 35**
Life (The biological environment) **L: 276**
Competition [economics]
See also Monopoly and competition *in this index*
Antitrust laws **A: 560**
Business (Competition) **B: 725**
Capitalism (Capitalism in its ideal form) **C: 194**; (Ensuring competition) **C: 195**
Conglomerate **Ci: 938**
Consumer protection (The right to choose) **Ci: 1018**
Economics **E: 58**
Free trade **F: 499**
Industry (Industrial organization) **I: 260**
Labor movement (Other possible origins) **L: 9**
Nationalization (Advantages and disadvantages) **N: 63**
Profit **P: 811**
Competitive local exchange carrier [company]
Telephone (In the United States) **T: 99**
Competitive service
Civil service (Federal civil service) **Ci: 612**
Compilation mapping [cartography]

Map (Observation and measurement) **M: 180**
Compiler [program]
Computer (Compiling or assembling a program) **Ci: 923**
Computer language (High-level languages) **Ci: 924h**
Complaint, The [book by Young]
Young, Edward **Y: 572**
Complaint letter
Letter writing (Complaint letters) **L: 212** *with picture*
Compleat Angler, The [book by Walton]
Walton, Izaak **W: 21**
Complement [biology]
Immune system (The humoral immune response) **I: 88**; (Other problems) **I: 88d**
Complement [mathematics]
Angle **A: 462**
Complementary and alternative medicine *See* Alternative medicine *in this index*
Complementary color
Color (Mixing colored lights) **Ci: 821-822** *with diagram*; (Producing color harmony) **Ci: 823-824** *with diagram*
Interior design (Using color) **I: 331**
Photography (Color reversal film) **P: 419**
Complementary metal-oxide semiconductor [electronics]
Camera **C: 80**, *picture on* **C: 82**
Photography (Capturing digital images) **P: 420**
Complete Far Side, The [book by Larson]
Larson, Gary **L: 78**
Complete flower
Flower (The parts of a flower) **F: 293**
Complete heat and power system
Gas [fuel] *diagram on* **G: 52**; (In industry) **G: 51**
Complete metamorphosis [biology]
Pupa **P: 904**
Complete protein
Kwashiorkor **K: 398**
Nutrition (Proteins) **N: 625**
Protein (Proteins in the diet) **P: 832**
Completed well
Petroleum (table) **P: 332**
Completely in-the-canal hearing aid
Hearing aid (Styles) **H: 130** *with picture*
Completely penetrant disease
Genetic testing (Genes associated with disease) **G: 84d**
Complex [psychology]
Oedipus complex **O: 676**
Psychoanalysis (Psychoanalytic theory) **P: 846**
Complex carbohydrate [chemistry]
Carbohydrate (Kinds of carbohydrates) **C: 203** *with diagram*
Nutrition (Carbohydrates) **N: 625**
Saccharides **S: 4**
Complex family
Family (Varieties of families) **F: 20**
Complex fraction [mathematics]
Fraction (Division) **F: 448**
Complex marriage [sociology]
Oneida Community **O: 762**
Complex number
Factor (Algebraic factors) **F: 4-5**
Number (Complex numbers) **N: 606**
Square root (Square roots of negative numbers) **So: 812**
Complex sentence
Sentence (Sentence classifications) **S: 303**
Complexity and Contradiction in Architecture [book by Venturi]
Venturi, Robert **V: 310**
Compliance audit [business]
Audit **A: 884**
Complimentary close
Letter writing (The complimentary close) **L: 211** *with picture*
Complin [religion]
Hour **H: 375**
Complutensian University of Madrid
Madrid (Education and cultural life) **M: 39**
Component system [electronics]
Stereophonic sound system (Types of systems) **So: 891**
Compony
Heraldry *picture on* **H: 195**
"Composed Upon Westminster Bridge, September 3, 1802" [poem by Wordsworth]
Poetry (Rhythm and meter) **P: 591-594**
Composer Ci: 904
See also the lists of composers in the Related articles in the Classical Music *article*
American Society of Composers, Authors and Publishers **A: 430**
Ballet (Music) **B: 50**
Motion picture (Adding music and sound effects)

M: 856
Television (Adding music and sound effects)
T: 112
Composers, Authors and Publishers, American Society of
American Society of Composers, Authors and
Publishers **A: 430**
Compositae [botany]
Composite family **Ci: 904**
Composite [cattle]
Cattle (Other beef cattle) **C: 309**
Composite [modeling]
Modeling (Careers) **M: 685**
Composite color video signal [electronics]
Television (Creating television signals) **T: 121-122**
Composite column [architecture]
Architecture (table) **A: 608** with picture
Column (The Roman orders) **Ci: 866** with picture
Composite family [botany] **Ci: 904**
Flower (table) **F: 300** with picture
Composite flower [botany]
Flower (Variations in flower structure) **F: 294**
with picture
Composite materials [manufacturing] **Ci: 904**
Materials **M: 300b**; (Composite materials)
M: 300d
Plastics (Making synthetic resins) **P: 556-557**
Composite number [mathematics]
Factor **F: 4**
Prime number **P: 780**
Composite object [physics]
Boson **B: 494**
Fermion **F: 74**
Composite particle [physics]
Quark **Q: 7**
Subatomic particle **So: 936**; (Composite particles)
So: 937
Composite photography
Photography (Artistic advances) **P: 424**
Compositing [cinematography]
Animation (Compositing) **A: 513** with pictures
Television (Adding special effects) **T: 112**
Composition [art material]
Doll (The 1800's) **D: 289**; (The early 1900's) **D: 291**
Composition [art]
Painting (The elements of painting) **P: 34-35**
Photography (Taking good photographs) **P: 409**
with pictures
Composition [painting by Mondrian]
Painting (Line) **P: 35**; (De Stijl) **P: 80** with picture
Composition [printing]
Printing [industry] (Typesetting) **P: 797**
Composition [writing] **Ci: 905**
See also Essay in this index
A Guide to Writing Skills **Research Guide: 6**
Composition B [explosive]
Ammunition (Artillery ammunition) **A: 435**
RDX **R: 154**
*Composition with Seven Figures and a Head (The
Forest)* [sculpture by Giacometti]
Giacometti, Alberto picture on **G: 183**
Compositor [career]
Printing (Typesetting) **P: 797**
Compost [gardening] **Ci: 905**
Environmental pollution (Environmental do's and
don'ts) **E: 337**
Fertilizer (Organic fertilizers) **F: 79**
Gardening (Analyzing the soil) **G: 31-32**
Lawn (Lawns and the environment) **L: 144**
Recycling (Uses for recycled materials) **R: 184**
Compound [chemistry] **Ci: 905**
Acid **A: 26**
Atom **A: 870**
Chemistry (Fundamental ideas of chemistry)
C: 398-399
Cobalt (Uses) **Ci: 741**
Element, Chemical **E: 219**
Isomer **I: 475**
Compound bow
Archery (Archery equipment) **A: 601**
Compound eye [zoology] **Ci: 906** with diagrams
Ant (Sense organs) **A: 522** with picture
Bee (Eyes) **B: 201**
Beetle (The bodies of beetles) **B: 215-216** with
diagram
Butterfly (The head) **B: 738** with diagram
Eye (Eyes of animals) **E: 469** with picture
Fly (Head) **F: 309** with pictures
Grasshopper (The body) **G: 327**
Insect (Eyes and antennae) **I: 287** with diagram;
(Sight) **I: 290** with pictures
Lobster (Body) **L: 405**
Wasp (Body) **W: 111**
Compound fracture
Fracture **F: 450** with diagram
Compound fruit
Fruit (Types of fruits in botany) **F: 544-546** with

pictures
Compound graph [character]
Chinese language (Written Chinese) **C: 509-510**
with picture
Compound interest
Interest (Compound interest) **I: 321**; (How
interest is calculated) **I: 321** with diagram
Compound leaf
Leaf (The blade) **L: 153-154** with pictures
Plant (Leaves) **P: 529-531** with picture
Tree (Leaves) **T: 417**
Compound lens [optics]
Photography (Lenses and focusing) **P: 410**
Compound lever
Lever (Classes of levers) **L: 217**
Compound microscope
Microscope (Optical microscopes) **M: 517** with
pictures
Compound motor
Electric motor (DC motors) **E: 181**
Compound ore
Ore **O: 825**
Compound predicate [grammar]
Sentence (Subject and predicate) **S: 303**
Compound sentence
Sentence (Sentence classifications) **S: 303**
Compound steam engine
Ship (Stronger, faster ships) **S: 425**
Compound subject [grammar]
Sentence (Subject and predicate) **S: 303**
Compound word [linguistics]
Language (Words and morphemes) **L: 62**
Compounding a felony [law]
Felony **F: 69**
Comprehension
Reading (Comprehending what is perceived)
R: 157; (Reading problems) **R: 161**
**Comprehensive Drug Abuse Prevention and
Control Act** [1970]
Drug (U.S. drug laws) **D: 357-358**
Drug abuse (Reducing demand) **D: 365**
Comprehensive Employment and Training Act
[1973]
Migrant labor **M: 538**
**Comprehensive Environmental Response,
Compensation, and Liability Act** [1980]
Environmental pollution (Government action)
E: 335 with picture
Environmental Protection Agency **E: 340**
Hazardous wastes (Disposal of hazardous wastes)
H: 122
Comprehensive insurance
Insurance (Automobile insurance) **I: 313**
Comprehensive Nuclear Test Ban Treaty See
Comprehensive Test Ban Treaty in this index
Comprehensive school
Education (Secondary education) **E: 92**
England (Education) **E: 297**
Germany (Education) **G: 151-153**
Scotland (Education) **S: 215**
United Kingdom (Education) **U: 56-57**
Vocational education (Public high schools) **V: 434**
Comprehensive Test Ban Treaty [1996]
Arms control (Arms control in the late 1900's and
early 2000's) **A: 722**
Nuclear weapon (Arms control) **N: 600**
United Nations (Arms control) **U: 92-93**
Compress [bandage]
Bandage **B: 75**
Compress warehouse [factory]
Cotton (Ginning and baling) **Ci: 1091**
Compressed air
Air (Air compression) **A: 172**
Compressed-air method [construction]
Tunnel (Earth tunnels) **T: 490**
Compression [electronics]
Computer (Research and development) **Ci: 924**
Photography (Storing digital images) **P: 421**
Compression [engine]
Gasoline engine (High and low compression)
G: 63
Compression [movement]
Massage **M: 295**
Compression-ignition engine
Diesel engine (How a diesel engine works) **D: 199**
Compression molding [industrial process]
Phenolic **P: 356**
Plastics picture on **P: 558**; (Making plastic
products) **P: 557**
Compression ratio
Diesel engine (How a diesel engine works) **D: 199**
Gasoline engine (High and low compression)
G: 63
Compression stroke
Automobile (The engine cycle) **A: 953**
Compression system [mechanism]
Refrigeration (Mechanical refrigeration) **R: 201**

Compressional boundary [geology] See
Convergent boundary in this index
Compressional wave [physics]
See also Longitudinal wave in this index
Earthquake diagram on **E: 34**; (Body waves) **E: 35**
Compressor [machine]
Refrigeration (The electric refrigerator) **R: 201**
with diagram
Compressor, Air See Air compressor in this index
Compressor station [industry]
Gas [fuel] (Transmitting and distributing gas)
G: 55
Compromise [politics]
Congress of the United States (Legislative
bargaining) **Ci: 944**
Compromise of 1850 [U.S. history] **Ci: 906**
African Americans (The deepening division over
slavery) **A: 136h**
Civil War, American (The Compromise of 1850)
Ci: 616
Clay, Henry (The Compromise of 1850) **Ci: 659**
Fillmore, Millard (Vice president) **F: 101-102**
Fugitive slave laws **F: 553**
Mexican War (Results of the war) **M: 447**
Taylor, Zachary (Sectional quarrels) **T: 60**
United States, History of the (The Compromise of
1850) **U: 175** with picture
Utah (Territorial days and statehood) **U: 246**
Compromise projection [cartography]
Map (The Robonson projection) **M: 183** with
diagram
Compromise Tariff [1833]
Tariff (United States tariffs) **T: 44**
Compsognathus [dinosaur] **Ci: 907**
Dinosaur picture on **D: 207**; (True dinosaurs)
D: 206b-211
Compton, Arthur Holly [American physicist]
Nobel Prizes (Physics: 1927) **N: 440**
Quantum mechanics (Wave-particle duality) **Q: 6**
Compton-Burnett, Ivy [British author] **Ci: 907**
Compton Gamma Ray Observatory [satellite]
Telescope (Gamma-ray telescopes) **T: 109**
Compton's Interactive Encyclopedia [software]
Encyclopedia (Today's encyclopedias) **E: 268b-
269**
Comptroller of the Currency [office]
Bank (Regulation of U.S. banks) **B: 92**
Bank of the United States (The Second Bank of
the United States) **B: 96-97**
Compulsion [psychology]
Hoarding **H: 271**
Mental illness (Anxiety disorders) **M: 405**
Obsessive-compulsive disorder **O: 646**
Overeaters Anonymous **O: 881**
Compulsive personality disorder
Mental illness (Personality disorders) **M: 406**
Compulsory arbitration
Arbitration (Industrial, or labor, arbitration)
A: 592
Compulsory dances
Ice skating (Ice dancing) **I: 12-13**
Compulsory military service See Draft, Military
in this index
Compulsory referendum [government]
Initiative and referendum (The referendum)
I: 272
Computational fluid dynamics
Aerodynamics (Computational fluid dynamics)
A: 88
Compute server [computer]
Computer (Local area networks [LAN's]) **Ci: 922**
Computed tomographic scanner [machine]
X rays (Uses of X rays) **X: 540**
Computed tomography [medicine] **Ci: 907** with
picture
Brain pictures on **B: 554**; (Imaging) **B: 551**;
(Disorders of the brain) **B: 557-558**
Cancer (Preliminary diagnosis) **C: 171**
Computer graphics (In medicine) **Ci: 924h**
Heart (Symptoms and diagnosis) **H: 137-138**
Positron emission tomography **P: 697** with picture
Radiology **R: 98**
X rays (Uses of X rays) **X: 540**
Computer [machine] **Ci: 908** with pictures
See also Personal computer in this index and the
list of Related articles in the Computer article
Bengaluru **B: 249**
Binary number (History) **B: 308**
Careers (Technical and mathematical
occupations) **C: 232** with picture
Crime (Computer crime) **Ci: 1136-1137**
Culture (Invention) **Ci: 1189** with picture
International Business Machines Corporation
I: 338
Invention (The early and middle 1900's) **I: 363**;
(Recent developments) **I: 364**
Repetitive strain injury **R: 242**

Search engine **S: 268**
Software **So: 572**
Systems analysis **So: 1077**
Technology (The computer age) **T: 75**
Terrorism (Computer-based terrorism) **T: 176**; (Security measures) **T: 177**
United States, History of the (The Information Age) **U: 196b** *with picture*
A Guide to Research Skills **Research Guide: 27**
Computer equipment
  Fax machine (Multifunction fax machines) **F: 57-58**
  Handheld computer **H: 45**
  Inkjet printer **I: 273**
  Keyboard **K: 308** *with picture*
  Modem **M: 685**
  Printer **P: 795**
Pioneers
  Babbage, Charles **B: 2**
  Dell, Michael **D: 116**
  Eckert, J. Presper, Jr. **E: 50**
  Gates, Bill **G: 67**
  Hopper, Grace Murray **H: 334**
  Jacquard, Joseph Marie **J: 20**
  Jobs, Steve **J: 129**
  Mauchly, John William **M: 312**
  Von Neumann, John **V: 448**
Uses
  Algebra (History) **A: 359**
  Archaeology *picture on* **A: 597**; (Evaluation) **A: 598-599**
  Artificial intelligence **A: 760**
  Astronomy (Computer modeling) **A: 846**; (Learning about astronomy) **A: 846**
  Audio-visual materials **A: 882**; (Multisensory materials) **A: 883**
  Automated teller machine **A: 944**
  Automation (Uses of automation) **A: 944**; (How automation works) **A: 945**
  Automobile (Building an automobile) **A: 956**
  Ballot **B: 63**
  Bank (Electronic banking) **B: 89-90**
  Biomedical engineering (Clinical engineering) **B: 325**
  Book (Modern books) **B: 468**
  Braille **B: 550** *with picture*
  Broadband communication **B: 635**
  Codes and ciphers (Cipher machines) **Ci: 750**
  Communication (The development of the Internet) **Ci: 886** *with picture*
  Computer-aided design **Ci: 924e**
  Database **D: 41**
  E-book **E: 2**
  Electricity (Recent developments) **E: 198**
  Electronic game **E: 204a**
  Electronic music **E: 205**
  Electronic publishing **E: 205**
  Electronics (Uses of electronics) **E: 207** *with picture*; (The development of electronics) **E: 215**
  Factory (Location and design) **F: 5**
  Fingerprinting (Types of fingerprints) **F: 106** *with picture*
  Geographic information system **G: 92**
  Greenhouse effect (Studying the greenhouse effect) **G: 383**
  Hobby (Other hobbies) **H: 273**
  Information retrieval **I: 268b**
  Information science **I: 269**
  Internet **I: 350** *with pictures*
  Iron and steel *picture on* **I: 452**
  Library *picture on* **L: 251**; (The growth of information and technology) **L: 237-238** *with picture*
  Magnetism (In the home) **M: 60a**
  Manufacturing (How science helps manufacturing) **M: 171**
  Map **M: 177**; (How maps are made) **M: 180** *with picture*; (Mapmaking and modern technology) **M: 185**
  Mathematics (Philosophies of mathematics) **M: 307**
  Mechanical drawing (Creating a drawing) **M: 354** *with picture*
  Motion picture (Shooting the movie) **M: 852-853**; (Editing the film) **M: 855** *with pictures*; (The computer revolution) **M: 872** *with pictures*
  Multimedia **M: 919**
  Newspaper *picture on* **N: 384**; (Writing and editing stories) **N: 383**; (Making up the pages) **N: 383**; (Recent trends) **N: 386-387**
  Occupational therapy (Helping people with physical disabilities) **O: 648**
  Ocean (Computers) **O: 664** *with picture*
  Photocomposition **P: 404**
  Photography (Processing digital images) **P: 422**

  Planetarium (Digital projectors) **P: 514c**
  Postal services (Technological advancements) **P: 707**
  Presentation software **P: 757**
  Printing (Typesetting) **P: 797**; (The electronic age) **P: 804**
  Projector (Digital data projectors) **P: 817**
  Radar (Continued progress) **R: 72**
  Railroad (Freight operations) **R: 109-110** *with picture*
  Reading (Individualized reading programs) **R: 159**
  Robot **R: 369**
  Satellite, Artificial (Performing the mission) **S: 150g**
  Science (Modeling with computers) **S: 195**
  Spreadsheet **So: 805**
  Stereophonic sound system (Parts of a stereo system) **So: 892**
  Teaching (Guiding and assisting student learning) **T: 66** *with picture*
  Telephone (Types of telephones) **T: 96-97**; (VoIP phone calls) **T: 97-98**
  Television (Adding special effects) **T: 112**
  Virtual reality **V: 426**
  Voting machine (Kinds of electoral voting machines) **V: 450**
  War (Recent developments) **W: 26**
  Weather (Mathematical models) **W: 166**
  Wireless communication (Wireless networking) **W: 345**
  Word processing **W: 403**
  World Wide Web **W: 499**
  X rays (Uses of X rays) **X: 540**
Computer, Personal [machine] *See* Personal computer *in this index*
Computer-aided design Ci: 924e
  Automobile (Planning the car) **A: 956** *with picture*
  Computer *picture on* **Ci: 920**; (Computer-aided design [CAD] programs) **Ci: 919** *with picture*
  Computer graphics (In engineering) **Ci: 924h**
  Industrial design (How an industrial designer works) **I: 244**
  Machine tool (Control of machine tools) **M: 19**
  Map (Production and reproduction) **M: 181** *with picture*
  Mechanical drawing (Creating a drawing) **M: 354**
Computer-aided design and drafting
  Computer-aided design **Ci: 924e**
  Mechanical drawing (Creating a drawing) **M: 354** *with picture*
Computer-aided machining
  Machine tool (Control of machine tools) **M: 19**
Computer-aided manufacturing
  Automobile (Manufacturing) **A: 958**
  Computer-aided design **Ci: 924e**
  Machine tool (Control of machine tools) **M: 19**
  Mechanical drawing (Creating a drawing) **M: 354**
Computer animation
  Animation **A: 512** *with picture*; (Computer animation) **A: 513** *with pictures*; (The computer revolution) **A: 514c**
Computer chip [electronics] **Ci: 924e** *with pictures*
  See also Integrated circuit; Microprocessor *in this index*
  California *picture on* **C: 56**
  Computer (Parts of computers) **Ci: 911**
  Copyright (Works protected) **Ci: 1046-1047**
  Electric meter (Digital meters) **E: 177**
  Electronics **E: 207**; (Types of electronic circuits) **E: 209-210** *with picture*
  Laser (Positioning) **L: 84**
  Microelectromechanical systems **M: 513**
  Noyce, Robert **N: 578**
  Semiconductor **S: 291**
  Smart card **S: 513**
  Telephone (The circuit board) **T: 95**
  Transistor **T: 372**
  Watch (Electronic watches) **W: 114**
Computer engineering
  Computer (Careers) **Ci: 924a**
  Engineering (Computer engineering) **E: 286**
Computer file [electronics] **Ci: 924g**
  Computer (Storage devices) **Ci: 915**
Computer game *See* Electronic game *in this index*
Computer-generated imagery
  Animation (Computer animation) **A: 513**; (The computer revolution) **A: 514c**
  Computer graphics (In entertainment and the arts) **Ci: 924g** *with picture*
  Motion picture (The computer revolution) **M: 872**
  Pixar Animation Studios **P: 503**
Computer graphics Ci: 924g *with pictures*
  Animation (Computer animation) **A: 513**
  Audio-visual materials (Video presentations) **A: 883**
  Computer (Graphics programs) **Ci: 918**

  Electronic game (Game design) **E: 204b** *with picture*
  Newspaper (Making up the pages) **N: 383**
Computer keyboard [electronics]
  Computer (Input devices) **Ci: 912** *with pictures*
  Keyboard **K: 308** *with picture*
  Laptop computer **L: 75**
Computer language Ci: 924h
  Computer (Programming a computer) **Ci: 923**
  Hopper, Grace Murray **H: 334**
  Internet (HTML) **I: 350d-350e**
  Software **So: 572**
Computer modeling
  See also Mathematical model *in this index*
  Animation (Modeling) **A: 513**
  Astronomy (Computer modeling) **A: 846**
  Climate (Climate models) **Ci: 679**
  Computer *pictures on* **Ci: 918, Ci: 920**; (Spreadsheet programs) **Ci: 917**
  Computer graphics (In engineering) **Ci: 924h**
  Meteorology (Computer modeling) **M: 433**
  Ocean (Computers) **O: 664**
  Pacific Ocean (Scientific research) **P: 15**
  Science (Modeling with computers) **S: 195**
  Tornado (Computer modeling) **T: 337**
  Weather (Mathematical models) **W: 166**
Computer monitor [electronic device]
  Computer *picture on* **Ci: 913**; (Output devices) **Ci: 916**
Computer network Ci: 924h
  See also Internet *in this index*
  Computer (Personal computers) **Ci: 909**; (Computer networks) **Ci: 920**
  Electronic game (The growth of computer gaming) **E: 204e**
  Internet **I: 350**
  Personal computer **P: 300f**
  Privacy, Right of **P: 808a**
  Technology (The computer age) **T: 75**
  Telecommunications **T: 89**
  Wireless communication (Wireless networking) **W: 345**
Computer program *See* Program *in this index*
Computer programmer [career] *See* Programmer *in this index*
Computer programming *See* Programming *in this index*
Computer security Ci: 925
  Computer (Computer security) **Ci: 924**
  Internet (Identity and privacy) **I: 350f**; (Internet crime) **I: 350f**
  Library (Security) **L: 238**
Computer simulation
  Aerodynamics *picture on* **A: 87**; (Computational fluid dynamics) **A: 88**
  Astronomy (Computer modeling) **A: 846**
  Audio-visual materials (Other computerized tools) **A: 883**
  Computer (Computer-aided design [CAD] programs) **Ci: 919** *with pictures*
  Electronic game (The growth of computer gaming) **E: 204e**
  Meteorology (Computer modeling) **M: 433**
  Science (Modeling with computers) **S: 195**
  Tornado (Computer modeling) **T: 337**
Computer Space [electronic game]
  Electronic game (Arcade games) **E: 204d**
Computer storage disk [electronics]
  Computer (Storage devices) **Ci: 915**
  DVD **D: 393**
Computer-to-plate [process]
  Magazine (Editing and assembling an issue) **M: 43-44**
  Newspaper (Making up the pages) **N: 383**
  Printing (Offset printing plates) **P: 798**
Computer virus [software] **Ci: 925**
  Computer (Computer security) **Ci: 924**
  Computer security **Ci: 925**
  Internet (Internet crime) **I: 350f**
  Terrorism (Computer-based terrorism) **T: 176**
Computerized axial tomography *See* Computed tomography *in this index*
Computerized tomography *See* Computed tomography *in this index*
Computerized tutorial
  Audio-visual materials (Other computerized tools) **A: 883**
Computerized typesetting [publishing]
  Printing (The electronic age) **P: 804**
  Type **T: 536**
Computing-Tabulating-Recording Company
  International Business Machines Corporation **I: 338**
COMSAT [company] *See* Communications Satellite Corporation *in this index*
COMSEC [cryptology] *See* Communications security *in this index*

Comstock, Anthony [American social reformer]
Comstock Law Ci: 926
Comstock, Henry T. P. [American prospector]
Comstock Lode Ci: 926
Nevada (The Comstock Lode) N: 174
Comstock, William A. [American political leader]
Michigan (table) M: 507
Comstock Law [1873] Ci: 926
Comstock Lode [U.S. history] Ci: 926
Nevada (The Comstock Lode) N: 174 with picture
Comte [title]
Count Ci: 1096
Comte, Auguste [French philosopher] Ci: 926
Positivism P: 697
Sociology (Early sociological thought) So: 566
Comtesse d'Haussonville [painting by Ingres]
Drawing picture on D: 343
Painting (Later neoclassicism) P: 67-68 with
picture
Comunidad Andina [organization] See Andean
Community in this index
Comus [play by Milton]
Milton, John (His early life and works) M: 557
Comyn, Red [Scottish nobleman]
Bruce, Robert B: 648
Con-con [convention]
Political convention (Other types of conventions)
P: 630
ConAgra Foods [company]
Nebraska (Service industries) picture on N: 109
Conakry [Guinea] Ci: 926
Guinea (Economy) G: 431 with picture
Conan, Laure [Canadian author]
Canadian literature (Fiction: 1850-1918) C: 157
Conant, Gordon D. [Canadian political leader]
Ontario (table) O: 783
Conant, James Bryant [American educator] Ci: 926
Conant, Roger [American settler]
Salem (History) S: 61
Concave lens [optics]
Eye (Nearsightedness) E: 464 with picture
Glasses (Prescription glasses) G: 224-225
Lens (A negative lens) L: 196 with diagrams
Concave mirror [light]
Mirror (Concave mirrors) M: 617 with diagrams
Concave polygon [geometry]
Polygon P: 650 with diagram
Conceit [poetry]
Donne, John (His poetry) D: 308
English literature (Metaphysical and Cavalier
poets) E: 317
Poetry (Renaissance poetry) P: 596
Concentrate [agriculture]
Dairying (Feeding) D: 7
Feed F: 67
Concentrate [food]
Soft drink (How soft drinks are made) So: 570
Concentrate [iron ore]
Iron and steel (Processing) I: 439
Concentration [industrial process]
Lead (Production) L: 149-150
Ore O: 825
Concentration camp Ci: 926 with picture
See also Labor camp in this index
Auschwitz A: 892
Bergen-Belsen B: 257
Buchenwald B: 663
Dachau D: 2
Himmler, Heinrich H: 234
Hitler, Adolf (The New Order) H: 266-267
Holocaust map on H: 297; (Before the Holocaust)
H: 296-296a; (The Holocaust) H: 296a with
picture
Holocaust Memorial Museum, United States
H: 298
Jews (The Holocaust) J: 124
Treblinka T: 409
World War II picture on W: 484; (Victory in Europe)
W: 486; (The Holocaust) W: 496
Concentrator [machine]
Telephone (Traditional phone calls) T: 96
Concepción [former name]
Grenada (History and government) G: 389
Concepción [Paraguay]
Paraguay picture on P: 147
Concepción [ship]
Magellan, Ferdinand (The voyage begins) M: 47
Concept car
Automobile (Planning the car) A: 956
Conception [biology]
See also Fertilization in this index
Abortion (Abortion history) A: 15
Pregnancy P: 734a
Reproduction, Human (Fertilization) R: 246
Sexuality (Before birth) S: 338
Conception, Immaculate [religion] See
Immaculate Conception in this index

Conceptismo [literature]
Spanish literature (The 1600's) So: 759-760
Concerned Women for America
Women's movement (Women's organizations)
W: 386
Concerning Children [book by Gilman]
Gilman, Charlotte Perkins G: 191
Concerning Faith [book by Saint Ambrose]
Ambrose, Saint A: 405
"Concerning Stones" [essay by Theophrastus]
Geology (The ancient Greeks) G: 97
Concerning Traditionalism [book by Unamuno]
Unamuno, Miguel de U: 19
Concert band [music]
Band (Concert bands) B: 74
Concert Champêtre [painting by Giorgione]
Giorgione G: 193
Concert flute in C
Flute F: 307
Concert grand piano
Piano (Grand pianos) P: 447 with picture
Concert of powers
International relations (From the 1500's to the
1900's) I: 345
Concert overture [music]
Overture O: 882
Concertina [musical instrument] Ci: 927 with
picture
Concerto [music] Ci: 928
Classical music (Orchestral music) Ci: 644
Orchestra (History) O: 822
Concerto for Left Hand [music by Ravel]
Ravel, Maurice R: 151
Concerto grosso
Classical music (Orchestral music) Ci: 644
Concerto C: 928
Corelli, Arcangelo Ci: 1052
Orchestra (History) O: 822
Concerto in F [music by Gershwin]
Gershwin, George G: 174
Conch [machine]
Chocolate (Milk chocolate) C: 519
Conch [sea animal] Ci: 928 with picture
Conch shell
Indian, American picture on I: 172
Shell picture on S: 386
Concha [anatomy]
Nose N: 548 with diagram
Smell S: 514; (How odors are detected) S: 514
Conchiolin [zoology]
Pearl (Characteristics of pearls) P: 217; (Care of
pearls) P: 218
Conchobar, King [legendary figure]
Irish literature (Heroic tales, romances, and sagas)
I: 430
Mythology (The Ulster cycle) M: 985
Conchology [hobby]
Shell (Collecting shells) S: 388
Concierge [occupation]
Careers (Personal services) C: 228
Concilium plebis [ancient Rome]
Rome, Ancient (The Roman Republic) R: 438
Concini, Concino [Italian public figure]
Marie de Médicis M: 200
Conclave [religion]
Pope (Present procedures) P: 662
Concluding Unscientific Postscript [book by
Kierkegaard]
Kierkegaard, Søren Aabye (His philosophy) K: 313
Conclusion
Deductive method D: 81
Geometry (Deductive reasoning) G: 101
Logic L: 425
Philosophy (Logic) P: 384
Concord [Massachusetts] Ci: 928
Concord [New Hampshire] Ci: 929
New Hampshire N: 209; (table: Average monthly
weather) N: 220
Concord, Battle of [1775] See Lexington and
Concord, Battles of in this index
Concord, Book of [religious book]
Lutheran Church-Missouri Synod L: 529
Lutherans (Doctrine) L: 529
Concord Academy
Vermont (Interesting facts) V: 319
Concord grape
Grape (North American grapes) G: 319
Concord Square [Greece]
Athens (Landmarks) A: 854 with map
Concordance
Information retrieval (History) I: 269
Concordat [religion]
Roman Catholic Church (Pius X) R: 410
Treaty T: 408
Concordat of Bologna [1516]
Francis I F: 480
Concordat of Worms [1122]

Church and state (History) C: 542
Concorde [airplane]
Airplane picture on A: 237; (Supersonic airplanes)
A: 238
Aviation (Recent developments) A: 991-992
Transportation picture on T: 391
Concorde, Place de la
Paris (Gardens, squares, and parks) P: 162 with
picture and map
Concourse [passage]
Airport (Terminal designs) A: 248
Concrete [building material]
Cement and concrete C: 343
Edison, Thomas Alva (Ore milling and cement)
E: 81
House (Building materials) H: 380
Rome, Ancient (Architecture and engineering)
R: 442
Concrete girder bridge
Bridge (Girder bridges) B: 600-601
Concrete mixer [machine]
Truck (Kinds of trucks) T: 457
Concrete noun [grammar]
Noun (Abstract and concrete nouns) N: 552
Concrete operations [psychology]
Child (The stages of childhood) C: 448
Piaget, Jean P: 445
Concubinage [practice]
Family (Development of the family) F: 21-22
Concurrent forces [physics]
Force (Concurrent forces) F: 370
Concurrent powers
Constitution of the United States (The supreme
law of the land) Ci: 998
Concurring opinion
Supreme Court of the United States (Written
opinions) So: 999
Concussion [injury] Ci: 929
Brain (From injury) B: 550d; (Injuries) B: 558
First aid (Concussion) F: 139
Condamine River [Australia]
Queensland (Land and climate) Q: 39
Conde [title]
Count Ci: 1096
Condé [diamond]
Diamond picture on D: 181
Condé, Alpha [Guinean political leader]
Guinea (History) G: 432
Condell, Henry [English actor]
Shakespeare, William (Shakespeare's plays)
S: 354; (Folios) S: 369
Condemnation [law]
Eminent domain E: 260
Urban renewal (The role of government) U: 220
Condensation [physics] Ci: 929
Air (Moisture in the air) A: 170
Dew D: 176
Dew point D: 176
Distillation D: 238
Heat (Changes in state) H: 153 with diagram
Natural gas liquids N: 64
Sound (table) So: 599; (The nature of sound)
So: 599 with diagram; (Beats) So: 604 with
diagram
Condensation trail See Contrail in this index
Condensed-matter physics
Solid-state physics So: 583
Condensed Novels [book by Harte]
Harte, Bret H: 77
Condenser [electricity]
Refrigeration (The electric refigerator) R: 201
with diagram
Condenser, Steam [mechanism]
Distillation D: 238
Electric power (Fossil-fueled steam electric power
plants) E: 183 with diagram
Nuclear energy (Steam production) N: 587 with
diagram
Watt, James W: 148
Condenser lens
Projector (Projector operation) P: 816
Condenser microphone
Microphone (Condenser microphones) M: 517
Condition of the Working Class in England, The
[book by Engels]
Engels, Friedrich E: 283
Conditional response [Pyschology]
Behavior (Learning) B: 220
Conditioned reflex [psychology]
Learning (Classical conditioning) L: 163
Pavlov, Ivan Petrovich P: 202
Reflex action (Conditioned reflex) R: 195
Conditioning [psychology]
Abnormal psychology (Cognitive-behavioral
theories) A: 12
Behavior (Learning) B: 220
Education (How people learn) E: 89

Learning (Classical conditioning) L: 163
Psychology (Behaviorism) P: 849-850
Conditioning process [industry]
Manufacturing (Making products) M: 170
Condom [birth control] Ci: 929
AIDS (Prevention) A: 165; (Education) A: 165
Birth control (Methods of birth control) B: 378-379
Condominium [dwelling] Ci: 929
Housing (Condominium housing) H: 390; (Housing since 1900) H: 391-392
Condor [bird] Ci: 929 *with pictures*
See also California condor *in this index*
Bird of prey *picture on* B: 374b; (Physical appearance) B: 374a
Condor of the Andes, National Order of the
Medals, decorations, and orders (The Americas) M: 358
Condorcet, Marquis de [French philosopher] Ci: 930
Enlightenment E: 326a
Philosophes P: 382
Women's movement (Forces of change) W: 384
Conduct
Behavior B: 220
Etiquette E: 374
Conducting [music]
See also the list of Related articles in the Orchestra *article*
Opera (The conductor) O: 793 *with picture*
Orchestra (The conductor) O: 821
Conduction [physics]
Heat (How heat travels) H: 151 *with diagram*
Insulation (Insulation to control heat flow) I: 306
Conductive hearing loss
Deafness (Types of hearing loss) D: 57; (Medical treatment) D: 58
Conductive keratoplasty [surgery]
Farsightedness F: 48
Myopia M: 971
Conductive plastics
Plastics (Growth of the plastics industry) P: 560
Conductive support
Electrophoresis E: 218
Conductivity [physical property]
See also Superconductivity *in this index*
Alloy (Characteristics of alloys) A: 377
Aluminum (Electrical conduction) A: 392
Gold (Physical properties) G: 249
Conductor, Electrical [electricity]
Cable (Cable construction) C: 4 *with diagrams*
Coaxial cable Ci: 740
Copper (Conductivity) Ci: 1041
Electric current (Conductors and insulators) E: 168
Electric motor (Parts of an electric motor) E: 179
Electricity (Conductors and insulators) E: 193 *with diagram*
Electrode E: 200
Electrolysis (How electrolysis works) E: 200
Electronics (Electronic circuits) E: 208-209
Insulator, Electric I: 308
Ohm O: 706
Transistor (Transistor materials) T: 372
Conductor, Railroad [career]
Careers (Transportation) C: 235
Railroad (Railroad workers) R: 113
Conductus [music]
Classical music (The Middle Ages) Ci: 645-646
Conduit [construction]
Cable (Cable installation) C: 5
House (table) H: 380
Conduit [geology]
Volcano *diagram on* V: 442a
Cone [anatomy]
Color (The roles of the eyes and brain) Ci: 818
Color blindness Ci: 827
Eye (The retina) E: 462 *with picture*
Mammal (Senses) M: 120-121
Perception (Receptors) P: 283
Cone [biology] *See* Conifer *in this index*
Cone [electronics]
Radio (The speaker) R: 89
Cone [geology]
Paricutín P: 159 *with picture*
Vesuvius V: 342
Cone [geometry] Ci: 931 *with diagrams*
See also Conic section *in this index*
Geometry *picture on* G: 104
Cone, Fred P. [American political leader]
Florida (table) F: 260
Cone-bearing plant *See* Conifer; Cycad *in this index*
Cone cluster [botany]
Welwitschia W: 196
Cone snail
Snail (Snails and people) S: 523 *with picture*
Coneflower

Echinacea E: 49
Flower (Flowers of prairies and dry plains) F: 286 *with picture*
Conestoga wagon [vehicle] Ci: 931
Pennsylvania Dutch P: 270
Pioneer life in America (How the pioneers traveled) P: 478
Westward movement in America *picture on* W: 244
Conexus Arts Centre
Regina (Education and cultural life) R: 205
Coney [animal] *See* Hyrax *in this index*
Coney Island [New York City]
New York City (Brooklyn) N: 326-328
Coney Island of the Mind, A [poem by Ferlinghetti]
Ferlinghetti, Lawrence F: 73
Confabulation [psychology]
Memory (Constructive processes) M: 393
Confection [food]
Candy C: 175
Confederación Española de Derechas Autónomas [political party]
Spain (The Spanish republic) So: 750
Confederacy *See* Confederate States of America *in this index*
Confederacy, First White House of the
Alabama (Places to visit) A: 266 *with picture*
Confederate currency
Money *picture on* M: 709; (Money in the American Civil War) M: 713
Confederate flag [U.S. history]
Flag F: 210 *with pictures*
Georgia (The late 1900's) G: 134; (The early 2000's) G: 134-135
Confederate Gulch [region]
Montana (The gold rush) M: 758
Confederate Memorial Day [custom]
Davis, Jefferson (His last years) D: 48
Memorial Day M: 392
Confederate States of America [U.S. history] Ci: 931 *with map*
Alabama (The Civil War and Reconstruction) A: 276
Buchanan, James (Prelude to war) B: 661
Choctaw Indians C: 519
Civil War, American (Secession) Ci: 617
Davis, Jefferson (Spokesman for the South) D: 48
Flag *pictures on* F: 210
Reconstruction R: 176
Richmond (History) R: 333
South Carolina (The Civil War) So: 660
United States, History of the (Secession) U: 177; (Reconstruction) U: 178
Confederate Veterans, United [organization]
Veterans' organizations (In the United States) V: 344
Confederation [government]
Federalism F: 66
Confederation [treaty]
Treaty (Kinds of treaties) T: 408-409
Confederation, Articles of *See* Articles of Confederation *in this index*
Confederation Bridge
New Brunswick (Economic developments) N: 199
Prince Edward Island (The late 1900's) P: 793
Confederation Building [St. John's]
Newfoundland and Labrador *picture on* N: 362
Confederation Centre of the Arts
Prince Edward Island (Places to visit) P: 788 *with picture*
Confederation Congress [U.S. history] *See* Congress of the Confederation *in this index*
Confederation of Canada Ci: 933 *with pictures*
Confederation of Chiefs of the United Tribes of New Zealand [New Zealand history]
New Zealand (Early European contact) N: 354
Confederation of National Trade Unions [labor federation]
Labor movement (In Canada) L: 14
Confederation of North, Central American and Caribbean Association Football
Soccer (International competition) So: 548
Confederation of the Rhine [German history]
Napoleon I (Dominates Europe) N: 15
Napoleonic Wars (The alliance of Prussia and Russia) N: 18 *with map*
Confederation poets
Canadian literature (Poetry: 1850-1918) C: 157
Conference [politics]
House of Representatives (Organization of the U.S. House) H: 387
Conference committee
Congress of the United States (From bill to law) Ci: 945-946
House of Representatives (Committees) H: 387
Conference of Catholic Bishops, United States
Ci: 936

Conference on Security and Co-operation in Europe *See* Organization for Security and Co-operation in Europe *in this index*
Confessio Amantis [poems by Gower]
English literature (The age of Chaucer) E: 316
Confession [book by Saint Patrick]
Patrick, Saint (Writings) P: 197
Confession [law] Ci: 936
Confession [religion] *See* Penance *in this index*
Confessional poetry
American literature ("Confessional" poetry) A: 423
Lowell, Robert L: 510
Poetry (Poetry of the 1900's) P: 597
Confessions [book by Rousseau]
French literature (The Enlightenment) F: 520-521
Rousseau, Jean-Jacques (Early life) R: 492
Confessions [book by Saint Augustine]
Augustine, Saint (His life) A: 888
Autobiography A: 942
Confessions of an English Opium Eater [book by De Quincey]
De Quincey, Thomas D: 151
English literature (Romantic prose) E: 320
Confessions of Felix Krull, Confidence Man [book by Mann]
Mann, Thomas M: 164
Confessions of Nat Turner, The [book by Styron]
Novel (The novel today) N: 575
Styron, William So: 898
Confidence-Man, The [book by Melville]
Melville, Herman (His literary career) M: 390-391
Confined animal feeding operation [agriculture]
See Factory farming *in this index*
Confinement [agriculture]
Agriculture (Raising livestock) A: 150-151
Dairying (Housing) D: 7
Farm and farming (Confinement operations) F: 40 *with picture*
Confirmation [religion] Ci: 936
Bar mitzvah B: 102
Christianity (Sacraments) C: 522h
Eastern Orthodox Churches (Sacraments) E: 46-47
Judaism (Special occasions) J: 182
Religious education (Private education) R: 225
Roman Catholic Church (Worship) R: 403-404
Confirmatory method
Statistics (Analyzing the data) So: 868
Conflict [sociology]
Human relations H: 428
Conflict diamond [gem]
Africa (Mining) A: 127
Conflict of interest [politics] Ci: 936
Confocal microscope
Light (Light in medicine) L: 292
Conformal projection
Map (The Mercator projection) M: 182 *with diagram*
Confrérie de la Passion [theater group]
Drama (The French theater) D: 333
Confucianism [religion] Ci: 936
Asia (Way of life in East Asia) A: 785; (Life in China) A: 786-787
China (Religion) C: 485; (The Song dynasty) C: 501
Chinese literature (Beginnings) C: 511
Government (Asia and the Middle East) G: 289
Han dynasty H: 38
Korea, North (Religion) K: 371
Korea, South (Religion) K: 378
Mencius M: 397
Philosophy (Eastern philosophy) P: 386
Religion R: 215; (How the major religions are organized) R: 218; (Confucianism) R: 220 *with picture*
Saint (Non-Christian saints) S: 29
Song dynasty So: 592
Taoism T: 36
World, History of the (The unification of China) W: 431
Confucius [Chinese philosopher] Ci: 937
Confucianism Ci: 936
Golden rule G: 256
Government (Asia and the Middle East) G: 289
I Ching I: 2
Religion (Confucianism) R: 220
Conga drum Ci: 937 *with picture*
Hispanic Americans *picture on* H: 247
Congaree National Park [South Carolina] Ci: 937
National Park System (table: National parks) N: 48
Congaree Swamp National Monument [South Carolina]
South Carolina (The early 2000's) So: 663
Congenital blindness
Blindness B: 401
Congenital defect *See* Birth defect *in this index*

Congenital disease
Heart (Birth defects) H: 140 *with picture*
Congenital dislocation [disorder]
Dislocation D: 235
Hip H: 238
Congenital hyperinsulinism [disease]
Hypoglycemia (Causes) H: 481
Congenital muscular dystrophy [disease]
Muscular dystrophy (Other muscular dystrophies)
M: 937
Conger eel [fish]
Eel E: 114
Congestion [traffic]
Traffic (Traffic problems) T: 365
Transportation (Overcrowding of streets and
highways) T: 397 *with picture*
Congestive cardiomyopathy [disorder]
Heart (Cardiomyopathy) H: 142-143
Congestive heart failure
Heart (Valve disease) H: 141-142
Congkak [game]
Malaysia (Recreation) M: 98d
Conglomerate [economics] Ci: 938
Business (Corporations) B: 726
Corporation (Business corporations) Ci: 1069
Merger M: 417
Conglomerate [geology]
Rock (Clastic sediments) R: 372
Sedimentary rock S: 280
Congo, Democratic Republic of the Ci: 940 *with
pictures and maps*
See also the list of Related articles in the Congo,
Democratic Republic of the *article*
Africa *picture on* A: 116
Army (Prevention of war) A: 725
Clothing *picture on* Ci: 692
Cold War (Africa) Ci: 768
Diamond (Where natural diamonds are found)
D: 181-182
Luba L: 512
Rwanda (History) R: 571-572
Sculpture (Royal and public sculpture) S: 240
with picture
Uganda (History) U: 3-4
Congo, Republic of the Ci: 940d *with picture and
map*
Flag *picture on* F: 198
French Equatorial Africa F: 514
"Congo, The" [poem by Lindsay]
Lindsay, Vachel L: 333
Congo buffalo [animal]
Water buffalo W: 133
Congo Free State
Belgium (Independence) B: 233
Berlin Conference B: 266
Congo, Democratic Republic of the (Belgian rule)
Ci: 940b
Stanley and Livingstone (Stanley's explorations)
So: 837-838
Congo-Ocean Railway
Congo, Republic of the (Economy) Ci: 940e
Congo River [Africa] Ci: 940f *with map*
Congo, Democratic Republic of the *picture on*
Ci: 940b; (Rivers and lakes) Ci: 940a *with map*;
(Transportation and communication) Ci: 940a
Congo, Republic of the (Land) Ci: 940d-940e
with map
River (table) R: 352
Stanley and Livingstone (Stanley's explorations)
So: 837-838
Ubangi River U: 2
Congolese Labor Party
Congo, Republic of the (History) Ci: 940e
Congolese Rally for Democracy [political party]
Congo, Democratic Republic of the (Cease-fires
and power sharing) Ci: 940c
Congregación [village]
Indian, American (In Latin America) I: 178
Congregate care
Foster care F: 428
Congregatio de Propaganda Fide [organization]
Propaganda (History) P: 824
Congregation of ...
Congregations appear under their key words, as in
Index, Congregation of the
Congregational Christian Churches [U.S.]
Baptists (Early history) B: 101
United Church of Christ U: 47
Congregational polity [religion]
Christianity (Church leadership) C: 522g
Congregationalists [religious group] Ci: 940f
Protestantism (The radical reform and free
church movements) P: 835
Congress [meeting] Ci: 941
Congress for Democracy and Progress [political
party]
Burkina Faso (History) B: 706-707

Congress Hall [Philadelphia]
Philadelphia (Downtown Philadelphia) P: 359
Congress-I Party [political party]
Gandhi, Rajiv G: 26
India (India under Indira Gandhi) I: 133-134
Indian National Congress I: 185
Rao, P. V. Narasimha R: 141
Congress of Aix-la-Chapelle [1818]
Aix-la-Chapelle, Congress of A: 253
Congress of Berlin [1878] *See* Berlin, Congress of
in this index
Congress of Cities
National League of Cities N: 40
Congress of Industrial Organizations [labor
history] Ci: 941
American Federation of Labor and Congress of
Industrial Organizations (History) A: 410
Bridges, Harry B: 607
Dubinsky, David D: 370
Hillman, Sidney H: 232
Labor movement (Formation of the CIO) L: 12
Lewis, John L. L: 221
Murray, Philip M: 931
United Automobile Workers U: 46
Congress of Paris [1856]
Congress Ci: 941
Congress of Racial Equality [organization] Ci: 941
Farmer, James Leonard F: 46
Freedom riders F: 508
McKissick, Floyd Bixler M: 342
Congress of the Confederation [U.S. history]
Ci: 941
Articles of Confederation A: 758
Federal Hall F: 64
Maryland (Statehood) M: 258
United States capitals U: 199
Congress of the People [political party]
African National Congress A: 137
Congress of the United States Ci: 942 *with
pictures*
Apportionment A: 574
Black Caucus, Congressional B: 386
Capitol, United States C: 197
Checks and balances C: 391
Citizenship (U.S. citizenship laws) Ci: 571
Congressional page Ci: 949
Congressional Record Ci: 949
Constitution of the United States (Article
I) Ci: 1004; (Amendment 12) Ci: 1013;
(Amendment 27) Ci: 1016
Electoral College E: 161
Franking and penalty privileges F: 485
House of Representatives H: 385 *with picture*
Impeachment (Procedure) I: 90
Iran-contra affair (Background) I: 406b
Library of Congress L: 263
National budget (Creating a budget) N: 30
Political party (Organizing the government)
P: 632
Reconstruction (Early congressional reaction)
R: 177
Senate S: 294 *with pictures*
State, Department of (Relationship with the
president and Congress) So: 860
Supreme Court of the United States (How the
Supreme Court is organized) So: 998
Television (Regulating U.S. television) T: 115
United States, Government of the (The legislative
branch) U: 138; (How a bill becomes law in the
United States) U: 141; (Current issues in U.S.
government) U: 146
United States, History of the (The nation divided
[1850-1869]) U: 174 *with picture*
United States capitals U: 199
Veto V: 346
Washington, D.C. (Capitol Hill) W: 71
Congress of Vienna *See* Vienna, Congress of *in
this index*
Congress Party [political party]
India (Politics) I: 111; (India under Indira Gandhi)
I: 133-134; (Religious and ethnic unrest) I: 134
Congressional Black Caucus *See* Black Caucus,
Congressional *in this index*
**Congressional Budget and Impoundment
Control Act** [1974]
Congressional Budget Office Ci: 949
Congressional Budget Office [U.S.] Ci: 949
Budget (Preparation of the U.S. budget) B: 671
Congressional Caucus for Women's Issues
Heckler, Margaret Mary H: 164
Congressional committee
Congress of the United States (Working
in committees) Ci: 944; (Conducting
investigations) Ci: 946
Congressional Debates [publication]
Congressional Record Ci: 949
Congressional district

Electoral college E: 164
House of Representatives (Size) H: 385
Congressional election
House of Representatives (Size) H: 385
Senate (Qualifications and election) S: 294
Congressional Globe [publication]
Congressional Record Ci: 949
Congressional Government [book by Wilson]
Wilson, Woodrow (Graduate student) W: 320
Congressional immunity
Constitution of the United States (Article I,
Section 6) Ci: 1006
Congressional investigation
Congress of the United States (Conducting
investigations) Ci: 946
Congressional Library *See* Library of Congress *in
this index*
Congressional Medal of Honor *See* Medal of
Honor *in this index*
Congressional page [messenger] Ci: 949
Congressional Record [publication] Ci: 949
Congressional Space Medal of Honor
Medals, decorations, and orders (table) M: 357
with picture
Congressman [office] Ci: 949
Address, Forms of (Officials of the United States)
A: 53
Congress of the United States (How Congress is
organized) Ci: 942; (Members of Congress at
work) Ci: 946
Congresswoman *See* Congressman *in this index*
Congreve [match]
Match (The first matches) M: 300
Congreve, William [English dramatist] Ci: 949
Congreve, Sir William [British engineer] Ci: 950
Guided missile (Early development) G: 426-427
Rocket (History) R: 390
Congreve rocket [weapon]
Rocket (History) R: 390
Congruence [mathematics]
Geometry (Properties of geometric figures)
G: 102
Triangle (Congruence) T: 438
Conibear [trap]
Fur (Trapping) F: 562
Trapping (Kinds of traps) T: 403 *with picture*
Conic section [mathematics]
Cone Ci: 931 *with diagram*
Ellipse E: 243
Geometry (Analytic geometry) G: 105-106
Hyperbola H: 476
Conidiophore [biology]
Fungi (Parts of a fungus) F: 558-559
Mold M: 690
Conie [animal]
Pika P: 461 *with picture*
Conifer [botany] Ci: 950
Earth (The Mesozoic Era) E: 27-28
Fir F: 119 *with pictures*
Lumber (Softwood lumber) L: 517
Pine P: 468 *with pictures*
Plant (Gymnosperms) P: 520; (Sexual
reproduction) P: 532-535 *with pictures*;
(Classification of plants) P: 546-547 *with picture*
Seed (Kinds of seeds) S: 280-281; (Seed
development in gymnosperms) S: 281-282
Taiga T: 14
Tree (Needleleaf trees) T: 414-415
Triassic Period T: 440
Wood (Kinds of wood) W: 389
Coniferous forest
Biome B: 322; (table) B: 323 *(with map)*
Plant (Temperate coniferous forests) P: 523 *with
map*
Conille, Garry [Haitian political leader]
Haiti (History) H: 15-17
Conjectures on Original Composition [book by
Young]
Young, Edward Y: 572
Conjoined twins [biology] Ci: 950 *with picture*
Multiple birth (How multiple births occur)
M: 919-920
Conjugation [biology]
Bacteria (How bacteria reproduce) B: 21
Paramecium P: 153
Conjugation [grammar] Ci: 950
Grammar (Inflection) G: 303
Inflection I: 268a
Conjunction [grammar] Ci: 951
Adverb (Conjunctive adverbs) A: 70
Conjunctiva [anatomy]
Conjunctivitis Ci: 951
Eye (The outer parts) E: 460 *with picture*;
(Diseases of the outer parts) E: 466
Conjunctive adverb [grammar]
Adverb (Conjunctive adverbs) A: 71
Conjunctivitis [disorder] Ci: 951

Allergy **A:** 373
Chlamydia **C:** 516
Eye *picture on* **E:** 466; (Diseases of the outer parts)
  E: 468
Trachoma **T:** 355
Conjure Woman, The [book by Chesnutt]
Chesnutt, Charles Waddell **C:** 411
Conjuring
Magician (Sleight of hand) **M:** 51
Conkling, Roscoe [American political leader]
Arthur, Chester Alan (Custom house collector)
  A: 755; (Election of 1880) **A:** 756
Hayes, Rutherford Birchard (Campaign of 1876)
  H: 120
Conlan, Jocko [American umpire]
Baseball (table: Hall of Fame) **B:** 134
Conley, Benjamin [American political leader]
Georgia (table) **G:** 130
Conley, William G. [American political leader]
West Virginia (table) **W:** 225
Conly, Robert Leslie [real name of]
O'Brien, Robert C. **O:** 643
Connally, John Bowden [American political
leader] **Ci:** 951
Kennedy, John Fitzgerald (The death of the
  President) **K:** 266 *with picture*
Texas (table) **T:** 203; (The mid-1900's) **T:** 208-209
Connaught and Strathearn, Duke of [British
general] **Ci:** 951
Connaught Place
New Delhi (The city) **N:** 202-203
Connecticut Ci: 952 *with pictures and maps*
See also the list of Related articles in the
  Connecticut *article*
Colonial life in America (Development of the
  Thirteen Colonies) **Ci:** 790 *with map*
United States, History of the (New England)
  U: 154
Western Reserve **W:** 241
Connecticut, University of Ci: 972
Connecticut Compromise *See* Great Compromise
in this index
Connecticut Courant [newspaper]
Connecticut (Communication) **Ci:** 966
Connecticut Land Company
Western Reserve **W:** 241
Connecticut River [river, U.S.] **Ci:** 972
New Hampshire (Rivers and lakes) **N:** 220 *with
  map*
Vermont (Land regions) **V:** 328
Connecticut River Valley [region, U.S.]
New Hampshire (Land regions) **N:** 218
Connecticut Yankee in King Arthur's Court, A
[book by Twain]
Twain, Mark (Productive years in Hartford) **T:** 529
Connecting rod [device]
Automobile *diagram on* **A:** 952
Gasoline engine *picture on* **G:** 63; (The pistons
  and connecting rods) **G:** 64
Machine *diagram on* **M:** 13
Connective tissue [anatomy] **Ci:** 972
Cancer (Classification by tissue) **C:** 168-169
Collagen **C:** 773
Human body (Cells and tissues) **H:** 417-418;
  (Organs and organ systems) **H:** 418
Marfan syndrome **M:** 198
Tissue (Animal tissues) **T:** 298
Connelly, Jennifer [American actress]
Motion picture (Best performance by an actress
  in a supporting role: 2001) **M:** 862b
Connelly, Marc [American author] **Ci:** 972
Conner, Martin Sennett [American political leader]
Mississippi (table) **M:** 640
Conner, Patrick E. [American military leader]
Utah (Territorial days and statehood) **U:** 246-248
Conner Prairie Interactive History Park
Indiana (Places to visit) **I:** 206
Indianapolis (Cultural life) **I:** 221-222
Connery, Sean [Scottish actor] **Ci:** 973 *with portrait*
Motion picture (Best performance by an actor in
  a supporting role: 1987) **M:** 862b
Connolly, Harold [Canadian political leader]
Nova Scotia (table) **N:** 567
Connolly, James B. [American athlete]
Olympic Games (The modern games) **O:** 750
Connolly, Maureen [American tennis player]
Tennis (Tennis tournaments) **T:** 165; (The mid-
  1900's) **T:** 166d
Connolly, Tom [American umpire]
Baseball (table: Hall of Fame) **B:** 134
Connor, Eugene "Bull" [American police
commissioner]
Alabama (The mid-1900's) **A:** 278
Connor, Fox [American general]
Eisenhower, Dwight David (Early military career)
  E: 149
Connor, John Thomas [American government

official]
Commerce, Department of (table) **Ci:** 871
Connor, Ralph [Canadian author]
Canadian literature (Fiction: 1850-1918) **C:** 157
Connor, Roger [American baseball player]
Baseball (table: Hall of Fame) **B:** 134
Connor, Seldon [American political leader]
Maine (table) **M:** 87
Connors, Jimmy [American tennis player] **Ci:** 973
ConocoPhillips [company]
Manufacturing (table) **M:** 170
Conon [pope]
Pope (table) **P:** 666
Conquest of Granada, The [play by Dryden]
Dryden, John **D:** 370
Conquistador [poem by MacLeish]
MacLeish, Archibald **M:** 24
Conquistadors [Latin American history] **Ci:** 973
Latin America (The conquest of the American
  Indians) **L:** 103
Peru (Spanish conquest and rule) **P:** 314
Conrad I [king of Germany]
Germany (The breakup of Charlemagne's empire)
  G: 162
Conrad II [king of Germany]
Henry III [of Germany] **H:** 186
Conrad, Charles, Jr. [American astronaut] **Ci:** 973
Astronaut (Achievements in space) **A:** 829-830;
  (table) **A:** 830 *with picture*
Cooper, Gordon **Ci:** 1034
Conrad, Charles M. [American government official]
Fillmore, Millard (table) **F:** 102
Conrad, Frank [American engineer]
Radio, Amateur (History) **R:** 96
Conrad, Joseph [Polish-British author] **Ci:** 973
English literature (Literature before World War
  I) **E:** 322
Ford, Ford Madox **F:** 371
Novel (New directions in the novel) **N:** 573-574
Conrad Hilton [hotel]
Hilton, Conrad Nicholson **H:** 233
Conrail
Railroad (Economic recovery-and decline) **R:** 118;
  (Railroads today) **R:** 118
Conscience of a Conservative, The [book by
Goldwater]
Goldwater, Barry Morris (Political career) **G:** 259
Conscientious objector Ci: 974
Pacifism **P:** 17
Consciousness [psychology]
Brain (Attention and consciousness) **B:** 554
Concussion **Ci:** 929
Mind **M:** 562
Phenomenology **P:** 356
Psychoanalysis (Psychoanalytic theory) **P:** 846
Subliminal **So:** 938
Conscription *See* Draft, Military *in this index*
Consensual union
Family (Varieties of families) **F:** 20
Consensus
Public opinion **P:** 858
Consent, Informed *See* Informed consent *in this
index*
Consenting Adult [book by Hobson]
Hobson, Laura Z. **H:** 273
Conservancy Act [1914]
Ohio (The early 1900's) **O:** 702
Conservation Ci: 974 *with pictures*
See also Wildlife conservation *in this index; and
  the list of Related articles in the* Conservation
  article
Audubon Society, National **A:** 885
Fish and Wildlife Service **F:** 175
Geography (Environmental conservation) **G:** 94
Greenpeace **G:** 386
Izaak Walton League of America **I:** 523
Land Management, Bureau of **L:** 57
Nature Conservancy **N:** 67
State government (Environment) **So:** 864-865
United States, History of the (Environmental and
  energy concerns) **U:** 196a
WWF **W:** 514
Energy conservation
  Conservation (Energy conservation) **Ci:** 983
    with picture
  Energy, Department of (Functions) **E:** 276
  Energy supply (Conserving energy) **E:** 282
  Light (Light and energy efficiency) **L:** 291
  Natural resources (Conservation and
    development) **N:** 64-65
  Petroleum (Falling prices) **P:** 349
Forest conservation
  Conservation (Kinds of conservation) **Ci:** 976;
    (Forest conservation) **Ci:** 981
  Forestry **F:** 404 *with pictures*
  Rain forest (Saving rain forests) **R:** 126d
  Soil (Soil conservation) **So:** 576

Tree farming **T:** 432
Soil conservation
  Conservation (Soil conservation) **Ci:** 979 *with
    pictures*
  Agronomy **A:** 162
  Coal (Strip mining) **Ci:** 722
  Conservation (Soil conservation) **Ci:** 979 *with
    pictures*; (Careers in conservation) **Ci:** 990
  Cropping system **Ci:** 1153
  Irrigation (History) **I:** 459
  Rye (Uses) **R:** 573
  Soil (Soil conservation) **So:** 576
Water conservation
  Conservation (Water conservation) **Ci:** 977
    with picture
  California (The mid-1900's) **C:** 62-63
  Dam (The effects of dams) **D:** 17
  Detergent and soap (The development of
    detergents) **D:** 165
  Ground water **G:** 401
  Irrigation **I:** 456
  Petroleum (Falling prices) **P:** 349
  Reservoir **R:** 258
  Tennessee Valley Authority **T:** 158
  Water (Water management and conservation)
    W: 122; (Fresh water from the sea) **W:** 127;
    (The challenge of today) **W:** 132
Conservation [acting]
Theater (Conservation and build) **T:** 238
Conservation biologist [occupation]
Biodiversity **B:** 310
Conservation (Careers in conservation) **Ci:** 990
Zoology (History) **Z:** 606-607
Conservation of energy [physics]
Energy (Conservation of energy) **E:** 274
Heat (Thermodynamics) **H:** 155
Helmholtz, Hermann Ludwig Ferdinand von
  H: 179
Joule, James Prescott **J:** 169
Mayer, Julius Robert von **M:** 327
Physics (Developments in the 1800's) **P:** 440
Thermodynamics **T:** 253
Conservation of mass, Law of [physics]
Chemical reaction **C:** 397
Chemistry (Lavoisier's contributions) **C:** 401
Lavoisier, Antoine Laurent **L:** 129
Science (The Enlightenment) **S:** 199
Conservation of matter, Law of *See* Conservation
of mass, Law of *in this index*
Conservation of momentum [physics]
Momentum **M:** 698 *with diagram*
Conservation tillage [agriculture]
Conservation (Soil conservation) **Ci:** 979-980
Farm and farming (Preparing the soil) **F:** 35
Conservationist [occupation]
Animal (How human beings protect animals)
  A: 505
Conservation **Ci:** 974
Conservatism [political science] **Ci:** 991
Heritage Foundation **H:** 210
Liberalism **L:** 228
Right wing **R:** 340
United States, Government of the (Current issues
  in U.S. government) **U:** 146
United States, History of the (The revival of
  conservatism) **U:** 196b
Conservative Judaism
Judaism (Conservative Judaism) **J:** 180; (Worship)
  J: 180
Religion (Judaism) **R:** 219-220
Conservative Party [Canada]
See also Conservative Party of Canada;
  Progressive Conservative Party *in this index*
Diefenbaker, John George (Member of
  Parliament) **D:** 197
Progressive Conservative Party **P:** 812
Quebec (Politics) **Q:** 30
Tupper, Sir Charles **T:** 493
Conservative Party [Norway]
Norway (Politics) **N:** 539
Conservative Party [United Kingdom] **Ci:** 991
Cameron, David **C:** 84
Disraeli, Benjamin **D:** 237
Liberal Democrats **L:** 226
Peel, Sir Robert (Starts Conservative Party) **P:** 229
Tory Party **T:** 345
United Kingdom (Politics) **U:** 54; (Political
  confusion) **U:** 69
Conservative Party of Canada [political party]
Ci: 992
See also Conservative Party [Canada] *in this index*
Canada, Government of (Political parties) **C:** 136
Canada, History of (Recent developments) **C:** 152
Harper, Stephen Joseph **H:** 66
Political party (Leading parties) **P:** 636
Progressive Conservative Party **P:** 812
Conservator [archaeology]

Archaeology (Recording and preserving
  evidence) A: 597
Conservator [career]
  Museum (Exhibition and care of materials)
  M: 939 *with picture*
Conservatory [school]
  Music (Careers in music) M: 957
Consideration [law]
  Contract Ci: 1023
Considerations of Representative Government
  [book by Mill]
  Mill, John Stuart M: 552
Consiglio [government]
  Italy (Local government) I: 499
Consistory [religion]
  Presbyterians P: 756a
  Reformed Church in America R: 199
Consolation of Philosophy [book by Boethius]
  Boethius, Anicius Manlius Severinus B: 436
Console [electronics] *See* Video game console *in
this index*
Console piano [musical instrument]
  Piano (Upright pianos) P: 447
Consolidated Aircraft Corporation
  Aviation (Aviation progress) A: 988
Consolidated city [government]
  Metropolitan area (Metropolitan federation)
  M: 443
**Consolidated Omnibus Budget and
  Reconciliation Act** [1986]
  Insurance (Greater regulation) I: 316
Consolidated school [education] Ci: 992
  School (Public schools) S: 182
Consolidation [political science]
  Local government (Conflicts in authority) L: 408
Consonance [music]
  Music (Harmony) M: 951-952
Consonance [poetry]
  Poetry (Sounds) P: 594-595
Consonant [language] Ci: 992
Consort [title]
  Prince consort P: 781
  Queen Q: 39
Conspiracy [law] Ci: 992
  Coup d'état Ci: 1099
Conspiracy of Catiline [book by Sallust]
  History (The ancient Greeks and Romans)
  H: 261-262
Constable [office]
  Police P: 620
Constable, John [British painter] Ci: 992
  Painting (Romanticism) P: 68 *with picture*
Constance, Council of [1414-1418]
  Hus, John H: 457
  John XXIII [antipope] J: 132
  Pope (The troubles of the papacy) P: 664
  Roman Catholic Church (The Great Schism)
  R: 407
  Sigismund S: 453
Constance, Lake [Europe] *See* Lake Constance *in
this index*
Constance, Peace of [1183]
  Frederick I F: 497
Constance of Castile [wife of]
  John of Gaunt J: 134
Constancy [psychology]
  Perception (Principles of perception) P: 284
Constans [Roman emperor]
  Rome, Ancient (table) R: 447
Constant [mathematics]
  Algebra (Sets and variables) A: 350-351
  Series (Working with infinite series) S: 317
Constant, Benjamin [French author]
  Staël, Madame de So: 820
Constant dollars [economics]
  Gross domestic product (Real GDP) G: 399
Constant of proportionality [mathematics]
  Geometry (Similarity) G: 103
  Proportion P: 828
Constant proportions, Law of [chemistry]
  Chemistry (Dalton's atomic theory) C: 402
  Proust, Joseph Louis P: 838
Constant Reader [book by Parker]
  Parker, Dorothy P: 170
Constant-speed propeller [device]
  Airplane (Propellers) A: 217
  Propeller (Airplane propellers) P: 826
Constant-volume gas thermometer
  Liquid air (Properties) L: 346
Constantine [antipope]
  Pope (table) P: 666
Constantine [Algeria] Ci: 993
Constantine I [pope]
  Pope (table) P: 666
Constantine I [Roman emperor] *See* Constantine
  the Great *in this index*
Constantine I [king of Greece] Ci: 993

Greece (George I) G: 362-363
Constantine II [Roman emperor]
  Rome, Ancient (table) R: 447
Constantine II [king of Greece] Ci: 993
  Greece (The revolt of 1967) G: 364; (The
  restoration of democracy) G: 365
Constantine III [king of Scotland]
  Scotland (Beginning of the Scottish kingdom)
  S: 219
Constantine, Arch of [ruins]
  Constantine the Great Ci: 993
  Rome (Other remains) R: 433 *with picture*
Constantine, Basilica of
  Vatican City (History) V: 288-289
Constantine the Great [Roman emperor] Ci: 993
  Arius A: 669
  Byzantine Empire (Religion) B: 753 *with picture*;
  (Beginnings) B: 753
  Christianity (Constantine) C: 523 *with picture*
  Church C: 541
  Eastern Orthodox Churches (History) E: 45
  Flag *picture on* F: 216
  Istanbul (History) I: 491
  Jerusalem (Roman rule) J: 101
  Julian J: 186
  Nicene Councils N: 402
  Praetorian Guard P: 729
  Rome, Ancient (The decline of the empire)
  R: 447-448
  Saint Peter's Basilica (History) S: 53
  Sylvester I, Saint So: 1065
Constantinescu, Emil [Romanian political leader]
  Romania (Recent developments) R: 426
Constantinople [former city]
  See also Istanbul *in this index*
  Architecture (Byzantine architecture) A: 617 *with
  picture*
  Byzantine Empire (Way of life) B: 752;
  (Beginnings) B: 753
  Christianity (Constantine) C: 523-524
  Crusades (The First Crusade) Ci: 1160
  Greece (Ottoman rule) G: 361
  Library (Libraries of the Middle Ages and the
  Renaissance) L: 259
  Ottoman Empire O: 877
  World, History of the (The Byzantine Empire)
  W: 434
Constantinople, Battle of [1453]
  Byzantine Empire (The late Byzantine period)
  B: 754
  Ottoman Empire (Expansion and decline) O: 878
Constantinople, Council of [381]
  Trinity T: 447
Constantius I [West Roman emperor]
  Constantine the Great Ci: 993
  Diocletian D: 214
  Rome, Ancient (table) R: 447
Constantius II [Roman emperor]
  Julian J: 187
  Rome, Ancient (table) R: 447
Constellation [astronomy] Ci: 993 *with picture*
  Astrology (History) A: 827
  Astronomy (Observing the sky) A: 835 *with maps*;
  (Locating objects in space) A: 838
  Star (Names of stars) So: 842 *with picture*
  Zodiac (The zodiac in astrology) Z: 597
Constellation [ship] Ci: 994 *with picture*
  Baltimore (Other interesting places to visit) B: 69
  Navy, United States (Undeclared war with France)
  N: 88
Constellation, U.S.S. [aircraft carrier]
  Warship *picture on* W: 40
Constipation [disorder] Ci: 994
  Laxative L: 148
  Nutrition (Include fiber) N: 628
Constituency [district]
  House of Commons H: 384
  Parliament P: 172
  United Kingdom (National government) U: 49
  Voting (Voting districts) V: 449
Constituent [government]
  United States, Government of the (Functions)
  U: 138
Constitution [document] Ci: 994
  Bill of rights (The Constitution of the United
  States) B: 301
  Civil rights Ci: 607
  Democracy (Constitutional government) D: 121
  Government G: 282; (Constitutional framework)
  G: 283; (Constitutional government) G: 291
  Judicial review J: 183
  Law (Public law) L: 130-131
  State government (State constitutions) So: 863
  Term limits T: 170
Constitution [ship] Ci: 995 *with picture*
  Hull, Isaac H: 412
  Massachusetts (Places to visit) M: 280

Navy, United States *picture on* N: 90; (Undeclared
  war with France) N: 88
Constitution Act [1867] *See* British North America
  Act *in this index*
Constitution Act [1982]
  British North America Act B: 632
  Canada, Government of (The constitution) C: 129
  Canada, History of (Constitutional changes)
  C: 151 *with picture*
  Trudeau, Pierre Elliott (The national scene)
  T: 464-465
Constitution Day [Japan]
  Holiday (In other countries) H: 291
Constitution Day and Citizenship Day [U.S.]
  Ci: 995
Constitution Gardens National Parkway
  [Washington, D.C.]
  National Park System (table: National parkways
  and other national parklands) N: 56
Constitution of 1795 [French history]
  French Revolution (The revolution ends) F: 527
Constitution of 1917 [Mexican history]
  Carranza, Venustiano C: 247
  Mexican Revolution of 1910 (Reforms) M: 445
  Mexico (The Constitution of 1917) M: 472
Constitution of Canada
  Bloc Québécois B: 404
  Campbell, Kim (The 1993 election) C: 90d
  Canada, Government of (The constitution) C: 129
  Canada, History of (Constitutional changes)
  C: 151
  Mulroney, Brian (Prime minister) M: 917
  Quebec (The late 1900's) Q: 32
  Trudeau, Pierre Elliott (Later years) T: 465
Constitution of Divine Revelation
  Vatican Council II (The work of the council) V: 289
Constitution of France
  French Revolution (The National Assembly)
  F: 525
Constitution of Pakistan
  Musharraf, Pervez M: 941
Constitution of South Africa
  South Africa (The dismantling of apartheid)
  So: 620; (Recent developments) So: 621
Constitution of South Korea
  Korea, South (A new constitution) K: 378c
Constitution of the Confederacy [document]
  Confederate States of America (Government)
  Ci: 931
Constitution of the United States [document]
  Ci: 996 *with pictures*
  See also the list of Related articles in the
  Constitution of the United States *article*
  Amendment A: 406
  American literature (The revolutionary period
  [1765-1787]) A: 415
  Census (Kinds of censuses) C: 346-347
  Checks and balances C: 391
  Citizenship (The Constitution) Ci: 571
  Civil rights (Civil rights in the United States)
  Ci: 608
  Democracy (Controls on power) D: 121;
  (American democracy) D: 123
  Election (Elections in the United States) E: 158
  Fletcher v. Peck F: 234
  Freedom (During the Enlightenment) F: 503
  Government (Constitutional framework) G: 283
  Impeachment (Procedure) I: 90
  Interstate commerce I: 350h
  Judicial review J: 184
  Law (Beginnings of U.S. law) L: 136
  Marshall, John (Chief justice) M: 230
  Massachusetts (The Revolutionary War)
  M: 291-292
  Money (Money in the new United States) M: 712
  National Archives and Records Administration
  N: 29
  Pinckney, Charles P: 467
  President of the United States (The founding of
  the presidency) P: 767
  State government (Relations with other
  governments) So: 865
  Territory (Territories in the United States) T: 174
  Treason T: 406
  Trial (The criminal defendant's rights) T: 436
  United States, Government of the (Principles of
  American government) U: 136; (Growth of the
  federal government) U: 145
  United States, History of the (Forming a
  new nation [1784-1819]) U: 160-161 *with
  picture*; (The Louisiana Purchase) U: 164;
  (Reconstruction) U: 178-179
  World, History of the (The rise of democracy and
  nationalism) W: 443
Constitution on the Liturgy
  Vatican Council II (The work of the council) V: 289
Constitution Plaza [Mexico City]

Mexico City (Downtown) **M: 476**
Constitution Square [Greece]
Athens (Landmarks) **A: 854** *with map*
Constitution State [name for]
Connecticut **Ci: 953**
Constitutional Act [1791]
Canada, History of (The United Empire Loyalists)
C: 142 *with map*
Constitutional convention [government]
Political convention (Other types of conventions)
P: 630
Constitutional Convention [U.S. history]
Congress of the United States (The founding of
Congress) **Ci: 947**
Constitution of the United States (The
Constitutional Convention) **Ci: 999**
Electoral College (History) **E: 164**
Franklin, Benjamin (The twilight years) **F: 491**
with picture
Madison, James (Constitutional Convention)
M: 33
United States, Government of the (Growth of the
federal government) **U: 145**
United States, History of the (Writing the
Constitution) **U: 161** *with picture*
Washington, George (Constitutional Convention)
W: 100 *with picture*
Constitutional Court
Russia (Courts) **R: 532**
South Africa (National government) **So: 608**
Constitutional law
Law (Public law) **L: 130-131**; (Beginnings of U.S.
law) **L: 136**
Constitutional monarchy [government]
French Revolution (The National Assembly)
F: 525
Government (Monarchy) **G: 286**
Monarchy **M: 700**
Puritans (Puritan influence) **P: 910**
Constitutional referendum [government]
Initiative and referendum (The referendum)
I: 272
Constitutional Reform Act [2005]
House of Lords **H: 385**
Constitutional Union Party [U.S. history] **Ci: 1016**
Civil War, American (Developments in the
political party system) **Ci: 616**
Lincoln, Abraham (Election of 1860) **L: 318**
Constitutionalism
Political science (Constitutionalism) **P: 639**
Constitutionality [law]
Supreme Court of the United States (Authority of
the Supreme Court) **So: 998**
Constitutive Act of the African Union [2000]
African Union **A: 137**
Constraint-induced movement therapy
Stroke (Rehabilitation) **So: 930**
Constrictor snake
Boa constrictor **B: 427**
Python **P: 922**
Snake (Feeding habits) **S: 530**
Construction [art]
Nevelson, Louise *picture on* **N: 178**
Sculpture (Assemblages) **S: 257** *with picture*
Construction [geometry]
Geometry (Some basic geometric constructions)
G: 103 *with diagrams*
Construction, Building *See* Building construction
in this index
Construction equipment
Dredging **D: 345**
Construction industry
Building trade **B: 685**
United States *picture on* **U: 131**
Construction survey
Survey (Other surveys) **So: 1011**
Constructional hill [geography]
Hill **H: 230**
Constructive interference [physics]
Diffraction (How diffraction occurs) **D: 201**
Interference **I: 324** *with diagram*
Light (Interference) **L: 288** *with diagram*
Sound (Beats) **So: 604** *with diagram*
Waves (Interference) **W: 153**
Constructive speech
Debate (Framework of a round) **D: 64**
Constructivism [art]
Abstract art **A: 18**
Gabo, Naum **G: 2**
Minimalism **M: 573**
Pevsner, Antoine **P: 351** *with picture*
Russia (Painting and sculpture) **R: 537**
Constructivist theory [psychology]
Developmental psychology (Constructivist
theory) **D: 174**
Emotion (The constructivist approach) **E: 261**
Consul [ancient Rome]

Consul **Ci: 1017**
Rome, Ancient (The Roman Republic) **R: 438**
Consul [government official] **Ci: 1017**
Diplomacy (Diplomatic representatives) **D: 216**
Foreign Service (Foreign Service careers) **F: 388**
International relations (Diplomacy) **I: 344**
Consul, The [opera by Menotti]
Menotti, Gian Carlo **M: 402**
Consulate [French history]
Napoleon I (First consul of France) **N: 15**
Consultative Council on Postal Studies
Postal Union, Universal **P: 708**
Consulting firm
Industrial design (How an industrial designer
works) **I: 244**
Consulting meteorologist
Weather (Careers in weather) **W: 170**
Consumer advocate
Consumer protection **Ci: 1017**
Consumer confidence measure [economics]
Economic indicator **E: 57**
Consumer cooperative [economics]
Cooperative (Supply, or purchasing,
cooperatives) **Ci: 1036**
Consumer credit [economics]
Credit (Types of credit) **Ci: 1124**
Consumer Credit Protection Act *See* Truth in
Lending Act *in this index*
Consumer Federation of America **Ci: 1017**
Consumer Financial Protection Bureau [U.S.]
Bank (Regulation of U.S. banks) **B: 92**
Mortgage **M: 821**
Consumer goods
Family and consumer sciences (Areas of study)
F: 25
Gross domestic product (Measuring GDP) **G: 399**
Industry (By the way goods are produced) **I: 277**
Manufacturing (Kinds of manufacturing) **M: 169**
Consumer magazine
Magazine (Consumer magazines) **M: 42**
Consumer movement *See* Consumerism *in this
index*
Consumer Price Index [economics] **Ci: 1017**
Cost of living **Ci: 1079** *with diagram*
Inflation (Measuring inflation) **I: 267**
Labor movement (Arranging contracts) **L: 4-5**
Consumer Product Safety Act [1972]
Consumer protection (The right to safety)
Ci: 1018
Consumer Product Safety Commission [U.S.]
Ci: 1017
Consumer protection (The right to safety)
Ci: 1018
Packaging (Packaging regulations) **P: 18**
Consumer protection [economics] **Ci: 1017**
Better Business Bureau **B: 275**
Class action **Ci: 642**
Consumer Federation of America **Ci: 1017**
Consumption **Ci: 1020**
Crime (White-collar crime) **Ci: 1136-1137**
Family and consumer sciences (Areas of study)
F: 25
Guaranty **G: 411**
Marketing **M: 214**
Nader, Ralph **N: 2**
National Consumers League **N: 32**
Price (What prices do) **P: 775**
Consumer Reports [publication]
Consumers Union **Ci: 1020**
Consumerism [movement]
See also Consumer protection *in this index*
Consumer protection **Ci: 1017**
Consumers League, National *See* National
Consumers League *in this index*
Consumers' Research, Inc. [organization]
Consumer protection (Beginnings of modern
consumerism) **Ci: 1019**
Consumers Union [organization] **Ci: 1020**
Consumer protection (The right to information)
Ci: 1018; (Beginnings of modern consumerism)
Ci: 1019
Consumption [disease] *See* Tuberculosis *in this
index*
Consumption [economics] **Ci: 1020**
Gross domestic product (Measuring GDP) **G: 399**
Inflation (Effects on consumer behavior) **I: 268**
Production **P: 810**
Standard of living (Other kinds of measures)
So: 834
Contact [cryptology]
Codes and ciphers (Communications
intelligence) **Ci: 750-751**
Contact [device]
Burglar alarm **B: 704**
Contact [filmmaking]
Motion picture (Shooting the movie) **M: 852-853**
Contact copying

Copying machine (Contact copying) **Ci: 1045**
Contact dermatitis [disease]
Eczema **E: 74**
Contact fuse [device]
Bomb (How bombs work) **B: 450**
Contact lens **Ci: 1020** *with pictures*
Eye (Defects of the eye) **E: 464**
Contact metamorphism [geology]
Metamorphic rock **M: 428**
Rock (Metamorphic rock) **R: 373**
Contact method [industrial process]
Sulfuric acid (How sulfuric acid is made) **So: 968**
Contact mine [device]
Mine warfare (Kinds of naval mines) **M: 565**
Contact poison
Insecticide **I: 301**
Contagious disease *See* Infectious disease *in this
index*
Contagious magic
Magic (Kinds of magic) **M: 49**
Contagiousness of Puerperal Fever, The [book by
Holmes]
Holmes, Oliver Wendell (His life) **H: 294**
Container
Bottle **B: 513**
Glass *picture on* **G: 211**; (Soda-lime glass) **G: 213**
Gutta-percha **G: 445**
Packaging **P: 18**
Tin can **T: 294**
Container car
Railroad *pictures on* **R: 105**; (Freight service)
R: 106
Container garden
Gardening (Container gardens) **G: 31**
Container ship
Containerization **Ci: 1021**
Saint Lawrence Seaway (The seaway today) **S: 45**
Ship **S: 402** *with picture*; (Kinds of ships) **S: 406-
407** *with pictures*
Containerization [transportation] **Ci: 1021** *with
picture*
Ship (Kinds of ships) **T: 406-408**
Transportation (Freight transportation) **T: 395**
Containment building
Nuclear energy (Power plant design) **N: 584**
Containment policy [international relations]
Cold War (The containment policy) **Ci: 764**
Europe (The Cold War) **E: 415**
Contamination *See* Environmental pollution *in
this index*
Conte [poem]
French literature (Narrative poetry) **F: 518-519**
Conté, Lansana [Guinean political leader]
Guinea (History) **G: 432**
Conte, Nicolas Jacques [French inventor]
Pencil (History) **P: 236**
Conte Di Savoia [ship]
Gyroscope (Mechanical gyroscopes) **G: 453-454**
Contemplation [religion]
Meditation **M: 380**
Contemplations, The [poems by Hugo]
Hugo, Victor (Exile and return) **H: 410**; (His works)
H: 410
Contemplative religious order [group]
Carthusians **C: 261**
Contemporary interior
Interior design (Style) **I: 327**
Contempt [law] **Ci: 1021**
Impeachment (History) **I: 91**
Trial (Presenting evidence) **T: 436**
Contender [boxing]
Boxing (Boxing in the United States) **B: 530**
Content [publishing]
Publishing (Preparing content for publication)
P: 866
Content word
English language (Grammar) **E: 312**
Contes [book by La Fontaine]
La Fontaine, Jean de **L: 29**
Context clue
Reading (Comprehending what is perceived)
R: 157
Contextual ad
Internet (Advertising) **I: 350b**
Contiguity, Law of [psychology]
Association **A: 819**
Continent **Ci: 1021**
Cretaceous Period **P: 1127**
Earth (The lithosphere) **E: 20**; (The shaping of the
continents) **E: 24**
Pangaea **P: 130**
Plate tectonics **P: 561** *with pictures and maps,
map on* **P: 564**
Races, Human (The geographical-race theory)
R: 54-55 *with map*
World *maps on* **W: 408, W: 413**; (Land) **W: 418**
Continental Army [U.S. history]

Army, United States (History) A: 737
Camden, Battle of C: 76
Revolution, American (The beginning of the war) R: 274; (The Continental Army) R: 275; (The fighting forces) R: 278-279; (Valley Forge) R: 283 *with picture*
Trumbull, Jonathan T: 473
Continental Association [U.S. history] Ci: 1021
Continental Board of War and Ordnance [U.S. history]
Adams, John (National politics) A: 36
Continental Colors [flag]
United States flag (The first American flags) U: 200
Continental Congress [U.S. history] Ci: 1021 *with picture*
Adams, John (National politics) A: 36
Adams, Samuel (The patriot) A: 44
Continental Association Ci: 1021
Declaration of Independence *picture on* D: 77; (The Continental Congress) D: 74
Money (Continental currency) M: 711
Pennsylvania (The Revolutionary War) P: 265
Randolph, Peyton R: 137
Revolution, American R: 270
United States capitals U: 198
United States flag U: 200
First Continental Congress
Continental Congress (The First Continental Congress) Ci: 1021-1022
Galloway, Joseph G: 16
Philadelphia (The Revolutionary War period) P: 366
Revolution, American (The First Continental Congress) R: 274
United States, History of the (The First Continental Congress) U: 159
Washington, George (First Continental Congress) W: 97
Second Continental Congress
Continental Congress (Second Continental Congress) Ci: 1022
Articles of Confederation A: 759
Congress of the Confederation Ci: 941
Franklin, Benjamin (The statesman) F: 490
Madison, James (Entry into politics) M: 33
Revolution, American (The Continental Army) R: 275; (The Declaration of Independence) R: 278
United States, History of the (The Revolutionary War begins) U: 159 *with picture*; (The Declaration of Independence) U: 160
Washington, George (Elected commander in chief) W: 97
Continental currency [money]
Dollar (The United States dollar) D: 295
Money *picture on* M: 708; (Continental currency) M: 711
Revolution, American (Financing the war) R: 280
Continental divide [geography] Ci: 1022
River (Divides) R: 353
Continental Divide [North America] *See* Great Divide *in this index*
Continental drift [geology]
Climate (Continental drift) Ci: 678
Earth (The shaping of the continents) E: 24
Fossil (Recording Earth's changes) F: 424
Indian Ocean (Ocean floor) I: 186-187
Mantle M: 168
Ocean (How the sea floor was formed) O: 662
Pangaea P: 130
Plate tectonics (Structure of tectonic plates) P: 561; (History of tectonic theory) P: 564 *with diagrams*
Prehistoric animal (The distribution of mammals) P: 741
Continental grip [tennis]
Tennis *picture on* T: 164
Continental island
Island *diagram on* I: 471; (Kinds of islands) I: 472
Continental margin [geology]
Atlantic Ocean (The Atlantic seafloor) A: 864
Ocean (The continental margin) O: 661
Continental Navy [U.S. history]
Flag *picture on* F: 209
Revolution, American (Maritime forces) R: 280
Continental rise [geology]
Atlantic Ocean (The continental margin) A: 864
Ocean (The continental rise) O: 662
Continental shelf [geology]
Arctic Ocean (The ocean floor) A: 643
Atlantic Ocean (The continental margin) A: 864
Earth (The lithosphere) E: 20
Fishing industry (Ocean fisheries) F: 181
Indian Ocean (Ocean floor) I: 186
Island *diagram on* I: 471

Ocean (The continental shelf) O: 661
Pacific Ocean (The ocean floor) P: 14
Continental slope [oceanography]
Atlantic Ocean (The continental margin) A: 864
Ocean (The continental slope) O: 662
Continental System [French history] Ci: 1022
Milan Decree M: 541
Napoleonic Wars (The Peninsular War) N: 18
Continentality [meteorology]
Europe (Climate) E: 395-397
Contingent truth [philosophy]
Metaphysics (Possibility and necessity) M: 430
Contino, Antonio [Italian architect]
Bridge of Sighs B: 606
Continuation War [1941-1944]
Finland (World War II) F: 117-118
Russo-Finnish wars (The Continuation War) R: 566a
Continuing education *See* Adult education *in this index*
Continuo [music] *See* Basso continuo *in this index*
Continuous casting [industrial process]
Iron and steel (Shaping and finishing steel) I: 445
Continuous freezer [machine]
Ice cream (How ice cream is made) I: 8-9
Continuous furnace
Furnace (Heating the charge) F: 567
Continuous mining machine
Coal (Continuous mining) C: 724 *with pictures*
Mining *picture on* M: 577
Continuous permafrost [geology]
Permafrost P: 289 *with map*
Continuous progress plan [education]
Education (Elementary education) E: 91
Continuous spectrum [light]
Light (The spectrum of light sources) L: 284
Continuous tank [furnace]
Glass (Melting) G: 215
Continuous tone copy [printing]
Printing (Preparing illustrations for reproduction) P: 797
Continuous-wave laser [device]
Laser (Kinds of lasers) L: 85
Continuous-wave radar [device]
Radar (Continuous-wave radar) R: 69
Continuously variable transmission [device]
Transmission (How a continuously variable transmission works) T: 378
Continuum mechanics [science]
Mechanics M: 354
Contour feather
Bird (Feathers) B: 362
Feather (Kinds and parts of feathers) F: 59
Contour map
Map (Thematic maps) M: 178
Photogrammetry *picture on* P: 405
Contour mining
Coal (Strip mining) Ci: 722
Mining (Area mining) M: 575
Contour plowing
Agronomy A: 162
Conservation (Soil conservation) Ci: 979-980 *with picture*
Dryland farming D: 370
Erosion (Controlling erosion) E: 355
Contour sawing
Machine tool (Sawing) M: 18
Contra bassoon [musical instrument]
Bassoon B: 158
Music (Wind instruments) M: 949
Contraband [commerce] Ci: 1023
High seas H: 229
Right of search R: 340
Contrabass [musical instrument] *See* Bass *in this index*
Contraception *See* Birth control *in this index*
Contraceptive [device]
Birth control (Methods of birth control) B: 378
Contraceptive implant
Birth control (Methods of birth control) B: 378-379
Contract [law] Ci: 1023
Incompetence I: 105
Labor movement (Arranging contracts) L: 4
Law (Private law) L: 130; (Beginnings of U.S. law) L: 136; (Law since 1900) L: 136
Lease L: 166
Minor M: 608
Publishing (Contracts and advances) P: 866
Teaching (Employment practices) T: 68
Tort T: 344
Treaty T: 408
Contract, Freedom of
Law (Law since 1900) L: 136; (Beginnings of U.S. law) L: 136
Contract, Liberty of [law]
Labor movement (The early 1900's) L: 11

Contract bridge [game]
Bridge B: 604
Contract builder [construction]
Housing (Private housing) H: 390
Contract carrier [transportation]
Truck (Industrial uses) T: 456
Contract farming
Agriculture (Industrialized agriculture) A: 150
Farm and farming (Marketing farm products) F: 42
Contract laborer
Asian Americans (The second wave) A: 812e
Western frontier life in America (Newcomers) W: 234
Contract market [economics] *See* Futures contract *in this index*
Contract performance bond
Insurance (Surety bonds) I: 314
Contract policing
Royal Canadian Mounted Police (Duties) R: 495-496
Contract with America [document]
Gingrich, Newt G: 191
Contract with God, A [book by Eisner]
Eisner, Will E: 155
Graphic novel G: 323
Contract with the American Family [social program]
Christian Coalition of America C: 522e
Contractile vacuole [biology]
Ameba A: 406
Paramecium P: 152
Contracting
Building trade (The contracting system) B: 685
Contraction [economics]
See also Recession *in this index*
Business cycle B: 728
Depression D: 150
Economics (Economic growth) E: 62
Contraction [physics]
Heat (Changes in size) H: 152
Contractionary monetary policy
Money (Monetary policy) M: 717
Contractual forfeiture [law]
Forfeiture F: 408
Contrail Ci: 1023 *with picture*
Contralto [music]
Opera (The singers) O: 792
Singing (Voice classification) S: 472
Contras [political group]
Honduras (Recent developments) H: 313
Iran-contra affair I: 406b
Latin America (Return to civilian government) L: 111
Nicaragua (The late 1900's) N: 400-401
Ortega, Daniel O: 859
Contrast [arts]
Classical music (Classical music forms) Ci: 644
Design (Contrast) D: 157
Contrast [photography]
Motion picture (Preparing to shoot) M: 852 *with picture*
Contrast, Law of [psychology]
Association A: 819
Contrast agent [medicine]
Computed tomography Ci: 907
Radiology R: 99
Contre Sainte-Beuve [book by Proust]
Proust, Marcel P: 839
Contreras, Battle of [1847]
Mexican War (Scott's campaign) M: 446-447
Contributor [publishing]
Encyclopedia (Selecting a contributor) E: 267 *with picture*
Contributory negligence [law]
Negligence N: 119
Control board [device]
Radio (Radio stations) R: 86; (From electric waves to radio waves) R: 86
Control center
Satellite, Artificial (Performing the mission) S: 150g
Control channel [electronics]
Telephone (Cellular phone calls) T: 97
Control circuit
Electronics (Digital circuits) E: 213-214
Control column
Helicopter (Piloting a helicopter) H: 171
Control Data Corporation
Computer (Miniaturization) Ci: 924c
Control group [science]
Placebo P: 505
Psychology (Experimentation) P: 849
Control-line model
Airplane, Model (Control-line models) A: 241 *with picture*
Control mode [aviation]

Automatic flight control system (How an AFCS works) **A:** 944
Control rod [nuclear energy]
Gadolinium **G:** 4
Nuclear energy (Power reactors) **N:** 584 *with diagrams*; (Chain reactions) **N:** 586 *with picture*
Control room
Radio (Radio stations) **R:** 86
Television (Live telecasts) **T:** 112 *with picture*
Control sample [criminology]
Crime scene investigation (Collecting evidence) **Ci:** 1140-1141
Control stick
Airplane (The controls and instruments) **A:** 217
Control system
Automobile (Controlling the car) **A:** 949
Guided missile (Guidance and control systems) **G:** 424
Control tower
Airport *picture on* **A:** 243; (The control tower) **A:** 245; (Air traffic control) **A:** 246
Control unit [electronics]
Computer (Microprocessors) **Ci:** 912
Controllable-pitch propeller
Airplane (Propellers) **A:** 217; (Engineering improvements) **A:** 237
Controlled access
Road (Primary highways) **R:** 358
Controlled-atmosphere storage
Food preservation (Other methods) **F:** 344
Controlled cross [agriculture]
Corn (Hybrid corn) **Ci:** 1059
Controlled environment agriculture
Greenhouse **G:** 382
Controlled experiment
Sociology (Methods of sociological research) **So:** 565
Statistics (Collecting the data) **So:** 868
Controlled mine [warfare]
Mine warfare (Land mines) **M:** 564
Controlled substance
Forensic science (What a forensic scientist analyzes) **F:** 389
Opiate **O:** 810
Controller [device]
Automation (How automation works) **A:** 945 *with diagram*
Computer (A controller) **Ci:** 915
Electronic game (Gameplay) **E:** 204a, *picture on* **E:** 204f; (Gameplay) **E:** 204b-204c
Transmission (The controller) **T:** 377 *with diagram*
Contusion [injury] *See* Bruise *in this index*
Conundrum
Riddle **R:** 335
Conure [bird]
Parrot (Kinds of parrots) **P:** 179
Conus arteriosus [anatomy]
Heart (Fish) **H:** 146
Convair XFY-1 [aircraft]
Airplane *picture on* **A:** 236
V/STOL **V:** 453
Convection [physics]
Cloud (How clouds form) **Ci:** 708-711 *with pictures*
Heat (How heat travels) **H:** 151 *with diagram*
Heating (Steam and hot-water heating systems) **H:** 159
Insulation (Insulation to control heat flow) **I:** 306
Radiator **R:** 82
Convection current
Air turbulence **A:** 200
Heat (Convection) **H:** 151
Jupiter (Zones and belts) **J:** 199
Plate tectonics (Causes of plate movement) **P:** 564
Convection oven
Range (Electric ranges) **R:** 137-138
Convection zone
Sun (Zones of the sun) **So:** 979-980 *with diagram*
Convective cloud
Rain (Characteristics of rain) **R:** 122-123
Convective heating
Air turbulence **A:** 200
Convective rise [geology]
Volcano (The violence of an eruption) **V:** 439
Convector [device]
Heating (Steam and hot-water heating systems) **H:** 159 *with diagrams*
Convenience, Flag of
Ship (Flags and registration) **S:** 412
Convenience food
Food (Sources of food) **F:** 329
Convent [religion] **Ci:** 1024
Monasticism **M:** 701
Nun **N:** 608
Women's movement (During the Middle Ages) **W:** 384

Convention [international relations]
Treaty **T:** 408
Convention [politics] *See* Political convention *in this index*
Convention for the Protection of the Mediterranean Sea Against Pollution [1976]
Mediterranean Sea (History of the Mediterranean) **M:** 382
Convention of London [1818]
Lake of the Woods **L:** 43
Convention on Cybercrime [2001]
Copyright (International agreements) **Ci:** 1048
Convention on International Trade in Endangered Species of Wild Fauna and Flora [international agreement]
Bird (Protective laws and treaties) **B:** 368
Elephant (Protecting elephants) **E:** 231-232
Endangered species (Protecting endangered species) **E:** 270
Ivory (Ivory today) **I:** 521
Poaching **P:** 588
Convention on the Conservation of Migratory Species of Wild Animals [agreement]
Bird (Protective laws and treaties) **B:** 368
Convention on the Law of the Sea [1982] *See* Law of the Sea Convention *in this index*
Convention on the Prohibition of the Development, Production, Stockpiling and Use of Chemical Weapons and on their Destruction [1997] *See* Chemical Weapons Convention *in this index*
Convention on the Prohibition of the Development, Production and Stockpiling of Bacteriological (Biological) and Toxin Weapons and on their Destruction [1972] *See* Biological Weapons Convention *in this index*
Convention on the Rights of the Child [1989]
United Nations (Aid to children) **U:** 88
Convention on Wetlands of International Importance [agreement] *See* Ramsar Convention *in this index*
Convention People's Party [political party]
Ghana (History) **G:** 179-180
Conventional aircraft
Navy (Aircraft carriers) **N:** 78
Conventional Armed Forces in Europe, Treaty of [1990]
Arms control (Arms control in the late 1900's and early 2000's) **A:** 722
Bush, George Herbert Walker (International affairs) **B:** 721-722
Conventional circuit [device]
Electronics (Types of electronic circuits) **E:** 209-210
Conventional mining
Coal (The room-and-pillar system) **Ci:** 723-724 *with pictures*
Conventuals [religion]
Franciscans **F:** 482
Convergence [mathematics]
Series (Working with infinite series) **S:** 317
Convergence [optics]
Lens (Convergence) **L:** 196a
Convergence zone [aviation]
Glider (Soaring) **G:** 229-230
Convergent boundary [geology]
Earthquake (Interplate quakes) **E:** 38
Plate tectonics (Plate interactions) **P:** 561
Convergent evolution [biology]
Ichthyosaur **I:** 24
Jerboa **J:** 92
Converging lens [optics] *See* Convex lens *in this index*
Conversation at Midnight [book by Millay]
Millay, Edna St. Vincent **M:** 552
Conversation in the Cathedral [book by Vargas Llosa]
Vargas Llosa, Mario **V:** 285
Conversation piece [art]
Gainsborough, Thomas **G:** 6
Converse, Julius [American political leader]
Vermont (table) **V:** 333
Conversion [industrial process]
Coal (Coal research) **Ci:** 730-731
Energy (Energy conversion) **E:** 274
Petroleum (Conversion) **P:** 344
Conversion [sports]
Rugby football (Rugby Union) **R:** 510; (Rugby League) **R:** 512
Conversion factor
Weights and measures (Conversion factors) **W:** 184
Conversion of Saint Paul [painting by Caravaggio]
Painting (Baroque) **P:** 58 *with picture*
Conversion of Saint Paul, The [painting by Michelangelo]
New Testament *picture on* **N:** 287

Conversion plant [industry]
Uranium (Refining and processing uranium ore) **U:** 215
Converter [device]
Radio (The tuner) **R:** 88-89 *with picture*
Convertibility [economics] **Ci:** 1024
Convex lens [optics]
Aberration (Point aberration) **A:** 10 *with diagram*
Eye (Farsightedness) **E:** 464 *with picture*
Glasses (Prescription glasses) **G:** 224-225
Lens (A positive lens) **L:** 196 *with diagrams*
Convex mirror [optics]
Mirror (Convex mirrors) **M:** 616 *with diagram*
Convex polygon [geometry]
Polygon **P:** 650 *with diagram*
Convex polyhedron [geometry]
Polyhedron **P:** 651
Conveyor belt [industry] **Ci:** 1024 *with pictures*
Assembly line **A:** 818
Coal (The room-and-pillar system) **Ci:** 723 *with diagram*
Convicts in Australia [Australian history]
Australia (History) **A:** 919-920
Convivio, Il [poems by Dante]
Dante Alighieri (His works) **D:** 34
Convoluted tubule [anatomy]
Kidney (How the kidneys produce urine) **K:** 311-312 *with diagram*
Convoy [warfare]
World War I (Mobilization) **W:** 462-463
World War II (The Battle of the Atlantic) **W:** 478
Convoy of Tears [Vietnamese history]
Vietnam War (The end of the war) **V:** 376
Convulsions [disorder] **Ci:** 1025
Anticonvulsant **A:** 553
First aid (Convulsion and epileptic seizure) **F:** 140
Conway, Elias Nelson [American political leader]
Arkansas (table) **A:** 712
Conway, Jack [American author]
Slang (Sources of slang) **S:** 500
Conway, James Sevier [American political leader]
Arkansas (table) **A:** 712
Conway, Moncure Daniel [American abolitionist]
Abolition movement **A:** 12
Conway, Thomas [American general]
Cabal **C:** 2
Washington, George (The army) **W:** 99
Conway cabal [U.S. history]
Cabal **C:** 2
Washington, George (The army) **W:** 99
Cony [animal]
See also Hyrax *in this index*
Pika **P:** 461 *with picture*
Cony, Samuel [American political leader]
Maine (table) **M:** 87
Conyers, John James, Jr. [American political leader]
Spingarn Medal (table: 2007) **So:** 794
Coochs Bridge, Battle of [1777]
Delaware (The American Revolution) **D:** 110
Coode, John [American colonial leader]
Maryland (Colonial days) **M:** 256-258
Cook, Frederick Albert [American explorer] **Ci:** 1025
Arctic (Race to the pole) **A:** 639
Exploration (The North Pole) **E:** 450
Mount McKinley **M:** 886
Peary, Robert Edwin (Arctic expeditions) **P:** 224; (Dispute with Cook) **P:** 224
Cook, George Cram [husband of]
Glaspell, Susan **G:** 210
Cook, James [British explorer] **Ci:** 1025 *with pictures and map*
Antarctica *map on* **A:** 538; (Early exploration) **A:** 536
Arctic (Search for the Northwest Passage) **A:** 638-639
Australia (Captain Cook) **A:** 920 *with map*
Botany Bay **B:** 510
British Columbia (European contact) **B:** 628 *with picture*
Cook Islands **Ci:** 1026
Exploration *map on* **E:** 451; (Exploring the Pacific) **E:** 447-448 *with map*
Hawaii **H:** 89; (European exploration) **H:** 106
Navigation (Explorers) **N:** 74
New Zealand (Early European contact) **N:** 354
Oregon (Exploration and settlement) **O:** 846
Pacific Islands (European explorers) **P:** 12
Pacific Ocean **P:** 14
Cook, John [American political leader]
Delaware (table) **D:** 109
Cook, John K. [American surveyor]
Sioux City **S:** 474
Cook, Sir Joseph [Australian statesman]
Australia (table) **A:** 923
Cook, Mount *See* Aoraki/Mount Cook *in this index*

Cook County [county, Illinois]
Chicago (Metropolitan area) **C: 425**
Cook Inlet
Alaska (Coastline) **A: 294**
Cook Islands [Pacific] **Ci: 1026**
New Zealand (Overseas territories) **N: 348**
Pacific Islands (Pacific alliances and independence movements) **P: 12**
Cookbook
Connecticut (Interesting facts) **Ci: 953**
Cooke, Hope [wife of Namgyal]
Sikkim (History) **S: 456**
Cooke, Jay [American financier] **Ci: 1026**
Philadelphia (Industrial beginnings) **P: 366-367**
Cooke, Lorrin A. [American political leader]
Connecticut (table) **C: 967**
Cooke, Nicholas [American political leader]
Rhode Island (table) **R: 311**
Cooke, Sam [American singer] **Ci: 1027**
Rock music (Soul music) **R: 380a**
Cooke, Terence James [American religious leader] **Ci: 1027**
Cooke, William [British physicist]
Telegraph (Development of the telegraph) **T: 90**
Wheatstone, Sir Charles **W: 278**
Cookie [computing]
Computer (The World Wide Web) **Ci: 921**
Internet (Glossary of Internet terms) **I: 350a**; (Advertising) **I: 350b**
Web browser **W: 175**
Cookie [food]
Baking picture on **B: 33**
Girl Scouts (Annual events) **G: 198**
Cooking Ci: 1027 with pictures
See also the list of Related articles in the Cooking article
Colonial life in America (Food and drink) **Ci: 802**
Gas [fuel] (In the home) **G: 51**
Herb **H: 196**
Meat (How meat is cooked) **M: 350**
Microwave oven **M: 520**
Pressure **P: 773**
Starch (Use in foods) **So: 855**
Cooktop [device]
Range **R: 137** with pictures
Cool jazz
Davis, Miles **D: 49**
Getz, Stan **G: 177**
Jazz (Cool jazz) **J: 72**
Coolant [chemical]
Automobile (The cooling system) **A: 953**
Nuclear energy (Power reactors) **N: 584-585** with picture
Cooley, Denton A. [American doctor]
Artificial heart **A: 759**
Cooley's anemia [disease]
Thalassemia **T: 228**
Coolidge, Abigail [sister of]
Coolidge, Calvin (Childhood) **Ci: 1030**
Coolidge, Calvin [U.S. president] **Ci: 1030** with pictures
Harding, Warren Gamaliel (table) **H: 58**
Hoover, Herbert Clark (Secretary of commerce) **H: 328-329**
Massachusetts (table) **M: 288**; (The early 1900's) **M: 293**
Roaring Twenties (Rising prosperity) **R: 363**
Vermont (Places to visit) **V: 326**
Vice president of the United States (Social duties) **V: 352**; (Growth of the vice presidency) **V: 353**
Coolidge, Calvin, Jr. [son of]
Coolidge, Calvin (Entry into politics) **Ci: 1031**; (Life in the White House) **Ci: 1033**
Coolidge, Carlos [American political leader]
Vermont (table) **V: 333**
Coolidge, Grace Goodhue [wife of Calvin Coolidge]
Coolidge, Calvin picture on **Ci: 1032**; (Entry into politics) **Ci: 1031**; (Later years) **Ci: 1033-1034**
First ladies of the United States (table) **F: 142**
Coolidge, John [son of]
Coolidge, Calvin (Entry into politics) **Ci: 1031**
Coolidge, John Calvin [father of]
Coolidge, Calvin (Childhood) **Ci: 1030**
Coolidge, Victoria Josephine Moor [mother of]
Coolidge, Calvin (Childhood) **Ci: 1030**
Cooling-off period [labor relations]
National Mediation Board **N: 40**
Cooling system
Air conditioning **A: 176**
Automobile diagram on **A: 948**; (The cooling system) **A: 953**
Thermostat (Uses) **T: 256**
Cooling tower
Electric power (Fossil-fueled steam electric power plants) **E: 183** with diagram
Nuclear energy (Steam production) **N: 587**

Cooling vent
Balloon (Operation of hot-air balloon) **B: 60**
Coomes, Jane [American educator]
Kentucky (Schools) **K: 276**
Coon [animal] See Raccoon in this index
Coon cat
Cat picture on **C: 289**; (Long-haired breeds) **C: 292**
Cooney, Barbara [American artist]
Literature for children picture on **L: 379**
Cooney, Frank H. [American political leader]
Montana (table) **M: 757**
Coonhound [dog]
Black and tan coonhound **B: 385**
Dog picture on **D: 271**
Coonskin Library [U.S. history]
Ohio (Libraries) **O: 685**
Co-op See Cooperative in this index
Co-op City
New York City (The Bronx) **N: 328-329**
Cooper [career]
Barrel **B: 118**
Cooper, Andy [American baseball player]
Baseball (table: Hall of Fame) **B: 134**
Cooper, Anthony Ashley [English political leader]
Locke, John (His life) **L: 413**
Cooper, Astley [British sportsman]
Commonwealth Games **Ci: 875**
Cooper, Chuck [American basketball player]
Basketball (The history of professional basketball) **B: 154a-155**
Cooper, Edward [son of]
Cooper, Peter **Ci: 1035**
Cooper, Frank James [birth name of]
Cooper, Gary **Ci: 1034**
Cooper, Gary [American actor] **Ci: 1034** with portrait
Motion picture (Best performance by an actor: 1941) **M: 862a**
Cooper, George [poet]
October (Quotations) **O: 671**
Cooper, Gordon [American astronaut] **Ci: 1034**
Space exploration (Vostok and Mercury: The first human beings in space) **So: 712-713** with picture
Cooper, James Fenimore [American author] **Ci: 1034**
American literature (The romance) **A: 418**
Novel (The United States) **N: 573**
Uncas **U: 19**
Cooper, Job A. [American political leader]
Colorado (table) **Ci: 844**
Cooper, John Sherman [American political leader]
Warren Report **W: 37**
Cooper, Leon Neil [American physicist]
Bardeen, John **B: 109**
Nobel Prizes (Physics: 1972) **N: 441**
Superconductivity **So: 992**
Cooper, Leroy Gordon, Jr. [American astronaut]
See Cooper, Gordon in this index
Cooper, Myers Y. [American political leader]
Ohio (table) **O: 699**
Cooper, Peter [American inventor] **Ci: 1035** with picture
Maryland (The War of 1812 and industrial development) **M: 258**
Railroad (Developments in the United States) **R: 115**
Cooper, Prentice [American political leader]
Tennessee (table) **T: 152**
Cooper, Susan [British author] **Ci: 1035**
Newbery Medal (table) **N: 359**
Cooper, William [American judge]
Cooperstown **Ci: 1037**
Cooper, William [American settler]
Camden **C: 76**
Cooper, William B. [American political leader]
Delaware (table) **D: 109**
Cooper-Hewitt, National Design Museum [New York City]
Smithsonian Institution (Museums) **S: 519**
Cooper pair [physics]
Superconductivity **So: 992**
Cooper Union [school]
Cooper, Peter **Ci: 1035**
Cooperative [economics] **Ci: 1035**
Collectivism **C: 775**
Cuba (Agriculture) **Ci: 1174**
Electric power (In the United States) **E: 186**
Farm and farming (Managing production costs) **F: 42**
Farm Credit System (Organization) **F: 45**
Fishing industry (Marketing) **F: 187**
Housing (Cooperative housing) **H: 390**
Milk (Marketing) **M: 547**
Owen, Robert **O: 882**
Truck farming (How truck farms operate) **T: 460**
Cooperative [education]

Universities and colleges (Residence) **U: 209**
Cooperative bank
Savings and loan association **S: 165**
Cooperative breeding [biology]
Bird (Caring for the young) **B: 359**
Co-operative Commonwealth Federation [political party]
Canada, Government of (Political parties) **C: 136-137**
New Democratic Party **N: 203**
Political party (Other parties) **P: 636-637**
Saskatchewan (Political changes) **S: 147**
Woodsworth, James Shaver **W: 396**
Cooperative education Ci: 1037
Career education **C: 213**
Careers (Preparing for a career) **C: 216**
Vocational education (Vocational teaching methods) **V: 434-435**
Cooperative Extension System [U.S.] **Ci: 1037**
4-H **F: 433**
Cooperative farm
Israel (Rural life) **I: 481**
Korea, North (Agriculture and fishing) **K: 372-373**
Ukraine (Agriculture) **U: 11**
Cooperative for Assistance and Relief Everywhere See CARE in this index
Cooperative game
Game theory **G: 23**
Cooperative insurance company
Insurance (Types of insurance companies) **I: 315**
Cooperative Marketing Act [1926]
Cooperative (History) **Ci: 1036**
Cooperative work experience
Cooperative education **Ci: 1037**
Cooper's Ferry [former name]
Camden **C: 76**
Cooperstown [New York] **Ci: 1037**
Doubleday, Abner **D: 312**
Coordinated Universal Time
Time (Coordinated Universal Time) **T: 292a**
Coordinates [geography]
Latitude **L: 117**
Coordinates [mathematics]
Algebra (Functions) **A: 356**
Geometry (Analytic geometry) **G: 105** with diagram
Coordinating conjunction [grammar]
Conjunction (Coordinating conjunctions) **Ci: 951**
Coordination [grammar]
Grammar (Grammatical relationships) **G: 303**
Coordination compound [chemistry]
Inorganic chemistry **I: 276**
Coot [bird] **Ci: 1038** with picture
Bird pictures on **B: 359**
Rail **R: 103**
Cootamundra wattle [tree]
Tree picture on **T: 427**
Cootie [insect]
Louse **L: 507**
Cop See Police in this index
"Cop Killer" [rap song]
Rock music (Rap) **R: 380d**
Copacabana Beach [Rio de Janeiro]
Brazil picture on **B: 574**
Rio de Janeiro (The city) **R: 345**
Copán [ancient city, Honduras] **Ci: 1038**
Honduras (The Indian period) **H: 312**
Maya (Government) **M: 324**; (The Maya heritage) **M: 326**
Co-payment [insurance]
Insurance (Insurance companies) **I: 311-312**
Medicine (The United States) **M: 367-368**
COPD [disease] See Chronic obstructive pulmonary disease in this index
Cope [manufacturing]
Cast and casting (How castings are made) **C: 278** with diagram
Cope, Edward Drinker [American paleontologist]
Dimetrodon **D: 204**
Copenhagen [Denmark] **Ci: 1038** with picture
Denmark **D: 132** with pictures; (Recreation) **D: 136-137** with picture
Copenhagen [horse]
Horse (table: Famous horses in history and legend) **H: 361**
Copenhagen, Battle of [1801]
Nelson, Horatio (Battle of Copenhagen) **N: 122**; (Victory at Trafalgar) **N: 122**
Copenhagen, University of
Copenhagen (The city) **Ci: 1038**
Denmark (Education) **D: 132**
Copepod [sea animal] **Ci: 1039**
Animal picture on **A: 486**
Ocean picture on **O: 656**; (Zooplankton) **O: 655**
Copernican theory [astronomy]
Astronomy (Sun-centered theories) **A: 835**; (Developing the modern view) **A: 847-848**

with diagram
Brahe, Tycho B: 548
Copernicus, Nicolaus Ci: 1039
Galileo (Early scientific interests) G: 11
Mathematics (Mathematics and the scientific revolution) M: 306
Physics (The Renaissance) P: 438-439
Planet (How planets move) P: 508-509
Copernicium [element]
Transuranium element T: 401
Copernicus [crater]
Moon (Craters) M: 789
Copernicus, Nicolaus [Polish astronomer] Ci: 1039
Astronomy (Sun-centered theories) A: 835; (Developing the modern view) A: 847-848 with picture
Evening star E: 423
Geology (The Renaissance) G: 98
Mathematics (Mathematics and the scientific revolution) M: 306
Moon (Ancient ideas) M: 791-792
Physics (The Renaissance) P: 438-439
Planet (How planets move) P: 508-509
Science (The rebirth of science) S: 197
Coping saw [tool]
Saw (Handsaws) S: 166 with picture
Woodworking (Cutting) W: 397 with picture
Copland, Aaron [American composer] Ci: 1040
Classical music (The 1900's) C: 649
Copley, John Singleton [American painter] Ci: 1040 with picture
Adams, Samuel picture on A: 44
Hancock, John picture on H: 39
Revere, Paul picture on R: 267
United States picture on U: 116
Copley Square [Boston]
Boston picture on B: 495
Copolymerization [chemistry]
Polyvinyl chloride P: 652
Coppélia [ballet]
Ballet (Kinds of ballet) B: 48
Delibes, Léo D: 116
Copper [butterfly]
Butterfly (Blues, coppers, and hairstreaks) B: 734 with picture
Copper [element] Ci: 1040 with picture
Aluminum (Properties of aluminum alloys) A: 391-392
Brass B: 565
Electrolysis (Uses of electrolysis) E: 200-201
Metal (Metals through the ages) M: 425
Metallurgy (Electrolysis) M: 427
Monel metal M: 703
Slag S: 499
Smelting S: 515
Statue of Liberty So: 872
Trace elements T: 355
Wire (Uses of wire) W: 344
Mining
Copper (Sources of copper) Ci: 1042 with diagrams
Arizona (Mining) A: 684
Chile (The Northern Desert) C: 464; (Mining) C: 466
Congo, Democratic Republic of the (Mining) Ci: 940s
Greater Sudbury G: 351
Lavender Pit L: 129
Michigan (Natural resources) M: 503
Zambia (Economy) Z: 585
Ores
Copper (Copper ores) Ci: 1042
Azurite A: 1004
Chalcocite C: 369
Chalcopyrite C: 369
Malachite M: 95
Mineral picture on M: 568
Copper [shield]
Indian, American (Before European contact) I: 162
Copper concentrate [material]
Copper (Milling) Ci: 1042-1043
Copper matte [material]
Copper (Smelting) Ci: 1043
Copper mine See Copper in this index
Copper River Basin
Alaska (Land regions) A: 292-294
Copperbelt [region]
Zambia (Economy) Z: 585
Copperfield, David [character] See David Copperfield in this index
Copperhead [snake] Ci: 1044
Snake picture on S: 534
Viper V: 391
Copperheads [U.S. history] Ci: 1044
Civil War, American (Government and politics) Ci: 622

Democratic Party (The slavery issue) D: 124-125
Ohio (The Civil War) O: 702
Sons of Liberty So: 594
Copperplate [writing]
Calligraphy picture on C: 68
Handwriting (Later writing styles) H: 50
Coppersmith barbet [bird]
Bird (Birds of Asia) B: 344f with picture
Coppola, Francis Ford [American director] Ci: 1044
Motion picture (Best achievement in directing: 1974) M: 862; (Changes in Hollywood) M: 871
Puzo, Mario P: 914
Coppola, Giovanni Carlo [Italian composer]
Opera picture on O: 797
Coppolani, Xavier [Mauritanian political leader]
Mauritania (History) M: 315
Copra [coconut] Ci: 1045
Coconut palm (The coconut) Ci: 746-747
Pacific Islands (Agriculture) P: 9
Co-processor [computing]
Computer (Personal computers) Ci: 909
Coptic Gospel of Thomas [document]
Gospels G: 278
Coptic language
Alphabet (Other alphabets) A: 383
Copts Ci: 1045
Rosetta stone R: 480
Copts [religious group] Ci: 1045
Africa (Religions) A: 106-107
Arabs (Religion) A: 586
Doll (Ancient times) D: 288
Eastern Catholic Churches E: 45
Egypt (Religion) E: 124
Copulative verb [grammar]
Verb (Linking, or copulative, verbs) V: 315
Copy [publishing]
Advertising (Creative work) A: 76b
Magazine (Editing and assembling an issue) M: 43
Newspaper (table) N: 383
Publishing (Preparing content for publication) P: 866
Copy camera
Copying machine (Projection copying) Ci: 1045
Copy editor [career]
Encyclopedia picture on E: 268
Newspaper (Writing and editing stories) N: 383
Publishing (Editors and fact checkers) P: 867
Copying machine Ci: 1045 with diagrams
Library (Photocopying) L: 239
Printing (Digital printing) P: 801
Xerox Corporation X: 544
Copyreader [career]
Newspaper (Writing and editing stories) N: 383
Copyright [law] Ci: 1046
Book (Inside a book) B: 464-465
Intellectual property I: 318
Library (Photocopying) L: 239
Library of Congress L: 264
Piracy P: 493
Plagiarism P: 505
Public domain P: 855
Copyright Office, United States
Copyright (How to obtain a copyright) Ci: 1048
Library (United States government libraries) L: 248
Copywriter [career]
Advertising (Creative work) A: 76b
Coquelles [France]
Channel Tunnel C: 375
Coquí [frog] Ci: 1048
Puerto Rico (Plant and animal life) P: 880
Coquina [rock]
Limestone picture on L: 307, L: 308
Coral [sea animal] Ci: 1048 with pictures
Animal picture on A: 487
Coral reef Ci: 1048b
Gem picture on G: 78
Global warming (Harm to ocean life) G: 232a
Great Barrier Reef G: 336
Ocean picture on O: 656
Rock (Organic sediments) R: 372
Sea fan S: 262a
Seven natural wonders of the world (The Great Barrier Reef) S: 324 with picture
Coral gall crab
Crab Ci: 1115
Coral Harbour
Southampton Island So: 686
Coral honeysuckle [plant]
Honeysuckle H: 316 with picture
Coral island
Island (Kinds of islands) I: 472 with diagram
Coral key [island]
Cuba (The land) Ci: 1172-1173
Coral reef Ci: 1048b with picture

Atoll A: 869 with picture
Australia (The Great Barrier Reef) A: 910 with picture
Coral Ci: 1048
Ecology picture on E: 53
Fish pictures on F: 154
Great Barrier Reef G: 336 with picture
Island (Coral islands) I: 472 with diagram
Pacific Islands (The low islands) P: 8 with picture
Pacific Ocean (Damage to reefs) P: 17
Coral Sea [South Pacific] Ci: 1049
Coral Sea, Battle of the [1942]
Air force (World War II) A: 185-186
Navy (World War II) N: 80
World War II (The Battle of the Coral Sea) W: 488
Coral snake Ci: 1050 with picture
Snake picture on S: 534
Coral tree Ci: 1050 with picture
Coral trout
Fish picture on F: 168
Coralbean [tree] See Coral tree in this index
Coralli, Jean [French choreographer]
Ballet (Romantic ballet) B: 51
Coralline algae [animals]
Coral reef (How coral reefs form) Ci: 1048b-1049
Coralline sponge [animal]
Sponge (Kinds of sponges) So: 800
Coranto [publication]
Communication (The effects of printing) Ci: 880
Corax [Greek orator]
Oratory (Beginnings) O: 818
Corbenic Castle
Holy Grail (Early history of the Grail) H: 299; (The search for the Grail) H: 299
Corbett, James John [American boxer] Ci: 1050
Boxing (Bare knuckles to gloves) B: 532 with picture
Solar plexus So: 579
Corbett, Tom [American political leader]
Pennsylvania (table) P: 263
Corbett National Park [India]
National park (table) N: 42f
Corbin, Abel R. [brother-in-law of]
Grant, Ulysses S. (Political corruption) G: 315-316
Corbin, Margaret Cochran [American patriot] Ci: 1051
Corbusier, Le [Swiss architect] See Le Corbusier in this index
Corcoran, William Wilson [American philanthropist]
Corcoran Gallery of Art Ci: 1051
Corcoran Gallery of Art [Washington, D.C.] Ci: 1051 with picture
Washington, D.C. map on W: 76; (Other Washington museums) W: 75
Corcovado Mountain [Brazil]
Rio de Janeiro (The city) R: 345
Corcyra [former name, Corfu]
Corinth Ci: 1053
Cord [glass]
Glass (Glass terms) G: 222
Cord [measurement]
Weights and measures (Miscellaneous weights and measures) W: 184
Cord and cordage
Macramé M: 26 with picture
Rope R: 472 with pictures
Cord blood [medicine]
Bone marrow transplant B: 458
Cord quilt
Quilt Q: 41
Corday, Charlotte [French patriot] Ci: 1051 with portrait
French Revolution (The National Convention) F: 526
Cordelia [literary figure]
Shakespeare, William: (King Lear) S: 363
Cordeliers Club [French history]
Danton, Georges-Jacques D: 34
Cordial [beverage] See Liqueur in this index
Cordillera [geography] Ci: 1051
Cordillera Central [mountains, Colombia]
Colombia (The Andes Mountains) Ci: 782
Cordillera Central [mountains, Puerto Rico]
Puerto Rico picture on P: 873
Cordillera Neo-Volcánica [region of Mexico]
Mexico (The Plateau of Mexico) M: 461
Cordillera Occidental [mountains, Colombia]
Colombia (The Andes Mountains) Ci: 782
Cordillera Oriental [mountains, Colombia]
Colombia (The Andes Mountains) Ci: 782
Cordillera Septentrional [region, Dominican Republic]
Dominican Republic (Land) D: 304
Cordless keyboard [electronic device]
Computer (A keyboard) Ci: 912-914
Cordless mouse [electronic device]

Computer (A mouse) **Ci: 912-914**
Cordless telephone
Telephone (Types of telephones) **T: 94**
Córdoba [Argentina] **Ci: 1051**
Córdoba [Spain] **Ci: 1051** *with picture*
Córdoba, Francisco Fernández de [Spanish explorer]
Mexico (The Spanish conquest) **M: 469**
Nicaragua (The colonial period) **N: 398**
Cordon offense [strategy]
Civil War, American (Grant in command) **Ci: 631**
Cordovan leather
Córdoba **Ci: 1051**
Corduroy [fabric] **Ci: 1052**
Corduroy road
Road (Early American roads) **R: 361-362**
Cordyceps [fungus]
Life *picture on* **L: 276**
Core [astronomy]
Jupiter (Core) **J: 200** *with diagram*
Mars (Physical features of Mars) **M: 225**
Moon (The interior of the moon) **M: 790**
Sun (Sun terms) **So: 976**; (Zones of the sun) **So: 979** *with diagram*
Uranus (Structure and composition) **U: 218**
Core [botany]
Root (The core) **R: 471**
Core [electrical device]
Electromagnet **E: 201**
Transformer **T: 371** *with diagram*
Core [fingerprinting]
Fingerprinting *picture on* **F: 106**
Core [geology]
Antarctica (Climate) **A: 534**
Climate (Determining past climates) **Ci: 678-679** *with picture*
Earth **E: 20** *with diagram*; (Earth's interior) **E: 23**
Geology *picture on* **G: 99**
Ice age (Evidence of ice ages and climates) **I: 6-7**
Mantle **M: 168**
Metal (Where metals are found) **M: 425**
Ocean (Research ships) **O: 662-663**
Ocean drilling programs **O: 667**
Petroleum (Geological studies) **P: 335**
Core [nuclear device]
Nuclear energy (Power reactors) **N: 584-585** *with picture*; (Hazards and safeguards) **N: 587-588**
CORE [organization] *See* Congress of Racial Equality *in this index*
Core-collapse supernova [astronomy]
Supernova **So: 994**
Core curriculum [education]
Education (What should be taught?) **E: 105**
Harvard University (History) **H: 80-81**
Core repository [library]
Ocean drilling programs **O: 667**
Core thread
Thread (Making thread from manufactured fibers) **T: 269**
Co-recreational sports
Intramural sports **I: 354**
Corelli, Arcangelo [Italian composer] **Ci: 1052**
Coreopsis [botany] **Ci: 1052** *with picture*
Coretta Scott King Awards [literary awards]
Literature for children (Awards) **L: 367**
McKissack, Patricia **M: 342**
Corey, Elias James [American chemist]
Nobel Prizes (Chemistry: 1990) **N: 444**
CORFO [Chilean history]
Chile (Years of progress) **C: 469**
Corfu [island, Greece]
Ionian Islands **I: 373** *with map*
Corgi [dog]
Cardigan Welsh corgi **C: 210** *with picture*
Dog *picture on* **D: 276**
Pembroke Welsh corgi **P: 233**
Cori, Carl Ferdinand [Czech-American physiologist]
Nobel Prizes (Physiology or medicine: 1947) **N: 445**
Cori, Gerty Theresa [Czech-American physiologist]
Nobel Prizes (Physiology or medicine: 1947) **N: 445**
Coriander [herb] **Ci: 1052** *with picture*
Corigliano, John [American composer]
Classical music (Classical music today) **Ci: 651**
"Corinna's Going A-Maying" [poem by Herrick]
Herrick, Robert **H: 215**
Corinth [ancient city] **Ci: 1053** *with picture*
Corinth [Mississippi]
Civil War, American (Battle of Shiloh) **Ci: 629**
Corinth Canal [waterway, Greece] **Ci: 1053**
Canal (table) **C: 164**
Corinthian column [architecture]
Acanthus **A: 21**
Architecture (table) **A: 608** *with picture*; (Classical Greek architecture) **A: 615**

Brunelleschi, Filippo *picture on* **B: 652**
Column (The Greek orders) **Ci: 865** *with pictures*
Corinthians, Epistles to the [New Testament] **Ci: 1053**
Bible (The Letters) **B: 284**
Coriolanus [play by Shakespeare]
Coriolanus, Gaius Marcius **Ci: 1053**
Shakespeare, William: (*Coriolanus*) **S: 364**
Coriolanus, Gaius Marcius [Roman general] **Ci: 1053**
Corioli [ancient city]
Coriolanus, Gaius Marcius **Ci: 1053**
Coriolis, Gaspard Gustave de [French scientist]
Coriolis effect **Ci: 1053**
Coriolis effect [physics] **Ci: 1053**
Air (Air movement) **A: 171-172**
Hurricane (How a hurricane forms) **H: 453**
Jupiter (Zones and belts) **J: 199**
Weather (Planetary-scale systems) **W: 158**
Corisco [island, Equatorial Guinea]
Equatorial Guinea **E: 346** *with map*
Cork [Ireland] **Ci: 1054**
Cork [bark] **Ci: 1054** *with pictures*
Bark (Outer bark) **B: 110** *with diagram*
Cell *picture on* **C: 337**
Interior design (Choosing patterns and textures) **I: 332-333**
Leaf (The leaf becomes fully grown) **L: 152**
Stem (Woody stems) **So: 887**
Tree (Trunk and branches) **T: 416-417** *with diagram*
Cork black [paint]
Cork (Uses) **Ci: 1055**
Cork cambium [botany]
Bark (Inner bark) **B: 110**
Root (Secondary tissues) **R: 471** *with diagram*
Stem (Woody stems) **So: 887** *with diagram*
Cork elm [tree]
Elm (Kinds) **E: 244-245**
Cork oak [tree]
Cork (The tree) **Ci: 1054** *with picture*
Oak (Other oaks) **O: 636**
Corliss, George Henry [American engineer] **Ci: 1055**
Corm [botany] **Ci: 1055**
Gladiolus **G: 206**
Cormack, Allan MacLeod [American physicist]
Nobel Prizes (Physiology or medicine: 1979) **N: 446**
Cormel [botany]
Corm **Ci: 1055**
Cormorant [bird] **Ci: 1055** *with pictures*
Corn [crop] **Ci: 1056** *with pictures and map*
Agriculture *picture on* **A: 153**
Arikara Indians **A: 661**
Colonial life in America (Food and drink) **Ci: 802**
Fertilizer *pictures on* **F: 79**
Gardening *picture on* **G: 37**
Genetically modified food (Production and consumption) **G: 85**
Grain **G: 301**
Grass (Cereals) **G: 326**
Heredity *picture on* **H: 205**
Hog **H: 284**
Hominy **H: 305**
Hybrid (Producing hybrid plants) **H: 461** *with picture*
Indian, American (The first farmers) **I: 152**
Indiana (Agriculture) **I: 211** *with picture*
Iowa *picture on* **I: 374**; (Agriculture) **I: 389**
Mexico (Food and drink) **M: 456**
Nutrition (Kinds of nutrients) **N: 625**
Pellagra **P: 229**
Pioneer life in America *picture on* **P: 482**; (Food) **P: 481**
Plant (How crops differ from wild plants) **P: 542** *with picture*
Popcorn **P: 659**
Root (Kinds of roots) **R: 469-470** *with diagram*
Corn [disorder] **Ci: 1064**
Callus **C: 69**
"Corn" [poem by Lanier]
Lanier, Sidney **L: 68**
Corn Belt [region, U.S.]
Corn (The corn plant) **Ci: 1057** *with picture*; (Corn production in the United States) **Ci: 1059**
Corn borer [insect] **Ci: 1064** *with map*
Corn crake [bird]
Rail **R: 103**
Corn earworm [insect] **Ci: 1064**
Insect *picture on* **I: 285**
Corn Is Green, The [play by Williams]
Williams, Emlyn **W: 310**
Corn Laws [British history] **Ci: 1064**
Cobden, Richard **Ci: 741**
Disraeli, Benjamin **D: 237**
Peel, Sir Robert (Prime minister) **P: 229**

United Kingdom (Establishment of free trade) **U: 69**
Corn meal [food]
Flour (Types of flour) **F: 268-269**
Pioneer life in America (Food) **P: 481**; (Tools) **P: 483**
Corn oil **Ci: 1064**
Vegetable oil **V: 294**
Corn Palace [Mitchell]
South Dakota (Places to visit) **So: 672**
Corn plaster [first aid]
Corn **Ci: 1064**
Corn root aphid
Insect *picture on* **I: 281**
Corn salad [plant]
Valerian **V: 265**
Corn smut [plant disease]
Fungi *picture on* **F: 559**
Smut **S: 522**
Corn State
Iowa **I: 374**
Corn syrup **Ci: 1064**
Sugar (Cornstarch and other starches) **So: 960**
Corn whiskey [beverage]
Pioneer life in America (Food) **P: 481-482**
Cornaro Chapel [Rome]
Bernini, Gian Lorenzo **B: 271**
Cornaros, Vitzentzos [Cretan poet]
Greek literature (Modern Greek literature) **G: 378**
Corncob pipe
Missouri (Interesting facts) **M: 651**
Cornea [anatomy]
Astigmatism **A: 825** *with picture*
Blindness (Diseases) **B: 401-402**
Cataract **C: 299**
Contact lens **Ci: 1020**
Eye (The sclera and the cornea) **E: 460** *with picture*; (Focusing) **E: 462**; (Astigmatism) **E: 464**; (Diseases of the cornea) **E: 466**
Eye bank **E: 470**
First aid (Eye injury) **F: 140**
LASIK surgery **L: 86**
Myopia **M: 971**
Corneal graft [surgery] *See* Corneal transplant *in this index*
Corneal opacity [disorder]
Blindness (Diseases) **B: 401-402**
Corneal transplant [surgery]
Blindness (Diseases) **B: 401-402**
Eye (Diseases of the cornea) **E: 466**
Eye bank **E: 470**
Transplant *picture on* **T: 380**; (Tissue transplants) **T: 379**
Corneille, Pierre [French dramatist] **Ci: 1065**
Drama (Neoclassical playwrights) **D: 333**
French literature (Classical drama) **F: 520**
Cornelia [wife of]
Caesar, Julius (Early life) **C: 13**
Cornelian [gem] *See* Carnelian *in this index*
Cornelius, Saint [pope]
Pope (table) **P: 666**
Cornell, Alonzo B. [American political leader]
New York (table) **N: 313**
Cornell, Eric Allin [American physicist]
Nobel Prizes (Physics: 2001) **N: 442**
Cornell, Ezra [American philanthropist] **Ci: 1065**
Cornell University **Ci: 1065**
Cornell, Ezra **Ci: 1065**
New York *picture on* **N: 295**
Corner Brook [Newfoundland and Labrador] **Ci: 1065**
Newfoundland and Labrador (Population) **N: 364**
Corner kick [soccer]
Soccer (Restarts) **So: 546**
Cornerback [football]
Football (The defensive team) **F: 357-358** *with diagrams*
Cornering the market [economics] **Ci: 1065**
Black Friday **B: 387**
Cornet [musical instrument] **Ci: 1065**
Cornfield ant
Insect *picture on* **I: 283**
Cornflower [plant] *See* Bachelor's-button; Bluebonnet *in this index*
Cornforth, John Warcup [Australian chemist]
Nobel Prizes (Chemistry: 1975) **N: 444**
Cornhusk
Corn (Appearance) **Ci: 1057**
Cornhusker State [name for]
Nebraska **N: 94**
Cornice
Architecture (table) **A: 608-609** *with picture*; (Minoan architecture) **A: 615**
Corning Ewer [vessel]
Glass *picture on* **G: 219**
Corning Glass Center
New York (Places to visit) **N: 302**

Corning Glass Works
Fiberglass (History) F: 89
Glass (table) G: 218
Invention (Recent developments) I: 364
Cornish, Samuel [American journalist]
Russwurm, John Brown R: 566b
Cornish chicken
Chicken (English class chickens) C: 441; (table)
C: 443
Cornish rex cat
Cat (Short-haired breeds) C: 290
Corno Grande [mountain, Italy]
Apennines A: 564
Cornplanter [American Indian chief] Ci: 1066
Cornrows [hair style]
Hairdressing (The 1900's) H: 12-13
Cornstalk [American Indian chief] Ci: 1066
Shawnee Indians S: 379
Cornstarch [food] Ci: 1066
Corn (The wet-milling industry) Ci: 1061
Sugar (Cornstarch and other starches) So: 960
Cornu, Paul [French inventor]
Helicopter (Early designs and experiments)
H: 173 with picture
Cornucopia [container]
Paper bag P: 138
Cornucopia [symbol] Ci: 1066
Cornwall, Duke of [title]
Prince of Wales P: 794
Cornwallis, Charles [British general] Ci: 1066
Camden, Battle of C: 76
Clinton, Sir Henry Ci: 682h
North Carolina (Revolution and independence)
N: 492
Revolution, American (The war in the North)
R: 281-282; (The war in the South) R: 284-285;
(The end of the war) R: 286 with picture
Yorktown, Siege of Y: 569
Cornwallis, Edward [British colonial official]
Ci: 1066
Halifax (Government and history) H: 21
Cornwell, David John Moore [birth name of]
Le Carré, John L: 174
Cornwell, John J. [American political leader]
West Virginia (table) W: 225; (Labor
developments) W: 229
Cornwell, Patricia [American author] Ci: 1066
Corolla [botany]
Flower (The parts of a flower) F: 293 with picture
Plant (Flowers) P: 531 with picture
Corona [sun] Ci: 1066
Astronomy (Spectroscopy) A: 840-841
Eclipse (Solar eclipses) E: 51 with picture
Solar wind So: 581
Sun (Sun terms) So: 976; (Zones of the sun)
So: 979-980 with pictures; (Producing images)
So: 982 with picture
Corona [Venus]
Venus (Surface and atmosphere) V: 311-312
Coronado, Francisco Vásquez de [Spanish
explorer] Ci: 1067 with picture and map
Arizona (Spanish exploration) A: 688
Estevanico E: 360
Exploration map on E: 443; (Spain's conquests in
the New World) E: 445-446
Hispanic Americans (In the Southwest) H: 251
Indian, American (After European contact) I: 168
Kansas (Exploration) K: 235
Nebraska (Exploration) N: 111
New Mexico (Exploration, conquest, and
settlement) N: 273
Oklahoma (Early days) O: 731
Texas (Spanish exploration) T: 204
Coronado, Juan Vásquez de [Spanish colonial
official]
Costa Rica (Colonial period) Ci: 1083
Coronado National Memorial [Arizona]
National Park System (table: National memorials)
N: 54
Coronagraph [instrument]
Corona Ci: 1067
Sun (Studying the sun) So: 982-983 with picture
Coronal hole [astronomy]
Corona Ci: 1067
Magnetic storm M: 57
Coronal loop [astronomy]
Sun So: 984 with picture
Coronal mass ejection [astronomy]
Aurora A: 892
Corona Ci: 1067
Sun picture on So: 986; (Coronal mass ejections)
So: 982
Coronal streamer [astronomy]
Corona Ci: 1067
Coronary angiography [medicine]
Heart (Symptoms and diagnosis) H: 137-138;
(Development of heart surgery) H: 144-145

Stress test So: 928
Coronary angioplasty [medicine] See Angioplasty
in this index
Coronary artery [anatomy]
Aorta A: 562
Artery (Principal arteries) A: 751
Fat (Fats and disease) F: 53
Heart (Blood vessels) H: 135 with picture;
(Coronary artery disease) H: 137; (Heart attack)
H: 138 with pictures
Human body (table) H: 422 with diagram
Coronary artery bypass surgery
Angina pectoris A: 461
Circulatory system (Disorders of the circulatory
system) Ci: 561
DeBakey, Michael Ellis D: 63
Heart (Treatment) H: 138 with pictures;
(Development of heart surgery) H: 144-145
Surgery (Cardiac surgery) So: 1007
Coronary artery disease
Electrocardiograph E: 199
Heart (Coronary artery disease) H: 137; (Progress
in treatment and prevention) H: 145-146
Nutrition (Heart disease) N: 630
Physical fitness (Health-related fitness) P: 434
Statin So: 867
Stress test So: 927
Coronary care unit [medicine]
Heart (Diagnosis and treatment) H: 139
Intensive care unit I: 321
Coronary occlusion [disorder] See Coronary
thrombosis in this index
Coronary thrombosis [disorder] Ci: 1068
See also Heart attack in this index
Blood (Controlling bleeding) B: 411
Heart (Heart attack) H: 138
Coronary vasodilator [drug]
Drug (Vasodilators) D: 351
Coronation [ceremony] Ci: 1068
Elizabeth II picture on E: 240
Scone, Stone of S: 209
Coronation Chair
Westminster Abbey W: 243
Coronation of Poppea, The [opera by Monteverdi]
Monteverdi, Claudio M: 764a
Coronation of the Virgin [painting by Bellini]
Bellini, Giovanni picture on B: 243
Coronavirus [virus]
Cold, Common Ci: 760
SARS S: 127
Coroner [office]
Forensic pathology F: 389a
Inquest I: 277
Medical examiner M: 361
Coroner's inquest [law]
Inquest I: 277
Coroner's jury
Jury (Coroner's juries) J: 202
Coronis [Greek mythology]
Apollo A: 566
Corot, Camille [French painter] Ci: 1069 with
picture
Barbizon School B: 108
Painting (Romanticism) P: 68
Corporación de Fomento de la Producción
[Chilean history]
Chile (Years of progress) C: 469
Corporal [rank]
Rank, Military (table) R: 140
Corporal punishment
Child (Motivating the child's behavior) C: 451
Child abuse C: 454
Torture T: 345
Corporate bond
Investment (Bonds) I: 368
Corporate chain
Chain store C: 369
Corporate colony [U.S. history]
Colonial life in America (Changes in colonial
control) Ci: 791
Corporate farming
Factory farming F: 5
Farm and farming (Farm owners and farm
operators) F: 41
Corporate fraud [crime]
Fraud F: 496
Corporate income tax [economics]
Income tax (Types of income taxes) I: 102;
(Federal income taxes in the United States)
I: 104
Corporate plane
Airplane (General aviation planes) A: 211-212
Corporate university
Adult education (Types of adult education) A: 68
Corporation [economics] Ci: 1069
Business (Corporations) B: 726
Conglomerate Ci: 938

Globalization (Features of globalization) G: 233
Insider trading I: 303
Multinational corporation M: 919
Stock So: 903
Corporation for Public Broadcasting Ci: 1070
National Public Radio N: 59
Public Broadcasting Service P: 855
Television (Public stations) T: 114-115
Corporation law
Law (Private law) L: 130
Corporative state
Fascism (Economic life) F: 49
Corps [military] Ci: 1070
Army, United States (table) A: 737
Corps de ballet
Ballet (table) B: 45
Corps of Cadets
United States Military Academy (The student
body) U: 202
Corps of Engineers See Engineers, Corps of in this
index
Corpse
Funeral customs (Preparation of the body) F: 557
Zombie Z: 598
Corpus [law] See Trust fund in this index
Corpus callosum [anatomy]
Brain (Sensing the environment) B: 552-553
Corpus Christi [Texas] Ci: 1070
Texas (table: Average monthly weather) T: 198
Corpus Christi [custom]
Drama (Religious plays) D: 333 with picture
Corpus Christi plays
Mystery play M: 972
Corpus Juris Civilis [law] See Justinian Code in
this index
Corpus luteum [biology]
Menstruation (Luteal phase) diagram on M: 403
Corpuscle [philosophy]
Mechanist philosophy M: 355
Corpuscle [physiology] Ci: 1071
See also Red blood cell; White blood cell in this
index
Corpuscular theory [physics]
Huygens, Christiaan H: 460
Light (Modern study) L: 285
Corral [area]
Ranching (Life on a cattle ranch) R: 134-135
Correa, Charles [Indian architect]
India (Architecture and sculpture) I: 119
Correa, Rafael [Ecuadorean political leader]
Ecuador (Recent developments) E: 74
Correctional facility
Prison (Types of correctional institutions) P: 805
Correctional Service of Canada
Prison P: 805
Corrections [law]
Criminal justice system (The correctional system)
Ci: 1144
Social work (Fields of social work) So: 558
Corrective advertising
Consumer protection (The right to information)
Ci: 1018
Correggio [Italian artist] Ci: 1071 with picture
Corregidor [island, Philippines] Ci: 1071
Manila Bay M: 143
Correns, Carl [German botanist]
Cell (The 1900's) C: 337-338
Heredity (The birth of genetics) H: 208
Correspondence [geometry]
Geometry (Congruence) G: 102 with diagram
Correspondence [writing] See Letter writing in
this index
Correspondence, Committees of See Committees
of Correspondence in this index
Correspondence course
Correspondence school Ci: 1071
Correspondence school Ci: 1071
Adult education (Distance learning) A: 69
School (Other kinds of schools) S: 182
Correspondence theory [philosophy]
Philosophy (Epistemology) P: 384
"Correspondences" [poem by Baudelaire]
Baudelaire, Charles B: 173
Symbolism So: 1066
Correspondent [journalism]
Foreign correspondent F: 386
War correspondent W: 26
Correspondent bank
Clearinghouse Ci: 660
Corresponding secretary [office]
Parliamentary procedure (Officers) P: 175
Corrida
Bullfighting (Types of bullfights) B: 695
Corrida de toros
Bullfighting (Types of bullfights) B: 695
Corridor Train
Railroad (Intercity trains) R: 105-106

Corridos [songs]
Mexico (Music) M: 460
Corriedale sheep
Sheep (Crossbred-wooled sheep) S: 382
Corriere della Sera [newspaper]
Italy (Communication) I: 512
Corrigan, Mairead [Irish social reformer]
Nobel Prizes (Peace: 1976) N: 448b
Corrigan, Sharon Christa [American educator] *See* McAuliffe, Christa *in this index*
Corrosion [chemistry] Ci: 1071
Aluminum (Corrosion resistance) A: 392
Electrochemistry E: 200
Materials (Chemical properties) M: 300b
Rust R: 567
Titanium T: 300
Corrosive poison
Poison (Kinds of poisons) P: 600
Corrupt bargain [U.S. history]
Adams, John Quincy (Democratic-Republican Party split) A: 42
Jackson, Andrew (Election of 1824) J: 9-10
Corrupt practices [politics] Ci: 1072
Lobbying L: 404
Police (In the United States since the mid-1900's) P: 624-625
Corruption of blood [English law]
Attainder A: 878
Corsair [pirate]
Algeria (Ottoman rule) A: 364
Barbary States B: 105
Libya (Early days) L: 267
Morocco (Corsairs and sharifs) M: 814
Pirate P: 494
Corse *See* Corsica *in this index*
Corsica [island, Mediterranean] Ci: 1072 *with maps*
France (Local government) F: 455; (Language) F: 458-459 *with map*; (The land) F: 464-466
Napoleon I (Boyhood) N: 14
Corson, Dale R. [American physicist]
Astatine A: 823
Cort, Henry [British inventor]
Industrial Revolution (The revolution in ironmaking) I: 249-250
Cortázar, Julio [Argentine author]
Latin American literature (The "Boom") L: 114
Cortelyou, George B. [American government official]
Commerce, Department of (table) Ci: 871
Roosevelt, Theodore (table) R: 466
Cortes [Spanish government]
Spain (The parliament) So: 731; (The Christian kingdoms) So: 746
Cortés, Hernán [Spanish conqueror] Ci: 1072 *with map*
Alvarado, Pedro de A: 398
Aztec (The Spanish conquest) A: 1003
Conquistadors Ci: 973
Cuauhtémoc Ci: 1167
Exploration *map on* E: 443; (Spain's conquests in the New World) E: 445
Indian, American *picture on* I: 178a; (Indians of Middle America) I: 169-171
Latin America *map on* L: 105 ; (The conquest of the American Indians) L: 103
Latin American literature (Colonial literature) L: 112
Mexico (The Spanish conquest) M: 469 *with picture*
Mexico City (City of the Aztec) M: 478
Montezuma II M: 764b
Cortés, Sea of
Gulf of California G: 436
Cortex [anatomy]
Adrenal gland A: 67 *with diagram*
Hair (The root and shaft) H: 9-10 *with diagram*
Kidney (How the kidneys produce urine) K: 311 *with diagrams*
Cortex [botany]
Potato (The potato plant) P: 712 *with picture*
Root (The outer tissues) R: 470-471 *with diagrams*
Stem (Herbaceous stems) So: 887
Cortex, Cerebral [anatomy] *See* Cerebral cortex *in this index*
Cortez, Hernán [Spanish conqueror] *See* Cortés, Hernán *in this index*
Cortez, Viorica [Romanian singer]
Opera *picture on* O: 803
Corti, Organ of [anatomy] *See* Organ of Corti *in this index*
Cortiço [slum]
São Paulo (People) S: 118
Corticosteroid [hormone]
Asthma (Treatment) A: 825
Cortisone Ci: 1073
Eczema E: 74

Inflammation I: 266
Multiple sclerosis M: 921
Corticosterone [hormone]
Steroid (The adrenal steroids) So: 894
Cortina, Juan Nepomuceno [Mexican political leader] Ci: 1073
Cortina d'Ampezzo [Italy]
Italy *picture on* I: 496
Cortisol [hormone]
Adrenal gland A: 67
Drug (Chemical laboratories) D: 354-355
Hypoglycemia (Causes) H: 481
Steroid (The adrenal steroids) So: 894
Cortisone [hormone] Ci: 1073
Julian, Percy Lavon J: 187
Cortland apple
Apple (table) A: 571 *with picture*
Corum, L. L. [American race driver]
Automobile racing (table: Indianapolis 500 winners) A: 980
Corundum [mineral] Ci: 1074
Alumina A: 390
Mineral *pictures on* M: 570
Ruby R: 508
Sapphire S: 122
Corvair [automobile]
Automobile (The growth of government regulation) A: 971
Corvée [tax]
Egypt, Ancient (Government) E: 139-142
Corvette [automobile]
Plastics (Growth of the plastics industry) P: 560
Sports car *picture on* So: 802; (History) So: 803 *with picture*
Corvette [ship]
Warship (Frigates) W: 40
Corvisart, Jean Nicolas [French doctor]
Laënnec, René Théophile Hyacinthe L: 26
Corwin, Thomas [American political leader]
Fillmore, Millard (table) F: 102
Ohio (table) O: 699
Corydon [Indiana]
Indiana (The Civil War) I: 216
Coryell, Charles D. [American chemist]
Promethium P: 818
Corymb [botany]
Inflorescence I: 268a
Corythosaurus [dinosaur] Ci: 1074
Dinosaur (True dinosaurs) D: 206b-206c *with pictures*
Prehistoric animal *picture on* P: 739
Corzine, Jon Stevens [American political leader]
New Jersey (table) N: 249
Cos lettuce [plant]
Lettuce (Kinds of lettuce) L: 214 *with picture*
Cosa, Juan de la [Spanish explorer]
Columbus, Christopher (Ships and crews) Ci: 858-859
Cosby, Bill [American entertainer] Ci: 1074 *with portrait*
Advertising *picture on* A: 76b
Cosby, William [British colonial official]
Utica U: 251
Zenger, John Peter Z: 589
Cosby Show, The [television program]
Cosby, Bill Ci: 1074
Coscoraba swan
Swan (Kinds) So: 1016
Cosecant [trigonometry]
Trigonometry (Right triangles) T: 443
Cosgrave, Liam [Irish political leader]
Ireland I: 428
Cosgrave, William Thomas [Irish political leader]
Ireland (The Irish Free State) I: 427; (table) I: 428
Cosgrove, Samuel G. [American political leader]
Washington (table) W: 65
Cosi Fan Tutte [opera by Mozart]
Mozart, Wolfgang Amadeus (His style) M: 907
Cosimo, Piero di [Italian painter]
Leonardo da Vinci (Return to Florence) L: 199
Cosimo de' Medici [Florentine ruler] *See* Medici, Cosimo de' *in this index*
Cosindas, Marie [American photographer]
Photography (A diversity of styles) P: 426-427
Cosine [trigonometry]
Trigonometry (Right triangles) T: 443
Cosines, Law of [trigonometry]
Trigonometry (The law of cosines) T: 443
Cosmeceutical [cosmetics]
Cosmetics (Cosmetics regulations) Ci: 1074-1075
Cosmetic dentistry
Dentistry D: 143
Cosmetic dermatology [medicine]
Dermatology D: 153
Cosmetic surgery
Plastic surgery P: 553
Cosmetics Ci: 1074

See also Makeup *in this index*
Egypt, Ancient (Food, clothing, and shelter) E: 137
Pure food and drug laws (Cosmetics) P: 908
Cosmetologist [career]
Careers (Personal services) C: 228 *with picture*
Cosmetics Ci: 1074
Hairdressing H: 11
Cosmic Background Explorer [satellite]
Astronomy (Advances in astrophysics) A: 848
Cosmic microwave background (CMB) radiation Ci: 1075
Cosmic dust grains [astronomy]
Heliosphere (Magnetic field) H: 175
Cosmic microwave background (CMB) radiation [energy] Ci: 1075 *with picture*
Astronomy (Radio and microwave astronomy) A: 843
Big bang B: 296
Cosmology Ci: 1077; (Microwave radiation) Ci: 1078
Inflation theory I: 268a
Telescope (Microwave telescopes) T: 108
Universe (Changing views of the universe) U: 205-206
Cosmic-ray astronomy
Astronomy (Cosmic-ray astronomy) A: 846
Cosmic rays [physics] Ci: 1075 *with diagram*
Astronomy (Cosmic-ray astronomy) A: 846
Heliosphere (Magnetic field) H: 175
Millikan, Robert Andrews M: 555
Particle detector P: 186
Radiation (The sun and other stars) R: 77
Radiocarbon R: 97
Relativity (Time dilation) R: 211
Supernova (Results of supernovae) So: 994
Thermosphere T: 256
Universe U: 205
Van Allen belts V: 269
Cosmological constant [astronomy]
Dark energy D: 37
Gravitation (Expansion of the universe) G: 332; (Dark energy) G: 332
Cosmological redshift [physics]
Astronomy (Spectroscopy) A: 840-841
Cosmology (The movement of galaxies) Ci: 1078
Redshift R: 192
Universe (Size of the universe) U: 205
Cosmology [astronomy] Ci: 1077
Astronomy A: 834; (Advances in cosmology) A: 849
Gravitation (Expansion of the universe) G: 332
Inflation theory I: 268a
Supernova (Thermonuclear supernovae) So: 994
Cosmology [philosophy]
God (Ideas about God) G: 244
Philosophy (Metaphysics) P: 383
Cosmonaut [astronaut]
See also Space exploration *in this index*
Astronaut A: 828; (The cosmonauts) A: 833 *with pictures*
Cosmonaut researcher [occupation]
Astronaut A: 829
Cosmos [book by Humboldt]
Humboldt, Baron von H: 432
Cosmos [plant] Ci: 1078
Flower *picture on* F: 277
COSPAS-SARSAT satellite system
Navigation (Electronic navigation) N: 74
Cossacks [people] Ci: 1079
Russia (The Time of Troubles) R: 549
Ukraine (Lithuanian and Polish rule) U: 12
Cossacks, The [book by Tolstoy]
Tolstoy, Leo (Early life and works) T: 322
Cost [economics] *See* Price *in this index*
Cost accountant [occupation]
Accounting (Management accounting) A: 23
Cost-benefit analysis [economics] Ci: 1079
Utilitarianism U: 252
Cost of living [economics] Ci: 1079 *with diagram*
Economic indicator E: 57
Cost per click [measurement]
Advertising (The Internet) A: 74
Cost per million [measurement]
Advertising (The Internet) A: 74
Cost per unit [economics]
Farm and farming (Managing production costs) F: 40
Cost-push inflation [economics]
Inflation (The cost-push theory) I: 268
Costa [botany]
Moss (The structure of mosses) M: 834
Costa, Lúcio [Brazilian architect]
Brasília (History) B: 565
Costa Brava [region]
Spain *picture on* So: 742
Costa Rica Ci: 1080 *with pictures and maps*

See also Central America *in this index*
National park (Costa Rica) **N: 42c**
Costanoan Indians
San Francisco (History) **S: 97**
Costello, John Aloysius [Irish political leader]
Ireland (The Republic of Ireland) **I: 427**; (table)
I: 428
Coster, Dirk [Dutch chemist]
Hafnium **H: 5**
Costner, Kevin [American actor/director]
Motion picture (Best achievement in directing:
1990) **M: 862**
Costovertebral joint [anatomy]
Rib **R: 320**
Costumbrismo [literature]
Latin American literature (Realism) **L: 113**
Spanish literature (The 1800's) **So: 761-762**
Costume [clothing]
Ballet (Sets and costumes) **B: 49** *with pictures*
Clothing (Regional traditional costumes) **Ci: 696**
Halloween (Halloween customs and symbols)
H: 24a *with picture*
Motion picture (Assembling the production
team) **M: 850** *with pictures*
Opera (The designers) **O: 794** *with picture*
Shakespeare, William (Costumes and sound
effects) **S: 352**
Theater (Costumes and makeup) **T: 242** *with
pictures*
Costume designer [career]
Motion picture (Assembling the production
team) **M: 850** *with picture*
Costume doll
Doll (Costume dolls) **D: 286**
Costume Institute
Metropolitan Museum of Art (The Costume
Institute) **M: 444**
Costume jewelry
Jewelry (Modern jewelry) **J: 119**
Cosyns, Max [Swiss balloonist]
Piccard, Auguste **P: 450**
Cotangent [trigonometry]
Trigonometry (Right triangles) **T: 443**
Cote [garment]
Clothing (The Middle Ages) **Ci: 700-701**; (The
Renaissance) **Ci: 702**
Côte d'Ivoire Ci: 1084a *with pictures and map*
Flag *picture on* **F: 198**
French West Africa **F: 527** *with map*
Houphouët-Boigny, Félix **H: 379**
Yamoussoukro **Y: 550**
Coteau des Prairies [region]
South Dakota (Land regions) **So: 674** *with map*
Coteau-du-lac National Historic Site [Quebec]
Canada (table: National historic sites) **C: 114**
Coteau du Missouri [region]
South Dakota (Land regions) **So: 674** *with map*
Coterie [biology]
Prairie dog (Habits) **P: 732**
Cotillard, Marion [French actress]
Motion picture (Best performance by an actress:
2007) **M: 862a**
Cotillion [dance] **Ci: 1085**
Dance (Social dances) **D: 26-27**
Cotillon [dance]
Dance (Social dances) **D: 26-27**
Cotonou [Benin] **Ci: 1085**
Benin **B: 249** *with map*
Cotopaxi [volcano, Ecuador] **Ci: 1085**
Ecuador (The Andes Highland) **E: 70** *with picture*
Mountain (table) **M: 896** *with diagram*
Volcano (table) **V: 442b**
Cotrubas, Ileana [Romanian singer]
Opera *picture on* **O: 802**
Cotswold sheep
Sheep (Long-wooled sheep) **S: 382**
Cottage cheese
Cheese (Soft cheese) **C: 392** *with picture*
Cottage garden
Gardening *picture on* **G: 38**; (Flower gardens)
G: 30
Cottage industry [economics] **Ci: 1085**
Cotton (In England) **Ci: 1092**
Industrial Revolution *picture on* **I: 247**; (The textile
industry) **I: 248**; (The working class) **I: 251**
Textile (During the Middle Ages) **T: 218-219**
Cotton Ci: 1086 *with pictures and map*
African Americans (The growth of slavery)
A: 136f-136g *with picture*
Boll weevil **B: 448** *with pictures*
Cotton gin **Ci: 1094**
Egypt (Agriculture) **E: 128-129** *with picture*
Farm and farming *picture on* **F: 30**
Fiber (Plant fibers) **F: 87**
Mississippi (Agriculture) **M: 639** *with picture*;
(Statehood) **M: 642** *with picture*
Mumbai (History) **M: 925**

Pink bollworm **P: 473**
Plant *picture on* **P: 521**
Slavery (Functions of slaves) **S: 503** *with picture*
Sudan *picture on* **So: 952**
Textile (Natural fibers) **T: 212**
Thread **T: 269**
United States, History of the (Cotton and slavery)
U: 166
Cotton, John [American religious leader] **Ci: 1094**
Literature for children (The Puritans) **L: 362**
Cotton, Sir Robert [English historian]
History (Antiquarian research and the
philosophes) **H: 262**
Cotton, William [British inventor]
Knitting machine **K: 355**
Cotton Bowl [stadium]
Dallas (Recreation) **D: 14-15**
Cotton candy
Candy (Other candies) **C: 176**
Cotton Club [New York City]
Ellington, Duke **E: 242**
Cotton Comes to Harlem [book by Himes]
Himes, Chester **H: 234**
Cotton diplomacy
Civil War, American (Relations with Europe)
Ci: 623
Cotton dust
Brown lung **B: 644**
Cotton gin [machine] **Ci: 1094** *with picture*
African Americans (The growth of slavery)
A: 136f-136g *with picture*
Agriculture *picture on* **A: 158**; (Agricultural
advances) **A: 157**
Cotton (Ginning and baling) **Ci: 1091**; (American
colonists) **Ci: 1092**
Invention (Economic needs) **I: 355**
United States, History of the (Cotton and slavery)
U: 166
Whitney, Eli **W: 295**
Cotton Incorporated
Cotton (Synthetic fibers) **Ci: 1093**
Cotton picker [machine]
Cotton *picture on* **Ci: 1087**; (Harvesting) **Ci: 1090**
Cottonmouth [snake] *See* Water moccasin *in this
index*
Cottonseed oil Ci: 1094
Cotton (Cottonseeds) **Ci: 1086**
Cottontail
Rabbit **R: 47** *with picture*; (Cottontails) **R: 46**;
(Young) **R: 48**
Cottonwood [tree] **Ci: 1094** *with picture*
Leaf *picture on* **L: 154**
Tree *picture on* **T: 414**
Cottonwood borer [insect]
Beetle *picture on* **B: 218**
Cottony cushion scale [insect]
Insect *picture on* **I: 281**; (Insect control) **I: 284-285**
Ladybug **L: 25**
Scale insect **S: 170**
Coty, René [French political leader]
De Gaulle, Charles André Joseph Marie (The Fifth
Republic) **D: 91**
Cotyledon [botany] **Ci: 1095**
Dicotyledon **D: 191**
Monocotyledon **M: 731**
Plant (Angiosperms) **P: 520**; (Seeds) **P: 531** *with
picture*; (Germination) **P: 535-537** *with picture*
Seed (The parts of a seed) **S: 281** *with diagrams*
Tree (Broadleaf trees) **T: 414**
Coubertin, Pierre de [French sportsman]
International Olympic Committee **I: 343**
Olympic Games (The modern games) **O: 750**
Couch, William [American settler]
Oklahoma (Great land rushes) **O: 732**
Cougar [animal]
Mountain lion **M: 898** *with pictures*
Cough [disorder] **Ci: 1095**
Croup **Ci: 1157**
Tuberculosis (The disease) **T: 478**
Cough medication
Drug abuse (Over-the-counter drugs) **D: 361**
Menthol **M: 410**
Coughlin, Charles Edward [American religious
leader] **Ci: 1095**
Coulee [geography]
Washington (The Columbia Plateau) **W: 58**
Coulee Dam *See* Grand Coulee Dam *in this index*
Coulomb [measurement] **Ci: 1095**
Ampere **A: 438**
Coulomb, Charles Augustin de **Ci: 1095**
Force (The electromagnetic force) **F: 370**
Metric system (Electricity) **M: 440**
Volt **V: 446**
Coulomb, Charles Augustin de [French physicist]
Ci: 1095
Coulomb **Ci: 1095**
Electricity (Experiments with electric charge)

E: 196-197
Coulomb's Law [physics]
Coulomb, Charles Augustin de **Ci: 1095**
Coumbite [custom]
Haiti (People) **H: 14**
Council [League of Nations]
League of Nations (Powers and organization)
L: 159
Council, City [government]
City government **Ci: 595**; (The council-manager
form) **Ci: 596**
Council ...
*Most councils appear under their key words, as in
Mutual Economic Assistance, Council for; Trent,
Council of; or Europe, Council of*
Council Bluffs and Nebraska Ferry Company
[U.S. history]
Omaha (History) **O: 756**
Council flats [housing]
England (City life) **E: 296**
Council for Interior Design Accreditation
Interior design (Training) **I: 334**
Council-manager form of government
City government (The council-manager form)
Ci: 596 *with diagram*
Council Oak [tree]
Tulsa (History) **T: 483**
Council of government
Metropolitan area (Councils of goverment)
M: 443
Council of Trent, The [painting]
Roman Catholic Church *picture on* **R: 409**
Counseling Ci: 1096
Careers (Sources of information) **C: 216**
Guidance **G: 422**
Teaching (Duties outside the classroom) **T: 67**
Counseling psychology
Psychology (Major fields of psychology) **P: 848**
Counselor *See* Counseling; Lawyer *in this index*
Count [title] **Ci: 1096**
Count-all [sports]
Horseshoe pitching (Scoring) **H: 368**
Count Almaviva [opera character]
Opera: (Barber of Seville, The) **O: 801** *with picture*;
(Marriage of Figaro, The) **O: 805-806**
Count di Luna [opera character]
Opera: (Trovatore, Il) **O: 808**
Count Dracula [literary figure]
Stoker, Bram **So: 906**
Count Fleet [horse]
Kentucky Derby (table) **K: 296**
Count noun
Noun (Mass nouns and count nouns) **N: 552**
Count of Carmagnola, The [play by Manzoni]
Italian literature (Romanticism) **I: 495**
Count of Monte Cristo, The [book by Dumas]
Dumas, Alexandre, père **D: 382**
Montecristo **M: 762**
Counter air tactical mission [military]
Air force (Combat missions) **A: 182-183**
Counter-electromotive force [physics]
Electric motor (Parts of an electric motor)
E: 179-180
Counter Reformation [European history] **Ci: 1096**
with picture
Architecture (Baroque architecture) **A: 622**
Baroque **B: 117**
Christianity (The Counter Reformation) **C: 525**
Education (The Reformation) **E: 100-101**
Europe (The Reformation) **E: 410-411**
Germany (The Reformation) **G: 164**
Loyola, Saint Ignatius **L: 511**
Paul IV **P: 199**
Pius IV **P: 502**
Pope (Renaissance and Reformation) **P: 664**
Reformation (Religious influences) **R: 198**
Roman Catholic Church (The Counter
Reformation) **R: 408**
Spanish literature (The 1600's) **So: 759-760**
Trent, Council of **T: 434**
Counterclaim [law]
Court (How civil courts work) **Ci: 1102**
Counterculture
Jeans **J: 75**
Woodstock festival **W: 395**
Counterespionage
Espionage (Counterespionage) **E: 358**
Counterfeiters, The [book by Gide]
Gide, André **G: 188**
Counterfeiting [crime] **Ci: 1097**
Money (U.S. paper money) **M: 714**
Counterintelligence
Central Intelligence Agency **C: 356**
Countermelody [music]
Counterpoint **Ci: 1097**
Counterpoint [music] **Ci: 1097**
Canon **C: 182**

Music (Harmony) M: 951-952
Countershaft [device]
  Transmission (The gears) T: 378 with diagram
Counterspy
  Espionage (Counterespionage) E: 358
Countersubject [music]
  Fugue F: 553
Counterterrorism [policy]
  Civil defense (Preparedness for future
    emergencies) Ci: 605
  September 11 terrorist attacks S: 310
  Terrorism T: 175; (Fighting terrorism) T: 177;
    (Counterterrorism measures) T: 179
Counterweight [device]
  Crane Ci: 1119 with picture
  Elevator (How elevators work) E: 234 with
    diagram
Countess [title]
  Lady L: 25
  Nobility (In the United Kingdom) N: 450
Countess Cathleen, The [play by Yeats]
  Irish literature (The Irish literary revival) I: 431-
    432
  Yeats, William Butler Y: 555
Counting [mathematics]
  Addition (Addition by counting) A: 48
  Number (History) N: 606
  Roman numerals R: 413
  Subtraction (Subtraction terms) So: 944
  Writing system (Counting devices) W: 512
Counting board
  Calculator C: 22
Counting coup [warfare]
  Indian, American (Why the Indians fought) I: 144;
    (After European contact) I: 159
Counting number [mathematics] See Natural
  number in this index
Country [political unit] Ci: 1097
  Nation N: 26
  Patriotism (Foundations of patriotism) P: 198
  World map on W: 408; (table) W: 410
Country and western music See Country music
  in this index
Country Club Plaza [Kansas City]
  Shopping center S: 434
Country collector [occupation]
  Fur (Marketing fur) F: 562
Country elevator
  Grain elevator (Kinds of grain elevators) G: 301
Country music Ci: 1098
  Arnold, Eddy A: 742
  Atkins, Chet A: 858
  Branson B: 564
  "Grand Ole Opry" G: 308
  Music (Western music) M: 955
  Popular music (The rise of country music) P: 671
    with picture
  Rock music (Musical roots) R: 376
  United States picture on U: 118
Country Music Association
  Country music (Emergence of the country music
    industry) Ci: 1098b-1098c
Country rock [music]
  Country music (Modern country music) Ci: 1098c
  Popular music (New forms of rock) P: 671
Country School, The [painting by Homer]
  Education picture on E: 102
Country Wife, The [play by Wycherley]
  Wycherley, William W: 514
Countrywide Financial [company]
  Bank of America B: 96
County [political unit] Ci: 1099
  Colonial life in America (Local government)
    Ci: 795
  Local government L: 406
  Metropolitan area (County government) M: 443
  Township T: 353
County Championship [award]
  Cricket (History) Ci: 1134-1135
County extension faculty See Extension agent in
  this index
County fair
  Fair (Agricultural fairs) F: 7
County government
  County (Forms of county governments) Ci: 1099
  Local government L: 406
  Metropolitan area (County government) M: 443
County jail
  Prison (Types of correctional institutions) P: 805
County police
  Police (County police) P: 622
Coup, William Cameron [American businessman]
  Barnum, P. T. B: 115
Coup de Lance, Le [painting by Rubens]
  Jesus Christ picture on J: 108b
Coup d'état [political science] Ci: 1099
Coup d'État of Eighteenth Brumaire [1799]

Napoleon I (First consul of France) N: 15
Coup stick [weapon]
  Indian, American (Why the Indians fought) I: 144
Couperin, François [French composer] Ci: 1099
Couperus, Louis [Dutch author]
  Netherlands (Arts) N: 142-144
Coupland, Douglas [Canadian author]
  Generation X G: 84
Coupler [photography]
  Photography (Color reversal film) P: 419
Coupler [railroad]
  Locomotive diagram on L: 416
  Railroad (Passenger and freight cars) R: 107 with
    picture
Couples [book by Updike]
  Updike, John U: 213
Couplet [poetry] Ci: 1100
  Poetry (table) P: 594
Coupon
  Rationing R: 148
Courantyne [river, Guyana]
  Guyana (Land) G: 446 with map
Courbet, Gustave [French artist] Ci: 1100 with
  picture
  Cézanne, Paul C: 364
  Painting (Realism) P: 70 with picture
Coureurs de bois [Canadian history] Ci: 1100
Cournand, André Frédéric [American physician]
  Nobel Prizes (Physiology or medicine: 1956)
    N: 446
Cournault, Étienne [French artist]
  Engraving picture on E: 326
Course [textile]
  Textile (Knitted fabrics) T: 214
Course of Empire, The [paintings by Cole]
  Cole, Thomas Ci: 771
Course of Positive Philosophy, The [book by
  Comte]
  Comte, Auguste Ci: 926
Course of study
  Curriculum (Curriculum content) Ci: 1197
Courser [bird] Ci: 1100 with picture
Coursing [sport]
  Dog racing D: 282
Court [law] Ci: 1101
  Canada, Government of (The courts) C: 136
  Constitution of the United States (Article III)
    Ci: 1009
  Criminal justice system (The courts) Ci: 1143;
    (Problems in the courts) Ci: 1144
  District court D: 240
  Feudalism (Justice under feudalism) F: 82
  Government (Judicial) G: 285
  International Criminal Court I: 338
  International law (Courts and arbitration) I: 341
  Judicial review J: 183
  Law (Common law systems) L: 132; (How laws are
    changed) L: 132
  Law enforcement L: 141
  Star Chamber So: 853
  State government (Judicial branch) So: 864
  Supreme Court of Canada So: 996
  Supreme Court of the United States So: 998
  United Kingdom (Courts) U: 54
Court [sports]
  Handball H: 41 with pictures
  Honduras picture on H: 313
  Squash So: 813 with pictures
  Tennis diagram on T: 162; (The court and
    equipment) T: 161 with diagram
  Volleyball (The court) V: 445
Court, Inns of [English history] See Inns of Court
  in this index
Court, Margaret Smith [Australian tennis player]
  Ci: 1104
  Tennis (Tennis tournaments) T: 165; (The mid-
    1900's) T: 166d; (Tennis today) T: 166d-166e
Court cupboard
  Furniture (England) F: 573
Court dance
  Dance (Social dances) D: 26-27
Court fool
  Jester J: 103
Court-martial [military] Ci: 1104
  Court of Appeals for the Armed Forces, United
    States Ci: 1105
  Mitchell, Billy M: 677
  Uniform Code of Military Justice U: 27
Court of Appeal
  New Zealand (Courts) N: 347
Court of appeals [law] Ci: 1105 with map
  Court (Types of courts) Ci: 1101; (Federal courts)
    Ci: 1102
  State government (Judicial branch) So: 864
  Supreme Court of the United States (Authority of
    the Supreme Court) So: 998
  United States, Government of the (Lower court

system) U: 144
**Court of Appeals for the Armed Forces, United
  States** Ci: 1105
  Court-martial Ci: 1105
  Uniform Code of Military Justice U: 27
Court of Auditors
  European Union (Governing institutions) E: 419
Court of Cassation [law]
  France (Courts) F: 455
Court of chancery [law]
  Common law Ci: 875
  Equity E: 348
Court of claims [law] Ci: 1105
  Court (Federal courts) Ci: 1102
Court of Common Council
  London (The government of the City of London)
    L: 439
Court of equity [law]
  Equity E: 348
Court of International Trade, United States
  Ci: 1105
Court of Justice of the European Union
  European Union (Governing institutions) E: 419
  Luxembourg L: 532
Court of the Four Evangelists [courtyard]
  Escorial E: 357
Court of the Lions [courtyard]
  Alhambra A: 366
  Spain picture on So: 739
Courtesy See Etiquette in this index
Courtesy flag
  Flag (table) F: 193
Courtesy title
  Nobility (Privileges of the peerage) N: 450
Courtier [aristocrat]
  Renaissance (The ideal courtier) R: 235
Courtier, The [book by Castiglione] See Book of the
  Courtier, The in this index
Courtly love [European history]
  Chaucer, Geoffrey (Life) C: 388
  Minnesinger M: 583
  Poetry (Medieval poetry) P: 596
  Walther von der Vogelweide W: 21
Courtois, Bernard [French chemist]
  Iodine (Properties of iodine) I: 370-371
Courtrai, Battle of [1302]
  Feudalism (The decline of feudalism) F: 83
Courtroom
  Johnson, Andrew picture on J: 141
  Supreme Court of the United States picture on
    So: 998
Courtship
  See also Dating in this index
  Animal (Courtship behavior) A: 497 with picture
  Bird (Courtship and mating) B: 356 with picture
  Butterfly (The life cycle of butterflies) B: 739
  Dance (Social reasons) D: 24
  Insect (Courtship) I: 294
  Swan (Habits) So: 1016-1017
Courtship of Miles Standish, The [poem by
  Longfellow]
  Alden, John and Priscilla A: 339
  Longfellow, Henry Wadsworth (Narrative poems)
    L: 450
Couscous [food]
  Africa (Food and drink) A: 109
  Algeria (Foods) A: 361
  Arab Americans (Arab American
    accomplishments) A: 580b-581
  Morocco (Food and drink) M: 812
Cousin [family] Ci: 1105
  Family (Family relationships) F: 21
Cousteau, Jacques-Yves [French explorer] Ci: 1106
  with portrait
  Diving, Underwater (History) D: 247
  Exploration (Deep-sea exploration) E: 450-451
  Skin diving S: 494
Cousy, Bob [American basketball player] Ci: 1106
  Basketball picture on B: 153
Couteau Slope [North Dakota]
  North Dakota (Land regions) N: 506
Couture [clothing]
  Fashion (The fashion industry) F: 51
Couture, Thomas [French painter]
  Manet, Édouard M: 138
Couturier [occupation]
  Fashion (The fashion industry) F: 51
Couvade [custom]
  Folklore (Superstitions and customs) F: 324-325
Covalent bond
  Bond B: 454
  Electronics (Active components) E: 210
  Materials (The role of bonds) M: 301
Coveleski, Stan [American baseball player]
  Baseball (table: Hall of Fame) B: 134
Coven [group]
  Magic (Modern magic) M: 51

Witchcraft (Organization and practices) **W:** 371
Covenant [religion]
Abraham **A:** 16
Ark of the Covenant **A:** 693
Judaism (The covenant with God) **J:** 179
Mormons (Church doctrines and ordinances) **M:** 806-807
Moses (The covenant with God) **M:** 829
Covenant, Ark of the See Ark of the Covenant *in this index*
Covenanters [Scottish history] **Ci:** 1106
Scotland (War with the king) **S:** 220
Covent Garden Market
London (Trade) **L:** 438
Coventry [England] **Ci:** 1106 *with picture*
Coventry Cathedral [England]
Cathedral *picture on* **C:** 302
Coventry **Ci:** 1107 *with picture*
Cover [shelter]
Balance of nature (Competition) **B:** 35
Cover crop [agriculture]
Alfalfa (As a cover and rotation crop) **A:** 347
Erosion (Controlling erosion) **E:** 355
Farm and farming (Preparing the soil) **F:** 35
Rye (Uses) **R:** 573
Cover letter
Careers (Contacting employers) **C:** 218
Letter writing (Letters of application) **L:** 211 *with picture*
Writing (Preparing and submitting a manuscript) **W:** 512
Coverdale, Miles [English religious leader]
Bible (Early English translations) **B:** 285
Covered bridge
New Brunswick (Places to visit) **N:** 188 *with picture*
Covered smut [plant disease]
Smut **S:** 522
Covered wagon
Conestoga wagon **Ci:** 931
Pioneer life in America (How the pioneers traveled) **P:** 478-479; (Crossing the Plains) **P:** 485-486 *with picture*
Westward movement in America *picture on* **W:** 244
Covered Wagon, The [book by Hough]
Hough, Emerson **H:** 378
Covering [music]
Rock music (A variety of styles) **R:** 378-379
Coverley, Sir Roger [literary figure]
Addison, Joseph **A:** 47
Coverslip [slide]
Microtomy **M:** 520
Covert [feather]
Bird (Feathers) **B:** 362 *with picture*
Covert action
Central Intelligence Agency **C:** 356
Covert attention [physiology]
Brain (Attention and consciousness) **B:** 554-555
Covey [zoology]
Grouse (Habits) **G:** 403-404
Quail **Q:** 4
Covington [Kentucky] **Ci:** 1107
Covington, Leonard [American general]
Covington **Ci:** 1107
Cow [female animal] **Ci:** 1107
Dolphin (The life of dolphins) **D:** 298
Elephant (Kinds of elephants) **E:** 247
Moose (The life of a moose) **M:** 798 *with picture*
Cow [female cattle]
See also Cattle *in this index*
Cattle **C:** 306 *with pictures*
Cow **Ci:** 1107
Dairying **D:** 6 *with picture*
Lactation **L:** 25
Milk **M:** 545 *with picture*; (History of the milk industry) **M:** 549
Skeleton *diagram on* **S:** 481
Cow Ford [former name]
Jacksonville **J:** 17
Cow parsnip [plant] **Ci:** 1107
Cow Plain
Forum, Roman **F:** 421
Cow town [U.S. history]
Cowboy (The trail drive) **Ci:** 1111
Kansas (The great cattle towns) **K:** 237
Western frontier life in America (Ranching) **W:** 236
Cowan, Clyde [American physicist]
Neutrino **N:** 154
Cowan, Sheila Ann [wife of]
Martin, Paul *picture on* **M:** 234d; (College years and early career) **M:** 234b-234c
Coward, Noël [British dramatist] **Ci:** 1107 *with portrait*
Lean, David **L:** 162
Cowbane [plant]

Poisonous plant (Some poisonous plants) **P:** 602
Cowberry [fruit]
Lingonberry **L:** 335 *with picture*
Cowbird **Ci:** 1107 *with picture*
Bird *picture on* **B:** 336; (Feeding methods) **B:** 350; (Brood parasites) **B:** 359
Cowboy **Ci:** 1108 *with pictures*
See also Gaucho *in this index*
Abilene **A:** 11
Montana *picture on* **M:** 746
Ranching **R:** 134 *with picture*
Rodeo **R:** 397 *with picture*
Western frontier life in America (Ranching) **W:** 236 *with picture*; (Entertainment) **W:** 240
Westward movement in America (Cattle frontiers) **W:** 251
Cowboy boots
Cowboy (His clothing) **Ci:** 1108-1109 *with picture*
Cowboy Horse Race
Nebraska (Interesting facts) **N:** 95 *with picture*
Cowboy music
Country music (Cowboy music) **Ci:** 1098a
Cowboys, Dallas [team] *See* Dallas Cowboys *in this index*
Cowell, Henry [American composer] **Ci:** 1112
Classical music (Experimental music) **Ci:** 650
Piano (History) **P:** 447-448
Cowen, Brian [Irish political leader]
Ireland (table) **I:** 428
Cowgirl
Rodeo (All-women's rodeos) **R:** 398 *with picture*
Cowhand
See also Cowboy *in this index*
Cowboy (Cowhands today) **Ci:** 1112
Cowley, Abraham [English author] **Ci:** 1112
Cowley, Joy [New Zealand author]
Literature for children *picture on* **L:** 380
Cowley Fathers [Anglican religious group]
Religious life (table) **R:** 227
Cowpea [plant] **Ci:** 1113
Cowpens, Battle of [1781]
Morgan, Daniel **M:** 802
Revolution, American (table) **R:** 276; (Cowpens and Guilford Courthouse) **R:** 285 *with picture*
South Carolina (The Revolutionary War) **So:** 659
Cowpens National Battlefield [South Carolina]
National Park System (table: National battlefields) **N:** 55
Cowper, Steve [American political leader]
Alaska (table) **A:** 300
Cowper, William [British poet] **Ci:** 1113
February (Quotations) **F:** 61
Literature for children (The rise of illustration) **L:** 364
Cowpox [disease]
Jenner, Edward (Jenner's work) **J:** 91
Medicine (The development of immunology) **M:** 374-375
Cowrie [sea animal] **Ci:** 1113 *with picture*
Money (Kinds of money) **M:** 705
Shell *pictures on* **S:** 386
Cowrie shell [device]
Arithmetic (Calculation tools) **A:** 669
Cowry [sea animal] *See* Cowrie *in this index*
Cowslip [plant] **Ci:** 1113
Cowtown [nickname]
Fort Worth **F:** 417
Cox, Archibald [American lawyer]
Nixon, Richard Milhous (Events at home) **N:** 435-436
Watergate (The break-in and cover-up) **W:** 144; (The tape controversy) **W:** 144
Cox, Channing H. [American political leader]
Massachusetts (table) **M:** 288
Cox, Edward Finch [son-in-law of]
Nixon, Richard Milhous *picture on* **N:** 435
Cox, George B. [American political leader]
Ohio (The early 1900's) **O:** 702
Cox, Isabel [wife of]
Meighen, Arthur (Early life) **M:** 385
Cox, Jacob Dolson [American political leader]
Grant, Ulysses S. (table) **G:** 316
Interior, Department of the (table) **I:** 325
Ohio (table) **O:** 699
Cox, James Middleton [American political leader] **Ci:** 1113
Harding, Warren Gamaliel (The smoke-filled room) **H:** 57
Ohio (table) **O:** 699
Roosevelt, Franklin Delano (Candidate for vice president) **R:** 451
Cox, John I. [American political leader]
Tennessee (table) **T:** 152
Cox, Patricia Nixon [daughter of]
Nixon, Richard Milhous *picture on* **N:** 435
Cox-2 inhibitor [drug]
Arthritis (Osteoarthritis) **A:** 751-752

Aspirin (How aspirin works) **A:** 816
Coxey, Jacob Sechler [American labor leader] **Ci:** 1114
Coxey's Army [U.S. history]
Cleveland, Grover (Labor unrest) **Ci:** 672 *with picture*
Coxey, Jacob Sechler **Ci:** 1114
Coxswain [pilot]
Rowing (Types of rowing) **R:** 493-494
Coy, George W. [American inventor]
Connecticut (Interesting facts) **C:** 953
Coyle, Grace L. [American social worker]
Social work (History) **So:** 559
Coyote [animal] **Ci:** 1114 *with picture*
Animal *picture on* **A:** 483
Fur (table) **F:** 561
Coyote brush [plant]
Plant *picture on* **P:** 525
Coyote State [nickname]
South Dakota **So:** 665
Coyotes, Phoenix [team]
Hockey (table: National Hockey League) **H:** 281
Coypu [animal]
Nutria **N:** 623 *with picture*
Coysevox, Antoine [French sculptor] **Ci:** 1114
Sculpture (Form and treatment) **S:** 230-231; (European sculpture) **S:** 253-254 *with picture*
Cozad, Robert Henry [American artist] *See* Henri, Robert *in this index*
Cozzens, James Gould [American author] **Ci:** 1114
Cozzens, William C. [American political leader]
Rhode Island (table) **R:** 311
CPA [Iraqi history] *See* Coalition Provisional Authority *in this index*
CPA [occupation] *See* Certified public accountant *in this index*
CPB [corporation] *See* Corporation for Public Broadcasting *in this index*
CPI [measurement] *See* Consumer Price Index *in this index*
CPP [political party]
Ghana (History) **G:** 179-180
CPR [medicine] *See* Cardiopulmonary resuscitation *in this index*
CPU [electronics] *See* Microprocessor *in this index*
Cr [symbol]
Chromium **C:** 538
Crab [astrology]
Cancer **C:** 174 *with picture*
Crab [sea animal] **Ci:** 1115 *with pictures*
Animal *pictures on* **A:** 469, **A:** 486
Arthropod **A:** 752 *with picture*
Crustacean **Ci:** 1162 *with picture*; (The life of a crustacean) **Ci:** 1163-1165 *with pictures*
Deep sea (Invertebrates) **D:** 82a *with picture*
Ocean *picture on* **O:** 656
Crab apple [tree] **Ci:** 1116 *with pictures*
Crab-eating macaque [animal]
Macaque **M:** 2
Crab-eating raccoon
Raccoon **R:** 50
Crab grass [weed]
Lawn *picture on* **L:** 143
Crab Nebula
Astronomy (Gamma-ray astronomy) **A:** 845
Gamma rays **G:** 23
Supernova (Results of supernovae) **So:** 994
Crabbing [industrial process]
Wool (Making fabric) **W:** 401
Crabeater seal [sea animal]
Antarctica (Living things) **A:** 534-535 *with picture*
Seal (Enemies) **S:** 267
Crabtree, William [English astronomer]
Transit **T:** 374
Crack [drug]
African Americans (Social struggles) **A:** 136s-136t
Cocaine **C:** 742
Drug abuse (Cocaine) **D:** 362; (table: Some commonly abused drugs) **D:** 363
Crack-Up, The [book by Fitzgerald]
Fitzgerald, F. Scott **F:** 190
Cracking [industrial process]
Gasoline (Gasoline-powered automobiles) **G:** 62
Crackowe [shoe]
Shoe **S:** 430
Cracόw [Poland] *See* Kraków *in this index*
Cradle Mountain National Park [Australia]
National park (table) **N:** 42f
Cradle of Jazz [name for]
Louisiana **L:** 478
Cradle of Liberty [name for Boston]
Boston **B:** 495
Faneuil, Peter **F:** 27
Cradle of New France [name for]
Quebec **Q:** 34
Cradle of the Confederacy [name for]
Montgomery **M:** 765

Cradle of the Russian Empire [name for]
Nizhniy Novgorod N: 438
Cradle of the Union [name for]
Albany (Government and history) A: 309-310
Cradle Will Rock, The [opera by Blitzstein]
Blitzstein, Marc B: 403
Cradleboard [bed]
Baby *picture on* B: 4
Cradles of civilization [anthropology]
Asia (History) A: 804 *with map*
Craft *See* Handicraft *in this index*
Craft [religion]
Witchcraft W: 371
Craft guild [European history]
Guild (Craft guilds) G: 428
Craft union [labor union]
Industrial Workers of the World I: 255
Labor movement (Types of unions) L: 7
Crafts, Samuel C. [American political leader]
Vermont (table) V: 333
Craftworker
City (Ancient cities) Ci: 578-580; (Medieval cities)
Ci: 581-585 *with picture*; (Industrial cities)
Ci: 585-588
Folk art (Folk artists) F: 319 *with pictures*
Handicraft H: 46
Craig, George N. [American political leader]
Indiana (table) I: 214
Craig, Locke [American political leader]
North Carolina (table) N: 490
Craigie, Andrew [American pharmacist]
Drug (Growth of the drug industry) D: 359
Craigie House [estate]
Longfellow, Henry Wadsworth *picture on* L: 450
Craig's Wife [play by Kelly]
Kelly, George Edward K: 256
Craigslist [website]
Internet (Commerce) I: 350b; (Changing
industries) I: 350e; (The Web forms) I: 350g
Craik, James [American doctor]
Washington, George (Death) W: 107
Crail [Scotland]
Scotland *picture on* S: 213
Crailo [Rensselaer, New York]
Colonial life in America (Places to visit) Ci: 800
Crak [tile]
Mah-jongg M: 64 *with picture*
Cram, Donald James [American chemist]
Nobel Prizes (Chemistry: 1987) N: 444
Cramer, Charles F. [American public figure]
Harding, Warren Gamaliel (Government scandals)
H: 58
Cramer, Stuart W. [American engineer]
Air conditioning (History) A: 180
Cramp [disorder] Ci: 1116
Muscle (Disorders of the muscles) M: 935-936
Crampon [tool]
Mountain climbing (Basic mountaineering
equipment and methods) M: 897
Cranach, Lucas, the Elder [German painter]
Ci: 1116
Luther, Martin *picture on* L: 527
Cranberry [fruit] Ci: 1116 *with picture*
Fruit (Temperate fruits) F: 546 *with picture*
New Jersey *picture on* N: 234
Cranbrook Academy of Art [Bloomfield Hills,
Michigan]
Detroit (Other interesting places to visit) D: 170
Crandall, Prudence [American educator] Ci: 1117
with portrait
Crane [bird] Ci: 1117 *with pictures*
Animal *picture on* A: 485
Bird (Birds of Africa) B: 344h *with picture*
Whooping crane W: 296
Crane [machine] Ci: 1119 *with pictures*
Building construction (Constructing a skyscraper)
B: 683-684 *with picture*
Crane, Arthur Griswold [American political leader]
Wyoming (table) W: 532
Crane, Hart [American poet] Ci: 1120
American literature (Modernist poetry) A: 421
Lost Generation L: 472
Crane, Ichabod [literary figure]
Irving, Washington I: 460
Crane, Stephen [American author] Ci: 1120 *with
portrait*
American literature (Naturalists) A: 419-420
Novel (The United States) N: 573
Crane, Walter [British artist] Ci: 1120
Literature for children (The rise of illustration)
L: 364
Crane, Winthrop M. [American political leader]
Junior Achievement J: 196
Massachusetts (table) M: 288
Crane fly [insect]
Daddy longlegs D: 3
Crane's-bill [plant]

Geranium G: 136
Cranford [book by Gaskell]
Gaskell, Elizabeth G: 61
Cranial bone [anatomy]
Skull S: 495
Cranial capacity [biology]
Head H: 124
Cranial nerve [physiology]
Brain B: 550a
Taste T: 50
Cranium [anatomy]
Skull S: 495
Crank [device]
Gasoline engine (The crankshaft) G: 64
Starter (Automobile starters) So: 858-859
Crankcase [device]
Gasoline engine (The crankcase) G: 64 *with
diagrams*
Cranko, John [South African choreographer]
Ballet (Ballet in Europe) B: 54
Crankshaft [device]
Automobile (The engine block) A: 951 *with
diagram*
Gasoline engine (Kinds of gasoline engines) G: 63
with picture; (The crankshaft) G: 64
Ignition (The direct-fire ignition system) I: 49
Machine *diagram on* M: 13
Starter (Automobile starters) So: 858
Transmission (What a transmission does) T: 375
Cranmer, Thomas [English religious leader]
Ci: 1120
Boleyn, Anne B: 441
Henry VIII [of England] H: 188
Crannog [building]
Lake dwelling L: 37
Cranston, John [British scientist]
Protactinium P: 831
Crapo, Henry H. [American political leader]
Michigan (table) M: 507
Crapper, Sir Thomas [British plumber]
Plumbing (History) P: 580
Crappie [fish] Ci: 1121
Craps [gambling]
Dice D: 187
Gambling (Craps) G: 21
Crash [film]
Motion picture (Best picture: 2005) M: 861
Crash, The [book by Zola]
Zola, Émile Z: 598
Crash test dummy
Automobile *picture on* A: 956
Crash truck
Fire department (Special fire vehicles) F: 127
Crashaw, Richard [English poet]
Counter Reformation (Catholic reform) Ci: 1096-
1097
Crassus, Marcus Licinius [Roman political leader]
Ci: 1121
Caesar, Julius (Alliance with Pompey) C: 13
Pompey the Great P: 655
Rome, Ancient (The later years of the republic)
R: 445
Crater [geology] Ci: 1121 *with diagrams*
See also Impact crater *in this index*
Callisto C: 68
Mars (Craters and impact basins) M: 226 *with
picture*
Meteor *picture on* M: 431
Moon M: 782; (Surface features of the moon)
M: 788 *with picture*; (Determining the origin of
craters) M: 792
Crater ejecta blanket [astronomy]
Moon (Craters) M: 789
Crater Lake [Oregon] Ci: 1121
Lake (How lakes are formed) L: 32
Oregon *picture on* O: 836; (Land and climate)
O: 838-840
Crater Lake National Park [Oregon] Ci: 1122
National Park System (table: National parks) N: 48
Oregon (Places to visit) O: 836 *with picture*
Crater of Diamonds State Park [Arkansas]
Arkansas (Places to visit) A: 704 *with picture*
Crater ray [astronomy]
Moon (Craters) M: 789
Craters of the Moon National Monument [Idaho]
Idaho (Places to visit) I: 34 *with picture*
Lava (Kinds of lava) L: 128
National Park System (table: National
monuments) N: 50
Craters of the Moon National Preserve [Idaho]
National Park System (table: National preserves)
N: 58
Cratylus [book by Plato]
Plato (The dialogues) P: 567
Cravat [clothing]
Necktie N: 117
Crawfish *See* Crayfish *in this index*

Crawford, Adair [Irish chemist]
Strontium So: 930
Crawford, Broderick [American actor]
Motion picture (Best performance by an actor:
1949) M: 862a
Crawford, Christina [daughter of]
Crawford, Joan Ci: 1122
Crawford, Coe I. [American political leader]
South Dakota (table) So: 680
Crawford, George W. [American government
official]
Georgia (table) G: 130
Taylor, Zachary (table) T: 60
Crawford, Isabella Valancy [Canadian poet]
Canadian literature (Poetry: 1850-1918) C: 157
Crawford, Joan [American actress] Ci: 1122 *with
portrait*
Motion picture (Best performance by an actress:
1945) M: 862
Crawford, Sam [American baseball player]
Baseball (table: Hall of Fame) B: 134
Crawford, Samuel J. [American political leader]
Kansas (table) K: 234
Crawford, William Harris [American political
leader]
Adams, John Quincy (Election of 1824) A: 42
Jackson, Andrew (Election of 1824) J: 9-10
Crawford Square [housing development]
Pittsburgh (Housing) P: 500b
Crawl
Swimming *pictures on* So: 1044; (The basic
strokes) So: 1043
Crawler mounted crane [machine]
Crane Ci: 1119 *with picture*
Crawler tractor [machine]
Tractor (Types of tractors) T: 361 *with picture*
Craxi, Bettino [Italian political leader]
Italy (Political changes) I: 519
Cray, Seymour [American engineer]
Computer (Miniaturization) Ci: 924c
Crayfish [animal] Ci: 1122 *with picture*
Evolution (Vestigial organs) E: 431
Louisiana *picture on* L: 482
Crayon Ci: 1122
Drawing (Materials and techniques) D: 342 *with
picture*
Crazy bone [anatomy]
Funny bone F: 560
Crazy Horse [American Indian chief] Ci: 1123
Indian wars (Little Bighorn) I: 193
South Dakota So: 664; (Territorial days) So: 681-
683
Crazy Horse Memorial [South Dakota]
South Dakota (Places to visit) So: 672
Western frontier life in America (Settlers and
Native Americans) W: 239
Crazy Horse's Vision [book by Bruchac]
Literature for children *picture on* L: 360
Crazy Mountains
Montana (Land regions) M: 752
Crazy quilt [sewing]
Quilt Q: 41
Cré na Cille [book by Ó Cadhain]
Irish literature (Modern works in Gaelic) I: 431
Cream [food]
Butter (How butter is made) B: 730
Milk (table) M: 547
Cream [horse]
Horse (Light harness horses) H: 345
Cream [rock group]
Clapton, Eric Ci: 638
Rock music (Fresh directions) R: 380
Cream cheese
Cheese (Soft cheese) C: 392 *with picture*
Cream narcissus [plant]
Narcissus N: 20
Cream of tartar [chemical]
Tartaric acid T: 48
Creamery [factory]
Butter (How butter is made) B: 730
Creamware [china]
Colonial life in America (Furnishings) Ci: 797-798
Wedgwood ware W: 178 *with picture*
Creasey, John [British author]
Detective story (The pattern) D: 162
Creation
Creationism Ci: 1123
Evolution (Acceptance of evolution) E: 433
Genesis G: 84
Life (Religious explanations) L: 278
Mythology (Types of myths) M: 973 *with pictures*
Roman Catholic Church (The Trinity and creation)
R: 403
Creation [book by Vidal]
Vidal, Gore V: 359
Creation, The [music by Haydn]
Haydn, Joseph H: 117

Creation of Adam, The [painting by Michelangelo]
Painting (The High Renaissance) P: 54-55
Creation of the World, The [music by Milhaud]
Milhaud, Darius M: 543
Creation Story [document]
Babylonia (Language and literature) B: 13
Creationism [doctrine] Ci: 1123
Darwin, Charles Robert (The influence of Darwin's ideas) D: 40
Evolution (Acceptance of evolution) E: 433
Intelligent design I: 320
Creative destruction [economics]
Schumpeter, Joseph Alois S: 188
Creative writing
Writing (Preparing for a writing career) W: 511
Creativity
Imagination I: 79
Learning (Theories of learning) L: 163-164
Creator [religion]
God G: 243
Mormons (Church doctrines and ordinances) M: 806
Crèche [display]
Christmas *picture on* C: 528; (Religious practices) C: 533
Doll D: 286
Crécy, Battle of [1346] Ci: 1124
Archery (History) A: 603-604
Edward [the Black Prince] E: 111
Edward III E: 112
England (The Hundred Years' War) E: 306 *with picture*
Feudalism (The decline of feudalism) F: 83
Hundred Years' War H: 437
Credit [economics] Ci: 1124
See also Loan *in this index*
Bookkeeping (Double-entry bookkeeping) B: 472
Credit card Ci: 1124
Installment plan I: 304
Interest I: 320; (Degree of risk) I: 322
Women's movement (Legal gains) W: 386
Credit [education]
Universities and colleges (Curriculum) U: 209
Credit bureau [economics]
Credit Ci: 1124
Credit card Ci: 1124
Bank (Providing a means of payment) B: 89
Credit (Types of credit) Ci: 1124
Identity theft I: 46
Loan company L: 404
Money (The money supply) M: 715-717
Credit check [economics]
Installment plan I: 304
Credit life insurance
Insurance (Major types of life insurance) I: 309-310
Credit Mobilier of America [U.S. history] Ci: 1125
Garfield, James Abram (Congressman) G: 41
Grant, Ulysses S. (Grant's second administration) G: 317
Credit rating [economics]
Credit Ci: 1124
Mortgage M: 820
Credit union [economics] Ci: 1125
Bank (Credit unions) B: 91; (Regulation of U.S. banks) B: 92
Cooperative (Credit unions) Ci: 1036
Creditor [economics]
Bankruptcy B: 97
Collection agency Ci: 774
Debt D: 65
Creditors [play by Strindberg]
Strindberg, August So: 929
Cree Indians Ci: 1125
Manitoba (Precontact era) M: 160 *with picture*
North West Rebellion N: 520
Poundmaker P: 722
Quebec (Indian days) Q: 30
Regina (History) R: 206
Saskatchewan (Early days) S: 144; (Métis and American Indian troubles) S: 146-147 *with picture*
Creech, Sharon [American author]
Newbery Medal (table) N: 359
Creed [religion]
Christianity (Creeds and catechisms) C: 522h
Protestantism (Authority of the Bible) P: 834
Roman Catholic Church (Roman Catholic beliefs) R: 403
Creed, American's
American's Creed A: 431
Creed, Apostles' *See* Apostles' Creed *in this index*
Creed, Nicene [religion] *See* Nicene Creed *in this index*
Creek [stream] *See* Brook *in this index*
Creek chub [fish]
Chub C: 540 *with picture*

Fish *picture on* F: 158
Minnow M: 607
Creek Confederacy [U.S. history]
Creek Indians Ci: 1125
Creek Indians Ci: 1125
Alabama (Territorial days) A: 275
Black Seminole B: 391
Georgia (English colony) G: 131-132
Indian, American (Indians of the Southeast) I: 157 *with picture*
Indian Territory I: 189 *with map*
Indian wars (Conflicts in the South) I: 192
Jackson, Andrew (The Battle of Horseshoe Bend) J: 9
McGillivray, Alexander M: 334
Tulsa (History) T: 483
Creek Indians [drawing by Catlin]
Indian, American *picture on* I: 157
Creel [fishing]
Fishing (Bait) F: 178-179
Creeley, Robert [American poet] Ci: 1126
American literature (Poetry) A: 423
Creep [measurement]
Materials (Properties of materials) M: 300b
Creeper [bird] Ci: 1126
Bird *picture on* B: 363; (Birds of Europe) B: 344c *with picture*
Hawaiian honeycreeper *picture on* H: 110
Creeper [plant]
Virginia creeper V: 424 *with picture*
Creeping bentgrass [plant]
Bentgrass B: 279
Creeping buttercup [plant]
Buttercup B: 731 *with picture*
Creeping Charlie [plant]
Loosestrife L: 453
Creeping eruption [disorder]
Hookworm H: 325
Creeping Jennie [plant]
Loosestrife L: 453
Creeping thistle [plant] *See* Canada thistle *in this index*
Cremaster [entomology]
Butterfly (The pupa) B: 741
Chrysalis C: 539
Cremation Ci: 1126
Funeral customs (Burial) F: 557
Suttee So: 1013
Crematorium [building] *See* Crematory *in this index*
Crematory [building]
Cremation Ci: 1126
Holocaust (The camps) H: 296a
Crémazie, Octave [Canadian poet]
Canadian literature (Poetry: 1850-1918) C: 157
Cremer, Sir William Randal [British statesman]
Nobel Prizes (Peace: 1903) N: 448
Crenel [structure]
Castle (Structure) C: 280
Creole [language]
Aborigines, Australian A: 13
Haiti (People) H: 14-15
Mauritius (People) M: 316
Creole Jazz Band
Armstrong, Louis A: 723
Creoles [people] Ci: 1126
Louisiana L: 478; (Population) L: 482
Mauritius (People) M: 316
Mexico (Spanish rule) M: 469-470
Mulatto M: 912
New Orleans (Ethnic groups) N: 280-281
São Tomé and Príncipe (People) S: 119
Sierra Leone (People) S: 451
Creon [literary figure]
Antigone A: 564
Creosote bush [shrub] Ci: 1126
Crepe paper
Paperwork (Paper handicrafts) P: 138
Crepe rubber
Rubber (Processing crude rubber) R: 503
Crepitus [disorder]
Fracture F: 450
Crepúsculo de la Libertad, El [newspaper]
New Mexico (Communication) N: 271
Crerar, Henry Duncan Graham [Canadian military leader]
Canada, History of (World War II) C: 148
Crescendo [music]
Music (table) M: 954
Crescent [butterfly]
Butterfly (Brush-footed butterflies) B: 736
Crescent [symbol] Ci: 1127
Heraldry (Elements of a coat of arms) H: 195
Crescent City [name for]
New Orleans (The city) N: 278
Crescent City Connection [bridge, Louisiana]
Bridge (table: Cantilever) B: 603
Crescent moon

Moon (Phases) M: 783-784
Crespi, Juan [Spanish religious leader]
Los Angeles (Exploration) L: 469
Cress [plant] Ci: 1127
Cressent, Charles [French cabinetmaker]
Furniture (The Régence style) F: 576 *with picture*
Cressida [literary figure]
Shakespeare, William: (*Troilus and Cressida*) S: 362
Cresson, Edith [French political leader]
France (Socialists win power) F: 478
Crest [anatomy]
Chicken (Kinds of chickens) C: 441
Crest [heraldry]
Heraldry (Elements of a coat of arms) H: 196 *with picture*
Crest [physics]
Waves *diagram on* W: 150; (Measuring waves) W: 152
Crested auklet [bird]
Bird (Other means of communication) B: 354
Crested turaco [bird]
Turaco T: 495 *with picture*
Crested wheatgrass [plant]
Grass *picture on* G: 325
Creswell, John A. J. [American government official]
Grant, Ulysses S. (table) G: 316
Cretaceous Period [geology] Ci: 1127
Baryonyx B: 122
Chalk C: 370
Dinosaur (Kinds of dinosaurs) D: 206b
Earth (The Mesozoic Era) E: 27-28; (table) E: 30 *with map*
Extinction (The Cretaceous extinction) E: 457
Forest (Later forests) F: 398
Fossil (Tracing the development of life) F: 423-424
Plant (The evolution of plants) P: 544-545
Prehistoric animal (The Age of Reptiles) P: 737; (table) P: 739 *with picture*
Crete [island, Mediterranean] Ci: 1127
Aegean civilization (The Minoan culture) A: 83
Clothing (Crete) Ci: 696 *with pictures*
Greece (Crete) G: 358 *with picture*
Labyrinth L: 19 *with picture*
Painting (Aegean painting) P: 41 *with picture*
Ship (Early watercraft) S: 414-415
World, History of the (The Greeks) W: 428
Crete, Battle of [1941]
Mountbatten, Louis M: 899
Crete, Sea of [Greece]
Aegean Sea A: 83
Cretinism [disorder] Ci: 1128
Thyroid gland (Underactive thyroid) T: 274-275
Creutzfeldt, Hans G. [German physician]
Creutzfeldt-Jakob disease Ci: 1128
Creutzfeldt-Jakob disease Ci: 1128
Mad cow disease M: 26
Prion P: 804
Crevasse [geology]
Glacier *diagrams on* G: 204; (How glaciers move) G: 203
Iceberg (Antarctic icebergs) I: 17
Crèvecoeur, Michel-Guillaume Jean de [French author] Ci: 1129
American literature (The revolutionary period [1765-1787]) A: 415
Crew
Opera (The technical staff) O: 795-796 *with picture*
Ship (Officers and crew) S: 410
Crew cut
Hairdressing (The 1900's) H: 12-13
Crew Exploration Vehicle [spacecraft]
Space exploration (Developing new spacecraft) So: 727-728 *with picture*
Crewe, Albert [American scientist]
Electron microscope (Scanning transmission electron microscopes) E: 204
Crewel [handicraft] Ci: 1129 *with picture*
Bayeux Tapestry B: 176 *with picture*
Cria [animal]
Alpaca A: 380
Llama L: 401
Crib [game]
Cribbage Ci: 1129
Crib death *See* Sudden infant death syndrome *in this index*
Cribbage [game] Ci: 1129 *with picture*
Cribellum [zoology]
Spider (How spiders make silk) So: 786
Crichton, Michael [American author] Ci: 1130
Crick, Francis Harry Compton [British biologist] Ci: 1130
Biology (The growth of modern biology) B: 319-320
Cell (The 1900's) C: 337-338

Franklin, Rosalind Elsie **F: 492**
Heredity (The chemistry of genes) **H: 208-209**
Science (Achievements of the mid-1900's) **S: 202** *with picture*
Watson, James Dewey **W: 147**
Wilkins, Maurice Hugh Frederick **W: 306**
Cricket [insect] **Ci: 1130** *with pictures*
Ear *picture on* **E: 13**
Insect *pictures on* **I: 280;** (Hearing) **I: 290-291** *with picture*
Cricket [game] **Ci: 1131** *with pictures*
Australia (Recreation) **A: 903** *with picture*
England (Recreation) **E: 296-297** *with picture*
London (Recreation) **L: 434**
Samoa (People) **S: 80a**
United Kingdom (Recreation) **U: 55**
Cricket [magazine]
Literature for children (New children's magazines) **L: 365-366**
Crickets [band]
Holly, Buddy **H: 293**
Cricoid cartilage [anatomy]
Larynx **L: 79**
Crier [occupation]
Advertising (History) **A: 79**
Colonial life in America (Communication) **Ci: 806**
Crile, George Washington [American doctor] **Ci: 1135**
Crime Ci: 1135 *with diagrams*
See also Criminal law *in this index; the list of Related articles in the* Crime *article; and the Criminal law section of the Related articles in the* Law *article*
Burglary **B: 704**
City (Social problems) **Ci: 591**
Colonial life in America (Crime and punishment) **Ci: 796**
Computer (Computer security) **Ci: 924**
Confession **Ci: 936**
Criminal justice system (The police) **Ci: 1143**
Famine (Effects of famine) **F: 26a**
Gang **G: 26**
Hate crime **H: 85**
Hostage **H: 374a**
Insider trading **I: 303**
Internet (Internet crime) **I: 350f**
Mafia **M: 41**
Moscow (Social problems) **M: 825**
New York City (Social problems) **N: 332-333**
Police (In the United States since the mid-1900's) **P: 624-625**
Poverty (Effects on society) **P: 724**
Racketeering **R: 63**
Sentence **S: 304**
Shoplifting **S: 433**
Vigilante **V: 378**
Western frontier life in America (Life in the mining towns) **W: 236;** (Law and order) **W: 238**
Investigation
Ballistics (Forensic ballistics) **B: 56**
Crime scene investigation **Ci: 1140**
Criminology **Ci: 1145**
Fingerprinting **F: 106**
Footprinting **F: 369** *with picture*
Forensic pathology **F: 389a**
Forensic science **F: 388b**
Hypnosis (Enhancing memory) **H: 479**
Medical examiner **M: 361**
Wiretapping **W: 345**
Prevention
Crime (Crime prevention) **Ci: 1139**
Adolescent (Delinquency) **A: 64**
Capital punishment **C: 193**
Gun control **G: 440**
Juvenile delinquency **J: 205**
Lighting (On streets and highways) **L: 297**
Crime against humanity
Nuremberg Trials (The trials) **N: 613**
War (Changes in the rules of war) **W: 24**
Crime and Punishment [book by Dostoevsky]
Dostoevsky, Fyodor **D: 311**
Novel (Russia) **N: 573**
Russian literature (The 1860's and 1870's) **R: 562**
Crime deterrent [law]
Criminal justice system (The correctional system) **Ci: 1144**
Crime insurance
Insurance (Crime insurance) **I: 314**
Crime laboratory
Crime scene investigation (At the laboratory) **Ci: 1141**
Forensic science **F: 388b**
Police (Investigations of crimes) **P: 621**
Crime rate
Crime (The extent of crime) **Ci: 1137** *with diagram;* (Social conditions and crime) **Ci: 1138-1139**

Criminology (Statistical studies) **Ci: 1145**
Crime scene investigation Ci: 1140 *with pictures*
Fingerprinting **F: 106**
Forensic science (Crime scene investigations) **F: 388b**
Crime syndicate
Crime (Organized crime) **Ci: 1136**
Crimea [region, Ukraine] **Ci: 1142** *with picture and map*
Russo-Turkish wars **R: 566b**
Crimean Mountains [Crimean Peninsula]
Ukraine (The Crimean Mountains) **U: 10** *with map*
Crimean War [1853-1856] **Ci: 1142**
Balaklava, Battle of **B: 34**
Greece (Otto I) **G: 362**
Napoleon III (Foreign affairs) **N: 17**
Nicholas I **N: 402**
Nightingale, Florence (Service in Crimea) **N: 420**
Paris, Treaties of (The treaty of 1856) **P: 167**
Russia (Nicholas I) **R: 551**
Russo-Turkish wars **R: 566b**
War (Conflicts over resources) **W: 23**
Criminal
Crime **Ci: 1135**
Criminal justice system **Ci: 1143**
Criminology **Ci: 1145**
Criminal court [law]
Court (How courts work) **Ci: 1101**
Criminal Investigation Department
See also Scotland Yard *in this index*
Police (In other countries) **P: 623**
Criminal Justice Information Services [organization]
Federal Bureau of Investigation (Other services) **F: 62**
Criminal justice system Ci: 1143
Police **P: 620**
Criminal law
Confession **Ci: 936**
Crime **Ci: 1135**
Criminal justice system (The courts) **Ci: 1143**
Criminology (History) **Ci: 1145**
Insanity **I: 277**
Jury (Petit juries) **J: 202**
Law (Public law) **L: 130**
Law enforcement **L: 141**
Supreme Court of the United States (Criminal law) **So: 1001**
Treaty (Kinds of treaties) **T: 408-409**
Criminal Life of Archibaldo de la Cruz, The [film]
Latin America (Motion pictures) **L: 101**
Criminal Victimization in the United States [report]
Crime (Unreported crime) **Ci: 1138**
Criminalist
Criminology (What criminologists study) **Ci: 1145**
Criminology Ci: 1145 *with picture*
See also Crime *in this index*
Blood (The significance of blood groups) **B: 412**
Criminal justice system (The correctional system) **Ci: 1144**
DNA fingerprinting **D: 258**
Juvenile delinquency (What causes delinquency?) **J: 206**
Lie detector **L: 271**
Crimson clover [plant]
Clover (Crimson clover) **Ci: 713** *with picture*
Crinet [armor]
Armor *picture on* **A: 720**
Crinoid [animal]
Ocean *picture on* **O: 656**
Criollismo [poetry]
Argentina (The arts) **A: 651-652**
Criollo [people]
Argentina (The arts) **A: 651-652**
Latin America (Colonial discontent) **L: 106**
Crioulo [language]
Guinea-Bissau (People) **G: 432-433**
Crippen, Robert L. [American astronaut]
Astronaut (Achievements in space) **A: 829-830;** (table) **A: 830**
Cripple Creek [Colorado]
Colorado (Progress as a state) **Ci: 847**
Crisis [literature]
Drama (The structure of drama) **D: 325**
Crisis, The [magazine]
Du Bois, W. E. B. **D: 372**
National Association for the Advancement of Colored People (History) **N: 29**
Crisp, Donald [British actor]
Motion picture (Best performance by an actor in a supporting role: 1941) **M: 862a**
Crisp head lettuce
Lettuce (Kinds of lettuce) **L: 213** *with picture*
Crispin: The Cross of Lead [book by Avi]
Avi **A: 982**
Crispin and Scapin [painting by Daumier]

Daumier, Honoré *picture on* **D: 44**
Crist, Charlie [American political leader]
Florida (table) **F: 260**
Cristallo glass
Glass (The Middle Ages) **G: 218;** (Types of art glass) **G: 220**
Cristiani, Alfredo [El Salvadoran political leader]
El Salvador (The 1900's) **E: 252**
Cristóbal Colón [volcano, Colombia]
Andes Mountains (Physical features) **A: 452-453**
Colombia (The Andes Mountains) **Ci: 782**
Cristofori, Bartolomeo [Italian inventor]
Piano (History) **P: 447**
Criterion, The [magazine]
Eliot, T. S. (His life) **E: 237**
Critias [Greek political leader]
Plato (Plato's life) **P: 567**
Sophists **So: 595**
Thirty Tyrants **T: 259**
Critias [book by Plato]
Atlantis **A: 868**
Critic [career]
Book review **B: 470**
Criticism **Ci: 1146**
Critic, The [play by Sheridan]
Sheridan, Richard Brinsley **S: 396**
Critica, La [magazine]
Croce, Benedetto **Ci: 1148c**
Critical and Pronouncing Dictionary and Expositor of the English Language [book by Walker]
Dictionary (Early English dictionaries) **D: 194**
Critical day
Biorhythm **B: 326**
Critical density [cosmology]
Dark energy **D: 37**
Critical mass [physics]
Nuclear energy (Chain reactions) **N: 586**
Nuclear weapon (Fission weapons) **N: 596-597**
Critical Philosophy
Philosophy (The philosophy of Immanuel Kant) **P: 389**
Critical temperature
Gas [physics] (How gases behave) **G: 48**
Mendeleev, Dmitri Ivanovich **M: 398**
Superconductivity **So: 992**
Critical thinking [philosophy]
Education (How teachers guide learning) **E: 90**
Ethics (What can ethics do for us?) **E: 367**
Criticism Ci: 1146
Book review **B: 470**
French literature (The middle and late 1900's) **F: 523**
Literature (Judging literature) **L: 352-353**
New Testament (Critical studies) **N: 288**
Painting (The art world, 1850-1900) **P: 73**
Pulitzer Prizes (table) **P: 892**
Critique of Practical Reason [book by Kant]
Kant, Immanuel (Kant's ideas) **K: 244**
Philosophy (The philosophy of Immanuel Kant) **P: 389-390**
Critique of Pure Reason [book by Kant]
Kant, Immanuel **K: 243**
Philosophy (The philosophy of Immanuel Kant) **P: 389**
Crito [book by Plato]
Plato (The dialogues) **P: 567**
Critolaus [Greek philosopher]
Aristotle (Aristotle's place in Western thought) **A: 664**
Crittenden, John J. [American political leader]
Crittenden Compromise **Ci: 1147**
Fillmore, Millard (table) **F: 102**
Harrison, William Henry (table) **H: 76**
Justice, Department of (table) **J: 203**
Tyler, John (table) **T: 534**
Crittenden, Thomas T. [American political leader]
Missouri (table) **M: 668;** (Progress as a state) **M: 671**
Crittenden Compromise [U.S. history] **Ci: 1147**
Crivelli, Carlo [Italian painter]
Painting *picture on* **P: 38**
Cro-Magnons [anthropology] **Ci: 1147** *with pictures*
Cave dwellers **C: 321**
Europe (Prehistoric times) **E: 406**
Prehistoric people (The Stone Age) **P: 751;** (table) **P: 754**
Croaker [fish]
Drum **D: 367** *with picture*
Croatan Indians
Lumbee Indians **L: 516**
Croatia Ci: 1148 *with pictures and map*
Bosnia-Herzegovina (History) **B: 492-493**
Flag *picture on* **F: 205**
Serbia (History) **S: 314-316**
United Nations *picture on* **U: 92**

Yugoslavia **Y:** 576
Croatian language
  Croatia (People) **Ci:** 1148
Croatian Peasant Party [Croatian history]
  Croatia (History) **Ci:** 1148a-1148b
Croatoan [U.S. history]
  Lost Colony **L:** 472
Croats [people]
  Bosnia-Herzegovina (People) **B:** 492
  Croatia (People) **Ci:** 1148
Croce, Benedetto [Italian philosopher] **Ci:** 1148c
Crochet [handicraft] **Ci:** 1148c *with pictures*
Crochet hook
  Crochet **Ci:** 1148c *with pictures*
  Needle **N:** 117 *with picture*
Crochet lace
  Lace **L:** 20
Crocidolite [material]
  Asbestos (Types of asbestos) **A:** 765
Crock of Gold, The [book by Stephens]
  Stephens, James **So:** 890
Crocker, Charles [American businessman]
  California (Early statehood) **C:** 62
Crocker Art Museum
  Sacramento (Education and cultural life) **S:** 6
Crockett, Davy [American frontiersman] **Ci:** 1148d
  with picture
  Alamo (Early days) **A:** 280
  Folklore (Legends) **F:** 324
  Texas (The Texas revolution) **T:** 206
Crocodile Ci: 1149 *with pictures*
  Alligator (Alligators and crocodiles) **A:** 376
  Animal *picture on* **A:** 486; (Providing protection)
    A: 500
  Endangered species *picture on* **E:** 271; (table)
    E: 270
  Reptile (Crocodilians) **R:** 251 *with picture*
Crocodile bird
  Courser **C:** 1101
Crocodile River [river, Africa]
  Limpopo River **L:** 309
Crocodilian [zoology]
  Crocodile **Ci:** 1149 *with picture*
  Dinosaur **D:** 206a
  Gavial **G:** 71 *with picture*
Crocus [plant] **Ci:** 1150 *with picture*
  Flower *picture on* **F:** 274; (Garden perennials
    grown from bulbs) **F:** 280 *with picture*
  Plant **P:** 519 *with picture*
  Saffron **S:** 17
Crocus, Autumn [plant]
  Colchicum **Ci:** 760
Croesus [king of Lydia] **Ci:** 1150
  Cyrus the Great **Ci:** 1208
  Lydia **L:** 533
Croft [farm]
  Hebrides **H:** 163
  Highland Clearances **H:** 229
Croft, William [English composer]
  Hymn (Words and music) **H:** 475
Crofter [agriculture]
  Highland Clearances **H:** 229
Crofters' Holdings Act [1886]
  Highland Clearances **H:** 229
Crohn's disease Ci: 1150
  Colostomy **Ci:** 850
  Inflammatory bowel disease **I:** 266
Cromer, Betsy [birth name of]
  Byars, Betsy **B:** 746
Crompton, Samuel [British inventor] **Ci:** 1151
  Clothing (Factory-made clothing) **Ci:** 691
  Industrial Revolution (Spinning machines)
    I: 248-249
  Spinning (The mule) **So:** 794
Cromwell [play by Hugo]
  Hugo, Victor (Early life) **H:** 409
Cromwell, Oliver [English political leader] **Ci:** 1151
  with portrait
  Charles I [of England] **C:** 380
  Charles II [of England] **C:** 380
  England (The Civil War) **E:** 308
  Ireland (Religious persecution) **I:** 426
  London (War, plague, and fire) **L:** 441
  Long Parliament **L:** 448
  Parliament (Parliament gains strength) **P:** 174
  Puritans (History) **P:** 910
  Rump Parliament **R:** 519
  Scotland (War with the king) **S:** 220
  Virginia (Royal governors and Cromwell) **V:** 418
Cromwell, Richard [son of Oliver Cromwell]
  Ci: 1152
  Cromwell, Oliver (The Protectorate) **Ci:** 1152
  England (table) **E:** 308; (The Restoration) **E:** 309
  Restoration **R:** 263
Cromwell, Thomas [English political leader]
  Ci: 1152
  England (The English Reformation) **E:** 307

Henry VIII [of England] **H:** 188
  United Kingdom, History of the (The English
    Reformation) **U:** 14
Cromwell, Thomas A. [Canadian jurist]
  Supreme Court of Canada (table) **So:** 997 *with
    portrait*
Cronin, A. J. [British author] **Ci:** 1152
Cronin, James Watson [American physicist]
  Nobel Prizes (Physics: 1980) **N:** 441
Cronin, Joe [American baseball player]
  Baseball (table: Hall of Fame) **B:** 134
Cronkite, Walter [American newscaster] **Ci:** 1152
  with portrait
Cronstedt, Axel [Swedish chemist]
  Nickel **N:** 404
Cronus [Greek mythology] **Ci:** 1152
  See also Saturn [Roman mythology] *in this index*
  Hades **H:** 4
  Hestia **H:** 220
  Mythology (The Greek creation myth) **M:** 980;
    (table) **M:** 981; (Greek divinities) **M:** 982
  Rhea **R:** 290
  Titans **T:** 300
  Uranus **U:** 217
  Zeus **Z:** 590
Crook [device]
  Bassoon **B:** 158 *with diagram*
Crook, George [American general]
  Crazy Horse **Ci:** 1123
  Geronimo **G:** 173
  Indian wars (Apache warfare) **I:** 195
Crookedest Street in the World [San Francisco]
  San Francisco *picture on* **S:** 96; (Downtown San
    Francisco) **S:** 92-93
Crookes, Sir William [British chemist] **Ci:** 1153
  Crookes tube **Ci:** 1153
  Electronics (Early experiments) **E:** 215
Crookes tube [physics] **Ci:** 1153 *with diagram*
  Electronics (Early experiments) **E:** 215 *with picture*
  Roentgen, Wilhelm Conrad **R:** 400
Crookesite [mineral]
  Thallium **T:** 229
Crooklyn [film]
  Lee, Spike **L:** 180
Crop [agriculture] **Ci:** 1153
  Agriculture (Agricultural products) **A:** 147;
    (History) **A:** 153-154
  Food supply (Limited agricultural resources)
    F: 348
  Plant (How crops differ from wild plants) **P:** 542;
    (Loss of biodiversity) **P:** 543
Crop [zoology]
  Ant (Internal organs) **A:** 522 *with diagram*
  Bird (The digestive system) **B:** 365
  Chicken (The body of a chicken) **C:** 440-441
  Esophagus **E:** 358
  Hoatzin **H:** 272
  Insect (Digestive system) **I:** 289 *with diagram*
Crop-dusting
  Airplane (Special-purpose planes) **A:** 212 *with
    picture*
  Helicopter *picture on* **H:** 170
  Insecticide **I:** 301 *with picture*
Crop insurance Ci: 1153
Crop milk [zoology] *See* Pigeon's milk *in this index*
Crop Over [festival]
  July **J:** 188
Crop rotation [agriculture]
  Agriculture (Rome) **A:** 156
  Alfalfa (As a cover and rotation crop) **A:** 347
  Conservation (Soil conservation) **Ci:** 979-980
  Cotton (Diseases) **Ci:** 1090
  Cropping system **Ci:** 1153
  Environmental pollution (Agriculture) **E:** 337
  Nitrogen (Nitrogen in agriculture) **N:** 426
  Pest control (Natural pest control) **P:** 318
Crop storage [agriculture]
  Farm and farming (Processing and storage) **F:** 37
    with pictures
Cropping [surgery]
  Dog (Body structure) **D:** 263-265
  Dogfighting **D:** 282
Cropping system [agriculture] **Ci:** 1153
Croquet [game] **Ci:** 1154 *with pictures*
Crore [money]
  Rupee **R:** 521
Crosby, Bing [American entertainer] **Ci:** 1154
  Hope, Bob **H:** 333
  Motion picture (Best performance by an actor:
    1944) **M:** 862a
Crosby, Fanny [American hymnist]
  Hymn (History) **H:** 475
Crosby, Robert B. [American political leader]
  Nebraska (table) **N:** 110
Crosby, Sidney [Canadian hockey player]
  Canada *picture on* **C:** 108
Crosby, William G. [American political leader]

Maine (table) **M:** 87
Crosley Field [Cincinnati]
  Baseball (Depression and war) **B:** 136
Cross [symbol] **Ci:** 1155 *with pictures*
  Byzantine art *picture on* **B:** 751
  Easter (The crucifix and the cross) **E:** 43
  Ku Klux Klan **K:** 389 *with picture*
Cross, Burton M. [American political leader]
  Maine (table) **M:** 87
Cross, James R. [British government official]
  Canada, History of (The separatist threat) **C:** 150
  Montreal (The separatist movement) **M:** 779
  Quebec (The late 1900's) **Q:** 32
  Trudeau, Pierre Elliott (The national scene) **T:** 464
Cross, Wilbur L. [American political leader]
  Connecticut (table) **Ci:** 967
Cross-bracing [building construction]
  Earthquake (Building design) **E:** 35 *with picture*
Cross burning
  Hate crime **H:** 85
  Ku Klux Klan **K:** 389 *with picture*
Cross-country [sport] **Ci:** 1155
Cross-country event
  Horse *picture on* **H:** 357; (Eventing) **H:** 358
Cross-country flight
  Airplane (Learning to fly) **A:** 226
Cross-country skiing [sport]
  Olympic Games (Winter Olympic Games) **O:** 746d
  Skiing *diagrams on* **S:** 485; (Nordic skiing) **S:** 482
    with picture; (Ski equipment and clothing)
    S: 483; (Nordic competitions) **S:** 487
Cross-examination [law]
  Civil rights (Due process) **Ci:** 608
  Debate (Framework of a round) **D:** 64; (Forms of
    competitive debate) **D:** 64
Cross-eye [disorder] *See* Strabismus *in this index*
Cross Fell [mountain, England]
  Pennines **P:** 243
Cross fox [animal]
  Fox (Kinds of foxes) **F:** 440
Cross-linking [chemistry]
  Materials (Physical bonds) **M:** 301
  Plastics (Types of plastics) **P:** 555
Cross-match [blood test]
  Blood (The significance of blood groups) **B:** 412
  Blood transfusion (Types of transfusion) **B:** 417
Cross moline [symbol]
  Heraldry *picture on* **H:** 195
Cross of gold [U.S. history]
  Bryan, William Jennings (Early career) **B:** 654
  Cleveland, Grover (Saving the gold standard)
    Ci: 673
"Cross of Snow, The" [poem by Longfellow]
  Longfellow, Henry Wadsworth (Author and world
    celebrity) **L:** 450
Cross-pollination [botany]
  Flower (Cross-pollination) **F:** 295
  Plant (Sexual reproduction) **P:** 532-533
  Pollen (Methods of pollination) **P:** 644 *with
    diagrams*
Cross-reference [publishing] **Ci:** 1155
  Dictionary (What a dictionary tells you) **D:** 193
  Encyclopedia (Ease of use) **E:** 266; (Providing
    cross-references) **E:** 267; (Basic steps in the
    preparation of a World Book article) **E:** 268
    with picture
Cross stitch
  Needlepoint **N:** 118
Cross treble stitch
  Crochet **Ci:** 1148d
Crossbar [sports]
  Pole vault **P:** 618
Crossbill [bird] **Ci:** 1155 *with picture*
Crossbow [weapon] **Ci:** 1156 *with picture*
Crossbred [animal husbandry]
  Hog (Kinds of hogs) **H:** 285
  Horse (table: Horse terms) **H:** 343
  Livestock (Outbreeding) **L:** 398
Crossbred-wooled sheep
  New Zealand (Agriculture) **N:** 353
  Wool (Sources of wool) **W:** 399
Crosscut
  Mining (Mining terms) **M:** 577
Crosscut saw [tool]
  Saw (Handsaws) **S:** 166 *with picture*
  Woodworking (Cutting) **W:** 397
Crosse [sports]
  Lacrosse (The field and equipment) **L:** 23 *with
    picture*
Crosse check [sports]
  Lacrosse (Men's lacrosse) **L:** 23
Crossfire [debating]
  Debate (A public forum debate) **D:** 65
CrossGlobal Link [organization]
  Missionary (Organization) **M:** 621
Crossing [genetics]
  Breeding **B:** 592

Fruit (Developing new fruit cultivars) F: 548
Crossing over [genetics]
Heredity (Genetic recombination) H: 203
Crossing straight
Ice skating (Long-track skating) I: 14
Crossley, Archibald M. [American statistician]
Public opinion poll (History) P: 863
Crossmatch See Cross-match in this index
Crossover [fingerprinting]
Fingerprinting picture on F: 106
Crossover hit [recording]
Country music (Emergence of the country music industry) Ci: 1098b-1098c
Crossover vehicle
Sport utility vehicle So: 802
Crossroads of America [name for]
Indianapolis I: 220
Crossroads of America [state motto]
Indiana I: 196
Crossroads of the Pacific [name for]
Honolulu H: 320
Crossroads of the South [name for]
Jackson J: 4
Crossroads of the World [name for]
Panama P: 115
Crosstie [construction]
Railroad (The crossties and rails) R: 109
Crossword puzzle Ci: 1156 with picture
Croswell, Charles M. [American political leader]
Michigan (table) M: 507
Crothers, Austin L. [American political leader]
Maryland (table) M: 255
Croton [shrub] Ci: 1156
Croton Aqueduct [New York City]
Aqueduct (Present-day aqueducts) A: 580
Croton bug [insect]
Cockroach Ci: 745
Crouch, Eric [American football player]
Football (table) F: 363
Crouching Tiger; Hidden Dragon [film]
Motion picture (Motion pictures today) M: 872-873
Crounse, Lorenzo [American political leader]
Nebraska (table) N: 110
Croup [disorder] Ci: 1157
Croupier [gambling]
Roulette R: 491
Crouse, Russel [American dramatist]
Lindsay, Howard L: 333
Crow [bird] Ci: 1157 with picture
Jackdaw J: 4 with picture
Crow [butterfly]
Butterfly picture on B: 735
Crow [poems by Hughes]
English literature (Recent English poetry) E: 323
Hughes, Ted H: 409
Crow, Jim [U.S. history] See Jim Crow in this index
Crow, John [American football player]
Football (table) F: 363
Crow Indians Ci: 1158
Indian, American picture on I: 144
Crowbar [tool]
Fire department (Rescue trucks) picture on F: 127
Crowd control
Mace M: 11
Crowder, Enoch H. [American general]
Missouri (Progress as a state) M: 671
Crowe, Russell [New Zealand actor] Ci: 1158
Motion picture (Best performance by an actor: 2000) M: 862a
Crowe, William J., Jr. [American military leader]
Joint Chiefs of Staff (table) J: 156
Crowfoot [Canadian Indian chief] Ci: 1158
Crowfoot [plant] See Buttercup in this index
Crowley, Aleister [British author]
Witchcraft (Witchcraft in modern times) W: 373
Crown [anatomy]
See also Crowning in this index
Teeth (Kinds of teeth) T: 79; (Pulp) T: 80 with picture
Crown [botany]
Rain forest (Structure and growth) R: 126a
Sugar beet So: 962 with picture
Tree (Trunk and branches) T: 416
Crown [part of hat]
Hat H: 83
Crown [symbol] Ci: 1158 with pictures
Crown Center
Kansas City [Missouri] (History) K: 242-243
Crown colony [political unit]
Commonwealth of Nations (Dependencies) Ci: 876
Crown conch [animal]
Shell picture on S: 386
Crown dependency [political unit]
Commonwealth of Nations (Dependencies) Ci: 876

Crown gall [plant disease]
Bacteria (Harmful bacteria) B: 20
Gall G: 13
Crown glass
Glass (Early American glass) G: 222
Crown Hill Cemetery [Indianapolis]
Indianapolis (Cultural life) I: 221-222
Crown imperial [plant]
Fritillary F: 535
Crown Mountain [St. Thomas]
Virgin Islands, United States (Islands) V: 395
Crown of thorns [starfish]
Coral (Stony corals) Ci: 1048a
Great Barrier Reef G: 336
Shell picture on S: 384
Crown Point [region, New York]
Revolution, American (The evacuation of Boston) R: 275
Crown rot [plant disease]
Alfalfa (Diseases and pests) A: 347
Crowned crane [bird]
Crane (Kinds) Ci: 1117
Crowned eagle
Eagle (Other kinds of eagles) E: 5
Crowning [dentistry]
Teeth (Dental decay) T: 82-83 with diagrams
Crowning Privilege, The [book by Graves]
Graves, Robert G: 330
Crowning with Thorns [painting by Titian]
Painting (The Renaissance in Venice) P: 55-56 with picture
Crowninshield, B. W. [American government official]
Madison, James (table) M: 35
Crow's-nest [structure]
Ship (Nautical terms) S: 405
Crowther, Samuel [American author]
Ford, Henry (Political and charitable activities) F: 380-381
Crowther, William [American programmer]
Electronic game (Early computer games) E: 204d
Crozat, Antoine [American businessman]
Louisiana (French Louisiana) L: 497-498
Crozat, Pierre [French art collector]
Watteau, Antoine W: 149
CRP [medicine] See C-reactive protein in this index
CRP [U.S. history]
Watergate (The break-in and cover-up) W: 144
CRT [electronics] See Cathode-ray tube in this index
Cruce, Lee [American political leader]
Oklahoma (table) O: 730
Crucian carp [fish] See Goldfish in this index
Crucible [device]
Aluminum (Casting the molten aluminum) A: 394 with diagram
Iron and steel (The blast furnace process) I: 440
Crucible, The [play by Miller]
American literature (Drama) A: 426
Miller, Arthur M: 553
Crucible process [industry]
Iron and steel (The first steel) I: 450
Crucifix [symbol]
Cross Ci: 1155 with picture
Easter (The crucifix and the cross) E: 43
Crucifixion [religion]
Jesus Christ (The Crucifixion) J: 108b with pictures
Joseph of Arimathea J: 168
New Testament (Historical Jesus research) N: 288
Peter, Saint (Life as an apostle) P: 324
Crucifixion of Saint Peter, The [painting by Michelangelo]
Michelangelo picture on M: 485
Crude birth rate [statistics]
Birth and death rates B: 377
Crude death rate [statistics]
Birth and death rates B: 377
Crude oil
Bitumen B: 384
Energy supply (Fossil fuels) E: 277
Fuel (Petroleum) F: 550
Oil shale O: 707
Persian Gulf War of 1991 (Consequences of the war) P: 300e
Petroleum P: 330 with pictures
Crude rate
Vital statistics (Using vital statistics) V: 429
Crude rubber
Rubber (Natural rubber) R: 502; (Processing crude rubber) R: 503
Cruel Tales [stories by Villiers de l'Isle-Adam]
Villiers de l'Isle-Adam, Comte de V: 385
Cruikshank, George [British artist] Ci: 1158
Dickens, Charles picture on D: 189
English literature picture on E: 321
Cruikshank, William [British chemist]
Carbon monoxide C: 208
Cruise [lamp]

Lamp (Fat or oil lamps) L: 52
Cruise, Tom [American actor] Ci: 1158 with portrait
Kidman, Nicole K: 311
Cruise control
Automobile (The passenger compartment) A: 950-951
Cruise missile
Carter, Jimmy (Early programs) C: 257
Guided missile picture on G: 423; (Nonballistic missiles) G: 425 with diagram
Submarine (Attack submarines) So: 939-940
Cruise ship Ci: 1159
Ship picture on S: 410; (Passenger ships) S: 409; (Officers and crew) S: 410
Cruiser [ship] Ci: 1159
Navy (Cruisers) N: 78
Navy, United States (Combat ships) N: 84; (Ordnance) N: 84
Warship (Cruisers) W: 40
Cruiser bicycle
Bicycle (Road bikes) B: 289
Cruiserweight class [boxing]
Boxing (table) B: 527
Cruising sailboat
Boating picture on B: 431
Crumb, George [American composer] Ci: 1159
Crumb, Robert [American cartoonist]
Comics (Comic books) Ci: 869-870
Crumb rubber
Rubber (Processing crude rubber) R: 503
Crump, Diane [American jockey]
Horse racing (History) H: 366
Crump, E. H. [American political leader]
Memphis (History) M: 396-397
Tennessee (The mid-1900's) T: 156
Crumple zone [device]
Automobile (Safety problems) A: 961-962
Crupper [device]
Armor picture on A: 720
Harness diagram on H: 63
Crusade for Justice [organization]
Gonzales, Rodolfo G: 269
Hispanic Americans (The Chicano movement) H: 256
Crusade in Europe [book by Eisenhower]
Eisenhower, Dwight David (NATO commander) E: 150
Crusades [European history] Ci: 1159 with picture and map
Astrology (History) A: 827
Byzantine Empire (The middle period) B: 754
Christianity (The medieval church) C: 524
Clothing picture on Ci: 703
Flag picture on F: 216
Food (The Middle Ages) F: 336
Heraldry (The development of heraldry) H: 194
Jews (Jews in Christian Europe) J: 122
Knights Templars K: 353
Louis IX L: 474
Middle Ages (Economic recovery) M: 526
Middle East (The spread of Islam) M: 533-534
Painting (Medieval painting) P: 48
Palestine (Arab control) P: 104-105
Seljuks S: 290
Slavery (The Middle Ages) S: 501
War (Clashing ideologies) W: 23
1st Crusade (1096-1099)
Egypt (Muslim rule) E: 130
Insignia I: 303
Jerusalem (Muslim rule) J: 101
Peter the Hermit P: 325
Turkey (The Seljuk Turks) T: 509-510
Urban II U: 219
3rd Crusade (1189-1192)
Richard I R: 328
Saladin S: 59
4th Crusade (1201-1204)
Innocent III (Crusades) I: 275
Crushed stone
Building stone B: 685
Materials (Stone) M: 300c-300d
Quarrying Q: 7
Crusher [machine]
Wine (How wine is made) W: 337-338
Crusoe, Robinson [literary figure] See Robinson Crusoe in this index
Crust [geology]
Earth (The lithosphere) E: 20 with diagram
Earthquake (How an earthquake begins) E: 35 with diagram
Hot spot H: 374a
Mantle M: 168
Mars (Interior) M: 225
Moon (The interior of the moon) M: 790
Plate tectonics (Structure of tectonic plates) P: 561
San Andreas Fault S: 83

Crustacean [zoology] **Ci: 1162** *with pictures*
  See also the list of Related articles in the Crustacean *article*
  Aquaculture **A: 578**
  Compound eye **Ci: 906**
  Crab **Ci: 1115**
  Eye (Eyes of animals) **E: 469**
  Ocean (Zooplankton) **O: 655**
  Prehistoric animal (Invertebrates) **P: 737**
Crustal root [geology]
  Mountain (Forces that shape mountains) **M: 894** *with diagram*
Crustose lichen [plant]
  Lichen **L: 269**
Crutcher [machine]
  Detergent and soap (The kettle method) **D: 164**
Crutches
  Poliomyelitis *picture on* **P: 626**
Crutzen, Paul Josef [Dutch chemist]
  Nobel Prizes (Chemistry: 1995) **N: 444**
Crux [constellation]
  Southern Cross **So: 688**
Cruz, Celia [Cuban American singer] **Ci: 1165** *with portrait*
  Hispanic Americans (Entertainment and arts) **H: 249**
Cruz, Juana Inés de la [Mexican poet] *See* Juana Inés de la Cruz *in this index*
Cruz, Nilo [American playwright]
  Hispanic Americans *picture on* **H: 248**
Cruz, Penélope [Spanish actress]
  Motion picture (Best performance by an actress in a supporting role: 2008) **M: 862b**
Cruz, Ramón Ernesto [Honduran political leader]
  Honduras (Revolutions and reforms) **H: 313**
Cruzan v. Director, Missouri Department of Health [1990]
  Euthanasia (Termination of life-sustaining treatment) **E: 421**
Cry, the Beloved Country [book by Paton]
  Paton, Alan **P: 196**
Cry of Dolores [Mexican history] *See* Grito de Dolores *in this index*
"Cry of the Children" [poem by Browning]
  Browning, Elizabeth Barrett **B: 646**
Crying
  Baby (Crying) **B: 10**
  Tears **T: 72**
Crying of Lot 49, The [book by Pynchon]
  Pynchon, Thomas **P: 915**
Cryobiology [science] **Ci: 1165**
  Biology (table) **B: 317**
Cryogenic freezing
  Food, Frozen (Cryogenic freezing) **F: 338**
  Food preservation (Freezing) **F: 342-343**
Cryogenic pump [machine]
  Vacuum (Producing a vacuum) **V: 256**
Cryogenic refrigerator
  Refrigeration (Low-temperature refrigeration) **R: 202**
Cryogenics [physics] **Ci: 1165**
  Liquid air **L: 346**
  Physics (Heat) **P: 437**
Cryolite [mineral]
  Aluminum (Smelting the alumina) **A: 393**
Cryoprecipitate [substance]
  Blood transfusion (Types of transfusion) **B: 417**
Cryopump [machine]
  Vacuum (Producing a vacuum) **V: 256**
Cryosphere [geology]
  Earth (The hydrosphere) **E: 20**
Cryosurgery
  Cryobiology **Ci: 1165**
  Surgery (Technique) **So: 1005**
Cryotherapy
  Eye (Diseases of the retina) **E: 467-468**
Cryovolcanism [geology]
  Neptune (Satellites and rings) **N: 129**
  Satellite (Titan) **S: 150a**
  Volcano (Volcanoes in the solar system) **V: 442b-443**
Crypsis [insect]
  Animal *picture on* **A: 495**
Crypt of Civilization [time capsule]
  Time capsule **T: 293**
Cryptanalysis [study]
  Codes and ciphers **Ci: 749**
Cryptic coloration [zoology]
  Butterfly (How butterflies protect themselves) **B: 742**
  Protective coloration **P: 831** *with picture*
Cryptocrystalline quartz [mineral]
  Jasper **J: 64**
  Quartz (Types) **Q: 8**
Cryptocrystalline silica [mineral]
  Silica **S: 457**
Cryptogram [message] *See* Ciphertext *in this index*

Cryptographic algorithm [cryptology]
  Codes and ciphers **Ci: 749**
Cryptographic authentication [cryptology]
  Codes and ciphers (Modern applications of cryptography) **Ci: 752**
Cryptography [communications]
  Central Intelligence Agency (Functions) **C: 356-357**
  Codes and ciphers **Ci: 749**
  Computer security **Ci: 925**
  Electronics (Electronics today) **E: 216-217**
Cryptology [communications]
  Codes and ciphers **Ci: 749**
Cryptosporidium [parasite]
  Food poisoning **F: 340**
Cryptosystem [code]
  Codes and ciphers **Ci: 749**
Crystal [chemistry] **Ci: 1166** *with pictures*
  Diffraction (Uses of diffraction) **D: 201**
  Gem (Crystal shape) **G: 77**
  Ice **I: 4** *with diagram*
  Ion *pictures on* **I: 371**
  Ion microscope **I: 372** *with picture*
  Life *picture on* **L: 275**
  Liquid crystal **L: 347**
  Mineral (Mineral crystals) **M: 567** *with pictures;* (The scientific study of mineral crystals) **M: 571**
  Nanotechnology (Applications of nanotechnology) **N: 10**
  Quartz **Q: 8**
  Quasicrystal **Q: 9**
  Rock (Extrusive rock) **R: 371**
  Semiconductor (Semiconductor crystals) **S: 291**
  Silicate **S: 457** *with picture*
  Snow **S: 539** *with pictures*
  Solid-state physics **So: 583**
  Symmetry **So: 1066**
  X rays (In crystal research) **X: 541**
Crystal [drug] *See* Methamphetamine *in this index*
Crystal [glass]
  Glass (Types of art glass) **G: 220**
Crystal ball
  Fortunetelling (Methods of fortunetelling) **F: 419**
Crystal Cave [cave, Kentucky]
  Mammoth Cave National Park **M: 130**
Crystal Ice Cave [Idaho]
  Idaho (Interesting facts about Idaho) **I: 27**
Crystal laser
  Laser (Solid-state lasers) **L: 85**
Crystal microphone
  Microphone (Crystal microphones and ceramic microphones) **M: 516** *with diagram*
Crystal Palace [London]
  Architecture (The Industrial Revolution) **A: 625** *with picture*
  Shelter (The Industrial Revolution) **S: 394**
  World's fair **W: 500**
Crystal Palace National Sports Centre
  London (Recreation) **L: 434**
Crystal radio
  Radio *picture on* **R: 92**; (How radio programs are received) **R: 88**
Crystal rectifier [electronics]
  Radio (How radio programs are received) **R: 88**
Crystalline lens [anatomy]
  Eye (The uveal tract) **E: 460-461** *with picture*
Crystalline rock [geology]
  Igneous rock **I: 49**
Crystalline silica [mineral]
  Silica **S: 457**
Crystalline silicon cell [device]
  Solar energy (How a photovoltaic cell is made) **So: 577**
Crystalline structure [chemistry]
  Carbon (Forms of carbon) **C: 204** *with diagrams*
Crystallization *See* Crystal *in this index*
Crystallization nucleus [physics]
  Crystal (Crystallization) **Ci: 1166**
Crystallography [science]
  Crystal **Ci: 1166**
  Franklin, Rosalind Elsie **F: 492**
  Kepler, Johannes (His life) **K: 305**
  X rays (In crystal research) **X: 541**
Cs [symbol]
  Cesium **C: 364**
CSCE [organization] *See* Organization for Security and Co-operation in Europe *in this index*
CSI [criminology] *See* Crime scene investigation *in this index*
CSM [space exploration] *See* Command/service module *in this index*
CSPI [organization] *See* Center for Science in the Public Interest *in this index*
CSRS [organization] *See* Civil Service Retirement System *in this index*
CSX Corporation
  Railroad (Railroad systems) **R: 112**

CT scan [medicine] *See* Computed tomography *in this index*
CT scanner [machine] *See* Computed tomographic scanner *in this index*
CTC [transportation]
  Railroad (Automatic block signal systems) **R: 111**
CTD [injury] *See* Repetitive strain injury *in this index*
Ctenoid scale [zoology]
  Fish (Scales) **F: 160** *with picture*
Ctenophore [sea animal] **Ci: 1167**
  Animal (A classification of the animal kingdom) **A: 506** *with picture*
Ctesibius of Alexandria [Greek engineer]
  Invention (Ancient Greece) **I: 359**
  Organ (History) **O: 852**
  Pump (History) **P: 901**
Ctesiphon [ancient city]
  Parthia **P: 183** *with map*
Cu [symbol]
  Copper **Ci: 1041**
Cuarón, Alfonso [Mexican author]
  Latin America (Motion pictures) **L: 101**
Cuatro [musical instrument]
  Venezuela (Recreation) **V: 301**
Cuauhtémoc [Aztec emperor] **Ci: 1167**
  Aztec (The Spanish conquest) **A: 1003**
  Cortés, Hernán (Victory over the Aztec) **Ci: 1073**
  Mexico **M: 448**; (The Spanish conquest) **M: 469**
Cuauhtlatoatzin [Mexican saint] *See* Juan Diego, Saint *in this index*
Cub [animal]
  Bear *picture on* **B: 183**; (Cubs) **B: 184**
  Fox (Young) **F: 439** *with picture*
  Lion (The body of a lion) **L: 340-341** *with picture*
  Mammal *diagram on* **M: 124**
  Polar bear (Habits) **P: 616-617** *with picture*
  Tiger (The life of a tiger) **T: 284**
Cub Scout
  Boy Scouts (Cub Scouting) **B: 537** *with picture*
  Scouts Canada (Age groups) **S: 224**
Cuba Ci: 1168 *with pictures and maps*
  Angola (History) **A: 465-466**
  Bay of Pigs invasion **B: 175**
  Buchanan, James (Minister to United Kingdom) **B: 660**
  Carter, Jimmy (Later years) **C: 259**
  Castro, Fidel **C: 283**
  Castro, Raúl **C: 283**
  Clinton, Bill (International affairs) **Ci: 682e**
  Cold War (The Bay of Pigs) **Ci: 768**; (The Cuban missile crisis) **Ci: 768**
  Columbus, Christopher (The first landing) **Ci: 860**
  Communism (The spread of Communism) **Ci: 893-894**
  Cuban missile crisis **Ci: 1179**
  Exploration (Columbus reaches America) **E: 444**
  Guerrilla warfare (History) **G: 420**
  Guevara, Che **G: 421**
  Hispanic Americans (In Puerto Rico and Cuba) **H: 247**; (Cuban immigration) **H: 254**
  Kennedy, John Fitzgerald (Cuba) **K: 265**
  Latin America (The movement toward independence) **L: 106-107**; (United States involvement) **L: 109** *with picture*
  Literacy (Literacy in other countries) **L: 352**
  Organization of American States **O: 854**
  Ostend Manifesto **O: 866**
  Reno, Janet **R: 240**
  Spanish-American War **So: 753**
  Union of Soviet Socialist Republics (Relations with the United States) **U: 39**
  United States, History of the (The Spanish-American War) **U: 185**
  West Indies (Abolition and independence movements) **W: 205**
Cubagua [island]
  Venezuela (European exploration and settlement) **V: 304**
Cuban Americans
  Hispanic Americans **H: 244** *with pictures*
  Miami (The city) **M: 479**; (History) **M: 480**
  Minority group (Hispanic Americans) **M: 609**
Cuban Independence Day
  Hispanic Americans (Holidays) **H: 250**
Cuban missile crisis [1962] **Ci: 1179**
  Cold War (The Cuban missile crisis) **Ci: 768**
  Communism (The Cold War) **Ci: 895**
  Cuba (The Cuban missile crisis) **Ci: 1178**
  Kennedy, John Fitzgerald (Cuba) **K: 265**
  Khrushchev, Nikita Sergeyevich (Soviet dictator) **K: 309**
  Nuclear weapon (The Cold War) **N: 601**
  Union of Soviet Socialist Republics (Relations with the United States) **U: 39**
  United Nations (Arms control) **U: 92**
  World, History of the (The rise of Communism and the Cold War) **W: 446-448**

Cuban Revolutionary Party [Cuban history]
Cuba (Struggle against Spain) Ci: 1176
Cube [mathematics] Ci: 1180 *with picture*
Geometry *picture on* G: 104
Polyhedron P: 651 *with diagram*
Power P: 728
Cube root [mathematics] Ci: 1180
Cubeb [fruit] Ci: 1180
Cubi XIX [sculpture by Smith]
Sculpture (Varieties of abstraction) S: 258 *with picture*
Cubic centimeter [measurement]
Metric system (The metric system at a glance) M: 438 *with picture*
Cubic decimeter [measurement]
Metric system (Space and time) M: 437
Cubic foot [measurement]
Cube *picture on* Ci: 1180
Foot F: 352
Cubic measure
Metric system (Space and time) M: 437
Weights and measures (table: Volume and capacity) W: 186
Cubic meter [measurement]
Metric system (Space and time) M: 437; (The metric system at a glance) M: 438 *with picture*
Cubic zirconia [gem]
Gem (Imitation and synthetic gems) G: 79
Cubism [art] Ci: 1181 *with pictures*
Braque, Georges B: 564
Chagall, Marc C: 368
Duchamp, Marcel D: 373 *with picture*
Feininger, Lyonel *picture on* F: 67
Gris, Juan G: 395
Lipchitz, Jacques L: 344
Marin, John M: 202
Painting (Cubism) P: 77 *with picture*
Picasso, Pablo (Cubism) P: 448b
Sculpture (Cubism and futurism) S: 257 *with pictures*
Cubit [measurement] Ci: 1182
Weights and measures (Early units) W: 186
Cuboidal cell [physiology]
Epithelium E: 345
Cubs, Chicago [team] *See* Chicago Cubs *in this index*
Cuchilla Grande [region]
Uruguay (The interior lowlands) U: 225-226
Cuchulainn [legendary figure] Ci: 1182
Irish literature (Heroic tales, romances, and sagas) I: 430
Mythology (The Ulster cycle) M: 985
Cuckoo [bird] Ci: 1182 *with picture*
Ani A: 467
Bird (Birds of forests and woodlands) B: 334 *with picture*; (Birds of Europe) B: 344c; (Birds of Africa) B: 344h *with picture*; (Brood parasites) B: 359
Cuckoo bee [insect]
Bee (Solitary bees) B: 205-206 *with picture*
Cuckoo roller [bird]
Bird (Birds of Africa) B: 344h *with picture*
Cuckoo-shrike [bird] Ci: 1182 *with picture*
Cuckoo wasp
Wasp W: 111 *with picture*
Cuckoopint [plant]
Arum A: 764 *with picture*
Cucumber [plant] Ci: 1183 *with picture*
Pickle P: 451
Cucumber beetle
Beetle *picture on* B: 218
Insect *picture on* I: 283
Cucumber tree
Magnolia M: 63
Cud [zoology] Ci: 1183
Cattle (Stomach) C: 307
Deer (Food) D: 84-85
Goat (Digestive system) G: 240
Ranching (Life on a cattle ranch) R: 134-135
Ruminant R: 519 *with diagram*
Cudahy, Michael [American businessman] Ci: 1183
Cudahy Packing Company
Cudahy, Michael Ci: 1184
Cue [behavior]
Butterfly (The life cycle of butterflies) B: 739-740
Cue [riding]
Horse (To control a horse) H: 353
Cue [stick]
Billiards (Equipment) B: 304-305
Shuffleboard S: 441
Cue ball
Billiards B: 304
Cue giving and taking
Congress of the United States (Legislative bargaining) Ci: 944-945
Cued speech
Deafness (Special language techniques) D: 58

Cuenca [Ecuador]
Ecuador *picture on* E: 69
Cuervo y Valdés, Francisco [Spanish colonial official]
Albuquerque (Government and history) A: 333
Cueva, Juan de la [Spanish author]
Spanish literature (The 1500's) So: 758-759
Cuff, Sergeant [literary figure]
Collins, Wilkie Ci: 776
Detective story (The pattern) D: 162
Cuffe, Paul [American social reformer] Ci: 1184
Cugnot, Nicolas Joseph [French inventor]
Automobile *picture on* A: 962; (The steam car) A: 965
Truck (History) T: 458
Cui-ui [fish]
Nevada (Plant and animal life) N: 168
Cuicuilco [ancient Mexican village]
Mexico (The growth of villages) M: 467
Cuirass [armor]
Armor (In early times) A: 719-720
Cuisenaire, Emile-Georges [Belgian educator]
Cuisenaire Method Ci: 1184
Cuisenaire Method [education] Ci: 1184 *with diagrams*
Cuisine [food]
Cooking Ci: 1027
Cuisse [armor]
Armor *picture on* A: 720
Cukor, George [American director] Ci: 1184
Motion picture (Best achievement in directing: 1964) M: 862
Culberson, Charles A. [American political leader]
Texas (table) T: 203
Culebra Cut [waterway]
Panama Canal (The Gaillard Cut) P: 123
Culex **mosquito**
Mosquito M: 831 *with picture, pictures on* M: 833
Culiacán [city, Mexico]
Sinaloa S: 468
Cullen, Countee [American poet] Ci: 1184
American literature (The Harlem Renaissance) A: 422
Harlem Renaissance H: 61
Cullet [glass]
Glass (Mixing) G: 214 *with diagram*
Cullinan Stone [diamond]
Diamond *picture on* D: 181; (Famous diamonds) D: 182
Gem (Some famous gems) G: 79
Culloden, Battle of [1746]
Scotland (Union with England) S: 220
Cullom, Shelby Moore [American political leader]
Illinois (table) I: 71
Culm [botany]
Grass (The grass plant) G: 324 *with picture*
Culpeper, John [English rebel]
North Carolina (Colonial days) N: 492
Culpeper Flag [U.S. history]
Flag *picture on* F: 209
Culpeper's Rebellion [1678]
North Carolina (Colonial days) N: 492
Culp's Hill [Civil War]
Civil War, American (Battle of Gettysburg) Ci: 627-628
Gettysburg, Battle of G: 176
Cult Ci: 1184
See also Mysteries *in this index*
Brainwashing B: 560
Mythology (Greek divinities) M: 982
Cultch [industry]
Oyster (Oyster farming) O: 892
Culteranismo [literature]
Góngora, Luis de G: 268
Spanish literature (The 1600's) So: 759-760
Cultivar [agriculture]
Fruit (Developing new fruit cultivars) F: 548
Cultivating
Farm and farming (Pest control) F: 34; (Cultivating) F: 36 *with picture*
Fruit (Caring for the crop) F: 546
Plow P: 574 *with pictures*
Cultivator [machine]
Farm and farming (Cultivating) F: 36 *with picture*
Cultural anthropology
Anthropology (Cultural anthropology) A: 547 *with picture*
Careers (Life, physical, and social sciences) C: 225-226 *with picture*
Ethnography E: 373
Cultural assimilation [sociology]
Minority group (Assimilation) M: 609
Cultural diffusion [anthropology]
City (Population growth) Ci: 578
Culture (Contact with other cultures) Ci: 1189
Cultural geography
Geography (Human geography) G: 94

Cultural lag [anthropology]
Culture (How cultures change) Ci: 1189
Cultural literacy [education]
Education (What should be taught?) E: 105
Multiculturalism M: 919
Cultural pattern
Culture (Forming patterns) Ci: 1187
Cultural pluralism [sociology]
Ethnic group E: 373
United States (Ancestry) U: 109-110
Cultural rationalism [philosophy]
Rationalism R: 148
Cultural relativism
Anthropology A: 546
Culture (Ethnocentrism and cultural relativism) Ci: 1188
Cultural resource management [process]
Archaeology (Archaeology today) A: 600
Cultural Revolution [Chinese history] Ci: 1185
China (The Cultural Revolution) C: 505
Chinese literature (Modern Chinese literature) C: 512
Cold War (The great blocs split) Ci: 769
Jiang Qing J: 125
Cultural studies [education]
Communication (Communication and culture) Ci: 888
Cultural trait [anthropology]
Culture (Forming patterns) Ci: 1187
Culturally deaf [sociology]
Deafness (Deaf community and culture) D: 59
Culture [social science] Ci: 1186 *with pictures*
Anthropology A: 546; (Cultural anthropology) A: 547
Archaeology A: 594
Asian Americans (Asian influences on American culture) A: 812c
Campbell, Joseph C: 90a
Child (Cultural differences) C: 450
City (Cultural variety in cities) Ci: 593
Civilization Ci: 635
Clothing (Cultiral beliefs and values) Ci: 690
Communication (Communication and culture) Ci: 888
Ethics (Nietzsche) E: 367
Ethnocentrism E: 373
Ethnography E: 373
Etiquette E: 374
Hispanic Americans (Cultural backgrounds) H: 247; (Hispanic influences on American culture) H: 248
Human being H: 413; (Cultural characteristics) H: 414 *with pictures*; (Human cultural development) H: 415
Human rights (Human rights and cultural differences) H: 428a
Indian, American (The preservation of Indian culture) I: 180
Internet (The Internet culture) I: 350e
Library L: 234
Multiculturalism M: 918
Poverty (Effects on the poor) P: 723-724
Sexuality (Cultural factors) S: 338; (Cultural influences) S: 338a
Sociology (Cultural influences) So: 565
Culture [biology] Ci: 1190
Culture and Anarchy [book by Arnold]
Arnold, Matthew A: 742
Culture area [anthropology]
Culture (The boundaries of cultures) Ci: 1187-1188
Indian, American I: 136b, *map on* I: 137
Culture-fair test
Education (How can student performance be improved?) E: 105
Races, Human (Race and discrimination) R: 59-60
Testing (Current issues in testing) T: 182a
Culture-free test *See* Culture-fair test *in this index*
Culture shock [anthropology]
Culture (Culture and society) Ci: 1188
Cultured butter
Butter (Churning) B: 730
Cultured buttermilk
Buttermilk B: 744
Cultured pearl
Pearl (Kinds of pearls) P: 217 *with picture*
Culver, Chet [American political leader]
Iowa (table) I: 391
Culvert [pipe]
Road (Grading) R: 359
Cum laude
Degree, College (The bachelor's degree) D: 92
Cumaean Sibyl [legendary figure]
Sibyl S: 445
Cumann na nGaedheal [Irish history]
Ireland (The Irish Free State) I: 427
Cumberland Compact [U.S. history]

Tennessee (Territorial years) T: 153
Cumberland Falls
  Kentucky *picture on* K: 273
Cumberland Gap [Appalachian Mountains]
  Ci: 1190
  Pioneer life in America (Crossing the
    Appalachians) P: 477
Cumberland Gap National Historical Park
  National Park System (table: National historical
    parks) N: 56-57
Cumberland House [Canadian history]
  Saskatchewan (The coming of the fur traders)
    S: 146
Cumberland Island National Seashore [Georgia]
  Georgia *picture on* G: 112
  National Park System (table: National seashores)
    N: 57
Cumberland Mountains [mountains, U.S.] Ci: 1191
Cumberland Narrows
  Allegheny Mountains A: 371
Cumberland Plateau [region, U.S.]
  Alabama (Land regions) A: 268
  Cumberland Mountains Ci: 1191
  Kentucky (Land regions) K: 285
Cumberland River [Kentucky-Tennessee] Ci: 1191
Cumberland Road See National Road *in this index*
Cumbres and Toltec Scenic Railroad
  Colorado (Places to visit) C: 836
Cumhaill [legendary figure] See Finn MacCool *in
  this index*
Cumin [herb] Ci: 1191 *with picture*
Cumming, Alfred [American political leader]
  Utah (Territorial days and statehood) U: 246-248
Cumming plaid [pattern]
  Tartan *picture on* T: 47
Cummings, Bill [American race driver]
  Automobile racing (table: Indianapolis 500
    winners) A: 980
Cummings, Candy [American baseball player]
  Baseball (table: Hall of Fame) B: 134
Cummings, E. E. [American poet] Ci: 1191 *with
  portrait*
  American literature (Modernist poetry) A: 421
  Lost Generation L: 472
Cummings, Homer S. [American government
  official]
  Justice, Department of (table) J: 203
  Roosevelt, Franklin Delano (table) R: 454
Cummins, Albert B. [American political leader]
  Iowa (table) I: 391
Cumorah [hill, New York]
  Mormons (Revelations) M: 808
Cumulative poison
  Mercury (Mercury in the environment) M: 413
Cumulative trauma disorder [injury] See
  Repetitive strain injury *in this index*
Cumulonimbus cloud
  Cloud (Clouds that grow vertically) Ci: 708 *with
    picture*
  Hurricane (The life of a hurricane) H: 453
  Lightning (Types of lightning) L: 300
Cumulus cloud
  Cloud (Kinds of clouds) Ci: 707 *with picture*
Cumulus congestus cloud
  Cloud *picture on* Ci: 709
Cunard, Sir Samuel [British businessman] Ci: 1191
Cunard Line, Ltd. [ships]
  Ship (Passenger vessels) S: 426 *with picture*
Cunaxa, Battle of [401 B.C.]
  Xenophon X: 543
Cunctator [nickname]
  Fabius Maximus, Quintus F: 2
Cuneiform [writing] Ci: 1192 *with picture*
  Assyria (Language and literature) A: 821
  Babylonia B: 13
  Communication *picture on* Ci: 880
  Hittites (Way of life) H: 269
  Number (The Babylonians) N: 606
  Persia, Ancient (Language and literature) P: 297
  Semitic languages S: 293
  Sumer (Way of life) So: 972 *with picture*
  World, History of the (The Tigris-Euphrates Valley)
    W: 422-424
Cunha, Euclides da [Brazilian author] Ci: 1192
  Brazil (The arts) B: 576-577
  Latin American literature (The early 1900's) L: 113
Cunning man or woman
  Magic (The magician) M: 49
Cunningham, Merce [American choreographer]
  Ci: 1192
  Dance (Modern dance) D: 30-31
CUNY [education] See New York, City University of
  in this index
Cuomo, Andrew M. [American political leader]
  Clinton, Bill (table) Ci: 682d
  Cuomo, Mario Matthew Ci: 1193
  Housing and Urban Development, Department

of (table) H: 393
  New York (table) N: 313; (The early 2000's) N: 320
Cuomo, Mario Matthew [American political
  leader] Ci: 1192 *with portrait*
  New York (table) N: 313
Cup [container]
  Persia, Ancient *picture on* P: 298
  Shell *picture on* S: 390
Cupcake [food]
  Cake C: 19
Cupid [Roman mythology] Ci: 1193
  Psyche P: 845
  Venus V: 310
Cupid and Psyche [sculpture by Canova]
  Canova, Antonio C: 183
Cupola [architecture]
  Byzantine art *picture on* B: 750
Cuprammonium process
  Rayon (How rayon is made) R: 153
Cuquenán Falls [waterfall, Venezuela] Ci: 1193
  South America (Waterfalls) So: 628
  Waterfall (table: Famous waterfalls of the world)
    W: 143
Cur Deus Homo [book by Anselm]
  Anselm, Saint A: 519
Curaçao [island] Ci: 1193
  Netherlands Antilles N: 151
Curaçao [ship]
  Shipwreck (table: Major shipwrecks) S: 428
Curacas [American Indians]
  Latin America (Colonial rule) L: 104-105
Curare [poison] Ci: 1193
  Surgery (Anesthesia) Su: 1004
Curassow [bird] Ci: 1193 *with picture*
Curator [career]
  Museum (Exhibition and care of materials)
    M: 939
  Zoo (Zoo workers) Z: 603
Curb bit [riding equipment]
  Horse (The bridle) H: 352 *with picture*
Curb Exchange
  Stock exchange (History) So: 904
Curbside collection program
  Recycling (Collecting materials) R: 184
Curculio [insect]
  Plum (Diseases and pests) P: 577
Curd [food]
  Cheese *pictures on* C: 394; (Separating the curd)
    C: 392
  Tofu T: 309
Cure, The [book by Avicenna]
  Avicenna A: 992
Curecanti National Recreation Area [Colorado]
  National Park System (table: National recreation
    areas) N: 49
Curettage, Suction [surgery]
  Abortion (Abortion methods) A: 14
Curfew [book by Donoso]
  Latin American literature (The post-Boom) L: 114
Curfew [custom] Ci: 1193
Curia [religion]
  Roman Catholic Church (The pope) R: 404
Curia [ruins, Rome]
  Forum, Roman F: 421 *with picture*
Curia regis [European history] Ci: 1194
  England (The Norman Conquest) E: 305
Curie [measurement] Ci: 1194
Curie, Frédéric Joliot- [French physicist] See Joliot-
  Curie, Frédéric *in this index*
Curie, Irène [French physicist] See Joliot-Curie,
  Irène *in this index*
Curie, Jacques [French physicist]
  Curie, Pierre Ci: 1194
  Piezoelectricity P: 458
Curie, Marie Skłodowska [Polish-French physicist]
  Ci: 1194 *with picture*
  Becquerel, Antoine Henri B: 197
  Curie, Pierre Ci: 1194 *with picture*
  Medicine *picture on* M: 375; (The medical
    revolution) M: 376
  Physics (The beginning of modern physics)
    P: 440-441 *with picture*
  Polonium P: 649
  Radium R: 100
Curie, Pierre [French physicist] Ci: 1194 *with
  picture*
  Becquerel, Antoine Henri B: 197
  Curie, Marie Skłodowska Ci: 1194 *with picture*
  Magnetism (Magnetic properties of materials)
    M: 60d
  Medicine *picture on* M: 375; (The medical
    revolution) M: 376
  Physics (The beginning of modern physics)
    P: 440-441
  Piezoelectricity P: 458
  Polonium P: 649
  Radium R: 100

Curie point [physics] See Curie temperature *in
  this index*
Curie temperature [physics]
  Curie, Pierre Ci: 1194
  Magnetism (In materials) M: 60c; (Magnetic
    properties of materials) M: 60d-61
Curing [industrial process]
  Bacon B: 18
  Cement and concrete (Curing) C: 344
  Cheese (Ripening) C: 393
  Food preservation (Curing) F: 341
  Ham (Curing and smoking) H: 28
  Leather (Preparing the hides) L: 167
  Meat packing (Curing and smoking) M: 352
  Pork P: 679
  Tobacco (Kinds of tobacco) T: 305 *with picture*;
    (Curing tobacco) T: 306
Curing society [religion]
  Indian, American (Shamans) I: 147-148
Curiosity [spacecraft]
  Mars (Observation by spacecraft) M: 226c-227
Curium [element] Ci: 1194
  Transuranium element T: 401
Curl, Robert Floyd, Jr. [American chemist]
  Carbon (Fullerenes) C: 205
  Nobel Prizes (Chemistry: 1996) N: 444
Curlew [bird] Ci: 1195 *with picture*
Curley, James Michael [American political leader]
  Ci: 1195
  Boston (Rise of Irish politicians) B: 504
  Massachusetts (table) M: 288
Curling [game] Ci: 1195 *with pictures*
  Olympic Games (Winter Olympic Games) O: 746d
  Scotland (Recreation) S: 214-215
Curly-coated retriever [dog] Ci: 1196 *with picture*
Curly maple [wood]
  Maple (Sugar maple) M: 186
Curly top [disease]
  Sugar beet (Raising sugar beets) So: 962
Currant [plant] Ci: 1196
  Raisin (Varieties) R: 129
Currency See Money *in this index*
Currency changer
  Vending machine (How vending machines work)
    V: 297
Currency unit [economics]
  Standard of living (Measuring standard of living)
    So: 833-834
Current, Air
  Glider G: 228, *diagram on* G: 229
  Jet stream J: 115
Current, Electric See Electric current *in this index*
Current, Ocean
  Arctic Ocean (Waters) A: 643
  Atlantic Ocean (Moving ocean waters) A: 866
  Earth (Cycles on and in Earth) E: 22
  El Niño E: 245
  Gulf Stream G: 437
  Ocean (Temperature) O: 653 *with map*; (How the
    ocean moves) O: 658
  Pacific Ocean (Currents) P: 14
  Southern Ocean (Currents) So: 688a
  Tide T: 280
  Whirlpool W: 281
Current account [economics]
  Balance of payments (How the balance of
    payments is determined) B: 36
  Capital C: 192
Current events
  Journalism J: 170
Current rating [electricity]
  Fuse F: 589
Current River [Missouri]
  Missouri (Rivers and lakes) M: 662 *with picture*
Currents, Ocean See Current, Ocean *in this index*
Curriculum [education] Ci: 1197
  Community college (How community colleges
    operate) Ci: 898
  EdisonLearning, Inc. E: 83
  Education (What should be taught?) E: 105
  Elementary school (Elementary school
    instruction) E: 224
  School (Public schools) S: 182
  Teaching (Preparing to teach classes) T: 65
  Universities and colleges (Curriculum) U: 209
Currie, Sir Arthur [Canadian military leader]
  Ci: 1197
Currier, Moody [American political leader]
  New Hampshire (table) N: 223
Currier, Nathaniel [American lithographer]
  Currier and Ives Ci: 1198
Currier, William [American lithographer]
  Currier and Ives Ci: 1198
Currier and Ives [lithographers] Ci: 1198
  Baseball *picture on* B: 133
  Brooklyn Bridge *picture on* B: 640
  United States, History of the *picture on* U: 170

Currier Gallery of Art [museum]
New Hampshire (Museums) **N:** 213
Curry [seasoning] **Ci:** 1198
Curry, John Steuart [American painter] **Ci:** 1198 *with picture*
Painting (Regionalism) **P:** 83
Curse of Caste, or The Slave Bride, The [book by Collins]
African American literature (The 1800's) **A:** 136a
Cursive writing
Handwriting (Kinds of handwriting) **H:** 47 *with pictures*; (Learning cursive writing) **H:** 48 *with pictures*
Cursor [computing]
Computer (A keyboard) **Ci:** 912
Cursus honorum [Roman history]
Rome, Ancient (The Roman Republic) **R:** 438
Curtain wall [construction]
Building construction (Types of construction) **B:** 683
Curtin, Andrew Gregg [American political leader]
Pennsylvania (table) **P:** 263
Curtin, John Joseph [Australian political leader]
Australia (table) **A:** 923
Curtis, Benjamin R. [American jurist]
Johnson, Andrew (Impeachment) **J:** 140
Supreme Court of the United States (table) **So:** 1000
Curtis, Charles [American political leader] **Ci:** 1198
Hoover, Herbert Clark (Election of 1928) **H:** 329
Vice president of the United States portrait on **V:** 349; (Growth of the vice presidency) **V:** 353
Curtis, Charles G. [American inventor]
Turbine (History) **T:** 498-499
Curtis, Christopher Paul [American author]
Newbery Medal (table) **N:** 359
Curtis, Cyrus Hermann Kotzschmar [American publisher] **Ci:** 1199
Magazine (Magazines in the 1800's) **M:** 45
Curtis, Edwin U. [American public figure]
Coolidge, Calvin (As governor) **Ci:** 1031
Curtis, Kenneth M. [American political leader]
Maine (table) **M:** 87
Curtis, Louisa Knapp [American editor]
Magazine (Magazines in the 1800's) **M:** 45
Curtis, Oakley C. [American political leader]
Maine (table) **M:** 87
Curtis, Samuel R. [Union general]
Civil War, American (Battles of Fort Henry and Fort Donelson) **Ci:** 628-629
Curtis Act [1898]
Indian Territory **I:** 190
Curtis Cup [tournament]
Golf (Tournaments) **G:** 264
Curtis Publishing Company
Curtis, Cyrus Hermann Kotzschmar **Ci:** 1199
Curtiss, Glenn Hammond [American inventor] **Ci:** 1199
Airplane (Other pioneer planes and fliers) **A:** 233 *with picture*
Aviation (Beginnings) **A:** 986
Langley, Samuel Pierpont **L:** 61
Curtiss-Wright Corporation
Aviation (Aviation progress) **A:** 988-989
Curtiz, Michael [Hungarian-American director]
Motion picture (Best achievement in directing: 1943) **M:** 862
Curule [chair]
Furniture (Ancient Rome) **F:** 570 *with picture*
Curvature [engineering]
Railroad (The roadbed and route) **R:** 109
Curve
Circle **Ci:** 558 *with diagrams*
Parabola **P:** 141 *with diagram*
Curve ball
Baseball (Pitching) **B:** 127
Bernoulli's principle **B:** 271
Bowling (How to bowl) **B:** 521-522 *with diagram*
Curzon, George [British diplomat] *See* Curzon, Lord *in this index*
Curzon, Lord [British diplomat]
Curzon Line **Ci:** 1199
Curzon Line [Polish history] **Ci:** 1199
Cusco [Peru] **Ci:** 1199
Inca **I:** 95 *with picture*
Machu Picchu **M:** 20
Cuscus [animal] **Ci:** 1199 *with picture*
Possum **P:** 698
Cush [ancient country] *See* Kush *in this index*
Cushing, Caleb [American government official]
Justice, Department of (table) **J:** 203
Pierce, Franklin (table) **P:** 456
Cushing, Harvey [American doctor] **Ci:** 1200
Cushing, Richard James [American religious leader]
Cardinal (table: American cardinals) **C:** 211
Cushing, William [American jurist]

Supreme Court of the United States (table) **So:** 1000
Cushion comb [zoology]
Chicken (Kinds of chickens) **C:** 441 *with picture*
Cushman, Karen [American author]
Newbery Medal (table) **N:** 359
Cushnoc [U.S. history]
Augusta **A:** 888
Cusp [anatomy]
Teeth (Permanent teeth) **T:** 79-80 *with picture*
Cuspid [anatomy] *See* Canine teeth *in this index*
Custer, George Armstrong [American general] **Ci:** 1200 *with picture*
Black Kettle **B:** 389
Crazy Horse **Ci:** 1123
Gall **G:** 13
Indian wars (Washita River) **I:** 193
Little Bighorn, Battle of the **L:** 391
Montana (Indian fighting) **M:** 758 *with picture*
Reno, Marcus Albert **R:** 240
Sioux Indians **S:** 475
South Dakota (Territorial days) **So:** 681
Western frontier life in America (Settlers and Native Americans) **W:** 239
Custer Battlefield National Monument [Montana] *See* Little Bighorn Battlefield National Monument *in this index*
Custer Died for Your Sins [book by Deloria]
Deloria, Vine, Jr. **D:** 117
Custer National Forest [South Dakota]
South Dakota (Places to visit) **So:** 672
Custer State Park [South Dakota]
South Dakota (Places to visit) *picture on* **So:** 672
"Custer's Last Stand" *See* Little Bighorn, Battle of the *in this index*
Custis, Daniel Parke [husband of]
Washington, Martha Custis **W:** 109
Custis, Eleanor Parke [granddaughter of]
Washington, George (Life in the Executive Mansion) **W:** 101-102
Custis, George Washington Parke [American dramatist]
Washington, George *picture on* **W:** 107; (Life in the Executive Mansion) **W:** 101-102
Custis, John Parke [stepson of]
Washington, George (Marriage) **W:** 95-96
Custis, Martha [wife of George Washington] *See* Washington, Martha Custis *in this index*
Custis, Martha Parke [stepdaughter of]
Washington, George (Marriage) **W:** 95-96
Custis, Mary Anna Randolph [wife of Robert E. Lee] *See* Lee, Mary Anna Randolph Custis *in this index*
Custody [law]
Adoption (The adoption process) **A:** 66
Arrest **A:** 743
Divorce (Child custody arrangements) **D:** 254
Custom **Ci:** 1200
See also the list of Related articles in the Custom article
Culture **Ci:** 1186
Democracy (Constitutional government) **D:** 121
Etiquette **E:** 374
Family (Home life) **F:** 21
Fashion **F:** 324
Folklore (Superstitions and customs) **F:** 324
Food (Customs) **F:** 332
Law (The development of law) **L:** 133
Marriage (Origins of some wedding customs) **M:** 221
Mores **M:** 802
Custom-built home
Housing (Supported housing) **H:** 390
Custom of Paris [law]
Law (The development of Canadian law) **L:** 136
Custom publication
Magazine (Other magazines) **M:** 42-43
Customary system [measurement] *See* Inch-pound system *in this index*
Customer service representative
Careers *picture on* **C:** 219
Customs [government] **Ci:** 1201
Customs Service, United States **Ci:** 1201
Customs and Border Protection, United States [agency]
Customs Service, United States **Ci:** 1201
Homeland Security, Department of (Organization) **H:** 301
Immigration and Naturalization Service **I:** 86
Washington, D.C. *map on* **W:** 76
Customs Court, United States [law] *See* Court of International Trade, United States *in this index*
Customs duties
See also Tariff *in this index*
Foreign trade zone **F:** 388a
Smuggling **S:** 521
Customs Service, United States **Ci:** 1201

Customs union [economics] **Ci:** 1201
Cut [engineering]
Panama Canal (The Gaillard Cut) **P:** 123
Cut [meat]
Ham (Kinds of ham) **H:** 28 *with pictures*
Pork **P:** 679
Cut [mining]
Coal (Strip mining) **Ci:** 722
Cut-and-fill construction
Road (Grading) **R:** 359
Cut-and-fill technique
Mining (Supported mining) **M:** 576
Cut and loop rug
Rugs and carpets (Kinds of rugs and carpets) **R:** 514-515 *with picture*
Cut glass
Glass (Cutting) **G:** 217
Cut Knife Hill, Battle of [Canadian history]
Poundmaker **P:** 722
Cut man [boxing]
Boxing **B:** 526
Cut, tear, and curl method
Tea (Processing tea) **T:** 62
Cutaneous anthrax [disease]
Anthrax **A:** 545
Cutaneous diphtheria [disease]
Diphtheria (Cause, symptoms, and complications) **D:** 216
Cutaneous leishmaniasis [disease]
Leishmaniasis **L:** 187
Cutaneous sense *See* Touch *in this index*
Cutbank Pass [Rocky Mountains]
Divide **D:** 241
Cutch [tree product] *See* Catechu *in this index*
Cuticle [anatomy]
Hair *picture on* **H:** 10; (The root and shaft) **H:** 9 *with diagram*
Cuticle [botany]
Leaf (Obtaining the raw materials) **L:** 155
Cutler, John C. [American political leader]
Utah (table) **U:** 245
Cutler, Manasseh [American settler]
Ohio Company (The second Ohio Company) **O:** 704
Cutler, Nathan [American political leader]
Maine (table) **M:** 87
Cutoff sawing
Machine tool (Sawing) **M:** 18
Cutter [boat]
Coast Guard, United States (Safety) **Ci:** 734 *with picture*
Sailing (Catboats and sloops) **S:** 24
Ship *picture on* **S:** 411
Cutter grade [meat]
Beef (Grades of beef) **B:** 209
Cutter race [Wyoming]
Wyoming *picture on* **W:** 525
Cutterhead [tool]
Mining (Hybrid mining techniques) **M:** 576-577
Cutthroat trout [fish]
Trout (True trout) **T:** 453-454
Cutting [botany]
Fruit (Fruit production) **F:** 546
Gardening (Obtaining new plants from cuttings) **G:** 38
Grape (Planting and cultivating) **G:** 319
Tree (How trees reproduce) **T:** 419
Cutting [cultural practice]
Circumcision **Ci:** 561
Cutting [industrial process]
Diamond (How diamonds are cut to make jewels) **D:** 182
Glass (Cutting) **G:** 217
Cutting garden
Gardening (Production gardens) **G:** 31
Cutting head [machine]
Phonograph (How phonograph records are made) **P:** 401 *with diagram*
Cutting horse
Cowboy (The roundup) **Ci:** 1111
Cuttlebone [zoology]
Cuttlefish **Ci:** 1202
Shell **S:** 384
Cuttlefish [sea animal] **Ci:** 1201 *with picture*
Mollusk (Octopuses and squids) **M:** 695
Shell (Octopuses and squids) **S:** 388
Cuttlefish Bones [book by Montale]
Montale, Eugenio **M:** 741
Cutty Sark [ship]
Clipper ship **Ci:** 682i
Cutworm [insect]
Bogong moth **B:** 437
Cuvier, Baron [French zoologist] **Ci:** 1202
Biology *picture on* **B:** 320; (The origins of scientific classification) **B:** 318
Evolution (Early theories) **E:** 432
Zoology (History) **Z:** 606

Cuvier, Georges Léopold See Cuvier, Baron *in this index*

Cuvilliés, François [Flemish architect]
Architecture *picture on* A: 623

Cuyahoga River [Ohio]
Cleveland (The city) Ci: 663; (Shipping) Ci: 666 *with picture*
Cuyahoga Valley National Park Ci: 1202

Cuyahoga Valley National Park [Ohio] Ci: 1202
National Park System (table: National parks) N: 48

Cuyler, Kiki [American baseball player]
Baseball (table: Hall of Fame) B: 134

Cuyuna Range [Minnesota]
Minnesota (The early 1900's) M: 604

Cuza, Alexander John [prince of Romania]
Romania (The origins of modern Romania) R: 423

Cuzco [Peru] See Cusco *in this index*

Cvetković, Mirko [Serbian political leader]
Serbia (Recent developments) S: 316a

CVT [device] See Continuously variable transmission *in this index*

CW radar
Radar (Continuous-wave radar) R: 69

CX [procedure] See Cross-examination *in this index*

Cy Young Award [baseball]
Maddux, Greg M: 29

Cyan [color]
Printing (Process color printing) P: 802 *with picture*

Cyanidation [industrial process]
Gold *diagram on* G: 250

Cyanide [chemical] Ci: 1202
Laetrile L: 26

Cyanite [mineral]
Kyanite K: 398

Cyanoacrylate [adhesive]
Adhesive A: 56

Cyanobacteria [organisms] Ci: 1202
Air (Origin of the atmosphere) A: 174
Algae (Structure of algae) A: 349
Domain D: 300
Lichen L: 269
Prokaryote P: 817

Cyanogen [gas]
Gay-Lussac, Joseph Louis G: 71

Cyanolabe [anatomy]
Eye (The retina) E: 462

Cyanosis [disorder] Ci: 1202
Blue baby B: 419

Cyaxares [king of Media]
Media M: 360

Cybele [goddess]
Phrygia P: 431
Rhea R: 290

Cyberbullying [psychology]
Bullying B: 698

Cyberjaya [Malaysia]
Putrajaya P: 913

Cybernetics [biology] Ci: 1203
Wiener, Norbert W: 299

Cybernetics [book by Wiener]
Cybernetics Ci: 1203

Cyberpunk [literary genre]
Science fiction (Science fiction today) S: 206

Cyberterrorism
Terrorism (Computer-based terrorism) T: 176; (Security measures) T: 177

Cyberwar
War (Recent developments) W: 26

Cycad [plant] Ci: 1203 *with picture*
Plant (Gymnosperms) P: 520 *with picture*; (The evolution of plants) P: 544-545; (Classification of plants) P: 546-547 *with picture*
Tree *pictures on* T: 413; (Cycad trees) T: 415

Cyclades [islands, Aegean Sea]
Aegean Sea A: 83 *with map*

Cycladic culture [Greek history]
Aegean civilization A: 82
Painting (Aegean painting) P: 41
Sculpture (Aegean) S: 234 *with picture*

Cycle [biology]
See also Life cycle *in this index*
Environmental pollution (Water pollution) E: 334; (Soil pollution) E: 334

Cycle [literature]
Drama (Mystery plays) D: 328-329
George, Stefan G: 109
Mythology (The Irish cycles) M: 985

Cycle [physics]
Electric current (Direct and alternating current) E: 168
Electric generator (A simple generator) E: 170; (How AC generators work) E: 171
Gasoline engine (Cycle) G: 63
Sound (Frequency and pitch) So: 599 *with diagram*

Cycle of abuse

Child (Problems in the home) C: 453
Child abuse C: 454

Cycle of the West, The [poem by Neihardt]
Neihardt, John N: 121

Cyclic pitch control
Helicopter (Piloting a helicopter) H: 171

Cyclical unemployment
Unemployment (Types of unemployment) U: 22

Cycling See Bicycle; Bicycle racing; Motorcycle *in this index*

Cyclitis [disease]
Eye (Diseases of the uveal tract) E: 467

Cyclo-taxi [vehicle]
Vietnam *picture on* V: 368; (City life) V: 365

Cycloid scale [zoology]
Fish (Scales) F: 160 *with picture*

Cyclone [weather] Ci: 1203 *with diagram*
Air (Air movement) A: 171-172
Asia (Natural disasters) A: 812
Disaster (table) D: 223
Hurricane H: 452
Pacific Ocean (Tropical cyclones) P: 14
Storm (Cyclonic storms) So: 913
Tornado T: 333
Weather (Synoptic-scale systems) W: 159-161
Wind (Synoptic-scale circulations) W: 329

Cyclone Eline
Mozambique (History) M: 905-906

Cyclone Nargis
Myanmar (Recent developments) M: 970e
Yangon Y: 551

Cyclonite [explosive] See RDX *in this index*

Cyclooxygenase-1 [enzyme]
Aspirin (How aspirin works) A: 816

Cyclooxygenase-2 [enzyme]
Aspirin (How aspirin works) A: 816

Cyclopedia See Encyclopedia *in this index*

Cyclopedia [book by Chambers]
Encyclopedia (An age of experiment) E: 268a

Cyclops [Greek mythology] Ci: 1204
Odyssey: (Odysseus describes his wanderings) O: 675
Ulysses (Return to Ithaca) U: 18
Uranus U: 217

Cyclops [play by Euripides]
Drama (Satyr plays) D: 327

Cyclops [ship]
Bermuda Triangle B: 269

Cyclorama [exhibit]
Theater (Kinds of scenery) T: 239

Cyclosporine [drug] Ci: 1204
Heart (The first heart transplants and artificial hearts) H: 145
Transplant (Preventing rejection) T: 380-381

Cyclothymia [psychology]
Bipolar disorder B: 327

Cyclotron [machine]
Deuterium (Uses) D: 172
Lawrence, Ernest Orlando L: 145
Particle accelerator (How accelerators work) P: 184-185 *with diagram*

Cygnet [bird]
Swan So: 1016

Cylinder [engine]
Automobile (The engine block) A: 951
Gasoline engine *picture on* G: 63; (The cylinders) G: 64 *with diagrams*

Cylinder [geometry] Ci: 1204 *with diagram*
Geometry *picture on* G: 104

Cylinder [gun]
Handgun (Types of handguns) H: 43 *with picture*

Cylinder [printing]
Printing (Methods of printing) P: 798 *with diagrams*

Cylinder block [engine]
Automobile *diagram on* A: 952; (Powering an internal-combustion car) A: 951
Gasoline engine (Cylinder block) G: 64

Cylinder head [engine]
Gasoline engine (The cylinder head) G: 64 *with diagrams*

Cylinder lock
Lock (Types of locks) L: 410-411

Cylinder machine
Paper (Sheet formation) P: 135-136

Cylinder phonograph [machine]
Edison, Thomas Alva (The phonograph) E: 78-79; (Phonograph developments) E: 80 *with picture*

Cylindrical grinding
Grinding and polishing (Grinding methods) G: 395
Machine tool (Abrasive processes) M: 19

Cylindrical lens
Eye (Astigmatism) E: 464-465 *with picture*

Cylindrical seal [emblem]
Assyria (Art and architecture) A: 821
Persia, Ancient *picture on* P: 299

Cylindroid [cylinder]
Cylinder Ci: 1204

Cymbal [musical instrument] Ci: 1204

Cymbeline [play by Shakespeare]
Shakespeare, William: *(Cymbeline)* S: 365

Cyme [botany]
Inflorescence I: 268b

Cymric cat See Manx *in this index*

Cymru [name for]
Wales W: 7

Cynewulf [English poet]
English literature (Old English poetry) E: 314-315

Cynic philosophy [philosophy] Ci: 1205
Diogenes D: 214
Hellenistic Age H: 177

Cynic's Word Book, The [book by Bierce]
Bierce, Ambrose B: 295

Cynodont [prehistoric animal]
Mammal (The ancestors of mammals) M: 126

Cynosarges [ancient Greece]
Cynic philosophy Ci: 1205

CYO [organization] See Catholic Youth Organization *in this index*

Cypress [painting by Kano Eitoku]
Painting (Japanese painting) P: 47 *with picture*

Cypress [tree] Ci: 1205
Tree *pictures on* T: 424; (Needleleaf trees) T: 414-415

Cypress Gardens [Charleston]
South Carolina (Places to visit) So: 650

Cypress Swamp
Mississippi (Places to visit) M: 632 *with picture*

Cypriots [people]
Cyprus (People) Ci: 1205

Cypris [zoology]
Barnacle B: 114
Larva L: 78

Cyprus [island, Mediterranean Sea] Ci: 1205 *with picture and map*
Flag *picture on* F: 202
Ford, Gerald Rudolph (Early problems) F: 376 *with picture*
Greece (The 1950's) G: 364; (The restoration of democracy) G: 365
Middle East M: 530
Turkey (The Cyprus crisis) T: 512

Cyprus cedar [tree]
Cedar (Needle-leaved cedars) C: 324

Cyrano de Bergerac [play by Rostand]
Cyrano de Bergerac, Savinien de Ci: 1208
Rostand, Edmond R: 484

Cyrano de Bergerac, Savinien de [French author] Ci: 1208
Science fiction (Forerunners of science fiction) S: 205

Cyrenaic philosophy
Hedonism H: 165

Cyrenaica [former province]
Libya (Independence) L: 267

Cyril, Saint [Christian scholar]
Alphabet (Other alphabets) A: 383

Cyril of Alexandria, Saint [Egyptian religious leader] Ci: 1208
Hypatia H: 475

Cyrillic alphabet
Alphabet (Other alphabets) A: 383-384
Moldova (History) M: 690a
Russian language (Alphabet) R: 557 *with pictures*

Cyrnos [island]
Corsica (History) Ci: 1072

Cyrus the Great [emperor of Persia] Ci: 1208
Army (Ancient armies) A: 726
Bible (Historical contexts) B: 287
Iran (The Achaemenid Empire) I: 405
Jerusalem (Ancient times) J: 100
Jews (Foreign domination) J: 121
Media M: 360
Palestine (Invasions and conquests) P: 104
Persia, Ancient (The Achaemenid Empire) P: 298

Cyrus the Great Cylinder [document]
Persia, Ancient P: 296

Cyrus the Younger [Persian prince]
Xenophon X: 543

Cyst [biology]
Parasite (An endoparasite) P: 354
Pfiesteria P: 353

Cyst [disorder] Ci: 1208
Acne A: 28
Ear (Diseases) E: 12
Polycystic kidney disease P: 649
Trichina T: 441

Cystic duct [anatomy]
Gallbladder G: 14 *with diagram*

Cystic fibrosis [disease] Ci: 1208
Heredity (table) H: 204
Races, Human (Susceptibility to genetic diseases) R: 58

Cystic fibrosis transmembrane conductance regulator [genetics]
Cystic fibrosis Ci: 1208
Cystitis [disease]
Bladder B: 395
Cystoscope [instrument]
Bladder B: 395
Cythera [island, Greece]
Ionian Islands I: 373 *with map*
Cytisine [poison]
Laburnum L: 19
Cytokine [chemical]
Immune system (Autoimmune disorders) I: 88c
Inflammation I: 266
Virus (Infection) V: 428a
Cytokinesis [biology]
Cell (Cell division) C: 330 *with diagram*
Cytokinin [hormone]
Hormone (Plant hormones) H: 337
Plant (Hereditary factors) P: 538
Cytology [microbiology]
Biology (table) B: 317
Cell C: 326
Cytomegalovirus retinitis [disorder]
AIDS (Opportunistic illness) A: 164a
Cytoplasm [biology]
Bacteria (The structure of bacteria) B: 20 *with diagram*
Cell C: 326; (The cytoplasm) C: 329 *with diagrams*
Chloroplast C: 518
Heredity (How proteins are made) H: 206-208
Life (Cells) L: 277
Protoplasm P: 837
Cytosine [biochemistry]
Cell (DNA—the wondrous molecule) C: 334-335 *with diagram*
DNA D: 258
Heredity (The structure of DNA) H: 205
RNA R: 357
Cytoskeleton [biology]
Cell (The cytoplasm) C: 329
Cytotoxic T cell [physiology]
Immune system (The cell-mediated immune response) I: 88-88a
Thymus T: 274
Czar [title]
Ivan IV, the Terrible I: 520
Russia R: 525
Union of Soviet Socialist Republics (History) U: 35
Czar liberator [name for]
Alexander II A: 341
Czech [language]
Czech Republic (Language) Ci: 1210
Czech Republic Ci: 1209 *with picture and map*
See also Czechoslovakia *in this index and the list of Related articles in the* Czech Republic *article*
Bohemia B: 437
Clothing *picture on* Ci: 694
Havel, Václav H: 87
Moravia M: 800
North Atlantic Treaty Organization (History) N: 471
Slovakia S: 508b
Teaching (Teaching around the world) T: 70
Czech Social Democratic Party [political party]
Czech Republic (Politics) Ci: 1210
Czechoslovakia [former country] Ci: 1215 *with maps*
See also Czech Republic; Slovakia *in this index*
Beneš, Eduard B: 248
Bohemia B: 438
Cold War (Czechoslovakia) Ci: 769
Communism (In Eastern Europe) Ci: 896
Czech Republic Ci: 1209; (The creation of Czechoslovakia) Ci: 1213
Havel, Václav H: 87
Hitler, Adolf (The road to war) H: 267
Lidice L: 270
Masaryk, Tomáš Garrigue M: 262
Motion picture (Movies in the 1960's) M: 870-871
Munich Agreement M: 927
Slovakia S: 508b; (The formation of Czechoslovakia) S: 509
Sudetenland So: 957
Union of Soviet Socialist Republics (Brezhnev comes to power) U: 39
Warsaw Pact W: 39
World War II (The failure of appeasement) W: 472
Czechs [people]
Bohemia B: 437
Czech Republic Ci: 1209
Czechoslovakia Ci: 1215
Częstochowa [Poland]
Poland *picture on* P: 609
Czolgosz, Leon F. [American assassin]
McKinley, William (Assassination) M: 341 *with picture*

D

D [letter] D: 1 *with pictures*
D'...
Names beginning D' are alphabetized as single words: D'Arezzo, Guido, *appears after* Dare, Virginia
D and C [medicine]
Surgery (Some common surgical operations) So: 1006
D and E [medicine] See Dilation and evacuation *in this index*
D-day D: 2
See also Normandy Invasion *in this index*
Amphibious warfare (History of amphibious warfare) A: 442
Eisenhower, Dwight David (Operation Overlord) E: 150
World War II (D-Day) W: 483 *with picture*
D-lactic acid [chemical]
Lactic acid L: 24
D quark [physics] See Down quark *in this index*
D-type asteroid [astronomy]
Asteroid (Composition) A: 824-824a
Da ...
Names of persons beginning Da are alphabetized as single words: Da Gama, Vasco, *appears after* Daffodil
Da capo [music]
Handel, George Frideric (His work) H: 42-43
Opera (Opera seria and opera buffa) O: 797
Da Nang [Vietnam] D: 2
DAB [broadcasting] See Digital audio broadcasting *in this index*
Dab [fish]
Flounder F: 267
Dabbling duck [bird]
Duck (Food) D: 375 *with picture*; (Kinds of ducks) D: 376
Dacca [Bangladesh] See Dhaka *in this index*
Dace, Horned [fish]
Chub C: 540
Dachau [concentration camp] D: 2
Dachshund [dog] D: 2 *with picture*
Dog *picture on* D: 270
Dacia [former region]
Domitian D: 306
Romania (Ancestry) R: 417; (Early days) R: 423
Trajan T: 368
Dacko, David [Central African political leader]
Central African Republic (History) C: 353
Dacron [fiber]
Sailing (Sails) S: 24
Dactyl [poetry]
Poetry (table) P: 594
Dactyl [satellite]
Asteroid *picture on* A: 824; (History of study) A: 824b
Dactylic hexameter [poetry]
Latin literature (Early Latin literature) L: 115-116
Dadaism [art] D: 2 *with picture*
Breton, André B: 594
Duchamp, Marcel D: 373
Painting (Dadaism) P: 80 *with picture*
Ray, Man R: 152
Schwitters, Kurt S: 190
Sculpture (Assemblages) S: 257 *with pictures*
"Daddy" [poem by Plath]
Plath, Sylvia P: 566
Daddy longlegs [animal] D: 3 *with picture*
Daedalus [Greek mythology] D: 3
Airplane (History) A: 229 *with picture*
Labyrinth L: 19
Minos M: 611
Dæhlie, Bjørn [Norwegian skier]
Skiing (The middle and late 1900's) S: 487-488
Daffodil [plant] D: 3 *with picture*
Flower (Garden perennials grown from bulbs) F: 280 *with picture*
Narcissus N: 20
Daffy Duck [cartoon character]
Animation *picture on* A: 514c
Daffyd [Welsh religious leader] See David, Saint *in this index*
Dafne [opera by Peri]
Opera (The development of opera) O: 797
Dafydd ap Gwilym [Welsh poet]
Wales (The arts) W: 9-10
Da Gama, Vasco [Portuguese explorer] D: 4 *with picture and map*
Cape of Good Hope C: 189
Exploration *map on* E: 443; (The voyage around Africa) E: 444
Geography (Era of exploration) G: 95
India (The coming of the Europeans) I: 130
Dagger [reference]
Footnote F: 369

Dagger [weapon] D: 4 *with picture*
Dagger moth
Moth *picture on* M: 841
Dagon [former name]
Yangon Y: 551
Dagon [Philistine god]
Samson S: 82
"Dagon" [story by Lovecraft]
Lovecraft, H. P. L: 508
Daguerre, Louis Jacques Mandé [French inventor] D: 4
Communication (The 1800's) Ci: 881
Daguerreotype D: 5
Niépce, Joseph Nicéphore N: 406
Photography (The invention of photography) P: 422-423 *with picture*
Daguerreotype [photography] D: 5 *with picture*
Communication (The 1800's) Ci: 881-882 *with picture*
Daguerre, Louis Jacques Mandé D: 4
Photography (The invention of photography) P: 422-423 *with picture*
Dah [telegraphy]
Morse code M: 819
Dahl, Carl [German inventor]
Paper (History) P: 136-137
Dahl, Roald [British author] D: 5
Dahlem District [district]
Berlin (Libraries and museums) B: 262
Dahlia [plant]
Flower *picture on* F: 280
Gardening *picture on* G: 33
Dahlia anemone [sea animal]
Animal *picture on* A: 486
Dahomey [former name, Benin]
Benin B: 249
Cotonou Ci: 1085
French West Africa F: 527
Dai Co Viet [Vietnamese history]
Indochina (The Khmer) I: 225; (A new kingdom) I: 225
Dai Viet [Vietnamese history]
Indochina (A new kingdom) I: 225
Daibutsu [sculpture]
Buddhism *picture on* B: 668
Dáil Éireann [Irish government]
De Valera, Eamon D: 173
Ireland (Parliament) I: 417; (The Easter Rising) I: 427
Sinn Féin (History) S: 473
Dailies
Motion picture (Preliminary steps) M: 854-855
Daily double [betting]
Horse racing (Betting) H: 365
Daily Express [newspaper]
Beaverbrook, Lord B: 195
Daily fee course [golf]
Golf G: 260
Daily Reference Value
Nutrition (Nutrition guidelines) N: 626
Daily Telegraph [newspaper]
Wyoming (Communication) W: 531
Daily total energy expenditure [measurement]
Weight control (Energy expenditure) W: 181
Daily Value
Nutrition (Nutrition guidelines) N: 626
Daimler, Gottlieb [German engineer] D: 5
Automobile *picture on* A: 963; (The gasoline car) A: 965-966
Gasoline engine (Development of the gasoline engine) G: 66
Invention (The late 1800's) I: 362
Maybach, Wilhelm M: 327
Motorcycle (History) M: 879 *with picture*
Daimler AG [company] D: 5
Manufacturing (table) M: 170
Daimler-Benz AG [former company]
Daimler AG D: 5
Daimler Motor Company [former company]
Daimler AG D: 5
DaimlerChrysler AG [former company]
Daimler AG D: 6
Daimyo [Japanese history]
Japan (Warring states period) J: 54
Daino [song]
Lithuania (People) L: 388
Daintree National Park [Australia]
National park (table) N: 42f
Dairy Belt [region, U.S.]
Milk M: 545
Dairy farm
Milk *picture on* M: 545; (At a dairy farm) M: 546
Dairy products
Food (Food from animals) F: 330
Hormone (Agricultural uses) H: 337-338
Lactose intolerance L: 24
Milk M: 545 *with pictures*

Nutrition (Kinds of nutrients) N: 625; (Nutrition guidelines) N: 626
Dairying [agriculture] D: 6 *with pictures*
Cattle C: 306; (Dairy cattle) C: 309 *with pictures;* (Dual-purpose cattle) C: 311; (Breeding) C: 311-312; (Dairy cows) C: 314
Farm and farming (Specialized livestock farms) F: 31-32 *with picture*
Wisconsin (Changes in agriculture) W: 368
Dairying ant
Ant (Dairying ants) A: 526 *with picture*
Daisetsuzan National Park [Japan]
National park (table) N: 42f
Daisies, Girl Scout
Girl Scouts (Girl Scouts of the USA) G: 196
Daisy [plant] D: 8 *with picture*
Flower *picture on* F: 294
Gardening *picture on* G: 33
Daisy cutter [bomb]
Bomb (General-purpose [GP] bombs) B: 450
Daisy fleabane [plant]
Fleabane F: 232
Daisy Miller [book by James]
James, Henry (His works) J: 26
Daisy wheel
Typewriter (How a typewriter works) T: 538-539 *with picture*
Daisy-wheel printer [electronic device]
Printer (Impact printers) P: 795
Dakar [Senegal] D: 9 *with picture*
Africa *picture on* A: 111
French West Africa F: 527 *with map*
Senegal (Economy) S: 299 *with pictures*
Dakota *See* North Dakota; South Dakota *in this index*
Dakota Conflict *See* Great Sioux Uprising *in this index*
Dakota Democrat [newspaper]
South Dakota (Communication) So: 679
Dakota Indians *See* Sioux Indians *in this index*
Dakota Territory [U.S. history]
North Dakota (Territorial days) N: 514; (Statehood) N: 514
South Dakota (Territorial days) So: 681
Dakota Water Resources Act [2000]
North Dakota (Recent developments) N: 516
Dakwah movement [Malaysian history]
Malaysia (Religion) M: 98d
Dal [food]
Chickpea C: 446
India (Food and drink) I: 118
Daladier, Édouard [French political leader]
World War II (The failure of appeasement) W: 472
Dalai Lama [Tibetan religious leader] D: 9
Bodhisattva B: 434
China (Recent developments) C: 506-507
Lamaism L: 49
Lhasa L: 225
Tibet (Religion and culture) T: 277; (History and government) T: 277
Dalayrac, Nicholas [French composer]
Bell (Uses of bells) B: 239
Dale, Charles M. [American political leader]
New Hampshire (table) N: 223
Dale, Sir Henry Hallett [British physiologist]
Nobel Prizes (Physiology or medicine: 1936) N: 445
Dale, James [American public figure]
Boy Scouts (Organization) B: 538
D'Alembert, Jean [French mathematician]
Encyclopedia (An age of experiment) E: 268a
D'Alembert's Dream [book by Diderot]
Diderot, Denis D: 195
Dalén, Nils Gustaf [Swedish physicist]
Nobel Prizes (Physics: 1912) N: 440
Daley, Richard Joseph [American political leader] D: 9
Byrne, Jane Margaret B: 747
Chicago (Political developments in the late 1900's) C: 436
Daley, Richard M. [American political leader]
Chicago (Political developments in the late 1900's) C: 436-437
Daley, Richard Joseph D: 10
Daley, William M. [American political leader]
Clinton, Bill (table) Ci: 682d
Commerce, Department of (table) Ci: 871
Daley, Richard Joseph D: 10
Daley Plaza
Chicago (Places to visit) C: 430-431 *with picture*
Dalhart, Vernon [American singer]
Country music (The roots of country music) Ci: 1098a-1098b
Dalhousie University
King's College, University of K: 331
Nova Scotia *picture on* N: 558
Dalí, Salvador [Spanish painter] D: 10 *with pictures*

Painting (Surrealism) P: 81 *with picture*
Dalibard, Thomas-François [French scientist]
Lightning L: 299
Dalit [sociology] *See* Untouchable *in this index*
Dalla Chiesa, Carlo Alberto [Italian military leader]
Italy (Social problems) I: 518
Dallapiccola, Luigi [Italian composer] D: 10
Dallas [Texas] D: 11 *with pictures and map*
Metropolitan area *map on* M: 442
Texas (table: Average monthly weather) T: 198
Dallas, George Mifflin [American political leader] D: 16
Dallas (History) D: 15
Polk, James Knox (Election of 1844) P: 642
Vice president of the United States V: 348 *with portrait*
Dallas Black Dance Theatre
Dallas *picture on* D: 13
Dallas Cowboys [team]
Aikman, Troy A: 168
Dallas (Recreation) D: 14
Football (National Football League) F: 364
Dallas/Fort Worth International Airport
Airport (table) A: 245
Dallas D: 11
Dallas Mavericks [team]
Basketball B: 150
Dallas (Recreation) D: 14
Dallas Museum of Art
Dallas (Museums and libraries) D: 14
Dallas Stars [team]
Dallas (Recreation) D: 14
Hockey (table: National Hockey League) H: 281
Dallas Theater Center
Dallas (Cultural life) D: 14
Dalles [geology] D: 16 *with picture*
Dallin, Cyrus Edwin [American sculptor] D: 16 *with picture*
Kansas City *picture on* K: 241
Massasoit (Massasoit on) M: 295
Dall's porpoise [sea animal]
Porpoise P: 679
Dall's sheep [animal]
Bighorn B: 299
Dalmatia [region, Croatia]
Croatia (Land and climate) Ci: 1148a
Yugoslavia (A new country) Y: 576
Dalmatian [dog] D: 16
Dog *picture on* D: 275
Dalmatian pelican [bird]
Pelican (Pelicans and people) P: 231
Dalrymple, Jack [American political leader]
North Dakota (table) N: 513
Dalt [letter]
D D: 1 *with picture*
Dalton [measurement] *See* Relative atomic mass *in this index*
Dalton, John [British chemist] D: 16
Atom (The birth of the modern atomic theory) A: 875
Chemistry (Dalton's atomic theory) C: 402 *with picture*
Physics (Developments in the 1800's) P: 440
Dalton, John M. [American political leader]
Missouri (table) M: 668
Dalton, John N. [American political leader]
Virginia (table) V: 417
Daltonism *See* Color blindness *in this index*
Dalton's law of partial pressures
Dalton, John D: 16
Daltrey, Roger [British musician]
Who, The W: 296
Daly, John [American golfer]
Golf (British Open) G: 264
Daly, Marcus [American businessman]
Montana (Statehood) M: 760
Dam D: 17 *with picture*
See also the list of Related articles in the Dam *article*
Beaver (Building dams and canals) B: 195 *with picture*
Conservation (Water conservation) Ci: 977
Energy supply (Water power) E: 278
Flood (Flood control) F: 238
Inland waterway I: 274
Irrigation (Surface water) I: 456
Lake *picture on* L: 32
Reservoir R: 258
Tennessee Valley Authority (The dams) T: 158 *with picture*
Dam [animal]
Cattle C: 306
Dog (Kinds of dogs) D: 265
Horse (table: Horse terms) H: 343
Dam, Henrik [Danish physiologist]
Nobel Prizes (Physiology or medicine: 1943) N: 445

Dam Square [Amsterdam]
Netherlands *picture on* N: 141
Dama [role]
Quinceañera Q: 42
Damaged Goods [play by Brieux]
Brieux, Eugène B: 608
Damages [law] D: 20
Contract Ci: 1023
Insurance (Property and liability insurance) I: 312
Tort T: 344
Daman and Diu [territory, India]
India (India in the 1950's and early 1960's) I: 133
Damão [territory, India] *See* Daman and Diu *in this index*
Damaraland mole-rat [animal]
Mole-rat M: 691
Damascus [Syria] D: 20 *with picture*
Syria So: 1070 *with picture*
Trade route (Early trade routes) T: 363
Damascus steel
Iron and steel (The first steel) I: 450
Damask [fabric] D: 21
Damask rose
Rose *picture on* R: 475
Damasus I, Saint [pope]
Pope (table) P: 666
Damasus II [pope]
Pope (table) P: 666
Damavand, Mount [Iran]
Iran (The Mountains) I: 402
Dambo [area]
Mosquito (Egg) M: 832-833
D'Amboise, Jacques [American dancer] D: 21 *with portrait*
Dame [title]
Address, Forms of (Officials of the Commonwealth of Nations) A: 53
Knighthood, Orders of (Honorary orders) K: 347
Dame school [education]
Colonial life in America (Education) Ci: 803
Rhode Island (Schools) R: 300
Damian, Cyrillys [Austrian inventor]
Accordion A: 22
Damien, Father [Belgian religious leader] D: 21
Hawaii (Molokai) H: 100-102
Damnation of Theron Ware, The [book by Frederic]
Frederic, Harold F: 497
Damocles [Greek courtier] D: 21
Damon and Pythias [legendary figures] D: 21
Damp [gas] D: 21
Damper [musical instrument]
Piano (The action) P: 446
Dampier, William [English explorer] D: 22
Dampierre, Guy de [Flemish nobleman]
Feudalism *picture on* F: 82
Damping [motion]
Compass Ci: 902b
Damping-off [plant disease] D: 22
Damrosch, Leopold [German-born conductor] D: 22
Damrosch, Walter Johannes [American conductor] D: 22
Damselfly [insect]
Dragonfly D: 319
Insect *pictures on* I: 280; (Incomplete metamorphosis) I: 293
Dan [people]
Africa *picture on* A: 116
Dan Patch [horse]
Harness racing (History) H: 64
Dana, Charles Anderson [American editor] D: 22
Chicago (A city reborn) C: 435
Dana, Francis [American diplomat]
Adams, John Quincy (Education) A: 40
Dana, John W. [American political leader]
Maine (table) M: 87
Dana, Richard Henry, Jr. [American author] D: 22
Danae [painting by Rembrandt]
Rembrandt (Early Amsterdam years) R: 229
Danaë [Greek mythology]
Perseus P: 295
Danby, Gordon T. [American physicist]
Magnetic levitation train (Electrodynamic maglev) M: 55
Dance D: 23 *with pictures*
See also Ballet; Ballroom dancing *in this index; and the list of Related articles in the* Dance *article*
Art and the arts *picture on* A: 748
Asia *picture on* A: 783
Careers (Sports and entertainment) C: 230-231
Flamenco F: 225 *with picture*
Folk dancing F: 320 *with picture*
Ice skating (Ice dancing) I: 12 *with diagrams*
India (Music and dance) I: 120-121
Indian, American *picture on* I: 164; (Ceremonies) I: 148
Latin America (Dance) L: 101

Musical comedy (Elements of musical comedy) M: 959
Rhythm R: 319
Sculpture (Indus Valley) S: 235-236; (Royal and public sculpture) S: 240
Tango T: 27
United States picture on U: 119
Waltz W: 22
Dance [entomology]
Bee (Finding food) B: 204
Dance band [music]
Band (Dance bands) B: 75
Dance club
Dance picture on D: 28
Dance fly
Insect (Courtship) I: 294
Dance Hall of the Dead [book by Hillerman]
Hillerman, Tony H: 232
Dance Mania [recording]
Puente, Tito P: 871
Dance music
Disco music D: 224
Popular music (Ragtime, jazz, and blues) P: 670
Dance of the Happy Shades [book by Munro]
Munro, Alice M: 928
Dance of the NW Indians at the Mission of San Jose de California [painting by Stephens]
Indian, American picture on I: 164
"Dance of the Seven Veils"
Opera: (Salome) O: 807 with picture
Dance 1, The [painting by Matisse]
Painting (The Fauves) P: 77 with picture
Dance orchestra
Orchestra O: 820
Dance skating
Roller skating (Artistic skating) R: 402a
Dance song
Folk music (Kinds of folk music) F: 321
Dance stick [sculpture]
Sculpture (The European impact) S: 244 with picture
Dance Theatre of Harlem
Ballet (Ballet in the United States) B: 53-54
Mitchell, Arthur M: 677
Dance to the Music of Time, A [books by Powell]
English literature (Literature after World War II) E: 322-323
Powell, Anthony P: 726
Dancer, Stanley F. [American harness driver]
Harness racing (History) H: 64
Dancers in Blue Dress [painting by Severini]
Italy picture on I: 505
Dances with Wolves [film]
Motion picture (Best picture: 1990) M: 861
Westerns W: 242
DanceSport [competition] See Ballroom dancing in this index
Dancing See Dance in this index
Dancing at Lughnasa [play by Friel]
Friel, Brian F: 533
Dancing Class, The [painting by Degas]
Degas, Edgar picture on D: 90
Painting (New visual sources) P: 72
Dancing Rabbit Creek, Treaty of [U.S. history]
Choctaw Indians C: 519
Dandelion [plant] D: 32
Lawn picture on L: 143
Plant picture on P: 531
Root diagram on R: 470
Dandelion Wine [book by Bradbury]
Bradbury, Ray B: 542
Dandie Dinmont terrier [dog] D: 32
Dandridge, Ray [American baseball player]
Baseball (table: Hall of Fame) B: 134
Dandruff [disorder] D: 32
Hair (Disorders of the hair and scalp) H: 10
Keratin K: 305
Danegeld [English history]
William I, the Conqueror W: 308
Danelaw [English history]
Alfred the Great A: 349
Vikings (The Danish Vikings) V: 383
Danes [people]
See also Vikings in this index
Denmark D: 132
Danforth, John C. [American government official]
United Nations (table) U: 86
"Danger of an Unconverted Ministry, The" [sermon]
Tennent, Gilbert T: 133
Dangerous [film]
Davis, Bette D: 47
Dangerous Liaisons [book by Laclos]
Enlightenment (The orderliness of nature) E: 326a-326b
Dangling Man [book by Bellow]
Bellow, Saul B: 244

Diary D: 185
Daniel [Biblical figure]
Handwriting on the wall H: 50
Daniel, Book of [Bible] D: 33 with picture
Bible (The Writings) B: 281-282
Daniel, Peter V. [American jurist]
Supreme Court of the United States (table) So: 1000
Daniel, Price [American political leader]
Texas (table) T: 203
Daniel and Florence Guggenheim Foundation
Guggenheim, Meyer G: 421
Daniel Boone [book by Daugherty]
Daugherty, James Henry D: 43
Daniel Deronda [book by Eliot]
Eliot, George E: 237
Daniel in the Lions' Den [painting by Rubens]
Daniel, Book of picture on D: 33
Daniell, John F. [British chemist]
Battery (History) B: 171
Daniels, Josephus [American editor]
Roosevelt, Franklin Delano (Assistant secretary of the Navy) R: 450f-451
Wilson, Woodrow (table) W: 323
Daniels, Mitch [American political leader]
Indiana (table) I: 214
Danish East India Company [Danish history]
East India Company E: 40
Danish landrace [hog]
Hog (Other breeds) H: 286; (table) H: 286
Danish pastry [food]
Pastry P: 194
Danish-Swedish War [1657-1660]
Denmark (Wars with Sweden) D: 140
Danish West India Company
Virgin Islands, United States (Danish rule) V: 396
Danish West Indies
Virgin Islands (Danish rule) V: 396
Danjou, Jean [French military leader]
Foreign Legion (History) F: 386
"Danke Schoen" [record album]
Newton, Wayne N: 390
Dannay, Frederic [American author]
Queen, Ellery Q: 39
Dannebrog, Order of the
Medals, decorations, and orders (Europe) M: 358; (table) M: 359
D'Annunzio, Gabriele [Italian author] D: 33
Duse, Eleonora D: 390
Italian literature (Romanticism) I: 495
Danseur
Ballet (table) B: 45
Dante Alighieri [Italian author] D: 33
See also Divine Comedy in this index
Allegory A: 371
Italian literature (The Middle Ages) I: 494
Virgil (His influence) V: 392
Danton, Georges-Jacques [French political leader] D: 34
French Revolution (The National Convention) F: 526; (The revolution ends) F: 527
Reign of Terror R: 207
D'Antonguolla, Rodolfo [real name of]
Valentino, Rudolph V: 264
Danton's Death [play by Büchner]
Büchner, Georg B: 663
German literature (Other writers) G: 140
Danube River [Europe] D: 34 with map
Austria picture on A: 935; (Land and climate) A: 933
Budapest B: 666 with picture
Bulgaria (The land) B: 691 with picture
Hungary picture on H: 439; (Rivers and lakes) H: 443 with map
Inland waterway I: 274
River (table) R: 352
Romania (Surface features) R: 419
Serbia (Land and climate) S: 314 with picture and map
Water (The challenge of today) W: 132
Danvers [Massachusetts]
Salem witchcraft trials S: 61
Danville [Virginia]
Virginia (The Civil War and Reconstruction) V: 421
Danzig [Germany] See Gdańsk in this index
Danzig Trilogy [books by Grass]
German literature (Postwar German literature [1945-1990]) G: 142
Dao-Ji [Chinese artist]
Painting (Chinese painting) P: 44-46
Daodejing [book] See Classic of the Way and the Virtue, The in this index
Daoism [religion] See Taoism in this index
Daoud Khan, Muhammad [Afghan political leader]
Afghanistan (The mid-1900's) A: 96
Daphne [Greek mythology] D: 35

Apollo A: 566
Daphne [plant]
Poisonous plant (Some poisonous plants) P: 602
Daphnis and Chloë [ballet by Fokine]
Fokine, Michel picture on F: 315
Daphnis and Chloë [book by Longus]
Greek literature (The Greco-Roman Age) G: 378
Novel (Ancient Greek and Roman narratives) N: 572
Romance R: 415
Dapsang [mountain] See K2 in this index
Dapsone [drug]
Leprosy (Treatment) L: 205
D'Aquino, Iva Toguri [American public figure] See Tokyo Rose in this index
DAR [organization] See Daughters of the American Revolution in this index
Dar es Salaam [Tanzania] D: 35
Tanzania T: 30 with picture; (Transportation and communication) T: 34
Darazi, Muhammad al- [Egyptian religious leader]
Druses D: 368
Darby [tool]
Plaster (Plastering) P: 552
Darby, Abraham [British engineer]
Coal (Developments in England) Ci: 731
Industrial Revolution (The revolution in ironmaking) I: 249
Darby, Abraham, II [British engineer]
Industrial Revolution (The revolution in ironmaking) I: 249-250
Darby, William O. [American military leader]
Rangers R: 139
Dardanelles [strait, Turkey] D: 35 with map
See also Hellespont in this index
World War I (The Dardanelles) W: 459
Dardanus [ancient city]
Dardanelles D: 35
Darden, Colgate W., Jr. [American political leader]
Virginia (table) V: 417
Dare, Virginia [American colonist] D: 35
Lost Colony L: 472
North Carolina (Interesting facts) N: 473 with picture
"Darest Thou Now, O Soul" [poem by Whitman]
Poetry (Forms) P: 595
Darfur [region] D: 35
Sudan (Violence in Darfur) So: 954
Dari [language]
Afghanistan (Ethnic groups and languages) A: 92a
Darién Colony [Panamanian history]
Balboa, Vasco Núñez de map on B: 37; (Rise to fame) B: 38
Darién Gap [Central America]
Pan American Highway (Route) P: 114 with map
Darien National Park [Panama]
National park (table) N: 42g
Darío, Rubén [Nicaraguan poet] D: 36
Latin American literature (Modernism) L: 113
Spanish literature (Modernism) So: 762
Darius I [king of Persia] D: 36
Bosporus B: 494
Greece, Ancient (The Persian wars) G: 373
Iran (The Achaemenid Empire) I: 405
Marathon, Battle of (Causes of the battle) M: 191
Persia, Ancient (The Achaemenid Empire) P: 298 with picture
Darius III [king of Persia] D: 36
Alexander the Great (Invasion of Asia) A: 342-343; (Victory over Darius) A: 343
Darius the Great See Darius I in this index
Darius the Mede [Biblical figure]
Daniel, Book of D: 33
Darjeeling tea
Darjiling D: 36
Tea (Processing tea) T: 62
Darjiling [India] D: 36
Dark Age [Greek history]
Greece, Ancient (History) G: 372
Dark Ages [European history] D: 36
See also Middle Ages in this index
Dark at the Top of the Stairs, The [play by Inge]
Inge, William I: 270
Dark chocolate
Chocolate (Dark chocolate) C: 519
Dark comedy
Comedy Ci: 867
Dark Continent [Africa]
Africa A: 103
Dark energy [astronomy] D: 36
Astronomy (Advances in cosmology) A: 849
Big bang B: 297
Cosmology (The future of the universe) Ci: 1078
Gravitation (Dark energy) G: 332
Universe (Changing views of the universe) U: 205-206

Dark-eyed junco [bird]
Junco J: 191 *with picture*
Dark-field microscope
Microscope (Dark field microscopes) M: 519
Dark lady [English literature]
Shakespeare, William (The sonnets) S: 366-367
Dark mantle deposit [astronomy]
Moon (Rilles) M: 790
"Dark Materials" trilogy [books by Pullman]
Pullman, Philip P: 900
Dark matter [astronomy] D: 37 *with picture*
Big bang B: 297
Brown dwarf B: 644
Cosmology (The future of the universe) Ci: 1078
Galaxy G: 8
Gravitation (Dark energy) G: 332-333
Matter (Dark matter) M: 311
Milky Way (Size of the galaxy) M: 550-551
Shadow matter S: 341
Universe (Changing views of the universe)
U: 205-206
Dark nebula [astronomy]
Nebula (Diffuse nebulae) N: 116
Dark Night's Passing, A [book by Shiga]
Japanese literature (The modern period) J: 62
Dark Side of the Moon [recording]
Rock music (Progressive rock) R: 380b
Darkness at Noon [book by Koestler]
Koestler, Arthur K: 361
Darkness at Noon [play by Kingsley]
Kingsley, Sidney K: 331
Darley Arabian [horse]
Horse racing (Thoroughbred horses) H: 363
Darling, Ding [American cartoonist] D: 37
Darling River [Australia]
Australia (Rivers) A: 909 *with map*
Darling underwing moth
Moth *picture on* M: 841
Darlington, Jennie [American explorer]
Antarctica (Exploration by air) A: 537-538
Darmstadtium [element] D: 38
Transuranium element T: 401
Darner [insect]
Insect *picture on* I: 280
Darnley, Lord [husband of Mary, Queen of Scots]
Bothwell, Earl of B: 510
Mary, Queen of Scots (Her reign) M: 239
d'Arrest, Heinrich L. [German astronomer]
Neptune (Discovery) N: 129
Darrieus, Georges [French inventor]
Turbine (Wind turbines) T: 498 *with picture*
Darrieus wind turbine
Turbine (Wind turbines) T: 498 *with picture*
D'Arriola, Don Andres [Spanish military leader]
Pensacola P: 272
Darrow, Clarence Seward [American lawyer] D: 38
Bryan, William Jennings (Later years) B: 655
Idaho (Early statehood) I: 44
Scopes trial S: 209 *with picture*
Tennessee (The early 1900's) T: 154-156
Darshana [religion]
Philosophy (Eastern philosophy) P: 386
D'Arsonval, Jacques Arsène [French physiologist]
Electric meter (History) E: 177
D'Arsonval galvanometer [instrument]
Electric meter (History) E: 177
Dart
Blowgun B: 419
Darts D: 39
Inuit (Hunting and fishing) I: 354d-354e
Dart [sewing]
Sewing (Darts) S: 332
Dart, Raymond [Australian-born anthropologist]
Prehistoric people (table) P: 754
Dart leader [lightning]
Lightning (Lightning strokes) L: 300
Dart poison frog See Poison dart frog *in this index*
Darter [bird]
Anhinga A: 467
Darter [fish] D: 38 *with picture*
Conservation (Water conservation) Ci: 977-978
Perch P: 284
Dartmouth [Nova Scotia] D: 38
Dartmouth College D: 39
Artificial intelligence A: 760
New Hampshire (Schools) N: 212-213 *with picture*
Universities and colleges (The oldest U.S.
universities and colleges) U: 210
Dartmouth College case [U.S. history] D: 39
Supreme Court of the United States (table)
So: 1002
Dartmouth College v. Woodward See Dartmouth
College case *in this index*
Dartmouth-Lake Sunapee
New Hampshire (Visitor's guide) N: 216
Darts [game] D: 39 *with picture*
Darwell, Jane [American actress]

Motion picture (Best performance by an actress
in a supporting role: 1940) M: 862b
Darwin [Australia] D: 39
Northern Territory N: 526 *with picture*
Darwin, Charles Robert [British biologist] D: 39
with portrait
Anthropology (Early anthropological thought)
A: 548
Biology *picture on* B: 321; (The theory of
evolution) B: 319
Christianity (The 1800's) C: 526
Comparative psychology Ci: 902b
Creationism (Creationist beliefs) Ci: 1123
Emotion (The basic emotion approach) E: 261
English literature (Victorian literature) E: 320-321
Evolution E: 426; (History of the theory of
evolution) E: 432
Galapagos Islands G: 7
Galton, Sir Francis G: 17
Heredity (Early ideas about heredity) H: 208
Huxley, Thomas Henry H: 459
Intelligent design I: 321
Malthus, Thomas Robert M: 115
National park (Other interesting national parks)
N: 42h
Natural selection N: 65
Races, Human (Evolutionary theory) R: 53-54
Science (Scientific advances of the 1800's) S: 200
with picture
Social Darwinism So: 551
Zoology (History) Z: 606
Darwin, Emma Wedgewood [wife of]
Darwin, Charles Robert (Darwin's life) D: 40
Darwin, Marx, Wagner [book by Barzun]
Barzun, Jacques B: 123
Darwin D. Martin House
Buffalo (Other interesting places to visit) B: 678
Das ...
Titles beginning Das *appear under their key words,
as in* Kapital, Das
Das, Tulsi [Indian poet]
Ramayana R: 132
Daschle, Tom [American political leader] D: 41
Dash [communications]
Telegraph (The Morse telegraph) T: 90
Dash [punctuation]
Punctuation (The dash) P: 902
Dashboard
Automobile (The passenger compartment)
A: 950
Dasheen [plant]
Elephant's-ear E: 233
Dasht-e Kavir [region]
Iran (The Interior Plateau) I: 402; (Climate) I: 403
Dasht-e Lut [region]
Iran (The Interior Plateau) I: 402; (Climate) I: 403
Dasyurid [animal]
Mammal (table) M: 128 *with picture*
Marsupial (Kinds of marsupials) M: 232
Marsupial mouse M: 233
DAT cassette [recording medium] See Digital
audiotape cassette *in this index*
Data [information]
Broadband communication B: 634
Database D: 41
Radio (Data transmission) R: 85
Spreadsheet So: 805
Data center [computing]
Internet *picture on* I: 350d; (Hardware) I: 350c
Data compression [electronics] D: 41
Television (Broadcasting) T: 123; (Digital
television) T: 128
Data Encryption Standard
Codes and ciphers (Later developments) Ci: 751
Data mining
Information retrieval (Research) I: 268-269
Information science I: 269
Statistics (Careers in statistics) So: 870
Data processing
Computer (Careers) Ci: 924a
Data Protection Act 1998 [United Kingdom]
Privacy, Right of P: 808a
Data protection law
Privacy, Right of P: 808a
Data storage [computing]
Computer (Storage devices) Ci: 915
Database [information] D: 41 *with picture*
Computer (Personal computers) Ci: 909;
(Database management programs) Ci: 918;
(Computer security) Ci: 924
Information retrieval I: 268b
Map (Database development) M: 180
Database management system [software]
Database D: 41
Search engine S: 268
Database query language [computing]
Database D: 41

Date [fruit]
Date palm D: 42 *with picture*
Date line, International See International date line
in this index
Date palm [tree] D: 42 *with picture*
Food (picture on F: 332
Palm (Products of palms) P: 109 *with picture*
Date rape [crime]
Rape R: 141
Dateline
Newspaper (table) N: 383
Dating [archaeology]
Archaeology (Dating) A: 598
Fossil (Dating fossils) F: 427
Prehistoric people (Placing prehistoric people in
time) P: 754a
Radiocarbon R: 97 *with diagrams*
Radiogeology R: 98
Dating [custom]
Adolescent (Dating and sex) A: 62 *with picture*
Etiquette (Dating etiquette) E: 374
Marriage (The path to marriage) M: 219
Datis [Persian general]
Marathon, Battle of (The battle) M: 191
Dative case [grammar]
Case (Cases in Latin) C: 271-272
Datura [botany] D: 43
Daturine [drug] See Stramonine *in this index*
Dauberval, Jean [French choreographer]
Ballet (Ballet d'action) B: 51
D'Aubigné, Françoise [wife of Louis XIV]
Maintenon, Marquise de M: 93
Daudet, Alphonse [French author] D: 43
Daugaard, Dennis [American political leader]
South Dakota (table) So: 680
Daugava River [Latvia]
Dvina River D: 393
Latvia (Land and climate) L: 119 *with map*
Daugherty, Harry M. [American government
official]
Coolidge, Calvin (Corruption in government)
Ci: 1032; (table) Ci: 1032
Harding, Warren Gamaliel (Entry into politics)
H: 57; (table) H: 58; (Government scandals)
H: 58
Justice, Department of (table) J: 203
Daugherty, James Henry [American author] D: 43
Newbery Medal (table) N: 359
Daughter cell [biology]
Ameba A: 406
Chromosome C: 538
Heredity (Sex cells and reproduction) H: 201
Daughter of Fortune [book by Allende]
Allende, Isabel A: 372
Daughter of the Confederacy [nickname, Winnie
Davis]
Davis, Jefferson (Davis's family) D: 47
Daughter of the Regiment, The [opera by
Donizetti]
Opera *picture on* O: 792
Daughters of Edward Darley Boit, The [painting
by Sargent]
Sargent, John Singer *picture on* S: 126
Daughters of Fire, The [book by Nerval]
French literature (Gautier and Nerval) F: 521-522
Daughters of the American Revolution
[organization] D: 43
African Americans (The Great Depression)
A: 136n
Daughters of the Confederacy, United
[organization] D: 43
Daughters of the Nile [organization]
Masonry (Organization) M: 267
D'Aulaire [American authors] D: 43
D'Aulaire, Edgar Parin [American author]
Caldecott Medal (table: 1940) C: 26
D'Aulaire D: 43
Regina Medal (table: 1970) R: 206
D'Aulaire, Ingri Mortenson [American author]
Caldecott Medal (table: 1940) C: 26
D'Aulaire D: 43
Regina Medal (table: 1970) R: 206
Daum Glass
Glass (Types of art glass) G: 220
Daumier, Honoré [French artist] D: 43 *with picture*
Bronze *picture on* B: 638
Caricature C: 238
Cartoon *picture on* C: 265
Painting (People) P: 31 *with picture*
Realism *picture on* R: 171
Dauphin [title] D: 44
Louis XVII L: 476
Dauphin Island [island, Alabama]
Alabama *picture on* A: 270
Dauphin River [Manitoba]
Lake Manitoba L: 40 *with map*
Dauphiné [former province, France]

Dauphin D: 44

Dausset, Jean Baptiste Gabriel Joachim [French physician]
Nobel Prizes (Physiology or medicine: 1980) N: 446

Dauversière, Sieur de la See Le Royer, Jérôme in this index

DAV [organization] See Disabled American Veterans in this index

Dávalos, Felipe [Mexican illustrator]
Literature for children picture on L: 355

Davenant, Sir William [English playwright] D: 44

Davenport [Iowa] D: 44
Iowa picture on I: 375; (Exploration and early settlement) picture on I: 393

Davenport, George [English trader]
Davenport D: 44

Davenport, John [American colonial leader]
New Haven (History) N: 229

Davey, Marie Augusta [American actress]
Fiske, Minnie Maddern F: 189

Davey, Martin L. [American political leader]
Ohio (table) O: 699

David [Biblical figure] D: 44 with pictures
Amalekites A: 400
Bathsheba B: 165
Bible (The Prophets) B: 280
Chronicles, Books of C: 539
Goliath G: 267
Jews picture on J: 122; (The kingdom of Israel) J: 121
Palestine (Early history and settlement) P: 104
Parable P: 141
Psalms, Book of P: 844
Religion (Judaism) R: 219
Solomon So: 584

David [kings of Scotland] D: 45

David [sculpture by Donatello] D: 45
Donatello D: 307
Renaissance picture on R: 235; (Arts of the 1300's and early 1400's) R: 236
Sculpture (Early Renaissance) S: 252 with picture

David [sculpture by Michelangelo]
David picture on D: 45
Michelangelo (Early life) M: 483-484

David I [king of Scotland]
David (David I) D: 45

David II [king of Scotland]
David (David II) D: 46

David, Francis [Hungarian religious leader]
Unitarians (History) U: 42

David, Jacques Louis [French painter] D: 46 with picture
Clothing picture on Ci: 704
French Revolution picture on F: 526
Painting (History paintings) P: 33; (Neoclassicism) P: 66-67 with picture
Socrates picture on So: 568

David, Saint [Welsh religious leader] D: 46

David, Shield of See Shield of David in this index

David, Star of See Star of David in this index

David and Goliath [painting by Michelangelo]
David picture on D: 45

David and Lucile Salter Packard Foundation
See Packard Foundation, David and Lucille in this index

David Copperfield [book by Dickens]
Dickens, Charles (The second phase) D: 188 with picture
English literature (Early Victorian literature) E: 321

David Harum [book by Westcott]
Westcott, Edward Noyes W: 230

Davidovsky, Mario [American composer]
Classical music (Electronic music) Ci: 650

Davidson, James O. [American political leader]
Wisconsin (table) W: 365

Davidson, Jo [American sculptor] D: 46

Davidson, Robert [Scottish inventor]
Electric railroad (History) E: 188

Davie, Alexander E. [Canadian political leader]
British Columbia (table) B: 628

Davie, Theodore [Canadian political leader]
British Columbia (table) B: 628

Davie, W. R. [American political leader]
North Carolina (table) N: 490

Davies, Arthur Bowen [American artist] D: 46
Ashcan School A: 768

Davies, Sir Louis Henry [Canadian jurist]
Prince Edward Island (table) P: 791

Davies, Myrick [American political leader]
Georgia (table) G: 130

Davies, Robertson [Canadian author] D: 46
Canadian literature (Modern English-Canadian fiction) C: 160 with portrait

Da Vinci, Leonardo [Italian artist] See Leonardo da Vinci in this index

Davis, Benjamin Oliver [American general]

African Americans (World War II [1939-1945]) A: 136n-136o

Davis, Benjamin Oliver, Jr. D: 47

Davis, Benjamin Oliver, Jr. [American general] D: 47 with portrait
African Americans (World War II [1939-1945]) A: 136n-136o
Tuskegee Airmen T: 525

Davis, Bette [American actress] D: 47 with portrait
Motion picture (Best performance by an actress: 1935, 1938) M: 862

Davis, Cushman K. [American political leader]
Minnesota (table) M: 602

Davis, D. W. [American political leader]
Idaho (table) I: 42

Davis, Daniel F. [American political leader]
Maine (table) M: 87

Davis, David [American jurist] D: 47
Electoral Commission E: 164

Davis, Deane C. [American political leader]
Vermont (table) V: 333

Davis, Dwight Filley [American statesman]
Coolidge, Calvin (table) Ci: 1032
Davis Cup D: 50
Hoover, Herbert Clark (table) H: 330

Davis, Edmund J. [American political leader]
Texas (table) T: 203

Davis, Ernie [American football player]
Football (table) F: 363

Davis, Floyd [American race driver]
Automobile racing (table: Indianapolis 500 winners) A: 980

Davis, Geena [American actress]
Motion picture (Best performance by an actress in a supporting role: 1988) M: 862b

Davis, George [American baseball player]
Baseball (table: Hall of Fame) B: 134

Davis, Glenn [American football player]
Football (table) F: 363

Davis, Gray [American political leader]
California (table) C: 59; (The late 1900's) C: 63-64; (The beginning of the 2000's) C: 64

Davis, Harry L. [American political leader]
Ohio (table) O: 699

Davis, Henry Gassaway [American political leader] D: 47

Davis, Jacob W. [American businessman]
Jeans J: 75
Strauss, Levi So: 922

Davis, James J. [American government official]
Hoover, Herbert Clark (table) H: 330
Labor, Department of (table) L: 2

Davis, Jeff [American political leader]
Arkansas (table) A: 712

Davis, Jefferson [Confederate political leader] D: 47 with portrait
Alabama (Places to visit) A: 266 with picture
Civil War, American picture on Ci: 618; (Secession) Ci: 617; (Government and politics) Ci: 623
Confederate States of America (Government) Ci: 931
Mississippi (The American Civil War) M: 642

Davis, Jehu [American political leader]
Delaware (table) D: 109

Davis, Jimmie H. [American political leader]
Louisiana (table) L: 496

Davis, John [American hunter]
Antarctica (Early exploration) A: 536

Davis, John [American political leader]
Massachusetts (table) M: 288

Davis, John [English explorer] D: 48
Exploration (The search for a northern passage) E: 446
Falkland Islands F: 15

Davis, John Edward [American political leader]
North Dakota (table) N: 513

Davis, John William [1826-1907, American political leader]
Rhode Island (table) R: 311

Davis, John William [1873-1955, American political leader] D: 49
Liberty League L: 233
Political convention (The changing role of conventions) P: 630

Davis, Jonathan M. [American political leader]
Kansas (table) K: 234

Davis, Judy [Australian actress]
Australia picture on A: 906

Davis, Miles [American musician] D: 49 with picture
Jazz (Cool jazz) J: 72 with picture

Davis, Nancy [wife of Ronald Reagan] See Reagan, Nancy Davis in this index

Davis, Paulina Wright [American social reformer] D: 49 with portrait

Davis, Raymond, Jr. [American chemist]
Nobel Prizes (Physics: 2002) N: 441-442

Davis, Richard Harding [American journalist] D: 49

War correspondent W: 26

Davis, Robert A. [Canadian political leader]
Manitoba (table) M: 159

Davis, Sammy, Jr. [American entertainer]
Sinatra, Frank S: 468

Davis, Samuel [Confederate spy] D: 49

Davis, Stuart [American painter] D: 50
Corcoran Gallery of Art picture on Ci: 1051

Davis, Thomas [Irish poet]
Irish literature (Early works in English) I: 431

Davis, Varina Howell [wife of]
Davis, Jefferson (Davis's family) D: 47

Davis, Westmoreland [American political leader]
Virginia (table) V: 417

Davis, William [Canadian political leader]
Ontario (table) O: 783

Davis, Winnie [daughter of]
Davis, Jefferson (Davis's family) D: 47

Davis Cup D: 50
Tennis (Tennis tournaments) T: 165; (The spread of tennis) T: 165; (Tennis today) T: 166d-166e

Davis Lock
Soo Canals (The American canals) So: 594 with map

Davis Mountain [Texas]
Texas (Mountains) T: 198

Davis Strait
Davis, John D: 48
Exploration (The search for a northern passage) E: 446
Northwest Passage N: 528

Davison, Sir William [English government official]
Brewster, William B: 596

Davisson, Clinton [American physicist]
Nobel Prizes (Physics: 1937) N: 440

Davy, Edmund [English chemist]
Acetylene A: 25

Davy, Sir Humphry [British chemist] D: 50
Aluminum (History) A: 397
Anesthesia (History) A: 459
Chlorine C: 516
Heat (The study of heat) H: 154-155
Light bulb L: 293

Davy Jones [legendary figure] See Jones, Davy in this index

Davy Jones's locker
Jones, Davy J: 158

Davy lamp
Davy, Sir Humphry D: 51

Davys, John [English explorer] See Davis, John in this index

Da`wa, Al- [political party]
Maliki, Nouri Kamel al- M: 110

Dawes, Charles Gates [American political leader] D: 51
Coolidge, Calvin ("Keep Cool with Coolidge") Ci: 1033
Dawes Plan D: 51
Nobel Prizes (Peace: 1925) N: 448a
Vice president of the United States portrait on V: 349; (Growth of the vice presidency) V: 353

Dawes, James W. [American political leader]
Nebraska (table) N: 110

Dawes, William [American patriot] D: 51
Prescott, Samuel P: 757
Revere, Paul (Paul Revere's ride) R: 268
Revolution, American (Lexington and Concord) R: 274-275

Dawes Act [1887]
Indian, American (In the United States) I: 178a-178b
Indian Affairs, Bureau of I: 185
Indian Territory I: 190

Dawes Commission [U.S. history]
Oklahoma (Progress toward statehood) O: 732

Dawes Plan [German history] D: 51
Coolidge, Calvin (Foreign affairs) Ci: 1033
Ruhr (History) R: 518

Dawkins, Pete [American football player]
Football (table) F: 363

Dawkins, Richard [British biologist] D: 51
Internet (Spreading ideas) I: 350e

Dawn [book by Wiesel]
Wiesel, Elie W: 299

Dawn [sculpture by Michelangelo]
Michelangelo M: 486 with picture

Dawn [spacecraft]
Asteroid (History of study) A: 824b
Ceres C: 362

Dawn at the Alamo [painting by McArdle]
Alamo picture on A: 281

Dawn Patrol, The [film]
Hawks, Howard H: 114

Dawn redwood [tree]
Redwood R: 192

Dawson [Yukon]
Klondike K: 344 with picture

Yukon (History) **Y:** 581
Dawson, Andre [American baseball player]
Baseball (table: Hall of Fame) **B:** 134
Dawson, George Mercer [Canadian geologist]
D: 51
Dawson, Joe [American race driver]
Automobile racing (table: Indianapolis 500 winners) **A:** 980
Dawson, Sir John William [Canadian geologist]
D: 51
Dawson, William M. O. [American political leader]
West Virginia (table) **W:** 225
Dawson Charlie [Canadian prospector]
Yukon (History) **Y:** 581
Dawson City Buildings [Yukon Territory]
Canada (table: National historic sites) **C:** 114
Day *See* Day and night *in this index*
Day [sculpture by Michelangelo]
Sculpture (Michelangelo) **S:** 252-253
Day, Benjamin [American educator]
Morse, Samuel Finley Breese (Early years) **M:** 817
Day, Benjamin Henry [American publisher]
Journalism (The growth of U.S. newspapers) **J:** 174
Day, Clarence [American author] **D:** 52
Day, Dorothy [American social reformer] **D:** 52
Day, J. Edward [American government official]
Kennedy, John Fitzgerald (table) **K:** 266
Day, Leon [American baseball player]
Baseball (table: Hall of Fame) **B:** 134
Day, Stephen *See* Daye, Stephen *in this index*
Day, Stockwell [Canadian political leader] **D:** 52
Day, The [poem by Parini]
Italian literature (The Baroque period and the Enlightenment) **I:** 494-495
Day, William R. [American jurist]
McKinley, William (table) **M:** 342
Supreme Court of the United States (table) **So:** 1000
Day and night D: 52
Earth (How Earth moves) **E:** 17 *with diagram*
Sidereal time **S:** 448
Time (Astronomical cycles) **T:** 288; (Time in today's world) **T:** 292 *with diagram*
"Day and Night" [poem by Livesay]
Canadian literature (Literature between the world wars) **C:** 158-159
Day by Day [book by Lowell]
Lowell, Robert **L:** 511
Day care D: 52
Education (Early childhood education) **E:** 91
Preschool **P:** 756a
School (Preschools) **S:** 181
Women's movement (In Western societies) **W:** 386-387 *with picture*
Day-Lewis, Cecil [Irish-born poet] **D:** 53
English literature (Poetry between the wars) **E:** 322
Day-Lewis, Daniel [Irish actor]
Motion picture (Best performance by an actor: 1989, 2007) **M:** 862a
Day lily [plant] **D:** 53 *with picture*
Flower (Garden perennials) **F:** 278 *with picture*
Gardening *picture on* **G:** 33
Day-neutral plant
Plant (Environmental factors) **P:** 538
Day of Atonement *See* Yom Kippur *in this index*
Day of Doom, The [poem by Wigglesworth]
American literature (New England) **A:** 414
Wigglesworth, Michael **W:** 300
Day of Reconciliation [holiday]
December **D:** 69
Day of Rejoicing [U.S. history]
Holiday (In the United States) **H:** 291
Day of the Dead [holiday] *See* Día de los muertos *in this index*
Day of the Locust, The [book by West]
West, Nathanael **W:** 198
Day tank [furnace]
Glass (Melting) **G:** 215
Day with the Cow Column in 1843, A [journal by Applegate]
Pioneer life in America (Life on the trail) **P:** 486-487
Dayaks [people] **D:** 53
Borneo *picture on* **B:** 489; (The people and their work) **B:** 490
Indonesia (Rural life) **I:** 229
Dayan, Moshe [Israeli general] **D:** 53
Daydream
Imagination **I:** 79
Daye, Matthew [American printer]
Daye, Stephen **D:** 54
Daye, Stephen [American printer] **D:** 54
Book (The 1600's and 1700's) **B:** 467
Massachusetts (Communication) **M:** 287
Printing (Early printing in North America) **P:** 803

Dayfly *See* Mayfly *in this index*
Daylight
Day and night **D:** 52
Daylight saving time D: 54
Franklin, Benjamin (Other studies) **F:** 489
Standard time (Time zones) **So:** 835
Daymark
Lighthouse (Identifying lighthouses) **L:** 294 *with picture*
Dayne, Ron [American football player]
Football **F:** 363
"Days" [poem by Emerson]
Emerson, Ralph Waldo (His poetry) **E:** 259
Dayton [Ohio] **D:** 54
Bosnia-Herzegovina (The Dayton peace plan) **B:** 493
Dayton [Tennessee]
Tennessee (The early 1900's) **T:** 154-156
Dayton, Jonathan [American political leader] **D:** 54
Dayton **D:** 54
Dayton, Mark [American political leader]
Minnesota (table) **M:** 602; (The early 2000's) **M:** 602
Dayton, William Lewis [American political leader] **D:** 55
Dayton Aviation Heritage National Historical Park [Ohio]
National Park System (table: National historical parks) **N:** 56-57
Dayton Wright Aeroplane Company
Aviation (World War I [1914-1918]) **A:** 987; (Aviation progress) **A:** 988-989
Daytona Beach [Florida] **D:** 55
Automobile racing *picture on* **A:** 975
Dazzle paint
Camouflage **C:** 87
DBMS [computing] *See* Database management system *in this index*
DBS [electronics] *See* Direct-broadcast satellite *in this index*
D.C. [district] *See* District of Columbia *in this index*
DC [electricity] *See* Direct current *in this index*
DC-3 [airplane]
Airplane *picture on* **A:** 234; (Engineering improvements) **A:** 237
Aviation (The industry comes of age) **A:** 989
DC-10 [airplane]
Airplane (Commercial transport planes) **A:** 210 *with picture*
D.D.S [degree] *See* Dental Surgery, Doctor of *in this index*
DDT [insecticide] **D:** 55
Agriculture (Chemical pesticides) **A:** 159
Bird (Endangered species) **B:** 370
Conservation (Renewed interest in conservation) **Ci:** 986
Environmental pollution (Government action) **E:** 335-336
Insecticide (Chlorinated hydrocarbon insecticides) **I:** 302
De ...
Titles beginning with the Latin word De appear below. Personal names beginning De are alphabetized as single words: De Angeli, Marguerite Lofft *appears after* Dean.
De Amicitia [book by Cicero]
Cicero, Marcus Tullius (His works) **Ci:** 552
De facto segregation
African Americans (Economic and social progress) **A:** 136p
Segregation (De facto segregation) **S:** 285
De Finibus [book by Cicero]
Cicero, Marcus Tullius (His works) **Ci:** 552
De jure segregation
Segregation (Jim Crow laws) **S:** 285
De Legibus [book by Cicero]
Cicero, Marcus Tullius (His works) **Ci:** 552
De Natura Deorum [book by Cicero]
Cicero, Marcus Tullius (His works) **Ci:** 552
De Officiis [book by Cicero]
Cicero, Marcus Tullius (His works) **Ci:** 552
De Oratore [book by Cicero]
Cicero Marcus Tullius (His works) **Ci:** 552
Oratory (Classical orators) **O:** 819
De-orbit
Space exploration (Returning to the earth) **So:** 701
De Profundis [book by Wilde]
Wilde, Oscar **W:** 302
De re Metallica [book by Agricola]
Geology (The Renaissance) **G:** 98
De Republica [book by Cicero]
Cicero, Marcus Tullius (His works) **Ci:** 552
De rerum natura *See* On the Nature of Things *in this index*
De Stijl [art] *See* Stijl, De *in this index*
De Vulgari Eloquentia [essay by Dante]

Dante Alighieri (His works) **D:** 34
DEA [organization] *See* Drug Enforcement Administration *in this index*
Deacon [religious title] **D:** 55
Christianity (The early church) **C:** 523
Eastern Orthodox Churches (Clergy) **E:** 46
Deaconess [religious title]
Deacon **D:** 55
Dead-air space [construction]
House (Insulation) **H:** 382-383
Dead ball era
Baseball (Early strategy and stars) **B:** 134b
Dead End [play by Kingsley]
Kingsley, Sidney **K:** 331
Dead-leaf insect mantis [insect]
Animal *picture on* **A:** 495
Dead lift [weightlifting]
Weightlifting **W:** 183
Dead-line [sports]
Football (Canadian football) **F:** 364
Dead of the Desert, The [book by Bialik]
Bialik, Chaim Nachman **B:** 278
Dead reckoning [navigation]
Airplane (Dead reckoning) **A:** 226
Columbus, Christopher (Sailing west) **Ci:** 860
Navigation (Dead reckoning) **N:** 70
Dead Sea [lake, Israel-Jordan] **D:** 55 *with map*
Asia *picture on* **A:** 794
Israel (The Rift Valley) **I:** 482
Jordan River **J:** 167
West Bank *picture on* **W:** 199; (Land and climate) **W:** 200 *with map*
Dead Sea Scrolls [manuscripts] **D:** 56
Bible *picture on* **B:** 282; (Literary contexts) **B:** 287
Library (Ancient libraries of animal skin) **L:** 258
Dead Sea Works [company]
Dead Sea **D:** 56
Dead Souls [book by Gogol]
Gogol, Nikolai **G:** 248
Russian literature (Late Romanticism) **R:** 561-562
Dead wool
Wool (Types of wool) **W:** 399
Deadbolt
Lock (Types of locks) **L:** 410-411 *with picture*
Deadhead
Grateful Dead **G:** 329
Rock music (The San Francisco scene) **R:** 380a
Deadly nightshade [plant] *See* Belladonna [plant] *in this index*
Deadweight tonnage
Ship (Nautical measurements) **S:** 406
Deadwood [South Dakota]
Calamity Jane **C:** 20
South Dakota *picture on* **So:** 683; (Places to visit) **So:** 672 *with picture*; (Territorial days) **So:** 681
Deadwood Dick [frontier figure]
Love, Nat **L:** 508 *with picture*
Deaf, National Association of the *See* National Association of the Deaf *in this index*
Deaf community [sociology]
Deafness (Deaf community and culture) **D:** 59
Deafness D: 56 *with pictures*
Closed captioning **Ci:** 685
Disability (Hearing disabilities) **D:** 219
Language (Signed languages) **L:** 63
Lip reading **L:** 344
Deák, Francis [Hungarian political leader]
Hungary (Austria-Hungary) **H:** 446
Deakin, Alfred [Australian political leader]
Australia (table) **A:** 923
Deal, Nathan [American political leader]
Georgia (table) **G:** 130
Dealey Plaza
Dallas (Landmarks) **D:** 11
Dean, Dizzy [American baseball player] **D:** 60
Baseball (table: Hall of Fame) **B:** 134
Dean, Howard [American political leader]
Vermont (table) **V:** 333
Dean, James [American actor] **D:** 60 *with portrait*
Dean, Jay Hanna *See* Dean, Dizzy *in this index*
Dean, John W., III [American government official]
United States, History of the *picture on* **U:** 196b
Watergate (The break-in and cover-up) **W:** 144
Dean of students [title]
Universities and colleges (Administration) **U:** 208
Deane, Silas [American diplomat] **D:** 60
Paine, Thomas (American revolutionary) **P:** 22
De Angeli, Marguerite Lofft [American author] **D:** 60
Newbery Medal (table) **N:** 359
Regina Medal (table: 1968) **R:** 206
Dean's December, The [book by Bellow]
Bellow, Saul **B:** 244
Dear Abby [newspaper column]
Van Buren, Abigail **V:** 269
Dear Mr. Henshaw [book by Cleary]
Cleary, Beverly **Ci:** 660

Dearborn [Michigan] **D:** 60
  Ford, Henry (Political and charitable activities)
    F: 380
Dearborn, Henry [American military leader] **D:** 61
Dearborn Street
  Chicago (Places to visit) **C:** 430
Dearden, John Francis [American religious leader]
  Cardinal (table: American cardinals) **C:** 211
Death D: 61
  See also Burial; Funeral customs; Suicide *in this
    index*
  Día de los muertos **D:** 178
  Famine (Effects of famine) **F:** 26a
  Forensic pathology **F:** 389a
  Living will **L:** 398
  Medical examiner **M:** 361
  Mythology (Types of myths) **M:** 973-974
  Palliative care **P:** 108
  Reincarnation **R:** 208
  Safety **S:** 9
  Spiritualism **So:** 545
  Transplant (Sources of donor organs) **T:** 380
  War (Loss of life) **W:** 25
Death [Greek mythology]
  Sisyphus **S:** 477
Death adder [snake]
  Adder **A:** 47
"Death be not proud" [poem by Donne]
  Donne, John (His poetry) **D:** 308
Death benefit
  Insurance (Life insurance) **I:** 309
Death camas [plant]
  Poisonous plant (Some poisonous plants) **P:** 602
Death camp [European history] *See* Concentration
    camp *in this index*
Death cap [fungus]
  Mushroom *picture on* **M:** 944
Death certificate
  Vital statistics (Collecting and publishing vital
    statistics) **V:** 429
Death Comes for the Archbishop [book by Cather]
  Cather, Willa **C:** 302
Death in the Afternoon [book by Hemingway]
  Hemingway, Ernest (Rise to fame) **H:** 180
Death in Venice [book by Mann]
  Mann, Thomas **M:** 164
Death mask
  Mask (Burial masks and death masks) **M:** 265
    with picture
  Tutankhamun *picture on* **T:** 526
Death of a Salesman [play by Miller]
  American literature (Drama) **A:** 426
  Drama *picture on* **D:** 324
  Miller, Arthur **M:** 553
  United States *picture on* **U:** 119
Death of Artemio Cruz, The [book by Fuentes]
  Fuentes, Carlos **F:** 553
  Latin American literature (The "Boom") **L:** 114
Death of Cook [painting by Webber]
  Cook, James *picture on* **Ci:** 1025
Death of General Wolfe, The [painting by West]
  West, Benjamin **W:** 198
  Wolfe, James *picture on* **W:** 377
"Death of God" [theology]
  Nietzsche, Friedrich (Nietzsche and religion)
    N: 406
"Death of Ivan Ilyich, The" [story by L. Tolstoy]
  Tolstoy, Leo (Later works) **T:** 323
Death of Marat, The [painting by David]
  French Revolution *picture on* **F:** 526
Death of Socrates, The [painting by David]
  Socrates *picture on* **So:** 568
Death of the Heart, The [book by Bowen]
  Bowen, Elizabeth **B:** 519
Death of the Virgin [painting by Van der Goes]
  Van der Goes, Hugo *picture on* **V:** 280
Death on the Installment Plan [book by Céline]
  Céline, Louis-Ferdinand **C:** 325
Death penalty *See* Capital punishment *in this index*
Death rate [statistics]
  Birth and death rates **B:** 377
  Disease (Death rates from diseases in the United
    States) **D:** 233 *with diagram*
  Infant mortality **I:** 264
  Life expectancy **L:** 280
Death row
  Capital punishment (History of capital
    punishment) **C:** 193
Death Valley [region, California] **D:** 62 *with picture
    and map*
  California (The Basin and Range Region) **C:** 50;
    (Climate) **C:** 52
  North America *picture on* **N:** 464
  Rain (Some rainfall records) **R:** 124 *with map*
  United States (The Western Plateaus, Basins, and
    Ranges) **U:** 125; (Climate) **U:** 126 *with picture*
Death Valley National Park [California-Nevada]

D: 63
  Death Valley **D:** 62
  National Park System (Areas preserved for natural
    features) **N:** 43; (table: National parks) **N:** 48
Death's-head moth [insect] **D:** 63
Deathwatch [insect] **D:** 63
De Baca, Ezequiel C. [American political leader]
  New Mexico (table) **N:** 272
DeBakey, Michael Ellis [American doctor] **D:** 63
  Arab Americans (Arab American
    accomplishments) **A:** 580b
  Heart (Development of heart surgery) **H:** 144-145
Debasement [economics]
  Money (Objects used as money) **M:** 705
Debate [speech] **D:** 63 *with picture*
  Parliamentary procedure (Motions) **P:** 176
De Beers Consolidated Mines [South Africa]
  Rhodes, Cecil John (Gains Rhodesia) **R:** 317
Debenture [security]
  Bond (Kinds of bonds) **B:** 454
Debierne, André [French scientist]
  Actinium **A:** 30
Debit
  Bookkeeping (Double-entry bookkeeping) **B:** 472
Debit card [banking]
  Bank (Providing a means of payment) **B:** 89
  Credit card **Ci:** 1125
  E-commerce (Business-to-consumer
    transactions) **E:** 2
  Money **M:** 704
Deborah [Biblical figure] **D:** 65
Debouillet sheep
  Sheep (Fine-wooled sheep) **S:** 381-382
De Brazza's guenon [animal]
  Monkey *picture on* **M:** 728
Debrecen [Hungary] **D:** 65
Debreu, Gérard [American economist]
  Economics (Modern economics) **E:** 64-65
  Nobel Prizes (Economics: 1983) **N:** 449
De Broglie, Louis Victor [French physicist] **D:** 65
  Physics (Quantum theory) **P:** 441
  Quantum mechanics (Wave-particle duality) **Q:** 6
  Schrödinger, Erwin **S:** 186
Debs, Eugene Victor [American labor leader] **D:** 65
    with portrait
  Darrow, Clarence Seward **D:** 38
  Labor movement (Opposition to unions) **L:** 10-11
  Pullman Strike **P:** 900
  Socialism (Moderate socialism) **So:** 561 *with
    picture*
Debt D: 65
  See also Loan *in this index*
  Attachment **A:** 878
  Bankruptcy **B:** 97
  City government (Budget problems) **Ci:** 597
  Collection agency **Ci:** 774
  Guaranty **G:** 411
  I.O.U. **I:** 373
  Moratorium **M:** 800
Debt, National *See* National debt *in this index*
Debt ceiling [economics]
  National debt (Economic growth and rising
    national debt) **N:** 34
  Obama, Barack (Debt limit battle) **O:** 640h
Debt to asset ratio [economics]
  Farm and farming (Financing farm operations)
    F: 42
Debtor
  Bankruptcy **B:** 97
  Collection agency **Ci:** 774
  Debt **D:** 65
Debtors' prison
  Prison (Early prisons) **P:** 807
Debugging
  Computer (Programming a computer) **Ci:** 923
Debunking biography [literature]
  Biography (Modern biography) **B:** 314
Debussy, Claude [French composer] **D:** 66
  Classical music (The 1900's) **Ci:** 649
  Impressionism (Music, literature, and sculpture)
    I: 94
Deby, Idriss [Chadian political leader]
  Chad (History) **C:** 367-368
Debye, Peter Joseph William [Dutch chemist]
    D: 66
  Nobel Prizes (Chemistry: 1936) **N:** 443
Decade for Women [UN]
  Women's movement (In developing nations)
    W: 387
Decadents [literature]
  Symbolism **So:** 1066
Decaffeinated coffee
  Coffee (Kinds of coffee) **Ci:** 755
Decal [decoration] **D:** 66
Decalcomania [decoration]
  Decal **D:** 66
Decalogue *See* Ten Commandments *in this index*

Decameron [book by Boccaccio]
  Boccaccio, Giovanni **B:** 433
  French literature (The Renaissance) **F:** 519
  Italian literature (Humanism and the
    Renaissance) **I:** 494
  Renaissance (Petrarch and Giovanni Boccaccio)
    R: 234
Decanting [process]
  Olive oil **O:** 744
Decarchy [political science]
  Lysander **L:** 538
Decathlon [sports] **D:** 66
  Track and field (The decathlon, heptathlon, and
    pentathlon) **T:** 359
Decatur [Illinois] **D:** 67
  Jackson, Jesse Louis Jr. **J:** 15
Decatur, Stephen [American military leader] **D:** 67
    with portrait
Decatur Staleys [team]
  Halas, George Stanley **H:** 18
Decay [chemistry] **D:** 67
  Decomposition **D:** 80
Decay, Tooth *See* Tooth decay *in this index*
Decay series [radioactivity]
  Isotope (Radioactive isotopes) **I:** 476
Deccan [region]
  India (The land) **I:** 121-122 *with picture and map*
Deccan Traps [formations]
  Dinosaur (Why the dinosaurs died out) **D:** 213
Decelean War [413-404 B.C.]
  Peloponnesian War **P:** 232
Deceleration [physics]
  Space exploration (Returning to the earth)
    So: 701
December [month] **D:** 68 *with pictures*
  Calendar (The Romans) **C:** 31
December Rebellion [1837]
  Rebellions of 1837 (In Upper Canada) **R:** 174
Decembrist Uprising [1825]
  Russia (Alexander I) **R:** 550
Decembrists [Russian history]
  Nicholas I **N:** 402
Decemvirs [ancient Rome]
  Twelve Tables, Laws of the **T:** 531
Decency [law]
  Obscenity and pornography **O:** 643
Decentralization
  Local government (Conflicts in authority) **L:** 408
Deception Island [Antarctica]
  Antarctica (Land) **A:** 531-532 *with map*
Deceptive advertising
  Advertising (Advertising associations) **A:** 77
De Charnisay, D'Aulnay [French settler]
  New Brunswick (French rivals) **N:** 196
Deci [prefix]
  Metric system (Metric prefixes) **M:** 439; (Selection
    of SI prefixes) **M:** 440
Decibel [measurement] **D:** 70
  Ear (The sense of hearing) **E:** 9
  Sound (table) **So:** 599; (Intensity and loudness)
    So: 600-601
Deciduous teeth
  Teeth *picture on* **T:** 80; (Deciduous teeth) **T:** 79
    with picture
Deciduous tree [botany] **D:** 70
  Biome **B:** 322; (table) **B:** 323 *(with map)*
  Forest (Temperate deciduous forests) **F:** 393;
    (Forest succession) **F:** 397 *with picture*
  Leaf (A leaf begins its life) **L:** 152
  Lumber (Hardwood lumber) **L:** 517
  Plant (Temperate deciduous forests) **P:** 523
  Tree (Broadleaf trees) **T:** 414
  Wood (Kinds of wood) **W:** 389-390
Decimal currency
  Money (History of the pound) **M:** 709-710
  Penny **P:** 271
Decimal fraction [mathematics]
  Division (Division of decimal fractions) **D:** 250
  Fraction (In symbols) **F:** 444-445
Decimal numeral system *See* Decimal system *in
    this index*
Decimal point
  Decimal system (Decimals less than one) **D:** 71
    with diagrams
Decimal system [mathematics] **D:** 70
  Arabic numerals **A:** 584
  Arithmetic **A:** 665; (Written arithmetic methods)
    A: 669
  Binary number **B:** 307
  Division (Division of decimal fractions) **D:** 250
  Fraction (History) **F:** 449
  Mathematics (Early civilization) **M:** 303
  Metric system (Advantages of the metric system)
    M: 436
  Number (The decimal system) **N:** 605 *with
    picture*; (The Hindu-Arabic numeral system)
    N: 607

Percentage **P: 280**
Weights and measures (Comparison of measurement systems) **W: 185**
Zero **Z: 590**
Decimus Junius Juvenalis [Roman poet] *See* Juvenal *in this index*
Deciphering *See* Decryption *in this index*
Decision [sports]
Boxing (A decision) **B: 528**
Wrestling (High school and intercollegiate wrestling) **W: 505**
Decision in Germany [book by Clay]
Clay, Lucius Dubignon **Ci: 659**
Decision making
Automation (Uses of automation) **A: 944**
Brain (Making decisions) **B: 555**
Ethics (Ethical issues) **E: 366**
Existentialism (What is existentialism?) **E: 437**
Game theory **G: 23**
Simon, Herbert Alexander **S: 466**
Decitex [measurement]
Microfiber **M: 514**
Decius [Roman emperor]
Rome, Ancient (table) **R: 447**
Deck [ship]
Aircraft carrier **A: 206** *with pictures*
Ship (Basic structure) **S: 403**
Deck officer
Ship (Officers and crew) **S: 410**
Declaration [law]
Customs **Ci: 1201**
Declaration by United Nations [1942]
United Nations (The Atlantic Charter) **U: 94**
Declaration of Human Rights *See* Human Rights, Universal Declaration of *in this index*
Declaration of Independence [U.S. history] **D: 73** *with pictures*
American literature (The revolutionary period [1765-1787]) **A: 415**
Democracy (American democracy) **D: 123**
Hancock, John **H: 38**
Independence Day **I: 107**
Jefferson, Thomas (The Declaration of Independence) **J: 79** *with picture*
Law (Beginnings of U.S. law) **L: 136**
Mason, George **M: 265**
National Archives and Records Administration **N: 29**
Revolution, American (The Declaration of Independence) **R: 278** *with picture*
United States, History of the (The Declaration of Independence) **U: 160**
World, History of the (The rise of democracy and nationalism) **W: 443**
Declaration of Independence, The [painting by Trumbull]
Painting (History paintings) **P: 33**
Declaration of London [1909]
Blockade **B: 406**
Declaration of Paris [1856]
Blockade **B: 406**
Declaration of Rights [1774]
Continental Congress (The First Continental Congress) **Ci: 1021**
Declaration of Rights [1776]
Mason, George **M: 265**
Virginia (Independence and statehood) **V: 420**
Declaration of Sentiments [1848]
Mott, Lucretia Coffin **M: 880**
Woman suffrage (Beginnings of the movement) **W: 380**
Women's movement (The beginnings of women's movements) **W: 384-385**
"Declaration of the Causes and Necessity of Taking up Arms" [U.S. history]
Jefferson, Thomas (The Declaration of Independence) **J: 79**
Declaration of the Rights of Man *See* Rights of Man, Declaration of the *in this index*
Declaration on Liberated Europe
Cold War (The alliance breaks up) **Ci: 763**
Declaration on Religious Liberty
Vatican Council II (Other documents) **V: 290**
Declaration on the Granting of Independence to Colonial Countries and Peoples [UN]
United Nations (Working for self-government) **U: 93**
Declaration on the Relation of the Church to non-Christian Religions
Vatican Council II (Other documents) **V: 290**
Declarative sentence
Sentence (Sentence classifications) **S: 303**
Declaratory Act [1720]
Grattan, Henry **G: 329**
Declaratory Act [1766]
Revolution, American (The Quartering and Stamp acts) **R: 272-273**

Declawing
Cat (Training) **C: 294**
Declension [grammar] **D: 79**
Inflection **I: 268a**
Declination [astronomy]
Astronomy *diagrams on* **A: 842**; (Locating objects in space) **A: 838**
Declination [navigation]
Compass (Variation) **Ci: 902b**
Decline and Fall of the Roman Empire *See* History of the Decline and Fall of the Roman Empire *in this index*
Decline of the West, The [book by Spengler]
Civilization (Rise and fall) **Ci: 636**
Spengler, Oswald **So: 778**
Decoder Circuitry Act [1990]
Closed captioning **C: 685**
Decoding [cryptology] *See* Decryption *in this index*
Decomposer [organism]
Soil (Organic matter) **So: 573**
Decomposition [chemistry] **D: 80** *with diagram*
Bacteria (Helpful bacteria) **B: 19**
Decay **D: 67**
Ecology (Energy flow) **E: 54**
Forest (The cycling of chemicals) **F: 396**
Fungi (The importance of fungi) **F: 559**
Landfill **L: 57**
Soil **So: 573**
Soil pollution **So: 576**
Waste disposal (Land disposal) **W: 113**
Wetland (Water and soil) **W: 252a**
Decompression sickness *See* Bends *in this index*
Decompression table
Diving, Underwater (Dangers of underwater diving) **D: 246-247**
Deconditioning [disorder]
Space exploration (Microgravity) **So: 701-702**
Deconstruction [philosophy]
Criticism (History of literary criticism) **Ci: 1146-1147**
Derrida, Jacques **D: 153**
French literature (The middle and late 1900's) **F: 523**
Decorated initial [art]
Illuminated manuscript **I: 78**
Decorated style [architecture]
Gothic art (Gothic architecture in England) **G: 279**
Decoration, Interior *See* Interior design *in this index*
Decoration Day *See* Memorial Day *in this index*
Decorations *See* Medals, decorations, and orders *in this index*
Decorative arts D: 80 *with diagram*
See also the list of Related articles in the Decorative arts *article*
Antique **A: 557** *with pictures*
Colonial life in America (Decorative arts) **Ci: 807** *with pictures*
Fine arts **F: 104**
Flower (As decoration) **F: 272** *with picture*
Glass (How glass is decorated) **G: 217** *with pictures*
Illuminated manuscript **I: 78**
Painting (Decoration) **P: 34**
Porcelain (Decorating porcelain) **P: 676**
Wallpaper **W: 19**
Decorticating [process]
Sisal **S: 476**
Decorum, Doctrine of
Drama (The French theater) **D: 333**
De Cosmos, Amor [Canadian political leader]
British Columbia (table) **B: 628**
De Coster, Charles [Belgian author]
Belgium (The arts) **B: 230**
Decoupage [art] **D: 81** *with picture*
Decreasing term insurance
Insurance (Major types of life insurance) **I: 309-310**
Decrescendo
Music (table) **M: 954**
Decriminalization [law]
Drug abuse (The legalization debate) **D: 365**
Marijuana (History) **M: 201**
Decryption
Codes and ciphers **Ci: 749**
Decubitus ulcer
Bedsore **B: 199**
Ulcer **U: 15**
Dedicated computer
Computer (Dedicated computers) **Ci: 911**
Dedicated server [computer]
Computer (Local area networks [LAN's]) **Ci: 922**
Dedicated service [telephone]
Telephone (Business services) **T: 98**
Dedicated word processor [machine]
Word processing (History) **W: 404**
Deduced reckoning *See* Dead reckoning *in this*

index
Deductible
Insurance (Major medical expense benefits) **I: 312**
Deduction [reasoning] *See* Deductive method *in this index*
Deduction [taxation]
Flat tax **F: 228**
Income tax (Defining taxable income) **I: 102**; (Figuring the individual income tax) **I: 104**
Deductive method D: 81
Geometry (The study of geometry) **G: 101**; (Greek geometry) **G: 106**
Logic **L: 425**
Philosophy (Logic) **P: 384**; (Rationalism) **P: 388**
Science (Mathematics and logic) **S: 192-193**
Deductive phonics *See* Synthetic phonics *in this index*
De Durão, José de Santa Rita [Brazilian poet]
Latin American literature (Colonial literature) **L: 112**
De Duve, Christian Rene [Belgian physiologist]
Nobel Prizes (Physiology or medicine: 1974) **N: 446**
Dee, Ruby [American actress]
Spingarn Medal (table: 2008) **So: 794**
Deed [law] **D: 81**
Deenie [book by Blume]
Blume, Judy **B: 425**
Deep [oceanography] **D: 81**
Deep basin [geography]
Arctic Ocean (The ocean floor) **A: 643**
Deep Blue [computer]
Artificial intelligence (Planning and problem solving) **A: 760**
Kasparov, Garry **K: 248**
Deep brain stimulation system [medicine]
Parkinson disease (Other treatments) **P: 171**
Deep Creek Lake
Maryland (Rivers and lakes) **M: 252**
Deep drawing [process]
Aluminum (Deep drawing) **A: 396**
Deep-frying
Cooking (Frying) **Ci: 1028**
Deep Impact [spacecraft] *See* EPOXI *in this index*
Deep Ocean Engineering [company]
Earle, Sylvia Alice **E: 14**
Deep sea [habitat] **D: 82** *with pictures*
Exploration (Deep-sea exploration) **E: 450**
Ocean (The benthos) **O: 655** *with picture*; (The land at the bottom of the sea) **O: 659** *with map*
Deep-sea angler [fish]
Animal *picture on* **A: 487**
Fish *picture on* **F: 156**
Deep-sea diving *See* Diving, Underwater *in this index*
Deep Sea Drilling Project
Ocean drilling programs **O: 667**
Deep-sea lobster [sea animal]
Lobster **L: 405**
Deep sea vent [oceanography] *See* Hydrothermal vent *in this index*
Deep Space 1 [space probe]
Comet (Studying comets) **Ci: 868-869**
Rocket (Ion rockets) **R: 389**
Space exploration (Probes to asteroids) **So: 711**
Deepsea Challenger [submarine]
Diving, Underwater (Diving in vehicles) **D: 246**
Deepwater Horizon [oil rig]
BP **B: 542**
Gulf oil spill of 2010 **G: 437**
Oil spill (Notable spills) **O: 708** *with picture*
Deer D: 82d *with pictures*
Animal *pictures on* **A: 479, A: 481, A: 483, A: 495**
Zoo *picture on* **Z: 600**
Deer, Ada E. [American government official]
Indian, American (Political gains) **I: 182**
Deer fly [insect] **D: 86** *with picture*
Fly (table) **F: 310**
Insect *picture on* **I: 282**
Deer Hunter, The [film]
Motion picture (Best picture: 1978) **M: 861**
Deer mouse
Hantavirus **H: 54**
Deer Park, The [book by Mailer]
Mailer, Norman **M: 67**
Deer tick [animal] **D: 86** *with picture*
Deere, John [American inventor] **D: 87**
Plow (The sulky plow) **P: 575**
Western frontier life in America (Improvements in farming) **W: 233-234**
Deere and Company
Deere, John **D: 87**
Deerskin [leather]
Buckskin **B: 664**
Deerslayer, The [book by Cooper]
Cooper, James Fenimore **Ci: 1035**

Deerweed [plant]
Plant *picture on* **P:** 525
De Falla, Manuel [Spanish composer] *See* Falla, Manuel *de in this index*
Defamation [law]
Libel **L:** 226
Defassa waterbuck
Antelope (Kinds of antelope) **A:** 542
Default [economics]
City government (Budget problems) **Ci:** 597
Mortgage **M:** 820
Defecation [physiology]
Alimentary canal **A:** 369
Defence of Poesie, The [essay by Sidney]
Sidney, Sir Philip **S:** 449
Defence of Poetry, A [essay by Shelley]
Shelley, Percy Bysshe (His writings) **S:** 391
Defence Research and Development Canada
Canadian Armed Forces (Organization) **C:** 154
Defendant [law]
Court (How civil courts work) **Ci:** 1102
Criminal justice system (The courts) **Ci:** 1143
Defender [sports]
Soccer (The defenders) **So:** 545 *with diagram*
Defender, Chicago [newspaper]
Abbott, Robert Sengstacke **A:** 6
Defenestration of Prague [European history]
Thirty Years' War (The Bohemian period) **T:** 260
Defense [government]
Government (Defense) **G:** 283
National budget (Government spending) **N:** 30
Defense, Civil *See* Civil defense *in this index*
Defense, Department of [U.S.] **D:** 87 *with picture*
Civil service (Federal civil service) **Ci:** 612
Gulf War syndrome **G:** 438
Hoover Commission **H:** 332
Internet (The early Internet) **I:** 350g
Navy, Department of the **N:** 81
Pentagon Building **P:** 274
RAND Corporation **R:** 136
Defense, Secretary of [U.S.]
Defense, Department of (Organization) **D:** 87
Flag *picture on* **F:** 211
Defense and Glorification of the French Language [book by Bellay]
French literature (The Pléiade) **F:** 519-520
Defense Intelligence Agency [U.S.]
Central Intelligence Agency (Functions) **C:** 356-357
Defense Language Institute
Monterey **M:** 764
Defense mechanism [psychology]
Freud, Sigmund (On behavior) **F:** 530
Psychotherapy (Psychodynamic-interpersonal psychotherapy) **P:** 852
Defense of Marriage Act [1993]
Same-sex marriage **S:** 78
Defenseman [sports]
Hockey (The starting lineup) **H:** 275
Defensive back
Football (The defensive team) **F:** 357-358 *with diagrams*
Defensive driving
Automobile (Defensive driving) **A:** 956
Deferent [astronomy]
Astronomy *diagram on* **A:** 847; (Earth-centered theories) **A:** 835
De Ferran, Gil [Brazilian-born race driver]
Automobile racing (table: Indianapolis 500 winners) **A:** 980
Deferred annuity
Insurance (Annuities) **I:** 311
Deferred payment
Installment plan **I:** 304
Deferred retirement credit
Social security (How benefits are figured) **So:** 554
Defibrillator [device] **D:** 88
Arrhythmia **A:** 743
Heart (Abnormal heart rhythms) **H:** 142; (Progress in treatment and prevention) **H:** 145
Paramedic (Duties) **P:** 153
Deficiency disease
Anemia (Insufficient production of red blood cells) **A:** 457
Diet (Normal diet) **D:** 199
Malnutrition **M:** 111
Nutrition (Deficiency diseases) **N:** 630
Deficient demand unemployment
Unemployment (Types of unemployment) **U:** 22
Deficit [economics]
Balance of payments (How the balance of payments is determined) **B:** 36
Budget (Economic effects of the national budget) **B:** 671, **B:** 671
Bush, George Herbert Walker **B:** 716
Inflation **I:** 267
Money (Printing money and inflation) **M:** 717

National budget (Deficits and surpluses) **N:** 31
National debt **N:** 33
Deficit spending [economics]
Economics (Modern economics) **E:** 64-65
Great Depression (New government policies) **G:** 342
Defined-benefit pension plan
Pension Benefit Guaranty Corporation **P:** 274
Defined term [mathematics]
Geometry (Axiomatic system) **G:** 102
Definite article [grammar]
Article (The definite article) **A:** 758
Definite integral
Calculus (The definite integral) **C:** 24
Definite proportions, Law of [chemistry]
Chemistry (Dalton's atomic theory) **C:** 402
Definition
Dictionary (What a dictionary tells you) **D:** 193
Deflation [economics] **D:** 88
Inflation **I:** 267
Recession (Recession and inflation) **R:** 175
Deflection [aerodynamics]
Aerodynamics (Lift) **A:** 85-86
Airplane (Airplane and lift) **A:** 220-221
Defoe, Daniel [English author] **D:** 88
English literature (The rise of the novel) **E:** 318
Literature for children (The 1700's) **L:** 362
Novel (The first English novelists) **N:** 572
Pillory **P:** 464
Robinson Crusoe **R:** 369
Defoliant [chemical]
Cotton (Harvesting) **Ci:** 1090
Defoliation [botany]
Agent Orange **A:** 140
Forestry (Diseases and pests) **F:** 407
Herbicide (Hazards of herbicides) **H:** 198
De Forest, Lee [American inventor] **D:** 89
Communication (The development of electronics) **Ci:** 883-884
Electronics (Early experiments) **E:** 215 *with picture*
Radio (The start of broadcasting) **R:** 92
Vacuum tube (History) **V:** 259
Deforestation [botany] **D:** 89 *with picture*
Amazon rain forest **A:** 402 *with picture*
Animal (Animals of the temperate forests) **A:** 478; (How human beings endanger animals) **A:** 504 *with picture*
Conservation (Conservation around the world) **Ci:** 988
Coral reef (Coral reefs and people) **Ci:** 1049
Forest (Deforestation) **F:** 398 *with picture*
Forestry (History) **F:** 408
Rain forest (The future of rain forests) **R:** 126d *with picture*
Deformable mirror [astronomy]
Telescope (Adaptive optics systems) **T:** 106
Deformation bonding [industrial process]
Welding (Solid-state bonding) **W:** 190
Deformity
Birth defect **B:** 380
Plastic surgery (Cosmetic surgery) **P:** 553
Défricheur, Le [newspaper]
Laurier, Sir Wilfrid (Young lawyer) **L:** 123
Defrosting
Refrigeration (Defrosting) **R:** 203
Deganawida [American Indian leader]
Hiawatha **H:** 221
Degas, Edgar [French artist] **D:** 90 *with picture*
Cassatt, Mary **C:** 275 *with picture*
Impressionism (French Impressionism) **I:** 93; (Music, literature, and sculpture) **I:** 94
Painting (Edouard Manet and the Impressionists) **P:** 71
De Gasperi, Alcide [Italian political leader]
Italy (The Italian republic) **I:** 517-518
Degassing [process]
Aluminum (Casting the molten aluminum) **A:** 394
De Gaulle, Charles André Joseph Marie [French political leader] **D:** 90 *with pictures*
Cold War (The great blocs split) **Ci:** 769
Foreign Legion (History) **F:** 386
France **F:** 455; (World War II) **F:** 475; (The Fourth Republic) **F:** 475; (The Fifth Republic) **F:** 476; (France under de Gaulle) **F:** 476; (France after de Gaulle) **F:** 477 *with picture*
Kennedy, John Fitzgerald (Other developments) **K:** 266
Paris (Paris in wartime) **P:** 166
World War II (The fall of France) **W:** 475
De Gaulle, Place Charles [Paris]
Paris (Gardens, squares, and parks) **P:** 162
De Gaulle, Yvonne Vendroux [wife of]
De Gaulle, Charles André Joseph Marie (Early life) **D:** 90-91
De Gaulle Airport [Paris]
Paris (Economy) **P:** 165
Degaussing

Mine warfare (Kinds of naval mines) **M:** 565
Degeneration [disorder]
Spine **So:** 793
Degenerative joint disease *See* Osteoarthritis *in this index*
Degerming system
Corn (The dry-milling industry) **Ci:** 1061
Degradable plastics
Plastics (Plastics and the environment) **P:** 560-561
De Grasse, François Joseph Paul [French admiral] **D:** 91
Revolution, American (Surrender at Yorktown) **R:** 286
Degree [grammar]
Adjective (Comparison of adjectives) **A:** 57
Degree [measurement] **D:** 92
Angle **A:** 462
Circle **Ci:** 558
Compass **Ci:** 902b
Latitude **L:** 117
Longitude (Longitude and location) **L:** 451
Map (Geographic grids) **M:** 179
Minute **M:** 613
Degree [music]
Music (Tone) **M:** 950
Degree, College **D:** 92
School (Colleges and universities) **S:** 182
Universities and colleges (Degrees) **U:** 209
De Groot, Huig *See* Grotius, Hugo *in this index*
De Havilland, Olivia [British actress]
Motion picture (Best performance by an actress: 1946, 1949) **M:** 862
De Havilland Comet [airplane]
Airplane *picture on* **A:** 235; (The jet age) **A:** 238
Aviation (A new age of flight) **A:** 990
Transportation *picture on* **T:** 391
Dehmelt, Hans Georg [American physicist]
Nobel Prizes (Physics: 1989) **N:** 442
Dehorned cattle
Cattle (Horns) **C:** 307
Dehumanization of Art, The [book by Ortega y Gasset]
Ortega y Gasset, José **O:** 859
Dehumidifier [machine]
Air conditioning (Controlling the moisture) **A:** 178
Dehydrated food **D:** 93
Fishing industry (Methods of processing) **F:** 186
Food preservation (Drying) **F:** 342-343; (Freeze-drying) **F:** 343; (Modern food preservation) **F:** 344
Dehydration [disorder] **D:** 93
Cholera **C:** 520
Vomiting **V:** 447
Deianira [Greek mythology]
Hercules (The death of Hercules) **H:** 199
Mythology *picture on* **M:** 981
Deicer
Salt (As a deicer) **S:** 72 *with picture*
Deighton, John [Canadian pioneer]
Vancouver (History) **V:** 277
Deighton, Len [British author] **D:** 93
Deimos [moon]
Mars (Satellites) **M:** 226b
Satellite (Satellites of the terrestrial planets) **S:** 150
Deinococcus radiodurans [organism]
Extremophile **E:** 458
Deinonychus [dinosaur] **D:** 93
Dinosaur *picture on* **D:** 207; (True dinosaurs) **D:** 206b-211
Deiphobus [legendary figure]
Helen of Troy **H:** 168
Deir el-Bahri [temple]
Hatshepsut **H:** 86
Deirdre of the Sorrows [play by Synge]
Synge, John Millington **So:** 1068
Deisenhofer, Johann [German chemist]
Nobel Prizes (Chemistry: 1988) **N:** 444
Deism [philosophy] **D:** 94
Enlightenment (Deism) **E:** 326b
Paine, Thomas (French revolutionary) **P:** 22-23
Deity
See the God *article and the Deities section of the list of Related articles in the* Religion *article*
Déjà vu [psychology]
Memory (Deja vu) **M:** 394
DeJong, Meindert [American author]
Newbery Medal (table) **N:** 359
Regina Medal (table: 1972) **R:** 206
Deka [prefix]
Metric system (Metric prefixes) **M:** 439; (Selection of SI prefixes) **M:** 440
Deke
Hockey (Hockey terms) **H:** 275
Dekker, Eduard Douwes [Dutch author]

Netherlands (Arts) N: 142-144
Dekker, Thomas [British author] D: 94
De Klerk, Frederik Willem [South African political leader] D: 94 *with portrait*
  Mandela, Nelson M: 136
  South Africa (The dismantling of apartheid) So: 620
De Kooning, Willem [American painter] D: 94 *with picture*
  Painting (Abstract Expressionism) P: 84 *with picture*
De la Bruyère, Jean *See* La Bruyère, Jean de *in this index*
Delacroix, Eugène [French painter] D: 95
  Columbus, Christopher *picture on* Ci: 861
  Greece *picture on* G: 362
  Painting (Romanticism) P: 68-69 *with picture*
  Shakespeare, William *picture on* S: 361
DELAG [airline]
  Airship (The zeppelins) A: 252
De la Garza, Eligio [American political leader]
  Hispanic Americans (Political developments) H: 256
Delahanty, Ed [American baseball player]
  Baseball (table: Hall of Fame) B: 134
Delahay, Mark H. [American jurist]
  Impeachment (History) I: 91
De La Hoya, Oscar [Mexican boxer]
  Boxing (The late 1900's) B: 532b
  Pacquiao, Manny P: 19
De la Madrid Hurtado, Miguel [Mexican political leader] D: 95
  Mexico (The late 1900's) M: 473-474
De la Mar, José [Peruvian general]
  Peru (The early republic) P: 315
De la Mare, Walter [British author] D: 95
  Regina Medal R: 206
Delano, Columbus [American government official]
  Interior, Department of the (table) I: 325
Delany, Martin Robinson [American social reformer] D: 95 *with portrait*
  African American literature (The 1800's) A: 136a
De la Roche, Mazo [Canadian author] D: 95
  Canadian literature (Literature between the world wars) C: 158 *with pictures*
Delaroche, Paul [French artist]
  Painting (Art for a new public) P: 70
De la Rosa, Fabian [Filipino painter]
  Philippines (The arts) P: 375
De la Rua, Fernando [Argentine political leader]
  Argentina (The late 1900's) A: 658
De la Salle, Saint Jean Baptiste *See* Jean Baptiste de la Salle, Saint *in this index*
Delaunay, Robert [French painter]
  Cubism Ci: 1181
De Laval, Carl Gustaf [Swedish engineer]
  Butter (History) B: 731
  Milking machine M: 550
Delaware D: 96 *with pictures and maps*
  See also the list of Related articles in the Delaware article
  Colonial life in America (Development of the Thirteen Colonies) Ci: 790 *with map*
  Whipping post W: 281
Delaware [breed]
  Chicken (table) C: 443
Delaware, Lord *See* De La Warr, Lord *in this index*
Delaware, University of D: 113
  Delaware *picture on* D: 100
Delaware Basin Compact [1961]
  Delaware River D: 114
Delaware Bay [bay, Delaware-New Jersey] D: 113
  Delaware River D: 114
Delaware Indians [Indian]
  Indian, American *picture on* I: 156; (In the United States) I: 178-178a
  Indian reservation (History) I: 189
  New Jersey (Before European settlement) N: 250
  Pennsylvania (Colonial days) P: 264
Delaware National Scenic River
  National Park System (table: National parkways and other national parklands) N: 56
Delaware Prophet [American Indian leader]
  Delaware Indians D: 113
  Pontiac P: 657
Delaware River [U.S.] D: 114
  Delaware (Rivers, bays, and lakes) D: 104 *with map*
  New York (Rivers) N: 306
  Philadelphia (The city) P: 358
  Trenton, Battle of T: 435
Delaware Water Gap [valley, Pennsylvania] D: 114
  New Jersey (Places to visit) N: 240 *with picture*
  Pennsylvania (The Appalachian Ridge and Valley Region) P: 256 *with picture*
Delaware Water Gap National Recreation Area [New Jersey-Pennsylvania]

National Park System (table: National recreation areas) N: 49
  New Jersey *picture on* N: 241
De La Warr, Lord [American colonial leader] D: 114
  Delaware (History) D: 110
  Jamestown J: 29
  Virginia (The Jamestown settlement) V: 418
DeLay, Tom [American political leader] D: 114
Delay fuse
  Bomb (How bombs work) B: 450
Delayed fallout [radioactivity]
  Nuclear weapon (Residual nuclear radiation) N: 599-600
Delayed implantation [reproduction]
  Seal (Birth) S: 266
Delbrück, Max [German-born American bacteriologist]
  Nobel Prizes (Physiology or medicine: 1969) N: 446
Del Cano, Juan Sebastián [Portuguese explorer]
  Exploration *map on* E: 443; (Exploring the New World) E: 445-446
  Magellan, Ferdinand (The end of the voyage) M: 47
Deledda, Grazia [Italian author]
  Nobel Prizes (Literature: 1926) N: 447
Delegate
  Political convention (Delegate selection) P: 628 *with picture*
  Republic R: 253
  United Nations (Delegations) U: 86
Delegate primary [election]
  Political convention (Delegate selection) P: 628-629
Delegated powers
  Congress of the United States (Origin of power) Ci: 943
  Constitution of the United States (The supreme law of the land) Ci: 998
  Government (Presidential democracy) G: 285
De León, Alonso [Spanish explorer]
  Texas (French exploration) T: 204
De León, Juan Ponce *See* Ponce de León, Juan *in this index*
De León Carpio, Ramiro [Guatemalan political leader]
  Guatemala (Political developments) G: 417
De l'Epee, Charles Michel [French clergyman]
  Disability (Early beliefs) D: 221
De Lesseps, Ferdinand Marie [French engineer] D: 114
  Panama Canal (The French failure) P: 125
  Suez Canal (History) So: 958
Delete
  Proofreading (Proofreaders' marks) P: 822
Delfshaven [harbor, Netherlands]
  Rotterdam R: 489
Delft [pottery] D: 114 *with picture*
Delft [Netherlands] D: 115
  Delft D: 114
Delgado, José Matías [Salvadoran patriot] D: 115
  El Salvador (Independence) E: 252
Delhi [India] D: 115 *with picture*
Delhi Public Library [India]
  Library (South and Southeast Asia) L: 253
Delhi Sultanate [history of India] D: 115
  India (Period of invasions) I: 129
  Pakistan (The Islamic impact) P: 99
Delian League [ancient Greece]
  Aristides A: 662
  Athens (The Golden Age) A: 857
  Greece, Ancient (The rivalry between Athens and Sparta) G: 372
  Pericles (War with Sparta) P: 287
Delibes, Léo [French composer] D: 116
Delicate Arch [Utah]
  Earth *picture on* E: 23
Delicate Balance, A [play by Albee]
  Albee, Edward A: 310
Delicious apple
  Apple (Varieties of apples) A: 571 *with picture*
  Fruit (Developing new fruit cultivars) F: 548
Délie [poem by Scève]
  French literature (Lyon) F: 520
Delilah [Biblical figure]
  Samson S: 82
DeLillo, Don [American author]
  American literature (Experimental styles) A: 425
  Novel (The novel today) N: 575
Delinquency, Juvenile *See* Juvenile delinquency *in this index*
Delirium [disorder]
  Mental illness (Kinds of mental illnesses) M: 404
Delirium tremens [disorder] D: 116
  Alcoholism (Effects of alcoholism) A: 338
Delius, Frederick [British composer] D: 116
Deliverance [book by Dickey]

Dickey, James D: 190
Dell, Michael [American businessman] D: 116
Dell Inc. [company]
  Dell, Michael D: 116
Della Falls
  British Columbia (Rivers, waterfalls, and lakes) B: 624
  Waterfall (table: Famous waterfalls of North America) W: 142
Della Francesca, Piero [Italian painter] *See* Piero Della Francesca *in this index*
Della Gondola, Andrea di Pietro [Italian architect] *See* Palladio, Andrea *in this index*
Della Porta, Giacomo [Italian architect]
  Saint Peter's Basilica (History) S: 53-54
Della Robbia, Andrea [Italian sculptor]
  Della Robbia, Luca D: 117
Della Robbia, Luca [Italian sculptor] D: 116 *with picture*
Della Vos, Victor [Russian educator]
  Vocational education (Early vocational education in schools) V: 435
Dells [geology]
  Dalles D: 16 *with picture*
Delore, Terrence R. [New Zealand pilot]
  Glider (table) G: 230
Deloria, Vine, Jr. [American social reformer] D: 117 *with portrait*
Delorme, Claude [French aviator]
  Airplane (Notable airplane flights) A: 236
De los Angeles, Victoria [Spanish singer] D: 117
Delphi [ancient city] D: 117
  Apollo A: 566
  Greece, Ancient (Religion) G: 367
  Oracle O: 814
Delphine [book by Staël]
  Staël, Madame de So: 820
Delphinium [plant]
  Flower (Garden perennials) F: 278 *with picture*
  Larkspur L: 77 *with picture*
Delphinula shell
  Shell *picture on* S: 386
Del Río, Andrés [Mexican chemist]
  Vanadium V: 268
Del Sesto, Christopher [American political leader]
  Rhode Island (table) R: 311
Delta [geography] D: 117 *with maps*
  Netherlands (The Polders) N: 144
  River (Alluvial fans and deltas) R: 353 *with diagram*
Delta [letter]
  D D: 1 *with picture*
Delta [region] *See* Mississippi Alluvial Plain *in this index*
Delta [fingerprinting]
  Fingerprinting *picture on* F: 106
Delta 4 [rocket]
  Space exploration *picture on* So: 699
Delta blues [music]
  Popular music (The recording era) P: 671
Delta Blues Museum [Clarksdale]
  Mississippi (Places to visit) M: 632
Delta Cultural Center [Helena]
  Arkansas (Places to visit) A: 704
Delta kite
  Kite (Types of kites) K: 339 *with picture*
Delta wave [physiology]
  Aircraft, Military (Fighters) A: 203
  Electroencephalograph E: 200
Delta wing
  Airplane *picture on* A: 215; (The wing) A: 213
Deltoid muscle [anatomy]
  Human body (table) H: 422 *with diagram*
  Shoulder S: 437 *with picture*
Del Toro, Benicio [Puerto Rican-born actor]
  Motion picture (Best performance by an actor in a supporting role: 2000) M: 862b
Del Tredici, David [American composer]
  Classical music (Classical music today) Ci: 651
Deluge [Bible] D: 118
  Ararat A: 592
  Deucalion D: 171
  Noah N: 439
Deluge, The [drawings by Leonardo]
  Leonardo da Vinci *picture on* L: 201; (Last years) L: 200
Delusion [psychology]
  Mental illness (Schizophrenia) M: 405
  Postpartum depression P: 709
  Schizophrenia S: 176
Delvalle, Eric Arturo [Panamanian political leader]
  Panama (The Noriega years) P: 120-121
Demand *See* Supply and demand *in this index*
Demand deposit [banking]
  Money (The money supply) M: 715
Demand Note [money]
  Money (Money in the American Civil War) M: 713

Demand-pull inflation [economics]
Inflation (The quantity theory) I: 268
Demand regulator
Diving, Underwater (Ambient diving) D: 245
Skin diving (Scuba diving) S: 493 with picture
Demarcation, Line of See Line of Demarcation in
this index
Demarçay, Eugène [French scientist]
Europium E: 420
De Maupassant, Guy [French author] D: 118
French literature (Realism) F: 522
Deme [ancient Greece]
Athens (Democracy) A: 857
Demens, Peter A. [Russian engineer]
Saint Petersburg [Florida] (Government and
history) S: 56
Dementia [disorder] D: 118
AIDS (Symptoms) A: 164
Alzheimer's disease A: 398
Mental illness (Dementia) M: 405
Parkinson disease (Symptoms) P: 170
Demerara [river]
Guyana (Land) G: 446 with map
Demerol [medication]
Analgesic A: 448
Demeter [Greek mythology] D: 118
See also Ceres in this index
Mysteries M: 972
Mythology (Greek divinities) M: 982
Persephone P: 295
Demetrius [literary figure]
Shakespeare, William: (A Midsummer Night's
Dream) S: 357
Demetrius I [king of Macedonia]
Antigonid dynasty A: 555
Demetrius of Phaleron [Greek official]
Aesop's fables A: 90
Demigod [religion]
Mythology (Greek divinities) M: 982
Saint S: 29
Demilitarized zone
Korea, North (The land) K: 371; (North-South
relations) K: 373 with picture
De Mille, Agnes [American choreographer] D: 119
Ballet (Ballet in the United States) B: 53-54 with
picture
Dance (Musical comedy) D: 31
DeMille, Cecil B. [American director] D: 119
De Mille, James [Canadian author]
Canadian literature (Fiction: 1850-1918) C: 157
Demineralization [disorder]
Space exploration (Microgravity) So: 701-703
Deming, W. Edwards [American businessman]
D: 119
Demirel, Süleyman [Turkish political leader]
Turkey (History) T: 509-512
Demiurge
Gnosticism G: 238
Demme, Jonathan [American director]
Motion picture (Best achievement in directing:
1991) M: 862
Demobilization
Army, United States (World War II) A: 739
Democracy [political science] D: 119 with picture
See also the list of Related articles in the
Democracy article
Athens (Democracy) A: 857
Censorship C: 345
Civil rights Ci: 607
Constitution Ci: 995
Election (Elections in a democracy) E: 158
Europe (Revolution, democracy, and nationalism)
E: 412
Freedom of speech F: 506
Freedom of the press F: 507
French Revolution (Terror and equality) F: 526
Government G: 282; (Forms of government)
G: 285; (History of government) G: 289
Greece, Ancient (Government) G: 372
Journalism (Journalism in free societies) J: 174
Patriotism (Foundations of patriotism) P: 198
Political party P: 631
Political science (Democracy and socialism)
P: 861
Public opinion (Controlling public opinion)
P: 861
Republic R: 253
Town meeting T: 352
United States, Government of the
(Representative democracy) U: 137; (How
democratic is the government?) U: 146
Voting V: 449
World (Forms of government) W: 407
World, History of the (The Greeks) W: 428; (The
rise of democracy and nationalism) W: 443
Democracy in America [book by Tocqueville]
Tocqueville, Alexis de T: 308

Democracy wall [Chinese history]
China (Communication) C: 498-499
Democratic Action Party [political party]
Malaysia (Political parties) M: 98b
Democratic Alliance [political party]
South Africa (Political parties) So: 609
Democratic and Social Convention [political
party]
Niger (Government) N: 407
Democratic centralism [political theory]
Communism (The role of the party) Ci: 891
Vietnam (Government) V: 365
Democratic Constitutional Rally [political party]
Tunisia (Government) T: 487-488
Democratic Convention [1968]
Riot (During the 1900's) R: 349
Democratic Convention of Romania [political
party]
Romania (Recent developments) R: 426
Democratic-Farmer-Labor Party [political party]
Farmer-Labor Party F: 46
Minnesota (Politics) M: 602-603; (The mid-1900's)
M: 606
Democratic Labour Party [political party]
Barbados (History) B: 104
Democratic Left Alliance [political party]
Poland (Politics) P: 605; (Free elections) P: 614-
615
Democratic National Salvation Front [political
party]
Romania (Protests and political change) R: 425-
426
Democratic Opposition [political party]
Yugoslavia (The end of Yugoslavia) Y: 577
Democratic Party [U.S. political party] D: 124 with
pictures
Barnburners B: 114
Congress of the United States (How Congress is
organized) Ci: 942
Copperheads Ci: 1044
Dixiecrat Party D: 256
Hamer, Fannie Lou H: 29
Locofocos L: 413
New Deal (Results of the New Deal) N: 202
Political convention P: 628
Political party (The Democratic Party) P: 635
President of the United States (The presidential
election) P: 762-763
Reconstruction (The Republicans lose power)
R: 179; (Effects of Reconstruction) R: 179-180
Republican Party R: 253
Tammany, Society of T: 22
Democratic Party of Japan [political party]
Japan (Politics) J: 35; (Recent developments) J: 59
Democratic People's Republic of Korea See Korea,
North in this index
Democratic Progressive Party
Taiwan (History) T: 17-18
Democratic republic [government]
Democracy D: 119
Government (Democracy) G: 285
Democratic Republic of East Timor See East Timor
in this index
Democratic Republic of the Congo See Congo,
Democratic Republic of the in this index
Democratic Republic of Vietnam See North
Vietnam in this index
Democratic-Republican Party [U.S. history] D: 129
Adams, John Quincy (Democratic-Republican
Party split) A: 42
Bucktails B: 664
Democratic Party (Origin) D: 124
Federalist Party F: 67
Jefferson, Thomas (Secretary of state) J: 81-82
Monroe, James (U.S. Senator) M: 736
National Republican Party N: 60
Political convention (The history of national
conventions) P: 630
Political party (Early history) P: 635
United States, History of the (Establishing
political parties) U: 163
Washington, George (Rise of political parties)
W: 104
Democratic Russia Movement [reform
movement]
Russia (Politics) R: 531
Democratic socialism
Communism (European reality in the early
1900's) Ci: 890
Democratic Union [political party]
Poland (Free elections) P: 614-615
Democratic Union Coalition
Mongolia (History) M: 723
Democratic Unionist Party
Ulster Unionist Party U: 15
"Democratic Vistas" [essay by Whitman]
Whitman, Walt (His work) W: 294

Democrats [political party]
Brazil (Politics) B: 569
Democritus [Greek philosopher] D: 129
Atom (Development of the atomic theory) A: 874
Atomism A: 877
Chemistry (Beginnings) C: 400
Leucippus L: 215
Pre-Socratic philosophy (The teachings of
Parmenides) P: 772-773
Demography [sociology] D: 129
Magazine M: 42
Population (Census) P: 673
Sociology (Population characteristics) So: 564
Television (Measuring a program's success) T: 113
Demoiselle [airplane]
Airplane picture on A: 232
Demoiselle crane [bird]
Crane picture on Ci: 1118
Demoiselles d'Avignon, Les [painting by Picasso]
Cubism Ci: 1182 with picture
Painting (Cubism) P: 77
Picasso, Pablo: (Les Demoiselles d'Avignon) P: 448b
De Molay, Jacques [French religious leader]
DeMolay International D: 129
Knights Templars K: 353
DeMolay International [organization] D: 129
Masonry (Organization) M: 267
Demon See Devil in this index
Demon, The [poem by Lermontov]
Russian literature (Late Romanticism) R: 561-562
Demon stinger
Fish picture on F: 167
Demons Tormenting Me [drawing by Ensor]
Ensor, James picture on E: 327
Demonstration [politics]
Political convention (Making nominations) P: 629
Demonstrative pronoun [grammar]
Pronoun P: 819
De Moscoso, Luis [Spanish explorer]
De Soto, Hernando (Journey to the Mississippi)
D: 161 with map
Demosthenes [Greek orator] D: 129
Oratory (Classical orators) O: 819
Philip II [of Macedonia] P: 369
Demotic [writing]
Greece (Language) G: 353
Greek language (Later developments) G: 376-377
Greek literature (Modern Greek literature) G: 378
Hieroglyphics (Development of hieroglyphic
writing) H: 225-226
Rosetta stone R: 479
Dempsey, Jack [American boxer] D: 130 with
picture
Boxing picture on B: 532b; (Boxing's Golden Age)
B: 532-532a
Dempsey, John J. [American political leader]
New Mexico (table) N: 272
Dempsey, John N. [American political leader]
Connecticut (table) Ci: 967
Dempsey, Martin [American military leader]
Joint Chiefs of Staff (table) J: 156
Dempster, Arthur Jeffrey [American physicist]
Uranium (History of the use of uranium) U: 216
Demultiplexer [electronic device]
Radio (Stereophonic receivers) R: 89
Demuth, Charles [American painter] D: 130
Painting (Precisionism) P: 82 with picture
Den [animal home]
Animal picture on A: 501
Bear (Winter sleep) B: 183-184
Fox (Dens) F: 439
Wolf (Young) W: 376
Den [scouting]
Boy Scouts (Cub Scouting) B: 535
Denakil Depression [landform]
Ethiopia (The lowlands) E: 370
Denali [mountain] See Mount McKinley in this index
Denali National Park [Alaska] D: 130
Alaska (Places to visit) A: 290
National Park System (table: National parks) N: 48
Denali National Preserve [Alaska]
National Park System (table: National preserves)
N: 58
Denarius [money]
Coin collecting picture on Ci: 758
Denatured alcohol
Alcohol (Ethanol) A: 335
Camphor C: 91
Dench, Judi [British actress] D: 130
Motion picture (Best performance by an actress
in a supporting role: 1998) M: 862b
Dendrite [anatomy]
Brain (How neurons work) B: 557 with diagram
Nervous system (The dendrites) N: 134 with
diagram
Dendritic cell [physiology]
Immune system (Antigen-presenting cells) I: 88

Dendrobium **orchid** [plant]
Orchid *picture on* O: 824
Dendrochronology [archaeology]
Archaeology (Dating) A: 598
Dene [people]
Northwest Territories (People) N: 530
Deneen, Charles S. [American political leader]
Illinois (table) I: 71
De Nemours, Pierre Samuel du Pont *See* Du Pont
de Nemours, Pierre Samuel *in this index*
Deng Xiaoping [Chinese political leader] D: 131
with portrait
China (Deng Xiaoping) C: 506
Communism (China after Mao) Ci: 896
Hu Yaobang H: 402
Jiang Zemin J: 125
Dengue [disease] D: 131
Mosquito (Mosquitoes and people) M: 834
Denier [coin]
Coin collecting *picture on* Ci: 758
Denier [measurement]
Microfiber M: 514
Nylon (How nylon is made) N: 633
Denim [fabric] D: 131
Jeans J: 75
Twill T: 531
De Niro, Robert [American actor] D: 131 *with
portrait*
Motion picture (Best performance by an actor:
1980) M: 862a; (Best performance by an actor
in a supporting role: 1974) M: 862b
Denis, Jean-Baptiste [French physician]
Blood transfusion (History) B: 417
Denishawn dance company
Shawn, Ted S: 378
Denison, Merrill [Canadian author]
Canadian literature (Literature between the
world wars) C: 158-159
Denison Dam [Red River, Oklahoma-Texas]
Lake Texoma L: 47 *with map*
Denitrification
Nitrogen cycle N: 426
Denitrifying bacteria
Nitrogen cycle N: 426 *with diagram*
Denmark D: 132 *with pictures and maps*
See also the list of Related articles in the Denmark
article
Christmas (In Denmark, Norway, and Sweden)
C: 531
Civil union Ci: 613
Flag F: 194, *picture on* F: 206
Greenland G: 383
Norway (Union with Denmark) N: 545
Scandinavia S: 170 *with map*
Sweden (History) So: 1032-1033
Valentine's Day (In Europe) V: 261
Vikings (The Danish Vikings) V: 383
Virgin Islands, United States V: 393; (Danish rule)
V: 396
World War II (The conquest of Denmark and
Norway) W: 473
Denney, William D. [American political leader]
Delaware (table) D: 109
Dennis, Martin [American inventor]
Leather (History) L: 169
Dennis, Sandy [American actress]
Motion picture (Best performance by an actress
in a supporting role: 1966) M: 862b
Dennison, William [American government official]
Lincoln, Abraham (table) L: 323
Ohio (table) O: 699
Denny, Reginald [American public figure]
Los Angeles (Recent developments) L: 470-471
Denominate number [mathematics] D: 142
Unit U: 42
Denomination [cards]
Bridge (Bidding) B: 604
Denomination [religion]
Church C: 541
Denominator [mathematics]
Fraction (In symbols) F: 444
Denouement
Literature (Plot) L: 353
Density [physical property] D: 142 *with diagrams*
Hydrometer H: 471
Star (Mass) So: 845
Denslow, W. W. [American illustrator]
Literature for children *picture on* L: 358
Densmore, James [American businessman]
Sholes, Christopher Latham S: 433
Dent, Frederick B. [American government official]
Commerce, Department of (table) Ci: 871
Ford, Gerald Rudolph (table) F: 378
Dent, John Charles [Canadian author] D: 143
Dent, Julia [wife of Ulysses S. Grant] *See* Grant, Julia
Dent *in this index*
Dent corn

Corn (Kinds of corn) Ci: 1058 *with picture*
Dental assistant *See* Dental hygienist *in this index*
Dental Association, American *See* American
Dental Association *in this index*
Dental Association, Canadian
Dentistry (Organizations) D: 145
Dental floss
Teeth (Cleaning the teeth) T: 81
Dental hygiene D: 143
Health (Cleanliness) H: 126
Mouth M: 903
Teeth (Dental checkups) T: 82
Dental hygienist
Careers (Health care) C: 223-224 *with picture*
Dental hygiene D: 143
Dental Hygienists' Association, American
Dental hygiene (Career) D: 143
Dental insurance
Insurance (Other types of health insurance) I: 312
Dental Medicine, Doctor of
Dentistry (Educational requirements) D: 145
Dental pulp
Dentistry (Endodontics) D: 144
Teeth (Pulp) T: 80 *with picture*
Dental school
Dentistry (Educational requirements) D: 145
Dental Surgery, Doctor of
Degree, College (The doctor's degree) D: 93
Dentistry (Educational requirements) D: 145
Dentalia shells
Indian, American (Money) I: 149 *with picture*
Dentin
Ivory (Characteristics of ivory) I: 521
Teeth (Dentin) T: 80 *with diagram*
Dentistry [medicine] D: 143 *with pictures*
Address, Forms of (Other forms) A: 54
Anesthesia (History) A: 459
Careers (Health care) C: 223-224 *with picture*
Hypnosis H: 479
Orthodontics O: 859
Teeth (Dental checkups) T: 82; (Dental decay)
T: 82
Denture
Dentistry D: 143; (Prosthodontics) D: 144
Teeth (Dental decay) T: 82-84
Denver [Colorado] D: 145 *with picture and map*
Colorado (table: Average monthly weather)
Ci: 840
Denver, James W. [American political leader]
Denver D: 145
Denver Art Museum
Colorado (Places to visit) Ci: 836
Denver Broncos [team]
Football (National Football League) F: 364
Denver International Airport [Denver]
Airport (table) A: 245
Denver Nuggets [team]
Basketball (table) B: 150
Denver Performing Arts Complex
Denver (Cultural life and recreation) D: 146
Denver Post, The [newspaper]
Bonfils, Frederick Gilmer B: 458
Denver Technological Center
Denver (History) D: 147-148
Deodar cedar [tree]
Cedar (Needle-leaved cedars) C: 324
Deodorant D: 148
Deodorizer D: 148
De Oñate, Juan *See* Oñate, Juan de *in this index*
Deontology [philosophy]
Ethics (Modern ethics) E: 366
Deoxyribonucleic acid [biochemistry] *See* DNA
in this index
Deoxyribose [sugar]
Cell (DNA—the wondrous molecule) C: 334-335
with diagram
DNA D: 258
Heredity (The structure of DNA) H: 205
De Palma, Ralph [American race driver]
Automobile racing (table: Indianapolis 500
winners) A: 980
DePaola, Tomie [American artist/author] D: 148
Laura Ingalls Wilder Award (table) L: 121
Regina Medal (table: 1983) R: 206
De Paolo, Peter [American race driver]
Automobile racing (table: Indianapolis 500
winners) A: 980
De Pareja, Juan
Velázquez, Diego *picture on* V: 295
Departed, The [film]
Motion picture (Best picture: 2006) M: 861
Department [education]
Universities and colleges (Faculty) U: 208
Department [political unit]
France (Local government) F: 455
Department of ...
Departments appear under their key words, as in

Labor, Department of
Department store D: 148
England *picture on* E: 302
Interior design *picture on* I: 327
Retailing (Department stores) R: 265
De Paul, Vincent [French religious leader] *See*
Vincent de Paul, Saint *in this index*
Dependency [building]
Colonial life in America (Houses) Ci: 796-797
Dependency [government]
Commonwealth of Nations (Dependencies)
Ci: 876
World (table) W: 412
Dependency ratio
Population (Age) P: 673
Dependent [economics]
Income tax (Figuring the individual income tax)
I: 104
Dependent clause [grammar]
Clause Ci: 657
Dependent Pension Bill [1890]
Cleveland, Grover (Veterans' affairs) Ci: 671
Harrison, Benjamin (Domestic affairs) H: 72
Deperdussin Company [France]
Airplane *picture on* A: 232; (Other pioneer planes
and fliers) A: 233-234
Deperdussin racer [airplane]
Airplane *picture on* A: 232
Depersonalization disorder [psychology]
Mental illness (Dissociative disorders) M: 406
Dephlogisticated air
Chemistry (The phlogiston theory) C: 401
Depilatory [chemical] D: 149
Hair (Disorders of the hair and scalp) H: 10
Deportation [law] D: 149
Alien and Sedition Acts A: 368
Holocaust (The camps) H: 296a
Illegal alien I: 51
Deposit [banking]
Bank (Bank services) B: 88
Certificate of deposit C: 363
Federal Reserve System F: 65
Deposit [geology]
Coal (Where coal is found) Ci: 721
Gold (Gold deposits) G: 252
Deposit insurance *See* Federal Deposit Insurance
Corporation *in this index*
Deposit modifier [additive]
Gasoline (Gasoline blends and additives)
G: 61-62
Deposition [geology]
Geomorphology G: 106a
Deposition [law] D: 149
Deposition [physics]
Cloud (How clouds form) Ci: 708-709
Sublimation So: 938
**Depository Institutions Deregulation and
Monetary Control Act** [1980]
Bank (A boom in money market funds) B: 94
Usury U: 229
Depp, Johnny [American actor] D: 149 *with portrait*
Depreciation [economics] D: 149
Income (National income and gross domestic
product) I: 101
National income (Determining national income)
N: 37-38
Deprés, Josquin [French composer] *See* Desprez,
Josquin *in this index*
Depressant [medication] D: 149
See also Antianxiety and hypnotic drug *in this
index*
Drug abuse (table: Some commonly abused
drugs) D: 363
Depression [economics] D: 150 *with picture*
See also Great Depression *in this index*
Deflation D: 88
Economics (Economic growth) E: 62
Gay Nineties (The despair of poverty) G: 72
Germany (The Weimar Republic) G: 167
Keynes, John Maynard K: 308a
Recession R: 175
United States, History of the (The rich and the
poor) U: 182
Van Buren, Martin (The Panic of 1837) V: 272
Depression [geology]
Egypt (The Western Desert) E: 125
Depression [psychology] D: 151
See also Postpartum depression *in this index*
Antidepressant A: 553
Bipolar disorder B: 327
Child (Emotional problems) C: 452
Fatigue F: 71
Mental illness (Mood disorders) M: 405
Parkinson disease (Symptoms) P: 170
Seasonal affective disorder S: 272
Serotonin S: 318
Suicide (Causes) So: 964

Depression, Great See Great Depression *in this index*

Depressive episode [psychology]
Bipolar disorder **B: 327**
Depression **D: 151**

DePriest, Oscar [American political leader]
African Americans (The Harlem Renaissance and other achievements) **A: 136m-136n**

Deptford trilogy [books by Davies]
Davies, Robertson **D: 46**

Depth charge [weapon] **D: 151**
Bomb (Other bombs) **B: 451**
Torpedo (How a torpedo works) **T: 340d-341**

Depth finder [device]
Navigation (Piloting) **N: 70-71**

Depth indicator [water]
Fathometer **F: 54**

Depth of field [optics]
Eye (Depth perception) **E: 463** *with picture*
Photography (Lenses and focusing) **P: 410**; (Aperture size) **P: 412-413** *with pictures*

Depth perception
Eye (Depth perception) **E: 463**

Depths [oceanography] See Deep *in this index*

Deputies, Chamber of [government]
Italy (Parliament) **I: 499**

Deputy
Duma (The modern Duma) **D: 382**
Union of Soviet Socialist Republics (National government) **U: 29**

Deputy, The [play by Hochhuth]
German literature (Postwar German literature [1945-1990]) **G: 142**
Hochhuth, Rolf **H: 273**

Deputy sheriff [office]
Sheriff **S: 397**

De Quervain's disease
Repetitive strain injury **R: 242**

De Quincey, Thomas [British author] **D: 151**
English literature (Romantic prose) **E: 320**

Der ...
Titles beginning Der appear under their key words, as in Freischütz, Der

Derailleur [mechanism]
Bicycle (Power and speed) **B: 290** *with diagram*

Derain, André [French artist] **D: 152** *with picture*
Fauves **F: 56** *with picture*

Derbigny, Pierre [American political leader]
Louisiana (table) **L: 496**

Derby [race] **D: 152**

Derby, Earl of [British nobleman]
Derby **D: 152**

Derby, Earl of [British statesman [1799-1869]]
United Kingdom (table: British prime ministers) **U: 72**

Derby, Kentucky See Kentucky Derby *in this index*

Derby, Soap Box [race]
Soap Box Derby **So: 543**

Derby eland [animal]
Eland **E: 156**

Derecho [storm] **D: 152**

Deregulation
Aviation (Deregulation and mergers) **A: 991**
Interest (Regulation of interest rates) **I: 323**
Interstate commerce (Interstate commerce today) **I: 351**

Derek and the Dominos [rock group]
Clapton, Eric **Ci: 638**

Dergue [government]
Eritrea (History) **E: 353-354**

Deringer, Henry, Jr. [American inventor]
Handgun (Early handguns) **H: 45**

Derivation [language]
Dictionary (What a dictionary tells you) **D: 193**
Latin language (Latin and English) **L: 115**

Derivative [economics]
Bank (Other services) **B: 89**

Derivative [mathematics]
Calculus (Derivatives) **C: 23**; (The fundamental theorem of calculus) **C: 25**

Derived unit [measurement]
Metric system (Kinds of metric units) **M: 436**

Derleth, August [American author] **D: 152**

Dermaptera
Insect (table) **I: 299**

Dermatitis [disorder] **D: 153**
Eczema **E: 74**
Skin (Inflammation) **S: 490**

Dermatitis hepetiformis [disorder]
Celiac disease **C: 325**

Dermatology [medicine] **D: 153**

Dermis [anatomy]
Human body (The dermis) **H: 418**
Mammal (Skin and hair) **M: 118**
Skin (Structure of the skin) **S: 488** *with picture*

Dermoptera [zoology]
Mammal (table) **M: 128** *with picture*

Dern, George H. [American political leader]
Roosevelt, Franklin Delano (table) **R: 454**
Utah (table) **U: 245**

Derna [Libya]
Marine Corps, United States (The 1800's) **M: 208**

DeRolph v. State of Ohio [U.S. history]
Ohio (Recent developments) **O: 703**

De Rosset [ship]
Maryland (The War of 1812 and industrial development) **M: 258**

Derrick [machine]
See also Oil derrick *in this index*
Building construction (Constructing a skyscraper) **B: 683-684**
Dredging **D: 345**
Oklahoma *picture on* **O: 728**
Ship (Nautical terms) **S: 405** *with diagram*

Derrida, Jacques [French philosopher] **D: 153**
French literature (The middle and late 1900's) **F: 523**

Derringer [gun]
Handgun (Early handguns) **H: 45** *with picture*

Dervish [religious group] **D: 153** *with picture*
Dance (Why people dance) **D: 24**
Sufism **So: 959**

Derwinski, Edward J. [American government official]
Veterans Affairs, Department of (table) **V: 343**

Derzhavin, Gavriil [Russian poet]
Russian literature (The classical movement) **R: 559-560**

DES [cryptology] See Data Encryption Standard *in this index*

DES [hormone] **D: 153**
Hormone (Agricultural uses) **H: 337-338**

"Desafinado" [song]
Getz, Stan **So: 177**

Desaguadero River [river, Bolivia]
Lake Titicaca **L: 47** *with map*

Desalination [industrial process]
Arabs (Economy) **A: 589**
Conservation (Water conservation) **Ci: 977-978**
Ocean (Other products) **O: 654**
Water (Fresh water from the sea) **W: 127**

Desalinization See Desalination *in this index*

Desas [villages]
Indonesia (Rural life) **I: 229**

De Saussure, Ferdinand See Saussure, Ferdinand de *in this index*

Descartes, René [French philosopher] **D: 154** *with portrait*
Enlightenment **E: 326a**
French literature (Classical prose) **F: 520**
Geometry (Beginnings of modern geometry) **G: 106**
Mathematics (Mathematics and the scientific revolution) **M: 306-307**
Philosophy (Modern philosophy) **P: 388**
Physics (The Renaissance) **P: 438-439**
Psychology (Beginnings) **P: 849**
Science *picture on* **S: 200**; (The scientific revolution) **S: 198**

Descendant, The [book by Glasgow]
Glasgow, Ellen **G: 210**

Descending aorta [anatomy]
Aorta **A: 562**

Descending colon [anatomy]
Colon **Ci: 786**
Intestine (The large intestine) **I: 353** *with diagram*

Descent from the Cross, The [painting by Van der Weyden]
Painting (The northern Renaissance) **P: 57** *with picture*

Descent of Man, The [book by Darwin]
Darwin, Charles Robert (Darwin's theories) **D: 40**

Deschamps, Marie [Canadian jurist]
Supreme Court of Canada (table) **So: 997** *with portrait*

Deschutes National Forest [Oregon]
National forest *picture on* **N: 35**
Oregon (Interesting facts) **O: 827** *with picture*

Deschutes River
Oregon (Land and climate) **O: 838-840** *with map*

Description of New England, A [book by Smith]
Massachusetts (Early exploration) **M: 289**

Description of the World [book by Polo]
Polo, Marco (Later life) **P: 648**

Descriptive adjective [grammar]
Adjective (Classifying adjectives) **A: 57**

Descriptive bibliography
Bibliography **B: 288**

Descriptive linguistics
Language (The science of language) **L: 66**
Linguistics **L: 335**

Descriptive notation
Chess (Chess notation) **C: 413** *with picture*

Desdemona [literary figure]

Shakespeare, William: *(Othello)* **S: 363** *with picture*

Desegregation See Segregation *in this index*

Desensitization [medicine] See Hyposensitization *in this index*

Deseret [U.S. history] **D: 154**
Mormons (The Mormons in Utah) **M: 809**
Nevada (Early settlement) **N: 174**
Utah **U: 231**; (Territorial days and statehood) **U: 246**

Deseret News [newspaper]
Utah (Communication) **U: 245**

Desert [geography] **D: 154** *with pictures and map*
See also the list of Related articles in the Desert *article*
Animal (Animals of the deserts) **A: 482** *with pictures and map*
Arabs (Land of the Arabs) **A: 585-586**
Arctic (Land regions) **A: 636**
Asia *picture on* **A: 778**
Biome **B: 324**; (table) **B: 323** *with map*
Bird (Birds of the desert) **B: 339** *with pictures*
Climate (Semiarid and desert climates) **Ci: 676b**
Dust devil **D: 392**
Flower (Flowers of the desert) **F: 290** *with pictures*
Irrigation **I: 456** *with picture*
Plant (Deserts) **P: 523** *with picture and map*; (Movement of water) **P: 537** *with picture*
Rain (Rainfall distribution) **R: 124**
United States *picture on* **U: 124**
World (table) **W: 417** *with map*

Desert bluebell
Flower *picture on* **F: 291**

Desert chicory [plant]
Flower *picture on* **F: 291**

Desert Fox [nickname]
Rommel, Erwin **R: 450**

Desert iguana
Iguana **I: 50**

Desert lark [bird]
Desert *picture on* **D: 155**

Desert lily
Flower *picture on* **F: 291**

Desert mallow
Flower *picture on* **F: 291**

Desert marigold
Flower (Flowers of the desert) **F: 290** *with picture*
Plant *picture on* **P: 526**

Desert sand verbena [plant]
Flower *picture on* **F: 290**

Desert star [plant]
Flower *picture on* **F: 290**

Desert Storm, Operation [1991]
Persian Gulf War of 1991 **P: 300a**

Desert tortoise [animal]
Reptile *picture on* **R: 250**
Tortoise **T: 344**
Turtle (Tortoises) **T: 524**

Desertas [islands]
Madeira Islands **M: 30**

Deserted Village, The [poem by Goldsmith]
English literature (The Johnson circle) **E: 319**
Goldsmith, Oliver **G: 259**

Desertification [conservation]
Agriculture (Ecosystem destruction) **A: 153**
Desert (How deserts develop and change) **D: 156-157**

Desertion [law] **D: 157**
Abandonment **A: 4**
Divorce (Fault divorce) **D: 253**

De Seversky, Alexander Procofieff [Russian-American engineer] **D: 157**

Deshret [desert]
Egypt, Ancient (The land) **E: 135**

De Sica, Vittorio [Italian director] **D: 157**
Motion picture (Postwar Realism) **M: 869** *with picture*

Desiccant [chemical]
Potato (Growing potatoes) **P: 712-713**
Silica gel **S: 457**

Desiderio da Settignano [Italian sculptor]
Sculpture (Early Renaissance) **S: 252**

Desiderius, Abbot [Italian religious leader]
Monte Cassino **M: 762**

Design [art] **D: 157** *with pictures*
Automobile (Planning the car) **A: 956**
Careers (Art, design, and communications) **C: 220** *with picture*
Clothing (The clothing industry) **Ci: 705-706** *with picture*
Computer (Computer-aided design [CAD] programs) **Ci: 919** *with pictures*
Desktop publishing **D: 158** *with picture*
Industrial design **I: 244** *with picture*
Interior design **I: 326**
Magazine (Editing and assembling an issue) **M: 43** *with picture*
Manufacturing (The main steps in

manufacturing) M: 170
Publishing (Art and design) P: 867
Textile (Designing a fabric) T: 215 *with picture*
Design concept
Interior design (Developing a plan) I: 329-330
Design for Living [play by Coward]
Coward, Noël Ci: 1107
Design patent [law]
Patent P: 194
Designated hitter
Baseball (Players) B: 125
Designer [publishing]
Encyclopedia *picture on* E: 268
Designer clothing
Clothing (Marketing categories of fashion)
Ci: 705
Designer dog
Dog (Kinds of dogs) D: 265-266
Designer food
Health food (Types of health foods) H: 129
Designer jeans [clothing]
Jeans J: 75
Desilu Productions
Arnaz, Desi A: 741
Ball, Lucille B: 43
Desire Under the Elms [play by O'Neill]
O'Neill, Eugene (His plays) O: 762
De Sitter, Willem [Dutch astronomer] D: 158
Dark energy D: 37
Desizing [industrial process]
Cotton (Finishing) Ci: 1091
Desjardins, Alphonse [Canadian businessman]
Credit union Ci: 1125
Desktop calculator
Calculator C: 22
Desktop computer
Computer *picture on* Ci: 913; (Personal
computers) Ci: 909
Personal computer P: 300f
Desktop publishing D: 158 *with picture*
See also Electronic publishing *in this index*
Inkjet printer I: 273
Printer (Laser printers) P: 795
Printing (Electronic imagesetting) P: 797; (The
electronic age) P: 804
Teaching *picture on* T: 66
Desmarest, Nicolas [French geologist]
Geology (The rock dispute) G: 98-99
De Smet, Pierre Jean [Belgian missionary] D: 159
Des Moines [Iowa] D: 159
Iowa (Population) I: 378; (table: Average monthly
weather) I: 388
Des Moines Art Center [Des Moines]
Iowa (Museums) I: 379 *with picture*
Des Moines River
Iowa (Rivers and lakes) I: 386
Desmond, Paul [American saxophonist]
Brubeck, Dave B: 647
Jazz *picture on* J: 73
De Soto, Hernando [Spanish explorer] D: 160 *with
picture and map*
Alabama (European exploration and settlement)
A: 275
Chickasaw Indians C: 439
Creek Indians Ci: 1125
Exploration *map on* E: 443; (Spain's conquests in
the New World) E: 445
Florida (Exploration and Spanish settlement)
F: 261
Georgia (Spanish control) G: 131
Louisiana (Exploration) L: 497
Memphis (History) M: 396
Mississippi (Exploration and early settlement)
M: 641
North Carolina (Exploration and settlement)
N: 490
Oklahoma (Early days) O: 731
Tennessee (Exploration) T: 153
Texas (Spanish exploration) T: 204
De Soto National Memorial [Florida]
National Park System (table: National memorials)
N: 54
DeSoto National Wildlife Refuge
Iowa (Places to visit) I: 384
Desoxyn [drug] *See* Methamphetamine *in this
index*
Despair [island, Rhode Island]
Rhode Island (Islands) R: 306
Despotism [political science] D: 161
Desprez, Josquin [French composer] D: 161
Classical music (Franco-Flemish music) Ci: 646
Desroches Island
British Indian Ocean Territory B: 632
Dessalines, Jean-Jacques [Haitian political leader]
D: 162
Haiti (History) H: 15-16
Dessert wine

Wine (Fortified wines) W: 336
Destalinization [Soviet history]
Cold War (The spirit of Geneva) Ci: 766
Khrushchev, Nikita Sergeyevich (Rise as a
Communist) K: 309
De Stijl [art movement]
Furniture (De Stijl) F: 582
Destiny Laboratory Module [spacecraft]
International Space Station (History) I: 346b *with
picture*
Destiny's Child [musical group]
Beyoncé B: 276
Destouches, Henri-Louis [French author]
Céline, Louis-Ferdinand C: 325
Destroyer [ship] D: 162 *with picture*
Navy (Destroyers) N: 78 *with picture*
Navy, United States (Combat ships) N: 84;
(Ordnance) N: 84
Warship *pictures on* W: 43; (Destroyers) W: 40
Destroyer, The [Hinduism]
Shiva S: 429
Destroyer escort [ship]
Destroyer D: 162
Destroying angel [fungus]
Mushroom (Poisonous mushrooms) M: 945 *with
picture*
Destructional hill [geography]
Hill H: 230
Destructive distillation [chemistry]
Distillation (Destructive distillation) D: 239 *with
diagram*
Destructive interference [physics]
Diffraction (How diffraction occurs) D: 201
Interference I: 324 *with picture*
Light (Interference) L: 288 *with diagram*
Sound (Beats) So: 604 *with diagram*
Waves (Interference) W: 153
De Sucre, Antonio José [Bolivian political leader]
See Sucre, Antonio José de *in this index*
Detached retina
Blindness (Diseases) B: 401
Detection [psychology]
Perception (Types of perception) P: 283
Detective [career]
Police (Investigations of crimes) P: 621
Detective Comics
Batman B: 165
Detective story D: 162
See also the list of Related articles in the Detective
story *article*
American literature (Popular forms) A: 422
Literature for children (Mystery and detective
stories) L: 360
Novel (New directions in the novel) N: 573-574
Poe, Edgar Allan P: 589
Detective Story [play by Kingsley]
Kingsley, Sidney K: 331
Detector [electronics]
Radio (The intermediate-frequency amplifier and
detector) R: 89 *with picture*
Traffic (Signals, signs, and markings) T: 366
Vacuum tube (Kinds of vacuum tubes) V: 258-
259
Detector, Metal
Metal detector M: 425
Détente [international relations]
International relations (New patterns of
international relations) I: 345-346
Russia (The Cold War) R: 554
Union of Soviet Socialist Republics (History)
U: 35-39
Detention camp [prison]
Asian Americans (World War II and Japanese
Americans) A: 812f
Canada, History of (World War II) C: 148
Segregation (Other segregation in the United
States) S: 286
Detergent [additive]
Gasoline (Gasoline blends and additives)
G: 61-62
Detergent alcohol
Alcohol (Other alcohols) A: 335
Detergent and soap D: 163 *with pictures*
Phosphate P: 402
Determinant [mathematics] D: 166
Determinate inflorescence [botany]
Inflorescence I: 268b
Determinative [linguistics]
Hieroglyphics (Development of hieroglyphic
writing) H: 225-226
Determiner [grammar]
Adjective (Classifying adjectives) A: 57
Determinism [philosophy]
Einstein, Albert (Further scientific work) E: 146b
Fatalism F: 54
Free will F: 500
Metaphysics (Causality) M: 429-430

Philosophy (Stoic philosophy and Epicureanism)
P: 387; (Rationalism) P: 388
Determinism, Environmental [philosophy]
London, Jack L: 444
Deterrence [criminology]
Criminal justice system (The correctional system)
Ci: 1144
Prison (How prisons operate) P: 806
Sentence S: 304
Deterrence [warfare]
Army (Prevention of war) A: 725
North Atlantic Treaty Organization N: 470
Nuclear weapon (Nuclear strategy) N: 600
War (The Cold War era) W: 26
Detmer, Ty [American football player]
Football (table) F: 363
De Tocqueville, Alexis *See* Tocqueville, Alexis de
in this index
D'Étoiles, Charles-Guillaume Le Normant
[husband of]
Pompadour, Marquise de P: 653
Detonator [explosive] D: 167
Dynamite D: 397
Fuse F: 588
Detoxification
Drug abuse (Treatment of substance use
disorders) D: 364
Detroit [Michigan] D: 167 *with pictures and maps*
Arab Americans (Where Arab Americans live)
diagram on A: 580b
Lamothe, Antoine Laumet de, Sieur de Cadillac
L: 52
Michigan *picture on* M: 489; (Libraries) M: 492
with picture; (table: Average monthly weather)
M: 502
Riot (During the 1900's) R: 349
Windsor (Government and history) W: 335
Detroit Gazette [newspaper]
Michigan (Communication) M: 506
Detroit Institute of Arts
Michigan (Museums) M: 493 *with picture*
Detroit Lions [team]
Detroit (Sports) D: 170
Football (National Football League) F: 364
Detroit Pistons [team]
Basketball (table) B: 150
Detroit (Sports) D: 170
Detroit Public Library
Michigan (Libraries) M: 492-493
Detroit Red Wings [team]
Detroit (Sports) D: 170
Hockey (table: National Hockey League) H: 281
Detroit River [Michigan-Ontario] D: 171
Detroit D: 167; (Shipping) D: 168-169 *with map*
Detroit Tigers [team]
Baseball (table) B: 130
Detroit (Sports) D: 170
Detroit Zoological Park
Detroit (Parks) D: 170
Deucalion [Greek mythology] D: 171
Deuce
Tennis (Scoring) T: 162-163
Deuce set
Tennis (Scoring) T: 162-163
Deukmejian, George [American political leader]
California (table) C: 59
Deusdedit, Saint [pope]
Pope (table) P: 666
Deuterium [isotope] D: 172
Big bang B: 296
Energy supply (Nuclear energy) E: 278
Fusion F: 589
Hydrogen (Isotopes) H: 469; (Preparation) H: 469
Isotope I: 476
Nuclear energy (Nuclear fusion) N: 583 *with
diagram*
Nuclear weapon *diagram on* N: 599;
(Thermonuclear weapons) N: 597
Urey, Harold Clayton U: 37
Deuterium oxide *See* Heavy water *in this index*
Deutero-Isaiah [prophet]
Bible (The Prophets) B: 280-281
Deutero-Pauline letters
Bible (The Letters) B: 284
New Testament (Authorship) N: 288
Deuterocanonical books
Old Testament (Contents) O: 741
Deuteron [atomic particle]
Deuterium (Properties) D: 172
Isotope (Artificial radioisotopes) I: 477
Star (Hydrogen fusion) So: 846-847
Deuteronomistic History [books]
Bible (The Prophets) B: 280
Deuteronomy [Bible] D: 172
Pentateuch P: 274
Deutsche mark
Mark M: 213

Deutsches Museum [Munich]
  Planetarium (Early planetariums) **P:** 514a-514b;
    (Modern planetariums) **P:** 514b
Deutschland *See* Germany *in this index*
Deutschland [airship]
  Airship (The zeppelins) **A:** 252
Deutschland über Alles [song] **D:** 172
Deutzia [shrub] **D:** 172 *with picture*
De Vaca, Cabeza [Spanish explorer] *See* Cabeza de
  Vaca, Álvar Núñez *in this index*
Devadasi [dancer]
  Dance (Asian theatrical dance) **D:** 28-29
De Valera, Eamon [Irish political leader] **D:** 173
  Ireland (The Irish Free State) **I:** 427
  Irish Republican Army (Division in the IRA) **I:** 433
  Sinn Féin (History) **S:** 473
De Valois, Ninette [British choreographer] **D:** 173
Devaluation [economics] **D:** 173
Devanagari [alphabet]
  Hindi language **H:** 234
Devastation of the Indies: A Brief Account, The
  [book by Las Casas]
  Las Casas, Bartolomé de **L:** 80
  Latin American literature (Colonial literature)
    L: 112
Developable Column [sculpture by Pevsner]
  Pevsner, Antoine *picture on* **P:** 351
Developed country
  Industry (Government regulation) **I:** 261;
    (Industry in developing countries) **I:** 261
  World (How nations are grouped) **W:** 407
Developer [chemical]
  Photography (Developing the film) **P:** 419
Developing
  Photography (How a camera works) **P:** 407-408;
    (Developing the film) **P:** 419 *with pictures*
Developing country D: 173
  See also Less developed country; Third World *in
    this index*
  Bank (Multilateral development banks) **B:** 91
  Education (Vocational education) **E:** 88;
    (Education in other countries) **E:** 95
  Energy supply (The 1900s) **E:** 280
  Environmental pollution (Effect of population
    growth) **E:** 339
  Exports and imports (Import restrictions) **E:** 454
  Food (Economic reasons) **F:** 331-332
  Food supply **F:** 345
  Global warming (Government action on global
    warming) **G:** 232c
  Globalization (The debate over globalization)
    G: 233
  Hunger **H:** 449
  Income (International income comparisons)
    I: 101-102
  Industry (Industry in developing countries) **I:** 261
    with picture
  Medicine (Other countries) **M:** 368 *with picture*
  National park (Development of park resources)
    N: 42h
  Natural resources (Conservation and
    development) **N:** 64-65
  Teaching (Teaching around the world) **T:** 70
  Technical assistance **T:** 73
  Technology (Sharing the benefits of technology)
    T: 78
  Third World (The economic Third World) **T:** 258-
    259
  United Nations (Working for progress) **U:** 87
  United Nations Industrial Development
    Organization **U:** 97
  Women's movement (In developing nations)
    W: 387
Development [music]
  Classical music (Sonata) **Ci:** 645
Development economics
  Economics (Fields of economics) **E:** 64
Development of a Bottle in Space [sculpture by
  Boccioni]
  Futurism *picture on* **F:** 590
Development of Capitalism in Russia, The [book
  by Lenin]
  Lenin, V. I. (Young revolutionist) **L:** 192
Developmental bilingual education *See* Two-way
  bilingual education *in this index*
Developmental biology [science] **D:** 173
  Evolution (Contributions from other scientific
    fields) **E:** 433
Developmental genetics
  Genetics (Molecular genetics) **G:** 86
Developmental method
  Reading (The teaching of reading) **R:** 157
Developmental psychology D: 174
  Erikson, Erik Homburger **E:** 352
  Personality (Personality development) **P:** 302
  Pestalozzi, Johann Heinrich **P:** 318
  Piaget, Jean **P:** 445

  Psychology (Major fields of psychology) **P:** 848
Devens, Charles [American government official]
  Justice, Department of (table) **J:** 203
Dever, Paul A. [American political leader]
  Massachusetts (table) **M:** 288
De Verchères, Madeleine *See* Verchères, Marie
  Madeleine Jarret de *in this index*
Deverson, Jane [British author]
  Generation X **G:** 84
Deviated septum
  Nosebleed **N:** 549
Deviation
  Compass (Deviation) **Ci:** 903
Device [emblem]
  Flag (table) **F:** 193
Device [medicine]
  Pure food and drug laws (Drugs and devices)
    P: 908
Devil [religion] **D:** 174
  Angel **A:** 459
  Devil worship **D:** 175
  Exorcism **E:** 438
  Mephistopheles **M:** 411
  Witchcraft (History) **W:** 372
"Devil, The" [story by Tolstoy]
  Tolstoy, Leo (Later works) **T:** 323
Devil and Daniel Webster, The [opera by Moore]
  Moore, Douglas Stuart **M:** 796
"Devil and Daniel Webster, The" [story by Benét]
  Benét, Stephen Vincent **B:** 248
Devil facial tumor disease
  Tasmanian devil **T:** 49
Devil Finds Work, The [book by Baldwin]
  Baldwin, James **B:** 39
Devil World [poem by Espronceda]
  Spanish literature (The 1800's) **So:** 761
Devil worship [religion] **D:** 175
Deville, Henri Étienne Sainte-Claire [French
  chemist]
  Aluminum (The first aluminum) **A:** 397
Devils, New Jersey [team]
  Hockey (table: National Hockey League) **H:** 281
Devil's-darning-needle *See* Dragonfly *in this index*
Devil's Dictionary, The [book by Bierce]
  Bierce, Ambrose **B:** 295
Devil's food cake
  Cake **C:** 19
Devils Hole pupfish
  Endangered species (table) **E:** 270
  Pupfish **P:** 905 *with picture*
Devils Island
  French Guiana **F:** 515
  Penal colony **P:** 235
Devils Lake [North Dakota]
  North Dakota (Rivers and lakes) **N:** 508; (Recent
    developments) **N:** 516
Devil's Lake State Park [park, Wisconsin]
  Wisconsin *picture on* **W:** 357
Devil's paintbrush [plant] **D:** 175
Devil's Pool, The [book by Sand]
  French literature (Romantic fiction) **F:** 521
Devils Postpile National Monument [California]
  National Park System (table: National
    monuments) **N:** 50
Devil's-snuffbox
  Puffball **P:** 905
Devils Tower National Monument [Wyoming]
  D: 175
  National Park System (table: National
    monuments) **N:** 50; (History) **N:** 58
  Wyoming **W:** 516; (Places to visit) **W:** 524 *with
    picture*
Devil's Triangle [Atlantic ocean]
  Bermuda Triangle **B:** 269
Devil's Trill Sonata [music by Tartini]
  Tartini, Giuseppe **T:** 48
Devine, Grant [Canadian political leader]
  Saskatchewan (table) **S:** 144
Devine, Joseph M. [American political leader]
  North Dakota (table) **N:** 513
Devise [law]
  Will **W:** 306
Devisee [law]
  Heir **H:** 167
DeVito, Tommy [American musician]
  Valli, Frankie **V:** 267 *with picture*
Devoir, Le [newspaper]
  Bourassa, Henri **B:** 516
Devolution [government] **D:** 175
  Scotland (Government) **S:** 211-212
Devon rex cat
  Cat *picture on* **C:** 288; (Short-haired breeds)
    C: 290-291
Devonian Period [geology] **D:** 175
  Earth (The Paleozoic Era) **E:** 27; (table) **E:** 30
  Extinction (The Devonian extinction) **E:** 456
  Fish (The Age of Fishes) **F:** 171

  Plant (The evolution of plants) **P:** 544-545 *with
    picture*
  Prehistoric animal (The first animals with
    backbones) **P:** 736-737; (table) **P:** 738
Devonshire, Duke of [British colonial official]
  D: 175
Devonshire, Duke of [British prime minister]
  United Kingdom (table: British prime ministers)
    U: 72
De Voto, Bernard Augustine [American author]
  D: 176
De Vries, Hugo [Dutch botanist] **D:** 176
  Cell (The 1900's) **C:** 337
  Heredity (The birth of genetics) **H:** 208
De Vries, Peter [American author]
  Parody **P:** 178
DeVries, William C. [American doctor]
  Artificial heart **A:** 759
Dew [weather] **D:** 176
  Dew point **D:** 176
  Weather (Humidity) **W:** 158
DEW line [defense]
  North Warning System **N:** 519
Dew point [weather] **D:** 176
  Air (Moisture in the air) **A:** 170
  Cloud (How clouds form) **Ci:** 708
  Humidity **H:** 433
  Weather (Humidity) **W:** 158
Dew-point hygrometer [instrument]
  Hygrometer (Other hygrometers) **H:** 474
Dew-retting [industrial process]
  Flax (Growing and processing fiber flax) **F:** 230-
    231
  Linen (Preparing the fibers) **L:** 334
Dewan Negara [legislature]
  Malaysia (National government) **M:** 98a
Dewan Rakyat [legislature]
  Malaysia (National government) **M:** 98a
Dewar, James [Scottish chemist]
  Hydrogen (Properties) **H:** 468
  Vacuum bottle **V:** 257
Dewar flask [container]
  Liquid air (Making liquid air) **L:** 347
  Vacuum **V:** 256
  Vacuum bottle **V:** 256
De Warm, Jacobus [English general]
  Vermont (Exploration and settlement) **V:** 334
Dewatering [coal]
  Coal (Cleaning coal) **Ci:** 726-727
Dewaxing [process]
  Petroleum (Dewaxing) **P:** 344
Dewberry [plant] **D:** 176 *with picture*
  Boysenberry **B:** 541
Dewclaw
  Deer (Legs and hoofs) **D:** 83 *with picture*
  Dog (Body structure) **D:** 263-265
Dewey [Welsh religious leader] *See* David, Saint *in
  this index*
Dewey, George [American admiral] **D:** 176
  Navy, United States (The Spanish-American War
    [1898]) **N:** 88
  Spanish-American War (Manila Bay) **So:** 753
Dewey, John [American philosopher] **D:** 177
  James, William J: 27
  Pragmatism **P:** 729
  Progressive education (Progressive educators)
    P: 813
Dewey, Melvil [American librarian] **D:** 177
  Library (Libraries in the United States) **L:** 261-262
Dewey, Nelson [American political leader]
  Wisconsin (table) **W:** 365; (Statehood) **W:** 366
Dewey, Thomas Edmund [American political
  leader] **D:** 177
  New York (table) **N:** 313
  Public opinion poll (History) **P:** 863
  Roosevelt, Franklin Delano (Election of 1944)
    R: 458
  Truman, Harry S. (Election of 1948) **T:** 470
Dewey Decimal Classification [library] **D:** 177
  Dewey, Melvil **D:** 177
  Library (Libraries in the United States) **L:** 261-262
  A Guide to Research Skills **Research Guide:** 29,
    Research Guide: 38
Dewi [Welsh religious leader] *See* David, Saint *in
  this index*
De Witt Clinton [locomotive]
  Railroad (Developments in the United States)
    R: 115
Dewlap [biology]
  Anole **A:** 518 *with picture*
  Iguana **I:** 50
DeWolfe, Florence Kling [wife of Warren G.
  Harding] *See* Harding, Florence Kling *in this index*
Dexedrine [medication]
  Amphetamine **A:** 439
  Drug abuse (table: Some commonly abused
    drugs) **D:** 363

Dexter, Andrew [American settler]
Montgomery (Government and history) M: 766
Dexter, Darrell [Canadian political leader]
Nova Scotia (table) N: 567
Dexter, Samuel [American government official]
Adams, John (table) A: 38
Jefferson, Thomas (table) J: 83
Dexter, Walter F. [American educator]
Nixon, Richard Milhous (Education) N: 429-430
Dexter Avenue King Memorial Baptist Church
Alabama (Places to visit) A: 266
Dexter cattle
Cattle (Other dairy cattle) C: 311
Dexter side
Heraldry (Expansion) H: 194
Dextrin [chemical] D: 178
Starch (Use in foods) So: 855
Dextrose [sugar] D: 178
Glucose G: 236
Dezhnev, Semyon [Russian explorer]
Arctic (Search for the Northwest Passage)
A: 638-639
DH [baseball]
Baseball (Players) B: 125
Dhaka [Bangladesh] D: 178
Bangladesh *pictures on* B: 79, B: 80, B: 82
Dhaka, University of
Bangladesh (Education) B: 82
Dharma [religion] D: 178
Buddha (Later life) B: 667
Buddhism (Beliefs and practices) B: 667
Manu M: 168
Dharma Chakra [symbol]
India *picture on* I: 110
Dharma Commentaries [religion]
Dharma D: 178
Dharma Sutras [religion]
Dharma D: 178
Dhaulagiri [mountain, Nepal]
Himalaya (Peaks) H: 233
Dhiban [ancient city]
Moabite stone M: 681
Dhivehi Raajjeyge Jumhooriyyaa See Maldives
in this index
DHLPP [vaccine]
Dog (Medical care) D: 279
Dhofar [region]
Oman (Land and climate) O: 758
Dhoinine, Ikililou [Comoran political leader]
Comoros (History) Ci: 900-901
Dhole [dog] D: 178
Dhoti [clothing]
Bangladesh (Way of life) B: 80-81
Clothing (India) Ci: 699
India (Clothing) I: 117
Dhow [boat]
Ship (Sailing ships in the 1900's) S: 423 *with
picture*
Transportation (Ancient Rome) T: 387
DHS [organization] *See* Homeland Security,
Department of *in this index*
Dhūl-Hijja [month]
Calendar (The Islamic calendar) C: 29
'Īd al-Ad-hā I: 25
Día de la Raza [custom]
Columbus Day Ci: 865
Día de los muertos [holiday] D: 178
Halloween (Halloween around the world) H: 24b
Latin America (Recreation) L: 98
Mexico *picture on* M: 458
November N: 576
Día de los Reyes Magos [holiday]
January J: 30
Diabetes [disease] D: 179
African Americans (Health issues) A: 136s
Banting, Sir Frederick Grant B: 99
Blindness (Diseases) B: 401
C-reactive protein C: 2
Disease (Metabolic diseases) D: 226
Glucose G: 236
Heredity (Hereditary disorders) H: 204
Hypoglycemia (Causes) H: 481
Insulin I: 308
Multiple birth (Complications of multiple birth)
M: 920
Pancreas P: 128
Physical fitness (Glucose tolerance) P: 435
Diabetes insipidus [disease]
Diabetes (Diabetes insipidus) D: 180
Diabetes mellitus [disease] *See* Diabetes *in this
index*
Diabetic retinopathy [disorder]
Blindness (Diseases) B: 401
Eye (Diseases of the retina) E: 467
Diablada [dance]
Latin America (Recreation) L: 98 *with picture*
Diablo [game]

Top (History of tops) T: 331
Diachronic linguistics
Linguistics (Comparative and historical
linguistics) L: 336
Diaconate [religious office]
Deacon D: 55
Diacritical mark [language] D: 180
Diaghilev, Sergei Pavlovich [Russian ballet
director] D: 180
Ballet (Ballet in Russia) B: 52
Ballets Russes B: 55
Stravinsky, Igor (Early works) So: 922
Diagnosis [medicine]
Blood (Diagnostic tests) B: 413
Cancer (Cancer detection and diagnosis) C: 171
Disease (Medical treatment) D: 232
Internal medicine I: 336
Medicine (Diagnosis) M: 364
Oncology O: 761
Diagnosis related group [insurance]
Hospital (Recent developments) H: 374
Medicine (The United States) M: 367
Diagnostic mammography [medicine]
Mammography M: 129
Diagonal [chess]
Chess (The board and the men) C: 411-412 *with
diagram*
Diagonal [mathematics]
Geometry (Euclidean geometry) G: 104 *with
diagram*
Diagonal stride
Skiing *diagram on* S: 484
Diagraming [grammar]
Sentence (Diagraming) S: 304
Diaguita Indians
Argentina (Early inhabitants) A: 655
Dial
Clock (Kinds of clocks) Ci: 682i
Sundial So: 990 *with picture*
Dial, The [magazine]
Emerson, Ralph Waldo (His prose works) E: 259
Magazine (Magazines in the 1800's) M: 45
Dial tone
Telephone (Traditional phone calls) T: 96
Dial-up connection [electronics]
Computer (Internet service providers) Ci: 921
Internet (Hardware) I: 350c
Dial-up modem [electronic device]
Broadband communication B: 635
Dialect [language] D: 180
Arabs (Language) A: 586
Chinese language C: 509
Cockney Ci: 745
England (Language) E: 294-296
German language (German dialects) G: 138
Grammar (Grammar and usage) G: 304
Greek language (Development of ancient Greek)
G: 376
Hispanic Americans (Who Hispanic Americans
are) H: 245
Italian literature (The Middle Ages) I: 494
Pronunciation P: 820
Speech So: 773
Dialect [zoology]
Bird (Calls and songs) B: 354
Killer whale K: 316
Dialectic [philosophy]
Hegel, G. W. F. (Hegel's dialectic) H: 165
Philosophy (Philosophy in the 1800's) P: 390
Socrates (The Socratic method) So: 568
Dialectical materialism [philosophy]
Materialism M: 300b
Philosophy (Philosophy in the 1800's) P: 390
Dialing mechanism
Telephone (The dialing mechanism) T: 95
Dialogs of the Dead [work by Fénelon]
Fénelon, François de Salignac de la Mothe- F: 71
Dialogue [book by Catherine of Siena]
Catherine of Siena, Saint C: 303
Dialogue [literature]
Drama (Other parts of drama) D: 325
Plato (The dialogues) P: 567
*Dialogue Concerning the Two Chief World
Systems* [book by Galileo]
Galileo (Galileo and the Roman Catholic Church)
G: 12
Relativity (Galilean relativity) R: 209
Dialogues [book by Saint Gregory]
Benedict of Nursia, Saint B: 248
Dialogues Concerning Natural Religion [book by
Hume]
Hume, David (Hume's life) H: 432
Dialysis [medicine]
Kidney (Kidney diseases) K: 312
Nephritis N: 128
Uremia U: 221
Diamagnetism [physics]

Magnetism (In materials) M: 60c
Diameter [geometry] D: 180
Circle (Parts of a circle) Ci: 558 *with diagram*
Pi P: 445
Sphere So: 779 *with diagram*
Diamond [gem] D: 180 *with pictures*
Africa (Mining) A: 127
Arkansas (Places to visit) A: 704
Botswana (Economy) B: 512
Carbon (Forms of carbon) C: 204 *with diagram*
Gem (Crystal shape) G: 77 *with picture*; (Index of
refraction) G: 77; (Sources of gems) G: 77-79;
(Cutting and polishing) G: 79
Mining *picture on* M: 574
South Africa (Discovery of diamonds and gold)
So: 618
Diamond [road]
Road (Intersections) R: 358-359
Diamond [suit]
Card game (History) C: 209
Diamond, Peter A. [American economist]
Nobel Prizes (Economics: 2010) N: 450
Diamond Head [volcano, Hawaii]
Honolulu (The city) H: 320 *with picture*
Diamond Match Company
Match (The first matches) M: 300-300a
Ohio (Interesting facts) O: 681
Diamond point nail
Nail (The parts of a nail) N: 3
Diamond python
Snake *picture on* S: 533
Diamond Shoals [region, Atlantic]
Cape Hatteras C: 188
Diamond Sutra [book]
Book (The development of printed books) B: 466
with picture
Tang dynasty T: 25
Diamondback rattlesnake
Rattlesnake R: 149
Snake *picture on* S: 534
Diamondback terrapin [turtle]
Terrapin T: 173 *with picture*
Diamondbacks, Arizona [team] *See* Arizona
Diamondbacks *in this index*
Diamonds Are Forever [book by Fleming]
Fleming, Ian F: 233
Diana [literary figure]
Shakespeare, William: (*All's Well That Ends Well*)
S: 362
Diana [Roman mythology] D: 183
See also Artemis *in this index*
Mythology (table) M: 981
Diana, Princess of Wales [British princess] D: 183
with portrait
Charles, Prince C: 382
William, Prince W: 309
Diana of the Crossways [book by Meredith]
Meredith, George M: 416
DIAND [organization] *See* Indian Affairs and
Northern Development, Department of *in this
index*
Dianthus [botany]
Pink P: 473
Diapause [entomology]
Hibernation (Other kinds of dormancy) H: 222
Metamorphosis (The pupa) M: 428
Moth (Migration) M: 839
Diaper
Baby (Clothing the baby) B: 10
Environmental pollution (Weighing benefits and
risks) E: 339
Diaphragm [anatomy] D: 184 *with diagrams*
Hiccup H: 223
Human body (The respiratory system) H: 420;
(table) H: 422 *with diagram*
Mammal (Internal organ systems) M: 119-120
with diagram
Respiration (Structures of breathing) R: 260
Diaphragm [birth control]
Birth control (Methods of birth control) B: 378-
379
Diaphragm [photography] *See* Shutter *in this index*
Diaphragm [sound reproduction]
Microphone (Carbon microphones) M: 516 *with
diagrams*
Speaker So: 767
Telephone (The microphone) T: 95
Diaphysis [anatomy]
Bone (Structure of the bones) B: 456
Diarmuid [legendary figure]
Mythology (The Fionn cycle) M: 985
Diarrhea [disorder] D: 184
Campylobacter C: 97
Cholera C: 520
Dehydration D: 93
Dysentery D: 398
E. coli E: 2

Inflammatory bowel disease I: 266
Rotavirus R: 486
Diary [book by Pepys]
Diary D: 184
Pepys, Samuel P: 279
Diary [literature] D: 184
Diary of Anne Frank [book by Frank] D: 185
Frank, Anne F: 484
Dias, Antônio Gonçalves [Brazilian poet]
Brazil (The arts) B: 576-577
Latin American literature (Romanticism) L: 112-113
Dias, Bartolomeu [Portuguese explorer] D: 185
Cape of Good Hope C: 189
Exploration (Reaching the tip of Africa) E: 443-444 *with map*
Dia's Story Cloth [book by Cha]
Literature for children *picture on* L: 383
Diaspora [Jewish history]
Jews (Foreign domination) J: 121; (The Jews today) J: 124
Diaspore [mineral]
Bauxite (How bauxite forms) B: 174
Diastole [physiology]
Heart (Regulating the heart rate) H: 135 *with diagram*
Diastolic pressure [physiology]
Blood pressure B: 416
Heart (Regulating blood pressure) H: 136-137
Diastrophic dwarfism [disorder]
Dwarfism (Causes) D: 394-395
Diatom [microbiology] D: 185 *with pictures*
Algae A: 349
Ocean O: 656; (Phytoplankton) O: 655 *with picture*
Diatomaceous earth
Diatom D: 186
Diatomic molecule [chemistry]
Molecule (Individual molecules) M: 692-693
Diatomite [mineral]
Algae A: 349
Diatom D: 186
Diatonic scale
Music (Tone) M: 950 *with diagrams*
Diatryma [bird]
Prehistoric animal (The development of other animals) P: 741
Díaz, Adolfo [Nicaraguan political leader]
Nicaragua (The United States and Nicaragua) N: 400
Diaz, Bartolomeu *See* Dias, Bartolomeu *in this index*
Díaz, David [American illustrator] D: 186
Caldecott Medal (table: 1995) C: 26
Díaz, Porfirio [Mexican political leader] D: 186
Latin America (Political circumstances in the early to middle 1900's) L: 109
Madero, Francisco Indalecio M: 30
Mexican Revolution of 1910 (Causes) M: 444-445
Mexico (The dictatorship of Porfirio Díaz) M: 472; (The Revolution of 1910) M: 472
Mexico City (Independence) M: 478
Díaz de Vivar, Rodrigo *See* Cid, The [Spanish hero] *in this index*
Díaz del Castillo, Bernal [Spanish author]
Latin American literature (Colonial literature) L: 112
Diazepam [medication]
Benzodiazepine B: 256
Tranquilizer T: 369
Diazinon [insecticide]
Insecticide (Organophosphate insecticides) I: 302
Dibao [newspaper]
Journalism (The first newspapers) J: 174
Newspaper (History) N: 386
Dibdin, Charles [British performer]
Circus (The birth of the circus) Ci: 562b
Dibong [river, Asia]
Brahmaputra River B: 548
DiCamillo, Kate [American author] D: 186
Newbery Medal (table) N: 359
DiCaprio, Leonardo [American actor] D: 187 *with portrait*
Dice [game] D: 187
Game (Dice games) G: 22
Dicenta, Joaquín [Spanish dramatist]
Spanish literature (The 1800's) So: 761
Dichloro-diphenyl-trichloroethane [chemical]
See DDT *in this index*
Dichlorodifluoromethane [chemical]
Chlorofluorocarbon C: 517
Dichroic mirror
Television (Capturing the image) T: 122
Dichromatic vision
Color blindness C: 827
Dichtung und Wahrheit [book by Goethe]
Goethe, Johann Wolfgang von (Late years) G: 247

Dicing [cooking]
Cooking (Preparation of ingredients) Ci: 1029
Dick, Philip K. [American author] D: 187
Dickcissel [bird]
Bird (Birds of grasslands) B: 336 *with picture*
Dicke, Robert H. [American physicist]
Cosmic microwave background (CMB) radiation Ci: 1075
Dickens, Catherine Hogarth [wife of]
Dickens, Charles (Personal life) D: 188
Dickens, Charles [British author] D: 187 *with pictures*
Child labor C: 455
Christmas (Other customs) C: 536
Daudet, Alphonse D: 43
Detective story (History) D: 163
English literature (Early Victorian literature) E: 321
Ghost G: 182
Marx, Karl *(Das Kapital)* M: 237
Novel (Britain) N: 573
Poe, Edgar Allan (Fiction and theory of fiction) P: 590
Dickens, John [father of]
Dickens, Charles (Dickens's life) D: 187
Dickerson, Denver S. [American political leader]
Nevada (table) N: 173
Dickerson, Mahlon [American government official]
Jackson, Andrew (table) J: 11
New Jersey (table) N: 249
Van Buren, Martin (table) V: 273
Dickerson, Philemon [American political leader]
New Jersey (table) N: 249
Dickey, Bill [American baseball player]
Baseball (table: Hall of Fame) B: 134
Dickey, James [American poet] D: 190
Dickey, Robert Barry [Canadian political leader]
Confederation of Canada (Fathers of Confederation) Ci: 935 *with picture*
Dickinson, Anna Elizabeth [American orator] D: 190 *with portrait*
Dickinson, Charles [American lawyer]
Duel D: 378
Jackson, Andrew (Business and politics) J: 8
Dickinson, Don M. [American government official]
Cleveland, Grover (table) Ci: 671
Dickinson, Emily [American poet] D: 190 *with portrait*
American literature (Walt Whitman and Emily Dickinson) A: 419 *with portrait*
Poetry (Stress meters) P: 592; (Beginnings of modern poetry) P: 597
Dickinson, Jacob M. [American government official]
Taft, William Howard (table) T: 11
Dickinson, John [American political leader] D: 191
Articles of Confederation A: 759
Constitution of the United States (The Constitutional Convention) Ci: 999
Delaware (Places to visit) D: 102; (table) D: 109
Jefferson, Thomas (The Declaration of Independence) J: 79
Pennsylvania (table) P: 263
Revolution, American (The Declaration of Independence) R: 278
Dickinson, Luren D. [American political leader]
Michigan (table) M: 507
Dickinson Mansion
Delaware (Places to visit) D: 102
Dickson, Brian [Canadian jurist] D: 191
Dickson, W. K. L. [American inventor]
Edison, Thomas Alva (Motion pictures) E: 80
Dicloxacillin [medication]
Antibiotic (table) A: 551
Dicot *See* Dicotyledon *in this index*
Dicotyledon [botany] D: 191
Angiosperm A: 462
Cotyledon Ci: 1095
Gardening (Pruning) G: 36
Seed (The parts of a seed) S: 281 *with diagram*
Dicoumarol [drug]
Anticoagulant A: 553
Dicrocoelium dendriticum [worm]
Parasite (Life cycle) P: 154 *with diagram*; (Influence on behavior) P: 155
Dictation
Shorthand S: 435
Dictator [title] *See* Dictatorship *in this index*
Dictatorship [political science] D: 191
Absolutism A: 17
Autocracy A: 942
Censorship C: 345
Democracy (Features of democracy) D: 120-121
Government G: 282; (Totalitarianism) G: 286; (Totalitarianism and Communism) G: 291
Totalitarianism T: 346
World War II (The rise of dictatorships) W: 469
Dictatorship of the proletariat [political theory]

Communism (The ideas of Marx) Ci: 890; (Lenin's contributions) Ci: 890
Dictes or Sayings of the Philosophers, The [book]
Caxton, William C: 322
Diction
Drama (Other parts of drama) D: 325
Singing (Training the voice) S: 472
Dictionary [book] D: 192
Accent A: 22
Dictionary of American Biography
Ochs, Adolph Simon O: 668
Dictionary of the English Language, A [book by Johnson]
Dictionary (Early English dictionaries) D: 194
English literature (Samuel Johnson) E: 319
Johnson, Samuel (Later years) J: 153
Diddley, Bo [American musician]
Rock music (The first generation) R: 377
Didelphimorphia [zoology]
Mammal (table) M: 128 *with picture*
Diderot, Denis [French philosopher] D: 195
Drama (France) D: 335
Encyclopedia (An age of experiment) E: 268a
Enlightenment E: 326a
French literature (The Enlightenment) F: 520
Philosophes P: 382
Didgeridoo [musical instrument]
Australia *picture on* A: 906
Didion, Joan [American author] D: 195 *with portrait*
American literature (Essays) A: 426
Didius Julianus [Roman emperor]
Rome, Ancient (table) R: 447
Dido [legendary figure] D: 195
Aeneid A: 84
Carthage C: 260
Didrikson, Babe [American athlete] *See* Zaharias, Babe Didrikson *in this index*
Didymium [chemical]
Praseodymium P: 733
Didymus [apostle]
Thomas, Saint T: 262
Die [game]
Dice D: 187
Die ...
Titles beginning Die *appear under their key words, as in* Meistersinger, Die
Die and diemaking [industry] D: 195 *with diagram*
Embossing E: 256
Extrusion E: 459 *with diagram*
Forging (Machine forging) F: 409-410
Money *picture on* M: 711; (Modern coins) M: 707; (Minting coins) M: 714-715
Silver *picture on* S: 465
Tool (Metalworking tools) T: 330
Toolmaking T: 330
Wire (How wire is made) W: 343
Die casting [industrial process]
Cast and casting (Other types of casting) C: 278
Die and diemaking D: 195
Diefenbaker, Edna May Brower [wife of]
Diefenbaker, John George (Young lawyer) D: 197
Diefenbaker, John George [Canadian political leader] D: 196 *with pictures*
Canada, History of (The end of Liberal rule) C: 149; (Challenges of the 1960's) C: 149
Progressive Conservative Party P: 812
Diefenbaker, Lake
Saskatchewan (Rivers and lakes) S: 138-140
Diefenbaker, Mary Florence Bannerman [mother of]
Diefenbaker, John George (Boyhood and education) D: 196
Diefenbaker, Olive Freeman Palmer [wife of]
Diefenbaker, John George (Young lawyer) D: 197
Diefenbaker, William [father of]
Diefenbaker, John George (Boyhood and education) D: 196
Diego, Juan [Mexican public figure]
Guadalupe Day G: 407
Dielectric medium [insulation]
Capacitor C: 186
Insulator, Electric I: 308
Dielectric strength
Materials (Electrical properties) M: 300c
Diels, Otto [German chemist]
Nobel Prizes (Chemistry: 1950) N: 443
Diem, Ngo Dinh [Vietnamese political leader] *See* Ngo Dinh Diem *in this index*
Diemaking *See* Die and diemaking *in this index*
Dien Bien Phu [Vietnam]
Foreign Legion (History) F: 386
Indochina (Independence) I: 225
Dien Bien Phu, Battle of [1954] D: 198
Diener, Theodor O. [Swiss-born scientist]
Viroid V: 426
Dieppe [France]

World War II (D-Day) **W:** 483
Diesel, Rudolf [German engineer] **D:** 198
  Diesel engine (History) **D:** 199
  Transportation (The beginnings of modern
    transportation) **T:** 390
Diesel-electric locomotive
  Locomotive *diagram on* **L:** 415; (Diesel
    locomotives) **L:** 414 *with picture*
  Railroad (Rolling stock) **R:** 107
Diesel-electric ship
  Ship (Engine-driven ships) **S:** 406
Diesel engine D: 198
  Automobile (Powering an internal-combustion
    car) **A:** 950; (Where cars are made) **A:** 959
  Catalytic converter **C:** 298
  Diesel, Rudolf **D:** 198
  Electric power (Other sources of electric power)
    E: 184
  Fuel injection **F:** 552
  Ship (Engine-driven ships) **S:** 406; (Stronger,
    faster ships) **S:** 425-426
  Starter (Diesel starters) **So:** 859
  Submarine (The power plant) **So:** 941
  Transportation (The beginnings of modern
    transportation) **T:** 390
Diesel fuel
  Fuel (Petroleum) **F:** 550
  Petroleum *diagram on* **P:** 344; (Petroleum as a
    fuel) **P:** 332
Diesel-hydraulic locomotive
  Locomotive (Diesel locomotives) **L:** 414-416
  Railroad (Rolling stock) **R:** 107
Diesel locomotive
  Locomotive (Diesel locomotives) **L:** 414 *with
    picture*; (History) **L:** 417
  Railroad, Model (Locomotives) **R:** 120-121
Diesel-mechanical locomotive
  Locomotive (Diesel locomotives) **L:** 414-416
Diet [government]
  Japan (National government) **J:** 33
Diet [Hungarian history]
  Hungary (The Kingdom of Hungary) **H:** 445
Diet [nutrition] **D:** 199
  See also Food *in this index*
  Baby (Feeding procedures) **B:** 9
  Diabetes (Treatment) **D:** 179
  Dietary supplement **D:** 200
  Fat (Biological and nutritional importance)
    F: 52-53
  Fiber, Dietary **F:** 88
  Food (How diets differ around the world) **F:** 331
  Health (Nutrition) **H:** 125
  Milk (Milk in the human diet) **M:** 546
  Nutrition **N:** 624 *with pictures*
  Obesity (Causes of obesity) **O:** 642a
  Pellagra **P:** 232
  Teeth (A good diet) **T:** 81
  Vegetarianism **V:** 295
  Weight control (Maintaining a healthy body
    weight) **W:** 181
  Zoo (Caring for zoo animals) **Z:** 602
Diet of ...
  Diets appear under their key words, as in Worms,
    Diet of
Dietary Guidelines for Americans
  Obesity (Prevention of obesity) **O:** 642b
Dietary law [religion]
  Judaism (Customs and ceremonies) **J:** 181
Dietary supplement D: 200
  Health food (Types of health foods) **H:** 129
  Herbal medicine **H:** 197
  Nutrition (Evaluate claims about foods and
    dietary supplements carefully) **N:** 630
Dietetic technician
  Nutrition (Careers in nutrition) **N:** 631
Dietetics
  Diet **D:** 199
  Family and consumer sciences (Nutrition,
    dietetics, and food science) **F:** 26
Diethyl ether *See* Ether [chemistry] *in this index*
Diethylstilbestrol [hormone] *See* DES *in this index*
Dietitian [career]
  Hospital (Professional services departments)
    H: 371
  Nutrition (Careers in nutrition) **N:** 631
Dietrich, Charles H. [American political leader]
  Nebraska (table) **N:** 110
Dietrich, Marlene [German actress] **D:** 200
  Von Sternberg, Josef **V:** 448
Dietrich of Bern [legendary figure]
  Theodoric **T:** 252
Diez y Seis de Septiembre [holiday]
  Hispanic Americans (Holidays) **H:** 250
Difference [arithmetic]
  Subtraction (Subtraction questions) **So:** 944
Difference engine
  Babbage, Charles **B:** 2

Computer (Punched-card devices) **Ci:** 924a-924b
Differential [mechanism]
  Automobile (The drive system) **A:** 949 *with
    diagram*
  Transmission *diagram on* **T:** 376; (The differential)
    T: 378
Differential anesthetic [medication]
  Menthol **M:** 410
Differential association, Theory of
  Criminology (History) **Ci:** 1145-1146
Differential calculus
  Calculus **C:** 22
  Mathematics (Branches of mathematics) **M:** 303
Differential distillation *See* Fractional distillation
  in this index
Differential hoist [mechanism]
  Block and tackle (An endless chain hoist) **B:** 405
    with diagram
Differential white count test
  Blood (Blood tests) **B:** 413-414
Differentiated instruction D: 200
  Encyclopedia (Today's encyclopedias) **E:** 268b-
    269
Differentiated staffing system
  Teaching (Rewards of teaching) **T:** 69
Differentiation [biology]
  Cell (Growth and specialization) **C:** 332
  Growth (In living things) **G:** 404
  Reproduction, Human (Origin of tissues and
    organs) **R:** 247-248
  Stem cell **So:** 889
Diffie, Whitfield [American engineer]
  Codes and ciphers (Later developments) **Ci:** 751
Diffraction [physics] **D:** 201
  Acoustics **A:** 29
  Hubble Space Telescope (How the telescope
    works) **H:** 403
  Light (Diffraction) **L:** 288 *with pictures*
  Molecule (Studying molecules) **M:** 694
  Sound (Diffraction) **So:** 603 *with diagram*
  Waves *diagram on* **W:** 151; (Diffraction) **W:** 153
Diffraction grating [physics]
  Diffraction (Uses of diffraction) **D:** 201
  Light (Diffraction) **L:** 288
Diffuse cutaneous leishmaniasis [disease]
  Leishmaniasis **L:** 187
Diffuse ring [astronomy]
  Planetary ring **P:** 514d
Diffuse vent [oceanography]
  Hydrothermal vent **H:** 473
Diffusion [anthropology]
  Culture (Contact with other cultures) **Ci:** 1189
Diffusion [chemistry] **D:** 201 *with diagrams*
Diffusion bonding [industrial process]
  Welding (Solid-state bonding) **W:** 190
Diffusion pump
  Vacuum **V:** 256
Diffusionism
  Sociology (Development of social research)
    So: 566
Diffusionon bonding [industrial process]
  Welding (Solid-state bonding) **W:** 190
DiFrancesco, Donald T. [American political leader]
  New Jersey (table) **N:** 249
Dig, Archaeological
  Science *picture on* **S:** 191
Digamma [letter]
  F **F:** 1 *with picture*
Digest
  Magazine (Consumer magazines) **M:** 42
Digest [law]
  Justinian Code **J:** 204
Digester [machine]
  Aluminum (How aluminum is produced) **A:** 393
    with diagram
  Paper (Pulping processes) **P:** 134-135 *with
    diagram*
Digestion *See* Digestive system *in this index*
Digestive system D: 201 *with diagrams*
  See also the list of Related articles in the Digestive
    System *article*
  Amphibian (Digestive system) **A:** 440
  Antacid **A:** 529
  Bird (The digestive system) **B:** 365
  Blood (Transporting nutrients and wastes) **B:** 408
    with diagrams
  Butterfly (The internal organs) **B:** 739 *with
    diagram*
  Cancer (Classification by primary body site)
    C: 167-168
  Fiber, Dietary **F:** 88
  Fish (Digestive system) **F:** 162 *with diagram*
  Hoatzin **H:** 272
  Hormone (Metabolic hormones) **H:** 335
  Human body (The digestive system) **H:** 419;
    (table) **H:** 422 *with diagram*
  Inflammatory bowel disease **I:** 266

Insect (Digestive system) **I:** 289 *with diagram*
Lactose intolerance **L:** 24
Liver (Digestion and use of food) **L:** 394
Magnesia **M:** 54
Mammal (Internal organ systems) **M:** 119
Mastication **M:** 298
Michigan (Interesting facts) **M:** 489
Nutrition (How the body uses food) **N:** 624
Pancreatitis **P:** 128
Ruminant **R:** 519
Spider (Digestive system) **So:** 785 *with diagram*
Digestive tract *See* Alimentary canal *in this index*
Digger pine [tree]
  Pine (Western pines) **P:** 469
Digger wasp [insect]
  Animal (Providing food) **A:** 498
  Wasp **W:** 111 *with picture*
Digging [behavior]
  Dog (Why dogs do the things they do) **D:** 263
    with picture
Digging stick [tool]
  Indian, American (Farming) **I:** 141
Digit [number]
  Arabic numerals **A:** 584
  Arithmetic **A:** 665
  Multiplication (Multiplying by one digit) **M:** 922
  Number (The decimal system) **N:** 605
  Zero **Z:** 590
Digital audio broadcasting
  Radio (Digital audio broadcasting [DAB]) **R:** 87;
    (DAB receivers) **R:** 90; (Radio since the 1950's)
    R: 94
Digital audio tape
  Communication (The digital age) **Ci:** 885
  Tape recorder **T:** 37
Digital audiotape cassette
  Tape recorder (Kinds of tape recorders) **T:** 38
Digital camcorder
  Camcorder (The development of camcorders)
    C: 75
Digital camera
  Camera **C:** 80 *with pictures*
  Photography **P:** 406; (Digital photography) **P:** 420
    with pictures; (The digital revolution) **P:** 427
Digital code [electronics]
  Camcorder **C:** 75
  Data compression **D:** 41
  Digital video recorder **D:** 203
  Internet (Information and media) **I:** 350
  Printing (Preparing material for printing) **P:** 797
  Telecommunications **T:** 89
Digital computer
  Analog computer **A:** 448
  Computer **Ci:** 908
Digital display
  Clock (Kinds of clocks) **Ci:** 682i *with diagram*;
    (Electric clocks) **Ci:** 682k
  Watch (How watches work) **W:** 114
Digital image
  Motion picture (Shooting the movie) **M:** 852-853
Digital imaging
  Biometrics **B:** 325
  Photogrammetry **P:** 405
  X rays (Uses of X rays) **X:** 540
Digital inkjet printing
  Textile (Finishing the fabric) **T:** 217
Digital library
  Library (The growth of information and
    technology) **L:** 237-238
Digital light processing [electronics]
  Electronics (Electronics today) **E:** 216-217
Digital light processing projector
  Audio-visual materials (Projection devices)
    A: 882-883
  Projector (Digital projectors) **P:** 817
Digital logic unit [electronics]
  Computer (Microprocessors) **Ci:** 912
Digital meter
  Electric meter (Digital meters) **E:** 177
Digital music player *See* Portable media player *in
  this index*
Digital oscilloscope [instrument]
  Oscilloscope **O:** 862
Digital photography *See* Digital camera *in this
  index*
Digital planetarium [machine]
  Planetarium (Digital projectors) **P:** 514c
Digital plotter [electronic device]
  Mechanical drawing *picture on* **M:** 353
Digital printing
  Printing (Digital printing) **P:** 801; (Printing in
    color) **P:** 801
Digital projector
  Projector (Types of projectors) **P:** 816-817
Digital recording
  Compact disc **Ci:** 901
  Copyright (Users' rights) **Ci:** 1047

Recording industry (History) R: 182
Tape recorder T: 37; (History) T: 38-39
Digital rectal examination [medicine]
Prostate cancer P: 829
Digital rights management [electronics]
Internet (Changing industries) I: 350e
Digital signal [electronics]
Cellular telephone C: 340
Communications satellite (How communications satellites work) Ci: 888b
Deafness (Special language techniques) D: 58
Digital video recorder D: 203
Electronics (How electronic circuits process information) E: 213
Telephone (Traditional phone calls) T: 96
Television (Broadcasting) T: 123
Videotape recorder (How videotape recorders work) V: 360
Digital signature [computing]
Computer (Computer security) Ci: 924
Digital single-lens reflex camera
Photography *pictures on* P: 420; (Single-lens [SLR] reflex cameras) P: 409
Digital subscriber line [electronics]
AT&T Inc. A: 851
Broadband communication B: 634
Computer (Internet service providers) Ci: 921
Internet (Hardware) I: 350c
Telephone (VoIP phone calls) T: 97
Digital synthesizer [machine]
Synthesizer So: 1068
Digital technology D: 203
Animation A: 511
Electronics (The digital age) E: 216
Hearing aid (History) H: 131
Digital television
Electronics (The digital age) E: 216
Television (Camera scanning patterns) T: 122; (Tuner) T: 124; (Digital television) T: 128
Digital thermometer
Thermometer (Resistance thermometers) T: 255 *with diagram*
Digital-to-analog converter [electronics]
Compact disc (Playback) Ci: 901
Television (Tuner) T: 124-125
Digital type
Type T: 536
Digital video effects
Television (Adding special effects) T: 112
Digital video recorder [device] D: 203
Computer *picture on* Ci: 913
Television (Home entertainment system) T: 110c
Videotape recorder (History) V: 361
Digital xerography
Copying machine (Electrostatic copying) Ci: 1045
Digitalis [medication] D: 203
Heart (Heart failure) H: 143
Digitizing tablet [electronic device]
Computer (A digitizing tablet) Ci: 914
Digitoxin [compound]
Digitalis D: 203
Digoxin [compound]
Digitalis D: 203
Digraph [writing]
Alphabet (The English alphabet) A: 383
Dihedral angle [mathematics]
Geometry (Solid geometry) G: 104 *with diagram*
Dihedral wing
Airplane (The wing) A: 213
Dihigo, Martin [American baseball player]
Baseball (table: Hall of Fame) B: 134
Dihong [river, Asia]
Brahmaputra River B: 548
Dik-dik [animal] D: 203
Antelope (Habits and appearance) A: 542
Dike [construction]
Irrigation (Surface irrigation) I: 457 *with picture*
Levee L: 216
Netherlands (Climate) N: 145
Rice *pictures on* R: 322; (Preparing the ground) R: 325
Dike [geology]
Rock (Intrusive rock) R: 371
Dilacor [drug]
Calcium channel blocker C: 21
Dilantin [drug]
Anticonvulsant A: 553
Di Lasso, Orlando See Lasso, Orlando di *in this index*
Dilation and evacuation [medicine]
Abortion (Abortion methods) A: 14-15
Dilator muscle [anatomy]
Eye (The uveal tract) E: 460-461 *with picture*
"Dilbert" [comic strip]
Adams, Scott A: 44 *with picture*
Dili [East Timor]
East Timor E: 40 *with picture and map*

Dillinger, John Herbert [American criminal] D: 204
Federal Bureau of Investigation (History) F: 62
Dillingham, Paul [American political leader]
Vermont (table) V: 333
Dillingham, William P. [American political leader]
Vermont (table) V: 333
Dillingham Commission [U.S. history]
Immigration (The third wave) I: 82
Dillon, Clarence Douglas [American government official]
Johnson, Lyndon Baines (table) J: 151
Kennedy, John Fitzgerald (table) K: 266
Dillon, Diane [American artist] See Dillon, Leo and Diane *in this index*
Dillon, Leo and Diane [American artists] D: 204
Caldecott Medal (table: 1976, 1977) C: 26
Literature for children *pictures on* L: 373, L: 374, L: 382
Dillon, Richard C. [American political leader]
New Mexico (table) N: 272
Dilmun [mythical place]
Bahrain (History) B: 30
Mythology (The influence of Sumerian mythology) M: 977
Diltiazem [medication]
Calcium channel blocker C: 21
Di Luna, Count [opera character]
Opera: (*Trovatore, Il*) O: 808
Dim sum [food]
Asian Americans (Asian influences on American culture) A: 812c
DiMaggio, Joe [American baseball player] D: 204
Baseball (table: Hall of Fame) B: 134; (Depression and war) B: 136 *with picture*; (table: Modern major league records) B: 138
Diman, Byron [American political leader]
Rhode Island (table) R: 311
Dime [money] D: 204
Money (Dimes) M: 714
Dime novel
Book (The 1800's) B: 467-468
United States, History of the (The Gilded Age) U: 183 *with picture*
Dimenhydrinate [medication]
Dramamine D: 342
Dimension
Fourth dimension F: 438
Dimension stone [building material]
Building stone B: 685
Materials (Stone) M: 300c-300d
Mining (Quarrying) M: 575
Quarrying Q: 7
Dimeter [poetry]
Poetry (table) P: 594
Dimethyl sulfoxide See DMSO *in this index*
Dimetrodon [extinct animal] D: 204
Evolution *picture on* E: 429
Permian Period P: 289
Prehistoric animal *picture on* P: 738
Diminished capacity [law]
Insanity I: 277
Diminished interval
Music (Harmony) M: 951
Diminuendo
Music (table) M: 954
Dimitrov, Filip [Bulgarian political figure]
Bulgaria (Political changes) B: 693
Dimitrov, Georgi [Bulgarian political figure]
Bulgaria (Communist rule) B: 693
Dimmer
Theater (Lighting methods) T: 240-241
Dimmesdale, Arthur [literary figure]
Hawthorne, Nathaniel (His novels) H: 115
Dimmick, Mary [wife of]
Harrison, Benjamin (Life in the White House) H: 73; (Later years) H: 73
Dimon, Jaime [American banker]
JPMorgan Chase & Co. J: 177
Dimond, Francis M. [American political leader]
Rhode Island (table) R: 311
Dimorphodon [extinct animal]
Pterosaur P: 854
DiNardo, Daniel [American religious leader]
Cardinal (table: American cardinals) C: 211
Dinaric Alps [mountains, Europe]
Croatia (Land and climate) Ci: 1148a *with map*
Dindsenchas [literary work]
Irish literature (Heroic tales, romances, and sagas) I: 430-431
Diné [people]
Navajo Indians N: 69
Dine, Jim [American artist] D: 204
Painting (Pop Art) P: 86
Diné College
Arizona (Universities and colleges) A: 674
Diner [film]
Levinson, Barry L: 219

Dinesen, Isak [Danish author] D: 205
Dingley, Nelson, Jr. [American political leader]
Maine (table) M: 87
Dingley Act [1897]
Gay Nineties (Industrial growth) G: 72
Dingo [dog] D: 205
Animal *picture on* A: 482
Australia (Introduced species) A: 913
Conservation (Australia) Ci: 989
Dinh [dynasty]
Vietnam (Independence) V: 370
Dinitrogen monoxide [gas] See Nitrous oxide *in this index*
Dinka [people] D: 205
Sudan, South (People) So: 955
Dinkins, David Norman [American political leader] D: 205
New York City (A time of change) N: 343
Dinner Party, The [sculpture by Chicago]
Chicago, Judy C: 437
Sculpture (As a record of history) S: 228-229 *with picture*; (From the mid-1900's to the early 2000's) S: 259-260
Dinner Table, The [painting by Matisse]
Matisse, Henri M: 310
Dinnerware
Ceramics (Kinds of ceramic products) C: 359
Dinoflagellate [biology] D: 205
Algae A: 349
Barracuda B: 118
Ocean *picture on* O: 656; (Phytoplankton) O: 655
Pfiesteria P: 353
Red tide R: 190
Dinoponera grandis [ant]
Ant *picture on* A: 520
Dinos Painter [Greek artist]
Painting (Mythology paintings) P: 34 *with picture*; (Greek painting) P: 42
Dinosaur [extinct animal] D: 206 *with pictures*
See also the list of Related articles in the Dinosaur article
Alberta (Interesting facts) A: 313
Cretaceous Period P: 1127
Earth (The Mesozoic Era) E: 27
Evolution (Contributions from other scientific fields) E: 433
Extinction (Mass extinction) E: 456
Fossil *picture on* F: 422; (Understanding ancient plants and animals) F: 423; (Recording Earth's changes) F: 424
Jurassic Period J: 201
Prehistoric animal *pictures on* P: 739; (Dinosaurs) P: 737; (The Age of Mammals) P: 740; (The study of prehistoric animals) P: 741
Reptile (The evolution of reptiles) R: 252
Triassic Period T: 439
Dinosaur National Monument [Colorado-Utah]
National Park System (table: National monuments) N: 50
Dinosaur Provincial Park [Alberta]
Alberta (Places to visit) A: 320
Dinosaurs, Age of See Mesozoic Era *in this index*
Dinsmoor, Samuel [American political leader]
New Hampshire (table) N: 223
Dinsmoor, Samuel, Jr. [American political leader]
New Hampshire (table) N: 223
Dinwiddie, Robert [British colonial official]
Washington, George (Messenger to the French) W: 93
Diocese [religion]
Archbishop A: 601
Bishop B: 381
Roman Catholic Church (Church organization) R: 404
Diocletian [Roman emperor] D: 214
Rome, Ancient (The decline of the empire) R: 447
Sebastian, Saint S: 277
Diocletian, Baths of [ruins]
Rome (Baths) R: 433
Diocletianus, Gaius Aurelius Valerius [Roman emperor] See Diocletian *in this index*
Diode [electronics]
Computer chip (Structure) Ci: 924e
Electronics (Diodes) E: 210 *with diagram*
Vacuum tube (Kinds of vacuum tubes) V: 258
Diode laser [physics]
Laser (Semiconductor lasers) L: 85 *with diagram*
Diodorus of Tyre [Phoenician philosopher]
Phoenicia (Decline) P: 395
Dioecious plant
Flower (Variations in flower structure) F: 294
Diogenes [Greek philosopher] D: 214
Cynic philosophy Ci: 1205
Diol [chemistry]
Glycol G: 237
Diola [people]
Senegal (People) S: 297

Diomed [horse]
Horse (table: Famous horses in history and legend) **H:** 361
Diomedes [Greek mythology]
Hercules (The twelve labors) **H:** 198-199
Dion, Céline [Canadian singer] **D:** 214 *with portrait*
Dion, Stéphane [Canadian political leader] **D:** 214 *with porrait*
Liberal Party of Canada **L:** 227
Dionaea [plant] *See* Venus's-flytrap *in this index*
Dione [satellite]
Satellite (The middle-sized icy satellites of Saturn and Uranus) **S:** 150c
Saturn (Satellites) **S:** 151-152
Dionysia [custom]
Drama (Greek drama) **D:** 326
Dionysian drive [philosophy]
Nietzsche, Friedrich (Classical scholarship) **N:** 406
Dionysius II [king of Syracuse]
Damocles **D:** 21
Dionysius, Saint [pope]
Pope (table) **P:** 666
Dionysius Exiguus [Greek scholar]
A.D. **A:** 31
B.C. **B:** 178
Calendar (Some calendars today) **C:** 29
Christian Era **C:** 522e
Dionysius the Elder [Greek military leader] **D:** 214
Dionysus [Greek mythology] **D:** 215
See also Bacchus *in this index*
Bacchus **B:** 15
Midas **M:** 521
Mythology (table) **M:** 981; (Greek divinities) **M:** 982
Dionysus, Theater of [ancient Greece] *See* Theater of Dionysus *in this index*
Diophantus [mathematician]
Algebra (History) **A:** 359
Diopside [gem]
Gem *picture on* **G:** 78
Dior, Christian [French fashion designer] **D:** 215
Dior, House of [fashion house]
Dior, Christian **D:** 215
Diorama [exhibit]
Daguerre, Louis Jacques Mandé **D:** 4
Dioscorus [antipope]
Pope (table) **P:** 666
Diospyros insculpta [tree]
Plant *picture on* **P:** 527
Dioxin [chemical] **D:** 215
Agent Orange **A:** 140
Air pollution (Burning of solid wastes) **A:** 198
Herbicide (Hazards of herbicides) **H:** 198
Incinerator **I:** 100
Dip [astronomy]
Horizon **H:** 335
Dip [mining]
Mining (Mining terms) **M:** 577
Dipavali [festival] *See* Diwali *in this index*
Dipendra [Nepalese prince]
Nepal (History) **N:** 126-127
Diphenhydramine [drug]
Antihistamine **A:** 556
Diphtheria [disease] **D:** 215
Croup **Ci:** 1157
Löffler, Friedrich August Johannes **L:** 420
Diphtheria toxoid
Diphtheria (Prevention) **D:** 216
Diphthong [language] **D:** 216
Dipivali [festival]
Feasts and festivals (In Hinduism) **F:** 58
Diplocaulus [animal]
Prehistoric animal *picture on* **P:** 738
Diplodocus [dinosaur] **D:** 216
Dinosaur **D:** 206; (True dinosaurs) **D:** 206b-209 *with picture*
Reptile *picture on* **R:** 251
Diploid cell [biology]
Reproduction (How genes are transferred) **R:** 242
Diploma
Degree, College **D:** 92
Graduation **G:** 297
Diplomacy D: 216
See also the list of Related articles in the Diplomacy *article*
Foreign policy **F:** 386
Foreign Service (Foreign Service careers) **F:** 388
Herald **H:** 194
International relations (Diplomacy) **I:** 344
Logan Act **L:** 423
Peace (Diplomacy) **P:** 207
Petroleum (Petroleum and diplomacy) **P:** 346
Diplomat [career] *See* Diplomacy *in this index*
Diplomatic asylum
Asylum **A:** 851
Diplomatic immunity
Citizenship (The duties of citizens) **Ci:** 569-570

Diplomacy (Diplomatic immunity) **D:** 217
Diplomatic Reception Room
White House *picture on* **W:** 288
Diplopod [zoology]
Arthropod **A:** 752 *with picture*
Diplura [entomology]
Insect (table) **I:** 299
Dipole [antenna]
Antenna (Types of antennas) **A:** 543 *with pictures*
Dipole [physics]
Magnetic equator **M:** 55
Magnetism (How magnetism works) **M:** 60b-60c *with diagrams*
Diponegoro, Pangeran [Javanese political leader]
Indonesia (The rise of nationalism) **I:** 237
Dipper [bird] **D:** 217 *with picture*
Dipper dredge
Dredging **D:** 345
Dipper gourd *See* Calabash *in this index*
Dippers, Big and Little [constellations] *See* Big and Little Dippers *in this index*
Dipping [industrial process]
Rubber (Shaping) **R:** 505
Dipping needle [device]
Magnetic equator **M:** 55
Dipping the flag
Flag (Raising and lowering the flag) **F:** 219
DiPrete, Edward D. [American political leader]
Rhode Island (table) **R:** 311
Diprotodont [animal]
Mammal (table) **M:** 128 *with picture*
Marsupial (Kinds of marsupials) **M:** 232
Diptera [entomology]
Fly **F:** 309
Insect *pictures on* **I:** 282; (table) **I:** 300 *with picture*
Dipterocarp [tree]
Rain forest (Asia) **R:** 126b
Dirac, Paul Adrien Maurice [British physicist]
Antimatter **A:** 556
Nobel Prizes (Physics: 1933) **N:** 440
Dirce [Greek mythology]
Farnese Bull **F:** 46
Dire Dawa [Ethiopia]
Ethiopia (Local government) **E:** 368
Direct Action Day [1946]
India (Independence and partition) **I:** 133
Pakistan (The nationalist movement) **P:** 99
Direct-broadcast satellite
Communications satellite **Ci:** 888a
Television (Satellite television) **T:** 110c; (Satellites) **T:** 123
Direct chill method [process]
Aluminum (Casting the molten aluminum) **A:** 394-395
Direct Communications Link *See* Hot line *in this index*
Direct current [electricity]
Electric current (Direct and alternating current) **E:** 168
Electric generator **E:** 170; (Direct-current generators) **E:** 173
Electric motor **E:** 179
Electricity (Direct and alternating current) **E:** 193
Electronics (Diodes) **E:** 210-212
Inductance **I:** 240
Tesla, Nikola (The alternating current system) **T:** 181
Vacuum tube (Kinds of vacuum tubes) **V:** 258-259
Direct current generator
Electric generator **E:** 170; (Direct-current generators) **E:** 173 *with diagrams*
Direct current motor
Electric motor **E:** 179; (DC motors) **E:** 181 *with picture*
Direct current tach generator [machine]
Governor **G:** 294
Direct democracy
Democracy **D:** 119
Government (Democracy) **G:** 285; (Ancient Greece) **G:** 289
Direct distance dialing
Telephone (Improvements in telephone technology) **T:** 100
Direct drive
Transmission *picture on* **T:** 377
Direct drive system
Phonograph (Parts of a phonograph) **P:** 400-401
Direct election
Voting **V:** 449
Direct evidence
Evidence (Kinds of evidence) **E:** 426
Forensic science (General kinds of evidence) **F:** 388b
Direct expression [industrial process]
Perfume (Plant substances) **P:** 286
Direct extrusion [industrial process]

Extrusion **E:** 459
Direct-fired furnace
Furnace (Sources of heat) **F:** 567
Direct initiative [political science]
Initiative and referendum (The initiative) **I:** 271-272
Direct-injection engine
Automobile (The fuel system) **A:** 953
Diesel engine (How a diesel engine works) **D:** 199
Direct investment
Investment (Kinds of investments) **I:** 366
Direct-mail advertising
Advertising (Direct mail) **A:** 74 *with picture*
Election campaign (Campaign financing) **E:** 160
Direct marketing
Livestock (Marketing livestock) **L:** 398
Mail-order business **M:** 66
Meat packing (Marketing livestock and meat) **M:** 350
Direct melt process
Fiberglass (How fiberglass is made) **F:** 89
Direct piezoelectric effect [physics]
Piezoelectricity **P:** 458
Direct-port fuel injection system *See* Multiport fuel injection system *in this index*
Direct primary [political science]
Primary election (Direct and indirect) **P:** 776
Direct-recording electronic system
Voting machine (Kinds of electoral voting machines) **V:** 450
Direct reduction system [industrial process]
Iron and steel (How iron is made) **I:** 439 *with diagram*
Direct reward [psychology]
Aggression **A:** 141
Direct sales
Sales (Other types of selling) **S:** 62
Direct sampling [science]
Astronomy (Direct sampling) **A:** 846
Direct seeding [horticulture]
Vegetable (Planting) **V:** 293
Direct tax
Taxation (Property taxes) **T:** 53
Direct-to-plate [process] *See* Computer-to-plate *in this index*
Direct-vision viewfinder
Photography (Compact cameras) **P:** 408
Directed verdict
Trial (Reaching a verdict) **T:** 436
Direction
Photography (Direction) **P:** 415
Directional drilling
Petroleum (Directional drilling) **P:** 339 *with diagrams*
Directional selection [biology]
Evolution (Natural selection) **E:** 428
Directivity [electronics]
Antenna **A:** 543
Directly reduced iron
Iron and steel (The direct reduction process) **I:** 441 *with diagram*
Director [device]
Antenna *picture on* **A:** 543
Director [occupation]
See also the list of Related articles in the Motion picture *and* Theater *articles*
Drama (Early realism) **D:** 338
Foundation **F:** 429
Motion picture *picture on* **M:** 850; (How motion pictures are made) **M:** 848; (table: Best achievement in directing) **M:** 862
Opera (The stage director) **O:** 794
Television (Planning and preparation) **T:** 110c
Theater **T:** 232; (The director) **T:** 235
Universities and colleges (Administration) **U:** 208
Director system [instrument]
Rangefinder **R:** 139
Directorate
Homeland Security, Department of (Organization) **H:** 301
Directors, Board of
Corporation (Business corporations) **Ci:** 1069-1070
Directory [computing]
Computer file **Ci:** 924g
Information retrieval (Research) **I:** 268-269
Directory [French history]
France (The French Revolution) **F:** 474
French Revolution (The revolution ends) **F:** 527
Napoleonic Wars (The Army of Italy) **N:** 18
Directory assistance
Telephone (Operator services) **T:** 98
Directrix [geometry]
Cylinder **Ci:** 1204
Parabola **P:** 141 *with diagram*
Dirigible [airship] *See* Airship *in this index*
Dirksen, Everett McKinley [American political

leader) D: 217
Ford, Gerald Rudolph (House minority leader)
F: 375 *with picture*
Dirksen and Hart Senate Office Buildings
[Washington, D.C.]
Washington, D.C. *map on* W: 76
Dirndl [clothing]
Austria (Way of life) A: 931
Dirty bomb
Terrorism (Nuclear attacks) T: 176
Dirty Hands [play by Sartre]
French literature (Existentialism) F: 523
Dirty war [Argentine history]
Argentina (The "dirty war") A: 658
Di Rupo, Elio [Belgian political leader]
Belgium B: 235
Dis Pater [Roman mythology]
Pluto P: 581
Disability D: 218 *with pictures*
See also the list of Related articles in the Disability
article
Americans with Disabilities Act A: 431
Bus (Bus regulations) B: 715
Child (Physical disabilities and challenges) C: 453
Civil rights (Major changes in the field of civil
rights) Ci: 609-610
Education (Special education) E: 88 *with picture;*
(Education for children with disabilities) E: 107
Interior design *picture on* I: 331
Keller, Helen K: 255
Library (Services for special groups) L: 241
Medicaid M: 361
Multiple sclerosis M: 920
Physical education (During the 1900's) P: 433
Physical therapy P: 435
Poverty (Social welfare programs) P: 725
Reading (Reading problems) R: 161
Special education So: 770
Vocational rehabilitation V: 435
Disability Discrimination Act [Australia, 1992]
Disability (The 1900's) D: 221-222
Disability Discrimination Act [United Kingdom,
1995]
Disability (The 1900's) D: 221-222
Disability income insurance
Insurance (Other types of health insurance)
I: 312; (Social insurance) I: 314
Social security (Social Security in the United
States) So: 553
Workers' compensation W: 405
Disability rights movement
Disability (The 1900's) D: 221 *with picture*
Disability Services Act [Australia, 1986]
Disability (The 1900's) D: 221-222
Disability studies
Disability (Recent developments) D: 222
Disability Supports for Employment Fund
Vancouver Foundation V: 278
Disabled See Disability *in this index*
Disabled American Veterans [organization]
D: 223
Veterans' organizations (In the United States)
V: 344-345
Disaccharide [chemistry]
Carbohydrate (Kinds of carbohydrates)
C: 203 *with diagram;* (How the body uses
carbohydrates) C: 204
Saccharides S: 4
Disadvantaged group [sociology]
Minority group M: 608
DiSalle, Michael V. [American political leader]
Ohio (table) O: 699
Disallowance [law]
Colonial life in America (Colonial government)
Ci: 795
Disarmament See Arms control *in this index*
Disarmament, Committee on [UN]
United Nations (Arms control) U: 92
Disaster D: 223
Civil defense Ci: 605
Earthquake (table: Largest earthquakes) E: 38
Federal Emergency Management Agency F: 63
Flood (Flood) F: 236 *with pictures*
Hurricane (table) H: 455
Insurance (Insurance today) I: 316
Disaster area
Civil defense (Recovery) Ci: 605
Disaster relief
Army (Internal security and civilian aid) A: 725
CARE C: 213
Civil defense Ci: 605
National Guard N: 37
Public health (Supplying disaster services) P: 857
Red Cross (The American Red Cross) R: 185; (The
Canadian Red Cross) R: 186
United Nations (Disaster relief) U: 89
Disaster services See Civil defense *in this index*

Disasters of War, The [prints by Goya]
Goya, Francisco G: 295
Disc [electronic device] See Compact disc;
Computer storage disk; Hard disk; Videodisc *in
this index*
Disc brake
Automobile (The brake system) A: 950
Brake (Hydraulic brakes) B: 560-561 *with diagram*
Disc jockey [career]
Hip-hop H: 238
Radio *picture on* R: 83; (Entertainment) R: 85
Rap music R: 141
Disc player [machine]
Laser (Recording, storing, and transmitting
information) L: 82
Discalced Carmelites [religious group]
Religious life (Religious life in the 1500's and
1600's) R: 227
Discépolo, Enrique Santos [Argentine composer]
Argentina (The arts) A: 651
Discharge [economics]
Bankruptcy (Features of bankruptcy) B: 97
Discharge, Military
Military discharge M: 543
Disciple [religion]
Apostles A: 566
Disciples of Christ [religious group] D: 223
Disciplinae [book by Varro]
Encyclopedia (The first reference works) E: 268a
Discipline [education]
Curriculum (Curriculum content) Ci: 1197
Disclosing tablet [dental hygiene]
Teeth (Cleaning the teeth) T: 81-82
Discman [device]
Portable media player P: 681
Disco music D: 223
Popular music (New forms of rock) P: 671
Rock music (Disco) R: 380c
Discoid lupus erythematosus [disease]
Lupus L: 526
Discontinuous permafrost
Permafrost P: 289 *with map*
Discothèque [dance club]
Disco music D: 224
Discount [economics]
Installment plan I: 304
Rebate R: 173
Discount interest [economics]
Interest (Discount interest) I: 322
Discount market
Clothing (Marketing categories of fashion)
Ci: 705
Discount rate [economics]
Federal Reserve System (The discount rate) F: 66
Interest (The discount rate) I: 323
Discount store D: 224
Retailing (Discount stores) R: 265
Discounting [economics]
Cost-benefit analysis Ci: 1079
Discours [poems by Ronsard]
Ronsard, Pierre de R: 450b
Discourse on Method [book by Descartes]
Descartes, René D: 154
French literature (Classical prose) F: 520
**"Discourse on the Origin and Foundations of
Inequality"**
Rousseau, Jean-Jacques (His ideas) R: 493
"Discourse on the Sciences and the Arts"
Rousseau, Jean-Jacques (Early life) R: 492
Discourse on Two New Sciences [book by Galileo]
Galileo (Galileo and the Roman Catholic Church)
G: 12
Discourse on Woman [book by Mott]
Mott, Lucretia Coffin M: 880
Discourses [essays by Reynolds]
Reynolds, Sir Joshua R: 289
Discourses on Davila [book by Adams]
Adams, John (Vice president) A: 37
Discovery
Exploration E: 439
Discovery [law]
Court (How civil courts work) Ci: 1102
Discovery [program]
Camp Fire USA (Small group programs) C: 88
Discovery [ship]
Cook, James (Final voyage) Ci: 1026
Hudson, Henry (North American voyages)
H: 404-405
Jamestown J: 28
Discovery [space shuttle]
Bondar, Roberta B: 455
Glenn, John Herschel, Jr. (Later career) G: 227
International Space Station (History) I: 346b
Space exploration (Back into space) So: 725; (The
Columbia disaster) So: 725-726
Discovery degree
FFA (Degrees) F: 85

Discovery Encyclopedia
Encyclopedia (Today's encyclopedias) E: 268b-
269
Discovery Institute
Intelligent design I: 321
Discovery of the Mississippi [painting by Powell]
De Soto, Hernando *picture on* D: 161
Discovery space
Shakespeare, William (The stage) S: 351-352
with picture
Discreet Charm of the Bourgeoisie, The [film]
Buñuel, Luis B: 700
Discreet function [mathematics]
Algebra (Functions) A: 356-357
Discrete transistor [electronics]
Transistor T: 372
Discretionary income
Income (Disposable and discretionary income)
I: 100
Discrimination [psychology]
Perception (Types of perception) P: 283
Discrimination [sociology]
See also Ageism; Sex discrimination *in this index*
AIDS (Discrimination) A: 166
Americans with Disabilities Act A: 431
Bermuda (History) B: 268-269
City (The people) Ci: 589-590
Civil rights (Protecting the rights of minorities)
Ci: 609
Civil Rights Act of 1964 Ci: 611
Disability (Employment) D: 221; (The 1900's)
D: 221-222
Equal Employment Opportunity Commission
E: 345
Gray Panthers G: 335
Hispanic Americans (Immigration restrictions and
growing discrimination) H: 252; (Education
and employment) H: 256-257
Homosexuality (Attitudes toward homosexuality)
H: 307
Housing (Housing since 1900) H: 391-392
India (Social structure) I: 116
Latin America (Attitudes toward race) L: 94
Lévesque, René L: 218
March on Washington M: 196
Minority group M: 608
Open housing O: 789
Poverty (Social factors) P: 723
Segregation S: 284
Racial discrimination
Affirmative action A: 91
African Americans (The growth of
discrimination) A: 136k; (During the
early 1900's) A: 136lj; (The civil rights
movement) A: 136o; (Housing and lending
discrimination) A: 136s
Apartheid A: 563
Asian Americans (History of Asian immigration)
A: 812d
Civil rights (The struggle for the rights of
African Americans) Ci: 609; (Civil rights in
other countries) Ci: 610
Ghetto (Ghettos today) G: 181
Hispanic Americans (Who Hispanic Americans
are) H: 245; (Immigration restrictions and
growing discrimination) H: 252
Oriental Exclusion Acts O: 855
Prejudice P: 754b
Races, Human R: 53; (Race and discrimination)
R: 59
Slavery (Effects of slavery) S: 503-504
United States, History of the (Poverty and
discrimination) U: 195
Religious discrimination
Freedom of religion F: 505
Inquisition I: 277
Northern Ireland (The Troubles) N: 525
Discus fish
Fish *picture on* F: 157
Discus throw [sport] D: 224 *with pictures*
Track and field (Throwing events) T: 358 *with
picture*
Discus Thrower, The [statue]
Europe *picture on* E: 391
Discussion
Debate D: 63
Discussion group
Universities and colleges (Instruction) U: 209
Discussion show [television] See Talk show *in this
index*
Disease D: 225 *with pictures*
See also the list of Related articles in the Disease
article
Bacteria (Harmful bacteria) B: 20
Disability D: 218
Dog (Medical care) D: 279
Drug (Drugs that fight infection) D: 351; (Drugs

that prevent infectious diseases) **D:** 351
Enzyme (Structure) **E:** 341; (Uses) **E:** 341
Famine (Effects of famine) **F:** 26a
Fever **F:** 83
Fungal disease **F:** 558
Genetic testing **G:** 84d
Insect (Harmful insects) **I:** 284
Microbiology (Fields of microbiology) **M:** 513
Mosquito (Mosquitoes and people) **M:** 834
Pet (Preventing illness) **P:** 322
Public health **P:** 856
Virus (Disease) **V:** 428
Animal diseases
  Balance of nature (Disease and parasites) **B:** 35
  Livestock (Prevention of disease) **L:** 397
  Veterinary medicine **V:** 345
Diseases in human beings
  Animal (Animals and people) **A:** 471-472
  Blood (Protecting against disease) **B:** 410
  Brain (Infectious diseases) **B:** 558
  Circulatory system (Disorders of the circulatory
    system) **C:** 561
  City (Description) **Ci:** 578, **Ci:** 585-587
  Deafness (Causes of hearing loss) **D:** 57
  Epidemic **E:** 343
  Eye (Diseases of the eye) **E:** 466
  Health (Medical and dental care) **H:** 126
  Heredity (Hereditary disorders) **H:** 204
  Inoculation **I:** 276
  Nervous system (Disorders of the nervous
    system) **N:** 136
  Nutrition (Nutrition and disease) **N:** 630
  Palliative care **P:** 108
  Parasite (Effects) **P:** 153
  Quarantine **Q:** 7
  Races, Human (Susceptibility to genetic
    diseases) **R:** 58
History
  Colonial life in America (Health and medicine)
    Ci: 809
  Columbus, Christopher (Columbus's impact on
    history) **Ci:** 864
  Jenner, Edward **J:** 91
  Koch, Robert **K:** 360
  Pioneer life in America (Health) **P:** 483
Plant diseases. See Plant disease *in this index*
Research
  Bacteriology (Controlling bacterial diseases)
    B: 22
  Gnotobiotics **G:** 239
  Pathology **P:** 196
Disease Control and Prevention, Centers for
[U.S.] *See* Centers for Disease Control and
Prevention *in this index*
Disgrace [book by Coetzee]
  Coetzee, J. M. **Ci:** 753
Disguise
  Mask **M:** 263 *with pictures*
Disguised symbolism [art]
  Campin, Robert **C:** 91
  Van Eyck, Jan **V:** 282
Disgust [emotion]
  Emotion (The basic emotion approach) **E:** 261
Dish [electronics]
  Antenna (Types of antennas) **A:** 543 *with picture*
  Radio wave **R:** 97
  Telescope (Radio and microwave telescopes)
    T: 106
  Television (Satellites) **T:** 123; (Receiving television
    signals) **T:** 124
Dish [pottery]
  Stoneware **So:** 912
Dish [solar heating]
  Solar energy (Parabolic dish systems) **So:** 579
Dishcloth gourd [plant]
  Gourd **G:** 281 *with picture*
Dishonorable discharge
  Military discharge **M:** 543
Disinfectant D: 235
  Bacteria (Protection against harmful bacteria)
    B: 20
  Deodorizer **D:** 148
  Hypochlorous acid **H:** 480
  Ultraviolet rays (Uses of ultraviolet rays) **U:** 17
  Water (Purifying and treating water) **W:** 126
Disinflation [economics]
  Recession (Recession and inflation) **R:** 175
Disinformation
  Central Intelligence Agency (Functions) **C:** 356-
    357
Disjoint set [mathematics]
  Set theory (Kinds of sets) **S:** 321 *with diagram*
Disk [anatomy] *See* Intervertebral disk *in this index*
Disk [blood]
  See also Platelet *in this index*
  Osler, Sir William **O:** 863
Disk [electronic device] *See* Compact disc;

Computer storage disk; Hard disk; Videodisc *in
this index*
Disk and wheel [device]
  Transmission (How a continuously variable
    transmission works) **T:** 378
Disk brake *See* Disc brake *in this index*
Disk drive [electronic device]
  Computer (Storage devices) **Ci:** 915
Disk flower [botany]
  Composite family **Ci:** 904
Disk harrow [tool]
  Harrow **H:** 77
Disk herniation [disorder]
  Back **B:** 17
  Spine **So:** 793
Disk jellyfish [sea animal]
  Animal *picture on* **A:** 486
Disk plow
  Plow (Other types of plow bottoms) **P:** 576 *with
    picture*
Disk-tumbler lock
  Lock (Mechanical locks) **L:** 411
Dislocation [injury] **D:** 235
  First aid (Fractures and dislocations) **F:** 140
  Hip **H:** 238
  Joint **J:** 155
Dismal Swamp [region, North Carolina-Virginia]
  D: 235 *with picture*
  Peat **P:** 225
Dismal Swamp Canal [waterway, North Carolina-
  Virginia]
  Atlantic Intracoastal Waterway **A:** 863
Dismount
  Gymnastics (The horizontal bar) **G:** 449
Disney, Walt [American producer] **D:** 235 *with
  pictures*
  Animation (Walt Disney) **A:** 514b *with picture*
  United States *picture on* **U:** 118
  Walt Disney Company **W:** 20
Disney Music Group
  Walt Disney Company **W:** 21
Disney World Resort *See* Walt Disney World Resort
  in this index
Disneyland [painting by Lindner]
  Lindner, Richard *picture on* **L:** 332
  Painting (Mass) **P:** 35
Disneyland Park [Anaheim, California]
  Amusement park **A:** 446
  California (Places to visit) **C:** 46 *with picture*
  Disney, Walt (TV and theme park ventures)
    D: 237 *with picture*
  Walt Disney Company **W:** 20
Disneyland Resort [Anaheim]
  Walt Disney Company **W:** 20
Disneyland Resort Paris
  Walt Disney Company **W:** 21
Disney's California Adventure [park]
  California (Places to visit) **C:** 46
  Walt Disney Company **W:** 21
Disney's Hollywood Studios
  Walt Disney Company **W:** 21
Disorderly conduct [crime]
  Breach of the peace **B:** 587
  Crime (table) **Ci:** 1137
Dispatch and communication center
  Fire department (Fire department equipment
    and resources) **F:** 125
Dispatch office
  Airport (The passenger terminal) **A:** 244
Dispatcher [occupation]
  Fire department (Dispatch and communication
    centers) **F:** 125
Dispersant [chemical]
  Oil spill (Responses) **O:** 707
Dispersion [chemistry]
  Colloid **Ci:** 777
  Emulsion **E:** 264
Dispersion [optics]
  Gem (Index of refraction) **G:** 77
  Light (Dispersion) **L:** 288-290
Dispersive wave
  Waves (How waves move) **W:** 152
Displaced person
  Holocaust (After the Holocaust) **H:** 296b
  Immigration **I:** 80
  Refugee **R:** 203
  Stolen Generation **So:** 907
  World War II (Displaced persons) **W:** 497
Displacement [engineering]
  Aircraft carrier (The United States carrier fleet)
    A: 206
Displacement [physics]
  Vacuum (Producing a vacuum) **V:** 256
Displacement behavior D: 237
  Personality (Freud's psychoanalytic theory) **P:** 302
Displacement hull
  Motorboat racing (Hull designs) **M:** 876 *with*

picture
Displacement tonnage [engineering]
  Ship (Nautical measurements) **S:** 406
Displacer piston
  Stirling engine **So:** 902 *with diagrams*
Display
  Radar **R:** 64 *with picture;* (The display) **R:** 71 *with
    diagram*
  Telephone (The display) **T:** 95
Display ad
  Newspaper (Preparing advertisements) **N:** 383
Display calculator
  Calculator **C:** 22 *with picture*
Display device [electronics]
  See also Monitor *in this index*
  Television (Display devices) **T:** 125 *with diagram*
Disposable camera *See* Single-use camera *in this
  index*
Disposable contact lens
  Contact lens (Soft contact lenses) **Ci:** 1020
Disposable diaper
  Baby (Clothing the baby) **B:** 10
Disposable income
  Income (Disposable and discretionary income)
    I: 100
Disposable nonwoven [textile]
  Textile (Nonwovens) **T:** 215
Disposal, Garbage [machine]
  Garbage disposal **G:** 28
Disposal, Waste *See* Waste disposal *in this index*
Disputed question [philosophy]
  Scholasticism (The Scholastic method) **S:** 179
Disqualification [boxing]
  Boxing (A disqualification) **B:** 528
Disquisitiones Arithmeticae [book by Gauss]
  Number theory **N:** 607
Disraeli, Benjamin [British political leader] **D:** 237
  with portrait
  Conservative Party **Ci:** 992
  Gladstone, William Ewart (Gladstone's first term
    as prime minister) **G:** 206
  United Kingdom (Gladstone and Disraeli) **U:** 69
Disraeli: A Picture of the Victorian Age [book by
  Maurois]
  Maurois, André **M:** 317
Disruptive coloration [zoology]
  Protective coloration **P:** 831
Dissected Till Plains
  Missouri (Land regions) **M:** 662; (Natural
    resources) **M:** 665
Dissection [biology]
  Anatomy **A:** 448b
  Medicine (The Renaissance) **M:** 373
Dissent *See* Civil disobedience; Social protest *in
  this index*
Dissenting opinion
  Supreme Court of the United States (Written
    opinions) **So:** 999
Dissertation [education]
  Degree, College (The doctor's degree) **D:** 93
Dissipation [physics]
  Acoustics **A:** 29
Dissociation [chemistry]
  Acid (The strength of an acid) **A:** 27
  Base **B:** 123
Dissociative disorder [psychology]
  Hypnosis (Hypnotic penomena) **H:** 478;
    (Enhancing memory) **H:** 479
  Mental illness (Dissociative disorders) **M:** 406
Dissolve [photography]
  Television (Adding special effects) **T:** 112
Dissonance
  Classical music (The 1900's) **Ci:** 649
  Harmony **H:** 63
  Music (Harmony) **M:** 951-952
Distal muscular dystrophy [disease]
  Muscular dystrophy (Other muscular dystrophies)
    M: 937
Distance
  Astronomy (Units of distance) **A:** 837
  Calculus (Differential calculus) **C:** 22
  Metric system (The metric system at a glance)
    M: 438 *with pictures*
  Weights and measures (table: Length and
    distance) **M:** 185
  Work **W:** 404
Distance education *See* Distance learning *in this
  index*
Distance learning [education] **D:** 238
  Adult education (Distance learning) **A:** 69
  Audio-visual materials (Other computerized
    tools) **A:** 883-884
  Careers (Distance learning programs) **C:** 217
  Correspondence school **Ci:** 1071
Distemper [disease] **D:** 238
  Cat (Veterinary care) **C:** 295
Distillate

Distillation **D: 238**
Distillate oil
  Fuel (Petroleum) **F: 550**
  Petroleum (Petroleum as a fuel) **P: 332**
Distillation [chemistry] **D: 238** with diagrams
  Alcoholic beverage **A: 336**
  Corn (The fermentation and distilling industry)
    Ci: 1062
  Evaporation (Uses of evaporation) **E: 423**
  Perfume (Plant substances) **P: 286**
  Petroleum (Separation) **P: 343**
  Water (Distillation) **W: 127**
Distilled alcoholic vinegar
  Vinegar (Kinds of vinegar) **V: 387**
Distilled beverage See Distilling in this index
Distilled water
  Distillation **D: 238**
  Water (Distillation) **W: 127**
Distilling [manufacturing] **D: 239**
  Alcoholic beverage **A: 336**
  Corn (The fermentation and distilling industry)
    Ci: 1062
  Distillation (Simple distillation) **D: 238-239**
  Whiskey **W: 282**
Distinct evolutionary lineage [biology]
  Evolution (Evolution of new species) **E: 429**
Distinguished Flying Cross
  Earhart, Amelia **E: 14**
  Medals, decorations, and orders (table) **M: 357**
    with picture
Distinguished Military Graduate [education]
  Reserve Officers Training Corps (Army ROTC)
    R: 258; (Air Force ROTC) **R: 258**
Distinguished Service Cross
  Medals, decorations, and orders (table) **M: 357**
    with pictures
Distinguished Service Medal
  Medals, decorations, and orders (Civilian awards)
    M: 355-357; (table) **M: 357** with pictures
Distortion
  Aberration **A: 10**
  Map **M: 176**; (Map projections) **M: 180, M: 182**
    with diagrams
Distractibility [disorder]
  Learning disabilities (Types) **L: 165**
Distress signal
  Flag (Raising and lowering the flag) **F: 219**
  Signaling (Distress signals) **S: 455**
Distribution [economics]
  Economics **E: 58**
  Manufacturing (Distribution and sales) **M: 171**
  Marketing (Distribution) **M: 214**
Distribution [physics]
  Lighting (Quantity of light) **L: 297**
Distribution line
  Gas [fuel] (Transmitting and distributing gas)
    G: 55
Distribution of wealth [economics]
  Capitalism (Equalizing the distribution of wealth)
    C: 195
  Economics (Distribution of income) **E: 63**
  Income (Income inequality) **I: 101** with diagram
Distribution substation
  Electric power picture on **E: 182**; (Distribution)
    E: 185 with diagram
Distribution transformer
  Electric power (Distribution) **E: 185** with diagram
Distributive industry
  Industry (By stage of production) **I: 256-257**
Distributive Law of Multiplication over Addition
  Algebra (Basic algebra) **A: 354**
Distributor [business]
  Motion picture (Distribution) **M: 860**
Distributor [mechanism]
  Gasoline engine (The ignition system) **G: 65**
  Ignition (The conventional electronic ignition
    system) **I: 49**
District [elections]
  Voting (Voting districts) **V: 449**
District attorney **D: 240**
District court [law] **D: 240**
  Court (Federal courts) **Ci: 1102**
  Supreme Court of the United States (Authority of
    the Supreme Court) **So: 998-999**
  United States, Government of the (Lower court
    system) **U: 144**
District fair
  Fair (Agricultural fairs) **F: 7**
District of Columbia [books by Dos Passos]
  Dos Passos, John **D: 311**
District of Columbia [district, U.S.] **D: 240**
  Electoral College **E: 161**
  Flag picture on **F: 213**
  Washington, D.C. **W: 70**; (History) **W: 85-86**
Districting
  Apportionment **A: 574**
Disulfiram [drug] **D: 240**

  Alcoholism (Treatment) **A: 338**
  Drug abuse (Treatment of substance use
    disorders) **D: 364**
Dit [telegraphy]
  Morse code **M: 819**
Ditch
  Drainage (Surface drainage) **D: 320** with diagram
Ditko, Steve [American cartoonist]
  Lee, Stan **L: 180**
  Spider-Man **So: 791**
Diuretic [medication] **D: 240**
  Blood presssure **B: 510**
  Drug (Other kinds of drugs) **D: 352**
  Edema **E: 75**
Diurnal libration [astronomy]
  Moon (Libration) **M: 785** with diagram
Diurnal tide
  Tide (The equilibrium tide) **T: 280-282**
Diurnal torpidity [zoology]
  Hibernation (Other kinds of dormancy) **H: 222**
Divali [festival] See Diwali in this index
Divan [poem by Hafiz]
  Iran (The arts) **I: 402**
Dive [maneuver]
  Submarine (Diving) **So: 941**
Dive [water sport]
  Diving **D: 242** with pictures
Diver [bird] See Loon in this index
Divergence [mathematics]
  Series (Working with infinite series) **S: 317**
Divergence [physics]
  Laser (Characteristics of laser light) **L: 84**
Divergent boundary [geology]
  Earthquake (Interplate quakes) **E: 38**
  Plate tectonics (Plate interactions) **P: 561**
  Volcano (Where volcanoes form) **V: 441**
Diverging lens [optics]
  Lens (Creating an image) **L: 196**
Diversified farming
  Farm and farming (Mixed farms) **F: 32**
Diversified occupation
  Cooperative education **Ci: 1037**
Diversifying selection [biology]
  Evolution (Balancing or diversifying) **E: 429**
Diversion [law]
  Road (How roads and highways are paid for)
    R: 360
Diverticulitis [disease] **D: 240** with diagrams
  Colostomy **Ci: 850**
  Fiber, Dietary **F: 88**
Diverticulosis [disorder]
  Diverticulitis **D: 240**
  Fiber, Dietary **F: 88**
Diverticulum [anatomy]
  Diverticulitis **D: 240** with picture
"Diverting History of John Gilpin, The" [poem
  by Cowper]
  Literature for children (The rise of illustration)
    L: 364
Divertissement
  Ballet (table) **B: 45**; (Kinds of ballet) **B: 48**
Divestiture [economics]
  Nationalization **N: 63**
Divide [geology] **D: 241** with diagram
  River (Divides) **R: 353** with picture
  Valley **V: 265**
Divide-down [game]
  Division (Fun with division) **D: 252**
Divided government
  United States, Government of the (How effective
    is the government?) **U: 146**
Divided highway
  Road (Primary highways) **R: 358**
Dividend [economics]
  Bankruptcy (Features of bankruptcy) **B: 97**
  Economics (Distribution of income) **E: 63**
  Industry (Working capital) **I: 258**
  Insurance (Dividends) **I: 310**
  Investment (table) **I: 366**; (Stocks) **I: 368**
  Stock (Stockholders) **So: 903**
Dividend [mathematics]
  Arithmetic (Division) **A: 668**
  Division (Writing division) **D: 248**
Divider [instrument] **D: 241**
Divination [magic] **D: 241**
  Druids **D: 367**
  Inca (Religion) **I: 96-97**
  Magic (Magical actions) **M: 49**
  Rome, Ancient (Religion) **R: 441**
Divine, Father [American religious leader] **D: 241**
  with portrait
Divine Comedies [book by Merrill]
  Merrill, James **M: 419**
Divine Comedy [poem by Dante] **D: 242**
  Allegory **A: 371**
  Ciardi, John **Ci: 551**
  Dante Alighieri **D: 33**

  Italian literature (The Middle Ages) **I: 494**
  Italy (Literature) **I: 504**
  Longfellow, Henry Wadsworth (Translations, lyric
    poems and dramatic poems) **L: 451**
  Michelangelo (The Last Judgment) **M: 486**
  Poetry (Medieval poetry) **P: 596**
  Virgil (His influence) **V: 392**
Divine Liturgy [religion]
  Eastern Orthodox Churches (Services) **E: 46**
  Mass **M: 269**
Divine Office [religion]
  Benedictines **B: 248**
  Bible (The Bible in worship) **B: 286**
  Eastern Orthodox Churches (Services) **E: 46**
Divine proportion See Golden section in this index
Divine right of kings **D: 242**
  Absolutism **A: 17**
  Charles I [of England] **C: 380**
  England (The first Stuarts) **E: 308**
  French Revolution (Background) **F: 524-525**
  Government (Monarchy) **G: 286**; (Sovereignty)
    G: 288-289
  King **K: 319**
  Petition of Right **P: 327**
Diving [biology]
  Dolphin (Swimming and diving) **D: 299**
  Whale (Respiratory system) **W: 259-260**
Diving [sport] **D: 242** with pictures
  Olympic Games (Summer Olympic Games)
    O: 746e-747
Diving, Underwater **D: 245** with pictures
  Archaeology (Working underwater) **A: 597** with
    picture
  Helium picture on **H: 176**
  Hyperbaric oxygen therapy **H: 476**
  Skin diving **S: 492** with pictures
Diving beetle [insect]
  Beetle picture on **B: 218**; (Predacious diving
    beetles) **B: 217**
  Water beetle **W: 133**
Diving bell [diving vessel]
  Diving, Underwater (History) **D: 247** with picture
Diving mask
  Diving, Underwater (Ambient diving) **D: 245**
Diving plane
  Submarine **So: 939**; (Diving) **So: 941**
Diving suit
  Diving, Underwater (Ambient diving) **D: 245** with
    picture; (History) **D: 247**
  Helium picture on **H: 176**
Divining rod [magic]
  Hazel **H: 123**
Divinity school See Seminary in this index
"Divinity School Address" [speech by Emerson]
  Emerson, Ralph Waldo (His prose works) **E: 259**
  Unitarians (History) **U: 42**
Divino Afflante Spiritu [encyclical]
  Pius XII **P: 503**
Divinsky, Nathan J. [Canadian scholar]
  Campbell, Kim (Education and entry into political
    life) **C: 90c**
Division [astronomy]
  Planetary ring **P: 514d**
Division [biology]
  Classification, Scientific (Groups in classification)
    Ci: 655
Division [mathematics] **D: 248** with pictures
  Algebra (Division) **A: 355**
  Algorithm **A: 366**
  Arithmetic (Division) **A: 668** with picture;
    (Arithmetic of small fractions) **A: 668**;
    (Arithmetic of negative numbers) **A: 668-669**
  Decimal system (Division) **D: 72** with diagrams
  Fraction **F: 444**; (Equivalent fractions) **F: 446** with
    diagram; (Division) **F: 448**
  Logarithms (Division) **L: 424**
Division [military] **D: 247**
  Air force (The organization of air forces) **A: 183**
  Army, United States (table) **A: 737**
  Brigade **B: 608**
  Infantry (Divisions) **I: 264**
  Navy (The organization of navies) **N: 77**
Division of Chemistry [bureau]
  Food and Drug Administration **F: 340**
Division of church and state See Church and state
  in this index
Division of information services
  Library (Special libraries) **L: 250**
Division of labor
  Factory (Kinds of factories) **F: 5**
  Industrial Revolution diagram on **I: 248**
  Mass production **M: 269**
  Smith, Adam **S: 515**
  Technology (Agriculture and civilization) **T: 74**
  United States, History of the (Improved
    production methods) **U: 180**
  Women's movement (Origins of women's

traditional roles) W: 383
Division of Labor [book by Durkheim]
Durkheim, Émile D: 389
Division of the house
Debate (Adjudication) D: 64
Divisionism [art]
Painting (Postimpressionism) P: 75-76 *with picture*
Divisor [mathematics]
Division (Writing division) D: 248
Divorce [law] D: 253
Abandonment A: 4
Alimony A: 369
Annulment A: 518
Child (Problems in the home) C: 453
Desertion D: 157
Eastern Orthodox Churches (Marriage) E: 47
Family (Development of the family) F: 21-22; (Challenges and opportunities) F: 24
Marriage (Laws concerning marriage) M: 219-220
Nevada (Legal gambling and easy divorce) N: 176
Vital statistics (Collecting and publishing vital statistics) V: 429-430
Diwali [festival] D: 255
Feasts and festivals (In Hinduism) F: 58
India (Hinduism) I: 116
Dix, Dorothea Lynde [American social reformer] D: 255
Civil War, American (Hospitals) Ci: 630
Mental illness (Humane treatment) M: 408
Dix, John Adams [American political leader]
Buchanan, James (table) B: 661
New York (table) N: 313
Dix, John Alden [American political leader]
New York (table) N: 313
Dix, Otto [German artist]
Beckmann, Max B: 197
Dixie [nickname, southern U.S.] D: 255
"Dixie" [song] D: 255
Emmett, Daniel Decatur E: 260
Dixie Highway [U.S.] D: 255
Dixie Mountaineers [musical group]
Country music *picture on* Ci: 1098
Dixiecrat Party [U.S. history] D: 256
Democratic Party (The Fair Deal) D: 126-127
Thurmond, Strom T: 273
Dixieland [region] *See Dixie in this index*
Dixieland jazz
Jazz (Early jazz) J: 70
Dixon, Frank M. [American political leader]
Alabama (table) A: 274
Dixon, George [British explorer]
Queen Charlotte Islands Q: 39
Dixon, Jeremiah [British astronomer]
Mason-Dixon Line M: 266
Dixon, Joseph M. [American political leader]
Montana (table) M: 757
Dixon, Scott [New Zealand race driver]
Automobile racing (table: Indianapolis 500 winners) A: 980
Dixon, Sharon Pratt [American political leader] *See* Kelly, Sharon Pratt *in this index*
Dixon, Sheila [American political leader]
Baltimore (The early 2000's) B: 70
Dizaine [literature]
French literature (Lyon) F: 520
Dizygotic twins *See Fraternal twins in this index*
Dizziness [disorder] D: 256
Djakarta [Indonesia] *See Jakarta in this index*
Djénné [Mali] D: 256
Mali *picture on* M: 107
Djerma-Songhai [people]
Niger (People) N: 407
Djibouti [country] D: 256 *with picture and map*
Flag *picture on* F: 198
Djibouti [city] D: 257
Djibouti D: 256 *with picture*
Djugashvili, Iosif Vissarionovich [birth name of]
Stalin, Joseph (Early life) So: 825
Djukanovic, Milo [Montenegran political leader]
Montenegro (History) M: 763-764
DLP projector *See* Digital light processing projector *in this index*
Dmanisi [site]
Homo erectus H: 306
Prehistoric people (Migration from Africa) P: 747 *with picture*; (table) P: 754
D.M.D [degree] *See* Dental Medicine, Doctor of *in this index*
DME [instrument]
Airplane (Electronic navigation) A: 227
Dmitriy [Russian nobleman]
Russia (The rise of Moscow) R: 548; (The Time of Troubles) R: 549
Dmowski, Roman [Polish political leader]
Poland (The struggle against foreign rule) P: 612
DMSO [drug] D: 257

DMT [drug]
Hallucinogenic drug H: 26
DNA [genetics] D: 258
Antiviral drug A: 560
Bacteria (The structure of bacteria) B: 20; (How bacteria reproduce) B: 21
Biochemistry (Biochemical research) B: 310
Biology (The growth of modern biology) B: 319-320
Botany (Later developments) B: 509
Cancer (How damaged genes cause cancer) C: 169
Cell C: 326; (The nucleus) C: 328; (Producing proteins) C: 333-334 *with diagrams*; (DNA—the wondrous molecule) C: 334 *with diagrams*; (The 1900's) C: 337-338 *with picture*; (The future) C: 339
Cloning Ci: 682l
Crick, Francis Harry Compton Ci: 1130
DNA fingerprinting D: 258
Evolution (Mutation) E: 427; (Contributions from other scientific fields) E: 433
Franklin, Rosalind Elsie F: 492
Gene G: 81
Gene mapping G: 81
Genetic engineering (How genes are reintroduced into cells) G: 84b *with diagrams*
Genetic testing (How genes carry information) G: 84d
Genomics G: 90
Heredity H: 200; (The flow of genetic information) H: 205 *with picture*; (The chemistry of genes) H: 208; (The era of genetic engineering) H: 209
Human body (Chemical elements and molecules) H: 417
Human Genome Project (The structure and importance of genomes) H: 427
Jefferson, Thomas (Jefferson and Sally Hemings) J: 79
Life (Nucleic acids) L: 278; (The puzzle of replication) L: 279
Mitochondria M: 679
Molecular biology (The beginning of molecular biology) M: 691-692
Mutation M: 968
Prehistoric people (The single origin theory) P: 750-751; (Analysis of the genetic materials) P: 754b
Protein (How the body uses proteins) P: 832
Races, Human (Mutation) R: 58
Reproduction (How genes are transferred) R: 242
Retrovirus R: 266
Rhesus monkey R: 291
RNA R: 357
Time (Changes in living things) T: 292
Virus (Structure) V: 427
Vitamin (Vitamin B_{12}, folic acid, and choline) V: 432
Watson, James Dewey W: 147
DNA analysis *See* DNA fingerprinting *in this index*
DNA fingerprinting [criminology] D: 258
Fingerprinting F: 106
Forensic science (Class and individual evidence) F: 388b-389
DNA typing *See* DNA fingerprinting *in this index*
DNase [drug]
Cystic fibrosis Ci: 1208
D'Nealian handwriting
Handwriting (Handwriting systems) H: 48 *with picture*
Dnepr River *See* Dnieper River *in this index*
Dneproges Dam [Ukraine]
Dnieper River D: 259
Dnieper-Prypyat Lowland
Ukraine (The land) U: 9 *with map*
Dnieper River [Europe] D: 258
Ukraine *picture on* U: 5; (Rivers and lakes) U: 10 *with map*
Dniester River [Europe]
Moldova (Land and climate) M: 690-690a
Ukraine (Rivers and lakes) U: 10 *with map*
Dnipro River [Europe] *See* Dnieper River *in this index*
Dnipropetrovsk [Ukraine] D: 259
Dnister River [Ukraine] *See* Dniester River *in this index*
Dnyapro River [Europe] *See* Dnieper River *in this index*
D.O. [degree]
Medicine (A career as a doctor) M: 370
Osteopathic medicine (Careers in osteopathic medicine) O: 867
Do Androids Dream of Electric Sheep? [book by Dick]
Dick, Philip K. D: 187
Do-it-yourself divorce

Divorce (No-fault divorce) D: 253-254
Do-ne-ho-ga-wa [birth name of]
Parker, Ely Samuel P: 170
Do Quang Em [Vietnamese artist]
Vietnam (The arts) V: 366
Do the Right Thing [film]
Lee, Spike L: 179
Doak, Samuel [American religious leader]
Tennessee (Schools) T: 138
Doak, William N. [American government official]
Hoover, Herbert Clark (table) H: 330
Labor, Department of (table) L: 2
Dobbin [ship]
United States Coast Guard Academy (History) U: 199
Dobbin, James C. [American government official]
Pierce, Franklin (table) P: 456
Dobell, Sir William [Australian painter]
Australia (Painting) A: 905-906
Döbereiner, Johann [German chemist]
Furfural F: 566
Doberman pinscher [dog] D: 259 *with picture*
Dog *picture on* D: 281
Dobermann, Louis [German dog breeder]
Doberman pinscher D: 259
Dobie, J. Frank [American author] D: 259
Dobrovolsky, Georgi T. [Soviet cosmonaut]
Astronaut (table) A: 830; (Accidents in space) A: 830-831
Space exploration (Salyut and Skylab) So: 721
Dobruja [region, Romania]
Romania (Land regions) R: 419-420 *with map*
Dobson, John [British architect]
Architecture (The Industrial Revolution) A: 625
Dobsonfly [insect]
Hellgrammite H: 177 *with picture*
Doby, Larry [American baseball player]
Baseball (table: Hall of Fame) B: 134
Dobzhansky, Theodosius [Russian-born American biologist]
Evolution (The synthetic theory) E: 432
Docetaxel [drug]
Taxol T: 56
Dock [shipping]
Dry dock D: 369
Dockery, Alexander M. [American political leader]
Missouri (table) M: 668
Docket [law]
Clerk of court Ci: 662b
Docking [space exploration]
Space exploration (Working in space) So: 704; (Space stations) So: 721
Docking, George [American political leader]
Kansas (table) K: 234
Docking, Robert [American political leader]
Kansas (table) K: 234
Docking pilot
Ship (Navigating a ship) S: 410
Docking well
Warship (Amphibious warfare ships) W: 40
Docklands [area]
London (Dealing with problems) L: 442-443
Dockwra, William [English merchant]
Postal services (The creation of the Penny Post) P: 706
Doctor [degree]
Address, Forms of (Other forms) A: 54
Degree, College (The doctor's degree) D: 93
Education (Higher education) E: 92
Doctor [medicine] *See* Physician *in this index*
Doctor-assisted suicide *See* Physician-assisted suicide *in this index*
Doctor blade [machine]
Printing *diagram on* P: 800; (Flexographic printing) P: 799
Doctor Brodie's Report [book by Borges]
Borges, Jorge Luis B: 487
Doctor Dolittle [literary figure]
Lofting, Hugh L: 420 *with picture*
Doctor Faustus [book by Mann]
German literature (Postwar German literature [1945-1990]) G: 142
Mann, Thomas M: 164
Dr. Faustus [play by Mamet]
Mamet, David M: 115
Doctor Faustus [play by Marlowe] *See* Tragical History of Doctor Faustus, The *in this index*
Dr. J [nickname]
Erving, Julius E: 355
Dr. Jekyll and Mr. Hyde [book by Stevenson]
Stevenson, Robert Louis (Novels) So: 898
Dr. Martin Luther King, Jr. Library
San Jose (History) S: 101-102
Doctor No [book by Fleming]
Fleming, Ian F: 233
Doctor of ...
Doctors appear under the key words in their titles,

as in Chiropractic, Doctor of
Dr. Strangelove [film]
Kubrick, Stanley **K:** 391
Motion picture (Movies in the 1960's) **M:** 870
with picture
Doctor Thorne [book by Trollope]
Trollope, Anthony **T:** 449
Dr. Zhivago [book by Pasternak]
Pasternak, Boris **P:** 192
Russian literature (Modern Soviet literature)
R: 564
Doctorfish [fish] **D:** 259 *with picture*
Doctorow, E. L. [American novelist] **D:** 259
Doctors Without Borders D: 260
Nobel Prizes (Peace: 1999) **N:** 448b
Doctrine and Covenants [book by Smith]
Community of Christ **Ci:** 899
Mormons (Church doctrines and ordinances)
M: 806
Doctrine of decorum
Drama (The French theater) **D:** 333
Doctrine of implied powers [U.S. history]
Hamilton, Alexander (Secretary of the treasury)
H: 32
Doctrine of the Faith, Congregation of the
Roman Catholic Church (The church today)
R: 412-413
Documentary
Motion picture **M:** 847
Television (Commercial television) **T:** 110a
Documentary photography
Photography (Dramatic changes) **P:** 425-426
with pictures
Dodd, Sonora Louise Smart [American public figure]
Father's Day **F:** 54
Dodd-Frank Wall Street Reform and Consumer Protection Act [2010]
Obama, Barack (Wall Street reform) **O:** 640h
Dodder [plant] **D:** 260
Plant (Photosynthesis) **P:** 537-538
Dodecahedron [geometry]
Geometry (Solid geometry) **G:** 104-105
Polyhedron **P:** 651 *with diagram*
Dodecanese Islands [Aegean Sea] **D:** 260
Aegean Sea **A:** 83 *with map*
Rhodes **R:** 316
Dodecaphonic music *See* Twelve-tone music *in this index*
Dodge, David L. [American businessman]
Peace (The 1800's and early 1900's) **P:** 206
Dodge, Grenville M. [American engineer]
Cheyenne (History) **C:** 417
Dodge, Henry [American political leader]
Wisconsin (Territorial days) **W:** 366
Dodge, Horace Elgin [American businessman]
Dodge brothers **D:** 260
Dodge, John Francis [American businessman]
Dodge brothers **D:** 260
Dodge, Mary Elizabeth Mapes [American author] **D:** 260
Literature for children (Masterpieces of fiction) **L:** 363
Dodge, Nehemiah [American businessman]
Providence (Government and history) **P:** 840
Rhode Island (Industrial expansion) **R:** 313
Dodge, Seril [American businessman]
Rhode Island (Industrial expansion) **R:** 313
Dodge brothers [American businessmen] **D:** 260
Dodge City [Kansas] **D:** 260 *with picture*
Conservation *picture on* **Ci:** 986
Kansas **K:** 217; (Places to visit) **K:** 226 *with picture;* (The great cattle towns) **K:** 237
Dodge Company
Dodge brothers **D:** 260
Dodgers, Brooklyn [team] *See* Brooklyn Dodgers *in this index*
Dodgson, Charles Lutwidge [real name of]
Carroll, Lewis **C:** 248
Dodo [extinct bird] **D:** 261 *with picture*
Bird (Extinct birds) **B:** 369-370 *with picture*
Dodoma [Tanzania] **D:** 261
Dodona [ancient Greece]
Oracle **O:** 814
Dodsworth [book by Lewis]
Lewis, Sinclair **L:** 221
Dodsworth [play by Howard]
Howard, Sidney **H:** 400
Doe [animal]
Deer **D:** 82d *with picture*
Goat **G:** 239
Doe, Elizabeth "Baby" [American public figure]
Colorado (Statehood) **Ci:** 845-847
Doe, Samuel K. [Liberian military leader]
Liberia (History) **L:** 231-232
Doenitz, Karl [German admiral] *See* Dönitz, Karl *in this index*

Doer, Gary [Canadian political leader]
Manitoba (table) **M:** 159; (Other developments) **M:** 163
Doerr, Bobby [American baseball player]
Baseball (table: Hall of Fame) **B:** 134
Dog D: 262 *with pictures*
See also the list of breeds of purebred dogs in the Dog *article*
Canine parvovirus **C:** 177
Distemper **D:** 238
Dogfighting **D:** 282
Evolution (Artificial selection) **E:** 432
Flea (Controlling fleas) **F:** 232
Guide dog **G:** 422 *with picture*
Heart *diagram on* **H:** 146
Heredity (Chromosomes and genes) **H:** 201
Hunting (Kinds of hunting) **H:** 450
Mammal *diagrams on* **M:** 120
Pet **P:** 319 *with pictures*
Play **P:** 570
Dog-day cicada [insect]
Cicada (Types of cicadas) **Ci:** 551
Dog fighting *See* Dogfighting *in this index*
Dog flea
Insect *picture on* **I:** 282
Dog guide *See* Guide dog *in this index*
Dog paddle
Swimming (The basic strokes) **So:** 1043-1044
Dog racing [sport] **D:** 282 *with picture*
Sled dog **S:** 506
Dog-rose plant
Brier **B:** 608
Dog salmon *See* Chum salmon *in this index*
Dog show
Dog (Dog competitions) **D:** 280 *with picture*
Dog sled [vehicle]
Alaska (Visitor's guide) **A:** 290 *with picture*
Iditarod **I:** 47
Inuit *pictures on* **I:** 354d; (Transportation) **I:** 354c
Sled **S:** 505
Sled dog **S:** 505
Dog sport
Dog (Dog competitions) **D:** 280-281
Dog Star *See* Sirius *in this index*
Dog tick
Rocky Mountain spotted fever **R:** 394
Tick **T:** 279
Dog violet [plant]
Violet **V:** 388
Dog Years [book by Grass]
German literature (Postwar German literature [1945-1990]) **G:** 142
Dogbane [plants] **D:** 282 *with picture*
Doge [Italian history] **D:** 282
Dogen [Japanese religious leader]
Zen **Z:** 589
Doges' Palace
Venice (The city) **V:** 306-307 *with picture and map*
Dogfight [warfare]
Air force (World War I) **A:** 185
Air Force, United States (World War I) **A:** 194
Airplane (World War I [1914-1918]) **A:** 234
Korean War (The air war) **K:** 382
World War I (The war in the air) **W:** 460-461 *with picture*
Dogfighting [sport] **D:** 282
Dogfish [fish] *See* Bowfin *in this index*
Dogfish [shark] **D:** 283 *with picture*
Doggett, Thomas [British humorist]
Rowing (History) **R:** 494
Doggett Coat and Badge [award]
Rowing (History) **R:** 494
Doghouse [industry]
Glass (Glass shows) **G:** 222
Doghouse [shelter]
Dog (Sleeping quarters) **D:** 278
Dogma [religion]
Protestantism (Authority of the Bible) **P:** 834
Dogmatic Constitution on the Church [religion]
Vatican Council II (The work of the council) **V:** 289
Dogo Canario [dog] **D:** 283 *with picture*
Dogon [people]
Mask *picture on* **M:** 264
Dogpatch U.S.A. [fictional place]
Capp, Al **C:** 198
Dogtooth [anatomy]
Teeth (Permanent teeth) **T:** 79-80
Dogtooth violet [plant] **D:** 283 *with picture*
Flower *picture on* **F:** 285
Dogwood [botany] **D:** 284 *with picture*
Flower (Variations in flower structure) **F:** 294 *with picture*
Plant *picture on* **P:** 525
Tree *pictures on* **T:** 421
Dogwood Festival
Connecticut (Visitor's guide) **Ci:** 960
Doha [Qatar] **D:** 284

City *picture on* **Ci:** 575
Qatar **Q:** 2 *with picture and map*
Doheny, Edward L. [American businessman]
Teapot Dome **T:** 72
Doherty, Peter Charles [Australian immunologist] **D:** 284
Nobel Prizes (Physiology or medicine: 1996) **N:** 446
Dohyo [space]
Sumo **So:** 973
Doi moi [Vietnamese history]
Vietnam (Economy) **V:** 369; (Recent developments) **V:** 372
Doisy, Edward Adelbert [American chemist]
Nobel Prizes (Physiology or medicine: 1943) **N:** 445
Dolan, Timothy M. [American religious leader]
Cardinal (table: American cardinals) **C:** 211
Dolbear, Amos E. [American inventor] **D:** 284
Dolce stil nuovo [art movement]
Italian literature (The Middle Ages) **I:** 494
Dolce Vita, La [film]
Fellini, Federico **F:** 68
Doldrums [weather]
Atlantic Ocean (Winds) **A:** 866
Calms, Regions of (The doldrums) **C:** 69
Climate (Atmospheric circulation) **Ci:** 676a
Trade wind **T:** 364
Wind (General circulation) **W:** 329 *with diagram*
Dole, Elizabeth Hanford [American government official] **D:** 284 *with portrait*
Dole, Robert Joseph (Political career) **D:** 285
Dole, Robert Joseph [American political leader] **D:** 285 *with portrait*
Bush, George Herbert Walker (The Republican nomination) **B:** 719
Clinton, Bill (The 1996 election) **Ci:** 682f
Dole, Sanford Ballard [American businessman] **D:** 285
Hawaii (The Republic of Hawaii) **H:** 108
Dole, Vincent [American doctor]
Methadone **M:** 433
Dolgoruki, Yuri [Russian prince]
Moscow (History) **M:** 826
Dolin, Anton [British dancer] **D:** 285
Doline [geology] *See* Sinkhole *in this index*
Dolittle, Doctor [literary figure]
Lofting, Hugh **L:** 420 *with picture*
Doll [toy] **D:** 286 *with pictures*
Indiana (Interesting facts) **I:** 197 *with picture*
Kachina **K:** 208
Papier-mâché (How to make a papier-mâché doll) **P:** 139 *with pictures*
United States *picture on* **U:** 116
Doll collecting
Doll (Doll collecting) **D:** 294
Doll theater
Drama (Japan) **D:** 336-337
Dollar [money] **D:** 294 *with pictures*
Money *picture on* **M:** 709; (Money in the new United States) **M:** 712; (Dollar coins) **M:** 714; (U.S. paper money) **M:** 714
Dollar diplomacy [economics] **D:** 295
Taft, William Howard (Foreign affairs) **T:** 11
Dollar spot [plant disease]
Lawn *picture on* **L:** 143
Dollar store
Discount store **D:** 224
Dollfuss, Engelbert [Austrian political leader]
Austria (After World War I) **A:** 939
Dollhouse D: 295 *with picture*
Dollier de Casson, François [Canadian religious leader]
Saint Lawrence Seaway (Early canals) **S:** 44
Doll's House, A [play by Ibsen]
Ibsen, Henrik (His plays) **I:** 4
Dolly [sheep]
Biology (Current research and issues) **B:** 320-321
Cloning (Successes) **Ci:** 683 *with picture*
Heredity (The era of genetic engineering) **H:** 209
Dollywood [theme park]
Tennessee (Places to visit) **T:** 144
Dolmen [archaeology]
Megalithic monuments **M:** 383
Dolmuş [taxi]
Istanbul (Economy) **I:** 491
Dolomite [mineral] **D:** 296
Dolomites [mountains, Italy]
Alps (Chief ranges of the Alps) **A:** 385
Dolores, Mission [U.S. history]
San Francisco (Other neighborhoods) **S:** 93 *with map;* (Settlement by Europeans) **S:** 97
Dolostone [rock]
Dolomite **D:** 296
Dolphin [fish] *See* Dolphinfish *in this index*
Dolphin [mammal] **D:** 296 *with pictures*
See also River dolphin *in this index*

Animal (A table of animal intelligence) **A:** 493
  Ichthyosaur **I:** 24
  Killer whale **K:** 316
  Mammal *pictures on* **M:** 117, **M:** 128
  Porpoise **P:** 679
  Tuna **T:** 485
  Whale (Dolphins and porpoises) **W:** 258
  Zoo (Interesting facts about zoo animals) **Z:** 601
Dolphin, The [poem by Lowell]
  Lowell, Robert **L:** 511
Dolphin Hotel [Walt Disney World]
  Graves, Michael *picture on* **G:** 330
Dolphin kick
  Swimming (The basic kicks) **So:** 1043
Dolphinfish D: 300
  Fish *picture on* **F:** 152
Dolphins, Miami [team] *See* Miami Dolphins *in this index*
Dom Casmurro [book by Machado de Assis]
  Brazil (The arts) **B:** 576-577
  Latin American literature (Realism) **L:** 113
Dom Pedro IV Square
  Lisbon *picture on* **L:** 348
Domagk, Gerhard [German doctor] **D:** 300
Domain [algebra]
  Algebra (Sets and variables) **A:** 350-351;
    (Functions) **A:** 356
Domain [biology] **D:** 300
  Classification, Scientific (Groups in classification)
    Ci: 655
  Kingdom **K:** 328
  Prokaryote **P:** 817
Domain name [computing]
  Internet (HTTP) **I:** 350d
  Website **W:** 176
Dombey and Son [book by Dickens]
  Dickens, Charles (The second phase) **D:** 188
Dome [architecture]
  Architecture *picture on* **A:** 610; (Roman
    architecture) **A:** 616
  Byzantine art (Architecture) **B:** 749
  Vault **V:** 291
Dome, Church of the [Paris]
  Napoleon I (The Hundred Days and Waterloo)
    N: 16
Dome mountain [geology]
  Mountain (Dome mountains) **M:** 894
Dome of the Rock [Jerusalem]
  Jerusalem *picture on* **J:** 94a; (The Old City) **J:** 95
    with map; (Islamic sites) **J:** 96; (Muslim rule)
    J: 101
  Muslims *picture on* **M:** 964a
Dome tent
  Tent (Kinds of tents) **T:** 168
Domesday Book [English history] **D:** 300
  Book *picture on* **B:** 465
  Census (Early censuses) **C:** 349
  England (The Norman Conquest) **E:** 305
  Norman Conquest **N:** 455
  William I, the Conqueror **W:** 308
Domestic animal
  Animal (Animals and people) **A:** 471
  Cat **C:** 284
Domestic economy
  Family and consumer sciences (History) **F:** 26
Domestic ferret [animal]
  Ferret **F:** 76
Domestic intelligence service
  Intelligence service **I:** 320
Domestic Manners of the Americans [book by
  Frances Trollope]
  Trollope, Anthony **T:** 449
Domestic partnership [law]
  See also Civil union *in this index*
  Civil union **Ci:** 613
  Gay rights movement (History of gay rights) **G:** 73
  Marriage (Same-sex unions and marriages)
    M: 220
  Same-sex marriage **S:** 78
Domestic policy
  Foreign policy (Influences on foreign policy)
    F: 387
Domestic Policy Council
  President of the United States (The executive
    branch) **P:** 764
Domestic system [economics] *See* Cottage
  industry *in this index*
Domestic trade
  International trade **I:** 347
  Trade **T:** 362
Domestic tragedy
  Drama (England) **D:** 334-335
  Tragedy **T:** 366
Domestic violence D: 300
  Child (Problems in the home) **C:** 453
  Marriage (Marriage problems) **M:** 222
  Restraining order **R:** 263

Domestica [plum]
  Plum (Kinds of plums) **P:** 577
Domestication
  Agriculture (History) **A:** 153
  Animal (Animals and people) **A:** 471
  Civilization (Development) **Ci:** 635
  Dog (History) **D:** 281
  Mammal (How people use mammals) **M:** 118
  Plant (The domestication of plants) **P:** 541
Domiciliary
  Veterans Affairs, Department of (History) **V:** 344
Dominance [zoology] **D:** 301 *with picture*
  Animal (Group living) **A:** 502
  Balance of nature (Behavior) **B:** 35
  Dog (Behavior) **D:** 277
  Mammal (Group life) **M:** 125
  Wolf (Habits) **W:** 375
Dominance hierarchy
  Animal (Group living) **A:** 502
  Squirrel (Territories and groups) **So:** 815
Dominant [music]
  Music (Tone) **M:** 950; (Harmony) **M:** 951 *with
    diagram*
Dominant disease
  Genetic testing (Genes associated with disease)
    G: 84d
Dominant gene
  Heredity (Patterns of heredity) **H:** 202
Dominant gene abnormality
  Muscular dystrophy **M:** 936
Dominant group [sociology]
  Minority group **M:** 608
  Segregation (Causes and effects of segregation)
    S: 285
Domingo, Plácido [Spanish singer] **D:** 301
Domínguez, Francisco Atanasio [Spanish
  explorer]
  Utah (Early exploration) **U:** 246
Dominic, Saint [Italian religious leader] **D:** 301
  Dominicans **D:** 305
Dominica D: 302 *with picture and map*
  Flag *picture on* **F:** 201
Dominican *See* Dominicans *in this index*
Dominican Family *See* Dominicans *in this index*
Dominican Republic D: 303 *with pictures and maps*
  Flag *picture on* **F:** 201
  Organization of American States **O:** 854
**Dominican Republic-Central America-United
  States Free Trade Agreement** [2004]
  Central America (Developments since the mid-
    1900's) **C:** 356
  Costa Rica (Recent developments) **Ci:** 1084
  El Salvador (Recent developments) **E:** 253
Dominicans [religious group] **D:** 305
  Dominic, Saint **D:** 301
  Friar **F:** 532
  Religious life (Religious life in the Middle Ages)
    R: 226
Dominion Day [holiday] *See* Canada Day *in this
  index*
Dominion Educational Association
  Canadian Education Association **C:** 156
Dominion Foundries and Steel, Ltd.
  Hamilton (History) **H:** 31-32
Dominion of Canada *See* Canada, Dominion of *in
  this index*
Dominion of New England [U.S. history]
  Colonial life in America (Plymouth Colony)
    Ci: 789-790
Dominion Police
  Royal Canadian Mounted Police (History) **R:** 497
Dominique
  Chicken (table) **C:** 443
Domino, Fats [American musician]
  Rock music (The first generation) **R:** 377
Domino theory [international relations]
  Cold War (To the brink and back) **Ci:** 765
  Vietnam War **V:** 373
Dominoes [game] **D:** 306
Domitian [Roman emperor] **D:** 306
  Agricola, Gnaeus Julius **A:** 144
  Rome, Ancient (The Roman Empire) **R:** 446;
    (table) **R:** 447
Domitius Ahenobarbus, Gnaeus [father of]
  Nero **N:** 130
Domitius Ahenobarbus, Lucius [Roman emperor]
  See Nero *in this index*
Domo [rodeo]
  Uruguay (Recreation) **U:** 225
Domostroy [book]
  Russian literature (Muscovite literature) **R:** 559
Domtoren [church tower]
  Utrecht **U:** 252
Domus Aurea [ruins]
  Rome (Other remains) **R:** 433
Don Giovanni [opera by Mozart]
  Mozart, Wolfgang Amadeus (Operas) **M:** 906-907;

  (His style) **M:** 907
  Opera (Recitative and arias) **O:** 792; *(Don
    Giovanni)* **O:** 803 *with picture*
Don Gonzalo [literary figure]
  Don Juan **D:** 306
Don John [literary figure]
  Shakespeare, William: *(Much Ado About Nothing)*
    S: 360
Don José [opera character]
  Opera: *(Carmen)* **O:** 802
Don Juan [literary figure] **D:** 306
  See also Don Giovanni *in this index*
  Opera: *(Don Giovanni)* **O:** 803
  Tirso de Molina **T:** 298
Don Juan [play by Molière]
  Molière **M:** 694
Don Juan [poem by Byron]
  Byron, Lord (Byron's life) **B:** 748; (Byron's poetry)
    B: 748
Don Juan and the Love for Geometry [play by
  Frisch]
  Frisch, Max **F:** 535
Don Juan Tenorio [play by Zorrilla]
  Don Juan **D:** 306
Don Pasquale [opera by Donizetti]
  Donizetti, Gaetano **D:** 307
Don Pedro Dam [California]
  Dam (table) **D:** 18
Don Quixote [book by Cervantes] **D:** 306 *with
  picture*
  Amadís of Gaul **A:** 399
  Cervantes, Miguel de **C:** 363
  Novel (Early novels) **N:** 572
  Proverb **P:** 839
  Spanish literature (The 1600's) **So:** 759
Don River [Russia] **D:** 307
Don Segundo Sombra [book by Güiraldes]
  Latin American literature (The early 1900's) **L:** 113
Doña Bárbara [book by Gallegos]
  Latin American literature (The early 1900's) **L:** 113
Doña Paz [ship]
  Shipwreck (table: Major shipwrecks) **S:** 428
Donaghey, George Washington [American
  political leader]
  Arkansas (table) **A:** 712
Donahey, A. Victor [American political leader]
  Ohio (table) **O:** 699
Donald Duck [cartoon character]
  Disney, Walt (The first Disney cartoons) **D:** 235-
    236 *with picture*
Donaldson, Jesse M. [American government
  official]
  Truman, Harry S. (table) **T:** 469
Doñana National Park [Spain]
  National park (table) **N:** 42f; (Other interesting
    national parks) **N:** 42h
Donat, Robert [British actor]
  Motion picture *picture on* **M:** 868; (Best
    performance by an actor: 1939) **M:** 862a
Donatello [Italian sculptor] **D:** 307 *with picture*
  Dragon *picture on* **D:** 319
  Renaissance *picture on* **R:** 235; (Arts of the 1300's
    and early 1400's) **R:** 236
  Sculpture (Early Renaissance) **S:** 252 *with picture*
Donati, Gemma [wife of]
  Dante Alighieri (His life) **D:** 33
Donati, Giuseppe [Italian musician]
  Ocarina **O:** 646
Donation Land Law [1850]
  Oregon (Provisional and territorial governments)
    O: 848
Donation of Constantine [document]
  Sylvester I, Saint **So:** 1065
Donation of Pepin [European history]
  Pepin the Short **P:** 277
  Rome (Early days) **R:** 434
Donbas [region]
  Ukraine (The Central Plateau) **U:** 9
Donegall Square [district]
  Belfast **B:** 224d *with picture*
Donelson, Andrew Jackson [nephew of]
  Jackson, Andrew (Jackson's family) **J:** 8; (Life in
    the White House) **J:** 11
Donelson, Emily [niece of]
  Jackson, Andrew (Life in the White House) **J:** 11
    with picture
  White House hostesses **W:** 291
Donelson, John [American pioneer]
  Tennessee (Territorial years) **T:** 153
Donelson, John [nephew of]
  Jackson, Andrew (Jackson's family) **J:** 8
Donelson, Samuel [brother-in-law of]
  Jackson, Andrew (Jackson's family) **J:** 8
Donets River [Ukraine]
  Don River **D:** 307
  Donetsk **D:** 307
Donetsk [Ukraine] **D:** 307

Dong Son [people]
   Vietnam (History) V: 369
Doniphan, Alexander W. [American military leader]
   Mexican War (Doniphan's victories) M: 446
Dönitz, Karl [German admiral] D: 307
   Nuremberg Trials (The trials) N: 613
   World War II (Victory in Europe) W: 486
Donizetti, Gaetano [Italian composer] D: 307
   Opera: *(Lucia di Lammermoor)* O: 804
Donjon [defense]
   Castle (Structure) C: 280
Donkey D: 307 *with picture*
   Democratic Party *picture on* D: 125
Donkey Kong [electronic game]
   Nintendo N: 423
"Donkey Serenade, The" [music by Friml]
   Friml, Rudolf F: 534
Donna Anna [opera character]
   Opera: *(Don Giovanni)* O: 803
"Donna è mobile, La" [aria]
   Opera: *(Rigoletto)* O: 806
Donnchad [king of Scotland] *See* Duncan I *in this index*
Donne, Ann More [wife of]
   Donne, John (His life) D: 308
Donne, John [English poet] D: 308
   Brodsky, Joseph B: 636
   English literature (Metaphysical and Cavalier poets) E: 317; (Prose writings) E: 317
   Metaphysical poets M: 429
   Poetry (Imagery) P: 595
Donnell, Forrest C. [American political leader]
   Missouri (table) M: 668
Donnelly, Ignatius [American political leader] D: 308
Donnelly, Phil M. [American political leader]
   Missouri (table) M: 668
Donner, George [American pioneer]
   Donner party D: 308
Donner, Jacob [American pioneer]
   Donner party D: 308
Donner party [U.S. history] D: 308
Donner Pass [California]
   Donner party D: 309
Dono, Paolo di [birth name of]
   Uccello, Paolo U: 3
Donohue, Mark [American race car driver]
   Automobile racing (table: Indianapolis 500 winners) A: 980
Donor [law]
   Trust fund (How a trust fund works) T: 473
Donor, Blood *See* Blood donor *in this index*
Donor, Organ *See* Organ donation *in this index*
Donor nucleus [biology]
   Cloning (Nuclear transfer) Ci: 682l
Donor site [medicine]
   Skin grafting S: 494
Donoso, José [Chilean author]
   Latin American literature (The "Boom") L: 114
Donovan, Raymond J. [American government official]
   Labor, Department of (table) L: 2
   Reagan, Ronald Wilson (table) R: 169
Donovan, Shaun [American government official]
   Housing and Urban Development, Department of (table) H: 393
   Obama, Barack (table) O: 640h
"Don't Ask Don't Tell" [policy]
   Obama, Barack (Military ends gay ban) O: 640h
"Don't fire until you see the whites of their eyes" [quotation]
   Revolution, American (Bunker Hill) R: 275
"Don't give up the ship" [quotation]
   Lawrence, James L: 146
Donus [pope]
   Pope (table) P: 666
Doo-wop [music]
   Rock music (A variety of styles) R: 378 *with picture*
Doodlebug [insect]
   Ant lion A: 529 *with picture*
Dooley, Mr. [literary figure]
   Dunne, Finley Peter D: 386
Doolittle, Hilda [American poet] D: 309
   American literature (Modernist poetry) A: 421
Doolittle, James Harold [American military leader] D: 309
   Aviation (table: Aviation speed records) A: 990
   World War II (The tide turns) W: 488
Doolittle Raid [1942]
   World War II (The tide turns) W: 488
Doom palm [tree]
   Doum palm D: 314
Doomsday Book *See* Domesday Book *in this index*
"Doonesbury" [comic strip]
   Trudeau, Garry T: 460 *with picture*
Door

House (Interior construction) H: 382 *with diagram*
Pioneer life in America (A pioneer settlement) P: 479-481
Door chime
   Electric bell E: 165 *with diagram*
Door County [Wisconsin]
   Wisconsin (Places to visit) W: 356 *with picture*
Door in the Wall, The [book by De Angeli]
   De Angeli, Marguerite Lofft D: 60
Door of Hope doll
   Doll (Before World War I) D: 291
Doors [musical group]
   Rock music (Fresh directions) R: 380
Dopamine [biochemistry] D: 309
   Alcoholism (Causes of alcoholism) A: 337-338
   Brain (Parkinson disease) B: 559
   Drug abuse (Methamphetamine) D: 362
   Mental illness (Chemical imbalances in the brain) M: 406
   Nicotine N: 405
   Parkinson disease (Symptoms) P: 170
   Ritalin R: 350
   Schizophrenia S: 176
Dopamine receptor [biochemistry]
   Dopamine D: 309
Dopamine receptor agonist [drug]
   Parkinson disease (Treatment with drugs) P: 170
Dopant [electronics]
   Electronics (Types of electronic circuits) E: 209-210
   Semiconductor (Doped crystals) S: 291
Doping [crime] D: 309
   Blood doping B: 415
Doping [electronics]
   Computer chip (Structure) Ci: 924e
   Electronics (Active components) E: 210
   Semiconductor (Doped crystals) S: 291-292
   Transistor (Transistor materials) T: 372
Doppler, Christian [Austrian physicist]
   Doppler effect D: 310
Doppler effect [physics] D: 310
   Astronomy (Spectroscopy) A: 840-841
   Light (The Doppler effect) L: 290
   Log (The Doppler sonar speed log) L: 421
   Radar *diagram on* R: 67; (Pulse radar) R: 69
   Redshift (The Doppler redshift) R: 192
   Sonar (How sonar works) So: 591
   Sound (How sound behaves) So: 601-602 *with diagram*
   Sun (Analyzing electromagnetic radiation) So: 983-984
   Ultrasound (Animal uses of ultrasound) U: 16
   Weather (Weather radar) W: 162
Doppler radar
   Meteorology (How meteorologists measure the atmosphere) M: 433
   Radar (Pulse radar) R: 69
   Tornado (Field studies) T: 336 *with picture*
   Weather (Weather radar) W: 162 *with pictures*
   Wind shear W: 333
Doppler redshift [physics]
   Astronomy (Spectroscopy) A: 840-841
   Redshift R: 192
   Telescope (Analyzing spectra) T: 105-106
Doppler sonar speed log [measuring device]
   Log (The Doppler sonar speed log) L: 421 *with picture*
Dorado [fish] *See* Dolphinfish *in this index*
Dorais, Gus [American football player]
   Football (Changes in the game) F: 366-367
Dorand, René [French inventor]
   Helicopter (The first practical helicopters) H: 173
Dorcas gazelle [animal]
   Desert *picture on* D: 155
   Gazelle G: 74
Dorchester [district, Boston]
   Boston (The south side) B: 500
Dorchester, Baron *See* Carleton, Sir Guy *in this index*
Dorchester Heights [Massachusetts]
   Boston (Resistance and revolution) B: 503
Doré, Gustave [French artist] D: 310 *with picture*
Dore metal
   Assaying (Dry assaying) A: 817
Dorfman, Ariel [Chilean author]
   Chile (The arts) C: 463
Dorgan, T. A. [American cartoonist]
   Slang (Sources of slang) S: 500
Doria, Andrea [Genoese admiral]
   Barbarossa B: 105
Dorians [ancient people] D: 310
   Greece, Ancient (History) G: 372
   Sparta (History) So: 766
Doric column [architecture]
   Architecture (Classical Greek architecture) A: 615
   Column (The Greek orders) Ci: 865 *with picture*
Doric order [architecture]

Architecture (table) A: 608-609 *with picture*
Dorion, Marie [American Indian] D: 310
Dorion, Pierre [French explorer]
   Dorion, Marie D: 310
   South Dakota (Exploration and fur trade) So: 681
Doris [Greek mythology]
   Nereids N: 130
Dorking [chicken]
   Chicken (English class chickens) C: 441; (table) C: 443
Dormancy [biology]
   Estivation E: 361
   Germination G: 172
   Hibernation (Warm-blooded hibernators) H: 222
   Plant (Germination) P: 535
   Seed (How seeds are spread) S: 282
Dormant volcano
   Volcano (Predicting eruptions) V: 442a-442b
Dormer window
   Window W: 334
Dormition of the Virgin, Church of the [Greece]
   Byzantine art *picture on* B: 750
Dormitory
   Universities and colleges (Residence) U: 209
Dormouse [animal] D: 310 *with picture*
Dorn, Friedrich Ernst [German chemist]
   Radon (Chemical properties) R: 100-101
Dornier [airplane]
   Airplane *picture on* A: 233; (Engineering improvements) A: 237
Dörpfeld, Wilhelm [German archaeologist]
   Troy (The archaeological Troy) T: 455
Dorr, Thomas Wilson [American social reformer]
   Dorr Rebellion D: 311
   Rhode Island (The Dorr Rebellion) R: 313
Dorr Rebellion [U.S. history] D: 311
   Rhode Island (The Dorr Rebellion) R: 313
Dorris, Michael [American author]
   Indian, American (Achievements in the arts) I: 181
Dorsal fin [zoology]
   Dolphin (The bodies of dolphins) D: 297 *with pictures*
   Fish (Fins) F: 160-161 *with picture*
   Killer whale K: 316 *with picture*
Dorset [people]
   Exploration (The Tuniit) E: 441
   Nunavut (Early history) N: 611
Dorset sheep
   Sheep (Medium-wooled sheep) S: 382
Dorsett, Tony [American football player]
   Football (table) F: 363
Dorsey, Hugh M. [American political leader]
   Georgia (table) G: 130
Dorsey, Thomas A. [American composer]
   Gospel music G: 277
Dos Passos, John [American author] D: 311
   American literature (Realist fiction) A: 422
   Impressionism (Music, literature, and sculpture) I: 94
   Lost Generation L: 472
Dos Santos, José Eduardo [Angolan political leader]
   Angola (History) A: 465-466
Dosage indicator cap
   Packaging P: 18
Dosanjh, Ujjal [Canadian political leader]
   British Columbia (table) B: 628
Dose [radiology]
   Radiation (Effects of radiation) R: 79
Doshi, Balkrishna [Indian architect]
   India (Architecture and sculpture) I: 119
Dosimeter [instrument]
   Electroscope E: 218
Dossin Great Lakes Museum
   Detroit (Cultural life) D: 170
Dost Muhammad Khan [emir of Afghanistan]
   Afghanistan (United Afghanistan) A: 95
Dostoevsky, Fyodor [Russian author] D: 311 *with portrait*
   Nihilism N: 421
   Novel (Russia) N: 573
   Russian literature (The 1860's and 1870's) R: 562
Dostoyevsky [book by Frank]
   Biography (Biography today) B: 314
Dot [communications]
   Telegraph (The Morse telegraph) T: 90
Dot [tile]
   Mah-jongg M: 64 *with picture*
Dot-com bubble [computing]
   Internet (The Web forms) I: 350g
Dot-matrix printer [electronic device]
   Computer (Printers) Ci: 916
   Printer (Impact printers) P: 795
Dots per inch [measure]
   Type T: 536
Dotted blazing star [plant]

Flower *picture on* F: 286
Doty, James D. [American businessman]
Madison (Government and history) M: 31
Douala [Cameroon] D: 312
Cameroon (People) C: 85
Douala [people]
Douala D: 312
Douay Bible
Bible (Early English translations) B: 285
Vulgate V: 453
Double [baseball]
Baseball (Reaching base) B: 129
Double [mathematics]
Addition (Addition facts) A: 49
Double, The [book by Dostoevsky]
Dostoevsky, Fyodor D: 311
Double action
Harp H: 65
Double-action principle [engineering]
Steam engine (Watt's engine) So: 881
Watt, James W: 148
Double-action revolver [gun]
Handgun (Types of handguns) H: 43
Double-action semiautomatic pistol
Handgun (Types of handguns) H: 43
Double agent [spy]
Espionage (Counterespionage) E: 358
Double bass [musical instrument] *See* Bass *in this index*
Double-blind method [science]
Disease (Research) D: 234
Double burden [sociology]
Women's movement (In Eastern Europe and the former Soviet republics) W: 387; (Impact of women's movements) W: 387
Double coconut palm [plant] *See* Coco-de-mer *in this index*
Double-convex lens [optics]
Lens (A positive lens) *diagram on* L: 196
Magnifying glass M: 62
Double coverage
Football (The defensive team) F: 357-358
Double-cross hybrids [botany]
Corn (Development of hybrids) Ci: 1063
Double dagger [reference]
Footnote F: 369
Double-deck elevator
Elevator (Special kinds of elevators) E: 235
Double-digit inflation
Inflation (Severe inflation) I: 267
Double-entry bookkeeping
Bookkeeping (Double-entry bookkeeping) B: 472; (History) B: 473
Double escapement
Piano (History) P: 447-448
Double fault
Tennis (The serve) T: 163
Double fertilization [botany]
Flower (Fertilization) F: 296
Pollen (Fertilization) P: 645
Double helical gear
Gear G: 75
Double helix [biology]
Cell (DNA—the wondrous molecule) C: 334-335
DNA D: 258
Heredity (The structure of DNA) H: 205 *with picture*; (The chemistry of genes) H: 208-209
Molecular biology (The beginning of molecular biology) M: 691-692
Double Helix, The [book by Watson]
Watson, James Dewey W: 147
Double Hook, The [book by Watson]
Canadian literature (Modern English-Canadian fiction) C: 160
Double horn [musical instrument]
French horn F: 516
Double-hung window
Window W: 334
Double indemnity clause
Insurance (Riders) I: 311
Double jeopardy [law]
Constitution of the United States (Amendment 5) Ci: 1012
Fifth Amendment F: 95
Double knit
Textile (Knitted fabrics) T: 214
Double mini-trampoline [event]
Gymnastics (Trampoline and tumbling) G: 449-450
007 [literary figure]
Fleming, Ian F: 233
Double orange daisy [plant]
Fleabane F: 232
Double play
Baseball (Baseball terms) B: 124
Double Play [book by Parker]
Parker, Robert B. P: 170

Double rhyme
Poetry (table) P: 594
Rhyme R: 319
Double salt [chemistry]
Salt, Chemical S: 75
"Double Shuffle" [Canadian history]
Macdonald, Sir John Alexander (Associate provincial prime minister) M: 7
Double star *See* Binary star *in this index*
Double stitch
Crochet Ci: 1148d
Double-team
Basketball (Defensive strategies) B: 147 *with picture*
Double trailer [truck]
Truck T: 456, *picture on* T: 459
Double weave
Weaving (Fancy weaves) W: 173
Doubleday, Abner [American sportsman] D: 312
Baseball (The Abner Doubleday Theory) B: 132
Doubleday, Page, and Company
Dreiser, Theodore D: 346
Doublet [clothing]
Clothing (The Renaissance) Ci: 702
Tartan T: 47 *with picture*
Doublet [gem]
Gem (Imitation and synthetic gems) G: 79
Doubling [cards]
Bridge (Bidding) B: 604
Doubloon [money] D: 312
Doubting Thomas
Thomas, Saint T: 262
Douc langur [animal]
Monkey *picture on* M: 728
Doud, Mamie Geneva [wife of Dwight D. Eisenhower] *See* Eisenhower, Mamie Doud *in this index*
Douerlein, Fred [American glassblower]
Glass (table) G: 218
Dough
Baking (Baking ingredients) B: 33
Bread B: 588
Dough conditioner
Bread (How yeast bread is made) B: 588
Doughboy [soldier]
A.E.F. A: 81
United States, History of the (The United States in the war) U: 188-189 *with picture*
Dougherty, Dennis J. [American religious leader]
Cardinal (table: American cardinals) C: 211
Doughnut [food] D: 312
Doughty, Thomas [American painter]
Hudson River School H: 406 *with picture*
Doughty, Thomas [English sea captain]
Drake, Sir Francis (Voyage around the world) D: 321
Douglas [former city]
Juneau J: 194
Douglas [Isle of Man]
Man, Isle of M: 130
Douglas, Buster [American boxer]
Boxing (The late 1900's) B: 532b
Tyson, Mike T: 542
Douglas, Donald Wills [American businessman]
Aviation (Aviation progress) A: 988
Douglas, Gabby [American gymnast]
Olympic Games *picture on* O: 748
Douglas, Helen Gahagan [American political leader]
Nixon, Richard Milhous (U.S. senator) N: 430
Douglas, Sir James [Canadian government official] D: 312
British Columbia (The colonial period) B: 630
Douglas, Jim [American political leader]
Vermont (table) V: 333; (Recent developments) V: 337
Douglas, Melvyn [American actor]
Motion picture (Best performance by an actor in a supporting role: 1963, 1979) M: 862b
Douglas, Michael [American actor]
Motion picture (Best performance by an actor: 1987) M: 862a
Douglas, Norman [British author] D: 312
Douglas, Stephen Arnold [American political leader] D: 312 *with portrait*
Buchanan, James (The struggle over slavery) B: 660
Civil War, American (Developments in the political party system) Ci: 616
Davis, Jefferson (Secretary of war) D: 48
Democratic Party (The slavery issue) D: 124
Kansas-Nebraska Act K: 243
Lincoln, Abraham (Success in politics) L: 314; (Reentry into politics) L: 317; (The debates with Douglas) L: 317
Douglas, Thomas [British philanthropist] *See* Selkirk, Earl of *in this index*

Douglas, Thomas C. [Canadian political leader]
New Democratic Party N: 203
Saskatchewan (Political changes) S: 147
Douglas, William L. [American political leader]
Massachusetts (table) M: 288
Douglas, William Orville [American jurist] D: 313
Truman, Harry S. (Vice president) T: 468
Douglas Dam [Tennessee]
Tennessee *picture on* T: 135
Douglas-fir [tree] D: 313 *with picture*
Fir F: 119
Oregon (Natural resources) O: 841
Plant *pictures on* P: 521, P: 524
Tree *pictures on* T: 424
Douglas-Home, Sir Alec [British political leader]
United Kingdom (table: British prime ministers) U: 72
Douglass, Frederick [American social reformer] D: 313 *with portrait*
African American literature (The 1800's) A: 136a
African Americans (The antislavery movement) A: 136h *with picture*
American literature (Nonfiction prose) A: 418
National Park System (table: National historic sites) N: 52-53
Douglass Residential College
Rutgers, The State University of New Jersey R: 568
Doukhobors [religious group] D: 314
Doum palm [tree] D: 314
Douppioni [fiber]
Silk (Douppioni) S: 460
Douro River [Spain-Portugal]
Portugal (Rivers) P: 690
Douroucouli [monkey] *See* Night monkey *in this index*
Dove [bird] D: 314 *with picture*
Bird (Birds of Asia) B: 344f *with picture*
Pigeon P: 458 *with pictures*
Turtle dove T: 524 *with picture*
Dove [ship]
Maryland (Exploration and settlement) M: 256
Dove, Arthur Garfield [American artist] D: 315
Dove, Rita [American poet] D: 315
Poet laureate (table: Poets laureate of the United States) P: 590
Dovekie [bird]
Auk A: 890 *with picture*
Dover [Delaware] D: 315
Dover [England] D: 315
Dover, Cliffs of [England]
Dover D: 315
Earth (The Mesozoic Era) *picture on* E: 29
Rock (Organic sediments) R: 372-373
United Kingdom (The English Lowlands) U: 59-61
Dover, Strait of [channel, England-France] D: 315 *with map*
English Channel E: 311 *with map*
"Dover Beach" [poem by Arnold]
Arnold, Matthew A: 742
Dover Castle
Citadel *picture on* Ci: 567
Dover sole [fish]
Sole So: 582
Doves [U.S. history]
Johnson, Lyndon Baines (The widening Vietnam War) J: 150-151
Vietnam War (Reactions in the United States) V: 375
Dovetail [carpentry]
Log cabin L: 422
Dow, Charles H. [American journalist]
Dow Jones averages D: 316
Dow, Herbert Henry [American businessman] D: 315
Dow Chemical Company
Dow, Herbert Henry D: 315
Polystyrene P: 651
Dow Jones averages [economics] D: 315
Dow process [chemistry]
Magnesium (How magnesium is obtained) M: 54
Dower [law] D: 316
Dowland, John [English composer] D: 316
Down [feather]
Bird (As a source of food and raw materials) B: 330-331; (Feathers) B: 362
Camping (Sleeping bags) C: 93
Duck (The features of a duck) D: 374
Feather (Kinds and parts of feathers) F: 59 *with diagram*
Down [sports]
Football (Advancing the ball) F: 360
Rugby football (Playing the ball) R: 513
Down, John Langdon Haydon [British doctor]
Down syndrome D: 316
Down and Out in Paris and London [book by Orwell]

Orwell, George **O: 860**
Down East
 Maine **M: 68**
Down payment [economics]
 Installment plan **I: 304**
 Mortgage **M: 820**
Down quark [physics]
 Quark **Q: 7**
 Subatomic particle (Elementary particles)
  So: 937; (Theoretical research) **So: 938**
Down syndrome [disorder] **D: 316**
 Birth defect (Prevention and treatment) **B: 380**
 Brain (Genetic disorders) **B: 558**
 Intellectual disability (Causes) **I: 318**
 Mutation **M: 968**
Downers
 Drug (Antianxiety and hypnotic drugs) **D: 352**
Downey, John G. [American political leader]
 California (table) **C: 59**
Downforce
 Automobile racing (Formula One racing) **A: 976-977**; (Indy and Champ Car racing) **A: 977**
Downhill race
 Skiing (Alpine competitions) **S: 486-487**
Downhill skiing
 Skiing *diagrams on* **S: 484**; (Alpine skiing) **S: 482** *with picture*; (Ski equipment and clothing) **S: 483**
Downing the Nigh Leader [painting by Remington]
 Remington, Frederic **R: 230**
Downloading [communications]
 Computer (The Internet) **Ci: 920-921**
 Internet (Commerce) **I: 350b**
Downshift
 Transmission (How a manual transmission works) **T: 377-378**
Downstream face
 Dam (Buttress dams) **D: 17**
Downtown
 City (Description) **Ci: 589**
Downturn
 Business cycle **B: 728**
Downy hawthorn [tree]
 Hawthorn **H: 114**
Downy mildew [fungus]
 Mildew **M: 541** *with picture*
Downy woodpecker [bird]
 Animal *picture on* **A: 479**
Dowry [custom]
 Africa (Marriage and the family) **A: 108**
 India (Family life) **I: 114**
 Marriage (Other marriage laws and practices) **M: 220-221**
Dowser
 Divination **D: 241**
Doxorubicin [drug]
 Antibiotic (Other kinds of antibiotics) **A: 550**
Doxycycline [medication]
 Antibiotic **A: 551**
Doyle, Arthur Conan [British author] **D: 316** *with portrait*
 Holmes, Sherlock **H: 295**
Doyle, Jim [American political leader]
 Wisconsin (table) **W: 365**
Doyle, Roddy [Irish author]
 Irish literature (Fiction) **I: 432**
 Novel (The novel today) **N: 575**
D'Oyly Carte, Richard [British producer] **D: 317**
 Gilbert and Sullivan **G: 190**
D'Oyly Carte Opera Company
 D'Oyly Carte, Richard **D: 317**
Dozen
 Duodecimal system **D: 386**
DP *See* Displaced person *in this index*
DR [navigation] *See* Dead reckoning *in this index*
Dr. ...
 Names beginning with Dr. are alphabetized together with names beginning with Doctor
Drabble, Margaret [English author] **D: 317**
Drachma [money] **D: 317** *with pictures*
 Coin collecting *picture on* **Ci: 758**
Draco [Greek legislator] **D: 317**
 Law (The influence of ancient Greece) **L: 133**
Draco lizard *See* Flying dragon *in this index*
Draconian Code [ancient Greece]
 Draco **D: 317**
Draconid meteor shower
 Meteor (The parent comet) **M: 431**
Dracula [book by Stoker] **D: 317**
 Stoker, Bram **So: 906**
 Transylvania **T: 402**
 Vampire **V: 268**
Dracula [film]
 Lugosi, Bela **L: 515**
Draft [banking] **D: 317**
 Bill (In bookkeeping) **B: 300**
 Commercial paper **Ci: 872**

Negotiable instrument (Forms) **N: 119**
Draft [nautical term]
 Ship (Nautical terms) **S: 405** *with diagram*
Draft [sports]
 Baseball (Minor leagues) **B: 130-131**
 Football (Professional competition) **F: 364**
 Hockey (Professional leagues) **H: 278**
Draft, Military D: 318
 Army (The rise of modern armies) **A: 727**
 Army, United States (The Civil War [1861-1865]) **A: 738**; (World War I [1914-1918]) **A: 738-739**; (World War II [1939-1945]) **A: 739**
 Borden, Sir Robert Laird (Conscription crisis) **B: 486**
 Canada, History of (The conscription issue) **C: 147**
 Civil War, American (The draft) **Ci: 618**
 Conscientious objector **Ci: 974**
 King, William Lyon Mackenzie (Third term as prime minister) **K: 327**
 Military training (Required military training) **M: 544**
 Montreal (The war issue) **M: 778**
 New York (Growing prosperity) **N: 316-318** *with picture*
 Nixon, Richard Milhous (The national scene) **N: 433-434**
 Progressive Conservative Party **P: 812**
 Quebec (World War I) **Q: 32**
 Riot (During the 1800's) **R: 348-349**
 Selective Service System **S: 289**
 World War I (The United States enters the war) **W: 462**
 World War II (Mobilizing for the war) **W: 495**
Draft horse
 Horse (table: Some types and breeds of horses) **H: 343**; (Draft horses) **H: 346** *with pictures*
Draft riots [U.S. history]
 New York (Growing prosperity) **N: 316-318** *with picture*
Drafter [career]
 Careers (Technical and mathematical occupations) **C: 232**
 Mechanical drawing (Information in the drawing) **M: 353** *with picture*
Drafting *See* Mechanical drawing *in this index*
Drafting machine
 Mechanical drawing (Creating a drawing) **M: 354**
Drag [manufacturing]
 Cast and casting (How castings are made) **C: 278** *with diagram*
Drag [physics]
 Aerodynamics (Principles of aerodynamics) **A: 85** *with diagram*; (Shock waves) **A: 87** *with diagram*
 Airplane (Principles of flight) **A: 220**
 Guided missile **G: 423**
 Kite (How kites fly) **K: 339** *with diagram*
 Streamlining **So: 924**
Drag racing [sport]
 Automobile racing (Drag racing) **A: 978** *with picture*
 Hot rod **H: 374a**
 Motorboat racing (Types of racing) **M: 877**
Drag rope
 Balloon (Operation of a gas balloon) **B: 60**
Drag strip
 Automobile racing (Drag racing) **A: 978**
Dragging [computing]
 Computer (A mouse) **Ci: 912-914**
Dragline [cable]
 Lumber (Transporting logs) **L: 518**
Dragline [machine]
 Mining (Surface mining methods) **M: 575**
Dragline [zoology]
 Spider (How spiders use silk) **So: 786**
Drago, Luis María [Argentine statesman] **D: 318**
Drago Doctrine [international relations]
 Drago, Luis María **D: 318**
Dragon [legendary animal] **D: 318** *with picture*
 George, Saint **G: 108**
Dragon [tile]
 Mah-jongg **M: 64** *with picture*
Dragon Boat Festival
 May **M: 321**
Dragon in the Sea, The [book by Herbert]
 Herbert, Frank **H: 197**
Dragon of Komodo [reptile] *See* Komodo dragon *in this index*
"Dragon" series [books by Pilkey]
 Pilkey, Dav **P: 464**
Dragonfly [insect] **D: 319** *with picture*
 Animal *picture on* **A: 492**
 Insect *pictures on* **I: 280**; (Wings) **I: 288**; (Incomplete metamorphosis) **I: 293** *with picture*
Dragons of Eden, The [book by Sagan]
 Sagan, Carl **S: 18**
Dragon's Teeth [book by Sinclair]

Sinclair, Upton **S: 469**
Dragster [automobile]
 Automobile racing (Drag racing) **A: 978**
Drain [electronics]
 Transistor (Metal oxide semiconductor field effect transistors [MOSFET's]) **T: 374** *with diagram*
Drain [plumbing]
 House *diagram on* **H: 383**
Drain auger [tool]
 Plumbing (The drain-waste-vent system) **P: 578**
Drain terminal [device]
 Electronics (Transistors) **E: 212**
Drain tile [building construction]
 House *diagram on* **H: 383**
Drain-waste-vent system
 Plumbing **P: 577** *with diagram*
Drainage [agriculture] **D: 320** *with diagrams*
Drainage basin [geography]
 River (Drainage basins) **R: 353**
Drainage divide [geography]
 Basin **B: 141**
Drainage net
 River (Drainage basins) **R: 353**
Drainage system
 Plumbing (The drain-waste-vent system) **P: 578** *with diagram*
Drainpipe
 Plumbing (The drain-waste-vent system) **P: 578** *with diagram*
Drais, Karl von [German inventor]
 Bicycle (Early bicycles) **B: 291**
Draisienne [bicycle] *See* Draisine *in this index*
Draisine [bicycle]
 Bicycle (Early bicycles) **B: 291**, *picture on* **B: 293**
 Transportation (The beginnings of modern transportation) **T: 390**
Drake [bird]
 Duck **D: 374**
Drake, Edwin Laurentine [American businessman]
 Petroleum (Beginnings of the petroleum industry) **P: 347** *with picture*
Drake, Sir Francis [English sea captain] **D: 320** *with pictures and map*
 California (Spanish and English exploration) **C: 60**
 Exploration *map on* **E: 443**
 Oregon (Exploration and settlement) **O: 846**
 San Francisco (History) **S: 97**
 Spanish Armada (Background to battle) **So: 755**
Drake, Francis M. [American political leader]
 Iowa (table) **I: 391**
Drake, Frank [American astronomer]
 Extraterrestrial intelligence **E: 458**
Drakensberg [mountains, Africa] **D: 323** *with picture*
 Lesotho (Land) **L: 207**
 South Africa *picture on* **So: 611**
DRAM [electronics]
 Computer chip (Memory chips) **Ci: 924f**
Dram [measurement]
 Apothecaries' weight **A: 567**
Drama
 Irish literature **I: 430**
Drama [literature] **D: 324** *with pictures*
 See also Theater *in this index and the list of Related articles in the* Drama *article*
 American literature (The world wars and depression [1914-1945]) **A: 420-423**; (Literature from 1945 to the early 2000's) **A: 422-426**
 Arabic literature (Drama) **A: 584**
 Canadian literature (Modern Canadian drama) **C: 161**
 China (Theater) **C: 490** *with picture*
 Chinese literature (Drama and fiction) **C: 511**
 Comedy **Ci: 867**
 Copyright (Works protected) **Ci: 1046**
 English literature (Early English drama) **E: 316**; (Elizabethan drama) **E: 317**; (Jacobean drama) **E: 317**; (Restoration drama) **E: 318**; (Later Victorian literature) **E: 321**; (Literature after World War II) **E: 322-323**
 Expressionism (Expressionist writing) **E: 455**
 French literature **F: 518**
 Greek literature (Drama) **G: 377**
 Mask (Theatrical masks) **M: 265**
 Mystery play **M: 972**
 Pulitzer Prizes (Prizes in literature, drama, and music) **P: 886b**; (table) **P: 895**
 Realism (In drama) **R: 172**
 Tragedy **T: 366**
 United States *picture on* **U: 119**
Dramamine [medication] **D: 342**
Dramatic irony
 Irony **I: 455**
Dramatic monologue [poetry]
 English literature (Later Victorian literature) **E: 321**
 Poetry (Dramatic poetry) **P: 591**

Dramatic Order Knights of Khorassan
[organization]
Knights of Pythias K: 352
Dramatic poetry
Poetry (Dramatic poetry) P: 591; (Renaissance poetry) P: 596
Dramatic soprano
Opera (The singers) O: 792
Dramatic tenor
Opera (The singers) O: 792
Dramatist
See also the list of playwrights in the Related articles of the Drama *article*
Drama D: 324
Theater T: 233
Dramatists Guild Quarterly, The [magazine]
Writing (Scriptwriting) W: 512
Dramaturge [occupation]
Theater (Interpreting the script) T: 235-236
Draped Reclining Woman [sculpture by Moore]
Hirshhorn Museum and Sculpture Garden *picture on* H: 243
Draper, Charles S. [American scientist]
Inertial guidance (History) I: 264
Draper, Eben S. [American political leader]
Massachusetts (table) M: 288
Draper, William Henry [Canadian political leader]
Macdonald, Sir John Alexander (Early public career) M: 7
Drapery [geology]
Cave (Speleothems) C: 319 *with diagram*
Drapier's Letters [book by Swift]
Swift, Jonathan (Swift's other works) So: 1040-1041
Draughts [game]
Checkers C: 391
Drava River [Europe]
Croatia (Land and climate) Ci: 1148a *with map*
Dravidian [language]
Dravidians D: 342
India (Languages) I: 114
Language *map on* L: 65; (Other language families) L: 66
Dravidians [people] D: 342
Asia (The people) A: 781
India (Ancestry) I: 111; (The Aryans) I: 128
Religion (Hinduism) R: 220
Dravite [mineral]
Tourmaline T: 349
Draw [sports]
Boxing (A draw) B: 528
Football (table) F: 356
Hockey (Hockey terms) H: 275
Lacrosse (Women's lacrosse) L: 23
Draw Dominoes [game]
Dominoes D: 306
Draw-table
Furniture (England) F: 573 *with picture*
Draw weight
Archery (Bows) A: 601-602
Drawbridge
See also Moveable bridge *in this index*
Castle (Structure) C: 280 *with picture*
Drawing [art] D: 342 *with pictures*
Animation (Drawing on film) A: 514a
Cartoon (Developing the idea) C: 266 *with pictures*
Drawing [gambling]
Lottery L: 473
Drawing [industrial process]
Aluminum (Drawing) A: 396
Cotton (Spinning) Ci: 1091
Glass (Drawing) G: 215, *pictures on* G: 216
Nylon (How nylon is made) N: 633
Wire (How wire is made) W: 343
Drawing, Mechanical *See* Mechanical drawing *in this index*
Drawn game
Chess (How chess is played) C: 413
Drawn sliver [yarn]
Cotton (Spinning) Ci: 1091
Drawpoint [mining]
Mining (Mining terms) M: 577
Drayton, Michael [English poet] D: 344
DRC [country] *See* Congo, Democratic Republic of the *in this index*
Dreadlocks [hairstyle]
Hairdressing (The 1900's) H: 12-13
Rastafarians R: 146
Dreadnought [ship]
Battleship (The modern battleship) B: 172
Warship *picture on* W: 43; (The birth of the modern battleship) W: 41
Dreadnought [ship class]
Navy (Engineering advances) N: 79-80
World War I (A build-up of military might) W: 453-454

Dream D: 344
Brain (Memory and imagination) B: 554
Mythology (Psychological approaches) M: 990
Nightmare N: 420
Sleep (The structure of sleep) S: 506; (Sleep in animals) S: 506
Dream, The [book by Kepler]
Kepler, Johannes (His life) K: 305
Dream Days [book by Grahame]
Grahame, Kenneth G: 301
Dream of Gerontius, The [music by Elgar]
Elgar, Sir Edward E: 235
Dream of Oengus, The [story]
Irish literature (Heroic tales, romances, and sagas) I: 430
Dream of the Red Chamber [book by Cao Xueqin]
Chinese literature (Drama and fiction) C: 511-512
Dream Play, A [play by Strindberg]
Drama (Expressionism) D: 339
Strindberg, August So: 929
Dream Team
Basketball (The history of professional basketball) B: 154a-155
Olympic Games *picture on* O: 755; (The recent games) O: 753
Dreaming [religion]
Aborigines, Australian (Aboriginal life) A: 14
Dreamland and Other Poems [book by Mair]
Mair, Charles M: 93
Dreams From My Father [book by Obama]
Obama, Barack (Early career) O: 640d
Dreamtime [religion] *See* Dreaming [religion] *in this index*
DreamWorks SKG [film studio]
Animation (New diversity) A: 514c
Spielberg, Steven So: 792
Dred Scott Decision [U.S. history] D: 345 *with picture*
African Americans (The deepening division over slavery) A: 136h-136i
Civil War, American (The Dred Scott Decision) Ci: 616
Missouri (The American Civil War) M: 671
Supreme Court of the United States (Civil rights) So: 1001; (table) So: 1002
Taney, Roger Brooke T: 24
United States, History of the (Party splits) U: 176
Dredge [machine]
Mining (Dredging) M: 575
Dredge [net]
Oyster (Oyster harvesting) O: 892
Dredging D: 345
Mining (Dredging) M: 575
Dreifuss, Ruth [Swiss political leader]
Switzerland (Recent developments) So: 1061
Dreiser, Theodore [American author] D: 346
American literature (Naturalists) A: 419-420
Naturalism (Naturalism in fiction) N: 65
Novel (The United States) N: 573
Dresden [Germany] D: 346
Dresden china D: 346 *with picture*
Dresden D: 346
Porcelain (German porcelain) P: 677 *with picture*
Dresden Opera House
Germany *picture on* G: 155
Dreser, Heinrich [German scientist]
Aspirin (History) A: 816
Dress [clothing] *See* Clothing *in this index*
Dress Macpherson plaid
Tartan *picture on* T: 47
Dress Menzies plaid
Tartan *picture on* T: 47
Dress parade
Theater (Costume design) T: 242-243
Dress rehearsal
Opera (Rehearsing a production) O: 796
Television (Rehearsals) T: 111
Theater (Rehearsing) T: 236-237
Dress shoe
Shoe (Kinds of shoes) S: 431 *with pictures*
Dress Stewart plaid
Tartan *picture on* T: 47
Dressage
Horse (Dressage) H: 357 *with picture*
Dressage spur [riding equipment]
Horse (Spurs) H: 351
Dressed lumber
Lumber (Kinds of lumber) L: 517
Dresser, Paul [American composer]
Dreiser, Theodore D: 346
Dressing [bandage]
Bandage B: 75
Dressing [industrial process]
Fur (Dressing) F: 563
Meat packing (Slaughtering and dressing) M: 351
Dressler, Marie [American actress]
Motion picture (Best performance by an actress:

1930-31) M: 862
Sennett, Mack *picture on* S: 301
Drew, Adrian E. [American aviator]
Aviation (table: Aviation speed records) A: 990
Drew, Charles Richard [American physician] D: 347
Blood (History of blood research) B: 414
Drew, Daniel [American businessman]
Fisk, James F: 189
Gould, Jay G: 280
Drew, George A. [Canadian political leader]
Diefenbaker, John George (Member of Parliament) D: 197
Ontario (table) O: 783
Drew, George F. [American political leader]
Florida (table) F: 260
Drew, Georgianna [American actress]
Barrymore B: 119
Drew, John [Irish-born American actor]
Barrymore B: 119
Drew, Nancy [literary figure]
Keene, Carolyn K: 254
Stratemeyer, Edward So: 920
Drew, Thomas S. [American political leader]
Arkansas (table) A: 712
Drexel, Anthony Joseph [American financier]
Philadelphia (A growing city) P: 367
Drexel, Catherine Mary [American religious leader] *See* Drexel, Saint Katharine *in this index*
Drexel, Saint Katharine [American religious leader] D: 347 *with portrait*
Drexel, Morgan & Company [bank]
Morgan, J. P. M: 803
Drey [nest]
Squirrel (Obtaining shelter) So: 815
Dreyer, Carl [Danish director]
Denmark (Arts) D: 136
Motion picture (The movies talk) M: 867
Dreyfus, Alfred [French public figure] *See* Dreyfus affair *in this index*
Dreyfus, Lee S. [American political leader]
Wisconsin (table) W: 365
Dreyfus affair [French history] D: 347
Holocaust (Before the Holocaust) H: 296
Jews (The Zionist movement) J: 123
Zionism (Movement to Palestine) Z: 595
Zola, Émile Z: 598
Dreyfusards [French history]
Dreyfus affair (Efforts to clear Dreyfus's name) D: 347-348
Dreyfuss, Barney [American baseball club owner]
Baseball (table: Hall of Fame) B: 134
Dreyfuss, Richard [American actor]
Motion picture (Best performance by an actor: 1977) M: 862a
DRG [insurance] *See* Diagnosis related group *in this index*
Dribble [sports]
Basketball *picture on* B: 146
Soccer (The forwards) So: 545; (table) So: 546; (Dribbling) So: 548
Dried food *See* Dehydrated food *in this index*
Dried fruit [food]
Date palm (Uses) D: 42
Fig F: 96
Prune P: 841
Raisin R: 129
Drift [geology]
Minnesota (Land regions) M: 596; (Natural resources) M: 599
Drift [mining]
Mining (Mining terms) M: 577
Drift, Continental [geology] *See* Continental drift *in this index*
Drift fishing
Fishing F: 175
Drift mine
Coal (Underground mining) Ci: 723 *with diagram*
Mining (Underground mining methods) M: 576
Drift net
Fishing industry (Nets) F: 183-185
Porpoise P: 679
Drift Prairie [North Dakota]
North Dakota (Land regions) N: 506; (Rivers and lakes) N: 508
Drift tube [machine]
Particle accelerator (How accelerators work) P: 184-185 *with diagram*
Drifter [illustration by Kent]
Kent, Rockwell *picture on* K: 271
Drifting Apart [play by Herne]
Herne, James A. H: 212
Drifting Clouds [book by Futabatei]
Japanese literature (The modern period) J: 62
Driftless Area
Illinois (Land regions) I: 64
Drill [farm machine]

Agriculture *picture on* A: 158
Farm and farming *picture on* F: 34; (Planting)
   F: 35-36 *with picture*
Oats (Growing oats) O: 640-640a
Tull, Jethro T: 483
Wheat (Planting) W: 271 *with picture*
Drill [tool] D: 348
Diamond (Industrial uses) D: 182
Industrial Revolution (The steam engine) I: 249
Machine tool (Metal removal) M: 17
Screw (Uses) S: 225
Woodworking (Drilling) W: 398 *with pictures*
Drill bit [tool] *See* Bit *in this index*
Drill pipe
Ocean drilling programs O: 667 *with diagram*
Petroleum (A rotary drilling rig) P: 338 *with diagram*
Drill press [machine]
Drill D: 348
Machine tool (Hole machining) M: 17-18
Drilling [excavation]
See also Boring [excavation] *in this index*
Gas [fuel] (Producing gas) G: 55
Petroleum (Completing the well) P: 340-341 *with pictures*
Drilling mud
Petroleum (A rotary drilling rig) P: 338-339
Drillship
Ocean drilling programs O: 667 *with diagram*
Petroleum *picture on* P: 340; (A rotary drilling rig) P: 339
"Drink to Me Only With Thine Eyes" [song]
Jonson, Ben J: 160
Drinker, Philip [American inventor]
Iron lung I: 453
Drinking
Alcoholism A: 337
Crime (table) Ci: 1137
Drip irrigation
Gardening (Caring for the garden) G: 35
Irrigation (Trickle irrigation) I: 458 *with picture*
Vegetable (Irrigation) V: 293
Driscoll, Alfred E. [American political leader]
New Jersey (table) N: 249
Driskill Mountain
Louisiana (Land regions) L: 490
Drive [psychology]
See also Motivation *in this index*
Adler, Alfred A: 58
Hull, Clark Leonard H: 412
Sales (Characteristics needed) S: 65
Drive [sports]
Badminton (Playing) B: 24-25
Drive [system]
Transmission (Transmissions and drives) T: 375
Drive, The [sculpture]
Dallas *picture on* D: 14
Drive-in theater
New Jersey (Interesting facts) N: 231
Drive shaft
Automobile (The drive system) A: 949
Hybrid car H: 461
Transmission (Transmissions and drives) T: 375
Drive system
Automobile (The drive system) A: 949 *with diagram*
Phonograph (Parts of a phonograph) P: 400-401
Drive-through restaurant
Restaurant (Fast-service restaurants) R: 262
Drive-through zoo
Zoo (Cageless zoos) Z: 602
Drive train [device] *See* Power train *in this index*
Driver [club]
Golf (Golf clubs) G: 262 *with picture*
Driver, William [American sea captain]
Flag (Flags of the United States and Canada) F: 208
United States flag U: 200
Driver ant [insect]
Animal *picture on* A: 480
Driving
Automobile (Driving an automobile) A: 954
Breath testing B: 591
Safety (Safety in transportation) S: 14
Driving force [physics]
Aerodynamics (Lift and drag in a sailboat) A: 86-87 *with diagram*
Driving Miss Daisy [film]
Motion picture (Best picture: 1989) M: 861
Driving under the influence [crime] *See* Driving while intoxicated *in this index*
Driving while intoxicated [crime] D: 348
Drizzle
Rain (Characteristics of rain) R: 122
Drnovšek, Janez [Slovenian political leader]
Slovenia (History) S: 512
Droll Stories [book by Balzac]

Balzac, Honoré de B: 71
Drolleries [art]
Illuminated manuscript I: 78
Dromedary [animal] D: 348
Camel C: 76, *picture on* C: 78
Desert (Desert animals) D: 156
Dromio [literary figure]
Shakespeare, William: (*The Comedy of Errors*) S: 355
Drone [aircraft] *See* Unmanned aerial vehicle *in this index*
Drone [entomology]
Bee (The honey bee colony) B: 201 *with picture*; (Division of labor) B: 205 *with picture*
Bumble bee B: 698 *with picture*
Drone pipe [musical instrument]
Bagpipe B: 26 *with picture*
Drop [sports]
Badminton (Playing) B: 24-25
Drop ball
Soccer (table) So: 546; (Fouls) So: 546-547
Drop forging
Forging (Machine forging) F: 409-410
Drop-kicking
Rugby football (Scoring) R: 510
Drop-off center
Recycling (Collecting materials) R: 184
Dropout center [education]
Alternative school (Features of alternative schools) A: 388-389
Dropped goal
Rugby football (Scoring) R: 510
Dropper line [tackle]
Fishing industry (Hooks) F: 185 *with picture*
Dropwindsonde [instrument]
Weather (Weather balloons, airplanes, and ships) W: 163
Drosophila melanogaster [insect]
Fruit fly F: 549
Heredity (Chromosomes and genes) H: 201
Drought [weather] D: 349
Dust Bowl D: 391
Famine (Drought) F: 26
Sahara (History) S: 22
Sinkhole S: 473
Water (Water shortages) W: 122 *with picture*
Drown proofing
Swimming (Water safety) So: 1042-1043
Drowned valley [geography]
Valley (Kinds of valleys) V: 265
Drowning D: 349
Drug D: 350 *with pictures*
See also the list of Related articles in the Drug *article*
Allergy A: 373
Biological clock B: 315
Cancer (Drug therapy) C: 172
Deafness (Environmental factors) D: 57
Diabetes (Treatment) D: 179
Dietary supplement D: 200
Disease (Medical treatment) D: 232
Food and Drug Administration F: 340
Heart (Treatment) H: 138; (Heart failure) H: 143
Herbal medicine H: 196
Indian, American (Hunting, gathering, and fishing) I: 141
Marine biology (What marine biologists do) M: 204
MedicAlert M: 361
Mind (Alterations of the mind) M: 563
Ocean (Medicines) O: 654
Pain (Treatment) P: 22
Pharmacology P: 354
Placebo P: 505
Plant (As medicines) P: 517
Pure food and drug laws P: 907
Rain forest (Scientific value) R: 126c
Safety (In the bathroom) S: 10
Social security (Medicare) So: 555
Weight control (Drugs) W: 182
Drug abuse D: 361 *with pictures*
See also the list of Related articles in the Drug abuse *article*
Adolescent (Alcohol and drug abuse) A: 63; (Risk taking) A: 64
African Americans (Social struggles) A: 136s-136t
AIDS (How HIV is transmitted) A: 164b; (Prevention) A: 165; (Education) A: 165
Barbiturate (Dangers of barbiturates) B: 107
Blood doping B: 415
City (Social problems) Ci: 591
Cocaine (Use) C: 742
Crime (table) Ci: 1137
Depressant D: 150
Dopamine D: 309
Drug (Analgesics) D: 352; (Drugs today) D: 360
Drug Enforcement Administration D: 366

Drug testing D: 366
Ecstasy E: 66
Forensic science (Controlled substances) F: 389
Hashish H: 82
Health (Health hazards) H: 126-127
Heroin H: 213
Inhalant I: 271
Mental illness (Substance use disorders) M: 406
Methadone M: 433
Morphine M: 816
Narcotic N: 21
New York City (Social problems) N: 332-333
Olympic Games (Charges of steroid use) O: 753; (The recent games) O: 753-754
Opium (Opium addiction) O: 811
Prostitution P: 830
Tobacco T: 305
Drug Abuse Prevention and Control Act [1970]
Drug (U.S. drug laws) D: 357-358
Drug addiction
Drug (Effects on the body) D: 354
Drug abuse D: 361
Drug Amendments Act [1962]
Drug (U.S. drug laws) D: 357
Food and Drug Administration F: 340
Drug cartel
Mexico (Recent developments) M: 474-475
Drug dependence
Drug (Effect on the body) D: 354
Drug Enforcement Administration D: 366
Drug abuse (Combating drug abuse) D: 364-365
Drug injection [execution] *See* Lethal injection *in this index*
Drug metabolism
Drug (Action in the body) D: 353-354
Drug testing D: 366
Drug abuse (Reducing demand) D: 364-365
Drug therapy
Mental illness (Somatic therapy) M: 407
Psychiatry (Somatic therapy) P: 845
Drug tolerance
Drug (Effect on the body) D: 354
Drug trafficking
Colombia (Civil war) Ci: 784 *with picture*
Drug abuse (Combating drug abuse) D: 364-365
Drug Enforcement Administration D: 366
Medellín M: 360
Money laundering M: 718
Noriega, Manuel Antonio N: 455
Druggist [career]
Pharmacy P: 354
Drugstore beetle [insect]
Deathwatch D: 63
Druids [religious group] D: 367
Celts C: 342
Mistletoe M: 676
Drum [electronics]
Videotape recorder (Recording) V: 361 *with diagram*
Drum [fish] D: 367 *with pictures*
Kingfish K: 329
Weakfish W: 154
Drum [machine]
Tire (Assembling a tire) T: 296
Drum [musical instrument] D: 367
Bongo drums B: 458 *with picture*
Conga drum Ci: 937 *with picture*
Dance (Ritual ethnic dances) D: 25
Indian, American *pictures on* I: 156, I: 160
Inuit *picture on* I: 354f
Jazz (Drums) J: 69 *with picture*
Music *pictures on* M: 949; (Percussion instruments) M: 950
Drum brake
Automobile (The brake system) A: 950
Brake (Hydraulic brakes) B: 560-561 *with diagram*, B: 562
Drum corps [marching band] D: 368
Drum drying
Food preservation (Drying) F: 342-343
Drum majorette
Baton twirling B: 167
Drum Point Lighthouse [Maryland]
Lighthouse *picture on* L: 294
"Drum Taps" [poems by Whitman]
Whitman, Walt (His work) W: 294
Drumfish [fish]
Drum D: 367 *with picture*
Drumhead
Drum D: 367
Drumlin [geology]
Glacier (How glaciers shape the land) G: 203-204 *with diagram*
Hill H: 230
New York (Land regions) N: 304-306
Drummond, William [English colonial official]
North Carolina (Exploration and settlement)

N: 490-492
Drummond, William Henry [Canadian poet]
D: 368
Drums Along the Mohawk [book by Edmonds]
Edmonds, Walter Dumaux E: 83
Drums at Dusk [book by Bontemps]
Bontemps, Arna Wendell B: 463
"Drunken Boat, The" [poem by Rimbaud]
Rimbaud, Arthur R: 341
Drunken driving See Driving while intoxicated *in this index*
Drunkenness
Alcoholism A: 337
Breath testing B: 591
Crime (Types of crimes) Ci: 1136; (table) Ci: 1137
Driving while intoxicated D: 348
Drupe [botany] D: 368
Fruit (Simple fruits) F: 544 *with pictures*
Druplet [botany]
Blackberry B: 392
Loganberry L: 423 *with picture*
Raspberry R: 145 *with picture*
Drury, Ernest C. [Canadian political leader]
Ontario (table) O: 783
Drury Lane Theatre [London]
Garrick, David G: 45
Druses [people] D: 368
Lebanon (Ethnic groups and religion) L: 171;
(War and terrorism) L: 173
Syria (Religion) S: 1071
Druzes [people] See Druses *in this index*
DRV [nutrition] See Daily Reference Value *in this index*
Dry bean
Bean (Kinds of beans) B: 181
Dry beer
Beer B: 211
Dry bite
Snake (Snakebite) S: 533
Dry-bulb thermometer
Hygrometer (The psychrometer) H: 474
Dry bulk carrier
Ship (Dry bulk carriers) S: 408 *with picture*
Dry cell [device]
Battery (Battery structure) B: 168
Dry chemical extinguisher
Fire extinguisher (Dry chemical extinguishers) F: 130
Dry cleaning D: 368
Dry cow
Cattle (Breeding) C: 312
Dry dock [shipping] D: 369
Ship (Launching and outfitting) S: 413 *with picture*
Dry-erase board
Audio-visual materials (Chalkboards, dry-erase boards, and flip charts) A: 882
Eraser E: 349
Dry farming See Dryland farming *in this index*
Dry gangrene [disease]
Gangrene G: 27
Dry hole
Petroleum (table) P: 332
Dry ice D: 369
Carbon dioxide C: 207
Cloud seeding (Cloud-seeding methods) C: 711
Food, Frozen (Cryogenic freezing) F: 338
Refrigeration (Dry ice) R: 201
Weather (How people affect the weather) W: 170
Dry kiln
Lumber (Seasoning) L: 519
Dry lake
Nevada (Natural resources) N: 169
Dry macular degeneration [disorder]
Macular degeneration M: 26
Dry measure
Weights and measures (Volume and capacity) W: 186
Dry milling [agriculture]
Corn (Corn in industry) Ci: 1061
Dry milling [industrial process]
Leather *picture on* L: 168
Dry painting [art]
Sand painting S: 107
Dry permafrost
Permafrost P: 289
Dry-plate process
Photography (Technical improvements) P: 423
Dry point [art]
Engraving (Dry point) E: 326
Dry-press process [industrial process]
Brick (Forming bricks) B: 597-598 *with picture*
Dry roasting [process]
Peanut (Processing peanuts) P: 214
Dry rot [plant disease]
Rot R: 485
Dry rub [cooking]

Barbecue B: 106
Dry salting [food]
Fishing industry (Methods of processing) F: 186
"Dry Salvages, The" [poem by Eliot]
Eliot, T. S. (His works) E: 237-238
Dry sand mold [manufacturing]
Cast and casting (Types of molds) C: 278
Dry simple fruit [botany]
Fruit (Simple fruits) F: 544 *with pictures*
Dry snow avalanche
Avalanche A: 982
Dry-sump engine
Gasoline engine (The lubrication system) G: 66
Dry Tortugas National Park [Florida] D: 369
National Park System (table: National parks) N: 48
Dry valley
Antarctica (Land) A: 531-532 *with picture*
Dry wall [construction] See Drywall *in this index*
Dry wine
Wine (Types of wine) W: 336
Dryad [Greek mythology]
Mythology (Greek divinities) M: 982
Dryden, John [English author] D: 369
English literature (Restoration literature) E: 318
Poetry (Neoclassical poetry) P: 596-597
Dryden Flight Research Center [California]
Edwards Air Force Base E: 114
Drying
Food preservation (Drying) F: 343
Drying oil
Linseed oil L: 339
Oil (Fixed oils) O: 706
Dryland farming D: 369
Farm and farming (Water management) F: 33
Nebraska (The Great Plains) N: 104
Western frontier life in America (Improvements in farming) W: 233
Dryline [meteorology]
Tornado (Moisture) T: 334
Drysdale, Don [American baseball player]
Baseball (table: Hall of Fame) B: 134; (table: Modern major league records) B: 138
Drysdale, Sir Russell [Australian painter]
Australia (Painting) A: 905-906
Drywall [construction]
House (table) H: 380
Wallboard W: 17
DSL [electronics] See Digital subscriber line *in this index*
DSLR [camera] See Digital single-lens reflex camera *in this index*
DTP [communications] See Desktop publishing *in this index*
DT's [disorder] See Delirium tremens *in this index*
Du ...
Most names beginning with Du are alphabetized as single words: Du Maurier appears after Dumas
Du Fu [Chinese poet]
Chinese literature (Poetry) C: 511
Du You [Chinese scholar]
Encyclopedia (The first reference works) E: 268a
Dual [wrestling]
Wrestling W: 505
Dual citizenship
Citizenship (Dual citizenship) Ci: 570
Dual flush toilet
Plumbing (How toilets work) P: 579-580
Dual language education See Two-way bilingual education *in this index*
Dual-mode school
Distance learning D: 238
Dual Monarchy See Austria-Hungary *in this index*
Dual nationality See Dual citizenship *in this index*
Dual Power [Russian history]
Russian Revolution of 1917 (The February Revolution) R: 566
Dual presidency
Government (Dual presidency) G: 286
Dual-purpose cattle
Cattle (Dual-purpose cattle) C: 311
Dual rake [machine]
Rake (The side-delivery rake) R: 130
Dualism [philosophy]
Descartes, René (His philosophy) D: 154
Materialism M: 300a
Metaphysics (Mind and body) M: 430
Duane, William J. [American government official]
Jackson, Andrew (table) J: 11; (Jackson's second Administration) J: 12
Duarte, José Napoleón [Salvadoran political leader]
El Salvador (The 1900's) E: 252
Duarte, Maria Eva [Argentine political leader] See Perón, Eva Duarte de *in this index*
Duarte Frutos, Nicanor [Paraguayan political leader]
Paraguay (Recent developments) P: 150

Duarte Peak [mountain]
West Indies (Land and climate) W: 204
Dub [music]
Rap music R: 141
Dub [poetry]
English literature (Recent English poetry) E: 323
Dubai [state]
United Arab Emirates U: 43
Dubai [city, United Arab Emirates] D: 370 *with picture*
Asia *picture on* A: 770
Monorail *picture on* M: 733
United Arab Emirates U: 43
Dubai International Airport
Airport (table) A: 245
Du Barry, Madame [French public figure]
Fragonard, Jean Honoré F: 451
Dubayy [United Arab Emirates] See Dubai *in this index*
Dubček, Alexander [Czechoslovak political leader]
Communism (In Eastern Europe) Ci: 896
Czech Republic (The 1960's) Ci: 1214
Czechoslovakia (The 1960's) Ci: 1216
Slovakia (Communist rule) S: 509
Socialism (The New Left) So: 561
Du Bellay, Joachim [French poet] D: 370
French literature (The Pléiade) F: 519-520
Dubhe [star]
North Star *picture on* N: 519
Dubinsky, David [American labor leader] D: 370
Dublin [Ireland] D: 370 *with picture*
Ireland I: 416 *with picture, pictures on* I: 417,
I: 427, I: 428; (Surface features) I: 422
Dublin, University of See Trinity College Dublin *in this index*
Dubliners [book by Joyce]
Irish literature (Fiction) I: 432
Joyce, James J: 176
Dubnium [element] D: 371
Transuranium element T: 401
DuBois, Blanche [literary figure]
Williams, Tennessee W: 312
Dubois, Eugène [Dutch anthropologist] D: 372
Java fossils J: 65
Prehistoric people (table) P: 754
Dubois, François [French painter]
Huguenots *picture on* H: 411
Du Bois, Guy Pène [American painter] D: 372
Du Bois, W. E. B. [American historian] D: 372 *with portrait*
African Americans *picture on* A: 136k; (The rise of new black leaders) A: 136l
American literature (Nonfiction writers) A: 420
Niagara Movement N: 394
Washington, Booker T. (Opposition to Washington) W: 89
Du Bois, William Pène [American author]
Du Bois, Guy Pène D: 372
Newbery Medal (table) N: 359
Dubos, René Jules [French-American microbiologist] D: 372
Dubuffet, Jean [French painter] D: 372
Dubuque [Iowa] D: 373
Dubuque, Julien [French-Canadian frontiersman] D: 373
Iowa *picture on* I: 394; (Exploration and early settlement) I: 393
Du Buque Visitor [newspaper]
Iowa (Communication) I: 391
Ducat [money] D: 373
Duccio di Buoninsegna [Italian painter] D: 373
Pilate, Pontius *picture on* P: 462
Duce, Il [title] See Mussolini, Benito *in this index*
Duchamp, Marcel [French painter] D: 373 *with picture*
Dadaism D: 2
Mobile M: 682
Painting (Europeans in America) P: 84
Sculpture (Assemblages) S: 257 *with picture*
Ducharme, Réjean [Canadian author]
Canadian literature (Modern literature: 1945 to the present) C: 159-160
Du Châtelet, Marquise [French author] See Châtelet, Marquise du *in this index*
Duchenne muscular dystrophy [disease]
Heredity (table) H: 204
Muscular dystrophy (Duchenne muscular dystrophy) M: 936
Duchess [title]
Duke D: 380
Nobility (In the United Kingdom) N: 450
Duchess of Alba [painting by Goya]
Goya, Francisco *picture on* G: 295
Duchess of Malfi, The [play by Webster]
English literature (Jacobean drama) E: 317
Webster, John W: 177
Duck [bird] D: 374 *with pictures*

Bird *picture on* B: 363; (As a source of food and raw materials) B: 330
  Mallard M: 110 *with picture*
  Poultry P: 720
Duck [fabric]
  Canvas C: 184
Duck hawk [bird] *See* Peregrine falcon *in this index*
Duckbill *See* Platypus *in this index*
Duckbilled dinosaur *See* Hadrosaur *in this index*
Ducking
  Boxing *picture on* B: 529
Ducking stool [punishment] D: 377
  Colonial life in America (Crime and punishment) Ci: 796
Duckling [bird]
  Duck (The features of a duck) D: 374 *with picture*; (Ducklings) D: 375
Duckpins [game]
  Bowling (Other kinds of bowling) B: 524b
Ducktail
  Hairdressing (The 1900's) H: 12-13
Duckweed [plant] D: 377
  Plant *picture on* P: 517
Duclot, Louis [American journalist]
  Louisiana (Communication) L: 495
Duco [lacquer]
  Painting (Synthetic resins) P: 40
Ducommun, Élie [Swiss statesman]
  Nobel Prizes (Peace: 1902) N: 448
Duct [building construction]
  House (Heating and air conditioning) H: 383
Ducted propeller [engineering] D: 377
Ductility [physical property] D: 377
  Alloy (Characteristics of alloys) A: 377
  Copper (Ductility) Ci: 1042
  Gold (Physical properties) G: 249
  Metal (What metals are) M: 425
Ductless gland *See* Endocrine gland *in this index*
Ductus arteriosus [anatomy]
  Heart (Abnormal openings in the heart) H: 141
Dud [warfare]
  Bomb (Dangers to civilians) B: 452
Dude ranch D: 377
  Western frontier life in America (Improvements in transportation) W: 233
  Wyoming *picture on* W: 516
Dudley, E. B. [American political leader]
  North Carolina (table) N: 490
Dudley, Lord Guildford [husband of]
  Grey, Lady Jane G: 391
Dudley, Robert *See* Leicester, Earl of *in this index*
Dudley, Thomas [American colonial official] D: 377
Due process of law D: 377
  Civil rights (Due process) Ci: 608
  Constitution of the United States (Amendment 5) Ci: 1012; (Amendment 14) Ci: 1013
  Freedom (Social freedom) F: 501
  Holmes, Oliver Wendell, Jr. (Supreme Court justice) H: 295
  Magna Carta (Promises in the charter) M: 53
  Patriot Act P: 197
  Trial (The criminal defendant's rights) T: 436437
Duel [combat] D: 378
Du Fay, Charles François [French physicist]
  Electricity (Experiments with electric charge) E: 196
Dufay, Guillaume [French composer]
  Classical music (Secular music) Ci: 646
Duff, James H. [American political leader]
  Pennsylvania (table) P: 263
Dufferin and Ava, Marquess of [British statesman] D: 378
Dufferin Terrace
  Quebec (Upper Town) Q: 34
Duffy, Carol Ann [British poet] D: 378
Duffy, Hugh [American baseball player]
  Baseball (table: Hall of Fame) B: 134
Dufrost de Lajemmerais, Marie-Marguerite
  Youville, Saint Marguerite d' Y: 574
Dufy, Raoul [French painter] D: 379 *with picture*
  Painting (Color) P: 35
Dug Hill Ridge
  Maryland (Land regions) M: 250
Dugdale, Henrietta [Australian political leader]
  Woman suffrage (Australia) W: 381
Dugin, Andrej [German illustrator]
  Literature for children *picture on* L: 355
Dugina, Olga [German illustrator]
  Literature for children *picture on* L: 355
Dugong [sea animal] D: 379 *with picture*
Dugout [baseball]
  Baseball (Foul territory) B: 127
Dugout [boat]
  Canoeing (History) C: 182
  Indian, American (Indians of the Southeast) I: 157
  Ship *picture on* S: 416
  Transportation *picture on* T: 386; (Water

transportation) T: 384
Du Gua, Pierre, Sieur de Monts [French explorer] D: 379
  Canada, History of (Early settlements) C: 140
  New Brunswick (Exploration and settlement) N: 196
  New France (Exploration and settlement) N: 204
  Nova Scotia (Exploration and settlement) N: 567-568
  Poutrincourt, Jean de Biencourt de P: 722
Du Guillot, Pernette [French poet]
  French literature (Lyon) F: 520
Duhalde, Eduardo [Argentine political leader]
  Argentina (The economic crisis of 2001) A: 659
DUI [crime] *See* Driving while intoxicated *in this index*
Duiker [animal]
  Antelope A: 541
Duino Elegies [poems by Rilke]
  Rilke, Rainer Maria R: 341
Duisburg [Germany] D: 379
Dujardin, Jean [French actor]
  Motion picture (Best performance by an actor: 2011) M: 862a
Dukakis, Michael Stanley [American political leader] D: 379 *with portrait*
  Bush, George Herbert Walker (The Republican nomination) B: 719
  Democratic Party (The late 1900's) D: 127
  Massachusetts (table) M: 288
Dukakis, Olympia [American actress]
  Motion picture (Best performance by an actress in a supporting role: 1987) M: 862b
Dukas, Paul Abraham [French composer] D: 380
Duke [title] D: 380
  Nobility (In the United Kingdom) N: 450
Duke, James Buchanan [American businessman]
  Duke University D: 380
  North Carolina (Economic progress) N: 493
Duke, Patty [American actress]
  Motion picture (Best performance by an actress in a supporting role: 1962) M: 862b
Duke cherry [plant]
  Cherry C: 410 *with picture*
Duke of Gloucester Street
  Williamsburg *picture on* W: 313
Duke University D: 380
  Krzyzewski, Mike K: 389
  North Carolina *picture on* N: 477
Dukenfield, William Claude [birth name of]
  Fields, W. C. F: 95
Dukhobors [religious group]
  Doukhobors D: 314
Dukun [healer]
  Magic (Asia) M: 50
DUKW [military transport]
  World War II *picture on* W: 485
Dulbecco, Renato [American physiologist]
  Nobel Prizes (Physiology or medicine: 1975) N: 446
Dulcimer [musical instrument] D: 380 *with pictures*
  Piano (History) P: 447
Dulcy [play by Connelly and Kaufman]
  Connelly, Marc C: 972
Dulle Griete
  Cannon *picture on* C: 179
Dulles, Allen W. [American government official]
  Warren Report W: 37
Dulles, Avery [American religious leader]
  Cardinal (table: American cardinals) C: 211
Dulles, John Foster [American statesman] D: 381
  Cold War (To the brink and back) Ci: 765
  Diplomacy (History) D: 217
  Eisenhower, Dwight David (Foreign affairs) E: 152
Duluth [Minnesota] D: 381
  Minnesota (The early 1900's) M: 604
Duluth, Sieur [French explorer]
  Duluth D: 381
  Minnesota (Exploration) M: 603
Duma [legislature] D: 381
  Lenin, V. I. (Revolt) L: 192
  Russia (National government) R: 531 *with picture*; (The Revolution of 1905) R: 552
  Russian Revolution of 1917 (The 1905 Revolution) R: 566
  Union of Soviet Socialist Republics (The February Revolution) U: 35
Dumas, Alexandre, père [1802-1870, French author] D: 382
  Novel (France) N: 573
Dumas, Alexandre, fils [1824-1895, French author] D: 382
  French literature (Realism) F: 522
Du Maurier, Daphne [English author] D: 382
Du Maurier, George [English artist and author] D: 382
Du Maurier, Sir Gerald [English actor]

Du Maurier, Daphne D: 382
"Dumb Bunny" series [books by Pilkey]
  Pilkey, Dav P: 464
Dumb rabies [disease]
  Rabies (Symptoms in animals) R: 49
Dumb supper [custom]
  Halloween (Halloween in the United States) H: 25
Dumbarton Oaks [conference, 1944] D: 383
  United Nations (The Dumbarton Oaks Conference) U: 94
Dumdum bullet
  Bullet B: 695
Dumdum fever *See* Kala-azar *in this index*
Dumky [music by Dvořák]
  Dvořák, Antonín D: 394
Dummer, Henry E. [American lawyer]
  Lincoln, Abraham (Study) L: 314
Dummy [cards]
  Bridge (The play) B: 604 *with diagram*
Dummy [puppet]
  Puppet (Dummies) P: 907
  Ventriloquism V: 309 *with picture*
Dummy spur [riding equipment]
  Horse (Spurs) H: 351
Dumont, Gabriel [Canadian revolutionary] D: 383 *with portrait*
  North West Rebellion N: 520
DuMont Television Network
  Television (History of U.S. television broadcasting) T: 117-118
Dump [sanitation]
  Environmental pollution (Solid waste) E: 334
  Landfill L: 58
Dump rake [machine]
  Rake (The dump rake) R: 130
Dump truck
  Truck *pictures on* T: 459
Dumping [economics]
  Tariff (Why tariffs are levied) T: 43
Dumpling [food]
  Food (Interesting facts about food) F: 329
Dun [insect] *See* Mayfly *in this index*
Dún Laoghaire [Ireland] D: 383
Dunant, Jean Henri [Swiss social reformer] D: 383
  Red Cross (Beginnings) R: 187
Dunaway, Faye [American actress]
  Motion picture (Best performance by an actress: 1976) M: 862
Dunbar, Battles of [Scottish history]
  Scotland (Fight for independence) S: 219; (War with the king) S: 220
Dunbar, Paul Laurence [American author] D: 383 *with portrait*
  African American literature (The 1800's) A: 136a
  American literature (Realist poetry) A: 421
Duncan I [king of Scotland] D: 383
  Macbeth M: 5
Duncan, Arne [American government official]
  Education, Department of (table) E: 110
  Obama, Barack (table) O: 640h
Duncan, Charles W., Jr. [American government official]
  Carter, Jimmy (table) C: 257
  Energy, Department of (table) E: 276
Duncan, Donald F. [American inventor]
  Yo-yo Y: 566
Duncan, Isadora [American dancer] D: 384 *with picture*
  Dance (Modern dance) D: 30-31
Duncan, Joseph [American political leader]
  Illinois (table) I: 71
Duncan, Robert [American poet] D: 384
  American literature (Poetry) A: 423
Duncan, Sara Jeannette [Canadian author]
  Canadian literature (Fiction: 1850-1918) C: 157
Duncan Dam
  British Columbia (The mid-1900's) B: 630
Duncan Phyfe furniture
  Phyfe, Duncan D: 451
Dunciad, The [poem by Pope]
  English literature (Swift and Pope) E: 318
  Pope, Alexander P: 667
Dundee [Scotland] D: 384
Dunderdale, Kathy [Canadian political leader]
  Newfoundland and Labrador (table) N: 375; (Recent developments) N: 377-378
Dundurn Castle [Ontario]
  Hamilton (Cultural life) H: 31 *with map*
Dune [geology] D: 384
  Denmark (The Western Dune Coast) D: 137 *with picture*
  Desert (Desert climate and land) D: 155-156
  Sand S: 106
Dune trilogy [books by Herbert]
  Herbert, Frank H: 197
Dunes [Netherlands]
  Netherlands (The land) N: 144

Dung [biology]
Dung beetle **D: 384**
Dung beetle [insect] **D: 384** *with picture*
Animal (Providing food) **A: 498**
Scarab **S: 172**
Dungeness crab [sea animal]
Crab **Ci: 1115**
Dungeons and Dragons [game]
Game (Board games) **G: 21-22**
Dunham, Katherine [American dancer] **D: 385**
with picture
Dunham, Madelyn [grandmother of]
Obama, Barack (Early life) **O: 640b** *with picture*
Dunham, Stanley [grandfather of]
Obama, Barack (Early life) **O: 640b** *with picture*
Dunham, Stanley Ann [mother of]
Obama, Barack (Early life) **O: 640b** *with picture*
Duniway, Abigail Jane Scott [American social
reformer] **D: 385** *with portrait*
Oregon (The early 1900's) **O: 848**
Dunk
Basketball *picture on* **B: 147**; (Basketball terms)
B: 145
Dunkerque [France] **D: 385** *with picture*
Dunkerque, Battle of [1940]
Alexander of Tunis, Earl **A: 342**
Dunkerque **D: 385** *with picture*
World War II *pictures on* **W: 473**; (The invasion of
the Low Countries) **W: 474**
Dunkers [religious group]
Brethren, Church of the **B: 594**
Dunkirk [France] *See* Dunkerque *in this index*
Dunkleosteus [fish]
Fish (The first fish) **F: 171**
Prehistoric animal (The first animals with
backbones) **P: 736-737**
Dunklin, Daniel [American political leader]
Missouri (table) **M: 668**
Dunlap, Frances [wife of]
Lowell, James Russell (Teacher and editor) **L: 510**
Dunlap, Robert [American political leader]
Maine (table) **M: 87**
Dunlap, William [American dramatist] **D: 386**
Dunleary [Ireland] *See* Dún Laoghaire *in this index*
Dunlop, John Boyd [Scottish inventor] **D: 386**
Tire (History) **T: 297**
Dunlop, John T. [American government official]
Ford, Gerald Rudolph (table) **F: 378**
Labor, Department of (table) **L: 2**
Dunmore, Lord [British colonial official]
Cornstalk **Ci: 1066**
Revolution, American (Fighting in the
Chesapeake and Southern colonies) **R: 276-
278**
Washington, George (The coming revolution)
W: 96-97
Dunn, James [American actor]
Motion picture (Best performance by an actor in
a supporting role: 1945) **M: 862a**
Dunn, Winfield [American political leader]
Tennessee (table) **T: 152**
Dunnart [animal]
Marsupial mouse **M: 233**
Dunne, Edward F. [American political leader]
Illinois (table) **I: 71**
Dunne, Finley Peter [American journalist] **D: 386**
Dunning, Paris C. [American political leader]
Indiana (table) **I: 214**
Dunninger [American magician]
Magician (Mentalist magic) **M: 52**
Dunquerque *See* Dunkerque *in this index*
Duns Scotus, John [medieval theologian] **D: 386**
Dunsany, Lord [Irish author] **D: 386**
Dunsmuir, James [Canadian political leader]
British Columbia (table) **B: 628**
Dunstable [former name]
Nashua **N: 23**
Dunstable, John [English composer]
Classical music (Secular music) **Ci: 646**
Dunster, Henry [American educator]
Bay Psalm Book **B: 176**
Duodecimal system [mathematics] **D: 386**
Duodenal ulcer [disorder]
Stomach (Peptic ulcers) **So: 908**
Ulcer **U: 15** *with picture*
Duodenum [anatomy]
Pancreas **P: 128**
Stomach **So: 908** *with diagram*
Duong Thu Huong [Vietnamese author]
Vietnam (The arts) **V: 366-368**
Dupatta [clothing]
Clothing (India) **Ci: 699**
Pakistan (Clothing) **P: 96**
Duperrey, Louis [French explorer]
Chuuk Islands **T: 465**
Dupin, Amantine-Aurore-Lucile *See* Sand, George
in this index

Du Plessis, Armand Jean *See* Richelieu, Cardinal
in this index
Duplessis, Maurice [Canadian political leader]
Quebec (table) **Q: 29**; (Politics) **Q: 30**; (World War
II) **Q: 32**
Trudeau, Pierre Elliott (Entry into public life)
T: 462
Duplex
Housing (Kinds of housing) **H: 389-390**
Duplex system
Telegraph (Service expansion and improvement)
T: 91-92
Duplexer [electronics]
Radar (The duplexer) **R: 71** *with diagram*
Duplicate bridge [cards]
Bridge **B: 604**; (Duplicate bridge) **B: 605**
Duplicator [machine] *See* Copying machine *in
this index*
Du Pont, Éleuthère Irénée [American
businessman] **D: 387**
Delaware (Places to visit) **D: 102**; (Statehood)
D: 112
DuPont Company D: 387
Chlorofluorocarbon **C: 517**
Delaware (Manufacturing) **D: 106**
Du Pont, Éleuthère Irénée **D: 387**
Teflon **T: 87**
Wilmington **W: 315**
Du Pont de Nemours, Pierre Samuel [1739-1817,
French economist] **D: 387**
Louisiana Purchase (Trouble begins) **L: 502**
Physiocrats **P: 445**
Du Pont de Nemours, Pierre Samuel [1870-1954,
American philanthropist]
Delaware (The early 1900's) **D: 112**
Du Pont de Nemours, Pierre Samuel, IV
[American political leader]
Delaware (table) **D: 109**
Du Pont de Nemours, Thomas Coleman
[American businessman]
Delaware (Transportation) **D: 108**
Duppa, Darrel [American settler]
Phoenix **P: 395**
Du Pré, Jacqueline [British cellist] **D: 387**
Dupré, Jacques [American political leader]
Louisiana (table) **L: 496**
Dupuy, Michel [Canadian diplomat]
United Nations (table) **U: 86**
Duquesne University D: 387
Dura mater [anatomy]
Brain (From injury) **B: 550d**
Membrane (Fibrous membranes) **M: 391**
Durable goods
Gross domestic product (Measuring GDP) **G: 399**
Industry (By the way goods are used) **I: 257**
Manufacturing (Kinds of manufacturing) **M: 169**
Durable nonwoven [textile]
Textile (Nonwovens) **T: 215**
Durable power of attorney [law]
Death (The right to die) **D: 61**
Euthanasia (Termination of life-sustaining
treatment) **E: 421**
Durack, Fanny [Australian swimmer]
Swimming (History) **So: 1047**
Duran, Roberto [Panamanian boxer]
Boxing (The late 1900's) **B: 532b**
Durand, Asher B. [American artist]
Hudson River School **H: 406**
Durango [state, Mexico] **D: 387**
Durango [city, Mexico]
Durango **D: 387**
**Durango & Silverton Narrow Gauge Railroad
and Museum** [Colorado]
Colorado (Places to visit) **Ci: 836** *with picture*
Durant, Henry Fowle [American educator]
Wellesley College **W: 194**
Durant, Kevin [American basketball player]
Basketball *picture on* **B: 154b**
Durant, William Crapo [American businessman]
D: 388
General Motors Company **G: 83**
Duras, Marguerite [French author]
French literature (The middle and late 1900's)
F: 523; (Recent French literature) **F: 523**
Duration [philosophy]
Bergson, Henri **B: 258**
Durban [South Africa] **D: 388**
Durbin, Winfield T. [American political leader]
Indiana (table) **I: 214**
Dürer, Albrecht [German artist] **D: 388** *with
pictures*
Bookplate **B: 474** *with picture*
Four Horsemen of the Apocalypse **F: 437** *with
picture*
Germany (Painting and sculpture) **G: 155**
Horse *picture on* **H: 361**
Painting (Albrecht Dürer) **P: 58** *with picture*

Witchcraft *picture on* **W: 373**
Durga [Hindu goddess]
Hinduism (Deities) **H: 236** *with picture*
Durham [city, England] **D: 388**
Durham [North Carolina] **D: 388**
Durham, Earl of [British statesman] **D: 389**
Durham Report [Canadian history]
Durham, Earl of **D: 389**
Durkheim, Émile [French sociologist] **D: 389**
Sociology (Development of social research)
So: 566
Durkin, Martin P. [American government official]
Eisenhower, Dwight David (table) **E: 152**
Labor, Department of (table) **L: 2**
Durmast oak [tree]
Oak (Other oaks) **O: 636**
Duroc [animal]
Hog (Kinds of hogs) **H: 285** *with picture*; (table)
H: 286
Durocher, Leo [American baseball player]
Baseball (table: Hall of Fame) **B: 134**
Durra [grain]
Sorghum (Grain sorghums) **So: 596**
Durrani, Ahmad Shah [Afghan tribal leader]
Afghanistan (United Afghanistan) **A: 95**
Kandahar **K: 212**
Durrell, Gerald [English naturalist] **D: 389**
Durrell, Lawrence [British author] **D: 389**
Dürrenmatt, Friedrich [Swiss author] **D: 389**
Drama (Later German-language drama) **D: 340**
German literature (Postwar German literature
[1945-1990]) **G: 142**
Durum wheat [plant]
Grass (Cereals) **G: 326**
Wheat (Species of wheat) **W: 269** *with picture*
D'Urville, Jules Dumont [French explorer]
Antarctica (Early exploration) **A: 536**
Pacific Islands (Peoples of the Pacific Islands) **P: 4**
Duryea, Charles E. [American inventor]
Duryea brothers **D: 390**
Duryea, J. Frank [American inventor]
Automobile racing (Growth of organized
automobile racing) **A: 979**
Duryea brothers **D: 390**
Duryea brothers [American inventors] **D: 390**
Automobile *picture on* **A: 964**; (The birth of the
automobile industry) **A: 966**
Du Sable, Jean Baptiste Point [American pioneer]
D: 390 *with portrait*
Chicago (Exploration and early settlement)
C: 434
Du Sable Museum of African-American History
Chicago (Museums) **C: 428-429**
Dušan, Stefan [king of Serbia]
Serbia (History) **S: 314**
Duse, Eleonora [Italian actress] **D: 390**
Dushanbe [Tajikistan] **D: 390**
Dusk *See* Sunset *in this index*
Düsseldorf [Germany] **D: 390**
Dust [agriculture]
Tea (Grades of tea) **T: 63**
Dust Bowl [region, U.S.] **D: 391** *with picture and
map*
Conservation (The rise of the conservation
movement) **Ci: 985-986**
Drought **D: 349**
Kansas (The Great Depression) **K: 238** *with picture*
Oklahoma (The 1930's) **O: 732-734** *with picture*
Route 66 **R: 493**
United States, History of the (The United States in
the Great Depression) **U: 192-193** *with picture*
Water (Water shortages) **W: 122**
Dust devil [meteorology] **D: 392**
Fairy (Magic powers) **F: 10-11**
Mars (Dust storms) **M: 226b**
Dust jacket
Book (Inside a book) **B: 464**
Dust mite [animal] **D: 392** *with picture*
Dust storm D: 392
Dust Bowl **D: 391**
Mars (Dust storms) **M: 226b**
Dust tail [astronomy]
Comet (Parts of a comet) **Ci: 867**
Meteor (Meteor showers) **M: 431**
Dust trail [astronomy]
Meteor (Meteor showers) **M: 431**
Dusting [agriculture]
See also Crop-dusting *in this index*
Insecticide (Using insecticides) **I: 302** *with picture*
Dusting [behavior]
Bird (Feather care) **B: 354-355**
Dutch [people]
Netherlands **N: 138**
Dutch Antilles *See* Netherlands Antilles *in this index*
Dutch Belted cattle

Cattle (Other dairy cattle) C: 311
Dutch doll
Doll (Wooden dolls) D: 289
Dutch door [architecture]
Colonial life in America (Houses) Ci: 796-797
Dutch East India Company [Dutch history] D: 392
Africa (European colonization in Africa) A: 133-134
Cape Colony C: 188
Flag *picture on* F: 209
Hudson, Henry (North American voyages) H: 404
Indonesia (The coming of the Europeans) I: 237; (Dutch rule) I: 237
Netherlands (Prosperity and power) N: 148
South Africa (Arrival of Europeans) So: 617
Dutch East Indies [former name, Indonesia]
Indonesia (Dutch rule) I: 237
Dutch elm disease [plant disease] D: 392
Elm (Diseases) E: 245
Wilt W: 328
Dutch Harbor [Alaska]
Aleutian Islands A: 340
Dutch language
See also Afrikaans language *in this index*
Belgium (Languages) B: 229
Netherlands (Language) N: 139
Dutch literature
Netherlands (Arts) N: 142
Dutch oven [cookware] D: 393
Dutch pins
Bowling (Modern forms of bowling) B: 524b
Dutch-processed cocoa powder
Chocolate (Cocoa) C: 518
Dutch processing [industrial process]
Food additive (Acids and alkalis) F: 340
Dutch Reformed Church [religious group]
Netherlands (Religion) N: 142
Reformed Church in America R: 199
South Africa (Religion) So: 613
Dutch Republic [Dutch history]
Netherlands (Eighty Years' War) N: 148
William I, Prince of Orange W: 308
Dutch West India Company [Dutch history] D: 393
Minuit, Peter M: 613
Netherlands (Prosperity and power) N: 148-149
New Netherland N: 277
New York (Exploration and settlement) N: 314
Patroon system P: 199
Dutch West Indies *See* Netherlands Antilles *in this index*
Dutch windmill
Windmill W: 334
Dutchman [play by Baraka]
Baraka, Amiri B: 103
Dutchman's-breeches [plant] D: 393
Flower *picture on* F: 285
Plant *picture on* P: 525
Dutert, Ferdinand [French architect]
Architecture *picture on* A: 625
Dutra, Eurico Gaspar [Brazilian political leader]
Brazil (Return to constitutional government) B: 585
Dutton, Henry [American political leader]
Connecticut (table) Ci: 967
Duty [economics]
See also Tariff *in this index*
Customs Ci: 1201
Smuggling S: 521
Duval, David [American golfer]
Golf (British Open) G: 264
Duval, Gabriel [American jurist]
Supreme Court of the United States (table) So: 1000
DuVal, William P. [American political leader]
Florida (Territorial days) F: 262
Du Vigneaud, Vincent [American chemist]
Nobel Prizes (Chemistry: 1955) N: 443
Duvoisin, Roger Antoine [American artist] D: 393
Duxbury [Massachusetts]
Standish, Miles So: 836
Dvaravati [former country]
Thailand (Early years) T: 226
DVD [electronics] D: 393
Audio-visual materials (Video presentations) A: 883
Communication (In recording) Ci: 886
Compact disc (Other formats) Ci: 902 *with picture*
Computer *picture on* Ci: 913; (DVD drives) Ci: 916
Electronics (Digital circuits) E: 213-214; (The digital age) E: 216

Laser (Recording, storing, and transmitting information) L: 82
Motion picture (Distribution) M: 860
Stereophonic sound system (Parts of a stereo system) So: 892
Television (VCR's and DVR's) T: 110c
DVD-Audio [electronics]
Recording industry (In a recording studio) R: 181; (History) R: 182
DVD-ROM [electronics]
DVD D: 393
Electronic game (Gaming platforms) E: 204c
Dvina River [Russia] D: 393
See also Daugava River *in this index*
D.V.M. [degree]
Veterinary medicine (Careers in veterinary medicine) V: 346
Dvořák, Antonín [Czech composer] D: 393
Czech Republic (The arts) Ci: 1211
DVR [electronics] *See* Digital video recorder *in this index*
Dwarf [biology] *See* Dwarfism *in this index*
Dwarf Athletic Association of America
Dwarfism (Living with dwarfism) D: 395
Dwarf Cavendish [banana]
Banana B: 72
Dwarf cornel [plant] *See* Bunchberry *in this index*
Dwarf crocodile
Crocodile (Kinds of crocodiles) Ci: 1149-1150
Dwarf fireweed [plant]
Flower *picture on* F: 283
Dwarf galaxy [astronomy]
Andromeda Galaxy A: 457
Galaxy (Irregular galaxies) G: 8b
Local Group L: 409
Universe U: 205
Dwarf goby [fish] *See* Trimmatom nanus *in this index*
Dwarf mammoth [animal]
Mammoth M: 130
Dwarf nova [astronomy]
Nova N: 553 *with picture*
Dwarf planet [astronomy] D: 394
Asteroid A: 824
Astronomy (Finding new objects) A: 848
Ceres C: 362
Eris E: 352
Planet P: 507; (The dwarf planets) P: 512
Pluto P: 580
Solar system (Our solar system) So: 580
Dwarf poinciana [tree]
Poinciana P: 599
Dwarf star [astronomy]
See also Brown dwarf; White dwarf *in this index*
Star So: 840
Dwarf weaver [spider]
Spider (Linyphiids) So: 789
Dwarfism [biology] D: 394 *with picture*
Evolution (Genetic drift) E: 429
Stratton, Charles Sherwood So: 921
Tree *picture on* T: 411
Dwelling *See* Housing; Shelter *in this index*
DWI [crime] *See* Driving while intoxicated *in this index*
Dwight D. Eisenhower [ship]
Aircraft carrier (The United States carrier fleet) A: 206
Dwight D. Eisenhower Library *See* Eisenhower Library and Museum *in this index*
Dwight D. Eisenhower System of Interstate and Defense Highways *See* Federal Interstate Highway System *in this index*
Dwight Mission [Russellville]
Arkansas (Schools) A: 698
Dwinell, Lane [American political leader]
New Hampshire (table) N: 223
Dworshak Dam [Idaho]
Dam (table) D: 18
DWV system
Plumbing P: 577
Dy [symbol]
Dysprosium D: 398
Dyaks [people] *See* Dayaks *in this index*
Dye D: 395 *with picture*
See also the list of Related articles in the Dye *article*
Batik B: 165
Cell (Looking at a cell) C: 327
Color (Mixing colorants) Ci: 819-820
Fur (Dyeing) F: 563
Ink I: 272
Lake L: 35
Laser (Dye lasers) L: 85
Leather (Final processing) L: 168
Phoenicia (Trade and manufacturing) P: 393
Pigment P: 461
Silk (Dyeing) S: 460
Textile (Finishing the fabric) T: 217 *with picture*

Tie dyeing T: 282
Wool (Making fabric) W: 401
Dye laser
Laser (Dye lasers) L: 85
Dye-polymer [recording]
Compact disc (CD-R) Ci: 902
Dyer, Elisha [American political leader]
Rhode Island (table) R: 311
Dyer, Mary [American religious leader] D: 396
Dying Captive, The [sculpture by Michelangelo]
Michelangelo (The tomb of Julius II) M: 484
Dying Gaul [sculpture]
Galatia G: 8
"Dying Swan, The" [ballet]
Pavlova, Anna P: 202
Dylan, Bob [American musician] D: 397
Baez, Joan B: 25
Rock music (Bob Dylan) R: 380 *with picture*; (Fresh directions) R: 380
Dymaxion house
Fuller, Buckminster F: 554
Dynamic metamorphism
Metamorphic rock M: 428
Dynamic meteorologist
Weather (Careers in weather) W: 170
Dynamic microphone
Microphone (Ribbon microphones) M: 517 *with diagram*
Dynamic pump
Pump P: 900b
Dynamic range [photography]
Camera (Comparing digital and film cameras) C: 84
Dynamic simulation [computing]
Animation (Computer animation) A: 513
Dynamics [music]
Music (Indicating expression) M: 955
Dynamics [physics] D: 397
Mechanics M: 354
Physics (Mechanics) P: 437
Dynamics, Group *See* Group dynamics *in this index*
Dynamics of Living Matter, The [book by Loeb]
Loeb, Jacques L: 420
Dynamite [explosive] D: 397 *with picture*
Nitroglycerin N: 426
Nobel, Alfred Bernhard N: 439
Sweden (Growth of industry) So: 1034
Dynamo [machine]
Electric generator E: 170
Electricity *picture on* E: 197
Dynamoelectric
Electric generator E: 170
Dynamometer [instrument]
Horsepower (Brake horsepower) H: 367
Dyne [measurement] D: 397
Metric system (Non-SI metric units) M: 440
Dynode [electronics]
Photomultiplier tube P: 430
D'Youville, Saint Marguerite [Canadian religious leader] *See* Youville, Saint Marguerite d' *in this index*
Dysart, A. Allison [Canadian political leader]
New Brunswick (table) N: 195
Dysarthria [disorder]
Aphasia A: 565
Dyscolos [play by Menander]
Menander M: 397
Dysentery [disease] D: 398
Parasite (An endoparasite) P: 154
Dysgraphia [disorder]
Learning disabilities (Types) L: 165
Dyslexia [disorder] D: 398
Aphasia A: 565
Learning disabilities (Types) L: 165
Reading (Reading problems) R: 161
Dysmenorrhea [disorder]
Menstruation (Effects of menstruation) M: 404
Dysnomia [moon]
Eris E: 352
Solar system (Moons) So: 511
Dyspepsia [disorder]
Indigestion I: 223
Dysphagia [disorder]
Speech therapy (Types of disorders) So: 773
Dysphasia [disorder]
Learning disabilities (Types) L: 165
Dyspraxia [disorder]
Learning disabilities (Types) L: 165
Dysprosium [element] D: 398
Dystopia [literature]
Atwood, Margaret A: 880
Science fiction S: 205
Dystrophin [protein]
Muscular dystrophy (Duchenne muscular dystrophy) M: 936
Dystrophy, Muscular [disease] *See* Muscular dystrophy *in this index*

Dzanga-Ndoki National Park [Central African Republic/Republic of the Congo]
National park (table) N: 42f
Dzong [religion]
Bhutan (People) B: 277 *with picture*
Dzongkha [language]
Bhutan (People) B: 277
Dzongkhag [district]
Bhutan (Government) B: 277

E

E [letter] E: 1 *with pictures*
E-book [computer file] E: 2
Book (Modern books) B: 468
Library (The growth of information and technology) L: 237-238
Publishing (Books) P: 868
E-business See E-commerce *in this index*
E-cash See Electronic money *in this index*
E. coli [bacteria] E: 2
Food poisoning F: 340
Genetic engineering (Uses of genetic engineering) G: 84b-84c
E-commerce [business] E: 2
Codes and ciphers (Modern applications of cryptography) Ci: 752
Retailing (Nonstore retailing) R: 265
Sales tax S: 66
E. I. du Pont de Nemours and Company See DuPont Company *in this index*
"E lucevan le stelle" [aria]
Opera: *(Tosca)* O: 807
E-mail [communication] E: 2
Advertising (Recent developments) A: 80
Careers (Finding job opportunities) C: 217 *with picture*
Communication (The development of the Internet) Ci: 886 *with picture*
Etiquette (Internet etiquette) E: 374
Instant messaging I: 304
Internet (Communication) I: 350b; (The Internet culture) I: 350e
Medicine (Computers and electronic communication) M: 370
Postal services (Technological advancements) P: 707
E-mail bomb [program]
Computer (Computer security) Ci: 924
E=mc² [physics] E: 3
Einstein, Albert (Famous theories) E: 146-146b
Nuclear energy (Artificial fission) N: 590
Physics (Einstein and relativity) P: 441-442
Relativity (Mass-energy relationship) R: 211
E-money See Electronic money *in this index*
E Pluribus Unum [motto] E: 3
Great Seal of the United States (The face) G: 348
Money (U.S. coins) M: 713
E ring [astronomy]
Enceladus E: 265
Satellite (Enceladus) S: 150b
Saturn S: 150i
E Street Band [pop group]
Springsteen, Bruce So: 809
E-ticket
Airport (Airline passenger services) A: 246
E-trading
Investment (How investors buy stocks) I: 369
E-zine [publication]
Magazine M: 42
E10 [chemical]
Ethanol E: 365
E100 [chemical]
Ethanol E: 365
Eads, James Buchanan [American engineer]
New Orleans (Civic improvements) N: 284
Eads Bridge [Saint Louis]
Mississippi River (History) M: 648-649
Saint Louis (The metropolitan area) S: 47 *with map*
Eagle [bird] E: 3 *with pictures*
Bird (Birds of the desert) B: 339 *with picture*; (Birds of Australia and New Zealand) B: 346 *with picture*; (Kinds of food) B: 350 *with picture*
Bird of prey B: 374a
Eagle [coin] E: 6
Money *pictures on* M: 708, M: 709
Eagle [ship]
Coast Guard, United States *picture on* Ci: 737
United States Coast Guard Academy (The course of instruction) U: 199
Eagle [spacecraft]
Armstrong, Neil Alden A: 723
Astronaut (Achievements in space) A: 829-830 *with picture*
Space exploration (Landing on the moon) So: 717 *with pictures*
Eagle [sports]

Golf (table) G: 261
Eagle, James Philip [American political leader]
Arkansas (table) A: 712
Eagle Mountain
Minnesota (Land regions) M: 596
Eagle-owl [bird]
Bird of prey *picture on* B: 374b
Owl (Important owls) O: 884
Eagle Peak [mountain]
Yellowstone National Park Y: 557
Eagle Scout
Boy Scouts (Star Scouts, Life Scouts, and Eagle Scouts) B: 537
Eagleburger, Lawrence Sidney [American government official]
State, Department of (table) So: 861
Eagles, Fraternal Order of E: 6
Eagles, Philadelphia [team] See Philadelphia Eagles *in this index*
Eaglet [bird]
Eagle (Young eagles) E: 4
Eagleton, Thomas F. [American political leader]
McGovern, George Stanley (Presidential candidate) M: 335
Eagleton, Thomas Francis [American political leader] E: 6
Eakins, Thomas [American painter] E: 6 *with picture*
Painting (Painting outside France) P: 72-73
Tanner, Henry Ossawa T: 28
Whitman, Walt *picture on* W: 294
EAM [organization]
Greece (World War II) G: 363-364
Eames, Charles [American designer] E: 6
Furniture *picture on* F: 583; (The retro style) F: 584
Eames chair
Eames, Charles E: 6
Furniture *picture on* F: 583; (The retro style) F: 584
EAN code [standard]
Bar coding B: 102
Eanes, Gil [Portuguese explorer]
Henry the Navigator H: 191
Ear [anatomy] E: 7 *with pictures*
See also Hearing *in this index and the list of Related articles in the* Ear *article*
Animal *picture on* A: 469
Deafness (Types of hearing loss) D: 57
Insect *diagram on* I: 286
Reproduction, Human (Development of organs and organ systems) R: 248
Reptile (Sense organs) R: 251-252
Ear [botany]
Corn (Appearance) Ci: 1057
Ear canal [anatomy]
Ear (The outer ear) E: 7
Ear mites
Cat (Veterinary care) C: 295
Ear shell See Abalone *in this index*
Earbuds
Headphones H: 125
Eardrum [anatomy]
Ear *diagram on* E: 10, *picture on* E: 13; (The outer ear) E: 7; (The middle ear) E: 7-8 *with diagrams*
Deafness (Types of hearing loss) D: 57; (Medical treatment) D: 58
Otoscope O: 870
Eared seal
Seal (Eared seals) S: 265
Earhart, Amelia [American aviator] E: 14 *with picture*
Airplane (Fliers of the golden age) A: 237
Earl [title]
Nobility (In the United Kingdom) N: 450
Thane T: 229
Earl, Anthony S. [American political leader]
Wisconsin (table) W: 365
Earl of Leicester [painting]
Clothing *picture on* Ci: 702
Earle, George Howard [American political leader]
Pennsylvania (table) P: 263
Earle, Sylvia Alice [American biologist] E: 14
Exploration (Deep-sea exploration) E: 450-451 *with picture*
Earless seal [animal]
Seal (Earless seals) S: 266
Earlobe
Ear (The outer ear) E: 7
Early, Jubal Anderson [Confederate general] E: 15
Civil War, American (Cavalry maneuvers) Ci: 631
Maryland (The Civil War) M: 258-259
Early, Peter [American political leader]
Georgia (table) G: 130
Early American style
Furniture *picture on* F: 569; (Early American furniture) F: 579 *with picture*
Interior design (Style) I: 327
Early Autumn [book by Bromfield]

Bromfield, Louis B: 636
Early Bird [satellite]
Communications satellite (History) Ci: 888b-889
Television (Technological advances) T: 127
Early blind snake
Snake (Early blind snakes) S: 535
Early childhood
Child (The preschool years) C: 449
Early childhood education E: 15
Careers (Teaching) C: 231
Education (The organization of U.S. education) E: 90-91
Head Start H: 124
Intelligence (Modifying intelligence) I: 319
Kindergarten K: 317
Montessori method M: 764a
Preschool P: 756a
School (Preschools) S: 181; (Kindergartens) S: 181
Early fallout [radioactivity]
Nuclear weapon (Residual nuclear radiation) N: 599
Early Head Start [program]
Head Start H: 124
Early human being See Prehistoric people *in this index*
Early Hunters [U.S. history]
West Virginia (Indian days) W: 226
Early saxifrage [plant]
Saxifrage S: 168 *with picture*
Early school years
Child (The school-age years) C: 449 *with picture*
"Early to bed and early to rise" [quotation]
Poor Richard's Almanac P: 659
Early voting
Voting (Methods of voting) V: 449-450
Earmold [device]
Hearing aid (Styles) H: 130 *with picture*
Earmuffs
Maine (Interesting facts) M: 69 *with picture*
Earned Income Tax Credit [federal program]
Welfare (The Earned Income Tax Credit) W: 190
Earned-run average
Baseball (Baseball terms) B: 124
Earnhardt, Dale [American race driver] E: 15
Automobile racing (table: NASCAR Sprint Cup champions) A: 981
Earnings
Careers (Probable earnings) C: 216
Earp, Wyatt [American frontiersman] E: 15 *with portrait*
Masterson, Bat M: 297
Wichita (History) W: 298
Earphones
Headphones H: 125
Stereophonic sound system (Headphones) So: 892
Earring [ornament]
Jewelry J: 117 *with picture*
Ring R: 342
Earth [philosophy]
Empedocles E: 261
Earth [planet] E: 16 *with pictures and maps*
Animal (When animals developed on the earth) A: 503
Asteroid (Impacts on Earth) A: 824b *with map*
Astrology (Earth) A: 826
Astronomy *picture on* A: 838; (Observing the sky) A: 835
Earthquake (Using earthquakes to explore Earth's interior) E: 38b
Element, Chemical E: 219
Eratosthenes E: 349
Gaia G: 5
Geography G: 92; (Forces that change Earth) G: 93
Geology G: 97
Geomorphology G: 106a
Heat (Sources of heat) H: 149
Landform L: 58
Magnetism (Earth) M: 60d
Mantle M: 168
Moon M: 782
Pendulum (Other pendulums) P: 238
Planet P: 507 *with pictures*
Plate tectonics P: 561 *with diagram*
Satellite (Satellites of the terrestrial planets) S: 150
Sun So: 974
Tidal forces T: 280
Tide T: 280 *with diagrams*
World W: 406 *with pictures and maps*
Earth [soil] See Soil *in this index*
Earth-and-rock-fill dam
Dam (Embankment dams) D: 18
Earth Art
Sculpture (From the mid-1900's to the early 2000's) S: 259-260

Earth Day E: 32
Environmental pollution *picture on* E: 339
Earth-fill dam
Dam (Embankment dams) D: 18 *with picture*
Earth lodge [dwelling]
Indian, American *picture on* I: 138; (Shelter)
I: 136d; (Before European contact) I: 158-159
Omaha Indians O: 757
Earth-observing satellite
Satellite, Artificial (table) S: 150e; (Types of
artificial satellites) S: 150f *with picture*
Earth Observing System [satellites]
Air (The study of air) A: 175
Planet (Earth) P: 511
Earth oven
Pacific Islands (Food) P: 6
Earth science E: 32
Earth Star [diamond]
Diamond *picture on* D: 181
Earth Summit [conference] *See* United Nations
Conference on Environment and Development
in this index
Earth tunnel
Tunnel (Earth tunnels) T: 490
Eartha [globe]
Globe G: 233
Earthenware
Porcelain P: 675
Pottery (Earthenware) P: 716 *with picture*
Earthquake [geology] E: 33 *with pictures and map*
Earth (Earthquakes) E: 24
Flood (Seacoast floods) F: 237
Geophysics G: 106a
Geothermal energy G: 136
Insurance (Insurance today) I: 316-317
Moment magnitude M: 697
Plate tectonics (Plate interactions) P: 561-562;
(History of tectonic theory) P: 564-565
Richter magnitude R: 334
Ring of Fire R: 342
San Andreas Fault S: 83
Seismograph S: 287
Seismology S: 288
Tsunami T: 475
Volcano (Predicting eruptions) V: 442a
Earthquakes in history
Alaska (Statehood) A: 303-304 *with picture*
Armenia (Soviet rule) A: 718b
Asia (Natural disasters) A: 812
Beijing (History) B: 223-224
California (The late 1900's) C: 63 *with picture*
China (Recent developments) C: 506-507
Disaster (table) D: 223
Egypt (Recent developments) E: 133-134
El Salvador (The 1900's) E: 252; (Recent
developments) E: 253
Haiti (History) H: 15-17 *with picture*
India (Recent developments) I: 134-135
Indonesia (Recent developments) I: 239
Iran (Recent developments) I: 406b
Islamabad I: 466
Japan (Recent developments) J: 59
Java J: 65
Kashmir (History) K: 248
Kobe K: 360
Los Angeles (Recent developments) L: 470-471
with picture
Managua M: 131
Mexico (The late 1900's) M: 473-474
Mexico City (Recent developments) M: 478
Missouri (Settlement) M: 669
New Zealand (Earthquakes) N: 353
Nuclear energy (Safety concerns) N: 591-592
Oakland (Government and history) O: 637-638
Pakistan (Musharraf) P: 100
Peru (Recent developments) P: 316-317
Port-au-Prince P: 680
San Francisco (Earthquake and fire) S: 98 *with
picture*; (Another earthquake) S: 99
San Francisco earthquake of 1906 S: 99
San Jose (History) S: 102
Tokyo (Earthquake and reconstruction) T: 319
Tsunami of 2004 T: 476
Turkey (Recent developments) T: 512
Earthsea trilogy [books by Le Guin]
Le Guin, Ursula K. L: 184
Earthshine [astronomy]
Moon (Phases) M: 783-784
Earthworm E: 39 *with pictures*
Animal *picture on* A: 506
Egg (Other kinds of eggs) E: 116
Heart (Hearts of animals) H: 146 *with diagram*
Worm *picture on* W: 501
Earwax
Ear (The outer ear) E: 7
Earwicker, Humphrey Chimpden [literary figure]
Joyce, James J: 177

Earwig [insect] E: 39
Insect *picture on* I: 281; (Family life) I: 294-295
Easement [law]
Property P: 827
Easing
Sewing (Seams) S: 332
Easley, Mike [American political leader]
North Carolina (table) N: 490
East, The *See* Far East *in this index*
East African Community [alliance]
Kenya (International trade) K: 302
Rwanda (History) R: 571-572
Tanzania (The united republic and socialism)
T: 35
Uganda (History) U: 3-4
East African Rift [geology]
Plate tectonics (The rifting of continents) P: 562
with diagram
East Alabama [former city]
Montgomery (Government and history) M: 766
East Antarctica
Antarctica (Ice) A: 532 *with map*
East Asia
See also Far East *in this index*
Asia (Way of life in East Asia) A: 785 *with pictures*;
(The land) A: 792; (Climate) A: 796
East Avon [river, England]
Avon, River A: 994
East Bengal *See* Bangladesh *in this index*
East Berlin [Germany] *See* Berlin *in this index*
East Block [building]
Ottawa (The Parliament Buildings) O: 872
East Boston [district, Massachusetts]
Boston (East Boston) B: 498
East Carolina University [North Carolina]
North Carolina, University of N: 495
East Chicago [Indiana]
Gary G: 47
East China Sea
China Sea C: 508 *with map*
"East Coker" [poem by Eliot]
Eliot, T. S. (His works) E: 237-238
East End [district]
London (Outlying areas) L: 430 *with map*
East Falkland [island, Atlantic]
Falkland Islands F: 15
East Florida Gazette [newspaper]
Florida (Communication) F: 260
East Germany *See* Germany *in this index*
East Greenland Current
Arctic Ocean *map on* A: 642; (Currents) A: 643
East Gulf Coastal Plain [region, U.S.]
Georgia (Land regions) G: 124
Louisiana (Land regions) L: 490
Mississippi (Land regions) M: 634
East India Company [European history] E: 40
See also British East India Company; Dutch East
India Company *in this index*
Indian Rebellion I: 187
Mumbai (History) M: 925
Revolution, American (The Tea Act) R: 273
East Indiamen
Ship (East Indiamen) S: 420 *with picture*
East Indian lotus [plant]
Flower *picture on* F: 292
East Indies [islands, Southeast Asia] E: 40
East Jerusalem
Israel (City life) I: 481
Jerusalem (East Jerusalem) J: 95
West Bank W: 199
East Los Angeles
Los Angeles (East Los Angeles) L: 461 *with picture*
East of Eden [book by Steinbeck]
Steinbeck, John So: 885
East of Eden [film]
Dean, James D: 60
East Okoboji Lake
Iowa (Rivers and lakes) I: 386
East Pacific Rise [ocean ridge]
Ocean (Deep-sea peaks, valleys, and plains)
O: 662 *with map*
Pacific Ocean (The ocean floor) P: 14
East Pakistan *See* Bangladesh *in this index*
East River [New York]
New York City (The city) N: 323; (Transportation)
N: 334
East Roman Empire *See* Byzantine Empire *in this
index*
East Room
White House (Public rooms) W: 286-290 *with
diagram*
East Sea *See* Japan, Sea of *in this index*
East Shawnee Trail
Oklahoma (After the Civil War) O: 731-732
East Slavs [people]
Russia (Early days) R: 547
Slavs (East Slavs) S: 505

Ukraine (Ancestry) U: 6; (Kievan Rus) U: 12
East Texas oil field
Texas (Mining) T: 201-202
East Texas Oil Museum [Texas]
Texas (Places to visit) T: 194
East Timor E: 40 *with picture and map*
Dili D: 204
Flag *picture on* F: 202
Human rights (Peacekeeping) H: 428a
Indonesia (The Lesser Sunda Islands) I: 234 *with
map*; (Indonesia under Suharto) I: 238
United Nations (Working for self-government)
U: 93-94
East-West Center
Hawaii (Statehood) H: 108-109
Eastchester [New York]
Mount Vernon M: 890
Eastend Fossil Research Station
Saskatchewan (Places to visit) S: 136
Easter [religion] E: 42 *with pictures*
Greece (Religion) *picture on* G: 356
Holy Week H: 300
Lent L: 196b
Nicene Councils N: 402
Palm Sunday P: 110
Easter egg
Alberta (Interesting facts) A: 313 *with picture*
Decorative arts *picture on* D: 80
Easter (Easter customs) E: 44
Fabergé, Peter Carl F: 2 *with picture*
Ukraine (The arts) U: 8 *with picture*
Easter egg rolling [custom]
Hayes, Rutherford Birchard (Life in the White
House) H: 121
Easter Island E: 44 *with picture*
Sculpture (Pacific Islands sculpture) S: 241-242
Easter lily [plant] E: 45
Easter (Easter symbols) E: 43-44
Easter Monday [history] *See* Easter Rising *in this
index*
Easter Monday [painting by De Kooning]
De Kooning, Willem *picture on* D: 94
"Easter Parade" [song by Berlin]
Berlin, Irving B: 266
Easter Rising [1916]
Ireland (The Easter Rising) I: 427
Sinn Féin (History) S: 473
Easterly wind [weather]
Weather (Planetary-scale systems) W: 158-159
Eastern Band of Cherokee
Cherokee Indians C: 409
Eastern bar-tailed godwit [bird]
Bird *pictures on* B: 361
Eastern bloc [world history]
Cold War Ci: 762
Eastern bluebird
Bluebird B: 422 *with picture*
Eastern Catholic Churches [religion] E: 45
Arab Americans (Who Arab Americans are)
A: 580a
Roman Catholic Church (Split with the East)
R: 407
Trinity T: 447
Eastern chimpanzee
Chimpanzee C: 471
Eastern Conference
Hockey (table: National Hockey League) H: 281
National Basketball Association N: 30
Eastern coral snake
Coral snake Ci: 1050 *with picture*
Snake *picture on* S: 534
Eastern cottonwood [tree]
Cottonwood Ci: 1095
Tree *pictures on* T: 421
Eastern Desert *See* Arabian Desert *in this index*
Eastern diamondback rattlesnake
Rattlesnake R: 149
Snake *picture on* S: 534
Eastern Europe
See also the index entries under the names of
various Eastern European countries, such as
Bulgaria
Cold War Ci: 762; (The Cold War after 1980)
Ci: 770
Communism (In Eastern Europe) Ci: 896
Europe (The Cold War) E: 415; (The collapse of
Communism) E: 416
Germany (East Germany) G: 170; (West Germany)
G: 170
Helsinki Accords H: 179
Jews (Eastern European religious movements)
J: 123
Library (Eastern Europe and Russia) L: 252
North Atlantic Treaty Organization (History)
N: 471
Union of Soviet Socialist Republics (History)
U: 35-37; (Threats to unity) U: 40

Warsaw Pact **W:** 39
Women's movement (In Eastern Europe and the former Soviet republics) **W:** 387
Eastern Front [World War I]
Germany *picture on* **G:** 167
World War I *map on* **W:** 460; (The Eastern Front) **W:** 456
Eastern gray kangaroo
Kangaroo (Kinds of kangaroos) **K:** 213
Eastern gray squirrel
Squirrel (Tree squirrels) **So:** 814b *with picture*
Eastern grip
Tennis *pictures on* **T:** 164
Eastern Hemisphere [geography]
Hemisphere **H:** 181 *with diagram*
Eastern hemlock [tree]
Hemlock **H:** 182
Tree *pictures on* **T:** 425
Eastern Kentucky Coal Field
Kentucky (Mining) **K:** 289
Eastern Kentucky Coal Field [region, U.S.]
Kentucky (Land regions) **K:** 285 *with picture*
Eastern kingbird
Kingbird **K:** 328 *with picture*
Eastern larch [tree]
Larch **L:** 75
Tree *pictures on* **T:** 425
Eastern lowland gorilla
Gorilla **G:** 275
Eastern meadowlark [bird]
Bird *picture on* **B:** 358
Meadowlark **M:** 345 *with picture*
Eastern milk snake
Milk snake **M:** 550
Eastern mole [animal]
Mole (Kinds of moles) **M:** 690b
Eastern moon snail
Shell *picture on* **S:** 386
Eastern Mountains [region, British Columbia]
British Columbia (Land regions) **B:** 622 *with map*
Eastern Orthodox Churches E: 45
Belarus (People) **B:** 224a
Bulgaria (Religion) **B:** 691
Byzantine art **B:** 749
Christianity (Organization) **C:** 522g; (History) **C:** 523-524
Grace **G:** 295
Greece (Religion) **G:** 356 *with picture*
Icon **I:** 24 *with picture*
Marriage (Roman Catholic and Eastern Orthodox weddings) **M:** 221
Monasticism (Christian monasticism) **M:** 701
Painting (Early Christian and Byzantine art) **P:** 49
Patriarch **P:** 196
Religion (Christianity) **R:** 222-223
Religious life (The Eastern Orthodox Churches) **R:** 227
Roman Catholic Church (Conflict with the East) **R:** 406; (Split with the East) **R:** 407
Ukraine (Religion) **U:** 8
World, History of the (The Byzantine Empire) **W:** 434
Eastern Paper Bag Company
Paper bag **P:** 138
Eastern pasqueflower [plant]
Flower *picture on* **F:** 287
Pasqueflower **P:** 190
Eastern philosophy
Philosophy **P:** 383; (Eastern philosophy) **P:** 386
Eastern poison oak [plant]
Poison oak **P:** 602
Eastern quoll [animal]
Quoll *picture on* **Q:** 44
Eastern racer [snake]
Snake *picture on* **S:** 533
Eastern redbud [tree]
Tree *pictures on* **T:** 423
Eastern redcedar [tree]
Juniper **J:** 196
Tree *pictures on* **T:** 425
Eastern Rite Churches [religion] *See* Eastern Catholic Churches *in this index*
Eastern Rumelia [former province]
Berlin, Congress of **B:** 265
Thrace **T:** 268
Eastern Sami [people]
Sami **S:** 79
Eastern screech-owl [bird]
Owl (Important owls) **O:** 884
Eastern Shore [region, Maryland-Virginia]
Virginia (Land regions) **V:** 410
Eastern spinebill [bird]
Bird (Birds of Australia and New Zealand) **B:** 346 *with picture*
Eastern Star [organization] **E:** 47
Eastern tent caterpillar [insect]
Tent caterpillar **T:** 169

Eastern towhee [bird]
Bird *picture on* **B:** 358
Towhee **T:** 351 *with picture*
Eastern Townships [region, Quebec]
Quebec (Land regions) **Q:** 22; (Natural resources) **Q:** 27
Eastern Turkestan
Turkestan (Chinese Turkestan) **T:** 501
Eastern white pine [tree]
Pine (Eastern pines) **P:** 468, *picture on* **P:** 470
Plant *picture on* **P:** 530
Tree *pictures on* **T:** 425
Eastern wood-pewee [bird]
Pewee **P:** 352 *with picture*
Eastern Zhou period [Chinese history]
Zhou dynasty **Z:** 591
Eastern zodiac
Zodiac (The Eastern zodiac) **Z:** 598
Eastland [ship]
Chicago (Tragedy and racial conflict) **C:** 435
Shipwreck (table: Major shipwrecks) **S:** 428
Eastman, George [American businessman] **E:** 47
Eastman Kodak Company **E:** 47
Eastman School of Music **E:** 47
Photography (Technical improvements) **P:** 423-424 *with picture*
Rochester (Government and history) **R:** 370-371
Eastman, James G. [American farmer]
Western frontier life in America (Farming) **W:** 238
Eastman, Linda [wife of]
McCartney, Paul **M:** 332c
Eastman Kodak Company E: 47
Camcorder (The development of camcorders) **C:** 75
Light (Studying light) **L:** 292
Rochester (Economy) **R:** 370
Eastman School of Music E: 47
Eastman Symphonic Wind Ensemble
Band (Wind ensembles) **B:** 75
Eastwood, Clint [American actor/director] **E:** 47
Motion picture (Best achievement in directing: 1992, 2004) **M:** 862
"Easy Chair, The" [newspaper column]
De Voto, Bernard Augustine **D:** 176
Easy open/reseal cap
Packaging **P:** 18
Easy reader book *See* Beginning reader book *in this index*
Eating *See* Food; Restaurant *in this index*
Eating disorder E: 48
See also Binge eating; Bulimia *in this index*
Eating quality
Meat packing (Quality grading) **M:** 351
Eaton, Alden [American businessman]
Dude ranch **D:** 377
Eaton, Benjamin H. [American political leader]
Colorado (table) **Ci:** 844
Eaton, Cyrus [American philanthropist]
Pugwash Conferences on Science and World Affairs **P:** 886
Eaton, Dorman Bridgman [American government official]
Arthur, Chester Alan (Civil service reform) **A:** 756
Eaton, Horace [American political leader]
Vermont (table) **V:** 333
Eaton, Howard [American businessman]
Dude ranch **D:** 377
Eaton, John H. [American government official]
Jackson, Andrew (Split with Calhoun) **J:** 11; (table) **J:** 11
O'Neale, Peggy **O:** 761
Eaton, Peggy [American public figure] *See* O'Neale, Peggy *in this index*
Eaton, Theophilus [American colonial leader] **E:** 48
Eaton, Timothy [Canadian businessman] **E:** 48
Eaton, Willis [American businessman]
Dude ranch **D:** 377
Eaton Free School [U.S. history]
Virginia (Schools) **V:** 402
Eaton's of Canada Limited
Eaton, Timothy **E:** 48
Eatonville [Florida]
African Americans (During the late 1800's) **A:** 136k-136l
Eau de Cologne [perfume]
Cologne **Ci:** 777
Eau de parfum [perfume]
Perfume **P:** 286
Eau d'or [perfume]
Lily of the valley **L:** 304
Eaves [construction]
House (table) **H:** 380
Roof **R:** 450c
Eavesdropping
Wiretapping **W:** 345
Ebadi, Shirin [Iranian activist]
Nobel Prizes (Peace: 2003) **N:** 448b

eBay [company]
E-commerce (Business-to-consumer transactions) **E:** 2
Internet (Commerce) **I:** 350b; (The Web forms) **I:** 350g
Ebbo [French religious leader]
Painting (Early medieval painting in the West) **P:** 49-50
Ebenezer Baptist Church [Atlanta]
King, Martin Luther, Jr. (Early life) **K:** 320-321; (King's death) **K:** 323
Martin Luther King, Jr., National Historic Site **M:** 235
Ebenezer onion
Onion *picture on* **O:** 763
Ebenezer Society
Amanites **A:** 400
Eberhart, Adolph O. [American political leader]
Minnesota (table) **M:** 602
Eberhart, Richard [American poet] **E:** 48
Ebey's Landing National Historical Reserve [Washington]
National Park System (table: National parkways and other national parklands) **N:** 56
Ebla [ancient city] **E:** 48
Ebola hemorrhagic fever [disease]
Ebola virus **E:** 49
Ebola virus E: 49
Ebonics [dialect] *See* African American English *in this index*
Ebony [magazine]
Johnson, John Harold **J:** 143
Magazine (Magazines in the 1900's) **M:** 45
Ebony [wood] **E:** 49
Eboracum [former name]
York [England] **Y:** 568
Ebro, Battle of the [1938]
Spanish Civil War (Progress of the war) **So:** 756a-756b
Ebro River [Spain]
Spain (The Ebro Basin) **So:** 740 *with map*
EBV [disorder] *See* Epstein-Barr virus *in this index*
EC [organization] *See* European Community *in this index*
ECA [government agency]
Marshall Plan **M:** 232
Eccles, Sir John Carew [Australian biologist]
Nobel Prizes (Physiology or medicine: 1963) **N:** 446
Ecclesiastes [Bible] **E:** 49
Bible (The Writings) **B:** 281-282
Ecclesiastical History of the English People [book by Bede]
Bede, Saint **B:** 199
English literature (Old English prose) **E:** 315
Ecclesiastical treaty
Treaty (Ecclesiastical treaties) **T:** 409
Ecclesiasticus [Bible]
Bible (The Christian Old Testament) **B:** 282
Eccrine gland
Skin (Hair, nails, and glands) **S:** 489
Ecdysis [zoology] *See* Molting *in this index*
Ecevit, Bülent [Turkish political leader]
Turkey (Political changes) **T:** 512
ECG [medicine] *See* Electrocardiograph *in this index*
Ecgbehrt [king of Wessex] *See* Egbert *in this index*
Echegaray y Eizaguirre, José [Spanish dramatist]
Nobel Prizes (Literature: 1904) **N:** 447
Echenique, Alfredo Bryce [Peruvian author]
Latin American literature (The post-Boom) **L:** 114
Echeverría, Esteban [Argentine poet]
Latin American literature (Romanticism) **L:** 112-113
Echeverría Álvarez, Luis [Mexican political leader]
Mexico (The 1late 1900's) **M:** 473-474
Echidna [animal] **E:** 49
Animal *picture on* **A:** 479
Anteater **A:** 541
Australia (Native animals) **A:** 911
Echinacea [plant] **E:** 49
Herbal medicine **H:** 196
Echinoderm [zoology] **E:** 49
Animal (A classification of the animal kingdom) **A:** 506-507 *with picture*
Invertebrate **I:** 366
Echinus [architecture]
Column (The Greek orders) **Ci:** 865
Echo [Greek mythology]
Echo **E:** 50
Narcissus **N:** 20
Echo [sound]
Echo **E:** 50
Radar **R:** 64
Sonar (How sonar works) **So:** 591
Sound (Reflection) **So:** 602
Echo 1 [satellite]
Communications satellite (History) **Ci:** 888b-889
Echo boomer [demography] *See* Generation Y *in*

this index
Echo River [Kentucky]
  Mammoth Cave National Park **M:** 130
Echocardiography [medicine]
  Heart (Valve disease) **H:** 141-142
Echoes of Time and the River [music by Crumb]
  Crumb, George **Ci:** 1159
Echolalia [psychology]
  Autism (Symptoms) **A:** 941
Echolocation [zoology]
  Bat **B:** 159 *with picture*; (Water) **B:** 160
  Bird (Hearing) **B:** 365
  Dolphin (The bodies of dolphins) **D:** 297-298
  Ear (The ears of animals) **E:** 12-13
  Mammal (Senses) **M:** 120
  Sonar **So:** 591
  Ultrasound (Animal uses of ultrasound) **U:** 16
  Whale (Senses) **W:** 260
Echovirus 7 [virus]
  Amyotrophic lateral sclerosis **A:** 447
Eck, Johann [German theologian] **E:** 50
  Luther, Martin (The break with the Roman
    Catholic Church) **L:** 528
Eckersley, Dennis [American baseball player]
  Baseball (table: Hall of Fame) **B:** 134
Eckert, J. Presper, Jr. [American engineer] **E:** 50
  Computer (The first electronic computers)
    Ci: 924b *with picture*
  Electronics *picture on* **E:** 216; (The vacuum tube
    era) **E:** 215
  Mauchly, John William **M:** 312
Eckhart, Johannes [German theologian] **E:** 50
Eckhart, Meister *See* Eckhart, Johannes *in this
  index*
Eclampsia [disorder]
  Preeclampsia **P:** 734
  Pregnancy (Preeclampsia) **P:** 735
Eclectic Reader [book by McGuffey]
  McGuffey, William Holmes **M:** 335 *with picture*
Eclecticism [psychology]
  Psychology (Modern psychology) **P:** 850
Eclipse [astronomy] **E:** 51 *with pictures*
  Corona **Ci:** 1066
  Moon (Eclipses) **M:** 784
  Penumbra **P:** 276
  Sun (History of modern solar study) **So:** 986
Eclipse [horse]
  Horse (table: Famous horses in history and
    legend) **H:** 361
Eclipsing binary [astronomy]
  Eclipse **E:** 51
Ecliptic [astronomy]
  Astronomy (How the stars move) **A:** 835
  Planet (Observing the planets) **P:** 507-508
Ecliptic plane [astronomy]
  Jupiter (Orbit and rotation) **J:** 198
  Moon (Rotation and orbit) **M:** 783
  Oort cloud **O:** 788
Eclogues [poems by Virgil]
  Virgil (His works) **V:** 391
ECM [manufacturing]
  Machine tool (Electrochemical machining [ECM])
    M: 19
Eco, Umberto [Italian author]
  Novel (The novel today) **N:** 575
Ecofact [archaeology]
  Archaeology (What archaeologists study) **A:** 595
    with picture; (Evaluation) **A:** 598-599
École des Beaux-Arts [school, Paris] **E:** 52
  Painting (The 1800's) **P:** 67
École des Beaux-Arts de l'Indochine [school]
  Vietnam (The arts) **V:** 366
École Nationale Supérieure des Beaux-Arts
  [school, Paris] *See* École des Beaux-Arts *in this
  index*
Ecological anthropology
  Anthropology (Cultural anthropology) **A:** 547
Ecological efficiency
  Ecology (Energy flow) **E:** 54-55
Ecological equivalent [biology]
  Biome **B:** 324
Ecological niche
  Biome **B:** 324
  Ecology (The role of a species) **E:** 54
  Permian Period **P:** 289
Ecological succession
  Ecology (Changes in communities) **E:** 54
  Forest (Forest succession) **F:** 397 *with picture*
Ecology [science] **E:** 53 *with pictures*
  Biology **B:** 316 *with picture*; (The growth of
    modern biology) **B:** 319-320
  Botany (Plant habitats) **B:** 508; (Later
    developments) **B:** 509
  Elton, Charles Sutherland **E:** 253
  Environment (Abiotic environment) **E:** 329
  Habitat **H:** 3
  Limnology **L:** 308

Zoology (What zoologists study) **Z:** 606-607
Problems and solutions
  Environmental pollution **E:** 330
  Pest control (Effects of pesticide use) **P:** 318
  Wetland (Preservation) **W:** 252b
  Wildlife conservation (Methods of wildlife
    conservation) **W:** 304
Processes
  Adaptation **A:** 45
  Balance of nature **B:** 34
  Decay **D:** 67
  Forest (Competition and cooperation) **F:** 396
Ecology, Human
  Sociology (Population characteristics) **So:** 564
ECOMOG [military group]
  Sierra Leone (History) **S:** 452
Econometrics E: 57
  Frisch, Ragnar **F:** 535
  Tinbergen, Jan **T:** 294
Economic Advisers, Council of [U.S.] **E:** 57
  President of the United States (The executive
    branch) **P:** 764
Economic Analysis, Bureau of [U.S.]
  Commerce, Department of (Functions) **Ci:** 871
Economic and Monetary Union
  European Union (Internal affairs) **E:** 418
Economic and Social Council
  United Nations *picture on* **U:** 86; (The six major
    UN organs) **U:** 78; (Other main organs) **U:** 84
Economic anthropology
  Anthropology (Social anthropology) **A:** 547
Economic blindness
  Blindness **B:** 401
Economic Community of West African States
  Africa (Africa since independence) **A:** 135
Economic Consequences of the Peace, The [book
  by Keynes]
  Keynes, John Maynard **K:** 308a
Economic Cooperation Administration [U.S.
  history]
  Marshall Plan **M:** 232
Economic determinism E: 57
Economic Development Administration
  Puerto Rico (Puerto Rico today) **P:** 884
Economic Development Corporation
  Ottawa (The 1900's) **O:** 875
Economic entomology [science]
  Entomology (What entomologists study) **E:** 328
Economic freedom
  Freedom (Kinds of freedom) **F:** 501; (Limits on
    economic freedom) **F:** 502
Economic geography
  Geography (Human geography) **G:** 94
Economic growth
  City (Economy) **Ci:** 590
  Democracy (Economic development and
    agreement on fundamentals) **D:** 122
  Economics (Economic growth) **E:** 62
  National debt *diagrams on* **N:** 33; (Economic
    growth and rising national debt) **N:** 34
Economic history
  Economics (Fields of economics) **E:** 64
  History (Approaches to history) **H:** 261
Economic indicator [economics] **E:** 57
Economic liberalism
  Liberalism (Features of liberalism) **L:** 228
  Smith, Adam **S:** 515
Economic migrant
  Refugee (The rights of refugees) **R:** 203
Economic miracle [German history]
  Germany (Economy) **G:** 159; (West Germany)
    G: 170
Economic Opportunity Act [1964]
  Vocational education (The 1900's and early
    2000's) **V:** 435
Economic Recovery Tax Act [1981]
  Inheritance tax **I:** 271
  Reagan, Ronald Wilson (Events at home) **R:** 167
Economic rights
  Human rights (Types of human rights) **H:** 428
Economic sanctions [political science] *See*
  Sanctions, Economic *in this index*
Economic theory
  Economics (Fields of economics) **E:** 64
Economically active population
  Labor force **L:** 3
Economics E: 58 *with pictures*
  See also the list of Related articles in the Economics
  article
  Advertising (Effects of advertising) **A:** 78
  Automobile (Economic impact) **A:** 959
  Capitalism **C:** 194
  Communism (The centrally planned economy)
    Ci: 891
  Econometrics **E:** 57
  Economic determinism **E:** 57
  Globalization **G:** 232d

Great Depression **G:** 338
Inflation **I:** 266
Input-output analysis **I:** 276
Interest (Economic activity) **I:** 322
International relations (Treaties) **I:** 344
Money (Money and the economy) **M:** 715
National income **N:** 37
Physiocrats **P:** 444
Price **P:** 774
Science (The social sciences) **S:** 194
World (Economic systems) **W:** 412b
Economics: An Introductory Analysis [book by
  Samuelson]
  Samuelson, Paul Anthony **S:** 82
Economies of scale [economics]
  Industry (Expansion) **I:** 260
Economist [occupation]
  Careers (Life, physical, and social sciences)
    C: 225-226
  Economics **E:** 58; (Careers in economics) **E:** 65
Economy [economics]
  See also Economics *in this index*
  Economics **E:** 58
Ecosystem [ecology]
  Agriculture (Ecosystem destruction) **A:** 153
  Ant (The importance of ants) **A:** 528
  Balance of nature (Ecosystems) **B:** 35
  Biodiversity (Kinds of biodiversity) **B:** 310
  Butterfly (Butterflies and the environment) **B:** 742
  Coral reef **Ci:** 1048b
  Ecology (Ecosystems) **E:** 54 *with diagram*
  Environmental pollution **E:** 330
  Forest **F:** 390
  Global warming (Impact of global warming)
    G: 232a
  Iceberg (Ecology) **I:** 18
  Invasive species (Managing invasive species)
    I: 354k
  Lawn **L:** 142
  Marine biology (Biological oceanographers)
    M: 205
  National park (Canada) **N:** 42c
  Oyster (Oysters and ecosystems) **O:** 891
  Plant (In ecosystems) **P:** 518; (Conservation of
    plants) **P:** 543
  Rain forest (Scientific value) **R:** 126c
  Wetland (Preservation) **W:** 252b
Ecosystem diversity
  Biodiversity (Kinds of biodiversity) **B:** 310
Ecoterrorism
  Terrorism (Terrorist groups and movements)
    T: 178-179
ECSC [organization] *See* European Coal and Steel
  Community *in this index*
Ecstasy [drug] **E:** 66
  Drug abuse (Club drugs) **D:** 363; (table: Some
    commonly abused drugs) **D:** 363
  Hallucinogenic drug **H:** 26
Ecstasy [psychology]
  Dance (Why people dance) **D:** 24
Ecstasy of Rita Joe, The [play by Ryga]
  Canadian literature (Modern Canadian drama)
    C: 161
Ectoderm [biology]
  Coelom **Ci:** 753
  Reproduction, Human (Origin of tissues and
    organs) **R:** 247-248
Ectoparasite [biology]
  Parasite (Types) **P:** 154
Ectopic pregnancy [disorder]
  Fallopian tube **F:** 18
  Pelvic inflammatory disease **P:** 233
  Pregnancy (An ectopic pregnancy) **P:** 735
Ectothermic animal *See* Cold-blooded animal *in
  this index*
Écu [coin]
  Money *picture on* **M:** 708
Ecuador E: 67 *with pictures and maps*
  See also the list of Related articles in the Ecuador
  article
  Andean Community **A:** 450
  Bolívar, Simón **B:** 441
  Clothing *picture on* **Ci:** 695
  El Niño **E:** 245
  Galapagos Islands **G:** 7
  Indian, American (Indians of the Andes) **I:** 173
  Organization of the Petroleum Exporting
    Countries **O:** 854
Ecumenical council [religion]
  Constantine the Great **Ci:** 993
  Roman Catholic Church (The recognition of
    Christianity) **R:** 405
  Vatican Council I **V:** 289
  Vatican Council II **V:** 289
Ecumenical movement [religion]
  Anglican Communion (Christian unity) **A:** 463
  Protestantism (The ecumenical movement)

P: 835
Religion (Religion today) R: 223
World Council of Churches W: 450
Ecumenical patriarch [title]
Eastern Orthodox Churches (Organization) E: 46
Patriarch P: 196
Eczema [disorder] E: 74
Allergy A: 373
Asthma (Causes) A: 825
Dust mite D: 392
Skin (Inflammation) S: 490
Ed Koch Queensboro Bridge
New York City (Queens) N: 329
"Ed Sullivan Show, The" [TV program]
CBS C: 323
Edam cheese
Cheese (Hard cheese) C: 392 *with picture*
Edaphosaurus [reptile]
Prehistoric animal *picture on* P: 738
EDB [chemical compound]
Bromine B: 636
Edda [Icelandic literature] E: 74
Brunhild B: 652
Mythology (Teutonic mythology) M: 985
Nibelungenlied: (The background) N: 395
Scandinavian literature (Beginnings) S: 171
Eddington, Sir Arthur Stanley [British
astronomer] E: 74
Relativity (Distortions in space-time) R: 212
Eddo [plant]
Elephant's-ear E: 233
Eddy, Howard [Canadian lawyer]
Campbell, Kim (Provincial legislator) C: 90c
Eddy, Mary Baker [American religious leader] E: 75
with portrait
Christian Scientists C: 522e
Eddy, William A. [American inventor]
Kite (The bowed kite) K: 339
Eddy current [electromagnetism]
Foucault, Jean Bernard Léon F: 429
Eddy current [fluid mechanics]
Gulf Stream (The path of the Gulf Stream) G: 438
Eddy flow [fluid mechanics]
Streamlining So: 924
Edelman, Gerald Maurice [American physiologist]
Nobel Prizes (Physiology or medicine: 1972)
N: 446
Edelweiss [plant] E: 75 *with picture*
Edema [disorder] E: 75
Altitude sickness A: 390
Diuretic D: 240
Lymphatic system (Return of interstitial fluid)
L: 534
Protein (Proteins in the diet) P: 832
Eden [Bible] E: 76
Adam and Eve A: 32
Paradise P: 143
Eden, Sir Anthony [British political leader] E: 76
Macmillan, Harold M: 25
United Kingdom (Economic recovery—and
collapse) U: 72
Eden Park
Cincinnati (The arts) Ci: 555 *with map*; (Parks and
playgrounds) C: 556
Edentate [zoology] E: 76
Ederle, Gertrude Caroline [American swimmer]
E: 76
English Channel E: 311
Edgar [king of England]
England (table) E: 308
Edgar [opera by Puccini]
Puccini, Giacomo P: 870
Edgar, Jim [American political leader]
Illinois (table) I: 71
Edgar Allan Poe House and Museum
Baltimore (Other interesting places to visit) B: 69
Edgar Allan Poe Museum
Richmond (Other interesting places to visit)
R: 332
Virginia (Libraries and museums) V: 402-403
Edgar Allan Poe National Historic Site
[Pennsylvania]
National Park System (table: National historic
sites) N: 52
Edgar Huntly [book by Brown]
Brown, Charles Brockden B: 642
Edgardo di Ravenswood [opera character]
Opera: (*Lucia di Lammermoor*) O: 804
Edge, The [Irish musician]
Bono B: 462
U2 U: 2
Edge, Walter E. [American political leader]
New Jersey (table) N: 249
Edge Island [island, Arctic]
Svalbard So: 1014
Edge of the Storm, The [book by Yáñez]
Latin American literature (The mid-1900's) L: 114

Edge of the Sword, The [book by De Gaulle]
De Gaulle, Charles André Joseph Marie (Early life)
D: 90-91
Edger-feeder [machine]
Postal services *picture on* P: 704; (Sorting) P: 703
Edger saw [machine]
Lumber *picture on* L: 520; (Sawing logs) L: 519
Edgerton, Harold Eugene [American inventor]
E: 76
Edgerton, Sidney [American government official]
Montana (The gold rush) M: 758
Edgewater Park [district]
New York City (The Bronx) N: 328-329
Edgeworth, Kenneth E. [Irish scientist]
Kuiper belt K: 392
Edgeworth, Maria [Irish author]
Irish literature (Early works in English) I: 431
Edgeworth-Kuiper belt [astronomy] *See* Kuiper
belt *in this index*
Edging candytuft [plant]
Candytuft C: 177
EDI [process] *See* Kirlian photography *in this index*
Edible bolete [fungus]
Mushroom (Nonpoisonous mushrooms) M: 943-
945 *with picture*
Edible Woman, The [book by Atwood]
Atwood, Margaret A: 880
Edict of ...
Edicts appear under their key words, as in Worms,
Edict of
Edinburgh [Scotland] E: 76 *with picture*
Scotland S: 211 *with picture*
United Kingdom *picture on* U: 48; (table: Average
monthly weather) U: 62
Edinburgh [ship]
Salvage S: 76b
Edinburgh, Duke of *See* Philip, Prince *in this index*
Edinburgh, University of [Scotland] E: 77
Edinburgh Castle
Edinburgh E: 77 *with picture*
Edinburgh International Festival
Scotland (The arts) S: 215-217
United Kingdom (The arts) U: 58
Edinburgh Review [magazine]
Macaulay, Thomas Babington M: 5
Ediphone [dictating machine]
Edison, Thomas Alva (Phonograph
developments) E: 80-81
Edirne [Turkey] E: 77
Edison, Charles [American political leader]
Edison, Thomas Alva (Family and friends) E: 81
New Jersey (table) N: 249
Roosevelt, Franklin Delano (table) R: 454
Edison, Nancy Elliott [mother of]
Edison, Thomas Alva (Early life) E: 78
Edison, Samuel [father of]
Edison, Thomas Alva (Early life) E: 78
Edison, Thomas Alva [American inventor] E: 77
with pictures
Cable (Electric power cables) C: 6
Communication (Famous first words) Ci: 884
with picture
Doll (Inventions) D: 291
EdisonLearning, Inc. E: 83
Electric light (History) E: 176
General Electric Company G: 88
Goldenrod G: 256
Invention *picture on* I: 360; (The late 1800's) I: 362
Latimer, Lewis Howard L: 90
Light bulb L: 293
Motion picture (The invention of motion
pictures) M: 863
Phonograph (History) P: 401
Sound (The recording of sound) So: 606
Telegraph (Service expansion and improvement)
T: 91-92
Telephone (The Bell System) T: 100
Tesla, Nikola (The alternating-current system)
T: 181
Vacuum tube (History) V: 259
Western Union W: 241
Westinghouse Electric Corporation W: 242
Edison effect [physics]
Vacuum tube (History) V: 259
Edison Learning, Inc. *See* EdisonLearning, Inc. *in
this index*
Edison National Historic Site [New Jersey]
Edison, Thomas Alva (Honors) E: 82
National Park System (table: National historic
sites) N: 52
Edison Project
EdisonLearning, Inc. E: 83
Edison Schools *See* EdisonLearning, Inc. *in this
index*
EdisonLearning, Inc. E: 82
Edit decision list [computer file]
Motion picture (Mixing the sound) M: 856

EDITH [program]
Fire drill F: 130
Editing
Composition (Your final editing) Ci: 905
Encyclopedia (Editing the manuscript) E: 267
with picture
Magazine (How print magazines are produced)
M: 43 *with picture*
Motion picture M: 846; (Editing the film) M: 855
with picture
Newspaper (The editorial department) N: 381;
(Writing and editing stories) N: 383
Publishing (Editors and fact checkers) P: 867
Television (Post-production) T: 111
Edition
Newspaper (table) N: 383
Editor *See* Editing *in this index*
Editor in chief [occupation]
Newspaper (The editorial department) N: 381
Editorial [journalism] E: 83
Journalism (Influencing public opinion) J: 173
Newspaper (The editorial department) N: 381-
382; (Writing editorials and features) N: 383
Pulitzer Prizes (Prizes in journalism) P: 886b;
(table) P: 890
Editorial cartoon
Block, Herbert Lawrence B: 404 *with picture*
Carpetbaggers *picture on* C: 247
Cartoon (Editorial cartoons) C: 263 *with picture*;
(Developing the idea) C: 266
Nast, Thomas N: 24
Pulitzer Prizes (table) P: 892
Republican Party *pictures on* R: 254, R: 256
"Editor's Easy Chair" [column by Howells]
Howells, William Dean H: 401
"Editor's Study" [column by Howells]
Howells, William Dean H: 401
EDM [manufacturing]
Machine tool (Electrical discharge machining
[EDM]) M: 19 *with diagram*
Edmonds, Sarah Emma Evelyn [Union soldier]
E: 83
Edmonds, Walter Dumaux [American author]
E: 83
Newbery Medal (table) N: 359
Edmondson, J. Howard [American political leader]
Oklahoma (table) O: 730
Edmonton [Alberta] E: 83 *with pictures and map*
Alberta (table: Average monthly weather) A: 324
Edmonton City Centre Airport
Edmonton (Economy) E: 85
Edmonton Eskimos [team]
Football (Canadian Football League) F: 364
Edmonton Oilers [team]
Hockey (table: National Hockey League) H: 281
Edmontosaurus [extinct animal]
Dinosaur (True dinosaurs) D: 206b-206c
Edmund I [king of England]
England (table) E: 308
Edmund II [king of England]
England (table) E: 308
Edmund Pettus Bridge [Alabama]
African Americans *picture on* A: 136t
Selma marches S: 290
Edmunds Anti-Polygamy Act [1882]
Arthur, Chester Alan (Other legislation) A: 757
Edo [former name, Tokyo]
Tokugawa Ieyasu T: 311
Tokyo (Early development) T: 318 *with picture*
Edo [people]
Benin B: 250
Edo era [Japanese history] *See* Tokugawa *in this
index*
Edom [ancient country] E: 85
Esau E: 356
Obadiah, Book of O: 640a
Edred [king of England]
England (table) E: 308
Education E: 86 *with pictures*
See also Higher education; Teaching *in this index;
the list of Related articles in the* Education
*article; and the Education sections of specific
country articles, such as* Mexico (Education)
Academic freedom A: 20
Adolescent (Adjusting to school life) A: 63;
(Education) A: 64
African Americans (Developments since 1970)
A: 136r
AIDS (Education) A: 165
Audio-visual materials A: 882
Baby boom generation (Effects of the baby
boom) B: 11
Computer (Educational software) Ci: 920 *with
picture*
Curriculum Ci: 1197
Debate (Academic debate) D: 64
Democracy (Education and democracy) D: 121

Disability (Education) **D:** 220
Electronic game (Education) **E:** 205
Europe (Education) **E:** 390
Fire department (Public education programs) **F:** 125
Ford Foundation (Programs) **F:** 382
Foundation (Education) **F:** 430
Grading **G:** 296
Hispanic Americans (Education) **H:** 256
Indian, American (Social and economic progress) **I:** 180-181
Learning disabilities **L:** 165
Library (School libraries) **L:** 244
Literacy **L:** 350
Local government (Education and community welfare functions) **L:** 407
Motion picture **M:** 846
Multiculturalism **M:** 918
Museum (Special services) **M:** 939
Parent-teacher organizations **P:** 157
Physical fitness (Developing physical fitness) **P:** 435
Poverty (Social factors) **P:** 723; (Educational programs) **P:** 725
Public opinion (Educational agencies) **P:** 860
Reading (The importance of reading) **R:** 155-156; (The teaching of reading) **R:** 157
Rome, Ancient (Education) **R:** 442
School **S:** 180 *with pictures*
Sexual harassment (Sexual harassment in education) **S:** 337
Social change **So:** 550
Social work (Fields of social work) **So:** 558
State government (State services) **So:** 864
Teaching **T:** 65 *with pictures*
Women's movement (The beginnings of women's movements) **W:** 384-385
History
City (Description) **Ci:** 585-587
Coeducation **Ci:** 752
Colonial life in America (Education and religion) **Ci:** 803 *with picture*
Creationism (The 1900's) **Ci:** 1123
Egypt, Ancient (Education) **E:** 136-137
Greece, Ancient (Education) **G:** 367
High school **H:** 228
Laurier, Sir Wilfrid (The Manitoba school issue) **L:** 125
Mann, Horace **M:** 164
McGuffey, William Holmes **M:** 335 *with picture*
Pestalozzi, Johann Heinrich **P:** 318
Pioneer life in America (Education) **P:** 484 *with picture*
Progressive education **P:** 813
United States, History of the (Better education) **U:** 173
Types and programs
Alternative school **A:** 388
Bilingual education **B:** 300
Career education **C:** 213
Cooperative education **Ci:** 1037
Early childhood education **E:** 15
EdisonLearning, Inc. **E:** 82
Family and consumer sciences (Family and consumer sciences education and communications) **F:** 26
Head Start **H:** 124
Home schooling **H:** 301
Montessori method **M:** 764a
Moral education **M:** 799
New mathematics **N:** 255
No Child Left Behind Act **N:** 438
Parent education **P:** 156
Sex education **S:** 336
Special education **So:** 770
Suzuki method **So:** 1013
Education, Agricultural *See* Agricultural education *in this index*
Education, American Council on
American Council on Education **A:** 409
Education, Board of
Education (Control and support of U.S. education) **E:** 94
High school (High schools in the United States) **H:** 228
School (Public schools) **S:** 182; (The growth of the public school system) **S:** 183
Teaching (Employment practices) **T:** 68
Education, Department of [U.S.] **E:** 110 *with pictures*
Education (The federal government and education) **E:** 94
Washington, D.C. *map on* **W:** 76
Education, Doctor of
Degree, College (The doctor's degree) **D:** 93
Education, Early childhood *See* Early childhood education *in this index*

Education, Secretary of [U.S.]
Education, Department of **E:** 110
Flag *picture on* **F:** 211
Education, Society for the Advancement of
Society for the Advancement of Education **So:** 563
Education, Vocational *See* Vocational education *in this index*
Education Act [United Kingdom, 1870]
United Kingdom (Gladstone and Disraeli) **U:** 69
Education Act [United Kingdom, 1996]
Disability (The 1900's) **D:** 221-222
Education (Education for children with disabilities) **E:** 107
Education Amendments Act [1972]
Education (Nonsexist education) **E:** 107
Sexual harassment (Sexual harassment in education) **S:** 337
Women's movement (Legal gains) **W:** 386
Education Amendments Act [1976]
Vocational education (The 1900's and early 2000's) **V:** 435
Education Association, National *See* National Education Association *in this index*
Education for All Handicapped Children Act [1975]
Disability (The 1900's) **D:** 221-222
Special education **So:** 770
Education of Henry Adams, The [book by Adams]
Adams, Henry **A:** 33
American literature (Nonfiction writers) **A:** 420
Education of Young Children, National Association for the *See* National Association for the Education of Young Children *in this index*
Education Week, American E: 111
Educational blindness
Blindness **B:** 401
Educational Consolidation and Improvement Act [1981]
Elementary and Secondary Education Act **E:** 224
Educational guidance
Guidance (Educational guidance) **G:** 422
Educational psychology E: 111
See also the list of *Related articles in the Educational Psychology article*
Herbart, Johann Friedrich **H:** 197
Learning **L:** 162
Psychology (Major fields of psychology) **P:** 848
Educational software
Computer (Educational software) **Ci:** 920
Educational television
Television (Public television) **T:** 110a
Educational Testing Service [U.S.]
National Assessment of Educational Progress **N:** 29
Educational theory
Education (What should be taught?) **E:** 105
Eduskunta [government]
Finland (Government) **F:** 109 *with picture*
EDVAC [computer]
Computer (The first electronic computers) **Ci:** 924b-924c
Edward [1767-1820, British prince]
Victoria (Early years) **V:** 355
Edward [1964- , British prince] *See* Edward, Prince *in this index*
Edward [the Black Prince] **E:** 111 *with portrait*
Duke **D:** 380
England (The Hundred Years' War) **E:** 306
Poitiers, Battle of **P:** 603
Edward [ship]
Barry, John **B:** 119
Edward I [king of England] **E:** 112 *with portrait*
Bruce, Robert **B:** 648
England (The beginnings of Parliament) **E:** 306
Model Parliament **M:** 684
Plantagenet **P:** 550
Prince of Wales **P:** 794
Scotland (Fight for independence) **S:** 219
Wales (Revolts against England) **W:** 12
Wallace, Sir William **W:** 17
Edward II [king of England] **E:** 112
Plantagenet **P:** 550
Prince of Wales **P:** 794
Edward II [play by Marlowe]
Marlowe, Christopher **M:** 216
Edward III [king of England] **E:** 112
Bruce, Robert **B:** 648
Crécy, Battle of **Ci:** 1124
England (The Hundred Years' War) **E:** 306
France (A period of wars) **F:** 473
Garter, Order of the **G:** 46
Hundred Years' War **H:** 437
John of Gaunt **J:** 134
Plantagenet **P:** 550
Salic law **S:** 66
Edward IV [king of England] **E:** 112 *with portrait*

England (The Wars of the Roses) **E:** 306
Henry VI [of England] **H:** 187
Warbeck, Perkin **W:** 34
Wars of the Roses **W:** 38
Warwick, Earl of **W:** 44
York **Y:** 568
Edward IV [literary figure]
Shakespeare, William: *(Richard III)* **S:** 356
Edward V [king of England] **E:** 112
Richard III **R:** 329
Tower of London **T:** 351
Edward VI [king of England] **E:** 113
Cranmer, Thomas **Ci:** 1121
England (The English Reformation) **E:** 307
Grey, Lady Jane **G:** 391
Henry VIII [king of England] **H:** 188
Money *picture on* **M:** 710
Tudor, House of **T:** 481
Edward VII [king of Britain] **E:** 113 *with portrait*
Buchanan, James (Life in the White House) **B:** 661
Diamond (Famous diamonds) **D:** 182
Royal Canadian Mounted Police (History) **R:** 497
Windsor **W:** 334
Edward VII Peninsula [Antarctica]
Exploration (The exploration of Antarctica) **E:** 450
Edward VIII [king of Britain] **E:** 113 *with portrait*
United Kingdom ("Peace in our time") **U:** 70
Edward, Lake [Africa]
Lake Edward **L:** 37
Edward, Prince [1964- , British prince]
Elizabeth II (The royal family) **E:** 240
Edward C. Elliott Hall of Music
Purdue University **P:** 907
Edward the Confessor [king of England] **E:** 113
England (The Anglo-Saxon period) **E:** 304-305
London (The Middle Ages) **L:** 439-440
Norman Conquest **N:** 455
Westminster Abbey **W:** 243
William I, the Conqueror **W:** 308
Edward the Elder [king of England]
Edward I **E:** 112
England (table) **E:** 308
Edward the Martyr [king of England]
Edward I **E:** 112
England (table) **E:** 308
Edwardian literature
English literature (Literature before World War I) **E:** 322
Edwardians, The [book by Sackville-West]
Sackville-West, V. S: 5
Edwards, Edward I. [American political leader]
New Jersey (table) **N:** 249
Edwards, Edwin W. [American political leader]
Louisiana (table) **L:** 496
Edwards, Glen W. [American pilot]
Edwards Air Force Base **E:** 114
Edwards, Henrietta Muir [Canadian reformer]
Famous Five **F:** 26b
Edwards, Henry W. [American political leader]
Connecticut (table) **Ci:** 967
Edwards, James B. [American political leader]
Energy, Department of (table) **E:** 276
Reagan, Ronald Wilson (table) **R:** 169
South Carolina (The late 1900's) **So:** 662
Edwards, John [American political leader] **E:** 114 *with portrait*
Bush, George Walker (The election of 2004) **B:** 722i-722j
Edwards, John C. [American political leader]
Missouri (table) **M:** 668
Edwards, Jonathan [American theologian] **E:** 114 *with portrait*
American literature (New England) **A:** 414
Great Awakening **G:** 335
Missionary (History) **M:** 621
Edwards, Ninian [American political leader]
Illinois (table) **I:** 71; (Early national period) **I:** 72-74
Edwards, Robert G. [British physiologist]
Nobel Prizes (Physiology or medicine: 2010) **N:** 447
Edwards Air Force Base [California] **E:** 114
Edwards and Kirby [law firm]
Edwards, John **E:** 114
Edwig [king of England]
England (table) **E:** 308
Edwin of the Iron Shoes [book by Muller]
Muller, Marcia **M:** 915
EEA [trade agreement] *See* European Economic Area *in this index*
EEC [organization] *See* European Economic Community *in this index*
EEG [medicine] *See* Electroencephalograph *in this index*
Eel [fish] **E:** 114 *with picture*
Deep sea (Fish) **D:** 82b-82c *with picture*
Fish *pictures on* **F:** 149, **F:** 156
Sargasso Sea (Origin of the seaweed) **S:** 125-126

Eel River [Indiana]
  Indiana *picture on* I: 196
Eelcat [fish]
  Catfish C: 300
Eelgrass [plant] E: 115
Eells, Cushing [American educator]
  Washington (Schools) W: 50-51
Eelworm [animal] E: 115
  Roundworm R: 491
EEOC [organization] *See* Equal Employment
  Opportunity Commission *in this index*
EEPROM chip [electronics]
  Computer chip (Memory chips) Ci: 924f
EER [measurement] *See* Energy efficiency ratio *in
  this index*
Eesti Vabariik [name for]
  Estonia E: 361
Eeyore [literary figure]
  Milne, A. A. M: 556
EEZ [law] *See* Exclusive economic zone *in this index*
EF ratings [meteorology] *See* Enhanced Fujita scale
  in this index
Efate [island, Vanuatu]
  Vanuatu V: 284
Efe [people]
  Africa (Peoples of Africa) A: 104
Effective demand [economics]
  Keynes, John Maynard K: 308a
Effective horsepower [measurement]
  Horsepower (Brake horsepower) H: 367
Effector [anatomy]
  Nervous system *diagram on* N: 135; (How the
  nervous system works) N: 132 *with diagram*
Effi Briest [book by Fontane]
  Fontane, Theodor F: 327
Efficiency [business]
  Sales (Characteristics needed) S: 65
Efficiency [physics] E: 115
  Boiler B: 439
  Machine (Efficiency) M: 14
Efficient cause [philosophy]
  Aristotle (Philosophy of nature) A: 664
Effigy mound
  Mound builders M: 882
Effigy Mounds National Monument [Iowa] E: 115
  Iowa (Places to visit) I: 384
  National Park System (table: National
  monuments) N: 50
Effleurage [movement]
  Massage M: 295
Efflorescence [discoloration]
  Hydrate H: 462
Effluent
  Sewage S: 329
Effort arm [mechanism]
  Lever L: 217
Eft [animal]
  Newt N: 388 *with picture*
EFT [banking] *See* Electronic funds transfer *in this
  index*
EFTA [organization] *See* European Free Trade
  Association *in this index*
Egan, William A. [American political leader]
  Alaska (table) A: 294
Egbert [king of Wessex] E: 115
  England (The Anglo-Saxon period) E: 304
Egede, Hans [Norwegian religious leader]
  Greenland (History) G: 385
Egg [food]
  Bird (As a source of food and raw materials)
  B: 330
  Chicken (Producing eggs) C: 443 *with pictures*
  Easter (Easter symbols) E: 43-44
  Farm and farming *picture on* F: 40
  Food (Interesting facts about food) F: 329; (Food
  from animals) F: 330
  Minnesota *picture on* M: 601
  Nutrition (Proteins) N: 625
  Poultry (Marketing poultry and eggs) P: 721
  Vegetarianism V: 294
Egg [reproduction] E: 116 *with pictures*
  Ant (Reproduction) A: 524 *with picture*
  Cell (Sizes of cells) C: 328; (Meiosis) C: 331;
  (Before 1900) C: 337
  Cloning (Nuclear transfer) Ci: 682l *with picture*
  Corn (How the plant reproduces) Ci: 1058
  Evolution (Mutation) E: 427-428
  Fallopian tube F: 17
  Fertilization F: 78
  Instinct (How instinctive behavior works) I: 304-
  305
  Plant (Flowers) P: 531; (The reproduction of
  plants) P: 532 *with diagram*
    Animal reproduction
    Animal (Sexual reproduction) A: 496 *with
    diagram*
    Bird (Laying and hatching eggs) B: 357 *with*

  pictures; (The reproductive system) B: 366
  Butterfly (The egg) B: 740 *with picture*
  Dinosaur (Reproduction and growth) D: 211
  Fish (Spawning and care of the eggs) F: 169
    with pictures
  Fly (Egg) F: 310 *with picture*
  Frog (Eggs) F: 538 *with pictures*
  Ichneumon wasp I: 24 *with picture*
  Insect (Reproduction) I: 292 *with picture*
  Lobster (Young) L: 406
  Ostrich (How the ostrich lives) O: 868 *with
  picture*
  Prehistoric animal (The move onto land) P: 737
  Reproduction (Through sexual reproduction)
  R: 242; (How reproduction has evolved)
  R: 243 *with picture*
  Reptile *picture on* R: 251; (Reproduction) R: 252
  Sea turtle (Reproduction) S: 263
  Snake (Reproduction) S: 529-530 *with picture;*
  (Feeding habits) S: 530 *with picture*
  Spider (Eggs) So: 787 *with pictures*
  Tadpole *picture on* T: 6
  Tick T: 279 *with picture*
  Turtle (Reproduction) T: 521 *with pictures*
    Human reproduction
    Embryo E: 257
    Heredity (Chromosomes and genes) H: 201
    Human body (The reproductive system) H: 425
    with picture
    In vitro fertilization I: 95
    Menstruation (The menstrual cycle) M: 404
    with pictures
    Ovary O: 881
    Reproduction, Human (The human
    reproductive system) R: 244-245 *with
    pictures*; (Fertilization) R: 246; (Development
    of the embryo) R: 246-248 *with picture*
    Sexuality (Before birth) S: 338
Egg case [entomology]
  Praying mantis P: 734
Egg cell [botany]
  Seed (How seeds develop) S: 281
Egg-eater snake
  Snake *pictures on* S: 531
Egg-laying mammal
  Mammal (Reproduction) M: 123-124
Egg retrieval [fertility procedure]
  Multiple birth (Causes of multiple birth) M: 920
Egg sac [zoology]
  Spider (The life of a spider) So: 787 *with picture*
Egg shell [zoology]
  Egg (The shell) E: 116
Egg tempera [painting medium] *See* Tempera *in
  this index*
Egg timer
  Hourglass H: 379
Egg tooth [zoology]
  Bird (Laying and hatching eggs) B: 357-359
  Snake (Reproduction) S: 529-530
Egglayer [zoology]
  Aquarium, Home (Choosing fish and plants)
  A: 578-578a
Eggleston, Edward [American author] E: 118
Eggleston, William [American photographer]
  Photography (A diversity of styles) P: 426-427
Eggplant [plant] E: 118 *with picture*
  Vegetable (Fruits) V: 292 *with picture*
Egielski, Richard [American artist]
  Caldecott Medal (table: 1987) C: 26
Egigingwah [Inuit explorer]
  Exploration (The North Pole) E: 450
Eglantine [plant] E: 119
Église du Dôme [Paris]
  Napoleon I (The Hundred Days and Waterloo)
  N: 16
Egmont [play by Goethe]
  Goethe, Johann Wolfgang von (Middle years)
  G: 247
Ego [psychology] E: 119
  Freud, Sigmund (On the mind) F: 530
  Mythology (Psychological approaches) M: 990
  Personality (Freud's psychoanalytic theory) P: 302
  Psychoanalysis (Psychoanalytic theory) P: 846
Egocentrism [psychology]
  Adolescent (Intellectual development) A: 61-62
  Child (The school-age years) C: 449
Egoist, The [book by Meredith]
  Meredith, George M: 416
Egret [bird] E: 119 *with pictures*
  Louisiana *picture on* L: 488
Egypt E: 120 *with pictures and maps*
  See also the list of Related articles in the Egypt
  article
  Arab-Israeli conflict A: 582
  Arab League A: 582b
  Clothing *picture on* Ci: 692
  Cold War (The Suez crisis) Ci: 766

  Fraction (History) F: 449
  Gaza Strip G: 73
  Library (Africa) L: 252-253
  Middle East M: 530 *with picture*
  Muslims (Colonialism) M: 964d
  Napoleonic Wars (The Egyptian Campaigns)
  N: 18 *with map*
  Nile River N: 422 *with picture and map*
  Sudan (History) So: 952
  Suez Canal So: 958 *with map*
  Suez crisis So: 958
  United Arab Republic U: 46
  United Kingdom (European unity) U: 71-72
  United Nations (Peacekeeping operations)
  U: 90-91
  World War II (The Western Desert campaign)
  W: 476
Egypt, Ancient E: 135 *with pictures and map*
  See also the list of Related articles in the Egypt,
  Ancient *article*
  Book (Early books) B: 465
  Breasted, James Henry B: 591
  Clothing (Egypt) Ci: 696 *with picture*
  Education (The beginning of formal education)
  E: 97
  Family (Ancient families) F: 21-22
  Geometry (History) G: 106
  Mediterranean Sea (History of the
  Mediterranean) M: 382
  Pharaoh hound P: 353
  Pythagorean theorem (Origins) P: 921
  Shield S: 400
    Agriculture
    Agriculture (Mesopotamia and Egypt) A: 156
    with picture
    Egypt, Ancient (Agriculture) E: 138
    Food (Ancient times) F: 336
    Irrigation (History) I: 459
    World, History of the *picture on* W: 422
    Art and architecture
    Egypt, Ancient *pictures on* E: 140; (Arts and
    sciences) E: 139 *with picture*
    Alabaster *pictures on* A: 280
    Architecture (Egyptian architecture) A: 612
    with picture
    Bed (History) B: 198 *with picture*
    Bronze *picture on* B: 638
    Doll (Ancient times) D: 288
    Furniture (Ancient Egypt) F: 570 *with picture*
    Ivory (Ivory carving) I: 521
    Jewelry (Early jewelry) J: 117
    Paint (The history of paint) P: 26
    Painting (Egyptian painting) P: 40; (Aegean
    painting) P: 41
    Papyrus P: 141
    Pottery *picture on* P: 717
    Pyramids (Egyptian pyramids) P: 916 *with
    pictures*
    Relief *picture on* R: 213
    Sculpture (Kinds of sculpture) S: 230;
    (Egyptian) S: 234 *with picture*
    Shelter (Ancient times) S: 393
    Sphinx (Egyptian sphinxes) So: 780 *with picture*
    History
    Egypt, Ancient (History) E: 142
    Exploration (Ancient exploration) E: 440 *with
    map*
    Hittites (History) H: 269
    Joseph J: 167
    Kush K: 394
    Nubia N: 578
    Phoenicia (Foreign control) P: 394
    Tutankhamun T: 526
    World, History of the (The Nile Valley) W: 424
    Language and literature
    Egypt, Ancient (The people) E: 136
    Alphabet (Semitic scripts) A: 381 *with pictures*
    Hieroglyphics H: 225 *with pictures*
    Library (Ancient libraries of papyrus) L: 257
    Writing system (Phonetization) W: 513
    Religion and mythology
    Egypt, Ancient (Religion) E: 137-138
    Astrology (History) A: 827
    Cat (History) C: 296 *with picture*
    Embalming (Ancient embalming) E: 255
    Funeral customs (History) F: 558
    Linen (History) L: 335
    Mummy M: 925 *with pictures*
    Mythology *pictures on* M: 974, M: 977;
    (Egyptian mythology) M: 978 *with picture*
    Osiris O: 863 *with picture*
    Scarab S: 172
    Seth S: 322
    Social and cultural life
    Egypt, Ancient (Life of the people) E: 136-137
    Beard B: 186
    Clothing (Egypt) Ci: 696 *with picture*

Hairdressing (Ancient times) **H:** 11 *with picture*
Perfume (History) **P:** 286
Ring **R:** 342 *with picture*
Women's movement (In ancient societies)
  W: 384
Technology and science
Egypt, Ancient (Sciences) **E:** 139
Calendar (History) **C:** 30
Clock *picture on* **Ci:** 682j
Drug (Drugs in ancient times) **D:** 358
Glass (Early times) **G:** 217-218 *with picture*
Heart (Interesting facts about the heart) **H:** 133
  with picture
Invention (The first civilizations) **I:** 358;
  (Ancient Greece) **I:** 359
Leather (History) **L:** 169 *with picture*
Map (Ancient maps) **M:** 182
Mathematics (Early civilization) **M:** 303
Medicine (The ancient Middle East) **M:** 372
Number (The Egyptians) **N:** 606 *with picture*
Scale, Weighing (Balances) **S:** 169
Science (Early civilizations) **S:** 196
Surveying **So:** 1011
Transportation
Egypt, Ancient (Trade and transportation)
  E: 139
Ship *pictures on* **S:** 416; (Egyptian ships) **S:** 415
Transportation (The first great civilizations)
  T: 385
Egypt, Plagues of
Moses (The Exodus) **M:** 828-829
Egyptian cobra [snake]
Asp **A:** 814 *with picture*
Egyptian lotus
Lotus **L:** 473 *with picture*
Egyptian Mau cat
Cat (Short-haired breeds) **C:** 290-291
Egyptian Museum
Cairo *picture on* **C:** 18
Egyptian privet [shrub]
Henna **H:** 185
Egyptian vulture [bird]
Vulture (Old World vultures) **V:** 454
Egyptian water lily [plant]
Lotus **L:** 473 *with picture*
Egyptology
Egypt, Ancient (Learning about ancient Egypt)
  E: 144
Egypt's Liberation: The Philosophy of the
  Revolution [book by Nasser]
Nasser, Gamal Abdel **N:** 24
Ehlert, Lois [American author/illustrator]
Regina Medal (table: 2009) **R:** 206
Ehrenburg, Ilya [Russian author]
Russian literature (Modern Soviet literature)
  R: 564
Ehringhaus, J. C. B. [American political leader]
North Carolina (table) **N:** 490
Ehrlich, Paul [German bacteriologist] **E:** 145
Medicine (The medical revolution) **M:** 376
Ehrlich, Paul Ralph [American biologist] **E:** 145
Ehrlich, Robert, Jr. [American political leader]
Maryland (table) **M:** 255
Ehrlichman, John D. [American government
  official]
Watergate **W:** 144
Eichendorff, Joseph von [German poet]
German literature (Romanticism) **G:** 140
Eichmann, Adolf [Nazi leader] **E:** 145
Wallenberg, Raoul **W:** 17
War crime (World War II) **W:** 27
Eichmann in Jerusalem [book by Arendt]
Arendt, Hannah **A:** 645
Eider down [feathers]
Eider duck **E:** 145
Eider duck [bird] **E:** 145
Duck (Food) **D:** 375-376
Eidetic imagery
Memory (Exceptionally good memory) **M:** 393
Eielson, Carl Ben [American aviator] **E:** 145
Wilkins, Sir Hubert **W:** 306
Eiffel, Gustave [French engineer] **E:** 145
Eiffel Tower **E:** 146
Statue of Liberty *picture on* **So:** 875; (The statue)
  So: 873; (Construction and dedication) **So:** 876
Eiffel Tower [Paris] **E:** 145 *with picture*
Eiffel, Gustave **E:** 145
Paris *picture on* **P:** 161; (Gardens, squares, and
  parks) **P:** 162-163 *with map*
Eigen, Manfred [German chemist]
Nobel Prizes (Chemistry: 1967) **N:** 443
Eiger [mountain, Switzerland]
Alps *picture on* **A:** 385
Eight, The *See* Ashcan School *in this index*
8½ [film]
Fellini, Federico **F:** 68
Eight-ball [game]

Billiards (Pool) **B:** 305
Eight Comedies and Eight Entremeses [book by
  Cervantes]
Cervantes, Miguel de (His literary career) **C:** 363
Eight-hour day
Wages and hours (Hours) **W:** 3
Eight Hour Day [Australian holiday]
Labor Day **L:** 2
800 service
Telephone (Business services) **T:** 98
8-millimeter film
Motion picture (The film) **M:** 857
8-millimeter videotape
Camcorder (The development of camcorders)
  C: 75 *with picture*
Videotape recorder (History) **V:** 361
Eight-petaled mountain avens [plant]
Flower *picture on* **F:** 283
Mountain avens **M:** 897
Eight-spotted forester moth
Moth *picture on* **M:** 841
Eight-track tape system
Tape recorder (History) **T:** 38-39
Eighteen Poems [book by Thomas]
Thomas, Dylan **T:** 261
1837: The Farmers' Revolt [play by Salutin]
Canadian literature (Modern Canadian drama)
  C: 161
18-wheeler [vehicle] *See* Tractor-semitrailer *in this
  index*
Eighteenth Amendment [U.S. Constitution]
Constitution of the United States **Ci:** 1014
Prohibition (The movement toward prohibition)
  P: 815
Roaring Twenties (Changing attitudes) **R:** 363-
  364
United States, History of the (Prohibition) **U:** 189
Volstead Act **V:** 445
Woman's Christian Temperance Union **W:** 382
Eighteenth Dynasty [ancient Egypt]
Pharaoh **P:** 353
Eightfold way theory [physics]
Gell-Mann, Murray **G:** 77
Eighth Amendment [U.S. Constitution]
Bail **B:** 31
Citizenship (The Constitution) **Ci:** 571
Constitution of the United States **Ci:** 1012
Eighth Crusade [1270]
Louis IX **L:** 474
Eighth Day, The [book by Wilder]
Wilder, Thornton **W:** 303
Eijkman, Christiaan [Dutch physiologist]
Nobel Prizes (Physiology or medicine: 1929)
  N: 445
Vitamin (History) **V:** 432
Eikon [religion] *See* Icon *in this index*
Eilat [Israel] *See* Elat *in this index*
Ein ...
Titles beginning with the German words Ein
  and Eine appear under their key words, as in
  Deutsches Requiem, Ein
Ein Kerem [area]
Jerusalem (West Jerusalem) **J:** 95 *with map*
Einhard [Frankish government official]
Charlemagne **C:** 378
Einsatzgruppen [German history]
Babi Yar **B:** 3
Holocaust ("The Final Solution") **H:** 296a
Einstein, Albert [German-American physicist]
  E: 146 *with pictures*
See also Relativity *in this index*
Autograph *picture on* **A:** 943
Brain (Interesting facts about the brain) **B:** 550b
Dark energy **D:** 37
Dark matter **D:** 36
Democracy (Famous quotations about
  democracy) **D:** 120
Eclipse (The study of eclipses) **E:** 52
E=mc² **E:** 3
Energy (Energy and matter) **E:** 274
Force (Gravitation) **F:** 370
Gravitation (Einstein's theory of gravitation)
  G: 331; (Predictions of general relativity) **G:** 332
Gravitational wave **G:** 333
Laser (History) **L:** 86
Light (Photons) **L:** 286; (The speed of light) **L:** 290
Motion (Einstein's theories of relativity) **M:** 845
Newton, Sir Isaac (Personal characteristics) **N:** 390
Nuclear energy (Artificial fission) **N:** 590; (The
  development of nuclear weapons) **N:** 590
Photon **P:** 430
Physics *picture on* **P:** 442; (Quantum theory)
  P: 441; (Einstein and relativity) **P:** 441
Pugwash Conferences on Science and World
  Affairs **P:** 886
Quantum mechanics (Quantum nature of light)
  Q: 6

Radiation (The quantum theory) **R:** 81
Time (Time in relativity theory) **T:** 292b
Universe (The future of the universe) **U:** 206
Einstein, Eduard [son of]
Einstein, Albert (First marriage) **E:** 146
Einstein, Elsa [wife of]
Einstein, Albert (Second marriage) **E:** 146b
Einstein, Hans Albert [son of]
Einstein, Albert (First marriage) **E:** 146 *with picture*
Einstein, Maria [sister of]
Einstein, Albert (Early years) **E:** 146 *with picture*
Einstein, Mileva Maric [wife of]
Einstein, Albert (Early years) **E:** 146 *with picture*
Einstein on the Beach [opera by Glass and Wilson]
Glass, Philip **G:** 224
Einstein Tower [Potsdam, Germany]
Germany *picture on* **G:** 155
Mendelsohn, Eric **M:** 399
Einsteinium [element] **E:** 147
Transuranium element **T:** 401
Einthoven, Willem [Dutch physiologist] **E:** 147
Electrocardiograph **E:** 199
Nobel Prizes (Physiology or medicine: 1924)
  N: 445
Éire [name for]
Ireland **I:** 416
Eirik the Red [Viking explorer] *See* Erik the Red *in
  this index*
Eisai [Japanese religious leader]
Zen **Z:** 589
Eisenhower, David [American public figure]
Camp David **C:** 88
Eisenhower, Dwight David *picture on* **E:** 154;
  (Eisenhower's family) **E:** 148-149
Nixon, Richard Milhous *picture on* **N:** 435
Eisenhower, Dwight David [U.S. president] **E:** 148
  with pictures
Advertising (Political effects) **A:** 78 *with picture*
Camp David **C:** 88
Cold War (To the brink and back) **Ci:** 765; (The
  spirit of Geneva) **Ci:** 766; (New challenges)
  Ci: 767
D-Day **D:** 2
Dollar (The United States dollar) **D:** 295 *with
  picture*
Interstate Highway System **I:** 352
Lodge, Henry Cabot, Jr. **L:** 419
Money (Dollar coins) **M:** 714
Nixon, Richard Milhous **N:** 428; (The 1952
  campaign) **N:** 430 *with picture*
President of the United States *picture on* **P:** 766
Republican Party (The Eisenhower years) **R:** 256
Ridgway, Matthew Bunker **R:** 336
Roosevelt, Franklin Delano (The United States
  goes to war) **R:** 457 *with picture*
Truman, Harry S. (Foreign affairs) **T:** 471
Union of Soviet Socialist Republics (Relations
  with the United States) **U:** 39
United Nations (Peaceful uses of nuclear energy)
  U: 89
Vietnam War (The divided country) **V:** 373-374
World War II (The Tunisia Campaign) **W:** 481; (The
  invasion of Italy) **W:** 483 *with picture*; (D-Day)
  W: 483-484
Eisenhower, John Shelton Doud [son of]
Eisenhower, Dwight David *picture on* **E:** 154;
  (Eisenhower's family) **E:** 148-149
Eisenhower, Julie Nixon [daughter of]
Nixon, Richard Milhous *picture on* **N:** 435
Eisenhower, Mamie Doud [wife of Dwight D.
  Eisenhower]
Advertising *picture on* **A:** 79
Eisenhower, Dwight David *pictures on* **E:** 150;
  (Boyhood) **E:** 148 *with pictures*
First ladies of the United States (table) **F:** 142
Nixon, Richard Milhous *picture on* **N:** 431
Eisenhower Doctrine [international relations]
Cold War (The Eisenhower Doctrine) **Ci:** 767
Eisenhower, Dwight David (Crises in the Middle
  East and Asia) **E:** 154
Eisenhower Expressway
Chicago (The West Side) **C:** 424
Eisenhower Library and Museum
Kansas *picture on* **K:** 221; (Places to visit) **K:** 226
Eisenhower Memorial Tunnel [Colorado]
Rocky Mountains (History) **R:** 395-396
**Eisenhower National System of Interstate and
  Defense Highways** [name for]
Interstate Highway System **I:** 352
Eisenhower Theater [Washington, D.C.]
Kennedy Center for the Performing Arts **K:** 270
Eisenstaedt, Alfred [American photographer]
  E: 155 *with picture*
Eisenstein, Sergei Mikhailovich [Soviet director]
  E: 155
Motion picture (Filmmaking in Europe) **M:** 866
Eisner, Will [American author] **E:** 155

American literature (Popular genres) **A:** 425
Graphic novel **G:** 323
Eisteddfod [Welsh festival]
Bard **B:** 109
Wales (The arts) **W:** 9-10
EITC [federal program] *See* Earned Income Tax
Credit *in this index*
**Eiteljorg Museum of American Indians and
Western Art** [Indianapolis]
Indiana (Museums) **I:** 201 *with picture*
Eitoku, Kano [Japanese artist]
Painting (Japanese painting) **P:** 47 *with picture*
Ejaculation [physiology]
Reproduction, Human (The human reproductive
system) **R:** 244-246
Ejido [farm]
Mexico (Agriculture) **M:** 465
Ekaterinburg [Russia] *See* Yekaterinburg *in this
index*
Ekaterinoslav [former name]
Dnipropetrovsk **D:** 259
Ekeberg, Anders G. [Swedish chemist]
Tantalum **T:** 29
EKG [medicine] *See* Electrocardiogram *in this index*
El [railroad] *See* Elevated railroad *in this index*
El ...
Personal names beginning El *appear under their
key words, as in* Greco, El. *Place names are
alphabetized as single words:* El Paso *appears
after* Elon College
El Al [airline]
Israel (Transportation and communication) **I:** 486
El Aaiun [Western Sahara] **E:** 156
Elagabalus [Roman emperor]
Rome, Ancient (table) **R:** 447
Elaine [legendary figure]
Galahad, Sir **G:** 7
Lancelot, Sir **L:** 56
El Alamein [Egypt] **E:** 156
World War II (The Tunisia Campaign) **W:** 481
El Alto [Bolivia]
La Paz **L:** 72
Elam [ancient country]
Susa **So:** 1012
Elamites [ancient people]
Cuneiform **Ci:** 1192
Iran (Early days) **I:** 405
Persia, Ancient (Early times) **P:** 297
Eland [animal] **E:** 156
Animal *picture on* **A:** 476
Antelope (Habits and appearance) **A:** 542 *with
picture*
Elaphrothrips tuberculatus [insect]
Thrips **T:** 270
Elapid [snake]
Snake (Fangs and venom glands) **S:** 528; (Elapids)
S: 535
Snakebite (Types of venomous snakes) **S:** 536
Elara [satellite]
Jupiter (Outer satellites) **J:** 200a
ELAS [military]
Greece (World War II) **G:** 363-364
Elasmosaur [extinct animal]
Plesiosaur **P:** 573
Elastic clause [government]
Congress of the United States (Origin of power)
Ci: 943
Elastic fluid
Fluid **F:** 304
Elastic modulus
Elasticity **E:** 156
Elasticity [physical property] **E:** 156
Hooke, Robert **H:** 324
Materials (Rubber) **M:** 300d
Mechanics **M:** 354
Rubber **R:** 500; (The chemistry of rubber) **R:** 501
Spring **So:** 806
Textile (Knitted fabrics) **T:** 214
Elasticity, Principle of [economics]
Taxation (Elasticity) **T:** 54
Elastin [protein]
Connective tissue **Ci:** 972
Elastomer [material]
Materials (Rubber) **M:** 300d
Rubber (Synthetic rubber) **R:** 504
Elastomeric fiber
Textile (Manufactured fibers) **T:** 213
Elat [Israel] **E:** 156
Israel (The Six-Day War) **I:** 488
Elavil [drug]
Antidepressant **A:** 553
El Azúcar, Lake [Mexico]
Rio Grande (Lower course) **R:** 347
Elba [island, Mediterranean] **E:** 156
Napoleon I (Exile to Elba) **N:** 16
Napoleonic Wars (Napoleon's downfall) **N:** 19-20
Elbaite [mineral]

Tourmaline **T:** 349
ElBaradei, Mohamed Mostafa [Egyptian
diplomat]
International Atomic Energy Agency **I:** 337
Nobel Prizes (Peace: 2005) **N:** 449
Elbe River [Europe] **E:** 156
Hamburg **H:** 28 *with picture*
Elbert, Samuel [American political leader]
Georgia (table) **G:** 130
Elberta peach
Peach (Cultivars) **P:** 210
Elbow [anatomy] **E:** 157 *with diagrams*
Arm **A:** 717
Elbrus, Mount *See* Mount Elbrus *in this index*
Elburz Mountains [mountains, Iran]
Iran (The Mountains) **I:** 402
El Camino Real [road, California] **E:** 157
California (Transportation) **C:** 58
El Camino Real [road, Mexico-U.S.]
El Camino Real **E:** 157
Las Cruces **L:** 80
New Mexico (Interesting facts) **N:** 257;
(Transportation) **N:** 271
El Capitan
Yosemite National Park (Rock masses) **Y:** 570
Elchibey, Abulfaz [Azerbaijani political leader]
Azerbaijan (Independence) **A:** 997-998
El Chichón [volcano, Mexico]
Volcano (table) **V:** 442b
Elder [religion]
Presbyterians **P:** 756a
Elder [tree] **E:** 157
Elder Edda [poems]
Edda **E:** 74
Sigurd **S:** 455
Elder statesman
Statesman **So:** 867
Elderly *See* Geriatrics; Old age *in this index*
Elderly Couple [painting by Gossaert]
Clothing *picture on* **Ci:** 701
Eldest [book by Paolini]
Paolini, Christopher **P:** 132
El Dorado [legendary figure]
El Dorado **E:** 157
El Dorado [legendary place] **E:** 157
Exploration (Spain's conquests in the New World)
E: 445
Gold (History of gold) **G:** 253
"Eldorado" [poem by Poe]
Poe, Edgar Allan (Poetry and poetic theory)
P: 589-590
Eleanor of Aquitaine [member of English royal
family] **E:** 157
Henry II [of England] **H:** 185
Eleanor Roosevelt National Historic Site [New
York]
National Park System (table: National historic
sites) **N:** 52
Elect [religion]
Calvin, John (Calvinism) **C:** 71
Election [government] **E:** 158
City government (Influencing city government)
Ci: 597
Communism (The party state) **Ci:** 891
Corrupt practices **Ci:** 1072
Democracy *picture on* **D:** 119; (Free elections)
D: 120
Election campaign **E:** 159
House of Representatives (Size) **H:** 385
Parliamentary procedure (Electing officers) **P:** 175
President of the United States (The presidential
election) **P:** 762
Primary election **P:** 776
Proportional representation **P:** 828
Public opinion poll (History) **P:** 863
Recall **R:** 174
Senate (Qualifications and election) **S:** 294
Supreme Court of the United States (Election
issues) **So:** 1001; (table) **So:** 1002
Term limits **T:** 170
Watergate **W:** 144
Election [religion]
Predestination **P:** 734
Election Act of 1893 [New Zealand]
Woman suffrage (New Zealand) **W:** 381
Election Act of 1970 [Canada]
Trudeau, Pierre Elliott (The national scene) **T:** 464
Election campaign [politics] **E:** 159
Advertising (Political effects) **A:** 78 *with picture*
Federal Election Commission **F:** 63
Political action committee **P:** 627
Political convention (Convention activities) **P:** 629
Political party (Raising funds) **P:** 633
Prime minister of Canada (How the prime
minister is chosen) **P:** 778d-779
Television (Effects on society) **T:** 121
United States, Government of the (How

democratic is the government?) **U:** 146-147
Election Day E: 161
Election campaign (Getting out the vote) **E:** 160
Electoral College (The college in action) **E:** 164
November **N:** 576
Election of 2000 E: 161
Ballot **B:** 63
Bush, George Walker (The election of 2000)
B: 722g; (Election reform) **B:** 722h
Bush v. Gore **B:** 724 *with picture*
Christopher, Warren Minor **C:** 537
Florida (The early 2000's) **F:** 265
Green party **G:** 381
Supreme Court of the United States (Election
issues) **So:** 1001
United States, History of the (Election of 2000)
U: 196d
Elective Affinities [book by Goethe]
Goethe, Johann Wolfgang von (Late years) **G:** 247
Elective system [education]
Curriculum (Curriculum content) **Ci:** 1197
High school (High schools in the United States)
H: 228
Elector [office]
Election (Elections in a democracy) **E:** 158
Electoral College **E:** 161
Electoral College [U.S.] **E:** 161
Constitution of the United States (Article II,
Section 1) **Ci:** 1008; (Amendment 12) **Ci:** 1013;
(Amendment 23) **Ci:** 1015-1016
Election of 2000 (On Election Day) **E:** 161
Electoral Commission **E:** 164
Presidential succession **P:** 771
United States, History of the (Provisions of the
Constitution) **U:** 162
Vice president of the United States (Election)
V: 350
Electoral Commission [U.S. history] **E:** 164
Davis, David **D:** 47
Hayes, Rutherford Birchard (The election dispute)
H: 120
Electoral vote
Electoral College **E:** 161
Electra [legendary figure] **E:** 165
Electra complex [psychology]
Electra **E:** 165
Oedipus complex **O:** 677
Electret [electronics]
Microphone (Condenser microphones) **M:** 517
Telephone (The microphone) **T:** 95
Electric arc furnace
Iron and steel (The electric furnace process)
I: 442-443; (The birth of modern steelmaking)
I: 450-451
Electric automobile *See* Electric car *in this index*
Electric battery *See* Battery *in this index*
Electric bell E: 165 *with diagram*
Electric car [automobile] **E:** 165 *with picture*
Automobile *picture on* **A:** 963; (Power systems)
A: 947-948 *with picture*; (Powering electric
and hybrid cars) **A:** 954; (Other infrastructure)
A: 960; (The electric car) **A:** 965; (The 2000's)
A: 972-273 *with picture*
Battery *picture on* **B:** 168
Edison, Thomas Alva (Batteries) **E:** 81
Hybrid car **H:** 461
Electric catfish [fish]
Catfish **C:** 300
Electric fish **E:** 169
Electric chair [execution]
Electrocution **E:** 200
Electric charge [electricity]
Atom (Electric charge) **A:** 872
Battery (Electric charges) **B:** 168
Electricity (Electric charge) **E:** 191 *with diagram*
Electroscope **E:** 218
Lightning (How lightning occurs) **L:** 300 *with
diagrams*
Volt **V:** 446
Electric circuit E: 166 *with diagrams*
Battery (How batteries work) **B:** 170
Computer chip **Ci:** 924e
Electricity (Electric circuits) **E:** 194 *with diagram*
Electronics (How an electronic system works)
E: 208
Ground **G:** 401
House (Electrical wiring) **H:** 382
Telephone (How a telephone call travels) **T:** 95
Electric clock
Clock *diagram on* **Ci:** 682i; (Electric clocks)
Ci: 682k; (History) **Ci:** 682k
Electric current E: 167
Electric circuit **E:** 166
Electric generator (Basic principles) **E:** 170 *with
diagrams*
Electricity (Electric current) **E:** 193 *with diagram*;
(Electric circuits) **E:** 194

Electrode E: 200
Electrolysis E: 200
Electromagnet E: 201
Electromagnetism E: 202
Electronics E: 206
Fuel cell (How a fuel cell works) F: 551
Gold (Other uses) G: 251
Hall effect H: 22
Heat (Electric power) H: 150
Inductance I: 240
Lenz's law L: 197 *with diagram*
Magnetism M: 58
Magneto M: 62
Motion picture (The sound track) M: 857-858
Ohm's law O: 706
Photoelectric effect P: 405
Power P: 727
Superconductivity So: 992
Transistor T: 372
Electric-discharge lamp
Electric light (Gaseous-discharge lamps) E: 174
Electric eel [fish] E: 168 *with picture*
Electric fish E: 169
Fish *picture on* F: 166
Electric eye [electronics] E: 169 *with pictures*
Burglar alarm B: 704
Electronics (Light-sensing devices) E: 213
Electric field [physics]
Electricity (Electric charge) E: 191
Electrophoresis E: 218
Light (Electromagnetic waves) L: 286
Magnetism (Electromagnetic fields) M: 60
Motion (The motion of subatomic particles)
    M: 845
Particle accelerator (How accelerators work)
    P: 184-185
Polarized light (Understanding polarized light)
    P: 617 *with diagram*
Quantum field theory Q: 5
Radiation (Electromagnetic radiation) R: 75
Relativity (The Michelson-Morley experiment)
    R: 210
Tachometer T: 4
Transistor (Bipolar transistors) T: 373
Volt V: 446
Electric fish [zoology] E: 169
Electric force [physics]
Force (The electromagnetic force) F: 370
Quantum field theory Q: 5
Electric furnace [industry]
Iron and steel (How steel is made) I: 441 *with
    diagrams*; (The electric furnace process) I: 442
    with diagrams
Electric fuse See Fuse *in this index*
Electric generator [machine] E: 169 *with pictures*
Electric railroad (History) E: 188
Electricity (Sources of current) E: 194
Energy (Energy conversion) E: 274
Lenz's law L: 197
Locomotive (Diesel locomotives) L: 414-415
Magnetism (In industry and business) M: 60a
Magneto M: 62
Tesla, Nikola (The alternating-current system)
    T: 181
Electric guitar [musical instrument] E: 173
Guitar G: 435 *with diagram*
Music (Electronic instruments) M: 950
Electric heating
Heating (Electric power) H: 159 *with diagram*
Electric induction See Induction, Electric *in this
    index*
Electric insulator See Insulator, Electric *in this index*
Electric Kool-Aid Acid Test, The [book by Wolfe]
Wolfe, Tom W: 378
Electric light E: 174 *with pictures*
Edison, Thomas Alva E: 77 *with picture, picture
    on* E: 81
Environmental pollution (Individual efforts)
    E: 338
Fire (Light) F: 122
Flashlight F: 228
Fluorescent lamp F: 305
Lamp (Electric lamps) L: 54
Latimer, Lewis Howard L: 90
Light bulb L: 293
Lighthouse (Development of the lighthouse)
    L: 294-295
Lighting L: 296 *with pictures*
Neon N: 123 *with picture*
Electric lock
Lock (Electric locks) L: 412
Electric locomotive
Locomotive *picture on* L: 415; (Electric
    locomotives) L: 416 *with pictures*; (History)
    L: 417
Railroad (Rolling stock) R: 107
Electric meter [instrument] E: 176 *with pictures*

Electric motor [machine] E: 178 *with pictures*
Automobile (Power systems) A: 947-948; (Electric
    motors) A: 954
Electric generator (Electromagnetism) E: 170
Hybrid car H: 461
Magnetism (Electromagnets) M: 60a; (In the
    home) M: 60a
Starter (Automobile starters) So: 858
Tesla, Nikola (The alternating-current system)
    T: 181
Electric power E: 182 *with pictures*
Agriculture (Electric power) A: 158
Cable (Coaxial cables) C: 4-5; (Electric power
    cables) C: 6 *with picture*
Coal (Electric power production) Ci: 718; (Recent
    developments) Ci: 732
Dam D: 17; (Planning) D: 19 *with picture*
Decibel D: 70
Edison, Thomas Alva (Electric utilities and
    manufacturing) E: 79; (Personal life) E: 81
Energy E: 273
Fuel cell F: 551
Geothermal energy G: 136
Heat (Sources of heat): H: 149
Heating (Electric power) H: 159
Magnetic amplifier M: 54
Magnetism (In industry and business) M: 60a
Nuclear energy N: 579
Rural Electrification Administration R: 521
Solar energy So: 576
Telephone (The power source) T: 95
Tennessee Valley Authority (Electric power)
    T: 159
Transformer T: 371
Windmill W: 333
Electric railroad E: 187 *with pictures*
Elevated railroad E: 233
Locomotive (History) L: 417
Subway So: 949
Transportation *picture on* T: 394
Electric range [appliance]
Range (Electric ranges) R: 137 *with picture*;
    (History) R: 138
Electric ray [fish] E: 189 *with picture*
Electric razor
Razor (Electric razors) R: 154
Electric refrigerator
Refrigeration (The electric refrigerator) R: 201
    with diagram
Electric shock
Electricity (Electrical safety) E: 195
First aid (Removing the cause of breathing
    failure) F: 138
Shock treatment S: 429
Electric sign
Neon N: 123 *with picture*
Electric storage heater
Heating (Electric power) H: 159
Electric switch E: 189 *with diagram*
Electricity (Controlling electric current) E: 195
Telephone (Traditional phone calls) T: 96
Transistor (The bipolar transistor as a switch)
    T: 373
Electric traction elevator
Elevator (How elevators work) E: 234
Electric train See Electric railroad *in this index*
Electric transformer See Transformer *in this index*
Electric typewriter
Typewriter (Kinds of typewriters) T: 538
Electric utility
Electric power (The electric power industry)
    E: 186
Electric wave
Radio (From sound waves to electric waves) R: 86
Electrical burn [injury]
Burn (First-aid care) B: 708
Electrical discharge machining [industry]
Machine tool (Electrical discharge machining
    [EDM]) M: 19 *with diagram*
Electrical energy See Electric power *in this index*
Electrical engineering
Engineering (Electrical engineering) E: 286 *with
    picture*
Electrical hygrometer [instrument]
Hygrometer (Other hygrometers) H: 474
Electrical properties
Materials (Electrical properties) M: 300c
Electrical resistance
Materials (Electrical properties) M: 300c; (Physical
    bonds) M: 301
Ohm O: 706
Thermometer (Resistance thermometers) T: 255
Electrical thermometer See Resistance
    thermometer *in this index*
**Electrical Workers, International Brotherhood
    of** E: 189
Labor movement (table) L: 8

Electrical Workers, National Brotherhood of
Electrical Workers, International Brotherhood
    of E: 189
Electrically short antenna [device]
Antenna (Types of antennas) A: 543
Electrician [career]
Building trade (Career opportunities) B: 686
Electricity E: 190 *with pictures*
See also Electric circuit; Electric current; Electric
    power *in this index; and the list of Related
    articles in the* Electricity *article*
Ceramics (Kinds of ceramic products) C: 359
Electric generator E: 169
Electric meter E: 176
Electric railroad E: 187
Electrochemistry E: 199
Electromagnetic waves E: 201
Electromagnetism E: 202
Electromotive force E: 203
Electron E: 203
Electronics E: 206
Energy supply (The Industrial Revolution) E: 280
Engineering (Electrical engineering) E: 286
Fire prevention (In homes and schools) F: 131
    with picture
Franklin, Benjamin (The scientist) F: 488
Heating (Electric power) H: 159
Invention (The Industrial Revolution) I: 361-362
Lightning L: 299
Magnetism M: 58; (Electricity and magnetism)
    M: 60c
Materials (Electrical properties) M: 300c;
    (Semiconductors) M: 301
Metric system (Electricity) M: 440
Physics (Electricity and magnetism) P: 437;
    (Developments in the 1800's) P: 440
Piezoelectricity P: 458
Safety (Safety with electricity) S: 11
Skyscraper (Electrical systems) S: 498
Electrics [obsolete term]
Electricity (Early discoveries) E: 196
Electrification, Rural
Rural Electrification Administration R: 521
Electroanalysis [chemistry]
Electrochemistry E: 200
Electrolysis (Principles of electrolysis) E: 201
Electrocardiogram [medicine]
Electrocardiograph E: 199
Heart (Symptoms and diagnosis) H: 137
Stress test So: 927
Electrocardiograph [instrument] E: 199
Cardiology C: 212
Einthoven, Willem E: 147
Heart (Symptoms and diagnosis) H: 137;
    (Invention of new medical instruments) H: 144
Stress test So: 927
Electrochemical cell
Battery (Battery structure) B: 168
Electrochemical machining
Machine tool (Electrochemical machining [ECM])
    M: 19
Electrochemical series [chemistry] See
    Electromotive series *in this index*
Electrochemistry E: 199
Chemistry (Development of physical chemistry)
    C: 404-405
Nervous system (How neurons carry impulses)
    N: 134-135
Electroconvulsive therapy [medicine]
Depression D: 151
Mental illness (Somatic therapy) M: 407
Psychiatry (Somatic therapy) P: 845
Shock treatment S: 429
Electrocution [execution] E: 200
Capital punishment (table) C: 193
Electrocyte [muscle cell]
Electric eel E: 168
Electrode [electricity] E: 200
Battery (How batteries work) B: 168 *with diagram*
Brain (Scientific study of the brain) B: 551
Electricity (Sources of current) E: 194
Electrocardiograph E: 199
Electrolysis (How electrolysis works) E: 200
Fluorescent lamp F: 305 *with diagram*
Fuel cell F: 551 *with diagram*
Graphite G: 323
Iron and steel (The electric furnace process)
    I: 442-443 *with diagrams*
Machine tool (Electrical discharge machining
    [EDM]) M: 19 *with diagram*
Particle accelerator (How accelerators work)
    P: 184
Vacuum tube T: 258
Welding (Arc welding) W: 189 *with diagram*
Electrodialysis [electricity]
Water (Electrodialysis) W: 128 *with diagram*
Electrodynamic magnetic levitation train

Magnetic levitation train (Types of maglev technology) **M:** 55
Electrodynamic wattmeter [instrument]
Wattmeter **W:** 149
Electroencephalogram *See* Electroencephalograph *in this index*
Electroencephalograph [instrument] **E:** 200
Brain (Electrode experiments) **B:** 551; (Disorders of the brain) **B:** 557-558
Dream (The biology of dreams) **D:** 344
Sleep (The structure of sleep) **S:** 506
Electroforming [industrial process]
Electroplating **E:** 218
Electrogalvanizing [industrial process]
Galvanizing **G:** 17
Electroluminescence [physics]
Light (Luminescence and fluorescence) **L:** 283-284
Electroluminescent panel
Electric light (Electroluminescent panels) **E:** 176
Electrolysis [chemistry] **E:** 200 *with diagram*
Alkali metal **A:** 369
Aluminum (Smelting the alumina) **A:** 393
Anodizing **A:** 518
Clausius, Rudolf Julius Emmanuel **Ci:** 657
Copper (How copper metal is produced) **Ci:** 1041 *with diagrams;* (Electrolytic refining) **Ci:** 1043
Electrochemistry **E:** 199
Hydrogen (Preparation) **H:** 469
Magnesium (How magnesium is obtained) **M:** 54
Manganese (Sources) **M:** 139
Metallurgy (Electrolysis) **M:** 427
Ore **O:** 825
Silver (Extracting and refining silver) **S:** 464-465
Sodium (Extracting sodium) **So:** 569
Electrolysis [grooming]
Depilatory **D:** 149
Hair (Disorders of the hair and scalp) **H:** 10
Electrolyte [chemistry] **E:** 201
Battery (Battery structure) **B:** 168; (Secondary batteries) **B:** 170
Electricity (Sources of current) **E:** 194
Electrochemistry **E:** 199
Electrolysis (How electrolysis works) **E:** 200
Fuel cell (How a fuel cell works) **F:** 551 *(with diagram)*
Electrolytic cell [electricity]
Electrolysis (How electrolysis works) **E:** 200
Electrolytic reduction *See* Electrolysis *in this index*
Electromagnet E: 201
See also Electromagnetism *in this index*
Electric generator (Parts of a generator) **E:** 170-171; (How AC generators work) **E:** 171
Electric motor (Basic principles) **E:** 179
Electricity (Electricity and magnetism) **E:** 196
Linear electric motor **L:** 334 *with diagram*
Magnetic levitation train (Types of maglev technology) **M:** 55
Magnetism **M:** 58 *with picture;* (Electromagnets) **M:** 60a *with picture*
Microphone (Ribbon microphones) **M:** 517
Particle detector (Scintillators) **P:** 187
Quantum field theory **Q:** 5
Radio (Early development) **R:** 91
Tape recorder (Erasing and recording) **T:** 38
Telephone (Parts of a telephone) **T:** 95
Videotape recorder (Recording) **V:** 361
Electromagnetic discharge imaging *See* Kirlian photography *in this index*
Electromagnetic energy [physics] *See* Electromagnetic radiation *in this index*
Electromagnetic field [physics]
Kirlian photography **K:** 336
Magnetism (Electromagnetic fields) **M:** 60
Metal detector **M:** 425
Electromagnetic force [physics]
Force (The electromagnetic force) **F:** 370
Standard Model **So:** 833
String theory **So:** 929
Electromagnetic forming [industrial method]
Machine tool (High-energy rate forming [HERF]) **M:** 19 *with diagram*
Electromagnetic induction *See* Induction, Electromagnetic *in this index*
Electromagnetic lock
Lock (Electric locks) **L:** 412
Electromagnetic magnetic levitation train
Magnetic levitation train (Types of maglev technology) **M:** 55
Electromagnetic pump
Pump (Electromagnetic pumps) **P:** 900b
Electromagnetic radiation [physics]
Astronomy (Electromagnetic radiation) **A:** 838
Electricity (Electricity and magnetism) **E:** 196
Fluorescence **F:** 304
Gamma rays **G:** 23
Light **L:** 282

Magnetism **M:** 59
Observatory (Observatories with telescopes) **O:** 644
Photon **P:** 430
Physics (Electricity and magnetism) **P:** 437; (Developments in the 1800's) **P:** 440; (The beginning of modern physics) **P:** 440-441
Radiation **R:** 74; (Electromagnetic radiation) **R:** 75 *with pictures*
Spectrum **So:** 772
Telescope (What telescopes do) **T:** 102
Thermometer (Radiation thermometers) **T:** 255
Weather satellite **W:** 171
Electromagnetic spectrum [physics]
Astronomy (Electromagnetic radiation) **A:** 838-839
Color (The relation between color and light) **Ci:** 817
Electromagnetic waves (The electromagnetic spectrum) **E:** 202 *with diagram*
Light (The spectrum of light sources) **L:** 284 *with diagram*
Optics **O:** 813
Radiation (Electromagnetic radiation) **R:** 75-76
Star (Color and temperature) **So:** 843-844
Electromagnetic theory of light [physics]
Light (Electromagnetic waves) **L:** 286
Electromagnetic transducer [device]
Seismograph **S:** 288
Electromagnetic waves [physics] **E:** 201 *with diagram*
Antenna **A:** 543
Color (The relation between color and light) **Ci:** 817
Communication (The development of electronics) **Ci:** 883
Electricity (Electricity and magnetism) **E:** 196
Hertz, Heinrich Rudolf **H:** 217
Irradiation **I:** 455
Light **L:** 282; (Electromagnetic waves) **L:** 286 *with diagram*
Magnetism (Electromagnetic fields) **M:** 60; (Electromagnetism) **M:** 60c
Maxwell, James Clerk **M:** 319
Radar (How radar works) **R:** 68
Radiation (Electromagnetic radiation) **R:** 75
Radio **R:** 83
Redshift **R:** 191
Relativity (The Michelson-Morley experiment) **R:** 210
Television (Transmitting television signals) **T:** 123
Wireless communication **W:** 344
Electromagnetism [physics] **E:** 202
Ampère, André Marie **A:** 438
Electric generator (Electromagnetism) **E:** 170
Electricity **E:** 190; (Electricity and magnetism) **E:** 196, **E:** 197
Faraday, Michael **F:** 27
Henry, Joseph **H:** 189
Light (Electromagnetic waves) **L:** 286
Magnetism **M:** 59; (Electromagnetism) **M:** 60c
Oersted, Hans Christian **O:** 676
Subatomic particle (Fundamental forces) **So:** 936; (Theories of forces) **So:** 937-938
Electromechanical engraving [printing]
Printing (Gravure cylinders) **P:** 800
Electrometer [instrument]
Electroscope **E:** 218
Electromotive force [physics] **E:** 203
Electric circuit **E:** 166
Electric current (Conductors and insulators) **E:** 168
Electric generator (Basic principles) **E:** 170
Electronics (How a circuit works) **E:** 208
Inductance **I:** 240
Ohm's law **O:** 706
Photoelectric effect **P:** 405
Electromotive series [chemistry] **E:** 203
Electron [atomic particle] **E:** 203
Antimatter **A:** 556
Atom (The parts of an atom) **A:** 870 *with diagrams;* (Electric charge) **A:** 872; (Chemical behavior) **A:** 872; (The forces within an atom) **A:** 873 *with diagrams*
Baryon **B:** 122
Battery (How batteries work) **B:** 168 *with diagram*
Bond **B:** 454
Electricity (Electric charge) **E:** 191 *with diagram;* (The electronic age) **E:** 198
Electromotive series **E:** 203
Electronics (Electronic circuits) **E:** 208; (Early experiments) **E:** 215
Element, Chemical (Electron shells) **E:** 223
Faraday, Michael **F:** 27
Force (Kinds of force) **F:** 370
Gamma rays **G:** 23
Lepton **L:** 205

Light *diagram on* **L:** 287; (How light is produced) **L:** 283
Magnetism (In atoms) **M:** 60b
Materials (The role of bonds) **M:** 301
Matter (Structure of matter) **M:** 310
Millikan, Robert Andrews **M:** 555
Nuclear energy (Atoms and nuclei) **N:** 581 *with diagram*
Oxidation **O:** 888
Particle accelerator (Uses of accelerators) **P:** 184
Plasma **P:** 552
Quantum mechanics (Quantized orbits) **Q:** 6
Radiation (Radiation and radioactivity) **R:** 75; (Particle radiation) **R:** 76; (Causes of radiation) **R:** 78
Relativity (General relativity) **R:** 211
Rutherford, Ernest **R:** 569
Schrödinger, Erwin **S:** 186
Semiconductor (Semiconductor crystals) **S:** 291
Subatomic particle **So:** 936; (Kinds of subatomic particles) **So:** 937
Superconductivity **So:** 992
Television (Creating the video signals) **T:** 122
Thomson, Sir Joseph John **T:** 264
Transistor (Transistor materials) **T:** 372
Vacuum tube (How a vacuum tube works) **V:** 258
X rays (Penetrating power) **X:** 541; (How X rays are produced) **X:** 542
Zeeman effect **Z:** 588
Electron-antineutrino [subatomic particle]
Baryon **B:** 122
Electron beam
Electron microscope **E:** 203
Electron beam lithography [engineering]
Nanotechnology (Making nanoscale ojects) **N:** 11
Electron bombardment [physics]
Mass spectrometry **M:** 269
Electron cloud model [physics]
Atom *diagram on* **A:** 875
Electron diffraction [physics]
Molecule (Studying molecules) **M:** 694
Electron gun [electronics]
Oscilloscope **O:** 862
Television (Creating the video signals) **T:** 122; (Cathode-ray tube screens) **T:** 125
Vacuum tube (Cathode-ray tubes) **V:** 259
Electron microprobe [instrument]
Mineral (Determining the structure of crystals) **M:** 571
Electron microscope [instrument] **E:** 203 *with pictures*
Botany *picture on* **B:** 508
Cell *picture on* **C:** 338; (Looking at a cell) **C:** 327
Coal (Analyzing coal composition) **Ci:** 717-718
Electronics (Medicine and research) **E:** 207 *with picture*
Microscope (Other kinds of microscopes) **M:** 519
Mineral (Determining the structure of crystals) **M:** 571
Molecule (Studying molecules) **M:** 694
Zworykin, Vladimir Kosma **Z:** 610
Electron multiplier [electronics]
Image orthicon **I:** 79
Electron-neutrino [atomic particle]
Astronomy (Neutrino astronomy) **A:** 845-846
Lepton **L:** 206
Neutrino **N:** 154
Electron pair [physics]
Gamma rays **G:** 24
Electron pair acceptor [chemistry]
Acid **A:** 27
Electron shell [physics]
Atom *diagrams on* **A:** 872; (The electrons) **A:** 871
Electron **E:** 203
Element, Chemical (Electron shells) **E:** 223
Matter (Structure of matter) **M:** 310-311
Radiation (Causes of radiation) **R:** 78
X rays (In X-ray tubes) **X:** 542
Electron spin resonance dating
Prehistoric people (Placing prehistoric people in time) **P:** 754a-754b
Electron theory [physics]
Chemistry (Development of physical chemistry) **C:** 404-405
Lorentz, Hendrik Antoon **L:** 454
Electron transport chain [biochemistry]
Respiration (Cellular respiration) **R:** 261
Electroneutrality, Principle of [chemistry]
Ion (Behavior of ions) **I:** 371
Electronic atlas
Atlas (Electronic atlases) **A:** 868
Electronic benefit transfer
Supplemental Nutrition Assistance Program **So:** 996
Electronic billboard
Advertising (Outdoor signs) **A:** 75
Electronic book *See* E-book *in this index*

Electronic calculator
Arithmetic *picture on* A: 665; (Calculation tools)
A: 669
Calculator C: 22 *with picture*
Electronics (How an electronic system works)
E: 208 *with picture*
Electronic card catalog [reference]
A Guide to Research Skills **Research Guide: 27**
Electronic circuit
Electronics (Electronic circuits) E: 208 *with picture*;
(How electronic circuits process information)
E: 213
Electronic combination lock
Lock (Electric locks) L: 412
Electronic commerce *See* E-commerce *in this index*
Electronic Communications Privacy Act [1986]
Wiretapping (Laws concerning wiretapping)
W: 345
Electronic component
Electronics E: 206 *with pictures*
Electronic Control Company
Eckert, J. Presper, Jr. E: 50
Electronic control module
Ignition (The direct-fire ignition system) I: 49
Electronic controller
Electric car (How electric cars work) E: 165
Electronic digital computer
Computer Ci: 908
Electronic encyclopedia
Encyclopedia (Today's encyclopedias) E: 268b
Electronic engineering
Electronics (Careers in electronics) E: 214
Electronic flash [photography]
Camera (Providing additional light) C: 80
Edgerton, Harold Eugene E: 76
Photography (Direction) P: 415 *with picture*;
(Artificial lighting devices) P: 416
Electronic Freedom of Information Act
Amendments [1996]
Freedom of Information Act F: 505
Electronic funds transfer [banking]
Bank (Electronic banking) B: 89
Electronic game E: 204a *with pictures*
Computer (Dedicated computers) Ci: 911; (A
controller) Ci: 915; (Games software) Ci: 919
with picture
Computer graphics (In entertainment and the
arts) Ci: 924g
Game (Electronic games) G: 22
Internet (Online communities) I: 350b
Nintendo N: 423
Television (Home entertainment systems) T: 110c
Electronic ignition
Gasoline engine *picture on* G: 63; (The ignition
system) G: 65
Ignition (The conventional electronic ignition
system) I: 49
Electronic imagesetting
Printing (Typesetting) P: 797
Electronic mail *See* E-mail *in this index*
Electronic mailbox [computer file]
E-mail E: 2
Electronic meter
Water meter W: 135
Electronic money
Bank (Electronic banking) B: 89-90
Money M: 704
Electronic music E: 205
Berio, Luciano B: 259
Classical music (Electronic music) Ci: 650 *with
picture*
Jazz (Fusion) J: 74
Music (Electronic instruments) M: 950
Synthesizer So: 1068
Electronic navigation
Airplane (Electronic navigation) A: 227
Log (Electronic navigation devices) L: 421
Navigation (Electronic navigation) N: 72 *with
picture*; (History) N: 74
Electronic newspaper
Newspaper (Recent trends) N: 386-387
Electronic Numerical Integrator And Computer
See ENIAC *in this index*
Electronic organ [musical instrument]
Organ (Electronic organs) O: 852
Electronic page [publishing]
Encyclopedia (Preparing for the press) E: 267
Electronic printing
Printing (Digital printing) P: 801
Electronic publishing E: 205
See also Desktop publishing *in this index*
Publishing P: 866
Electronic sewing machine
Sewing machine (Kinds of sewing machines)
S: 333
Electronic signature
Contract Ci: 1023

Electronic stroboscope [instrument]
Edgerton, Harold Eugene E: 76
Electronic support aircraft
Aircraft, Military (Special-mission aircraft) A: 203
Electronic surveillance
Radio (Special uses) R: 85
Terrorism (Intelligence efforts) T: 177
Wiretapping W: 345
Electronic tagging [law enforcement] E: 205
Electronic typewriter
Typewriter (Kinds of typewriters) T: 538
Word processing W: 403
Electronic viewfinder
Photography (Compact cameras) P: 408
Electronic watch
Watch (Electronic watches) W: 114 *with pictures*
Electronics E: 206 *with pictures*
See also the list of Related articles in the Electronics
article and Circuit, Electronic, *in this index*
Computer (The first electronic computers)
Ci: 924b
Dallas (Manufacturing) D: 15 *with picture*
Electricity (Controlling electric current) E: 195
Electronic music E: 205
Industrial arts (Industrial arts courses) I: 242-243
Invention (The early and middle 1900's) I: 363
Massachusetts (The mid-1900's) M: 293
McLuhan, Marshall M: 343
Semiconductor S: 291
Transistor T: 372
Electronics industry
Electronics (The electronics industry) E: 214
Electronvolt [measurement]
Cosmic rays Ci: 1075
Electromagnetic waves (The electromagnetic
spectrum) E: 202
Particle accelerator (How accelerators work)
P: 184
Subatomic particle (Elementary particles) So: 937
Electrophoresis [process] E: 218
Biochemistry (Investigative methods) B: 310
Biophysics B: 326
Electrophysiological test
Audiology A: 882
Electroplaque [muscle cell]
Electric eel E: 168
Electroplating [industrial process] E: 218 *with
diagram*
Aluminum (Electrochemical finishes) A: 396
Electrolysis (Uses of electrolysis) E: 200-201
Electrotyping E: 219
Gold (Electrowinning) G: 253
Iron and steel (Finishing) I: 447
Phonograph (How phonograph records are
made) P: 401
Silver (Extracting and refining silver) S: 464
Electroscope [instrument] E: 218
Cosmic rays (Cosmic ray research) Ci: 1077
Electroshock *See* Electroconvulsive therapy *in
this index*
Electrospray ionization [physics]
Mass spectrometry M: 269
Electrostatic attraction [electricity]
Induction, Electric I: 240
Electrostatic copying
Copying machine (Electrostatic copying) Ci: 1045
with diagrams
Electricity (Static electricity) E: 192
Electrostatic microphone
Microphone (Condenser microphones) M: 517
Electrostatic precipitator
Air cleaner (Types of air cleaners) A: 175
Air conditioning *picture on* A: 180; (Cleaning the
air) A: 177-178
Deodorizer D: 148
Electricity (Static electricity) E: 192
Electrostatic reciprocator [machine]
Automobile *diagram on* A: 957
Electrotyping [printing] E: 219
Electroplating E: 218
Electroweak theory [physics]
Subatomic particle (The Standard Model) So: 938
Electrowinning [industrial process]
Gold *diagram on* G: 250; (Electrowinning) G: 253
Electrum [metal]
Gold (Gold deposits) G: 252
Money (Lydian coins) M: 706
**"Elegiac Stanzas Suggested by a Picture of Peele
Castle"** [poem by Wordsworth]
Wordsworth, William (Later career) W: 404
Elegiac verse [poetry]
Greek literature (Elegiac poetry) G: 377
Elegies [poems by Donne]
Donne, John (His poetry) D: 308
Elegies to the Spanish Republic [paintings by
Motherwell]
Motherwell, Robert M: 843 *with picture*

Painting (Abstract painting) P: 34; (Composition)
P: 35
Elegy [poetry]
Greek literature (Lyric poetry) G: 377
Poetry (Lyric poetry) P: 591
"Elegy Written in a Country Churchyard" [poem
by Gray]
Gray, Thomas G: 334
Elektra [opera by Strauss]
Strauss, Richard So: 922
Elektron [name for]
Amber A: 404
Element [computing]
HyperText Markup Language H: 477
Element [mathematics]
Determinant D: 166
Set theory S: 321
Element, Chemical E: 219 *with picture*
Atom A: 870; (The properties of atoms) A: 871
with diagrams
Chemistry (Fundamental ideas of chemistry)
C: 398-399
Compound Ci: 905
Geochemistry G: 91
Isotope I: 476
Life (The chemical basis of life) L: 277
Element 102 *See* Nobelium *in this index*
Element 104 *See* Rutherfordium *in this index*
Element 105 *See* Dubnium *in this index*
Element 106 *See* Seaborgium *in this index*
Element 107 *See* Bohrium *in this index*
Element 108 *See* Hassium *in this index*
Element 109 *See* Meitnerium *in this index*
Element 110 *See* Darmstadtium *in this index*
Element 111 *See* Roentgenium *in this index*
Element 112 *See* Copernicium *in this index*
Element 113 [chemistry]
Transuranium element T: 402
Element 114 [chemistry]
Transuranium element T: 401
Element 115 [chemistry]
Transuranium element T: 402
Element 116 [chemistry]
Transuranium element T: 401
Element 117 [chemistry]
Transuranium element T: 402
Element 118 [chemistry]
Transuranium element T: 401
Elemental analysis [geology]
Coal (Analyzing coal composition) Ci: 717
Elemental cycle
Oceanography O: 667
Elementary and Secondary Education Act [1965]
E: 224 *with picture*
Education (In the late 1900's) E: 104
No Child Left Behind Act N: 438
Parent-teacher organizations (Local parent
advisory committees) P: 158
Elementary backstroke
Swimming (The basic strokes) So: 1043-1044
Elementary Education Act [England, 1870]
Education (Development of British education)
E: 101
School (The development of British schools)
S: 185
Elementary particle [physics]
See also Subatomic particle *in this index*
String theory So: 929
Subatomic particle So: 936; (Elementary
particles) So: 937
Supersymmetry So: 995
Elementary school E: 224 *with pictures*
*See also the Education section of specific countries,
such as* France (Education)
Careers (Teaching) C: 231
Early childhood education (Formal education
programs) E: 15
Education (Elementary education) E: 91
Language arts L: 67
Library (Elementary school libraries) L: 244
Physical education (Elementary school programs)
P: 432 *with picture*
Rhythm band R: 320
School (Elementary schools) S: 181 *with picture*
Teaching (Teaching as a profession) T: 65;
(Becoming a teacher) T: 67-68; (Job
opportunities) T: 68
Elementary Treatise on Chemistry [book by
Lavoisier]
Lavoisier, Antoine Laurent L: 129
Elements [book by Euclid]
Euclid E: 377
Geometry (Greek geometry) G: 106
Mathematics (The Greeks) M: 306
Number theory N: 607
Elements, The [painting by MacDonald]
Group of Seven *picture on* G: 403

Painting (Composition) **P:** 35
Elements of Newton's Philosophy [book by Voltaire]
 Châtelet, Marquise Du **C:** 388
Elephant E: 226 *with pictures*
 Animal *pictures on* **A:** 469, **A:** 477, **A:** 486
 Brain (Interesting facts about the brain) **B:** 550b
 Circus (At the circus) **Ci:** 562 *with picture*
 Conservation *picture on* **Ci:** 989
 Ear (The ears of animals) **E:** 12-13 *with picture*
 Endangered species (Wildlife trade) **E:** 269-270
 Heart (Birds and mammals) **H:** 146-147
 Ivory **I:** 521
 Mammal *diagram on* **M:** 122; (table) **M:** 129 *with picture*
 Mastodon **M:** 298
 Zoo (Interesting facts about zoo animals) **Z:** 601
Elephant, Order of the [award]
 Knighthood, Orders of (Honorary orders) **K:** 347 *with pictures*
Elephant bird [extinct bird] **E:** 232 *with picture*
Elephant Butte Dam [Rio Grande, New Mexico]
 Rio Grande (Upper course) **R:** 346 *with map*
 Rio Grande Project **R:** 347
Elephant Butte Reservoir [lake, New Mexico]
 New Mexico (Land regions) **N:** 266-268
Elephant Cave [Spain]
 Cave dwellers **C:** 234
Elephant man's disease *See* Neurofibromatosis *in this index*
Elephant-nose mormyrid [fish]
 Fish *picture on* **F:** 157; (Bony fish) **F:** 147
Elephant seal [animal] **E:** 232 *with picture*
 Antarctica (Living things) **A:** 534-535 *with picture*
 Seal (The body of a seal) **S:** 266; (Diving) **S:** 267
Elephant shrew [animal] **E:** 233 *with picture*
 Mammal (table) **M:** 128 *with picture*
Elephanta Caves
 India (Architecture and sculpture) **I:** 119
Elephantiasis [disease] **E:** 233
 Edema **E:** 76
 Filaria **F:** 99
 Mosquito (Mosquitoes and people) **M:** 834
"Elephant's Child, The" [story by Kipling]
 Limpopo River **L:** 309
Elephant's-ear [plant] **E:** 233
 See also Taro *in this index*
Eleusinian Mysteries [religion]
 Demeter **D:** 118
 Mysteries **M:** 972
Eleuthera [island, Bahamas]
 Bahamas (Land and climate) **B:** 29 *with map*
Eleutherius, Saint [pope]
 Pope (table) **P:** 666
Elevated railroad E: 233
 Chicago *picture on* **C:** 428; (Downtown Chicago) **C:** 420-421
Elevating-platform truck
 Fire department (Ladder trucks) **F:** 126
Elevation [measurement]
 Climate (The role of altitude) **Ci:** 676
 Sea level **S:** 262a
Elevator [airplane part]
 Airplane *picture on* **A:** 214; (The tail) **A:** 214 *with pictures*; (Basic movements and controls) **A:** 222-223 *with diagrams*
 Airship (Control) **A:** 251
 Glider (The tail) **G:** 229
Elevator [machine] **E:** 233 *with diagrams*
 Otis, Elisha Graves **O:** 870
 Skyscraper (Elevators) **S:** 498
Elevator, Grain *See* Grain elevator *in this index*
Elevator stage
 Theater (Changing scenery) **T:** 240
11-plus examination
 England (Education) **E:** 297
Eleventh Amendment [U.S. Constitution]
 Constitution of the United States **Ci:** 1013
Elf [meteorology]
 Lightning (Jets, sprites, and elves) **L:** 301
Elf [Norse mythology] **E:** 235
ELF [political movement] *See* Eritrean Liberation Front *in this index*
Elf owl [bird]
 Animal *picture on* **A:** 483
 Bird (Birds of the desert) **B:** 339 *with picture*
 Owl *picture on* **O:** 885
Elfreth's Alley [street]
 Philadelphia (Downtown Philadelphia) **P:** 359
Elfstedentocht [race]
 Netherlands (Holidays and recreation) **N:** 141
Elgar, Sir Edward [British composer] **E:** 235
El Gezira [region, Sudan] *See* Gezira, El *in this index*
Elgin, Earl of [1766-1841, British diplomat]
 Elgin Marbles **E:** 236
Elgin, Earl of [1811-1863, British statesman] **E:** 236
Elgin Marbles [sculpture] **E:** 236

Parthenon **P:** 183
El Greco *See* Greco, El *in this index*
El Guettar, Battle of [1943]
 Patton, George Smith, Jr. (African invasion) **P:** 199
Elhanan [Biblical figure]
 David (Early life) **D:** 44-45
Elhuyar, Fausto de [Spanish chemist]
 Tungsten **T:** 487
Elhuyar, Juan José de [Spanish chemist]
 Tungsten **T:** 487
Eli Lilly [pharmaceutical company]
 Indiana (Manufacturing) **I:** 211
Elia [pen name]
 Lamb, Charles **E:** 50
Eliade, Mircea [Romanian scholar]
 Religion (Later theories) **R:** 219
Eliena skipper [butterfly]
 Butterfly *picture on* **B:** 734
Eliezer, Israel ben [Jewish religious leader] *See* Ba'al Shem Tov *in this index*
Elijah [Biblical figure] **E:** 236
 Malachi, Book of **M:** 95
Elijah [music by Mendelssohn]
 Mendelssohn, Felix (His music) **M:** 399
Elijah Muhammad *See* Muhammad, Elijah *in this index*
Elimination [physiology] **E:** 236
 Blood (Transporting nutrients and wastes) **B:** 408 *with diagram*
 Colostomy **Ci:** 850
 Drug (Elimination from the body) **D:** 354
 Fiber, Dietary **F:** 88
 Incontinence **I:** 106
 Space exploration (Meeting basic needs in space) **So:** 703
Elimination sample [criminology]
 Crime scene investigation (Collecting evidence) **Ci:** 1140-1141
Elion, Gertrude Belle [American biochemist] **E:** 236
Eliot, Charles William [American educator] **E:** 237
 Harvard University (History) **H:** 80-81
Eliot, George [British author] **E:** 237 *with portrait*
 English literature (Later Victorian literature) **E:** 321
 Novel (Britain) **N:** 573
Eliot, John [American missionary] **E:** 237
Eliot, T. S. [British poet] **E:** 237 *with portrait*
 American literature (Modernist poetry) **A:** 421
 English literature (Poetry between the wars) **E:** 322
 Metaphysical poets **M:** 429
 Poetry (Poetry of the 1900's) **P:** 597
Elisey [poem by Maykov]
 Russian literature (The classical movement) **R:** 559-560
Elisha [Biblical figure] **E:** 238
Elision [poetry]
 Poetry (table) **P:** 594
Elissa [legendary figure] *See* Dido *in this index*
Elite [sociology]
 Panama (Way of life) **P:** 116-117
 Pareto, Vilfredo **P:** 159
Eliza [literary figure]
 Uncle Tom's Cabin **U:** 20
Elizabeth [empress of Russia]
 Russia (Music) **R:** 536; (table: Czars and empresses) **R:** 549
 Seven Years' War (In Europe) **S:** 328
Elizabeth [wife of Albert I]
 Albert I **A:** 311
Elizabeth [wife of Franz Joseph]
 Franz Joseph **F:** 494
Elizabeth [New Jersey] **E:** 238
Elizabeth [ship]
 Drake, Sir Francis (Voyage around the world) **D:** 321
Elizabeth I [queen of England] **E:** 238 *with portrait*
 Boleyn, Anne **B:** 440
 Church of England (History) **C:** 542
 Drake, Sir Francis **D:** 320
 England (The reign of Elizabeth I) **E:** 307 *with picture*
 Handwriting *picture on* **H:** 50
 Henry VIII (king of England) **H:** 188
 India (The coming of the Europeans) **I:** 130
 Knox, John (Later career) **K:** 358
 Leicester, Earl of **L:** 186
 Mary, Queen of Scots (Her death) **M:** 239
 Mary I **M:** 239
 New Year's Day (Early customs) **N:** 289
 Protestantism (The conservative reform movements) **P:** 834-835
 Raleigh, Sir Walter (Raleigh and Elizabeth I) **R:** 131
 Shakespeare, William (England of Shakespeare's day) **S:** 349 *with picture*
 Spanish Armada (Background to battle) **So:** 755

Tudor, House of **T:** 481
 Virginia **V:** 398; (Early days) **V:** 418
Elizabeth II [queen of United Kingdom] **E:** 239 *with pictures*
 Canada, Government of **C:** 128
 Canada, History of *picture on* **C:** 151
 Charles, Prince **C:** 382
 Diefenbaker, John George *picture on* **D:** 197
 England (Government) **E:** 292-293
 Flag *picture on* **F:** 214; (Flags of individuals) **F:** 195 *with picture*
 Knighthood, Orders of *picture on* **K:** 347
 New Zealand (Government) **N:** 346
 Penny *picture on* **P:** 271
 Philip, Prince **P:** 371
 Trudeau, Pierre Elliott *picture on* **T:** 463
 United Kingdom *picture on* **U:** 50
Elizabeth, Saint [mother of John the Baptist] **E:** 241
Elizabeth, the Queen Mother [British public figure]
 Elizabeth II (Early life) **E:** 239
 George VI **G:** 107
Elizabeth and Essex [book by Strachey]
 Strachey, Lytton **So:** 917
Elizabeth City State University
 North Carolina, University of **N:** 495
Elizabeth Imagined an Iceberg [book by Raschka]
 Raschka, Chris **R:** 144
Elizabeth Islands [Massachusetts]
 Massachusetts (Islands) **M:** 282
Elizabeth of York [wife of]
 Henry VII [of England] **H:** 187
Elizabeth the Queen [play by Anderson]
 Anderson, Maxwell **A:** 452
Elizabeth Tower [London]
 Big Ben **B:** 297 *with picture*
Elizabethan Age [English history]
 Drama (Elizabethan, Jacobean, and Caroline drama) **D:** 331-332 *with picture*
 Elizabeth I **E:** 238
 England (The arts) **E:** 298
 English literature (The beginning of Modern English [1485-1603]) **E:** 316
 Furniture (England) **F:** 573
 Shakespeare, William (England of Shakespeare's day) **S:** 349; (The Elizabethan theater) **S:** 351 *with pictures*
Elizabethan Poor Law [1601]
 Welfare (History) **W:** 191
Elizabethan revival
 Furniture (Historical revivals) **F:** 581
Elizabethan theater
 Drama (Elizabethan theaters) **D:** 331
 English literature (Elizabethan drama) **E:** 317
 Globe Theatre **G:** 233
 Shakespeare, William (The Elizabethan theater) **S:** 351 *with pictures*
Elizabethtown [New Jersey]
 Elizabeth **E:** 238
Elk [animal] **E:** 241 *with picture*
 Moose **M:** 798
Elk Hills [California]
 Teapot Dome **T:** 72
Elk Island National Park [Alberta]
 Canada (table: National parks and national park reserves) **C:** 113
Elkington, Steve [American golfer]
 Golf (U.S. PGA Championship) **G:** 265
Elkins [West Virginia]
 West Virginia (table: Average monthly weather) **W:** 220
Elkins, Stephen B. [American government official]
 Harrison, Benjamin (table) **H:** 72
Elkins Act [1903]
 Roosevelt, Theodore (Domestic problems) **R:** 466
Elko [Nevada]
 Nevada (table: Average monthly weather) **N:** 169
Elks, Benevolent and Protective Order of E: 242
Elks National Foundation
 Elks, Benevolent and Protective Order of **E:** 242
Elks National Home [Bedford, Virginia]
 Elks, Benevolent and Protective Order of **E:** 242
Ellery, William [American patriot] **E:** 242
Ellery Queen's Mystery Magazine [magazine]
 Queen, Ellery **Q:** 39
Ellesmere Island [Nunavut] **E:** 242
 Nunavut (Land and resources) **N:** 609 *with map*
 Peary, Robert Edwin ("The Pole at last!") **P:** 224
Ellice Islands [former name]
 Kiribati (History) **K:** 335
 Tuvalu **T:** 527
Ellicott, Andrew [American surveyor]
 Washington, D.C. (Building the city) **W:** 85-86
Elling, Lars [Norwegian illustrator]
 Literature for children *picture on* **L:** 354
Ellington, Buford [American political leader]

Tennessee (table) **T:** 152
Ellington, Duke [American musician] **E:** 242 *with picture*
African Americans *picture on* **A:** 136l
Jazz (The 1920's) **J:** 70 *with picture*; (The swing era) **J:** 70-71 *with picture*
Popular music *picture on* **P:** 670
Ellington, Edward Kennedy [birth name of]
Ellington, Duke **E:** 242
Ellington, Mercer [American trumpeter]
Ellington, Duke **E:** 243
Elliot, Gilbert John Murray Kynynmond [British statesman]
Minto, Earl of **M:** 613
Elliot Lake
Ontario (The mid-1900's) **O:** 786-787
Elliott [ship]
Destroyer *picture on* **D:** 162
Elliott, Andrew C. [Canadian political leader]
British Columbia (table) **B:** 628
Elliott, Bill [American race car driver]
Automobile racing (table: NASCAR Sprint Cup champions) **A:** 981
Ellipse [mathematics] **E:** 243 *with diagrams*
Astronomy (Sun-centered theories) **A:** 835-836
Climate (Changes in the earth's orbit) **Ci:** 677
Gravitation (Newton's law of gravitation) **G:** 331
Kepler, Johannes (Kepler's laws) **K:** 305
Orbit **O:** 819 *with diagram*
Planet (How planets move) **P:** 508-509
Ellipse, The [Washington, D.C.]
Washington, D.C. *map on* **W:** 76
Elliptical galaxy [astronomy]
Galaxy (Types of galaxies) **G:** 8a *with picture*
Local Group **L:** 409
Elliptical geometry *See* Riemannian geometry *in this index*
Elliptical orbit
Jupiter (Orbit and rotation) **J:** 198
Kepler, Johannes (Kepler's laws) **K:** 305
Planet (How planets move) **P:** 508-509 *with diagram*
Space exploration (Kinds of earth orbits) *diagram on* **So:** 697
Ellis, Havelock [British psychologist] **E:** 243
Ellis, John W. [American political leader]
North Carolina (table) **N:** 490
Ellis, Joseph J. [American historian]
Biography (Biography today) **B:** 314
Ellis, Samuel [American merchant]
Ellis Island **E:** 243
Ellis, Trey [American author]
African American literature (Recent developments) **A:** 136a
Ellis, William Webb [English rugby player]
Rugby football (History) **R:** 513
Ellis Island E: 243 *with picture*
Immigration *picture on* **I:** 80; (The first wave) **I:** 82
Photography (Artistic advances) **P:** 424-425 *with picture*
Races, Human *picture on* **R:** 59
Ellis Island Immigration Museum [New York]
Ellis Island **E:** 244 *with picture*
Ellis-Van Creveld syndrome [disorder]
Evolution (Genetic drift) **E:** 429
Ellison, Harlan [American author] **E:** 244
Ellison, Ralph [American author] **E:** 244
African American literature (The 1900's) **A:** 136a
American literature (Fiction and other prose) **A:** 424 *with portrait*
Novel (After World War II) **N:** 574
Ellora [India]
India (Architecture and sculpture) **I:** 119 *with picture*
Ellsworth, Lincoln [American explorer] **E:** 244
Antarctica (Exploration by air) **A:** 537-538 *with map*
Exploration (The North Pole) **E:** 450
Ellsworth, Oliver [American jurist] **E:** 244
Ellsworth, William W. [American political leader]
Connecticut (table) **Ci:** 967
Elm [tree] **E:** 244 *with picture*
Dutch elm disease **D:** 392
Plant *picture on* **P:** 525
Tree *pictures on* **T:** 421
Wood *picture on* **W:** 389
El Malpais National Monument [New Mexico]
National Park System (table: National monuments) **N:** 50
Elmen, G. W. [American engineer]
Permalloy **P:** 289
Elmer Gantry [book by Lewis]
Lewis, Sinclair **L:** 221
Elmira System
Prison (During the 1800's) **P:** 807
El Misti [volcano, Peru] **E:** 245
El Morro Fortress [San Juan]

Puerto Rico (Places to visit) **P:** 877 *with picture*
San Juan **S:** 103
El Morro National Monument [New Mexico]
National Park System (table: National monuments) **N:** 51
ELN [military group] *See* National Liberation Army *in this index*
El Niño [current] **E:** 245 *with maps*
Atlantic Ocean (Climate) **A:** 864
Climate (Changes in ocean circulation) **Ci:** 676d
Ocean (Discoveries) **O:** 664
Pacific Islands (Climate) **P:** 8
Pacific Ocean (Climate) **P:** 14
South America (Climate) **So:** 629-631
El norte [wind]
Norther **N:** 520
Elobey Chico [island]
Equatorial Guinea **E:** 346 *with map*
Elobey Grande [island]
Equatorial Guinea **E:** 346 *with map*
Elodea [plant] **E:** 246
Elohim [Hebrew god] **E:** 246
God **G:** 243
Jehovah **J:** 89
El Paso [Texas] **E:** 246
Juárez **J:** 178
El Petén [Guatemala]
Maya (The Preclassic Period) **M:** 325
El Rastro [Madrid]
Spain *picture on* **So:** 737
Elrod, Samuel H. [American political leader]
South Dakota (table) **So:** 680
Els, Ernie [South African golfer]
Golf (British Open) **G:** 264
Elsa [lioness]
Adamson, Joy **A:** 45
El Salvador E: 248 *with pictures and maps*
Hispanic Americans (Central American migration) **H:** 255
Romero, Oscar Arnulfo **R:** 450
War (Stalemates) **W:** 24-25
Elssler, Fanny [Austrian dancer]
Ballet (Romantic ballet) **B:** 51
El Teniente [mine, Chile]
Chile (Mining) **C:** 466
Elthon, Leo [American political leader]
Iowa (table) **I:** 391
Elton, Charles Sutherland [British biologist] **E:** 253
Éluard, Paul [French poet]
French literature (Surrealism) **F:** 522-523
Elul [month]
Calendar (The Hebrew calendar) **C:** 29
Elver [fish]
Eel (Life cycle) **E:** 114-115
Elves *See* Elf *in this index*
Elvis Presley Birthplace [Tupelo]
Mississippi (Places to visit) **M:** 632 *with picture*
Ely, Eugene [American aviator]
Navy, United States ("The Great White Fleet") **N:** 88
Ely, Joseph B. [American political leader]
Massachusetts (table) **M:** 288
Ely Cathedral
Norman architecture *picture on* **N:** 455
Élysée Palace
Paris (Famous buildings) **P:** 163-164 *with map*
Elysian Fields [Greek mythology] *See* Elysium *in this index*
Elysium [Greek mythology] **E:** 253
Hades **H:** 4
Elytis, Odysseus [Greek poet]
Greek literature (Modern Greek literature) **G:** 378
Nobel Prizes (Literature: 1979) **N:** 448
Elyton Land Company [U.S. history]
Birmingham **B:** 375
Elytra [entomology]
Beetle **B:** 214; (The thorax) **B:** 216 *with diagram*
Firefly (Body) **F:** 134
El Yunque [mountain, Puerto Rico]
Puerto Rico (Places to visit) **P:** 877; (Climate) **P:** 880 *with picture*
Emancipation [U.S. history]
Proslavery movement **P:** 828
Slavery (The decline of slavery) **S:** 504
Emancipation Day [holiday]
August **A:** 886
Emancipation Proclamation [U.S. history] **E:** 253 *with pictures*
African Americans (The American Civil War) **A:** 136i-136j *with picture*
Civil War, American (The Emancipation Proclamation) **Ci:** 621
Executive order **E:** 436
Lincoln, Abraham (The Emancipation Proclamation) **L:** 323
United States, History of the (Abolition of slavery) **U:** 178

Emancipator, The [newspaper]
Tennessee **T:** 135 *with picture*
Emancipists [Australian history]
Australia (Macquarie's administration) **A:** 921
Macquarie, Lachlan **M:** 26
Emanuel, David [American political leader]
Georgia (table) **G:** 130
Emanuel, Rahm [American political leader]
Chicago (Political developments in the late 1900's) **C:** 436-437
Embalming [funeral] **E:** 255
Funeral customs (Preparation of the body) **F:** 557
Mummy (Egyptian mummies) **M:** 925
Embankment dam
Dam (Types of dams) **D:** 17
Embarcadero [street]
San Francisco (Downtown San Francisco) **S:** 92-93
Embargo [law] **E:** 255
Bush, George Herbert Walker (Persian Gulf crisis) **B:** 721
Embargo Act **E:** 256
Hong Kong (British control) **H:** 319-320
International relations (Nonmilitary sanctions) **I:** 345
Iraq (The Persian Gulf War of 1991) **I:** 414
Sanctions, Economic **S:** 106
United States, History of the (Jefferson's foreign policy) **U:** 164
"Embargo, The" [poem by Bryant]
Bryant, William Cullen (His early works) **B:** 655
Embargo Act [1807] **E:** 256
Jefferson, Thomas (The embargo) **J:** 87
Madison, James (Secretary of state) **M:** 34
Maine (The Revolutionary War) **M:** 89
Massachusetts (Progress as a state) **M:** 292
War of 1812 (American reaction) **W:** 29
Embarkation for Cythera, The [painting by Watteau] *See* Island of Cythera, The *in this index*
Embassy [diplomacy]
Ambassador **A:** 404
Diplomacy (Diplomatic duties) **D:** 216-217
Government (Foreign affairs) **G:** 283
State, Department of **So:** 859
Embden [bird]
Goose (Kinds of geese) **G:** 270 *with picture*
Embedded computer
Computer (Embedded computers) **Ci:** 911
Embedded journalist
War correspondent **W:** 27
Emberley, Ed [American artist]
Caldecott Medal (table: 1968) **C:** 26
Embezzlement [law] **E:** 256
Insurance (Crime insurance) **I:** 314
Embioptera [entomology]
Insect (table) **I:** 300
Emblem
Girl Scouts **G:** 196 *with picture*
Symbol **So:** 1065
Embolism [disorder] **E:** 256
Diving, Underwater (Dangers of underwater diving) **D:** 246
Stroke (Causes) **So:** 930
Embolismic month
Calendar (The Hebrew calendar) **C:** 29
Embolus [physiology]
Embolism **E:** 256
Embossing [decoration] **E:** 256
Aluminum (Mechanical finishes) **A:** 396
Embrace at Maipú, The [painting by Subercaseaux]
Argentina *picture on* **A:** 657
Embree, Elihu [American journalist]
Tennessee **T:** 135
Embriaci Tower
Genoa *picture on* **G:** 89
Embroidered rug
Rugs and carpets (Other methods) **R:** 516
Embroidery [handicraft] **E:** 256 *with picture*
Crewel **Ci:** 1129 *with picture*
Mexico *picture on* **M:** 457
Needlepoint **N:** 118 *with pictures*
Sampler **S:** 81 *with picture*
Embryo [biology] **E:** 257
Abortion **A:** 14
Animal (Sexual reproduction) **A:** 496-497
Baby (The developing baby) **B:** 4
Bioethics **B:** 311
Cloning (Nuclear transfer) **Ci:** 682l; (Ethical concerns) **Ci:** 683
Corn (How the plant develops) **Ci:** 1057 *with diagram*
Cotyledon **Ci:** 1095
Developmental biology **D:** 174
Egg (How embryos develop) **E:** 117-118
Evolution (Embryology) **E:** 431
Fish (How fish live) **F:** 165 *with picture*
Germination **G:** 173
Growth (Early development) **G:** 404-405

Haeckel, Ernst Heinrich **H:** 5
Heart (Interesting facts about the heart) **H:** 133 *with picture*
In vitro fertilization **I:** 95
Plant (Seeds) **P:** 531 *with pictures*; (Sexual reproduction) **P:** 532-535 *with diagrams*; (Germination) **P:** 536-537
Pregnancy **P:** 734a
Reproduction, Human **R:** 244 *with picture*; (Development of the embryo) **R:** 246-247 *with diagrams*
Seed (The parts of a seed) **S:** 281 *with diagrams*
Stem cell **So:** 889
Surrogate birth **So:** 1010
Embryo transfer [biology]
Breeding (Animal breeding) **B:** 592-593
Infertility (Treatment) **I:** 265
Embryology [biology]
See also Developmental biology *in this index*
Baer, Karl Ernst von **B:** 25
Biology (table) **B:** 317
Evolution (Embryology) **E:** 431
Zoology (What zoologists study) **Z:** 606-607
Embryonic stem cell [biology]
Bioethics **B:** 311
Bush, George Walker (Other domestic issues) **B:** 723
Medical ethics **M:** 361
Stem cell **So:** 889
Emcee [performer]
Hip-hop **H:** 238
Emerald [gem] **E:** 257 *with picture*
Colombia (Mining) **Ci:** 783
Gem *picture on* **G:** 78; (Value of gems) **G:** 79
Emerald ash borer [beetle] **B:** 258
Emerald Buddha, Temple of the [Bangkok]
Bangkok (The city) **B:** 77
Thailand *picture on* **T:** 226
Emerald cuckoo
Bird (Birds of Africa) **B:** 344h *with picture*
Emerald Isle [nickname, Ireland]
Ireland **I:** 416 *with picture*
Emerald tree boa [snake]
Boa **B:** 426
Emergency
Civil defense **Ci:** 605
Emergency room **E:** 258
Fire department **F:** 123
First aid **F:** 136 *with pictures*
Homeland Security, Department of (Organization) **H:** 301
Trauma center **T:** 405
Emergency Banking Act [1933]
New Deal (Helping savers and investors) **N:** 200
Emergency brake
Brake (Mechanical brakes) **B:** 560
Emergency contraception
Birth control (Methods of birth control) **B:** 378
Emergency core cooling system
Nuclear energy (Hazards and safeguards) **N:** 587-588
Emergency Economic Stabilization Act [2008]
Bush, George Walker (Economy) **B:** 722j-723
Emergency Events Database
Flood (Reducing flood losses) **F:** 238
Emergency management *See* Civil defense *in this index*
Emergency Management Agency, Federal [U.S.] *See* Federal Emergency Management Agency *in this index*
Emergency Medical Services E: 258
Fire department (Emergency medical operations) **F:** 124
Trauma center **T:** 405
Emergency medical technician
Emergency Medical Services **E:** 258
Fire department (Emergency medical operations) **F:** 124
Medicine *picture on* **M:** 377; (Other careers in medicine) **M:** 371
Emergency medical technician-paramedic
Emergency Medical Services **E:** 258
Medicine (Other careers in medicine) **M:** 371
Paramedic **P:** 153
Emergency medicine
Emergency Medical Services **E:** 258
Emergency operating center
Civil defense (Civil defense in action) **Ci:** 605
Emergency powers
President of the United States (Chief executive) **P:** 764
Emergency Preparedness Canada [agency]
Civil defense (How civil defense is administered) **Ci:** 605
Emergency room [medicine] **E:** 258
Hospital (Hospital units) **H:** 372 *with picture*
Emergent [tree]

Rain forest (Structure and growth) **R:** 126a
Emergent literacy
Reading (Developing good readers) **R:** 159-160
Emerging market country *See* Developing country *in this index*
Emerson, Frank C. [American political leader]
Wyoming (table) **W:** 532
Emerson, John [American doctor]
Dred Scott Decision (The background of the case) **D:** 345
Emerson, Lee E. [American political leader]
Vermont (table) **V:** 333
Emerson, Ralph Waldo [American author] **E:** 258
American literature (Nonfiction prose) **A:** 418 *with portrait*
April (Quotations) **A:** 577
Brown, John (Harpers Ferry) **B:** 643
Essay (Formal essays) **E:** 359
Revolution, American **R:** 270
Thoreau, Henry David (His life) **T:** 266
Transcendentalism **T:** 370
Unitarians (History) **U:** 42
Emery [rock] **E:** 259
Emetic [medication] **E:** 259
Emetic russula [mushroom]
Mushroom *picture on* **M:** 944
Emetine [chemical]
Ipecac **I:** 397
Emf [physics] *See* Electromotive force *in this index*
Emi Koussi [mountain, Chad]
Chad (Land and climate) **C:** 366 *with map*
Emigration
Immigration **I:** 80
Ireland (Ancestry and population) **I:** 418
Émigrés [French history]
French Revolution (The revolution begins) **F:** 525; (The Legislative Assembly) **F:** 526
Émile [book by Rousseau]
French literature (The Enlightenment) **F:** 520-521
Rousseau, Jean-Jacques (His ideas) **R:** 493
Emin Pasha [German explorer] **E:** 259
Stanley and Livingstone (Stanley's explorations) **So:** 837-838
Eminent domain [law] **E:** 260
City planning (Governmental authority) **Ci:** 601
Urban renewal (The role of government) **U:** 220
Eminent Victorians [book by Strachey]
Biography (Modern biography) **B:** 314
Strachey, Lytton **So:** 917
Emir [title]
Bahrain (Government) **B:** 29
Kuwait (Government) **K:** 395
United Arab Emirates (Government) **U:** 44
Emission control
Air pollution (Control of air pollution) **A:** 199
Automobile (The exhaust system) **A:** 953; (Testing the car) **A:** 956; (Air pollution) **A:** 964
Global warming (Government action on global warming) **G:** 232c
Emission credit
Global warming (Types of policies) **G:** 232c
Emission line [physics]
Astronomy (Spectroscopy) **A:** 840
Star (Color and temperature) **So:** 843-844
Sun (Analyzing electromagnetic radiation) **So:** 983; (History of modern solar study) **So:** 986
Telescope (Analyzing spectra) **T:** 105
Emission nebula [astronomy]
Nebula (Diffuse nebulae) **N:** 116
Emission standards [law]
Air pollution (Effects of air pollution) **A:** 199
Emissions permit
Environmental pollution (Government action) **E:** 335
Emitter [electronics]
Transistor (How transistors work) **T:** 372-373 *with diagram*
Vacuum tube (How a vacuum tube works) **V:** 258
Emma [queen of the Netherlands]
Wilhelmina **W:** 306
Emma [book by Austen]
Austen, Jane **A:** 892
English literature (Romantic prose) **E:** 320
Literature (Judging literature) **L:** 352-353
Emma Willard School
Willard, Emma Hart **W:** 307
Emmentaler [cheese]
Cheese (Kinds of cheese) **C:** 392
Emmerson, Henry R. [Canadian political leader]
New Brunswick (table) **N:** 195
Emmerson, Louis L. [American political leader]
Illinois (table) **I:** 71; (Prohibition and the Great Depression) **I:** 75
Emmet, Robert [Irish patriot] **E:** 260
Emmett, Daniel Decatur [American composer] **E:** 260

"Dixie" **D:** 255
Emmett Till case [U.S. history] **E:** 260 *with picture*
African Americans (The civil rights movement) **A:** 136o
Emmy Awards
Television (Television awards) **T:** 116
Emotion E: 260
Brain (Regulating emotions) **B:** 554
Child (Special challenges and concerns) **C:** 452
Dream (The content of dreams) **D:** 344
Lie detector **L:** 271
Literature (Theme) **L:** 353
Perception (Learning, emotion, and motivation) **P:** 283
Personality **P:** 300f
Trauma **T:** 404
Weight control (How body weight is determined) **W:** 181
Emotion and Personality [book by Magda]
Emotion (The appraisal approach) **E:** 261
Emotional cycle
Biorhythm **B:** 326
Emotional lability [disorder]
Learning disabilities (Types) **L:** 165
Emotional memory [acting]
Theater (Observation and imagination) **T:** 238
Emotionally disturbed child
Special education (Children with emotional disturbances) **So:** 771
Emotivism
Philosophy (Philosophy in the 1900's) **P:** 390
Empathy
Sales (Characteristics needed) **S:** 65
Empedocles [Greek philosopher] **E:** 261
Air (The study of air) **A:** 175
Chemistry (Beginnings) **C:** 400
Color (Early theories of color vision) **Ci:** 825
Geology (The ancient Greeks) **G:** 97
Pre-Socratic philosophy (The teachings of Parmenides) **P:** 772-773
Empennage [airplane part]
Airplane (The tail) **A:** 214
Glider (The tail) **G:** 229
Emperor [title] **E:** 261
Emperor Franz Joseph at a Ball in Vienna [painting by Gause]
Dance *picture on* **D:** 27
Emperor Jones, The [play by O'Neill]
O'Neill, Eugene (His plays) **O:** 762
Emperor penguin [bird] **E:** 262 *with picture*
Animal *picture on* **A:** 484; (Incubation) **A:** 498-500 *with picture*
Antarctica (Living things) **A:** 534-535 *with picture*
Bird (Birds of the ocean and the Antarctic) **B:** 344 *with picture*
Penguin (The body of a penguin) **P:** 238 *with picture*
Emperor snapper [fish]
Fish *picture on* **F:** 155
Emphatic form [grammar]
Conjugation **Ci:** 951
Tense **T:** 168
Emphysema [disease] **E:** 262 *with diagrams*
Bronchodilator **B:** 637
Chronic obstructive pulmonary disease **C:** 539
Smoking (Why smoking is dangerous) **S:** 520
Empire [apple]
Apple (table) **A:** 571 *with picture*
Empire [political unit]
See also Emperor; Imperialism *in this index*
Indian, American (Empires and states) **I:** 144
"Empire Builder" [name for]
Hill, James Jerome **H:** 230
Empire State [name for]
New York **N:** 291; (Growing prosperity) **N:** 316
Empire State Building [New York City] **E:** 263
New York City (A visitor's guide) **N:** 338
Empire State of the South [name for]
Georgia **G:** 112
Empire State Plaza
Albany (Description) **A:** 309
New York *picture on* **N:** 291
Empire style
Clothing (The 1800's) **Ci:** 704-705
Furniture (The Empire style) **F:** 580 *with picture*
White House *picture on* **W:** 288
Empiricism [philosophy] **E:** 263
Bacon, Francis **B:** 18
Hume, David **H:** 432
Locke, John (His philosophy) **L:** 413
Philosophy (Epistemology) **P:** 384; (Empiricism) **P:** 389
Positivism **P:** 697
Psychology (Beginnings) **P:** 849
Employee benefit *See* Benefit *in this index*
Employee relations [business] *See* Personnel management *in this index*

Employee Retirement Income Security Act [1974]
Bentsen, Lloyd Millard, Jr. **B: 255**
Pension Benefit Guaranty Corporation **P: 274**
Personnel management (Development of personnel management) **P: 303**
Employer of last resort [economics]
Unemployment (Programs and policies) **U: 23**
Employers' liability
Workers' compensation **W: 405**
Employment
See also Unemployment in this index and the Related articles in the Careers article
Affirmative action **A: 91**
Career education **C: 213**
Careers **C: 214**
City **Ci: 574**
Civil service **Ci: 611**
Cooperative education **Ci: 1037**
Disability (Employment) **D: 221**
Drug testing **D: 366**
Family (Changes) **F: 23** with picture
Hispanic Americans (Employment) **H: 258**
Job Corps **J: 129**
Labor, Department of (Functions) **L: 2**
Occupational medicine **O: 647**
Old age (Employment and other activities) **O: 739**
Pension **P: 272**
Sex discrimination (Origins of sex discrimination) **S: 335**
Sexual harassment (Types of sexual harassment) **S: 337**
Universities and colleges (Working during school) **U: 207L**
Women's movement **W: 383**
Employment agency [economics] **E: 263**
Careers (Finding job opportunities) **C: 217-218**
Employment Assistance Program
Indian, American (In the United States) **I: 179**
Employment Equity Act [South Africa, 1998]
Disability (The 1900's) **D: 221-222**
Employment interview
Careers (Being interviewed) **C: 219**
Employment Service, United States
Labor force (The government and the labor force) **L: 5**
Employment Standards Administration [U.S.]
Fair Labor Standards Act **F: 8**
Emporia Gazette [newspaper]
White, William Allen **W: 285**
Empresa Mexicana de Lucha Libre [company]
Lucha libre **L: 514**
Empresario [colonist]
Texas (American settlement) **T: 206**
Empress [title]
Emperor **E: 262**
Empress Hotel
Victoria **V: 358**
Empress of Heaven [Taoist deity]
Religion picture on **R: 222**
Empress of Ireland [ship]
Shipwreck (table: Major shipwrecks) **S: 428**
"Empty calorie" food
Nutrition (Limit intake of sodium and sugar) **N: 628**
Empty-nest family
Family (Varieties of families) **F: 20**
Empty Quarter [region, Arabia]
Yemen (Land) **Y: 562-563**
Empty set [mathematics]
Set theory (Kinds of sets) **S: 321**
EMS [medicine] See Emergency Medical Services in this index
EMS [organization] See European Monetary System in this index
EMT-Paramedic See Emergency medical technician in this index
Emu [bird] **E: 263** with picture
Australia picture on **A: 915**
EMU [organization] See Economic and Monetary Union in this index
Emulation program
Computer (Compiling or assembling a program) **Ci: 923**
Emulsification [chemistry]
Alcohol (Other alcohols) **A: 335**
Margarine (How margarine is made) **M: 198**
Emulsifier See Emulsifying agent in this index
Emulsifying agent [chemical]
Emulsion **E: 264**
Food additive (Kinds of additives) **F: 339**
Emulsion [chemistry] **E: 264**
Photography (Exposing the film) **P: 416**; (Making prints) **P: 419**; (Technical improvements) **P: 423**
En passant rule
Chess (The moves) **C: 412-413**
Enabling Act [Germany, 1933]
Hitler, Adolf (The New Order) **H: 266-267-**

Enabling act [law]
South Dakota (Statehood) **So: 683**
Enamel [paint]
Enamel **E: 264**
Enamel [porcelain] **E: 264** with picture
Porcelain (Painting) **P: 676**
Enamel [tooth]
Ivory (Characteristics of ivory) **I: 521**
Teeth (Enamel) **T: 81** with diagram
Enamels and Cameos [poems by Gautier]
French literature (Gautier and Nerval) **F: 521**
Gautier, Théophile **G: 70**
Enamelware [metal]
Enamel **E: 264** with picture
Enantiornithine [bird]
Bird (The first known birds) **B: 369**
Encampment Among the Islands of Lake Huron [painting by by Kane]
Indian, American picture on **I: 154**
Encaustic painting
Painting picture on **P: 39**; (Encaustic painting) **P: 36**
Enceladus [satellite] **E: 265**
Satellite picture on **S: 150a**; (Enceladus) **S: 150b**
Saturn (Satellites) **S: 151**
Encephalitis [disease] **E: 265**
Brain (From injury) **B: 550d**; (Infectious diseases) **B: 558**
Nervous system (Disorders of the nervous system) **N: 136**
West Nile virus **W: 205**
Enchilada [food]
Mexico (Food and drink) **M: 456**
Enciphering See Encryption in this index
Encke gap [astronomy]
Saturn (Rings) **S: 150j** with diagram
Encke's Comet [astronomy]
Comet (table) **Ci: 868**
Enclave [political unit] **E: 265**
Enclosed seed [botany]
Plant (Seeds) **P: 531** with pictures
Seed (Kinds of seeds) **S: 280**
Encoder [electronics]
Digital video recorder **D: 203**
Television diagram on **T: 124**; (Encoding the color signals) **T: 123**
Encoding [cryptology] See Encryption in this index
Encomienda system
Hispanic Americans (In the Southwest) **H: 251**
Indian, American (In Latin America) **I: 178**
Latin America (Colonial rule) **L: 104**
Peru (Spanish conquest and rule) **P: 314**
Encounter group
Sensitivity training **S: 302**
Encryption [electronics]
Codes and ciphers **Ci: 749**
Computer (Computer security) **Ci: 924**
Enculturation
Child (Cultural differences) **C: 450**
Culture **Ci: 1186**
Encyclical [religion]
Pope (The 1900's and 2000's) **P: 665**
Encyclopedia E: 265 with pictures
Enlightenment (Influence of the Enlightenment) **E: 326b**
Encyclopedia [book by Diderot] See Encyclopédie in this index
Encyclopedia Americana
Encyclopedia (Encyclopedias of the 1800's and 1900's) **E: 268b**
Encyclopædia Britannica
Encyclopedia (An age of experiment) **E: 268a-268b**; (Encyclopedias of the 1800's and 1900's) **E: 268b**
Encyclopedia of Associations [reference]
A Guide to Research Skills **Research Guide: 34**
Encyclopedia of the Philosophical Sciences [book by Hegel]
Hegel, G. W. F. (Hegel's writings) **H: 165**
Encyclopédie [book by Diderot]
Diderot, Denis **D: 195**
Encyclopedia (An age of experiment) **E: 268a**
Enlightenment (Influence of the Enlightenment) **E: 326b**
French literature (The Enlightenment) **F: 520**
End [sports]
Curling (The game) **Ci: 1195**
Football (The offensive team) **F: 356** with diagrams; (The defensive team) **F: 357** with diagrams
End, The [etching by Kollwitz]
Kollwitz, Käthe picture on **K: 363**
End moraine [geology]
Glacier (How glaciers shape the land) **G: 203** with diagram
End of the Chapter [book by Galsworthy]
Galsworthy, John **G: 17**

End of the Pier, The [book by Grimes]
Grimes, Martha **G: 393**
End of the Trail, The [sculpture by Fraser]
Oklahoma picture on **O: 723**
End-of-train device
Railroad (Rolling stock) **R: 107-108** with picture
End paper
Book (Inside a book) **B: 464-465**
Paperwork (End papers) **P: 138**
End rhyme
Rhyme **R: 319**
End zone
Football (The field) **F: 354-355** with diagram
Endangered species [conservation] **E: 269**
See also Rare species; Threatened species in this index
African hunting dog **A: 137** with picture
Animal (Animals of the grasslands) **A: 476**; (Animals of the temperate forests) **A: 478**; (Animals of the tropical forests) **A: 480**; (The future of animals) **A: 504**
Aquarium, Public (Conservation) **A: 578b**
Biodiversity (Protecting biodiversity) **B: 311**
Bird (Endangered species) **B: 370** with pictures
Blue whale **B: 421**
Chimpanzee (The life of a chimpanzee) **C: 472-473**
Condor **Ci: 929**
Conservation (To maintain the quality of life) **Ci: 976**; (Biodiversity conservation) **Ci: 976**
Deer (Endangered species) **D: 86**
Eagle (The bald eagle) **E: 5**
Elephant **E: 226**
Global warming (Effect on plant and animal life) **G: 232a**
Hunting (Laws and conservation) **H: 450**
Invasive species **I: 354j**
Mammal (The future of mammals) **M: 127**
National Wildlife Refuge System **N: 61**
Panda (Protecting pandas) **P: 129**
Poaching **P: 587**
Rhinoceros (Protecting the rhinoceros) **R: 295**
Wildlife conservation **W: 303**; (Classifications of scarce wildlife) **W: 304**
WWF **W: 514**
Zoo **Z: 599**; (Wildlife conservation) **Z: 600**
Endangered Species Act [1973]
Animal (Laws) **A: 505**
Conservation (Renewed interest in conservation) **Ci: 986-987**
Endangered species (Protecting endangered species) **E: 270**
Fish and Wildlife Service **F: 175**
Grizzly bear (Grizzly bears and people) **G: 397**
Trapping (Trapping and wildlife conservation) **T: 403-404**
Wetland (Conservation) **W: 253**
Wildlife conservation (Wildlife conservation today) **W: 305**
Endara, Guillermo [Panamanian political leader]
Panama (The Noriega years) **P: 1120-21**
Endeavour [ship]
Cook, James (First Pacific voyage) **Ci: 1025**
Endeavour [space shuttle]
Astronaut (Achievements in space) **A: 829-830**
International Space Station (History) **I: 346b**
Jemison, Mae Carol **J: 90**
Space exploration picture on **So: 695**; (Repair missions) **So: 724**
Endeavour Crater [Mars]
Mars (Observation by spacecraft) **M: 226c-226d**
Endecott, John [American colonial leader] **E: 271**
Massachusetts Bay Colony **M: 295**
Salem (History) **S: 61**
Endemic disease
Disease (Spread of infectious diseases) **D: 228**
Epidemic **E: 343**
Endemic typhus [disease]
Typhus (Murine typhus) **T: 541**
Enderby Land [region, Antarctica] **E: 272**
Antarctica (Early exploration) **A: 536**
Enders, John Franklin [American bacteriologist] **E: 272**
Measles **M: 346**
Endicott, William C. [American government official]
Cleveland, Grover (table) **Ci: 671**
Endive [plant] **E: 272** with pictures
Endless chain [mechanism]
Block and tackle (An endless chain hoist) **B: 405** with diagram
Endnote [reference]
Footnote **F: 369**
Endocarditis [disease]
Heart (Inflammatory heart disease) **H: 142**
Mitral valve prolapse **M: 679**
Endocardium [anatomy]

Heart (Chambers, valves, and inner lining) **H: 133**; (Inflammatory heart disease) **H: 142**
Endocarp [botany]
Fruit (Types of fruits in botany) **F: 544**
Endochronal bone formation [anatomy]
Bone (Structure of the bones) **B: 456**
Endocrine gland [anatomy]
Disease (Metabolic diseases) **D: 229**
Gland **G: 207** *with diagram*
Hormone (Human hormones) **H: 335**
Human body (table) **H: 422** *with diagram*; (The endocrine system) **H: 425**
Immune system (The cell-mediated immune response) **I: 88-88a**
Infertility (Causes) **I: 265**
Endoderm [biology]
Coelom **Ci: 753**
Reproduction, Human (Origin of tissues and organs) **R: 247-248**
Endodermis [botany]
Root (The outer tissues) **R: 470-471** *with diagrams*
Endodontics
Dentistry (Endodontics) **D: 144**
Endogamy
Marriage (Other marriage laws and practices) **M: 220**
Endogenous pyrogen [physiology]
Fever **F: 83**
Endometriosis [disease] **E: 272**
Infertility (Causes) **I: 265**
Endometrium [anatomy]
Pelvic inflammatory disease **P: 232**
Reproduction, Human (The human reproductive system) **R: 244-245**
Endoparasite [biology]
Parasite (Types) **P: 154**
Endoplasmic reticulum [biology]
Cell (The cytoplasm) **C: 329** *with diagrams*
Endorphin [physiology] **E: 272**
Acupuncture **A: 31**
Brain (Regulating body processes) **B: 554**
Narcotic **N: 21**
Placebo **P: 505**
Endorsement [banking]
Check (How the checking system works) **C: 390-391**
Negotiable instrument (Endorsement) **N: 119**
Note (Liability of the maker) **N: 550**
Endorsement [marketing]
Publishing (Marketing) **P: 867**
Endoscope [instrument] **E: 272** *with pictures*
Fiber optics (Uses of optical fibers) **F: 88-89**
Inflammatory bowel disease (Diagnosis and treatment) **I: 266**
Endosperm [botany]
Bran **B: 562**
Corn (How the plant develops) **Ci: 1057** *with diagram*
Flour (How white flour is milled) **F: 269**
Germination **G: 173**
Plant (Seeds) **P: 531-532** *with pictures*
Seed (The parts of a seed) **S: 281** *with diagram*
Wheat (Food for people) **W: 266-267** *with diagram*; (Structure) **W: 267-268** *with diagram*
Endothermic animal *See* Warm-blooded animal *in this index*
Endothermic mixture [physics]
Refrigeration (Ice refrigeration) **R: 200-201**
Endothermic reaction [chemistry]
Chemical reaction **C: 397**
Refrigeration (Ice refrigeration) **R: 200**
Endotoxin [poison]
Toxin **T: 353**
Endowment [fund] **E: 273**
Foundation **F: 429**
Private school **P: 808b**
Endowment [religion]
Mormons (Church doctrines and ordinances) **M: 806-807**
Endowment for International Peace
Carnegie, Andrew (Carnegie's contributions to society) **C: 242**
Endsheet
Bookbinding (Tipping) **B: 470-471**
Endurance [ship]
Exploration *picture on* **E: 450**
Endurance exercise
Aerobics **A: 84**
Endurance racing
Automobile racing (Sports car racing) **A: 977**
Motorboat racing (Types of racing) **M: 877**
Enduring Love [book by McEwan]
McEwan, Ian **M: 334**
Enduro [race]
Motorcycle (Motorcycling as a sport) **M: 879**
Endymion [Greek mythology] **E: 273**

Endymion [poem by Keats]
Keats, John (His life) **K: 253**; (His work) **K: 253**
Enemy alien [U.S. history]
World War II (Treatment of enemy aliens) **W: 496**
Enemy of the People, An [play by Ibsen]
Ibsen, Henrik (His plays) **I: 4**
Energia [rocket]
Space exploration (The Soviet space shuttle) **So: 723**
Energization [psychology]
Motivation **M: 875**
Energy [physics] **E: 273** *with diagram*
See also Dark energy; Nuclear energy; Solar energy *in this index*
Astronomy (Electromagnetic radiation) **A: 838**
Biomass **B: 322**
Calorie **C: 70**
Cell (The work of a cell) **C: 332** *with diagram*
Chemical reaction **C: 397**
$E=mc^2$ **E: 3**
Ecology (Energy flow) **E: 54**
Efficiency **E: 115**
Einstein, Albert (Famous theories) **E: 146-146b**
Electricity **E: 190**
Energy supply **E: 277** *with pictures*
Entropy **E: 328**
Food (Producing energy) **F: 330**
Foot-pound **F: 353**
Fuel **F: 550**
Heat **H: 148, H: 150** *with diagram*; (Heat and energy) **H: 155**
Joule **J: 169**
Krebs cycle **K: 386**
Light **L: 282**; (Energy and brightness) **L: 290** *with diagram*
Machine (Principles of machines) **M: 13**
Matter **M: 310**
Metric system (Mechanics) **M: 437-440**
Nutrition (Kinds of nutrients) **N: 625**
Particle detector (How particle detectors work) **P: 186**
Perpetual motion machine **P: 293**
Physics (Developments in the 1800's) **P: 440**
Planck, Max Karl Ernst Ludwig **P: 507**
Power **P: 726**
Quantum mechanics (Quanta of energy) **Q: 6**
Radiation **R: 74**
Relativity (Mass-energy relationship) **R: 211**; (General relativity) **R: 211-212**
Solar energy **So: 576**
Star (Converting mass to energy) **So: 846**
Sun **So: 975**; (Energy output) **So: 976**
Thermodynamics **T: 253**
Thermography **T: 253**
Uranium **U: 214**
Water power **W: 139**
Waves **W: 150**
Weight control **W: 181**
Work **W: 405**
Energy, Conservation of *See* Conservation of energy; Energy conservation *in this index*
Energy, Department of [U.S.] **E: 276** *with pictures*
Conservation (Renewed interest in conservation) **Ci: 986-987**
Electronics (Research and development) **E: 214**
Idaho National Laboratory **I: 46**
National laboratory **N: 40**
Strategic Petroleum Reserve **So: 920**
Washington, D.C. *map on* **W: 76**
Energy, Pyramid of
Ecology (Energy flow) **E: 54-55**
Energy, Secretary of [U.S.]
Energy, Department of **E: 276**
Flag *picture on* **F: 211**
Energy Administration, Federal [U.S.] *See* Federal Energy Administration *in this index*
Energy assistance [program]
Welfare (Other public assistance programs) **W: 190**
Energy conservation *See* Conservation *in this index*
Energy crisis [U.S. history]
Automobile *picture on* **A: 970**; (Demand for petroleum) **A: 961**; (The rise of international automaking) **A: 972**
California (The beginning of the 2000's) **C: 64**
Coal **Ci: 716**
Conservation (Renewed interest in conservation) **Ci: 986-987** *with picture*
Daylight saving time **D: 54**
Ford, Gerald Rudolph (Energy policy) **F: 377**
Nixon, Richard Milhous (Events at home) **N: 435-436**
Petroleum (The energy crisis) **P: 349**
United States, History of the (Environmental and energy concerns) **U: 196a**
Energy diagram [chemistry]

Chemical reaction **C: 397** *with diagram*
Energy Efficiency Ratio
Air conditioning (Electric power requirements) **A: 180**
Energy-equivalent of mass [physics]
Energy (Energy and matter) **E: 274**
Energy level [physics]
Atom (The forces within an atom) **A: 873** *with diagrams*
Element, Chemical (The periodic table of the elements) **E: 219**
Light *diagram on* **L: 287**
Energy Policy Act [1992]
Nuclear energy (The spread of nuclear capability) **N: 591**
Energy Reorganization Act [1974]
Nuclear Regulatory Commission **N: 596**
Energy Research and Development Administration [U.S.]
Energy, Department of (History) **E: 276**
Nuclear energy (The spread of nuclear capability) **N: 591**
Energy Resource Tribes, Council of
Indian, American (In the United States) **I: 179**; (Social and economic progress) **I: 180-181**
Energy supply **E: 277** *with pictures*
Coal **Ci: 716**; (Recent developments) **Ci: 732**
Conservation (Energy conservation) **Ci: 983**
Electricity (Recent developments) **E: 198**
Energy, Department of (Functions) **E: 276**
Geothermal energy **G: 136**
Ocean (The importance of the ocean) **O: 653-654**
United States, History of the (Environmental and energy concerns) **U: 196a**
Waste disposal (Incineration) **W: 113**
Wind power **W: 331**
Enesco, Georges [Romanian composer]
Romania (The arts) **R: 419**
Enevoldson, Einar [American pilot]
Glider (table) **G: 230**
Enewetak [atoll, Pacific] **E: 283**
World War II (Island hopping in the Central Pacific) **W: 489-490**
Enfants terribles, Les [book by Cocteau]
Cocteau, Jean **Ci: 747**
Enfleurage [industrial process]
Perfume (Plant substances) **P: 286**
Enflurane [drug]
Halothane **H: 27**
Enforcement Acts *See* Force bill *in this index*
Enforcement of law *See* Law enforcement *in this index*
Enfranchisement [Canadian history]
Indian, American (In Canada) **I: 178**
"Enfranchisement of Women" [essay by Mill]
Mill, Harriet Taylor **M: 552**
Eng [conjoined twin]
Conjoined twins **Ci: 950** *with picture*
Engagement ring
Ring **R: 342** *with picture*
Engel v. Vitale [U.S. history]
Religious education (Public schools) **R: 225**
Supreme Court of the United States (table) **So: 1002**
Engelmann spruce [tree]
Plant *pictures on* **P: 521, P: 524**
Tree *pictures on* **T: 425**
Engels, Friedrich [German philosopher] **E: 283** *with portrait*
Communism (The ideas of Marx) **Ci: 890**
Marx, Karl (Marx's life) **M: 236**
Materialism **M: 300b**
Socialism (Karl Marx) **So: 560**
Engine **E: 283**
See also Gasoline engine; Internal-combustion engine *in this index; and the list of Related articles in the Engine article*
Airplane *picture on* **A: 219**; (Power for flight) **A: 217**
Automobile (Power systems) **A: 947-948** *with diagram*
Flywheel **F: 313**
Motorboat racing (Engine designs) **M: 876**
Rotary engine **R: 485**
Ship *picture on* **S: 412**; (Propulsion and steering) **S: 406**
Starter **So: 858**
Thermodynamics **T: 253**
Transmission **T: 375**
Transportation **T: 382**
Turbine **T: 495**
Engine [firefighting]
Fire department (Firefighting) **F: 123**; (Trucks and vehicles) **F: 126** *with picture*
Engine [railroad] *See* Locomotive *in this index*
Engine analyzer [machine] **E: 283**
Engine block *See* Cylinder block *in this index*

Engine company
  Fire department (Firefighting) F: 123
Engine instruments
  Airplane *picture on* A: 222
Engine 382 [locomotive]
  Locomotive *picture on* L: 415
Engineer [profession]
  Army, United States (Engineers) A: 735
  Engineering E: 284; (Engineering careers) E: 288
  National Society of Professional Engineers N: 61
  Railroad (Railroad workers) R: 113
  Recording industry (In a recording studio) R: 181
    with picture
  Ship (Officers and crew) S: 410
Engineer Heartfield, The [painting by Grosz]
  Grosz, George *picture on* G: 401
Engineered lumber [material]
  Lumber (Engineered lumber) L: 518
Engineered materials
  Materials M: 300b
Engineering E: 284 *with pictures*
  See also the list of Related articles in the
    Engineering *article*
  Automobile (Engineering the parts) A: 956
  Biomedical engineering B: 324
  Careers (Technical and mathematical
    occupations) C: 232
  Computer graphics (In engineering) Ci: 924h
  Electronics (Careers in electronics) E: 214
  Ergonomics E: 350
  Manufacturing (The main steps in
    manufacturing) M: 170
  Photography (Scientific photographers) P: 428
  Rome, Ancient (Architecture and engineering)
    R: 442 *with picture*; (The Roman heritage)
    R: 448
Engineering, National Academy of *See* National
  Academy of Engineering *in this index*
Engineering Institute of Canada
  Engineering (table) E: 289
Engineering technician
  Engineering (Education and training) E: 289
Engineering technologist
  Engineering (Education and training) E: 289
Engineers, Corps of [U.S.] E: 291 *with picture*
  Everglades (Saving the Everglades) E: 424
  Washington (The late 1900's) W: 68-69
Engineers, International Union of Operating
  E: 291
  Labor movement (table) L: 8
Engineers and the Price System, The [book by
  Veblen]
  Veblen, Thorstein Bunde V: 291
England E: 292 *with pictures and maps*
  See also Great Britain; United Kingdom *in this
    index; and the list of Related articles in the*
    England *article*
  Ballet (Ballet in England) B: 53
  Bank B: 88
  Christmas (In England, Ireland, Scotland, and
    Wales) C: 530 *with picture*
  Classical music (History) Ci: 645-646
  Coal (Developments in England) Ci: 731
  Cotton (History) Ci: 1092
  English Channel E: 311
  Flag *picture on*s F: 216, F: 217
  Furniture (England) F: 573 *with picture*
  Glass (The Middle Ages) G: 218-219 *with picture*
  Halloween (Halloween customs and symbols)
    H: 24a; (History) H: 25
  John Bull J: 133
  New Year's Day (Early customs) N: 289
  Painting (Romanticism) P: 68; (The Pre-
    Raphaelite Brotherhood) P: 71
  Porcelain (English porcelain) P: 677
  Pottery *picture on* P: 717
  Road (The first roads) R: 361
  United Kingdom U: 48 *with picture*
  Valentine's Day (Early Valentine customs) V: 261
England, Bank of *See* Bank of England *in this index*
England, Commonwealth of [English history]
  Cromwell, Oliver (Rise to power) C: 1151-1152
  England (The Civil War) E: 308-309
England, History of
  See also the list of Related articles in the England
    article and specific topics, such as Civil War
    [England], *in this index*
  England (History) E: 303 *with pictures*
  Anglo-Saxon Chronicle A: 464
  Anglo-Saxons A: 464 *with maps*
  Bill of rights (English Bill of Rights) B: 301
  Coal (History of coal use) Ci: 731
  Coffee house Ci: 755
  Domesday Book D: 300
  East India Company E: 40
  Equity E: 348
  Exploration (The French and English in North

America) E: 446
  Glorious Revolution G: 234
  Gunpowder Plot G: 442
  Hampton Court Conference H: 36
  Hastings, Battle of H: 83
  Hudson's Bay Company H: 407
  Hundred Years' War H: 437
  Lancaster L: 55
  Laud, William L: 121
  Law (The Middle Ages) L: 134-135
  Long Parliament L: 448
  Magna Carta M: 52
  Model Parliament M: 684
  Netherlands (Wars with England and France)
    N: 149
  Norman Conquest N: 455
  Petition of Right P: 327
  Plantagenet P: 550
  Restoration R: 263
  Shakespeare, William (England of Shakespeare's
    day) S: 349 *with picture*
  Spanish Armada So: 755
  Stuart, House of So: 931
  Wales (History) W: 11-12
  Wars of the Roses W: 38
  Wat Tyler's Rebellion W: 113
  Welfare (History) W: 191
  York Y: 568
**"England expects that every man will do his
  duty"** [quotation]
  Nelson, Horatio (Victory at Trafalgar) N: 122
Engle, Robert F. [American economist]
  Nobel Prizes (Economics: 2003) N: 449
Engler, John [American political leader]
  Michigan (table) M: 507
Englert, François [Belgian physicist]
  Higgs, Peter Ware H: 227
English, George W. [American jurist]
  Impeachment (History) I: 91
English, James E. [American political leader]
  Connecticut (table) Ci: 967
English, National Council of Teachers of
  Teaching (Teachers organizations) T: 69
English, William Hayden [American political
  leader] E: 311
English Bards and Scotch Reviewers [poem by
  Byron]
  Byron, Lord (Byron's life) B: 748; (Byron's poetry)
    B: 748
English bond
  Brick (Bonds) B: 599 *with picture*
English Channel [England-France] E: 311 *with map*
  Channel Tunnel C: 375
  Dover, Strait of D: 315
  Ederle, Gertrude Caroline E: 76
  England (The land) E: 299
  Great Britain G: 337
  Tunnel (History) T: 491-492
  United Kingdom U: 49, *picture on* U: 73
English Civil War *See* Civil War, English *in this index*
English class [breeds]
  Chicken (Kinds of chickens) C: 441; (table) C: 443
English cocker spaniel [dog] E: 311
  Dog *picture on* D: 269
English Congregational Church [religious group]
  Baptists B: 101
English East India Company *See* British East India
  Company *in this index*
English elm [tree]
  Elm (Kinds) E: 244-245
English Fairy Tales [book by Jacobs]
  Jacobs, Joseph J: 20
English foxhound [dog] E: 312 *with picture*
English grammar
  Grammar G: 303
English hawthorn [tree]
  Hawthorn H: 114 *with picture*
English history *See* England, History of *in this index*
English holly [tree]
  Holly H: 292
English horn [musical instrument] E: 312
  Music (Wind instruments) M: 949 *with picture*
English ivy [plant]
  Gardening *picture on* G: 37
  Ivy (Common, or English, ivy) I: 522 *with pictures*
English language E: 312
  Accent A: 22
  Alphabet (The English alphabet) A: 383 *with
    pictures*
  Anglo-Saxons A: 464
  Australia (Language) A: 900
  Canada (Languages) C: 106
  Closed captioning Ci: 685
  Cockney Ci: 745
  Dialect D: 180
  England (Language) E: 294; (The Norman
    Conquest) E: 305

French language F: 516
  German language G: 137
  India (Languages) I: 114
  Indian, American (Native Americans and the
    English language) I: 150
  Inflection I: 268a
  Irish literature I: 430
  Language (Language change) L: 64
  Latin language (Latin and English) L: 115
  Phonetics (An international phonetic alphabet)
    P: 400; (Phonetics and spelling) P: 400
  Pidgin English P: 452
  Pronunciation P: 820
  Shakespeare, William S: 344; (Shakespeare's style)
    S: 367
  United Kingdom (Language) U: 55
  Universal language U: 205
  Vocabulary V: 434
  Vowel V: 452
English Language Acquisition Act [2001]
  Hispanic Americans (Education) H: 256-257
English literature E: 314 *with pictures*
  See also the list of Related articles in the English
    literature *article*
  Bible (Translations of the Bible) B: 284-285
  Classicism (England) Ci: 653
  Drama (England) D: 334; (British drama) D: 338;
    (Later British drama) D: 340
  Novel (The rise of the English novel) N: 572; (The
    1800's) N: 572
  Realism (In fiction) R: 171-172
English neoclassical style
  Furniture (English neoclassical furniture) F: 579
    with picture
English notation
  Chess (Chess notation) C: 413 *with picture*
English oak [tree]
  Oak (Other oaks) O: 636 *with picture*
  Tree *picture on* T: 427
English Patient, The [film]
  Motion picture (Best picture: 1996) M: 861
English round hand
  Handwriting (Later writing styles) H: 50
English Rugby Union
  Rugby football (History) R: 513
English saddle
  Horse (The saddle) H: 351 *with picture*
  Saddle S: 7 *with picture*
English setter [dog] E: 325
  Dog *picture on* D: 268
  Setter S: 323
English sonnet
  Poetry (Forms) P: 595
English sparrow [bird] *See* House sparrow *in this
  index*
English springer spaniel [dog] E: 325
  Dog *picture on* D: 269
English Stage Company [organization]
  Theater (Britain) T: 247-248
English system [measurement] *See* Inch-pound
  system *in this index*
English toy spaniel [dog] E: 325 *with picture*
English Traits [book by Emerson]
  Emerson, Ralph Waldo (His prose works) E: 259
English walnut [tree]
  Nut (Kinds of nuts) *picture on*N: 621
  Walnut W: 19 *with picture*
English yew [tree]
  Yew Y: 565
Engraving [art] E: 325 *with pictures*
  See also Photoengraving *in this index*
  Etching E: 364
  Glass (Copper-wheel engraving) G: 217 *with
    picture*
  Graphic arts G: 322
  Schongauer, Martin S: 179
Engraving and Printing, Bureau of [U.S.] E: 326a
  Money *pictures on* M: 712; (How money is
    manufactured) M: 714
  Washington, D.C. *map on* W: 76, *picture on* W: 78;
    (South of the Mall) W: 75
Enhanced Fujita scale [measurement]
  Tornado (Damage by tornadoes) T: 335
Enhanced recovery [industrial process]
  Petroleum (Secondary and tertiary recovery)
    P: 342
ENI [company]
  Manufacturing (table) M: 170
ENIAC [computer]
  Computer (The first electronic computers)
    Ci: 924b *with picture*
  Eckert, J. Presper, Jr. E: 50
  Electronics *picture on* E: 216; (The vacuum tube
    era) E: 215
  Mauchly, John William M: 312
Enid [Oklahoma] E: 326a
Enigma [machine]

Codes and ciphers (Cipher machines) **Ci: 750**
Enigma Variations, The [music by Elgar]
Elgar, Sir Edward **E: 235**
Enkephalin [physiology]
Endorphin **E: 272**
Narcotic **N: 21**
Enki [god]
Mythology (Middle Eastern mythology) **M: 976-977**
Enkidu [literary figure]
Gilgamesh, Epic of **G: 190**
Enlarger [machine]
Photography (Making prints) **P: 419** *with picture*
Enlightened despot [political science]
Despotism **D: 161**
Enlightenment [European history] **E: 326a**
Christianity (The 1600's and 1700's) **C: 525**
Diderot, Denis **D: 195**
Education (The Enlightenment) **E: 101**
Europe (The scientific revolution and the Enlightenment) **E: 412**
Exploration (Linking the globe) **E: 446**
France (Literature) **F: 461-462**
Freedom (During the Enlightenment) **F: 503**
Freedom of speech (History) **F: 507**
French literature (The Enlightenment) **F: 520**
German literature (The Enlightenment) **G: 139**
Government (The Enlightenment) **G: 290**
Invention (The Enlightenment) **I: 360**
Italian literature (The Baroque period and the Enlightenment) **I: 494**
Jefferson, Thomas **J: 76**
Philosophes **P: 382**
Philosophy (The Enlightenment) **P: 389**
Roman Catholic Church (The Enlightenment) **R: 409**
Rousseau, Jean-Jacques **R: 492**
Science (The Enlightenment) **S: 199**
Women's movement (From the Renaissance to the 1800's) **W: 384**
Enlil [mythology]
Mythology (Sumerian mythology) **M: 976-977**
Enlisted personnel
Rank, Military (table) **R: 140**
Ennead [Egyptian mythology]
Mythology (The Great Ennead) **M: 979** *with pictures*
Enneads [lectures by Plotinus]
Plotinus **P: 574**
Ennius, Quintus [Roman poet]
Latin literature (Early Latin literature) **L: 115-116**
Enobarbus [literary figure]
Shakespeare, William: (*Antony and Cleopatra*) **S: 364**
Enoch Pratt Free Library [Baltimore]
Baltimore (Education) **B: 68-69**
Maryland (Libraries) **M: 244**
Enola Gay [airplane]
World War II (The atomic bomb) **W: 493**
Enormous Room, The [book by Cummings]
Cummings, E. E. **Ci: 1191**
Enquiry Concerning Human Understanding, An [book by Hume]
Hume, David (Hume's life) **H: 432**
Enquiry Concerning Political Justice, An [book by Godwin]
Godwin, William **G: 245**
Enquiry Concerning the Principles of Morals, An [book by Hume]
Hume, David (Hume's life) **H: 432**
Enriched bread
Bread (The food value of bread) **B: 589**; (History) **B: 589**
Enriched flour
Flour (How white flour is milled) **F: 269**
Wheat (Food for people) **W: 266-267**
Enriched pasta [food]
Pasta **P: 192**
Enriched rice
Rice (Food) **R: 323**
Enriched uranium
Iran (Recent developments) **I: 406b**
Uranium (Refining and processing uranium ore) **U: 215**
Enrichment plant
Nuclear energy (Fuel preparation) **N: 586**
Enright, Elizabeth [American author] **E: 327**
Newbery Medal (table) **N: 359**
Enríquez de Harana, Beatriz [mistress of]
Columbus, Christopher (Years of waiting) **Ci: 858**
Enrobing [process]
Candy (Chocolate candies) **C: 176**
Enrolled nurse
Nursing (Practical nursing courses) **N: 619**
Enrollment Act [1863]
Army, United States (The Civil War [1861-1865]) **A: 738**

Enron Corporation **E: 327**
Accounting (The history of accounting) **A: 23**
Bush, George Walker (Corporate wrongdoing) **B: 722h**
Business (Recent developments) **B: 727**
United States, History of the (Financial troubles) **U: 196f**
Ensemble [music]
Chamber music **C: 370**
Classical music (Chamber music) **Ci: 643**
Opera (Ensembles) **O: 792** *with picture*
Ensemble playing [drama]
Theater (Creating a role) **T: 238**
Ensign [flag]
Flag (table) **F: 193**; (Military flags) **F: 195-208** *with pictures*
Ensign [rank]
Coast Guard, United States (Training an officer) **Ci: 736**
Rank, Military (table) **R: 140**
Ensign staff
Flag (table) **F: 193**
Ensor, James [Belgian painter] **E: 327** *with picture*
Entablature [architecture]
Architecture (table) **A: 608-609** *with picture*; (Minoan architecture) **A: 615**
Column **Ci: 865**
Entail [law]
Jefferson, Thomas (Virginia lawmaker) **J: 80**
Entailment [semantic relation]
Semantics **S: 291**
Entebbe [Uganda] **E: 327**
Commando **Ci: 871**
Kampala **K: 212**
Entente Cordiale [alliance]
France (The Third Republic) **F: 474-475**
Germany (Foreign policy) **G: 166**
Russia (World War I) **R: 552**
United Kingdom (Gladstone and Disraeli) **U: 69**
World War I (The Triple Entente) **W: 455**
Entered Apprentice
Masonry (The lodges and degrees of Masonry) **M: 267**
Enterococcus [bacteria]
Antibiotic (Resistance to antibiotics) **A: 551**; (History) **A: 552**
Enterprise [aircraft carrier]
Aircraft carrier (The United States carrier fleet) **A: 206**
Navy, United States (The nuclear age Navy) **N: 89-90** *with picture*
Virginia (Interesting facts) **V: 399**
Enterprise [space shuttle]
Space exploration (The shuttle era begins) **So: 723**
Enterprise [steamboat]
Kentucky (Transportation) **K: 289**
Enterprise union [labor]
Labor movement (In other countries) **L: 14-15**
Enterprise zone [government]
United Kingdom (City life) **U: 55**
Entertainer, The [play by Osborne]
Osborne, John **O: 861**
Entertainment
See also Recreation *in this index*
Careers (Sports and entertainment) **C: 230** *with picture*
Public speaking (Purpose) **P: 864**
Radio (Radio programming) **R: 85**
Television **T: 110**
Entertainment Software Rating Board
Electronic game (Fighting games) **E: 204e**
Entisol [soil]
Soil *map on* **So: 575**; (How soils are classified) **So: 576**
Entomologist
Entomology (What entomologists study) **E: 328**
Entomology **E: 328**
See also Insect *in this index*
Biology (table) **B: 317**
Zoology (What zoologists study) **Z: 606-607**
Entrapment [physics]
Vacuum (Producing a vacuum) **V: 256**
Entrechat
Ballet (table) **B: 45**
Entreprenant balloon, L' [aircraft]
Aircraft, Military *picture on* **A: 204**
Entrepreneur [economics]
Economics (Life) **E: 60**
Industrial Revolution (Life before the Industrial Revolution) **I: 246-247**
Schumpeter, Joseph Alois **S: 188**
Entrepreneurial system [economics]
Capitalism (How capitalism differs from central planning) **C: 194**
Entropy [physics] **E: 328**
Heat (Disorder) **H: 151** *with diagram*; (The second law of thermodynamics) **H: 151**
Time (Arrows of time) **T: 292b-292c**
Entry
Space exploration (table) **So: 696**
Entry barrier [economics]
Capitalism (Ensuring competition) **C: 195**
Monopoly and competition (Causes and effects of monopolies) **M: 732**
Entry of Christ into Brussels, The [painting by Ensor]
Ensor, James **E: 327**
Entwistle, John [British musician]
Who, The **W: 296**
Enuma Elish [poem]
Mythology (Sumerian mythology) **M: 976**
Enumerator
Census (United States censuses) **C: 346**; (Conducting censuses) **C: 347-348**
Enunciation [speech]
Pronunciation **P: 820**
Envelope [communication]
Letter writing (The envelope address) **L: 211** *with pictures*
Postal Service, United States (Stamps and other mailing materials) **P: 699**
Postal services (The creation of the Penny Post) **P: 706**
Envelope [aircraft]
Airship (Nonrigid airships) **A: 250** *with diagram*
Envelope [electronics]
Vacuum tube **V: 258**
Environment **E: 329**
See also Environmental pollution *in this index*
Adaptation **A: 45**
Agriculture (Agriculture and the environment) **A: 152**
Animal (The bodies of animals) **A: 488**
Baby (Growth and development) **B: 6**
Balance of nature (Ecosystems) **B: 35**
Behavior (Environment) **B: 220**
Child (Individual differences among children) **C: 450**; (The influence of the child's environment) **C: 452**
City (Physical environment) **Ci: 577**
Conservation **Ci: 974**
Deafness (Environmental factors) **D: 57**
Ecology **E: 53**
Extinction **E: 456**
Gaia **G: 5**
Genetic engineering (Concerns about genetic engineering) **G: 84c**
Geography (Environmental conservation) **G: 94**
Heredity (Heredity and natural selection) **H: 203**; (Heredity and environment) **H: 205** *with picture*
Intellectual disability (Causes) **I: 318**
Intelligence (The roles of heredity and environment) **I: 319**
Lawn (Lawns and the environment) **L: 144**
Life (Living things and their environment) **L: 275**
Motivation **M: 875**
National park (Changes in the environment) **N: 42h**
Ocean (As an influence on climate) **O: 654**
Personality (Personality and environment) **P: 302**
Plant (Where plants live) **P: 520**; (Effects of heredity and environment) **P: 538**
Public health (Ensuring environmental safety) **P: 856** *with picture*
Races, Human (Climatic adaptations) **R: 58**
Racism (The science of race) **R: 62**
Standard of living (Standard of living and the environment) **So: 834**
State government (State services) **So: 864**
Territoriality **T: 174**
United Nations (Controlling the environment) **U: 89**
Environmental acoustics [science]
Acoustics **A: 29**
Sound (Modern acoustics) **So: 606**
Environmental art
Christo **C: 537**
Environmental assessment
Conservation (Renewed interest in conservation) **Ci: 986-987**
Environmental Control Law [1970]
Vermont (The late 1900's) **V: 337**
Environmental Defense Fund [organization] **E: 329**
Environmental determinism *See* Determinism, Environmental *in this index*
Environmental education
Camp Fire USA (Camping and environmental education programs) **C: 89**
Environmental engineering
Engineering (Environmental engineering) **E: 286** *with picture*
Environmental Hazards, Bureau of

Public health (Ensuring environmental safety) P: 856
Environmental impact statement E: 329
Conservation (Renewed interest in conservation) Ci: 986-987
Dam (Planning) D: 19
Landscape architecture (Land planning) L: 59
Road (Planning) R: 358
Environmental injustice
Racism (Types of racism) R: 62
Environmental Policy, Office on
Conservation (Recent developments) Ci: 988
Environmental Protection Agency E: 340
Environmental Policy Act, National [1970]
Conservation (Renewed interest in conservation) Ci: 986-987
Environmental impact statement E: 329
Environmental pollution E: 330 *with pictures*
See also Air pollution; Soil pollution; Water pollution *in this index*
Agriculture (Pollution) A: 153
Algae A: 349
Animal (Pollution) A: 504
Automobile (Automobiles and the environment) A: 963 *with picture*
Cancer (Genes damaged by substances in the environment) C: 170
Chemistry (The chemical industry) C: 405-406
City (The people) Ci: 586-587 *with picture*; (Description) Ci: 589; (City problems) Ci: 590-591
Coast Guard, United States (Protection of the environment) Ci: 735
Coral reef (Coral reefs and people) Ci: 1049
Detergent and soap (The development of detergents) D: 165-166
Disease (Environmental and occupational diseases) D: 230
Earth Day E: 32
Ecology E: 53
Electric power (Fossil-fueled steam electric power plants) E: 183-184
Energy supply (Environmental effects) E: 281
Engineering (Environmental engineering) E: 286
Environmental Defense Fund E: 329
Environmental impact statement E: 329
Environmental Protection Agency E: 340
Forest (Deforestation) F: 398
Fossil fuel (Concerns) F: 428
Foundation (Environment and animals) F: 431
Green party G: 381
Greenpeace G: 386
Hazardous wastes H: 122
Health (Environmental health hazards) H: 127
Industry (Social costs) I: 261
Insecticide (Chlorinated hydrocarbon insecticides) I: 302
Landfill L: 58
Mediterranean Sea (History of the Mediterranean) M: 382
Mercury (Mercury in the environment) M: 413
Moscow (Social problems) M: 825
Natural resources (Conservation and development) N: 64-65
Nuclear energy (The industry and the environment) N: 589
Oil spill O: 707
Oregon (The late 1900's) O: 849
Oxide O: 889
Pest control (Effects of pesticide use) P: 318
Petroleum (Environmental problems) P: 345
Plant (Pollution) P: 544
Plastics (Plastics and the environment) P: 560
Radon R: 100
Rain (Characteristics of rain) R: 122-123
Recycling R: 184
Sanitation S: 111
Seal (Threats to seal populations) S: 268
Ship (Pollution) S: 413 *with picture*
Sierra Club S: 450
Smog S: 519
Technology (Challenges of technology) T: 77 *with picture*
Transportation (Environmental problems) T: 398
United States, History of the (Environmental and energy concerns) U: 196a
Waste disposal W: 112
Wildlife conservation (Scientific value) W: 304
World (Threats to the environment) W: 418 *with picture*
Environmental Protection Agency [U.S.] E: 340
Asbestos (History) A: 765-766
Coal (Coal research) Ci: 730
Conservation (Renewed interest in conservation) Ci: 986-987
Environmental pollution (Government action) E: 335

Gasoline engine (Air pollution controls) G: 66
Herbicide (Hazards of herbicides) H: 198
Incinerator I: 100
Industry (Social costs) I: 261
Natural resources (Conservation and development) N: 64-65
Nixon, Richard Milhous (The national scene) N: 433-434
Oil spill (Responses) O: 707-708
Environmental Quality, Council on
President of the United States (The executive branch) P: 764
Environmental racism
Racism (Types of racism) R: 62
Environmental scientist
Careers (Life, physical, and social sciences) C: 225-226
Environmentalist *See* Conservationist *in this index*
Envoi
Ballade B: 43
Envoy [diplomat]
Treaty (Negotiation) T: 409
Envoy extraordinary [diplomat]
Diplomacy (Diplomatic representatives) D: 216
Enzyme [biology] E: 340 *with diagram*
Antiviral drug A: 560
Biochemistry (Biochemical research) B: 310
Biosynthesis B: 326
Blood (Red blood cells) B: 408
Catalysis C: 297
Cell (Growth and specialization) C: 332; (Producing proteins) C: 333
Cloning (Nuclear transfer) Ci: 682l
Digestive system D: 202
Disease (Bacterial diseases) D: 227
Food (Regulating body processes) F: 331
Fungi (How a fungus lives) F: 559
Genetics (Molecular genetics) G: 86
Heredity H: 200; (The flow of genetic information) H: 205
Human body (Chemical elements and molecules) H: 417
Nutrition (Proteins) N: 625
Protein P: 832
Reptile (Skin) R: 251
Stomach (The stomach's work) So: 908
Trace elements T: 355
Vitamin (How vitamins work) V: 432
Enzyme replacement therapy [treatment]
Gaucher's disease G: 68
Eocene Epoch [geology]
Earth (The Cenozoic Era) E: 28-29; (table) E: 30
Prehistoric animal (table) P: 740
Eohippus [extinct animal]
Horse (Origins of the horse) H: 360 *with picture*
Prehistoric animal (The development of placentals) P: 741
EOKA [organization]
Cyprus (History) Ci: 1207
E.ON [company]
Manufacturing (table) M: 170
Eon [geology]
Earth (Age of Earth) E: 26
Eoraptor [dinosaur] E: 341
Eos [Greek mythology]
Aurora A: 891 *with picture*
EOS [satellites] *See* Earth Observing System *in this index*
Eosin [dye]
Resorcinol R: 259
Eosinophil [cell]
Blood (Protecting against disease) B: 410
Immune system (Other white blood cells) I: 88
Eötvös, Loránd [Hungarian physicist]
Relativity (Principle of equivalence) R: 211-212
EPA [organization] *See* Environmental Protection Agency *in this index*
Epaminondas [Greek general]
Boeotia B: 436
Messenia M: 423
Pelopidas P: 232
Thebes T: 251
Epaphus [Greek mythology]
Io I: 370
Epcot [Florida]
Florida (Places to visit) F: 252 *with picture*
Walt Disney Company W: 20
Epee [weapon]
Fencing F: 71 *with picture*
Ephedra [herb]
Dietary supplement D: 200
Ephedrine [chemical]
Dietary supplement D: 200
Ephemeroptera [entomology]
Insect (table) I: 299
Ephesians, Epistle to the [New Testament] E: 341
Bible (The Letters) B: 284

Ephesus [ancient city] E: 341
Turkey (Tourism) T: 509 *with picture*
Ephesus, Council of [431]
Cyril of Alexandria, Saint Ci: 1208
Roman Catholic Church (Conflict with the East) R: 406
Ephialtes [Greek political leader]
Pericles P: 287
Ephod [clothing]
High priest H: 228
Ephor [official]
Greece, Ancient (Sparta) G: 372
Ephraim [Biblical figure]
Joseph (Settling his family in Egypt) J: 168
Ephrata Cloister [Pennsylvania]
Colonial life in America (Places to visit) Ci: 800 *with picture*
Pennsylvania (Places to visit) P: 254 *with picture*
Ephron, Nora [American author] E: 342
Epibatae [ancient Greece]
Marine (History) M: 204
Epibenthic sled [machine]
Deep sea (Deep-sea exploration) D: 82c
Epic [literary form] E: 342
See also the list of *Related articles in the* Epic *article*
Fiction (History) F: 90
French literature (Narrative poetry) F: 518
German literature (The Germanic epic) G: 138
Greek literature (Greek poetry) G: 377
Literature for children (Epics) L: 358
Mythology (Mythical beings) M: 975
Novel (Ancient Greek and Roman narratives) N: 572
Poetry (Narrative poetry) P: 591; (Medieval poetry) P: 596
Spanish literature (The 1400's) So: 758-759
Storytelling (Myths, epics, and legends) So: 914
Epic Center [Wichita]
Wichita (History) W: 298
Epic of Gilgamesh See Gilgamesh, Epic of *in this index*
Epic of the Wheat [novels]
Norris, Frank N: 457
Epic theater
Brecht, Bertolt B: 591
Drama (Epic theater) D: 339
Epicanthic fold [anatomy]
Races, Human (The three-race theory) R: 53
Epicardium [anatomy]
Heart (Outer lining and muscle) H: 133
Epicenter [geology]
Earthquake (How an earthquake begins) E: 35-36 *with diagram*
Epicondylitis, Lateral [disorder]
Repetitive strain injury R: 242
Epicotyl [botany]
Germination G: 173
Plant (Germination) P: 535-537 *with picture*
Seed (How seeds sprout) S: 283-283
Epictetus [Greek philosopher] E: 342
Greek literature (The Greco-Roman Age) G: 378
Epicureanism [philosophy]
Epicurus E: 342
Hedonism H: 165
Hellenistic Age H: 177
Lucretius L: 514
Philosophy (Stoic philosophy and Epicureanism) P: 387
Epicurus [Greek philosopher] E: 342
Atom (Development of the atomic theory) A: 874
Atomism A: 877
Materialism M: 300b
Philosophy (Stoic philosophy and Epicureanism) P: 387
Radiation (History) R: 80
Epicycle [astronomy]
Astronomy *diagram on* A: 847; (Earth-centered theories) A: 835
Epicyclic gear
Gear G: 75
Epidaurus [ruins, Greece] E: 342
Epidemic [medicine] E: 343
AIDS (History) A: 166-167
Centers for Disease Control and Prevention C: 351
Disease (Spread of infectious diseases) D: 228
Influenza (Flu epidemics) I: 268b
Leprosy (History) L: 205
Plague P: 506
Public health (History) P: 857
Epidemic typhus [disease]
Rickettsia R: 335
Typhus (Epidemic typhus) T: 540
Epidemiologic study [medicine]
Disease (Research) D: 234
Epidemiologist [occupation]
Careers (Life, physical, and social sciences)

C: 225-226
Epidemic E: 343
Epidemiology
Occupational medicine O: 647
Epidermis [biology]
Human body (The epidermis) H: 418
Keratin K: 305
Leaf (Obtaining the raw materials) L: 155
Plant (Leaves) P: 529-531 *with picture*
Root (The outer tissues) R: 470 *with diagrams*
Skin (Structure of the skin) S: 488 *with picture*
Stem (Herbaceous stems) So: 887
Epididymis [anatomy]
Testicle T: 182
Epidural anesthesia
Childbirth (Methods of childbirth) C: 456-457
Epigenetics [biology]
Cloning (Differences among clones) Ci: 683
Epiglottis [anatomy]
Croup Ci: 1157
Hiccup H: 223
Throat T: 270
Trachea T: 355
Epigram [poetry] E: 343
Greek literature (The Hellenistic Age) G: 378
Epigraphy [writing]
Paleography P: 102
Epilepsy [disorder] E: 343
Brain (Genetic disorders) B: 558
First aid (Convulsion and epileptic seizure) F: 140
Nervous system (Disorders of the nervous system) N: 136
Epimetheus [Greek mythology]
Pandora P: 130
Epinephrine [hormone] E: 343
See also Adrenalin *in this index*
Anaphylactic shock A: 448
Inhalant I: 271
Stress (How stress affects the body) So: 926-927
Epinikion [poetry]
Greek literature (Lyric poetry) G: 377
Epiphanes [Seleucid king] *See* Antiochus IV *in this index*
Epiphany [literary device]
Short story S: 434
Epiphany [religion] E: 344
Christianity (Forms of worship) C: 522h-523
Christmas *picture on* C: 532; (Religious practices) C: 533-534
January J: 30
Epiphragm [zoology]
Snail (Where snails live) S: 522
Epiphyseal cartilage [anatomy]
Giant G: 183
Epiphyseal growth plate [anatomy]
Bone (Development of bones) B: 456 *with diagram*
Epiphysis [anatomy]
Bone (Structure of the bones) B: 456 *with diagram*
Epiphyte [botany] E: 344 *with picture*
Amazon rain forest A: 401
Bromeliad B: 636
Rain forest (Structure and growth) R: 126a
Spanish moss So: 764
Epipsychidion [poem by Shelley]
Shelley, Percy Bysshe (His writings) S: 391
Epipubic bone
Marsupial (Characteristics of marsupials) M: 232
Epirus [region]
Greece (Epirus) G: 358
Episcopal Church [religious group] E: 344
Anglican Communion A: 463
Protestantism (The conservative reform movements) P: 834
Roman Catholic Church (The church today) R: 412-413
Episiotomy [surgery]
Childbirth (Methods of childbirth) C: 456-457
Episode
Drama (Tragedy) D: 326
Fugue F: 553
Episodic tremor and slip earthquake
Earthquake (Why a quake begins) E: 36
Episodios nacionales [book by Galdós]
Spanish literature (The 1800's) So: 761-762
Epistaxis [disorder]
Nosebleed N: 549
Epistemology
Philosophy (Epistemology) P: 384
Epistle [literature] E: 344
Epistle of James [New Testament] *See* James, Epistle of *in this index*
"Epistle to Doctor Arbuthnot, An" [poem by Pope]
Pope, Alexander P: 667
Epistle to Philemon [New Testament] *See*

Philemon, Epistle to *in this index*
Epistle to the Clergy of the Southern States [pamphlet by Grimké]
Grimké (Sarah Moore Grimké) G: 394
Epistle to the Ephesians [New Testament] *See* Ephesians, Epistle to the *in this index*
Epistle to the Galatians [New Testament] *See* Galatians, Epistle to the *in this index*
Epistle to the Hebrews [New Testament] *See* Hebrews, Epistle to the *in this index*
Epistle to the Philippians [New Testament] *See* Philippians, Epistle to the *in this index*
Epistle to the Romans [book by Barth]
Barth, Karl B: 120
Epistle to the Romans [New Testament] *See* Romans, Epistle to the *in this index*
Epistles [book by Horace]
E Pluribus Unum E: 3
Horace H: 334
Latin literature (The Augustan Age) L: 116
Epistles [New Testament]
Bible (table) B: 281; (The Letters) B: 284
New Testament (Letters) N: 287; (Authorship) N: 288
Epistles of Paul [New Testament] *See* Paul, Epistles of *in this index*
Epistles of Peter [New Testament] *See* Peter, Epistles of *in this index*
Epistles to the Corinthians [New Testament] *See* Corinthians, Epistles to the *in this index*
Epistles to the Thessalonians [New Testament] *See* Thessalonians, Epistles to the *in this index*
Epistolary novel [literature]
Epistle E: 344
Epitaph of a Small Winner [book by Machado de Assis]
Latin American literature (Realism) L: 113
Epithalamion [poem by Spenser]
Spenser, Edmund (Spenser's other poems) So: 778
Epithelial tissue [anatomy]
Cancer (Classification by tissue) C: 168-169
Human body (Cells and tissues) H: 417-418
Epithelioma [disorder] E: 345
Epithelium [anatomy] E: 345
Biopsy B: 326
Cervical cancer C: 364
Epithelioma E: 345
Tissue (Animal tissues) T: 298
Epizeuxis [language]
Shakespeare, William (Rhetoric) S: 368
Epizootic [disease]
Veterinary medicine (On farms and ranches) V: 345
EPLF [political party] *See* Eritrean People's Liberation Front *in this index*
EPO [hormone] *See* Erythropoietin *in this index*
Epoch [geology]
Earth (Age of Earth) E: 26
Prehistoric animal (The world of prehistoric animals) P: 736
Epode [poetry]
Ode O: 673
Poetry (Lyric poetry) P: 591
Epodes [poems by Horace]
Horace H: 334
Epoetin alfa [drug]
Anemia (Anemia of renal disease) A: 458
EPOXI [spacecraft]
Comet (Studying comets) Ci: 868-869
Space exploration (Probes to comets) So: 711
Epoxy [plastic]
Adhesive A: 56
Plastics (table) P: 556; (Growth of the plastics industry) P: 560
Epps, Meave Gillian [British-born zoologist] *See* Leakey, Meave Gillian *in this index*
EPR paper [physics]
Einstein, Albert (Further scientific work) E: 146b
Epsilon [letter]
E E: 1 *with picture*
Epsilon Lyrae [star]
Lyra L: 537
Epsom Derby [race]
Derby D: 152
Horse racing (Types of horse races) H: 364
Epsom salt [medication] E: 345
Laxative L: 148
Epstein, Brian [British businessman]
Beatles B: 190
Epstein, Sir Jacob [British sculptor] E: 345
Epstein-Barr virus E: 345
Mononucleosis M: 731
Virus (Infection) V: 428-428a
Equal area projection [map]
Map (The Mollweide projection) M: 183 *with diagram*

Equal-arm balance
Scale, Weighing (Balances) S: 169
Equal Credit Opportunity Act [1974]
Bank (Changes in banking laws) B: 94
Women's movement (Legal gains) W: 386
Equal Employment Opportunity Act [1972]
Equal Employment Opportunity Commission E: 345
Equal Employment Opportunity Commission [U.S.] E: 345
Americans with Disabilities Act A: 431
Civil Rights Act of 1964 Ci: 611
Thomas, Clarence T: 261
Equal Pay Act [1963]
Fair Labor Standards Act F: 8
Sex discrimination (Changes in laws) S: 335
Women's movement (Legal gains) W: 386
Equal protection of the laws
Constitution of the United States (Amendment 14) Ci: 1013
Freedom (Social freedom) F: 501
Equal Rights Amendment E: 345
Civil rights (The struggle for women's rights) Ci: 609
National Organization for Women N: 42
Paul, Alice P: 200
Schlafly, Phyllis Stewart S: 177
Sex discrimination (Changes in laws) S: 335
Women's movement (Legal gains) W: 386
Equal rights feminists
Women's movement (The beginnings of women's movements) W: 384-385
Equal Rights Party [U.S. history]
Lockwood, Belva Ann Bennett L: 413
Equal set [mathematics]
Set theory (Kinds of sets) S: 321 *with diagram*
Equality [law]
Democracy D: 120
Liberalism L: 227
Equality League of Self-Supporting Women
Blatch, Harriot Eaton Stanton B: 398
Equality State [name for]
Wyoming W: 517
Equals sign
Addition (Writing addition) A: 49
Equant [astronomy]
Astronomy *diagram on* A: 847
Equation
Algebra (Statements and equations) A: 351
Geometry (Analytic geometry) G: 105-106
Mathematics M: 302
Equator [geography] E: 346 *with maps*
Earth (Earth's size and shape) E: 18
Ecuador E: 67
Latitude L: 117 *with diagram*
Magnetic equator M: 55 *with map*
Map (Geographic grids) M: 179 *with diagram*
Rain (Rainfall distribution) R: 124
Weather (Planetary-scale systems) W: 158-159
Equatorial Countercurrent
Atlantic Ocean (Moving ocean waters) A: 866
Equatorial electrojet [electricity]
Magnetic equator M: 55
Equatorial Guinea E: 346 *with map*
Flag *picture on* F: 198
Guinea G: 429
Equatorial Islands *See* Line Islands *in this index*
Equatorial jet [wind]
Jet stream J: 115 *with map*
Equatorial mount [astronomy]
Telescope (Controlling a telescope) T: 105
Equatorial Star, Order of the [Gabon]
Medals, decorations, and orders (table) M: 359
Equestrian order [ancient Rome] E: 347
Equestrian sports
See also Horseback riding *in this index*
Circus (The birth of the circus) Ci: 562b
Horse (Horse shows and sports) H: 356 *with pictures*
Olympic Games (Summer Olympic Games) O: 746e-746f
Equiangular polygon [geometry]
Polygon P: 650 *with diagram*
Equiano, Olaudiah [British abolitionist]
Abolition movement A: 12
Equilateral polygon [geometry]
Polygon P: 650 *with diagram*
Equilateral triangle
Triangle (Kinds of triangles) T: 437 *with diagram*
Equilibrium [physics]
Fahrenheit scale F: 6
Force (Concurrent forces) F: 370
Gravity, Center of G: 334
Lever (Law of equilibrium) L: 217
Statics So: 867
Equilibrium, Chemical [chemistry] E: 347
Equilibrium, Law of [physics]

Lever (Law of equilibrium) **L:** 217
Equilibrium price [economics]
Economics (The free market) **E:** 59
Price (Demand and supply) **P:** 774
Supply and demand **So:** 996
Equilibrium theory, General [economics] *See*
General equilibrium theory *in this index*
Equilibrium tide [geology]
Tide (The equilibrium tide) **T:** 280 *with diagrams*
Equinoctial year
Year **Y:** 554
Equinox [astronomy] **E:** 348 *with diagram*
Hipparchus **H:** 239
March **M:** 194
Season (The four seasons) **S:** 270-271
September **S:** 308
Equitation competition
Horse (Horse shows) **H:** 356
Equites [ancient Rome]
Equestrian order **E:** 347
Rome, Ancient (The people) **R:** 437
Equity [bookkeeping]
Bookkeeping (Double-entry bookkeeping) **B:** 472
Equity [law] **E:** 348
Common law **Ci:** 875
Mortgage **M:** 820
Taxation (Equity) **T:** 54
Trial (History) **T:** 437
Equity, Court of [law]
Equity **E:** 348
Equity account
Bookkeeping (Accounts) **B:** 472
Equivalence [topology]
Topology (Invariance and equivalence) **T:** 332
with picture
Equivalence, Principle of [physics]
Gravitation (The principle of equivalence) **G:** 332
Relativity (Principle of equivalence) **R:** 211
Equivalent dose [radiology]
Radiation (Dose) **R:** 79-80
Equivalent fraction [mathematics]
Fraction (Equivalent fractions) **F:** 446 *with
diagrams*
Equivalent projection [cartography] *See* Equal
area projection *in this index*
Equivalent sets [mathematics]
Set theory (Kinds of sets) **S:** 321
Equus [animal]
Horse (Origins of the horse) **H:** 360
Equus [play by Shaffer]
Shaffer, Peter **S:** 342
ER [medicine] *See* Emergency room *in this index*
Er [symbol]
Erbium **E:** 349
ERA [baseball]
Baseball (Baseball terms) **B:** 124
Era [time]
Earth (Age of Earth) **E:** 26
Prehistoric animal (The world of prehistoric
animals) **P:** 736
Era of Good Feeling [U.S. history]
Madison, James (The growth of nationalism)
M: 36
Monroe, James (Monroe's administration) **M:** 736
United States, History of the (The Era of Good
Feeling) **U:** 165
Eragon [book by Paolini]
Paolini, Christopher **P:** 132
Érard, Sébastien [French piano maker]
Piano (History) **P:** 447-448
Eraser E: 349
Rubber (First uses) **R:** 500-501
Erasmus, Desiderius [Dutch philosopher] **E:** 349
Etiquette (Books on etiquette) **E:** 375
Holbein, Hans, the Younger **H:** 289
Humanism (The spread of humanism) **H:** 431
Luther, Martin (Reformation leader) **L:** 528
Renaissance (Desiderius Erasmus and Saint
Thomas More) **R:** 238 *with picture*
Spanish literature (The 1500's) **So:** 758
Zwingli, Huldreich (His life) **Z:** 610
Erato [Greek mythology]
Muses **M:** 937
Eratosthenes [Greek mathematician] **E:** 349
Geography (Early study) **G:** 95
Map (Ancient maps) **M:** 182-183
Physics (The Greeks) **P:** 438
Sieve of Eratosthenes **S:** 452
Erbakan, Necmettin [Turkish political leader]
Turkey (Political changes) **T:** 512
Erbe, Norman A. [American political leader]
Iowa (table) **I:** 391
Erbium [element] **E:** 349
Ercilla y Zúñiga, Alonso de [Spanish poet]
Chile (The arts) **C:** 463
Latin American literature (Colonial literature)
L: 112

Spanish literature (The 1500's) **So:** 758-759
ERDA [agency] *See* Energy Research and
Development Administration *in this index*
Erdogan, Recep Tayyip [Turkish political leader]
Turkey (Recent developments) **T:** 512
Erdrich, Louise [American author]
Indian, American (Achievements in the arts)
I: 181
Literature for children *picture on* **L:** 360
Erebus [ship]
Exploration (The exploration of Antarctica) **E:** 450
Erebus, Mount *See* Mount Erebus *in this index*
Erec and Enide [poem by Chrétien de Troyes]
Hartmann von Aue **H:** 79
Erechtheum [ruins, Athens]
Acropolis **A:** 29
Athens (The Acropolis and its buildings) **A:** 856
Erectile dysfunction [disorder] **E:** 349
Erection [physiology]
Erectile dysfunction **E:** 349
Reproduction, Human (The human reproductive
system) **R:** 244-246
Eremetical religious life
Religious life (The Eastern Orthodox Churches)
R: 227
Erevan [Armenia] *See* Yerevan *in this index*
Erewhon [book by Butler]
Utopia **U:** 252
Erg [geography]
Desert (Desert climate and land) **D:** 155-156
Sahara (Land and climate) **S:** 20-21
Ergogenic aid [sports]
Blood doping **B:** 416
Ergonomic keyboard
Keyboard **K:** 309
Ergonomics [science] **E:** 350
Disease (Environmental and occupational
diseases) **D:** 230
Repetitive strain injury **R:** 242
Ergonovine [medication]
Ergot **E:** 350
Ergot [fungus] **E:** 350
Migraine **M:** 538
Plant (Diseases) **P:** 539-540
Rye (Ergot) **R:** 574
Ergotamine [medication]
Ergot **E:** 350
Ergotism [disease]
Ergot **E:** 350
Plant (Diseases) **P:** 539-540
Rye (Ergot) **R:** 574
Ergotoxine [medication]
Ergot **E:** 350
Erhard, Ludwig [German political leader]
Germany (West Germany) **G:** 170
Eric the Red [Viking explorer] *See* Erik the Red *in
this index*
Erickson, Arthur Charles [Canadian architect]
E: 350
Architecture *picture on* **A:** 607
Canada (Architecture) **C:** 112
Erickson, Hattie [American farmer]
Western frontier life in America (Hardships and
challenges) **W:** 239
Erickson, John E. [American political leader]
Montana (table) **M:** 757
Erickson, Milton H. [American scientist]
Hypnosis (Scientific studies) **H:** 480
Ericson, Leif [Norse explorer] *See* Leif Eriksson *in
this index*
Ericsson, John [Swedish-American engineer]
E: 350
Monitor and *Merrimack* **M:** 724
Propeller **P:** 826
Ship (The first propeller-driven ships) **S:** 425
Erie [Pennsylvania] **E:** 350
Erie, Lake *See* Lake Erie *in this index*
Erie Canal [waterway, New York] **E:** 351 *with map*
Buffalo (History) **B:** 678-679
Canal (table) **C:** 164; (History) **C:** 164-165
Cement and concrete (History) **C:** 345
Hudson River **H:** 406
Michigan (Territorial period) **M:** 509
New York (Waterways) **N:** 311; (Growing
prosperity) **N:** 316 *with picture*
New York State Canal System **N:** 345 *with map*
Pioneer life in America (Crossing the
Appalachians) **P:** 477-478
Rochester (Government and history) **R:** 370
Saint Lawrence Seaway (Early canals) **S:** 44
Transportation (Development of inland
transport) **T:** 388-389
United States, History of the (The American
System) **U:** 165-166
Westward movement in America (The Old
Northwest) **W:** 247-248
Erie Railroad

Gould, Jay **G:** 280
Railroad (Expansion in the United States) **R:** 115
Erigeron [medication]
Fleabane **F:** 232
Erik Chronicle [epic]
Sweden (Literature) **So:** 1026
Erik Dorn [book by Hecht]
Hecht, Ben **H:** 164
Erik the Red [Norse explorer] **E:** 351
Arctic (Arctic exploration) **A:** 638
Exploration (Viking exploration) **E:** 442
Greenland (History) **G:** 385
Iceland (Early days) **I:** 23
Norway (The Viking period) **N:** 545
Vikings (The Norwegian Vikings) **V:** 382
Erikson, Erik Homburger [American
psychoanalyst] **E:** 351
Erikson, T. A. (Dad) [American educator]
4-H (The first 4-H program) **F:** 436
Eriksson, Leif [Norse explorer] *See* Leif Eriksson *in
this index*
Erin *See* Ireland *in this index*
Erinaceomorph [mammal]
Mammal (table) **M:** 128 *with picture*
Erinyes [Greek mythology] *See* Furies *in this index*
Eris [astronomy] **E:** 352
Kuiper belt **K:** 392
Planet (The outer dwarf planets) **P:** 512
Eris [Greek mythology]
Trojan War (The beginning of the war) **T:** 449
Eritrea E: 352 *with picture and map*
Ethiopia (Haile Selassie) **E:** 371; (Military take-
over) **E:** 372 *with picture*
Flag *picture on* **F:** 198
Eritrean Liberation Front [political movement]
Eritrea (History) **E:** 353-354
Eritrean People's Liberation Front [political party]
Eritrea (History) **E:** 353-354
Erlach, Johann Bernhard Fischer von [Austrian
architect] *See* Fischer von Erlach, Johann
Bernhard *in this index*
Erlanger, Joseph [American physiologist]
Nobel Prizes (Physiology or medicine: 1944)
N: 445
Ermine [animal] **E:** 354
Fur (table) **F:** 561
Heraldry *picture on* **H:** 195
Weasel **W:** 155
Ernaux, Annie [French author]
French literature (Recent French literature) **F:** 523
Ernest Augustus [duke of Brunswick]
Brunswick **B:** 652
Ernst, Max [German painter] **E:** 354
Painting (Europeans in America) **P:** 84
Surrealism **So:** 1010 *with picture*
Ernst, Richard Robert [Swiss chemist]
Nobel Prizes (Chemistry: 1991) **N:** 444
Ernst-Reuter-Platz [landmark]
Berlin (Downtown Berlin) **B:** 260-261
Erofeev, Venedikt [Russian author]
Russian literature (Modern Soviet literature)
R: 564-565
Erofeev, Viktor [Russian author]
Russian literature (Modern Russian literature)
R: 565
Eroica [music by Beethoven]
Beethoven, Ludwig van (The second period)
B: 214
Eros [asteroid] **E:** 354
Eros [Greek mythology] *See* Cupid *in this index*
Erosion [geology] **E:** 355
Conservation (Soil conservation) **Ci:** 976-979
Dam (The effects of dams) **D:** 17
Desert (How deserts develop and change)
D: 156-157
Dust storm **D:** 392
Earth *picture on* **E:** 22; (Sedimentary rocks) **E:** 21
Farm and farming (Soil management) **F:** 33
Geomorphology **G:** 106a
Glacier (How glaciers shape the land) **G:** 203
Gold (Types of deposits) **G:** 252
Grass **G:** 324
Humus **H:** 437
Landform **L:** 58
Lyell, Sir Charles **L:** 533
Mountain (Forces that shape mountains) **M:** 894
with diagram
Soil (Soil conservation) **So:** 576
Water (How water shapes Earth) **W:** 121
Erosion-corrosion [process]
Corrosion **Ci:** 1072
Erosion mountain [geology]
Mountain (Erosion mountains) **M:** 894
Erotocritos [poem by Cornaros]
Greek literature (Modern Greek literature) **G:** 378
Erratic [rock]
Earth *picture on* **E:** 29

Erromango [island, Vanuatu]
Vanuatu V: 284
Error [sports]
Baseball (Reaching base) B: 129
Bowling (Scoring) B: 521-522
Error correction [information theory]
Information theory I: 269
Error signal
Servomechanism S: 320
Ershad, H. M. [Bangladeshi political leader]
Bangladesh (The new nation) B: 86
Ertegun, Ahmet [American recording executive]
Rock music (Soul music) R: 380a
Ertl, Gerhard [German chemist]
Nobel Prizes (Chemistry: 2007) N: 444
Erudite and Interesting Letters [book by Feijoo]
Spanish literature (The 1700's) So: 760
Eruption [anatomy]
Teeth (Deciduous teeth) T: 79
Eruption [geology]
Mount Saint Helens M: 888 *with picture*
Volcano V: 438 *with pictures*
Eruption column [geology]
Volcano (The violence of an eruption) V: 439
Ervin, Sam J., Jr. [American government official]
Watergate (The break-in and cover-up) W: 144
Erving, Julius [American basketball player] E: 355
Basketball *picture on* B: 154a
Erymanthus, Boar of [Greek mythology]
Hercules (The twelve labors) H: 198-199
Eryops [extinct animal] E: 355
Prehistoric animal *picture on* P: 738; (The move onto land) P: 737
Erysipelas [disease] E: 355
Erythema [disorder] E: 356
Erythroblastosis fetalis [disorder]
Rh factor R: 290
Erythrocyte [biology] *See* Red blood cell *in this index*
Erythrolabe [anatomy]
Eye (The retina) E: 462
Erythromycin [medication] E: 356
Whooping cough (Treatment and prevention) W: 296
Erythropoietin [hormone]
Anemia (Anemia of renal disease) A: 458
Blood (How the body maintains its blood supply) B: 410-411
Blood doping B: 415
Cancer (Biological response modifiers) C: 172-173
Kidney (Other functions of the kidneys) K: 312
Erzberg [mountain, Austria]
Austria (Natural resources) A: 935
Es [symbol]
Einsteinium E: 147
ESA [organization] *See* European Space Agency *in this index*
Esaki, Leo [Japanese physicist]
Nobel Prizes (Physics: 1973) N: 441
Esarhaddon [king of Assyria]
Assyria (History) A: 822
Babylon (The Old Babylonian period) B: 11-12
Esau [Biblical figure] E: 356
Edom E: 85
Hittites (History) H: 269-270
Isaac I: 461
Jacob J: 19
Escalante, Silvestre Velez de [Spanish religious leader]
Utah (Early exploration) U: 246
Escalante Desert
Utah (Deserts) U: 242 *with map*
Escalator [machine] E: 356 *with diagrams*
Conveyor belt (Uses) Ci: 1024
New York (Interesting facts) N: 291
Escalator clause
Labor movement (Arranging contracts) L: 4-5
Escales [music by Ibert]
Ibert, Jacques I: 3
Escamillo [opera character]
Opera: (Carmen) O: 802 *with picture*
Escanaba [Michigan]
Michigan (table: Average monthly weather) M: 502
Escape [books by Bromfield]
Bromfield, Louis B: 636
Escape [wrestling]
Wrestling *picture on* W: 506
Escape from Freedom [book by Fromm]
Fromm, Erich F: 541
Escape velocity
Orbit O: 819
Escape wheel
Clock (Mechanical clocks) Ci: 682j
Watch (Mechanical watches) W: 114
Escapement [conservation]

Salmon (Salmon conservation) S: 70
Escapement [device]
Clock (Mechanical clocks) Ci: 682j *with diagram*
Pendulum (Clock pendulums) P: 237
Watch (Mechanical watches) W: 114
Escargot [food]
Snail (Snails and people) S: 523
Escarole [plant]
Endive E: 272 *with picture*
Esch-Cummins Act [1920]
Railroad (Regulation and control of U.S. railroads) R: 118
Eschatological Messiah [Judaism]
Messiah M: 423
Eschatology [geology]
Mythology (The end of the world) M: 987
Escheat [law]
Feudalism (The principles of feudalism) F: 82
Heir H: 167
Will W: 307
Eschenbach, Wolfram von [German poet] *See* Wolfram von Eschenbach *in this index*
Escher, M. C. [Dutch artist] E: 357 *with picture*
Escherichia coli [bacteria] *See* E. coli *in this index*
Escobar, Marisol [American sculptor] *See* Marisol *in this index*
Escobedo, Danny [American public figure]
Escobedo v. Illinois E: 357
Escobedo v. Illinois [U.S. history] E: 357
See also Miranda v. Arizona *in this index*
Escorial [Spain] E: 357
Architecture (Later Renaissance architecture) A: 621
Spain (Architecture) So: 738
Escrima [sport]
Martial arts (Martial arts in other countries) M: 234a
Escutcheon
Heraldry (Elements of a coat of arms) H: 196 *with pictures*
Esdaile, James [British doctor]
Hypnosis (Scientific studies) H: 480
Esdraelon, Plain of [region, Israel]
Israel (The Coastal Plain) I: 482
Esdras [Bible]
Bible (The Christian Old Testament) B: 282
ESEA [law] *See* Elementary and Secondary Education Act *in this index*
Esfahan *See* Isfahan *in this index*
Eshkol, Levi [Israeli political leader] E: 357
Esker [geology]
Glacier (How glaciers shape the land) G: 203-204 *with diagram*
Eskie [dog] *See* American Eskimo dog *in this index*
Eskimo [people] *See* Inuit *in this index*
Eskimo curlew [bird]
Curlew Ci: 1195
Eskimo dog *See* American Eskimo dog *in this index*
Esophagus [anatomy] E: 357
Acid reflux A: 27
AIDS (Opportunistic illness) A: 164a
Alimentary canal A: 368 *with diagram*
Heartburn H: 147
Human body (The mouth, esophagus, and stomach) H: 419; (table) H: 422 *with diagram*
Mouth M: 903 *with diagram*
Stomach S: 907 *with diagram*
Throat T: 270
Esoteric writings
Aristotle (Aristotle's writings) A: 663
ESP [mental power] *See* Extrasensory perception *in this index*
España *See* Spain *in this index*
Esparto [plant]
Atlas Mountains A: 869
Espectador, El [newspaper]
Colombia (Transportation and communication) Ci: 783
Espenschied, Lloyd [American engineer]
Cable (Telephone cables) C: 6
Coaxial cable (History) Ci: 740
Esperanto [language] E: 358
Esperpento [literature]
Spanish literature (The Generation of 1898) So: 762
Espinel, Vicente [Spanish author]
Spanish literature (The 1600's) So: 759
Espionage E: 358
War (Information and intelligence) W: 24
World War II (Spies and saboteurs) W: 494
Espionage Act [1917]
Flynn, Elizabeth Gurley F: 313
Schenck v. United States S: 174
Sedition S: 280
Espiritu Santo [island, Vanuatu]
Vanuatu V: 284
Espoo [Finland]

Tapiola T: 41
Esposito, Phil [Canadian hockey player] E: 358
Esposito, Raffaele [Italian baker]
Pizza P: 505
Esposizione Universale di Roma [world's fair]
Rome (Period of construction) R: 435 *with picture*
Exposure mode [photography]
Photography (Exposure meters) P: 413
Espressivo
Music (table) M: 954
Espronceda, José de [Spanish poet]
Spanish literature (The 1800's) So: 761
Espy, Mike [American government official] E: 358
Esquiline Hill
Rome R: 429
Esquivel, Laura [Mexican author]
Latin America (Motion pictures) L: 101
Latin American literature (The post-Boom) L: 114
Esquivel, Manuel [Belize political leader]
Belize (History) B: 238
ESRO [alliance]
European Space Agency E: 418
Essais [book by Montaigne]
Essay (Personal essays) E: 359
Essay [literature] E: 359
American literature (Essays) A: 426
Composition Ci: 905
English literature (Addison and Steele) E: 318
French literature (Michel de Montaigne) F: 520
Essay Concerning Human Understanding, An [book by Locke]
Locke, John (His philosophy) L: 413
Philosophy (Empiricism) P: 389
Essay of Dramatic Poesy, An [essay by Dryden]
Dryden, John D: 370
Essay on Criticism, An [poem by Pope]
Poetry (Stress meters) P: 593-594
Pope, Alexander P: 667
Essay on General Grammar [book by Proudhon]
Proudhon, Pierre Joseph P: 838
Essay on Man, An [poem by Pope]
English literature (Swift and Pope) E: 318
Pope, Alexander P: 667
Essay on the Principle of Population [book by Malthus]
Birth control (The birth control movement) B: 378
Malthus, Thomas Robert M: 115
Essay Towards the Present and Future Peace of Europe [book by Penn]
Peace (From the 1400's to the 1700's) P: 206
Penn, William (Arrested again) P: 242
Essays [book by Emerson]
Emerson, Ralph Waldo (His prose works) E: 259
Essays in Criticism [book by Arnold]
Arnold, Matthew A: 742
Essays of Elia [book by Lamb]
Lamb, Charles (His essays) L: 50
Essays on the Generation of Animals [book by Harvey]
Harvey, William H: 81
Essen [Germany] E: 359
Essence [chemistry]
Extract E: 457
Oil (Volatile oils) O: 707
Perfume P: 286
Essence [magazine]
Parks, Gordon P: 171
Essence [philosophy]
Santayana, George S: 115
Essence d'orient [animal product]
Pearl (Imitation pearls) P: 218
Essence of Christianity, The [book by Feuerbach]
Feuerbach, Ludwig Andreas F: 83
Essenes [religious group] E: 359
Dead Sea Scrolls D: 56
Jews (The Hellenistic period) J: 121-122
Library (Ancient libraries of animal skin) L: 258-259
Essential amino acid
Nutrition (Proteins) N: 625
Protein (The structure of proteins) P: 832
Essential fatty acid
Fat (Biological and nutritional importance) F: 52-53
Milk (Fats) M: 546
Essential hypertension [disorder]
Blood pressure B: 416
Hypertension (Causes) H: 476
Essential oil [botany]
Oil (Volatile oils) O: 707
Perfume (Plant substances) P: 286
Essequibo [river]
Guyana (Land) G: 446 *with map*
Essex [ship]
Porter, David P: 682
Essex, Earl of [English nobleman [1566-1601]]

Elizabeth I (Later years) E: 239
Essex Steam Train and Riverboat
Connecticut (Places to visit) Ci: 960
Essex Transcript [newspaper]
Liberty Party L: 233
Essien-Udom, E. U. [Nigerian anthropologist]
Anthropology (The middle and late 1900's)
A: 549
Established Church See Church of England *in this index*
Established church [U.S. history]
Colonial life in America (Religion) Ci: 804
Establishment, The
Power (Systems of power) P: 727-728
Estaing, Comte d' [French admiral]
Revolution, American (Stalemate in the North)
R: 283; (Savannah and Charleston) R: 284-285
Estancia [ranch]
Argentina (Rural life) A: 650
Uruguay (Way of life) U: 223-224
Estate [law] E: 359
Executor E: 436
Estate by curtesy [law]
Dower D: 316
Estate plan [law]
Will (Estate plan) W: 307
Estate tax
Estate E: 359
Inheritance tax I: 271
Taxation (Other taxes) T: 54
Estates-General [French history] E: 360
Philip IV P: 370
Estéban [Moorish explorer] See Estevanico *in this index*
Estébanez Calderón, Serafín [Spanish author]
Spanish literature (The 1800's) So: 761-762
Ester [chemistry] E: 360
Methanol M: 434
Esterhazy von Galantha, Nikolaus Joseph [Austrian nobleman]
Haydn, Joseph H: 117
Estes, Eleanor [American author]
Newbery Medal (table) N: 359
Estevanico [Moroccan explorer] E: 360
African Americans (The years of slavery) A: 136d
Cíbola, Seven Cities of Ci: 551
Esther [Biblical figure]
Esther, Book of E: 360
Purim P: 909
Esther, Additions to the Book of [Bible]
Bible (The Christian Old Testament) B: 282
Esther, Book of [Bible] E: 360
Bible (The Writings) B: 281-282
Esthetic dentistry
Dentistry D: 143
Esthetics See Aesthetics *in this index*
Estienne family [French history]
Book (The spread of printed books) B: 467
Estimate, Board of
New York City (Government) N: 339-340
Estimated tax
Income tax (Paying the individual income tax)
I: 104
Estimating [mathematics]
Addition (Estimating) A: 51
Subtraction (How to borrow) So: 947
Estivation [zoology] E: 361
Bat (Hibernation and migration) B: 160-161
Fish (How fish rest) F: 166-167
Hibernation (Other kinds of dormancy) H: 222
Lungfish L: 525
Mammal (Hibernation) M: 125-126
Reptile (Hibernation) R: 252
Snail (Where snails live) S: 522
Snake (Regulation of body temperature) S: 530
Toad (The life of a toad) T: 304
Estonia E: 361 *with pictures and map*
Environmental pollution *picture on* E: 330
Flag *picture on* F: 206
Tallinn T: 21
Union of Soviet Socialist Republics (World War II)
U: 37; (Threats to unity) U: 40-41
World War II (The invasion of the Soviet Union)
W: 477
Estonia [ship]
Shipwreck (table: Major shipwrecks) S: 428
Estournelles de Constant, Paul Henri d' [French statesman]
Nobel Prizes (Peace: 1909) N: 448
Estrada, Joseph Ejercito [Filipino political leader]
Philippines (Recent developments) P: 380-381
Estrada Palma, Tomás [Cuban political leader]
Cuba (The Platt Amendment) Ci: 1177
Estradiol [hormone]
Estrogen E: 363
Estrangement [psychology] See Alienation *in this index*

Estrela [mountain]
Portugal (Land regions) P: 690
Estrogen [hormone] E: 363
Adolescent (Physical development) A: 60-61
Breast cancer B: 591
DES D: 153
Hormone (Growth and sex hormones) H: 336
Hormone replacement therapy H: 338
Menopause M: 402
Menstruation (The menstrual cycle) M: 404
Osteoporosis (Causes) O: 867-868
Ovary O: 881
Pregnancy (How pregnancy affects women)
P: 734b
Steroid (The sex steroids) So: 894
Tamoxifen T: 23
Estrogen receptor [protein]
Tamoxifen T: 23
Estrous cycle [reproduction] E: 363
Mammal (Mating) M: 122
Estrus [reproduction]
Cat (Reproduction) C: 293
Dog (Social and moral responsibilities) D: 279
Estrous cycle E: 363
Estuary [geography] E: 364
River (Estuaries) R: 352 *with diagram*
E.T. The Extra-Terrestrial [electronic game]
Electronic game (The rise and fall of Atari)
E: 204d
E.T.: The Extra-Terrestrial [film]
Motion picture *picture on* M: 847; (A new generation of filmmakers) M: 871
Eta [letter]
H H: 1 *with picture*
ETA [political group]
Basques B: 156
Bilbao B: 300
Spain (Growth and discontent) So: 751; (Recent developments) So: 751-752 *with picture*
"État c'est moi, L'" [quotation]
Louis XIV L: 474
États Belgiques Unis [Belgian history]
Belgium (The Brabant Revolution) B: 233
Etch [finish]
Aluminum (Chemical finishes) A: 396
Etchemin Indians
Maine (Early days) M: 89
Etching [art] E: 364 *with pictures*
Glass (Etching) G: 217
Graphic arts G: 322
Etching [electronics]
Microelectromechanical systems M: 513
Etching [printing]
Printing (Gravure cylinders) P: 800
Eteocles [literary figure]
Antigone A: 554
Eternal City [name for]
Rome R: 428
"Ethan Brand" [story by Hawthorne]
Hawthorne, Nathaniel (His stories and sketches)
H: 115
Ethane [gas] E: 364
Hydrogenation H: 470
Natural gas liquids N: 64
Ethanediol [chemical] See Ethylene glycol *in this index*
Ethanol [chemical] E: 364
Alcohol (Ethanol) A: 335
Alcoholic beverage A: 336
Automobile racing (Indy and Champ car racing)
A: 977
Biofuel B: 312
Brazil (Energy sources) B: 581 *with picture*
Distillation (Simple distillation) D: 238
Environmental pollution (Scientific efforts) E: 336
Grain (Other uses) G: 301
Ethelbald [king of England]
England (table) E: 308
Ethelbert [king of England]
Augustine of Canterbury, Saint A: 888
England (The Germanic invasions) E: 304; (table)
E: 308
Ethelred I [king of England]
England (table) E: 308
Ethelred II [king of England]
England (The Anglo-Saxon period) E: 304-305;
(table) E: 308
Vikings (The Danish Vikings) V: 383
Ethelwulf [king of England]
England (table) E: 308
Ether [chemistry] E: 365
Anesthesia (History) A: 459
Gasoline (Gasoline blends and additives)
G: 61-62
Long, Crawford Williamson L: 446
Morton, William Thomas Green M: 821
Oil O: 706

Ether [physics] E: 365
Light (Electromagnetic waves) L: 286
Lorentz, Hendrik Antoon L: 454
Physics (Developments in the 1800's) P: 440
Relativity (The Michelson-Morley experiment)
R: 210; (Special relativity) R: 210
Ethereal match
Match (Early fire-making devices) M: 300
Etherege, Sir George [English author] E: 365
Ethical and Political Science, Academy of
Institute of France I: 305
Ethics [philosophy] E: 365
Aristotle (Ethics and politics) A: 664
Business ethics B: 727
Hume, David (Hume's thought) H: 432
Kant, Immanuel (Kant's ideas) K: 244
Medical ethics M: 361
Medicine (Current issues in medicine) M: 377
Moore, G. E. M: 796
Philosophy (Ethics and political philosophy)
P: 385
Plato (Ethics) P: 568
Religion (A code of conduct) R: 217
Ethics, Congressional
Congress of the United States (Congressional ethics) Ci: 948
Ethics, The [book by Spinoza]
Spinoza, Baruch So: 795
Ethiopia E: 368 *with pictures and maps*
Bruce, James B: 647
Christmas (In Africa) C: 533 *with picture*
Clothing *picture on* Ci: 692
Eritrea E: 352
Flag *picture on* F: 198
Haile Selassie I H: 8
Italo-Ethiopian War I: 495
League of Nations (The League's greatest failure)
L: 160
Somalia (History) So: 589
World War II (Aggression on the march) W: 470-472
Ethiopian lily [plant]
Calla C: 67
Ethiopian Orthodox Church
Africa (Religions) A: 106-107 *with picture*
Christmas (In Africa) C: 533 *with picture*
Ethiopia (Religion) E: 369
Old Testament (Contents) O: 741
Ethiopian People's Democratic Revolutionary Front [political party]
Ethiopia (The late 1900's) E: 372
"Ethiopian songs" [music by Foster]
Foster, Stephen Collins F: 428
Ethmoid bone [anatomy]
Face F: 3
Nose N: 548
Ethmoid sinus [anatomy]
Sinus S: 474 *with diagram*
Ethnic area of choice
Segregation (Other segregation in the United States) S: 286
Ethnic cleansing [Balkan history]
Bosnia-Herzegovina (History) B: 492-493
Milošević, Slobodan M: 556
Ethnic dancing
Dance (Ritual ethnic dances) D: 25, D: 25 *with pictures*
Ethnic group [sociology] E: 373
See also Minority group *in this index*
Asia (People) A: 772
Culture (Culture and society) Ci: 1188
Europe *picture on* E: 387; (Ethnic groups) E: 382
Flag *pictures on* F: 218
Minority group M: 608
New York City (Ethnic groups) N: 331
Races, Human (Race and ethnic or national identity) R: 59
Segregation (Other segregation in the United States) S: 286
Stereotyping So: 893
Tribe T: 440
Ethnic pluralism See Cultural pluralism *in this index*
Ethnic stratification
Minority group (Relationships between groups)
M: 609
Ethnocentrism [anthropology] E: 373
Anthropology A: 546
Culture (Ethnocentrism and cultural relativism)
Ci: 1188
Education (Unification through education) E: 103
Mores M: 802
Sumner, William Graham So: 973
Ethnography E: 373
Culture (How people study culture) Ci: 1189
Ethnology [anthropology]
Ethnography E: 373
Ethogram [zoology]

Comparative psychology **Ci: 902a**
Ethology **E: 373**
Ethology [zoology] **E: 373**
Biology (table) **B: 317**
Lorenz, Konrad Zacharias **L: 454**
Sociobiology **So: 563**
Zoology (History) **Z: 606-607**
Ethyl alcohol [chemical] *See* Ethanol *in this index*
Ethyl cellulose [chemical]
Cellulose (Industrial uses) **C: 341**
Ethyl ether [chemical] *See* Ether [chemistry] *in this index*
Ethyl-tert-butyl ether [chemical]
Gasoline (Gasoline blends and additives) **G: 61-62**
Ethylbenzene [chemical]
Plastics (Making synthetic resins) **P: 556**
Ethylene [chemical] **E: 373**
Banana (How bananas grow) **B: 73**
Butane and propane **B: 729**
Ethanol **E: 365**
Hormone (Other growth regulators) **H: 337**
Hydrogenation **H: 470**
Polyethylene **P: 650**
Tomato (Growing, harvesting, and processing) **T: 325**
Ethylene dibromide [chemical]
Bromine **B: 636**
Ethylene glycol [chemical]
Alcohol (Ethanediol) **A: 335**
Antifreeze **A: 554**
Glycol **G: 237**
Etiquette **E: 374**
Address, Forms of **A: 53**
Letter writing **L: 209**
Post, Emily **P: 698**
Etiquette [book by Post]
Etiquette (Books on etiquette) **E: 375**
Post, Emily **P: 698**
Etna, Mount *See* Mount Etna *in this index*
Étoile, Place de l' [area, Paris]
Paris (Gardens, squares, and parks) **P: 162**
Eton College [English secondary school] **E: 375**
United Kingdom *picture on* **U: 56**
Etosha Game Park [Namibia]
Namibia (Land and climate) **N: 8**
National park (table) **N: 42f**
Etowah Indian Mounds
Georgia (Places to visit) **G: 122**
Etrog [tree]
Citron **Ci: 573**
Etruria [ancient region]
Etruscans **E: 375** *with map*
Etruscan [language]
Etruscans (Language and culture) **E: 375**
Etruscans [ancient people] **E: 375** *with picture and map*
Alphabet (The Etruscans) **A: 383** *with pictures*
Italy (End of the Roman Empire) **I: 512-513**
Painting (Etruscan painting) **P: 42**
Rome, Ancient (History) **R: 444** *with picture*
Sculpture (Etruscan sculpture) **S: 246**
Ets, Marie Hall [American artist]
Caldecott Medal (table: 1960) **C: 26**
Étude [music] **E: 376**
Etymologist [career]
Etymology **E: 376**
Etymology [language] **E: 376**
Etymon [language]
Etymology (Etymons and cognates) **E: 376**
Etzel [legendary figure]
Nibelungenlied **N: 395**
Eu [symbol]
Europium **E: 420**
Euboea [region]
Greece (Central Greece and Euboea) **G: 358**
Eucalyptus [tree] **E: 376** *with picture*
Australia *pictures on* **A: 915**; (Native plants) **A: 911**; (Forestry and fishing) **A: 918**
Eucharist [religion] *See* Communion *in this index*
Eucharist, Celebration of the *See* Mass *in this index*
Eucharistic liturgy [religion]
Roman Catholic Church (The Eucharist or Mass) **R: 404**
Eucken, Rudolf [German philosopher]
Nobel Prizes (Literature: 1908) **N: 447**
Euclid [Greek mathematician] **E: 377**
Geometry (Euclidean geometry) **G: 104**; (Greek geometry) **G: 106**
Lobachevsky, Nikolai **L: 404**
Mathematics (Branches of mathematics) **M: 303**; (The Greeks) **M: 306**
Number theory **N: 607**
Prime number (Facts about primes) **P: 780**
Radiation (History) **R: 80**
Riemann, Georg Friedrich Bernhard **R: 337**
Euclidean geometry [mathematics]

Geometry (Types of geometry) **G: 103**
Mathematics (Branches of mathematics) **M: 303**
Trigonometry **T: 442**
Euclid's algorithm [mathematics]
Algorithm **A: 366**
Euclid's fifth axiom [geometry] *See* Parallel axiom *in this index*
Eucoelomate [biology]
Coelom **Ci: 753**
Eudicotyledon [botany]
Angiosperm **A: 462**
Flower (The classifying of flowers) **F: 298**; (The evolution of flowering plants) **F: 299**; (table) **F: 300** *with pictures*
Plant *picture on* **P: 530**; (Angiosperms) **P: 520**; (Classification of plants) **P: 546-547** *with picture*
Stem *picture on* **So: 888**; (Herbaceous stems) **So: 887**
Tree (Broadleaf trees) **T: 414**
Eudoxus of Cnidus [Greek mathematician]
Mathematics (The Greeks) **M: 306**
Eugene [Oregon] **E: 377**
Eugène [play by Jodelle]
French literature (The Pléiade) **F: 519-520**
Eugene I, Saint [pope]
Pope (table) **P: 666**
Eugene II [pope]
Pope (table) **P: 666**
Eugene III [pope]
Pope (table) **P: 666**
Eugene IV [pope]
Pope (table) **P: 666**
Eugene of Savoy, Prince [Austrian prince]
Blenheim, Battle of **B: 400**
Eugene Onegin [poem by Pushkin]
Pushkin, Alexander (His works) **P: 911-912**
Russian literature (Early Romanticism) **R: 560-561**
Eugene O'Neill National Historic Site [California]
National Park System (table: National historic sites) **N: 52**
Eugenics [science] **E: 377**
Galton, Sir Francis **G: 17**
Genetic testing (Promises and challenges of genetic testing) **G: 85**
Eugenist [occupation]
Eugenics **E: 377**
Eugenius [Roman emperor]
Rome, Ancient (table) **R: 447**
Euglena [microorganism] **E: 377** *with picture*
Protozoan (Flagellates) **P: 837**
Euhedral crystal
Crystal (Crystallization) **Ci: 1166**
Euhemerus [Greek scholar]
Mythology (Allegorical approaches) **M: 988**
Eukaryota [classification]
Domain **D: 300**
Kingdom **K: 328**
Eukaryote [organism]
Archaea **A: 593**
Flagellum **F: 224**
Kingdom **K: 328**
Protist **P: 836**
Eukaryotic cell [biology]
Archaea **A: 593**
Cell (table) **C: 327**
Classification, Scientific (Groups in classification) **Ci: 655**
Domain **D: 300**
Kingdom **K: 328**
Life (Cells) **L: 277**
Prokaryote **P: 817**
Eulalius [antipope]
Pope (table) **P: 666**
Euler, Leonhard [Swiss mathematician] **E: 377**
Geometry (Solid geometry) **G: 104**
Mathematics (Developments in the 1700's) **M: 307**
Euler, Ulf Svante von [Swedish physiologist]
Nobel Prizes (Physiology or medicine: 1970) **N: 446**
Euler characteristic [mathematics]
Topology (Algebraic topology) **T: 332**
Euler-Chelpin, Hans Karl August Simon von [German chemist]
Nobel Prizes (Chemistry: 1929) **N: 443**
Euler Crater
Moon *picture on* **M: 789**
Euler's number [mathematics]
Euler, Leonhard **E: 378**
Euler's polyhedral formula [mathematics]
Geometry (Solid geometry) **G: 104**
Eulogy
Funeral customs (The funeral) **F: 557**
"Eulogy of Saint Columba, The" [poem by Forgaill]
Irish literature (Early Irish literature) **I: 430**
Eumenides [play by Aeschylus]

Furies **F: 566** *with picture*
Eunuch [person]
Zheng He **Z: 591**
Euphonium [musical instrument]
Tuba **T: 477**
Euphoria [psychiatry]
Bipolar disorder **B: 327**
Cocaine (Physical and psychological effects) **Ci: 742**
Opium (Opium addiction) **O: 811**
Euphrates River [Asia] **E: 378** *with map*
Fertile Crescent **F: 78** *with map*
Iraq (The southern plain) **I: 411** *with map*
River (table) **R: 352**
Euphrosyne [Greek mythology]
Graces **G: 296** *with picture*
Euphues: The Anatomy of Wit [book by Lyly]
Lyly, John **L: 533**
Novel (Early novels) **N: 572**
Euphuism [literature]
Lyly, John **L: 533**
Euphyllophyte [plant]
Plant (Classification of plants) **P: 546-547** *with pictures*
E.U.R. [world's fair]
Rome (Period of construction) **R: 435** *with picture*
Eurafricans [people]
Swaziland (People) **So: 1017-1018**
Eurasia [continent]
See also Asia; Europe *in this index*
Asia (The land) **A: 792**
Continent **Ci: 1021**
Europe (The land) **E: 393**
Eurasian Basin [geography]
Arctic Ocean (The deep basin) **A: 643**
Eurasian blackbird
Thrush **T: 271**
Eurasian eagle-owl [bird]
Bird of prey *picture on* **B: 374b**
Owl (Important owls) **O: 884**
Eurasian green woodpecker [bird]
Bird *picture on* **B: 344d**; (Birds of Europe) **B: 344c**
Eurasian hobby [bird]
Bird (Birds of Europe) **B: 344c** *with picture*
Eurasian lynx [animal]
Lynx **L: 536** *with picture*
Eurasian musk thistle [plant]
Invasive species (Managing invasive species) **I: 354k**
Eurasian nutcracker [bird]
Nutcracker **N: 622**
Eurasian plate [geology]
Plate tectonics (Convergent plate boundaries) **P: 562-563** *with diagram*
Eurasian red squirrel [animal]
Squirrel **So: 814b** *with picture*
Eurasian rook [bird]
Rook **R: 450c**
Eurasian sevenspotted lady beetle [insect]
Invasive species (Managing invasive species) **I: 354k**
Euratom [organization] *See* European Atomic Energy Community *in this index*
Eureka: A Prose Poem [essay by Poe]
Poe, Edgar Allan (Poe's life) **P: 589**
Eureka Springs [Arkansas]
Arkansas (Places to visit) **A: 704**; (Springs) **A: 708**
Euripides [Greek dramatist] **E: 378**
Drama (Tragedy) **D: 326-327**
Greek literature (Drama) **G: 377**
Sophocles **So: 595**
Euro [currency] **E: 378** *with pictures*
Balance of payments (Balance of payments and exchange rates) **B: 36**
Europe (Recent developments) **E: 416**
European Economic and Monetary Union **E: 417**
European Union (Internal affairs) **E: 418**; (History) **E: 420**
Germany (Political changes) **G: 171-172**
Greece (Recent developments) **G: 365**
Netherlands (Recent developments) **N: 150**
Peseta **P: 317**
Eurobank [economics]
Eurodollar **E: 379**
Eurodollar [economics] **E: 379**
Euronext Amsterdam stock exchange [building]
Architecture (Early modern architecture in Europe) **E: 627-628** *with picture*
Europa [Greek mythology] **E: 379** *with picture*
Cadmus **C: 12**
Europa [satellite] **E: 379** *with picture*
Astrobiology **A: 826**
Galileo **G: 13**
Jupiter (Galilean satellites) **J: 200a**
Life (In our solar system) **L: 280**
Satellite (Physical characteristics) **S: 149-150**
Europe **E: 380** *with pictures and maps*

See also the list of Related articles in the Europe *article*
Asia (The land) A: 792
Conservation (Europe) Ci: 989
Continent Ci: 1021
Language (Indo-European) L: 65 *with map*
Agriculture
Europe (Agriculture) E: 400
Wheat (Europe) W: 272 *with map*
Art and architecture
Europe (The arts) E: 391 *with pictures*
Painting (Medieval painting) P: 48 *with pictures*;
(The Renaissance) P: 51 *with pictures*; (The 1600's and 1700's) P: 58 *with pictures*; (The 1800's) P: 67 *with pictures*; (The 1900's in Europe) P: 77 *with pictures*
Porcelain (European porcelain) P: 677
Sculpture (The European impact) S: 244
Communications and mass media
Advertising (Advertising in other countries) A: 77
Newspaper (In Europe) N: 386
Television (In Europe) T: 117 *with picture*
Education
Library (Libraries of the world) L: 252
Finance and banking
Bank (Europe) B: 92
Health and welfare
Welfare (Welfare throughout the world) W: 191
History
Europe (History) E: 406 *with pictures and maps*
Arabs (Ottoman and European rule) A: 590;
(Relations with Europe and the United States) A: 590a
Christianity (History) C: 523-524
Classicism C: 653
Communism (European reality in the early 1900's) Ci: 890
Feudalism F: 81
Great Depression (Effects in Europe) G: 342
Immigration (Immigration to the United States)
I: 81; (Europe) I: 85
Indian, American I: 136
Industrial Revolution I: 246
Luther, Martin (Luther's place in history) L: 528
Magic (Europe) M: 50
Minority group (Other European immigrants)
M: 610
Muslims (Colonialism) M: 964d
Plague (History of plague) P: 506
Radicalism (In Europe) R: 82
Reformation R: 195
Slavery (The Middle Ages) S: 501
Tariff (Modern tariff policies) T: 44
Trade route (Early trade routes) T: 363
United States, History of the (America before colonial times) U: 149
World, History of the (Medieval Europe)
W: 432; (The spread of Western civilization)
W: 438 *with pictures and map*
Manufacturing
Europe (Manufacturing) E: 401
Automobile (Where cars are made) A: 959
Manufacturing (In Europe) M: 169
Textile (In Europe) T: 218
Natural resources
Bird (Birds of Europe) B: 344c *with pictures*
National park (table) N: 42f
People
Europe (People) E: 382 *with pictures and maps*;
(Ways of life) E: 387 *with pictures and maps*
Clothing *pictures on* Ci: 694; (Regional traditional costumes) Ci: 696; (Clothing of Europe) Ci: 700 *with pictures*
Population (World population) P: 672
Prehistoric people (Migration from Africa)
P: 747; (The origin of *Homo sapiens*) P: 748-749
Physical features
Europe (The land) E: 393 *with pictures and maps*
Continental divide Ci: 1022
Transportation
Europe (Transportation) E: 405 *with picture*
Railroad (In Europe) R: 114
Europe [ship]
Ship *picture on* S: 422
Europe, Council of [alliance] E: 417
Flag *picture on* F: 216
Switzerland (After the wars) So: 1061
Europe After the Rain [painting by Ernst]
Surrealism *picture on* So: 1010
European Aeronautic Defence and Space Company
Aviation (Aircraft manufacturing) A: 984
European Article Number code
Bar coding B: 102

European asp [snake]
Snake *picture on* S: 534
European aspen [tree]
Aspen A: 815
European Atomic Energy Community
European Union (Formation of the European Community) E: 420
Monnet, Jean M: 731
Nuclear energy (The first peaceful uses) N: 591
European Bank for Reconstruction and Development
Foreign aid (Regional development programs)
F: 385
European bark beetle [insect]
Dutch elm disease D: 392
European Baseball Federation
Baseball (Baseball around the world) B: 132
European bee-eater [bird]
Bird (Birds of Europe) B: 344c *with picture*
European bison [animal] *See* Wisent *in this index*
European bream [fish]
Bream B: 590
European Central Bank
European Union (Governing institutions) E: 419;
(Formation of the European Union) E: 420
European Coal and Steel Community [alliance]
European Union (Beginnings) E: 420
Monnet, Jean M: 731
European Commission
European Union (Governing institutions) E: 419
Prodi, Romano P: 810
European Community [alliance]
See also European Economic Community;
European Union *in this index*
Cold War (The growing strength of Europe)
Ci: 769; (The Cold War in the 1970's) Ci: 770
De Gaulle, Charles André Joseph Marie (The Fifth Republic) D: 91
Europe (Toward European unity) E: 415-416
European Free Trade Association E: 417
European Union E: 418; (Formation of the European Community) E: 420
France (France under de Gaulle) F: 476-477
Greenland (History) G: 385-386
Monnet, Jean M: 731
Norway (Social and economic changes) N: 547
United Kingdom (Economic recovery—and collapse) U: 72-73
European corn borer [insect]
Corn borer Ci: 1064
European Council
European Union (Governing institutions) E: 419
European cowslip [plant]
Cowslip Ci: 1113
European cranberry bush [plant] *See* Snowball *in this index*
European Economic and Monetary Union E: 417
European Economic Area [trade agreement]
Common market C: 875
European Economic and Monetary Union E: 418
European Economic Community [alliance]
Cold War (The shifting Cold War background)
Ci: 769
Europe (Toward European unity) E: 415
France (France under de Gaulle) F: 476-477
International relations (Treaties) I: 344
United Kingdom (European unity) U: 71-72;
(Economic recovery—and collapse) U: 72
European eel [fish]
Eel E: 114 *with picture*
Sargasso Sea (Origin of the seaweed) S: 125-126
European elk [animal]
Elk (The European elk) E: 242
European Federation for Animal Science
Dairying (Improvements in dairy farming) D: 7-8
European flea
Flea (Kinds of fleas) F: 232 *with picture*
European Free Trade Association [alliance] E: 417
Austria (International trade) A: 936
Common market C: 875
Europe (International trade) E: 402-403
Iceland (Recent developments) I: 24
European goldfinch [bird]
Bird *picture on* B: 344d; (Birds of Europe) B: 344c
Goldfinch G: 256 *with picture*
European gooseberry [fruit]
Gooseberry G: 271
European hornet [insect]
Hornet H: 340 *with picture*
European horsechestnut [tree]
Horsechestnut H: 366 *with picture*
Tree *pictures on* T: 422
European house spider
House spider H: 388
European Investment Bank
Foreign aid (Regional development programs)
F: 385

European Laboratory for Particle Physics *See* CERN *in this index*
European larch [tree]
Larch L: 75
Tree *picture on* T: 426
European mole [animal]
Mole (Kinds of moles) M: 690b
European Monetary System [economics]
European Union (Increasing cooperation) E: 420
European Organization for Nuclear Research *See* CERN *in this index*
European Parliament
European Union (The European Parliament)
E: 419
Luxembourg L: 532
European pear
Pear (Varieties) P: 215
European Plain [region, Europe]
Europe (The Great European Plain) E: 394 *with picture*
Russia (The European Plain) R: 539 *with picture*
European plan [travel]
Hotel (Kinds of hotels) H: 376
European plum
Plum (Kinds of plums) P: 577 *with picture*
European polecat
Ferret F: 76
European rabbit
Rabbit (European rabbits) R: 46
European race [theory]
Races, Human (The geographical-race theory)
R: 54
European Recovery Program *See* Marshall Plan *in this index*
European red mite [animal]
Apple (Pests and diseases) A: 572
European robin [bird]
Bird *picture on* B: 344d
Robin R: 367
Thrush T: 271
European roller [bird]
Bird (Birds of Europe) B: 344c *with picture*
European Space Agency E: 418
Hubble Space Telescope (How the telescope works) H: 403
International Space Station I: 346b
Mars (Observation by spacecraft) M: 226c-226d
Space exploration (Space probes) So: 708-710;
(Spacelab missions) So: 724; (European nations) So: 726
European Space and Research Organization
European Space Agency E: 418
European sparrowhawk [bird]
Sparrowhawk So: 765
European Union [organization] E: 418
See also European Community; European Economic Community *in this index*
Antitrust laws A: 560
Austria (International trade) A: 936
Balance of payments (Balance of payments and exchange rates) B: 36
Bosnia-Herzegovina (The Dayton peace plan)
B: 493-494
Bulgaria (Recent developments) B: 693
Cyprus (History) Ci: 1207
Denmark (The late 1900's) D: 141
Estonia (Independence regained) E: 363
Euro E: 378
Europe (International trade) E: 402; (Toward European unity) E: 415-416
European Economic and Monetary Union E: 417
Exports and imports (Export promotion) E: 454
Flag *picture on* F: 216
Foreign aid (Regional development programs)
F: 385
Foreign policy (Alliances) F: 387
France (International trade) F: 470
Germany (Economy) G: 159-160
Greece (The restoration of democracy) G: 365
Hungary (Recent developments) H: 448
Immigration (Europe) I: 85-86
International trade (Government trade policies)
I: 348-349
Italy (Economy) I: 509
Kosovo (History) K: 384b-385
Latvia (Recent developments) L: 120-121
Luxembourg L: 532
Malta (History) M: 113-114
Microsoft Corporation M: 520
Monopoly and competition (History) M: 732
Norway (Political changes) N: 547
Portugal (Foreign trade) P: 692
Poverty (Poverty standards) P: 723
Serbia (Recent developments) S: 316a
Turkey (Recent developments) T: 512
United Kingdom (Thatcher resigned) U: 73
Western European Union W: 231

European Union, Council of the
European Union (Governing institutions) E: 419
European Union, Treaty on [1992]
Europe (Toward European unity) E: 415-416 with picture
European Union (Formation of the European Union) E: 420
European viper [snake]
Adder A: 46 with picture
Reptile (Lizards and snakes) R: 250-251
European water spider
Animal picture on A: 491
Spider So: 782 with picture; (Respiratory system) So: 785
European white birch [tree]
Birch (Paper birch) B: 327
Europeans [people]
Africa (Peoples of Africa) A: 104-105
Europe E: 380; (People) E: 382
Races, Human (The geographical-race theory) R: 54-55 with map
Europium [element] E: 420
Europoort
Rotterdam R: 489
Eurotunnel Group [company]
Channel Tunnel C: 375
Eurovision [television]
Europe (Communication) E: 406
Euryale [Greek mythology]
Gorgons G: 274
Eurydice [Greek mythology] E: 420
Orpheus O: 858
Eurystheus [Greek mythology]
Hercules (The twelve labors) H: 198
Eusden, Laurence [English poet]
Poet laureate (table: Poets laureate of the United Kingdom) P: 590
Eusebius, Saint [pope]
Pope (table) P: 666
Euskadi ta Askatasuna [political group] See ETA in this index
Euskara [language]
Basques B: 156
Eusociality [biology]
Naked mole-rat N: 5
Eustachian tube [anatomy]
Cleft palate Ci: 661
Ear (The middle ear) E: 7-8 with diagram; (Diseases) E: 12
Mastoid M: 298
Eustis, William [American political leader]
Massachusetts (table) M: 288
Euterpe [Greek mythology]
Muses M: 937
Euthanasia E: 421
Death (The right to die) D: 61
Disability (The 1900's) D: 221
National Right to Life Committee N: 60
Palliative care P: 109
Euthyphro [book by Plato]
Plato (The dialogues) P: 567; (The early dialogues) P: 568; (The theory of forms) P: 568
Eutrophication [biology] E: 421
Environmental pollution (Water pollution) E: 334
Phosphorus P: 403
Water pollution diagram on W: 137; (Disruption of natural processes) W: 138
Eutychian, Saint [pope]
Pope (table) P: 666
Euwe, Max [Dutch chess player]
Chess (World chess champions) C: 414
eV [measurement] See Electronvolt in this index
"Ev and Jerry Show"
Ford, Gerald Rudolph (House minority leader) F: 375 with picture
EVA [space exploration] See Extravehicular activity in this index
Eva Luna [book by Allende]
Latin American literature (The post-Boom) L: 114
Evacuation
Civil defense (Evacuation) Ci: 605
Evangelical and Reformed Church [religious group]
United Church of Christ U: 47
Evangelical Lutheran Church [religious group]
Denmark (Religion) D: 136
Evangelical Lutheran Church in America [religious group] E: 421
Lutherans (Lutheranism in America) L: 529
Evangelical United Brethren [religious group]
United Methodist Church U: 75
Evangelicalism [religion] E: 422
Christianity (Christianity today) C: 526-527 with picture
Protestantism (The modern evangelical and Pentecostal movements) P: 835
Wilberforce, Samuel W: 300

Evangeline [poem by Longfellow]
Acadia A: 21
Grand Pré G: 309
Longfellow, Henry Wadsworth (Author and world celebrity) L: 450; (Narrative poems) L: 450
Nova Scotia N: 555
Evangeline Trail
Nova Scotia (Places to visit) N: 560
Evangelization of Peoples, Congregation for the [organization]
Missionary (Organization) M: 621
Evans, Sir Arthur John [British archaeologist] E: 422
Knossos K: 355
Evans, Billy [American umpire]
Baseball (table: Hall of Fame) B: 134
Evans, Dale [American actress]
Rogers, Roy R: 401
Evans, Daniel J. [American political leader]
Washington (table) W: 65
Evans, David [Irish musician] See Edge, The in this index
Evans, Donald L. [American government official]
Bush, George Walker (table) B: 722h
Commerce, Department of the (table) Ci: 871
Evans, Edmund [British engraver]
Caldecott, Randolph C: 25
Literature for children (The rise of illustration) L: 364
Evans, Gil [American musician]
Jazz (Cool jazz) J: 72
Evans, John V. [American political leader]
Idaho (table) I: 42
Evans, Sir Martin John [British biologist]
Nobel Prizes (Physiology or medicine: 2007) N: 447
Evans, Mary Ann See Eliot, George in this index
Evans, Melvin H. [American government official]
Virgin Islands, United States (United States rule) V: 397
Evans, Oliver [American inventor] E: 422
Automobile (The steam car) A: 965
Flour (History) F: 269
Steam engine (Modern steam engines) So: 881
Evans, Timothy [American political leader]
Chicago (Political developments in the late 1900's) C: 436-437
Evans, Walker [American photographer] E: 422
Agee, James A: 139
Photography (Dramatic changes) P: 425-426 with picture
Evans and Sutherland Corporation
Planetarium (Digital projectors) P: 514c
Evans-Pritchard, Edward Evan [British anthropologist]
Anthropology (Entering the community) A: 547
Ethnography (table) E: 373
Evanston [Illinois]
Northwestern University N: 535
Evansville [Indiana]
Indiana (Average monthly weather) I: 210
Evaporated milk
Milk (table) M: 547
Evaporating pond
Salt (Salt from the sea) S: 72-73
Evaporation [physics] E: 422 with diagrams
Heat (Changes in state) H: 153
Ocean (Composition) O: 654; (Sediments) O: 654
Vapor V: 285
Evaporator [machine]
Refrigeration (The electric refrigerator) R: 201 with diagram
Evaporator [pan]
Maple syrup (Production) M: 187-188
Evapotranspiration [botany]
Air (Moisture in the air) A: 170
Evaristus, Saint [pope]
Pope (table) P: 666
Evarts, William Maxwell [American lawyer] E: 423
Eve [Biblical figure] See Adam and Eve in this index
"Eve of Saint Agnes, The" [poem by Keats]
Keats, John (His work) K: 253
Evelina [book by Burney]
Burney, Fanny B: 709
Evelyn, John [English author]
English literature (Restoration prose) E: 318
Evening [sculpture by Michelangelo]
Michelangelo M: 486 with picture
Evening grosbeak [bird]
Grosbeak G: 398
Evening on Karl Johans Gate [painting by Munch]
Norway picture on N: 540
Evening Post [newspaper]
Bryant, William Cullen (His later career) B: 656
Evening primrose [plant] E: 423
Flower pictures on F: 286, F: 291; (table) F: 300 with picture

Evening shoe
Shoe (Kinds of shoes) S: 431
Evening star [astronomy] E: 423
Evening trumpetflower [plant] See Yellow jessamine in this index
Evenings on a Farm near Dikanka [book by Gogol]
Gogol, Nikolai G: 248
Event, The [book by Ernaux]
French literature (Recent French literature) F: 523
Event horizon [physics]
Black hole (Characteristics of black holes) B: 388
Eventing
Horse picture on H: 357; (Eventing) H: 358
Everblooming hybrid [plant]
Rose (Types of roses) R: 474
Everest, Frank K., Jr. [American aviator]
Aviation (table: Aviation speed records) A: 990
Everest, Sir George [British colonial leader]
Mount Everest M: 884
Everest, Mount See Mount Everest in this index
Everett, Edward [American political leader] E: 424
Fillmore, Millard (table) F: 102
Gettysburg Address G: 176
Lincoln, Abraham (The Gettysburg Address) L: 323
Massachusetts (table) M: 288
Everglades [region, Florida] E: 424 with map
Florida picture on F: 242; (Land regions) F: 254
Python P: 922
Everglades National Park [Florida] E: 424
Florida picture on F: 256; (Places to visit) F: 252
National Park System (table: National parks) N: 48
United States picture on U: 121
Evergreen [tree] E: 424
See also the list of Related articles in the Evergreen article
Forest picture on F: 397; (Temperate evergreen forests) F: 393; (Mountain evergreen forests) F: 395; (Boreal forests) F: 396
Plant (Gymnosperms) P: 520
Pruning P: 841
Tree (Broadleaf trees) T: 414
Evergreen huckleberry [shrub]
Huckleberry H: 404
Evergreen State [name for]
Washington W: 46
Everlasting flower [plant]
Immortelle I: 86
Everman, Jason [American guitarist]
Nirvana N: 424
Evers, Charles [American civil rights leader]
Evers, Medgar E: 425
Mississippi (The mid-1900's) M: 644-645
Evers, Johnny [American baseball player]
Baseball (table: Hall of Fame) B: 134
Evers, Medgar [American civil rights leader] E: 425
Evers-Williams, Myrlie E: 425
Mississippi (The mid-1900's) M: 644 with picture
Evers-Williams, Myrlie [American civil rights leader] E: 425
Spingarn Medal (table: 1998) So: 794
Evert, Chris [American tennis player] E: 425
Tennis (Tennis today) T: 166d-166e with picture
Every, Henry [British pirate]
Pirate picture on P: 495
Every Child a Reader [organization]
Book Week B: 470
Every Good Boy Deserves Favor [play by Stoppard]
Stoppard, Tom So: 912
"Every Man a King" [slogan]
Long (Huey Pierce Long) L: 445-446
Every Man in his Humour [play by Jonson]
Jonson, Ben J: 160
Everybody's Magazine
Magazine (Magazines in the 1800's) M: 45
Everyman [play by Hofmannsthal]
Hofmannsthal, Hugo von H: 284
Everything Book, The [book by Fleming]
Literature for children picture on L: 366
Everything That Rises Must Converge [book by O'Connor]
O'Connor, Flannery O: 668
Eves, Ernie [Canadian political leader]
Ontario (table) O: 783; (Recent developments) O: 787
Evesham, Battle of [1265]
Henry III H: 186
Eviction [law] E: 425
Evidence E: 425
Crime scene investigation Ci: 1140
Criminal justice system (Pretrial procedures) Ci: 1143
Debate (Froms of competitive debate) D: 64
Forensic science F: 388b
Evidential breath tester [machine]
Breath testing B: 591
Evil eye [magic] E: 426

Clothing (Protection) **Ci: 687**
Witchcraft (Witchcraft as sorcery) **W: 371**
Evil spirit
Devil **D: 174**
Exorcism **E: 438**
Evita [Argentine political leader] *See* Perón, Eva
Duarte *de in this index*
Evita [musical]
Lloyd Webber, Andrew **L: 403**
Evo-devo [biology]
Developmental biology **D: 174**
Evolution E: 426 *with pictures*
See also the list of Related articles in the Evolution
article
Adaptation **A: 45**
Anaximander **A: 449**
Animal (The origin and development of animals)
A: 503
Anning, Mary **A: 517**
Anthropology (Early anthropological thought)
A: 548
Biology (Current research and issues) **B: 320**
Bird (The evolution of birds) **B: 369**
Christianity (The 1800's) **C: 526**
Creationism (Creationist beliefs) **Ci: 1123**
Darwin, Charles Robert **D: 39**
Dawkins, Richard **D: 51**
Developmental biology **D: 173**
Evolutionary psychology **E: 434**
Extinction **E: 456**
Flower (The evolution of flowering plants) **F: 299**
Fossil (Tracing the development of life) **F: 423**
Genetics (Population genetics) **G: 87**
Gould, Stephen Jay **G: 281**
Haeckel, Ernst Heinrich **H: 5**
Hamilton, William Donald **H: 33**
Hand (Animal hands) **H: 40**
Heredity (Heredity and natural selection) **H: 203**
Horse (Origins of the horse) **H: 360** *with picture*
Human being (Human physical development)
H: 414
Intelligent design **I: 320**
Island (How life develops on islands) **I: 473**
Lamarck, Chevalier de **L: 50**
Life (Adaptation) **L: 275**; (The origin of life) **L: 278**
Mammal (The evolution of mammals) **M: 126**
Mayr, Ernst **M: 330**
Morgan, Lewis Henry **M: 804**
Mutation **M: 968**
Natural selection **N: 65**
Paleontology **P: 103**
Plant (The evolution of plants) **P: 544** *with
pictures*
Pragmatism **P: 729**
Prehistoric animal (Evolution and extinction)
P: 742
Prehistoric people **P: 743**
Primate (The evolution of primates) **P: 778b** *with
diagram*
Races, Human (Evolutionary theory) **R: 53**;
(Natural selection) **R: 57**
Reproduction (How reproduction has evolved)
R: 243
Reptile (The evolution of reptiles) **R: 252**
Science (To philosophical thought) **S: 192**;
(Scientific advances of the 1800's) **S: 200**
Scopes trial **S: 209**
Social Darwinism **So: 551**
Sociology (Early sociological thought) **So: 566**
Spencer, Herbert **So: 777**
Teilhard de Chardin, Pierre **T: 88**
Time (Changes in living things) **T: 292**
Wallace, Alfred Russel **W: 15**
Evolutionary biology
Biology (table) **B: 317**
Evolutionary developmental biology
Developmental biology **D: 174**
Evolutionary psychology E: 434
Psychology (Major fields of psychology) **P: 848**
Evtushenko, Evgeny [Russian poet] *See*
Yevtushenko, Yevgeny *in this index*
Evzone [soldier]
Athens (Landmarks) **A: 854**
Ewald, Johannes [Danish dramatist]
Denmark (Arts) **D: 136**
Scandinavian literature (The 1700's) **S: 171**
Ewe [animal]
Sheep (The body of the sheep) **S: 380**
Ewe [people]
Togo (People) **T: 309**; (History) **T: 310**
Ewell, Richard Stoddert [Confederate general]
E: 434
Ewing, Buck [American baseball player]
Baseball (Hall of Fame) **B: 134**
Ewing, Patrick [American basketball player] **E: 435**
Ewing, Patrick, Jr. [American basketball player]
Ewing, Patrick **E: 435**

Ewing, Thomas [American government official]
Harrison, William Henry (table) **H: 76**
Interior, Department of the (table) **I: 325**
Taylor, Zachary (table) **T: 60**
Tyler, John (table) **T: 534**
Ewing, William L. D. [American political leader]
Illinois (table) **I: 71**
Ewing's sarcoma [disease]
Cancer (Cancer in children) **C: 169**
Ex parte Milligan [U.S. history] **E: 435**
Supreme Court of the United States (table)
So: 1002
Ex post facto [law] **E: 435**
Civil rights (Due process) **Ci: 608**
Constitution of the United States (Article I,
Section 9) **Ci: 1007-1008**
Exa [prefix]
Metric system (Metric prefixes) **M: 439**
Exaltation [religion]
Mormons (Church doctrines and ordinances)
M: 806-807
Examination [testing] *See* Testing *in this index*
Examination, Physical
Cancer (Cancer checkups) **C: 171**
Medicine (Diagnosis) **M: 364** *with pictures*
Examiner [newspaper, U.S.]
Clay, Cassius Marcellus **Ci: 658**
Examiner, The [newspaper, England]
Hunt, Leigh **H: 449**
Excalibur [legendary sword] **E: 435** *with picture*
Arthur, King **A: 757**
Excavation [archaeology]
Archaeology (Excavating sites) **A: 597** *with
pictures*
Excavation [construction]
Building construction (Constructing a skyscraper)
B: 683
House (The foundation) **H: 380**
**Excellence in Education, National Commission
on**
Education (What should be taught?) **E: 105**
Excelsior State [name for]
New York **N: 291**
Except for Me and Thee [book by West]
West, Jessamyn **W: 198**
Except the Lord [book by Cary]
Cary, Joyce **C: 270**
Excepted service
Civil service (Federal civil service) **Ci: 612**
Exceptional children *See* Gifted children *in this
index*
Exchange, Stock *See* Stock exchange *in this index*
Exchange rate [economics] **E: 435**
Balance of payments (Balance of payments and
exchange rates) **B: 36**
Devaluation **D: 173**
Economics (The world economy) **E: 61**
Gold standard **G: 254**
Inflation (Severe inflation) **I: 267**
Money *picture on* **M: 715**; (Money and
international finance) **M: 717**
Standard of living (Measuring standard of living)
I:So: 833-834
Exchange student [education]
Fulbright scholarship **F: 554**
Scholarship (International scholarships) **S: 179**
Exchange-traded fund [investment]
American Stock Exchange **A: 430**
Excimer laser [physics]
Laser (Other kinds of lasers) **L: 85**
LASIK surgery **L: 86**
Excipient [ingredient]
Drug (Developing the finished product) **D: 356**
Excise [tax] **E: 436**
Inland revenue **I: 273**
Internal revenue **I: 336**
Sales tax **S: 66**
Taxation (Taxes on transactions) **T: 53**
Excitation [physics]
Radiation (Effects of radiation) **R: 79**
Excitatory postsynaptic potential
Nervous system (Transmission across synapses)
N: 135
Excited state [physics]
Atom (Electron energy levels) **A: 873** *with
diagram*
Laser (Producing laser light) **L: 84** *with diagrams*
Light (How light is produced) **L: 283**
Exciter [machine]
Electric generator (How AC generators work)
E: 171
Electric power (Sources of electric power) **E: 182**
with diagram
Exciter lamp
Motion picture (The projector) **M: 858-859** *with
diagram*
Exclamation point [punctuation]

Punctuation (The exclamation point) **P: 902**
Exclamatory sentence
Sentence (Sentence classifications) **S: 303**
Exclusion [economics]
Income tax (Figuring the individual income tax)
I: 104
Exclusion Acts *See* Oriental Exclusion Acts *in this
index*
Exclusion principle [physics]
Pauli, Wolfgang **P: 201**
Exclusionary practice [economics]
Consumer protection (The right to choose)
Ci: 1018
Exclusive agent
Insurance (How insurance is sold) **I: 315**
Exclusive economic zone
Fishing industry **F: 181**; (Government regulation)
F: 187
High seas **H: 229**
Law of the Sea Convention **L: 141**
Ocean (Who owns the ocean?) **O: 665-666**
Territorial waters **T: 173**
Exclusive jurisdiction, Principle of
Labor movement (Organizing workers) **L: 4**
Excommunication [religion] **E: 436**
City (The people) **Ci: 582-584**
Middle Ages (The power of the church) **M: 525**
Excretion [physiology]
Elimination **E: 236**
Excursion, The [poem by Wordsworth]
Wordsworth, William (Later career) **W: 404**
Executable file [computing]
Computer file **Ci: 924g**
Execution [civil law]
Debt **D: 65**
Execution [criminal law] *See* Capital punishment
in this index
Executioner's Song, The [book by Mailer]
Mailer, Norman **M: 67**
Executions of 3rd May, 1808, The [painting by
Goya]
Goya, Francisco **G: 295**
Painting (Social expression) **P: 34**; (Romanticism)
P: 68-69 *with picture*
Executive [government] **E: 436**
See also Executive department *in this index*
Government (Executive) **G: 284**
President **P: 757**
Executive agreement [international relations]
Treaty (Negotiation) **T: 409**
**Executive Branch of the Government,
Commission on Organization of the** *See*
Hoover Commission *in this index*
Executive department [U.S.]
Constitution of the United States (Article II)
Ci: 1008
Executive **E: 436**
President of the United States (The executive
departments) **P: 764**
United States, Government of the (The executive
branch) **U: 140**
Executive editor [occupation]
Newspaper (The editorial department) **N: 381**
Executive Mansion [U.S.] *See* White House *in this
index*
Executive Office [U.S.]
President of the United States (The executive
branch) **P: 764**
United States, Government of the (The Executive
Office of the President) **U: 140**
Washington, D.C. *map on* **W: 76**
Executive order E: 436
President of the United States (Chief executive)
P: 764
Executive Order 9066 [U.S. history]
Asian Americans (World War II and Japanese
Americans) **A: 812f**
Executive president
President **P: 757**
Executive privilege
President of the United States (The Watergate
scandal) **P: 769**
Presidential assistant **P: 771**
Supreme Court of the United States (table)
So: 1002
Executive producer
Motion picture (How motion pictures are made)
M: 848
Executor [law] **E: 436**
Administrator **A: 58**
Probate **P: 809**
Will (Administration) **W: 307**
Exekias [Greek painter]
Painting (Greek painting) **P: 42** *with picture*
Exemplar fingerprint
Fingerprinting (Types of fingerprints) **F: 106**
Exemplary Novels [stories by Cervantes]

Cervantes, Miguel de (His literary career) C: 363
Exempt carrier
Truck (Industrial uses) T: 456
Exemption [economics]
Bankruptcy (Features of bankruptcy) B: 97
Customs Ci: 1201
Flat tax F: 228
Income tax (Figuring the individual income tax) I: 104
Exercise
Aerobics A: 84
Aging (Overcoming aging) picture on A: 142
Dance (Recreational reasons) D: 24
Diabetes (Treatment) D: 179
Dog (Exercise and play) D: 279
Fibromyalgia F: 90
Gymnastics G: 447 with pictures
Health (Exercise) H: 125
Isometrics I: 475
Jogging J: 131
Muscle (Skeletal muscles) M: 933-934
Obesity (Causes of obesity) O: 642a
Physical education (Physical education) P: 432 with picture
Physical fitness (Developing physical fitness) P: 435 with pictures
Physical therapy (Aids in physical therapy) P: 435
Running R: 520
Space exploration (Microgravity) So: 701-703
Weight control (Physical activity) W: 182
Exercise stress test See Stress test in this index
Exeter Book [book]
Riddle R: 335
Exhaust manifold
Automobile diagram on A: 948; (The exhaust system) A: 953
Gasoline engine (The exhaust system) G: 65
Exhaust stroke
Automobile (The engine cycle) A: 953
Exhaust system
Automobile diagram on A: 948; (The exhaust system) A: 953
Catalytic converter C: 298
Exhaust trail
Contrail Ci: 1023
Exhaust valve
Gasoline engine (The valves) G: 64 with diagrams
Exhaustion [physiology]
Stress (How stress affects the body) So: 926-927
Exhaustion, Method of [mathematics]
Mathematics (The Greeks) M: 306
Exhibit, Science
Science projects (Preparing an exhibit) S: 207
Exhibition
Fair F: 7
Museum (Exhibition and care of materials) M: 939
Exhibition Hall
National Archives and Records Administration N: 29
Exhibitor
Motion picture (Exhibition) M: 860
Exile [punishment] E: 437
Existence [philosophy] See Being in this index
Existential psychotherapy
Psychotherapy (Humanistic-experiential psychotherapy) P: 852
Existentialism [philosophy] E: 437
American literature (Southern fiction) A: 424-425
Beauvoir, Simone de B: 191
Dostoevsky, Fyodor D: 312
French literature (Existentialism) F: 523
Heidegger, Martin H: 166
Jaspers, Karl J: 65
Kierkegaard, Søren Aabye K: 313
Novel (Existentialism) N: 574
Ortega y Gasset, José O: 859
Philosophy (Philosophy in the 1900's) P: 390
Sartre, Jean-Paul S: 127
Existentialism and Humanism [book by Sartre]
Sartre, Jean-Paul S: 127
Existing light [photography] See Natural light in this index
Exit Drills in the Home [program]
Fire drill F: 130
Exit poll
Public opinion poll (History) P: 863
Exocarp [botany]
Fruit (Types of fruits in botany) F: 544
Exocrine gland [anatomy]
Gland G: 207 with diagram
Exodus [Bible] E: 438
Bible (The Law) B: 280
Jews (The Exodus) J: 121
Moses (The Exodus) M: 828-829
Passover P: 192
Pentateuch P: 274
Red Sea R: 190

Exoduster [U.S. history]
Western frontier life in America (Newcomers) W: 234 with picture
Exogamy
Marriage (Other marriage laws and practices) M: 220
Exon, J. James [American political leader]
Nebraska (table) N: 110
Exophthalmos [disorder]
Goiter G: 248
Graves' disease G: 331
Exopolysaccharide [molecule]
Biofilm B: 311
Exorcism [ritual] E: 438
Jesus Christ (The miracles) J: 107
Exoskeleton [zoology]
Ant (The bodies of ants) A: 521
Arthropod A: 753
Beetle B: 214; (The life cycle of beetles) B: 216
Butterfly (The bodies of butterflies) B: 738; (The larva) B: 741
Crayfish Ci: 1122 with picture
Crustacean Ci: 1162
Insect (Skeleton) I: 286
Molting M: 696
Skeleton (Animal skeletons) S: 480
Exosphere [atmosphere]
Air diagram on A: 173; (The thermosphere) A: 174
Moon M: 783; (The exosphere of the moon) M: 788
Exosystem [psychology]
Child (The influence of the child's environment) C: 452
Exoteric writings
Aristotle (Aristotle's writings) A: 663
Exothermic reaction [chemistry]
Chemical reaction C: 397
Exotic cat
Cat (Short-haired breeds) C: 290-291
Exotic river
River (Sources of river water) R: 351
Exotoxin [poison]
Toxin T: 353
Expandable balloon
Balloon (Gas balloons) B: 58 with picture
Expandable clay
Clay Ci: 658
Expanded Very Large Array [New Mexico]
Astronomy pictures on A: 840; (Radio and microwave astronomy) A: 843
National Radio Astronomy Observatory N: 59
Observatory (Ground-based observatories) O: 644-645
Telescope (Types of radio telescopes) T: 106-107 with picture
Expanding universe
Astronomy (Advances in cosmology) A: 849
Big bang B: 297
Gravitation (Expansion of the universe) G: 332
Inflation theory I: 268a
Redshift (Cosmological redshift) R: 192
Universe (Size of the universe) U: 205; (Changing views of the universe) U: 205-206
Expansion [economics]
Business cycle B: 728
Depression D: 150
Recession R: 175
Expansion [mathematics]
Binomial theorem B: 309
Expansion [physics] E: 438
Heat (Changes in size) H: 152
Expansion bolt [hardware]
Bolt B: 449 with picture
Climbing (Technical climbing) Ci: 680 with picture
Expansion joint [construction]
Heat (Changes in size) H: 152-153 with diagrams
Expansion of the universe See Expanding universe in this index
Expansion slot [electronics]
Computer (Parts of computers) Ci: 911-912
Expansionary monetary policy
Money (Monetary policy) M: 717
Expatriation
Citizenship (Expatriation) Ci: 571
Expedition of Humphry Clinker, The [book by Smollett]
English literature (The rise of the novel) E: 318-319
Novel (The first English novelists) N: 572
Smollett, Tobias George S: 521
Expedition style
Mountain climbing (Styles of mountain climbing) M: 897
Expeller pressing [industrial process]
Vegetable oil (Production) V: 294
Expenditure [economics]

Budget (Estimating expenditures) B: 670
Recession (Causes of recession) R: 175
"Experience" [essay by Emerson]
Emerson, Ralph Waldo (His prose works) E: 259
Experience [philosophy]
Dewey, John D: 177
Empiricism E: 263
Hume, David (Hume's thought) H: 432
Kant, Immanuel (Kant's ideas) K: 244
Locke, John (His philosophy) L: 413
Phenomenology P: 356
Experience chart
Reading (The language-experience method) R: 158
Experiential therapy
Psychotherapy (Humanistic-experiential psychotherapy) P: 852
Experiment [science]
See also Animal experimentation in this index
Drug (Creating a new drug) D: 355 with picture
Psychology (Experimentation) P: 849
Science S: 191; (Conducting experiments) S: 195
Science projects (Kinds of science projects) S: 206
Experiment station
Agricultural experiment station A: 145
Experimental Aircraft Association
Wisconsin picture on W: 357
Experimental cuisine
Cooking (Other cooking methods) Ci: 1028
Experimental economics
Economics (Fields of economics) E: 64
Experimental group
Psychology (Experimentation) P: 849
Experimental Novel, The [book by Zola]
Naturalism (Naturalism in fiction) N: 65
Experimental test pilot [aviation]
Test pilot T: 182
Experimental theater
Drama (Modern drama since World War II) D: 340
Experiments in Art and Technology [project]
Rauschenberg, Robert R: 150
Expert system [computer science]
Artificial intelligence (Knowledge representation and reasoning) A: 760
Computer (Artificial intelligence [AI] software) Ci: 920
Expiration [physiology]
Diaphragm D: 184
Lung (Gas exchange in the lungs) L: 523-524
Respiration (The process of breathing) R: 260 with diagram
Explanatory myth
Mythology (Types of myths) M: 973
Exploits River [Newfoundland and Labrador]
Newfoundland and Labrador (Rivers and lakes) N: 370 with map
Exploration E: 439 with pictures and maps
See also the list of Related articles in the Exploration article
Deep sea (Deep-sea exploration) D: 82c
Geography (Era of exploration) G: 95
Ocean (Exploring the ocean) O: 662 with pictures
Portugal (The age of exploration) P: 693
Transportation (The age of overseas expansion) T: 388
United States, History of the (America before colonial times) U: 149 with picture
Vikings (Exploration and conquest) V: 382 with map
World, History of the (The age of exploration) W: 440
Exploration, Age of [European history]
Portugal P: 686; (The age of exploration) P: 693
Exploration geochemistry
Geochemistry G: 91
Exploration of Space, The [book by Clarke]
Clarke, Arthur C. Ci: 642
Exploration Place [Wichita]
Kansas (Places to visit) K: 226
Explorationist [career]
Gold (Gold deposits) G: 252
Prospecting P: 829
Exploratory method
Statistics (Analyzing the data) So: 868
Explorer
Exploration E: 439
Explorer 1 [spacecraft]
Eisenhower, Dwight David (The space age) E: 154
Rocket (The space age) R: 391
Space exploration (The space race begins) So: 707-708
Van Allen belts V: 269
Von Braun, Wernher V: 448
Explosion
Explosive E: 453
Fallout F: 18
Fire (Kinds of fire) F: 120-121

Explosive E: 453
See also the list of Related articles in the Explosive *article*
  Bomb B: 450
  Coal (Strip mining) Ci: 722; (The conventional mechanized method) Ci: 724
  Mine warfare M: 563
  Plastic explosive P: 553
Explosive train
  Ammunition (How shells explode) A: 436
Expo 67 [Montreal, Quebec]
  Architecture *picture on* A: 610
  Quebec *picture on* Q: 31
Expo 86 [Vancouver, British Columbia]
  British Columbia (The late 1900's) B: 630-631
Expo 2005 [Aichi, Japan]
  World's fair W: 500
Exponent [mathematics]
  Algebra (Terms used in algebra) A: 351; (Multiplication) A: 355
  Decimal system (The decimal system and number words) D: 70-71
  Logarithms L: 423
  Number (The decimal system) N: 605
  Power P: 728
  Scientific notation S: 207
Export [economics] *See* Exports and imports *in this index*
Export Pipeline
  Pipeline (In other countries) P: 491
Export processing zone
  South America (Manufacturing) So: 635
Export subsidy [trade]
  Tariff (Offsetting unfair trade practices) T: 43
Exports and imports [economics] E: 454
  Balance of payments (How the balance of payments is determined) B: 36
  Customs Ci: 1201
  Devaluation D: 173
  Export-Import Bank of the United States E: 454
  Free trade F: 499
  Free trade zone F: 499
  Gross domestic product (Net exports) G: 399
  Tariff (Offsetting unfair trade practices) T: 43
  World Trade Organization W: 451
Exposition [fair]
  Fair F: 7
Exposition [literature]
  Drama (The structure of drama) D: 325
  Literature (Plot) L: 353
Exposition [music]
  Classical music (Sonata) Ci: 645; (Fugue) Ci: 645
  Fugue F: 553
Exposition of the System of the Universe [book by Laplace]
  Laplace, Marquis de L: 73
Exposure [photography]
  Camera C: 80
  Photography (Exposure) P: 411 *with pictures*; (Exposing the film) P: 416
Exposure [psychology]
  Phobia P: 392
Exposure [social practice]
  Family (Development of the family) F: 21-22
Exposure meter [instrument]
  Light meter L: 294
  Photography (Exposure meters) P: 413
Exposure mode
  Photography (Exposure meters) P: 413
Exposure sheet [film]
  Animation (Preliminary steps in animation) A: 511-512; (Traditional animation) A: 512
"Express, The" [poem by Spender]
  Spender, Stephen So: 778
Express authority [law]
  Agent A: 140
Express mail
  Postal Service, United States (Classes of mail) P: 699
Express repeal [law]
  Repeal R: 241
Express service
  Airmail A: 207
  Wells, Fargo & Company W: 195
Expressed powers *See* Delegated powers *in this index*
Expression [mathematics]
  Algebra (Terms used in algebra) A: 351
Expression [music]
  Music (Indicating expression) M: 955
Expression [psychology]
  Emotion (The basic emotion approach) E: 261
  Instinct (Human instincts) I: 305
Expression, Freedom of
  Academic freedom A: 20
Expression of the Emotions in Man and Animals, The [book by Darwin]

Comparative psychology Ci: 902b
  Darwin, Charles Robert (Darwin's theories) D: 40
  Emotion (The basic emotion approach) E: 261
Expressionism [arts] E: 455 *with picture*
  See also Abstract Expressionism *in this index*
  Drama (Expressionism) D: 339 *with picture*
  German literature (Expressionism) G: 141
  Germany (Painting and sculpture) G: 155 *with picture*; (Motion pictures) G: 156
  Motion picture (Filmmaking in Europe) M: 866 *with picture*
  Munch, Edvard M: 927 *with picture*
  Opera (The search for new forms) O: 799-800
  Painting (Expressionism) P: 78 *with picture*
  Photography (A diversity of styles) P: 426-427
Expressive criticism
  Criticism (Kinds of literary criticism) Ci: 1146
Expressway [road]
  See also Freeway *in this index*
  Automobile (Roads) A: 959-960
  City (Description) Ci: 589 *with picture*
  Road (Primary highways) R: 358
  Traffic (Traffic problems) T: 365-366
Expropriation [law]
  Eminent domain E: 260
Exsanguination [industrial process]
  Meat packing (Slaughtering and dressing) M: 351
Extended deterrence [arms control]
  Nuclear weapon (Inducements) N: 601
Extended family
  Africa (Marriage and the family) A: 108
  Arabs (Family life) A: 587
  Arctic (Traditional ways of life) A: 638
  Family (Varieties of families) F: 20 *with picture*; (Non-Western families) F: 24
  Indian, American (Family life) I: 136b-136c
  Latin America (Family life) L: 96
Extended spectrum penicillin [drug]
  Penicillin (Forms of penicillin) P: 240
Extended-wear contact lens
  Contact lens (Soft contact lenses) Ci: 1020
Extension [hairstyle]
  Hairdressing (The 1900's) H: 12-13
Extension agent [occupation]
  Agricultural experiment station A: 145
  Farm and farming (Obtaining management assistance) F: 43-44
Extension programs [education]
  Adult education (History of adult education in the United States) A: 69
  Cooperative Extension System Ci: 1037
  Education (Adult education) E: 88-89
Extension service [education]
  Agricultural education (Colleges and universities) A: 144
  Farm and farming (Obtaining management assistance) F: 43-44
Extensional boundary [geology] *See* Divergent boundary *in this index*
Extensor
  Muscle (Skeletal muscles) M: 933
Extensor pollicis brevis [anatomy]
  Human body (table) H: 422 *with diagram*
Exterminating trap
  Trapping (Kinds of traps) T: 403 *with pictures*
External auditory canal [anatomy]
  Ear *diagrams on* E: 8, E: 10; (The outer ear) E: 7
External beam radiotherapy [medicine]
  Cancer (Radiation therapy) C: 172
External-combustion engine
  Heat (Changing heat into motion) H: 153
  Internal-combustion engine I: 336
External defibrillator [device]
  Defibrillator D: 88
External fertilization [biology]
  Animal (Sexual reproduction) A: 496 *with diagram*
  Fertilization F: 78
  Fish (How fish reproduce) F: 169
  Reproduction (How reproduction has evolved) R: 243
External insulin pump [device]
  Diabetes (Treatment) D: 179
External parasite [organism]
  Cattle (Diseases) C: 312-314
External senses [anatomy]
  Senses (External senses) S: 301 *with diagrams*
Extinct volcano
  Volcano (Predicting eruptions) V: 442a-442b
Extinction [biology] E: 456 *with picture*
  See also Endangered species *in this index*
  Animal (Why species become extinct) A: 503
  Biodiversity (Protecting biodiversity) B: 311
  Bird (Extinct birds) B: 369 *with pictures*
  Conservation (Biodiversity conservation) Ci: 976
  Dinosaur (Why dinosaurs died out) D: 213
  Earth (The Paleozoic Era) E: 27

Endangered species E: 269
Evolution (Contributions from other scientific fields) E: 433
  Fossil F: 422 *with pictures*
  Mammal (The future of mammals) M: 127
  Prehistoric animal (Evolution and extinction) P: 742
  Reptile (The evolution of reptiles) R: 252
  Triassic Period T: 439
  Wildlife conservation W: 303
Extortion [crime] E: 457
Extra [sports]
  Cricket (Scoring) Ci: 1132
Extra point
  Football (Scoring) F: 362
Extra-virgin olive oil
  Olive oil O: 744
Extract E: 457
  Herbal medicine H: 196
  Meat extract M: 350
  Perfume P: 286
Extracted materials
  Materials (Extracted materials) M: 300d
Extraction [chemistry]
  Solvent So: 587
Extraction [dentistry]
  Dentistry D: 143
  Orthodontics O: 859
Extraction unit [industry]
  Gas [fuel] (Transmitting and distributing gas) G: 55
Extractive
  Wood (The composition of wood) W: 390
Extractive industry
  Industry (By stage of production) I: 256-257
Extractive reserve [area]
  Rain forest (Saving rain forests) R: 126d
Extracts from the Virginia Charters [book by Mason]
  Mason, George (Early life) M: 266
Extracurricular activities
  Curriculum (Curriculum content) Ci: 1197
  High school (High schools in the United States) H: 228
  School (Public schools) S: 182
  Universities and colleges (Extracurricular activities) U: 210
Extradition [law] E: 457
  Constitution of the United States (Article IV, Section 2) Ci: 1010
  Political prisoner P: 638
  Treaty (Kinds of treaties) T: 408-409
Extradition treaty
  Terrorism (Diplomatic, economic, and military pressure) T: 177
Extragalactic nebula [astronomy]
  Nebula N: 116
Extrajudicial confession [law]
  Confession Ci: 936
Extramural jurisdiction [government]
  Metropolitan area (Metropolitan area plans) M: 443
Extranet [computing]
  Computer (Extranets) Ci: 923
  E-commerce (Business-to-business transactions) E: 2
Extraordinary rendition [policy]
  Central Intelligence Agency (History) C: 357
Extrasensory perception E: 457
  Clairvoyance Ci: 636
  Parapsychology P: 153
  Psychical research P: 846
  Telepathy T: 93
Extrasolar planet
  Planet (Planets in other solar systems) P: 513 *with picture*
Extraterrestrial [being] *See* Alien *in this index*
Extraterrestrial intelligence E: 458
  SETI Institute S: 323
Extraterrestrial life
  Astrobiology A: 826
  Extraterrestrial intelligence E: 458
  Life (The search for life on other worlds) L: 280
  Mars (Possibility of life) M: 226c *with picture*; (Observation by spacecraft) M: 226c
  Satellite S: 149
Extraterrestrial state
  Spiritualism (Beliefs) So: 796
Extraterritorial powers [government] *See* Extramural jurisdiction *in this index*
Extraterritoriality [law]
  Diplomacy (Diplomatic immunity) D: 217
Extratropical cyclone
  Storm (Extratropical cyclones) So: 913
Extravehicular activity [space exploration]
  Aldrin, Buzz A: 339
  Space exploration (Leaving the spacecraft)

So: 704 *with pictures*; (Voskhod and Gemini: The first multiperson space flights) So: 714
White, Edward Higgins, II W: 284
World, History of the *picture on* W: 448b
Extreme skiing
Skiing (Alpine competitions) S: 486-487
Extreme Ultraviolet Explorer [satellite]
Astronomy (Ultraviolet astronomy) A: 844
Extreme ultraviolet rays [physics]
Astronomy (Ultraviolet astronomy) A: 844
Telescope (Ultraviolet telescopes) T: 108-109
Extreme unction See Anointing of the sick *in this index*
Extremophile [biology] E: 458
Astrobiology A: 826
Life (The physical environment) L: 275
Extrovert [psychology] E: 459
Jung, Carl Gustav (His theories) J: 195
Extruder [machine]
Gelatin G: 77
Extrusion [industrial process] E: 459 *with diagram*
Aluminum (Extruding) A: 396
Ceramics (Making ceramics) C: 360
Die and diemaking D: 195
Iron and steel (Extruding) I: 447
Plastics (Extrusion) P: 558 *with picture*
Polypropylene P: 651
Polystyrene P: 652
Polyvinyl chloride P: 652
Rubber (Shaping) R: 505
Soybean (Soy meal) So: 690
Extrusive rock [geology]
Igneous rock I: 49
Rock (Extrusive rock) R: 371
Exudative macular degeneration [disorder]
Macular degeneration M: 26
Exus [spirit]
Devil worship D: 175
Exxon Corporation See Exxon Mobil Corporation *in this index*
Exxon Mobil Corporation E: 459
Exxon Valdez oil spill E: 459
Manufacturing (table) M: 170
Exxon Valdez **oil spill** [U.S. history] E: 459
Alaska (Recent developments) A: 304
Bush, George Herbert Walker (National affairs) B: 720
Coast Guard, United States (The Coast Guard since World War II) Ci: 738-739
Exxon Mobil Corporation E: 459
Oil spill (Notable spills) O: 708
Petroleum (Spills and seeps) P: 345
ExxonMobil [company] See Exxon Mobil Corporation *in this index*
Eyadéma, Gnassinbé [Togolese political leader]
Togo (History) T: 310-311
Eyass [bird]
Eagle (Young eagles) E: 4
Eyck, Hubert van [brother of]
Van Eyck, Jan V: 282
Eyck, Jan van [Flemish painter] See Van Eyck, Jan *in this index*
Eye [anatomy] E: 460 *with pictures*
See also Vision *in this index and the list of Related articles in the Eye article*
Alhazen A: 366
Allergy A: 373
Animal *picture on* A: 469
Artificial eye A: 759
Blind spot B: 400
Cat (Head) C: 286-287 *with pictures*
Color (The roles of the eyes and brain) Ci: 818-819
Compound eye Ci: 906 *with diagrams*
Contact lens Ci: 1020 *with picture*
Farsightedness F: 48
First aid (Eye injury) F: 140
Fish (Sight) F: 164
Frog (Senses) F: 537 *with picture*
Human body *picture on* H: 417
Insect (Eyes and antennae) I: 287 *with diagrams*
Iritis I: 434
Light (Light in medicine) L: 292
Lighting (What is good lighting) L: 297
Macular degeneration M: 26
Myopia M: 971
Ophthalmology O: 810
Optometry O: 814
Owl (Appearance) O: 884
Perception (Receptors) P: 283
Planarian P: 506 *with picture*
Races, Human (The three-race theory) R: 53 *with picture*
Reading (How we read) R: 156
Reproduction, Human (Development of organs and organ systems) R: 248
Reptile (Sense organs) R: 251 *with pictures*

Sun lamp So: 987
Tears T: 72 *with picture*
Eye [meteorology]
Hurricane H: 452 *with pictures*
Typhoon T: 540 *with picture*
Eye agate [mineral]
Agate A: 139 *with picture*
Eye bank [medicine] E: 470
Eye bolt [hardware]
Bolt B: 449 *with picture*
Eye disease
See also the Related articles in the Eye *article*
Allergy A: 373
Eye (Diseases of the eye) E: 466
Eye of Providence [emblem]
United States, Government of the *picture on* U: 137
Eye rhyme See Visual rhyme *in this index*
Eye transplant
Eye bank E: 470
Eyed click beetle
Beetle *picture on* B: 218
Eyeglasses See Glasses *in this index*
Eyelash
Eye (The outer parts) E: 460
Eyelid
Eye (The outer parts) E: 460; (Diseases of the outer parts) E: 468
Eyepiece
Microscope (Tube and lenses) M: 517-518 *with pictures*
Eyes of the Interred, The [book by Asturias]
Asturias, Miguel Angel A: 850
Eyeshine
Cat (Head) C: 286-287
Eyesight See Vision *in this index*
Eyespot [zoology]
Eye (Eyes of animals) E: 469 *with picture*
Moth *picture on* M: 837; (Giant silkworm moths and royal moths) M: 841 *with pictures*
Protozoan (Structure) P: 837
Starfish (The body of a starfish) So: 856
Eyestrain [disorder]
Lighting (Lighting problems) L: 297-298
Eyetooth
Teeth (Permanent teeth) T: 79-80
Eyewall [meteorology]
Hurricane H: 452, *picture on* H: 454
Typhoon T: 540 *with picture*
Eyjafjallajökull glacier
Iceland (The inland plateau) I: 22
Eylau, Battle of [1807]
Army *picture on* A: 727
Eyre, Edward John [British explorer]
Australia *map on* A: 921
Exploration (Exploring Australia's interior) E: 448 *with map*
Eyre, Lake See Lake Eyre *in this index*
Eyrie [nest] See Aerie *in this index*
Eysturoy [island]
Faroe Islands F: 47
Ezana [king of Aksum]
Aksum A: 371
Ethiopia (The Aksum Kingdom) E: 371
Ezekiel [Biblical figure]
Ezekiel, Book of E: 470
Ezekiel, Book of [Bible] E: 470
Bible (The Prophets) B: 280-281
Ezra [Biblical figure]
Ezra, Book of E: 470
Scribe S: 226
Ezra, Book of [Bible] E: 470

F

F [letter] F: 1 *with pictures*
F [symbol]
Fluorine F: 306
F-5E Tiger II [military aircraft]
Jet propulsion *picture on* J: 113
F-14 Tomcat [aircraft]
Aircraft, Military *picture on* A: 205
F-15 [airplane]
Air Force, United States (Fighters) A: 191
F-15 Eagle [airplane]
Air Force, United States *picture on* A: 191
F-16 [airplane]
Air Force, United States *picture on* A: 193; (Fighters) A: 191
Airplane *picture on* A: 211
F-22 [airplane]
Air Force, United States *picture on* A: 192
F-86 Sabre [airplane]
Korean War (The air war) K: 382
F-100 Super Sabre [airplane]
Airplane *picture on* A: 235; (Supersonic airplanes) A: 238
F-104 [airplane]

Lawrence, Robert Henry Jr. L: 146
F-111, The [painting by Rosenquist]
Rosenquist, James Albert R: 479
F-117 [airplane]
Air Force, United States (Fighters) A: 191; (The Persian Gulf War of 1991) A: 196
Aircraft, Military (Bombers) A: 202 *with picture*
F clef
Music (Indicating pitch) M: 952-953 *with picture*
F-stop [photography]
Camera (Controlling the exposure) C: 80
Photography (Aperture size) P: 412 *with diagram*
Fa [god]
Mythology (Babylonian mythology) M: 978
Fa Ngum [Laotian political leader]
Indochina (A new kingdom) I: 225
FAA [agency] See Federal Aviation Administration *in this index*
Fa'a Samoa [customs]
Pacific Islands (Ways of life) P: 6
Faber, Eberhard [American businessman] F: 2
Faber, Red [American baseball player]
Baseball (table: Hall of Fame) B: 134
Fabergé, Peter Carl [Russian jeweler] F: 2 *with picture*
Decorative arts *picture on* D: 80
Fabian, Saint [pope]
Pope (table) P: 666
Fabian Society [British history] F: 2
Shaw, George Bernard (Early life) S: 378
Socialism (Moderate socialism) So: 561
Webb, Sidney and Beatrice W: 175
Fabius Maximus, Quintus [Roman military leader] F: 2
Fabian Society F: 2
Fable [literature] F: 2 *with picture*
See also Allegory; Parable *in this index*
Aesop's fables A: 90
Fiction (History) F: 90
Folklore (Folk tales) F: 323
German literature (Popular literature) G: 139
La Fontaine, Jean de L: 29 *with picture*
Literature for children (Fables) L: 359 *with picture*
Storytelling (Fables) So: 914
Fable, A [book by Faulkner]
Faulkner, William F: 55
Fable for Critics, A [poem by Lowell]
Lowell, James Russell (Literary success) L: 510
Fable of Polifemo and Galatea, The [poem by Góngora]
Góngora, Luis de G: 268
Fables [book by La Fontaine]
La Fontaine, Jean de L: 29
Fables [book by Lobel]
Lobel, Arnold L: 404
Fables in Slang [essays by Ade]
Ade, George A: 54
Fabliaux [poetry]
French literature (Narrative poetry) F: 518-519
Fabre, Jean Henri Casimir [French naturalist] F: 3
Fabric See Textile *in this index*
Fabric brightener
Bleach F: 399
Fabrica [book by Vesalius]
Vesalius, Andreas V: 341
Fabricating industry
Industry (By stage of production) I: 256-257
Fabricating ingot [metallurgy]
Aluminum (Casting the molten aluminum) A: 394
Fabrication [meat packing]
Meat packing (Slaughtering and dressing) M: 351-352
Facade [architecture]
Architecture (table) A: 608-609 *with picture*
Façade [music by Walton]
Walton, Sir William W: 22
Façade [poems by Sitwell]
Sitwell, Edith S: 478
Façade theater
Drama (The Roman stage) D: 328; (The Italian stage) D: 330 *with picture*
Face [anatomy] F: 3
Face [geometry]
Geometry (Solid geometry) G: 104 *with pictures*
Polyhedron P: 651 *with diagram*
Face [printing]
Type T: 537 *with pictures*
Face [weaving]
Rugs and carpets (Materials used in rugs and carpets) R: 514
Face brick
Brick (Building bricks) B: 597
Face fly [insect] F: 4 *with picture*
Face mask
Skin diving (Kinds of skin diving) S: 493 *with pictures*
Face-off [sports]

Hockey (The rink) **H: 274-275**; (Playing the game) **H: 277** *with picture*
Lacrosse (Men's lacrosse) **L: 23**
Face value [economics]
Investment (table) **I: 366**; (Corporate bonds) **I: 368**
Money (Prvately issued bank notes) **M: 713**
Facebook [website] **F: 4**
Internet (Social networking websites) **I: 350b**; (The evolving Internet) **I: 350g-350h**
Zuckerberg, Mark **Z: 608**
Facelift [surgery]
Plastic surgery (Cosmetic surgery) **P: 553**
Facemash [website]
Zuckerberg, Mark **Z: 608**
Facer-canceler [machine]
Postal services *picture on* **P: 704**; (Sorting) **P: 703**
Facet [gem]
Diamond (How diamonds are cut to make jewels) **D: 182** *with pictures*
Gem (Cutting and polishing) **G: 79**
Lapidary **L: 73**
Facial disk [anatomy]
Northern harrier **N: 520**
Owl (Appearance) **O: 884** *with picture*
Facing [sewing]
Sewing (Facings) **S: 333**
Facioscapulohumeral muscular dystrophy [disease]
Muscular dystrophy (Facioscapulohumeral and limb-girdle muscular dystrophies) **M: 937**
Facsimile machine *See* Fax machine *in this index*
Fact
Addition (Addition facts) **A: 49**
Debate (Types of resolutions) **D: 63**
Fact checker [occupation]
Publishing (Editors and fact checkers) **P: 867**
Factionalism
Communism (The role of the party) **Ci: 891**
Factor [mathematics] **F: 4**
Algebra (Multiplication) **A: 355**
Factor analysis [statistics]
Thurstone, Louis Leon **T: 273**
Factorial [mathematics]
Permutations and combinations (By using symbols and formulas) **P: 291**
Series **S: 316b**
Factorial series [mathematics]
Series **S: 316b**
Factoring
Algebra (Factoring) **A: 356**
Factory **F: 5**
Culture (Invention) **Ci: 1189**
Industrial Revolution **I: 246** *with picture*
Lighting (In offices, stores, and factories) **L: 296**
Sweatshop **So: 1019**
Technology (The Industrial Revolution) **T: 75**
United States, History of the (Economic growth) **U: 169-170**
World, History of the (The Industrial Revolution) **W: 444** *with picture*
Factory Act [1833]
United Kingdom (The era of reform) **U: 68**
Factory and shop lumber
Lumber (Softwood lumber) **L: 517**
Factory farming [agriculture] **F: 5**
Agriculture (Raising livestock) **A: 150-151**; (Reforming agricultural practices) **A: 151**
People for the Ethical Treatment of Animals **P: 277**
Factory ship
Fishing industry *pictures on* **F: 186**
Whale (Hunting techniques) **W: 263** *with picture*
Factory trawler [ship]
Ship (Specialized vessels) **S: 410**
Faculae [astronomy]
Climate (Activity on the sun's surface) **Ci: 676d**
Faculty [education]
Universities and colleges (Faculty) **U: 208**
Fad
Custom **Ci: 1200**
Fashion **F: 50**
Fadden, Sir Arthur [Australian political leader]
Australia (table) **A: 923**
Fading scarlet waxy cap [mushroom]
Mushroom *picture on* **M: 944**
Fado [music]
Portugal (The arts) **P: 689-690**
FAE [weapon]
Bomb (Fuel-air explosives [FAE's]) **B: 451**
Faena
Bullfighting (The order of the bullfight) **B: 696-697** *with picture*
Faenza [Italy] *See* Faïence *in this index*
Faerie Queene, The [poem by Spenser]
English literature (Elizabethan poetry) **E: 316-317**
Poetry (Renaissance poetry) **P: 596**

Spenser, Edmund **So: 778**
Faero Islands [Atlantic] *See* Faroe Islands *in this index*
Fafnir [legendary figure] **F: 6**
Fagg, Bernard [British archaeologist]
Nok **N: 451**
Fagundes, João Alvarez [Portuguese explorer]
Nova Scotia (Exploration and settlement) **N: 567**
Fagus Works [building]
Gropius, Walter *picture on* **G: 398**
Fahd [king of Saudi Arabia] **F: 6** *with portrait*
Abdullah **A: 9**
Saudi Arabia (Continued progress) **S: 161-162**
Fahlberg, Constantin [American chemist]
Saccharin **S: 4**
Fahrenheit, Gabriel Daniel [German physicist] **F: 6**
Fahrenheit scale **F: 6**
Fahrenheit 451 [book by Bradbury]
Bradbury, Ray **B: 542**
Fahrenheit scale **F: 6**
Celsius scale **C: 342**
Fahrenheit, Gabriel Daniel **F: 6**
FAI [French government]
Aviation (The first flying regulations) **A: 987**
Faïence [pottery] **F: 6** *with picture*
Failure
Learning (Motivation) **L: 164**
Fainting [disorder] **F: 6** *with picture*
First aid (Fainting) **F: 140**
Fair **F: 7** *with picture*
Fair, A. A. [pen name]
Gardner, Erle Stanley **G: 39**
Fair ball
Baseball (Outs by batters) **B: 128-129**
Fair catch
Football (table) **F: 356**
Fair-comment doctrine [law]
Libel **L: 226**
Fair Deal [U.S. history] **F: 8**
Democratic Party (The Fair Deal) **D: 126**
Truman, Harry S. (Problems at home) **T: 472**
Fair employment practices
Equal Employment Opportunity Commission **E: 345**
Fair Employment Practices Committee [U.S.]
World War II (Producing for the war) **W: 495**
Fair Housing Act [1968] *See* Civil Rights Act of 1968 *in this index*
Fair housing laws [U.S.]
Open housing **O: 789**
Fair Labor Standards Act [1938] **F: 8**
Child labor (U.S. federal laws) **C: 455**
Minimum wage **M: 574**
New Deal (The final measures) **N: 202**
Fair Lane [estate]
Dearborn **D: 60**
Fair Maid of February [plant]
Snowdrop **S: 541** *with picture*
Fair Oaks, Battle of [1862]
Civil War, American (table) **Ci: 624**; (The peninsular campaign) **Ci: 626**
Lee, Robert E. (Opening campaigns) **L: 178**
Fair Packaging and Labeling Act [1966]
Consumer protection (The right to information) **Ci: 1018**
Fair Park [Dallas]
Dallas (Cultural life) **D: 14**
Texas (Places to visit) **T: 194**
Fair preponderance [law]
Evidence (Burden of proof) **E: 426**
Fair territory
Baseball (The field) **B: 126** *with diagram*
Fair-trade laws [law] **F: 8**
Fair use principle
Copyright (Users' rights) **Ci: 1047**
Fair Wages Resolution
King, William Lyon Mackenzie (Education) **K: 325**
Fairbanks [Alaska] **F: 8** *with picture*
Fairbanks, Charles Warren [American political leader] **F: 9** *with portrait*
Fairbanks **F: 8**
Wilson, Woodrow (Election of 1916) **W: 324**
Fairbanks, Douglas, Sr. [American actor] **F: 9** *with picture*
Fairbanks, Erastus [American political leader]
Vermont (table) **V: 333**
Fairbanks, Horace [American political leader]
Vermont (table) **V: 333**
Fairbanks, Richard [American businessman]
Massachusetts (Interesting facts) **M: 271**
Postal services (Postal service in the United States) **P: 706**
Fairburn, William Armstrong [American inventor]
Match (The first matches) **M: 300-300a**
Fairchild, Charles S. [American government official]
Cleveland, Grover (table) **Ci: 671**

Fairchild, Lucius [American political leader]
Wisconsin (table) **W: 365**
Fairchild, Sherman Mills [American inventor] **F: 9**
Fairfax, George William [American colonist]
Washington, George (Washington the surveyor) **W: 93**
Fairfield, Cicily Isabel [British author] *See* West, Rebecca *in this index*
Fairfield, John [American political leader]
Maine (table) **M: 87**
Fairless, Benjamin Franklin [American businessman] **F: 9**
Fairly Good Time, A [book by Gallant]
Gallant, Mavis **G: 13**
Fairly Honourable Defeat, A [book by Murdoch]
Murdoch, Iris **M: 930**
Fairmount Park
Park (Kinds of parks) **P: 167-168**
Philadelphia (Downtown Philadelphia) **P: 359**; (Recreation) **P: 364** *with picture*
Fairway
Golf (The course) **G: 260-261** *with picture*
Fairway wood [golf]
Golf (Golf clubs) **G: 262** *with picture*
Fairweather Mountain [Alaska-British Columbia]
Alaska (Land regions) **A: 292** *with map*
British Columbia (Land regions) **B: 622** *with map*
Fairy **F: 9** *with pictures*
Elf **E: 235**
Halloween (Halloween symbols) **H: 24b**
Fairy-bluebird [bird]
Bird (Birds of Asia) **B: 344f** *with picture*
Fairy Falls [falls, Washington]
Waterfall (table: Famous waterfalls of North America) **W: 142**
Fairy fly
Insect *picture on* **I: 278**
Fairy lantern [plant]
Mariposa lily **M: 212** *with picture*
Fairy mound
Fairy (Trooping fairies) **F: 10**
Fairy penguin
Penguin (The body of a penguin) **P: 238**
Fairy ring [botany]
Fairy (Magic powers) **F: 10**
Mushroom (Fairy rings) **M: 943**
Redwood (The coast redwood) **R: 193**
Fairy-ring mushroom
Mushroom (Nonpoisonous mushrooms) **M: 943-945** *with picture*
Fairy sight
Fairy (Magic powers) **F: 10**
Fairy slipper [plant]
Flower *picture on* **F: 284**
Fairy tale
Andersen, Hans Christian **A: 451**
Fairy (Fairy tales) **F: 11**
Literature for children (Traditional literature) **L: 357** *with picture*
Fairy tern [bird]
Tern **T: 172**
Fairyland [mythical place]
Fairy (Trooping fairies) **F: 10**
Fairywren [bird]
Bird (Birds of Australia and New Zealand) **B: 346** *with picture*
Faisal [king of Saudi Arabia] **F: 11**
Saudi Arabia (The new kingdom) **S: 161**; (Continued progress) **S: 161-162**
Faisal I [king of Iraq] **F: 12**
Iraq (British rule) **I: 413**
Faisal II [king of Iraq]
Iraq (Independence) **I: 413**; (The 1950's) **I: 413**
Faith
See also Religion *in this index*
Luther, Martin (Justification by faith) **L: 527**
Protestantism (Faith and grace) **P: 834**
Faith 7 [spacecraft]
Cooper, Gordon **Ci: 1034**
Faith healing [religion] **F: 12**
Eddy, Mary Baker **E: 75**
Faithless elector [government]
Electoral College (The college in action) **E: 164**
Fake fur *See* Artificial fur *in this index*
Fakir [person] **F: 12**
Dervish **D: 153**
Fala [dog]
Franklin Delano Roosevelt Memorial **F: 493** *with picture*
Falabella [horse]
Horse (Kinds of horses) **H: 343**
Falange Española [political party] **F: 12**
Fascism (Fascism in other countries) **F: 50**
Spain (Civil war) **So: 750**
Spanish Civil War **So: 756**
Falcon [bird] **F: 12** *with pictures*
Animal *pictures on* **A: 489, A: 505**

Bird *pictures on* B: 329, B: 365
Bird of prey B: 374a, *picture on* B: 374b
Falconry F: 14
Falcon Dam [Rio Grande, Mexico-U.S.]
  Rio Grande (Lower course) R: 347
Falconer, Ian [American artist/author] F: 14
Falconet [bird]
  Bird of prey (Physical appearance) B: 374a
Falconry [sport] F: 14
Falcons, Atlanta [team]
  Football (National Football League) F: 364
Faldo, Nick [British golfer]
  Golf (British Open) G: 264
Fale [dwelling]
  Samoa *picture on* S: 80b; (People) S: 80a
Faleiro, Ruy [Portuguese geographer]
  Magellan, Ferdinand (Planning the expedition)
  M: 46
Falkenhayn, Erich von [German general]
  World War I (The Western Front) W: 455-456; (The
  Battle of Verdun) W: 458
Falkland, Viscount [English government official]
  Falkland Islands F: 15
Falkland Current
  Atlantic Ocean (Currents) A: 866
Falkland Islands [Atlantic] F: 15
  Argentina (The "dirty war") A: 658
  United Kingdom (Thatcher) U: 73
Falklands War [1982]
  Argentina (The "dirty war") A: 658
Fall [accident]
  Safety (Safety at home) S: 9-10
Fall [season] *See* Autumn *in this index*
Fall [wrestling]
  Wrestling *picture on* W: 506; (High school and
  intercollegiate wrestling) W: 505
Fall, Albert Bacon [American government official]
  F: 15
  Harding, Warren Gamaliel (table) H: 58;
  (Government scandals) H: 58
  Interior, Department of the (table) I: 325
  Teapot Dome T: 72
Fall, The [book by Camus]
  Camus, Albert C: 97
Fall cankerworm [insect]
  Cankerworm C: 177 *with picture*
Fall line [geography] F: 15 *with map*
  Piedmont Region P: 453
  United States (The Coastal Lowlands) U: 121
  Waterfall W: 141
Fall of America: Poems of These States, The
  [poems by Ginsberg]
  Ginsberg, Allen G: 192
"Fall of Hyperion, The" [poem by Keats]
  Keats, John (His work) K: 253-254
Fall of the Alamo [painting by Onderdonk]
  Crockett, Davy *picture on* Ci: 1148d
"Fall of the House of Usher, The" [story by Poe]
  Poe, Edgar Allan (Fiction and theory of fiction)
  P: 590
Fall River [Massachusetts] F: 16
Fall River, Battle of [1778]
  Fall River F: 16
Fall River Legend [ballet]
  De Mille, Agnes D: 119
Falla, Manuel de [Spanish composer] F: 16
Fallacy [logic] F: 16
Fallen Angels [book by Myers]
  Myers, Walter Dean M: 970f
Fallen arch [disorder]
  Flatfoot F: 229
Fallen Timbers, Battle of [1794]
  Indian wars (Conflicts in the Midwest) I: 191-192
  with map
  Indiana (Territorial days) I: 215
  Little Turtle L: 392
  Ohio (Exploration and settlement) O: 700
  Wayne, Anthony W: 154
Faller [job]
  Lumber (Cutting down trees) L: 518
Fallersleben, Hoffmann von [German composer]
  Deutschland über Alles D: 172
Fallin, Mary [American political leader]
  Oklahoma (table) O: 730
Falling bodies, Law of [physics] F: 16 *with
  diagrams*
  Calculus (Differential calculus) C: 22
  Galileo (Mature scientific career) G: 11
Falling star *See* Meteor *in this index*
Falling Up [book by Silverstein]
  Silverstein, Shel S: 465
Fallingwater house
  Pennsylvania (Places to visit) P: 254
  United States *picture on* U: 117
  Wright, Frank Lloyd (Later career) W: 508
Fallopian tube [anatomy] F: 17
  Human body (table) H: 422 *with diagram*; (The

reproductive system) H: 425
  Hysterectomy H: 482
  Infertility (Causes) I: 265
  Menstruation (The menstrual cycle) M: 404 *with
  diagrams*
  Pelvic inflammatory disease P: 232
  Pregnancy (An ectopic pregnancy) P: 735
  Reproduction, Human (The human reproductive
  system) R: 244-245 *with diagram*
Fallot, Étienne-Louis [French physician]
  Heart (Blockage of blood flow) H: 141
Fallout [radioactivity] F: 18 *with map*
  Chernobyl disaster C: 409
  Civil defense (History of civil defense in the
  United States) Ci: 606
  Nuclear weapon (Residual nuclear radiation)
  N: 599
Fallout shelter
  Civil defense (History of civil defense in the
  United States) Ci: 606
  Fallout (The fallout hazard) F: 19
Fallow deer
  Deer (table) D: 85; (Asian and European deer)
  D: 86
Fallow land [farming]
  Dryland farming D: 370
Falls [botany]
  Iris I: 429 *with picture*
Falls [geology] *See* Waterfall *in this index*
Falls City [name for]
  Louisville L: 504
Falls of Saint Anthony [falls, Mississippi River]
  Hennepin, Louis H: 185
Fallujah [Iraq]
  Iraq (The Iraq War) I: 414a-414b
  Iraq War (Resistance to the coalition) I: 414e-414f
Falmouth [former name]
  Portland [Maine] P: 683
Falmouth Gazette [newspaper]
  Maine (Communication) M: 87
False Antipathy, The [play by La Chaussée]
  Drama (France) D: 335
False color [electronics]
  Remote sensing R: 231
False Dmitriy [czar of Russia]
  Russia (table: Czars and empresses) R: 549; (The
  Time of Troubles) R: 549
False dogwood [plant]
  Soapberry So: 543
False Face Society
  Indian, American (Shamans) I: 147-148; (Before
  European contact) I: 154-156
  Mask (Ceremonial masks) M: 264
False imprisonment [law] F: 19
False killer whale [sea animal]
  Killer whale K: 316
False Messiah
  Messiah M: 423
False rib [anatomy]
  Rib R: 320
False teeth
  Dentistry (Prosthodontics) D: 144
  Teeth (Dental decay) T: 82-84
Falstaff [opera by Verdi]
  Opera (Giuseppe Verdi) O: 798
  Verdi, Giuseppe V: 316
Falstaff, Sir John [literary figure]
  Drama *picture on* D: 324
  Shakespeare, William: *(Henry IV)* S: 358-359; *(The
  Merry Wives of Windsor)* S: 361
Falun Gong [spiritual movement]
  Beijing (History) B: 223-224
  China (Religion) C: 485-486
Falwell, Jerry [American religious leader]
  Evangelicalism E: 422
Fame, Hall of *See* Hall of Fame *in this index*
Famenne [region, Belgium]
  Belgium (The Ardennes) B: 231
Familia, La [family]
  Family (Varieties of families) F: 20-21
Familiar [spirit]
  Witchcraft (Witchcraft as sorcery) W: 371
Familiar Quotations [book by Bartlett]
  Bartlett, John B: 120
Family [astronomy]
  Asteroid (Orbital groups) A: 824a
Family [biology] F: 19
  Animal (The scientific classification of animals)
  A: 472-473
  Classification, Scientific (Groups in classification)
  Ci: 655
Family [criminal organization]
  Mafia M: 41
Family [sociology] F: 20 *with pictures*
  See also the list of Related articles in the Family
  article
  Adolescent (Family relationships) A: 62

Arabs (Family life) A: 587
Asian Americans (Who Asian Americans are)
  A: 812b
Birth control B: 378
Budget (Personal and family budgets) B: 669
Child (The role of the family) C: 451
China (Family life) C: 482
City (The people) Ci: 582-584
Disability (Family life) D: 220
Early childhood education (Activities planned by
  families) E: 15
Europe (The family) E: 389
Family and consumer sciences F: 25
Income *diagrams on* I: 101
Indian, American (Family life) I: 136b; (The
  preservation of Indian culture) I: 180
Juvenile delinquency (What causes
  delinquency?) J: 206
Latin America *picture on* L: 94
Marriage M: 219
Parent P: 156
Parent education P: 156
Social work (Family and child welfare) So: 558
Socialization So: 562
Welfare (Criticism of the welfare system) W: 191
Women's movement (On attitudes and values)
  W: 388
Family and consumer sciences F: 25
  Beecher, Catharine Esther B: 209
Family and Court of Ludovico Gonzaga II [painting
  by Mantegna]
  Renaissance *picture on* R: 232
Family child-care home
  Day care (Day care for children) D: 52
Family compact [Canadian history]
  Canada, History of (Growing discontent) C: 143
  Rebellions of 1837 (In Upper Canada) R: 174
Family Computer
  Electronic game (The Nintendo revolution)
  E: 204d
Family-couples psychotherapy
  Psychotherapy (Family-couples psychotherapy)
  P: 852
Family Group [sculpture by Moore]
  Moore, Henry M: 797
**Family History Library of the Church of Jesus
  Christ of Latter-day Saints** [Salt Lake City]
  Genealogy G: 82
Family law
  Law (Private law) L: 130
Family name
  Name N: 5; (Family names) N: 5; (The history of
  names) N: 7
Family of Charles IV, The [painting by Goya]
  Goya, Francisco G: 295
"Family of Man, The" [photography exhibit]
  Steichen, Edward So: 884
Family of Saltimbanques, The [painting by Picasso]
  Picasso, Pablo (The Rose Period) P: 448a *with
  picture*
Family planning *See* Birth control *in this index*
Family practice
  Medicine (Primary care physicians) M: 366;
  (Canada) M: 367
Family resource program *See* Family support
  program *in this index*
Family restaurant
  Restaurant (Full-service restaurants) R: 262
Family Support Act [1988]
  Clinton, Bill (Steps to the presidency) Ci: 682c
Family support program
  Early childhood education (Activities planned by
  families) E: 15
  Parent education (Family support programs)
  P: 157
Family tree [ancestry]
  Genealogy G: 82
  Pedigree P: 228
Famine F: 26 *with pictures*
  Africa (Agriculture) A: 125-126
  Ethiopia (Military take-over) E: 372
  Great Irish Famine G: 343
Famine [book by O'Flaherty]
  O'Flaherty, Liam O: 678
Famine Emergency Commission [U.S.]
  Hoover, Herbert Clark (Elder statesman) H: 330-
  331
Famous Five [Canadian history] F: 26b
Famous Men [work by St. Jerome]
  Jerome, Saint J: 93
Fan F: 26b *with picture*
Fan-in-fin system
  Helicopter (Single-rotor helicopters) H: 170-171
Fan Kuan [Chinese artist]
  Painting (Landscapes and seascapes) P: 32-33
  with picture
Fan Si Pan [mountain, Vietnam]

Vietnam (Northern Vietnam) V: 368
Fan worm [sea animal]
Animal *picture on* A: 486
Fancher, Frederick B. [American political leader]
North Dakota (table) N: 513
Fancy Free [ballet]
Ballet (Ballet in the United States) B: 53-54
Fandango [dance]
Folk dancing F: 320
Faneuil, Peter [American businessman] F: 27
Faneuil Hall
Boston *picture on* B: 498; (Downtown Boston)
B: 496
Faneuil, Peter F: 27
Faneuil Hall Marketplace
Boston *picture on* B: 500
Massachusetts *picture on* M: 271
Fang [people]
Equatorial Guinea (People) E: 346; (History)
E: 347
Gabon (People) G: 3
Fang [zoology]
See also Canine teeth *in this index*
Animal *picture on* A: 494
Rattlesnake R: 149
Snake (Fangs and venom glands) S: 528 *with
picture*
Snakebite S: 536
Spider (Chelicerae) So: 784 *with picture*
Fangio, Juan M. [Argentine race driver]
Automobile racing (table: Formula One World
Drivers' Championship) A: 980
Fanjet [airplane] *See* Turbofan *in this index*
Fannie Mae [agency] *See* Federal National
Mortgage Association *in this index*
Fannin, J. W. [American military leader]
Alamo (Early days) A: 280
Fannin, Paul [American political leader]
Arizona (table) A: 687
Fanny and Alexander [film]
Bergman, Ingmar B: 257
Fanon, Frantz Omar [Algerian author] F: 27
Fantail [bird]
Bird *picture on* B: 348
Fantail pigeon [bird]
Pigeon *picture on* P: 458
Fantasia [music] F: 27
Classical music (Free form) Ci: 645
Fantastic Four [cartoon characters]
Comics (Comic books) Ci: 869-870
Fantasy [literature]
Literature for children (Fiction) L: 359 *with
picture*; (The middle and late 1900's) L: 365
with picture
Fantasy piece [music]
Fantasia F: 27
Fantasy variations [philosophy]
Phenomenology P: 357
Fante [people]
Ghana (People) G: 178
Fantin-Latour, Henri [French painter]
Manet, Édouard *picture on* M: 138
Fantus, Bernard [American physician]
Blood (History of blood research) B: 414
FAO [organization] *See* Food and Agriculture
Organization *in this index*
Faqih [title]
Iran (Government) I: 399
Far Away and Long Ago [book by Hudson]
Hudson, William Henry H: 405
Far East [region, Asia] F: 27
Asia (Way of life in East Asia) A: 785 *with pictures*
Cat (History) C: 296
Cold War (Communist expansion in Asia) Ci: 764
Orient O: 855
Far from the Madding Crowd [book by Hardy]
Hardy, Thomas H: 59
Far Oceania [region]
Pacific Islands (Peoples of the Pacific Islands) P: 4
Far side
Moon *map on* M: 787; (Rotation and orbit) M: 783
"Far Side, The" [cartoon]
Cartoon *picture on* C: 264
Larson, Gary L: 77
Far ultraviolet rays
Astronomy (Ultraviolet astronomy) A: 844
Far Ultraviolet Spectroscopic Explorer [satellite]
Astronomy (Ultraviolet astronomy) A: 844
Far West [Missouri]
Mormons (Mormons in the Middle West) M: 808-
809
Young, Brigham (Mormon leader) Y: 571
Far West [U.S. history]
Westward movement in America (Exploring and
settling the Far West) W: 248 *with pictures*
Farabundo Martí National Liberation Front
[political group]

El Salvador (The 1900's) E: 252
Farad [measurement] F: 27
Capacitor (Capacitance) C: 186
Farad, Wali [American religious leader] *See* Fard,
Wallace D. *in this index*
Faraday, Michael [British physicist] F: 27
Battery (History) B: 171
Electric generator (Basic principles) E: 170
Electric motor (History) E: 181
Electricity (Electricity and magnetism) E: 197
Electrolysis (Principles of electrolysis) E: 201
Gas [physics] (History) G: 49
Invention (The Industrial Revolution) I: 361-362
Magnetism (Electricity and magnetism) M: 60d
Physics (Developments in the 1800's) P: 440
Radio (Early development) R: 91
Rubber (The chemistry of rubber) R: 501
Science *picture on* S: 201
Farallon Islands [San Francisco]
California (Coastline) C: 50
FARC [military group] *See* Revolutionary Armed
Forces of Colombia *in this index*
Farce [literature]
Comedy Ci: 867
Drama (Comedy) D: 325; (Farces and interludes)
D: 330
French literature (Early drama) F: 519
Farcy [disease]
Glanders G: 210
Fard, Wallace D. [American religious leader]
Black Muslims B: 389
Nation of Islam N: 27
"Farewell Address"
Washington, George (Farewell Address) W: 106
Farewell to Arms, A [book by Hemingway]
Hemingway, Ernest (Rise to fame) H: 180
Farewell-to-spring [plant]
Godetia G: 245
Fargo [North Dakota] F: 28 *with picture*
North Dakota *picture on* N: 497; (table: Average
monthly weather) N: 509
Fargo, William George [American businessman]
F: 28
Wells, Fargo & Company W: 195
Fargo Air Museum
North Dakota *picture on* N: 505
Farina, Giuseppe [Italian race driver]
Automobile racing (table: Formula One World
Drivers' Championship) A: 980
Fariña, Mimi [American musician]
Baez, Joan B: 25
Farjeon, Eleanor [British author] F: 28
Regina Medal (table: 1959) R: 206
Farley, James Aloysius [American political leader]
F: 28
Roosevelt, Franklin Delano (Election of 1932)
R: 452
Farley, John M. [American religious leader]
Cardinal (table: American cardinals) C: 211
Farley, Walter [American author] F: 28
Farm and farming F: 29 *with pictures*
See also Agriculture *in this index*
Agribusiness A: 143
Aquaculture A: 578
Bird (The importance of birds) B: 330 *with picture*
Careers (Farming, fishing, and forestry) C: 222
with picture
Dairying (Dairy farming) D: 6
Deere, John D: 87
FFA F: 84
Housing (Farm housing) H: 390
Livestock L: 344
Pet (Farm pets) P: 320 *with picture*
Slavery (Development of slavery) S: 501
Farm life in the United States
Agriculture, Department of A: 161
Cooperative (History) Ci: 1036
Grange, National G: 310
National Farmers Union N: 34
United States *picture on* U: 98; (Rural life)
U: 112
Farm life outside the United States
Africa (Rural life) A: 110-111 *with picture*;
(Agriculture) A: 125
Arabs (Economy) A: 589
China (Rural life) C: 474 *with picture*; (Rural life) C: 482
with picture; (Agriculture) C: 496 *with picture*
Collective farm Ci: 774
Europe (Rural life) E: 388 *with picture*;
(Agriculture) E: 400
Inca (Food, clothing, and shelter) I: 95
Middle East (Ways of life) M: 530; (Economy)
M: 531 *with picture*
Nigeria *picture on* N: 410
Women's movement (In developing nations)
W: 387
Farming methods

Farm and farming (Modern crop production)
F: 33 *with pictures*
Drainage D: 320
Dryland farming D: 370
Factory farming F: 5
Food (Geographic reasons) F: 331; (Production)
F: 334
Food supply (Limited agricultural resources)
F: 348; (Methods to increase the food
supply) F: 349
Irrigation I: 456 *with pictures*
Manure M: 172
Soybean (Soybean farming) So: 691
Water (Water for irrigation) W: 118 *with picture*
Farming problems
Farm and farming (Farm management) F: 41
Drought D: 349
Fungicide F: 560
Insect (Harmful insects) I: 284; (Insect control)
I: 284-285
Locust L: 419 *with picture*
Soil (Soil conservation) So: 576
History
City (Advances in technology) Ci: 577
Colonial life in America (Farming) Ci: 809 *with
picture*
Dust Bowl D: 391 *with picture and map*
Gay Nineties (Industrial growth) G: 72
Great Depression (The farm depression and
bank failures) G: 339
Indian, American (Farming) I: 141; (The first
farmers) I: 152; (Before European contact)
I: 169
New Deal (Helping the farmers) N: 201
Pioneer life in America (Stages of settlement)
P: 477; (Food) P: 481
Plant (The domestication of plants) P: 541
Townshend, Viscount T: 352
United States, History of the (Economic
growth) U: 169 *with picture*; (The South and
white supremacy) U: 183-185; (Early reform
efforts) U: 185; (The economy--boom and
bust) U: 191
Western frontier life in America (Improvements
in farming) W: 233; (Farming) W: 238
Farm cooperative
Cuba (Agriculture) Ci: 1174
Farm Credit Administration [U.S.]
Farm Credit System F: 45
Farm Credit System [U.S.] F: 45
Farm Credit System Insurance Corporation
Farm Credit System (Organization) F: 45-46
Farm machinery
Agriculture (Technological advances) A: 157;
(The industrialization of agriculture) A: 157
with pictures
Farm and farming *pictures on* F: 34
Illinois (Manufacturing) I: 69 *with picture*
Farm Security Administration [U.S. history]
Health and Human Services, Department of
(History) H: 128
New Deal (table) N: 201
Farm Service Agency [U.S.]
Agricultural Stabilization and Conservation
Service A: 145
Farm Show, The [drama]
Canadian literature (Modern Canadian drama)
C: 161
Farm system [baseball]
Rickey, Branch R: 335
Farm Workers Association, National
Chavez, Cesar Estrada C: 389
Farm Workers of America, United *See* United
Farm Workers of America *in this index*
Farm Workers Organizing Committee, United
Chavez, Cesar Estrada C: 389
Farman, Henri [French aviator]
Airplane (Other pioneer planes and fliers) A: 233
Aviation (The first airlines) A: 988
Farman, Joseph C. [British scientist]
Ozone hole O: 894
Farman, Maurice [French aviator]
Aviation (The first airlines) A: 988
Farmer *See* Farm and farming *in this index*
Farmer, James Leonard [American social reformer]
F: 46 *with portrait*
Farmer-Labor Party [U.S. history] F: 46
Humphrey, Hubert Horatio (Early life) H: 436
Minnesota (Politics) M: 602; (The early 1900's)
M: 604-606
Farmers' Alliance [U.S. history]
Kansas (Spirit of Reform) K: 237
Lease, Mary Elizabeth L: 166
Populism (Origins) P: 674
United States, History of the (Early reform efforts)
U: 185
Farmers' Educational and Cooperative Union of

America
National Farmers Union N: 35
Farmers Home Administration [U.S.] F: 46
Housing (The United States) H: 391
Farmers' market
Food (Marketing) F: 335
Farmers Market [Los Angeles]
Los Angeles picture on L: 467; (Visitor's guide)
L: 468
Farmers' Museum [Cooperstown, New York]
New York (Places to visit) N: 302
Farmers of America, Future See FFA in this index
Farmers Organization, National See National
Farmers Organization in this index
Farmers Union, National See National Farmers
Union in this index
Farming See Farm and farming in this index
Farnese, Alessandro [pope] See Paul III in this index
Farnese Bull [sculpture] F: 46 with picture
Farnham, Roswell [American political leader]
Vermont (table) V: 333
Farnsworth, Daniel D. T. [American political
leader]
West Virginia (table) W: 225
Farnsworth, Philo Taylor [American inventor] F: 46
Baird, John Logie B: 31
Television (Early development) T: 127
Faroe Islands [islands, Atlantic] F: 47 with map
Denmark D: 132
Farouk I [king of Egypt] See Faruk I in this index
Farquhar, George [English author] F: 47
Farquhar Islands
British Indian Ocean Territory B: 632
Farquharson, Donald [Canadian political leader]
Prince Edward Island (table) P: 791
Farragut, David Glasgow [American admiral] F: 47
with portrait
Admiral A: 59
Alabama picture on A: 277; (The Civil War and
Reconstruction) A: 276
Civil War, American (Capture of New Orleans)
Ci: 629; (Battle of Mobile Bay) Ci: 632
Lincoln, Abraham (Election of 1864) L: 323-324
Louisiana picture on L: 497
Porter, David P: 682
Farrakhan, Louis [American religious leader] F: 47
with portrait
African Americans (Politics) A: 136s
Black Muslims B: 389
Nation of Islam N: 27
Farrar, Frank L. [American political leader]
South Dakota (table) So: 680
Farrell, James T. [American author] F: 48
American literature (Realist fiction) A: 422
Farrow [zoology]
Hog (table) H: 284; (Farrowing) H: 287
Farsi [language]
Iran (Language) I: 401
Farsightedness [disorder] F: 48
Contact lens Ci: 1020 with picture
Eye (Farsightedness) E: 464 with pictures
Glasses (Prescription glasses) G: 224-225
Farthing [money] F: 48
Penny P: 271
Faruk I [king of Egypt] F: 48
Egypt (Republic) E: 132
Farwell, Leonard J. [American political leader]
Wisconsin (table) W: 365
FAS [disorder] See Fetal alcohol syndrome in this
index
FASB [organization] See Financial Accounting
Standards Board in this index
Fasces [symbol] F: 48 with picture
Fascia [building construction]
House diagram on H: 383
Fascism [political science] F: 49
Europe (Europe between the wars) E: 414
Government (Fascism) G: 288
Italy (Italy under Mussolini) I: 517 with picture
Mussolini, Benito (Fascist dictator) M: 967
Nazism N: 92
Spanish Civil War So: 756
World War II (Economic problems) W: 469; (The
rise of dictatorships) W: 469
Fashion F: 50 with pictures
See also Clothing in this index
Clothing (The globalization of fashion) Ci: 695;
(The clothing industry) Ci: 705-706 with picture
Custom Ci: 1200
Hairdressing H: 11 with pictures
Hip-hop H: 238
Italy picture on I: 510
Fashion doll
Doll (Modern dolls) D: 292 with picture
Fashion model [career]
Clothing picture on Ci: 706
Modeling (Kinds of models) M: 684

Fashion show
Modeling (Kinds of models) M: 684
Fashionable doll
Doll (Porcelain dolls) D: 290
Fast [religion] F: 52
Islam (The Five Pillars of Islam) I: 463-464
Ramadan R: 132
Fast ball
Baseball (Pitching) B: 127
Fast break
Basketball (Offensive strategies) B: 146
Fast breeder reactor
Nuclear energy (Nuclear fission) N: 582-583
Fast fashion
Clothing (The clothing industry) Ci: 705-706
Fast-food restaurant
McDonald's Corporation M: 332h
United States (Food) U: 115
Fast nova [astronomy]
Nova N: 553
Fast-pitch softball
Softball (Types of softball) So: 571
Fast reactor [nuclear reactor]
Nuclear energy (Nuclear fission) N: 582-583;
(Advanced fission reactors) N: 594
Fast-service restaurant
Restaurant (Kinds of restaurants) R: 262
Fastnacht [custom]
Mardi Gras M: 198
Shrove Tuesday S: 441
Fat [substance] F: 52 with diagram
Cancer (Nutrition) C: 171
Cholesterol (Factors that cause high cholesterol
levels) C: 520
Cooking (Cooking with fat) Ci: 1029
Detergent and soap (How soap is made) D: 164
Fat substitute F: 53
Food (Producing energy) F: 330
Heart (Risk factors) H: 137
Lipid L: 344
Liver (Digestion and use of food) L: 394
Lymphatic system (Absorption of fats) L: 535
Milk (Fats) M: 546
Nutrition (Fats) N: 625; (Nutrition guidelines)
N: 626
Obesity O: 642
Oil (Fixed oils) O: 706
Physical fitness (Body fat) P: 434
Tallow T: 21
Trans fats T: 369
Weight control W: 181
Fat-free milk See Skim milk in this index
Fat lamp
Lamp (Fat or oil lamps) L: 52 with pictures
Fat liquoring [industrial process]
Leather (Final processing) L: 168
Fat-soluble vitamin
Lipid (Kinds of lipids) L: 345
Nutrition (Vitamins) N: 626
Vitamin (Kinds of vitamins) V: 430
Fat substitute [nutrition] F: 53
Fat Tuesday See Mardi Gras in this index
Fata Morgana [mirage]
Mirage M: 615
Fatah [political group] F: 54
Arafat, Yasir A: 591
Hamas H: 28
Palestine Liberation Organization P: 106
Fatal familial insomnia [disorder]
Insomnia I: 303
Fatalism [belief] F: 54
Fatback [fish]
Menhaden M: 400
Fates [mythology] F: 54
Mythology (Greek divinities) M: 982
Fathead [fish]
Redfish R: 191
Father See Parent in this index
Father [religion] See God the Father in this index
Father, The [play by Strindberg]
Strindberg, August So: 929
Father Abraham [nickname]
Lincoln, Abraham (Assassination) L: 326
Father Christmas [legendary figure]
Christmas (In England, Ireland, Scotland, and
Wales) C: 530
Santa Claus (How the Santa Claus legend began)
S: 113
Father Divine [American religious leader] See
Divine, Father in this index
Father Frost [legendary figure]
Jack Frost J: 2
Father of bluegrass music [name for]
Monroe, Bill M: 733
Father of English history [name for]
Bede, Saint B: 199
Father of history [name for]

Herodotus H: 213
Father of medicine [name for]
Hippocrates H: 239
Father of New France [name for]
Champlain, Samuel de C: 373
**Father of Psyche Sacrificing at the Temple of
Apollo, The** [painting by Claude]
Classicism picture on Ci: 653
Painting (Composition) P: 35; (Classicism) P: 61
Father of the Blues [name for]
Handy, W. C. H: 50
Father of the Constitution [name for]
Madison, James M: 32
Father of the Country [name for]
Washington, George W: 90
Father of the Waltz [name for]
Strauss, Johann, Sr. So: 921
Fatherland Front [Bulgarian history]
Bulgaria (The world wars) B: 693
Fathers and Sons [book by Turgenev]
Nihilism N: 421
Russian literature (Early realism) R: 562
Turgenev, Ivan T: 500
Father's Day [custom] F: 54
Washington (Interesting facts about Washington)
W: 47
Fathers of Confederation
Confederation of Canada (Moves toward
confederation) Ci: 933-934
Mowat, Sir Oliver M: 903
Quebec Conference Q: 38
Tupper, Sir Charles T: 493
Fathers of Confederation [painting by Woods]
Canada, History of picture on C: 139
Fathom [measurement]
Fathom Five National Park [Ontario]
Canada (table: National marine conservation
areas) C: 114
National park (Canada) N: 42c
Fathometer [instrument] F: 54
Fatigue [disorder] F: 54
Chronic fatigue syndrome C: 538
Lactic acid L: 24
Fatigue strength [engineering]
Materials (Mechanicical properties) M: 300b
Fātiha [religion]
Islam (The Five Pillars of Islam) I: 463
Fátima, Our Lady of [religion] F: 55
Fātimah [daughter of Muhammad]
Fātimid dynasty F: 55
Muhammad (Early life) M: 910
Qom Q: 4
Fātimid dynasty [Muslim history] F: 55
Cairo (History) C: 17
Egypt (Muslim rule) E: 130
Muslims (The fall of the Abbāsids) M: 964c-964d
Fattening [agriculture] See Finishing in this index
Fatty acid [chemical]
See also Trans fats in this index
Cell (Producing energy) C: 332-333 with diagram
Fat (Structure) F: 52
Fat substitute F: 54
Food (Producing energy) F: 330
Lard L: 75
Life diagram on L: 277
Metabolism (Catabolism) M: 424
Nutrition (Fats) N: 625
Tallow T: 21
Triglyceride T: 442
Fatty oil
Oil (Fixed oils) O: 706
Fatty streak [physiology]
Arteriosclerosis (Causes) A: 750
Faubus, Orval E. [American political leader]
Arkansas (table) A: 712; (The mid-1900's) A: 714
Eisenhower, Dwight David (Civil rights) E: 153-
154
Little Rock (History) L: 392
Faucet [plumbing]
Plumbing (How faucets work) P: 579 with
diagram
Fauchard, Pierre [French scientist]
Dentistry (Early dentistry) D: 144-145
Faulds, Henry [Scottish doctor]
Fingerprinting (History) F: 107
Faulkner, William [American author] F: 55 with
portrait
American literature (Modernist fiction) A: 421-
422 with portrait
Mississippi, University of M: 646
Novel (New directions in the novel) N: 573-574
Fault [geology]
California (Land regions) C: 48
Earth (Earthquakes) E: 24
Earthquake (The cracking of ground) E: 33-34
with diagram; (Building location) E: 35; (How an
earthquake begins) E: 35-36 with pictures

Geothermal energy G: 136
Hot springs H: 374b
Lake (How lakes are formed) L: 32
Mountain (Tectonic mountains) M: 893 *with diagrams*
Petroleum *diagram on* P: 337; (Migration) P: 333-334
Plate tectonics (Transform plate boundaries) P: 563
Fault [sports]
Horse (Jumping) H: 357 *with picture*
Tennis (The serve) T: 163
Fault-block mountain [geology]
Mountain (Fault-block mountains) M: 893 *with diagram*
Fault divorce
Divorce (Fault divorce) D: 253
Fault plain [geology]
Earthquake (Why a quake begins) E: 36
Faun [Roman mythology] F: 56
Satyr S: 153
Faun, House of the [Pompeii]
Atrium *picture on* A: 877
Fauna [biology] F: 56
Fauna [Roman mythology]
Fauna F: 56
Fauntleroy, Betsy [American colonist]
Washington, George (Only foreign trip) W: 93
Faunus [Roman mythology]
Faun F: 56
Mythology (Roman divinities) M: 982-983
Fauquier, Francis [American political leader]
Jefferson, Thomas (Education) J: 77-78
Fauré, Gabriel Urbain [French composer] F: 56
Faure Gnassingbé [Togolese political leader]
Togo (History) T: 310-311
Fauset, Jesse Redmon [American author]
American literature (The Harlem Renaissance) A: 422
Faust [German magician] F: 56
Faust [literary figure]
See also Doctor Faustus *in this index*
Mephistopheles M: 412
Faust [opera by Gounod]
Gounod, Charles G: 281
Opera: *(Faust)* O: 804
Faust [play by Goethe]
Faust F: 56
German literature (Other writers) G: 140
Goethe, Johann Wolfgang von (Late years) G: 247
Gounod, Charles G: 281
Mephistopheles M: 411
Faustulus [legendary figure]
Romulus and Remus R: 450a
Faustus [German magician] *See* Faust *in this index*
Fauves [art movement] F: 56 *with picture*
Derain, André D: 152
Matisse, Henri M: 309 *with picture*
Painting (The Fauves) P: 77 *with picture*
Fauvism *See* Fauves *in this index*
Favaloro, René [Argentine physician]
Heart (Development of heart surgery) H: 144-145
Favela [slum]
Brazil (City life) B: 573 *with picture*
Latin America *picture on* L: 97
Favre, Brett [American football player] F: 56
Favrile glass [glassware]
Tiffany, Louis Comfort T: 283
Fawkes, Guy [English public figure] F: 57
Gunpowder Plot G: 442
Fawkner, John Pascoe [Australian colonist]
Melbourne (History) M: 389
Fawn [animal]
Deer D: 82d
Fax [document]
Fax machine F: 57
Fax board [electronics]
Fax machine (Multifunction fax machines) F: 57-58
Fax machine [communications] F: 57
Communication *picture on* Ci: 887
Telephone *picture on* T: 94
United States, History of the (The Information Age) U: 196b
Fayetteville State University
North Carolina, University of N: 495
Fayetteville Street Mall
Raleigh R: 130
Faymann, Werner [Austrian political leader]
Austria (Recent developments) A: 940
Fazenda [estate]
Brazil (The Central and Southern Plateaus) B: 580
FBI [agency] *See* Federal Bureau of Investigation *in this index*
FBI Academy
Federal Bureau of Investigation (Other services) F: 62

FBI Identification Division
Federal Bureau of Investigation (Other services) F: 62
FBI Laboratory
Federal Bureau of Investigation (Other services) F: 62
FC-2 [airplane]
Fairchild, Sherman Mills F: 9
FC Barcelona [team]
Ronaldinho R: 450a
FCA [government agency]
Farm Credit System F: 45
FCA [organization]
Fellowship of Christian Athletes F: 69
FCC [agency] *See* Federal Communications Commission *in this index*
FCIC [agency] *See* Federal Crop Insurance Corporation *in this index*
FCSIC [agency]
Farm Credit System (Organization) F: 45-46
FDA [agency] *See* Food and Drug Administration *in this index*
FDD [political group]
Burundi (History) B: 713-714
FDIC [agency] *See* Federal Deposit Insurance Corporation *in this index*
FDR Memorial [Washington, D.C.] *See* Franklin Delano Roosevelt Memorial *in this index*
Fe [symbol]
Iron (Properties) I: 435
Fear [emotion]
See also Anxiety *in this index*
Brain (Regulating emotions) B: 554
Child (Emotional problems) C: 452-453
Emotion (The basic emotion approach) E: 261
Instinct (Human instincts) I: 305
Mental illness (Anxiety disorders) M: 405
Panic disorder P: 130
Phobia P: 392
Fear and Trembling [book by Kierkegaard]
Kierkegaard, Søren Aabye (His philosophy) K: 313
Fearful Symmetry: A Study of William Blake [book by Frye]
Frye, Northrop F: 549
Fearn, John [British explorer]
Nauru (History) N: 68
Feast in the House of Levi [painting by Veronese]
Painting (The Renaissance in Venice) P: 55-56 *with picture*
Feast of Dedication *See* Hanukkah *in this index*
Feast of Fast-Breaking *See* `Id al-Fitr *in this index*
Feast of King Belshazzar, The [play by Calderón de la Barca]
Spanish literature (The 1600's) So: 759-760
Feast of Lights *See* Hanukkah *in this index*
Feast of Sacrifice *See* `Id al-Ad-hā *in this index*
Feast of Saint Nicholas *See* Saint Nicholas, Feast of *in this index*
Feast of Saint Nicholas, The [painting by Steen]
Steen, Jan *picture on* So: 883
Feast of Santa Lucia
December D: 68
Feast of Tabernacles
Sukkot So: 965
Feast of the Assumption
Assumption A: 820
Feast of the Chrysanthemums
Chrysanthemum C: 540
Feast of the Redeemer
Venice (The people) V: 307
Feast of the Rose Garlands, The [painting by Dürer]
Dürer, Albrecht D: 388
Feast of Weeks
Shavuot S: 377
Feasts and festivals F: 58
See also the list of Related articles in the Feasts and Festivals *article*
Doll (Doll festivals and customs) D: 287 *with picture*
Feather F: 59 *with pictures*
Bird (As a source of food and raw materials) B: 330-331, *diagram on* B: 352; (Feather care) B: 354; (Feathers) B: 362 *with picture*
Chicken (Kinds of chickens) C: 441
Indian, American *pictures on* I: 138, I: 144
Peacock *picture on* P: 212
Pigeon (The body of a pigeon) P: 458
Skin (Animal skin) S: 491
Feather art
Indian, American *picture on* I: 146
Feather moss [plant]
Moss M: 834
Feather star [sea animal]
Deep sea (Invertebrates) D: 82a-82b
Feather-winged beetle [insect]
Beetle B: 215

Feathering propeller
Airplane (Propellers) A: 217 *with pictures*
Propeller (Airplane propellers) P: 826
Feathers and Tails [book by Kherdian]
Literature for children *picture on* L: 358
Featherstonhaugh, George W. [American explorer]
Minnesota (The Louisiana Purchase) M: 603-604
Featherweight class
Boxing (table) B: 527
Feathery [ball]
Golf (Beginnings) G: 264
Feature [archaeology]
Archaeology (What archaeologists study) A: 595 *with picture*; (Evaluation) A: 598
Feature story
Newspaper (Writing editorials and features) N: 383
Feature syndicate
Journalism (News services) J: 171
Newspaper (Writing editorials and features) N: 383
Feboldson, Febold [legendary figure] F: 59
Febres Cordero, León [Ecuadorean political leader]
Ecuador (The 1900's) E: 73-74
Febronianism [religion]
Pope (The 1700's and 1800's) P: 665
February [month] F: 60 *with pictures*
Calendar (The Romans) C: 31
Julian calendar J: 187
Leap year L: 162
February Revolution [1848]
France (The revolutions of 1830 and 1848) F: 474
Revolution of 1848 R: 288
February Revolution [1917]
Lenin, V. I. (The road to power) L: 193
Russia (The February Revolution) R: 553
Russian Revolution of 1917 (The February Revolution) R: 566
Union of Soviet Socialist Republics (The February Revolution) U: 35
Februus [Roman mythology]
Mythology (Roman divinities) M: 982-983
Fecal occult blood test
Cancer (Cancer checkups) C: 171
Feces [physiology]
Alimentary canal A: 369
Digestive system (In the small intestine) D: 202-203
Incontinence I: 106
Fechino, Esteban [Argentinian pilot]
Glider (table) G: 230
Fed [agency] *See* Federal Reserve System *in this index*
Federal Aid Highway Act [1956]
Interstate Highway System I: 352
Federal Aid in Wildlife Restoration Act [1937]
Conservation (The rise of the conservation movement) Ci: 985-986
Federal Alliance of Land Grants [organization]
Hispanic Americans (Political developments) H: 256
Federal Assembly
Russia (National government) R: 531
Federal Aviation Administration [U.S.] F: 62
Airplane (Learning to fly) A: 226; (Building an airplane) A: 228
Airport A: 242; (Kinds of airports) A: 243
Aviation (Aviation agencies) A: 985; (A new age of flight) A: 990-991; (Careers in aviation) A: 992
Transportation, Department of (Agencies) T: 400; (History) T: 400
Washington, D.C. *map on* W: 76
Federal Board for Vocational Education [U.S. history]
Veterans Affairs, Department of (History) V: 344
Federal budget *See* National budget *in this index*
Federal Bureau of Investigation [U.S.] F: 62
Crime (Crime in the United States) Ci: 1138
Forensic science F: 388b
Hoover, J. Edgar H: 331
Police (Federal law enforcement agencies) P: 622
Reno, Janet R: 240
Washington, D.C. *map on* W: 76
Federal chancellor [office]
Germany (Executive) G: 147
Federal Civil Defense Act [1950]
Civil defense (History of civil defense in the United States) Ci: 606
Federal Communications Commission [U.S.] F: 63
Monitoring station M: 725
Radio (Government regulation of radio) R: 90-91
Radio, Amateur (Licenses) R: 95
Telephone (Competition in the U.S. telephone industry) T: 101
Television (Regulating U.S. television) T: 115;

(Digital television) T: 128
Federal Constitutional Court [government]
Germany (Courts) G: 147
Federal Council on the Arts and the Humanities
[U.S.]
National Foundation on the Arts and the
Humanities N: 36
Federal court
Court picture on Ci: 1103; (Federal courts)
Ci: 1102
United States, Government of the (The judicial
branch) U: 141
Federal Court [Malaysia]
Malaysia (Courts) M: 98b
Federal Court of Canada
Canada, Government of (The courts) C: 136
Federal Crop Insurance Corporation [U.S.]
Insurance (Other government insurance
programs) I: 314
Federal Deposit Insurance Corporation [U.S.]
F: 63
Bank (Regulation of U.S. banks) B: 92; (The
savings and loan crisis) B: 94
Great Depression (The New Deal) G: 341-342
New Deal (Helping savers and investors) N: 200-
201
Savings and loan association S: 165
Federal Deposit Insurance Corporation
Improvement Act [1991]
Bank (The savings and loan crisis) B: 94
Federal detention center
Prison (Types of correctional institutions) P: 805
Federal disaster area
Federal Emergency Management Agency F: 63
Federal district [political unit] F: 63
Federal District, Department of the [government]
Mexico City (City government) M: 478
Federal Election Campaign Act [1974]
Federal Election Commission F: 63
Hatch Political Activities Act H: 85
Federal Election Commission [U.S.] F: 63
Federal Emergency Management Agency [U.S.]
F: 63
Civil defense (How civil defense is administered)
Ci: 605-606
Fire department (The 1900's) F: 129
Hurricane Katrina (The aftermath) H: 456
Federal Emergency Relief Administration [U.S.
history]
Great Depression (The New Deal) G: 341
New Deal (Helping the needy) N: 201
Federal Employees, National Federation of
American Federation of Government Employees
A: 409
Federal Employees' Compensation Act [1916]
Workers' compensation W: 405
Federal Employees' Retirement System
Pension (Federal pension plans) P: 272-273
Federal Energy Administration [U.S.]
Energy, Department of (History) E: 276
Federal Farm Board [U.S.]
Hoover, Herbert Clark (Champion of prosperity)
H: 329
Federal Farm Credit Administration [U.S.]
Farm Credit System F: 45
Federal Farm Credit Banks Funding Corporation
Farm Credit System (Organization) F: 45-46
Federal Food, Drug, and Cosmetic Act [1938]
Drug (U.S. drug laws) D: 357
Food additive (Government regulations) F: 340
Food and Drug Administration F: 340
Pure food and drug laws P: 907
Federal funds rate
Economics (Government intervention) E: 59
Interest (The federal funds rate) I: 323
Federal government See Federalism; United
States, Government of the in this index
Federal government debt See National debt in
this index
Federal Hall [New York City] F: 64
L'Enfant, Pierre Charles L: 191
National Park System (table: National memorials)
N: 54
Federal Highway Administration [U.S.] F: 64
Transportation, Department of (Agencies) T: 400
Federal Home Loan Mortgage Corporation [U.S.]
F: 64
Bush, George Walker (Economy) B: 722j
Mortgage M: 821
Federal Housing Administration [U.S.] F: 64
Housing and Urban Development, Department
of (History) H: 393
Mortgage M: 821
Federal Insecticide, Fungicide, and Rodenticide
Act [1947]
Pest control (Effects of pesticide use) P: 318
Federal Insurance Contributions Act [1937]

Pension (Federal pension plans) P: 272
Social security (Financing Social Security) So: 555
Federal Interstate Highway System
Road (How roads and highways are paid for)
R: 360
Federal Investment Review Agency [Canada]
Trudeau, Pierre Elliott (The national scene) T: 464
Federal Job Information Centers
Civil service (Federal civil service) Ci: 612
Federal Land Bank
Farm Credit System (History) F: 46
Federal Library and Information Center
Committee
Library (United States government libraries)
L: 248-249
Federal Lighthouse Service
Coast Guard, United States (New duties) Ci: 737
Federal Maritime Commission [U.S.] F: 64
Federal means-tested pension
Pension (Pensions in other countries) P: 273
Federal National Mortgage Association [U.S.]
F: 64
Bush, George Walker (Economy) B: 722j
Mortgage M: 821
Federal Open Market Committee [U.S.]
Federal Reserve System (Organization) F: 65
Federal Power Commission [U.S.]
Energy, Department of (History) E: 276
Federal president [office]
Germany (Executive) G: 147
Federal prison
Prisons, Federal Bureau of P: 808
Federal Property and Administrative Services
Act [1949]
General Services Administration G: 83
Federal Railroad Administration [U.S.]
Railroad (The role of the federal government)
R: 113
Federal Reports Act [1942]
Census (Conducting censuses) C: 347
Federal Republic of Germany See Germany in
this index
Federal Reserve Act [1913]
Bank (The national banking system) B: 93
Federal Reserve System (History) F: 66
Glass, Carter G: 223
Federal Reserve Bank [U.S.]
Federal Reserve System (Organization) F: 65
Federal Reserve Note
Money pictures on M: 709, M: 710; (Federal
Reserve Notes) M: 713; (Modern U.S. currency)
M: 713
Federal Reserve System [U.S.] F: 65 with map
Bank (Central banks) B: 91; (Regulation of U.S.
banks) B: 92; (The national banking system)
B: 93; (Crisis in finance) B: 95
Clearinghouse Ci: 660
Deflation D: 88
Depression (Depressions since World War II)
D: 150
Economics (Government intervention) E: 59
Greenspan, Alan G: 386
Inflation (Monetary policy) I: 268
Interest (Government policy) I: 322; (The federal
funds rate) I: 322
Money (Federal Reserve Notes) M: 713
Washington, D.C. map on W: 76
Wilson, Woodrow (Legislative program) W: 322-
323
Federal Savings and Loan Insurance Corporation
[U.S.]
Bank (The savings and loan crisis) B: 94
Federal Security Agency [U.S.]
Health and Human Services, Department of
(History) H: 128
Federal Security Service [agency]
Russia (Courts) R: 532
Federal style
Architecture (Neoclassical architecture) A: 623-
624
Furniture picture on F: 569; (Early American
furniture) F: 579 with picture
Phyfe, Duncan P: 431
Federal system [political science] See Federalism
in this index
Federal Trade Commission [U.S.] F: 66
Advertising (Regulation of advertising) A: 77
Antitrust laws A: 560
Consumer protection (The right to information)
Ci: 1018
Industry (Monopolies) I: 261
Monopoly and competition (History) M: 732
Packaging (Packaging regulations) P: 18
Washington, D.C. map on W: 76
Wilson, Woodrow (Legislative program) W: 322-
323
Federal Trade Commission Act [1914]

Antitrust laws A: 560
Federal Triangle
Washington, D.C. (Executive branch buildings)
W: 75
Federal Unemployment Tax Act [1939]
Unemployment insurance (United States plan)
U: 24
Federal waterfowl refuges [Wyoming]
Wyoming (Places to visit) W: 524
Federalism [political science]
Constitution of the United States (The supreme
law of the land) Ci: 998
Democracy (Controls on power) D: 121
Devolution D: 175
Government (Levels of government) G: 285
Local government L: 406; (Federal systems)
L: 408
Political party (Organizing the government)
P: 632
State government So: 862
Supreme Court of the United States (Federalism)
So: 1000
United States, Government of the (Federalism)
U: 137
Federalist, The [book by Hamilton, Madison, and
Jay] F: 66
Essay (Formal essays) E: 359
Hamilton, Alexander (Early political career) H: 32
Jay, John J: 67
Madison, James (Constitutional Convention)
M: 33-34
United States, History of the (Adopting the
Constitution) U: 162
Federalist Party [U.S. history] F: 66
Adams, John (Vice president) A: 37; (Difficulties
with France) A: 38
Constitution of the United States (Ratifying the
Constitution) Ci: 1001
Democratic-Republican Party D: 129
Hamilton, Alexander (Secretary of the treasury)
H: 32-33
Jefferson, Thomas (Election of 1800) J: 83; (New
policies) J: 83-84
Madison, James (Congressman) M: 34; (Progress
of the war) M: 35-36
Political party (Early history) P: 635
United States, History of the (Establishing
political parties) U: 163; (Decline of the
Federalists) U: 165
Washington, George (Rise of political parties)
W: 104
Federated city
Metropolitan area (Metropolitan federation)
M: 443
Federated States of Micronesia See Micronesia,
Federated States of in this index
Federation [political unit]
See also Federalism in this index
Indian, American (Federations) I: 143
Fédération Aéronautique Internationale
[organization]
Aviation (The first flying regulations) A: 987
National Aeronautic Association N: 27
Federation Council
Duma D: 381
Russia (National government) R: 531
Federation Cup
Tennis (Tennis tournaments) T: 165
Fédération Internationale de Football
Association [organization]
Soccer (Soccer competition) So: 548
World Cup W: 450
Fédération Internationale de l'Automobile
[organization]
Automobile racing (Racing organizations) A: 976;
(Formula One racing) A: 976; (Growth of
organized automobile racing) A: 979
Fédération Internationale de Natation
[organization]
Diving (Diving meets) D: 243
International Olympic Committee I: 343
Swimming (Swimming as a sport) So: 1044
Fédération Internationale de Ski [organization]
Snowboarding S: 541
Fédération Internationale des Échecs
[organization]
Chess (Tournament competition) C: 413;
(History) C: 414
Kasparov, Garry K: 248
Fédération Internationale des Luttes Associées
[organization]
Wrestling W: 505
Fédération Internationale des Sociétés d'Aviron
[organization]
Rowing (Competition) R: 494
Federation of ...
Federations appear under their key words, as in

South Arabia, Federation of
Federer, Roger [Swiss tennis player] **F:** 67
FedEx Corporation [company]
Postal services *picture on* **P:** 707
FedEx Cup [tournament]
Golf (Tournaments) **G:** 264
Fedor I [czar]
Russia (The Time of Troubles) **R:** 549; (table: Czars and empresses) **R:** 549
Fedor II [czar]
Russia (table: Czars and empresses) **R:** 549
Fedor III [czar]
Russia (table: Czars and empresses) **R:** 549
Fee [law] **F:** 67
Fee-for-service plan [medicine]
Medicine (The United States) **M:** 367
Fee simple [law]
Estate **E:** 360
Fee **F:** 67
Fee tail [law]
Estate **E:** 360
Fee **F:** 67
Feed [agriculture] **F:** 67
Alfalfa (As livestock feed) **A:** 346 *with picture*
Beef (Food value) **B:** 211
Cattle (Feeding) **C:** 312
Corn (Livestock feed) **Ci:** 1057 *with picture*; (The mixed-feed industry) **Ci:** 1061
Dairying (Feeding) **D:** 7
Grain (Uses) **G:** 301
Hay **H:** 115
Livestock (Feed) **L:** 397
Silo **S:** 462
Soybean **So:** 689
Vetch **V:** 343
Wheat (Livestock feed) **W:** 267 *with picture*
Feed bunk [manger]
Dairying (Feeding) **D:** 7
Feed crop
Farm and farming (Processing and storage) **F:** 37
Feed lot [agriculture]
Agriculture (Raising livestock) **A:** 150-151
Cattle *picture on* **C:** 313
Farm and farming (Livestock finishing) **F:** 40
Food supply (Reducing the demand for feed grain) **F:** 350
Livestock (Feed) **L:** 397
Feedback
Automation (How automation works) **A:** 945 *with diagram*
Cybernetics **Ci:** 1203
Rock music (Psychedelic rock) **R:** 380a
Feeder [agriculture]
Cattle (Feeder cattle) **C:** 314
Feeder [machine]
Glass (Glass terms) **G:** 222
Feeder cattle [animal]
Cattle (Feeder cattle) **C:** 314
Ranching (Life on a cattle ranch) **R:** 134
Feeding center [anatomy]
Weight control (How body weight is determined) **W:** 181
Feedlot *See* Feed lot *in this index*
Feedstocks [manufacturing]
Recycling (Uses for recycled materials) **R:** 184
Feeler [entomology] *See* Antennae *in this index*
Feet *See* Foot *in this index*
Fei qian [money]
Money (Paper money) **M:** 708
Feijoada [food]
Brazil (Food and drink) **B:** 574
Feijoo, Benito Jerónimo [Spanish author]
Spanish literature (The 1700's) **So:** 760
Feingold, Russell Dana [American political leader]
McCain, John (Political life) **M:** 332a
Feininger, Lyonel [American painter] **F:** 67 *with picture*
Painting (Expressionism) **P:** 78-79
Feinstein, Dianne [American political leader] **F:** 68 *with portrait*
Feint [boxing]
Boxing (Boxing skills) **B:** 529
Feira [market]
Brazil (Food and drink) **B:** 574
Feisal [king of Saudi Arabia] *See* Faisal *in this index*
Feitsui Dam [Taiwan]
Dam *picture on* **D:** 18
Feke, Robert [American painter] **F:** 68
Colonial life in America (Painting) **Ci:** 807 *with picture*
Felafel [food]
Israel (Food and drink) **I:** 481
Felch, Alpheus [American political leader]
Michigan (table) **M:** 507
Feldberg [mountain, Germany]
Black Forest **B:** 386
Feldspar [mineral] **F:** 68

Crystal (Classifying crystals) **Ci:** 1166-1167 *with picture*
Granite **G:** 311
Mineral *picture on* **M:** 566
Felibrige [French literature]
Mistral, Frédéric **M:** 676
Feliciana Country [region]
Louisiana (Places to visit) **L:** 488
Feline enteritis [disorder] *See* Panleukopenia *in this index*
Feline immunodeficiency virus
Cat (Veterinary care) **C:** 295
Feline leukemia [disease]
Cat (Veterinary care) **C:** 295
Felix I, Saint [pope]
Pope (table) **P:** 666
Felix II [antipope]
Pope (table) **P:** 666
Felix III, Saint [pope]
Pope (table) **P:** 666
Felix IV, Saint [pope]
Pope (table) **P:** 666
Felix V [antipope]
Pope (table) **P:** 666
Felix the Cat [cartoon]
Animation (Pioneers of American animation) **A:** 514a-515b
Television (History of U.S. television broadcasting) **T:** 117 *with picture*
Felker, Samuel D. [American political leader]
New Hampshire (table) **N:** 223
Fellahin [people]
Egypt (Rural life) **E:** 123 *with picture*
Feller, Bob [American baseball player] **F:** 68
Baseball (table: Hall of Fame) **B:** 134; (Depression and war) **B:** 136
Fellini, Federico [Italian director] **F:** 68
Motion picture (The art film revival) **M:** 870
Fellow [education] *See* Fellowship *in this index*
Fellow travelers [literary group]
Russian literature (The period of rebirth) **R:** 564
Fellowcraft
Masonry (The lodges and degrees of Masonry) **M:** 267
Fellowship [education] **F:** 69
Scholarship **S:** 178
Universities and colleges (Faculty) **U:** 208
Fellowship of Christian Athletes [organization] **F:** 69
Fellowship of the Ring, The [book by Tolkien]
Tolkien, J. R. R. **T:** 321
Fells Point [Baltimore]
Baltimore (Other interesting places to visit) **B:** 69
Felon [European history]
Feudalism (Justice under feudalism) **F:** 82-83
Felony [law] **F:** 69
Burglary **B:** 704
Crime (Felonies and misdemeanors) **Ci:** 1136
Felony murder [law]
Murder **M:** 929
Felt [fabric] **F:** 69
Felt pause [poetry]
Poetry (Rhythm and meter) **P:** 591-593
Felt-tip pen
Pen (Soft-tip pens) **P:** 234 *with picture*
Felting [characteristic]
Wool **W:** 399
Felton, John [English military leader]
Buckingham, Duke of **B:** 663
Felton, Rebecca L. [American political leader]
Georgia (The early 1900's) **G:** 134
FEMA [agency] *See* Federal Emergency Management Agency *in this index*
Female
See also Girl *in this index*
Fragile X syndrome **F:** 451
Growth (Growth rate) **G:** 405
Heredity (Chromosomes and sexual determination) **H:** 202; (Sex-linked genes) **H:** 202
Reproduction, Human (The human reproductive system) **R:** 244 *with diagram*
Sex ratio **S:** 336
Sexuality (Biological factors) **S:** 337
Steroid (The sex steroids) **So:** 894
Female circumcision [surgery]
Circumcision **Ci:** 561
Female Eunuch, The [book by Greer]
Greer, Germaine **G:** 387
Female genital mutilation
Circumcision **Ci:** 561
Female Nude [book by Duffy]
Duffy, Carol Ann **D:** 378
Female pattern baldness
Baldness **B:** 38
Female Review, The [book about Sampson]
Sampson, Deborah **S:** 81

Feminine gender [grammar]
Gender **G:** 80
Noun (Gender) **N:** 552-553
Feminine Mystique, The [book by Friedan]
Friedan, Betty **F:** 532
National Organization for Women **N:** 42
Women's movement (Decline after 1920) **W:** 385-386
Femininity
Sexuality (Sex and gender) **S:** 338; (Gender roles) **S:** 338a
Feminism **F:** 69 *with picture*
French literature (The middle and late 1900's) **F:** 523
Friedan, Betty **F:** 532
Greer, Germaine **G:** 387
Grimké **G:** 393
History (Approaches to history) **H:** 261
Walker, Alice **W:** 13
Women's movement **W:** 383
Feminist literary criticism
Criticism (History of literary criticism) **Ci:** 1146-1147
Femoral artery [anatomy]
Artery (Principal arteries) **A:** 751
Human body (table) **H:** 422 *with diagram*
Leg (Blood and nerve supply) **L:** 182
Femoral nerve [anatomy]
Human body (table) **H:** 422 *with diagram*
Femto [prefix]
Metric system (Metric prefixes) **M:** 439
Femur [anatomy]
Frog *picture on* **F:** 537
Hip **H:** 238 *with diagram*
Human body (table) **H:** 422 *with diagram*
Knee **K:** 345
Leg **L:** 181 *with diagram*
Pelvis **P:** 233
Fen [geography]
Wetland **W:** 252a; (Bogs and fens) **W:** 252b
Fen [money]
Yuan **Y:** 575
Fence rider
Cowboy (On the ranch) **Ci:** 1110-1111
Fences [play by Wilson]
Drama *picture on* **D:** 341
Wilson, August **W:** 316
Fencing [sport] **F:** 70 *with pictures*
Olympic Games (Summer Olympic Games) **O:** 746e-746f
Fend
Rugby football (Rugby Union) **R:** 510
Fender, Leo [American inventor]
Electric guitar **E:** 174
Fénelon, François de Salignac de la Mothe- [French author] **F:** 71
Fenestron [device]
Helicopter (Single-rotor helicopters) **H:** 170-171
Fengxian cave [China]
China *picture on* **C:** 489
Fenian cycle [Irish literature] *See* Fionn cycle *in this index*
Fenian movement [Irish history] **F:** 71
Confederation of Canada (Approval of confederation) **Ci:** 934-935
Fenian Ram [submarine]
Holland, John Philip **H:** 292
Fenian Society [organization]
Holland, John Philip **H:** 292
Fenn, John Bennett [American chemist]
Nobel Prizes (Chemistry: 2002) **N:** 444
Fennec [animal] **F:** 71
Fox (Fennecs) **F:** 440 *with picture*
Fennel [plant] **F:** 72 *with picture*
Fennell, Frederick [American musician]
Band (Wind ensembles) **B:** 75
Fenner, Arthur [American political leader]
Rhode Island (table) **R:** 311
Fenner, James [American political leader]
Rhode Island (table) **R:** 311
Fennoscandia [region, Europe]
Scandinavia **S:** 170
Fens [region, England]
England (The English Lowlands) **E:** 300-301
United Kingdom (The English Lowlands) **U:** 59-61 *with map*
Fenton, Reuben Eaton [American political leader]
New York (table) **N:** 313
Fenton, Roger [British journalist]
Photography (Artistic advances) **P:** 424-425
Feodor [brother of]
Peter I, the Great (Early life) **P:** 323
Feoktistov, Konstantin P. [Soviet cosmonaut]
Space exploration (Voskhod and Gemini: The first multiperson space flights) **So:** 714
Fer-de-lance [snake] **F:** 72 *with picture*
Viper **V:** 391

FERA [agency] See Federal Emergency Relief Administration in this index
Ferber, Edna [American author] **F:** 72
  Show Boat **S:** 438
Ferdinand [literary figure]
  Shakespeare, William: (The Tempest) **S:** 365
Ferdinand I [Holy Roman emperor]
  Austria (The Habsburgs) **A:** 937
  Habsburg, House of **H:** 3
Ferdinand I [king of Romania]
  Romania (The origins of modern Romania)
  R: 423; (Depression and fascism) **R:** 424
Ferdinand I [king of the Two Sicilies]
  Bourbon (In Naples and Sicily) **B:** 517
  Sicilies, Kingdom of the Two Sicilies **S:** 446
Ferdinand II [Holy Roman emperor] **F:** 72
  Thirty Years' War (The Bohemian period) **T:** 260
Ferdinand III [Holy Roman emperor] **F:** 72
Ferdinand IV [king of Spain] See Ferdinand I [king of the Two Sicilies] in this index
Ferdinand V [king of Castile and Aragon] **F:** 73
  Boabdil **B:** 427
  Castile and Aragon **C:** 279
  Columbus, Christopher (Years of waiting) **Ci:** 858; (Trouble, settlement, and exploration) **Ci:** 862; (Third voyage westward) **Ci:** 862; (Fourth voyage westward) **Ci:** 863; (Final days) **Ci:** 864
  Granada **G:** 304
  Isabella I **I:** 461
  Ponce de León, Juan (Florida expeditions) **P:** 655
  Spain (Union of the Spanish kingdoms) **So:** 746
Ferdinand VII [king of Spain]
  Latin America (The movement toward independence) **L:** 106
  Mexico (Revolt against the Spaniards) **M:** 470
  Napoleon I (Fall from power) **N:** 15-16
  Spain (Loss of the empire) **So:** 748
Fergana Valley [region, Uzbekistan]
  Uzbekistan (Land and climate) **U:** 254
Ferguson, Emily Gowan [birth name of]
  Murphy, Emily Gowan **M:** 931
Ferguson, George H. [Canadian political leader]
  Ontario (table) **O:** 783
Ferguson, James E. [American political leader]
  Texas (table) **T:** 203; (The early 1900's) **T:** 207-208
Ferguson, Miriam A. [American political leader]
  Texas (table) **T:** 203; (The early 1900's) **T:** 207-208
Ferguson plaid
  Tartan picture on **T:** 47
Feria [festival]
  Peru (Recreation) **P:** 310
Ferlinghetti, Lawrence [American poet] **F:** 73
Fermat, Pierre de [French mathematician] **F:** 73
  Geometry (Beginnings of modern geometry) **G:** 106
  Insurance (The growth of insurance) **I:** 315
  Mathematics (Mathematics and the scientific revolution) **M:** 306-307
Fermat's last theorem [mathematics]
  Fermat, Pierre de **F:** 73
Ferment [chemistry]
  Fermentation **F:** 73
Fermentation [chemistry] **F:** 73
  Alcoholic beverage **A:** 336
  Antibiotic (Production) **A:** 552 with diagram
  Bacteria (Helpful bacteria) **B:** 19-20
  Beer **B:** 211
  Brewing **B:** 595 with picture
  Cider **Ci:** 552
  Distilling **D:** 239
  Ethanol **E:** 365
  Food preservation (Other methods) **F:** 344; (Early methods) **F:** 344
  Fungi (The importance of fungi) **F:** 559-560
  Silo **S:** 463
  Tea (Processing tea) **T:** 62
  Vinegar (Making vinegar) **V:** 386
  Whiskey **W:** 282
  Wine (Types of wine) **W:** 336 with picture; (How wine is made) **W:** 337-338 with pictures
Fermented beverage See Fermentation in this index
Fermi, Enrico [American physicist] **F:** 73
  Chicago, University of (Research program) **C:** 438
  Physics (Uncovering the secrets of the atom) **P:** 442
  Radiation (The nuclear age) **R:** 81
  Science picture on **S:** 203; (Achievements of the mid-1900's) **S:** 202 with picture
  Szilard, Leo **So:** 1077
  Uranium (History of the use of uranium) **U:** 216-217
Fermi Gamma-ray Space Telescope
  Astronomy (Gamma-ray astronomy) **A:** 845
  Telescope (Gamma-ray telescopes) **T:** 109
Fermi National Accelerator Laboratory [Batavia, Illinois] **F:** 74

Chicago (Industry) **C:** 431-432
  Electricity picture on **E:** 198
  Illinois picture on **I:** 53; (The mid-1900's) **I:** 75-76
  Neutrino **N:** 154
  Particle accelerator (How accelerators work) **P:** 184-186
  Particle detector picture on **P:** 187
Fermi Research Alliance, LLC [corporation]
  Fermi National Accelerator Laboratory **F:** 74
Fermilab [Batavia, Illinois] See Fermi National Accelerator Laboratory in this index
Fermion [subatomic particle] **F:** 74
  Boson **B:** 494
  Supersymmetry **So:** 995
Fermium [element] **F:** 74
  Transuranium element **T:** 401
Fern [plant] **F:** 74 with pictures
  Coal picture on **Ci:** 716
  Evolution (Evolution of new species) **E:** 429-430
  Fossil picture on **F:** 425
  Fractal **F:** 443
  Plant pictures on **P:** 522, **P:** 524; (Vascular plants) **P:** 518; (Sexual reproduction) **P:** 532-533 with pictures; (Classification of plants) **P:** 546-547 with pictures
  Spore (Plant spores) **So:** 801 with diagram
  Tree (Tree ferns) **T:** 415
Fern-tree jacaranda [tree]
  Jacaranda **J:** 2
Fernald, Bert M. [American political leader]
  Maine (table) **M:** 87
Fernandez, Dolores Clara [American activist] See Huerta, Dolores Fernandez in this index
Fernández de Kirchner, Cristina [Argentine political leader]
  Argentina (Recent developments) **A:** 659
  Latin America (In the early 2000's) **L:** 111
Fernández de Lizardi, José Joaquín [Mexican author]
  Latin American literature (The 1800's) **L:** 112
  Mexico (Literature) **M:** 460
Fernández Reyna, Leonel [Dominican political leader]
  Dominican Republic (History) **D:** 304-305
Fernández y Félix, Miguel [Mexican political leader] See Victoria, Guadalupe in this index
Fernandina Island
  Galapagos Islands **G:** 7 with map
Fernandinos [people]
  Equatorial Guinea (People) **E:** 346
Fernando Po [island, Equatorial Guinea] See Bioko in this index
Ferney [estate]
  Voltaire (Later years) **V:** 447
Ferrara, Duke of [Italian nobleman] See Alfonso II d'Este in this index
Ferraro, Geraldine Anne [American political leader] **F:** 76 with portrait
  Democratic Party (The late 1900's) **D:** 127
  Mondale, Walter Frederick (Political career) **M:** 702
Ferré, Luis A. [Puerto Rican political leader]
  Puerto Rico (Puerto Rico today) **P:** 884
Ferre, Maurice [American political leader] **F:** 76 with portrait
  Miami (History) **M:** 480
Ferrell, Rick [American baseball player]
  Baseball (table: Hall of Fame) **B:** 134
Ferrer, José [American actor]
  Motion picture (Best performance by an actor: 1950) **M:** 862a
Ferret [animal] **F:** 76 with picture
Ferric alum [chemical]
  Invisible ink **I:** 369
Ferric chloride [chemical]
  Invisible ink **I:** 369
Ferric oxide [chemical] See Iron oxide in this index
Ferrimagnetic material [physics]
  Magnetism (In materials) **M:** 60c with diagram
Ferris, G. W. Gale [American engineer]
  Ferris wheel **F:** 77
Ferris, Jean Leon Gerome [American painter]
  Penn, William picture on **P:** 243
  Plymouth Colony picture on **P:** 583
Ferris, Woodbridge N. [American political leader]
  Michigan (table) **M:** 507
Ferris wheel [ride] **F:** 77 with picture
Ferrite [alloy]
  Magnetism picture on **M:** 60
Ferromagnetic material [physics]
  Magnetism (In materials) **M:** 60c with diagram
  Materials (Magnetic properties) **M:** 300c
Ferromanganese [metal]
  Manganese (Industrial uses) **M:** 139
Ferrosilicon process [chemistry]
  Magnesium (How magnesium is obtained) **M:** 54
Ferrous alloy [chemistry]

Alloy (Alloys of iron) **A:** 377
Ferrous sulfate [chemical] **F:** 77
Ferrovanadium [alloy]
  Vanadium **V:** 268
Ferry [boat] **F:** 77 with picture
  Transportation picture on **T:** 390
Ferry, Elisha P. [American political leader]
  Washington (table) **W:** 65
Ferry Building
  San Francisco (Downtown San Francisco) **S:** 92-93
Ferry Farm
  Washington, George (Boyhood) **W:** 92
Ferryland [settlement]
  Newfoundland and Labrador (Colonization) **N:** 375
FERS [organization] See Federal Employees' Retirement System in this index
Fert, Albert [French physicist]
  Nobel Prizes (Physics: 2007) **N:** 442
Fertile Crescent [region, Asia] **F:** 78 with map
  Agriculture picture on **A:** 156; (Centers of domestication) **A:** 154
  Arabs (Land of the Arabs) **A:** 585
  Asia (The Tigris-Euphrates Valley) **A:** 804
  Prehistoric people (The rise of agriculture) **P:** 752
Fertility control See Birth control in this index
Fertility doll
  Doll (Doll festivals and customs) **D:** 287-288 with picture
Fertility drug
  Fertilization **F:** 78
  Infertility (Treatment) **I:** 265
  Multiple birth (Causes of multiple births) **M:** 920
Fertility program [agriculture]
  Cotton (Diseases) **Ci:** 1090
Fertility rate [statistics]
  Birth and death rates **B:** 377
Fertilization [biology] **F:** 78
  Animal (Sexual reproduction) **A:** 496
  Baby (Before birth) **B:** 4
  Cell (Meiosis) **C:** 331-332
  Corn (How the plant reproduces) **Ci:** 1058
  Embryo **E:** 257
  Evolution (Mutation) **E:** 427-428
  Fallopian tube **F:** 17
  Fish (How fish reproduce) **F:** 169
  Flower (Fertilization) **F:** 296
  Fruit (Caring for the crop) **F:** 546
  Heredity (Sex cells and reproduction) **H:** 201
  Human body (The reproductive system) **H:** 425
  In vitro fertilization **I:** 95
  Infertility (Treatment) **I:** 265
  Pollen (Fertilization) **P:** 645
  Reproduction (Through sexual reproduction) **R:** 242; (How reproduction has evolved) **R:** 243
  Reproduction, Human **R:** 244 with pictures; (Fertilization) **R:** 246
  Seed (Seed development in angiosperms) **S:** 281
Fertilized egg [reproduction]
  Heredity (Sex cells and reproduction) **H:** 201
Fertilizer [agriculture] **F:** 78 with pictures
  See also the list of Related articles in the Fertilizer article
  Agriculture (Artificial fertilizers) **A:** 158; (Chemical pesticides) **A:** 159
  Compost **Ci:** 905
  Conservation (Soil conservation) **Ci:** 979-980
  Cropping system **Ci:** 1153
  Environmental pollution picture on **E:** 333; (Soil pollution) **E:** 334; (Agriculture) **E:** 337
  Farm and farming (Soil management) **F:** 33
  Food supply (Limited agricultural resources) **F:** 348; (Making farmland more productive) **F:** 349
  Gardening (Fertilizing) **G:** 32; (Fertilizer) **G:** 37
  Indian, American (Farming) **I:** 141-142
  Lawn (Maintenance) **L:** 144; (Lawns and the environment) **L:** 144
  Phosphate **P:** 402
  Soil (Soil conservation) **So:** 576
  Soil pollution **So:** 576
Fès [Morocco] See Fez in this index
Fescue [plant] **F:** 80
  Lawn (Types of lawns) **L:** 142
Fessenden, Reginald Aubrey [Canadian-born physicist]
  Communication (The development of electronics) **Ci:** 883-884
  Radio (Early development) **R:** 91
  Wireless communication (History) **W:** 345
Fessenden, William Pitt [American political leader]
  Lincoln, Abraham (table) **L:** 323
Feste [literary figure]
  Shakespeare, William: (Twelfth Night) **S:** 360-361
Festival See Feasts and festivals in this index
Festival of Light
  Sweden (Holidays) **So:** 1026

Festival of Pacific Arts
Pacific Islands (Arts) **P:** 7
Festival of the Sun
Indian, American *picture on* **I:** 174
Festival of Two Worlds [arts festival]
Menotti, Gian Carlo **M:** 403
Festival USA
Bicentennial Celebration, American **B:** 288
Festive mask
Mask (Festive masks) **M:** 264
Fetal alcohol syndrome [disorder] **F:** 80
Intellectual disability (Environmental factors)
I: 318
Fetal monitor [medicine]
Childbirth (Methods of childbirth) **C:** 456-457
Fête galante [painting]
Painting (Rococo painting) **P:** 65
Rococo **R:** 396
Fêtes Galantes [poems by Verlaine]
Verlaine, Paul **V:** 317
Fetid horehound [plant]
Horehound **H:** 335
Fetish [magic] **F:** 81 *with picture*
Doll **D:** 286
Fetish [psychology]
Fetish **F:** 81
Fetterman, William J. [American soldier]
Western frontier life in America (Settlers and
Native Americans) **W:** 239
Wyoming (Indian and settler conflicts) **W:** 534
Fetus [reproduction]
Abortion **A:** 14
Baby (The developing baby) **B:** 4 *with pictures*
Embryo **E:** 257
Growth (Early development) **G:** 404-405
Preeclampsia **P:** 734
Pregnancy **P:** 734a
Reproduction, Human **R:** 244 *with picture;*
(Development of the embryo) **R:** 246-248 *with
picture;* (Growth of the fetus) **R:** 248
Toxoplasmosis **T:** 353
Ultrasound (Medical uses) **U:** 16
Umbilical cord **U:** 18
Feud [quarrel] **F:** 81
Feudal aid [European history]
Feudalism (The principles of feudalism) **F:** 82
Feudal incident [European history]
Feudalism (The principles of feudalism) **F:** 82
Feudalism [European history] **F:** 81 *with picture*
Army (Armies in the Middle Ages) **A:** 727
Castle **C:** 280
Charlemagne (Administration and influence)
C: 379
City (Government) **C:** 585
Democracy (The Middle Ages) **D:** 122
Estate **E:** 360
Europe (The Franks) **E:** 409
Freedom (The Middle Ages) **F:** 502
Government (Feudalism) **G:** 290
Homage **H:** 300
Hundred Years' War **H:** 437
Knights and knighthood **K:** 348
Law (The Middle Ages) **L:** 134-135
Middle Ages (Feudal Europe) **M:** 524
Painting (Medieval painting) **P:** 48
Primogeniture **P:** 781
World, History of the (Medieval Europe) **W:** 432
Feuerbach, Ludwig Andreas [German
philosopher] **F:** 83
Feulner, Edwin [American political figure]
Heritage Foundation **H:** 211
Fever [disorder] **F:** 83
Disease (Immune responses) **D:** 231-232
Fever blister [disorder] *See* Cold sore *in this index*
Feverfew [plant] **F:** 83
Pyrethrum **P:** 920
Few, William [American political leader] **F:** 83
Few Figs from Thistles, A [book by Millay]
Millay, Edna St. Vincent **M:** 552
Fey, Charles A. [American inventor]
Slot machine **S:** 508a
Feynman, Richard Phillips [American physicist]
F: 83 *with diagram*
Nanotechnology **N:** 10
Feynman diagram
Feynman, Richard Phillips **F:** 84 *with diagram*
Fez [city, Morocco] **F:** 84
Morocco (Arab conquest) **M:** 814
Fez [hat] **F:** 84
Morocco (Way of life) **M:** 811-812
Fez, Treaty of [1912]
Morocco (French and Spanish control) **M:** 814-
815
Fezzan [former province]
Libya (Independence) **L:** 267
FFA [organization] **F:** 84 *with pictures*
Agricultural education (Youth programs and

organizations) **A:** 145
FHA [agency] *See* Federal Housing Administration
in this index
Fhima, Lamen Khalifa [Libyan public figure]
Libya (United Nations sanctions) **L:** 268
FHWA [U.S.] *See* Federal Highway Administration
in this index
FIA [organization] *See* Fédération Internationale de
l'Automobile *in this index*
Fianna [Irish legend]
Mythology (The Fionn cycle) **M:** 985
Fianna Fáil [political party]
De Valera, Eamon **D:** 173
Ireland (Politics) **I:** 417; (The Irish Free State)
I: 427; (The Republic of Ireland) **I:** 427-428
Sinn Féin (History) **S:** 473
Fiat [law] **F:** 86
Fiat money
Money **M:** 704
Fiat S.p.A. [company]
Automobile (The birth of the automobile
industry) **A:** 966
Italy (Manufacturing) **I:** 511-512 *with picture*
Manufacturing (table) **M:** 170
Fiber F: 86 *with pictures*
Acetate **A:** 25
Acrylic **A:** 29
Agriculture (Raw materials) **A:** 148
Clothing (Clothing materials) **Ci:** 695
Composite materials **Ci:** 904
Cotton **Ci:** 1153
Materials (Biological materials) **M:** 300d
Microfiber **M:** 514
Plastics (To replace natural fibers and hides)
P: 555
Polyester **P:** 649
Spandex **So:** 753
Textile (Sources of textile fibers) **T:** 212
Fiber, Dietary [nutrition] **F:** 88
Colon cancer **C:** 786
Diverticulitis **D:** 240
Food (How the body uses food) **F:** 330
Laxative **L:** 148
Nutrition (Include fiber) **N:** 628
Fiber amplifier [machine]
Laser (Recording, storing, and transmitting
information) **L:** 82
Fiber crop [agriculture]
Crop **Ci:** 1153
Fiber flax
Flax (Growing and processing fiber flax) **F:** 230
with picture
Fiber hemp [plant]
Hemp **H:** 183
Fiber-optic bronchoscope [instrument]
Bronchoscope **B:** 637
Fiber-optic gyro [device]
Inertial guidance (Strap-down systems) **I:** 263
Fiber optics [physics] **F:** 88 *with pictures*
Cable *diagram on* **C:** 7; (Fiber-optic cables) **C:** 5
with diagram; (Telephone cables) **C:** 7
Communication (The digital age) **Ci:** 885 *with
picture*
Electronics (Light-emitting devices) **E:** 213
Endoscope **E:** 273
Glass (Specialty glasses) **G:** 212
Gyroscope (Optical gyroscopes) **G:** 454
Invention (Recent developments) **I:** 364
Laser (Recording, storing, and transmitting
information) **L:** 82
Light *picture on* **L:** 292; (Refraction) **L:** 288;
(Photonics) **L:** 291
Optics **O:** 813
Physics (Physics today) **P:** 442-443
Planetarium (Modern planetariums)
P: 514b-514c
Telephone (Traditional phone calls) **T:** 96-97;
(Improvements in telephone technology)
T: 100-101
Television (Coaxial cable and fiber-optic cable)
T: 123
Fiber-to-the-premises technology
Telephone (Improvements in telephone
technology) **T:** 100-101
Fiberboard [building material]
Wallboard **W:** 17
Fiberglass [material] **F:** 89 *with diagram*
Energy supply *picture on* **E:** 281
Glass *picture on* **G:** 211; (Kinds of glass) **G:** 212;
(Drawing) **G:** 215
Interior design (Choosing patterns and textures)
I: 332
Fiberglass-reinforced plastics
Materials (Composite materials) **M:** 300d
Fiberglass wool
Fiberglass (How fiberglass is made) **F:** 89
Fibiger, Johannes Andreas Grib [Danish

bacteriologist]
Nobel Prizes (Physiology or medicine: 1926)
N: 445
Fibonacci, Leonardo [Italian mathematician] **F:** 89
Decimal system (Spread of the decimal system)
D: 73
Mathematics (Arab mathematics) **M:** 306
Fibonacci sequence [mathematics]
Fibonacci, Leonardo **F:** 89
Fibrillation [disorder]
Defibrillator **D:** 88
Digitalis **D:** 203
Drug (Antiarrhythmics) **D:** 351
Heart (Diagnosis and treatment) **H:** 139;
(Abnormal heart rhythms) **H:** 142
Fibrillin [protein]
Marfan syndrome **M:** 198
Fibrin [physiology] **F:** 90
Anticoagulant **A:** 553
Blood *picture on* **B:** 412; (Controlling bleeding)
B: 411
Fibrinogen [protein]
Blood (Platelets) **B:** 408; (Controlling bleeding)
B: 411
Fibrin **F:** 90
Liver (Other functions) **L:** 394
Plasma (Functions of plasma) **P:** 551 *with picture*
Fibroid [disorder]
Hysterectomy **H:** 482
Fibrolite [mineral]
Sillimanite **S:** 462
Fibromyalgia [disorder] **F:** 90
Fibrous glass *See* Fiberglass *in this index*
Fibrous membrane [anatomy]
Membrane **M:** 391
Fibrous root [botany]
Plant (Roots) **P:** 528 *with picture*
Root (Kinds of roots) **R:** 469-470 *with diagram*
Vegetable (Roots) **V:** 292
Fibula [anatomy]
Human body (table) **H:** 422 *with diagram*
Leg (The leg) **L:** 182 *with diagram*
Fibula [ornament]
Clothing (Greece) **Ci:** 697
Pin **P:** 466 *with picture*
FICA [law] *See* Federal Insurance Contributions Act
in this index
Ficciones [stories by Borges]
Borges, Jorge Luis **B:** 487
Latin American literature (The mid-1900's) **L:** 114
Fichte, Johann Gottlieb [German philosopher]
F: 90
Political science (Liberalism) **P:** 639
Ficino, Marsilio [Italian philosopher]
Renaissance (The revival of Platonism) **R:** 234
Fiction [literature] **F:** 90
Arabic literature (Fiction) **A:** 583
English literature (Elizabethan fiction) **E:** 317
Literature **L:** 352
Literature for children (Fiction) **L:** 359
Novel **N:** 571
Poe, Edgar Allan (Fiction and theory of fiction)
P: 590
Pulitzer Prizes (table) **P:** 894
Romance **R:** 414
Writing (Fiction) **W:** 511
Fictional biography
Biography (Forms of biography) **B:** 312
Fictive kin
Family (Family relationships) **F:** 21
Fiddle [violin]
Country music (The instruments) **Ci:** 1098
Violin (History) **V:** 390
Fiddlehead [botany]
Fern (Parts of a fern) **F:** 74-75
Fiddleneck [plant]
Flower (Flowers of summer-dry regions) **F:** 288
with picture
Fiddler crab [sea animal] **F:** 91 *with picture*
Biological clock (Other rhythms) **B:** 315
Crab **Ci:** 1115
Crustacean *pictures on* **Ci:** 1164
Fiddler on the Roof [musical]
Musical comedy (The modern musical emerges)
M: 960
FIDE [organization] *See* Fédération Internationale
des Échecs *in this index*
Fidelio [opera by Beethoven]
Beethoven, Ludwig van (The second period)
B: 214
Fidelity bond [insurance]
Bonding **B:** 455
Insurance (Crime insurance) **I:** 314
Fidesz-Hungarian Civic Union [political party]
Hungary (Politics) **H:** 439
Fiduciary bond
Bonding **B:** 455

Insurance (Surety bonds) **I:** 314
Fiedler, Arthur [American conductor] **F:** 91
Fief [European history]
Fee **F:** 67
Feudalism **F:** 81
Middle Ages (The Carolingian Empire) **M:** 524
Field [database]
Database **D:** 41 *with picture*
Field [flag]
Flag *diagram on* **F:** 194
Field [physics]
Quantum field theory **Q:** 5
Waves **W:** 152
Field, Ben [American businessman]
Pullman, George Mortimer **P:** 900
Field, Cyrus West [American businessman] **F:** 91
Cable (Telegraph cables) **C:** 5-6
Field, David Dudley, Jr. [American lawyer] **F:** 91
Field, Eugene [American author] **F:** 91
Field, Frederick W. [American businessman]
Field, Marshall, I (His family) **F:** 92
Field, James G. [American political leader]
Populism (The People's Party) **P:** 675
Field, Marshall, I [American merchant] **F:** 92
Field, Marshall, II [son of]
Field, Marshall, I (His family) **F:** 92
Field, Marshall, III [American publisher]
Field, Marshall, I (His family) **F:** 92
Field, Marshall, IV [American publisher]
Field, Marshall, I (His family) **F:** 92
Field, Marshall, V [American businessman]
Field, Marshall, I (His family) **F:** 92
Field, Rachel [American author] **F:** 92
Newbery Medal (table) **N:** 359
Field, Richard [English printer]
Shakespeare, William (His first poems) **S:** 347
Field, Sally [American actress]
Motion picture (Best performance by an actress:
1979, 1984) **M:** 862, **M:** 862a
Field, Stephen Johnson [American jurist] **F:** 92
Field archery
Archery (Field archery) **A:** 603
Field artillery
Artillery (Field artillery) **A:** 762 *with picture*
Field coil
Electric motor (Parts of an electric motor) **E:** 179
Field cradle
United States *picture on* **U:** 113
Field cricket [insect]
Cricket **Ci:** 1130 *with picture*
Insect *picture on* **I:** 280
Field crop [agriculture]
Farm and farming (Specialized crop farms) **F:** 30
Field effect transistor [electronics]
Electronics (Transistors) **E:** 212
Transistor (Metal oxide semiconductor field effect
transistors [MOSFET's]) **T:** 374 *with diagram*
Field-emission display [electronics]
Television (Flat-panel displays) **T:** 126
Field-emission microscope [instrument]
Atom (How scientists study atoms) **A:** 874
Field Enterprises, Inc.
Field, Marshall, I (His family) **F:** 92
Field glasses
Binoculars **B:** 309
Field goal
Football (Scoring) **F:** 362
Rugby football (Rugby League) **R:** 512
Field guide [book]
Bird (Bird watching) **B:** 367
Field Guide to the Birds [book by Peterson]
Peterson, Roger Tory **P:** 326
Field hand [person]
Slavery (Conditions of slavery) **S:** 503
Field hockey [sport] **F:** 92 *with picture*
Hockey (Beginnings) **H:** 280-281
Indian, American (Recreation) **I:** 142
Field Hockey Association, United States
Field hockey (History) **F:** 93
Field Hockey Association of America
Field hockey (History) **F:** 93
Field holler
Blues **B:** 425
Field-ion microscope *See* Ion microscope *in this
index*
Field judge [sports]
Football (The officials) **F:** 362
Field line [physics]
Cosmic rays (The travel of primary cosmic rays)
Ci: 1076
Magnetism *diagram on* **M:** 59; (Magnetic fields)
M: 60
Van Allen belts **V:** 269
Field magnet
Electric motor (Parts of an electric motor) **E:** 179
Field mouse
Mouse (Field mice) **M:** 902

Field Museum [Chicago] **F:** 93
Chicago (Museums) **C:** 428
Dinosaur *picture on* **D:** 210
Field mushroom
Mushroom (Nonpoisonous mushrooms) **M:** 943-
945 *with picture*
Field observation
Sociology (Field observation) **So:** 566
Field of vision
Blindness **B:** 401
Field painting
Painting (Abstract Expressionism) **P:** 84-85
Field particle [physics]
Quantum field theory **Q:** 6
Field position [sports]
Football (table) **F:** 356
Field research *See* Field study *in this index*
Field round [contest]
Archery (Field archery) **A:** 603
Field sobriety test [law enforcement]
Driving while intoxicated **D:** 348
Field spaniel [dog] **F:** 94 *with picture*
Field strength [physics]
Weber **W:** 175
Field structure
Electric generator (Parts of a generator) **E:** 170
with diagrams; (How AC generators work)
E: 171
Electric motor (Parts of an electric motor) **E:** 179
Field study
Anthropology (How anthropologists work)
A: 547-548
Boas, Franz **B:** 427
Geography (How geographers work) **G:** 94
Mythology (Anthropological approaches)
M: 989-990
Tornado (Studying tornadoes) **T:** 336
Zoology (How zoologists work) **Z:** 606
Field trial
Dog (Dog competitions) **D:** 280-281
Fielder [position]
Baseball (Player positions) **B:** 127; (Fielding)
B: 128
Cricket (The fielding side) **Ci:** 1134
Fielder, James E. [American political leader]
New Jersey (table) **N:** 249
Fielder's choice
Baseball (Reaching base) **B:** 129
Fielder's glove
Baseball (Equipment) **B:** 125 *with picture*
Glove *picture on* **G:** 235
Fielding, Henry [British author] **F:** 94 *with portrait*
English literature (The rise of the novel) **E:** 318-
319
Novel (The first English novelists) **N:** 572
Police (Early law enforcement in England) **P:** 624
Fielding, William S. [Canadian political leader]
Nova Scotia (table) **N:** 567
Fields, W. C. [American actor] **F:** 95 *with picture*
Fieldstone Center
Battle Creek **B:** 172
Fieldwork *See* Field study *in this index*
Fiery searcher beetle
Beetle *picture on* **B:** 218
Fieschi, Sinobaldo [birth name of]
Innocent IV **I:** 275
Fiesta [celebration]
Latin America (Recreation) **L:** 98
Mexico (Holidays) **M:** 457
Fiesta de los Vaqueros, La [rodeo]
Arizona *picture on* **A:** 678
FIFA [organization] *See* Fédération Internationale
de Football Association *in this index*
FIFA World Cup [soccer] *See* World Cup *in this index*
Fife [musical instrument] **F:** 95 *with pictures*
Fifer, Joseph W. [American political leader]
Illinois (table) **I:** 71
Fifteenth Amendment [U.S. Constitution] **F:** 95
Constitution of the United States **Ci:** 1014
Force bill **F:** 371
Reconstruction (The impeachment of Johnson)
R: 178
Voting (Who may vote) **V:** 449
Voting Rights Act of 1965 **V:** 451
Fifth Amendment [U.S. Constitution] **F:** 95
Constitution of the United States **Ci:** 1012
Due process of law **D:** 378
Privacy, Right of **P:** 808a
Fifth Avenue [street]
New York City *picture on* **N:** 330; (Manhattan)
N: 323-325
Fifth Business [book by Davies]
Davies, Robertson **D:** 46
Fifth column [military] **F:** 96
Guerrilla warfare (Types of guerrilla movements)
G: 420
Propaganda **P:** 823

Underground **U:** 20
Fifth Crusade [1217-1221]
Crusades (Other Crusades) **Ci:** 1161
Fifth of July, The [play by Wilson]
Wilson, Lanford **W:** 317
Fifth Republic
De Gaulle, Charles André Joseph Marie (The Fifth
Republic) **D:** 91
France (Government) **F:** 455; (The Fifth Republic)
F: 476
Fifth wheel [mechanism]
Truck (Kinds of trucks) **T:** 457
Fifth-wheel trailer [vehicle]
Trailer (Recreational trailers) **T:** 367
50° July isotherm [meteorology]
Arctic (Land and climate) **A:** 636 *with map*
Fifty-Four Forty or Fight [U.S. history] **F:** 96
British Columbia (The border dispute) **B:** 630
Polk, James Knox (Election of 1844) **P:** 642
51 Pegasi [star]
Planet (The first discoveries) **P:** 513
50 State Quarters program
Money (Quarters) **M:** 714
Fig [fruit] **F:** 96 *with picture*
Fruit (Types of fruit in botany) **F:** 544-546 *with
picture*
Invasive species (How species become invasive)
I: 354j
Tree *picture on* **T:** 427
Fig wasp [insect]
Fig **F:** 96
Figari, Pedro [Uruguayan artist]
Uruguay (The arts) **U:** 225
Figaro [literary figure]
Opera: (*Barber of Seville, The*) **O:** 801 *with picture*;
(*Marriage of Figaro, The*) **O:** 805-806
Figg, James [British boxer]
Boxing (The revival of boxing) **B:** 532
Figgis, Mike [British director]
Motion picture (The computer revolution) **M:** 872
Fight-or-flight response [physiology]
Brain (Regulating body processes) **B:** 553
Stress **So:** 926
Fighter [airplane]
Air force (Aircraft and missiles) **A:** 183 *with picture*
Air Force, United States (Fighters) **A:** 191
Aircraft, Military (Fighters) **A:** 203 *with pictures*
Airplane (Military planes) **A:** 212
De Seversky, Alexander Procofieff **D:** 157
Fighter [career]
Boxing **B:** 526 *with picture*
Fighter-bomber
Aircraft, Military (Bombers) **A:** 202 *with picture*
Bomber (Kinds of bombers) **B:** 453 *with picture*
Fighting game
Electronic game (Fighting games) **E:** 204e
Fighting Irish [team]
Notre Dame, University of (The campus) **N:** 551
Fightingfish F: 96 *with picture*
Fish *picture on* **F:** 157; (Hatching and care of the
young) **F:** 170 *with picture*
Figueiredo, João Baptista [Brazilian political
leader]
Brazil (Under military rule) **B:** 586
Figueres, José [Costa Rican political leader]
Costa Rica (Revolutions and reforms) **Ci:** 1084
Figurate number [mathematics]
Series (Working with odd numbers) **S:** 317
Figurative painting [art]
Painting (New image painting) **P:** 87 *with picture*
Figure [wood]
Wood **W:** 389 *with pictures*
Figure-ground perception
Gestalt psychology **G:** 175
Figure of speech [language] **F:** 97
Slang (Figures of speech) **S:** 500
Figure skating
Ice skating **I:** 10; (Figure skating) **I:** 11 *with
pictures*; (History) **I:** 16
Olympic Games (Winter Olympic Games) **O:** 746d
Roller skating (Artistic skating) **R:** 402a
Figured bass [music]
Bach, Johann Sebastian (His works) **B:** 16
Figurehead
Folk art *picture on* **F:** 319; (Sculpture) **F:** 317
Figwort family [botany] **F:** 97
Fiji F: 97 *with pictures and map*
Flag *picture on* **F:** 202
Pacific Islands *pictures on* **P:** 6, **P:** 7; (Pacific
alliances and independence movements) **P:** 12
Filament [astronomy]
Universe **U:** 205
Filament [biology]
Flower (The stamens) **F:** 293 *with pictures*
Plant (Flowers) **P:** 531 *with picture*
Filament [electricity]
Edison, Thomas Alva (The electric light) **E:** 79

Electric light *picture on* E: 176; (The filament)
   E: 174
Electricity (A simple circuit) E: 194
Light bulb L: 293
Vacuum tube (How a vacuum tube works) V: 258
Filament [textile]
   Fiber F: 87
   Textile (Sources of textile fibers) T: 212; (Making
      the yarn) T: 215
   Thread T: 269 *with picture*
Filament winding [industrial process]
   Composite materials (Polymer composites)
      Ci: 904
Filaria [animal] F: 99 *with picture*
   Manson, Sir Patrick M: 167
   Mosquito (Mosquitoes and people) M: 834
Filature [factory]
   Silk (Reeling) S: 460
Filbert [tree] F: 99 *with pictures*
   Hazel H: 122
   Nut (Kinds of nuts) N: 621 *with picture*
Fildes, Sir Luke [British artist]
   Painting (Painting outside France) P: 72
File [chess]
   Chess (The board and the men) C: 411-412 *with
      diagram*
File [computing] *See* Computer file *in this index*
File [heraldry]
   Heraldry *picture on* H: 195
File [tool]
   Woodworking (Cutting) W: 397-398 *with pictures*
File allocation table [computing]
   Computer file Ci: 924g
File clam [animal]
   Biology *picture on* B: 316
File name [computing]
   Computer file Ci: 924g
File snake
   Snake (Other snake families) S: 535
File transfer protocol [electronics]
   Computer (Internet software) Ci: 922
   Internet (Software) I: 350c-350d
File virus [software]
   Computer virus Ci: 925
Filefish
   Fish *picture on* F: 155
   Triggerfish T: 442
Filene, Edward Albert [American businessman]
   Credit union Ci: 1125
Filfla [island, Mediterranean]
   Malta M: 113 *with map*
Filibuster [pirate]
   Pirate P: 494
Filibustering [politics] F: 99
   Cloture Ci: 707
   Senate (Considering legislation) S: 295
Filibusterismo, El [book by Rizal]
   Rizal, José R: 357
Filid [poets]
   Irish literature (Early Irish literature) I: 430
Filion, Herve [Canadian harness driver]
   Harness racing (History) H: 64
Filioque [religion]
   Eastern Orthodox Churches (Doctrines) E: 46
Filipepi, Allesandro [birth name of]
   Botticelli, Sandro B: 513
Filipino [language]
   Philippines (Languages) P: 374
Filipinos [people]
   Asian Americans A: 812b; (History of Asian
      immigration) A: 812d *with picture*
   Philippines P: 372
Fill dam
   Dam (Embankment dams) D: 18 *with picture*
Fill flash [photography]
   Photography (Back lighting) P: 415
Fille mal gardée, La [ballet]
   Ballet (Ballet d'action) B: 51
Filled-system thermometer
   Thermometer (Thermal expansion
      thermometers) T: 254
Filler
   Plastics (Making synthetic resins) P: 556
   Rubber (Compounding and mixing) R: 505
Filler metal
   Welding (Fusion welding) W: 189
Filles du Feu, Les [poems by Nerval]
   Nerval, Gérard de N: 131
Fillet [architecture]
   Column (The Greek orders) Ci: 865 *with diagram*
Fillet [fish]
   Fishing industry (Methods of processing) F: 186
Fillet [hairdressing]
   Hairdressing (Ancient times) H: 11 *with picture*
Filling [dentistry]
   Teeth (Dental decay) T: 82-83 *with pictures*
Filling [food processing]

Food preservation (Canning) F: 341-342 *with
   picture*
Filling [weaving]
   Textile (Woven fabrics) T: 214
   Velvet V: 297
Fillmore, Abigail Powers [wife of Millard Fillmore]
   Fillmore, Millard (Fillmore's family) F: 101 *with
      picture*; (Life in the White House) F: 102 *with
      portrait*
   First ladies of the United States (table) F: 142
Fillmore, Caroline Carmichael McIntosh [wife of
   Millard Fillmore]
   Fillmore, Millard (Later years) F: 102
Fillmore, Mary Abigail [daughter of]
   Fillmore, Millard (Fillmore's family) F: 101; (Life in
      the White House) F: 102
   White House hostesses W: 291
Fillmore, Millard [U.S. president] F: 100 *with
   pictures*
Fillmore, Millard Powers [son of]
   Fillmore, Millard (Fillmore's family) F: 101
Fillmore, Nathaniel [father of]
   Fillmore, Millard (Early life) F: 100
Fillmore, Phoebe Millard [mother of]
   Fillmore, Millard (Early life) F: 100
Fillon, François [French political leader]
   France (Recent developments) F: 478
Filly [animal]
   Horse (table: Horse terms) H: 343
   Horse racing (Thoroughbred horses) H: 363-364
Film
   See also Motion picture *in this index*
   Camera C: 80
   Eastman Kodak Company E: 47
   Edison, Thomas Alva (Motion pictures) E: 80
   Motion picture (The film) M: 857 *with pictures*
   Photography (How a camera works) P: 407; (Film
      photography) P: 416 *with pictures*
   Polyester P: 649
   Silver nitrate S: 465
   Videotape recorder V: 360
Film advance [mechanism]
   Camera (Preparing for the next exposure) C: 80
Film City [name for]
   Rochester (Government and history) R: 370-371
Film festival
   Motion picture (Festivals and awards) M: 861
Film music
   India (Music and dance) I: 120
   Motion picture (Adding music and sound effects)
      M: 856
Film scanner [electronic device]
   Computer (A scanner) Ci: 915
   Photography (Processing digital images) P: 422
Film Society of Lincoln Center
   Lincoln Center for the Performing Arts L: 327
Film speed
   Photography (Speed) P: 416
Filmon, Gary [Canadian political leader]
   Manitoba (table) M: 159; (Other developments)
      M: 163
Filmstrip F: 103
   Audio-visual materials (Projection devices) A: 882
Filo, David [American businessman]
   Yahoo! Inc. Y: 548
Filocolo [book by Boccaccio]
   Boccaccio, Giovanni B: 433
Filostrato [poem by Boccaccio]
   Boccaccio, Giovanni B: 433
Filter [mechanical device] F: 103
   See also Polarizing filter *in this index*
   Air cleaner (Types of air cleaners) A: 175
   Air conditioning *picture on* A: 180; (Cleaning the
      air) A: 177
   Aquarium, Home (Basic equipment) A: 578 *with
      picture*
   Photography (Filters) P: 416
Filter factor [measurement]
   Photography (Filters) P: 416
Filter feeding [zoology]
   Animal (Filtering mechanisms) A: 490
Filtering
   Information retrieval (Research) I: 268-269
Filtration [water treatment]
   Water *diagram on* W: 124; (Purifying and treating
      water) W: 126
Filtration air cleaner
   Air cleaner (Types of air cleaners) A: 175
Fimbriation [part of flag]
   Flag (table) F: 193
Fin [airplane part]
   Airplane (The tail) A: 214 *with pictures*
   Airship (Control) A: 251 *with diagram*
   Glider (The tail) G: 229
Fin [zoology]
   Animal (Fins, tails, and flippers) A: 490 *with
      picture*

Fish (Fins) F: 160 *with picture*
   Tetrapod (Early tetrapods) T: 182b
Fin ray [zoology]
   Tetrapod (Early tetrapods) T: 182b
Fin whale F: 103
   Antarctica (Living things) A: 534 *with picture*
   Whale *diagram on* W: 259; (Rorquals) W: 255-258
      with picture; (Reproduction) W: 260-261
FINA [organization] *See* Fédération Internationale
   de Natation *in this index*
Final Act [treaty]
   See also Helsinki Accords *in this index*
   Helsinki Accords H: 179
   Union of Soviet Socialist Republics (Détente)
      U: 39
Final cause [philosophy]
   Aristotle (Philosophy of nature) A: 664
Final cut
   Motion picture (The rough and final cuts)
      M: 855-856
Final drive
   Transmission *diagram on* T: 376; (The final drive)
      T: 378
**Final Settlement With Respect to Germany,
   Treaty on the** [1990]
   Germany (The unification of East and West
      Germany) G: 171
Final solution [German history]
   Heydrich, Reinhard H: 220
   Holocaust ("The Final Solution") H: 296a
   Nazism (Expansion, war, and collapse) N: 92
Finance
   Budget B: 669
   Business (Specialized departments) B: 726
   Money (Money and international finance) M: 717
Finance charge [economics]
   Installment plan I: 304
Finance company [economics] F: 103
   Installment plan I: 304
Finance Corporation, International *See*
   International Finance Corporation *in this index*
Financial accounting
   Accounting (Fields of accounting) A: 23
Financial Accounting Standards Board
   Accounting (Financial reports) A: 22
Financial aid
   Education (The federal government and
      education) E: 94; (Financial support) E: 97
Financial audit [business]
   Audit A: 884
Financial capital
   Capital C: 192
Financial Center Development Act [1981]
   Delaware (The late 1900's) D: 113
Financial Consumer Agency of Canada
   Interest (Regulation of interest rates) I: 323
Financial Control Board
   Washington, D.C. (Government changes)
      W: 87-88
Financial Crimes Enforcement Network
   [organization]
   Money laundering M: 718
Financial crisis [2007-]
   Automobile (The 2000's) A: 972
   Bank (Crisis in finance) B: 95
   Bush, George Walker (Economy) B: 722j
   Europe (Recent developments) E: 416
   Federal Home Loan Mortgage Corporation F: 65
   Federal National Mortgage Association F: 65
   Mortgage M: 820
   Obama, Barack (Domestic issues) O: 640f
   United States, History of the (Financial troubles)
      U: 196f
Financial crisis [economics]
   Depression D: 150
Financial District
   New York City (Manhattan) N: 323-324; (Finance)
      N: 334; (A visitor's guide) N: 338
Financial futures [economics]
   Commodity exchange (Financial futures) Ci: 874
**Financial Institutions Reform, Recovery and
   Enforcement Act** [1989]
   Bank (The savings and loan crisis) B: 94
Financial report
   Accounting (Financial reports) A: 22
Financial services
   Bank (Diversification and mergers) B: 94
   Insurance (Insurance today) I: 316-317
Financial Services Modernization Act [1999]
   Bank (Diversification and mergers) B: 94
   Insurance (Insurance today) I: 316-317
Financial Times Stock Exchange Index
   [economics]
   Stock exchange (Stock prices and indexes)
      So: 904
Financier, The [book by Dreiser]
   Dreiser, Theodore D: 346

Finasteride [drug]
Baldness B: 39
Finca [plantation]
El Salvador (Economy) E: 251
Finch [bird] F: 103
Bird *picture on* B: 335; (As pets) B: 331 *with
picture*; (Birds of Australia and New Zealand)
B: 346 *with picture*; (Birds of the Pacific Islands)
B: 349 *with picture*
Evolution (Geographic distribution of species)
E: 430-431 *with picture*
Island (How life develops on islands) I: 473
Linnet L: 338
Finch, Cliff [American political leader]
Mississippi (table) M: 640
Finch, Peter [Australian actor]
Motion picture (Best performance by an actor:
1976) M: 862a
Finch, Robert Hutchison [American government
official]
Health and Human Services, Department of
(table) H: 128
Finch, Stanley W. [American government official]
Federal Bureau of Investigation (History) F: 62
Findlay, William [American political leader]
Pennsylvania (table) P: 263
Findley, John [American frontiersman]
Boone, Daniel (Tales of a hunter's paradise)
B: 477; (Boone in Kentucky) B: 477
Fine [law] F: 104
Fine, John S. [American political leader]
Pennsylvania (table) P: 263
Fine art photography
Photography (Fine art photographers) P: 428
Fine arts F: 104
Aesthetics A: 90
Antique A: 557
Art and the arts A: 745
Fine Arts, Academy of [France]
Institute of France I: 305
Fine Arts, Palace of
San Francisco *picture on* S: 95
Fine cut
Motion picture (The rough and final cuts) M: 855
Fine Gael [political party]
Ireland (Politics) I: 417; (The Republic of Ireland)
I: 427
Fine-wooled sheep
Sheep (Fine-wooled sheep) S: 381
Wool (Sources of wool) W: 399
Fineness [metallurgy]
Gold (Gold alloys) G: 251
Fingal's Cave [music by Mendelssohn]
Mendelssohn, Felix (His life) M: 399
Finger [anatomy]
Hand H: 39; (Parts of the hand) H: 40 *with
diagram*
Finger [botany]
Banana (How bananas grow) B: 73
Finger, Bill [American author]
Batman B: 165
Finger, Charles Joseph [American author] F: 104
Newbery Medal (table) N: 359
Finger board
Guitar G: 436 *with pictures*
Violin (Parts of the violin) V: 389 *with pictures*
Finger Lakes [New York] F: 104
New York (Lakes) N: 306-307
Finger painting [art] F: 105 *with pictures*
Finger puppet
Puppet (Hand puppets) P: 906
Finger spelling
Deafness (Special language techniques) D: 58
Finger weaving
Weaving (Weaving without a loom) W: 174
Fingered limpet [sea animal]
Animal *picture on* A: 486
Fingernail
Nail N: 4
Fingerprinting [criminology] F: 106 *with pictures*
Biometrics B: 325
Crime scene investigation (Collecting evidence)
Ci: 1140
Federal Bureau of Investigation (Other services)
F: 62
Forensic science (What a forensic scientist
analyzes) F: 389
Fingers, Rollie [American baseball player]
Baseball (table: Hall of Fame) B: 134
Finial [ornament]
Flag *picture on* F: 194
Fininvest [company]
Berlusconi, Silvio B: 267
Finish carpentry
Carpentry C: 246
Woodworking W: 396
Finished floor

House (Interior construction) H: 382
Finished market lumber
Lumber (Hardwood lumber) L: 517-518
Finishing [agriculture]
Farm and farming (Livestock care) F: 39;
(Livestock finishing) F: 40
Finishing [industrial process]
Cotton (Finishing) Ci: 1091 *with pictures*
Iron and steel (Shaping and finishing steel) I: 445
with diagrams
Leather (Final processing) L: 168-169 *with picture*
Finishing [weaving]
Basket making (Methods) B: 141
Finishing [woodworking]
Woodworking (Sanding and finishing) W: 398
Finishing the Picture [play by Miller]
Miller, Arthur M: 553
Finite series [mathematics]
Series S: 316b; (Working with finite series)
S: 316b
Finite set [mathematics]
Set theory (Kinds of sets) S: 321
Finite verb
Verb (Finite and nonfinite verbs) V: 315
Fink, Mike [American frontiersman] F: 107 *with
picture*
Finland F: 108 *with pictures and maps*
See also the list of Related articles in the Finland
article
Euro E: 379
Flag *picture on* F: 206
Lapland L: 74
Russo-Finnish wars R: 566a
Sami S: 78
Scandinavia S: 170 *with map*
Union of Soviet Socialist Republics (World War
II) U: 37
World War II (The invasion of the Soviet Union)
W: 477
Finland, Gulf of
Baltic Sea B: 65 *with map*
Finlandia [music by Sibelius]
Sibelius, Jean S: 443
Finlay, Carlos Juan [Cuban biologist] F: 118
Yellow fever (History) Y: 556
Finlay Park [Columbia]
South Carolina *picture on* So: 649
Finless porpoise
Porpoise P: 679
Finn cycle [literature] *See* Fionn cycle *in this index*
Finn MacCool [legendary figure] F: 119
Giant's Causeway G: 184
Irish literature (Heroic tales, romances, and sagas)
I: 430
Mythology (The Fionn cycle) M: 985
Finnegans Wake [book by Joyce]
Fable F: 3
Joyce, James J: 177
Finney, Charles G. [American religious leader]
Revivalism R: 269
Finney, Joan [American political leader]
Kansas (Economic and political changes) K: 238-
239
Finnish spitz [dog] F: 119 *with picture*
Finns [people]
Finland (Early years) F: 117
Sami (History) S: 80
Finsen, Niels Ryberg [Danish doctor]
Nobel Prizes (Physiology or medicine: 1903)
N: 444
Fionn cycle [Irish literature]
Finn MacCool F: 119
Irish literature (Heroic tales, romances, and sagas)
I: 430-431
Mythology (The Irish cycles) M: 985
Fiord [geography] F: 119
Canada (The Pacific Ranges and Lowlands) C: 115
Denmark (Land regions) D: 137-138 *with picture*
Europe *picture on* E: 395
Glacier (How glaciers shape the land) G: 203
Ice age (Extent of the Pleistocene glaciers) I: 6
Iceland (The inland plateau) I: 22
Norway N: 536 *with picture*; (Coast and islands)
N: 542 *with map*
Fiordland [park, New Zealand]
National park (New Zealand) N: 42d; (table)
N: 42f
Fiorelli, Giuseppe [Italian archaeologist]
Pompeii (Excavations) P: 654
Fiqh [religion]
Islam (The Shari`ah) I: 465
Shari`ah S: 374
Fir [tree] F: 119 *with pictures*
See also Douglas-fir *in this index*
Plant *picture on* P: 524
Tree *pictures on* T: 424
Firbolgs [legendary people]

Mythology (The Irish cycles) M: 985
Fire F: 120 *with pictures*
Arson A: 745
Bomb (Incendiary bombs) B: 451
Camping (Building a campfire) C: 94 *with picture*
Combustion C: 866
Earthquake (Fire) E: 34
Empedocles E: 261
Fire department F: 123 *with picture*
Heat (Sources of heat) H: 149
Heraclitus H: 194
National park (Management of fire and wildlife)
N: 42j
Prehistoric people (The use of fire) P: 747
Pyromania P: 920
Vulcan V: 453
Disastrous fires
Arizona (The early 2000's) A: 692
Baltimore (The 1900's) B: 70
California (The beginning of the 2000's) C: 64
Chicago (The Great Chicago Fire) C: 435 *with
picture*
Chicago Fire C: 438
Colorado (The early 2000's) Ci: 847-848
Disaster (table) D: 223
Florida (The late 1900's) F: 264-265
London (War, plague, and fire) L: 441
Los Angeles (Recent developments) L: 470-471
New Mexico (Recent developments) N: 276
Persian Gulf War of 1991 (Consequences of the
war) P: 300e *with picture*
San Diego (Other recent developments) S: 91
San Francisco (Earthquake and fire) S: 98 *with
picture*
San Francisco earthquake of 1906 S: 99
Triangle Shirtwaist Factory Fire T: 438
Wisconsin (History) W: 365-366
Fire, Andrew Zachary [American biologist]
Nobel Prizes (Physiology or medicine: 2006)
N: 447
Fire, Ring of [region, Pacific Ocean] *See* Ring of Fire
in this index
Fire Administration, United States
Fire department (The 1900's) F: 129
Fire ant F: 122
Ant (The importance of ants) A: 528
Conservation (Biodiversity conservation) Ci: 976-
977
Fire blight [plant disease]
Apple (Pests and diseases) A: 572
Bacteria (Harmful bacteria) B: 20
Blight B: 400
Pear (Diseases and pests) P: 216
Fire clay
Clay Ci: 658
Fire Club [organization]
Fire department (The 1700's) F: 128
Fire curing
Tobacco (Kinds of tobacco) T: 305; (Curing
tobacco) T: 307
Fire department F: 123 *with pictures*
Franklin, Benjamin (Civic leader) F: 487-488
Fire drill F: 129
Fire extinguisher F: 130 *with picture*
Fire department (Fire prevention and fire safety)
F: 125
Fire fighter *See* Firefighter *in this index*
Fire Fighters, International Association of
Labor movement (table) L: 8
Fire fighting *See* Firefighting *in this index*
Fire hydrant [device]
Fire department (Firefighting) F: 123-124; (Water
systems) F: 126
Fire Island National Seashore [New York]
National Park System (table: National seashores)
N: 57
New York (Places to visit) N: 302
Fire laws
Fire prevention (Fire prevention laws) F: 132
Fire Next Time, The [book by Baldwin]
Baldwin, James B: 39
Fire opal [gem]
Opal O: 789
Fire-over
Glass (Glass terms) G: 222
Fire poppy
Flower (Flowers of summer-dry regions) F: 288
with picture
Fire prevention F: 130 *with pictures*
Building construction (Classification of buildings)
B: 683
Fire department (Fire prevention and fire safety)
F: 125; (Fire protection in North America)
F: 128
Fireproofing F: 134
Forestry (Fire and forests) F: 407
Safety (Safety from fire) S: 11

Fire Prevention and Control Administration, National [U.S.]
Fire department (The 1900's) F: 129
Fire-refining furnace
Copper (Smelting) Ci: 1043
Fire retardant
Fireproofing F: 134
Fire safety See Fire prevention in this index
Fire safety code
Fire department (Fire prevention and fire safety) F: 125
Fire ship
Spanish Armada (The battle) So: 756
Fire-stick elder [African leader]
Maasai M: 2
Fire stop [building construction]
House diagram on H: 383
Fire test
Building construction (Classification of buildings) B: 683
Fire prevention picture on F: 132
Fire truck
Fire department (Firefighting) F: 123 with picture; (Trucks and vehicles) F: 126 with pictures
Fire wheel [flower]
Gaillardia G: 6 with picture
Fire worship [religion] F: 132
Firearm [weapon] F: 132 with pictures
Browning, John Moses B: 646
Flintlock F: 236 with picture
Forensic science (What a forensic scientist analyzes) F: 389 with picture
Infantry (Equipment) I: 265
War (Technological advancements) W: 25
Weapon (Firearms) W: 154b
Whitney, Eli (Arms manufacturer) W: 295
Fireball [astronomy] F: 133
Meteor M: 430
Fireball [nuclear energy]
Fallout (How fallout is produced) F: 18
Nuclear weapon (Blast wave) N: 599
Firebird [bird] See Baltimore oriole; Scarlet tanager in this index
Firebird, The [ballet]
Classical music picture on Ci: 651; (Igor Stravinsky) Ci: 649
Stravinsky, Igor (Early works) So: 922
Fireboat company
Fire department (Additional operations) F: 124
"Firebombing, The" [poem by Dickey]
Dickey, James D: 190
Firebox
Locomotive (Steam locomotives) L: 417
Firebrick
Refractory R: 200
Firebugs, The [play by Frisch]
Frisch, Max F: 535
Firecracker
Fireworks F: 135
Firecracker flower [plant] F: 134 with picture
Firedamp [gas]
Damp D: 21
Safety lamp S: 16
Firefighter [occupation]
Clothing picture on Ci: 688
Fire department F: 123; (Careers) F: 129
Forestry (Fire and forests) F: 407 with picture
Radio (In public safety) R: 84
Firefly [insect] F: 134 with pictures
Beetle (Fireflies) B: 217
Insect picture on I: 283; (Courtship) I: 294 with picture
Firefly, The [operetta by Friml]
Friml, Rudolf F: 534
Fireline
Forestry (Fire and forests) F: 407
Fireman
See also Firefighter in this index
Railroad (Railroad workers) R: 113
Ship (Officers and crew) S: 410
Firenze [Italy] See Florence in this index
Fireplace
Colonial life in America (Furnishings) Ci: 797
Heating (Fireplaces) H: 160
Pioneer life in America (A pioneer settlement) P: 479-480
Fireproof Building
South Carolina (Interesting facts about South Carolina) So: 641 with picture
Fireproofing F: 134
Fire (Fireproof materials) F: 121
Fireside chats [U.S. history]
President of the United States picture on P: 765
Radio (The Golden Age of Broadcasting) R: 92-93 with picture
Roosevelt, Franklin Delano (The banking crisis) R: 452-453 with picture

Fireside Poets
American literature (Poetry) A: 418
Firestone, Harvey Samuel [American businessman] F: 135
Edison, Thomas Alva (Family and friends) E: 81-82
Firestone Tire & Rubber Company
Firestone, Harvey Samuel F: 135
Firestorm
Storm (Other storms) So: 913
Firewall [computing]
Computer (Intranets) Ci: 923
Computer network Ci: 925
Computer security Ci: 925
Internet (Glossary of Internet terms) I: 350a
Fireweed [plant] F: 135
Flower (Flowers of the Arctic tundra) F: 283 with picture
Firewing [book by Oppel]
Literature for children picture on L: 377
Firewood
Camping (Building a campfire) C: 94-96
Fireworks F: 135
Firing [business]
Unemployment (How people become unemployed) U: 21
Firing [industrial process]
Brick (Firing bricks) B: 598 with picture
Ceramics (Making ceramics) C: 360
Glass (Fired decorations) G: 217
Pottery (Firing) P: 718
Firing chamber
Rifle (How a rifle works) R: 338
Firing mechanism
Firearm (Mechanism) F: 132-133 with picture
Firing pin
Ammunition (The primer) A: 435
Firearm (Mechanism) F: 132-133 with diagrams
Handgun picture on H: 44; (Single-action revolvers) H: 43
Rifle (How a rifle works) R: 338
Firing post [defense]
Pioneer life in America (Defending a settlement) P: 485
Firing squad [execution]
Capital punishment (table) C: 193
Firm, The [book by Grisham]
Grisham, John G: 396
Firmin, Geoffrey [literary figure]
Lowry, Malcolm L: 511
Firn [geology]
Glacier (How glaciers form) G: 202
First African Baptist Church
Georgia (Places to visit) G: 122
First aid F: 136 with pictures
See also the list of Related articles in the First aid article
Bandage B: 75
Barbiturate (Dangers of barbiturates) B: 107
Bleeding (First aid for bleeding) B: 399
Blister B: 403
Bruise B: 650
Burn (First-aid care) B: 708
Cardiopulmonary resuscitation C: 212 with pictures
Drowning (Giving first aid) D: 349
Emetic E: 259
Fainting F: 7 with picture
Frostbite F: 543
Hyperthermia (Treatment) H: 477
Nosebleed N: 549 with pictures
Poison ivy (Control and treatment) P: 601
Rabies (Treatment) R: 49
Red Cross (Health and safety training) R: 185
Shock S: 429
Snakebite (First aid) S: 536
Sunburn So: 989
Tourniquet T: 350
First Amendment [U.S. Constitution]
Christianity (Growth in the United States) C: 526
Church and state C: 542
Civil rights (The First Amendment) Ci: 608
Comstock Law C: 926
Constitution of the United States Ci: 1011
Democracy D: 120
Freedom of assembly (In the United States) F: 504
Freedom of religion (In the United States) F: 505
Freedom of speech (In the United States) F: 506
Libel L: 226
Religious education (Public schools) R: 225
Schenck v. United States S: 174
School prayer S: 186
United States (Religion) U: 114
Wiretapping (Laws concerning wiretapping) W: 345
First American Bankshares, Inc.
Clifford, Clark McAdams Ci: 674

First Balkan War See Balkan Wars in this index
First Bank of the United States See Bank of the United States in this index
First Baptist Meeting House
Providence (Description) P: 839-840 with picture
First baseman
Baseball (Player positions) B: 127
First baseman's glove
Baseball (Equipment) B: 125 with picture
First Book of Architecture, The [book by Serlio]
Drama on D: 331
First cause [philosophy]
Philosophy (Aristotle) P: 387
First Circle, The [book by Solzhenitsyn]
Russian literature (Modern Soviet literature) R: 564
Solzhenitsyn, Alexander So: 587
First-class lever
Lever L: 218; (Classes of levers) L: 217
First-class mail
Postal Service, United States (Classes of mail) P: 699
Postal services (Technological advancements) P: 707
First Class Scout
Boy Scouts (First-Class Scout) B: 537
First Continental Congress See Continental Congress in this index
First cousin
Cousin Ci: 1105
Family (Family relationships) F: 21
First cousin once removed
Family (Family relationships) F: 21
First-degree burn
Burn (Classification of burns) B: 708
First aid (Burns) F: 138
Skin (Burns) S: 490
First-degree murder
Murder M: 930
First edition
Book collecting (Author collections) B: 469
First estate [French history]
Estates-General E: 360
First Fleet [Australian history]
Australia (British settlement) A: 920 with picture
First Folio
Shakespeare, William (Shakespeare's plays) S: 354; (Folios) S: 369 with picture
First gear
Automobile (The transmission) A: 948-949
Transmission (How a manual transmission works) T: 377-378 with diagram
"First in war, first in peace, and first in the hearts of his countrymen" [quotation]
Washington, George W: 90
First Indochina War See Indochina War in this index
First intermediate period [Egyptian history]
Egypt, Ancient (The Old Kingdom) E: 142-143
First International, The [organization]
Socialism (The First International) So: 560
First Ladies National Historic Site [Ohio]
National Park System (table: National historic sites) N: 52
First ladies of the United States [U.S. history] F: 142 with pictures
White House hostesses W: 291
First law of motion
Motion (Newton's laws of motion) M: 844
First Love [book by Turgenev]
Russian literature (Early realism) R: 562
First Love, Last Rites [book by McEwan]
McEwan, Ian M: 334
First National Center [Omaha]
Omaha (The city) O: 756
First Nations See Indian, American in this index
First Navigation Act [1651]
Navigation Acts N: 75
First New Deal [U.S. history] See Hundred Days [U.S. history] in this index
First overtone
Harmonics H: 62 with diagram
First person [literature]
Literature (Style) L: 353
First-person game
Electronic game (Gameplay) E: 204b-204c
First Punic War [264-241 B.C.] See Punic Wars in this index
First quarter
Moon (Phases) M: 783-784
First Quorum of the Seventy
Mormons (Church organization) M: 807
First responder [occupation]
Crime scene investigation Ci: 1140
Fire department (Emergency medical operations) F: 124
First Riel Rebellion See Red River Rebellion in this index

First-run syndication
  Television (Syndicated programming) **T: 114**
First Seminole War See Seminole Wars in this index
First sergeant [rank]
  Rank, Military (table) **R: 140**
First State [name for]
  Delaware **D: 96**
First Stories-The Power of a Horse [film]
  Canada *picture on* **C: 112**
First Temple See Temple in Jerusalem in this index
First Triumvirate See Triumvirate in this index
First United States Volunteer Cavalry See Rough Riders in this index
First Vatican Council See Vatican Council I in this index
First violin [music]
  Orchestra (The musicians) **O: 820**
First Virginia Convention [1774]
  Jefferson, Thomas (Revolutionary leader) **J: 79**
  Virginia (The course toward independence) **V: 420**
First World
  Third World (The political Third World) **T: 258**
First World War See World War I in this index
First Zionist Congress [1897]
  Zionism (Movement to Palestine) **Z: 595**
FirstGov [information service]
  Library (United States government libraries) **L: 248-249**
Firth [geography]
  Fiord **F: 119**
  Scotland (Rivers and lakes) **S: 217** with map
Firth, Colin [British actor]
  Motion picture (Best performance by an actor: 2010) **M: 862a**
Firth of Forth [Scotland] **F: 143**
  Scotland (Rivers and lakes) **S: 217**
FIS [political party] See Front Islamique du Salut in this index
Fiscal policy
  Depression (Depressions since World War II) **D: 150**
  Economics (Government intervention) **E: 59**
  Government (Commerce) **G: 283**
  Inflation (Weapons against inflation) **I: 268**
  Keynes, John Maynard **K: 308a**
  Recession (Fighting recession) **R: 175**
  Unemployment (Programs and policies) **U: 23**
Fiscal year [accounting]
  National budget **N: 30**
Fischer, Bobby [American chess player] **F: 143**
  Chess (World chess champions) **C: 414**; (History) **C: 414**
Fischer, Edmond Henri [American physiologist]
  Nobel Prizes (Physiology or medicine: 1992) **N: 446**
Fischer, Emil [German chemist]
  Nobel Prizes (Chemistry: 1902) **N: 442**
Fischer, Ernst Otto [German chemist]
  Nobel Prizes (Chemistry: 1973) **N: 444**
Fischer, Hans [German biochemist]
  Nobel Prizes (Chemistry: 1930) **N: 443**
Fischer, Helmut H. [German pilot]
  Glider (table) **G: 230**
Fischer, Jan [Czech political leader]
  Czech Republic (Recent developments) **Ci: 1214**
Fischer-Dieskau, Dietrich [German singer] **F: 143**
Fischer von Erlach, Johann Bernhard [Austrian architect]
  Architecture (Baroque architecture) **A: 622**
  Austria (Architecture) **A: 932**
  Vienna (The city) **V: 361-362**
Fischinger, Oskar [German filmmaker]
  Animation (Animation in Europe) **A: 514b**
Fischl, Eric [American artist]
  Painting (Postmodernism) **P: 88**
Fisgard Lighthouse [British Columbia]
  Canada (table: National historic sites) **C: 114**
Fish F: 144 with pictures
  See also the list of Related articles in the Fish article
  Animal (table: Length of life of animals) **A: 473**; (A table of animal intelligence) **A: 493**
  Aquaculture **A: 578**
  Aquarium, Home **A: 578** with picture
  Aquarium, Public **A: 578b**
  Balance of nature (Upsetting the balance) **B: 36**
  Brain (Among vertebrates) **B: 560** with diagram
  Cell *picture on* **C: 330**
  Coral reef (Life on coral reefs) **Ci: 1048b-1049**
  Deep sea (Fish) **D: 82b** with pictures
  Ear (The ears of animals) **E: 12-13**
  Egg (Other kinds of eggs) **E: 116**
  Food (Interesting facts about food) **F: 329**
  Food supply (Livestock and fish) **F: 347**
  Heart (Fish) **H: 146** with diagram
  Ichthyology **I: 24**
  Nutrition (Kinds of nutrients) **N: 625**

Ocean (The importance of the ocean) **O: 654**; (Life in the ocean) **O: 655** with pictures
Pet **P: 320**
Pfiesteria **P: 353**
Prehistoric animal (The first animals with backbones) **P: 736-737**; (Fish) **P: 738** with picture
Seafood **S: 264**
Sushi **So: 1012**
Tetrapod (Early tetrapods) **T: 182b**
Thermal pollution **T: 253**
Tiktaalik **T: 286** with picture
Tropical fish **T: 450**
Fish, Hamilton [American political leader] **F: 175**
  New York (table) **N: 313**
Fish, Morris J. [Canadian jurist]
  Supreme Court of Canada (table) **So: 997** with portrait
Fish and chips [food]
  England (Food and drink) **E: 295-296**
Fish and Wildlife Service [U.S.] **F: 175**
Fish community
  Fish (Fish in the balance of nature) **F: 147**
Fish crow [bird]
  Crow (Kinds of crows) **Ci: 1157**
Fish-eagle [bird]
  Bird (Birds of Africa) **B: 344h** with picture
Fish farm See Aquaculture in this index
Fish glue
  Glue (Types of glue) **G: 236**
Fish hawk [bird]
  Osprey **O: 866** with picture
Fish House [aquarium]
  Aquarium, Public (History) **A: 579**
Fish ladder [conservation]
  Bonneville Dam **B: 462**
  Salmon (The life of a salmon) **S: 69-70**
  Washington (The late 1900's) **W: 68-69**
Fish market
  Asia *picture on* **A: 787**
Fish meal
  Fishing industry (Methods of processing) **F: 186-187**
Fish net
  Net **N: 137** with picture
Fish oil
  Fishing industry (Methods of processing) **F: 186-187**
Fish trap
  Fishing industry (Traps) **F: 185** with diagram
Fishback, William Meade [American political leader]
  Arkansas (table) **A: 712**
Fisher [animal]
  Fur (table) **F: 561**
  Marten **M: 233**
Fisher, Andrew [Australian statesman]
  Australia (table) **A: 923**
Fisher, Anna L. [American astronaut]
  Astronaut (A look at the astronauts) **A: 831**
Fisher, Carl Graham [American businessman]
  Dixie Highway **D: 255**
  Lincoln Highway **L: 327**
Fisher, Charles [Canadian political leader]
  Confederation of Canada (Fathers of Confederation) **Ci: 935**
Fisher, John Stuchell [American political leader]
  Pennsylvania (table) **P: 263**
Fisher, Leonard Everett [American author]
  Regina Medal (table: 1991) **R: 206**
Fisher, Sir Ronald [British statistician]
  Evolution (The synthetic theory) **E: 432**
  Statistics (History) **So: 869-870**
Fisher, Saint John [English religious leader] **F: 175**
Fisher, Vardis [American author] **F: 175**
Fisher, Walter L. [American government official]
  Interior, Department of the (table) **I: 325**
  Taft, William Howard (table) **T: 11**
Fisherman See Fishing; Fishing industry in this index
Fisherman's ring [ornament]
  Pope (Titles, clothing, and symbols) **P: 661-662**
Fisherman's Wharf
  San Francisco (Downtown San Francisco) **S: 92-93** with map
Fishermen's Memorial [statue]
  Gloucester **G: 234**
Fishery [conservation]
  Fish *pictures on* **F: 146**
  Fishing industry (Where fish are caught) **F: 181** with pictures
Fishery conservation zone See Exclusive economic zone in this index
Fishes, Age of See Devonian Period in this index
Fisheye lens
  Photography (Types of lenses) **P: 411**
Fishhook

Fishing (Hooks) **F: 178** with pictures
Fishing industry (Hooks) **F: 185**
Indian, American *picture on* **I: 139**
Fishing F: 175 with pictures
  See also Fishing industry in this index
  Animal (Hunting and fishing) **A: 505**
  Fish (Food and game fish) **F: 146**
  Indian, American (Hunting, gathering, and fishing) **I: 141**
  Inuit (Hunting and fishing) **I: 354d** with picture
  Maine *picture on* **M: 72**
  Nunavut *picture on* **N: 611**
  Salmon (Salmon fishing) **S: 70**
Fishing admiral
  Newfoundland and Labrador (Colonization) **N: 375**
Fishing industry F: 180 with pictures and maps
  See also the list of Related articles in the Fishing industry article
  Grand Banks **G: 306**
  Pictures
    Canada *picture on* **C: 99**
    Coast Guard, United States *picture on* **Ci: 736**
    England *picture on* **E: 303**
    Europe *picture on* **E: 403**
    Net *picture on* **N: 137**
    Oyster (The oyster industry) **O: 892** with picture
    United Kingdom *picture on* **U: 65**
  Text
    Alabama (Fishing industry) **A: 273**
    Canada (Fishing industry) **C: 125** with picture
    Careers (Farming, fishing, and forestry) **C: 222**
    Cod **Ci: 748**
    Colonial life in America (Fishing and whaling) **Ci: 810**
    Conservation (Ocean conservation) **Ci: 978**
    Coral reef (Coral reefs and people) **Ci: 1049**
    Dolphin (Dolphin conservation) **D: 299**
    England (Agriculture and fishing) **E: 302** with picture
    Fish (Food and game fish) **F: 146** with pictures
    Herring **H: 215** with picture
    Iceland (Fishing industry) **I: 22** with picture; (Independence) **I: 23-24**
    Norway (Fishing) **N: 544**
    Nova Scotia (Fishing) **N: 565**
    Ocean (The importance of the ocean) **O: 654**; (Fisheries) **O: 665**
    Portugal (Way of life) **P: 687** with picture
    Russia (Fishing industry) **R: 546**
    Seafood **S: 265**
    Seal (Seals and fishing crews) **S: 267**
    Ship (Specialized vessels) **S: 410**
    Thailand (Economy) **T: 225** with picture
Fishing laws
  Fishing (Fishing tips) **F: 179**
  Fishing industry (Fishery conservation) **F: 187**
Fishing-owl [bird]
  Owl (Important owls) **O: 884-886**
Fishing pole
  Fishing (Rods) **F: 176** with pictures
Fishing spider See Nursery-web spider in this index
Fishplate
  Railroad (The crossties and rails) **R: 109**
Fishworm See Earthworm in this index
Fisk, Carlton [American baseball player]
  Baseball (table: Hall of Fame) **B: 134**
Fisk, James [American financier] **F: 188**
  Black Friday **B: 387**
  Gould, Jay **G: 280**
Fisk Jubilee Singers
  Gospel music **G: 277**
Fiske, John [American philosopher] **F: 189**
Fiske, Minnie Maddern [American actress] **F: 189**
Fiske, Robert B. [American attorney]
  Clinton, Bill (National affairs) **Ci: 682d-682e**
Fission [biology]
  Ameba **A: 406**
  Protozoan (Reproduction) **P: 837**
  Reproduction (Through asexual reproduction) **R: 242-243** with picture
Fission [physics] **F: 189**
  Atom (Studying the nucleus) **A: 876**
  Electric power (Nuclear power plants) **E: 184**
  $E=mc^2$ **E: 3**
  Energy supply (Nuclear energy) **E: 278**
  Fermi, Enrico **F: 74**
  Hahn, Otto **H: 7**
  Isotope (Artificial radioisotopes) **I: 477**
  Neutron **N: 155**
  Nuclear energy (Nuclear fission) **N: 582** with diagram; (Artificial fission) **N: 590**
  Nuclear physics **N: 595**
  Nuclear weapon (Fission weapons) **N: 596**
  Petroleum (The future of petroleum) **P: 349**
  Physics (Nuclear physics) **P: 437**; (Uncovering the secrets of the atom) **P: 442**

Radiation (In industry) **R:** 75; (Artificial radioactive substances) **R:** 77 *with picture*
Transmutation of elements **T:** 379
Uranium (Fissionability) **U:** 215
Fission fragment [physics]
Nuclear energy (Nuclear fission) **N:** 582 *with diagram*
Fission weapon *See* Nuclear weapon *in this index*
Fissure [anatomy]
Brain *diagram on* **B:** 550c
Fist puppet
Puppet (Hand puppets) **P:** 906
Fitch [fur]
Fur (table) **F:** 561
Polecat **P:** 619
Fitch, Clyde [American dramatist] **F:** 189
Fitch, John [American inventor] **F:** 189 *with picture*
Propeller **P:** 826
Ship (The first steamboats) **S:** 424
Fitch, Val Logsdon [American physicist]
Nobel Prizes (Physics: 1980) **N:** 441
Fitness [biology]
Evolution (Main ideas of evolutionary theory) **E:** 426-427; (Natural selection) **E:** 428
Fitness [health] *See* Physical fitness *in this index*
Fitter's model
Modeling (Kinds of models) **M:** 684
Fittipaldi, Emerson [Brazilian race driver]
Automobile racing (table: Formula One World Drivers' Championship) **A:** 980; (table: Indianapolis 500 winners) **A:** 980
Fitzgerald, Barry [Irish actor]
Motion picture (Best performance by an actor in a supporting role: 1944) **M:** 862a
FitzGerald, Edward [British author] **F:** 190
Rubaiyat **R:** 499
Fitzgerald, Ella [American singer] **F:** 190 *with portrait*
Fitzgerald, F. Scott [American author] **F:** 190 *with portrait*
American literature (The Lost Generation) **A:** 421
Lost Generation **L:** 472
Novel (New directions in the novel) **N:** 573-574
United States, History of the (The Lost Generation and Flaming Youth) **U:** 190
Fitzgerald, Frank D. [American political leader]
Michigan (table) **M:** 507
FitzGerald, Garret [Irish government official]
Ireland (table) **I:** 428
United Kingdom (Thatcher) **U:** 73
Fitzgerald, George [Irish physicist]
Relativity (Lorentz-Fitzgerald contraction) **R:** 211
Fitzgerald, John F. [American political leader]
Boston (Rise of Irish politicians) **B:** 504
Kennedy, John Fitzgerald (Family background) **K:** 260
FitzGerald, L. L. [Canadian painter]
Group of Seven **G:** 402
Fitzgerald, Rose [American public figure] *See* Kennedy, Rose Fitzgerald *in this index*
Fitzgerald, Zelda [wife of]
Fitzgerald, F. Scott **F:** 190
Fitzgerald contraction [physics] *See* Lorentz-Fitzgerald contraction *in this index*
Fitzgerald v. Nixon [U.S. history]
Supreme Court of the United States (table) **So:** 1002
Fitzhugh, Louise [American author]
Literature for children (New frankness) **L:** 365
Fitzooth, Robert
Robin Hood **R:** 367
Fitzpatrick, Benjamin [American political leader]
Alabama (table) **A:** 274
Fitzpatrick, Thomas [American frontiersman] **F:** 190
Westward movement in America (Exploration) **W:** 248-249
Fitzsimmons, Bob [British boxer] **F:** 191
Boxing *picture on* **B:** 532; (Boxing in Australia and New Zealand) **B:** 531
Solar plexus **So:** 579
Fitzsimmons, Frank Edward [American labor leader] **F:** 191
FitzSimons, Thomas [American political leader] **F:** 191
Fitzwilliam Virginal Book [music]
Byrd, William **B:** 747
Virginal **V:** 397
FIV [virus] *See* Feline immunodeficiency virus *in this index*
Five, The [music]
Rimsky-Korsakov, Nikolai **R:** 342
Five Books of Moses *See* Pentateuch; Torah *in this index*
Five-cent piece [money] *See* Nickel *in this index*
Five Civilized Tribes [U.S. history] **F:** 191
Choctaw Indians **C:** 519

Indian, American (After European contact) **I:** 158
Indian Territory **I:** 189 *with map*
Oklahoma (The Indian nations) **O:** 731; (Progress toward statehood) **O:** 732
Seminole Indians **S:** 292
Five Classics [religious book]
Chinese literature (Beginnings) **C:** 511
Confucianism (Early Confucianism) **Ci:** 936-937
I Ching **I:** 2
Religion (Confucianism) **R:** 220-221
Five-finger [plant]
Cinquefoil **Ci:** 557
500 Index, Standard & Poor's [stock market]
Standard & Poor's indexes **So:** 833
Five-leaved ivy [plant]
Virginia creeper **V:** 424 *with picture*
Five Letters [book by Cortés]
Latin American literature (Colonial literature) **L:** 112
Five Nations [U.S. history] *See* Five Civilized Tribes; Iroquois League *in this index*
Five Pillars of Islam
Islam (Teachings and practices) **I:** 463
"Five Points" [essay by Le Corbusier]
Le Corbusier **L:** 175
Five-Power Naval Limitation Treaty
Washington Conference **W:** 109
Five-spot
Flower *picture on* **F:** 288
Five-step delivery
Bowling (Delivering the ball) **B:** 522
Five Weeks in a Balloon [book by Verne]
Verne, Jules **V:** 338
Five-year plan [economics] **F:** 191
China (The beginning of Communist rule) **C:** 505
Communism (Under Stalin) **Ci:** 892
India (India in the 1950's and early 1960's) **I:** 133
Russian literature (The period of industrial literature) **R:** 564
Stalin, Joseph (The five-year plan) **So:** 826
Union of Soviet Socialist Republics (History) **U:** 35-36
5f subshell [chemistry]
Actinide **A:** 30
Fivefold symmetry [mathematics]
Quasicrystal **Q:** 9
Fivepins [sport]
Bowling (Canadian fivepins) **B:** 524
Fixation
Reading (How we read) **R:** 156-157
Speed reading **So:** 774
Fixative
Painting (Pastel) **P:** 39
Perfume (Animal substances) **P:** 286
Fixed ammunition
Ammunition (Artillery ammunition) **A:** 435-436
Fixed Base Operator
Airport (Small aircraft services) **A:** 246
Fixed Calendar
Calendar (Calendar reform) **C:** 32
Fixed capital [economics]
National income (Changes in national income) **N:** 38
Fixed-focus camera
Camera (Fixed-focus cameras) **C:** 82
Photography (Compact cameras) **P:** 408-409
Fixed income [economics]
Inflation (Effects on income) **I:** 268
Fixed joint [anatomy]
Human body (The skeletal system) **H:** 418
Joint **J:** 155 *with diagram*
Fixed landing gear
Airplane (The landing gear) **A:** 216-217
Fixed nitrogen
Nitrogen cycle **N:** 426
Fixed oil
Oil (Fixed oils) **O:** 706
Fixed-pitch propeller
Airplane (Propellers) **A:** 217
Propeller (Airplane propellers) **P:** 826
Fixed-position manufacturing
Factory (Kinds of factories) **F:** 5
Fixed-rate mortgage
Mortgage **M:** 820
Fixed sentence [law]
Parole **P:** 178
Sentence **S:** 304
Fixed-wing craft [machine]
Unmanned aerial vehicle **U:** 212
Fixer [chemical]
Photography (Black-and-white negative film) **P:** 419
Fixer, The [book by Malamud]
Malamud, Bernard **M:** 95
Fixture [device]
Toolmaking **T:** 330
Fixture [law] **F:** 191

Fizeau, Armand H. L. [French physicist]
Optics (History) **O:** 813
Fjord [geography] *See* Fiord *in this index*
Flaccid paralysis [disease]
Paralysis (Paralysis of central nervous system origin) **P:** 152
Flaccus, Quintus Horatius [full name of]
Horace **F:** 334
Flaccus, Valerius [Roman political leader]
Cato, Marcus Porcius, the Elder **C:** 304
Latin literature (The Imperial Period) **L:** 116-117
Flag F: 192 *with pictures*
Heraldry (Beginnings) **H:** 194
Mississippi (The early 2000's) **M:** 645
Pirate (A pirate's life) **P:** 494-495 *with pictures*
Semaphore **S:** 291
Ship *pictures on* **S:** 426; (Flags and registration) **S:** 412
Union Jack **U:** 27
Flag [music]
Music (Indicating time values) **M:** 953
Flag, Canadian
Canada, History of (The return of the Liberals) **C:** 149-150
Flag (Displaying the flag) **F:** 218; (Manufacturing flags) **F:** 222-223
Flag, United States *See* United States flag *in this index*
Flag burning
Flag (Interesting facts about flags) **F:** 193
Supreme Court of the United States (table) **So:** 1002
Flag code
Flag (Honoring a national flag) **F:** 218; (Permitted and prohibited uses) **F:** 222
Flag Code, International
Flag *picture on* **F:** 196; (Flags that talk) **F:** 208
Flag Day [custom] **F:** 223
Sweden (Holidays) **So:** 1026
Flag football [sport]
Football **F:** 354
Flag hoist
Signaling (Visual and sound signals) **S:** 454
Flag of convenience
Ship (Flags and registration) **S:** 412
Flag of truce
Truce **T:** 456
Flag officer [rank] **F:** 224
Flagellate [zoology]
Protozoan (Flagellates) **P:** 837 *with picture*
Flagellum [biology] **F:** 224 *with picture*
Algae **A:** 349
Bacteria (How bacteria move) **B:** 21 *with picture*
Reproduction, Human (The human reproductive system) **R:** 244-246
Sponge (Special cells) **So:** 799
Flageolet [musical instrument] **F:** 224 *with picture*
Flagg, James Montgomery [American artist]
Uncle Sam *picture on* **U:** 19
Flagler, Henry Morrison [American businessman] **F:** 224
Florida (Progress as a state) **F:** 262
Miami (History) **M:** 480
Flagrant foul
Basketball (Fouls) **B:** 147-148
Flagstad, Kirsten [Norwegian singer] **F:** 224
Flagstaff [Arizona] **F:** 224 *with picture*
Radar *picture on* **R:** 69
Flagstaff [boat]
Hydrofoil (Modern hydrofoil development) **H:** 468
Flaherty, Pat [American race driver]
Automobile racing (table: Indianapolis 500 winners) **A:** 980
Flaherty, Robert Joseph [American director] **F:** 225
Flahiff, George Bernard [Canadian religious leader]
Cardinal (table: Canadian cardinals) **C:** 211
Flail [tool]
Wheat (The mechanization of wheat farming) **W:** 276
Flaking grits
Corn (The dry-milling industry) **Ci:** 1061-1062
Flamboyant tracery [architecture]
Tracery **T:** 355
Flame *See* Fire *in this index*
Flame azalea [plant]
Flower *picture on* **F:** 281
Flame of Liberty [nickname]
Gadsden (Christopher Gadsden) **G:** 4
Flame of Life, The [book by D'Annunzio]
D'Annunzio, Gabriele **D:** 33
Flame scallop [animal]
Mollusk *picture on* **M:** 695
Flame thrower [weapon] **F:** 225 *with picture*
Flamefish

Fish *picture on* **F:** 155
Flamenco [dance] **F:** 225 *with picture*
Spain (Music) **So:** 739 *with picture*
Flames, Calgary [team]
Hockey (table: National Hockey League) **H:** 281
Flaming Gorge Dam [Green River, Utah]
Utah *picture on* **U:** 247
Wyoming (Rivers and lakes) **W:** 528-529
Flaming Gorge National Recreation Area [Utah]
Utah *picture on* **U:** 240
Flaming Youth [U.S. history]
United States, History of the (The Lost Generation and Flaming Youth) **U:** 190
Flamingo F: 226 *with pictures*
Bird *picture on* **B:** 351
Zoo (Interesting facts about zoo animals) **Z:** 601 *with picture*
Flamingo [sculpture by Calder]
Chicago (Places to visit) **C:** 430-431
Flamingo lily [plant]
Anthurium **A:** 550
"Flammonde" [poem by Robinson]
Robinson, Edwin Arlington **R:** 368
Flanagan, Edward Joseph [American social reformer] **F:** 227 *with portrait*
Boys Town **B:** 541
Flanagin, Harris [American political leader]
Arkansas (table) **A:** 712
Flanders [region, Europe] **F:** 227 *with maps*
Belgium (Regions and language communities) **B:** 227
City *picture on* **Ci:** 583
Classical music (Franco-Flemish music) **Ci:** 646
Flemings **F:** 233
Painting (The northern Renaissance) **P:** 57 *with pictures*
Renaissance (The Renaissance outside Italy) **R:** 237
Walloons **W:** 18
Flanders, Benjamin [American political leader]
Louisiana (table) **L:** 496
Flanders Field [Belgium] **F:** 227
Flange [biology]
Orangutan **O:** 817 *with picture*
Flanged wheel
Railroad (History) **R:** 114
Flanker
Football (The offensive team) **F:** 356-357 *with diagrams*
Flannel [fabric] **F:** 227
Flap [surgery]
Plastic surgery (Reconstructive plastic surgery) **P:** 553
Flapper [plumbing]
Plumbing (How toilets work) **P:** 579 *with diagrams*
Flapper [U.S. history]
Held, John, Jr. **H:** 168 *with picture*
United States, History of the (The Lost Generation and Flaming Youth) **U:** 190 *with picture*
Flaps [airplane]
Aerodynamics (Creating extra lift) **A:** 86
Airplane (The wing) **A:** 213-214 *with picture*
Glider (The wings) **G:** 228
Flare [device]
Cloud seeding (Cloud-seeding methods) **C:** 711
Fireworks (Other uses of fireworks) **F:** 135
Flare, Solar *See* Solar flare *in this index*
Flaring [process]
Gas [fuel] (Storing gas) **G:** 55
Flash burn [injury]
Nuclear weapon (Thermal radiation) **N:** 599
Flash camera
Camera (Providing additional light) **C:** 80
Flash disk [electronic device]
Computer (Flash drives) **Ci:** 916
Flash distillation
Distillation (Simple distillation) **D:** 238-239
Water *diagram on* **W:** 128; (Distillation) **W:** 127
Flash drive [electronic device]
Computer (Flash drives) **Ci:** 916
Flash flood F: 227
Flood (River floods) **F:** 236 *with picture*
Flash lamp
Laser (Parts of a laser) **L:** 83
Flash memory [electronics]
Camera *picture on* **C:** 82
Computer (Flash drives) **Ci:** 916
Computer chip (Memory chips) **Ci:** 924f
Photography (Storing digital images) **P:** 421
Flash point [chemistry]
Combustion **C:** 867
Flash synchronizer [device]
Photography (Artificial lighting devices) **P:** 416
Flash unit [photography] *See* Electronic flash *in this index*
Flashback [psychology]

Hallucinogenic drug **H:** 26
LSD **L:** 512
Post-traumatic stress disorder **P:** 710
Flashing [building material]
House (The roof) **H:** 382 *with diagram*
Flashlight F: 228 *with diagram*
Flashover
Fire (How fires behave) **F:** 121
Flask [manufacturing]
Cast and casting (How castings are made) **C:** 278 *with diagram*
Flat [horticulture]
Transplanting **T:** 381 *with picture*
Vegetable (Planting) **V:** 293
Flat [music]
Music (Tone) **M:** 950; (Indicating pitch) **M:** 952-953
Flat [scenery]
Theater (Kinds of scenery) **T:** 239
Flat-bed press
Printing (Letterpress printing) **P:** 799-800
Flat bread
Bread (Kinds of bread) **B:** 588 *with pictures*
Flat-coated retriever [dog] **F:** 228 *with picture*
Flat color printing
Printing (Flat color printing) **P:** 802
Flat-file database [software]
Database **D:** 42
Flat glass
Glass (Flat glass) **G:** 212; (Drawing) **G:** 215 *with picture*
Flat kite
Kite (Types of kites) **K:** 339 *with picture*
Flat paint
Paint (Selecting the paint) **P:** 25
Flat panel screen [electronics]
Computer (Monitors) **Ci:** 916
Television (Flat-panel displays) **T:** 126 *with picture*
Flat-plate collector [instrument]
Energy supply (Solar energy) **E:** 278
Solar energy (Solar heating) **So:** 579 *with picture*
Flat stitch
Embroidery (Embroidery stitches) **E:** 257 *with picture*
Flat tax F: 228
Income tax (Defining taxable income) **I:** 102-103
Flat Tax, The [book by Hall and Rabushka]
Flat tax **F:** 228
Flat-topped inflorescence [botany]
Inflorescence **I:** 268a
Flat water racing
Canoeing (Flat water racing) **C:** 182 *with picture*
Flat yard [railroad]
Railroad (At classification yards) **R:** 110
Flatbed scanner [electronic device]
Computer (A scanner) **Ci:** 915
Photography (Processing digital images) **P:** 422
Flatbed truck [vehicle]
Transportation *picture on* **T:** 396
Truck *picture on* **T:** 459; (On-highway trucks) **T:** 457
Flatboat [boat] **F:** 228 *with picture*
Pioneer life in America (How the pioneers traveled) **P:** 478-479 *with picture*
Raft **R:** 102
Flatbottom [motorboat]
Motorboat racing (Hull designs) **M:** 876 *with picture*
Flatbush [district]
New York City (Brooklyn) **N:** 326-328
Flatfish [fish] **F:** 228
Flatfoot [disorder] **F:** 229
Flathead Indians
De Smet, Pierre Jean **D:** 159
Flathead Lake Marine Trail
Montana (Places to visit) **M:** 750; (Rivers and lakes) **M:** 752
Flathead Mountains
Montana (Land regions) **M:** 752
Flatiron Building
New York City (Architecture) **N:** 336
Flats [region, Alaska]
Yukon River (Upper Yukon) **Y:** 582 *with map*
Flatt, Lester [American musician]
Country music (Bluegrass music) **Ci:** 1098a *with picture*
Flatt and Scruggs [American musicians]
Country music (Bluegrass music) **Ci:** 1098a *with picture*
Flattop [ship] *See* Aircraft carrier *in this index*
Flatwater kayak [boat]
Kayaking **K:** 250a
Flatworm [animal] **F:** 229 *with diagram*
Animal *picture on* **A:** 486; (A classification of the animal kingdom) **A:** 506 *with picture*
Disease (Other infectious diseases) **D:** 227-228
Eye *picture on* **E:** 468

Invertebrate **I:** 365
Worm (Flatworms) **W:** 500 *with pictures*
Flaubert, Gustave [French author] **F:** 230 *with portrait*
De Maupassant, Guy **D:** 118
French literature (Realism) **F:** 522
Novel (France) **N:** 573
Flaugergues, Comet [astronomy]
Comet (table) **Ci:** 868
Flavedo [botany]
Orange (The fruit and the tree) **O:** 814
Flavian Amphitheater *See* Colosseum *in this index*
Flavian emperors
Rome, Ancient (The Roman Empire) **R:** 446
Flavonoid [chemical] **F:** 230
Citrin **Ci:** 573
Flavor
Spice **So:** 781
Taste **T:** 50
Flavoring agent
Food additive (Kinds of additives) **F:** 339
Flawless diamond
Diamond (How diamonds can be judged) **D:** 182
Flax [plant] **F:** 230 *with pictures*
Fiber (Plant fibers) **F:** 87
Linen **L:** 334
Linseed oil **L:** 339
Materials (Biological materials) **M:** 300d
Flaxman, John [British sculptor]
Sculpture (European sculpture) **S:** 253-254
Flaxseed
Flax **F:** 230; (Growing and processing seed flax) **F:** 231 *with picture*
Flea [insect] **F:** 231 *with picture*
Cat (Veterinary care) **C:** 295
Disease (Spread of infectious diseases) **D:** 228
Dog (Grooming) **D:** 278
Insect *picture on* **I:** 282
Flea circus
Flea **F:** 232
Fleabane [plant] **F:** 232 *with picture*
Flower *picture on* **F:** 286
Fledermaus, Die [operetta by Strauss]
Operetta **O:** 809
Fleece
Hair **H:** 9
Karakul **K:** 245
Wool **W:** 399 *with picture*
Fleece flower [plant]
Knotweed **K:** 357
Fleet [ships]
Navy (The organization of navies) **N:** 77
Fleet, Thomas [American printer]
Mother Goose (Who was Mother Goose?) **M:** 842
Fleet admiral
Admiral **A:** 58
Fleet Forces Command
Navy, United States (The Operating Forces) **N:** 85
Fleet Marine Forces, United States
Camp Lejeune **C:** 90
Marine Corps, United States (The purpose of the Marine Corps) **M:** 206; (Operating forces) **M:** 208
Navy, United States (The Operating Forces) **N:** 85
Fleet marriage
Fleet Prison **F:** 232
Fleet Prison [London] **F:** 232
Fleet Street
London (Communication) **L:** 438
Fleet support ship
Navy, United States (Auxiliary ships) **N:** 84
Fleet system [Spanish history]
Cuba (Early years) **Ci:** 1175
Fleischer, Dave [American cartoonist]
Animation (Pioneers of American animation) **A:** 514a-514b
Fleischer, Max [American cartoonist]
Animation (Pioneers of American animation) **A:** 514a-514b
Fleischman, Paul [American author]
Newbery Medal (table) **N:** 359
Fleischman, Sid [author]
Newbery Medal (table) **N:** 359
Fleischmann Planetarium and Science Center [Reno]
Nevada (Places to visit) **N:** 164
Fleming, Sir Alexander [British bacteriologist]
F: 232 *with portrait*
Antibiotic (History) **A:** 552
Chain, Ernst Boris **C:** 369
Penicillin **P:** 240
Fleming, Aretas B. [American political leader]
West Virginia (table) **W:** 225
Fleming, Denise [American author/illustrator]
Literature for children *picture on* **L:** 366
Fleming, Francis P. [American political leader]
Florida (table) **F:** 260

Fleming, Ian [British author] F: 232
Fleming, John Ambrose [British engineer]
Vacuum tube (History) V: 259
Fleming, Renée [American singer] F: 233 *with portrait*
Fleming, Sir Sandford [Canadian engineer] F: 233
Fleming, Victor [American director]
Motion picture (Best achievement in directing: 1939) M: 862
Fleming, Walter M. [American doctor]
Shriners International S: 440
Fleming, William [American political leader]
Virginia (table) V: 417
Flemings [people] F: 233
Belgium B: 226; (Population and ancestry) B: 229; (Independence) B: 233-234; (After World War II) B: 235
Flanders F: 227
Walloons W: 18
Flemish bond
Brick (Bonds) B: 599 *with picture*
Flemish language and literature
Belgium (Languages) B: 229; (The arts) B: 230
Flemming, Arthur Sherwood [American government official]
Eisenhower, Dwight David (table) E: 152
Health and Human Services, Department of (table) H: 128
Flemming, Hugh John [Canadian political leader]
New Brunswick (table) N: 195
Flemming, James K. [Canadian political leader]
New Brunswick (table) N: 195
Flemming, Walter [German scientist]
Chromosome C: 538
Flenser [job]
Whale (Processing whale products) W: 263
Flesh F: 233
Flesh-eating animal See Carnivore *in this index*
Flesh-eating plant See Carnivorous plant *in this index*
Fleshing [industrial process]
Leather (Preparing the hides) L: 167
Fleshy-finned fish
Fish (Bony fish) F: 147-148 *with pictures*
Fleshy fruit
Fruit *pictures on* F: 545
Seed (Kinds of seeds) S: 280-281
Fletcher, Allen M. [American political leader]
Vermont (table) V: 333
Fletcher, Ernie [American political leader]
Kentucky (table) K: 290; (The 2000's) K: 294
Fletcher, John [English dramatist] F: 234
Beaumont, Francis B: 191
Shakespeare, William (His last years) S: 348; (Shakespeare's plays) S: 354; (The fourth period [1609-1614]) S: 365
Fletcher, Joseph [American military leader]
Iceberg (Northern Hemisphere icebergs) I: 17
Fletcher, Louise [American actress]
Motion picture (Best performance by an actress: 1975) M: 862
Fletcher, Ryland [American political leader]
Vermont (table) V: 333
Fletcher, Thomas C. [American political leader]
Missouri (table) M: 668
Fletcher v. Peck [U.S. history] F: 234
Marshall, John (Chief justice) M: 230
Supreme Court of the United States (table) So: 1002
Fletching [arrow part]
Archery (Arrows) A: 602 *with diagram*
Fleur-de-lis [symbol] F: 234 *with picture*
Heraldry *picture on* H: 195
Iris I: 430
Fleurs du mal, Les [poems by Baudelaire] See Flowers of Evil, The *in this index*
Fleury, André Hercule de [French clergyman]
Louis XV L: 475
Flexibility
Physical fitness (Performance-related fitness) P: 433-434; (Health-related fitness) P: 434
Flexible divisor [investment]
Dow Jones averages D: 316
Flexible exchange rate [economics]
Money (Money and international finance) M: 717
Flexible fuel vehicle
Alcohol (Ethanol) A: 335
Ethanol E: 365
Flexible kite
Kite (The flexible kite) K: 340 *with picture*
Flexible manufacturing system
Machine tool M: 17
Flexible spending account
Insurance (Other types of health insurance) I: 312
Flexible theater
Theater (The stage) T: 233-235
Flexitime See Flextime *in this index*

Flexner, Abraham [American educator] F: 234
Medicine (Professional organizations and medical reform) M: 376
Flexographic printing
Printing *diagram on* P: 800; (Relief printing) P: 799
Flexography See Flexographic printing *in this index*
Flexor [muscle]
Hand *diagrams on* H: 40
Muscle (Skeletal muscles) M: 933
Flextime
Wages and hours (Hours) W: 3
Flextrack
Railroad, Model (Track) R: 120
Flick, Elmer [American baseball player]
Baseball (table: Hall of Fame) B: 134
Flicker [bird] F: 234 *with picture*
Bird *picture on* B: 367; (Birds of forests and woodlands) B: 334 *with picture*
Woodpecker (Kinds) W: 394
Yellowhammer Y: 557
Flickertail State [name for]
North Dakota N: 496
Flight See Aviation; Flying *in this index*
Flight [military unit]
Air force (The organization of air forces) A: 183
Flight 93 National Memorial [Pennsylvania]
National Park System (table: National memorials) N: 54
September 11 terrorist attacks (Pennsylvania) S: 310c
Flight archery [contest]
Archery (Flight archery) A: 603
Flight deck [airplane]
Airplane *picture on* A: 219
Flight deck [ship]
Aircraft carrier A: 206 *with pictures*
Flight engineer [occupation]
Astronaut A: 828
Aviation (Jobs with airlines and airports) A: 992
Flight envelope [aviation]
Test pilot (Experimental test pilots) T: 182
Flight feather [biology]
Bird (Feathers) B: 362
Flight instruments
Airplane *picture on* A: 222
Flight into Egypt [sculpture]
Sculpture *picture on* S: 250
Flight of Ashes [book by Maron]
German literature (Recent German literature) G: 142
Flight of Daedalus and Fall of Icarus [woodcut]
Airplane *picture on* A: 229
Flight of the Bumblebee, The [music by Rimsky-Korsakov]
Rimsky-Korsakov, Nikolai R: 342
Flight of the Moth, The [book by Post]
Post, Emily P: 698
Flight recorder [electronic device]
Airplane (The controls and instruments) A: 217
Flight simulator [aviation]
Audio-visual materials (Other computerized tools) A: 883
Wind shear W: 332
Flight surgeon
Aerospace medicine (Aviation medicine) A: 89
Flight Test Center
Edwards Air Force Base E: 114
Flightless bird
Bird (How birds move) B: 350 *with picture*
Flin Flon [Manitoba-Saskatchewan] F: 235
Flinders, Matthew [British explorer]
Australia *map on* A: 921; (Mapping the continent) A: 922 *with map*
Franklin, Sir John F: 492
South Australia (History) So: 639
Flinders Island [Australia]
Tasmania (Land and climate) T: 48
Flint [city, Michigan] F: 235 *with picture*
Flint [mineral] F: 236 *with picture*
Fire (Methods of starting fires) F: 121
Quartz (Types) Q: 8
Rock (table) R: 373 *with picture*
Flint corn
Corn (Kinds of corn) Ci: 1058
Flint Cultural Center
Flint F: 235
Flint Hills
Kansas (Land regions) K: 228
Flintknapping [technique]
Archaeology (Evaluation) A: 598
Flintlock [gun] F: 236 *with picture*
Handgun (Early handguns) H: 45 *with picture*
Revolution, American (Weapons and tactics) R: 279 *with pictures*
Rifle *picture on* R: 339
Weapon (Firearms) W: 154b

"Flintstones, The" [cartoon]
Animation (Animation in the mid-1900's) A: 514b
Flip book
Animation A: 511
Flip chart
Audio-visual materials (Chalkboards, dry-erase boards, and flip charts) A: 882
Flip turn
Swimming (Starts and turns) So: 1046
Flipper [zoology]
Animal (Fins, tails, and flippers) A: 490
Dolphin (The bodies of dolphins) D: 297 *with pictures*
Seal (Flippers) S: 266
Whale (Body shape) W: 259 *with picture*
FLIR [electronic device] See Forward-Looking Infrared system *in this index*
Flitch [wood]
Plywood (Making plywood) P: 586
FLN [political group, Algeria] See Front de Libération Nationale *in this index*
Float [fishing]
Fishing (Floats) F: 178 *with picture*
Float [parade]
Flower *picture on* F: 274
Float [plumbing]
Plumbing (How toilets work) P: 579 *with diagrams*
Float [tool]
Plaster (Plastering) P: 552-553 *with picture*
Float bath [furnace]
Glass (Drawing) G: 215
Floating
Drowning D: 349
Swimming (Water safety) So: 1042-1043
Floating dock [shipping]
Dry dock D: 369
Floating exchange rate [economics]
Balance of payments (Balance of payments and exchange rates) B: 36
Economics (The world economy) E: 61
Exchange rate E: 436
Money (Money and international finance) M: 717
Floating Gardens of Xochimilco [Mexico]
Lake Xochimilco L: 48
Floating market
Myanmar *picture on* M: 970c
Floating Opera, The [book by Barth]
Barth, John B: 120
Floating rib [anatomy]
Rib R: 320 *with diagrams*
Floating soap
Detergent and soap (Bar soaps) D: 164
Floating sorrel [plant]
Endangered species (table) E: 270
Floatplane
Airplane (Seaplanes) A: 212
Flock
Bird *picture on* B: 360
Duck (Habits) D: 376
Flock, Tim [American race driver]
Automobile racing (table: NASCAR Sprint Cup champions) A: 981
Flodden Field, Battle of [1513]
Scotland (The House of Stuart) S: 219
Flong [paper]
Stereotyping So: 893
Flood F: 236 *with pictures*
Conservation (Water conservation) Ci: 977
Dam (The effects of dams) D: 17
Disaster (table) D: 223
Dominican Republic (History) D: 304-305
Famine (Causes of famine) F: 26a
Flash flood F: 227
Global warming (Rise in sea level) G: 232a
Hurricane (Hurricane damage) H: 455
Hurricane Katrina H: 456 *with picture*
Iowa (The mid-1900's) I: 396
Johnstown J: 155
Johnstown Flood J: 155
Levee L: 216
Mississippi River (Floods and flood control) M: 647
Missouri (The late 1900's) M: 672
Missouri River (Dams and reservoirs) M: 675; (History) M: 675-676
Monsoon M: 740
Netherlands (Climate) N: 145
New Orleans (The early 2000's) N: 285 *with picture*
Ohio (The early 1900's) O: 702 *with picture*
Pakistan (Musharraf) P: 100
Rapid City R: 144
Rio de Janeiro (History) R: 346
Safety (During a flood) S: 15
South Dakota (The mid-1900's) So: 684 *with picture*

Swamp So: 1015
Tennessee Valley Authority (Flood control) T: 159
Water *picture on* W: 116
Flood, Great *See* Deluge *in this index*
Flood basalt [geology]
Volcano (Flood basalts) V: 442a *with picture*
Flood irrigation
Irrigation (Surface irrigation) I: 457 *with picture*
Flood plain [geography]
Flood (River floods) F: 237; (Reducing flood losses) F: 238 *with diagram*
Plain P: 506 *with picture*
River (Flood plains) R: 353 *with diagram*
Valley V: 265
Floodgate
Flood (Flood control) F: 238
Floodlight
Lighting (For outdoor events) L: 297 *with picture*
Floodwater mosquito [insect]
Mosquito (Egg) M: 832-833
Floodway
Flood (Reducing flood losses) F: 238
Mississippi River (Floods and flood control) M: 647-648
Floor [geography]
Rain forest (Structure and growth) R: 126a
Valley V: 265
Floor broker [economics]
Commodity exchange Ci: 873
Floor covering *See* Rugs and carpets *in this index*
Floor exercise [gymnastics]
Gymnastics *picture on* G: 450; (Men's events) G: 448; (Women's events) G: 449
Floor joist [construction] *See* Joist *in this index*
Floor leader [office]
Political party (Organizing the government) P: 632
United States, Government of the (Party leadership) U: 138-140
Floor loom
Weaving (Kinds of looms) W: 174
Floor plan
Interior design (Planning on paper) I: 330
Flooring [building material] F: 239
House (The frame) H: 382 *with diagram*
Interior design (Choosing patterns and textures) I: 332-333
Linoleum L: 338
Lumber (table) L: 518
Mosaic M: 822
Flora [biology] F: 239
Fauna F: 56
Floral bract [botany]
Pineapple (The pineapple plant) P: 472
Floral organ [botany]
Grass (The grass plant) G: 324
Floralia [custom]
May Day M: 322
Flore et Zéphire [painting by Chalon and Lane]
Ballet *picture on* B: 53
Floreana Island
Galapagos Islands G: 7 *with map*
Florence [Italy] F: 239 *with pictures*
Florin F: 266
Leonardo da Vinci (Early career) L: 199
Medici M: 362
Michelangelo (Early life) M: 483; (The Last Judgment) M: 486
Painting (The 1300's) P: 51-52
Renaissance (The Italian Renaissance) R: 233 *with map*
Florence, Cathedral of [Italy]
Architecture (Early Renaissance architecture) A: 620 *with picture*
Brunelleschi, Filippo B: 651
Campanile C: 90a
Florence, Council of [1438]
Roman Catholic Church (The close of the Middle Ages) R: 407-408
Florence, William J. [American actor]
Shriners International S: 440
Florentine *Pietà* [sculpture by Michelangelo]
Michelangelo (Later years) M: 487 *with picture*
Flores, Pedro [Filipino inventor]
Yo-yo Y: 566
Flores de Mayo [festival]
May M: 320
Flores Island [island, Azores] F: 241
Homo floresiensis H: 306
Florey, Lord [British bacteriologist] F: 241
Chain, Ernst Boris C: 369
Penicillin (Early history) P: 240
Floria Tosca [opera character]
Opera: (Tosca) O: 807
Florian [Roman emperor]
Rome, Ancient (table) R: 447
Floribunda [plant]

Rose (Types of roses) R: 474 *with picture*; (table) R: 474
Floriculture [botany] F: 241
Horticulture (The horticulture industry) H: 369
Florida F: 242 *with pictures and maps*
See also the list of Related articles in the Florida *article*
Bush v. Gore B: 724
Election of 2000 (On Election Day) E: 161
Gálvez, Bernardo de G: 18
Hispanic Americans (In the Southeast) H: 250; (Cuban immigration) H: 254
Menéndez de Avilés, Pedro M: 400
Ponce de León, Juan P: 655
United States, History of the *map on* U: 184
Florida, University of F: 266
Florida East Coast Railway
Flagler, Henry Morrison F: 224
Florida Keys [islands, Florida] F: 266 *with picture*
Florida (Land regions) F: 254 *with picture*
Florida Marlins [team] *See* Miami Marlins *in this index*
Florida panther [wild cat] F: 266 *with picture*
Florida Panthers [team]
Hockey (table: National Hockey League) H: 281
Florida parishes [region, Louisiana]
Louisiana (Land regions) L: 490
Florida pompano [fish]
Fish *picture on* F: 153
Pompano P: 653 *with picture*
Florida Purchase [U.S. history]
Monroe, James (War with the Seminole) M: 737
Florida softshell turtle
Turtle (Softshell turtles) T: 523
Florida Southern College
Florida *picture on* F: 246
Florida State University F: 266
Florida Supreme Court
Election of 2000 (Court challenges) E: 161
Florida Times-Union [newspaper]
Florida (Communication) F: 260
Florin [money] F: 266
Guilder G: 429
Florio, James J. [American political leader]
New Jersey (table) N: 249
Florissant Fossil Beds National Monument [Colorado] F: 266 *with picture*
National Park System (table: National monuments) N: 51
Florist [occupation]
Flower (As decoration) F: 272
Florizel [literary figure]
Shakespeare, William: (The Winter's Tale) S: 365
Flory, Paul John [American chemist]
Nobel Prizes (Chemistry: 1974) N: 444
Flotation cell
Copper (Milling) Ci: 1042-1043
Flotation process [chemistry] F: 267
Copper (Milling) Ci: 1042
Lead (Production) L: 149
Flotsam, jetsam, and lagan [wreckage] F: 267
Flounder [fish] F: 267 *with picture*
Fish *pictures on* F: 149, F: 153, F: 166
Flour [food] F: 267 *with pictures*
Africa *picture on* A: 113
Bran B: 562
Bread B: 588
Sago S: 19
Wheat (Food for people) W: 266
Flour beetle [insect] F: 269 *with picture*
Flour City [nickname]
Rochester (Government and history) R: 370
Flour corn
Corn (Kinds of corn) Ci: 1058-1059
Flow chart
Computer (Preparing a program) Ci: 923
"Flow my tears" [song by Dowland]
Dowland, John D: 316
Flower F: 270 *with pictures*
See also the table in the Flower *article*
Angiosperm A: 462 *with picture*
Bud B: 666
Cotton *picture on* Ci: 1088
Floriculture F: 241
Gardening (Ornamental gardens) G: 30 *with pictures*; (table) G: 33 *with diagram*
Grass (The grass plant) G: 324 *with picture*
Netherlands (Holidays and recreation) N: 141
Perfume (Plant substances) P: 286
Plant (Angiosperms) P: 520 *with pictures*; (Parts of plants) P: 528; (Flowers) P: 531 *with pictures*; (Sexual reproduction) P: 532-533 *with pictures*
Seed (Seed development in angiosperms) S: 281
Tree (Seeds) T: 417
Vegetable (Flower buds) V: 292 *with picture*
Flower [fireworks]
Fireworks (How fireworks work) F: 135

Flower [tile]
Mah-jongg M: 64 *with picture*
Flower, Roswell Pettibone [American political leader]
New York (table) N: 313
Flower arranging [art]
Flower *picture on* F: 298; (Flower arranging) F: 297
Flower child
Hippies H: 239
Flower Fables [book by Alcott]
Alcott, Louisa May A: 338
Flower garden
Gardening (Kinds of outdoor gardens) G: 30 *with picture*; (Planting an informal flower garden) G: 32 *with picture*; (Cultivating an outdoor garden) G: 34
"Flower Song" [aria]
Opera: (Carmen) O: 802-803
Flower-visiting bat [animal]
Bat (Fruit bats and flower-visiting bats) B: 161
Flowering dogwood [plant]
Dogwood D: 284 *with picture*
Tree *pictures on* T: 421
Flowering maple [shrub] F: 303 *with picture*
Flowering of New England, The [book by Brooks]
Brooks, Van Wyck B: 641
Flowering plant *See* Angiosperm *in this index*
Flowering quince [plant]
Quince Q: 42
Flowering tobacco [plant] F: 303 *with picture*
Flowerpecker [bird] F: 303
Flowers of Evil, The [poems by Baudelaire]
Baudelaire, Charles B: 173
French literature (Symbolism) F: 522
Flowers of sulfur [chemistry]
Sulfur (Forms) So: 966-967
Flowfield [physics]
Aerodynamics (Applying aerodynamic principles) A: 88
Flowing tracery [architecture]
Tracery T: 355
Flowstone
Cave (Speleothems) C: 319 *with diagram*
Floyd, Charles [American explorer]
Iowa (Territorial days) I: 393
Lewis and Clark expedition (Up the Missouri) L: 222a-222b
Sioux City S: 474
Floyd, Charles M. [American political leader]
New Hampshire (table) N: 223
Floyd, John [American political leader]
Virginia (table) V: 417
Floyd, John Buchanan [American government official]
Buchanan, James (table) B: 661
Virginia (table) V: 417
Floyd, William [American patriot] F: 303
FLQ [political group] *See* Front de Libération du Québec *in this index*
FLSA [U.S. history] *See* Fair Labor Standards Act *in this index*
Flu *See* Influenza *in this index*
Fluconazole [drug]
Antibiotic (table) A: 551
Flue curing
Tobacco (Kinds of tobacco) T: 305; (Flue curing) T: 307
Flue pipe [musical instrument]
Organ (Pipe organs) O: 851-852
Fluency [speech]
Speech therapy (Types of disorders) So: 773
Stuttering So: 934
Fluffer [machine]
Cotton (Cleaning and blending) Ci: 1091
Flügelhorn [musical instrument] F: 304
Music *picture on* M: 949
Fluid [physics] F: 304
Friction (Kinds of friction) F: 532
Liquid L: 346
Physics (Fluid and plasma physics) P: 438
Viscosity V: 428b *with picture*
Fluid dynamics
Mechanics M: 354
Fluid film bearing [machine]
Bearing (Plain bearings) B: 188 *with diagram*
Fluid mechanics [physics] F: 304
Fluid ounce [measure]
Ounce O: 879
Fluid statics [physics]
Fluid mechanics (Fluid statics) F: 304
Fluidic engine
Hydraulic engine H: 462
Fluidics [engineering]
Coanda, Henri-Marie Ci: 733
Fluidized-bed combustion
Coal (Coal research) Ci: 730

Fluidized bed freezing [process]
  Food, Frozen (Air-blast freezing) F: 338
Fluke [animal] F: 304
  Animal *picture on* A: 468
  Flatworm F: 229 *with diagram*
  Parasite (Life cycle) P: 154 *with diagram*
  Worm (Flatworms) W: 500 *with picture*
Fluke [fin]
  Dolphin (The bodies of dolphins) D: 297 *with pictures*
  Whale (Body shape) W: 259 *with picture*
Fluke [fish]
  Flounder F: 267
Flume [New Hampshire]
  New Hampshire (Places to visit) N: 216 *with picture*
Flunitrazepam [drug] *See* Rohypnol *in this index*
Fluor [mineral] *See* Fluorite *in this index*
Fluorescein [medicine]
  Light (Light in medicine) L: 292
Fluorescence [physics] F: 304 *with pictures*
  Light (Luminescence and fluorescence) L: 283
Fluorescence microscopy [science]
  Microscope (Specialized optical microscopes and techniques) M: 518
Fluorescent lamp [lighting] F: 305 *with diagram*
  Electric light (Gaseous-discharge lamps) E: 174 *with picture*
  Interior design (Selecting accessories) I: 333
  Invention *picture on* I: 356
  Light bulb L: 293
  Lighting (Lighting devices) L: 298
Fluorescent light *See* Fluorescent lamp *in this index*
Fluoridation [water treatment] F: 305
  Dentistry (Modern dentistry) D: 144-145
  Teeth (A good diet) T: 81
Fluoride [chemistry]
  Dentistry (Modern dentistry) D: 144-145
  Fluoridation F: 305
  Fluorine F: 306
  Hydrofluoric acid H: 465
Fluorine [element] F: 306
  Atom *diagram on* A: 872
  Halogen H: 26
Fluorite [mineral] F: 306
  Fluorine F: 306
  Mineral *picture on* M: 569
Fluorophore [medicine]
  Light (Light in medicine) L: 292
Fluoroscope [instrument]
  Fluoroscopy F: 306 *with picture*
Fluoroscopy [medicine] F: 306 *with pictures*
  Radiology R: 98
Fluorspar [mineral] *See* Fluorite *in this index*
Fluothane [drug]
  Halothane H: 27
Fluoxetine [drug]
  Antidepressant A: 553
  Depression D: 151
Flush [botany]
  Tea (Growing tea) T: 62 *with picture*
Flush [poker]
  Poker P: 603
Flushing Institute [school]
  Muhlenberg, Henry Melchior M: 912
Flushing Meadows Corona Park [district]
  New York City (Queens) N: 329
Flute [musical instrument] F: 307 *with pictures*
  Music (Wind instruments) M: 949 *with picture*
  Piccolo P: 450 *with pictures*
Fluted armor
  Armor (During the Middle Ages) A: 719-720
Fluted point [archery]
  Indian, American (The first Americans) I: 151
Flutie, Doug [American football player]
  Football (table) F: 363
Flutter kick
  Swimming (The basic kicks) So: 1043
Flux [chemistry] F: 307
  Gold (Smelting) G: 253
  Welding (Fusion welding) W: 189
Flux lines [physics]
  See also Field lines *in this index*
  Sun (Magnetic field) So: 977
  Weber W: 175
Fluxing [industrial process]
  Aluminum (Fabricating ingots) A: 394
Fly [flag]
  Flag *diagram on* F: 194
Fly [insect] F: 308 *with pictures*
  See also the list of Related articles in the Fly *article*
  Biology *picture on* B: 319
  Bot fly B: 507
  Flower (Beetles and flies) F: 295
  Insect *pictures on* I: 282; (Wings) I: 288; (Touch) I: 291
  Lovebug L: 508

Midge M: 535 *with picture*
  Typhoid fever (Cause and spread) T: 539
Fly, Artificial
  Fishing *picture on* F: 177; (Bait) F: 178 *with picture*
Fly agaric [fungus]
  Mushroom (Poisonous mushrooms) M: 945 *with picture*
Fly ash
  Cement and concrete (Materials) C: 343
  Coal (Coal as a fuel) Ci: 718
Fly-by-wire system [aviation]
  Automatic flight control system (How an AFCS works) A: 944
Fly end
  Flag *diagram on* F: 194
Fly out
  Baseball (Outs by batters) B: 128-129; (Rule changes) B: 133
Fly reel
  Fishing (Reels) F: 176-177 *with picture*
Fly shuttle [machine]
  Cotton (In England) Ci: 1092
  Hargreaves, James H: 60
  Industrial Revolution (Weaving machines) I: 249
  Invention (Economic needs) I: 355
Fly-up [ceremony]
  Girl Scouts (Girl Scout Juniors) G: 197
Flyball governor [machine]
  Automation (History of automation) A: 945
Flyby craft [spacecraft]
  Comet (Studying comets) Ci: 868-869
Flycatcher [bird] F: 311 *with picture*
  Bird *picture on* B: 358; (Birds of grasslands) B: 336 *with picture*
  Pewee P: 352 *with picture*
Flyer [airplane]
  Airplane (The Wright brothers) A: 231 *with picture*
  Wright brothers W: 508 *with picture*
Flyer [circus]
  Circus (At the circus) Ci: 562 *with picture*
Flyers, Philadelphia [team]
  Hockey (table: National Hockey League) H: 281
Flying
  See also Aviation *in this index*
  Airplane (Principles of flight) A: 220 *with diagrams*
  Animal (Wings) A: 488
  Bird (How birds move) B: 350 *with diagrams*
  Insect (Wings) I: 288
Flying [scenery]
  Theater (Changing scenery) T: 240
Flying boat [airplane]
  Airplane *picture on* A: 233; (Seaplanes) A: 212; (Engineering improvements) A: 237
  Aviation (The industry comes of age) A: 989 *with picture*
Flying buttress [architecture]
  Architecture (Architectural terms) A: 608 *with picture*; (Gothic architecture) A: 618-619 *with pictures*
  Gothic art (Early Gothic architecture) G: 278
  Notre Dame, Cathedral of N: 551
Flying Cloud [ship]
  McKay, Donald M: 337
  Ship *picture on* S: 422
Flying crane [aircraft]
  Helicopter (For transportation and construction work) H: 170
Flying Doctor Service, Royal *See* Royal Flying Doctor Service of Australia *in this index*
Flying dragon [reptile] F: 311 *with picture*
  Animal *picture on* A: 469
  Lizard (How lizards move) L: 399
Flying Dutchman [legendary ship] F: 311
Flying Dutchman, The [opera by Wagner]
  Flying Dutchman F: 311
  Opera (Richard Wagner) O: 798-799
Flying fish *See* Flyingfish *in this index*
Flying Fortress [airplane]
  Air Force, United States (Between world wars) A: 195
  Aircraft, Military *picture on* A: 205
  Airplane *picture on* A: 234
  Bomber (History) B: 453
  World War II (The air war) W: 482
Flying fox [animal] F: 311
  Bat B: 159; (Fruit bats and flower bats) B: 161
  Global warming (Effect on plant and animal life) G: 232a
Flying gurnard [fish]
  Gurnard G: 443
Flying hatchetfish
  Fish *picture on* F: 145
Flying lemur [animal] F: 312 *with picture*
  Mammal *picture on* M: 116; (table) M: 128 *with picture*
Flying lizard [animal]

Flying dragon F: 311 *with picture*
Flying saucer *See* Unidentified flying object *in this index*
Flying squirrel [animal] F: 312 *with picture*
  Animal *picture on* A: 479
  Squirrel (Types of squirrels) So: 814b
Flying Tigers [World War II] F: 312
  Chennault, Claire Lee C: 408
  World War II (China) W: 492
Flying top [toy]
  Helicopter (Early designs and experiments) H: 173
Flyingfish [fish] F: 312
  Animal *picture on* A: 487
  Fish *pictures on* F: 145, F: 152
Flynn, Edmund J. [Canadian political leader]
  Quebec (table) Q: 29
Flynn, Elizabeth Gurley [American labor leader] F: 313
Flynn, William S. [American political leader]
  Rhode Island (table) R: 311
Flytrap [plant] *See* Venus's-flytrap *in this index*
Flyway [route]
  Bird (Where birds migrate) B: 360
Flyweight [mechanism]
  Governor G: 293 *with diagram*
Flyweight class
  Boxing (table) B: 527
Flywheel [device] F: 313
  Automobile *diagrams on* A: 952; (The transmission) A: 948
  Gasoline engine *picture on* G: 63; (The flywheel) G: 64
  Machine *diagram on* M: 13
  Starter (Automobile starters) So: 858 *with diagram*
  Transmission (What a transmission does) T: 375; (The clutch) T: 378
FM [radio] *See* Frequency modulation *in this index*
Fm [symbol]
  Fermium F: 74
FM-CW radar
  Radar (Continuous-wave radar) R: 69
FM screening
  Printing (Preparing illustrations for reproduction) P: 797
FMLN [political organization]
  El Salvador (The 1900's) E: 252
FMS [manufacturing]
  Machine tool M: 17
FNL [political group]
  Burundi (History) B: 713-714
FNLA [political group] *See* National Front for the Liberation of Angola *in this index*
FNM [political party] *See* Free National Movement *in this index*
Fo, Dario [Italian dramatist]
  Drama (Drama in other countries) D: 341
  Nobel Prizes (Literature: 1997) N: 448
Foal [animal]
  Horse (Life history) H: 351; (Training horses) H: 359 *with picture*
  Horse racing (Thoroughbred horses) H: 363-364
  Zebra Z: 587 *with picture*
Foam extinguisher
  Fire extinguisher (Foam extinguishers) F: 130
Foam glass
  Glass (Specialty glasses) G: 212
Foam rubber
  Rubber (Sponge rubber) R: 505
Foaming [industrial process]
  Plastics (Foaming) P: 558 *with picture*
Focal length [optics]
  Lens (The focal length) L: 196a *with diagrams*
  Magnifying glass M: 62
  Photography (Lenses and focusing) P: 410; (Aperture size) P: 412-413
Focal plane [optics]
  Lens (The focal plane) L: 196a
  Telescope (Optical telescopes) T: 103
Foch, Ferdinand [French military leader] F: 313 *with portrait*
  World War I (The last campaigns) W: 463
Foci *See* Focus *in this index*
Focke, Henrich [German inventor]
  Helicopter (The first practical helicopters) H: 173 *with picture*
Focus [astronomy]
  Kepler, Johannes (Kepler's laws) K: 305
  Planet (How planets move) P: 508-509
Focus [geology]
  Earthquake (How an earthquake begins) E: 35-36
Focus [geometry]
  Ellipse E: 243 *with diagram*
  Parabola P: 141 *with diagram*
Focus [optics]
  Aberration A: 10

Camera (How a camera works) **C:** 80 *with diagram*
Eye (Focusing) **E:** 462 *with diagrams*
Lens (Convergence) **L:** 196a *with diagrams*
Mirror (Convex mirrors) **M:** 616-617; (Concave mirrors) **M:** 617 *with diagram*
Photography (How a camera works) **P:** 407-408 *with diagram*; (Lenses and focusing) **P:** 410 *with pictures*
Focus group
Public opinion poll (Designing the questionnaire) **P:** 862
Focusing screen [device]
Camera *picture on* **C:** 82
F.O.E. [organization] *See* Eagles, Fraternal Order of *in this index*
Foehn [weather] **F:** 313
Alps (Climate) **A:** 385
Austria (Climate) **A:** 934
Chinook **C:** 513
Switzerland (Climate) **So:** 1056
Wind (Local winds) **W:** 329-330
Foetus *See* Fetus *in this index*
FOG [navigation] *See* Fiber-optic gyro *in this index*
Fog [weather] **F:** 314 *with diagrams*
United Kingdom (Climate) **U:** 61-62
Weather (Humidity) **W:** 158
Fogel, Robert William [American economist]
Nobel Prizes (Economics: 1993) **N:** 449
Fogg, Phileas [literary figure]
Verne, Jules **V:** 338
Foggy Bottom [area]
State, Department of **So:** 860
Washington, D.C. (Executive branch buildings) **W:** 75
Fogo [island]
Cape Verde **C:** 189 *with map*
FOIA *See* Freedom of Information Act *in this index*
Foie gras [food]
Goose (Raising geese) **G:** 271
Foil [boat]
Hydrofoil **H:** 465 *with pictures*
Missile boat **M:** 618 *with diagram*
Foil [weapon]
Fencing **F:** 70 *with picture*
Foix, Count of [French nobleman]
Andorra (History) **A:** 455
Fokine, Michel [Russian choreographer] **F:** 314 *with picture*
Ballet (Ballet in Russia) **B:** 52
Fokine, Vera [wife of]
Fokine, Michel *picture on* **F:** 315
Fokker, Anthony Herman Gerard [Dutch engineer] **F:** 315
Air Force, United States (World War I) **A:** 194
Fokker D VII [airplane]
Airplane *picture on* **A:** 233
Fokker DR-1 triplane
Aircraft, Military *picture on* **A:** 204
Folacin [vitamin] *See* Folic acid *in this index*
Folate [vitamin] *See* Folic acid *in this index*
Fold [geology]
Hot springs **H:** 374b
Mountain (Fold-thrust mountains) **M:** 893 *with diagram*
Fold of the axis [geometry]
Symmetry (An axis of symmetry) **So:** 1066-1067
Fold-thrust mountain
Mountain (Fold-thrust mountains) **M:** 893 *with diagram*
Folding camping trailer [vehicle]
Recreational vehicle (Folding camping trailers) **R:** 184
Trailer (Recreational trailers) **T:** 367
Folding fan
Fan **F:** 26b *with picture*
Folding kayak [boat]
Kayaking **K:** 250a
Folding machine
Bookbinding (Forming a book) **B:** 470
Foley, John P. [American religious leader]
Cardinal (table: American cardinals) **C:** 211
Foley, Larry [Australian boxer]
Boxing (Boxing in Australia and New Zealand) **B:** 531
Foley, Thomas Stephen [American political leader] **F:** 315 *with portrait*
Folger, Charles J. [American government official]
Arthur, Chester Alan (table) **A:** 756; (Election of 1884) **A:** 757
Folger, Henry Clay [American bibliophile]
Folger Shakespeare Library **F:** 315
Folger Shakespeare Library [Washington, D.C.] **F:** 315
Washington, D.C. *map on* **W:** 76, *picture on* **W:** 83; (Folger Shakespeare Library) **W:** 71
Folic acid [vitamin] **F:** 315
Anemia (Insufficient production of red blood

cells) **A:** 457
Diet (Normal diet) **D:** 199
Nutrition (Vitamins) **N:** 626
Spina bifida **So:** 792
Vitamin (table) **V:** 431; (Vitamin B$_{12}$, folic acid, and choline) **V:** 432
Folio [publishing] **F:** 315
Shakespeare, William (Publishing history) **S:** 369 *with picture*
Foliose lichen [plant]
Lichen **L:** 269 *with picture*
Folk [sociology]
Folklore **F:** 322
Folk, Joseph W. [American political leader]
Missouri (table) **M:** 668; (Progress as a state) **M:** 671
Folk art F: 316 *with pictures*
See also Folk dancing; Folk music; Folklore; Handicraft *in this index*
Sculpture (American sculpture) **S:** 255 *with pictures*
Folk costume *See* Regional traditional costume *in this index*
Folk dancing F: 320 *with picture*
China *picture on* **C:** 481
Dance (Dances to take part in) **D:** 25 *with pictures*
Folklore *picture on* **F:** 325
Square dancing **So:** 811 *with picture*
Folk doll
Doll (Traditional dolls) **D:** 287 *with picture*
Folk high school
Denmark (Education) **D:** 136
Folk literature *See* Folklore *in this index*
Folk meter [poetry]
Poetry (Rhythm and meter) **P:** 591-592
Folk music F: 321
Country music (The roots of country music) **Ci:** 1098a
Folklore *picture on* **F:** 323; (Folk songs) **F:** 324
Jazz (The roots of jazz) **J:** 70
Music (Western music) **M:** 955
Opera (Nationalism) **O:** 799
Popular music **P:** 669; (The folk music revival) **P:** 671
Folk narrative [story]
Legend **L:** 183
Folk rock
Rock music (Bob Dylan) **R:** 380 *with picture*
Folk song *See* Folk music *in this index*
Folk tale
Folklore (Folk tales) **F:** 323
Literature for children (Traditional literature) **L:** 357
Storytelling (Kinds of stories for telling) **So:** 914
Folkeskole [school]
Denmark (Education) **D:** 136
Folkestone [United Kingdom]
Channel Tunnel **C:** 375
Folketing [parliament]
Denmark (Government) **D:** 132-133
Folklore F: 322 *with pictures*
See also the list of Related articles in the Folklore article
Fairy **F:** 9
Literature for children (Traditional literature) **L:** 357; (Fractured folklore) **L:** 365
Storytelling **So:** 914
Folkmoot
Vikings (Ancestry and population) **V:** 378-379
Folkway [anthropology]
Mores **M:** 802
Sumner, William Graham **So:** 973
Folkways [book by Sumner]
Sumner, William Graham **So:** 973
Follicle [anatomy]
Acne **A:** 27 *with diagram*
Hair (The structure and growth of hair) **H:** 9 *with diagram*
Follicle [zoology]
Egg (Development of the bird's egg) **E:** 117
Follicle-stimulating hormone
Hormone (Growth and sex hormones) **H:** 336
Menstruation (Follicular phase) *diagram on* **M:** 403
Follow-on
Cricket (The game) **Ci:** 1132
Follow-up letter
Letter writing (Letters of application) **L:** 211-212 *with picture*
Following the Equator [book by Twain]
Twain, Mark (Later works) **T:** 530
Folsom, Frances [wife of Grover Cleveland] *See* Cleveland, Frances Folsom *in this index*
Folsom, James E. [American political leader]
Alabama (table) **A:** 274
Folsom, Jim, Jr. [American political leader]
Alabama (table) **A:** 274

Folsom, Marion B. [American government official]
Eisenhower, Dwight David (table) **E:** 152
Health and Human Services, Department of (table) **H:** 128
Folsom point [archaeology] **F:** 326 *with picture*
Indian, American (Early days) **I:** 151 *with picture*
New Mexico (Indian peoples) **N:** 272
Fomento [organization]
Puerto Rico (Puerto Rico today) **P:** 884
Fomorians [legendary people]
Mythology (The Irish cycles) **M:** 985
Fon [people]
Benin (People) **B:** 249
Fonck, René [French aviator]
Ace **A:** 24
Fond [cooking]
Cooking (Methods) **Ci:** 1029
Fond du Lac [Minnesota]
Duluth **D:** 381
Fonda, Henry [American actor] **F:** 326 *with portrait*
Motion picture (Best performance by an actor: 1981) **M:** 862a
Fonda, Jane [American actress] **F:** 326 *with portrait*
Motion picture (Best performance by an actress: 1971, 1978) **M:** 862
Fong, Hiram Leong [American political leader] **F:** 326
Fonio [plant]
Burkina Faso (Economy) **B:** 706
Fono [parliament]
Samoa (Government) **S:** 80
Fonseca, Gulf of [gulf, Honduras]
Honduras (The Southern Coast) **H:** 310 *with map*
Fonseca, Manoel Deodoro da [Brazilian political leader]
Brazil (Birth of the republic) **B:** 585
Font [printing]
Photocomposition **P:** 404
Printing (Electronic imagesetting) **P:** 797
Proofreading (Proofreaders' marks) **P:** 822
Type **T:** 536
Fontaine, Joan [British actress]
Motion picture (Best performance by an actress: 1941) **M:** 862
Olivier, Laurence *picture on* **O:** 744
Fontainebleau [France] **F:** 326 *with picture*
Architecture (Later Renaissance architecture) **A:** 621 *with picture*
Fontainebleau, Treaty of [1762]
Louisiana (French Louisiana) **L:** 497-498
Fontanarossa, Susanna [mother of]
Columbus, Christopher (Early years) **Ci:** 857
Fontane, Theodor [German author] **F:** 327
Fontanne, Lynn [British actress] **F:** 327
Lunt, Alfred **L:** 526
Fonteyn, Margot [British dancer] **F:** 327 *with picture*
Nureyev, Rudolf **N:** 613 *with picture*
Fonvizin, Denis [Russian dramatist]
Russian literature (The classical movement) **R:** 559-560
Fonyo, Steve [Canadian public figure]
Fox, Terry **F:** 442
Foochow [China]
Fuzhou **F:** 590
Food F: 328 *with pictures*
See also Cooking; Diet; Food, Frozen; Food preservation; Food supply; Nutrition *in this index; the list of Related articles in the* Food *article; and the* Way of life *or* People *sections of various country articles, such as* England (People)
Adolescent (Eating disorders) **A:** 63
Agriculture (Agricultural products) **A:** 147
Allergy **A:** 373
Animal (Animals and people) **A:** 471; (Adaptations for eating) **A:** 490; (Providing food) **A:** 498
Balance of nature (Ecosystems) **B:** 35; (Competition) **B:** 35
Bird (As a source of food and raw materials) **B:** 330
Cancer (Genes damaged by substances in the environment) **C:** 170
Colonial life in America (Food and drink) **Ci:** 802
Consumer protection **Ci:** 1017
Disease (Spread of infectious diseases) **D:** 228
Family and consumer sciences (Nutrition, dietetics, and food science) **F:** 26
Flower (Other uses) **F:** 273
Food and Drug Administration **F:** 340
Fungi (The importance of fungi) **F:** 559
Genetically modified food **G:** 85
Grain **G:** 301
Greece, Ancient (Food, clothing, and shelter) **G:** 367
Health food **H:** 129

Hunger H: 449
Indian, American (Food) I: 136d *with picture*
Inuit (Food) I: 354b
Ocean (The importance of the ocean) O: 654
Organic food O: 853
Pioneer life in America (Food) P: 481 *with picture*
Plant (The importance of plants) P: 516; (Loss of biodiversity) P: 543
Potato P: 711
Protein P: 832
Pure food and drug laws (Foods) P: 907
Restaurant R: 262
Rice (Food) R: 323
Rome, Ancient (Food) R: 440
Seed (How people use seeds) S: 283
Soybean So: 689
Space exploration (Meeting basic needs in space) So: 703
Starvation So: 859
Weight control W: 181
Western frontier life in America (Food) W: 238
Food, Frozen F: 338 *with picture*
Birdseye, Clarence B: 375
Food preservation (Freezing) F: 342; (Freeze-drying) F: 343
Nitrogen (Uses of nitrogen) N: 425-426
Refrigeration R: 200
Food additive F: 339
Bread (How yeast bread is made) B: 588
Cancer (Genes damaged by substances in the environment) C: 170
Cattle (Feeding) C: 312
Food (Processing) F: 334
Food preservation (Additives) F: 343
Health food (Types of health foods) H: 129
Pure food and drug laws (Food additives) P: 907
Food Administration [U.S. history]
Hoover, Herbert Clark (Food administrator) H: 328
World War I (The United States enters the war) W: 462
Food Aid Convention
Food supply (Food aid programs) F: 351
Food and Agriculture Organization [UN] F: 340
Dairying (Improvements in dairy farming) D: 7-8
Food supply (Food supply programs) F: 350
Globalization (Features of globalization) G: 233
United Nations (Fighting hunger) U: 89
Food and Commercial Workers International Union, United See United Food and Commercial Workers International Union *in this index*
Food and Drug Administration [U.S.] F: 340
Antibiotic (Testing) A: 551
Artificial sweetener A: 761
Consumer protection (The right to safety) Ci: 1018
Cosmetics (Cosmetics regulations) Ci: 1074
Dietary supplement D: 200
Drug (Drug regulation) D: 357
Food additive (Government regulations) F: 340
Genetic engineering (History) G: 84c
Health and Human Services, Department of (Organization) H: 128
Herbal medicine H: 196
Industry (Lack of information) I: 261
Nutrition (Nutrition guidelines) N: 626
Packaging (Packaging regulations) P: 18
Pure food and drug laws P: 907
Sanitation (Food processing and distribution) S: 111
Thalidomide T: 229
Food and drug laws See Pure food and drug laws *in this index*
Food and Drugs Act [1920]
Pure food and drug laws (Food and drug laws in Canada) P: 909
Food and Drugs Act, Federal [1906]
Adams, Samuel Hopkins A: 44
Consumer protection (Beginnings of modern consumerism) Ci: 1019
Drug abuse (History) D: 365
Pure food and drug laws (History) P: 909
Roosevelt, Theodore (Domestic problems) R: 466-467
Food chain [biology]
Animal (Adaptations for eating) A: 490
Botany (The importance of botany) B: 508-509
Deep sea (Environment) D: 82
Ecology (Energy flow) E: 54
Environmental pollution (Water pollution) E: 334
Fish (Fish in the balance of nature) F: 147 *with diagram*
Forest (The flow of energy) F: 396
Hydrothermal vent H: 473
Ocean (The food cycle) O: 655; (Discoveries) O: 664
Pest control (Effects of pesticide use) P: 318

Food coloring
Food additive (Kinds of additives) F: 339
Food crop [agriculture]
Crop Ci: 1153
Food for Peace [federal program] F: 340
Food supply (Food aid programs) F: 351
Humphrey, Hubert Horatio (Senator and Vice President) H: 437
Food Guide Pyramid [nutrition]
Nutrition (Nutrition guidelines) N: 626
Food inspection
Pure food and drug laws (Enforcement) P: 908-909
Sanitation (Food processing and distribution) S: 111 *with picture*
Food laws See Pure food and drug laws *in this index*
Food pellet
Zoo (Diet) Z: 602
Food poisoning F: 340
Botulism B: 514
Camping (Safety) C: 96
Campylobacter C: 97
E. coli E: 2
Listeria L: 349
Mycotoxin M: 970f
Poison (Kinds of poisons) P: 600
Salmonellosis S: 71
Food preservation F: 341 *with picture*
See also Preservative *in this index*
Cold storage Ci: 761
Dehydrated food D: 93
Food, Frozen F: 338
Fruit (Harvesting) F: 547-548
Irradiation I: 455
Meat packing (Curing and smoking) M: 352
Pasteurization P: 193
Refrigeration R: 200
Food processing
See also Food preservation *in this index*
Air conditioning (In business and industry) A: 176-177
Food (Processing) F: 334
Health food (Types of health foods) H: 129
Meat packing (Meat-packing processes) M: 350 *with picture*
Omaha O: 756
Food Safety Modernization Act [2010]
Food and Drug Administration F: 340
Pure food and drug laws (History) P: 909
Food science
Family and consumer sciences (Nutrition, dietetics, and food science) F: 26
Food service industry
Careers (Tourism and hospitality) C: 233-234 *with picture*
Hospital *picture on* H: 372; (Professional services departments) H: 371
Restaurant R: 262
Food Stamp Act [1964]
Supplemental Nutrition Assistance Program So: 996
Food Stamp Program See Supplemental Nutrition Assistance Program *in this index*
Food storage tissue [botany]
Plant (Seeds) P: 531
Food supply F: 345 *with pictures*
Agribusiness A: 143
Balance of nature (Ecosystems) B: 35; (Competition) B: 35
Famine F: 26
Hunger H: 449
Malthus, Thomas Robert M: 115
Ocean (The importance of the ocean) O: 654
Population (Effects) P: 674
United Nations (Fighting hunger) U: 89
Women's movement (In developing nations) W: 387
Food vacuole [biology]
Ameba A: 406
Food value See Nutrition *in this index*
Food web [ecology]
Animal (Adaptations for eating) A: 490
Ecology (Energy flow) E: 54
Fish (Fish in the balance of nature) F: 147
Fool [food] *See* Ful *in this index*
Fool hen [bird]
Grouse (Habits) G: 404
Fool's gold *See* Pyrite *in this index*
Foot [anatomy] F: 352 *with diagram*
Bunion B: 700
Flatfoot F: 229
Shoe S: 430
Foot [measurement] F: 352
Weights and measures (Measurement systems) W: 184
Foot [poetry]
Poetry (Rhythm and meter) P: 591-594

Foot [zoology]
Animal (Legs and feet) A: 488 *with pictures*
Bird *pictures on* B: 363; (Legs and feet) B: 364
Clam (The body of a clam) Ci: 637
Conch Ci: 928
Mollusk (Gastropods) M: 695; (Bivalves) M: 695
Oyster (Young) O: 891
Snail S: 522 *with pictures*
Foot, Michael [British political leader] F: 353 *with portrait*
Foot, Samuel A. [American political leader]
Connecticut (table) Ci: 967
Foot-and-mouth disease F: 353
Cattle (Diseases) C: 312-314
Foot-candle [measurement] F: 353
Lighting (Quantity of light) L: 297
Foot cavalry
Civil War, American (The peninsular campaign) Ci: 626
Foot fault
Tennis (The serve) T: 163
Foot launching [aviation]
Hang gliding H: 51
Foot-pound [measurement] F: 353
Energy (Units of work and energy) E: 274
Horsepower H: 367
Work W: 405
Foot survey [archaeology]
Archaeology (Locating sites) A: 595-596
Football [sport] F: 354 *with pictures*
See also Rugby football; Soccer *in this index; and the list of Related articles in the* Football *article*
Hall of fame (Sports halls of fame) H: 23
Heisman Memorial Trophy H: 167
National Football League N: 35
Football, Australian Rules See Australian Rules football *in this index*
Football, Canadian [sport]
Grey Cup G: 391
Football Hall of Fame [Ohio] See Pro Football Hall of Fame *in this index*
Football helmet
Helmet *picture on* H: 178
Foote, Andrew Hull [Union military leader] F: 368
Foote, Henry S. [American political leader]
Mississippi (table) M: 640
Foothill paloverde [tree]
Paloverde P: 112
Footing [construction]
Building construction (Constructing a skyscraper) B: 683-684
House *diagram on* H: 383; (The foundation) H: 380
Footnote [reference] F: 369
A Guide to Writing Skills **Research Guide: 21**
Footprinting [criminology] F: 369 *with picture*
Footwall
Mining (Mining terms) M: 577
For a Morality of Ambiguity [book by Beauvoir]
French literature (Existentialism) F: 523
For-hire carrier
Truck (Industrial uses) T: 456
For-profit university
Universities and colleges (For-profit universities) U: 211
"For the Anniversary of My Death" [poem by Merwin]
Merwin, W. S. M: 420
For the Little One [painting by Chase]
Chase, William Merritt *picture on* C: 387
For the Love of Imabelle [book by Himes]
Himes, Chester H: 234
For the Term of His Natural Life [book by Clarke]
Australia (Literature) A: 904-905
For the Union Dead [book by Lowell]
Lowell, Robert L: 511
For Whom the Bell Tolls [book by Hemingway]
Hemingway, Ernest (Rise to fame) H: 180-181
Forage [food]
Alfalfa A: 345
Cattle (Feeding) C: 312
Conservation (Conservation of grazing lands) Ci: 981
Dairying (Feeding) D: 7
Farm and farming (Livestock care) F: 39
Grass (Grazing and forage grasses) G: 324
Forage fish [ecology]
Minnow M: 607
Forage harvester [machine]
Corn (Harvesting) Ci: 1061
Hay H: 116
Foraker, Joseph B. [American political leader]
Ohio (table) O: 699
Foraker Act [1900]
Puerto Rico (United States rule) P: 883
Foraminifera [zoology]
Ice age (Evidence from oceans) I: 7

Protozoan (Sarcodines) **P:** 837-838
Rock (Organic sediments) **R:** 372
Foras Feasa ar Éirinn [book by Keating]
Irish literature (Modern works in Gaelic) **I:** 431
Forbes, Charles R. [American government official]
Harding, Warren Gamaliel (Government scandals) **H:** 58
Forbes, Edward Waldo [American artist]
Shell *picture on* **S:** 390
Forbes, Esther [American author] **F:** 369 *with portrait*
Newbery Medal (table) **N:** 359
Forbes, Kenneth [Canadian artist]
Borden, Sir Robert Laird *picture on* **B:** 483
Forbidden City [district, Beijing]
Architecture *picture on* **A:** 612
Beijing (The city) **B:** 222 *with picture and map*
Ming dynasty **M:** 572
Forbidden City, The [Tibet] *See* Lhasa *in this index*
Forbidden Island [nickname]
Hawaii (Niihau) **H:** 102
Forbush effect [astronomy]
Magnetic storm **M:** 57
Force [physics] **F:** 369 *with diagrams*
See also the list of Related articles in the Force *article*
Foot-pound **F:** 353
G **G:** 2
Mass **M:** 268
Metric system (Mechanics) **M:** 437-440
Motion (The second law) **M:** 844
Power **P:** 727
Relativity (General relativity) **R:** 211
Standard Model **So:** 833
Weight **W:** 180
Work **W:** 404
Force bill [law] **F:** 371
African Americans (The first years of freedom) **A:** 136j-136k
Grant, Ulysses S. (Reconstruction policies) **G:** 315
Ku Klux Klan (Birth of the Klan) **K:** 390
Nullification **N:** 603
United States, History of the (Jackson as president) **U:** 171
Force of Circumstances [book by Beauvoir]
Beauvoir, Simone de **B:** 191
Force-out
Baseball (Base runners--advancing and outs) **B:** 129-130
Force pump
Pump (Force pumps) **P:** 901
Force situation
Baseball (Base runners—advancing and outs) **B:** 129
Forced convection [engineering]
Heat (Convection) **H:** 151 *with diagram*
Forces for the Defense of Democracy [political group]
Burundi (History) **B:** 713-714
Forcible entry tool
Fire department (Ladder trucks) **F:** 126 *with pictures*
Ford [automobile]
Automobile *pictures on* **A:** 967, **A:** 969; (The birth of the automobile industry) **A:** 966
Ford, Henry (Industrial accomplishments) **F:** 380 *with pictures*
Ford [geography] **F:** 371
Ford, Betty [wife of Gerald Ford]
First ladies of the United States (table) **F:** 142
Ford, Gerald Rudolph *picture on* **F:** 376; (Marriage) **F:** 374; (Life in the White House) **F:** 378 *with picture*; (Later years) **F:** 379
Ford, Dorothy [mother of]
Ford, Gerald Rudolph *picture on* **F:** 374; (Family background) **F:** 372
Ford, Edsel [American businessman]
Ford Foundation (History) **F:** 382
Ford, Elizabeth Bloomer [wife of Gerald Ford] *See* Ford, Betty *in this index*
Ford, Ford Madox [British author] **F:** 371
English literature (Fiction between the wars) **E:** 322
Novel (New directions in the novel) **N:** 573-574
Ford, Gayle [daughter-in-law of]
Ford, Gerald Rudolph *picture on* **F:** 378
Ford, Gerald R. [stepfather of Gerald Ford]
Ford, Gerald Rudolph *picture on* **F:** 374; (Family background) **F:** 372
Ford, Gerald Rudolph [U.S. president] **F:** 372 *with pictures*
Nixon, Richard Milhous (Events at home) **N:** 435-437 *with picture*
Presidential succession **P:** 771
Republican Party (The Watergate scandal) **R:** 257
Vice president of the United States (Growth of the vice presidency) **V:** 353

Vietnam War (The end of the war) **V:** 376
Warren Report **W:** 37
Ford, Hannibal Choate [American inventor] **F:** 379
Ford, Harrison [American actor] **F:** 379 *with portrait*
Ford, Henry [American businessman] **F:** 380 *with pictures*
Airplane (The golden age) **A:** 235
Assembly line **A:** 818
Automobile (The birth of the automobile industry) **A:** 966
Aviation (Aviation progress) **A:** 988
Dearborn **D:** 60
Edison, Thomas Alva (Family and friends) **E:** 81-82 *with picture*; (Honors) **E:** 82
Ford Foundation (History) **F:** 382
Ford Motor Company **F:** 382
Michigan *picture on* **M:** 510; (The early 1900's) **M:** 509
Ford, Henry, II [American businessman] **F:** 381
Ford, James [half-brother of]
Ford, Gerald Rudolph *picture on* **F:** 374
Ford, John [English dramatist] **F:** 381
Ford, John [American director] **F:** 381
Motion picture (Best achievement in directing: 1935, 1940, 1941, 1952) **M:** 862
Ford, John Gardner [son of]
Ford, Gerald Rudolph *picture on* **F:** 378; (Marriage) **F:** 374-375
Ford, Michael Gerald [son of]
Ford, Gerald Rudolph *picture on* **F:** 378; (Marriage) **F:** 374-375
Ford, Richard [American author]
American literature (Fiction and other prose) **A:** 424
Ford, Richard [half-brother of]
Ford, Gerald Rudolph *picture on* **F:** 374
Ford, Robert [American bandit]
James, Jesse **J:** 26
Ford, Sam C. [American political leader]
Montana (table) **M:** 757
Ford, Seabury [American political leader]
Ohio (table) **O:** 699
Ford, Steven Meigs [son of]
Ford, Gerald Rudolph *picture on* **F:** 378; (Marriage) **F:** 374-375
Ford, Susan Elizabeth [daughter of]
Ford, Gerald Rudolph *picture on* **F:** 378; (Marriage) **F:** 374-375
Ford: The Times, the Man, the Company [book by Nevins]
Nevins, Allan **N:** 178
Ford, Thomas [American political leader]
Illinois (table) **I:** 71
Ford, Thomas [half-brother of]
Ford, Gerald Rudolph *picture on* **F:** 374
Ford, W. Kent, Jr. [American astrophysicist]
Dark matter **D:** 37
Ford, Wendell Hampton [American political leader] **F:** 381
Ford, Whitey [American baseball player]
Baseball (table: Hall of Fame) **B:** 134
Ford County [book by Grisham]
Grisham, John **G:** 396
Ford Foundation [organization] **F:** 381
Ford Motor Company **F:** 382
Foundation (table) **F:** 430; (Education) **F:** 430-431; (International affairs) **F:** 431
Ford Instrument Company
Ford, Hannibal Choate **F:** 379
Ford Motor Company F: 382
Automobile (Economic impact) **A:** 959; (War and depression) **A:** 968; (The postwar years) **A:** 970-971
Dearborn **D:** 60
Firestone, Harvey Samuel **F:** 135
Ford, Henry **F:** 380
Ford, Henry, II **F:** 381
Manufacturing (table) **M:** 170
Michigan (The early 1900's) **M:** 509
Sports car (History) **So:** 803
Ford Tri-Motor [airplane]
Airplane *picture on* **A:** 233; (The golden age) **A:** 235
Aviation *picture on* **A:** 989
Forde, Francis [Australian political leader]
Australia (table) **A:** 923
Fordham University F: 383
Fordice, Kirk [American political leader]
Mississippi (table) **M:** 640
Fordney-McCumber Tariff Act [1922]
United States, History of the (The economy--boom and bust) **U:** 191
Ford's Theatre [Washington, D.C.]
Booth, John Wilkes **B:** 480
Lincoln, Abraham *picture on* **L:** 325; (Assassination) **L:** 326
Washington, D.C. *map on* **W:** 76; (Ford's Theatre)

W: 75
Ford's Theatre National Historic Site [Washington, D.C.]
National Park System (table: National historic sites) **N:** 52
Fordson [Michigan]
Dearborn **D:** 60
Fore! [golf term]
Golf (The course) **G:** 260
Fore [ship]
Sailing (Hull) **S:** 23
Forearm [anatomy]
Arm **A:** 717 *with diagram*
Forebrain *See* Cerebrum *in this index*
Forecasting, Weather *See* Weather forecasting *in this index*
Forecastle [ship]
Caravel **C:** 202
Galleon **G:** 15
Ship (Nautical terms) **S:** 405 *with diagram*; (The cog) **S:** 407
Foreclosure [law]
Bush, George Walker (Economy) **B:** 722j
Federal Home Loan Mortgage Corporation **F:** 64
Federal National Mortgage Association **F:** 65
Mortgage **M:** 820
Receiver **R:** 174
Forefathers' Day [custom]
Holiday (In the United States) **H:** 291
Foregut [entomology]
Insect (Digestive system) **I:** 289
Forehand drive
Tennis *pictures on* **T:** 164; (The ball in play) **T:** 163
Foreign Affairs, Department of [former name]
State, Department of (Establishment) **So:** 860-861
Foreign Affairs, Ministry of [Canada]
Foreign policy (The executive) **F:** 387
Foreign aid F: 383 *with pictures*
See also the list of Related articles in the Foreign Aid *article*
Africa (Foreign aid, debt, and investment) **A:** 129
Cold War (The containment policy) **Ci:** 764
Technical assistance **T:** 73
Truman, Harry S. (Foreign affairs) **T:** 471
United Nations (Economic and technical aid) **U:** 87
Foreign correspondent [journalism] **F:** 386
Foreign exchange control
Exports and imports (Import restrictions) **E:** 454
Foreign exchange market
Money (Money and international finance) **M:** 717
Foreign exchange rate *See* Exchange rate *in this index*
Foreign film
Motion picture (Postwar Realism) **M:** 869 *with pictures*; (The New Wave in France) **M:** 870 *with picture*
Foreign intelligence service
Intelligence service **I:** 320
Foreign Intelligence Service [agency]
Russia (Courts) **R:** 532
Foreign Intelligence Surveillance Act [1978]
Wiretapping (Laws concerning wiretapping) **W:** 345
Foreign Intelligence Surveillance Court
Wiretapping (Laws concerning wiretapping) **W:** 345
Foreign Investment Review Agency
Canada, History of (Foreign affairs) **C:** 150
Foreign Legion [military] **F:** 386
Foreign office [government]
Diplomacy (Diplomatic representatives) **D:** 216
Foreign policy [political science] **F:** 386
See also United States foreign policy *in this index*
Foreign aid **F:** 383
International law **I:** 340
International relations **I:** 343
International trade (Government trade policies) **I:** 348
Foreign relations *See* Foreign policy; International relations *in this index*
Foreign Service [diplomacy] **F:** 388
Ambassador **A:** 404
Attaché **A:** 878
Consul **Ci:** 1017
Foreign Service Act [1946]
Foreign Service (Additional changes) **F:** 388a
Foreign Service Act [1980]
Foreign Service (Additional changes) **F:** 388a
Foreign Service Institute [Washington, D.C.]
Foreign Service (Foreign Service careers) **F:** 388
Foreign Service officer [career]
Foreign Service (Personnel) **F:** 388
Foreign Service specialist [career]
Foreign Service (Personnel) **F:** 388
Foreign trade *See* International trade *in this index*

Foreign trade zone F: 388a
Free trade zone F: 499
Foreign-Trade Zones Board [U.S.]
Foreign trade zone F: 388a
Free trade zone F: 499
Foreman [manager]
Careers picture on C: 227
Foreman, George [American boxer] **F: 388a** with portrait
Foremast [ship]
Galleon G: 15
Sailing (Spars) S: 23
Ship (The full-rigged ship) S: 418-419
Forensic anthropologist [scientist]
Crime scene investigation (Collecting evidence) Ci: 1140-1141
Forensic science picture on F: 389
Forensic ballistics [criminology]
Ballistics (Forensic ballistics) B: 56
Forensic data analysis
Computer security Ci: 925
Forensic dentistry
Dentistry (Oral pathology) D: 144
Forensic entomologist [scientist]
Crime scene investigation (Collecting evidence) Ci: 1140-1141
Forensic fingerprint identification
Fingerprinting (Fingerprint identification) F: 106-107
Forensic pathology [medicine] **F: 389a**
Crime scene investigation (Beginning an investigation) Ci: 1140
Medical examiner M: 361
Forensic science F: 388a with pictures
Crime scene investigation (Beginning an investigation) Ci: 1140
Foreordination See Predestination in this index
Foreskin [anatomy] See Prepuce in this index
Forest F: 390 with pictures and maps
See also Deforestation; Forest products; Forestry; Rain forest; Taiga in this index
Animal (Animals of the temperate forests) A: 478 with pictures and map; (Animals of the tropical forests) A: 480 with pictures; (Destruction of habitat) A: 504 with picture
Biome B: 322; (table) B: 323 with map
Bird (Birds of forests and woodlands) B: 334 with pictures
Climate (Human activity) Ci: 678
Conservation (Forest conservation) Ci: 981
Flower (Flowers of woodlands and forests) F: 284 with pictures
Jungle J: 195
National forest N: 35
Plant (Where plants live) P: 520 with pictures and map
Forest, National See National forest in this index
Forest, Petrified See Petrified forest in this index
Forest City [Ontario]
London L: 444
Forest conservation See Conservation in this index
Forest elephant
Elephant (Kinds of elephants) E: 227
Forest entomology [science]
Entomology (What entomologists study) E: 328
Forest-falcon [bird]
Bird of prey picture on B: 374b
Forest fire
Airplane (Special-purpose planes) A: 212
Drought D: 349
Fire (How fires behave) F: 121
Fire department (Additional operations) F: 124 with picture
Forestry (Fire and forests) F: 407 with picture
National Park System (Preserving the parklands) N: 47
Forest floor
Forest (The forest floor) F: 392 with picture
Forest Hills Gardens [district]
New York City (Queens) N: 329
Forest History Center [Grand Rapids]
Minnesota (Places to visit) M: 594
Forest horse See Tarpan in this index
"Forest Hymn, A" [poem by Bryant]
Bryant, William Cullen (His early works) B: 655-656
Forest management
Forestry F: 404; (History) F: 408
Lumber (Cutting down trees) L: 518
Forest Park [park]
Saint Louis (Parks) S: 48
Forest products F: 400 with pictures
See also Forestry in this index
Bark (How people use bark) B: 110-111
Lumber L: 517 with pictures
Tree farming T: 432
Wood W: 389 with pictures

Forest ranger [career]
Forest Service F: 403
National forest (Administration) N: 36
Forest reserve [U.S. history]
Forestry (History) F: 408
National forest (History) N: 36
Forest Sami [people]
Sami S: 79
Forest Service [U.S.] **F: 403**
Forestry (History) F: 408
National forest N: 35
National Trails System N: 61
Pinchot, Gifford P: 467
Forest supervisor [office]
National forest (Administration) N: 36
Forester [career]
Forestry F: 404 with picture
Lumber (Cutting down trees) L: 518
Forester, Cecil Scott [British author] **F: 403**
Forestry F: 404 with pictures
See also Forest; Forest products in this index
Botany (Uses of plants) B: 508
Careers (Farming, fishing, and forestry) C: 222 with picture
Conservation (Careers in conservation) Ci: 990
National forest (Uses) N: 35
Forever... [book by Blume]
Blume, Judy B: 425
Forever Free [book by Adamson]
Adamson, Joy A: 45
Forfeiture [law] **F: 408**
Forge [furnace]
Forging (Hand forging) F: 409 with picture
Forgery [crime] **F: 408**
Graphology G: 323
Forges du Saint-Maurice National Historic Site [Quebec]
Canada (table: National historic sites) C: 114
Forget-me-not [plant] **F: 408** with picture
Flower picture on F: 289
Plant picture on P: 524
Forging [industrial process] **F: 409** with pictures
Aluminum (Forging) A: 396
Automobile (Manufacturing) A: 958
Die and diemaking D: 195
Iron and steel (Forging) I: 447
Forging hammer
Forging (Machine forging) F: 409
Forging press
Forging (Machine forging) F: 409 with picture
Machine tool (Metal forming operations) M: 19
Forgiveness Sunday
Easter (The beginning of Lent) E: 42
Forillon National Park [Quebec]
Canada (table: National parks and national park reserves) C: 113
Fork [riding equipment]
Saddle diagram on S: 7
Forked lightning
Lightning (Appearance) L: 300
Forks, The [historic area]
Canada (table: National historic sites) C: 114
Winnepeg (History) W: 341-342
Forlanini, Enrico [Italian inventor]
Hydrofoil (History) H: 468
Form [aesthetics]
Art and the arts (The reasons for art) A: 745
Interior design (Elements of design) I: 327 with pictures
Form [animal home]
Hare H: 59
Rabbit (Homes) R: 48
Form [psychology]
Gestalt psychology G: 175
Form class [grammar]
English language (Grammar) E: 312
Parts of speech P: 189
Form drag [physics]
Aerodynamics (Form drag) A: 86
Formal cause [philosophy]
Aristotle (Philosophy of nature) A: 664
Formal censorship
Censorship (Censorship methods) C: 346
Formal criticism
Criticism (Kinds of literary criticism) Ci: 1146
Formal education
Education E: 86
Formal essay [literature]
Essay E: 359
Formal fallacy
Fallacy F: 16
Formal garden
Gardening (Flower gardens) G: 30
Formal invitation
Letter writing (Formal invitations) L: 212 with pictures
Formal operations [psychology]

Child (The stages of childhood) C: 448
Piaget, Jean P: 445
Formaldehyde [chemical] **F: 410**
Disinfectant D: 235
Methanol M: 434
Phenolic P: 356
Formalin [chemical]
Formaldehyde F: 410
Formalism [mathematics]
Mathematics (Philosophies of mathematics) M: 307
Forman, Milos [Czechoslovak director]
Motion picture (Best achievement in directing: 1975, 1984) M: 862; (Movies in the 1960's) M: 870-871
Format [photography]
Photography (Other types of cameras) P: 409; (Film characteristics) P: 416
Formed element [physiology]
Blood (The composition of blood) B: 407
Circulatory system (The blood) Ci: 559
Former Prophets [Bible]
Bible (The Prophets) B: 280
Former Yugoslav Republic of Macedonia See Macedonia in this index
Formic acid [chemical] **F: 410**
Formosa See Taiwan in this index
Formosus [pope]
Pope (table) P: 666
Forms, Theory of [philosophy]
Neoplatonism N: 124
Philosophy (Plato) P: 387
Plato (The theory of forms) P: 568
Formula [food]
Baby (The first month) B: 6; (Feeding procedures) B: 9
Formula [mathematics]
Algebra (Writing formulas) A: 353
Calculus (Functions) C: 23
Formula Atlantic [automobile]
Automobile racing (Other kinds of racing) A: 978
Formula One car
Automobile racing (Formula One racing) A: 976 with picture
Føroyar Islands See Faroe Islands in this index
Forrest [Australian explorers]
Australia map on A: 921
Forrest, Edwin [American actor] **F: 410** with portrait
Macready, William Charles M: 26
Forrest, Nathan Bedford [Confederate general] **F: 410**
Civil War, American (Raids) Ci: 629
Mississippi (The American Civil War) M: 642
Forrest Gump [film]
Hanks, Tom H: 51
Motion picture (Best picture: 1994) M: 861
Forrestal [ship]
Aircraft carrier (History) A: 207
Forrestal, James Vincent F: 410
Forrestal, James Vincent [American government official] **F: 410**
Truman, Harry S. (table) T: 469
Fors Clavigera [book by Ruskin]
Ruskin, John R: 523
Forssmann, Werner [German physician]
Nobel Prizes (Physiology or medicine: 1956) N: 446
Forster, E. M. [British author] **F: 410**
Forsterite [mineral]
Olivine O: 744
Forsyte Saga, The [book by Galsworthy]
Galsworthy, John G: 16
Forsyth, Alexander [Scottish inventor]
Handgun (Early handguns) H: 45
Forsyth, John [American government official]
Georgia (table) G: 130
Jackson, Andrew (table) J: 11
Van Buren, Martin (table) V: 273
Forsyth, William [British botanist]
Forsythia F: 411
Forsythia [shrub] **F: 411** with picture
Flower (Flowering shrubs) F: 281 with picture
Fort [fortification] **F: 411**
Crusades picture on Ci: 1160
Fort, George F. [American political leader]
New Jersey (table) N: 249
Fort, John Franklin [American political leader]
New Jersey (table) N: 249
Fort Amsterdam [New York]
Minuit, Peter M: 613
New York City (Settlement) N: 341
Fort Ancient [Ohio]
Mound builders (Mississippian Period) M: 883
Ohio (Places to visit) O: 690
Fort Anne National Historic Site [Nova Scotia]
Canada (table: National historic sites) C: 114

Fort Atkinson [Nebraska]
Indian wars (Wars on the Plains) **I:** 192
Nebraska (American exploration and settlement) **N:** 111-112
Fort Battleford [Saskatchewan]
Canada (table: National historic sites) **C:** 114
Fort Beauséjour National Historic Site [New Brunswick]
Canada (table: National historic sites) **C:** 114
Fort Belvoir [Virginia] **F:** 411
Fort Benning [Georgia] **F:** 411 *with picture*
Fort Benton [Montana]
Montana (Exploration) **M:** 758
Fort Bliss [Texas] **F:** 411
El Paso (History) **E:** 247
Fort Boonesborough State Park [Lexington]
Kentucky *picture on* **K:** 283
Fort Bowie National Historic Site [Arizona]
National Park System (table: National historic sites) **N:** 52
Fort Bragg [North Carolina] **F:** 411
Fort Bridger [fort, Wyoming]
Wyoming (Exploration) **W:** 533
Fort Brooke [Florida]
Tampa (History) **T:** 23
Fort Calgary [Alberta]
Calgary (History) **C:** 34
Fort Caroline [Florida]
Florida (Exploration and Spanish settlement) **F:** 261 *with picture*
Jacksonville (Cultural life and recreation) **J:** 18
Fort Caroline National Memorial [Florida]
National Park System (table: National memorials) **N:** 54
Fort Casimir [Delaware]
Delaware (Exploration and early settlement) **D:** 110
Fort Chambly National Historic Site [Quebec]
Canada (table: National historic sites) **C:** 114
Fort Chipewyan [Alberta]
Mackenzie, Roderick **M:** 23
Fort Christina [Delaware]
Delaware (Exploration and early settlement) **D:** 110
Minuit, Peter **M:** 613
Wilmington (History) **W:** 315
Fort Clatsop [Oregon]
Astoria **A:** 826
Lewis and Clark expedition (Crossing the mountains) **L:** 222c-222d
Fort Clatsop National Memorial [Oregon]
Oregon (Places to visit) **O:** 836
Fort Condé [Alabama]
Alabama (European exploration and settlement) **A:** 275
Fort Crèvecoeur [Illinois]
La Salle, René-Robert Cavelier, Sieur de (First explorations) **L:** 79-80 *with map*
Peoria **P:** 277
Tonty, Henri de **T:** 330
Fort D. A. Russell [Wyoming]
Cheyenne (History) **C:** 417
Fort Davis National Historic Site [Texas]
National Park System (table: National historic sites) **N:** 52
Fort-de-France [Martinique] **F:** 412
Martinique **M:** 235
Fort Dearborn [Illinois] **F:** 412 *with picture*
Chicago (Birth of the city) **C:** 434
Fort Dearborn Massacre [1812]
Chicago (Indian troubles) **C:** 434
Fort Dearborn **F:** 412
Illinois (Early national period) **I:** 72-74
Potawatomi Indians **P:** 714
Fort Delaware
Delaware *picture on* **D:** 112; (Places to visit) **D:** 102 *with picture*
Fort Des Moines [Iowa]
Des Moines (Government and history) **D:** 159-160
Fort Donelson, Battle of [1862]
Civil War, American (table) **Ci:** 624; (Battles of Fort Henry and Fort Donelson) **Ci:** 628
Foote, Andrew Hull **F:** 368
Fort Donelson National Battlefield [Tennessee]
National Park System (table: National battlefields) **N:** 55
Fort Dummer [Vermont]
Vermont (Exploration and settlement) **V:** 334
Fort Duquesne [Pennsylvania] **F:** 412
Braddock, Edward **B:** 542
French and Indian wars (The French and Indian War) **F:** 512-513
Washington, George (Surrender of Fort Necessity) **W:** 94; (Braddock's defeat) **W:** 94; (Frontier commander) **W:** 95
Fort Edmonton [Alberta]

Edmonton (History) **E:** 85
Fort Edmonton Park [Alberta]
Edmonton (Culture and recreation) **E:** 84-85
Fort Edward National Historic Site [Nova Scotia]
Canada (table: National historic sites) **C:** 114
Fort Eustis [Virginia] **F:** 413
Fort Fincastle [Bahamas]
Bahamas (History) **B:** 29
Fort Francis E. Warren [Wyoming]
Cheyenne (History) **C:** 417
Fort Frederica National Monument [Georgia] **F:** 413
National Park System (table: National monuments) **N:** 51
Fort Garry [Manitoba]
Winnipeg (History) **W:** 341
Fort George [Belize]
Belize City **B:** 238
Fort George [former name]
Prince George **P:** 794
Fort George G. Meade [Maryland] **F:** 413
Fort George National Historic Site [Ontario]
Canada (table: National historic sites) **C:** 114
Fort Gibraltar [Manitoba]
Winnipeg (History) **W:** 341
Fort Gordon [Georgia] **F:** 413
Fort Hall Replica [Idaho]
Idaho (Places to visit) **I:** 34
Fort Hawkins [Georgia]
Macon **M:** 25
Fort Henry, Battle of [1862]
Civil War, American (table) **Ci:** 624; (Battles of Fort Henry and Fort Donelson) **Ci:** 628
Foote, Andrew Hull **F:** 368
Fort Hood [Texas] **F:** 413
Fort Industry [Ohio]
Toledo (History) **T:** 321
Fort Jefferson National Monument
Dry Tortugas National Park **D:** 369
Fort Kent [Maine]
Maine *picture on* **M:** 90
Fort King George [Georgia]
Colonial life in America (Places to visit) **Ci:** 800
Fort Knox [Kentucky] **F:** 413 *with picture*
Kentucky (Interesting facts about Kentucky) **K:** 273 *with picture*
Fort-Lamy [former name]
N'Djamena **N:** 93
Fort Langley National Historic Site [British Columbia]
Canada (table: National historic sites) **C:** 114
Fort Laramie [city, Wyoming]
Wyoming (Schools) **W:** 520
Fort Laramie [fort, Wyoming]
Wyoming (Exploration) **W:** 533
Fort Laramie, Treaty of [1851]
Indian wars (Wars on the Plains) **I:** 192
Wyoming (Indian and settler conflicts) **W:** 534
Fort Laramie, Treaty of [1868]
Crazy Horse **Ci:** 1123
Indian wars (Red Cloud's War [1866-1868]) **I:** 193
South Dakota (Territorial days) **So:** 681
Spotted Tail **So:** 804
Fort Laramie National Historic Site [Wyoming]
National Park System (table: National historic sites) **N:** 52
Wyoming (Places to visit) **W:** 524
Fort Larned National Historic Site [Kansas]
Kansas (Places to visit) **K:** 226
National Park System (table: National historic sites) **N:** 52
Fort Lauderdale [Florida] **F:** 413
Fort Leavenworth [Kansas] **F:** 414
Fort Le Boeuf [Pennsylvania]
Washington, George (Messenger to the French) **W:** 93-94
Fort Lee [Virginia] **F:** 414
Fort Lee [West Virginia]
Charleston (Government and history) **C:** 384
Fort Lennox National Historic Site [Quebec]
Canada (table: National historic sites) **C:** 114
Fort Leonard Wood [Missouri] **F:** 414
Fort Lernoult [Michigan]
Detroit (Early settlement) **D:** 170
Fort Lisa [Nebraska]
Nebraska (American exploration and settlement) **N:** 111
Fort Little Niagara [Ontario]
Fort Niagara **F:** 415
Fort Louis [Alabama]
Alabama (European exploration and settlement) **A:** 275
Mobile **M:** 681
Fort Mackinac [Michigan]
Mackinac Island **M:** 24
Fort Macleod [Alberta]
Alberta (Early settlement) **A:** 329

Fort Madison [Iowa]
Iowa (Territorial days) **I:** 393
Fort Malden National Historic Site [Ontario]
Canada (table: National historic sites) **C:** 114
Fort Mandan [North Dakota]
North Dakota (Places to visit) **N:** 504; (Exploration and early settlement) **N:** 513
Fort Marion National Monument [Florida]
Castillo de San Marcos National Monument **C:** 280
Fort Massachusetts [Mississippi]
Mississippi (Places to visit) **M:** 632
Fort Matanzas National Monument [Florida] **F:** 414
National Park System (table: National monuments) **N:** 51
Fort McHenry National Monument and Historic Shrine [Maryland] **F:** 414
Baltimore (Other interesting places to visit) **B:** 69
Key, Francis Scott **K:** 308
Maryland (Places to visit) **M:** 248 *with picture*; (The War of 1812 and industrial development) **M:** 258
National Park System (table: National monuments) **N:** 51
"Star-Spangled Banner" (How the song came to be written) **So:** 854
Fort McPherson [Georgia] **F:** 414
Fort Meade [Maryland]
Fort George G. Meade **F:** 413
Fort Michilimackinac [Michigan]
Michigan (Places to visit) **M:** 498
Fort Mims [Alabama]
Alabama *picture on* **A:** 276; (Territorial days) **A:** 275
Fort Monmouth [New Jersey] **F:** 414
Fort Monroe National Monument [Virginia] **F:** 415
National Park System (table: National monuments) **N:** 51
Fort Moultrie [South Carolina] **F:** 415
South Carolina (Places to visit) **So:** 650
Fort Museum of the North West Mounted Police [Fort Macleod]
Alberta (Places to visit) **A:** 320
Fort Nashborough [Tennessee]
Nashville **N:** 23; (History) **N:** 23
Tennessee (Territorial years) **T:** 153
Fort Navidad [Haiti]
Haiti (History) **H:** 15
Fort Necessity [Pennsylvania] **F:** 415
National Park System (table: National battlefields) **N:** 55
Washington, George (Surrender of Fort Necessity) **W:** 94
Fort Nelson [British Columbia]
British Columbia (table: Average monthly weather) **B:** 624
Fort Niagara [New York] **F:** 415
Colonial life in America (Places to visit) **Ci:** 801
New York (Places to visit) **N:** 302
Fort Orange [New York]
Albany (Government and history) **A:** 309-310
New York (Exploration and settlement) **N:** 314
Fort Peck Dam [Missouri River, Montana] **F:** 415
Montana (Places to visit) **M:** 750; (Depression years) **M:** 760
Fort Peck Lake
Montana (Rivers and lakes) **M:** 752-754
Fort Pelly National Historic Site [Saskatchewan]
Canada (table: National historic sites) **C:** 114
Fort Phil Kearny [Wyoming]
Wyoming (Indian and settler conflicts) **W:** 534
Fort Pickens [Florida] **F:** 415
Fort Pitt [Pennsylvania]
Pittsburgh **P:** 500a; (Early days) **P:** 501
Fort Point National Historic Site [California]
National Park System (table: National historic sites) **N:** 52
Fort Pontchartrain [Michigan]
Detroit (Early settlement) **D:** 170
Lamothe, Antoine Laumet de, Sieur de Cadillac **L:** 52
Pontiac **P:** 657
Fort Prince of Wales National Historic Park [Manitoba]
Manitoba (Places to visit) **M:** 152
Fort Pueblo [Colorado]
Pueblo **P:** 870
Fort Pulaski National Monument [Georgia] **F:** 415
National Park System (table: National monuments) **N:** 51
Fort Raleigh National Historic Site [North Carolina]
National Park System (table: National historic sites) **N:** 52
Fort Randall Dam [Missouri River, South Dakota] **F:** 415

South Dakota *picture on* So: 679
Fort Recovery [Ohio]
   Ohio (Places to visit) O: 690
Fort Richardson [Alaska]
   Anchorage A: 450
Fort Riley [Kansas] F: 415
   Kansas (Places to visit) K: 226
Fort Rodd Hill National Historic Site [British Columbia]
   Canada (table: National historic sites) C: 114
Fort Rosalie [Mississippi]
   Natchez N: 26
Fort Rouge [Manitoba]
   Winnipeg (History) W: 341
Fort Rucker [Alabama] F: 416
Fort Sackville [Indiana]
   Indiana *picture on* I: 217
   Vincennes V: 386
Fort Saint Anthony
   Minneapolis (Early days) M: 582-583
   Minnesota (The Louisiana Purchase) M: 603
Fort Saint Joseph [Niles]
   Michigan (British control) M: 508
Fort Saint Joseph National Historic Site [Ontario]
   Canada (table: National historic sites) C: 114
Fort Saint Louis [Illinois]
   La Salle, René-Robert Cavelier, Sieur de (Expeditions to the Gulf of Mexico) L: 80 *with map*
Fort Saint Louis [Quebec]
   Quebec (Early days) Q: 36
Fort Saint Louis [Texas]
   Texas (French exploration) T: 204
Fort Sainte Marie [Ontario]
   Ontario (Early settlement) O: 784
Fort Sam Houston [Texas] F: 416
Fort San Antonio de Bexar [Texas]
   Texas (The mission period) T: 204
Fort Schuyler [New York]
   Utica U: 251
Fort Scott National Historic Site [Kansas]
   Kansas (Places to visit) K: 226
   National Park System (table: National historic sites) N: 52
Fort Shafter [Hawaii] F: 416
Fort Sill [Oklahoma] F: 416
   Oklahoma (Places to visit) O: 722 *with picture*
Fort Smith [city, Arkansas] F: 416
   Arkansas (Average monthly weather) A: 708; (Territorial years) A: 712
Fort Smith National Historic Site [Arkansas-Oklahoma]
   National Park System (table: National historic sites) N: 52
Fort Snelling [Minnesota]
   Minnesota (Schools) M: 588; (Places to visit) M: 594; (The Louisiana Purchase) M: 603-604 *with picture*
Fort Snelling, Sioux Scalp Dance [painting by Kane]
   Minnesota *picture on* M: 603
Fort Stanwix [New York]
   Rome R: 435
Fort Stanwix, Treaty of [1768]
   Indian wars (Lord Dunmore's War [1774]) I: 191
Fort Stanwix National Monument [New York] F: 416
   National Park System (table: National monuments) N: 51
Fort Sullivan [South Carolina]
   Fort Moultrie F: 415
Fort Sumter [South Carolina] F: 416
   Buchanan, James (Prelude to war) B: 661
   Civil War, American (Secession) Ci: 617 *with picture*; (Fort Sumter) Ci: 624
   Lincoln, Abraham (Fort Sumter and war) L: 321
   South Carolina (Places to visit) So: 650 *with picture*
Fort Sumter National Monument [South Carolina] F: 416
   National Park System (table: National monuments) N: 51
   South Carolina (Places to visit) So: 650
Fort Supply Dam [Wolfe Creek, Oklahoma] F: 416
Fort Témiscamingue National Historic Site [Quebec]
   Canada (table: National historic sites) C: 114
Fort Ticonderoga [New York] F: 416 *with picture*
   Allen, Ethan A: 371
   New York (Places to visit) N: 302 *with picture*
   Revolution, American (The evacuation of Boston) R: 275; (Victory at Saratoga) R: 282
   Saint Clair, Arthur S: 32
   Vermont (The Revolutionary War in America) V: 334
Fort Union National Monument [New Mexico] F: 416

National Park System (table: National monuments) N: 51
Fort Union Trading Post National Historic Site [North Dakota-Montana]
   National Park System (table: National historic sites) N: 52-53
Fort Vancouver National Historic Site [Washington]
   National Park System (table: National historic sites) N: 52-53
Fort Walsh National Historic Site [Saskatchewan]
   Canada (table: National historic sites) C: 114
Fort Washington, Battle of [1776]
   Corbin, Margaret Cochran Ci: 1051
   Revolution, American (The campaign in New York) R: 281-282
Fort Washington Park [Maryland]
   National Park System (table: National parkways and other parklands) N: 56
Fort Wayne [Indiana] F: 417
   Indiana (Places to visit) I: 206 *with picture*
Fort Western [Maine]
   Augusta A: 888
Fort William [former name]
   Thunder Bay T: 272
Fort William [fort, Wyoming]
   Wyoming (Exploration) W: 533
Fort William Henry [New York]
   French and Indian wars (The French and Indian War) F: 512-513 *with map*
Fort Wood [New York]
   Liberty Island L: 233
   Statue of Liberty (Description) So: 873 *with picture*
Fort Worth [Texas] F: 417 *with picture*
   Metropolitan area *map on* M: 442
Fort Worth Zoological Park
   Fort Worth (Education and cultural life) F: 418
Fort Yuma Reservation [California and Arizona]
   Quechan Indians Q: 38
Fortaleza [Brazil] F: 419
Fortas, Abe [American jurist] F: 419
   Nixon, Richard Milhous (The national scene) N: 434
Forte [music]
   Music (table) M: 954
Forten, James [American abolitionist] F: 419
Forth Bridge [Scotland]
   Bridge (table: Cantilever) B: 603
   Firth of Forth F: 143
Fortier, Michael [American public figure]
   Oklahoma City bombing O: 737
Fortier, Yves [Canadian diplomat]
   United Nations (table) U: 86
Fortification See Castle; Fort; Walled city *in this index*
Fortifications of Quebec
   Canada (table: National historic sites) C: 114
Fortified cereal
   Cereal C: 361
Fortified milk
   Milk (Fortification) M: 548
Fortified wine
   Grape (European grapes) G: 318
   Wine (Clarifying and aging the wine) W: 338
Fortissimo [music]
   Music (table) M: 954; (Indicating expression) M: 955 *with picture*
Fortress of Louisbourg See Louisbourg, Fortress of *in this index*
Fortress of Louisbourg National Historic Site [Nova Scotia]
   Canada (table: National historic sites) C: 114
Fortuna [Roman mythology] F: 419
Fortune [ship]
   Plymouth Colony (Expansion of the colony) P: 583
Fortune and Men's Eyes [play by Herbert]
   Canadian literature (Modern Canadian drama) C: 161
Fortune Teller, The [painting by Caravaggio]
   Caravaggio, Michelangelo Merisi da *picture on* C: 201
Fortunetelling F: 419
   Divination D: 241
   Halloween (Fortunetelling) H: 24b
Fortuño, Luis G. [Puerto Rican political leader]
   Puerto Rico (Puerto Rico today) P: 884
Forty Immortals [members of]
   French Academy F: 511
Forty Mile [mining camp]
   Klondike K: 344
Forty-Mile Creek
   Yukon River (Upper Yukon) Y: 582 *with map*
Forty-Niners [U.S. history] F: 420
   California (The gold rush) C: 62
   Taylor, Zachary *picture on* T: 59

Westward movement in America (California) W: 249
49ers, San Francisco [team] See San Francisco 49ers *in this index*
42nd Parallel, The [book by Dos Passos]
   Dos Passos, John D: 311
Forty-Two Articles [religion]
   Ridley, Nicholas R: 336
Forty-two-line Bible
   Book (The development of printed books) B: 466-467
Forum, Roman [ancient Rome] F: 420 *with picture*
   Rome (Forums) R: 433 *with picture*
   Rome, Ancient *picture on* R: 436; (City life) R: 438
Forum des Halles, Le [Paris]
   Paris (Renewal and new construction) P: 166-167
Forward [sports]
   Basketball (The players) B: 144
   Hockey (The starting lineup) H: 275
   Soccer (The forwards) So: 545 *with diagram*
Forward, Walter [American government official]
   Tyler, John (table) T: 534
Forward bias [electronics]
   Electronics (Diodes) E: 210-211 *with diagram*
Forward contract [economics]
   Commodity exchange (Forward and futures contracts) Ci: 873
   Cotton (Selling) Ci: 1091
   Livestock (Direct markets) L: 398
Forward extrusion [industrial process]
   Extrusion E: 459
Forward-Looking Infrared system [electronic device]
   Night vision systems N: 419
Forward pass [football]
   Football (Changes in the game) F: 366
Forward stroke
   Cricket (The batting side) Ci: 1133 *with picture*
Forza Italia [political party]
   Berlusconi, Silvio B: 267
Fosbury, Dick [American athlete]
   High jump H: 227
   Track and field (Jumping events) T: 357-358
Fosbury flop
   High jump H: 227 *with picture*
Foscolo, Ugo [Italian author] F: 421
   Italian literature (The Baroque period and the Enlightenment) I: 494-495
Fosdick, Harry Emerson [American religious leader] F: 421
Foss, Eugene N. [American political leader]
   Massachusetts (table) M: 288
Foss, Joseph Jacob [American military leader]
   South Dakota (table) So: 680
Fosse, Bob [American director/choreographer]
   Dance (Musical comedy) D: 31-32 *with picture*
   Motion picture (Best achievement in directing: 1972) M: 862
Fossett, Steve [American adventurer]
   Airplane (table: Notable airplane flights) A: 236
   Balloon (Long-distance balloon flights) B: 62
   Glider (table) G: 230
Fossey, Dian [American zoologist] F: 421 *with picture*
Fossil [geology] F: 422 *with pictures*
   Ant *picture on* A: 521
   Cambrian Period C: 74
   Climate (Fossils) Ci: 679
   Coal *picture on* C: 716
   Dinosaur D: 206a; (Working with dinosaur fossils) D: 210 *with pictures*; (Dinosaur discoveries) D: 213
   Earth (Life on Earth) E: 27 *with picture*
   Evolution (The fossil record) E: 430
   Fish (The development of fish) F: 171 *with picture*
   Gem G: 77
   Geology (Experimental geology) G: 99
   Insect *picture on* I: 279
   La Brea tar pits L: 18 *with picture*
   Nebraska (Interesting facts) N: 95 *with picture*
   Ocean *picture on* O: 651
   Olduvai Gorge O: 742
   Paleobotany P: 102
   Paleontology P: 103
   Prehistoric animal P: 736; (The study of prehistoric animals) P: 741 *with picture*
   Prehistoric people P: 743; (table) P: 754; (Studying prehistoric people) P: 754a *with pictures*
   Radiocarbon R: 97
   Sedimentary rock S: 280
   Tree (Fossil trees) T: 455
Fossil Butte National Monument [Wyoming] F: 427
   National Park System (table: National monuments) N: 51
   Wyoming (Places to visit) W: 524

Fossil fuel F: 427
  Agriculture (Biofuels) **A:** 148
  Automobile (Automobiles and the environment) **A:** 963
  Biofuel **B:** 312
  Carbon cycle **C:** 206
  Climate **Ci:** 675; (Human activity) **Ci:** 678
  Coal (The composition of coal) **Ci:** 717
  Conservation (Energy conservation) **Ci:** 983
  Coral reef (Coral reefs and people) **Ci:** 1049
  Electric power (Fossil-fueled steam electric power plants) **E:** 183
  Energy supply **E:** 277; (Depletion of fuel reserves) **E:** 281
  Fuel **F:** 550
  Global warming (Causes of global warming) **G:** 232; (Ways to limit global warming) **G:** 232b
  Greenhouse effect (Increases in greenhouse gases) **G:** 383
  Hydrogen (Uses) **H:** 469
  Nuclear energy (The role of nuclear energy in power production) **N:** 580
  Soil pollution **So:** 576
  Technology (Challenges of technology) **T:** 77
Fossil record See Geological record *in this index*
Fossiliferous limestone
  Rock (Organic sediments) **R:** 372
Fossorial mammal
  Mammal (Underground) **M:** 122
Foster, Bill [American baseball player]
  Baseball (table: Hall of Fame) **B:** 134
Foster, Charles [American government official]
  Ohio (table) **O:** 699
Foster, Sir George Eulas [Canadian political leader] **F:** 428
Foster, Jane McDowell [wife of]
  Foster, Stephen Collins **F:** 428
Foster, Jodie [American actress/director] **F:** 428
  Motion picture (Best performance by an actress: 1988, 1991) **M:** 862a
Foster, Murphy J. [American political leader]
  Louisiana (table) **L:** 496
Foster, Murphy J., Jr. [American political leader]
  Louisiana (table) **L:** 496
Foster, Rube [American baseball player]
  Baseball (table: Hall of Fame) **B:** 134
Foster, Stephen Collins [American composer] **F:** 428 *with portrait*
  Folk music (Characteristics of folk music) **F:** 321
  Popular music (1840's to the Civil War) **P:** 669
Foster, Walter E. [Canadian political leader]
  New Brunswick (table) **N:** 195
Foster Botanical Gardens
  Honolulu (Cultural life) **H:** 321-322
Foster care F: 428
  Adoption (The adoption process) **A:** 66
  Children's home **C:** 457
Foster Care [program]
  Children's Bureau **C:** 457
Foster Grandparent Program
  Old age (Employment and other activities) **O:** 739
Foster person
  Foster care **F:** 428
Foucault, Jean Bernard Léon [French physicist] **F:** 429
  Gyroscope (History) **G:** 454
  Optics (History) **O:** 813
  Pendulum (Other pendulums) **P:** 238
Foucault, Michel [French philosopher] **F:** 429
Foucault pendulum
  Pendulum (Other pendulums) **P:** 238
Fouché, Joseph [French government official]
  Secret police **S:** 278
Foucher, Adèle [wife of]
  Hugo, Victor (Early life) **H:** 409
Foul [sports]
  Boxing (Fight rules) **B:** 527
  Lacrosse (Men's lacrosse) **L:** 23
  Soccer (Fouls) **So:** 546
Foul ball
  Baseball (Outs by batters) **B:** 128-129
Foul territory
  Baseball (The infield) **B:** 126 *with diagram*; (Foul territory) **B:** 127 *with diagram*
Foul tip
  Baseball (Outs by batters) **B:** 128-129
Foulbrood [disease]
  Bee (Enemies) **B:** 205
Found space
  Theater (The stage) **T:** 233-235
Foundation [construction]
  Building construction (Parts of a building) **B:** 681-682; (Constructing a skyscraper) **B:** 683
  House *diagram on* **H:** 383; (The foundation) **H:** 380
  Pile **P:** 462
  Skyscraper (Building skyscrapers) **S:** 497

Foundation [organization] **F:** 429
  Endowment **E:** 273
Foundation Center [organization]
  Foundation **F:** 429
Foundation degree [education]
  Degree, College (The associate's degree) **D:** 91
Foundation Directory
  Foundation **F:** 430
Foundation for Interior Design Research
  Interior design (Training) **I:** 334
Foundation of the Complete Theory of Knowledge [book by Fichte]
  Fichte, Johann Gottlieb **F:** 90
Foundation series [books by Asimov]
  Asimov, Isaac **A:** 814
Foundations of Economic Analysis [book by Samuelson]
  Samuelson, Paul Anthony **S:** 82
Founder
  Horse (Medical care) **H:** 356
Founder effect [genetics]
  Races, Human (The founder effect) **R:** 59
Founding [industrial process]
  Foundry **F:** 432
Founding Brothers [book by Ellis]
  Biography (Biography today) **B:** 314
Founding Fathers [U.S. history] **F:** 432
  United States, History of the (Writing the Constitution) **U:** 161-162
Foundry [industry] **F:** 432
  Aluminum (Casting the molten aluminum) **A:** 394-395
Foundry ingot [metallurgy]
  Aluminum (Casting the molten aluminum) **A:** 394
Fountain [art by Duchamp]
  Duchamp, Marcel **D:** 373
Fountain [water] **F:** 432 *with picture*
  Rome *picture on* **R:** 430
  Taft, Lorado *picture on* **T:** 7
Fountain of Neptune [Rome]
  Neptune *picture on* **N:** 128
  Rome *picture on* **R:** 430
Fountain of the Four Rivers [sculpture by Bernini]
  Italy *picture on* **I:** 505
Fountain of the Great Lakes [sculpture by Taft]
  Taft, Lorado **T:** 7 *with picture*
Fountain of Youth [legendary spring] **F:** 433
  Ponce de León, Juan **P:** 655
Fountain Paint Pots
  Yellowstone National Park (The Lower Loop) **Y:** 558
Fountain pen
  Ink (Writing inks) **I:** 273
  Pen **P:** 233 *with picture*
Fountainhead, The [book by Rand]
  Rand, Ayn **R:** 136
Fountains of Rome, The [music by Respighi]
  Respighi, Ottorino **R:** 259
Fouquet, Jean [French artist]
  France *picture on* **F:** 463
Four-angled mountain heather [plant]
  Flower *picture on* **F:** 283
Four Apostles [painting by Dürer]
  Dürer, Albrecht **D:** 388
Four Books [religious books]
  Religion (Confucianism) **R:** 220-221
Four Books of Architecture [book by Palladio]
  Palladio, Andrea **P:** 108
Four Books of Sentences [book by Lombard]
  Duns Scotus, John **D:** 386
  Lombard, Peter **L:** 427
  Scholasticism (The Scholastic method) **S:** 179
"Four Branches of the Mabinogi" [stories]
  Mythology (Celtic mythology) **M:** 984
Four-color theorem [mathematics]
  Topology (History) **T:** 333
Four Corners [region, U.S.] **F:** 433
  Anasazi **A:** 448a
Four Corners virus See Pulmonary syndrome hantavirus *in this index*
Four-eyed fish See Anableps *in this index*
4f subshell [chemistry]
  Lanthanide **L:** 69
Four Freedoms [paintings by Rockwell]
  Rockwell, Norman **R:** 394
4G [communications]
  Cellular telephone (History) **C:** 341
Four Gospels, The [books by Zola]
  Zola, Émile **Z:** 598
4-H [organization] **F:** 433 *with pictures*
  Agricultural education (Youth programs and organizations) **A:** 145
4-H Mall
  4-H (The National 4-H Council) **F:** 434
4-H National Youth Science Day
  4-H (National, state, and county events) **F:** 435-436

Four-horned antelope [animal]
  Antelope (Kinds of antelope) **A:** 542
Four Horsemen [football]
  Football *picture on* **F:** 367
Four Horsemen of the Apocalypse [New Testament] **F:** 437 *with picture*
Four Horsemen of the Apocalypse, The [book by Blasco Ibáñez]
  Blasco Ibáñez, Vicente **B:** 398
Four Horsemen of the Apocalypse, The [film]
  Valentino, Rudolph **V:** 264 *with picture*
Four Hundred, Council of the [ancient Greece]
  Areopagus **A:** 645
400 Blows, The [film]
  Motion picture (The New Wave in France) **M:** 870
400-meter hurdles [race]
  Hurdling **H:** 452
Four-in-hand
  Necktie **N:** 117
Four Little Girls [film]
  Lee, Spike **L:** 180
Four Masters [Chinese history]
  Painting (Chinese painting) **P:** 44-46
Four Noble Truths [religion]
  Buddhism (Buddha) **B:** 667-668
Four-o'clock [plant] **F:** 437 *with picture*
  Flower *picture on* **F:** 291
401(k) plan
  Pension (Private pension plans) **P:** 273
Four-of-a-kind
  Poker **P:** 603
Four-poster bed [furniture]
  Colonial life in America (Furnishings) **Ci:** 797-799
Four-Power Treaty
  Washington Conference **W:** 109
Four Quartets [poem by Eliot]
  Eliot, T. S. (His works) **E:** 237-238
Four Rivers, Fountain of the [Rome]
  Fountain **F:** 432
Four Saints in Three Acts [opera by Thomson]
  Thomson, Virgil **T:** 265
Four Seasons [singing group]
  Valli, Frankie **V:** 266 *with picture*
Four Seasons, The [music by Vivaldi]
  Vivaldi, Antonio **V:** 433
Four-step delivery
  Bowling (Delivering the ball) **B:** 522 *with pictures*
Four-stroke cycle engine
  Automobile (The engine cycle) **A:** 953
  Diesel engine (Kinds of diesel engines) **D:** 199
  Gasoline engine *diagrams on* **G:** 65; (Cycle) **G:** 63; (Development of the gasoline engine) **G:** 66
421 chair
  Furniture *picture on* **F:** 583; (The retro style) **F:** 584
Four-wheel drive
  Automobile (The drive system) **A:** 949
  Sport utility vehicle **So:** 802
  Transmission (Transmissions and drives) **T:** 375
Fourdrinier papermaking machine
  Paper (Sheet formation) **P:** 135
Foureye butterflyfish
  Butterflyfish **B:** 744 *with picture*
Fourier, Charles [French social reformer] **F:** 437
  Collectivism **Ci:** 775
  Marx, Karl (Early development) **M:** 237
Fourier, Jean Baptiste [French mathematician] See Fourier, Joseph, Baron *in this index*
Fourier, Joseph, Baron [French mathematician]
  Mathematics (In the 1800's) **M:** 307
Fourier series [mathematics]
  Series **S:** 316b
Fourment, Hélène [wife of Rubens]
  Rubens, Peter Paul (His life) **R:** 506 *with picture*
Fourneyron, Benoît [French engineer]
  Turbine (History) **T:** 498-499
Fournier, Pierre-Simon [French type designer]
  Book (The 1600's and 1700's) **B:** 467
Fourragère [emblem]
  Insignia **I:** 303
Foursquare Gospel, International Church of the [religious group]
  McPherson, Aimee Semple **M:** 344
Fourteen Points [U.S. history] **F:** 437
  Atlantic Charter **A:** 862
  House, Edward Mandell **H:** 384
  Lippmann, Walter **L:** 346
  United States, History of the (The peace treaty) **U:** 189
  Wilson, Woodrow (The Fourteen Points) **W:** 325
  World War I (The Fourteen Points) **W:** 465
Fourteenth Amendment [U.S. Constitution] **F:** 438
  Black codes **B:** 386
  Citizenship (The Constitution) **Ci:** 571
  Civil rights (The First Amendment) **Ci:** 608; (The struggle for the rights of African Americans) **Ci:** 609
  Constitution of the United States **Ci:** 1013

Dred Scott Decision **D:** 345
Due process of law **D:** 378
Holmes, Oliver Wendell, Jr. (Supreme Court justice) **H:** 295
Johnson, Andrew (Break with Congress) **J:** 140
Privacy, Right of **P:** 808a
Reconstruction (The 14th Amendment) **R:** 178
Supreme Court of the United States (Federalism) **So:** 1000-1001
Trumbull, Lyman **T:** 473
Fourth Amendment [U.S. Constitution]
Constitution of the United States **Ci:** 1012
Privacy, Right of **P:** 808a
Search warrant **S:** 269
Wiretapping (Laws concerning wiretapping) **W:** 345
Fourth dimension [mathematics] **F:** 438
Fourth estate F: 438
Fourth Hand, The [book by Irving]
Irving, John **I:** 459
Fourth of July *See* Independence Day *in this index*
Fourth Republic [French history]
France (The Fourth Republic) **F:** 475
Fous de Bassan, Les [book by Hébert]
Canadian literature (Modern literature: 1945 to the present) **C:** 159-160
Fouta Djallon [region]
Guinea (Land and climate) **G:** 431 *with map*; (History) **G:** 432
Fouta Djallon mountains
Senegal (Land and climate) **S:** 299
Fovea centralis [anatomy]
Eye *picture on* **E:** 461; (Focusing) **E:** 462 *with picture*
Fowl
Chicken **C:** 440; (Producing meat) **C:** 445
Poultry **P:** 720
Fowle, D. G. [American political leader]
North Carolina (table) **N:** 490
Fowler, Robert [Canadian diplomat]
United Nations (table) **U:** 86
Fowler, William Alfred [American physicist]
Astronomy (Advances in astrophysics) **A:** 848
Nobel Prizes (Physics: 1983) **N:** 442
Fowling in the Marshes [painting]
Painting (Egyptian painting) **P:** 40-41 *with picture*
Fox [animal] **F:** 438 *with pictures*
Animal *picture on* **A:** 483
Fox hunting **F:** 442
Fur *picture on* **F:** 562; (table) **F:** 561
Mammal *diagram on* **M:** 121
Fox [movie studio]
Motion picture (Movies become big business) **M:** 865-866
Fox [television network] **F:** 441
Television (The national networks) **T:** 113; (The early 2000's) **T:** 120
Fox, Billy [American boxer]
Boxing (The controversy over boxing) **B:** 530
Fox, Charles James [British statesman] **F:** 441
Hastings, Warren **H:** 83
North, Lord **N:** 457
Radicalism (In Europe) **R:** 82
Fox, George [English religious leader] **F:** 441
Peace (From the 1400's to the 1700's) **P:** 206
Quakers (History) **Q:** 5
Fox, George L. [American pantomimist]
Pantomime **P:** 132
Fox, Harry [American entertainer]
Ballroom dancing **B:** 63
Fox, Katherine [American religious leader]
Spiritualism **So:** 796
Fox, Margaret [American religious leader]
Spiritualism **So:** 796
Fox, Nelson [American baseball player]
Baseball (table: Hall of Fame) **B:** 134
Fox, Paula [American author] **F:** 441
Newbery Medal (table) **N:** 359
Fox, Terry [Canadian athlete] **F:** 441 *with picture*
Fox, Vicente [Mexican political leader] *See* Fox Quesada, Vicente *in this index*
"Fox and the Grapes, The" [fable]
Fable **F:** 2 *with picture*
Fox grape
Grape (North American grapes) **G:** 319
Fox hunting [sport] **F:** 442
England (Recreation) **E:** 296-297
Fox **F:** 438
Virginia *picture on* **V:** 402
Fox Indians
Iowa (Indian days) **I:** 393
Sauk Indians **S:** 163
Wisconsin (Struggle for control) **W:** 366
FOX network [television] *See* Fox *in this index*
Fox Quesada, Vicente [Mexican political leader] **F:** 442
Calderón Hinojosa, Felipe **C:** 27

Mexico (Opposition to the PRI) **M:** 474
Fox River [Wisconsin]
Lake Winnebago **L:** 48
Fox squirrel [animal]
Squirrel (Tree squirrels) **So:** 814b
Fox Talbot, William Henry [British scientist]
Communication (The 1800's) **Ci:** 881-882
Photography (The invention of photography) **P:** 422-423
Printing (Developments in platemaking) **P:** 803-804
Talbotype **T:** 19
Fox terrier [dog]
Dog *pictures on* **D:** 272, **D:** 273
Smooth fox terrier **S:** 521
Toy fox terrier **T:** 354
Wire fox terrier **W:** 344
Fox trot [dance]
Ballroom dancing **B:** 63
Foxberry [fruit]
Lingonberry **L:** 335 *with picture*
Foxe, John [English teacher]
Biography (The Renaissance) **B:** 313
Foxe, Luke [English seaman]
Manitoba (Newcomers) **M:** 160
Foxglove [plant] **F:** 442
Digitalis **D:** 203
Flower *picture on* **F:** 277
Foxhound [dog]
American foxhound **A:** 411 *with picture*
Dog *picture on* **D:** 270
English foxhound **E:** 312 *with picture*
Foxtail [weed]
Lawn *picture on* **L:** 143
Foxtail barley [plant] **F:** 443
Foxtail millet [hay]
Millet **M:** 555
Foxx, Jamie [American actor]
Motion picture (Best performance by an actor: 2004) **M:** 862a
Foxx, Jimmie [American baseball player] **F:** 443
Foyn, Svend [Norwegian whaler]
Whale (Hunting techniques) **W:** 263
Foyt, A. J. [American race car driver] **F:** 443
Automobile racing (table: Indianapolis 500 winners) **A:** 980
Fr [symbol]
Francium **F:** 482
FRA [agency]
Railroad (The role of the federal government) **R:** 113
Fra Angelico [Italian painter] *See* Angelico, Fra *in this index*
Fra Filippo Lippi [Italian painter]
Lippi, Filippo **L:** 345 *with picture*
Fra Giovanni da Fiesole [Italian painter] *See* Angelico, Fra *in this index*
"Fra Lippo Lippi" [poem by Browning]
Browning, Robert (Browning's poems) **B:** 646-647
Fractal [geometry] **F:** 443 *with diagram*
Fractal geometry
Mathematics (Philosophies of mathematics) **M:** 307
Fraction [industry]
Gas oil **G:** 60
Petroleum (Uses of petroleum) **P:** 331
Fraction [mathematics] **F:** 444 *with pictures*
Arithmetic (Arithmetic of small fractions) **A:** 668
Decimal system (Decimals and fractions) **D:** 72 *with diagrams*
Number (Rational numbers) **N:** 605-606
Percentage **P:** 280
Ratio **R:** 147
Fractional distillation [chemistry]
Distillation (Simple distillation) **D:** 238
Paraffin **P:** 143
Petroleum (Separation) **P:** 343
Fractionating column
Distillation (Rectification) **D:** 239
Fractionating tower
Petroleum *picture on* **P:** 330, *diagram on* **P:** 344; (Separation) **P:** 343
Fractionation [medicine]
Plasma (Uses in medicine) **P:** 551
Fracture [injury] **F:** 450 *with diagrams*
Bone (Broken bones) **B:** 457 *with diagram*
First aid (Fractures and dislocations) **F:** 140
Osteoporosis **O:** 867
Rib **R:** 321
Fracture [mineralogy]
Gem (Cleavage) **G:** 77
Fractured folklore [literature]
Literature for children (Fractured folklore) **L:** 365
Fragile river mussel [animal]
Shell *picture on* **S:** 387
Fragile X mental retardation protein [genetics]
Fragile X syndrome **F:** 451

Fragile X syndrome [genetics] **F:** 450
Brain (Genetic disorders) **B:** 558
Intellectual disability (Causes) **I:** 318
Fragment, Sentence [grammar]
Sentence (Sentence fragments) **S:** 304
Fragmentation [munitions] **F:** 451
Fragmentation bomb [weapon]
Bomb (Fragmentation bombs) **B:** 451 *with diagram*
Fragmentation **F:** 451
Fragmentation grenade [weapon]
Grenade **G:** 390 *with diagram*
Fragmentation shell [weapon]
Fragmentation **F:** 451
Fragonard, Jean Honoré [French painter] **F:** 451
Painting (Rococo painting) **P:** 65-66 *with picture*
Frahm, Herbert Ernst Karl *See* Brandt, Willy *in this index*
Frail, Dale A. [American astronomer]
Planet (The first discoveries) **P:** 513
Fram [ship]
Amundsen, Roald (The race to the South Pole) **A:** 445
Nansen, Fridtjof **N:** 11
Oslo **O:** 864
Frambesia [disease] *See* Yaws *in this index*
Frame [bowling]
Bowling (table) **B:** 521
Frame [film]
Motion picture (How motion pictures work) **M:** 856
Frame [television]
Television (Camera scanning patterns) **T:** 122
Frame, Frederick [American race driver]
Automobile racing (table: Indianapolis 500 winners) **A:** 980
Frame construction [architecture]
Building construction (Frame construction) **B:** 683
Colonial life in America (Houses) **Ci:** 796-797
House (Building materials) **H:** 380; (The frame) **H:** 382 *with diagram*
Skyscraper (Building skyscrapers) **S:** 497
Frame-dragging [physics]
Gravitation (Bending of light rays) **G:** 332
Relativity (Distortions in space-time) **R:** 212
Frame of Government [document]
Pennsylvania (Colonial days) **P:** 264
Frame sled
Inuit *picture on* **I:** 354d; (Transportation) **I:** 354c
Framework silicate
Silicate **S:** 458
Framing lumber
Lumber (Softwood lumber) **L:** 517
Framingham Heart Study [medicine] **F:** 451
Heart (Progress in treatment and prevention) **H:** 145-146
Framley Parsonage [book by Trollope]
Trollope, Anthony **T:** 449
Franc [money] **F:** 451
Franca, Celia [British dancer]
Ballet (Ballet in Canada) **B:** 54
France F: 452 *with pictures and maps*
See also the list of Related articles in the France *article*
English Channel **E:** 311
Euro **E:** 379
Flag *pictures on* **F:** 206, **F:** 209, **F:** 216
Food *picture on* **F:** 328
Arts
France (Arts) **F:** 461 *with pictures*
Ballet (History) **B:** 50-51
Classical music (History) **Ci:** 645-646
Fleur-de-lis **F:** 234
Furniture (France) **F:** 572 *with picture*
"Marseillaise" **M:** 227
Modernism **M:** 686
Motion picture (The New Wave in France) **M:** 870 *with picture*
Painting (The 1600's and 1700's) **P:** 58-61; (The 1800's) **P:** 67; (The 1900's in Europe) **P:** 77
Porcelain (French porcelain) **P:** 677
Sculpture (European sculpture) **S:** 253-254 *with picture*
Statue of Liberty **So:** 872
Theater (France) **T:** 248
Communications and mass media
France (Communication) **F:** 470
Newspaper (In Europe) **N:** 386
Education
France (Education) **F:** 460
Education (Control) **E:** 96-97
Library (France) **L:** 261
Government
France (Government) **F:** 455
Air force (The French Air Force) **A:** 184
Army (The French Army) **A:** 726

Bill of rights (French bill of rights) **B:** 301
Communism (In non-Communist countries)
  Ci: 897
Estates-General **E:** 360
Foreign aid (Other countries' aid programs)
  F: 384
Foreign Legion **F:** 386
Law (The first modern law codes) **L:** 135-136
Maginot Line **M:** 52
Navy (Major navies of the world) **N:** 78-79
Police (In other countries) **P:** 623 *with picture*,
  P: 623 *[with picture]*
Right wing **R:** 340
Zouaves **Z:** 607
History
France (History) **F:** 471
Africa (European colonization in Africa)
  A: 133-134
Air force (History) **A:** 184 *with picture*
Algeria (French rule) **A:** 364
Alsace-Lorraine **A:** 387
Arabs (Ottoman and European rule) **A:** 590
Belgium (The Brabant Revolution) **B:** 233
Berlin Airlift **B:** 266
Bourbon (In France) **B:** 516
Canada, History of **C:** 138
Cold War (The great blocs split) **Ci:** 769
Colonialism (Later colonialism) **Ci:** 813-814
Comoros (History) **C:** 900
Continental System **Ci:** 1022
Côte d'Ivoire (History) **Ci:** 1084b
Dauphin **D:** 44
Dien Bien Phu, Battle of **D:** 198
Emancipation Proclamation (Effects of the
  proclamation) **E:** 254
Exploration (The French and English in North
  America) **E:** 446
Franco-Prussian War **F:** 483
Franklin, Benjamin (Serving in France) **F:** 491
  with picture
Franks **F:** 494
French and Indian wars **F:** 511
French Revolution **F:** 524
French West Africa **F:** 527
Fronde **F:** 541
Fur trade (The early fur trade) **F:** 564
Geneva Accords **G:** 87
Holy Roman Empire **H:** 299 *with map*
Huguenots **H:** 410
Hundred Years' War **H:** 437
Indian, American (In Canada) **I:** 178
Indian wars (The French and Indian wars [1689-
  1763]) **I:** 191
Italy (The French Revolution and Napoleon)
  I: 514-515
Jackson, Andrew (Foreign affairs) **J:** 13-14
Jefferson, Thomas (Minister to France) **J:** 81
July Revolution **J:** 190
League of Nations (The League in action)
  L: 160
Louisiana Purchase **L:** 502
Madagascaar (History) **M:** 29
Mali (History) **M:** 108-109
Mexico (The French invasion) **M:** 471
Mississippi Scheme **M:** 649
Monroe Doctrine (Origins) **M:** 739
Netherlands (Wars with England and France)
  N: 149
New France **N:** 204 *with picture*
New Zealand (International tensions) **N:** 355-
  356
Pacific Islands (Colonial rule) **P:** 12; (Nuclear
  testing) **P:** 12
Reign of Terror **R:** 207
Renaissance (The Renaissance outside Italy)
  R: 237
Revolution, American **R:** 270; (Diplomacy)
  R: 280; (France's entry into the Revolutionary
  War) **R:** 283; (Costs of the war) **R:** 287
Revolution of 1848 **R:** 288
Roman Catholic Church (Growth of the church
  in Europe) **R:** 406
Seigneurial system **S:** 287
Senegal (History) **S:** 299
Seven Years' War **S:** 328
Seychelles (History) **S:** 340
Slavery (The decline of slavery) **S:** 504
Spanish Civil War (Foreign assistance) **So:** 756a
Suez Canal (History) **So:** 958
Suez crisis **So:** 958
Syndicalism **So:** 1067
Toronto (History) **T:** 340b
United Kingdom (The growing empire) **U:** 67
United States, History of the (The English and
  French) **U:** 151; (Problems in foreign affairs)
  U: 163; (The Louisiana Purchase) **U:** 164
Vietnam **V:** 364; (History) **V:** 369-370

War of 1812 **W:** 28
Waterloo, Battle of (Napoleon returns to
  France) **W:** 145
World War I **W:** 452; (Destruction and
  casualties) **W:** 464
World War II (The fall of France) **W:** 475 *with
  picture*
Language and literature See French language;
  French literature *in this index*
People
France (People) **F:** 455
Christmas (In France) **C:** 530 *with picture*
Clothing *picture on* Ci: 694
Technology and science
Industrial Revolution (France) **I:** 253
Metric system (Creation of the metric system)
  M: 441
France, Anatole [French author] **F:** 480
France, Institute of [organization]
  Institute of France **I:** 305
France, La [airship]
  Airship (The first airships) **A:** 251
France, Marie de [French poet]
  Launfal, Sir **L:** 121
France, William H. G. (Bill) [American race car
  driver]
  NASCAR **N:** 21
France and England in the New World [book by
  Parkman]
  Parkman, Francis **P:** 171
France-Soir [newspaper]
  Paris (Economy) **P:** 165
France Telecom [company]
  Manufacturing (table) **M:** 170
Francesca, Piero della [Italian painter] *See* Piero
  della Francesca *in this index*
Franche-Comté [former province]
  Burgundy **B:** 705
Franchise [law] **F:** 480
  Chain store **C:** 369
  Hotel (History) **H:** 376-377
  Motel **M:** 836
  Restaurant (Chains and franchises) **R:** 262
  Soft drink (How soft drinks are made) **So:** 570-
    571
Franchise tax
  Taxation (Taxes on transactions) **T:** 53
Franchitti, Dario [Scottish race driver]
  Automobile racing (table: Indianapolis 500
    winners) **A:** 980
Francia, José Gaspar Rodríguez de [Paraguayan
  political leader]
  Paraguay (Independence) **P:** 149
Francis I [emperor of Austria] *See* Francis II [Holy
  Roman emperor] *in this index*
Francis I [Holy Roman emperor]
  Habsburg, House of **H:** 3
  Maria Theresa **M:** 199
Francis I [king of France] **F:** 480
  Cartier, Jacques (Exploration of Canada) **C:** 262
  Exploration (The search for a northern passage)
    E: 446
  France (A period of wars) **F:** 473
  Leonardo da Vinci (Last years) **L:** 200
  Louvre **L:** 507
  Renaissance (Political background) **R:** 237
Francis II [Holy Roman emperor] **F:** 480
  Austria (Wars in the 1700's and 1800's) **A:** 937-
    938 *with picture*
  Holy Roman Empire (The House of Habsburg)
    H: 300
Francis II [king of France]
  Catherine de Médicis **C:** 303
Francis, David R. [American government official]
  Cleveland, Grover (table) **Ci:** 672
  Missouri (table) **M:** 668
Francis, Dick [British author] **F:** 481
Francis, Felix [British author]
  Francis, Dick **F:** 481
Francis, James B. [English inventor]
  Turbine (History) **T:** 498-499
Francis, John Brown [American political leader]
  Rhode Island (table) **R:** 311
Francis, Thomas, Jr. [American doctor]
  Salk, Jonas Edward (His life) **S:** 68
Francis Case, Lake
  South Dakota (Rivers and lakes) **So:** 676 *with map*
Francis de Sales, Saint [French religious leader]
  F: 481
  Religious life (Religious life in the 1500's and
    1600's) **R:** 227
Francis Ferdinand [archduke of Austria] *See* Franz
  Ferdinand *in this index*
Francis Joseph [emperor of Austria] *See* Franz
  Joseph *in this index*
Francis of Assisi, Saint [Italian religious leader]
  F: 481 *with picture*

Christianity (The medieval church) **C:** 524 *with
  picture*
Franciscans **F:** 482
Italian literature (The Middle Ages) **I:** 494
Religious life (Religious life in the Middle Ages)
  R: 226
Francis turbine
  Turbine (Water turbines) **T:** 497
Francis Xavier [Spanish missionary] *See* Xavier,
  Saint Francis *in this index*
Franciscana [animal] *See* La Plata dolphin *in this
  index*
Franciscans [religious group] **F:** 482
  California (The California missions) **C:** 60
  Capuchins **C:** 199
  Christianity (The medieval church) **C:** 524 *with
    picture*
  Francis of Assisi, Saint **F:** 481
  Friar **F:** 532
  Hispanic Americans (In the Southwest) **H:** 251
  Mission life in America (Eastern missions) **M:** 618
  Religious life (Religious life in the Middle Ages)
    R: 226
Francium [element] **F:** 482
  Alkali metal **A:** 369
Franck, César [French composer] **F:** 482
Franck, James [German physicist]
  Nobel Prizes (Physics: 1925) **N:** 440
Franco, Federico [Paraguayan political leader]
  Paraguay (Recent developments) **P:** 150 *with
    picture*
Franco, Francisco [Spanish political leader] **F:** 482
  Falange Española **F:** 12
  Fascism (Fascism in other countries) **F:** 50
  Juan Carlos I **J:** 177
  Madrid (History) **M:** 40
  Spain (Civil war) **So:** 750 *with picture*; (Recent
    developments) **So:** 751-752
  Spanish Civil War (Rebellion leads to civil war)
    So: 756a; (Progress of the war) **So:** 756a;
    (Results of the war) **So:** 756b
Franco, Itamar [Brazilian political leader]
  Brazil (Return to civilian government) **B:** 586
Franco, Jean [French mountain climber]
  Mount Makalu **M:** 886
Franco-Flemish school [art]
  Sculpture (European sculpture) **S:** 253 *with
    picture*
Franco-Ontarian Festival [Ottawa]
  Ottawa (Annual events) **O:** 873
Franco-Prussian War [1870-1871] **F:** 483
  Balloon (Balloons in war) **B:** 61
  France (The Franco-Prussian War) **F:** 474
  Germany (The unification of Germany) **G:** 165
  Homing pigeon (History) **H:** 305
  Paris (Paris in wartime) **P:** 166
Franconia [former state, Germany]
  Germany (The breakup of Charlemagne's empire)
    G: 162
Franconia Range
  New Hampshire (Mountains) **N:** 220 *with map*
Francophone school
  Alberta (Schools) **A:** 317
Frangipani [plant]
  Flower *picture on* **F:** 273
Frank, Anne [German public figure] **F:** 484 *with
  portrait*
  Diary **D:** 184
  Diary of Anne Frank **D:** 185
Frank, Clint [American football player]
  Football (table) **F:** 363
Frank, Ilya M. [Russian physicist]
  Nobel Prizes (Physics: 1958) **N:** 441
Frank, Joseph [American historian]
  Biography (Biography today) **B:** 314
Frank, Michael [American educator]
  Wisconsin (Schools) **W:** 350
Frank, Otto [father of Anne Frank]
  Diary of Anne Frank **D:** 185
Frank, Robert [American photographer]
  Photography (A diversity of styles) **P:** 426
Frank Slide Interpretive Centre [Alberta]
  Alberta (Places to visit) **A:** 320 *with picture*
Franken, Al [American political leader]
  Minnesota (The early 2000's) **M:** 606
Frankenmuth [Michigan]
  Michigan (Places to visit) **M:** 498
Frankenstein [book by Shelley] **F:** 484
  Shelley, Mary Wollstonecraft **S:** 391
Frankenstein [film]
  Karloff, Boris **K:** 246
Frankenthaler, Helen [American painter] **F:** 484
  Painting (Abstract painting) **P:** 34 *with picture*;
    (Color-field painting) **P:** 85
Frankfort [Kentucky] **F:** 484
Frankfurt [Germany] **F:** 484
Frankfurt, Treaty of [1871]

Franco-Prussian War (The end of the war) **F: 483**
Frankfurt Airport
Airport (table) **A: 245**
Frankfurt Assembly [German history]
Germany (The Revolution of 1848) **G: 165**
Frankfurter [food]
Food (Interesting facts about food) **F: 329**
Iowa picture on **I: 395**
Meat packing picture on **M: 351**; (Sausage making) **M: 352**
Sausage **S: 163**
Frankfurter, Felix [American jurist] **F: 485**
Frankie and Johnny in the Clair de Lune [play by McNally]
McNally, Terrence **M: 344**
Frankincense [tree product] **F: 485**
Franking and penalty privileges [law] **F: 485**
Frankish kingdom [European history]
Charlemagne (Military conquests) **C: 379** *with map*
France (History) **F: 471** *with map*
Franks **F: 494** *with map*
Frankland, Sir Edward [British chemist]
Helium **H: 176**
Franklin [Idaho]
Idaho (Exploration and early settlement) **I: 42**
Franklin, Aretha [American singer] **F: 485**
Franklin, Barbara H. [American government official]
Commerce, Department of (table) **Ci: 871**
Franklin, Battle of [1864]
Civil War, American (table) **Ci: 624**; (North to Nashville) **Ci: 632**
Franklin, Benjamin [American statesman] **F: 486** *with pictures*
Adams, John (Diplomat) **A: 36**
Adult education (History of adult education in the United States) **A: 69**
Albany Congress **A: 310**
American literature (Philadelphia) **A: 415**
Autobiography **A: 942**
Bath (History) **B: 164**
Cent **C: 350**
Colonial life in America (Furnishings) **Ci: 797-798**; (Literature) **Ci: 806-807**; (Science) **Ci: 808-809**
Declaration of Independence picture on **D: 77**; (The Continental Congress) **D: 74**
Electricity (Experiments with electric charge) **E: 196**
Fire department (The 1700's) **F: 128**
Foundation (History) **F: 431**
Glasses **G: 224**
Gulf Stream **G: 437**
Harmonica **H: 62**
Insurance (Insurance in the United States) **I: 315**
Jefferson, Thomas (The Declaration of Independence) **J: 79** *with picture*
Kite (History) **K: 340**
Library (Libraries in the United States) **L: 261**
Lightning **L: 299**
Paine, Thomas (Early life) **P: 22**
Pennsylvania, University of **P: 269**
Philadelphia (Libraries and museums) **P: 363**; (Early colonial days) **P: 365-366**
Poor Richard's Almanac **P: 658**
Postal Service, United States (Colonial times) **P: 700** *with picture*
Postal services (Postal service in the United States) **P: 706**
Proverb **P: 839**
Quebec (Communication) **Q: 29**
Rebus picture on **R: 174**
Revolution, American picture on **R: 278**; (The Treaty of Paris) **R: 286**
State, Department of (Establishment) **So: 860-861**
Westward movement in America (Regional conflict) **W: 245**
Franklin, Francis Folger [son of]
Franklin, Benjamin (Printer) **F: 487**
Franklin, James [brother of]
Franklin, Benjamin (Student and apprentice) **F: 487**
Franklin, James [publisher]
Rhode Island (Communication) **R: 310**
Franklin, Jesse [American political leader]
North Carolina (table) **N: 490**
Franklin, Sir John [British explorer] **F: 492**
Arctic (Arctic exploration) **A: 638-639**
Exploration (Arctic exploration) **E: 449** *with map*
Northwest Passage **N: 528**
Franklin, John Hope [American historian] **F: 492**
Franklin, Rosalind Elsie [British chemist] **F: 492**
Franklin, Shirley [American political leader]
Atlanta (Recent developments) **A: 861**
Franklin, State of [U.S. history] **F: 493** *with map*
Sevier, John **S: 328**

Tennessee **T: 135**; (Territorial years) **T: 153**
Watauga Association **W: 113**
Franklin, William [son of]
Franklin, Benjamin (Printer) **F: 487**
Franklin D. Roosevelt Lake [Washington]
Grand Coulee Dam **G: 308**
Irrigation (Surface water) **I: 456**
Washington (Land regions) **W: 58-60** *with map*
Franklin D. Roosevelt National Historic Site, Home of [New York]
National Park System (table: National historic site) **N: 52-53**
New York (Places to visit) **N: 302** *with picture*
Franklin Delano Roosevelt Memorial [Washington, D.C.] **F: 493** *with picture*
National Park System (table: National memorials) **N: 54**
Washington, D.C. map on **W: 76**; (The Tidal Basin) **W: 73** *with picture*
Franklin Institute
Franklin Institute Science Museum **F: 494**
Franklin Institute Science Museum [Philadelphia] **F: 493**
Franklin, Benjamin (The twilight years) **F: 491-492**; (His place in history) **F: 492**
Pennsylvania (Museums) **P: 248-249**
Philadelphia (Libraries and museums) **P: 363-364**
Franklin Lake
Nevada (Rivers and lakes) **N: 166-168** *with map*
Franklin Mountains [Canada]
Northwest Territories (The Mackenzie Valley) **N: 531**
Franklin Park
Boston (Recreation) **B: 502**
Franklin stove
Franklin, Benjamin picture on **F: 490**; (Other studies) **F: 490**
Heating (Wood-burning stoves) picture on **H: 160**
Franklin Technical Institute [Boston]
Franklin, Benjamin (The twilight years) **F: 491-492**
Franklinite [mineral]
Zinc **Z: 594**
Franklinton [former name]
Columbus (History) **Ci: 856**
Franks [people] **F: 494** *with map*
Belgium (The Middle Ages) **B: 232**
Charlemagne (Military conquests) **C: 379**
Europe (The Franks) **E: 409** *with map*
Frankfurt **F: 485**
Germany (History) **G: 162**
Lombards **L: 427**
Merovingian dynasty **M: 418**
Netherlands (Early days) **N: 148**
Switzerland (Early days) **So: 1058-1059**
Franks, Bobby [American public figure]
Darrow, Clarence Seward **D: 38**
Franz Ferdinand [archduke of Austria] **F: 494**
Austria (Austria-Hungary) **A: 939**
Austria-Hungary **A: 941**
Bosnia-Herzegovina (History) **B: 492-493**
Franz Joseph **F: 494**
Germany (World War I) **G: 166**
World War I (The assassination of an archduke) **W: 455** *with picture*
Franz Josef II, Prince [Liechtenstein ruler]
Liechtenstein (History) **L: 273**
Franz Josef Land [islands, Russia] **F: 494**
Franz Joseph [emperor of Austria] **F: 494**
Beard **B: 187**
Franz Josef Land **F: 494**
Maximilian **M: 319**
Rampolla del Tindaro, Mariano **R: 133**
Frasch, Herman [American scientist]
Sulfur (How sulfur is obtained) **So: 967**
Frasch method
Mining diagram on **M: 578**; (Pumping methods) **M: 577**
Sulfur (How sulfur is obtained) **So: 967**
Fraser, Dawn [Australian swimmer]
Swimming (History) **So: 1047**
Fraser, Gretchen [American skier]
Skiing (The middle and late 1900's) **S: 487**
Fraser, James Earle [American sculptor]
Oklahoma picture on **O: 723**
Fraser, John J. [Canadian political leader]
New Brunswick (table) **N: 195**
Fraser, Malcolm [Australian political leader]
Australia (table) **A: 923**; (Political upheavals) **A: 925**
Fraser, Simon [Canadian explorer] **F: 494**
British Columbia (The overland fur traders) **B: 628-630**
Fraser River **F: 495**
Prince George **P: 794**
Fraser fir [tree]
Fir **F: 119**

Fraser River [river, British Columbia] **F: 495**
British Columbia (The colonial period) **B: 630**
Canada (The Pacific Basin) **C: 120**
Fraser Valley
British Columbia (Land regions) **B: 622**; (Agriculture) **B: 625**
Frashëri, Midhat [Albanian political leader]
Albania (World War II) **A: 307-308**
Fraternal benefit society
Insurance (Types of insurance companies) **I: 315**
Fraternal Order of Eagles [organization] See Eagles, Fraternal Order of in this index
Fraternal organization **F: 495**
Fraternal twins
Behavior (The nature/nurture debate) **B: 221**
Multiple birth **M: 919**
Reproduction, Human (Multiple birth) **R: 246**
Fraternity [organization] **F: 495**
Universities and colleges (Fraternities and sororities) **U: 209**
Fraud [crime] **F: 496**
Bush, George Walker (Corporate wrongdoing) **B: 722h**
Business (Recent developments) **B: 727**
Identity theft **I: 46**
United States, History of the (Financial troubles) **U: 196f**
Fraunhofer, Joseph von [German physicist]
Astronomy (Spectroscopy) **A: 840**
Fraunhofer lines [light]
Sun (Analyzing electromagnetic radiation) **So: 983**
Fravashirs [spirits]
Zoroastrianism (Beliefs) **Z: 607**
Frazer, Sir James George [Scottish anthropologist] **F: 496**
Magic (Kinds of magic) **M: 49**
Mythology (Anthropological approaches) **M: 989**
Frazier, Edward Franklin [American sociologist] **F: 497**
Frazier, James B. [American political leader]
Tennessee (table) **T: 152**
Frazier, Lynn J. [American political leader]
North Dakota (table) **N: 513**; (The early 1900's) **N: 514-516**
Frazier-Lyde, Jacqui [American boxer]
Boxing (Women's boxing) **B: 532b-533** *with picture*
Fréchette, Louis-Honoré [Canadian poet]
Canadian literature (Poetry: 1850-1918) **C: 157**
Laurier, Sir Wilfrid (Early public career) **L: 124**
Frechette, Louise [Canadian diplomat]
United Nations (table) **U: 86**
Freckled darter [fish]
Darter **D: 38**
Freckles
Skin (Skin color) **S: 490**
Freddie Mac [agency] See Federal Home Loan Mortgage Corporation in this index
Frederic, Harold [American author] **F: 497**
Frederick [Danish kings] See under Frederik in this index
Frederick [king of Bohemia]
Thirty Years' War (The Bohemian period) **T: 260**
Frederick I [Holy Roman emperor] **F: 497**
Adrian IV **A: 67**
Alexander III **A: 341**
Bohemia **B: 437**
Crusades (The Third Crusade) **Ci: 1160** *with map*
Frederick I [king of Prussia]
Berlin (Prussian capital) **B: 264**
Germany (The rise of Prussia) **G: 164**
Hohenzollern **H: 289**
Frederick II [Holy Roman emperor] **F: 497**
Crusades (Other Crusades) **Ci: 1161**
Czech Republic (The rise of Bohemia) **Ci: 1213**
Gregory IX **G: 388**
Innocent III (Imperial power) **I: 274**
Innocent IV **I: 275**
Frederick II [king of Prussia] **F: 497**
Army (The rise of modern armies) **A: 727-728**
Espionage (History) **E: 358**
Frederick William I **F: 498**
Germany (The rise of Prussia) **G: 164**
Hohenzollern **H: 289**
Maria Theresa **M: 199**
Prussia (Frederick II, or Frederick the Great) **P: 843**
Seven Years' War (In Europe) **S: 328**
Succession wars (The War of the Austrian Succession) **So: 950**
Voltaire (Later years) **V: 447**
Frederick III [king of Prussia] **F: 497**
Wilhelm II **W: 305**
Frederick Barbarossa See Frederick I [Holy Roman emperor] in this index
Frederick Douglass [paintings by Lawrence]
Lawrence, Jacob **L: 145**

Frederick Douglass National Historic Site
[Washington, D.C.]
National Park System (table: National historic sites) **N:** 52-53
Frederick Law Olmsted National Historic Site
[Massachusetts]
National Park System (table: National historic sites) **N:** 52-53
Frederick of Hohenzollern [ruler of Prussia]
Prussia (Early history) **P:** 843
Frederick the Great *See* Frederick II [king of Prussia] *in this index*
Frederick the Great [book by Carlyle]
Carlyle, Thomas (Later career) **C:** 240
Frederick Valley
Maryland (Land regions) **M:** 250
Frederick William [ruler of Brandenburg] **F:** 497
Berlin (Prussian capital) **B:** 264
Germany (The rise of Prussia) **G:** 164
Hohenzollern **H:** 289
Frederick William I [king of Prussia] **F:** 498
Hohenzollern **H:** 289
Frederick William III [king of Prussia]
Aix-la-Chapelle, Congress of **A:** 253
Louise of Mecklenburg-Strelitz **L:** 477
Napoleonic Wars (The alliance of Prussia and Russia) **N:** 18
Wilhelm (Wilhelm I) **W:** 305
Frederick William IV [king of Prussia]
Germany (The Revolution of 1848) **G:** 165
Wilhelm (Wilhelm I) **W:** 305
Fredericksburg [Virginia] **F:** 498
Fredericksburg, Battle of [1862]
Civil War, American (table) **Ci:** 624; (Battle of Fredericksburg) **Ci:** 627
Lee, Robert E. (Later battles) **L:** 178
Fredericksburg and Spotsylvania County Battlefields Memorial [Virginia]
National Park System (table: National military parks) **N:** 55
Fredericton [New Brunswick] **F:** 498
New Brunswick *pictures on* **N:** 185, N: 187
Frederik II [king of Denmark and Norway]
Christian IV **C:** 522d
Frederik VII [king of Denmark]
Denmark (The Schleswig wars) **D:** 140
Frederik VIII [king of Denmark] **F:** 498
Frederik IX [king of Denmark]
Denmark (Postwar years) **D:** 141
Frederik Meijer Gardens and Sculpture Park
[Grand Rapids]
Michigan (Places to visit) **M:** 498 *with picture*
Frederika [wife of]
Paul I **P:** 199
Fredonia [New York]
Gas [fuel] (Development of the natural gas industry) **G:** 57
Free Academy [former name]
New York, City University of **N:** 321
Free Aceh Movement [Indonesian history]
Sumatra **So:** 972
Free African Society [organization]
Allen, Richard **A:** 372
Jones, Absalom **J:** 157
Free and Accepted Masons *See* Masonry [organization] *in this index*
Free association [government]
Marshall Islands (History) **M:** 231
Pacific Islands (Pacific alliances and independence movements) **P:** 12-13
Pacific Islands, Trust Territory of the **P:** 13
Palau (Government) **P:** 101
Free association [psychology]
Freud, Sigmund (On treatment) **F:** 531
Psychoanalysis (Psychoanalytic treatment) **P:** 846
Psychology (Psychoanalysis) **P:** 850
Psychotherapy (Psychodynamic-interpersonal psychotherapy) **P:** 852
Free Association, Compact of [government]
Marshall Islands (History) **M:** 231
Micronesia, Federated States of (History) **M:** 515
Free Churches
England (Religion) **E:** 297-298
Free city [political unit] **F:** 498
Free dancing
Ice skating (Ice dancing) **I:** 13
Free Democratic Party [political party]
Germany (Politics) **G:** 147
Free Education Act [1852]
Prince Edward Island (Schools) **P:** 786
Free electron [physics]
Electronics (How a circuit works) **E:** 208-209
Light (How light is produced) **L:** 283
Semiconductor (Semiconductor crystals) **S:** 291; (Using doped crystals) **S:** 292
Free-electron laser [physics]
Laser (Other kinds of lasers) **L:** 85

Light (How light is produced) **L:** 283
Free Enquirer [magazine]
Wright, Frances **W:** 507
Free enterprise system [economics]
See also Capitalism *in this index*
Business (Business in a free enterprise system) **B:** 725
Capitalism (How capitalism differs from central planning) **C:** 194
Chamber of Commerce, United States **C:** 371
Dartmouth College case **D:** 39
Freedom (Economic freedom) **F:** 501
Laissez faire **L:** 31
Lenin, V. I. **L:** 191
United States (Economy) **U:** 128
World (Economic systems) **W:** 412b
Free-fall
Skydiving **S:** 496
Free-flight model
Airplane, Model (Free-flight models) **A:** 241 *with picture*
Free-floating balloon
Balloon **B:** 57
Free-flowing agent
Salt (How table salt is made) **S:** 74
Free form [music]
Classical music (Free form) **Ci:** 645
Free French [World War II]
De Gaulle, Charles André Joseph Marie (Leader of the Free French) **D:** 91
Foreign Legion (History) **F:** 386
France (World War II) **F:** 475
World War II (The fall of France) **W:** 475
Free jazz
Coltrane, John **Ci:** 850
Mingus, Charles **M:** 573
Free Jazz [recording]
Jazz (New directions) **J:** 73
Free kick
Soccer (Fouls) **So:** 546
Free-lance [employment]
Commercial art **Ci:** 872
Photography (Careers) **P:** 427-428
Writing **W:** 511
Free Libraries Act [1882]
Ontario (Libraries) **O:** 769
Free market [economics]
Capitalism (How capitalism differs from central planning) **C:** 194
Economics (The free market) **E:** 59
Price **P:** 774
Free Methodist Church F: 498
Methodists (Social change and division) **M:** 435
Free morpheme [linguistics]
Language (Words and morphemes) **L:** 62
Free mount [paleontology]
Fossil (Working with fragments) **F:** 426
Free National Movement [political party]
Bahamas (History) **B:** 29
Free Officers [political group]
Egypt (Republic) **E:** 132
Free Papua Movement [political group]
Indonesia (Indonesia under Suharto) **I:** 238-239
Free port [trade]
Foreign trade zone **F:** 388a
Free trade zone **F:** 499
Hong Kong (Economy) **H:** 318
Free position [sports]
Diving *picture on* **D:** 244; (Kinds of dives) **D:** 243
Lacrosse (Women's lacrosse) **L:** 23-24
Free radical [molecule]
Aging (How aging occurs) **A:** 141
Antioxidant **A:** 557
Herzberg, Gerhard **H:** 217
Free-range chicken
Agriculture *picture on* **A:** 151
Free school
Alternative school **A:** 388
Colonial life in America (Education) **Ci:** 803
Education (What should be taught?) **E:** 105
Ontario (Schools) **O:** 769
School (Growth and reform) **S:** 184
Free silver [economics] **F:** 499
Bryan, William Jennings (Early career) **B:** 654
Cleveland, Grover (Saving the gold standard) **Ci:** 673
Democratic Party (After the Civil War) **D:** 125
Gay Nineties (Industrial growth) **G:** 72
McKinley, William (Congressman) **M:** 339
Populism (Origins) **P:** 674
Free skating
Ice skating (Singles skating) **I:** 11-12; (Pairs skating) **I:** 12
Roller skating (Artistic skating) **R:** 402a *with picture*
Free Soil Party [U.S. history] **F:** 499
Adams, Charles Francis **A:** 33

Liberty Party **L:** 233
Taylor, Zachary (Nomination for President) **T:** 59-60
Free Speech Movement [organization]
California (The mid-1900's) **C:** 62-63
New Left **N:** 255
Free stall barn
Dairying (Housing) **D:** 7
Free stall housing [agriculture]
Dairying (Housing) **D:** 7
Free-standing sculpture [art]
Sculpture (Kinds of sculpture) **S:** 230
Free State [name for]
Maryland (The early 1900's) **M:** 259
Free State of Panama [Panamanian history]
Herrera, Tomás **H:** 214
Free State party [U.S. history]
Kansas ("Bleeding Kansas") **K:** 235
Free Synagogue [New York]
Wise, Stephen Samuel **W:** 370
Free-tailed bat [animal]
Bat (Brazilian free-tailed bats) **B:** 161
Free Thai Movement [Thai history]
Thailand (In World War II [1939-1945]) **T:** 227
Free throw
Basketball *picture on* **B:** 147
Free trade [economics] **F:** 499
Customs union **Ci:** 1201
Economics (The world economy) **E:** 61
European Union **E:** 418
Globalization (Features of globalization) **G:** 233
North American Free Trade Agreement **N:** 470
Smith, Adam **S:** 515
United Kingdom (Establishment of free trade) **U:** 69
Free Trade Agreement, North American [1992]
See North American Free Trade Agreement *in this index*
Free trade area [economics]
Customs union **Ci:** 1201
Free trade zone F: 499
Foreign trade zone **F:** 388a
Free Traders [Australian history]
Australia (Building a nation) **A:** 923
Free University of Brussels
Belgium (Education) **B:** 229-230
Free verse [poetry] **F:** 500
American literature (Walt Whitman and Emily Dickinson) **A:** 419
Meter **M:** 433
Poetry (table) **P:** 594; (Forms) **P:** 595
Free will [philosophy] **F:** 500
Metaphysics (Causality) **M:** 429-430
Freebase [drug]
Cocaine **Ci:** 742
Freebooter
Pirate **P:** 494
Freecall service
Telephone (Business services) **T:** 98
Freed, Alan [American disc jockey]
Rock music (Musical roots) **R:** 376; (Setbacks) **R:** 379
Freedman [person]
African Americans (Free blacks) **A:** 136g; (The first years of freedom) **A:** 136j
Rome, Ancient (The people) **R:** 437
Freedman, Russell [American author] **F:** 500
Laura Ingalls Wilder Award (table) **L:** 121
Newbery Medal (table) **N:** 359
Regina Medal (table: 1996) **R:** 206
Freedmen's Bureau [U.S. history] **F:** 500
African Americans (The first years of freedom) **A:** 136j *with picture*
Georgia (Reconstruction and recovery) **G:** 132
Reconstruction (Early congressional reaction) **R:** 177
Freedom F: 501
Bill of rights **B:** 301
Civil rights **Ci:** 607
Communism (Restrictions on personal freedom) **Ci:** 891
Declaration of Independence (A Declaration of Rights) **D:** 76
Democracy **D:** 120
Existentialism (What is existentialism?) **E:** 437
Fascism (Personal liberty) **F:** 49
Freedom of religion **F:** 505
Freedom of speech **F:** 506
Freedom of the press **F:** 507
Liberalism **L:** 252
Sartre, Jean-Paul **S:** 127
Union of Soviet Socialist Republics (Personal freedom) **U:** 31
Freedom [proposed space station]
International Space Station (History) **I:** 346b
Freedom, Academic *See* Academic freedom *in this index*

Freedom, Statue of
Capitol, United States C: 197
Columbia Ci: 851
Freedom and Justice Party
Egypt (Recent developments) E: 133
Freedom Council
Denmark (World War II) D: 140-141
Freedom Day, National [custom] F: 503
Freedom dues [U.S. history]
Colonial life in America (The lower class) Ci: 794
Freedom fighter [Hungarian history]
Cold War (Unrest in Eastern Europe) Ci: 766
Freedom of a Christian, The [book by Luther]
Luther, Martin (The break with the Roman Catholic Church) L: 528
Freedom of Access to Clinic Entrances Act [1994]
Abortion (Abortion in the United States) A: 15-16
Freedom of assembly F: 504
Constitution of the United States (Amendment 1) Ci: 1011
Freedom (Social freedom) F: 501
Freedom of contract
Law (Beginnings of U.S. law) L: 136; (Law since 1900) L: 136
Freedom of Information Act [1966] F: 505
Freedom of religion F: 505
Calvert, Cecilius C: 70
Church and state C: 542
Colonial life in America (Religious and political reasons) Ci: 788; (Religion) C: 804
Communism (Restrictions on personal freedom) Ci: 891-892
Constitution of the United States (Amendment 1) Ci: 1011
Indian, American (Political gains) I: 182
Maryland (Colonial days) M: 256
Nantes, Edict of N: 11
Pennsylvania (Colonial days) P: 264
Pennsylvania Dutch P: 270
Philadelphia (Early colonial days) P: 365-366
Providence (Government and history) P: 840
Religious education (Public schools) R: 225
School prayer S: 185
Toleration Act T: 321
Union of Soviet Socialist Republics (Personal freedom) U: 31
United States, History of the (Virginia and Maryland) U: 153
Vatican Council II (Other documents) V: 390
Freedom of speech F: 506
Civil rights (Limits of civil rights) Ci: 608
Communism (Restrictions on personal freedom) Ci: 891-892
Constitution of the United States (Amendment 1) Ci: 1011
Freedom (Social freedom) F: 501
Obscenity and pornography (Legal history for obscenity) SO: 643
Riot R: 348
Schenck v. United States S: 174
Supreme Court of the United States (Freedom of speech) So: 1001; (table) So: 1002
Freedom of the City [play by Friel]
Friel, Brian F: 533
Freedom of the press F: 507
Constitution of the United States (Amendment 1) Ci: 1011
Journalism (The role of U.S. journalism) J: 172; (Major issues in journalism) J: 173; (Journalism in free societies) J: 174; (Journalism in government-controlled societies) J: 174
New York (Under English rule) N: 314-315
Newspaper (Newspapers in other countries) N: 385-386
Supreme Court of the United States (table) So: 1002
Freedom of thought and expression
Academic freedom A: 20
Freedom of Will [book by Edwards]
American literature (New England) A: 414
Edwards, Jonathan E: 114
Freedom Party [political party]
Austria (Recent developments) A: 940
Freedom riders [U.S. history] F: 508 *with picture*
African Americans (The growing movement) A: 136o
Kennedy, John Fitzgerald (Civil rights) K: 264
Rustin, Bayard R: 567
Freedom school [education]
Alternative school (History) A: 389
Freedom 7 [spacecraft]
Shepard, Alan Bartlett, Jr. S: 395
Freedom to farm law [1996]
Farm and farming (Federal farm programs) F: 44
Freedom Trail
Boston *map on* B: 499; (Downtown Boston) B: 496

Freedom's Journal [newspaper]
Russwurm, John Brown R: 566b
Walker, David W: 13
Freeh, Louis J. [American government official]
Federal Bureau of Investigation (History) F: 62-63
Freehold [law]
Estate E: 360
Freeholder [U.S. history]
Colonial life in America (Economic reasons) Ci: 788
New Jersey (Local government) N: 249
Freeman, Daniel [American settler]
Nebraska (Statehood) N: 112
Freeman, Frankie Muse [American attorney]
Spingarn Medal (table: 2011) So: 794
Freeman, Mary Eleanor Wilkins [American author] F: 509
Freeman, Morgan [American actor]
Motion picture (Best performance by an actor in a supporting role: 2004) M: 862b
Freeman, Orville Lothrop [American political leader]
Agriculture, Department of (table) A: 161
Kennedy, John Fitzgerald (table) K: 266
Minnesota (table) M: 602
Mondale, Walter Frederick (Political career) M: 702
Freeman, R. Austin [English author]
Detective story (History) D: 162-163
Freeman, Walter [American psychiatrist]
Lobotomy L: 405
Freeman-Thomas, Freeman [British colonial official]
Willingdon, Marquess of W: 314
Freeman's Farm, Battles of [1777] *See* Saratoga, Battle of *in this index*
Freeman's Oath, The [book]
Daye, Stephen D: 54
Freemasonry *See* Masonry [organization] *in this index*
Freephone service
Telephone (Business services) T: 98
Freeport Doctrine [U.S. history]
Davis, Jefferson (Secretary of war) D: 48
Lincoln, Abraham (The debates with Douglas) L: 317
Freer, Charles Lang [American businessman]
Freer Gallery of Art F: 509
Freer Gallery of Art [Washington, D.C.] F: 509
Smithsonian Institution (Museums) S: 519
Washington, D.C. *map on* W: 76; (Smithsonian museums) W: 71-72
Freesia [plant] F: 509 *with picture*
Freeskiing [competition]
Skiing (Alpine competitions) S: 486-487
Freestall barn
Barn B: 113
Freestone [rock]
Limestone L: 308
Freestone peach [fruit]
Peach (Cultivars) P: 210
Freestyle competition
Olympic Games (Winter Olympic Games) O: 746d
Swimming (Kinds of races) So: 1044
Freestyle wrestling
Wrestling (Chief forms of wrestling) W: 505
Freethinker [philosophy] F: 509
Freetown [Sierra Leone] F: 510
Sierra Leone S: 450 *with picture*
Freeway [road]
See also Expressway *in this index*
Automobile *picture on* A: 968
Los Angeles (Transportation) L: 465
Road (Primary highways) R: 358
Traffic (Traffic problems) T: 365-366
Freeze-drying [industrial process] F: 510
Coffee (Instant coffee) Ci: 754
Dehydrated food D: 93
Food preservation (Freeze-drying) F: 343
Taxidermy (Process of mounting) T: 56
Freezer
Food, Frozen F: 338
Ice cream (How ice cream is made) I: 8 *with diagram*
Freezer burn
Food, Frozen (Packaging) F: 339
Freezing
Cryobiology Ci: 1165
Fishing industry (Methods of processing) F: 186
Food, Frozen F: 337
Food preservation (Freezing) F: 342
Frost F: 542
Ice I: 4
Water (Other desalting processes) W: 128
Freezing nucleus
Cloud (How clouds form) Ci: 708-709
Rain (The ice-crystal process) R: 124

Freezing point F: 510
Heat (Changes in state) H: 153 *with diagram*
Freezing rain
Ice storm I: 16
Freezing tip [medicine]
Cryobiology Ci: 1165
Frei Montalva, Eduardo [Chilean political leader]
Chile (Years of progress) C: 469
Freie Bühne [theater group]
Drama (Early realism) D: 338
Freight [shipping] F: 510
Containerization Ci: 1021
Railroad (Freight service) R: 106; (Rolling stock) R: 107-108 *with pictures*; (Freight operations) R: 109; (Leading countries in railroad transportation) R: 114
Transportation (Freight transportation) T: 395
Freight elevator
Elevator E: 234
Freight forwarder
Aviation (Aviation support industries) A: 985
Freight train
Locomotive (Kinds of locomotives) L: 414
Railroad (Freight service) R: 106 *with picture*; (Rolling stock) R: 107-108 *with pictures*
Freighter [ship]
See also Cargo ship *in this index*
Ship (Roman ships) S: 416
Freischütz, Der [opera by Weber]
Opera (Romanticism) O: 798
Weber, Carl Maria von W: 175
Fréjus Peak [mountain, France-Italy]
Fréjus Tunnels F: 510
Fréjus Tunnels [France-Italy] F: 510
France (Transportation) F: 470
Tunnel (table) T: 491
Frelimo [political organization]
Mozambique (Government) M: 904; (History) M: 905-906
Frelinghuysen, Frederick T. [American government official]
Arthur, Chester Alan (table) A: 756
Frelinghuysen, Theodore [American political leader]
Polk, James Knox (Election of 1844) P: 642
Frelinghuysen, Theodore J. [German-American religious leader]
Great Awakening G: 335
Fremantle, Sir Charles Howe [British explorer]
Australia (Mapping the continent) A: 922
Frémont, Jessie Benton [wife of]
Frémont, John Charles F: 511
Frémont, John Charles [American explorer] F: 511 *with portrait*
California (The Mexican War) C: 60
Carson, Kit (Rise to prominence) C: 250
Civil War, American (Developments in the political party system) Ci: 616
Lake Tahoe L: 46
Nevada (Exploration) N: 173-174
Republican Party (The election of 1856) R: 253
Westward movement in America (Exploration) W: 248
Wyoming (Exploration) W: 533
Fremont Bridge [Oregon]
Bridge (table: Steel arch) B: 603
French, Augustus C. [American political leader]
Illinois (table) I: 71
French, Daniel Chester [American sculptor] F: 511
Lincoln Memorial L: 328 *with picture*
French, John Denton Pinkstone [British general]
Edward VIII E: 113
French Academy [organization] F: 511
Institute of France I: 305
Metric system (Creation of the metric system) M: 441
Weights and measures (The metric system) W: 187
French-American Committee for the Restoration of the Statue of Liberty
Statue of Liberty (Repairs and changes) So: 878
French and Indian War [1754-1763]
See also Seven Years' War *in this index*
French and Indian wars (The French and Indian War) F: 512 *with picture and map*
Acadia A: 21
Braddock, Edward B: 542 *with picture*
Canada, History of (The colonial wars) C: 141
Fort Duquesne F: 412
Fort Stanwix National Monument F: 416
France (The age of absolutism) F: 473
Franklin, Benjamin (The Plan of Union) F: 489
Indiana (Exploration and settlement) I: 215
Maine (Indian wars) M: 89
New France (The British conquest) N: 205
Ohio (Exploration and settlement) O: 700
Pontiac P: 657

Quebec, Battle of **Q**: 37
Revolution, American (Background and causes of the revolution) **R**: 271
Rogers's Rangers **R**: 401
Tennessee (Exploration) **T**: 153
United Kingdom (The growing empire) **U**: 67
United States, History of the (The French and Indian War) **U**: 158
Washington, George (Messenger to the French) **W**: 93-94 *with picture*
French and Indian wars [1689-1763] **F**: 511 *with picture and map*
Canada, History of (The colonial wars) **C**: 141
Colonial life in America (The struggle for land) **Ci**: 793
France (The age of absolutism) **F**: 473
Indian, American (In Canada) **I**: 178
Indian wars (The French and Indian wars [1689-1763]) **I**: 191
Massachusetts (The French and Indian wars) **M**: 291
Michigan (British control) **M**: 508
New Hampshire (French and Indian wars) **N**: 224
New York (Under English rule) **N**: 314-315
Smallpox **S**: 513
French bulldog [dog] **F**: 513
Dog *picture on* **D**: 275
French Cameroun [former colony]
British Cameroons **B**: 611
Cameroon (History) **C**: 86
French Canadian cattle
Cattle (Other dairy cattle) **C**: 311
French Canadians [people]
Canada (Ancestry) **C**: 105
Civil rights (Civil rights in other countries) **Ci**: 610
Flag *picture on* **F**: 218
Laurier, Sir Wilfrid **L**: 123
Montreal (Ethnic groups) **M**: 772
Quebec (Population) **Q**: 14
French chalk
Soapstone **So**: 543
French coach horse
Horse (table: Some types and breeds of horses) **H**: 343
French combing length
Wool (Sorting and grading) **W**: 400
French Communist Party
France (Politics) **F**: 455
French Community
French West Africa (History) **F**: 528
French Connection, The [film]
Motion picture (Best picture: 1971) **M**: 861
French Dickens [name for]
Daudet, Alphonse **D**: 43
French East India Company [French history]
East India Company **E**: 40
French Equatorial Africa [former colony] **F**: 514 *with map*
Central African Republic **C**: 352
Chad (History) **C**: 367
Gabon (History) **G**: 3
French Foreign Legion
Foreign Legion **F**: 386
French Guiana [territory, South America] **F**: 514 *with pictures and map*
Indian, American (Indians of the Tropical Forest) **I**: 175
French Guinea [former colony]
French West Africa **F**: 527
Guinea (History) **G**: 432
French horn [musical instrument] **F**: 516 *with pictures*
Horn **H**: 339
Music *picture on* **M**: 949; (Wind instruments) **M**: 949
French Indochina [former colony]
Indochina **I**: 224
Vientiane **V**: 363
French language F: 516
Canada (Languages) **C**: 106
Civil rights (Civil rights in other countries) **Ci**: 610
Congo, Democratic Republic of the (Languages) **Ci**: 938-939
Dialect **D**: 180
English language (Middle English) **E**: 313
French Academy **F**: 511
Manitoba (Language rights) **M**: 163
Montreal (Social problems) **M**: 773
Phonetics (Phonetics and spelling) **P**: 400
Quebec (The people) **Q**: 35
French Language, Charter of the
Quebec (The late 1900's) **Q**: 32
French literature F: 518 *with pictures*
See also the list of Related articles in the French Literature *article*
Classicism (France) **Ci**: 653
Drama (French neoclassical drama) **D**: 333;

(France) **D**: 335; (Romanticism) **D**: 337; (French drama) **D**: 339
Novel (France) **N**: 573; (The modern novel) **N**: 573-574
French marigold [plant]
Flower *picture on* **F**: 276
French National Committee [World War II]
De Gaulle, Charles André Joseph Marie (Leader of the Free French) **D**: 91
French Open [tournament]
Tennis (table: French Open) **T**: 166a
French overture [music]
Lully, Jean-Baptiste **L**: 516
Overture **O**: 882
French pastry [food]
Pastry **P**: 194
French Polynesia [territory, Pacific] **F**: 524
Marquesas Islands **M**: 217
Society Islands **So**: 563
Tuamotu Islands **T**: 476
French provincial style
Furniture *picture on* **F**: 576
French Quarter [district]
Louisiana (Population) *picture on* **L**: 482; (Visitor's guide) **L**: 488
New Orleans (Downtown New Orleans) **N**: 278 *with picture*
French Revolution [1789-1799] **F**: 524 *with pictures*
Adams, John (Difficulties with France) **A**: 38
Bastille **B**: 158
Charles X [of France] **C**: 382
Clothing (Protection) **Ci**: 686-687; (The 1700's) **Ci**: 703-704
Danton, Georges-Jacques **D**: 34
Democracy (French contributions to democracy) **D**: 122-123
Estates-General **E**: 360
Europe (Revolution, democracy, and nationalism) **E**: 412
Fashion (Why fashions change) **F**: 51
France (The French Revolution) **F**: 474 *with picture*
Freedom (During the Enlightenment) **F**: 503
Girondists **G**: 200
Government (The Enlightenment) **G**: 290-291
Guillotine **G**: 429
Italy (The French Revolution and Napoleon) **I**: 514
Jacobins **J**: 20
Jefferson, Thomas (Minister to France) **J**: 81
Lafayette, Marquis de (The revolution at home) **L**: 28
Louis XV **L**: 475
Louis XVI **L**: 476
Marie Antoinette (The revolution) **M**: 200
"Marseillaise" **M**: 227
Mirabeau, Comte de **M**: 614
Napoleonic Wars (Background) **N**: 18
Paine, Thomas (French revolutionary) **P**: 22
Paris (The Renaissance) **P**: 166
Pitt, William, the Younger **P**: 500
Radicalism (In Europe) **R**: 82
Reign of Terror **R**: 207
Rights of Man, Declaration of the **R**: 340
Robespierre **R**: 366
Roland de la Platière, Marie Jeanne **R**: 401
Roman Catholic Church (The decline of church influence) **R**: 410
Terrorism (The beginnings of modern terrorism) **T**: 178
Tuileries **T**: 481
United Kingdom (The Napoleonic Wars) **U**: 68
Versailles, Palace of **V**: 339
Washington, George (Neutrality proclamation) **W**: 105
Women's movement (Forces of change) **W**: 384
World, History of the (The rise of democracy and nationalism) **W**: 443-444 *with picture*
French Revolution, The [book by Carlyle]
Carlyle, Thomas (Early career) **C**: 240
French Revolutionary calendar
Month **M**: 767
French Royal Banner
Flag *picture on* **F**: 216
French Shore [region]
Newfoundland and Labrador (War with France) **N**: 375
French Somaliland
Djibouti **D**: 256
Somaliland **So**: 590
French style ice cream
Ice cream (The composition of ice cream) **I**: 8
French Sudan [African history]
French West Africa **F**: 528; (History) **F**: 528
Mali (History) **M**: 108-109
French Territory of the Afars and Issas
Djibouti **D**: 256

French Togoland [African history]
Togo (History) **T**: 310-311
French Union [African history]
French West Africa (History) **F**: 528
French West Africa [African history] **F**: 527 *with map*
Senegal (History) **S**: 299
French West Indies [territory, Caribbean] **F**: 528
Frenchman Butte National Historic Site [Sakatchewan]
Canada (table: National historic sites) **C**: 114
Frenchtown [former name]
War of 1812 (Raisin River) **W**: 33
Freneau, Philip [American author] **F**: 528
Columbia **Ci**: 851
Frenette, Ray [Canadian political leader]
New Brunswick (table) **N**: 195
Frenulum [zoology]
Moth **M**: 837
Freon [compound]
Chlorofluorocarbon **C**: 517
FREPASO [political party]
Argentina (Politics) **A**: 647
Frequency [marketing]
Advertising (Media selection) **A**: 76a
Frequency [physics]
Acoustics **A**: 28
Antenna **A**: 543
Astronomy (Frequency) **A**: 839
Ear (The sense of hearing) **E**: 9; (How sounds reach the brain) **E**: 10
Electric current (Direct and alternating current) **E**: 168
Electric generator (A simple generator) **E**: 170
Electronics (Transistors) **E**: 212
Hertz **H**: 217
Kilohertz **K**: 317
Light (How light is produced) **L**: 283; (The spectrum of light sources) **L**: 284 *with diagram*; (Light and measurement) **L**: 290
Metric system (Space and time) **M**: 437
Pitch **P**: 498
Radiation (Electromagnetic radiation) **R**: 75
Radio (From sound waves to electric waves) **R**: 86
Radio, Amateur **R**: 95
Radio wave **R**: 97
Sound (table) **So**: 599; (Frequency and pitch) **So**: 599 *with diagrams*
Television (Broadcasting) **T**: 123
Ultrasound **U**: 16
Vibration **V**: 347
Waves (Measuring waves) **W**: 152
Weather (Weather radar) **W**: 162-163
Frequency analysis
Codes and ciphers (Communications intelligence) **Ci**: 750
Frequency band [radio]
Broadband communication **B**: 635
Communications satellite (How communications satellites work) **Ci**: 888b
Frequency-modulated continuous-wave radar
Radar (Continuous-wave radar) **R**: 69
Frequency modulation [radio] **F**: 528
Antenna **A**: 543
Radio (Transmitting radio waves) **R**: 86 *with diagram*
Static **So**: 867
Wireless communication (How wireless communication works) **W**: 344
Frère Jean [literary figure]
Rabelais, François **R**: 49
Fresco [art] **F**: 529 *with picture*
Architecture (Medieval architecture) **A**: 617
Byzantine art (Frescoes and mosaics) **B**: 750 *with picture*
Catacombs **C**: 297
Greece, Ancient *picture on* **G**: 373
Leonardo da Vinci (Paintings) **L**: 200b-201
Michelangelo (The Sistine Chapel) **M**: 484
Mural **M**: 929 *with picture*
Painting (Fresco painting) **P**: 38
Renaissance (Arts of the 1300's and early 1400's) **R**: 236
Fresco secco
Painting (Fresco painting) **P**: 38
Fresh air
Ventilation **V**: 309
Fresh cow
Cattle (Breeding) **C**: 312
Fresh 1 [boat]
Hydrofoil (History) **H**: 468
"Fresh Prince of Bel Air" [TV show]
Smith, Will **So**: 518
Fresh water
Hydrosphere **H**: 472
Water **W**: 116
Freshness labeling

Consumer protection (The right to information)
Ci: 1018
Freshwater crocodile
Crocodile (Kinds of crocodiles) Ci: 1149-1150
Freshwater eel
Eel E: 114
Freshwater eelgrass [plant]
Eelgrass E: 115
Freshwater fish
Fish (Freshwater environments) F: 150; (How fish adjust to change) F: 168
Freshwater marsh
Marsh M: 228
Freshwater snail
Snail (Where snails live) S: 522 *with picture*
Fresnel, Augustin J. [French physicist]
Lighthouse (Development of the lighthouse)
L: 294-295
Optics (History) O: 813
Physics (Developments in the 1800's) P: 440
Radiation (History) R: 80
Fresnel lens
Lighthouse (Development of the lighthouse)
L: 294-295
Fresno [California] F: 529
Fret [musical instrument]
Guitar G: 436 *with pictures*
Sitar S: 477
FRETILIN [organization]
East Timor E: 41
Freud, Anna [Austrian psychiatrist] F: 530
Freud, Sigmund [Austrian psychiatrist] F: 530 *with portrait*
See also Freudian theory *in this index*
Abnormal psychology (Psychodynamic theories)
A: 12; (History) A: 12
Autograph A: 943
Biography (Modern biography) B: 314
Doolittle, Hilda D: 309
Dream (The meaning and function of dreams)
D: 345
Enlightenment (Criticism of the Enlightenment)
E: 326b
Erikson, Erik Homburger E: 352
Horney, Karen H: 340
Hypnosis (Scientific studies) H: 480
Jung, Carl Gustav J: 194
Memory (Motivated forgetting) M: 393
Mental illness (Medical approaches) M: 409
Mythology (Psychological approaches)
M: 990
Neurosis N: 153
Oedipus complex O: 677
Painting (Surrealism) P: 81
Personality (Freud's psychoanalytic theory) P: 302 *with picture*
Psychoanalysis P: 846
Psychology (Psychoanalysis) P: 850
Psychotherapy (Psychodynamic-interpersonal psychotherapy) P: 852
Religion (Earlier theories) R: 218
Unconscious U: 20
Freudenthal, Dave [American political leader]
Wyoming (table) W: 532
Freudian theory [psychology]
See also Psychoanalysis *in this index*
Personality (Freud's psychoanalytic theory)
P: 302
Psychoanalysis (Psychoanalytic theory) P: 846
Frey [Norse mythology] F: 531
Vikings (Religion) V: 380
Freyja [Norse mythology] F: 531
Vikings (Religion) V: 380
Freyr [Norse mythology]
Frey F: 531
Freyssinet, Eugene [French engineer]
Cement and concrete (History) C: 345
Friar [religion] F: 531
Capuchins C: 199
Dominicans D: 305
Franciscans F: 482
Friar Bacon and Friar Bungay [play by Greene]
Drama (Elizabethan playwrights) D: 331-332
Greene, Robert G: 382
Friar Tuck [literary figure]
Robin Hood R: 367
Friars Minor [religious group]
Franciscans F: 482
Friar F: 532
Fricative sound
Lisping L: 349
Frick, Ford [American baseball commissioner]
Baseball (table: Hall of Fame) B: 134
Frick, Henry Clay [American businessman]
Carnegie, Andrew (Rise to wealth) C: 242; (The Homestead Strike) C: 242
Frick Collection F: 532

Goldman, Emma G: 258
Frick, Wilhelm [Nazi official]
Hitler, Adolf (Rise of the Nazis) H: 266
Frick Art Reference Library
Frick Collection F: 532
Frick Collection [New York City] F: 532
New York City (Museums) N: 338
Fricka [opera character]
Opera: *(Ring of the Nibelung, The)* O: 806-807
Fricker, Brenda [Irish actress]
Motion picture (Best performance by an actress in a supporting role: 1989) M: 862b
Friction [movement]
Massage M: 295
Friction [physics] F: 532
Aerodynamics (Friction drag) A: 86
Brake B: 560
Fire (Methods of starting fires) F: 121
Heat (Sources of heat) H: 149
Machine (Efficiency) M: 14
Motion (Motion in everyday life) M: 844
Friction drag
Aerodynamics (Friction drag) A: 86
Friction ridge [forensic science]
Forensic science (Fingerprints) F: 389
Frictional unemployment
Unemployment (Types of unemployment) U: 22
Friday [day] F: 532
Islam (The Five Pillars of Islam) I: 463-464
Friday [literary figure]
Robinson Crusoe R: 369
Friday Harbor Laboratory [California]
Marine biology (What marine biologists do)
M: 204-205
Friday Island
Torres Strait Islands T: 343
Friday mosque [building]
Mosque M: 830
"Friday Night Fights" [television program]
Boxing (The 1950's) B: 532a
Fried, Alfred Hermann [Austrian author]
Nobel Prizes (Peace: 1911) N: 448
Friedan, Betty [American social reformer] F: 532 *with portrait*
Feminism F: 70
National Organization for Women N: 42
Women's movement (Decline after 1920)
W: 385-386
Friedkin, William [American director]
Motion picture (Best achievement in directing: 1971) M: 862
Friedland, Battle of [1807]
Napoleon I (Dominates Europe) N: 15
Friedland, Duke of [Bohemian military leader]
See Wallenstein, Albrecht Wenzel Eusebius von *in this index*
Friedlander, Lee [American photographer]
Photography (A diversity of styles) P: 426-427
Friedman, Jerome Isaac [American physicist]
Kendall, Henry Way K: 258
Nobel Prizes (Physics: 1990) N: 442
Friedman, Milton [American economist] F: 533
Chicago, University of (Research program) C: 438
Economics (Modern economics) E: 64-65
Laissez faire L: 31
Voucher V: 451
Friedrich, Caspar David [German artist]
Painting (Romanticism) P: 68 *with picture*
Friedrichstrasse, Berlin [painting by Kirchner]
Expressionism *picture on* E: 455
Painting (Expressionism) P: 78-79
Friel, Brian [Irish dramatist] F: 533
Irish literature (Drama) I: 432
Friending [computing]
Facebook (Uses) F: 4
Internet (Social networking websites) I: 350b
Friendly Island
Hawaii (Molokai) H: 100
Friendly Islands
Tonga T: 327
Friendly Persuasion [film]
Cooper, Gary Ci: 1034
Friendly Persuasion, The [book by West]
West, Jessamyn W: 198
Friendly society [economics]
Fraternal organization (History) F: 495
Friendly take-over [business]
Business (Recent developments) B: 727
Merger M: 417
Friends, Religious Society of [religious group] See Quakers *in this index*
Friends of the Library
Library (Supporting the public library) L: 242-243
Friends Service Council [organization]
Nobel Prizes (Peace: 1947) N: 448a
Friends World Committee for Consultation [organization]

Quakers (Worship) Q: 5
Friendship Bridge [Brazil-Paraguay]
Paraguay (Transportation and communication)
P: 148
Friendship Hill National Historic Site [Pennsylvania]
National Park System (table: National historic sites) N: 52-53
Friendship Pipeline
Pipeline (In other countries) P: 491-492
Friendship 7 [spacecraft]
Glenn, John Herschel, Jr. G: 226; (Glenn's historic flight) G: 226 *with picture*
Friesland [province]
Netherlands (Language) N: 139
Frietchie, Barbara [literary figure] F: 533
Frieze [decoration]
Architecture (table) A: 608-609 *with picture;* (Minoan architecture) A: 615
Parthenon P: 183
Frieze rug
Rugs and carpets (Kinds of rugs and carpets)
R: 514-515 *with picture*
Frigate [ship] F: 533 *with diagram*
Destroyer D: 162
Navy (Frigates) N: 78
Navy, United States (Combat ships) N: 84
Warship (Frigates) W: 40
Frigatebird F: 534 *with picture*
Bird *picture on* B: 356; (Birds of the ocean and the Antarctic) B: 344 *with picture*
Frigg [Norse mythology]
Balder B: 38
Friday F: 532
Frijoles [food]
Mexico (Food and drink) M: 456
Frill [anatomy]
Triceratops T: 441
Frilled lizard
Lizard (Defenses) L: 400 *with picture*
Friml, Rudolf [Austrian-American composer] F: 534
Musical comedy (The first musicals) M: 959
Fringe [light] See Interference fringe *in this index*
Fringe benefit [compensation]
Careers (Probable earnings) C: 216
Labor movement (Arranging contracts) L: 4-5
Medicine (The United States) M: 367
Pension P: 272
Profit sharing P: 811
Wages and hours (Wages) W: 2-3
Fringe-toed lizard
Desert *picture on* D: 155
Fringed gentian [plant]
Flower *picture on* F: 285, *picture on* F: 285
Fringed lizard
Lizard (How lizards move) L: 399-400
Fringing reef
Coral reef (Kinds of coral reefs) Ci: 1048b
Frisbee F: 534
Frisch, Frankie [American baseball player]
Baseball (table: Hall of Fame) B: 134
Frisch, Karl von [Austrian zoologist] F: 534
Frisch, Max [Swiss author] F: 535
German literature (Postwar German literature [1945-1990]) G: 142
Frisch, Otto R. [Austrian physicist]
Fermi, Enrico F: 74
Hahn, Otto H: 7
Meitner, Lise M: 387
Nuclear energy (Artificial fission) N: 590
Strassmann, Fritz So: 918
Frisch, Ragnar [Norwegian economist] F: 535
Econometrics E: 57
Tinbergen, Jan T: 294
Frisian [language]
Netherlands (Language) N: 139
Frist, Bill [American political leader] F: 535
Fritchie, Barbara [American public figure]
Frietchie, Barbara F: 533
Frith, William Powell [British artist]
Painting (Painting outside France) P: 72
Fritillary [butterfly]
Butterfly (Brush-footed butterflies) B: 736
Fritillary [plant] F: 535
Flower (Garden perennials grown from bulbs)
F: 280 *with picture*
Frito-Lay, Inc.
PepsiCo, Inc. P: 279
Fritz, Jean [American author]
Laura Ingalls Wilder Award (table) L: 121
Literature for children (Biography and autobiography) *picture on* L: 378
Regina Medal (table: 1985) R: 206
FRMP [genetics]
Fragile X syndrome F: 451
Fröbel, Friedrich Wilhelm August [German educator] F: 535

Kindergarten K: 317; (Early kindergartens) K: 319
Frobisher, Sir Martin [English explorer] **F: 535**
  Arctic (Search for the Northwest Passage)
    A: 638-639
  Exploration *map on* E: 443; (The search for a
    northern passage) E: 446
  Inuit (The arrival of Europeans) I: 354g
  Iqaluit I: 397
  Northwest Passage N: 528
  Nunavut (Arrival of the Europeans) N: 612
  Spanish Armada (The two fleets) So: 755-756
  Thanksgiving Day (Thanksgiving Day in Canada)
    T: 230
Frobisher Bay [former name]
  Iqaluit I: 397
  Northwest Passage N: 528
Frock coat
  Clothing *picture on* Ci: 705
Froebel, Friedrich [German educator] *See* Fröbel,
  Friedrich Wilhelm August *in this index*
Frog [anatomy]
  Horse (table: Horse terms) H: 343; (Legs and
    hoofs) H: 349
Frog [animal] **F: 536** *with pictures*
  Amphibian (Kinds of amphibians) A: 440 *with
    pictures*
  Animal *pictures on* A: 478, A: 490, A: 507
  Bullfrog B: 697
  Ear (The ears of animals) E: 12-13 *with picture*
  Egg (How embryos develop) E: 117
  Heart *diagram on* H: 146
  Larva L: 78 *with picture*
  Metamorphosis (Other examples) M: 428 *with
    pictures*
  Sound *picture on* So: 598
  Tadpole T: 6
  Tree frog T: 432 *with picture*
  Wetland *picture on* W: 253
Frogner Park [park, Oslo]
  Norway (Arts) N: 541 *with picture*
Frogs [play by Aristophanes]
  Aristophanes A: 663
Froissart, Jean [French historian] **F: 541**
  French literature (Early prose) F: 519
Frolic [party]
  Colonial life in America (Recreation) Ci: 802
Frolinat [group]
  Chad (History) C: 367
From Dawn to Decadence [book by Barzun]
  Barzun, Jacques B: 123
"From Greenland's Icy Mountains" [hymn]
  Mason, Lowell M: 266
From Here to Eternity [film]
  Motion picture (Best picture: 1953) M: 861
  Zinnemann, Fred Z: 595
From Immigrant to Inventor [book by Pupin]
  Pupin, Michael Idvorsky P: 905
From Madrigal to Modern Music [book by Moore]
  Moore, Douglas Stuart M: 796
From Morn to Midnight [play by Kaiser]
  Drama (Expressionism) D: 339
  Kaiser, Georg K: 210
From Slavery to Freedom [book by Franklin]
  Franklin, John Hope F: 492
*From the Dictatorship of Porfirio Díaz to the
  Revolution* [painting by Siqueiros]
  Painting *picture on* P: 40
From the Fifteenth District [book by Gallant]
  Gallant, Mavis G: 14
From the Founding of the City [book by Livy]
  History (The ancient Greeks and Romans)
    H: 261-262
From the Greeks to Darwin [book by Osborn]
  Osborn, Henry Fairfield O: 861
*From the Mixed-Up Files of Mrs. Basil E.
  Frankweiler* [book by Konigsburg]
  Konigsburg, Elaine K: 365
From the New World [music by Dvořák]
  Dvořák, Antonín D: 393
Fromm, Erich [German-American psychoanalyst]
  F: 541
Fromme, Lynette Alice [American public figure]
  Ford, Gerald Rudolph (Two attempted
    assassinations) F: 378
Frond [botany]
  Fern (Parts of a fern) F: 74-75 *with pictures*
  Plant (Ferns and related plants) P: 518-520
  Seaweed (Kinds) S: 276
Fronde [French history] **F: 541**
  Louis XIV L: 475
Frondizi, Arturo [Argentine political leader]
  Argentina (Argentina under Perón) A: 657-658
Front [weather]
  Air turbulence A: 200
  Bjerknes, Vilhelm B: 385
  Climate (Atmospheric circulation) Ci: 676a
  Cloud (How clouds form) Ci: 708-711

Derecho D: 152
Fog F: 314
Tornado (Air temperature) T: 334
Weather (table: Weather terms) W: 157;
  (Planetary-scale systems) W: 158-159;
  (Synoptic-scale systems) W: 159-160 *with
  diagrams*
Front bench [politics]
  Parliament (How the House of Commons works)
    P: 173
Front crawl
  Swimming *pictures on* So: 1044; (The basic
    strokes) So: 1043
Front de Libération du Québec [political group]
  Canada, History of (The Quebec separatist
    movement) C: 149; (The separatist threat)
    C: 150
  Montreal (The separatist movement) M: 779
  Quebec (The late 1900's) Q: 32
  Trudeau, Pierre Elliott (The national scene) T: 464
Front de Libération Nationale [political group]
  Algeria (Government) A: 360-361; (History)
    A: 364-365
Front for a Country in Solidarity [political party]
  Argentina (Politics) A: 647
Front for Liberation of Mozambique [political
  group] *See* Frelimo *in this index*
**Front for the Liberation of Occupied South
  Yemen** [political group]
  Yemen (Formation of South Yemen) Y: 563
Front fork
  Motorcycle (The parts of a motorcycle) M: 878
    with picture
Front group [organization]
  Money laundering M: 718
Front Islamique du Salut [political party]
  Algeria (Recent developments) A: 365
Front lighting
  Photography (Direction) P: 415 *with picture*
Front line [music]
  Jazz (The sound of jazz) J: 68 *with picture*
Front-line trench [warfare]
  World War I (The deadlock on the Western Front)
    W: 457
Front Page, The [play by Hecht and MacArthur]
  Hecht, Ben H: 164
"Front Page Challenge" [television program]
  Berton, Pierre B: 272
Front porch campaign [U.S. history]
  McKinley, William (The front-porch campaign)
    M: 340
Front Range [mountains]
  Colorado (Land regions) Ci: 838 *with map*
Front Street [Dodge City]
  Kansas (Places to visit) K: 226 *with picture*
Front-wheel drive
  Automobile (The drive system) A: 949
  Transmission (Transmissions and drives) T: 375
Frontal bone [anatomy]
  Face F: 3
  Head *diagram on* H: 123
  Human body (table) H: 422 *with diagram*
  Skull S: 495
Frontal cortex [brain]
  Mind (The mind/body problem) M: 563
Frontal fog [weather]
  Fog F: 314 *with diagram*
Frontal lifting [weather]
  Cloud (How clouds form) Ci: 708-711
Frontal lobe [anatomy]
  Brain (The cerebrum) B: 550a-550b *with diagram*
  Dream (The biology of dreams) D: 344-345
  Lobotomy L: 405
Frontal muscle [anatomy]
  Human body (table) H: 422 *with diagram*
Frontal sinus [anatomy]
  Sinus S: 474 *with diagram*
Frontenac [racing car]
  Chevrolet, Louis C: 415
Frontenac, Comte de [Canadian political leader]
  F: 541 *with picture*
  Canada, History of (The royal province) C: 140-
    141
  Jolliet, Louis (Discovery and exploration) J: 156
  Marquette, Jacques (Exploration and discovery)
    M: 218
Frontier [U.S. history]
  Boom town B: 475
  Pioneer life in America P: 476
  Turner, Frederick Jackson T: 515
  West, The W: 199
  Western frontier life in America W: 232
  Westward movement in America W: 244; (Closing
    of the frontier) W: 252; (The frontier influence)
    W: 252
Frontier Scout [newspaper]
  North Dakota (Communication) N: 512

Frontispiece
  Book (Inside a book) B: 464-465
Fronto [Roman scholar]
  Latin literature (The Imperial Period) L: 116-117
Fronto-temporal dementia [disorder]
  Alzheimer's disease (Causes) A: 399
Frosch, Paul [German bacteriologist]
  Löffler, Friedrich August Johannes L: 420
  Virus (Discovery) V: 427
Frost [weather] **F: 542** *with pictures*
  Fruit (Caring for the crop) F: 546-547
  Jack Frost J: 2
Frost, Jack [legendary figure]
  Jack Frost J: 2
Frost, Leslie M. [Canadian political leader]
  Ontario (table) O: 783
Frost, Robert [American poet] **F: 542** *with portrait*
  American literature (Realist poetry) A: 421 *with
    portrait*
  Autograph *picture on* A: 943
  Blank verse B: 398
Frostbite [injury] **F: 543**
  Dry ice D: 369
  First aid (Frostbite) F: 141
  Weather (Reporting the weather) W: 169-170
Frosting [hairdressing]
  Hairdressing (The 1900's) H: 12
Frostline [geology]
  House (The foundation) H: 380
Froude, James Anthony [British historian]
  Biography (The 1800's) B: 314
Frozen Charlotte [doll]
  Doll (Porcelain dolls) D: 290
Frozen food *See* Food, Frozen *in this index*
Frozen smoke [chemistry] *See* Carbon aerogel *in
  this index*
Frozen yogurt [food]
  Ice cream (The composition of ice cream) I: 8
FRS [organization] *See* Federal Reserve System *in
  this index*
Fructose [sugar] **F: 543**
  Carbohydrate (Kinds of carbohydrates) C: 203;
    (How the body uses carbohydrates) C: 204
  Corn syrup C: 1065
  Hydrolysis H: 471
  Jerusalem artichoke J: 102
  Nutrition (Carbohydrates) N: 625
  Sugar (Kinds of sugar) So: 960
Fruit F: **544** *with pictures*
  See also the list of Related articles in the Fruit *article*
  Angiosperm A: 462 *with picture*
  Antioxidant A: 557
  Farm and farming (Specialized crop farms) F: 30-
    31 *with picture*
  Flavonoid F: 230
  Food (Food from plants) F: 329
  Food, Frozen (Freezing food at home) F: 338-339
  Horticulture (Pomology) H: 369
  Lake (Climate) L: 33
  Nutrition (Carbohydrates) N: 625; (Nutrition
    guidelines) N: 626
  Plant (Seeds) P: 531
  Pruning P: 841
  Tree (Food products) T: 412; (Seeds) T: 417 *with
    pictures*
  Vegetable V: 292; (Fruits) V: 292 *with picture*
  Vegetarianism V: 294
  Wine W: 336
Fruit bat [animal]
  Bat (Fruit bats and flower-visiting bats) B: 161
    with picture
  Flying fox F: 312
Fruit-dove [bird]
  Bird (Birds of Asia) B: 344f *with picture*
Fruit fly [insect] **F: 549** *with picture*
  Apple maggot A: 573
  Compound eye *picture on* Ci: 906
  Genetic engineering (History) G: 84c
  Heredity (Chromosomes and genes) H: 201; (The
    birth of genetics) H: 208
  Insect *picture on* I: 291; (Wings) I: 288
  Mediterranean fruit fly M: 380 *with picture*
Fruit juice [drink]
  Wine W: 336
Fruit of Islam [organization]
  Nation of Islam N: 27
Fruit pigeon *See* Asian fruit pigeon *in this index*
Fruit sugar *See* Fructose *in this index*
Fruiting body
  Fungi (Parts of a fungus) F: 558-559 *with pictures*
  Mold M: 689
  Mushroom M: 941
Fruitlands [social reform]
  Alcott, Bronson A: 338
Frunze [former name]
  Bishkek B: 381
Frustration tolerance [psychology]

Baby (From 1 to 6 months) **B:** 7
Frustule [biology]
Diatom **D:** 186
Frustum [geometry]
Cone **Ci:** 931 *with diagram*
Fruticose lichen
Lichen **L:** 269
Fry [zoology]
Fish (How fish live) **F:** 165 *with picture*
Fry, Christopher [British dramatist] **F:** 549
Fry, Elizabeth Gurney [British social reformer]
F: 549
Newgate Prison **N:** 378
Fry, Joseph [American sea captain]
Virginius Affair **V:** 425
Fry, Joshua [English surveyor]
Map (Mapping the Americas) **M:** 184-185
Fry, Roger [English art critic]
Postimpressionism **P:** 709
Frye, Northrop [Canadian critic] **F:** 549
Mythology (Literary approaches) **M:** 990-991
Fryer [food]
Poultry (Raising poultry) **P:** 720
Frying
Cooking (Frying) **Ci:** 1028
Frying Pan-Arkansas Project [water system]
Colorado (The mid-1900's) **Ci:** 847
FSA [insurance]
Insurance (Other types of health insurance) **I:** 312
FSA [U.S. history] *See* Farm Security Administration
in this index
FSH [hormone] *See* Follicle-stimulating hormone
in this index
FSLIC [agency] *See* Federal Savings and Loan
Insurance Corporation *in this index*
FSM [country] *See* Micronesia, Federated States of
in this index
FSO [career]
Foreign Service (Personnel) **F:** 388
FT [train]
Locomotive *picture on* **L:** 416
Ft-lb [measurement] *See* Foot-pound *in this index*
FTC [agency] *See* Federal Trade Commission *in
this index*
FTP [computing] *See* File transfer protocol *in this
index*
Fu-chou [China]
Fuzhou **F:** 590
Fuad I [king of Egypt]
Faruk I **F:** 48
Fuchs, Leonhard [German botanist]
Fuchsia **F:** 550
Fuchs, Sir Vivian Ernest [British geologist] **F:** 549
Antarctica (The International Geophysical Year)
A: 538 *with map*
Exploration (The exploration of Antarctica) **E:** 450
with map
Fuchsia [plant] **F:** 549 *with picture*
Fudge-A-Mania [book by Blume]
Blume, Judy **B:** 425
Fuegians [people]
Tierra del Fuego **T:** 283
Fuel F: 550
See also the list of *Related articles* in the Fuel *article*
Agriculture (Fuel and raw materials) **A:** 148
Automobile (Power systems) **A:** 947-948
Environmental pollution *picture on* **E:** 333; (Air
pollution) **E:** 331
Ethanol **E:** 364
Fire (How fire is produced) **F:** 121
Fuel cell **F:** 551
Gas [fuel] (Gas as a fuel) **G:** 51
Global warming (Ways to limit global warming)
G: 232b
Guided missile (The engine) **G:** 424 *with diagrams*
Hydrogen (Uses) **H:** 469
Jet propulsion **J:** 110
Light **L:** 282
Methanol **M:** 434
Natural gas liquids **N:** 64
Petroleum **P:** 330
Plant (As raw materials) **P:** 517
Rocket (Kinds of rocket engines) **R:** 387-388 *with
diagrams*
Uranium **U:** 214
Western frontier life in America (Fuel) **W:** 238
Fuel-air explosive
Bomb (Fuel-air explosives [FAE's]) **B:** 451
Fuel assembly [device]
Nuclear energy (Power reactors) **N:** 584-585 *with
diagram*; (Fuel preparation) **N:** 586 *with picture*;
(Wastes and waste disposal) **N:** 588
Fuel cell [device] **F:** 551 *with diagram*
Automobile (The 2000's) **A:** 972-973 *with picture*
Automobile racing (Safety measures) **A:** 975-976
Cooper, Gordon **Ci:** 1034
Electric car **E:** 165

Electrochemistry **E:** 199
Electrolysis (Uses of electrolysis) **E:** 200-201
Energy supply (Fuel cells) **E:** 279
Gas [fuel] (The modern gas industry) **G:** 59
Global warming (Increased fuel efficiency)
G: 232b
Hybrid car **H:** 461
Hydrogen (Uses) **H:** 469
Fuel fabrication plant
Nuclear energy (Fuel preparation) **N:** 586
Uranium (Refining and processing uranium ore)
U: 215
Fuel injection [engineering] **F:** 552 *with diagram*
Automobile (The fuel system) **A:** 953 *with
diagram*
Catalytic converter **C:** 298
Gasoline engine *picture on* **G:** 63
Fuel line
Carburetor **C:** 208
Gasoline engine *picture on* **G:** 63; (The fuel
system) **G:** 65
Fuel nozzle
Carburetor **C:** 208
Fuel oil
Heating (Oil) **H:** 159
Fuel reservoir
Carburetor **C:** 208
Fuel rod
Nuclear energy (Power reactors) **N:** 584-585 *with
diagram*
Fuel shortage
Automobile (The rise of international
automaking) **A:** 972
Energy supply **E:** 277
Petroleum (The energy crisis) **P:** 349
Transportation (Declining fuel reserves) **T:** 397
Fuel system
Automobile *diagram on* **A:** 948; (The fuel system)
A: 953
Gasoline engine (The fuel system) **G:** 65
Fuentes, Carlos [Mexican author] **F:** 552
Latin American literature (The "Boom") **L:** 114
Fugard, Athol [South African author] **F:** 553
Drama (Drama in other countries) **D:** 341
Fugio cent
Cent **C:** 350
Fugitive slave laws [U.S. history] **F:** 553
Cary, Mary Ann Shadd **C:** 270
Civil War, American (The Compromise of 1850)
Ci: 616
Compromise of 1850 **Ci:** 907
Mississippi (The American Civil War) **M:** 642
Still, William **So:** 900
Underground railroad **U:** 20
United States, History of the (The Compromise of
1850) **U:** 175
Fugitives [literary group]
American literature (Modernist poetry) **A:** 421
Fugu [fish]
Puffer **P:** 885
Fugue [music] **F:** 553
Classical music (Fugue) **Ci:** 645
Counterpoint **Ci:** 1097
Fugue [psychology] *See* Psychogenic fugue *in this
index*
Fuhlrott, Johann K. [German anthropologist]
Prehistoric people (table) **P:** 754
Führer [title]
Hitler, Adolf (The New Order) **H:** 266-267
Fuji [apple]
Apple (Varieties of apples) **A:** 571
Fuji, Mount *See* Mount Fuji *in this index*
Fuji-Hakone-Izu National Park [Japan]
National park *picture on* **N:** 42c; (Japan) **N:** 42d;
(table) **N:** 42f
Fuji-san *See* Mount Fuji *in this index*
Fuji-yama *See* Mount Fuji *in this index*
Fujimori, Alberto [Peruvian political leader]
Peru (Peru under Fujimori) **P:** 316; (Recent
developments) **P:** 316
Fujimori, Keiko [Peruvian political leader]
Peru (Recent developments) **P:** 316-317
Fujita scale [measurement]
Tornado (Damage by tornadoes) **T:** 335; (table)
T: 336
Fujiwara [Japanese history]
World, History of the (The rise of Japanese
civilization) **W:** 435-436
Fukuda, Yasuo [Japanese political leader]
Japan (Recent developments) **J:** 59
Fukui, Kenichi [Japanese chemist]
Nobel Prizes (Chemistry: 1981) **N:** 444
Fukushima Daiichi Nuclear Power Station
Fallout (History) **F:** 19
Nuclear energy (Safety concerns) **N:** 591-592
Ful [food]
Egypt (Food and drink) **E:** 124

Sudan (Food and drink) **So:** 951
Sudan, South (People) **So:** 955
Fula [people] *See* Fulani *in this index*
Fulani [people] **F:** 553 *with picture*
Cameroon (People) **C:** 85
Gambia (People) **G:** 18
Guinea (People) **G:** 430; (History) **G:** 432
Hausa **H:** 86
Mali (People) **M:** 106
Niger (People) **N:** 407
Senegal (People) **S:** 297
Fulbright, J. William [American political leader]
F: 554
Fulbright Act [1946]
Fulbright scholarship **F:** 554
Fulbright scholarship [education] **F:** 554
Scholarship (International scholarships) **S:** 179
Fulcrum [mechanism]
Lever **L:** 217
Machine (Six simple machines) **M:** 14 *with
pictures*; (Mechanical advantage) **M:** 14 *with
picture*
Fuld, William [American inventor]
Ouija board **O:** 879
Fulgurite [rock]
Glass (Early times) **G:** 217-218
Fulks, Joe [American basketball player]
Basketball (Changes in the game) **B:** 151-152
Full bridle [riding equipment]
Horse (The bridle) **H:** 352
Full-fashioned fabric
Knitting machine **K:** 355
Full field digital mammography [medicine]
Mammography **M:** 130
Full house
Poker **P:** 603
Full moon
Blue moon **B:** 420
Moon (Phases) **M:** 783-784 *with picture*
Full retirement age
Social security (Benefits) **So:** 553
Fullback [sports]
Football (The offensive team) **F:** 356 *with
diagrams*
Soccer (The defenders) **So:** 545
Fuller, Alvin T. [American political leader]
Massachusetts (table) **M:** 288
Fuller, Buckminster [American engineer] **F:** 554
with picture
Architecture *picture on* **A:** 610
Fuller, Levi K. [American political leader]
Vermont (table) **V:** 333
Fuller, Margaret [American author] **F:** 554
American literature (Nonfiction prose) **A:** 418
Magazine (Magazines in the 1800's) **M:** 45
Fuller, Melville Weston [American jurist] **F:** 555
Fuller, Sarah [American educator]
Bell, Alexander Graham (The Boston teacher)
B: 240
Fullerene [molecule]
Carbon (Fullerenes) **C:** 205 *with diagram*
Fuller's earth [earth] **F:** 555
Fulling [industrial process]
Broadcloth **B:** 635
Fuller's earth **F:** 555
Wool (Making fabric) **W:** 401
Fullmoon maple [tree]
Maple (Other maples) **M:** 187
Fully submerged hydrofoil [boat]
Hydrofoil (Kinds of hydrofoils) **H:** 466-467 *with
diagram*
Fulmar [bird] **F:** 555
Fulton, Robert [American inventor] **F:** 555 *with
picture*
Clermont **Ci:** 662b
Pennsylvania (Industrial growth) **P:** 267
Ship (The first steamboats) **S:** 424
Submarine (Early submarines) **So:** 942
Torpedo (History) **T:** 341
Fulton, Robert D. [American political leader]
Iowa (table) **I:** 391
Fulton the First [ship]
Fulton, Robert (Builds the *Clermont*) **F:** 556
Fulton II [ship]
Perry, Matthew Calbraith **P:** 294
Fumarole [geology] **F:** 556
Fumble
Football (Advancing the ball) **F:** 360-362
Fumigant insecticide
Fumigation **F:** 556
Insecticide (Using insecticides) **I:** 302 *with picture*
Fumigation F: 556
Food preservation (Other methods) **F:** 344
Fuming sulfuric acid [chemical]
Sulfuric acid (Uses and properties) **So:** 968
Funafuti [island, Pacific] **F:** 556
Tuvalu **T:** 527 *with map*

Funan [ancient kingdom]
Cambodia (History) C: 72
Funchal [Madeira] F: 556
Madeira Islands (The island of Madeira) M: 30
Function [mathematics]
Algebra (Functions) A: 356
Calculus (Functions) C: 23; (The fundamental theorem of calculus) C: 25
Function key
Computer (A keyboard) Ci: 912
Keyboard K: 308 with picture
Function word [grammar]
Adjective (Comparison of adjectives) A: 57
English language (Grammar) E: 312
Grammar (Principles of English grammar) G: 303
Parts of speech P: 189
Functional constituency
Hong Kong (Government) H: 319
Functional food
Health food (Types of health foods) H: 129
Functional hypoglycemia [disorder]
Hypoglycemia H: 481
Functional illiteracy
Education (Literacy programs) E: 106
Literacy L: 350
Functional jurisdiction [law]
Government (Jurisdiction) G: 289
Functional learning [education]
Handwriting (Learning manuscript writing) H: 47
Functional literacy
Reading (The importance of reading) R: 155; (Reading and society) R: 162-163
Functional magnetic resonance imaging [medicine]
Brain (Imaging) B: 551
Magnetic resonance imaging M: 56 with picture
Functional murmur [physiology]
Heart murmur H: 147
Functional protein
Metabolism (Anabolism) M: 424
Functional type [classification]
Archaeology (Classification) A: 597-598
Functionalism
Anthropology (The early 1900's) A: 548
Sociology (Development of social research) So: 566
Fund [economics]
Endowment E: 273
Foundation F: 429
Fund-raising event
Election campaign (Campaign financing) E: 160
Fundamental boson [physics]
Boson B: 494
Subatomic particle (Elementary particles) So: 937
Fundamental force
Force (Kinds of force) F: 370
Subatomic particle (Fundamental forces) So: 936; (Theories of forces) So: 937-938
Fundamental frequency [sound]
Harmonics H: 62 with diagram
Pitch P: 498
Sound (Sound quality) So: 601
Fundamental Orders [U.S. history]
Connecticut Ci: 952; (Constitution) Ci: 967; (English settlement) Ci: 968
Hartford (Government and history) H: 78
Hooker, Thomas H: 324
Fundamental theorem of arithmetic
Gauss, Carl Friedrich G: 70
Number theory N: 607
Prime number (Facts about primes) P: 780
Fundamental theorem of calculus
Calculus (The fundamental theorem of calculus) C: 25; (History) C: 25
Fundamentalism [religion] F: 556
Evangelicalism E: 422
Islam (Divisions of Islam) I: 466
Protestantism (The modern evangelical and Pentecostal movements) P: 835
Religion (Religion today) R: 223
Fundamentals, The [religious history]
Evangelicalism E: 422
Fundamentalism (Development of Protestant fundamentalism) F: 556-557
Fundo [farm]
Chile (Rural life) C: 460-462
Fundy, Bay of See Bay of Fundy in this index
Fundy National Park [New Brunswick]
Canada (table: National parks and national park reserves) C: 113
National park (table) N: 42g
Funeral at Ornans, The [painting by Courbet] See Burial at Ornans, A in this index
Funeral customs F: 557
See also Burial in this index
Bell (Uses of bells) B: 239
Cremation Ci: 1126

Embalming E: 255
Flag (Permitted and prohibited uses) F: 222
Maya (Religion) M: 322-323
Mummy M: 925
Necropolis N: 117
Painting (Egyptian painting) P: 40-41
Pyramids (Egyptian pyramids) P: 916
Suttee So: 1013
Wake W: 5
Funeral home
Funeral customs (The funeral) F: 557
Funeral march
March M: 193
Funes, Mauricio [Salvadoran political leader]
El Salvador (Recent developments) E: 253
Fungal disease F: 558
See also the list of Related articles in the Fungal disease article
Disease (Other infectious diseases) D: 227
Lawn pictures on L: 143
Fungi [organisms] F: 558 with pictures
See also the list of Related articles in the Fungi article
Animal A: 468
Antibiotic (Other kinds of antibiotics) A: 550
Booklouse B: 474
Classification, Scientific (Groups in classification) Ci: 655
Disease (Other infectious diseases) D: 227
Forestry (Diseases and pests) F: 407
Fungal disease F: 558
Fungicide F: 560
Hay fever (Causes and prevention) H: 116
Kingdom K: 328
Lichen L: 269 with pictures
Life picture on L: 276
Mushroom M: 941 with pictures
Mycotoxin M: 970f
Plant (Roots) P: 528; (Diseases) P: 539
Rust So: 566b
Saprophyte S: 122
Spore (Algal and fungal spores) So: 802 with diagram
Fungicide [chemical] F: 560
Agriculture (Chemical pesticides) A: 159
Mildew M: 542
Pest control (Pesticides) P: 318
Potato (Potato pests) P: 713
Fungus See Fungi in this index
Fungus-growing ant
Ant pictures on A: 520, A: 528; (Fungus-growing ants) A: 527
Funj Sultanate [former empire] F: 560
Sudan (History) So: 952-953
Funk, Casimir [Polish biochemist]
Vitamin (History) V: 432
Funky jazz
Jazz (Hard bop) J: 72
Funnel [smokestack]
Ship diagram on S: 405, pictures on S: 426
Funnel [zoology]
Squid (The body of a squid) So: 814 with diagram
Funnel cloud
Tornado T: 333 with pictures
Funnel gauge [meteorology]
Rain (Measuring rainfall) R: 125
Funnel weaver [spider]
House spider H: 388
Spider (Funnel weavers) So: 789
Funnel-web spider
Spider (Dangerous spiders) So: 790
Funnies See Comics in this index
Funny bone [anatomy] F: 560
Funny Car
Automobile racing (Drag racing) A: 978
Funny Girl [musical]
Brice, Fanny B: 597
Funny Thing Happened on the Way to the Forum, A [musical]
Sondheim, Stephen So: 591
Funston, Frederick [American general] F: 560
Fuqua, Henry L. [American political leader]
Louisiana (table) L: 496
Fur F: 561 with pictures
See also Coat [zoology]; Fur trade in this index
Camel (Camels and people) C: 77; (The body of a camel) C: 77
Hair H: 9
Fur [people]
Sudan (People) So: 951
Fur Products Labeling Act [1952]
Fur (Cutting and sewing) F: 563
Fur ranch
Fur F: 561; (Fur ranching) F: 562
Fur seal [sea animal]
Alaska (Plant and animal life) A: 295-296 with picture

Animal picture on A: 500
Antarctica (Living things) A: 534-535 with picture
Mammal picture on M: 116
Pribilof Islands P: 774
Seal (Eared seals) S: 265 with picture; (Seals in captivity) S: 267
Fur trade [American history] F: 563 with picture and map
Alaska (Fur industry) A: 298
Alberta (The fur trade) A: 329
Astor, John Jacob A: 825
Canada, History of (Start of the fur trade) C: 140 with pictures; (Exploration of the West) C: 143
Hudson's Bay Company H: 407
Indian, American (After European contact) I: 154
Indiana (Exploration and settlement) I: 215
New France (Colonial life) N: 204
North West Company N: 519
Fur Trade, Museum of the [Chadron]
Nebraska (Places to visit) N: 102
Furchgott, Robert Francis [American pharmacologist]
Nobel Prizes (Physiology or medicine: 1998) N: 446
Furcolo, Foster [American political leader]
Massachusetts (table) M: 288
Furfural [chemical] F: 566
Grain (Other uses) G: 301
Furfuraldehyde [chemical] See Furfural in this index
Furfuryl alcohol [chemical]
Furfural F: 566
Furies [mythology] F: 566 with pictures
Hades H: 4
Furies, The [play by Aeschylus]
Aeschylus A: 90
Furious [ship]
Aircraft carrier (History) A: 207
Furious Seasons [book by Carver]
Carver, Raymond C: 269
Furka Pass [Switzerland]
River R: 351 with picture
Furlong [measurement] F: 566
Horse racing (At the races) H: 365
Weights and measures (Miscellaneous weights and measures) W: 184; (Inch-pound units) W: 187
Furlough
Criminal justice system (Problems in the correctional system) Ci: 1144
Furman v. Georgia [U.S. history]
Capital punishment (History of capital punishment) C: 193
Supreme Court of the United States (Criminal law) So: 1001; (table) So: 1002
Furnace F: 567 with diagram
Heating (Warm-air heating) H: 157
Iron and steel I: 436 with picture; (How steel is made) I: 441 with diagrams
Steam engine (How steam engines work) So: 880
Furnas, Robert W. [American political leader]
Nebraska (table) N: 110
Furness, H. H. [American author]
Shakespeare, William (Editions of the 1700's and 1800's) S: 369
"Furnished Room, The" [story by O. Henry]
Henry, O. (His works) H: 189
Furniture F: 568 with pictures
See also the list of Related articles in the Furniture article
Antique (Furniture) A: 558 with picture
Bauhaus picture on B: 173
Colonial life in America (Furnishings) Ci: 797; (Decorative arts) Ci: 807 with picture
Folk art (Household objects) F: 318 with picture
Grand Rapids G: 309
Interior design I: 326 with pictures
Ironwork, Decorative picture on I: 454
Lacquer L: 22
Mahogany M: 66
Paint (Industrial paints) P: 24
Pioneer life in America (Furniture and household utensils) P: 481 with picture
Sweden (Industrial design) So: 1027
White House pictures on W: 288
Wicker W: 298
Furniture City [name for]
Grand Rapids G: 309
Furrow irrigation
Irrigation (Surface irrigation) I: 457-458 with picture
Vegetable (Irrigation) V: 293
Furrow mining
Mining (Surface mining methods) M: 575 with diagram
Furtwängler, Wilhelm [German conductor] F: 588
Furze [shrub] F: 588 with picture
Fus-hā [dialect] See Modern Standard Arabic in

this index
Fusarium wilt [fungus]
Pea (Diseases and pests) **P: 205**
Watermelon **W: 146**
Fuse [explosives] **F: 588**
Ammunition (How shells explode) **A: 436**
Bomb (How bombs work) **B: 450** *with diagrams*
Depth charge **D: 151**
Fireworks (How fireworks work) **F: 135**
Mine warfare (Land mines) **M: 564**
Fuse [electricity] **F: 589** *with diagrams*
Electric circuit **E: 166**
Electricity (Controlling electric current) **E: 195**
House (Electrical wiring) **H: 382**
Fused silica glass
Glass (Fused silica glass) **G: 213**
Fusee [flare]
Fireworks (Other uses of fireworks) **F: 135**
Fuselage [aviation]
Airplane (The fuselage) **A: 214** *with picture*
Glider (The fuselage) **G: 228**
Fusible metal
Bismuth **B: 383**
Fusil [symbol]
Heraldry *picture on* **H: 195**
Fusion [optics]
Eye (Depth perception) **E: 463-464**
Fusion [physics] **F: 589**
Alpha particle **A: 381**
E=mc² **E: 3**
Energy supply *picture on* **E: 282**; (Nuclear energy) **E: 278**
Fuel (Nuclear fuels) **F: 551**
Glass (Specialty glasses) **G: 212-213**
Hydrogen (Occurrence) **H: 469**
Laser (Heating) **L: 82-83**
Nova **N: 553**
Nuclear energy (Nuclear fusion) **N: 583** *with diagram*; (Experimental fusion devices) **N: 592** *with pictures*
Nuclear physics **N: 595**
Nuclear weapon (Thermonuclear weapons) **N: 597**
Petroleum (The future of petroleum) **P: 349**
Physics (Nuclear physics) **P: 437**
Plasma **P: 552**
Radiation (In industry) **R: 75**; (The sun and other stars) **R: 77** *with diagram*
Star (Fusion in stars) **So: 846**; (Evolution of stars) **So: 848**; (High-mass stars) **So: 849-850**
Sun (Nuclear fusion) **So: 978**
Supernova (Thermonuclear supernovae) **So: 994**
Transmutation of elements **T: 379**
White dwarf **W: 285**
Fusion inhibitor [drug]
AIDS (Treatment) **A: 164b-165**
Fusion jazz
Davis, Miles **D: 49**
Jazz (Fusion) **J: 73**
Fusion Party [political party]
Australia (Building a nation) **A: 923**
Fusion reactor
Hydrogen (Uses) **H: 469-470**
Magnetohydrodynamics **M: 62**
Nuclear energy (Experimental fusion devices) **N: 592** *with pictures*
Fusion weapon *See* Nuclear weapon *in this index*
Fusion welding
Welding (Fusion welding) **W: 189** *with picture*
Fussell, Jacob [American businessman]
Ice cream (History) **I: 9**
Fust, Johannes [German printer]
Gutenberg, Johannes **G: 444**
Futabatei, Shimei [Japanese author]
Japanese literature (The modern period) **J: 62**
Futebol [sport]
Brazil (Recreation) **B: 575**
Futon [quilt]
Japan (Way of life) **J: 38**
Tokyo (Visitor's guide) **T: 316**
Futrell, Junius Marion [American political leader]
Arkansas (table) **A: 712**
Futrelle, Jacques [American author]
Detective story (History) **D: 162-163**
Future *See* Time *in this index*
Future Eve, The [book by Villiers de l'Isle Adam]
Villiers de l'Isle-Adam, Comte de **V: 385**
Future Farmers of America *See* FFA *in this index*
Future Farmers of Virginia
FFA (History) **F: 86**
Future perfect tense [grammar]
Tense **T: 168**
Future Shock [recording]
Hancock, Herbie **H: 38**
Future tense [grammar]
Tense **T: 168**
Futures contract [economics]

Commodity exchange (Forward and futures contracts) **Ci: 873**; (Financial futures) **Ci: 874**
Cotton (Selling) **Ci: 1091**
Wheat (Buying and selling wheat) **W: 274**
Futurism [art] **F: 589** *with pictures*
Boccioni, Umberto **B: 434**
Italian literature (The 1900's) **I: 495**
Italy (Arts) **I: 504-505** *with picture*
Russian literature (Post-symbolism) **R: 563**
Sculpture (Cubism and futurism) **S: 257**
Fuze [munitions] *See* Fuse *in this index*
Fuzhou [China] **F: 590**
Treaty port **T: 409**
Fuzing system
Guided missile (The warhead) **G: 423-424**
Torpedo (How a torpedo works) **T: 340d**
FXS [disorder] *See* Fragile X syndrome *in this index*
FYROM [country] *See* Macedonia *in this index*

G

G [letter] **G: 1** *with pictures*
C **C: 1**
G [physics] **G: 2**
Space exploration (Getting into space and back) **So: 698**
G [rating]
Motion picture (Censorship and self-regulation) **M: 860-861**
G-7 [organization]
Group of Twenty **G: 402**
G-8 [organization]
Group of Twenty **G: 403**
G-20 [organization] *See* Group of Twenty *in this index*
G clef [music]
Music (Indicating pitch) **M: 952-953** *with picture*
Treble **T: 409**
G-Men [FBI agents]
Federal Bureau of Investigation (History) **F: 62**
G scale
Railroad, Model (Scale and size) **R: 120**
GA [hormone]
Gibberellin **G: 185**
G.A. [organization] *See* Gamblers Anonymous *in this index*
Ga [people]
Accra **A: 24**
Ga [symbol]
Gallium **G: 16**
GAAP [accounting]
Accounting (Financial reports) **A: 22**
Gabbro
Rock (table) **R: 373** *with picture*
Gaberones [former name]
Gaborone **G: 4**
Gabirol, Solomon ibn [Hebrew poet]
Hebrew literature (Medieval works) **H: 162**
Gable, Clark [American actor] **G: 2** *with portrait*
Autograph *picture on* **A: 943**
Motion picture (Best performance by an actor: 1934) **M: 862a**
Gable roof
Roof **R: 450b** *with picture*
Gabo, Naum [Russian-born sculptor] **G: 2**
Pevsner, Antoine **P: 351**
Gabon **G: 2** *with map*
Flag *picture on* **F: 198**
French Equatorial Africa **F: 514**
Rain forest *picture on* **R: 126d**
Gabonese Democratic Party
Gabon (Government) **G: 3**
Gaboon adder [snake] *See* African Gaboon viper *in this index*
Gaboon viper [snake] *See* African Gaboon viper *in this index*
Gabor, Dennis [British engineer] **G: 4**
Holography **H: 298**
Gaborone [Botswana] **G: 4**
Gabriel [American slave revolt leader] **G: 4**
Gabriel [Biblical figure]
Annunciation **A: 518**
Islam **I: 463**
Jesus Christ (The Nativity) **J: 105**
Kaaba **K: 208**
Qur'ān **Q: 44**
Gabriel, Peter [British musician]
Rock music (World music) **R: 380d**
Gabrieli, Andrea [Italian composer]
Classical music (The Baroque period) **Ci: 647**
Gabrieli, Giovanni [Italian composer]
Classical music (The Baroque period) **Ci: 647**
Gaceta de Texas [newspaper]
Texas (Communication) **T: 203**
Gades [ancient city]
Phoenicia (Language) **P: 393**
Gadhafi, Mu'ammar Muhammad al- [Libyan political leader] *See* Qadhāfī, Mu'ammar

Muhammad al- *in this index*
Gadolin, Johan [Finnish chemist]
Gadolinium **G: 4**
Gadolinite [mineral]
Gadolinium **G: 4**
Rhenium **R: 290**
Ytterbium **Y: 574**
Gadolinium [element] **G: 4**
Gadsby's Tavern
Alexandria **A: 345**
Gadsden [American colonial leaders] **G: 4**
Gadsden, Christopher [American government official]
Gadsden (Christopher Gadsden) **G: 4**
Gadsden, James [American government official]
Gadsden (James Gadsden) **G: 4**
Gadsden Purchase **G: 4**
Gadsden Purchase [1853] **G: 4** *with map*
Arizona (Spanish exploration) **A: 688-690**
Gadsden (James Gadsden) **G: 4**
Mexico (Difficulties of the early republic) **M: 471**
New Mexico (Territorial days) **N: 275**
United States, History of the *map on* **U: 184**; (The Mexican War) **U: 169**
Westward movement in America (The Southwest) **W: 249**
Gadwall [duck] **G: 5** *with picture*
Gaea [Greek mythology]
Cronus **Ci: 1152**
Hesperides **H: 218**
Mythology (The Greek creation myth) **M: 980**
Titans **T: 300**
Uranus **U: 217**
Gaekkebrev [custom]
Valentine's Day (In Europe) **V: 261**
Gaelic football
Ireland (Recreation) **I: 420**
Gaelic languages **G: 5**
Ireland (Language) **I: 418**
Irish literature **I: 430**; (Modern works in Gaelic) **I: 431**
Northern Ireland (Language) **N: 522**
Scotland (Language) **S: 213**
United Kingdom (Language) **U: 55**
Gaelic League [Irish history]
Irish literature (Modern works in Gaelic) **I: 431**
Gaelic literature
Irish literature **I: 430**; (Modern works in Gaelic) **I: 431**
Gaels [Celtic-speaking people] **G: 5**
Gaetani, Benedetto [birth name of]
Boniface VIII **B: 459**
Gaff [fishing equipment]
Fishing (Bait) **F: 178-179**
Gaff [sailing]
Sailing (Spars) **S: 23-24**
Gaffer [glassmaking]
Glass (Glass terms) **G: 222**
Gaffer [photography]
Motion picture (Preparing to shoot) **M: 852**
Gag cartoon
Cartoon (Single panel cartoons) **C: 265-266** *with picture*; (Developing the idea) **C: 266-267**
Gag order [law]
Freedom of the press (In the United States) **F: 507-508**
Gag Rules [U.S. history]
Adams, John Quincy (The Gag Rules) **A: 43**
Gagaku [music]
Music (Japanese music) **M: 956**
Gagarin, Yuri Alekseyevich [Russian cosmonaut] **G: 5**
Astronaut (Achievements in space) **A: 829** *with picture*; (table) **A: 830**
Exploration (Human space travel) **E: 452**
Korolev, Sergei Pavlovich **K: 384**
Space exploration (Vostok and Mercury: The first human beings in space) **So: 712-713** *with picture*
Union of Soviet Socialist Republics *picture on* **U: 33**
Gage [instrument]
Gauge **G: 69**
Gage, Henry T. [American political leader]
California (table) **C: 59**
Gage, Jack R. [American political leader]
Wyoming (table) **W: 532**
Gage, Lyman J. [American government official]
McKinley, William (table) **M: 342**
Roosevelt, Theodore (table) **R: 466**
Gage, Thomas [British general] **G: 5**
Revere, Paul (Paul Revere's ride) **R: 268**
Revolution, American (The Intolerable Acts) **R: 274**; (Lexington and Concord) **R: 274**
Gagil-Tamil [island, Pacific]
Yap Islands **Y: 553**
Gagnan, Émile [French diver]

Diving, Underwater (History) D: 247
Exploration (Deep-sea exploration) E: 450-451
Skin diving (History) S: 494
Gagnon, Édouard [Canadian religious leader]
Cardinal (table: Canadian cardinals) C: 211
Gagnon, Madeleine [Canadian poet]
Canadian literature (Modern Canadian poets)
C: 161
Gagnon, Rene A. [American soldier]
Iwo Jima, Battle of picture on I: 523
Gahagan, Helen [American political leader]
Nixon, Richard Milhous (U.S. senator) N: 430
Gahn, Johan Gottlieb [Swedish chemist]
Manganese M: 139
Gaia [biology] G: 5
Gaillard, David DuBose [American engineer]
Panama Canal (The Gaillard Cut) P: 123
Gaillard Cut
Panama Canal (The Gaillard Cut) map on P: 123;
(Cutting through the isthmus) P: 126; (The
canal since 1920) P: 126
Gaillardia [plant] G: 6 with picture
Flower picture on F: 287
Gaiman, Neil [British-American author]
Newbery Medal (table) N: 359
Gain medium [electronics] See Active medium in
this index
Gainsborough, Thomas [British painter] G: 6 with
picture
Painting (People) P: 31 with picture; (Landscapes
and seascapes) P: 32-33
Rococo R: 396
Siddons, Sarah Kemble picture on S: 448
Gainsborough hat
Hat H: 83, picture on H: 84
Gairy, Sir Eric [Grenada political leader]
Grenada (History and government) G: 389
Gaiseric [Vandal king]
Vandals V: 279
Gait
Horse (Gaits) H: 353 with pictures
Gaitán, Jorge Eliécer [Colombian political leader]
Colombia (The early to middle 1900's) Ci: 784
Latin America (Political circumstances in the early
to middle 1900's) L: 109
Gaîté Parisienne [ballet]
Massine, Léonide M: 296
Gaius Caesar Augustus Germanicus [Roman
emperor] See Caligula in this index
Gaius Marius [Roman general]
Sulla, Lucius Cornelius So: 968
Gaius Plinius Caecilius Secundus [Roman author]
See Pliny the Younger in this index
Gaius Plinius Secundus [Roman author] See Pliny
the Elder in this index
Gaius Verres [Roman political leader]
Cicero, Marcus Tullius (His life) Ci: 552
Gaiwiio [message]
Handsome Lake H: 46
Gajdusek, Daniel Carleton [American
physiologist]
Nobel Prizes (Physiology or medicine: 1976)
N: 446
Gal [measurement]
Metric system (Non-SI metric units) M: 440
Gala [apple]
Apple (Varieties of apples) A: 571 with picture
Galabiyyah [clothing]
Arabs (Clothing) A: 588
Egypt (Clothing) E: 124
Galactic cluster [astronomy]
Milky Way (Shape of the galaxy) M: 550
Galactic cosmic rays
Astronomy (Cosmic-ray astronomy) A: 846
Cosmic rays (Galactic cosmic rays) Ci: 1076
Galactic halo
Halo H: 26
Galactose
Carbohydrate (Kinds of carbohydrates) C: 203;
(How the body uses carbohydrates) C: 204
Cell (Metabolic diseases) C: 336
Galactosemia [disorder]
Cell (Metabolic diseases) C: 336
Galago [animal] G: 7 with picture
Primate (Galagos and lorises) P: 778
Galah [bird]
Parrot (Kinds of parrots) P: 179
Galahad, Sir [legendary figure] G: 7
Holy Grail (The search for the Grail) H: 299
Lancelot, Sir L: 56
Round Table (Origin) R: 491
Galant style [music]
Classical music (The Classical period) Ci: 647
Galapagos Islands [islands, Pacific] G: 7 with
picture and map
Ecuador E: 67; (The Galapagos Islands) E: 70 with
picture

Evolution (Geographic distribution of species)
E: 430-431 with picture; (Darwin's theory)
E: 432
Island (How life develops on islands) I: 473
Galapagos Marine Reserve
Galapagos Islands G: 8
Galapagos National Park [Ecuador]
Galapagos Islands G: 8
National park (table) N: 42g; (Other interesting
national parks) N: 42h
Galapagos penguin
Penguin (The life of penguins) P: 238
Galapagos tortoise
Tortoise T: 344
Turtle (Tortoises) T: 524
Galarza, Ernesto [Mexican-American historian]
G: 8
Galatea, La [book by Cervantes]
Cervantes, Miguel de (His literary career) C: 363
Galatia [former region, Turkey] G: 8
Galatians [people]
Galatia G: 8
Galatians, Epistle to the [New Testament] G: 8
Bible (The Letters) B: 284
Galaxy [astronomy] G: 8 with pictures
Andromeda Galaxy A: 457 with picture
Astronomy (Modern astronomy) A: 836-837;
(Discovering other galaxies) A: 848
Cosmology Ci: 1077
Dark matter D: 37
Hubble, Edwin Powell H: 403
Inflation theory I: 268a
Interstellar medium I: 352
Local Group L: 409
Magellanic Clouds M: 48
Milky Way M: 550 with picture
Nebula N: 116
Star So: 840
Star cluster So: 853
Universe U: 205
Galaxy cluster [astronomy]
Dark matter D: 37
Galaxy (Interactions between galaxies) G: 8b-9;
(Galaxy groups, clusters, and beyond) G: 9
Universe U: 205
Galba [Roman emperor]
Rome, Ancient (table) R: 447
Galba, Martí Joan de [Spanish author]
Spanish literature (The 1400's) So: 758
Galbraith, John Kenneth [American economist]
G: 9
Galdhøpiggen [mountain, Norway]
Norway (Land regions) N: 541 with map
Galdikas, Biruté [Lithuanian-born anthropologist]
G: 10
Galdós, Benito Pérez [Spanish author]
Spanish literature (The 1800's) So: 761-762
Gale [weather]
Wind (table) W: 330
Gale, Leonard D. [American inventor]
Morse, Samuel Finley Breese (Morse as inventor)
M: 818
Telegraph (The Morse telegraph) T: 90
Gale warning [meteorology]
Boating (Warning signals) picture on B: 430
Flag picture on F: 197
Galego [language]
Portuguese language P: 695
Galen [Greek doctor] G: 10
Anatomy A: 448b
Biology (Beginnings) B: 317-318 with picture
Color (Early theories of color vision) Ci: 825-826
Heart (Early beliefs about the heart) H: 143
Medicine (Greece and Rome) M: 372-373
Occupational therapy (History) O: 649
Science (Ancient Rome) S: 197
Vesalius, Andreas V: 341
Zoology (History) Z: 606
Galena [Illinois]
Illinois (Places to visit) I: 62 with picture
Galena [mineral] G: 10
Lead (Production) L: 149; (Properties) L: 149
Mineral picture on M: 568
Galerius [Roman emperor]
Diocletian D: 214
Rome, Ancient (table) R: 447
Gali Gali [Egyptian magician]
Magician (Sleight of hand) M: 51
Galicia [province]
Spain (Language) So: 733; (The Northern
Mountains) So: 740 with map
Galicia [region, Europe] G: 10
Ukraine (History) U: 11-12
Galician [language]
Portuguese language P: 695
Spain (Language) So: 733
Spanish language (Castilian Spanish) So: 757

Galigaï, Leonora [Italian public figure]
Marie de Médicis M: 200
Galilean relativity [physics]
Motion (Galileo's principle of relativity) M: 845
Relativity (Galilean relativity) R: 209
Galilean satellite [astronomy]
Jupiter (Galilean satellites) J: 200a
Solar system (Moons) So: 580-581
Galilean transformation [physics]
Relativity (Galilean transformations) R: 210
Galilee [region, Israel]
Israel (The Judeo-Galilean Highlands) I: 482
Jesus Christ (Public life) J: 106 with map
Galilee, Sea of [lake, Israel-Syria] G: 11
Galilei, Galileo [Italian astronomer] See Galileo in
this index
Galileo [Italian astronomer] G: 11 with portrait
Academic freedom (Beginnings) A: 20
Astronomy (Developing the modern view)
A: 847-848
Callisto C: 69
Copernicus, Nicolaus (Theories of heavenly
motion) Ci: 1039
Europa E: 379
Falling bodies, Law of F: 16
Ganymede G: 27
Gravitation G: 331
Io I: 370
Italian literature (The Baroque period and the
Enlightenment) I: 494
Jupiter (History of Jupiter study) J: 200b
Leaning Tower of Pisa L: 162
Light (The speed of light) L: 290
Mathematics (Mathematics and the scientific
revolution) M: 306-307
Meteorology (History) M: 433
Moon (Early observations with telescopes)
M: 792
Motion (Galileo's principle of relativity) M: 845
Pendulum P: 237
Physics picture on P: 440; (The Renaissance)
P: 438-439
Relativity (Galilean relativity) R: 209
Satellite (Exploration by spacecraft) S: 150c
Saturn (History of study) S: 153
Science (The scientific revolution) S: 198 with
picture
Sound (The study of waves) So: 605
Telescope T: 102; (Refracting telescopes) T: 103-
104
World, History of the picture on W: 442
Galileo [navigation system]
Navigation (Satellite navigation) N: 73
Galileo [space probe] G: 12 with picture
Asteroid (History of study) A: 824b
Europa E: 379
Jupiter (History of Jupiter study) J: 200b
Satellite (Exploration by spacecraft) S: 150c
Space exploration (Probes to Jupiter and beyond)
So: 711
Galileo Galilei [opera by Glass]
Glass, Philip G: 224
Gall [American Indian leader] G: 13
Gall [botany] G: 13
Eelworm E: 115
Gall, Franz Joseph [German anatomist]
Phrenology P: 430
Gall bladder [anatomy] See Gallbladder in this
index
Gall mite [animal]
Mite M: 678
Galla Placidia, Mausoleum of [Italy]
Ravenna R: 151
Galland, Isaac [American doctor]
Iowa (Schools) I: 378
Galland, Jean Antoine [French scholar]
Arabian Nights A: 582b
Gallant, Mavis [Canadian author] G: 13
Gallant Fox [horse]
Kentucky Derby (table) K: 296
Gallatin, Albert [American statesman] G: 14
Jefferson, Thomas (New policies) J: 83
Madison, James (The growth of nationalism)
M: 36
Gallatin Mountains
Montana (Land regions) M: 752
Gallaudet [American educators] G: 14
Gallaudet, Edward Miner [American educator]
Gallaudet G: 14
Gallaudet, Thomas [American educator]
Gallaudet G: 14
Gallaudet, Thomas Hopkins [American educator]
Connecticut (Schools) Ci: 956
Gallaudet G: 14
Gallaudet University G: 14
Gallaudet University G: 14
Deafness (Education) D: 59 with picture; (Deaf

community and culture) D: 59-60
Gallbladder [anatomy] G: 14 *with diagram*
  Bile B: 300
  Human body (table) H: 422 *with diagram*
  Liver L: 393
Gallé, Emile [French artist]
  Art Nouveau A: 750
Galle, Johann G. [German astronomer]
  Astronomy (Finding new objects) A: 848
  Neptune (Discovery) N: 129
Gallé glass
  Glass (Types of art glass) G: 220 *with picture*
Gallego, Juan Nicasio [Spanish poet]
  Spanish literature (The 1800's) So: 761
Gallegos, Rómulo [Venezuelan political leader]
  Latin American literature (The early 1900's) L: 113
  Venezuela (The arts) V: 301; (The road to democracy) V: 305
Gallen, Hugh J. [American political leader]
  New Hampshire (table) N: 223
Gallen-Kallela, Akseli [Finnish painter]
  Finland (The arts) F: 112 *with picture*
Galleon [ship] G: 15 *with picture*
  Navy (The beginning of modern navies) N: 79
  Ship (The galleon) S: 419 *with picture*
  Transportation *picture on* T: 388
  Warship *picture on* W: 42; (The age of sailing ships) W: 41
Galleria [Houston]
  Houston *picture on* H: 397; (The city) H: 394
Galleria Vittorio Emanuele II
  Milan (People) M: 540 *with picture*
Gallery [theater]
  Shakespeare, William (The stage) S: 351-352 *with picture*
Galley [kitchen]
  Sailing *picture on* S: 25
Galley [printing]
  Linotype (How the linotype works) L: 338-339
Galley [ship] G: 15 *with picture*
  Navy (Ancient navies) N: 79
  Ship (Phoenician and Greek ships) S: 415 *with picture*; (Lateen-rigged ships) S: 417-418
  Warship *picture on* W: 42; (Early warships) W: 41
Gallic Wars [European history]
  Gaul G: 70
Gallicanism [religion]
  Pope (The 1700's and 1800's) P: 665
  Roman Catholic Church (Gallicanism) R: 408
Gallienus [Roman emperor] G: 15
Gallinule [bird] G: 16
  Rail R: 103
Gallio [Roman governor]
  New Testament (The life of Paul) N: 288
Gallipoli, Battle of [1915]
  Atatürk, Kemal A: 852
  World War I (The Dardanelles) W: 459
Gallipolis [Ohio]
  Ohio *picture on* O: 694
Gallium [element] G: 16
Gallium arsenide [chemical]
  Light-emitting diode L: 293
Gallon [measurement] G: 16 *with picture*
Gallop
  Horse (Gaits) H: 353 *with picture*
  Mammal (On land) M: 121-122
Galloping cavalry charge
  Cavalry C: 318 *with picture*
Galloping Ghost [nickname]
  Grange, Red G: 310
Galloway [breed]
  Cattle (The bodies of cattle) C: 306-307
Galloway, Joseph [American political leader] G: 16
Gallstone [disorder]
  Gallbladder G: 14
Gallup [New Mexico] G: 16
Gallup, George Horace [American statistician] G: 16
  Public opinion poll (History) P: 863
Gallup Poll
  Gallup, George Horace G: 16
Gallus [Roman emperor]
  Rome, Ancient (table) R: 447
Galsworthy, John [British author] G: 16
  Democracy (Famous quotations about democracy) D: 120
Galt, Sir Alexander Tilloch [Canadian government official] G: 17
  Confederation of Canada (Fathers of Confederation) Ci: 935 *with picture*
Galt, Edith Bolling [wife of Woodrow Wilson] *See* Wilson, Edith Bolling *in this index*
Galtier, Lucian [American settler]
  Saint Paul (History) S: 52
Galton, Sir Francis [British scientist] G: 17
  Fingerprinting (History) F: 107
  Heredity (Early ideas about heredity) H: 208

Intelligence (Theories of intelligence) I: 319
Galusha, Jonas [American political leader]
  Vermont (table) V: 333
Galvani, Luigi [Italian anatomist] G: 17
  Electricity (Experiments with electric charge) E: 196-197
  Telegraph (Development of the telegraph) T: 90
Galvanism [physics]
  Galvani, Luigi G: 17
  Telegraph (Early discoveries) T: 90
Galvanized iron and steel
  Zinc Z: 594
Galvanizing [industrial process] G: 17
  Cadmium C: 12
  Iron and steel (Finishing) I: 447 *with diagram*
Galvanometer [instrument]
  Ampère, André Marie A: 438
  Electric meter (History) E: 177 *with picture*
  Kelvin, Lord K: 258
  Motion picture *diagram on* M: 859; (The sound track) M: 857
Galvanoplasty [industrial process]
  Electroplating E: 218
Galveston [Texas] G: 17
Galveston Island [Gulf of Mexico]
  Galveston G: 17
  Laffite, Jean L: 29
Gálvez, Bernardo de [Spanish colonial official] G: 18
  Galveston G: 18
  Louisiana (Spanish Louisiana) L: 498
Galvin, Pud [American baseball player]
  Baseball (table: Hall of Fame) B: 134
Galway [Ireland] G: 18
  Ireland (Surface features) I: 422
Gama, José Basílio da [Brazilian poet]
  Latin American literature (Colonial literature) L: 112
Gama, Vasco da [Portuguese explorer] *See* Da Gama, Vasco *in this index*
Gamaliel [Biblical figure] G: 18
Gambang [musical instrument]
  Orchestra *picture on* O: 823
Gambel's quail [bird]
  Bird (Birds of the desert) B: 339 *with picture*
  Quail Q: 4
Gambetta, Léon [French political leader]
  Franco-Prussian War (The siege and Commune of Paris) F: 483
Gambia G: 18 *with picture and map*
  Flag *picture on* F: 198
  Senegal (History) S: 299-300
Gambia River [Africa]
  Gambia (Land) G: 19 *with map*
Gambian giant rat [animal]
  Monkeypox (Outbreaks) M: 730
Gambier Islands [islands, Pacific]
  French Polynesia F: 524
Gamble, Hamilton R. [American political leader]
  Missouri (table) M: 668
Gamble, John [American military leader]
  Marine Corps, United States (The early Marine Corps) M: 247
Gamble, Kenny [American recording executive]
  Rock music (Soul music) R: 380a-380b
Gamblers Anonymous G: 20
Gambling G: 20
  Atlantic City A: 862
  Gamblers Anonymous G: 20
  Horse racing (Betting) H: 365
  Indian, American (Social and economic progress) I: 180-181
  Las Vegas L: 87
  Lottery L: 473
  Nevada *picture on* N: 171; (Service industries) N: 169; (Legal gambling and easy divorce) N: 176
  Slot machine S: 508a
Gambrel roof
  Roof R: 450b *with picture*
Game [animals] G: 21
  Meat M: 346
  Poaching P: 588 *with picture*
Game [game theory]
  Game theory G: 23
Game [psychiatry]
  Sensitivity training S: 302
Game [recreation] G: 21 *with picture*
  See also the list of Related articles in the Game [recreation] *article*
  Colonial life in America (Recreation) Ci: 802 *with picture*
  Hobby (Games and sports) H: 273
  Indian, American (Recreation) I: 142 *with picture*
Game, Computer *See* Electronic game *in this index*
Game Boy [machine]
  Electronic game (The Nintendo revolution)

E: 204d-204e
  Nintendo N: 424
Game bred dog
  Dogfighting D: 282
Game designer [career]
  Electronic game (Game design) E: 204b *with picture*
Game fish
  Fish (Food and game fish) F: 146
Game fishing *See* Fishing *in this index*
Game laws
  Hunting (Laws and conservation) H: 450
  Wildlife conservation (History) W: 304-305
Game Management [book by Leopold]
  Leopold, Aldo L: 204
Game of chance
  Card game C: 209
  Dice D: 187
  Roulette R: 490
Game of Silence, The [book by Erdrich]
  Literature for children *picture on* L: 360
Game plan
  Football (The coaches) F: 358
Game point
  Tennis (table) T: 162; (Scoring) T: 162-163
Game preserve
  Buffalo *picture on* B: 674
  Lion L: 340
Game song
  Folk music (Kinds of folk music) F: 321
Game theory G: 23
  Economics (Modern economics) E: 64-65
  Industry (Industrial organization) I: 260
  Nash, John Forbes, Jr. N: 22
  Von Neumann, John V: 448
Gamecock [bird]
  Cockfighting Ci: 744
  South Carolina (The Revolutionary War) So: 659-660
Gamelan [orchestra]
  Indonesia (The arts) I: 232-233
  Malaysia (The arts) M: 99
  Music (Indonesian music) M: 956 *with picture*
Gamemaster
  Game (Board games) G: 22
Gameplay [recreation]
  Electronic game E: 204a; (Gameplay) E: 204b
Gamete [reproduction]
  See also Egg cell; Egg [reproduction]; Sperm *in this index*
  Alternation of generations A: 388
  Developmental biology D: 174
  Fungi (How a fungus lives) F: 559
  Heredity (Sex cells and reproduction) H: 201; (Sources of genetic variation) H: 203
  Moss (How mosses live) M: 834-835
  Plant (Sexual reproduction) P: 532
  Reproduction R: 242
  Reproduction, Human R: 244
  Spore (Plant spores) So: 801
Gamete intrafallopian transfer [reproduction]
  Infertility (Treatment) I: 265
Gametophyte [botany]
  Alternation of generations A: 388
  Bryophyte B: 656
  Fern (Life cycle of a fern) F: 75 *with picture*
  Hornwort H: 341
  Liverwort L: 396
  Moss (How mosses live) M: 834-835
  Plant (Sexual reproduction) P: 532 *with diagrams*
  Seed (How seeds develop) S: 281
  Spore (Plant spores) So: 801
Gamines [people]
  Colombia (Way of life) Ci: 779-781
Gamio, Manuel [Mexican anthropologist] G: 23
Gaml [letter]
  C C: 1 *with picture*
  G G: 1 *with picture*
Gamla Stan [district, Stockholm]
  Stockholm (The city) So: 905
  Sweden *pictures on* So: 1020, So: 1024
Gamma [letter]
  C C: 1 *with picture*
  G G: 1 *with picture*
Gamma globulin [physiology] G: 23
  Hepatitis (Hepatitis A) H: 192
  Immune system (Passive immunity) I: 88b
  Kawasaki disease K: 250
  Measles (Prevention) M: 346
  Plasma (Functions of plasma) P: 551
  Serum S: 319
Gamma hydroxybutyrate [drug] *See* GHB *in this index*
Gamma interferon [drug]
  Interferon I: 324
Gamma Phi Beta
  Sorority So: 597

Gamma-ray astronomy
Astronomy (Gamma-ray astronomy) **A:** 845
Gamma-ray burst [astronomy]
Astronomy (Gamma-ray astronomy) **A:** 845
Supernova (Results of supernovae) **So:** 994
Gamma Ray Observatory [satellite] *See* Compton
Gamma Ray Observatory *in this index*
Gamma rays [radiation] **G:** 23
Astronomy (table: The electromagnetic
spectrum) **A:** 839; (Gamma-ray astronomy)
A: 845
Atom (Radioactivity) **A:** 873
Cancer (Radiation therapy) **C:** 172
Electromagnetic waves (The electromagnetic
spectrum) **E:** 202 *with diagram*
Light (The spectrum of light sources) **L:** 284 *with
diagram*
Lightning (Emissions) **L:** 301
Nuclear energy (Radioactive decay) **N:** 582
Nuclear weapon (Prompt nuclear radiation)
N: 599
Positron emission tomography **P:** 698
Radiation *picture on* **R:** 78; (Electromagnetic
radiation) **R:** 75-76 *with picture*
Telescope (Gamma-ray telescopes) **T:** 109
Gammell, Stephen [American artist]
Caldecott Medal (table: 1989) **C:** 26
Gammon, Warren [American farmer]
Cattle (Hereford) **C:** 309
Gamow, George [Russian-born physicist]
Big bang **B:** 297
Gamp, Sairy [literary figure]
Dickens, Charles (The first phase) **D:** 188
Gamsakhurdia, Zviad K. [Georgian political
leader]
Georgia (History) **G:** 111
Gan Island
Maldives (History) **M:** 104-105
Gance, Abel [French director]
Motion picture (The movies talk) **M:** 867
Gand [Belgium]
Ghent **G:** 181
Ganda [people] **G:** 24
Uganda (People) **U:** 3
Gander [goose] *See* Goose *in this index*
Gander International Airport
Newfoundland and Labrador (Libraries and
museums) **N:** 364
Gandharan school [art]
Kanishka **K:** 215
Gandhi [film]
Motion picture (Best picture: 1982) **M:** 861
Gandhi, Indira [Indian political leader] **G:** 24 *with
portrait*
Gandhi, Rajiv **G:** 25
India (India under Indira Gandhi) **I:** 133-134 *with
picture*
Indian National Congress **I:** 185
Rao, P. V. Narasimha **R:** 141
Gandhi, Mohandas Karamchand [Indian political
leader] **G:** 24 *with portrait*
Asia (The end of colonialism) **A:** 807 *with picture*
Civil disobedience (History of civil disobedience)
Ci: 607
Clothing (Political influences) **Ci:** 690-691
Fast **F:** 52
India (Rise of Indian nationalism) **I:** 131;
(Independence and partition) **I:** 133 *with
picture*
Indian National Congress **I:** 185
Pacifism **P:** 18
South Africa (The Union of South Africa) **So:** 618-
619
Gandhi, Rajiv [Indian political leader] **G:** 25
Gandhi, Indira **G:** 24
Gandhi, Sonia **G:** 26
India (India under Indira Gandhi) **I:** 133-134;
(Religious and ethnic unrest) **I:** 134
Indian National Congress **I:** 185
Rao, P. V. Narasimha **R:** 141
Gandhi, Sanjay [Indian political leader]
Gandhi, Indira **G:** 24
Gandhi, Sonia [Indian political leader] **G:** 26
Gandhi, Rajiv **G:** 26
India (Recent developments) **I:** 134-135
Gandy Bridge [Saint Petersburg-Tampa]
Saint Petersburg [Florida] (Government and
history) **S:** 56
Ganesa [Hindu god]
India (Hinduism) **I:** 116
Ganesh [Hindu god] *See* Ganesa *in this index*
Gang [sociology] **G:** 26
Hip-hop **H:** 238
Gang of Four [Chinese history]
China (Deng Xiaoping) **C:** 506
Gang Plank [region]
Wyoming (Land regions) **W:** 526

Gang plow
Plow (The gang plow) **P:** 575 *with picture*
Gang saw [machine]
Lumber (Sawing logs) **L:** 519
Ganges dolphin
Mammal *picture on* **M:** 117
River dolphin **R:** 354
Ganges River [India] **G:** 26 *with picture*
Asia *picture on* **A:** 782
Bangladesh **B:** 78; (Rivers and streams) **B:** 83
Brahmaputra River **B:** 548
India (The Northern Plains) **I:** 121-122
River (table) **R:** 352
Varanasi **V:** 285
Yamuna River **Y:** 550
Ganglion [biology]
Brain (Invertebrates) **B:** 559
Insect (Nervous system) **I:** 289 *with diagram*
Nervous system (The cell body) **N:** 133
Spider (Digestive system) **So:** 785 *with diagram*
Ganglioside [physiology]
Tay-Sachs disease **T:** 56
Gangrene [disease] **G:** 27
Gangster
Gang **G:** 26
Gangster film
Motion picture (Movies in the 1930's) **M:** 867
Gangster Funeral [painting by Levine]
Levine, Jack *picture on* **L:** 219
Gangster rap [music]
Rap music **R:** 141
Gangue [mineral]
Metallurgy (Mineral dressing) **M:** 426
Mining (Mining terms) **M:** 577
Ore **O:** 825
Gannet [bird] **G:** 27
Newfoundland and Labrador (Places to visit)
N: 368
Gannett Company
Newspaper (Newspapers in the 1990's) **N:** 387
USA Today **U:** 229
Gannett Peak
Rocky Mountains (Chief ranges of the Rockies)
R: 394-395
Wyoming (Land regions) **W:** 526
Ganoid scale [zoology]
Fish (Scales) **F:** 160 *with picture*
Gantos, Jack [American author]
Newbery Medal (table) **N:** 359
Gantry [machine]
Computed tomography **Ci:** 907
Gantt, Harvey [American political leader]
Charlotte (Government and history) **C:** 385
Ganwa [people]
Burundi (History) **B:** 713
Ganymede [Greek mythology] **G:** 27
Ganymede [satellite] **G:** 27 *with picture*
Galileo **G:** 13
Jupiter (Galilean satellites) **J:** 200a
Gao [African history]
Africa (The empires of west Africa) **A:** 131
Mali (History) **M:** 108-109 *with map*
Niger (History) **N:** 409
Songhai Empire **So:** 593 *with map*
GAO [agency] *See* Government Accountability
Office *in this index*
Gao Xingjian [Chinese author]
Chinese literature (Modern Chinese literature)
C: 512
Nobel Prizes (Literature: 2000) **N:** 448
Gaol [institution] *See* Jail *in this index*
Gap [astronomy]
Planetary ring **P:** 514d
Gap [electronics]
Videotape recorder (Recording) **V:** 361
Gap [geography] **G:** 27
Gaposchkin, Cecilia Payne [British astronomer]
See Payne-Gaposchkin, Cecilia Helena *in this
index*
Gaposchkin, Sergei [Russian astronomer]
Payne-Gaposchkin, Cecilia Helena **P:** 204
G.A.R. [abbreviation]
Grand Army of the Republic **G:** 305 *with picture*
Gar [fish] **G:** 28 *with picture*
Fish (Bony fish) **F:** 147-148
Pike **P:** 461
Gar [Tibet]
Tibet **T:** 276
Gar pike [fish]
Pike **P:** 461
Garage rock [music]
Rock music (Garage rock) **R:** 380a
Garamba National Park [Democratic Republic of
the Congo]
National park (table) **N:** 42f
Garand, John C. [American engineer]
Garand rifle **G:** 28

Garand rifle G: 28
Garay, Juan de [Spanish soldier]
Buenos Aires (History) **B:** 673
Garbage
Culture (How people study culture) **Ci:** 1189-
1190 *with picture*
Environmental pollution (Types of pollution)
E: 331
Fly (Head) **F:** 309; (Larva) **F:** 310
Middle Ages (Medieval towns) **M:** 527
Ocean (Marine pollution) **O:** 664
Waste disposal **W:** 112
Garbage disposal [machine] **G:** 28
See also Waste disposal *in this index*
Garbanzo *See* Chickpea *in this index*
Garber, Silas [American political leader]
Nebraska (table) **N:** 110
Garbo, Greta [Swedish-American actress] **G:** 28
with portrait
Steichen, Edward *picture on* **So:** 884
Garcelon, Alonzo [American political leader]
Maine (table) **M:** 87
Garcés, Francisco [Spanish missionary]
Nevada (Exploration) **N:** 173
García, Héctor P. [American diplomat]
American GI Forum of the United States **A:** 411
Hispanic Americans (Political developments)
H: 256
Garcia, Jerry [American singer]
Grateful Dead **G:** 329
Rock music (Psychedelic rock) **R:** 380a
García Gutiérrez, Antonio [Spanish author]
Opera (*Trovatore, Il*) **O:** 808
García Íñiguez, Calixto [Cuban general] **G:** 29
García Lorca, Federico [Spanish author] **G:** 29
Spanish literature (Drama) **So:** 763
García Márquez, Gabriel José [Colombian author]
G: 29
Colombia (The arts) **Ci:** 781
Latin American literature (The "Boom") **L:** 114
Novel (The novel today) **N:** 575
García Moreno, Gabriel [Ecuadorean political
leader]
Ecuador (Independence) **E:** 73
García Pérez, Alan [Peruvian political leader]
Bolivia (Recent developments) **B:** 423-424
Peru (Return to civilian government) **P:** 316;
(Recent developments) **P:** 316-317
García Robles, Alfonso [Mexican diplomat]
Nobel Prizes (Peace: 1982) **N:** 448b
García Sarmiento, Félix Rubén [Nicaraguan poet]
See Darío, Rubén *in this index*
Garciaparra, Nomar [American baseball player]
Hamm, Mia **H:** 34
Garcilaso de la Vega [1503-1536, Spanish poet]
Spanish literature (The 1500's) **So:** 758
Garcilaso de la Vega [1539-1616, Latin American
author]
Latin American literature (Colonial literature)
L: 112
Garden *See* Gardening *in this index*
Garden, Mary [American singer] **G:** 29
Garden balsam [plant]
Flower *picture on* **F:** 277
Garden canna [plant]
Flower *picture on* **F:** 279
Garden cress [plant]
Cress **Ci:** 1127
Garden croton [plant]
Croton **Ci:** 1156
Garden district
New Orleans (Residential districts) **N:** 279
Garden egg [plant]
Eggplant **E:** 118
Garden fork [tool]
Gardening (Cultivating an outdoor garden) **G:** 34
Garden Island [nickname]
Hawaii (Kauai) **H:** 102
Garden loosestrife [plant]
Loosestrife **L:** 453
Garden morning-glory [plant]
Morning-glory *picture on* **M:** 809
Garden Next Door, The [book by Donoso]
Latin American literature (The post-Boom) **L:** 114
Garden of Earthly Delights, A [book by Oates]
Oates, Joyce Carol **O:** 639
Garden of Earthly Delights, The [painting by
Bosch]
Bosch, Hieronymus **B:** 491
Garden of Eden [Bible] *See* Eden *in this index*
Garden of Gethsemane *See* Gethsemane *in this
index*
Garden of Intelligence
Zoo (History) **Z:** 604
Garden of the Gods [Colorado] **G:** 29
Colorado (Places to visit) **Ci:** 836
Rock (table) **R:** 374

Garden of the Gulf [nickname]
Prince Edward Island **P: 783**
Garden sage [plant]
Sage **S: 18**
Garden spider
Spider picture on **So: 785**
Garden State [nickname]
New Jersey **N: 231**
Garden State Parkway [road]
New Jersey (The mid-1900's) **N: 253**
Garden thyme [plant]
Thyme **T: 274**
Gardenia [plant] **G: 29**
Flower picture on **F: 292**
Gardening G: 30 with pictures
See also the list of Related articles in the Gardening article
Bonsai **B: 463**
Cold frame **Ci: 761**
Fertilizer **F: 78**
Greenhouse **G: 382**
Hotbed **H: 375**
Landscape architecture **L: 59** with picture
Peat moss **P: 225**
Pruning **P: 841** with picture
Rose (Reproducing and growing roses) **R: 475**
Safety (In the yard) **S: 11**
Transplanting **T: 381** with pictures
United Kingdom picture on **U: 56**
Gardening, Landscape See Landscape architecture in this index
Gardiner, David [American political leader]
Tyler, John (Life in the White House) **T: 534**
Gardiner, Julia [wife of John Tyler] See Tyler, Julia Gardiner in this index
Gardiner, William Tudor [American political leader]
Maine (table) **M: 87**
Gardner, Alexander [American photographer]
Civil War, American (The home front) **Ci: 622**
Photography (Artistic advances) **P: 424-425**
Gardner, Booth [American political leader]
Washington (table) **W: 65**
Gardner, Erle Stanley [American author] **G: 39** with portrait
Gardner, Frederick D. [American political leader]
Missouri (table) **M: 668**
Gardner, Gerald B. [British religious leader]
Witchcraft (Witchcraft as a religion) **W: 371**; (Witchcraft in modern times) **W: 373**
Gardner, Henry J. [American political leader]
Massachusetts (table) **M: 288**
Gardner, Howard E. [American psychologist]
Child (Psychological differences) **C: 450**
Intelligence (Theories of intelligence) **I: 319**
Teaching (Guiding and assisting student learning) **T: 66**
Gardner, John William [American government official] **G: 39**
Common Cause **Ci: 874**
Gardner, Newport [American musician]
African Americans (Free blacks) **A: 136g-136h**
Gardner, O. Max [American political leader]
North Carolina (table) **N: 490**
Gardnerella vaginalis [bacterium]
Vaginitis **V: 260**
Garfield, Abram [father of]
Garfield, James Abram (Childhood) **G: 40**
Garfield, Eliza Ballou [mother of]
Garfield, James Abram (Childhood) **G: 40**
Garfield, Harry Augustus [son of]
Garfield, James Abram (Garfield's family) **G: 40-41**
Garfield, James Abram [U.S. president] **G: 40** with pictures
Arthur, Chester Alan (Election of 1880) **A: 756**
Bell, Alexander Graham (His later life) **B: 241**
Blaine, James Gillespie **B: 396**
Civil service (History) **Ci: 613**
Republican Party (Political inactivity) **R: 255**
Garfield, James R. [American government official]
Garfield, James Abram (Garfield's family) **G: 40-41**
Interior, Department of the (table) **I: 325**
Roosevelt, Theodore (table) **R: 466**
Garfield, Lucretia Rudolph [wife of James A. Garfield]
First ladies of the United States (table) **F: 142**
Garfield, James Abram picture on **G: 41**; (Garfield's family) **G: 40**
Garfunkel, Art [American singer]
Simon, Paul **S: 466**
Gargantua and Pantagruel [book by Rabelais]
French literature (François Rabelais) **F: 519**
Humanism (The spread of humanism) **H: 431**
Rabelais, François **R: 49**
Gargle [liquid] **G: 43**
Gargoyle [architecture] **G: 43** with picture
Garibaldi, Giuseppe [Italian military leader] **G: 43**

Italy (Italy united) **I: 515-516** with picture
Sicilies, Kingdom of the Two **S: 446**
Garies and Their Friends, The [book by Webb]
African American literature (The 1800's) **A: 136a**
Garifuna [people]
Honduras (Ancestry) **H: 309**
Garland, Augustus Hill [American political leader]
Arkansas (table) **A: 712**
Cleveland, Grover (table) **Ci: 671**
Justice, Department of (table) **J: 203**
Garland, Hamlin [American author] **G: 43**
American literature (Naturalists) **A: 419**
Garland, Judy [American entertainer] **G: 43** with picture
Motion picture picture on **M: 846**
Wizard of Oz, The **W: 374**
Garlic [plant] **G: 44** with picture
Gardening (Planting and transplanting) **G: 34**
Garment See Clothing in this index
Garment District
New York City (Manhattan) **N: 323-324**; (Industry) **N: 333**
Garment industry
Textile **T: 212**
Garn, Edwin J. [American political leader]
Astronaut (A look at the astronauts) **A: 831**
Bank (A boom in money market funds) **B: 94**
Garn-St. Germain Depository Institutions Act [1982]
Bank (A boom in money market funds) **B: 94**
Garneau, Alfred [Canadian poet]
Canadian literature (Poetry: 1850-1918) **C: 157**
Garneau, François Xavier [Canadian historian]
Canadian literature (Early Québécois literature) **C: 157**
Garneau, Marc [Canadian astronaut] **G: 44** with portrait
Astronaut (table) **A: 830**; (A look at the astronauts) **A: 831**
Garner, John Nance [American political leader] **G: 44** with portrait
Hoover, Herbert Clark (Election of 1932) **H: 330**
Roosevelt, Franklin Delano (Election of 1932) **R: 452** with picture
Vice president of the United States (Social duties) **V: 352**
Garnet [gem] **G: 45** with picture
Gem picture on **G: 78**
Ruby **R: 508**
Ytterbium **Y: 574**
Garnier, Charles [French architect]
Architecture (Combined styles) **A: 626** with picture
Garnish [food]
Cooking picture on **Ci: 1028**
Garnishment [law] **G: 45**
Garrahy, J. Joseph [American political leader]
Rhode Island (table) **R: 311**
Garrett, Mike [American football player]
Football (table) **F: 363**
Garrett, Pat [American frontiersman] **G: 45**
Underground railroad **U: 20**
Garrett, Thomas [American social reformer]
Underground railroad **U: 20**
Garrick, David [British actor] **G: 45**
Drama (England) **D: 334** with picture
Garrick Gaieties, The [musical]
Hart, Lorenz **H: 77**
Garrick Year, The [book by Drabble]
Drabble, Margaret **D: 317**
Garrison [military]
Flag (table) **F: 193**
Garrison, Lindley M. [American government official]
Wilson, Woodrow (table) **W: 323**
Garrison, Lucy McKim [American publisher]
Spiritual **So: 796**
Garrison, Nicholas [British artist]
Colonial life in America picture on **Ci: 792**
Garrison, William Lloyd [American social reformer] **G: 45** with portrait
Abolition movement **A: 12**
Massachusetts (Progress as a state) **M: 292**
United States, History of the (The abolition movement) **U: 173-174**
Garrison Dam [Missouri River, North Dakota] **G: 46**
North Dakota (The mid-1900's) **N: 516**
Garrison Diversion Project
Canada, History of (Foreign affairs) **C: 150**
North Dakota (The mid-1900's) **N: 516**; (Late 1900's) **N: 516**
Garrison flag
Flag (table) **F: 193**
Garrote [execution] **G: 46**
Garson, Greer [British actress]
Motion picture (Best performance by an actress: 1942) **M: 862**
Garson, Stuart S. [Canadian political leader]

Manitoba (table) **M: 159**
Garst, Warren [American political leader]
Iowa (table) **I: 391**
Garter, Order of the [award] **G: 46** with picture
George, Saint **G: 108**
Insignia **I: 303**
Knighthood, Orders of (Honorary orders) **K: 347**
Medals, decorations, and orders (table) **M: 359**
Garter snake [reptile] **G: 46** with picture
Snake picture on **S: 533**
Garter stitch
Knitting picture on **K: 354**
Garth Brooks [recording]
Brooks, Garth **B: 641**
Garum [food]
Rome, Ancient (Food) **R: 440**
Garvey, Dan E. [American political leader]
Arizona (table) **A: 687**
Garvey, Marcus [American social reformer] **G: 47** with portrait
African Americans (The Garvey movement) **A: 136m** with picture
Malcolm X **M: 103**
Garvin, Lucius F. C. [American political leader]
Rhode Island (table) **R: 311**
Gary [Indiana] **G: 47**
Gary, Elbert Henry [American businessman] **G: 47**
Gary **G: 47**
Gary, James [American government official]
McKinley, William (table) **M: 342**
Gary, Raymond D. [American political leader]
Oklahoma (table) **O: 730**; (The mid-1900's) **O: 734**
Gary goldenrod [plant]
Flower picture on **F: 285**
Gary School Plan [education]
Indiana (Schools) **I: 200-201**
Gas [physics] **G: 47** with pictures
See also the list of Related articles in the Gas article
Aerosol **A: 89**
Air (Gases of the air) **A: 166** with diagram
Avogadro, Amedeo **A: 994**
Chemistry (The phlogiston theory) **C: 401**
Cohesion **Ci: 756**
Condensation **Ci: 929**
Density **D: 142**
Electricity (Conductors) **E: 193**
Expansion **E: 438**
Interstellar medium **I: 352**
Matter (States of matter) **M: 311**
Molecule (Molecules and matter) **M: 693**
Solution (Gaseous solutions) **So: 587**
Volcano diagram on **V: 442a**; (Gases) **V: 439**; (Dangerous gases) **V: 440** with diagram
Gas [fuel] **G: 50** with pictures and map
See also Manufactured gas and Natural gas in this index and the list of Related articles in the Gas [fuel] article
Fuel (Gas fuels) **F: 551**
Heating (Gas) **H: 159**
Gas [weapon] See Poison gas in this index
Gas, Manufactured See Manufactured gas in this index
Gas, Natural See Natural gas in this index
Gas, Poison See Poison gas in this index
Gas, Tear See Tear gas in this index
Gas balloon
Balloon (Gas balloons) **B: 58** with pictures; (Operation of a gas balloon) **B: 60**; (Sport ballooning) **B: 60**
Gas burner See Burner in this index
Gas chamber G: 59
Auschwitz **A: 892**
Capital punishment (table) **C: 193**
Holocaust (The camps) **H: 296a**
Gas chromatography [chemistry]
Chromatography (Gas chromatography) **C: 538**
Gas chromatography/mass spectrometry [test]
Drug testing **D: 366**
Gas-discharge tube [electronic component]
Electronics (Early experiments) **E: 215**
Gas engine See Gasoline engine in this index
Gas fuel cell [device]
Gas [fuel] (The modern gas industry) **G: 59**
Gas gangrene [disease]
Gangrene **G: 27**
Hyperbaric oxygen therapy **H: 476**
Gas giant [planet]
Hydrogen (Occurrence) **H: 469**
Planet **P: 507**
Satellite **S: 149**; (Satellites of the gas giants) **S: 150** with picture
Gas hydrate
Gas [fuel] (From well to user) **G: 52-53**
Ice (Ice "cages") **I: 5**
Gas infrared heater
Gas [fuel] (In industry) **G: 51**
Gas laser [physics]

Laser (Gas lasers) L: 85
Noble gas N: 451
Gas lighting
Gas [fuel] (First uses of manufactured gas) G: 57
Invention *picture on* I: 356
Lamp (Gas lamps) L: 53 *with picture*
Gas mask G: 60 *with picture*
Morgan, Garrett Augustus M: 802
Gas metal arc welding
Welding (Arc welding) W: 189
Gas meter G: 60 *with picture*
Gas oil [petroleum] G: 60
Gas permeable contact lens
Contact lens (Hard contact lenses) Ci: 1020
Gas poisoning
Chemical-biological-radiological warfare
(Chemical) C: 396
Gas range
Range (Gas ranges) R: 138 *with pictures*
Gas refrigerator
Refrigeration (The gas refrigerator) R: 202 *with diagram*
Gas scrubber
Iron and steel (The blast furnace process) I: 440 *with diagram*
Gas system [mechanism]
Machine gun (Operation) M: 15-16
Gas-to-liquid technology
Gas [fuel] (Gas as a raw material) G: 52
Gas tungsten arc welding
Welding (Arc welding) W: 189
Gas turbine [machine]
Electric power (Other sources of electric power) E: 184
Turbine (Gas turbine systems) T: 497
Gas-turbine electric locomotive
Railroad (Rolling stock) R: 107
Gas turbine engine
Warship (Warships in the nuclear age) W: 42-43
Gas warfare *See* Chemical-biological-radiological warfare *in this index*
Gas welding
Welding (Gas welding) W: 189
Gas well
Gas [fuel] (Exploring for gas) G: 53; (Producing gas) G: 55 *with picture*; (Transmitting and distributing gas) G: 55
Well (Oil and natural gas wells) W: 193
Gascoigne, George [English author] G: 60
Gascons [people]
Gascony G: 60
Gascony [France] G: 60
Gascony, Gulf of *See* Gulf of Gascony *in this index*
Gascoyne-Cecil, Robert Arthur Talbot *See* Salisbury, Marquess of *in this index*
Gaseous diffusion [chemistry]
Isotope (Separating isotopes) I: 476
Uranium (Separating uranium isotopes) U: 215 *with diagram*
Gaseous-discharge lamp
Electric light (Gaseous-discharge lamps) E: 174 *with pictures*
Gaseous nebula [astronomy]
Nebula N: 116 *with picture*
Gaseous waste
Waste disposal W: 112
Gasification [industrial process]
Coal (Coal as a raw material) Ci: 719-720; (Coal research) Ci: 730-731; (Recent developments) Ci: 732
Gas [fuel] *picture on* G: 51
Gaskell, Elizabeth [British author] G: 61
Gaslight
Gas [fuel] (First uses of manufactured gas) G: 57
Lamp (Gas lamps) L: 53 *with picture*
Gasohol [chemical]
Ethanol E: 365
Gasoline [fuel] G: 61 *with picture*
Automobile (Power systems) A: 947-948; (Other infrastructure) A: 960; (The gasoline car) A: 965
Bromine B: 636
Bush, George Walker (Economy) B: 722j
Fuel (Petroleum) F: 550
Petroleum (Refining petroleum) P: 342-343 *with diagram*
Gasoline engine G: 63 *with pictures*
See also the list of Related articles in the Gasoline engine *article*
Automobile (Power systems) A: 947-948; (Powering an internal-combustion car) A: 951 *with diagrams*
Catalytic converter C: 298
Engine E: 283
Filter F: 103
Fuel injection F: 552
Gasoline G: 61
Heat (Chemical reactions) H: 149; (Internal-

combustion engines) H: 154
Rotary engine R: 486 *with diagrams*
Gasoline filter
Gasoline engine (The fuel system) G: 65
Gasoline shortage *See* Energy crisis *in this index*
Gasoline tax G: 66
Road (How roads and highways are paid for) R: 360
Gaspar [Biblical figure]
Magi M: 48
Gaspé Peninsula [Quebec] G: 66
Quebec *picture on* Q: 10; (Visitor's guide) Q: 20; (Land regions) Q: 22 *with map*; (Natural resources) Q: 27
Gaspee [ship]
Rhode Island (The Revolutionary War) R: 313
Gaspra [asteroid]
Asteroid (History of study) A: 824b
Gass, Patrick [American explorer]
Lewis and Clark expedition (Up the Missouri) L: 222a-222b
Gassan, Ogata [Japanese artist]
Japan *picture on* J: 55
Gassendi, Pierre [French philosopher]
Materialism M: 300b
Gasser, Herbert Spencer [American physiologist]
Nobel Prizes (Physiology or medicine: 1944) N: 445
Gassion, Edith Giovanna [French singer] *See* Piaf, Edith *in this index*
"Gassy Jack" [city history]
Vancouver (History) V: 277
Gaster [entomology]
Ant (The abdomen) A: 522 *with picture*
Gaston, William [American political leader]
Massachusetts (table) M: 288
Gastown [district]
British Columbia (Places to visit) B: 620 *with picture*
Vancouver (The city) V: 274-275
Gastrectomy
Surgery (Some common surgical operations) So: 1006
Gastric bypass surgery
Bariatric surgery B: 109 *with diagram*
Weight control (Surgery) W: 183
Gastric juice [physiology]
Digestive system (From mouth to stomach) D: 202
Stomach (The stomach's work) So: 908
Gastric ulcer
Stomach (Peptic ulcers) So: 908
Ulcer U: 15 *with picture*
Gastrin [hormone]
Gland (Exocrine glands) G: 207-208
Stomach (The stomach's work) So: 908
Gastritis [disorder] G: 66
Gastrocnemius [anatomy]
Leg (The leg) L: 182 *with diagram*
Gastroesophageal reflux [physiology] *See* Acid reflux *in this index*
Gastroesophageal reflux disease
Acid reflux A: 27
Gastrointestinal anthrax
Anthrax A: 545
Gastrointestinal tract *See* Alimentary canal *in this index*
Gastrolith [stone]
Seismosaurus S: 288
Gastropod [zoology]
Mollusk (Gastropods) M: 695
Shell (Kinds of mollusk shells) S: 385 *with diagram*
Gastroscope [instrument]
Endoscope E: 273 *with pictures*
Gate [structure]
Airport (The passenger terminal) A: 244
Gate City of the South [name for]
Atlanta (Gate City of the South) A: 861
Gate of Heavenly Peace
Beijing (The city) B: 222 *with map*
Gate region [electronics]
Transistor (Metal oxide semiconductor field effect transistors [MOSFET's]) T: 374 *with diagram*
Gatehouse
Castle (Structure) C: 280 *with picture*
Gatekeeper [medicine]
Medicine (The United States) M: 367-368
Gates, Bill [American businessman] G: 67
Computer (The personal computer) Ci: 924c-924d
Gates Foundation G: 67
Microsoft Corporation M: 519
Gates, Charles W. [American political leader]
Vermont (table) V: 333
Gates, Henry Louis, Jr. [American educator]
African Americans (Race relations) A: 136t

Gates, Horatio [American general] G: 67
Arnold, Benedict (A disappointed officer) A: 741
Burgoyne, John *picture on* B: 704
Camden, Battle of C: 76
Revolution, American (Victory at Saratoga) R: 282-283 *with picture*; (Camden) R: 285
Saratoga, Battle of S: 123
South Carolina (The Revolutionary War) So: 659
Washington, George (The army) W: 99
Gates, Melinda [wife of Bill Gates]
Gates Foundation G: 67
Gates, Ralph F. [American political leader]
Indiana (table) I: 214
Gates, Robert M. [American government official]
Bush, George Walker (table) B: 722h
Defense, Department of (table) D: 87
Obama, Barack (table) O: 640h
Gates, The [sculpture by Christo]
Christo C: 537
Gates, Thomas S., Jr. [American government official]
Defense, Department of (table) D: 87
Eisenhower, Dwight David (table) E: 152
Gates, William [American businessman] *See* Gates, Bill *in this index*
Gates Foundation G: 67
Foundation (table) F: 430
Gates of Ivory, The [book by Drabble]
Drabble, Margaret D: 317
Gates of Paradise [sculptures by Ghiberti]
Ghiberti, Lorenzo D: 182
Gates of the Arctic National Park [Alaska] G: 67
National Park System (table: National parks) N: 48; (table: National preserves) N: 58
Gateway [communications]
Communications satellite Ci: 888a
Gateway, The [Salt Lake City]
Utah (Places to visit) U: 238
Gateway Arch [Saint Louis] G: 67
Missouri *picture on* M: 651; (Places to visit) M: 660
Saint Louis (The city) S: 46 *with picture*
Gateway Center
Minneapolis (Downtown redevelopment) M: 583
Gateway National Recreation Area [New Jersey-New York]
National Park System (table: National recreation areas) N: 49
New York City (Parks) N: 338
Gateway State [former nickname]
Ohio O: 680
Gateway to China [name for]
Lanzhou L: 69
Gateway to the North [nickname]
Edmonton E: 83
Gateway to the West [name for]
Pittsburgh P: 500a
Gathas [hymns]
Persia, Ancient (Religion) P: 297
Zoroastrianism (Beliefs) Z: 607
Gather [glassmaking]
Glass (Glass terms) G: 222
"Gather ye rosebuds while ye may" [line by Herrick]
Herrick, Robert H: 215
Gathering line [pipeline]
Gas [fuel] (Transmitting and distributing gas) G: 55
Gathering machine
Bookbinding (Gathering) B: 471
Gathering Place [nickname]
Hawaii (Oahu) H: 102
Gatineau [Quebec] G: 68
Gatineau Park [Quebec]
Quebec *picture on* Q: 19
Gatineau River [Quebec]
Quebec *picture on* Q: 11
Gatling, Richard Jordan [American inventor] G: 68
Indiana (Early statehood) I: 216
Gatling gun
Gatling, Richard Jordan G: 68
Machine gun (History) M: 16 *with picture*
Gator Bowl [sports]
Jacksonville (Cultural life and recreation) J: 18-19
'Gator hole
Alligator (Habits) A: 375-376
Gatornationals [race]
Automobile racing (Drag racing) A: 978
Gatsby Charitable Foundation
Foundation (table) F: 430
GATT [agreement] *See* General Agreement on Tariffs and Trade *in this index*
Gattamelata [sculpture by Donatello]
Donatello D: 307
Gatun Dam [Chagres River]
Panama Canal (Gatun Lake) P: 123 *with map*
Gatun Lake [Panama Canal]
Panama Canal *diagram on* P: 124; (Gatun Lake)

P: 123 *with map*
Gatun locks [Panama Canal]
Panama Canal *pictures on* P: 124; (The Gatun Locks) P: 123 *with map*
Gatwick Airport
London (Transportation) L: 438
Gaucher's disease G: 68
Gauchesca [poetry]
Argentina (The arts) A: 651-652
Gaucho [cowboy] G: 68
See also Cowboy *in this index*
Argentina (Rural life) A: 650; (The arts) A: 651-652
Brazil (Clothing) B: 574
Indian, American (After European contact) I: 177 *with picture*
Latin America (Clothing) L: 97
Latin American literature (Romanticism) L: 112-113
Uruguay *picture on* U: 223; (Way of life) U: 223-224
Gaudí, Antonio [Spanish architect] G: 68
Barcelona B: 108
Gaudio, Bob [American musician]
Valli, Frankie V: 267 *with picture*
Gaugamela, Battle of [331 B.C.] *See* Arbela, Battle of *in this index*
Gauge [instrument] G: 69
Gauge [knitting]
Knitting (Knitting the fabric) K: 354
Gauge [measurement]
Railroad (The crossties and rails) R: 109; (Invention of the locomotive) R: 115
Railroad, Model (Scale and size) R: 120
Shotgun S: 438
Wire (Sizes of wire) W: 344
Woodworking (Planning and design) W: 396
Gauge boson [physics] *See* Fundamental boson *in this index*
Gauge theory [physics]
Subatomic particle (The Standard Model) So: 938
Gauguin, Paul [French artist] G: 69 *with picture*
Derain, André D: 152
Marquesas Islands M: 217
Painting (Postimpressionism) P: 75 *with picture*
Picasso, Pablo (Early sculptures) P: 448a-448b
Postimpressionism P: 709
Van Gogh, Vincent V: 282
Gaul [former region] G: 70 *with map*
Belgium (History) B: 232
Caesar, Julius (Campaigns in Gaul) C: 13
France (Early days) F: 471
French language (Beginnings) F: 517
Rubicon R: 507
Gauley River [West Virginia]
Kanawha River K: 212
Gauley River National Recreation Area [West Virginia]
National Park System (table: National recreation areas) N: 49
Gaulish [language]
French language (Beginnings) F: 517
Gaulle, Charles André Joseph Marie de [French political leader] *See* De Gaulle, Charles André Joseph Marie *in this index*
Gauls [ancient people]
France (Ancestry) F: 455
Galatia G: 8
Gaul G: 70
Gault decision [law]
Juvenile court (In the United States) J: 205
Gaultier, François [French businessman]
Doll (Rivalry in the doll industry) D: 291
Gaungbaung [garment]
Myanmar (Way of life) M: 970a
Gauntlet [clothing] G: 70
Armor (During the Middle Ages) A: 719-720 *with picture*
Glove G: 234 *with picture*
Gaur [animal] G: 70
Gause, Wilhelm [German painter]
Dance *picture on* D: 27
Gauss [measurement] G: 70
Magnetism (Strength of a magnetic field) M: 60
Gauss, Carl Friedrich [German mathematician] G: 70
Ceres [asteroid] C: 362
Gauss G: 70
Geometry (Rise of non-Euclidean geometry) G: 106
Lobachevsky, Nikolai L: 404
Mathematics (In the 1800's) M: 307
Number theory N: 607
Topology (History) T: 333
Gautama [religious leader] *See* Buddha *in this index*
Gautier, Louis Adolphe [French artist]
United States, History of the *picture on* U: 174

Gautier, Théophile [French author] G: 70
French literature (Gautier and Nerval) F: 521
Gauze [weaving]
Weaving (Fancy weaves) W: 173
Gavarnie Falls [falls, France]
Waterfall (table: Famous waterfalls of the world) W: 143 *with picture*
Gavel
Parliamentary procedure (table) P: 176
Gavial [reptile] G: 71 *with picture*
Crocodile C: 1149
Reptile (Crocodilians) R: 251
Gawain, Sir [legendary figure] G: 71
Round Table (The knights of the Round Table) R: 491
Gay [sexuality] *See* Homosexuality *in this index*
Gay, John [English author] G: 71
Gay-Lussac, Joseph Louis [French chemist] G: 71
Boron B: 490
Gas [physics] (Gas laws) G: 48-49
Iodine (Properties of iodine) I: 370-371
Gay-Lussac's Law [chemistry]
Gas [physics] (Gas laws) G: 48-49 *with pictures*
Gay marriage *See* Same-sex marriage *in this index*
Gay Nineties [U.S. history] G: 71
Gay rights movement G: 73
California (The beginning of the 2000's) C: 64
Civil rights (Major changes in the field of civil rights) Ci: 609-610
Civil union C: 613
Homosexuality (Attitudes toward homosexuality) H: 307
Marriage (Laws concerning marriage) M: 219-220
Obama, Barack (Military ends gay ban) O: 640h
Vermont (Recent developments) V: 337
Gaye, Marvin [American musician] G: 73
Gayfeather [plant]
Blazing star B: 398
Gayle, John [American political leader]
Alabama (table) A: 274
Gaylord, Frank C. II [American sculptor]
Korean War Veterans Memorial K: 384
Gaynor, Janet [American actress]
Motion picture (Best performance by an actress: 1927-28) M: 862
Gaza Strip [region, Middle East] G: 73 *with map*
Abbas, Mahmoud A: 4
Arab-Israeli conflict (The 1948 war) A: 582; (The 1967 war) A: 582a; (The first intifada) A: 582a; (Peacemaking) A: 582a; (The second intifada) A: 582a
Arafat, Yasir A: 590b
Egypt (Republic) E: 132
Hamas H: 28
Intifada I: 353
Israel I: 478; (History) I: 486-488; (The early 2000's) I: 489-490
Kadima K: 208
Middle East (History) M: 533-534
Palestine (The continuing conflict and peace efforts) P: 106
Palestine Liberation Organization P: 106
Palestinian Authority P: 107
Palestinians P: 107
Rabin, Yitzhak R: 50
Sharon, Ariel S: 377
Gazehound *See* Sight hound *in this index*
Gazelle [animal] G: 74 *with picture*
Antelope (Habits and appearance) A: 542
Gazelle hound [dog] *See* Saluki *in this index*
Gazetteer [reference]
Dictionary (Specialized dictionaries) D: 192
Gazprom [company]
Manufacturing (table) M: 170
Gbagbo, Laurent [Ivorian political leader]
Côte d'Ivoire (History) Ci: 1084b-1085
Gbowee, Leymah [Liberian political leader]
Nobel Prizes (Peace: 2011) N: 449
GBU-43 massive ordnance air blast [bomb]
Bomb (General-purpose [GP] bombs) B: 450
GBU-57 massive ordnance penetrator [bomb]
Bomb (General-purpose [GP] bombs) B: 450
Gd [symbol]
Gadolinium G: 4
Gdańsk [Poland] G: 74
Poland (World War I and independence) P: 612; (Rebuilding the Polish nation) P: 612-613; (Antigovernment protests) P: 614
GDP [measurement] *See* Gross domestic product *in this index*
Gdynia [Poland]
Poland *picture on* P: 615
GE [company] *See* General Electric Company *in this index*
Ge [Greek mythology] *See* Gaea *in this index*
Ge [symbol]
Germanium G: 143

Gê Indians
Indian, American (Indians of the Marginal Regions) I: 176-177
Gê-Pano-Carib [language group]
Indian, American (Language groups) I: 147-150
Gear [mechanism] G: 75
Automobile (The transmission) A: 948-949
Bicycle (Power and speed) B: 290 *with diagram*
Transmission (What a transmission does) T: 375; (How an automatic transmission works) T: 376 *with diagrams*; (How a manual transmission works) T: 377 *with diagrams*
Truck T: 456
Gear, John H. [American political leader]
Iowa (table) I: 391
Gear pump
Pump (Rotary pumps) P: 900b
Gear ratio [mechanism]
Transmission (Gears) T: 375
Gearbox [device] *See* Transmission *in this index*
Geared-drive ship
Ship (Engine-driven ships) S: 406
Geared traction elevator
Elevator (How elevators work) E: 234
Gearless traction elevator
Elevator (How elevators work) E: 234 *with diagram*
Gearshift
Automobile (The transmission) A: 948-949
Transmission (How a manual transmission works) T: 377-378 *with diagram*
Geary, John White [American political leader]
Pennsylvania (table) P: 263
Geb [Egyptian god]
Mythology *picture on* M: 974; (The Great Ennead) M: 979; (The Osiris myth) M: 979
Gebel-Williams, Gunther [American animal trainer]
Circus (The middle and late 1900's) Ci: 564
Gecko [reptile] G: 75 *with picture*
Lizard (How lizards move) L: 399
Gediminas [Lithuanian ruler]
Vilnius V: 385
Geechee [people] *See* Gullah *in this index*
Geer, T. T. [American political leader]
Oregon (table) O: 845
Geertz, Clifford James [American anthropologist]
Anthropology (The middle and late 1900's) A: 549
Geese *See* Goose *in this index*
Ge'ez [language]
Africa (Literature) A: 116b
Ethiopia (People) E: 368
Geffen, David [American businessman]
Spielberg, Steven So: 792
Gehenna [ancient region]
Hell H: 177
Gehrig, Lou [American baseball player] G: 75
Baseball (table: Hall of Fame) B: 134; (The Babe Ruth Era) B: 135-136
Gehringer, Charley [American baseball player]
Baseball (table: Hall of Fame) B: 134
Gehry, Frank [American architect] G: 75 *with picture*
Architecture (Architecture today) A: 632-633
Furniture *picture on* F: 587
Guggenheim Museum G: 421
Los Angeles *picture on* L: 466
Geiger, Hans [German physicist]
Geiger counter G: 76
Geiger counter [instrument] G: 76 *with pictures*
Prospecting P: 829
Geiger-Müller counter *See* Geiger counter *in this index*
Geim, Andre [Dutch physicist]
Nobel Prizes (Physics: 2010) N: 442
Geisel, Ernesto [Brazilian political leader]
Brazil (Under military rule) B: 586
Geisel, Theodor Seuss [American author] *See* Seuss, Dr. *in this index*
Geisha [entertainer]
Clothing (Cultural beliefs and values) Ci: 691 *with picture*
Geithner, Timothy F. [American government official]
Obama, Barack (table) O: 640h
Treasury, Department of the (table) T: 407
Gelada [monkey]
Baboon B: 3
Gelasius I, Saint [pope] G: 76
Church and state (History) C: 542
Pope (table) P: 666
Gelasius II [pope]
Pope (table) P: 666
Gelatin [explosive]
Dynamite (Kinds of dynamite) D: 397
Gelatin [protein] G: 76

Bone (Composition of bone) **B: 456**
Glue **G: 236**
Photography (Technical improvements) **P: 423**
Printing (Gravure cylinders) **P: 800**; (Collotype printing) **P: 801**
Gelding [horse]
Horse (Selecting a horse) **H: 353**
Horse racing (Thoroughbred horses) **H: 363-364**
Gelisol [soil]
Soil *map on* **So: 575**; (How soils are classified) **So: 576**
Gell-Mann, Murray [American physicist] **G: 77**
Atom (Recent discoveries) **A: 876**
Physics (Advances in the mid-1900's) **P: 442**
Quark **Q: 7**
Gellée, Claude [French painter] *See* Claude *in this index*
Gellius, Aulus [Roman author]
Latin literature (The Imperial Period) **L: 116-117**
Gelsemium [plant]
Poisonous plant (Some poisonous plants) **P: 602**
Gelugpa order [religious group]
Dalai Lama **D: 9**
Gem G: 77 *with pictures*
See also the list of Related articles in the Gem *article*
Jewelry **J: 117**
Lapidary **L: 73**
Gem, Harry [British sportsman]
Tennis (Beginnings) **T: 165**
Gem of the Ocean [play by Wilson]
Wilson, August **W: 316**
Gem State [nickname]
Idaho **I: 27**
Gemara [religious book]
Jews (The Talmudic period) **J: 122**
Judaism (The Talmud) **J: 180**
Talmud **T: 21**
Gemayel, Amin [Lebanese political leader]
Lebanon (Political struggle) **L: 174**
Gemayel, Bashir [Lebanese political leader]
Lebanon (War and terrorism) **L: 173**
Gemfibrozil [drug]
Cholesterol (Treatment of high blood cholesterol) **C: 520**
Gemini [astrology] **G: 80** *with picture*
Zodiac (The zodiac in astrology) **Z: 597** *with picture*
Gemini [constellation] **G: 80**
Castor and Pollux **C: 282**
Gemini program [space exploration]
Astronaut (Achievements in space) **A: 829**
Grissom, Virgil Ivan **G: 396**
Space exploration (Voskhod and Gemini: The first multiperson space flights) **So: 714** *with picture*
Gemini 3
Space exploration (Voskhod and Gemini: The first multiperson space flights) **So: 714**
Gemini 4
Space exploration (Voskhod and Gemini: The first multiperson space flights) **So: 714** *with picture*
Gemini 5
Conrad, Charles, Jr. **Ci: 973**
Cooper, Gordon **Ci: 1034**
Space exploration (Voskhod and Gemini: The first multiperson space flights) **So: 714**
Gemini 6
Borman, Frank **B: 488**
Schirra, Walter Marty, Jr. **S: 176**
Space exploration (Voskhod and Gemini: The first multiperson space flights) **So: 714**
Gemini 7
Lovell, James Arthur, Jr. **L: 509**
Schirra, Walter Marty, Jr. **S: 176**
Space exploration (Voskhod and Gemini: The first multiperson space flights) **So: 714**
Gemini 8
Armstrong, Neil Alden **A: 723**
Space exploration (Voskhod and Gemini: The first multiperson space flights) **So: 714**
Gemini 12
Aldrin, Buzz **A: 339**
Gemmule [reproduction]
Sponge (Asexual reproduction) **So: 800**
Gempei War [1180-1185]
Minamoto Yoritomo **M: 562**
Gemsbok [animal] **G: 80**
Antelope (Kinds of antelope) **A: 542-543** *with picture*
Gemsbok National Park [Botswana]
National park (South Africa) **N: 42e**; (table) **N: 42f**
Gemsbuck [animal] *See* Gemsbok *in this index*
Gen Xer [demography] *See* Generation X *in this index*
Gendai budo [sport]
Martial arts (Japanese martial arts) **M: 234-234a**

Gendarmerie [police]
Police (In other countries) **P: 623** *with picture*
Gender [grammar] **G: 80**
German language (Nouns) **G: 137**
Noun (Gender) **N: 552**
Gender [sexuality]
Gay rights movement **G: 73**
History (Approaches to history) **H: 261**
Reproduction, Human (How sex is determined) **R: 246**
Sexuality (Sex and gender) **S: 338**; (Gender identity) **S: 338**; (Gender roles) **S: 338a**
Gender discrimination *See* Sex discrimination *in this index*
Gender role [behavior]
Aggression **A: 141**
Etiquette (The origins of etiquette) **E: 374**; (Etiquette today) **E: 375**
Indian, American (Family life) **I: 136b-136c**
Parent (The role of parents) **P: 156**
Sex discrimination (Views on sex discrimination) **S: 335**
Sexuality (Sex and gender) **S: 338**; (Gender roles) **S: 338a**
Women's movement (Origins of women's traditional roles) **W: 383**
Gene [genetics] **G: 81**
See also Heredity *in this index*
Adaptation **A: 45**
Alcoholism (Causes of alcoholism) **A: 337**
Allergy (The development of allergies) **A: 374**
Antibiotic (Resistance to antibiotics) **A: 551**
Apoptosis **A: 566**
Biodiversity (Kinds of biodiversity) **B: 310**
Brain (Genetics) **B: 551**; (Genetic disorders) **B: 558**
Breast cancer **B: 591**
Cancer **C: 167**; (How damaged genes cause cancer) **C: 169**; (Genetics) **C: 173**
Cell (The code of life) **C: 334** *with diagrams*; (Before 1900) **C: 337**
Chromosome **C: 538**
Cloning **Ci: 682l** *with picture*; (Gene and cell cloning) **Ci: 684**
Colon cancer **Ci: 786**
Conservation (Biodiversity conservation) **Ci: 976**
Cystic fibrosis **Ci: 1208**
Dawkins, Richard **D: 51**
Developmental biology **D: 174**
Diabetes (Type 2 diabetes) **D: 179**
Disease **D: 225**; (Noninfectious diseases) **D: 228**
DNA **D: 258**
Down syndrome **D: 316**
Dwarfism (Causes) **D: 394-395**
Evolution (Mutation) **E: 427**; (History of the theory of evolution) **E: 432-433**
Gene mapping **G: 81**
Genetic counseling **G: 84a**
Genetic engineering **G: 84b**
Genetic testing **G: 84d**
Genetically modified food **G: 85**
Genetics **G: 86**
Genomics **G: 90**
Hamilton, William Donald **H: 33**
Heredity **H: 200**
Human Genome Project (The structure and importance of genomes) **H: 427**
Intelligence (The roles of heredity and environment) **I: 319**
Life (Adaptation) **L: 275**
Medicine (Medical researchers) **M: 369**; (The medical revolution) **M: 376-377**; (The challenge of genetics) **M: 378**
Mental illness (Genetic factors) **M: 407**
Molecular biology (The beginning of molecular biology) **M: 691-692**; (Molecular biology today) **M: 692**
Molecular medicine **M: 692**
Muscular dystrophy **M: 936**
Mutation **M: 968**
Plant (The reproduction of plants) **P: 532**
Prehistoric people (Analysis of the genetic materials) **P: 754b**
Prion **P: 804**
Proteomics **P: 833**
Psoriasis **P: 844**
Races, Human (How human populations develop and change) **R: 57**; (Susceptibility to genetic diseases) **R: 58**
Reproduction (How genes are transferred) **R: 242**
Reproduction, Human (How sex is determined) **R: 246**
Syphilis **So: 1069**
Tay-Sachs disease *diagram on* **T: 56**
Tuberculosis (Prevention of tuberculosis) **T: 479**
Virus (Structure) **V: 427**
Wilson, Edward Osborne **W: 316**
Gene bank [agriculture]

Agriculture (Preserving genetic diversity) **A: 160**
Horticulture (Research in horticulture) **H: 370**
Gene expression
Heredity (Mutation) **H: 200**; (How proteins are made) **H: 206**
Gene flow [genetics]
Heredity (Gene pools and allele frequency) **H: 203-204**
Races, Human (Migration and gene flow) **R: 59**
Gene frequency [genetics]
Races, Human (How human populations develop and change) **R: 57**
Gene mapping [genetics] **G: 81** *with diagram*
Genetics (Transmission genetics) **G: 87**
Heredity (Hereditary disorders) **H: 204**; (The Human Genome Project) **H: 210**
Human Genome Project (The work of the Human Genome Project) **H: 427**
Gene Marshall doll
Doll (The 1990's) **D: 293**
Gene mutation [genetics]
Heredity (Mutation) **H: 203**
Gene pool [genetics]
Evolution (Contributions from other scientific fields) **E: 433**
Heredity (Gene pools and allele frequency) **H: 203**
Races, Human (How human populations develop and change) **R: 57**
Gene splicing
Genetic engineering (How genes are reintroduced into cells) **G: 84b** *with diagram*
Gene therapy [medicine] **G: 81**
Cell (The 1900's) **C: 337-338**
Cystic fibrosis **Ci: 1208**
Genetic engineering (In medicine) **G: 84c**
Heredity (Hereditary disorders) **H: 204**; (The era of genetic engineering) **H: 209**
Immune system (Recent advances) **I: 88d**
Genealogical and Heraldic Dictionary of the Peerage and Baronetage of the United Kingdom [book]
Burke's *Peerage* **B: 705**
Genealogy [study] **G: 82**
Heraldry **H: 194** *with picture*
Genealogy of Morals, The [book by Nietzsche]
Nietzsche, Friedrich (Nietzsche and religion) **N: 406-407**
General [locomotive]
Civil War, American (Raids) **Ci: 629**
Locomotive *picture on* **L: 415**
General [rank] **G: 82**
Army, United States *picture on* **A: 732**
Marine Corps, United States *pictures on* **M: 207**
Rank, Military (table) **R: 140**
General, The [film]
Keaton, Buster **K: 253** *with picture*
General Accounting Office *See* Government Accountability Office *in this index*
General adaptation syndrome [physiology]
Stress (How stress affects the body) **So: 926**
General Agreement on Tariffs and Trade [1947] **G: 83**
Clinton, Bill (International affairs) **Ci: 682e**
Globalization (Features of globalization) **G: 233**
International trade (Government trade policies) **I: 348**
Reciprocal trade agreement **R: 175**
Tariff (The 1900's) **T: 45**
World Trade Organization **W: 451**
General anesthesia [medicine]
Anesthesia (General anesthesia) **A: 458**
Dentistry (Modern dentistry) **D: 144-145**
Drug (Anesthetics) **D: 352**
Ether **E: 365**
Surgery (Anesthesia) **So: 1004**
General assembly
Kibbutz **K: 310**
General Assembly [UN]
International law (After World War II) **I: 342**
United Nations (The six major UN organs) **U: 78** *with picture*; (The General Assembly) **U: 78**; (Membership questions) **U: 95**
World *picture on* **W: 412a**
General Assembly of the Church of Scotland [religious group]
Scotland (Religion) **S: 215**
General assignment editor [occupation]
Newspaper (Gathering information) **N: 382**
General Authorities
Mormons (Church organization) **M: 807**
General aviation airport
Airport (General aviation airports) **A: 243**
General aviation plane
Aviation (The aviation industry) **A: 984**
General Chronicle of Spain [book]
Spanish literature (Early medieval literature) **So: 757-758**

General Church of the New Jerusalem [religious group]
Swedenborgians So: 1035
General Conference
United Nations (Amending the charter) U: 78
General Conference on Weights and Measures
Light (The speed of light) L: 290
General contractor
Building trade (The contracting system) B: 685
General Convention
Episcopal Church E: 344
General Convention of the New Jerusalem [religious group]
Swedenborgians So: 1035
General council [religion] *See* Ecumenical council *in this index*
General Council of the Valleys
Andorra (Government) A: 454
General court-martial
Court-martial Ci: 1104
General damages [law]
Damages D: 20
General dentistry
Dentistry D: 143
General discharge
Military discharge M: 543
General Dynamics Corporation
Holland, John Philip H: 292
General education
Education (Kinds of education) E: 87
General election
Government (Parliamentary democracy) G: 286
Parliament (How members are selected) P: 173
General Electric Company G: 83
Business (Conglomerates) B: 726
Edison, Thomas Alva (Electric utilities and manufacturing) E: 79-80
Manufacturing (table) M: 170
Reagan, Ronald Wilson (Television star) R: 166
Schenectady S: 174
General Electric Research Laboratory
Diamond (Synthetic diamonds) D: 183 *with pictures*
General Epistles [New Testament]
James, Epistle of J: 26
General equilibrium theory [economics]
Arrow, Kenneth Joseph A: 743
General Giant [tree]
Sequoia (Size) S: 310d
General Grand Chapter [organization]
Eastern Star E: 47
General Grant National Memorial [New York]
Grant, Ulysses S. (Later years) G: 317-318 *with picture*
National Park System (table: National memorials) N: 54
General Grant Tree [tree, California]
Kings Canyon National Park K: 330
General History [book]
Spanish literature (Early medieval literature) So: 757-758
General History of Connecticut, A [book by Peters]
Blue laws B: 420
General History of Quadrupeds, A [book by Bewick]
Bewick, Thomas B: 276
General illumination [lighting]
Theater (Lighting methods) T: 240-241
General jurisdiction [law]
Court (Types of courts) Ci: 1101; (State courts) Ci: 1102
General Lee Tree [tree, California]
Kings Canyon National Park K: 330
General Letters [New Testament]
Bible (The Letters) B: 284
General lien [law]
Lien L: 273
General manager
Opera (The general manager) O: 794
General Medical Council [agency]
Medicine (A career as a doctor) M: 370-371
General mobile radio service
Walkie-talkie W: 14
General Motors Company G: 83
Automobile (Economic impact) A: 959; (The rise of the Big Three) A: 968; (The 2000's) A: 972
Durant, William Crapo D: 388
Flint F: 235
Ford, Henry (Industrial accomplishments) F: 380
Kettering, Charles Franklin K: 307
Manufacturing (table) M: 170
Nash, Charles William N: 22
Plastics (Growth of the plastics industry) P: 560
Sports car (History) So: 803
General of the Air Force [rank]
General G: 82
General of the Armies of the United States

Washington, George (Death) W: 107-108
General of the Army [rank]
General G: 82
General practitioner [medicine]
Medicine (Primary care physicians) M: 366; (The United Kingdom) M: 366-367
General Product Safety Regulations
Consumer protection (The right to safety) Ci: 1018
General-purpose bomb
Bomb (General-purpose [GP] bombs) B: 450 *with diagram*
General Radio Service [Canada]
Citizens band radio Ci: 568
General reference map
Map (General reference maps) M: 177 *with picture*
General Services Administration [U.S.] G: 83
Washington, D.C. *map on* W: 76
General Sherman Tree [California]
Sequoia (Size) S: 310d *with picture*
Sequoia National Park S: 311
Tree (Interesting facts about trees) T: 411
General Slocum Norge [ship]
Shipwreck (table: Major shipwrecks) S: 428
General staff [military]
Army (The rise of modern armies) A: 727-728
General Strike [British history]
Baldwin, Stanley B: 40
General strike [labor]
Labor movement (Handling labor disputes) L: 6-7
General Synod of the Reformed Church in America
Reformed Church in America R: 199
General Theory of Employment, Interest, and Money, The [book by Keynes]
Capitalism (Changing attitudes toward capitalism) C: 196
Keynes, John Maynard K: 308a
General theory of relativity [physics]
Dark energy D: 36
Dark matter D: 37
Einstein, Albert E: 146
Force (Einstein's theory of general relativity) F: 370
Gravitation (Einstein's theory of gravitation) G: 331; (Predictions of general relativity) G: 332
Gravitational wave G: 333
Motion (Einstein's theories of relativity) M: 845
Relativity R: 209; (General relativity) R: 211
Riemann, Georg Friedrich Bernhard R: 337
General Tom Thumb *See* Stratton, Charles Sherwood *in this index*
General transport airport
Airport (General aviation airports) A: 243
General utility airport
Airport (General aviation airports) A: 243
Generalization [logic]
Inductive method I: 240
Generalization [psychology]
Personality (Emotional reactions) P: 302
Generalized anxiety disorder [psychology]
Anxiety disorder A: 562
Generall Historie of Virginia, New England and the Summer Isles, The [book by Smith]
American literature (Virginia) A: 414
Generally accepted accounting principles
Accounting (Financial reports) A: 22
Generation [biology]
Races, Human (Mutation) R: 58; (Genetic drift) R: 58-59
Generation name
Name (The history of names) N: 7
Generation of 1898 [literary group]
Spanish literature (The Generation of 1898) So: 762
Generation of 1927 [literary group]
Spanish literature (The Generation of 1927) So: 763
Generation X [book by Deverson and Hamblett]
Generation X G: 84
Generation X [demography] G: 84
Generation X; Tales for an Accelerated Culture [book by Coupland]
Generation X G: 84
Generation Y [demography] G: 84
Generations, Alternation of *See* Alternation of generations *in this index*
Generative grammar
Chomsky, Noam C: 520
Grammar G: 303
Language (The science of language) L: 66-67
Linguistics (The generative theory of language) L: 337
Generator [cloud seeding]
Cloud seeding (Cloud-seeding methods) C: 711
Generator [refrigeration]

Refrigeration (The gas refrigerator) R: 202 *with diagram*
Generator [vat]
Vinegar (Making vinegar) V: 386
Generator, Electric *See* Electric generator *in this index*
Generic name
Drug (The United States Adopted Name) D: 356
Wine (Where wine comes from) W: 336-337
Genesee River [New York]
New York (Rivers) N: 306
Rochester (Description) R: 370
Genesis [book] G: 84
Bible (The Law) B: 280
Deluge D: 118
Eden E: 76
Joseph J: 167
Life (Religious explanations) L: 278
Pentateuch P: 274
Genesis [spacecraft]
Astronomy (Direct sampling) A: 846
Sun (Space-based studies) So: 986
Genesis [wallhanging]
Rugs and carpets *picture on* R: 517
Genêt, Edmond Charles Édouard [French diplomat] G: 84
Adams, John Quincy (Lawyer and writer) A: 40-41
Washington, George (Relations with France) W: 105
Genet, Jean [French dramatist] G: 84a
Drama (Theater of the Absurd) D: 340
French literature (Developments in drama) F: 523
Genetic code
Cell (The genetic code) C: 336
Heredity (How proteins are made) H: 206
Molecular biology (The beginning of molecular biology) M: 691-692
RNA R: 357
Genetic counseling G: 84a
Birth defect (Prevention and treatment) B: 380
Heredity (Hereditary disorders) H: 204-205
Genetic diversity
Agriculture (Preserving genetic diversity) A: 160
Biodiversity (Kinds of biodiversity) B: 310
Genetic drift
Evolution (Genetic drift) E: 429; (The synthetic theory) E: 432-433
Heredity (Gene pools and allele frequency) H: 203-204
Races, Human (Genetic drift) R: 58
Genetic engineering G: 84b *with diagrams*
Agriculture (Recent developments) A: 159-160
Bacteriology (Controlling bacterial diseases) B: 22
Biology (Current research and issues) B: 320-321 *with picture*
Biotechnology B: 327
Corn (Controlling pests and diseases) Ci: 1061
Fruit (Developing new fruit cultivars) F: 548
Gene mapping G: 81
Genetically modified food G: 85
Genetics (Molecular genetics) G: 86-87
Heredity (The era of genetic engineering) H: 209
Horticulture (Research in horticulture) H: 370
Technology (Emerging technologies) T: 76
Genetic medicine
Medicine (The challenge of genetics) M: 378
Genetic testing [medicine] G: 84d
Genetic variation
Heredity (Sources of genetic variation) H: 203
Genetically modified food G: 85 *with picture*
Plant (Breeding and genetics) P: 542
Genetically modified organism
Agriculture *picture on* A: 153; (Genetic engineering) A: 160
Cotton (Recent developments) Ci: 1093
Cropping system Ci: 1154
Fruit (Developing new fruit cultivars) F: 548
Genetically modified food G: 85
Geneticist [career]
Genetics G: 86
Heredity H: 200
Genetics G: 86
See also Heredity *in this index*
Agriculture (Agricultural genetics) A: 158
Biology (table) B: 317; (The growth of modern biology) B: 319-320
Botany (How plants function) B: 508; (Later developments) B: 509
Cell (The code of life) C: 334
Developmental biology D: 173
Evolution (History of the theory of evolution) E: 432
Genetic counseling G: 84a
Genetic engineering G: 84b
Heredity H: 200; (The birth of genetics) H: 208
Medicine (table) M: 369
Mendel, Gregor Johann M: 398

Molecular biology M: 691
Plant (Breeding and genetics) P: 542
Races, Human (How human populations develop and change) R: 57; (Genetic drift) R: 58
Science (Science in the early 1900's) S: 201-202
Sociobiology So: 563
Zoology (What zoologists study) Z: 606-607
Geneva [Switzerland] G: 87
Calvin, John (His life) C: 70
Presbyterians (History) P: 756a
Geneva, Lake [France-Switzerland] See Lake Geneva in this index
Geneva Accords [international relations] G: 87
Indochina (The Geneva Accords) I: 225
Vietnam V: 364; (The First Indochina War) V: 371
Vietnam War (The Indochina War) V: 373
Geneva Agreements [1954] See Geneva Accords in this index
Geneva Arbitration [1871-1872]
Alabama A: 255
Washington, Treaty of W: 109
Geneva conference [1954]
Cold War (To the brink and back) Ci: 765
Geneva conference [1955]
Cold War (The spirit of Geneva) Ci: 766
Geneva Conventions [international law] G: 88
International law (In the 1800's) I: 342
Prisoner of war P: 808
Red Cross (The Red Cross in other lands) R: 187; (In the United States) R: 187
War crime W: 27
Geneva Phonogram Convention [1974]
Copyright (International agreements) Ci: 1048
Genève [Switzerland] See Geneva in this index
Geneviève, Sainte [French religious leader]
Paris (Famous buildings) P: 163-164
Genf [Switzerland] See Geneva in this index
Genfer See [lake, Switzerland]
Lake Geneva L: 38 with map
Genghis Khan [Mongol conqueror] G: 88 with picture and map
Asia (The people) A: 791; (Nomadic invasions) A: 805-806
India (The Mughal Empire) I: 129
Mongol Empire (Early empire) M: 719
Genie [Arab mythology] G: 89
Genie [mythical being] G: 89
See also Jinni in this index
Aladdin A: 280
Genin, John Nicholas [American businessman]
Hat (History) H: 84-85
Genital herpes [disease] See Herpes, Genital in this index
Genital organs [anatomy]
Menstruation M: 404 with pictures
Reproduction, Human (The human reproductive system) R: 244-245 with diagrams
Sexuality (Biological factors) S: 337
Sterility So: 893
Genital phase [psychology]
Libido L: 233
Genitive case [grammar]
Case (Cases in Latin) C: 271-272
Genius [Roman mythology] G: 89
Genius of Universal Emancipation, The [magazine]
Lundy, Benjamin L: 523
United States, History of the (The abolition movement) U: 173-174
Genji, Prince [literary figure]
Murasaki Shikibu M: 929
Genn, James [American surveyor]
Washington, George (First expedition) W: 93
Gennes, Pierre-Gilles de [French physicist]
Nobel Prizes (Physics: 1991) N: 442
Gennesaret [name for]
Galilee, Sea of G: 11
Genoa [Italy] G: 89 with picture
Columbus, Christopher (Early years) Ci: 857
Venice (History) V: 308
Genoa [Nevada]
Nevada (Early settlement) N: 174 with picture
Genoa, Gulf of
Genoa G: 89 with picture
Genoa jib
Sailing (Sails) S: 24
Genocide [crime] G: 89
Armenian Genocide A: 719
Holocaust ("The Final Solution") H: 296a
International Criminal Court I: 338
Minority group (The creation of minority groups) M: 609
Racism (History) R: 62
War (Changes in the rules of war) W: 24
Genocide Convention [1948]
Genocide G: 90
Holocaust (The Nuremberg Trials) H: 297
Genome [genetics]

Ape A: 563
Biology (Current research and issues) B: 320-321
Classification, Scientific Ci: 653
Gene mapping G: 81
Genomics G: 90
Heredity (Chromosomes and genes) H: 201; (The Human Genome Project) H: 210
Human Genome Project H: 427
Medicine (The challenge of genetics) M: 378
Molecular medicine M: 692
Neandertals N: 93
Prehistoric people (The single origin theory) P: 750-751
Proteomics P: 833
Science (Recent developments) S: 203
Typhus (Treatment) T: 541
Virus (Structure) V: 427
Genome sequencing [genetics]
Genomics G: 90
Genomic medicine See Molecular medicine in this index
Genomics [science] G: 90
Genotype [genetics]
Heredity (Heredity and environment) H: 205
Molecular medicine M: 692
Races, Human (How human populations develop and change) R: 57
Genre film
Motion picture (Movies become big business) M: 865-866
Genre painting [art]
Painting (People) P: 31 with picture
Teniers, David, the Younger picture on T: 133
Genro [Japanese government]
Statesman So: 867
Genseric [Vandal king]
Vandals V: 279
Gent [Belgium]
Ghent G: 181
Gentamicin [medication]
Antibiotic (table) A: 551
Gentian [botany] G: 90
Flower pictures on F: 285, P: 289; (table) F: 300 with picture
Gentile [people] G: 90
Gentileschi, Artemisia [Italian painter] G: 90
Painting (Baroque) P: 58
Gentle Art of Making Enemies, The [book by Whistler]
Whistler, James Abbott McNeill W: 283
Gentleman Boss [nickname]
Arthur, Chester Alan A: 754
"Gentleman from San Francisco, The" [story by Bunin]
Russian literature (Symbolism) R: 563
Gentleman Jim [nickname]
Corbett, James John Ci: 1050
Gentleman's Agreement [book by Hobson]
Hobson, Laura Z. H: 273
Gentleman's Agreement [film]
Hart, Moss H: 77
Motion picture (Best picture: 1947) M: 861
Gentleman's Magazine
Magazine (History) M: 44
Gentlemen's agreement [1908] G: 90
Asian Americans (The second wave) A: 812e
Roosevelt, Theodore (Friction with Japan) R: 467
Gentoo penguin
Antarctica (Living things) A: 534-535 with picture
Gentry [social class]
Colonial life in America (The structure of colonial society) Ci: 793
Genuine Risk [horse]
Kentucky Derby K: 297
Genus [biology]
Animal (The scientific classification of animals) A: 472-473
Classification, Scientific (Groups in classification) Ci: 655
Geocentric theory
Astronomy (Earth-centered theories) A: 835; (History) A: 846-847 with diagram
Geocentric zenith [astronomy]
Zenith Z: 589
Geochemical Ocean Section Studies
Atlantic Ocean (New techniques) A: 867
Geochemistry G: 91
Geode [geology]
Fluorite F: 306
Quartz Q: 8
Geodesic dome
Architecture picture on A: 610
Carbon (Fullerenes) C: 205
Fuller, Buckminster F: 554 with picture
Geodesy [surveying] G: 91
Geodetic center of North America G: 91
Kansas K: 216

Geodetic control point
Survey (Types of surveys) So: 1011
Geodetic effect [physics]
Gravitation (Bending of light rays) G: 332
Relativity (Distortions in space-time) R: 212
Geodetic survey
Geodesy G: 91
Surveying (Types of surveys) So: 1011
Geoduck [clam] G: 91 with picture
Geoengineering
Global warming (Ways to limit global warming) G: 232b
Geoffrey, Count of Anjou [French nobleman]
Henry II [king of England] H: 185
Plantagenet P: 550
Geoffrey of Monmouth [Welsh historian] G: 91
Gawain, Sir G: 71
Geographic center of North America G: 92
North Dakota (Interesting facts) N: 497
Geographic center of the United States G: 92
United States map on U: 120
Geographic grid
Map (Geographic grids) M: 179 with diagram
Geographic information system G: 92
Geography G: 92
Map M: 177; (Production and reproduction) M: 181 with picture
Geographic Names, United States Board on G: 92
Geographical Magazine
Royal Geographical Society R: 498
Geographical mile [measurement]
Mile M: 542
Geographical-race theory
Races, Human (The geographical-race theory) R: 54-55 with map
Geographical Society, Royal
Royal Geographical Society R: 498
Geography G: 92 with pictures and map
See also the list of Related articles in the Geography article
Botany (Plant habitats) B: 508
Evolution (Evolution of new species) E: 429-430; (Geographic distribution of species) E: 430
Geographic information system G: 92
Geomorphology G: 106a
Races, Human (The geographical-race theory) R: 54-55 with map
World (Physical features of the world) W: 415
Geography [book by Ptolemy]
Map picture on M: 176; (Ancient maps) M: 182-183
Ptolemy P: 854
Geography [book by Strabo]
Geology (The ancient Greeks) G: 97
Strabo So: 917
Geography III [poetry by Bishop]
American literature (Poetry) A: 423
Geological catastrophe [zoology]
Cuvier, Baron Ci: 1202
Geological engineer
Mining (Mining careers) M: 577-578
Geological oceanography
Oceanography O: 668
Geological record
Fossil F: 422
Time (The formation of rock) T: 292
Geological Survey [Canada]
Geological Survey, United States G: 96
Geological Survey, United States G: 96
Map (Database development) M: 180; (Mapping the Americas) M: 184-185
Moon (Describing lunar evolution) M: 794
Geological time scale
Earth (Age of Earth) E: 26; (table) E: 30
Geology G: 97 with pictures
See also the list of Related articles in the Geology article
Careers (Life, physical, and social sciences) C: 225-226
Earth E: 16
Gas [fuel] (Exploring for gas) G: 53
Geomorphology G: 106a
Hutton, James H: 459
Lyell, Sir Charles L: 533
Mining (Mining careers) M: 577-578
Petroleum (Geological studies) P: 335
Prehistoric people P: 744
Prospecting P: 829
Radiogeology R: 98
Science (The physical sciences) S: 193
Geomagnetic field
Magnetism (Earth) M: 60d
Geomagnetic north pole
North Pole N: 517
Geomagnetic south pole
South Pole So: 685

Geometric fractal
 Fractal F: 443 *with diagrams*
Geometric model
 Computer graphics (In engineering) Ci: 924h
Geometric progression [mathematics]
 Progression (Geometric progressions) P: 812
 Series S: 316b; (Working with infinite series)
  S: 317
Geometric series [mathematics]
 Series S: 316b; (Working with infinite series)
  S: 317
Geometric style [art] G: 101
 Painting (Greek painting) P: 42
Geometric tracery [architecture]
 Tracery T: 355
Geometrical optics [physics]
 Optics O: 813
 Physics (Light) P: 437
Geometry G: 101 *with diagrams*
 See also the list of Related articles in the Geometry
  article
 Axiom A: 994
 Euclid E: 377
 Fourth dimension F: 438
 Mathematics (Branches of mathematics) M: 303
 Philosophy (Rationalism) P: 388-389
 Riemann, Georg Friedrich Bernhard R: 337
 Symmetry So: 1066
 Topology T: 332
Geomorphology [geology] G: 106a
 Geography (Physical geography) G: 94
 Geology (Areas of specialization) G: 100-101
Geophone [instrument]
 Acoustics A: 29
 Gas [fuel] (Exploring for gas) G: 53
 Petroleum (Seismic studies) P: 337
Geophysics G: 106a
 Careers (Life, physical, and social sciences)
  C: 225-226
 Gas [fuel] (Exploring for gas) G: 53
 Geology (Areas of specialization) G: 100-101
 Petroleum (Geophysical studies) P: 336
 Seismology S: 288
Geopolitics G: 106b
 War (Conflicts over resources) W: 23
Georg II [duke of Saxe-Meiningen]
 Drama (Early realism) D: 338
George [city, Washington]
 Washington (Interesting facts about Washington)
  W: 47
George I [king of England] G: 106b
 South Carolina (Colonial days) So: 659
 United Kingdom (The beginning of cabinet
  government) U: 67
 Walpole, Sir Robert W: 20
George I [king of Greece] G: 106b
 Greece (George I) G: 362
George II [king of England] G: 106b *with portrait*
 United Kingdom (The beginning of cabinet
  government) U: 67
George II [king of Greece] G: 106b
 Greece (Between world wars) G: 363
George III [king of Britain] G: 107 *with portrait*
 Buckingham Palace B: 664
 North, Lord N: 457
 Pitt, William, the Younger P: 500
 Pound P: 721
 Revolution, American (British policy changes)
  R: 271-272; (The Declaration of Independence)
  R: 278
 United Kingdom (The beginning of cabinet
  government) U: 67; (The Revolutionary War in
  America) U: 67
 United States, History of the (Policy changes)
  U: 158; (The Revolutionary War begins)
  U: 159-160
George IV [king of United Kingdom] G: 107
George V [king of United Kingdom] G: 107 *with
 portrait*
George VI [king of United Kingdom] G: 107 *with
 portrait*
George, David Lloyd [British political leader] *See*
 Lloyd George, David *in this index*
George, Eddie [American football player]
 Football (table) F: 363
George, Elizabeth [American author] G: 108
George, Francis Eugene [American religious
 leader] G: 108
George, Henry [American social reformer] G: 108
 Ricardo, David R: 321
 Single tax S: 472
George, James Zachariah [American political
 leader] G: 108
George, Jean Craighead [American author] G: 108
 Newbery Medal (table) N: 359
 Regina Medal (table: 2003) R: 206
George, John L. [husband of]

George, Jean Craighead G: 108
George, Saint [legendary figure] G: 108
 Dragon D: 319 *with picture*
George, Stefan [German poet] G: 108
George-Barden Act [1946]
 Agricultural education (History) A: 145
George Bush Intercontinental Airport
 Airport (table) A: 245
George Bush Presidential Library and Museum
 Bush, George Herbert Walker (Later years)
  B: 722a
George C. Marshall Space Flight Center
 Alabama A: 256; (Population) A: 260; (The mid-
  1900's) A: 278
 Huntsville H: 451
George Cross
 Medals, decorations, and orders (table) M: 359
George F. Getty, Inc.
 Getty, J. Paul G: 175
George H. W. Bush [ship]
 Aircraft carrier (The United States carrier fleet)
  A: 206
George Land [island, Arctic]
 Franz Josef Land F: 494
George Rogers Clark National Historical Park
 [Indiana]
 National Park System (table: National historical
  parks) N: 56-57
George Town [Cayman Islands]
 Cayman Islands C: 323
George Town [Malaysia] G: 109
George Tupou I [king of Tonga]
 Fiji (History) F: 98
 Tonga (History) T: 328
George Tupou II [king of Tonga]
 Tonga (History) T: 328
George Tupou V [king of Tonga]
 Tonga (History) T: 328-329
George Tupou VI [king of Tonga]
 Tonga (History) T: 328-329
George W. Bush Presidential Center
 Bush, George Walker (Later years) B: 724
George Washington [sculpture by Greenough]
 Sculpture (American sculpture) S: 255 *with
  picture*
George Washington [ship]
 Aircraft carrier (The United States carrier fleet)
  A: 206
**George Washington Birthplace National
 Monument** [Virginia] G: 109
 National Park System (table: National
  monuments) N: 51
George Washington Bridge [New York City] G: 109
 Bridge (table: Suspension) B: 603
 New Jersey (Transportation) N: 248 *with picture*
George Washington Carver National Monument
 [Missouri] G: 109
 Carver, George Washington (Awards and honors)
  C: 269
 National Park System (table: National
  monuments) N: 51
**George Washington Carver Research
 Foundation** [Alabama]
 Carver, George Washington (Tuskegee instructor
  and researcher) C: 268-269
George Washington Memorial Parkway
 [Maryland-Virginia]
 National Park System (table: National parkways
  and other national parklands) N: 56
George Washington of South America
 [nickname]
 Bolívar, Simón B: 441
Georges, Hurricane *See* Hurricane Georges *in this
 index*
**Georges Pompidou National Center of Art and
 Culture** [Paris]
 France (Museums and libraries) F: 461
 Paris (Museums and art galleries) P: 164 *with
  picture*
Georgetown [Guyana] G: 109
 Guyana G: 445, *picture on* G: 447
Georgetown [Washington, D.C.]
 Washington, D.C. *picture on* W: 81; (Architectural
  styles) W: 78; (Northwest) W: 79; (History)
  W: 85
Georgetown University G: 109
 Carroll C: 248
Georgia [country] G: 109 *with picture and map*
 Abkhazia A: 11
 Caucasus C: 317
 Flag *picture on* F: 203
 Shevardnadze, Eduard Amvrosiyevich S: 399
 Union of Soviet Socialist Republics (History) U: 35
Georgia [state, U.S.] G: 112 *with pictures and maps*
 See also the list of Related articles in the Georgia
  article
 Colonial life in America (Development of the

 Thirteen Colonies) Ci: 790 *with map*
 South Carolina (Colonial days) So: 659
 Trail of Tears T: 367
 United States, History of the (North Carolina,
  South Carolina, and Georgia) U: 156
Georgia, Strait of [Washington]
 Puget Sound P: 886
Georgia, University of G: 135
 Georgia (Schools) G: 116 *with picture*
Georgia Aquarium
 Atlanta *picture on* A: 860b
Georgia Institute of Technology G: 135
"Georgia On My Mind" [song]
 Carmichael, Hoagy C: 241
"Georgia Peach, The" [nickname]
 Cobb, Ty Ci: 741
Georgia Tech [school] *See* Georgia Institute of
 Technology *in this index*
Georgia Warm Springs Foundation
 Roosevelt, Franklin Delano (Battle with polio)
  R: 451
Georgian architecture G: 135
 Australia (Architecture) A: 906
 Colonial life in America (Houses) Ci: 796-797
 England (The arts) E: 298-299
 House *picture on* H: 381
 White House (The original building) W: 290 *with
  picture*
Georgian Bay [bay, Ontario] G: 136
 Lake Huron L: 39 *with map*
 Ontario *picture on* O: 764
Georgian Bay Islands National Park [Ontario]
 Canada (table: National parks and national park
  reserves) C: 113
Georgian language
 Alphabet (Other alphabets) A: 383
 Georgia (People) G: 109
Georgian poets [English literature]
 Brooke, Rupert B: 639
 English literature (Literature before World War
  I) E: 322
Georgians [people]
 Georgia (People) G: 109
Georgics [poems by Virgil]
 Latin literature (The Augustan Age) L: 116
 Virgil (His works) V: 391-392
GEOSAT [satellite] *See* Geostationary orbit satellite
 in this index
Geoscientist
 Careers (Life, physical, and social sciences)
  C: 225-226
**Geostationary Operational Environmental
 Satellite**
 Satellite, Artificial *picture on* S: 150f
Geostationary orbit satellite
 Antenna (Types of antennas) A: 543
 Communications satellite (Types of satellites)
  Ci: 888a
 Weather (Weather satellites) W: 163-164
 Weather satellite W: 172 *with picture*
Geosynchronous orbit
 Satellite, Artificial (Satellite orbits) S: 150d *with
  picture*
 Space exploration (Kinds of earth orbits) *diagram
  on* So: 697
Geotextile [fabric]
 Textile (Nonwovens) T: 215
Geothermal energy G: 136
 Electric power (Other sources of electric power)
  E: 184
 Energy supply (Geothermal power) E: 279
 Global warming (Alternative energy sources)
  G: 232b
 Heat (Earth) H: 149
 Hot springs H: 374b
 Volcano V: 438
Geothermal reservoir
 Geothermal energy G: 136
Geotropism [botany]
 Plant (Environmental factors) P: 538 *with picture*
 Tropism T: 451
Gephardt, Richard Andrew [American political
 leader] G: 136
Ger [tent]
 Family *picture on* F: 24
 Mongolia (The people) M: 722 *with picture*
Gerald R. Ford Museum
 Grand Rapids G: 309
Geraniol [chemical]
 Citronella Ci: 573
Geranium [plant] G: 136
 Flower *picture on* F: 292; (table) F: 300 *with
  picture*
 Plant *pictures on* P: 525, P: 547
Gerard, Forrest [American government official]
 Indian, American (Political gains) I: 182
Gerbil [animal] G: 136

Gerhardt, Charles [French chemist]
Aspirin (History) A: 816
Geriatrics [medicine] G: 137
See also Old age in this index
Senility S: 300
Géricault, Théodore [French painter] G: 137
Painting (Romanticism) P: 68-69 with picture
Geringer, Jim [American political leader]
Wyoming (table) W: 532
Germ [food]
Bran B: 563
Egg (The yolk) E: 117
Flour (How white flour is milled) F: 269
Wheat (Food for people) W: 266-267 with
diagram; (Structure) W: 267-268 with diagram
Germ [microorganism] See Microorganism in this
index
Germ cell [biology]
Cell (Meiosis) C: 331
Germ plasm [genetics]
Weismann, August W: 188
Germ theory [medicine]
Biology (Materialistic physiology and the cell
theory) B: 319
Drug (The drug revolution) D: 359
Medicine (Scientific study of the effects of
disease) M: 375
Germ warfare
Biological Weapons Convention B: 315
Chemical-biological-radiological warfare
(Biological) C: 396
Terrorism (Biological attacks) T: 176
Germain, Sophie [French mathematician]
Prime number (Special primes) P: 780
Germain prime [mathematics]
Prime number (Special primes) P: 780
German cockroach
Cockroach Ci: 745
Insect picture on I: 285
German Confederation [German history]
Austria (Metternich and revolution) A: 938
Germany (The German Confederation) G: 165;
(The unification of Germany) G: 165
Liechtenstein (History) L: 273
German Democratic Republic
Germany (East Germany) G: 170
German Dictionary [book by Grimm]
Grimm G: 394
German East Africa [former colony]
Rwanda (History) R: 571
German Empire [German history]
Berlin (Prussian capital) B: 264
Germany (The unification of Germany) G: 165
with map; (The German Empire) G: 166
Prussia (German empire) P: 843 with map
German Expressionism [art]
Painting (Expressionism) P: 78
German Grammar [book by Grimm]
Grimm G: 394
German language G: 137
Belgium (Regions and language communities)
B: 227
English language (The development of English)
E: 313
Phonetics (Phonetics and spelling) P: 400
Yiddish language Y: 566
German literature G: 138 with pictures
See also the list of Related articles in the German
literature article
Drama (Germany) D: 336; (Romanticism) D: 337
Mythology (Teutonic mythology) M: 985 with
picture
German measles See Rubella in this index
German Museum
Munich (The city) M: 927
German Pavilion [Barcelona, Spain]
Mies van der Rohe, Ludwig M: 537
German pinscher [dog] G: 143
Dog picture on D: 267
German Requiem, A [music by Brahms]
Brahms, Johannes (His music) B: 549
German shepherd dog G: 143 with picture
Dog picture on D: 262
Police dog P: 625
German shorthaired pointer [dog] G: 143
Dog picture on D: 269
German silver [metal]
Alloy (Costly and ornamental alloys) A: 378
German Society [organization]
Legal aid L: 182
German State Library [Berlin]
Berlin (Downtown Berlin) B: 260; (Libraries and
museums) B: 262
German Togoland [former region]
Lomé L: 427
Togo (History) T: 310-311
German Village [district]

Columbus (History) Ci: 856
German wirehaired pointer [dog] G: 143 with
picture
German Workers' Party [German history]
Hitler, Adolf (Birth of the Nazi Party) H: 265
Nazism (The birth of Nazism) N: 92
Germani [ancient people]
Germany (Ancient times) G: 162
Germania [book by Tacitus]
Tacitus, Cornelius T: 5
Germanic languages
Language (Indo-European) L: 65-66
Germanicus, Gaius Caesar Augustus [Roman
emperor] See Caligula in this index
Germanium [element] G: 143
Metalloid M: 426
Germanium oxide [chemical]
Germanium G: 143
Germans [people]
Germany G: 144
Middle Ages (The Germanic invasions) M: 523;
(The Germanic kingdoms) M: 523
Germans, Buffalo [team]
Basketball (The history of professional basketball)
B: 154a
Germantown [district, Philadelphia]
Pastorius, Francis Daniel P: 193
Philadelphia (Residential districts) P: 360-362
Germantown, Battle of [1777]
Pennsylvania picture on P: 267
Revolution, American (table) R: 276; (Brandywine
and Germantown) R: 282
Germanus, Saint [French religious leader]
Patrick, Saint (Life) P: 197
Germany G: 144 with pictures and maps
See also the list of Related articles in the Germany
article
Art and architecture
Germany (Arts) G: 153
Architecture pictures on A: 619
Classical music (History) Ci: 645-646
Doll (Rivalry in the doll industry) D: 291; (The
early 1900's) D: 291
Motion picture (Filmmaking in Europe) M: 866
with picture
Painting (The northern Renaissance) P: 57;
(The 1800's) P: 67-68; (The 1900's in Europe)
P: 77-78
Porcelain (German porcelain) P: 677
Theater (Germany) T: 248
Communications and mass media
Germany (Transportation) G: 162
German language G: 137
Newspaper (In Europe) N: 386
Defense
Germany (Armed forces) G: 147
Air force (The German air force) A: 184
Education
Germany (Education) G: 151
Academic freedom (Beginnings) A: 20
Library (History) L: 261
Finance and banking
Bankruptcy (In other countries) B: 97-98
Euro E: 379
Government
Germany (Government) G: 147
Green party G: 381
Police (In other countries) P: 623
Health and welfare
Police (In other countries) P: 623
Social security (History) So: 556-557
Unemployment (Unemployment throughout
the world) U: 23
History
Germany (History) G: 162 with pictures and
maps
Air force (History) A: 184-185
Alsace-Lorraine A: 387
Armor (During the Middle Ages) A: 719-720
with picture
Aviation (World War II [1939-1945]) A: 989
Belgium (The world wars) B: 234
Berlin Airlift B: 266
Berlin Wall B: 266
Bulge, Battle of the B: 695
Cameroon (History) C: 86
City-state Ci: 603
Cold War Ci: 762; (Germany) Ci: 767; (The Cold
War in the 1970's) Ci: 770; (The Cold War
after 1980) Ci: 770
Colonialism (Later colonialism) Ci: 813-814
Communism (In Eastern Europe) Ci: 896-897
Czech Republic (The Munich Agreement)
Ci: 1213
Dawes Plan D: 51
Fascism (Fascism in Germany) F: 49
Feudalism F: 81

Flag picture on F: 206, F: 217
Franco-Prussian War F: 483
Free city F: 498
Greece (World War II) G: 363
Hitler Youth H: 268
Holy Roman Empire H: 299 with map
India (Rise of Indian nationalism) I: 131; (World
War II [1939-1945]) I: 132
Industrial Revolution (Germany) I: 254
Inflation (Hyperinflation) I: 267 with picture
Jews (Beginnings of Nazi persecution) J: 124
Latvia (History) L: 119
League of Nations (The League in action)
L: 160
Lenin, V. I. (Outcast) L: 193
Leningrad, Siege of L: 195
Lithuania (History) L: 389-390
Money (Printing money and inflation) M: 717
Napoleon III (His defeat) N: 17
Nazism N: 92
Netherlands (World War II) N: 149
Norway (World War II) N: 546
Nuremberg Trials N: 613
Pacific Islands (Colonial rule) P: 12
Potsdam Conference P: 715
Prussia P: 842 with map
Renaissance (The Renaissance outside Italy)
R: 237
Revolution of 1848 R: 288
Russia (World War II) R: 554
Rwanda (History) R: 571
Samoa (History) S: 80a-80b
Spanish Civil War (Foreign assistance) So: 756a
Stalin, Joseph (World War II) So: 827; (The Cold
War) So: 827
Sudetenland So: 957
Tanzania (Colonial rule) T: 35
Underground U: 20
Union of Soviet Socialist Republics (History)
U: 35
United Kingdom ("Peace in our Time") U: 70
United States, History of the (Immigration)
U: 172
Warsaw (History) W: 38
Warsaw Pact W: 39
World War I W: 452 with pictures and maps
World War II W: 468 with pictures and maps
Language and literature See German language;
German literature in this index
People
Germany (People) G: 147
Social and cultural life
Germany (Way of life) G: 150 with pictures
Christmas (In Germany) C: 530
Clothing picture on Ci: 694
Technology and science
Automobile (Where cars are made) A: 959
Space exploration (European nations) So: 726
Germany, A Winter's Tale [poem by Heine]
German literature (The Young Germany)
G: 140-141
**Germany, Treaty on the Final Settlement With
Respect to** [1990]
Germany (The unification of East and West
Germany) G: 171
Germany Over All [song]
Deutschland über Alles D: 172
Germicidal lamp
Sun lamp So: 988
Ultraviolet rays (Uses of ultraviolet rays) U: 17
Germicide
Antiseptic A: 559
Disinfectant D: 235
Germinal mutation [genetics]
Heredity (Mutation) H: 203
Mutation M: 968
Germination [botany] G: 172
Plant (Germination) P: 535 with picture
Seed (How seeds sprout) S: 282 with pictures
Tree (How seeds sprout into trees) T: 418
Germinie Lacerteux [book by Goncourt brothers]
French literature (Naturalism) F: 522
Germline gene therapy
Gene therapy G: 82
Germont, Alfredo [opera character]
Opera: (Traviata, La) O: 807-808 with picture
Gernsback, Hugo [American journalist]
Science fiction (The early 1900's) S: 205
Geronimo [American Indian chief] G: 173 with
portrait
Apache Indians A: 562
Arizona (Indian fighting) A: 690 with picture
Autograph picture on A: 943
Fort Sill F: 416
Indian wars (Apache warfare) I: 195
New Mexico (Territorial days) N: 275
Oklahoma picture on O: 723

Gerontology [science]
Geriatrics G: 137
Old age O: 738
Gerousia [council]
Greece, Ancient (Sparta) G: 372
Gerry, Elbridge [American political leader] G: 173
Constitution of the United States (The Constitutional Convention) Ci: 999-1000
Gerrymander G: 174
Massachusetts (table) M: 288
Vice president of the United States V: 348 with portrait
XYZ Affair X: 546
Gerrymander [politics] G: 174 with picture
Gerry, Elbridge G: 173
Hispanic Americans (Political developments) H: 256
House of Representatives (Size) H: 385
Voting (Voting districts) V: 449
Gershwin, George [American composer] G: 174
Classical music (Third-stream music) Ci: 650
Gershwin, Ira G: 174
Musical comedy (Musical comedy matures) M: 960
Opera (American opera) O: 800; (Porgy and Bess) O: 806
Roaring Twenties (Cultural trends) R: 364
Gershwin, Ira [American lyricist] G: 174
Gershwin, George G: 174
Opera: (Porgy and Bess) O: 806
Gerstein, Mordicai [American author/artist]
Caldecott Medal (table: 2004) C: 26
Gertie the Dinosaur [film]
Animation (Pioneers of American animation) A: 514a-514b with picture
Gerund [grammar]
Participle P: 184
Geryon [Greek mythology]
Hercules (The twelve labors) H: 198-199
Geschichte der Kunst des Altertums [book by Winckelmann]
Winckelmann, Johann Joachim W: 329
Gesland [dollmakers]
Doll (Porcelain dolls) D: 290
Gesner, Abraham [Canadian geologist]
Kerosene (History) K: 306
Museum (Early Canadian museums) M: 940
Gesso [art material]
Painting (Grounds) P: 36
Gestalt psychology G: 175
Köhler, Wolfgang K: 361
Psychology (Gestalt psychology) P: 850
Gestalt therapy
Psychotherapy (Humanistic-experiential psychotherapy) P: 852
Gestapo [German history] G: 175
Himmler, Heinrich H: 234
Hitler, Adolf (The New Order) H: 266-267
Nazism (The rise to power) N: 92
World War II (Civilian life) W: 496
Gestation [biology]
See also Pregnancy in this index
Mammal (Reproduction) M: 123-124
Gestational diabetes
Diabetes (Symptoms) D: 179
Multiple birth (Complications of multiple birth) M: 920
Gestational surrogacy [medicine]
Surrogate birth So: 1010
Gesture
Dance (Asian theatrical dance) D: 28
Gethsemane [garden] G: 175
Jesus Christ (The trial) J: 108 with picture
Getting Out [play by Norman]
Norman, Marsha N: 455
Getty, Donald R. [Canadian political leader]
Alberta (History) A: 328
Getty, J. Paul [American businessman] G: 175
Getty Center [California] G: 176
Meier, Richard M: 384 with picture
Getty Museum, J. Paul [California] G: 176
Getty Oil [company]
Getty, J. Paul G: 175
Getty Research Institute
Getty Center G: 176
Getty Trust, J. Paul [foundation]
Foundation (table) F: 430
Gettys, James [American businessman]
Gettysburg G: 176
Gettysburg [Pennsylvania] G: 176
Pennsylvania picture on P: 255
Gettysburg, Battle of [1863] G: 176
Civil War, American picture on C: 614; (table) Ci: 624; (Battle of Gettysburg) Ci: 627 with map
Ewell, Richard Stoddert E: 435
Gettysburg G: 176
Gettysburg Address G: 176

Lee, Robert E. (Later battles) L: 178
Longstreet, James L: 452
Meade, George Gordon M: 345
Pennsylvania picture on P: 266
Pickett, George Edward P: 451
United States, History of the picture on U: 176
Gettysburg Address [U.S. history] G: 176
Everett, Edward E: 424
Lincoln, Abraham (The Gettysburg Address) L: 323
Gettysburg National Cemetery [Pennsylvania]
National cemetery N: 31
Gettysburg National Military Park [Pennsylvania]
Gettysburg G: 176
National Park System (table: National military parks) N: 55
Pennsylvania (Places to visit) P: 254 with picture
Getz, Stan [American musician] G: 177
Jazz picture on J: 71; (Cool jazz) J: 72
GeV [measurement]
Particle accelerator (How accelerators work) P: 184
Geyser [geology] G: 177 with pictures
Enceladus E: 265
Iceland (The inland plateau) I: 22
Satellite (Physical characteristics) S: 149
Yellowstone National Park (Touring Yellowstone) Y: 558 with map
Geysers Geothermal Field [power plant]
California (Electric power and utilities) C: 57-58
Geothermal energy G: 136
Geysir [hot spring, Iceland]
Iceland (The inland plateau) I: 22
Géza [Magyar leader]
Hungary (The Kingdom of Hungary) H: 445
Gezelligheid [trait]
Netherlands (Way of life) N: 139
Gezira, El [region, Sudan]
Sudan (Southern Sudan) So: 951 with picture
GH [hormone] See Growth hormone in this index
Ghali, Boutros Boutros- [Egyptian diplomat] See Boutros-Ghali, Boutros in this index
Ghana G: 178 with pictures and map
Africa pictures on A: 111, A: 113
Ashanti A: 767
Clothing picture on Ci: 692
Doll (Dolls in festivals and customs) D: 287-288 with picture
Flag picture on F: 198
Police picture on P: 623
Ghana Empire [African history] G: 180 with map
Africa (The empires of west Africa) A: 131
African Americans (The cultural heritage) A: 136c
French West Africa (History) F: 528
Mali (History) M: 108
Mali Empire M: 109
Mauritania (History) M: 315
World, History of the (African civilizations) W: 437
Gharb Darfur [state]
Darfur D: 35
Gharial [reptile] See Gavial in this index
Ghats [stairs]
Ganges River G: 26
Ghazi [king of Iraq]
Iraq (Independence) I: 413
GHB [drug]
Drug abuse (table: Some commonly abused drugs) D: 363; (Club drugs) D: 363
Ghedi, Ali Mohamed [Somali political leader]
Somalia (History) So: 589-590
Ghee [food]
Butter B: 730
India (Food and drink) I: 118
Ghegs [people]
Albania (People) A: 306
Ghent [Belgium] G: 181
Ghent, Battle of [1411]
Cannon picture on C: 179
Ghent, Treaty of [1814] G: 181
New Orleans, Battle of N: 286
United States, History of the (The War of 1812) U: 165
War of 1812 (Treaty of Ghent) W: 31
Ghent, University of
Belgium (Education) B: 229-230
Ghent Altarpiece [painting by Van Eyck]
Van Eyck, Jan V: 282
Gheorghiu-Dej, Gheorghe [Romanian political leader]
Romania (Opposition to the Soviet Union) R: 425
Gherarducci, Silvestro dei [Italian artist]
Illuminated manuscript picture on I: 78
Gherkin [food]
Cucumber Ci: 1183
Ghetto [sociology] G: 181
African Americans (The black migration to the North) A: 136m; (Unrest in the cities) A: 136q

Anti-Semitism A: 559
Holocaust (Before the Holocaust) H: 296
Housing H: 389
Jews (Jews in Christian Europe) J: 122-123
Segregation (Other segregation in the United States) S: 286
Ghibellines [Italian history] See Guelphs and Ghibellines in this index
Ghiberti, Lorenzo [Italian sculptor] G: 181
Donatello D: 307
Relief picture on R: 213
Ghiordes knot
Rugs and carpets (Oriental rugs) R: 516 with diagram
Ghiorso, Albert [American physicist]
Americium A: 432
Californium C: 66
Curium Ci: 1195
Fermium F: 74
Ghirlandajo, Domenico [Italian painter] G: 182
Michelangelo (Early life) M: 483
Ghislanzoni, Antonio [Italian librettist]
Opera: (Aida) O: 801
Ghislieri, Michele [birth name of]
Pius V, Saint P: 567
Ghiz, Joseph [Canadian political leader]
Prince Edward Island (table) P: 791
Ghiz, Robert [Canadian political leader]
Prince Edward Island (table) P: 791; (Recent developments) P: 793
Ghor [Israel-Jordan]
Dead Sea D: 56
Ghost G: 182
Ghost story G: 182
Halloween (Halloween symbols) H: 24b
Ghost crab [sea animal]
Crab picture on Ci: 1115
Ghost Dance [religious movement] G: 182
Indian, American (After European contact) I: 159-160
Indian wars (Wovoka) I: 194; (Wounded Knee) I: 194
Sioux Indians S: 475
South Dakota (Territorial days) So: 681-683
Western frontier life in America (Settlers and Native Americans) W: 239
Wounded Knee (The 1890 massacre) W: 502
Wovoka W: 502
Ghost flower
Flower picture on F: 291
Ghost shirt [ceremonial garment]
Ghost Dance G: 182
Ghost story [literature] G: 182
Ghost town G: 182
Boom town B: 475
Ghost Writer, The [book by Roth]
Roth, Philip R: 487
Ghosts [play by Ibsen]
Ibsen, Henrik (His plays) I: 4
GI [military] G: 182
Gi [uniform]
Karate (Karate training) K: 245-246
GI Bill [U.S.]
Roosevelt, Franklin Delano (The home front) R: 457-458
Veterans Affairs, Department of (Benefits and other services) V: 343
Vocational education (The 1900's and early 2000's) V: 435
GI Forum, American [organization] See American GI Forum of the United States in this index
G.I. Joe doll
Doll (The 1960's) D: 293
Gia Long [emperor of Vietnam]
Vietnam (Independence) V: 368-370
Giacconi, Riccardo [Italian-born physicist]
Nobel Prizes (Physics: 2002) N: 440-442
Giacobini-Zinner, Comet
Meteor (The parent comet) M: 431
Giacometti, Alberto [Swiss sculptor] G: 183 with picture
Sculpture (Assemblages) S: 257-258 with picture
Giacosa, Giuseppe [Italian librettist]
Opera: (Bohème, La) O: 801; (Madama Butterfly) O: 804; (Tosca) O: 807
Giaever, Ivar [American physicist]
Nobel Prizes (Physics: 1973) N: 441
Giamatti, A. Bartlett [American baseball official]
Rose, Pete R: 476
Giambologna [Italian sculptor]
Mercury picture on M: 416
Giannini, Amadeo Peter [American businessman]
Bank of America B: 96
Giant [biology] G: 183 with picture
Giant [film]
Dean, James D: 60
Giant [mythology] G: 183

Giant African snail
Invasive species (Managing invasive species)
I: 354k
Snail (Snails and people) S: 523
Giant anteater
Anteater A: 540 *with picture*
Giant armadillo [animal]
Armadillo A: 717
Giant cactus *See* Saguaro *in this index*
Giant City State Park [Illinois]
Illinois *picture on* I: 64
Giant clam
Clam (Types of clams) Ci: 637 *with picture*
Shell S: 384 *with picture*
Giant corporation
Business (Corporations) B: 726
Giant desert centipede
Centipede C: 351
Giant four-o'clock
Flower *picture on* F: 291
Giant Hercules moth
Moth M: 837 *with picture*; (Giant silkworm moths and royal moths) M: 841-842
Giant house spider
House spider H: 388
Giant hummingbird
Hummingbird (Size) H: 433-435 *with picture*
Giant Impact [theory]
Moon (Origin and evolution of the moon) M: 788 *with picture*
Giant Jaguar, Temple of the [Guatemala]
Latin America *picture on* L: 104
Giant kelp [plant]
Kelp K: 257 *with picture*
Ocean *picture on* O: 651
Seaweed (Kinds) S: 276
Giant mimivirus [biology]
Virus (Structure) V: 427
Giant otter
Otter O: 875
Giant owl moth
Moth M: 837
Giant panda
Animal *picture on* A: 475
Bear (Kinds of bears) B: 184
Endangered species (table) E: 270
Evolution (Contributions from other scientific fields) E: 433
National park *picture on* N: 42g
Panda P: 128 *with picture*
Giant protea [tree]
Protea P: 831 *with picture*
Giant ragweed [plant]
Ragweed R: 103
Giant sable antelope
Antelope (Antelope and people) A: 542-543
Giant salamander
Amphibian *picture on* A: 441
Salamander S: 59
Giant scavenger beetle
Beetle *picture on* B: 218
Giant schnauzer [dog] G: 184
Giant sequoia [tree] *See* Sequoia *in this index*
Giant silkworm moth
Moth (Giant silkworm moths and royal moths) M: 841-842 *with pictures*
Giant slalom [race]
Skiing (Alpine competitions) S: 486-487 *with picture*
Snowboarding S: 541
Giant sloth [extinct animal]
Biology *picture on* B: 320
Giant spider crab
Crab Ci: 1115
Crustacean Ci: 1162 *with picture*
Giant Springs
Montana (Interesting facts) M: 743
Giant squid G: 184 *with picture*
Squid (Kinds of squids) So: 814a
Giant stag beetle
Stag beetle So: 821
Giant swallowtail [butterfly]
Butterfly *picture on* B: 736
Giant toad *See* Cane toad *in this index*
Giant tortoise
Animal *picture on* A: 469
Ecuador *picture on* E: 70
Giant water bug
Water bug W: 133
Giantess Geyser
Geyser (How geysers form) G: 177-178
Giants [mythical beings]
Mythology *picture on* M: 979; (The Greek creation myth) M: 980-982; (The construction of the world) M: 986
Giants, New York [team] *See* New York Giants *in this index*

Giants, San Francisco [team] *See* San Francisco Giants *in this index*
Giant's Causeway [Ireland] G: 184 *with picture*
Giants in the Earth [book by Rölvaag]
American literature (Realist fiction) A: 422
Giants in the Earth [opera by Moore]
Moore, Douglas Stuart M: 796
Giardia [parasite]
Giardiasis G: 184
Giardiasis [disorder] G: 184
Giauque, William Francis [American chemist]
Nobel Prizes (Chemistry: 1949) N: 443
Gibberellic acid [hormone]
Gibberellin G: 185
Gibberellin [hormone] G: 185
Hormone (Plant hormones) H: 337
Plant (Hereditary factors) P: 538
Gibbon [animal] G: 185 *with picture*
Animal *picture on* A: 468
Ape A: 563 *with picture*
Mammal *diagram on* M: 122
Primate (Lesser apes) P: 778a *with picture*
Siamang S: 443
Gibbon, Edward [British historian] G: 185
History (Antiquarian research and the philosophes) H: 262
Rome, Ancient (Learning about ancient Rome) R: 448
Gibbon, John H. [American doctor]
Heart (Development of heart surgery) H: 144
Gibbons, Gail [American author]
Regina Medal (table: 2010) R: 206
Gibbons, Grinling [Dutch sculptor]
Woodcarving W: 391
Gibbons, James [American religious leader]
Cardinal (table: American cardinals) C: 211
Gibbons, Jim [American political leader]
Nevada (table) N: 173
Gibbons, Orlando [English composer] G: 185
Gibbons, Thomas [American businessman]
Gibbons v. Ogden G: 186
Gibbons v. Ogden [U.S. history] G: 185
Interstate commerce (The commerce clause) I: 351
Supreme Court of the United States (table) So: 1002
Gibbous moon
Moon (Phases) M: 783-784
Gibbs, A. C. [American political leader]
Oregon (table) O: 845
Gibbs, Josiah Willard [American physicist]
Chemistry (Development of physical chemistry) C: 404
Gibbs, William C. [American political leader]
Rhode Island (table) R: 311
Gibbsite [mineral]
Bauxite (How bauxite forms) B: 174
Gibraltar [British territory] G: 186 *with picture and map*
Barbary ape B: 105
Treaty T: 408
Gibraltar, Rock of
Gibraltar G: 186 *with picture*
Rock (table) R: 374
Gibraltar, Strait of [Africa-Spain] G: 187
Gibraltar of America [nickname]
Quebec Q: 34
Gibran, Kahlil [Lebanese author] G: 187
Gibson, Althea [American tennis player] G: 187
Tennis (The mid-1900's) T: 166d
Gibson, Bob [American baseball player]
Baseball (table: Hall of Fame) B: 134
Gibson, Charles Dana [American artist] G: 187 *with picture*
Hairdressing (The 1800's) H: 12
Gibson, Edward [American astronaut]
Astronaut *picture on* A: 831
Gibson, Ernest W. [American political leader]
Vermont (table) V: 333
Gibson, Josh [American baseball player] G: 187
Baseball (table: Hall of Fame) B: 134; (Postwar baseball) B: 136
Gibson, Kenneth A. [American political leader]
Newark (History) N: 357-358
Gibson, Mel [Australian actor/director] G: 187 *with portrait*
Motion picture (Best achievement in directing: 1995) M: 862
Gibson, Paris [American settler]
Great Falls G: 343
Gibson, William [American-born author]
Science fiction (Science fiction today) S: 206
Gibson, William F. [American civil rights leader]
Evers-Williams, Myrlie E: 425
Gibson Desert [Australia]
Australia (Deserts) A: 908 *with map*
Australian Desert A: 927

Gibson girl
Gibson, Charles Dana G: 187 *with picture*
Hairdressing (The 1800's) H: 12 *with picture*
Gide, André [French author] G: 188
French literature (The early years) F: 522
Nobel Prizes (Literature: 1947) N: 447
Gideon [Biblical figure] G: 188
Gideon, Clarence [American public figure]
Gideon v. Wainwright G: 188
Gideon, Inspector [literary figure]
Detective story (The pattern) D: 162
Gideon v. Wainwright [U.S. history] G: 188
Supreme Court of the United States (Criminal law) So: 1001; (table) So: 1002
Gideons International [organization]
Montana (Interesting facts) M: 743
Gidzenko, Yuri [Russian cosmonaut]
International Space Station (History) I: 346b *with picture*
Gielgud, John [British actor] G: 188
Motion picture (Best performance by an actor in a supporting role: 1981) M: 862b
Gierek, Edward [Polish political leader]
Poland (Antigovernment protests) P: 614
Giessbach Falls [Switzerland]
Switzerland (The Swiss Alps) So: 1055-1056
Giffard, Henri [French engineer]
Airship (The first airships) A: 251
Giffords, Gabrielle [American political leader]
Arizona (The early 2000's) A: 692
GIFT [reproduction] *See* Gamete intrafallopian transfer *in this index*
Gift from the Sea [book by Lindbergh]
Lindbergh, Anne Morrow L: 330
Gift of Giving, A [program]
Camp Fire USA (Service learning programs) C: 89
"Gift of the Magi, The" [story by O. Henry]
Henry, O. H: 189
"Gift Outright, The" [poem by Frost]
Frost, Robert F: 542
Gift tax
Inheritance tax I: 271
Taxation (Other taxes) T: 54
Gifted children G: 188
Special education (Gifted children) So: 771
Giga [prefix]
Metric system (Metric prefixes) M: 439
Gigabyte [measurement]
Computer (Computer code) Ci: 911
Giganotosaurus [dinosaur] G: 188
Gigantic jet [meteorology]
Lightning (Jets, sprites, and elves) L: 301
Gigantism [disorder]
Giant G: 183
Human growth hormone H: 427
Gigantomachy [war]
Mythology (The Greek creation myth) M: 980-982
Gigantopithecus [extinct animal] G: 189
Gigawatt [measurement]
Watt W: 148
Gigi [film]
Motion picture (Best picture: 1958) M: 861
Gihon River [Bible]
Eden E: 76
Gikuyu [people] *See* Kikuyu *in this index*
Gil, Gilberto [Brazilian musician]
Brazil (The arts) B: 576-577
Gil Blas [book by Lesage]
French literature (The Enlightenment) F: 520-521
Gila Cliff Dwellings National Monument [New Mexico] G: 189
National Park System (table: National monuments) N: 51
Gila monster [lizard] G: 189
Animal *picture on* A: 483
Lizard (Defenses) L: 400
Reptile R: 250 *with picture*
Gila River [Arizona-New Mexico]
Phoenix (The city) P: 395 *with map*
Gila Wilderness
New Mexico (Places to visit) N: 264
Gila woodpecker [bird]
Bird (Birds of the desert) B: 339 *with picture*
Gilani, Yousaf Raza [Pakistani political leader]
Musharraf, Pervez M: 941
Pakistan (Musharraf) P: 100
Gilbert, Grove Karl [American geologist]
Moon (Determining the origin of craters) *diagram on* M: 793-794
Gilbert, Sir Humphrey [English explorer] G: 189
Newfoundland and Labrador (Colonization) N: 375
Gilbert, Rufus [American inventor]
Elevated railroad E: 233
Gilbert, Walter [American chemist]
Nobel Prizes (Chemistry: 1980) N: 444

Sanger, Frederick **S:** 110
Gilbert, William [English doctor] **G:** 189
 Electricity (Early discoveries) **E:** 196
 Electroscope **E:** 219
Gilbert, Sir William Schwenck [British author] **G:** 189
 Gilbert and Sullivan **G:** 190
 Sullivan, Sir Arthur Seymour **So:** 969
Gilbert and Ellice Islands [islands, Pacific]
 Kiribati (History) **K:** 335
 Tuvalu (History) **T:** 528
Gilbert and Sullivan G: 190
 D'Oyly Carte, Richard **D:** 317
 Gilbert, Sir William Schwenck **G:** 189
 Operetta **O:** 809
 Sullivan, Sir Arthur Seymour **So:** 969
Gilbert Islands [Pacific]
 Kiribati **K:** 335
 World War II (Island hopping in the Central Pacific) **W:** 489 with picture
Gilbert Stuart Birthplace [North Kingstown, Rhode Island]
 Rhode Island (Places to visit) **R:** 304 with picture
Gilberto, João [Brazilian musician]
 Latin America (Music) **L:** 100
Gilbreth, Frank and Lillian [American engineers] **G:** 190
Gilchrist, Albert W. [American political leader]
 Florida (table) **F:** 260
Gilcrease Museum [Tulsa]
 Oklahoma (Places to visit) **O:** 722
Gilda [opera character]
 Opera: (Rigoletto) **O:** 806
Gilded Age [U.S. history]
 Rhode Island (The Gilded Age) **R:** 313
 Twain, Mark (Productive years in Hartford) **T:** 529
 United States, History of the (The Gilded Age) **U:** 183
Gilded Age, The [book by Twain and Warner]
 Twain, Mark (Productive years in Hartford) **T:** 529
Gilder's tip [tool]
 Gold leaf **G:** 254
Gilding [art]
 Gold leaf **G:** 253
Gilding metal
 Ammunition (The bullet) **A:** 435
Giles, Ernest [Australian explorer]
 Australian Desert **A:** 927
Giles, Herbert A. [British scholar]
 Chinese language (Development) **C:** 510-511
Giles, Warren [American baseball executive]
 Baseball (table: Hall of Fame) **B:** 134
Giles, William Branch [American political leader]
 Virginia (table) **V:** 417
Giles Goat-Boy [book by Barth]
 Barth, John **B:** 120
Gilgamesh, Epic of [poem] **G:** 190
 Babylonia (Language and literature) **B:** 13
 Deluge **D:** 118
 Mythology picture on **M:** 976; (Symbols) **M:** 975; (Babylonian mythology) **M:** 978
Gill [botany]
 Mushroom (Parts of a mushroom) **M:** 942 with picture
Gill [zoology]
 Amphibian (Breathing) **A:** 440
 Animal (Adaptations for breathing) **A:** 491-492 with picture
 Fish **F:** 145, diagrams on **F:** 162; (Respiratory system) **F:** 161 with picture
 Oyster (Body organs) **O:** 890 with diagram
 Respiration (Breathing in animals without lungs) **R:** 261
Gill net
 Fishing industry (Nets) **F:** 183-184 with diagram
Gill-over-the-ground [plant]
 Ivy (Ground ivy) **I:** 522
Gill raker [organ]
 Basking shark **B:** 155
Gillard, Julia [Australian political leader] **G:** 190 with portrait
 Australia (table) **A:** 923
Gillars, Mildred [American public figure]
 World War II (Propaganda) **W:** 494-495
Gillespie, Dizzy [American musician] **G:** 190
 Hines, Earl **H:** 237
Gillett, James N. [American political leader]
 California (table) **C:** 59
Gilliam, Terry [American animator]
 Cleese, John **Ci:** 661
 "Monty Python's Flying Circus" **M:** 780
Gillick, Pat [American baseball executive]
 Baseball (table: Hall of Fame) **B:** 134
Gilligan, John J. [American political leader]
 Ohio (table) **O:** 699
Gillray, James [British artist]
 Caricature **C:** 238 with picture

Gillyflower [plant] See Wallflower in this index
Gilman, Alfred Goodman [American physiologist]
 Nobel Prizes (Physiology or medicine: 1994) **N:** 446
Gilman, Charlotte Perkins [American social reformer] **G:** 191
Gilman, George F. [American businessman]
 Hartford, George Huntington **H:** 79
Gilman, John T. [American political leader]
 New Hampshire (table) **N:** 223
Gilman, Nicholas [American political leader] **G:** 191
Gilmer, George R. [American political leader]
 Georgia (table) **G:** 130
Gilmer, Thomas Walker [American political leader]
 Tyler, John (table) **T:** 534
 Virginia (table) **V:** 417
Gilmore, James S., III [American political leader]
 Virginia (table) **V:** 417
Gilmore, Joseph A. [American political leader]
 New Hampshire (table) **N:** 223
Gilmore, Patrick Sarsfield [American bandleader] **G:** 191
Gilpatric, Guy [American diver]
 Diving, Underwater (History) **D:** 247
Gilpin, Henry D. [American government official]
 Justice, Department of (table) **J:** 203
 Van Buren, Martin (table) **V:** 273
Gilpin, William [American government official]
 Colorado (The gold rush) **Ci:** 845
Gilsemans, Isaac [Dutch artist]
 New Zealand picture on **N:** 356
Gilsonite [mineral]
 Asphalt (Asphalt production) **A:** 815
Gilt [hog]
 Hog (table) **H:** 284
Gimbal [navigation]
 Compass (Deviation) **Ci:** 903
 Gyroscope (Mechanical gyroscopes) **G:** 454 with diagram
Gimble, Johnny [American musician]
 Country music (Western swing music) **Ci:** 1098a
Gimenez, Carlos [American political leader]
 Miami (History) **M:** 480-481
Gin [drink]
 Alcoholic beverage (Gin) **A:** 336; (History) **A:** 337
Gin, Cotton [machine] See Cotton gin in this index
Ginaca machine
 Pineapple (Cultivation and production) **P:** 472-473
Ginastera, Alberto [Argentine composer]
 Opera (Opera today) **O:** 800 with picture
Ginevra de' Benci [painting by Leonardo]
 Leonardo da Vinci picture on **L:** 200
Ginger [plant]
 Flower picture on **F:** 292
 Ginger **G:** 191
Ginger [spice] **G:** 191
Gingerbread hornbook
 Hornbook **H:** 339
Gingerbread tree
 Doum palm **D:** 314
Gingham [fabric] **G:** 191
Gingivitis [disease]
 Periodontitis **P:** 287
 Teeth (Periodontal diseases) **T:** 85 with picture
 Trench mouth **T:** 434
Gingrich, Newt [American political leader] **G:** 191
 Congress of the United States (Congressional ethics) **Ci:** 948
Ginkgo [tree] **G:** 192
 Dietary supplement **D:** 200
 Herbal medicine **H:** 196
 Plant (Gymnosperms) **P:** 520 with picture; (The evolution of plants) **P:** 544-545; (Classification of plants) **P:** 546-547 with picture
 Tree pictures on **T:** 413; (Ginkgo trees) **T:** 415
Ginnie Mae [agency] See Government National Mortgage Association in this index
Ginning [industrial process]
 Cotton (Ginning and baling) **Ci:** 1091
Ginnungagap [Norse mythology]
 Mythology (The creation of life) **M:** 985
Ginsberg, Allen [American poet] **G:** 192
 American literature (Variations on Modernist poetry) **A:** 423
 Beat movement **B:** 189
Ginsburg, Ruth Bader [American jurist] **G:** 192
 Supreme Court of the United States picture on **So:** 999
Ginseng [plant] **G:** 192 with pictures
 Herbal medicine **H:** 196
Gintl, Wilhelm Julius [Austrian inventor]
 Telegraph (Service expansion and improvement) **T:** 91-92
Ginza district
 Advertising picture on **A:** 72

Tokyo picture on **T:** 312
Ginzberg, Asher [Hebrew poet]
 Hebrew literature (Modern Hebrew literature) **H:** 162-163
Ginzburg, Vitaly L. [Russian physicist]
 Nobel Prizes (Physics: 2003) **N:** 442
Gio [people]
 Liberia (Civil war) **L:** 232
Gioconda, La [opera by Ponchielli]
 Boito, Arrigo **B:** 440
Gioconda, La [painting by Leonardo da Vinci] See Mona Lisa in this index
Giocondo, Lisa del [Italian public figure]
 Mona Lisa **M:** 698
Giorgione [Italian painter] **G:** 193
 Jesus Christ picture on **J:** 104
 Painting (The Renaissance in Venice) **P:** 55-56 with picture
Giorno di Regno, Un [opera by Verdi]
 Verdi, Giuseppe **V:** 316
Giotto [Italian artist] **G:** 193 with picture
 Christianity picture on **C:** 524
 Italy (Painting and sculpture) **I:** 506
 Jesus Christ picture on **J:** 106
 Mural **M:** 928-929 with picture
 Painting (The 1300's) **P:** 51 with picture
 Renaissance (Arts of the 1300's and early 1400's) **R:** 236
Giotto [space probe]
 European Space Agency **E:** 418
 Space exploration (Probes to comets) **So:** 711
Giovanni, Nikki [American poet] **G:** 193
Giovanni da Fiesole, Fra [Italian artist] See Angelico, Fra in this index
Giovanni's Room [book by Baldwin]
 Baldwin, James **B:** 39
Gipsies [people] See Roma in this index
Gir Forest [region, India]
 Lion **L:** 340; (Hunting lions) **L:** 342-343
Giraffe G: 194 with pictures and map
 Animal pictures on **A:** 469, **A:** 476
 Mammal picture on **M:** 119
 Zoo (Interesting facts about zoo animals) **Z:** 601 with picture
Giralda [Seville Cathedral]
 Seville **S:** 329
Girard, Marc A. [Canadian political leader]
 Manitoba (table) **M:** 159
Girard, Rodolphe [Canadian author]
 Canadian literature (Fiction: 1850-1918) **C:** 157
Giraudoux, Jean [French dramatist] **G:** 195
 French literature (Developments in drama) **F:** 523
Girder [construction]
 Bridge (Girder bridges) **B:** 600 with diagram
 Building construction (Beams, girders, and columns) **B:** 682-683
Girder bridge
 Bridge (Girder bridges) **B:** 600 with diagram
Girdle [zoology]
 Reptile (Skeleton) **R:** 251
Girl
 See also Female in this index
 Adolescent (Physical development) **A:** 60-61
 Baby **B:** 4
 Child **C:** 448
 Rett syndrome **R:** 266
 Sexuality (Biological factors) **S:** 337
"Girl from Ipanema, The" [song]
 Getz, Stan **G:** 177
Girl Guides [organization] **G:** 195
 See also Girl Scouts in this index
 Baden-Powell, Lord **B:** 23
 Girl Scouts **G:** 196
Girl Guides and Girl Scouts, World Association of See World Association of Girl Guides and Girl Scouts in this index
Girl Guides Association of South Africa
 Girl Scouts (South Africa) **G:** 199
Girl Guides Australia
 Girl Scouts (Australia) **G:** 199
Girl Guides of Canada
 Girl Scouts (Girl Guides of Canada-Guides du Canada) **G:** 198
Girl Holding a Cat [sculpture by Segal]
 Segal, George picture on **S:** 284
Girl of the Golden West, The [opera by Puccini]
 Puccini, Giacomo **P:** 869
Girl Scout Gold Award
 Girl Scouts (Girl Scout Seniors) **G:** 197
Girl Scout Silver Award
 Girl Scouts (Girl Scout Cadettes) **G:** 197
Girl Scout Week
 Girl Scouts (Annual events) **G:** 198
Girl Scouts [organization] **G:** 196 with pictures
 See also Girl Guides in this index
 Low, Juliette Gordon **L:** 509
Girl with the Dragon Tattoo, The [book by Larsson]

Detective story (History) **D:** 162-163
GirlGuiding New Zealand
  Girl Scouts (New Zealand) **G:** 199
GirlGuiding UK
  Girl Scouts (United Kingdom) **G:** 199 *with picture*
Girls and Boys Town [organization] *See* Boys Town *in this index*
Girls Clubs of America, Inc. [former name]
  Girls Incorporated **G:** 200
Girls' Day
  Doll (Dolls in festivals) **D:** 287
Girls Incorporated G: 200
Girls Nation [meeting]
  Girls State **G:** 200
Girls State [meeting] **G:** 200
  American Legion Auxiliary **A:** 413
Gironde [French history]
  Girondists **G:** 200
Girondists [French history] **G:** 200
  French Revolution (The National Convention) **F:** 526
  Marat, Jean-Paul **M:** 190
  Robespierre (Revolutionary leader) **R:** 366
  Roland de la Platière, Marie Jeanne **R:** 401
Girth [riding equipment]
  Harness *diagram on* **H:** 63
  Horse (table: Riding equipment) **H:** 351; (The saddle) **H:** 351-352 *with picture*
  Saddle **S:** 7 *with pictures*
Girty, Simon [American military leader] **G:** 201
GIS [cartography] *See* Geographic information system *in this index*
Giscard d'Estaing, Valéry [French political leader]
  France (France after de Gaulle) **F:** 477-478
Giselle [ballet]
  Ballet (Romantic ballet) **B:** 51
  Moscow *picture on* **M:** 825
Gish, Dorothy [American actress] **G:** 201 *with picture*
Gish, Lillian [American actress] **G:** 201 *with picture*
Gist, Christopher [American frontiersman]
  Frankfort **F:** 484
  Ohio (Exploration and settlement) **O:** 700
  Washington, George (Messenger to the French) **W:** 93-94
Gist's Plantation [U.S. history]
  Ohio Company (The first Ohio Company) **O:** 704
Giuliani, Rudolph William [American political leader] **G:** 201 *with portrait*
  New York City (A time of change) **N:** 343
  September 11 terrorist attacks (Moving forward) **S:** 310b
Giunta [government]
  Italy (Local government) **I:** 499
Givat Ram [area]
  Jerusalem (West Jerusalem) **J:** 95 *with map*
"Give me liberty or give me death" [quotation]
  Henry, Patrick **H:** 189
  Revolution, American (Fighting in the Chesapeake and Southern colonies) **R:** 276-278
  Richmond (Other interesting places to visit) **R:** 332
Given name
  Name **N:** 5
Giver, The [book by Lowry]
  Lowry, Lois **L:** 511
Giving Tree, The [book by Silverstein]
  Silverstein, Shel **S:** 465
Giza [Egypt] **G:** 202
  Cairo **C:** 15
  Egypt, Ancient (Arts and sciences) **E:** 139
  Pyramids (The Pyramids of Giza) **P:** 917 *with pictures*
  Sphinx (Egyptian sphinxes) **So:** 780 *with picture*
Gizikis, Phaidon [Greek political leader]
  Greece (The restoration of democracy) **G:** 365
Gizzard [zoology] **G:** 202 *with diagram*
  Bird (The digestive system) **B:** 365 *with diagram*
  Chicken (The body of a chicken) **C:** 440-441
  Insect (Digestive system) **I:** 289
Gjellerup, Karl [Danish author]
  Nobel Prizes (Literature: 1917) **N:** 447
Gjøa [ship]
  Amundsen, Roald *picture on* **A:** 445
  Northwest Passage **N:** 529 *with picture*
Glacial acetic acid [chemical]
  Acetic acid **A:** 25
Glacial advance [geology] *See* Ice age *in this index*
Glacial epoch [geology]
  Carboniferous Period **C:** 208
  Ice age **I:** 6
  Pleistocene Epoch **P:** 572
Glacial ice
  Arctic Ocean (Ice) **A:** 641 *with picture*
Glacial lake
  Lake (How lakes are formed) **L:** 32 *with picture*

Glaciated valley [geography]
  Valley (How valleys are formed) **V:** 266
Glaciation [geology]
  Ice age **I:** 6
Glacier [geography] **G:** 202 *with pictures*
  Alaska (Glaciers) **G:** 295 *with picture*
  Alps (How the Alps were formed) **A:** 384
  Antarctica (Ice) **A:** 532; (Climate) **A:** 534
  Arctic Ocean (Ice) **A:** 641 *with picture*
  Canyon **C:** 185
  Climate (Glaciers) **Ci:** 679 *with picture*
  Earth *picture on* **E:** 23; (Earth's changing climate) **E:** 24
  Erosion (How erosion occurs) **E:** 355
  Glacier National Park **G:** 205
  Global warming *pictures on* **G:** 232a
  Ice age **I:** 6 *with picture and map*
  Ice formation **I:** 9
  Iceberg **I:** 17 *with picture*
  Island (Kinds of islands) **I:** 472
  Lake (How lakes are formed) **L:** 32
  Moraine **M:** 799
  Plate tectonics (History of tectonic theory) **P:** 564
  Pleistocene Epoch **P:** 572
  Prehistoric people (Migration from Africa) **P:** 747
  River (Sources of river water) **R:** 351 *with picture*
  Water (How water shapes Earth) **W:** 121
  Wisconsin (Land and climate) **W:** 358
Glacier Bay National Park [Alaska] **G:** 204
  Flower *picture on* **F:** 270
  National Park System (table: National parks) **N:** 48
Glacier Bay National Preserve [Alaska]
  National Park System (table: National preserves) **N:** 58
Glacier bear
  Bear (American black bears) **B:** 184
Glacier National Park [British Columbia]
  Canada (table: National parks and national park reserves) **C:** 113
Glacier National Park [Montana] **G:** 205 *with maps*
  Divide **D:** 241
  Global warming *pictures on* **G:** 232a
  Montana *picture on* **M:** 742; (Places to visit) **M:** 750
  National park (table) **N:** 42g
  National Park System (table: National parks) **N:** 48
  Rocky Mountains (Chief ranges of the Rockies) **R:** 394-395
Glacier Point
  Yosemite National Park (Rock masses) **Y:** 570
Glackens, William James [American artist] **G:** 205
  Ashcan School **A:** 768
Gladden, Washington [American clergyman]
  Christianity (The 1800's) **C:** 526
Glade Creek [West Virginia]
  United States *picture on* **U:** 120
Gladesville Bridge [Sydney, Australia]
  Bridge (table: Concrete arch) **B:** 603
Gladiator [film]
  Crowe, Russell **Ci:** 1158
  Motion picture (Best picture: 2000) **M:** 861
Gladiator [warrior] **G:** 206
  Colosseum **Ci:** 850
  Helmet *picture on* **H:** 178
  Rome, Ancient (Recreation) **R:** 440 *with picture*
Gladiolus [plant] **G:** 206
  Flower (Garden perennials grown from bulbs) **F:** 280 *with picture*
Gladstone, James [Canadian political leader]
  Alberta (The mid-1900's) **A:** 329-331
Gladstone, William Ewart [British political leader] **G:** 206 *with portrait*
  Liberal Democrats (A major party) **L:** 227
  United Kingdom (Gladstone and Disraeli) **U:** 69
Gladstonian Liberals [British history]
  United Kingdom (Gladstone and Disraeli) **U:** 69
Glagolitic alphabet
  Alphabet (Other alphabets) **A:** 383
Gland [anatomy] **G:** 207 *with diagram*
  See also the list of Related articles in the Gland *article*
  Bird (Why birds migrate) **B:** 360
  Blood (Carrying hormones) **B:** 410
  Disease (Metabolic diseases) **D:** 229
  Frog *pictures on* **F:** 537
  Hormone (Metabolic hormones) **H:** 335-336
  Human body (table) **H:** 422 *with diagram*
  Mammal (Skin and hair) **M:** 118
Glanders [disease] **G:** 210
Glans [anatomy]
  Circumcision **Ci:** 561
Glanville, Bartholomew de [French scholar]
  Encyclopedia (From the 1200's to the 1600's) **E:** 268a
Glare
  Lighting (Lighting problems) **L:** 297-298
Glaser, Donald Arthur [American physicist]

  Nobel Prizes (Physics: 1960) **N:** 441
Glasgow [Montana]
  Montana (table: Average monthly weather) **M:** 754
Glasgow [Scotland] **G:** 210
Glasgow, Ellen [American author] **G:** 210
Glasgow, University of [Scotland] **G:** 210
Glashow, Sheldon Lee [American physicist]
  Nobel Prizes (Physics: 1979) **N:** 441
  Subatomic particle (The Standard Model) **So:** 938
Glasnost [Soviet history]
  Communism (The Soviet Union under Gorbachev) **Ci:** 895-896
  Gorbachev, Mikhail Sergeyevich (Domestic policies) **G:** 272
  Russian literature (Modern Soviet literature) **R:** 564-565
  Union of Soviet Socialist Republics (Gorbachev's reforms) **U:** 40
Glaspell, Susan [American dramatist] **G:** 210
Glass G: 211 *with pictures*
  Antique (Glass) **A:** 558 *with picture*
  Bottle **B:** 513
  Ceramics (Kinds of ceramic products) **C:** 359
  Composite materials **Ci:** 904
  Gem (Imitation and synthetic gems) **G:** 79
  Plastics (To replace glass and ceramics) **P:** 555
  Quartz (Uses) **Q:** 8
  Tempering **T:** 130
  Textile (Manufactured fibers) **T:** 213-214
Glass, Carter [American political leader] **G:** 223
  Bank (The crisis of 1933) **B:** 93-94
  Wilson, Woodrow (Legislative program) **W:** 322-323
Glass, Hugh [American frontiersman] **G:** 223
Glass, Philip [American composer] **G:** 224
  Classical music (Minimalism) **Ci:** 651
Glass-beaded screen
  Projection screen **P:** 816
Glass blowing
  Glass (Blowing) **G:** 215 *with picture, pictures on* **G:** 216
Glass building block
  Glass (Specialty glasses) **G:** 212
Glass Capital of the World [nickname]
  Toledo **T:** 321
Glass catfish
  Catfish **C:** 300 *with picture*
Glass ceiling [sociology]
  Sex discrimination (The persistence of sex discrimination) **S:** 335
Glass-ceramics
  Glass *picture on* **G:** 211; (Specialty glasses) **G:** 212-213
Glass family [literary figures]
  Salinger, J. D. **S:** 66
Glass harmonica [musical instrument]
  Harmonica **H:** 62
Glass House [Connecticut]
  Johnson, Philip Cortelyou **J:** 152
Glass industry
  Glass (Modern glassmaking) **G:** 222
Glass laser
  Laser (Solid-state lasers) **L:** 85
Glass lizard G: 224 *with picture*
  Lizard (How lizards move) **L:** 399-400; (Defenses) **L:** 400
Glass marbles
  West Virginia (Interesting facts) **W:** 207 *with picture*
Glass Menagerie, The [play by Williams]
  Drama (Later United States drama) **D:** 340
  Williams, Tennessee **W:** 312
Glass snake *See* Glass lizard *in this index*
Glass solder
  Glass (table) **G:** 218
Glass sponge [sea animal]
  Deep sea (Invertebrates) **D:** 82a-82b *with picture*
  Sponge (Kinds of sponges) **So:** 800
Glass-Steagall Banking Act [1933]
  Bank (The crisis of 1933) **B:** 93-94
  Glass, Carter **G:** 223
  New Deal (Helping savers and investors) **N:** 200-201
Glass tubing
  Glass (Specialty glasses) **G:** 212-213; (Drawing) **G:** 215-216 *with diagram*
Glasscock, William E. [American political leader]
  West Virginia (table) **W:** 225; (Labor developments) **W:** 229
Glasses [vision] **G:** 224 *with picture*
  See also Eye; Vision *in this index*
  Eye (Defects of the eye) **E:** 464
Glasshouse [gardening] *See* Greenhouse *in this index*
Glassmaking
  Glass (Composition of glass) **G:** 213; (How glass

is made) G: 214 *with diagrams;* (How glass is shaped and finished) G: 215 *with pictures;* (How glass is decorated) G: 217
West Virginia *picture on* W: 223
Glassware
Colonial life in America (Decorative arts) Ci: 807-808 *with picture*
Islamic art (Glassware) I: 470
Glasswort [plant] G: 225
Glassy [marble]
Marbles M: 193
Glassy carbon *See* Amorphous carbon *in this index*
Glastonbury [England] G: 225
Glaswegians [people]
Glasgow G: 210
Glatiramer acetate [drug]
Multiple sclerosis M: 921
Glauber, Roy Jay [American physicist]
Nobel Prizes (Physics: 2005) N: 442
Glaucoma [disease] G: 226
Beta-blocker B: 274
Blindness (Diseases) B: 401
Eye (Glaucoma) E: 466
Glauconite [mineral] G: 226
Glaucus [Greek mythology]
Scylla S: 261
Glauert's seadragon [animal]
Seadragon S: 264
Glaze [industrial process]
Ceramics (Making ceramics) C: 360
Enamel E: 264
Pottery (Decorating and glazing) P: 718
Tile T: 287
Gleason, Henry A. [American ecologist]
Botany (Later developments) B: 509
Gleason, Jean Berko [American linguist]
Language (Words and morphemes) L: 62-63
Gleevec [drug]
Leukemia (Cause) L: 215
Gleizes, Albert [French painter]
Cubism Ci: 1181
Glen [geography]
Scotland (Land regions) S: 217
Glen Canyon Dam [Colorado River, Arizona] G: 226
Arizona *picture on* A: 686
Dam (table) D: 18
Lake Powell L: 45 *with map*
Glen Canyon National Recreation Area [Arizona-Utah]
National Park System (table: National recreation areas) N: 49
Glen More [region, Scotland]
Scotland (The land) S: 217 *with map*
Glendenin, Lawrence E. [American chemist]
Promethium P: 818
Glendening, Parris N. [American political leader]
Maryland (table) M: 255
Glendower, Owen [Welsh prince]
Wales (Revolts against England) W: 12
Glengarry Glen Ross [play by Mamet]
Mamet, David M: 115
Glenn, John Herschel, Jr. [American astronaut] G: 226 *with pictures*
Astronaut (Achievements in space) A: 829 *with picture;* (A look at the astronauts) A: 831; (Selecting the NASA astronauts) A: 831
Exploration (Human space travel) E: 452
Space exploration (Vostok and Mercury: The first human beings in space) So: 712-713 *with picture*
Glenn, R. B. [American political leader]
North Carolina (table) N: 490
Glennon, John J. [American religious leader]
Cardinal (table: American cardinals) C: 211
Glensheen [Duluth]
Minnesota (Places to visit) M: 594 *with picture*
Glenville [district]
Cleveland (Social problems) Ci: 665; (Downturn and racial tensions) Ci: 667
Glessner House [Chicago]
Architecture (Early modern architecture in America) A: 629
Richardson, Henry Hobson R: 330 *with picture*
Glia [anatomy]
Brain (Brain cells) B: 550c
Myelin M: 970f
Nervous system (Parts of a neuron) N: 133-134
Gliadin [protein]
Gluten G: 237
Glick, George Washington [American political leader] G: 227
Kansas (table) K: 234
Glickman, Dan [American government official]
Agriculture, Department of (table) A: 161
Clinton, Bill (table) Ci: 682d
Glidden, Carlos [American inventor] G: 227
Sholes, Christopher Latham S: 433

Typewriter (History) T: 539
Glidden, Joseph F. [American inventor]
Barbed wire B: 106
Glide ratio [physics]
Glider (Parts of a glider) G: 228
Glider [aircraft] G: 228 *with pictures*
Airplane A: 209; (First human flights) A: 230 *with pictures*
Hang gliding H: 51 *with picture*
Wright brothers (Gliding experiments) W: 509
Glider [animal] G: 231 *with picture*
Possum P: 698
Gliding [sport] *See* Glider [aircraft]; Hang gliding *in this index*
Gliding possum [animal] *See* Glider [animal] *in this index*
Gliese 581 [star]
Planet (The first discoveries) P: 513-514
Glima [sport]
Iceland (Recreation) I: 22
Glinka, Mikhail Ivanovich [Russian composer] G: 231
Russia (Music) R: 536-537
Glioma [disorder]
Tumor T: 484
Glitter [film]
Carey, Mariah C: 236
Global heat conveyor [geology]
Earth (Cycles in and on Earth) E: 22
Global ocean *See* World ocean *in this index*
Global Oscillation Network Group Project
National Optical Astronomy Observatories N: 42
Sun (Earth-based studies) So: 987
Global Positioning System [navigation] G: 231 *with diagram*
Airplane (Electronic navigation) A: 227
Airport (Air traffic control) A: 246-247
Altimeter A: 390
Antenna A: 543
Archaeology (Surveying sites) A: 596; (The 1900's) A: 599
Automatic flight control system (How an AFCS works) A: 944
Cellular telephone (Features) C: 341
Electronics (Automation) E: 207
Geography (Study of geography) G: 93
Guided missile (Preset guidance) G: 426
Map (Navigation maps) M: 178; (Observation and measurement) M: 180; (Mapmaking and modern technology) M: 185 *with picture*
Mountain (Measuring mountains) M: 896b
Navigation (Satellite navigation) N: 73; (Electronic navigation) N: 75 *with diagram*
Railroad (Other train controls) R: 112
Rocket (Launching probes and satellites) R: 386
Satellite, Artificial *picture on* S: 150f
Seismograph S: 288
Surveying (Surveying tools) So: 1011
Time T: 288
Global Programme against Money Laundering
Money laundering M: 718
Global reference frame
Geodesy G: 91
Global Security and Sustainability, Program on
MacArthur Foundation M: 4
Global Trade Item Number
Bar coding B: 102
Global warming G: 232 *with pictures*
Agriculture (Pollution) A: 153
Air (Changes in the atmosphere) A: 175
Antarctica (Scientific research) A: 539-540
Arctic (Climate change) A: 640
Arctic Ocean (Climate) A: 641; (Disappearance of ice) A: 641-642 *with pictures;* (Threats) A: 644
Automobile (Global warming) A: 964
Butterfly (Butterflies and environmental change) B: 743
Carbon footprint C: 207
Climate Ci: 675; (Causes of climate change) Ci: 676d
Coal (Recent developments) Ci: 732
Deforestation D: 89
Desert (How deserts develop and change) D: 156
Extinction (Modern extinction) E: 456-457
Gas [fuel] (Gas and the environment) G: 56
Glacier National Park (Glaciers) G: 205
Greenhouse effect (Increases in greenhouse gases) G: 383
Housing (Sustainable housing) H: 392
National Park System (Changes in the environment) N: 42h-42i
Nunavut (Establishment of Nunavut) N: 612
Ocean (Climate change) O: 665
Pacific Ocean (Scientific research) P: 15
Petroleum (Global warming) P: 345
Plant (Global warming) P: 544
Ship (Pollution) S: 413

Soil So: 573
Southern Ocean (Scientific research) So: 688b
Technology (Challenges of technology) T: 77
Globalism
World (Cooperation among nations) W: 412b
Globalization G: 232d
Clothing (The globalization of fashion) Ci: 695
Democracy (Democracy today) D: 123
Economics (The world economy) E: 61
Government (Recent developments) G: 291
Group of Twenty G: 403
Human rights H: 428
International relations (Globalization) I: 346
Latin America (In the early 2000's) L: 111
New Democratic Party N: 203
Radicalism (In the United States) R: 82
Trade T: 362
World Trade Organization W: 451
Globe [map] G: 233
Great-circle route G: 338 *with diagram*
Map M: 176; (Map projections) M: 180; (Advances in European cartography) M: 184
Globe artichoke [plant]
Artichoke A: 758 *with picture*
Globe candytuft [plant]
Candytuft C: 177
Globe mallow [plant]
Flower (Flowers of prairies and dry plains) F: 286 *with picture*
Globe Shakespeare, The [book]
Shakespeare, William (Editions of the 1700's and 1800's) S: 369-370
Globe Theatre [English history] G: 233
London (Expansion beyond the walls) L: 440 *with picture*
Shakespeare, William *picture on* S: 352; (The Globe Theatre) S: 348
Globe tulip [plant]
Mariposa lily M: 212 *with picture*
Globular cluster [astronomy]
Cosmology (The ages of stars) Ci: 1078
Milky Way (Shape of the galaxy) M: 550
Pulsar P: 900a
Shapley, Harlow S: 373
Star cluster (Kinds of clusters) So: 853 *with picture*
Universe (Changing views of the universe) U: 205-206
Globulin [protein] G: 234
Blood (Protecting against disease) B: 410
Drug (Antiserums and globulins) D: 351
Gamma globulin G: 23
Liver (Other functions) L: 394
Plasma (Functions of plasma) P: 551
Glochidia [zoology]
Larva L: 78
Glockenspiel [musical instrument] G: 234 *with picture*
Music (Percussion instruments) M: 950
Glögg [drink]
Christmas (Christmas feasting) C: 534-535
Glomar Challenger [ship]
Mediterranean Sea (Formation) M: 382
Ocean drilling programs O: 667
Plate tectonics (History of tectonic theory) P: 564-565
Glomerulonephritis [disease]
Kidney (Kidney diseases) K: 312
Nephritis N: 127
Glomerulus [anatomy]
Kidney (How the kidneys produce urine) K: 311 *with diagram*
GLONASS [navigation system]
Navigation (Satellite navigation) N: 73
Glooscap [legendary figure]
Mi'kmaq Indians M: 513
New Brunswick (Interesting facts) N: 181
Prince Edward Island P: 783
Glooscap Trail
Nova Scotia (Places to visit) N: 560
Gloriosa lily
Flower *picture on* F: 272
Glorious beetle [insect]
Beetle *picture on* B: 218
Glorious Flight: Across the Channel with Louis Blériot, The [book by Provensen]
Literature for children (Bibliography) *picture on* L: 382
Glorious Revolution [1688] G: 234
England (The Restoration) E: 309
James II J: 25
Restoration R: 263
William III W: 308
Glory [film]
Washington, Denzel W: 89
Glory hole [glassmaking]
Glass (Glass terms) G: 222
Gloss paint

Paint (Selecting the paint) **P: 25**
Glossa [entomology]
  Insect *diagram on* **I: 287**
Glossary [reference]
  Dictionary (History) **D: 194**
Glossopharyngeal nerve [anatomy]
  Neuralgia **N: 152**
Glossopharyngeal neuralgia [disorder]
  Neuralgia **N: 152**
Glottis [anatomy]
  Larynx **L: 79**
Gloucester [Massachusetts] **G: 234**
Gloucester, Battle of [1777]
  Lafayette, Marquis de (Service to the United
    States) **L: 28**
Gloucester, Duke of [former name] *See* Richard III
  in this index
Gloucester, Duke of [literary figure]
  Shakespeare, William: *(Richard III)* **S: 356**;
    (Rhetoric) **S: 368**
Gloucester, Earl of [literary figure]
  Shakespeare, William: *(King Lear)* **S: 363**
Glove [clothing] **G: 234** *with pictures*
  Baseball (Equipment) **B: 125** *with pictures*
  Boxing (Equipment) **B: 526-527**; (Bare knuckles
    to gloves) **B: 532**
  Virtual reality **V: 426**
Glove puppet
  Puppet (Hand puppets) **P: 906**
Glover, Joseph [British religious leader]
  Daye, Stephen **D: 54**
Glowworm [insect]
  Beetle (Fireflies) **B: 217-219**
  Firefly **F: 134**
Gloxinia [plant] **G: 235** *with picture*
  Flower *picture on* **F: 292**
GLTP [park] *See* Great Limpopo Transfrontier Park
  in this index
Glucagon [hormone]
  Hormone (Metabolic hormones) **H: 335**
  Hypoglycemia (Treatment) **H: 481**
  Pancreas **P: 128**
Gluck, Christoph Willibald [German composer]
  G: 235
  Opera (Gluck and opera reform) **O: 798**
  Overture **O: 882**
Glück, Louise [American poet] **G: 236**
  Poet laureate (table: Poets laureate of the United
    States) **P: 590**
Glückauf [ship]
  Ship (Tankers) **S: 408**
Glucocerebrosidase [enzyme]
  Gaucher's disease **G: 68**
Glucocerebroside [chemical]
  Gaucher's disease **G: 68**
Glucocorticoid [hormone]
  Adrenal gland **A: 67**
  Allergy (Treatment) **A: 374**
  Hormone (Metabolic hormones) **H: 335-336**
Glucose [sugar] **G: 236**
  Carbohydrate (Kinds of carbohydrates)
    C: 203 *with diagram*; (How the body uses
    carbohydrates) **C: 204**
  Cellulose (Biological importance) **C: 341**
  Dextrose **D: 178**
  Diabetes **D: 179**
  Glycogen **G: 237**
  Hunger **H: 449**
  Hydrolysis **H: 471**
  Hypoglycemia **H: 480**
  Liver (Digestion and use of food) **L: 394**
  Physical fitness (Glucose tolerance) **P: 435**
  Starch **So: 855**
  Sugar (Kinds of sugar) **So: 960**
Glucose catabolism
  Metabolism (Catabolism) **M: 424**
Glucose tolerance [physiology]
  Physical fitness (Glucose tolerance) **P: 435**
Glue **G: 236**
  Woodworking (Gluing) **W: 398**
Glue gesso
  Painting (Grounds) **P: 36**
Gluon [physics] **G: 236**
  Boson **B: 494**
  Matter (Quark-gluon plasmas) **M: 311**
  Physics (Physics today) **P: 442**
  Subatomic particle (Elementary particles) **So: 937**
Glutamate [neurotransmitter]
  Taste **T: 50**
Glutamic acid [chemical]
  Monosodium glutamate **M: 733**
  Wheat (Other uses) **W: 267**
Glutaraldehyde [chemical]
  Disinfectant **D: 235**
Gluten [protein] **G: 237**
  Baking (Baking ingredients) **B: 33**
  Celiac disease **C: 325**

Corn (The wet-milling industry) **Ci: 1061**
Flour (The chemistry of flour) **F: 268**; (Types of
  flour) **F: 268**
Grass (Cereals) **G: 326**
Wheat (Food for people) **W: 266**
Yeast (How yeast is used) **Y: 554-555**
Gluten sensitive enteropathy [disorder] *See* Celiac
  disease *in this index*
Glutenin [protein]
  Gluten **G: 237**
Glutton [animal]
  Wolverine **W: 380** *with picture*
Glycerin [chemical] *See* Glycerol *in this index*
Glycerius [Roman emperor]
  Rome, Ancient (table) **R: 447**
Glycerol [chemical] **G: 237**
  Detergent and soap (The kettle method) **D: 164**
  Fat (Structure) **F: 52**
  Fat substitute **F: 54**
  Food (Producing energy) **F: 330**
  Lard **L: 75**
  Lipid (Kinds of lipids) **L: 345**
  Nitroglycerin **N: 426**
  Nutrition (Fats) **N: 625**
  Triglyceride **T: 442**
Glycogen [physiology] **G: 237**
  Bernard, Claude **B: 270**
  Carbohydrate (Kinds of carbohydrates) **C: 203**
  Glucose **G: 236**
  Liver (Digestion and use of food) **L: 394**
  Metabolism (Anabolism) **M: 424**
Glycogen storage disease [disorder]
  Hypoglycemia (Causes) **H: 481**
Glycol [chemistry] **G: 237**
  Butterfly (Hibernation) **B: 742**
  Food, Frozen (Liquid immersion freezing) **F: 338**
Glycolipid [chemical]
  Lipid (Kinds of lipids) **L: 345**
Glycolysis [biochemistry]
  Metabolism (Catabolism) **M: 424**
  Respiration (Cellular respiration) **R: 261**
Glycoside [compound]
  Digitalis **D: 203**
Glycyrrhizin [chemical]
  Licorice **L: 270**
Glynn, Martin Henry [American political leader]
  New York (table) **N: 313**
Glyph [symbol]
  Indian, American (Writing) **I: 150** *with picture*
  Writing system (Phonetization) **W: 513**
GM [company] *See* General Motors Company *in
  this index*
GM food *See* Genetically modified food *in this index*
GM Renaissance Center
  Detroit (The city) **D: 167-168**
GMO [genetics] *See* Genetically modified organism
  in this index
GMO corn
  Corn (Controlling pests and diseases) **Ci: 1061**;
    (Development of hybrids) **Ci: 1063**
Gmünd Roadster [car]
  Porsche AG **P: 680**
Gnat [insect] **G: 237** *with picture*
Gnatcatcher [bird] **G: 238** *with picture*
Gnathostomata [biology]
  Fish (A classification of fish) **F: 172**
Gneiss [rock] **G: 238** *with picture*
  Rock (table) **R: 373** *with picture*; (Metamorphic
    rock) **R: 373**
Gnetophyte [plant]
  Plant (Gymnosperms) **P: 520**; (Classification of
    plants) **P: 546-547** *with picture*
Gnetum [plant]
  Plant (Angiosperms) **P: 520**
GNMA [agency] *See* Government National
  Mortgage Association *in this index*
Gnome [legendary creature] **G: 238**
Gnomon [instrument]
  Sundial **So: 990** *with picture*
Gnomonic projection
  Great-circle route **G: 338** *with diagram*
Gnosis [religion]
  Gnosticism **G: 238**
Gnosticism [religion] **G: 238**
  Irenaeus, Saint **I: 429**
  Roman Catholic Church (The first 300 years)
    R: 405
Gnotobiotics [biology] **G: 239**
GNP [economics] *See* Gross national product *in
  this index*
Gnu [animal] *See* Wildebeest *in this index*
Go [game]
  Game (Board games) **G: 22**
Go-away bird
  Turaco **T: 495**
Go Down, Moses [stories by Faulkner]
  Faulkner, William **F: 55**

Go-kart [automobile]
  Kart racing **K: 247**
Go Tell It On the Mountain [book by Baldwin]
  Baldwin, James **B: 39**
  Novel (After World War II) **N: 574**
"Go West, young man" [quotation]
  Greeley, Horace (His publications) **G: 379**
Goa [state, India]
  India (India in the 1950's and early 1960's) **I: 133**
  Xavier, Saint Francis **X: 543**
Goal [sports]
  Lacrosse **L: 23**
  Rugby football (Rugby Union) **R: 510**; (Rugby
    League) **R: 512**
  Soccer (The field) **So: 544**
Goal area
  Soccer (The field) **So: 544**
Goal judge
  Hockey (The officials) **H: 278**
Goal kick
  Soccer (Restarts) **So: 546**
Goal line [sports]
  Field hockey (The field and equipment) **F: 92**
    with diagram
  Football (The field) **F: 354-355** *with diagram*
  Rugby football (Rugby Union) **R: 510**; (Rugby
    League) **R: 512**
  Soccer (The field) **So: 544**
Goal post [sports]
  Football (The field) **F: 354-355** *with picture*
  Rugby football (Rugby Union) **R: 510**
Goalie [hockey] *See* Goalkeeper *in this index*
Goalkeeper [sports]
  Hockey (The starting lineup) **H: 275**; (Equipment)
    H: 276
  Lacrosse **L: 23**
  Soccer (The goalkeeper) **So: 545** *with diagram*
Goaltending
  Basketball (Basketball terms) **B: 145**
Goanna [lizard]
  Monitor **M: 724**
Goat [animal] **G: 239** *with pictures*
  Animal *picture on* **A: 474**
Goat, The [astrology]
  Capricorn **C: 198** *with picture*
Goat antelope [animal]
  Chamois **C: 372**
  Goat (Wild goats) **G: 239**
  Mountain goat **M: 898**
Goat of the fan [animal]
  Springbok **So: 807** *with picture*
Goat tying
  Rodeo (All-women's rodeos) **R: 398**
Goatee
  Beard **B: 186**
Goatsbeard [plant] **G: 241**
Goatsucker [bird] **G: 242** *with picture*
Gobat, Charles Albert [Swiss statesman]
  Nobel Prizes (Peace: 1902) **N: 448**
Gobelin [French history]
  Tapestry (History) **T: 39-40**
Gober, Hershel W. [American government official]
  Clinton, Bill (table) **Ci: 682d**
Gobi [region, Asia] **G: 242** *with picture and map*
  Andrews, Roy Chapman **A: 456**
  Camel *picture on* **C: 77**
  China (The Xinjiang-Mongolian Uplands) **C: 491**
    with picture; (Climate) **C: 494**
  Mongolia (Land) **M: 722**
  Plant (Deserts) **P: 523-525**
Gobind Singh [Indian religious leader]
  Sikhism (History) **S: 455**
Goble, Paul [British author]
  Caldecott Medal (table: 1979) **C: 26**
  Regina Medal (table: 2006) **R: 206**
Goblin
  Fairy **F: 10**
"Goblin Market" [poem by Rossetti]
  Rossetti, Christina Georgina **R: 482**
Goby [fish] **G: 243** *with picture*
  Fish **F: 144**
God **G: 243**
  See also the list of Related articles in the God *article
    and the articles on specific religions, such as*
    Hinduism
  Agnosticism **A: 143**
  Anselm, Saint **A: 519**
  Aquinas, Saint Thomas (His thought) **A: 580-580a**
  Aristotle (Metaphysics) **A: 664**
  Atheism **A: 853**
  Augustine, Saint (His beliefs) **A: 888**
  Bible **B: 279**
  Christianity (Beliefs) **C: 522g**
  Creationism **Ci: 1123**
  Deism **D: 94**
  Enlightenment (Deism) **E: 326b**
  Hinduism (Deities) **H: 236**

Intelligent design **I:** 320
Islam **I:** 463
Judaism (The teachings of Judaism) **J:** 179
Kant, Immanuel (Kant's ideas) **K:** 244
Mormons (Church doctrines and ordinances)
 M: 806
Mysticism **M:** 972
Mythology **M:** 973; (Mythical beings) **M:** 975
Philosophy (Philosophy and religion) **P:** 386;
 (Neoplatonism) **P:** 388; (Medieval philosophy)
 P: 388; (Rationalism) **P:** 388-389; (The
 philosophy of Immanuel Kant) **P:** 389-390
Polytheism **P:** 652
Protestantism (Protestant beliefs) **P:** 833-834;
 (Worship) **P:** 834
Religion **R:** 214
Spinoza, Baruch **So:** 795
Theism **T:** 251
Theology **T:** 252
Theosophy **T:** 252
Trinity **T:** 447
Witchcraft (Witchcraft as a religion) **W:** 371-372
God, Kingdom of [religion]
 Christianity (Origins) **C:** 523
 Jesus Christ (Public life) **J:** 106; (The early
 Christians) **J:** 108b
God and Man at Yale [book by Buckley]
 Buckley, William F., Jr. **B:** 664
"God Bless America" [song] **G:** 244
 Berlin, Irving **B:** 266
"God helps them that help themselves"
 [quotation]
 Poor Richard's Almanac **P:** 659
"God is dead" [philosophy]
 God (Ideas about God) **G:** 244
 Nietzsche, Friedrich (Nietzsche and religion)
 N: 406
 Philosophy (Philosophy in the 1800's) **P:** 390
God Knows [book by Heller]
 Heller, Joseph **H:** 177
God of Small Things, The [book by Roy]
 Novel (The novel today) **N:** 575
God of Vengeance [play by Asch]
 Asch, Sholem **A:** 766
"God Save the King" [song]
 "God Save the Queen" **G:** 244
 National anthem **N:** 29
"God Save the Queen" [song] **G:** 244
 National anthem **N:** 29
God Sends Sunday [book by Bontemps]
 Bontemps, Arna Wendell **B:** 463
God That Failed, The [anthology]
 Wright, Richard **W:** 508
God the Father [religion]
 Christianity (The Trinity) **C:** 522g
 Mormons (Church doctrines and ordinances)
 M: 806
 Trinity **T:** 447
God the Son [religion]
 See also Jesus Christ *in this index*
 Christianity (The Trinity) **C:** 522g
 Trinity **T:** 447
Godard, Jean-Luc [French director] **G:** 244
 Motion picture (The New Wave in France) **M:** 870
 with picture
Godavari River [India]
 Religion *picture on* **R:** 214
Godbody [book by Sturgeon]
 Sturgeon, Theodore **S:** 934
Godbout, Adélard [Canadian political leader]
 Quebec (table) **Q:** 29
Goddard, Mary Katherine [American publisher]
 G: 244
Goddard, Robert Hutchings [American physicist]
 G: 244
 Lindbergh, Charles Augustus (His historic flight)
 L: 330
 Rocket (Rockets of the early 1900's) **R:** 390 *with
 picture*
 Space exploration (Early dreams of space flight)
 So: 706 *with picture*
Goddard, Samuel P., Jr. [American political leader]
 Arizona (table) **A:** 682
Goddard, William [American publisher] **G:** 245
Goddess
 Mythology (Mythical beings) **M:** 975
 Witchcraft (Witchcraft as a religion) **W:** 371-372
Goddess of Democracy [statue]
 China *picture on* **C:** 506
Godefroy, Alexandre F. [French hairdresser]
 Hairdressing (The 1800's) **H:** 12
Gödel, Kurt [Austrian-born American
 mathematician]
 Mathematics (Philosophies of mathematics)
 M: 307
Goderich, Viscount [British political leader]
 United Kingdom (table: British prime ministers)

U: 72
Godetia [plant] **G:** 245 *with picture*
Godey, Louis Antoine [American publisher] **G:** 245
 Magazine (Magazines in the 1800's) **M:** 45
Godey's Lady's Book [magazine]
 Godey, Louis Antoine **G:** 245
 Magazine (Magazines in the 1800's) **M:** 45
Godfather, Part II, The [film]
 Coppola, Francis Ford **Ci:** 1044
 De Niro, Robert **D:** 131
 Motion picture (Best picture: 1974) **M:** 861
 Pacino, Al **P:** 18
 Puzo, Mario **P:** 914
Godfather, Part III, The [film]
 Pacino, Al **P:** 18
 Puzo, Mario **P:** 914
Godfather, The [book by Puzo]
 Puzo, Mario **P:** 913
Godfather, The [film]
 Brando, Marlon **B:** 563
 Coppola, Francis Ford **Ci:** 1044
 Motion picture (Best picture: 1972) **M:** 861;
 (Changes in Hollywood) **M:** 871 *with picture*
 Pacino, Al **P:** 18
 Puzo, Mario **P:** 914
Godfather of Soul [nickname]
 Brown, James **B:** 642
Godfrey, Thomas [American inventor]
 Sextant **S:** 337
Godfrey of Bouillon [French crusader]
 Crusades (The First Crusade) **Ci:** 1160 *with map*
Godiva, Lady [English public figure] **G:** 245
Godkin, Edward Lawrence [American editor]
 G: 245
Gododdin [poem by Aneirin]
 Wales (The arts) **W:** 9
Godolphin Arabian [horse]
 Horse racing (Thoroughbred horses) **H:** 363
Godparent [religion]
 Baptism **B:** 101
 Family (Family relationships) **F:** 21
Gods *See* God *in this index*
Gods Are Athirst, The [book by France]
 France, Anatole **F:** 480
God's Gift to Poland [weather]
 Indian summer **I:** 189
God's Man [engravings by Ward]
 Ward, Lynd Kendall **W:** 36
God's Trombones [book by Johnson]
 Johnson, James Weldon **J:** 143
Godse, Nathuram [Indian public figure]
 Gandhi, Mohandas Karamchand (Freedom and
 death) **G:** 25
Godspeed [ship]
 Jamestown **J:** 28
Godthåb [Greenland] *See* Nuuk *in this index*
Godunov, Boris [czar of Russia]
 Russia (table: Czars and empresses) **R:** 549; (The
 Time of Troubles) **R:** 549
Godwin, Mary [British author] *See* Shelley, Mary
 Wollstonecraft *in this index*
Godwin, Mary Wollstonecraft [British author] *See*
 Wollstonecraft, Mary *in this index*
Godwin, Mills E., Jr. [American political leader]
 Virginia (table) **V:** 417
Godwin, William [British author] **G:** 245
Godwin Austen, Henry Haversham [British
 surveyor]
 K2 **K:** 208
Godwin Austen, Mount *See* K2 *in this index*
Godwine, Earl of Wessex [English nobleman]
 Edward the Confessor **E:** 113
 Harold II **H:** 65
Godwit [bird] **G:** 246 *with picture*
 Bird *pictures on* **B:** 361
Goebbels, Joseph [Nazi government official]
 G: 246
 Kristallnacht **K:** 388
 World War II (Propaganda) **W:** 494
Goebel, William [American political leader]
 Kentucky **K:** 272; (The early 1900's) **K:** 293
Goeppert-Mayer, Maria [American physicist] *See*
 Mayer, Maria Goeppert *in this index*
Goering, Hermann Wilhelm [Nazi general] *See*
 Göring, Hermann Wilhelm *in this index*
Goes, Hugo van der [Flemish painter] *See* Van der
 Goes, Hugo *in this index*
Goethals, George Washington [American
 engineer] **G:** 246
 Panama Canal (Cutting through the isthmus)
 P: 126
Goethals Bridge [New Jersey-New York]
 Elizabeth **E:** 238
 New York City (Transportation) **N:** 334
Goethe, Johann Wolfgang von [German author]
 G: 246 *with portrait*
 Classicism (Germany) **Ci:** 653

 Color (Newton and Goethe) **Ci:** 826
 Drama (Romanticism) **D:** 337
 German literature (German Preromanticism)
 G: 139; (German Classicism) **G:** 139; (Other
 writers) **G:** 140
 Herder, Johann Gottfried von **H:** 199
 Mephistopheles **M:** 411
Goff, Nathan, Jr. [American government official]
 Hayes, Rutherford Birchard (table) **H:** 121
Gogarty, Deirdre [Irish boxer]
 Boxing (Women's boxing) **B:** 532b-533
Goggles
 Inuit (Clothing) **I:** 354b-354c
 Night vision systems *picture on* **N:** 419
 Skin diving (History) **S:** 494
Gogh, Vincent Van [Dutch painter] *See* Van Gogh,
 Vincent *in this index*
Gogol, Nikolai [Russian author] **G:** 248
 Drama (Russian drama and Chekhov) **D:** 338
 Russian literature (Late Romanticism) **R:** 561
Goh Chok Tong [Singapore political leader] **G:** 248
 Singapore (History) **S:** 471
Goidelic Celts [language]
 Gaels **G:** 5
Going My Way [film]
 Crosby, Bing **Ci:** 1154
 Motion picture (Best picture: 1944) **M:** 861
Going public [investment]
 Initial public offering **I:** 271
Going to Meet the Man [stories by Baldwin]
 Baldwin, James **B:** 39
Goiter [disorder] **G:** 248
 Iodine (Uses of iodine) **I:** 370
 Nutrition (Deficiency diseases) **N:** 630-631
 Physiology **P:** 411
Gokarne Aunsi [holiday]
 August **A:** 886
Gola [people]
 Mask (Ceremonial masks) **M:** 264-265
Golan [ancient city]
 Cities of refuge **Ci:** 568
Golan Heights [region, Middle East] **G:** 248
 Israel (The Yom Kippur War) **I:** 488
 Middle East (Cold War alliances) **M:** 534-534a
 Syria (The continuing Arab-Israeli conflict)
 So: 1075-1076
 United Nations (Peacekeeping operations)
 U: 90-91
Golconda [painting by Magritte]
 Magritte, René **M:** 63
Gold [element] **G:** 249 *with pictures*
 Alchemy **A:** 334
 Alloy (Costly and ornamental alloys) **A:** 378
 Carat **C:** 201
 Colonial life in America (Decorative arts) **Ci:** 807
 El Dorado **E:** 157
 Gold leaf **G:** 253
 Gold rush **G:** 254
 Gresham's law **G:** 391
 Hong Kong (Service industries) **H:** 318
 Mercantilism **M:** 411
 Metallurgy (Leaching) **M:** 426
 Mineral *picture on* **M:** 568
 Money (Modern coins) **M:** 707; (Money in the
 new United States) **M:** 712
 Montana (Interesting facts) **M:** 743
 South Africa (Mining) **So:** 616 *with picture*;
 (Discovery of diamonds and gold) **So:** 618
 South Dakota *picture on* **So:** 682
 Teeth (Dental decay) **T:** 82-83
"Gold-Bug, The" [story by Poe]
 Poe, Edgar Allan (Poe's life) **P:** 589
Gold certificate [money]
 Money *picture on* **M:** 709; (Money in the
 American Civil War) **M:** 713
Gold Coast [Africa]
 Ghana **G:** 178
Gold Coast [district, Chicago]
 Chicago (The North Side) **C:** 423 *with picture*
 Shelter *picture on* **S:** 393
Gold crew
 Submarine (Life aboard a submarine) **So:** 941
Gold Cup race
 Motorboat racing (Types of racing) **M:** 877
Gold depository
 Fort Knox **F:** 413 *with picture*
Gold Diggers of 1933 [film]
 Motion picture (Movies in the 1930's) **M:** 867
 with picture
Gold eagle [money]
 Money *picture on* **M:** 708
Gold filling
 Gold (Jewelry) **G:** 251
Gold film
 Gold (Other uses) **G:** 251 *with picture*
Gold leaf **G:** 253
 Gold (Other uses) **G:** 251

Gold-leaf electroscope
Electroscope E: 218
Gold mine
Gold (Mining) G: 252
Nevada (Mining) N: 171 *with picture*
Gold piece
Money *pictures on* M: 708, M: 709
Gold plating
Gold (Jewelry) G: 251
Gold record
Recording industry (Recording industry awards)
R: 182
Gold rush [Australian history]
Australia (The discovery of gold) A: 922
Gold rush [Canadian history]
Klondike K: 344 *with picture*
Royal Canadian Mounted Police (History) R: 497
Yukon (History) Y: 581 *with picture*
Gold rush [U.S. history] G: 254 *with picture*
Alaska *picture on* A: 302; (The gold rush) A: 301
Asian Americans (The first wave of Asian
immigration) A: 812d
California *picture on* C: 61; (The gold rush) C: 62
with picture
Colorado *picture on* Ci: 846; (The gold rush)
Ci: 845
Forty-Niners F: 420
Gold (History of gold) G: 253
Goldfield G: 256
Indian wars (Wars on the Plains) I: 192
Jefferson Territory J: 88
Juneau J: 194
Marshall, James Wilson M: 229
Montana (The gold rush) M: 758 *with picture*
Murieta, Joaquín M: 930
Pioneer life in America (Crossing the Plains)
P: 485-486
San Francisco (The gold rush) S: 97
South Dakota (Territorial days) So: 681
Taylor, Zachary *picture on* T: 59
Western frontier life in America *picture on* W: 236;
(The shifting frontier) W: 232; (Mining) W: 234
with picture; (Settlers and Native Americans)
W: 239
Westward movement in America (California)
W: 249 *with picture*
Gold standard [economics] G: 254
Cleveland, Grover (The currency and the tariff)
Ci: 671; (Saving the gold standard) Ci: 673
Exchange rate E: 436
Gold (History of gold) G: 253
Great Depression (The beginning of the Great
Depression) G: 339
McKinley, William (The front-porch campaign)
M: 340
Money M: 704; (History of the pound) M: 709-
710
Republican Party (The money issue) R: 255
Gold Standard Act [1900]
McKinley, William (McKinley's first administration
[1897-1901]) M: 340
Goldberg, Arthur Joseph [American statesman]
G: 254
Kennedy, John Fitzgerald (table) K: 266
United Nations (table) U: 86
Goldberg, Ephraim Owen [birth name of]
Gehry, Frank G: 76
Goldberg, Rube [American cartoonist]
Cartoon *picture on* C: 263
Goldberg, Whoopi [American actress]
Motion picture (Best performance by an actress
in a supporting role: 1990) M: 862b
Goldberg Variations [music by Bach]
Canon C: 183
Goldberger, Joseph [American doctor] G: 255
Pellagra P: 232
Vitamin (History) V: 432
Golden Age [world history] G: 255
Elizabeth I E: 238
England (The reign of Elizabeth I) E: 307
Greek literature (The Golden Age) G: 377
Gupta dynasty G: 442
India (The golden age) I: 129
Jews (The Jews under Islam) J: 122
Latin literature (The Golden Age) L: 116
Netherlands N: 139; (Prosperity and power)
N: 148 *with picture*
Russian literature (Early Romanticism) R: 560
Spanish literature (The Golden Age) So: 758
World, History of the (The Greeks) W: 428 *with
picture*
Golden Age, The [book by Grahame]
Grahame, Kenneth G: 301
Golden Age, The [film]
Buñuel, Luis B: 700
Golden Age of Athens [ancient Greece]
Athens (The Golden Age) A: 857

Golden Age G: 255
Greek literature (The Golden Age) G: 377
Pericles P: 287
Golden Age of Broadcasting
Radio R: 83; (Putting a show on the air) R: 86;
(The Golden Age of Broadcasting) R: 92 *with
pictures*
Golden Age of Jazz, The
Jazz (The 1920's) J: 70
Golden Age of Piracy
Pirate P: 494
Golden apples [Greek mythology]
Hercules (The twelve labors) H: 198-199
Hesperides H: 218
Golden bell [plant]
Forsythia F: 411 *with picture*
Golden Bough, The [book by Frazer]
Frazer, Sir James George F: 496
Magic (Kinds of magic) M: 49
Mythology (Anthropological approaches) M: 989
Golden-brown algae [organisms] *See* Diatom *in
this index*
Golden chain [tree]
Laburnum L: 19
Golden chanterelle [fungus]
Mushroom (Mushroomlike fungi) M: 945
Golden Cockerel, The [opera by Rimsky-Korsakov]
Rimsky-Korsakov, Nikolai R: 341
Golden Compass, The [book by Pullman]
Pullman, Philip P: 900
Golden-crowned kinglet
Bird *picture on* B: 358
Kinglet K: 330 *with picture*
Golden crucian carp [fish] *See* Goldfish *in this index*
Golden Delicious
Apple (Varieties of apples) A: 571 *with picture*
Golden eagle
Bird (Birds of the desert) B: 339 *with picture*
Eagle E: 3; (Food) E: 5; (The golden eagle) E: 5
with picture
Golden Fleece [Greek mythology] G: 255
Argonauts A: 660
Jason J: 64
Medea M: 360
Golden Fleece, Order of the
Knighthood, Orders of (Honorary orders) K: 347
Golden-fronted leafbird
Bird (Birds of Asia) B: 344f *with picture*
Golden Gate [bay]
San Francisco (History) S: 97
Golden Gate Bridge [San Francisco] G: 255
Bridge *picture on* B: 600; (table: Suspension)
B: 603
California *picture on* C: 37; (Transportation) C: 58
United States *picture on* U: 98
Golden Gate International Exposition [1939-
1940]
California (Progress as a state) C: 62
Golden Gate National Recreation Area
[California]
National Park System (table: National recreation
areas) N: 49
Golden Gate Park
San Francisco (Other neighborhoods) S: 93-94
with map
Golden Gate Quartet [musical group]
Gospel music G: 277
Golden Gateway Center
San Francisco (Downtown San Francisco) S: 92-93
Golden Gloves tournament
Boxing (Amateur boxing) B: 530
Golden hamster
Hamster H: 37 *with picture*
Golden Hind [ship]
Drake, Sir Francis (Voyage around the world)
D: 321 *with picture*
Golden Horde [Russian history]
Mongol Empire (Breakup) M: 721
Russia (Mongol rule) R: 548
Golden Horn [inlet, Istanbul]
Istanbul (The city) I: 490-491
Golden Horseshoe [region, Ontario]
Ontario O: 764
Golden Legend, The [book by James of Voragine]
George, Saint G: 109
Golden Lotus [book]
Chinese literature (Drama and fiction) C: 511-512
Golden mahseer [fish]
Minnow M: 607
Golden Notebook, The [book by Lessing]
Lessing, Doris L: 208
Golden Pavilion [Kyoto, Japan]
Kyoto K: 398
Golden pheasant
Pheasant (Kinds of pheasants) P: 355 *with picture*
Golden-plover [bird]
Animal *picture on* A: 485

Bird (Birds of the Arctic) B: 343 *with picture*
Golden poison dart frog
Poison dart frog P: 601
Golden-rain tree
New Harmony N: 229
Golden rectangle [geometry]
Golden section G: 256 *with diagram*
Golden retriever [dog] G: 255
Dog *picture on* D: 268
Golden rice
Plant (Breeding and genetics) P: 542
Golden robin [bird] *See* Baltimore oriole *in this
index*
Golden rule [religion] G: 256
Confucianism (Early Confucianism) Ci: 936
Jesus Christ (His teaching) J: 107
Religion (A code of conduct) R: 217
Golden Sebright bantam rooster
Chicken *picture on* C: 442
Golden section [geometry] G: 256 *with diagram*
Golden shiner [fish]
Minnow M: 607
Roach R: 357
Golden Spike National Historic Site [Utah]
National Park System (table: National historic
sites) N: 52-53
Golden State [name for]
California C: 36
Golden State Warriors [team]
Basketball (table) B: 150
Golden Temple [India]
Amritsar A: 444
India (India under Indira Gandhi) I: 133-134
Sikhism *picture on* S: 455
Golden tortoise beetle
Beetle *picture on* B: 218
Golden Triangle [district, Pittsburgh]
Pittsburgh (The city) P: 500a *with picture*
Golden trout [fish]
Trout *picture on* T: 453
Golden-winged woodpecker *See* Yellow-shafted
flicker *in this index*
Goldeneyed lacewing [insect]
Insect *picture on* I: 281
Goldenrod [plant] G: 256
Flower (Flowers of woodlands and forests) F: 284
with picture
Goldfield [Nevada] G: 256
Goldfield [plant]
Flower *picture on* F: 288
Goldfinch [bird] G: 256 *with pictures*
Bird *pictures on* B: 344d, B: 358; (Birds of Europe)
B: 344c
Goldfish [fish] G: 257 *with pictures*
Goldin, Horace [American magician]
Magician (Illusions) M: 51
Golding, Bruce [Jamaican political leader]
Jamaica (History) J: 24-25
Golding, William [British author] G: 258
Lord of the Flies L: 454
Goldman, Edwin Franko [American bandleader]
G: 258
Goldman, Emma [Russian-American social
reformer] G: 258 *with portrait*
Goldman, Ronald [American public figure]
Simpson, O. J. S: 468
Goldman Band
Goldman, Edwin Franko G: 258
Goldman Sachs Tower [building]
Jersey City (Description) J: 94 *with picture*
Goldmann, Max [Austrian director]
Reinhardt, Max R: 209
Goldoni, Carlo [Italian dramatist] G: 258
Drama (Italy) D: 335
Italian literature (The Baroque period and the
Enlightenment) I: 494-495
Goldrick, Q. J. [American educator]
Colorado (Schools) Ci: 832
Goldsborough, Charles [American political leader]
Maryland (table) M: 255
Goldsborough, Phillips Lee [American political
leader]
Maryland (table) M: 255
Goldschmidt, Neil E. [American government
official]
Carter, Jimmy (table) C: 257
Oregon (table) O: 845
Transportation, Department of (table) T: 400
Goldsmith, Deborah [American painter]
Folk art *picture on* F: 317
Goldsmith, Oliver [Canadian poet]
Canadian literature (Early English-Canadian
literature) C: 157
Goldsmith, Oliver [Irish author] G: 259
English literature (The Johnson circle) E: 319
with picture
Irish literature (Early works in English) I: 431

Newbery, John **N:** 358
Goldstein, Joseph Leonard [American physiologist]
Nobel Prizes (Physiology or medicine: 1985) **N:** 446
Goldwater, Barry Morris [American political leader] **G:** 259 *with portrait*
Arizona (Politics) **A:** 687-688
Johnson, Lyndon Baines (Full-term president) **J:** 149-150
Nixon, Richard Milhous (New York City lawyer) **N:** 432
Goldwyn, Samuel [American producer] **G:** 259
Goles [English jester]
Jester **J:** 103
Golf [sport] **G:** 260 *with pictures*
Japan *picture on* **J:** 41
Ryder Cup **R:** 573
Scotland (Recreation) **S:** 214 *with picture*
United Kingdom *picture on* **U:** 57
Zaharias, Babe Didrikson **Z:** 584
Golf ball
Golf (Golf balls) **G:** 261 *with picture*
Golf club
Golf (Golf clubs) **G:** 262 *with pictures*
Golf course
Golf **G:** 260 *with pictures*
Golfers' Association, Professional *See* Professional Golfers' Association *in this index*
Golgi, Camillo [Italian physiologist] **G:** 267
Golgi apparatus [biology]
Cell (The cytoplasm) **C:** 329 *with diagrams*
Golgi cell [biology]
Golgi, Camillo **G:** 267
Golgi complex [biology]
Cell (The cytoplasm) **C:** 329 *with diagrams*
Golgotha [New Testament] *See* Calvary *in this index*
Goliad [Texas]
Texas (The Texas revolution) **T:** 206
Goliath [Biblical figure] **G:** 267
David (Early life) **D:** 44-45 *with picture*
Giant **G:** 183
Goliath beetle
Beetle **B:** 215
Insect *picture on* **I:** 278; (The variety of insects) **I:** 280-281
Goliath birdeater tarantula [spider]
Spider *picture on* **So:** 783
Tarantula **T:** 42
Goliath frog
Frog (The body of a frog) **F:** 536
Goliath grouper [fish] **G:** 267
Bass (Sea bass) **B:** 157 *with picture*
Fish *picture on* **F:** 153
Golkar [political organization]
Indonesia (Politics) **I:** 227
Golubac Castle
Serbia *picture on* **S:** 314
Goma [Democratic Republic of the Congo]
Congo, Democratic Republic of the *picture on* **Ci:** 940a
Gombu, Nawang [Nepalese mountain climber]
Mount Everest **M:** 884
Gomera [Canary Islands]
Columbus, Christopher (Sailing west) **Ci:** 860
Gómez, Esteban [Portuguese explorer]
Nova Scotia (Exploration and settlement) **N:** 567
Gómez, General [Mexican military leader]
Maximilian **M:** 319
Gómez, Juan Vicente [Venezuelan political leader]
Venezuela (Rule by dictatorships) **V:** 304
Gomez, Lefty [American baseball player]
Baseball (table: Hall of Fame) **B:** 134a
Gómez de Espinosa, Gonzalo [Spanish sailor]
Magellan, Ferdinand (The end of the voyage) **M:** 47
Gómez Farías, Valentín [Mexican political leader]
Mexico (Difficulties of the early republic) **M:** 471
Gomorrah [ancient city] *See* Sodom and Gomorrah *in this index*
Gompers, Samuel [American labor leader] **G:** 268
Coolidge, Calvin (As governor) **Ci:** 1031-1032
Labor movement (The first nationwide labor organizations) **L:** 9-10
United States, History of the (Early reform efforts) **U:** 185
Gomułka, Władysław [Polish political leader]
Cold War (Unrest in Eastern Europe) **Ci:** 766
Poland (History) **P:** 611-613
Gona [site]
Prehistoric people (The Stone Age) **P:** 751
Gonad [anatomy]
Hormone (Growth and sex hormones) **H:** 336
Gonadotropin [hormone]
Steroid (The adrenal steroids) **So:** 894-895
Gonarezhou National Park [Zimbabwe]
Great Limpopo Transfrontier Park **G:** 346

Gonçalves, Nuno [Portuguese painter]
Portugal (The arts) **P:** 689
Gonçalves Dias, Antônio [Brazilian poet] *See* Dias, Antônio Gonçalves *in this index*
Gonçalves Zarco, João [Portuguese explorer]
Henry the Navigator **H:** 191
Goncharov, Ivan [Russian author]
Russian literature (Early realism) **R:** 562
Goncharova, Natalya [Russian artist]
Painting (Nonobjective painting in Russia) **P:** 79
Pushkin, Alexander (His life) **P:** 912
Goncourt, Edmond de [French author]
French literature (Naturalism) **F:** 522
Impressionism (Music, literature, and sculpture) **I:** 94
Goncourt, Jules de [French author]
French literature (Naturalism) **F:** 522
Impressionism (Music, literature, and sculpture) **I:** 94
Göncz, Árpád [Hungarian political leader]
Hungary (Multiparty elections) **H:** 448
Gondola [boat] **G:** 268
Europe *picture on* **E:** 395
Italy *picture on* **I:** 510
Gondola [compartment]
Airship (Thrust) **A:** 250-251 *with diagram*
Piccard, Auguste **P:** 450
Gondola car [railroad]
Railroad *picture on* **R:** 108
Gondolier [career]
Gondola **G:** 268
Gondwanaland [geology]
Antarctica (Climate) **A:** 532
Cretaceous Period **Ci:** 1127
Earth *map on* **E:** 31; (The shaping of the continents) **E:** 24
Jurassic Period **J:** 201
Pangaea **P:** 130
Plate tectonics *map on* **P:** 564; (Plate movement) **P:** 563
Gone with the Wind [book by Mitchell] **G:** 268
Mitchell, Margaret **M:** 677
Gone with the Wind [film]
Gable, Clark **G:** 2
Gone with the Wind [book] **G:** 268
McDaniel, Hattie **M:** 332g *with picture*
Mitchell, Margaret **M:** 678
Motion picture (Best picture: 1939) **M:** 861; (Movies in the 1930's) **M:** 868
United States *picture on* **U:** 118
Goneril [literary figure]
Shakespeare, William: (*King Lear*) **S:** 363
Gong [musical instrument]
Music *picture on* **M:** 949
GONG [program]
National Optical Astronomy Observatories **N:** 42
Gongfu [martial art] *See* Kung fu *in this index*
Góngora, Luis de [Spanish poet] **G:** 268
Spanish literature (The 1600's) **So:** 759-760
Gongorismo [literature]
See also Culteranismo *in this index*
Góngora, Luis de **G:** 268
Gonne, Maud [Irish public figure]
Yeats, William Butler **Y:** 555
Gonorrhea [disease] **G:** 268
Chlamydia **C:** 516
Penicillin (Resistance) **P:** 241
Sexually transmitted disease **S:** 338b
Gonzaga, Tomás Antônio [Brazilian poet]
Latin American literature (Colonial literature) **L:** 112
Gonzales, Alberto R. [American government official] **G:** 268
Bush, George Walker (table) **B:** 722h; (Other domestic issues) **B:** 723
Gonzales, Corky [American social reformer] *See* Gonzales, Rodolfo *in this index*
Gonzales, José [American Indian leader]
New Mexico (Mexican rule) **N:** 273-275
Gonzales, Rodolfo [American social reformer] **G:** 269
Hispanic Americans (The Chicano movement) **H:** 256
González, Elián [Cuban public figure]
Miami (History) **M:** 480-481
Reno, Janet **R:** 240
Gonzalez, Henry B. [American political leader]
Hispanic Americans (Political developments) **H:** 255
González, José Victoriano [Spanish painter]
Gris, Juan **G:** 395
González, Lázaro [Cuban public figure]
Hispanic Americans (Cuban immigration) **H:** 253-254
González Videla, Gabriel [Chilean political leader]
Chile (Years of progress) **C:** 469
Gonzalo, Don [literary figure]

Don Juan **D:** 306
Gonzalo de Berceo [Spanish poet]
Spanish literature (Early medieval literature) **So:** 757-758
Goober [food] *See* Peanut *in this index*
Goober State [nickname]
Georgia **G:** 112
Good, James W. [American government official]
Hoover, Herbert Clark (table) **H:** 330
Good As Gold [book by Heller]
Heller, Joseph **H:** 177
Good-bye, Mr. Chips [book by Hilton]
Hilton, James **H:** 233
Good Companions, The [book by Priestley]
Priestley, John Boynton **P:** 776
Good Earth, The [book by Buck]
Buck, Pearl S. **B:** 663
Good Friday [religion] **G:** 269
Easter (Good Friday) **E:** 43 *with picture*
Holy Week **H:** 300
Philippines *picture on* **P:** 373
"Good Friday, 1613. Riding Westward" [poem by Donne]
Donne, John (His poetry) **D:** 308
Good Friday Agreement [1998]
Northern Ireland (The Good Friday Agreement) **N:** 525
Troubles **T:** 453
Ulster Unionist Party **U:** 15
Good Hope, Cape of *See* Cape of Good Hope *in this index*
Good luck charm
Fetish **F:** 81
Good Man Is Hard to Find, A [stories by O'Connor]
O'Connor, Flannery **O:** 668
Good Morning Blues [book by Basie]
Basie, Count **B:** 140
Good-Natur'd Man, The [play by Goldsmith]
Goldsmith, Oliver **G:** 259
Good Neighbor Policy [American history]
Monroe Doctrine (The Good Neighbor Policy) **M:** 740
Pan-American conferences (Good Neighbor Policy) **P:** 113
Roosevelt, Franklin Delano (Foreign policy) **R:** 454
Good News Bible
Bible (Modern English translations) **B:** 286
"Good Rockin' Tonight" [song]
Rock music (Musical roots) **R:** 376
Good Samaritan [Bible]
Samaritans **S:** 78
Good Shepherd, The [mosaic]
Mosaic *pictures on* **M:** 822
Good Soldier, The [book by Ford]
Ford, Ford Madox **F:** 371
Novel (New directions in the novel) **N:** 573-574
Goodall, Jane [British zoologist] **G:** 269
Chimpanzee (Chimpanzees and people) **C:** 473 *with picture*
Primate (The study of nonhuman primates) **P:** 778c
Goodbye, Columbus [book by Roth]
Roth, Philip **R:** 487
Goodbye to All That [book by Graves]
Graves, Robert **G:** 330
Goodbye to Berlin [book by Isherwood]
Isherwood, Christopher **I:** 462
Goode, W. Wilson [American political leader]
Philadelphia (Continued growth) **P:** 367
Goodell, David H. [American political leader]
New Hampshire (table) **N:** 223
Goodfellas [film]
Scorsese, Martin **S:** 210
Goodfellow, Robin
Puck **P:** 870
Goodhue, Grace Anna [wife of Calvin Coolidge]
See Coolidge, Grace Goodhue *in this index*
Goodhue, James Madison [American publisher]
Minnesota (Communication) **M:** 601
Gooding, Cuba, Jr. [American actor]
Motion picture (Best performance by an actor in a supporting role: 1996) **M:** 862b
Gooding, Frank R. [American political leader]
Idaho (table) **I:** 42
Goodland, Walter S. [American political leader]
Wisconsin (table) **W:** 365
Goodman, Benny [American clarinet player] **G:** 269
Jazz (The swing era) **J:** 71 *with picture*
Goodman Theatre
Theater *pictures on* **I:** 236T; 237, **T:** 239, **T:** 240, **T:** 241
Goodreau Doll [company]
Doll (The 2000's) **D:** 294
Goodrich, Benjamin Franklin [American businessman] **G:** 269
Goodrich, James P. [American political leader]

Indiana (table) I: 214
Goodrich Company, B. F.
Goodrich, Benjamin Franklin G: 269
Zipper Z: 596
Goods and services
Consumer Price Index Ci: 1017
Economics E: 58, *diagram on* E: 61
Gross domestic product G: 399
Income (Nominal and real income) I: 100
Trade T: 362
Goods and services tax [Canada]
Mulroney, Brian (Other economic developments)
M: 917-918
Goodwin, Archie [literary figure]
Stout, Rex So: 916
Goodwin, Ichabod [American political leader]
New Hampshire (table) N: 223
Goodwin, John N. [American political leader]
Arizona (Territorial days) A: 690
Goodwin, W. A. R. [American historian]
Williamsburg (Restoration) W: 313
Goodyear, Charles [American inventor] G: 269
Connecticut (The 1800's) Ci: 970
Invention (The inventive process) I: 355-357
Rubber (Discovery of vulcanization) R: 501
Goodyear, Miles [American frontiersman] G: 270
Goodyear Airdock [building]
Akron (The city) A: 254
Goodyear blimp
Advertising *picture on* A: 73
Airship *picture on* A: 250
Goofballs
Drug (Antianxiety and hypnotic drugs) D: 352
Google Inc. G: 270
Internet (The Web forms) I: 350g; (Ongoing
controversies) I: 350h
Search engine *picture on* S: 269
United States *picture on* U: 133
Goose G: 270 *with pictures*
Bird *picture on* B: 329, *picture on* B: 360; (As a
source of food and raw materials) B: 330; (Birds
of the Arctic) B: 343 *with picture*
Brant B: 564 *with picture*
Canada goose C: 154
Instinct (Imprinting) I: 305
Life *picture on* L: 275
Poultry P: 720
Goose, Elizabeth [American author]
Mother Goose (Who was Mother Goose?) M: 842
Goose barnacle [sea animal]
Barnacle B: 113 *with pictures*
Goose bumps
Hair (Glands and muscles) H: 10
Gooseberry [fruit] G: 271
"Goosebumps" novels [books by Stine]
Stine, R. L. So: 902
Goosefoot [plant]
Lamb's-quarters L: 51
Goosen, Retief [South African golfer]
Golf (U.S. Open) G: 265
G.O.P. [political party]
Republican Party R: 253
Gopher [animal] G: 271 *with picture*
Gopher State [nickname]
Minnesota M: 584
Gopher tortoise
Tortoise T: 344
Turtle *picture on* T: 523; (Tortoises) T: 524
Gorbachev, Mikhail Sergeyevich [Soviet political
leader] G: 272 *with portrait*
Armenia (Independence) A: 719
Bush, George Herbert Walker (U.S.-Soviet
relations) B: 721
Cold War (The Cold War after 1980) Ci: 770
Communism (The Soviet Union under
Gorbachev) Ci: 895
Estonia (History) E: 362-363
Europe (The collapse of Communism) E: 416
International relations (The Cold War ends) I: 346
Latvia (History) L: 119-120
Lithuania (History) L: 389-390
Moscow (Revolution and Soviet rule) M: 827
Politburo P: 627
Russia (The rise of Gorbachev) R: 554
Russian literature (Modern Soviet literature)
R: 564-565
Saint Petersburg [Russia] (History) S: 55
Shevardnadze, Eduard Amvrosiyevich S: 399
Union of Soviet Socialist Republics (History)
U: 35-40 *with picture*
United States, History of the (The end of the Cold
War) U: 196d
World, History of the (The end of the Cold War)
W: 448-448a
Yeltsin, Boris Nikolayevich Y: 560
Gordian I [Roman emperor]
Rome, Ancient (table) R: 447

Gordian II [Roman emperor]
Rome, Ancient (table) R: 447
Gordian III [Roman emperor]
Rome, Ancient (table) R: 447
Gordian knot [Greek mythology]
Alexander the Great (Invasion of Asia) A: 342-343
Gordillo, Francisco [Spanish explorer]
Ayllón, Lucas Vásquez de A: 995
South Carolina (Exploration and settlement)
So: 659
Gordimer, Nadine [South African author] G: 273
Gordium [ancient city, Asia Minor]
Alexander the Great (Invasion of Asia) A: 342-343
Gordon, Alexander [Scottish nobleman]
Gordon setter G: 273
Gordon, Charles George [British soldier]
Emin Pasha E: 260
Gordon, James W. [American political leader]
Michigan (table) M: 507
Gordon, Jeff [American race car driver] G: 273
Automobile racing (table: NASCAR Sprint Cup
champions) A: 981
Gordon, Joe [American baseball player/manager]
Baseball (table: Hall of Fame) B: 134a
Gordon, John Brown [Confederate general]
Georgia (table) G: 130
Gordon, John Campbell Hamilton- [British
statesman] *See* Aberdeen and Temair, Marquess
of *in this index*
Gordon, Ruth [American actress]
Motion picture (Best performance by an actress
in a supporting role: 1968) M: 862b
Gordon, Yehudah Leib [Hebrew poet]
Hebrew literature (Modern Hebrew literature)
H: 162
Gordon setter [dog] G: 273
Dog *picture on* D: 269
Setter S: 323
Gordy, Berry, Jr. [American businessman] G: 273
Gaye, Marvin G: 73
Rock music (Independent producers) R: 379
Gore, Al [American political leader] G: 273 *with
portrait*
Bush, George Walker B: 722b; (Election as
president) B: 722f
Bush v. Gore B: 724
Clinton, Bill (The Democratic nomination)
Ci: 682c-682d; (table) Ci: 682d *with picture*
Democratic Party (The early 2000's) D: 128 *with
picture*
Election of 2000 E: 161
Global warming (How scientists study global
warming) G: 232d
Lieberman, Joseph Isadore L: 271
Vice president of the United States (Growth of
the vice presidency) V: 353-354
Gore, Albert, Sr. [American political leader]
Gore, Al (Early life) G: 273
Gore, Albert Arnold, Jr. [American political leader]
See Gore, Al *in this index*
Gore, Charles [British religious leader]
Oxford Movement O: 888
Gore, Christopher [American political leader]
Massachusetts (table) M: 288
Gore, Howard M. [American government official]
Agriculture, Department of (table) A: 161
Coolidge, Calvin (table) Ci: 1032
West Virginia (table) W: 225
Gore, Mary Elizabeth Aitcheson "Tipper" [wife
of Al Gore]
Gore, Al (Early life) G: 274
Gorée [Senegal] G: 274
Gorgas, William Crawford [American doctor]
G: 274
Panama Canal (Victory over disease) P: 126
Yellow fever (History) Y: 556
Gorge [geology]
Canyon C: 185
Dalles D: 16
Gorgeana [former name, York]
Maine (Ownership disputes) M: 89
Gorges, Sir Ferdinando [English colonial official]
Maine (Exploration and settlements) M: 89
New Hampshire (Settlement) N: 224
Gorgias [book by Plato]
Plato (The dialogues) P: 567
Gorgias [Greek orator]
Oratory (Beginnings) O: 818
Sophists So: 595
Gorgonian [coral]
Coral (Other kinds of corals) Ci: 1048a
Gorgons [Greek mythology] G: 274
Medusa M: 383
Gorham, Nathaniel [American political leader]
G: 274
Gorilla G: 275 *with pictures and map*
Africa *picture on* A: 122

Animal *picture on* A: 481
Ape A: 563 *with picture*
Fossey, Dian F: 421
Human being (Prehuman ancestors) H: 414 *with
diagram*
Primate (Great apes) P: 778a
Skeleton *diagram on* S: 481
Zoo (Interesting facts about zoo animals) Z: 601
Gorillas in the Mist [book by Fossey]
Fossey, Dian F: 421
Göring, Hermann Wilhelm [Nazi general] G: 276
with portrait
Hitler, Adolf *picture on* H: 268
Luftwaffe L: 515
Nuremberg Trials (The trials) N: 613
World War II *picture on* W: 497
Gorkha [former kingdom]
Kathmandu K: 249
Gorkhas [Nepalese soldiers] *See* Gurkhas *in this
index*
Gorki [Russia] *See* Nizhniy Novgorod *in this index*
Gorki, Maxim [Russian author] G: 276
Russian literature (Late realism) R: 562-563
Gorki Park
Moscow (Entertainment and recreation) M: 825
with picture
Gorky, Arshile [American painter] G: 277 *with
picture*
Gorrie, John [American inventor]
Air conditioning (History) A: 180
Food preservation (Modern food preservation)
F: 344
Gorse [shrub]
Furze F: 588
Gorsky, Alexander [Russian choreographer]
Bolshoi Ballet B: 449
Gorton, John Grey [Australian political leader]
Australia (table) A: 923
Gorton, Samuel [American colonial leader]
Rhode Island (Settlement) R: 312
Goshawk [bird]
Hawk H: 111, *picture on* H: 112
Goshenite [mineral]
Gem *picture on* G: 78
Goshman, Albert [American magician]
Magician (Close-up magic) M: 51
Goslin, Goose [American baseball player]
Baseball (table: Hall of Fame) B: 134a
Gosling [bird]
Goose (The life of a wild goose) G: 271
Gosling Memorial Library [St. John's]
Newfoundland and Labrador (Libraries and
museums) N: 364
Gosnold, Bartholomew [English explorer]
Cape Cod C: 188
Martha's Vineyard M: 234
Massachusetts (Early exploration) M: 289
Gospel music G: 277
Jackson, Mahalia J: 15
Popular music (Soul music) P: 561
Gospel of ... *See under key word, as in* John, Gospel
of
Gospels [New Testament] G: 278
Bible (table) B: 281; (The Gospels) B: 283;
(Historical contexts) B: 287
Biography (Early biographies) B: 312-313
Jesus Christ (Sources of information about Jesus)
J: 104
New Testament (Contents) N: 287
Gossaert, Jan [Flemish painter]
Clothing *picture on* Ci: 701
Gossamer ring [astronomy]
Jupiter (Rings) J: 200a-200b *with picture*
Gosse, William [Australian explorer]
Uluru U: 17
Gossett, Charles C. [American political leader]
Idaho (table) I: 42
Gossett, Louis, Jr. [American actor]
Motion picture (Best performance by an actor in
a supporting role: 1982) M: 862b
Gossip column
Winchell, Walter W: 328
Gösta Berling's Saga [book by Lagerlöf]
Lagerlöf, Selma L: 30
Göta Canal [waterway, Sweden]
Sweden (Recreation) So: 1025
Götaland Plateau
Sweden (The South Swedish Highland) So: 1029
with map
Göteborg [Sweden] G: 278
Gotha [airplane]
Bomber (History) B: 453
Gothic architecture
Architecture (Gothic architecture) A: 618 *with
pictures*
Chartres Cathedral C: 386 *with picture*
Europe (Medieval art) E: 391-392 *with picture*

Gargoyle **G: 43** *with picture*
Gothic art **G: 278** *with picture*
Notre Dame, Cathedral of *picture on* **N: 551**
Reims **R: 208** *with picture*
Gothic armor
Armor (During the Middle Ages) **A: 719-720**
Gothic art G: 278 *with picture*
Furniture (The Middle Ages) **F: 571**; (Historical revivals) **F: 581**
Painting (Gothic painting) **P: 50** *with picture*
Tracery **T: 355**
Gothic lettering
Handwriting (Later writing styles) **H: 50**
Paleography **P: 103**
Gothic novel G: 279
American literature (The romance) **A: 418**
English literature (Romantic prose) **E: 320**
Novel (Gothic novels) **N: 572**
Romance **R: 415**
Romanticism (Romanticism in literature) **R: 427**
Gothic Quarter [Barcelona]
Barcelona **B: 108**
Gothic revival [architecture]
Architecture (The Gothic Revival) **A: 626** *with picture*
New York City (Architecture) **N: 336**; (Saint Patrick's Cathedral) **N: 339** *with picture*
Goths [ancient people] **G: 279**
Russia (Early days) **R: 547**
Gotland [island, Baltic Sea]
Lombards **L: 427**
Sweden (The land) **So: 1028** *with map*
Goto Optical Manufacturing Company
Planetarium (Modern planetariums) **P: 514b-514c**
Götterdämmerung, Die [opera by Wagner]
Opera: (Ring of the Nibelung, The) **O: 806-807**
Wagner, Richard (Later career) **W: 4**
Gottes Zeit [music by Bach]
Bach, Johann Sebastian (His works) **B: 16**
Gottfried von Strassburg [German poet]
German literature (The romance) **G: 138**
Gotthard tunnels [Switzerland] *See* Saint Gotthard tunnels *in this index*
Gottlieb, Adolph [American painter] **G: 280** *with picture*
Gottmann, Jean [French geographer]
Megalopolis **M: 384**
Gottorp Globe [device]
Planetarium *picture on* **P: 514b**; (Early planetariums) **P: 514a**
Gottschalk, Louis Moreau [American composer] **G: 280**
Gottsched, Johann [German dramatist]
Drama (Germany) **D: 336**
Gottwald, Klement [Czechoslovak political leader]
Czechoslovakia (Communist rule) **Ci: 1216**
Götz von Berlichingen [play by Goethe]
Goethe, Johann Wolfgang von (Early years) **G: 247**
Gou-Gu theorem
Mathematics (Chinese mathematics) **M: 306**
Gouache [art]
Painting (Water-color painting) **P: 39-40**
Gouda [Netherlands]
Netherlands *picture on* **N: 141**
Goudy, Frederic William [American printer]
Book (The 1800's) **B: 467-468**
Gouge [tool]
Woodcarving **W: 391** *with diagram*
Gouin, Lomer [Canadian political leader]
Quebec (table) **Q: 29**
Goujon, Jean [French sculptor]
Louvre **L: 507**
Goukouni Oueddei [Chadian political leader]
Chad (History) **C: 367-368**
Goulart, João [Brazilian political leader]
Brazil (Return to constitutional government) **B: 585-586**
Latin America (The rise of military regimes) **L: 110**
Goulash [food]
Hungary (Food and drink) **H: 441**
Gould, Sir Francis Carruthers [British artist]
John Bull **J: 133**
Gould, Glenn [Canadian pianist] **G: 280**
Gould, Gordon [American inventor]
Laser (History) **L: 86**
Gould, Jay [American businessman] **G: 280**
Black Friday **B: 387**
Fisk, James **F: 189**
Grant, Ulysses S. (Political corruption) **G: 315**
Labor movement (The first nationwide labor organizations) **L: 9-10**
Gould, Stephen Jay [American naturalist] **G: 281**
Essay (Formal essays) **E: 359**
Gouldian finch [bird]
Bird (Birds of Australia and New Zealand) **B: 346**

with picture
Gounod, Charles [French composer] **G: 281**
Opera: (Faust) **O: 804**
Gourd [botany] **G: 281** *with pictures*
Africa *picture on* **A: 116**
Gourmet restaurant
Restaurant (Kinds of restaurants) **R: 262**
Gout [disease] **G: 281**
Arthritis (Other forms of arthritis) **A: 752**
Gouty arthritis [disease]
Gout **G: 281**
Goux, Jules [American race driver]
Automobile racing (table: Indianapolis 500 winners) **A: 980**
Government G: 282 *with pictures*
See also Government regulation *in this index and the list of Related articles in the Government article*
Capitalism (Protecting the public interest) **C: 195**
Church and state **C: 542**
City (Government) **Ci: 590**; (Political culture) **Ci: 593**
Colonial life in America (Government and law enforcement) **Ci: 795**
Economics (Government intervention) **E: 59**
Flag *pictures on* **F: 211**; (Kinds of flags) **F: 195**
Freedom of the press **F: 507**
Gross domestic product (Measuring GDP) **G: 399**
Internet (The Internet and politics) **I: 350f** *with picture*; (Ongoing controversies) **I: 350h**
Journalism (Journalism in government-controlled societies) **J: 174**
Metropolitan area (Problems of metropolitan areas) **M: 442**
Nationalization **N: 63**
Pension **P: 272**
Political science **P: 638**
Privatization **P: 808b**
State government **So: 862** *with pictures*
Truck (Governmental uses) **T: 457**
Unemployment (Government and unemployment) **U: 22**
World (Forms of government) **W: 407**
Diplomacy and foreign relations
Diplomacy **D: 216**
Foreign policy **F: 386**
International relations **I: 343**
Forms of government
Absolutism **A: 17**
Aristocracy **A: 662**
Authoritarianism **A: 941**
Autocracy **A: 942**
Communism **Ci: 889**
Democracy **D: 120** *with picture*
Despotism **D: 161**
Fascism **F: 49**
Federalism **F: 66**
Monarchy **M: 700**
Nazism **N: 92**
Oligarchy **O: 742**
Police state **P: 626**
Provisional government **P: 840**
Republic **R: 253**
Theocracy **T: 251**
Totalitarianism **T: 346**
Organization
Citizenship **Ci: 568**
City planning **Ci: 598**
Country **Ci: 1097**
Government regulation **G: 293**
Law **L: 130**
Taxation **T: 52**
Voting **V: 449**
Theories and philosophies
Anarchism **A: 448**
Civil disobedience **Ci: 606**
Conservatism **Ci: 991**
Enlightenment (The orderliness of nature) **E: 326a-326b**
Europe (The role of government) **E: 390**
Liberalism **L: 228**
United States, History of the (Colonial government) **U: 158**; (Government and the people) **U: 185**
Government [parliament]
Parliament (How the House of Commons works) **P: 173**
Government, Commission of [1934]
Newfoundland and Labrador (Ruin and recovery) **N: 377**
Government Accountability Office [U.S.] **G: 292**
Budget (Preparation of the U.S. budget) **B: 671**
Government bond
Savings bond **S: 166**
Government Center
Boston (Downtown Boston) **B: 496**
Government corporation

United States, Government of the (Executive departments and agencies) **U: 140**
Government Employees, American Federation of *See* American Federation of Government Employees *in this index*
Government Employees, National Association of
Labor movement (table) **L: 8**
Government hospital
Hospital (Type of ownership) **H: 371**
Government House [Ottawa]
Ottawa (Rideau Hall) **O: 872**
Government in the Sunshine Act [1976]
Sunshine laws **So: 991**
Government library
Library (Government libraries) **L: 248** *with picture*
Government National Mortgage Association [U.S.] **G: 292**
Housing and Urban Development, Department of (Functions) **H: 393**
Mortgage **M: 821**
Government of India Act [1935]
India (New Constitution) **I: 132**
Government of Ireland Act [1920]
Ireland (The Irish Free State) **I: 427**
Irish Republican Army (Beginnings) **I: 433**
Northern Ireland (The division of Ireland) **N: 524**
Government ownership
See also Nationalization *in this index*
Communism **Ci: 889**
Corporation (Other corporations) **Ci: 1070**
Public utility **P: 865**
Socialism **So: 560**
Government Printing Office [U.S.] **G: 292**
Washington, D.C. *map on* **W: 76**
Government regulation G: 293
Agriculture (Government regulation) **A: 152**
Automobile (The growth of government regulation) **A: 971**
Business (Government regulation of business) **B: 727**
City (Solving city problems) **Ci: 592**
Environmental pollution (Government action) **E: 335**; (Weighing benefits and risks) **E: 339**
Industry (Government regulation) **I: 261**
Insurance (Government regulation) **I: 315**; (Greater regulation) **I: 316**
Nuclear energy (Government regulation) **N: 589**
President of the United States (The independent agencies) **P: 764**
Public utility (Government regulation) **P: 865**
Radio (Government regulation of radio) **R: 90**
Railroad (The role of the federal government) **R: 113**
Sales (Regulation of selling) **S: 64**
Television (Regulating U.S. television) **T: 115**
Transportation (Government and transportation) **T: 397**
Truck (Regulation of trucks) **T: 458**
United States (Economy) **U: 128**
Government securities
Federal Reserve System (Open market operations) **F: 65-66**
Investment (Indirect investments) **I: 367**
Government service *See* Civil service *in this index*
Government shutdown
National budget (Creating a budget) **N: 30**
Governments, Census of
Census (United States censuses) **C: 346-347**
Governor [machine] **G: 293** *with diagram*
Corliss, George Henry **Ci: 1055**
Governor [office] **G: 293**
See also the tables of governors in the state articles
Address, Forms of (Officials of the United States) **A: 53**
Lieutenant governor **L: 273**
State government (Executive branch) **So: 863**
Veto (Governors' veto power) **V: 346**
Governor [penology]
Prison (The prison staff) **P: 806**
Governor general [office] **G: 294**
Address, Forms of (Officials of the Commonwealth of Nations) **A: 53**
Australia (The federal government) **A: 895**
Canada, Government of **C: 128**; (The governor general) **C: 129**; (How a bill becomes law in Canada) **C: 132** *with diagram*; (The courts) **C: 136**
Flag *picture on* **F: 214**
Prime minister of Canada **P: 778c**
Supreme Court of Canada (Organization) **So: 996**
Governor General's Literary Awards G: 294
Governorate [political unit]
Egypt (Local government) **E: 121**
Governors, Palace of the [Santa Fe]
New Mexico (Interesting facts) **N: 257** *with picture*
Governors Island [New York]
New York City (Small islands) **N: 330**

Governors Island National Monument [New York]
  National Park System (table: National
  monuments) **N: 51**
Gowda, Kempe [Indian ruler]
  Bengaluru **B: 249**
Gower, John [English poet]
  English literature (The age of Chaucer) **E: 316**
Gown [clothing]
  Graduation **G: 297**
Gowon, Yakubu [Nigerian political leader]
  Nigeria (Civil war) **N: 418**
Goya, Francisco [Spanish painter] **G: 294** *with
  picture*
  Painting (Social expression) **P: 34**; (Romanticism)
  P: 68-69 *with picture*
  Realism (In painting) **R: 172**
Gozo [island, Mediterranean]
  Malta **M: 113** *with map*
Gozzi, Carlo [Italian dramatist]
  Drama (Italy) **D: 335**
Gozzoli, Benozzo [Italian painter]
  Italy *picture on* **I: 514**
  Roman Catholic Church *picture on* **R: 406**
GP [medicine] *See* General practitioner *in this index*
GP bomb *See* General-purpose bomb *in this index*
GPA [education]
  Grading **G: 296**
GPO [organization] *See* Government Printing Office
  in this index
GPS [navigation] *See* Global Positioning System *in
  this index*
Gracchi [ancient Rome]
  Gracchus family **G: 295**
Gracchus, Gaius Sempronius [Roman political
  leader]
  Gracchus family **G: 295**
  Rome, Ancient (The later years of the republic)
  R: 445
Gracchus, Tiberius Sempronius [Roman political
  leader]
  Gracchus family **G: 295**
  Rome, Ancient (The later years of the republic)
  R: 445
Gracchus family [Roman political leaders] **G: 295**
Grace [princess of Monaco] *See* Kelly, Grace *in this
  index*
Grace [religion] **G: 295**
  Augustine, Saint (His beliefs) **A: 888**
  Luther, Martin (Justification by faith) **L: 527-528**
  Protestantism (Faith and grace) **P: 834**
Graceland [estate, Memphis] **G: 296**
  Memphis (The city) **M: 394**
  Presley, Elvis **P: 772**
  Tennessee (Places to visit) **T: 144** *with picture*
Graces [Greek mythology] **G: 296** *with picture*
Gracile australopithecine [hominid]
  Australopithecus **A: 927**
  Prehistoric people (Types of australopithecines)
  P: 745
Gracioso [literature]
  Spanish literature (The 1600's) **So: 759**
Grackle [bird] **G: 296** *with picture*
Grade [agriculture]
  Agriculture (Grades and labels) **A: 152**
Grade [education]
  Grading **G: 296**
  Teaching (Checking student progress) **T: 67**
Grade [employment]
  Civil service (Federal civil service) **Ci: 612**
Grade [engineering]
  Railroad (The roadbed and route) **R: 109**
  Road (Grading) **R: 359**
Grade [horse]
  Horse (table: Horse terms) **H: 343**
Grade [rank]
  Rank, Military **R: 139**
Grade A
  Milk (At a dairy farm) **M: 546-547**
Grade cow
  Dairying (Dairy cattle) **D: 6**
Grade point average [education]
  Grading **G: 296**
Grade school *See* Elementary school *in this index*
Grade separation
  Road (Primary highways) **R: 358**
Grading [education] **G: 296**
Grading [engineering]
  Railroad (The roadbed and route) **R: 109**
  Road (Grading) **R: 359** *with picture*
Grading [industry]
  Beef (Grades of beef) **B: 209**
  Cotton (Classing) **Ci: 1091**
  Lumber (Grading lumber) **L: 519**
  Meat (How to select meat) **M: 347**
  Rice (Grading) **R: 326**
  Wool (Processing of wool) **W: 400**
Gradualism [biology]

Evolution (Main ideas of evolutionary theory)
  E: 426-427
Graduate [student]
  Universities and colleges (The student body)
  U: 208; (Graduate study) **U: 209**
Graduate, The [film]
  Nichols, Mike **N: 403**
Graduate school [education]
  Careers (Professional and graduate schools)
  C: 217
  Universities and colleges (Graduate study) **U: 209**
Graduated-payment mortgage [economics]
  Mortgage **M: 820**
Graduation [education] **G: 297**
  Rite of passage **R: 350**
Graduation Week [custom]
  United States Military Academy (The student
  body) **U: 202**
Gradus ad Parnassum [music by Clementi]
  Clementi, Muzio **Ci: 662a**
Grady, Henry Woodfin [American editor] **G: 297**
Graf, Steffi [German tennis player] **G: 297**
  Agassi, Andre **A: 139**
  Tennis (Tennis today) **T: 166d-166f** *with picture*
Graf Spee [ship] **G: 297**
Graf Zeppelin [airship]
  Airship (Between world wars) **A: 252**
  Ellsworth, Lincoln **E: 244**
Graffenried, Cristoph von [Swiss colonial leader]
  New Bern **N: 179**
Graffiti [markings] **G: 297** *with picture*
  Dubuffet, Jean **D: 372**
  Hip-hop **H: 238**
  Painting (Recent painting) **P: 87-88**
Graft [politics] **G: 298**
Graft-versus-host disease
  Bone marrow transplant **B: 457**
Grafting [horticulture] **G: 298** *with pictures*
  Forestry (Tree improvement) **F: 405**
  Fruit (Fruit production) **F: 546**
  Grape (Diseases and pests) **G: 320**
  Nursery **N: 614**
  Pear (Planting and care) **P: 215-216**
  Rose (Reproducing and growing roses) **R: 475**
Grafting [medicine]
  See also Skin grafting *in this index*
  Plastic surgery (Reconstructive plastic surgery)
  P: 553
  Transplant (Tissue transplants) **T: 379**
Grafton, Duke of [British statesman]
  United Kingdom (table: British prime ministers)
  U: 72
Grafton, Sue [American author] **G: 299** *with
  portrait*
Grafton Street [Dublin]
  Ireland *picture on* **I: 420**
Graham, A. B. [American educator]
  4-H (The first 4-H program) **F: 436**
Graham, Bill [Canadian political leader]
  Liberal Party of Canada **L: 227**
Graham, Billy [American religious leader] **G: 300**
  with portrait
  Revivalism **R: 269**
Graham, Bob [American political leader]
  Florida (table) **F: 260**
Graham, Donald E. [American publisher]
  Graham, Katharine **G: 300**
Graham, Evarts [American doctor]
  Surgery (History) **So: 1007**
Graham, Franklin [American Religious Leader]
  Graham, Billy **G: 300**
Graham, Horace F. [American political leader]
  Vermont (table) **V: 333**
Graham, Katharine [American businesswoman]
  G: 300 *with portrait*
Graham, Martha [American dancer] **G: 300** *with
  picture*
  Dance (Modern dance) **D: 30-31** *with picture*
  United States *picture on* **U: 119**
Graham, Shawn [Canadian political leader]
  New Brunswick (table) **N: 195**
Graham, Sylvester [American minister]
  Health food (History) **H: 129**
Graham, William A. [American political leader]
  Fillmore, Millard (table) **F: 102**
  North Carolina (table) **N: 490**
  Pierce, Franklin (Election of 1852) **P: 456**
Graham Bell Island
  Franz Josef Land **F: 494**
Graham Island
  Queen Charlotte Islands **Q: 39**
Graham Land [peninsula]
  Antarctica (Early exploration) **A: 536**
Graham plaid
  Tartan *picture on* **T: 47**
Grahame, Gloria [American actress]
  Motion picture (Best performance by an actress

in a supporting role: 1952) **M: 862b**
Grahame, Kenneth [British author] **G: 301**
GRAIL [satellites]
  Moon (Recent exploration) **M: 795**
Grail, Holy *See* Holy Grail *in this index*
Grain [book by Stead]
  Canadian literature (Literature between the
  world wars) **C: 158-159**
Grain [food] **G: 301**
  Agriculture (Cereal grains) **A: 147** *with picture*
  Demeter **D: 118**
  Farm and farming (Specialized crop farms) **F: 30**
  Food (Food from plants) **F: 329**
  Food supply (Cereal grains) **F: 347**; (Making
  farmland more productive) **F: 349-350**;
  (Reducing the demand for feed grain) **F: 350**
  Grass (Cereals) **G: 326**
  Livestock (Feed) **L: 397**
  Nutrition (Nutrition guidelines) **N: 626**
  Reaper **R: 173**
  Threshing machine **T: 270**
  Triticale **T: 448**
  Vegetarianism **V: 294**
Grain [fuel]
  Guided missile (The engine) **G: 424**
  Rocket (Solid-propellant rockets) **R: 387** *with
  diagram*
Grain [measurement]
  Apothecaries' weight **A: 567**
  Avoirdupois **A: 994**
Grain [metallurgy]
  Alloy (Characteristics of alloys) **A: 377**
Grain alcohol *See* Ethanol *in this index*
Grain Coast
  Liberia (History) **L: 231**
Grain drill [machine]
  Oats (Growing oats) **O: 640-640a**
Grain elevator [building] **G: 301**
  Buffalo (Economy) **B: 677**
  Wheat *picture on* **W: 275**; (Transporting and
  storing wheat) **W: 273**
Grain exchange [economics]
  Wheat (Buying and selling wheat) **W: 274** *with
  picture*
Grain sorghum [plant] **G: 302**
  Sorghum (Grain sorghums) **So: 596** *with picture*
  Sudan grass **So: 956**
Grain weevil [insect] **G: 302** *with picture*
Grainger, Percy [Australian-American composer]
  G: 302
Graininess [photography]
  Photography (Graininess) **P: 417**
Grainne [legendary figure]
  Mythology (The Fionn cycle) **M: 985**
Gram [measurement] **G: 302**
  Metric system (Mechanics) **M: 437**; (The metric
  system at a glance) **M: 438-439** *with picture*;
  (Creation of the metric system) **M: 441**
Gram, Hans C. J. [Danish bacteriologist]
  Antibiotic (Antibacterial antibiotics) **A: 550**
Gram-negative bacteria
  Antibiotic (Antibacterial antibiotics) **A: 550**
Gram-positive bacteria
  Antibiotic (Antibacterial antibiotics) **A: 550**
Grama grass [plant]
  Grass *picture on* **G: 325**
Grambling State University [Louisiana]
  Robinson, Eddie **R: 368**
Grameen Bank
  Nobel Prizes (Peace: 2006) **N: 449**
Gramm, Phil [American political leader] **G: 302**
  with portrait
Gramm-Rudman-Hollings Act [1985]
  Gramm, Phil **G: 303**
Grammar [language] **G: 303**
  See also specific language articles, such as French
  language, *and the lists of Related articles in the*
  Grammar *and* English language *articles*
  English language (Grammar) **E: 312**
  Language (Grammar) **L: 63**
  Latin language (Grammar) **L: 114**
  Liberal arts **L: 226**
  Linguistics (Constructing a grammar) **L: 335**
  Parts of speech **P: 189**
Grammar of Assent, The [book by Newman]
  Newman, John Henry **N: 379**
Grammar of Science [book by Pearson]
  Pearson, Karl **P: 219**
Grammar school [education]
  See also Elementary school *in this index*
  Education (The Renaissance) **E: 100**
  England (Education) **E: 297**
  United Kingdom (Education) **U: 56**
Grammatical transformation
  Linguistics (The generative theory of language)
  L: 337
Grammaticus [teacher]

Education (Ancient Roman education) E: 98
Gramme, Zénobe Théophile [Belgian engineer]
Electric motor (History) E: 181
Grammy Awards [music]
Recording industry (Recording industry awards)
R: 182
Gramophone [machine]
Phonograph P: 400; (History) P: 401
Grampian Mountains [Scotland]
Scotland (Land regions) S: 217 *with map*
Gran Chaco [region, South America] G: 304
Argentina (Northern Argentina) A: 652 *with map*
Bolivia (Territorial losses) B: 447
Paraguay (The land and climate) P: 148; (The land and
climate) P: 147 *with map*
South America *picture on* So: 626; (The Central
Plains) So: 628
Gran Colombia [Latin American history]
Bolívar, Simón (His victories) B: 441
Colombia (Independence) Ci: 783
Ecuador (Spanish rule) E: 73
Venezuela (The struggle for independence)
V: 304
Gran Paradiso National Park [Italy]
National park (table) N: 42f
Gran Sabana, La [region, Venezuela]
Angel Falls A: 460
Gran Sasso Tunnel [Italy]
Tunnel (table) T: 491
Gran Vía [street]
Madrid (The city) M: 38 *with picture*
Granada [city, Nicaragua] G: 304
Granada [city, Spain] G: 304 *with picture and map*
Alhambra A: 366
Granada [Spanish history] G: 304 *with map*
Isabella I I: 461
Granada, Luis de [Spanish author]
Spanish literature (The 1500's) So: 758-759
Granadilla [plant] *See* Passion-flower *in this index*
Granary of the Confederacy
Virginia (The Civil War and Reconstruction) V: 421
Granary weevil [insect]
Weevil W: 180
Grand [airplane]
Airplane *picture on* A: 232; (Other pioneer planes
and fliers) A: 233-234
Grand Alliance [European history] G: 305
Succession wars (The War of the Spanish
Succession) So: 950
Grand American Road Racing Association
Automobile racing (Racing organizations) A: 976
Grand Army [French history]
Napoleonic Wars (Renewed hostilities) N: 18
Grand Army of the Republic [organization] G: 305
with picture
Memorial Day (History) M: 392
Veterans' organizations (In the United States)
V: 344
Woman's Relief Corps, National W: 382
Grand Atlas Mountains [Africa]
Atlas Mountains A: 869
Grand Bahama Island
Bahamas B: 28 *with map*
Grand Banks [Newfoundland and Labrador] G: 305
with map
Newfoundland and Labrador (Plant and animal
life) N: 372
Grand Canal [waterway, China]
Canal *picture on* C: 162; (table) C: 164; (Major
canals in other countries) C: 164; (History)
C: 164-165
China (Transportation) C: 497-498
Sui dynasty So: 964
Grand Canal [waterway, Venice]
Venice (The city) V: 306 *with map*
Grand Canyon [Arizona] G: 306 *with picture and
map*
See also Grand Canyon National Park *in this index*
Arizona (Visitor's guide) A: 678; (Places to visit)
A: 678 *with picture*
Colorado River Ci: 848 *with map*
Fossil (Tracing the development of life) F: 423
Grand Canyon National Park G: 307 *with map*
Seven natural wonders of the world (The Grand
Canyon) S: 324 *with picture*
Grand Canyon National Park [Arizona] G: 307
with map
National park (Changes in the environment)
N: 42h
National Park System (table: National parks) N: 48
Grand Canyon of the Yellowstone [region,
Wyoming]
Yellowstone National Park (The Lower Loop)
Y: 558-559 *with map*
Grand Canyon State [name for]
Arizona A: 670
Grand Canyon Suite, The [music by Grofé]

Grofé, Ferde G: 397
Grand Cayman Island [Caribbean]
Cayman Islands C: 323
Grand Central Station
New York City (Transportation) N: 334-335
Grand Concourse [street]
New York City (The Bronx) N: 328-329
Grand Coulee Dam [Columbia River, Washington]
G: 308
Columbia River (Hydroelectric power and
irrigation) Ci: 853 *with map*
Irrigation (Surface water) I: 456
Washington (Places to visit) W: 56; (Electric
power and utilities) W: 64 *with picture*
Grand crossfire [debating]
Debate (A public forum debate) D: 65
Grand Design [European history]
Peace (From the 1400's to the 1700's) P: 206
Grand dictionaire historique, Le [book]
Encyclopedia (From the 1200's to the 1600's)
E: 268a
Grand Dictionnaire Universel du XIXᵉ siècle, Le
[book by Larousse]
Encyclopedia (Encyclopedias of the 1800's and
1900's) E: 268a
Grand Dixence Dam [Dixence River, Switzerland]
Dam (table) D: 18
Grand Falls [former name, Churchill Falls]
Churchill River C: 550
Grand Falls [waterfall, New Brunswick]
New Brunswick (Rivers and lakes) N: 192
Grand fir [tree]
Fir F: 120
Grand Forks [North Dakota]
North Dakota (Late 1900's) N: 516
Grand Gallery
Pyramids (The pyramids of Giza) P: 917
Grand Hotel [film]
Motion picture (Best picture: 1931-32) M: 861
Grand Illusion [film]
Motion picture (Movies in the 1930's) M: 867-868
with picture
Renoir, Jean R: 240
Grand Island [island, New York]
Niagara River (Description) N: 394
Grand Isle
Louisiana (Places to visit) L: 488
Grand jeté [movement]
Ballet (table) B: 45 *with picture*
Grand Junction [Colorado]
Colorado (table: Average monthly weather)
Ci: 840
Grand jury G: 308
Court (How courts work) Ci: 1101
Criminal justice system (Pretrial procedures)
Ci: 1143
Indictment I: 223
Jury (Grand juries) J: 202
Law enforcement (Trial) L: 141
Grand Kremlin Palace
Moscow (Famous landmarks) M: 823-824 *with
map*
Grand Lake [Colorado]
Colorado (Rivers and lakes) Ci: 840
Grand Lake [New Brunswick]
New Brunswick (Rivers and lakes) N: 192
Grand Lake [Newfoundland and Labrador]
Newfoundland and Labrador (Rivers and lakes)
N: 370-372 *with map*
Grand Lake [Nova Scotia]
Nova Scotia (Rivers and lakes) N: 562-564
Grand Lake O' The Cherokees [Oklahoma]
Oklahoma (Land regions) O: 724-727 *with map*
Grand larceny [crime]
Larceny L: 75
Grand Lodge
Masonry (Organization) M: 267
Grand Lodge of England
Masonry (History) M: 267
Grand Loop [road]
Yellowstone National Park (Touring Yellowstone)
Y: 558
Grand mal seizure [disease]
Epilepsy E: 343
Grand Master
Masonry (Organization) M: 267
Grand Monarch [name for]
Louis XIV L: 474
Grand Mosque [Khartoom]
Sudan *picture on* So: 954
Grand Nain
Banana B: 72
Grand National [race] G: 308
Steeplechasing So: 883
Grand National Champion
Motorcycle (Motorcycling as a sport) M: 879
Grand National Consolidated Trades Union

[labor history]
Owen, Robert (Cooperatives) O: 882-883
"Grand Ole Opry" [radio program] O: 308
Country music (History) Ci: 1098a-1098b
Nashville (Cultural life and recreation) N: 23
Tennessee (Places to visit) T: 144 *with picture*
Grand opera [music]
Opera (table) O: 791; (Grand opera) O: 798
Grand Palace [Bangkok]
Bangkok (The city) B: 77
Thailand *picture on* T: 221
Grand piano
Piano (Grand pianos) P: 447 *with picture*
Grand' Place
Belgium *picture on* B: 229
Grand Portage National Monument [Minnesota]
G: 309
Minnesota (Places to visit) M: 594
National Park System (table: National
monuments) N: 51
Grand Pré [Nova Scotia] G: 309
Canada (table: National historic sites) C: 114
Grand Prismatic Spring
Yellowstone National Park (The Lower Loop)
Y: 558
Grand Prix [horse show]
Horse (Jumping) H: 357
Grand Prix [race]
Automobile racing (Formula One racing) A: 976-
977; (Growth of organized automobile racing)
A: 979; (Grand Prix world champions) A: 980
Grand Rapids [Michigan] G: 309
Furniture (The furniture industry) F: 586
Grand River
Michigan (Rivers, waterfalls, and lakes) M: 500
with map
South Dakota (Rivers and lakes) So: 676 *with map*
Grand slam [bowling]
Carter, Don C: 251
Grand slam [cards]
Bridge (Bidding) B: 604
Grand slam [golf]
Golf (Tournaments) G: 264
Grand slam [tennis]
Laver, Rod L: 129
Tennis (Tennis tournaments) T: 165
Williams, Serena W: 311
Grand Slam [warfare]
Bomb (History) B: 452
Grand Strand [northern coastline]
South Carolina (Coastline) So: 652
Grand Terre [island, Pacific]
New Caledonia N: 200
Grand Testament [poem by Villon]
French literature (Lyric poetry) F: 518
Grand Teton [mountain, Wyoming]
Grand Teton National Park G: 309
Grand Teton National Park [Wyoming] G: 309
with picture
National Park System (table: National parks) N: 48
Teton Range T: 182b
Wyoming W: 516; (Places to visit) W: 524
Grand Theatre [Quebec]
Quebec (The arts) Q: 36
Grand Traverse Bay
Lake Michigan (Surface features) L: 41
Grand Trianon [palace, Versailles]
Trianon, Treaty of T: 439
Versailles, Palace of V: 339
Grand Trunk Canal [England]
Industrial Revolution (Waterways) I: 250
Grand Turk [island, Caribbean Sea]
Turks and Caicos Islands T: 514b
Grand unified theories [physics]
Physics (Physics today) P: 443
Subatomic particle (Theoretical research) So: 938
Grand Union Flag
Flag (First United States flags) F: 208-210 *with
picture*
Grand Vizier [title]
Vizier V: 433
Grand Wizard [office]
Ku Klux Klan (Birth of the Klan) K: 390
Grande batterie [army unit]
Army (The rise of modern armies) A: 727-728
Grande Chartreuse, La [monastery, France]
Carthusians C: 261
Grande Comore [island, Comoros]
Comoros Ci: 899
Grande Jatte, La [painting by Seurat] *See* Sunday
Afternoon on the Island of La Grande Jatte *in
this index*
Grande-Terre Island [Caribbean Sea]
Guadeloupe G: 408
Grandes écoles [education]
France (Education) F: 460-461
Grandfather clause [U.S. history] G: 310

Fifteenth Amendment **F:** 95
Grandfather clock
 Colonial life in America (Furnishings) **Ci:** 797-798
Grandfather Mountain
 North Carolina (Places to visit) **N:** 482 *with picture*
Grandfather paradox [physics]
 Time (Time travel) **T:** 292b
Grandiflora [plant]
 Rose (Types of roses) **R:** 474; (table) **R:** 474
Grandissimes, The [book by Cable]
 Cable, George Washington **C:** 7
Grandma Moses [American artist] *See* Moses,
 Grandma *in this index*
Grandparent
 Family (Family relationships) **F:** 21
GrandPre, Mary [American artist]
 Literature for children *picture on* **L:** 377
Grands Ballets Canadiens, Les
 Ballet (Ballet in Canada) **B:** 54
 Canada (Ballet and opera) **C:** 111
Grange, Harold Edward [real name of]
 Grange, Red **G:** 311
Grange, National [organization] **G:** 310
 Cooperative (History) **Ci:** 1036
 Rural delivery **R:** 521
 United States, History of the (Early reform efforts)
 U: 185
Grange, Red [American football player] **G:** 310
 Football (The rise of professional football) **F:** 367
 with picture
Granger, Clive W. J. [British economist]
 Nobel Prizes (Economics: 2003) **N:** 449
Granger, Francis [American government official]
 Harrison, William Henry (table) **H:** 76
 Tyler, John (table) **T:** 534
Granger cases [U.S.] **G:** 311
 Waite, Morrison Remick **W:** 5
Granholm, Jennifer [American political leader]
 Michigan (table) **M:** 507; (The early 2000's)
 M: 512
Granit, Ragnar Arthur [Swedish physiologist]
 Nobel Prizes (Physiology or medicine: 1967)
 N: 446
Granite [rock] **G:** 311
 Building stone **B:** 685
 Earth *picture on* **E:** 21
 Igneous rock **I:** 49
 Mineral *picture on* **M:** 566
 Ocean (How the sea floor was formed) **O:** 662
 Rhode Island (Minerals) **R:** 310
 Rock (table) **R:** 373 *with picture*; (Metamorphic
 rock) **R:** 373
 Vermont (Places to visit) **V:** 326; (Mining) **V:** 332
 with picture
Granite moss
 Moss **M:** 834 *with picture*
Granite Mountains
 Wyoming (Land regions) **W:** 526
Granite Peak [mountain]
 Montana (Land regions) **M:** 752
 Rocky Mountains (Chief ranges of the Rockies)
 R: 394-395 *with map*
Granite Plateau [region, Austria]
 Austria (Land regions) **A:** 933 *with map*
Granite State [nickname]
 New Hampshire **N:** 208
Granma [newspaper]
 Cuba (Transportation and communication)
 Ci: 1175
Granny knot
 Knots, hitches, and splices (Useful knots) **K:** 356
 with diagram
Granny Smith
 Apple (Varieties of apples) **A:** 571 *with picture*
Grant
 Fellowship **F:** 69
 Ford Foundation **F:** 382
 Foundation (Arts and humanities) **F:** 431
 Scholarship **S:** 178
Grant, Cary [American actor] **G:** 311 *with portrait*
 Motion picture (Movies in the 1930's) **M:** 867-868
 with picture
Grant, Ellen Wrenshall [daughter of]
 Grant, Ulysses S. *picture on* **G:** 316; (Grant's family)
 G: 313-314
Grant, Frank [American baseball player]
 Baseball (Hall of Fame) **B:** 134a
Grant, Frederick Dent [son of]
 Grant, Ulysses S. *picture on* **G:** 316; (Grant's family)
 G: 313-314
Grant, George Monro [Canadian educator] **G:** 311
Grant, Hiram Ulysses [birth name]
 Grant, Ulysses S. (Boyhood) **G:** 312
Grant, James B. [American political leader]
 Colorado (table) **C:** 844
Grant, Jesse Root, Jr. [son of]
 Grant, Ulysses S. *picture on* **G:** 316; (Grant's family)

 G: 313-314
Grant, Julia Dent [wife of Ulysses S. Grant]
 First ladies of the United States (table) **F:** 142
 Grant, Ulysses S. (Early Army career) **G:** 313,
 picture on **G:** 314
Grant, Kathryn [American actress]
 Crosby, Bing **Ci:** 1154
Grant, Lee [American actress]
 Motion picture (Best performance by an actress
 in a supporting role: 1975) **M:** 862b
Grant, Richard [American settler]
 Montana (The cattle industry) **M:** 758
Grant, Ulysses S. [U.S. president] **G:** 312 *with*
 pictures
 Army, United States (The Civil War [1861-1865])
 A: 738
 Black Friday **B:** 387
 Civil War, American (Battles of Fort Henry and
 Fort Donelson) **Ci:** 628-629; (The Vicksburg
 campaign) **Ci:** 629; (The final year–1864-1865)
 Ci: 631
 Hayes, Rutherford Birchard **H:** 118
 Illinois (Places to visit) **I:** 62
 Kentucky (The Civil War) **K:** 293
 Lee, Robert E. (Final engagements) **L:** 179
 Liberal Republican Party **L:** 227
 Lincoln, Abraham (Building the army) **L:** 321-322
 Republican Party (The Radical Republicans and
 Reconstruction) **R:** 254
 Saint Louis (Places to visit) **S:** 49
 Sheridan, Philip Henry **S:** 396
 United States, History of the (Government and
 the people) **U:** 185
 Whiskey Ring **W:** 282
Grant, Ulysses S., Jr. [son of]
 Grant, Ulysses S. (Grant's family) **G:** 313-314;
 (Later years) **G:** 317 *with picture*
Grant & Ward [bank]
 Grant, Ulysses S. (Later years) **G:** 317
Grant Grove
 Kings Canyon National Park **K:** 330
Grant-in-aid
 City government (City finances) **Ci:** 597
 Local government (Relations with higher levels of
 government) **L:** 407
 State government (State finances) **So:** 865
Grant-Kohrs Ranch National Historic Site
 [Montana]
 National Park System (table: National historic
 sites) **N:** 52-53
Grant-maintained school
 Charter school **C:** 386
Grant Park
 Chicago (Downtown Chicago) **C:** 420-421;
 (Cultural life and places to visit) **C:** 428
Grant's gazelle
 Gazelle **G:** 74
Grant's tomb *See* General Grant National Memorial
 in this index
Granulation [chemistry]
 Honey (Kinds of honey) **H:** 314
Granule [sun]
 Sun (Zones of the sun) **So:** 979-980
Granulomatous colitis *See* Crohn's disease *in this*
 index
Granville-Barker, Harley [British author] **G:** 318
Granville Island [Vancouver]
 British Columbia (Places to visit) **B:** 620
Grape [fruit] **G:** 318 *with pictures*
 Europe *picture on* **E:** 403
 France (Agriculture) **F:** 469
 Fruit (Simple fruits) **F:** 544 *with picture*
 Italy (Agriculture) **I:** 511 *with picture*
 Phylloxera **P:** 431 *with picture*
 Portugal *picture on* **P:** 692
 Raisin **R:** 129
 Wine **W:** 336 *with picture*
Grape phylloxera [insect]
 Grape (Diseases and pests) **G:** 320
Grape sugar
 Glucose **G:** 236
Grapefruit [plant] **G:** 320 *with picture*
 Fruit (Subtropical fruits) **F:** 546 *with picture*
 Tangelo **T:** 26
Grapes of Wrath, The [book by Steinbeck] **G:** 321
 American literature *picture on* **A:** 416; (Realist
 fiction) **A:** 422
 Dust Bowl **D:** 391
 Steinbeck, John **So:** 885
Grapes of Wrath, The [film]
 Ford, John **F:** 381
Grapevine
 Grape (Growing grapes) **G:** 319
 Raisin (Growing grapes) **R:** 129
Graph [mathematics] **G:** 321 *with pictures*
 Computer graphics (In science) **Ci:** 924f-924g
 Geometry (Analytic geometry) **G:** 105 *with*

 diagram
Grapheme [linguistics]
 Reading (Phonics instruction) **R:** 159
Graphene [mineral]
 Carbon (Graphite) **C:** 205
Graphic arts G: 322
 See also the list of Related articles in the Graphic
 arts *article*
 Industrial arts (Industrial arts courses) **I:** 242-243
Graphic Communications Council of the
 International Brotherhood of Teamsters
 Labor movement (table) **L:** 8
Graphic design
 Careers *picture on* **C:** 220
 Desktop publishing **D:** 158 *with picture*
 Map (Planning and graphic design) **M:** 181 *with*
 picture
 Publishing (Graphic designers) **P:** 867
Graphic novel [literature] **G:** 322 *with picture*
 American literature (Popular genres) **A:** 425
 Literature for children (The early 2000's) **L:** 366
Graphical user interface [computing]
 Apple Inc. **A:** 573
 Computer (Input devices) **Ci:** 912
 Microsoft Corporation **M:** 520
 World Wide Web **W:** 500
Graphics, Computer *See* Computer graphics *in*
 this index
Graphics co-processor [electronics]
 Computer (Personal computers) **Ci:** 909
Graphics file [computing]
 Computer (Storage devices) **Ci:** 915
 Computer file **Ci:** 924g
 Newspaper (Making up the pages) **N:** 383
Graphing calculator
 Calculator **C:** 22
Graphite [mineral] **G:** 323
 Carbon (Forms of carbon) **C:** 204 *with diagram*
 Cast iron **C:** 279
 Charcoal **C:** 317
 Interstellar medium **I:** 352
 Mineral *picture on* **M:** 568
 Pencil **P:** 236
 Powder metallurgy **P:** 725
Graphology [writing] **G:** 323
Grapnel
 Anchor **A:** 449 *with picture*
Grappling [sports]
 Mixed martial arts **M:** 680
Grason, William [American political leader]
 Maryland (table) **M:** 255
Grass [drug] *See* Marijuana *in this index*
Grass [plant] **G:** 324 *with pictures*
 See also the list of Related articles in the Grass
 article
 Artificial turf **A:** 761
 Bluegrass **B:** 424
 Dog (Why dogs do the things they do) **D:** 263
 with picture
 Lawn **L:** 142 *with pictures*
 Plant *pictures on* **P:** 521, **P:** 530; (Grasslands)
 P: 527 *with picture*; (Roots) **P:** 528 *with picture*
Grass, Günter [German author] **G:** 326
 German literature (Postwar German literature
 [1945-1990]) **G:** 142
 Novel (The novel today) **N:** 575
Grass carp [fish]
 Carp **C:** 245 *with picture*
Grass frog
 Frog *picture on* **F:** 537
Grass Is Blue, The [recording]
 Parton, Dolly **P:** 188
Grass Is Singing, The [book by Lessing]
 Lessing, Doris **L:** 208
Grass Lake
 Illinois (Rivers and lakes) **I:** 64-66
Grass line
 Baseball (The outfield) **B:** 126
Grass pickerel [fish]
 Fish *picture on* **F:** 159
 Pickerel **P:** 450
 Pike **P:** 461
Grass skirt
 Hawaii (Growth of constitutional government)
 H: 106-108
Grass tree [plant]
 Australia *picture on* **A:** 915
Grasse, Comte de [French admiral] *See* De Grasse,
 François Joseph Paul *in this index*
Grasshopper [insect] **G:** 327 *with pictures*
 Insect *pictures on* **I:** 280, **I:** 286; (Muscular system)
 I: 289 *with diagram*; (Hearing) **I:** 290-291
 Katydid **K:** 249
 Plant (Pests) **P:** 540 *with picture*
Grasshopper Glacier [Montana]
 Montana (Interesting facts) **M:** 743
Grasshopper mouse

Mouse (Grasshopper mice) M: 902
Grassland [geography] G: 329 *with picture*
Africa (Deserts, grasslands, and forests) A: 117
Animal (Animals of the grasslands) A: 476 *with pictures and map*
Biome B: 324; (table) B: 323 *with map*
Colorado *picture on* Ci: 841
Forestry (Rangeland) F: 407
Pampas P: 113
Plant *map on* P: 523; (Grasslands) P: 527 *with picture*
Prairie P: 730 *with picture and map*
Savanna S: 164 *with picture*
Steppe So: 891
Grasslands National Park [Saskatchewan]
Canada (table: National parks and national park reserves) C: 113
Grasso, Ella Tambussi [American political leader] G: 329 *with portrait*
Connecticut (table) Ci: 967
Grassy buttercup [plant]
Buttercup B: 731
Grateau, Marcel [French hairdresser]
Hairdressing (The 1800's) H: 12
Grateful Dead [musical group] G: 329
Rock music (Psychedelic rock) R: 380a
Gratian [Roman emperor]
Rome, Ancient (table) R: 447
Theodosius I T: 252
Graticule [map]
Map (Geographic grids) M: 179 *with diagram*
Grating [optics]
Diffraction (Uses of diffraction) D: 201
Spectrometer So: 772
Grating cheese
Cheese (Kinds of cheese) C: 392 *with pictures*
Grattan, Henry [Irish political leader] G: 329
Ireland (Union with Britain) I: 426
Grattan fight [U.S. history]
Wyoming (Indian and settler conflicts) W: 534
Grau San Martín, Ramón [Cuban government official]
Cuba (History) Ci: 1175-1177
Graupel [weather]
Rain (The ice-crystal process) R: 124
Snow (How snow forms) S: 539
Grave goods
Funeral customs (The funeral) F: 557
Indian, American (Indians of the Southeast) I: 157-158
Sculpture (Later Indian sculpture) S: 243
Tomb T: 326
Gravel [rock] G: 329
Gravenhage, 's [Netherlands] *See* Hague, The *in this index*
Graves, Abner [friend of Doubleday]
Baseball (The Abner Doubleday Theory) B: 132-133
Graves, Bibb [American political leader]
Alabama (table) A: 274
Graves, Bill [American political leader]
Kansas (table) K: 234
Graves, Michael [American architect] G: 330 *with picture*
Architecture *picture on* A: 633
Graves, Morris [American painter] G: 330 *with picture*
Graves, Richard [American colonial businessman]
Pewter (History) P: 352-353
Graves, Robert [British author] G: 330
Mythology (Literary approaches) M: 990-991
Graves' disease [disease]
Immune system (Organ-specific autoimmune diseases) I: 88c
Thyroid gland (Overactive thyroid) T: 275
Gravestone [sculpture by Collins]
Sculpture (American sculpture) S: 255 *with picture*
Graveyard of the Atlantic
Cape Hatteras C: 188
North Carolina N: 472
Nova Scotia N: 554
Sable Island S: 3
Gravimeter [instrument]
Petroleum (Geophysical studies) P: 336
Prospecting P: 829
Graving dock [shipping]
Dry dock D: 369
Gravitation [physics] G: 331
See also the list of Related articles in the Gravitation *article*
Airplane (Gravity and lift) A: 220 *with diagram*
Antigravity A: 555
Black hole B: 388
Boson B: 494
Dark matter D: 37
Ear (The response to gravity) E: 11

Earth (Earth's size and shape) E: 18
Falling bodies, Law of F: 17 *with diagrams*
Force (Kinds of force) F: 370
G G: 2
Gravitational wave G: 333
Gravity, Center of G: 333
Hawking, Stephen William H: 113
Local Group L: 409
Mars (Gravitational force) M: 225
Mass (Mass and weight) M: 268
Moon M: 762
Newton, Sir Isaac (The theories of motion and gravitation) N: 388
Petroleum (Geophysical studies) P: 336
Physics (Newton) P: 439; (Einstein and relativity) P: 441-442
Relativity (General relativity) R: 211
Satellite (Formation) S: 150
Satellite, Artificial (Satellite orbits) S: 150d
Space exploration (Getting into space and back) So: 698; (Microgravity) So: 701
Star (Fusion in stars) So: 846
String theory So: 929
Subatomic particle (Fundamental forces) So: 936; (Theories of forces) So: 937-938
Tidal forces T: 280
Tide T: 280 *with diagrams*
Time (Time travel) T: 292b
Weight W: 180
Gravitational constant [physics]
Force (Gravitation) F: 370
G G: 2
Gravitational force [physics]
Quantum field theory Q: 6
Gravitational lensing [physics]
Astronomy *diagram on* A: 841; (Radio and microwave astronomy) A: 843-844
Dark matter *picture on* D: 37
Gravitational mass [physics]
Relativity (General relativity) R: 211-212
Gravitational observatory
Observatory (Gravitational observatories) O: 645
Gravitational wave [physics] G: 333
Astronomy (Gravitational-wave astronomy) A: 846
Gravitation (Gravitational waves) G: 332
Observatory (Gravitational observatories) O: 645
Physics (Einstein and relativity) P: 441-442
Relativity (Gravitational waves) R: 212
Gravitational-wave astronomy
Astronomy (Gravitational-wave astronomy) A: 846
Gravitometer [instrument]
Pipeline (How pipelines work) P: 491
Graviton [physics]
Boson B: 494
Gravitropism [botany] *See* Geotropism *in this index*
Gravity *See* Gravitation *in this index*
Gravity, Center of [physics] G: 333 *with diagram*
Archimedes (His discoveries) A: 605
Automobile (Safety problems) A: 961-962
Gravity, Specific [physics]
Density D: 143
Galileo (Early scientific interests) G: 11
Gem (Specific gravity) G: 77
Mineral (Specific gravity) M: 567
Water (The properties of water) W: 129-130
Gravity bomb
Bomb (Kinds of bombs) B: 450
Gravity dam
Dam (Masonry dams) D: 17
Gravity meter *See* Gravimeter *in this index*
Gravity Probe B [spacecraft]
Gravitation (Bending of light rays) G: 332
Relativity (Distortions in space-time) R: 212
Gravity's Rainbow [book by Pynchon]
American literature (Experimental styles) A: 425
Pynchon, Thomas P: 915
Gravure [printing]
Magazine (Editing and assembling an issue) M: 43-44
Printing (Recess printing) P: 800 *with diagram*
Gravure cylinder [printing]
Printing (Recess printing) P: 800 *with diagram*
Gravure screen
Printing (Gravure cylinders) P: 800
Gray [color]
Color *diagram on* Ci: 822
Gray [horse]
Horse (Light harness horses) H: 345
Gray [unit of measurement]
Radiation (Dose) R: 79
Gray, Asa [American botanist] G: 334
Gray, Elisha [American inventor] G: 334
Telephone (The Bell System) T: 100
Gray, Elizabeth Janet [American author]
Newbery Medal (table) N: 359

Gray, Horace [American jurist]
Supreme Court of the United States (table) So: 1000
Gray, Isaac P. [American political leader]
Indiana (table) I: 214
Gray, John Hamilton [1812-1887, Canadian political leader]
Confederation of Canada (Fathers of Confederation) Ci: 935 *with picture*
Gray, John Hamilton [1814-1889, Canadian political leader]
Confederation of Canada (Fathers of Confederation) Ci: 935 *with picture*
Gray, Louis H. [British biologist]
Radiation (Dose) R: 79
Gray, Robert [American explorer] G: 334
Oregon *picture on* O: 847
Washington (Discovery and exploration) W: 66
Gray, Simon [British dramatist] G: 334
Gray, Thomas [British poet] G: 334
Gray, William H. [American religious leader]
Whitman, Marcus W: 293
Gray birch [tree]
Birch (Gray birch) B: 327
Gray catbird [bird]
Bird B: 358
Catbird C: 299 *with picture*
Gray Eagle
Speaker, Tris So: 768
Gray fox
Fox F: 438 *with picture*; (Dens) F: 439; (Kinds of foxes) F: 440
Gray friars [religious group]
Friar F: 532
Gray ghost [dog]
Weimaraner W: 188
Gray goods [fabric] *See* Gray-state cloth *in this index*
Gray jay [bird]
Jay J: 66
Gray kangaroo
Kangaroo (Kinds of kangaroos) K: 213
Gray limestone [rock]
Limestone L: 307 *with picture*
Gray market [economics]
Black market B: 389
Gray matter [anatomy]
Brain (The cerebrum) B: 550a-550b
Nervous system (The axon) N: 133-134
Schizophrenia S: 176
Gray nurse shark [fish]
Nurse shark N: 614
Gray Panthers [organization] G: 335
Old age (Employment and other activities) O: 739
Gray parrot
Parrot (Kinds of parrots) P: 179
Gray squirrel
Animal *picture on* A: 478
Invasive species (How invasive species affect habitats) I: 354j
Squirrel (Tree squirrels) So: 814b *with picture*
Gray-state cloth
Cotton (Spinning) Ci: 1091
Gray whale G: 335
Animal *picture on* A: 491
Whale *picture on* W: 256; (Gray whales) W: 255
Gray wolf
Wildlife conservation (Vulnerable species) W: 304
Wolf W: 375
Graybeard [plant] *See* Spanish moss *in this index*
Graylag goose
Goose G: 270; (Kinds of geese) G: 270
Grayling [fish] G: 335 *with picture*
Gray's Inn [London]
Inns of Court I: 275
Grays Lake National Wildlife Refuge [Idaho]
Whooping crane W: 297
Grayson, Dick [fictional character]
Batman B: 166 *with picture*
Graz [Austria] G: 335
Graziano, Rocky [American boxer]
Boxing (Boxing's Golden Age) B: 532-532a
Grazing
Farm and farming (Livestock grazing) F: 40 *with picture*
Forestry (Grazing land) F: 407
Grass (Grazing and forage grasses) G: 324
Ranching (Life on a cattle ranch) R: 134-135
Grazing incidence
Telescope (Ultraviolet telescopes) T: 108-109
Grazing incidence angle [physics]
X rays (Penetrating power) X: 541
Grazing land
Conservation (Conservation of grazing lands) Ci: 981 *with picture*
Grease [musical]
Musical comedy (During the late 1900's) M: 960

Rock music (The early 1970's) R: 380b
Travolta, John T: 406
Greasewood [shrub] G: 335
Creosote bush Ci: 1126
Greasy spot [plant disease]
Orange (Pests and diseases) O: 815
Great Abaco Island
Bahamas (Land and climate) B: 29 with map
"Great African Americans" series [books]
McKissack, Patricia M: 342
Great American Desert [nickname, Great Plains]
Westward movement in America (Exploration)
W: 248
Great American Fraud, The [book by Adams]
Adams, Samuel Hopkins A: 44
Great American Tea Company
Chain store C: 369
Hartford, George Huntington H: 79
Great American Tower [building]
Cincinnati (The city) Ci: 554
Great ape [animal]
Ape A: 563
Primate (Anthropoids) P: 778; (Conservation)
P: 778c
Great Apes, The [book by Yerkes]
Yerkes, Robert Mearns Y: 564
Great Artesian Basin
Australia (Underground water) A: 910
Great Atlantic and Pacific Tea Company
Chain store C: 369
Hartford, George Huntington H: 79
Great auk [extinct bird]
Auk A: 890 with picture
Bird (Extinct birds) B: 369-370 with picture
Great Awakening [U.S. history] G: 335
Christianity (The 1600's and 1700's) C: 525
Colonial life in America (Religion) Ci: 804-805
with picture
Edwards, Jonathan E: 114
Revivalism R: 269
Tennent, Gilbert T: 133
Great Baltimore Fire [1904]
Baltimore (The 1900's) B: 70
Great barracuda [fish]
Barracuda B: 117
Fish F: 153
Great Barrier Reef [Australia] G: 336 with picture
Australia (The Great Barrier Reef) A: 910 with
picture
Coral reef (Kinds of coral reefs) Ci: 1048b with
picture
Queensland Q: 39
Seven natural wonders of the world (The Great
Barrier Reef) S: 324 with picture
Great Barrier Reef Marine Park [Australia]
National park (Australia) N: 42b with picture;
(table) N: 42f
Great Barrier Reef Marine Park Authority
[Australia]
Great Barrier Reef G: 336
Great Basin [region, U.S.] G: 336 with map
Indian, American (Indians of the Great Basin)
I: 164 with picture and map
United States (The Western Plateaus, Basins, and
Ranges) U: 125 with picture
Great Basin bristlecone pine [tree]
Bristlecone pine B: 610 with pictures
Great Basin National Park [Nevada] G: 336 with
picture
National Park System (table: National parks) N: 48
Great Bear [constellation]
Big and Little Dippers (The Big Dipper) B: 296
Great Bear Lake [Northwest Territories] G: 336
with map
Lake (table) L: 34
Great black-backed gull [bird]
Bird picture on B: 330
Gull (Kinds of gulls) G: 439 with picture
Great blue heron
Bird (Birds of inland waters and marshes) B: 340
with picture
Heron picture on H: 213; (Kinds of herons) H: 214
Great Bridge, Battle of [1775]
Revolution, American (Fighting in the
Chesapeake and Southern colonies) R: 276-
278
Great Britain [island] G: 337
See also United Kingdom in this index
United Kingdom U: 48; (The land) U: 58 with map
Great Britain [ship]
Brunel, Isambard Kingdom B: 651
Ship (The first propeller-driven ships) S: 425 with
picture
**Great Britain and Northern Ireland, United
Kingdom of** See United Kingdom in this index
Great Buddha [sculpture]
Japan (Sculpture) J: 43 with picture

Great Buddha, Hall of the [temple]
Temple picture on T: 131
Great Charter See Magna Carta in this index
Great circle [geometry]
Azimuth A: 998
Geometry (Non-Euclidean geometry) G: 105 with
diagram
Sphere So: 780 with diagram
Trigonometry (Spherical trigonometry) T: 444
with diagram
Great-circle route [geography] G: 338 with maps
Globe G: 233
Great City of Tenochtitlan [painting by Rivera]
Aztec picture on A: 1004
Indian, American picture on I: 136
Great Code: The Bible and Literature, The [book
by Frye]
Frye, Northrop F: 549
Great Comet [astronomy]
Comet (table) Ci: 868
Great Compromise [U.S. history]
Congress of the United States (The founding of
Congress) C: 947
Connecticut (Statehood) Ci: 970
Constitution of the United States (The
compromises) Ci: 1000-1001
Franklin, Benjamin (The twilight years) F: 491
New Jersey (The American Revolution) N: 250-
251
Great Council [English history]
Parliament (History) P: 174
Great crested flycatcher [bird]
Flycatcher F: 311
Yellowhammer Y: 557
Great Dane [dog] G: 338 with picture
Great Dark Spot [astronomy]
Neptune (Surface and atmosphere) N: 128-129
Planet (Neptune) P: 512
Great Depression [1929-1942] G: 338 with pictures
African Americans (The Great Depression)
A: 136n
Argentina (Military dictatorships) A: 657
Australia (Between the wars) A: 924
Automobile (The Great Depression) A: 970
Baby boom generation (Causes of the baby
boom) B: 11
Bank (The crisis of 1933) B: 93
Birmingham (History) B: 376
Canada, History of (The Great Depression) C: 148
Capitalism (Changing attitudes toward
capitalism) C: 196
Chicago (Ending a century of progress) C: 436
Conservation (The rise of the conservation
movement) Ci: 985-986
Deflation D: 88
Democratic Party (The New Deal) D: 126
Depression (U.S. depressions) D: 150 with picture
Economics (Modern economics) E: 64
Family (Changes) F: 23
Grapes of Wrath, The G: 321
Hispanic Americans (Immigration restrictions and
growing restrictions) H: 252
Hoover, Herbert Clark (The Great Depression)
H: 329
Hopkins, Harry Lloyd H: 333
Housing (Housing since 1900) H: 391
Insurance (Greater regulation) I: 316
Kansas (The Great Depression) K: 238
Kentucky (The early 1900's) K: 293-294
Lange, Dorothea L: 61 with picture
Michigan (Depression and recovery) M: 509
Minnesota (The early 1900's) M: 604-606
Motion picture (Movies in the 1930's) M: 867
New Deal N: 200
New Zealand (The Great Depression) N: 355
Photography (Dramatic changes) P: 425-426
with picture
Railroad (The 1920's and the Great Depression)
R: 118
Roaring Twenties (The end of an era) R: 364
Roosevelt, Franklin Delano (Governor of New
York) R: 452; (Roosevelt's first administration
[1933-1937]) R: 452
Saskatchewan (The Great Depression) S: 147
United States, Government of the (The rise of big
government) U: 146
United States, History of the (Depression and
world conflict [1930-1959]) U: 192 with picture
Washington, D.C. (Continued growth) W: 87
Welfare (National welfare systems) W: 191
Welfare W: 192
Works Progress Administration W: 405
World War II (Economic problems) W: 469
Great Dictator, The [film]
Chaplin, Charlie C: 376
Great Dismal Swamp National Wildlife Refuge
Dismal Swamp D: 235

Great Dissenter [name for]
Holmes, Oliver Wendell, Jr. (Supreme Court
justice) H: 295
Great Divide [geography] G: 342
Colorado (Land regions) Ci: 838
Continental divide Ci: 1022
North America (Rivers) N: 464
Rocky Mountains R: 394
Wyoming (Land regions) W: 526
Great Divide, The [play by Moody]
Moody, William Vaughn M: 781
Great Dividing Range [region, Australia]
Australia (Land regions) A: 907 with picture and
map
Queensland (Land and climate) Q: 39
Great Eastern [ship]
Brunel, Isambard Kingdom B: 651
Ship (Ships of iron) S: 424-425 with picture
Great Egg Harbor Scenic and Recreational River
[New Jersey]
National Park System (table: National parkways
and other national parklands) N: 56
Great egret [bird]
Egret (Kinds) E: 119 with picture
Great Elector [name for]
Frederick William F: 497
"Great Elegy for John Donne" [poem by Brodsky]
Brodsky, Joseph B: 636
Great Enclosure [structure]
Great Zimbabwe G: 350
Great English Vowel Shift
Vowel V: 452
Great Ennead [Egyptian mythology]
Mythology (The Great Ennead) M: 979
Great Escarpment [region]
South Africa (The Plateau) So: 614 with map
Great Exhibition of 1851 [London]
Architecture (The Industrial Revolution) A: 625
with picture
Victoria and Albert Museum V: 358
World's fair W: 500
Great Expectations [book by Dickens]
Dickens, Charles (The second phase) D: 188-189
Great Exuma Island
Bahamas (Land and climate) B: 29 with map
Great Fall [waterfall, Guyana]
Guyana (Land) G: 446 with map
Great Falls [city, Montana] G: 343
Montana (Interesting facts) M: 743
Great Falls [falls, Guyana]
Guyana (Land) G: 446
Great Falls [falls, Montana]
Great Falls G: 343
Lewis and Clark expedition (West to the Rockies)
L: 222b-222c with picture
Great Fire of London [1666]
Fire department (Fire protection in Europe)
F: 127-128
London (War, plague, and fire) L: 441
Urban renewal (History) U: 220
Wren, Sir Christopher W: 504
Great Flood [Biblical history] See Deluge in this
index
Great Fountain Geyser
Yellowstone National Park (The Lower Loop)
Y: 558
Great frigatebird [bird]
Bird picture on B: 356
Great Gatsby, The [book by Fitzgerald]
American literature (The Lost Generation) A: 421
Fitzgerald, F. Scott F: 190
Novel (New directions in the novel) N: 573-574
Great Go-Between, The [play by Echegaray]
Spanish literature (The 1800's) So: 761
Great God Brown, The [play by O'Neill]
O'Neill, Eugene (His plays) O: 762
Great-grandparent
Family (Family relationships) F: 21
Great grey owl
Owl (Important owls) O: 884-886
Great hall [castle]
Castle (Life in a castle) C: 281 with picture
Great Hall [temple]
Egypt, Ancient (Religion) E: 137
Great Hall of the People
China picture on C: 477
Great horned owl
Owl (Important owls) O: 884 with picture
Great household
Babylonia (Way of life) B: 13
Great Inagua Island
Bahamas (Land and climate) B: 29 with map
Great Irish Famine [1845-1848] G: 343
Ireland (The potato famine) I: 426 with picture
Potato (History) P: 713
Great Lakes [Canada-U.S.] G: 343 with map
See also the list of Related articles in the Great

Lakes *article*
Canada (The Atlantic Basin) **C:** 116; (Waterways and ports) **C:** 126
Environmental pollution (Progress in controlling pollution) **E:** 338
Erie Canal **E:** 351 *with map*
Inland waterway **I:** 274
Lake (Travel and trade routes) **L:** 34
Lake Erie **L:** 37 *with map*
Lake Huron **L:** 38 *with map*
Lake Michigan **L:** 40 *with map*
Lake Ontario **L:** 43 *with map*
Lake Superior **L:** 45 *with map*
Lamprey (Destructiveness) **L:** 55
North America (Lakes) **N:** 464
Ruffe **R:** 509
Saint Lawrence River **S:** 41
Saint Lawrence Seaway **S:** 42 *with picture and map*
Ship (Dry bulk carriers) **N:** 408
Zebra mussel **Z:** 587
Great Lakes Aquarium [Duluth]
Minnesota (Places to visit) **M:** 594
Great Lakes Lowland
Ontario (Land regions) **O:** 776 *with map*
Great Lakes of South Dakota
South Dakota (Places to visit) **So:** 672
Great Lakes-Saint Lawrence Basin Agreement [1941]
Saint Lawrence Seaway (Agreements of 1941 and 1954) **S:** 45
Great Lakes-Saint Lawrence Seaway *See* Saint Lawrence Seaway *in this index*
Great Lakes Science Center [Cleveland]
Cleveland (Museums and libraries) **Ci:** 666
Great Lakes Water Quality Agreement [1972]
Environmental pollution (Progress in controlling pollution) **E:** 338
Great Lakes (Water quality) **G:** 345
Great laurel [shrub]
Rhododendron **R:** 318 *with picture*
Great Leap Forward [Chinese history]
China (The Great Leap Forward) **C:** 505
Mao Zedong (His leadership) **M:** 175
Great Limpopo Transfrontier Park [Africa] **G:** 346
National park (South Africa) **N:** 42e *with picture*; (table) **N:** 42f
South Africa (The Plateau) **So:** 614 *with picture*
Great Mahele [Hawaiian history]
Hawaii (Growth of constitutional government) **H:** 106
Great Meadows, Battle of the [1754]
Fort Duquesne **F:** 412
Great Migration [U.S. history]
African Americans *picture on* **A:** 136b; (The black migration to the North) **A:** 136m
Great Migration, The [book by Lawrence]
Literature for children *picture on* **L:** 359
Great Moravian Empire [European history]
Czechoslovakia (Early history) **Ci:** 1215
Moravia **M:** 801
Slavs **S:** 505
Great Mormon [butterfly]
Butterfly *picture on* **B:** 737
Great Mosque [Saudi Arabia]
Islam (The Five Pillars of Islam) **I:** 463-464 *with picture*
Kaaba **K:** 208
Mecca (The city) **M:** 352 *with picture*
Saudi Arabia *picture on* **S:** 154
Great Mughals, Kingdom of the
Mongol Empire (Breakup) **M:** 721
Great National Pike
National Road **N:** 60
Great Nebula in Andromeda [galaxy] *See* Andromeda Galaxy *in this index*
Great Nebula in Orion
Nebula *picture on* **N:** 116
Orion **O:** 856
Great northern diver [bird]
Loon **L:** 453
Great Northern Peninsula
Newfoundland and Labrador (Land regions) **N:** 370 *with map*
Great Northern Railway
Hill, James Jerome **H:** 231
Great Northern War [1700-1721]
Charles XII **C:** 382
Denmark (Wars with Sweden) **D:** 140
Finland (Swedish rule) **F:** 116
Great Palace [Petrodvorets]
Russia (Architecture) **R:** 536
Great Peace [U.S. history] *See* Iroquois League *in this index*
Great Philippine eagle [bird]
Eagle (Other kinds of eagles) **E:** 5
Great Plains [region, North America] **G:** 346 *with map*
Colorado (Land regions) **Ci:** 838 *with map*
Dust Bowl **D:** 391 *with picture*
Indian, American (Indians of the Plains) **I:** 158 *with pictures*
Indian Territory **I:** 189
North America (Agriculture) **N:** 468
Pioneer life in America (Crossing the Plains) **P:** 485
South Dakota (Land regions) **So:** 674 *with map*
Switchgrass **So:** 1049
United States (The Interior Plains) **U:** 124
United States, History of the (The United States moves west) **U:** 168
Westward movement in America (Settling the Great Plains) **W:** 250
Great Platte River Road Archway Monument [Nebraska]
Nebraska (Places to visit) **N:** 102
Great Purge [Soviet history]
Communism (Under Stalin) **Ci:** 892-893
Russia (Stalin) **R:** 553
Stalin, Joseph (Rule by terror) **So:** 826-827
Union of Soviet Socialist Republics (Stalin's policies) **U:** 36-37
Great purple hairstreak [butterfly]
Butterfly (Blues, coppers, and hairstreaks) **B:** 734 *with picture*
Great Pyramid [Egypt]
Egypt, Ancient (Arts and sciences) **E:** 139
Pyramids *diagram on* **P:** 919; (The pyramids of Giza) **P:** 917 *with picture*
Great Pyrenees [dog] **G:** 347
Dog *picture on* **D:** 267
Great Railway Bazaar, The [book by Theroux]
Theroux, Paul **T:** 257
Great Red Spot [astronomy]
Jupiter (Ovals) **J:** 199 *with picture*
Planet *picture on* **P:** 510
Space exploration *picture on* **So:** 709
Great Republic [ship]
Clipper ship **Ci:** 682i *with picture*
McKay, Donald **M:** 337
Ship (Clipper ships) **S:** 422
Great rhododendron [shrub]
Rhododendron **R:** 318 *with picture*
Great Rift Valley [Africa-Asia] **G:** 347
Ethiopia (The Ethiopian Plateau) **E:** 369-370
Israel (The Rift Valley) **I:** 482
Kenya (Land regions) **K:** 301 *with map*
Malawi (Land) **M:** 97
Red Sea **R:** 189
Rwanda (Land) **R:** 571
Tanzania (Land and climate) **T:** 32
Uganda (Land) **U:** 3
Great Saint Bernard Hospice [shelter]
Saint Bernard Passes (Great St. Bernard) **S:** 32 *with picture*
Great Saint Bernard Pass [Switzerland]
Alps (Chief ranges of the Alps) **A:** 385 *with picture*
Saint Bernard Passes (Great St. Bernard) **S:** 32
Great Saint Bernard Tunnel [Switzerland]
Alps (Alpine travel) **A:** 386
Switzerland (Transportation) **So:** 1058
Great Salt Lake [Utah] **G:** 347 *with maps*
United States (The Western Plateaus, Basins, and Ranges) **U:** 125
Utah (Interesting facts) **U:** 231; (Places to visit) **U:** 238 *with picture*; (Land regions) **U:** 240 *with map*; (Rivers and lakes) **U:** 242
Great Salt Lake City [former name]
Salt Lake City (History) **S:** 76a
Great Salt Lake Desert [region, Utah]
Utah (Land regions) **U:** 240 *with map*; (Deserts) **U:** 242
Great Salt Water [name for]
Chesapeake Bay **C:** 411
Great Sand Dunes National Park [Colorado] **G:** 347
Colorado (Interesting facts) **Ci:** 829 *with picture*
National Park System (table: National parks) **N:** 48
Great Sand Dunes National Preserve [Colorado]
National Park System (table: National preserves) **N:** 58
Great Sandy Desert [Australia]
Australia (Deserts) **A:** 908 *with map*
Australian Desert **A:** 927
Great Schism [1378-1417]
See also Schism *in this index*
John XXIII [antipope] **J:** 132
Pope (The troubles of the papacy) **P:** 664
Roman Catholic Church (The Great Schism) **R:** 407
Sigismund **S:** 453
Urban VI **U:** 219
Great Seal of the United States [emblem] **G:** 348
E Pluribus Unum **E:** 3
Flag (The colors) **F:** 210
United States, Government of the *picture on* **U:** 137
Great September Comet [astronomy]
Comet (table) **Ci:** 868
Great Serpent Mound [Ohio]
Mound builders *picture on* **M:** 881
Ohio (Places to visit) **O:** 690 *with picture*
Great shearwater [bird]
Shearwater **S:** 379
Great Siberian Way
Trans-Siberian Railroad **T:** 401
Great Silk Road [trade route] *See* Silk Road *in this index*
Great Sioux Reservation
Crazy Horse **Ci:** 1123
South Dakota (Territorial days) **So:** 681
Great Sioux Uprising [1862]
Indian wars (The Great Sioux Uprising [1862]) **I:** 192
Minnesota (Statehood) **M:** 604
Great skua [bird]
Antarctica *picture on* **A:** 535
Great Slave Lake [Northwest Territories] **G:** 348 *with map*
Hearne, Samuel **H:** 131
Great Smoky Mountains [North Carolina-Tennessee] **G:** 348 *with picture*
Clingmans Dome **Ci:** 681
Tennessee *picture on* **T:** 134
Great Smoky Mountains National Park [North Carolina-Tennessee] **G:** 348
National Park System (table: National parks) **N:** 48 *with picture*
Tennessee (Places to visit) **T:** 144 *with picture*
Great Socialist People's Libyan Arab Jamahiriya [official name]
Libya **L:** 264
Great Society [U.S. history] **G:** 349
Democratic Party (The Great Society) **D:** 127
Johnson, Lyndon Baines (The Great Society) **J:** 150
Great Sphinx [Giza, Egypt]
Egypt, Ancient (Painting and sculpture) **E:** 139
Sphinx (Egyptian sphinxes) **So:** 780 *with picture*
Great spirit [religion]
Indian, American (Beliefs) **I:** 147
Great Star Cloud in Sagittarius [astronomy]
Milky Way (The center of the galaxy) **M:** 551
Great Star Flag [U.S. history]
Flag *picture on* **F:** 209; (Changes in the United States flag) **F:** 214
Great Stone Face [White Mountains]
New Hampshire (Places to visit) **N:** 216
White Mountains **W:** 291
Great Sun [ruler]
Indian, American (Indians of the Southeast) **I:** 157
Great Swamp Fight [1675]
Indian wars (King Philip's War [1675-1676]) **I:** 191
Rhode Island (King Philip's War) **R:** 312-313
Great-tailed grackle [bird]
Grackle **G:** 296
Great Temple [Mexico City]
Aztec (The Aztec heritage) **A:** 1006
Great Theater of the World, The [play by Calderón de la Barca]
Spanish literature (The 1600's) **So:** 759-760
Great Train Robbery, The [film] **G:** 349
Motion picture (Early motion pictures) **M:** 863 *with picture*
Westerns **W:** 242
Great Trek [South African history]
Afrikaners **A:** 138
South Africa (British rule) **So:** 618
Great Valley [region, California]
California (Land regions) **C:** 48
Great Valley [region, eastern U.S.]
Appalachian Mountains (Physical features) **A:** 568
Pennsylvania (The Appalachian Ridge and Valley Region) **P:** 256
United States (The Appalachian Highlands) **U:** 120-121
Virginia (Land regions) **V:** 410
Great vessels [anatomy]
Heart (Blood vessels) **H:** 135
Great Victoria Desert [region, Australia] **G:** 349
Australia (Deserts) **A:** 908 *with map*
Great Wall of China **G:** 349
Asia (Agriculture) on **A:** 786; (The Huang He and Yangtze valleys) **A:** 805
China (The Qin dynasty) **C:** 500 *with picture*
Gobi **G:** 242
Shi Huangdi **S:** 399
World, History of the *picture on* **W:** 431
Great Western [ship]
Brunel, Isambard Kingdom **B:** 651
Ship (Ships of iron) **S:** 424-425

Great Western Railroad [Canada]
Hamilton (History) **H:** 31-32
Great wheel [machine]
Spinning (Early spinning wheels) **So:** 794
Great White Fleet [U.S. history]
Navy, United States ("The Great White Fleet")
N: 88
Roosevelt, Theodore (Friction with Japan) **R:** 467
Great White Hope, The [play]
Jones, James Earl **J:** 158
Great white pelican
Bird *picture on* **B:** 328
Great white shark [fish] **G:** 350 *with picture*
Animal *picture on* **A:** 471
Shark (Kinds of sharks) **S:** 375 *with pictures*; (How people use sharks) **S:** 376
Great White Way, The [name for]
Broadway **B:** 635
Great World and Timothy Colt, The [book by Auchincloss]
Auchincloss, Louis **A:** 880
Great Wrath [Finnish history]
Finland (Swedish rule) **F:** 116
Great Ziegfeld, The [film]
Motion picture (Best picture: 1936) **M:** 861
Great Zimbabwe [ancient city] **G:** 350
Africa (States and kingdoms) **A:** 131 *with picture*
Zimbabwe (History) **Z:** 592-593
Greater Antilles [islands, Caribbean Sea]
Caribbean Sea **C:** 237
West Indies **W:** 201
Greater bird-of-paradise
Bird-of-paradise **B:** 374 *with picture*
Greater Columbus Arts Festival
Columbus (Cultural life and recreation) **Ci:** 855
Greater East Asia Co-Prosperity Sphere [Japanese history]
World War II (Japan attacks) **W:** 479; (Propaganda) **W:** 494-495
Greater flamingo [bird]
Flamingo **F:** 226
Greater glider [animal]
Glider [animal] **G:** 231
Greater grison [animal]
Weasel **W:** 155
Greater jihad [religion]
Jihad **J:** 126
Greater kudu [animal]
Antelope *picture on* **A:** 542
Greater London
London *map on* **L:** 429; (Greater London) **L:** 428
Greater London Authority [government]
London (The Greater London Authority) **L:** 439; (Recent developments) **L:** 443
Greater Los Angeles [area]
Los Angeles (Metropolitan area) **L:** 462 *with map*
Greater prairie-chicken
Bird *picture on* **B:** 337
Prairie-chicken **P:** 731
Greater roadrunner [bird]
Bird *picture on* **B:** 339
Roadrunner **R:** 362
Greater scaup [bird]
Duck *picture on* **D:** 375
Greater sooty-owl [bird]
Owl (Important owls) **O:** 884
Greater Sudbury [Ontario] **G:** 350
Greater Sunda Islands
Indonesia (The Greater Sunda Islands) **I:** 233 *with map*
Greater Syria
Syria (History) **So:** 1074
Greater Texas and Pan American Exposition [1937]
Texas (The early 1900's) **T:** 207-208
Greater Toronto Area
Toronto (The metropolitan area) **T:** 339
Greatest common factor [mathematics]
Factor (Common factors) **F:** 4-5
Greatest Show on Earth [circus]
Barnum, P. T. **B:** 115
Circus (History) **Ci:** 562-563
Greatest Show on Earth, The [film]
DeMille, Cecil B. **D:** 119
Motion picture (Best picture: 1952) **M:** 861
Greave [armor]
Armor *picture on* **A:** 720; (In early times) **A:** 719-720
Greb, Harry [American boxer]
Boxing (Boxing's Golden Age) **B:** 532-532a
Grebe [bird] **G:** 351
Bird *picture on* **B:** 357; (Birds of inland waters and marshes) **B:** 340 *with picture*; (In the water) **B:** 353-354
Grebel, Conrad [Swiss religious leader]
Reformation (Zwingli and the Anabaptists) **R:** 197-198

Gréber, Jacques [French architect]
Ottawa (The 1900's) **O:** 875
Gréboun, Mount [Niger]
Niger (Land and climate) **N:** 408
Grecian Archipelago
Aegean Sea **A:** 83 *with map*
Grecian stock [plant]
Stock **So:** 903
Greco, El [Spanish painter] **G:** 351 *with picture*
Art and the arts (The aesthetic experience) **A:** 745-746 *with picture*
Greece (Arts) **G:** 356
Philosophy *picture on* **P:** 388
Resurrection *picture on* **R:** 263
Greco-Roman Age
Greek literature (The Greco-Roman Age) **G:** 378
Greco-Roman wrestling
Wrestling (Chief forms of wrestling) **W:** 505
Greece **G:** 352 *with pictures and maps*
See also the list of Related articles in the Greece *article*
Balkans (The First Balkan War) **B:** 42; (The Second Balkan War) **B:** 42
Clothing *picture on* **Ci:** 694
Cold War (The containment policy) **Ci:** 764
Cyprus **Ci:** 1205
Euro **E:** 379
Europe (Recent developments) **E:** 416
Macedonia **M:** 11 *with map*
Macedonia [country] (History) **M:** 12a
Otto I **O:** 876
Philip, Prince **P:** 371
World War II (Fighting in the Balkans) **W:** 477
Greece, Ancient **G:** 366 *with pictures and maps*
See also the list of Related articles in the Greece, Ancient *article*
Armor *picture on* **A:** 720; (In early times) **A:** 719-720
Bell (History) **B:** 239
Book (Early books) **B:** 465
Classicism (Greece) **G:** 653
Communication (During ancient times) **Ci:** 879 *with picture*
Europe (Ancient Greece) **E:** 407
Family (Ancient families) **F:** 21-22
Golden Age **G:** 255
Hellenistic Age **H:** 177
Ionians **I:** 373
Mental illness (Early attitudes) **M:** 408
Money (Lydian coins) **M:** 706-707 *with picture*
Olympiad **O:** 746
Art and architecture
Greece, Ancient (The arts) **G:** 369 *with pictures*
Acropolis **A:** 29
Architecture (Classical Greek architecture) **A:** 615 *with pictures*
Column (The Greek orders) **Ci:** 865 *with pictures*
Doll (Ancient times) **D:** 288 *with picture*
Europe (The arts) **E:** 391 *with pictures*
Geometric style **G:** 101
Jewelry (Early jewelry) **J:** 117-118
Lyre **L:** 537
Painting (Greek painting) **P:** 42 *with picture*; (Roman painting) **P:** 42
Pottery *picture on* **P:** 717
Ring *picture on* **R:** 342
Sculpture (The importance of sculpture) **S:** 228 *with picture*; (As part of architecture) **S:** 229; (Greek sculpture) **S:** 245 *with pictures*
Sphinx (The Greek sphinx) **So:** 781 *with picture*
Education
Greece, Ancient (Education) **G:** 367
Atomism **A:** 877
Education (Ancient Greek education) **E:** 98
Physical education (Early history) **P:** 433
Zoo (History) **Z:** 604
Government
Greece, Ancient (Government) **G:** 372
Democracy (Origins of democracy) **D:** 122
Freedom (In ancient Greece and Rome) **F:** 502
Government *picture on* **G:** 290; (Ancient Greece) **G:** 289
Law (The influence of ancient Greece) **L:** 133
Peace (Ancient Greece and Rome) **P:** 206
History
Greece, Ancient (History) **G:** 372 *with pictures and maps*
Army (Ancient armies) **A:** 726
Barbarian **B:** 104
Citizenship (History) **Ci:** 572
Exploration (The Greeks) **E:** 441
History (The ancient Greeks and Romans) **H:** 261
Library (Greece) **L:** 258
Marathon, Battle of **M:** 191
Navy (Ancient navies) **N:** 79

Philosophy **P:** 383; (Ancient philosophy) **P:** 386
Rome, Ancient (Architecture and engineering) **R:** 442; (The Roman Republic) **R:** 444-445
Slavery **S:** 501
Women's movement (In ancient societies) **W:** 384
World, History of the (The Greeks) **W:** 428 *with picture*
Language and literature See Greek language; Greek literature *in this index*
Parks and monuments
Park (History) **P:** 168
Recreation and sports
Boxing (Ancient history) **B:** 531
Olympic Games **O:** 746; (The ancient games) **O:** 750 *with picture*
Religion and mythology
Greece, Ancient (Religion) **G:** 367
Butterfly **B:** 732
Greece, Ancient (Religion) **G:** 367
Helen of Troy **H:** 168
Mythology **M:** 973, *picture on* **M:** 979; (Greek mythology) **M:** 980 *with pictures*; (Roman mythology) **M:** 982
Poetry (Ancient poetry) **P:** 595
Social and cultural life
Greece, Ancient (Life of the people) **G:** 367 *with picture*
Bed (History) **B:** 198
Classical music (Early music) **Ci:** 645
Clothing (Greece) **Ci:** 697 *with picture*
Cremation **Ci:** 1126
Food (Ancient times) **F:** 336
Furniture (Ancient Greece) **F:** 570 *with picture*
Gymnasium **G:** 447
Hairdressing (Ancient times) **H:** 11 *with picture*
Homosexuality (Attitudes toward homosexuality) **H:** 307
Technology and science
Greece, Ancient (Science) **G:** 369
Anatomy **A:** 448b
Aqueduct (Ancient aqueducts) **A:** 580
Astrology (History) **A:** 827
Astronomy (History) **A:** 846-847
Drug (Drugs in ancient times) **D:** 358
Electricity (Early discoveries) **E:** 196
Fraction (History) **F:** 449-450
Geography (Early study) **G:** 95
Geology (The ancient Greeks) **G:** 97
Geometry (Greek geometry) **G:** 106
Heart (Early beliefs about the heart) **H:** 143
Invention (Ancient Greece) **I:** 359
Map (Ancient maps) **M:** 182
Mathematics (The Greeks) **M:** 306
Medicine (Greece and Rome) **M:** 372 *with picture*
Moon (Ancient ideas) **M:** 791-792
Number (The Greeks) **N:** 606
Physics (The Greeks) **P:** 438
Science (Ancient Greece) **S:** 196 *with picture*
Screw (History) **S:** 226
Ship (Phoenician and Greek ships) **S:** 415 *with pictures*
Transportation (Ancient Greece) **T:** 386
Greece Expiring on the Ruins of Missolonghi [painting by Delacroix]
Greece *picture on* **G:** 362
Greek alphabet
Alphabet (The Greeks) **A:** 383 *with pictures*
Greek language (Alphabet) **G:** 376
Greek Anthology, The [poems]
Masters, Edgar Lee **M:** 297
Greek architecture *See* Greece, Ancient *in this index*
Greek art *See* Greece, Ancient *in this index*
Greek cross [architecture]
Architecture (Later Renaissance architecture) **A:** 621
Cross **Ci:** 1155 *with picture*
Saint Peter's Basilica (History) **S:** 53-54
Greek drama
Drama (Greek drama) **D:** 326 *with pictures*
Greek fire [chemistry] **G:** 376
Greek gods *See* Greece, Ancient *in this index*
Greek language **G:** 376
Alphabet (The Greeks) **A:** 383 *with pictures*
Language (Indo-European) **L:** 65-66
Linguistics (Comparative reconstruction) **L:** 336; (Comparative and historical research) **L:** 337
New Testament (Textual criticism) **N:** 288
Old Testament (Ancient translations) **O:** 741
Greek-letter society [organization] *See* Fraternity; Sorority *in this index*
Greek literature **G:** 377
See also the list of Related articles in the Greek literature *article*
Biography (Early biographies) **B:** 312

Drama (Greek drama) **D: 326** *with pictures*
Fable **F: 3**
Greece, Ancient (The arts) **G: 369**
Mask (Theatrical masks) **M: 265**
Novel (Ancient Greek and Roman narratives)
    N: 572
Romance **R: 414**
Greek mythology *See Greece, Ancient in this index*
Greek Myths, The [book by Graves]
Mythology (Literary approaches) **M: 990-991**
Greek Orthodox Archdiocese of America
[religious group] **G: 379**
Greek Orthodox Church
Bible (The Christian Old Testament) **B: 282**
Eastern Orthodox Churches **E: 45**
Greece (Religion) **G: 356** *with picture*
Greek Orthodox Archdiocese of America **G: 379**
Old Testament (Contents) **O: 741**
Greek Orthodox Church of the Annunciation
Milwaukee (Annual events and places of interest)
    M: 560-561
Greek philosophy
Mythology (The study of myths) **M: 988**
Philosophy (Ancient philosophy) **P: 386**
Greek process
Olive (Harvesting and preparation for market)
    O: 743
Greek Revival style [architecture]
Architecture (The Greek Revival) **A: 625**
House *picture on* **H: 381**
Latrobe, Benjamin Henry **L: 118**
Greek Slave [sculpture by Powers]
Powers, Hiram **P: 728**
Greek tragedy
Drama (Tragedy) **D: 326**
Greek literature (Drama) **G: 377**
Tragedy **T: 366**
Greek War of Independence [1821-1829]
Greece (Independence) **G: 362**
Greeks [people]
Greece (Population) **G: 353**
Greece, Ancient (The people) **G: 367**
Greeley, Horace [American publisher] **G: 379** *with portrait*
Colorado (Territorial days) **Ci: 845**
Davis, Jefferson (Confederate leader) **D: 48**
Grant, Ulysses S. (Election of 1872) **G: 316-317**
Journalism (The growth of U.S. newspapers)
    J: 174
Liberal Republican Party **L: 227**
Lincoln, Abraham (Second inauguration) **L: 324-325**
Nast, Thomas **N: 25**
Green
Color (Mixing colorants) **Ci: 819-820** *with diagrams*
Green [sports]
Bowling *picture on* **B: 524**
Golf (The green) **G: 261** *with diagram*
Lawn bowling **L: 144**
Green, Bartholomew [Canadian printer]
Printing (Early printing in North America) **P: 803**
Green, Dwight H. [American political leader]
Illinois (table) **I: 71**
Green, Fred W. [American political leader]
Michigan (table) **M: 507**
Green, Nehemiah [American political leader]
Kansas (table) **K: 234**
Green, Paul Eliot [American dramatist] **G: 379**
Green, Project
Dion, Stéphane **D: 215**
Green, Robert S. [American political leader]
New Jersey (table) **N: 249**
Green, Samuel [American doctor]
Ku Klux Klan (Mid-1900's) **K: 390**
Green, Samuel [American printer]
Almanac *picture on* **A: 379**
Green, Theodore Francis [American political leader] **G: 379**
Rhode Island (table) **R: 311**
Green, Warren [American political leader]
South Dakota (table) **So: 680**
Green, William [American labor leader] **G: 380**
Congress of Industrial Organizations **Ci: 941**
Labor movement (Reunification of the AFL and the CIO) **L: 13**
Green algae [organism]
Algae (Kinds of algae) **A: 349** *with picture*
Seaweed (Kinds) **S: 276** *with picture*
Green almond [nut]
Pistachio nut **P: 497**
Green anaconda [snake]
Boa **B: 426**
Snake *picture on* **S: 526**
Green-backed heron [bird]
Bird (Birds of inland waters and marshes) **B: 340** *with picture*

Green Bank Telescope [West Virginia] **G: 380** *with picture*
National Radio Astronomy Observatory **N: 59**
Observatory (Ground-based observatories)
    O: 644-645
West Virginia *picture on* **W: 227**
Green Bay [Wisconsin] **G: 380**
Wisconsin (table: Average monthly weather)
    W: 360
Green-Bay Intelligencer [newspaper]
Wisconsin (Communication) **W: 364**
Green Bay Packers [team]
Favre, Brett **F: 56**
Football (National Football League) **F: 364**
Lombardi, Vince **L: 427**
Wisconsin *picture on* **W: 350**
Green Belt
London (Outlying areas) **L: 430**; (Rebuilding)
    L: 442
Moscow *map on* **M: 824**; (Layout of Moscow)
    M: 823
Green Berets [army unit] *See Special Forces in this index*
Green broadbill [bird]
Bird *picture on* **B: 344g**
Green chain [machine]
Lumber (Grading lumber) **L: 519**
Green corn dance
Indian, American (Ceremonies) **I: 148**; (Before European contact) **I: 157-158**
Green Day [rock group]
Rock music (Alternative rock) **R: 381**
Green frog
Wetland *picture on* **W: 253**
Green Gables House
Prince Edward Island (Places to visit) **P: 788** *with picture*
Green Henry [book by Keller]
German literature (Realism) **G: 141**
Green heron [bird]
Heron (Kinds of herons) **H: 214** *with picture*
Green Hills of Africa [book by Hemingway]
Hemingway, Ernest (Rise to fame) **H: 180**
Green House, The [book by Vargas Llosa]
Latin American literature (The "Boom") **L: 114**
Vargas Llosa, Mario **V: 285**
Green iguana
Iguana **I: 50** *with picture*
Green jay [bird]
Jay **J: 66** *with picture*
Green Knight [legend]
Round Table (The knights of the Round Table)
    R: 491
Green lumber [wood]
Lumber (Sawing logs) **L: 519**
Green manure
Fertilizer (Organic fertilizers) **F: 79**
Legume **L: 185**
Manure **M: 172**
Green moray eel
Fish *picture on* **F: 155**
Green Mountain Boys [U.S. history] **G: 380**
Allen, Ethan **A: 371**
Vermont *picture on* **V: 335**; (Land disputes) **V: 334**; (The Revolutionary War in America) **V: 334**
Warner, Seth **W: 36**
Green Mountain National Forest
Vermont (Places to visit) **V: 326**
Green Mountains [Vermont] **G: 380**
Vermont *picture on* **V: 318**; (Land regions) **V: 328** *with map*
Green olive [fruit]
Olive (Harvesting and preparation for market)
    O: 743
Green onion
Onion (Cultivation) **O: 763** *with picture*
Green Party [Germany]
Germany (Politics) **G: 147**; (West Germany) **G: 170**
Green party **G: 381**
Green party [political party] **G: 381**
Environmental pollution (Environmental organizations) **E: 338**
Green Party [United States]
Green party **G: 381**
Nader, Ralph **N: 2**
Green pasta [food]
Pasta **P: 192**
Green Pastures, The [play by Connelly]
Bradford, Roark **B: 544**
Connelly, Marc **Ci: 972**
Green pepper [plant]
Pepper **P: 278** *with picture*
Green Revolution [agriculture]
Agriculture (The Green Revolution) **A: 159**
Borlaug, Norman Ernest **B: 488**
Food supply (Making farmland more productive)

F: 349 *with picture*
India (Agriculture) **I: 125**
Plant (Industrialized agriculture) **P: 542**
Population (Effects) **P: 674**
Wheat (Breeding new varieties of wheat) **W: 277**
Green River [Utah-Wyoming]
Utah *picture on* **U: 240**; (Rivers and lakes) **U: 242** *with map*
Wyoming (Rivers and lakes) **W: 528**
Green Room
White House (Public rooms) **W: 286-290** *with pictures*
Green sand [manufacturing]
Cast and casting (Types of molds) **C: 278**
Green screen [cinematography]
Animation (Lighting and rendering) **A: 513-514a**
Green shell bean [plant]
Bean (Kinds of beans) **B: 181**
Green snake
Snake *picture on* **S: 533**
Green tea
Tea (Processing tea) **T: 62**
Green tree python [snake]
Python **P: 922**
Green turtle
Magnetism *picture on* **M: 60c**
Turtle **T: 520** *with picture*; (Reproduction) **T: 521**
Green Water, Green Sky [book by Gallant]
Gallant, Mavis **G: 13**
Green-winged teal [bird]
Teal **T: 71**
Green woodpecker [bird]
Bird *picture on* **B: 344d**; (Birds of Europe) **B: 344c**
Woodpecker *picture on* **W: 394**
Greenaway, Kate [British artist] **G: 381**
Literature for children *picture on* **L: 361**; (The rise of illustration) **L: 364**
Valentine's Day *picture on* **V: 262**; (Commercial valentines) **V: 264** *with picture*
Greenback [money] **G: 381**
Hayes, Rutherford Birchard (Money problems)
    H: 121
Money (Money in the American Civil War) **M: 713**
Greenback Party [U.S. history] **G: 381**
Cooper, Peter **Ci: 1035**
Political party (Third parties) **P: 636**
Greenbelt [area]
Conservation (Urban conservation) **Ci: 984**
Greenbelt [Maryland]
Washington, D.C. (Metropolitan area) **W: 80-81**
Greenbelt Park [Maryland]
National Park System (table: National parkways and other national parklands) **N: 56**
Greenberg, Hank [American baseball player]
Baseball (table: Hall of Fame) **B: 1134a**
Greenbottle fly [insect]
Fly (The body of a fly) **F: 309** *with picture*
Greenbrier [plant] **G: 381**
Greenbrier Hotel
White Sulphur Springs **W: 292**
Greene, Catherine Littlefield [American social reformer]
Whitney, Eli (The cotton gin) **W: 295**
Greene, Freddie [American musician]
Basie, Count **B: 140**
Greene, Graham [British author] **G: 381**
English literature (Fiction between the wars)
    E: 322
Novel (After World War II) **N: 574**
Greene, Nathanael [American general] **G: 382**
Greensboro **G: 386**
Revolution, American (Cowpens and Guilford Courthouse) **R: 285**
Rhode Island (Places to visit) **R: 304**
South Carolina (The Revolutionary War) **So: 659**
Trenton, Battle of **T: 435**
Greene, Robert [English author] **G: 382**
Drama (Elizabethan playwrights) **D: 331-332**
Shakespeare, William (Early career in London)
    S: 347
Greene, William [American political leader]
Rhode Island (table) **R: 311**
Greene's Groats-Worth of Wit Bought with a Million of Repentance [pamphlet by Greene]
Greene, Robert **G: 382**
Shakespeare, William (Early career in London)
    S: 347
Greenfield, Herbert [Canadian political leader]
Alberta (table) **A: 328**
Greenfield Village [Dearborn, Michigan]
Dearborn **D: 60**
Detroit (Other interesting places to visit) **D: 170**
Edison, Thomas Alva *picture on* **E: 81**; (Honors) **E: 82**
Ford, Henry (Political and charitable activities)
    F: 380
Michigan (Museums) **M: 493**; (Places to visit)

M: 498 *with picture*
Greengard, Paul [American neurobiologist]
Nobel Prizes (Physiology or medicine: 2000)
N: 447
Greenglass, David [American public figure]
Rosenberg, Julius and Ethel R: 479
Greenhalge, Frederic T. [American political leader]
Massachusetts (table) M: 288
Greenhand degree
FFA (Degrees) F: 85
Greenhouse [gardening] G: 382
Floriculture F: 241
Greenhouse effect [physics] G: 382
Agriculture (Pollution) A: 153
Air pollution (Atmosphere) A: 199
Animal (Pollution) A: 504
Biodiversity (Protecting biodiversity) B: 311
Coal (Recent developments) Ci: 732
Conservation (International problems) Ci: 990
Earth (The atmosphere) E: 18-19
Energy supply (Environmental effects) E: 281
Environmental pollution (Air pollution) E: 331
Forest (Deforestation) F: 398-399
Global warming (Causes of global warming)
G: 232; (Ways to limit global warming) G: 232b
Greenhouse G: 382
Marine biology (Biological oceanographers)
M: 205
Ocean (Climate change) O: 665
Pacific Ocean (Scientific research) P: 15-17
Paleobotany P: 102
Petroleum (Global warming) P: 345
Planet (Venus) P: 511
Remote sensing R: 231
Soil So: 573
Venus (Temperature) V: 312
Weather (Air temperature) W: 157
Greenhouse gas
See also Greenhouse effect
Carbon footprint C: 207
Greenhouse effect G: 382
Greenhouse range [agriculture]
Greenhouse G: 382
Greenhouse whitefly [insect]
Whitefly W: 292
Greenland [province, Denmark] G: 383 *with
pictures and map*
See also the list of Related articles in the Greenland
article
Climate (Glaciers) Ci: 679 *with picture*
Denmark D: 132; (Postwar years) D: 141
Erik the Red E: 351
Ice age (Evidence from modern glaciers and from
caves) I: 6-7
Iceberg (Northern Hemisphere icebergs) I: 17-18
with map
Inuit I: 354 *with map*; (History) I: 354g; (The Inuit
today) I: 354h-354i
Leif Erikkson L: 186
Peary, Robert Edwin (Arctic expeditions) P: 224
Greenland cod [fish]
Cod Ci: 748
Greenland halibut [fish]
Halibut H: 20
Greenland National Park [Greenland]
National park (table) N: 42g
Greenlandic [language]
Greenland (People) G: 384
Greenly, William L. [American political leader]
Michigan (table) M: 507
Greenough, Horatio [American sculptor] G: 386
Sculpture (American sculpture) S: 255 *with
picture*
Greenpeace [organization] G: 386
New Zealand (International tensions) N: 355-356
Greensand [mineral]
Glauconite G: 226
Greensboro [North Carolina] G: 386
Greensburg [Kansas]
Kansas (The early 2000's) K: 239
Greenspan, Alan [American government official]
G: 386
Greenstick fracture
Fracture F: 450 *with diagram*
Greenville [South Carolina]
South Carolina (Population) So: 644
Greenville, Treaty of [1795]
Indian wars (Conflicts in the Midwest) I: 191-192
with picture
Northwest Territory (Settlement) N: 535
Westward movement in America (Indian
conflicts) W: 247 *with picture*
Greenway, John Campbell [American engineer]
G: 386
Greenway, Thomas [Canadian political leader]
Manitoba (table) M: 159
Greenwich [London]

London (Other places of interest) L: 437
Greenwich Hospital [England]
Wren, Sir Christopher W: 504 *with picture*
Greenwich meridian [geography] G: 386
International date line I: 339
London (Other places of interest) L: 437
Longitude (Longitude and location) L: 451 *with
diagram*
Map (Geographic grids) M: 178
Time (International time zones) T: 292a
Greenwich Observatory, Royal [England] G: 387
Greenwich meridian G: 386
Greenwich Tea Burning [U.S. history]
New Jersey (The American Revolution) N: 250
Greenwich Village [district]
New York City (Manhattan) N: 323-324; (A
visitor's guide) N: 338
Greenwood, Chester
Maine (Interesting facts) M: 69 *with picture*
Greenwood field [region, Colorado-Kansas]
Helium (Production) H: 176
Greer, Germaine [Australian author] G: 387
Greeting
Address, Forms of A: 53
Greeting cards G: 387
Valentine's Day V: 261 *with pictures*
Gregg, Hugh [American political leader]
New Hampshire (table) N: 223
Gregg, John Robert [Irish-American educator]
Shorthand S: 435
Gregg, Judd Alan [American political leader]
New Hampshire (table) N: 223
Gregg method
Shorthand S: 435
Gregg v. Georgia [U.S. history]
Capital punishment (History of capital
punishment) C: 193
Supreme Court of the United States (Criminal
law) So: 1001; (table) So: 1002
Gregoire, Christine [American political leader]
Washington (table) W: 65; (The late 2000's) W: 69
Gregoire, Paul [Canadian religious leader] G: 387
Gregor, William [English scientist]
Titanium T: 300
Gregori, Johann [German author]
Russian literature (Western influences) R: 559
Gregorian calendar G: 387
Calendar (Some calendars today) C: 29; (The
Gregorian calendar) C: 32
Julian calendar J: 187
Month M: 767
Gregorian chant [music]
Classical music (The Middle Ages) Ci: 645
Song So: 592
Gregorius [poem by Hartmann von Aue]
Hartmann von Aue H: 79
Gregory [antipope]
Pope (table) P: 666
Gregory I, Saint [pope] G: 387
Archbishop of Canterbury A: 601
Augustine of Canterbury, Saint A: 888
Benedict of Nursia, Saint B: 248
Classical music (The Middle Ages) Ci: 645
Pope (The early Middle Ages) P: 663 *with picture*
Gregory III, Saint [pope]
All Saints' Day A: 370
Gregory VII, Saint [pope] G: 387
Germany (The Holy Roman Empire) G: 162
Henry IV [of Germany] H: 187
Pope (The peak of papal power) P: 663
Gregory IX [pope] G: 388
Inquisition I: 277
Gregory X [pope] G: 388
Pope (Early days) P: 662
Gregory XIII [pope] G: 388
Calendar (The Gregorian calendar) C: 32
Julian calendar J: 187
Gregory XVI [pope]
Pope (table) P: 666
Gregory, Dick [American entertainer] G: 388
Gregory, Hanson [American sea captain]
Doughnut D: 312
Gregory, John Munford [American political leader]
Virginia (table) V: 417
Gregory, Lady [Irish dramatist] G: 388
Irish literature (The Irish literary revival) I: 431
Yeats, William Butler Y: 555
Gregory, Thomas W. [American government
official]
Justice, Department of (table) J: 203
Gregory, William [American political leader]
Rhode Island (table) R: 311
Greider, Carol W. [American biologist]
Nobel Prizes (Physiology or medicine: 2009)
N: 447
Greige [fabric]
Cotton (Spinning) Ci: 1091

Textile (Finishing the fabric) T: 217
Grein, Jacob T. [British producer]
Drama (Early realism) D: 338
Greiner, Ludwig [German dollmaker]
Doll (Papier-mâché and composition dolls)
D: 289-290
Gremlin [legendary creature] G: 388
Grenada [country] G: 388 *with picture and map*
Flag *picture on* F: 201
Grenadines G: 390
Reagan, Ronald Wilson (Foreign affairs) R: 168
War correspondent W: 26
West Indies *picture on* W: 204
Grenada [Mississippi]
Mississippi M: 623
Grenade [weapon] G: 390 *with diagram*
Grenadier [fish]
Deep sea (Fish) D: 82b-82c
Grenadier [soldier]
Grenade G: 390
Grenadines [islands, Caribbean Sea] G: 390
Grenada G: 388
Saint Vincent and the Grenadines S: 56
Grendel [literary figure]
Beowulf B: 256
Grenfell, Sir Wilfred Thomason [British doctor]
G: 390
Grenoble [France] G: 390
Grenville, George [British political leader]
Revolution, American (The Sugar Act) R: 272
United Kingdom (table: British prime ministers)
U: 72
Grenville, Lord [British political leader]
United Kingdom (table: British prime ministers)
U: 72
Grenville, Sir Richard [English military leader]
G: 390
Grès [pottery]
Stoneware So: 912
Gresham, Sir Thomas [English economist]
Gresham's law G: 391
Gresham, Walter Q. [American government
official]
Arthur, Chester Alan (table) A: 756
Cleveland, Grover (table) Ci: 672
Gresham's law [economics] G: 391
Gretzky, Wayne [Canadian hockey player] G: 391
with portrait
Greve, Félix Paul [Canadian author]
Grove, Frederick Philip G: 404
Grevy's zebra [animal]
Mammal *picture on* M: 116
Zebra Z: 587
Grew, Nehemiah [English botanist]
Botany (The development of modern botany)
B: 509
Grey, Albert Henry George [British statesman] *See*
Grey, Earl [1851-1917] *in this index*
Grey, Earl [1764-1845, British prime minister]
United Kingdom (table: British prime ministers)
U: 72
Grey, Earl [1851-1917, British statesman] G: 391
Grey Cup G: 391
Grey, Sir George [British colonial official]
New Zealand (The New Zealand Wars) N: 355
Grey, Henry [English nobleman]
Grey, Lady Jane G: 391
Grey, Lady Jane [queen of England] G: 391
Edward VI E: 113
Mary I M: 239
Ridley, Nicholas R: 336
Tower of London T: 351
Grey, Joel [American actor]
Motion picture (Best performance by an actor in
a supporting role: 1972) M: 862b
Grey, Zane [American author] G: 391
American literature (Popular forms) A: 422
Grey butcherbird [bird]
Bird (Birds of Australia and New Zealand) B: 346
with picture
Grey Cup [trophy] G: 391
Football (Canadian football) F: 364
Grey Glacier
Chile *picture on* C: 458
Grey heron [bird]
Heron (Kinds of herons) H: 214
Grey King, The [book by Cooper]
Cooper, Susan Ci: 1035
Grey Nuns [religious order]
Youville, Saint Marguerite d' Y: 574
Grey owl [bird]
Owl (Important owls) O: 884-886
Grey Owl [Canadian naturalist] G: 392
Greyhound [dog] G: 392
Dog *picture on* D: 270
Dog racing D: 282 *with picture*
Italian greyhound I: 492 *with picture*

Greyhound Bus Lines
 Minnesota (Transportation) M: 601
Greystoke, Lord [literary figure]
 Burroughs, Edgar Rice B: 711
Griboyedov, Alexander [Russian dramatist]
 Russian literature (Early Romanticism) R: 560-561
Grid [electrical device]
 Battery (Lead-acid batteries) B: 170
Grid [electronics]
 Vacuum tube (How a vacuum tube works) V: 258
Grid, Geographic [cartography] *See* Geographic grid *in this index*
Gridiron
 Football (The field) F: 354-355
Gridiron pattern
 City (Description) Ci: 585-586
Gridiron pendulum [instrument]
 Pendulum (Clock pendulums) P: 237-238 *with diagram*
Gridley, Reuel C. [American businessman]
 Nevada (Interesting facts about Nevada) N: 157 *with picture*
Grieg, Edvard [Norwegian composer] G: 392
 Grainger, Percy G: 302
Grier, Robert C. [American jurist]
 Supreme Court of the United States (table) So: 1000
Grievance process
 Industrial relations (The settlement of disputes) I: 245
 Labor movement (Arranging contracts) L: 4-6 *with pictures*
 Labor union L: 16
Griffey, Ken, Sr. [American baseball player]
 Griffey, Ken, Jr. G: 393
Griffey, Ken, Jr. [American baseball player] G: 393
Griffin [Greek mythology] G: 393
Griffin, Archie [American football player]
 Football (table) F: 363
Griffin, Charles [American educator]
 North Carolina (Schools) N: 476-477
Griffin, Marvin [American political leader]
 Georgia (table) G: 130
Griffin, Robert, III [American football player]
 Football (table) F: 363
Griffin, Walter Burley [American architect]
 Canberra (History) C: 166
Griffith, Arthur [Irish political leader] G: 393
 Ireland (The Easter Rising) I: 427
 Sinn Féin (History) S: 473
Griffith, Clark C. [American baseball player]
 Baseball (table: Hall of Fame) B: 134a
Griffith, D. W. [American director] G: 393
 Gish, Lillian G: 201
 Motion picture (D. W. Griffith) M: 864 *with picture*
Griffith, Hugh [British actor]
 Motion picture (Best performance by an actor in a supporting role: 1959) M: 862b
Griffith Foundation [organization]
 McConnell Family Foundation M: 332e
Griffith Park
 Los Angeles (Recreation) L: 467 *with picture*
Griffith Water Project [conservation]
 Nevada (The mid-1900's) N: 176
Griffon [dog]
 Dog *picture on* D: 274
 Wirehaired pointing griffon W: 344
Griffon [ship]
 Hennepin, Louis H: 185
Griggs, David [American geologist]
 Plate tectonics (History of tectonic theory) P: 564-565
Griggs, John W. [American government official]
 Justice, Department of (table) J: 203
 McKinley, William (table) M: 342
 New Jersey (table) N: 249
Grignard, François Auguste Victor [French chemist]
 Nobel Prizes (Chemistry: 1912) N: 443
Grigny, Nicolas de [French composer]
 Classical music (The Baroque period) Ci: 647
Grijalva, Juan de [Spanish explorer]
 Mexico (The Spanish conquest) M: 469
Grilling
 Cooking (Grilling and broiling) Ci: 1028
Grillparzer, Franz [Austrian dramatist]
 Austria (Literature) A: 933
Grimaldi, Francesco M. [Italian mathematician]
 Moon (Early observations with telescopes) M: 792
Grimaldi, Joseph [British actor]
 Clown Ci: 713
Grimaldi, Rainier Louis Henri Maxence Bertrand de [prince of Monaco] *See* Rainier III *in this index*
Grimaldi family [European history]
 Monaco (History) M: 700
Grimes, Burleigh [American baseball player]

 Baseball (table: Hall of Fame) B: 134a
Grimes, George [American prospector]
 Idaho (Exploration and early settlement) I: 42
Grimes, James W. [American political leader]
 Iowa (table) I: 391
Grimes, Martha [American author] G: 393
Grimké [American social reformers] G: 393 *with portraits*
Grimké, Angelina Emily [American social reformer]
 Grimké G: 393 *with portrait*
Grimké, John F. [American jurist]
 Grimké G: 393
Grimké, Sarah Moore [American social reformer]
 Grimké G: 393 *with portrait*
 Feminism F: 69
Grimm [German linguists] G: 394 *with portrait*
 See also Grimm's Fairy Tales *in this index*
 Folklore (Origins of folklore) F: 322
 Grimm's Fairy Tales G: 394
 Storytelling (The 1800's) So: 915
Grimm, Jakob Ludwig [German linguist]
 See also Grimm *in this index*
 Grimm G: 394
 Language (The science of language) L: 66-67
 Linguistics (Comparative and historical research) L: 337
 Mythology (Comparative approaches) M: 989
Grimm, Wilhelm Karl [German linguist]
 See also Grimm *in this index*
 Grimm G: 394
 Mythology (Comparative approaches) M: 989
Grimmelshausen, Johann Jakob Christoffel von [German author]
 German literature (Baroque literature) G: 139
Grimm's Fairy Tales G: 394
 Fairy (Fairy tales) F: 11 *with picture*
 Folklore (Origins of folklore) F: 322
 Grimm G: 394
 Mythology (Comparative approaches) M: 989
 Romanticism (Romanticism in literature) R: 427
 Storytelling (The 1800's) So: 915
Grímsvötn volcano
 Iceland (The inland plateau) I: 22
Grinding and polishing [industrial process] G: 394 *with pictures*
 Machine tool (Abrasive processes) M: 19
Grinding belt
 Grinding and polishing (Grinding tools) G: 395
Grinding stone
 Indian, American *pictures on* I: 140
Grinding wheel [tool]
 Grinding and polishing (Grinding tools) G: 395
 Machine tool *picture on* M: 17; (Abrasive processes) M: 18-19
Grinnell Glacier
 Global warming *pictures on* G: 232a
Grinnell Point
 Montana *picture on* M: 742
Griot [storyteller]
 Africa (Dance and music) A: 116a-116b
 Guinea (People) G: 430-431
Grippe [disease] *See* Influenza *in this index*
Gripper [printing]
 Offset O: 678
Gripping beast [art]
 Vikings (Cultural life and recreation) V: 381
Gris, Juan [Spanish painter] G: 395
 Collage Ci: 773
 Cubism Ci: 1181 *with picture*
 Modigliani, Amedeo *picture on* M: 686
 Painting (Still-life paintings) P: 33; (Cubism) P: 77-78
Griscom, Samuel [father of]
 Ross, Betsy R: 481
Griseofulvin [medication]
 Athlete's foot A: 858
Grisham, John [American author] G: 396
Grison [animal] G: 396 *with picture*
 Weasel W: 155
Grissini [food]
 Bread *picture on* B: 588
Grissom, Virgil Ivan [American astronaut] G: 396
 Astronaut (Accidents in space) A: 830-831
 Space exploration (Vostok and Mercury: The first human beings in space) So: 712-713 *with picture*; (Making ready) So: 715
Gristle *See* Cartilage *in this index*
Griswold, Dwight [American political leader]
 Nebraska (table) N: 110
Griswold, Matthew [American political leader]
 Connecticut (table) Ci: 967
Griswold, Morley [American political leader]
 Nevada (table) N: 173
Griswold, Roger [American political leader]
 Connecticut (table) Ci: 967
Griswold, Rufus [Poe's literary executor]

 Poe, Edgar Allan P: 589
Grit chamber
 Sewage (Primary treatment) S: 329
Grito de Dolores [Mexican history]
 Hidalgo y Costilla, Miguel H: 224
 Mexico (Revolt against the Spaniards) M: 470
Grits [food]
 Hominy H: 305
 Indian, American (Indians of the Southeast) I: 157
Grizzlies, Memphis [team]
 Basketball (table) B: 150
Grizzly bear G: 396 *with picture*
 Bear (Brown bears) B: 184 *with pictures*
 Lewis and Clark expedition (West to the Rockies) L: 222b
Grizzly Giant [tree]
 Yosemite National Park Y: 569
Groat [botany]
 Buckwheat B: 665
 Oatmeal O: 640
Groce, Jared [American farmer]
 Texas (Agriculture) T: 202
Grocery
 Food (Marketing) F: 335
Groenendael [dog]
 Belgian sheepdog B: 225 *with picture*
Groesbeck, Alexander J. [American political leader]
 Michigan (table) M: 507
Grofé, Ferde [American composer] G: 397
Grog Shop, The [book by Zola]
 Zola, Émile Z: 598
Grohl, Dave [American drummer]
 Nirvana N: 424
Groin [engineering]
 Jetty J: 116
Groined vault [architecture]
 Vault V: 291
Grolier Multimedia Encyclopedia, The
 Encyclopedia (Today's encyclopedias) E: 268b-269
Gromyko, Andrei Andreyevich [Soviet political leader] G: 397
Grønland [official name]
 Greenland G: 383
Gronouski, John Austin, Jr. [American government official]
 Johnson, Lyndon Baines (table) J: 151
 Kennedy, John Fitzgerald (table) K: 266
Groom
 Marriage (Wedding ceremonies) M: 220
Groome, James Black [American political leader]
 Maryland (table) M: 255
Grooming
 Chimpanzee (The life of a chimpanzee) C: 472 *with picture*
 Dog (Grooming) D: 278 *with picture*
 Hairdressing H: 11
 Horse (Grooming) H: 355 *with picture*
Groomsman
 Marriage (Wedding ceremonies) M: 220
Groot, Huig de [Dutch lawyer] *See* Grotius, Hugo *in this index*
Grooved terrain [geology]
 Satellite (Ganymede) S: 150a
Gropius, Walter [German architect] G: 397 *with picture*
 Architecture (Early modern architecture in Europe) A: 627-629; (Walter Gropius) A: 630 *with picture*
 Bauhaus B: 173
Gros, Antoine-Jean [French artist]
 Army *picture on* A: 727
Gros Bourdon, Le [bell]
 Montreal (Churches) M: 773
Gros Morne National Park [Newfoundland and Labrador]
 Canada (table: National parks and national park reserves) C: 113
 National park (table) N: 42g
 Newfoundland and Labrador (Places to visit) N: 368
Gros point [handicraft]
 Needlepoint N: 118
Gros Ventre Indians G: 398
Grosbeak [bird] G: 398 *with picture*
 Bird *picture on* B: 358; (Bills) B: 362 *with picture*
Groseilliers, Médard Chouart, Sieur des [French explorer] G: 398
 Hudson's Bay Company (Beginnings) H: 407
 Minnesota (Exploration) M: 603
 Radisson, Pierre Esprit R: 99
 Wisconsin (European exploration and settlement) W: 365
Gross, David J. [American physicist]
 Gluon G: 237
 Nobel Prizes (Physics: 2004) N: 442

Subatomic particle (The Standard Model) **So: 938**
Gross, Robert E. [American doctor]
Heart (Development of heart surgery) **H: 144**
Gross anatomy
Anatomy **A: 448b**
Gross combination weight rating [measure]
Truck (Kinds of trucks) **T: 457**
Gross domestic product [economics] **G: 399** *with diagrams*
See also individual country, state, and province articles
Depression **D: 150**
Economic indicator **E: 57**
Economics (The standard of living) **E: 62**
Income (National income and gross domestic product) **I: 101**; (International income comparisons) **I: 101-102**
National budget (Government spending) **N: 30**
National debt (National debt and GDP) **N: 33** *with diagrams*; (Economic growth and rising national debt) **N: 34**
Recession **R: 175**
Standard of living (Measuring standard of living) **So: 833**
Taxation (Taxes in the United States) **T: 53**
Gross Domestic Product Deflator [economics]
Inflation (Measuring inflation) **I: 267**
Gross income [economics]
Income (Gross and net income) **I: 100**
Income tax (Figuring the individual income tax) **I: 104**
Gross national income [economics]
World, History of the *map on* **W: 447**
Gross national product [economics]
Economic indicator **E: 57**
Gross domestic product (GDP versus GNP) **G: 399**
National income (Determining national income) **N: 37-38**
Gross tonnage [shipping]
Merchant marine **M: 413**
Ship (Nautical measurements) **S: 406**; (Flags and registration) **S: 412**
Grosse, Hans Werner [German aviator]
Glider (table) **G: 230**
Grosseteste, Robert [English scholar]
Physics (The Middle Ages) **P: 438**
Radiation (History) **R: 80**
Grossglockner [mountain, Austria]
Alps **A: 384** *with pictures*
Austria (Land and climate) **A: 933** *with map*
Grossmünster Church [Zurich]
Zurich *picture on* **Z: 609**
Grossularite [gem]
Garnet **G: 45**
Grosz, George [German painter] **G: 400** *with picture*
Beckmann, Max **B: 197**
Grósz, Károly [Hungarian political leader]
Hungary (Beginnings of change) **H: 448**
Grote Markt [square]
Antwerp (Chief buildings) **A: 561**
Grotesque [literature]
Anderson, Sherwood **A: 452**
Grotius, Hugo [Dutch lawyer] **G: 400**
International law (In early days) **I: 342**
Peace (From the 1400's to the 1700's) **P: 206**
Political science (Secularism) **P: 639**
Grotowski, Jerzy [Polish director]
Drama (Experimental theater) **D: 340**
Grotto of the Agony
Gethsemane **G: 175**
Grouch, The [play by Menander]
Drama (New Comedy) **D: 327**
Ground [art]
Painting (Grounds) **P: 36**
Ground [construction]
Plaster (Plastering) **P: 552**
Ground [electricity] **G: 401**
Ground [flag]
Flag *diagram on* **F: 194**
Ground beetle [insect]
Beetle *picture on* **B: 218**; (Ground beetles) **B: 217**
Ground-dove [bird]
Pigeon (The life of a pigeon) **P: 459**
Ground effect machine *See* Air cushion vehicle *in this index*
Ground-effects panel
Automobile racing (Indy and Champ car racing) **A: 977**
Ground-effects underbody
Automobile racing (Indy and Champ car racing) **A: 977**
Ground-finch [bird]
Bird (Birds of the Pacific Islands) **B: 349** *with picture*
Ground Forces of the Russian Federation
Army (The Russian army) **A: 726**

Ground hemlock [tree]
Yew **Y: 565** *with picture*
Ground-hog [animal] *See* Groundhog *in this index*
Ground iguana
Iguana **I: 50**
Ground ivy [plant]
Ivy **I: 522**
Lawn *picture on* **L: 143**
Ground-launched missile
Air force (Missiles) **A: 183**
Ground moraine [geology]
Glacier (How glaciers shape the land) **G: 203**
Ground pearl [shell]
Scale insect **S: 170**
Ground-penetrating radar
Archaeology (Locating sites) **A: 595-596**
Radar (In scientific research) **R: 68**
Ground rod
Lightning (Protection from lightning) **L: 301**
Ground sloth [extinct animal] **G: 401** *with picture*
Prehistoric animal *picture on* **P: 736**
Ground speed
Airplane (Measuring flying speed) **A: 225**
Ground squirrel [animal] **G: 401** *with picture*
Animal (Animals of the polar regions) **A: 484**
Squirrel (Types of squirrels) **So: 814b**
Ground state [physics]
Atom (Electron energy levels) **A: 873** *with diagram*
Laser (Producing laser light) **L: 84**
Ground station [astronomy]
Telephone *diagram on* **T: 96**
Ground stroke
Tennis (The ball in play) **T: 163**
Ground-to-cloud lightning
Lightning (Origin and destination) **L: 300**
Ground water [geology] **G: 401**
Environmental pollution (Water pollution) **E: 334**
Forest (Environmental value) **F: 391**
Hazardous wastes (Effects of hazardous wastes) **H: 122**
Hydrology **H: 470**
Irrigation (Ground water) **I: 456**
Landfill **L: 58** *with diagram*
River (Sources of river water) **R: 351**
Sinkhole **S: 473**
Spring **So: 806**
Thermal pollution **T: 253**
Water (Precipitation) **W: 120-121** *with diagram*; (Sources of supply) **W: 124**
Well (Water wells) **W: 193**
Wetland **W: 252a**
Ground wave [radio]
Radio (Transmitting AM band signals) **R: 87** *with diagram*
Ground zero
Nuclear weapon (Blast wave) **N: 599**
Groundhog [animal] *See* Woodchuck *in this index*
Groundhog Day [custom] **G: 402**
February **F: 60**
Woodchuck **W: 392**
Groundnut *See* Peanut *in this index*
Groundout
Baseball (Outs by batters) **B: 128-129**
Group [astronomy]
Galaxy (Interactions between galaxies) **G: 8b**
Group [mathematics]
Mathematics (Philosophies of mathematics) **M: 307**
Group [military unit]
Air force (The organization of air forces) **A: 183**
Navy (The organization of navies) **N: 77**
Group [scouting]
Girl Scouts (Girls Scouts of the USA) **G: 196**
Group [sociology]
Clothing (Identity) **Ci: 687**
Collective behavior **Ci: 774**
Community **Ci: 898**
Game theory **G: 23**
Group dynamics **G: 402**
Mammal (Group life) **M: 125**
Primate **P: 777**
Sociology **So: 564**
Group, The [book by McCarthy]
McCarthy, Mary **M: 332b**
Group A beta-hemolytic streptococcus [bacteria]
Erysipelas **E: 355**
Scarlet fever (Causes) **S: 173**
Strep throat **So: 925**
Streptococcus **So: 926**
Group annuity plan
Pension (Private pension plans) **P: 273**
Group dynamics [psychology] **G: 402**
Human relations **H: 428**
Lewin, Kurt **L: 220**
Morale **M: 800**
Social psychology **So: 552**

Group 47 [literary group]
Grass, Günter **G: 326**
Group health insurance
Insurance (How private health insurance is provided) **I: 311**
Group home
Children's home **C: 457**
Foster care **F: 428**
Group life insurance
Insurance (Major types of life insurance) **I: 309-310**
Group of Eight [organization]
Group of Twenty **G: 403**
Group of Seven [Canadian artists] **G: 402** *with picture*
Canada *picture on* **C: 110**; (Painting and sculpture) **C: 109**
Canadian literature (Literature between the world wars) **C: 158**
Jackson, Alexander Young **J: 5**
Thomson, Tom **T: 265**
Group of Seven [organization]
Group of Twenty **G: 402**
Group of Twenty [organization] **G: 402**
Group Portrait with Lady [book by Böll]
Böll, Heinrich **B: 448**
Group suicide
Suicide (Types) **So: 964**
Group Theatre
Method acting **M: 434**
Odets, Clifford **O: 674**
Group therapy
Drug abuse *picture on* **D: 364**
Mental illness (Psychotherapy) **M: 407-408**
Psychiatry (Psychotherapy) **P: 845**
Psychology *picture on* **P: 847**
Speech therapy (Treatment) **So: 774**
Group work
Social work (Methods of social work) **So: 558**
Grouper [fish] **G: 403** *with picture*
Goliath grouper **G: 267**
Grouse [bird] **G: 403** *with picture*
Bird (Other means of communication) **B: 354**
Ruffed grouse **R: 509** *with picture*
Grout [engineering]
Dam (Embankment dams) **D: 18**
Grout, Josiah [American political leader]
Vermont (table) **V: 333**
Grove, Frederick Philip [Canadian author] **G: 404**
Canadian literature (Literature between the world wars) **C: 158-159**
Grove, Lefty [American baseball player]
Baseball (table: Hall of Fame) **B: 134a**
Grover, La Fayette [American political leader]
Oregon (table) **O: 845**
Grover Cleveland [book by Nevins]
Nevins, Allan **N: 178**
Groves, Leslie R. [American military leader]
Manhattan Project **M: 141**
Growing-equity mortgage
Mortgage **M: 820**
Growth [biology] **G: 404**
Adolescent (Physical development) **A: 60-61**
Baby **B: 4** *with pictures, diagram on* **B: 8**
Hormone (Plant hormones) **H: 337**
Human growth hormone **H: 427**
Kwashiorkor **K: 398**
Life (Growth) **L: 275**
Life cycle **L: 280**
Plant (The growth of plants) **P: 535** *with diagrams*
Regeneration **R: 203**
Tropism **T: 451**
Growth, Economic *See* Economic growth *in this index*
Growth by accretion [geology]
Growth (In nonliving things) **G: 404**
Growth fund [economics]
Mutual fund **M: 969**
Growth hormone
DES **D: 153**
Dwarfism (Causes) **D: 394**
Genetic engineering (In agriculture) **G: 84c**
Giant **G: 183**
Heredity (The era of genetic engineering) **H: 209**
Hormone (Metabolic hormones) **H: 335-336**; (Growth and sex hormones) **H: 336**
Pituitary gland **P: 502**
Growth of the Soil, The [book by Hamsun]
Hamsun, Knut **H: 37**
Growth rate
Child (Physical differences) **C: 450**
Growth regulator herbicide
Herbicide (How herbicides work) **H: 198**
Growth ring [botany] *See* Annual ring *in this index*
Growth theory
Economics (Fields of economics) **E: 64**
Groznyy [Chechnya]

Chechnya C: **390** with map
Grub [entomology] G: **406**
Beetle (The life cycle of beetles) B: **216**
Insect (Complete metamorphosis) I: **293**
Lawn picture on L: **143**
Grubbs, Robert Howard [American chemist]
Nobel Prizes (Chemistry: 2005) N: **444**
Gruber, Eberhard [German religious leader]
Amanites A: **400**
Gruelle, Johnny [American cartoonist]
Doll (Before World War I) D: **291**
Indiana (Interesting facts) I: **197** with picture
Gruen, Victor [Austrian architect]
Gehry, Frank G: **76**
Gruening, Ernest [American political leader]
G: **406**
Gruentzig, Andreas [Swiss physician]
Heart (Progress in treatment and prevention)
H: **145**
Grumman Aircraft Corporation
Aviation (Aviation progress) A: **988-989**
Grünberg, Peter A. [German physicist]
Nobel Prizes (Physics: 2007) N: **442**
Grundtvig, Nicolai Frederik Severin [Danish poet]
Scandinavian literature (The Golden Age) S: **171**
Grundy, Felix [American government official]
Justice, Department of (table) J: **203**
Polk, James Knox (Education) P: **641**
Van Buren, Martin (table) V: **273**
Grunewald [district, Berlin]
Berlin (Recreation) B: **262**
Grünewald, Matthias [German painter] G: **406**
with picture
Grunge rock [music]
Nirvana N: **424**
Rock music (Alternative rock) R: **381**
Grunion [fish] G: **407** with picture
Biological clock (Other rhythms) B: **315**
Grunitzky, Nicolas [Togolese political leader]
Togo (History) T: **310-311**
Grunt [fish] G: **407**
Fish pictures on F: **155**
Grunting ox [animal]
Yak Y: **548**
Gruyère [cheese]
Cheese (Hard cheese) C: **392** with picture
Grybauskaite, Dalia [Lithuanian political leader]
Lithuania (Recent developments) L: **390-391**
Gryphius, Andreas [German author]
German literature (Baroque literature) G: **139**
GSA [organization] See General Services
Administration in this index
GS1 system
Bar coding B: **102**
GST [tax] See Goods and services tax in this index
Gstaad [Switzerland]
Europe picture on E: **381**
GTIN [code]
Bar coding B: **102**
GTL technology
Gas [fuel] (Gas as a raw material) G: **52**
Gu Kaizhi [Chinese painter] G: **407**
Painting (Chinese painting) P: **44** with picture
Guacamole [food]
Avocado A: **993**
Guácharo [bird]
Oilbird O: **708** with picture
Guácharo, Cave of the
Venezuela (The Andean Highlands) V: **302**
Guadalajara [Mexico] G: **407**
Guadalcanal, Battle of [1942]
World War II (The South Pacific) W: **489**
Guadalcanal Island [island, Coral Sea] G: **407**
Guadalupe bass [fish]
Bass (Black bass) B: **156**
Guadalupe Day [custom] G: **407**
Mexico (Holidays) M: **457-458**
Guadalupe Hidalgo, Treaty of [1848] G: **408**
Arizona (Spanish exploration) A: **688**
California (The Mexican War) C: **60-62**
Hispanic Americans (Conflict) H: **252**
Latin America (Early years of independence)
L: **107-108**
Mexican War (The peace treaty) M: **447**
State, Department of (Changing responsibilities)
So: **861**
Texas (Statehood and early progress) T: **207**
United States, History of the (The Mexican War)
U: **169**
Westward movement in America (The
Southwest) W: **249**
Guadalupe Mountains
Texas (Mountains) T: **198**
Guadalupe Mountains National Park [Texas]
G: **408**
National Park System (table: National parks) N: **48**
Guadalupe Peak [mountain]

Texas (Mountains) T: **198**
Guadeloupe [islands, Caribbean Sea] G: **408** with
maps
Guadiana River [Portugal-Spain]
Portugal (Rivers) P: **690**
Guajardo, Jesús [Mexican assassin]
Zapata, Emiliano Z: **587**
Guajira Peninsula [Colombia]
Colombia (The Coastal Lowlands) Ci: **782**
Guam [territory, Pacific] G: **408** with pictures and
map
Exploration (Magellan's globe-circling
expedition) E: **445**
Flag picture on F: **213**
Mariana Islands M: **199**
Territory (Territories in the United States) T: **174**
World War II (Island hopping in the Central
Pacific) W: **489-490**
Guan [bird] G: **409**
Guan [public official]
Mandarin M: **135**
Guan Hanqing [Chinese dramatist]
Chinese literature (Drama and fiction) C: **511**
Guanabara Bay [Brazil]
Rio de Janeiro R: **344** with picture
South America picture on So: **622**
Guanaco [animal] G: **409** with picture
Alpaca A: **381**
Argentina picture on A: **653**
Guanahani [island]
Columbus, Christopher (The first landing) Ci: **860**
Guanahatabey Indians
Cuba (Early years) Ci: **1175**
Guanajuato [state, Mexico]
Fox Quesada, Vicente F: **442**
Guanajuato [city, Mexico]
Mexico picture on M: **448**
Guangzhou [China] G: **410** with picture
City picture on Ci: **583**
Treaty port T: **409**
Guangzhou Baiyun International Airport
Airport (table) A: **245**
Guangzhou International Finance Center [China]
Skyscraper (table) S: **498**
Guanine [biochemistry]
Cell (DNA—the wondrous molecule) C: **334-335**
with diagram
DNA D: **258**
Heredity (The structure of DNA) H: **205**
RNA R: **357**
Guano [fertilizer] G: **411** with picture
Bird (As a source of food and raw materials)
B: **330-331**
Peru (Mining) P: **313**
Guantánamo [Cuba] G: **411**
Guantánamo Naval Base
Bush, George Walker (Homeland security)
B: **722g**
Cuba (History) Ci: **1175-1176**
Guantánamo G: **411**
Guar [plant] G: **411**
Guarani [language]
Paraguay (Languages) P: **145**; (The arts) P: **147**
Tupi-Guarani Indians T: **492**
Guarani Indians
Argentina (Early inhabitants) A: **655**
Brazil (History) B: **583**
Paraguay P: **144**; (People) P: **145**; (The arts)
P: **147**; (Early days) P: **148-149**
Tupi-Guarani Indians T: **492**
Guaranty G: **411**
Guaranty Building [Buffalo]
Architecture (Early modern architecture in
America) A: **629**
Sullivan, Louis Henri So: **970** with picture
Guard [sports]
Basketball (The players) B: **144**
Football (The offensive team) F: **356** with
diagrams
Guard, Changing of the [ceremony]
United Kingdom picture on U: **63**
Guard cell [botany]
Leaf (Obtaining the raw materials) L: **155** with
diagram
Guard hairs [zoology]
Fur F: **561** with picture
Mammal (Skin and hair) M: **118**
Guard of Honor [book by Cozzens]
Cozzens, James Gould Ci: **1114**
Guardhouse, The [painting by Teniers]
Teniers, David, the Younger picture on T: **133**
Guardia, Tomás [Costa Rican military leader]
Costa Rica (Revolutions and reforms) Ci: **1084**
Guardian [law] G: **411**
Guardian ad litem [law]
Guardian G: **411**
Guardian spirit [religion]

Indian, American (The guardian spirit) I: **147**
Guarini, Guarino [Italian architect]
Architecture (Baroque architecture) A: **622**
Guarneri [Italian violinmakers] G: **411**
Guarneri, Andrea [Italian violinmaker]
Guarneri G: **411**
Guarneri, Giuseppe [Italian violinmaker]
Guarneri G: **411**
Guarneri, Giuseppe Antonio [Italian violinmaker]
Guarneri G: **411**
Violin (History) V: **390**
Guarneri, Pietro [Italian violinmaker]
Guarneri G: **411**
Guatemala G: **412** with pictures and maps
See also Central America in this index and the list
of Related articles in the Guatemala article
Alvarado, Pedro de A: **398**
Belize (History) B: **238**
Clothing picture on Ci: **695**
Indian, American (Indians of Middle America)
I: **169**; (Current issues) I: **182-183**
Latin America picture on L: **104**; (Political
circumstances in the early to middle 1900's)
L: **109-110**
Valle, José Cecilio Del V: **265**
Guatemala City [Guatemala] G: **418**
Guatemala G: **412** with picture; (Population)
G: **414**; (Colonial period) G: **416**
Guava [fruit] G: **418** with picture
Guayacan [tree] See Lignum-vitae in this index
Guayaquil [Ecuador] G: **418**
Ecuador E: **67**
Guayas River
Ecuador (The Coastal Lowland) E: **69**
Guaymí Indians
Indian, American picture on I: **140**
Guayule [shrub] G: **418**
Rubber (The rubber tree) R: **502**
Gubbrud, Archie [American political leader]
South Dakota (table) So: **680**
Guden River
Denmark (Lakes and rivers) D: **138**
Gudrun [legendary figure]
Brunhild B: **652**
Gudvanga Tunnel [Norway]
Tunnel (table) T: **491**
Guebuza, Armando [Mozambican political leader]
Mozambique (History) M: **905-906**
Gueï, Robert [Ivorian political leader]
Côte d'Ivoire (History) Ci: **1084b-1085**
Guelder rose [plant]
Snowball S: **541** with picture
Guelphs and Ghibellines [Italian history] G: **418**
Italy (Rise of the city-states) I: **513-514**
Guenevere [legendary figure]
Arthur, King A: **757**
Lancelot, Sir L: **56**
Round Table (Origin) R: **491**; (The decline of the
Round Table) R: **491**
Guenon [animal] G: **419** with picture
Monkey diagram on M: **727**, picture on M: **728**
Guérin, Jules [American artist]
Lincoln Memorial L: **328**
Guermantes Way, The [book by Proust]
Proust, Marcel P: **838**
Guernica [painting by Picasso]
Picasso, Pablo (The 1920's and 1930's) P: **448b-
449** with picture
Spanish Civil War (Progress of the war) So: **756a**
Guernica [Spain]
Spanish Civil War (Progress of the war) So: **756a**
Guernsey [cattle]
Cattle (Guernsey) C: **310** with picture; (table)
C: **313**
Dairying (Dairy cattle) D: **6**
Guernsey [island, English Channel] G: **419**
Channel Islands C: **375** with map
Guerrero, Vicente [Mexican patriot]
Mexico (Independence) M: **470**
Guerrière [ship]
Constitution Ci: **995**
Hull, Isaac H: **412**
Guerrilla warfare G: **419** with picture
Commando Ci: **871**
Marion, Francis M: **211**
McKinley, William (America becomes a world
power) M: **341**
Palestine Liberation Organization P: **106**
Revolution (Features of revolution) R: **269**
Terrorism T: **175**
World War II (Resistance groups) W: **494**
Guerrillas [play by Hochhuth]
Hochhuth, Rolf H: **273**
Guest, Edgar Albert [American poet] G: **421**
Guest worker
Berlin (People) B: **262**
Germany (Ancestry) G: **147**

Immigration (Europe) I: 85
Guevara, Angel Anibal [Guatemalan political leader]
Guatemala (Political developments) G: 417
Guevara, Che [Argentine military leader] G: 421 *with portrait*
Bolivia (Return to military rule) B: 447
Cuba *picture on* Ci: 1168; (The Castro revolution) Ci: 1177-1178
Guerrilla warfare (History) G: 420
Latin America (Political circumstances in the early to middle 1900's) L: 109-110
Guevara, Ernesto "Che" *See* Guevara, Che *in this index*
Guggenheim, Daniel [American businessman]
Guggenheim, Meyer G: 421
Guggenheim, Meyer [American businessman] G: 421
Guggenheim, Murry [American businessman]
Guggenheim, Meyer G: 421
Guggenheim, Simon [American philanthropist]
Guggenheim, Meyer G: 421
Guggenheim, Solomon R. [American philanthropist]
Guggenheim, Meyer G: 422
Guggenheim Museum G: 421
Guggenheim foundations
Guggenheim, Meyer G: 421
Guggenheim Museum G: 421
Guggenheim Memorial Foundation, John Simon
Guggenheim, Meyer G: 422
Guggenheim Museum [New York City] G: 421
New York *picture on* N: 297
New York City (Museums) N: 338
Wright, Frank Lloyd (Later career) W: 508
Guggenheim Museum [Spain]
Bilbao B: 299
Gehry, Frank G: 76 *with picture*
GUI [computing] *See* Graphical user interface *in this index*
Guiana [region, South America] G: 422
Guiana Current [ocean current]
Caribbean Sea (Currents) C: 237
Guiana Highlands [region]
South America (The Eastern Highlands) So: 628 *with picture*
Guicciardini, Francesco [Italian historian]
History (The Humanist movement) H: 262
Guiccioli, Teresa [mistress of]
Byron, Lord (Byron's life) B: 748
Guidance [education] G: 422 *with picture*
Counseling Ci: 1096
Guidance eruption [dentistry]
Orthodontics O: 859
Guidance system
Guided missile (Guidance and control systems) G: 424; (Kinds of guidance systems) G: 426 *with diagrams*
Guide dog G: 422 *with pictures*
Tennessee T: 135 *with picture*
Guide for the Perplexed [book by Maimonides]
Hebrew literature (Medieval works) H: 162
Maimonides, Moses M: 67
Guided ammunition
Ammunition (Guided ammunition) A: 436
Guided bomb
Bomb (Kinds of bombs) B: 450 *with diagram*
Weapon (Recent developments) W: 154b
Guided democracy [Indonesian history]
Indonesia (Indonesia under Sukarno) I: 238
Guided missile [weapon] G: 423 *with pictures*
See also the list of Related articles in the Guided missile *article*
Air force (Aircraft and missiles) A: 183; (History) A: 184-186
Air Force, United States (Missiles) A: 191-192
Army, United States (Missiles) A: 735
Ballistics B: 56
Cuban missile crisis Ci: 1179
Laser (Guiding) L: 83
Missile boat M: 618
Navy, United States (Ordnance) N: 84
Nuclear weapon (Strategic nuclear weapons) N: 598; (Nuclear defense) N: 600
Radar (In the military) R: 65, R: 65
Rocket (Military use) R: 386
Guided missile cruiser [ship]
Cruiser Ci: 1159
Navy, United States (Combat ships) N: 84
Warship *picture on* W: 43; (Cruisers) W: 40
Guides [scouting]
Girl Scouts (Guides) G: 199
Guideway [train track]
Magnetic levitation train M: 55 *with picture*
Guido d'Arezzo [Italian musician]
Classical music (The Middle Ages) Ci: 645-646 *with picture*

Guidon [flag]
Flag (Military flags) F: 195-196 *with picture*
Guild [European history] G: 428
City (Economy) Ci: 584-585
Education (Christian education in the Middle Ages) E: 99
Industrial Revolution I: 246
Insurance (Earliest insurance) I: 315
Labor movement (Origins of the labor movement) L: 9
Middle Ages (Medieval towns) M: 527
Mystery play M: 972
Textile (During the Middle Ages) T: 218-219
Guild, Curtis, Jr. [American political leader]
Massachusetts (table) M: 288
Guilder [money] G: 429
Guilford, Earl of [British statesman]
North, Lord N: 457
Guilford Courthouse, Battle of [1781]
North Carolina (Revolution and independence) N: 492
Revolution, American (table) R: 276; (Cowpens and Guilford Courthouse) R: 285
Guilford Courthouse National Military Park [North Carolina]
National Park System (table: National military parks) N: 55
Guilin [China]
China *pictures on* C: 484, C: 494
Guillaume, Charles Édouard [French physicist]
Nobel Prizes (Physics: 1920) N: 440
Guillaume de Lorris [French poet]
French literature (Narrative poetry) F: 518
Guillemin, Roger Charles Louis [American physiologist]
Nobel Prizes (Physiology or medicine: 1977) N: 446
Guillemot [bird] G: 429 *with picture*
Auk A: 890
Guillén, Nicolás [Cuban poet]
Latin American literature (The mid-1900's) L: 114
Guillén, Rafael [Mexican political leader] *See* Marcos, Subcomandante *in this index*
Guillotin, Joseph Ignace [French doctor]
Guillotine G: 429
Guillotine [machine] G: 429 *with picture*
Capital punishment (History of capital punishment) Ci: 193
French Revolution (Terror and equality) F: 526-527
Paris (Gardens, squares, and parks) P: 162-163
Reign of Terror R: 207
Guinand, Pierre-Louis [French chemist]
Glass (table) G: 218
Guinea [region, Africa] G: 429
Guinea [country] G: 430 *with pictures and map*
Flag *picture on* F: 199
French West Africa F: 528 *with map*
Guinea [money] G: 432
Money (History of the pound) M: 709-710
Guinea-Bissau G: 432 *with picture and map*
Flag *picture on* F: 199
Guinea G: 429
Portugal (Empire and wealth) P: 693-694 *with map*
Guinea fowl [bird]
Poultry P: 720
Guinea pig [animal] G: 434 *with picture*
Cavy C: 322
Guineafowl [bird] G: 435 *with picture*
Bird (Birds of Africa) B: 344h *with picture*
Guinée, République de [official name]
Guinea G: 430
Guinevere [legendary figure] *See* Guenevere *in this index*
Guinizelli, Guido [Italian poet]
Italian literature (The Middle Ages) I: 494
Guinn, Kenny [American political leader]
Nevada (table) N: 173
Guinness, Alec [British actor] G: 435 *with portrait*
Motion picture (Best performance by an actor: 1957) M: 862a
Guion, John I. [American political leader]
Mississippi (table) M: 640
Güiraldes, Ricardo [Argentine author]
Latin American literature (The early 1900's) L: 113
Guiscard, Robert [Norman conqueror]
Normans N: 456
Guiscard, Roger [Norman conqueror]
Normans N: 456
Guise, Henry of [French nobleman] *See* Henry of Guise *in this index*
Guise, Mary of [historic figure] *See* Mary of Guise *in this index*
Guise family [French history]
Huguenots H: 410
Guitar [musical instrument] G: 435 *with pictures*

See also Electric guitar *in this index*
Christian, Charlie C: 522d
Country music (The instruments) Ci: 1098
Jazz (The guitar) J: 69
Segovia, Andrés S: 284
Guitar [sculpture by Picasso]
Picasso, Pablo (Cubism) P: 448b
Sculpture (Cubism and futurism) S: 257 *with picture*
Guitar Hero [electronic game]
Electronic game (Broadening audiences) E: 204f
Guiteau, Charles J. [American assassin]
Arthur, Chester Alan (Assassination of Garfield) A: 756
Garfield, James Abram (Assassination) G: 42
Guittone d'Arezzo [Italian poet]
Italian literature (The Middle Ages) I: 494
Guizot, François Pierre Guillaume [French historian]
History (History in the universities) H: 262-263
Gujarat [state, India]
India (Recent developments) I: 134-135
Mumbai (History) M: 925
Gujarati [language]
India (Languages) I: 114
Gulab Singh [ruler of Kashmir]
Kashmir (History) K: 248
Gulag [prison]
Concentration camp (Other concentration camps) Ci: 927
Gulag Archipelago, 1918-1956, The [book by Solzhenitsyn]
Solzhenitsyn, Alexander So: 587
Gulden [money]
Guilder G: 429
Gules [color]
Heraldry (Expansion) H: 194 *with picture*
Gulf [geography] G: 436
Ocean (The world ocean) O: 651
Gulf and Ship Island Railroad
Gulfport G: 439
Gulf Between, The [film]
Technicolor T: 73
Gulf Coast [Alabama]
Alabama (Coastline) A: 268
Gulf Coastal Plain [region, North America]
United States (The Gulf Coastal Plain) U: 124
Gulf Cooperation Council
Oman (History) O: 759
United Arab Emirates (History) U: 45
Gulf Intracoastal Waterway [North America] G: 436 *with map*
Louisiana (Transportation) L: 495
Texas (Transportation) T: 202-203
Gulf Islands National Park Reserve [British Columbia]
Canada (table: National parks and national park reserves) C: 113
Gulf Islands National Seashore [Florida-Mississippi]
National Park System (table: National seashores) N: 57
Gulf of Alaska
Alaska (Coastline) A: 294
Exxon Valdez oil spill E: 459
Gulf of Aqaba
Arab-Israeli conflict (The 1967 war) A: 582a
Red Sea R: 189
Gulf of Bothnia
Baltic Sea B: 65 *with map*
Sweden (The Mountain Range) So: 1028 *with picture and map*
Gulf of California G: 436 *with map*
Gulf of California harbor porpoise [sea animal]
Porpoise P: 679
Gulf of Carpentaria [Australia]
Exploration (Exploring Australia's interior) E: 448
Gulf of Finland
Baltic Sea B: 65 *with map*
Gulf of Fonseca
Honduras (The Southern Coast) H: 310 *with map*
Gulf of Gascony
Bay of Biscay B: 176
Gulf of Genoa
Genoa G: 89 *with picture*
Gulf of Mexico G: 436 *with map*
See also Gulf oil spill of 2010 *in this index*
Flood (Seacoast floods) F: 237
Florida *picture on* F: 243
Gulf oil spill of 2010 G: 437
Hurricane Katrina (The storm) H: 456
La Salle, René-Robert Cavelier, Sieur de (Expeditions to the Gulf of Mexico) L: 80 *with map*
Tornado (How a tornado forms) T: 334
Gulf of Oman

Persian Gulf **P:** 300 *with map*
Gulf of Riga
Estonia (Land and climate) **E:** 361 *with map*
Gulf of Saint Lawrence G: 437
Gulf of Suez
Red Sea **R:** 189
Gulf of Taganrog
Azov, Sea of **A:** 998
Gulf of Thailand
China Sea **C:** 508 *with map*
Gulf of Tonkin
China Sea **C:** 508 *with map*
Gulf of Tonkin Resolution [U.S. history]
Johnson, Lyndon Baines (Foreign affairs) **J:** 149
Vietnam War (The Gulf of Tonkin incident) **V:** 375
Gulf oil spill of 2010 G: 437
Alabama (The 2000's) **A:** 279
BP **B:** 542
Florida (The early 2000's) **F:** 265
Louisiana (The early 2000's) **L:** 501
Mississippi (The early 2000's) **M:** 645
Obama, Barack (Oil rig disaster) **O:** 640h
Oil spill (Notable spills) **O:** 708 *with picture*
Petroleum (Spills and seeps) **P:** 345
United States, History of the (Environmental
disaster) **U:** 196f
Gulf porpoise [sea animal]
Porpoise **P:** 679
Gulf Stream [Atlantic] **G:** 437 *with picture and map*
Arctic Ocean (Glacial ice) **A:** 641
Atlantic Ocean (Currents) **A:** 866
Europe (Climate) **E:** 395-397
Franklin, Benjamin (Other studies) **F:** 489
Gulf of Mexico **G:** 437
Ocean (Circulation) **O:** 658
Gulf War [1991] *See* Persian Gulf War of 1991 *in
this index*
Gulf War syndrome [disorder] **G:** 438
Persian Gulf War of 1991 (Consequences of the
war) **P:** 300e
Gulfport [Mississippi] **G:** 438
Gulfweed [plant]
Seaweed (Kinds) **S:** 276 *with picture*
Gulick, Charlotte Vetter [American educator]
Camp Fire USA (History) **C:** 90
Gulick, Luther Halsey [American educator]
Camp Fire USA (History) **C:** 90
Gulistan [book by Saadi]
Islamic art *picture on* **I:** 469
Gull [bird] **G:** 439 *with pictures*
Bird *pictures on* **B:** 330, **B:** 353; (Birds of inland
waters and marshes) **B:** 340 *with picture*; (Birds
of the seacoasts) **B:** 342 *with picture*
Instinct (How instinctive behavior works) **I:** 304-
305
Gullah [people] **G:** 439
Gullet [anatomy]
Esophagus **E:** 357
Paramecium **P:** 152
Gulliver, Lemuel [literary figure]
Gulliver's Travels **G:** 440
Swift, Jonathan: (*Gulliver's Travels*) **So:** 1040 *with
picture*
Gulliver's Travels [book by Swift] **G:** 440
English literature (Swift and Pope) **E:** 318
Literature for children (The 1700's) **L:** 362
Swift, Jonathan **So:** 1039 *with picture*
Gull's Hornbook, The [book by Dekker]
Dekker, Thomas **D:** 94
Gullstrand, Allvar [Swedish ophthalmologist]
Nobel Prizes (Physiology or medicine: 1911)
N: 445
Gully [natural feature]
Mars (Channels, valleys, and gullies) **M:** 226 *with
picture*
GUM [department store]
Moscow (Famous landmarks) **M:** 823-824 *with
map*
Gum [industrial product] **G:** 440
See also Bubble gum; Chewing gum *in this index*
Gum arabic [tree product]
Acacia **A:** 20
Gum **G:** 440
Lithography (How lithography works) **L:** 387
Gum elastic [compound]
Invention (The inventive process) **I:** 355-357
Gum eraser [compound]
Eraser **E:** 349
Gum resin
Resin (Natural resins) **R:** 259
Gum rosin [by-product]
Rosin **R:** 480
Gum tissue
Dentistry (Periodontics) **D:** 144
Gum tree G: 440
Australia (Native plants) **A:** 911-912
Gum turpentine [tree product]

Turpentine **T:** 519
Gumbo [plant] *See* Okra *in this index*
Gumm, Frances [birth name of]
Garland, Judy **G:** 44
Gums [anatomy]
Teeth (Periodontal diseases) **T:** 85
Gun G: 440
Ballistics (Interior ballistics) **B:** 56
Flintlock (Flintlock) **F:** 236 *with picture*
Forensic science (Firearms) **F:** 389 *with picture*
Navy (The history of navies) **N:** 79
Weapon (Firearms) **W:** 154b
Whitney, Eli (Arms manufacturer) **W:** 295
Gun control [law] **G:** 440
National Rifle Association of America **N:** 60
Second Amendment **S:** 278
Gun director [equipment]
Warship (Warships in the two world wars) **W:** 41
Gun-type method
Nuclear weapon *diagram on* **N:** 598; (Fission
weapons) **N:** 596-597
Gunboat diplomacy [U.S. history]
Latin America (United States involvement) **L:** 109
Guncotton [explosive] **G:** 441
Gunpowder (History) **G:** 441
Gunderson, Carl [American political leader]
South Dakota (table) **So:** 680
Gundog *See* Sporting dog *in this index*
Gunn, Thomas [American poet]
American literature (Diverse voices) **A:** 424
Gunnbjørn Fjeld [mountain, Greenland]
Greenland (The land) **G:** 385 *with map*
Gunnbjörn Ulfsson [Norse explorer]
Exploration (Viking exploration) **E:** 442
Gunnison River [Colorado]
Black Canyon of the Gunnison National Park
B: 385
Gunpowder [explosive] **G:** 441
Army (Ancient armies) **A:** 726-727; (Armies in the
Middle Ages) **A:** 727
Firearm (History) **F:** 133
Fireworks **F:** 135
Invention (The Renaissance) **I:** 360
Weapon (Gunpowder weapons) **W:** 154b
Gunpowder Plot [English history] **G:** 442
Fawkes, Guy **F:** 57
Guns of August, The [book by Tuchman]
Tuchman, Barbara Wertheim **T:** 480
Gunship
Air force (Aircraft and missiles) **A:** 183
Aircraft, Military (Helicopters) **A:** 203-204
Helicopter (Further improvements) **H:** 171-174
Gunston Hall [estate]
Virginia (Places to visit) **V:** 408
Gunter, Julius C. [American political leader]
Colorado (table) **Ci:** 844
Gunter's chain [measuring device]
Surveying (Early tools) **So:** 1011
Guntersville Dam [Alabama]
Alabama (Rivers and lakes) **A:** 270
Guntersville Lake [Alabama]
Alabama (Rivers and lakes) **A:** 270
Gunther [legendary figure]
Nibelungenlied **N:** 395
Gunther, Fritz [German chemist]
Detergent and soap (The development of
detergents) **D:** 165
Gunung Agung [mountain, Bali]
Bali **B:** 41
Gunung Leuser National Park [Indonesia]
Conservation *picture on* **Ci:** 975
National park (table) **N:** 42f
Gunwale
Canoeing (Entering and leaving a canoe) **C:** 180
Günz ice age [geology]
Ice age (Evidence of ice ages and their climates)
I: 6-7
Guoyu [language]
Chinese language (Spoken Chinese) **C:** 510
Taiwan (People) **T:** 16
Guppy [fish] **G:** 442 *with picture*
Animal *picture on* **A:** 490
Fish *picture on* **F:** 157
Tropical fish **T:** 451
Guppy, R. J. L. [British scientist]
Guppy **G:** 442
Gupta dynasty [history of India] **G:** 442 *with picture*
India (The golden age) **I:** 129 *with map*
World, History of the (The Mauryan Empire in
India) **W:** 430-431 *with picture*
Gurdwara [religion]
Sikhism (Beliefs and practices) **S:** 455
Gurik, Robert [Canadian dramatist]
Canadian literature (Modern Canadian drama)
C: 161
Gurkhas [people] **G:** 443
Nepal (People) **N:** 125

Gurnard [fish] **G:** 443
Guru [person]
Buddhism (The Vajrayana) **B:** 669
Hinduism (Veneration of holy people) **H:** 237
Sikhism (History) **S:** 455
Yoga **Y:** 566
Guru Granth Sahib [book]
Sikhism (Beliefs and practices) **S:** 455
Gurunsi [people]
Burkina Faso (People) **B:** 706
Gusenbauer, Alfred [Austrian political leader]
Austria (Recent developments) **A:** 940
Gusev Crater [Mars]
Mars (Observation by spacecraft) **M:** 226c-226d
Mars Exploration Rover Mission **M:** 227
Space exploration *picture on* **So:** 709
Gusher [oil well]
Petroleum (table) **P:** 332; (Growth of the
petroleum industry) **P:** 347
Gusmão, José Alexandre [Timorese political
leader]
East Timor (History) **E:** 41-42
Gusset [fold]
Paper bag **P:** 138
Gustafsson, Greta Lovisa [birth name of]
Garbo, Greta **G:** 28
Gustav I Vasa [king of Sweden] **G:** 443
Helsinki **H:** 179
Sweden (The beginnings of modern Sweden)
So: 1033
Gustav Line [World War II]
World War II (The invasion of Italy) **W:** 483
Gustavo Capanema Palace
Niemeyer, Oscar **N:** 406
Gustavus II [king of Sweden] *See* Gustavus
Adolphus *in this index*
Gustavus Adolphus [king of Sweden] **G:** 443
Army (The rise of modern armies) **A:** 727
Sweden *picture on* **So:** 1033; (The age of
expansion) **So:** 1034
Thirty Years' War (The Swedish period) **T:** 260
Guston, Philip [American painter] **G:** 444
Gutenberg, Johannes [German printer] **G:** 444
Bible *picture on* **B:** 280
Book (The development of printed books) **B:** 466
Communication (The invention of movable type)
Ci: 880
Invention (The Renaissance) **I:** 360-361
Library (Paper, printing, and libraries) **L:** 260
Printing **P:** 796; (The invention of movable type)
P: 803 *with picture*
Printing press **P:** 804
Type (History) **T:** 537
Gutenberg Bible
Bible *pictures on* **B:** 280, **B:** 286
Book (The development of printed books) **B:** 466
Gutenberg, Johannes **G:** 444
Library of Congress **L:** 263
Guth, Alan H. [American physicist]
Inflation theory **I:** 268a
Guthrie [Oklahoma]
Oklahoma (Interesting facts) **O:** 713
Guthrie, A. B., Jr. [American author] **G:** 444
Guthrie, Arlo [American singer]
Guthrie, Woody **G:** 445
Guthrie, James [American government official]
Pierce, Franklin (table) **P:** 456
Guthrie, Janet [American race driver]
Automobile racing (Automobile racing today)
A: 980
Guthrie, Samuel [American chemist]
Chloroform **C:** 517
Guthrie, Tyrone [British director] **G:** 444
Guthrie, Woody [American singer] **G:** 444
Popular music (The folk music revival) **P:** 671
Guthrie Theater [Minneapolis]
Guthrie, Tyrone **G:** 444
Minneapolis (Cultural life) **M:** 582
Minnesota (Places to visit) **M:** 594 *with picture*
Guthrum [Danish military leader]
Alfred the Great **A:** 349
Gutians [ancient people]
Babylonia (The Akkadian and Neo-Sumerian
periods) **B:** 14
Gutiérrez, Antonio García [Spanish dramatist]
Spanish literature (The 1800's) **So:** 761
Gutierrez, Carlos M. [American government
oficial]
Commerce, Department of (table) **Ci:** 871
Gutiérrez, Gustavo [Peruvian clergyman]
Latin America (The rise of military regimes) **L:** 110
Liberation theology **L:** 228
Gutiérrez, José Ángel [American social reformer]
G: 445 *with portrait*
Hispanic Americans (The Chicano movement)
H: 256
Gutiérrez, Lucio [Ecuadorean political leader]

Ecuador (The 1900's) **E:** 73-74
GUT's [physics] *See* Grand unified theories *in this index*
Gutta-percha [tree product] **G:** 445
Gutter [bowling]
Bowling (The lane) **B:** 523
Guttero, Alfredo [Argentine painter]
Argentina (The arts) **A:** 651-652
Gutty [ball]
Golf (Beginnings) **G:** 264
Guy, John [English settler]
Newfoundland and Labrador (Colonization) **N:** 375
Guy, William L. [American political leader]
North Dakota (table) **N:** 513
Guy Fawkes Day [custom]
Fawkes, Guy **F:** 57
Guy line
Crane **Ci:** 1120 *with pictures*
Guy Mannering [book by Scott]
Dandie Dinmont terrier **D:** 32
Guy of Warwick [legendary figure] **G:** 445
Guyana G: 445 *with picture and map*
Flag *picture on* **F:** 201
Indian, American (Indians of the Tropical forest) **I:** 175
Guyana, University of
Guyana (People) **G:** 445-446
Guyenne [province, France]
Hundred Years' War **H:** 437
Guyot [oceanography]
Seamount **S:** 268
Guyot, Mount [North Carolina-Tennessee]
Great Smoky Mountains **G:** 348
Guys and Dolls [musical]
Loesser, Frank **L:** 420
Runyon, Damon **R:** 521
Guy's Hospital [London]
Addison, Thomas **A:** 48
Guzmán, Antonio [Dominican Republic political leader]
Dominican Republic (History) **D:** 304-305
Guzmán Blanco, Antonio [Venezuelan political leader]
Venezuela (Rule by dictatorships) **V:** 304
Guzmán de Alfarache [book by Alemán]
Spanish literature (The 1600's) **So:** 759
Guzmán Huerta, Rodolfo [Mexican wrestler] *See* Santo, El *in this index*
Guzmán Reynoso, Abimael [Peruvian political leader]
Peru (Peru under Fujimori) **P:** 316
Gwaii Haanas National Park [British Columbia]
Canada (table: National parks and national park reserves) **C:** 113
Gwenn, Edmund [British actor]
Motion picture (Best performance by an actor in a supporting role: 1947) **M:** 862a
Gwin, William M. [American political leader]
Pony express **P:** 657
Gwinnett, Button [American patriot] **G:** 447
Gwoyeu Romatzyh [Chinese language]
Lin Yutang **L:** 309
Gwyn, Nell [English actress] **G:** 447
Gwynn, Tony [American baseball player]
Baseball (table: Hall of Fame) **B:** 134a
Gyanendra [king of Nepal]
Nepal (History) **N:** 126-127
Gymnasium [secondary school]
Education (Ancient Greek education) **E:** 98
Germany (Education) **G:** 151-152
Hungary (Education) **H:** 441
Gymnasium [sports] **G:** 447
Physical education (Early history) **P:** 433
Safety (Safety at school) **S:** 11-12
Gymnastics [sport] **G:** 447 *with pictures*
Comaneci, Nadia **Ci:** 866
Olympic Games (Summer Olympic Games) **O:** 746e-746f *with picture*
Gymnopédies [music by Satie]
Satie, Erik **S:** 150h
Gymnosperm [botany] **G:** 451 *with picture*
Angiosperm **A:** 462
Cotyledon **Ci:** 1095
Earth (The Mesozoic Era) **E:** 27-28
Flower **F:** 271; (The evolution of flowering plants) **F:** 299
Plant (Gymnosperms) **P:** 520 *with pictures*; (The evolution of plants) **P:** 544-545; (Classification of plants) **P:** 546-547 *with pictures*
Seed **S:** 280 *with diagram*
Tree *pictures on* **T:** 417; (Needleleaf trees) **T:** 414-415
Gynecology [medicine]
Medicine (table) **M:** 369
Obstetrics and gynecology **O:** 646
Surgery (Obstetrics and gynecology) **So:** 1007

Győr [Hungary] **G:** 451
Gypsies [people] *See* Roma *in this index*
Gypsum [mineral] **G:** 451
Alabaster **A:** 280
Cement and concrete (Raw materials) **C:** 344
Crystal (Classifying crystals) **Ci:** 1166-1167 *with picture*
Mineral *picture on* **M:** 569
Plaster of Paris **P:** 553
Wallboard **W:** 17
Gypsum flower [geology]
Cave (Speleothems) **C:** 319
Gypsum Hills [Oklahoma]
Oklahoma (Land regions) **O:** 724-726 *with map*
Gypsy [musical]
Merman, Ethel **M:** 418
Gypsy moth [insect] **Ci:** 452 *with picture*
Insect *picture on* **I:** 285
Moth *picture on* **M:** 839; (Tussock moths) **M:** 841 *with picture*
Tussock moth **T:** 526
Gyre [oceanography]
Atlantic Ocean (Moving ocean waters) **A:** 866
Ocean (Circulation) **O:** 658
Pacific Ocean (Currents) **P:** 14-15
Gyrfalcon [bird]
Falcon (The gyrfalcon) **F:** 14 *with picture*
Gyro [tool]
Gyroscope **G:** 453 *with pictures*
Gyrocompass [instrument] **G:** 452
Compass (Deviation) **Ci:** 903
Inertial guidance (History) **I:** 264
Sperry, Elmer Ambrose **So:** 779
Gyronny [symbol]
Heraldry *picture on* **H:** 195
Gyroscope [tool] **G:** 453 *with pictures*
Automatic flight control (How an AFCS works) **A:** 944
Foucault, Jean Bernard Léon **F:** 429
Gyrocompass **G:** 452
Inertial guidance **I:** 263; (Gyroscopic systems) **I:** 263; (History) **I:** 264
Laser (Guiding) **L:** 83
Sperry, Elmer Ambrose **So:** 779
Top (Kinds of tops) **T:** 331
Gyroscopic compass *See* Gyrocompass *in this index*
Gyroscopic inertia [physics]
Gyroscope (Gyroscopic properties) **G:** 453
Gyroscopic precession [physics]
Ballistics (Exterior ballistics) **B:** 56
Gyroscope (Gyroscopic properties) **G:** 453-454 *with diagram*
Gyurcsány, Ferenc [Hungarian political leader]
Hungary (Recent developments) **H:** 448

H

H [letter] **H:** 1 *with pictures*
H [slang]
Heroin **H:** 213
H [symbol]
Henry **H:** 185
Hydrogen **H:** 468
H1N1 virus
Swine flu **So:** 1048
H₂ [element]
Hydrogen **H:** 468
H-2 [rocket]
Space exploration *picture on* **So:** 699; (Japan) **So:** 726-727
H-2A [rocket]
International Space Station **I:** 346b
H₂O [compound]
Compound **Ci:** 906
Water (The chemistry of water) **W:** 129 *with diagram*
H. M. Pulham, Esq. [book by Marquand]
Marquand, John Phillips **M:** 217
H-R-R test
Color blindness **Ci:** 827
H. W. Lay Company
PepsiCo, Inc. **P:** 279
Ha-am, Ahad [Hebrew poet]
Hebrew literature (Modern Hebrew literature) **H:** 162-163
Ha Ha Bay [Quebec]
Saguenay River **S:** 20
Haab [calendar]
Calendar (The Maya) **C:** 31
Haakon IV [king of Norway]
Norway (The Viking period) **N:** 545
Haakon VI [king of Norway]
Denmark (A great power) **D:** 139
Haakon VII [king of Norway]
Norway (Independence) **N:** 546; (World War II) **N:** 546
Ha'apai [islands]
Tonga (Land) **T:** 328 *with map*

Haarde, Geir [Icelandic political leader]
Iceland (Recent developments) **I:** 24
HAART [medicine]
AIDS (Treatment) **A:** 164b-165
Haas, Ernst [Austrian-American photographer]
Photography *picture on* **P:** 428; (A diversity of styles) **P:** 426-427
Haavelmo, Trygve [Norwegian economist]
Nobel Prizes (Economics: 1989) **N:** 449
Habakkuk [Biblical figure]
Habakkuk, Book of **H:** 2
Habakkuk, Book of [Bible] **H:** 2
Habana, La [Cuba] *See* Havana *in this index*
"Habañera" [aria]
Opera: *(Carmen)* **O:** 802-803
Habeas corpus [law] **H:** 2 *with pictures*
Civil rights (Due process) **Ci:** 608
Civil War, American (Government and politics) **Ci:** 622
Freedom (Social freedom) **F:** 501
Law (The Middle Ages) **L:** 134-135
Habeas Corpus Amendment Act [1679]
Habeas corpus **H:** 2
Haber, Fritz [German chemist]
Chemistry (Growth of industrial chemistry) **C:** 405
Haber process **H:** 2
Nobel Prizes (Chemistry: 1918) **N:** 443
Haber-Bosch process *See* Haber process *in this index*
Haber process [chemistry] **H:** 2
Hydrogen (Uses) **H:** 469
Nitrogen (Production of nitrogen compounds) **N:** 426
Habibie, Bacharuddin Jusuf [Indonesian political leader]
Indonesia (The fall of Suharto) **I:** 239
Habibullah Khan [emir of Afghanistan]
Afghanistan (The Anglo-Afghan wars) **A:** 95
Habichtsburg [Aargau, Switzerland]
Habsburg, House of **H:** 3
Habimah [theater]
Israel (The arts) **I:** 482
Habit [clothing]
Friar **F:** 532
Habit [geology]
Mineral (Other identification tests) **M:** 567
Habit [psychology] **H:** 2
Learning (Theories of learning) **L:** 163-164
Habitable zone [astronomy]
Planet (The first discoveries) **P:** 513-514
Habitant [Canadian history]
Canada *picture on* **C:** 110; (Painting and sculpture) **C:** 109
Drummond, William Henry **D:** 368
Habitant, The [poems by Drummond]
Drummond, William Henry **D:** 368
Habitant Farm, The [painting by Krieghoff]
Canada *picture on* **C:** 110
Habitat [biology] **H:** 3
Animal (Where animals live) **A:** 473; (How human beings endanger animals) **A:** 504; (Habitat restoration) **A:** 505
Aquarium, Public (Displaying exhibits) **A:** 578b
Automobile (Damage to natural habitats) **A:** 963
Endangered species (Loss of habitat) **E:** 269
Extinction (Modern extinction) **E:** 456-457
Flower (Wildflowers) **F:** 282
Invasive species (How invasive species affect habitats) **I:** 354j
Lake (The lake habitat) **L:** 33
Ocean (Habitat modification) **O:** 665
Plant (Where plants live) **P:** 520; (Habitat destruction) **P:** 543
Raccoon (The life of a raccoon) **R:** 50
Habitat [laboratory]
Diving, Underwater (History) **D:** 247
Habitat 67 [housing development, Montreal]
Montreal (Housing) **M:** 772
Safdie, Moshe **S:** 8
Habitat for Humanity [organization]
Atlanta (Social problems) **A:** 860a
Carter, Jimmy (Later years) **C:** 259
Habitat fragmentation [biology]
Butterfly (Butterflies and environmental change) **B:** 743
Plant (Habitat destruction) **P:** 543
Habitat management
Wildlife conservation (Methods of wildlife conservation) **W:** 304
Habits of adjustment [psychology]
Habit (Kinds of habits) **H:** 3
Habré, Hissene [Chadian political leader]
Chad (History) **C:** 367-368
Habsburg, House of [European history] **H:** 3
Austria (The Habsburgs) **A:** 937 *with map*
Belgium (Habsburg rule) **B:** 233
Bohemia **B:** 437

Croatia (History) Ci: 1148a-1148b
Czech Republic (Habsburg rule) Ci: 1213
Franz Ferdinand F: 494
Germany (The Holy Roman Empire) G: 162-163
Holy Roman Empire (The House of Habsburg) H: 300
Hungary (History) H: 445
Italy (Spanish and Austrian rule) I: 514
Magyars M: 64
Maximilian I M: 319
Prague (History) P: 730
Richelieu, Cardinal (Thirty Years' War) R: 331
Switzerland (The struggle for freedom) So: 1059
Thirty Years' War (The Swedish-French period) T: 260
Vienna (History) V: 362
Habyarimana, Juvénal [African military leader]
Burundi (History) B: 713
Rwanda (History) R: 571
HACE [illness]
Altitude sickness A: 390
Hacienda [estate]
Bolivia (Colonial rule) B: 447
Ecuador (Way of life) E: 69
Mexico (Agriculture) M: 465; (Spanish rule) M: 469-470
Peru (Spanish conquest and rule) P: 314
Hacienda Buena Vista [Puerto Rico]
Puerto Rico (Places to visit) P: 877
Hack [sports]
Curling *diagram on* Ci: 1196; (The game) Ci: 1195
Hackamore [riding equipment]
Horse (table: Riding equipment) H: 351
Hackberry [tree] H: 3
Tree *pictures on* T: 421
Hacker [computing]
Crime (Computer crime) Ci: 1357
Library (Security) L: 238-239
Hackled band [zoology]
Spider (How spiders make silk) So: 786
Hackley, Robert J. [American settler]
Tampa (History) T: 23
Hackman, Gene [American actor]
Motion picture (Best performance by an actor: 1971) M: 862a; (Best performance by an actor in a supporting role: 1992) M: 862b
Hackmatack [tree]
Larch L: 75
Hackney [breed]
Horse (table: Some types and breeds of horses) H: 343; (Light harness horses) H: 345
Hackney pony
Horse (table: Some types and breeds of horses) H: 343; (Ponies) H: 347 *with picture*
Hacksaw [tool]
Saw (Handsaws) S: 166-167 *with picture*
Had bush [plant]
Desert *picture on* D: 155
Hadassah [organization]
Szold, Henrietta So: 1078
Hadassah Medical Center
Jerusalem (West Jerusalem) J: 95 *with map*
Hadden, Briton [American publisher]
Journalism (The age of sensationalism) J: 175
Haddock [fish] H: 3 *with picture*
Fish *picture on* F: 153
Hader, Berta Hoerner [American artist]
Caldecott Medal (table: 1949) C: 26
Hader, Elmer [American artist]
Caldecott Medal (table: 1949) C: 26
Hades [Greek mythology] H: 4
See also Pluto [god] *in this index*
Asclepius A: 767
Eurydice E: 420
Mythology (Mythical places) M: 975; (table) M: 981; (Greek divinities) M: 982
Orpheus O: 858
Persephone P: 295
Tartarus T: 48
Hadi, Abd-Rabbu Mansour [Yemeni political leader]
Yemen (Formation of North Yemen) Y: 563
Hadid, Zaha [Iraqi-British architect] H: 4 *with picture*
Hadith [religion]
Islam (The Sunnah of Muhammad) I: 463
Shari'ah S: 374
Wahhabis W: 5
Hadj [religion] *See* Hajj *in this index*
Hadley, Herbert S. [American political leader]
Missouri (table) M: 668
Hadley, John [British inventor]
Sextant S: 337
Hadley, Ozra A. [American political leader]
Arkansas (table) A: 712
Hadrian [popes] *See* Adrian *in this index*
Hadrian [Roman emperor] H: 4

Jerusalem (Roman rule) J: 101
Library (Rome) L: 58
Hadrianopolis [ancient city]
Edirne E: 77
Hadrian's Library [Athens]
Library (Rome) L: 58
Hadrian's Wall [England]
England (The Roman conquest) E: 303-304 *with picture*
Roman walls R: 414 *with picture*
Scotland (The Roman invasion) S: 219
Hadron [physics] H: 5
Gluon G: 237
Quark Q: 7
Subatomic particle (Composite particles) So: 937
Hadrosaur [dinosaur] H: 5
Dinosaur *picture on* D: 209; (True dinosaurs) D: 206b-206c; (Reproduction and growth) D: 211
Hadrosaurid [dinosaur] *See* Hadrosaur *in this index*
Haeckel, Ernst Heinrich [German zoologist] H: 5
Haema...
Words beginning Haema or Haemo appear under Hema or Hemo, as in Hemoglobin
Hafey, Chick [American baseball player]
Baseball (table: Hall of Fame) B: 134a
Hafiz [Persian poet] H: 5
Iran (The arts) I: 402
Hafnium [element] H: 5
Hafsah [wife of Muhammad]
Muslims (The early caliphs) M: 964a
Haft [handle]
Ax A: 994
Hagaman, Frank L. [American political leader]
Kansas (table) K: 234
Haganah [organization]
Dayan, Moshe D: 53
Eshkol, Levi E: 357
Hagar [Biblical figure]
Abraham A: 16
Ishmael I: 462
Islam (The Five Pillars of Islam) I: 463-464
Muslims (Before Muhammad) M: 964
Hagåtña [Guam] H: 5
Guam G: 408 *with picture*
Hagelin, Boris C. W. [Swedish engineer]
Codes and ciphers (Cipher machines) Ci: 750
Hagen [legendary figure]
Nibelungenlied N: 395
Hagen, Walter [American golfer] H: 6
Hagenbeck, Carl [German animal trainer]
Zoo (The evolution of zoos) Z: 605
Hagerman Fossil Beds National Monument [Idaho]
Idaho (Places to visit) I: 34
National Park System (table: National monuments) N: 51
Hagerstown Valley
Maryland (Land regions) M: 250
Hägerstrand, Torsten [Swedish geographer]
Geography (The growth of geography) G: 96
Hagfish [sea animal]
Animal *picture on* A: 507
Fish (Lampreys and hagfish) F: 148 *with picture*
Haggadah [religion]
Passover P: 192
Religion *picture on* R: 217
Haggai, Book of [Bible] H: 6
Haggard, H. Rider [British author] H: 6
Haggis [food]
Scotland (Food and drink) S: 214
Hägglund, Joel [Swedish American songwriter] *See* Hill, Joe *in this index*
Hagia Sophia [museum, Istanbul] H: 6
Architecture *picture on* A: 618; (Byzantine architecture) A: 617
Byzantine art (Architecture) B: 749-750
Byzantine Empire *picture on* B: 753
Istanbul (The city) I: 490-491 *with picture*
Hagiography [literature]
Biography (The Middle Ages) B: 313
Hagley Museum and Library [Wilmington]
Delaware (Places to visit) D: 102
Hague, Frank [American political leader]
Jersey City (Government and history) J: 94
Hague, The [The Netherlands] H: 6
Netherlands (National government) N: 139
Hague Convention on Intercountry Adoption [1993]
Adoption (International adoptions) A: 66
Hague Conventions H: 7
Hijacking H: 230
War crime W: 27
Hague Peace Conference [1899]
Hague, The (History) H: 7
International law (In the 1800's) I: 342
Prisoner of war P: 808

Hague Peace Conference [1907]
Hague, The (History) H: 7
International law (In the 1800's) I: 342
Neutrality N: 153
Prisoner of war P: 808
Right of search R: 340
Hahajima [island, Japan]
Bonin Islands B: 460
Hahn, Kurt [German educator]
Outward Bound O: 880
Hahn, Michael [American political leader]
Louisiana (table) L: 496
Hahn, Otto [German chemist] H: 7
Meitner, Lise M: 387
Nuclear energy (Artificial fission) N: 590
Physics (Uncovering the secrets of the atom) P: 442
Protactinium P: 831
Strassmann, Fritz So: 918
Uranium (History of the use of uranium) U: 216
Hahnemann, Samuel [German doctor]
Homeopathy H: 303
Haida Indians H: 7
Alaska *picture on* A: 300; (Population) A: 286
Canada *picture on* C: 110; (Painting and sculpture) C: 109
Indian, American *picture on* I: 162; (Shelter) I: 136d
Tlingit Indians T: 303
Haider, Jörg [Austrian political leader]
Austria (After World War II) A: 939-940
Haider, Sign of [Pakistan]
Medals, decorations, and orders (table) M: 359
Haifa [Israel] H: 7
Haig, Alexander Meigs, Jr. [American government official] H: 7
Haig, Douglas [British military leader] H: 8
World War I (The Battle of the Somme) W: 458; (Allied failures) W: 461
Haig, Earl *See* Haig, Douglas *in this index*
Haight, Henry H. [American political leader]
California (table) C: 59
Haik [garment]
Algeria (Clothing) A: 361
Haiku [poetry] H: 8
Japanese literature (The Tokugawa period) J: 62
Poetry (Lyric poetry) P: 591
Hail [weather] H: 8 *with picture*
Rain (The ice-crystal process) R: 124
Tornado (The life of a tornado) T: 335
Weather (Synoptic-scale systems) W: 159-161
Hail insurance
Crop insurance Ci: 1153
Hail Mary [prayer]
Annunciation A: 518
Rosary R: 474
Hail the Conquering Hero [film]
Sturges, Preston So: 934
"Hail to the Chief" [song] H: 8
Haile, William [American political leader]
New Hampshire (table) N: 223
Haile-Mariam, Mengistu [Ethiopian political leader] *See* Mengistu Haile-Mariam *in this index*
Haile Selassie I [emperor of Ethiopia] H: 8
Eritrea (History) E: 353-354
Ethiopia (Haile Selassie) E: 371; (Military takeover) E: 372 *with picture*
Italo-Ethiopian War I: 495
Jamaica (People) J: 23
Rastafarians R: 146
Hailstone
Hail H: 8 *with picture*
Haines, Daniel [American political leader]
New Jersey (table) N: 249
Haines, Jackson [American skater]
Ice skating (History) I: 16
Haines, Jesse [American baseball player]
Baseball (table: Hall of Fame) B: 134a
Haines, John M. [American political leader]
Idaho (table) I: 42
Haines, William T. [American political leader]
Maine (table) M: 87
Haiphong [Vietnam] H: 8
Vietnam War (Invasion of the south) V: 376
Hair H: 9 *with pictures*
See also Fur *in this index*
Baldness B: 38
Cosmetics (Kinds of cosmetics) Ci: 1074
Depilatory D: 149
Fur F: 561 *with pictures*
Hairdressing H: 11 *with pictures*
Head lice H: 123
Mammal M: 117; (Skin and hair) M: 118 *with picture*
Races, Human R: 52 *with picture, pictures on* R: 54
Skin (Hair, nails, and glands) S: 489
Wig W: 299

Hair [musical]
  Musical comedy (During the late 1900's) M: 960
  Rock music (Fresh directions) R: 380
Hair cell [anatomy]
  Ear (The inner ear) E: 8; (How sounds reach the brain) E: 10 *with diagram*; (The response to gravity) E: 11 *with diagram*
Hair dye
  Hairdressing (Ancient times) H: 11
Hair hygrometer [instrument]
  Hygrometer (The hair hygrometer) H: 474
Hair setting
  Hairdressing H: 11 *with pictures*
Hair snake [animal]
  Horsehair worm H: 367
Hair transplanting
  Baldness B: 39
Hair weaving
  Baldness B: 39
Hairball [disorder]
  Cat (Grooming) C: 294
Hairbell [plant]
  Bluebell B: 422
Haircap moss [plant]
  Moss M: 834 *with picture*
Hairdresser
  Hairdressing H: 11; (Careers in hairdressing) H: 13 *with picture*
Hairdressing H: 11 *with pictures*
  See also Barber *in this index*
  Barber B: 106
  Colonial life in America (Clothing) Ci: 799
Hairdryer
  Hairdressing (Caring for the hair) H: 13
Hairless Chinese crested [dog]
  Chinese crested C: 509 *with picture*
Hairspring
  Watch (Mechanical watches) W: 114
Hairstreak [butterfly]
  Butterfly (Blues, coppers, and hairstreaks) B: 734 *with picture*
Hairstyle
  Egypt, Ancient *picture on* E: 138
  Hairdressing H: 11 *with pictures*
Hairworm
  Horsehair worm H: 367
Hairy Ape, The [play by O'Neill]
  O'Neill, Eugene (His plays) O: 762
Hairy mammoth [extinct animal]
  Mammoth M: 130
Hairy-nosed wombat [animal]
  Wombat W: 382
Hairy woodpecker
  Woodpecker *picture on* W: 394
Hairystem gooseberry [fruit]
  Gooseberry G: 271
Haise, Fred Wallace, Jr. [American astronaut] H: 13 *with portrait*
  Lovell, James Arthur Jr. L: 509
  Space exploration (The flight of Apollo 13) So: 718
Haiti H: 14 *with pictures and map*
  Aristide, Jean-Bertrand A: 662
  Bush, George Walker (Later years) B: 724
  Christophe, Henri C: 537
  Clinton, Bill (International affairs) Ci: 682e
  Duvalier, François D: 393
  Earthquake *picture on* E: 33
  Flag *picture on* F: 201
  Hispaniola H: 259
  Latin America (The movement toward independence) L: 106-107
  Toussaint Louverture T: 350
  Vodou V: 436 *with picture*
  Zombie Z: 598
Haitian Creole [language]
  West Indies (Languages) W: 201
Hajj [religion] H: 17
  Id al-Ad-hā I: 25
  Islam (The Five Pillars of Islam) I: 463-464
  Mecca (Economy) M: 358-353
Hajji [religion] *See* Hajj *in this index*
Hakama [garment]
  Clothing (Japan) Ci: 699
Hake [fish] H: 17 *with picture*
Hakkinen, Mika [Finnish race driver]
  Automobile racing (table: Formula One World Drivers' Championship) A: 980
Hakkoda Tunnel [Japan]
  Tunnel (table) T: 491
Hal, Prince [literary figure]
  Henry V [of England] H: 187
  Shakespeare, William: *(Henry IV)* S: 358-359
Halal [religion]
  Meat packing (Meat-packing processes) M: 351
Halas, George Stanley [American football coach] H: 17

Halberstam, David [American journalist]
  War correspondent W: 26
Halcion [drug]
  Benzodiazepine B: 256
Hald, Jens [Danish physician]
  Disulfiram D: 240
Haldane, J. B. S. [British biologist]
  Evolution (The synthetic theory) E: 432
  Life (Modern explanations) L: 278-279
Haldane, William [American cabinetmaker]
  Furniture (The furniture industry) F: 586
Haldeman, H. R. [American government official]
  Watergate W: 144
Hale, Edward Everett [American author] H: 18
Hale, George Ellery [American astronomer] H: 18
  Mount Wilson Observatory M: 890
  Palomar Observatory P: 112
  Sun (History of modern solar study) So: 986
  Yerkes Observatory Y: 565
Hale, John Parker [American political leader] H: 18
  Free Soil Party F: 499
Hale, Nathan [American editor]
  Hale, Edward Everett H: 18
Hale, Nathan [American patriot] H: 18 *with picture*
  Connecticut (The Revolutionary War) C: 570
  Revolution, American (The campaign in New York) R: 281-282
Hale, Samuel W. [American political leader]
  New Hampshire (table) N: 223
Hale, Sarah Josepha [American editor] H: 19
  Magazine (Magazines in the 1800's) M: 45
  Thanksgiving Day (Later thanksgiving days in the United States) T: 230
Hale, William [British engineer]
  Rocket (History) R: 390
Hale-Bopp, Comet
  Comet (table) Ci: 868; (Studying comets) Ci: 868-869
Hale rocket [weapon]
  Rocket (History) R: 390
Hale Telescope [California]
  Astronomy *picture on* A: 849
  Palomar Observatory P: 112
  Telescope (Reflecting telescopes) T: 104-105
Haleakala [volcano]
  Hawaii (Maui) H: 100
Haleakala National Park [Hawaii] H: 19 *with picture*
  Hawaii (Places to visit) H: 98 *with picture*
  National Park System (table: National parks) N: 48
Halemaumau [crater, Hawaii]
  Kilauea K: 315
Hales, Stephen [British scientist]
  Heart (Discovery of circulation) H: 144
Hales Bar Dam [Tennessee River, Alabama]
  Tennessee River T: 158
Halevi, Judah [Hebrew poet] H: 19
  Hebrew literature (Medieval works) H: 162
Halévy, Ludovic [French librettist]
  Opera: *(Carmen)* O: 802
Haley, Alex [American author] H: 19 *with portrait*
  American literature (Works by minority writers) A: 425
  Roots R: 472
Haley, Bill [American singer]
  Rock music (A variety of styles) R: 378 *with picture*
Haley, Gail E. [American artist]
  Caldecott Medal (table: 1971) C: 26
Haley, Jack [American actor]
  Garland, Judy *picture on* G: 44
Haley, Nikki [American political leader]
  Asian Americans (Notable Asian American "firsts") A: 812f
  South Carolina (table) So: 658
Haley, W. D. [American author]
  Appleseed, Johnny A: 574
Half-and-half [dairy product]
  Milk (table) M: 547
Half-Breeds [U.S. history]
  Garfield, James Abram (Congressman) G: 41-42
  Hayes, Rutherford Birchard (Campaign of 1876) H: 120
  Republican Party (The Radical Republicans and Reconstruction) R: 254-255
Half brother
  Family (Family relationships) F: 21
Half-camp [dwelling]
  Lincoln, Abraham (Boyhood) L: 312
Half-cell reaction [chemistry]
  Battery (Half-cell reactions) B: 170 *with diagram*
Half dollar [money] H: 20 *with pictures*
  Money (Half dollars) M: 714
Half Dome
  Yosemite National Park (Rock masses) Y: 570
Half-hour glass [measuring device]
  Hourglass H: 379
Half-life [physics]

  Isotope (Radioactive isotopes) I: 476
  Nuclear energy (Radioactive decay) N: 582
  Radiation (Radiation and radioactivity) R: 75
  Radiocarbon (Radiocarbon dating) R: 97
  Radiogeology R: 98
  Uranium (Radioactivity) U: 214-215
Half-mast [custom]
  Flag (Raising and lowering the flag) F: 219
Half moon [astronomy]
  Moon (Phases) M: 783-784
Half Moon [ship]
  Hudson, Henry (North American voyages) H: 404-405
Half-pipe [competition]
  Snowboarding S: 541
Half shaft
  Automobile (The drive system) A: 949 *with diagram*
Half sister
  Family (Family relationships) F: 21
Half stitch [embroidery]
  Petit point P: 326
Half-timbered house
  Shelter (The Middle Ages) S: 393
Half-title page
  Book (Inside a book) B: 464-465
Half tone [music]
  Tone T: 327
Halfback [sports]
  Football (The offensive team) F: 356 *with diagrams*
  Soccer (The midfielders) So: 545
Halfpenny [money]
  Penny P: 271
Halftone image [printing]
  Photography (Technical improvements) P: 423
  Printing (Preparing illustrations for reproduction) P: 797; (Process color printing) P: 802
Halftone screen [printing]
  Printing (Preparing illustrations for reproduction) P: 797
Halfway house
  Criminal justice system (Problems in the correctional system) Ci: 1144
  Prison (Reforms in the 1900's) P: 807-808
Halfway line [sports]
  Rugby football (Rugby Union) R: 510
Haliburton, Thomas Chandler [Canadian author]
  Canadian literature (Early English-Canadian literature) C: 157
Halibut [fish] H: 20 *with picture*
  Fish *picture on* F: 153
Halicarnassus, Mausoleum at [Persia]
  Seven Wonders of the Ancient World *picture on* S: 327; (The Mausoleum at Halicarnassus) S: 325
Halide [chemistry]
  Halogen H: 26
Halifax [Nova Scotia] H: 20 *with picture*
  Halifax explosion H: 22
  Nova Scotia *picture on* N: 555; (Population) N: 558; (table: Average monthly weather) N: 564; (The struggle in Acadia) N: 568 *with picture*
Halifax, Earl of [British nobleman]
  Halifax H: 20
Halifax Citadel National Historic Site [Nova Scotia]
  Canada (table: National historic sites) C: 114
Halifax explosion [Canadian history] H: 22
  Nova Scotia (The early to middle 1900's) N: 570
Halifax Gazette [newspaper]
  Nova Scotia (Communication) N: 567
Halite [mineral]
  Mineral (Mineral crystals) M: 567-570 *with pictures*
  Salt S: 72
Hall, Asaph [American astronomer]
  Mars (Satellites) M: 226b
Hall, Sir Benjamin [British government official]
  Big Ben B: 297
Hall, Charles Martin [American chemist]
  Alcoa Inc. A: 334
  Aluminum (Smelting the alumina) A: 393; (Growth of the aluminum industry) A: 397
Hall, David [American political leader]
  Delaware (table) D: 109
  Oklahoma (table) O: 730
Hall, Donald [American poet]
  Poet laureate (table: Poets laureate of the United States) P: 590
Hall, Edward T. [American anthropologist]
  Communication (The study of communication) Ci: 887
Hall, Edwin H. [American physicist]
  Hall effect H: 22
Hall, Fred [American political leader]

Kansas (table) K: 234
Hall, G. Stanley [American educator] H: 22
Progressive education (Progressive educators)
P: 813
Hall, Hiland [American political leader]
Vermont (table) V: 333
Hall, Sir James [Scottish geologist]
Geology (Experimental geology) G: 99
Hall, James Norman [American author]
Nordhoff and Hall N: 453
Hall, John H. [American political leader]
Oregon (table) O: 845
Hall, John Louis [American physicist]
Nobel Prizes (Physics: 2005) N: 442
Hall, John W. [American political leader]
Delaware (table) D: 109
Hall, Joshua [American political leader]
Maine (table) M: 87
Hall, Luther E. [American political leader]
Louisiana (table) L: 496
Hall, Lyman [American patriot] H: 22
Georgia (table) G: 130
Hall, Nathan K. [American government official]
Fillmore, Millard (table) F: 102
Hall, Prince [American social leader] H: 22
Masonry (History) M: 267-268
Hall, Robert E. [American economist]
Flat tax F: 228
Hall, Samuel Read [American educator]
Vermont (Schools) V: 322
Hall, Stuart [British cultural critic]
Communication (Communication and culture)
Ci: 888
Hall, Willard P. [American political leader]
Missouri (table) M: 668
Hall, William [American political leader]
Tennessee (table) T: 152
Hall effect [electricity] H: 22
Hall-Héroult process [industrial process]
Aluminum (Smelting the alumina) A: 393;
(Growth of the aluminum industry) A: 397
Hall of Fame H: 22 with pictures
Hall of Fame, Baseball See Baseball Hall of Fame
in this index
Hall of Fame, Basketball See Naismith Memorial
Basketball Hall of Fame in this index
Hall of Fame, Hockey See Hockey Hall of Fame in
this index
Hall of Fame for Great Americans [New York City]
Hall of fame (The Hall of Fame for Great
Americans) H: 22 with picture
Hall of Memory [Birmingham, England]
Birmingham B: 376 with picture
Hall of Mirrors
Versailles, Palace of V: 339
Hall of One Hundred Columns [Persepolis]
Architecture (Mesopotamian architecture)
A: 611-612
Hall of the Great Buddha [temple]
Temple picture on T: 131
Hall of the Slain [Norse mythology]
Valhalla V: 265
Hall voltage [electricity]
Hall effect H: 22
Halla-san [mountain, South Korea]
Korea, South (The land) K: 378-378a with
diagram
Hallaca [food]
Christmas (In Latin America) C: 532
Venezuela (Food) V: 301
Hallam, Arthur Henry [friend of]
Tennyson, Lord (His life) T: 166f
Halle, Adam de la [French dramatist]
French literature (Early drama) F: 519
Halleck, Henry Wager [Union general] H: 24
Civil War, American (The war in the West--1862-
1864) Ci: 628
Grant, Ulysses S. ("Unconditional Surrender"
Grant) G: 314
"Hallelujah Chorus" [music by Handel]
Handel, George Frideric (His work) H: 42
Halles, Les [district]
Paris (Renewal and new construction) P: 166-167
Halley, Edmond [English astronomer] H: 24
Greenwich Observatory, Royal G: 387
Halley's Comet H: 24
Insurance (The growth of insurance) I: 315
Map (Advances in European cartography) M: 184
Newton, Sir Isaac (The *Principia*) N: 388-389
Transit T: 374
Halley-type comet
Meteor (The parent comet) M: 431
Halley's Comet [astronomy] H: 24 with diagram
Comet (Studying comets) Ci: 868 with picture;
(table) Ci: 868
Halley, Edmond H: 24
Space exploration (Probes to comets) So: 711

Halliburton, Richard [American author] H: 24a
Hallidie, Andrew S. [American engineer]
Cable car C: 7
San Francisco (Continued prosperity) S: 97-98
Halliwell, James [British author]
Nursery rhyme (History) N: 615-616
Halloween H: 24a with picture
Mask (Festive masks) M: 264
October O: 670
Pumpkin P: 901
Hallstatt [Austria]
Celts C: 342
Necropolis N: 117
Hallucination [psychology] H: 25
Alcoholism (Effects of alcoholism) A: 338
Amphetamine (Amphetamine abuse) A: 439
Hallucinogenic drug H: 26
Mental illness (Schizophrenia) M: 405
Narcolepsy N: 20
Postpartum depression P: 709
Sleep (What happens without sleep) S: 507
Hallucinogenic drug H: 25
Drug (Hallucinogens) D: 352
Drug abuse (Abuse of illegal drugs) D: 362; (table:
Some commonly abused drugs) D: 363
LSD L: 511
Halmahera [island, Indonesia]
Indonesia (The Molucca Islands) I: 234
Halo [astronomy]
Galaxy (Spiral galaxies) G: 8a-8b
Milky Way (Shape of the galaxy) M: 550
Halo [light] H: 26 with picture
Madonna and Child (Types of Madonna
paintings) M: 38
Halo ring [astronomy]
Jupiter (Rings) J: 200a with picture
Halogen [chemistry] H: 26
Halogen lamp See Tungsten-halogen lamp in this
index
Halogen oven [appliance]
Range (Electric ranges) R: 137-138
Haloid Company [former name]
Xerox Corporation X: 544
Halon extinguisher
Fire extinguisher (Liquefied gas extinguishers)
F: 130
Halonen, Tarja [Finnish political leader]
Finland (Recent developments) F: 118
Halophile [biology]
Extremophile E: 458
Halothane [drug] H: 27
Hals, Frans [Dutch painter] H: 27 with picture
Painting (The Dutch masters) P: 62 with picture
Halsall, William F. [American painter]
Pilgrims picture on P: 463
Halsey, William Frederick, Jr. [American admiral]
H: 27
World War II (The liberation of the Philippines)
W: 491
Halsted, William [American doctor]
Dentistry (Modern dentistry) D: 144-145
Mastectomy M: 297
Surgery (History) So: 1007
Halteres [entomology]
Fly (Thorax) F: 309 with diagram
Insect (Wings) I: 288
Mosquito (Thorax) M: 832 with diagram
Halva [food]
Pakistan (Food and drink) P: 96
Halyard [rope]
Flag (table) F: 193; (Raising and lowering the
flag) F: 219
Sailing (Rigging) S: 24
Ham [Biblical figure]
Noah N: 439
Ham [food] H: 28 with pictures
Meat pictures on M: 349
Ham [radio]
Radio, Amateur R: 95
Hamadryad [mythology]
Nymph N: 633
Hamadryas [animal]
Baboon B: 3
Hamakua Coast [region]
Hawaii (Places to visit) H: 98
Hamamelin [medication]
Witch hazel W: 371
Haman [Biblical figure]
Esther, Book of E: 360
Purim P: 909
Hamas [political group] H: 28
Gaza Strip G: 74
Middle East (The 1970's and 1980's) M: 534a; (The
2000's) M: 534b
Palestine picture on P: 105; (The continuing
conflict and peace efforts) P: 106
Palestinian Authority (History) P: 107

Hamate bone [anatomy]
Hand (Parts of the hand) H: 40
Wrist diagram on W: 510
"Hamatreya" [poem by Emerson]
Emerson, Ralph Waldo (His poetry) E: 259
Hambletonian [horse]
Harness racing (Harness horses) H: 63
Hamblett, Charles [British author]
Generation X G: 84
Hamburg [Germany] H: 28 with picture
Drama (Germany) D: 336
Lessing, Gotthold Ephraim L: 209
Hamburg Dramaturgy, The [essays by Lessing]
Drama (Germany) D: 336
Lessing, Gotthold Ephraim L: 209
Hamburg parsley [plant]
Parsley P: 181
Hamburg State [Germany]
Hamburg H: 29
Hamburger [food]
Food (Interesting facts about food) F: 329
Hame tug [device]
Harness diagram on H: 63
Hamelin [Germany]
Pied Piper of Hamelin P: 4532
Hamer, Fannie Lou [American civil rights leader]
H: 29
Hames [device]
Harness H: 63 with diagram
Hamilcar Barca [Carthaginian general] H: 29
Barcelona B: 108
Hannibal (His early life) H: 52
Hamilton [Bermuda] H: 29
Hamilton [Ontario] H: 30 with picture and map
Hamilton, Alexander [American statesman] H: 32
with portrait
Adams, John (Vice president) A: 37; (The
Federalist split) A: 37-38; (Difficulties with
France) A: 38
Bank (History of U.S. banking) B: 92
Bank of the United States B: 96
Burr, Aaron (Gains recognition) B: 711
Clinton, George Ci: 682g
Constitution of the United States Ci: 998
Democratic-Republican Party D: 129
Federalist, The F: 66
Federalist Party F: 67
Jefferson, Thomas (Secretary of state) J: 81 with
picture; (Election of 1804) J: 86
Madison, James (Congressman) M: 34
Paterson P: 195
United States, Government of the (Early years)
U: 145
United States, History of the (Establishing
a government) U: 161-162 with picture;
(Problems in foreign affairs) U: 163
Washington, D.C. (Choosing the capital) W: 85
Washington, George (Cabinet) W: 102 with
picture; (Finances) W: 103; (Constitutional
debate) W: 103
Hamilton, Alice [American doctor] H: 33
Hull House H: 412
Hamilton, Andrew [American lawyer]
Postal Service, United States (Colonial times)
P: 700
Zenger, John Peter Z: 589
Hamilton, Andrew J. [American political leader]
Texas (table) T: 203
Hamilton, Billy [American baseball player]
Baseball (table: Hall of Fame) B: 134a
Hamilton, Charles [American author]
Carmichael, Stokely C: 241
Hamilton, Emma Lady [British public figure]
Nelson, Horatio (Battle of the Nile) N: 122
Hamilton, George [Canadian pioneer]
Hamilton H: 30; (History) H: 31
Hamilton, Gordon [American social worker]
Social work (History) So: 559
Hamilton, Jimmy [American clarinetist]
Ellington, Duke picture on E: 242
Hamilton, John M. [American political leader]
Illinois (table) I: 71
Hamilton, Lewis [British race driver]
Automobile racing (table: Formula One World
Drivers' Championship) A: 980
Hamilton, Mount [California]
Lick Observatory L: 270
Hamilton, Paul [American political leader]
Madison, James (table) M: 35
Hamilton, Todd [American golfer]
Golf (British Open) G: 264
Hamilton, Virginia [American author] H: 33
Literature for children picture on L: 374
Newbery Medal (table) N: 359
Regina Medal (table: 1990) R: 206
Hamilton, William Donald [British biologist] H: 33
Hamilton, William T. [American political leader]
Maryland (table) M: 255
Hamilton Fish [book by Nevins]

Nevins, Allan **N:** 178
Hamilton-Gordon, John Campbell [British statesman] *See* Aberdeen and Temair, Marquess of *in this index*
Hamilton Grange National Memorial [New York]
National Park System (table: National memorials) **N:** 54
Hamilton Harbour [Canada]
Hamilton (The city) **H:** 30 *with map*
Hamilton River [former name]
Churchill River **C:** 550
Hamilton Tiger-Cats [team]
Football (Canadian Football League) **F:** 364
Hamlet [film]
Motion picture (Best picture: 1948) **M:** 861
Olivier, Laurence **O:** 744
Hamlet [play by Shakespeare]
Gielgud, John **G:** 188
Shakespeare, William: *(Hamlet)* **S:** 361 *with picture*; (Rhetoric) **S:** 368
Hamlet, The [book by Faulkner]
Faulkner, William **F:** 55
Hamlet council
Nunavut (Government) **N:** 611
Hamlin, Hannibal [American political leader] **H:** 33
Lincoln, Abraham (Election of 1860) **L:** 318 *with picture*
Maine (table) **M:** 87; (Statehood) **M:** 89-91
Vice president of the United States **V:** 348 *with portrait*
Hamlisch, Marvin [American composer]
Musical comedy (The modern musical emerges) **M:** 960
Hamm, John F. [Canadian political leader]
Nova Scotia (table) **N:** 567
Hamm, Mia [American soccer player] **H:** 33 *with portrait*
Hammann [ship]
Midway, Battle of **M:** 536
Hammarskjöld, Dag [Swedish statesman] **H:** 34
Pearson, Lester Bowles *picture on* **P:** 223
United Nations (The secretary-general) **U:** 83 *with portrait*
Hammer [anatomy]
Ear (The middle ear) **E:** 7-8 *with diagram*
Hammer [gun]
Rifle (How a rifle works) **R:** 338
Hammer [tool] **H:** 34 *with pictures*
Woodworking (Steps in woodworking) **W:** 396 *with picture*
Hammer, Edward E. [American inventor]
Light bulb **L:** 293
Hammer throw [sport] **H:** 34 *with pictures*
Track and field (Throwing events) **T:** 358
Hammered dulcimer
Dulcimer **D:** 380 *with picture*
Hammerhead shark [fish] **H:** 35 *with picture*
Shark (Kinds of sharks) **S:** 375
Hammerkop [bird]
Bird (Birds of Africa) **B:** 344h *with picture*
Hammerstein, Oscar, II [American dramatist] **H:** 35
Musical comedy (Musical comedy matures) **M:** 960
Rodgers, Richard **R:** 398
Show Boat **S:** 438
Hammett, Dashiell [American author] **H:** 35
American literature (Popular forms) **A:** 422-423
Detective story (History) **D:** 162-163
Hammill, John [American political leader]
Iowa (table) **I:** 391
Hammock [bed]
Indian, American *picture on* **I:** 140
Hammon, Jupiter [American poet]
African Americans (Free blacks) **A:** 136g-136h
Hammond [Indiana]
Gary **G:** 47
Hammond, Abram A. [American political leader]
Indiana (table) **I:** 214
Hammond, Jay S. [American political leader]
Alaska (table) **A:** 300
Hammond, John [American businessman]
Basie, Count **B:** 140
Hammond, John Hays, Jr. [American inventor] **H:** 35
Hammond, Winfield S. [American political leader]
Minnesota (table) **M:** 602
Hammond Island
Torres Strait Islands **T:** 343
Hammurabi [king of Babylonia] **H:** 35 *with picture*
Babylon (The Old Babylonian period) **B:** 11
Babylonia (The dynasties of Babylon) **B:** 14
World, History of the (The Tigris-Euphrates Valley) **W:** 422-424
Hammurabi, Code of [law]
Adoption (History) **A:** 67
Government (Early forms of government) **G:** 289
Hammurabi **H:** 35

Insurance (Earliest insurance) **I:** 315
Law (Early developments in the East) **L:** 133
Theocracy **T:** 251
World, History of the (The Tigris-Euphrates Valley) **W:** 422-424
Hammurapi [king of Babylonia] *See* Hammurabi *in this index*
Hampshire [hog]
Hog (Kinds of hogs) **H:** 285 *with picture*; (table) **H:** 286
Hampshire sheep
Sheep (Medium-wooled sheep) **S:** 382
Hampton [Virginia] **H:** 36
Hampton, Lionel [American musician] **H:** 36
Jazz (The swing era) **J:** 71 *with picture*
Hampton, Wade [American general]
War of 1812 (Campaigns of 1813) **W:** 31
Hampton, Wade [Confederate general] **H:** 36
South Carolina (Reconstruction) **So:** 660
Hampton Beach
New Hampshire (Places to visit) **N:** 216 *with picture*
Hampton Court Conference [1604] **H:** 36
Puritans (History) **P:** 910
Hampton National Historic Site [Maryland]
National Park System (table: National historic sites) **N:** 52-53
Hampton Normal and Agricultural Institute [former name]
Hampton University **H:** 37
Hampton Roads [harbor, Virginia] **H:** 36
Hampton Roads, Battle of [1862]
Civil War, American (First battle between ironclads) **Ci:** 626 *with picture*
Hampton Roads Conference [1865] **H:** 37
Stephens, Alexander Hamilton **So:** 890
Hampton University **H:** 37
Hamster [animal] **H:** 37 *with picture*
Hamstring [anatomy]
Leg (The thigh) **L:** 181-182
Hamsun, Knut [Norwegian author] **H:** 37
Hamzah ibn Ali [Egyptian religious leader]
Druses **D:** 368
Han [Japanese history]
Japan (Tokugawa period) **J:** 55
Han [people]
China (Nationalities) **C:** 481 *with picture*
Han dynasty [Chinese history] **H:** 37 *with map*
Asia (The Huang He and Yangtze valleys) **A:** 805 *with map*
China (The arts) **C:** 487 *with picture*; (The Han dynasty) **C:** 500 *with map*
Clothing (China) **Ci:** 699
Liu Bang **L:** 393
Painting (Chinese painting) **P:** 44
Porcelain (Oriental porcelain) **P:** 676
Sculpture (China) **S:** 238
World, History of the (The unification of China) **W:** 431 *with picture*
Han Gaozu [Chinese emperor] *See* Liu Bang *in this index*
Han Kao-tsu [emperor of China] *See* Liu Bang *in this index*
Han River [South Korea]
Seoul **S:** 304
Hanbok [garment]
Clothing (Korea) **Ci:** 699 *with picture*
Hancock, George W. [American sportsman]
Softball (History) **So:** 572
Hancock, Herbie [American musician] **H:** 38
Hancock, John [American patriot] **H:** 38 *with pictures*
Declaration of Independence *picture on* **D:** 77; (Adoption of the Declaration) **D:** 74
Massachusetts (table) **M:** 288
Revere, Paul **R:** 267
Shays's Rebellion **S:** 379
Hancock, Thomas [British inventor]
Rubber (The rubber industry begins) **R:** 501
Hancock, Thomas [uncle of]
Hancock, John **H:** 39
Hancock, Walker Kirtland [American sculptor]
Stone Mountain **So:** 910
Hancock, Winfield Scott [Union general] **H:** 39
Arthur, Chester Alan (Election of 1880) **A:** 756
Hancock Center [Chicago] *See* John Hancock Center *in this index*
Hancock Park [Los Angeles]
La Brea tar pits **L:** 18
Hancock Tower [Boston] *See* John Hancock Tower *in this index*
Hand [anatomy] **H:** 39 *with diagrams*
Brain (Controlling movement) **B:** 553
Carpal tunnel syndrome **C:** 245
Rett syndrome **R:** 266
Skeleton *diagrams on* **S:** 480
Wrist **W:** 510 *with diagram*

Hand [botany]
Banana (How bananas grow) **B:** 73
Hand [measurement]
Horse (Size) **H:** 348
Weights and measures (table: Miscellaneous weights and measures) **W:** 184
Hand, Learned [American jurist] **H:** 40
Hand axe [tool]
Prehistoric people *picture on* **P:** 752; (How the first people lived) **P:** 746-747
Hand brake
Brake (Mechanical brakes) **B:** 560
Hand cannon [gun]
Harquebus **H:** 67
Hand drill [tool]
Woodworking (Drilling) **W:** 398 *with picture*
Hand game
Indian, American (Recreation) **I:** 142-143
Hand loom [weaving]
Textile *picture on* **T:** 218
Hand organ [musical instrument] **H:** 40
Hand prop
Theater (Properties and set dressing) **T:** 240
Hand puppet
Puppet (Hand puppets) **P:** 906
Hand scanner [electronic device]
Computer (A scanner) **Ci:** 915
Hand tool
Woodworking (Steps in woodworking) **W:** 396 *with pictures*
Handball [sport] **H:** 41 *with pictures*
Team handball **T:** 71
Handball court
Handball **H:** 41 *with diagrams*
Handbook of a Christian Soldier [book by Erasmus]
Erasmus, Desiderius **E:** 349
Handcuffs **H:** 42 *with picture*
Handel, George Frideric [German composer] **H:** 42
Classical music (Oratorios) **Ci:** 644; (The Baroque period) **Ci:** 647
Oratorio **O:** 818
Handforth, Thomas [American artist]
Caldecott Medal (table: 1939) **C:** 26
Handgun [weapon] **H:** 43 *with pictures*
Firearm *picture on* **F:** 133
Gun control (Approaches to gun control) **G:** 440-441
Handheld computer **H:** 45
Computer (Personal computers) **Ci:** 909-910 *with picture*
Handheld game system
Electronic game (Handheld game systems) **E:** 204d; (Handheld games) **E:** 204f
Handheld vacuum cleaner [machine]
Vacuum cleaner **V:** 258
Handicap [sports] **H:** 45
Golf (table) **G:** 261
Polo (Handicaps) **P:** 647
Sailing (Handicap races) **S:** 27
Trapshooting **T:** 404
Handicapped *See* Disability *in this index*
Handicraft **H:** 45 *with pictures*
Embossing **E:** 256
Hobby (Handicrafts) **H:** 272
Indian, American *pictures on* **I:** 138; (Arts and crafts) **I:** 145 *with pictures*
Mexico (Manufacturing) **M:** 464-465
Handke, Peter [German author]
Drama (Later German-language drama) **D:** 340
German literature (Postwar German literature [1945-1990]) **G:** 142
Handkerchief **H:** 46
Handlebars
Bicycle (Steering and stopping) **B:** 290 *with diagrams*
Handler [boxing]
Boxing **B:** 526
Handler, Daniel [American author] *See* Snicket, Lemony *in this index*
Handley, George [American political leader]
Georgia (table) **G:** 130
Handley, Harold W. [American political leader]
Indiana (table) **I:** 214
Handmaid's Tale, The [book by Atwood]
Atwood, Margaret **A:** 880
Handoff [electronics]
Cellular telephone (How cellular telephones work) **C:** 340-341
Telephone (Cellular phone calls) **T:** 97
Handover [electronics] *See* Handoff *in this index*
Hands *See* Hand *in this index*
Hands-on practice [education] *See* Learning by doing *in this index*
Hands-only CPR [first aid]
Cardiopulmonary resuscitation **C:** 212
Handsaw [tool]

Saw (Handsaws) S: 166 *with pictures*
Handset
Telephone (How a telephone works) T: 94 *with picture*
Handshape [gesture]
Language (Signed languages) L: 63 *with diagram*
Handsome Lake [American Indian leader] H: 46
Indian, American (Prophets) I: 148
Iroquois Indians I: 455
Red Jacket R: 188
Handwriting H: 46 *with pictures*
See also the list of Related articles in the Handwriting article
Charlemagne (Administration and influence) C: 379
Graphology G: 323
Handwriting analysis
Graphology G: 323
Handwriting on the wall H: 50
Handwriting-recognition software [computing]
Computer (A touch screen) Ci: 914-915
Handheld computer H: 45
Handy, W. C. [American composer] H: 50
African Americans (The Harlem Renaissance and other achievements) A: 136m
Blues B: 425
Memphis (The city) M: 394
Haneda Airport [Tokyo] *See* Tokyo International Airport *in this index*
Hanes, Horace A. [American aviator]
Aviation (Table: Aviation speed records) A: 990
Hanford Project [Washington]
DuPont Company D: 387
Washington (The mid-1900's) W: 68
Hang-chou [China] *See* Hangzhou *in this index*
Hang gliding [sport] H: 51 *with picture*
Glider (Gliding today) G: 231
Hangar
Airport (Hangars) A: 245
Hangar deck
Aircraft carrier A: 206 *with diagram*
Hangbird *See* Baltimore oriole *in this index*
Hanging [execution] H: 51
Capital punishment (table) C: 193
Lynching L: 535
Western frontier life in America (Law and order) W: 238
Hanging Gardens of Babylon
Seven Wonders of the Ancient World *picture on* S: 327; (The Hanging Gardens of Babylon) S: 325
Babylon (The Neo-Babylonian Empire) B: 12
Gardening (History of gardening) G: 38-39
World, History of the (Civilizations of southwest Asia) W: 426
Hanging parrot
Parakeet P: 151
Parrot (Kinds of parrots) P: 179
Hanging valley [geology]
Valley (How valleys are formed) V: 266
Hanging wall
Mining (Mining terms) M: 577
Han'gul [alphabet]
Alphabet (Other alphabets) A: 383-384
Korea, North (Language) K: 369
Korea, South (Language) K: 376
Hangzhou [China] H: 51
Hangzhou Bay Bridge [China]
Bridge (table: Cable-stayed) B: 603
Shanghai (History) S: 372
Hanington, Daniel L. [Canadian political leader]
New Brunswick (table) N: 195
Haniwa [sculpture]
Japan (Sculpture) J: 43; (Early days) J: 52-53
Sculpture (Japan) S: 239
Haniyeh, Ismail [Palestinian political leader]
Hamas H: 28
Hankou [China]
Wuhan W: 514
Hanks, Horatio [American inventor]
Connecticut (The 1800's) Ci: 970
Hanks, Lucy [grandmother of]
Lincoln, Abraham (Family background) L: 311-312
Hanks, Nancy [mother of]
Lincoln, Abraham (Family background) L: 311-312
Hanks, Rodney [American inventor]
Connecticut (The 1800's) Ci: 970
Hanks, Sam [American race driver]
Automobile racing (table: Indianapolis 500 winners) A: 980
Hanks, Tom [American actor] H: 51
Motion picture (Best performance by an actor: 1993, 1994) M: 862a
Hanlon, Ned [American baseball player]
Baseball (table: Hall of Fame) B: 134a

Hanly, J. Frank [American political leader]
Indiana (table) I: 214
Hanna, L. B. [American political leader]
North Dakota (table) N: 513
Hanna, Mark [American political leader] H: 51
McKinley, William (Governor) M: 340
Ohio (The early 1900's) O: 702
Hanna, William [American animator]
Animation (Animation in the mid-1900's) A: 514b
Hannah and Her Sisters [film]
Allen, Woody A: 372
Hannegan, Robert E. [American government official]
Truman, Harry S. (table) T: 469
Hannett, Arthur T. [American political leader]
New Mexico (table) N: 272
Hannibal [Carthaginian general] H: 52 *with picture*
Fabius Maximus, Quintus F: 2
Hamilcar Barca H: 29
Punic Wars (The Second Punic War) P: 903
Rome, Ancient (The Roman Republic) R: 444-445
Scipio Africanus, Publius Cornelius S: 208
Hannibal [Missouri] H: 53
Missouri *pictures on* M: 654, M: 661
Twain, Mark (Boyhood) T: 528
Hanno [Carthaginian explorer]
Exploration (The Phoenicians) E: 441
Hannover [Germany] *See* Hanover *in this index*
Hannuka [religion] *See* Hanukkah *in this index*
Hanoi [Vietnam] H: 53
Vietnam W: 364
Hanover [city, Germany] H: 53
Hanover [region, Germany] H: 53
Hanover, House of [British history]
Brunswick B: 652
George I G: 106b
Windsor W: 334
HANS [device]
Automobile racing (Safety measures) A: 975-976
Hans-Adam II [Liechtenstein ruler]
Liechtenstein (History) L: 273
Hans Brinker [book by Dodge]
Dodge, Mary Elizabeth Mapes D: 260
Literature for children (Masterpieces of fiction) L: 363
Hans Christian Andersen Award
Literature for children (Awards) L: 367
Hansa [German history]
Hanseatic League H: 54
Hansa Quarter [district]
Berlin (Downtown Berlin) B: 260-261
Hansberry, Lorraine [American dramatist] H: 53
African American literature (The 1900's) A: 136a
American literature (Drama) A: 426
Drama (Later United States drama) D: 340
Hänsch, Theodor Wolfgang [German physicist]
Nobel Prizes (Physics: 2005) N: 442
Hanseatic League [German history] H: 53
Flag *picture on* F: 217
Gdańsk G: 74
Germany (The rise of cities) G: 163
Lübeck L: 513
Middle Ages (Economic recovery) M: 526-527
Trade route (Medieval routes) T: 363
Hansel and Gretel [opera by Humperdinck]
Humperdinck, Engelbert H: 436
"Hansel and Gretel" [story]
Grimm's Fairy Tales G: 394
Hansen, Clifford P. [American political leader]
Wyoming (table) W: 532
Hansen, Gerhard H. Armauer [Norwegian doctor]
Leprosy (Causes) L: 204
Hansen's bacillus [bacteria]
Leprosy (Causes) L: 204 *with picture*
Hansen's disease *See* Leprosy *in this index*
Hanson, Duane [American sculptor]
Sculpture (From the mid-1900's to the early 2000's) S: 259 *with picture*
Hanson, Howard [American composer] H: 54
Hanson, John [American political leader] H: 54
Hantavirus [virus] H: 54
Hantavirus pulmonary syndrome [disease]
Hantavirus H: 54
Hanukkah [religion] H: 54
December D: 69
Judah Maccabee J: 179
Judaism (Other holidays) J: 182
Hanukkiyah [symbol]
Hanukkah H: 55
Hanuman langur [monkey]
Langur L: 68 *with picture*
Hanyang [China]
Wuhan W: 514
Haora Bridge [India]
Bridge (table: Cantilever) B: 603
HAPE [illness]
Altitude sickness A: 390

Hapgood [play by Stoppard]
Stoppard, Tom So: 912
Haploid cell [biology]
Reproduction (How genes are transferred) R: 242
Happening [performance art]
Performance art P: 285
Happiness [philosophy]
Aristotle (Ethics and politics) A: 664
Bentham, Jeremy B: 254
Cynic philosophy Ci: 1205
Declaration of Independence (A Declaration of Rights) D: 76
Emotion (The basic emotion approach) E: 261
Ethics (Bentham and Mill) E: 367
Nirvana N: 424
Philosophy (Plato) P: 387
Plato (Ethics) P: 568
Utilitarianism U: 251
Happy Feet [film]
Computer graphics *picture on* Ci: 924g
Happy Prince and Other Tales, The [stories by Wilde]
Wilde, Oscar W: 301
Happy Warrior [nickname]
Smith, Alfred Emanuel S: 515
Hapsburg, House of *See* Habsburg, House of *in this index*
Hara-kiri [suicide] H: 55
World War II (The South Pacific) W: 489
Harald I [king of Norway] H: 55
Norway (The Viking period) N: 545
Harald III [king of Norway] H: 55
Harald V [king of Norway]
Norway (Political changes) N: 547
Harald Bluetooth [king of Denmark]
Denmark (Early days) D: 139
Harald Fairhair [king of Norway] *See* Harald I *in this index*
Harald Finehair [king of Norway] *See* Harald I *in this index*
Harald Sigurdsson [king of Norway] *See* Harald III *in this index*
Haram al-Sharif [area] *See* Temple Mount *in this index*
Harambee school [education]
Kenya (Education) K: 300 *with picture*
Harappa [ancient city]
India (Earliest times) I: 128
Indus Valley civilization I: 241
Pakistan (Early civilizations) P: 98
World, History of the (The Indus Valley) W: 425
Harappan civilization *See* Indus Valley civilization *in this index*
Harare [Zimbabwe] H: 55
Zimbabwe *picture on* Z: 593
Haras du Pin, Le [painting by Dufy]
Dufy, Raoul *picture on* D: 379
Painting (Color) P: 35
Harassment, Sexual *See* Sexual harassment *in this index*
Harbin [China] H: 55
Harbor [geography] H: 55
Breakwater B: 589 *with picture*
Ship (Navigation) S: 410
Harbor pilot
Ship (Navigating a ship) S: 410
Harbor porpoise [sea animal]
Porpoise P: 679 *with picture*
Harbourfront Jubilee Theatre [Summerside]
Prince Edward Island (Places to visit) P: 788
Harburg, E. Y. [American lyricist]
Wizard of Oz, The W: 374
Harcourt, Michael [Canadian political leader]
British Columbia (table) B: 628
Hard alcohol *See* Alcoholic beverage *in this index*
Hard-boiled detective story
American literature (Popular forms) A: 422
Detective story (History) D: 162-163
Hard bop [music]
Jazz (Hard bop) J: 72
Hard candy
Candy (Hard candies) C: 176
Hard cider [drink]
Alcoholic beverage (Other fermented beverages) A: 336
Cider Ci: 552
Hard consonant
Russian language (Pronunciation) R: 557
Hard contact lens
Contact lens Ci: 1020
Hard-core pornography
Obscenity and pornography (Regulating pornography) O: 644
Hard Day's Night, A [film]
Beatles B: 190
Hard disk [electronic device]
Computer (Hard drives) Ci: 915

Hard drive [electronic device]
Computer *picture on* Ci: 913; (Storage devices) Ci: 915
Digital video recorder D: 203
Magnetism (In the home) M: 60a
Hard good [merchandising]
Retailing (Department stores) R: 265
Hard lander [space probe]
Space exploration (Space probes) So: 708
Hard money [fund-raising]
Election campaign (Campaign financing) E: 160
Hard of hearing See Deafness *in this index*
Hard palate [anatomy]
Cleft palate Ci: 661
Mouth M: 903 *with diagram*
Palate P: 101 *with diagram*
Hard-paste porcelain
Porcelain (Kinds of porcelain) P: 675
Hard-rock mining
Gold (Mining) G: 252
Hard science fiction
Science fiction (The New Wave) S: 206
Hard-shell clam
Clam (Types of clams) Ci: 637 *with picture*
Hard Times [book by Dickens]
Dickens, Charles (The second phase) D: 188-189
Hard to Be a God [book by Strugatsky brothers]
Science fiction (Growing popularity) S: 205-206
Hard water
Detergent and soap D: 164
Water (Purifying and treating water) W: 126
Hard X ray
X rays (Wavelength) X: 541
Hardanger Plateau
Norway (Land regions) N: 541 *with map*
Hardboard
Forest products (Fiber products) F: 401-402 *with picture*
Wallboard W: 17
Hardecanute [Danish king]
England (table) E: 308
Harald III H: 55
Hardee, Cary A. [American political leader]
Florida (table) F: 260
Harden, Sir Arthur [British chemist]
Nobel Prizes (Chemistry: 1929) N: 443
Harden, Marcia Gay [American actress]
Motion picture (Best performance by an actress in a supporting role: 2000) M: 862b
Hardenberg, Friedrich von [German poet] *See* Novalis *in this index*
Hardening of the arteries See Arteriosclerosis *in this index*
Hardin, Charles H. [American political leader]
Missouri (table) M: 668
Hardin, Clifford M. [American government official]
Agriculture, Department of (table) A: 161
Nixon, Richard Milhous (table) N: 433
Hardin, Lil [American pianist]
Armstrong, Louis A: 723
Harding, Florence Kling [wife of Warren G. Harding]
First ladies of the United States (table) F: 142
Harding, Warren Gamaliel (Marriage) H: 56; (Death) H: 58-59 *with picture*
Harding, Warren Gamaliel [U.S. president] H: 56 *with pictures*
Coolidge, Calvin (As governor) Ci: 1031-1032
Hoover, Herbert Clark (Secretary of commerce) H: 328
President of the United States *picture on* P: 769
Teapot Dome T: 72
United States, History of the (Looking backward) U: 191
Harding, William L. [American political leader]
Iowa (table) I: 391
Hardinge, Sam Wylde [husband of]
Boyd, Belle B: 539
Hardman, Lamartine G. [American political leader]
Georgia (table) G: 130
Hardness [physical property] H: 59
Diamond D: 180; (Industrial uses) D: 182
Gem (Qualities of gem minerals) G: 77
Mineral (Hardness) M: 567
Quartz Q: 8
Rock (Hardness) R: 375
Hardouin-Mansart, Jules [French architect]
Architecture (Baroque architecture) A: 622
Hardscrabble [farm]
Grant, Ulysses S. (Business failures) G: 314
Hardtack [food]
Civil War, American (The enlisted men) Ci: 619-620
Hardware [electronics]
Computer Ci: 908
Internet I: 350; (How the Internet works) I: 350b

Software So: 572
Hardwick, Philip [British architect]
Architecture (The Industrial Revolution) A: 625
Hardwick, Thomas W. [American political leader]
Georgia (table) G: 130
Hardwood
Forest products (Lumber) F: 400
Lignum-vitae L: 302
Lumber (Hardwood lumber) L: 517
Plywood (Kinds of plywood) P: 585
Tree (Broadleaf trees) T: 414; (Broadleaf forests) T: 428 *with picture*
Wood (Kinds of wood) W: 389 *with pictures*
Woodworking (Wood for woodworking) W: 398
Hardwood dimension parts
Lumber (Hardwood lumber) L: 517
Hardy, Alexandre [French dramatist]
Drama (The French theater) D: 333
Hardy, Arthur S. [Canadian political leader]
Ontario (table) O: 783
Hardy, Harriet [birth name of]
Mill, Harriet Taylor M: 552
Hardy, James D. [American doctor]
Mississippi M: 623
Hardy, Oliver [American actor]
Laurel and Hardy L: 122 *with picture*
Hardy, Thomas [British author] H: 59
English literature (Later Victorian literature) E: 321
Novel (Britain) N: 573
Hardy chrysanthemum [plant]
Flower *picture on* F: 279
Hardy-Rand-Rittler test
Color blindness C: 827
Hare [animal] H: 59 *with picture*
Rabbit R: 46
Snowshoe hare S: 542 *with picture*
Taiga T: 14
Hare, David [British dramatist]
English literature (Recent English drama) E: 323
Hare, Thomas [British lawyer]
Proportional representation (The Hare System) P: 828
"Hare and the Tortoise, The" [story] *See* "Tortoise and the Hare, The" *in this index*
Hare Krishna
Cult (Modern cults) Ci: 1185
Yoga Y: 567
Hare System [political science]
Proportional representation (The Hare System) P: 828
Hare-wallaby [animal]
Wallaby W: 15
Harebell [plant]
Bluebell B: 422
Haredim [people]
Jerusalem (The people of Jerusalem) J: 96-98
Harefoot [son of Canute] *See* Harold I *in this index*
Harelip [birth defect]
Cleft palate Ci: 661
Harem [anthropology] H: 60
Ottoman Empire (People) O: 877
Persia, Ancient (The people) P: 296-297
Harem [zoology]
Elephant seal E: 232
Elk (The American elk) E: 241
Mammal (Mating) M: 122-123
Harem herd [zoology]
Impala I: 90
Hargobind, Guru [Sikh religious leader]
Diwali D: 255
Hargrave, Lawrence [Australian inventor]
Kite (The box kite) K: 339; (History) K: 340-341
Hargreaves, James [British inventor] H: 60 *with picture*
Industrial Revolution (Spinning machines) I: 248-249
Spinning (The spinning jenny) So: 794
Spinning jenny So: 795
Hari, Mata [German spy]
Mata Hari M: 298
Hari Singh [ruler of Kashmir]
Kashmir (History) K: 248
Harijan [sociology] *See* Untouchable *in this index*
Haring, Keith [American artist]
Painting (Recent painting) P: 87-88
Hariri, Rafik [Lebanese political leader]
Lebanon (After the civil war) L: 174
Syria (The early 2000's) So: 1076
"Hark, the Herald Angels Sing" [hymn]
Hymn (Words and music) H: 475
Harken Oil and Gas, Incorporated
Bush, George Walker (Business career) B: 722e
Harkness, Edward Stephen [American philanthropist]
Yale University (The Yale campus) Y: 548-549
Harkness Tower [New Haven]

New Haven *picture on* N: 229
Harlan, James [American political leader] H: 61
Harlan, John Marshall [1833-1911, American jurist] H: 61
Harlan, John Marshall [1899-1971, American jurist]
Harlan, John Marshall H: 61
Harlem [district]
Harlem Renaissance H: 61
New York City (Manhattan) N: 323-326 *with picture*
Harlem Globetrotters [team]
Basketball *picture on* B: 152; (The history of professional basketball) B: 154a-155
Harlem Hit Parade [recordings]
Rhythm and blues R: 320
Harlem Renaissance [arts] H: 61
African American literature (The 1900's) A: 136a
African Americans (The Harlem Renaissance and other achievements) A: 136m
American literature (The Harlem Renaissance) A: 422
Hughes, Langston H: 409
Locke, Alain LeRoy L: 412
Harlem River
New York City (The city) N: 323; (Transportation) N: 334
Harlequin [clown]
Drama (Commedia dell' arte) D: 331 *with picture*
Pantomime P: 132
Harlequin bug [insect]
Insect *picture on* I: 281
Stink bug So: 902
Harlequin hat
Hat (History) H: 84-85
Harlequin tuskfish
Fish *picture on* F: 155
Harlow, Harry Frederick [American psychologist] H: 61
HARM [missile]
Guided missile (Air-to-surface missiles) G: 426
Harmar, Josiah [American general]
Indian wars (Conflicts in the Midwest) I: 191
Little Turtle L: 392
Harmattan [weather]
Harmon, Judson [American government official]
Cleveland, Grover (table) Ci: 672
Justice, Department of (table) J: 203
Ohio (table) O: 699
Harmon, Tom [American football player]
Football (table) F: 363
Harmonic minor scale [music]
Music (Tone) M: 950 *with diagram*
Harmonic progression [mathematics]
Progression P: 812
Series (Working with infinite series) S: 317
Harmonic sound
Noise N: 451
Harmonic telegraph
Telephone (Bell's invention) T: 99
Harmonica [musical instrument] H: 61 *with pictures*
Harmonics [sound] H: 62 *with diagrams*
Pitch P: 498
Harmonists [religious group]
New Harmony N: 228
Harmonium [musical instrument] H: 62
Harmony [aesthetics]
Art and the arts (Enjoying the arts) A: 748
Design (Harmony) D: 157
Harmony [music] H: 62
Music (Harmony) M: 951
Rameau, Jean-Philippe R: 133
Variation V: 286
Harmony, Color
Color (Producing color harmony) Ci: 823 *with diagrams*
Harmony, Inc. [organization]
Barbershop quartet singing B: 107
Harmsworth, Alfred Charles William [British publisher]
Northcliffe, Viscount N: 520
Harnack, Adolf von [German theologian]
Max Planck Society for the Advancement of Science M: 318
Harness [machine]
Weaving (How a loom works) W: 173-174
Harness [parachute]
Parachute (Parts of a parachute) P: 142-143 *with picture*
Harness [riding equipment] H: 63 *with diagram*
Transportation (The Middle Ages) T: 387
Harness, Henry D. [British cartographer]
Map (Development of thematic and inventory mapping) M: 185
Harness horse
Horse (table: Some types and breeds of horses) H: 343; (Light harness horses) H: 345 *with*

picture

Harness racing [sport] **H: 63** *with picture*
Harnessed antelope
Antelope (Kinds of antelope) **A: 542**
Harnett, William Michael [American painter] **H: 64**
with picture
Harney, William [American general]
Wyoming (Indian and settler conflicts) **W: 534**
Harney Peak [mountain]
Black Hills **B: 387**
South Dakota (Land and Climate) **So: 675-676**
with map
Harnick, Sheldon [American lyricist]
Musical comedy (The modern musical emerges)
M: 960
Harold [kings of Norway] *See under Harald in this*
index
Harold I [king of England]
England (table) **E: 308**
Harold II [king of England] **H: 65**
Bayeux Tapestry **B: 176** *with picture*
Edward the Confessor **E: 113**
England (The Norman Conquest) **E: 305**
Hastings, Battle of **H: 83**
Norman Conquest **N: 455**
William I, the Conqueror **W: 308**
Harold, Earl of Wessex *See Harold II in this index*
Harold Washington Library Center
Chicago (New construction) **C: 437**
Harp [constellation] *See Lyra in this index*
Harp [musical instrument] **H: 65** *with pictures*
Harp of Zion, The [hymnal]
Gospel music **G: 277**
Harper, Benjamin [son of]
Harper, Stephen Joseph (Reform Party pioneer)
H: 66a *with picture*
Harper, Frances Ellen Watkins [American author]
H: 65 *with portrait*
African American literature (The 1800's) **A: 136a**
Harper, Joseph [father of]
Harper, Stephen Joseph (Childhood) **H: 66**
Harper, Margaret Johnston [mother of]
Harper, Stephen Joseph (Childhood) **H: 66**
Harper, Rachel [daughter of]
Harper, Stephen Joseph (Reform Party pioneer)
H: 66a *with picture*
Harper, Stephen Joseph [Canadian political
leader] **H: 66** *with pictures*
Canada, Government of *picture on* **C: 133**
Canada, History of (The return of the
Conservatives) **C: 152**
Conservative Party of Canada **Ci: 992**
Harper, William Rainey [American educator]
Chicago, University of (History) **C: 438**
Correspondence school **Ci: 1071**
Harpers Ferry [West Virginia] **H: 66b**
Brown, John (Harpers Ferry) **B: 643**
Civil War, American (Raid at Harpers Ferry)
Ci: 616; (Battle of Antietam) **Ci: 627**
United States, History of the (The "irrepressible
conflict") **U: 176**
West Virginia *picture on* **W: 227**; (Civil War and
statehood) **W: 226**
Harpers Ferry National Historical Park
[Maryland-West Virginia]
National Park System (table: National historical
parks) **N: 56-57**
West Virginia (Places to visit) **W: 216** *with picture*
Harper's Weekly [magazine]
Civil War, American (The home front) **Ci: 622**
with picture
Homer, Winslow **H: 304**
Magazine (Magazines in the 1800's) **M: 45**
Harpoon [weapon] **H: 66b**
Fishing industry (Harpoons) **F: 186**
Inuit (Hunting and fishing) **I: 354d**
Whale (Hunting techniques) **W: 263**
Harpsichord [musical instrument] **H: 66b** *with*
picture
Classical music (The Baroque period) **Ci: 647**
Orchestra *picture on* **O: 822**
Piano (History) **P: 447**
Harpy [mythology] **H: 67**
Harpy eagle [bird] **H: 67** *with picture*
Eagle (Other kinds of eagles) **E: 5**
Harquebus [gun] **H: 67** *with picture*
Harridge, Will [American baseball executive]
Baseball (table: Hall of Fame) **B: 134a**
Harrier [aircraft]
V/STOL **V: 452**
Harrier [bird] **H: 67**
Hawk *picture on* **H: 112**
Northern harrier **N: 520** *with picture*
Harrier [dog] **H: 68** *with picture*
Harriet the Spy [book by Fitzhugh]
Literature for children (New frankness) **L: 365**
Harriet Tubman Home

Tubman, Harriet **T: 480**
Harriman, Averell [American statesman] *See*
Harriman, W. Averell *in this index*
Harriman, Edward Henry [American financier]
Hill, James Jerome **H: 231**
Harriman, W. Averell [American statesman] **H: 68**
Truman, Harry S. (table) **T: 469**
Harriman, Walter [American political leader]
New Hampshire (table) **N: 223**
Harrington, Emerson C. [American political
leader]
Maryland (table) **M: 255**
Harrington, Gordon S. [Canadian political leader]
Nova Scotia (table) **N: 567**
Harrington, Michael [American political scientist]
Socialism (The New Left) **So: 561**
Harris, Andrew L. [American political leader]
Ohio (table) **O: 699**
Harris, Benjamin [American publisher] **H: 68**
Journalism (Early American journalism) **J: 174**
Literature for children (The Puritans) **L: 362**
Newspaper (Development of U.S. newspapers)
N: 386
Harris, Bucky [American baseball player]
Baseball (table: Hall of Fame) **B: 134a**
Harris, Chapin [American dentist]
Dentistry (Early dentistry) **D: 144-145**
Harris, Elisha [American political leader]
Rhode Island (table) **R: 311**
Harris, Eric [American public figure]
Columbine High School shooting (The attack)
Co: 853
Harris, Isham G. [American political leader]
Tennessee (table) **T: 152**
Harris, Joe Frank [American political leader]
Georgia (table) **G: 130**
Harris, Joel Chandler [American author] **H: 68**
with portrait
American literature (Realists) **A: 419**
Literature for children (Traditional literature)
L: 357-358
Harris, John [English theologian]
Encyclopedia (An age of experiment) **E: 268a**
Harris, John, Jr. [American businessman]
Harrisburg **H: 69**
Harris, Katherine [American government official]
Election of 2000 (Court challenges) **E: 161**
Harris, Lawren [Canadian painter]
Group of Seven **G: 402**
Harris, Louis [American pollster]
Public opinion poll *picture on* **P: 862**
Harris, Mary [American social reformer] *See Jones,*
Mary Harris in this index
Harris, Michael D. [Canadian political leader]
Ontario (table) **O: 783**; (The late 1900's) **O: 787**
Harris, Nathaniel E. [American political leader]
Georgia (table) **G: 130**
Harris, Patricia Roberts [American government
official] **H: 68** *with portrait*
African Americans (Politics) **A: 136s**
Harris, Paul P. [American lawyer]
Rotary International **R: 486**
Harris, Robert [Canadian painter] **H: 69** *with picture*
Harris, Roy [American composer] **H: 69**
Harris, Sarah [American public figure]
Crandall, Prudence **Ci: 1117**
Harris, Townsend [American diplomat]
Japan (Renewed relations with the West) **J: 56**
Harris, William Beasley [American educator]
Harris, Patricia Roberts **H: 69**
Harris, William J. [American political leader]
Russell, Richard Brevard **R: 524**
Harris, William Torrey [American educator]
Education (New theories of education) **E: 104**
Harris, Wynonie [American singer]
Rock music (Musical roots) **R: 376**
Harris Papyrus 1 [manuscript]
Library (Ancient libraries of papyrus) **L: 257**
Harrisburg [Pennsylvania] **H: 69**
Harrisburg Pennsylvanian [newspaper]
Public opinion poll (History) **P: 863**
Harrison, Albertis S., Jr. [American political leader]
Virginia (table) **V: 417**
Harrison, Anna Symmes [wife of William H.
Harrison]
First ladies of the United States (table) **F: 142**
Harrison, William Henry *picture on* **H: 76**;
(Harrison's family) **H: 74**
Harrison, Benjamin [American patriot] **H: 69**
Harrison, William Henry **H: 74**
Virginia (table) **V: 417**
Harrison, Benjamin [U.S. president] **H: 70** *with*
pictures
Cleveland, Grover (Election of 1888) **Ci: 671**
Harrison, Caroline Scott [wife of Benjamin
Harrison]
First ladies of the United States (table) **F: 142**

Harrison, Benjamin (Education) **H: 70**; (Life in the
White House) **H: 73** *with picture*
Harrison, David H. [Canadian political leader]
Manitoba (table) **M: 159**
Harrison, George [British musician]
Beatles **B: 189**
Rock music *picture on* **R: 380**; (The Beatles) **R: 379**
Harrison, Henry B. [American political leader]
Connecticut (table) **Ci: 967**
Harrison, Jane Irwin [daughter-in-law of]
Harrison, William Henry (Harrison's
administration (1841)) **H: 76** *with picture*
White House hostesses **W: 291**
Harrison, John [British clockmaker]
Chronometer **C: 539**
Map (Advances in European cartography) **M: 184**
Harrison, Mary [daughter of]
Harrison, Benjamin (Harrison's family) **H: 70**
Harrison, Mary Dimmick [wife of]
Harrison, Benjamin (Later years) **H: 73**
Harrison, Rex [British actor]
Motion picture (Best performance by an actor:
1964) **M: 862a**
Harrison, Russell Benjamin [son of]
Harrison, Benjamin (Harrison's family) **H: 70**
Harrison, William Henry [U.S. president] **H: 74**
with pictures
Harrison, Benjamin **H: 70**
Indian wars (Conflicts in the Midwest) **I: 191-192**
Indiana (Places to visit) **I: 206**; (Territorial days)
I: 215 *with picture*
Northwest Territory (Settlement) **N: 535**
United States, History of the (Politics after
Jackson) **U: 171**
Van Buren, Martin (Election of 1836) **V: 272**;
(Election of 1840) **V: 273**
Whig Party (In the 1840's) **W: 280**
Harrison Act [1914]
Drug abuse (History) **D: 365**
Opium (History) **O: 811**
Harrods [department store]
England *picture on* **E: 302**
Harroun, Ray [American race driver]
Automobile racing (table: Indianapolis 500
winners) **A: 980**
Harrow [tool] **H: 76**
Farm and farming (Preparing the soil) **F: 35** *with*
pictures
Harrow School [London] **H: 77**
Harry, Prince [British prince]
Charles, Prince **C: 382**
Diana, Princess of Wales **D: 183**
William, Prince **W: 309**
Harry Potter [literary figure] *See Potter, Harry in*
this index
Harry Potter and the Chamber of Secrets [book
by Rowling]
Rowling, J.K. **R: 494**
Harry Potter and the Deathly Hallows [book by
Rowling]
Literature for children (The early 2000's) **L: 366**
Rowling, J. K. **R: 494**
Harry Potter and the Goblet of Fire [book by
Rowling]
Literature for children *picture on* **L: 377**
Rowling, J.K. **R: 494**
Harry Potter and the Half-Blood Prince [book by
Rowling]
Rowling, J. K. **R: 494**
Harry Potter and the Order of the Phoenix [book
by Rowling]
Rowling, J. K. **R: 494**
Harry Potter and the Philosopher's Stone [book
by Rowling]
Potter, Harry **P: 715**
Rowling, J.K. **R: 494**
Harry Potter and the Prisoner of Azkaban [book
by Rowling]
Rowling, J.K. **R: 494**
Harry Potter and the Sorcerer's Stone [book by
Rowling]
Potter, Harry **P: 715**
Rowling, J.K. **R: 494**
Harry S. Truman [ship]
Aircraft carrier (The United States carrier fleet)
A: 206
Harry S. Truman Library and Museum
[Independence, Missouri]
Independence **I: 106**
Missouri (Museums) **M: 655** *with picture*; (Places
to visit) **M: 660**
Harry S. Truman National Historic Site [Missouri]
National Park System (table: National historic
sites) **N: 52-53**
Harry S. Truman Reservoir
Missouri (Rivers and lakes) **M: 662**
Harsanyi, John Charles [American economist]

Nobel Prizes (Economics: 1994) N: 449
Harsha [king of India] H: 77
Harsha-vardhana See Harsha in this index
Harshacraita [book]
Biography (The Middle Ages) B: 313
Hart [animal]
Deer D: 82d
Red deer R: 188
Hart, Isaiah D. [American settler]
Jacksonville J: 17
Hart, John [American patriot] H: 77
Hart, John [Canadian political leader]
British Columbia (table) B: 628
Hart, Johnny [American cartoonist]
Cartoon *pictures on* C: 267
Hart, Julia Catherine Beckwith [Canadian author]
New Brunswick (Interesting facts) N: 181
Hart, Leon [American football player]
Football (table) F: 363
Hart, Lorenz [American lyricist] H: 77
Musical comedy (Musical comedy matures)
M: 960
Rodgers, Richard R: 398
Hart, Louis F. [American political leader]
Washington (table) W: 65
Hart, Mickey [American musician]
Grateful Dead G: 329
Hart, Moss [American dramatist] H: 77
Kaufman, George S. K: 250
Hart, Ossian B. [American political leader]
Florida (table) F: 260
Hart, Steve [Australian outlaw]
Kelly, Ned K: 257
Hart, William Aaron [American businessman]
Gas [fuel] (Development of the natural gas
industry) G: 57-58
Hart-Dole-Inouye Federal Center
Battle Creek B: 172
Hart Memorial Trophy
Hockey (Professional leagues) H: 278-279
Hartack, Bill [American jockey]
Kentucky Derby K: 297
Harte, Bret [American author] H: 77
American literature (Realists) A: 419
Hartebeest [animal] H: 78 *with picture*
Hartford [Connecticut] H: 78
Connecticut *picture on* Ci: 953; table: Average
monthly weather Ci: 964
Hartford [ship]
Civil War, American (Battle of Mobile Bay) Ci: 632
Hartford, George Huntington [American
businessman] H: 79
Hartford Convention [U.S. history] H: 79
Madison, James (Progress of the war) M: 35-36
United States, History of the (Decline of the
Federalists) U: 165
Hartford Courant, The [newspaper]
Connecticut (Interesting facts) Ci: 953;
(Communication) Ci: 966
Hartford (Description) H: 78
Hartford School for the Deaf
Gallaudet G: 14
Harthacnut [Danish king] See Hardecanute in this
index
Hartley, Fred [American political leader]
Taft-Hartley Act T: 12
Hartley, Marsden [American painter] H: 79 *with
picture*
Hartley, Roland H. [American political leader]
Washington (table) W: 65
Hartline, Haldan Keffer [American physiologist]
Nobel Prizes (Physiology or medicine: 1967)
N: 446
Hartmann, Erich [German aviator]
Ace A: 24
Hartmann von Aue [German poet] H: 79
Hartnell, Nathaniel [Canadian artist]
Canada, History of *picture on* C: 144
Hartness, James [American political leader]
Vermont (table) V: 333
Hartnett, Gabby [American baseball player]
Baseball (table: Hall of Fame) B: 134a
Hartog, Dirk [Dutch explorer]
Western Australia (History) W: 231
Hartranft, John Fredrick [American political
leader]
Pennsylvania (table) P: 263
Hartsfield-Jackson Atlanta International Airport
Airport (table) A: 245
Hartwell, Leland Harrison [American geneticist]
Nobel Prizes (Physiology or medicine: 2001)
N: 447
Hārūn al-Rashīd [Muslim ruler] H: 79 *with portrait*
Harunobu [Japanese artist] H: 80
Japanese print (The master print artists) J: 63
with picture
Haruspice [religious leader]

Etruscans (Language and culture) E: 375-376
Harvard, John [English philanthropist] H: 80
Harvard University (History) H: 80
Library (Libraries in the United States) L: 261
Harvard Law School
Law (Law education) L: 138
Harvard-Smithsonian Center for Astrophysics
Smithsonian Institution (Other facilities) S: 519
Harvard University H: 80 *with picture*
Cambridge C: 74
Colonial life in America (Education) Ci: 803-804
with picture
Eliot, Charles William E: 237
Facebook (History) F: 4
Football (The history of football) F: 365
Law (Law education) L: 138
Massachusetts (Libraries) M: 274 *with picture*;
(Places to visit) M: 280
Radcliffe College R: 73
Rowing (History) R: 494
Universities and colleges (First universities in the
Americas) U: 210
Harvard University Herbarium
Gray, Asa G: 334
Harvard University Library
Library (Libraries in the United States) L: 261
Harvard Yard
Harvard University (The Harvard campus) H: 80
with picture
Harvest festival [custom]
Thanksgiving Day T: 230
Harvest-home celebration [custom]
Thanksgiving Day T: 230
Harvest mite [insect]
Chigger C: 447 *with picture*
Harvest moon H: 81
Harvest mouse
Mouse (Harvest mice) M: 901 *with picture*
Harvester [machine]
Hay H: 115
Reaper R: 173
Harvester ant [insect]
Ant *pictures on* A: 521, A: 524; (Castes) A: 523;
(Harvester ants) A: 526 *with picture*
Insect (Family life) I: 294-295
Harvester-conveyor [machine]
Pineapple (Cultivation and production) P: 472-
473
Harvesting [agriculture]
Farm and farming (Harvesting) F: 37 *with picture*
Combine Ci: 866
Cotton (Harvesting) Ci: 1090
Fruit (Harvesting) F: 547
Gardening (Harvesting) G: 36
Hay H: 115 *with picture*
Rice (Harvesting) R: 326 *with picture*
Vegetable (Harvesting and marketing
vegetables) V: 294
Harvestman [animal] See Daddy longlegs in this
index
Harvey, Charles T. [American inventor]
Elevated railroad E: 233
Harvey, Doug [American umpire]
Baseball (table: Hall of Fame) B: 134a
Harvey, Gabriel [English poet]
Nashe, Thomas N: 22
Harvey, George B. M. [American political leader]
Wilson, Woodrow (Governor of New Jersey)
W: 321
Harvey, James M. [American political leader]
Kansas (table) K: 234
Harvey, Louis P. [American political leader]
Wisconsin (table) W: 365
Harvey, Matthew [American political leader]
New Hampshire (table) N: 223
Harvey, William [English physician] H: 81
Biology (The Renaissance) B: 318
Heart (Discovery of circulation) H: 144 *with
picture*
Medicine (The beginnings of modern research)
M: 374
Science (Conducting experiments) S: 195
Haryana [state, India]
Punjab P: 903
Hasa [region]
Saudi Arabia (The Eastern Lowlands) S: 158 *with
picture*
Hash mark
Football (The field) F: 354-355 *with diagram*
Hashemite family
Jordan (Government) J: 160
Hashish [drug] H: 81
Assassination A: 817
Drug abuse (table: Some commonly abused
drugs) D: 363
Hashshashins [Middle Eastern history]
Assassination A: 817

Terrorism (Early terrorism) T: 178
Hasidism [religion] H: 82
Ba'al Shem Tov B: 2
Jews (Eastern European religious movements)
J: 123
Kabbalah K: 208
New York City *picture on* N: 332
Hasina Wajed, Sheikh [Bangladeshi political
leader]
Bangladesh (Recent developments) B: 86
Hasinai Confederacy [American Indians]
Texas (Indian days) T: 204
Haskalah [religious-cultural movement] H: 82
Hebrew literature (Modern Hebrew literature)
H: 162
Jews (Emergence into freedom) J: 123
Mendelssohn, Moses M: 399
Haskall, John [American inventor]
Combine Ci: 866
Haskell, Charles N. [American political leader]
Oklahoma (table) O: 730; (Early statehood)
O: 732
Haskell, Coburn [American golfer]
Golf (Beginnings) G: 264
Haskell, Robert [American political leader]
Maine (table) M: 87
Haskell Indian Nations University
Kansas (Schools) K: 220
Haslam, Bill [American political leader]
Tennessee (table) T: 152
Haslet, Joseph [American political leader]
Delaware (table) D: 109
Hasmoneans [ancient people]
Jerusalem (Ancient times) J: 100-101
Jews (The Hellenistic period) J: 121
Hass, Robert [American poet]
Poet laureate (table: Poets laureate of the United
States) P: 590
Hassall, William [American inventor]
Nail (How nails are made) N: 4
Hassam, Childe [American painter] H: 82
Impressionism (American Impressionism) I: 94
Hassan I [sultan of Morocco]
Morocco (French and Spanish control) M: 814
Hassan II [king of Morocco]
Morocco (Constitutional monarchy) M: 815
Hassel, Odd [Norwegian chemist]
Nobel Prizes (Chemistry: 1969) N: 443
Hassium [element] H: 82
Transuranium element T: 401
Hastert, J. Dennis [American political leader] H: 83
Hastie, William Henry [American jurist] H: 83
African Americans (The Great Depression)
A: 136n
Hasting, Daniel Hartman [American political
leader]
Pennsylvania (table) P: 263
Hastings, Alcee L. [American jurist]
Impeachment (History) I: 91-92
Hastings, Battle of [1066] H: 83
Norman Conquest N: 455
William I, the Conqueror W: 308
Hastings, Jonathan [American farmer]
Yankee Y: 552
Hastings, Warren [British political leader] H: 83
India (The rise of the East India Company) I: 130
Haston, Dougal [British mountain climber]
Mount Everest M: 884
Hasty generalization
Fallacy F: 16
Haszard, Francis L. [Canadian political leader]
Prince Edward Island (table) P: 791
Hat H: 83 *with pictures*
Clothing *pictures on* Ci: 704
Colonial life in America (Clothing) Ci: 799
Indian, American *pictures on* I: 145, I: 162
Hat trick [hockey]
Hockey (Hockey terms) H: 275
Hatch
Ship (Nautical terms) S: 405 *with diagram*
Space exploration (Space stations) So: 721
Hatch, Carl [American political leader]
Hatch Political Activities Act H: 85
Hatch, Fred L. [American farmer]
Silo S: 463
Hatch Act [1887]
Agricultural education (History) A: 145
Hatch Act [1939-40] See Hatch Political Activities
Act in this index
Hatch Act Reform Amendments [1993]
Hatch Political Activities Act H: 85
Hatch Memorial Shell
Boston (The arts) B: 501 *with picture*
Hatch Political Activities Act [1939-1940] H: 85
Hatcher, Richard Gordon [American political
leader] H: 85
Gary G: 47

Hatchery
Fish *pictures on* F: 146
Poultry (Raising poultry) P: 720
Salmon (Salmon conservation) S: 70
Hatchet [book by Paulsen]
Paulsen, Gary P: 202
Hatchetfish
Fish *pictures on* F: 145, F: 156, F: 157
Hatchett, Charles [British chemist]
Niobium N: 424
Hatching [art]
Painting (Tempera) P: 38-39 *with picture*
Hatching [biology]
Bird (Laying and hatching eggs) B: 357-359 *with pictures*
Chicken (Breeding and hatching) C: 443
Incubator (Incubators for eggs) I: 106
Hate crime H: 85
Crime (Hate crime) Ci: 1137
Hatfield [American family]
Feud F: 81
Hatfield, Henry D. [American political leader]
West Virginia (table) W: 225; (Labor developments) W: 229
Hatfield, Mark O. [American political leader]
Oregon (table) O: 845
Hatfield, Richard [Canadian political leader]
New Brunswick (table) N: 195
Hath Not a Jew… [book by Klein]
Klein, A. M. K: 343
Hatha-yoga
Yoga Y: 567
Hathaway, Anne [wife of William Shakespeare]
Shakespeare, William (Marriage) S: 346
Hathaway, Stanley K. [American political leader]
Ford, Gerald Rudolph (table) F: 378
Interior, Department of the (table) I: 325
Wyoming (table) W: 532
Hatheway, George L. [Canadian political leader]
New Brunswick (table) N: 195
Hathor [Egyptian goddess]
Isis I: 462
Mythology *picture on* M: 977; (Other Egyptian divinities) M: 980
Hathorne, John [American jurist]
Hawthorne, Nathaniel (His stories and sketches) H: 115
Hatoyama, Yukio [Japanese political leader]
Japan (Recent developments) J: 59
Hatshepsut [queen of ancient Egypt] H: 86
Architecture (Egyptian architecture) A: 612 *with picture*
Egypt, Ancient (The New Kingdom) E: 143
Exploration (Ancient exploration) E: 440
Thutmose III T: 273
Hatteras, Cape *See* Cape Hatteras *in this index*
Hatter's Castle [book by Cronin]
Cronin, A. J. Ci: 1152
Hatto [literary figure]
Mouse Tower M: 902
Hatton, Frank [American government official]
Arthur, Chester Alan (table) A: 756
Hatton, Ricky [British boxer]
Boxing *picture on* B: 526
Hattusas [ancient city]
Hittites (History) H: 269
Haughey, Charles James [Irish political leader]
Ireland (table) I: 428
Haughton, William R. [American harness driver]
Harness racing (History) H: 64
Haumea [dwarf planet]
Dwarf planet D: 394
Planet (The outer dwarf planets) P: 512
Haunch [architecture]
Arch *diagram on* A: 593
Haun's Mill, Massacre at [1838]
Mormons (Mormons in the Middle West) M: 808-809
"Haunted Mind, The" [story by Hawthorne]
Hawthorne, Nathaniel (His stories and sketches) H: 115
Haunting of Hill House, The [book by Jackson]
Jackson, Shirley J: 16
Hauptman, Herbert Aaron [American chemist]
Nobel Prizes (Chemistry: 1985) N: 444
Hauptmann, Bruno Richard [American public figure]
Lindbergh, Charles Augustus (The Lindbergh kidnapping) L: 330
Hauptmann, Gerhart [German author] H: 86
German literature (Naturalism) G: 141
Naturalism (Naturalism in drama) N: 66
Hauptschule [education]
Germany (Education) G: 151-152
Hausa [language]
Africa (Languages) A: 105
Niger (People) N: 407-408

Hausa [people] H: 86
Niger (People) N: 407 *with picture*
Nigeria *picture on* N: 414; (People) N: 411
Hausen, Harald zur [German biologist]
Nobel Prizes (Physiology or medicine: 2008) N: 447
Haushofer, Karl [German geopolitician]
Geopolitics G: 106b
Haussmann, Georges Eugene [French government official]
City planning (The Renaissance) Ci: 602
Haute couture [fashion]
Clothing (Marketing categories of fashion) Ci: 706
Haute cuisine [food]
France (Food and drink) F: 459
Haüy, René J. [French scientist]
Mineral (The scientific study of mineral crystals) M: 571
Havana [Cuba] H: 86 *with picture*
Cuba Ci: 1168 *with picture*; (History) Ci: 1175
Havana, University of
Havana (Education and cultural life) H: 86-87
Havana brown cat
Cat *picture on* C: 288; (Short-haired breeds) C: 290-291
Havanese [dog] H: 87 *with picture*
Havasupai Indians
Grand Canyon (History) G: 307
Havel, Václav [Czech political leader] H: 87
Czech Republic (History) Ci: 1213-1214
Czechoslovakia (The Velvet Revolution) Ci: 1216
Havel River [Germany]
Berlin *picture on* B: 262
Haven, C. D. [American chemist]
Glass (table) G: 218
Havers, Clopton [English biologist]
Haversian canals H: 87
Haversian canals [anatomy] H: 87
Haviland, David [American businessman]
Porcelain (French porcelain) P: 677
Haviland, Thomas Heath [Canadian political leader]
Confederation of Canada (Fathers of Confederation) Ci: 935
Haviland, Virginia [American author]
Regina Medal (table: 1976) R: 206
Havlicek, John [American basketball player]
Basketball *picture on* B: 154
Haw [fruit]
Hawthorn H: 114
Hawaii H: 88 *with pictures and maps*
See also the list of Related articles in the Hawaii *article*
Bird (Birds of the Pacific Islands) B: 349 *with picture*; (Endangered species) B: 370
Civil union Ci: 613
Mythology (Pacific Islands divinities) M: 984
United States (Climate) U: 126-128 *with picture*
Agriculture
Pineapple (History) P: 473
Government
City government Ci: 595
History
Asian Americans (The second wave) A: 812e; (Arrivals of the early 1900's) A: 812e
Cleveland, Grover (Foreign affairs) Ci: 673
Cook, James (Final voyage) Ci: 1026
Dole, Sanford Ballard D: 285
Harrison, Benjamin (International affairs) H: 73
Public lands (Acquisition of public lands) P: 858
United States, History of the *map on* U: 184
Physical features
Hot spot H: 374a
Mountain (Above a hot spot) M: 893
Pacific Islands (The high islands) P: 7-8 *with picture*
Plate tectonics (Evidence of plate movement) P: 563
Seamount S: 269
Hawaii, Kingdom of
Hawaii (The kingdom of Hawaii) H: 106
Hawaii, Republic of
Hawaii (The Republic of Hawaii) H: 108
Hawai'i, University of H: 110
Hawaii *picture on* H: 95
Hawaii-loa [legendary figure]
Hawaii (Early days) H: 106
Hawai'i Volcanoes National Park [Hawaii] H: 110
Cave *picture on* C: 321
Kilauea K: 315
National Park System (table: National parks) N: 48
Hawaiian eruption [geology]
Volcano (Describing eruptions) V: 442b
Hawaiian goose [bird] *See* Nene *in this index*
Hawaiian honeycreeper [bird] H: 110 *with pictures*
Hawaiian Islands *See* Hawaii *in this index*

Hawaiian language
Hawaii (Language) H: 93
Hawaiian sling
Spearfishing So: 768 *with picture*
Hawaiians [people]
Hawaii (Population) H: 92-93
Hawaiki [Hawaiian legend]
Hawaii (Early days) H: 106
Hawes, Charles Boardman [American author]
Newbery Medal (table) N: 359
Hawi, Khalil [Lebanese author]
Arabic literature (Poetry) A: 583
Hawikuh [ancient city]
Gallup G: 16
Hawk [bird] H: 111 *with pictures*
Bird of prey B: 374a
Buzzard B: 745
Falconry F: 14
Hawk [tool]
Plaster *picture on* P: 553
Hawk [weapon]
Artillery *picture on* A: 763
Hawk, Tony [American skateboarder] H: 113 *with picture*
Hawk in the Rain, The [poems by Hughes]
Hughes, Ted H: 409
Hawk moth H: 113
Animal *picture on* A: 490
Moth (Migration) M: 839; (Hawk moths) M: 841 *with pictures*
Hawk Mountain Sanctuary [Kittatinny Mountains]
Pennsylvania (Places to visit) P: 254
Hawke, Robert James Lee [Australian political leader]
Australia (table) A: 923; (Political upheavals) A: 925
Hawkes, Graham [American engineer]
Earle, Sylvia Alice E: 14
Hawkes, Kevin [American artist]
Literature for children *picture on* L: 375
Hawkeye State [nickname]
Iowa I: 374
Hawking, Stephen William [British physicist] H: 113
Hawking glove
Glove *picture on* G: 235
Hawking radiation [physics]
Hawking, Stephen William H: 113
Hawkins, Alvin [American political leader]
Tennessee (table) T: 152
Hawkins, Coleman [American saxophonist] H: 113
Hawkins, George [American dollmaker]
Doll (Cloth dolls) D: 289
Hawkins, Jim [literary figure]
Stevenson, Robert Louis (Novels) So: 898
Hawkins, Sir John [English sea captain] H: 114
Drake, Sir Francis (Early life) D: 321; (Later life) D: 323
Galleon G: 15
Spanish Armada (The two fleets) So: 755-756
Hawkins, William [American political leader]
North Carolina (table) N: 490
Hawks [U.S. history]
Johnson, Lyndon Baines (The widening Vietnam War) J: 150-151
Vietnam War (Reactions in the United States) V: 375
Hawks, Atlanta [team]
Basketball (table) B: 150
Hawks, Howard [American director] H: 114
Hawksbill turtle
Sea turtle (Types) S: 262b *with picture*
Hawkweed [plant]
Devil's paintbrush D: 175
Hawkyns, Sir John [English sea captain] *See* Hawkins, Sir John *in this index*
Hawley, James H. [American political leader]
Idaho (table) I: 42
Hawley, Joseph R. [American political leader]
Connecticut (table) Ci: 967
Hawn, Goldie [American actress]
Motion picture (Best performance by an actress in a supporting role: 1969) M: 862b
Haworth, Sir Walter Norman [British chemist]
Nobel Prizes (Chemistry: 1937) N: 443
Hawthorn [tree] H: 114 *with picture*
Holly H: 293
Tree *pictures on* T: 421
Hawthorn, Mike [British race driver]
Automobile racing (table: Formula One World Drivers' Championship) A: 980
Hawthorne [book by James]
American literature (Mark Twain and Henry James) A: 420
Hawthorne, Nathaniel [American author] H: 114
American literature (The romance) A: 418 *with portrait*

Novel (The United States) N: 573
Pierce, Franklin (Early life) P: 454
Poe, Edgar Allan (Fiction and theory of fiction)
P: 590
Romance R: 415
Romanticism (Romanticism in literature) R: 427
Hay [feed] H: 115 *with picture*
Alfalfa (As livestock feed) A: 346 *with picture*
Horse (Food) H: 355
Rake R: 130 *with picture*
Timothy T: 292d
Hay, George D. [American radio broadcaster]
Country music (Early commercial success)
Ci: 1098b
"Grand Ole Opry" G: 308
Hay, John Milton [American statesman] H: 116
Hay-Pauncefote Treaty H: 117
Open-Door Policy O: 789
Panama Canal (The United States and the canal)
P: 125
Hay, Marion E. [American political leader]
Washington (table) W: 65
Hay, Merle [American soldier]
Iowa (The early 1900's) I: 395
Hay-Bunau-Varilla Treaty [1903]
Panama Canal (The United States and the canal)
P: 125-126
Hay conditioner [machine]
Hay H: 115
Hay fever [disorder] H: 116
Allergy A: 373
Goldenrod G: 256
Immune system (The humoral immune response)
I: 88-
Pollen P: 644
Ragweed R: 103
Sneezing S: 538
Hay Fever [play by Coward]
Coward, Noël Ci: 1107
Hay-Herrán Treaty [1903]
Panama Canal (The United States and the canal)
P: 125
Hay millet [grain]
Millet M: 555
Hay-Pauncefote Treaty [1901] H: 116
Clayton-Bulwer Treaty Ci: 659
Panama Canal (The United States and the canal)
P: 125
Haya de la Torre, Víctor Raúl [Peruvian political
leader]
Latin America (Political circumstances in the early
to middle 1900's) L: 109
Peru (The rise of APRA) P: 316
Hayabusa [space probe]
Asteroid (History of study) A: 824b
Space exploration (Probes to asteroids) So: 711
Hayden, Carl Trumbull [American political leader]
H: 117
Hayden, Ferdinand V. [American explorer]
Yellowstone National Park (History) Y: 559-560
Hayden, Horace [American dentist]
Dentistry (Early dentistry) D: 144-145
Hayden, Melissa [Canadian dancer] H: 117
Hayden, Mike [American political leader]
Kansas (table) K: 234
Hayden Planetarium [New York City]
Planetarium *picture on* P: 514a; (Modern
planetariums) P: 514b-514c *with picture*
Haydn, Franz Joseph See Haydn, Joseph *in this
index*
Haydn, Joseph [Austrian composer] H: 117
Austria (Music) A: 932
Beethoven, Ludwig van (Beethoven's life) B: 213
Classical music (The Classical period) Ci: 647-648
Music box M: 958
Symphony So: 1067
Hayek, Friedrich August von [Austrian-born
economist]
Economics (Modern economics) E: 64-65
Nobel Prizes (Economics: 1974) N: 449
Hayes, Denis [American attorney]
Earth Day E: 32
Hayes, Helen [American actress] H: 117 *with
portrait*
Motion picture (Best performance by an actress:
1931-32) M: 862; (Best performance by an
actress in a supporting role: 1970) M: 862b
Hayes, Ira H. [American soldier]
Iwo Jima, Battle of *picture on* I: 523
Hayes, Lord [British admiral]
Pekingese P: 231
Hayes, Lucy Webb [wife of Rutherford B. Hayes]
First ladies of the United States F: 143; (table)
F: 142
Hayes, Rutherford Birchard (Hayes's family)
H: 119; (Life in the White House) H: 121 *with
portrait*

Hayes, Patrick Joseph [American religious leader]
Cardinal (table: American cardinals) C: 211
Hayes, Roland [American singer] H: 117
Hayes, Rutherford, Jr. [father of]
Hayes, Rutherford Birchard (Early life) H: 118
Hayes, Rutherford Birchard [U.S. president]
H: 118 *with pictures*
Electoral Commission E: 164
Ohio (table) O: 699
Reconstruction (The 1876 presidential election)
R: 179
Republican Party (The Radical Republicans and
Reconstruction) R: 254
Hayes, Sophia Birchard [mother of]
Hayes, Rutherford Birchard (Early life) H: 118
Hayes Library [Fremont]
Ohio (Places to visit) O: 690
Hayman Fire
Colorado (The early 2000's) Ci: 847-848
Haymarket Riot [1886] H: 121
Altgeld, John Peter A: 389
Chicago (A city reborn) C: 435
Illinois (Industrial development) I: 74 *with picture*
Labor movement (Opposition to unions) L: 10
Riot (During the 1800's) R: 348-349
United States, History of the (Early reform efforts)
U: 185-186
Hayne, Robert Young [American political leader]
H: 122
Jackson, Andrew (The nullification crisis) J: 12
Nullification N: 603
Webster, Daniel (The U.S. senator) W: 177
Haynes, Elwood [American inventor] H: 122
Indiana (Progress as a state) I: 216 *with picture*
Haynsworth, Clement F., Jr. [American jurist]
Nixon, Richard Milhous (The national scene)
N: 433-434
Hays, George Washington [American political
leader]
Arkansas (table) A: 712
Hays, William [husband of]
Pitcher, Molly P: 499
Hayter, Andrew [American settler]
Arlington A: 716
Hayward, Susan [American actress]
Motion picture (Best performance by an actress:
1958) M: 862
Haywood, William Dudley [American labor leader]
Idaho *picture on* I: 43; (Early statehood) I: 44
Hazanavicius, Michel [French film director]
Motion picture (Best achievement in directing:
2011) M: 862
Hazard of New Fortunes, A [book by Howells]
Howells, William Dean H: 401
Hazardous wastes H: 122
See also Hazmat *in this index*
Electric power (Nuclear power plants) E: 184
Engineering (Environmental engineering) E: 286
with picture
Environmental pollution (Hazardous waste)
E: 334
Greenpeace G: 386
New York (The late 1900's) N: 319-320
Haze [weather]
Fog F: 314
Haze droplet
Rain (Formation of rain) R: 123
Hazel [tree] H: 122 *with picture*
Hazelnut [nut]
Filbert F: 99 *with pictures*
Hazel H: 122 *with picture*
Hazelwood, Joseph J. [American ship captain]
Exxon Valdez oil spill E: 459
Hazen, John D. [Canadian political leader]
New Brunswick (table) N: 195
Hazer [person]
Rodeo (Steer wrestling) R: 397
Hazing
Fraternity (Membership) F: 495-496
Hazlitt, William [British author] H: 123
English literature (Romantic prose) E: 320
Essay (Formal essays) E: 359
Hazmat [materials]
Fire department *picture on* F: 128; (Special fire
vehicles) F: 127; (Protective clothing) F: 127
Hazzard, David [American political leader]
Delaware (table) D: 109
HCE [literary figure]
Joyce, James J: 177
HCG [hormone] *See* Human chorionic
gonadotropin *in this index*
H.D. [pen name]
American literature (Modernist poetry) A: 421
HD-4 [boat]
Hydrofoil (History) H: 468
HD 168443 [star]
Planet (The first discoveries) P: 513

HD 209458 [star]
Planet (The first discoveries) P: 513
HD Radio
Radio (Radio since the 1950's) R: 94
HDHP [insurance]
Insurance (Other types of health insurance) I: 312
HDL [biochemistry] *See* High-density lipoprotein
in this index
HDPE [plastic] *See* High density polyethylene *in
this index*
HDTV [electronics] *See* High-definition television
in this index
He [letter]
E E: 1 *with picture*
He [symbol]
Helium (Properties) H: 176
Head [anatomy] H: 123 *with diagrams*
See also Skull *in this index*
Human body (Anatomy of the human body)
H: 422 *with diagrams*
Phrenology P: 430
Head [botany]
Flower (Variations in flower structure) F: 294
Inflorescence I: 268a
Head [computing]
HyperText Markup Language H: 477
Head [magnetic recording]
Tape recorder (How tape recorders work) T: 37
with diagrams
Videotape recorder (Recording) V: 361 *with
diagrams*
Head, Natt [American political leader]
New Hampshire (table) N: 223
Head Hunters [recording]
Hancock, Herbie H: 38
Head lettuce
Lettuce (Kinds of lettuce) L: 213 *with pictures*
Head lice [insects] H: 123
Hair (Disorders of the hair and scalp) H: 10
Louse L: 507
Head linesman [sports]
Football (The officials) F: 362
Head-mounted display [electronics]
Virtual reality V: 426 *with picture*
Head of household
Income tax (Figuring the individual income tax)
I: 104
Head of state [government]
Government (Heads of government) G: 283
Prime minister P: 778c
Head shrinking
Headhunter H: 125
Indian, American (Why the Indians fought)
I: 144-145
Jívaro Indians J: 128
Head-Smashed-in Buffalo Jump [cliff]
Alberta (Interesting facts) A: 313 *with picture*
Head Start [education] H: 124
Children and Families, Administration for C: 457
Preschool (History) P: 756b-757
Head tax *See* Poll tax *in this index*
Head wind [weather]
Wind shear W: 332
Headache H: 124
Allergy A: 373
Migraine M: 537
Whiplash W: 281
Headdress
See also Hairdressing; Hat *in this index*
Clothing (The Renaissance) Ci: 702 *with picture*
Egypt, Ancient (Food, clothing, and shelter)
E: 137
Indian, American *picture on* I: 160
Sioux Indians *picture on* S: 475
Header [construction]
Brick (Bonds) B: 599
House (table) H: 380
Headhunter [anthropology] H: 125
Heading [fabric]
Flag (Manufacturing flags) F: 222-223
Heading [letter writing]
Letter writing (The heading) L: 210 *with picture*
Heading [soccer]
Soccer (Heading) So: 547
Headland [geography]
Cape C: 186
Headline [advertising]
Advertising (Attention-getting headlines) A: 76
Headline News [television network]
Cable News Network C: 7
Headman [leader]
Blackfeet Indians B: 393
Headphones H: 125
Stereophonic sound system (Speakers) So: 892
Headrig [machine]
Lumber (From sawmill to lumberyard) L: 518
Headrights [law]

Colonial life in America (Economic reasons)
Ci: 788
Heads-up display map [navigation]
Map (Navigation maps) M: 178
Headsaw [machine]
Lumber *pictures on* L: 520, L: 524; (Sawing logs)
L: 519
Headstart [education] *See* Head Start *in this index*
Headwaters [geography]
Divide D: 241 *with diagram*
River (River systems) R: 351
Heald, Nathan [American military leader]
Fort Dearborn F: 412
Healey-Kay, Sydney Francis [British dancer]
Dolin, Anton D: 285
Healing, Faith [religion] *See* Faith healing *in this index*
Health H: 125 *with pictures*
See also Public health *in this index; and the list of Related articles in the* Health *article*
African Americans (Health issues) A: 136s
Air pollution (Effects of air pollution) A: 199
Careers (Health) C: 223 *with pictures*
Cigarette Ci: 553
Colonial life in America (Health and medicine)
Ci: 809
Environmental pollution E: 330
Fat (Fats and disease) F: 53
Foundation (Health) F: 431
Homelessness (Causes and conditions) H: 302
Indian reservation (Description) I: 188-189
Mythology (Symbols) M: 975
Obesity (Consequences of obesity) O: 642a
Physical education (During the 1900's) P: 433
Physical fitness P: 433
Poverty (Effects of poverty) P: 723
Shoe (Shoes and health) S: 431
Smoking S: 520
Social work (Fields of social work) So: 558
Tea (Tea and health) T: 63
World, History of the (Scientific and technological achievements) W: 448a
Health, Board of [U.S.] H: 127
Health, National Institutes of *See* National Institutes of Health *in this index*
Health, Public *See* Public health *in this index*
Health and Human Services, Department of
[U.S.] H: 127 *with picture*
Hoover Commission H: 332
National Institute for Occupational Safety and Health N: 39
Obesity (Prevention of obesity) O: 642b
Public health P: 855
Washington, D.C. *map on* W: 76
Health and Human Services, Secretary of [U.S.]
Flag *picture on* F: 211
Health and Human Services, Department of (Organization) H: 128
Health care
See also Health insurance *in this index*
Disability (Health care and assistive devices)
D: 221
Infant mortality I: 264
Old age (Health care) O: 739
Health care reform *See* Health insurance, National *in this index*
Health Council, National [organization] H: 129
Health, Education, and Welfare, Department of
Health and Human Services, Department of
H: 128
Health food H: 129
Food (Recent developments) F: 337
Health insurance
See also Health insurance, National *in this index*
Blue Cross and Blue Shield B: 420
Genetic testing (Promises and challenges of genetic testing) G: 85
Insurance (Health insurance) I: 311 *with diagram;* (Greater regulation) I: 316
Maine (The early 2000's) M: 92
Managed care plans M: 131
Medicaid M: 361
Medicare M: 362
Medicine (Providing medical care) M: 366; (Financing advanced medical care) M: 377-378
Obama, Barack (Health insurance reform)
O: 640g; (Health care law upheld) O: 641
Poverty (Social welfare programs) P: 725
Social security (Medicare) So: 555
Health insurance, National H: 129
Clinton, Bill (National affairs) Ci: 682d
Clinton, Hillary Rodham Ci: 682h
Medicine (Other countries) M: 368
Health insurance exchange
Obama, Barack (Health insurance reform)
O: 640g-640h
Health Insurance Portability and Accountability

Act [1996]
Insurance (Greater regulation) I: 316
Health maintenance organization
Insurance (Managed care plans) I: 312
Managed care plans (In the United States) M: 131
Medicine (The United States) M: 367-368
Health Organization, World *See* World Health Organization *in this index*
Health resort
Bath (Medical bathing) B: 163
Health Resources and Services Administration
[U.S.]
Health and Human Services, Department of (Organization) H: 128
Health Statistics, National Center for
Vital statistics (Collecting and publishing vital statistics) V: 429-430
Healy, George Peter Alexander [American artist]
Buchanan, James *picture on* B: 658
Calhoun, John Caldwell *picture on* C: 35
Pierce, Franklin *picture on* P: 454
Polk, James Knox *picture on* P: 640
Tyler, John *picture on* T: 532
Van Buren, Martin *picture on* V: 270
Webster, Daniel *picture on* W: 177
Healy, James Augustine [American religious leader] H: 129
Heaney, Seamus [Irish poet] H: 130
Heap o' Living, A [poems by Guest]
Guest, Edgar Albert G: 421
Heard, Stephen [American political leader]
Georgia (table) G: 130
Heard, William W. [American political leader]
Louisiana (table) L: 496
Hearing [sense]
Animal (Adaptations for sensing the environment) A: 492-493 *with picture*
Audiology A: 882
Bird (Hearing) B: 365
Deafness D: 56
Dog (Senses) D: 265
Ear E: 7; (The sense of hearing) E: 9
Fish (Hearing) F: 164
Hearing aid H: 130
Insect (Hearing) I: 290-291 *with picture*
Mammal (Senses) M: 120
Mastoid M: 298
Reading (Physical disabilities) R: 162
Reptile (Sense organs) R: 251-252
Senses S: 301
Tinnitus T: 294
Hearing aid [instrument] H: 130 *with pictures*
Deafness (Assistive technology) D: 58
Hearing disorder
See also Deafness *in this index*
Closed captioning Ci: 685
Disability (Hearing disabilities) D: 219
Hearing ear dog
Deafness (Assistive technology) D: 58-59
Hearing fan
Hearing aid (History) H: 131
Hearing loss *See* Deafness *in this index*
Hearne, Samuel [British explorer] H: 131
Canadian literature (Beginnings of Canadian literature) C: 156-157
Exploration (Crossing North America) E: 447 *with map*
Great Slave Lake G: 348
Northwest Territories (European exploration) N: 533
Saskatchewan (The coming of the fur traders) S: 146
Hearnes, Warren E. [American political leader]
Missouri (table) M: 668
Hearsay evidence [law]
Evidence (Rules) E: 426
Hearse [vehicle]
Funeral customs (The funeral) F: 557
Hearst, George [father of]
Hearst, William Randolph H: 131
Hearst, Patricia [American public figure]
Hearst, William Randolph H: 131
Hearst, Phoebe Apperson [American educator]
H: 131
Birney, Alice Josephine McLellan B: 377
Hearst, William Randolph H: 131
Hearst, Randolph A. [American publisher]
Hearst, William Randolph H: 131
Hearst, William H. [Canadian political leader]
Ontario (table) O: 783
Hearst, William Randolph [American publisher]
H: 131
Citizen Kane Ci: 568
Constitution Day and Citizenship Day Ci: 572
Spanish-American War (Background to the war)
So: 753
Welles, Orson W: 194

Hearst Castle [estate]
California (Places to visit) C: 46 *with picture*
Heart [anatomy] H: 132 *with pictures*
See also the list of Related articles in the Heart *article*
Angina pectoris A: 461
Aorta A: 562
Arrhythmia A: 743
Artery A: 750
Artificial heart A: 759 *with picture*
Blood (What blood does in the body) B: 408
Blood pressure B: 416
Calcium channel blocker C: 21
Cardiology C: 212
Circulatory system (The heart) Ci: 559 *with picture*
Death (Defining death) D: 61
Defibrillator D: 88
Electrocardiograph E: 199
Frog *picture on* F: 537
Human body *picture on* H: 417; (The heart)
H: 421; (table) H: 422 *with diagram*
Insect (Circulatory system) I: 288 *with diagram*
Life (Tissues, organs, and organ systems) L: 277 *with diagram*
Mitral valve prolapse M: 679
Muscle (Cardiac muscle) M: 935
Nuclear physics N: 595
Stress test So: 927
Vein V: 295
Heart [suit]
Card game (History) C: 209
Heart Association, American *See* American Heart Association *in this index*
Heart attack [disorder]
Aspirin (Health benefits) A: 816
C-reactive protein C: 2
Disease (Diseases associated with aging) D: 230
First aid (Heart attack) F: 141
Heart H: 132; (Coronary artery disease) H: 137; (Heart attack) H: 138 *with pictures*
Hypertension H: 476
Heart block [disorder]
Arrhythmia A: 743
Heart (Abnormal heart rhythms) H: 142
Heart disease
Heart H: 132; (Coronary artery disease) H: 137
Beta-blocker B: 274
C-reactive protein C: 2
Cholesterol (Cholesterol and heart disease)
C: 520
Digitalis D: 203
Disability D: 218
Drug (Drugs that affect the heart and blood vessels) D: 351
Fat (Fats and disease) F: 53
Framingham Heart Study F: 451
Hormone replacement therapy H: 338
Lidocaine L: 270
Menopause M: 402
Nutrition (Heart disease) N: 630
Rheumatic fever R: 291
Smoking (Why smoking is dangerous) S: 520
Triglyceride T: 442
United Kingdom (Food and drink) U: 55
Heart failure
Heart (Diagnosis and treatment) H: 139; (Valve disease) H: 141-142; (Heart failure) H: 143
Inhalant I: 271
Myocarditis M: 971
Heart Fund
Heart Association, American H: 147
Heart Is a Lonely Hunter, The [book by McCullers]
McCullers, Carson M: 332g
Heart-lung machine
Heart (Treatment) H: 138 *with picture;* (Development of heart surgery) H: 144 *with picture*
Heart murmur [disorder] H: 147
Heart (Birth defects) H: 140-141
Rheumatic fever R: 291
"Heart of Darkness" [story by Conrad]
Conrad, Joseph Ci: 973
Heart of Dixie [nickname]
Alabama A: 256
Heart of the Matter, The [book by Greene]
Greene, Graham G: 382
Novel (After World War II) N: 574
Heart rate
Heart (Regulating the heart rate) H: 135; (Abnormal heart rhythms) H: 142
Heart scan [medicine]
Heart (Symptoms and diagnosis) H: 137-138
Heart transplant [surgery]
Barnard, Christiaan Neethling B: 114
Heart (Heart failure) H: 143 *with picture;* (The first heart transplants and artificial hearts) H: 145
Shumway, Norman Edward S: 443

Surgery (History) **So:** 1007-1008
Transplant (Organ transplants) **T:** 379
Heartbeat
Heart (Regulating the heart rate) **H:** 135-136
Pulse **P:** 900a
"Heartbreak Hotel" [song]
Rock music (Elvis Presley) **R:** 376-377
Heartburn [book by Ephron]
Ephron, Nora **E:** 342
Heartburn [disorder] **H:** 147
Acid reflux **A:** 27
Antacid **A:** 529
Indigestion **I:** 223
Heartfield, John [German artist]
Photography (Dramatic changes) **P:** 425-426
Hearth [ironmaking]
Iron and steel (The blast furnace process) **I:** 440
Hearth bread
Bread (Kinds of bread) **B:** 588
Hearth furnace
Iron and steel (The Iron Age) **I:** 449-450
Heartland
Geopolitics **G:** 106b
Heartsease [plant] *See* Pansy *in this index*
Heartwood [botany]
Sap (Vascular sap) **S:** 121
Tree (How trunks and branches grow thicker)
T: 418 *with diagram*
Heartworm [parasite]
Dog (Medical care) **D:** 279
Heat H: 148 *with pictures*
See also the list of Related articles in the Heat
article
Blood (Distributing body heat) **B:** 410
British thermal unit **B:** 632
Calorie **C:** 70
Combustion **Ci:** 866
Decomposition **D:** 80
Energy (Conservation of energy) **E:** 274
Expansion **E:** 438
Gas [fuel] (The composition of natural gas) **G:** 50
Geothermal energy **G:** 136
Heat pipe **H:** 156
Joule, James Prescott **J:** 169
Light (Incandescence) **L:** 283
Materials (Thermal properties) **M:** 300c
Metric system (Heat) **M:** 440
Physics (Heat) **P:** 437; (Developments in the
1800's) **P:** 440
Radiator **R:** 82
Sun **So:** 974; (Energy output) **So:** 976
Temperature **T:** 130
Thermodynamics **T:** 253
Thermography **T:** 253
Vacuum bottle **V:** 257
Water (The properties of water) **W:** 129-130
Heat [biology]
Cat (Reproduction) **C:** 293
Dog (Social and moral responsibilities) **D:** 279
Estrous cycle **E:** 363
Heat [sports]
Harness racing (The race) **H:** 63
Ice skating (Pack skating) **I:** 14-15
Heat, Miami [team] *See* Miami Heat *in this index*
Heat capacity [physics]
Materials (Thermal properties) **M:** 300c
Water (The properties of water) **W:** 129-130
Heat cramps [disorder]
Hyperthermia (Forms of hyperthermia) **H:** 477
Heat energy
Energy (Energy conversion) **E:** 274
Heat engine
Engine **E:** 283
Heat (Changing heat to motion) **H:** 153
Thermodynamics **T:** 253
Heat exchanger [engineering]
Solar energy (Central receiver systems) **So:** 579
Heat exhaustion [disorder]
First aid (Heatstroke and heat exhaustion) **F:** 141
Hyperthermia (Forms of hyperthermia) **H:** 477
Heat flow
Insulation **I:** 306
Heat index [weather] **H:** 155 *with diagram*
Weather (Reporting the weather) **W:** 169-170
Heat lightning
Lightning (Appearance) **L:** 300
Heat of adsorption
Absorption and adsorption (Adsorption) **A:** 18
Heat of combustion
Combustion **Ci:** 867
Heat of fusion [physics]
Heat (Changes in state) **H:** 153
Heat of vaporization [physics]
Heat (Changes in state) **H:** 153
Steam **So:** 880
Heat pipe H: 156
Heat prostration [disorder]

First aid (Heatstroke and heat exhaustion) **F:** 141
Heat pump H: 156
Heating *diagram on* **H:** 158; (Heat pumps) **H:** 157
Heat rash [disorder]
Prickly heat **P:** 776
Heat rays [light] *See* Infrared rays *in this index*
Heat-resistant glass
Glass (Specialty glasses) **G:** 212; (Borosilicate
glass) **G:** 213
Heat-seeking missile
Guided missile (Homing guidance) **G:** 426 *with
diagram*
Heat shield [spacecraft]
Space exploration (Returning to the earth)
So: 701
Heat transfer [physics]
Refrigeration (Principles of refrigeration) **R:** 200
Thermodynamics **T:** 253
Heat transfer printing
Textile (Finishing the fabric) **T:** 217
Heat wave [weather]
Heat index **H:** 156
Heater, Electric
Heating (Room heaters) **H:** 160
Heath [geography]
Heath **H:** 156
Scotland (Land regions) **S:** 217
Heath [shrub] **H:** 156
Heath, Edward [British political leader] **H:** 157
United Kingdom (Economic recovery—and
collapse) **U:** 72-73
Heath, Sir Robert [English political leader]
North Carolina (Exploration and settlement)
N: 490
South Carolina (Exploration and settlement)
So: 659
Heath hen [extinct bird]
Bird (Extinct birds) **B:** 369-370
Prairie-chicken **P:** 732
"Heathen Chinee, The" [poem by Harte]
Harte, Bret **H:** 78
Heather [shrub]
Flower *picture on* **F:** 283
Heath **H:** 156
Heather bell [flower]
Heath **H:** 156
Heathrow Airport
Airport (table) **A:** 245
London (Transportation) **L:** 438
Heating H: 157 *with pictures*
Automation (How automation works) **A:** 945 *with
diagram*
Coal (Other uses of coal as a fuel) **Ci:** 719
Furnace **F:** 567
Gas [fuel] (Uses of gas) **G:** 51
Heat pipe **H:** 156
House (Heating and air conditioning) **H:** 383
Solar energy (Solar heating) **So:** 579 *with picture*
Heating unit
Range (Electric ranges) **R:** 137
Heating value
Coal (How composition affects value) **Ci:** 717
Heatstroke [disorder]
First aid (Heatstroke and heat exhaustion) **F:** 141
Hyperthermia (Forms of hyperthermia) **H:** 477
Heaven [religion] **H:** 161
Mythology *picture on* **M:** 974
Heaven, Temple of
Beijing (The city) **B:** 222 *with picture*
Heavens [theater]
Shakespeare, William (The stage) **S:** 351-352
with picture
Heaves [disease] **H:** 161
Heavy crude
Petroleum (The composition of petroleum)
P: 331
Heavy harness horse
Horse (Heavy harness horses) **H:** 347
Heavy horse
Horse (Kinds of horses) **H:** 343; (table: Some
types and breeds of horses) **H:** 343
Heavy hydrogen *See* Deuterium *in this index*
Heavy Ion Research Center
Bohrium **B:** 438
Darmstadtium **D:** 38
Hassium **H:** 83
Meitnerium **M:** 387
Roentgenium **R:** 400
Heavy metal [physics]
Environmental pollution (Hazardous waste)
E: 334-335
Heavy metal [rock music]
Led Zeppelin **L:** 175
Rock music (The heavy metal sound) **R:** 380a
Heavy metal fluoride glass
Glass (Specialty glasses) **G:** 212-213
Heavy rain

Rain (Characteristics of rain) **R:** 122-123
Heavy spar [mineral] *See* Barite *in this index*
Heavy truck
Truck *pictures on* **T:** 459; (Kinds of trucks) **T:** 457
Heavy water [chemistry] **H:** 161
Astronomy (Neutrino astronomy) **A:** 845
Deuterium (Properties) **D:** 172
Nuclear energy (Nuclear fission) **N:** 582-583;
(Power reactors) **N:** 584-586
Observatory (Neutrino observatories) **O:** 645
Sun (Analyzing neutrinos) **So:** 984-985
Water (The chemistry of water) **W:** 129
Heavyweight
Boxing (table) **B:** 527
Hebbian synaptic plasticity [neurology]
Brain (Synapses) **B:** 557
Hebe [Greek mythology] **H:** 161
Hebern, Edward H. [American businessman]
Codes and ciphers (History) **Ci:** 751
Hébert, Anne [Canadian poet]
Canadian literature (Modern literature: 1945 to
the present) **C:** 159-160
Hébert, Louis [Canadian pioneer]
Quebec (Early days) **Q:** 36
Hebert, Paul O. [American political leader]
Louisiana (table) **L:** 496
Hebrew Association, Young Men's and Women's
[organization]
Jewish community centers **J:** 119
Hebrew Bible
See also Old Testament *in this index*
Bible **B:** 279; (The Hebrew Bible) **B:** 279; (table)
B: 281; (The Christian Old Testament) **B:** 282;
(Translations of the Bible) **B:** 284; (Literary
contexts) **B:** 287
Dead Sea Scrolls **D:** 56
Habakkuk, Book of **H:** 2
Judaism **J:** 179; (The sacred writings of Judaism)
J: 180
Old Testament **O:** 740
Hebrew calendar
Calendar (The Hebrew calendar) **C:** 29
Hebrew language H: 161
Alphabet (Aramaic, Hebrew, and Arabic) **A:** 383
Israel (Language) **I:** 480
Name (Hebrew names) **N:** 5
Yiddish language **Y:** 566
Hebrew literature H: 162
See also the list of Related articles in the Hebrew
literature *article*
Hebrew University
Jewish Women, National Council of **J:** 119
Hebrews [people]
See also Israelites *in this index*
Jews **J:** 120; (Beginnings) **J:** 120-121
Law (Early developments in the East) **L:** 133
Middle East (Early civilizations) **M:** 533
Palestine (Early history and settlement) **P:** 104
Tribe **T:** 440
World, History of the (Civilizations of southwest
Asia) **W:** 426
Hebrews, Epistle to the [New Testament] **H:** 163
Bible (The Letters) **B:** 284
New Testament (Letters) **N:** 287
Hebrides [islands, Scotland] **H:** 163 *with maps*
Hebrides, The [music by Mendelssohn]
Mendelssohn, Felix (His life) **M:** 399
Hebron [West Bank] **H:** 163
Cities of refuge **C:** 568
Hecate [Greek mythology] **H:** 164
Hecatompylos [ancient city]
Parthia **P:** 183 *with map*
Heceta, Bruno [Spanish explorer]
Washington (Discovery and exploration) **W:** 66
Hecht, Ben [American author] **H:** 164
Heck, Richard F. [American chemist]
Nobel Prizes (Chemistry: 2010) **N:** 444
Heckart, Eileen [American actress]
Motion picture (Best performance by an actress
in a supporting role: 1972) **M:** 862b
Heckel, Erich [German painter]
Painting (Expressionism) **P:** 78
Hecker, Isaac Thomas [American religious leader]
Paulists **P:** 202
Heckler, Margaret Mary [American government
official] **H:** 164
Heckman, James Joseph [American economist]
Economics (Modern economics) **E:** 64-65
Nobel Prizes (Economics: 2000) **N:** 449
Hecla [ship]
Parry, Sir William Edward **P:** 181
Hecla Island [Canada]
Lake Winnipeg **L:** 48 *with map*
Hectare [measurement]
Metric system (The metric system at a glance)
M: 438 *with picture*; (Non-SI metric units)
M: 440

Hecto [prefix]
Metric system (Metric prefixes) **M: 439**; (Selection of SI prefixes) **M: 440**
Hector [legendary figure] **H: 164**
Achilles **A: 26**
Iliad **I: 51**
Priam **P: 774**
Trojan War (The siege of Troy) **T: 449**
Hector, Charles [French admiral] *See* Estaing, Comte d' *in this index*
Hecuba [legendary figure] **H: 164**
Paris **P: 159**
Heda, Willem Claesz. [Dutch painter]
Painting (Still-life paintings) **P: 33**; (The Dutch masters) **P: 62-63** *with picture*
Hedda Gabler [play by Ibsen]
Drama (Ibsen) **D: 338**
Ibsen, Henrik (His plays) **I: 4**
Heddles [mechanism]
Weaving (How a loom works) **W: 173-174**
Hedge apple *See* Osage orange *in this index*
Hedge bindweed [plant]
Bindweed **B: 308**
Hedgehog [animal] **H: 164** *with picture*
Hedgehog cactus [plant]
Leaf *picture on* **L: 157**
Hedgehog tenrec [animal]
Tenrec **T: 167** *with picture*
Hedging [economics]
Commodity exchange (Forward and futures contracts) **Ci: 873**
Livestock (Direct markets) **L: 398**
Hedonism [philosophy] **H: 165**
Nietzsche, Friedrich (Psychological ideas) **N: 407**
Philosophy (Stoic philosophy and Epicureanism) **P: 387**
Heeger, Alan Jay [American physicist]
Nobel Prizes (Chemistry: 2000) **N: 444**
Heel-and-toe
Walking **W: 14**
Heel fly
Bot fly **B: 507**
Warble fly **W: 34**
Heeling force [physics]
Aerodynamics (Lift and drag in a sailboat) **A: 86-87** *with diagram*
Heemstra Hepburn-Ruston, Edda van [birth name of]
Hepburn, Audrey **H: 192**
Heenan, John C. [American boxer]
Boxing *picture on* **B: 531**
Heflin, Van [American actor]
Motion picture (Best performance by an actor in a supporting role: 1942) **M: 862a**
Hegel, G. W. F. [German philosopher] **H: 165**
Civilization (Rise and fall) **Ci: 636**
Existentialism (What is existentialism?) **E: 437**
Feuerbach, Ludwig Andreas **F: 83**
Germany (Literature and philosophy) **G: 153**
Idealism **I: 46**
Marx, Karl (Early development) **M: 237**
Philosophy (Philosophy in the 1800's) **P: 390**
Political science (Liberalism) **P: 639**
Schelling, Friedrich Wilhelm Joseph von **S: 174**
Hegenberger, A. F. [American military leader]
Hawaii (The Territory of Hawaii) **H: 108**
Hegira [Islamic history] *See* Hijrah *in this index*
Heian-kyo [ancient city]
Japan (Heian era) **J: 53**
Kyoto **K: 398**
Heian period [Japanese history]
Clothing (Japan) **Ci: 699**
Japan (Heian era) **J: 53**
Japanese literature (The Heian period) **J: 61**
Painting (Japanese painting) **P: 47**
Sculpture (Japan) **S: 239**
Heidegger, Martin [German philosopher] **H: 165**
Phenomenology **P: 357**
Heidelberg [Germany] **H: 166**
Germany *picture on* **G: 152**
Heidelberg, University of [Germany] **H: 166**
Heidelberg Catechism [religion]
Presbyterians (Teaching and worship) **P: 756a**
Heidelberg School [art school]
Australia (Painting) **A: 905-906**
Heiden, Eric [American speedskater] **H: 166**
Ice skating (History) **I: 16**
Olympic Games (Boycotts) **O: 753**
Heidenstam, Verner von [Swedish author]
Nobel Prizes (Literature: 1916) **N: 447**
Heidi [book by Spyri]
Spyri, Johanna **So: 810**
Heidi Chronicles, The [play by Wasserstein]
Drama (Later United States drama) **D: 340-341**
Wasserstein, Wendy **W: 112**
Heifer [animal]
Cattle **C: 306**; (Breeding) **C: 311-312**

Heifetz, Jascha [Lithuanian-American violinist] **H: 166**
Heiffelfinger, William "Pudge" [American football player]
Football (The rise of professional football) **F: 367**
Height [geometry]
Cylinder **Ci: 1204**
Height and weight tables
Baby **B: 8**
Growth (Growth rate) **G: 405**
Heike [family] *See* Taira *in this index*
Heil, Julius P. [American political leader]
Wisconsin (table) **W: 365**; (The La Follette Progressives) **W: 368**
Heiligenblut [village, Austria]
Austria *picture on* **A: 928**
Heilmann, Harry [American baseball player]
Baseball (table: Hall of Fame) **B: 134a**
Heimaey [island, Iceland]
Iceland (The inland plateau) **I: 22**
Heimlich maneuver
First aid (Choking) **F: 139** *with pictures*
Heimskringla [book by Snorri Sturluson]
Snorri Sturluson **S: 538**
Hein, Christoph [German author]
German literature (Recent German literature) **G: 142**
Heinbecker, Paul [Canadian diplomat]
United Nations (table) **U: 86**
Heine, Heinrich [German author] **H: 166**
German literature (The Young Germany) **G: 140**
Heinecken, Robert [American photographer]
Photography (A diversity of styles) **P: 426-427**
Heineman, Dave [American political leader]
Nebraska (table) **N: 110**
Heinemann, Barbara [American religious leader]
Amanites **A: 400**
Heinkel Company
Aviation (World War II [1939-1945]) **A: 989**
Turbine (History) **T: 498-500**
Heinkel He-178 [aircraft]
Jet propulsion (Development of jet propulsion) **J: 114** *with picture*
Heinlein, Robert A. [American author] **H: 167**
Science fiction (The Golden Age) **S: 205**
Heinz, Teresa [wife of]
Kerry, John Forbes **K: 307**
Heinz Hall for the Performing Arts
Pittsburgh (Cultural life) **P: 500c** *with picture*
Heinze, F. Augustus [American businessman]
Montana (Statehood) **M: 760**
Heir [law] **H: 167**
Inheritance tax **I: 271**
Heiress, The [film]
Copland, Aaron **Ci: 1040**
Heisei Emperor *See* Akihito *in this index*
Heisenberg, Werner [German physicist] **H: 167**
Physics (Quantum theory) **P: 441**
Quantum mechanics (The uncertainty principle) **Q: 6**
Heisman, John W. [American football coach]
Heisman Memorial Trophy **H: 167**
Heisman Memorial Trophy [sports] **H: 167**
Football (table) **F: 363**
Hejaz [region, Saudi Arabia]
Ibn Saud **I: 4**
Saudi Arabia (The Western Highlands) **S: 158** *with map*
Hekla [volcano, Iceland] **H: 167**
Iceland (The inland plateau) **I: 22**
Hel [Norse mythology]
Balder **B: 38**
Mythology (Mythical places) **M: 975**; (The construction of the world) **M: 986**
Held, John, Jr. [American cartoonist] **H: 167** *with picture*
Heldentenor [singer]
Opera (The singers) **O: 792**
Helderberg Escarpment
New York (Mountains) **N: 306**
Helen [Georgia]
Georgia (Places to visit) **G: 122** *with picture*
Helen Keller Endowment Fund
Keller, Helen (She helps others) **K: 255**
Helen of Troy [legendary figure] **H: 168**
Cassandra **C: 275**
Mythology (Greek heroes) **M: 982**
Trojan War (The beginning of the war) **T: 449**
Troy (The legendary Troy) **T: 454**
Helena [literary figure]
Shakespeare, William: (*A Midsummer Night's Dream*) **S: 357**; (*All's Well That Ends Well*) **S: 362**
Helena [Montana] **H: 168**
Helena Public Library
Arkansas (Libraries) **A: 699**
Helene [satellite]
Saturn (Satellites) **S: 151-152**

Hélène Fourment and Her Children [painting by Rubens]
Rubens, Peter Paul *picture on* **R: 507**
Helgoland [island, North Sea] **H: 168** *with map*
Heliarc welding
Helium (Uses) **H: 176** *with picture*
Helical gear
Gear **G: 75**
Helical symmetry [biology]
Virus (Structure) **V: 427-428** *with picture*
Helicobacter pylori [bacteria]
Gastritis **G: 67**
Stomach (Peptic ulcers) **So: 908**
Ulcer **U: 15**
Heliconius [butterfly]
Mimicry **M: 561**
Helicopter [aircraft] **H: 169** *with pictures*
Air force (Aircraft and missiles) **A: 183**
Aircraft, Military (Helicopters) **A: 203** *with picture*; (The jet age) **A: 205**
Autogiro **A: 942**
Coast Guard, United States *picture on* **Ci: 738**; (Aircraft) **Ci: 736**
Connecticut (Manufacturing) **Ci: 966** *with picture*
Korean War (The air war) **K: 382**
Transportation *picture on* **T: 391**; (Air transportation) **T: 384-385**
V/STOL **V: 452**
Vietnam War (The opposing forces) **V: 375**
Warship (Amphibious warfare ships) **W: 40**
Helicopter gunship [aircraft]
Aircraft, Military (Helicopters) **A: 203-204**
Helictite [geology]
Cave (Speleothems) **C: 319-320** *with diagram*
Heliocentric theory
Astronomy (Developing the modern view) **A: 847-848** *with picture*; (Sun-centered theories) **A: 835**
Kepler, Johannes (His life) **K: 305**
Science (The rebirth of science) **S: 197** *with diagram*
Heliograph [communications] **H: 174**
Communication (The 1800's) **Ci: 881**
Niépce, Joseph Nicéphore **N: 406**
Heliopause [astronomy]
Heliosphere (Shock waves) **H: 175**
Solar system (The heliosphere) **So: 581**
Voyager **V: 452**
Heliopolis [ancient city, Egypt]
Cleopatra's Needles **Ci: 662b**
Phoenix **P: 399**
Re **R: 154**
Helios [Greek mythology] **H: 174**
Mythology (Symbols) **M: 975**
Rhodes **R: 317**
Selene **S: 289**
Helios [space probes]
Space exploration (European nations) **So: 726**
Helioseismology [science]
Sun (Sun terms) **So: 976**; (Analyzing electromagnetic radiation) **So: 983-984**
Heliosheath [astronomy]
Heliosphere (Shock waves) **H: 175**
Heliosphere [astronomy] **H: 174**
Cosmic rays (Anomalous component cosmic rays) **Ci: 1076**
Solar system (The heliosphere) **So: 581**
Heliospheric magnetic field [astronomy]
Heliosphere (Magnetic field) **H: 175**
Heliostat [machine]
Solar energy (Central receiver systems) **So: 579**
Sun *picture on* **So: 978**
Heliotrope [plant] **H: 175** *with picture*
Heliport
Airport (General aviation airports) **A: 243**
Helicopter (For transportation and construction work) **H: 170**
Helium [element] **H: 175** *with pictures*
See also Liquid helium *in this index*
Airship (Lift) **A: 250**
Balloon (Gas balloons) **B: 58**
Big bang **B: 296**
Cosmology (Abundant helium) **Ci: 1078**
Jupiter (Chemical composition) **J: 198**
Nuclear weapon (Thermonuclear weapons) **N: 597**
Star (Fusion in stars) **So: 846**
Helium 3 [physics]
Superfluid **So: 993**
Helium 4 [physics]
Superfluid **So: 993**
Helium flash [physics]
Star (Intermediate-mass stars) **So: 848**
Helix garden snail
Snail (Snails and people) **S: 523**
Hell [religion] **H: 176**
Divine Comedy **D: 242**

Hell-diver [bird]
  Grebe G: 351
Helladic civilization [ancient Greece]
  Aegean civilization (The Mycenaean culture)
    A: 83
Hellas [name for]
  Greece, Ancient G: 366
Hellas Planitia [crater]
  Mars (Craters and impact basins) M: 226
Hellbender [animal]
  Salamander S: 59
Hellebore [plant] H: 177
Hellen [Greek mythology]
  Deucalion D: 172
Hellenes [ancient people]
  Deucalion D: 172
  Greece, Ancient G: 366
Hellenic Trough
  Mediterranean Sea (The seabed) M: 381
Hellenica [book by Xenophon]
  Xenophon X: 544
Hellenistic Age [ancient Greece] H: 177
  Alexander the Great A: 342
  Greece, Ancient (The Hellenistic Age) G: 374
  Greek literature (The Hellenistic Age) G: 378
  Middle East (Early civilizations) M: 533
  Sculpture (Hellenistic sculpture) S: 246 with
    picture
  World, History of the (The Greeks) W: 428-429
Heller, Joseph [American author] H: 177
  American literature (Experimental styles) A: 425
  Novel (The middle and late 1900's) N: 575
Hellespont [former name, Dardanelles]
  Hero and Leander H: 212
Hellfire missile
  Guided missile with pictureG: 425
Hellgrammite [insect] H: 177 with pictures
Hellman, Lillian [American dramatist] H: 178
  American literature (Drama) A: 422-423
Hellman, Martin [American engineer]
  Codes and ciphers (Later developments) Ci: 751
Hello, Goodbye Window, The [book by Juster]
  Raschka, Chris R: 144 with picture
Hell's Angels [gang]
  Rock music (Outdoor rock festivals) R: 380b
Hells Canyon [Idaho-Oregon]
  Idaho (Places to visit) I: 34 with picture
  Snake River S: 536
Helm
  Ship (Propulsion and steering) S: 406
Helmand River
  Afghanistan (The Southwestern Lowlands) A: 94
Helmet [clothing] H: 178 with pictures
  Armor (During the Middle Ages) A: 719-720 with
    pictures; (Later developments) A: 720-721 with
    picture
  Automobile racing (Safety measures) A: 975-976
  Diving, Underwater (Ambient diving) D: 245
    with picture
  Fire department (Protective clothing) F: 127 with
    picture
  Heraldry (Elements of a coat of arms) H: 196 with
    picture
  Space exploration (Leaving the spacecraft)
    So: 704-705 with pictures
  Vikings (Weapons and armor) V: 382 with picture
Helmet vanga [bird]
  Bird (Birds of Africa) B: 344h with picture
Helmeted guineafowl [bird]
  Bird picture on B: 345
Helmholtz, Hermann Ludwig Ferdinand von
  [German physicist] H: 178
  Color (The three-component theory) Ci: 826
  Heat (Heat and energy) H: 155
  Ophthalmoscope O: 810
  Physics (Developments in the 1800's) P: 440
  Psychology (Psychology becomes a science)
    P: 849
Helmont, Jan Baptista van [Belgian chemist]
  Botany (The development of modern botany)
    B: 509
  Gas [fuel] (First uses of manufactured gas) G: 57
  Gas [physics] (History) G: 49
Helms, Jesse Alexander [American political
  leader] H: 179
  North Carolina (The late 1900's) N: 493-494
Helms-Burton Act [1996]
  Cuba (Foreign relations) Ci: 1178-1179
Héloïse [French nun]
  Abelard, Peter A: 9
Helots [ancient Greece]
  Sparta (The people) So: 766
Help! [film]
  Beatles B: 190
Helping verb
  Tense T: 168
Helpmates [film]

Laurel and Hardy picture on L: 122
Helquist, Brett [American artist]
  Literature for children picture on L: 374
Helsinki [Finland] H: 179 with picture
  Finland F: 108 with picture; (Ancestry and
    population) F: 111 with picture
Helsinki, University of
  Finland (Education) F: 112
Helsinki Accords H: 179
  Europe (The Cold War) E: 415
  Ford, Gerald Rudolph (Meetings with foreign
    leaders) F: 378
  Human Rights Watch H: 430
  Organization for Security and Co-operation in
    Europe O: 854
Helsinki Watch [former name]
  Human Rights Watch H: 430
Helvetia [name for]
  Switzerland So: 1050
Helvetians [people] H: 180
  Switzerland (Early days) So: 1058
Helvetic Republic [Swiss history]
  Switzerland (French control) So: 1060
Helvétius, Claude [French philosopher]
  Law (Beginnings of U.S. law) L: 136
  Philosophes P: 382
Hem
  Sewing (Hems) S: 333
Hemangioma [disorder]
  Birthmark B: 380
Hematite [mineral] H: 180
  Iron and steel (Kinds of iron ore) I: 438
  Mars Exploration Rover Mission M: 227
  Taconite T: 5
Hematocrit [test]
  Blood (Blood tests) B: 413
  Blood doping B: 415
Hematology [medicine]
  See also Blood in this index
  Ehrlich, Paul E: 145
Hematopoietic growth factor [physiology]
  Blood (How the body maintains its blood supply)
    B: 410; (History of blood research) B: 414
Hemicellulose [material]
  Wood (The composition of wood) W: 390
Hemicyon [animal]
  Prehistoric animal picture on P: 740
Heminge, John [English actor]
  Shakespeare, William (Shakespeare's plays)
    S: 354; (Folios) S: 369
Hemings, Eston [American public figure]
  Jefferson, Thomas (Jefferson and Sally Hemings)
    J: 79
Hemings, Madison [American public figure]
  Jefferson, Thomas (Jefferson and Sally Hemings)
    J: 79
Hemings, Sally [American public figure]
  Jefferson, Thomas (Jefferson and Sally Hemings)
    J: 79
Hemingway, Ernest [American author] H: 180
  American literature picture on A: 417; (The Lost
    Generation) A: 421 with portrait
  Lost Generation L: 472
  Novel (New directions in the novel) N: 573-574
Hemipene [zoology]
  Snake (Reproduction) S: 529-530
Hemiptera [entomology]
  Bug B: 680
  Insect pictures on I: 281; (table) I: 300 with picture
Hemispatial neglect [disorder]
  Brain (Attention and consciousness) B: 554-555
Hemisphere [geography] H: 180 with pictures
Hemisphere [geometry]
  Sphere So: 780
Hemlock [herb] H: 181 with picture
  Alkaloid A: 360
Hemlock [tree] H: 181 with pictures
  Plant picture on P: 524
  Tree pictures on T: 425
Hemlock and After [book by Wilson]
  Wilson, Angus W: 316
Hemodialysis [medicine]
  Kidney (Kidney diseases) K: 312
Hemoglobin [physiology] H: 182
  Anemia (Excessive destruction of red blood cells)
    A: 458
  Blood (Red blood cells) B: 408; (What blood does
    in the body) B: 408
  Blood count B: 415
  Cyanosis Ci: 1202
  Genetic testing (How genes carry information)
    G: 84d
  Hemolysis H: 182
  Inorganic chemistry I: 276
  Iron (How bodies use iron) I: 435
  Kendrew, Sir John Cowdery K: 259
  Light (Light in medicine) L: 292

Liver (Purification of the blood) L: 394
Protein (How the body uses proteins) P: 832
Respiration (Gas transport between the lungs
  and tissues) R: 261
Sickle cell anemia S: 447
Thalassemia T: 228
Trace elements T: 355
Hemoglobin S [physiology]
  Sickle cell anemia S: 447
Hemolysis [physiology] H: 182
  Anemia (Excessive destruction of red blood cells)
    A: 458
  Streptococcus So: 926
Hemolytic anemia [disorder]
  Anemia (Excessive destruction of red blood cells)
    A: 458
Hemolytic jaundice [disorder]
  Jaundice J: 65
Hémon, Louis [French author]
  Canadian literature (Literature between the
    world wars) C: 158
Hemophilia [disease] H: 182 with diagram
  Blood (Bleeding disorders) B: 414
  Blood transfusion B: 416
  Genetic testing (Genes associated with disease)
    G: 84d
  Heredity (Hereditary disorders) H: 204
  Plasma (Uses in medicine) P: 551
  Von Willebrand's disease V: 448
Hemorrhage [disorder] H: 183
  See also Bleeding in this index
  First aid (First aid for bleeding) F: 136 with
    pictures
  Stroke (Causes) So: 930
Hemorrhage, Cerebral See Cerebral hemorrhage
  in this index
Hemorrhagic fever [disorder]
  Ebola virus E: 49
  Hantavirus H: 54
Hemorrhoids [disorder] H: 183
  Varicose vein V: 286
Hemostat [instrument]
  Surgery (A typical operation) So: 1006
Hemotoxin [poison]
  Snake (Fangs and venom glands) S: 528
Hemp [plant] H: 183
  Hashish H: 81
  Marijuana M: 201 with picture
  Philippines picture on P: 379
  Rope (Natural-fiber rope) R: 473
Hempstead, Stephen P. [American political leader]
  Iowa (table) I: 391
Hen [bird]
  Chicken C: 440
  Poultry (Raising poultry) P: 720
  Turkey T: 513
Hen harrier [bird] See Northern harrier in this index
Henbane [plant] H: 183
Hench, Philip Showalter [American physician]
  Nobel Prizes (Physiology or medicine: 1950)
    N: 445
Henday, Anthony [British explorer] H: 183
Hendee, George W. [American political leader]
  Vermont (table) V: 333
Henderson, Arthur [British statesman]
  Nobel Prizes (Peace: 1934) N: 448a
Henderson, Charles [American political leader]
  Alabama (table) A: 274
Henderson, Fletcher [American musician] H: 183
  Jazz (The 1920's) J: 70
Henderson, James Pinckney [American political
  leader]
  Texas (table) T: 203
Henderson, Richard [American jurist]
  Boone, Daniel (The Wilderness Road) B: 477
Henderson, Rickey [American baseball player]
  H: 184
  Baseball (table: Hall of Fame) B: 134a; (table:
    Modern major league records) B: 138
Henderson, Robert [American prospector]
  Klondike K: 344
Henderson the Rain King [book by Bellow]
  Bellow, Saul B: 244
Hendricks, Thomas Andrews [American political
  leader] H: 184
  Cleveland, Grover (Election of 1884) Ci: 670
  Hayes, Rutherford Birchard (Campaign of 1876)
    H: 120
  Indiana (table) I: 214
  Vice president of the United States V: 348 with
    portrait
Hendricks, William [American political leader]
  Indiana (table) I: 214
Hendricksen, Cornelius [Dutch explorer]
  Pennsylvania (Exploration and settlement) P: 264
Hendrix, Jimi [American musician] H: 184 with
  portrait

Rock music (The heavy metal sound) R: 380a
Henequen [plant]
Mexico (The Yucatán Peninsula) M: 463
Rope (Natural-fiber rope) R: 473
Henge [archaeology]
Megalithic monuments M: 383
Stonehenge So: 911
Henie, Sonja [Norwegian skater] H: 184
Ice skating (History) I: 16
Olympic Games *picture on* O: 752; (Between the wars) O: 751
Henkes, Kevin [American illustrator/author] H: 184
Caldecott Medal (table: 2005) C: 26
Henley Royal Regatta [race]
Rowing (Competition) R: 494
Henna [dye] H: 185
Dye (Natural dyes) D: 396
Hennepin, Louis [Belgian explorer] H: 185
Iowa (Exploration and early settlement) I: 393
Minneapolis (Early days) M: 582
Minnesota (Exploration) M: 603
Hennin [hat]
Clothing (The Renaissance) Ci: 702 *with picture*
Hat H: 83, *picture on* H: 84
Henotheism
Religion (Belief in a deity) R: 215
Henri [grand duke of Luxembourg]
Luxembourg (History) L: 531-532
Henri, Robert [American artist] H: 185
Ashcan School A: 768
Davies, Arthur Bowen D: 46
Lawson, Ernest L: 147
Prendergast, Maurice Brazil P: 756
Henriade, La [poem by Voltaire]
Voltaire (Imprisonment and early success) V: 446
Henrietta Maria [wife of Charles I]
Maryland M: 240; (Exploration and settlement) M: 256
Henry [British prince] *See* Harry, Prince *in this index*
Henry [measurement] H: 185
Henry, Joseph H: 189
Inductance I: 240
Henry I [king of England] H: 185
England (Struggles for power) E: 305
Stephen So: 890
Henry I [king of Germany]
Germany (The breakup of Charlemagne's empire) G: 162
Otto I, the Great O: 877
Henry II [king of England] H: 185
Becket, Saint Thomas B: 196
Eleanor of Aquitaine E: 157
England (Struggles for power) E: 305-306
Ireland (The Norman invaders) I: 425
Plantagenet P: 550
Henry II [king of France] H: 186
France (A period of wars) F: 473
Paré, Ambroise P: 156
Henry III [Holy Roman emperor] H: 186
Henry III [king of England] H: 186
England (table) E: 308
Plantagenet P: 550
Wales (Revolts against England) W: 12
Westminster Abbey W: 243
Henry III [king of France] H: 186
Ballet *picture on* B: 52
Catherine de Médicis C: 303
Huguenots (The massacre) H: 410
Henry IV [Holy Roman Emperor] H: 187
Germany (The Holy Roman Empire) G: 162
Gregory VII, Saint G: 387
Urban II U: 219
Henry IV [king of England] H: 186
England (The Hundred Years' War) E: 306
Lancaster L: 55
Lollards L: 427
Richard II R: 329
Henry IV [king of France] H: 186 *with portrait*
Bourbon (In France) B: 516
Champlain, Samuel de (Early life) C: 373
Henry III [of France] H: 186
Marie de Médicis M: 200
Nantes, Edict of N: 11
Nova Scotia (Exploration and settlement) N: 567-568
Henry IV [play by Pirandello]
Pirandello, Luigi P: 493
Henry IV [play by Shakespeare]
Drama *picture on* D: 324
Henry V [of England] H: 187
Shakespeare, William: (Henry IV) S: 358
Henry V [Holy Roman emperor]
Paschal II P: 190
Henry V [king of England] H: 187 *with portrait*
England (The Hundred Years' War) E: 306
Hundred Years' War H: 437
Lancaster L: 55

Henry V [literary figure]
Shakespeare, William: (Henry IV) S: 358-359; (Henry V) S: 359 *with picture*
Henry V [play by Shakespeare]
Olivier, Laurence O: 744
Shakespeare, William: (Henry V) S: 359 *with picture*
Henry VI [Holy Roman emperor] H: 187
Henry VI [king of England] H: 187
England (The Hundred Years' War) E: 306; (The Wars of the Roses) E: 306
Lancaster L: 55
Wars of the Roses W: 38
Warwick, Earl of W: 44
York Y: 568
Henry VI [plays by Shakespeare]
Shakespeare, William (Early career in London) S: 347; (Henry VI) S: 355
Henry VII [king of England] H: 187 *with portrait*
Arctic (Search for the Northwest Passage) A: 638
Cabot, John C: 8
England (The Wars of the Roses) E: 306-307
Exploration (Exploring the New World) E: 444
Renaissance (Political background) R: 237-238
Richard III R: 329
Tudor, House of T: 481
Wales (Union with England) W: 12
Warbeck, Perkin W: 34
Wars of the Roses W: 38
Westminster Abbey W: 243
Wolsey, Thomas W: 379
Henry VIII [king of England] H: 188 *with portrait*
Boleyn, Anne B: 440
Catherine of Aragon C: 303
Christianity (The Church of England) C: 525
Church of England (History) C: 542
Cranmer, Thomas C: 1120
Cromwell, Thomas Ci: 1152
England (The English Reformation) E: 307
Hairdressing (The Renaissance) H: 11-12
Holbein, Hans, the Younger H: 289
Ireland (The conquest of Ireland) I: 426
More, Sir Thomas (His life) M: 801
Postal services (The growth of public mail systems) P: 703
Protestantism (The conservative reform movements) P: 834-835
Reformation (In England) R: 198
Tudor, House of T: 481
Wales (Union with England) W: 12
Wolsey, Thomas W: 379
Henry VIII [play by Shakespeare]
Fletcher, John F: 234
Shakespeare, William (Religion) S: 350; (The fourth period [1609-1614]) S: 365; (Henry VIII) S: 366
Henry, Alexander [Canadian explorer] H: 188
Henry, Barbara [American educator]
Bridges, Ruby B: 607
Henry, Brad [American political leader]
Oklahoma (table) O: 730
Henry, George S. [Canadian political leader]
Ontario (table) O: 783
Henry, Gregory W. [American astronomer]
Planet (The first discoveries) P: 513
Henry, John [American political leader]
Maryland (table) M: 255
Henry, John [legendary figure] H: 188
Folklore (Legends) F: 324
Henry, Joseph [American physicist] H: 189
Electromagnet E: 201
Electromagnetism E: 203
Energy supply (The Industrial Revolution) E: 280
Faraday, Michael F: 27
Magnetism (Electricity and magnetism) M: 60d
Physics (Developments in the 1800's) P: 440
Radio (Early development) R: 91
Henry, Lou [wife of Herbert Hoover] *See* Hoover, Lou Henry *in this index*
Henry, Marguerite Breithaupt [American author]
Newbery Medal (table) N: 359
Henry, O. [American author] H: 189
Short story S: 434
Henry, Patrick [American political leader] H: 189 *with picture*
Constitution of the United States (The Constitutional Convention) Ci: 999-1000
Madison, James (Virginia assemblyman) M: 33
Revolution, American (Fighting in the Chesapeake and Southern colonies) R: 276-278
Richmond (Other interesting places to visit) R: 332
Virginia (table) V: 417
Henry, Prince [British prince] *See* Harry, Prince *in this index*
Henry, William Alexander [Canadian political

leader]
Confederation of Canada (Fathers of Confederation) Ci: 935 *with picture*
Henry Doorly Zoo [Omaha]
Nebraska (Places to visit) N: 102 *with picture*
Zoo *picture on* Z: 599
Henry E. Huntington Library and Art Gallery [San Marino, California]
Los Angeles (Museums) L: 466
Henry Esmond [book by Thackeray]
Thackeray, William Makepeace (Later career) T: 220
Henry Ford Museum [Dearborn, Michigan]
Detroit (Other interesting places to visit) D: 170
Ford, Henry (Political and charitable activities) F: 380-381
Henry Francis Du Pont Winterthur Museum [Delaware] *See* Winterthur Museum & Country Estate *in this index*
Henry Huggins [book by Cleary]
Cleary, Beverly Ci: 660
Henry James [book by West]
West, Rebecca W: 199
Henry Mountains
Utah (Land regions) U: 240-242 *with map*
Henry of Bolingbroke [ling of England] *See* Henry IV [king of England] *in this index*
Henry of Burgundy [French knight]
Portugal (Founding the Portuguese nation) P: 693
Henry of Guise [French nobleman]
Henry III [king of France] H: 186
Huguenots H: 410
Saint Bartholomew's Day, Massacre of S: 31
Henry of Luxembourg [German ruler]
Luxembourg (History) L: 531
Henry of Mecklenburg-Schwerin [husband of]
Wilhelmina W: 306
Henry of Navarre [king of France] *See* Henry IV [king of France] *in this index*
Henry Street Settlement [New York City]
Wald, Lillian D. W: 6
Henry the Fowler [king of Germany] *See* Henry I [king of Germany] *in this index*
Henry the Lion [duke of Saxony]
Brunswick B: 652
Munich (History) M: 927
Henry the Navigator [Portuguese geographer] H: 191
Exploration (Reaching the tip of Africa) E: 443
Portugal (The age of exploration) P: 693
Henry Whitfield State Museum [Guilford, Connecticut]
Colonial life in America (Places to visit) Ci: 800
Henshaw, David [American government official]
Tyler, John (table) T: 534
Hensley, Cindy [wife of]
McCain, John (Early life) M: 332-332a
Hensley, Virginia Patterson [birth name of]
Cline, Patsy Ci: 681
Henson, Jim [American puppeteer] H: 191
Puppet (Hand puppets) P: 906
Henson, Josiah [American public figure]
Slavery (Conditions of slavery) S: 503
Henson, Matthew Alexander [American explorer] H: 191 *with portrait*
Exploration (The North Pole) E: 450
Peary, Robert Edwin P: 224
Henson, William S. [British inventor]
Airplane (Powered flight) A: 230 *with picture*
Henze, Hans Werner [German composer] H: 191
HEPA filter
Air cleaner (Types of air cleaners) A: 175-176
Hepatic artery [anatomy]
Liver *picture on* L: 394; (Structure of the liver) L: 393
Hepatic duct [anatomy]
Bile B: 300
Gallbladder G: 14 *with diagram*
Liver (Structure of the liver) L: 393
Hepatic vein [anatomy]
Liver *picture on* L: 394; (Structure of the liver) L: 393
Hepatica [plant] H: 192
Flower *picture on* F: 285
Plant *picture on* P: 530
Hepatitis [disease] H: 192
Blood transfusion (How blood is collected) B: 416-417
Cirrhosis Ci: 566
Disease (table) D: 226
Liver (Diseases of the liver) L: 394-395
Hepatocellular jaundice [disorder]
Jaundice J: 65
Hepburn, Audrey [British actress] H: 192 *with portrait*
Motion picture (Best performance by an actress:

1953) M: 862
Hepburn, James [Scottish nobleman]
Bothwell, Earl of B: 510
Hepburn, Katharine [American actress] H: 193
with portrait
Motion picture (Best performance by an actress: 1932-33, 1967, 1968, 1981) M: 862; (Movies in the 1930's) M: 867-868 *with picture*
Tracy, Spencer T: 362 *with picture*
Hepburn, Mitchell F. [Canadian political leader]
Ontario O: 783
Hepburn Railway Rate Act [1906]
Roosevelt, Theodore (Domestic problems) R: 466
Hepburn system
Japanese language J: 61
Hephaestus [Greek mythology] H: 193
Aphrodite A: 565
Ares A: 645
Mythology (Greek mythology) M: 882; (table) M: 981
Pandora P: 130
Vulcan V: 453
Hephaestus, Temple of [Athens]
Architecture *picture on* A: 615
Hepplewhite, George [British furniture designer] H: 193
Heppner [Oregon]
Oregon (The early 1900's) O: 848
Heptaméron [work by Marguerite of Navarre]
French literature (The Renaissance) F: 519
Heptameter [poetry]
Poetry (table) P: 594
Heptane [chemical]
Gasoline (Octane ratings) G: 61
Natural gas liquids N: 64
Octane number O: 669
Heptanesos [islands] *See* Ionian Islands *in this index*
Heptarchy [English history]
Anglo-Saxons A: 464
England (The Anglo-Saxon period) E: 304
Heptathlon [sports] H: 193
Joyner-Kersee, Jackie J: 177
Track and field (The decathlon, heptathlon, and pentathlon) T: 359
Hepworth, Barbara [English sculptor] H: 193 *with picture*
Her Majesty's Opposition [government]
United Kingdom (National government) U: 49
HER2 [medicine]
Breast cancer B: 591
Cancer (Monoclonal antibodies) C: 172-173
Hera [Greek mythology] H: 194
See also Juno *in this index*
Argus A: 661
Big and Little Dippers (The Little Dipper) B: 296
Hercules (Early life) H: 198; (The twelve labors) H: 198
Hesperides H: 218
Io I: 369 *with picture*
Mythology (table) M: 981; (Greek divinities) M: 982
Zeus Z: 590
Heraclean stone [rock]
Lodestone L: 419
Heracles [Greek mythology] *See* Hercules *in this index*
Heraclitus [Greek philosopher] H: 194
Pre-Socratic philosophy (The first pre-Socratics) P: 772
Herald [European history] H: 194
Heraldry (Expansion) H: 194
Herald of Holiness [newspaper]
Church of the Nazarene C: 543
Heraldic achievement *See* Coat of arms *in this index*
Heraldry H: 194 *with pictures*
Flag F: 194
Herald H: 194
Heralds' College
Heraldry (Heraldry today) H: 196
Herb [botany] H: 196
Dietary supplement D: 200
Flower (Garden flowers) F: 274
Gardening (Production gardens) G: 31
Herbal medicine H: 196
Herb layer [forest]
Forest (The herb layer) F: 392 *with picture*
Herb Robert [plant]
Geranium G: 136
Herbaceous perennial [botany]
Flower (Garden flowers) F: 274
Herbaceous stem
Plant (Stems) P: 529 *with pictures*
Stem *pictures on* So: 888; (Kinds of stems) So: 887
Herbal medicine H: 196
Cancer (Alternative medicine) C: 173
Herbalism [medicine]

Alternative medicine A: 388
Herbart, Johann Friedrich [German psychologist] H: 197
Herbert, Frank [American author] H: 197
Herbert, Gary R. [American political leader]
Utah (table) U: 245; (The early 2000's) U: 249-250
Herbert, George [English poet] H: 197
Poetry (Stress meters) P: 592
Herbert, Hilary A. [American government official]
Cleveland, Grover (table) Ci: 672
Herbert, John [Canadian dramatist]
Canadian literature (Modern Canadian drama) C: 161
Herbert, Thomas J. [American political leader]
Ohio (table) O: 699
Herbert, Victor [American composer] H: 197
American Society of Composers, Authors and Publishers A: 430
Musical comedy (The first musicals) M: 959
Herbert Hoover Library [Iowa]
Hoover, Herbert Clark (Elder statesman) H: 330-331
Herbert Hoover National Historic Site [Iowa]
National Park System (table: National historic sites) N: 52-53
Herbicide H: 198
Agent Orange A: 140
Agriculture (Chemical pesticides) A: 159
Cotton (Weeds) Ci: 1090
Farm and farming (Pest control) F: 34
Pest control (Pesticides) P: 318
Potato (Potato pests) P: 713
Vegetable (Pest control) V: 293
Herbivore [zoology] H: 198
Forest (The flow of energy) F: 396
Mammal (What mammals eat) M: 121 *with diagrams*
Herblock [pen name]
Block, Herbert Lawrence B: 404 *with picture*
Herbs *See* Herb *in this index*
Hercegovina [region] *See* Bosnia-Herzegovina *in this index*
Herceptin [drug]
Breast cancer B: 591
Herculaneum [ancient city] H: 198
Architecture (Neoclassical architecture) A: 623
Library (Rome) L: 258
Painting (Roman painting) P: 42-43; (Neoclassicism) P: 66
Hercules [Greek mythology] H: 198
Alexander the Great (His youth) A: 342
Atlas A: 868
Cornucopia Ci: 1066
Hebe H: 161
Hydra H: 461
Mythology *pictures on* M: 979, M: 981; (Greek divinities) M: 982
Prometheus P: 817
Renaissance *picture on* R: 237
Hercules [constellation] H: 199
Hercules, Pillars of
Gibraltar, Strait of G: 187
Hercules, Tower of [lighthouse]
Lighthouse (Notable lighthouses) L: 295
Hercules and Antaeus [sculpture by Pollaiuolo]
Pollaiuolo, Antonio del P: 644
Hercules beetle [insect] H: 199
Beetle *picture on* B: 215
Hercules's-club [tree]
Prickly-ash P: 775
Herd [zoology]
Animal (Group living) A: 502
Dolphin *picture on* D: 297
Whale (Group life) W: 261
Herd of Horses [cave painting]
Painting *picture on* P: 41
Herdbook [book]
Cattle C: 306
Herder, Johann Gottfried von [German author] H: 199
German literature (German Preromanticism) G: 139
Goethe, Johann Wolfgang von (Early years) G: 247
Herding dog
Dog *pictures on* D: 276; (Herding dogs) D: 266
Herd's-grass [plant]
Timothy T: 292d
Herdsman [constellation]
Boötes B: 480
HERE [labor union]
UNITE HERE U: 43
Here and Now [poems by Layton]
Layton, Irving L: 148
Here Come the Clowns [play by Barry]
Barry, Philip B: 119
Heredia, José María [Cuban poet]

Latin American literature (Romanticism) L: 112
Hereditary disease
Allergy (The development of allergies) A: 374
Alzheimer's disease (Causes) A: 399
Anemia (Excessive destruction of red blood cells) A: 458
Attention deficit disorder A: 879
Birth defect (Causes) B: 380
Brain (Genetic disorders) B: 558
Cancer (Inheriting damaged genes) C: 170
Diabetes (Type 2 diabetes) D: 179
Disease (Inherited diseases) D: 228
Ear (Birth defects) E: 11
Eugenics E: 377
Fragile X syndrome F: 450
Framingham Heart Study F: 451
Gene mapping G: 81
Genetic counseling G: 84a
Genetic testing G: 85
Genetics (Transmission genetics) G: 87
Hemophilia (How hemophilia is inherited) H: 182 *with diagram*
Heredity (Sex-linked genes) H: 202; (Hereditary disorders) H: 204
Inflammatory bowel disease (Causes) I: 266
Intellectual disability (Causes) I: 318
Medicine (The medical revolution) M: 376-377; (The challenge of genetics) M: 378
Mental illness (Genetic factors) M: 407
Molecular medicine M: 692
Muscular dystrophy M: 936
Polycystic kidney disease P: 649
Races, Human (Susceptibility to genetic diseases) R: 58
Sickle cell anemia S: 447
Tay-Sachs disease T: 56
Thalassemia T: 228
Hereditary material *See* DNA *in this index*
Hereditary peerage
Nobility (In the United Kingdom) N: 450
Parliament (The House of Lords) P: 173
Heredity H: 200 *with pictures*
See also the list of Related articles in the Heredity article
Alcoholism (Causes of alcoholism) A: 337
Baby (Growth and development) B: 6
Baldness B: 39
Behavior (Heredity) B: 220
Bioethics B: 311
Cell (The nucleus) C: 328; (Meiosis) C: 331
Child (Individual differences among children) C: 450
Chromosome C: 538
Dislocation D: 235
DNA D: 258
Eugenics E: 377
Evolution (Mutation) E: 427
Genetic counseling G: 84a
Genetic testing G: 84d
Genetics G: 86
Growth (In living things) G: 404; (Factors affecting human growth) G: 406
Intelligence (The roles of heredity and environment) I: 319
Life (Adaptation) L: 275
Mendel, Gregor Johann M: 398
Mutation M: 968
Plant (Effects of heredity and environment) P: 538
Races, Human (How human populations develop and change) R: 57
Rh factor R: 290
Science (Science in the early 1900's) S: 201-202
Zoology (What zoologists study) Z: 606-607
Hereford cattle
Cattle *picture on* C: 306; (Hereford) C: 309 *with picture*; (table) C: 312
Herenton, Willie [American political leader]
Memphis (History) M: 396-397
Herero [people]
Namibia (People) N: 8
Heresy [religion] H: 210
Inquisition I: 277
Roman Catholic Church (The first 300 years) R: 405
Witchcraft (Middle Ages to the 1700's) W: 372
HERF [industrial method]
Machine tool (High-energy rate forming [HERF]) M: 19 *with diagram*
Hering, Ewald [German physiologist]
Color (The opponent color theory) Ci: 826
Hering, Frank E. [American public figure]
Mother's Day M: 843
Heritage Foundation H: 210
Heritage park
Pennsylvania (Recovery) P: 268
Heritage '76

Bicentennial Celebration, American **B:** 288
Herjolfsson, Bjarni [Norse explorer]
Exploration (Viking exploration) **E:** 442
Vikings (The Norwegian Vikings) **V:** 382
Herkomer, Sir Hubert von [British artist]
Painting (Painting outside France) **P:** 72
Herland [book by Gilman]
Gilman, Charlotte Perkins **G:** 191
Herman, Alexis M. [American government official]
Clinton, Bill (table) **Ci:** 682d
Labor, Department of (table) **L:** 2
Herman, Billy [American baseball player]
Baseball (table: Hall of Fame) **B:** 134a
Herman, Robert [American physicist]
Big bang **B:** 297
Herman, Woody [American musician] **H:** 211
Jazz (The swing era) **J:** 71 *with picture*
Herman Ottó Museum [Hungary]
Miskolc **M:** 618
Hermann [Missouri]
Missouri *picture on* **M:** 651
Hermann and Dorothea [book by Goethe]
Goethe, Johann Wolfgang von (Middle years) **G:** 247
Hermaphrodite [zoology] **H:** 211
Earthworm **E:** 39
Flatworm **F:** 229
Oyster (The life of an oyster) **O:** 890
Hermeias [Greek ruler]
Aristotle (Aristotle's life) **A:** 663
Hermes [Greek mythology] **H:** 211
See also Mercury [Roman mythology] *in this index*
Argus **A:** 660
Io **I:** 370
Mercury **M:** 415
Mythology (Greek mythology) **M:** 882; (table) **M:** 981
Praxiteles **P:** 734 *with picture*
Hermia [literary figure]
Shakespeare, William: (*A Midsummer Night's Dream*) **S:** 357
Herminius [Roman legend]
Horatius **H:** 334
Hermione [literary figure]
Shakespeare, William: (*The Winter's Tale*) **S:** 365
Hermit H: 211
Hermit crab [sea animal] **H:** 211
Animal *picture on* **A:** 501
Hermit Kingdom
Korea, History of (The Choson dynasty) **K:** 366-367
Hermit thrush [bird]
Bird *picture on* **B:** 358
Hermitage [museum]
Russia (Museums and libraries) **R:** 536 *with picture*
Saint Petersburg [Russia] (The city) **S:** 54; (Education and cultural life) **S:** 55
Hermitage [religion]
Hermit **H:** 211
Hermitage, The [estate]
Jackson, Andrew (Business and politics) **J:** 8; (Later years) **J:** 14 *with picture*
Tennessee (Places to visit) **T:** 144
Hermon, Mount [Lebanon-Syria]
Jordan River **J:** 167
Hernández, José [Argentine author]
Argentina (The arts) **A:** 651-652
Latin American literature (Romanticism) **L:** 112-113
Hernández Colón, Rafael [Puerto Rican political leader]
Puerto Rico (Puerto Rico today) **P:** 884
Hernández Martínez, Maximiliano [Salvadoran political leader]
El Salvador (The 1900's) **E:** 252
Hernani [play by Hugo]
Drama (Romanticism) **D:** 337
Hugo, Victor (Early life) **H:** 409
Herndon, Ellen Lewis [wife of]
Arthur, Chester Alan *picture on* **A:** 756; (Arthur's family) **A:** 755
Herndon, Hugh [American aviator]
Airplane (Fliers of the golden age) **A:** 237
Herndon, William Henry [American lawyer] **H:** 212
Lincoln, Abraham (Early practice) **L:** 315
Herne, James A. [American dramatist] **H:** 212
Hernia [disorder] **H:** 212
Hernia cerebri [disorder]
Hernia **H:** 212
Hernial sac [disorder]
Hernia **H:** 212
Herniated disk [disorder] *See* Disk herniation *in this index*
Hero [Greek scientist]
Invention (Ancient Greece) **I:** 359
Jet propulsion (Development of jet propulsion) **J:** 114

Steam engine (History) **So:** 881
Hero [mythology]
Mythology (Mythical beings) **M:** 975; (Greek heroes) **M:** 982; (Literary approaches) **M:** 990
Hero and Leander [Greek mythology] **H:** 212
Hero and Leander [poem by Marlowe]
Marlowe, Christopher **M:** 216
Hero and the Crown, The [book by McKinley]
McKinley, Robin **M:** 337
Hero of Israel
Medals, decorations, and orders (table) **M:** 359
Hero of Our Times, A [book by Lermontov]
Russian literature (Late Romanticism) **R:** 561-562
Hero of Two Worlds [nickname]
Kościuszko, Tadeusz **K:** 384
Hero with a Thousnd Faces [book by Campbell]
Mythology (Literary approaches) **M:** 990
Herod [Palestinian rulers] **H:** 212
Herod, King [opera character]
Opera: (*Salome*) **O:** 807 *with picture*
Herod Agrippa I [Palestinian ruler]
Herod (Harod Agrippa I) **H:** 212
James the Greater, Saint **J:** 28
Herod Agrippa II [Palestinian ruler]
Herod (Herod Agrippa II) **H:** 213
Herod Antipas [Palestinian ruler]
Jesus Christ (The trial) **J:** 108
John the Baptist, Saint **J:** 134
Salome **S:** 71
Herod Archelaus [Palestinian ruler]
Herod (Herod the Great) **H:** 212
Herod Philip [Palestinian ruler]
Herod (Herod the Great) **H:** 212
Herod the Great [Palestinian ruler]
Herod (Herod the Great) **H:** 212
Jerusalem (Roman rule) **J:** 101
Jesus Christ (The Nativity) **J:** 105
Masada **M:** 262
New Testament (Historical Jesus research) **N:** 2288
Samaria **S:** 77
Herodotus [Greek historian] **H:** 213
Amazons **A:** 404
Geology (The ancient Greeks) **G:** 97
Greek literature (Historical literature) **G:** 377
History (The ancient Greeks and Romans) **H:** 261
Lake dwelling **L:** 37
Mummy (Egyptian mummies) **M:** 925-926
Phoenicia (Decline) **P:** 395
Postal services (Ancient times) **P:** 703
Pyramids (The pyramids of Giza) **P:** 917
Heroes' Square [Budapest]
Hungary *picture on* **H:** 438
Heroic Captive, The [sculpture by Michelangelo]
Michelangelo (The tomb of Julius II) **M:** 484
Heroic couplet [poetry]
Couplet **Ci:** 1100
English literature (Restoration drama) **E:** 318; (Swift and Pope) **E:** 318
Poetry (table) **P:** 594; (Neoclassical poetry) **P:** 596
Heroic drama
Drama (England) **D:** 334
Heroic scale [art]
Sculpture (Kinds of sculpture) **S:** 230
Heroic tragedy
English literature (Restoration drama) **E:** 318
Heroides [book by Ovid]
Ovid **O:** 882
Heroin [drug] **H:** 213
Drug abuse (Abuse of illegal drugs) **D:** 362; (table: Some commonly abused drugs) **D:** 363; (History) **D:** 365
Methadone **M:** 433
Morphine **M:** 816
Opium **O:** 811
Herold, David E. [American public figure]
Lincoln, Abraham (The trial of the conspirators) **L:** 326
Heron [bird] **H:** 213 *with pictures*
Bird (Birds of inland waters and marshes) **B:** 340 *with pictures*
Bittern **B:** 383 *with picture*
Egret **E:** 119
Heron's-bill [plant]
Geranium **G:** 136
Héroult, Paul L. T. [French chemist]
Aluminum (Smelting the alumina) **A:** 393; (Growth of the aluminum industry) **A:** 397
Iron and steel (The birth of modern steelmaking) **I:** 450-451
Herpes, Genital [disease] **H:** 214
Sexually transmitted disease **S:** 338b
Herpes simplex virus
Cold sore **Ci:** 761
Eye (Diseases of the cornea) **E:** 466
Herpes simplex virus, type 2
Herpes, Genital **H:** 214

Herpes zoster [disease] *See* Shingles *in this index*
Herpesvirus [virus] **H:** 214
Antiviral drug **A:** 560
Epstein-Barr virus **E:** 345
Herpes, Genital **H:** 214
Virus (Structure) **V:** 427-428 *with picture*
Herpetologist [occupation]
Snake (The life of snakes) **S:** 528
Herpetology [zoology] **H:** 214
Herr Eugen Dühring's Revolution in Science [book by Engels]
Engels, Friedrich **E:** 283
Herrán, Tomás [Colombian diplomat]
Panama Canal (The United States and the canal) **P:** 125
Herreid, Charles N. [American political leader]
South Dakota (table) **So:** 680
Herrenchiemsee Palace
Ludwig II **L:** 515
Herrenhausen Gardens
Hanover **H:** 53
Herrera, Juan de [Spanish architect]
Architecture (Later Renaissance architecture) **A:** 621
Herrera, Tomás [Panamanian political leader] **H:** 214
Herrerasaurus [dinosaur]
Dinosaur *picture on* **D:** 206
Herrick, James B. [American doctor]
Heart (Development of heart surgery) **H:** 144
Herrick, Myron T. [American political leader]
Ohio (table) **O:** 699
Herrick, Robert [English poet] **H:** 215
Herries Chronicles [books by Walpole]
Walpole, Hugh Seymour **W:** 19
Herriman, George [American cartoonist]
Cartoon *picture on* **C:** 264
Herring [fish] **H:** 215 *with pictures*
Animal (Providing food) **A:** 498
Fish *picture on* **F:** 152
Sardine **S:** 124 *with picture*
Whitefish **W:** 292
Herring, Clyde L. [American political leader]
Iowa (table) **I:** 391
Herring gull [bird]
Gull (Kinds of gulls) **G:** 439 *with picture*
Herring rake [tool]
Indian, American (Hunting, gathering, and fishing) **I:** 141
Herringbone [weaving]
Basket making (Methods) **B:** 141
Herringbone gear
Gear **G:** 75
Herringbone stride
Skiing (Nordic skiing) **S:** 482-483
Herrington, John Bennett [American astronaut]
Astronaut (table) **A:** 830
Herrington, John S. [American government official]
Energy, Department of (table) **E:** 276
Reagan, Ronald Wilson (table) **R:** 169
Herriot, James [British veterinarian] **H:** 216
Herrmann, Adelaide [British magician]
Magician (Illusions) **M:** 51-52
Herrnhut [Germany]
Moravian Church **M:** 801
Herrold, David [American businessman]
California (Communication) **C:** 58
Herron, Helen [wife of William H. Taft] *See* Taft, Helen Herron *in this index*
Herschbach, Dudley Robert [American chemist]
Nobel Prizes (Chemistry: 1986) **N:** 444
Herschel [crater]
Saturn (Satellites) **S:** 151-152
Herschel, Caroline Lucretia [British astronomer] **H:** 216
Herschel, Sir John Frederick William [British astronomer] **H:** 216
Photography (The invention of photography) **P:** 422-423
Herschel, Sir William [British astronomer] **H:** 216
Astronomy (Finding new objects) **A:** 848
Enceladus **E:** 265
Infrared rays **I:** 270
Uranus **U:** 217
Herschel, Sir William J. [British government official]
Fingerprinting (History) **F:** 107
Herschel Space Observatory
Astronomy (Infrared astronomy) **A:** 842-843
European Space Agency **E:** 418
Herschler, Edgar J. [American political leader]
Wyoming (table) **W:** 532
Herself Surprised [book by Cary]
Cary, Joyce **C:** 270
Herseth, Ralph [American political leader]
South Dakota (table) **So:** 680

Hersey, John [American author] **H:** 216
Hershey [Pennsylvania]
Pennsylvania (Interesting facts) **P:** 245
Hershey, Alfred Day [American biologist]
Nobel Prizes (Physiology or medicine: 1969)
N: 446
Hershey, Milton Snavely [American businessman]
H: 216
Hershey Chocolate Company
Hershey, Milton Snavely **H:** 216
Hershey millet [grain]
Millet **M:** 555
Hershiser, Orel [American baseball player]
Baseball (table: Modern major league records)
B: 138
Hershko, Avram [Israeli chemist]
Nobel Prizes (Chemistry: 2004) **N:** 444
Herstmonceux Castle [England]
Greenwich meridian **G:** 387
Herter, Christian Archibald [American
government official]
Eisenhower, Dwight David (table) **E:** 152
Massachusetts (table) **M:** 288
Hertz [measurement] **H:** 217
Acoustics **A:** 28
Ear (The sense of hearing) **E:** 9
Electric current (Direct and alternating current)
E: 168
Electric generator (A simple generator) **E:** 170
Electromagnetic waves (The electromagnetic
spectrum) **E:** 202
Kilohertz **K:** 317
Light (Light and measurement) **L:** 290
Metric system (Space and time) **M:** 437
Radio (Broadcasting power and frequency)
R: 87-88
Sound (table) **So:** 599; (Frequency and pitch)
So: 599 with diagram
Hertz, Gustav [German physicist] **H:** 217
Hertz, Heinrich Rudolf [German physicist] **H:** 217
Antenna (History) **A:** 544
Communication (The development of
electronics) **Ci:** 883
Electricity (Electricity and magnetism) **E:** 197
Hertz **H:** 217
Marconi, Guglielmo (Early life) **M:** 197
Physics (Developments in the 1800's) **P:** 440
Radar (The development of radar) **R:** 71
Radio (Early development) **R:** 91
Relativity (The Michelson-Morley experiment)
R: 210
Hertzberg Circus Collection and Museum [Texas]
Circus (Places to visit and annual events) **Ci:** 566
Hertzog, James Barry Munnik [South African
political leader] **H:** 217
South Africa (The rise of Afrikaner nationalism)
So: 619
Hertzsprung, Ejnar [Danish astronomer]
Star (The Hertzsprung-Russell diagram) **So:** 845
Hertzsprung-Russell diagram [astronomy]
Star diagram on **So:** 849; (Characteristics of stars)
So: 842; (The Hertzsprung-Russell diagram)
So: 845 with diagram
Hervey, Walter L. [American educator]
Teachers College, Columbia University (History)
T: 64
Herzberg, Gerhard [Canadian physicist] **H:** 217
Nobel Prizes (Chemistry: 1971) **N:** 443
Herzegovina [region] See Bosnia-Herzegovina in
this index
Herzen, Alexander Ivanovich [Russian publisher]
H: 217
Herzl, Theodor [Austrian author] **H:** 217
Duel **D:** 378
Jews (The Zionist movement) **J:** 123
Zionism (Movement to Palestine) **Z:** 595
Herzog [book by Bellow]
Bellow, Saul **B:** 244
Herzog, Émile [French author]
Maurois, André **M:** 317
Herzog, Maurice [French mountain climber]
Annapurna **A:** 517
Herzog, Whitey [American baseball player/
manager]
Baseball (table: Hall of Fame) **B:** 134a
Hesburgh, Theodore Martin [American educator]
H: 217
Heseltine, Michael Ray Dibdin [British political
leader] **H:** 218 with portrait
Heshvan [month]
Calendar (The Hebrew calendar) **C:** 29
Hesiod [Greek poet] **H:** 218
Greek literature (Epic poetry) **G:** 377
Mythology (Interweaving relationships) **M:** 976;
(Greek mythology) **M:** 980
Hesperian Period
Mars (Periods of evolution) **M:** 226b-226c

Hesperides [Greek mythology] **H:** 218
Hesperides [poems by Herrick]
Herrick, Robert **H:** 215
Hesperidium [botany]
Citrus **Ci:** 573
Fruit (Simple fruits) **F:** 544
Lemon **L:** 188
Orange (The fruit and the tree) **O:** 814
Hesperis [Greek mythology]
Hesperides **H:** 218
Hesperornis [extinct bird] **H:** 218
Bird (The first known birds) **B:** 369
Hesperus [Greek mythology]
Venus **V:** 310
Hess, Myra [British pianist] **H:** 218
Hess, Rudolf [Nazi leader] **H:** 218 with portrait
Hitler, Adolf (Rise of the Nazis) **H:** 266
Nuremberg Trials (The trials) **N:** 613
World War II picture on **W:** 497
Hess, Victor Franz [Austrian physicist]
Anderson, Carl David **A:** 451
Cosmic rays (Cosmic ray research) **Ci:** 1077
Nobel Prizes (Physics: 1936) **N:** 440
Hess, Walter Richard Rudolf [Swiss physiologist]
Nobel Prizes (Physiology or medicine: 1949)
N: 445
Hesse [region, Germany]
Hessians **H:** 219
Hesse, Hermann [German author] **H:** 219
Hesse, Karen [American author] **H:** 219
Newbery Medal (table) **N:** 359
Hessian cloth [fabric]
Burlap **B:** 707
Hessian fly [insect] **H:** 219
Gnat **G:** 238
Insect picture on **I:** 285
Wheat (Care during growth) **W:** 271
Hessians [soldiers] **H:** 219 with picture
Revolution, American (The fighting forces) **R:** 278
Trenton, Battle of **T:** 435
Hestia [Greek mythology] **H:** 220
Mythology (table) **M:** 981; (Greek divinities)
M: 982
Vesta **V:** 342
Heston, Charlton [American actor] **H:** 220
Motion picture (Best performance by an actor:
1959) **M:** 862a
Hetch Hetchy Valley [region, California]
Yosemite National Park (Hetch Hetchy Valley)
Y: 570
Heterocyclic antidepressant [drug]
Mental illness (Somatic therapy) **M:** 407
Heterodont teeth [anatomy]
Teeth (Teeth of animals) **T:** 86
Heterodontosaurus [dinosaur]
Dinosaur picture on **D:** 206d; (True dinosaurs)
D: 206b-206c
Heteroecious rust [fungus]
Rust **R:** 567
Heterogeneous catalysis [chemistry]
Catalysis **C:** 298
Heterogeneous society
City (The people) **Ci:** 578-580
Heterosexuality
Adolescent (Establishing a sexual identity) **A:** 63
Homosexuality **H:** 307
Sexuality (Sexual orientation) **S:** 338b
Heterotroph [botany]
Plant (Photosynthesis) **P:** 537-538
Heterotrophic bacteria
Bacteria (How bacteria obtain food) **B:** 21
Heterotropia [disorder]
Strabismus **So:** 916
Hetty Dorval [book by Wilson]
Wilson, Ethel **W:** 317
Heureaux, Ulises [Dominican political leader]
Dominican Republic (History) **D:** 304-305
Heuristics [science]
Artificial intelligence (Planning and problem
solving) **A:** 760
Hevea [tree]
Latex **L:** 90
Rubber (The rubber tree) **R:** 502
Hevelius, Johannes [Polish astronomer]
Moon (Early observations with telescopes)
M: 792 with picture
Hevesy, Georg von [Hungarian-Danish chemist]
Hafnium **H:** 5
Nobel Prizes (Chemistry: 1943) **N:** 443
HEW [organization] See Health and Human
Services, Department of in this index
Hewes, Joseph [American patriot] **H:** 220
Hewish, Antony [British astronomer]
Nobel Prizes (Physics: 1974) **N:** 441
Pulsar **P:** 900a
Hewitt, Abram [American businessman]
Cooper, Peter **Ci:** 1035

Hewlett Foundation, William and Flora
Foundation (table) **F:** 430
Hewlett-Packard Company
Manufacturing (table) **M:** 170
Hewson, Paul David [birth name of]
Bono **B:** 462
Hex sign [art]
Folklore picture on **F:** 323
Pennsylvania Dutch **P:** 271
Hexagon [geometry] **H:** 220 with diagram
Hexagonal system [chemistry]
Crystal (Classifying crystals) **Ci:** 1166 with picture
Hexagonal wind system [astronomy]
Saturn (History of study) **S:** 153 with picture
Hexagone Poets [group]
Canadian literature (Modern Canadian poets)
C: 161
Hexagram [figure]
I Ching **I:** 2
Hexameter [poetry]
Greek literature (Lyric poetry) **G:** 377
Poetry (table) **P:** 594
Hexane [gas]
Natural gas liquids **N:** 64
Hexosaminidase A [physiology]
Tay-Sachs disease **T:** 56
Hexylresorcinol [medication]
Resorcinol **R:** 259
Heydrich, Reinhard [Nazi leader] **H:** 220
Lidice **L:** 270
Heye, George Gustav [American art collector]
National Museum of the American Indian **N:** 41
Heyer, Georgette [British author] **H:** 220
Heyerdahl, Thor [Norwegian adventurer] **H:** 220
with picture
Raft **R:** 102
Heymans, Corneille Jean-François [Belgian
physiologist]
Nobel Prizes (Physiology or medicine: 1938)
N: 445
Heyrovský, Jaroslav [Czech chemist]
Nobel Prizes (Chemistry: 1959) **N:** 443
Heyse, Paul von [German author]
Nobel Prizes (Literature: 1910) **N:** 447
Heyward, DuBose [American author] **H:** 221
Gershwin, Ira **G:** 175
Opera: (Porgy and Bess) **O:** 806
Heyward, Thomas, Jr. [American patriot] **H:** 221
Heywood, Thomas [English dramatist] **H:** 221
Hezbollah [political group] **H:** 221
Arab-Israeli conflict (The second intifada)
A: 582a-582b
Israel (The early 2000's) **I:** 489
Lebanon (After the civil war) **L:** 174
Middle East (The 1970's and the 1980's) **M:** 534a;
(The 2000's) **M:** 534b
Hezekiah [Biblical figure] **H:** 221
Hf [symbol]
Hafnium **H:** 5
Hg [symbol]
Mercury **M:** 413
hGH [homone] See Human growth hormone in
this index
HHFA [agency] See Housing and Home Finance
Agency in this index
HHS [organization] See Health and Human Services,
Department of in this index
HI [measurement] See Heat index in this index
Hiawatha [American Indian leader] **H:** 221
Indian, American (Federations) **I:** 143-144;
(Prophets) **I:** 148
Longfellow, Henry Wadsworth (Narrative poems)
L: 450
Hiawatha [poem by Longfellow] See Song of
Hiawatha, The in this index
Hiawatha National Forest
Michigan (Places to visit) **M:** 498
Hibbing [Minnesota] **H:** 222
Hibernaculum [zoology]
Snake (Regulation of body temperature) **S:** 530
Hibernation [zoology] **H:** 222 with picture
Animal (Animals of the polar regions) **A:** 484
with picture
Bear (Winter sleep) **B:** 183-184
Butterfly (Hibernation) **B:** 742
Frog (The life of a frog) **F:** 538
Insect (Hibernation and migration) **I:** 296 with
picture
Lizard (Where lizards live) **L:** 399
Mammal (Hibernation) **M:** 125
Raccoon (The life of a raccoon) **R:** 50-51
Reptile (Hibernation) **R:** 252
Snake (Regulation of body temperature) **S:** 530
Temperature, Body (Warm-blooded animals)
T: 130
Turtle (Hibernation) **T:** 522
Hibernia [former name, Ireland] **H:** 223

Hibernia [region]
  Grand Banks **G: 306** *with map*
Hibiscus [plant] **H: 223** *with picture*
  Flower (Self-pollination) **F: 296** *with picture*
Hiccough *See* Hiccup *in this index*
Hiccup [disorder] **H: 223**
Hickel, Walter J. [American government official]
  Alaska (table) **A: 300**
  Interior, Department of the (table) **I: 325**
Hickenlooper, Bourke B. [American political leader]
  Iowa (table) **I: 391**
Hickenlooper, John [American political leader]
  Colorado (table) **Ci: 844**
Hickey, J. J. [American political leader]
  Wyoming (table) **W: 532**
Hickok, Wild Bill [American frontiersman] **H: 223** *with portrait*
  Abilene **A: 11**
  South Dakota (Territorial days) **So: 681**
Hickory [tree] **H: 223** *with pictures*
  Plant *picture on* **P: 525**
  Tree *pictures on* **T: 421**
  Wood *pictures on* **W: 389**
Hicks, Edward [American painter] **H: 224**
  Folk art *picture on* **F: 316**; (Folk artists) **F: 319**
Hicks, Henry D. [Canadian political leader]
  Nova Scotia (table) **N: 567**
Hicks, Sir John Richard [British economist]
  Arrow, Kenneth Joseph **A: 743**
  Nobel Prizes (Economics: 1972) **N: 449**
Hicks, Thomas Holliday [American political leader]
  Maryland (table) **M: 255**
Hidalgo [state, Mexico] **H: 224**
Hidalgo y Costilla, Miguel [Mexican patriot] **H: 224**
  Hidalgo **H: 224**
  Latin America (The movement toward independence) **L: 106-107**
  Mexico (Revolt against the Spaniards) **M: 470** *with picture*
Hidatsa Indians
  Gros Ventre Indians **G: 398**
  Indian, American *picture on* **I: 160**
  Mandan Indians **M: 135**
Hidden curriculum
  Curriculum **Ci: 1197**
Hidden Persuaders, The [book by Packard]
  Consumer protection (Growth of the movement) **Ci: 1019**
Hide [leather]
  Leather **L: 166**
  Tannic acid **T: 29**
Hide boat
  Indian, American *picture on* **I: 138**
  Ship *pictures on* **S: 416, S: 419**
Hide glue
  Glue (Types of glue) **G: 236**
Hideyoshi [Japanese political leader] **H: 225**
  Japan (Warring states period) **J: 54-55**; (Tokugawa period) **J: 55**
  Tokugawa Ieyasu **T: 311**
Hiding
  Animal (How animals protect themselves) **A: 493**
Hiedler, Johann Georg [grandfather of]
  Hitler, Adolf (Boyhood) **H: 264-265**
Hierarchy [behavior]
  Dominance **D: 301**
  War (Organization and control) **W: 24**
Hierarchy [religion]
  Religion (How the major religions are organized) **R: 218**
Hieratic writing
  Egypt, Ancient (The people) **E: 136**
  Hieroglyphics (Development of hieroglyphic writing) **H: 225-226** *with picture*
Hiero [king of Syracuse]
  Archimedes (His discoveries) **A: 605**
Hieroglyphics [writing] **H: 225** *with pictures*
  Alphabet (The Egyptians) *pictures on* **A: 382**
  Egypt, Ancient (The people) **E: 136**
  Hittites (Way of life) **H: 269**
  Maya (Communication and learning) **M: 324** *with picture*
  Mythology (The Great Ennead) **M: 979**
  Number (The Egyptians) **N: 606** *with picture*
  Rosetta stone **R: 479** *with picture*
  Writing system (Phonetization) **W: 513**
Hiester, Joseph [American political leader]
  Pennsylvania (table) **P: 263**
Higginbotham, A. Leon, Jr. [American jurist]
  Spingarn Medal (table: 1996) **So: 794**
Higginbotham, William [American physicist]
  Electronic game (History) **E: 204d**
Higgins, Frank Wayland [American political leader]
  New York (table) **N: 313**

Higgins, James H. [American political leader]
  Rhode Island (table) **R: 311**
Higgins, Marguerite [American journalist]
  War correspondent **W: 26**
Higgins, Mary [American author] *See* Clark, Mary Higgins *in this index*
Higgins Armory Museum [Worcester]
  Massachusetts (Places to visit) **M: 280**
Higgs, Peter Ware [British physicist] **H: 227**
  Higgs boson **H: 227**
Higgs boson [physics] **H: 227**
  Boson **B: 494**
  Higgs, Peter Ware **H: 227**
  Subatomic particle (The Standard Model) **So: 938**
Higgs mechanism [physics]
  Higgs, Peter Ware **H: 227**
High [drugs]
  Cocaine **Ci: 742**
  Marijuana (Effects) **M: 201**
High [meteorology]
  Calms, Regions of (The horse latitudes) **C: 69**
  Weather (Air pressure) **W: 157**; (table: Weather terms) **W: 157**; (Synoptic-scale systems) **W: 159-161**
  Wind (Synoptic-scale circulations) **W: 329**
High-altitude cerebral edema [illness]
  Altitude sickness **A: 390**
High-altitude pulmonary edema [illness]
  Altitude sickness **A: 390**
High-altitude rocket
  Rocket (High-altitude rockets) **R: 390**
High-altitude sickness *See* Altitude sickness *in this index*
High Atlas Mountains [Africa] *See* Grand Atlas Mountains *in this index*
High blood pressure *See* Hypertension *in this index*
High Bridge
  New York City (Transportation) **N: 334**
High Bridge [painting by Lawson]
  Lawson, Ernest *picture on* **L: 147**
High Coast Bridge
  Bridge (table: Suspension) **B: 603**
High-compression engine
  Gasoline engine (High and low compression) **G: 63**
High Council
  Mormons (Church organization) **M: 807**
High Court
  Australia (The federal government) **A: 895**
  New Zealand (Courts) **N: 347**
High Court of Justice [British law]
  Equity **E: 348**
High Court of Justiciary [Scottish law]
  United Kingdom (Courts) **U: 54**
High dam [engineering]
  Tennessee Valley Authority (The dams) **T: 158-159**
High deductible health plan
  Insurance (Other types of health insurance) **I: 312**
High-definition television
  Electronics (The digital age) **E: 216**
  Television *picture on* **T: 127**; (High-definition television) **T: 128**
High-definition video
  Motion picture (Shooting the movie) **M: 852-853**
High-density lipoprotein [biochemistry]
  Cholesterol **C: 520**
  Physical fitness (Cholesterol levels) **P: 434**
High density polyethylene [plastic]
  Pipe (Kinds of pipe) **P: 489**
  Polyethylene **P: 650**
High-early-strength concrete
  Cement and concrete (High-early-strength concrete) **C: 343**
High-efficiency condensing boiler
  Boiler **B: 439**
High-energy rate forming [industrial process]
  Machine tool (High-energy rate forming [HERF]) **M: 19** *with diagram*
High Energy Transient Explorer-2 [satellite]
  Astronomy (Gamma-ray astronomy) **A: 845**
  Telescope (Gamma-ray telescopes) **T: 109**
High explosive
  Ammunition (Artillery ammunition) **A: 435**
  Explosive (High explosives) **E: 453**
High Falls [Minnesota]
  Minnesota (Lakes, rivers, and waterfalls) **M: 598-599**
High-fidelity system *See* Stereophonic sound system *in this index*
High-fructose corn syrup
  Dextrose **D: 178**
High German [language]
  German language (High German) **G: 138**
  Germany (Language) **G: 150**
High-hat [fish]
  Drum **D: 367**

High Holidays [religion]
  Judaism (Holy days and festivals) **J: 181**
High hurdles [race]
  Hurdling **H: 452** *with picture*
High-intensity focused ultrasound
  Ultrasound (Medical uses) **U: 16**
High island [geography]
  Pacific Islands (The land and climate) **P: 7** *with picture*
High jump [sport] **H: 227** *with picture*
  Track and field (Jumping events) **T: 357** *with picture*
High King, The [book by Alexander]
  Alexander, Lloyd **A: 342**
High-lead logging
  Lumber (Transporting logs) **L: 518**
High-level language [computing]
  Computer (Using programming languages) **Ci: 923**
  Computer language (High-level languages) **Ci: 924h**
High-lift devices
  Aerodynamics (Creating extra lift) **A: 86**
High magic
  Witchcraft (Role of magic) **W: 372**
High-mass star
  Star (High-mass stars) **So: 849**
High Middle Ages [European history]
  Middle Ages (The High Middle Ages) **M: 526**
High Museum of Art [Atlanta]
  Georgia (Museums) **G: 117** *with picture*
High Park Fire
  Colorado (The early 2000's) **Ci: 847-848**
High Plains
  Oklahoma (Land regions) **O: 724-726** *with map*
High-pressure sodium vapor lamp
  Electric light (High-pressure sodium lamps) **E: 175**
  Lighting (Efficient use of lighting) **L: 297**
High-pressure tire
  Tire (History) **T: 297-298**
High priest [religion] **H: 228**
High-protein cereal
  Cereal **C: 361**
High Renaissance
  Painting (The High Renaissance) **P: 54** *with picture*
High-rise [dwelling]
  Prison (Prison buildings) **P: 806**
  Shelter *picture on* **S: 393**
High school H: 228
  See also Secondary education *in this index*
  Agricultural education (High schools) **A: 144**
  Careers (Teaching) **C: 231**
  Curriculum (Curriculum content) **Ci: 1197**
  Education (Vocational education) **E: 88**; (Secondary education) **E: 92**
  Library (High school libraries) **L: 245**
  Parochial school **P: 177**
  Physical education (Secondary school programs) **P: 432**
  School (High schools) **S: 181**
  Student government **So: 932**
  Teaching (Teaching as a profession) **T: 65** *with picture*; (Becoming a teacher) **T: 67-68**
  Vocational education (Public high schools) **V: 434**
High seas [international law] **H: 228**
  Ocean (Who owns the ocean?) **O: 665-666**
High seat [furniture]
  Vikings (Housing) **V: 380**
High Sierra [region, California]
  Yosemite National Park **Y: 569**
High Society [film]
  Jazz *picture on* **J: 72**
High-speed Anti-Radiation Missile
  Guided missile (Air-to-surface missiles) **G: 426**
High-speed disperser [machine]
  Paint (Grinding) **P: 24**
High-speed train
  Electric railroad **E: 188** *with picture*
  Europe *picture on* **E: 405**
  Magnetic levitation train **M: 55** *with picture*
High-sulfur coal
  Coal (Coal as a fuel) **C: 718**
High Tatras [mountain range]
  Slovakia (Land and climate) **S: 508d**
High technology
  United States, History of the (Economic changes) **U: 196b**
High-temperature gas-cooled reactor
  Nuclear energy (Advanced fission reactors) **N: 594**
High-temperature short-time method
  Milk (Pasteurization) **M: 548**
High tide
  Ocean (Tides) **O: 659**
  Tide **T: 280** *with diagram*

High vacuum diffusion pump
Pump (Jet pumps) **P: 900b**
High volume instrument [machine]
Cotton (Classing) **Ci: 1091**
High-wheeler
Bicycle *picture on* **B: 293**; (Early bicycles) **B: 291**
High wire performer
Circus *picture on* **Ci: 565**
High-yield bond
Bond (Bond ratings) **B: 454**
High-yield variety [agriculture]
Agriculture (The Green Revolution) **A: 159**
Highboy [furniture]
Colonial life in America (Furnishings) **Ci: 797-798**
Higher animal *See* Vertebrate *in this index*
Higher education
Community college **Ci: 898**
Education (Higher education) **E: 92**
Universities and colleges **U: 206** *with pictures*
Higher order determinant [mathematics]
Determinant (Using higher order determinants)
D: 166
Highholder [bird] *See* Flicker *in this index*
Highhole [bird] *See* Flicker *in this index*
Highland [region, Scotland]
Highland Clearances **H: 229**
Inverness **I: 365**
Scotland (Population) **S: 213**; (Land regions)
S: 217 *with map*
United Kingdom (The Scottish Highlands) **U: 59**
with picture and map
Highland Clearances [Scottish history] **H: 229**
Highland climate
Climate (Highland climates) **Ci: 676d**
Highland fling [dance]
Scotland (The arts) **S: 215-217**
Highland games
Nova Scotia (Visitor's guide) **N: 560**
Scotland (Recreation) **S: 214**
Highland Park [community]
Dallas (The city) **D: 11**
Highlanders [people]
Gaels **G: 5**
Scotland (Union with England) **S: 220**
Highlands [region, Scotland] *See* Highland *in this
index*
Highly Active Antiretroviral Therapy [medicine]
AIDS (Treatment) **A: 164b-165**
Highly saturated fat
Fat (Structure) **F: 52**
Highsmith, Patricia [American author] **H: 229**
Highveld [region]
South Africa (The Plateau) **So: 614** *with map*
Highwall mining
Mining (Hybrid mining techniques) **M: 576**
Highway
Automobile **A: 946** *with picture, picture on* **A: 965**;
(Demand for services and facilities) **A: 959**
Interstate Highway System **I: 352**
Road **R: 357**
Route 66 **R: 493**
Traffic **T: 365**
Transportation (Development of inland
transport) **T: 388-389**; (Private transportation)
T: 392
Highway Administration, Federal [U.S.] *See*
Federal Highway Administration *in this index*
Highway engineer
Road (Planning) **R: 358**
Highway maintenance
Road (How roads and highways are maintained)
R: 360
Highway planner
Road (Planning) **R: 358**
Highway robbery [crime]
Robbery **R: 365**
"Highwayman, The" [poem by Noyes]
Noyes, Alfred **N: 578**
Highwaymen [singers]
Country music *picture on* **Ci: 1098d**
Nelson, Willie **N: 123**
Higuchi Ichiyo [Japanese author] **H: 229**
Hijāb [clothing]
Arabs *picture on* **A: 586**; (Clothing) **A: 588**
Clothing (Clothing under Islam) **Ci: 697-698**
Hijacking [crime] **H: 229**
Airport (Airport security) **A: 247**
Aviation (Airline safety concerns) **A: 991**
September 11 terrorist attacks **S: 310**
Terrorism (Hijackings) **T: 176**
Hijar [community] *See* Hujar *in this index*
Hijo del Santo, El [Mexican wrestler]
Luchas libre **L: 514**
Hijrah [Islamic history]
Calendar (The Islamic calendar) **C: 29**
Muhammad (The Hijrah) **M: 911**
Muslims (Muhammad) **M: 964a**

Religion (Islam) **R: 223**
Saudi Arabia (The rise of Islam) **S: 160**
Hiking [sport] **H: 230**
England (Recreation) *picture on* **E: 297**
Sweden *picture on* **So: 1026**
Hiking boot
Camping (Clothing) **C: 94**
Hilary, Saint [pope]
Pope (table) **P: 666**
Hilbert, David [German mathematician]
Mathematics (Philosophies of mathematics)
M: 307
Hildebrand [Italian religious leader] *See* Gregory
VII, Saint *in this index*
Hildebrand [legendary figure]
Nibelungenlied **N: 395**
Hildreth, Horace A. [American political leader]
Maine (table) **M: 87**
Hill [geography] **H: 230**
Mountain **M: 891**
Hill, A. P. [Confederate general]
Civil War, American (Battle of Antietam) **Ci: 627**
Hill, Anita F. [American law professor]
Thomas, Clarence **T: 261**
Hill, Sir Archibald Vivian [British physiologist]
Nobel Prizes (Physiology or medicine: 1922)
N: 445
Hill, Damon [British race car driver]
Automobile racing (table: Formula One World
Drivers' Championship) **A: 980**
Hill, David Bennett [American political leader]
New York (table) **N: 313**
Hill, David Octavius [Scottish painter]
Europe *picture on* **E: 411**
Hill, Faith [American singer]
Country music (Modern country music)
Ci: 1098c-1099 *with picture*
Hill, Geoffrey [British poet]
English literature (Recent English poetry) **E: 323**
Hill, George Roy [American director]
Motion picture (Best achievement in directing:
1973) **M: 862**
Hill, Graham [British race driver] **H: 230**
Automobile racing (table: Formula One World
Drivers' Championship) **A: 980**; (table:
Indianapolis 500 winners) **A: 980**
Hill, Isaac [American political leader]
Kitchen Cabinet **K: 337**
New Hampshire (table) **N: 223**
Hill, James Jerome [American businessman]
H: 230
Saint Paul (History) **S: 52**
Hill, Joe [Swedish-American songwriter] **H: 231**
Hill, John Fremont [American political leader]
Maine (table) **M: 87**
Hill, Octavia [British social reformer] **H: 231**
Hill, Oliver W. [American social reformer]
Spingarn Medal (table: 2005) **S: 794**
Hill, Pete [American baseball player]
Baseball (table: Hall of Fame) **B: 134a**
Hill, Phil [American race driver]
Automobile racing (table: Formula One World
Drivers' Championship) **A: 980**
Hill, Philip C. [Canadian political leader]
Nova Scotia (table) **N: 567**
Hill, Sir Rowland [British educator]
Postal services (The creation of the Penny Post)
P: 706
Hill-Burton Act [1946]
Hospital (The 1900's) **H: 374**
Hill Cipher [cryptology]
Codes and ciphers (Substitution) **Ci: 750**
Hill Complex [structure]
Great Zimbabwe **G: 350**
Hill of Ares [ancient Greece]
Areopagus **A: 645**
Hill peoples
Myanmar (People) **M: 970a**
"Hill Wife, The" [poem by Frost]
Frost, Robert (His poems) **F: 543**
Hillaby, Mount
Barbados (Land) **B: 104**
Hillary, Sir Edmund Percival [New Zealand
mountain climber] **H: 231** *with picture*
Antarctica (The International Geophysical Year)
A: 538
Mount Everest **M: 884**
Tenzing Norgay **T: 169**
Hillbilly music
Popular music (The rise of country music) **P: 671**
Hillel [organization]
Hillel I **H: 232**
Hillel I [Jewish religious leader] **H: 232**
Hillel the Elder [Jewish religious leader] *See* Hillel
I *in this index*
Hiller, Wendy [British actress]
Motion picture (Best performance by an actress

in a supporting role: 1958) **M: 862b**
Hillerman, Tony [American author] **H: 232**
Hilliard, Nicholas [English painter]
Elizabeth I *picture on* **E: 239**
Hillman, John [American prospector]
Crater Lake **Ci: 1122**
Hillman, Sidney [American labor leader] **H: 232**
Hills, Carla Anderson [American government
official]
Ford, Gerald Rudolph (table) **F: 378**
Housing and Urban Development, Department
of (table) **H: 393**
Hillsborough Bay
Prince Edward Island (Land and climate) **P: 790**
Hillsborough Convention [1788]
North Carolina (Statehood) **N: 492**
Hillside Home School
Wisconsin (Places to visit) **W: 356**
Hilltopping [zoology]
Butterfly (The life cycle of butterflies) **B: 739-740**
Hillyer, Robert Silliman [American poet] **H: 232**
Hilo [Hawaii] **H: 232**
Hawaii (table: Average monthly weather) **H: 102**
Mauna Loa **M: 313**
Hilt
Knife **K: 345**
Sword **So: 1061** *with pictures*
Hilton, Conrad Nicholson [American
businessman] **H: 232**
Hilton, Edward [English colonist]
New Hampshire (Settlement) **N: 224**
Hilton, James [British author] **H: 233**
Hilton, Paris [American actress]
Hilton, Conrad Nicholson **H: 233**
Hilton Head Island [South Carolina]
South Carolina *pictures on* **So: 641, So: 650**
Hilton Hotel Systems
Hilton, Conrad Nicholson **H: 232**
Him [play by Cummings]
Cummings, E. E. **Ci: 1191**
Himachal Pradesh [state, India]
Punjab **P: 903**
Himalaya [mountains, Asia] **H: 233** *with map*
Bird (Birds of Asia) **B: 344f**
India (The land) **I: 121** *with picture*
Mountain (Plate flexing) **M: 894**
Mountain climbing (Challenge of the Himalaya)
M: 897
Nepal (Land and climate) **N: 126**
Plate tectonics (Convergent plate boundaries)
P: 562-563 *with diagram*
Tibet (The land) **T: 276**
World War II *picture on* **W: 491**
Himalayan bear
Bear (Asiatic black bears) **B: 185**
Himalayan blue poppy [plant]
Flower *picture on* **F: 279**
Himalayan ibex [animal]
Animal *picture on* **A: 475**
Ibex **I: 3**
Himalayan monal [bird]
Bird (Birds of Asia) **B: 344f** *with picture*
Himalia [satellite]
Jupiter (Outer satellites) **J: 200a**
Himation [clothing]
Clothing (Greece) **Ci: 697**
Himes, Chester [American author] **H: 233**
Himmelfarb, Alex [Canadian political leader]
Martin, Paul *picture on* **M: 235**
Himmler, Heinrich [Nazi leader] **H: 234**
Gestapo **G: 175**
Hitler, Adolf (Rise of the Nazis) **H: 266**
Hina-Matsuri [festival]
March **M: 194**
Hinchinbrook [ship]
Nelson, Horatio (Joins the navy) **N: 121**
Hinckley, Gordon B. [American religious leader]
Mormons (Mormons today) **M: 809**
Hinckley, John W., Jr. [American public figure]
Reagan, Ronald Wilson (Events at home) **R: 167-
168**
Hind [animal]
Red deer **R: 188**
Hind, Henry Y. [Canadian geologist]
Saskatchewan (North-West Territories) **S: 146**
Hind and the Panther, The [poem by Dryden]
Dryden, John **D: 370**
English literature (John Dryden) **E: 318**
Hindemith, Paul [German composer] **H: 234**
Hindenburg [airship]
Airship (The *Hindenburg*) **A: 252** *with picture*
Hindenburg, Paul von [German political leader]
H: 234
Germany (The Weimar Republic) **G: 167**
Hitler, Adolf (Rise of the Nazis) **H: 266-267**; (The
New Order) **H: 266-267** *with picture*
Junkers **J: 197**

Ludendorff, Erich Friedrich Wilhelm L: 515
Papen, Franz von P: 133
World War I (The Eastern Front) W: 456; (The Battle of Verdun) W: 458
Hindenburg Line
Siegfried Line S: 449
World War I (Allied failures) W: 461
Hindgut [biology]
Insect (Digestive system) I: 289 *with diagram*
Hindi language H: 234
India (Languages) I: 114
Urdu language U: 220
Hindi-Urdu [languages]
Hindi language H: 234
Urdu language U: 220
Hindu-Arabic numerals *See* Arabic numerals *in this index*
Hindu Kush [mountains, Asia] H: 235
Afghanistan (The Central Highlands) A: 94
Pakistan *picture on* P: 92
Hinduism [religion] H: 235 *with pictures*
See also the list of Related articles in the Hinduism article
Asia (Religions) A: 773; (The people) A: 781 *with picture*
Bangladesh (Religion) B: 82
Bhagavad-Gita B: 276
Dance (Asian theatrical dance) D: 28
Dharma D: 178
Divorce (In other countries) D: 254
Education (Early Chinese and Indian education) E: 99
Feasts and festivals (In Hinduism) F: 58
Food (Religious reasons) F: 332
Fundamentalism (Fundamentalism in other religions) F: 557
Ganges River G: 26 *with picture*
God G: 243
Heaven H: 161
India (Hinduism) I: 116 *with picture*; (History) I: 128
Manu M: 168
Marriage *picture on* M: 219; (Wedding ceremonies) M: 220
Meditation M: 380
Monasticism (Non-Christian monasticism) M: 701
New Age movement N: 178
Rammohun Roy R: 133
Religion R: 215 *with picture*; (How the major religions are organized) R: 218; (Hinduism) R: 220; (Buddhism) R: 220
Saint (Non-Christian saints) S: 29
Sculpture (India) S: 236 *with pictures*
Suttee So: 1013
Upanishads U: 212
Vishnu V: 429 *with picture*
World, History of the (The Mauryan Empire in India) W: 430 *with picture*
Yoga Y: 567
Hindustani [language] *See* Hindi-Urdu *in this index*
Hine, Lewis W. [American photographer]
Photography (Artistic advances) P: 424-425
Hines, Earl [American pianist] H: 237
Jazz (The 1920's) J: 70
Hines, Edward N. [American businessman]
Michigan (Interesting facts) M: 489
Hines, "Fatha" [American pianist] *See* Hines, Earl *in this index*
Hinge joint [anatomy]
Joint J: 155 *with diagram*
Hinged window
Window W: 334
Hingis, Martina [Swiss tennis player] H: 237
Hinkle, James F. [American political leader]
New Mexico (table) N: 272
Hinny [animal]
Donkey D: 308
Mule M: 913
Hinode spacecraft
Astronomy (X-ray astronomy) A: 845
Corona Ci: 1067
Sun (Space-based studies) So: 986-987
Hinrichs, Gustavus D. [Danish-American scientist]
Derecho D: 152
Hinshelwood, Sir Cyril [British chemist]
Nobel Prizes (Chemistry: 1956) N: 443
Hinter Rhine [river, Switzerland]
Rhine River (The course of the Rhine) R: 292
Hinton, S. E. [American author] H: 237
Hip [anatomy] H: 238 *with diagram*
Human body (table) H: 422 *with diagram*
Hip-hop [culture] H: 238
Clothing (Japan) Ci: 699
Rap music R: 141
Hip roof
Roof R: 450b *with picture*
Hip straps

Harness *diagram on* H: 63
HIPAA [law] *See* Health Insurance Portability and Accountability Act *in this index*
Hipparchus [Greek ruler] H: 238
Hipparchus [Greek astronomer] H: 239
Magnitude M: 62
Ptolemy P: 854
Star (Magnitude and luminosity) So: 842
Hippias [Greek ruler]
Cleisthenes Ci: 661
Hipparchus H: 238
Hippies [social movement] H: 239
Hippo [former city]
Augustine, Saint (His life) A: 888
Hippocampus [physiology]
Bird (The nervous system) B: 366
Brain *diagram on* B: 553; (Memory and imagination) B: 554
Memory M: 392
Hippocrates [Greek doctor] H: 239
Blood (History of blood research) B: 414
Medicine (Greece and Rome) M: 372-373 *with picture*
Mental illness (Early attitudes) M: 408
Personality (Personality types) P: 301
Hippocratic oath
Hippocrates H: 239
Medicine (Greece and Rome) M: 372-373
Hippodamus [Greek architect]
City planning (Ancient times) Ci: 602 *with diagram*
Piraeus P: 493
Hippodrome [New York City]
Hippodrome H: 240
Hippodrome [sports] H: 240
Byzantine Empire *pictures on* B: 753
Olympia O: 745
Hippolyta [Greek mythology]
Hercules (The twelve labors) H: 198-199
Hippolytus, Saint [antipope]
Pope (table) P: 666
Hippopotamus [animal] H: 240 *with pictures and map*
Animal *picture on* A: 477
Hips [fruit]
Rose R: 474
Hira, Mount [Saudi Arabia]
Religion (Islam) R: 223
Hiragana [character]
Japanese language J: 61
Writing system (Phonetization) W: 513
Hiram [king of Tyre]
Phoenicia (The spread of Phoenician influence) P: 394-395
Solomon So: 584
Hire purchase system [economics]
Installment plan I: 304
Hired Girl Washer [machine]
Washing machine (History) W: 45
Hireling Shepherd, The [painting by Hunt]
Pre-Raphaelite Brotherhood *picture on* P: 756
Hiring hall [labor]
Labor movement (Other union activities) L: 7 *with picture*
Hirohito [emperor of Japan] H: 242 *with portrait*
Japan (World War II) J: 58 *with picture*; (Postwar boom) J: 58-59
World War II (The rise of dictatorships) W: 469-470
Hiroshige [Japanese artist] H: 242 *with picture*
Japanese print (The master print artists) J: 63
Tokyo *picture on* T: 319
Hiroshima [Japan] H: 242
Nuclear weapon N: 596, *picture on* N: 598; (World War II) N: 601
World War II (The atomic bomb) W: 493 *with picture*
Hiroshima [book by Hersey]
Hersey, John H: 216
Hiroshima No Pika [book by Maruki]
Literature for children *picture on* L: 355
Hirschman, Susan [American editor]
Regina Medal (table: 2004) R: 206
Hirshhorn, Joseph H. [American financier]
Hirshhorn Museum and Sculpture Garden H: 243
Hirshhorn Museum and Sculpture Garden [Washington, D.C.] H: 243 *with picture*
Washington, D.C. *map on* W: 76
Hirst, A. R. [American engineer]
Road (Modern roads) R: 362
Hirst, Damien [British artist] H: 243 *with picture*
Hirudin [chemical]
Leech L: 180
His House in Order [play by Pinero]
Pinero, Arthur Wing P: 473
His Majesty's Opposition [government]
United Kingdom (National government) U: 49

His Toy, His Dream, His Rest [book by Berryman]
Berryman, John B: 272
Hisatsinom [American Indians] *See* Anasazi *in this index*
Hisinger, Wilhelm von [Swedish geologist]
Cerium C: 362
Hismanal [drug]
Antihistamine A: 556
Hispania
Spain (Roman conquest) So: 745
Hispanic Americans [people] H: 244 *with pictures and map*
See also Cuban Americans; Mexican Americans; Puerto Ricans *in this index*
Chicago (Ethnic groups) C: 426
Education (Bilingual education) E: 107
Minority group (Hispanic Americans) M: 609
Name (Hispanic names) N: 6
National Council of La Raza N: 33
Racial profiling R: 61
United States *picture on* U: 111
Western frontier life in America (Early occupants) W: 234
Hispanics *See* Hispanic Americans *in this index*
Hispaniola [island, Caribbean Sea] H: 259
Ayllón, Lucas Vásquez de A: 995
Balboa, Vasco Núñez de *map on* B: 37; (Early life) B: 38
Columbus, Christopher (The first landing) Ci: 860-861; (Trouble, settlement, and exploration) Ci: 862; (Problems in Hispaniola) Ci: 862; (Fourth voyage westward) Ci: 863
Dominican Republic (Land) D: 304
Exploration (Columbus reaches America) E: 444
Haiti H: 14; (History) H: 15
Las Casas, Bartolomé de L: 80
Ponce de León, Juan (Early life and career) P: 655
United States, History of the (European discoveries) U: 150
Hiss, Alger [American public figure] H: 259 *with picture*
Chambers, Whittaker C: 372
Nixon, Richard Milhous (U.S. representative) N: 430
Truman, Harry S. (Problems at home) T: 472
Un-American Activities Committee U: 19
Hissarlik [ruins]
Troy (The archaeological Troy) T: 455
Histadrut [labor union]
Eshkol, Levi E: 357
Israel (Economy) I: 485
Histamine [physiology]
Allergy (Allergic reactions) A: 373-374
Antihistamine A: 556
Histocompatibility antigen [physiology]
Doherty, Peter Charles D: 284
Histology [biology] H: 260
Anatomy A: 448b
Bichat, Marie François Xavier B: 289
Histone [protein]
Chromosome C: 538
Histoplasma capsulatum [fungus]
Bird (In nature) B: 330
Histoplasmosis H: 260
Histoplasmosis [disease] H: 260
Bird (In nature) B: 330
Fungal disease (In people) F: 558
Historia Naturalis [book by Pliny the Elder]
Encyclopedia (The first reference works) E: 268a
Geology (The Romans) G: 98
Historia Regum Britanniae [book by Geoffrey of Monmouth] *See* History of the Kings of Britain *in this index*
Historiae ab Urbe Condita [book by Livy]
Livy L: 399
Historian [career]
See also the list of Related articles in the History article
History H: 260
Historian [office]
Parliamentary procedure (Officers) P: 175
Historiated initial [art]
Illuminated manuscript I: 78 *with picture*
Manuscript (Illustrated manuscripts) M: 174
Historic Arkansas Museum
Little Rock (Description) L: 392
Historic Doubts on the Life and Reign of King Richard the Third [book by Walpole]
Biography (The 1700's) B: 313
Historic house
Museum (History museums) M: 938 *with picture*
Historic Jamestowne [Virginia]
Colonial life in America (Places to visit) Ci: 800
Historic peace church [religious group]
Brethren B: 593
Historic Roscoe Village [Coshocton]
Ohio (Places to visit) O: 690 *with picture*

Historic Saint Mary's City [Maryland] *See* Saint Mary's City *in this index*
Historic Savannah
Georgia (Places to visit) G: 122
Historic Sites Act [1935]
National Park System (History) N: 58
Historic trail
National Trails System N: 61
Historic village
Museum (History museums) M: 938 *with picture*
Historical Association, American [organization] H: 260
Historical biography
Biography (Forms of biography) B: 312
Historical books [Bible]
Bible (table) B: 281; (The Christian Old Testament) B: 282
Old Testament (Contents) O: 741
Historical cycle [Irish literature]
Irish literature (Heroic tales, romances, and sagas) I: 430-431
Historical geology
Geology G: 97
Historical linguistics
Linguistics L: 335; (Comparative and historical linguistics) L: 336; (Comparative and historical research) L: 337
Historical novel [literature]
Literature for children (Historical fiction) L: 360 *with picture*
Novel (Britain) N: 573
Historical Register for the Year 1736, The [book by Fielding]
Fielding, Henry (His life) F: 94
Histories [book by Tacitus]
History (The ancient Greeks and Romans) H: 261-262
Latin literature (The Imperial Period) L: 116-117
Tacitus, Cornelius T: 4
Histories [books by Herodotus]
Herodotus H: 213
History (The ancient Greeks and Romans) H: 261
Histories or Tales of Past Times, with Morals [book by Perrault]
Mother Goose (The history of Mother Goose literature) M: 842
Historis Naturalis [book by Pliny the Elder] *See* Natural History *in this index*
History H: 260
See also the list of Related articles in the World, History of the *article*
Bible (Historical contexts) B: 287
Greek literature (Historical literature) G: 377
Mythology (Historical relationships) M: 976; (Allegorical approaches) M: 988
Painting (History paintings) P: 33 *with picture*
Pulitzer Prizes (table) P: 895
World, History of the W: 420
History [drama]
Shakespeare, William (The English ruler) S: 350; (Shakespeare's plays) S: 354-355
History and Present State of Virginia, The [book by Beverley]
American literature (Virginia) A: 414
History and Technology, National Museum of
See National Museum of American History *in this index*
History museum
Museum (History museums) M: 938 *with picture*
History of British India, The [book by Mill]
Mill, James M: 552
History of Canada [book by Roberts]
Roberts, Charles G. D. R: 365
History of economic thought
Economics (Fields of economics) E: 64
History of England from the Accession of James II, The [book by Macaulay]
Macaulay, Thomas Babington M: 5
History of King Richard III [book by More]
Biography (The Renaissance) B: 313
History of Little Goody Two-Shoes, The [book]
Literature for children (The 1700's) L: 362-363
History of New York from the Beginning of the World to the End of the Dutch Dynasty, A [book by Irving] *See* Knickerbocker's History of New York *in this index*
History of Plymouth Plantation [book by Bradford]
Bradford, William [1590-1657] B: 544
History of Rome [book by Mommsen]
Rome, Ancient (Learning about ancient Rome) R: 448
History of Sexuality, The [book by Foucault]
Foucault, Michel F: 429
History of the Decline and Fall of the Roman Empire [book by Gibbon]
Gibbon, Edward G: 185
History (Antiquarian research and the

philosophes) H: 262
Rome, Ancient (Learning about ancient Rome) R: 448
History of the Dividing Line [book by Byrd]
American literature (Virginia) A: 414
History of the English Law [book by Maitland]
Maitland, Frederic William M: 93
History of the French Revolution [book by Thiers]
Thiers, Louis Adolphe T: 258
History of the Hoppers, The [book by Parker]
Literature for children *picture on* L: 354
History of the Kings of Britain [book by Geoffrey of Monmouth]
Gawain, Sir G: 71
Geoffrey of Monmouth G: 91
History of the Peloponnesian War [book by Thucydides]
History (The ancient Greeks and Romans) H: 261
Oratory (Classical orators) O: 819
Thucydides T: 271
History of the Russian State [book by Karamzin]
Russian literature (Sentimentalism) R: 560
History of the United States [book by Adams]
Adams, Henry A: 33
History of Tom Jones, The [book by Fielding] *See* Tom Jones *in this index*
History of Woman Suffrage [book]
Anthony, Susan Brownell A: 545
History Portraits [photographs by Sherman]
Sherman, Cindy S: 396
Histosol [soil]
Soil *map on* So: 575; (How soils are classified) So: 576
Histotoxic anoxia [disorder]
Anoxia A: 519
Hit [baseball] *See* Base hit *in this index*
Hit-and-run play
Baseball (Baseball terms) B: 124
Hit-to-kill missile
Guided missile (The warhead) G: 423-424
Hitachi, Ltd. [company]
Manufacturing (table) M: 170
Hitchcock, Alfred [British director] H: 263
Motion picture (Movies in the 1930's) M: 867-868 *with picture*
Hitchcock, Ethan A. [American government official]
Interior, Department of the (table) I: 325
McKinley, William (table) M: 342
Roosevelt, Theodore (table) R: 466
Hitchcock, Frank H. [American government official]
Taft, William Howard (table) T: 11
Hitchcock, Henry-Russell [American author]
Johnson, Philip Cortelyou J: 152
Hitches
Knots, hitches, and splices K: 355
Hitchings, George Herbert [American biochemist]
Elion, Gertrude Belle E: 236
Nobel Prizes (Physiology or medicine: 1988) N: 446
Hitler, Adolf [German dictator] H: 264 *with pictures*
Austria (After World War I) A: 939 *with picture*
Bonhoeffer, Dietrich B: 459
Bormann, Martin B: 488
Braun, Eva B: 566
Czechoslovakia (The Munich Agreement) Ci: 1215
Dönitz, Karl D: 307
Fascism (Fascism in Germany) F: 49-50
Germany (Nazi Germany) G: 167; (World War II) G: 168
Goebbels, Joseph G: 246
Göring, Hermann Wilhelm G: 276
Government (Fascism) G: 288
Hess, Rudolf H: 218
Hindenburg, Paul von H: 234
Hitler Youth H: 268
Holocaust H: 296
Hungary (World War II) H: 446
Italy (World War II) I: 517
Jodl, Alfred J: 130
Mein Kampf M: 386
Minority group (The creation of minority groups) M: 609
Munich Agreement (Background) M: 928
Nazism N: 92
Olympic Games (Between the wars) O: 751
Owens, Jesse O: 883
Papen, Franz von P: 133
Propaganda *pictures on* P: 823; (Simplicity and repetition) P: 824; (Between the wars) P: 825
Prussia (Decline of Prussia) P: 843
Stalin, Joseph (World War II) So: 827
Union of Soviet Socialist Republics (Stalin's policies) U: 36-37
United Kingdom ("Peace in our time") U: 70

Volkswagen AG V: 444
World War II (The rise of dictatorships) W: 469-470 *with picture*
Hitler, Alois [father of]
Hitler, Adolf (Boyhood) H: 264-265
Hitler Youth [German history] H: 268
Hitler, Adolf (The New Order) H: 266-267
Hitleriad, The [book by Klein]
Klein, A. M. K: 343
Hittites [ancient people] H: 269 *with picture*
Cuneiform Ci: 1192
Hieroglyphics (Other hieroglyphic writing) H: 227 *with picture*
Iron and steel (The Iron Age) I: 449-450
Mitanni M: 676
Ramses II R: 134
Turkey (History) T: 509
Hitty, Her First Hundred Years [book by Field]
Field, Rachel F: 92
HIV [virus] *See* Human immunodeficiency virus *in this index*
Hiva Oa [island, Pacific]
Marquesas Islands M: 217
Hive [biology]
Bee *pictures on* B: 204; (The honey bee colony) B: 201 *with picture*; (As an industry) B: 206-207 *with picture*
Hives [disorder] H: 270
Allergy A: 373
Hizbollah [political group] *See* Hezbollah *in this index*
Hkakabo Razi [mountain]
Myanmar (Land regions) M: 970c *with map*
HLA antigen [medicine]
Blood (The significance of blood groups) B: 412
Bone marrow transplant B: 457
Transplant (Preventing rejection) T: 380-381
HLN [network]
Cable News Network C: 7
HMD [electronics] *See* Head-mounted display *in this index*
HMG-coA reductase [enzyme]
Statin So: 867
HMO [health care] *See* Health maintenance organization *in this index*
Hmong [people] H: 270
French Guiana *picture on* F: 515
Laos (People) L: 70
Hnatyshyn, Ramon John [Canadian political leader] H: 270
Ho [symbol]
Holmium H: 296
Ho Chi Minh [Vietnamese political leader] H: 270 *with portrait*
Asia (The spread of Communism) A: 807
Communism (Expansion in Southeast Asia) Ci: 894
Geneva Accords G: 87
Indochina (Independence) I: 225
Vietnam (The August Revolution of 1945) V: 370; (The First Indochina War) V: 371
Vietnam War (The Indochina War) V: 373
Ho Chi Minh City [Vietnam] H: 270
Vietnam V: 364, *picture on* V: 368
Vietnam War (The end of the war) V: 376-377
Ho Chi Minh Mausoleum
Hanoi H: 53
Ho Chi Minh Trail [road]
Laos (History) L: 71-72
Vietnam War (The Viet Cong rebellion) V: 374
Ho-Chunk Indians H: 271
Winnebago Indians W: 339
HO gauge [size]
Railroad, Model (Scale and size) R: 120 *with picture*
Ho Quy Ly [Vietnamese ruler]
Vietnam (Independence) V: 370
Hoadly, George [American political leader]
Ohio (table) O: 699
Hoan, Daniel W. [American political leader]
Milwaukee (The 1900's) M: 561
Hoar, Ebenezer Rockwood [American government official]
Grant, Ulysses S. (table) G: 316
Justice, Department of (table) J: 203
Hoard, William Dempster [American political leader]
Wisconsin (Agriculture) W: 363; (table) W: 365
Hoarding [disorder] H: 271
Hoare-Laval Agreement [1935]
Laval, Pierre L: 128
Hoarfrost [weather]
Frost F: 542 *with pictures*
Hoary bat [animal]
Bat (Red bats and hoary bats) B: 161
Hoary redpoll [bird]
Redpoll R: 191

Hoatzin [bird] H: 271 *with picture*
  Bird *picture on* B: 344b; (Birds of Central and South America) B: 344a
Hob [device] *See* Cooktop *in this index*
Hoban, James [American architect]
  Adams, John *picture on* A: 38
  White House (The original building) W: 290
Hobart [Australia] H: 272
  Australia *picture on* A: 901
  Tasmania (People) T: 48 *with picture*
Hobart, Garret Augustus [American political leader] H: 272
  McKinley, William (Crisis and triumph) M: 340
  Vice president of the United States V: 348 *with portrait*
Hobbes, Thomas [English philosopher] H: 272
  Enlightenment (Criticism of the Enlightenment) E: 326b
  Government (The rise of monarchies and nation-states) G: 290
  Materialism M: 300b
  Political science (Secularism) P: 639
  Psychology (Beginnings) P: 849
Hobbit [anthropology] *See* Homo floresiensis *in this index*
Hobbit, The [book by Tolkien]
  Fairy (Fairies in literature) F: 11
  Tolkien, J. R. R. T: 321
Hobby H: 272
  Bee (As a hobby) B: 207
  Book collecting B: 468
  Button (Button collecting) B: 745
  Handicraft H: 46
  Horticulture (Horticulture as a hobby) H: 370
  Library (Library services) L: 235-236
  Railroad, Model R: 119
  Recreation (Kinds of recreation) R: 183
  Rock (Rocks as a hobby) R: 373
  Rocket, Model R: 391
  Weaving W: 173
  Woodworking W: 396
Hobby [bird]
  Bird (Birds of Europe) B: 344c *with picture*
Hobby, Oveta Culp [American government official] H: 273
  Eisenhower, Dwight David (Eisenhower's methods) E: 151-152
Hobby, William Pettus [American political leader]
  Texas (table) T: 203
Hobby magazine
  Magazine (Consumer magazines) M: 42
Hobgoblin [legendary figure]
  Puck P: 870
Hobo clown
  Clown Ci: 713
Hobson, Laura Z. [American author] H: 273
Hoch, Edward Wallis [American political leader]
  Kansas (table) K: 234
Hochdeutsch [dialect] *See* High German *in this index*
Hochelaga [former village]
  Montreal (Exploration) M: 777
Hochhuth, Rolf [German dramatist] H: 273
  German literature (Postwar German literature [1945-1990]) G: 142
Höchstädt, Battle of [1704]
  Blenheim, Battle of B: 400
Hock [zoology]
  Horse (Legs and hoofs) H: 349-350
Hockenhull, A. W. [American political leader]
  New Mexico (table) N: 272
Hockey [sport] H: 274 *with pictures*
  Canada (Recreation and sports) C: 108 *with picture*
  Field hockey F: 92
  Glove *picture on* G: 235
  Ice skating I: 10 *with picture*
  Olympic Games *picture on* O: 754; (Winter Olympic Games) O: 746d
  Ringette R: 343
  Roller skating (Competitive roller skating) R: 402a
  Stanley Cup So: 838
Hockey Canada [organization]
  Hockey (Amateur organization) H: 279; (Amateur development) H: 281
Hockey Hall of Fame [Canada]
  Hall of fame (Sports halls of fame) H: 23
  Hockey (Famous players and All-Star teams) H: 281
  Stanley Cup So: 838
Hockey Hall of Fame [U.S.]
  Hockey (Famous players and All-Star teams) H: 281
Hockney, David [British artist] H: 282 *with picture*
Hod Carriers' Union
  Laborers' International Union of North America L: 16

Hodeida [Yemen]
  United Arab Republic U: 46
Hodel, Donald P. [American government official]
  Energy, Department of (table) E: 276
  Interior, Department of the (table) I: 325
  Reagan, Ronald Wilson (table) R: 169
Hoder [Norse mythology]
  Balder B: 38
  Loki L: 426
Hodges, George Hartshorn [American political leader]
  Kansas (table) K: 234
Hodges, Johnny [American saxophonist]
  Ellington, Duke *picture on* E: 242
Hodges, Luther Hartwell [American political leader]
  Commerce, Department of (table) Ci: 871
  Johnson, Lyndon Baines (table) J: 151
  Kennedy, John Fitzgerald (table) K: 266
  North Carolina (table) N: 490
Hodgkin, Sir Alan Lloyd [British biophysicist]
  Nobel Prizes (Physiology or medicine: 1963) N: 446
Hodgkin, Dorothy Crowfoot [British chemist] H: 283
Hodgkin, Thomas [British doctor]
  Hodgkin's disease H: 283
Hodgkin's disease H: 283
  Cancer (Classification by primary body site) C: 167-168
Hodgson, James D. [American government official]
  Labor, Department of (table) L: 2
  Nixon, Richard Milhous (table) N: 433
Hoe [tool]
  Gardening (Cultivating an outdoor garden) G: 34
Hoe, Richard March [American businessman]
  Printing (New presses and typecasting machines) P: 803
Hoegh, Leo A. [American political leader]
  Iowa (table) I: 391
Hoehling, A. A. [American jurist]
  Coolidge, Calvin (Vice president) Ci: 1032
Hoes, Hannah [wife of]
  Van Buren, Martin (Van Buren's family) V: 271
Hoeven, John [American political leader]
  North Dakota (table) N: 513; (Recent developments) N: 513
Hoey, Clyde R. [American political leader]
  North Carolina (table) N: 490
Hoff, Philip H. [American political leader]
  Vermont (table) V: 333
Hoffa, James Phillip [American labor leader] H: 283
Hoffa, James Riddle [American labor leader] H: 283
  Hoffa, James Phillip H: 283
Hoffer, Eric [American philosopher] H: 283
Hoffman, Dustin [American actor] H: 283
  Motion picture (Best performance by an actor: 1979, 1988) M: 862a
Hoffman, Harold G. [American political leader]
  New Jersey (table) N: 249
Hoffman, John Thompson [American political leader]
  New York (table) N: 313
Hoffman, Philip Seymour [American actor]
  Motion picture (Best performance by an actor: 2005) M: 862a
Hoffmann, E. T. A. [German author] H: 283
  German literature (Romanticism) G: 140
  Nutcracker, The N: 622
Hoffmann, Josef [Austrian architect]
  Architecture (Early modern architecture in Europe) A: 627-628 *with picture*
Hoffmann, Jules A. [Luxembourg-born physiologist]
  Nobel Prizes (Physiology or medicine: 2011) N: 447
Hoffmann, Roald [American chemist]
  Nobel Prizes (Chemistry: 1981) N: 444
Hoffmannsthal, Hugo von [German poet]
  German literature (Impressionism, Neoromanticism, and Symbolism) G: 141
Hofmann, Albert [Swiss chemist]
  LSD L: 512
Hofmann, August Wilhelm von [German chemist]
  Formaldehyde F: 410
Hofmann, Hans [German-American painter] H: 284
  Drawing *picture on* D: 343
  Krasner, Lee K: 386
Hofmannsthal, Hugo von [Austrian author] H: 284
  Austria (Literature) A: 933
  Opera (Richard Strauss) O: 799; (*Rosenkavalier, Der*) O: 807
  Strauss, Richard So: 922
Hofstadter, Robert [American physicist]

  Nobel Prizes (Physics: 1961) N: 441
Hog [animal] H: 284 *with pictures*
  See also the list of Related articles in the Hog *article*
  Farm and farming *picture on* F: 39
  Iowa (Agriculture) I: 389
  Meat packing M: 350
  Swine flu S: 1048
  Wart hog W: 44 *with picture*
  Xenotransplant X: 544
Hog line
  Curling *diagram on* Ci: 1196
Hog millet [grain]
  Millet M: 555
Hog-nosed bat [animal] *See* Kitti's hog-nosed bat *in this index*
Hog-nosed skunk
  Skunk S: 496
Hogan [dwelling] H: 288
  Indian, American *picture on* I: 139; (Shelter) I: 136d; (Before European contact) I: 166-168
  Navajo Indians N: 69
Hogan, Ben [American golfer] H: 288
  Golf *picture on* G: 266; (U.S. Open) G: 265
"Hogan's Alley" [comic strip]
  Outcault, Richard Felton O: 879
Hogarth, Mary [sister-in-law of]
  Dickens, Charles (Personal life) D: 188
Hogarth, William [English artist] H: 288 *with picture*
  Fielding, Henry *picture on* F: 94
Hogarth Press [publisher]
  Woolf, Virginia W: 401
Hogchoker [fish]
  Sole So: 582 *with picture*
Hoge, James [American inventor]
  Ohio (Interesting facts) O: 681
Hogfish
  Fish *picture on* F: 155
Hogg, Frank [Canadian astronomer]
  Hogg, Helen Sawyer H: 288
Hogg, Helen Sawyer [American-Canadian astronomer] H: 288
Hogg, James S. [American political leader]
  Texas (table) T: 203; (Conquering the frontier) T: 207
Hognose snake
  Adder A: 47
  Animal (Playing dead) A: 496
  Snake *picture on* S: 526; (Protection against predators) S: 531
Hogrogian, Nonny [American artist]
  Caldecott Medal (table: 1966, 1972) C: 26
  Literature for children *picture on* L: 358
Hogweed [plant]
  Ragweed R: 103
Hohensalzburg Fortress [Salzburg]
  Austria *picture on* A: 931
Hohenstaufen [German history]
  Germany (The Holy Roman Empire) G: 162-163
  Guelphs and Ghibellines G: 419
Hohenzollern [German history] H: 289
  Berlin (History) B: 264
  Germany (The rise of Prussia) G: 164
  Prussia (The Prussian people) P: 842; (Early history) P: 843
Hohokam Indians
  Arizona (Early days) A: 688
  Indian, American *picture on* I: 151; (Farming) I: 141; (Indians of the Southwest) I: 166
  Phoenix (History) P: 398
  Pima Indians P: 465
Hohokam Pima National Monument [Arizona]
  National Park System (table: National monuments) N: 51
Hoist [flag part]
  Flag *diagram on* F: 194; (Flags that talk) F: 208
Hoist [machine]
  Block and tackle (An endless chain hoist) B: 405 *with diagram*
Hoit, Albert Gallatin [American painter]
  Harrison, William Henry *picture on* H: 74
Hoitsu, Sakai [Japanese artist]
  Painting (Landscapes and seascapes) P: 32-33 *with picture*
Hojo family [Japanese history]
  Japan (Rise of the shogun) J: 54
Hokan [language group]
  Indian, American (Language groups) I: 149-150
Hokkaido [island, Japan]
  Japan *picture on* J: 33; (Hokkaido) J: 46 *with picture and map*
Hokku [poetry]
  Haiku H: 8
Hokulea [canoe]
  Hawaii (Renewed interest in Hawaiian culture) H: 109
Hokusai [Japanese artist] H: 289 *with picture*

Japanese print (The master print artists) J: 63
Holbein, Hans, the Elder [German painter] H: 289
Holbein, Hans, the Younger [German painter]
H: 289 *with picture*
Clothing *picture on* Ci: 702
Erasmus, Desiderius *picture on* E: 349
Germany (Painting and sculpture) G: 155
Henry VIII *picture on* H: 188
More, Sir Thomas *picture on* M: 801; (Character and writings) M: 802
Renaissance *picture on* R: 238
Holberg, Ludvig [Danish dramatist] H: 290
Denmark (Arts) D: 136
Holbrook, Frederick [American political leader]
Vermont (table) V: 333
Holbrook, Josiah [American educator]
Lyceum L: 532
Holbrooke, Richard C. [American diplomat]
United Nations (table) U: 86
HOLC [agency] *See* Home Owners Loan Corporation *in this index*
Holcomb, Marcus H. [American political leader]
Connecticut (table) C: 967
Holcomb, Silas A. [American political leader]
Nebraska (table) N: 110
Hold [wrestling]
Wrestling W: 504 *with picture*
Holdback straps
Harness *diagram on* H: 63
Holden, Bob [American political leader]
Missouri (table) M: 668
Holden, Phyllis [wife of]
Dole, Robert Joseph (Early life) D: 285
Holden, William [American actor]
Motion picture (Best performance by an actor: 1953) M: 862a
Holden, William W. [American political leader]
North Carolina (Interesting facts) N: 473; (table) N: 490
Holder [banking]
Note (Liability of the maker) N: 550
Holder, Eric Himpton, Jr. [American government official] H: 290 *with portrait*
Justice, Department of (table) J: 203
Hölderlin, Friedrich [German poet]
German literature (German Classicism) G: 139
Holding [sports]
Football (Violations and penalties) F: 363
Holding company [economics] H: 292
United States, History of the (The rise of "trusts") U: 181
Hole [electronics]
Electronics (Active components) E: 210
Transistor (Transistor materials) T: 372
Hole [golf]
Golf G: 260
Hole, William [Scottish painter]
Scotland *picture on* S: 220
Hole-in-one
Golf G: 261
Hole machining
Machine tool (Metal removal) M: 17 *with pictures*
Holes [book by Sachar]
Sachar, Louis S: 5
Holgate, Edwin [Canadian painter]
Group of Seven G: 402
Holi [festival] H: 290
Feasts and festivals (In Hinduism) F: 58
India (Hinduism) I: 116 *with picture*
Holiday H: 291
See also the list of Related articles in the Holiday article
Colonial life in America (Recreation) Ci: 802-803
Folklore (Holidays) F: 325
Holiday [play by Barry]
Barry, Philip B: 119
Holiday, Billie [American singer] H: 291 *with portrait*
Holiday World & Splashin' Safari [Santa Claus]
Indiana (Places to visit) I: 206 *with picture*
Holiness Code [Bible]
Leviticus L: 219
Holiness movement [religion]
Church of God in Christ, The C: 543
Churches of God C: 543
Pentecostal churches (Major Pentecostal churches) P: 275
Protestantism (The modern evangelical and Pentecostal movements) P: 835
Holinshed, Raphael [English historian]
Holinshed's Chronicles H: 291
Holinshed's Chronicles [book] H: 291
Macbeth M: 5
Shakespeare, William *picture on* S: 351; (Shakespeare's plays) S: 354-355
Holistic medicine H: 292
New Age movement N: 178

Holker, John [British businessman]
Industrial Revolution (Spread of the Industrial Revolution) I: 252
Holl, Frank [British artist]
Painting (Painting outside France) P: 72
Holladay, Benjamin [American businessman]
Wells, Fargo & Company W: 195
Holland [country] *See* Netherlands *in this index*
Holland [breed]
Chicken (table) C: 443
Holland [Michigan] H: 292
Michigan (Visitor's guide) M: 498 *with picture*
Holland [submarine]
Holland, John Philip H: 292
Submarine (Early submarines) So: 942-943 *with picture*
Holland, John Philip [Irish-American inventor]
H: 292
Submarine (Early submarines) So: 942-943
Holland, Kingdom of [Dutch history]
Netherlands (Independence) N: 149
Holland, Spessard L. [American political leader]
Florida (table) F: 260
Holland, William [American race driver]
Automobile racing (table: Indianapolis 500 winners) A: 980
Holland Tunnel [New Jersey-New York]
Hudson River tunnels (The Holland Tunnel) H: 407
Tunnel (Motor-traffic tunnels) T: 491
Hollande, François [French political leader]
France (Recent developments) F: 478
Hollerith, Herman [American inventor]
Computer *picture on* Ci: 924a; (Foundations of data processing) Ci: 924b
Holley, Alexander H. [American political leader]
Connecticut (table) C: 967
Holley, Charles Hardin [birth name of]
Holly, Buddy H: 293
Holley, Robert William [American physiologist]
Nobel Prizes (Physiology or medicine: 1968) N: 446
Holliday, Doc [American gunfighter]
Earp, Wyatt E: 15
Holliday, Frederick W. M. [American political leader]
Virginia (table) V: 417
Holliday, Judy [American actress]
Motion picture (Best performance by an actress: 1950) M: 862
Hollister, Meridian [American political leader]
Ohio (table) O: 699
Hollow stalk bolete [mushroom]
Mushroom *picture on* M: 944
Holloway, William J. [American political leader]
Oklahoma (table) O: 730; (The 1920's) O: 732
Holly [tree] *picture on* F: 277
Christmas (Christmas decorations) C: 535
Tree *pictures on* T: 422
Holly, Buddy [American musician] H: 293 *with portrait*
Rock music (A variety of styles) R: 378
Holly Hobbie [doll]
Doll (The 1970's) D: 293
Hollyhock [plant] H: 293 *with picture*
Flower *picture on* F: 277
Gardening *picture on* G: 33
Hollywood [California] H: 293 *with picture*
California *picture on* C: 55
Los Angeles *picture on* L: 461; (Recent developments) L: 470-471
Motion picture (The birth of Hollywood) M: 864
Hollywood Africans [painting by Basquiat]
Painting (Recent painting) P: 87-88 *with picture*
Hollywood Boulevard
Los Angeles *picture on* L: 457; (Central Los Angeles) L: 460
Hollywood Bowl
Hollywood H: 293
Hollywood Cemetery [Virginia]
Richmond (Other interesting places to visit) R: 332
Hollywood Pictures [company]
Walt Disney Company W: 21
Holm, Celeste [American actress]
Motion picture (Best performance by an actress in a supporting role: 1947) M: 862b
Holm, Hanya [German-American choreographer]
H: 294
Holm oak
Oak (Other oaks) O: 636 *with picture*
Holmes, Arthur [Scottish geologist]
Geology (Experimental geology) G: 99
Holmes, Comet
Comet (table) Ci: 868
Holmes, David [American political leader]
Mississippi (table) M: 640; (Statehood) M: 642

Holmes, Don [American journalist]
Feboldson, Febold F: 59
Holmes, Gabriel [American political leader]
North Carolina (table) N: 490
Holmes, Larry [American boxer]
Ali, Muhammad (Later years) A: 367
Holmes, Oliver Wendell [American author] H: 294 *with portrait*
American literature (Poetry) A: 418
Essay (Personal essays) E: 359
Holmes, Oliver Wendell, Jr. [American jurist]
H: 295 *with portrait*
Civil rights (Limits of civil rights) Ci: 608
Lochner v. New York L: 410
Schenck v. United States S: 174
Holmes, Robert D. [American political leader]
Oregon (table) O: 845
Holmes, Sherlock [literary figure] H: 295
Detective story (History) D: 162-163
Doyle, Arthur Conan D: 316
Holmes, Simon H. [Canadian political leader]
Nova Scotia (table) N: 567
Holmes v. Walton [U.S. history]
Brearley, David B: 590
Holmium [element] H: 296
Holness, Andrew [Jamaican political leader]
Jamaica (History) J: 24-25
Holocaust [European history] H: 296 *with pictures and map*
Bielski partisans B: 295
Germany (World War II) G: 168-169
Holocaust Memorial Museum, United States H: 298
Human rights (The development of human rights) H: 428-428a
Jerusalem *picture on* J: 100
Jews (The Holocaust) J: 124
Nazism (Expansion, war, and collapse) N: 92
Schindler, Oskar S: 175
Wallenberg, Raoul W: 17
Whiteread, Rachel W: 293
World War II (The Holocaust) W: 496
Zionism (The Balfour Declaration) Z: 595-596
Holocaust Memorial Museum, United States [Washington, D.C.] H: 298
Washington, D.C. *map on* W: 76; (South of the Mall) W: 75
Holocaust Project, The [art]
Chicago, Judy C: 437
Holocene Epoch [geology]
Earth (table) E: 30
Prehistoric animal (table) P: 740
Holofernes [Biblical figure]
Judith J: 184
Hologram [photography]
Holography H: 298 *with picture*
Holographic will [law]
Will W: 307
Holography [photography] H: 298 *with diagrams*
Gabor, Dennis G: 4
Laser (Recording, storing, and transmitting information) L: 82
Holoku [clothing]
Hawaii (Clothing) H: 94
Holoplankton [organisms]
Plankton P: 515
Holshouser, James E., Jr. [American political leader]
North Carolina (table) N: 490; (The late 1900's) N: 493-494
Holst, Gustav [British composer] H: 298
Holstein [region, Germany]
Denmark (The Schleswig wars) D: 140
Holstein [breed]
Cattle *picture on* C: 307; (Holstein-Friesian) C: 310 *with picture*
Holstein-Friesian [cattle]
Cattle (Holstein-Friesian) C: 310 *with picture*; (table) C: 313
Dairying (Dairy cattle) D: 6
Holt, Harold [Australian political leader]
Australia (table) A: 923
Holt, Homer A. [American political leader]
West Virginia (table) W: 225
Holt, Joseph [American government official]
Buchanan, James (table) B: 661
Holt, Thomas M. [American political leader]
North Carolina (table) N: 490
Holt, W. Elmer [American political leader]
Montana (table) M: 757
Holton, A. Linwood, Jr. [American political leader]
Virginia (table) V: 417; (Politics) V: 418; (Political changes) V: 422
Holtzman, Elizabeth [American political leader]
Heckler, Margaret Mary H: 164
Holubtsi [food]
Ukraine (Food and drink) U: 8

Holwell, John [British colonial official]
Black Hole of Calcutta B: 389
Holy Alliance [European history] H: 298
Alexander I [czar] A: 341
Monroe Doctrine (Origins) M: 739
Holy Apostles, Church of the [Greece]
Byzantine art (Architecture) B: 749-750
Holy Ark [religion] *See* Ark of the Covenant *in this index*
Holy Bible *See* Bible *in this index*
Holy Communion [religion] *See* Communion *in this index*
Holy day of obligation [religion]
Roman Catholic Church (The Eucharist or Mass) R: 404
Holy Eucharist [religion] *See* Communion *in this index*
Holy Family on the Steps [painting by Poussin]
Classicism (The qualities of Classicism) Ci: 653
Painting (Classicism) P: 61 *with picture*
Holy Ghost [religion] *See* Holy Spirit *in this index*
Holy Grail [religion] H: 299 *with picture*
Arthur, King A: 757
Chrétien de Troyes C: 522d
Galahad, Sir G: 7
Knights and knighthood *picture on* K: 348
Lancelot, Sir L: 56
Mythology (Welsh myths) M: 985
Round Table (Origin) R: 491
Holy Land
Israel I: 478
Palestine P: 103
Holy League [European history]
Pius V, Saint P: 502
Holy of Holies [religion]
Tabernacle T: 2
Holy Office, Congregation of the [religion]
Inquisition I: 277
Holy orders [religion]
See also Ordination *in this index*
Eastern Orthodox Churches (Sacraments) E: 46-47
Roman Catholic Church (Worship) R: 403-404
Holy Place [religion]
Tabernacle T: 2
Holy Roman Empire [European history] H: 299 *with map*
See also the list of Related articles in the Holy Roman Empire *article*
Austria (Early years) A: 936
Charlemagne C: 378
Czech Republic (The rise of Bohemia) Ci: 1213
Czechoslovakia (Early history) Ci: 1215
Europe (The Franks) E: 409 *with map*
Flag *picture on* F: 217
Germany (The Holy Roman Empire) G: 162; (Conflicts with France) G: 164-165
Habsburg, House of H: 3
Italy (The Middle Ages) I: 513 *with map*
Middle Ages (Feudal government) M: 524-525 *with map*
Holy Saturday [religion]
Easter (Holy Saturday) E: 43
Holy Week H: 300
Holy Scriptures *See* Bible *in this index*
Holy See [religion]
Pope P: 660
Holy Sepulcher, Church of the [Jerusalem]
Jerusalem (Christian sites) J: 96 *with picture and map*
Holy Sonnets [poems by Donne]
Donne, John (His poetry) D: 308
Holy Spirit [religion]
Christianity (The Trinity) C: 522g
Protestantism (Protestant beliefs) P: 833-834
Trinity T: 447
Holy Thursday [religion] *See* Maundy Thursday *in this index*
Holy tradition [religion]
Eastern Orthodox Churches E: 45
Holy Trinity, Cathedral of the
Quebec (Churches) Q: 36
Holy Trinity Church [Stratford-on-Avon]
Shakespeare, William (His last years) S: 348 *with picture*
Holy Trinity with the Virgin and Saint John, The [painting by Masaccio]
Masaccio M: 261 *with picture*
Holy unction [religion] *See* Anointing of the sick *in this index*
Holy Wars
Crusades (The First Crusade) Ci: 1160
Holy Week [religion] H: 300
Easter (Holy Week) E: 42 *with picture*
Lent L: 196b
Palm Sunday P: 110
Spain (Holidays) So: 736

Holy Wisdom, Church of the *See* Hagia Sophia *in this index*
Holyfield, Evander [American boxer]
Boxing (The late 1900's) B: 532b *with picture*
Tyson, Mike T: 542
Homage [European history] H: 300
Feudalism (The principles of feudalism) F: 82
Homage to Catalonia [book by Orwell]
Orwell, George O: 860
Homage to Mistress Bradstreet [poem by Berryman]
Berryman, John B: 272
Homage to the Square [paintings by Albers]
Albers, Josef A: 311 *with picture*
Homalopsid [snake]
Snake (Homalopsids) S: 535
Hombori Tondo [mountain, Mali]
Mali (Land and climate) M: 107 *with map*
Hombre [book by Leonard]
Leonard, Elmore L: 198
Home
Animal (Animal homes and communities) A: 501 *with pictures*
Colonial life in America (Colonists at home) Ci: 796 *with picture*
Early childhood education (Activities planned by families) E: 15
Electricity (In homes) E: 191
Family (Home life) F: 21
House H: 380 *with pictures*
Lighting (In the home) L: 296 *with picture*
Reading (Learning in the home) R: 160
Safety (Safety at home) S: 9 *with pictures*
Shelter S: 392
Solar energy *picture on* So: 578
"Home, Sweet Home" [song]
Payne, John Howard P: 204
Popular music (Revolutionary War to 1840) P: 669
Home, The [book by Gilman]
Gilman, Charlotte Perkins G: 191
Home and School Association
Parent-teacher organizations (Home and School Associations) P: 158
Home-built airplane
Airplane (Special-purpose planes) A: 212-213
"Home Burial" [poem by Frost]
Frost, Robert (His poems) F: 543
Home-care aide
Day care (Day care for the elderly) D: 53
Medicine *picture on* M: 365
Home-delivery service
Restaurant (Fast-service restaurants) R: 262
Home Department [former name]
Interior, Department of the (History) I: 325
Home economics *See* Family and consumer sciences *in this index*
Home entertainment system
Television (Home entertainment systems) T: 110c
Home Insurance Building [Chicago]
Architecture (Early modern architecture in America) A: 629
Arthur, Chester Alan *picture on* A: 755
Chicago (A city reborn) C: 435
Illinois *picture on* I: 53
Jenney, William Le Baron J: 92
Skyscraper (History) S: 498-499
Home meal replacement
Restaurant (Kinds of restaurants) R: 262
Home network
Computer (Personal computers) Ci: 909
Home of Franklin D. Roosevelt [New York]
National Park System (table: National historic sites) N: 52-53
Home Owners Loan Corporation [U.S.]
New Deal (table) N: 201
Home page [computing]
Internet (HTTP) I: 350d
Website W: 176
Home plate
Baseball (The infield) B: 126 *with diagrams;* (Umpires) B: 130
Home range [biology]
Animal (Home range) A: 501
Deer (Life of a deer) D: 84
Mammal (Territoriality) M: 125
Orangutan O: 817
Raccoon (The life of a raccoon) R: 50
Home rule [Irish history]
Gladstone, William Ewart (Later political career) G: 206-207
Ireland (The Easter Rising) I: 427
Northern Ireland (Union with Britain) N: 524
Parnell, Charles Stewart P: 177
United Kingdom (Gladstone and Disraeli) U: 69
Home rule [political science]
City (Governmental problems) Ci: 592
City government (The) Ci: 594

Greenland (Government) G: 383
Local government (Units of local government) L: 407
Progressive Era (Political reforms) P: 814
Home Rule Bill [British history]
Gladstone, William Ewart (Later political career) G: 206-207
Home run
Baseball (Reaching base) B: 129; (table: Modern major league records) B: 138
Home schooling H: 301
Education (Control and support of U.S. education) E: 94
School (Other kinds of schools) S: 182
Home study [social work]
Adoption (The adoption process) A: 66
Home-study school *See* Correspondence school *in this index*
Home theater personal computer
Computer (Personal computers) Ci: 909
Home theater system [electronics]
Stereophonic sound system (Types of systems) So: 891
Home to Harlem [book by McKay]
McKay, Claude M: 337
Home Truths [book by Gallant]
Gallant, Mavis G: 14
Home visitors [education]
Parent education (Home visitation) P: 157
Homecoming, The [play by Pinter]
Pinter, Harold P: 475
Homeland
South Africa (Provincial government) So: 609; (Ways of life) So: 611
Homeland Security, Department of [U.S.] H: 301 *with picture*
Bush, George Walker (Homeland security) B: 722g
Citizenship and Immigration Services, United States Ci: 572
Coast Guard, United States (The Coast Guard since World War II) Ci: 738-739
Customs Service, United States Ci: 1201
Immigration and Naturalization Service I: 86
Naturalization N: 67
Ridge, Tom R: 336
September 11 terrorist attacks (Protecting the homeland) S: 310b
Transportation Security Administration T: 400
United States, History of the (September 11 terrorist attacks) U: 196d
Washington, D.C. *map on* W: 76
Homeland Security, Office of [U.S.]
Homeland Security, Department of (History) H: 301
September 11 terrorist attacks (Protecting the homeland) S: 310b
Homeland security, Secretary of
Flag F: 192
Homeland Security, Department of H: 301
Homeland Security Advisory System
Homeland Security, Department of H: 301
Homelessness H: 302 *with picture*
Colombia (Way of life) Ci: 779-781
Homeopathic magic
Magic (Kinds of magic) M: 49
Homeopathy [medicine] H: 303
Alternative medicine A: 388
Cancer (Alternative medicine) C: 173
Homeostasis [biology] H: 303
Motivation (Kinds of motives) M: 875
Homeowner insurance
Insurance *diagram on* I: 310; (Homeowners' insurance) I: 313
Homer [Greek poet] H: 303
Epic E: 342
Golden Age G: 255
Greece, Ancient *picture on* G: 373
Greek literature (Epic poetry) G: 377
Iliad I: 51
Mythology (Greek mythology) M: 980
Odyssey O: 675
Poetry (Narrative poetry) P: 591
Homer [bird] *See* Homing pigeon *in this index*
Homer, Winslow [American painter] H: 304
Civil War, American (The war on the home front) Ci: 622
Education *picture on* E: 102
Painting (Painting outside France) P: 72
United States *picture on* U: 117
Homeric Greek
Greek language (Development of ancient Greek) G: 376
Homeric question [literature]
Homer (Analysts and unitarians) H: 304
Homestake mine
Gold rush (Gold rushes in the United States) G: 254

Lead **L:** 150
South Dakota **So:** 664; (Natural resources) **So:** 677
Homestead [agriculture]
Homestead Act **H:** 304
Pioneer life in America (Establishing a homestead) **P:** 479
Ranching (History) **R:** 136
United States, History of the *picture on* **U:** 169
Western frontier life in America (Farming) **W:** 238
Westward movement in America (Homesteading on the Great Plains) **W:** 251
Homestead [Florida]
Miami (History) **M:** 480-481
Homestead Act [1862] **H:** 304
Civil War, American (Economy) **Ci:** 623
Johnson, Andrew (U.S. senator) **J:** 138
Public lands (Disposal of public lands) **P:** 858
Ranching (History) **R:** 136
United States, History of the (The end of the Western frontier) **U:** 185
Western frontier life in America (Newcomers) **W:** 234
Westward movement in America (Homesteading on the Great Plains) **W:** 251
Homestead association *See* Savings and loan association *in this index*
Homestead National Monument [Nebraska]
National Park System (table: National monuments) **N:** 51
Homestead Strike [1892] **H:** 305
Carnegie, Andrew (The Homestead Strike) **C:** 242
Goldman, Emma **G:** 258
Labor movement (Opposition to unions) **L:** 10
Homicide [crime] **H:** 305
Manslaughter **M:** 167
Homing behavior [zoology]
Duck (The life of a duck) **D:** 374
Homing guidance
Guided missile (Homing guidance) **G:** 426 *with diagram*
Homing instinct
Salmon (The life of a salmon) **S:** 69
Homing pigeon **H:** 305
Pigeon (Domestic pigeons) **P:** 460
Hominid [zoology]
Australopithecus **A:** 927
Human being (Scientific classification) **H:** 413; (Prehuman ancestors) **H:** 414
Laetoli fossil site **L:** 26
Prehistoric people *picture on* **P:** 749; (Prehuman ancestors) **P:** 744 *with pictures*
Primate (The evolution of primates) **P:** 778b-778c
Hominin [zoology] *See* Hominid *in this index*
Hominoidea [biology]
Human being (Scientific classification) **H:** 413
Hominy [food] **H:** 305
Homma, Masaharu [Japanese military leader]
Bataan Death March **B:** 162
Homo erectus [anthropology] **H:** 305
Fossil (Understanding ancient plants and animals) **F:** 423
Homo floresiensis **H:** 306
Human being (Early human beings) **H:** 415
Java fossils **J:** 65
Leakey, Richard Erskine Frere **L:** 161
Peking fossils **P:** 230
Prehistoric people *picture on* **P:** 743; (The first human beings) **P:** 746 *with pictures*; (How the first people lived) **P:** 746; (The origin of *Homo sapiens*) **P:** 748 *with picture*; (table) **P:** 754 *with map*
Homo ergaster [anthropology]
Homo erectus **H:** 306
Leakey, Richard Erskine Frere **L:** 161
Prehistoric people (Migration from Africa) **P:** 747; (The origin of *Homo sapiens*) **P:** 748-750
Homo Faber [book by Frisch]
Frisch, Max **F:** 535
Homo floresiensis [anthropology] **H:** 306 *with picture*
Dwarfism **D:** 394
Prehistoric people (Migration from Africa) **P:** 747
Homo habilis [anthropology] **H:** 306
Johanson, Donald Carl **J:** 131
Leakey, Louis Seymour Bazett **L:** 161
Leakey, Richard Erskine Frere **L:** 161
Olduvai Gorge **O:** 742
Prehistoric people *picture on* **P:** 748; (The first human beings) **P:** 746 *with picture*; (How the first people lived) **P:** 746; (table) **P:** 754 *with map*
Homo heidelbergensis [anthropology]
Prehistoric people (The single origin theory) **P:** 750
Homo Ludens [book by Huizinga]
Huizinga, Johan **H:** 411

Homo rudolfensis [anthropology]
Homo habilis **H:** 306
Leakey, Richard Erskine Frere **L:** 161
Prehistoric people (The first human beings) **P:** 746; (How the first people lived) **P:** 746
Homo sapiens [anthropology]
Human being (Scientific classification) **H:** 413; (Human beings of today) **H:** 415
Neandertals **N:** 93
Prehistoric people (The origin of *Homo sapiens*) **P:** 748 *with pictures*; (table) **P:** 754 *with map*
Races, Human **R:** 53 *with pictures*
Homo sapiens sapiens [anthropology]
Human being (Scientific classification) **H:** 413
Races, Human **R:** 53 *with pictures*
Homocysteine [biochemistry]
Folic acid **F:** 315
Homodont teeth [anatomy]
Teeth (Teeth of animals) **T:** 86
Homogeneous catalysis [chemistry]
Catalysis **C:** 298
Homogeneous society
City (The people) **Ci:** 578-580
Homogenization [process]
Milk (At a processing plant) **M:** 547-548 *with diagram*
Homograft [medicine]
Skin grafting **S:** 494
Homology [biology] **H:** 306
Homophile organization
Gay rights movement (History of gay rights) **G:** 73
Homophone [language]
Spelling (Spelling demons) **So:** 777
Homosexuality **H:** 307
See also Gay rights movement *in this index*
Adolescent (Establishing a sexual identity) **A:** 63
AIDS (How HIV is transmitted) **A:** 164a; (History) **A:** 166
Boy Scouts (Organization) **B:** 538
Family (Varieties of families) **F:** 20
Sexuality (Sexual orientation) **S:** 338b
Honda ATC90 [vehicle]
All-terrain vehicle **A:** 370
Honda knot
Cowboy (His rope) **Ci:** 1109
Honda Motor Company
Manufacturing (table) **M:** 170
Sports car (History) **So:** 804
Transportation *picture on* **T:** 398
Hondo [book by L'Amour]
L'Amour, Louis **L:** 52
Honduras **H:** 308 *with pictures and maps*
See also the list of Related articles in the Honduras *article*
El Salvador (The 1900's) **E:** 252
Indian, American (Indians of Middle America) **I:** 169
Honduras, British [former name] *See* Belize *in this index*
Honecker, Erich [German political leader] **H:** 314
Germany (East Germany) **G:** 170
Honegger, Arthur [French composer] **H:** 314
Honest Abe [nickname]
Lincoln, Abraham (Search for a career) **L:** 314
Honey [food] **H:** 314 *with picture*
Bear (Food) **B:** 184
Bee (Making honey) **B:** 204
Beeswax **B:** 212
Honey ant
Ant (Protection against enemies) **A:** 524-525 *with picture*; (Honey ants) **A:** 527 *with picture*
Honey badger
Ratel **R:** 147 *with picture*
Honey bear *See* Sloth bear *in this index*
Honey bee
Bee **B:** 200 *with pictures*
Beeswax **B:** 212
Deseret **D:** 154
Honey **H:** 314 *with picture*
Insect *picture on* **I:** 295; (Legs) **I:** 287-288; (Reproduction) **I:** 292
Pollen (Cross-pollination) **P:** 645 *with pictures*
Honey bee mite [insect]
Bee (Enemies) **B:** 205
Honey eater [bird] *See* Honeyeater *in this index*
Honey extractor [machine]
Honey (The honey industry) **H:** 315
Honey locust [tree] **H:** 315 *with picture*
Leaf *picture on* **L:** 154
Tree *pictures on* **T:** 422
Honey mesquite [shrub]
Mesquite **M:** 422
Tree *pictures on* **T:** 422
Honey possum [animal]
Possum **P:** 698
Honey stomach [anatomy]
Bee **B:** 200; (Making honey) **B:** 204

Honey tangerine [fruit]
Tangor **T:** 27
Honeybloom [plant]
Dogbane **D:** 282 *with picture*
Honeycomb
Bee (The honey bee colony) **B:** 201 *with picture*; (Making wax) **B:** 204-205 *with picture*
Beeswax **B:** 212
Honey **H:** 314 *with picture*; (The honey industry) **H:** 315
Insect *picture on* **I:** 295
Honeycomb mirror
Telescope (Reflecting telescopes) **T:** 104-105
Honeycreeper [bird]
Hawaiian honeycreeper **H:** 110 *with pictures*
Honeydew [entomology]
Ant (Dairying ants) **A:** 526 *with picture*
Aphid **A:** 565
Butterfly (Blues, coppers, and hairstreaks) **B:** 734-736
Caddisfly **C:** 11
Pear (Diseases and pests) **P:** 216
Honeydew melon [fruit]
Muskmelon **M:** 963
Honeyeater [bird] **H:** 315 *with picture*
Bird (Birds of Australia and New Zealand) **B:** 346 *with picture*
Honeyguide [bird]
Bird (Feeding methods) **B:** 350
Honeypot ant *See* Honey ant *in this index*
Honeysuckle [shrub] **H:** 316 *with picture*
Flower (Flowering shrubs) **F:** 281 *with picture*
Honeywell, Ira [Canadian settler]
Ottawa (Early days) **O:** 874
Hong Kong [administrative region, China] **H:** 316 *with pictures and map*
Asia *picture on* **A:** 788
China (Hong Kong and Macau) **C:** 506
Hong Kong [city, Hong Kong]
Skyscraper *picture on* **S:** 497
Hong Kong, University of
Hong Kong (Education) **H:** 317-318
Hong Kong Disneyland
Walt Disney Company **W:** 21
Hong Kong flu [disease]
Influenza (Flu epidemics) **I:** 268b
Hong Kong International Airport
Airport (table) **A:** 245
Hong Kong (The land) **H:** 318
Honi soit qui mal y pense [inscription]
Garter, Order of the **G:** 46
Honiara [Solomon Islands] **H:** 320
Honing [industrial process]
Machine tool (Abrasive processes) **M:** 19
Honiton lace [fabric]
Lace *picture on* **L:** 21
Honky-tonk [music]
Country music (Honky-tonk music) **Ci:** 1098a; (History) **Ci:** 1098a-1098b; (Modern country music) **Ci:** 1098c-1098d
Honolulu [Hawaii] **H:** 320 *with pictures and maps*
Hawaii **H:** 88 *with picture*; (Population) **H:** 92 *with picture and map*; (table: Average monthly weather) **H:** 102
Honolulu Academy of Arts
Honolulu (Cultural life) **H:** 321
Honor *See* Medals, decorations, and orders *in this index*
Honor code
United States Air Force Academy (Cadet life) **U:** 197
United States Military Academy (The student body) **U:** 202
Honor feather
Indian, American *pictures on* **I:** 144
Honor society
Fraternity (Honor and recognition societies) **F:** 496
Honorable discharge
Military discharge **M:** 543
Honorary degree
Degree, College (Honorary degrees) **D:** 93
Honoré I [prince of Monaco]
Monaco (History) **M:** 700
Honoria [Roman noblewoman]
Attila **A:** 879
Honorius [Roman emperor]
Gladiator **G:** 206
Rome, Ancient (table) **R:** 447
Theodosius I **T:** 252
Honorius I [pope] **H:** 323
Pope (table) **P:** 666
Honorius II [antipope]
Pope (table) **P:** 666
Honorius II [pope]
Pope (table) **P:** 666
Honorius III [pope] **H:** 323

Pope (table) P: 666
Honorius IV [pope]
Pope (table) P: 666
Honshu [island, Japan]
Japan (The land) J: 45 *with map*
Hood [ship]
Bismarck B: 382
Hood, Harrison [American chemist]
Glass (table) G: 218
Hood, James [American public figure]
Alabama (The mid-1900's) A: 278
Hood, John Bell [Confederate general] H: 323
Civil War, American (The Atlanta campaign)
Ci: 632; (North to Nashville) Ci: 632
Tennessee (The American Civil War) T: 154
Hood, Mount *See* Mount Hood *in this index*
Hood, Robin *See* Robin Hood *in this index*
Hood, Samuel [British admiral]
Mount Hood M: 885
Hooded merganser [duck]
Merganser M: 416
Hooded pitohui [bird]
Animal *picture on* A: 469
Pitohui P: 499 *with picture*
Hooded seal [animal]
Seal (Head) S: 266
Hooded warbler [bird]
Warbler *picture on* W: 34
Hoodoos, The [natural feature]
Yellowstone National Park (The Upper Loop)
Y: 559 *with map*
Hoof H: 324
Deer (Legs and hoofs) D: 83 *with picture*
Horse (Legs and hoofs) H: 349 *with pictures*
Ungulate U: 25 *with picture*
Hoof-and-mouth disease
Foot-and-mouth disease F: 353
Hooghly River [India] H: 324
Kolkata K: 362
Hook [fishing] *See* Fishhook *in this index*
Hook [geography]
Beach B: 178
Hook [sports]
Bowling (How to bowl) B: 521-522 *with diagram*
Hook, Captain [literary figure]
Peter Pan P: 325
Hookah
Pipe P: 489
Hooke, Robert [English physicist] H: 324
Biology (Early discoveries with the microscope)
B: 318 *with picture*
Botany (The development of modern botany)
B: 509
Cell (Before 1900) C: 337 *with picture*
Gas [physics] (Gas laws) G: 48
Jupiter (Ovals) J: 199-200
Microscope (History) M: 519
Mineral (The scientific study of mineral crystals)
M: 571
Hooked rug
Rugs and carpets (Other methods) R: 516;
(History) R: 517
Hooker [player]
Rugby football (Rugby Union) R: 510-511
Hooker, Joseph [Union general] H: 324 *with
portrait*
Civil War, American (Battle of Chancellorsville)
Ci: 627
Hooker, Thomas [American colonial leader] H: 324
Connecticut (English settlement) Ci: 968
Hartford H: 78
Hooke's law [physics]
Hooke, Robert H: 324
Hookham, Margaret [British dancer] *See* Fonteyn,
Margot *in this index*
Hooks, Benjamin Lawson [American social
reformer] H: 324 *with portrait*
Hookworm [animal] H: 324 *with diagram*
Animal *picture on* A: 506
Worm (Roundworms) W: 501 *with picture*
Hoolock gibbon [animal]
Gibbon G: 185
Hoop [croquet]
Croquet Ci: 1154 *with diagram*
Hoop-and-pole game
Indian, American (Recreation) I: 142-143 *with
picture*
Hoop skirt
Clothing (The 1700's) Ci: 703
Hoopa Valley Reservation
Yurok Indians Y: 582
Hooper, Ben W. [American political leader]
Tennessee (table) T: 152
Hooper, Harry [American baseball player]
Baseball (table: Hall of Fame) B: 134a
Hooper, Tom [British film director]
Motion picture (Best achievement in directing:
2010) M: 862
Hooper, William [American patriot] H: 325
Hoopoe [bird] H: 325 *with picture*
Hoosac Mountains [mountains, U.S.]
Green Mountains G: 381
Hoosac tunnel [Massachusetts] H: 325
Hoosic River [Massachusetts-Vermont]
Massachusetts (Rivers and lakes) M: 284
Hoosier Poet
Riley, James Whitcomb R: 341
Hoosier Schoolmaster, The [book by Eggleston]
Eggleston, Edward E: 118
Hoosier State [nickname]
Indiana I: 196
Hoover, Allan [uncle of]
Hoover, Herbert Clark (Boyhood) H: 326
Hoover, Herbert Clark [U.S. president] H: 326 *with
pictures*
African Americans (The Great Depression)
A: 136n
Democratic Party (During the 1920's) D: 126
Edison, Thomas Alva *picture on* E: 81
Great Depression G: 338
Harding, Warren Gamaliel (Return to normalcy)
H: 58
Hoover Commission H: 332
Iowa (Places to visit) I: 384
Republican Party (During the RoaringTwenties)
R: 255-256
Roosevelt, Franklin Delano (Election of 1932)
R: 452
World War I (The United States enters the war)
W: 462
Hoover, Herbert Clark, Jr. [American government
official]
Hoover, Herbert Clark (Hoover's family) H: 327-
328
Hoover, J. Edgar [American government official]
H: 331 *with portrait*
Federal Bureau of Investigation (History) F: 62
Hoover, Lou Henry [wife of Herbert Hoover]
First ladies of the United States F: 143; (table)
F: 142
Hoover, Herbert Clark *picture on* H: 328; (Hoover's
family) H: 327
Hoover Commission [U.S. history] H: 332
Hoover, Herbert Clark (Elder statesman) H: 330-
331
Hoover Dam [Colorado River, Arizona-Nevada]
H: 332
Arizona *picture on* A: 689
California (Progress as a state) C: 62
Colorado River Ci: 849 *with map*
Dam (table) D: 18
Hoover, Herbert Clark (Recovery efforts) H: 329
Nevada N: 156; (Places to visit) N: 164 *with picture*
**Hoover Institution on War, Revolution, and
Peace** [library]
Hoover, Herbert Clark (Elder statesman) H: 330
Hoover Moratorium [U.S. history]
Hoover, Herbert Clark (The Great Depression)
H: 329
Hooverize [U.S. history]
Hoover, Herbert Clark (Food administrator)
H: 328
Hooverville [U.S. history]
Great Depression *picture on* G: 339; (Human
suffering) G: 340-341
Hoover, Herbert Clark (The Great Depression)
H: 329
United States, History of the (The United States in
the Great Depression) U: 192-193
Hop [plant] H: 332
Brewing (Boiling) B: 595
Hop hornbeam [tree]
Ironwood I: 454 *with picture*
Hop, step, and jump [sports]
Track and field (Jumping events) T: 357-358
Hopak [dance]
Ukraine (The arts) U: 9
Hope, Bob [American entertainer] H: 332 *with
portrait*
Hope, John [American educator] H: 333
Hope diamond
Diamond *picture on* D: 181; (Famous diamonds)
D: 182
Hopewell [ship]
Hudson, Henry (Northern voyages) H: 404
Hopewell Cape
New Brunswick *picture on* N: 192
Hopewell Culture National Historical Park [Ohio]
National Park System (table: National historical
parks) N: 56-57
Hopewell Furnace National Historic Site
[Pennsylvania]
National Park System (table: National historic
sites) N: 52-53
Hopewell Indians
Indian, American (The first farmers) I: 152
Mound builders (Woodland Period) M: 882
Hopewell Rocks [Hopewell Cape]
New Brunswick (Places to visit) N: 188
Hopi Ceremonial Dance [painting by Kabotie]
Indian, American *picture on* I: 169
Hopi Indians H: 333
Doll (Dolls in religion) D: 288
Indian, American *pictures on* I: 139, I: 167, I: 169;
(Hunting, gathering, and fishing) I: 141
Kachina K: 208
Mask (Ceremonial masks) M: 264
Navajo Indians N: 70
Rain dance R: 125
Sculpture (The European impact) S: 244 *with
picture*
Snake dance S: 536
United States *picture on* U: 116
Wupatki National Monument W: 514
Hopkins, Anthony [British-American actor] H: 333
Motion picture (Best performance by an actor:
1991) M: 862a
Hopkins, Esek [American military leader]
Navy, United States (The earliest colonial
warships) N: 85
Hopkins, Sir Frederick [British biochemist]
Nobel Prizes (Physiology or medicine: 1929)
N: 445
Vitamin (History) V: 432
Hopkins, Gerard Manley [British poet] H: 333
English literature (Later Victorian literature)
E: 321
Poetry (Sounds) P: 594
Rhyme R: 319
Hopkins, Harry Lloyd [American government
official] H: 333
Hopkins, Johns [American philanthropist] H: 334
Johns Hopkins University J: 135
Hopkins, Mark [American businessman]
California (Early statehood) C: 62
Hopkins, Mark [American educator]
Garfield, James Abram (Education and early
career) G: 40
Hopkins, Stephen [American patriot] H: 334
Providence (Description) P: 839
Hopkinson, Francis [American patriot] H: 334
Flag (First United States flags) F: 208-210
United States flag (The first American flags)
U: 200
Hopley-Woolrich, Cornell George [American
author] *See* Woolrich, Cornell *in this index*
Hoplite [soldier]
Weapon (Metal weapons) W: 154a
Hopper [device]
Railroad *pictures on* R: 108
Hopper, Edward [American painter] H: 334
Drawing *picture on* D: 344
Roaring Twenties (Cultural trends) R: 364
Hopper, Grace Murray [American computer
scientist] H: 334
Hoppin, William W. [American political leader]
Rhode Island (table) R: 311
Hops [plants] *See* Hop *in this index*
Hopscotch [book by Cortázar]
Latin American literature (The "Boom") L: 114
Hora [dance]
Dance (Folk dances) D: 26
Horace [Roman poet] H: 334
Epistle E: 344
Latin literature (The Augustan Age) L: 116
Satire S: 150h
Horace [play by Corneille]
French literature (Classical drama) F: 520
Horatian ode [poetry]
Ode O: 673
Horatian satire
Satire S: 150h
Horatius [Roman legend] H: 334
Horeb *See* Mount Sinai *in this index*
Horehound [plant] H: 334
Horemheb [king of ancient Egypt]
Egypt, Ancient (The New Kingdom) E: 143
Tutankhamun T: 526
Horicon Marsh [Wisconsin]
Wisconsin *picture on* W: 360
Horizon [astronomy] H: 335 *with diagram*
Azimuth A: 998
Navigation (Celestial navigation) N: 71
Horizon [geology] *See* Soil horizon *in this index*
Horizon [organization]
Camp Fire USA (Small group programs) C: 88
Horizon glass [measuring device]
Sextant S: 336
Horizon problem [cosmology]
Inflation theory I: 268a
Horizons '76

Bicentennial Celebration, American **B: 288**
Horizontal bar [sports]
Gymnastics (Men's events) **G: 448-449** *with picture*
Horizontal-branch phase [astronomy]
Star (Intermediate-mass stars) **So: 848**
Horizontal opposed engine
Gasoline engine (Cylinder arrangement) **G: 64** *with diagram*
Horizontal well
Petroleum (Directional drilling) **P: 339** *with diagram*
Horlick, William [American businessman]
Wisconsin (Interesting facts) **W: 347**
Hormisdas, Saint [pope]
Pope (table) **P: 666**
Hormone [biology] **H: 335**
Acne **A: 27**
Adolescent (Physical development) **A: 60-61**
Agriculture (Reforming agricultural practices) **A: 151**
Bird (Why birds migrate) **B: 360**
Blood *diagram on* **B: 409**; (Plasma) **B: 407**; (Carrying hormones) **B: 410**
Brain (Regulating body processes) **B: 553**
Cell (Producing proteins) **C: 333**
Cholesterol **C: 520**
Disease (Metabolic diseases) **D: 229**
Drug (Other kinds of drugs) **D: 352**
Dwarf (Causes) **D: 395**
Endorphin **E: 272**
Epinephrine **E: 343**
Estrogen **E: 364**
Farm and farming (Livestock care) **F: 39**
Food (Regulating body processes) **F: 331**
Gland (Endocrine glands) **G: 207**
Growth (In living things) **G: 404**
Hypothalamus **H: 481**
Instinct (Motivation) **I: 305**
Lipid (Kinds of lipids) **L: 345**
Liver (Other functions) **L: 394**
Menopause **M: 402**
Metabolism (Control of metabolism) **M: 424**
Migration (What triggers migrations) **M: 539**
Ovary **O: 881**
Placenta **P: 505**
Plant (Hereditary factors) **P: 538**
Pregnancy (How pregnancy affects women) **P: 734b**
Prostaglandin **P: 829**
Protein (How the body uses proteins) **P: 832**
Reproduction, Human (The human reproductive system) **R: 244**
Hormone receptor [physiology]
Breast cancer **B: 591**
Hormone replacement therapy [medicine] **H: 338**
Osteoporosis (Prevention and treatment) **O: 868**
Hormuz, Strait of
Persian Gulf **P: 300** *with map*
Horn [growth] **H: 338** *with pictures*
Animal *picture on* **A: 494**
Rhinoceros **R: 293** *with picture*
Horn [musical instrument] **H: 339**
French horn **F: 516** *with pictures*
Horn [saddle]
Horse (The saddle) **H: 351-352** *with picture*
Horn, Cape [South America]
Cape Horn **C: 188** *with maps*
Horn antenna [device]
Antenna *picture on* **A: 543**
Horn Island [island, Australia]
Torres Strait Islands **T: 343**
Horn Island [island, Chile]
Cape Horn **C: 188** *with map*
Horn Lake [Mississippi]
United States *picture on* **U: 112**
Horn of plenty [symbol]
Cornucopia **Ci: 1066**
Hornaday, William Temple [American zoologist]
Buffalo (Protection of bison) **B: 675**
Hornbeam *See* Ironwood *in this index*
Hornbein, Thomas F. [American mountain climber]
Mount Everest **M: 884**
Hornbill [bird] **H: 339**
Bird (Birds of Asia) **B: 344f** *with picture*; (Bills) **B: 362**
Hornblende [mineral] **H: 339**
Mineral *picture on* **M: 566**
Hornblower, Horatio [literary figure]
Forester, Cecil Scott **F: 403**
Hornbook [education] **H: 339** *with picture*
Colonial life in America (Education) **Ci: 803-804**
Horne, Lena [American entertainer] **H: 339** *with portrait*
Horne, Marilyn [American opera singer] **H: 340**
Horned dace [fish]

Chub **C: 540**
Horned grebe [bird]
Bird (Birds of inland waters and marshes) **B: 340** *with picture*
Horned lark [bird]
Bird (Birds of grasslands) **B: 336** *with picture*
Lark **L: 76** *with picture*
Horned lizard **H: 340** *with picture*
Lizard (Defenses) **L: 400**
Horned owl
Owl (Important owls) **O: 884** *with picture*
Horned pout [fish] *See* Bullhead *in this index*
Horned puffin [bird]
Puffin **P: 885** *with picture*
Horned rattlesnake *See* Sidewinder *in this index*
Horned toad
Horned lizard **H: 340** *with picture*
Horned viper [snake]
Asp **A: 814**
Desert *picture on* **D: 155**
Horner, Henry [American political leader]
Illinois (table) **I: 71**
Hornet [aircraft carrier]
Aircraft carrier (History) **A: 207**
Doolittle, James Harold **D: 309**
Hornet [aircraft]
Air force *picture on* **A: 182**
Hornet [insect] **H: 340** *with picture*
Insect *picture on* **I: 283**
Wasp **W: 111**
Hornets, New Orleans [team] *See* New Orleans Hornets *in this index*
Hornet's nest
Hornet **H: 340**
Horney, Karen [German-American psychiatrist] **H: 340**
Hornigold, Benjamin [English pirate]
Pirate (Other regions) **P: 495**
Hornish, Sam, Jr. [American race driver]
Automobile racing (table: Indianapolis 500 winners) **A: 980**
Hornsby, Rogers [American baseball player] **H: 341**
Baseball (table: Hall of Fame) **B: 134a**; (The Babe Ruth Era) **B: 135-136**
Hornung, Paul [American football player]
Football (table) **F: 363**
Hornussen [sport]
Switzerland (Sports) **So: 1054** *with picture*
Hornworm [insect]
Hawk moth **H: 113**
Moth (Hawk moths) **M: 841** *with picture*
Hornwort [plant] **H: 341**
Bryophyte **B: 656**
Plant *picture on* **P: 522**; (Nonvascular plants) **P: 518**; (Classification of plants) **P: 546** *with picture*
Horny toad [animal]
Horned lizard **H: 340** *with picture*
Höröldt, Johann [German painter]
Dresden china **D: 347**
Porcelain (German porcelain) **P: 677**
Horoscope [astrology] **H: 341**
Astrology (Principles of astrology) **A: 826** *with picture*
House **H: 384**
Horowitz, Vladimir [Russian-American pianist] **H: 341**
Horrocks, Jeremiah [English astronomer]
Transit **T: 374**
Horror comics
Comics (Comic books) **Ci: 869**
Horror film
Motion picture *picture on* **M: 853**; (Filmmaking in Europe) **M: 866** *with picture*; (Movies in the 1930's) **M: 867-868**
Horse [animal] **H: 342** *with pictures*
Distemper **D: 238**
Hand (Animal hands) **H: 40**
Harness **H: 63** *with picture*
Horse racing **H: 363**
Kentucky (Agriculture) **K: 289**
Polo **P: 646** *with picture*
Rodeo **R: 397** *with picture*
Saddle **S: 7**
Show jumping **S: 438**
Skull **S: 495** *with picture*
Horse [gymnastics] *See* Pommel horse *in this index*
Horse [slang]
Heroin **H: 213**
Horse, Master of the
Royal Household of the United Kingdom **R: 498**
Horse bean [plant] *See* Broad bean *in this index*
Horse bot fly [insect]
Bot fly **B: 507**
Horse brier [plant]
Greenbrier **G: 381**
Horse chestnut *See* Horsechestnut *in this index*

Horse Fair, The [painting by Bonheur]
Bonheur, Rosa **B: 459** *with picture*
Painting (Women artists) **P: 73-74**
Horse Feathers [film]
Marx Brothers **M: 238** *with picture*
Horse fly [insect] **H: 363** *with picture*
Fly *picture on* **F: 308**; (table) **F: 310**
Insect *picture on* **I: 282**; (Mouth parts) **I: 286-287**
Horse latitudes [geography] **H: 363**
Calms, Regions of (The horse latitudes) **C: 69**
Wind (General circulation) **W: 329** *with diagram*
Horse racing [sport] **H: 363** *with pictures*
Derby **D: 152**
Furlong **F: 566**
Gambling (Types of gambing) **G: 20**
Harness racing **H: 63**
Ireland (Recreation) **I: 420** *with picture*
Steeplechasing **So: 883**
United Kingdom *picture on* **U: 57**
Horse show
Horse (Horse shows) **H: 356**
Horseback riding
Horse (Saddle horses) **H: 343**; (Riding equipment) **H: 351**; (How to ride) **H: 353** *with pictures*
Indian, American (Indians of the Plains) **I: 158**
Olympic Games (Summer Olympic Games) **O: 746e-746f**
Horsebean [plant] *See* Broad bean *in this index*
Horsecar [vehicle]
Streetcar **So: 925**
Transportation *picture on* **T: 389**
Horsechestnut **H: 366** *with picture*
Bud *picture on* **B: 665**
Horsefly *See* Horse fly *in this index*
Horsehair
Horse (Coat and skin) **H: 348**
Horsehair worm [animal] **H: 367**
Horsehead Nebula
Orion **O: 856**
Horsehides
Baseball (Equipment) **B: 125** *with diagram*
Hörselberg [mountain, Germany]
Tannhäuser **T: 29**
Horsemanship
Horse (How to ride) **H: 353** *with pictures*
Horsepower [measurement] **H: 367**
Air conditioning (Capacity of air conditioners) **A: 179-180**
Energy (Energy and power) **E: 295**
Metric system (Mechanics) **M: 437-440**
Power **P: 727**
Horseradish [plant] **H: 367** *with picture*
Horse's Mouth, The [book by Cary]
Cary, Joyce **C: 270**
Horseshoe
Horse (Shoes) **H: 356**
Transportation (The Middle Ages) **T: 387**
Horseshoe Bay [bay, Canada]
British Columbia *picture on* **B: 621**
Horseshoe Bend, Battle of [1814]
Alabama (Territorial days) **A: 275**
Creek Indians **Ci: 1125**
Indian wars (The Red Sticks) **I: 192**
Jackson, Andrew (The Battle of Horseshoe Bend) **J: 9**
Westward movement in America (Indian conflicts) **W: 247**
Horseshoe Bend National Military Park [Alabama]
Alabama (Places to visit) **A: 266**
National Park System (table: National military parks) **N: 55**
Horseshoe crab [sea animal] **H: 368** *with picture*
Horseshoe Falls [Canada]
Niagara Falls **N: 391** *with picture*; (Description) **N: 391-392** *with picture*; (History) **N: 392-393**
Ontario (Places to visit) **O: 774** *with picture*; (Rivers, waterfalls, and lakes) **O: 778**
Horseshoe pitching [game] **H: 368** *with diagram*
Horsetail [plant] **H: 369** *with picture*
Plant *pictures on* **P: 522, P: 524**; (Ferns and related plants) **P: 518-520**; (Classification of plants) **P: 546-547** *with picture*
Tree (Fossil trees) **T: 415**
Horsley, John Callcott [British artist]
Christmas (Christmas cards) **C: 536**
Greeting cards **G: 387**
Horthy, Nicholas [Hungarian political leader]
Hungary (Between world wars) **H: 446**
Horticulture [agriculture] **H: 369**
Farm and farming (Modern crop production) **F: 33**
FFA (Training) **F: 84**
Fruit **F: 544**
Gardening **G: 30**
Vegetable **V: 292**
Horton, Alonzo E. [American businessman]

San Diego (The city) S: 88
Horton, Henry H. [American political leader]
Tennessee (table) T: 152
Horton, Lester [American choreographer]
Ailey, Alvin A: 168
Horus [Egyptian god] H: 370
Egypt, Ancient picture on E: 140; (Religion) E: 137
Isis I: 462
Mythology picture on M: 977; (The Great Ennead)
M: 979; (The Osiris myth) M: 979-980
Osiris O: 863
Pharaoh P: 353
Phoenicia picture on P: 393
Relief picture on R: 213
Sphinx (Egyptian sphinxes) So: 780
Horvath, Les [American football player]
Football (table) F: 363
Horvitz, H. Robert [American biologist]
Nobel Prizes (Physiology or medicine: 2002)
N: 447
Hose [clothing]
Clothing (The Renaissance) Ci: 703
Hose [tool]
Fire department (Firefighting) F: 123; (Trucks and
vehicles) F: 126
Hosea [Biblical figure]
Hosea, Book of H: 370
Hosea, Book of [Bible] H: 370
Hosiery [clothing]
Stockings So: 906
Hospice [health care] H: 370
AIDS (Providing medical care) A: 166
Medicare M: 362
Palliative care P: 109
Social security (Medicare) So: 555
Hospice [travel]
Hospice H: 370
Hospital H: 371 with pictures
Civil War, American (Behind the lines) Ci: 630
with picture
Emergency room E: 258 with picture
Hospice H: 370
Incubator (Hospital incubators) I: 106
Medicine (The United Kingdom) M: 366-367;
(During the Middle Ages) M: 373; (Financing
advanced medical care) M: 377-378
Mental illness (Treatment settings) M: 408
Nightingale, Florence (Service in Crimea) N: 420
with picture
Nursing (Hospital nurses) N: 616 with picture
Trauma center T: 405
Hospital insurance
Insurance (Basic types of health insurance) I: 312;
(Medicare) I: 314
Medicare M: 362
Social security (Medicare) So: 555
**Hospital of St. John of Jerusalem, Order of
the** [military and religious order] See Knights
Hospitallers in this index
Hospital Sketches [book by Alcott]
Alcott, Louisa May A: 338
Hospitality careers
Careers (Tourism and hospitality) C: 233 with
pictures
Hospitality management
Family and consumer sciences (Hospitality
management) F: 26
Hospitallers [order] See Knights Hospitallers in
this index
Host [biology]
Ant (Reproduction) A: 524
Balance of nature (Disease and parasites) B: 35
Bird (Brood parasites) B: 359
Clownfish Ci: 714
Flatworm F: 229
Life (The biological environment) L: 276
Parasite P: 153
Remora R: 230
Tapeworm T: 40
Virus V: 427 with diagram
Host [computer] See Server in this index
Host cell [biology]
Antiviral drug A: 560
Host country [international relations]
Peace Corps (How the corps works) P: 207
Hostage [law] H: 374a
Iran (Revolution and the Islamic Republic) I: 406a
with picture
Iran-contra affair (Administration actions) I: 407
Iran-Iraq War I: 407
Lebanon (War and terrorism) L: 173
Terrorism (Assassinations and kidnappings)
T: 175-176
Treaty (Enforcement of treaties) T: 409
United States, History of the (The hostage crisis)
U: 196b
Hostage, The [play by Behan]

Behan, Brendan B: 220
Irish literature (Drama) I: 432
Hostage negotiating team
Police (Other activities) P: 621-622
Hostel
Youth hostel Y: 574
Hostelling International [organization]
Youth hostel Y: 574
Hostile environment [law]
Sexual harassment (Types of sexual harassment)
S: 337
Hostile take-over [business]
Business (Recent developments) B: 727
Merger M: 417
Hosting [computing]
Internet (Hardware) I: 350c
Website W: 176
Hot-air balloon
Air picture on A: 169
Balloon (Hot-air balloons) B: 57 with diagram;
(Operation of a hot-air balloon) B: 60; (Sport
ballooning) B: 60
Bomb (History) B: 452 with picture
Montgolfier brothers M: 765
Hot-air oven
Range (Electric ranges) R: 137-138
Hot August Nights [festival]
Nevada (Visitor's guide) N: 164
Hot cereal
Cereal C: 360
Hot cross bun [food]
Easter (Other foods) E: 44
Hot-dip galvanizing [industrial process]
Galvanizing G: 17
Iron and steel (Finishing) I: 447
Hot dog [food] See Frankfurter in this index
Hot Five [band]
Armstrong, Louis A: 723
Jazz (The 1920's) J: 70
Hot flash [physiology]
Hormone replacement therapy H: 338
Menopause M: 402
Hot l Baltimore, The [play by Wilson]
Wilson, Lanford W: 317
Hot line [communications] H: 374a
Cold War (Easing Cold War tensions) Ci: 769
Union of Soviet Socialist Republics (Relations
with the United States) U: 39
Hot link [computing] See Hyperlink in this index
Hot-melt adhesive
Adhesive A: 56
Hot-metal car
Iron and steel (The blast furnace process)
I: 440-441
Hot-metal typesetting
Printing (Typesetting) P: 797
Hot rod [automobile] H: 374a
Heat picture on H: 148
Iron and steel (Rolling) I: 445 with diagram
Hot Seven [band]
Armstrong, Louis A: 723
Jazz (The 1920's) J: 70
Hot shoe [photography]
Photography (Artificial lighting devices) P: 416
Hot spot [computing]
World Wide Web W: 500
Hot spot [geology] H: 374a with map
Geothermal energy G: 136
Hydrothermal vent H: 473
Mountain (Volcanic mountains) M: 892
Plate tectonics (Evidence of plate movement)
P: 563
Volcano (Where volcanoes form) V: 441
Hot spot [radioactivity]
Fallout (How fallout is distributed) F: 18
Hot Springs [Arkansas] H: 374b
Arkansas A: 694; (Visitor's guide) A: 704 with
picture; (Springs) A: 708
Hot springs [geology] H: 374b
Hot Springs National Park [Arkansas] H: 374b
with picture
Arkansas (Places to visit) A: 704
National Park System (table: National parks) N: 48
Hot tub
Bath (Bathing for relaxation or pleasure) B: 163
Hot type [printing]
Type T: 536 with picture
Hot vent [oceanography]
Hydrothermal vent H: 473
Hot-water heating
Heating (Steam and hot-water heating systems)
H: 159 with diagram
Plumbing (The water supply system) P: 577-578
with diagram
Hotbed [gardening] H: 375 with diagram
Cold frame Ci: 761

Hotbox
Railroad (Rolling stock) R: 107-108
Hotbox detector
Railroad (Rolling stock) R: 107-108
Hotchkiss gun
World War I picture on W: 457
Hotel H: 375 with pictures
See also Motel in this index
Hotel chain [business]
Hotel (History) H: 376-377
Hôtel de Bourgogne [Paris]
Drama (The French theater) D: 333
Hôtel de Ville [Paris]
Paris (Famous buildings) P: 163-164 with map
Hôtel des Invalides [Paris]
Paris (Museums and art galleries) P: 164-165
Hôtel Dieu [hospital, Paris]
Hospital (Early hospitals) H: 373
**Hotel Employees and Restaurant Employees
International Union**
UNITE HERE U: 43
Hotel New Hampshire, The [book by Irving]
Irving, John I: 459
Hotel Universe [play by Barry]
Barry, Philip B: 119
Hothouse [gardening]
Greenhouse G: 382
Hotspot [communication]
Wireless communication (Wireless networking)
W: 345
Hotspot [computing] See Hot spot in this index
Hotspot [geology] See Hot spot in this index
Hotspur [literary figure]
Shakespeare, William: (Henry IV) S: 358-359
Hottentot [people] See Khoikhoi in this index
Houdan [breed]
Chicken (Other classes) C: 441
Houde, Camillien [Canadian political leader]
Montreal (The war issue) M: 778
Houdin, Jean Eugène Robert [French magician]
See Robert-Houdin, Jean Eugène in this index
Houdini, Harry [American magician] H: 377 with
picture
Magician (Escape magic) M: 52 with picture
Houdon, Jean Antoine [French sculptor] H: 378
with picture
Richmond (The city) R: 332
Sculpture (European sculpture) S: 253-254 with
picture
Virginia (Interesting facts) V: 399 with picture
Hough [district]
Cleveland (Social problems) Ci: 665; (Downturn
and racial tensions) Ci: 667
Hough, Emerson [American author] H: 378
Houllebecq, Michel [French author]
French literature (Recent French literature) F: 523
Houma Indians
Baton Rouge (Government and history) B: 166
Hound H: 378 with picture
Dog pictures on D: 270; (Hounds) D: 266
Fox hunting F: 442
Houngan [religion]
Haiti (People) H: 14
Hounsfield, Sir Godfrey [British engineer]
Nobel Prizes (Physiology or medicine: 1979)
N: 446
Houphouët-Boigny, Félix [Ivorian political leader]
H: 379
Côte d'Ivoire (History) Ci: 1084b
Yamoussoukro Y: 550
Houppelande [garment]
Clothing (The Renaissance) Ci: 702
Hour [time] H: 379
Hourglass [measuring device] H: 379 with picture
Hourglass style
Clothing picture on Ci: 704
Hours [employment] See Wages and hours in this
index
Hours, The [film]
Kidman, Nicole K: 311
Hours of Idleness [poems by Byron]
Byron, Lord (Byron's life) B: 748; (Byron's poetry)
B: 748
Housatonic [ship]
Submarine (Early submarines) So: 942
Housatonic River [Connecticut-Massachusetts]
H: 379
Massachusetts (Rivers and lakes) M: 284
House [building] H: 380 with pictures
See also Shelter in this index and the list of Related
articles in the House article
Colonial life in America (Houses) Ci: 796 with
picture
Indian, American pictures on I: 138; (Shelter)
I: 136d
Indonesia (Rural life) I: 229 with picture
Inuit (Shelter) I: 354c

Log cabin **L:** 422 *with picture*
Mobile home **M:** 682
Pioneer life in America (A pioneer settlement)
  P: 479 *with pictures*
Prehistoric people (Changes in lifestyle) **P:** 753
Radon (Protection against radon) **R:** 100
Rome, Ancient (Way of life) **R:** 438 *with picture*
Shelter *pictures on* **S:** 392
Solar energy *picture on* **So:** 578
Thermography *picture on* **T:** 254
Western frontier life in America (Life on the
  ranches) **W:** 237 *with picture;* (Shelter) **W:** 238
House [astrology] **H:** 384
Astrology (The houses) **A:** 827
Horoscope (Parts of a horoscope) **H:** 341
House [curling]
Curling *diagram on* **Ci:** 1196; (The game) **Ci:** 1195
House [gambling]
Gambling (Types of gambling) **G:** 20
House, Edward Mandell [American statesman]
  H: 384
House and Garden [play]
Ayckbourn, Alan **A:** 995
House at Pooh Corner, The [book by Milne]
Milne, A. A. **M:** 556
House by the Medlar Tree, The [book by Verga]
Verga, Giovanni **V:** 317
House Chamber [U.S.]
Capitol, United States **C:** 197
House Committee on Un-American Activities
  [U.S.] *See* Un-American Activities Committee *in
  this index*
House cricket [insect]
Cricket **Ci:** 1130 *with picture*
House crow [bird]
Crow (Kinds of crows) **Ci:** 1157
"House Divided, A" [speech by Lincoln]
Lincoln, Abraham (The debates with Douglas)
  L: 317
House dust mite [animal] *See* Dust mite *in this
  index*
House finch [bird]
Linnet **L:** 338
House flag
Flag (Flags of the sea) **F:** 208
Ship *pictures on* **S:** 426
House fly [insect]
Fly **F:** 308 *with pictures;* (table) **F:** 310
Insect (Kinds of insects) **I:** 282; (Wings) **I:** 288
Metamorphosis *pictures on* **M:** 428
House for Mr. Biswas, A [book by Naipaul]
Naipaul, V. S. **N:** 4
House in Paris, The [book by Bowen]
Bowen, Elizabeth **B:** 519
House Journal [publication]
Constitution of the United States (Article I,
  Section 5) **Ci:** 1006
House Made of Dawn [book by Momaday]
American literature (Works by minority writers)
  A: 425
Indian, American (Achievements in the arts)
  I: 181
House mouse [animal]
Mouse **M:** 900 *with picture*
House of Burgesses [U.S. history] **H:** 384
Colonial life in America (Colonial government)
  Ci: 795 *with picture*
Jamestown **J:** 29
London Company **L:** 445
Virginia (The course toward independence)
  V: 420
House of Chiefs [government]
Botswana (Government) **B:** 510-511
House of Commons [Canada]
Canada, Government of (The House of
  Commons) **C:** 130 *with picture;* (How a bill
  becomes law in Canada) **C:** 132-133 *with
  diagrams*
Prime minister of Canada (Roles of the prime
  minister) **P:** 778c-778d
House of Commons [United Kingdom] **H:** 384
Address, Forms of (Officials of the
  Commonwealth of Nations) **A:** 53
England (Government) **E:** 292-293
Parliament (The Parliament of the United
  Kingdom) **P:** 172 *with picture*
Speaker (In the United Kingdom) **So:** 768
United Kingdom (Government) **U:** 49 *with picture*
House of Connelly, The [play by Green]
Green, Paul Eliot **G:** 379
House of Earth, The [books by Buck]
Buck, Pearl S. **B:** 663
House of Fame, The [poem by Chaucer]
Chaucer, Geoffrey (Poetry) **C:** 388
House of Freedoms [political party]
Berlusconi, Silvio **B:** 267
House of Hope [fort]

Connecticut (Dutch exploration) **Ci:** 968
House of Intellect, The [book by Barzun]
Barzun, Jacques **B:** 123
House of Life, The [poems by Rossetti]
Rossetti, Dante Gabriel **R:** 483
House of Lords [United Kingdom] **H:** 383
Address, Forms of (Officials of the
  Commonwealth of Nations) **A:** 53
England (Government) **E:** 292-293
Lady **L:** 25
Nobility (Privileges of the peerage) **N:** 450
Parliament (The Parliament of the United
  Kingdom) **P:** 172 *with picture*
United Kingdom (Government) **U:** 49-50;
  (Gladstone and Disraeli) **U:** 69
House of Mirth, The [book by Wharton]
American literature (Women writers) **A:** 420
House of Representatives [Australia]
Australia (The federal government) **A:** 895
House of Representatives [state government]
State government (Organization) **So:** 863
House of Representatives [U.S.] **H:** 385 *with
  picture*
Address, Forms of (Officials of the United States)
  A: 53
Capitol, United States **C:** 197
Congress of the United States (The House of
  Representatives) **Ci:** 943 *with picture;* (table)
  Ci: 943; (Passing a bill) **Ci:** 945; (Congressional
  ethics) **Ci:** 948
Constitution of the United States (Article I)
  Ci: 1004; (Amendment 12) **Ci:** 1013
Electoral College (The college in action) **E:** 164
Impeachment (Procedure) **I:** 90
Mace **M:** 11
Speaker (In the United States) **So:** 768
United States, Government of the (The legislative
  branch) **U:** 138; (How a bill becomes law in the
  United States) **U:** 141
United States, History of the (The election of
  1824) **U:** 170-171
Washington, D.C. *map on* **W:** 76
House of Slaves [building, Gorée]
Gorée **G:** 274
House of Spirits, The [book by Allende]
Allende, Isabel **A:** 372
House of the Faun [Pompeii]
Atrium *picture on* **A:** 877
House of the Seven Gables, The [book by
  Hawthorne]
Hawthorne, Nathaniel (His novels) **H:** 115
House of the Spirits, The [book by Allende]
Latin American literature (The post-Boom) **L:** 114
House of Wisdom [library]
Muslims (The Abbāsids) **M:** 964c
House on the Rock [Wisconsin]
Wisconsin (Places to visit) **W:** 356
House-raising [custom]
Pioneer life in America (A pioneer settlement)
  P: 479-480; (Social activities) **P:** 485
House slave
Slavery (Conditions of slavery) **S:** 503
House sparrow [bird] **H:** 388 *with picture*
Bird *pictures on* **B:** 344d, **B:** 358; (Birds of urban
  areas) **B:** 333 *with picture;* (Birds of Europe)
  B: 344c
Sparrow **So:** 765 *with picture*
Weaver **W:** 172
House spider H: 388
Spider (table) *picture on* **So:** 785
House style [publishing]
Publishing (Copy editors) **P:** 867
House swift [bird]
Animal *picture on* **A:** 475
House That Ruth Built [nickname]
Ruth, Babe **R:** 568
House training
Pet (House training) **P:** 320
House wrap [building construction]
House (The frame) **H:** 382
House wren [bird]
Bird *picture on* **B:** 358; (Birds of urban areas)
  B: 333 *with picture*
Wren *picture on* **W:** 503: **W:** 504
Houseboat H: 388 *with picture*
Boating *picture on* **B:** 431; (Sailboats) **B:** 429
Shelter *picture on* **S:** 392
Housebreaking [pets] *See* House training *in this
  index*
Household [economics]
Economics (The organization of economies) **E:** 58
Household budget
Budget (Personal and family budgets) **B:** 669
Household Management [book]
Russian literature (Muscovite literature) **R:** 559
Household paint
Paint (Kinds of paint) **P:** 23

Housekeeping functions
Local government (Functions of local
  government) **L:** 407
Houseleek [plant] **H:** 389 *with picture*
Houseman, John [American actor]
Motion picture (Best performance by an actor in
  a supporting role: 1973) **M:** 862b
Houses of Parliament [London]
Architecture (The Gothic Revival) **A:** 626
Big Ben **B:** 297 *with picture*
London *picture on* **L:** 431; (The Houses of
  Parliament) **L:** 435
Parliament (The Parliament of the United
  Kingdom) **P:** 172 *with pictures*
Housetraining [pets]
Dog (Housetraining) **D:** 280
Housewife [career]
Women's movement (Decline after 1920)
  W: 385-386
Housing H: 389 *with pictures*
See also Public housing; Shelter *in this index and
  sections on the people and their way of life in
  specific country articles, such as Philippines
  (Way of life)*
African Americans (Housing and lending
  discrimination) **A:** 136s
Bush, George Walker (Economy) **B:** 722j
Chicago (Housing) **C:** 427 *with pictures;* (Dealing
  with aging infrastructure) **C:** 437
City (The people) **Ci:** 582; (City problems) **Ci:** 590
  with picture
City planning **Ci:** 598 *with pictures*
Condominium **C:** 929
Disability (Housing and transportation) **D:** 221
Federal Housing Administration **F:** 64
Homelessness **H:** 302
Indian reservation (Description) **I:** 188-189
Levitt, William Jaird **L:** 219
Mortgage **M:** 820
New York City (Housing) **N:** 332
Old age (Housing) **O:** 739
Open housing **O:** 789
Poverty (Social welfare programs) **P:** 725
Russia (Way of life) **R:** 533
Segregation (De facto segregation) **S:** 285
Tenement **T:** 133
United States, History of the (Suburban growth)
  U: 195 *with picture*
Urban renewal (History) **U:** 220
Housing, Census of
Census (Kinds of censuses) **C:** 346-347
Housing and Home Finance Agency [U.S. history]
Housing and Urban Development, Department
  of (History) **H:** 393
**Housing and Urban Development, Department
  of H:** 393
**Housing and Urban Development, Department
  of** [U.S.] **H:** 393 *with picture*
Government National Mortgage Association
  G: 292
Housing (Housing since 1900) **H:** 391
Johnson, Lyndon Baines (The Great Society)
  J: 150
Urban renewal (History) **U:** 220
Washington, D.C. *map on* **W:** 76
**Housing and urban development, Secretary
  of** [U.S.]
Flag *picture on* **F:** 211
Housing and Urban Development, Department
  of **H:** 393
Housing authority [government]
Housing (Public housing) **H:** 391
Housing Authority, U.S. [U.S. history]
Housing (Housing since 1900) **H:** 391
Housing Choice Vouchers [program]
Housing (Housing subsidy programs) **H:** 391
Housing cooperative
Cooperative (Housing cooperatives) **Ci:** 1036
Housing estate
Singapore (The city of Singapore) **S:** 470
Housing project
Housing (Private housing projects) **H:** 390
Housman, A. E. [British poet] **H:** 393
Houssay, Bernardo Alberto [Argentine
  physiologist]
Nobel Prizes (Physiology or medicine: 1947)
  N: 445
Houston [Texas] **H:** 394 *with pictures and map*
Texas *picture on* **T:** 185; (Population) **T:** 188;
  (Transportation) **T:** 202
Houston, David F. [American government official]
Agriculture, Department of (table) **A:** 161
Wilson, Woodrow (table) **W:** 323
Houston, George Smith [American political
  leader]
Alabama (table) **A:** 274
Houston, Sam [American political leader] **H:** 399
  with portrait
Alamo (The siege) **A:** 280-281

Fort Sam Houston **F: 416**
San Jacinto, Battle of **S: 99**
Santa Anna, Antonio López de (War with Texas) **S: 113**
Tennessee (table) **T: 152**
Texas (table) **T: 203**; (The Texas revolution) **T: 206** *with picture*; (The Republic of Texas) **T: 206**; (The Civil War and Reconstruction) **T: 207**
Texas Rangers (Early days) **T: 210-211**
Houston Astros [team]
Baseball (table) **B: 130**
Houston (Recreation) **H: 397**
Houston Livestock Show and Rodeo
Houston (Recreation) **H: 397-398**
Houston Museum of Natural Science
Houston (Museums and libraries) **H: 397** *with picture*
Houston Public Library
Houston (Museums and libraries) **H: 397**
Houston Rockets [team]
Basketball (table) **B: 150**
Houston (Recreation) **H: 397**
Houston Ship Channel [waterway]
Houston (Commercial city) **H: 398**
Texas *picture on* **T: 202**
Houston Texans [team]
Football (National Football League) **F: 364**
Houston (Recreation) **H: 397**
Houstoun, John [American political leader]
Georgia (table) **G: 130**
Houx, Frank L. [American political leader]
Wyoming (table) **W: 532**
Houyhnhnm [fictional animal]
Gulliver's Travels **G: 440**
Swift, Jonathan: (*Gulliver's Travels*) **So: 1040**
Hove [former city] *See* Brighton and Hove *in this index*
Hovell, William [Australian explorer]
Australia *map on* **A: 921**; (Mapping the continent) **A: 922** *with map*
Hovenweep National Monument [Colorado-Utah]
National Park System (table: National monuments) **N: 51**
Hovercraft [aircraft] *See* Air cushion vehicle *in this index*
Hoverla, Mount [Ukraine]
Ukraine (The Eastern Carpathian Mountains) **U: 9** *with map*
Hoveve-Zion [organization]
Zionism (Movement to Palestine) **Z: 595**
Hovey, Alvin P. [American political leader]
Indiana (table) **I: 214**
Hovey, Richard [American poet]
Carman, Bliss **C: 240**
Hovhaness, Alan [American composer] **H: 399**
Hovland, Carl I. [American psychologist]
Communication (The effects of media) **Ci: 887**
How Does a Poem Mean? [book by Ciardi]
Ciardi, John **Ci: 551**
How Green Was My Valley [film]
Ford, John **F: 381**
Motion picture (Best picture: 1941) **M: 861**
How the Other Half Lives [book by Riis]
Urban renewal (History) **U: 220**
"How to Make Our Ideas Clear" [essay by Peirce]
Peirce, Charles Sanders **P: 230**
How to Succeed In Business Without Really Trying [musical]
Loesser, Frank **L: 420**
How to Win Friends and Influence People [book by Carnegie]
Carnegie, Dale **C: 242**
Howard, Sir Albert [British scientist]
Organic food (History) **O: 853**
Howard, Catherine [wife of]
Henry VIII [of England] **H: 188**
Howard, Charles [English admiral]
England (The reign of Elizabeth I) **E: 307-308**
Spanish Armada (The two fleets) **So: 755-756**
Howard, Desmond [American football player]
Football **F: 363**
Howard, Ebenezer [British architect]
City *picture on* **Ci: 587**
Howard, George [American political leader]
Maryland (table) **M: 255**
Howard, Henry [American political leader]
Rhode Island (table) **R: 311**
Howard, Henry [English poet] *See* Surrey, Earl of *in this index*
Howard, John [British explorer]
West Virginia (White settlement) **W: 226**
Howard, John [British social reformer] **H: 399**
Howard, John Eager [American political leader]
Maryland (table) **M: 255**
Howard, John Winston [Australian political leader] **H: 399**
Australia (table) **A: 923**; (Political upheavals)

A: 925
Howard, Oliver Otis [American general]
Cochise **Ci: 743**
Freedmen's Bureau **F: 500**
Howard, Ron [American actor/director]
Motion picture (Best achievement in directing: 2001) **M: 862**
Howard, Sidney [American dramatist] **H: 400**
Howard, Lord Thomas [English sea captain]
Grenville, Sir Richard **G: 390**
Howard University [Washington, D.C.] **H: 400**
Howards End [book by Forster]
Forster, E. M. **F: 410**
Howe, Earl [British admiral] *See* Howe, Richard *in this index*
Howe, Elias [American inventor] **H: 400**
Sewing machine (History) **S: 333**
Singer, Isaac Merrit **S: 472**
Howe, Gordie [Canadian hockey player] **H: 400**
Howe, Irving [American critic]
American literature (Essays) **A: 426**
Howe, John Ireland [American inventor]
Pin **P: 466**
Howe, Joseph [Canadian political leader] **H: 400**
Halifax (Government and history) **H: 21**
Nova Scotia (Progress as a province) **N: 568-570**
Tupper, Sir Charles (Confederation) **T: 494**
Howe, Julia Ward [American author] **H: 400** *with portrait*
"Battle Hymn of the Republic" **B: 172**
Civil War, American (The home front) **Ci: 622**
Mother's Day **M: 843**
Howe, Louis [American political leader]
Roosevelt, Franklin Delano (Entry into politics) **R: 450f**
Howe, Neil [American author]
Generation Y **G: 84**
Howe, Octavius T. [American pioneer]
Pioneer life in America (Life on the trail) **P: 486-487**
Howe, Oscar [American painter]
Indian, American *picture on* **I: 160**
Howe, Richard [British admiral] **H: 401**
Maryland (The Revolutionary War) **M: 258**
Howe, Samuel Gridley [American social reformer] **H: 401**
Bridgman, Laura Dewey **B: 607**
Howe, Timothy O. [American government official]
Arthur, Chester Alan (table) **A: 756**
Howe, Viscount *See* Howe, William *in this index*
Howe, William [British general] **H: 401**
Hale, Nathan (The fateful mission) **H: 18**
Revolution, American (Lexington and Concord) **R: 274-275**; (The campaign in New York) **R: 281**; (Trenton and Princeton) **R: 282**
Howell, Richard [American political leader]
New Jersey (table) **N: 249**
Howell, Troy [American artist]
Literature for children *picture on* **L: 377**
Howell, Varina [wife of]
Davis, Jefferson (Davis's family) **D: 47**
Howells, William Dean [American author] **H: 401**
American literature (Realists) **A: 419**
August (Quotations) **A: 887**
Novel (The United States) **N: 573**
Howitzer [weapon]
Army, United States (Artillery) **A: 734**
Artillery (Kinds of artillery) **A: 762** *with pictures*
Firearm *picture on* **F: 133**
Mortar **M: 862**
Nuclear weapon *picture on* **N: 597**
"Howl" [poem by Ginsberg]
American literature (Variations on Modernist poetry) **A: 423**
Beat movement **B: 189**
Ginsberg, Allen **G: 192**
Howland, Esther A. [American businesswoman]
Valentine's Day (Commercial valentines) **V: 264**
Howler [animal] **H: 402**
Animal *picture on* **A: 480**
Howley, Richard [American political leader]
Georgia (table) **G: 130**
Hoxha, Enver [Albanian political leader] **H: 402**
Albania (World War II) **A: 307-308**
Hoyle, Edmond [English whist player] **H: 402**
Hoyle, Fred [British astronomer] **H: 402**
Astronomy (Advances in astrophysics) **A: 848**
Hoyt, Henry Martyn [American political leader]
Pennsylvania (table) **P: 263**
Hoyt, Waite [American baseball player]
Baseball (table: Hall of Fame) **B: 134a**
Hoyte, Hugh Desmond [Guyana political leader]
Guyana (History) **G: 446-447**
Hozier, Clementine [wife of]
Churchill, Sir Winston Leonard Spencer (Churchill's family) **C: 547** *with portrait*
HPV [virus] *See* Human papillomavirus *in this index*

HR 8799 [star]
Planet *picture on* **P: 513**
Hradčany [hill]
Prague (The city) **P: 730**
Hrawi, Elias [Lebanese political leader]
Lebanon (Political struggle) **L: 174**
Hrolf [Norman chieftan] *See* Rollo *in this index*
HRT [medicine] *See* Hormone replacement therapy *in this index*
Hrungnir [Norse mythology]
Thor **T: 265**
Hsen-Hsu Hu [Chinese botanist]
Redwood (The dawn redwood) **R: 192**
Hsi Chiang [river, China] *See* Xi Jiang *in this index*
Hsuan-tsang [Chinese explorer]
Exploration (Chinese exploration) **E: 442**
Hsuehshan Tunnel [Taiwan]
Tunnel (table) **T: 491**
Hsun-tzu [Chinese philosopher] *See* Xunzi *in this index*
HSV-2 [virus] *See* Herpes simplex virus, type 2 *in this index*
HTGR [nuclear reactor] *See* High-temperature gas-cooled reactor *in this index*
HTML [computing] *See* HyperText Markup Language *in this index*
HTST method [pasteurization]
Milk (Pasteurization) **M: 548**
HTTP [electronics] *See* HyperText Transfer Protocol *in this index*
Hu Jintao [Chinese political leader] **H: 402** *with portrait*
China (Recent developments) **C: 506-507**
Hu Yao-pang *See* Hu Yaobang *in this index*
Hu Yaobang [Chinese government official] **H: 402**
China (Deng Xiaoping) **C: 506**; (Protests) **C: 506**
Hua Guofeng [Chinese government official]
China (Deng Xiaoping) **C: 506**
HUAC [committee] *See* Un-American Activities Committee *in this index*
Huaca [religion]
Inca (Religion) **I: 96-97**
Hualalai [volcano]
Hawaii (Hawaii) **H: 100**
Huang Chao [Chinese military leader]
Tang dynasty (The fall of the dynasty) **T: 26**
Huang Hai *See* Yellow Sea *in this index*
Huang He [river, China] **H: 402**
Asia (Rivers) **A: 794**
China (The land) **C: 490-491** *with map*
Famine (Too much rainfall) **F: 26a**
Flood (River floods) **F: 236-237**
River (table) **R: 352**
Huang He [region, China]
Asia (The Huang He and Yangtze valleys) **A: 805**
World, History of the (The Huang He Valley) **W: 472**
Huang Ho [river, China] *See* Huang He *in this index*
Huang Kungwang [Chinese artist]
Painting (Chinese painting) **P: 44-46**
Huangdi [emperor of China]
Calendar (The Chinese calendar) **C: 30**
Silk (Discovery of silk) **S: 460**
Huanglongbong [plant disease]
Orange (Pests and diseases) **O: 815**
Huánuco coca [tree]
Coca **Ci: 742**
Huaraches [clothing]
Mexico (Clothing) **M: 456**
Huari Indians
Indian, American (Indians of the Andes) **I: 173-174**
Nazca **N: 92**
Huarte, John [American football player]
Football **F: 363**
Huascar [Inca emperor]
Inca (The empire) **I: 98-99**
Huascarán [mountain, Peru]
Andes Mountains (Physical features) **A: 452**
Peru (The highlands) **P: 311** *with map*
Huaso [cowboy]
Chile (Clothing) **C: 462**
Huayna Capac [Inca emperor]
Inca (The empire) **I: 98-99**
Hub [money]
Money *picture on* **M: 711**; (Minting coins) **M: 714-715**
Hub and spoke system
Aviation (Deregulation and mergers) **A: 991**
Hub of the Universe [nickname]
Boston **B: 495**
Hubbard, Cal [American umpire]
Baseball (table: Hall of Fame) **B: 134a**
Hubbard, Elbert [American publisher]
García Íñiguez, Calixto **G: 29**
Hubbard, Gardiner Green [American lawyer]
Bell, Alexander Graham (The Boston teacher)

B: 240
Telephone (The Bell System) T: 100
Hubbard, Henry [American political leader]
New Hampshire (table) N: 223
Hubbard, John [American political leader]
Maine (table) M: 87
Hubbard, L. Ron [American religious leader]
Scientology S: 208
Hubbard, Lucius F. [American political leader]
Minnesota (table) M: 602
Hubbard, Mabel [wife of]
Bell, Alexander Graham (The Boston teacher)
B: 240
Hubbard, Mina Benson [Canadian author]
Canadian literature (Other literature) C: 158
Hubbard, Richard B. [American political leader]
Texas (table) T: 203
Hubbard, Richard D. [American political leader]
Connecticut (table) Ci: 967
Hubbard, Samuel D. [American government
official]
Fillmore, Millard (table) F: 102
Hubbard squash [plant]
Squash (Winter squashes) So: 813 with picture
Hubbell, Carl [American baseball player]
Baseball (table: Hall of Fame) B: 134a
Hubbell Trading Post National Historic Site
[Arizona]
National Park System (table: National historic
sites) N: 52-53
Hubble, Edwin Powell [American astronomer]
H: 403
Astronomy (Spectroscopy) A: 840-841;
(Discovering other galaxies) A: 848 with picture
Dark energy D: 37
Galaxy G: 8
Gravitation (Expansion of the universe) G: 332
Mount Wilson Observatory M: 890
Redshift (Cosmological redshift) R: 192
Hubble constant [astronomy]
Redshift (Cosmological redshift) R: 192
Hubble Space Telescope H: 403 with picture
Astronaut (Achievements in space) A: 829-830
Astronomy picture on A: 834; (Optical astronomy)
A: 8339-840
Exploration (Robotic spacecraft) E: 452
Pluto P: 581 with pictures
Space exploration (Repair missions) So: 724
Hubble's law [astronomy]
Redshift (Cosmological redshift) R: 192
Hubel, David Hunter [American physiologist]
Nobel Prizes (Physiology or medicine: 1981)
N: 446
Huber, Andrew [American settler]
Hoover, Herbert Clark (Boyhood) H: 326
Huber, Robert [German chemist]
Nobel Prizes (Chemistry: 1988) N: 444
Hubertusburg, Treaty of [1763]
Seven Years' War (In Europe) S: 328
Hubley, Faith [American animator]
Animation (Animation in the mid-1900's) A: 514b
Hubley, John [American animator]
Animation (Animation in the mid-1900's) A: 514b
Hübner, Johann [German educator]
Encyclopedia (An age of experiment) E: 268a
Huckabee, Mike [American political leader]
Arkansas (table) A: 712
Huckleberry [shrub] H: 404
Huckleberry Finn [book by Twain] H: 404
American literature (Mark Twain and Henry
James) A: 420
Novel (The United States) N: 573
Twain, Mark (Productive years in Hartford) T: 529
HUD [organization] See Housing and Urban
Development, Department of in this index
Huddle [group]
Fellowship of Christian Athletes F: 69
Hudson, Henry [English explorer] H: 404 with map
Arctic (Search for the Northwest Passage)
A: 638-639
Canada, History of (Start of the fur trade) C: 140
Delaware (Exploration and early settlement)
D: 110
Exploration (The French and English in North
America) E: 446-447 with map
Flag picture on F: 209
New York (Exploration and settlement) N: 314
Northwest Passage N: 528
Pennsylvania (Exploration and settlement) P: 264
Hudson, Jennifer [American actress]
Motion picture (Best performance by an actress
in a supporting role: 2006) M: 862b
Hudson, John [son of]
Hudson, Henry (Northern voyages) H: 404
Hudson, William Henry [British naturalist] H: 405
Hudson Bay [bay, Canada] H: 405 with map
Canada (The Hudson Bay and Hudson Strait

Basin) C: 120
Exploration (The French and English in North
America) E: 446-447
Hudson Bay Lowlands [Canada]
Canada map on C: 118; (The Hudson Bay
Lowlands) C: 118
Manitoba (Land regions) M: 154 with picture
Ontario (Land regions) O: 776 with map
Quebec (Land regions) Q: 22 with map
Hudson River [New York] H: 405
Lincoln Tunnel L: 329
New York picture on N: 290
Hudson River Railroad
Vanderbilt, Cornelius V: 279
Hudson River School [art] H: 406 with picture
Church, Frederic Edwin C: 541
Cole, Thomas Ci: 771
Hudson River tunnels [New Jersey-New York]
H: 406
Lincoln Tunnel L: 329
New York City (Transportation) N: 334-335
Hudson seal [fur]
Muskrat M: 963
Hudsonian curlew [bird]
Curlew C: 1195
Hudsonian godwit [bird]
Godwit G: 246
Hudson's Bay Company H: 407 with picture
British Columbia (Schools) B: 616; (The border
dispute) B: 630; (The colonial period) B: 630
Canada, History of (Exploration of the West)
C: 143
Douglas, Sir James D: 312
Fur trade (The early fur trade) F: 564
Groseilliers, Médard Chouart, Sieur des G: 398
Hudson, Henry (North American voyages)
H: 404-405
Manitoba (Newcomers) M: 160; (The Red River
Colony) M: 160
Nevada (Exploration) N: 173
North West Company N: 519
Northwest Territories (Political development)
N: 533
Nunavut (Arrival of the Europeans) N: 612
Ontario (Early settlement) O: 784
Prairie Provinces (History) P: 733
Radisson, Pierre Esprit R: 99
Saskatchewan (The coming of the fur traders)
S: 146
Simpson, Sir George S: 467
Trading post T: 365 with picture
Victoria V: 358
Winnipeg (History) W: 341
Hue [city, Vietnam] H: 407
Vietnam (Independence) V: 370
Hue [color]
Color (Characteristics of color) Ci: 824 with
diagrams
Hueffer, Ford Madox [birth name of]
Ford, Ford Madox F: 371
Huemul [animal]
Deer (table) D: 85; (Central and South American
deer) D: 85-86
Huerta, Adolfo de la [Mexican political leader]
Ávila Camacho, Manuel A: 993
Huerta, Dolores Fernandez [American activist]
H: 408
Huerta, Victoriano [Mexican political leader]
Carranza, Venustiano C: 247
Mexican Revolution of 1910 (The revolution)
M: 445
Mexico (The Revolution of 1910) M: 472
Mexico City (Revolution and growth) M: 478
Wilson, Woodrow (Crisis in Mexico) W: 323
Huey P. Long Bridge [New Orleans]
Louisiana (Transportation) L: 495
Huey tlatoani [emperor]
Aztec (The Aztec empire) A: 999
Huff, Leon [American recording executive]
Rock music (Soul music) R: 380a-380b
Hufnagel, Charles [American doctor]
Heart (Development of heart surgery) H: 144
Hufstedler, Shirley Mount [American government
official] H: 408
Hug, Wendelin [German pilot]
Glider (table) G: 230
Huggins, Charles Brenton [American physiologist]
Nobel Prizes (Physiology or medicine: 1966)
N: 446
Huggins, Miller [American baseball player]
Baseball (table: Hall of Fame) B: 134a
Hugh Capet [king of France] H: 408
Capetian dynasty C: 191
France (The Capetian dynasty) F: 471
Hugh Keenleyside Dam
British Columbia (The mid-1900's) B: 630
"Hugh Selwyn Mauberley" [poem by Pound]

Pound, Ezra P: 722
Hughes, Charles [British performer]
Circus (The birth of the circus) Ci: 562b
Hughes, Charles Evans [American jurist] H: 408
with portrait
Fairbanks, Charles Warren F: 9
Harding, Warren Gamaliel (Return to normalcy)
H: 58
New York (table) N: 313
Wilson, Woodrow (Election of 1916) W: 324
Hughes, Chris [American programmer]
Facebook (History) F: 4
Hughes, Edward David [British chemist]
Ingold, Sir Christopher I: 270
Hughes, Harold E. [American political leader]
Iowa (table) I: 391
Hughes, Harry R. [American political leader]
Maryland (table) M: 255
Hughes, Howard Robard [American businessman]
H: 408
Nevada (The mid-1900's) N: 176
Hughes, John [American religious leader]
Fordham University F: 383
Hughes, Langston [American author] H: 409
African Americans picture on A: 136l
American literature (The Harlem Renaissance)
A: 422
Harlem Renaissance H: 61
Hughes, Richard J. [American political leader]
New Jersey (table) N: 249
Hughes, Sarah T. [American jurist]
Kennedy, John Fitzgerald (The new President)
K: 267
Hughes, Simon P. [American political leader]
Arkansas (table) A: 712
Hughes, Ted [British poet] H: 409
English literature (Recent English poetry) E: 323
Plath, Sylvia P: 566
Hughes, Thomas [British author] H: 409
Hughes, William Morris [Australian political
leader]
Australia (table) A: 923
Hughes Tool Company
Hughes, Howard Robard H: 409
Hugo, Victor [French author] H: 409
Drama (Romanticism) D: 337
French literature (Romantic poetry) F: 521;
(Romantic drama) F: 521
Marx, Karl: *(Das Kapital)* M: 237
Hugoton field [region, Kansas]
Helium (Production) H: 176
Kansas (Mining) K: 233
Huguenots [French history] H: 410 with picture
Calvin, John (Calvinism) C: 71
Florida (Exploration and Spanish settlement)
F: 261
France (Religious wars) F: 473
Henry II [king of France] H: 186
Henry III [king of France] H: 186
Henry IV [king of France] H: 186
La Rochelle L: 77
Louis XIV L: 475
Nantes, Edict of N: 11
Reformation (John Calvin) R: 198
Richelieu, Cardinal (Strengthening the monarchy)
R: 331
Saint Bartholomew's Day, Massacre of S: 31
Huguenots, Les [opera by Meyerbeer]
Meyerbeer, Giacomo M: 479
*Hui Neng, the Sixth Patriarch, Chopping Bamboo
at the Moment of Enlightenment* [painting by
Liang Kai]
Painting (Chinese painting) P: 44-46 with picture
Hui-Tsung [Chinese emperor] See Huizong in this
index
Huichol [American Indian]
Mexico picture on M: 457
Huidobro, Vicente [Chilean poet]
Latin American literature (The early 1900's) L: 113
Huipil [clothing]
Clothing (Handmade clothing) Ci: 691; (Clothing
of Native Americans) Ci: 700
Huipil grande [clothing]
Mexico (Clothing) M: 456-457
Huis ten Bosch [palace, The Netherlands]
Hague, The (The city) H: 6
Huitzilopochtli [Aztec god]
Mythology (Aztec mythology) M: 987
Huizinga, Johan [Dutch historian] H: 411
Huizong [Chinese emperor] H: 411
Hukbong Magpapalayang Bayan [Philippine
history] See Huks in this index
Huks [Philippine history]
Guerrilla warfare (History) G: 420-421
Philippines (Independence) P: 380
Hula [dance]
Hawaii H: 88; (Dancing and music) H: 94 with

picture
Hula, Lake [former lake]
  Jordan River **J: 167**
Hulbert, William [American sportsman]
  Baseball (table: Hall of Fame) **B: 134a**
Hull [England] **H: 411**
  Humberside **H: 431**
Hull [botany]
  Cotton (Cottonseeds) **Ci: 1086**
  Rice (Structure) **R: 323** *with diagram*
Hull [ship]
  Motorboat racing (Hull designs) **M: 876** *with pictures*
  Sailing (Hull) **S: 23** *with diagram*
  Ship **S: 402;** (Basic structure) **S: 403;** (Environmental controls) **S: 414**
  Submarine **So: 939**
Hull, Albert W. [American engineer]
  Electronics (The vacuum tube era) **E: 215**
Hull, Bobby [Canadian hockey player] **H: 411**
  Hull, Brett **H: 412**
Hull, Brett [Canadian hockey player] **H: 411**
Hull, Charles J. [American businessman]
  Hull House **H: 412**
Hull, Clark Leonard [American psychologist] **H: 412**
  Hypnosis (Scientific studies) **H: 480**
Hull, Cordell [American statesman] **H: 412**
  Bennett, Richard Bedford *picture on* **B: 253**
Hull, Dennis [Canadian hockey player]
  Hull, Brett **H: 412**
Hull, Isaac [American military leader] **H: 412**
  Constitution **Ci: 995**
Hull, Jane Dee [American political leader]
  Arizona (table) **A: 687;** (The late 1900's) **A: 691-692**
Hull, Josephine [American actress]
  Motion picture (Best performance by an actress in a supporting role: 1950) **M: 862b**
Hull, William [American military leader] **H: 412**
  War of 1812 (Land campaign of 1812) **W: 31**
Hull House [Chicago] **H: 412**
  Addams, Jane **A: 46**
  Chicago (A city reborn) **C: 435**
  King, William Lyon Mackenzie (Education) **K: 325**
  Lathrop, Julia Clifford **L: 90**
  Progressive Era *picture on* **P: 813**
Hull-Rust mine [Minnesota]
  Hibbing **H: 221**
Hulling [agriculture]
  Rice (Cleaning and hulling) **R: 326** *with picture*
Hulme, Denis [New Zealand race driver]
  Automobile racing (table: Formula One World Drivers' Championship) **A: 980**
Hulme, Keri [New Zealand author]
  New Zealand (The arts) **N: 349**
Hulse, Russell Alan [American physicist]
  Gravitational wave **G: 333**
  Nobel Prizes (Physics: 1993) **N: 442**
Hum [historical region]
  Bosnia-Herzegovina (History) **B: 492**
Humai [religion]
  Sikhism (Beliefs and practices) **S: 455**
Humala, Ollanta [Peruvian political leader]
  Peru (Recent developments) **P: 316-317**
Human and Community Development, Program on
  MacArthur Foundation **M: 4**
Human behavior *See* Behavior *in this index*
Human being H: 413 *with pictures*
  See also Female; Human body; Male *in this index*
  Animal (Animals and people) **A: 471;** (The future of animals) **A: 504**
  Anthropology **A: 545**
  Cloning (Ethical concerns) **Ci: 683**
  Heidegger, Martin **H: 165**
  Human Genome Project **H: 427**
  Instinct (Human instincts) **I: 305**
  Mind **M: 562**
  Primate (Anthropoids) **P: 778** *with picture;* (The evolution of primates) **P: 778b-778c** *with diagram*
  Psychology **P: 847**
Human body [anatomy] **H: 416** *with pictures*
  Anatomy **A: 448b**
  Death (Medical aspects of death) **D: 61**
  Growth (Human growth) **G: 404**
  Human being (Characteristics of human beings) **H: 413**
  Leonardo da Vinci (Leonardo's works) **L: 200a** *with picture*
  Mind (The mind/body problem) **M: 563**
  Nutrition **N: 624**
  Water (Water in living things) **W: 118**
Human cannonball [circus act]
  Circus *picture on* **Ci: 562a**
Human capital [economics]

Capital **C: 192**
  Economics (Economic growth) **E: 62-63**
  Industry (Labor) **I: 259**
Human chorionic gonadotropin [hormone]
  Pregnancy (Confirming pregnancy) **P: 734a**
  Testicular cancer **T: 182**
Human Comedy, The [books by Balzac]
  Balzac, Honoré de **B: 71**
  French literature (Romantic fiction) **F: 521**
  Novel (France) **N: 573**
Human development
  See also the list of Related articles in the Human body *article*
  Aging **A: 141**
  Baby (The developing baby) **B: 4** *with diagrams;* (Growth and development) **B: 6** *with pictures*
  Cartilage **C: 263**
  Child (The stages of childhood) **C: 448** *with pictures*
  Developmental psychology **D: 174**
  Family and consumer sciences (Human development and family studies) **F: 25**
  Growth (Human growth) **G: 404**
  Human being (Human physical development) **H: 414**
  Intelligence **I: 319**
  Language **L: 62**
  Learning **L: 162**
  Learning disabilities **L: 165**
  Lisping **L: 349**
  Nutrition **N: 624**
  Personality **P: 300f**
  Piaget, Jean **P: 445**
  Play **P: 570**
  Progeria **P: 811**
  Psychology **P: 847**
  Sleep (The need for sleep) **S: 507**
  Teeth (Kinds of teeth) **T: 79**
Human ecology
  Family and consumer sciences **F: 25**
  Sociology (Population characteristics) **So: 564**
Human engineering *See* Ergonomics *in this index*
Human environmental sciences *See* Family and consumer sciences *in this index*
Human factors engineering *See* Ergonomics *in this index*
Human Genome Project [genetics] **H: 427**
  Bioethics **B: 311**
  Biology (Current research and issues) **B: 320-321**
  Gene mapping **G: 81**
  Heredity (The Human Genome Project) **H: 210**
  Medicine (The challenge of genetics) **M: 378**
  Molecular medicine **M: 692**
  Watson, James Dewey **W: 147**
  Wellcome Trust **W: 193**
Human geography
  Geography (Human geography) **G: 94**
Human growth hormone H: 427
  Heredity (The era of genetic engineering) **H: 209**
Human immunodeficiency virus
  AIDS **A: 164**
  Disease *picture on* **D: 229**
  Evolution (Direct observation of evolution) **E: 431**
  Retrovirus **R: 266**
  Transplant (Sources of donor organs) **T: 380**
Human intelligence [data]
  Intelligence service **I: 320**
Human papillomavirus H: 427
  Cancer (Viruses) **C: 171**
  Cervical cancer **C: 364**
Human races *See* Races, Human *in this index*
Human relations [psychology] **H: 428**
  Group dynamics **G: 402**
  Industrial relations **I: 245**
  Personnel management **P: 303**
  Psychology **P: 847**
  Segregation **S: 284**
  Social psychology **So: 552**
Human reproduction *See* Reproduction, Human *in this index*
Human resources [economics]
  Labor force **L: 3**
Human resources management [business] *See* Personnel management *in this index*
Human rights H: 428
  See also Civil rights *in this index*
  Bill of rights **B: 301**
  Bosnia-Herzegovina (History) **B: 492-493**
  Ford Foundation (Programs) **F: 382**
  Helsinki Accords **H: 179**
  Human Rights, Universal Declaration of **H: 428b**
  Human Rights Watch **H: 430**
  Pinochet Ugarte, Augusto **P: 474**
  Refugee (The rights of refugees) **R: 203**
  Slavery (Views of slavery) **S: 502**
  Truth commission **T: 474**
  United Nations (Human rights) **U: 88**

  United Nations Human Rights Council **U: 97**
  United States, History of the (The Declaration of Independence) **U: 160**
Human Rights, Universal Declaration of [1948] **H: 428b**
  Bill of rights (The United Nations General Assembly) **B: 301**
  Civil rights (Civil rights in other countries) **Ci: 610**
  Freedom of assembly (In other countries) **F: 504**
  Human rights (The development of human rights) **H: 428-428a**
  Privacy, Right of **P: 808a**
  United Nations (Human rights) **U: 88**
  War crime (New accords) **W: 27**
Human Rights Act [United Kingdom, 1998]
  Bill of rights (English Bill of Rights) **B: 301**
Human Rights Watch [organization] **H: 430**
  Human rights (Independent organizations) **H: 428a**
Human sacrifice
  Aztec (Religion) **A: 1000** *with picture*
  Funeral customs (Burial) **F: 557-558**
  Inca (Religion) **I: 96-97**
  Indian, American (Why the Indians fought) **I: 144-145;** (Ceremonies) **I: 148** *with picture*
  Maya (Religion) **M: 322-323**
  Mythology (Aztec mythology) **M: 987**
  Phoenicia (Religion) **P: 393**
Human sciences *See* Family and consumer sciences *in this index*
Human Sexual Response [book by Masters and Johnson]
  Masters and Johnson **M: 297**
Human Stain, The [book by Roth]
  Roth, Philip **R: 487**
Human Zoo, The [book by Morris]
  Morris, Desmond **M: 816**
Humana Building
  Louisville (Changes during the 1900's) **L: 506**
Humanae Vitae [encyclical, 1968]
  Paul VI **P: 200**
Humane Association, American *See* American Humane Association *in this index*
Humane society H: 430
  Society for the Prevention of Cruelty to Animals **So: 563** *with picture*
Humane Society of the United States [organization]
  Animal rights movement **A: 510**
Humanism [philosophy] **H: 430**
  Biography (The Middle Ages) **B: 313**
  Education (The Renaissance) **E: 100**
  French literature (The Renaissance) **F: 519**
  German literature (The Renaissance) **G: 139**
  History (The Humanist movement) **H: 262**
  Italian literature (Humanism and the Renaissance) **I: 494**
  Middle Ages (The growth of humanism) **M: 528**
  Nicholas V **N: 403**
  Painting (The Renaissance) **P: 51**
  Petrarch **P: 327**
  Philosophy (Modern philosophy) **P: 388**
  Renaissance (Humanism) **R: 233;** (Christian humanism) **R: 238**
  Sculpture (Italian Renaissance sculpture) **S: 251**
  Women's movement (From the Renaissance to the 1800's) **W: 384**
  World, History of the (The Renaissance) **W: 438**
Humanistic-experiential psychotherpy
  Psychotherapy (Humanistic-experiential psychotherapy) **P: 852**
Humanistic psychology
  Maslow, Abraham Harold **M: 265**
  Psychology (Modern psychology) **P: 850**
Humanistic script
  Paleography **P: 103**
Humanistic theory [psychology]
  Education (How people learn) **E: 89-90**
Humanities
  Foundation (Arts and humanities) **F: 431**
  Humanism **H: 430**
  Liberal arts **L: 226**
  Social science (Relationship to humanities) **So: 553**
Humanities and Social Sciences Library [New York]
  New York Public Library **N: 344**
Humanity Asleep [painting by Schnabel]
  Schnabel, Julian **S: 177**
Humber, River [England]
  Humberside **H: 431**
Humber Bridge [England]
  Bridge (table: Suspension) **B: 603**
  Humberside **H: 431**
Humberside [region, England] **H: 431**
Humbert [Italian nobleman]
  Savoy **S: 166**

"Humble-Bee, The" [poem by Emerson]
Emerson, Ralph Waldo (His poetry) **E: 259**
Humboldt, Alexander von See Humboldt, Baron von in this index
Humboldt, Baron von [German scientist] **H: 432**
Botany (Later developments) **B: 509**
Geography (The growth of geography) **G: 96**
Geology (The rock dispute) **G: 98-99**
Humboldt Current
Peru Current **P: 317**
Humboldt National Forest
Great Basin National Park **G: 336**
Humboldt River [Nevada]
Nevada (Rivers and lakes) **N: 166** with map
Humboldt Sink [region, Nevada]
Great Basin **G: 336** with map
Humboldt University
Berlin (Downtown Berlin) **B: 260**
Germany (Education) **G: 151**
Humboldt's Gift [book by Bellow]
Bellow, Saul **B: 244**
Humboldt's woolly monkey
Woolly monkey **W: 402**
Hume, David [Scottish philosopher] **H: 432**
Freethinker **F: 509**
Kant, Immanuel **K: 243**
Philosophy (Empiricism) **P: 389**
Political science (Liberalism) **P: 639**
Psychology (Beginnings) **P: 849**
Hume, Hamilton [Australian explorer]
Australia map on **A: 921**; (Mapping the continent) **A: 922**
Hume, John [Irish political leader]
Nobel Prizes (Peace: 1998) **N: 448b**
Humectant [chemical]
Food preservation (Additives) **F: 343**
Humerus [anatomy]
Arm **A: 717** with diagram
Bird (Skeleton and muscles) **B: 364** with diagram
Elbow **E: 157** with diagrams
Frog picture on **F: 537**
Human body (table) **H: 422** with diagram
Rotator cuff **R: 486**
Shoulder **S: 437** with picture
Humid continental climate
Climate (Humid continental climates) **Ci: 676c**
Humid oceanic climate
Climate (Humid oceanic climates) **Ci: 676c**
Humid subtropical climate
Climate (Humid subtropical climates) **Ci: 676c**
Humidifier [machine] **H: 432**
Heating **H: 157**; (Warm-air heating) **H: 157**
Humidity [weather] **H: 433** with diagram
Air (Moisture in the air) **A: 170**
Air conditioning (Controlling the moisture) **A: 178**
Heating (Warm-air heating) **H: 157**
Humidifier **H: 432**
Hygrometer **H: 474**
Rain (Rainfall distribution) **R: 124**
Weather (table: Weather terms) **W: 157**; (Humidity) **W: 158**
Hummer [vehicle]
Automobile picture on **A: 969**
Jeep **J: 75**
Hummingbird [bird] **H: 433** with pictures
Animal picture on **A: 469**
Bird (In nature) pictures on **B: 329, B: 330, B: 358**; (Feeding methods) **B: 350**
Evolution picture on **E: 427**
Flower (Other agents) **F: 295-296**
Heart (Birds and mammals) **H: 146-147**
Pollen (Cross-pollination) **P: 645**
Hummingbird moth See Hawk moth in this index
Hummus [food]
Chickpea **C: 446**
Humor H: 435
See also the list of Related articles in the Humor article
Humor [physiology]
Blood (History of blood research) **B: 414**
Drama (Elizabethan playwrights) **D: 331-332**
Humoral immune response [physiology]
Immune system diagram on **I: 88b**; (The immune response) **I: 88**
Virus (Immune response) **V: 428a**
Humorous Phases of Funny Faces [film]
Animation (Early animation) **A: 514a**
Hump [engineering]
Railroad (At classification yards) **R: 110** with diagram
Hump [zoology]
Camel **C: 76**; (The hump) **C: 78** with pictures
Hump, The [military history]
Air force (World War II) **A: 185-186**
World War II (The China-Burma-India theater) **W: 491-492**

Hump yard [railroad]
Railroad (At classification yards) **R: 110** with pictures
Humpback [disorder]
Hunchback **H: 437**
Humpback salmon See Pink salmon in this index
Humpback whale H: 436
Animal (Animal travelers) **A: 502**
Antarctica (Living things) **A: 534** with picture
Whale (Rorquals) **W: 255-258** with picture; (Group life) **W: 261**
Humperdinck, Engelbert [German composer] **H: 436**
Humphrey, Doris [American dancer]
Dance (Modern dance) **D: 30-31**
Humphrey, George Magoffin [American government official]
Eisenhower, Dwight David (table) **E: 152**
Humphrey, Hubert Horatio [American political leader] **H: 436** with portrait
Johnson, Lyndon Baines (Full-term president) **J: 149**
Minneapolis picture on **M: 580**
Minnesota (Politics) **M: 602-603**
Nixon, Richard Milhous (The 1968 election) **N: 432**
Political convention (Further reforms of the convention system) **P: 630**
Vice president of the United States (Growth of the vice presidency) **V: 353**
Humphrey, Lyman Underwood [American political leader]
Kansas (table) **K: 234**
Humphrey, Muriel Buck [wife of]
Humphrey, Hubert Horatio (Early life) **H: 436**
Humphreys, Benjamin G. [American political leader]
Mississippi (table) **M: 640**
Humphreys, West H. [American jurist]
Impeachment (History) **I: 91**
Humphreys Peak
Arizona (Land regions) **A: 680**
Humuhumu-nukunuku-a-pua'a [fish]
Fish picture on **F: 154**
Humus [earth] **H: 437**
Plumbing (The drain-waste-vent system) **P: 578-579**
Sewage (Rural sewerage systems) **S: 330-331**
Soil (Organic matter) **So: 573**
Hun Sen [Cambodian political leader] **H: 437**
Cambodia (History) **C: 72-74**
Hunchback [disorder] **H: 437**
Hunchback of Notre Dame, The [book by Hugo]
French literature (Romantic fiction) **F: 521**
Hugo, Victor (His works) **H: 410**
Hundred [English history]
Delaware (Local government) **D: 109**
Shire **S: 429**
Hundred Acre Wood [fictional place]
Milne, A. A. **M: 556**
Hundred Days [French history]
Louis XVIII **L: 477**
Napoleon I (The Hundred Days and Waterloo) **N: 16**
Napoleonic Wars (The Hundred Days) **N: 20**
Hundred Days [U.S. history]
Great Depression (The New Deal) **G: 341**
New Deal (The Hundred Days) **N: 200**
Roosevelt, Franklin Delano (The Hundred Days) **R: 453**
Hundred Years' War [1337-1453] **H: 437**
Agincourt, Battle of **A: 141**
England (The Hundred Years' War) **E: 306** with picture
France (A period of wars) **F: 473**
Henry V [of England] **H: 187**
Joan of Arc, Saint **J: 128**
Middle Ages (A halt in progress) **M: 528**
Philip VI **P: 370**
Poitiers, Battle of **P: 603**
Salic law **S: 66**
Hung jury
Jury (Petit juries) **J: 202**
Trial (Reaching a verdict) **T: 436**
Hungarian Democratic Forum [political party]
Hungary (Multiparty elections) **H: 448**
Hungarian language See Magyar in this index
Hungarian oak [tree]
Oak (Other oaks) **O: 636**
Hungarian partridge [bird]
Partridge **P: 189**
Hungarian pointer [dog]
Vizsla **V: 433** with picture
Hungarian Revolution [1956]
Cold War (Unrest in Eastern Europe) **Ci: 766** with picture
Hungary (Unsuccessful revolution) **H: 447** with

picture
Hungarian Socialist Party
Hungary (Politics) **H: 439**; (History) **H: 445-448**
Hungary H: 438 with pictures and maps
See also the list of Related articles in the Hungary article
Clothing picture on **Ci: 694**
Cold War (Unrest in Eastern Europe) **Ci: 766** with picture
Communism (In Eastern Europe) **Ci: 896**
Croatia (History) **Ci: 1148a-1148b**
Czech Republic (Habsburg rule) **Ci: 1213**
Germany (East Germany) **G: 170**
Magyars **M: 63**
North Atlantic Treaty Organization (History) **N: 471**
Slovakia (Hungarian rule) **S: 509**
Transylvania **T: 402**
Trianon, Treaty of **T: 439**
Warsaw Pact **W: 39**
Hunger H: 449
See also Starvation in this index
Population (Effects) **P: 674**
United Nations (Fighting hunger) **U: 89**
Hunger strike
Strike **So: 928**
Hungry Horse Dam [Montana]
Dam (table) **D: 18**
Hunkpapa Sioux Indians
Gall **G: 13**
Hunlen Falls
British Columbia (Rivers, waterfalls, and lakes) **B: 624**
Hunley [submarine]
Submarine (Early submarines) **So: 942**
Hunn, John [American political leader]
Delaware (table) **D: 109**
Huns [people] **H: 449**
Asia (Nomadic invasions) **A: 805**
Attila **A: 879**
Europe (Germanic invasions) **E: 408**
Goths **G: 280**
Russia (Early days) **R: 547**
Hunsdon, Lord [English political leaders]
Shakespeare, William (Acting companies) **S: 352**
Hunt, E. Howard [American public figure]
Watergate (The break-in and cover-up) **W: 144**
Hunt, Frank W. [American political leader]
Idaho (table) **I: 42**
Hunt, George Wylie Paul [American political leader]
Arizona (table) **A: 687**; (Progress as a state) **A: 690**
Hunt, Guy [American political leader]
Alabama (table) **A: 274**; (The late 1900's) **A: 278-279**
Hunt, Helen [American actress]
Motion picture (Best performance by an actress: 1997) **M: 862a**
Hunt, Holman [British painter] See Hunt, William Holman in this index
Hunt, Irene [American author]
Newbery Medal (table) **N: 359**
Hunt, James [British race driver]
Automobile racing (table: Formula One World Drivers' Championship) **A: 980**
Hunt, James B., Jr. [American political leader]
North Carolina (table) **N: 490**
Hunt, Sir John [British mountain climber]
Mount Everest **M: 884**
Hunt, Leigh [British editor] **H: 449**
Keats, John (His life) **K: 253**
Hunt, Lester C. [American political leader]
Wyoming (table) **W: 532**
Hunt, Linda [American actress]
Motion picture (Best performance by an actress in a supporting role: 1983) **M: 862b**
Hunt, Richard Morris [American architect] **H: 449**
Statue of Liberty (The pedestal) **So: 873**; (Inspiration and preparations) **So: 876**
Hunt, Timothy [British biologist]
Nobel Prizes (Physiology or medicine: 2001) **N: 447**
Hunt, Walter [American inventor]
Pin **P: 466**
Hunt, Ward [American jurist]
Supreme Court of the United States (table) **So: 1000**
Hunt, Washington [American political leader]
New York (table) **N: 313**
Hunt, William H. [American government official]
Arthur, Chester Alan (table) **A: 756**
Garfield, James Abram (table) **G: 42**
Hunt, William Holman [British painter]
Painting (The Pre-Raphaelite Brotherhood) **P: 71**
Pre-Raphaelite Brotherhood **P: 756** with picture
Hunt Family Cabin
South Carolina picture on **So: 645**

Hunt of the Unicorn, The [tapestries]
  Tapestry *picture on* T: 39
Hunter, Catfish [American baseball player]
  Baseball (table: Hall of Fame) B: 134a
Hunter, Evan [pen name of]
  McBain, Ed M: 332
Hunter, Holly [American actress]
  Motion picture (Best performance by an actress:
    1993) M: 862a
Hunter, John [British doctor]
  Surgery (History) So: 1007
Hunter, Kim [American actress]
  Motion picture (Best performance by an actress
    in a supporting role: 1951) M: 862b
Hunter, Matthew A. [American chemist]
  Titanium T: 300
Hunter, Rielle [American public figure]
  Edwards, John E: 114
Hunter Mountain [New York]
  Catskill Mountains C: 305
Hunting H: 450
  Animal (Hunting and fishing) A: 505
  Bird (As a source of food and raw materials)
    B: 330
  Conservation (Biodiversity conservation) Ci: 976;
    (Conservation in the United States) Ci: 985;
    (Africa) Ci: 990
  Egypt, Ancient (Recreation) E: 137
  Elephant E: 226
  Endangered species (Overhunting) E: 270
  Falconry F: 14
  Fox hunting F: 442
  Game G: 21
  Hound H: 378
  Indian, American (Hunting, gathering, and
    fishing) I: 141; (The first Americans) I: 151
  Inuit (Hunting and fishing) I: 354d
  Peregrine falcon P: 284
  Poaching P: 587
  Pointer P: 600
  Prehistoric people (How the first people lived)
    P: 746-747; (How the Neandertals lived) P: 751;
    (The Stone Age) P: 751
  Retriever R: 266
  Rifle R: 338 *with pictures*
  Safari S: 8
  Shotgun S: 436
  Wildlife conservation (Methods of wildlife
    conservation) W: 304
Hunting and gathering
  Agriculture (History) A: 153
  Arctic (Traditional ways of life) A: 638
  Human being (Hunting and gathering societies)
    H: 415
  Indian, American (Hunting, gathering, and
    fishing) I: 141
Hunting dog
  Dog (Sporting dogs) D: 268 *with pictures*
  Hunting (Kinds of hunting) H: 450
Hunting gull [bird] *See* Jaeger *in this index*
Hunting knife
  Knife (Types of knives) K: 345-346 *with pictures*
"Hunting of the Snark, The" [poem by Carroll]
  Carroll, Lewis (Other works) C: 249
Hunting spider
  Spider So: 783; (Hunting spiders) So: 790
Hunting Stewart plaid
  Tartan *picture on* T: 47
Hunting whip
  Horse (The whip) H: 351
Huntington [West Virginia] H: 450
Huntington, Collis Potter [American businessman]
  California (Early statehood) C: 62
  Huntington H: 450
Huntington, George [American physician]
  Huntington's disease H: 451
Huntington, Samuel [1731-1796, American
    patriot] H: 450
  Connecticut (table) Ci: 967
Huntington, Samuel [American political leader]
  Ohio (table) O: 699
Huntington Library [San Marino, California]
  Los Angeles (Museums) L: 466
Huntington's chorea [disease] *See* Huntington's
  disease *in this index*
Huntington's disease H: 451
  Brain (Making decisions) B: 555; (Genetic
    disorders) B: 558
  Genetic testing (Genes associated with disease)
    G: 84d
  Heredity (table) H: 204
Hunton, Jonathan [American political leader]
  Maine (table) M: 87
Huntsman [sports]
  Fox hunting F: 442
Huntsman, Benjamin [British inventor]
  Iron and steel (The first steel) I: 450

Huntsman, Jon M. [American political leader]
  Utah (table) U: 245; (The early 2000's) U: 249-250
Huntsman, Jon M., Jr. [American political leader]
  Utah (table) U: 245
Huntsman Marine Science Centre [St. Andrews]
  New Brunswick (Places to visit) N: 188
Huntsman's-cup [plant]
  Pitcher plant P: 499
Huntsville [Alabama] H: 451
  Alabama A: 256; (Population) A: 260; (Early
    statehood) A: 275
Hunyadi, John [Hungarian nobleman]
  Hungary (The Kingdom of Hungary) H: 445
Hupa Indians
  California (Early days) C: 60
  Indian, American *pictures on* I: 139
Huppa [canopy]
  Judaism (Special occasions) J: 182
Hurd, Earl [American cartoonist]
  Animation (Pioneers of American animation)
    A: 514a-514b
Hurdle [movement]
  Diving D: 243 *with diagram*
Hurdling [sport] H: 451 *with picture*
  Track and field (Track events) T: 356 *with picture*
Hurdy-gurdy [musical instrument]
  Hand organ H: 41
Hurley, Charles F. [American political leader]
  Massachusetts (table) M: 288
Hurley, Patrick Jay [American diplomat]
  Hoover, Herbert Clark (table) H: 330
Hurley, Robert A. [American political leader]
  Connecticut (table) Ci: 967
Hurling [sport]
  Ireland (Recreation) I: 420
Huron, Lake [Canada-U.S.] *See* Lake Huron *in this
  index*
Huron Indians
  Canada, History of (Early settlements) C: 140
  Champlain, Samuel de (The founding of Quebec)
    C: 373
  Indian, American (Indians of the Northeast)
    I: 154-155
  Ontario (Original inhabitants) O: 784
Huron National Forest
  Michigan (Places to visit) M: 498
Huronia [Canadian history]
  Ontario (Early settlement) O: 784
Hurricane [airplane]
  World War II (The Battle of Britain) W: 476
Hurricane [drawing by Leonardo]
  Leonardo da Vinci *picture on* L: 201
Hurricane [weather] H: 452 *with pictures and map*
  Arctic Ocean (Climate) A: 641
  Boating *picture on* B: 431
  Cuba (Climate) Ci: 1173
  Cyclone Ci: 1204
  Disaster (table) D: 223
  Galveston G: 18
  Insurance (Insurance today) I: 316-317
  Pacific Ocean (Tropical cyclones) P: 14
  Safety (During a hurricane) S: 15
  Storm (Tropical cyclones) So: 913
  Weather *pictures on* W: 166, W: 167
  Wind (table) W: 330
Hurricane Andrew
  Florida (The late 1900's) F: 264-265
  Hurricane *picture on* H: 452; (Hurricane damage)
    H: 455
  Miami (History) M: 480-481
Hurricane Camille
  Hurricane (Hurricane damage) H: 455
Hurricane Charley
  Florida (The early 2000's) F: 265
Hurricane Floyd
  North Carolina (Recent developments) N: 494
Hurricane Georges
  Puerto Rico (Puerto Rico today) P: 884
Hurricane Gilbert
  Hurricane (Hurricane damage) H: 455
Hurricane Gustav
  Cuba (Recent developments) Ci: 1179
  New Orleans (The early 2000's) N: 285
Hurricane Hugo
  Antigua and Barbuda (History) A: 556
  Charleston (Government and history) C: 383-384
  South Carolina (The late 1900's) So: 662-663
    with picture
Hurricane hunter [airplane]
  Hurricane (Forecasting hurricanes) H: 456
Hurricane Ike
  Galveston G: 18
  Houston (The early 2000's) H: 398
Hurricane Iniki
  Hawaii (Economic changes) H: 109
Hurricane Irene
  Flood (River floods) F: 236

Hurricane Ivan
  Alabama (The 2000's) A: 279
  Grenada (History and government) G: 389-390
Hurricane Katrina H: 456 *with picture*
  Baton Rouge (Government and history) B: 166-
    167
  Biloxi B: 307
  Bush, George Herbert Walker (Later years)
    B: 722a
  Bush, George Walker (Domestic issues) B: 722j
  Civil defense (Recent developments) Ci: 606
  Federal Emergency Management Agency F: 64
  Florida (The early 2000's) F: 265
  Gulfport G: 439
  Hurricane *picture on* H: 453; (Hurricane damage)
    H: 455
  Louisiana (The early 2000's) L: 501
  Mississippi (The early 2000's) M: 645
  New Orleans N: 278; (The early 2000's) N: 285
    with picture
  Red Cross (In the United States) R: 187-188
  United States, History of the (Hurricane Katrina)
    U: 196e *with picture*
Hurricane Luis
  Antigua and Barbuda (History) A: 556
Hurricane Mitch
  Honduras (Recent developments) H: 313
  Nicaragua (The late1900's) N: 400-401
Hurricane Sandy
  United States, History of the (Hurricane Sandy)
    U: 196f
Hurricane warning
  Flag *picture on* F: 197
  Hurricane (Forecasting hurricanes) H: 456
Hurricane watch [meteorology]
  Hurricane (Forecasting hurricanes) H: 456
Hurricane Wilma
  Florida (The early 2000's) F: 265
Hurricanes, Carolina [team]
  Hockey (table: National Hockey League) H: 281
Hurston, Zora Neale [American author] H: 457
  American literature (The Harlem Renaissance)
    A: 422
  Harlem Renaissance H: 61
Hurstwood, George [literary figure]
  Dreiser, Theodore D: 346
Hurt, William [American actor]
  Motion picture (Best performance by an actor:
    1985) M: 862a
Hurt Locker, The [film]
  Motion picture (Best picture: 2009) M: 861
Hurtado, Miguel de la Madrid [Mexican political
  leader] *See* De la Madrid Hurtado, Miguel *in this
  index*
Hurwicz, Leonid [Russian economist]
  Nobel Prizes (Economics: 2007) N: 449
Hus, John [Bohemian religious leader] H: 457
  Czech Republic (The rise of Bohemia) Ci: 1213
  Eck, Johann E: 50
  Hussites H: 457
  Lollards L: 427
  Moravian Church M: 801
  Prague (The city) P: 730
  Sigismund S: 453
Husain [grandson of Muhammad] *See* Husayn *in
  this index*
Husain, Maqbool F. [Indian painter]
  India (Painting) I: 119-120
Husák, Gustáv [Czechoslovak political leader]
  Czech Republic (The 1960's) Ci: 1214
  Czechoslovakia (The 1960's) Ci: 1216; (The Velvet
    Revolution) Ci: 1216
  Slovakia (Communist rule) S: 509
Husayn [Muslim ruler]
  Muslims (The Muslim Empire) M: 964c
  Shi'ites S: 400
Husayn-Ali, Mírza [Persian religious leader] *See*
  Bahá'u'lláh *in this index*
Husband
  See also Divorce; Parent *in this index*
  Marriage M: 219
Husband, Rick [American astronaut]
  Columbia disaster H: 852
  Space exploration (The Columbia disaster)
    So: 725
Husbandry, Patrons of *See* Grange, National *in
  this index*
Hush money [crime]
  Extortion E: 457
Husk [botany]
  Coconut palm (The coconut) Ci: 746
  Corn (Appearance) Ci: 1057
Husky [dog]
  Siberian husky S: 445 *with picture*
Huss, John [Bohemian religious leader] *See* Hus,
  John *in this index*
Hussein [ruler of Mecca]

Ibn Saud I: 4
Jordan (Independence) J: 164
Hussein I [king of Jordan] H: 457
Abdullah II A: 9
Israel *picture on* I: 489
Jordan (History) J: 164
Hussein, Muna al- [Jordanian princess]
Abdullah II A: 9
Hussein, Nur Hassan [Somali political leader]
Somalia (History) So: 589-590
Hussein, Qusay [Iraqi political leader]
Hussein, Saddam H: 458
Iraq (The Iraq War) I: 414a-414b
Iraq War (After the fall of the Hussein regime)
I: 414d-414e
Hussein, Saddam [Iraqi political leader] H: 457
with portrait
Air Force, United States (The Iraq War) A: 196
Army, United States (The Iraq War [2003-2010])
A: 740
Bush, George Walker (Iraq) B: 722i
Iran-Iraq War I: 407
Iraq I: 408
Iraq War I: 414c, *picture on* I: 414e
Kuwait (History) K: 396
Maliki, Nouri Kamel al- M: 110
Middle East (History) M: 533-534a
Persian Gulf War of 1991 P: 300b
Terrorism (The Iraq War [2003-2011]) T: 180
War (Recent developments) W: 26
War crime (Wars in Iraq) W: 27
Hussein, Uday [Iraqi political leader]
Hussein, Saddam H: 458
Iraq (The Iraq War) I: 414a-414b
Iraq War (After the fall of the Hussein regime)
I: 414d-414e
Husserl, Edmund [German philosopher]
Existentialism E: 437
Phenomenology P: 356
Philosophy (Philosophy in the 1900's) P: 390
Hussites [European history] H: 458
Bohemia B: 437
Hus, John H: 457
Prague (History) P: 730
Huston, Anjelica [American actress]
Motion picture (Best performance by an actress
in a supporting role: 1985) M: 862b
Huston, John [American director] H: 458
Motion picture (Best achievement in directing:
1948) M: 862
Huston, Walter [American actor]
Motion picture (Best performance by an actor in
a supporting role: 1948) M: 862a
Hutch [cage]
Rabbit (Cage) R: 48
Hutchings, Andrew Jackson [nephew of]
Jackson, Andrew (Jackson's family) J: 8
Hutchings, John [nephew of]
Jackson, Andrew (Jackson's family) J: 8
Hutchins, Robert Maynard [American educator]
Democracy (Famous quotations about
democracy) D: 120
Hutchinson, Anne Marbury [American colonial
leader] H: 458
Rhode Island (Settlement) R: 312
Hutchinson, Sir Jonathan [English physican]
Progeria P: 811
Hutchinson, Sara [sister-in-law of Wordsworth]
Coleridge, Samuel Taylor (His life) Ci: 771-772
Hutchinson, Thomas [British colonial official]
H: 458
Boston Tea Party B: 506
Hutchinson, William [husband of]
Hutchinson, Anne Marbury H: 458
Hutchinson Family [singing group]
Popular music *picture on* P: 670; (1840's to the
Civil War) P: 669
Hutchinson-Gilford progeria syndrome [disease]
Progeria P: 811
Hutchinsonite [mineral]
Thallium T: 229
Hutong [street]
Beijing (The city) B: 222
Hutspot [food]
Netherlands (Food and drink) N: 141
Hutt, William [Canadian actor]
Drama *picture on* D: 324
Hutter, Jacob [Moravian religious leader]
Hutterites H: 459
Hutterian Brethren [religious group] *See*
Hutterites *in this index*
Hutterites [religious group] H: 459
Alberta (Population) A: 316
Anabaptists A: 447
Hutton, James [Scottish philosopher] H: 459
Geology (The rock dispute) G: 98-99
Lyell, Sir Charles L: 533

Hutton, Timothy [American actor]
Motion picture (Best performance by an actor in
a supporting role: 1980) M: 862b
Hutu [people] H: 459
Burundi B: 712; (People) B: 713; (History) B: 713
Congo, Democratic Republic of the (The fall of
Mobutu) Ci: 940c
Ruanda-Urundi R: 499
Rwanda R: 570
Tutsi T: 527
Huxley, Aldous [British author] H: 459
English literature (Fiction between the wars)
E: 322
Huxley, Andrew Fielding [British biologist]
Nobel Prizes (Physiology or medicine: 1963)
N: 446
Huxley, Thomas Henry [British zoologist] H: 459
Agnosticism A: 143
Darwin, Charles Robert (The influence of Darwin's
ideas) D: 40
Huxman, Walter A. [American political leader]
Kansas (table) K: 234
Huygens [space probe]
Cassini C: 276
European Space Agency E: 418
Huygens, Christiaan H: 460
Titan T: 299 *with picture*
Huygens, Christiaan [Dutch physicist] H: 460
Diffraction (How diffraction occurs) D: 201
Light (Modern study) L: 285
Optics (History) O: 813
Pendulum P: 237
Physics (Newton) P: 439
Radiation (Electromagnetic waves) R: 80
Saturn (History of study) S: 153
Titan T: 299
Huygens, Constantijn [Dutch playwright]
Netherlands (Arts) N: 142
HVI [machine] *See* High volume instrument *in this
index*
Hwange National Park [Zimbabwe]
National park (table) N: 42f
Hyacinth [plant] H: 460
Flower (Garden perennials grown from bulbs)
F: 280 *with picture*
Plant *picture on* P: 525
Poisonous plant (Some poisonous plants) P: 602
Water hyacinth W: 134
Hyacinth bean
Bean (Kinds of beans) B: 181
Hyacinth macaw [bird]
Parrot (Kinds of parrots) P: 179
Hyakutake, Comet
Comet (table) Ci: 868
Hyaline membrane disease *See* Respiratory
distress syndrome *in this index*
Hyannis [Massachusetts]
Cape Cod C: 188 *with map*
Hyatt, Gilbert [Canadian settler]
Sherbrooke S: 396
Hyatt, Isaiah [American inventor]
Plastics (The invention of Celluloid) P: 559
Hyatt, John W. [American inventor]
Plastics (The invention of Celluloid) P: 559
Hyatt's Mills
Sherbrooke S: 396
Hybrid [biology] H: 460 *with picture*
Agriculture (Agricultural genetics) A: 158
Breeding B: 592
Corn (Hybrid corn) Ci: 1059; (Development of
hybrids) Ci: 1063
Flower (Flower breeding) F: 297-298
Grafting (Uses of grafting) G: 298
Hog (Kinds of hogs) H: 285
Rice (Kinds of rice) R: 323-324
Rose (Types of roses) R: 474 *with picture*;
(Reproducing and growing roses) R: 475
Hybrid adjustable-rate mortgage
Mortgage M: 820
Hybrid bicycle
Bicycle (Hybrids) B: 290
Hybrid breed
Dog (Kinds of dogs) D: 265-266
Hybrid car H: 461
Automobile A: 946; (Providing electric power)
A: 951; (Powering electric and hybrid cars)
A: 954 *with diagram*; (The 2000's) A: 972-973
with picture
Electric car (History) E: 165-166
Global warming (Increased fuel efficiency)
G: 232b
Toyota Motor Corporation T: 355
Transportation (Declining fuel reserves) T: 397-
398 *with picture*
Hybrid derecho [storm]
Derecho D: 152
Hybrid magnet [electromagnet]

Magnetism *picture on* M: 60
Hybrid perpetual rose
Rose (Types of roses) R: 474
Hybrid rocket
Rocket (Hybrid rockets) R: 388
Hybrid tea rose
Flower *picture on* F: 281
Rose (Types of roses) R: 474 *with pictures*; (table)
R: 474
Hybrid vigor [agriculture]
Corn (Hybrid corn) Ci: 1059
Hybridization [horticulture]
Breeding B: 592
Hybridoma [cell]
Monoclonal antibody M: 731
Hydathode [botany]
Leaf (The blade) L: 153
Hyde, Arthur M. [American political leader]
Agriculture, Department of (table) A: 161
Hoover, Herbert Clark (table) H: 330
Missouri (table) M: 668
Hyde, Douglas [Irish poet]
Irish literature (Modern works in Gaelic) I: 431
Hyde, Edward [birth name of]
Clarendon, Earl of Ci: 638
Hyde Amendment [law]
Abortion (Abortion in the United States) A: 15-16
Hyde Park [district, Boston]
Boston (Hyde Park and West Roxbury) B: 500
Hyde Park [park, London]
London (Parks) L: 435
Hyderabad [city, India] H: 461
Passion play *picture on* P: 191
Hydra [Greek mythology] H: 461
Hercules (The twelve labors) H: 198-199
Renaissance *picture on* R: 237
Hydra [animal] H: 461 *with picture*
Animal *picture on* A: 497
Hydra [satellite]
Planet (Pluto) P: 512
Pluto P: 581
Hydrangea [shrub] H: 462 *with picture*
Flower (Flowering shrubs) F: 281 *with picture*
Hydrate [chemistry] H: 462
Hydrated aluminum hydroxide [mineral]
Bauxite B: 174
Hydrated aluminum silicate [mineral]
Fuller's earth F: 555
Hydrated lime [chemical]
Lime L: 306
Hydrated silicate [mineral]
Asbestos (Types of asbestos) A: 765
Hydration melting [geology]
Volcano (Subduction zones) V: 441
Hydraulic brake
Brake (Hydraulic brakes) B: 560 *with diagram*
Hydraulic cement
Cement and concrete C: 343
Hydraulic dredge
Dredging D: 346
Hydraulic elevator
Elevator (How elevators work) E: 234 *with
diagram*
Hydraulic engine H: 462
Engine E: 283
Hydraulic engineering
Hydraulics H: 463
Hydraulic fracturing [mining]
Coal (Recent developments) Ci: 732
Hydraulic oil
Transmission (The controller) T: 377
Hydraulic press [machine]
Hydraulics H: 463; (Use of hydrostatic principles)
H: 463 *with diagram*
Hydraulic rescue tool
Fire department (Rescue trucks) F: 126-127 *with
picture*
Hydraulic system
Tractor (Parts of a tractor) T: 360
Hydraulic turbine *See* Water turbine *in this index*
Hydraulicking [mining]
Mining (Placer mining) M: 575
Hydraulics [physics] H: 463 *with diagrams*
Automobile (Automobile systems) A: 947
Fluid mechanics F: 304
Levee L: 216
Hydraulus [musical instrument]
Organ (History) O: 852
Hydrazine [chemical]
Fuel (Chemical fuels) F: 551
Hydric soil
Wetland (Water and soil) W: 252a
Hydro-Drome [boat]
Hydrofoil (History) H: 468 *with picture*
Hydro-Electric Power Commission [Canada]
Ontario (In the early 1900's) O: 786
Saint Lawrence Seaway (The hydroelectric power

project) S: 44
Hydrocarbon [chemistry] H: 465
  Catalytic converter C: 298
  Coal (The composition of coal) Ci: 717
  Gas [fuel] (The composition of natural gas) G: 50
  Gasoline (Gasoline production) G: 61
  Hydrogen (Compounds) H: 469
  Natural gas liquids N: 64
  Petrochemicals (How petrochemicals are made) P: 329
  Petroleum (The composition of petroleum) P: 331
  Rubber (The chemistry of rubber) R: 501
  Saturn (Satellites) S: 151
  Smog (Photochemical smog) S: 519
Hydrocephalus [disease]
  Spina bifida So: 792
Hydrochloric acid [chemical] H: 465
  Acid A: 26; (The strength of an acid) A: 27
  Chlorine (Uses of chlorine) C: 516-517
  Halogen H: 27
  Hydrogen (Compounds) H: 469
  Neutralization N: 154
  Stomach (The stomach's work) So: 908; (Peptic ulcers) So: 908
Hydrocortisone [hormone] See Cortisol in this index
Hydrocracking [industrial process]
  Petroleum (Cracking processes) P: 344
Hydrocyanic acid
  Prussic acid P: 843
Hydrocyanic acid gas
  Gas chamber G: 59
Hydrodynamics [physics]
  Fluid mechanics (External fluid mechanics) F: 304
  Hydraulics H: 463; (Liquids in motion) H: 464 with diagrams
Hydroelectric power
  See also the Electric Power sections of specific state and province articles, such as Arizona (Electric Power)
  Columbia River Ci: 852
  Electric power (Hydroelectric power plants) E: 184 with diagram
  Fall line F: 16
  Niagara River (Water power) N: 394
  Water power W: 139
Hydroelectric power plant
  Nuclear energy (The role of nuclear energy in power production) N: 580
  Turbine (Water turbines) T: 496
Hydrofluoric acid [chemical] H: 465
Hydrofoil [vehicle] H: 465 with pictures
  Boating picture on B: 431; (Sailboats) B: 429
  Missile boat M: 618
  Transportation (Water transportation) T: 384
Hydrogen [element] H: 468
  See also the list of Related articles in the Hydrogen article
  Acid A: 26
  Airship (Lift) A: 250
  Atom A: 870 with diagram; (The atomic mass number) A: 871 with diagrams
  Battery (Metal hydride batteries) E: 200
  Deuterium D: 172
  Electrolysis (How electrolysis works) E: 200
  Energy supply (Hydrogen) E: 279
  Fire (Gases) F: 122
  Fusion F: 589
  Haber process H: 2
  Isotope I: 476
  Jupiter (Chemical composition) J: 198
  Life (The chemical basis of life) L: 277 with diagram
  Moon picture on M: 792
  Nuclear weapon (Thermonuclear weapons) N: 597
  Relativity (General relativity) R: 211
  Star (Fusion in stars) So: 846; (Evolution of stars) So: 848
  Tritium T: 448
Hydrogen balloon
  Balloon (Gas balloons) B: 58; (The hydrogen balloon) B: 61
Hydrogen bomb [weapon]
  Bomb diagram on B: 452
  Cold War (To the brink and back) Ci: 765; (The great blocs split) Ci: 769
  Deuterium D: 172
  Einsteinium E: 147
  Nuclear weapon N: 596
  Teller, Edward T: 129
Hydrogen bond [chemistry]
  Bond (Other linkages) B: 454
  Ice (The structure of ice) I: 5 with diagram
  Water (How water is held together) W: 131
Hydrogen chloride [chemical]

Chlorine (Uses of chlorine) C: 516
Hydrochloric acid H: 465
Hydrogen cyanide [chemical]
  Cyanide Ci: 1202
Hydrogen fluoride [chemical]
  Fluorine F: 306
  Hydrofluoric acid H: 465
Hydrogen ion
  Acid A: 26
Hydrogen peroxide [chemical] H: 470
  Bleach B: 399
Hydrogen sulfide [gas] H: 470
  Damp D: 22
Hydrogenated oil
  Hydrogen (Uses) H: 469
Hydrogenated tallow alcohol [chemical]
  Detergent and soap (How detergents are made) D: 165
Hydrogenation [chemistry] H: 470
  Coal (Coal research) Ci: 730-731
  Fat (Structure) F: 52
  Hydrogen (Uses) H: 469
  Nickel (Industrial uses) N: 404
  Trans fats T: 369
Hydrographic survey
  Surveying (Other surveys) So: 1011
Hydrography [geography] H: 470
  Geology picture on G: 100
Hydrolase [enzyme]
  Malt M: 112
Hydrologic cycle [geology]
  Earth (Cycles on and in Earth) E: 22
  Hydrology H: 470
  Rain R: 122
  Water (Nature's water cycle) W: 120 with diagram
Hydrological Decade, International
  Water (The challenge of today) W: 132
Hydrology [science] H: 470
  Flood (Reducing flood losses) F: 238
  Geophysics G: 106a
Hydrolysis [chemistry] H: 471
  Energy supply (Hydrogen) E: 279
Hydrolyzer [machine]
  Detergent and soap (Continuous processing) D: 164
Hydromagmatic eruption [geology]
  Volcano (The violence of an eruption) V: 439
Hydromedusa [animal]
  Ocean picture on O: 656
Hydrometallurgy
  Metallurgy (Leaching) M: 426
Hydrometer [measuring device] H: 471
Hydronic system
  Boiler B: 439
Hydronium ion [chemistry]
  Acid A: 26
  Hydrolysis H: 471
Hydrophobia [disease]
  Rabies R: 49
Hydrophobia [psychology]
  Phobia P: 392
Hydrophone [instrument]
  Acoustics A: 29
  Fathometer F: 54
  Ocean drilling programs diagram on O: 667
  Petroleum (Seismic studies) P: 336-337
  Sonar (How sonar works) So: 571
  Torpedo (How a torpedo works) T: 340d-341
Hydrophyte [plant] See Water plant in this index
Hydroplane [boat] H: 471
  Motorboat racing (Hull designs) M: 876 with picture
Hydroponics [botany] H: 471 with diagrams
  Farm and farming (Special crop-growing methods) F: 37-38
Hydropower See Water power in this index
Hydrosol [chemistry]
  Colloid Ci: 777
Hydrosphere [geography] H: 472
  Earth (Earth's spheres) E: 18-20 with picture
Hydrostatic balance [instrument]
  Galileo (Early scientific interests) G: 11
Hydrostatics [physics]
  Archimedes (His discoveries) A: 605
  Hydraulics H: 463
Hydrosulfuric acid [chemical]
  Hydrogen sulfide H: 470
Hydrotherapy [treatment] H: 472 with picture
Hydrothermal metamorphism [geology]
  Metamorphic rock M: 428
Hydrothermal vent [oceanography] H: 473 with pictures
  Archaea A: 593
  Atlantic Ocean (The Mid-Atlantic Ridge) A: 864; (Ocean life) A: 866
  Ballard, Robert Duane B: 43
  Deep sea (The deep-sea floor) D: 82a with picture;

(Deep-sea life) D: 82a-82b
  Ocean (Sediments) O: 654; (The food cycle) O: 655-658; (Discoveries) O: 664
  Pacific Ocean (The ocean floor) P: 14
Hydrotreating [process]
  Petroleum (Chemical treatment) P: 345
Hydrotropism [botany]
  Plant (Environmental factors) P: 538
Hydrous silica [mineral]
  Silica S: 457
Hydroxide [chemistry] H: 474
  Base B: 123
  Hydrolysis H: 471
Hydroxyl [chemistry]
  Alcohol A: 335
Hydroxyurea [drug]
  Sickle cell anemia S: 447
Hydrozoan [zoology]
  Jellyfish J: 90
Hyena [animal] H: 474 with picture
  Aardwolf A: 2 with picture
Hyères, France, 1930 [photograph by Cartier-Bresson]
  Cartier-Bresson, Henri picture on C: 263
Hygiene, Dental See Dental hygiene in this index
Hygiene, Public
  Epidemic E: 343
  Public health P: 855
Hygiene hypothesis [physiology]
  Allergy (The development of allergies) A: 374
Hygienic Laboratory [former name]
  National Institutes of Health N: 39
Hyginus, Saint [pope]
  Pope (table) P: 666
Hygrometer [instrument] H: 474
  Humidity diagram on H: 433
  Weather (Land-based observation stations) W: 162
Hygroscopic seeding agent [chemical]
  Cloud seeding (Cloud-seeding methods) C: 711
Hyksos [ancient people] H: 475
  Egypt, Ancient (The Middle Kingdom) E: 143
Hyman, Trina Schart [American artist]
  Caldecott Medal (table: 1985) C: 26
  Literature for children picture on L: 378
Hymen [anatomy]
  Vagina V: 260
Hymenoptera [entomology]
  Insect pictures on I: 283; (table) I: 300 with picture
Hymn [song] H: 475
  Chorale C: 522
  Greek literature (Medieval literature) G: 378
"Hymn to Adversity" [poem by Gray]
  Gray, Thomas G: 378
Hymn to the Rising Sun [play by Green]
  Green, Paul Eliot G: 379
Hymn tune
  Hymn (Words and music) H: 475
Hymnes [poems by Ronsard]
  Ronsard, Pierre de R: 450b
Hymnody [music]
  Hymn (History) H: 475
Hymns, Collection of [book by Wesley]
  Wesley, Charles W: 197
Hymns to the Night [poems by Novalis]
  German literature (Romanticism) G: 140
  Novalis N: 571
Hymnus [music by Dvořák]
  Dvořák, Antonín D: 394
Hyoid bone [anatomy]
  Woodpecker diagram on W: 394
Hyoscyamine [medication]
  Henbane H: 183
Hypatia [Egyptian mathematician] H: 475
Hyperactivity [disorder]
  Attention deficit disorder A: 878
  Child (Obstacles to learning) C: 453
  Learning disabilities (Types) L: 165
  Special education (Children with learning disabilities) So: 770-771
Hyperacute rejection [medicine]
  Xenotransplant X: 544
Hyperbaric chamber [device]
  Hyperbaric oxygen therapy H: 475 with picture
Hyperbaric oxygen therapy H: 475 with picture
  Oxygen tent O: 890
Hyperbola [mathematics] H: 476
  Orbit O: 819 with diagram
Hyperbole [language]
  Figure of speech F: 97
  Humor (The humor of words) H: 435
Hyperbolic geometry [mathematics]
  Geometry (Non-Euclidean geometry) G: 105
Hypercholesterolemia [disorder]
  Cholesterol (Factors that cause high cholesterol levels) C: 520
Hyperglycemia [disorder]

Diabetes **D:** 179
Hypergol [fuel]
Rocket (Liquid-propellant rockets) **R:** 388
Hyperhidrosis [disorder]
Perspiration **P:** 305
Hypericum [plant]
Saint-John's-wort **S:** 37 *with picture*
Hyperinflation [economics]
Inflation (Hyperinflation) **I:** 267 *with picture*
Money (Printing money and inflation) **M:** 717
World War II (Economic problems) **W:** 469
"Hyperion" [poem by Keats]
Keats, John (His work) **K:** 253
Hyperion [satellite]
Saturn (Satellites) **S:** 151-153
Hyperkinesis [disorder]
Amphetamine (Medical uses) **A:** 439
Hyperlink [computing]
See also Hypertext *in this index*
Computer (The World Wide Web) **Ci:** 921
HyperText Markup Language **H:** 477
Internet (HTTP) **I:** 350d
Search engine **S:** 269
Website **W:** 176
World Wide Web **W:** 500
Hypermnesia [disorder]
Hypnosis (Hypnotic phenomena) **H:** 478
Hyperopia [disorder] *See* Farsightedness *in this index*
Hypersonic speed
Aerodynamics (Supersonic aerodynamics) **A:** 87
Airplane (Supersonic airplanes) **A:** 238
Wind tunnel **W:** 333
Hypertension [disorder] **H:** 476
Blood pressure **B:** 416
Cerebral hemorrhage **C:** 361
Circulatory system (Disorders of the circulatory system) **Ci:** 561
Disease (Diseases associated with aging) **D:** 230
Drug (Antihypertensives) **D:** 352
Framingham Heart Study **F:** 451
Heart (Risk factors) **H:** 137; (Progress in treatment and prevention) **H:** 145-146
Nutrition (Heart disease) **N:** 630
Stroke (Causes) **So:** 930
Hypertensive crisis [medicine]
Hypertension **H:** 476
Hypertensive emergency [medicine]
Hypertension **H:** 476
Hypertext [computing]
See also Hyperlink *in this index*
Berners-Lee, Tim **B:** 270
HyperText Markup Language **H:** 477
Website **W:** 176
World Wide Web **W:** 500
Hypertext Markup Language [computing] **H:** 477
Berners-Lee, Tim **B:** 270
Computer (The World Wide Web) **Ci:** 921
Internet (Glossary of Internet terms) **I:** 350a; (HTML) **I:** 350d; (The Web forms) **I:** 350g
Website **W:** 176
HyperText Transfer Protocol [electronics]
Berners-Lee, Tim **B:** 270
Computer (Internet software) **Ci:** 922
Internet (HTTP) **I:** 350d; (The Web forms) **I:** 350g
Hyperthermia [disorder] **H:** 477
Weather (Reporting the weather) **W:** 169-170
Hyperthyroidism [disorder]
Goiter **G:** 248
Graves' disease **G:** 331
Thyroid gland (Overactive thyroid) **T:** 275
Hypertrophic cardiomyopathy [disorder]
Heart (Cardiomyopathy) **H:** 142-143
Hyperurbanization [sociology]
Local government (Local governments in less developed countries) **L:** 409
Hyperventilation [disorder] **H:** 477
Skin diving (Breath-hold diving) **S:** 493
Hyphae [biology]
Fungi (Parts of a fungus) **F:** 558 *with picture*
Mold **M:** 690
Mushroom (Parts of a mushroom) **M:** 942 *with picture*
Hyphen
Punctuation (The hyphen) **P:** 903
Hypnagogic hallucination [dream]
Narcolepsy **N:** 20
Hypnos [Greek mythology] **H:** 477
Morpheus **M:** 816
Mythology (table) **M:** 981
Hypnosis **H:** 478
Mesmer, Franz Anton **M:** 421
Hypnotic drug
Depressant **D:** 149
Drug (Drugs that affect the nervous system) **D:** 352
Narcotic **N:** 21

Sedative **S:** 279
Hypnotic state
Hypnosis **H:** 478
Hypnotism *See* Hypnosis *in this index*
Hypo [chemical]
Herschel, Sir John Frederick William **H:** 216
Hypo [photography]
Photography (Black-and-white negative film) **P:** 419
Hypocaust [heating system]
Heating (History) **H:** 160
Hypocenter [seismology] *See* Focus [earthquake] *in this index*
Hypochlorite [chemistry]
Disinfectant **D:** 235
Hypochlorous acid **H:** 480
Hypochlorous acid [chemical] **H:** 480
Hypochondria [psychology] **H:** 480
Mental illness (Somatoform disorders) **M:** 406
Hypocotyl [botany]
Cotyledon **Ci:** 1095
Germination **G:** 173
Plant (Germination) **P:** 535-536 *with picture*
Seed (How seeds sprout) **S:** 282-283
Hypocretin [chemical]
Narcolepsy **N:** 20
Hypodermic injection **H:** 480
Drug *picture on* **D:** 350
Intravenous injection **I:** 354
Hypoglycemia [disorder] **H:** 480
Diabetes (Treatment) **D:** 179
Insulin (Diabetes) **I:** 308
Hypomanic episode [psychology]
Bipolar disorder **B:** 327
Hyponatremia [disorder]
Dehydration **D:** 93
Hyponymy [semantic relation]
Semantics **S:** 291
Hypophysis [anatomy] *See* Pituitary gland *in this index*
Hyposensitization [medicine]
Allergy (Treatment) **A:** 374
Hay fever (Treatment) **H:** 116
Hypotension [disorder]
Blood pressure **B:** 416
Hypotenuse [geometry]
Triangle (Right triangles and the Pythagorean theorem) **T:** 437-438
Hypothalamus [anatomy] **H:** 481
Brain *diagram on* **B:** 551; (Regulating body processes) **B:** 553; (Regulating emotions) **B:** 554
Fever **F:** 83
Gland (Endocrine glands) **G:** 207 *with diagram*; (table) **G:** 208
Hormone (Growth and sex hormones) **H:** 336; (Endocrine control hormones) **H:** 336
Human body (The endocrine system) **H:** 425
Hunger **H:** 449
Perspiration **P:** 305
Steroid (The adrenal steroids) **So:** 894-895
Stress (How stress affects the body) **So:** 926
Temperature, Body (Warm-blooded animals) **T:** 130
Thirst **T:** 259
Hypothermia [medicine] **H:** 481
Safety (In winter sports) **S:** 12
Weather (Reporting the weather) **W:** 169-170
Hypothesis [science]
Crime scene investigation (Reconstructing the crime) **Ci:** 1142
Popper, Karl Raimund **P:** 668
Psychology (Methods of psychological research) **P:** 847
Science (Forming a hypothesis) **S:** 195
Zoology (How zoologists work) **Z:** 606
Hypothyroidism [disorder]
Goiter **G:** 248
Thyroid gland (Underactive thyroid) **T:** 274
Hypotonic cerebral palsy [disorder]
Cerebral palsy (Types) **C:** 361
Hypoxia [disorder] *See* Anoxia *in this index*
Hyracoidea [zoology]
Mammal **M:** 128 *with picture*
Hyracotherium [extinct animal] *See* Eohippus *in this index*
Hyrax [animal] **H:** 482 *with picture*
Mammal *picture on* **M:** 117; (table) **M:** 128 *with picture*
Hyssop [shrub] **H:** 482 *with picture*
Hysterectomy [medicine] **H:** 482
Cervical cancer **C:** 364
Surgery (Some common surgical operations) **So:** 1006
Hysteria [psychology] **H:** 482

I
I [letter] **I:** 1 *with pictures*
I [symbol]
Iodine (Properties of iodine) **I:** 370
I ...
Titles beginning with the Italian word I *appear under their key words, as in* Pagliacci, I
I. C. Sorosis [organization]
Sorority **So:** 597
I Am a Cat [book by Natsume Soseki]
Natsume Soseki **N:** 64
"I Am Joaquín" [poem by Gonzales]
Gonzales, Rodolfo **G:** 269
I and the Village [painting by Chagall]
Chagall, Marc *picture on* **C:** 368
I-bond
Investment (Bonds) **I:** 368
"I came, I saw, I conquered" [quotation]
Caesar, Julius (Last victories) **C:** 13
I Ching [ancient book] **I:** 2
I, Claudius [book by Graves]
Graves, Robert **G:** 330
"I Have a Dream" [speech by King]
King, Martin Luther, Jr. (The growing movement) **K:** 321
March on Washington **M:** 196
I-head engine
Gasoline engine (Valve arrangement) **G:** 64
"I Heard a Fly Buzz" [poem by Dickinson]
Dickinson, Emily (Her poems) **D:** 190-191
Poetry (Stress meters) **P:** 592
"I Heard It Through the Grapevine" [song]
Gaye, Marvin **G:** 73
I-it relationship [philosophy]
Buber, Martin **B:** 657
I-Kiribati [people]
Kiribati (People) **K:** 335
I Know Why the Caged Bird Sings [book by Angelou]
Angelou, Maya **A:** 460
"I Love Lucy" [TV program]
Arnaz, Desi **A:** 741
Ball, Lucille **B:** 43
CBS **C:** 323
"I Love You Truly" [song by Bond]
Bond, Carrie Jacobs **B:** 455
"I only regret that I have but one life to lose for my country" [quotation]
Hale, Nathan (The fateful mission) **H:** 18-19
I, Rigoberta Menchú [book by Menchú]
Menchú, Rigoberta **M:** 397
"I think, therefore I am" [proposition]
Descartes, René (His philosophy) **D:** 154
I-thou relationship [philosophy]
Buber, Martin **B:** 657
IAAF [organization] *See* International Amateur Athletic Federation *in this index*
Iachimo [literary figure]
Shakespeare, William: (*Cymbeline*) **S:** 365
Iacocca, Lee [American businessman] **I:** 2 *with portrait*
Automobile (Challenges to the Big Three) **A:** 972
IAEA [agency] *See* International Atomic Energy Agency *in this index*
Iago [literary figure]
Shakespeare, William: (*Othello*) **S:** 363
Iamb [poetry]
Poetry (Foot-verse meters) **P:** 593
Iambic pentameter [poetry]
Blank verse **B:** 398
English literature (The age of Chaucer) **E:** 316
Poetry (Foot-verse meters) **P:** 593
Shakespeare, William (The third period [1601-1608]) **S:** 361
Iambic verse
Greek literature (Elegiac poetry) **G:** 377
Iapetus [satellite] **I:** 2
Satellite (Iapetus) **S:** 150c
Saturn (Satellites) **S:** 151-152 *with picture*
IATA [organization] *See* International Air Transport Association *in this index*
Iatrochemistry
Chemistry (Alchemy) **C:** 400-401
IAU [organization] *See* International Astronomical Union *in this index*
Ibadan [Nigeria] **I:** 2
Ibadis [Muslim sect]
Oman (History) **O:** 759
Ibáñez, Vicente Blasco *See* Blasco Ibáñez, Vicente *in this index*
Ibáñez del Campo, Carlos [Chilean political leader]
Chile (Era of changes) **C:** 469
Ibans [people]
Dayaks **D:** 53
Malaysia (People) **M:** 98b-98c
Ibarbourou, Juana de [Uruguayan poet]

Latin American literature (The early 1900's) **L:** 113
Ibarra, Francisco de [Spanish explorer]
  Durango **D:** 387
Ibbotson, Eva [Austrian-born author]
  Literature for children *picture on* **L:** 375
IBD [disorder] *See* Inflammatory bowel disease *in this index*
Ibeji [Nigeria]
  Sculpture *picture on* **S:** 229
Iberia [region, Europe] **I:** 2
  Spanish language (Beginnings) **So:** 757
Iberia [music by Albéniz]
  Albéniz, Isaac **A:** 311
Iberian lynx [animal]
  Lynx **L:** 536
Iberians [ancient people]
  Iberia **I:** 2
  Portugal (Population and ancestry) **P:** 687; (Early days) **P:** 692
Ibert, Jacques [French composer] **I:** 2
Iberville, Sieur d' [French-Canadian explorer] *See* Le Moyne, Pierre, Sieur d'Iberville *in this index*
IBEW [union] *See* Electrical Workers, International Brotherhood of *in this index*
Ibex [animal] **I:** 3
  Animal *picture on* **A:** 475
  Goat *picture on* **G:** 240; (Wild goats) **G:** 239
IBEX [space probe]
  Heliosphere (Probing the heliosphere) **H:** 175
Ibirapuera Park
  São Paulo (The city) **S:** 117-118 *with picture*
Ibis [bird] **I:** 3
  Bird (Birds of Central and South America) **B:** 344a *with picture*
Ibizan hound **I:** 3 *with picture*
Iblis [religion]
  Devil **D:** 174
IBM [company] *See* International Business Machines Corporation *in this index*
IBM clone [computer]
  International Business Machines Corporation **I:** 338
Ibn Abd al-Wahhab, Muhammad [Saudi religious leader] *See* Abd al-Wahhab, Muhammad Ibn *in this index*
Ibn al-Haytham [Arab scientist] *See* Alhazen *in this index*
Ibn Battūta [Arab explorer] **I:** 3
  Exploration (Muslim exploration) **E:** 442
Ibn Khaldūn [Arab historian] **I:** 3
Ibn Qutaiba [Arabian scholar]
  Encyclopedia (The first reference works) **E:** 268a
Ibn Saud [king of Saudi Arabia] **I:** 3
  Saudi Arabia (The founding of Saudi Arabia) **S:** 161
Ibn Saud, Muhammad [Saudi ruler]
  Saudi Arabia (The Saud dynasty) **S:** 160-161
Ibn-Sina [Arab philosopher] *See* Avicenna *in this index*
Ibn Tashfin, Yusuf [Berber leader]
  Marrakech **M:** 218
Ibo [people] *See* Igbo *in this index*
Ibsen, Henrik [Norwegian dramatist] **I:** 4
  Drama (Ibsen) **D:** 338
  Grieg, Edvard **G:** 392
  Realism (In drama) **R:** 172
  Shaw, George Bernard (Early life) **S:** 378
Ibuka, Masaru [Japanese businessman]
  Sony Corporation **So:** 594
Ibuprofen [drug] **I:** 4
ICANN [corporation] *See* Internet Corporation for Assigned Names and Numbers *in this index*
ICAO [organization] *See* International Civil Aviation Organization *in this index*
Icaria [former name]
  Nauvoo **N:** 69
Icarius [legendary figure]
  Ulysses (The Trojan War) **U:** 17-18
Icarus [Greek mythology]
  Airplane (History) **A:** 229 *with picture*
  Daedalus **D:** 3
Icaza, Jorge [Ecuadorean author]
  Latin American literature (The early 1900's) **L:** 113
ICBM [missile] *See* Intercontinental ballistic missile *in this index*
ICC [agency] *See* Interstate Commerce Commission *in this index*
ICC [court] *See* International Criminal Court *in this index*
Ice [drug] **I:** 4 *with pictures*
  See also Dry ice *in this index*
  Antarctica (Geography) **A:** 531 *with pictures*
  Arctic Ocean **A:** 641 *with picture;* (Ice) **A:** 641 *with picture*
  Freezing point **F:** 510
  Global warming (Impact of global warming) **G:** 232a *with pictures*

Hail **H:** 8 *with pictures*
Ice formation **I:** 9
Ice storm **I:** 16 *with picture*
Iceberg **I:** 17 *with pictures*
Refrigeration (Ice refrigeration) **R:** 200
Snow **S:** 539 *with pictures*
Water (The properties of water) **W:** 129
ICE [agency] *See* Immigration and Customs Enforcement, United States *in this index*
ICE [commodity exchange]
  Commodity exchange **Ci:** 873
Ice [drug] *See* Methamphetamine *in this index*
Ice age [geology] **I:** 6 *with picture and map*
  Climate (Causes of climate change) **Ci:** 676d
  Earth (Earth's changing climate) **E:** 24
  Glacier **G:** 202
  Indian, American (Early days) **I:** 151
  La Brea tar pits **L:** 18
  Lake Agassiz **L:** 35
  Prehistoric animal (The ice ages) **P:** 741
  Prehistoric people (Migration from Africa) **P:** 747
Ice Age, The [book by Drabble]
  Drabble, Margaret **D:** 317
Ice Age National Scientific Reserve [Wisconsin]
  Wisconsin (Places to visit) **W:** 356
Ice core [geology]
  Antarctica (Climate) **A:** 534
Ice cream **I:** 8 *with diagram*
  Pennsylvania (Interesting facts) **P:** 245
Ice cream cone
  Food (Interesting facts about food) **F:** 329
Ice-crystal process [meteorology]
  Rain (Formation of rain) **R:** 123-124 *with diagram*
Ice dancing
  Ice skating (Ice dancing) **I:** 12 *with diagrams*
Ice fishing
  Fishing **F:** 175
Ice floe [geology]
  Antarctica (Ocean) **A:** 532-534
  Ice formation **I:** 9
Ice formation [geology] **I:** 9
  Glacier **G:** 202
Ice-formed pond
  Pond (Kinds of ponds) **P:** 656
Ice hockey *See* Hockey *in this index*
Ice Hockey Federation, International *See* International Ice Hockey Federation *in this index*
Ice house
  Food preservation (Modern food preservation) **F:** 344
Ice island [geography]
  Arctic Ocean (Glacial ice) **A:** 641
Ice Island 3T
  Iceberg (Northern Hemisphere icebergs) **I:** 17
Ice nucleus
  Air (Moisture in the air) **A:** 170
  Rain (The ice-crystal process) **R:** 124
Ice plant **I:** 9 *with picture*
Ice sheet
  Antarctica (Ice) **A:** 532; (Climate) **A:** 534
  Climate (Icecap climates) **Ci:** 676d
  Glacier (Kinds of glaciers) **G:** 202
  Greenland (The land) **G:** 385
  Ice age **I:** 6 *with map*
  Ice formation **I:** 9
  Icecap **I:** 19
  Pleistocene Epoch **P:** 572
Ice shelf
  Antarctica (Ocean) **A:** 532-534
  Climate (Icecap climates) **Ci:** 676d
  Ice formation **I:** 9
  Iceberg **I:** 17
Ice show
  Ice skating *picture on* **I:** 10
Ice skating [sport] **I:** 10 *with pictures*
  Netherlands (Holidays and recreation) **N:** 141
  Olympic Games (Winter Olympic Games) **O:** 746d-746e *with picture*
Ice storm **I:** 16 *with picture*
Ice-T [American rapper]
  Rock music (Rap) **R:** 380d
Ice yachting
  Iceboating **I:** 18 *with pictures*
Iceberg **I:** 17 *with pictures and map*
  Antarctica (Ocean) **A:** 532-534
  Arctic Ocean *picture on* **A:** 641; (Glacial ice) **A:** 641
  Glacier (How glaciers form) **G:** 202-203
  Ice formation **I:** 9
  Water *picture on* **W:** 117
Iceberg Lake [Montana]
  Glacier National Park (Lakes) **G:** 205
Iceberg lettuce
  Lettuce (Kinds of lettuce) **L:** 213 *with picture*
Icebergia [nickname]
  Alaska **A:** 283
Iceboating **I:** 18 *with pictures*
Icebox

Refrigeration (Ice) **R:** 200 *with picture*
Icebreaker [ship] **I:** 19 *with picture*
  Antarctica (Scientific research) **A:** 539-540
  Arctic Ocean (Use) **A:** 644
  Canada *picture on* **C:** 120
  Coast Guard, United States (Mobility) **Ci:** 735 *with picture*
Icecap **I:** 19
  See also Ice sheet *in this index*
  Climate (Icecap climates) **Ci:** 676d
  Glacier (Kinds of glaciers) **G:** 202
  Ice formation **I:** 9
IceCube Neutrino Detector [machine]
  Neutrino **N:** 154-155
Iced tea
  Tea (Brewing tea) **T:** 63; (History) **T:** 63-64
Icefields Parkway [Alberta]
  Jasper National Park **J:** 64
Iceland **I:** 20 *with pictures and map*
  See also the list of Related articles in the Iceland *article*
  Flag *picture on* **F:** 206
  Scandinavia **S:** 170 *with map*
  Vikings (Viking influence) **V:** 383
Iceland poppy
  Poppy **P:** 668
Iceland poppy [plant]
  Flower *picture on* **F:** 277
Icelandic language
  Iceland (People) **I:** 21
Icelandic literature
  Saga **S:** 17
  Skald **S:** 478
Iceman [anthropology]
  Mummy (Other mummies) **M:** 926
Iceman Cometh, The [play by O'Neill]
  O'Neill, Eugene (His life) **O:** 762
"Ichabod" [poem by Whittier]
  Whittier, John Greenleaf **W:** 295
Ichiyo, Higuchi [Japanese author] *See* Higuchi Ichiyo *in this index*
Ichneumon wasp [insect] **I:** 24 *with picture*
  Insect *picture on* **I:** 294; (The variety of insects) **I:** 280-281
Ichthyology [zoology] **I:** 24
  Biology (table) **B:** 317
  Fish (Kinds of fish) **F:** 147
  Zoology (What zoologists study) **Z:** 606-607
Ichthyornis [extinct bird]
  Bird (The first known birds) **B:** 369
Ichthyosaur [extinct animal] **I:** 24 *with picture*
  Anning, Mary **A:** 517
  Prehistoric animal (Other reptiles) **P:** 737
Ichthyostega [extinct animal]
  Fossil (Tracing the development of life) **F:** 423
Icibemba [language and culture] *See* Bemba *in this index*
Icing the puck [hockey]
  Hockey (Defensive play) **H:** 278 *with picture*
Ickes, Harold Le Claire [American government official]
  Interior, Department of the (table) **I:** 325
  Roosevelt, Franklin Delano **R:** 454
  Truman, Harry S. (table) **T:** 469
Icon [computing]
  Computer (A mouse) **Ci:** 912-914
Icon [religion] **I:** 24 *with picture*
  Byzantine art (Other art forms) **B:** 751 *with picture*
  Eastern Orthodox Churches (Church buildings) **E:** 46
  Painting (Medieval painting) **P:** 48-49 *with picture*
  Russia (Painting and sculpture) **R:** 537 *with picture*
Iconoclast [religion]
  Byzantine art (Frescoes and mosaics) **B:** 750
  Byzantine Empire (Loss and transition) **B:** 754
  Idolatry **I:** 47
Iconoclastic controversy [Byzantine history]
  Byzantine art (Frescoes and mosaics) **B:** 750
Iconoscope [television] **I:** 25
  Television (Early development) **T:** 127
  Zworykin, Vladimir Kosma **Z:** 610
Iconostasis [religion]
  Altar **A:** 388
  Eastern Orthodox Churches (Church buildings) **E:** 46
Icosahedral symmetry [biology]
  Virus (Structure) **V:** 427-428 *with picture*
Icosahedron [geometry]
  Geometry (Solid geometry) **G:** 104-105
  Polyhedron **P:** 651 *with diagram*
  Topology (Algebraic topology) **T:** 332 *with picture*
ICSI [reproduction] *See* Intracytoplasmic sperm injection *in this index*
ICSU [organization] *See* International Council for Science *in this index*
Ictinus [Greek architect]
  Parthenon **P:** 183

ICU [medicine] *See* Intensive care unit *in this index*
Id [psychology]
Ego E: 119
Freud, Sigmund (On the mind) F: 530
Mythology (Psychological approaches) M: 990
Personality (Freud's psychoanalytic theory) P: 302
Psychoanalysis (Psychoanalytic theory) P: 846
`Id al-Ad-hā [festival] I: 25
Feasts and festivals (In Islam) F: 58
Islam (Holidays and celebrations) I: 465
`Id al-Fitr [festival] I: 25
Feasts and festivals (In Islam) F: 58
Islam (Holidays and celebrations) I: 465
Ramadan R: 132
Ida [asteroid]
Asteroid *picture on* A: 824; (History of study)
A: 824b
IDA [organization] *See* International Development
Association *in this index*
Ida, Mount
Crete (Land and climate) Ci: 1127
Idaho I: 26 *with pictures and maps*
See also the list of Related articles in the Idaho
article
Idaho, University of I: 45
Idaho I: 30 *with picture*
Idaho Falls [Idaho] I: 45
Idaho National Laboratory I: 45
Idaho (Postwar changes) I: 44
Idaho, University of I: 45
Idaho Power Company
Idaho (Postwar changes) I: 44-45
Idaho State University I: 46
IDE [computing] *See* Integrated development
environment *in this index*
Idea [philosophy]
See also Forms, Theory of *in this index*
Hume, David (Hume's thought) H: 432
Idealism I: 46
Philosophy (Plato) P: 387; (Empiricism) P: 389
"Idea of a University, The" [lecture]
Newman, John Henry N: 378
Ideal Husband, An [play by Wilde]
Wilde, Oscar W: 301
Ideal type [sociology]
Sociology (Development of social research)
So: 566
Idealism [philosophy] I: 46
Berkeley, George B: 259
Fichte, Johann Gottlieb F: 90
Materialism M: 300b
Moore, G. E. M: 796
Philosophy (Metaphysics) P: 383-384; (Plato)
P: 387
Plato (The theory of forms) P: 568
Royce, Josiah R: 499
Ideas, Comedy of
Comedy Ci: 867
Ideas, Theory of [philosophy] *See* Forms, Theory
of *in this index*
Ideas and Integrities [book by Fuller]
Fuller, Buckminster F: 554
Ideas of Madame Aubray, The [play by Dumas]
Dumas, Alexandre, fils D: 382
Ideas on the Philosophy of the History of Mankind
[book by Herder]
Herder, Johann Gottfried von H: 199
Identical twins
Cloning (Differences among clones) Ci: 683
Conjoined twins Ci: 950 *with picture*
Heredity (Heredity and environment) H: 205
Multiple birth M: 919
Reproduction, Human (Multiple birth) R: 246
Identification [criminology]
Fingerprinting F: 106
Footprinting F: 369 *with picture*
Identity [psychology]
Adolescent (Psychological development) A: 62
Clothing (Identity) C: 687
Erikson, Erik Homburger E: 351
Internet (Identity and privacy) I: 350f
Identity crisis [psychology]
Adolescent (The "invention" of adolescence)
A: 60; (Identity and self-esteem) A: 62
Erikson, Erik Homburger E: 352
Identity group [sociology]
Minority group M: 609
Social class (How people are categorized)
So: 550-551
Identity theft [crime] I: 46
Fraud F: 496
Internet (Internet crime) I: 350f
Identity: Youth and Crisis [book by Erikson]
Erikson, Erik Homburger E: 352
Ideogram [writing]
Hieroglyphics (Development of hieroglyphic
writing) H: 225-226

Writing system (Ideograms) W: 512
Ideography *See* Ideogram *in this index*
Ideology [philosophy] I: 46
War (Clashing ideologies) W: 23
Ides [Roman calendar]
Month M: 767
Ides of March, The [book by Wilder]
Wilder, Thornton W: 303
Idiographic study
Abnormal psychology (Studies in abnormal
psychology) A: 12
Idiom [language]
Dictionary (What dictionaries contain) D: 192
Slang S: 499
Idiorrhythmic religious life
Religious life (The Eastern Orthodox Churches)
R: 227
Idiot's Delight [play by Sherwood]
Sherwood, Robert Emmet S: 398
Iditabike [race]
Bicycle racing (Road races) B: 292-293
Iditarod [sled dog race] I: 47
Alaska (Visitor's guide) A: 290 *with picture*
Bicycle racing (Road races) B: 292-293
Nome N: 452
IDL [geography] *See* International date line *in this
index*
Idlak [weapon]
Inuit (Hunting and fishing) I: 354d
Idle, Eric [British actor]
Cleese, John Ci: 661 *with picture*
"Monty Python's Flying Circus" M: 780
Idler gear
Transmission (The gears) T: 378 *with diagram*
Ido [language]
Universal language U: 205
Idol of the Mind [philosophy]
Bacon, Francis (His philosophy) B: 18
Idolatry [religion] I: 47
Idris I [king of Libya]
Libya (Independence) L: 267
Idris ibn Abd Allah [Arab leader]
Morocco (Arab conquest) M: 814
Muslims (The fall of the Abbāsids) M: 964c
Idrisī, al- [Arab geographer] *See* Al-Idrisī *in this
index*
Idrisid dynasty
Morocco (Arab conquest) M: 814
IDS Center [Minneapolis]
Architecture *picture on* A: 606
Minneapolis (The city) M: 580-581
Minnesota *picture on* M: 585
Idumea [ancient region]
Edom E: 85
Idyl [poetry] I: 47
Tennyson, Lord (His poems) T: 166f-167
Idylls of the King [book by Tennyson]
Lancelot, Sir L: 56
IEA [agency]
International Energy Agency I: 339
IED [weapon] *See* Improvised explosive device *in
this index*
Ieper [Belgium]
Ypres Y: 574
IES [organization]
Lighting (In offices, stores, and factories) L: 296-
297
Ieyasu Tokugawa [Japanese political leader] *See*
Tokugawa Ieyasu *in this index*
If He Hollers Let Him Go [book by Himes]
Himes, Chester H: 234
"If We Must Die" [poem by McKay]
Poetry (Stress meters) P: 593-594
IFAD [organization] *See* International Fund for
Agricultural Development *in this index*
IFC [organization] *See* International Finance
Corporation *in this index*
Ife [city, Nigeria]
Ife I: 47
Ife [former country] I: 47
Benin B: 251
Pottery *picture on* P: 717; (Early pottery) P: 718
IFLA [organization]
Library (International library programs) L: 254
IFP [political party] *See* Inkatha Freedom Party *in
this index*
IFR [aviation]
Airplane (Electronic navigation) A: 227; (Safety)
A: 227
Map (Navigation maps) M: 178
Iftar [meal]
Ramadan R: 132
IG [office]
Inspector General I: 304
Igal [clothing] *See* Iqal *in this index*
Igbo [people] I: 47
Nigeria (People) N: 411

IgE [physiology]
Allergy (Allergic reactions) A: 373
IgE receptor [physiology]
Allergy (The development of allergies) A: 374
Igitur [poem by Mallarmé]
Mallarmé, Stéphane M: 111
Iglesia de la Compañía de Jesús [cathedral]
Latin America *picture on* L: 100
Igloo [dwelling] I: 48 *with diagrams*
See also Snowhouse *in this index*
Ignarro, Louis Joseph [American pharmacologist]
Nobel Prizes (Physiology or medicine: 1998)
N: 446
Ignatieff, George [Canadian diplomat]
United Nations (table) U: 86
Ignatieff, Michael [Canadian political leader] I: 48
with portrait
Liberal Party of Canada L: 227
Ignatius, Saint [early Christian] I: 48
Ignatius Loyola, Saint *See* Loyola, Saint Ignatius
in this index
Igneous rock [geology] I: 49
Earth (Earth's rocks) E: 20-21 *with picture*
Gem (Sources of gems) G: 78
Mountain (Volcanic mountains) M: 892
Rock (Igneous rock) R: 371 *with pictures*; (The
rock cycle) R: 373
Ignition [engineering] I: 49
Automobile (Powering an internal-combustion
car) A: 951 *with diagram*; (Providing electric
power) A: 951
Diesel engine (How a diesel engine works) D: 199
Gasoline engine *picture on* G: 63; (The ignition
system) G: 65
Induction coil I: 240
Magneto M: 62
Rocket (Solid-propellant rockets) R: 387
Ignition coil
Ignition (Parts of an ignition system) I: 49
Ignition switch [battery ignition]
Ignition (Parts of an ignition system) I: 49
Ignition system
Rocket (Liquid-propellant rockets) R: 388
Ignition temperature
Combustion Ci: 867
Fire (How fire is produced) F: 121
Igrayne [legendary figure]
Arthur, King A: 757
Iguaçu Falls [falls, Argentina-Brazil] I: 50
Argentina (Northern Argentina) A: 652-653 *with
map*
Brazil *picture on* B: 579
National park (Argentina) N: 42b *with picture*
South America (Waterfalls) So: 628
Iguaçu National Park [Brazil]
National park (Argentina) N: 42b *with picture*;
(table) N: 42g
Iguaçu River [Argentina-Brazil]
Brazil (The Central and Southern Plateaus) B: 580
Iguaçu Falls I: 50
Iguala, Plan of [Mexican history]
Iturbide, Agustín de I: 520
Iguana [reptile] I: 50 *with picture*
Animal *picture on* A: 480
Galapagos Islands G: 7 *with picture*
Iguanodon [dinosaur] I: 50 *with picture*
Dinosaur *picture on* D: 207; (True dinosaurs)
D: 206b-206c; (Dinosaur discoveries) D: 213
Iguazú Falls [falls, Argentina-Brazil] *See* Iguaçu Falls
in this index
Iguazú National Park [Argentina]
National park (Argentina) N: 42b; (table) N: 42g
IGY [program] *See* International Geophysical Year
in this index
Ihara Saikaku [Japanese author]
Japanese literature (The Tokugawa period) J: 62
Ihram [garment]
Islam (The Five Pillars of Islam) I: 463-464
IIHF [organization] *See* International Ice Hockey
Federation *in this index*
Ijma [religion]
Sharī`ah S: 374
IJsselmeer [region, Netherlands]
Netherlands N: 138
Ike [nickname]
Eisenhower, Dwight David E: 148
IKEA [company]
Sweden *picture on* So: 1032; (Industrial design)
So: 1027
Ikeda, Kikunae [Japanese chemist]
Monosodium glutamate M: 733
Ikeya-Seki, Comet [astronomy]
Comet (table) Ci: 868
Ikhwan [religious group]
Saudi Arabia (The founding of Saudi Arabia)
S: 161
Ikhwān al-Muslimūn [movement] *See* Muslim

Brotherhood *in this index*

Il ...
Titles beginning Il *appear under their key words, as in* Trovatore, Il

ILA [labor union]
Bridges, Harry B: 607

Île de Bourbon [former name]
Nova Scotia (Exploration and settlement) N: 567-568

Île-de-France [French history]
Middle Ages (Feudal government) M: 524 *with map*

Île de France [Mauritian history]
Mauritius (History) M: 317

Île de la Cité [island]
Paris *picture on* P: 160; (The city) P: 161-162 *with map*

Île d'Orléans [island]
Quebec (Places to visit) Q: 20 *with picture*
Quebec, Battle of (Bombardment of Quebec) Q: 37

Ile Saint Jean [former name]
Prince Edward Island (Exploration and early history) P: 791

Ileitis [disorder] *See* Crohn's disease *in this index*

Ileum [anatomy]
Crohn's disease Ci: 1150

Iliac artery [anatomy]
Artery (Principal arteries) A: 751
Human body (table) H: 422 *with diagram*

Iliac vein [anatomy]
Human body (table) H: 422 *with diagram*

Iliad [poem by Homer] I: 51
See also the list of Related articles in the Iliad *article*
Achaeans A: 25
Epic E: 342
Greek language (Development of ancient Greek) G: 376
Greek literature (Epic poetry) G: 377
Hector H: 164
Homer H: 303
Literature for children (Epics) L: 358
Mythology (Greek mythology) M: 980
Odyssey O: 675
Poetry (Narrative poetry) P: 591; (Ancient poetry) P: 595
Schliemann, Heinrich S: 177
Trojan War (The siege of Troy) T: 449
Troy T: 454
Ulysses U: 17

Iliamna Lake [Alaska]
Alaska (Rivers and lakes) A: 294-295

Iliescu, Ion [Romanian political leader]
Romania (Protests and political change) R: 425

Ilium [anatomy]
Dinosaur *picture on* D: 206c
Frog *picture on* F: 537
Hip H: 238 *with diagram*
Human body (table) H: 422 *with diagram*
Pelvis P: 233 *with diagram*

Ilium [ancient city] *See* Troy *in this index*

Ilkhans [Mongol history]
Mongol Empire (Breakup) M: 721

Illecillewaet Glacier [British Columbia]
Selkirk Mountains S: 290

Illegal alien I: 51
Alien A: 368
Amnesty (Since the early 1900's) A: 437-438
Deportation D: 149
Fourteenth Amendment F: 438
Hispanic Americans (Immigration restrictions and growing discrimination) H: 252; (Effects of World War II) H: 253; (Hispanic American immigration today) H: 255
Immigration (The fourth wave) I: 83
Immigration and Naturalization Service I: 86
United States, History of the (Immigration) U: 196f

Illegal procedure
Football (Violations and penalties) F: 363

Illica, Luigi [Italian librettist]
Opera (*Bohème, La*) O: 801; (*Madama Butterfly*) O: 804; (*Tosca*) O: 807

Illilouette Falls
Yosemite National Park (Waterfalls) Y: 570

Illimani [mountain, Bolivia]
Andes Mountains (Physical features) A: 452

Illini Indians *See* Illinois Indians *in this index*

Illiniwek Indians *See* Illinois Indians *in this index*

Illinoian ice age [geology]
Ice age (Evidence of ice ages and their climates) I: 6-7

Illinois I: 52 *with pictures and maps*
See also the list of Related articles in the Illinois *article*
Capital punishment (History of capital punishment) C: 193-194

Revolution, American (The Illinois campaign) R: 284

Illinois, University of I: 77
Chicago (Education) C: 427
Illinois *picture on* I: 56

Illinois and Michigan Canal [Illinois]
Chicago (Growth as a city) C: 434
Illinois (Early statehood) I: 74

Illinois and Michigan National Heritage Corridor [historic area]
Illinois (Places to visit) I: 62

Illinois Confederacy [American Indians]
Illinois (Indian days) I: 72

Illinois ex rel. McCollum v. Board of Education [U.S. history]
Religious education (Public schools) R: 225

Illinois Indians I: 78
Illinois I: 53; (Indian days) I: 72

Illinois Institute of Technology
Architecture *picture on* A: 632
Mies van der Rohe, Ludwig M: 537

Illinois Medical District
Chicago (The West Side) C: 424

Illinois River I: 78
Illinois (Rivers and lakes) I: 64-66 *with picture*

Illinois Waterway
Illinois (Rivers and lakes) I: 64-66

Illiteracy *See* Literacy *in this index*

Illness *See* Disease *in this index*

Illuminance [light] *See* Illumination *in this index*

Illuminated manuscript I: 78 *with picture*
Book (The Middle Ages) B: 466
Byzantine art (Other art forms) B: 751 *with picture*
Calligraphy C: 68
Manuscript (European manuscripts of the Middle Ages) M: 173 *with picture*
Painting (Medieval painting) P: 48-49 *with pictures*
Scribe S: 226
Pictures
  Bible *picture on* B: 283
  Book *picture on* B: 464
  Communication *picture on* Ci: 881
  Crossbow *picture on* Ci: 1156
  England *picture on* E: 307
  Europe *picture on* E: 409
  Gothic art *picture on* G: 279
  Joan of Arc, Saint *pictures on* J: 128
  Law *picture on* L: 135
  Middle Ages *pictures on* M: 522, M: 523

Illuminated printing [engraving]
Blake, William B: 397

Illuminating Engineering Society of North America
Lighting (In offices, stores, and factories) L: 296-297

Illuminating grenade
Grenade G: 390

Illuminating shell [ammunition] *See* Star shell *in this index*

Illumination [art] *See* Illuminated manuscript *in this index*

Illumination [light]
Foot-candle F: 353

Illuminations [poems by Rimbaud]
Rimbaud, Arthur R: 341

Illusion [vision]
See also Optical illusion *in this index*
Magician (Illusions) M: 51
Perception (Principles of perception) P: 284 *with pictures*
Ventriloquism V: 309

Illusionist
Magician (Illusions) M: 51

Illusionistic surrealism [art]
Painting (Surrealism) P: 81

Illustrated London News [British magazine]
Magazine (Magazines in the 1800's) M: 45

Illustration [art]
Encyclopedia (Illustrations) E: 266; (Illustrating the article) E: 267 *with picture*
Literature for children (The rise of illustration) L: 364
Printing (Preparing illustrations for reproduction) P: 797
Publishing (Art and design) P: 867

Illustration award
Caldecott Medal C: 26
Literature for children (Awards) L: 367

Illustration model
Modeling (Kinds of models) M: 684

Illustrations of the Huttonian Theory [book by Playfair]
Geology (The rock dispute) G: 98-99

"Illustrations of the Logic of Science" [essays by Peirce]
Pragmatism P: 729

Illustrative cartoon
Cartoon (Illustration) C: 266 *with picture*; (Developing the idea) C: 266-267

Illyrians [ancient people]
Albania (History) A: 307
Bosnia-Herzegovina (History) B: 492

Ilmen, Lake [Russia]
Lake Ilmen L: 39

Ilmenite [mineral] I: 78
Titanium T: 300

ILO [organization] *See* International Labour Organization *in this index*

Iloilo [Philippines] I: 79

Ilopango Lake [El Salvador]
El Salvador *picture on* E: 248

Ilus [legendary figure]
Troy T: 454

ILWU [labor union]
Bridges, Harry B: 607

IM [communication] *See* Instant messaging *in this index*

I'm No Angel [film]
West, Mae W: 199

I'm Not Stiller [book by Frisch]
Frisch, Max F: 535

Image [light]
Lens (Creating an image) L: 196 *with diagrams*
Mirror M: 616 *with diagrams*
Photography P: 406
Telescope (Producing detailed images) T: 103
Television (Creating television signals) T: 121

Image [religion]
Icon I: 24
Idolatry I: 47

Image assembly [printing] *See* Page makeup *in this index*

Image dissector [electronics]
Farnsworth, Philo Taylor F: 46

Image intensifier
Fluoroscopy F: 306
Night vision systems N: 419

Image object
Projector (Projector operation) P: 816

Image orthicon [electronic device] I: 79
Iconoscope I: 25

Image sensor [electronics]
Camera C: 80
Photography (How a camera works) P: 407

Imager [instrument]
Hubble Space Telescope (How the telescope works) H: 403

Imagery [language]
Poetry (Imagery) P: 595
Shakespeare, William (Imagery) S: 368

Imaginary Landscape No. 4 [music by Cage]
Cage, John C: 14

Imaginary number
Gauss, Carl Friedrich G: 70
Mathematics (Branches of mathematics) M: 303
Number (Beyond real numbers) N: 607
Square root (Square roots of negative numbers) So: 812

Imaginary unit [mathematics]
Euler, Leonhard E: 378
Number (Complex numbers) N: 606

Imagination I: 79
Brain (Memory and imagination) B: 554

Imagine Canada [organization]
Foundation F: 430

Imaging software
Photography (Processing digital images) P: 422

Imagists [art]
Painting (New image painting) P: 87

Imagists [literature]
American literature (Modernist poetry) A: 421
Doolittle, Hilda D: 309
Free verse F: 500
Lowell, Amy L: 509
Poetry (Poetry of the 1900's) P: 597

Imago [entomology] I: 79
Metamorphosis (The adult) M: 428

Imām [religious leader]
Islam (The Five Pillars of Islam) I: 463-464; (Divisions of Islam) I: 466
Mullah M: 914
Muslims (Ali) M: 964b
Shī`ites S: 400

Imāmi Shī`ah [religion]
Islam (Divisions of Islam) I: 466

IMAP [electonics]
Internet (Software) I: 350c-350d

Imari porcelain
Porcelain (Oriental porcelain) P: 676-677

Imbolc [holiday]
Witchcraft (Witchcraft as a religion) W: 371-372

IMF [organization] *See* International Monetary Fund *in this index*

Imhotep [ancient Egyptian doctor] **I:** 79
Pyramids (The first pyramids) **P:** 916
Imitation [music]
Bach, Johann Sebastian (His works) **B:** 16
Imitation [psychology]
Education (History) **E:** 97
Personality (Personality development) **P:** 302
Imitation diamond
Diamond (Imitation diamonds) **D:** 183
Imitation of Christ [book by Thomas à Kempis]
Thomas à Kempis **T:** 262
Imitations of Horace [book by Pope]
Pope, Alexander **P:** 667
Imitative magic
Magic (Homeopathic magic) **M:** 49
Immaculate Conception [religion] **I:** 79
Annunciation **A:** 518
Duns Scotus, John **D:** 386
Pius IX **P:** 503
Immaculate Conception, The [painting by Murillo]
Murillo, Bartolomé Esteban **M:** 930
Immersion [religious rite]
Baptism **B:** 101
Baptists **B:** 101
Immersion Cinema [exhibit]
National Museum of Natural History *picture on*
N: 41
Immersion education
Bilingual education (Immersion education)
B: 300
Immersion experience
Aquarium, Public (Displaying exhibits) **A:** 578b-
579
Immersion foot [disorder] **I:** 79
Immigrant *See* Immigration *in this index*
Immigration **I:** 80 *with pictures*
Alien **A:** 367
Arab Americans (History of Arab immigration)
A: 581
Arizona (The early 2000's) **A:** 692
Asian Americans (History of Asian immigration)
A: 812d
Bush, George Walker (Immigration) **B:** 722j
Canada (Population) **C:** 105
Chicago (People) **C:** 426; (Growth as a city) **C:** 435
Citizenship and Immigration Services, United
States **Ci:** 572
City (Cultural variety in cities) **Ci:** 593
Colonial life in America (Population growth)
Ci: 791
Cuba (Foreign relations) **Ci:** 1178-1179
Deportation **D:** 149
Ellis Island **E:** 243
Family and consumer sciences (History) **F:** 26
Hispanic Americans **H:** 244; (History) **H:** 250 *with
pictures*
Illegal alien **I:** 51
Kindergarten (Kindergartens today) **K:** 319
London (Ancestry) **L:** 430
McCain, John (Political career) **M:** 332a
Minority group (The creation of minority groups)
M: 609
Multiculturalism **M:** 919
New York City (The growing city) **N:** 341-342
with picture
Obama, Barack (Immigration policy) **O:** 641
Roaring Twenties (Changing attitudes) **R:** 363
Statue of Liberty (Growth as a symbol) **So:** 877-
878
United States (Ancestry) **U:** 108-109
United States, History of the *pictures on* **U:** 182;
(Immigration) **U:** 172; (A growing population)
U: 180; (Immigration) **U:** 196f
Immigration Act [1924]
Asian Americans (Asian immigration halted)
A: 812e-812f
Oriental Exclusion Acts **O:** 855
United States, History of the (Looking backward)
U: 191
Immigration Act [1990]
Citizenship (Laws passed by Congress) **Ci:** 571
**Immigration and Customs Enforcement, United
States** [agency]
Customs Service, United States **Ci:** 1201
Homeland Security, Department of
(Organization) **H:** 301
Immigration and Naturalization Service **I:** 86
Immigration and Nationality Act [1952]
Asian Americans (Restrictions lifted) **A:** 813
Citizenship (Laws passed by Congress) **Ci:** 571
Immigration (A temporary decline) **I:** 83; (The
fourth wave) **I:** 83
McCarran, Patrick Anthony **M:** 332a
Oriental Exclusion Acts **O:** 855
Immigration and Naturalization Service [U.S.]
I: 86
Citizenship and Immigration Services, United

States **Ci:** 572
Immigration Reform and Control Act [1986]
Hispanic Americans (Stricter immigration laws)
H: 255
Immigration (The fourth wave) **I:** 83
Immigration Restriction Act [1901]
Australia (Social policies) **A:** 924
Immoralist, The [book by Gide]
Gide, André **G:** 188
Immortal Thirty-Three [Uruguayan history]
Uruguay (Independence) **U:** 227
Immortality [religion] **I:** 86
Death **D:** 61
Egypt, Ancient (Religion) **E:** 137-138
Mythology (Mythical beings) **M:** 975
Plato (Immortality of the soul) **P:** 568
Immortals, The [members of]
French Academy **F:** 511
Immortelle [plant] **I:** 86 *with picture*
Immovable feast [religion]
Calendar (The Christian church calendar) **C:** 29
Immune deficiency disease
(Other disorders of the immune system) **I:** 89c
Immune globulins [physiology]
Gamma globulin **G:** 23
Immune memory [physiology]
Virus (Immune response) **V:** 428a
Immune reaction *See* Immune response *in this
index*
Immune response [physiology]
C-reactive protein **C:** 2
Disease (Immune responses) **D:** 231
Immune system **I:** 87; (The immune response)
I: 88 *with diagrams*
Interferon **I:** 324
Interleukin **I:** 335
Immune system [physiology] **I:** 87 *with pictures*
Addison's disease **A:** 48
AIDS **A:** 164
Allergy **A:** 373
Biology (Current research and issues) **B:** 320
Blood (Protecting against disease) **B:** 410
Cancer (Biological response modifiers) **C:** 172
Chronic fatigue syndrome **C:** 539
Cyclosporine **C:** 1204
Disease (Disorders of the immune system)
D: 229; (Immune responses) **D:** 231
Doherty, Peter Charles **D:** 284
Heredity (The era of genetic engineering) **H:** 209
Inoculation **I:** 276
Interleukin **I:** 335
Lupus **L:** 526
Monoclonal antibody **M:** 731
Pasteur, Louis (His work in medicine) **P:** 193
Prophylaxis **P:** 827
Stress (Stress-related illnesses) **So:** 927
Thymus **T:** 274
Transplant (Preventing rejection) **T:** 380
Virus (Immune response) **V:** 428a
Immunity [physiology]
See also Immune system *in this index*
Disease (Immune responses) **D:** 231-232
Immune system **I:** 87
Immunization (Active immunization) **I:** 89;
(Passive immunization) **I:** 89
Immunity, Congressional
Constitution of the United States (Article I,
Section 6) **Ci:** 1006
House of Representatives (Salary and privileges)
H: 386
Senate (Salary and privileges) **S:** 294
Immunity, Diplomatic *See* Diplomatic immunity
in this index
Immunization [medicine] **I:** 89
Child (Understanding the child's basic needs)
C: 451
Drug (Vaccines) **D:** 351
Hay fever (Treatment) **H:** 116
Health (Public health) **H:** 127
Immune system (Active immunity) **I:** 88a
Medicine (The medical revolution) **M:** 376-377
Public health (Providing preventice health care
services) **P:** 856 *with picture*
Immunoassay [test]
Drug testing **D:** 366
Immunoglobulin [physiology]
Allergy (Allergic reactions) **A:** 373
Immune system (The humoral immune response)
I: 88
Immunology [medicine]
Biology (table) **B:** 317
Immune system **I:** 87
Medicine (The development of immunology)
M: 374
Prophylaxis **P:** 827
Immunosuppressive drug
Drug (Immunosuppressive drugs) **D:** 353

Immune system (The cell-mediated immune
response) **I:** 88-88a
Myasthenia gravis **M:** 970f
Transplant (Preventing rejection) **T:** 380-381
Immunotherapy [medicine]
Allergy (Treatment) **A:** 374
Cancer (Biological response modifiers) **C:** 172
IMO [organization]
International Maritime Organization **I:** 342
Imo [ship]
Halifax explosion **H:** 22
Imogen [literary figure]
Shakespeare, William: (*Cymbeline*) **S:** 365
Impact basin [geology]
Mars (Craters and impact basins) **M:** 226
Meteor (Impact craters and basins) **M:** 432
Impact crater
Asteroid (Origin and development) **A:** 824a
Crater **Ci:** 1121 *with diagrams*
Meteor (Impact craters and basins) **M:** 432
Satellite (Physical characteristics) **S:** 149;
(Formation) **S:** 150
Saturn (Satellites) **S:** 151-152
Venus (Surface and atmosphere) **V:** 311-312 *with
picture*
Impact extrusion [industrial process]
Extrusion **E:** 459
Impact fuze [device]
Guided missile (The warhead) **G:** 423-424
Impact printer [electronic device]
Printer (Impact printers) **P:** 795
Impact vehicle
Comet (Studying comets) **Ci:** 868-869
Space exploration (Space probes) **So:** 708
Impacted wisdom tooth [anatomy]
Dentistry (Oral surgery) **D:** 144
Teeth (Permanent teeth) **T:** 79-80
Impactor [spacecraft] *See* Impact vehicle; Impact
vehicle *in this index*
Impala [animal] **I:** 90 *with picture*
Animal *picture on* **A:** 494
Antelope *picture on* **A:** 542
Impasto [art]
Painting (Other materials) **P:** 36; (The Dutch
masters) **P:** 62-64
Impatiens [plant] **I:** 90
Impeachment [government] **I:** 90
Arizona (The late 1900's) **A:** 691-692
Clinton, Bill (Domestic events) **Ci:** 682f
Congress of the United States (Impeaching and
trying federal officials) **Ci:** 946
Constitution of the United States (Article I,
Section 2) **Ci:** 1004-1005; (Article I, Section 3)
Ci: 1005; (Article II, Section 4) **Ci:** 1009
House of Representatives (Other powers and
duties) **H:** 387
Johnson, Andrew (Impeachment) **J:** 140
Nixon, Richard Milhous (Events at home) **N:** 435-
437
President of the United States (Term of office)
P: 758-762; (The impeachment of Bill Clinton)
P: 769
Reconstruction (The impeachment of Johnson)
R: 178
Senate (Other powers and duties) **S:** 295
United States, History of the (The Clinton
impeachment) **U:** 196d
Watergate (The resignation of Nixon) **W:** 145
Impedance [electricity]
Ohm's law **O:** 706
Impeller [device]
Pump (Centrifugal pumps) **P:** 900b *with diagram*
Transmission (A torque converter) **T:** 376
Imperative mood [grammar]
Conjugation **Ci:** 951
Mood (Imperative mood) **M:** 781
Sentence (Sentence classifications) **S:** 303
Imperfect flower
Flower (Variations in flower structure) **F:** 294
Plant *picture on* **P:** 530
Pollen (Self-pollination) **P:** 645
Imperforate stamp
Stamp collecting *picture on* **So:** 831; (Separations)
So: 830
Imperial [hair]
Beard **B:** 187
Imperial Airways
Aviation (The first airlines) **A:** 988
Imperial angelfish
Fish *picture on* **F:** 155
Imperial British East Africa Company
Kenya (British rule) **K:** 303
Imperial City [district]
Beijing (The city) **B:** 222 *with map*
Imperial Conference [British history]
Canada, History of (Independence) **C:** 147
Commonwealth of Nations (History) **Ci:** 876

Imperial Council Shrine Guilds of America, Inc.
Masonry (Organization) **M: 267**
Imperial gallon [measurement]
Gallon **G: 16**
Weights and measures (Inch-pound units) **W: 187**
Imperial Hotel [Tokyo]
Wright, Frank Lloyd (Early career) **W: 507-508**
Imperial Mosque [Isfahan, Iran]
Architecture *diagram on* **A: 614**
Imperial Palace [Tokyo]
Tokyo *picture on* **T: 320**; (The Imperial Palace)
T: 316
Imperial parrot [animal]
Endangered species (table) **E: 270**
Imperial Period [literature]
Latin literature (The Imperial Period) **L: 116**
Imperial pint [measurement]
Pint **P: 475**
Weights and measures (Miscellaneous weights
and measures) **W: 184**
Imperial Russian Nuptial Crown
Crown *picture on* **Ci: 1158**
Imperial standard gauge
Wire (Sizes of wire) **W: 344**
Imperial Technical School [Moscow]
Vocational education (Early vocational education
in schools) **V: 435**
Imperial University [ancient China]
Confucianism (Early Confucianism) **Ci: 936-937**
Imperial Valley [region, California] **I: 92**
Irrigation *map on* **I: 457**
Mexico (The Pacific Northwest) **M: 460**
Imperial War Cabinet [British history]
Borden, Sir Robert Laird *picture on* **B: 484**; (War
leader) **B: 486**
Imperialism [political science] **I: 92**
Colonialism **Ci: 813**
Communism (Lenin's contributions) **Ci: 890**
Government (The rise of monarchies and nation-
states) **G: 290**
United Kingdom (Gladstone and Disraeli) **U: 69**
World, History of the (Imperialism) **W: 445**
Imperialist, The [book by Duncan]
Canadian literature (Fiction: 1850-1918) **C: 157**
Impermeable rock [geology]
Petroleum (Migration) **P: 333-334**
Impetigo [disease]
Skin (Infections) **S: 490**
Implantable defibrillator [medicine]
Defibrillator **D: 88**
Implantable pump [medicine]
Drug (Entrance into the body) **D: 353**
Implantation [pregnancy]
Reproduction, Human (The first days of
pregnancy) **R: 246-247**
Implicit Price Deflator [economics]
Inflation (Measuring inflation) **I: 267**
Implicit Price Index [economics]
Inflation (Measuring inflation) **I: 267**
Implied authority [law]
Agent **A: 140**
Implied line
Photography (Line) **P: 409**
Implied powers
Congress of the United States (Origin of power)
Ci: 943
Constitution of the United States (The supreme
law of the land) **Ci: 998**
Executive order **E: 436**
Government (Presidential democracy) **G: 285**
Marshall, John (Chief justice) **M: 230**
McCulloch v. Maryland **M: 332g**
United States, History of the (The power of the
federal government) **U: 164**
Implosion method
Nuclear weapon *diagram on* **N: 598**; (Fission
weapons) **N: 596-597**
Impluvium [architecture]
Atrium **A: 877** *with picture*
Import *See* Exports and imports *in this index*
Import quota
Economics (The world economy) **E: 61**
Exports and imports (Import restrictions) **E: 454**
International trade (Government trade policies)
I: 348
World Trade Organization **W: 451**
Importance of Being Earnest, The [play by Wilde]
Wilde, Oscar **W: 302**
Imported cabbageworm [insect]
Insect (Quarantine systems) **I: 285** *with picture*
Impossibility theorem [economics]
Arrow, Kenneth Joseph **A: 743**
Impotence [physiology] *See* Erectile dysfunction
in this index
Impression [mark]
Engraving (Printing the engraving) **E: 325**
Forensic science (What a forensic scientist

analyzes) **F: 389**
Fossil (How fossils form) **F: 425** *with picture*
Impression [philosophy]
Hume, David (Hume's thought) **H: 432**
Philosophy (Empiricism) **P: 389**
Impression: Sunrise [painting by Monet]
Monet, Claude **M: 703**
Impression cylinder [printing]
Printing (Offset presses) **P: 798-799**
Impressionism [arts] **I: 93** *with pictures*
Cézanne, Paul **C: 364**
Classical music (The 1900's) **Ci: 649**
Expressionism **E: 455**
France (Painting) **F: 462**
German literature (Impressionism,
Neoromanticism, and Symbolism) **G: 141**
Matisse, Henri **M: 309**
Monet, Claude **M: 703** *with picture*
Morisot, Berthe **M: 805**
Painting (Edouard Manet and the Impressionists)
P: 71; (Painting outside France) **P: 72-73**
Pissarro, Camille **P: 496** *with picture*
Postimpressionism **P: 708**
Realism (In painting) **R: 172**
Renoir, Pierre Auguste **R: 241** *with picture*
Impressment Act [1863]
Civil War, American (Economy) **Ci: 623**
Impressment of seamen [American history]
War of 1812 (Impressment of seamen) **W: 29**
Imprint
Fossil (Formation of impressions, molds, and
casts) **F: 425**
Imprinting [psychology]
Instinct (Imprinting) **I: 305**
Imprisonment, False
False imprisonment **F: 19**
Impromptu speech
A Guide to Speaking Skills **Research Guide: 22**
Improper fraction
Fraction (Improper fractions) **F: 448**
Improvisation [arts]
Classical music (Solo music) **Ci: 643**
Drama (Commedia dell' arte) **D: 331**
Jazz **J: 68**
Improvised explosive device **I: 95**
Army, United States (The Iraq War [2003-2010])
A: 740
Impulse [physiology]
Nervous system (How the nervous system works)
N: 132 *with diagram*; (How neurons carry
impulses) **N: 134** *with diagrams*
Impulse buying
Advertising (Other ways of advertising) **A: 75**
Impulse turbine
Turbine (Kinds of turbines) **T: 496** *with picture*
Impulsive sound
Sound (Noises) **So: 599**
IMRT [medicine]
Radiation (Refining the uses of radiation) **R: 81**
Imu [cooking]
Hawaii (Food) **H: 94**
IMU [device]
Guided missile (Preset guidance) **G: 426**
In [symbol]
Indium **I: 224**
In a Green Night: Poems, 1948-1960 [poems by
Walcott]
Walcott, Derek **W: 6**
In a Mist [music by Beiderbecke]
Beiderbecke, Bix **B: 222**
In Abraham's Bosom [play by Green]
Green, Paul Eliot **G: 379**
In Chancery [book by Galsworthy]
Galsworthy, John **G: 16**
In Cold Blood [book by Capote]
Capote, Truman **C: 198**
Novel (The novel today) **N: 575**
In commission [military]
Commission, Military **Ci: 872**
In communion [religion]
Eastern Catholic Churches **E: 45**
In Dahomey [play]
Williams, Bert **W: 310**
In Dubious Battle [book by Steinbeck]
Steinbeck, John **So: 885**
"In Flanders Fields" [poem by McCrae]
McCrae, John **M: 332f**
In-goal [sports]
Rugby football (Rugby Union) **R: 510**; (Rugby
League) **R: 512**
In God We Trust [motto]
National Motto, United States **N: 40**
In-ground pool
Swimming pool **So: 1047** *with picture*
In-house agency
Advertising (Advertising departments) **A: 77**
In-laws

Family (Family relationships) **F: 21**
In-line engine
Automobile (The engine block) **A: 951-953**
Gasoline engine (Cylinder arrangement) **G: 64**
with diagram
In-line skate
Roller skating (Roller skates) **R: 402** *with picture*
"In Living Color" [television program]
Fox **F: 441**
In Memoriam [poem by Tennyson]
English literature (Later Victorian literature)
E: 321
Tennyson, Lord (His life) **T: 166f**; (His poems)
T: 166f-167
In Our Time [stories by Hemingway]
Hemingway, Ernest (Early life) **H: 180**
In Praise of Folly [book by Erasmus] *See Praise of
Folly in this index*
In print [publishing]
Publishing (Going out of print) **P: 869**
**In Retrospect: The Tragedy and Lessons of
Vietnam** [book by McNamara]
McNamara, Robert Strange **M: 344**
In Search of Myself [book by Grove]
Grove, Frederick Philip **G: 404**
In-service training
Education (Who should teach?) **E: 106-107**
Teaching (Continuing professional development)
T: 69
In situ solution mining
Uranium (Mining uranium) **U: 215**
In the Blood [play by Parks]
Parks, Suzan-Lori **P: 172**
In-the-canal hearing aid
Hearing aid (Styles) **H: 130**
"In the City of Slaughter" [poem by Bialik]
Bialik, Chaim Nachman **B: 278**
In the Clearing [poems by Frost]
Frost, Robert (His life) **F: 542-543**
In-the-ear hearing aid
Hearing aid (Styles) **H: 130**
In the Heart of the Country [book by Coetzee]
Novel (The novel today) **N: 575**
In the Heat of the Night [film]
Motion picture (Best picture: 1967) **M: 861**
In the Park [painting by Laurencin]
Laurencin, Marie *picture on* **L: 122**
In the Shadow of the Glen [play by Synge]
Synge, John Millington **So: 1067**
In the Shadow of Tomorrow [essays by Huizinga]
Huizinga, Johan **H: 411**
In the Steppes of Central Asia [music by Borodin]
Borodin, Alexander **B: 490**
In-vehicle navigation system
Map (Navigation maps) **M: 178**
In vitro fertilization [medicine] **I: 95**
Fallopian tube **F: 18**
Fertilization **F: 78**
Infertility (Treatment) **I: 265**
Multiple birth (Causes of multiple birth) **M: 920**
Pregnancy (Becoming pregnant) **P: 734a**
Surrogate birth **So: 1010**
"In Westminster Abbey" [poem by Betjeman]
Betjeman, John **B: 275**
In Which We Serve [film]
Lean, David **L: 162**
Inactivated vaccine [medicine]
Virus (Vaccines) **V: 428a**
Inadmissible Evidence [play by Osborne]
Osborne, John **O: 861**
Inalienable rights [philosophy]
United States, History of the (The Declaration of
Independence) **U: 160**
Inarching
Grafting (Other kinds of grafting) **G: 299**
Inauguration [ceremony]
President of the United States (The inauguration)
P: 762-763 *with picture*
Vice president of the United States (Inauguration)
V: 350
Inboard engine
Boating (Motorboats) **B: 428**
Motorboat racing (Hull designs) **M: 876**
Inboard-outboard [boat]
Boating *picture on* **B: 430**
Inboard-outboard motor
Boating (Motorboats) **B: 428**
Inbreeding [genetics]
Hybrid (Producing hybrid plants) **H: 461**
Livestock (Breeding livestock) **L: 398**
Zoo (Wildlife conservation) **Z: 600**
Inca [people] **I: 95** *with pictures and maps*
Architecture (Pre-Columbian architecture) **A: 614**
Bolivia (History) **B: 446-447**
Clothing (Inca) **Ci: 700**
De Soto, Hernando **D: 160**
Ecuador (History) **E: 73**

Indian, American *pictures on* **I: 140, I: 143, I: 144**; (Pottery) **I: 145**; (Weaving) **I: 146** *with picture*; (Beliefs) **I: 147**; (Shamans) **I: 148**; (Writing) **I: 150**; (Indians of the Andes) **I: 173-174** *with pictures*
Jewelry (Pre-Columbian jewelry) **J: 118**
Latin America *picture on* **L: 91**; (Architecture) **L: 99**; (Early inhabitants) **L: 102-103**
Machu Picchu **M: 20**
Mummy (Other mummies) **M: 926**
Panama (The Spanish colonial period) **P: 120**
Peru *picture on* **P: 311**; (History) **P: 314**
Pizarro, Francisco (Conquest of Peru) **P: 504** *with pictures*
Potato (History) **P: 713**
Quinoa **Q: 42**
Road (From the 500's to the 1800's) **R: 361**
Vicuña **V: 359**
World, History of the (Civilizations in the Americas) **W: 437** *with picture*
Inca, El [Latin American author] *See* Garcilaso de la Vega *in this index*
Incandescence [physics]
Light (Incandescence) **L: 283**
Luminescence **L: 522**
Incandescent lamp
Edison, Thomas Alva *picture on* **E: 81**; (The electric light) **E: 79**
Electric light (Incandescent lamps) **E: 174** *with picture*
Electric power (Early developments) **E: 186**
Interior design (Selecting accessories) **I: 333**
Invention *picture on* **I: 356**
Latimer, Lewis Howard **L: 90**
Light (Incandescence) **L: 283**
Light bulb **L: 293**
Lighting (Lighting devices) **L: 298**
Incantation
Magic (Magical words) **M: 49**
Incapacitation
Prison (How prisons operate) **P: 806**
Incarnation [religion]
Annunciation **A: 518**
Roman Catholic Church (Sin, the Incarnation, and salvation) **R: 403**
Incendiary bomb
Bomb (Incendiary bombs) **B: 451** *with diagram*
Incendiary weapon
Weapon **W: 154a**
Incense I: 99
Frankincense **F: 485**
Incentive [psychology]
Fatigue **F: 55**
Inceptisol [soil]
Soil *map on* **So: 575**; (How soils are classified) **So: 576**
Incest
Abortion (Arguments for abortion) **A: 15**
Family (Ancient families) **F: 21-22**
Marriage (Other marriage laws and practices) **M: 220**
Inch [measurement] **I: 99** *with pictures*
Inch-pound system [measurement]
Fraction (History) **F: 449-450**
Metric system **M: 436**; (The inch-pound system) **M: 437**
Weights and measures (Measurement systems) **W: 184**; (Comparison of measurement systems) **W: 185**; (Inch-pound units) **W: 187**
Inchcape Rock [reef, Scotland] **I: 99**
"Inchcape Rock, The" [poem by Southey]
Inchcape Rock **I: 99**
Inchon [South Korea] **I: 99**
Inchon landing [Korean War]
Amphibious warfare (History of amphibious warfare) **A: 442**
Korean War (The Inchon landing) **K: 381** *with map*
Inchworm [insect]
See also Measuring worm *in this index*
Insect *picture on* **I: 297**
Incident light meter
Photography (Exposure meters) **P: 413**
Incidental music
Classical music (Orchestral music) **Ci: 644**
Opera **O: 790**
Incidents from the Massacre at Chios [painting by Delacroix]
Delacroix, Eugène **D: 95**
Incidents in the Life of a Slave Girl [book by Jacobs]
African American literature (The 1800's) **A: 136a**
Child, Lydia Maria **C: 454**
Incineration
Waste disposal (Incineration) **W: 113**
Incinerator [furnace] **I: 99** *with picture*
Waste disposal (Incineration) **W: 113**
Incision

Surgery (A typical operation) **So: 1006**
Incisor [anatomy]
Beaver (Teeth) **B: 193** *with picture*
Elephant (Tusks and teeth) **E: 228**
Rodent **R: 397** *with picture*
Squirrel (The origin and development of squirrels) **So: 814b**
Teeth (Deciduous teeth) **T: 79**; (Permanent teeth) **T: 79** *with pictures*
Incitatus [horse]
Horse (table: Famous horses in history and legend) **H: 361**
Inclined orbit
Space exploration *diagrams on* **So: 697**
Inclined plane I: 100 *with picture*
Machine (Inclined plane) **M: 15** *with pictures*
Simple machines **S: 467**
Inclinometer [measuring device] **I: 100**
Inclusion [gem]
Emerald **E: 257**
Inclusive education
Disability (Education) **D: 220-221**
Inclusive fitness [biology]
Hamilton, William Donald **H: 33**
Inco Limited
Thompson **T: 262**
Incoherent light
Laser (Characteristics of laser light) **L: 84-85**
Income I: 100 *with diagrams*
Budget (Estimating income) **B: 670**; (Economic effects of the national budget) **B: 671-672**
Capitalism (Capitalism in its ideal form) **C: 194**
Careers (Probable earnings) **C: 216**
Communism (The centrally planned economy) **Ci: 891**
Cost of living **C: 1079**
Economics (Government intervention) **E: 59-61**; (Distribution of income) **E: 63**
Gross domestic product (Another way to measure GDP) **G: 399**
Inflation (Effects on income) **I: 268**
Investment **I: 366**; (table) **I: 366**; (Direct investments) **I: 367**
National income **N: 37**
Pension **P: 272**
Poverty (Poverty standards) **P: 723**
Social security (Old-age, survivors, and disability insurance) **So: 553**
Standard of living (Measuring standard of living) **So: 833**
Income-Based Repayment Plan [2007]
Universities and colleges (Student loan debt) **U: 211**
Income bond
Bond (Kinds of bonds) **B: 454**
Income fund
Mutual fund **M: 969**
Income inequality
Income (Income inequality) **I: 101**
Income statement
Accounting (Financial reports) **A: 22-23**
Bookkeeping (Bookkeeping and financial statements) **B: 473** *with picture*
Income tax I: 102 *with diagrams*
Capital gains tax **C: 192**
Constitution of the United States (Article I, Section 9) **Ci: 1007-1008**; (Amendment 16) **Ci: 1014**
Flat tax **F: 228**
Friedman, Milton **F: 533**
Government (Taxation) **G: 283**
Internal revenue (History) **I: 337**
Internal Revenue Service **I: 337**
Progressive Era (Economic reforms) **P: 813-814**
Recession (Fighting recession) **R: 175**
Tax Court, United States **T: 52**
Taxation (Income taxes) **T: 53**
Incompatibility
Divorce (No-fault divorce) **D: 253**
Incompetence [law] **I: 105**
Insanity **I: 277**
Incomplete flower
Flower (The parts of a flower) **F: 293**
Incomplete metamorphosis [biology]
Metamorphosis (Other examples) **M: 428**
Incomplete protein
Nutrition (Proteins) **N: 625**
Protein (Proteins in the diet) **P: 832**
Incompletely penetrant disease
Genetic testing (Disorders involving more than one gene) **G: 85**
Incompressible fluid
Fluid **F: 304**
Incongruity
Humor (The humor of situation) **H: 435**
Incontinence [disorder] **I: 106**
Bladder **B: 395**

Prostate cancer **P: 829**
Inconvenient Truth, An [film and book]
Gore, Al (Later years) **G: 274**
Incorporated territory
Territory (Territories in the United States) **T: 174**
Incorporation [law]
Corporation **Ci: 1069**
Delaware (Economy) **D: 106**
Incorporation [sociology]
Minority group (The creation of minority groups) **M: 609**
Rite of passage **R: 350**
Incorporation, Articles of
Charter **C: 385**
Corporation **Ci: 1069**
Incubation [biology]
Animal (Incubation) **A: 498** *with picture*
Bird (Laying and hatching eggs) **B: 357-359**
Reptile (Reproduction) **R: 252**
Incubation period [disease]
Disease (table) **D: 226**
Incubator [machine] **I: 106**
Chicken *picture on* **C: 444**; (Breeding and hatching) **C: 443**
Egg (How embryos develop) **E: 117-118**
Hospital *picture on* **H: 373**
Inculcation [teaching]
Moral education (Methods of moral education) **M: 799**
Incunabula [books]
Book (The development of printed books) **B: 466-467**
Library of Congress **L: 263**
Incus [anatomy]
Ear *diagram on* **E: 10**; (The middle ear) **E: 7-8** *with diagram*
IND [subway]
New York City (Transportation) **N: 334-335**
Indecent Obsession, An [book by McCullough]
McCullough, Colleen **M: 332g**
Indefatigable Island
Galapagos Islands **G: 7** *with map*
Indefinite, The [philosophy]
Anaximander **A: 448b**
Indefinite article
Article (The indefinite articles) **A: 758**
Indefinite pronoun
Pronoun **P: 820**
Indemnity
Insurance **I: 309**
Managed care plans **M: 131**
Indemnity benefit
Insurance (Insurance companies) **I: 311**
Indemnity Only [book by Paretsky]
Paretsky, Sara **P: 159**
Indenture [contract]
Indentured servant **I: 106**
Indentured servant I: 106
African Americans (Colonial times) **A: 136d**
Colonial life in America (The lower class) **Ci: 794**
Immigration (The first wave) **I: 82**
Plantation (Slave-labor plantations) **P: 550**
Transportation of convicts **T: 400**
United States, History of the (Why the colonists came) **U: 157**
West Indies (People) **W: 201**
Westward movement in America (The earliest settlements) **W: 244-245**
Independence [Missouri] **I: 106**
Mormons (Mormons in the Middle West) **M: 808-809**
Young, Brigham (Mormon leader) **Y: 571**
Independence [child development]
Adolescent (Independence and responsibility) **A: 62**
Baby (From 6 to 12 months) **B: 7**
Parent (The role of parents) **P: 156**; (Changes in parenthood) **P: 156**
Independence [ship]
Aircraft carrier (History) **A: 207**
Independence, Declaration of *See* Declaration of Independence *in this index*
Independence, War for *See* Revolution, American *in this index*
Independence Day I: 106
Independence Day [film]
Smith, Will **So: 518**
Independence Day [Mexico]
Hidalgo y Costilla, Miguel **H: 225**
Independence Day [Philippines]
Independence Day **I: 107**
Independence Day [U.S.]
Independence Day **I: 106**
July **J: 188**
United States, History of the *picture on* **U: 156**
Independence Hall [Philadelphia] **I: 107**
National Park System (table: National historical

parks) N: 56-57
Pennsylvania *picture on* P: 265
Philadelphia *picture on* P: 361; (Downtown
    Philadelphia) P: 359
Independence Medal [Turkey]
Medals, decorations, and orders (table) M: 359
Independence movements [political science]
*See also the History section of specific country
    articles, such as Peru (History)*
Africa (Struggles for independence) A: 134
Asia (The end of colonialism) A: 807
Latin America (The movement toward
    independence) L: 106
Nationalism (The rise of nationalism) N: 62-63
Union of Soviet Socialist Republics (Threats to
    unity) U: 40-41
Independence National Historical Park
[Pennsylvania]
National Park System (table: National historical
    parks) N: 56-57
Philadelphia (Downtown Philadelphia) P: 359
Independence Plaza
Montevideo M: 764b *with picture*
Independent [voter]
Voting (Voter turnout) V: 450
Independent agency [government]
President of the United States (The independent
    agencies) P: 764
United States, Government of the (Executive
    departments and agencies) U: 140
Independent agent
Insurance (How insurance is sold) I: 315
Independent assortment [genetics]
Heredity (Independent assortment) H: 203;
    (Mendel's laws) H: 208
Independent Assortment, Law of [biology]
Heredity (Mendel's laws) H: 208
Mendel, Gregor Johann (His work) M: 398
Independent clause
Clause Ci: 657
**Independent Community Authority of South
Africa**
South Africa (Communication) So: 617
Independent counsel [law] I: 107
Grand jury G: 308
Independent Counsel, Office of [U.S.]
Independent counsel I: 107
Independent foundation
Foundation (Kinds of foundations) F: 430
Independent living program
Children's Bureau C: 457
Foster care F: 429
Independent National Party [U.S. history]
Greenback Party G: 381
Independent National Patriotic Front of Liberia
[political group]
Liberia (Civil war) L: 232
Independent Order of ...
*Independent orders appear under their key words,
    as in Odd Fellows, Independent Order of*
Independent power producer
Electric power (The electric power industry)
    E: 186
Independent prosecutor [law] *See* Independent
counsel *in this index*
Independent-Republicans [political party]
Minnesota (Politics) M: 602-603; (The mid-1900's)
    M: 606
Independent school
Education (Education in the United Kingdom)
    E: 95
United Kingdom (Education) U: 56-57
Independent Smallholders' and Peasants' Party
[political party]
Hungary (Multiparty elections) H: 448
Independent station
Television (Commercial stations) T: 114
Independent study
Library (High school libraries) L: 245
Independent Television Commission
London (Communication) L: 438-439
Independent Theatre Society [theater group]
Drama (Early realism) D: 338
Independent treasury [U.S. history]
Van Buren, Martin (The independent treasury)
    V: 272
Independent Treasury Act [1846]
Polk, James Knox (An independent treasury)
    P: 643
Indeterminate inflorescence [botany]
Inflorescence I: 268a
Raceme R: 51
Indeterminate sentence [law]
Sentence S: 304
Index [economics]
Inflation (Measuring inflation) I: 267
Mortgage M: 820

Index [mathematics]
Root R: 469
Index [reference] I: 107
Book (Inside a book) B: 464-465
Encyclopedia (Arrangement of content) E: 266;
    (Ease of use) E: 266; (Indexing) E: 267 *with
    picture*
Map *picture on* M: 179; (Map indexes) M: 180
Search engine S: 268
Index, Stock *See* Stock index *in this index*
Index, The [church publication] *See* Index of
Forbidden Books *in this index*
Index fund
Mutual fund M: 969
Index glass [instrument]
Sextant S: 336
Index of Forbidden Books I: 107
Paul IV P: 200
Index of refraction [physics] *See* Refractive index
in this index
Indexation [economics]
Cost of living Ci: 1079
Income tax (Effects of inflation) I: 103
Inflation (Effects on income) I: 268
Indexes, Standard & Poor's [stock market]
Standard & Poor's indexes So: 833
Indexing [economics] *See* Indexation *in this index*
Indexing [information science]
Information retrieval (How information retrieval
    works) I: 268b
India I: 108 *with pictures and maps*
See also the list of Related articles in the India
    article
Asia (Way of life in South Asia) A: 781 *with picture*
Agriculture
Cotton (Leading cotton-producing countries)
    Ci: 1089
India (Agriculture) I: 125 *with picture and map*
Irrigation *picture on* I: 458
Tea T: 62
Art and architecture
India (The arts) I: 119
Bell *picture on* B: 239
Furniture (India) F: 572
Gupta dynasty (Cultural life under the guptas)
    G: 442
Music (Indian music) M: 956
Painting (Indian painting) P: 44 *with picture*
Sculpture (India) S: 236 *with pictures*
Communications and mass media
Television (In Asia) T: 116
Defense
Air force (The Indian Air Force) A: 184
Army (The Indian Army) A: 726
Independence Day I: 107
Navy (Major navies of the world) N: 78-79
Education
Education (Early Chinese and Indian education)
    E: 99
Government
India (Government) I: 109
Indian National Congress I: 185
Parliament (Parliaments in other countries)
    P: 174
Territory (Territories in other countries)
    T: 174-175
Health and welfare
Birth control (Birth control today) B: 379
Social security (Social security in other
    countries) So: 556
History
India (History) I: 128 *with pictures*
Asia (Other struggles) A: 810
Asian Americans (History of Asian immigration)
    A: 812d-812e
Bangladesh B: 78
Besant, Annie Wood B: 273
Bhopal disaster B: 276
Clinton, Bill (International affairs) Ci: 682f
Cold War (The great blocs split) Ci: 769
Da Gama, Vasco (Voyage to India) D: 4
Enclave E: 265
Famine (Causes of famine) F: 26
Gandhi, Mohandas Karamchand G: 24
Kashmir K: 247
Medicine (China and India) M: 372
Money (Indian coins) M: 707 *with picture*
Mountbatten, Louis M: 899
Muslim League M: 964
Nehru N: 120 *with picture*
Nuclear weapon (The end of the Cold War)
    N: 601-602
Pakistan (History) P: 98-99
Philosophy (Eastern philosophy) P: 386
Roma R: 402a
Seven Years' War (In North America and India)
    S: 328

Tsunami of 2004 T: 476
United Kingdom *picture on* U: 68
United Nations (Arms control) U: 92-93
World, History of the (The Mauryan Empire
    in India) W: 430 *with picture*; (The age of
    invasions of India) W: 436; (The Islamic
    empires) W: 441-442
World War II (The China-Burma-India theater)
    W: 491
Language and literature
Hindi language H: 234
Sanskrit literature S: 112
Urdu language U: 220
Manufacturing
India (Manufacturing) I: 125
Textile (In Asia) T: 218
People
India (People) I: 111
Caste C: 279
Clothing *pictures on* Ci: 689, Ci: 693;
    (Protection) Ci: 687 *with picture*; (India)
    Ci: 699
Divorce (In other countries) D: 254
Family *picture on* F: 20
Suttee So: 1013
Religion
India (Religion) I: 116 *with pictures*
Hinduism H: 235 *with pictures*
Social and cultural life
India (Way of life) I: 114 *with pictures*
Dance (Asian theatrical dance) D: 28-29
Drama (India) D: 336 *with picture*
Fable F: 3
Girl Scouts (India) G: 199
Technology and science
Fishing industry (Inland fisheries) F: 182
Nuclear energy (The spread of nuclear
    capability) N: 591
Space exploration (India) So: 727
Transportation
India (Transportation) I: 127
Railroad (In Asia) R: 113-114
India, Star of [gem]
Sapphire S: 122
India rubber
Goodyear, Charles G: 269
Indian, American I: 136 *with pictures and maps*
See also the list of Related articles in the Indian,
    American, *article*
Agriculture (In the Americas) A: 157
Alaska (Land-use issues) A: 304
American Indian Movement A: 411
Arizona (The mid-1900's) A: 691
Black Seminole B: 391
Bolivia (Population and ancestry) B: 443
Canada (The territories) C: 104; (Ancestry) C: 105-
    106 *with picture*; (Arctic life) C: 107
Carson, Kit (Military career) C: 250
Catlin, George C: 304
Clothing (Clothing of Native Americans) Ci: 700
Columbus, Christopher (The first landing) Ci: 860;
    (Columbus' impact on history) Ci: 864
Education *picture on* E: 108
Exploration (Columbus reaches America) E: 444
Fur trade F: 564
Girty, Simon G: 201
Guerrilla warfare (History) G: 420
Hispanic Americans (In Mexico) H: 248
Interior, Department of the I: 324
La Farge, Oliver L: 27
Menchú, Rigoberta M: 397
Minority group (American Indians) M: 610
Mission life in America M: 618 *with picture*
Name (Native American names) N: 6
National Congress of American Indians N: 32
National Museum of the American Indian N: 41
North America (People) N: 458
Northwest Territories (People) N: 530;
    (Government) N: 532-533
Ontario (Population) O: 768 *with picture*
Segregation (Other segregation in the United
    States) S: 286
Tribe T: 440
Culture
Arrowhead A: 744 *with pictures*
Buffalo ceremonials B: 679
Corn Ci: 1056; (Kinds of corn) Ci: 1058-1059
    with picture
Curare Ci: 1193
Dance (Ritual ethnic dances) D: 25 *with picture*
Doll (Traditional dolls) D: 287
Folk music (American folk music) F: 321
Food *picture on* F: 329; (Foods of the New
    World) F: 336
Ghost Dance G: 182
Gila Cliff Dwellings National Monument G: 189
Horse (Horses and people) H: 360-361

Indian reservation I: 188
Lacrosse (History) L: 24
Lévi-Strauss, Claude L: 218
Mask M: 263
Mound builders M: 881 *with pictures*
Music (American Indian music) M: 957 *with picture*
Mythology (Aztec mythology) M: 987 *with picture*
Peace pipe P: 209
Pemmican P: 233
Pyramids (American pyramids) P: 917-919 *with picture*
Raccoon (People and raccoons) R: 51
Rain dance R: 125
Rubber (First uses) R: 500
Sand painting S: 107
Science (Early civilizations) S: 196
Sculpture (Indian sculpture of the Americas) S: 242 *with pictures*
Slavery (The Middle Ages) S: 501-502
Sun dance So: 987
Tomahawk T: 324 *with pictures*
Totem T: 346 *with picture*
Wampum W: 22
History
American literature (Beginnings of American literature) A: 414
Canoeing (History) C: 182
Code talkers Ci: 749
Colonial life in America Ci: 787; (Before the arrival of the European settlers) Ci: 788; (Early English settlements) Ci: 789; (Colonists and Indians) Ci: 792
Cotton (History) Ci: 1092
Coureurs de bois Ci: 1100
Five Civilized Tribes F: 191
French and Indian wars F: 511 *with picture and map*
Guatemala (Indians) G: 413
Harrison, William Henry (Entry into politics) H: 74
Indian Territory I: 189 *with map*
Indian wars I: 190 *with pictures*
Jackson, Andrew (The Indian issue) J: 13
Jefferson, Thomas (Policies toward the American Indians) J: 86
Las Casas, Bartolomé de L: 80
Latin America (Ancestry) L: 92 ; (The first inhabitants) L: 102 *with picture*; (The conquest of the Indians) L: 103
Pioneer life in America (Before the arrival of the pioneers) P: 477; (Pioneers and Indians) P: 485; (Indians on the Plains) P: 487
Quanah Q: 5
Revolution, American (The war in the West) R: 283
Trading post T: 365
United States, History of the (America before colonial times) U: 149 *with pictures*; (Policy changes) U: 158; (Indian removal) U: 172 *with picture*; (The end of the Western frontier) U: 185
Western frontier life in America (Early occupants) W: 234; (Settlers and Native Americans) W: 239
Westward movement in America (Indian conflicts) W: 247 *with picture*
Whale (American whaling) W: 262
World, History of the (Civilizations in the Americas) W: 437 *with pictures*
Indian, American race [theory]
Races, Human (The geographical-race theory) R: 54
Indian, Asian race [theory]
Races, Human (The geographical-race theory) R: 54
Indian, Cigar store [sculpture]
Folk art (Sculpture) F: 317 *with picture*
Indian, The [book by Fuentes]
Latin American literature (The early 1900's) L: 113
Indian Act [1876]
Indian, American (In Canada) I: 178
Indian Affairs, Bureau of [U.S.] I: 184
American Indian Movement A: 411
Indian, American (In the United States) I: 178-178a, I: 179
Indian reservation I: 188; (History) I: 189
Indian Affairs and Northern Development, Department of [Canada]
Indian, American (In Canada) I: 178b
Indian bean [tree]
Catalpa C: 297
Indian blanket
Indian, American *pictures on* I: 162, I: 167, I: 168
Indian braiding
Weaving (Weaving without a loom) W: 174

Indian-Bridge Town [former name]
Bridgetown B: 607
Indian chief *See* Chief *in this index*
Indian Citizenship Act [law]
Indian, American (In the United States) I: 179
Indian Claims Commission [U.S.] I: 185
Indian cobra
Cobra Ci: 742 *with picture*
Indian Desert [region, India-Pakistan]
Thar Desert T: 231
Indian dipper [plant]
Pitcher plant P: 499
Indian elephant *See* Asian elephant *in this index*
Indian Empire, Order of the [organization]
Knighthood, Orders of *picture on* K: 347
Indian fig *See* Prickly pear *in this index*
Indian Gaming Regulatory Act [1988]
Indian, American (Social and economic progress) I: 180-181
Indian grass
Plant *picture on* P: 526
Indian Head [rock, Colorado]
Garden of the Gods G: 29
Indian head cent [money]
Cent *pictures on* C: 350
Coin collecting *picture on* Ci: 758
Indian Health Service
Health and Human Services, Department of (Organization) H: 128
Indian hemp [plant]
Dogbane D: 282
Indian Hunters Pursuing the Buffalo [painting by Rindisbacher]
Indian, American *picture on* I: 141
Indian Law, Institute for the Development of
Deloria, Vine, Jr. D: 117
Indian mallow [plant] *See* Velvetleaf *in this index*
Indian Mills [U.S. history]
Indian reservation (History) I: 189
Indian National Congress [political party] I: 185
India (Rise of Indian nationalism) I: 131; (World War II [1939-1945]) I: 132; (Independence and partition) I: 133
Muslim League M: 964
Indian Ocean I: 185 *with map*
See also Tsunami of 2004 *in this index*
Bay of Bengal B: 175 *with map*
Deep sea (The deep-sea floor) D: 82a
Fishing industry (Where fish are caught) F: 181-182
Flood (Seacoast floods) F: 237
Hurricane H: 452
Ocean (The world ocean) O: 651 *with picture*
Indian Opinion [newspaper]
Gandhi, Mohandas Karamchand (Gandhi's early life) G: 25
Indian paintbrush [plant] I: 187
Flower *picture on* F: 284
Indian peafowl [bird]
Peacock P: 211
Indian pipe [plant] I: 187 *with picture*
Flower *picture on* F: 284
Plant (Photosynthesis) P: 537-538 *with picture*
Indian pitta [bird]
Bird *picture on* B: 344g
Indian poke [plant]
Hellebore H: 177
Indian python
Python P: 922 *with picture*
Indian Rebellion [1857-1859] I: 187
India (The Indian Rebellion) I: 130
Indian Removal Act [1830]
Choctaw Indians C: 519
Indian, American (In the United States) I: 178-178a
Indian wars (Conflicts in the South) I: 192
Jackson, Andrew (The Indian issue) J: 13
Trail of Tears T: 367
Indian Reorganization Act [1934]
Indian Affairs, Bureau of I: 184
Indian reservation I: 188 *with map*
Indian, American (In the United States) I: 178-178a; (The preservation of Indian culture) I: 180 *with picture*
Indian wars I: 190
Indian rhinoceros
Animal *picture on* A: 477
Rhinoceros (Kinds of rhinoceroses) R: 294 *with picture*
Indian rice *See* Wild rice *in this index*
Indian rug
Rugs and carpets (Oriental rugs) R: 516-517
Indian Self-Determination and Education Assistance Act [1975]
Indian, American (Political gains) I: 182
Indian Affairs, Bureau of I: 185
Indian-shot canna [plant]

Canna C: 178
Indian Society of Lighting Engineers
Lighting (In offices, stores, and factories) L: 296-297
Indian Summer [book by Stifter]
German literature (Realism) G: 141
Indian summer [weather] I: 189
Indian Territory [former region, U.S.] I: 189 *with map*
Five Civilized Tribes F: 191
Indian, American (In the United States) I: 178-178a
Indian wars (The Seminole) I: 192
Oklahoma (Progress toward statehood) O: 732
Pioneer life in America (Pioneers and Indians) P: 485
Trail of Tears T: 367 *with map*
Westward movement in America (Closing of the frontier) W: 252
Indian tobacco
Lobelia L: 405
Indian tribe
Indian, American (Tribes) I: 143
Indian turnip [plant]
Jack-in-the-pulpit J: 3
Indian wars [U.S. history] I: 190 *with pictures and map*
See also specific Indian wars, such as Seminole wars *or* Modoc War *in this index*
Buffalo Soldiers B: 680
Colonial life in America (Colonists and Indians) Ci: 792
Pioneer life in America (Pioneers and Indians) P: 485
Smallpox S: 513
United States, History of the (Indian removal) U: 172
Western frontier life in America (Early occupants) W: 234; (Settlers and Native Americans) W: 239
Westward movement in America (Indian conflicts) W: 247 *with picture*; (The last Indian wars) W: 250 *with picture*
Wounded Knee W: 502
Indiana I: 196 *with pictures and maps*
See also the list of Related articles in the Indiana article
Labor movement (Recent developments) L: 14
Vincennes V: 385
Indiana [book by Sand]
Sand, George S: 106
Indiana, Port of
Indiana I: 218
Indiana Dunes National Lakeshore [Indiana]
Indiana *picture on* I: 208
National Park System (table: National lakeshores) N: 58
Indiana Gazette [newspaper]
Indiana (Communication) I: 213
Indiana Jones and the Kingdom of the Crystal Skull [film]
Lucas, George L: 513
Indiana Jones and the Last Crusade [film]
Lucas, George L: 513
Indiana Jones and the Temple of Doom [film]
Lucas, George L: 513
Indiana Pacers [team]
Basketball (table) B: 150
Indiana State University I: 219
Indiana Territory [U.S. history]
Indiana (Territorial days) I: 215
Michigan (Territorial period) M: 509
Indiana University I: 220 *with picture*
Knight, Bob K: 346
Indiana University Art Museum
Indiana University *picture on* I: 220
Indianapolis [Indiana] I: 220 *with pictures and map*
Indiana *picture on* I: 197; (Average monthly weather) I: 210
Indianapolis Colts [team]
Football (National Football League) F: 364
Manning, Peyton M: 165
Indianapolis 500 [race]
Automobile racing (Indy and Champ car racing) A: 977; (Growth of organized automobile racing) A: 979; (Indianapolis 500 winners) A: 980
Indiana *picture on* I: 218; (Visitor's guide) I: 206 *with picture*
Indianapolis Motor Speedway and Hall of Fame Museum [Indianapolis]
Indianapolis (Recreation) I: 222 *with map*
Indians *See* Indian, American *in this index*
Indians, Cleveland [team] *See* Cleveland Indians *in this index*
Indians Bartering [painting by Smyth]
Indian, American *picture on* I: 149
Indians Hunting Buffalo with Bows and Lances

[painting by Catlin]
   Indian, American *picture on* I: 136a
Indicated horsepower [measurement]
   Horsepower (Indicated horsepower) H: 367
Indicative mood [grammar]
   Conjugation Ci: 951
   Mood M: 780
Indictment [law] I: 223
   Grand jury G: 308
   Jury (Grand juries) J: 202
   Law enforcement (Trial) L: 141
Indies [islands] I: 223
   East Indies E: 40
   Indian, American I: 136
   West Indies W: 201
Indifference analysis [economics]
   Pareto, Vilfredo P: 159
Indigenismo [Peruvian history]
   Peru (The early 1900's) P: 315-316
Indigestion I: 223
   Antacid A: 529
Indigo [dye] I: 223
   Dye (Natural dyes) D: 396
   Pinckney, Eliza Lucas P: 467
Indigo [plant]
   Flower *picture on* F: 287
Indigo bunting [bird] I: 223 *with picture*
   Bunting B: 700
Indigo lactarius [fungus]
   Mushroom (Nonpoisonous mushrooms) M: 943-945
Indigotin [dye]
   Indigo I: 223
Indinavir [drug]
   AIDS (Treatments) A: 164b-165
Indirect-contact freezing *See* Plate freezing *in this index*
Indirect democracy
   Democracy D: 119
Indirect election
   Electoral College E: 161
   Voting V: 449
Indirect evidence *See* Circumstantial evidence *in this index*
Indirect-fired furnace
   Furnace (Sources of heat) F: 567
Indirect induction [hypnosis]
   Hypnosis (Inducing hypnosis) H: 478
Indirect-injection engine
   Diesel engine (How a diesel engine works) D: 199
Indirect investment
   Investment (Kinds of investments) I: 366
Indirect piezoelectric effect [physics]
   Piezoelectricity P: 458
Indirect primary
   Primary election (Direct and indirect) P: 776
Indirect tax
   National income (Determining national income) N: 37-38
   Taxation (Taxes on transactions) T: 53-54
Indium [element] I: 224
Indium tin oxide [compound]
   Indium I: 224
Individual [philosophy]
   Existentialism (What is existentialism?) E: 437
Individual differences
   Personality P: 300f
Individual evidence
   Forensic science (Class and individual evidence) F: 388b
Individual income tax
   Income tax (Types of income taxes) I: 102; (Federal income taxes in the United States) I: 104
Individual insurance mandate [law]
   Insurance (Health care reform) I: 316
Individual medley race
   Swimming (Kinds of races) So: 1044
Individual pension plan
   Pension P: 272; (Individual pension plans) P: 273
Individual psychology
   Adler, Alfred A: 58
Individual racism
   Racism (Types of racism) R: 62
Individual retirement account
   Bank (Commercial banks) B: 90
   Pension (Individual pension plans) P: 273
Individualism [philosophy]
   Political science (Liberalism) P: 639
Individualists [Chinese history]
   Painting (Chinese painting) P: 44-46
Individualized instruction
   Curriculum (Curriculum planning) Ci: 1197
   Middle school M: 535
   Reading (Individualized reading programs) R: 159
   Universities and colleges (Instruction) U: 209-210

Vocational education (Vocational teaching methods) V: 434
Individually quick frozen food
   Food, Frozen (Air-blast freezing) F: 338
Indo-Aryan [languages]
   Aryans A: 764
Indo-Aryans [people]
   Asia (The people) A: 781
   India (Ancestry) I: 111
Indo-European languages
   Africa (Languages) A: 105
   English language (Origins) E: 313
   India (Languages) I: 114
   Language (Indo-European) L: 65 *with map*
   Linguistics (Comparative and historical research) L: 337
Indo-Europeans [people]
   Mythology (Genetic relationships) M: 976; (Roman mythology) M: 982
   World, History of the (The advance of civilization) W: 426
Indo-Iranian [language]
   Language (Indo-European) L: 65-66
Indo-Iranians [people]
   Aryans A: 764
Indochina [Asian history] I: 224 *with maps*
   Cold War (To the brink and back) Ci: 765
   Foreign Legion (History) F: 386
   France (The Fourth Republic) F: 475-476
   Geneva Accords G: 87
   Guerrilla warfare (History) G: 420
   Vietnam War (The Indochina War) V: 373
Indochina War [1946-1954]
   Dien Bien Phu, Battle of D: 198
   Indochina (Independence) I: 225; (The Geneva Accords) I: 225
   Vietnam (The First Indochina War) V: 371
   Vietnam War (The Indochina War) V: 373
Indochinese forest ox
   Kouprey K: 385 *with picture*
Indonesia I: 226 *with pictures and maps*
   See also the list of Related articles in the Indonesia *article*
   Asia *picture on* A: 784; (Education) A: 785; (The arts) A: 785
   Batik B: 165
   Borneo B: 489 *with map*
   Clothing *picture on* Ci: 693
   Dance (Asian theatrical dance) D: 28-29 *with picture*
   Dili D: 204
   East Timor E: 40; (History) E: 41
   Exploration (Exploring the Pacific) E: 447
   Food *picture on* F: 332
   Java J: 65
   Music (Indonesian music) M: 956 *with picture*
   Netherlands (History) N: 148-150
   Orchestra *picture on* O: 823
   Timor T: 292d
   United Nations (Membership questions) U: 95-96
Indonesian Democratic Party of Struggle [political party]
   Indonesia (Politics) I: 227
Indonesian National Party
   Indonesia (The rise of nationalism) I: 237
   Sukarno So: 965
Indoor air pollution
   Environmental pollution *picture on* E: 333; (Air pollution) E: 331
Indoor archery
   Archery (Indoor archery) A: 603
Indoor Radon Abatement Act [1988]
   Radon (Protection against radon) R: 100
Indoor relief
   Welfare (History) W: 191
Indoxyl [chemical]
   Indigo I: 223
Indra [Hindu god]
   Mythology (Genetic relationships) M: 976
Indri [animal]
   Lemur L: 190
Induced abortion
   Abortion A: 14
Induced drag
   Aerodynamics (Induced drag) A: 86
Induced labor
   Childbirth (Methods of childbirth) C: 456-457
Inductance [electricity] I: 240
   Electronics (Passive components) E: 212
   Henry H: 185
Inductance coil [electricity] *See* Inductor *in this index*
Induction [reasoning] *See* Inductive method *in this index*
Induction, Electric [electricity] I: 240
Induction, Electromagnetic [physics]
   Electric generator (Basic principles) E: 170

Electricity (Electricity and magnetism) E: 196
Electromagnetism E: 203
Energy supply (The Industrial Revolution) E: 280
Faraday, Michael F: 27
Henry, Joseph H: 189
Induction coil I: 240
Invention (The Industrial Revolution) I: 361-362
Lenz's law L: 197
Linear electric motor L: 334
Magnetometer M: 62
Radio (Early development) R: 91
Transformer T: 371
Induction, Military
   Draft, Military D: 318
Induction coil [electricity] I: 240
   Gasoline engine (The ignition system) G: 65
Induction motor
   Electric motor (AC motors) E: 181
Induction telegraph [machine]
   Railroad (Engineering improvements) R: 117
Inductive balance [electronics]
   Metal detector M: 425
Inductive method [reasoning] I: 240
   Bacon, Francis (His philosophy) B: 18
   Deductive method D: 81
   Geometry (The study of geometry) G: 101-102
   Logic L: 425
   Philosophy (Logic) P: 384; (Modern philosophy) P: 388
   Reason R: 173
   Science (Mathematics and logic) S: 192-193
Inductor [device]
   Electronics (Passive components) E: 212
   Inductance I: 240
Indulgence [religion] I: 240
   Christianity (The Reformation) C: 524
   Luther, Martin (The Ninety-Five Theses) L: 527
   Reformation (Martin Luther) R: 197 *with picture*
   Roman Catholic Church (The Reformation) R: 408
   Tetzel, Johann T: 183
Indus River [Pakistan] I: 240
   Asia (The Indus Valley) A: 805
   Lake (Irrigation) L: 34
   Punjab (The land) P: 903
   River (table) R: 352
   Tarbela Dam T: 42
Indus River dolphin [animal]
   River dolphin R: 354
Indus Valley civilization I: 241 *with picture and map*
   Asia (History) A: 804
   Clothing (India) Ci: 699
   Cotton (History) Ci: 1092
   Cymbal Ci: 1205
   India (Earliest times) I: 128
   Pakistan (History) P: 98
   Punjab (History) P: 903
   Sculpture (Indus Valley) S: 235 *with pictures*
   World, History of the (The Indus Valley) W: 425 *with picture*
Indus Valley Railway [India]
   Indus River I: 241
Indusium [botany]
   Fern (Parts of a fern) F: 74-75
Industrial arbitration
   Arbitration (Industrial, or labor, arbitration) A: 592
Industrial arts I: 242
   See also the list of Related articles in the Industrial Arts *article*
   Safety (In other school areas) S: 12
Industrial Average [investment]
   Dow Jones averages D: 315
Industrial capitalism
   Industrial Revolution (The role of capital) I: 251
Industrial chemistry
   Chemistry (Growth of industrial chemistry) C: 405
Industrial city
   City (Industrial cities) Ci: 585 *with pictures*
Industrial design I: 244 *with picture*
   Packaging P: 18
   Sweden (Industrial design) So: 1027
Industrial diamond
   Diamond D: 181; (Industrial uses) D: 182 *with pictures*; (Synthetic diamonds) D: 183
Industrial Disputes Investigation Act [1907]
   King, William Lyon Mackenzie (Early political and public career) K: 325
Industrial drawing
   Industrial arts (Industrial arts courses) I: 242-243
Industrial economics *See* Industrial organization *in this index*
Industrial education
   Industrial arts I: 242
Industrial engineering
   Engineering (Industrial engineering) E: 287 *with picture*

Industrial Estates Limited
Nova Scotia (The early to middle 1900's) N: 570
Industrial health nurse
Nursing (Occupational and industrial health nursing) N: 617
Industrial Light & Magic [company]
Animation (The computer revolution) A: 514c
Industrial literature
Russian literature (The period of industrial literature) R: 564
Industrial medicine
Hamilton, Alice H: 33
Industrial organization
Economics (Fields of economics) E: 64
Industry (Industrial organization) I: 260
Industrial paint
Paint (Industrial paints) P: 24
Industrial pollution See Environmental pollution in this index
Industrial psychology I: 244
Psychology (Major fields of psychology) P: 848
Industrial radiography [manufacturing]
Radiation (In industry) R: 75
Industrial relations I: 245
See also Labor-management relations; Personnel management in this index
Industrial research
Manufacturing (How science helps manufacturing) M: 171
Industrial Revolution I: 246 with pictures
Adult education (History of adult education in the United States) A: 69
Architecture (The Industrial Revolution) A: 625; (Early modern architecture in Europe) A: 627
Army (The rise of modern armies) A: 727-728
Automobile (Early automobiles) A: 964
Child labor (Abuses of child labor) C: 455
City (Industrial cities) C: 585 with picture
City planning (The Industrial Revolution) Ci: 603
Coal (Developments in England) Ci: 731
Communism (The ideas of Marx) Ci: 890
Conservation (The Industrial Revolution) Ci: 984 with picture
Democracy (The spread of democracy) D: 123
Energy supply (The Industrial Revolution) E: 280
Environmental pollution (The growth of pollution) E: 338
Europe (The Industrial Revolution) E: 413
Family and consumer sciences (History) F: 26
Fashion (Why fashions change) F: 51
Housing (The Industrial Revolution) H: 391
Invention I: 359; (The Industrial Revolution) I: 361
Labor movement (Other possible origins) L: 9
London (The world's largest city) L: 441
Marx, Karl (Early development) M: 237
Sales (History) S: 64
Shelter (The Industrial Revolution) S: 394
Social security (History) So: 556
Socialism So: 560
Sweatshop So: 1019 with picture
Technology (The Industrial Revolution) T: 75
Textile (The Industrial Revolution) T: 219
United Kingdom (The Industrial Revolution) U: 67
Wages and hours (Hours) W: 3
War (Technological advancements) W: 25
Weaving (History) W: 174
Women's movement (Forces of change) W: 384
World, History of the (The Industrial Revolution) W: 444
Industrial Revolution, The [book by Toynbee]
Toynbee, Arnold T: 354
Industrial technology
Human being (Industrial societies) H: 415
Industrial union
Industrial Workers of the World I: 255
Labor movement (Types of unions) L: 7
Industrial Workers of the World [U.S. history] I: 255
Hill, Joe H: 231
Labor movement (The Industrial Workers of the World) L: 11 with picture
Industrialism See Industrial Revolution in this index
Industrialized agriculture
Agriculture (Agricultural practices) A: 148-149; (Industrialized agriculture) A: 150; (The industrialization of agriculture) A: 157 with pictures
Plant (Industrialized agriculture) P: 542
Industry I: 256 with pictures
See also Industrial Revolution in this index and the list of Related articles in the Industry article
Air conditioning (In business and industry) A: 176
Automation A: 944
Careers (Production) C: 229
Cartel C: 251
Colonial life in America (The economy) Ci: 809
Communication (Communications systems)

Ci: 878-879
Electricity (In industry) E: 191
Environmental pollution picture on E: 332; (Business and industry) E: 336; (Wastefulness in the industrialized world) E: 339
Gay Nineties (Industrial growth) G: 72
Global warming (Causes of global warming) G: 232
Human being (Industrial societies) H: 415
Industrial relations I: 245
Input-output analysis I: 276
Lighting (In offices, stores, and factories) L: 296-297
Mathematics (In industry) M: 302
Nationalization N: 63
Occupational medicine O: 647
Radiation (In industry) R: 75
Safety (Safety on the job) S: 13
Tariff (Why tariffs are levied) T: 43; (Arguments against tariffs) T: 43
United States, History of the (Industrialization and reform [1870-1916]) U: 179 with picture
Water (Water for industry) W: 118 with pictures
Water pollution (Industrial wastes) W: 136
X rays (In industry) X: 541
Industry and Humanity [book by King]
King, William Lyon Mackenzie (Early political and public career) K: 325
Industry Canada [agency]
Monitoring station M: 725
Radio, Amateur (The Amateur Extra class license) R: 96
Indy car
Automobile racing (Indy and Champ car racing) A: 977
Indy Racing League
Automobile racing (Racing organizations) A: 976; (Indy and Champ car racing) A: 977-978
Inert gas [chemistry]
Helium H: 175
Noble gas N: 451
Radon R: 100
Inertia [physics] I: 262 with pictures
Centripetal force C: 358
Force (Overcoming inertia) F: 369
Gyroscope (Gyroscopic inertia) G: 453 with diagram
Inertial guidance I: 263
Kilogram K: 316
Mass M: 268
Matter M: 310
Motion (The first law) M: 844
Relativity (Inertial frames) R: 210
Inertial air cleaner
Air cleaner (Inertial air cleaners) A: 176
Inertial confinement [physics]
Fusion F: 589
Nuclear energy (Experimental fusion devices) N: 592-593
Inertial frame [physics]
Relativity (Inertial frames) R: 210; (Special relativity) R: 210
Inertial guidance [navigation] I: 262 with diagram
Airplane (Inertial guidance) A: 227
Gyroscope (History) G: 454
Navigation (Inertial guidance) N: 73
Submarine (Ballistic missile submarines) So: 941
Inertial mass [physics]
Relativity (General relativity) R: 211-212
Inertial measurement unit [device]
Guided missile (Preset guidance) G: 426
Navigation (Inertial guidance) N: 73
Inertial navigation system See Inertial guidance in this index
Inertial reference system See Inertial guidance in this index
Inertinite [geology]
Coal (Analyzing coal composition) Ci: 717-718
Inés of My Soul [book by Allende]
Allende, Isabel A: 372
Inexhaustible resource
Conservation Ci: 974
Infallibility, Papal [religion] See Papal infallibility in this index
Infancy Gospel of James [document]
Jesus Christ (Other gospels) J: 105; (Early life) J: 105
Infancy Gospel of Thomas [document]
Jesus Christ (Other gospels) J: 105; (Childhood) J: 106
Infant See Baby in this index
Infant and toddler book
Literature for children (Picture books) L: 356
Infant botulism
Botulism B: 514
Infant mortality I: 264
Baby B: 4

Birth and death rates B: 377
Infant school
Alternative school (History) A: 389
Preschool (History) P: 356b
Infante, Guillermo Cabrera [Cuban author]
Latin American literature (The post-Boom) L: 114
Infanticide [crime] I: 264
National Right to Life Committee N: 60
Infantile paralysis See Poliomyelitis in this index
Infantry [military] I: 264
Army A: 724
Army, United States (Infantry) A: 734
Rangers R: 139
Infection [disorder]
Abscess A: 17
Blood (Infections) B: 414
Boil B: 438 with diagrams
Disease (Infectious diseases) D: 227
Gamma globulin G: 23
Inflammation I: 266
Lister, Sir Joseph L: 349
Lymphatic system (Fighting infection) L: 535
Sexually transmitted disease (Factors in the spread of STD's) S: 338b
Surgery (Antiseptics and asepsis) So: 1004
Virus diagram on V: 427; (Infection) V: 428
Infectious disease
Blood transfusion (Risks of transfusion) B: 417
Brain (Infectious diseases) B: 558
Disease D: 225 with picture; (Infectious diseases) D: 227; (Spread of infectious diseases) D: 228
Public health (Health planning) P: 856; (Furnishing support services for health workers) P: 857
Water pollution (Human illness) W: 138
Infectious hepatitis [disease]
Hepatitis (Hepatitis A) H: 192
Infectious mononucleosis [disease]
Mononucleosis M: 731
Infective endocarditis [disorder]
Mitral valve prolapse M: 679
Inference [philosophy]
Philosophy (Logic) P: 384
Inferior vena cava [anatomy]
Heart (Blood vessels) H: 135 with picture
Human body (The blood vessels) H: 421; (table) H: 422 with diagram
Vein V: 295
Infernal Machine, The [play by Cocteau]
Cocteau, Jean Ci: 747
Inferno [work by Dante]
Divine Comedy D: 242
Infertility [biology] I: 265
Fallopian tube F: 18
Sterility So: 893
Infidelity
Marriage (Marriage problems) M: 221
Infield
Baseball (The infield) B: 126 with diagrams
Infielder
Baseball (Player positions) B: 127
Infinite series [mathematics]
Binomial theorem B: 310
Mathematics (Branches of mathematics) M: 303
Series S: 316b; (Working with infinite series) S: 317
Infinite set [mathematics]
Set theory (Kinds of sets) S: 321
Infinitesimal [mathematics]
Mathematics (Branches of mathematics) M: 303
Infinitive [grammar] I: 265
Adverb (Adverbs that split an infinitive) A: 71
Verb (Finite and nonfinite verbs) V: 315
Infinity [mathematics] I: 266
Calculus (Finding areas) C: 24; (The definite integral) C: 24-25
Inflammable air
Cavendish, Henry C: 322
Inflammation [disorder] I: 266
Aspirin (How aspirin works) A: 816
C-reactive protein C: 2
Heart (Inflammatory heart disease) H: 142
Inflammatory bowel disease [disorder] I: 266
Inflammatory colitis [disease]
Colitis Ci: 772
Inflammatory heart disease
Heart (Inflammatory heart disease) H: 142
Inflation [economics] I: 266 with picture
Capital gains tax C: 192
Capitalism (Stabilizing the economy) C: 195
Consumer Price Index Ci: 1017
Cost of living Ci: 1079
Credit (Credit and the economy) Ci: 1124
Deflation D: 88
Depreciation D: 149
Economics (Modern economics) E: 64-65
Federal Reserve System (Organization) F: 65

Ford, Gerald Rudolph (The economy) F: 377
Germany (The Weimar Republic) G: 167 *with picture*
Great Depression (The beginning of the Great Depression) G: 339
Gross domestic product (Real GDP) G: 399
Income (Nominal and real income) I: 100
Income tax (Current issues) I: 102
Insurance (Annuities) I: 311
Interest (Inflation) I: 322
Investment (Direct investments) I: 367
Money (Paper money) M: 708; (Printing money and inflation) M: 717
National debt N: 33
National income (Determining national income) N: 37-38
Nixon, Richard Milhous (The national scene) N: 433-434
Poverty (Economic factors) P: 724
Price control P: 775
Rationing R: 148
Recession (Recession and inflation) R: 175
Taxation (Elasticity) T: 54
Inflation [physics] *See* Inflation theory *in this index*
Inflation-indexed bond
Investment (Bonds) I: 368
Inflation theory [physics] I: 268a
Big bang B: 297
Cosmic microwave background (CMB) radiation Ci: 1075
Cosmology (Other theories) Ci: 1078
Inflection [grammar] I: 268a
Case C: 271
Comparison Ci: 902b
Declension D: 80
English language (Grammar) E: 312
Grammar (Principles of English grammar) G: 303
Parts of speech P: 189
Inflorescence [botany] I: 268a
Flower *picture on* F: 272; (Variations in flower structure) F: 294
Pineapple (The pineapple plant) P: 472
Raceme R: 51
Influence
Power (Forms of power) P: 727
Influence of Sea Power upon History, The [book by Mahan]
Mahan, Alfred Thayer M: 64
Influenza [disease] I: 268b *with picture*
Avian influenza A: 982
Disease (table) D: 226; (Death rates from diseases in the United States) D: 233 *with picture*
Hospital *picture on* H: 374
Swine flu So: 1048
Virus *diagram on* V: 427; (Antiviral drugs) V: 428a
Infomercial [advertising]
Television (Infomercials) T: 114
Informal adult education
Adult education (Informal adult education) A: 69
Informal censorship
Censorship (Censorship methods) C: 346
Informal economy [economics]
Pacific Islands (Economy) P: 8-9
South America (Service industries) So: 637
Informal education
Education E: 86 *with picture*
Informal fallacy
Fallacy F: 16
Informal garden
Gardening (Flower gardens) G: 30
Informal settlement
Housing H: 389
Information
Public speaking (Purpose) P: 864
Information [law]
Law enforcement (Trial) L: 141
Information, Bureau of [U.S. history]
Espionage (History) E: 358
Information, Freedom of
Freedom of Information Act F: 505
Information Age
United States, History of the (The Information Age) U: 196b
Information assurance
National Security Agency/Central Security Service N: 60
Information asymmetry [economics]
Industry (Lack of information) I: 261
Information book
Literature for children (Information books) L: 361
Information extraction [computing]
Information retrieval (Research) I: 268-269
Information for Playwrights [magazine]
Writing (Scriptwriting) W: 512
Information professional [librarian]
Library (Careers for librarians) L: 255 *with picture*
Information resource center

Library (United States government libraries) L: 248
Information retrieval I: 268b
Database D: 41 *with picture*
Index I: 107
Laser (How lasers are used) L: 82
Library (Information science) L: 251
Microfilm M: 514
Information science I: 269
See also Information theory *in this index*
Information retrieval I: 268b
Library (Information science and technology) L: 251; (Educational requirements) L: 256
Information Science and Technology, American Society for
Library (Information science) L: 251
Information service
Library (Assisting patrons) L: 236
Information services, Division of
Library (Special libraries) L: 250
Information technology
Information science I: 269
Information theory I: 269
Informational appeal
Advertising (Basic appeals) A: 76
Informational defect [law]
Product liability suit P: 810
Informed consent
Genetic testing (Promises and challenges of genetic testing) G: 85
Transplant (Sources of donor organs) T: 380
Informer, The [book by O'Flaherty]
Irish literature (Fiction) I: 432
O'Flaherty, Liam O: 678
Informer, The [film]
Ford, John F: 381
InfoTrac [reference]
A Guide to Research Skills **Research Guide: 31**
Infrared Astronomical Satellite
Telescope (Infrared telescopes) T: 108
Infrared astronomy
Astronomy (Infrared astronomy) A: 842
Infrared autofocus
Photography (Types of lenses) P: 411
Infrared energy [physics]
Thermography T: 254
Infrared photography
Geography (Scientific instruments) G: 95
Infrared radiation thermometer
Thermometer (Radiation thermometers) T: 255 *with picture*
Infrared rays [radiation] I: 269 *with picture*
Astronomy (table: The electromagnetic spectrum) A: 839; (Infrared astronomy) A: 842
Camera (Automatic focusing) C: 82
Color *diagram on* Ci: 818
Electromagnetic waves (The electromagnetic spectrum) E: 202 *with diagram*
Gas [fuel] (In industry) G: 51
Gold (Other uses) G: 251 *with picture*
Greenhouse effect (The natural greenhouse effect) G: 382
Heat *diagram on* H: 151; (Radiation) H: 152
Heating (Steam and hot-water heating systems) H: 159
Hubble Space Telescope (How the telescope works) H: 403
Laser (Gas lasers) L: 85
Light (The spectrum of light sources) L: 284 *with diagram*
Night vision systems N: 419
Radiation (Electromagnetic radiation) R: 75-76 *with picture*
Remote control (The parts of a remote control system) R: 230
Remote sensing R: 231
Spectroscopy So: 772
Telescope (Infrared telescopes) T: 108
Thallium T: 229
Weather (Air temperature) W: 157; (Weather satellites) W: 163-164
Infrared telescope
Astronomy (Infrared astronomy) A: 842
Telescope (Infrared telescopes) T: 108 *with picture*
Infrared Telescope Facility [Mauna Kea]
Astronomy (Infrared astronomy) A: 842-843
Infrasound [physics]
Acoustics A: 28
Elephant (Senses) E: 229
Infraspinatus [muscle]
Rotator cuff R: 486
Infrastructure
Automobile (Demand for services and facilities) A: 959
City planning (The master plan) Ci: 599
Industry (Capital goods) I: 258
Local government (Population changes)

L: 407-408
Infringement [law]
Copyright (Owners' rights) Ci: 1047
Patent (How patents protect inventors) P: 194
Trademark (In the United States) T: 365
Inge, William [American dramatist] I: 270
Ingersoll, Charles R. [American political leader]
Connecticut (table) Ci: 967
Ingersoll, Jared [American political leader] I: 270
Ingersoll, Robert Green [American lawyer] I: 270
Blaine, James Gillespie B: 396
Ingham, Samuel D. [American government official]
Jackson, Andrew (table) J: 11; (Split with Calhoun) J: 11
Ingold, Sir Christopher [British chemist] I: 270
Ingólfur Arnason [Norse explorer]
Iceland (Early days) I: 23
Ingot [metal]
Aluminum (Casting the molten aluminum) A: 394 *with picture*
Gold (Money) G: 251
Iron and steel (Ingot casting) I: 445 *with diagram*
Magnesium (How magnesium is obtained) M: 54
Ingraham, Hubert [Bahamian political leader]
Bahamas (History) B: 29
Ingraham, Joseph [American sea captain]
Marquesas Islands M: 217
Ingram, Mark [American football player]
Football (table) F: 363
Ingres, Jean Auguste Dominique [French painter] I: 271
Drawing *picture on* D: 343
Painting (Later neoclassicism) P: 67 *with picture*
Philip V *picture on* P: 370
Inguri Dam [Inguri River, Georgia]
Dam (table) D: 18
INH [drug]
Isoniazid I: 475
Tuberculosis (Treatment of tuberculosis) T: 479
Inhalant [drug] I: 271
Drug *picture on* D: 350
Drug abuse (Abuse of legal drugs) D: 361
Inhalation [physiology] *See* Inspiration *in this index*
Inhalational anthrax [disease]
Anthrax A: 545
Inhaler [medicine]
Bronchodilator B: 637
Inheritance [biology] *See* Heredity *in this index*
Inheritance [law]
Dower D: 316
Genealogy G: 82
Law (Private law) L: 130
Nobility N: 450
Primogeniture P: 781
Will W: 306
"Inheritance Cycle" [books by Paolini]
Paolini, Christopher P: 132
Inheritance tax I: 271
Taxation (Other taxes) T: 54
Inhibitory postsynaptic potential [physiology]
Nervous system (Transmission across synapses) N: 135
INI [laboratory] *See* Idaho National Laboratory *in this index*
Initial [letter]
Illuminated manuscript I: 78 *with picture*
Initial public offering [investment] I: 271
Initial side [geometry]
Angle A: 462
Initial velocity
Ballistics (Interior ballistics) B: 56
Initiating system [device]
Bomb (How bombs work) B: 450
Initiation ceremony
Indian, American (Children) I: 136c
Mysteries M: 972
Initiative 200 [law]
Affirmative action A: 91
Initiative 300 [law]
Nebraska (The late 1900's) N: 115
Initiative and referendum [political science] I: 271
Law (By direct action of the people) L: 132
Populism (Influences of populism) P: 675
Progressive Era (Political reforms) P: 814
State government (Initiative and referendum) So: 864
Injection [mechanical device] *See* Fuel injection *in this index*
Injection [medicine] *See* Hypodermic injection; Intravenous injection; Lethal injection *in this index*
Injection method [food processing]
Bacon B: 18
Injection molding [industrial process]
Plastics *picture on* P: 558; (Making plastic products) P: 557
Polypropylene P: 651

Polyvinyl chloride **P:** 652
Injera [food]
Ethiopia (Way of life) **E:** 368-369
Injunction [law] **I:** 272
Equity **E:** 348
Norris-La Guardia Act **N:** 457
Pure food and drug laws (Enforcement) **P:** 908-909
Injury
Bleeding **B:** 399
Blindness (Causes of blindness) **B:** 401-402
Blister **B:** 403
Brain (Injuries) **B:** 558
Bruise **B:** 650
Burn **B:** 708
Concussion **Ci:** 929
First aid **F:** 136
Frostbite **F:** 543
Mayhem **M:** 328
Nosebleed **N:** 549
Paralysis **P:** 152
Repetitive strain injury **R:** 242
Safety **S:** 9
Scar **S:** 172
Sports medicine **So:** 804
Sprain **So:** 805
Trauma center **T:** 405
Whiplash **W:** 281
Workers' compensation **W:** 405
Injustice to Tou O [play by Guan Hanqing]
Chinese literature (Drama and fiction) **C:** 511
Ink I: 272
Drawing (Materials and techniques) **D:** 342
Engraving (Printing the engraving) **E:** 325
Painting (Chinese painting) **P:** 44; (Japanese painting) **P:** 47
Pen **P:** 233
Printing (Process color printing) **P:** 802
Ink sac [zoology]
Squid (The body of a squid) **So:** 814 *with diagram*
Inkatha Freedom Party [political party] **I:** 273
South Africa (Political parties) **So:** 609
Xhosa **X:** 544
Zulu **Z:** 608
Inkberry [plant]
Pokeweed **P:** 603 *with picture*
Inkjet copying
Copying machine (Inkjet copying) **Ci:** 1045
Inkjet printer [electronic device] **I:** 273
Computer (Printers) **Ci:** 916
Mechanical drawing (Creating a drawing) **M:** 354
Microelectromechanical systems **M:** 513
Photography (Printing digital images) **P:** 422
Printing (Digital printing) **P:** 801
Inky cap [fungus]
Mushroom (Nonpoisonous mushrooms) **M:** 943-945
Inlaid linoleum
Linoleum **L:** 338
Inland marine insurance
Insurance (Marine insurance) **I:** 313-314
Inland navigation
Inland waterway **I:** 273
Lake (Travel and trade routes) **L:** 34
Inland revenue [taxation] **I:** 273
Inland Rules
Boating (Boating regulations) **B:** 429
Inland Voyage, An [book by Stevenson]
Stevenson, Robert Louis (Early life) **So:** 897
Inland waterway I: 273
Inland wetland
Wetland (Water and soil) **W:** 252a
Inlay [decoration] **I:** 274
INMARSAT [satellite system]
Communications Satellite Corporation **Ci:** 889
Inmate
Prison **P:** 805
Inn
Hotel (History) **H:** 376
Innate immunity [physiology]
Immune system **I:** 87
Inner bark
Tree (Trunk and branches) **T:** 416 *with diagram*
Inner city [district]
City (Description) **Ci:** 589; (The people) **Ci:** 589-590
Inner City Mother Goose, The [book by Merriam]
Diaz, David **D:** 186
Inner core [geology]
Earth *diagram on* **E:** 20; (Earth's interior) **E:** 23
Inner ear [anatomy]
Deafness (Sensorineural hearing loss) **D:** 57
Dizziness **D:** 256
Ear *diagram on* **E:** 7; (The inner ear) **E:** 8 *with diagram*; (How sounds travel to the inner ear) **E:** 9
Inner Harbor [Baltimore]

Baltimore (The city) **B:** 67 *with picture*
Maryland (Places to visit) **M:** 248 *with picture*
Inner Hebrides [islands, Scotland]
Hebrides **H:** 163
Inner Light [religion]
Quakers (History) **Q:** 5
Inner Mongolia *See* Mongolia, Inner *in this index*
Inner Temple [London]
Inns of Court **I:** 275
Inner tube
Tire (History) **T:** 297-298
Innes plaid
Tartan *picture on* **T:** 47
Inness, George [American painter] **I:** 274 *with picture*
Inning
Baseball (The game) **B:** 128; (Rule changes) **B:** 133
Innings
Cricket (The game) **Ci:** 1132
Innocent III [antipope]
Pope (table) **P:** 666
Innocent III [pope] **I:** 274
Christianity *picture on* **C:** 524
Crusades (The Fourth Crusade) **Ci:** 1161
John **J:** 132
Langton, Stephen **L:** 61
Pope *picture on* **P:** 663; (The peak of papal power) **P:** 663
Roman Catholic Church (Innocent III) **R:** 407 *with picture*
Innocent IV [pope] **I:** 275
Innocent XI [pope]
Roman Catholic Church (Gallicanism) **R:** 408-409
Innocent Man, The [book by Grisham]
Grisham, John **G:** 396
Innocents Abroad, The [book by Twain]
Twain, Mark (Return to the East) **T:** 529
Innovation
Economics (Modern economics) **E:** 64-65
Invention **I:** 354l
Inns of Court [English history] **I:** 275
London (The Inns of Court) **L:** 437
Innsbruck [Austria] **I:** 275
Innsbruck Cathedral
Austria *picture on* **A:** 933
Innu Indians I: 276
Indian, American *pictures on* **I:** 138
Newfoundland and Labrador (Early European exploration) **N:** 375
Quebec (Indian days) **Q:** 30
Ino [legendary figure]
Golden Fleece **G:** 255
Inoculation [medicine] **I:** 276
Inönü, Ismet [Turkish political leader]
Turkey (The Republic of Turkey) **T:** 511
Inorganic chemistry I: 276
Inorganic compound
Compound **C:** 906
Inorganic fertilizer
Fertilizer (Inorganic fertilizers) **F:** 79
Inositol [vitamin]
Lipid (Kinds of lipids) **L:** 345
Inouye, Daniel Ken [American political leader]
Asian Americans (World War II and Japanese Americans) **A:** 812f; (Notable Asian American "firsts") **A:** 812f
Input [economics]
Business (Productive resources) **B:** 725
Economics (Economic growth) **E:** 62
Industry (The needs of industry) **I:** 257 *with diagram*; (Management) **I:** 259
Input [information]
Automation (How automation works) **A:** 945
Input device [electronics]
Computer (Input devices) **Ci:** 912 *with picture*
Input equipment [electronics]
Electronics (How an electronic system works) **E:** 208
Input-output analysis [economics] **I:** 276 *with diagram*
Input shaft [mechanical device]
Transmission (A torque converter) **T:** 376
Inquest [law] **I:** 277
Jury (Coroner's juries) **J:** 202
Inquilinos [people]
Chile (Rural life) **C:** 460-462
Inquisition [European history] **I:** 277
Counter Reformation (Counteracting Protestantism) **Ci:** 1096
Galileo (Galileo and the Roman Catholic Church) **G:** 12
Jews (Jews in Christian Europe) **J:** 122-123
Paul IV **P:** 200
Portugal (Years of decline) **P:** 694
Roman Catholic Church (Innocent III) **R:** 407
Spain (Union of the Spanish kingdoms) **So:** 746

Spanish literature (The 1500's) **So:** 758
Torquemada, Tomás de **T:** 341
Witchcraft (Middle Ages to the 1700's) **W:** 372
INS [organization] *See* Immigration and Naturalization Service *in this index*
Insane asylum
Abnormal psychology (History) **A:** 12
Insanity [law] **I:** 277
Mental illness **M:** 404
Inscriptions and Belles Lettres, The Academy of
Institute of France **I:** 305
Insect I: 278 *with pictures*
See also Insecticide *in this index*; the list of Related articles in the Insect *article*
Arthropod **A:** 752 *with picture*
Compound eye **Ci:** 906 *with diagram*
Cotton (Insect pests) **Ci:** 1090 *with picture*
Disease (Spread of infectious diseases) **D:** 228
Entomology **E:** 327
Flower (Cross-pollination) **F:** 295 *with picture*
Forestry (Diseases and pests) **F:** 407
Gardening (Pests) **G:** 35
Insecticide **I:** 301
Lawn *pictures on* **L:** 143
Molting **M:** 697
Nervous system (In invertebrates) **N:** 136
Plant (Environmental factors) **P:** 538 *with picture*; (Pests) **P:** 540 *with picture*; (How plants protect themselves) **P:** 540
Plant quarantine **P:** 550
Prehistoric animal (The move onto land) **P:** 737
Protective coloration **P:** 831
Rain forest (Plants and animals) **R:** 126a
Insect bite
First aid (Injected poisons) **F:** 137; (Animal bites or stings) **F:** 138
Insect Comedy, The [play by Čapek]
Čapek, Karel **C:** 191
Insect growth regulator [insecticide]
Insecticide **I:** 301
Insectary [agriculture]
Alfalfa (Beneficial insects) **A:** 348
Insecticide I: 301 *with picture*
Agriculture (Chemical pesticides) **A:** 159
DDT **D:** 55
Gulf War syndrome **G:** 438
Insect (Insect control) **I:** 284-285
Pest control (Pesticides) **P:** 318
Potato (Potato pests) **P:** 713
Typhus (Treatment) **T:** 541
Vegetable (Pest control) **V:** 293
Insectivore [zoology]
Mammal (What mammals eat) **M:** 121
Tree shrew **T:** 433
Insectivorous plant *See* Carnivorous plant *in this index*
Insensible perspiration
Perspiration **P:** 305
Insensitive explosive
Bomb (The explosive material) **B:** 450
Insert [advertising]
Newspaper (Preparing advertisements) **N:** 383
Insertion device [physics]
X rays (Synchrotron radiation) **X:** 542-543
Inside Passage [waterway, North America] **I:** 303
Alaska (Visitor's guide) **A:** 290
British Columbia (Places to visit) **B:** 620 *with picture*
Juneau **J:** 194
Inside the Third Reich [book by Speer]
Speer, Albert **So:** 775
Insider, The [film]
Crowe, Russell **Ci:** 1158
Insider trading [crime] **I:** 303
Insight [psychology]
Education (How people learn) **E:** 89
Learning (Insight learning) **L:** 163
Mysticism **M:** 972
Insignia [emblems] **I:** 303
Air Force, United States *pictures on* **A:** 189
Army, United States *pictures on* **A:** 732
Boy Scouts *pictures on* **B:** 536
Canadian Armed Forces *pictures on* **C:** 155
Girl Scouts **G:** 196 *with picture*
Knighthood, Orders of *pictures on* **K:** 347
Marine Corps, United States *pictures on* **M:** 207
Navy, United States *pictures on* **N:** 86
Insitu Group [company]
Automatic flight control system (History) **A:** 944
Insolvency [law]
Bankruptcy (Features of bankruptcy) **B:** 97
Insomnia [disorder] **I:** 303
Health (Rest and sleep) **H:** 125-126
Inspector General [military officer] **I:** 304
Inspector-General, The [play by Gogol]
Drama (Russian drama and Chekhov) **D:** 338
Gogol, Nikolai **G:** 248

Russian literature (Late Romanticism) R: 561-562
Inspiration [physiology]
Diaphragm D: 184
Lung (Gas exchange in the lungs) L: 523-524
Respiration (The process of breathing) R: 260 *with diagram*
Installation [art]
Sculpture (From the mid-1900's to the early 2000's) S: 259-260
Video art V: 359
Installment contract [economics]
Great Depression (The stock market crash) G: 340
Installment plan [economics] I: 304
Credit (Types of credit) Ci: 1124
Instant camera
Camera (Instant cameras) C: 83 *with picture*
Photography (Other types of cameras) P: 409
Instant coffee
Coffee (Instant coffee) Ci: 754
Instant gratification [sociology]
Generation Y G: 84
Instant messaging I: 304
Internet (Communication) I: 350b
Instant oatmeal [food]
Oatmeal O: 640
Instant replay
Television (Recording the program) T: 113
Instant-start lamp
Fluorescent lamp F: 305
Instant tea
Tea (Grades of tea) T: 62-63; (History) T: 63-64
Instantaneous north pole
North Pole N: 517
Instantaneous rate of change
Calculus (Limits) C: 23
Instantaneous south pole
South Pole So: 685
Instantaneous speed
Calculus (Limits) C: 23
Instauratio Magna [book by Bacon]
Bacon, Francis B: 18
Instep [anatomy]
Foot (The bones) F: 352
Soccer (Kicking) So: 547
Instinct [psychology] I: 304
Behavior (Heredity) B: 220
Dog (Behavior) D: 277
Ethology E: 373
Institute for Advanced Study [Princeton, New Jersey] I: 305
Einstein, Albert (Einstein in the United States) E: 147
Flexner, Abraham F: 234
Institute for Heavy Ion Research [Darmstadt, Germany] *See* Heavy Ion Research Center *in this index*
Institute for Scientific and Technical Information, Canada
Library (Canadian government libraries) L: 249
Institute for the Development of Indian Law
Deloria, Vine, Jr. D: 117
Institute for Theoretical Physics [Copenhagen, Denmark]
Bohr, Niels B: 438
Institute of Applied Optics
Light (Studying light) L: 292-293
Institute of Electrical and Electronics Engineers
Engineering (table) E: 289
Institute of France I: 305
Institute of International Education
Scholarship (International scholarships) S: 179
Institute of International Law
Nobel Prizes (Peace: 1904) N: 448
Institute of Medicine
National Academies N: 27
National Academy of Sciences N: 27
National Research Council N: 60
Institute of Optics
Light (Studying light) L: 292-293
Institute of Public Opinion, American
Gallup, George Horace G: 16
Institutes [book by Justinian]
Justinian Code J: 204
Institutes of the Christian Religion [book by Calvin]
Calvin, John (His life) C: 70
Institutio Oratoria [book by Quintilian] *See Training of an Orator, The in this index*
Institution
Foster care F: 428
Sociology (Social institutions) So: 564
Institution, Public
Library L: 234 *with pictures*
School S: 180 *with pictures*
Institution of Lighting Engineers
Lighting (In offices, stores, and factories) L: 296-297

Institutional racism
Racism (Types of racism) R: 62
Institutional Revolutionary Party *See* Partido Revolucionario Institucional *in this index*
Instruction set [electronics]
Computer chip (Instruction sets) Ci: 924f
Instructional materials center
Library (School libraries) L: 244
Instructional media *See* Audio-visual materials *in this index*
Instructor [occupation]
Universities and colleges (Faculty) U: 208
Instrument [spiritualism] *See* Medium [spiritualism] *in this index*
Instrument, Musical *See* Musical instrument *in this index*
Instrument Flight Rules *See* IFR *in this index*
Instrument Landing System
Airplane (Safety) A: 227-228
Airport (Air traffic control) A: 246-247 *with diagram*
Instrument transformer [electricity]
Transformer T: 372
Instrumental conditioning [psychology]
Education (How people learn) E: 89
Learning (Instrumental conditioning) L: 163
Mouse *picture on* M: 902
Instrumental music
Classical music (Instrumental music) Ci: 643
Instrumentalism [philosophy]
Dewey, John D: 177
Pragmatism P: 729
Insufficiency [disorder]
Heart (Other heart disorders) H: 141
Insular Cases [1901]
McKinley, William (McKinley's second Administration [1901]) M: 341
Territory (Territories in the United States) T: 174
Insular Mountains [North America]
British Columbia (Land regions) B: 622 *with map*
Insulation I: 306 *with pictures*
Aerogel A: 89
Cable (Cable construction) C: 4
Camping (Sleeping bags) C: 93
Cork (Uses) Ci: 1055
Energy supply *picture on* E: 281
Environmental pollution (Environmental do's and don'ts) E: 337
Fiberglass (Uses) F: 89
Heat (Insulation) H: 152
House (Insulation) H: 382 *with diagram*
Tantalum T: 29
Insulation board [building material]
Forest products (Fiber products) F: 401-402
Insulator, Electric I: 308 *with picture*
Capacitor C: 186
Electric current (Conductors and insulators) E: 168
Electricity (Conductors and insulators) E: 193
Electronics (Electronic circuits) E: 208-209
Insulin [hormone] I: 308
Best, Charles Herbert B: 274
Biology (Current research and issues) B: 320-321
Diabetes (Causes) D: 179; (Treatment) D: 179
Drug (Animals) D: 355; (The drug revolution) D: 359
Genetic engineering (In medicine) G: 84c; (History) G: 84c
Hormone (Metabolic hormones) H: 335
Human body (The endocrine system) H: 425
Hypoglycemia (Causes) H: 481
Pancreas P: 128
Insulin-dependent diabetes [disease] *See* Type 1 diabetes *in this index*
Insulin infusion pump [device]
Diabetes (Treatment) D: 179
Insulin pump [device]
Diabetes (Treatment) D: 179
Insulin receptor [anatomy]
Insulin (How insulin acts in the body) I: 308
Insulin resistance
Diabetes (Type 2 diabetes) D: 179
Insulin (Treatment) I: 308
Insulin shock therapy
Shock treatment S: 429
Insulinoma [disorder]
Hypoglycemia (Causes) H: 481
Insurability
Insurance (How life insurance premiums are determined) I: 310
Insurance I: 309 *with picture and diagram*
See also Health insurance; Life insurance *in this index*
Connecticut (Service industries) Ci: 966
Investment (Life insurance policies) I: 369
Malpractice suit M: 112
Medicine (Providing medical care) M: 366

Nebraska (Service industries) N: 107
No-fault insurance N: 438
Postal Service, United States (Extra protection) P: 700
Railway brotherhoods R: 122
Underwriting U: 21
Unemployment insurance U: 24
Workers' compensation W: 405
Insurance agent
Insurance (How insurance is sold) I: 315
Sales (Steps in selling) S: 62-63
Insurance City [nickname]
Hartford H: 78
Insurance Institute for Highway Safety
Safety (Private organizations) S: 15
Insurgent [warfare]
Guerrilla warfare (Types of guerrilla movements) G: 420
United States, History of the (Iraq War [2003-2010]) U: 196e-196f
Insurgente, L' [ship]
Constellation Ci: 994
Insurrection, The [book by Skármeta]
Latin American literature (The post-Boom) L: 114
Intact dilation and extraction *See* Partial-birth abortion *in this index*
Intaglio [engraving] I: 317
Offset O: 677
Printing (Recess printing) P: 800 *with diagram*
Relief R: 212
Sculpture (Kinds of sculpture) S: 230
Stamp collecting (Printing) So: 830
Intake manifold
Carburetor C: 208
Gasoline engine *picture on* G: 63; (The fuel system) G: 65
Intake port [engine]
Fuel injection F: 552
Intake stroke
Automobile (The engine cycle) A: 953
Intake valve
Gasoline engine (The valves) G: 64 *with diagrams*
Intangible product
Intellectual property I: 318
Integer [mathematics] I: 317
Logarithms (Common logarithms) L: 424
Number (Integers) N: 605
Rational number R: 148
Integral [mathematics]
Calculus (The definite integral) C: 24
Integral [satellite]
Astronomy (Gamma-ray astronomy) A: 845
Telescope (Gamma-ray telescopes) T: 109
Integral appreciation [anthropology]
Gamio, Manuel G: 23
Integral calculus
Calculus C: 22; (Integral calculus) C: 23
Mathematics (Branches of mathematics) M: 303
Torricelli, Evangelista T: 343
Integral train
Railroad (Rolling stock) R: 107-108
Integrase inhibitor [drug]
AIDS (Treatment) A: 164b-165
Integrated Automated Fingerprint Identification System
Forensic science (Fingerprints) F: 389
Integrated circuit [electronics]
Computer *picture on* Ci: 914; (Miniaturization) Ci: 924c
Computer chip Ci: 924e
Electricity (Controlling electric current) E: 195
Electronics E: 206; (Types of electronic circuits) E: 209-210; (Passive components) E: 212; (The solid-state revolution) E: 215-216
Invention (Recent developments) I: 364
Kilby, Jack K: 315
Noyce, Robert N: 578
Integrated development environment [computing]
Computer (Compiling or assembling a program) Ci: 923
Integrated Ocean Drilling Program
Ocean drilling programs O: 667
Integrated pest management [agriculture]
Environmental pollution (Agriculture) E: 337-338
Farm and ranch (Pest control) F: 34
Fruit (Caring for the crop) F: 546-547
Insect (Chemical control) I: 285
Pest control P: 318
Plant (Disease and pest control) P: 541
Integrated steel mill
Iron and steel (The steel industry) I: 447-448
Integration [economics]
Economics (The world economy) E: 61
Integration [sociology]
See also Segregation *in this index*
Immigration (Effects of immigration) I: 81

Integumentary system [anatomy]
Human body (The skin) H: 418
Intel Corporation
New Mexico *picture on* N: 269
Noyce, Robert N: 578
Intellect [psychology]
Plato (Psychology and politics) P: 568
Intellectual cycle
Biorhythm B: 326
Intellectual disability I: 317
Autism (Causes) A: 942
Capital punishment (History of capital
punishment) C: 193-194
Disability (Mental illness and cognitive
disabilities) D: 219
Down syndrome D: 316
Fragile X syndrome F: 450
Gaucher's disease G: 68
Intelligence quotient I: 319
Lesch-Nyhan syndrome L: 206
Phenylketonuria P: 357
Rett syndrome (Symptoms) R: 266
Special education (Children with intellectual
disabilities) So: 770
Special Olympics So: 771
Intellectual play [recreation]
Play P: 570
Intellectual property [law] I: 318
Copyright Ci: 1046
Piracy P: 493
Public domain P: 855
Trade secret T: 364
Intelligence [information]
Central Intelligence Agency C: 356
Codes and ciphers Ci: 749; (Communications
intelligence) Ci: 750
Espionage E: 358
Federal Bureau of Investigation F: 62
Homeland Security, Department of H: 301
Intelligence service I: 320
Police (Criminal intelligence) P: 621
Radar (In the military) R: 65
Terrorism T: 175; (Intelligence efforts) T: 177
War (Information and intelligence) W: 24
Intelligence [psychology] I: 319
See also Intelligence quotient *in this index*
Animal (A table of animal intelligence) A: 493
Child (Psychological differences) C: 450
Extraterrestrial intelligence E: 458
Heredity (Heredity and environment) H: 205
Intellectual disability I: 317
Mammal (Intelligence) M: 121
Mensa International M: 402
Races, Human (Race and discrimination) R: 59-60
Teaching (Guiding and assisting student
learning) T: 66
Testing (Tests of learning ability) T: 182a
Intelligence quotient [psychology] I: 320
Child (Psychological differences) C: 450
Intellectual disability (Diagnosis) I: 317
Testing (Tests of learning ability) T: 182a
**Intelligence Reform and Terrorist Prevention
Act** [2004]
Central Intelligence Agency (History) C: 357
Federal Bureau of Investigation (History) F: 62-63
September 11 terrorist attacks (Protecting the
homeland) S: 310b
Intelligence service [military] I: 320
Central Intelligence Agency C: 356
Intelligence test *See* Intelligence quotient *in this
index*
Intelligencer [newspaper]
West Virginia (Communication) W: 224
Intelligent design [theory] I: 320
Creationism (Recent developments) Ci: 1124
Evolution (Acceptance of evolution) E: 433-434
Intelligent disobedience
Guide dog G: 422
Intelligent materials [engineering] *See* Smart
materials *in this index*
Intelligent transportation system
Transportation (Challenges of modern
transportation) T: 397
INTELSAT [organization]
Communications Satellite Corporation Ci: 889
Intelsat 1 [satellite]
Communications satellite (History) Ci: 888b-889
Intendant [office]
Canada, History of (The royal province) C: 140
Intensifier [grammar]
Adverb (Intensifiers) A: 71
Intensity
Ear (The sense of hearing) E: 9; (How sounds
reach the brain) E: 10
Lighting (Quantity of light) L: 297
Photography (Intensity) P: 415
Sound (table) So: 599; (Intensity and loudness)

So: 600-601 *with diagram*
Intensity modulated radiation therapy
[medicine]
Radiation (Refining the uses of radiation) R: 81
Intensity of rainfall [meteorology]
Rain (Characteristics of rain) R: 122-123
Intensive care unit [medicine] I: 321
Heart (Diagnosis and treatment) H: 139
Hospital (Hospital units) H: 372
Neonatology N: 124
Intensive pronoun
Pronoun P: 819
Intentionality [philosophy]
Phenomenology P: 356
Interaction
Sociology (Social behavior) So: 564
Interactive environment [computer]
Computer (Educational software) Ci: 920
Electronic game E: 204a
Interactive mapping websites
Map (Mapmaking and modern technology)
M: 185
Interactive television
Television (Digital television) T: 128
Inter-Allied Declaration [1941]
United Nations (The founding of the UN) U: 94
Inter-American conferences
Monroe Doctrine (The Good Neighbor Policy)
M: 740
Pan-American conferences P: 113
Interamerican Cup [award]
Soccer (International competition) So: 548
Inter-American Development Bank
Foreign aid (Regional development programs)
F: 385
Inter-American Highway
Pan American Highway (Development) P: 114
Inter-American Treaty of Reciprocal Assistance
[1947]
Pan-American conferences (Stronger ties) P: 113
Intercalated Games
Olympic Games (The modern games) O: 750-751
Intercardinal points [navigation]
Compass Ci: 902b
Intercellular material [anatomy]
Collagen Ci: 773
Interception
Football (Advancing the ball) F: 360-361
Interchange
Railroad (Freight operations) R: 109
Road (Primary highways) R: 358; (Intersections)
R: 358-359
Interchangeable parts [manufacturing]
Automobile (The birth of the automobile
industry) A: 966
Mass production M: 269
Intercity train
Electric railroad E: 188
Railroad (Passenger service) R: 105
Intercloud lightning *See* Cloud-to-cloud lightning
in this index
**Intercollegiate Athletics, National Association
of** *See* National Association of Intercollegiate
Athletics *in this index*
Intercolonial Railway [Canada]
Fleming, Sir Sandford F: 233
Intercontinental ballistic missile
Air force (Missiles) A: 183; (Major air forces of the
world) A: 184
Air Force, United States (Missiles) A: 191
Cold War (The missile gap) Ci: 767
Guided missile *picture on* G: 423; (Surface-to-
surface missiles) G: 425
Nuclear weapon (Strategic nuclear weapons)
N: 598; (The Cold War) N: 601
Rocket (Military use) R: 386
IntercontinentalExchange [commodity exchange]
Commodity exchange Ci: 873
Intercostal space [anatomy]
Rib R: 320
Intercourse, Sexual *See* Sexual intercourse *in this
index*
Intercropping [agriculture]
Forestry (Community forestry) F: 406
Interdependence
World, History of the (A turbulent and
interdependent world) W: 448a
Interdependence of animals
Symbiosis So: 1065
Interdependence of plants
Symbiosis So: 1065
Interdict [religion]
Middle Ages (The power of the church) M: 525-
526
Interdiction attack [warfare]
Air force (Combat missions) A: 182-183
Interdigital ringworm [disease]

Ringworm R: 344
Interest [economics] I: 321
Bond B: 454
Certificate of deposit C: 363
Check (Checks and the economy) C: 391
Credit (Lending institutions) Ci: 1124
Depression (Depressions since World War II)
D: 150
Federal Reserve System (Monetary policy) F: 65
Great Depression (The stock market crash) G: 340
Income tax (Effects of inflation) I: 103
Investment (table) I: 366; (Indirect investments)
I: 367; (Bonds) I: 368; (Life insurance policies)
I: 369
Mortgage M: 820
Percentage (Interest) P: 282
Recession (Fighting recession) P: 282
Usury U: 229
Interest, Conflict of *See* Conflict of interest *in this
index*
Interest inventory [test]
Testing (Tests of aptitude and interest) T: 182a
Interest-only mortgage [economics]
Mortgage M: 820
Interest rate [economics] *See* Interest *in this index*
Interest test
Testing (Tests of aptitude and interest) T: 182a
Interests [psychology]
Careers (Interests) C: 215
Differentiated instruction D: 200
Interexchange carrier
Telephone (Traditional phone calls) T: 96 *with
diagram*
Interface [computing]
Computer (Operating system software) Ci: 917
Software (Kinds of software) So: 572
Interface [geology]
Tide (The study of the tides) T: 282
Interference [physics] I: 323 *with pictures*
Acoustics A: 29
Cable (Cable construction) C: 4
Diffraction (How diffraction occurs) D: 201
Light (Modern study) L: 285; (Interference) L: 288
with diagram
Newton's rings N: 390 *with picture*
Optics (History) O: 813
Sound (Beats) So: 604 *with diagrams*
Waves *diagram on* W: 151; (Interference) W: 153
Interference [sports]
Football (Violations and penalties) F: 363
Interference fringe [physics]
Interference I: 324 *with diagram*
Interference pattern [physics]
Astronomy (Interferometry) A: 841
Inertial guidance (Strap-down systems) I: 263-
264
Light (Interference) L: 288 *with diagram*
Interferometer [instrument]
Astronomy (Interferometry) A: 841; (Radio and
microwave astronomy) A: 843
Gravitational wave G: 333
Keck Observatory K: 254
Michelson, Albert Abraham M: 487
Interferometry [science]
Astronomy (Interferometry) A: 841; (Radio and
microwave astronomy) A: 843
Interferon [protein] I: 324
AIDS (Treatment) A: 164b-165
Cold, Common (Prevention) Ci: 761
Disease (Immune responses) D: 231-232
Genetic engineering (In medicine) G: 84c
Multiple sclerosis M: 921
Virus (Immune response) V: 428a
Interfraternity council
Fraternity (Organization) F: 496
Interglacial period [geology]
Glacier (How glaciers form) G: 202-203
Ice age I: 6
Interglossa [language]
Universal language U: 205
**Inter-Governmental Maritime Consultative
Organization** [UN]
International Maritime Organization I: 343
Intergovernmental Panel on Climate Change
Global warming (How scientists study global
warming) G: 232d
Intergovernmental Relations, Commission on
[U.S.]
States' rights (Later developments) So: 866
Interim committee
State government (Organization) So: 863-864
Interior, Department of the [U.S.] I: 324 *with
picture*
National Park Service N: 42j
Washington, D.C. *map on* W: 76
Interior, Secretary of the [office]
Flag *picture on* F: 211

Interior, Department of the I: 324
Interior architecture
Interior design I: 326
Interior decoration *See* Interior design *in this index*
Interior design I: 326 *with pictures*
Furniture F: 568 *with pictures*
House (Interior design) H: 383
Lighting (In the home) L: 296; (Lighting devices) L: 298
Painting (Decoration) P: 34
Interior Design Educators Council
Interior design (Training) I: 334
Interior designer [career]
Interior design I: 326; (Careers in interior design) I: 334
Interior environment
Interior design I: 326
Interior monologue [literature] *See* Stream of consciousness *in this index*
Interior of the Hut of a Mandan Chief, The
[painting by Bodmer]
Indian, American *picture on* I: 159
Interior Plains
Canada (The Interior Plains) C: 117 *with map*
North America (Land regions) N: 462
United States *picture on* U: 121, *map on* U: 122; (The Interior Plains) U: 124
Interior Salish [American Indians]
Salish Indians (The Interior Salish) S: 67
Interjection [grammar] I: 335
Interlaced scanning [electronics]
Television (Camera scanning patterns) T: 122
Interleukin [protein] I: 335
Oncology O: 761
Interlibrary loan system
Library (State libraries) L: 249
Interlingua [language] I: 335
Universal language U: 205
Interlining [sewing]
Quilt Q: 41
Interlock knit
Textile (Weft knitting) T: 214
Interlocking control
Railroad (Automatic block signal systems) R: 111
Interlude
Drama (Farces and interludes) D: 330
Opera (The orchestra) O: 793
Intermediate [chemistry]
Chemical reaction C: 397
Intermediate care facility
Nursing home (Intermediate care facilities) N: 620
Intermediate color
Color (Producing color harmony) Ci: 823-824 *with diagram*
Intermediate frequency [electronics]
Radio (The tuner) R: 88-89
Intermediate-range ballistic missile [weapon]
Air force (Missiles) A: 183; (Major air forces of the world) A: 184
Guided missile (Surface-to-surface missiles) G: 425-426
Intermediate-Range Nuclear Forces Treaty [1987]
Congress of the United States (Approving treaties) Ci: 946
Intermediate school *See* Middle school *in this index*
Intermediate-term loan
Interest (Length of a loan) I: 323
Intermezzo [music] I: 335
Drama (Intermezzi and operas) D: 330
Opera (Opera seria and opera buffa) O: 797
Pergolesi, Giovanni Battista P: 287
"Intermezzo" [music by Mascagni]
Opera: (Cavalleria Rusticana) O: 803
Intermittent motion
Motion picture (The camera) M: 856-857
Intermodal train
Railroad (At interchanges) R: 110
Intermodal transport
Transportation (Freight transportation) T: 395 *with picture*
Intermolecular force [chemistry]
Bond (Other linkages) B: 454
Intermontane Basin
Colorado (Land regions) Ci: 838
Internal auditor
Accounting (Auditing) A: 23
Internal chemoreceptor [physiology]
Hunger H: 449
Internal colonialism
Minority group (Relationships between groups) M: 609
Internal-combustion engine I: 336 *with diagrams*
Automobile A: 946; (Power systems) A: 947-948; (Powering an internal-combusion car) A: 950 *with diagrams*; (Automobiles and the environment) A: 963; (The gasoline car) A: 965-966
Carburetor C: 208
Diesel engine D: 198
Gasoline engine G: 63 *with diagrams*
Heat (Changing heat into motion) H: 154 *with diagram*
Hybrid car H: 461
Invention (The late 1800's) I: 362
Lenoir, Jean Joseph Étienne L: 196
Rotary engine R: 485 *with pictures*
Internal energy [physics]
Heat H: 148; (Temperature and heat) H: 150 *with diagram*
Thermodynamics T: 253
Internal fertilization
Animal (Sexual reproduction) A: 496 *with diagram*
Fertilization F: 78
Fish (How fish reproduce) F: 169
Reproduction (Reptiles and birds) R: 243
Internal gear
Transmission (Planetary gears) T: 377 *with diagrams*
Internal medicine I: 336
Medicine (table) M: 369
Internal memory *See* Random-access memory *in this index*
Internal parasite [organism]
Cattle (Diseases) C: 312-314
Internal reconstruction
Linguistics (Internal reconstruction) L: 336
Internal revenue I: 336
Inland revenue I: 273
Internal Revenue Service I: 337
Internal Revenue Service [U.S.] I: 337
Income tax (Paying the individual income tax) I: 104; (Processing income tax returns) I: 105
Internal revenue (The Internal Revenue Service) I: 337
Tax Court, United States T: 52
Washington, D.C. *map on* W: 76
Internal revenue stamp
Stamp So: 829
Internal rhyme
Rhyme R: 319
Internal Security, Committee on
Un-American Activities Committee U: 18
Internal Security Act [1950]
McCarran, Patrick Anthony M: 332a
Internal senses
Senses *diagrams on* S: 301; (Internal senses) S: 302
Internal short circuit [electricity]
Battery (Battery structure) B: 168
Internal tide [geology]
Tide (The study of the tides) T: 282
Internal waters
Territorial waters T: 173
Internally displaced person
Refugee (The rights of refugees) R: 203
International Advertising Association
Advertising (Advertising in other countries) A: 77-78
International Afro-American Museum [former name]
Museum of African American History M: 940
International Air Transport Association I: 337
Aviation (Other aviation organizations) A: 986
International airport
Airport (Commercial service airports) A: 243; (World's 25 busiest airports) A: 245
International Amateur Athletic Federation
Track and field T: 356; (Organizations) T: 359
International Amateur Radio Union
Radio, Amateur (Amateur radio organizations) R: 96
International America's Cup Class
America's Cup A: 431
International arbitration
Arbitration (International arbitration) A: 592
International Archery Federation
Archery (Target archery) A: 602-603
International Association of Bridge, Structural and Ornamental Iron Workers
Labor movement (table) L: 8
International Association of Fire Fighters
Labor movement (table) L: 8
International Association of Lions Clubs *See* Lions Clubs International *in this index*
International Association of Machinists and Aerospace Workers *See* Machinists and Aerospace Workers, International Association of *in this index*
International Astronautical Federation
Astronautics A: 833
International Astronomical Union
Asteroid A: 823
Astronomy (Astronomy associations) A: 849
Dwarf planet D: 394
Eris E: 352
Planet P: 507
Pluto P: 580
Solar system (Our solar system) So: 580
Star (Names of stars) So: 842
International Atomic Energy Agency [UN] I: 337
Eisenhower, Dwight David (Foreign affairs) E: 152-153
Nobel Prizes (Peace: 2005) N: 449
Nuclear energy (The first peaceful uses) N: 591
Nuclear Nonproliferation Treaty N: 595
United Nations (Peaceful uses of nuclear energy) U: 89
International Balloon Fiesta [Albuquerque]
New Mexico (Annual events) N: 265 *with picture*
International Bank for Reconstruction and Development [UN]
World Bank W: 450
International Bowling Campus
Bowling (The 1900's) B: 524b
International Bowling Federation
Bowling (The 1900's) B: 524b
International Boxing Association
Boxing (Regulation) B: 530
International Boxing Federation
Boxing (Boxing today) B: 533
International Bridge [Michigan-Ontario]
Soo Canals (The Canadian canal) So: 595 *with map*
International Brigade [Spanish history]
Spain (Civil war) So: 750
International Broadcasting Bureau
Voice of America V: 437
International Brotherhood of Electrical Workers *See* Electrical Workers, International Brotherhood of *in this index*
International Brotherhood of Magicians
Magician (Becoming a magician) M: 52
International Brotherhood of Painters and Allied Trades
Labor movement (table) L: 8
International Brotherhood of Teamsters, Chauffeurs, Warehousemen, and Helpers of America *See* Teamsters Union *in this index*
International Bureau
Postal Union, Universal P: 708
International Bureau of Weights and Measures I: 338
Weights and measures (Measurement systems) W: 184
International Business Machines Corporation I: 338
Computer (Personal computers) Ci: 909-910; (Manufacturing) Ci: 924; (Foundations of data processing) Ci: 924b; (The personal computer) Ci: 924c-924d *with picture*
Encyclopedia: (World Book) E: 268b-269
Gates, Bill G: 67
Manufacturing (table) M: 170
Microsoft Corporation M: 519
Watson, Thomas John W: 148
International Campaign to Ban Landmines [organization]
Mine warfare (Efforts to ban land mines) M: 565
Nobel Prizes (Peace: 1997) N: 448b
International Centre for the Settlement of Investment Disputes [UN]
World Bank W: 450
International Chamber of Commerce [organization]
Chamber of commerce C: 371
International Church of the Foursquare Gospel [religious group]
McPherson, Aimee Semple M: 344
International Circus Festival of Monte Carlo [Monaco]
Circus (Places to visit and annual events) Ci: 566 *with picture*
International Civil Aviation Organization [UN] I: 338
Airport A: 242
Aviation (The International Civil Aviation Organization) A: 986
International Civil Rights Center & Museum
North Carolina (Museums) N: 477
International code
Flag (Flags that talk) F: 208 *with pictures*
Morse code M: 820 *with picture*
Radio, Amateur R: 95
International Coffee Agreement [1963]
Coffee (History) Ci: 755
International Cometary Explorer [space probe]
Space exploration (Probes to comets) So: 711

International Commerce Centre [building, Hong Kong]
Skyscraper (table) **S: 498**
International Commission for the Protection of the Danube River
Water (The challenge of today) **W: 132**
International Commission on Radiological Protection
Radiation (Dose) **R: 79-80**
International Committee of the Red Cross [organization]
Nobel Prizes (Peace: 1963) **N: 448b**
Red Cross (The Red Cross in other lands) **R: 187**
International Composers' Guild
Varèse, Edgard **V: 285**
International Confederation of Autonomous Chapters of the American Indian Movement
American Indian Movement **A: 412**
International Confederation of Free Trade Unions
Labor movement (International organizations) **L: 15**
International Convention on the Elimination of All Forms of Racial Discrimination [1969]
United Nations (Human rights) **U: 88**
International copyright
Copyright (International agreements) **Ci: 1048**
International Correspondence Schools
Correspondence school **Ci: 1071**
International Council for Science I: 338
International Council for the Exploration of the Sea [organization]
Fishing industry (International commissions and treaties) **F: 187**
International Court of Justice [UN] **I: 338**
Court (International courts) **Ci: 1102**
International law (Courts and arbitration) **I: 341**
International relations (International law) **I: 344-345**
United Nations (The six major UN organs) **U: 78**; (Other main organs) **U: 84**
War crime (The United Nations and war crimes) **W: 27**
International Covenant on Civil and Political Rights [1966]
Human rights (Treaties) **H: 428a**
International Covenant on Economic, Social, and Cultural Rights [1966]
Human rights (Treaties) **H: 428a**
International Criminal Court I: 338
Court (Courts around the world) **Ci: 1102-1104**
Genocide **G: 90**
International relations (International law) **I: 345**
Sudan (Violence in Darfur) **So: 954**
United Nations (Human rights) **U: 88**
War crime (The United Nations and war crimes) **W: 27**
International Criminal Police Organization
Interpol **I: 350h**
International Criminal Tribunal for the former Yugoslavia
Milošević, Slobodan **M: 556**
International culture
Culture (The boundaries of cultures) **Ci: 1187-1188**
International DanceSport Federation
Ballroom dancing **B: 63**
International date line [geography] **I: 339** *with map*
Time (International time zones) **T: 292a** *with diagram*
International Development Association [UN] **I: 339**
Foreign aid (Worldwide lending programs) **F: 385**
World Bank **W: 450**
International Development Cooperation Agency [U.S.]
Agency for International Development **A: 140**
State, Department of (Since World War II) **So: 862**
International economics
Economics (Fields of economics) **E: 64**
International Education, Institute of
Scholarship (International scholarships) **S: 179**
International Electrical Congress
Metric system (Evolution of the metric system) **M: 441**
International Electrotechnical Commission
Metric system (Evolution of the metric system) **M: 441**
International Energy Agency I: 339
International Expositions, Bureau of
World's fair **W: 500**
International Falls [Minnesota]
Minnesota (table: Average monthly weather) **M: 598**
International Farm Youth Exchange
4-H (Expansion) **F: 436**

International Federation of Library Associations and Institutions
Library (International library programs) **L: 254**
International Federation of Red Cross and Red Crescent Societies
Red Cross (The Red Cross in other lands) **R: 187**
International Fencing Federation
Fencing (Fencing organizations) **F: 71**
International Finance Corporation I: 340
Foreign aid (Worldwide lending programs) **F: 385**
World Bank **W: 450**
International Fisherman's race
Bluenose **B: 424**
International flag code
Flag (Flags that talk) **F: 208** *with pictures*
International foot [measurement]
Mile **M: 542**
International Fund for Agricultural Development [UN] **I: 340**
International Geographical Union
Geography (Careers in geography) **G: 96**
International Geophysical Year
Antarctica (The International Geophysical Year) **A: 538**
International gold standard [economics]
Exchange rate **E: 436**
International Grand Championship Horse Show
Tennessee *picture on* **T: 138**
International Gymnastics Federation
Gymnastics (Organization) **G: 451**
International Hang Gliding and Paragliding Commission
Hang gliding **H: 51**
International Harvester Company
McCormick, Cyrus Hall **M: 332f**
International Hydrographic Organization
Southern Ocean **So: 688**
International Hydrological Programme
Water (The challenge of today) **W: 132**
International Ice Hockey Federation
Hockey (Amateur organization) **H: 279**; (Amateur development) **H: 281**
International Ice Patrol [organization]
Iceberg (Icebergs and people) **I: 18**
International Interior Design Association
Interior design (Training) **I: 334**
International Jazz Festival [Montreal]
Quebec *picture on* **Q: 14**
International Joint Commission I: 340
Saint Lawrence Seaway (First construction plans) **S: 44**
International Labour Conference
International Labour Organization **I: 340**
International Labour Organization I: 340
Foreign aid (Technical assistance and relief) **F: 385**
Freedom of assembly (In other countries) **F: 504**
Unemployment (Measuring unemployment) **U: 22-23**
International Ladies' Garment Workers' Union
UNITE HERE **U: 43**
International language
Esperanto **E: 358**
Universal language **U: 205**
International Latin style
Ballroom dancing **B: 63**
International law I: 340
See also the list of Related articles in the International Law *article*
Grotius, Hugo **G: 400**
International relations (International law) **I: 344**
Law (Public law) **L: 130-131**; (Developments in international law) **L: 137**
Peace (From the 1400's to the 1700's) **P: 206**
Treaty port **T: 409**
War crime (The United Nations and war crimes) **W: 27**
International Law, Institute of [organization]
Nobel Prizes (Peace: 1904) **N: 448**
International Law Association
Field, David Dudley, Jr. **F: 91**
International Law Commission [UN]
War crime (The United Nations and war crimes) **W: 27**
International Longshoremen's and Warehousemen's Union
Bridges, Harry **B: 607**
International Longshoremen's Association
Bridges, Harry **B: 607**
Labor movement (table) **L: 8**
International Maritime Organization [UN] **I: 342**
International Meteorological Organization
World Meteorological Organization **W: 451**
International Military Tribunal
Nuremberg Trials (The trials) **N: 613**
International Monetary Conference [1944]
Bretton Woods **B: 594**

Morgenthau, Henry, Jr. **M: 805**
New Hampshire (The mid-1900's) **N: 226-227**
International Monetary Fund [UN] **I: 343**
Balance of payments (How the balance of payments is determined) **B: 36**
Bretton Woods **B: 594**
Globalization (Features of globalization) **G: 233**
Latin America (In the early 2000's) **L: 111**
New Hampshire (The mid-1900's) **N: 226-227**
Special Drawing Rights **So: 770**
International money order
Money order **M: 718**
International Morse Code
Morse code **M: 820** *with picture*
International Motor Sports Association
Automobile racing (Racing organizations) **A: 976**
International nautical mile [measurement]
Knot **K: 355**
Mile **M: 542**
International Negotiation Network Council
Carter, Jimmy (Later years) **C: 259**
International Network for the Improvement of Banana and Plantain [organization]
Banana (The banana industry) **B: 73-74**
International News Service
Hearst, William Randolph **H: 131**
International Nickel Company
Manitoba (The mid-1900's) **M: 162-163**
Thompson **T: 262**
International Olympic Committee I: 343
Blood doping **B: 415**
Doping **D: 309**
Olympic Games (The International Olympic Committee) **O: 746a**; (Olympic competition) **O: 746b**
International Order of the Rainbow for Girls [organization]
Rainbow for Girls **R: 128**
International Organization for Standardization
International standard book number **I: 347**
Smart card **S: 513**
Television (Digital television) **T: 128**
International Pacific Halibut Commission
Fishing industry (International commissions and treaties) **F: 187**
International Peace Bureau
Nobel Prizes (Peace: 1910) **N: 448**
International Peace Garden [Manitoba-North Dakota] **I: 343**
North Dakota (Places to visit) **N: 504** *with picture*
International Peace Park
Waterton-Glacier International Peace Park **W: 147**
International Phonetic Alphabet
Phonetics (An international phonetic alphabet) **P: 400**
International Physicians for the Prevention of Nuclear War
Nobel Prizes (Peace: 1985) **N: 448b**
International Planned Parenthood Federation
Planned Parenthood Federation of America **P: 515**
International Polar Year 2007-2008 [study]
Antarctica (Scientific research) **A: 539-540**
Arctic (Climate change) **A: 640**
International Political Science Association
Political science (Contemporary ideas) **P: 639**
International Pro Hockey League
Hockey (Professional hockey) **H: 281**
International prototype kilogram [measurement]
Metric system (Evolution of the metric system) **M: 441**
Weights and measures **W: 184**
International quarantine
Quarantine **Q: 7**
International Red Cross and Red Crescent Movement
Red Cross (The Red Cross in other lands) **R: 187**
International Red Cross Conference [organization]
Red Cross (The Red Cross in other lands) **R: 187**
International Refugee Organization
Refugee (Efforts to help refugees) **R: 203**
United Nations (Aid to refugees) **U: 88**
International relations I: 343 *with pictures*
See also the list of Related articles in the International relations *article*
Balance of power **B: 36**
Cold War **Ci: 762**
Foreign policy **F: 386**
Foundation (International affairs) **F: 431**
Government (Foreign affairs) **G: 283**
Petroleum (Petroleum and international relations) **P: 346**
Political science (International relations) **P: 638**
State, Department of **So: 859**
Technical assistance **T: 73**
Treaty **T: 408**

Treaty port T: 409
International Rice Research Institute
[Philippines]
Rice (History) R: 326-327
International Romani Union Parliament
Roma (History) R: 402b
International Rugby Board [organization]
Rugby football (History) R: 513
International Rules
Boating (Boating regulations) B: 429
International Rules of the Road
Ship (Safety) S: 411
International Safety of Life at Sea conventions
Ship (Safety) S: 411
International Seabed Authority [organization]
Law of the Sea Convention L: 142
International Skating Union
Ice skating (Figure skating) I: 11-12; (History) I: 16
International Olympic Committee I: 343
International Society for Krishna Consciousness
See Hare Krishna in this index
International Softball Federation
Softball (History) So: 572
International Space Station I: 346a with pictures
Space exploration (The International Space
Station) So: 722; (The Columbia disaster)
So: 725-726; (Completing the station) So: 726
International Special Olympic Games
Special Olympics So: 771
International Species Information System
[database]
Zoo (Wildlife conservation) Z: 600
International standard book number I: 347
International standard style
Ballroom dancing B: 63
International statute mile [measurement]
Mile M: 542
International Style [design]
Architecture picture on A: 632; (The International
Style) A: 630
Furniture (Recent developments) F: 584
House picture on H: 381
Jahn, Helmut J: 21
Johnson, Philip Cortelyou J: 152
Le Corbusier L: 151
International Style of Buddhist art
Sculpture (Korea) S: 238; (Japan) S: 239
International System of Units See Metric system
in this index
International Telecommunication Union [UN]
I: 347
International Telegraph Union
International Telecommunication Union I: 347
Telegraph (Service expansion and improvement)
T: 91
International Tennis Federation
Tennis (Amateur tennis) T: 165
International trade I: 347 with picture
See also Trade in this index
Convertibility Ci: 1024
Economics (The world economy) E: 61
Exchange rate E: 435
Exports and imports E: 454
Free trade F: 499
General Agreement on Tariffs and Trade G: 83
Globalization G: 232d
Great Depression G: 338
Japan (Postwar boom) J: 58
Money (Money and international finance) M: 717
North American Free Trade Agreement N: 470
Reciprocal trade agreement R: 175
Sanctions, Economic S: 106
Tariff T: 43
World Trade Organization W: 451
International Trade, U.S. Court of
Court of International Trade, United States
Ci: 1105
International Trade Commission, United States
I: 349
International Trade Organization
General Agreement on Tariffs and Trade G: 83
**International Union, United Automobile,
Aerospace and Agricultural Implement
Workers of America** See United Automobile
Workers in this index
**International Union for the Conservation of
Nature and Natural Resources**
Endangered species (Protecting endangered
species) E: 270
National park (International concern for national
parks) N: 42j
Wildlife conservation (International cooperation)
W: 305
**International Union of Bricklayers and Allied
Craftsmen**
Labor movement (table) L: 8
International Union of Electronic, Electrical,

Salaried, Machine, Furniture Workers
Labor movement (table) L: 8
International Union of Operating Engineers
Engineers, International Union of Operating
E: 291
Labor movement (table) L: 8
**International Union of Pure and Applied
Chemistry**
Bohrium B: 438
Dubnium D: 371
Element, Chemical E: 219
Hassium H: 83
Meitnerium M: 387
Mendelevium M: 398
Nobelium N: 450
Roentgenium R: 400
Rutherfordium R: 569
Seaborgium S: 264
Transuranium element T: 401
International Union of Pure and Applied Physics
Bohrium B: 438
Dubnium D: 371
Hassium H: 83
Meitnerium M: 387
Mendelevium M: 398
Rutherfordium R: 569
Seaborgium S: 264
International war
War W: 23
International waters
High seas H: 228
International Whaling Commission
Conservation (Ocean conservation) Ci: 978-979
Whale (The future of whales) W: 264
International Wildlife Conservation Park [zoo]
New York City (The Bronx) N: 328; (Parks) N: 338
International Women's Day
March M: 195
International Woodworkers of America
Carpenters and Joiners of America, United
Brotherhood of C: 246
International Workingmen's Association
[European history]
Marx, Karl (Move to London) M: 237; (The
Communist Manifesto) M: 237
International Youth Hostel Federation
Youth hostel Y: 574
"Internationale, The" [song] I: 349
Internationalization
Aviation (Internationalization) A: 991
Internet I: 350 with pictures
See also World Wide Web in this index
Africa (Communication) A: 129
Business (Recent developments) B: 727
Careers (Finding job opportunities) C: 217 with
picture
Computer (Web browsers) Ci: 919; (The Internet)
Ci: 920
Copyright (Users' rights) Ci: 1047-1048
Etiquette (Internet etiquette) E: 374
Globalization G: 233
HyperText Markup Language H: 477
Information retrieval I: 268b
Intellectual property I: 318
Invention (Recent developments) I: 364
Obscenity and pornography (Regulating
pornography) O: 643
Privacy, Right of P: 808a
Remote control (History) R: 231
Sales tax S: 66
Search engine S: 268
Slang (Sources of slang) S: 500
Technology (The computer age) T: 75-76
Television (Television and the Internet) T: 128
Website W: 176
Uses
Adult education (Distance learning) A: 69
Advertising picture on A: 76; (The Internet)
A: 74; (Recent developments) A: 80
Auction A: 881
Bank (Providing a means of payment) B: 89;
(Electronic banking) B: 89-90
Blog B: 406
Book (Modern books) B: 468
Censorship (Censorship methods) C: 346
Codes and ciphers (Modern applications of
cryptography) Ci: 752
Communication (The development of the
Internet) Ci: 886
Database D: 41
E-book E: 2
E-commerce E: 2
Election campaign (Internet contributions)
E: 160
Electronic game (Personal computers) E: 204c
Electronic publishing E: 205
Gambling (Modern gambling) G: 21

Game (Internet games) G: 22
Instant messaging I: 304
Investment (How investors buy stocks) I: 369
Journalism (Fields of journalism) J: 170
Library (The growth of information and
technology) L: 237-238; (Information science
and technology) L: 251
Manufacturing (How science helps
manufacturing) M: 171-172
Map (Mapmaking and modern technology)
M: 185
Marketing (Market research) M: 214;
(Distribution) M: 214
Medicine (Computers and electronic
communication) M: 370
Museum (Museums today) M: 940
North America (Transportation and
communication) N: 469
Popular music (New technologies) P: 671
Postal Service, United States (Electronic
services) P: 700
Postal services (Technological advancements)
P: 707
Publishing P: 866
Radio (Webcasting and podcasting) R: 87
Recording industry (History) R: 182
Remote control (History) R: 231
Sales (Current trends in sales) S: 65
School (Growth and reform) S: 184
Storytelling (The 2000's) S: 915
Teaching (Guiding and assisting student
learning) T: 66
Technology (The computer age) T: 75
Telephone (How a telephone call travels)
T: 95-96
Television (Television and the Internet) T: 128
Text messaging T: 211
Universities and colleges (Online learning)
U: 211
Wireless communication (Wireless networking)
W: 345
Internet cafe
Internet picture on I: 350
**Internet Corporation for Assigned Names and
Numbers** [computing]
Internet (ICANN) I: 350e
Website W: 176
Internet game
Game (Internet games) G: 22
Internet library
Library (The growth of information and
technology) L: 237-238
Internet Message Access Protocol [electonics]
Internet (Software) I: 350c-350d
Internet Protocol address
Computer (Internet software) Ci: 922
Internet (How the Internet works) I: 350c
Internet service provider
Computer (Internet service providers) Ci: 921
E-mail E: 2
Internet (Hardware) I: 350c; (Net neutrality)
I: 350g
Internist [medicine]
Internal medicine I: 336
Medicine (Primary care physicians) M: 366
Internment camp
Asian Americans picture on A: 812e; (World War II
and Japanese Americans) A: 812f
Concentration camp (Other concentration
camps) Ci: 927
Japanese American internment J: 60
Mineta, Norman Yoshio M: 572
World War II (Treatment of enemy aliens) W: 496
Internship
Cooperative education Ci: 1037
Interpersonal relations See Human relations in
this index
Interphase [biology]
Cell (Mitosis) C: 330
Interplanetary medium [astronomy]
Solar system So: 580
Interplanetary space [astronomy]
Space exploration (Space between the planets)
So: 696
Interplanting
Gardening (Planning a kitchen garden) G: 34
Interplate earthquake
Earthquake (Where earthquakes occur) E: 38
Interpointing [printing]
Braille B: 550
Interpol [police] I: 350h
Police (Interpol) P: 623
Interpolation [electronics]
Photography (Capturing digital images) P: 420-
421 with picture
Interposition [chess]
Chess (How chess is played) C: 413

Interposition [U.S. history]
States' rights (Later developments) **So:** 866
Interpretation of Dreams, The [book by Freud]
Mythology (Psychological approaches) **M:** 990
Interpreter [computing]
Computer (Interpreting a program) **Ci:** 923
Interpretive photogrammetry [cartography]
Photogrammetry **P:** 405
Interpretive reporting
Journalism (Informing the public) **J:** 172-173
Interprovincial Pipeline
Pipeline (In Canada) **P:** 491
Interpublic Group of Companies
Advertising (The advertising industry) **A:** 77
Interregnum [European history]
Holy Roman Empire (Problems of the empire)
H: 299-300
Interrogation point
Punctuation (The question mark) **P:** 902
Interrogative [grammar]
Adjective (Classifying adjectives) **A:** 57
Pronoun **P:** 819
Sentence (Sentence classifications) **S:** 303
Interrupted Sleep, The [painting by Boucher]
Boucher, François *picture on* **B:** 515
Interscholastic sports
Physical education (Secondary school programs)
P: 432
Intersection [mathematics]
Set theory (Using set theory) **S:** 322 *with diagram*
Intersection [road]
Road (Intersections) **R:** 358
Interstate commerce **I:** 350h
Gibbons v. Ogden **G:** 185
Granger cases **G:** 311
Insurance (Greater regulation) **I:** 315
Interstate Commerce Act [1887]
Cleveland, Grover (Other actions) **Ci:** 671
Interstate commerce (The Interstate Commerce
Act) **I:** 351
Railroad (Regulation and control of U.S. railroads)
R: 118
Interstate Commerce Commission [U.S.] **I:** 352
Government regulation **G:** 293
Interstate commerce (The Interstate Commerce
Act) **I:** 351
Public utility (History) **P:** 865
Interstate Highway System **I:** 352
Road (How roads and highways are paid for)
R: 360
United States *map on* **U:** 134
Interstate 35 bridge collapse
Minneapolis (Recent developments) **M:** 583
Interstellar cloud [astronomy]
Heliosphere **H:** 175
Hydrogen (Occurrence) **H:** 469
Interstellar dust [astronomy]
Galaxy (Types of galaxies) **G:** 8a
Interstellar medium **I:** 352
Milky Way (Shape of the galaxy) **M:** 550
Interstellar medium [astronomy] **I:** 352
Spitzer, Lyman, Jr. **So:** 797
Interstellar neutral [astronomy]
Heliosphere (Magnetic field) **H:** 175
Interstellar space [astronomy]
Cosmic rays **Ci:** 1075
Heliosphere **H:** 175
Space exploration (Space between the stars)
So: 696
Voyager **V:** 451
Interstitial fluid [physiology]
Human body (The lymphatic system) **H:** 424
Lymphatic system **L:** 533; (Return of interstitial
fluid) **L:** 534
Interstitial pneumonia [disorder]
Pneumonia (How pneumonia develops) **P:** 586
Intertidal zone [geology]
Tide **T:** 280
Interval
Music (Harmony) **M:** 951
Intervention [international relations] **I:** 352
Monroe Doctrine **M:** 739
Roosevelt, Franklin Delano (The road to war)
R: 455
World War II (The United States enters the war)
W: 478
Intervertebral disk [anatomy]
Back **B:** 17
Sciatica **S:** 190
Spine **So:** 792 *with picture*
Interview
Careers (Being interviewed) **C:** 219
Geography (Interviewing) **G:** 95
Newspaper (Gathering information) **N:** 382 *with
picture*
Public opinion poll (Interviewing the sample)
P: 862 *with picture*

A Guide to Research Skills **Research Guide:** 34
Inter-vivos trust [economics]
Trust fund (Kinds of trusts) **T:** 474
Intestate [law]
Heir **H:** 167
Will **W:** 307
Intestinal autointoxication [disorder]
Intoxication **I:** 354
Intestinal juice [physiology]
Digestive system (In the small intestine) **D:** 202
Intestine [anatomy] **I:** 352 *with diagram*
Alimentary canal **A:** 368 *with diagram*
Campylobacter **C:** 97
Catgut **C:** 301
Celiac disease **C:** 325
Colon **Ci:** 786
Colon cancer **Ci:** 786
Colonoscopy **Ci:** 815
Colostomy **Ci:** 850
Crohn's disease **Ci:** 1150
Diarrhea **D:** 184
Digestive system (In the small intestine) **D:** 202
with diagrams
Giardiasis **G:** 184
Gland (table) **G:** 209
Human body (table) **H:** 422 *with diagram*
Incontinence **I:** 106
Inflammatory bowel disease **I:** 266
Laxative **L:** 147
Inthanon Mountain
Thailand (The Mountainous North) **T:** 224 *with
picture*
Inti Raymi [festival]
Argentina (Recreation) **A:** 650
Inca (Religion) **I:** 96-97
Intifada [uprising] **I:** 353
Arab-Israeli conflict (The first intifada) **A:** 582a
Gaza Strip **G:** 74
Israel (The early 2000's) **I:** 489-490
Jerusalem (Israeli control) **J:** 102
Middle East (History) **M:** 533-534a
Palestine (The continuing conflict and peace
efforts) **P:** 106
Palestine Liberation Organization (History)
P: 106-107
Intima [anatomy]
Vein **V:** 295
"Intimations of Immortality" [poem by
Wordsworth]
Wordsworth, William (Later career) **W:** 404
Intolerable Acts [1774] **I:** 353
Adams, Samuel (The patriot) **A:** 44
Boston Port Act **B:** 505
Quebec Act **Q:** 38
Revolution, American (The Intolerable Acts)
R: 274
United States, History of the (Renewed conflict)
U: 158-159
Intolerance [film]
Griffith, D. W. **G:** 393
Intoxication [disorder] **I:** 353
Driving while intoxicated **D:** 348
Intracartilaginous bone formation
Bone (Development of bones) **B:** 456
Intracloud lightning
Lightning (Origin and destination) **L:** 300 *with
diagram*
Intracytoplasmic sperm injection [reproduction]
Infertility (Treatment) **I:** 265
Intradermal injection
Hypodermic injection **H:** 480
Intramembranous bone formation
Bone (Development of bones) **B:** 456
Intramural sports **I:** 354
Football **F:** 354
Physical education (Secondary school programs)
P: 432
Intramuros [district]
Manila (Description) **M:** 142
Intramuscular injection
Hypodermic injection **H:** 480
Intranet [computing]
Computer (Intranets) **Ci:** 922
Intransitive verb
Verb (Transitive and intransitive verbs) **V:** 315
Intraocular lens [medicine]
Cataract **C:** 299
Eye (Cataract) **E:** 466
Intraplate earthquake
Earthquake (Intraplate quakes) **E:** 38a
Intrapsychic conflict [psychology]
Abnormal psychology (Psychodynamic theories)
A: 12
Intrastate commerce
Interstate commerce **I:** 350h
Intra-urban service
Electric railroad **E:** 188

Intrauterine device
Birth control (Methods of birth control) **B:** 378-
379
Intravenous injection **I:** 354
Hypodermic injection **H:** 480
Intensive care unit **I:** 321
Intrepid [spacecraft]
Conrad, Charles, Jr. **Ci:** 973
Intrinsic criticism
Criticism (Kinds of literary criticism) **Ci:** 1146
Intrinsically photosensitive retinal ganglion cell
[anatomy]
Eye (The retina) **E:** 462
Introduced species [biology]
Invasive species **I:** 354j
Introduction
Public speaking (Introduction) **P:** 865
Introduction and Allegro [music by Elgar]
Elgar, Sir Edward **E:** 235
Introduction to the Devout Life, An [book by
Francis de Sales]
Francis de Sales, Saint **F:** 481
Introduction to the Method of Leonardo da Vinci
[essay by Valéry]
Valéry, Paul **V:** 265
Introduction to the Science of Sociology [book by
Burgess and Park]
Collective behavior **Ci:** 774
*Introduction to the Study of Experimental
Medicine* [book by Bernard]
Bernard, Claude **B:** 270
Introductions [customs]
Address, Forms of **A:** 53
Etiquette (Introduction etiquette) **E:** 374
Introspection
Psychology (Structuralism) **P:** 849
Introvert [psychology] **I:** 354
Jung, Carl Gustav (His theories) **J:** 195
Testing (Personality tests) **T:** 182a
Intruder, The [play by Maeterlinck]
Maeterlinck, Maurice **M:** 41
Intrusion [geology]
Rock (Intrusive rock) **R:** 371
Intrusive rock
Igneous rock **I:** 49
Rock (Intrusive rocks) **R:** 371
Intubation [medical procedure]
Croup **Ci:** 1157
Intuitionism [philosophy]
Mathematics (Philosophies of mathematics)
M: 307
Intumescent coating
Fireproofing **F:** 135
Inuit [people] **I:** 354 *with pictures*
Alaska (Population) **A:** 286; (Land-use issues)
A: 304
Aleuts **A:** 340
Arctic (Groups) **A:** 638
Canada (The territories) **C:** 104 *with picture*;
(Ancestry) **C:** 105-106; (Arctic life) **C:** 107
Clothing *pictures on* **Ci:** 690, **Ci:** 695
Exploration (The Tuniit) **E:** 441; (Inuit exploration)
E: 442
Greenland (People) **G:** 384 *with picture*
Igloo **I:** 48
Indian, American *pictures on* **I:** 138; (Shelter)
I: 136d; (Peoples of the Arctic) **I:** 152; (Current
issues) **I:** 182-183
Indian reservation **I:** 188
Iqaluit **I:** 397
Manitoba (Interesting facts) **M:** 145
Mask *picture on* **M:** 264
Mythology (Mythical places) **M:** 975
Newfoundland and Labrador (Early European
exploration) **N:** 375
North America (People) **N:** 458-459
Northwest Territories (People) **N:** 530; (The late
1900's) **N:** 534
Nunavut **N:** 608; (People) **N:** 609
Quebec (Indian days) **Q:** 30
Races, Human (Climatic adaptations) **R:** 58
Seal (Hunting of seals) **S:** 267
Tundra **T:** 486
United States, History of the (America before
colonial times) **U:** 149
Walrus **W:** 20
Whale (The future of whales) **W:** 264
Inuit-Inupiaq [language]
Inuit **I:** 354; (Language) **I:** 354f
Inuit Tapirisat of Canada [organization]
Indian, American (In Canada) **I:** 178b
Inuk [person] *See* Inuit *in this index*
Inuktitut [language]
Nunavut **N:** 609; (People) **N:** 609; (Education)
N: 611
Inuvialuit [people]
Northwest Territories (People) **N:** 530

Inuvik [Northwest Territories] I: 354j *with picture*
Invalid argument
  Logic L: 425
Invalides, Hôtel des [Paris]
  Paris (Museums and art galleries) P: 164-165
Invar [metal]
  Nickel (Industrial uses) N: 404
Invar tape [measuring device]
  Surveying (Surveying tools) So: 1011
Invariance [topology]
  Topology (Invariance and equivalence) T: 332
    with picture
Invasive cervical cancer [disorder]
  Cervical cancer C: 364
Invasive species [biology] I: 354j *with picture*
  Animal (Introduction of new species) A: 505
  Coquí Ci: 1048
  Flower (Wildflowers) F: 282
  Forestry (Invasive species) F: 408
  Great Lakes (Invasive species) G: 345
  Plant (Invasive species) P: 543
  Ship (Invasive species) S: 414
  Snake (Snakes as invasive species) S: 532
  Wetland (Threats) W: 252b
Invention I: 354l *with pictures*
  See also the list of Related articles in the Invention
    article
  Culture (How cultures change) Ci: 1189
  Edison, Thomas Alva E: 77
  Leonardo da Vinci (Drawings and scientific
    studies) L: 200-200a; (Leonardo's importance)
    L: 201
  Patent P: 194
  Public domain P: 855
  United States, History of the (New products)
    U: 180
Inventory [manufacturing]
  Publishing (Going out of print) P: 869
Inventory map
  Map (Types of maps) M: 177-178 *with picture*;
    (Development of thematic and inventory
    mapping) M: 185
Inverness [Scotland] I: 365
Inverse of fraction [mathematics]
  Fraction (Division) F: 448
Inverse square law [physics]
  Light (Energy and brightness) L: 290
Inversion [biochemistry]
  Honey H: 314
Inversion [weather]
  Smoke S: 520
  Weather (How people affect the weather) W: 170
Invert sugar
  Candy (Types of candies) C: 175-176
Invertebrate [zoology] I: 365 *with picture*
  Animal (Kinds of animals) A: 472; (Invertebrates
    and vertebrates) A: 488 *with diagram*; (A table
    of animal intelligence) A: 493
  Brain (The brain in other animals) B: 559
  Circulatory system (Invertebrates) Ci: 561
  Deep sea (Deep-sea life) D: 82a *with pictures*
  Heart (Hearts of animals) H: 146 *with diagram*
  Nervous system (In invertebrates) N: 136
  Prehistoric animal (The earliest animals) P: 736;
    (Invertebrates) P: 737
  Sleep (Sleep in animals) S: 506
Invertebrate paleontology [geology]
  Lamarck, Chevalier de L: 50
  Paleontology P: 103
Inverted U hypothesis [economics] *See* Kuznets
  hypothesis *in this index*
Investigation, Crime
  Criminal justice system (The police) Ci: 1143
Investigative reporting
  Journalism (Investigating wrongdoing) J: 173
  Newspaper (Gathering information) N: 382
Investigator [ship]
  Northwest Passage *picture on* N: 529
Investigatory grand jury
  Grand jury G: 308
Investiture [ceremony]
  Feudalism (The principles of feudalism) F: 82
  Girl Scouts (Girl Scout Daisies) G: 197
  Knighthood, Orders of (Honorary orders) K: 347
    with picture
  Netherlands (National government) N: 139
Investiture, Right of [Church history]
  Gregory VII, Saint G: 387
  Paschal II P: 190
Investment [economics] I: 366 *with picture*
  Certificate of deposit C: 363
  Economics (Economic growth) E: 62
  Gross domestic product (Measuring GDP) G: 399
  Income tax (Effects on the economy) I: 104
  Industry (Capital) I: 258
  Inflation (Effects on investment) I: 268
  Insider trading I: 303

Mutual fund M: 969
United States, History of the (Investment and
  banking) U: 181
Investment banking I: 369
  Bank (Investment banks) B: 91
  Initial public offering I: 271
Investment Canada [agency]
  New Democratic Party N: 203
Investment casting [industrial process]
  Cast and casting (Other types of casting) C: 278
Investment credit
  Credit (Types of credit) Ci: 1124
Investment-grade rating
  Bond (Bond ratings) B: 454
Investment Review Agency, Federal [Canada]
  Trudeau, Pierre Elliott (The national scene) T: 464
Invincible Armada *See* Spanish Armada *in this
  index*
Invisible glass
  Glass (Specialty glasses) G: 212-213
Invisible hand [economics]
  Economics (The free market) E: 59
Invisible ink I: 369
Invisible light *See* Infrared rays; Ultraviolet rays *in
  this index*
Invisible Man [book by Ellison]
  African American literature (The 1900's) A: 136a
  Ellison, Ralph E: 244
  Novel (After World War II) N: 574
Invitation [custom]
  Etiquette (Invitation etiquette) E: 374
  Letter writing (Personal letters) L: 212 *with
    pictures*
Invitation to the Sideshow [painting by Seurat]
  Postimpressionism *picture on* P: 709
Invocation [magic]
  Magic (Magical words) M: 49
Invoice
  Bill (In commerce) B: 300
Involucre [botany]
  Four-o'clock F: 437 *with picture*
Involuntary act *See* Reflex action *in this index*
Involuntary bankruptcy
  Bankruptcy (Features of bankruptcy) B: 97
Involuntary immigrant
  Immigration (Causes of immigration) I: 80
Involuntary manslaughter
  Manslaughter M: 167
Involuntary muscle
  Human body (Smooth muscles) H: 419
  Muscle (Smooth muscles) M: 934-935
Inwood [district]
  New York City (Manhattan) N: 323-326
Inyangani, Mount
  Zimbabwe (Land and climate) Z: 592 *with map*
Io [Greek mythology] I: 369 *with picture*
  Bosporus B: 494
  Hera H: 194
Io [satellite] I: 370 *with picture*
  Galileo G: 13
  Jupiter (Magnetic field) J: 198-199; (Galilean
    satellites) J: 200a
  Mountain (On Io) M: 895
  Satellite (Satellites of the gas giants) S: 150-150a
  Space exploration *picture on* So: 694
  Volcano (Volcanoes in the solar system) V: 442b
  Voyager V: 451
Io moth
  Moth *picture on* M: 840
IOC [organization] *See* International Olympic
  Committee *in this index*
Iodine [element] I: 370
  Disinfectant D: 235
  Goiter G: 242
  Halogen H: 26
Iodized salt [food]
  Iodine (Uses of iodine) I: 370
  Salt (How table salt is made) S: 74
Iodophor [chemical]
  Disinfectant D: 235
  Iodine (Uses of iodine) I: 370
IODP [program]
  Ocean drilling programs O: 667
Ioffe, Abram F. [Russian physicist]
  Electron E: 203
Iolani Palace
  Honolulu (The city) H: 320
Iole [Greek mythology]
  Hercules (The death of Hercules) H: 199
Ion [book by Plato]
  Plato (The early dialogues) P: 568
Ion [chemistry] I: 371 *with pictures*
  Atom (Electric charge) A: 872
  Base B: 123
  Battery (Electric charges) B: 168
  Bond (An ionic bond) B: 454
  Brain (Action potentials) B: 557

Comet (Parts of a comet) Ci: 867
Cosmic rays (Galactic cosmic rays) Ci: 1076
Electricity (Ions) E: 192 *with diagram*
Electrolyte E: 201
Electron E: 203
Fuel cell (How a fuel cell works) F: 551
Halogen H: 26
Hydroxide H: 474
Ionosphere I: 373
Matter (Structure of matter) M: 310-311
Molecule (Polar molecules and ionic substances)
  M: 693
Nervous system (The beginning of an impulse)
  N: 135
Ocean (Composition) O: 654
Particle accelerator P: 184
Particle detector (Cloud chambers) P: 186
Plasma P: 552
Reduction R: 192
Sun (Composition) So: 975-976
Superconductivity So: 992
Ion channel [anatomy]
  Brain (Action potentials) B: 557 *with diagram*
Ion-exchange process
  Water softening W: 140
Ion microscope I: 372 *with picture*
  Microscope (Ion microscopes) M: 519
Ion propulsion [physics]
  Rocket (Ion rockets) R: 389 *with diagram*
Ion rocket
  Rocket R: 384; (Ion rockets) R: 389 *with diagram*
  Space exploration (Developing more efficient
    rockets) So: 728
Ion tail [astronomy]
  Comet (Parts of a comet) Ci: 867
  Solar wind So: 582
Ionesco, Eugène [French dramatist] I: 372
  Drama (Theater of the Absurd) D: 340
  French literature (Developments in drama) F: 523
  Romania (The arts) R: 419
Ionia [ancient region]
  Ionians I: 373
Ionian Islands [Greece] I: 372 *with map*
  Greece (The Ionian Islands) G: 358 *with map*
Ionian Sea [Mediterranean] I: 373
Ionian War [413-404 B.C.]
  Peloponnesian War P: 232
Ionians [ancient people] I: 373
  Greece, Ancient (The people) G: 367
Ionic bond
  Bond B: 454
  Materials (The role of bonds) M: 301
Ionic column [architecture]
  Architecture (table) A: 608-609 *with picture*;
    (Classical Greek architecture) A: 615
  Column (The Greek orders) Ci: 865 *with picture*
Ionic compound [chemistry]
  Bond B: 454
Ionic crystal
  Ion (Ions in solids) I: 371 *with pictures*
Ionic lattice [chemistry]
  Salt, Chemical S: 75
Ionisation [music by Varèse]
  Varèse, Edgard V: 285
Ionization [physics]
  Fluorescent lamp F: 305
  Gamma rays G: 24
  Ion I: 371
  Irradiation I: 455
  Isotope (Separating isotopes) I: 476
  Kirlian photography K: 336
  Physics (Fluid and plasma physics) P: 438
  Radiation (Effects of radiation) R: 79
  Radiation sickness R: 81
  X rays (Uses of X rays) X: 541-542
Ionization detection
  Smoke alarm S: 520
Ionization grid
  Rocket (Ion rockets) R: 389 *with diagram*
Ionizing radiation
  Cancer (Radiation) C: 170
  Food preservation (Irradiation) F: 343
  Radiation (Ionizing ability) R: 79
Ionosphere [atmosphere] I: 373
  Air (The thermosphere) A: 174
  Arecibo Observatory A: 645
  Ion I: 371
  Magnetic equator M: 55
  Radar (In scientific research) R: 68; (The first uses
    of radar) R: 71
  Radio (Transmitting AM band signals) R: 87 *with
    diagram*
  Short waves S: 435
  Thermosphere T: 256
"Ionych" [story by Chekhov]
  Russian literature (Late realism) R: 562-563
Iota [letter]

I **I:** 1 *with picture*
J **J:** 1 *with picture*
I.O.U. [debt] **I:** 373
Iowa I: 374 *with pictures and maps*
  See also the list of Related articles in the Iowa
  article
Iowa [ship]
  Battleship (The modern battleship) **B:** 172
Iowa, Territory of [U.S. history]
  Iowa (Territorial days) **I:** 393-395
Iowa, University of I: 396
Iowa Indians I: 397
Iowa River
  Iowa (Rivers and lakes) **I:** 386
Iowa State Historical Museum [Des Moines]
  Iowa (Places to visit) **I:** 384
Iowa State University of Science and Technology
  I: 397
  Iowa *picture on* **I:** 379
IP address [computing] *See* Internet Protocol
  address *in this index*
iPad [computer]
  Apple Inc. **A:** 573
IPC [organization] *See* Intergovernmental Panel on
  Climate Change *in this index*
Ipcress File, The [book by Deighton]
  Deighton, Len **D:** 93
Ipecac [medication] **I:** 397
Ipellie, Alootook [Canadian poet]
  Canadian literature (Modern Canadian poets)
  C: 161
IPEX syndrome[disease]
  Immune system (The cell-mediated immune
  response) **I:** 88-88a
Iphigenia [legendary figure] **I:** 397
Iphigenia in Aulis [opera by Gluck]
  Gluck, Christoph Willibald **G:** 235
Iphigenia in Aulis [play by Euripides]
  Euripides **E:** 378
Iphigenia in Tauris [opera by Gluck]
  Gluck, Christoph Willibald **G:** 235
Iphigenia in Tauris [play by Goethe]
  Goethe, Johann Wolfgang von (Middle years)
  G: 247
iPhone [device]
  Apple Inc. **A:** 573
  Cellular telephone (History) **C:** 341
IPM [agriculture] *See* Integrated pest management
  in this index
IPO [investment] *See* Initial public offering *in this
  index*
iPod [device]
  Apple Inc. **A:** 573
  United States, History of the *picture on* **U:** 196c
ipRGC [anatomy]
  Eye (The retina) **E:** 462
I.Q. [measurement] *See* Intelligence quotient *in
  this index*
Iqaluit [Nunavut] **I:** 397
  Nunavut **N:** 608 *with picture*
Iqbal, Sir Muhammad [Pakistani philosopher]
  I: 397
Ir [symbol]
  Iridium **I:** 429
IR thermometer *See* Infrared radiation
  thermometer *in this index*
IRA [finance] *See* Individual retirement account *in
  this index*
IRA [Irish history] *See* Irish Republican Army *in this
  index*
Iraklion [Crete]
  Crete **Ci:** 1127
Irala, Domingo Martínez de [Spanish colonial
  official]
  Paraguay (Early days) **P:** 148-149
Iran I: 398 *with pictures and maps*
  See also Persia, Ancient, *and the list of Related
  articles in the* Iran *article*
  Aryans **A:** 764
  Asia *picture on* **A:** 811
  Bush, George Walker (Iran) **B:** 723
  Carter, Jimmy (The Iranian crisis) **C:** 258
  Hostage **H:** 374a
  Internet *picture on* **I:** 350f
  Iran-contra affair **I:** 406b
  Iran-Iraq War **I:** 407
  Journalism (Journalism today) **J:** 175
  Khamenei, Ali **K:** 308a
  Khomeini, Ruhollah **K:** 308b
  Kurds **K:** 392
  Kuwait (History) **K:** 396
  Middle East **M:** 530 *with picture*; (The 1970's and
  1980's) **M:** 534a
  Mohammad Reza Pahlavi **M:** 687
  Muslims (The Safavid dynasty) **M:** 964d
  Nuclear Nonproliferation Treaty **N:** 595
  Obama, Barack (Syria and Iran) **O:** 642

Organization of the Petroleum Exporting
  Countries **O:** 854
Persian Gulf War of 1991 (Background to the war)
  P: 300b
Safavid dynasty **S:** 8
State, Department of (Since World War II) **So:** 862
Theocracy **T:** 251
United Arab Emirates (History) **U:** 45
United States, History of the (The hostage crisis)
  U: 196b
Iran-contra affair [U.S. history] **I:** 406b
  Bush, George Herbert Walker (Election as
  president) **B:** 719
  Reagan, Ronald Wilson (The Iran-contra affair)
  R: 170
  Weinberger, Caspar Willard **W:** 188
Iran-Iraq War [1980-1988] **I:** 407
  Iran (The war with Iraq) **I:** 406a
  Iraq (War with Iran) **I:** 414
  Persian Gulf War of 1991 (Background to the war)
  P: 300b
  War (Stalemates) **W:** 24
Iran Liberation Movement
  Iran (Politics) **I:** 399
Iranian language *See* Persian language *in this index*
Iraq I: 408 *with pictures and maps*
  See also the list of Related articles in the Iraq *article*
  Air Force, United States (The Iraq War) **A:** 196;
  (The Persian Gulf War of 1991) **A:** 196
  Arabs *picture on* **A:** 585; (Arabs today) **A:** 590-
  590a
  Army, United States (The Persian Gulf War of
  1991) **A:** 739; (The Iraq War [2003-2010]) **A:** 740
  Bush, George Herbert Walker (Persian Gulf crisis)
  B: 721
  Bush, George Walker **B:** 722g *with picture*
  Chemical-biological-radiological warfare
  (History) **C:** 396-397
  Clinton, Bill (International affairs) **Ci:** 682e,
  Ci: 682f
  Cold War (The Eisenhower Doctrine) **Ci:** 767
  Egypt (Recent developments) **E:** 133-134
  Flag *picture on* **F:** 203
  Gulf War syndrome **G:** 438
  Hussein, Saddam **H:** 457
  Iran-Iraq War **I:** 407
  Iraq War **I:** 414c
  Jordan (Recent developments) **J:** 165
  Kurds **K:** 392
  Kuwait (History) **K:** 396
  Map *picture on* **M:** 184; (Ancient maps) **M:** 182
  Mesopotamia **M:** 421
  Organization of the Petroleum Exporting
  Countries **O:** 854
  Persian Gulf War of 1991 **P:** 300a
  Qatar (History) **Q:** 3
  Saudi Arabia (The Persian Gulf War of 1991)
  S: 162
  United Nations (Military actions) **U:** 91-92; (Policy
  disagreements) **U:** 96
  United States, History of the (The Persian Gulf
  War) **U:** 196d; (Iraq War [2003-2010]) **U:** 196e
  War crime (Wars in Iraq) **W:** 27
  World, History of the (The war on terrorism)
  W: 448b
Iraq Study Group
  Baker, James Addison, III **B:** 32
Iraq Survey Group
  Iraq (The Iraq War) **I:** 414a-414b
Iraq War [2003-2011] **I:** 414c *with pictures and map*
  Air force (In the Iraq War) **A:** 187
  Air Force, United States (Fighters) **A:** 191; (The
  Iraq War) **A:** 196
  Arab Americans (Arab Americans today) **A:** 581
  Arab League **A:** 582b
  Arabs (Relations with Europe and the United
  States) **A:** 590a
  Army, United States (The Iraq War [2003-2010])
  A: 740
  Australia (Iraq War and counterterrorism) **A:** 925
  Baghdad (History) **B:** 26
  Bahrain (History) **B:** 31
  Basra **B:** 156
  Bush, George Walker **B:** 722b *with picture*
  Central Intelligence Agency (History) **C:** 357
  Democratic Party (The early 2000's) **D:** 128
  Gas mask **G:** 60
  Guided missile (Postwar developments) **G:** 427-
  428
  Howard, John Winston **H:** 400
  Hussein, Saddam **H:** 457
  Improvised explosive device **I:** 95
  International law (Efforts by the UN) **I:** 342
  International relations (The Iraq War) **I:** 346a
  Iraq (The Iraq War) **I:** 414a
  Kuwait (History) **K:** 396-397
  Marine Corps, United States (Recent Marine

operations) **M:** 210
Middle East (The 2000's) **M:** 534b
Mosul **M:** 836
Navy, United States (Wars in Iraq and
  Afghanistan) **N:** 89
North Atlantic Treaty Organization (History)
  N: 471
Nuclear weapon (After the terrorist attacks of
  Sept. 11, 2001) **N:** 602
Obama, Barack (Presidential nomination)
  O: 640e; (Foreign affairs) **O:** 641
Persian Gulf War of 1991 (Consequences of the
  war) **P:** 300e
Petroleum (Petroleum and war) **P:** 346; (Wars
  against Iraq) **P:** 349
Prisoner of war **P:** 808
Qatar (History) **Q:** 3
Saudi Arabia (Recent developments) **S:** 162
September 11 terrorist attacks (Global war on
  terrorism) **S:** 310a-310b
Terrorism (The Iraq War [2003-2011]) **T:** 180
United Kingdom (Recent developments) **U:** 74
United Nations (Arms control) **U:** 92-93
United States, History of the (The Iraq War)
  U: 196e
War (table) **W:** 25; (Recent developments) **W:** 26
War correspondent **W:** 27
War crime (Wars in Iraq) **W:** 27
World, History of the (The war on terrorism)
  W: 448b-449
IRAS [satellite] *See* Infrared Astronomical Satellite
  in this index
Irawadi River *See* Irrawaddy River *in this index*
Irazú [volcano, Costa Rica]
  Costa Rica (Revolutions and reforms) **Ci:** 1084
Irazú National Park [Costa Rica]
  National park (Costa Rica) **N:** 42c-42d
IRB [Irish history]
  Ireland (The Easter Rising) **I:** 427
IRBM [weapon] *See* Intermediate-range ballistic
  missile *in this index*
Iredell, James, Jr. [American political leader]
  North Carolina (table) **N:** 490
Ireland I: 416 *with pictures and maps*
  See also Irish literature *in this index and the list of*
  Related articles in the Ireland *article*
  Boston (Ethnic groups) **B:** 501
  British-Irish Council **B:** 632
  Christmas (In England, Ireland, Scotland, and
  Wales) **C:** 530
  De Valera, Eamon **D:** 173
  Euro **E:** 379
  Europe (Recent developments) **E:** 416
  Fenian movement **F:** 71
  Flag *pictures on* **F:** 206, **F:** 217
  Freedom of speech (In other countries) **F:** 507
  Gaelic languages **G:** 5
  Girl Scouts (Ireland) **G:** 199
  Great Irish Famine **G:** 343
  Halloween (Halloween customs and symbols)
  H: 24a; (Halloween around the world) **H:** 24b
  Lloyd George, David (Prime minister) **L:** 403
  Mythology (Celtic mythology) **M:** 984
  North-South Ministerial Council **N:** 518
  Northern Ireland **N:** 521
  Parliament (Parliaments in other countries) **P:** 174
  Patrick, Saint **P:** 197
  School (In other countries) **S:** 183
  Senate (Senates in other countries) **S:** 296
  Steeplechasing **So:** 883
  United Kingdom (Troubles with Ireland) **U:** 68;
  (Gladstone and Disraeli) **U:** 69; (Postwar
  problems) **U:** 70
  United States, History of the (Immigration) **U:** 172
  Vikings (The Norwegian Vikings) **V:** 382
Ireland, John [American political leader]
  Texas (table) **T:** 203
Ireland, John [American religious leader]
  Saint Paul (History) **S:** 52
Ireland, Plantation of [Irish history]
  Ireland (The conquest of Ireland) **I:** 426
Ireland, Republic of
  See also Ireland *in this index*
  Ireland (The Republic of Ireland) **I:** 427
Ireland, Ward Stone [American inventor]
  Shorthand machine **S:** 435
Irenaeus, Saint [Christian theologian] **I:** 429
Irene [Byzantine empress]
  Nicene Councils **N:** 402
Irene [early Christian]
  Sebastian, Saint **S:** 277
Irène [play by Voltaire]
  Voltaire (Later years) **V:** 447
Irgun Zvai Leumi [Israeli history]
  Begin, Menachem **B:** 219
Irhil M'Goun [mountain, Africa]
  Atlas Mountains **A:** 869

Irian Barat [former name]
Indonesia (Papua) I: 234
Irian Jaya [province, Indonesia] See Papua in this index
Iridium [element] I: 429
Iris [anatomy]
Eye (The uveal tract) E: 460 with picture
Iritis I: 434
Iris [plant] I: 429
Fleur-de-lis F: 234
Flower (Garden perennials) F: 278 with picture; (table) F: 301 with picture
Gardening picture on G: 33
Orrisroot O: 859
Iris borer [insect]
Iris I: 429
Irish, William [pen name]
Woolrich, Cornell W: 402
Irish Amateur Boxing Association
Boxing (Amateur boxing) B: 531
Irish Christian Brothers [religious group]
Religious life (table) R: 227
Irish Church Act [1869]
United Kingdom (Gladstone and Disraeli) U: 69
Irish elk
Elk (The European elk) E: 242
Irish Famine, Great [1845-1848] See Great Irish Famine in this index
Irish Free State
De Valera, Eamon D: 173
Ireland (The Irish Free State) I: 427
Irish Republican Army (Division in the IRA) I: 433
Northern Ireland (The division of Ireland) N: 524
United Kingdom (Postwar problems) U: 70
Irish Girl Guides
Girl Scouts (Ireland) G: 199
Irish language
Gaelic languages G: 5
Irish Literary Revival
Drama (Irish drama) D: 339
Ireland (The arts) I: 421
Russell, George William R: 524
Yeats, William Butler Y: 555
Irish Literary Theatre [Dublin]
Yeats, William Butler Y: 555
Irish literature I: 430
See also the list of Related articles in the Irish Literature article
Drama (Irish drama) D: 339
Mythology (The Irish cycles) M: 985
Irish Melodies [poems by Moore]
Irish literature (Early works in English) I: 431
Popular music (Revolutionary War to 1840) P: 669
Irish moss [plant] I: 433
Prince Edward Island (Interesting facts) P: 783 with picture
Seaweed picture on S: 277
Irish potato
Potato (History) P: 713
Irish Republican Army [Irish history] I: 433
Adams, Gerry A: 33
Ireland (The Irish Free State) I: 427
Mountbatten, Louis M: 899
Northern Ireland (The Troubles) N: 525
Sinn Féin S: 473
Trimble, David T: 445
Troubles T: 452
United Kingdom (Recent developments) U: 74
Irish Republican Brotherhood [Irish history]
Ireland (The Easter Rising) I: 427
Irish Sea I: 434
England (The land) E: 299
Irish setter [dog] I: 434 with picture
Setter S: 323
Irish stew
Ireland (Food and drink) I: 420
Irish terrier I: 434
Dog picture on D: 272
Irish tweed [fabric]
Ireland picture on I: 425
Irish water spaniel I: 434
Dog picture on D: 268
Irish whiskey
Whiskey W: 282
Irish wolfhound I: 434
Dog pictures on D: 265, D: 270
Wolfhound W: 378
Iritis [disorder] I: 434
Eye (Diseases of the uveal tract) E: 467
Leprosy (Symptoms) L: 204
Irkutsk [Russia] I: 434
Russia picture on R: 534
IRO [organization] See International Refugee Organization in this index
[element] I: 435
also Iron and steel in this index
Insufficient production of red blood

cells) A: 457
Baby (Vitamins and iron) B: 9
Nutrition (Minerals) N: 625-626; (Deficiency diseases) N: 630-631
Iron [sports]
Golf (Golf clubs) G: 262 with pictures
Iron Age [anthropology] I: 435
Iron and steel (The Iron Age) I: 449
Lake dwelling L: 37
Iron and steel I: 436 with pictures and maps
See also Iron; Iron ore in this index; and the list of Related articles in the Iron and steel article
Alabama (State prosperity) A: 276
Edison, Thomas Alva (Ore milling and cement) E: 81
Galvanizing G: 17
Materials (Metals and alloys) M: 300d with picture
Nickel (Industrial uses) N: 404
Ship (Ships of iron) S: 424
Iron
Alloy (Alloys of iron) A: 377
Cast iron C: 279
Colonial life in America (Ironmaking) Ci: 811
Electromagnet E: 201
Hematite H: 180
Hibbing H: 222
Industrial Revolution (Coal and iron) I: 249 with picture
Iron Age I: 435
Slag S: 499
Taconite T: 5
United States, History of the picture on U: 179
Steel
Alabama picture on A: 273
Alloy (Characteristics of alloys) A: 377 with pictures
China picture on C: 497
Fireproofing F: 134
Great Lakes (Commerce) G: 344-345
Heat picture on H: 148
Indiana picture on I: 211
Invention (China) I: 359
Pennsylvania picture on P: 261
Pittsburgh P: 500a; (Manufacturing) P: 500d with picture
Railroad (The crossties and rails) R: 109
Recycling R: 184
Rust R: 567
Tempering T: 130
Vanadium V: 268
Iron and Steel, Amalgamated Association of
Homestead Strike H: 305
Iron and Steel Association, American
Iron and Steel Institute, American I: 453
Iron and Steel Institute, American I: 453
Iron Chancellor [name for]
Bismarck, Otto von (Bismarck's wars) B: 382
Iron Cross
Medals, decorations, and orders (table) M: 359 with picture
Iron cross [gymnastics]
Gymnastics (The still rings) G: 448
Iron Curtain [international relations] I: 453
Churchill, Sir Winston Leonard Spencer (Leader of the opposition) C: 549
Cold War (The Iron Curtain descends) Ci: 763
Communism (World War II) Ci: 893
Union of Soviet Socialist Republics (Beginnings of the Cold War) U: 38
World War II (New power struggles) W: 497
Iron-deficiency anemia [disorder]
Iron (How bodies use iron) I: 435
Iron Duke [name for]
Wellington, Duke of W: 194
Iron Gate [region, Romania-Serbia]
Danube River D: 34
Iron Gate Dam
Serbia (Land and climate) S: 314 with map
Iron Guard [political party]
Romania (Depression and fascism) R: 424
Iron lung [machine] I: 453 with picture
Respirator R: 262
Iron Market
Haiti picture on H: 16
Iron meteorite
Meteor (Meteorites) M: 432
Iron Molders, National Union of
Labor movement (The first nationwide labor organizations) L: 9
Iron notch
Iron and steel (The blast furnace process) I: 440
Iron ore
Brazil (Mining) B: 581
Hematite H: 180
Iron and steel (Sources of iron ore) I: 437 with picture; (Mining and processing iron ore) I: 438

Michigan (Natural resources) M: 503; (Mining) M: 506
Minnesota (Natural resources) M: 599; (Mining) M: 601; (Industrial development) M: 604; (The early 1900's) M: 604; (The mid-1900's) M: 606
Taconite T: 5
Iron Ore Company of Canada
Mulroney, Brian (Business executive) M: 917
Iron oxide [chemical]
Iron (Properties) I: 435
Iron and steel (Processing) I: 439
Rust R: 567
Iron plant
Aspidistra A: 816
Iron pyrite [mineral]
Mineral picture on M: 568
Pyrite P: 920
Iron rust [chemistry]
Rust R: 567
Iron triangle
Korean War map on K: 383
Ironclad [ship]
Battleship (Development of the battleship) B: 172
Civil War, American (First battle between ironclads) Ci: 626 with picture
Monitor and Merrimack M: 724
Warship picture on W: 42; (Warships of the 1800's) W: 41
Ironman [sports competition]
Triathlon T: 440
Irons, David [American psychologist]
Emotion (The appraisal approach) E: 261
Irons, Jeremy [British actor]
Motion picture (Best performance by an actor: 1990) M: 862a
Ironsides [English history]
Cromwell, Oliver (Rise to power) Ci: 1151
Ironsides, Old [ship] See Constitution [ship] in this index
Ironwood [tree] I: 453 with picture
Ironwork, Decorative I: 454 with pictures
Ironworker
Building trade (Career opportunities) B: 686
Irony [humor] I: 454
Humor (The types of humor) H: 435-436
Iroquoian [languages]
Iroquois Indians I: 455
Iroquois [horse]
Horse (table: Famous horses in history and legend) H: 361
Iroquois Confederacy See Iroquois League in this index
Iroquois Indians I: 455
Canada, History of (Threats to expansion) C: 140
Cayuga Indians C: 323
Champlain, Samuel de (The founding of Quebec) C: 373
Handsome Lake H: 46
Hiawatha H: 221
Indian, American pictures on I: 138, I: 156; (Shelter) I: 136d; (Federations) I: 143-144; (Shamans) I: 147-148; (Indians of the Northeast) I: 154 with picture
Indian wars (Lord Dunmore's War [1774]) I: 191
Mask (Ceremonial masks) M: 264
Montreal (French settlement) M: 777
New York (Statehood) N: 315
Ontario (Original inhabitants) O: 784
Quebec (Early days) Q: 36
Revolution, American (Invasion of the Iroquois country) R: 284
Seneca Indians S: 296
United States, History of the (The first Americans) U: 149
Verchères, Marie Madeleine Jarret de V: 315
Iroquois League
Cayuga Indians C: 323
Hiawatha H: 221
Indian, American (Federations) I: 143-144; (Indians of the Northeast) I: 154
Iroquois Indians I: 455
Mohawk Indians M: 688
Seneca Indians S: 296
Iroquois long house [dwelling]
Cayuga Indians C: 323
Indian, American (Shelter) I: 136d
Iroquois Long House [federation]
Iroquois Indians I: 455
Iroquois Steeplechase [Nashville]
Tennessee picture on T: 145
Iroquois Theater Fire [1903]
Chicago (Tragedy and racial conflict) C: 435
Irradiance [physics]
Light (Energy and brightness) L: 290
Irradiation [physics] I: 455
See also Radiation in this index

Food preservation (Irradiation) **F:** 343
Irrational number
Decimal system (Decimals and fractions) **D:** 72
Mathematics (The Greeks) **M:** 306
Number (Irrational numbers) **N:** 606; (The Greeks) **N:** 606
Pi **P:** 445
Quasicrystal **Q:** 9
Rational number **R:** 148
Square root (Square roots of positive numbers) **So:** 812
Irrawaddy River [Myanmar] **I:** 455
Myanmar (Land regions) **M:** 970c *with map*
Irreconcilable differences [law]
Divorce (No-fault divorce) **D:** 253
Irregular galaxy [astronomy]
Galaxy (Types of galaxies) **G:** 8a *with picture*
Magellanic Clouds **M:** 48
Irregular satellite [astronomy]
Satellite **S:** 149; (Satellites of the gas giants) **S:** 150-150a
Irregular verb [grammar]
Verb (Regular and irregular verbs) **V:** 314
Irregulars [Irish history]
Irish Republican Army (Division in the IRA) **I:** 433
Irrevocable trust [law]
Trust fund (Kinds of trusts) **T:** 474
Irrigation [agriculture] **I:** 456 *with pictures and map*
Agriculture (Ancient civilizations) **A:** 155-156 *with picture*
Arabs (Economy) **A:** 589
Egypt (Agriculture) **E:** 128
Environmental pollution (Soil pollution) **E:** 334
Farm and farming (Water management) **F:** 33 *with picture*
Food supply (Making farmland more productive) **F:** 349
Fruit (Caring for the crop) **F:** 546
Grand Coulee Dam **G:** 308 *with picture*
Indian, American (Farming) **I:** 141
Oasis *picture on* **O:** 638
Vegetable (Irrigation) **V:** 293
Water (Water for irrigation) **W:** 118 *with picture*; (Water and civilization) **W:** 132
Irritant poison
Poison (Kinds of poisons) **P:** 600
IRS [organization] *See* Internal Revenue Service *in this index*
IRT [transportation]
New York City (Transportation) **N:** 334-335
Irvin, Monte [American baseball player]
Baseball (table: Hall of Fame) **B:** 134a
Irving, Clifford [American author]
Hughes, Howard Robard **H:** 409
Irving, John [American author] **I:** 459
Irving, Washington [American author] **I:** 460 *with portrait*
American literature (Literature of a young nation [1788-1830]) **A:** 415
Ghost **G:** 182
Rip Van Winkle **R:** 349
United States, History of the (A national culture) **U:** 166
Irving, William [brother of]
Irving, Washington (Early career) **I:** 460
Irvington [New Jersey] **I:** 461
Irwin, James Benson [American astronaut] **I:** 461 *with portrait*
Invention *picture on* **I:** 362
Space exploration *picture on* **So:** 720; (Other moon landings) **So:** 719
Irwin, Jared [American political leader]
Georgia (table) **G:** 130
Irwin, Lord [history of India]
India (New Constitution) **I:** 132
Irwin, Walter W. [American aviator]
Aviation (table: Aviation speed records) **A:** 990
Irwin, William [American political leader]
California (table) **C:** 59
Isa bin Salman Al-Khalifa [emir of Bahrain]
Bahrain (History) **B:** 30-31
Isaa [Japanese poet]
Poetry (Lyric poetry) **P:** 591
Isaac [Biblical figure] **I:** 461
Abraham **A:** 17
Ishmael **I:** 462
Jacob **J:** 19
Isaac, Bobby [American race driver]
Automobile racing (table: NASCAR Sprint Cup champions) **A:** 981
Isaacs, Alick [British biochemist]
Interferon **I:** 324
Isaacs, Jorge [Colombian author]
Colombia (The arts) **Ci:** 781
Latin American literature (Romanticism) **L:** 112-113
Isabela [Spanish colony]

Columbus, Christopher (Trouble, settlement, and exploration) **Ci:** 862
Isabela Island
Galapagos Islands **G:** 7 *with map*
Isabella [literary figure]
Shakespeare, William: (*Measure for Measure*) **S:** 362
Isabella I [queen of Castile and Aragon] **I:** 461 *with picture*
Boabdil **B:** 427
Castile and Aragon **C:** 279
Columbus, Christopher (Years of waiting) **Ci:** 858; (Trouble, settlement, and exploration) **Ci:** 862; (Third voyage westward) **Ci:** 862; (Fourth voyage westward) **Ci:** 863; (Final days) **Ci:** 864
Exploration (Columbus reaches America) **E:** 444
Ferdinand V **F:** 73
Granada **G:** 304
Spain (Union of the Spanish kingdoms) **So:** 746
Torquemada, Tomás de **T:** 341
Isabella II [queen of Spain]
Spain (The reign of Isabella II) **So:** 748
Isabella moth [insect]
Woollybear **W:** 402
Isabella Stewart Gardner Museum
Massachusetts (Museums) **M:** 275
Isabella tiger moth
Insect *picture on* **I:** 282
Moth *picture on* **M:** 840
Isacks, Bryan L. [American geologist]
Plate tectonics (History of tectonic theory) **P:** 564-565
Isaiah [Biblical figure]
Isaiah, Book of **I:** 462 *with picture*
Lucifer **L:** 514
Isaiah, Book of [Bible] **I:** 461 *with picture*
Bible (The Prophets) **B:** 280-281
Lucifer **L:** 514
Isan [region] *See* Khorat Plateau *in this index*
Isapo-muxika [birth name of]
Crowfoot **Ci:** 1158
ISBN [number]
International standard book number **I:** 347
Iscariot, Judas [apostle] *See* Judas Iscariot *in this index*
Ischium [anatomy]
Dinosaur *picture on* **D:** 206c
Hip **H:** 238 *with diagram*
Human body (table) **H:** 422 *with diagram*
Pelvis **P:** 233 *with diagram*
Isenheim altarpiece [paintings by Grünewald]
Grünewald, Matthias **G:** 406
Isfahan [Iran] **I:** 462
Abbas I **A:** 4
Architecture *diagram on* **A:** 614
Iran *picture on* **I:** 398; (The Safavid dynasty) **I:** 405-406
Safavid dynasty **S:** 8
Isherwood, Christopher [British-American author] **I:** 462
Auden, W. H. **A:** 881
Ishiguro, Kazuo [British author]
English literature (Recent English fiction) **E:** 323
Novel (The novel today) **N:** 575
Ishihara test
Color blindness **Ci:** 827
Ishmael [Biblical figure] **I:** 462
Abraham **A:** 16
`Id al-Ad-ha **I:** 25
Kaaba **K:** 208
Muslims (Before Muhammad) **M:** 964
Ishmaelites [ancient people]
Joseph **J:** 167
Ishtar [Assyrian goddess]
Assyria (Religion) **A:** 821
Astarte **A:** 823
Ishtar Gate [Babylon]
Babylon (The Neo-Babylonian Empire) **B:** 12
Isidia [biology]
Lichen (How lichens grow) **L:** 269
Isidore [Spanish religious leader]
Encyclopedia (The first reference works) **E:** 268a
Isidorus of Miletus [Byzantine architect]
Architecture (Byzantine architecture) **A:** 617
IsiNdebele [language]
Zimbabwe (People) **Z:** 592
Isinglass [animal product] **I:** 462
ISIS [database] *See* International Species Information System *in this index*
Isis [Egyptian goddess] **I:** 462
Egypt, Ancient *picture on* **E:** 140; (Religion) **E:** 137
Hieroglyphics *picture on* **H:** 225
Horus **H:** 370
Mythology *picture on* **M:** 977; (The Great Ennead) **M:** 979; (The Osiris myth) **M:** 979
Iskandar Visiting a Hermit [painting by Bihzad]
Bihzad, Kamal ad-Din *picture on* **B:** 299

Iskra [newspaper]
Lenin, V. I. (Beginnings of revolution) **L:** 192
Isla, José Francisco de [Spanish author]
Spanish literature (The 1700's) **So:** 760
Isla Española, La [name for]
Hispaniola **H:** 259
Islam [religion] **I:** 463 *with pictures*
See also Muslims *in this index*
Abduh, Muhammad **A:** 9
Afghanistan *picture on* **A:** 93; (The coming of Islam) **A:** 95
Africa (The rise of Islam) **A:** 131
Algeria (Religion) **A:** 362
Allah **A:** 370
Angel **A:** 459
Arabs **A:** 585; (Religion) **A:** 586; (The rise and spread of Islam) **A:** 589
Asia (Religions) **A:** 773
Clothing *picture on* **Ci:** 687; (Clothing under Islam) **Ci:** 697 *with picture*; (India) **Ci:** 699
Dervish **D:** 153
Education (Religion and early Western education) **E:** 98-99
Egypt (Religion) **E:** 124
Feasts and festivals (In Islam) **F:** 58
Flag *picture on* **F:** 216
Fundamentalism (Fundamentalism in other religions) **F:** 557
Government (Asia and the Middle East) **G:** 289-290
Harem **H:** 60
Heaven **H:** 161
`Id al-Ad-ha **I:** 25
`Id al-Fitr **I:** 25
Jerusalem **J:** 94a
Jews (The Jews under Islam) **J:** 122
Jihad **J:** 126
Jinni **J:** 127
Middle Ages (The rise of Islam) **M:** 524
Middle East (Religion) **M:** 531; (The spread of Islam) **M:** 533
Muhammad **M:** 910
Mullah **M:** 914
Ottoman Empire (People) **O:** 877
Qa`ida, Al- **Q:** 2
Qur'ān **Q:** 44
Ramadan **R:** 132
Religion **R:** 215 *with picture*; (How the major religions are organized) **R:** 218; (Islam) **R:** 223
Resurrection **R:** 264
Saint (Non-Christian saints) **S:** 29
Saudi Arabia **S:** 155; (Religion) **S:** 158
Sculpture (Asian sculpture) **S:** 236
Shari`ah **S:** 373
Shi`ites **S:** 400
Sufism **So:** 959
Sunnis **So:** 991
Taliban **T:** 19
Turkey **T:** 502 *with picture*
Wahhābis **W:** 5
World, History of the (The Islamic world) **W:** 434; (The Islamic empires) **W:** 441
Yemen (History) **Y:** 563
Islam, Nation of *See* Black Muslims; Nation of Islam *in this index*
Islamabad [Pakistan] **I:** 466
Asia *picture on* **A:** 779
Pakistan (Provincial and local government) **P:** 93
Islamic architecture
Architecture (Islamic architecture) **A:** 613
Asia (The arts) **A:** 780
Sculpture (Asian sculpture) **S:** 236
World, History of the *picture on* **W:** 436
Islamic art **I:** 467 *with pictures*
Africa (Fine arts) **A:** 115-116
Arabs (Literature and the arts) **A:** 587
Asia (The arts) **A:** 780 *with picture*
Painting (Islamic painting) **P:** 48 *with picture*
Sculpture (Asian sculpture) **S:** 236
World, History of the (The Islamic world) **W:** 434-435 *with picture*
Islamic Association
Indonesia (The rise of nationalism) **I:** 237
Islamic bank
Bank (Africa) **B:** 91
Islamic calendar
Calendar (The Islamic calendar) **C:** 29
Ramadan **R:** 132
Islamic Courts Union
Somalia (History) **So:** 589-590
Islamic Development Bank
Foreign aid (Regional development programs) **F:** 385
Islamic Empire **I:** 470
Agriculture (In China and the Middle East) **A:** 157
Egypt (Muslim rule) **E:** 130
Feudalism (The beginnings of feudalism) **F:** 81-82

Middle East (The spread of Islam) M: 533
Islamic miniature paintings
Islamic art (Books) I: 470
Islamic Party of Malaysia
Malaysia (Political parties) M: 98b
Islamic Republic of Pakistan See Pakistan in this index
Islamic Salvation Army [military group]
Algeria (Recent developments) A: 365
Islamic Salvation Front [political party] See Front Islamique du Salut in this index
Islamism [movement]
Middle East (Struggles for independence) M: 534
Islamist Justice and Development Party
Middle East (The 2000's) M: 534b
Islamization [policy]
Pakistan (Struggle for democracy) P: 100
Island I: 471 with diagrams
Atlantic Ocean (The Atlantic seafloor) A: 864
Evolution (Geographic distribution of species) E: 430
Island [fingerprinting]
Fingerprinting picture on F: 106
Island [road]
Road (Intersections) R: 358
Island [ship]
Aircraft carrier A: 206 with pictures
Island arc
Deep sea (The deep-sea floor) D: 82a
Island (Volcanic islands) I: 472
Mountain (At subduction zones) M: 893
Island Beach State Park [New Jersey]
New Jersey picture on N: 241
Island bed
Gardening (Planting an informal flower garden) G: 32
Island hopping [warfare]
Nimitz, Chester William N: 423
World War II (Island hopping in the Central Pacific) W: 489
Island of Cythera, The [painting by Watteau]
Painting (Rococo painting) P: 65 with picture
Watteau, Antoine W: 149
Island Range [mountains, British Columbia]
Vancouver Island (Location, size, and features) V: 278
Island white bear
Bear (American black bears) B: 184
Islanders, New York [team] See New York Islanders in this index
Islands of Langerhans [anatomy] See Islets of Langerhans in this index
Islands of the Blessed [Greek mythology]
Elysium E: 253
Islas de los Ladrones [name for]
Mariana Islands M: 199
Islas Malvinas [name for] See Falkland Islands in this index
Isle of Man [island, Irish Sea] See Man, Isle of in this index
Isle of Pines [Pacific]
New Caledonia N: 200
Isle of Wight [island, England]
Wight, Isle of W: 300
Isle Royale [Michigan]
Ecology E: 53
Michigan (Islands) M: 500
Isle Royale National Park [Michigan] I: 474
Lake Superior (Description) L: 45 with map
National Park System (table: National parks) N: 48
Isles, Council of the See British-Irish Council in this index
Isles of Shoals [islands, New Hampshire]
New Hampshire (Coastline) N: 220
Islet transplant [surgery]
Diabetes (Research) D: 180
Islets of Langerhans [anatomy]
Gland (table) G: 208
Insulin I: 308
Pancreas P: 128
Ismaelillo [poems by Martí]
Martí, José Julián M: 234
Ismail I [king of Iran]
Iran (The Safavid dynasty) I: 405
Muslims (The Safavid dynasty) M: 964d
Safavid dynasty S: 8
Ismail Pasha [Egyptian government official]
Egypt (Muhammad Ali and modernization) E: 131
Ismāʻ īlī Shiʻah [sect]
Islam (Divisions of Islam) I: 466
Isn't It Romantic [play by Wasserstein]
Wasserstein, Wendy W: 112
ISO [organization] See International Organization for Standardization in this index
ISO number
Photography (Speed) P: 416-417; (Capturing

digital images) P: 420-421
Isobar [meteorology] I: 474 with map
Hurricane (Tropical depression) H: 453
Map (Thematic maps) M: 178
Isobar [physics]
Atom (The atomic mass number) A: 871-872
Isobutane [gas]
Butane and propane B: 729
Isomer I: 475
Isocrates [Greek orator] I: 474
Isoetopsid [plant] See Quillwort in this index
Isoflurane [drug]
Halothane H: 27
Isograft [medicine]
Skin grafting S: 494
Isogram [cartography]
Map (Thematic maps) M: 178
Isolated soy protein
Soybean (Soy meal) So: 690
Isolationism [political science] I: 475
America First Committee A: 407
Iron Curtain I: 453
Monroe Doctrine (The Monroe doctrine and isolationism) M: 740
Roosevelt, Franklin Delano (The road to war) R: 455
United Kingdom (Gladstone and Disraeli) U: 69
World War II (The United States enters the war) W: 478
Isolator [cage]
Gnotobiotics G: 239
Isolde [legendary figure]
Tristan T: 448
Isoline [cartography]
Map (Thematic maps) M: 178
Isolt [legendary figure]
Tristan T: 448
Isomer [chemistry] I: 475
Chemistry (Development of organic chemistry) C: 404
Isomeric transition [physics]
Gamma rays G: 23
Isometric drawing
Mechanical drawing diagram on M: 354
Isometric system
Crystal (Classifying crystals) Ci: 1166 with picture
Gem (Crystal shape) G: 77
Isometrics [exercise] I: 475
Isomorphism [chemistry]
Mineral (Mineral composition and structure) M: 570-571
Isoniazid [medication] I: 475
Tuberculosis (Treatment of tuberculosis) T: 479
Isonicotinic acid hydrazide See Isoniazid in this index
Isooctane [chemical]
Gasoline (Octane ratings) G: 61
Octane O: 669
Isopod [animal]
Pill bug P: 464
Isoprene [chemical]
Rubber (The chemistry of rubber) R: 501
Isopropanol [chemical]
Alcohol (Propanol) A: 335
Isoptera [entomology] I: 475
See also Termite in this index
Insect picture on I: 281; (table) I: 299
Isosceles triangle [geometry]
Triangle (Kinds of triangles) T: 437 with diagram
Isostasy [geology]
Mountain (Forces that shape mountains) M: 894
Isostatic equilibrium [geology]
Mountain (Forces that shape mountains) M: 894
Isotherm [geography] I: 475 with map
Arctic (Land and climate) A: 636
Humboldt, Baron von H: 432
Isothermal line [meteorology]
Isotherm I: 475 with map
Isotope [physics] I: 476 with diagrams
See also Radioisotope in this index
Atom (The atomic mass number) A: 871; (Relative atomic mass) A: 872
Cobalt (Uses) Ci: 741
Element, Chemical (The periodic table of the elements) E: 219
Fallout F: 18
Hydrogen (Isotopes) H: 469
Ice age (Evidence from oceans) I: 7
Nuclear energy (Isotopes) N: 581
Radiation (Naturally radioactive substances) R: 77
Soddy, Frederick So: 568
Uranium (Uranium isotopes) U: 214; (Separating uranium isotopes) U: 215
Urey, Harold Clayton U: 221
Isotope geology
Geochemistry G: 91
Isotretinoin [drug]

Acne A: 28
ISP [business] See Internet service provider in this index
Israel [Biblical figure] See Jacob in this index
Israel [country] I: 478 with pictures and maps
See also Arab-Israeli Wars and Palestine in this index, and the Related articles in the Israel article
Air force (The Israeli Air Force) A: 184
Arab-Israeli conflict A: 582 with map
Arab League A: 582b
Arabs (Arabs today) A: 590
Arafat, Yasir A: 591
Army picture on A: 726
Asia (The people) A: 778
B'nai B'rith B: 426
Citizenship (Naturalization) Ci: 570
Cooperative (In other countries) Ci: 1036
Dance picture on D: 25
Gaza Strip G: 73
Hamas H: 28
Hebrew language H: 161
Hezbollah H: 221
Holocaust (After the Holocaust) H: 296b-297
Hussein I: H: 457
Immigration (Asia) I: 85
Intifada I: 353
Jericho J: 93
Jerusalem (History) J: 100-101
Jews (The rebirth of Israel) J: 124; (The Jews today) J: 124
Jordan (History) J: 164
Kibbutz K: 310
Lebanon (War and terrorism) L: 173
Middle East M: 530; (History) M: 533-534
Olympic Games (Terrorism in Munich) O: 752
Palestine (World War II and the division of Palestine) P: 105-106 with map; (The continuing conflict and peace efforts) P: 106
Palestine Liberation Organization P: 106
Palestinian Authority P: 107
Palestinians P: 107
Persian Gulf War of 1991 (Iraq's response) P: 300d
Rabin, Yitzhak R: 50
Red Cross R: 185
Sadat, Anwar el- S: 7
Saudi Arabia (Continued progress) S: 161-162
Suez crisis So: 958
Syria (History) So: 1074-1075
United Nations (Peacekeeping operations) U: 90-91
West Bank W: 199
Zionism Z: 595
Israel, Ancient
Jews (The kingdom of Israel) J: 121 with map
David D: 44
Education (The beginning of formal education) E: 97
Jacob J: 19
Joshua J: 169
Moses M: 828
Palestine (Early history and settlement) P: 104
Prophet P: 827
Solomon So: 584
Israel Broadcasting Authority
Israel (Transportation and communication) I: 486
Israel Labor Party
Israel (Politics) I: 479; (Unity government) I: 489
Peres, Shimon P: 285
Shamir, Yitzhak S: 371
Israel Museum
Jerusalem (Culture) J: 99
Israel Potter [book by Melville]
Melville, Herman (His literary career) M: 390-391
Israel Workers' Party See Mapai in this index
Israeli-Arab wars See Arab-Israeli conflict in this index
Israelites [people]
See also Hebrews in this index
Bible (The Law) B: 280; (The Prophets) B: 280
Canaanites C: 97
Exodus E: 438
Jews (Beginnings) J: 120-121
Judaism (The covenant with God) J: 179
Moses M: 828
Old Testament (Origins) O: 740
Philistines P: 382
Religion (Judaism) R: 219
Tabernacle T: 2 with picture
"Israfel" [poem by Poe]
Poe, Edgar Allan (Poe's life) P: 589
Issas [people]
Djibouti (People) D: 256
Issue fee [law]
Patent (How patents protect inventors) P: 194
Istanbul [Turkey] I: 490 with picture
See also Constantinople in this index
Architecture picture on A: 618

Bosporus **B:** 494
  Muslims (The Ottoman Empire) **M:** 964d
  Turkey **T:** 502 *with picture*
Istanbul University
  Istanbul (Education and cultural life) **I:** 491
Isthmian Games [ancient Greece] **I:** 492
  Corinth **Ci:** 1053
  Olympic Games (The ancient games) **O:** 750
Isthmus [geography] **I:** 492 *with map*
Isthmus of ...
  Isthmuses appear under their key words, as in Panama, Isthmus of
Istiqlal Party
  Morocco (Independence) **M:** 815
Istria [region]
  Croatia (Communist rule) **Ci:** 1148a-1148b
ISU [organization] *See* International Skating Union *in this index*
It Happened One Night [film]
  Motion picture (Best picture: 1934) **M:** 861
"It Was a Lover and His Lass" [song]
  Morley, Thomas **M:** 805
Itaipú Dam [Brazil]
  Brazil *picture on* **B:** 583; (The Central and Southern Plateaus) **B:** 580; (Energy sources) **B:** 581
  Paraguay (Energy sources) **P:** 148
  South America (Rivers) **So:** 628
  Water power (World water power production) **W:** 140
Italia [name for]
  Italy **I:** 496
Italian, The [book by Radcliffe]
  Gothic novel **G:** 279
Italian corn salad [plant]
  Valerian **V:** 265
Italian greyhound [dog] **I:** 492 *with picture*
Italian Journey [book by Goethe]
  Goethe, Johann Wolfgang von (Middle years) **G:** 247
Italian language I: 492
  Italian literature **I:** 494
  Italy (Language) **I:** 502
  Phonetics (Phonetics and spelling) **P:** 400
Italian literature I: 494
  See also the list of Related articles in the Italian Literature article
  Drama (Italian Renaissance drama) **D:** 330; (Italy) **D:** 335; (Italian drama) **D:** 339
  Italy (Literature) **I:** 494
Italian millet [grain]
  Millet **M:** 555
Italian overture [music]
  Overture **O:** 882
Italian Peninsula [Europe]
  Rome, Ancient (The land) **R:** 436
Italian Republic, Order of Merit of the
  Medals, decorations, and orders (table) **M:** 359 *with picture*
Italian Somaliland
  Somalia (History) **So:** 589
  Somaliland **So:** 590
Italian sonnet
  Poetry (Forms) **P:** 595
Italian Symphony [music by Mendelssohn]
  Mendelssohn, Felix (His music) **M:** 399
Italian Tyrol [region, Italy]
  Tyrol **T:** 542 *with map*
Italics [printing] **I:** 495
  Handwriting (Early forms of writing) **H:** 49-50
  Proofreading (Proofreaders' marks) **P:** 822
  Type (Classes of type) **T:** 537 *with picture*
Italicus, Silius [Roman poet]
  Latin literature (The Imperial Period) **L:** 116-117
Italo-Ethiopian War [1935-1936] **I:** 495
Italy I: 496 *with pictures and maps*
  See also the list of Related articles in the Italy article
  Art and architecture
    Italy (Arts) **I:** 504-506 *with pictures*
    Classical music (History) **Ci:** 645-646
    Furniture (Italy) **F:** 572 *with picture*; (The early 1600's) **F:** 574 *with picture*
    Opera (The development of opera) **O:** 797 *with pictures*
    Painting (The Renaissance) **P:** 51 *with pictures*
    Pottery *picture on* **P:** 717
    Sculpture (Italian Renaissance sculpture) **S:** 251 *with pictures*
    Theater (Italy) **T:** 248
  Education
    Library (Italy) **L:** 261
  Finance and banking
    Euro **E:** 379
  Government
    Italy (Government) **I:** 497
    Communism (In non-Communist countries) **Ci:** 897

History
  Italy (History) **I:** 512
  Albania (World War II) **A:** 307
  Bank **B:** 88 *with picture*
  Bomb (History) **B:** 452 *with picture*
  City-state **Ci:** 603
  Colonialism (Later colonialism) **Ci:** 813-814
  Eritrea (History) **E:** 353-354
  Ethiopia (Haile Selassie) **E:** 371
  Fascism (Fascism in Italy) **F:** 49
  Garibaldi, Giuseppe **G:** 43
  Greece (World War II) **G:** 363
  Holy Roman Empire **H:** 299 *with map*
  Italo-Ethiopian War **I:** 495
  League of Nations (The League in action) **L:** 160
  Libya (Italian control) **L:** 267
  Mussolini, Benito **M:** 966
  Napoleon III (Foreign affairs) **N:** 17
  Renaissance (The Italian Renaissance) **R:** 233
  Revolution of 1848 **R:** 288
  San Marino [country] (History) **S:** 104
  Spanish Civil War (Foreign assistance) **So:** 756a
  Tyrol **T:** 542 *with map*
  Victor Emmanuel II **V:** 355
  World War I (The Italian Front) **W:** 459 *with map*; (The fighting ends) **W:** 463
  World War II **W:** 468 *with pictures and maps*
  Language and literature See Italian language; Italian literature *in this index*
  Social and cultural life
    Christmas (In Italy) **C:** 531
    Clothing (The Renaissance) **Ci:** 702 *with picture*
    Valentine's Day (In Europe) **V:** 261
Italy, Kingdom of [European history]
  Italy (The Kingdom of Italy) **I:** 515-516 *with map*
Itatiaia National Park [Brazil]
  National park (table) **N:** 42g
ITC hearing aid
  Hearing aid (Styles) **H:** 130
Itch mite [animal]
  Mite *picture on* **M:** 678
  Scabies **S:** 169
Itching Parrot, The [book by Fernández de Lizardi]
  Latin American literature (The 1800's) **L:** 112
  Mexico (Literature) **M:** 460
ITE hearing aid
  Hearing aid (Styles) **H:** 130
ITF [organization]
  Tennis (Amateur tennis) **T:** 165
Ithaca [island, Greece]
  Ionian Islands **I:** 373 *with map*
  Odyssey: (The *Odyssey* begins) **O:** 675
Ithna Ashari [sect] *See* Imāmī Shī'ah *in this index*
Itjawy [ancient city]
  Egypt, Ancient (The Middle Kingdom) **E:** 143
Itokawa [asteroid]
  Asteroid (Sizes and shapes) **A:** 824 *with picture*; (History of study) **A:** 824b
  Space exploration (Probes to asteroids) **So:** 711
It's a Wonderful Life [film]
  Capra, Frank **C:** 198
It's Too Late Now [book by Milne]
  Milne, A. A. **M:** 556
ITU [union] *See* International Telecommunication Union *in this index*
iTunes Music Store
  Apple Inc. **A:** 573
Iturbide, Agustín de [emperor of Mexico] **I:** 520
  Mexico (Independence) **M:** 470
  Santa Anna, Antonio López de (Young soldier) **S:** 112
IUCN [organization] *See* International Union for the Conservation of Nature and Natural Resources *in this index*
IUD [device]
  Birth control (Methods of birth control) **B:** 378-379
IUPAC [organization] *See* International Union of Pure and Applied Chemistry *in this index*
Ivan I, the Moneybag [Russian nobleman]
  Russia (The rise of Moscow) **R:** 548
Ivan III, the Great [grand prince of Moscow] **I:** 520
  Moscow (History) **M:** 826-827
  Russia (The rise of Moscow) **R:** 548
Ivan IV, the Terrible [czar of Russia] **I:** 520
  Romanov **R:** 426
  Russia (Ivan the Terrible) **R:** 548 *with picture*; (table: Czars and empresses) **R:** 549
Ivan V [czar of Russia]
  Peter I, the Great (Early life) **P:** 323
  Russia (Peter the Great) **R:** 549; (table: Czars and empresses) **R:** 549
Ivan VI [czar of Russia]
  Russia (table: Czars and empresses) **R:** 549
Ivan Susanin [opera by Glinka]
  Glinka, Mikhail Ivanovich **G:** 231

Ivanhoe [book by Scott]
  Robin Hood **R:** 367
  Scott, Sir Walter (The Waverley novels) **S:** 222
Ivanov, Lev Ivanovich [Russian choreographer]
  Nutcracker, The **N:** 622
Ivanovsky, Dimitri [Russian biologist]
  Virus (Discovery) **V:** 427
"I've Got You Under My Skin" [song by Porter]
  Porter, Cole **P:** 682
Iverson, Allen [American basketball player] **I:** 520
Ives, Burl [American actor]
  Motion picture (Best performance by an actor in a supporting role: 1958) **M:** 862a
Ives, Charles [American composer] **I:** 520
Ives, James Merritt [American lithographer]
  Currier and Ives **Ci:** 1198
Ivesia [plant]
  Flower *picture on* **F:** 289
IVF [medicine] *See* In vitro fertilization *in this index*
Ivins, Bruce E. [American scientist]
  September 11 terrorist attacks (Anthrax attacks) **S:** 310b
Ivins, Marsha S. [American astronaut]
  International Space Station *picture on* **I:** 346b
Ivory I: 520 *with pictures*
  Byzantine art (Other art forms) **B:** 751
  Conservation (Africa) **Ci:** 990
  Elephant **E:** 226
  National park *picture on* **N:** 42h
Ivory, Vegetable *See* Vegetable ivory *in this index*
Ivory-billed woodpecker
  Woodpecker (Kinds) **W:** 394 *with picture*
Ivory black [pigment] **I:** 521
Ivory Coast *See* Côte d'Ivoire *in this index*
Ivory-nut palm
  Ivory palm **I:** 522
Ivory palm [tree] **I:** 522 *with pictures*
Ivvavik National Park [Yukon]
  Canada (table: National parks and national park reserves) **C:** 113
Ivy [plant] **I:** 522 *with pictures*
  Gardening *picture on* **G:** 37
Ivy geranium
  Flower *picture on* **F:** 292
Ivy Green [house]
  Alabama (Places to visit) **A:** 266
Iwan [architecture]
  Architecture (Islamic architecture) **A:** 613-614 *with diagram*
  Islamic art (Madrasahs) **I:** 468
  Mosque **M:** 831
Iwane, Matsui [Japanese general]
  Nanking Massacre **N:** 10
Iwate Ichinohe Tunnel [Japan]
  Tunnel (table) **T:** 467
IWC [organization] *See* International Whaling Commission *in this index*
Iwein [poem by Hartmann von Aue]
  Hartmann von Aue **H:** 79
Iwo Jima [former name]
  Iwo Jima, Battle of **I:** 523
Iwo Jima, Battle of [1945] **I:** 523 *with picture*
  World War II *picture on* **W:** 491; (Closing in on Japan) **W:** 492
Iwo Jima Statue [Arlington, Virginia]
  Marine Corps, United States *picture on* **M:** 206
  Washington, D.C. (Marine Corps War Memorial) **W:** 78 *with picture*
Iwo To [island, Japan]
  Iwo Jima, Battle of **I:** 523
IWW [union] *See* Industrial Workers of the World *in this index*
Ix Chel [Maya god]
  Maya (Religion) **M:** 322
Ixtacihuatl [volcano, Mexico] **I:** 523 *with picture*
  Mexico (The Plateau of Mexico) **M:** 461 *with map*
  Mountain (table) **M:** 896 *with diagram*
Ixtacihuatl-Popocatepetl National Park [Mexico]
  National park (table) **N:** 42g
Iyar [month]
  Calendar (The Hebrew calendar) **C:** 29
IYHF [organization]
  Youth hostel **Y:** 574
Izaak Walton League of America [conservation organization] **I:** 523
Izabal, Lake
  Guatemala (The Northern Plain) **G:** 414 *with map*
Izenour, Steven [American author]
  Venturi, Robert **V:** 310
İzmir [Turkey] **I:** 524 *with picture*
  Turkey (Tourism) **T:** 509
İzmit [Turkey]
  Earthquake (Long-term forecasts) **E:** 38b
Iztaccihuatl [volcano, Mexico] *See* Ixtacihuatl *in this index*
Izu Islands [islands, Pacific]
  Tokyo (The Tokyo Metropolitan Prefecture)

T: 313-314
Izvestia [newspaper]
  Kennedy, John Fitzgerald (Other developments)
    K: 266
  Moscow (Communications) M: 826
Izz al-Din al-Qassam Brigades [military group]
  Hamas H: 28
Izzard [letter]
  Z Z: 583

J

J [letter] J: 1 *with pictures*
  I I: 1
J. C. Penney Company
  Penney, James Cash P: 243
J-Class yacht
  America's Cup A: 431
J. Edgar Thomson Works
  Carnegie, Andrew (Rise to wealth) C: 242
J.Lo [recording]
  Lopez, Jennifer L: 453
J. P. Morgan & Company
  JPMorgan Chase & Co. J: 177
  Morgan, J. P. M: 803
J. P. Morgan Chase & Co. *See* JPMorgan Chase &
  Co. *in this index*
J particle [nuclear particle] *See* Psi particle *in this*
  index
J. S. Fry and Sons
  Chocolate (History) C: 519
J. S. Morgan and Company
  Morgan, Junius Spencer M: 804
J-stroke [canoeing]
  Canoeing (Paddling and steering) C: 181
J. W. McConnell Foundation *See* McConnell Family
  Foundation *in this index*
JA [organization] *See* Junior Achievement *in this*
  index
Jäätteenmäki, Anneli [Finnish political leader]
  Finland (Recent developments) F: 118
Jab [boxing]
  Boxing (Boxing skills) B: 529 *with picture*
Jabal ad Duruz [mountain, Syria]
  Syria (The mountains) So: 1073 *with map*
Jabal Katrinah [mountain]
  Egypt (The Sinai Peninsula) E: 126 *with map*
Jabara, James [American pilot]
  Ace A: 24
Jabbar, Kareem Abdul- [American basketball
  player] *See* Abdul-Jabbar, Kareem *in this index*
Jabès, Edmond [French author]
  French literature (Recent French literature) F: 523
Jabiru [bird] J: 2 *with picture*
  Stork So: 913
Jacana [bird] J: 2 *with picture*
  Bird (Birds of Africa) B: 344h *with picture*
Jacaranda [tree] J: 2 *with picture*
J'Accuse [letter]
  Dreyfus, Alfred (Efforts to clear Dreyfus's name)
    D: 347
  Zola, Émile Z: 598
Jack [animal]
  Donkey D: 308
  Mule M: 913
Jack [flag]
  Flag (Military flags) F: 195-208
  Union Jack U: 27
Jack [imaginary person]
  Halloween (Jack-o'-lanterns) H: 24b
Jack [machine] *See* Jackscrew *in this index*
Jack [sports]
  Lawn bowling L: 144
Jack Frost [legendary figure] J: 2
Jack-in-the-pulpit [plant] J: 2 *with picture*
  Plant *picture on* P: 525
Jack Miner Migratory Bird Foundation
  Miner, Jack M: 565
Jack-o'-lantern J: 3
  Halloween (Jack-o'-lanterns) H: 24b *with picture*
  Pumpkin P: 901
Jack-o'lantern mushroom
  Mushroom (Poisonous mushrooms) M: 945 *with*
  picture
Jack pine [tree]
  Pine *picture on* P: 470; (Eastern pines) P: 468
Jack Pine, The [painting by Thomson]
  Thomson, Tom T: 265 *with picture*
Jack rabbit J: 3 *with picture*
  Animal *picture on* A: 483
  Hare H: 59 *with picture*
Jack Russell terrier *See* Parson Russell terrier *in*
  this index
Jack the Giant Killer [legendary figure]
  Giant G: 183
Jack the Ripper [British criminal] J: 3
Jack-up rig
  Petroleum *picture on* P: 340

Jackal [animal] J: 3 *with picture*
Jackass hare
  Jack rabbit *picture on* J: 3
Jackdaw [bird] J: 4 *with picture*
Jacketed bullet
  Rifle (History) R: 339-340
Jackhammer [tool]
  Drill (Rock drills) D: 348
  Pneumatic tool P: 586
Jackknife [scenery]
  Theater (Changing scenery) T: 240
Jackknife-fish
  Drum D: 367
Jackling, Daniel C. [American engineer]
  Copper (Industrial developments) Ci: 1044
Jackpot [money]
  Slot machine S: 508a
Jacks [game] J: 4 *with picture*
Jackscrew [tool]
  Machine (Screw) M: 15 *with picture*
  Screw (Uses) S: 225
Jackson [Mississippi] J: 4
  Mississippi *pictures on* M: 623, M: 627; (table:
    Average monthly weather) M: 636
Jackson, Alan [American musician]
  Country music (Modern country music)
    Ci: 1098c-1099 *with picture*
Jackson, Alexander Young [Canadian painter] J: 5
  with picture
  Group of Seven G: 402
Jackson, Alphonso R. [American government
  official]
  Housing and Urban Development, Department
    of (table) H: 393
Jackson, Amelia [wife of]
  Holmes, Oliver Wendell (His life) H: 294
Jackson, Andrew [U.S. president] J: 6 *with pictures*
  Adams, John Quincy (Election of 1824) A: 42
  Alabama (Territorial days) A: 275
  Bank (The Second Bank of the United States)
    B: 93
  Biddle, Nicholas B: 294
  Calhoun, John Caldwell (Early career) C: 35
  Cherokee Indians C: 409
  Congress of the United States (Growth and
    conflict) Ci: 948
  Creek Indians Ci: 1126
  Democratic Party (Origin) D: 124; (Jacksonian
    policies) D: 124
  Democratic-Republican Party D: 129
  Duel D: 378
  Electoral College (History) E: 164
  Florida (The second Spanish period) F: 262
  Indian wars (Conflicts in the South) I: 192
  Kitchen Cabinet K: 337
  Memphis (History) M: 396
  New Orleans (The early 1800's) N: 283
  New Orleans, Battle of N: 285
  Oklahoma (The American Civil War) O: 731
  O'Neale, Peggy O: 761
  Polk, James Knox (Lawyer and legislator) P: 641
  President of the United States (Strengthening the
    office) P: 768
  Public opinion poll (History) P: 863
  Taney, Roger Brooke T: 25
  Tennessee (Building the state) T: 153
  Trail of Tears T: 367
  Tyler, John (Governor and senator) T: 533
  United States, History of the (Jackson as
    president) U: 171; (Politics after Jackson)
    U: 171
  Webster, Daniel (The U.S. senator) W: 177
  Western frontier life in America (Settlers and
    Native Americans) W: 239
  Whig Party (The Whig Party of the 1800's) W: 280
Jackson, Bo [American athlete]
  Football (table) F: 363
Jackson, Charles [American political leader]
  Rhode Island (table) R: 311
Jackson, Charles T. [American chemist]
  Long, Crawford Williamson L: 446
  Morton, William Thomas Green M: 821
Jackson, Claiborne F. [American political leader]
  Missouri (table) M: 668; (The American Civil War)
    M: 671
Jackson, Ed [American political leader]
  Indiana (table) I: 214
Jackson, Elihu E. [American political leader]
  Maryland (table) M: 255
Jackson, Frank D. [American political leader]
  Iowa (table) I: 391
Jackson, Glenda [British actress]
  Motion picture (Best performance by an actress:
    1970, 1973) M: 862
Jackson, Hancock Lee [American political leader]
  Missouri (table) M: 668
Jackson, Helen Hunt [American author] J: 14

  November (Quotations) N: 577
  September (Quotations) S: 309
Jackson, Howell E. [American jurist]
  Supreme Court of the United States (table)
    So: 1000
Jackson, Jacob B. [American political leader]
  West Virginia (table) W: 225
Jackson, James [American military leader]
  Indian wars (The Modoc War [1872-1873]) I: 194
Jackson, James [American political leader]
  Georgia (table) G: 130
Jackson, Jesse Louis [American social reformer]
  J: 14 *with portrait*
  African Americans *picture on* A: 136q; (Politics)
    A: 136s
Jackson, Joseph Jefferson [American baseball
  player] *See* Jackson, Shoeless Joe *in this index*
Jackson, Mahalia [American singer] J: 15
Jackson, Maynard H., Jr. [American political
  leader]
  Atlanta (The mid-1900's) A: 861
  Georgia (The late 1900's) G: 134
Jackson, Michael [American singer] J: 15 *with*
  portrait
  Rock music (Madonna and Michael Jackson)
    R: 380c
  Television *picture on* T: 119
Jackson, Peter [New Zealand director] J: 15
  Motion picture (Best achievement in directing:
    2003) M: 862
Jackson, Rachel Robards [wife of]
  Jackson, Andrew *picture on* J: 9; (Jackson's family)
    J: 8; (Election of 1828) J: 10
Jackson, Reggie [American baseball player]
  Baseball (table: Hall of Fame) B: 134a
Jackson, Sir Robert G. A. [husband of]
  Ward, Barbara W: 35
Jackson, Robert Houghwout [American jurist]
  J: 16
Jackson, Samuel [American businessman]
  West Virginia (Early industries) W: 226
Jackson, Sarah Yorke [daughter-in-law of]
  White House hostesses W: 291
Jackson, Shirley [American author] J: 16
Jackson, Shoeless Joe [American baseball player]
  J: 16
Jackson, Stonewall [Confederate general] J: 16
  with portrait
  Civil War, American (The commanding officers)
    Ci: 618 *with portrait*; (First Battle of Bull Run)
    Ci: 625; (The peninsular campaign) Ci: 626;
    (Battle of Chancellorsville) Ci: 627
  Ewell, Richard Stoddert E: 434
  Frietchie, Barbara F: 533
  Lee, Robert E. (Opening campaigns) L: 178
Jackson, Thomas Jonathan *See* Jackson, Stonewall
  in this index
Jackson, Travis [American baseball player]
  Baseball (table: Hall of Fame) B: 134a
Jackson, William [American political leader]
  Constitution of the United States (The
    Constitutional Convention) Ci: 999-1000
Jackson, William Henry [American photographer]
  J: 17
  Fur trade *picture on* F: 565
  Photography (Artistic advances) P: 424-425
  Pioneer life in America *picture on* P: 476
  Wyoming *picture on* W: 534
Jackson Five [singers]
  Jackson, Michael J: 15
Jackson Hole [region, Wyoming]
  Grand Teton National Park G: 309
Jackson Lake [Wyoming]
  Grand Teton National Park G: 309
Jackson Park
  Chicago *picture on* C: 426
Jackson Square [district]
  New Orleans (Downtown New Orleans) N: 278
Jackson State University
  Mississippi (The early 2000's) M: 645
Jackson's Mill [farm, Weston]
  West Virginia (Places to visit) W: 216
Jacksonville [Florida] J: 17 *with picture and map*
  Florida *picture on* F: 243
Jacksonville Jaguars [team]
  Football (National Football League) F: 364
Jackstaff
  Flag (table) F: 193
Jackstones [game]
  Jacks J: 4 *with picture*
Jacob [Biblical figure] J: 19
  Abraham A: 16
  Esau E: 356
  Isaac I: 461
  Jews (Beginnings) J: 120
  Joseph J: 167
  Rachel R: 60

Jacob, François [French geneticist]
Nobel Prizes (Physiology or medicine: 1965) N: 446
Jacob, John Edward [American social reformer] J: 19
Jacob, John J. [American political leader]
West Virginia (table) W: 225
Jacob Blessing the Sons of Joseph [painting by Rembrandt]
Rembrandt (The last years: 1640-1669) R: 229
Jacob Have I Loved [book by Paterson]
Paterson, Katherine P: 196
Jacob Wrestling with the Angel [painting by Gauguin] *See* Vision After the Sermon, The *in this index*
Jacobean drama
Drama (Jacobean and Caroline drama) D: 332
English literature (Jacobean drama) E: 317
Jacobin pigeon [bird]
Pigeon *picture on* P: 459
Jacobins [French history] J: 20
French Revolution (The National Convention) F: 526; (Terror and equality) F: 526; (The revolution ends) F: 527
Marat, Jean-Paul M: 190
Mirabeau, Comte de M: 615
Robespierre R: 366
Roland de la Platière, Marie Jeanne R: 402
Jacobite [British history]
Scotland (Union with England) S: 220
Jacobite Rebellion [1715]
George I G: 106b
Rob Roy R: 364
Jacobite Rebellion [1745]
Tartan T: 47
Jacobs, Harriet Ann [American author]
African American literature (The 1800's) A: 136a
Jacobs, Joseph [British author] J: 20
Literature for children (Collections of tales) L: 363
Storytelling (The 1800's) So: 915
Jacob's Pillow Dance Festival
Shawn, Ted S: 379
Jacobsen, Arne [Danish architect]
Denmark (Arts) D: 136
Jacobsen, Erik [Danish physician]
Disulfiram D: 240
Jacobson, Eddie [American businessman]
Truman, Harry S. (Businessman) T: 467
Jacobson's organ [zoology]
Amphibian (Sense organs) A: 440
Reptile (Sense organs) R: 251-252
Snake (Sense organs) S: 527-528 *with diagram*
Jacquard, Joseph Marie [French inventor] J: 20
Computer (Punched-card devices) Ci: 924a
Weaving (History) W: 174-175
Jacquard loom [machine]
Computer (Punched-card devices) Ci: 924a
Jacquard, Joseph Marie J: 20
Rugs and carpets (Weaving) R: 515-516; (History) R: 517
Weaving (History) W: 174-175
Jacques, Brian [British author] J: 20
Jacques Cartier, Mount [Quebec]
Gaspé Peninsula G: 66
Jacques the Fatalist [book by Diderot]
Diderot, Denis D: 195
Jade [gem] J: 20
China (The arts) C: 487 *with picture*
Gem *picture on* G: 78
World, History of the *picture on* W: 431
Jade Emperor [Taoist deity]
Religion *picture on* R: 222
Jade Sea [name for]
Lake Turkana L: 47
Jadeite [mineral]
Jade (Jadeite) J: 20
Jadwiga [queen of Poland]
Poland (The Polish empire) P: 612
Jaeger [bird] J: 20
Bird (Birds of the Arctic) B: 343 *with picture*
Jaeger [gun]
Rifle (History) R: 339
Jafari, Ibrahim al- [Iraqi political leader]
Iraq (A new government) I: 414b *with picture*
Jaffa [Israel]
Tel Aviv T: 88
Jagan, Cheddi B. [Guyanan political leader]
Guyana (History) G: 446-447
Jagan, Janet [Guyanan political leader]
Guyana (History) G: 446-447
Jagannath temple *See* Juggernaut *in this index*
Jagdeo, Bharrat [Guyana political leader]
Guyana (History) G: 446-447
Jaggard, Isaac [English printer]
Shakespeare, William (Shakespeare's plays) S: 354; (Folios) S: 369
Jagger, Dean [American actor]

Motion picture (Best performance by an actor in a supporting role: 1949) M: 862a
Jagger, Mick [British musician]
Rock music *picture on* R: 380d; (The Rolling Stones) R: 380
Rolling Stones R: 402a
Jagiełło, Władysław [ruler of Lithuania and Poland]
Lithuania L: 389
Poland (The Polish empire) P: 612
Jagiellonian dynasty [Polish history]
Poland (The Polish empire) P: 612
Jagiellonian University [Poland]
Kraków K: 386
Poland (Education) P: 605
Jaguar [animal] J: 21
Animal *pictures on* A: 472, A: 481
Rain forest *picture on* R: 126c
Sculpture (Early sculpture) S: 243 *with picture*
Jaguars, Jacksonville [team] *See* Jacksonville Jaguars *in this index*
Jaguarundi [animal] J: 21
Jahan, Shah [Mughal emperor] *See* Shah Jahan *in this index*
Jahangir [Mughal emperor]
India (The coming of the Europeans) I: 130
Mughal Empire M: 910
Muslims (The Mughal Empire) M: 964d
Jahn, Friedrich Ludwig [German educator]
Gymnastics G: 448
Jahn, Helmut [American architect] J: 21 *with picture*
Jahre Viking [ship]
Tanker (Kinds of tankers) T: 28
Jai alai [sport] J: 21 *with picture*
Jail
Prison (Jails) P: 806
Jailhouse Rock [film]
Rock music *picture on* R: 377
Jainism [religion] J: 22 *with picture*
India (Jainism) I: 117
Mahavira M: 65
Monasticism (Non-Christian monasticism) M: 701
Religion R: 215; (Hinduism) R: 220
Jakarta [Indonesia] J: 22
Indonesia *pictures on* I: 226, I: 227
Jakeš, Miloš [Czechoslovak political leader]
Czechoslovakia (The Velvet Revolution) Ci: 1216
Jakob, Alfons M. [German physician]
Creutzfeldt-Jakob disease Ci: 1128
Jalap [plant]
Morning-glory M: 809
Jalna [book by De la Roche]
De la Roche, Mazo D: 95
Jam [food] *See* Jelly and jam *in this index*
Jama Masjid [temple]
Delhi (The city) D: 115
Jama Musjid [mosque]
Allahabad A: 370
Jamā`at-i-Islāmī [political movement]
Muslims (Reform and renewal) M: 964d-965
Jamahiriya, Great Socialist People's Libyan Arab [official name]
Libya L: 264
Jamaica [country] J: 23 *with picture and map*
Flag *picture on* F: 201
Morgan, Sir Henry (Early career) M: 803
Rap music R: 141
Reggae R: 204
Jamaica [district]
New York City (Queens) N: 329-330
Jamaica mignonette [shrub]
Henna H: 185
Jamaica pepper [spice] *See* Allspice *in this index*
Jamaica Plain [district, Boston]
Boston (The south side) B: 500
Jambalaya [food]
Cajuns C: 19
Jamboree
Boy Scouts (Scouting throughout the world) B: 538
James [kings of England and Scotland] J: 25
James I [king of England]
James (James I) J: 25
Baron B: 116
Bible (The King James Version) B: 285
Buckingham, Duke of B: 663
England (The first Stuarts) E: 308; (table) E: 308
English literature (The early and middle 1600's) E: 317
Fawkes, Guy F: 57
Hampton Court Conference H: 36
Horse racing (History) H: 366
Ireland (Religious persecution) I: 426
London Company L: 445
Mary, Queen of Scots (Her reign) M: 239
Northern Ireland (Protestant settlement) N: 524
Nova Scotia (The struggle in Acadia) N: 568

Shakespeare, William (The King's Men) S: 348; (Elizabethan society) S: 349
Tudor, House of T: 481
Virginia (The Jamestown settlement) V: 418; (Royal governors and Cromwell) V: 418
James I [king of Scotland]
James (Five kings named James) J: 25
James II [king of England]
James (James II) J: 25
Boyne, Battle of the B: 539
England (table) E: 308; (The Restoration) E: 309
Ireland (Religious persecution) I: 426
Monmouth, Duke of M: 730
New England, Dominion of N: 203
Northern Ireland (Protestant settlement) N: 524
Penn, William (Arrested again) P: 242
United States, History of the (The Middle Colonies) U: 154-155
William III W: 308
James II [king of Scotland]
James (Five kings named James) J: 25
James III [king of Scotland]
James (Five kings named James) J: 25
James IV [king of Scotland]
Henry VII [of England] H: 188
James (Five kings named James) J: 25
Scotland (The House of Stuart) S: 219
James V [king of Scotland]
James (Five kings named James) J: 25
Mary, Queen of Scots M: 239
Scotland (The House of Stuart) S: 219
James VI [king of Scotland] *See* James I [king of England] *in this index*
James, Arthur Horace [American political leader]
Pennsylvania (table) P: 263
James, "Chappie" *See* James, Daniel, Jr. *in this index*
James, Daniel, Jr. [U.S. general] J: 25 *with portrait*
James, Epistle of [New Testament] J: 26
Bible (The Letters) B: 284
James, Saint J: 27
James, Fob, Jr. [American political leader]
Alabama (table) A: 274
James, Forrest H., Jr. [American political leader]
Alabama (table) A: 274
James, Frank [American bandit]
James, Jesse J: 26
James, Henry [1843-1916, American author] J: 26
American literature (Mark Twain and Henry James) A: 420 *with portrait*
Novel (The United States) N: 573
Ozick, Cynthia O: 893
James, Jesse [American bandit] J: 26 *with portrait*
Missouri *picture on* M: 670
Northfield N: 528
James, LeBron [American basketball player] J: 26
James, P. D. [English writer] J: 27
James, Ralph A. [American physicist]
Americium A: 432
Curium Ci: 1195
James, Saint [Biblical figure] J: 27
James, Epistle of J: 26
James, Thomas [English explorer]
James Bay J: 27
Manitoba (Newcomers) M: 160
James, Thomas L. [American government official]
Garfield, James Abram (table) G: 42
James, W. H. [American political leader]
Nebraska (table) N: 110
James, Will [American author]
Newbery Medal (table) N: 359
James, William [American philosopher] J: 27
American literature (Nonfiction writers) A: 420
Emotion (The constructivist approach) E: 261
James, Henry (His life) J: 26
Peace Corps (History) P: 208
Pragmatism P: 729
Psychology (Psychology becomes a science) P: 849
James A. Garfield National Historic Site [Ohio]
National Park System (table: National historic sites) N: 52-53
James Bay [bay, Canada] J: 27
Hudson Bay H: 405 *with map*
James Buchanan Brady Urological Institute
Brady, Diamond Jim B: 546
James E. Sullivan Award
Amateur Athletic Union A: 401
James Forrestal campus
Princeton University (Campus buildings) P: 795
James Herriot's Yorkshire [book by Herriot]
Herriot, James H: 216
James Island [Galapagos Islands]
Galapagos Islands G: 7 *with map*
James Island [Gambia]
Gambia G: 18
James Madison Memorial Building [Washington, D.C.]

Washington, D.C. map on **W: 76**
James Peak [mountain, Colorado]
Moffat Tunnel **M: 686**
James R. Thompson Center [Chicago]
Jahn, Helmut **J: 21** with picture
James River [South Dakota]
South Dakota (Land regions) **So: 674** with map
James River [Virginia] **J: 28**
Jamestown **J: 28** with picture
James Stuart: Duke of Richmond and Lennox
[painting by Van Dyck]
Clothing picture on **Ci: 703**
James the Greater, Saint [apostle] **J: 28**
James the Less, Saint [apostle] **J: 28**
James Webb Space Telescope
Hubble Space Telescope (History) **H: 404**
James Whitcomb Riley Museum Home
[Indianapolis]
Indianapolis (Cultural life) **I: 221-222** with map
James Whitcomb Riley Old Home and Museum
[Greenfield]
Indiana (Places to visit) **I: 206**
Jameson, Sir Leander Starr [British colonial
leader]
Anglo-Boer Wars **A: 463**
Jameson Raid [South African history]
Rhodes, Cecil John (Conflict with the Boers)
R: 317
Jamestown [Virginia] **J: 28** with picture
Colonial life in America (Why the colonists came
to America) **Ci: 788** with picture; (Early English
settlements) **Ci: 789**; (Places to visit) **Ci: 800**
with picture
Exploration (The French and English in North
America) **E: 446-447**
Indian wars (Jamestown) **I: 190**
London Company **L: 445**
Newport, Christopher **N: 379**
Rolfe, John **R: 402**
Smith, John **S: 516**
United States, History of the (The American
Colonies [1607-1753]) **U: 152** with picture
Virginia picture on **V: 419**; (Places to visit) **V: 408**
Jamestown Colonial National Historical Park See
Colonial National Historical Park in this index
Jammeh, Yahya [Gambian political leader]
Gambia (History) **G: 19-20**
Jammu and Kashmir See Kashmir in this index
Jamuna River See Brahmaputra River in this index
Janáček, Leoš [Czech composer]
Czech Republic (The arts) **Ci: 1211**
Opera (The search for new forms) **O: 799-800**
Janata Party [political party]
India (India under Indira Gandhi) **I: 133-134**
Janco, Marcel [Romanian artist]
Dadaism **D: 3** with picture
Jane Eyre [book by Brontë]
Brontë sisters (The sisters' works) **B: 637**
Jane Frances de Chantal, Saint [French religious
leader]
Francis de Sales, Saint **F: 481**
Religious life (Religious life in the 1500's and
1600's) **R: 227**
Janes, Elizabeth [American artist]
Cherokee Indians picture on **C: 409**
Janiculum Hill [park]
Rome (Parks and gardens) **R: 429**
Janin, Louis [American businessman]
Hoover, Herbert Clark (Engineer and
businessman) **H: 328**
Janissaries [soldiers] **J: 29**
Army (Armies in the Middle Ages) **A: 727**
Muslims (The Ottoman Empire) **M: 964d**
Ottoman Empire (The beginning of the empire)
O: 878
Janjaweed [militia]
Darfur **D: 36**
Sudan (Violence in Darfur) **So: 954**
Janklow, William J. [American political leader]
South Dakota (table) **So: 680**; (The early 2000's)
So: 685
Janney, Eli [American inventor]
Railroad (Engineering improvements) **R: 117**
Jannings, Emil [German actor]
Motion picture (Best performance by an actor:
1927-28) **M: 862a**
Jannus, Tony [American aviator]
Airplane (The golden age) **A: 235**
Aviation (The first airlines) **A: 988**
Janowicz, Vic [American football player]
Football (table) **F: 363**
Jansen, Cornelius [Belgian religious leader] **J: 29**
Roman Catholic Church (Jansenism) **R: 409**
Jansenism [religion]
Jansen, Cornelius **J: 29**
Pascal, Blaise **P: 190**
Roman Catholic Church (Jansenism) **R: 409**

Jansky, Karl Guthe [American engineer] **J: 29**
Radio wave **R: 97**
Janson, Eric [Swedish settler]
Illinois (Places to visit) **I: 62**
Janssen, Jules [French astronomer]
Sun (History of modern solar study) **So: 986**
Janssen, Pierre J. [French astronomer]
Helium **H: 176**
Janssen, Zacharias [Dutch optician]
Microscope (History) **M: 519**
Jansz, Willem [Dutch explorer]
Australia (European explorations) **A: 920** with
map
Exploration (Exploring the Pacific) **E: 447**
January [month] **J: 30** with pictures
Calendar (The Romans) **C: 31**
Janub Darfur [state]
Darfur **D: 35**
Janus [Roman mythology] **J: 31**
New Year's Day (Early customs) **N: 289**
Janzen, Lee [American golfer]
Golf (U.S. Open) **G: 265**
Japan J: 32 with pictures and maps
See also the list of Related articles in the Japan
article
Asia (Way of life in East Asia) **A: 785**
Flag pictures on **F: 203, F: 217**
Agriculture
Japan (Agriculture) **J: 49**
Art and architecture
Japan (The arts) **J: 43** with pictures
Architecture (Japanese architecture) **A: 613**
with picture
Asia (The arts) **A: 789**
Bell picture on **B: 239**
Dance picture on **D: 23**; (Asian theatrical dance)
D: 28-29
Doll (Traditional dolls) **D: 287**; (Doll festivals
and customs) **D: 287** with picture
Drama (Japan) **D: 336** with picture
Fan **F: 26b**
Flower (Flower arranging) **F: 297**
Furniture picture on **F: 571**; (Japan) **F: 572**
Gardening picture on **G: 38**
Haiku **H: 8**
Ivory (Ivory carving) **I: 521** with picture
Lacquerware **L: 22**
Music (Japanese music) **M: 956** with picture
Painting (Landscapes and seascapes) **P: 33** with
picture; (Japanese painting) **P: 47** with picture
Sculpture (Japan) **S: 239** with picture
Communications and mass media
Japan (Transportation) **J: 51**
Newspaper (In Asia) **N: 386**
Television (In Asia) **T: 116-117**
Education
Japan (Education) **J: 42** with picture
Asia (Education) **A: 789**
Government
Japan (Government) **J: 33**
Clinton, Bill (International affairs) **Ci: 682e**
Government (Asia and the Middle East)
G: 289-290
Local government (Unitary systems) **L: 408**
Health and welfare
Abortion (In other countries) **A: 16**
Social security (Social security in other
countries) **So: 556**
Unemployment (Unemployment throughout
the world) **U: 23-24**
History
Japan (History) **J: 52** with pictures
Air force (World War II) **A: 185-186**
Asia (History of the; (The rise of the
Japanese Empire) **A: 806**
Asian Americans (History of Asian immigration)
A: 812d-812e
Aviation (World War II [1939-1945]) **A: 989-990**
Bataan Death March **B: 162**
Bush, George Herbert Walker (International
trade) **B: 722**
China (Nationalist rule) **C: 504**; (War with
Japan) **C: 504** with map
Colonialism (Later colonialism) **Ci: 813-814**
Deming, W. Edwards **D: 119**
Gentlemen's agreement **G: 90**
Hong Kong (British control) **H: 320**
India (World War II [1939-1945]) **I: 132**
Indonesia (Independence) **I: 237**
Kamakura period **K: 212**
Korea, History of (The Choson dynasty) **K: 366-
367**; (Korea under Japan) **K: 367**
Korea, North (Way of life) **K: 369-370**
Korea, South (Way of life) **K: 376**
League of Nations (The League's shortcomings)
L: 160
MacArthur, Douglas (World War II) **M: 3**; (The

occupation of Japan) **M: 3**
Manchuria (History) **M: 134**
Midway, Battle of **M: 536**
Myanmar (World War II) **M: 970d**
Nanking Massacre **N: 10**
Nuclear energy (Safety concerns) **N: 591-592**
Oriental Exclusion Acts **O: 855**
Palau (History) **P: 102**
Pearl Harbor **P: 218**
Perry, Matthew Calbraith **P: 294**
Philippines (Japanese control) **P: 380**
Russo-Japanese War **R: 566a**
Ryukyu Islands (History) **R: 574**
Seoul (History) **S: 306-307**
Shogun **S: 433**
Sino-Japanese War of 1894-1895 **S: 473**
Sino-Japanese War of 1937-1945 **S: 473**
Thailand (In World War II [1939-1945]) **T: 227**
Union of Soviet Socialist Republics (History)
U: 35-37
Vietnam (The August Revolution of 1945)
V: 370
World, History of the (The rise of Japanese
civilization) **W: 435-436**; (Developments in
China and Japan) **W: 442-443**
World War I (Fighting elsewhere) **W: 457**
World War II **W: 468** with pictures and maps
Manufacturing
Automobile pictures on **A: 970, A: 971**;
(Where cars are made) **A: 959**; (The rise
of international automaking) **A: 972**;
(Challenges to the Big Three) **A: 972**
Electronics (Manufacturing and sales) **E: 214**
Iron and steel (In Japan) **I: 448**
Natural resources
National park (Japan) **N: 42d**
People
Japan (People) **J: 35** with pictures
Ainu **A: 168**
Asia (Life in Japan) **A: 788**
Clothing picture on **Ci: 693**; (Cultural beliefs
and values) **Ci: 691** with picture; (Japan)
Ci: 699; (The 1900's and 2000's) **Ci: 705**
Judo **J: 184**
Karate **K: 245**
Tattooing **T: 51**
Recreation and sports
Baseball (Baseball around the world) **B: 132**
with picture
Martial arts **M: 234**
Religion
Japan (Religion) **J: 40** with pictures
Asia (Religions) **A: 786**
Feasts and festivals (In Buddhism) **F: 58**
Religion (Shinto) **R: 221** with picture
Shinto **S: 401**
Social and cultural life
Japan (Way of life) **J: 38** with pictures
Birth control (In other countries) **B: 379**
Chrysanthemum **C: 540**
Library (Australia and East Asia) **L: 253**
Paperwork (Paper handicrafts) **P: 138**
Segregation (Segregation in other countries)
S: 286
Technology and science
International Space Station **I: 346b**
Moon (Recent exploration) **M: 795**
Space exploration (Japan) **So: 726**
Transportation
Railroad (Intercity trains) **R: 105**; (In Asia) **R: 114**
Japan, Sea of J: 60
Japan Current See Kuroshio in this index
Japan Railways Group
Japan (Transportation) **J: 51**
Japan Sinks [book by Komatsu]
Science fiction (Growing popularity) **S: 205-206**
Japan Tobacco [company]
Manufacturing (table) **M: 170**
Japanese Aerospace Exploration Agency
Sun (Space-based studies) **So: 986-987**
Japanese Alps
Japan (Honshu) **J: 45**
Japanese American internment [U.S. history] **J: 60**
Asian Americans picture on **A: 812e**; (World War II
and Japanese Americans) **A: 812f**
Concentration camp (Other concentration
camps) **C: 927**
Roosevelt, Franklin Delano (The home front)
R: 457-458
World War I picture on **W: 495**; (Treatment of
enemy aliens) **W: 496**
Japanese Americans
Asian Americans (History of Asian immigration)
A: 812d-812e with picture
Japanese American internment **J: 60**
Minority group (Asian Americans) **M: 610**
Oriental Exclusion Acts **O: 855**

Japanese barberry [plant]
Barberry **B:** 106

Japanese beetle [insect] **J:** 60
Beetle (Scarabs) **B:** 217
Insect *picture on* **I:** 285

Japanese bobtail [cat]
Cat (Short-haired breeds) **C:** 290-291 *with picture*

Japanese boxwood [tree]
Box **B:** 524b

Japanese Canadians [people]
Canada, History of (World War II) **C:** 148

Japanese cherry tree
Taft, William Howard (Life in the White House)
T: 11
Washington, D.C. *picture on* **W:** 74; (The Tidal
Basin) **W:** 73-74 *with picture*

Japanese chin [dog] **J:** 61 *with picture*

Japanese ivy [plant]
Ivy **I:** 522

Japanese language J: 61
Japan (Language) **J:** 38
Writing system (Phonetization) **W:** 513

Japanese literature J: 61
Drama (Japan) **D:** 336

Japanese macaque [animal] *See* Snow monkey *in this index*

Japanese maple [tree]
Maple (Other maples) **M:** 187 *with picture*

Japanese pear
Pear (Varieties) **P:** 215

Japanese persimmon [tree]
Persimmon **P:** 300e *with picture*

Japanese plum
Plum (Kinds of plums) **P:** 577 *with picture*

Japanese print [art] **J:** 62 *with picture*
Drama *picture on* **D:** 337

Japanese river fever [disease]
Chigger **C:** 447

Japanese spaniel [dog]
Japanese chin **J:** 61 *with picture*

Japanese-wood oil [tree product]
Tung oil **T:** 486

Japanese yew [plant]
Plant *picture on* **P:** 521
Yew **Y:** 565

Japheth [Biblical figure]
Noah **N:** 439

Japurá River [river, Brazil]
Amazon River (The course of the Amazon) **A:** 403

Jar
City *picture on* **Ci:** 577
Glass (Glass containers) **G:** 212
Pottery *picture on* **P:** 717

Jarabe tapatío [dance]
Mexico (Clothing) **M:** 456-457 *with picture*

Jarcha [poetry]
Spanish literature (Early medieval literature)
So: 757

Jardin Botanique [botanical garden]
Montreal *picture on* **M:** 776; (Parks) **M:** 774

Jardine, Al [American musician]
Beach Boys **B:** 179 *with picture*

Jardine, William M. [American government
official]
Agriculture, Department of (table) **A:** 161
Coolidge, Calvin (table) **Ci:** 1032
Hoover, Herbert Clark (table) **H:** 330

Jargon [language]
Slang **S:** 499

Jarl, Birger [Swedish statesman]
Stockholm (History) **So:** 905

Jarlshof [ancient city]
City *picture on* **Ci:** 577

Jarrah [tree]
Eucalyptus **E:** 376

Jarrell, Randall [American poet] **J:** 63

Jarret de Verchères, Marie Madeleine [French-
Canadian public figure]
Verchères, Marie Madeleine Jarret de **V:** 315

Jarrett, Dale [American race driver]
Automobile racing (table: NASCAR Sprint Cup
champions) **A:** 981

Jarrett, Keith [American pianist]
Jazz *picture on* **J:** 68

Jarrett, Ned [American race driver]
Automobile racing (table: NASCAR Sprint Cup
champions) **A:** 981

Jaruzelski, Wojciech [Polish political leader]
Poland (History) **P:** 611-614

Jarves, Deming [American businessman]
Glass (Early American glass) **G:** 222

Jarvik, Robert K. [American doctor]
Artificial heart **A:** 759
Heart (The first heart transplants and artificial
hearts) **H:** 145

Jarvik-7 [artificial heart]
Artificial heart **A:** 759

Jarvis, Anna [American public figure]
Mother's Day **M:** 843 *with portrait*

Jarvis, Gregory B. [American astronaut]
Challenger disaster **C:** 370
Space exploration (The Challenger disaster)
So: 725

Jarvis, T. J. [American political leader]
North Carolina (table) **N:** 490

Jasmine [plant] **J:** 64 *with picture*

Jason [Greek mythology] **J:** 64
Argonauts **A:** 660
Golden Fleece **G:** 255
Medea **M:** 360
Mythology (Greek heroes) **M:** 982

Jason and Medea [ballet]
Ballet *picture on* **B:** 52

Jasper [mineral] **J:** 64
Gem *picture on* **G:** 78

Jasper National Park [Alberta] **J:** 64
Canada *picture on* **C:** 115; (table: National parks
and national park reserves) **C:** 113

Jasper ware
Pottery (Decorating and glazing) **P:** 718
Wedgwood ware **W:** 179 *with picture*

Jaspers, Karl [German philosopher] **J:** 65

Jataka [story]
Buddha (Later life) **B:** 667

Jatis [sociology]
Caste **C:** 279
India (Social structure) **I:** 116

Jatiya Dal [political party]
Bangladesh (Politcal parties) **B:** 79; (The new
nation) **B:** 86

Jaundice [disorder] **J:** 65
Hepatitis **H:** 192
Liver (Diseases of the liver) **L:** 394
Yellow fever **Y:** 556

Java [island, Indonesia] **J:** 65
Asia (The arts) **A:** 785
Dance (Asian theatrical dance) **D:** 28-29
Indonesia *picture on* **I:** 232; (City life) **I:** 229;
(The Greater Sunda Islands) **I:** 233 *with map*;
(Agriculture) **I:** 235; (Dutch rule) **I:** 237
Quinine **Q:** 42
Raffles, Sir Thomas Stamford **R:** 101

Java [breed]
Chicken (table) **C:** 443

Java [coffee]
Coffee (Kinds of coffee) **Ci:** 755

Java [computer language]
Computer (Using programming languages)
Ci: 923

Java fossils J: 65
Dubois, Eugène **D:** 372
Homo erectus **H:** 306
Prehistoric people (Migration from Africa) **P:** 747;
(table) **P:** 754

Java man [fossil] *See* Java fossils *in this index*

Java Sea, Battle of the [1942]
World War II (Early Japanese victories) **W:** 487

Java sparrow [bird]
Bird (Birds of Asia) **B:** 344f *with picture*

Java Trench
Indian Ocean (Boundaries and size) **I:** 185
Ocean (Depth) **O:** 651-652

Javacheff, Christo [birth name of]
Christo **C:** 537

Javan, Ali [American physicist]
Laser (History) **L:** 86

Javan rhinoceros
Rhinoceros (Kinds of rhinoceroses) **R:** 294

Javanese [people]
Indonesia (People) **I:** 227
Java **J:** 65

Javanese cat
Cat (Long-haired breeds) **C:** 292

Javanese dancing
Indonesia (The arts) **I:** 232 *with picture*

Javelin [missile]
Guided missile (Surface-to-air missiles) **G:** 426

Javelin [weapon] **J:** 65 *with picture*
Track and field (Throwing events) **T:** 358 *with
picture*

Javelina [animal]
Peccary **P:** 226

Jaw [anatomy]
Animal (Teeth and jaws) **A:** 491 *with picture*
Face **F:** 3
Head *diagram on* **H:** 123

Jawa [island, Indonesia] *See* Java *in this index*

Jawara, Sir Dawda [Gambian political leader]
Gambia (History) **G:** 19

Jawbone *See* Mandible *in this index*

Jawed fish
Fish (Kinds of fish) **F:** 147

Jawfish
Fish *picture on* **F:** 170

Jawhar [Egyptian military leader]
Cairo (History) **C:** 17

Jawless fish
Fish (Kinds of fish) **F:** 147

Jaworski, Leon [American lawyer]
Nixon, Richard Milhous (Events at home) **N:** 435-
436
Watergate (The tape controversy) **W:** 144

Jaws [film]
Motion picture (A new generation of filmmakers)
M: 871

Jaws of Life [tool]
Fire department (Rescue trucks) **F:** 126-127 *with
picture*

Jay [bird] **J:** 66 *with picture*
See also Blue jay *in this index*

Jay, John [American statesman] **J:** 67 *with portrait*
Adams, John (Diplomat) **A:** 36
Constitution of the United States (The
background of the Constitution) **Ci:** 1000
Federalist, The **F:** 66
Jay Treaty **J:** 67
New York (table) **N:** 313
Revolution, American (The Treaty of Paris) **R:** 286
United States, History of the (Adopting the
Constitution) **U:** 162; (Problems in foreign
affairs) **U:** 163

Jay Treaty [1794] **J:** 67
Monroe, James (Opposition to Washington)
M: 736
United States, History of the (Problems in foreign
affairs) **U:** 163
Washington, George (Relations with Britain)
W: 106; (Cabinet scandal) **W:** 106
Westward movement in America (The Northwest
Ordinance) **W:** 247
XYZ Affair **X:** 546

Jay-Z [American singer] **J:** 67 *with portrait*
Beyoncé **B:** 276

Jaya, Puncak [mountain, New Guinea]
Indonesia (Papua) **I:** 234
New Guinea (Land and climate) **N:** 206 *with map*

Jayakarta [former name]
Jakarta (History) **J:** 22

Jayapura [Indonesia]
Indonesia (Papua) **I:** 234

Jaycees [organization] **J:** 67

Jayewardene, J. R. [Sri Lankan political leader]
Sri Lanka (History) **So:** 819

Jayhawker State [name for]
Kansas **K:** 216

Jayhawkers [U.S. history]
Kansas **K:** 216

Jayne, William [American government official]
South Dakota (Territorial days) **So:** 681

Jazirah, Al [region, Sudan] *See* Gezira, El *in this
index*

Jazz [book by Morrison]
Morrison, Toni **M:** 817

Jazz [music] **J:** 68 *with pictures*
See also the list of Related articles in the Jazz *article*
Band (Jazz bands) **B:** 75
Music (Western music) **M:** 955
New Orleans (Ethnic groups) **N:** 280; (The arts)
N: 281 *with picture*
Popular music (Ragtime, jazz, and blues) **P:** 670
with picture; (The recording era) **P:** 671
United States *picture on* **U:** 118
United States, History of the (The Lost Generation
and Flaming Youth) **U:** 190 *with picture*

Jazz, Utah [team]
Basketball (table) **B:** 150

Jazz Age *See* Roaring Twenties *in this index*

Jazz at Lincoln Center
Lincoln Center for the Performing Arts **L:** 327

Jazz dab [hair]
Beard **B:** 187

Jazz dance
Dance (Other forms of theatrical dance) **D:** 32

Jazz Epistles [musical group]
Masekela, Hugh **M:** 263

Jazz festival
Jazz (The spread of jazz) **J:** 72-73

Jazz Messengers [band]
Blakey, Art **B:** 397

Jazz Singer, The [film]
Jolson, Al **J:** 157
Motion picture (The movies talk) **M:** 867

Jazz Workshop
Mingus, Charles **M:** 573

J.B. [play by MacLeish]
MacLeish, Archibald **M:** 24

JCC [organizations]
Jewish community centers **J:** 119

JCC Association
Jewish community centers **J:** 119

JCS [organization] *See* Joint Chiefs of Staff *in this*

index
J.D. [degree]
Law (Law education) **L:** 138
Je t'aime [paintings by Motherwell]
Motherwell, Robert **M:** 843
Jealousy [book by Robbe-Grillet]
Novel (After World War II) **N:** 574
Jean [grand duke of Luxembourg]
Luxembourg (History) **L:** 531-532
Jean II [prince of Monaco]
Monaco (History) **M:** 700
Jean, Michaëlle [Canadian political leader] **J:** 74
Harper, Stephen Joseph (Prime minister) **H:** 66a
Jean Baptiste de la Salle, Saint [French educator]
J: 75
Jean-Christophe [book by Rolland]
Rolland, Romain **R:** 402
Jean Lafitte National Historical Park and Preserve [Louisiana]
Louisiana (Places to visit) **L:** 488
National Park System (table: National historical parks) **N:** 56-57
New Orleans (Libraries and museums) **N:** 281-282
Jean Santeuil [book by Proust]
Proust, Marcel **P:** 839
Jeanmaire, Renée "Zizi" [French dancer]
Petit, Roland **P:** 326
Jeanne-Claude [American artist]
Christo **C:** 537
Sculpture (From the mid-1900's to the early 2000's) **S:** 259-260 *with picture*
Jeanne d'Arc [French patriot] *See* Joan of Arc, Saint *in this index*
Jeanneret-Gris, Charles Édouard [birth name of]
Le Corbusier **L:** 175
Jeans [clothing] **J:** 75
Fashion (Why fashions change) **F:** 51
Strauss, Levi **So:** 922
Jebel Toubkal [mountain, Africa]
Atlas Mountains **A:** 869
Jebusites [ancient people]
Jerusalem (Ancient times) **J:** 100
Jeddah [Saudi Arabia] *See* Jiddah *in this index*
Jeep [vehicle] **J:** 75
Automobile *picture on* **A:** 971
Sport utility vehicle **So:** 802
Jeepney [vehicle]
Philippines *picture on* **P:** 375
Jeffers, Robinson [American poet] **J:** 75
Jefferson, Arthur Stanley [birth name of Stan Laurel]
Laurel and Hardy **L:** 122
Jefferson, Jane Randolph [mother of]
Jefferson, Thomas (Boyhood) **J:** 76-77
Jefferson, Joseph [American actor] **J:** 75
Jefferson, Martha [daughter of Thomas Jefferson]
See Randolph, Martha Jefferson *in this index*
Jefferson, Martha Skelton [wife of]
Jefferson, Thomas (Jefferson's family) **J:** 78; (Delegate to the Congress) **J:** 80
Jefferson, Mount [New Hampshire]
New Hampshire (Mountains) **N:** 220
Jefferson, Peter [English surveyor]
Map (Mapping the Americas) **M:** 184-185
Jefferson, Peter [father of]
Jefferson, Thomas (Boyhood) **J:** 76-77
Jefferson, State of [U.S. history] **J:** 75
Jefferson, Thomas [U.S. president] **J:** 76 *with pictures*
American literature (The revolutionary period [1765-1787]) **A:** 415
Architecture (Colonial architecture in America) **A:** 624
Astrology *picture on* **A:** 827
Bank (History of U.S. banking) **B:** 92
Banneker, Benjamin **B:** 98
Book collecting **B:** 468
Burr, Aaron (Gains recognition) **B:** 711
Democracy (American democracy) **D:** 123
Democratic Party (Origin) **D:** 124
Electoral College (History) **E:** 164
Jefferson Memorial **J:** 88
Liberalism (History) **L:** 228
Library (Libraries in the United States) **L:** 261
Library of Congress **L:** 264
Monroe, James (Soldier) **M:** 734
Monticello **M:** 767
Mount Rushmore National Memorial *picture on* **M:** 887
Nickel **N:** 404 *with picture*
Revolution, American *picture on* **R:** 278
Richmond (The city) **R:** 332
Slavery (Views of slavery) **S:** 502-503
Virginia (table) **V:** 417; *(The Mother of Presidents)* **V:** 421
Washington, D.C. (Choosing the capital) **W:** 85

Early years
Adams, John (National politics) **A:** 36; (Vice president) **A:** 37; (Later years) **A:** 39
Bank of the United States **B:** 96
Declaration of Independence *picture on* **D:** 77
Democratic-Republican Party **D:** 129
Hamilton, Alexander **H:** 32
Jouett, Jack **J:** 169
Mazzei, Philip **M:** 331
State, Department of (Establishment) **So:** 860-861
United States, History of the (The Declaration of Independence) **U:** 160; (Forming a new nation [1784-1819]) **U:** 161-162
Vice president of the United States (Early days) **V:** 352-353
Washington, George (Cabinet) **W:** 102 *with picture*
President
Adams, John (Later years) **A:** 39
Gallatin, Albert **G:** 14
Lewis and Clark expedition (Jefferson's plans) **L:** 222; (Up the Missouri) **L:** 222a-222b
Louisiana Purchase **L:** 502
Madison, Dolley Payne **M:** 31
Marshall, John **M:** 229
President of the United States (Strengthening the office) **P:** 768
Spoils system **So:** 798
United States, History of the (Forming a new nation [1784-1819]) **U:** 161-163
Westward movement in America (The Louisiana Purchase) **W:** 248
White House (The original building) **W:** 290
Jefferson City [Missouri] **J:** 88
Jefferson Memorial [Washington, D.C.] **J:** 88
National Park System (table: National memorials) **N:** 54
Washington, D.C. *map on* **W:** 76, *picture on* **W:** 82; (The Tidal Basin) **W:** 73 *with picture*
Jefferson National Expansion Memorial [Saint Louis]
National Park System (table: National memorials) **N:** 54
Saint Louis (The city) **S:** 46; (Museums) **S:** 48
Jefferson Territory [U.S. history] **J:** 88
Colorado (The gold rush) **Ci:** 845
Jeffersonian democracy
Democracy (American democracy) **D:** 123
Jefferson, Thomas **J:** 76
United States, History of the (The Jeffersonian triumph) **U:** 163
Jefferys, C. W. [Canadian painter]
Macdonald, Sir John Alexander *picture on* **M:** 9
Jeffords, James Merrill [American political leader] **J:** 89
Democratic Party (The early 2000's) **D:** 128
Republican Party (The early 2000's) **R:** 257
Jeffreys, Alec [British geneticist]
DNA fingerprinting **D:** 258
Jeffreys, Sir Harold [British physicist]
Plate tectonics (History of tectonic theory) **P:** 564
Jeffreys, Lord [English jurist]
Monmouth, Duke of **M:** 730
Jeffries, James Jackson [American boxer] **J:** 89
Boxing (Boxing's Golden Age) **B:** 532
Jeffries, John [American doctor]
Balloon (The growth of ballooning) **B:** 61
Blanchard, Jean-Pierre **B:** 398
Jehoram [king of ancient Israel]
Elisha **E:** 238
Jehovah [religion] **J:** 89
Jehovah's Witnesses [religious group] **J:** 89
Jehu [Biblical figure]
Elisha **E:** 238
Jekyll, Gertrude [British landscape architect]
Lutyens, Sir Edwin Landseer **L:** 530
Jelinek, Elfriede [Austrian author]
Austria (Literature) **A:** 933
Nobel Prizes (Literature: 2004) **N:** 448
Jelks, William Dorsey [American political leader]
Alabama (table) **A:** 274
Jellaba [clothing]
Morocco (Way of life) **M:** 811-812
Jellicoe, John Rushworth [British admiral] **J:** 89
Jutland, Battle of **J:** 204
World War I (The war at sea) **W:** 460
Jelly and jam [food] **J:** 89
Pectin **P:** 227
Jellybean
Candy (Other candies) **C:** 176
Jellyfish [sea animal] **J:** 89 *with pictures*
Animal *picture on* **A:** 486; (Fins, tails, and flippers) **A:** 490
Cnidarian **Ci:** 715
Light *picture on* **L:** 284
Sea wasp **S:** 264

Jemaah Islamiya [terror group]
Terrorism (Recent developments) **T:** 180
Jemison, Mae Carol [American astronaut] **J:** 90 *with portrait*
Astronaut (table) **A:** 830
Jemison, Mary [American settler] **J:** 91
Jena, Battle of [1806]
Napoleon I (Dominates Europe) **N:** 15
Napoleonic Wars (The alliance of Prussia and Russia) **N:** 18 *with map*
Jenever [drink]
Netherlands (Food and drink) **N:** 141
Jenghis Khan [Mongoliam conqueror] *See* Genghis Khan *in this index*
Jenifer, Daniel of St. Thomas [American political leader] **J:** 91
Jenkins, Charles J. [American political leader]
Georgia (table) **G:** 130
Jenkins, Ferguson [American baseball player]
Baseball (table: Hall of Fame) **B:** 134a
Jenks, Joseph, Jr. [American settler]
Pawtucket **P:** 204
Jenna's Beach Boy [horse]
Harness racing (History) **H:** 64
Jenne [Mali] *See* Djénné *in this index*
Jennens, Charles [British scholar]
Handel, George Frideric (His work) **H:** 42
Jenner, Edward [British doctor] **J:** 91 *with pictures*
Immune system (The study of the immune system) **I:** 88d
Medicine *picture on* **M:** 373; (The development of immunology) **M:** 374
Jennet [animal]
Donkey **D:** 308
Jenney, Neil [American artist]
Painting (New image painting) **P:** 87
Jenney, William Le Baron [American architect] **J:** 92
Architecture (Early modern architecture in America) **A:** 629
Chicago (Architecture) **C:** 428
Skyscraper (History) **S:** 498-499
Jennie Gerhardt [novel by Dreiser]
Dreiser, Theodore **D:** 346
Jennifer Lorn [book by Wylie]
Wylie, Elinor **W:** 515
Jennings, Hugh [American baseball player]
Baseball (table: Hall of Fame) **B:** 134a
Jennings, Jonathan [American political leader]
Indiana (table) **I:** 214; (Early statehood) **I:** 216
Jennings, Sarah [wife of the Duke of Marlborough]
See Churchill, Sarah Jennings *in this index*
Jennings, Waylon [American singer]
Country music (Modern country music) **Ci:** 1098c-1098d *with picture*
Nelson, Willie **N:** 123
Jennings, William S. [American political leader]
Florida (table) **F:** 260
Jennison, Silas H. [American political leader]
Vermont (table) **V:** 333
Jenny [animal]
Donkey **D:** 308
Jenny [book by Undset]
Undset, Sigrid **U:** 21
Jenny [machine] *See* Spinning jenny *in this index*
Jenny wren [bird] *See* House wren *in this index*
Jensen, J. Hans [German physicist] **J:** 92
Jensen, James A. [American scientist]
Supersaurus **So:** 994
Jensen, Johannes Vilhelm [Danish author]
Denmark (Arts) **D:** 136
Jensen, Leslie [American political leader]
South Dakota (table) **So:** 680
Jenson, Nicolas [French printer]
Book (The spread of printed books) **B:** 467
Jephtha [music by Handel]
Handel, George Frideric (His life) **H:** 42
Jerboa [animal] **J:** 92 *with picture*
Desert *picture on* **D:** 155
Jerboa marsupial mouse [animal] *See* Kultarr *in this index*
Jeremiah [Hebrew prophet]
Jeremiah, Book of **J:** 92 *with picture*
Jeremiah, Book of [Bible] **J:** 92 *with picture*
Bible (The Prophets) **B:** 280-281
Jeremiah, Letter of [Bible]
Bible (The Christian Old Testament) **B:** 282
Jeria, Ángela [Chilean political activist]
Bachelet, Michelle **B:** 17
Jericho [West Bank] **J:** 93
Arab-Israeli conflict (Peacemaking) **A:** 582a
Joshua **J:** 169
Jerimoth Hill
Rhode Island (Land regions) **R:** 306 *with map*
Jerne, Niels Kaj [British-born physiologist]
Nobel Prizes (Physiology or medicine: 1984) **N:** 446

Jernigan, Aaron [American businessman]
  Orlando **O:** 857
Jeroboam [Biblical figures] **J:** 93
Jeroboam I [Biblical figure]
  Jeroboam **J:** 93
  Solomon **So:** 584
Jeroboam II [Biblical figure]
  Jeroboam **J:** 93
Jerome, David H. [American political leader]
  Michigan (table) **M:** 507
Jerome, Saint [Christian scholar] **J:** 93 *with portrait*
  Bible (The first translations) **B:** 284-285 *with picture*
  Old Testament (Translations) **O:** 741
  Vulgate **V:** 453
Jersey [island, English Channel] **J:** 93
  Channel Islands **C:** 375 *with map*
Jersey [animal]
  Cattle (Jersey) **C:** 310 *with picture*; (table) **C:** 313
  Dairying (Dairy cattle) **D:** 6
Jersey [fabric] **J:** 94
  Textile (Knitted fabrics) **T:** 214
Jersey Boys [musical]
  Musical comedy (Musical comedy today) **M:** 961
  Valli, Frankie **V:** 267
Jersey City [New Jersey] **J:** 94 *with picture*
  Freedom of assembly (In the United States) **F:** 504
Jersey Giant [breed]
  Chicken (table) **C:** 443
Jersey Lily, The [nickname]
  Langtry, Lillie **L:** 62
Jersey Zoological Park [England]
  Durrell, Gerald **D:** 389
Jerusalem [Israel] **J:** 94a *with pictures and map*
  Army *picture on* **A:** 726
  David (King of Israel) **D:** 45
  Hezekiah **H:** 221
  Israel **I:** 478 *with picture*; (City life) **I:** 481
  Jeremiah, Book of **J:** 93
  Jesus Christ (Entry into Jerusalem) **J:** 108
  Jews (The kingdom of Israel) **J:** 121 *with map*; (Roman rule) **J:** 122
  Judea **J:** 183
Jerusalem [book by Lagerlöf]
  Lagerlöf, Selma **L:** 30
Jerusalem [book by Mendelssohn]
  Mendelssohn, Moses **M:** 399
Jerusalem, Temple in *See* Temple in Jerusalem *in this index*
Jerusalem artichoke [plant] **J:** 102 *with picture*
  Artichoke **A:** 758
Jerusalem Conquered [book by Tasso]
  Tasso, Torquato **T:** 50
Jerusalem cricket [insect]
  Cricket **Ci:** 1131
Jerusalem Delivered [book by Tasso]
  Italian literature (Humanism and the Renaissance) **I:** 494
  Tasso, Torquato **T:** 50
Jervas, Charles [English painter]
  Swift, Jonathan *picture on* **So:** 1040
Jervis, Sir John [British admiral]
  Nelson, Horatio (Wounded at Calvi) **N:** 121-122
Jess [falconry]
  Falconry **F:** 14
Jessamine [plant] *See* Jasmine; Yellow jessamine *in this index*
Jester [clown] **J:** 102
Jester, Beauford H. [American political leader]
  Texas (table) **T:** 203
Jesuits [religious group] **J:** 103
  Christianity (The Counter Reformation) **C:** 525
  Counter Reformation (Catholic reform) **Ci:** 1096
  Fordham University **F:** 383
  Loyola, Saint Ignatius **L:** 511
  Mission life in America (Eastern missions) **M:** 618
  Pope (Renaissance and Reformation) **P:** 664
  Religious life (Religious life in the 1500's and 1600's) **R:** 227; (table) **R:** 227
  Roman Catholic Church (The Counter Reformation) **R:** 408; (Suppression of the Jesuits) **R:** 409
  Xavier, Saint Francis **X:** 543
Jesuits' bark [plant product]
  Cinchona **Ci:** 553
Jesup, Thomas [American general]
  Seminole Indians **S:** 293
Jesus Christ J: 104 *with pictures*
  See also Christianity *in this index*
  A.D. **A:** 31
  Antichrist **A:** 553
  Arianism **A:** 661
  Barabbas **B:** 102
  B.C. **B:** 118
  Bible (The New Testament) **B:** 282
  Byzantine art *pictures on* **B:** 749, **B:** 750, **B:** 751

Candlemas Day **C:** 175
Christianity **C:** 522f *with picture*
Christmas **C:** 528 *with picture*
Easter **E:** 42
Faith healing **F:** 12
God **G:** 243
Golden rule **G:** 255
Gospels **G:** 278
Grace **G:** 295
Holy Grail **H:** 299
Holy Week **H:** 300
Icon *picture on* **I:** 25
Jerusalem (Christian sites) **J:** 96; (Roman rule) **J:** 101
Jews (Roman rule) **J:** 122
Joseph **J:** 167
Judas Iscariot **J:** 182
Last Supper, The **L:** 87
Madonna and Child **M:** 37 *with picture*
Mary **M:** 238
Messiah **M:** 423
Millennium **M:** 552
Mormons (Church doctrines and ordinances) **M:** 806
New Testament (Gospels) **N:** 287; (Historical Jesus research) **N:** 287
Painting (Religious subjects) **P:** 32
Parable **P:** 141
Peter, Saint **P:** 324
Pilate, Pontius **P:** 462
Protestantism (Protestant beliefs) **P:** 833-834
Qur'ān **Q:** 44
Religion (Christianity) **R:** 222
Resurrection **R:** 264 *with picture*
Roman Catholic Church (Roman Catholic beliefs) **R:** 403
Samaritans **S:** 78
Shroud of Turin **S:** 440 *with pictures*
Thomas, Saint **T:** 262
Transfiguration **T:** 371
Vatican Council II (The Constitution of Divine Revelation) **V:** 289
Wandering Jew **W:** 22
Jesus Christ Superstar [musical]
  Lloyd Webber, Andrew **L:** 403
Jesus Heals a Blind Man [sculpture]
  Jesus Christ *picture on* **J:** 107
Jésus Island [Quebec]
  Laval **L:** 128
Jet [coal] **J:** 109
  Gem *picture on* **G:** 78
Jet [magazine]
  Johnson, John Harold **J:** 143
Jet [meteorology]
  Lightning (Jets, sprites, and elves) **L:** 301
Jet airplane
  Air force (The development of jet aircraft) **A:** 186
  Aircraft, Military (The jet age) **A:** 205
  Airplane (Types of airplanes) **A:** 210 *with pictures*; (History) **A:** 229-238
  Aviation (A new age of flight) **A:** 990
  Jet propulsion **J:** 110 *with pictures*
  Korean War (The air war) **K:** 382
Jet engine
  Airplane (Jet engines) **A:** 220 *with picture*
  Automobile racing (Other kinds of racing) **A:** 978-979
  Guided missile (The engine) **G:** 424
  Invention (The early and middle 1900's) **I:** 363
  Jet propulsion **J:** 110 *with diagrams*
  Kerosene (Uses) **K:** 306
  Rocket **R:** 384
Jet exhaust
  Airplane (Jet engines) **A:** 220
Jet piercing machine
  Taconite **T:** 5
Jet propulsion J: 110 *with pictures*
  See also Jet airplane; Jet engine *in this index*
  Turbine (Gas turbines) **T:** 497-498
Jet Propulsion Laboratory [Pasadena, California] **J:** 115
Jet pump
  Pump (Jet pumps) **P:** 900b
Jet stream [atmosphere] **J:** 115 *with map*
  Air (Air movement) **A:** 171-172
  Air turbulence **A:** 200
  Weather (Planetary-scale systems) **W:** 158-159
Jeté [ballet]
  Ballet (table) **B:** 45 *with picture*
Jeter, Derek [American baseball player] **B:** 116
Jethro [Biblical figure]
  Moses (Early life) **M:** 828-829
Jets, New York [team] *See* New York Jets *in this index*
Jets, Winnipeg [team]
  Hockey (table: National Hockey League) **H:** 281
Jetsam [wreckage]

Flotsam, jetsam, and lagan **F:** 267
Jetty [wall] **J:** 116 *with picture*
Jetway
  Airport (The passenger terminal) **A:** 244
Jeu de Paume [museum]
  Paris (Museums and art galleries) **P:** 164-165
Jeune Belgique, La [magazine]
  Belgium (The arts) **B:** 230
Jeux [music by Debussy]
  Debussy, Claude **D:** 66
Jew *See* Jews *in this index*
Jew of Malta, The [play by Marlowe]
  Marlowe, Christopher **M:** 216
Jewel [award]
  Knighthood, Orders of (Honorary orders) **K:** 347 *with pictures*
Jewel [ornament]
  See also Jewelry *in this index and the list of Related articles in the Gem article*
  Gem **G:** 77
  Jewelry **J:** 117
Jewel Cave National Monument [South Dakota] **J:** 117
  National Park System (table: National monuments) **N:** 51
"Jewel Song" [aria]
  Opera: *(Faust)* **O:** 804
Jeweler [occupation]
  Careers (Production) **C:** 229
Jewelers' rouge
  Grinding and polishing (Polishing) **G:** 395
Jewell, Marshall [American government official]
  Connecticut (table) **Ci:** 967
  Grant, Ulysses S. (table) **G:** 316
Jewelry [ornament] **J:** 117 *with pictures*
  See also the list of Related articles in the Gem article
  Fabergé, Peter Carl **F:** 2
  Gem **G:** 77
  Gold (Jewelry) **G:** 251
  Indian, American *picture on* **I:** 146
  Providence (Economy) **P:** 839
  Rhode Island (Manufacturing) **R:** 310 *with picture*; (Industrial expansion) **R:** 313
  Watch **W:** 114
Jewelweed [plant]
  Impatiens **I:** 90 *with picture*
Jewett, Charles Coffin [American librarian]
  Library (Libraries in the United States) **L:** 261
Jewett, Sarah Orne [American author] **J:** 119
  American literature (Realists) **A:** 419
Jewfish [fish] *See* Goliath grouper *in this index*
Jewish Agency [organization]
  Zionism (The Balfour Declaration) **Z:** 595-596
Jewish Antiquities [book by Josephus]
  Josephus, Flavius **J:** 169
Jewish Bible *See* Hebrew Bible *in this index*
Jewish calendar
  Calendar (The Hebrew calendar) **C:** 29
Jewish community centers J: 119
Jewish Congress, American
  Wise, Stephen Samuel **W:** 370
Jewish Congress, World [organization]
  World Jewish Congress **W:** 450
Jewish Documentation Center [Vienna]
  Wiesenthal, Simon **W:** 299
Jewish Institute of Religion
  Wise, Stephen Samuel **W:** 370
Jewish law
  Hillel I **H:** 232
  Talmud **T:** 21
Jewish literature
  Hebrew literature **H:** 162
  Yiddish literature **Y:** 566
Jewish Publication Society of America
  Bible (Modern English translations) **B:** 286
Jewish State [book by Herzl]
  Herzl, Theodor **H:** 217
Jewish Theological Seminary of America J: 119
Jewish War Veterans [organization]
  Veterans' organizations (In the United States) **V:** 344
Jewish Women, National Council of J: 119
Jews [people] **J:** 120 *with pictures and maps*
  See also Israel; Judaism *in this index; and the list of Related articles in the* Jews *article*
  Abraham **A:** 16
  Anti-Semitism **A:** 559
  Arab-Israeli conflict **A:** 582
  Ashkenazim **A:** 769
  Asia (The people) **A:** 778
  Babi Yar **B:** 1
  Black Death **B:** 386
  B'nai B'rith **B:** 426
  Circumcision **Ci:** 561
  Concentration camp **Ci:** 926
  Cossacks **Ci:** 1079

Czech Republic (People) **Ci:** 1210
Europe (Religions) **E:** 386
Food (Religious reasons) **F:** 332
Germany (Religion) **G:** 151; (Nazi Germany) **G:** 167-168
Ghetto (Early ghettos) **G:** 181
Haskalah **H:** 82
Hebrew language **H:** 161
Hitler, Adolf **H:** 264
Holocaust **H:** 296
Immigration (Asia) **I:** 85 *with picture*
Israel (Jews) **I:** 480
Jerusalem (The people of Jerusalem) **J:** 96
Kristallnacht **K:** 388
Minority group (Effects of subordinate status) **M:** 609; (Jews) **M:** 610
Moses **M:** 828
Netherlands (World War II) **N:** 149-150
New York City (Ethnic groups) **N:** 331 *with picture*
Old Testament **O:** 740
Palestine **P:** 103
Peter, Saint (Life as an apostle) **P:** 324-325
Races, Human (Race and discrimination) **R:** 59
Russia (People) **R:** 532
Schindler, Oskar **S:** 175
Segregation (Other segregation in the United States) **S:** 286; (Segregation in other countries) **S:** 286
Sephardim **S:** 307
Spain (Union of the Spanish kingdoms) **So:** 746-747
Union of Soviet Socialist Republics (People) **U:** 31
Vatican Council II (Other documents) **V:** 290
Wallenberg, Raoul **W:** 17
Wandering Jew **W:** 22
Warsaw (History) **W:** 38
Western Wall **W:** 241
World War II (The Holocaust) **W:** 496
Yiddish language **Y:** 565
Yiddish literature **Y:** 566
Zunz, Leopold **Z:** 609
Jew's-harp [musical instrument] **J:** 125 *with pictures*
Jezebel [butterfly]
Butterfly *picture on* **B:** 737
Jezebel [film]
Davis, Bette **D:** 47
Jharkhand [state]
India (Recent developments) **I:** 134
Jiang Qing [Chinese political leader] **J:** 125
China (Deng Xiaoping) **C:** 506
Jiang Zemin [Chinese political leader] **J:** 125
China (Recent developments) **C:** 506-507
Hu Jintao **H:** 402
Jiangxi province [China]
Mao Zedong (His life) **M:** 174
Jib [device]
Crane **Ci:** 1120
Sailing (Sails) **S:** 24 *with diagram*
Jibing
Sailing (Trimming and tacking) **S:** 26
Jicama [plant] **J:** 125 *with picture*
Jicarilla Apache [American Indians]
Apache Indians **A:** 562
Jiddah [Saudi Arabia] **J:** 126
Jig [device]
Toolmaking **T:** 330
Jig [lure]
Fishing *picture on* **F:** 177; (Artificial bait) **F:** 177-178
Jigger [animal] *See* Chigger *in this index*
Jiggering [industrial process]
Ceramics (Making ceramics) **C:** 360
Pottery (Shaping the clay) **P:** 716-717
Jigme Dorji Wangchuk [king of Bhutan]
Bhutan (History) **B:** 278
Jigme Singye Wangchuk [king of Bhutan]
Bhutan (History) **B:** 278
Jigsaw [tool]
Saw (Power saws) **S:** 167 *with picture*
Jihad [religion] **J:** 126
Qutb, Sayyid **Q:** 44
Jim Crow [U.S. history] **J:** 126
Brown v. Board of Education of Topeka **B:** 645
Segregation (Jim Crow laws) **S:** 285
Jim-suit [diving]
Exploration (Deep-sea exploration) **E:** 450-451
Jiménez, Juan Ramón [Spanish poet] **J:** 126
Jiménez de Quesada, Gonzalo [Spanish explorer] **J:** 127
Colombia (Early days) **Ci:** 783
Latin America *map on* **L:** 105
Jimi Hendrix Experience [musical group]
Hendrix, Jimi **H:** 184
Rock music (The heavy metal sound) **R:** 380a
Jimmu [legendary figure] **J:** 127
Jimmy Carter National Historic Site [Georgia]

National Park System (table: National historic sites) **N:** 52-53
Jimson weed [plant] **J:** 127 *with picture*
Datura **D:** 43
Nightshade **N:** 421 *with picture*
Jin Mao Building [Shanghai, China]
Shanghai (History) **S:** 372
Jina [Indian religious leader] *See* Mahavira *in this index*
Jindal, Bobby [American political leader]
Asian Americans (Notable Asian American "firsts") **A:** 812f
Louisiana (table) **L:** 496; (The early 2000's) **L:** 501
Jingdezhen [China]
Porcelain (Oriental porcelain) **P:** 676
"Jingle Bells" [song]
Buchanan, James **B:** 658
Jingoism [politics] **J:** 127
Patriotism (Abuses of patriotism) **P:** 198
Jingxi [theater] *See* Beijing opera *in this index*
Jinmen [island] *See* Quemoy *in this index*
Jinnah, Mohammad Ali [Pakistani political leader] **J:** 127 *with portrait*
India (New Constitution) **I:** 132
Muslim League **M:** 964
Pakistan (The nationalist movement) **P:** 99; (Independence) **P:** 99
Jinni [mythical being] **J:** 127
See also Genie *in this index*
Jinrikisha [vehicle]
Pedicab **P:** 228
Jirga [tribal council]
Afghanistan (Government) **A:** 92-92a *with picture*
Pashtuns **P:** 190
Jiří of Poděbrady [king of Bohemia]
Czech Republic (The rise of Bohemia) **Ci:** 1213
Jitney [play by Wilson]
Wilson, August **W:** 316
Jitterbug [dance]
Ballroom dancing **B:** 63
Dance *picture on* **D:** 28
Jiu Zhang Suan Shu [book]
Mathematics (Chinese mathematics) **M:** 306
Jiva [religion]
Jainism **J:** 22
Jívaro Indians **J:** 128 *with picture*
Indian, American (Before European contact) **I:** 175-176 *with picture*
Jive [dance]
Ballroom dancing **B:** 63
J.Lo [recording]
Lopez, Jennifer **L:** 453
Joachim [Biblical figure]
Anne, Saint **A:** 517
Joachim, Joseph [German violinist]
Brahms, Johannes (His life) **B:** 548
Joachim with the Shepherds [painting by Giotto]
Painting (The 1300's) **P:** 51-52 *with picture*
Joachimsthaler [money]
Dollar **D:** 295
Joan of Arc, Saint [French patriot] **J:** 128 *with picture*
Charles VII (France) **C:** 381
England (The Hundred Years' War) **E:** 306
Hundred Years' War **H:** 437
Orléans **O:** 857
Joan of Arc Chapel
Milwaukee (Annual events and places of interest) **M:** 560-561
Joan of Arc's Day
Holiday (In other countries) **H:** 291
Joanna of Castile [mother of Charles V] *See* Juana of Castile *in this index*
João [king of Kongo]
Nzinga Nkuwu **N:** 633
Job [Biblical figure]
Job, Book of **J:** 129
Job [work] *See* Career education; Careers; Employment *in this index*
Job, Book of [Bible] **J:** 129
Bible (The Writings) **B:** 281-282
Devil **D:** 174
Job Corps [U.S.] **J:** 129
Labor force (The government and the labor force) **L:** 3
Job discrimination
Civil rights (Major changes in the field of civil rights) **Ci:** 609-610
Job fair
Careers *picture on* **C:** 214
Job Opportunities and Basic Skills Training Program
Children and Families, Administration for **C:** 457
Job performance evaluation
Industrial psychology (Industrial psychologists) **I:** 245
Job safety

Safety (Safety on the job) **S:** 13
Job satisfaction
Industrial psychology (Organizational psychologists) **I:** 245
Job shadowing
Careers (Sources of information) **C:** 216
Job training
Cooperative education **Ci:** 1037
Job Training Partnership Act [1982]
Vocational education (The 1900's and early 2000's) **V:** 435
Jobim, Antônio Carlos [Brazilian musician]
Latin America (Music) **L:** 100
Jobs, Steve [American engineer] **J:** 129
Apple Inc. **A:** 573
Computer (The personal computer) **Ci:** 924c *with picture*
Pixar Animation Studios **P:** 503
Job's Daughters [organization] **J:** 130
Masonry (Organization) **M:** 267
Jocasta [Greek mythology]
Oedipus **O:** 676
Jochanaan [opera character]
Opera: (*Salome*) **O:** 807
Jocho [Japanese sculptor]
Sculpture (Japan) **S:** 239
Jockey [career]
Horse racing (Thoroughbred horses) **H:** 363-364; (Jockeys) **H:** 364 *with picture*; (History) **H:** 366
Jockey Club
Horse racing (Regulation) **H:** 365
Jodelle, Étienne [French dramatist]
French literature (The Pléiade) **F:** 519-520
Jodhpurs [clothing]
Horse (Clothes for riding) **H:** 351
Jodl, Alfred [Nazi general] **J:** 130
World War II (Victory in Europe) **W:** 486
Jodrell Bank Observatory [England] **J:** 130
Lovell, Sir Bernard **L:** 509
Joe Turner's Come and Gone [play by Wilson]
Wilson, August **W:** 316
Joel, Book of [Bible] **J:** 130
Joersz, Eldon W. [American aviator]
Aviation (table: Aviation speed records) **A:** 990
Joey [clown]
Kangaroo (The life of a kangaroo) **K:** 214 *with picture*
Marsupial *picture on* **M:** 232
Wallaby **W:** 15
Joey [clown]
Clown **Ci:** 713
Joffre, Joseph Jacques Césaire [French general] **J:** 130
World War I (The Western Front) **W:** 455-456; (The Battle of Verdun) **W:** 458
Joffre Falls
Quebec (Rivers, waterfalls, and lakes) **Q:** 24
Joffrey, Robert [American choreographer] **J:** 130
Arpino, Gerald **A:** 743
Ballet (Ballet in the United States) **B:** 53-54
Joffrey Ballet of Chicago
Arpino, Gerald **A:** 743
Ballet (Ballet in the United States) **B:** 53-54
Joffrey, Robert **J:** 131
Jog Falls [waterfall, India]
Waterfall (table: Famous waterfalls of the world) **W:** 143
Jogaila [Lithuanian ruler] *See* Jagiełło, Władysław *in this index*
Jogging **J:** 131
Running **R:** 520
Jogues, Saint Isaac [French missionary] **J:** 131
Jóhanna Sigurðardóttir [Icelandic political leader]
Iceland (Recent developments) **I:** 24
Johannesburg [South Africa] **J:** 131 *with picture*
Gold rush (Gold rushes in other countries) **G:** 254
Johannine Letters
New Testament (Letters) **N:** 287
Johanns, Mike [American political leader]
Agriculture, Department of (table) **A:** 161
Bush, George Walker (table) **B:** 722h
Nebraska (table) **N:** 110; (The early 2000's) **N:** 115
Johansen, Hjalmar [Norwegian explorer]
Nansen, Fridtjof **N:** 11
Johanson, Donald Carl [American anthropologist] **J:** 131
Prehistoric people (table) **P:** 754
Johansson, Erik [father of]
Gustav I Vasa **G:** 443
John [antipope]
Pope (table) **P:** 666
John [king of England] **J:** 131
England (Magna Carta) **E:** 306; (table) **E:** 308
Innocent III (Imperial power) **I:** 274-275
Langton, Stephen **L:** 62
Magna Carta **M:** 52
Parliament (History) **P:** 174

Philip II [king of France] **P: 369**
Plantagenet **P: 550**
John I [king of France]
France (table) **F: 471**
John I [king of Kongo]
Nzinga Nkuwu **N: 633**
John I [king of Portugal]
Portugal (Founding the Portuguese nation) **P: 693**
John II [king of Portugal]
Cape of Good Hope **C: 189**
Columbus, Christopher (Presentation of the plan to Portugal) **Ci: 858**
Dias, Bartolomeu **D: 185**
John II, the Good [king of France]
Charles V [of France] **C: 381**
France (table) **F: 471**
Poitiers, Battle of **P: 603**
John III [pope]
Pope (table) **P: 666**
John III Sobieski [king of Poland] **J: 132** with portrait
John III [king of Portugal]
Xavier, Saint Francis **X: 543**
John IV [king of Portugal]
Portugal (Spanish conquest) **P: 694**
John VI [king of Portugal] **J: 132**
Portugal (A weakening monarchy) **P: 694**
Rio de Janeiro (History) **R: 346**
John XVI [antipope]
Pope (table) **P: 666**
John XXII [pope] **J: 132**
John XXIII [antipope] **J: 132**
John XXIII [pope] **J: 132**
Pope (The 1900's and 2000's) **P: 665** with picture
Roman Catholic Church (Vatican Council II) **R: 410**
Vatican Council II **V: 289**
John, Elton [British singer] **J: 133**
John, Epistles of [New Testament] **J: 133**
Bible (The Letters) **B: 284**
John, Gospel of [New Testament]
Bible (The Gospels) **B: 283** with picture
Gospels **G: 278**
Jesus Christ (Sources of information about Jesus) **J: 104**; (Public life) **J: 106**
New Testament (Gospels) **N: 287**
John, Saint [apostle] **J: 133**
See also John, Gospel of in this index
James the Greater, Saint **J: 28**
Revelation, Book of **R: 267**
John Adams Building [Washington, D.C.]
Washington, D.C. map on **W: 76**
John and Mabel Ringling Museum of Art [Sarasota]
Circus (Places to visit and annual events) **Ci: 566**
Florida (Museums) **F: 247** with picture
John Brown House
Providence (Description) **P: 839**
John Brown's Body [poem by Benét]
Benét, Stephen Vincent **B: 248**
"John Brown's Body" [song]
"Battle Hymn of the Republic" **B: 172**
Brown, John (Harpers Ferry) **B: 643**
John Bull [symbol] **J: 133** with picture
John Bull [locomotive]
Railroad (Developments in the United States) **R: 115**
John Bull's Other Island [play by Shaw]
Irish literature (Drama) **I: 432**
John C. Stennis [ship]
Aircraft carrier (The United States carrier fleet) **A: 206**
John Chrysostom, Saint [Syrian religious leader]
See Chrysostom, Saint John in this index
John Crerar Library [Chicago]
Chicago, University of (Research program) **C: 438**
John D. and Catherine T. MacArthur Foundation
See MacArthur Foundation in this index
John D. Rockefeller [book by Nevins]
Nevins, Allan **N: 178**
John D. Rockefeller, Jr. Memorial Parkway [Wyoming]
National Park System (table: National parkways and other national parklands) **N: 56**
John Day Fossil Beds National Monument [Oregon] **J: 133**
National Park System (table: National monuments) **N: 51**
John F. Kennedy Center for the Performing Arts
See Kennedy Center for the Performing Arts in this index
John F. Kennedy Federal Office Building
Boston (Downtown Boston) **B: 496**
John F. Kennedy International Airport
Airport (table) **A: 245**
New York City (Queens) **N: 329-330**

John F. Kennedy Library [Boston]
Pei, I. M. **P: 230** with picture
John F. Kennedy Space Center [Florida] See Kennedy Space Center in this index
John Fitzgerald Kennedy National Historic Site [Massachusetts]
National Park System (table: National historic sites) **N: 52-53**
John Gabriel Borkman [play by Ibsen]
Ibsen, Henrik (His plays) **I: 4**
John H. Glenn Research Center [Cleveland]
Ohio (The mid-1900's) **O: 703**
John Hancock Center [Chicago]
Chicago (Downtown Chicago) **C: 420-421**
John Hancock Tower [Boston]
Boston picture on **B: 495**; (Back Bay) **B: 497** with picture
John Hay Library [Brown University]
Rhode Island (Libraries) **R: 300**
John Henry [legendary figure] See Henry, John, in this index
John Howard Association J: 133
John James Audubon Memorial Museum, The
Kentucky (Museums) **K: 277** with picture
John Lackland See John [king of England] in this index
John Mark [saint] See Mark, Saint in this index
John Marshall House
Virginia (Places to visit) **V: 408**
John Martin Reservoir [Arkansas River]
Colorado (Rivers and lakes) **Ci: 840-841**
John Muir National Historic Site [California]
National Park System (table: National historic sites) **N: 52-53**
John of Gaunt [English nobleman] **J: 134**
Chaucer, Geoffrey (Life) **C: 388**
Henry IV [king of England] **H: 186**
Lancaster **L: 55**
Richard II **R: 329**
John of Montecorvino [Italian missionary]
Mongol Empire (European contacts) **M: 720-721**
John of Plano Carpini [Italian explorer]
Exploration (Medieval European exploration) **E: 442**
John of the Cross, Saint [Christian religious leader]
Spanish literature (The 1500's) **So: 758-759**
John on Patmos, Saint [painting by Fouquet]
France picture on **F: 463**
John P. Robarts Research Library [Toronto]
Library picture on **L: 247**
John Paul I [pope] **J: 134**
Pope (table) **P: 666**
John Paul II [pope] **J: 134**
Galileo (Galileo and the Roman Catholic Church) **G: 12**
Poland (Antigovernment protests) **P: 614**
Pope **P: 661**; (The 1900's and 2000's) **P: 665-667** with picture; (table) **P: 666**
Roman Catholic Church (John Paul II) **R: 411**
Rosary **R: 474**
John Paul Jones [book by Morison]
Morison, Samuel Eliot **M: 805**
John Pennekamp Coral Reef State Park [Key Largo]
Florida (Places to visit) **F: 252** with picture
John Simon Guggenheim Memorial Foundation
Guggenheim, Meyer **G: 421**
John the Baptist, Saint [Biblical figure] **J: 134** with picture
Baptism **B: 101**
Elizabeth, Saint **E: 241**
Herod (Herod Antipas) **H: 212**
Jesus Christ (Public life) **J: 106** with picture
Opera: (Salome) **O: 807**
Verrocchio, Andrea del **V: 339** with picture
John the Good [king of France] See John II, the Good in this index
John Wesley Harding [recording]
Rock music (Fresh directions) **R: 380**
Johncock, Gordon [American race driver]
Automobile racing (table: Indianapolis 500 winners) **A: 980**
Johnny Appleseed [American frontiersman] See Appleseed, Johnny in this index
Johnny Crow's Garden [book by Brooke]
Brooke, Leonard Leslie **B: 639**
Johnny darter [fish]
Darter picture on **D: 38**
Johnny Panic and the Bible of Dreams [book by Plath]
Plath, Sylvia **P: 566**
Johnny Tremain [book by Forbes]
Forbes, Esther **F: 369**
Johnnycake [food]
Pioneer life in America (How the pioneers traveled) **P: 478**
Johns, Charley E. [American political leader]

Florida (table) **F: 260**
Johns, Jasper [American artist] **J: 135** with picture
Painting (The revival of subject matter) **P: 86** with picture
Johns Hopkins Hospital [Baltimore]
Hopkins, Johns **H: 334**
Johns Hopkins University J: 135
Hopkins, Johns **H: 334**
Maryland picture on **M: 241**
Johnson, Andrew [U.S. president] **J: 136** with pictures
Grant, Ulysses S. (National hero) **G: 315**
Impeachment (History) **I: 91**
Lincoln, Abraham (Election of 1864) **L: 323-324**
Nebraska (Statehood) **N: 112**
President of the United States (Term of office) **P: 758-762**; (The decline of the presidency) **P: 768**
Reconstruction (Johnson's plan) **R: 177**; (The impeachment of Johnson) **R: 178**
Stanton, Edwin McMasters **So: 839**
Tennessee (table) **T: 152**; (Building the state) **T: 153**; (The American Civil War) **T: 154**
United States, History of the (Reconstruction) **U: 178**
Johnson, Ban [American sportsman]
Baseball (table: Hall of Fame) **B: 134a**
Johnson, Ben [American actor]
Motion picture (Best performance by an actor in a supporting role: 1971) **M: 862b**
Johnson, Ben [Canadian athlete]
Olympic Games (Charges of steroid use) **O: 753**
Johnson, Benj. F., of Boone [pen name]
Riley, James Whitcomb **R: 341**
Johnson, Byron I. [Canadian political leader]
British Columbia (table) **B: 628**
Johnson, Cave [American government official]
Polk, James Knox (table) **P: 643**
Johnson, Charles Spurgeon [American sociologist] **J: 142**
Johnson, Coffin Ed [fictional character]
Himes, Chester **H: 234**
Johnson, Daniel [Canadian political leader]
Quebec (table) **Q: 29**
Johnson, David Moffat [Canadian diplomat]
United Nations (table) **U: 86**
Johnson, Earvin, Jr. [American basketball player]
See Johnson, Magic in this index
Johnson, Edwin C. [American political leader]
Colorado (table) **Ci: 844**
Johnson, Eliza McCardle [wife of Andrew Johnson]
First ladies of the United States (table) **F: 142**
Johnson, Andrew (Johnson's family) **J: 137**
Johnson, Esther [friend of]
Swift, Jonathan (His life) **So: 1039**
Johnson, Eyvind [Swedish author]
Nobel Prizes (Literature: 1974) **N: 448**
Johnson, Gary E. [American political leader]
New Mexico (table) **N: 272**
Johnson, Henry [American political leader]
Louisiana (table) **L: 496**
Johnson, Herschel Vespasian [American political leader] **J: 142**
Georgia (table) **G: 130**
Johnson, Hiram Warren [American political leader] **J: 142**
California (table) **C: 59**; (Progress as a state) **C: 62**
Harding, Warren Gamaliel (The smoke-filled room) **H: 57**
Taft, William Howard (Election of 1912) **T: 12**
Johnson, Hugh Samuel [American government official] **J: 143**
National Recovery Administration **N: 59**
Johnson, Isaac [American political leader]
Louisiana (table) **L: 496**
Johnson, Jack [American boxer] **J: 143**
Boxing (Bare knuckles to gloves) **B: 532** with picture; (Boxing's Golden Age) **B: 532**
Jeffries, James Jackson **J: 89**
Johnson, James [American political leader]
Georgia (table) **G: 130**
Johnson, James P. [American pianist] **J: 143**
Jazz (The 1920's) **J: 70**
Johnson, James Weldon [American poet] **J: 143** with portrait
American literature (The Harlem Renaissance) **A: 422**
Harlem Renaissance **H: 61**
Johnson, Jimmie [American race driver]
Automobile racing (table: NASCAR Sprint Cup champions) **A: 981**
Johnson, John A. [American political leader]
Minnesota (table) **M: 602**
Johnson, John Arthur [American boxer] See Johnson, Jack in this index
Johnson, John Harold [American publisher] **J: 143**

Magazine (Magazines in the 1900's) **M:** 45
Johnson, John Mercer [Canadian political leader]
Confederation of Canada (Fathers of
Confederation) **Ci:** 935 *with picture*
Johnson, John Neely [American political leader]
California (table) **C:** 59
Johnson, Joseph [American political leader]
Virginia (table) **V:** 417
Johnson, Joseph B. [American political leader]
Vermont (table) **V:** 333
Johnson, Judy [American baseball player]
Baseball (table: Hall of Fame) **B:** 134a
Johnson, Kevin [American political leader]
Sacramento (History) **S:** 6
Johnson, Lady Bird [wife of Lyndon B. Johnson]
First ladies of the United States (table) **F:** 142
Johnson, Lyndon Baines (Marriage) **J:** 146 *with
picture*
Johnson, Linton Kwesi [British poet]
English literature (Recent English poetry) **E:** 323
Johnson, Louis A. [American government official]
Defense, Department of (table) **D:** 87
Truman, Harry S. **T:** 469
Johnson, Louisa [wife of John Quincy Adams] *See*
Adams, Louisa Johnson *in this index*
Johnson, Luci Baines [daughter of]
Johnson, Lyndon Baines (Marriage) **J:** 146
Johnson, Lynda Bird [daughter of]
Johnson, Lyndon Baines (Marriage) **J:** 146
Johnson, Lyndon Baines [U.S. president] **J:** 144
with pictures
African Americans (The civil rights movement)
A: 136o-136p
Cold War (Soviet-American relations) **Ci:** 769
Congress of the United States (Continued
struggle for power) **Ci:** 948
Democratic Party (The Great Society) **D:** 127 *with
picture*
Fortas, Abe **F:** 419
Great Society **G:** 349
Hispanic Americans (Expanding influence) **H:** 256
Kennedy, John Fitzgerald *picture on* **K:** 264;
(Steps to the White House) **K:** 263; (The new
President) **K:** 267
March on Washington **M:** 196
Nixon, Richard Milhous (Defeat by Kennedy)
N: 431
President of the United States (The Vietnam War)
P: 769
Republican Party (Defeat, then victory) **R:** 256
Texas (The mid-1900's) **T:** 208-209
United States, History of the (The civil rights
movement) **U:** 196a; (The Vietnam War)
U: 196a
Vice president of the United States (Growth of
the vice presidency) **V:** 353
Vietnam War (The Gulf of Tonkin incident) **V:** 375
Washington, D.C. (Government changes) **W:** 87
Johnson, Magic [American basketball player]
J: 152 *with portrait*
Basketball *picture on* **B:** 154a
Bird, Larry **B:** 373
Johnson, Marguerite [birth name of]
Angelou, Maya **A:** 460
Johnson, Michael [American athlete]
Olympic Games (The recent games) **O:** 753-754
Johnson, Middleton Tate [American political
leader]
Arlington **A:** 716
Johnson, Paul B. [American political leader]
Mississippi (table) **M:** 640
Johnson, Pauline [Canadian author] **J:** 152
Canadian literature (Poetry: 1850-1918) **C:** 157
Johnson, Philip Cortelyou [American architect]
J: 152
Architecture *picture on* **A:** 606; (The International
Style) **A:** 630; (Ludwig Mies van der Rohe)
A: 631-632; (Architecture today) **A:** 632-633
Johnson, Pierre Marc [Canadian political leader]
Quebec (table) **Q:** 29; (The late 1900's) **Q:** 32-33
Johnson, Randy [American baseball player] **J:** 152
Johnson, Reverdy [American government official]
Justice, Department of (table) **J:** 203
Taylor, Zachary (table) **T:** 60
Johnson, Richard L. [American aviator]
Aviation (table: Aviation speed records) **A:** 990
Johnson, Richard Mentor [American political
leader] **J:** 153
Vice president of the United States **V:** 348 *with
portrait*; (Election) **V:** 350
Johnson, Robert [American musician] **J:** 153
Johnson, Samuel [British author] **J:** 153
Biography (The 1700's) **B:** 313
Boswell, James **B:** 506
Dictionary (Early English dictionaries) **D:** 194
English literature (The Age of Johnson) **E:** 319
with picture

Idealism **I:** 46
Metaphysical poets **M:** 429
Shakespeare, William (Editions of the 1700's and
1800's) **S:** 369
Johnson, Samuel Ealy, Jr. [father of]
Johnson, Lyndon Baines (Boyhood) **J:** 145
Johnson, Thomas [American political leader]
Maryland (table) **M:** 255; (The Revolutionary
War) **M:** 258
Supreme Court of the United States (table)
So: 1000
Johnson, Tom L. [American political leader]
Cleveland (Continued growth and progress)
Ci: 667
Progressive Era (Political reforms) **P:** 814
Johnson, Uwe [German author]
German literature (Postwar German literature
[1945-1990]) **G:** 142
Johnson, Virginia Eshelman [American
researcher]
Masters and Johnson **M:** 297
Johnson, Walter [American baseball player] **J:** 153
Baseball (table: Hall of Fame) **B:** 134a; (The early
1900's) **B:** 135; (table: Modern major league
records) **B:** 138
Johnson, Walter W. [American political leader]
Colorado (table) **Ci:** 844
Johnson, William [American jurist]
Supreme Court of the United States (table)
So: 1000
Johnson, Sir William [British general]
Brant, Joseph **B:** 564
Johnson, William Freame [American political
leader]
Pennsylvania (table) **P:** 263
Johnson, William Samuel [American political
leader] **J:** 154
Johnson & Johnson [company]
Manufacturing (table) **M:** 170
Johnson County War [1892]
Wyoming *picture on* **W:** 535; (The Johnson
County War) **W:** 536
Johnson Foundation
Foundation (table) **F:** 430; (Health) **F:** 431
Johnson grass
Sorghum (Grassy sorghums) **So:** 596
Johnson Library [Austin] *See* Lyndon Baines
Johnson Library and Museum *in this index*
Johnson Publishing Company
Johnson, John Harold **J:** 143
Johnson-Sirleaf, Ellen [Liberian political leader]
J: 154
Liberia (Recent developments) **L:** 232
Johnson Space Center [Texas] **J:** 154
Astronaut (Training the astronauts) **A:** 831
Electronics *picture on* **E:** 207
Houston (Landmarks) **H:** 395
Texas **T:** 184; (Places to visit) **T:** 194 *with picture*;
(The late 1900's) **T:** 209
Johnson Wax Building [Racine, Wisconsin]
Architecture (Frank Lloyd Wright) **A:** 629-630
Wright, Frank Lloyd (Later career) **W:** 508
Johnston, Albert Sidney [Confederate general]
J: 154
Civil War, American (The commanding officers)
Ci: 618; (The war in the West--1862-1864)
Ci: 628
Johnston, David Lloyd [Canadian political leader]
J: 154
Johnston, Franz [Canadian painter]
Group of Seven **G:** 402
Johnston, Henry S. [American political leader]
Oklahoma (table) **O:** 730; (The 1920's) **O:** 732
Johnston, Joseph Eggleston [Confederate
general] **J:** 154
Civil War, American (The commanding officers)
Ci: 618; (The Atlanta campaign) **Ci:** 632; (The
South surrenders) **Ci:** 633
Lee, Robert E. (Opening campaigns) **L:** 178
Johnston, Joseph Forney [American political
leader]
Alabama (table) **A:** 274
Johnston, Philip [American engineer]
Code talkers **Ci:** 749
Johnston, Rita [Canadian political leader]
British Columbia (table) **B:** 628
Johnston, Samuel [American political leader]
North Carolina (table) **N:** 490
Johnston, Sarah Bush [stepmother of]
Lincoln, Abraham (Boyhood) **L:** 312
Johnstone-Wilson, Angus Frank [British author]
See Wilson, Angus *in this index*
Johnstown [Pennsylvania] **J:** 155
Johnstown Flood [1889] **J:** 155
Johnstown Flood National Memorial
[Pennsylvania]
National Park System (table: National memorials)

N: 54
Johor-Riau Malay language
Malay language **M:** 98
JOIDES Resolution [research ship]
Ocean drilling programs **O:** 667
"Join or Die" [cartoon by Franklin]
Cartoon *picture on* **C:** 265
Franklin, Benjamin (The Plan of Union) **F:** 489
"Join the Revolution of Responsibility"
[campaign]
4-H (Expansion) **F:** 436
Joint [anatomy] **J:** 155 *with pictures*
Ankle **A:** 515 *with diagram*
Ankylosis **A:** 516
Arthritis **A:** 751 *with diagrams*
Arthroscopy **A:** 753 *with picture*
Bursitis **B:** 711
Dislocation **D:** 235
Hip **H:** 238 *with diagram*
Human body (The skeletal system) **H:** 418
Knee **K:** 345
Orthopedics **O:** 860
Rheumatism **R:** 291
Rheumatology **R:** 291
Shoulder **S:** 437 *with picture*
Sprain **So:** 805
Joint [animation]
Animation (Making the model move) **A:** 513
Joint [botany]
Prickly pear **P:** 776
Joint administration [political unit]
Commonwealth of Nations (Dependencies)
Ci: 876
Joint Air-to-Surface Standoff Missile
Guided missile (Air-to-surface missiles) **G:** 426
Joint and survivorship annuity
Insurance (Annuities) **I:** 311
Joint bar [construction]
Railroad (The crossties and rails) **R:** 109
Joint Base Elmendorf-Richardson [Alaska]
Anchorage **A:** 450
Joint Base Langley-Eustis [Virginia]
Langley Air Force Base **L:** 61
Joint Base Pearl Harbor-Hickam [Hawaii]
Pearl Harbor (Pearl Harbor as a naval base) **P:** 219
Joint Base San Antonio [Texas]
Fort Sam Houston **F:** 416
Lackland Air Force Base **L:** 22
Joint Chiefs of Staff J: 156
Defense, Department of (Organization) **D:** 87
Joint command
Air Force, United States (Organization of the Air
Force) **A:** 193
Joint committee
Congress of the United States (Working in
committees) **Ci:** 944
House of Representatives (The speaker and other
leaders) **H:** 387; (Committees) **H:** 387
State government (Organization) **So:** 863-864
United States, Government of the (Committee
system) **U:** 138
Joint Forces Command
Army, United States (Army service component
commands) **A:** 736
Joint Global Ocean Flux Study
Atlantic Ocean (New techniques) **A:** 867
Marine biology (Biological oceanographers)
M: 205
Joint Institute for Nuclear Research
Bohrium **B:** 438
Dubnium **D:** 371
Hassium **H:** 83
Meitnerium **M:** 387
Nobelium **N:** 450
Rutherfordium **R:** 569
Seaborgium **S:** 264
Transuranium element **T:** 401
Joint operation [warfare]
Army **A:** 724
Joint session
Congress of the United States (When Congress
meets) **Ci:** 943 *with picture*
Joint Staff
Joint Chiefs of Staff **J:** 156
Joint-stock company
Colonial life in America (Why the colonists came
to America) **Ci:** 788
Joinville, Jean de [French author]
French literature (Early prose) **F:** 519
Joist [construction]
Building construction (Beams, girders, and
columns) **B:** 682-683
House (The frame) **H:** 382 *with diagram*
Jojoba [plant]
Nut (Uses of nuts) **N:** 621
Jókai, Mor [Hungarian author]
Hungary (The arts) **H:** 442

Joke
 Humor H: 435
Jokul [Norse mythology]
 Jack Frost J: 2
Jola [people]
 Gambia (People) G: 18
Jolie, Angelina [American actress]
 Motion picture (Best performance by an actress in a supporting role: 1999) M: 862b
Jolie Rouge [flag]
 Pirate (A pirate's life) P: 494-495
Joliet Junior College
 Community college Ci: 898
Joliot-Curie, Frédéric [French physicist]
 Joliot-Curie, Irène J: 156
 Nobel Prizes (Chemistry: 1935) N: 443
Joliot-Curie, Irène [French physicist] J: 156
 Nobel Prizes (Chemistry: 1935) N: 443
Jolliet, Louis [French-Canadian explorer] J: 156
 Arkansas A: 713
 Chicago (Exploration and early settlement) C: 434
 Exploration (The French and English in North America) E: 446 *with map*
 Illinois (French and British control) I: 72
 Iowa (Exploration and early settlement) I: 393
 Marquette, Jacques M: 217
 Michigan (French exploration and settlement) M: 508
 Missouri (Exploration) M: 669
 Missouri River (History) M: 575-676
 Peoria P: 277
Jolly Roger [flag]
 Pirate (A pirate's life) P: 494-495 *with picture*
Jolson, Al [American singer] J: 157
 Communication (Famous first words) Ci: 884
 Motion picture (The movies talk) M: 867
Jolthead porgy [fish]
 Porgy P: 678 *with picture*
Joly, Henri-G. [Canadian political leader]
 Quebec (table) Q: 29
Jomon [Japanese history]
 Japan (Ancestry) J: 35; (Early days) J: 52
Jonah [Biblical figure]
 Jonah, Book of J: 157
Jonah, Book of [Bible] J: 157
Jonathan [Jewish leader]
 Masada M: 262
Jonathan, Brother [U.S. history] *See* Brother Jonathan *in this index*
Jonathan, Goodluck [Nigerian political leader]
 Nigeria (Internal conflict) N: 418
Jonathan, Leabua [Lesotho political leader]
 Lesotho (History) L: 208
Jonathan apple
 Apple (table) A: 571 *with picture*
Joncaire, Daniel de [French frontiersman]
 Buffalo (History) B: 678
Jones, Absalom [American religious leader] J: 157
 African Methodist Episcopal Church A: 137
Jones, Alan [Australian race driver]
 Automobile racing (table: Formula One World Drivers' Championship) A: 980
Jones, Ben A. [American horse trainer]
 Kentucky Derby K: 297
Jones, Bob, Sr. [American religious leader]
 Bob Jones University B: 432
Jones, Bobby [American golfer] J: 157
Jones, Brian [British musician]
 Rolling Stones R: 402a
Jones, Brian [British pilot]
 Balloon (Long-distance balloon flights) B: 62
Jones, Casey [American railroad engineer] J: 157
 Locomotive *picture on* L: 415
 Tennessee (Places to visit) T: 144
Jones, Christopher [English navigator]
 Mayflower M: 327
Jones, D. G. [Canadian poet]
 Canadian literature (Modern Canadian poets) C: 161
Jones, Daniel Webster [American political leader]
 Arkansas (table) A: 712
Jones, David C. [American military leader]
 Joint Chiefs of Staff (table) J: 156
Jones, Davy [legendary figure] J: 158
Jones, Donald F. [American geneticist]
 Corn (Development of hybrids) Ci: 1063
Jones, Elizabeth Orton [American artist]
 Caldecott Medal (table: 1945) C: 26
Jones, Fearless [fictional character]
 Mosley, Walter M: 830
Jones, Grave Digger [fictional character]
 Himes, Chester H: 234
Jones, Inigo [English architect] J: 158 *with picture*
 Architecture (Later Renaissance architecture) A: 621-622
 England (The arts) E: 298-299

 Masque M: 268
Jones, J. Walter [Canadian political leader]
 Prince Edward Island (table) P: 791
Jones, James C. [American political leader]
 Tennessee (table) T: 152
Jones, James Earl [American actor] J: 158 *with portrait*
 Drama *picture on* D: 341
Jones, Jennifer [American actress]
 Motion picture (Best performance by an actress: 1943) M: 862
Jones, Jesse Holman [American government official]
 Commerce, Department of (table) Ci: 871
 Roosevelt, Franklin Delano (table) R: 454
Jones, Jim [American public figure]
 Cult (Modern cults) Ci: 1185
 Guyana (History) G: 446-447
Jones, Jo [American musician]
 Basie, Count B: 140
Jones, John E. [American political leader]
 Nevada (table) N: 173
Jones, John Paul [American military leader] J: 158
 Hewes, Joseph H: 220
Jones, John Paul [British bassist]
 Led Zeppelin L: 175
Jones, Joseph T. [American businessman]
 Gulfport G: 439
Jones, Kenney [British musician]
 Who, The W: 296
Jones, LeRoi [American author] *See* Baraka, Amiri *in this index*
Jones, Mary Harris [American social reformer] J: 159 *with portrait*
 West Virginia (Labor developments) W: 229
 Western frontier life in America (Life in the mining towns) W: 236
Jones, Parnelli [American race driver]
 Automobile racing (table: Indianapolis 500 winners) A: 980
Jones, Paula Corbin [American public figure]
 Clinton, Bill (Domestic events) Ci: 682f
Jones, Quincy [American musician] J: 159 *with portrait*
Jones, Robert T. [American political leader]
 Arizona (table) A: 687
Jones, Robert Tyre [American golfer] *See* Jones, Bobby *in this index*
Jones, Sam H. [American political leader]
 Louisiana (table) L: 496
Jones, Samuel M. [American political leader]
 Progressive Era (Political reforms) P: 814
Jones, Shirley [American actress]
 Motion picture (Best performance by an actress in a supporting role: 1960) M: 862b
Jones, Steve [American golfer]
 Golf (U.S. Open) G: 265
Jones, Terry [British actor]
 Cleese, John Ci: 661
 "Monty Python's Flying Circus" M: 780
Jones, Thomas Goode [American political leader]
 Alabama (table) A: 274
Jones, Tom [literary figure] *See* Tom Jones *in this index*
Jones, Tommy Lee [American actor]
 Motion picture (Best performance by an actor in a supporting role: 1993) M: 862b
Jones, William [American political leader]
 Madison, James (table) M: 35
 Rhode Island (table) R: 311
Jones Act [1916]
 Wilson, Woodrow (Foreign affairs) W: 323
Jones Act [1917]
 Puerto Rico (United States rule) P: 883
Jonestown [Guyana]
 Cult (Modern cults) Ci: 1185
 Guyana (History) G: 446-447
Jongleur [minstrel]
 French literature (Early French literature) F: 518
Jonker [diamond]
 Diamond (Famous diamonds) D: 182
Jonny spielt auf [opera by Křenek]
 Opera (The search for new forms) O: 799-800
Jonquil [plant] J: 159 *with picture*
 Daffodil D: 3
 Narcissus N: 20
Jonson, Ben [English dramatist] J: 159
 Drama (Elizabethan playwrights) D: 331-332
 English literature (Jacobean drama) E: 317
 Humor (Puns) H: 435
 Masque M: 268
Jonsson, Erik [American political leader]
 Dallas (Commercial growth) D: 15
Joola [ship]
 Shipwreck (table: Major shipwrecks) S: 428
Joplin [Missouri]
 Missouri (The early 2000's) M: 672

Joplin, Janis [American singer]
 Rock music *picture on* R: 380b
Joplin, Scott [American composer] J: 160
Jordan J: 160 *with pictures and maps*
 Flag *picture on* F: 203
 Jerusalem J: 94a
 Middle East M: 530
 Palestine Liberation Organization (History) P: 106
 West Bank (History and government) W: 200
Jordan, Barbara Charline [American political leader] J: 166
Jordan, Chester B. [American political leader]
 New Hampshire (table) N: 223
Jordan, Hamilton [American government official]
 Carter, Jimmy (The national scene) C: 257
Jordan, I. King [American educator]
 Deafness (Deaf community and culture) D: 59-60
Jordan, Len B. [American political leader]
 Idaho (table) I: 42
Jordan, Michael [American basketball player] J: 166 *with portrait*
 Basketball *picture on* B: 154b
Jordan, Vernon Eulion, Jr. [American social reformer] J: 167
Jordan River [Israel-Jordan] J: 167
 Dead Sea D: 55
 Israel (The Rift Valley) I: 482-484
 Jordan (The Jordan River Valley) J: 163
 River (table) R: 352
 West Bank (Land and climate) W: 200 *with map*
Joropo [dance]
 Venezuela (Recreation) V: 301
José, Don [opera character]
 Opera: (*Carmen*) O: 802
José Batlle y Ordóñez Park [Montevideo]
 Uruguay (table) U: 228
Joseph [husband of Mary] J: 167
 Jesus Christ (The Nativity) J: 105 *with picture*
Joseph [son of Jacob] J: 167
 Jews (Beginnings) J: 120-121
 Judah J: 179
 Rachel R: 60
Joseph I [Holy Roman emperor]
 Succession wars (The War of the Spanish Succession) So: 950
Joseph II [Holy Roman emperor]
 Belgium (The Brabant Revolution) B: 233
 Roman Catholic Church (Gallicanism) R: 408-409
Joseph, Chief [American Indian chief] J: 168 *with portrait*
 Idaho *picture on* I: 43
 Indian wars (The Nez Perce War [1877]) I: 194
 Montana (Indian fighting) M: 758
 Nez Perce Indians N: 391
 Oregon (Indian treaties and conflicts) O: 846-848
Joseph, Lake [Ontario]
 Muskoka Lakes M: 963
Joseph and His Brothers [book by Mann]
 Mann, Thomas M: 164
Joseph and the Amazing Technicolor Dreamcoat [musical]
 Lloyd Webber, Andrew L: 403
Joseph Andrews [book by Fielding]
 Fielding, Henry (His novels) F: 94
Joseph of Arimathea [Biblical figure] J: 168
 Galahad, Sir G: 7
 Holy Grail (Early history of the Grail) H: 299; (The search for the Grail) H: 299
 Jesus Christ (The Crucifixion) J: 108-108b
Josephine [wife of Napoleon I] J: 168 *with portrait*
 Napoleon I (Marriage) N: 14; (Divorce and remarriage) N: 15
Josephism [religion]
 Pope (The 1700's and 1800's) P: 665
Josephson, Brian [British physicist]
 Nobel Prizes (Physics: 1973) N: 441
Josephson, Matthew [American historian]
 United States, History of the (The rich and the poor) U: 182
Josephus, Flavius [Jewish historian] J: 169
Joshua [Biblical figure] J: 169
 Amalekites A: 400
 Jericho J: 93
 Jordan River J: 167
Joshua, Book of
 Bible (The Prophets) B: 280
 Joshua J: 169
Joshua Then and Now [book by Richler]
 Richler, Mordecai R: 331
Joshua tree
 Joshua Tree National Park J: 169
 Tree *picture on* T: 430
 Yucca Y: 169
Joshua Tree, The [recording]
 Rock music (New wave and mainstream rock) R: 380c
Joshua Tree National Park [California] J: 169

National Park System (table: National parks) N: 48
Tree *picture on* T: 430
Josiah [king of Judah] J: 169
Joslyn Art Museum
Nebraska (Museums) N: 98
Omaha (Cultural life and recreation) O: 756 *with picture*
Jospin, Lionel Robert [French government official]
France (Recent developments) F: 478
Joss, Addie [American baseball player]
Baseball (table: Hall of Fame) B: 134a
Jost van Dyke [island]
Virgin Islands V: 392 *with map*
Jostedalsbreen Glacier [Norway]
Glacier (Famous glaciers) G: 204
Icecap I: 19
Norway (Land regions) N: 541 *with map*
Jotunheim [Norse mythology]
Mythology (The construction of the world) M: 986
Jouett, Jack [American patriot] J: 169
Jouhaux, Léon [French statesman]
Nobel Prizes (Peace: 1951) N: 448a
Joule [measurement] J: 169
British thermal unit B: 632
Calorie C: 70
Energy (Units of work and energy) E: 274-275
Heat (Temperature and heat) H: 150
Light (Energy and brightness) L: 290
Metric system (Mechanics) M: 437-440
Power P: 727
Work W: 405
Joule, James Prescott [British physicist] J: 169
Energy (Conservation of energy) E: 274
Heat (Heat and energy) H: 155
Mayer, Julius Robert von M: 327
Physics (Developments in the 1800's) P: 440
Science (Scientific advances of the 1800's) S: 200
Joule-Thomson effect [physics]
Liquid air (Making liquid air) L: 347
Joule-Thomson expansion [physics]
Liquid air (Making liquid air) L: 347
Joule's Law [physics]
Joule, James Prescott J: 169
Journal [book by Goncourt brothers]
French literature (Naturalism) F: 522
Journal [book by Mansfield]
Mansfield, Katherine M: 167
Journal [book by Woolman]
Woolman, John W: 402
Journal [literature]
Diary D: 184
Journal [magazine]
Magazine (Magazines in the 1800's) M: 45
Publishing (Magazines and journals) P: 869
Journal bearing [machine]
Bearing B: 188 *with diagrams*
Journal box
Railroad (Rolling stock) R: 107-108
Journal de Montréal, Le [newspaper]
Quebec (Communication) Q: 29
Journal of a Residence on a Georgian Plantation in 1838-1839 [book by Kemble]
Kemble, Fanny K: 258
Journal of a Tour to the Hebrides [book by Boswell]
Boswell, James B: 506
Journal of a Voyage to Lisbon, The [book by Fielding]
Fielding, Henry (His life) F: 94
Journal of Negro Education
Howard University H: 400
Journal of Religious Thought
Howard University H: 400
Journal of the Franklin Institute
Franklin Institute Science Museum F: 494
Journal of Travels Over the Rocky Mountains [book by Palmer]
Palmer, Joel P: 110
Journal Square Transportation Center [Jersey City]
Jersey City (Government and history) J: 94
Journal to Stella [book by Swift]
Swift, Jonathan (His life) So: 1039
Journalism J: 170 *with pictures*
See also Magazine; Newspaper *in this index*
Editorial E: 83
Foreign correspondent F: 386
Freedom of the press F: 507
Missouri (Interesting facts) M: 651
Pulitzer Prizes (Prizes in journalism) P: 886b; (table) P: 886b
War correspondent W: 26
Writing (Preparing for a writing career) W: 511
Journalist
See also the list of *Related articles* in the Journalism article
Journalism J: 170 *with picture*; (Careers in

journalism) J: 176
Radio (Careers) R: 90
Journals of Lewis and Clark
Lewis and Clark expedition (Results of the expedition) L: 223 *with picture*
Journey [scouting]
Girl Scouts (Journeys) G: 198
Journey of the Magi [fresco by Gozzoli]
Italy *picture on* I: 514
Journey to Parnassus [poem by Cervantes]
Cervantes, Miguel de (His literary career) C: 363
Journey to the End of the Night [book by Céline]
Céline, Louis-Ferdinand C: 325
Journey to the West, The [book by Wu Cheng'en]
Chinese literature (Drama and fiction) C: 511
Journeyman [labor]
Apprentice A: 575
Guild (Craft guilds) G: 428
Labor movement (Craft guilds) L: 9
Joust [combat]
Knights and knighthood (Tournaments) K: 350 *with picture*
Maryland (Interesting facts) M: 241 *with picture*
Jove [mythology] *See* Jupiter [Roman mythology] *in this index*
Jovian [Roman emperor]
Rome, Ancient (table) R: 447
Jovian asteroid
Asteroid (Orbital groups) A: 824a
Jovian planet [astronomy] *See* Gas giant *in this index*
Jovian system [astronomy]
Jupiter J: 197
Joy Luck Club, The [book by Tan]
Novel (The novel today) N: 575
Joyce, James [Irish author] J: 176
Fable F: 3
Irish literature (Fiction) I: 432
Novel (New directions in the novel) N: 573-574
Obscenity and pornography (Legal history for obscenity) O: 643
Pound, Ezra P: 721
Joyce, William [British public figure]
Old Bailey O: 740
Joyeuse Entrée [Belgian history]
Belgium (The Middle Ages) B: 232-233
Joyner-Kersee, Jackie [American athlete] J: 177
Joystick [electronic device]
Computer (A controller) Ci: 915
Electronic game (Gameplay) E: 204b-204c
József, Attila [Hungarian poet]
Hungary (The arts) H: 442
JPEG [format]
Photography (Storing digital images) P: 421
JPMorgan Chase & Co. J: 177
Bank (Diversification and mergers) B: 94-95; (Crisis in finance) B: 95
JSOW [missile]
Guided missile (Air-to-surface missiles) G: 426
Juan, Don [father of]
Juan Carlos I J: 177
Juan, Don [literary figure] *See* Don Juan *in this index*
Juan Carlos I [king of Spain] J: 177
Franco, Francisco (As dictator) F: 483
Spain (Political changes) So: 751 *with picture*
Juan de Fuca, Strait of [Washington]
Puget Sound P: 886
Juan Diego, Saint [Mexican saint] J: 177
Juana Inés de la Cruz [Mexican poet] J: 178
Latin American literature (Colonial literature) L: 112
Juana of Castile [mother of Charles V]
Maximilian I M: 319
Juárez [Mexico] J: 178
El Paso (History) E: 247
Texas *picture on* T: 208
Juárez, Benito Pablo [Mexican political leader] J: 178
Latin America (Early years of independence) L: 107-108
Maximilian M: 319
Mexico (Reform) M: 471; (The French invasion) M: 471
Juárez Law [Mexican history]
Juárez, Benito Pablo J: 178
Juba [king of Numidia]
Numidia N: 608
Juba [South Sudan] J: 178
Sudan, South So: 954 *with map*
Jubba River
Somalia (Land and climate) So: 588 *with map*
Jubilee Jim [nickname]
Fisk, James F: 189
Jubilee quartet style [music]
Gospel music G: 277
Jubilee Singers

Spiritual So: 796
Juchereau de Saint Denis, Louis [French frontiersman]
Louisiana (French Louisiana) L: 497-498
Judah [Biblical figure] J: 178
Joseph J: 167
Judah [ancient country]
See also Judea *in this index*
David (Early life) D: 44-45
Jerusalem (Ancient times) J: 100
Jews (The divided kingdom) J: 121 *with map*
Palestine (Early history and settlement) P: 104
Judah ha-Nassi [Jewish religious leader]
Judaism (The Talmud) J: 180
Judah Halevi [Hebrew poet] *See* Halevi, Judah *in this index*
Judah Maccabee [Jewish leader] J: 179
Daniel, Book of D: 33
Jerusalem (Ancient times) J: 100-101
Jews (The Hellenistic period) J: 121
Judaism [religion] J: 179 *with pictures*
See also Jews *in this index*
Abraham A: 16
Angel A: 459
Assumption A: 820
Bar mitzvah B: 102
Bat mitzvah B: 162
Bible B: 279; (table) B: 281; (Translations of the Bible) B: 284; (The Bible in worship) B: 286
Christianity (The early church) C: 523; (Relations between Jews and Christians) C: 526
Devil D: 174
Divorce (The divorce rate) D: 254-255
Education (Religion and early Western education) E: 98
Fast F: 52
Feasts and festivals (In Judaism) F: 58
Fundamentalism (Fundamentalism in other religions) F: 557
Galilee G: 11
Heaven H: 161
High priest H: 228
Israel (Religion) I: 481
Jerusalem J: 94a
Kabbalah K: 208
Kosher K: 384
Marriage (Wedding ceremonies) M: 220
Name (Other family names) N: 7
New Testament N: 287
Old Testament O: 740
Parochial school P: 201
Paul, Saint (Paul's letters and ideas) P: 201
Pharisees P: 354
Priest P: 776
Rabbi R: 46
Rashi R: 144
Religion R: 215; (How the major religions are organized) R: 218; (Judaism) R: 219
Resurrection R: 264
Sabbath S: 2
Sadducees S: 8
Saint (Non-Christian saints) S: 29
Star of David So: 854
Talmud T: 21
Ten Commandments T: 132
World, History of the (Civilizations of southwest Asia) W: 426
Judas, Gospel of
Judas Iscariot J: 182
Judas Iscariot [apostle] J: 182
Jesus Christ (The trial) J: 108 *with picture*
Potter's field P: 715
Judas Maccabaeus [Jewish religious leader] *See* Judah Maccabee *in this index*
Judas tree
Redbud R: 190
Juddah [Saudi Arabia] *See* Jiddah *in this index*
Jude, Epistle of [New Testament]
Bible (The Letters) B: 284
Jude, Saint [apostle] J: 183
Jude the Obscure [book by Hardy]
Hardy, Thomas H: 59
Judea [ancient country] J: 183
See also Judah [ancient country] *in this index*
Christianity (Origins) C: 523
Jerusalem (Roman rule) J: 101
Jesus Christ (Public life) J: 106 *with map*
Palestine (Roman rule) P: 104
Judean Hills
Israel (The Judeo-Galilean Highlands) I: 482
Judge [competition]
Boxing (Officials) B: 527
Judge [Jewish history]
Judges, Book of J: 183
Judge [office] J: 183
Address, Forms of (Officials of the Commonwealth of Nations) A: 53

Court Ci: 1101
Law (Common law systems) L: 132; (How laws are changed) L: 132
State government (Judicial branch) So: 864
United States, Government of the (Judges) U: 145
Judge, The [book by West]
West, Rebecca W: 199
Judge, Thomas L. [American political leader]
Montana (table) M: 757
Judges, Book of [Bible] J: 183
Bible (The Prophets) B: 280
Judgment [law]
Clerk of court Ci: 662b
Judgment [psychology]
Ethics (Aristotle) E: 366
Judgment [text]
I Ching I: 2
Judgment Day
Resurrection R: 264
Judgment Day [book by Farrell]
Farrell, James T. F: 48
Judgment of Paris [myth]
Venus V: 310
Judicial Committee of the Privy Council
Supreme Court of Canada (History) So: 997
Judicial Conference of the United States J: 183
Judicial confession [law]
Confession Ci: 936
Judicial Department
Constitution of the United States (Article III) Ci: 1009
Justice, Department of J: 202
Judicial duel
Duel D: 378
Judicial methodology
Supreme Court of the United States (Controversy on the court) So: 1001
Judicial oath [law]
Oath O: 639
Judicial restraint [law]
Holmes, Oliver Wendell, Jr. (Supreme Court justice) H: 295
Judicial review [law] J: 183
Constitution Ci: 995
Constitution of the United States (Article III, Section 2) Ci: 1009
Government (Judicial) G: 285
Jefferson, Thomas (The courts) J: 84
Law (Public law) L: 130-131; (Beginnings of U.S. law) L: 136
Marbury v. Madison M: 193
Marshall, John (Chief justice) M: 230
Supreme Court of the United States (Authority of the Supreme Court) So: 998
United States, Government of the (Authority of the courts) U: 141
Judicial Yuan [court]
Taiwan (Government) T: 15-16
Judiciary
Government *diagram on* G: 287; (Judicial) G: 285
Judiciary Act [1789]
Ellsworth, Oliver E: 244
Jefferson, Thomas (The courts) J: 84
Supreme Court of the United States (How the Supreme Court is organized) So: 998
Judiciary Act [1801]
Jefferson, Thomas (The courts) J: 84
Judiciary Act [1925]
Taft, William Howard (Chief justice) T: 12
Judith [Biblical figure] J: 184
Bible (The Christian Old Testament) B: 282
Judith [ship]
Drake, Sir Francis (Early life) D: 321
Judith Mountains
Montana (Land regions) M: 752
Judith with the Head of Holofernes [painting by Klimt]
Painting (Symbolism) P: 76 *with picture*
Judo [sport] J: 184 *with pictures*
Asian Americans (Asian influences on American culture) A: 812c
Martial arts M: 234
Olympic Games (Summer Olympic Games) O: 746e-746f
Judo Federation, United States
Judo (Learning judo) J: 184-185
Judogi [costume]
Judo (Learning judo) J: 184
Judoka [instruction]
Judo (Learning judo) J: 184
Judson, Adoniram [American missionary] J: 185
Baptists (Early history) B: 101
Judson, Clara Ingram [American author]
Laura Ingalls Wilder Award (table) L: 121
Judson, Whitcomb L. [American inventor]
Zipper Z: 596

Juggernaut [image] J: 185 *with picture*
Juggling J: 186 *with picture*
Jugnauth, Aneerood [Mauritian political leader]
Mauritius (History) M: 317
Jugoslavia See Yugoslavia *in this index*
Jugular vein [anatomy] J: 186 *with diagram*
Human body (table) H: 422 *with diagram*
Jugurtha [king of Numidia]
Numidia N: 608
Juice [drink]
Wine W: 336
Juilliard School J: 186
Lincoln Center for the Performing Arts L: 327
New York *picture on* N: 296
Jujitsu [sport] See Judo *in this index*
Jujutsu [sport] See Judo *in this index*
Jukebox musical
Musical comedy M: 961
Julenissen [legendary figure]
Christmas (In Denmark, Norway, and Sweden) C: 531
Julgröt [food]
Christmas (In Denmark, Norway, and Sweden) C: 531
Julia [literary figure]
Shakespeare, William: (*The Two Gentlemen of Verona*) S: 356
Julia [wife of]
Pompey the Great P: 655
Julian [book by Vidal]
Vidal, Gore V: 359
Julian [Roman emperor] J: 186
Rome, Ancient (The decline of the empire) R: 447-448
Julian, Percy Lavon [American chemist] J: 187 *with portrait*
Julian calendar J: 187
Calendar (The Julian calendar) C: 31
Gregorian calendar G: 387
Juliana [queen of the Netherlands] J: 187 *with portrait*
Netherlands (Holidays and recreation) N: 141; (Political changes) N: 150
Ottawa (Annual events) O: 873
Wilhelmina W: 306
Julie of the Wolves [book by George]
George, Jean Craighead G: 108
Juliet [literary figure]
Shakespeare, William: (*Romeo and Juliet*) S: 357-358
Juliette Low World Friendship Fund
Girl Scouts (History) G: 200
Juliettes, Girl Scout
Girl Scouts (Girl Scout Juliettes) G: 198
Julio-Claudian emperors
Rome, Ancient (The Roman Empire) R: 446
Julius I, Saint [pope]
Pope (table) P: 666
Julius II [pope] J: 187
Architecture (Later Renaissance architecture) A: 621
Michelangelo (Early life) M: 483-484; (The Sistine Chapel) M: 484; (The tomb of Julius II) M: 484
Pope (Renaissance and Reformation) P: 664; (table) P: 666
Raphael (His life) R: 142-143
Swiss Guard So: 1049
Julius III [pope]
Pope (table) P: 666
Julius Caesar [opera by Handel]
Handel, George Frideric (His work) H: 42-43
Julius Caesar [play by Shakespeare]
Blank verse B: 398
Caesar, Julius (Assassination) C: 14
Shakespeare, William: (*Julius Caesar*) S: 360
Julius Nepos [Roman emperor]
Rome, Ancient (table) R: 447
Jultomten [legendary figure]
Christmas (In Denmark, Norway, and Sweden) C: 531
July [month] J: 188 *with pictures*
Julian calendar J: 187
July Hay [painting by Benton]
Painting *picture on* P: 38
July Ordinances [French history]
July Revolution J: 190
July Revolution [1830] J: 190 *with picture*
France (The revolutions of 1830 and 1848) F: 474
Jumada I [month]
Calendar (The Islamic calendar) C: 29
Jumada II [month]
Calendar (The Islamic calendar) C: 29
Jumanji [book by Van Allsburg]
Literature for children *picture on* L: 364
Van Allsburg, Chris V: 269
Jumbo [elephant]
Barnum, P. T. B: 115

Elephant E: 226
Jumbo jet [airplane]
Aviation *picture on* A: 983; (Aircraft manufacturing) A: 984
Jumeau, Emile [French businessman]
Doll (Porcelain dolls) D: 290-291; (Rivalry in the doll industry) D: 291
Jumhurii Tojikiston See Tajikistan *in this index*
Jumna River [India] See Yamuna River *in this index*
Jump shot
Basketball *picture on* B: 147; (Changes in the game) B: 151-152
Luisetti, Hank L: 516
Jumping
Frog (Legs) F: 536
Jumping bean [toy] J: 190 *with pictures*
Jumping cholla cactus [plant]
Cactus (Kinds of cactuses) C: 11
Plant *picture on* P: 526
Jumping competition
Horse (Jumping) H: 357 *with picture*
Long jump L: 448
Jumping events [sports] See Long jump; Triple jump *in this index*
Jumping jack [toy]
Doll (The 1600's and 1700's) D: 289
Jumping mouse [animal] J: 190 *with pictures*
Jumping spider
Spider So: 783 *with picture, picture on* So: 785; (Jumping spiders) So: 790
Junco [bird] J: 191 *with picture*
Junction [electronics]
Semiconductor (Using doped crystals) S: 292
Thermocouple T: 253
Junction [road]
Road (Bypasses) R: 358
June [month] J: 192 *with pictures*
June beetle See Junebug *in this index*
June Bug [airplane]
Airplane (Other pioneer planes and fliers) A: 233 *with picture*
Curtiss, Glenn Hammond Ci: 1199
June bug [insect] See Junebug *in this index*
June War [1967]
Arab-Israeli conflict (The 1967 war) A: 582a
Juneau [Alaska] J: 194 *with picture*
Alaska A: 282 *with picture*
Juneau, Solomon [American settler]
Milwaukee M: 558; (Early development) M: 561
Junebug [insect] J: 194
Antennae *picture on* A: 544
Beetle (Scarabs) B: 217
Insect *picture on* I: 283; (Hearing) I: 290-291
Juneteenth [holiday]
Galveston G: 18
June Jr. J: 192
Jung, Carl Gustav [Swiss psychologist] J: 194 *with portrait*
Electra E: 165
Extrovert E: 459
Freud, Sigmund (His life) F: 530
Introvert I: 354
Mythology (Psychological approaches) M: 990
Personality (Personality types) P: 301 *with picture*
Jungfrau [mountain, Switzerland]
Alps A: 384 *with pictures*
Mountain (table) M: 896 *with diagram*
Jungle J: 195
Indian, American (Indians of the Tropical Forest) I: 175
Jungle, The [book by Sinclair]
Consumer protection (Beginnings of modern consumerism) Ci: 1019
Muckrakers M: 908
Novel (The United States) N: 573
Publishing (The power of published ideas) P: 869
Roosevelt, Theodore (Domestic problems) R: 466
Sinclair, Upton S: 468
United States, History of the (Theodore Roosevelt) U: 187
Jungle Book, The [book by Kipling]
Kipling, Rudyard (Kipling in America) K: 334
Jungle cycle [medicine]
Yellow fever Y: 556
Jungle Fever [film by Lee]
Lee, Spike L: 179
Jungle fowl [bird] See Junglefowl *in this index*
Jungle music [jazz sound]
Ellington, Duke E: 242
Junglefowl [bird] J: 195 *with picture*
Chicken (History) C: 445
Junior [education]
Universities and colleges (The student body) U: 208
Junior Achievement [organization] J: 195
Junior bantamweight [boxing]
Boxing (table) B: 527

Junior Chamber of Commerce
Jaycees J: 67
Junior Citizens [former name]
Jaycees J: 67
Junior college See Community college in this index
Junior featherweight [boxing]
Boxing (table) B: 527
Junior flyweight
Boxing (table) B: 527
Junior high school J: 196
Education (Intermediate education) E: 91
Library (Middle school and junior high school libraries) L: 244
School (Intermediate schools) S: 181; (High schools) S: 181
Junior League [baseball]
Little League Baseball L: 391
Junior Leagues [organizations] J: 196
Junior lightweight
Boxing (table) B: 527
Junior middleweight
Boxing (table) B: 527
Junior Order Knights of Pythias
Knights of Pythias K: 352
Junior Sports and Junior Olympic Games
Amateur Athletic Union A: 401
Junior welterweight
Boxing (table) B: 527
Juniors, Girl Scout
Girl Scouts (Girl Scouts of the USA) G: 196 with picture
Juniper [shrub] J: 196 with picture
Tree pictures on T: 425
Juniper titmouse [bird]
Titmouse T: 302
Junípero Serra [Spanish missionary] See Serra, Junípero in this index
Junius [month]
Calendar (The Romans) C: 31
Junk [ship]
Houseboat H: 389
Ship picture on S: 423; (Chinese ships) S: 419
Transportation picture on T: 388; (Water transportation) T: 384
Junk bond
Bond (Bond ratings) B: 454
Junkers [airplane]
Airplane picture on A: 232; (World War I [1914-1918]) A: 234-235; (The golden age) A: 235
Junkers [German history] J: 196
Prussia (The Prussian people) P: 842
Junkers, Hugo [German inventor]
Airplane (World War I [1914-1918]) A: 234
Junket [mission]
Congress of the United States (Congressional travel) Ci: 947
Juno [asteroid]
Asteroid (History of study) A: 824b
Juno [Roman mythology] J: 197
See also Hera in this index
June J: 192
Mythology (table) M: 981; (Roman divinities) M: 982
Venus V: 310
Juno I [rocket]
Rocket (The space age) R: 391
Juno and the Paycock [play by O'Casey]
Irish literature (The Irish literary revival) I: 432
O'Casey, Sean O: 646
Junta [government] J: 197
Chile (Independence) C: 468; (Marxism and military rule) C: 470
Junta de Defensa Nacional [Spanish history]
Spanish Civil War (Rebellion leads to civil war) So: 756a
Junto [U.S. history]
Adult education (History of adult education in the United States) A: 69
Junzi [philosophy]
Confucianism (Early Confucianism) Ci: 936
Jupiter [planet] J: 197 with pictures
Astronomy (How the planets move) A: 835
Callisto C: 68
Cassini, Giovanni Domenico C: 277
Europa E: 379
Galileo [astronomer] (Mature scientific career) G: 11
Galileo [space probe] G: 12
Ganymede G: 27
Io I: 370
Light (The speed of light) L: 290
Lightning (Extraterrestrial lightning) L: 301
Meteor (The parent comet) M: 431; (Other planets and moons) M: 432
Mountain (On Io) M: 895
Planet P: 507 with pictures
Planetary ring P: 514d

Satellite S: 149; (Satellites of the gas giants) S: 150; (table: Major satellites of the solar system) S: 150b
Space exploration picture on So: 709; (Probes to Jupiter and beyond) So: 711
Jupiter [Roman god] J: 201
See also Zeus in this index
Diana D: 183
God (Cosmic Gods) G: 243
Juno J: 197
Mercury M: 417
Mythology (table) M: 981; (Roman divinities) M: 982
Quirinal Hill Q: 43
R R: 46
Thursday T: 273
Venus V: 310
Jupiter [rocket]
Rocket (High-altitude rockets) R: 390-391
Space exploration picture on So: 698
Voyager V: 451
Jupiter, Temple of
Pompeii (Remains) P: 654
Jupiter family comet
Meteor (The parent comet) M: 431
Jupiter Symphony [music by Mozart] See Symphony No. 41 in this index
Juppé, Alain [French political leader]
France (Socialists win power) F: 478
Jura [canton]
Switzerland (After the wars) So: 1061
Jura [mountains, Europe] J: 201
Switzerland (The Jura Mountains) So: 1054
Jurassic Park [book by Crichton]
Crichton, Michael Ci: 1130
Jurassic Park [film]
Animation (The computer revolution) A: 514c
Motion picture (The computer revolution) M: 872 with picture
Jurassic Period [geology] J: 201
Dinosaur (Kinds of dinosaurs) D: 206b
Earth (table) E: 30 with map
Forest picture on F: 398
Prehistoric animal (Birds) P: 738; (table) P: 739
Jurchen [people]
Manchus M: 135
Jurgen [book by Cabell]
Cabell, James Branch C: 3
Jurisdiction [law]
Government (Jurisdiction) G: 289
Jurisdictional strike [labor]
Labor movement (Handling labor disputes) L: 6-7
Strike (Kinds of strikes) So: 928
Taft-Hartley Act T: 13
Jurisprudence
Law (Ancient Roman law) L: 133
Jurisprudence, Doctor of [degree]
Law (Law education) L: 138
Lawyer L: 147
Jurist See Judge [office] in this index
Juror [law] See Jury in this index
Juruá River [river, Brazil]
Amazon River (The course of the Amazon) A: 403
Jury [law] J: 201
See also Trial in this index
Constitution of the United States (Article III, Section 2) Ci: 1009-1010; (Amendment 6) Ci: 1012; (Amendment 7) Ci: 1012
Court (How courts work) Ci: 1101
England (Struggles for power) E: 305
Grand jury G: 308
Henry II [of England] H: 185
Judge J: 183
Magna Carta (Promises in the charter) M: 53
Jury, Richard [literary character]
Grimes, Martha G: 393
Jus civile [Roman Empire]
Law (Ancient Roman law) L: 133-134
Jus gentium [Roman Empire]
Law (Ancient Roman law) L: 133-134
Rome, Ancient (The law) R: 438
Jus sanguinis [law]
Citizenship (Birth) Ci: 570; (U.S. citizenship laws) Ci: 571
Nationality N: 63
Jus soli [law]
Citizenship (Birth) Ci: 570
Nationality N: 63
Just, Ernest Everett [American biologist] J: 202
Just Around the Corner [film]
Temple, Shirley picture on T: 131
Just One Flick of the Finger [book by Lorbiecki]
Diaz, David D: 186
Just school
Moral education (Moral development) M: 799
Just So Stories [book by Kipling]
Kipling, Rudyard (Later career) K: 334

Just war
War (Ethical and legal aspects of war) W: 24
Juster, Norton [American architect]
Raschka, Chris R: 144 with picture
Justice [office]
Court of appeals Ci: 1105
Judge J: 183
Supreme Court of the United States (Membership) So: 998; (table) So: 1000
Justice [philosophy]
Ethics (Plato) E: 366
Law L: 130
Justice [play by Galsworthy]
Galsworthy, John G: 17
Justice, Department of [U.S.] J: 202 with picture
Antitrust laws A: 560
Federal Bureau of Investigation (Criminal investigation) F: 62
Immigration and Naturalization Service I: 86
Police (Federal law enforcement agencies) P: 622
Washington, D.C. map on W: 76
Justice, Minister of [office]
Attorney general A: 880
Justice, Palace of [Paris]
Paris (Famous buildings) P: 163-164 with map
Justice of the peace [office] J: 203
Breach of the peace B: 588
Justice Statistics, Bureau of [U.S.]
Police (Federal law enforcement agencies) P: 622
Justicialist Party
Argentina (Politics) A: 647; (Argentina under Perón) A: 657
Justifiable homicide [law]
Homicide H: 305
Justification [typography]
Linotype (How the linotype works) L: 338
Justification by faith [religion]
Luther, Martin (Justification by faith) L: 527
Lutherans (Doctrine) L: 529
Paul, Saint (Paul's letters and ideas) P: 201
Reformation (Martin Luther) R: 197
Justification by grace [religion]
Protestantism (Faith and grace) P: 834
Justin I [Byzantine emperor]
Justinian I J: 204
Justin the Martyr, Saint [Christian author] J: 204
Justine [book by Durrell]
Durrell, Lawrence D: 389
Justinian I [Byzantine emperor] J: 204
Byzantine Empire (The late Roman period) B: 753 with picture
Clothing picture on Ci: 701
Istanbul (History) I: 491
Italy (The Middle Ages) I: 513
Justinian Code J: 204
Law (Civil law systems) L: 132; (Ancient Roman law) L: 133-134
Plato (Plato's place in Western thought) P: 569
Rome (Early days) R: 434
Theodora T: 252
World, History of the (The Byzantine Empire) W: 434
Justinian Code [Roman law] J: 204
Civil law Ci: 607
Justinian I J: 204
Law (Civil law systems) L: 132; (Ancient Roman law) L: 133-134
Library (Medieval collections) L: 259
World, History of the (The Byzantine Empire) W: 434
Jute [fiber] J: 204
Materials (Biological materials) M: 300d
Rope (Natural-fiber rope) R: 473
Jute [plant]
Bangladesh (Agriculture) B: 84
Jute J: 204
Jutes [ancient people] J: 204
Anglo-Saxons A: 464 with map
England (The Germanic invasions) E: 304
Jutland [region]
Denmark D: 132; (The land) D: 137 with picture and map
Jutes J: 204
Jutland, Battle of [1916] J: 204
Battleship (The modern battleship) B: 172
Jellicoe, John Rushworth J: 89
Navy (World War I) N: 80
World War I (The war at sea) W: 460
Juvenal [Roman poet] J: 205
Latin literature (Early Latin literature) L: 115-116
Satire S: 150h
Juvenalian satire
Satire S: 150h
Juvenile [law]
Juvenile delinquency J: 205
Juvenile correctional institution
Prison (Juvenile correctional institutions) P: 806

Juvenile court [law] J: 205
Juvenile delinquency J: 205
 Adolescent (Delinquency) **A:** 64
 City (Social problems) **Ci:** 591
 Juvenile court J: 205
 Reformatory R: 199
Juvenile Delinquent Acts [1908]
 Juvenile court (In Canada) J: 205
Juvenile detention center
 Prison (Types of correctional institutions) P: 805
 Reformatory R: 199
Juvenile diabetes [disease] *See* Type 1 diabetes *in this index*
Juvenile officer
 Police (Juvenile work) P: 621
Juvenile water [geology]
 Mineral water M: 572
Juvigny, Sieur [French musician]
 Flageolet F: 224
JWB [organization]
 Jewish community centers J: 119

K

K [letter] **K: 207** *with pictures*
K [symbol]
 Potassium P: 710
K-gun [weapon]
 Depth charge D: 151
K. of C. [abbreviation]
 Knights of Columbus **K: 352** *with picture*
K2 [mountain, Kashmir] **K: 208**
 Mountain (table) **M: 896** *with diagram*
 Pakistan (Land and climate) P: 96
Kaaba [shrine, Mecca] **K: 208**
 Hajj H: 17
 Islam (The Five Pillars of Islam) **I: 463-464** *with picture*
 Mecca (The city) M: 352
 Muhammad (His religious life) M: 910
 Muslims (Before Muhammad) M: 964-964a
Ka`ba [shrine, Mecca] *See* Kaaba *in this index*
Kabaka [title]
 Ganda G: 24
 Uganda (History) U: 3-4
Kabalega Falls [Uganda]
 National park (table) N: 42f
 Nile River *picture on* N: 423
Kabat, Elvin A. [American biochemist]
 Immune system (Further breakthroughs) I: 88d
Kabbah, Ahmad Tejan [Sierra Leone political leader]
 Sierra Leone (History) S: 452
Kabbalah [religion] **K: 208**
 Hebrew literature (Medieval works) H: 162
 Jews (Jews in Christian Europe) J: 122-123
Kabila, Joseph [Congolese political leader]
 Congo, Democratic Republic of the (Cease-fires and power sharing) **Ci: 940c;** (New government) **Ci: 940d**
Kabila, Laurent Désiré [Congolese political leader]
 Congo, Democratic Republic of the (The fall of Mobutu) **Ci: 940c;** (Cease-fires and power sharing) **Ci: 940c**
Kabotie, Fred [American painter]
 Indian, American *picture on* I: 169
Kabui, Joseph [Papuan political leader]
 Papua New Guinea (History) P: 141
Kabuki [drama]
 Dance (Asian theatrical dance) D: 28-29
 Drama (Japan) **D: 336-337** *with picture*
 Japan (Theater) **J: 43** *with picture*
 Japanese literature (The Tokugawa period) J: 62
 Music (Japanese music) M: 956
Kabul [Afghanistan] **K: 208**
 Afghanistan **A: 92** *with picture*
Kabyè [people]
 Togo (People) **T: 309;** (History) T: 310-311
Kabyle [people]
 Berbers B: 256
Kachin [people]
 Myanmar (Early days) M: 970d
Kachina [ceremony] **K: 208**
 Indian, American *picture on* **I: 169;** (Ceremonies) I: 148
 Mask (Ceremonial masks) M: 264
 Pueblo Indians (Early history and way of life) P: 871
Kachina [doll]
 Doll (Dolls in religion) D: 288
 Hopi Indians H: 333
 Indian, American *picture on* I: 168
 Kachina K: 208
 Sculpture (The European impact) **S: 244** *with picture*
 United States *picture on* U: 116
Kachina mask
 Indian, American *picture on* I: 167

Kaczyński, Lech [Polish political leader]
 Poland (Recent developments) P: 615
Kaczynski, Theodore J. [American terrorist]
 Terrorism (Terrorist groups and movements) T: 178-179
Kádár, János [Hungarian political leader]
 Hungary (Beginnings of change) H: 448
Kadazan Harvest Festival
 May M: 320
Kadazans [people]
 Malaysia (People) M: 98b-98c
Kaddafi, Mu'ammar Muhammad al- [Libyan political leader] *See* Qadhâfî, Mu'ammar Muhammad al- *in this index*
Kaddish [prayer]
 Judaism (Special occasions) J: 182
Kaddoumi, Farouk [Palestinian political leader]
 Fatah F: 54
Kadesh, Battle of [1285 B.C.]
 Ramses II R: 134
Kadesh, Battle of [c. 1274 B.C.]
 Hittites (History) H: 269
Kadima [political party] **K: 208**
 Israel (Politics) **I: 479;** (The early 2000's) I: 489-490
 Olmert, Ehud O: 745
Kadohadacho Indians *See* Caddo Indians *in this index*
Kadohata, Cynthia [American author]
 Newbery Medal (table) N: 359
Kadooment Day [holiday]
 August A: 886
KADU [political party] *See* Kenya African Democratic Union *in this index*
Kadyrov, Akhmad [Chechen political leader]
 Chechnya C: 390
Kadyrov, Ramzan [Chechen political leader]
 Chechnya C: 390
 Russia (Recent developments) R: 555-556
Kaesong [North Korea]
 Korean War (The truce talks) K: 382
Kaffir [racial term]
 South Africa (Arrival of Europeans) So: 617-618
Kaffiyyeh [clothing]
 Arabs (Clothing) A: 588
 Jordan (Way of life) **J: 162-163** *with picture*
Kafir [food] K: 209
Kafka, Franz [Czech author] **K: 209** *with portrait*
 Expressionism (Expressionist writing) E: 455
 German literature (Expressionism) **G: 141-142**
 Novel (New directions in the novel) N: 573-574
Kaftan [garment] *See* Caftan *in this index*
Kagame, Paul [Rwandan political leader]
 Rwanda (History) R: 571-572
Kagan, Elena [American jurist] **K: 209**
 Obama, Barack (Kagan appointed) O: 640h
 Supreme Court of the United States *picture on* So: 999
Kagera River [Africa]
 Rwanda (Land) **R: 571** *with map*
Kagu [bird]
 Bird (Birds of the Pacific Islands) **B: 349** *with picture*
Kahlo, Frida [Mexican artist] **K: 209**
 Latin America (Painting) L: 99-100
 Painting (Modern Mexican painting) **P: 83** *with picture*
Kahn, Louis Isadore [American architect] **K: 209**
 Architecture (Architecture today) **A: 632-633** *with picture*
 Bangladesh *picture on* B: 79
Kahneman, Daniel [Israeli-born psychologist]
 Nobel Prizes (Economics: 2002) N: 449
Kahoolawe [island, Hawaii]
 Hawaii (Kahoolawe) H: 100
Kahului [Hawaii]
 Hawaii (Maui) H: 100
Kai-shek, Chiang [Chinese political leader] *See* Chiang Kai-shek *in this index*
Kaibab Plateau [Arizona]
 Balance of nature (Upsetting the balance) B: 36
Kaien Island [British Columbia]
 Prince Rupert P: 794
Kaieteur Fall [waterfall, Guyana]
 Guyana (Land) G: 446
 Waterfall (table: Famous waterfalls of the world) W: 143
Kaieteur National Park [Guyana]
 National park (table) N: 42g
Kailas, Mount [Tibet]
 Himalaya (Peaks) H: 233
Kain [clothing]
 Indonesia (Clothing) I: 229
Kainah Indians
 Blackfeet Indians B: 393
Kaine, Timothy M. [American political leader]
 Virginia (table) V: 417
Kaing Guek Eav [Cambodian political leader]

 Cambodia (History) C: 72-74
 Khmer Rouge K: 308b
Kainga [family]
 Pacific Islands (Food) P: 6
Kainji Dam [Nigeria]
 Niger River N: 409
Kainji Lake [Nigeria]
 Niger River N: 409
Kaiser [title] K: 210
Kaiser, Georg [German dramatist] **K: 210**
 Drama (Expressionism) D: 339
Kaiser, Henry John [American engineer] **K: 210**
Kaiser, Ray [American architect]
 Eames, Charles E: 6
Kaiser-Frazer Corporation
 Kaiser, Henry John K: 210
Kaiser Jeep Corporation
 Kaiser, Henry John K: 210
Kaiser Wilhelm Canal [Germany] *See* Kiel Canal *in this index*
Kaiser Wilhelm Memorial Church [Berlin]
 Berlin (Downtown Berlin) **B: 260-261** *with picture*
 Germany *picture on* G: 152
Kaiser Wilhelm Society
 Max Planck Society for the Advancement of Science M: 318
Kaivalya [religion]
 Yoga Y: 567
Kaka [bird]
 Bird *picture on* B: 348
 Parrot (Kinds of parrots) P: 179
Kakadu National Park [Australia]
 National park (Australia) **N: 42b;** (table) N: 42f; (The rights of original inhabitants) N: 42i
Kakapo [bird]
 Bird *picture on* B: 370
 Parrot (Kinds of parrots) P: 179
Kaki [tree]
 Persimmon **P: 300e** *with picture*
Kakiemon porcelain
 Porcelain (Oriental porcelain) P: 676
Kala-azar [disease] K: 210
Kalaallisut [language]
 Greenland (People) G: 384
Kalaallit [people]
 Greenland (People) G: 384
Kalaallit Nunaat [official name] *See* Greenland *in this index*
Kalahari Desert [region, Africa] **K: 210** *with map*
 Botswana (Land and climate) **B: 511-512** *with picture*
 San S: 83
 South Africa (The Namib and Kalahari deserts) So: 615 *with map*
Kalahari Gemsbok National Park [South Africa]
 National park (South Africa) **N: 42e;** (table) N: 42f
Kalakaua [king of Hawaii]
 Hawaii (Growth of constitutional government) H: 106-108
 Pearl Harbor (Pearl Harbor as a naval base) P: 219
Kalanga [people]
 Botswana (People) B: 511
Kalanianaole, Jonah Kuhio [American political leader]
 Hawaii (Statehood) H: 108
Kalaupapa National Historical Park [Hawaii]
 National Park System (table: National historical parks) N: 56-57
Kalb, Johann [German-American general] **K: 211**
Kale [plant] K: 211
Kaleidoscope [toy] **K: 211** *with pictures*
Kalevala [poem]
 Finland (The arts) **F: 112** *with picture;* (Control by Russia) F: 116
 Sibelius, Jean S: 443
Kali [Hindu goddess]
 Hinduism (Deities) **H: 236** *with picture*
 India (Hinduism) I: 116
 Thug T: 271
Kalidasa [Indian author]
 Gupta dynasty (Cultural life under the guptas) G: 442-443
 India (The golden age) I: 129
 Sanskrit literature (The Classical period) S: 112
Kalila and Dimna [book]
 Islamic art (Books) I: 470
Kalimantan [region, Borneo]
 Borneo (The land and its resources) B: 489
 Indonesia (The Greater Sunda Islands) **I: 233** *with map*
Kaline, Al [American baseball player]
 Baseball (table: Hall of Fame) B: 134a
Kalinga, Conquest of [history of India]
 Ashoka A: 769
 India (The Mauryan Empire) I: 128-129
Kaliningrad [Russia] K: 211
Kalita Humphreys Theater

Dallas (Cultural life) **D:** 14
Kálmán [king of Hungary]
Croatia (History) **Ci:** 1148a-1148b
Kalmar, Union of [1397]
Denmark (A great power) **D:** 139-140
Sweden (Union with Norway and Denmark)
So: 1033
Kalmia [plant]
Mountain laurel **M:** 898
Kalmus, Herbert T. [American engineer]
Technicolor **T:** 73
Kalogeropoulos, Cecilia Sophia Anna Maria
[birth name of]
Callas, Maria **C:** 67
Kaloko-Honokohau National Historical Park
[Hawaii]
National Park System (table: National historical
parks) **N:** 56-57
Kaltenbrunner, Ernst [German military leader]
Nuremberg Trials (The trials) **N:** 613
Kalua pig [food]
Hawaii (Food) **H:** 94
Kama [river, Russia]
Volga River **V:** 444
Kama [Hinduism]
Manu **M:** 168
Kamakura [Japan]
Buddhism *picture on* **B:** 668
Japan (Sculpture) **J:** 43 *with picture*
Kamakura period [Japanese history] **K:** 212
Sculpture (Japan) **S:** 239 *with picture*
Kamarinskaya [music by Glinka]
Glinka, Mikhail Ivanovich **G:** 231
Kamayura Indians
Indian, American *picture on* **I:** 176
Kamchatka Peninsula [region, Russia] **K:** 212
Exploration (The Russians in Siberia) **E:** 447
Russia (The East Siberian Uplands) **R:** 541 *with
map*
Kame [formation]
Glacier *diagram on* **G:** 204
Kameez [clothing]
India (Clothing) **I:** 117
Kamehameha I [king of Hawaii] **K:** 212
Hawaii (The kingdom of Hawaii) **H:** 106 *with
picture*
Honolulu (History) **H:** 322 *with picture*
Kamehameha II [king of Hawaii]
Hawaii (The kingdom of Hawaii) **H:** 106
Kamehameha III [king of Hawaii]
Hawaii (Schools) **H:** 94; (Growth of constitutional
government) **H:** 106
Kamehameha IV [king of Hawaii]
Hawaii (Growth of constitutional government)
H: 106-108
Kamehameha V [king of Hawaii]
Hawaii (Niihau) **H:** 102; (Growth of constitutional
government) **H:** 106-108
Kamen, Martin D. [American chemist]
Radiocarbon (Radiocarbon in biology) **R:** 98
Kamenev, Lev [Soviet political leader]
Union of Soviet Socialist Republics (Stalin gains
power) **U:** 36
Kamerlingh Onnes, Heike [Dutch physicist]
Nobel Prizes (Physics: 1913) **N:** 440
Superconductivity **So:** 992
Kamerun [former colony]
British Cameroons **B:** 611
Kamet, Mount [Asia]
Himalaya (Peaks) **H:** 233
Kami [religion]
Religion (Belief in a deity) **R:** 215
Shinto **S:** 401
Kamiakin [American Indian chief]
Washington (Territorial days) **W:** 66
Kamikaze [pilot] **K:** 212
World War II *picture on* **W:** 489; (The liberation of
the Philippines) **W:** 491
Kamloops [British Columbia] **K:** 212
British Columbia (Places to visit) **B:** 620
Kamouraska [book by Hébert]
Canadian literature (Modern literature: 1945 to
the present) **C:** 159-160
Kampala [Uganda] **K:** 212
Uganda *picture on* **U:** 3
Kampong [district]
Jakarta (The city) **J:** 22
Malaysia (Way of life) **M:** 98c
Kampuchea *See* Cambodia *in this index*
Kan, Naoto [Japanese political leader]
Japan (Recent developments) **J:** 59
Kana [symbol]
Japanese language **J:** 61
Kanaks [people] *See* Melanesians *in this index*
Kanamori, Hiroo [Japanese seismologist]
Moment magnitude **M:** 697
Kanawha [former name]

West Virginia (Civil War and statehood) **W:** 226-
228
Kanawha mine [West Virginia]
West Virginia (Labor developments) **W:** 229
Kanawha River [West Virginia] **K:** 212
Kanchenjunga, Mount *See* Mount Kanchenjunga
in this index
Kandahar [Afghanistan] **K:** 212
Kandel, Eric Richard [American biologist]
Nobel Prizes (Physiology or medicine: 2000)
N: 446
Kandinsky, Wassily [Russian painter] **K:** 213 *with
picture*
Painting (Expressionism) **P:** 78-79 *with picture*;
(Nonobjective painting in Russia) **P:** 79
Kändler, Johann [German sculptor]
Dresden china **D:** 347 *with picture*
Porcelain (German porcelain) **P:** 677 *with picture*
Kane, Bob [American cartoonist]
Batman **B:** 165
Kane, Paul [Canadian painter] **K:** 213
Indian, American *pictures on* **I:** 154, **I:** 155, **I:** 162,
I: 166
Minnesota *picture on* **M:** 603
Kanem [former empire] **K:** 213
Nigeria (Early kingdoms) **N:** 417
Kang [bed]
Furniture (China) **F:** 571
Kang Rimpoche [mountain, Tibet]
Himalaya (Peaks) **H:** 233
Kangaba [former state]
Mali Empire **M:** 109 *with map*
Sundiata Keita **So:** 990
Kangaroo K: 213 *with pictures*
Animal *picture on* **A:** 477
Australia *picture on* **A:** 915; (Native animals)
A: 911
Conservation (Australia) **Ci:** 989
Marsupial (Kinds of marsupials) **M:** 232
Kangaroo court [U.S. history] **K:** 215
Kangaroo rat [animal] **K:** 215 *with picture*
Animal *picture on* **A:** 482
Jerboa **J:** 92
Kanha National Park [India]
National park (table) **N:** 42f
Kania, Stanisław [Polish political leader]
Poland (Antigovernment protests) **P:** 614
Kanishka [Asian ruler] **K:** 215
Kanji [writing]
Writing system (Phonetization) **W:** 513
Kankan Mousa [Mali ruler] *See* Mansa Musa *in
this index*
Kannada [language]
Dravidians **D:** 342
Kannekuk [American Indian] *See* Kennekuk *in this
index*
Kanner, Leo [American psychiatrist]
Autism **A:** 941
Kannon Temple
Tokyo (Shrines and temples) **T:** 316
Kano, Jigoro [Japanese sportsman]
Judo (History) **J:** 185
Kano School [Japanese history]
Painting (Japanese painting) **P:** 47
Kanon [poetry]
Greek literature (Medieval literature) **G:** 378
Kanpur [India] **K:** 215
Kansa Indians K: 215
Kansas **K:** 216
Kansas City [Missouri] (History) **K:** 242
Kansai [dialect]
Japanese language **J:** 61
Kansai International Airport [Osaka]
Japan (Transportation) **J:** 51-52
Osaka **O:** 861
Kansan ice age [geology]
Ice age (Evidence of ice ages and their climates)
I: 6-7
Kansas K: 216 *with pictures and maps*
See also the list of *Related articles in the* Kansas
article
Brown, John (The abolitionist) **B:** 643
Buchanan, James (The struggle over slavery)
B: 660
Kansas-Nebraska Act **K:** 243
Missouri (The American Civil War) **M:** 671
United States *picture on* **U:** 121
United States, History of the (The "irrepressible
conflict") **U:** 176
Kansas, University of K: 240
Kansas (Museums) **K:** 221 *with picture*
Kansas City [Kansas] **K:** 240 *with picture*
Kansas City [Missouri] **K:** 240 *with picture and map*
Missouri (table: Average monthly weather)
M: 664
Pendergast, Thomas Joseph **P:** 236
United States, History of the *picture on* **U:** 170

Kansas City Board of Trade
Wheat (Buying and selling wheat) **W:** 274
Kansas City Chiefs [team]
Football (National Football League) **F:** 364
Kansas City Royals [team]
Baseball (table) **B:** 130
Kansas City Star [newspaper]
Nelson, William Rockhill **N:** 122
Kansas Cosmosphere and Space Center
[Hutchinson]
Kansas (Places to visit) **K:** 226 *with picture*
Kansas-Nebraska Act [1854] **K:** 243
African Americans (The deepening division over
slavery) **A:** 136h-136i *with picture*
Civil War, American (The Kansas-Nebraska Act)
Ci: 616; (Developments in the political party
system) **Ci:** 616
Democratic Party (The slavery issue) **D:** 124
Missouri Compromise **M:** 674
Nebraska (Territorial days) **N:** 112
Pierce, Franklin (The Kansas-Nebraska Act) **P:** 456
Popular sovereignty **P:** 672
Republican Party (Origin) **R:** 253
United States, History of the (The Kansas-
Nebraska Act) **U:** 175
Wisconsin (Statehood) **W:** 366
Kansas River
Kansas *picture on* **K:** 228; (Rivers and lakes) **K:** 230
Kant, Immanuel [German philosopher] **K:** 243
Ethics (Kant) **E:** 367
Existentialism (What is existentialism?) **E:** 437
Fichte, Johann Gottlieb **F:** 90
Germany (Literature and philosophy) **G:** 153
Idealism **I:** 46
Philosophy (The philosophy of Immanuel Kant)
P: 389; (Philosophy in the 1800's) **P:** 390
Political science (Liberalism) **P:** 639
Schopenhauer, Arthur **S:** 186
Kantemir, Antioch [Russian author]
Russian literature (Western influences) **R:** 559
Kantor, Mickey [American government official]
Clinton, Bill (table) **Ci:** 682d
Commerce, Department of (table) **Ci:** 671
Kantorovich, Leonid Vitaliyevich [Russian
economist]
Nobel Prizes (Economics: 1975) **N:** 449
Kantrowitz, Adrian [American doctor]
Heart (Development of heart surgery) **H:** 144-145
KANU [political party] *See* Kenya African National
Union *in this index*
Kanuri [people]
Niger (People) **N:** 407
Kao, Charles K. [American physicist]
Nobel Prizes (Physics: 2009) **N:** 442
Kaolin [clay] **K:** 244
Alumina **A:** 390
Clay **Ci:** 658
Feldspar **F:** 68
Macon **M:** 25
Porcelain **P:** 675
Pottery (Porcelain) **P:** 716
Kap [letter]
K **K:** 207 *with picture*
Kapiolani Park
Hawaii (Places to visit) **H:** 98
Kapital, Das [book by Marx]
Engels, Friedrich **E:** 283
Marx, Karl (Move to London) **M:** 237; *(Das Kapital)*
M: 237
Kapitsa, Pyotr [Soviet physicist]
Nobel Prizes (Physics: 1978) **N:** 441
Superfluid **So:** 993
Kaplan, Dora [Russian assassin]
Lenin, V. I. (Rule by terror) **L:** 194
Kaplan, Victor [Austrian inventor]
Turbine (History) **T:** 498-499
Kaplan turbine
Turbine (Water turbines) **T:** 497 *with pictures*
Kapok [fiber] **K:** 244 *with picture*
Forest products (Other forest products) **F:** 402-
403
Kapok tree
Kapok **K:** 244
Kapoor, Anish [Indian sculptor]
Sculpture (From the mid-1900's to the early
2000's) **S:** 259-260
Kaposi's sarcoma [disease]
AIDS (Opportunistic illness) **A:** 164a
Kappa [letter]
K **K:** 207 *with picture*
Kappa Alpha Society
Fraternity **F:** 495
Kappa Alpha Theta
Sorority **So:** 597
Kaprow, Allan [American artist]
Performance art **P:** 285
Kapuas Range

Borneo (The land and its resources) **B: 489** *with map*
Kapuas River
Borneo (The land and its resources) **B: 489** *with map*
Kara Sea [Arctic Ocean] **K: 244**
Exploration (The search for a northern passage) **E: 446**
Karabiner [tool]
Climbing (Technical climbing) **Ci: 680**
Mountain climbing (Basic mountaineering equipment and methods) **M: 897**
Karachi [Pakistan] **K: 244**
Muslims *picture on* **M: 966**
Pakistan **P: 92** *with picture*
Karadjordjević, Peter [king of Serbia] *See* Peter I *in this index*
Karadžić, Radovan [Serbian political leader]
Srebrenica massacre **So: 816**
Karagiye Depression [Kazakhstan]
Kazakhstan (Land and climate) **K: 250b** *with map*
Karajan, Herbert von [Austrian conductor] **K: 245**
Karakatsanis, Andromache [Canadian jurist]
Supreme Court of Canada (table) **So: 997** *with portrait*
Karakoram Range [mountains, India-Pakistan]
Himalaya **H: 233**
Karakul [animal] **K: 245**
Sheep *picture on* **S: 381**; (Coarse-wooled sheep) **S: 382**
Karakum [desert, Turkmenistan] **K: 245**
Turkmenistan (Land and climate) **T: 514a** *with map*
Karakum Canal [Turkmenistan]
Karakum **K: 245**
Karamanlis, Konstantinos [Greek political leader]
Greece (The 1950's) **G: 364**; (The restoration of democracy) **G: 365**
Karamanlis, Kostas [Greek political leader]
Greece (Recent developments) **G: 365**
Karami, Rashid [Lebanese political leader]
Lebanon (War and terrorism) **L: 173**
Karamojong [people]
Uganda (People) **U: 2-3**
Karamu [feast]
Kwanzaa **K: 398**
Karamu House
Cleveland (The arts) **Ci: 665**
Karamzin, Nikolai [Russian author]
Russian literature (Sentimentalism) **R: 560**
Karan, Donna [American fashion designer] **K: 245**
Karanga [people]
Zimbabwe (History) **Z: 592-593**
Karat [measurement]
See also Carat *in this index*
Carat **C: 202**
Gold (Gold alloys) **G: 251**
Weights and measures (Miscellaneous weights and measures) **W: 184**
Karate [sport] **K: 245** *with picture*
Martial arts **M: 234**
Karatepe-Aslantas National Park [Turkey]
National park (table) **N: 42f**
Karelia [republic, Russia] **K: 246**
Finland (The new republic) **F: 117**; (World War II) **F: 117-118**
Karelian Isthmus [region, Soviet Union]
Russo-Finnish wars (The Winter War) **R: 566a**
Karen [people]
Myanmar (Early days) **M: 970d**
Karenga, Maulana [American educator]
Kwanzaa **K: 397**
Kariba Dam [Zambezi River]
Zambezi River **Z: 584**
Zambia **Z: 584**
Zimbabwe (Economy) **Z: 592**
Kariba Lake [Zambia-Zimbabwe]
Zambia **Z: 584**
Zimbabwe (Economy) **Z: 592**
Karimov, Islam [Uzbek political leader]
Uzbekistan (History) **U: 254**
Kariye Camii, Church of [Istanbul]
Byzantine art (Frescoes and mosaics) **B: 750-751** *with picture*
Karl-Franzens University
Graz **G: 335**
Karl-Marx-Stadt [Germany] *See* Chemnitz *in this index*
Karl Marx University [Leipzig]
Germany (Education) **G: 151**
Karl of Hohenzollern [German prince] *See* Carol I *in this index*
Karle, Jerome [American chemist]
Nobel Prizes (Chemistry: 1985) **N: 444**
Karlfeldt, Erik Axel [Swedish author]
Nobel Prizes (Literature: 1931) **N: 447**
Karloff, Boris [British actor] **K: 246**

Karlovy Vary [Czech Republic] **K: 246**
Czech Republic (The Bohemian Mountains) **Ci: 1211**
Karlowitz, Treaty of [1699]
Croatia (History) **Ci: 1148a-1148b**
Karlsbad [Czech Republic] *See* Karlovy Vary *in this index*
Karlskirche [church]
Vienna (The city) **V: 361-362**
Karluk [ship]
Bartlett, Robert Abram **B: 121**
Karma [religion] **K: 247**
Hell **H: 177**
Hinduism (Reincarnation and karma) **H: 236**
Reincarnation **R: 208**
Witchcraft (Role of magic) **W: 372**
Karman, Tawakul [Yemeni political leader]
Nobel Prizes (Peace: 2011) **N: 449**
Karnak, Temple of [Egypt]
Hatshepsut **H: 86**
Seti I **S: 323**
Sphinx (Egyptian sphinxes) **So: 780**
Thutmose III **T: 274**
Karolinska Institute [Sweden]
Nobel Prizes **N: 439**
Károlyi, Mihály [Hungarian political leader]
Hungary (Between world wars) **H: 446**
Karoo [region, South Africa]
South Africa (The Cape Mountains Region) **So: 615** *with map*
Karpov, Anatoly [Russian chess player]
Chess *picture on* **C: 412**; (World chess champions) **C: 414**; (History) **C: 414**
Kasparov, Garry **K: 248**
Karrer, Paul [Swiss chemist]
Nobel Prizes (Chemistry: 1937) **N: 443**
Karsh, Yousuf [Canadian photographer] **K: 247**
Karst [region, Slovenia]
Slovenia (Land and climate) **S: 511**
Karstens, Harry P. [American mountain climber]
Mount McKinley **M: 886**
Kart racing [sport] **K: 247**
Automobile racing (Other kinds of racing) **A: 978**
Karume, Sheik Abeid [Tanzanian political leader]
Tanzania (The united republic and socialism) **T: 35**
Karyotype [genetics]
Down syndrome **D: 316**
Karzai, Hamid [Afghan political leader] **K: 247** *with portrait*
Afghanistan (Government) **A: 92-92a**; (Recent developments) **A: 96** *with picture*
Kasai [province, Democratic Republic of the Congo]
Congo, Democratic Republic of the (Civil disorder) **Ci: 940c**
Kasavubu, Joseph [Congolese political leader]
Congo, Democratic Republic of the (Independence) **Ci: 940b-940c**
Käsebier, Gertrude [American photographer]
Photography (Artistic advances) **P: 424-425**
Kasem, George A. [American political leader]
Arab Americans (Arab American accomplishments) **A: 580b**
Kasha [food]
Buckwheat **B: 665**
Kashi [India] *See* Varanasi *in this index*
Kashmir [region, Asia] **K: 247**
India (Independence and partition) **I: 133**; (India under Indira Gandhi) **I: 133-134**; (Religious and ethnic unrest) **I: 134**; (Recent developments) **I: 134-135**
Pakistan (Independence) **P: 99**; (Struggle for democracy) **P: 100**
Kasich, John [American political leader]
Ohio (table) **O: 699**
Kasimdzhanov, Rustam [Uzbek chess player]
Chess (World chess champions) **C: 414**
Kaskaskia [Illinois]
Illinois (Early national period) **I: 72-74**
Kasner, Angela Dorothea [birth name of]
Merkel, Angela **M: 417**
Kasparov, Garry [Russian chess player] **K: 248**
Artificial intelligence **A: 760**
Chess *picture on* **C: 412**; (World chess champions) **C: 414**; (History) **C: 414**
Kass, Deborah [American artist]
Painting (Postmodernism) **P: 88**
Kassebaum, Nancy Landon [American political leader] **K: 249**
Kassem, Abdul Karim [Iraqi political leader]
Hussein, Saddam **H: 458**
Iraq (The republic) **I: 414**
Kasserine Pass [Tunisia]
World War II (The Tunisia Campaign) **W: 481-482**
Kassites [ancient people]
Babylonia (The dynasties of Babylon) **B: 14**

Kastler, Alfred [French physicist]
Nobel Prizes (Physics: 1966) **N: 441**
Kastrup Airport [Copenhagen]
Denmark (Transportation) **D: 139**
Kata [sports]
Judo (Judo contests) **J: 185**
Karate (Karate styles) **K: 246**
Katabatic wind
Southern Ocean (Winds) **So: 688a**
Kataev, Valentin [Russian author]
Russian literature (The period of industrial literature) **R: 564**
Katainen, Jyrki [Finnish political leader]
Finland (Recent developments) **F: 118**
Katakana
Japanese language **J: 61**
Writing system (Phonetization) **W: 513**
Katamewaza
Judo (Judo techniques) **J: 185**
Katanga [former province]
Cold War (Africa) **Ci: 768**
Congo, Democratic Republic of the (Civil disorder) **Ci: 940c**; (Rebuilding the nation) **Ci: 940c**
Katchina [ceremony] *See* Kachina *in this index*
Katcina [ceremony] *See* Kachina *in this index*
Katerina Ismailova [opera by Shostakovich]
Shostakovich, Dimitri **S: 436**
Kathak [dance]
Dance (Asian theatrical dance) **D: 28-29**
India (Music and dance) **I: 120-121**
Kathakali [dance]
Dance (Asian theatrical dance) **D: 28-29**
Katharevousa [language]
Greek language (Later developments) **G: 376-377**
Greek literature (Modern Greek literature) **G: 378**
Katherine [literary figure]
Shakespeare, William: (The Taming of the Shrew) **S: 356**
Kathina [festival]
Feasts and festivals (In Buddhism) **F: 58**
Kathmandu [Nepal] **K: 249**
Nepal (People) **N: 125-126** *with picture*
Katipunan [political group]
Philippines (Revolt against the Spaniards) **P: 379-380**
Rizal, José **R: 357**
Katmai National Park [Alaska] **K: 249**
National Park System (table: National parks) **N: 48**
Katmai National Preserve [Alaska]
National Park System (table: National preserves) **N: 58**
Katmandu [Nepal] *See* Kathmandu *in this index*
Katowice [Poland]
Poland (Land regions) **P: 608**
Katrina, Hurricane *See* Hurricane Katrina *in this index*
Katydid [insect] **K: 249**
Grasshopper *picture on* **G: 327**; (Long-horned grasshoppers) **G: 328**
Insect *pictures on* **I: 280, I: 291**
Katyn Massacre [European history] **K: 249**
Katz, Sir Bernard [British physiologist]
Nobel Prizes (Physiology or medicine: 1970) **N: 446**
Katz v. United States [U.S. history]
Wiretapping (Laws concerning wiretapping) **W: 345**
Katzenbach, Nicholas deBelleville [American government official]
Johnson, Lyndon Baines (table) **J: 151**
Justice, Department of (table) **J: 203**
Katzenberg, Jeffrey [American businessman]
Spielberg, Steven **So: 792**
KAU [political party]
Kenya (Opposition to the British) **K: 303**
Kauai [island, Hawaii]
Hawaii (Kauai) **H: 102**
Kauffmann, Angelica [Swiss-born painter] **K: 249**
Kaufman, George S. [American dramatist] **K: 250**
Ferber, Edna **F: 72**
Hart, Moss **H: 77**
Kaufman, Irving [American jurist]
Rosenberg, Julius and Ethel **R: 479**
Kaufmann Fallingwater house *See* Fallingwater house *in this index*
Kaumualii [Hawaiian ruler]
Hawaii (The kingdom of Hawaii) **H: 106**
Kaunakes [clothing]
Clothing *picture on* **Ci: 696**
Kaunas [Lithuania] **K: 250**
Kaunda, Kenneth David [Zambian political leader] **K: 250**
Zambia (History) **Z: 585-586**
Kaunitz, Wenzel Anton von [Austrian statesman]
Maria Theresa **M: 199**
Seven Years' War (In Europe) **S: 328**

Kauravas [legendary figures]
  Mahabharata **M: 64**
Kauri [tree]
  New Zealand (Plant life) **N: 353**
Kava [drink]
  Fiji (People) **F: 98**
  Kava **K: 250**
  Pacific Islands (Food) **P: 6**
Kava [shrub] **K: 250**
Kavaic acid [juice]
  Kava **K: 250**
Kavanagh, Edward [American political leader]
  Maine (table) **M: 87**
Kavanagh, Patrick [Irish poet]
  Irish literature (Poetry) **I: 433**
Kaw Indians See Kansa Indians in this index
Kaw-Kaw [former kingdom]
  Songhai Empire **So: 593**
Kaw River See Kansas River in this index
Kawabata, Yasunari [Japanese author]
  Japanese literature (The modern period) **J: 62**
  Nobel Prizes (Literature: 1968) **N: 448**
Kawaii style
  Clothing (Japan) **Ci: 699**
Kawasaki disease [disease] **K: 250**
Kay, John [British inventor]
  Cotton (In England) **Ci: 1092**
  Hargreaves, James **H: 60**
  Industrial Revolution (Weaving machines) **I: 249**
  Invention (Economic needs) **I: 355**
Kayak [boat]
  Kayaking **K: 250** with picture
  Greenland (People) **G: 384-385** with picture
  Inuit picture on **I: 354d**; (Transportation) **I: 354c** with pictures
Kayak Island
  Exploration (The Russians in Siberia) **E: 447**
Kayaking [sport] **K: 250** with picture
  Olympic Games (Summer Olympic Games) **O: 746e-746f**
Kayapó Indians
  Indian, American picture on **I: 183**
Kaye, Danny [American entertainer] **K: 250a**
Kaye, Nora [American dancer] **K: 250a**
Kayibanda, Grégoire [Rwandese political leader]
  Rwanda (History) **R: 571**
Kayuga [spacecraft]
  Moon (Recent exploration) **M: 795**
Kazakhs [people]
  China (Nationalities) **C: 481**
  Kazakhstan (People) **K: 250b**
  Union of Soviet Socialist Republics (People) **U: 31**
Kazakhstan K: 250a
  Almaty **A: 379**
  Astana **A: 823**
  Flag picture on **F: 203**
  Russia (The new nation) **R: 555**
  Strategic Arms Reduction Treaty **So: 919**
Kazan [Russia] **K: 252**
Kazan, Elia [American director] **K: 252**
  Motion picture (Best achievement in directing: 1947, 1954) **M: 862**
Kazantzakis, Nikos [Greek author] **K: 252**
Kazembe [former kingdom]
  Lunda **L: 523**
Kaziranga National Park [India]
  National park (table) **N: 42f**
Kazmaier, Dick [American football player]
  Football (table) **F: 363**
KBO [astronomy] See Kuiper belt object in this index
KC-10 [aircraft]
  Air Force, United States picture on **A: 192**
  Aircraft, Military (Tankers) **A: 203** with picture
KC-135 [aircraft]
  Aircraft, Military (Tankers) **A: 203**
KCA tribes
  Kiowa Indians **K: 333**
KDKA [radio station, Pittsburgh]
  Journalism (Radio journalism) **J: 175**
  Radio (The start of broadcasting) **R: 92**
  Westinghouse Electric Corporation **W: 242**
Kea [bird] **K: 252**
  Bird picture on **B: 348**
  Parrot (Kinds of parrots) **P: 179**
  Sheep (Enemies of sheep) **S: 383**
Kealakekua Bay
  Hawaii (Places to visit) **H: 98**
Kean, Edmund [English actor] **K: 252**
Kean, Thomas H. [American political leader]
  Bush, George Walker (Homeland security) **B: 722g**
  New Jersey (table) **N: 249**
  September 11 terrorist attacks (Investigations) **S: 310b**
Keane, John B. [Irish dramatist]
  Irish literature (Drama) **I: 432**
Kearney, Denis [American labor leader]

Immigration (The second wave) **I: 82**
Kearny, Philip [American general] **K: 252**
Kearny, Stephen Watts [American general] **K: 253**
  Mexican War (The occupation of New Mexico and California) **M: 446**
Kearsarge [ship]
  Alabama **A: 255** with picture
Kearsarge, Mount
  New Hampshire (Mountains) **N: 220** with map
Keating, Frank [American political leader]
  Oklahoma (table) **O: 730**
Keating, Geoffrey [Irish author]
  Irish literature (Modern works in Gaelic) **I: 431**
Keating, Paul [Australian political leader]
  Australia (table) **A: 923**; (Political upheavals) **A: 925**
Keating, William H. [American explorer]
  Minnesota (The Louisiana Purchase) **M: 603-604**
Keaton, Buster [American actor] **K: 253** with picture
Keaton, Diane [American actress]
  Motion picture (Best performance by an actress: 1977) **M: 862**
Keats, Ezra Jack [American artist]
  Caldecott Medal (table: 1963) **C: 26**
  Literature for children picture on **L: 369**
Keats, John [British poet] **K: 253**
  Chapman, George **C: 377**
  English literature (Romantic poetry) **E: 320**
  Poetry (Imagery) **P: 595**
Kebara Cave [Israel]
  Prehistoric people (The single origin theory) **P: 750-751**
Keble, John [British religious leader]
  Oxford Movement **O: 888**
Kebnekaise, Mount
  Sweden (The Mountain Range) **So: 1028** with map
Keck Foundation, W. M. [organization]
  Foundation (Science and technology) **F: 431**
Keck Interferometer [instrument]
  Keck Observatory **K: 254**
Keck Observatory [Hawaii] **K: 254**
  Mauna Kea **M: 313**
  Observatory (Ground-based observatories) **O: 644-645** with picture
  Telescope picture on **T: 109**; (Reflecting telescopes) **T: 104-105**
Kedesh [ancient city]
  Cities of refuge **Ci: 568**
Kedrova, Lila [Russian-French actress]
  Motion picture (Best performance by an actress in a supporting role: 1964) **M: 862b**
Keech, Ray [American race driver]
  Automobile racing (table: Indianapolis 500 winners) **A: 980**
Keefe, Tim [American baseball player]
  Baseball (table: Hall of Fame) **B: 134a**
Keek-wilie house
  British Columbia (Early days) **B: 628**
Keel [ship]
  Sailing (Hull) **S: 23**; (Controlling direction) **S: 25**
  Ship (Basic structure) **S: 403-404**; (Sailing ships) **S: 406**
  Vikings (The Vikings as shipbuilders) **V: 381**
Keel-billed toucan [bird]
  Bird (Birds of Central and South America) **B: 344a** with picture
  Rain forest picture on **R: 126c**
Keelboat [boat]
  Flatboat **F: 228**
  Lewis and Clark expedition (Preparation) **L: 222a**
Keeler, Wee Willie [American baseball player]
  Baseball (table: Hall of Fame) **B: 134a**; (Early strategy and stars) **B: 134b**
Keeler, William H. [American religious leader]
  Cardinal (table: American cardinals) **C: 211**
Keenan, Philip C. [American astronomer]
  Star (The Hertzsprung-Russell diagram) **So: 845-846**
Keene, Carolyn [pen name] **K: 254**
  Stratemeyer, Edward **So: 920**
Keep [defense]
  Castle (Structure) **C: 280**
Keeper [occupation]
  Zoo (Caring for zoo animals) **Z: 602**
Keeshond [dog] **K: 254**
  Dog picture on **D: 275**
Kefauver, Estes [American political leader] **K: 254**
  Television (Early programs) **T: 118**
  Tennessee (The mid-1900's) **T: 156** with picture
Kegel exercise
  Incontinence **I: 106**
Keglers [sport]
  Bowling (Modern forms of bowling) **B: 524b**
Keikogi [uniform]
  Karate (Karate training) **K: 245-246**
Keillor, Garrison [American humorist] **K: 254**

Keita, Modibo [Malian political leader]
  Mali (History) **M: 108-109**
Keitel, Wilhelm [German military leader]
  Nuremberg Trials (The trials) **N: 613**
  World War II picture on **W: 497**
Keith, Harold Verne [American author]
  Newbery Medal (table) **N: 359**
Keizersgracht [canal]
  Amsterdam (The city) **A: 443-444** with picture
Kejimkujik Lake
  Nova Scotia (Rivers and lakes) **N: 562-564**
Kejimkujik National Park and National Historic Site
  Canada (table: National parks and national park reserves) **C: 113**
  Nova Scotia picture on **N: 561**
Kékes, Mount
  Hungary (The land) **H: 442** with map
Kekkonen, Urho Kaleva [Finnish political leader]
  Finland (Postwar developments) **F: 118**; (The late 1900's) **F: 118**
Kekuku, Joseph [Hawaiian musician]
  Hawaii (Dancing and music) **H: 94**
Kekulé von Stradonitz, Friedrich August [German chemist]
  Benzene **B: 255**
  Chemistry (Development of organic chemistry) **C: 404**
Kell, George [American baseball player]
  Baseball (table: Hall of Fame) **B: 134a**
Kellar, Harry [American magician]
  Magician (Illusions) **M: 51-52**
Keller, Gottfried [Swiss author] **K: 254**
  German literature (Realism) **G: 141**
Keller, Helen [American public figure] **K: 255** with picture
  Alabama (Places to visit) **A: 266**
  American literature (Nonfiction writers) **A: 420**
  Autograph picture on **A: 943**
  Sullivan, Anne Mansfield **So: 968**
Keller Endowment Fund
  Keller, Helen (She helps others) **K: 255**
Kelley, Clarence M. [American government official]
  Federal Bureau of Investigation (History) **F: 62**
Kelley, Florence [American social reformer] **K: 255**
  Hull House **H: 412**
  Wald, Lillian D. **W: 7**
Kelley, Joe [American baseball player]
  Baseball (table: Hall of Fame) **B: 134a**
Kelley, Larry [American football player]
  Football (table) **F: 363**
Kelley, Oliver Hudson [American government official]
  Grange, National **G: 310**
Kelleys Island [Lake Erie]
  Ohio (Places to visit) **O: 690**
Kellogg, Frank Billings [American political leader] **K: 256**
  Kellogg-Briand Pact **K: 256**
Kellogg, John Harvey [American businessman]
  Battle Creek **B: 172**
  Health food (History) **H: 129**
  Michigan (Interesting facts) **M: 489**
Kellogg, Steven [author]
  Regina Medal (table: 1989) **R: 206**
Kellogg, W. K. [American businessman] **K: 256**
  Battle Creek **B: 172**
  Health food (History) **H: 129**
  Kellogg Foundation **K: 256**
  Michigan (Interesting facts) **M: 489**
Kellogg, William P. [American political leader]
  Louisiana (table) **L: 496**
Kellogg Bird Sanctuary
  Michigan (Places to visit) **M: 498**
Kellogg-Briand Pact [1928] **K: 256**
  Briand, Aristide **B: 597**
  France (Between World Wars) **F: 475**
  International law (After World War I) **I: 342**
Kellogg Company
  Battle Creek **B: 172**
Kellogg Foundation K: 256
  Foundation (table) **F: 430**
Kells, Book of See Book of Kells in this index
Kelly [ship]
  Mountbatten, Louis **M: 899**
Kelly, Dan [Australian outlaw]
  Kelly, Ned **K: 257**
Kelly, Edward [Australian outlaw] See Kelly, Ned in this index
Kelly, Ellsworth [American artist]
  Painting (Abstract artists) **P: 88**
Kelly, Eric Philbrook [American author]
  Newbery Medal (table) **N: 359**
Kelly, Eugene Curran See Kelly, Gene in this index
Kelly, Gene [American dancer] **K: 256**
Kelly, George [American baseball player]
  Baseball (table: Hall of Fame) **B: 134a**

Kelly, George Edward [American dramatist] **K: 256**
Kelly, George "Machine Gun" [American criminal]
　Federal Bureau of Investigation (History) **F: 62**
Kelly, Grace [American actress] **K: 256**
　Monaco (History) **M: 700**
　Motion picture (Best performance by an actress:
　　1954) **M: 862**
　Rainier III **R: 129**
Kelly, Harry F. [American political leader]
　Michigan (table) **M: 507**
Kelly, J. D. [Canadian painter]
　Macdonald, Sir John Alexander *picture on* **M: 8**
Kelly, King [American baseball player]
　Baseball (table: Hall of Fame) **B: 134a**; (Early
　　strategy and stars) **B: 134b**
Kelly, Ned [Australian outlaw] **K: 257**
　Australia (Language) **A: 900**
Kelly, Sharon Pratt [American political leader]
　K: 257 *with portrait*
Kelly, William [American metallurgist]
　Iron and steel (The birth of modern steelmaking)
　　I: 450
Kelly Air Force Base [Texas]
　Lackland Air Force Base **L: 22**
Kelly Air Mail Act [1925]
　Aviation (Aviation progress) **A: 988**
Kelly gang [Australian criminals]
　Kelly, Ned **K: 257**
Kelmscott Chaucer [book]
　Book *picture on* **B: 464**
Kelmscott Press
　Book *picture on* **B: 464**; (The 1800's) **B: 467-468**
　Morris, William **M: 817**
Keloid [disorder] **K: 257**
　Scar **S: 172**
Kelp [plant] **K: 257** *with picture*
　Algae (Kinds of algae) **A: 349**
　Balance of nature (Upsetting the balance) **B: 36**
　Ocean *pictures on* **O: 651, O: 656**; (The
　　importance of the ocean) **O: 654**
　Seaweed (Kinds) **S: 276** *with picture*
Kelp gull [bird]
　Gull (Kinds of gulls) **G: 439**
Kelsey, Henry [British explorer]
　Manitoba (Newcomers) **M: 160**
　Saskatchewan *picture on* **S: 145**; (The coming of
　　the fur traders) **S: 146**
Kelso, Jack [American frontiersman]
　Lincoln, Abraham (Life on his own) **L: 314**
Keltic *See* Celtic language *in this index*
Kelvin, Lord [British physicist] **K: 258**
　Cable (Telegraph cables) **C: 5-6**
　Physics (Developments in the 1800's) **P: 440**
Kelvin scale [temperature]
　Gas [physics] (Gas laws) **G: 48-49**
　Kelvin, Lord **K: 258**
　Metric system (Structure of the metric system)
　　M: 437; (Heat) **M: 440**
　Star (Color and temperature) **So: 843**
　Sun **So: 975**
　Temperature **T: 130**
Kemakeza, Sir Allan [Solomon Islands political
　leader]
　Solomon Islands (History) **So: 585-586**
Kemal Atatürk *See* Atatürk, Kemal *in this index*
Kemari [game]
　Religion *picture on* **R: 222**
Kemble, Fanny [British actress] **K: 258**
Kemet [name for]
　Egypt, Ancient **E: 135**
Kemijoki [river, Finland]
　Finland (Rivers) **F: 114**
Kemp, Jack French [American political leader]
　K: 258
Kemp, Will [English actor]
　Shakespeare, William (Acting companies)
　　S: 352-353
Kempe, C. Henry [American doctor]
　Child abuse **C: 455**
Kempenland [region]
　Belgium (The Kempenland) **B: 230**
Kemper, James L. [American political leader]
　Virginia (table) **V: 417**
Kempis, Thomas à [German author]
　Thomas à Kempis **T: 262**
Kemp's ridley sea turtle
　Endangered species (table) **E: 270**
　Sea turtle (Types) **S: 262b**
　Turtle (Sea turtles) **T: 522**
Kempthorne, Dirk Arthur [American political
　leader]
　Idaho (table) **I: 42**
　Interior, Department of the (table) **I: 325**
Kenai Fjords National Park [Alaska] **K: 258**
　National Park System (table: National parks) **N: 48**
Kendall, Amos [American political leader]
　Jackson, Andrew (table) **J: 11**

Kitchen Cabinet K: 337
Kendall, Edward Calvin [American biochemist]
　Nobel Prizes (Physiology or medicine: 1950)
　　N: 445
Kendall, George W. [American publisher]
　War correspondent **W: 26**
Kendall, Henry Way [American physicist] **K: 258**
　Nobel Prizes (Physics: 1990) **N: 442**
Kendall, N. E. [American political leader]
　Iowa (table) **I: 391**
Kendrew, Sir John Cowdery [British physicist]
　K: 259
　Nobel Prizes (Chemistry: 1962) **N: 443**
Kendrick, John B. [American political leader]
　Wyoming (table) **W: 532**
Keneally, Thomas [Australian author] **K: 259**
　Australia (Literature) **A: 904-905**
Kenekuk [American Indian] *See* Kennekuk *in this
　index*
Kennan, George Frost [American diplomat] **K: 259**
Kennebec River [river, Maine]
　Maine (Rivers and lakes) **M: 82**
Kennebunkport [Maine]
　Maine *picture on* **M: 84**
Kennedy, Anthony McLeod [American jurist]
　K: 259
　Supreme Court of the United States *picture on*
　　So: 999
Kennedy, Cape *See* Cape Canaveral *in this index*
Kennedy, Caroline [daughter of John F. Kennedy]
　See Schlossberg, Caroline Kennedy *in this index*
Kennedy, Edward Moore [American political
　leader] **K: 259** *with portrait*
　Kennedy, John Fitzgerald (Boyhood) **K: 260-261**
Kennedy, Eunice [sister of John F. Kennedy] *See*
　Shriver, Eunice Kennedy *in this index*
Kennedy, George [American actor]
　Motion picture (Best performance by an actor in
　　a supporting role: 1967) **M: 862b**
Kennedy, Jacqueline Lee Bouvier [wife of John
　F. Kennedy] *See* Onassis, Jacqueline Kennedy *in
　this index*
Kennedy, Jean [sister of John F. Kennedy] *See*
　Smith, Jean Kennedy *in this index*
Kennedy, John Fitzgerald [U.S. president] **K: 260**
　with pictures
　Affirmative action **A: 91**
　African Americans (The growing movement)
　　A: 136o-136p
　Alliance for Progress **A: 375**
　Arlington National Cemetery **A: 717**
　Bay of Pigs invasion **B: 176**
　Cabinet (Membership) **C: 3**
　Clinton, Bill (School life) **Ci: 682b** *with picture*
　Cold War *picture on* **Ci: 762**; (The Cuban missile
　　crisis) **Ci: 768**; (Easing Cold War tensions)
　　Ci: 769
　Consumer protection (Growth of the movement)
　　Ci: 1019
　Cuba (The Cuban missile crisis) **Ci: 1178**
　Cuban missile crisis **Ci: 1180**
　Dallas (Landmarks) **D: 11**
　Debate (Political debate) **D: 63**
　Democratic Party (The New Frontier) **D: 127**
　Great Society (Development) **G: 349**
　Guantánamo **G: 411**
　Johnson, Lyndon Baines **J: 144**; (Vice President)
　　J: 148
　Journalism (Television journalism) **J: 175**
　March on Washington **M: 196**
　Massachusetts (The mid-1900's) **M: 293**
　Nixon, Richard Milhous (Defeat by Kennedy)
　　N: 431 *with picture*
　Onassis, Jacqueline Kennedy **O: 761**
　Oswald, Lee Harvey **O: 869**
　Peace Corps (History) **P: 208**
　Pearson, Lester Bowles *picture on* **P: 223**
　President of the United States *picture on* **P: 767**
　Space exploration (Apollo: Mission to the moon)
　　So: 714
　Television (The 1960's) **T: 119**
　Texas (The mid-1900's) **T: 208-209**
　Union of Soviet Socialist Republics (Relations
　　with the United States) **U: 39**
　United States, History of the (The civil rights
　　movement) **U: 196a**
　Vietnam War (The Viet Cong rebellion) **V: 374**
　Warren Report **W: 37**
　West Virginia (An era of change) **W: 229**
　White House (Rebuilding and redecorating)
　　W: 290
　World, History of the *picture on* **W: 448a**
Kennedy, John Fitzgerald, Jr. [son of John F.
　Kennedy]
　Kennedy, John Fitzgerald *picture on* **K: 265**;
　　(Kennedy's family) **K: 262**
　Kennedy, Joseph Patrick (His family) **K: 269-270**

　Onassis, Jacqueline Kennedy **O: 761**
Kennedy, John Pendleton [American government
　official]
　Fillmore, Millard (table) **F: 102**
　Poe, Edgar Allan (Poe's life) **P: 589**
Kennedy, Joseph P., II [American political leader]
　Kennedy, Joseph Patrick (His family) **K: 269**
Kennedy, Joseph P., Jr. [brother of John F.
　Kennedy]
　Kennedy, John Fitzgerald (Boyhood) **K: 260**
　Kennedy, Joseph Patrick (His family) **K: 269**
Kennedy, Joseph Patrick [American financier]
　K: 269
　Kennedy, John Fitzgerald (Family background)
　　K: 260
Kennedy, Joseph William [American chemist]
　Plutonium **P: 581**
Kennedy, Kathleen [sister of John F. Kennedy]
　Kennedy, John Fitzgerald (Boyhood) **K: 260-261**
　Kennedy, Joseph Patrick (His family) **K: 269**
Kennedy, Patricia [sister of] *See* Lawford, Patricia
　Kennedy *in this index*
Kennedy, Patrick [American political leader]
　Kennedy, Joseph Patrick (His family) **K: 269-270**
Kennedy, Patrick [great-grandfather of]
　Kennedy, John Fitzgerald (Family background)
　　K: 260
Kennedy, Patrick J. [grandfather of]
　Kennedy, John Fitzgerald (Family background)
　　K: 260
Kennedy, Robert Francis [American political
　leader] **K: 270**
　Freedom riders **F: 509**
　Johnson, Lyndon Baines (The widening Vietnam
　　War) **J: 150-151**
　Kennedy, John Fitzgerald *picture on* **K: 263**;
　　(Boyhood) **K: 260-261**
Kennedy, Rose Fitzgerald [mother of John F.
　Kennedy]
　Kennedy, John Fitzgerald (Family background)
　　K: 260
　Kennedy, Joseph Patrick (His family) **K: 269**
Kennedy, Rosemary [sister of John F. Kennedy]
　Kennedy, John Fitzgerald (Boyhood) **K: 260-261**
　Kennedy, Joseph Patrick (His family) **K: 269**
Kennedy, Ted [American political leader] *See*
　Kennedy, Edward Moore *in this index*
Kennedy, Thomas L. [Canadian political leader]
　Ontario (table) **O: 783**
Kennedy Center for the Performing Arts
　[Washington, D.C.] **K: 270**
　Kennedy, John Fitzgerald (The world mourns)
　　K: 267-268
　Smithsonian Institution (Affiliated institutions)
　　S: 519
　Washington, D.C. (John F. Kennedy Center for the
　　Performing Arts) **W: 75**
Kennedy International Airport *See* John F.
　Kennedy International Airport *in this index*
Kennedy Library [Boston] *See* John F. Kennedy
　Library *in this index*
Kennedy Space Center [Florida] **K: 270** *with map*
　Cape Canaveral **C: 187**
　Florida (Places to visit) **F: 252**
　Kennedy, John Fitzgerald (The world mourns)
　　K: 267-268
Kennedy's mariposa lily [flower]
　Flower *picture on* **F: 290**
Kennekuk [American Indian]
　Kickapoo Indians **K: 310**
Kennelly-Heaviside layer [atmosphere]
　Radio (Transmitting AM band signals) **R: 87**
Kennesaw Mountain, Battle of [1864]
　Civil War, American (table) **Ci: 624**; (The Atlanta
　　campaign) **Ci: 632**
Kennesaw Mountain National Battlefield Park
　National Park System (table: National battlefields)
　　N: 55
Kenneth I MacAlpin [king of Scotland]
　Scotland (Beginning of the Scottish kingdom)
　　S: 219
Kenneth III [king of Scotland]
　Scotland (Beginning of the Scottish kingdom)
　　S: 219
Kennicott, Carol [literary figure]
　Lewis, Sinclair **L: 221**
Kennon, Robert F. [American political leader]
　Louisiana (table) **L: 496**
Kenny, Elizabeth [Australian nurse] **K: 271**
Kenny, Enda [Irish political leader]
　Ireland (table) **I: 428**
Kenseth, Matt [American race driver]
　Automobile racing (table: NASCAR Sprint Cup
　　champions) **A: 981**
Kensington and Chelsea [borough, London]
　London (Residential areas and housing) **L: 432**
　　with picture

Kensington Gardens [park]
London *picture on* L: 429; (Parks) L: 435-436
Kensington rune stone [archaeology] K: 271
Kent [county, England]
United Kingdom (Agriculture) U: 65
Kent, Clark [fictional character]
Superman So: 993
Kent, Edward [American political leader]
Maine (table) M: 87
Kent, James [American jurist] K: 271
Kent, Joseph [American political leader]
Maryland (table) M: 255
Kent, Rockwell [American artist] K: 271 *with picture*
Kent, Samuel B. [American jurist]
Impeachment (History) I: 91-92
Kent, William [American political leader]
Muir Woods National Monument M: 912
Kent, William [English architect]
Architecture (The Palladian Revival) A: 623 *with picture*
Kent Falls
Connecticut (Rivers, waterfalls, and lakes) Ci: 964
Kent State Shooting [U.S. history]
Nixon, Richard Milhous (Foreign policy) N: 432-433
Vietnam War (The invasion of Cambodia) V: 376
Kente cloth [fabric]
Africa *picture on* A: 129
Ashanti A: 767
Clothing (Clothing of Africa) Ci: 698
Kentish Guards [U.S. history]
Greene, Nathanael G: 382
Kenton, Stan [American bandleader] K: 271
Kentucky K: 272 *with pictures and maps*
See also the list of Related articles in the Kentucky *article*
Boone, Daniel B: 476 *with pictures*
Kentucky and Virginia Resolutions K: 295
Westward movement in America (Crossing the Appalachians) W: 246
Kentucky, University of K: 295
Kentucky (Libraries) K: 276-277 *with picture*
Kentucky and Virginia Resolutions [1798] K: 295
Adams, John (The Alien and Sedition Acts) A: 38
Alien and Sedition Acts A: 368
Jefferson, Thomas (Vice president) J: 82-83
Nullification N: 603
States' rights (Early history) So: 866
United States, History of the (The Alien and Sedition Acts) U: 163
Kentucky bass [fish]
Bass (Black bass) B: 156 *with picture*
Kentucky bluegrass [plant]
Bluegrass B: 424
Grass *picture on* G: 325
Lawn (Types of lawns) L: 142
Kentucky coffeetree [tree] K: 295
Kentucky Dam [Tennessee River]
Kentucky Lake K: 297 *with map*
Tennessee Valley Authority (The dams) T: 158-159 *with map*
Kentucky Derby [race] K: 295
Kentucky *picture on* K: 292; (Interesting facts about Kentucky) K: 273 *with picture*
Louisville L: 504
Kentucky Derby Museum [Louisville]
Kentucky (Places to visit) K: 282
Kentucky Fair and Exposition Center
Louisville (Recreation) L: 505-506
Kentucky Gazette, The [newspaper]
Kentucky (Communication) K: 289
Kentucky Horse Park [Lexington]
Kentucky (Places to visit) K: 282
Kentucky Lake [Kentucky-Tennessee] K: 297 *with map*
Kentucky *picture on* K: 283
Tennessee (Rivers and lakes) T: 148 *with map*
Kentucky rifle [gun]
Rifle (History) R: 339-340
Westward movement in America (The Old West) W: 245
Kenya K: 297 *with pictures and maps*
Clinton, Bill (International affairs) Ci: 682f
Clothing *picture on* Ci: 692
Kikuyu K: 314
Mau Mau M: 312
National park (Kenya) N: 42d
Kenya, Mount *See* Mount Kenya *in this index*
Kenya African Democratic Union [political party]
Kenya (History) K: 303
Kenya African National Union [political party]
Kenya (Politics) K: 298; (History) K: 303
Moi, Daniel Toroitich arap M: 688
Kenya African Union [political party]
Kenya (Opposition to the British) K: 303
Kenya People's Union [political party]
Kenya (Building the new nation) K: 303-304

Kenyanthropus platyops [hominid]
Leakey, Meave Gillian L: 161
Prehistoric people (Types of australopithecines) P: 745-746
Kenyatta, Jomo [Kenyan political leader] K: 304 *with portrait*
Kenya (History) K: 303
Mau Mau M: 312
Kenyatta, Uhuru [Kenyan political leader]
Kenya (Building the new nation) K: 303-304
Kenyon Review [magazine]
Ransom, John Crowe R: 140
Keogh plan
Pension (Individual pension plans) P: 273
Keokuk [American Indian chief]
Black Hawk B: 387
Keokuk Dam [Mississippi River]
Iowa (The development of the railroads) I: 395
Keoladeo National Park [India]
National park (table) N: 42f
Kepi [clothing]
Foreign Legion (Uniform and traditions of the Legion) F: 386
Kepler [opera by Glass]
Glass, Philip G: 224
Kepler, Johannes [German astronomer] K: 305
Astronomy (Sun-centered theories) A: 835-836; (Developing the modern view) A: 847
Brahe, Tycho B: 548
Copernicus, Nicolaus (Theories of heavenly motion) Ci: 1039
Ellipse E: 243
Physics (The Renaissance) P: 438-439
Planet (How planets move) P: 508-509
Science (The rebirth of science) S: 197
Space exploration (The dawn of the space age) So: 706
Kepler's laws [astronomy]
Astronomy (Sun-centered theories) A: 835-836
Kepler, Johannes K: 305
Planet (How planets move) P: 508-509 *with diagram*
Keppler, Joseph [American cartoonist]
Cartoon (Editorial cartoons) C: 263-265
Kerala [state, India]
India (Christianity) I: 117
Keratin [protein] K: 305
Hair (The root and shaft) H: 9
Horn H: 338
Skin (Epidermis) S: 489; (Hair, nails, and glands) S: 489
Keratinization [zoology]
Hair (The root and shaft) H: 9 *with diagram*
Keratinocyte [biology]
Skin (Epidermis) S: 489
Keratoconus [disorder]
Contact lens (Hard contact lenses) Ci: 1020
Eye (Diseases of the cornea) E: 466
Keratohyaline [chemical]
Skin (Epidermis) S: 489
Keratotic ringworm [disease]
Ringworm R: 344
Kerch Strait
Black Sea B: 390 *with map*
Kerekou, Mathieu [Benin political leader]
Benin (History) B: 250
Kerensky, Alexander Feodorovich [Russian political leader] K: 305
Lenin, V. I. (Return from exile) L: 193; (The October Revolution) L: 193
Russian Revolution of 1917 (The February Revolution) R: 566
Union of Soviet Socialist Republics (History) U: 35
Kerf [groove]
Saw S: 166
Kermis [fair]
Netherlands (Holidays and recreation) N: 141
Kermit the Frog [puppet]
Henson, Jim H: 191
Kermode's bear
Bear (American black bears) B: 184
Kern, Jerome [American composer] K: 305
Hammerstein, Oscar, II H: 35
Musical comedy (Musical comedy matures) M: 960
Show Boat S: 438
Kern, John Worth [American political leader] K: 306
Kern County [California]
Oil spill (Notable spills) O: 708
Kernan, Joseph E. [American political leader]
Indiana (table) I: 214
Kernel [botany]
Corn Ci: 1056
Nut N: 620
Rice (Structure) R: 323
Seed (Kinds of seeds) S: 280-281

Wheat (Food for people) W: 266; (Structure) W: 267-268 *with diagram*
Kernel [grammar]
Sentence (Sentence patterns) S: 303
Kerner, Otto [American political leader]
Illinois (table) I: 71
Johnson, Lyndon Baines (Problems at home) J: 151
Kerner Commission Report [U.S. history]
African Americans (Unrest in the cities) A: 136q
Johnson, Lyndon Baines (Problems at home) J: 151
Riot (During the 1900's) R: 349
Kernite [mineral]
Borax B: 481
Kerogen [geology]
Fuel (Synthetic liquid fuels) F: 550
Oil shale O: 707
Petroleum (How petroleum deposits form) P: 333
Kerosene [fuel] K: 306
Fuel (Petroleum) F: 550
Petroleum (Beginnings of the petroleum industry) P: 347
Kerosene lamp
Fire (Light) F: 122
Invention *picture on* I: 356
Lamp (Fat or oil lamps) L: 52-53 *with picture*
Kerosine *See* Kerosene *in this index*
Kerouac, Jack [American author] K: 306
American literature (Fiction and other prose) A: 424
Beat movement B: 189
Kerr, Sir John [Australian political leader]
Australia (Political upheavals) A: 925
Kerr, Robert S. [American political leader]
Oklahoma (table) O: 730; (The mid-1900's) O: 734
Kerr Reservoir [lake, North Carolina-Virginia]
Virginia (Rivers and lakes) V: 412-413
Kerrey, Bob [American political leader]
Nebraska (table) N: 110
Kerry [cattle]
Cattle (Other dairy cattle) C: 311
Kerry, John Forbes [American political leader] K: 306 *with portrait*
Bush, George Walker (The election of 2004) B: 722i-722j
Democratic Party (The early 2000's) D: 128
Edwards, John E: 114
Kerry, Julia Thorne [wife of]
Kerry, John Forbes K: 306
Kerry, Teresa Heinz [wife of]
Kerry, John Forbes K: 307
Kerry blue terrier [dog] K: 307
Dog *picture on* D: 273
Kertész, André [Hungarian-American photographer]
Photography (Dramatic changes) P: 425-426
Kertész, Imre [Hungarian writer]
Nobel Prizes (Literature: 2002) N: 448
Kervella, Pierre [French astronomer]
Betelgeuse B: 274
Kerwin, Joseph P. [American astronaut]
Astronaut (Achievements in space) A: 829-830; (table) A: 830 *with picture*
Kesey, Ken [American author] K: 307
American literature (Experimental styles) A: 425
Kesselring, Albert [German general]
World War II (The invasion of Italy) W: 483
Kestrel [bird] K: 307
Bird (Birds of grasslands) B: 336 *with picture*
Bird of prey *picture on* B: 374a
Falcon (The American kestrel) F: 14 *with picture*
Keta [fish] *See* Chum salmon *in this index*
Ketamine [drug]
Drug abuse (Club drugs) D: 363
Ketch [boat]
Sailing (Yawls, ketches, and schooners) S: 24 *with picture*
Ketchikan [Alaska]
Alaska (Places to visit) A: 290 *with picture*
Ketchup [food] K: 307
Ketoacidosis [disorder]
Diabetes (Symptoms) D: 179
Keton [clothing]
Phoenicia (Trade and manufacturing) P: 393
Ketone [chemical]
Diabetes (Symptoms) D: 179
Kettering, Charles Franklin [American inventor] K: 307
Automobile (Technological advances) A: 968
Starter (Automobile starters) So: 858-859
Kettering Laboratories
Kettering, Charles Franklin K: 307
Ketterle, Wolfgang [German physicist]
Nobel Prizes (Physics: 2001) N: 442
Kettle Hill, Battle of [1898]
Rough Riders R: 490

Spanish-American War *picture on* **So: 754**
Kettle hole [geology]
  Glacier (How glaciers shape the land) **G: 203-204**
    with diagram
Kettledrum [musical instrument] *See* Timpani *in
  this index*
Ketubim [Bible] *See* Writings, The *in this index*
Ketubim [Old Testament]
  Old Testament **O: 740**
keV [measurement]
  Particle accelerator (How accelerators work)
    P: 184
Kevala [religion]
  Mahavira **M: 65**
Kevlar [fiber] *See* Aramid *in this index*
Kevorkian, Jack [American physician]
  Euthanasia (Physician-assisted suicide) **E: 421**
Kew-blas glass
  Glass (Types of art glass) **G: 220**
Kew Gardens [London]
  London (Parks) **L: 435-436**
Keweenaw National Historical Park [Michigan]
  National Park System (table: National historical
    parks) **N: 57**
Keweenaw Peninsula [region, Michigan]
  Lake Superior (Description) **L: 45** *with map*
Kewpie doll
  Doll (Before World War I) **D: 291** *with picture*
Key [botany]
  Maple **M: 186** *with pictures*
Key [construction]
  Plaster (Plaster bases) **P: 552**
Key [cryptology]
  Codes and ciphers **Ci: 749**
Key [electrical device]
  Telegraph (The Morse telegraph) **T: 90** *with
    picture*
  Typewriter (How a typewriter works) **T: 538** *with
    picture*
Key [geography]
  Florida Keys **F: 266**
Key [lock]
  Lock **L: 410** *with pictures*
Key [musical instrument]
  Key **K: 307**
Key [music] **K: 307**
  Music (Harmony) **M: 951-952**
Key, David M. [American government official]
  Hayes, Rutherford Birchard (Civil service reform)
    H: 121
Key, Francis Scott [American poet] **K: 307**
  Baltimore **B: 66**
  National anthem **N: 29**
  "Star-Spangled Banner" **So: 854**
  United States flag **U: 200**
  War of 1812 (Campaigns of 1814) **W: 31**
Key, John [New Zealand political leader] **K: 308**
    with portrait
  New Zealand (Political changes) **N: 356**
Key channel
  Organ (Pipe organs) **O: 851-852**
Key-in-knob lock
  Lock (Types of locks) **L: 410** *with picture*
Key Largo [play by Anderson]
  Anderson, Maxwell **A: 452**
Key ring
  Ring *picture on* **R: 342**
Key school
  China (Education) **C: 486**
Key signature [music]
  Music (Indicating pitch) **M: 952-953** *with pictures*
Key Tower
  Ohio *picture on* **O: 681**
Key West [Florida] **K: 308**
  Florida (Places to visit) **F: 252**
  Florida Keys **F: 266** *with picture*
Key word [cryptology]
  Codes and ciphers (Substitution) **Ci: 750**
Key word search [reference] *See* Keyword search
  in this index
Keyboard [machine] **K: 308** *with picture*
  See also Computer keyboard *in this index*
  Electronic game (Personal computers)
    E: 204c-204d
  Telephone (The dialing mechanism) **T: 95**
  Typewriter (How a typewriter works) **T: 538** *with
    pictures*; (History) **T: 539**
Keyboard instrument
  Classical music (Solo music) **Ci: 643**
  Music *pictures on* **M: 949**; (Keyboard instruments)
    M: 950
  Piano **P: 445** *with pictures*
Keyboard Practice [music by Bach]
  Bach, Johann Sebastian (His works) **B: 16**
Keyes, Henry W. [American political leader]
  New Hampshire (table) **N: 223**
Keyes field [region, Oklahoma]

Helium (Production) **H: 176**
Keyframe animation
  Animation (Making the model move) **A: 513**
Keyhole saw [tool]
  Saw (Handsaws) **S: 166-167** *with picture*
Keying [television] *See* Matting *in this index*
Keynes, John Maynard [British economist] **K: 308a**
  Capitalism (Changing attitudes toward
    capitalism) **C: 196**
  Consumption **C: 1020**
  Economics (Modern economics) **E: 64-65**
  Inflation (The Keynesian Theory) **I: 268**
Keynesian economics
  Friedman, Milton **F: 533**
  Inflation (The Keynesian Theory) **I: 268**
  Keynes, John Maynard **K: 308a**
  Robinson, Joan Violet **R: 369**
Keynote [music]
  Key **K: 307**
Keynote address
  Political convention (Organizing the convention)
    P: 629
Keypad
  Computer (A keyboard) **Ci: 912**
  Keyboard **K: 308** *with picture*
  Telephone (The dialing mechanism) **T: 95**
Keys of the Kingdom, The [book by Cronin]
  Cronin, A. J. **Ci: 1152**
Keyser, F. Ray, Jr. [American political leader]
  Vermont (table) **V: 333**
Keystone [architecture]
  Arch **A: 593** *with diagram*
Keystone Cops [film characters]
  Sennett, Mack **S: 301**
Keystone Province [name for]
  Manitoba **M: 145**
Keystone State [name for]
  Pennsylvania **P: 245**
Keyword search [reference]
  Internet (Search engines) **I: 350a**
  Search engine **S: 268**
  A Guide to Research Skills **Research Guide: 29**
KGB [Soviet history] **K: 308a**
  Union of Soviet Socialist Republics (National
    government) **U: 29**
Kha [people]
  Indochina (The Viets) **I: 224-225**
Khachaturian, Aram Ilich [Soviet composer]
  K: 308a
Khadija [wife of]
  Muhammad (Early life) **M: 910**
Khafji [Saudi Arabia]
  Persian Gulf War of 1991 (The ground war)
    P: 300d
Khafre [king of ancient Egypt]
  Egypt, Ancient (Painting and sculpture) **E: 139**
  Pyramids (The pyramids of Giza) **P: 917**
  Sphinx (Egyptian sphinxes) **So: 780**
Khair-ed-Din [Barbary pirate]
  Barbarossa **B: 105**
Khalid [king of Saudi Arabia]
  Saudi Arabia (Continued progress) **S: 161-162**
Khalifa bin Zayid al-Nahyan, Sheik [United Arab
  Emirates political leader]
  (History) **U: 29**
Khalifman, Alexander [Russian chess player]
  Chess (World chess champions) **C: 414**
Khalilzad, Zalmay [American diplomat]
  United Nations (table) **U: 86**
Khalkha Mongolian [language]
  Mongolia (The people) **M: 722**
Khalsa [religion]
  Sikhism (History) **S: 455**
Khama, Ian [Botswanan political leader]
  Botswana (History) **B: 512**
Khama, Sir Seretse [Botswanan political leader]
  Botswana (History) **B: 512**
Khamenei, Ali [Iranian political leader] **K: 308a**
  Iran (After Khomeini) **I: 406a**
Khamsin [weather]
  Egypt (Climate) **E: 127**
  Israel (Climate) **I: 484**
Khan, Genghis [Mongol conqueror] *See* Genghis
  Khan *in this index*
Khan, Kublai [Mongol ruler] *See* Kublai Khan *in
  this index*
Khan, Yahya [Pakistani military leader] *See* Yahya
  Khan, Agha Muhammad *in this index*
Khanate [Asian kingdom]
  Kyrgyzstan (History) **K: 400**
  Uzbekistan (History) **U: 254**
Khao Yai National Park [Thailand]
  National park (table) **N: 42f**
Kharg Island [island, Iran]
  Iran *picture on* **I: 405**
Kharijites [religious group]
  Islam (Divisions of Islam) **I: 466**

Muslims (Ali) **M: 964b**
Kharkiv [Ukraine] **K: 308a**
  Ukraine (Climate) **U: 10**
Kharkov [Ukraine] *See* Kharkiv *in this index*
Khartoum [Sudan] **K: 308b**
  Sudan *picture on* **So: 954**
Khat [plant]
  Africa (Agriculture) **A: 125-126**
  Ethiopia (Agriculture) **E: 370**
  Yemen (Food, clothing, and customs) **Y: 562**
Khatami, Mohammad [Iranian political leader]
  Iran (Political change) **I: 406a**
Khatchkar [monument]
  Armenia (People) **A: 718-718a**
Khayyam, Omar [Persian poet] *See* Omar Khayyam
  in this index
Khazari, al- [book by Halevi]
  Halevi, Judah **H: 19**
Khazars [ancient people]
  Russia (Early days) **R: 547**
Khedive [title]
  Egypt (Muhammad Ali and modernization)
    E: 131
Kheer [food]
  Pakistan (Food and drink) **P: 96**
Kherdian, David [American author]
  Literature for children *picture on* **L: 358**
Khin Kyi, Daw [Burmese diplomat]
  Aung San Suu Kyi **A: 890**
Khirbat Qumran [ruins]
  Essenes **E: 359**
Khirbet Qumran [site]
  Dead Sea Scrolls **D: 56**
Khitans [people]
  Beijing (History) **B: 223**
  Cathay **C: 301**
Khmer [people]
  Cambodia (People) **C: 71**
  Thailand (History) **T: 226**
Khmer Empire [Cambodian history]
  Cambodia (History) **C: 72**
  Indochina (The Khmer) **I: 225**
Khmer Rouge [Cambodian political group] **K: 308b**
  Cambodia (History) **C: 72-73** *with picture*
  Hun Sen **H: 437**
  Norodom Sihanouk **N: 457**
  Phnom Penh **P: 391**
  Pol Pot **P: 603**
  Vietnam (Invasion of Cambodia) **V: 372**
Khnum [Egyptian god]
  Egypt, Ancient (Religion) **E: 137**
Khodorkovsky, Mikhail [Russian businessman]
  Russia (Recent developments) **R: 555-556**
Khoikhoi [people] **K: 308b**
  Africa (Peoples of Africa) **A: 104-105**
  South Africa (History) **So: 617**
Khoisan [people]
  South Africa (History) **So: 617**
Khoisan language
  Africa (Languages) **A: 105**
  Language *map on* **L: 65**; (Other language
    families) **L: 66**
  San **S: 83**
Khomeini, Ruhollah [Iranian religious leader]
  K: 308b
  Asia *picture on* **A: 811**
  Carter, Jimmy (The Iranian crisis) **C: 258** *with
    picture*
  Iran **I: 398**; (Revolution and the Islamic Republic)
    I: 406a *with picture*; (After Khomeini) **I: 406a**
  Iran-Iraq War **I: 407**
  Middle East (The 1970's and 1980's) **M: 534a**
  Mohammad Reza Pahlavi **M: 687**
  Qom **Q: 4**
  Rafsanjani, Ali Akbar Hashemi **R: 102**
  Rushdie, Salman **R: 522**
Khons [Egyptian god]
  Amun **A: 445**
Khons, Temple of [Egypt]
  Architecture *picture on* **A: 611**
Khorana, Har Gobind [American physiologist]
  Nobel Prizes (Physiology or medicine: 1968)
    N: 446
Khorat Plateau
  Thailand (The land) **T: 224-225**
Khorezm [kingdom]
  Genghis Khan (Conquests) **G: 88** *with map*
Khorsabad [ancient city]
  Architecture (Mesopotamian architecture) **A: 611**
Khosrow I [Sasanian ruler]
  Persia, Ancient (The Sasanian dynasty) **P: 299-
    300**
Khrushchev, Nikita Sergeyevich [Soviet political
  leader] **K: 308b** *with portrait*
  Brezhnev, Leonid Ilyich (Rise to power) **B: 596**
  Cold War (The spirit of Geneva) **Ci: 766**; (New
    challenges) **Ci: 766**

Communism (Under Stalin's successors) **Ci: 893**
Cuban missile crisis **Ci: 1180**
Eisenhower, Dwight David (U-2 incident) **E: 154**
Kennedy, John Fitzgerald (Cuba) **K: 265**
Malenkov, Georgi Maximilianovich **M: 105**
Nixon, Richard Milhous (Overseas missions) **N: 431** *with picture*
Russia (The Cold War) **R: 554**
Union of Soviet Socialist Republics (History) **U: 35-38** *with picture*
Zhukov, Georgi Konstantinovich **Z: 591**
Khufu [king of ancient Egypt] **K: 309**
Pyramids (The pyramids of Giza) **P: 917**
Khuzistan Plain [Iran]
Iran (The Khuzistan Plain) **I: 403**; (Climate) **I: 403**
Khyber Pakhtunkhwa [province, Pakistan]
Pakistan (Provincial and local government) **P: 93**
Khyber Pass [region, Asia] **K: 309** *with map*
Afghanistan (Transportation and communication) **A: 95**
Pakistan (Land and climate) **P: 96** *with picture and map*
Ki [energy]
Aikido **A: 167**
Ki [mythology]
Mythology (Middle Eastern mythology) **M: 976-977**
Kiai [sound]
Karate (Karate styles) **K: 246**
Kiang [animal]
Donkey **D: 308**
Kiangya [ship]
Shipwreck (table: Major shipwrecks) **S: 428**
Kibaki, Mwai [Kenyan political leader]
Kenya (Building the new nation) **K: 303-304**; (Recent developments) **K: 304**
Kibbutz [community] **K: 310**
Asia (Country life) **A: 779-780**
Education (Education in other countries) **E: 96**
Israel (Rural life) **I: 481**
Kibo [mountain summit]
Kilimanjaro **K: 315** *with picture*
Kick [sports]
See also Kickoff *in this index*
Karate (Karate styles) **K: 246** *with picture*
Soccer (Kicking) **So: 547**
Kick at goal *See* Conversion [sports] *in this index*
Kickapoo Indians **K: 310**
Kickapoo Prophet [nickname]
Kickapoo Indians **K: 310**
Kickboxing [sport] **K: 310** *with picture*
Boxing (Boxing in Asia) **B: 531**
Martial arts **M: 234**
Thailand (Recreation) **T: 224** *with picture*
Kicker [machine]
Fur (Dressing) **F: 563**
Kickoff [sports]
Football (How football is played) **F: 358-359** *with picture*
Soccer (Starting the game) **So: 546**
Kid [animal]
Goat **G: 239**
Kidd, William [Scottish pirate] **K: 311**
Pirate (Other regions) **P: 495**
Kidman, Nicole [Australian actress] **K: 311** *with portrait*
Motion picture (Best performance by an actress: 2002) **M: 862a**
Kidnapped [book by Stevenson]
Stevenson, Robert Louis (Novels) **So: 898**
Kidnapping [law] **K: 311**
Iraq War (Resistance to the coalition) **I: 414e-414f**
Lindbergh, Charles Augustus (The Lindbergh kidnapping) **L: 330**
Terrorism (Assassinations and kidnappings) **T: 175**
Kidney [anatomy] **K: 311** *with diagrams*
Bladder **B: 395** *with diagram*
Blood *diagram on* **B: 409**
Circulatory system (In removal of wastes and poisons) **Ci: 560** *with picture*
Diuretic **D: 240**
Elimination **E: 236**
Evolution (Embryology) **E: 431**
Frog *picture on* **F: 537**
Gland (table) **G: 208**
Hantavirus **H: 54**
Human body (table) **H: 422** *with diagram*
Hypertension **H: 476**
Kidney stone **K: 312**
Nephritis **N: 127**
Polycystic kidney disease **P: 649**
Urine **U: 221**
Kidney bean
Bean (Kinds of beans) **B: 181** *with picture*
Kidney stone **K: 312**
Kidney transplant

Organ donation **O: 852**
Surgery (History) **So: 1007-1008**
Transplant (Organ transplants) **T: 379** *with picture*; (Survival rates) **T: 381**
Kidwell, John [British horticulturist]
Hawaii (Growth of constitutional government) **H: 106-108**
Kiefer, Anselm [German painter] **K: 313** *with picture*
Germany (Painting and sculpture) **G: 155**
Painting (Neoexpressionism) **P: 87** *with picture*
Kiel, Treaty of [1814]
Denmark (Wars with Sweden) **D: 140**
Norway (Union with Sweden) **N: 545**
Kiel Canal [waterway, Germany] **K: 313**
Canal (table) **C: 164**
Kiely, Benedict [Irish author]
Irish literature (Fiction) **I: 432**
Kierkegaard, Søren Aabye [Danish philosopher] **K: 313**
Existentialism **E: 437**
Kieschner, Sidney [American dramatist]
Kingsley, Sidney **K: 331**
Kieselguhr [earth]
Dynamite (History) **D: 397**
Kiesinger, Kurt Georg [German political leader]
Germany (West Germany) **G: 170**
Kiev [Ukraine] **K: 314** *with picture*
Ukraine **U: 5** *with picture*; (Way of life) **U: 8**
Kievan Rus [historic region]
Belarus (History) **B: 224b-224c**
Russia (Ancestry) **R: 532**; (The state of Kievan Rus) **R: 547**
Ruthenia **R: 568**
Ukraine (History) **U: 11-12**
Kigali [Rwanda] **K: 314**
Rwanda **R: 570**
Kigo [literature]
Haiku **H: 8**
Kikuyu [people] **K: 314**
Africa (Peoples of Africa) **A: 104**
Bantu **B: 99** *with picture*
Kenya *picture on* **K: 300**; (Population and ethnic groups) **K: 298**; (Opposition to the British) **K: 303**
Mau Mau **M: 312**
Kikuyu grass [plant]
Lawn (Types of lawns) **L: 142**
Kikwete, Jakaya [Tanzanian political leader]
Tanzania (After socialism) **T: 35-36**
Kilauea [volcano, Hawaii] **K: 315**
Hawaii *picture on* **H: 89**; (Hawaii) **H: 100**
Hawai'i Volcanoes National Park **H: 110**
Pacific Islands *picture on* **P: 8**
Volcano *picture on* **V: 438**
Kilbourn, Byron [American settler]
Milwaukee (Early development) **M: 561**
Kilbourntown House
Milwaukee (Annual events and places of interest) **M: 560-561**
Kilby, Jack [American engineer] **K: 315**
Computer chip (History) **Ci: 924f**
Electronics (The solid-state revolution) **E: 215-216**
Invention (Recent developments) **I: 364**
Nobel Prizes (Physics: 2000) **N: 442**
Noyce, Robert **N: 578**
Kilby, Thomas Erby [American political leader]
Alabama (table) **A: 274**
Kildare, Monastery of [Ireland]
Brigid, Saint **B: 609**
Kilgour, Geills McCrae [wife of]
Turner, John Napier (Entry into politics) **T: 516-517** *with picture*
Kilimanjaro [volcano, Tanzania] **K: 315** *with picture*
Africa (Mountains) **A: 119** *with picture*
Mountain (table) **M: 896** *with diagram*
National park (Kenya) **N: 42d**
Tanzania **T: 30** *with picture*
Kilimanjaro National Park [Tanzania]
National park (table) **N: 42f**
Tanzania *picture on* **T: 30**
Kill Devil Hill [North Carolina]
Wright brothers (Early gliders) **W: 509**
Kill fee [payment]
Publishing (Kill fees) **P: 867**
Kill switch [safety device]
Motorboat racing (Safety equipment) **M: 877**
Kill Van Kull [waterway]
New York City (The city) **N: 323**; (Transportation) **N: 334**
Killarney [Ireland] **K: 315**
Killarney, Lakes of [Ireland] *See* Lakes of Killarney *in this index*
Killdeer [bird] **K: 316**
Bird *pictures on* **B: 355, B: 357, B: 363**
Protective coloration (Disruptive coloration)

P: 831
"Killdozer" [story by Sturgeon]
Sturgeon, Theodore **So: 934**
Killebrew, Harmon [American baseball player]
Baseball (table: Hall of Fame) **B: 134a**
Killen, Jacob A. [American publisher]
Delaware (Communication) **D: 108**
Killer bee
Bee (Sting) **B: 202**
Killer cell *See* Cytotoxic T cell *in this index*
Killer smog [pollution]
Air pollution (Health) **A: 199**
Killer whale **K: 316** *with picture*
Animal *picture on* **A: 486**
Antarctica (Living things) **A: 534-535** *with picture*
Balance of nature (Upsetting the balance) **B: 36**
Dolphin *picture on* **D: 298**; (Other species) **D: 297**; (Swimming and diving) **D: 299**
Whale *picture on* **W: 257**; (Life span) **W: 261**
Killington Mountain [Vermont]
Vermont *picture on* **V: 327**
Killy, Jean-Claude [French skier]
Olympic Games (The 1968 games) **O: 752**
Skiing (The middle and late 1900's) **S: 487**
Kilmer, Joyce [American author] **K: 316**
Kiln [industry]
Brick (Firing bricks) **B: 598**
Cement and concrete (Burning) **C: 344**
Ceramics (Making ceramics) **C: 360**
Clay **Ci: 658**
Pottery (Firing) **P: 718**
Kilo [prefix]
Metric system (Use of standard prefixes) **M: 437**; (Metric prefixes) **M: 439**
Kiloampere [measurement]
Ampere **A: 438**
Kilobit [measurement]
Broadband communication **B: 634**
Kilobyte [measurement]
Computer (Computer code) **Ci: 911**
Kilocalorie [measurement]
Calorie **C: 70**
Weight control **W: 181**
Kilogram [measurement] **K: 316**
Metric system (Structure of the metric system) **M: 437**; (The metric system at a glance) **M: 438-439** *with picture*; (Evolution of the metric system) **M: 441**
Weight **W: 181**
Weights and measures **W: 184**
Kilogram calorie [measurement]
Calorie **C: 70**
Kilogram-force [measurement]
Metric system (Non-SI metric units) **M: 440**
Kilohertz [measurement] **K: 317**
Radio (Broadcasting power and frequency) **R: 87-88**
Kilometer [measurement] **K: 317**
Metric system (Kinds of metric units) **M: 436**; (The metric system at a glance) **M: 438** *with pictures*
Kilopascal [measurement]
Aerodynamics (Principles of aerodynamics) **A: 85**
Pascal **P: 189**
Kilowatt [measurement] **K: 317**
Electric generator **E: 170**
Watt **W: 148**
Kilowatt-hour [measurement]
Electric meter (Utility meters) **E: 177**
Kilowatt **K: 317**
Kilpatrick, Kwame [American political leader]
Detroit (The early 2000's) **D: 171**
Kilrain, Jake [American boxer]
Boxing (Bare knuckles to gloves) **B: 532**
Mississippi *picture on* **M: 623**
Kilroy, Thomas [Irish dramatist]
Irish literature (Drama) **I: 432**
Kilt [clothing]
Scotland *picture on* **S: 214**
Tartan **T: 47**
Kiltartan [language]
Gregory, Lady **G: 388**
Kim [book by Kipling]
Kipling, Rudyard (Later career) **K: 334**
Kim Chong-il [Korean political leader] *See* Kim Jong-il *in this index*
Kim Dae-jung [Korean political leader]
Kim Jong-il **K: 317**
Korea, North (Nuclear tensions) **K: 374**
Korea, South (Recent developments) **K: 378d** *with picture*
Nobel Prizes (Peace: 2000) **N: 448b**
Kim Il-sung [Korean political leader] **K: 317**
Kim Jong-il **K: 317**
Korea, North *picture on* **K: 369**; (History) **K: 373**
Kim Jae Kyu [Korean assassin]
Korea, South (South Korea under Park) **K: 378c**
Kim Jong-il [Korean political leader] **K: 317**

Korea, North (Nuclear tensions) K: 374
Korea, South (Recent developments) K: 378d
  with picture
Kim Jong-un [Korean political leader]
  Kim Jong-il K: 317
Korea, North (Recent developments) K: 374
Kim Sung-ju [Korean political leader] See Kim
  Il-sung in this index
Kim Young Sam [Korean political leader]
Korea, South (Recent developments) K: 378d
Kim Yu-Na [Korean skater]
  Olympic Games picture on O: 746d
Kimax [glass]
  Glass (Borosilicate glass) G: 213
Kimball, Charles D. [American political leader]
  Rhode Island (table) R: 311
Kimbanguists [people]
  Congo, Democratic Republic of the (Religion)
  Ci: 939
Kimberley [South Africa] K: 317
Kimberlite [geology]
  Diamond (Where natural diamonds are found)
  D: 181-182
Kimchi [food]
  Asian Americans (Asian influences on American
  culture) A: 812c
Korea, North (Food and drink) K: 371
Kimeu, Kamoya [Kenyan anthropologist]
  Prehistoric people (table) P: 754
Kimono [clothing]
  Clothing (Cultiral beliefs and values) Ci: 691;
  (Japan) Ci: 699
Japan (Clothing) J: 39
Kin, Next of [law]
  Next of kin N: 390
Kin selection [biology] See Inclusive fitness in this
  index
Kinabalu, Mount [Borneo]
  Malaysia (Land and climate) M: 99 with picture
Kinabalu National Park [Malaysia]
  National park (table) N: 42f
Kinchinjunga, Mount See Mount Kanchenjunga
  in this index
Kindergarten [education] K: 317 with picture
  Careers (Teaching) C: 231
  Early childhood education (Formal education
  programs) E: 15
  Education (Early childhood education) E: 91
  Fröbel, Friedrich Wilhelm August F: 535
  Hearst, Phoebe Apperson H: 131
  Missouri (Interesting facts) M: 651
  School (Kindergartens) S: 181
  Teaching picture on T: 65
Kindertotenlieder [music by Mahler]
  Mahler, Gustav M: 65
Kindle [device]
  Book (Modern books) B: 468
  E-book E: 2
Kindling temperature
  Camping (Building a campfire) C: 94-96
Kinect [electronic device]
  Electronic game (Broadening audiences) E: 204f
Kiner, Ralph [American baseball player]
  Baseball (table: Hall of Fame) B: 134a
Kinescope [television]
  Television (Early development) T: 127
  Zworykin, Vladimir Kosma Z: 610
Kinesics [science] K: 319
  Body language B: 435
  Communication (The study of communication)
  Ci: 887
Kinetic energy [physics]
  Energy E: 273; (Kinetic energy) E: 275 with
  diagram
  Evaporation (How evaporation occurs) E: 422
  Wind power W: 331
Kinetic friction [physics]
  Friction (Kinds of friction) F: 532
Kinetic sculpture
  Sculpture (Form and treatment) S: 230-231
Kinetic theory of gases [physics]
  Chemistry (Development of physical chemistry)
  C: 404
  Gas [physics] (How gases behave) G: 48
  Maxwell, James Clerk M: 319
Kinetophone [machine]
  Edison, Thomas Alva (Motion pictures) E: 80
Kinetoscope [machine]
  Edison, Thomas Alva (Motion pictures) E: 80
  Motion picture (The invention of motion
  pictures) M: 863
King [chess]
  Chess (The board and the men) C: 411-412 with
  diagram; (The moves) C: 412
King [entomology]
  Termite (The termite colony) T: 171
King [title] K: 319

Address, Forms of (Officials of the
  Commonwealth of Nations) A: 53
Crown Ci: 1158
Divine right of kings D: 242
Emperor E: 261
Parliament (The Parliament of the United
  Kingdom) P: 172
Primogeniture P: 781
Sovereignty S: 688b
King, Alvin O. [American political leader]
  Louisiana (table) L: 496
King, Angus [American political leader]
  Maine (table) M: 87
King, Austin A. [American political leader]
  Missouri (table) M: 668
King, B. B. [American singer] K: 320 with portrait
King, Billie Jean [American tennis player] K: 320
  Tennis (Tennis today) T: 166d-166e
King, Bruce [American political leader]
  New Mexico (table) N: 272
King, Coretta Scott [American social reformer]
  K: 320 with portrait
  King, Martin Luther, Jr. (Early life) K: 320-321
  Selma marches picture on S: 290
King, Dorothy Gardner [mother of Gerald Ford]
  See Ford, Dorothy in this index
King, Edward J. [American political leader]
  Dukakis, Michael Stanley (Political career) D: 380
  Massachusetts (table) M: 288
King, Ernest Joseph [American admiral]
  Navy, United States (World War II [1939-1945])
  N: 89
King, Franklin Hiram [American agriculturist]
  Silo S: 463
King, George E. [Canadian political leader]
  New Brunswick (table) N: 195
King, Horatio [American government official]
  Buchanan, James (table) B: 661
King, Isabel [sister of]
  King, William Lyon Mackenzie (Boyhood) K: 324
King, Isabel Grace Mackenzie [mother of]
  King, William Lyon Mackenzie (Boyhood) K: 324
King, Janet [sister of]
  King, William Lyon Mackenzie (Boyhood) K: 324
King, John [father of]
  King, William Lyon Mackenzie (Boyhood) K: 324
King, John [grandfather of]
  King, William Lyon Mackenzie (Boyhood) K: 324
King, John Alsop [American political leader]
  New York (table) N: 313
King, John W. [American political leader]
  New Hampshire (table) N: 223
King, Karl [American composer] K: 320
King, Leslie Lynch [father of]
  Ford, Gerald Rudolph (Family background) F: 372
King, Macdougall [brother of]
  King, William Lyon Mackenzie (Boyhood) K: 324;
  (Early political and public career) K: 325
King, Martin Luther, Jr. [American social reformer]
  K: 320 with pictures
  African Americans (The civil rights movement)
  A: 136o with picture
  Alabama (Interesting facts) A: 257; (The mid-
  1900's) A: 278 with picture
  Atlanta picture on A: 860; (The mid-1900's) A: 861
  Civil disobedience (History of civil disobedience)
  Ci: 607
  King, Coretta Scott K: 320
  Malcolm X M: 103
  March on Washington M: 196
  Martin Luther King, Jr., Day M: 235
  Martin Luther King, Jr., National Historic Site
  M: 235
  Mays, Benjamin Elijah M: 330
  Memphis (The people) M: 394
  Montgomery bus boycott M: 767
  Nobel Prizes (Peace: 1964) N: 448b with picture
  Selma marches S: 291 with picture
  Tennessee (The mid-1900's) T: 156-157
  United States, History of the (Poverty and
  discrimination) U: 195; (The civil rights
  movement) U: 196a
King, Richard [American steamboat captain]
  King Ranch K: 328
King, Riley B. [American singer] See King, B. B. in
  this index
King, Rodney G. [American public figure]
  African Americans (Race relations) A: 136t
  Bush, George Herbert Walker (National affairs)
  B: 720-721
  Christopher, Warren Minor C: 537
  Los Angeles (Recent developments) L: 470
  Riot (During the 1900's) R: 349
King, Rufus [American political leader] K: 323
  Louisiana Purchase (Trouble begins) L: 502
  Monroe, James (Secretary of state) M: 736
  Northwest Ordinance N: 528

Van Buren, Martin (U.S. senator) V: 271
King, Samuel Ward [American political leader]
  Rhode Island (table) R: 311
King, Stephen [American author] K: 323
King, Thomas [American author]
  Indian, American (Achievements in the arts)
  I: 181
King, Tom [British bandit]
  Turpin, Dick T: 519
King, William [American political leader]
  Maine (table) M: 87; (Statehood) M: 89
King, William Lyon Mackenzie [Canadian political
  leader] K: 324 with pictures
  Canada, History of (World War I and
  independence [1914-1931]) C: 146-147
  Great Depression (Effects in Canada) G: 341-342
  Liberal Party of Canada L: 227
  Meighen, Arthur M: 385; (First term) M: 386
  Saint Laurent, Louis Stephen (Entry into public
  life) S: 39-40
King, William Rufus Devane [American political
  leader] K: 327 with portrait
King and I, The [musical]
  Mongkut M: 719
  Rodgers, Richard R: 398
King Arthur See Arthur, King in this index
King bird-of-paradise [bird]
  Bird-of-paradise B: 374 with picture
King Center [Atlanta, Georgia]
  King, Coretta Scott K: 320
King Charles [dog]
  English toy spaniel E: 325
King cobra [snake]
  Cobra Ci: 742
  Snake picture on S: 534
King crab [sea animal]
  See also Red king crab in this index
  Horseshoe crab H: 368
King cycle [Irish literature]
  Irish literature (Heroic tales, romances, and sagas)
  I: 430-431
King Edward's Chair
  Coronation (The British coronation) Ci: 1068
King Fahd Causeway
  Bridge (table: Combination bridges) B: 600-603
King Fahd International Airport [Saudi Arabia]
  Airport A: 242
King George's War [1744-1748]
  Canada, History of (The colonial wars) C: 141
  French and Indian wars (King George's War)
  F: 512
  Louisbourg L: 477
  Succession wars (The War of the Austrian
  Succession) So: 950
King Hedley II [play by Wilson]
  Wilson, August W: 316
King Island [Pacific]
  Tasmania (Land and climate) T: 48
King James Version [Bible]
  Bible (The King James Version) B: 285 with
  picture; (Modern English translations) B: 286
  English literature (Prose writings) E: 317
  Hampton Court Conference H: 36
  James (James I) J: 25
  Prose P: 828
King John [play by Shakespeare]
  Shakespeare, William (Religion) S: 350; (King
  John) S: 356
King Kong [film]
  Animation (Stop-motion animation) A: 514a
  with picture
King Lear [play by Shakespeare]
  Shakespeare, William: (King Lear) S: 363;
  (Rhetoric) S: 368
King mackerel [fish]
  Kingfish K: 329 with picture
  Mackerel M: 24
King Memorial Library, Martin Luther
  [Washington, D.C.]
  Washington, D.C. map on W: 76
King of kings [title]
  Persia, Ancient (The Achaemenid Empire) P: 298
King of Kings, The [film]
  DeMille, Cecil B. D: 119
King of Mambo [name for]
  Puente, Tito P: 871
King of Saxony bird-of-paradise [bird]
  Bird-of-paradise B: 374 with picture
King of the Cowboys [nickname]
  Rogers, Roy R: 401
King Peak [mountain, Yukon] K: 328
King penguin K: 328
  Penguin picture on P: 239
King Philip [Indian chief] See Philip, King in this
  index
King Philip's War [1675-1678]
  Indian wars (King Philip's War [1675-1676]) I: 191

Maine (Indian wars) **M:** 89
Massachusetts (King Philip's War) **M:** 291
Philip, King **P:** 370
Rhode Island (King Philip's War) **R:** 312
King protea [tree]
Protea **P:** 831 *with picture*
King Pym [English history]
Pym, John **P:** 915
King Ranch [Texas] **K:** 328
King salmon [fish] *See* Chinook salmon *in this index*
King snake *See* Kingsnake *in this index*
King Solomon's Mines [book by Haggard]
Haggard, H. Rider **H:** 6
King vulture [bird]
Bird *picture on* **B:** 344b; (Birds of Central and South America) **B:** 344a
Vulture (New World vultures) **V:** 454
King William's School
Maryland (Schools) **M:** 244
King William's War [1689-1697]
Canada, History of (The colonial wars) **C:** 141
French and Indian wars (King William's War) **F:** 512
Le Moyne, Pierre, Sieur d'Iberville **L:** 189
Kingbird [bird] **K:** 328 *with picture*
Bird (Birds of grasslands) **B:** 336 *with picture*
Kingdom [biology] **K:** 328
Classification, Scientific (Groups in classification) **Ci:** 655
Kingdom of ...
Kingdoms appear under their key words, as in Sardinia, Kingdom of
Kingdom of God in America, The [book by Niebuhr]
Niebuhr, H. Richard **N:** 405
Kingfish [fish] **K:** 329 *with picture*
Kingfish [nickname]
Long (Huey Pierce Long) **L:** 445-446
Kingfisher [bird] **K:** 329 *with picture*
Bird (Birds of inland waters and marshes) **B:** 340 *with picture*; (Birds of Africa) **B:** 344h *with picture*
Kinghead [plant]
Ragweed **R:** 103
Kingkey 100 [building, China]
Skyscraper (table) **S:** 498
Kinglet [bird] **K:** 330 *with picture*
Bird *picture on* **B:** 358; (Birds of forests and woodlands) **B:** 334 *with picture*
Kingmaker [nickname]
Warwick, Earl of **W:** 44
Kings, Books of [Bible] **K:** 330
Bible (The Prophets) **B:** 280
Kings, Los Angeles [team]
Hockey (table: National Hockey League) **H:** 281
Kings, Sacramento [team]
Basketball (table) **B:** 150
Kings, Valley of the *See* Valley of the Kings *in this index*
King's Bench, Court of
Law *picture on* **L:** 135
Kings Canyon [canyon, California]
Kings Canyon National Park **K:** 330
Kings Canyon National Park [California] **K:** 330 *with picture*
National Park System (table: National parks) **N:** 48
King's Chamber
Pyramids (The pyramids of Giza) **P:** 917
King's College, University of K: 331
Universities and colleges (First universities in the Americas) **U:** 210
King's County [Irish history]
Ireland (The conquest of Ireland) **I:** 426
King's Court [European history]
Curia regis **Ci:** 1194
Kings Dominion [Virginia]
Virginia (Places to visit) **V:** 408
Kings Landing Historical Settlement [Prince William]
New Brunswick (Places to visit) **N:** 188
King's Men [theater group]
Shakespeare, William (The King's Men) **S:** 348
Kings Mountain, Battle of [1780]
Revolution, American (table) **R:** 276; (Kings Mountain) **R:** 285
South Carolina (The Revolutionary War) *picture on* **So:** 659-660
Kings Mountain National Military Park [South Carolina]
National Park System (table: National military parks) **N:** 55
Kings Peak [mountain]
Rocky Mountains (Chief ranges of the Rockies) **R:** 394-395 *with map*
Utah (Land regions) **U:** 240 *with map*
Kings Point
United States Merchant Marine Academy **U:** 200

Kings River [river, California]
Kings Canyon National Park **K:** 330
King's Speech, The [film]
Motion picture (Best picture: 2010) **M:** 861
Kingsley, Ben [British actor]
Motion picture (Best performance by an actor: 1982) **M:** 862a
Kingsley, Charles [British author] **K:** 331
Kingsley, Henry [Australian author]
Australia (Literature) **A:** 904-905
Kingsley, Mary Henrietta [British explorer] **K:** 331
Kingsley, Sidney [American dramatist] **K:** 331
Kingsley, Zephaniah [American settler]
Jacksonville (Cultural life and recreation) **J:** 18
Kingsley Plantation [Florida]
Jacksonville (Cultural life and recreation) **J:** 18
Kingsmere [estate]
King, William Lyon Mackenzie (Retirement and death) **K:** 327
Kingsnake K: 331
Milk snake **M:** 550
Snake *picture on* **S:** 533
Kingston [Jamaica] **K:** 331 *with picture*
Jamaica **J:** 32 *with map*
Kingston [Tennessee]
Tennessee **T:** 135
Kingston, Maxine Hong [American author]
American literature (Works by minority writers) **A:** 425
Kingston upon Hull [England]
Hull **H:** 411
Kingstown [St. Vincent and the Grenadines] **K:** 332
Saint Vincent and the Grenadines **S:** 57 *with picture*
Kinich Ahau [Maya god]
Maya (Religion) **M:** 322
Kinkajou [animal] **K:** 332 *with picture*
Kinkead, John H. [American political leader]
Nevada (table) **N:** 173
Kinneret, Lake [name for]
Galilee, Sea of **G:** 11
Kinnick, Nile [American football player]
Football (table) **F:** 363
Kinnock, Neil Gordon [British political leader] **K:** 332
Kino, Eusebio Francisco [Italian priest and explorer] **K:** 332
Arizona (Spanish exploration) **A:** 688
Mission life in America (Western missions) **M:** 618-619
Kinsella, Thomas [Irish poet]
Irish literature (Poetry) **I:** 433
Kinsey, Alfred Charles [American biologist] **K:** 332
Kinsey Report, The [books by Kinsey]
Kinsey, Alfred Charles **K:** 333
Kinshasa [Democratic Republic of the Congo] **K:** 333 *with picture*
Congo, Democratic Republic of the **Ci:** 938 *with picture*
Kinship [sociology]
Family **F:** 20; (Non-Western families) **F:** 24
Kinte, Kunta [literary figure]
Haley, Alex **H:** 19
Kintpuash [American Indian leader] *See* Captain Jack *in this index*
Kinyarwanda [language]
Rwanda (People) **R:** 570
KIO Towers [Madrid]
Spain *picture on* **So:** 731
Kiowa Indians K: 333
Kipfer, Paul [Swiss balloonist]
Balloon (Balloon explorations) **B:** 62
Kipling, Rudyard [British author] **K:** 333 *with portrait*
Limpopo River **L:** 309
Kippered herring [food]
Herring (Uses) **H:** 216
Scotland (Food and drink) **S:** 214
Kirby, Jack [American cartoonist]
Comics (Comic books) **Ci:** 869
Lee, Stan **L:** 180
Kirby-Smith, Edmund [Confederate general] *See* Smith, Edmund Kirby *in this index*
Kirchhoff, Gustav Robert [German physicist]
Cesium **C:** 364
Optics (History) **O:** 813
Rubidium **R:** 507
Kirchhoff's laws [physics]
Electric circuit (Circuit mathematics) **E:** 167
Kirchner, Ernst Ludwig [German artist]
Expressionism *picture on* **E:** 455
Painting (Expressionism) **P:** 78
Kirchner, Néstor [Argentine political leader]
Argentina (Recent developments) **A:** 659
Latin America (In the early 2000's) **L:** 111
Kiribati K: 335 *with picture and map*
Flag *picture on* **F:** 203

Line Islands **L:** 333
Kirilenko, Andrei Pavlovich [Soviet political leader] **K:** 336
Kiritimati Atoll K: 336 *with map*
Kiriyat Arba [settlement, West Bank]
Hebron **H:** 163
Kiriyenko, Sergei Vladilenovich [Russian political leader]
Russia (The new nation) **R:** 555
Kirk, Claude R., Jr. [American political leader]
Florida (table) **F:** 260
Kirk, Ron [American political leader]
Dallas (Commercial growth) **D:** 15
Kirke, Sir David [English settler]
Newfoundland and Labrador (Colonization) **N:** 375
Quebec (Early days) **Q:** 36
Kirker, Thomas [American political leader]
Ohio (table) **O:** 699
Kirkland, Gelsey [American ballerina]
Baryshnikov, Mikhail *picture on* **B:** 123
Kirkland, Lane [American labor leader] **K:** 336
Kirkpatrick, Jeane Jordan [American government official] **K:** 336
United Nations (table) **U:** 86
Kirkwall [Orkney Islands]
Orkney Islands **O:** 699
Kirkwood, Samuel Jordan [American political leader] **K:** 336
Garfield, James Abram (table) **G:** 42
Iowa (table) **I:** 391
Kirlian photography K: 336 *with picture*
Kirman, Richard, Sr. [American political leader]
Nevada (table) **N:** 173
Kirov, Sergey [Russian political leader]
Saint Petersburg [Russia] (History) **S:** 55
Kirov Ballet
Ballet (The rise of professional ballet) **B:** 51; (Ballet in Russia) **B:** 52-53
Bolshoi Ballet **B:** 449
Russia (Ballet) **R:** 537
Kirov Theater
Saint Petersburg [Russia] (Education and cultural life) **S:** 55
Kirstein, Lincoln Edward [American director] **K:** 337
Kirtland [Ohio]
Mormons (Mormons in the Middle West) **M:** 808
Young, Brigham (Mormon leader) **Y:** 571
Kisatchie National Forest [Louisiana]
Louisiana (Places to visit) **L:** 488
Kishinev [Moldova] *See* Chisinau *in this index*
Kiska [island]
Alaska (Interesting facts) **A:** 283; (World War II) **A:** 301
Kislev [month]
Calendar (The Hebrew calendar) **C:** 29
Kiss of the Spider Woman, The [book by Puig]
Novel (The novel today) **N:** 575
Kissimmee [Florida]
Aviation (The first flying regulations) **A:** 987
Kissimmee River [Florida]
Everglades (Environmental problems) **E:** 424
Florida (The late 1900's) **F:** 264-265
Kissinger, Henry Alfred [American government official] **K:** 337
Diplomacy (History) **D:** 217
Ford, Gerald Rudolph (Foreign affairs) **F:** 378
International relations *picture on* **I:** 344
Vietnam War (Invasion of the south) **V:** 376
Kistler, Steven [American chemical engineer]
Aerogel **A:** 89
Kiswahili [language] *See* Swahili *in this index*
Kit [animal]
Beaver (Raising young) **B:** 194 *with picture*
Fox (Young) **F:** 439 *with picture*
Rabbit (Young) **R:** 48
Kit Carson House
Taos **T:** 36
Kit fox [animal]
Animal *picture on* **A:** 483
Fox (Kinds of foxes) **F:** 440
Kitāb al-Manāzir [book by Alhazen]
Alhazen **A:** 366
Optics (History) **O:** 813
Kitasato, Shibasaburo [Japanese bacteriologist]
Immune system (The study of the immune system) **I:** 88d
Kitbashing [hobby]
Railroad, Model (Cars) **R:** 121
Kitchen
Interior design *picture on* **I:** 330
Mount Vernon *picture on* **M:** 889
Safety (In the kitchen) **S:** 10
Sailing (Places to visit) **S:** 25
Zoo *picture on* **Z:** 604; (Diet) **Z:** 602
Kitchen Cabinet [U.S. history] **K:** 337

Cabinet (Development of the Cabinet) **C:** 3
Jackson, Andrew (The spoils system) **J:** 10-11
"Kitchen debate" [U.S. history]
  Nixon, Richard Milhous (Overseas missions)
  N: 431 *with picture*
Kitchen garden
  Gardening (Production gardens) **G:** 31 *with
  picture*; (Planning a kitchen garden) **G:** 34;
  (Cultivating an outdoor garden) **G:** 34
Kitchen garden portulaca [plant]
  Portulaca **P:** 696
Kitchener [Ontario] **K:** 337
Kitchener, Horatio Herbert [British military leader]
  K: 338
  Anglo-Boer Wars **A:** 463
Kitchin, W. W. [American political leader]
  North Carolina (table) **N:** 490
Kite [bird] **K:** 338 *with picture*
  Bird of prey **B:** 374a
Kite [toy] **K:** 338 *with pictures*
  Airplane (Early experiments and ideas) **A:** 229
  Franklin, Benjamin (The scientist) **F:** 488
Kite, Tom [American golfer]
  Golf (U.S. Open) **G:** 265
Kite spider
  Spider *picture on* **So:** 788
Kithara [musical instrument]
  Classical music *picture on* **Ci:** 647; (Early music)
  Ci: 645
Kitimat [British Columbia] **K:** 341
Kitt Peak National Observatory [Arizona]
  Arizona **A:** 671; (Places to visit) **A:** 678
  National Optical Astronomy Observatories **N:** 42
  National Radio Astronomy Observatory **N:** 59
  Sun (Earth-based studies) **So:** 986 *with picture*
Kittatinny Mountains [New Jersey-Pennsylvania]
  Delaware Water Gap **D:** 114
  New Jersey (Land regions) **N:** 242
Kitten [animal]
  See also Cat
  Cat *picture on* **C:** 284; (Growth and development)
  C: 293 *with pictures*
  Pet (Training your pet) **P:** 320
Kitten's First Full Moon [book by Henkes]
  Henkes, Kevin **H:** 184
Kittinger, Joseph W., Jr. [American balloonist]
  Balloon (Balloon explorations) **B:** 62; (Long-
  distance balloon flights) **B:** 62
Kitti's hog-nosed bat [animal]
  Bat **B:** 159
  Mammal *picture on* **M:** 117
Kittiwake [bird] **K:** 341 *with picture*
  Gull (Kinds of gulls) **G:** 439
Kitty Hawk [North Carolina]
  Airplane (The Wright brothers) **A:** 231
  Wright brothers **W:** 508
Kitty Hawk [ship]
  Aircraft carrier (The United States carrier fleet)
  A: 206
Kitzhaber, John [American political leader]
  Oregon (table) **O:** 845, **O:** 845
Kiva [architecture]
  Anasazi (Way of life) **A:** 448a
  Archaeology *picture on* **A:** 597
  Architecture (Pre-Columbian architecture) **A:** 614
  Mesa Verde National Park **M:** 420
  Pueblo Indians (Early history and way of life)
  P: 871
Kivi, Aleksis [Finnish author]
  Scandinavian literature (The Golden Age) **S:** 171
Kiviniemi, Mari [Finnish political leader]
  Finland (Recent developments) **F:** 118
Kivu, Lake [Rwanda-Zaire]
  Lake Tanganyika **L:** 46 *with map*
  Rwanda (Land) **R:** 571 *with map*
Kiwanis International [organization] **K:** 341 *with
picture*
Kiwi [bird] **K:** 342 *with picture*
  Bird *picture on* **B:** 348; (Smell, taste, and touch)
  B: 365
  New Zealand (Animal life) **N:** 353
Kiwi fruit K: 342 *with picture*
  Fruit (Temperate fruits) **F:** 546 *with picture*
Kjellen, Rudolf [Swedish scholar]
  Geopolitics **G:** 106b
Kjølen Mountains
  Norway (Land regions) **N:** 541 *with map*
  Sweden (The Mountain Range) **So:** 1028
KKK [organization] *See* Ku Klux Klan *in this index*
KLA [political group] *See* Kosovo Liberation Army
in this index
Klaipėda [Lithuania] **K:** 342
Klamath Indians K: 343
Klamath Mountains [mountains, California-
Oregon]
  California (Land regions) **C:** 48
  Oregon (Land regions) **O:** 838 *with map*

Klan [organization] *See* Ku Klux Klan *in this index*
Klaproth, Martin Heinrich [German chemist]
  Cerium **C:** 362
  Titanium **T:** 300
  Uranium **U:** 214
  Zirconium **Z:** 597
Klaus, Josef [Austrian political leader]
  Austria (After World War II) **A:** 939-940
Klaus, Karl [Russian chemist]
  Ruthenium **R:** 568
Klaus, Václav [Czech political leader]
  Czech Republic (Recent developments) **Ci:** 1214
Kleberg, Richard M. [American political leader]
  Johnson, Lyndon Baines (Entry into politics)
  J: 146
Klebold, Dylan [American public figure]
  Columbine High School shooting (The attack)
  Co: 853
Klebs, Edwin [German pathologist]
  Löffler, Friedrich August Johannes **L:** 420
Klee, Paul [Swiss painter] **K:** 343
Klee Wyck [book by Carr]
  Carr, Emily **C:** 247
Kleefisch, Rebecca [American political leader]
  Wisconsin (A battle over collective bargaining)
  W: 369
Klein, A. M. [Canadian author] **K:** 343
  Canadian literature (Literature between the
  world wars) **C:** 158
Klein, Calvin [American fashion designer] **K:** 343
Klein, Chuck [American baseball player]
  Baseball (table: Hall of Fame) **B:** 134a
Klein, F. A. [Prussian missionary]
  Moabite stone **M:** 681
Klein, Lawrence Robert [American economist]
  K: 343
Klein, Ralph [Canadian political leader]
  Alberta (table) **A:** 328
Klein, William [American photographer]
  Photography (A diversity of styles) **P:** 426
Kleindienst, Richard G. [American government
official]
  Justice, Department of (table) **J:** 203
  Nixon, Richard Milhous (table) **N:** 433
  Watergate **W:** 144
Kleist, Heinrich von [German author] **K:** 343
  German literature (Other writers) **G:** 140
Klem, Bill [American umpire]
  Baseball (table: Hall of Fame) **B:** 134a
Klemperer, Otto [German conductor] **K:** 344
Kleopatra [asteroid]
  Asteroid (Sizes and shapes) **A:** 824 *with picture*
Kleppe, Thomas S. [American government official]
  Ford, Gerald Rudolph (table) **F:** 378
  Interior, Department of the (table) **I:** 325
Kleptomania [psychology] **K:** 344
Klima, Viktor [Austrian political leader]
  Austria (After World War II) **A:** 939-940
Klimt, Gustav [Austrian artist] **K:** 344
  Austria (Painting) **A:** 933
  Painting (Symbolism) **P:** 76 *with picture*
Kline, Franz [American painter] **K:** 344
  Abstract Expressionism *picture on* **A:** 18
Kline, Kevin [American actor]
  Motion picture (Best performance by an actor in
  a supporting role: 1988) **M:** 862b
Kling, Florence [wife of William G. Harding] *See*
  Harding, Florence Kling *in this index*
Klint, Kaare [Danish architect]
  Furniture *picture on* **F:** 584; (Modern
  Scandinavian design) **F:** 583
Klipspringer [animal]
  Antelope (Kinds of antelope) **A:** 542
Klismos [chair]
  Furniture (Ancient Greece) **F:** 570 *with picture*
Klitzing, Klaus von [German physicist]
  Nobel Prizes (Physics: 1985) **N:** 442
KLM Royal Dutch Airlines
  Netherlands (Transportation) **N:** 147-148
Klompen [clothing]
  Netherlands (Rural life) **N:** 141
Klondike [region, Yukon] **K:** 344 *with picture and
map*
  Yukon (Service industries) **Y:** 579-580 *with map*
Klondike Fever [book by Berton]
  Berton, Pierre **B:** 272
Klondike Gold Rush [1897-1898]
  Alaska (The gold rush) **A:** 361
  Gold rush (Gold rushes in other countries) **G:** 254
  Klondike **K:** 344 *with picture*
  Yukon (History) **Y:** 581 *with picture*
Klondike Gold Rush National Historical Park
[Alaska-Washington]
  National Park System (table: National historical
  parks) **N:** 56-57
Klondike River [Yukon]
  Klondike **K:** 344 *with map*

Yukon (History) **Y:** 581
Yukon River (Upper Yukon) **Y:** 582 *with map*
Klondike solitaire [card game]
  Solitaire **So:** 584
Klossowski de Rola, Balthasar [birth name of]
  Balthus **B:** 65
Kluane National Park [Yukon]
  Canada (table: National parks and national park
  reserves) **C:** 113
Klug, Sir Aaron [South African chemist]
  Nobel Prizes (Chemistry: 1982) **N:** 444
Klutznick, Philip M. [American government
official]
  Carter, Jimmy (table) **C:** 257
  Commerce, Department of (table) **Ci:** 871
Klystron [electronic part]
  Particle accelerator (How accelerators work)
  P: 184-185
  Radar (Continued progress) **R:** 72
  Vacuum tube (Microwave tubes) **V:** 259
Klyuchevskaya [volcano]
  Russia (The East Siberian Uplands) **R:** 541
  Siberia (The land and climate) **S:** 443-444
Kmart Holding Corp.
  Sears, Roebuck and Co. **S:** 269
Knapweed [plant]
  Spotted knapweed **K:** 804
Knebel, John A. [American government official]
  Agriculture, Department of (table) **A:** 161
  Ford, Gerald Rudolph (table) **F:** 378
Knecht Ruprecht [legendary figure]
  Christmas (Gift giving) **C:** 534
Knee [anatomy] **K:** 345 *with diagrams*
  Anterior cruciate ligament **A:** 544
  Arthroscopy **A:** 753 *with picture*
Knee jerk [physiology]
  Nervous system (Simple pathways) **N:** 134
  Reflex action **R:** 194
Kneecap [anatomy]
  Knee **K:** 345
  Leg (The knee joint) **L:** 182 *with diagram*
Kneeling archer [sculpture]
  Sculpture (China) **S:** 238 *with picture*
Kneip, Richard F. [American political leader]
  South Dakota (table) **So:** 680
Knesset [legislature]
  Israel (National government) **I:** 479 *with picture*
Knickerbocker, Diedrich [pen name]
  Irving, Washington (Early career) **I:** 460
Knickerbocker Base Ball Club of New York [team]
  Baseball (Alexander Cartwright) **B:** 133 *with
  picture*
Knickerbockers, New York [team] *See* New York
  Knickerbockers *in this index*
Knickerbocker's History of New York [book by
Irving]
  American literature (Literature of a young nation
  [1788-1830]) **A:** 415
  Irving, Washington (Early career) **I:** 460
  Santa Claus (Santa's appearance) **S:** 114
Knife [tool] **K:** 345 *with pictures*
  Indian, American *picture on* **I:** 175
Knife in the Water [film]
  Motion picture (Movies in the 1960's) **M:** 870-871
Knife River Indian Villages National Historic Site
[North Dakota]
  National Park System (table: National historic
  sites) **N:** 52-53
Knifefish
  Fish *picture on* **F:** 157
Knight *See* Knights and knighthood *in this index*
Knight [chess]
  Chess (The board and the men) **C:** 411-412 *with
  diagram*; (The moves) **C:** 412
Knight, Bob [basketball coach] **K:** 346
Knight, Eric [British-American author] **K:** 346
Knight, Etheridge [American author]
  African American literature (The 1900's) **A:** 136a
Knight, Goodwin J. [American political leader]
  California (table) **C:** 59
Knight, Margaret [American inventor]
  Paper bag **P:** 138
Knight, Nehemiah R. [American political leader]
  Rhode Island (table) **R:** 311
Knight, Robert Montgomery *See* Knight, Bob *in
this index*
Knight bachelor [title]
  Knighthood, Orders of (Honorary orders) **K:** 347
Knight Commander [title]
  Knighthood, Orders of (Honorary orders) **K:** 347
Knight Grand Cross [title]
  Knighthood, Orders of (Honorary orders) **K:** 347
Knight of the Burning Pestle, The [play by
Beaumont]
  Beaumont, Francis **B:** 191
  English literature (Jacobean drama) **E:** 317
Knighthood, Orders of [awards] **K:** 346 *with*

pictures
Bath, Order of the **B:** 165
Knights, Teutonic See Teutonic Knights in this index
Knights and knighthood [European history]
K: 348 with pictures
Address, Forms of (Officials of the
Commonwealth of Nations) **A:** 53
Armor (During the Middle Ages) **A:** 719
Army (Armies in the Middle Ages) **A:** 727
Cavalry **C:** 318
Etiquette (The origins of etiquette) **E:** 374
Feudalism (Knighthood under feudalism) **F:** 82
with picture
Helmet **H:** 179
Heraldry (The development of heraldry) **H:** 194
with pictures
Medals, decorations, and orders (History) **M:** 359
Middle Ages (Life of the people) **M:** 526
Knights Hospitallers [religious and military order]
K: 351
Crusades picture on **Ci:** 1160
Knights Templars **K:** 353
Malta (History) **M:** 113-114
Rhodes **R:** 317
Valletta **V:** 265
Knights of Ak-Sar-Ben
Omaha (Cultural life and recreation) **O:** 756;
(History) **O:** 756-757
Knights of Columbus K: 352 with picture
Knights of Labor [union] **K:** 352
Cleveland, Grover (Labor problems) **Ci:** 670
Cooperative (History) **Ci:** 1036
Labor movement (The first nationwide labor
organizations) **L:** 9-10 with picture
United States, History of the (Early reform efforts)
U: 185-186
Knights of Malta See Knights Hospitallers in this
index
Knights of Peter Claver [organization] **K:** 352
Knights of Pythias [organization] **K:** 352 with
picture
Knights of Rhodes [military and religious order]
See Knights Hospitallers in this index
Knights of St. John of Jerusalem [religious and
military order] See Knights Hospitallers in this
index
Knights of the Bath [award] See Bath, Order of the
in this index
Knights of the Round Table See Round Table in
this index
Knights Templars [European history] **K:** 353
Cyprus (History) **Ci:** 1207
Masonry (The lodges and degrees of Masonry)
M: 267 with picture
Knit [stitch]
Knitting (Knitting the fabric) **K:** 354
Textile **T:** 212; (Knitted fabrics) **T:** 214 with picture;
(The age of modern textiles) **T:** 219
Knitted rug
Rugs and carpets (Other methods) **R:** 516
Knitting [handicraft] **K:** 353 with pictures
Knitting machine K: 354 with picture
Rugs and carpets (Other methods) **R:** 516
Textile picture on **T:** 216
Knob [disorder]
Rickets **R:** 334
Knoblock, Edward [British author]
Bennett, Arnold **B:** 251
Knock [noise]
Gasoline (Engine requirements) **G:** 61
Octane number **O:** 669
Knock Nevis [ship]
Tanker (Kinds of tankers) **T:** 28
Knockout
Boxing (Scoring a fight) **B:** 527
Kickboxing **K:** 310
Mixed martial arts **M:** 680
Knoll, Hans [German designer]
Furniture (Recent developments) **F:** 584
Knoll International
Furniture (Recent developments) **F:** 584
Knopf, Alfred A. [American publisher] **K:** 355
Knorr [ship]
Ship picture on **S:** 419
Vikings (The Vikings as shipbuilders) **V:** 381
Knossos [ancient Greece] **K:** 355
Architecture (Minoan architecture) **A:** 615 with
picture
Crete picture on **Ci:** 1128
Minotaur **M:** 611
Painting (Aegean painting) **P:** 41 with picture
Knot [measurement] **K:** 355
Weights and measures (Miscellaneous weights
and measures) **W:** 184
Knotmeter [measuring device]
Log (A tachometer) **L:** 421
Knots, hitches, and splices K: 355 with diagrams

Fishing pictures on **F:** 178
Macramé **M:** 26 with picture
Knotted stitch
Embroidery (Embroidery stitches) **E:** 257 with
picture
Needlepoint **N:** 118
Knott's Berry Farm
California (Places to visit) **C:** 46
Los Angeles (Metropolitan area) **L:** 462
Knotweed [plant] **K:** 357
Knous, W. Lee [American political leader]
Colorado (table) **Ci:** 844
Know-Nothings [U.S. history] **K:** 357
Buchanan, James (Election of 1856) **B:** 660
Civil War, American (Developments in the
political party system) **Ci:** 616
Immigration (The second wave) **I:** 82
Johnson, Andrew (Governor) **J:** 138
Pierce, Franklin **P:** 454
Riot (During the 1800's) **R:** 348-349
United States, History of the (Party splits) **U:** 176
Washington Monument **W:** 110
Knowledge
See also Truth in this index
Artificial intelligence (Knowledge representation
and reasoning) **A:** 760
Empiricism **E:** 263
Existentialism (What is existentialism?) **E:** 437
Hume, David **H:** 432
Kant, Immanuel (Kant's ideas) **K:** 244
Philosophy (Epistemology) **P:** 384
Knowledge management center [special library]
Library (Special libraries) **L:** 250
Knowles, Beyoncé Giselle [birth name of]
Beyoncé **B:** 276
Knowles, Tony [American political leader]
Alaska (table) **A:** 300
Knowles, Warren P. [American political leader]
Wisconsin (table) **W:** 365
Knowles, William Standish [American chemist]
Nobel Prizes (Chemistry: 2001) **N:** 444
Knowlton cactus [plant]
Endangered species picture on **E:** 271; (table)
E: 270
Known fingerprint
Fingerprinting (Types of fingerprints) **F:** 106
Knox, Frank [American political leader] **K:** 357
Roosevelt, Franklin Delano (The road to war)
R: 455
Knox, Henry [American general] **K:** 358
Revolution, American (The evacuation of Boston)
R: 275 with picture
United States, History of the picture on **U:** 162
Veterans' organizations (In the United States)
V: 344
Washington, George (Cabinet) **W:** 102 with
picture
Knox, John [Scottish religious leader] **K:** 358
Edinburgh **E:** 77
Presbyterians (History) **P:** 756a
Protestantism (The conservative reform
movements) **P:** 834-835
Scotland (The Scottish Reformation) **S:** 219
Knox, Philander Chase [American political leader]
Roosevelt, Theodore (table) **R:** 466
Taft, William Howard (Foreign affairs) **T:** 11
Knox, William Franklin [American political leader]
See Knox, Frank in this index
Knox class [ship]
Frigate picture on **F:** 533
Knoxville [Tennessee] **K:** 358 with picture
Tennessee (table) **T:** 139
Tennessee, University of **T:** 158
Knoxville World's Fair
Knoxville (Government and history) **K:** 359 with
picture
Tennessee (The late 1900's) **T:** 157 with picture
Knuckle ball
Baseball (Pitching) **B:** 127-128
Knuckle walking [locomotion]
Chimpanzee (The life of a chimpanzee) **C:** 472
Knuckling down
Marbles **M:** 193
KO [sports] See Knockout in this index
Koala [animal] **K:** 359 with picture
Animal picture on **A:** 479
Australia picture on **A:** 915
Marsupial (Kinds of marsupials) **M:** 232
Koan [religion]
Zen **Z:** 589
Kobayashi, Makoto [Japanese physicist]
Nobel Prizes (Physics: 2008) **N:** 442
Kobe [Japan] **K:** 360
København [Denmark] See Copenhagen in this
index
Kobuk Valley National Park [Alaska] **K:** 360
National Park System (table: National parks) **N:** 48

Kobzar [book by Shevchenko]
Ukraine (The arts) **U:** 9
Koch, Edward I. [American political leader]
New York City (A time of change) **N:** 343
Koch, Robert [German doctor] **K:** 360
Antibiotic (History) **A:** 552
Bacteria (History) **B:** 22
Bacteriology (Studying bacteria) **B:** 22; (History)
B: 22
Medicine (Scientific study of the effects of
disease) **M:** 375 with picture
Tuberculosis **T:** 477
Koch, Rudolph [German printer]
Book (The 1800's) **B:** 467-468
Koch snowflake [geometry]
Fractal **F:** 443 with diagram
Kochanowski, Jan [Polish poet]
Poland (The arts) **P:** 607
Kocharian, Robert [Armenian political leader]
Armenia (Recent developments) **A:** 719
Köchel, Ludwig [German cataloger]
Mozart, Wolfgang Amadeus (His style) **M:** 907-
908
Köchel number [music]
Mozart, Wolfgang Amadeus (His style) **M:** 907-
908
Kocher, Emil Theodor [Swiss physician]
Nobel Prizes (Physiology or medicine: 1909)
N: 445
Koch's postulates [biology]
Bacteriology (Studying bacteria) **B:** 22
Kodak [camera]
Eastman, George **E:** 47
Photography (Technical improvements) **P:** 423-
424 with picture
Kodály, Zoltán [Hungarian composer] **K:** 360
Kodiak bear
Animal picture on **A:** 485
Bear (Brown bears) **B:** 184
Kodiak Island
Exploration (The Russians in Siberia) **E:** 447
Koerner, W. H. D. [artist]
Cowboy picture on **Ci:** 1108
Koestler, Arthur [Hungarian-British author] **K:** 361
Koffka, Kurt [German-born psychologist]
Gestalt psychology **G:** 175
Kofun era [Japanese history] **K:** 361
Japan (Early days) **J:** 52-53
Kogawa, Joy [Canadian author]
Canadian literature (Modern English-Canadian
fiction) **C:** 160
Koguryo [former region]
Korea, History of (Early years) **K:** 366 with map
Koh-i-noor [gem]
Diamond picture on **D:** 181; (Famous diamonds)
D: 182
Gem (Some famous gems) **G:** 79
Kohala [volcano]
Hawaii (Hawaii) **H:** 100
Kohemp [fiber]
Kudzu **K:** 391
Kohl, Helmut [German political leader] **K:** 361
Germany (West Germany) **G:** 170; (The
unification of East and West Germany) **G:** 171
Köhler, Georges Jean Franz [German physiologist]
Immune system (Further breakthroughs) **I:** 88d
Nobel Prizes (Physiology or medicine: 1984)
N: 446
Kohler, Walter J., Jr. [American political leader]
Wisconsin (table) **W:** 365
Köhler, Wolfgang [German-American
psychologist] **K:** 361
Education (How people learn) **E:** 86
Learning (Insight learning) **L:** 163
Kohlrabi [plant] **K:** 361 with picture
Evolution (Artificial selection) **E:** 432 with picture
Kohn, Walter [Austrian-born American chemist]
Nobel Prizes (Chemistry: 1998) **N:** 444
Kohoutek, Comet [astronomy]
Comet (table) **Ci:** 868
Koinē [language]
Greek language (Development of ancient Greek)
G: 376
Koirala, Girija Prasad [Nepaese political leader]
Nepal (History) **N:** 126-127
Koivisto, Mauno [Finnish political leader]
Finland (The late 1900's) **F:** 118
Koizumi, Junichiro [Japanese political leader]
Japan (Recent developments) **J:** 59
Kojiki [book]
Jimmu **J:** 127
Shinto **S:** 401
Kokanee [fish]
Fish picture on **F:** 159
Salmon (Kinds of salmon) **S:** 70
Koko [gorilla]
Gorilla (Gorillas in captivity) **G:** 276

Kokoro [book by Natsume Soseki]
Natsume Soseki N: 64
Kokoschka, Oskar [Austrian painter] K: 362 *with picture*
Austria (Painting) A: 933
Painting (People) P: 31 *with picture*
Kokpar [sport]
Kazakhstan K: 250a-250b
Kokytos [legendary river]
Hades H: 4
Kola nut K: 362 *with picture*
Kola Peninsula [Russia]
Sami S: 78
Kola Sami [people]
Sami S: 79
Kolamba [former name]
Colombo Ci: 785
Kolas, Yakub [Belarusian poet]
Belarus (People) B: 224a-224b
Kolélas, Bernard [Congolese political leader]
Congo, Republic of the (History) Ci: 940e-940f
Kölen Mountains [mountains, Norway-Sweden]
Sweden (The land) So: 1028
Kolingba, André [Central African political leader]
Central African Republic (History) C: 353
Kolkata [India] K: 362 *with pictures*
Black Hole of Calcutta B: 389
Kolkhozy [agriculture] *See* Collective farm *in this index*
Kölln [former village]
Berlin (Early days) B: 264
Kollwitz, Käthe [German artist] K: 363 *with picture*
Köln [Germany] *See* Cologne *in this index*
Kolokol [newspaper]
Herzen, Alexander Ivanovich H: 217
Kolonia [Federated States of Micronesia]
Palikir P: 108
Komar [ship]
Missile boat M: 618
Komarov, Vladimir M. [Russian cosmonaut]
Astronaut (Accidents in space) A: 830-831
Space exploration (Voskhod and Gemini: The first multiperson space flights) So: 714
Komatsu, Sakyo [Japanese author]
Science fiction (Growing popularity) S: 205-206
Komenský, Jan Amos [Czech educator] *See* Comenius, John Amos *in this index*
Komodo dragon [reptile] K: 364 *with picture*
Lizard (Sizes of lizards) L: 399
Monitor M: 724
National park *picture on* N: 42g
Komodo National Park [Indonesia]
National park *picture on* N: 42g; (table) N: 42f; (Other interesting national parks) N: 42h
Komondor [dog] K: 364 *with picture*
Komorowski, Bronisław [Polish political leader]
Poland (Recent developments) P: 615
Komos [part of play]
Drama (Old Comedy) D: 327
Kompendium der Psychiatrie [book by Kraepelin]
Abnormal psychology (History) A: 12
Kompong Som [Cambodia]
Cambodia (Economy) C: 72
Komunyakaa, Yusef [American author]
African American literature (The 1900's) A: 136a
Kon-Tiki [book by Heyerdahl]
Heyerdahl, Thor H: 221
Kon-Tiki [raft]
Heyerdahl, Thor H: 221 *with picture*
Oslo O: 864
Raft R: 102
Konaré, Alpha Oumar [Malian political leader]
Mali (History) M: 108-109
Konaté, Sékouba [Guinean political leader]
Guinea (History) G: 432
Kong Qiu [Chinese philosopher] *See* Confucius *in this index*
Kongo [former kingdom] K: 364
Africa (States and kingdoms) A: 132
Congo, Democratic Republic of the (Early days) Ci: 940b
Nzinga Nkuwu N: 633
Kongo [people]
Congo, Republic of the (People) Ci: 940d
König, Friedrich [German inventor]
Communication (The 1800's) Ci: 881
Printing (New presses and typecasting machines) P: 803
Königgrätz, Battle of [1866]
Seven Weeks' War S: 325
Königsberg [former name]
Kaliningrad K: 212
Königsberg, Allen Stewart [birth name of]
Allen, Woody A: 372
Konigsburg, Elaine [American author] K: 365
Newbery Medal (table) N: 359
Regina Medal (table: 2001) R: 206

Konitz, Lee [American saxophonist]
Jazz (Cool jazz) J: 72
Konoe, Prince Fumimaro [Japanese political leader] K: 365
Kontakion [hymn]
Greek literature G: 378
Konversations-Lexikon [book]
Encyclopedia (Encyclopedias of the 1800's and 1900's) E: 268b
Koobi Fora National Park [Kenya]
Lake Turkana L: 47
Kookaburra [bird] K: 365 *with picture*
Australia (Native animals) A: 911
Bird (Birds of Australia and New Zealand) B: 346 *with picture*
Kingfisher K: 329
Koolau Range [mountains]
Hawaii (Oahu) H: 102
Koolhaas, Rem [Dutch architect]
Seattle (Museums and libraries) S: 275 *with picture*
Koons, Jeff [American sculptor]
Sculpture (From the mid-1900's to the early 2000's) S: 259-260 *with picture*
Koontz, Dean [American author] K: 365
Koopmans, Tjalling Charles [American economist]
Nobel Prizes (Economics: 1975) N: 449
Kooser, Ted [American poet]
Poet laureate (table: Poets laureate of the United States) P: 590
Kootenai Indians *See* Kutenai Indians *in this index*
Kootenay National Park
Canada (table: National parks and national park reserves) C: 113
Kootenay River [Canada-U.S.]
British Columbia (Rivers, waterfalls, and lakes) B: 624
Kopechne, Mary Jo [American public figure]
Kennedy, Edward Moore K: 259
Koplik's spots [disorder]
Measles (Cause and effects) M: 346
Kopp, Elisabeth [Swiss political leader]
Switzerland (After the wars) So: 1061
Koppel, Ted [American newscaster] K: 365
Köppen, Wladimir [German climatologist]
Climate (Kinds of climates) Ci: 676a
Köppen Hill [hill, Germany]
Pied Piper of Hamelin P: 453
Korab, Mount *See* Mount Korab *in this index*
Korai [carvings]
Sculpture (Archaic sculpture) S: 245
Korakuen Garden [Tokyo]
Tokyo (Parks and gardens) T: 316
Koran [religious book] *See* Qur'ān *in this index*
Korat cat
Cat *picture on* C: 288; (Short-haired breeds) C: 290-291
Korbel, Madeleine [birth name of]
Albright, Madeleine Korbel A: 333
Korbut, Olga [Soviet gymnast]
Union of Soviet Socialist Republics *picture on* U: 33
Kore [Greek mythology]
Persephone P: 295
Kore [sculpture]
Sculpture (Archaic sculpture) S: 245 *with picture*
Korea, Democratic People's Republic of *See* Korea, North *in this index*
Korea, History of K: 366 *with picture and map*
Asian Americans (History of Asian immigration) A: 812d-812e
Clothing *picture on* Ci: 693; (Korea) Ci: 699 *with picture*
Folklore *picture on* F: 324
Han dynasty H: 38
Japan (Imperialism) J: 57
Karate K: 245
Martial arts M: 234a
Russo-Japanese War (Underlying causes) R: 566a
Sculpture (Korea) S: 238 *with picture*
Sino-Japanese War of 1894-1895 S: 473
Korea, North K: 368 *with pictures and maps*
Air force (The North Korean Air Force) A: 184
Army (The North Korean Army) A: 726
Asia (Korea and Taiwan) A: 789; (The spread of Communism) A: 807
Bush, George Walker (North Korea) B: 723
Carter, Jimmy (Later years) C: 259
Cold War (The Korean War) Ci: 764
Cooperative (In other countries) Ci: 1036
Flag *picture on* F: 203
Korea, South (History) K: 378c
Korean War K: 379
Nuclear Nonproliferation Treaty N: 595
Nuclear weapon (After the terrorist attacks of Sept. 11, 2001) N: 602
United Nations (Military actions) U: 91

Korea, Republic of *See* Korea, South *in this index*
Korea, South K: 375 *with pictures and maps*
Asia (Korea and Taiwan) A: 789; (The spread of Communism) A: 807
Automobile (Where cars are made) A: 959
Cold War (The Korean War) Ci: 764
Inchon I: 99
Korea, North (History) K: 373
Korean War K: 379
United Nations (Military actions) U: 91
Korea Strait
Yellow Sea Y: 557
Korea Train Express
Korea, South *picture on* K: 378b
Korean language
Alphabet (Other alphabets) A: 383-384
Korea, North (Language) K: 369
Korea, South (Language) K: 376
Korean pear
Pear (Varieties) P: 215
Korean Peninsula
Korea, History of K: 366
Korean War [1950-1953] K: 379 *with pictures and maps*
Ace A: 24
Air force (Air forces in limited wars) A: 186
Air Force, United States (The Korean War) A: 195
Army (Armies in the nuclear age) A: 728
Army, United States (The Korean War) A: 739
Asia (The spread of Communism) A: 807
Brainwashing B: 560
Cold War (The Korean War) Ci: 764 *with picture*
Communism (The Cold War) Ci: 895
Eisenhower, Dwight David (Presidential candidate) E: 151; (Foreign affairs) E: 152
International law (After World War II) I: 342
International relations (Collective security) I: 345
Korea, North (History) K: 373
Korea, South (A divided peninsula) K: 378c
Korean War Veterans Memorial K: 384
MacArthur, Douglas (The Korean War) M: 3
Marine Corps, United States (The 1900's) M: 209
Navy (Navies during the Cold War) N: 80
Navy, United States (The Korean War [1950-1953]) N: 89
Prisoner of war P: 808
Ridgway, Matthew Bunker R: 336
Seoul (History) S: 306-307
Stalin, Joseph (The Cold War) So: 827
Truman, Harry S. (The Korean War) T: 471
United Nations (Military actions) U: 91
United States, History of the (The Korean War) U: 196
Unknown soldier U: 212
War (table) W: 25
War crime (The Korean War) W: 27
World, History of the (The rise of Communism and the Cold War) W: 446-448
Korean War Veterans Memorial [Washington, D.C.] K: 384
National Park System (table: National memorials) N: 54
Washington, D.C. (The Korean War Veterans Memorial) W: 73 *with picture*
Korean Workers' Party [Korea, North]
Korea, North (Government) K: 368
Koresh, David [American public figure]
Cult (Modern cults) Ci: 1185
Reno, Janet R: 240
Kornberg, Arthur [American biochemist]
Cell (The 1900's) C: 337-338
Nobel Prizes (Physiology or medicine: 1959) N: 445
Kornberg, Roger David [American chemist]
Nobel Prizes (Chemistry: 2006) N: 444
Kornilov, Lavr [Russian general]
Russia (The October Revolution) R: 553
Russian Revolution of 1917 (The February Revolution) R: 566
Union of Soviet Socialist Republics (The October Revolution) U: 35
Korolev, Sergei Pavlovich [Russian engineer] K: 384
Koroma, Ernest Bai [Sierra Leone political leader]
Sierra Leone (History) S: 452
Koror [Palau]
Palau P: 101
Korotkoff, Nikolai [Russian physician]
Heart (Invention of new medical instruments) H: 144
Kortright, Elizabeth [wife of James Monroe] *See* Monroe, Elizabeth Kortright *in this index*
Koryo [Korean history]
Korea, History of (Early years) K: 366
Seoul (History) S: 306
Korzeniowski, Józef Teodor Konrad Nalecz [birth name of]

Conrad, Joseph Ci: 973
Košava [wind]
  Croatia (Land and climate) Ci: 1148a
Kosciuszko, Mount See Mount Kosciuszko in this index
Kościuszko, Tadeusz [Polish patriot] K: 384
  Poland (The partitions) P: 612
Kosciuszko National Park
  Mount Kosciuszko M: 885
Kosher [religion] K: 384
  Judaism (Dietary laws) J: 182
  Meat packing (Meat-packing processes) M: 351
Koshiba, Masatoshi [Japanese physicist]
  Nobel Prizes (Physics: 2002) N: 441-442
Košice [Slovakia] K: 384a
Kosode with Plum Tree and Flowering Plants
  [painting by Hoitsu]
  Painting (Landscapes and seascapes) P: 32-33
  with picture
Kosova See Kosovo in this index
Kosovo K: 384a with picture and map
  Albania (Recent developments) A: 309
  Clinton, Bill (International affairs) Ci: 682f
  Europe picture on E: 387; (The new nationalism) E: 416
  Flag picture on F: 206
  Milošević, Slobodan M: 556
  Priština P: 808a
  Serbia S: 312; (Kosovo crisis) S: 316 with picture; (Recent developments) S: 316a
  United States, History of the (The Balkan conflicts) U: 196d
  Yugoslavia (Kosovo crisis) Y: 577
Kosovo Liberation Army [political group]
  Kosovo (History) K: 384b
  Serbia (Kosovo crisis) S: 316-316a
  Yugoslavia (Kosovo crisis) Y: 577
Kosrae [island, Pacific]
  Caroline Islands C: 244
  Micronesia, Federated States of (Government) M: 515
  Pacific Islands, Trust Territory of the P: 13
Koss, Johann Olav [Norwegian skater]
  Ice skating (History) I: 16
Kossel, Albrecht [German physiologist]
  Nobel Prizes (Physiology or medicine: 1910) N: 445
Kossuth, Lajos [Hungarian patriot] K: 385
  Debrecen D: 65
  Hungary (Habsburg rule) H: 445-446
Kostov, Ivan [Bulgarian political leader]
  Bulgaria (Recent developments) B: 693
Koštunica, Vojislav [Serbian political leader]
  Milošević, Slobodan M: 556
  Serbia (The fall of Milošević) S: 316a; (Recent developments) S: 316a
  Yugoslavia (The end of Yugoslavia) Y: 577
Kosygin, Aleksei Nikolaevich [Soviet political leader] K: 385
  Cold War (Soviet-American relations) Ci: 769
  Johnson, Lyndon Baines (Other developments) J: 151
  Russia (The Cold War) R: 554
  Trudeau, Pierre Elliott picture on T: 462
  Union of Soviet Socialist Republics (History) U: 35-39
Koto [musical instrument]
  Music (Japanese music) M: 956 with picture
Kotoku [emperor of Japan]
  Japan (Chinese influence) J: 53
Kotte [Sri Lanka] See Sri Jayewardenepura Kotte in this index
Kotzebue Sound
  Alaska (Coastline) A: 294
Kouchibouguac National Park [New Brunswick]
  Canada (table: National parks and national park reserves) C: 113
Koufax, Sandy [American baseball player] K: 385
  Baseball (table: Hall of Fame) B: 134a; (Recent developments) B: 137
Kouloura [food]
  Bread picture on B: 588
Koulouri [island, Greece] See Salamis in this index
Kountché, Seyni [Niger political leader]
  Niger (History) N: 409
Kouprey [animal] K: 385 with picture
Kouroi [carvings]
  Sculpture (Archaic sculpture) S: 245
Koussevitzky, Serge [Russian-American conductor] K: 385
  Maynor, Dorothy M: 329
Kowloon Peninsula [region, Hong Kong]
  Hong Kong H: 316 with picture
Koxinga [Chinese military leader]
  Taiwan (History) T: 17-18
Kozhedub, Ivan [Russian pilot]
  Ace A: 24

Kozhikode [city, India]
  Da Gama, Vasco (Voyage to India) D: 4
Kpelle [people]
  Liberia (People) L: 229
KPU [political party]
  Kenya (Building the new nation) K: 303-304
Kr [symbol]
  Krypton K: 389
Kraepelin, Emil [German psychiatrist]
  Abnormal psychology (History) A: 12
  Mental illness (Medical approaches) M: 409
Kraft, J. L. [American businessman]
  Cheese (History) C: 394
Kraft Nabisco Championship
  Golf (Tournaments) G: 264
Kraft process [industrial process]
  Paper (Pulping processes) P: 134-135
Krahn [people]
  Liberia (Civil war) L: 232
Krai [government unit]
  Russia (Local government) R: 531
Krait [snake]
  Snake picture on S: 534
Krak des Chevaliers [castle, Syria]
  Crusades picture on Ci: 1160
Krakatau [volcanic island, Indonesia] K: 386
  Indonesia (Java) I: 233
  Volcano (table) V: 442b
Krakatoa [volcanic island, Indonesia] See Krakatau in this index
Kraków [Poland] K: 386
  Galicia G: 10
  Poland picture on P: 608
Kramer vs. Kramer [film]
  Motion picture (Best picture: 1979) M: 861
Kramnik, Vladimir [Russian chess player]
  Chess (History) C: 414; (World chess champions) C: 414
Kraschel, Nelson G. [American political leader]
  Iowa (table) I: 391
Krasner, Lee [American painter] K: 386 with picture
  Pollock, Jackson P: 646
Kraus, Karl [Austrian author]
  Austria (Literature) A: 933
Krauss, Alison [American musician]
  Country music (Bluegrass music) Ci: 1098a
Kravchuk, Leonid Makarovich [Ukrainian political leader]
  Ukraine (Independence) U: 13
"Krazy Kat" [cartoon]
  Cartoon picture on C: 264
Krebs, Arthur [French engineer]
  Airship (The first airships) A: 251
Krebs, Edwin Gerhard [American physiologist]
  Nobel Prizes (Physiology or medicine: 1992) N: 446
Krebs, Sir Hans Adolf [German biochemist] K: 386
  Krebs cycle K: 387
Krebs cycle [biochemistry] K: 386
  Metabolism (Catabolism) M: 424
  Respiration (Cellular respiration) R: 261
Kreisky, Bruno [Austrian political leader]
  Austria (After World War II) A: 939-940
Kreisler, Fritz [Austrian violinist] K: 387
Kremlin [Moscow] K: 387
  Moscow picture on M: 823; (The city) M: 823 with picture and map
  Russia picture on R: 525; (Architecture) R: 536
Krems [city, Austria]
  Austria picture on A: 935
Křenek, Ernst [Austrian composer]
  Opera (The search for new forms) O: 799-800
Krenz, Egon [German political leader]
  Germany (East Germany) G: 170
Kreps, Juanita Morris [American government official] K: 387
Kretschmer, Ernst [German psychiatrist]
  Personality (Personality types) P: 301
Kreuger, Ivar [Swedish businessman]
  Match (The first safety matches) M: 300a
Kreutzmann, Bill [American musician]
  Grateful Dead G: 329
Krewe [organization]
  Mardi Gras M: 198
  New Orleans (Annual events) N: 282
Krieghoff, Cornelius [Canadian artist]
  Canada picture on C: 110; (Painting and sculpture) C: 109
Kriemhild [legendary figure]
  Nibelungenlied N: 395
Krikalev, Sergei [Russian cosmonaut]
  International Space Station (History) I: 346b with picture
Krill [sea animal] K: 388 with picture
  Animal picture on A: 485
  Antarctica picture on A: 531; (Living things) A: 534

Blue whale B: 421
Fin whale F: 103
Humpback whale H: 436
Southern Ocean (Commercial resources) So: 688b
Krimml Falls [waterfall, Austria]
  Waterfall (table: Famous waterfalls of the world) W: 143
Kringle [food]
  Denmark (Food and drink) D: 135
Kringle, Kris [legendary figure]
  Santa Claus (Santalike characters in other countries) S: 114
Krio [language]
  Sierra Leone (People) S: 451
Krios [people]
  Sierra Leone (People) S: 451
Kris [dagger]
  Indonesia (The arts) I: 232-233
Kris [leader]
  Roma (Language and culture) R: 402b
Kris Kringle [legendary figure]
  Santa Claus (Santalike characters in other countries) S: 114
Krishna [Hindu god] K: 388
  Bhagavad-Gita B: 276
  God (Personal Gods) G: 243
  Hinduism (The Ramayana and the Mahabharata) H: 236
  Holi H: 291
  India picture on I: 121; (Hinduism) I: 116
  Juggernaut J: 185 with picture
  Painting (Indian painting) P: 44
  Vishnu V: 429
Kristall [space exploration]
  Mir M: 614 with picture
Kristallnacht [German history] K: 388
  Germany (Nazi Germany) G: 167-168
  Holocaust (Before the Holocaust) H: 296-296a with picture
Kristin Lavransdatter [book by Undset]
  Undset, Sigrid U: 21
Kristofferson, Kris [American singer]
  Country music picture on Ci: 1098d
  Nelson, Willie N: 123
Krk Bridge [Croatia]
  Bridge (table: Concrete arch) B: 603
Krkonoše Mountains [Czech Republic]
  Czech Republic (The Sudeten Mountains) Ci: 1211
Kroc, Ray [American businessman]
  McDonald's Corporation M: 332h
Kroemer, Herbert [American physicist]
  Nobel Prizes (Physics: 2000) N: 442
Kroetsch, Robert [Canadian author]
  Canadian literature (Modern English-Canadian fiction) C: 160
Kroetz, Franz Xaver [German dramatist]
  Drama (Later German-language drama) D: 340
Krogh, Schack August Steenberg [Danish physiologist]
  Nobel Prizes (Physiology or medicine: 1920) N: 445
Krohn Conservatory
  Cincinnati (Parks and playgrounds) Ci: 556
Krol, John Joseph [American religious leader]
  Cardinal (table: American cardinals) C: 211
Kroll, Wilhelm J. [Luxembourg inventor]
  Titanium T: 300
Krommes, Beth [American illustrator]
  Caldecott Medal (table: 2009) C: 26
Krone, Julie [American jockey]
  Horse racing (History) H: 366
Kronos [Greek mythology] See Cronus in this index
Kropotkin, Peter [Russian prince]
  Anarchism A: 448
Kroto, Sir Harold [British chemist]
  Carbon (Fullerenes) C: 205
  Nobel Prizes (Chemistry: 1996) N: 444
Kru [people]
  Côte d'Ivoire (People) Ci: 1084a
Krug, Julius A. [American government official]
  Interior, Department of the (table) I: 325
  Truman, Harry S. (table) T: 469
Kruger, Paul [South African political leader] K: 388
Kruger, Stephanus Johannes Paulus See Kruger, Paul in this index
Kruger National Park [South Africa]
  Great Limpopo Transfrontier Park G: 346
  National park (South Africa) N: 42e
  South Africa (The Plateau) So: 614 with picture
Krugman, Paul [American economist]
  Nobel Prizes (Economics: 2008) N: 450
Krumgold, Joseph [American author]
  Newbery Medal (table) N: 359
Krung Thep [Thailand] See Bangkok in this index
Krupa, Gene [American drummer] K: 388

Krupp [family] K: 388
Krupp, Alfred [German industrialist]
  Industrial Revolution (Spread of the Industrial Revolution) I: 252-253
  Krupp K: 388
Krupp, Alfried [German industrialist]
  Krupp K: 389
Krupp, Friedrich [German industrialist]
  Krupp K: 388
Krupp, Gustav [German industrialist]
  Krupp K: 389
Krupp works
  Essen E: 359
  Krupp K: 388
Krupskaya, Nadezhda Konstantinovna [Russian political leader] K: 389
  Lenin, V. I. (Young revolutionist) L: 192
Krylov, Ivan [Russian author]
  Fable F: 3
  Russian literature (The classical movement) R: 559-560
Krypton [element] K: 389
Krzyzewski, Mike [American basketball coach] K: 389
'Ksan Historical Village and Museum [British Columbia]
  British Columbia (Places to visit) B: 620 *with picture*
Kshatriya
  Caste C: 279
  Hinduism (Caste) H: 236
K_-band [communications]
  Communications satellite (How communications satellites work) Ci: 888b
Ku K'ai-chih [Chinese painter] *See* Gu Kaizhi *in this index*
Ku Klux Klan [organization] K: 389 *with picture*
  African Americans (The first years of freedom) A: 136j-136k *with picture*; (During the early 1900's) A: 136l
  Alabama (World War I and the Great Depression) A: 276
  Nazism (Neo-Nazism) N: 92-93
  Oklahoma (The 1920's) O: 732
  Reconstruction (Violence against blacks) R: 177
  Roaring Twenties (Changing attitudes) R: 363
  Terrorism (Terrorist groups and movements) T: 178 *with picture*
  Texas (The Civil War and Reconstruction) T: 207
  United States, History of the (Reconstruction) U: 178-179; (Looking backward) U: 191
Ku Klux Klan Act [1871]
  Force bill F: 371
Kuala Lumpur [Malaysia] K: 390 *with picture*
  Malaysia M: 98a *with picture*
  Petronas Towers P: 350
Kuala Lumpur International Airport
  Malaysia (Transportation) M: 100
Kuba [former kingdom]
  Congo, Democratic Republic of the (Early days) Ci: 940b
Kubasov, Valery N. [Soviet cosmonaut]
  Astronaut (Achievements in space) A: 829-830
Kubelsky, Benjamin [birth name of]
  Benny, Jack B: 254
Kubitschek, Juscelino [Brazilian political leader]
  Brasília B: 565
  Brazil (Return to constitutional government) B: 585
"Kubla Khan" [poem by Coleridge]
  Coleridge, Samuel Taylor (His writing) Ci: 772
Kublai Khan [Mongol ruler] K: 391 *with map*
  China (Mongol rule) C: 501
  Exploration (Medieval European exploration) E: 442-443
  Mongol Empire (Kublai Khan) M: 720
  Myanmar (Early days) M: 970d
  Polo, Marco (Early life) P: 648; (Journey to China) P: 648; (Later life) P: 648
  Postal services (Ancient times) P: 703
  World, History of the (China) W: 435
Kubrick, Stanley [American director] K: 391
  Motion picture (Movies in the 1960's) M: 870
Kuchma, Leonid Danylovich [Ukrainian political leader]
  Ukraine (Independence) U: 13-14; (Political changes) U: 14
Kudu [animal] K: 391
  Antelope *picture on* A: 542
Kudzu [plant] K: 391
  Plant (Interesting facts about plants) P: 519 *with picture*
Kufah, Al [Iraq]
  Islamic art (Calligraphy) I: 468
Kufic [writing]
  Islamic art (Calligraphy) I: 468
Kufri Jyoti [potato]

Potato *picture on* P: 711
Kufuor, John A. [Ghanaian political leader]
  Ghana (History) G: 179-180
Kugelhupf [food]
  Bread *picture on* B: 588
Kuhn, Franz Felix Adalbert [German linguist]
  Mythology (Comparative approaches) M: 989
Kuhn, Richard [German chemist]
  Nobel Prizes (Chemistry: 1938) N: 443
Kuiper, Gerard Peter [American astronomer]
  Kuiper belt K: 392
  Neptune (Satellites and rings) N: 129
Kuiper Airborne Observatory
  Observatory (Airborne observatories) O: 645
Kuiper belt [astronomy] K: 392
  Astronomy (Finding new objects) A: 848
  Comet (The parts of a comet) Ci: 867 *with diagram*
  Dwarf planet D: 394
  Oort cloud O: 788
  Triton T: 448
Kuiper belt object [astronomy]
  Kuiper belt K: 392
  Planet P: 508
  Planetary ring P: 514d
  Pluto P: 580
  Satellite S: 149; (Nonplanetary satellites) S: 150b
  Solar system (Dwarf planets) So: 580
Kujala Kadphises [Kushan emperor]
  Kushan Empire K: 394
Kukenaam Falls [Venezuela]
  Cuquenán Falls Ci: 1193
Kukis [people]
  India (Religious and ethnic unrest) I: 134
Kukulkan [Maya god]
  Chichén Itzá C: 439
Kulbak, Moshe [Yiddish author]
  Yiddish literature Y: 566
Kulick, Kelly [American bowler]
  Bowling (The 1900's) B: 524b
Kulikovo, Battle of [1380]
  Russia (The rise of Moscow) R: 548 *with picture*
Kulongoski, Ted [American political leader]
  Oregon (table) O: 845
Kultarr [animal]
  Marsupial mouse M: 233
Kulwicki, Alan [American race driver]
  Automobile racing (table: NASCAR Sprint Cup champions) A: 981
Kumaratunga, Chandrika Bandaranaike [Sri Lankan political leader]
  Bandaranaike, Sirimavo B: 76
  Sri Lanka (History) So: 819-820
Kumasi [Ghana]
  Ashanti A: 767
Kumbh Mela [Hindu religious festival]
  Religion *picture on* R: 214
Kumbi Saleh [ancient city]
  Ghana Empire G: 181 *with map*
  Mauritania (History) M: 315
Kumite [contest]
  Karate (Karate shows and exhibitions) K: 246
Kump, Herman G. [American political leader]
  West Virginia (table) W: 225
Kumquat [fruit] K: 392 *with picture*
Kun, Béla [Hungarian political leader]
  Hungary (Between world wars) H: 446
Kuna Indians
  Indian, American (Indians of the Caribbean) I: 172
  Latin America (Handicrafts) L: 102 *with picture*
  Panama (Way of life) P: 116-117 *with picture*
  Rain forest (The Americas) R: 126b
Kundera, Milan [Czech author]
  Novel (The novel today) N: 575
Kung fu [martial art] K: 392
  Martial arts (Chinese martial arts) M: 234
Kunin, Madeleine M. [American political leader]
  Vermont (table) V: 333
Kunitz, Stanley [American poet]
  Poet laureate (table: Poets laureate of the United States) P: 590
Kunqu [theater]
  China (Theater) C: 490
Kunta Kinte [literary figure]
  Haley, Alex H: 19
Kuomintang Party [Chinese history]
  Chiang Kai-shek C: 418
  China (History) C: 499-503
  Mao Zedong (His life) M: 174
  Sun Yat-sen (The Kuomintang Party) So: 988; (His later years) So: 989
  Taiwan (Government) T: 15-16; (History) T: 17-18
Kupala [Belarusian poet]
  Belarus (People) B: 224a-224b
Kupi, Abas [Albanian political leader]
  Albania (World War II) A: 307-308
Kur River [Asia]

Azerbaijan (Land and climate) A: 996-997 *with map*
  Georgia *picture on* G: 111
Kur Valley [Caucasus Mountains]
  Georgia (Land and climate) G: 110
Kurdish Autonomous Region
  Iraq (The republic) I: 414
Kurdistan [historic region]
  Kurds K: 392
Kurds [people] K: 392
  Arabs (Religious and ethnic clashes) A: 590a
  Bush, George Herbert Walker (Persian Gulf crisis) B: 721
  Hussein, Saddam H: 457
  Iraq (History) I: 413-414
  Persian Gulf War of 1991 (Consequences of the war) P: 300d
  Turkey (People) T: 505 *with picture*; (Recent developments) T: 512
Kurfürstendamm [street, Berlin]
  Berlin (Downtown Berlin) B: 260-261
  Germany *picture on* G: 152
Kurgan [ancient culture]
  Linguistics (Comparative and historical research) L: 337
Kuril Islands [Pacific] K: 393
Kurosawa, Akira [Japanese director] K: 393
  Motion picture (Postwar Realism) M: 869
Kuroshio [current, Pacific] K: 393 *with map*
  Alaska (Climate) A: 296
  Japan (Climate) J: 48
  Ocean (Circulation) O: 658
  Pacific Ocean (Currents) P: 14-15
Kursk [ship]
  Shipwreck (table: Major shipwrecks) S: 428
Kursk, Battle of [1943]
  World War II (The Soviet advance) W: 486
Kurtzman, Harvey [American artist]
  Comics (Comic books) Ci: 869
Kusaie Island [Pacific] *See* Kosrae *in this index*
Kusch, Polykarp [German-American physicist]
  Lamb, Willis Eugene, Jr. L: 51
  Nobel Prizes (Physics: 1955) N: 441
Kush [ancient country] K: 393 *with map*
  Africa (Early civilizations) A: 130
  Nubia N: 578
Kushan dynasty [history of India]
  India (The Mauryan Empire) I: 128-129
Kushan Empire [ancient country] K: 394
  Kanishka K: 215
  Pakistan (Invasions and conquests) P: 98
Kushans [people]
  Afghanistan (Early invasions) A: 95
Kushner, Tony [American dramatist]
  American literature (Drama) A: 426
  Drama (Later United States drama) D: 340-341
Kuskokwim River [river, Alaska]
  Alaska (Rivers and lakes) A: 295
Kutenai Indians K: 394
Kutta, Martin W. [German mathematician]
  Aerodynamics (Lift) A: 85-86
Kutta condition [physics]
  Aerodynamics (Lift) A: 85
Kuuarmuon [title]
  Nuer N: 602
Kuujjuaq [Quebec]
  Labrador Peninsula *picture on* L: 17
Kuvasz [dog] K: 394 *with picture*
Kuwait [country] K: 394 *with pictures and map*
  Arab League A: 582b
  Arabs (Economic inequality) A: 590a
  Army, United States (The Persian Gulf War of 1991) A: 739
  Asia *picture on* A: 778
  Bush, George Herbert Walker (Persian Gulf crisis) B: 721
  Clinton, Bill (International affairs) Ci: 682e
  Egypt (Recent developments) E: 133-134
  Flag *picture on* F: 203
  Hussein, Saddam H: 457
  Hussein I H: 457
  International relations (The Persian Gulf War of 1991) I: 346
  Iraq (The Persian Gulf War of 1991) I: 414
  Middle East M: 530
  Organization of the Petroleum Exporting Countries O: 854
  Persian Gulf War of 1991 P: 300a
  Qatar (History) Q: 3
  Saudi Arabia (The Persian Gulf War of 1991) S: 162
  United Nations (Military actions) U: 91-92
  United States, History of the (The Persian Gulf War) U: 196d
Kuwait [city] K: 397
  Kuwait K: 395; (History) K: 396 *with picture*
  Persian Gulf War of 1991 *picture on* P: 300d

Kuwait Oil Company
Kuwait (History) K: 396
Kuybyshev [Russia] See Samara in this index
Kuznets, Simon [American economist] K: 397
Economics (Modern economics) E: 64-65
Kuznets cycles [economics]
Kuznets, Simon K: 397
Kuznets hypothesis [economics]
Kuznets, Simon K: 397
Kvant laboratories [space exploration]
Mir M: 614 with picture
Kwahu Plateau
Ghana (Land) G: 179 with map
Kwajalein [islands, Pacific]
Marshall Islands (History) M: 231
World War II (Island hopping in the Central
Pacific) W: 489-490
Kwakiutl Indians K: 397
Indian, American picture on I: 162
Kwame Nkrumah [Ganaian political leader] See
Nkrumah, Kwame in this index
Kwanzaa [holiday] K: 397
Christmas (In the United States and Canada)
C: 529
Kwashiorkor [disorder] K: 398
Disease (Metabolic diseases) D: 229
Famine (Death and disease) F: 26a
Malnutrition M: 111
Nutrition (Deficiency diseases) N: 630 with picture
Protein (Proteins in the diet) P: 832
Kwaśniewski, Aleksander [Polish political leader]
Poland (Free elections) P: 614-615
KwaZulu-Natal [province, South Africa]
Pietermaritzburg P: 458
Kyanite [mineral] K: 398
Mineral picture on M: 569
Kyd, Thomas [English dramatist] K: 398
Drama (Elizabethan playwrights) D: 331
English literature (Elizabethan drama) E: 317
Kydland, Finn E. [Norwegian economist]
Nobel Prizes (Economics: 2004) N: 449
Kylián, Jiří [Czech choreographer]
Ballet (Ballet in Europe) B: 54
Kynopolis [ancient city]
Anubis A: 562
Kyoto [Japan] K: 398
Religion picture on R: 222
Kyoto Protocol [1997]
Bush, George Walker (Environmental issues)
B: 722g
Global warming (Government action on global
warming) G: 232c
Nuclear energy (The industry and the
environment) N: 589
Petroleum (Environmental issues) P: 347
Kyphosis [disorder] See Hunchback in this index
Kyrenia Mountains [Cyprus]
Cyprus (Land and climate) Ci: 1206 with picture
and map
Kyrgyz [people]
Kazakhstan (History) K: 251
Kyrgyzstan (People) K: 398
Union of Soviet Socialist Republics (People) U: 31
Kyrgyzstan K: 398 with picture and map
Flag picture on F: 203
Kyushu [island, Japan]
Japan (Kyushu) J: 46 with picture and map
Kyzylkum [desert, Kazakhstan-Uzbekistan] K: 400
Uzbekistan (Land and climate) U: 254

L

L [letter] L: 1 with pictures
L′ ...
Titles beginning L′ appear under their key words, as
in Après-midi d'un faune, L′
**L. M. Montgomery's Cavendish National Historic
Site** [Prince Edward Island]
Canada (table: National historic sites) C: 114
L-1 [spacecraft]
Space exploration (Soviet attempts to reach the
moon) So: 720
L-band [communications]
Communications satellite (How communications
satellites work) Ci: 888b
L-dopa [chemical]
Dopamine D: 309
Parkinson disease (Treatment with drugs) P: 170
L-head engine
Gasoline engine (Valve arrangement) G: 64
L-lactic acid [chemical]
Lactic acid L: 24
L-tryptophan [biochemistry] See Tryptophan in
this index
La [symbol]
Lanthanum L: 69
La ...
Titles beginning with La appear under their key
words, as in Bohème, La. Place names beginning
La are alphabetized as single words: La Brea tar
pits appears after Labrador
La Amistad National Park [Costa Rica-Panama]
National park (table) N: 42g
Laayoune [Western Sahara] See El Aaiun in this
index
Laban [Biblical figure]
Jacob J: 19
Laban, Rudolf von [German dancer]
Ballet (Preserving a ballet) B: 50
Labanotation [choreography]
Ballet diagram on B: 49; (Preserving a ballet) B: 50
Labarum [Roman Empire]
Flag picture on F: 216
Labe River
Elbe River E: 156
Label [heraldry]
Heraldry picture on H: 195
Labeling [industry]
Agriculture (Grades and labels) A: 152
Bar coding B: 102
Consumer protection (The right to information)
Ci: 1018
Genetically modified food (Regulation) G: 86
Nutrition (Nutrition guidelines) N: 626
Packaging (Packaging regulations) P: 18
Pure food and drug laws (Labeling of foods)
P: 908
Labella [entomology]
Fly (Head) F: 309 with diagram
La Belle [shipwreck]
Archaeology (Working underwater) A: 597
Laberge, Albert [Canadian author]
Canadian literature (Fiction: 1850-1918) C: 157
Labium [entomology]
Insect (Mouthparts) I: 286 with diagrams
Mosquito (How a mosquito "bites") M: 831-832
with diagram
La Boétie, Étienne de [French author]
Montaigne, Michel Eyquem de M: 741
LaBonte, Terry [American race driver]
Automobile racing (table: NASCAR Sprint Cup
champions) A: 981
Labor [birth]
Baby (Birth) B: 6
Childbirth (The birth process) C: 456
Pregnancy (Changes in the uterus) P: 734b
Reproduction, Human (Birth) R: 248 with pictures
Labor [economics]
Economics (Economic growth) E: 62
Industry (Labor) I: 259 with pictures
Labor force L: 3
Marx, Karl: (Das Kapital) M: 237
Productivity P: 810
State government (Business and labor) So: 865
Labor [unions] See Labor movement in this index
Labor, Department of [U.S.] L: 2 with picture
Washington, D.C. map on W: 76
Labor, Division of See Division of labor in this index
Labor, Knights of See Knights of Labor in this index
Labor, Secretary of [office]
Flag picture on F: 211
Labor, Department of L: 2
Labor arbitration
Arbitration (Industrial, or labor, arbitration)
A: 592
Labor camp
Communism (Under Stalin) Ci: 892-893
Labor Day [holiday] L: 2
Labor economics
Economics (Fields of economics) E: 64
Labor force L: 3
Economic indicator E: 57
Industry (Labor) I: 259
Unemployment U: 21
Labor income [economics]
Flat tax F: 228
Labor-intensive industry
Industry (Labor) I: 259
Labor legislation
Child labor (Early child labor laws) C: 455
Strike (Kinds of strikes) So: 928
Workers' compensation W: 405
Labor-management relations
See also Industrial relations in this index
Lockout L: 413
National Mediation Board N: 40
Strike So: 928
Taft-Hartley Act T: 12
Workers' compensation W: 405
Labor-Management Relations Act See Taft-
Hartley Act in this index
**Labor-Management Reporting and Disclosure
Act**
Labor movement (Charges of corruption) L: 13
Labor movement L: 4 with pictures

See also the list of Related articles in the Labor
movement article
City (Description) Ci: 585-587; (Government)
Ci: 588
Cleveland, Grover (Labor problems) Ci: 670
Haymarket Riot H: 121
Industrial Revolution (Life during the Industrial
Revolution) I: 251
New Deal (Helping industry and labor) N: 201
Roosevelt, Theodore (Friend of labor) R: 464
Syndicalism So: 1067
United States, History of the (Social reform)
U: 173; (Early reform efforts) U: 185; (The
economy—boom and bust) U: 191
Workers' compensation W: 405
World, History of the (The Industrial Revolution)
W: 444-445
Labor Party [Australia] See Australian Labor Party
in this index
Labor Party [Israel] See Israel Labor Party in this
index
Labor Party [Norway]
Norway (Politics) N: 539
Labor Party of Australia See Australian Labor
Party in this index
Labor relations [business] See Personnel
management in this index
Labor riot
Riot (Major riots in the United States) R: 349 with
picture
Labor Statistics, Bureau of [U.S.] L: 15
Consumer Price Index Ci: 1017
Cost of living L: 1079
Unemployment (Measuring unemployment)
U: 22
Labor theory of value [economics]
Ricardo, David R: 321
Labor union L: 15
Labor movement L: 4
American Federation of Labor and Congress of
Industrial Organizations A: 409
Boycott B: 539
Coal (Mineworkers) Ci: 728-729
Election E: 158
Gay Nineties (Industrial growth) G: 72
Homestead Strike H: 305
Industrial Revolution (The working class) I: 251
Labor, Department of (Functions) L: 2
National Labor Relations Act N: 39
Norris-La Guardia Act N: 457
Railroad (Rail unions) R: 113
Strike So: 928
Taft-Hartley Act T: 12
Teamsters Union T: 72
United States, History of the (Early reform efforts)
U: 185
Western frontier life in America (Life in the
mining towns) W: 236
Laboratory L: 16
Edison, Thomas Alva E: 77 with pictures
Electronics picture on E: 213
Hospital (Professional services departments)
H: 371
Safety (In other school areas) S: 12
Universities and colleges (Research and
laboratory work) U: 210
Laboratory glassware
Glass picture on G: 211; (Specialty glasses) G: 212
Laboratory school [education] L: 16
Preschool (History) P: 756b-757
Laboratory technician
Medicine (Other careers in medicine) M: 371
Public health picture on P: 856
Laborers' International Union of North America
L: 16
American Federation of Labor and Congress of
Industrial Organizations (History) A: 410
Labor movement (table) L: 8
Laboulaye, Édouard-René Lefebvre de [French
historian]
Statue of Liberty picture on So: 875; (Inspiration
and preparations) So: 876
Labour Day
Holiday (In Canada) H: 291
Labour Gazette [newspaper]
King, William Lyon Mackenzie (Early political and
public career) K: 325
Labour Organization, International See
International Labour Organization in this index
Labour Party [New Zealand]
Clark, Helen Elizabeth Ci: 639
New Zealand (Political parties) N: 347
Labour Party [United Kingdom] L: 16
Blair, Tony B: 396
Brown, Gordon B: 642
Callaghan, James C: 67
Fabian Society F: 2

Foot, Michael **F:** 353
Labor movement (In other countries) **L:** 14
Liberal Democrats **L:** 226
MacDonald, James Ramsay **M:** 5
Socialism (World Wars I and II) **So:** 561
United Kingdom (Politics) **U:** 54; (The rise of the Labour Party) **U:** 70
Labour Representation Committee
Labour Party (History) **L:** 16
La Bourgogne and Cromartyshire [ship]
Shipwreck (table: Major shipwrecks) **S:** 428
Labradoodle [dog]
Dog (Kinds of dogs) **D:** 265-266
Labrador [Canada] *See* Labrador Peninsula; Newfoundland and Labrador *in this index*
Labrador Current [Arctic Ocean] **L:** 17 *with map*
Arctic Ocean *map on* **A:** 642; (Currents) **A:** 643
Atlantic Ocean (Currents) **A:** 866
Maine (Climate) **M:** 83
Ocean (Circulation) **O:** 658
Labrador duck
Bird (Extinct birds) **B:** 369-370
Duck (Sea ducks) **D:** 376
Labrador Peninsula L: 17 *with map* and picture
Labrador retriever L: 18 *with picture*
Dog *picture on* **D:** 268
Retriever *on* **R:** 266
Labrador tea [plants] **L:** 18
Flower *picture on* **F:** 284
Labradorite [mineral]
Feldspar **F:** 68
La Brea tar pits [California] **L:** 18 *with picture*
Los Angeles (Visitor's guide) **L:** 468 *with picture*
Labrouste, Henri [French architect]
Architecture (The Industrial Revolution) **A:** 625
Labrum [zoology]
Insect (Mouthparts) **I:** 286 *with diagrams*
La Bruyère, Jean de [French author] **L:** 19
French literature (Classical prose) **F:** 520
Laburnum [tree] **L:** 19
Labyrinth [anatomy]
Ear (The inner ear) **E:** 8 *with diagram*
Labyrinth [Greek mythology] **L:** 19 *with picture*
Daedalus **D:** 3
Minos **M:** 611
Minotaur **M:** 611
Labyrinth of Fate, The [book by Mena]
Spanish literature (The 1400's) **So:** 758
Labyrinth of Solitude [book by Paz]
Paz, Octavio **P:** 205
Labyrinthine organs [anatomy]
Ear (The inner ear) **E:** 8
Labyrinthodont [extinct animal]
Amphibian *picture on* **A:** 441
Lac [animal product] **L:** 19
Lacquer **L:** 22
Resin (Natural resins) **R:** 259
Lac [money]
Rupee **R:** 521
Lac du Chat [former name]
Lake Erie **L:** 37
Lac Laronge III [painting by Stella]
Stella, Frank *picture on* **So:** 886
Lac Léman [lake, France-Switzerland]
Lake Geneva **L:** 38 *with map*
Lac Vieux Desert [region, Michigan-Wisconsin]
Wisconsin River **W:** 370
Lacalle, Luis Alberto [Uruguayan political leader]
Uruguay (The late 1900's) **U:** 228
Laccolith [geology]
Rock (Intrusive rock) **R:** 371
Lace [fabric] **L:** 19 *with pictures*
Crochet *picture on* **Ci:** 1148c
Paraguay (The arts) **P:** 147
Textile (Other textiles) **T:** 215
Lacedaemon [ancient city] *See* Sparta *in this index*
La Ceiba [Honduras] **L:** 20
Lacemaker, The [painting by Vermeer]
Vermeer, Jan **V:** 317
Lacertid lizard
Lizard (Reproduction) **L:** 400-401
Lacewing [insect] **L:** 22 *with picture*
Insect *picture on* **I:** 281
Larva *picture on* **L:** 78
Lacey Bird and Game Act [1900]
Conservation (The rise of the conservation movement) **Ci:** 985
La Chaussée, Pierre de [French dramatist]
Drama (France) **D:** 335
Laches [book by Plato]
Plato (The early dialogues) **P:** 568; (The theory of forms) **P:** 568
Lachesis [mythology]
Fates **F:** 54
Lachine Canal [waterway, Quebec]
Canada (table: National historic sites) **C:** 114
Montreal (The early 1800's) **M:** 778

Quebec (Transportation) **Q:** 28
Lachmann, Hedwig [German librettist]
Opera: (*Salome*) **O:** 807
Lackland, John [king of England] *See* John *in this index*
Lackland Air Force Base [Texas] **L:** 22
Laclède Liguest, Pierre [French frontiersman]
Missouri (Settlement) **M:** 669
Saint Louis (Early settlement) **S:** 49
Laclos, Pierre de [French author]
Enlightenment (The orderliness of nature) **E:** 326a-326b
Lacombe, Albert [Canadian religious leader]
Alberta (Missionary activity) **A:** 329
La Condamine, Charles Marie de [French explorer]
Rubber (First uses) **R:** 500-501
Laconia [department, Greece]
Sparta **So:** 766
Laconia [New Hampshire]
New Hampshire *picture on* **N:** 217
La Coruña [Spain]
Lighthouse (Notable lighthouses) **L:** 295
Lacquer [finish] **L:** 22
Lacquerware **L:** 22 *with picture*
Paint (Industrial paints) **P:** 24
Varnish **V:** 286
Lacquer [recording]
Phonograph (How phonograph records are made) **P:** 401
Lacquer tree [tree]
Lacquer **L:** 22
Lacquerware [decoration] **L:** 22 *with pictures*
Lacrimal bone [anatomy]
Face **F:** 3
Lacrimal gland [anatomy]
Eye (The outer parts) **E:** 460 *with picture*
Gland (Exocrine glands) **G:** 207-208 *with diagram;* (table) **G:** 209
Tears **T:** 72 *with picture*
Lacrimal sac [anatomy]
Eye (The outer parts) **E:** 460 *with picture*
Tears **T:** 72 *with picture*
La Crosse [Wisconsin] **L:** 23
Lacrosse [sport] **L:** 23 *with picture*
Indian, American *picture on* **I:** 156; (Recreation) **I:** 142
Lactalbumin [protein]
Albumin **A:** 333
Lactarius [fungus]
Mushroom (Nonpoisonous mushrooms) **M:** 943-945
Lactase [enzyme]
Lactose intolerance **L:** 25
Milk (Milk in the human diet) **M:** 546
Lactate ester [chemical]
Lactic acid **L:** 24
Lactation [zoology] **L:** 25
Breast **B:** 590
Pregnancy (Changes in breasts) **P:** 734b
Lacteal [anatomy]
Intestine (The small intestine) **I:** 353
Lymphatic system (Absorption of fats) **L:** 535
Lactic acid [chemical] **L:** 24
Lacto-ovo-vegetarian
Vegetarianism **V:** 294
Lacto-vegetarian
Vegetarianism **V:** 294
Lactobacillus [bacteria]
Fermentation **F:** 73
Yogurt **Y:** 567
Lactometer [measuring device]
Hydrometer **H:** 471
Lactose [sugar]
Carbohydrate (Kinds of carbohydrates) **C:** 203; (How the body uses carbohydrates) **C:** 204
Lactic acid **L:** 24
Lactose intolerance **L:** 25
Milk (Carbohydrates) **M:** 546
Nutrition (Carbohydrates) **N:** 625
Sugar (Kinds of sugar) **So:** 960
Lactose intolerance [disorder] **L:** 24
Milk (Milk in the human diet) **M:** 546
Ladd, Herbert W. [American political leader]
Rhode Island (table) **R:** 311
Ladd & Company
Hawaii (The kingdom of Hawaii) **H:** 106
Ladd Memorial Stadium [Mobile]
Mobile (The city) **M:** 681
Ladder [unit]
Fire department (Firefighting) **F:** 123
Ladder truck
Fire department (Firefighting) **F:** 123 *with picture;* (Trucks and vehicles) **F:** 126 *with picture*
La Défense [Paris]
Paris (Renewal and new construction) **P:** 166-167 *with picture*

Laden, Osama bin [Saudi-born Muslim leader] *See* Bin Laden, Osama *in this index*
Ladewig, Marion [American bowler] **L:** 25 *with portrait*
Ladies Auxiliary to the Veterans of Foreign Wars
Veterans of Foreign Wars of the United States **V:** 344
Ladies-delight [plant]
Pansy **P:** 131
Ladies Oriental Shrine of North America
Masonry (Organization) **M:** 267
Ladies Pro Bowlers Tour
Bowling (Professional bowling) **B:** 524
Ladies Professional Golf Association
Golf (Tournaments) **G:** 264; (Women's golf) **G:** 266
Sorenstam, Annika **So:** 596
Zaharias, Babe Didrikson **Z:** 584
La Digue [island]
Seychelles **S:** 339
Ladin [language]
Italy (Language) **I:** 502
Ladinos [people]
Guatemala (People) **G:** 413
Ladoga, Lake [Russia] *See* Lake Ladoga *in this index*
Ladrone [pirate]
Pirate **P:** 494
Ladrones, Islas de los
Mariana Islands **M:** 199
Lady [title] **L:** 25
Duke **D:** 380
Knighthood, Orders of (Honorary orders) **K:** 347
Middle Ages (Life of the people) **M:** 526
Nobility (Privileges of the peerage) **N:** 450
"Lady, or the Tiger?, The" [story by Stockton]
Stockton, Frank Richard **So:** 906
Lady Amherst's pheasant
Bird (Birds of Asia) **B:** 344f *with picture*
Lady and the Tramp [film by Disney]
Disney, Walt (Full-length movies) **D:** 236 *with picture*
Lady beetle [insect] *See* Ladybug *in this index*
Lady Byng Memorial Trophy
Hockey (Professional leagues) **H:** 278-279
Lady Byron Vindicated [book by Stowe]
Stowe, Harriet Beecher (Other works) **So:** 916
Lady Chatterley's Lover [book by Lawrence]
Lawrence, D. H. **L:** 145
Lady Godiva [English public figure] *See* Godiva, Lady *in this index*
Lady in waiting
Lady **L:** 25
Lady Jean [painting by Bellows]
Bellows, George Wesley *picture on* **B:** 245
Lady Macbeth of Mtsensk [opera by Shostakovich]
Shostakovich, Dimitri **S:** 436
Lady mayoress [title]
Lady **L:** 25
Lady Murasaki [Japanese author] *See* Murasaki Shikibu *in this index*
Lady of Lyons, The [play by Bulwer-Lytton]
Bulwer-Lytton, Edward George Earle Lytton **B:** 698
Lady of the bedchamber [title]
Royal Household of the United Kingdom **R:** 498
Lady of the Camellias, The [play by Dumas]
Dumas, Alexandre, fils **D:** 382
Opera: (*Traviata, La*) **O:** 807-808
Lady of the Lake [legendary figure]
Excalibur **E:** 435 *with picture*
Lancelot, Sir **L:** 56
Merlin **M:** 418
Lady of the Lake, The [poem by Scott]
"Hail to the Chief" **H:** 8
Scott, Sir Walter (His life) **S:** 222
Lady Oracle [book by Atwood]
Atwood, Margaret **A:** 880
Lady Sings the Blues [book by Holiday]
Holiday, Billie **H:** 291
Lady Windermere's Fan [play by Wilde]
Wilde, Oscar **W:** 301
Lady with a Pink [painting by Memling]
Clothing *picture on* **Ci:** 702
Lady with an Ermine [painting by Leonardo]
Leonardo da Vinci *picture on* **L:** 200
Lady with the Unicorn, The [tapestries]
Tapestry (History) **T:** 39-40
Unicorn *picture on* **U:** 26
Ladybird [insect] *See* Ladybug *in this index*
Ladybug [insect] **L:** 25 *with picture*
Beetle (Ladybugs) **B:** 217
Insect *pictures on* **I:** 283, I; 296; (Insect control) **I:** 284-285 *with picture*
Lady's eardrop [plant]
Fuchsia **F:** 549
Lady's Magazine, The [magazine]
Magazine (Early magazines) **M:** 44-45

Lady's Not for Burning, The [play by Fry]
Fry, Christopher **F:** 549
Lady's-slipper [plant] **L:** 25 *with picture*
Orchid **O:** 825
Ladysmith Black Mambazo [musical group] **L:** 26
South Africa (The arts) **So:** 614
Laënnec, René Théophile Hyacinthe [French doctor] **L:** 26
Stethoscope **S:** 895
Lærdal Tunnel [Norway]
Tunnel (table) **T:** 491; (History) **T:** 491-492
Laertes [legendary figure]
Ulysses (The Trojan War) **U:** 17
Laertes [literary figure]
Shakespeare, William: *(Hamlet)* **S:** 361-362
Laetare Medal [award]
Notre Dame, University of (Programs) **N:** 551
Laetoli fossil site [Tanzania] **L:** 26
Leakey, Mary Douglas **L:** 161
Prehistoric people (Types of australopithecines) **P:** 745 *with picture*; (table) **P:** 754
Laetrile [drug] **L:** 26
La Farge, John [American painter] **L:** 26 *with picture*
Stained glass (Decline and revival) **So:** 823
La Farge, Oliver [American author] **L:** 26
La Fayette, François de [husband of]
La Fayette, Madame de **L:** 27
La Fayette, Madame de [French author] **L:** 27
French literature (Classical prose) **F:** 520
Novel (Early novels) **N:** 572
Lafayette, Marquis de [French general] **L:** 27 *with portrait*
Monroe, James (Life in the White House) **M:** 737
Morse, Samuel Finley Breese (Morse as artist) **M:** 818 *with portrait*
Revolution, American (Valley Forge) **R:** 283; (The end of the war) **R:** 285
"Lafayette, we are here" [quotation]
Pershing, John Joseph (World War I) **P:** 296
Lafayette Escadrille [military unit]
Air Force, United States (World War I) **A:** 194
Lafayette Square [Buffalo]
Buffalo *picture on* **B:** 677
Laffin, Julie [American performance artist]
Art and the arts *picture on* **A:** 746
Laffite, Jean [American pirate] **L:** 28
Jackson, Andrew (Glory at New Orleans) **J:** 9
New Orleans (The early 1800's) **N:** 283
Laffite, Pierre [brother of]
Laffite, Jean **L:** 28
Lafitte, Jean [American pirate] *See* Laffite, Jean *in this index*
Lafkenche [people]
Mapuche **M:** 189
La Flesche, Susan [American doctor]
Picotte, Susan La Flesche **P:** 452
La Follette [American family] **L:** 29 *with portrait*
La Follette, Belle Case [American journalist]
La Follette (Belle Case La Follette) **L:** 29
La Follette, Philip Fox [American political leader]
La Follette (Philip Fox La Follette) **L:** 29
Progressive Party (The La Follette Progressives) **P:** 814
Wisconsin (table) **W:** 365; (The La Follette Progressives) **W:** 368
La Follette, Robert Marion, Sr. [American political leader]
La Follette (Robert Marion La Follette, Sr.) **L:** 29 *with portrait*
Progressive Era (Political reforms) **P:** 814
Progressive Party (The La Follette Progressives) **P:** 814
Wisconsin (table) **W:** 365; (The Progressive Era) **W:** 366
La Follette, Robert Marion, Jr. [American political leader]
La Follette (Robert Marion La Follette, Jr.) **L:** 29
Progressive Party (The La Follette Progressives) **P:** 814
Wisconsin (The La Follette Progressives) **W:** 368; (Decline of La Follette Progressivism) **W:** 368
La Follette Progressives *See* Progressive Party *in this index*
La Follette's Magazine
La Follette (Belle Case La Follette) **L:** 29
La Fontaine, Henri [Belgian statesman]
Nobel Prizes (Peace: 1913) **N:** 448a
La Fontaine, Jean de [French poet] **L:** 29 *with picture*
Fable **F:** 3
French literature (Classical poetry) **F:** 520
Literature for children (Fables) **L:** 359
Lafontaine, Sir Louis Hippolyte [Canadian political leader]
Baldwin, Robert **B:** 40
Canada, History of (The beginning of self-

government) **C:** 144
La Fontaine, Zöe [wife of]
Laurier, Sir Wilfrid (Young lawyer) **L:** 123
La Fortaleza [palace]
San Juan **S:** 103
La Framboise, Joseph [French explorer]
South Dakota (Exploration and fur trade) **So:** 681
Lag bolt
Bolt **B:** 449 *with picture*
Lagan [wreckage]
Flotsam, jetsam, and lagan **F:** 267
Lagash [ancient city]
Babylonia (Sumerian city-states) **B:** 14
Lager [drink]
Alcoholic beverage (Beer) **A:** 336
Beer **B:** 211
Lagerfeld, Karl [German-born fashion designer] **L:** 30
Lagerkvist, Pär Fabian [Swedish author] **L:** 30
Lagerlöf, Selma [Swedish author] **L:** 30
Sweden (Arts) **So:** 1026-1027
Lagomorph [zoology]
Mammal (table) **M:** 128 *with picture*
Lagoon [geography] **L:** 30
Atoll **A:** 870 *with pictures*
Coral reef (Kinds of coral reefs) **Ci:** 1048b
Lagos [Nigeria] **L:** 30 *with picture*
Abuja **A:** 19
Africa *picture on* **A:** 98
City *picture on* **Ci:** 575
Nigeria *picture on* **N:** 413
Lagos Escobar, Ricardo [Chilean political leader]
Bachelet, Michelle **B:** 17
Chile (Recent developments) **C:** 470
Lagosuchus [extinct animal]
Dinosaur (Dinosaur ancestors) **D:** 206b
La Grande River [Quebec]
Hudson Bay **H:** 405
Lagrange, Joseph-Louis [French mathematician] **L:** 31
Lagrange point [physics]
Star (Binary stars) **So:** 852
Lagting [government]
Faroe Islands **F:** 47
Norway (National government) **N:** 537-539
La Guardia, Fiorello Henry [American political leader] **L:** 31 *with portrait*
New York City (Formation of Greater New York) **N:** 342
Norris-La Guardia Act **N:** 457
La Guardia Airport [New York City]
New York City (Queens) **N:** 329-330
Lahar [geology]
Volcano (Lahars) **V:** 440 *with diagram*
La Have River
Nova Scotia (Rivers and lakes) **N:** 562 *with map*
Lahontan, Lake [geology]
Nevada (Rivers and lakes) **N:** 166-168
LaHood, Ray [American government official]
Obama, Barack (table) **O:** 640h
Transportation, Department of (table) **T:** 400
Lahore [Pakistan] **L:** 31
Pakistan (The Islamic impact) **P:** 99
Lahoud, Emile [Lebanese political leader]
Lebanon (After the civil war) **L:** 174
Lahr, Bert [American actor]
Drama *picture on* **D:** 340
Garland, Judy *picture on* **G:** 44
Lai [poem]
French literature (Narrative poetry) **F:** 518-519
Lai de Lanval [poem by de France]
Launfal, Sir **L:** 121
Laika [dog]
Space exploration (The space race begins) **So:** 707
Laing, Alexander Gordon [Scottish explorer]
Exploration (The exploration of Africa) **E:** 448 *with map*
Laird, Melvin Robert [American political leader] **L:** 31
Laissez faire [economics] **L:** 31
Capitalism (How capitalism differs from central planning) **C:** 194; (The development of capitalism) **C:** 196
Democratic Party (After the Civil War) **D:** 125
Depression **D:** 150
Economics (History of economic thought) **E:** 63
Freedom (Economic freedom) **F:** 501
Greenspan, Alan **G:** 386
Keynes, John Maynard **K:** 308a
Lochner v. New York **L:** 410
Mercantilism **M:** 411
Welfare state **W:** 192
Laity [religion]
Protestantism (The laity) **P:** 834
Religion (How the major religions are organized) **R:** 218

Roman Catholic Church (Pastor and parish) **R:** 404
Vatican Council II (The Dogmatic Constitution on the Church) **V:** 289
Laius [Greek mythology]
Oedipus **O:** 676
Lajeunesse, Gabriel [literary figure]
Longfellow, Henry Wadsworth (Narrative poems) **L:** 450
Lajoie, Napoleon [American baseball player]
Baseball (table: Hall of Fame) **B:** 134a; (table: Modern major league records) **B:** 138
Lakandula [Manilan ruler]
Manila (History) **M:** 143
Lakatoi [ship]
Ship (Sailing ships in the 1900's) **S:** 423 *with picture*
Lake [geography] **L:** 32 *with pictures*
See also the list of Related articles in the Lake article
Climate (Oceans and large lakes) **Ci:** 676a
World (Water) **W:** 415
Lake [substance] **L:** 35
Mordant **M:** 801
Lake, Everett J. [American political leader]
Connecticut (table) **Ci:** 967
Lake, Simon [American inventor]
Submarine (Early submarines) **So:** 942-943
Lake, Veronica [American actress]
Hairdressing (The 1900's) **H:** 12
Lake Agassiz [former lake] **L:** 35
Lake Ainslie [Nova Scotia]
Nova Scotia (Rivers and lakes) **N:** 562-564
Lake Albano [Italy] **L:** 35
Lake Albert [Africa] **L:** 35
Exploration (The exploration of Africa) **E:** 448-449
Lake Argyle [Australia]
Australia (Lakes) **A:** 909
Lake Arresø [Denmark]
Denmark (Lakes and rivers) **D:** 138
Lake Athabasca [Canada] **L:** 35 *with map*
Alberta (Rivers and lakes) **A:** 322-324
Exploration (Crossing North America) **E:** 447
Lake Atitlán [Guatemala]
Guatemala *picture on* **G:** 414
Lake Baikal [Siberia] **L:** 35 *with map*
Exploration (The Russians in Siberia) **E:** 447
Lake (table) **L:** 34
Russia (Rivers and lakes) **R:** 541 *with picture*
Siberia (The land and climate) **S:** 444-444 *with picture and map*
Lake Balaton [Hungary]
Hungary *picture on* **H:** 442; (Rivers and lakes) **H:** 443 *with map*
Lake Balkhash [Kazakhstan] **L:** 36
Lake Bangweulu [Zambia] **L:** 36
Lake Baykal [Siberia] *See* Lake Baikal *in this index*
Lake Bonneville [former lake]
Flood (Other floods) **F:** 237
Great Salt Lake **G:** 348
Utah (Rivers and lakes) **U:** 242
Lake Buena Vista Resort [Florida]
Graves, Michael *picture on* **G:** 330
Lake Burley Griffin [Australia]
Canberra *picture on* **Ci:** 166
Lake Chad [Africa] **L:** 36
Lake Champlain [Canada-U.S.] **L:** 36 *with map*
Vermont (Rivers and lakes) **V:** 335; (Rivers and lakes) **V:** 328-330 *with map*
Lake Champlain, Battle of [1814]
Macdonough, Thomas **M:** 11
War of 1812 (Lake Champlain) **W:** 32
Lake Chapala [Mexico]
Mexico (The Plateau of Mexico) **M:** 461 *with map*
Lake Charles [Louisiana] **L:** 36
Lake Chaubunagungamaug [Massachusetts]
Massachusetts (Rivers and lakes) **M:** 284-285
Lake Chelan [Washington]
Washington (Land regions) **W:** 58-60 *with map*
Lake Chelan National Recreation Area [Washington]
National Park System (table: National recreation areas) **N:** 49
Lake Chicot [Arkansas]
Arkansas (Rivers and lakes) **A:** 706-708
Lake Chilwa [Mozambique]
Stanley and Livingstone (Livingstone's discoveries) **So:** 837 *with map*
Lake Clark National Park [Alaska] **L:** 36
National Park System (table: National parks) **N:** 48
Lake Clark National Preserve [Alaska]
National Park System (table: National preserves) **N:** 58
Lake Coeur d'Alene [Idaho]
Idaho (Rivers, waterfalls, springs, and lakes) **I:** 38
Lake Como [Italy] **L:** 37 *with map*
Lake Constance [Europe] **L:** 37
Switzerland (The Swiss Plateau) **So:** 1055 *with*

map
Lake Country [region, Chile]
Chile (The Central Valley) C: 464-465
Lake Diefenbaker [Saskatchewan]
Saskatchewan (Rivers and lakes) S: 138-140
Lake District [region, England]
England (The Pennines) E: 300 *with picture*
United Kingdom (The Pennines) U: 59
Lake District [region, Finland]
Finland (Land regions) *map on* F: 113
Lake District National Park [England]
National park *picture on* N: 42e; (Other interesting
national parks) N: 42f; (table) N: 42g
Lake Drummond [Virginia]
Virginia (Rivers and lakes) V: 412-413
Lake dwelling [archaeology] L: 37
Lake Edward [Africa] L: 37
Lake-effect snow [meteorology]
Winter W: 342
Lake El Azúcar [Mexico]
Rio Grande (Lower course) R: 347
Lake Erie [Canada-U.S.] L: 37 *with map*
Cleveland (Economy) Ci: 666
Great Lakes G: 343 *with map*
Ohio (Shoreline) O: 692 *with map*
Lake Erie, Battle of [1813]
Ohio *picture on* O: 700, O: 702
Perry, Oliver Hazard P: 294 *with picture*
War of 1812 (Lake Erie) W: 32
Lake Eyre [Australia] L: 38
Australia (Land regions) A: 907 *with map*
Lake Forest College L: 38
Lake Francis Case [South Dakota]
South Dakota (Rivers and lakes) So: 676 *with map*
Lake Geneva [France-Switzerland] L: 38 *with map*
Rhône River R: 318
Switzerland (The Swiss Plateau) So: 1055 *with
map*
Lake George [New York]
New York (Lakes) N: 306
Lake Gordon [Tasmania]
Australia (Lakes) A: 909-910
Lake Guanoco [Venezuela]
Asphalt (Asphalt production) A: 815
Lake Havasu City [Arizona]
London Bridge L: 445
Lake Hula [former lake]
Jordan River J: 167
Lake Huron [Canada-U.S.] L: 38 *with map*
Great Lakes G: 343 *with map*
Lake (table) L: 34
Lake Ilmen [Russia] L: 39
Lake Itasca [Minnesota] L: 39
Minnesota (Lakes, rivers, and waterfalls) M: 598;
(The Louisiana Purchase) M: 603-604
Mississippi River *picture on* M: 648; (The course of
the Mississippi) M: 646
Lake Izabal [Guatemala]
Guatemala (The Northern Plain) G: 414 *with map*
Lake Joseph [Ontario]
Muskoka Lakes M: 963
Lake Kinneret [name for]
Galilee, Sea of G: 11
Lake Kivu [Africa]
Lake Tanganyika L: 46 *with map*
Rwanda (Land) R: 571 *with map*
Lake Ladoga [Russia] L: 39
Lake Onega L: 43
Leningrad, Siege of L: 195
Russia (Rivers and lakes) R: 541
Lake Lahontan [former lake]
Nevada (Rivers and lakes) N: 166-168
Lake Louise [Alberta] L: 39 *with map*
Alberta *picture on* A: 312
Lake Lugano [Italy-Switzerland] L: 40
Lake Macquarie [Australia] L: 40
Lake Maggiore [Italy-Switzerland] L: 40
Lake Malawi [Africa]
Exploration (The exploration of Africa) E: 448-449
Malawi M: 96 *with picture and map*
Lake Malawi National Park [Malawi]
National park (table) N: 42f
Lake Manapouri [New Zealand] L: 40
Lake Manasarowar [Tibet]
Himalaya (Peaks) H: 233
Lake Manitoba [Manitoba] L: 40 *with map*
Lake Maracaibo [Venezuela] L: 40 *with map*
South America (Lakes) So: 628
Venezuela *picture on* V: 304; (The Maracaibo
Basin) V: 302
Lake Marion [South Carolina]
South Carolina (Rivers, waterfalls, and lakes)
So: 652-654 *with map*
Lake Mattamuskeet [North Carolina]
North Carolina (Rivers, waterfalls, and lakes)
N: 484 *with map*
Lake McConaughy [Nebraska]

Nebraska (Rivers and lakes) N: 106-107
Lake McDonald [Montana]
Glacier National Park (Lakes) G: 205
Lake Mead [Arizona-Nevada] L: 40 *with map*
Hoover Dam H: 332
Las Vegas (Metropolitan area) L: 88
National Park System (Areas preserved for
recreational use) N: 46
Nevada (Rivers and lakes) N: 166-168 *with map*
Lake Mead National Recreation Area [Arizona-
Nevada]
National Park System (Areas preserved for
recreational use) N: 46; (table: National
recreation areas) N: 49
Lake Melville [Newfoundland and Labrador]
Newfoundland and Labrador (Rivers and lakes)
N: 370 *with map*
Lake Memphremagog [Canada-U.S.]
Vermont (Rivers and lakes) V: 328-330 *with map*
Lake Mendota [Wisconsin]
Madison M: 30
Lake Meredith National Recreation Area [Texas]
National Park System (table: National recreation
areas) N: 49
Lake Merritt [California]
Oakland (Description) O: 637 *with picture*
Lake Michigan [U.S.] L: 40 *with map*
Chicago *pictures on* Ci: 420, Ci: 424
Chicago Sanitary and Ship Canal C: 438
Great Lakes G: 343 *with map*
Lake (Climate) L: 33; (table) L: 34
Lake Missoula [Montana]
Flood (Other floods) F: 237
Lake Mistassini [Quebec]
Quebec (Rivers, waterfalls, and lakes) Q: 24 *with
map*
Lake Mohave [Nevada]
Nevada *picture on* N: 166
Lake Monona [Wisconsin]
Madison M: 30
Lake Mungo archaeological site [Australia]
Prehistoric people (table) P: 754
Lake Muskoka [Ontario]
Muskoka Lakes M: 963
Lake Nasser [Egypt-Sudan] L: 41 *with map*
Aswan High Dam A: 851
Lake Neagh [Northern Ireland] *See* Lough Neagh
in this index
Lake Nemi [Italy] L: 42
Lake Ngami [Botswana]
Stanley and Livingstone (Livingstone's
discoveries) So: 837 *with map*
Lake Ngardok [Palau]
Melekeok M: 389
Lake Nicaragua [Nicaragua] L: 42
Lake Nyasa [Africa] L: 42 *with map*
Exploration (The exploration of Africa) E: 448-449
Lake (table) L: 34
Malawi M: 96 *with picture and map*
Stanley and Livingstone (Livingstone's
discoveries) So: 837 *with map*
Lake Oahe [South Dakota]
South Dakota (Rivers and lakes) So: 676
Lake of Bays [Ontario]
Muskoka Lakes M: 963
Lake of Lucerne [Switzerland] L: 42
Lake of the Clouds [Michigan]
Michigan *picture on* M: 488
Lake of the Ozarks [Missouri] L: 42 *with map*
Missouri (Places to visit) M: 660; (Rivers and lakes)
M: 662; (Progress as a state) M: 671
Lake of the Woods [Canada-U.S.] L: 42 *with map*
Lake of Thun [Switzerland] L: 43
Lake Ohrid [Albania-Yugoslavia]
Albania (Land) A: 306
Lake Okeechobee [Florida] L: 43
Florida (Rivers, lakes, and springs) F: 256
Lake Onega [Russia] L: 43
Lake Ontario [Canada-U.S.] L: 43 *with map*
Great Lakes G: 343 *with map*
Lake (Climate) L: 33
Lake Oroville [California]
Oroville Dam O: 858
Lake Ouachita [Arkansas] L: 44 *with map*
Lake Peipus [Estonia-Russia] L: 44
Estonia (Land and climate) E: 361 *with map*
Lake Placid [city, New York]
Lake Placid L: 44
Lake Placid [lake, New York] L: 44
New York *picture on* N: 308; (Places to visit) N: 302
Olympic Games (Boycotts) O: 753
Lake Poets [English literature] L: 44
Lake Pontchartrain [Louisiana] L: 44 *with map*
Louisiana (Rivers, bayous, and lakes) L: 490-492
New Orleans (The city) N: 278
Lake Pontchartrain Causeway [bridge, Louisiana]
Bridge (table: Combination) B: 603

Lake Pontchartrain L: 45 *with map*
Louisiana (Transportation) L: 495
Lake Poopó [Bolivia]
Andes Mountains (Glaciers, lakes, and rivers)
A: 453
Lake Powell [Arizona-Utah] L: 45 *with map*
Fossil *picture on* F: 424
Glen Canyon Dam G: 226
Lake Roosevelt National Recreation Area
[Washington]
National Park System (table: National recreation
areas) N: 49
Lake Rossignol [Nova Scotia]
Nova Scotia (Rivers and lakes) N: 562 *with map*
Lake Rudolf *See* Lake Turkana *in this index*
Lake Saint Clair [Michigan-Ontario] L: 45
Lake Saint Clair National Park [Australia]
National park (table) N: 42f
Lake Saint Francis [Canada]
Saint Lawrence River (The course of the St.
Lawrence) S: 41
Lake Saint Lawrence [New York]
Saint Lawrence Seaway (The seaway system)
S: 43; (The hydroelectric power project) S: 44;
(Construction of the seaway) S: 45
Lake Saint Louis [Canada]
Saint Lawrence River (The course of the St.
Lawrence) S: 41
Lake Sakakawea [North Dakota]
Garrison Dam G: 46
North Dakota (Places to visit) N: 504; (Rivers and
lakes) N: 508 *with picture*
Lake Scutari [Europe]
Albania (Land) A: 306
Lake Sevan [Armenia]
Armenia (Land and climate) A: 718a *with map*
Lake Sharpe [South Dakota]
South Dakota (Rivers and lakes) So: 676
Lake Siskiwit [Michigan]
Isle Royale National Park I: 474
Lake Springfield [Illinois]
Springfield So: 807
Lake States
North Central States N: 495
Lake sturgeon [fish]
Sturgeon So: 934
Lake Superior [Canada-U.S.] L: 45 *with map*
Great Lakes G: 343 *with map*
Lake (table) L: 34
Minnesota *picture on* M: 584
Lake Superior Marine Museum [Duluth]
Minneapolis (Museums) M: 580
Lake Superior National Park [Ontario]
Canada (table: National marine conservation
areas) C: 114
Lake Superior Railroad Museum [Duluth]
Minnesota (Museums) M: 589
Lake Tahoe [California-Nevada] L: 46 *with map*
California (Rivers, waterfalls, and lakes) C: 50-51
Nevada *picture on* N: 157; (Rivers and lakes)
N: 166-168 *with map*
Washoe Indians W: 110
Lake Tana [Ethiopia] L: 46
Lake Taneycomo [Missouri]
Branson B: 564
Lake Tanganyika [Africa] L: 46 *with map*
Exploration (The exploration of Africa) E: 448
Lake (table) L: 34
Lake Taupo [New Zealand]
New Zealand (Lakes, rivers, and waterfalls) N: 353
with map
Lake Texcoco [Mexico]
Aztec (The Aztec empire) A: 999
Mexico (The growth of villages) M: 467
Mexico City (The city) M: 476
Tenochtitlan T: 167
Lake Texoma [Oklahoma-Texas] L: 46 *with map*
Lake Tiberias [Israel-Syria]
Galilee, Sea of G: 11
Lake Titicaca [Bolivia-Peru] L: 47 *with map*
Bolivia (The Andean Highlands) B: 444-445 *with
map*
Peru (The highlands) P: 311 *with map*
South America (Lakes) So: 628 *with picture*
Lake Torrens [Australia] L: 47
Lake Trasimeno, Battle of [217 B.C.]
Hannibal (His military campaigns) H: 52
Lake trout [fish]
Lake Superior (Recreation and commerce)
L: 45-46
Trout (Other trout) T: 454 *with picture*
Lake Tsana [Ethiopia]
Lake Tana L: 46
Lake Turkana [Kenya-Ethiopia] L: 47
Africa *picture on* A: 120
Homo erectus H: 306
Homo habilis H: 306

Kenya (Rivers and lakes) **K:** 301 *with map*
Leakey, Richard Erskine Frere **L:** 161
Prehistoric people (The first human beings)
  P: 746
Lake Ullswater [England]
  National park *picture on* **N:** 42e
Lake Vänern [Sweden]
  Sweden (The Swedish Lowland) **So:** 1029 *with map*
Lake Vättern [Sweden]
  Sweden (The Swedish Lowland) **So:** 1029 *with map*
Lake Victoria [Africa] **L:** 47 *with map*
  Exploration (The exploration of Africa) **E:** 448-449
  Kenya (Rivers and lakes) **K:** 301 *with map*
  Lake (table) **L:** 34
Lake Volta [Ghana] **L:** 48 *with map*
  Ghana (Land) **G:** 179 *with map*
Lake Washington Ship Canal [waterway, Washington]
  Washington (Transportation) **W:** 64-65
Lake whitefish [fish]
  Whitefish **W:** 292
Lake Windermere [England]
  Windermere **W:** 333
Lake Winnebago [Wisconsin] **L:** 48
  Wisconsin (Rivers, waterfalls, and lakes) **W:** 358-360
Lake Winnipeg [Manitoba] **L:** 48 *with map*
  Manitoba (Rivers and lakes) **M:** 154 *with map*
Lake Winnipegosis [Manitoba] **L:** 48
Lake Winnipesaukee [New Hampshire]
  New Hampshire (Places to visit) **N:** 216 *with picture*; (Rivers and lakes) **N:** 220-221
Lake Wobegon [fictional place]
  Keillor, Garrison **K:** 254
Lake Wolfgang [Austria]
  Austria *picture on* **A:** 932
Lake Xochimilco [Mexico] **L:** 48
Lakehurst [New Jersey]
  Airship (The *Hindenburg*) **A:** 252
Lakeland terrier [dog] **L:** 48 *with picture*
Laker [ship]
  Canada (Waterways and ports) **C:** 126
Lakers, Los Angeles [team]
  Basketball (table) **B:** 150
Lakes of Killarney [Ireland] **L:** 49 *with map*
Lakes-to-Gulf Waterway
  Illinois (Transportation) **I:** 70
Lakmé [opera by Delibes]
  Delibes, Léo **D:** 116
Lakota Indians
  Crazy Horse **Ci:** 1123
  North Dakota (History) **N:** 513
  Sioux Indians **S:** 475
  Spotted Tail **S:** 804
  Wounded Knee **W:** 502
Lakshmi [Hindu goddess]
  Diwali **D:** 255
  Hinduism (Deities) **H:** 236
Lalawethika [former name]
  Shawnee Prophet **S:** 379
La Leche League International L: 49
Lallement, Pierre [French inventor]
  Bicycle *picture on* **B:** 293; (Early bicycles) **B:** 291
Lalo, Édouard [French composer] **L:** 49
Lam, Wilfredo [Cuban painter]
  Cuba (The arts) **Ci:** 1171-1172
  Latin America (Painting) **L:** 99-100
Lama [title]
  Lamaism **L:** 49
Lamaism [religion] **L:** 49
  Asia (Religion) **A:** 791
  Bhutan (People) **B:** 277
  Mongolia (The people) **M:** 722
  Tibet (Religion and culture) **T:** 277
  Ulaanbaatar **U:** 14
Lamar, Joseph R. [American jurist]
  Supreme Court of the United States (table)
    So: 1000
Lamar, Lucius Quintus Cincinnatus [American political leader] **L:** 49
Lamar Hunt U.S. Open Cup [award]
  Soccer (In North America) **So:** 548
Lamarck, Chevalier de [French biologist] **L:** 49
  Evolution **E:** 426; (Early theories) **E:** 432
  Heredity (Early ideas about heredity) **H:** 208
  Zoology (History) **Z:** 606
Lamartine, Alphonse de [French author] **L:** 50
  French literature (Romantic poetry) **F:** 521
La Mauricie National Park [Quebec]
  Canada (table: National parks and national park reserves) **C:** 113
Lamaze method
  Childbirth (Methods of childbirth) **C:** 456-457
Lamb [animal]
  See also Sheep *in this index*

Easter (Easter symbols) **E:** 43-44
Lamb [food] **L:** 50
Lamb [food] **L:** 50
  Easter (Easter symbols) **E:** 43-44
  Meat *pictures on* **M:** 348; (Kinds of meat) **M:** 347
  Mutton **M:** 969
Lamb, Charles [British author] **L:** 50 *with portrait*
  English literature (Romantic prose) **E:** 320
  Essay (Personal essays) **E:** 359
  February (Quotations) **F:** 61
Lamb, Mary Ann [British author]
  Lamb, Charles **L:** 50
"Lamb, The" [poem by Blake]
  Blake, William **B:** 397
Lamb, Willis Eugene, Jr. [American physicist] **L:** 51
Lamb of God
  Easter (Easter symbols) **E:** 43-44
Lambaréné [Gabon]
  Gabon **G:** 2 *with map*
Lambda [letter]
  L **L:** 1 *with picture*
Lambert, John [American political leader]
  New Jersey (table) **N:** 249
Lambert crazyweed [plant]
  Locoweed **L:** 418
Lambeth Conferences [religion]
  Anglican Communion (Organization) **A:** 463
Lamborghini Gallardo [automobile]
  Sports car *picture on* **So:** 803
Lamb's-quarters [plant] **L:** 51
Lamb's wool
  Wool (Types of wool) **W:** 399
Lambton, John George [British statesman] *See*
  Durham, Earl of *in this index*
Lamd [letter]
  L **L:** 1 *with picture*
Lame duck [politics]
  Lame Duck Amendment **L:** 51
Lame Duck Amendment [U.S. Constitution] **L:** 51
  Constitution of the United States (Amendment 20) **Ci:** 1015
  Hoover, Herbert Clark (Election of 1932) **H:** 330
Lamellar layer [zoology]
  Shell (How shells are formed) **S:** 385
Lament for Art O'Leary, The [poem by O'Leary]
  Irish literature (Modern works in Gaelic) **I:** 431
Lament for Ignacio Sanchez Mejías [poem by García Lorca]
  García Lorca, Federico **G:** 29
Lamentations [Bible] **L:** 51
  Tishah be-Av **T:** 298
Lamer, Antonio [Canadian jurist] **L:** 51
LaMettrie, Julien de [French philosopher]
  Materialism **M:** 300b
"Lamia" [poem by Keats]
  Keats, John (His work) **K:** 253
Lamin A [protein]
  Progeria **P:** 811
Lamina [botany] *See* Blade *in this index*
Laminar flow [atmosphere]
  Aerodynamics (Friction drag) **A:** 86
Laminate flooring
  Flooring **F:** 239
Laminated glass
  Glass (Specialty glasses) **G:** 212; (table) **G:** 218
Laminating [industrial process] **L:** 51
  Bamboo (How bamboo is used) **B:** 72
  Plastics (Laminating) **P:** 558 *with picture*
Laminitis [disease]
  Horse (Medical care) **H:** 356
Lamizana, Sangoulé [African general]
  Burkina Faso (History) **B:** 706-707
Lamm, Richard D. [American political leader]
  Colorado (table) **Ci:** 844
Lammas [holiday]
  Witchcraft (Witchcraft as a religion) **W:** 371-372
Lammas Day [festival]
  August **A:** 886
Lammergeier [bird] **L:** 52 *with picture*
Lamoille Lake [Nevada]
  Nevada (Rivers and lakes) **N:** 166-168
Lamona
  Chicken (table) **C:** 443
Lamont, Daniel S. [American government official]
  Cleveland, Grover (table) **Ci:** 672
Lamont, Robert P. [American government official]
  Commerce, Department of (table) **Ci:** 871
  Hoover, Herbert Clark (table) **H:** 330
LaMoore, Louis Dearborn [birth name of]
  L'Amour, Louis **L:** 52
Lamothe, Antoine Laumet de, Sieur de Cadillac [French colonial official] **L:** 52
  Detroit (Early settlement) **D:** 170
  Michigan (French exploration and settlement) **M:** 508
Lamothe, Laurent [Haitian political leader]
  Haiti (History) **H:** 15-17

La Motta, Jake [American boxer]
  Boxing (The controversy over boxing) **B:** 530; (The 1950's) **B:** 532a
Lamour, Dorothy [American actress]
  Hope, Bob **H:** 333
L'Amour, Louis [American author] **L:** 52
Lamp L: 52 *with pictures*
  Electric light **E:** 174 *with pictures*
  Interior design (Selecting accessories) **I:** 333
  Light bulb **L:** 293
  Lighting (Lighting problems) **L:** 297-298; (Lighting devices) **L:** 298
  Projector (Projector operation) **P:** 816
  Safety lamp **S:** 16 *with picture*
Lamp chimney
  Lamp (Fat or oil lamps) **L:** 52 *with pictures*
Lamp reflector [device]
  Projector (Projector operation) **P:** 816
Lamp shade
  Lighting (Quantity of light) **L:** 297
Lamp shell [animal] *See* Brachiopoda *in this index*
Lampblack
  Soot **So:** 595
Lamper eel [sea animal]
  Lamprey (Destructiveness) **L:** 55
Lampman, Archibald [Canadian poet] **L:** 54
  Canadian literature (Poetry: 1850-1918) **C:** 157
Lamprey [fish] **L:** 54 *with pictures*
  Animal *picture on* **A:** 507
  Fish (Lampreys and hagfish) **F:** 148 *with picture*
  Hagfish **H:** 6
  Lake Superior (Recreation and commerce) **L:** 45-46
Lampworking [industrial process]
  Glass (Lampworking) **G:** 216 *with picture*
LAN [computing] *See* Local area network *in this index*
Lan-chou [China] *See* Lanzhou *in this index*
Lan Xang [Laotian history]
  Indochina (A new kingdom) **I:** 225
  Laos (History) **L:** 71
  Vientiane **V:** 363
Lana [chimpanzee]
  Chimpanzee (Chimpanzees and people) **C:** 473
Lanai [island]
  Hawaii (Lanai) **H:** 102
Lancaster [English history] **L:** 55
  England (The Wars of the Roses) **E:** 306; (table) **E:** 308
  Henry IV [of England] **H:** 186
  Henry VI [of England] **H:** 187
  Plantagenet **P:** 550
  Wars of the Roses **W:** 38
  York **Y:** 568
Lancaster [Pennsylvania] **L:** 55
  Pennsylvania *picture on* **P:** 244
  United States capitals **U:** 199
Lancaster, Burt [American actor]
  Motion picture (Best performance by an actor: 1960) **M:** 862a
Lancaster, Duke of *See* John of Gaunt *in this index*
Lancaster, Joseph [British educator]
  School (The development of British schools) **S:** 185
Lancaster County [Pennsylvania]
  Evolution (Genetic drift) **E:** 429
  Pennsylvania Dutch **P:** 270
Lancaster Sound [Canada]
  Exploration (Arctic exploration) **E:** 449
Lancaster Turnpike [U.S. history]
  Road (Early American roads) **R:** 361
Lance [fireworks]
  Fireworks (How fireworks work) **F:** 135
Lance [industry]
  Iron and steel (The basic oxygen process [BOP]) **I:** 441-442 *with diagram*; (The open-hearth process) **I:** 443-444 *with diagram*
Lance [weapon]
  Knights and knighthood (Armor) **K:** 350 *with picture*
  Spear **So:** 768
Lance corporal
  Rank, Military (table) **R:** 140
Lanceleaf lungwort [plant]
  Lungwort **L:** 525
Lancelet [sea animal] *See* Amphioxus *in this index*
Lancelot, Sir [legendary figure] **L:** 56 *with picture*
  Arthur, King **A:** 757
  Galahad, Sir **G:** 7
  Round Table (The decline of the Round Table) **R:** 491
Lancet fluke [animal]
  Parasite (Life cycle) **P:** 154 *with diagram*
Lancet window
  Window **W:** 334
L'Ancienne-Lorette [Quebec]
  Quebec (Recent developments) **Q:** 37

Land *See* Landform; Property; Real estate *in this index*
Land, Edwin Herbert [American inventor] L: 56
  Photography (Dramatic changes) P: 425-426
Land, Frank S. [American businessman]
  DeMolay International D: 129
Land, The [film]
  Flaherty, Robert Joseph F: 225
Land-based observation station [weather]
  Weather (Land-based observation stations)
  W: 162
Land Between the Lakes [recreation area]
  Kentucky (Places to visit) K: 282
Land bridge [geology]
  Indian, American (Early days) I: 151
  Pleistocene Epoch P: 572
  Prehistoric people (The spread of settlement)
  P: 752
Land captain [Russian history]
  Russia (Alexander III) R: 551
Land disposal
  Waste disposal (Land disposal) W: 113
Land-Grant Act [1862]
  Land-grant university L: 56
  Reserve Officers Training Corps (History) R: 258
Land-grant university [U.S. history] L: 56
  Adult education (History of adult education in
  the United States) A: 69
  Agricultural education (Colleges and universities)
  A: 144
  Agricultural experiment station A: 145
  Cooperative Extension System Ci: 1037
  4-H F: 433
Land hemisphere [geography]
  Hemisphere H: 181 *with diagram*
Land iguana
  Iguana I: 50
Land League [Irish history]
  Parnell, Charles Stewart P: 177
Land management
  Land Management, Bureau of L: 57
  Public lands (Management of public lands) P: 858
Land Management, Bureau of [U.S.] L: 57
  National Trails System N: 61
Land mile
  Mile M: 542
Land mine
  Arms control (Arms control in the late 1900's and
  early 2000's) A: 722
  Mine warfare (Land mines) M: 564 *with pictures*
  United Nations *picture on* U: 90
Land of Enchantment [name for]
  New Mexico N: 256
Land of Evangeline [region]
  Nova Scotia N: 555
Land of Green Plums, The [book by Müller]
  German literature (Recent German literature)
  G: 142
Land of Infinite Variety [name for]
  South Dakota So: 664
Land of Lincoln [name for]
  Illinois I: 52
Land of Shining Mountains [name for]
  Montana M: 742
Land plaster
  Gypsum G: 451
Land Purchase Act [1875]
  Prince Edward Island (Member of the union)
  P: 791
Land reform [economics] L: 57
  George, Henry G: 108
  Mexico (Agriculture) M: 465
Land snail [animal]
  Snail (Where snails live) S: 522 *with picture*
Land speculator [U.S. history]
  Pioneer life in America (How the pioneers
  obtained land) P: 479
Land survey
  Surveying (Types of surveys) So: 1011
Land tenure [European history]
  Feudalism (The beginnings of feudalism) F: 81-82
Land turtle
  Turtle T: 520 *with pictures*
Land-use map
  City planning *picture on* Ci: 600
  United States *map on* U: 130
Landau [vehicle]
  Carriage C: 248
Landau, Lev Davidovich [Russian physicist]
  Nobel Prizes (Physics: 1962) N: 441
Landau, Martin [American actor]
  Motion picture (Best performance by an actor in
  a supporting role: 1994) M: 862b
Lander, Richard Lemon [British explorer]
  Exploration (The exploration of Africa) E: 448
  with map
Landers, Ann [American journalist] L: 57 *with*

portrait
  Van Buren, Abigail V: 269
Landes, Bertha Knight [American political leader]
  L: 57
Landfill L: 57 *with diagram*
  Environmental pollution (Solid waste) E: 334
  Hazardous wastes (Disposal of hazardous wastes)
  H: 122
  Incinerator I: 99
  Plastics (Plastics and the environment) P: 560
  Recycling R: 184
  Waste disposal (Land disposal) W: 113
Landform [geography] L: 58
  Soil (Influence of land surface features) So: 574
Landing [aviation]
  Aircraft carrier (Flight operations) A: 206
  Airplane *diagram on* A: 224
  Space exploration (Returning to the earth)
  So: 701
Landing [logging]
  Lumber (table) L: 518; (Transporting logs) L: 518
Landing craft [ship]
  Amphibious ship A: 442 *with picture*
  Warship (Amphibious warfare ships) W: 40
Landing gear
  Airplane *pictures on* A: 215, A: 219; (The landing
  gear) A: 216
Landing of Columbus [painting by Vanderlyn]
  Columbus, Christopher *picture on* Ci: 860
Landing of William Penn [painting by Ferris]
  Penn, William *picture on* P: 243
Landing radar
  Radar (In space travel) R: 67-68
Landing ship—tank
  Warship (Warships in the two world wars) W: 41-
  42 *with picture*
Landing strip
  Airport (Runways) A: 245
Landis, Kenesaw Mountain [American jurist] L: 57
  Baseball (table: Hall of Fame) B: 134a; (The Black
  Sox Scandal) B: 135
  Jackson, Shoeless Joe J: 16
Ländler [dance]
  Folk dancing F: 320
Landline [electronics]
  Telephone (How a telephone call travels) T: 95
Landlord
  Lease L: 166
  Middle Ages (Barbarian Europe) M: 523
  Tenant T: 132
Landmark movement [religion]
  American Baptist Association A: 408
Landmark status [law]
  Architecture (Architecture today) A: 632-633
Lando [pope]
  Pope (table) P: 666
Landolphia [vine]
  Rubber (The rubber tree) R: 502
Landon, Alfred Mossman [American political
  leader] L: 57
  Kansas (table) K: 234; (The Great Depression)
  K: 238
  Kassebaum, Nancy Landon K: 249
  Knox, Frank K: 357
  Public opinion poll (History) P: 863
  Roosevelt, Franklin Delano (Election of 1936)
  R: 454
Landrace [hog]
  Hog (Kinds of hogs) H: 285 *with picture*
Landrieu, Mitch [American political leader]
  New Orleans (The early 2000's) N: 285
Landrieu, Moon [American government leader]
  Carter, Jimmy (table) C: 257
  Housing and Urban Development, Department
  of (table) H: 393
Landrum-Griffin Act [1959]
  Labor movement (Charges of corruption) L: 13
Landry, Bernard [Canadian political leader]
  Quebec (table) Q: 29; (Recent developments)
  Q: 33
Lands, Public *See* Public lands *in this index*
Landscape [painting by Cole]
  Cole, Thomas *picture on* Ci: 771
Landscape and ornamental horticulture
  Horticulture (The horticulture industry) H: 369
Landscape Architects, American Society of
  Landscape architecture (History) L: 59
Landscape architecture L: 59 *with picture*
  Flower (In landscaping) F: 273
  Gardening G: 30
  House (Landscaping) H: 383
  Le Nôtre, André L: 196
  Olmsted, Frederick Law O: 745
  Road (Roadside improvement) R: 360
Landscape contractor [occupation]
  House (Landscaping) H: 383
Landscape painting

  China (The arts) C: 487 *with picture*
  Church, Frederic Edwin C: 541 *with picture*
  Painting (Landscapes and seascapes) P: 32
  with picture; (Chinese painting) P: 44-45;
  (Romanticism) P: 68 *with picture*
Landscape with Polyphemus and Galatea
  [painting]
  Painting (Roman painting) P: 42-43
Landscape with Satyr [drawing by Titian]
  Drawing *picture on* D: 344
Landscape with the Fall of Icarus [painting by
  Bruegel]
  Painting (The northern Renaissance) P: 57 *with
  picture*
Landscaping *See* Gardening; Landscape
  architecture *in this index*
Landseer, Sir Edwin [British painter]
  Painting (Art for a new public) P: 70 *with picture*
Landsgemeinde [government]
  Switzerland (Cantonal and local government)
  So: 1051
Landside [tool]
  Plow (The moldboard plow bottom) P: 575
Landslide [geology] L: 60
  Earthquake (Landslides or avalanches) E: 34
  Tsunami T: 475
  Volcano (Avalanches and landslides) V: 440 *with
  diagram*
Landsmål [language]
  Norway (Language) N: 539
Landspout [meteorology]
  Tornado (The life of a tornado) T: 335
Landsteiner, Karl [Austrian-American physiologist]
  L: 60
  Blood (History of blood research) B: 414
  Blood transfusion (History) B: 417
  Nobel Prizes (Physiology or medicine: 1930)
  N: 445
  Rh factor R: 289
Landtag [legislature]
  Austria (The Federal Assembly) A: 929-930
Lane
  Bowling (The lane) B: 523
Lane, Fitz Hugh [American artist]
  Painting (Landscapes and seascapes) P: 32 *with
  picture*
Lane, Franklin K. [American government official]
  Interior, Department of the (table) I: 325
  Wilson, Woodrow (table) W: 323
Lane, Harriet [niece of]
  Buchanan, James (Life in the White House) B: 661
  with picture
  White House hostesses W: 291
Lane, Henry Smith [American political leader]
  Indiana (table) I: 214
Lane, Joseph [American political leader]
  Washington (Territorial days) W: 66
Lane, William Preston, Jr. [American political
  leader]
  Maryland (table) M: 255
Laney, Benjamin T. [American political leader]
  Arkansas (table) A: 712
Lanfranc [English religious leader] L: 60
Lang, Andrew [Scottish author]
  Literature for children (Collections of tales) L: 363
Lang, Fritz [German-American director] L: 60
  Motion picture (The movies talk) M: 867
Langdell, Christopher Columbus [American
  educator]
  Case method C: 272
Langdon, John [American political leader] L: 60
  New Hampshire (table) N: 223
Langdon, Olivia [wife of]
  Twain, Mark (Return to the East) T: 529
Lange, Carl [Danish physiologist]
  Emotion (The constructivist approach) E: 261
Lange, Christian Louis [Norwegian statesman]
  Nobel Prizes (Peace: 1921) N: 448a
Lange, David Russell [New Zealand political
  leader] L: 60
  New Zealand (International tensions) N: 355-356
Lange, Dorothea [American photographer] L: 60
  with picture
  Photography (Dramatic changes) P: 425-426
  with picture
Lange, Jessica [American actress]
  Motion picture (Best performance by an actress:
  1994) M: 862a; (Best performance by an
  actress in a supporting role: 1982) M: 862b
Langen, Eugen [German inventor]
  Gasoline engine (Development of the gasoline
  engine) G: 66
Langer, William [American political leader]
  North Dakota (table) N: 513
Langevin, Hector-Louis [Canadian patriot]
  Abbott, Sir John Joseph Caldwell (Prime minister)
  A: 6

Confederation of Canada (Fathers of
Confederation) **Ci: 935** *with picture*
Langevin, Paul [French physicist]
Piezoelectricity **P: 458**
Zworykin, Vladimir Kosma **Z: 610**
Langhorne, Nancy [British political leader] *See*
Astor, Lady *in this index*
Langland, William [English poet] **L: 61**
English literature (The age of Chaucer) **E: 316**
Langlet, Nils [Swedish chemist]
Helium **H: 176**
Langley [ship]
Aircraft carrier (History) **A: 207**
Langley, Samuel Pierpont **L: 61**
Langley, Samuel Pierpont [American engineer]
L: 61
Airplane (Powered flight) **A: 230-231**
Bell, Alexander Graham (His later life) **B: 241**
Bolometer **B: 449**
Langley Air Force Base [Virginia] **L: 61**
Langlie, Arthur B. [American political leader]
Washington (table) **W: 65**
Langmuir, Irving [American chemist]
Nobel Prizes (Chemistry: 1932) **N: 443**
Langrenus [Dutch astronomer]
Moon (Early observations with telescopes)
M: 792
Langshan
Chicken (Asiatic class chickens) **C: 441**; (table)
C: 443
Langton, Stephen [English religious leader] **L: 61**
Langtry [Texas]
Bean, Judge Roy **B: 182** *with picture*
Langtry, Lillie [British actress] **L: 62**
Bean, Judge Roy **B: 182**
Language **L: 62** *with pictures and map*
See also the list of Related articles in the Language
article
Alphabet **A: 381**
Artificial intelligence (Speech and natural
language processing) **A: 760**
Autism (Symptoms) **A: 941**
Bilingual education **B: 300**
Brain (Language) **B: 556**
Chimpanzee (Chimpanzees and people) **C: 473**
Communication (Interpersonal communication)
Ci: 878; (Prehistoric times) **Ci: 879**; (The study
of communication) **Ci: 887**
Culture (Using symbols) **Ci: 1187**
Education (History) **E: 97**
Etymology **E: 376**
Europe (Languages) **E: 382** *with map*
Grammar **G: 303**
Human being (Cultural characteristics) **H: 414**
Indian, American (Language) **I: 149**
Linguistics **L: 335**
Mythology (Comparative approaches) **M: 989**
Philosophy (The philosophy of language) **P: 385**;
(Medieval philosophy) **P: 388**; (Philosophy in
the 1900's) **P: 390-391**
Prehistoric people (The development of speech)
P: 752
Races, Human (The social significance of race)
R: 59
Reading **R: 155**
Rhythm **R: 319**
Richards, I. A. **R: 329**
Sign language **S: 453**
Speech **So: 773**
United States (Language) **U: 110**
Wittgenstein, Ludwig **W: 374**
Women's movement (On attitudes and values)
W: 388
World (Languages) **W: 414**
Writing system **W: 512**
Language, Programming *See* Computer language
in this index
Language arts **L: 67**
See also Language *in this index*
Language discrimination
Civil rights (Civil rights in other countries) **Ci: 610**
Language-experience method
Reading (The language-experience method)
R: 158
Language family
Language (Language families) **L: 65** *with map*
Language-game [philosophy]
Philosophy (Philosophy in the 1900's) **P: 390-391**
Language minority [sociology]
Hispanic Americans **H: 244**
Langue d'oc and langue d'oïl [French language]
French language (Old French) **F: 517**
Troubadour **T: 452**
Trouvère **T: 454**
Languedoc [region, France]
Paris, Treaties of (The treaty of 1229) **P: 167**
Langur [animal] **L: 67** *with picture*

Monkey *picture on* **M: 728**
Primate (Old World monkeys) **P: 778a**
Lanham, S. W. T. [American political leader]
Texas (table) **T: 203**
Lanier, Jaron [American artist/scientist]
Virtual reality **V: 427**
Lanier, Sidney [American poet] **L: 68**
La Niña [current]
El Niño **E: 245**; (Climate with La Niña) **E: 246**
Ocean (Discoveries) **O: 664**
Pacific Ocean (El Niño) **P: 14**
Lanolin [animal product]
Wax (Animal wax) **W: 153**
LANSCE [organization]
Los Alamos National Laboratory **L: 455**
Lansdowne, Marquess of [Canadian statesman]
L: 68
L'Anse aux Meadows National Historic Site
[Newfoundland and Labrador]
Canada (table: National historic sites) **C: 114**
Newfoundland and Labrador (Places to visit)
N: 368 *with picture*
Vikings *picture on* **V: 380**
Lansing [Michigan] **L: 68**
Lansing, Robert [American government official]
State, Department of (table) **So: 861**
Lanston, Tolbert [American inventor]
Printing (New presses and typecasting machines)
P: 803
Lanternfish **L: 68** *with picture*
Fish *picture on* **F: 156**
Lanthanide [chemistry] **L: 69**
Actinide **A: 30**
Element, Chemical *diagram on* **E: 221**
Magnetism (Permanent magnets) **M: 60**
Rare earth **R: 144**
Lanthanide oxide [chemical]
Fluorescent lamp **F: 305**
Lanthanoid [chemistry] *See* Lanthanide *in this
index*
Lanthanum [element] **L: 69**
Lantz, Walter [American animator]
Animation (Animation in the mid-1900's) **A: 514b**
Lanugo [hair]
Reproduction, Human (Stages of growth) **R: 248**
Lanzhou [China] **L: 69**
Lao Lum [people]
Laos (People) **L: 70**
Lao People's Revolutionary Party [Laotian
political party]
Laos (Government) **L: 70**
Lao Sung [people]
Laos (People) **L: 70**
Lao Thoeng [people]
Laos (People) **L: 70**
Lao Tzu [Chinese philosopher] *See* Laozi *in this
index*
Laocoön [Greek mythology] **L: 69** *with picture*
Troy (The legendary Troy) **T: 454**
Laocoön [sculpture]
Vatican City (Vatican Palace) **V: 287**
Laokoön [essay by Lessing]
Lessing, Gotthold Ephraim **L: 209**
Laos **L: 70** *with pictures and map*
Cold War (To the brink and back) **Ci: 765**; (The
Vietnam War) **Ci: 769**
Flag *picture on* **F: 203**
France (The Fourth Republic) **F: 475-476**
Geneva Accords **G: 87**
Indochina **I: 224** *with map*
Vientiane **V: 363**
Vietnam War *map on* **V: 374**; (Other effects in
Southeast Asia) **V: 377**
Laozi [Chinese philosopher] **L: 72**
Religion *picture on* **R: 222**
Laparoscope [instrument]
Surgery (Instruments) **So: 1005**
Laparoscopic sterilization
Birth control (Methods of birth control) **B: 378**
La Paz [Bolivia] **L: 72** *with picture*
Bolivia **B: 442** *with picture*
Latin America *picture on* **L: 96**
La Paz [Mexico]
Baja California Sur **B: 32**
Lapel button
Button **B: 745** *with picture*
Lapel microphone *See* Lavalier microphone *in
this index*
Lapidary [handicraft] **L: 73**
Diamond (How diamonds are cut to make jewels)
D: 182
Gem (Cutting and polishing) **G: 79**
Lapilli [geology]
Volcano (Pyroclasts) **V: 439**; (Pyroclastic hazards)
V: 440
Lapis lazuli [mineral] **L: 73** *with picture*
Afghanistan (Mining) **A: 94-95**

Gem *picture on* **G: 78**
Lapita [people]
Exploration *picture on* **E: 441**
Lapiths [ancient people]
Centaur **C: 350** *with picture*
Laplace, C. P. T. [French sea captain]
Hawaii (The kingdom of Hawaii) **H: 106**
Laplace, Marquis de [French astronomer] **L: 73**
Nebular hypothesis **N: 116**
Tide (The study of the tides) **T: 282**
Laplace, Pierre Simon de *See* Laplace, Marquis de
in this index
Lapland [region, Scandinavia] **L: 74** *with map*
Sami (Land and climate) **S: 79**
Lapland rosebay
Flower *picture on* **F: 283**
Lapland rosebay [shrub]
Flower *picture on* **F: 283**
Laplas [assistant]
Vodou **V: 436**
La Plata [Argentina]
Argentina *picture on* **A: 654**
La Plata, Río de [bay] *See* Río de la Plata *in this
index*
La Plata, United Provinces of [Argentine history]
Argentina (Road to becoming a nation) **A: 656**
with map
La Plata, Viceroyalty of [Argentine history]
Argentina (Settlement and colonial life) **A: 655-
656** *with map*
La Plata dolphin
River dolphin **R: 354** *with picture*
Lapointe, Ernest [Canadian political leader]
Saint Laurent, Louis Stephen (Entry into public
life) **S: 39**
Laporte, Pierre [Canadian government official]
Canada, History of (The separatist threat) **C: 150**
Montreal (The separatist movement) **M: 779**
Quebec (The late 1900's) **Q: 32**
Trudeau, Pierre Elliott (The national scene) **T: 464**
Lapping [industrial process]
Machine tool (Abrasive process) **M: 19**
Lapps [people] *See* Sami *in this index*
Laptop computer **L: 74** *with picture*
Computer *pictures on* **Ci: 913, Ci: 921**; (Personal
computers) **Ci: 909-910** *with picture*
Lapwai Mission Station
Idaho (Exploration and early settlement) **I: 42**
Lapwing [bird] **L: 75**
Bird *picture on* **B: 344e**
Lar [Roman mythology]
Lares and penates **L: 76**
Laramie [Wyoming] **L: 75**
Laramie, Jacques [American explorer]
Laramie **L: 75**
Laramie Mountains [mountains, Wyoming]
Wyoming (Land regions) **W: 526**
Larceny [crime] **L: 75**
Crime (table) **Ci: 1137**
Embezzlement **E: 256**
Robbery **R: 365**
Larch [tree] **L: 75**
Tree *pictures on* **T: 425, T: 426**; (Needleleaf trees)
T: 414-415
Larch suillus [mushroom]
Mushroom *picture on* **M: 944**
Lard [food] **L: 75**
Hog (Food) **H: 286**
Lardner, Ring [American author] **L: 75**
Laredo [Texas] **L: 76**
Lares and penates [Roman mythology] **L: 76**
Vesta **V: 342**
La Reunion [U.S. history]
Dallas (History) **D: 15**
Large Binocular Telescope
Telescope (Reflecting telescopes) **T: 104-105**
Large Blue Horses, The [painting by Marc]
Germany *picture on* **G: 155**
Painting (Expressionism) **P: 78-79**
Large-eddy simulation modeling [meteorology]
Tornado (Vortex chambers) **T: 337**
Large Electron-Positron collider [machine] *See*
LEP2 synchrotron *in this index*
Large-firm sector [economics]
Japan (Manufacturing) **J: 49**
Large-format camera
Photography (Other types of cameras) **P: 409**
Large ground-finch [bird]
Bird (Birds of the Pacific Islands) **B: 349** *with
picture*
Large Hadron Collider [machine]
CERN **C: 363**
Fermi National Accelerator Laboratory **F: 74**
Particle accelerator (How accelerators work)
P: 184-186
Large intestine [anatomy]
Intestine (The large intestine) **I: 353** *with diagram*

Colon [anatomy] **Ci:** 786
Colon cancer **Ci:** 786
Colonoscopy **Ci:** 815
Frog *picture on* **F:** 537
Human body (The small intestine and large intestine) **H:** 420; (table) **H:** 422 *with diagram*
Large-leaf linden [tree]
Linden **L:** 332
Large Magellanic Cloud [astronomy]
Magellanic Clouds **M:** 48
Supernova (Results of supernovae) **So:** 994
Large numbers, Law of [mathematics]
Insurance **I:** 309
Large-scale map
Map (Scale) **M:** 178
Large skipper [butterfly]
Butterfly *picture on* **B:** 734
Large White
Hog (Other breeds) **H:** 286
Largemouth bass
Bass (Black bass) **B:** 156 *with picture*
Fish *picture on* **F:** 158
Largillière, Nicolas de [French painter]
Clothing *picture on* **Ci:** 703
Largo
Music (table) **M:** 954
"Largo al factotum" [aria]
Opera: *(Barber of Seville, The)* **O:** 801
Lariat
Cowboy (His rope) **Ci:** 1109
Larionov, Mikhail [Russian artist]
Painting (Nonobjective painting in Russia) **P:** 79
Larisa [Greece]
Thessaly **T:** 258
Lark [bird] **L:** 76 *with picture*
Bird *picture on* **B:** 344d; (Birds of grasslands) **B:** 336 *with pictures*; (Birds of Europe) **B:** 344c
Lark, The [play by Anouilh]
Anouilh, Jean **A:** 519
Lark, The [play by Fry]
Fry, Christopher **F:** 549
Lark bunting [bird]
Bird (Birds of grasslands) **B:** 336 *with picture*
Bunting **B:** 700
Lark sparrow [bird]
Sparrow **So:** 764 *with picture*
Larkin, Barry [American baseball player]
Baseball (table: Hall of Fame) **B:** 134a
Larkin, Philip [British poet] **L:** 76
English literature (Literature after World War II) **E:** 322-323
Larkin Building [Buffalo, New York]
Architecture (Frank Lloyd Wright) **A:** 629-630
Wright, Frank Lloyd (Early career) **W:** 507
Larkspur [plant] **L:** 77 *with picture*
Flower *picture on* **F:** 277
La Roche-Mesgouez, Marquis de [French nobleman]
Nova Scotia (Exploration and settlement) **N:** 567-568
La Rochefoucauld, Duc de [French author] **L:** 77
French literature (Classical prose) **F:** 520
La Rochelle [France] **L:** 77
La Rocque, Jean-François de [French explorer] *See* Roberval, Jean François de La Roque, Sieur de *in this index*
Larousse, Pierre [French publisher]
Encyclopedia (Encyclopedias of the 1800's and 1900's) **E:** 268b
Larra, Mariano José de [Spanish author]
Spanish literature (The 1800's) **So:** 761
Larrabee, William [American political leader]
Iowa (table) **I:** 391
Larrazolo, Octaviano Ambrosio [American political leader] **L:** 77
New Mexico (table) **N:** 272
Larrey, Dominique-Jean [French physician]
Ambulance **A:** 406
L'Arroseur Arrosé [motion picture]
Motion picture *picture on* **M:** 864
Larsen, Nella [American author]
African American literature (The 1900's) **A:** 136a
Larson, Gary [American cartoonist] **L:** 77
Cartoon *picture on* **C:** 264
Larson, John A. [American inventor]
Lie detector **L:** 271
Larson, Morgan F. [American political leader]
New Jersey (table) **N:** 249
Larsson, Stieg [Swedish author]
Detective story (History) **D:** 162-163
Lartet, Louis [French anthropologist]
Prehistoric people (table) **P:** 754
Lartius [Roman legend]
Horatius **H:** 334
Larva [zoology] **L:** 78 *with pictures*
See also the list of *Related articles in the* Larva article

Ant *picture on* **A:** 520; (Reproduction) **A:** 524 *with picture*
Ant lion **A:** 529 *with picture*
Barnacle **B:** 114
Beetle (The life cycle of beetles) **B:** 216 *with diagram*
Bot fly **B:** 507
Butterfly (The larva) **B:** 741 *with pictures*
Cocoon **Ci:** 747
Fish (How fish live) **F:** 165 *with picture*
Fly (Larva) **F:** 310 *with picture*
Grub **G:** 406
Insect *picture on* **I:** 282; (Complete metamorphosis) **I:** 293
Metamorphosis (The larva) **M:** 428 *with picture*
Moth (The life cycle of moths) **M:** 838-839 *with pictures*
Pupa **P:** 904
Tadpole **T:** 6
Tapeworm **T:** 40
Laryngitis [disorder] **L:** 79
Voice (Straining the voice) **V:** 437
Laryngotracheitis [disease]
Poultry (Raising poultry) **P:** 720-721
Larynx [anatomy] **L:** 79 *with diagram*
Cancer (Classification by primary body site) **C:** 167-168
Frog (Voice) **F:** 537-538
Hiccup **H:** 223
Human body (The air passages) **H:** 420-421; (table) **H:** 422 *with diagram*
Language (The sounds of language) **L:** 62 *with diagram*
Laryngitis **L:** 79
Respiration (Structures of breathing) **R:** 260
Voice (The human voice) **V:** 436 *with diagram*
LAS [chemical]
Detergent and soap (The development of detergents) **D:** 165-166
Las ...
Titles beginning Las *appear under their key words, as in* Meninas, Las. *Names beginning* Las *are alphabetized as single words:* Las Charcas *appears after* Lascaux Cave
La Sal Mountains
Utah (Land regions) **U:** 240-242 *with map*
La Salle, Jean Baptiste de *See* Jean Baptiste de la Salle, Saint *in this index*
La Salle, René-Robert Cavelier, Sieur de [French explorer] **L:** 79 *with picture and map*
Arkansas (Exploration and settlement) **A:** 712
Colorado (Exploration and settlement) **C:** 845
Exploration (The French and English in North America) **E:** 446-447 *with map*
Hennepin, Louis **H:** 185
Indiana (Exploration and settlement) **I:** 215
Iowa (Exploration and early settlement) **I:** 393
Louisiana **L:** 478; (Exploration) **L:** 497
Memphis (History) **M:** 396
Michigan (French exploration and settlement) **M:** 508
Mississippi (Exploration and early settlement) **M:** 641
Missouri (Exploration) **M:** 669
Nebraska (Exploration) **N:** 111
New Orleans (History) **N:** 283
New York (Under English rule) **N:** 314-315
North Dakota (Exploration and early settlement) **N:** 513
Ohio (Exploration and settlement) **O:** 700
Ohio River (History) **O:** 705
Oklahoma (Early days) **O:** 731
South Dakota (Exploration and fur trade) **So:** 681
Tennessee (Exploration) **T:** 153
Texas (French exploration) **T:** 204
Tonty, Henri de **T:** 330
LaSalle Street
Chicago (Downtown Chicago) **C:** 420-421
La Scala [opera house]
Abbado, Claudio **A:** 4
Italy *picture on* **I:** 505
Toscanini, Arturo **T:** 346
Las Casas, Bartolomé de [Spanish missionary] **L:** 80
Latin America (Colonial rule) **L:** 104; (Protecting the Indians) **L:** 105
Latin American literature (Colonial literature) **L:** 112
Lascaux Cave [France] **L:** 80 *with picture*
Cave (table) **C:** 320
Horse *picture on* **H:** 360
Painting (Prehistoric painting) **P:** 40 *with picture*
Las Charcas [community]
Guatemala (Indian period) **G:** 416
Las Cruces [New Mexico] **L:** 80
Laser [machine] **L:** 81 *with pictures*
Biomedical engineering (Bioinstrumentation)

B: 324
Birthmark **B:** 380
Compact disc (Audio CD's) **Ci:** 901 *with diagram*
Electric light (Lasers) **E:** 176
Electronics *picture on* **E:** 206; (Light-emitting devices) **E:** 213
Extraterrestrial intelligence **E:** 458
Forensic science *picture on* **F:** 388b
Guided missile (Beam-riding guidance) **G:** 426
Holography **H:** 298 *with diagram*
Hospital *picture on* **H:** 373
Invention (Recent developments) **I:** 364
Light *picture on* **L:** 284; (Lasers) **L:** 291
Machine tool (Beam cutting) **M:** 19
Nuclear energy (Experimental fusion devices) **N:** 592-593
Photocomposition **P:** 404 *with diagram*
Physics (Advances in the mid-1900's) **P:** 442 *with picture*
Printing (Electronic imagesetting) **P:** 797; (Digital printing) **P:** 801
Radar (The antenna) **R:** 71; (Continued progress) **R:** 72-73
Science *picture on* **S:** 193
Uranium (Separating uranium isotopes) **U:** 215-216 *with diagram*
Laser altimeter [instrument]
Altimeter **A:** 389
Laser glass
Glass (Specialty glasses) **G:** 212-213
Laser gyroscope [tool]
Gyroscope (Optical gyroscopes) **G:** 454 *with picture*
Laser (Guiding) **L:** 83
Laser in situ keratomileusis [surgery] *See* LASIK surgery *in this index*
Laser Interferometer Gravitational-Wave Observatory
Observatory (Gravitational observatories) **O:** 645-646
Relativity (Gravitational waves) **R:** 212
Laser isotope separation
Uranium (Separating uranium isotopes) **U:** 215-216 *with diagram*
Laser platesetter [machine]
Magazine (Editing and assembling an issue) **M:** 43-44
Printing (Electronic imagesetting) **P:** 797
Laser printer
Computer (Printers) **Ci:** 916 *with picture*
Ink (Printing inks) **I:** 273
Magazine (Editing and assembling an issue) **M:** 43-44
Photography (Printing digital images) **P:** 422
Printer (Laser printers) **P:** 795
Printing (Digital printing) **P:** 801
Laser radar
Radar (How radar works) **R:** 68
Laser range finder [instrument]
Rangefinder **R:** 139
Laser ranging [measurement]
Mountain (Measuring mountains) **M:** 896b
Laser welding
Welding (Laser welding) **W:** 189
LaserWriter [printer]
Desktop publishing **D:** 158
LASIK surgery **L:** 86
Eye (Defects of the eye) **E:** 464
Myopia **M:** 971
Lasker, Emanuel [German chess player]
Chess (World chess champions) **C:** 414
Lasorda, Tom [American baseball manager]
Baseball (table: Hall of Fame) **B:** 134a
Las Palmas [Canary Islands]
Canary Islands **C:** 165
Laspeyresia saltitans [insect]
Jumping bean **J:** 190 *with picture*
Lassalle, Ferdinand [German socialist]
Bebel, August **B:** 196
Duel **D:** 378
Lassen, Peter [American frontiersman]
Lassen Peak **L:** 87
Lassen Peak [volcano, California] **L:** 86
Cascade Range **C:** 271
Mountain (table) **M:** 896 *with diagram*
Volcano (table) **V:** 442b
Lassen Volcanic National Park [California] **L:** 87
National Park System (table: National parks) **N:** 48
Lasseter, John [American animator]
Animation (The computer revolution) **A:** 514c
Lassi [drink]
Pakistan (Food and drink) **P:** 96
Lasso, Orlando di [Flemish composer] **L:** 87
Classical music (Instrumental music) **Ci:** 646
Lassone, J. M. F. de [French chemist]
Carbon monoxide **C:** 208
Lassus, Roland de [Flemish composer] *See* Lasso,

Orlando di *in this index*
Lasswell, Harold D. [American political scientist]
  Communication (Communication and politics)
    Ci: 888
Last [tool]
  Shoe (The shoe industry in the United States)
    S: 431
Last and First Men [book by Stapledon]
  Science fiction (The early 1900's) **S: 205**
Last Barrier and Other Stories, The [book by Roberts]
  Roberts, Charles G. D. **R: 365**
Last Chance Gulch [Montana]
  Helena **H: 168**
Last Chronicle of Barset, The [book by Trollope]
  Trollope, Anthony **T: 449**
Last Days of Pompeii, The [book by Bulwer-Lytton]
  Bulwer-Lytton, Edward George Earle Lytton
    B: 698
Last Emperor, The [film]
  Motion picture (Best picture: 1987) **M: 861**
Last Forty Years, The [book by Dent]
  Dent, John Charles **D: 143**
Last Judgment, The [painting by Bosch]
  Bosch, Hieronymus *picture on* **B: 491**
Last Judgment, The [painting by Michelangelo]
  Michelangelo *picture on* **M: 483**; (The Last
    Judgment) **M: 486**
  Painting (Religious subjects) **P: 32**
  Religion *picture on* **R: 216**
  Sistine Chapel **S: 477**
Last Laugh, The [film]
  Motion picture (Filmmaking in Europe) **M: 866**
Last name
  Name **N: 5**
Last Night in Twisted River [book by Irving]
  Irving, John **I: 459**
Last of Mr. Norris, The [book by Isherwood]
  Isherwood, Christopher **I: 462**
Last of the Mohicans, The [book by Cooper]
  Cooper, James Fenimore **Ci: 1035**
  Mahican Indians **M: 65**
  Novel (The United States) **N: 573**
  Uncas **U: 19**
Last Poems [book by Housman]
  Housman, A. E. **H: 393**
Last quarter
  Moon (Phases) **M: 783-784**
Last September, The [book by Bowen]
  Irish literature (Fiction) **I: 432**
Last Supper [religion]
  Holy Grail **H: 299**
  Jesus Christ (The Last Supper) **J: 108** *with picture*
  Mass **M: 269**
Last Supper, The [painting by Leonardo da Vinci]
  L: 87
  Jesus Christ *picture on* **J: 108**
  Leonardo da Vinci (Paintings) **L: 200b-201**
Last Supper, The [painting by Tintoretto]
  Painting (Mannerism) **P: 56-57** *with picture*
  Tintoretto **T: 294**
Last Tycoon, The [book by Fitzgerald]
  Fitzgerald, F. Scott **F: 190**
Lastex [fiber]
  Fiber (Synthetic fibers) **F: 87-88**
Lasting machine
  Shoe (The shoe industry in the United States)
    S: 431
Lastman, Pieter [Dutch artist]
  Rembrandt (Early years) **R: 228**; (Leiden years)
    R: 228
Las Vegas [Nevada] **L: 87** *with picture and map*
  Nevada (In **L: 156** *with picture*; (Population) **N: 160**;
    (Visitor's guide) **N: 164**; (table: Average
    monthly weather) **N: 169**
  Presley, Elvis **P: 772**
Las Vegas Convention Center
  Las Vegas (Industry) **L: 89**
Las Vegas Strip [area]
  Las Vegas **L: 87** *with picture*
Latchstring [door]
  Pioneer life in America (A pioneer settlement)
    P: 479-481
Late blight [plant disease]
  Rot **R: 485**
Late George Apley, The [book by Marquand]
  Marquand, John Phillips **M: 217**
Late Mattia Pascal, The [book by Pirandello]
  Pirandello, Luigi **P: 493**
Lateen sails [ship]
  Caravel **C: 202**
  Exploration (Medieval exploration) **E: 441-442**;
    (The age of European exploration) **E: 442**
  Galleon **G: 15**
  Invention (The Middle Ages) **I: 359-360**
  Ship *picture on* **S: 420**; (Lateen-rigged ships)
    S: 417 *with picture*; (The full-rigged ship) **S: 419**

Transportation (Ancient Rome) **T: 387**
Latency [human development]
  Psychoanalysis (Psychoanalytic theory) **P: 846**
La Tène style [art]
  Celts **C: 342** *with picture*
Latent fingerprint
  Fingerprinting (Types of fingerprints) **F: 106**
Latent heat [physics]
  Heat (Changes in state) **H: 153**
  Refrigeration (Effects of heat transfer) **R: 200**
  Water (The properties of water) **W: 129-130**
Latent image
  Photography (How a camera works) **P: 407-408**;
    (Exposing the film) **P: 416**
Lateral [waterway]
  Irrigation (Bringing irrigation water to farms)
    I: 457
Lateral arch [anatomy]
  Foot (The arches) **F: 352**
Lateral bud [botany]
  Bud **B: 665** *with diagram*
  Plant (Stems) **P: 529** *with picture*
Lateral chromatic aberration [optics]
  Aberration (Chromatic aberration) **A: 11**
Lateral collateral ligament [anatomy]
  Anterior cruciate ligament **A: 544**
Lateral epicondylitis [injury]
  Repetitive strain injury **R: 242**
Lateral line [zoology]
  Amphibian (Sense organs) **A: 440**
  Fish (The senses of fish) **F: 164** *with diagram*;
    (Touch and the lateral line system) **F: 164**
Lateral moraine [geology]
  Glacier (How glaciers shape the land) **G: 203** *with
    diagram*
  Moraine **M: 799**
Lateral surface [geometry]
  Cylinder **Ci: 1204**
Lateran Councils [religion]
  Alexander III **A: 341**
  Innocent III (Spiritual authority) **I: 275**
  Nicholas II [pope] **N: 402**
  Pope (Early days) **P: 662**
  Roman Catholic Church (Innocent III) **R: 407**
Lateran Palace [Rome]
  Pope (The 1700's and 1800's) **P: 665**
  Vatican City (History) **V: 288-289**
Lateran Treaty [1929]
  Papal States **P: 133**
  Pope (The 1700's and 1800's) **P: 665**
  Vatican City (History) **V: 288-289**
Latex [synthetic product]
  Rubber (General-purpose synthetic rubbers)
    R: 504
Latex [tree product] **L: 90**
  Chewing gum (History) **C: 416**
  Chicle **C: 446**
  Forest products (Other forest products) **F: 402-
    403**
  Rubber (First uses) **R: 500**; (Natural rubber) **R: 502**
Latex paint
  Paint (Household paints) **P: 23**
Lath [construction]
  House (Interior construction) **H: 382**
  Plaster (Plaster bases) **P: 552**
Latham, Jean Lee [American author]
  Newbery Medal (table) **N: 359**
Latham, Milton S. [American political leader]
  California (table) **C: 59**
Lathe [machine]
  Machine tool (Metal removal) **M: 17**
  Phonograph (How phonograph records are
    made) **P: 401** *with diagram*
  Plywood (Making plywood) **P: 586**
  Woodworking (Cutting) **W: 397-398**
Lathrop, Dorothy P. [American artist]
  Caldecott Medal (table: 1938) **C: 26**
Lathrop, Julia Clifford [American government
    official] **L: 90** *with portrait*
  Hull House **H: 412**
Latifundio [property]
  South America (Agriculture) **So: 634**
Latifundium [estate]
  Rome, Ancient (Rural life) **R: 438**
Latimer, Hugh [English religious leader] **L: 90**
  Puritans (History) **P: 910**
Latimer, Lewis Howard [American inventor] **L: 90**
Latin [language] *See* Latin language *in this index*
Latin America L: 91 *with pictures and maps*
  See also Central America; South America *in this
    index; and the list of Related articles in the* Latin
    America *article*
  Alliance for Progress **A: 374**
  Bank (Latin America) **B: 92**
  Conservation (Latin America) **Ci: 988**
  Immigration (Latin America) **I: 85**
  Indian, American (In Latin America) **I: 178**;

(Indians in the early and mid-1900's) **I: 178b**;
    (Current issues) **I: 182-183**
  Liberation theology **L: 228**
  Library (Latin America) **L: 254**; (Libraries in Latin
    America) **L: 261**
  Manufacturing (In Latin America) **M: 170**
  Newspaper (In Latin America) **N: 386**
  Population (World population) **P: 672**
  Railroad (In other countries) **R: 113**
  Roman Catholic Church (In Latin America) **R: 411**
  Spanish America **So: 753**
  Television (In Latin America) **T: 117**
  Textile (In Latin America) **T: 218**
  Welfare (Welfare throughout the world) **W: 191**
  World, History of the (The colonization of
    America) **W: 441**; (Imperialism) **W: 445**
Latin American literature L: 112
Latin cross
  Cross **Ci: 1155** *with picture*
  Saint Peter's Basilica (History) **S: 53-54**
Latin language L: 114
  Alphabet (The Roman alphabet) **A: 383** *with
    pictures*
  Case (Cases in Latin) **C: 271**
  English language (The development of English)
    E: 313
  Italian language (Development) **I: 493**
  Italian literature (Humanism and the
    Renaissance) **I: 494**
  Latin literature (Language and form) **L: 115**
  Linguistics (Comparative reconstruction) **L: 336**
  Name (Greek and Latin names) **N: 5**
  Old Testament (Ancient translations) **O: 741**
  Romance languages **R: 415**
  Romania (Language) **R: 417**
  Rome, Ancient (The Roman heritage) **R: 448**
  Spanish literature **So: 757**
Latin League [ancient Rome]
  Rome, Ancient (The Roman Republic) **R: 444**
Latin literature L: 115
  See also the list of Related articles in the Latin
    literature *article*
  Classicism (Rome) **Ci: 653**
  Drama (Roman drama) **D: 328**
Latin Quarter [district]
  Paris (Schools and libraries) **P: 165**
Latin rite [religion]
  Vatican Council II (The Constitution of the
    Liturgy) **V: 289**
Latinos [people] *See* Hispanic Americans *in this
    index*
Latins [people]
  Rome, Ancient (The regal period) **R: 444**
Latinus [legendary figure]
  Aeneid **A: 84**
Latitude [geography] **L: 117** *with pictures*
  Climate (Why climates vary) **Ci: 676**
  Map (Geographic grids) **M: 178** *with diagram*
  Moon (Libration) **M: 785** *with diagram*
  Sextant **S: 336**
  Weather (Planetary-scale systems) **W: 158-159**
Latitudinal migration
  Migration (Types of migration) **M: 538**
Latium [former region] **L: 117**
  Rome, Ancient (The regal period) **R: 444**
La Tour, Charles de [French settler]
  New Brunswick (French rivals) **N: 196**
La Tour, Marie de [wife of Charles de la Tour]
  New Brunswick (French rivals) **N: 196**
La Tour, Maurice Quentin de [French artist]
  Voltaire *picture on* **V: 446**
Latrobe, Benjamin Henry [American architect]
  L: 118
  Architecture (Neoclassical architecture) **A: 623-
    624**
  White House (The original building) **W: 290**
Latter-Day Pamphlets [book by Carlyle]
  Carlyle, Thomas (Later career) **C: 240**
Latter-day Saints [religious group] *See* Mormons
    in this index
**Latter Day Saints, Reorganized Church of Jesus
    Christ of** [religious group] *See* Community of
    Christ *in this index*
Latter Prophets [Bible]
  Bible (The Prophets) **B: 280**
Lattice top pie [food]
  Pie (Baking a pie) **P: 452**
Latticino [glass]
  Glass (Types of art glass) **G: 220**
Latting, Patience S. [American political leader]
  Oklahoma City (Government) **O: 736**
Lattner, Johnny [American football player]
  Football (table) **F: 363**
Latvia L: 118 *with pictures and map*
  Flag *picture on* **F: 206**
  Union of Soviet Socialist Republics (World War II)
    U: 37; (Threats to unity) **U: 40-41**

World War II (The invasion of the Soviet Union) W: 477
Latvian [language]
Latvia (The people) L: 118
Latvians [people]
Latvia (The people) L: 118
Latynina, Larissa [Ukrainian gymnast]
Olympic Games (The postwar games) O: 751-752
Lau v. Nichols [1974]
Education (Bilingual education) E: 107
Laubach Literacy International
Literacy (Illiteracy in the United States) L: 351-352
Laud, William [English religious leader] L: 121
Long Parliament L: 448
Lauda, Niki [Austrian race driver]
Automobile racing (table: Formula One World Drivers' Championship) A: 980
Laudanum [drug]
Opium (History) O: 811
Lauderdale, William [American military leader]
Fort Lauderdale F: 413
Laudonnière, René Goulaine de [French settler]
Jacksonville (History) J: 19
Lauds [religion]
Hour H: 379
Laue, Max Theodor Felix von [German physicist]
Mineral (Determining the structure of crystals) M: 571
Nobel Prizes (Physics: 1914) N: 440
Laugh
Humor H: 435
Laughing Boy [book by La Farge]
La Farge, Oliver L: 27
Laughing comedy
Drama (England) D: 334-335
Laughing gas See Nitrous oxide *in this index*
Laughing gull
Bird (Birds of the seacoasts) B: 342 *with picture*
Laughing jackass See Kookaburra *in this index*
Laughing kookaburra [bird]
Bird (Birds of Australia and New Zealand) B: 346 *with picture*
Kookaburra K: 365 *with picture*
Laughlin, Robert B. [American physicist]
Nobel Prizes (Physics: 1998) N: 442
Laughter
Humor H: 435
Laughton, Charles [British actor] L: 121
Motion picture (Best performance by an actor: 1932-33) M: 862a
Lauha Bhasma [medicine]
Iron (How iron is used in medicine) I: 435
Laulau [food]
Hawaii (Food) H: 94
Laumet, Antoine [French colonial official] *See* Lamothe, Antoine Laumet de, Sieur de Cadillac *in this index*
Launch pad
Space exploration (Overcoming gravity) So: 699-700
Launch service
Space exploration (Private launch services) So: 728
Launch vehicle
Rocket (Launching probes and satellites) R: 386; (Space travel) R: 387 *with picture*
Space exploration (Getting into space and back) So: 698
Launch window
Space exploration (table) So: 696
Launching
Guided missile *picture on* G: 423; (Launching equipment) G: 424 *with diagrams*
Rocket (Launching probes and satellites) R: 386 *with pictures*
Rocket, Model (Building and flying model rockets) R: 392-393 *with pictures*
Ship (Launching and outfitting) S: 413
Laundry
Washing machine W: 45
Launfal, Sir [legendary figure] L: 121
Launoy [French inventor]
Helicopter (Early designs and experiments) H: 173
Laura [literary figure]
Petrarch P: 327
Laura Ingalls Wilder Award L: 121
Literature for children (Awards) L: 367
Laura Z.: A Life [book by Hobson]
Hobson, Laura Z. H: 273
Laurasia [geology]
Cretaceous Period Ci: 1127
Earth *map on* E: 31; (The shaping of the continents) E: 24
Jurassic Period J: 201
Pangaea P: 130

Plate tectonics *map on* P: 564; (Plate movement) P: 563
Laurel [tree] L: 121 *with pictures*
Daphne D: 35
Greece, Ancient *picture on* G: 371
Medals, decorations, and orders (History) M: 359
Plant *picture on* P: 524
Laurel, José Paciano [Filipino political leader]
Roxas y Acuña, Manuel R: 494
Laurel, Stan [American actor]
Laurel and Hardy L: 122 *with picture*
Laurel and Hardy [American actors] L: 122 *with picture*
Lauren, Ralph [American fashion designer] L: 122
Laurence, Friar [literary figure]
Shakespeare, William: (Romeo and Juliet) S: 357-358
Laurence, Margaret [Canadian author] L: 122
Canadian literature (Modern English-Canadian fiction) C: 160
Laurencin, Marie [French painter] L: 122 *with picture*
Laurent, François [French balloonist] See Arlandes, Marquis d' *in this index*
Laurentian Library [Florence, Italy]
Library (Renaissance collections) L: 259
Michelangelo (The Medici Chapel) M: 486
Laurentian Mountains
Quebec (Land regions) Q: 22 *with map*
Laurentian Plateau
Canadian Shield C: 162
Laurentide Ice Sheet [geology]
Glacier (How glaciers form) G: 202-203
Laurentides [mountains]
Quebec (Land regions) Q: 22 *with map*
Laurentides Provincial Park
Quebec (Land regions) Q: 22 *with map*
Laurier, Carolus [father of]
Laurier, Sir Wilfrid (Boyhood and education) L: 123
Laurier, Sir Wilfrid [Canadian political leader] L: 123 *with pictures and map*
Borden, Sir Robert Laird (Conservative leader) B: 484; (A new Conservative program) B: 485
Canada, History of (Growth of the Dominion [1868-1913]) C: 145
Liberal Party of Canada L: 227
Quebec (Politics) Q: 30; (Early years as a province) Q: 30-32
Laurier, Zöe Lafontaine [wife of]
Laurier, Sir Wilfrid (Young lawyer) L: 123
Laurier House [museum, Ottawa]
Canada (table: National historic sites) C: 114
King, William Lyon Mackenzie (Retirement and death) K: 327
Laurier, Sir Wilfrid *picture on* L: 125; (Death) L: 126
Ottawa (Museums) O: 872
Laurium [ancient city]
Themistocles T: 251
Lausanne [Switzerland] L: 127 *with picture*
Lausanne, Treaty of [1923]
Atatürk, Kemal A: 852
Bosporus B: 494
Dardanelles D: 36
Greece (Between world wars) G: 363
Lausche, Frank John [American political leader]
Ohio (table) O: 699
Laussedat, Aimé [French military leader]
Photogrammetry P: 405
Lautarite [mineral]
Iodine (Sources of iodine) I: 370
Lauterbur, Paul Christian [American physiologist]
Magnetism (Magnetic resonance) M: 61
Nobel Prizes (Physiology or medicine: 2003) N: 447
Lava [geology] L: 127 *with pictures*
Basalt B: 123
Igneous rock I: 49
Magnetism (Earth) M: 60d
Planet *picture on* P: 510
Pumice P: 900a
Rock (Extrusive rock) R: 371
Seamount S: 268
Volcano V: 438 *with pictures*
Lava Beds National Monument [California] L: 128
Cave (table) C: 320
National Park System (table: National monuments) N: 51
Lava cave
Cave (How caves are formed) C: 319 *with picture*
Lava dome [geology]
Volcano (Lava) V: 439
Lava flow [geology]
Volcano (Lava) V: 439; (Lava flows) V: 440 *with diagram*
Lava flow front [lunar feature]
Moon (Rilles) M: 790

Lava forest
Oregon (Interesting facts) O: 827
Lava Hot Springs [Idaho]
Idaho (Interesting facts about Idaho) I: 27
Lava-lava [clothing]
Pacific Islands (Clothing) P: 7
Lava tube [geology]
Cave *picture on* C: 321; (How caves are formed) C: 319
Laval [Quebec] L: 128
Laval, Pierre [French political leader] L: 128 *with portrait*
Laval de Montmorency, François Xavier de [French religious leader] L: 128
Frontenac, Comte de F: 541
Quebec (Early days) Q: 36
Laval University L: 128
Quebec (Libraries) Q: 15 *with picture*
Universities and colleges (First universities in the Americas) U: 210
Lavalier microphone
Microphone M: 516
Lavallée, Calixa [Canadian composer]
"O Canada" O: 635
Lavender [color]
Lavender L: 129
Lavender [plant] L: 129 *with picture*
Lavender, Harrison M. [American businessman]
Lavender Pit L: 129
Lavender Pit [Bisbee, Arizona] L: 129
La Venta [Mexico]
Indian, American (Before European contact) I: 169
Laver, Rod [Australian tennis player] L: 129
Tennis (Tennis tournaments) T: 165; (The mid-1900's) T: 166d *with picture*
Laveran, Charles Louis Alphonse [French doctor] L: 129
La Vérendrye, François [French-Canadian explorer]
Exploration (Crossing North America) E: 447
South Dakota (Exploration and fur trade) So: 681
La Vérendrye, Louis-Joseph [French-Canadian explorer]
Exploration (Crossing North America) E: 447
South Dakota (Exploration and fur trade) So: 681
La Vérendrye, Pierre Gaultier de Varennes, Sieur de [French-Canadian explorer] L: 129
Canada, History of (The growing French-English rivalry) C: 141
Exploration (Crossing North America) E: 447 *with map*
Manitoba (Newcomers) M: 160
North Dakota (Exploration and early settlement) N: 513
Winnipeg (History) W: 341
La Vergne, Marie Madelaine Pioche de [French author] See La Fayette, Madame de *in this index*
Lavinia [Greek mythology]
Aeneid A: 84
Lavoisier, Antoine Laurent [French chemist] L: 129
Biology *picture on* B: 320; (Materialistic physiology and the cell theory) B: 319
Chemistry (Lavoisier's contributions) C: 401 *with picture*
Element, Chemical (Discovery of elements) E: 219
Hydrogen H: 468
Oxygen (History) O: 890
Science (The Enlightenment) S: 199
Law L: 130 *with pictures*
See also the list of Related articles in the Law *article*
American Bar Association A: 408
Blood (The significance of blood groups) B: 412
Careers (Law) C: 225
Civil disobedience Ci: 606
Civil law C: 607
Civil rights Ci: 608
Criminal justice system (The police) Ci: 1143
Draco D: 317
Family (Home life) F: 21
Government (Lawmaking and law enforcement) G: 282
Gun control G: 440
Homosexuality (Attitudes toward homosexuality) H: 307
Intellectual property I: 318
Islam (Ethics and morals) I: 465
Lie detector L: 271
Martial law M: 234a
Muslims (Colonialism) M: 964d
Pioneer life in America (Government) P: 484
Sex discrimination (Sex-based laws) S: 335; (Changes in laws) S: 335
Law, Andrew Bonar [British political leader] L: 140
New Brunswick N: 180
Law, Bernard Francis [American religious leader]

L: 140
Law, Due process of See Due process of law *in this index*
Law, John [Scottish public figure] L: 140
  Arkansas (Exploration and settlement) A: 712
  Illinois (French and British control) I: 72
  Louisiana (French Louisiana) L: 497-498
  Mississippi Scheme M: 649
Law, Scout See Scout Law *in this index*
Law, The [religion] See Pentateuch; Torah *in this index*
Law and Justice [political party]
  Poland (Politics) P: 605; (Recent developments) P: 615
"Law & Order" [television program]
  Television *picture on* T: 111
Law Day, U.S.A. [custom] L: 141
Law enforcement L: 141
  Ammunition (Riot control ammunition) A: 435
  Colonial life in America (Government and law enforcement) Ci: 795
  Criminal justice system (The police) Ci: 1143
  Electronic tagging E: 205
  Government (Lawmaking and law enforcement) G: 282
  Local government (Functions of local government) L: 407
  Racial profiling R: 61
  Radar (In controlling automobile speed and traffic) R: 67 *with pictures*
  Vigilante V: 378
  Western frontier life in America (Law and order) W: 238
Law library
  Library (State libraries) L: 249
Law lord [office]
  House of Lords H: 384
  Parliament (The House of Lords) P: 173-174
Law of ...
  Most laws appear under their key words, as in Return, Law of
Law of Civilization and Decay, The [book by Adams]
  Adams, Brooks A: 33
Law of the Sea Convention [1982] L: 141
  High seas H: 229
  Ocean (Who owns the ocean?) O: 665
  United Nations (Peaceful uses of outer space and the seabed) U: 93
  Water pollution (Laws) W: 138
Law school [education]
  Law (Law education) L: 138
Lawes, Henry [English composer]
  Milton, John (His early life and works) M: 557
Lawford, Patricia Kennedy [sister of John F. Kennedy]
  Kennedy, John Fitzgerald (Boyhood) K: 261
  Kennedy, Joseph Patrick (His family) K: 269
Lawford, Peter [British-born actor]
  Sinatra, Frank S: 468
Lawless, Luke [American lawyer]
  Impeachment (History) I: 91
Lawless, Theodore Kenneth [American doctor] L: 142
Lawmaking
  Canada, Government of (How a bill becomes law in Canada) C: 132 *with diagrams*
  Congress of the United States (Congress's power to make laws) Ci: 943
  Legislature L: 184
  Lobbying L: 404
  McCulloch v. Maryland M: 332g
  United States, Government of the (The lawmaking process) U: 140; (How a bill becomes law in the United States) U: 141
Lawn [grass] L: 142 *with pictures*
Lawn bowling L: 144 *with picture*
  Bowling *picture on* B: 524
Lawn mower
  Lawn (Lawns and the environment) L: 144
  Safety (In the yard) S: 11 *with picture*
Lawn tennis
  Tennis (The court) T: 161
Lawrence [antipope]
  Pope (table) P: 666
Lawrence [Kansas]
  Kansas (Statehood) K: 237 *with picture*
Lawrence [ship]
  Perry, Oliver Hazard P: 294 *with picture*
Lawrence, D. H. [British author] L: 145
  English literature (Fiction between the wars) E: 322
  Novel (New directions in the novel) N: 573-574
Lawrence, David Leo [American political leader]
  Pennsylvania (table) P: 263
Lawrence, Ernest Orlando [American physicist] L: 145

Lawrence Berkeley National Laboratory L: 146
Lawrence Livermore National Laboratory L: 147
Lawrencium L: 147
Lawrence, Jacob [American painter] L: 145 *with picture*
  African Americans *picture on* A: 136b
  Literature for children *picture on* L: 359
Lawrence, James [American military leader] L: 146
  Navy, United States N: 83
Lawrence, Robert Henry Jr. [American scientist] L: 146
Lawrence, T. E. [British soldier] L: 146
  Allenby, Lord A: 372
Lawrence Berkeley National Laboratory L: 146
  Dubnium D: 371
  Mendelevium M: 398
  Nobelium N: 450
  Rutherfordium R: 569
  Seaborgium S: 264
  Transuranium element T: 401
Lawrence Livermore National Laboratory L: 147
  Nuclear energy (Experimental fusion devices) N: 592-593
  Seaborgium S: 264
Lawrence of Arabia [British soldier] See Lawrence, T. E. *in this index*
Lawrence of Arabia [film]
  Lean, David L: 162
  Motion picture (Best picture: 1962) M: 861
Lawrence Radiation Laboratory See Lawrence Berkeley National Laboratory *in this index*
Lawrence v. Texas [U.S. history]
  Homosexuality (Attitudes toward homosexuality) H: 307
  Supreme Court of the United States (table) So: 1002
Lawrence's goldfinch [bird]
  Goldfinch G: 256
Lawrencium [element] L: 147
  Transuranium element T: 401
Laws, Doctor of
  Degree, College (Honorary degrees) D: 93
Laws, The [book by Plato]
  Plato (The dialogues) P: 567
Laws of ...
  Laws appear under their key words, as in Motion, Laws of
Lawson, Ernest [American painter] L: 147 *with picture*
  Ashcan School A: 768
Lawson, Robert [American artist] L: 147
  Newbery Medal (table) N: 359
Lawsuit See Suit *in this index*
Lawyer L: 147
  Address, Forms of (Other forms) A: 54
  Careers (Law) C: 225 *with picture*
  Escobedo v. Illinois E: 357
  Gideon v. Wainwright G: 188
  Inns of Court I: 275
  Law (A career as a lawyer) L: 138
  Law enforcement L: 141
  Public defender P: 855
Laxalt, Paul [American political leader]
  Nevada (table) N: 173
Laxative [medication] L: 147
  See also the list of Related articles in the Laxative *article*
  Constipation Ci: 994
  Epsom salt E: 345
Laxness, Halldór [Icelandic author]
  Nobel Prizes (Literature: 1955) N: 447
  Scandinavian literature (The modern period in Scandinavian literature) S: 171
Lay, Herman [American businessman]
  PepsiCo, Inc. P: 279
Lay, Kenneth L. [American businessman]
  Enron Corporation E: 327
Lay-down [agriculture]
  Cotton (Cleaning and blending) Ci: 1091
Lay investiture [religion]
  Gregory VII, Saint G: 387
  Henry IV [of Germany] H: 187
  Nicholas II [pope] N: 402
  Pope (The peak of papal power) P: 663
Lay judge [office]
  Cuba (Courts) Ci: 1170
Lay midwife
  Midwife M: 536
"Lay of Igor's Campaign, The" [poem]
  Russian literature (Nonreligious literature) R: 559
Lay of the Last Minstrel, The [poem by Scott]
  Scott, Sir Walter (His life) S: 222
Lay people [religion] See Laity *in this index*
Lay-up shot
  Basketball (Basketball terms) B: 145
Layamon [English poet]
  Round Table (Origin) R: 491

Layard, Sir Austen [British archaeologist]
  Archaeology (The 1800's) A: 599
Layari River [Pakistan]
  Karachi (The city) K: 244
Laying hen
  Poultry (Raising poultry) P: 720
Laying house [poultry]
  Chicken (Producing eggs) C: 443 *with picture*
  Poultry (Raising poultry) P: 720
Layla and Other Assorted Love Songs [recording]
  Clapton, Eric Ci: 638
Layoff
  Unemployment (How people become unemployed) U: 21
Layout [art]
  Advertising (Creative work) A: 76b
  Desktop publishing D: 158 *with picture*
  Magazine (How print magazines are produced) M: 43
  Newspaper (Making up the pages) N: 383
  Publishing (Graphic designers) P: 867
Layout artist
  Animation (Traditional animation) A: 512
  Encyclopedia *picture on* E: 268
Lays of Ancient Rome [book by Macaulay]
  Horatius H: 334
  Macaulay, Thomas Babington M: 5
Laysan finch [bird]
  Hawaiian honeycreeper *picture on* H: 110
Layton, Irving [Canadian poet] L: 148
Lazarillo de Tormes [book]
  Novel (Early novels) N: 572
  Spanish literature (The 1500's) So: 758-759
Lazarists [Roman Catholic order] See Vincentians *in this index*
Lazarovitch, Pincu [birth name of]
  Layton, Irving L: 148
Lazarsfeld, Paul F. [American sociologist]
  Communication (The effects of media) Ci: 887
Lazarus [Biblical figure] L: 148
Lazarus, Emma [American author] L: 148
  Statue of Liberty *picture on* So: 875; (The statue as a symbol) So: 872-873
Lazear, Jesse William [American doctor] L: 148
  Reed, Walter R: 194
Lazier, Buddy [American race driver]
  Automobile racing (table: Indianapolis 500 winners) A: 980
Lazuli bunting [bird]
  Bunting B: 700
Lazurite [gem]
  Lapis lazuli L: 73
Lazy eye [disorder]
  Eye (Strabismus) E: 466
Lazzeri, Tony [American baseball player]
  Baseball (table: Hall of Fame) B: 134a
Lb [abbreviation]
  Pound P: 721
LBJ Ranch [estate]
  Johnson, Lyndon Baines (The "whirlwind president") J: 149
LBT [telescope] See Large Binocular Telescope *in this index*
LBW [cricket]
  Cricket (Outs) Ci: 1132-1133 *with picture*
LCD [electronics] See Liquid crystal display *in this index*
LD debate
  Debate (Forms of competitive debate) D: 64
LDL [biochemistry] See Low-density lipoprotein *in this index*
LDP [political party] See Liberal Democratic Party *in this index*
Le ...
  Titles beginning with Le appear under their key words, as in Nozze di Figaro, Le. *Most names beginning with Le are alphabetized as single words:* Le Carré, John, *appears after* Lebanon
Le [dynasty]
  Vietnam (Independence) V: 370
Le Duc Tho [Vietnamese diplomat]
  International relations *picture on* I: 344
  Nobel Prizes (Peace: 1973) N: 448b
  Vietnam War (Invasion of the south) V: 376
Le Loi [Vietnamese ruler]
  Vietnam (Independence) V: 370
Lea, Preston [American political leader]
  Delaware (table) D: 109
Lea, Tom [American painter]
  Reconstruction *picture on* R: 176
Lea, Walter M. [Canadian political leader]
  Prince Edward Island (table) P: 791
Leach, Alexander Archibald [birth name of]
  Grant, Cary G: 311
Leachate [pollution]
  Landfill *diagram on* L: 58
Leaching [chemistry]

Copper (Leaching) **Ci: 1043**
Gold *diagram on* **G: 250**; (Leaching) **G: 253**
Irrigation (Providing artificial drainage) **I: 459**
Metallurgy (Leaching) **M: 426**
Leaching field
Sewage (Rural sewerage systems) **S: 330**
Leachman, Cloris [American actress]
Motion picture (Best performance by an actress in a supporting role: 1971) **M: 862b**
Leacock, Stephen Butler [Canadian author] **L: 148**
Canadian literature (Other literature) **C: 158** *with portrait*
Lead [element] **L: 148** *with pictures*
Brass **B: 565**
Environmental pollution (Hazardous waste) **E: 334-335**
Galena **G: 10**
Lead poisoning **L: 150**
Litharge **L: 386**
Metallurgy (History) **M: 427**
Paint (Household paints) **P: 23-24**
Pewter **P: 352**
Radiogeology **R: 98**
X rays (Penetrating power) **X: 541**
Lead [South Dakota] **L: 150**
Lead [sports]
Curling (The rink) **Ci: 1196**
Lawn bowling **L: 145**
Lead [ice]
Arctic Ocean (Sea ice) **A: 641**
Lead [journalism]
Newspaper (Writing and editing stories) **N: 383**
Lead-acid battery
Battery (Secondary batteries) **B: 170** *with diagram*
Lead (Uses) **L: 149** *with picture*
Lead-chamber method
Sulfuric acid (How sulfuric acid is made) **So: 968**
Lead chromate [pigment]
Ink **I: 272**
Lead climber
Climbing (Technical climbing) **Ci: 680** *with picture*
Lead colic [disorder]
Painter's colic **P: 27**
Lead glass
Glass (Soda-lead glass) **G: 213**; (The Middle Ages) **G: 218-222**
"Lead, Kindly Light" [hymn]
Newman, John Henry **N: 379**
Lead monoxide [chemical]
Litharge **L: 386**
Lead oxide [chemical]
Glass (Soda-lead glass) **G: 213**
Lead pencil
Pencil (Cased pencils) **P: 236**
Lead poisoning L: 150
Lead **L: 149**
Painter's colic **P: 27**
Leader [fishing]
Fishing (Leaders) **F: 177**
Leader [meteorology]
Lightning (Lightning strokes) **L: 300**
Leader, George Michael [American political leader]
Pennsylvania (table) **P: 263**
Leading tone
Music (Tone) **M: 950-951**
Leading truck [wheels]
Railroad (Developments in the United States) **R: 115**
Leadville [Colorado] **L: 150**
Leadwort [plant]
Plumbago **P: 577**
Leaf [botany] **L: 151** *with pictures*
Bud **B: 665** *with pictures*
Deciduous tree **D: 70**
Fern (Parts of a fern) **F: 74** *with pictures*
Grass (The grass plant) **G: 324**
Leafminer **L: 159**
Photosynthesis **P: 430**
Plant (Leaves) **P: 529** *with pictures*
Tree **T: 410**; (Leaves) **T: 417** *with diagrams*
Vegetable (Leaves) **V: 292** *with picture*
Leaf beetle
Beetle (Leaf beetles) **B: 217**
Leaf butterfly
Insect (Protection from enemies) **I: 297**
Leaf collecting
Leaf (How to collect leaves) **L: 157**
Leaf curl [plant disease]
Peach (Diseases) **P: 211**
Leaf-cutter ant
Ant *picture on* **A: 520**, **A: 528**; (Fungus-growing ants) **A: 527**
Leaf grade
Tea (Grades of tea) **T: 63**
Leaf insect L: 158 *with picture*
Leaf lettuce

Lettuce (Kinds of lettuce) **L: 214** *with picture*
Leaf merchant
Tobacco (Marketing tobacco) **T: 307**
Leaf-monkey
Colobus **Ci: 777**
Langur **L: 67** *with picture*
Leaf-nosed snake
Snake *picture on* **S: 526**
Leaf pressing
Leaf (How to preserve leaves) **L: 158**
Leaf print
Leaf (How to make leaf rubbings and prints) **L: 158**
Leaf rubbing
Leaf (How to make leaf rubbings and prints) **L: 158**
Leaf scar [botany]
Leaf (The leaf dies) **L: 153**
Leaf spot disease
Alfalfa (Diseases and pests) **A: 347**
Lawn *picture on* **L: 143**
Pea (Diseases and pests) **P: 205**
Sugar beet (Raising sugar beets) **So: 962**
Leafcutting bee [insect]
Bee (Solitary bees) **B: 205-206** *with picture*
Leafhopper [insect] **L: 158** *with picture*
Leaflet [anatomy]
Mitral valve prolapse **M: 679**
Leaflet [botany]
Leaf (The blade) **L: 153-154** *with pictures*
Leaflet bomb
Bomb (Other bombs) **B: 451**
Leafminer [insect] **L: 159** *with picture*
Moth **M: 837** *with picture*
Leafroller [insect]
Beetle *picture on* **B: 215**
Leafy liverwort [plant]
Plant *picture on* **P: 546**
Leafy seadragon [animal]
Seadragon **S: 264**
Leafy spurge [plant]
Spurge **So: 810**
League [measurement] **L: 159**
League Covenant [constitution]
League of Nations (Powers and organization) **L: 159**
League of Arab States *See* Arab League *in this index*
League of Augsburg, War of the [1689-1697]
French and Indian wars (King William's War) **F: 512**
Grand Alliance **G: 305**
League of Corinth [Greek history]
Philip II [of Macedonia] **P: 369**
League of Nations [organization] **L: 159** *with picture*
Democratic Party (Wilsonian democracy) **D: 125-126**
Geneva **G: 87**
Harding, Warren Gamaliel (The front porch campaign) **H: 57**
International law (After World War I) **I: 342**
International relations (Collective security) **I: 345**
Law (Developments in international law) **L: 137**
Lodge, Henry Cabot **L: 419**
Mandated territory **M: 136**
Peace (The 1800's and early 1900's) **P: 206**
Refugee (Efforts to help refugees) **R: 203**
Roaring Twenties (Changing attitudes) **R: 363**
Smuts, Jan Christiaan **S: 522**
United Nations **U: 76**
United States, History of the (The peace treaty) **U: 189**
Versailles, Treaty of (Background of the treaty) **V: 340**
War (Preventing war) **W: 25**
Wilson, Woodrow (The peace settlement) **W: 325-326**; (Opposition to the League) **W: 327**; (Wilson's collapse) **W: 327**
World War I (The Fourteen Points) **W: 465**; (The postwar world) **W: 466**
World War II (Nationalism) **W: 469**; (Allies) **W: 470-472**
League of Red Cross Societies
Nobel Prizes (Peace: 1963) **N: 448b**
Red Cross (The Red Cross in other lands) **R: 187**
League of the Physically Handicapped
Disability (The 1900's) **D: 221**
League of Three Cantons [Swiss history]
Saint Gotthard Pass **S: 34**
League of Twelve Cities [European history]
Etruscans (Government and economy) **E: 375**
League of United Latin American Citizens L: 161
Hispanic Americans (The early 1900's) **H: 252**
League of Women Voters [organization] **L: 161**
Catt, Carrie Chapman **C: 305**
Women's movement (Decline after 1920) **W: 385**

League of Youth, The [play by Ibsen]
Drama (Ibsen) **D: 338**
Leah [Biblical figure]
Jacob **J: 19**
Leahy, Patrick Joseph [American political leader]
Vermont (The late 1900's) **V: 337**
Leake, Walter [American political leader]
Mississippi (table) **M: 640**
Leakey, Jonathan [Kenyan anthropologist]
Prehistoric people (table) **P: 754**
Leakey, Louis Seymour Bazett [British anthropologist] **L: 161**
Homo habilis **H: 306**
Olduvai Gorge **O: 742**
Leakey, Mary Douglas [British anthropologist] **L: 161**
Laetoli fossil site **L: 26**
Olduvai Gorge **O: 742**
Prehistoric people (table) **P: 754**
Leakey, Meave Gillian [British zoologist] **L: 161**
Leakey, Richard Erskine Frere [Kenyan scientist] **L: 161**
Prehistoric people (table) **P: 754**
Leal, Fernando [Mexican artist]
Latin America *picture on* **L: 108**
Lean, David [British director] **L: 162**
Motion picture (Best achievement in directing: 1957, 1962) **M: 862**
Lean-to [structure]
Roof **R: 450b** *with picture*
Leander [legendary figure]
Hero and Leander **H: 212**
Leane, Lough [lake, Ireland]
Lakes of Killarney **L: 49** *with map*
Leaner [plant]
Liana **L: 226**
Leaner [sports]
Horseshoe pitching (Scoring) **H: 368**
Leaning Tower of Pisa [Italy] **L: 162** *with picture*
Campanile **C: 90a**
Leap second [measurement]
Year (The calendar year) **Y: 554**
Leap year L: 162
Calendar (Some calendars today) **C: 29**
Gregorian calendar **G: 387**
Year (The calendar year) **Y: 554**
Leap-year day
Calendar (Calendar reform) **C: 32**
Leaphorn, Joe [literary figure]
Hillerman, Tony **H: 232**
Lear, Edward [British author] **L: 162**
Limerick **L: 307**
Literature for children (Masterpieces of poetry) **L: 364**
Lear, King [literary figure]
Shakespeare, William: (*King Lear*) **S: 363**
Learjet Corporation
Wichita (History) **W: 298**
Learner literacy
Reading (The importance of reading) **R: 155-156**
Learning L: 162
See also the list of Related articles in the Learning *article*
Animal (Learning and play) **A: 500**
Behavior (Learning) **B: 220**
Comparative psychology **Ci: 902a**
Culture (Learning) **Ci: 1187**
Differentiated instruction **D: 200**
Distance learning **D: 238**
Early childhood education **E: 15**
Education (How people learn) **E: 89**
Educational psychology **E: 111**
Habit (How we learn habits) **H: 2**
Instinct **I: 304**
Language **L: 62**
Learning disabilities **L: 165**
Memory **M: 392**
Perception (Learning, emotion, and motivation) **P: 283** *with picture*
Reading (The teaching of reading) **R: 157**; (Developing good readers) **R: 159**
Socialization **So: 562**
Study **So: 932**
Teaching **T: 65**
Television (Effects on learning and perception) **T: 120**
Learning by doing
Vocational education (Vocational teaching methods) **V: 434**
Learning disabilities L: 165 *with picture*
Child (Obstacles to learning) **C: 453**
Dyslexia **D: 398**
Occupational therapy (Helping people with physical disabilities) **O: 648**
Reading (Reading problems) **R: 161**
Special education (Children with learning disabilities) **So: 770**

Learning from Las Vegas [book by Venturi, Izenour, and Brown]
Venturi, Robert V: 310
Learning resources center
Library (School libraries) L: 244
Learning style [education]
Differentiated instruction D: 200
Learning theory [psychology]
Developmental psychology (Learning theory) D: 174
Learning Tree, The [film]
Parks, Gordon P: 171
Lease [law] L: 166
Estate E: 360
Tenant T: 132
Lease, Mary Elizabeth [American social reformer]
L: 166 *with portrait*
Leasehold [law]
Estate E: 360
Leash
Dog (Social and moral responsibilities) D: 279
Least bittern [bird]
Bittern B: 383
Least darter [fish]
Darter D: 38
Least tern [bird]
Tern T: 172
Least weasel [animal]
Weasel W: 155
Leather L: 166 *with pictures*
Buckskin B: 664
Materials (Biological materials) M: 300d
Leather-Stocking Tales, The [books by Cooper]
Cooper, James Fenimore Ci: 1034
Leatherback turtle
Animal (How animals raise their young) A: 498
Sea turtle (Types) S: 262b *with picture*
Turtle (Sea turtles) T: 522 *with picture*
Leathercraft [handicraft] L: 169 *with picture*
Leathernecks [nickname]
Marine Corps, United States M: 206
Leave of absence
Teaching (Rewards of teaching) T: 69
Leaven [bread]
Baking (Baking ingredients) B: 33
Baking powder B: 33
Bread (Kinds of bread) B: 588
Flour (The chemistry of flour) F: 268
Leavenworth [Kansas] L: 170
Leavenworth, Henry [American general]
Kansas (Settlement) K: 235
South Dakota (Exploration and fur trade) So: 681
Leavenworth Prison [Kansas] L: 170
Leaves *See* Leaf *in this index*
Leaves of Grass [poems by Whitman]
American literature (Walt Whitman and Emily Dickinson) A: 419
Whitman, Walt W: 294
Leavis, F. R. [English literary critic] L: 170
Leavis, Queenie Roth [English journalist]
Leavis, F. R. L: 170
Leavitt, Henrietta Swan [American astronomer]
L: 170
Leavitt, Michael O. [American political leader]
Bush, George Walker (table) B: 722h
Health and Human Services, Department of (table) H: 128
Utah (table) U: 245; (The early 2000's) U: 249-250
Lebanese Christians [religious group]
Lebanon (War and terrorism) L: 173
Lebanon L: 170 *with pictures and maps*
Arab Americans (Who Arab Americans are) A: 580a
Arab-Israeli conflict (The Israeli invasion of Lebanon) A: 582a; (The second intifada) A: 582a-282b
Arabs (Religious and ethnic clashes) A: 590a
Cold War (The Eisenhower Doctrine) Ci: 767
Flag *picture on* F: 203
Hezbollah H: 221
Iran-contra affair (Administration actions) I: 407
Israel (Invasion of Lebanon) I: 489
Middle East M: 530; (The 1970's and 1980's) M: 534a
Militia M: 544
Palestine Liberation Organization (History) P: 106
Reagan, Ronald Wilson (Foreign affairs) R: 168
Syria (Other conflicts) So: 1076; (The early 2000's) So: 1076
Lebanon Mountains
Lebanon (Land and climate) L: 172
Lebanon oak [tree]
Oak (Other oaks) O: 636
LeBel, Louis [Canadian jurist]
Supreme Court of Canada (table) So: 997 *with portrait*
Lebensraum [German history]

Geopolitics G: 106b
Germany (Nazi Germany) G: 167-168
Lebkuchen [food]
Christmas (In Germany) C: 530
Leblanc, Nicolas [French chemist]
Detergent and soap (Early soap) D: 165
LeBlanc, Roméo [Canadian political leader] L: 174
Le Bon, Gustave [French scientist]
Collective behavior Ci: 774
Group dynamics G: 402
Lebor Gabala [stories]
Irish literature (Heroic tales, romances, and sagas) I: 430
Mythology (Celtic mythology) M: 984
Le Bourget Field [Paris]
Lindbergh, Charles Augustus (His historic flight) L: 330
Le Breton, Emilie Charlotte [British actress] *See* Langtry, Lillie *in this index*
Le Brun, Charles [French artist]
Furniture (Louis XIV furniture) F: 575
Versailles, Palace of V: 339
Lebrun, Jean Baptiste [French art dealer]
Vigée-Lebrun, Elisabeth V: 378
Le Carré, John [British author] L: 174
Lech River, Battle of the [955]
Otto I, the Great O: 877
Leche, Richard W. [American political leader]
Louisiana (table) L: 496
Lechuguilla Cave [New Mexico]
Cave *picture on* C: 319
Lechwe [animal]
Antelope A: 542
Lecithin [biochemistry]
Food additive (Kinds of additives) F: 339
Soybean (Soy oil) So: 690-691
LeClaire, Antoine [American pioneer]
Davenport D: 44
Le Clézio, J.-M. G. [French author]
French literature (Recent French literature) F: 523
Nobel Prizes (Literature: 2008) N: 448
Lecompton Constitution [U.S. history]
Buchanan, James (The struggle over slavery) B: 660
Johnson, Andrew (U.S. senator) J: 138
Le Conte, Mount [North Carolina-Tennessee]
Great Smoky Mountains G: 348
Lecoq de Boisbaudran, Paul Émile [French chemist]
Dysprosium D: 398
Gallium G: 16
Samarium S: 78
Le Corbusier [Swiss architect] L: 175
Architecture *picture on* A: 632; (Le Corbusier) A: 631
Lecter, Hannibal [fictional character]
Hopkins, Anthony H: 333
Lectionary [book]
Bible (The Bible in worship) B: 286
Byzantine art (Other art forms) B: 751 *with picture*
Lecture
Universities and colleges (Instruction) U: 209
LED [electronics] *See* Light-emitting diode *in this index*
Led Zeppelin [musical group] L: 175
Rock music (The heavy metal sound) R: 380a
Leda [Greek mythology]
Helen of Troy H: 168
Leda [satellite]
Jupiter (Outer satellites) J: 200a
Lederberg, Joshua [American physiologist] L: 175
Lederer, Esther Pauline Friedman [real name of]
Landers, Ann L: 57 *with portrait*
Lederman, Leon Max [American physicist]
Neutrino N: 154
Nobel Prizes (Physics: 1988) N: 442
Ledger, Heath [British actor]
Motion picture (Best performance by an actor in a supporting role: 2008) M: 862b
Ledger line
Music (Indicating pitch) M: 952-953
Ledo Road
Burma Road B: 708
Lee, Alice Hathaway [wife of]
Roosevelt, Theodore (First marriage) R: 462 *with picture*
Lee, Andrew E. [American political leader]
South Dakota (table) So: 680
Lee, Arthur [American government official]
Adams, John (Diplomat) A: 36
Deane, Silas D: 60
Lee, Charles [American general] L: 175
Washington, George (The army) W: 99
Lee, Charles [American government official]
Adams, John (table) A: 38
Justice, Department of (table) J: 203
Washington, George (table) W: 102

Lee, David Morris [American physicist]
Nobel Prizes (Physics: 1996) N: 442
Lee, Dixie [American actress]
Crosby, Bing Ci: 1154
Lee, Don L. [American author]
African American literature (The 1900's) A: 136a
Lee, Doris Emrick [American painter]
Thanksgiving Day *picture on* T: 230
Lee, Fitzhugh [American political leader]
Virginia (table) V: 417
Lee, Francis Lightfoot [American patriot] L: 176
Lee, George Washington Custis [son of]
Lee, Robert E. (In the Corps of Engineers) L: 177
Lee, Harper [American author] L: 176
Lee, Henry [American military leader] L: 176
Lee, Robert E. L: 176
Virginia (table) V: 417
Washington, George W: 90
Lee, J. Bracken [American political leader]
Utah (table) U: 245
Lee, James M. [Canadian political leader]
Prince Edward Island (table) P: 791
Lee, Jason [Canadian-born missionary] L: 176
Oregon (Schools) O: 830
Lee, Li-Young [American poet]
American literature (Diverse voices) A: 424
Lee, Manfred B. [American author]
Queen, Ellery Q: 39
Lee, Mary Anna Randolph Custis [wife of]
Lee, Robert E. (In the Corps of Engineers) L: 177; (Other duties) L: 178
Lee, Mother Ann [British religious leader]
Shakers S: 343
Lee, Richard Henry [American patriot] L: 176
Adams, John (National politics) A: 36
Articles of Confederation A: 759
Declaration of Independence (The Continental Congress) D: 74
Jefferson, Thomas (The Declaration of Independence) J: 79
Revolution, American (The Declaration of Independence) R: 278
Lee, Robert E. [Confederate general] L: 176 *with pictures*
Arlington National Cemetery A: 717
Autograph *picture on* A: 943
Civil War, American (Raid at Harpers Ferry) Ci: 616; (The commanding officers) Ci: 618 *with picture*; (The final year—1864-1865) Ci: 631 *with picture*
Fort Monroe National Monument F: 415
Gettysburg, Battle of G: 176
Grant, Ulysses S. (Grant in command) G: 315
Jackson, Stonewall J: 16
Maryland (The Civil War) M: 258-259
Lee, Sammy [American diver]
Asian Americans (Notable Asian American "firsts") A: 812f
Lee, Shelton Jackson [American director] *See* Lee, Spike *in this index*
Lee, Spike [American film director] L: 179 *with portrait*
Motion picture (A new generation of filmmakers) M: 871-872
Lee, Stan [American cartoonist] L: 180
Comics (Comic books) Ci: 869
Spider-Man So: 791
Lee, Thomas Sim [American political leader]
Maryland (table) M: 255
Lee, Tsung Dao [Chinese-American physicist] L: 180
Yang, Chen Ning Y: 551
Lee, William [English inventor]
Knitting machine K: 355
Lee, Yuan Tseh [American chemist]
Nobel Prizes (Chemistry: 1986) N: 444
Lee Hsien Loong [Singapore political leader]
Singapore (History) S: 471
Lee Kuan Yew [Singapore political leader]
Singapore (History) S: 471
Lee Myung-bak [Korean political leader]
Korea, South (Recent developments) K: 378d
Leeboard [boat]
Sailing (Hull) S: 23; (Controlling direction) S: 25
Leech [animal] L: 180 *with picture*
Worm (Segmented worms) W: 501 *with picture*
Leechee [tree]
Litchi L: 350 *with picture*
Leeds [England] L: 180
Leeds, University of [England]
Leeds L: 180
Leedy, John W. [American political leader]
Kansas (table) K: 234
Leek [food] L: 180
Leerdam glass
Glass (Types of art glass) G: 220
Lee's Legion [U.S. history]

Lee, Henry **L:** 176
Leeuwenhoek, Anton van [Dutch biologist] **L:** 181
Bacteria (History) **B:** 21
Bacteriology (History) **B:** 22
Biology (Early discoveries with the microscope) **B:** 318
Medicine (The beginnings of modern research) **M:** 374
Microscope (History) **M:** 520
Leeward Islands [islands, Caribbean Sea] **L:** 181
Leeward Maroons [people]
Maroons **M:** 217
Leeward side
Climate (The role of topography) **Ci:** 676a
Sailing (Why a boat sails) **S:** 25
Le Fanu, Sheridan [Irish author]
Ghost story **G:** 182
Lefranc, Hervé [German pilot]
Glider (table) **G:** 230
Left- and right-handedness
Handwriting (Learning manuscript writing) **H:** 47; (Left-handedness) **H:** 49
Left Bank [district, Paris]
Paris (The city) **P:** 161-162 with map
Left-handed whelk
Shell picture on **S:** 386
Left hook
Boxing picture on **B:** 528
Left jab
Boxing picture on **B:** 528
Left-ventricular assist device [medicine]
Heart (The first heart transplants and artificial hearts) **H:** 145
Left wing [political science] **L:** 181
Liberalism **L:** 228
Leg [biology] **L:** 181 with diagram
Animal (Legs and feet) **A:** 488 with picture
Butterfly (Legs) **B:** 739 with diagram
Frog (Legs) **F:** 536 with pictures
Reproduction, Human (Development of organs and organ systems) **R:** 248
Skeleton (The appendicular skeleton) **S:** 480 with diagrams
Leg before wicket
Cricket (Outs) **Ci:** 1132-1133 with picture
Leg bye
Cricket (Scoring) **Ci:** 1132
Leg-hold trap
Fur (Trapping) **F:** 562
Leg ulcer
Ulcer **U:** 15
Legacy [law] **L:** 182
Executor **E:** 437
Will **W:** 306
Legal age
Minor **M:** 607
Legal aid L: 182
Public defender **P:** 855
Legal Aid and Defender Association, National
Legal aid **L:** 182
Legal assistance
Law (The right to legal assistance) **L:** 137
Legal blindness
Blindness **B:** 401
Legal clinic
Law (The right to legal assistance) **L:** 137-138
Legal holiday
Holiday (In the United States) **H:** 291
Legal name
Name **N:** 5, **N:** 5
Legal profession See Lawyer in this index
Legal separation [law]
Alimony **A:** 369
Divorce **D:** 253
Marriage (Marriage problems) **M:** 222
Legal Services Corporation
Legal aid **L:** 182
Legal tender L: 182
Money picture on **M:** 709; (Money in the American Civil War) **M:** 713
Legal Tender Act [1933]
Legal tender **L:** 182
Legalism [Chinese history]
China (The first dynasties) **C:** 499-500
Legalization, Drug
Drug abuse (The legalization debate) **D:** 365
Legaré, Hugh S. [American government official]
Justice, Department of (table) **J:** 203
Tyler, John (table) **T:** 534
Legate [diplomat]
Vatican City (Diplomatic corps) **V:** 288
Legatee [law]
Heir **H:** 167
Legation [international relations]
Diplomacy (Diplomatic duties) **D:** 216-217
Legato [music]
Music (table) **M:** 954; (Indicating expression)

M: 955 with diagram
Legazpi, Miguel López de [Spanish explorer]
Manila (History) **M:** 143
Philippines (Spanish settlement and rule) **P:** 379
Legend [map]
Map (Reading a map) **M:** 178 with picture
Legend [story] **L:** 182
See also the lists of Related articles in the Folklore and Mythology articles
Fairy **F:** 10
Folklore (Legends) **F:** 324
Indian, American (Legends) **I:** 148
Mythology **M:** 973
Religion (The use of sacred stories) **R:** 217
Storytelling (Myths, epics, and legends) **So:** 914
Legend of Good Women, The [poem by Chaucer]
Chaucer, Geoffrey (Poetry) **C:** 388
Legend of Sigurd & Gudrún, The [book by Tolkien]
Tolkien, J. R. R. **T:** 322
"Legend of Sleepy Hollow, The" [story by Irving]
Ghost **G:** 182
Irving, Washington **I:** 460
Legend of the Centuries, The [poem by Hugo]
Hugo, Victor (Exile and return) **H:** 410; (His works) **H:** 410
Legend of the Invisible City of Kitezh and the Maiden Fevroniia, The [opera by Rimsky-Korsakov]
Rimsky-Korsakov, Nikolai **R:** 341
Legend of the True Cross, The [painting by Piero della Francesca]
Piero della Francesca **P:** 457
Legend of Ulenspiegel, The [book by De Coster]
Belgium (The arts) **B:** 230
Legend of Zelda, The [electronic game]
Electronic game (The Nintendo revolution) **E:** 204d-204e; (Renewed interest in consoles) **E:** 204e
Legendre, Adrien Marie [French mathematician]
Mathematics (In the 1800's) **M:** 307
Léger, Fernand [French painter] **L:** 183 with picture
Cubism **C:** 1181
Léger, Jules [Canadian government official] **L:** 183
Léger, Paul-Émile [Canadian religious leader]
Cardinal (table: Canadian cardinals) **C:** 211
Legerdemain [magic]
Magician (Sleight of hand) **M:** 51
Leggett, Anthony J. [British-American physicist]
Nobel Prizes (Physics: 2003) **N:** 442
Leghorn [bird]
Chicken (Mediterranean class chickens) **C:** 441; (Commercially important breeds) **C:** 443 with picture
Legion [Roman Empire] **L:** 183
Army (Ancient armies) **A:** 726
Rome, Ancient (The army) **R:** 438
Legion, American See American Legion in this index
Legion, Foreign [military]
Foreign Legion **F:** 386
Légion étrangère [name for]
Foreign Legion **F:** 386
Legion of Honor
Knighthood, Orders of (Honorary orders) **K:** 347
Medals, decorations, and orders (Europe) **M:** 358; (table) **M:** 359
Legion of Merit
Medals, decorations, and orders (table) **M:** 357 with pictures
Legionella micdadei [bacteria]
Pneumonia (How pneumonia develops) **P:** 586-587
Legionella pneumophila [bacteria]
Legionnaires' disease **L:** 184
Legionnaires' disease L: 184
Pneumonia (How pneumonia develops) **P:** 586
Legislative Assembly [government]
French Revolution (The Legislative Assembly) **F:** 526
Quebec (Legislature) **Q:** 29
Legislative calendar
Congress of the United States (Passing a bill) **Ci:** 945
Legislative Council [government]
Quebec (Legislature) **Q:** 29
Legislative council [government]
State government (Organization) **So:** 863-864
Legislative Department of the United States Government See Congress of the United States in this index
Legislative reference and research service
Library (State libraries) **L:** 249
Legislative voting machine
Voting machine **V:** 450
Legislature [government] **L:** 184
See also the list of Related articles in the Legislature article

Colonial life in America (Colonial government) **Ci:** 795 with picture
Foreign policy (The legislature) **F:** 387
Government diagrams on **G:** 287; (Branches of government) **G:** 284
Law (Civil law systems) **L:** 132; (How laws are changed) **L:** 132
Proportional representation **P:** 828
State government (Legislative branch) **So:** 863
United States, Government of the (The legislative branch) **U:** 138
Legitimacy [political science]
Government (Legitimacy) **G:** 289
Legitimist [French history]
Louis Philippe **L:** 477
Legnano, Battle of [1176]
Alexander III **A:** 341
Frederick I **F:** 497
Legree, Simon [literary figure]
Uncle Tom's Cabin **U:** 20
Leguía, Augusto B. [Peruvian political leader]
Peru (The early 1900's) **P:** 315
Le Guin, Ursula K. [American author] **L:** 184
Legume [botany] **L:** 185
Alfalfa (The alfalfa plant) **A:** 346
Fertilizer (Organic fertilizers) **F:** 79
Flower (table) **F:** 201 with picture
Food supply (Other major food sources) **F:** 348
Manure **M:** 172
Nitrogen (Nitrogen and life) **N:** 425
Nutrition (Proteins) **N:** 625
Pea **P:** 205
Peanut **P:** 213
Prairie (Life on the prairie) **P:** 731
Lehár, Franz [Hungarian composer] **L:** 185
Le Havre [France] **L:** 185
Lehman, Herbert Henry [American political leader]
New York (table) **N:** 313
Lehman, Tom [American golfer]
Golf (British Open) **G:** 264
Lehman Caves National Monument
Great Basin National Park **G:** 336
Lehn, Jean-Marie [French chemist]
Nobel Prizes (Chemistry: 1987) **N:** 444
Lei [decoration]
Flower (As decoration) **F:** 272 with picture
Hawaii (Clothing) **H:** 94
Leib, Mani [American author]
Yiddish literature **Y:** 566
Leibniz, Gottfried Wilhelm [German philosopher] **L:** 185
Binary number (History) **B:** 308
Calculus (History) **C:** 25
Computer (History) **Ci:** 924a
Mathematics (Mathematics and the scientific revolution) **M:** 306-307
Number (Binary numbers) **N:** 607
Philosophy (Rationalism) **P:** 388
Physics (Newton) **P:** 439
Leibowitz, Samuel S. [American lawyer]
Scottsboro case **S:** 223
Leica [camera]
Photography (Dramatic changes) **P:** 425-426
Leicester [England] **L:** 185
Leicester, Earl of [English nobleman] **L:** 186
Elizabeth I (Problems at home and abroad) **E:** 238-239
Leicester sheep
Sheep (Long-wooled sheep) **S:** 382
Leichhardt, Ludwig [German-born explorer]
Australia map on **A:** 921
Leiden [Netherlands] **L:** 186
Pilgrims **P:** 462
Leiden, University of
Netherlands (Education) **N:** 142
Leif Eriksson [Norse explorer] **L:** 186
Exploration (Viking exploration) **E:** 442
Greenland (History) **G:** 385
United States, History of the (European discoveries) **U:** 150
Vikings (The Norwegian Vikings) **V:** 382
Leigh, Augusta [sister of]
Byron, Lord (Byron's life) **B:** 748
Leigh, Vivien [British actress]
McDaniel, Hattie picture on **M:** 332g
Motion picture (Best performance by an actress: 1939, 1951) **M:** 862
Leighton, Frederic [British artist]
Painting (Later neoclassicism) **P:** 67-68
Leila Arboretum [Battle Creek]
Michigan (Places to visit) **M:** 498
Leinart, Matt [American football player]
Football (table) **F:** 363
Leipzig [Germany] **L:** 186 with picture
Leipzig, Battle of [1813] See Nations, Battle of the in this index

Leipzig, University of
Leipzig (History) **L:** 186
Leipzig Gewandhaus Orchestra
Masur, Kurt **M:** 298
Leishmania [microorganism]
Kala-azar **K:** 210
Leishmaniasis **L:** 187
Leishmaniasis [disease] **L:** 187
Leister [spear]
Inuit (Hunting and fishing) **I:** 354d-354e
Leisure
Hobby **H:** 272
Play **P:** 570
Recreation **R:** 182
Television (Effects of television) **T:** 120
Leitmotif [music]
Opera (table) **O:** 791; (The orchestra) **O:** 793;
(Richard Wagner) **O:** 798-799
Lejeune, John A. [American general]
Camp Lejeune **C:** 90
Lek [zoology]
Bird (Courtship and mating) **B:** 356
Manakin **M:** 132
Leland, Henry M. [American businessman]
Automobile (Mass production) **A:** 966
Lelang [former region]
Korea, History of (Early years) **K:** 366
Lélia [book by Sand]
Sand, George **S:** 106
Leloir, Luis Federico [Argentine chemist]
Nobel Prizes (Chemistry: 1970) **N:** 443
Lem, Stanisław [Polish author]
Science fiction (Growing popularity) **S:** 205
Le Maire, Jacob [Dutch explorer]
Admiralty Islands **A:** 59
Tonga (History) **T:** 328
Léman, Lac [lake] *See* Lake Geneva *in this index*
Le Mans [France] **L:** 187
Lemass, Sean [Irish government official]
Ireland (table) **I:** 428
LeMay, Curtis Emerson [American general] **L:** 187
Nixon, Richard Milhous (The 1968 election)
N: 432
World War II (Closing in on Japan) **W:** 492
Lemay, Léon-Pamphile [Canadian poet]
Canadian literature (Poetry: 1850-1918) **C:** 157
Lemberg [former name] *See* Lviv *in this index*
Lemberg, Battles of [1914]
Russia (World War I) **R:** 552
Lemieux, Mario [Canadian hockey player] **L:** 187
Lemmer [career]
Whale (Processing whale products) **W:** 263-264
Lemming [animal] **L:** 188
Animal *picture on* **A:** 485
Lemmon, Jack [American actor]
Motion picture (Best performance by an actor:
1973) **M:** 862a; (Best performance by an actor
in a supporting role: 1955) **M:** 862a
Lemnitzer, Lyman L. [American military leader]
Joint Chiefs of Staff (table) **J:** 156
Lemon [food] **L:** 188 *with picture*
Citric acid **Ci:** 573
Fruit (Subtropical fruits) **F:** 546 *with picture*
Lemon, Bob [American baseball player]
Baseball (table: Hall of Fame) **B:** 134a
Lemon balm *See* Balm *in this index*
Lemon day lily [plant]
Day lily *picture on* **D:** 53
Lemon shark L: 189
Fish *pictures on* **F:** 168, **F:** 170
Lemon Sky [play by Wilson]
Wilson, Lanford **W:** 317
Lemon verbena [plant]
Verbena **V:** 315
LeMond, Greg [American cyclist]
Bicycle racing (Road races) **B:** 292-293
**Le Moyne, Charles, Sieur de Longueil et de
Châteauguay** [Canadian colonist] **L:** 189
Le Moyne, Jean Baptiste, Sieur de Bienville
[French-Canadian explorer] **L:** 189
Le Moyne, Charles, Sieur de Longueil et de
Châteauguay **L:** 189
Le Moyne, Pierre, Sieur d'Iberville **L:** 189
Louisiana (French Louisiana) **L:** 497
Mississippi (Exploration and early settlement)
M: 641
Mobile (History) **M:** 681
Natchez **N:** 26
New Orleans (French and Spanish rule) **N:** 283
Le Moyne, Pierre, Sieur d'Iberville [French-
Canadian explorer] **L:** 189
Le Moyne, Charles, Sieur de Longueil et de
Châteauguay **L:** 189
Louisiana (French Louisiana) **L:** 497
Mississippi (Exploration and early settlement)
M: 641
Lempa River [El Salvador]

El Salvador (The Interior Highlands) **E:** 251 *with
map*
Lemur [animal] **L:** 189 *with picture*
Madagascar (Animal and plant life) **M:** 28 *with
picture*
Mammal *picture on* **M:** 116
Potto **P:** 719
Primate *diagram on* **P:** 778b; (Kinds of primates)
P: 777 *with picture*
Lemur, Flying [animal]
Flying lemur **F:** 312
Lena River [Russia] **L:** 190
River (table) **R:** 352
Russia (Rivers and lakes) **R:** 541
Lenape [American Indians] *See* Delaware Indians
in this index
Lenard, Philipp Eduard Anton von [German
physicist]
Nobel Prizes (Physics: 1905) **N:** 440
Lenca Indians
Indian, American (Indians of the Caribbean)
I: 172
Lend-Lease [U.S. history] **L:** 190
Foreign aid (World War II aid) **F:** 383
Neutrality (World War II) **N:** 154
Roosevelt, Franklin Delano (Roosevelt's third
administration [1941-1945]) **R:** 456
World War II (The arsenal of democracy) **W:** 478-
479
Lend-Lease Act [1941]
Lend-Lease **L:** 190
Lender of last resort
Bank (Central banks) **B:** 91
Federal Reserve System (Other Fed activities)
F: 66
Lendl, Ivan [Czech-American tennis player] **L:** 190
L'Enfant, Pierre Charles [French architect] **L:** 190
Washington, D.C. (Building the city) **W:** 85 *with
picture*
L'Engle, Madeleine [American author] **L:** 191
Newbery Medal (table) **N:** 359
Regina Medal (table: 1984) **R:** 206
Lenglen, Suzanne [French tennis player]
Tennis (The spread of tennis) **T:** 165-166d
Lengon [fruit]
Lingonberry **L:** 335 *with picture*
Length [measurement]
Metric system (Space and time) **M:** 437; (The
metric system at a glance) **M:** 438 *with pictures*;
(Metric conversion table) **M:** 439 *with pictures*
Weights and measures (table: Length and
distance) **W:** 185
Lenin, V. I. [Soviet dictator] **L:** 191 *with pictures*
Bolsheviks **B:** 449
Communism **Ci:** 889; (Lenin's contributions)
Ci: 890; (Before 1917) **Ci:** 892; (Under Lenin)
Ci: 892 *with picture*
Krupskaya, Nadezhda Konstantinovna **K:** 389
Marx, Karl (Marx's influence) **M:** 238
Plekhanov, Georgi Valentinovich **P:** 572
Propaganda (History) **P:** 824-825
Russia (Nicholas II) **R:** 551-552 *with picture*
Russian Revolution of 1917 (Background to the
revolution) **R:** 565; (The February Revolution)
R: 566
Socialism (World Wars I and II) **So:** 561
Stalin, Joseph (Young revolutionist) **So:** 825
Trotsky, Leon **T:** 452
Union of Soviet Socialist Republics *picture on*
U: 28; (History) **U:** 35
World War I (The Russian Revolution) **W:** 461-462
World War II (The rise of dictatorships) **W:** 469
Lenin Mausoleum [Moscow]
Lenin, V. I. (Death) **L:** 195 *with picture*
Lenin State Library [Moscow] *See* Russian State
Library *in this index*
Leningrad [former name] *See* Saint Petersburg
[Russia] *in this index*
Leningrad, Siege of [Soviet history] **L:** 195
World War II (The Siege of Leningrad) **W:** 481
Lennon, John [British musician] **L:** 195 *with portrait*
Beatles **B:** 189
Rock music *picture on* **R:** 380; (The Beatles) **R:** 379
Lennox Island [Malpeque Bay]
Prince Edward Island (Places to visit) **P:** 788
Lenoir, Jean Joseph Étienne [French inventor]
L: 196
Automobile (The gasoline car) **A:** 965-966
Gasoline engine (Development of the gasoline
engine) **G:** 66
Invention (The late 1800's) **I:** 362
Lenormand, Sébastien [French physicist]
Parachute (History) **P:** 143
Le Normant d'Étoiles, Charles-Guillaume
[husband of]
Pompadour, Marquise de **P:** 653
Le Nôtre, André [French landscape designer]

L: 196
Versailles, Palace of **V:** 339
Lenovo Group Limited [company]
International Business Machines Corporation
I: 338
Lens [anatomy]
Cataract **C:** 299
Eye (The uveal tract) **E:** 460-461 *with picture*;
(Focusing) **E:** 462; (Cataract) **E:** 466
Lens [optics] **L:** 196 *with diagrams*
Aberration **A:** 10 *with diagrams*
Binoculars **B:** 309 *with diagram*
Camera (How a camera works) **C:** 80 *with
diagram*
Lighthouse (Development of the lighthouse)
L: 294-295
Magnifying glass **M:** 62
Microscope (Optical microscopes) **M:** 517 *with
pictures*
Photography (How a camera works) **P:** 407 *with
diagram*; (Lenses and focusing) **P:** 410 *with
pictures*; (The invention of photography)
P: 422-423
Projector **P:** 816
Telescope (Optical telescopes) **T:** 103
Television *diagram on* **T:** 124; (Capturing the
image) **T:** 122
Lens, Contact *See* Contact lens *in this index*
Lens element [device]
Photography (Lenses and focusing) **P:** 410
Lens equation
Lens (The lens equation) **L:** 196a
Lenski, Lois [American author]
Newbery Medal (table) **N:** 359
Regina Medal (table: 1969) **R:** 206
Lent [religion] **L:** 196b
Ash Wednesday **A:** 767
Carnival **C:** 243
Christianity (Forms of worship) **C:** 522h-523
Easter (Religious observances of Easter) **E:** 42
Lent, Blair [American artist]
Caldecott Medal (table: 1973) **C:** 26
Lenticel [botany] **L:** 196b
Bark (Outer bark) **B:** 110-111
Lenticular cloud [meteorology]
Glider (Soaring) **G:** 229
Lenticular screen
Projection screen **P:** 816
Lentil [plant] **L:** 196b *with picture*
Lentivirus [organism]
Retrovirus **R:** 266
Lenz, Heinrich F. E. [German physicist]
Lenz's law **L:** 197
Lenz's law [physics] **L:** 197 *with diagram*
Leo [astrology] **L:** 197 *with picture*
Zodiac (The zodiac in astrology) **Z:** 597 *with
picture*
Leo [constellation]
Leonids **L:** 202
Leo I, Saint [pope] **L:** 197
Roman Catholic Church (The recognition of
Christianity) **R:** 405-406
Leo III, Saint [pope] **L:** 197
Leo IX, Saint [pope] **L:** 198
Eastern Orthodox Churches (History) **E:** 45-46
Leo X [pope] **L:** 198
Luther, Martin (The Ninety-Five Theses) **L:** 527
Raphael (His life) **R:** 142-143
Wolsey, Thomas **W:** 379
Leo XI [pope]
Medici **M:** 362
Leo XIII [pope] **L:** 198
Christianity (The 1800's) **C:** 526
Rampolla del Tindaro, Mariano **R:** 133
Roman Catholic Church (Leo XIII) **R:** 410
Vatican City (Vatican Palace) **V:** 287
Leo, Melissa [American actress]
Motion picture (Best performance by an actress
in a supporting role: 2010) **M:** 862b
Leochares [Greek sculptor]
Seven Wonders of the Ancient World (The
Mausoleum at Halicarnassus) **S:** 325
Leodegan, King [legendary figure]
Round Table (Origin) **R:** 491
León [Nicaragua] **L:** 198
León, Alonso de [Spanish explorer]
Texas (French exploration) **T:** 204
León, Luis de [Spanish author]
Spanish literature (The 1500's) **So:** 758-759
León, Ponce de [Spanish explorer] *See* Ponce de
León, Juan *in this index*
Leon II [king of Abkhazia]
Abkhazia **A:** 11
Leonard, Benny [American boxer]
Boxing *picture on* **B:** 532b
Leonard, Buck [American baseball player]
Baseball (table: Hall of Fame) **B:** 134a

Leonard, Elmore [American author] **L:** 198
  American literature (Popular genres) **A:** 425
Leonard, Helen Louise [birth name of]
  Russell, Lillian **R:** 524
Leonard, Ray Charles See Leonard, Sugar Ray in this index
Leonard, Sugar Ray [American boxer] **L:** 198
  Boxing (The late 1900's) **B:** 532b
Leonardo da Vinci [Italian artist] **L:** 199 with pictures
  Air conditioning (History) **A:** 180
  Airplane (Early experiments and ideas) **A:** 229-230 with picture
  Biology (The Renaissance) **B:** 318
  Heart picture on **H:** 144
  Helicopter (Early designs and experiments) **H:** 173 with picture
  Jesus Christ picture on **J:** 108
  John the Baptist, Saint picture on **J:** 135
  Last Supper, The **L:** 87
  Medicine (The Renaissance) **M:** 373-374
  Michelangelo (Early life) **M:** 483-484
  Mona Lisa **M:** 698
  Painting (The 1400's) **P:** 52-53 with picture
  Parachute picture on **P:** 143
  Physics (The Renaissance) **P:** 438-439
  Raphael (His life) **R:** 142-143
  Renaissance (Arts of the 1400's and early 1500's) **R:** 236 with picture
  Sonar (History) **So:** 5901
Leonardo da Vinci [book by Freud]
  Biography (Modern biography) **B:** 314
Leonardo da Vinci International Airport [Rome]
  Italy (Transportation) **I:** 512
Leonardo of Pisa [Italian mathematician] See Fibonacci, Leonardo in this index
Leoncavallo, Ruggiero [Italian composer] **L:** 202
  Opera picture on **O:** 805; (Pagliacci) **O:** 806
Leone, Sergio [Italian director]
  Eastwood, Clint **E:** 47
Leonidas I [king of Sparta] **L:** 202
  Thermopylae **T:** 256
Leonidas of Rhodes [Greek runner]
  Olympic Games (The ancient games) **O:** 750
Leonids [astronomy] **L:** 202
  Meteor (Meteor showers) **M:** 431
Léonin [French composer]
  Classical music (Church music) **Ci:** 645
Leonora [opera character]
  Opera: (Trovatore, Il) **O:** 808
Leonov, Alexei A. [Soviet cosmonaut]
  Astronaut picture on **A:** 833; (Achievements in space) **A:** 829; (table) **A:** 830
  Space exploration (Voskhod and Gemini: The first multiperson space flights) **So:** 714 with picture; (The Apollo-Soyuz Test Project) **So:** 721 with picture
Leonov, Leonid [Russian author]
  Russian literature (The period of rebirth) **R:** 564
Leonowens, Anna [British educator]
  Mongkut **M:** 719
Leontes [literary figure]
  Shakespeare, William: (The Winter's Tale) **S:** 365
Leontief, Wassily [American economist]
  Input-output analysis **I:** 276
  Nobel Prizes (Economics: 1973) **N:** 449
Leopard [animal] **L:** 202 with pictures
  Africa (Native animals) **A:** 122 with picture
  Animal pictures on **A:** 472, **A:** 475, **A:** 481
  Endangered species (table) **E:** 270
Leopard [ship]
  Barron, James **B:** 119
  Jefferson, Thomas (The struggle for neutrality) **J:** 86-87
  War of 1812 (Impressment of seamen) **W:** 29
Leopard cat See Ocelot in this index
Leopard frog L: 203 with picture
  Amphibian picture on **A:** 441
  Frog (Other frogs) **F:** 536; (True frogs) **F:** 540
Leopard lily
  Lily **L:** 304
Leopard seal L: 203 with picture
  Antarctica (Living things) **A:** 534-535 with picture
Leopard shark L: 204 with picture
Leopard-skin chief
  Nuer **N:** 602
Leopard tortoise
  Turtle picture on **T:** 520
Leopardi, Giacomo [Italian poet]
  Italian literature (Romanticism) **I:** 495
Leopold [German prince]
  Franco-Prussian War (Background to the war) **F:** 483
Leopold I [king of Belgium]
  Belgium (Independence) **B:** 233
Leopold I [Austrian nobleman]
  Austria (Early years) **A:** 936

Leopold II [Holy Roman emperor]
  Marie Antoinette (The revolution) **M:** 200
Leopold II [king of Belgium]
  Belgium (Independence) **B:** 233
  Berlin Conference **B:** 266
  Congo, Democratic Republic of the (Belgian rule) **Ci:** 940b
  Emin Pasha **E:** 260
  Stanley and Livingstone (Stanley's explorations) **So:** 837-838
Leopold III [king of Belgium]
  Belgium (The world wars) **B:** 234; (After World War II) **B:** 235
Leopold V [duke of Austria]
  Flag **F:** 194
  Richard I **R:** 328
Leopold, Aldo [American naturalist] **L:** 204
  Conservation (The rise of the conservation movement) **Ci:** 985-986
Leopold, Nathan F., Jr. [American public figure]
  Darrow, Clarence Seward **D:** 38
Leopold, Order of
  Medals, decorations, and orders (table) **M:** 359
Leopold of Anhalt-Cöthen [German prince]
  Bach, Johann Sebastian (His life) **B:** 15
Leopold of Saxe-Coburg-Saalfeld [king of Belgium] See Leopold I in this index
Léopoldville [former name] See Kinshasa in this index
LEOSAT [satellite] See Low earth orbit satellite in this index
LEP2 synchrotron [machine]
  Particle accelerator (How accelerators work) **P:** 184-186
LePage, Paul [American political leader]
  Maine (table) **M:** 87
Lepage, Robert [Canadian dramatist]
  Canadian literature (Modern Canadian drama) **C:** 161
Lepanto, Battle of [1571]
  Cervantes, Miguel de (His early life) **C:** 363
  Navy picture on **N:** 80
  Philip II [of Spain] **P:** 369
  Turkey (The Ottoman decline) **T:** 510
Lepchas [people]
  Sikkim (People) **S:** 456
Lepidolite [mineral]
  Mica **M:** 482
Lepidoptera [entomology]
  Butterfly **B:** 732 with pictures
  Insect pictures on **I:** 282; (table) **I:** 300
  Moth **M:** 837 with pictures
Lepidus, Marcus Aemilius [Roman general]
  Antony, Mark **A:** 561
  Augustus (Rise to power) **A:** 889
  Pompey the Great **P:** 655
  Rome, Ancient (The later years of the republic) **R:** 445-446
Leporello [opera character]
  Opera: (Don Giovanni) **O:** 803-804
Leprechaun
  Fairy (Solitary fairies) **F:** 10
Leprohon, Rosanna [Canadian author]
  Canadian literature (Fiction: 1850-1918) **C:** 157
Lepromatous leprosy [disease]
  Leprosy (Symptoms) **L:** 204 with picture
Leprosarium [medicine]
  Leprosy (Treatment) **L:** 205
Leprosy [disease] **L:** 204 with pictures
  Medicine (During the Middle Ages) **M:** 373
  Thalidomide **T:** 229
Leptocephalus [larva]
  Eel (Life cycle) **E:** 114-115
Leptoceratops [dinosaur]
  Dinosaur (True dinosaurs) **D:** 206b-208
Leptodactylid frog
  Frog (Other frogs) **F:** 540
Lepton [physics] **L:** 205
  Fermion **F:** 74
  Muon **M:** 928
  Neutrino **N:** 154
  Subatomic particle (Kinds of subatomic particles) **So:** 937
Leptorynchoides thecatus [animal]
  Animal picture on **A:** 506
Lermontov, Mikhail [Russian author]
  Russian literature (Late Romanticism) **R:** 561
Lernaean Hydra [Greek mythology]
  Hydra **H:** 461
Lerner, Alan Jay [American lyricist] **L:** 206
  Musical comedy (The modern musical emerges) **M:** 960
Lerner, Daniel [American political analyst]
  Communication (Communication and politics) **Ci:** 888
LeRoy, Pierre [French watchmaker]
  Chronometer **C:** 539

Le Royer, Jérôme [French businessman]
  Montreal (French settlement) **M:** 777
Les ...
  Titles beginning Les appear under their key words, as in Sylphides, Les
Lesage, Alain René [French author]
  French literature (The Enlightenment) **F:** 520-521
Lesage, Jean [Canadian political leader]
  Canada, History of (The Quebec separatist movement) **C:** 149
  Quebec (table) **Q:** 29; (Postwar Quebec) **Q:** 32
Lesbia [literary figure]
  Catullus, Gaius Valerius **C:** 316
Lesbianism
  See also Gay rights movement in this index
  Adolescent (Establishing a sexual identity) **A:** 63
  Gay rights movement **G:** 73
  Homosexuality **H:** 307
Lesbos [island, Aegean] **L:** 206
  Aeolians **A:** 84
Lesch, Michael [American physician]
  Lesch-Nyhan syndrome **L:** 206
Lesch-Nyhan syndrome [disorder] **L:** 206
  Uric acid **U:** 221
Leschetizky, Theodor [Polish musician]
  Paderewski, Ignace Jan (Child prodigy) **P:** 19
Lescot, Pierre [French architect]
  Louvre **L:** 507
Le Seur, Lucille [birth name of]
  Crawford, Joan **Ci:** 1122
Lesh, Phil [American musician]
  Grateful Dead **G:** 329
Lesion [disorder]
  Leprosy (Symptoms) **L:** 204 with picture
  Yaws **Y:** 553
Leslie, Harry G. [American political leader]
  Indiana (table) **I:** 214
Leslie, Lisa [American basketball player]
  Basketball picture on **B:** 154b
Lesotho L: 206 with pictures and map
  Flag picture on **F:** 199
Lesotho Congress for Democracy [political party]
  Lesotho (History) **L:** 208
Less Deceived, The [poems by Larkin]
  Larkin, Philip **L:** 77
Less developed country [economics]
  See also Developing country in this index
  AIDS (AIDS around the world) **A:** 166
  Industry (Industry in developing countries) **I:** 261-262
  International Development Association **I:** 339
  Local government (Local governments in less developed countries) **L:** 409
  World (How nations are grouped) **W:** 407
Less Than One [essays by Brodsky]
  Brodsky, Joseph **B:** 636
Lessee [law]
  Lease **L:** 166
Lesseps, Ferdinand Marie de [French engineer]
  See De Lesseps, Ferdinand Marie in this index
Lesser Antilles [islands, Caribbean Sea]
  Caribbean Sea **C:** 237
  French West Indies **F:** 528
  Leeward Islands **L:** 181
  West Indies **W:** 201
Lesser ape [animal]
  Ape **A:** 563
  Gibbon **G:** 185
  Primate (Anthropoids) **P:** 778
Lesser golden-plover [bird]
  Bird (Birds of the Arctic) **B:** 343 with picture
Lesser jihad [religion]
  Jihad **J:** 126
Lesser panda See Red panda in this index
Lesser prairie-chicken
  Prairie-chicken **P:** 732
Lesser redpoll [bird]
  Redpoll **R:** 191
Lesser roadrunner [bird]
  Roadrunner **R:** 362
Lesser Sunda Islands [Indonesia]
  Indonesia (The Lesser Sunda Islands) **I:** 234 with map
Lesser wives
  Egypt, Ancient (Government) **E:** 139
Lessing, Doris [British author] **L:** 208
  English literature (Literature after World War II) **E:** 322-323
Lessing, Gotthold Ephraim [German author] **L:** 208
  Drama (Germany) **D:** 336
  German literature (The Enlightenment) **G:** 139
Lesson, The [play by Ionesco]
  Ionesco, Eugène **I:** 372
Lesson plan
  Teaching (Preparing to teach classes) **T:** 65-66
Lesson-sermon

Christian Scientists (Beliefs) C: 522e
Lessor [law]
Lease L: 166
Lester, Jeeter [literary figure]
Caldwell, Erskine C: 28
Lesvos [island, Aegean] *See* Lesbos *in this index*
Leszczyńska, Maria [wife of]
Louis XV L: 476
Leszczyński, Stanislas [king of Poland]
Succession wars (The War of the Polish
Succession) So: 950
Let [tennis]
Tennis (The serve) T: 163
"Let them eat cake" [quotation]
Marie Antoinette M: 200
"Let Us Beat Swords into Plowshares" [sculpture]
United Nations *picture on* U: 80
Let Us Now Praise Famous Men [book by Agee
and Evans]
Evans, Walker E: 422
Letcher, John [American political leader]
Virginia (table) V: 417
Letchworth [England]
City *picture on* Ci: 587
Letchworth State Park
New York (Places to visit) N: 302
Leterme, Yves [Belgian political leader]
Belgium B: 235
Lethal injection L: 209
Capital punishment C: 193; (table) C: 193
Euthanasia E: 421
Lethal yellowing [tree disease]
Coconut palm (Growing coconut palms) Ci: 747
Lethbridge [Alberta] L: 209
Lethbridge, John [British inventor]
Diving, Underwater (History) D: 247
Lethbridge, University of L: 209
Erickson, Arthur Charles E: 350
Lethe [mythology] L: 209
Leto [Greek mythology]
Niobe N: 424
Letrozole [drug]
Tamoxifen T: 23
Let's Get It On [recording]
Gaye, Marvin G: 73
Letsie III [king of Lesotho]
Lesotho (History) L: 208
Letter [character]
See also Alphabet *in this index and articles on
specific letters, such as* A
Braille *pictures on* B: 550
Flag *pictures on* F: 196
Morse code *pictures on* M: 819
Letter [correspondence] *See* Letter writing *in this
index*
Letter carrier [occupation]
Postal Service, United States *picture on* P: 699
Postal services *pictures on* P: 704, P: 705; (How
mail is delivered) P: 702-703
**Letter Carriers of the United States of America,
National Association of**
Labor movement (table) L: 8
Letter of application *See* Application, Letter of *in
this index*
Letter to Coroticus [letter by Saint Patrick]
Patrick, Saint (Writings) P: 197
Letter to Louis XIV [book by Fénelon]
Fénelon, François de Salignac de la Mothe- F: 71
Letter to the World [dance]
Graham, Martha *picture on* G: 300
Letter writing L: 209 *with pictures*
Address, Forms of A: 53
Etiquette (Invitation etiquette) E: 374
Letterhead [stationery]
Letter writing (The heading) L: 210
Lettering pen
Pen (Specialty pens) P: 234 *with picture*
Letterpress [printing]
Printing (Letterpress printing) P: 799
Letters [Bible] *See* Epistles *in this index*
Letters [book by Pliny the Younger]
Pliny the Younger P: 574
Letters, Doctor of
Degree, College (Honorary degrees) D: 93
Letters Concerning the English Nation [book by
Voltaire]
Voltaire (Exile and return to France) V: 446
Letters from a Farmer in Pennsylvania [book by
Dickinson]
Dickinson, John D: 191
Letters from an American Farmer [book by
Crèvecoeur]
American literature (The revolutionary period
[1765-1787]) A: 415
Crèvecoeur, Michel-Guillaume Jean de Ci: 1129
Letters from Rifka [book by Hesse]
Hesse, Karen H: 219

Letters of a Russian Traveler [book by Karamzin]
Russian literature (Sentimentalism) R: 560
Letters of marque and reprisal [warfare]
Privateer P: 808b
Letters of the alphabet *See* Letter *in this index*
Letters on Dancing and Ballet [book by Noverre]
Ballet (Ballet d'action) B: 51
*Letters on the Equality of the Sexes and the
Condition of Woman* [book by Grimké]
Feminism F: 69
Grimké (Sarah Moore Grimké) G: 394
Letters patent [document]
Communication (The 1700's) Ci: 880-881
Nobility (The creation of peerages) N: 450
Letters to Atticus [manuscript by Cicero]
Renaissance (Petrarch and Giovanni Boccaccio)
R: 234
Letters to Judy [book by Blume]
Blume, Judy B: 431
Lettre à M. Dacier [pamphlet by Champollion]
Rosetta stone R: 480
"Lettre du voyant" [poem by Rimbaud]
Rimbaud, Arthur R: 341
Letts [people] *See* Latvians *in this index*
Lettuce L: 213 *with pictures*
California (Vegetables) C: 57 *with picture*
Letzburgesch [language]
Luxembourg (People) L: 530-531
Leucas [island, Greece]
Ionian Islands I: 373 *with map*
Leucippus [Greek philosopher] L: 214
Atomism A: 877
Materialism M: 300b
Pre-Socratic philosophy (The teachings of
Parmenides) P: 772-773
Leuctra, Battle of [371 B.C.]
Messenia M: 423
Pelopidas P: 232
Sparta (History) So: 766
Leukemia [disease] L: 215
Bone marrow transplant B: 457
Cancer (Classification by primary body site)
C: 167-168; (Cancer in children) C: 169
Cat (Veterinary care) C: 295
Gene therapy G: 82
Leukocyte [biology] *See* White blood cell *in this
index*
Leukocyte pyrogen [physiology]
Fever F: 83
Leukopenia [disorder]
Blood (White-cell abnormalities) B: 414
Leukosis [disease]
Poultry (Raising poultry) P: 720-721
Leutnant Gustl [book by Schnitzler]
Schnitzler, Arthur S: 178
Leutze, Emanuel Gottlieb [American painter]
L: 216 *with picture*
Rivers, Larry *picture on* R: 355
State, Department of *picture on* So: 862
Lev [Galician leader]
Lviv L: 532
Levada, William J. [American religious leader]
Cardinal (American cardinals) C: 211
LeVander, Harold E. [American political leader]
Minnesota (table) M: 602
Levant cotton
Cotton (Kinds of cotton) Ci: 1087
Levassor, Émile Constant [French inventor]
Automobile *picture on* A: 963; (The gasoline car)
A: 965-966
Le Vau, Louis [French architect]
Architecture (Baroque architecture) A: 622
Versailles, Palace of V: 339
Levee [engineering] L: 216
Flood (Flood control) F: 238 *with diagram*
Irrigation (Surface irrigation) I: 457
Mississippi (Statehood) M: 642
Mississippi River (Floods and flood control)
M: 647-648
New Orleans *map on* N: 285; (The city) N: 278
Levee, Natural [geography]
River (Flood plains) R: 353 *with diagram*
Level [mining]
Mining (Mining terms) M: 577
Level [tool] L: 216 *with pictures*
Level designer [career]
Electronic game (Game design) E: 204b
Level loop rug
Rugs and carpets (Kinds of rugs and carpets)
R: 514 *with picture*
Level one nurse
Nursing (Nursing careers) N: 616
Level two nurse
Nursing (Practical nursing courses) N: 619
Levellers [English history] L: 217
Leven, River [England]
Windermere W: 333

Lever [machine] L: 217 *with diagrams*
Archimedes (His discoveries) A: 605
Machine (Efficiency) M: 14; (Lever) M: 14 *with
pictures*
Simple machines S: 467
Wheel and axle W: 278
Wheelbarrow W: 279
Lever-action rifle
Rifle (Kinds of rifles) R: 338
Lever House [New York City]
New York City (Architecture) N: 336
Lever lock
Lock (Types of locks) L: 410
Lever machine
Voting (Methods of voting) V: 449
Voting machine (Kinds of electoral voting
machines) V: 450
Lever safety valve
Safety valve S: 17 *with diagram*
Lever-tumbler lock
Lock (Mechanical locks) L: 411-412
Leveraged buyout [business]
Merger M: 417
Leveret [animal]
Hare H: 60
Le Verrier, Urbain [French astronomer]
Astronomy (Finding new objects) A: 848
Neptune (Discovery) N: 129
Levertov, Denise [American poet]
American literature (Poetry) A: 423
Lévesque, René [Canadian political leader] L: 218
Canada, History of (The separatist threat) C: 150
Parti Québécois P: 183
Quebec (Postwar Quebec) Q: 32; (The late 1900's)
Q: 32
Levi [apostle] *See* Matthew, Saint *in this index*
Levi [son of Jacob]
Levites L: 219
Levi-Montalcini, Rita [Italian-American biologist]
Nobel Prizes (Physiology or medicine: 1986)
N: 446
Lévi-Strauss, Claude [French anthropologist]
L: 218
Mythology (Structuralist approaches) M: 991
Levi Strauss & Co.
Strauss, Levi So: 922
Leviathan [book by Hobbes]
Government (The rise of monarchies and nation-
states) G: 290
Hobbes, Thomas H: 272
Levin, Karen [birth name of]
Hesse, Karen H: 219
Levine, David [American artist]
Caricature *picture on* C: 238
Levine, Jack [American painter] L: 218 *with picture*
Levine, James [American musician] L: 219
Levine, Philip [American physiologist]
Rh factor R: 289
Levine, Philip [American poet]
Poet laureate (table: Poets laureate of the United
States) P: 590
Levine, Sherrie [American artist]
Painting (Postmodernism) P: 88
Levinson, Barry [American director] L: 219
Motion picture (Best achievement in directing:
1988) M: 862
Levi's [jeans]
Strauss, Levi So: 922
Lévis, François de [French general]
Quebec, Battle of (Bombardment of Quebec)
Q: 37
Lévis Forts National Historic Site [Quebec]
Canada (table: National historic sites) C: 114
Levites [Bible] L: 219
Leviticus [Bible] L: 219
Pentateuch P: 274
Levitt, William Jaird [American businessman]
L: 219
Levittown [New York] L: 219
Levitt, William Jaird L: 219
Levittown [Pennsylvania]
Levitt, William Jaird L: 219
Levodopa [drug] *See* L-dopa *in this index*
Levulose [sugar] *See* Fructose *in this index*
Levy, David H. [Canadian-born American
astronomer]
Jupiter (History of Jupiter study) J: 200b
Levy, Louis [American inventor]
Printing (Developments in platemaking) P: 803-
804
Levy, Max [American inventor]
Printing (Developments in platemaking) P: 803-
804
Lewelling, Lorenzo D. [American political leader]
Kansas (table) K: 234
Lewes [Delaware]
Delaware (Places to visit) D: 102

Lewes, George Henry [British author]
Eliot, George E: 237
Lewin, Kurt [German-American psychologist]
L: 219
Group dynamics G: 402
Sensitivity training S: 302
Lewinsky, Monica [American public figure]
Clinton, Bill (Domestic events) Ci: 682f
Reno, Janet R: 240
Starr, Kenneth Winston So: 857
United States, History of the (The Clinton impeachment) U: 196d
Lewis, Andrew L., Jr. [American government official]
Reagan, Ronald Wilson (table) R: 169
Transportation, Department of (table) T: 400
Lewis, Sir Arthur [British economist] L: 220
Lewis, C. S. [British author] L: 220
Lewis, Carl [American athlete] L: 220 with picture
Lewis, David Peter [American political leader]
Alabama (table) A: 274
Lewis, Edward B. [American physiologist]
Nobel Prizes (Physiology or medicine: 1995)
N: 446
Lewis, Elizabeth Foreman [American author]
Newbery Medal (table) N: 359
Lewis, Francis [American patriot] L: 220
Lewis, Gilbert Newton [American chemist]
Chemistry (Development of physical chemistry)
C: 404-405
Deuterium (Discovery) D: 172
Heavy water H: 161
Lewis, James T. [American political leader]
Wisconsin (table) W: 365
Lewis, Jerry Lee [American singer]
Rock music (The first generation) R: 377
Lewis, John Aaron [American composer] L: 220
Jazz (New directions) J: 73
Lewis, John L. [American labor leader] L: 221
Labor movement (Formation of the CIO) L: 12
United Mine Workers of America U: 75
Lewis, Matthew G. [British author]
Gothic novel G: 279
Lewis, Meriwether [American explorer] L: 221
Clark, William Ci: 642
Exploration (Crossing North America) E: 447 with map
Lewis and Clark expedition L: 222 with portrait
Rocky Mountains (History) R: 395-396
South Dakota (Exploration and fur trade) So: 681
Westward movement in America (Exploration)
W: 248
Lewis, Morgan [American political leader]
New York (table) N: 313
Lewis, Ray [American football player]
Football picture on F: 368
Lewis, Robert [American author]
Method acting M: 434
Lewis, Sinclair [American author] L: 221
American literature (Satirists) A: 422
Nobel Prizes (Literature: 1930) N: 447
Novel (New directions in the novel) N: 573-574
Roaring Twenties (Cultural trends) R: 364
United States, History of the (The Lost Generation and Flaming Youth) U: 190
Lewis, Stephen [Canadian diplomat]
United Nations (table) U: 86
Lewis, William B. [American government official]
Kitchen Cabinet K: 337
Lewis and Clark expedition [U.S. history] L: 222 with pictures and maps
Clark, William Ci: 642
Exploration (Crossing North America) E: 447 with map
Idaho (Exploration and early settlement) I: 42
Indian, American (After European contact) I: 166
Jefferson, Thomas (Exploration and expansion)
J: 85
Lewis, Meriwether L: 221
Missouri picture on M: 670
Montana (Exploration) M: 758
Navigation (Explorers) N: 74
Sacagawea S: 4
South Dakota (Exploration and fur trade) So: 681
Washington picture on W: 67
Lewis and Clark Interpretive Center
North Dakota (Places to visit) N: 504
Washington (Places to visit) W: 56
Lewis and Clark Lake
South Dakota (Rivers and lakes) So: 676 with map
Lewis and Clark National Historic Trail Interpretive Center [Great Falls]
Montana (Places to visit) M: 750
Lewis and Clark National Historical Park
[Oregon/Washington]
National Park System (table: National historical parks) N: 57

Lewis and Harris [Scotland] See Lewis with Harris in this index
Lewis Hills
Newfoundland and Labrador (Mountains) N: 370 with map
Lewis Overthrust [ridge]
Glacier National Park (Lewis Overthrust) G: 205
Lewis with Harris [island, Scotland]
Hebrides H: 163
Lewisia [plant]
Flower picture on F: 289
Lewis's mock orange [plant]
Syringa So: 1077
Lewiston [Idaho]
Idaho (table: Average monthly weather) I: 39;
(Transportation) I: 41
Lewiston [Maine] L: 224
Lex de imperio Vespasiani
Vespasian V: 341
Lexicon See Dictionary in this index
Lexicon Technicum [book by Harris]
Encyclopedia (An age of experiment) E: 268a
Lexington [Kentucky] L: 224
Kentucky (table: Average monthly weather)
K: 286
Lexington [ship]
Barry, John B: 119
Lexington and Concord, Battles of [1775] L: 224
Concord Ci: 928
Gage, Thomas G: 5
Revolution, American (Lexington and Concord)
R: 274 with map; (table) R: 276
United States, History of the (The Revolutionary War begins) U: 159
Lexington Public Library [Lexington]
Kentucky (Libraries) K: 276
Leyden [Netherlands]
Leiden L: 186
Leyster, Judith [Dutch painter] L: 225
Painting (The Dutch masters) P: 62-63
Leyte [island, Philippines]
MacArthur, Douglas (World War II) M: 3 with picture
Philippines (The main islands) P: 376-378 with map
World War II (The liberation of the Philippines)
W: 491
Leyte Gulf, Battle for [1944]
Navy (World War II) N: 80
World War II (The liberation of the Philippines)
W: 491
Lezama Lima, José [Cuban author]
Cuba (The arts) Ci: 1171-1172
LH [hormone] See Luteinizing hormone in this index
Lhamo Dhondup [Tibetan religious leader] See Dalai Lama in this index
Lhasa [Tibet] L: 225
Tibet picture on T: 278; (Cities) T: 277 with picture
Lhasa apso [dog] L: 225 with picture
Dog picture on D: 275
LHC [machine] See Large Hadron Collider in this index
Lhotse [mountain, Nepal-Tibet]
Mount Everest M: 884
Li [philosophy]
Confucianism (Later Confucianism) Ci: 937
Li [symbol]
Lithium L: 386
Li Bai [Chinese poet] See Li Bo in this index
Li Bo [Chinese poet] L: 225
Chinese literature (Poetry) C: 511
Li Cheng [Chinese artist]
China picture on C: 488
Li Ning [Chinese gymnast]
Olympic Games (Boycotts) O: 753
Li Peng [Chinese political leader] L: 225 with portrait
China (Recent developments) C: 506
Li Po [Chinese poet] See Li Bo in this index
Li River [river, China]
China picture on C: 494
Li Shimin [emperor of China]
Li Yuan L: 226
Tang dynasty (The rise of the dynasty) T: 25
Li Tsung-jen [Chinese political leader]
Chiang Kai-shek (Communist triumph) C: 419
Li Yuan [emperor of China] L: 225
Tang dynasty (The rise of the dynasty) T: 25
Liability [bookkeeping]
Bookkeeping (Double-entry bookkeeping) B: 472
Liability, Product
Product liability suit P: 810
Liability account
Bookkeeping (Accounts) B: 472
Liability coverage
Insurance (Automobile insurance) I: 313
Liability insurance

Insurance diagram on I: 310; (Property and liability insurance) I: 312
Liana [plant] L: 226 with picture
Plant picture on P: 527
Rain forest (Structure and growth) R: 126a
Liang Bua [cave]
Homo floresiensis H: 306
Liang Kai [Chinese artist]
Painting (Chinese painting) P: 44-46 with picture
Liao dynasty [Chinese history]
Beijing (History) B: 223
Liaodong Peninsula [region, China]
Russo-Japanese War (Underlying causes) R: 566a
Liard River
Yukon (Location, size, and description) Y: 578 with map
Libation Bearers, The [play by Aeschylus]
Aeschylus A: 90
Libbeus [apostle] See Jude, Saint in this index
Libbey, Edward Drummond [American engineer]
Fiberglass (History) F: 89
Toledo (History) T: 321
Libbey Glass Company
Toledo (History) T: 321
Libby, Willard Frank [American chemist]
Radiocarbon (Radiocarbon dating) R: 97
Libby Dam [Montana]
British Columbia (The mid-1900's) B: 630
Montana (Rivers and lakes) M: 752-754; (The mid-1900's) M: 760
Libel [law] L: 226
Damages D: 20
Freedom of speech (Limitations) F: 506
Journalism (Restrictions on freedom of the press)
J: 173
Slander S: 499
Liber Abaci [book by Fibonacci]
Fibonacci, Leonardo F: 89
Liber Chronicarum [book]
Library picture on L: 239
Liber Quadratorum [book by Fibonacci]
Fibonacci, Leonardo F: 89
Liberal arts L: 226
Fine arts F: 104
Universities and colleges U: 206; (Vocational study and the liberal arts) U: 211
Liberal constitutionalists [Russian history]
Russia (Nicholas II) R: 551-552
Liberal Democratic Party [Japan]
Japan (Politics) J: 35; (Postwar boom) J: 58
Liberal Democratic Party [Russia]
Russia (Politics) R: 531
Liberal Democrats [United Kingdom] L: 226
See also Liberal Party [United Kingdom] in this index
United Kingdom (Politics) U: 54
Liberal education
Education (General education) E: 87
Liberal Party [Australia]
Australia (Political parties) A: 897; (Building a nation) A: 923
Menzies, Sir Robert Gordon M: 410
Liberal Party [Denmark]
Denmark (Politics) D: 133; (Recent developments) D: 141
Liberal Party [Japan]
Japan (Politics) J: 35; (Recent developments) J: 59
Liberal Party [New Zealand]
New Zealand (Depression and social reform)
N: 355
Liberal Party [South Africa]
Paton, Alan P: 196
Liberal Party [United Kingdom]
See also Liberal Democrats in this index
Ireland (The Easter Rising) I: 427
United Kingdom (Political confusion) U: 69
Liberal Party of Canada L: 227
See also Canada, History of in this index
Canada, Government of (Political parties) C: 136
Chrétien, Jean C: 522a; (The 1993 election)
C: 522c
Dion, Stéphane D: 214
Ignatieff, Michael I: 48
Laurier, Sir Wilfrid (Early public career) L: 124
Martin, Paul M: 234b
Mulroney, Brian (Election as party leader) M: 917
Ontario (Politics) O: 784
Political party (Leading parties) P: 636
Quebec (Politics) Q: 30
Saint Laurent, Louis Stephen (Prime minister [1948-1957]) S: 40
Saskatchewan (Politics) S: 144
Liberal Republican Party [U.S. history] L: 227
Grant, Ulysses S. (Election of 1872) G: 316
Liberal Unionists [British history]
United Kingdom (Gladstone and Disraeli) U: 69
Liberalism [political science] L: 227

Conservatism **Ci: 991**
Political science (Liberalism) **P: 639**
Smith, Adam **S: 515**
United States, Government of the (Current issues in U.S. government) **U: 146**
Liberation Day [Italy]
Holiday (In other countries) **H: 291**
Liberation theology [religion] **L: 228**
Christianity (Other Christian writings) **C: 522h**
Roman Catholic Church (In Latin America) **R: 411-412**
Liberation Tigers of Tamil Eelam [political group]
Gandhi, Rajiv **G: 25**
Sri Lanka (History) **So: 819**
Liberator, The [newspaper]
Abolition movement **A: 12**
Garrison, William Lloyd **G: 45**
Massachusetts (Progress as a state) **M: 292**
Liberator, The [nickname]
Bolívar, Simón **B: 441**
Liberia L: 228 *with pictures and map*
African Americans (Free blacks) **A: 136g-136h**
Flag *picture on* **F: 199**
Liberians United for Reconciliation and Democracy [political group]
Liberia (Recent developments) **L: 232**
Liberius [pope]
Pope (table) **P: 666**
Libero [player]
Volleyball (The court) **V: 445**
Libertador, El [nickname]
Bolívar, Simón **B: 441**
Libertarian Party [political party] **L: 232**
Liberty *See* Freedom *in this index*
Liberty [airplane engine]
Aviation (World War I [1914-1918]) **A: 987**
Liberty [ship]
Hancock, John **H: 39**
Rhode Island (The Revolutionary War) **R: 313**
Liberty, Age of [Swedish history]
Sweden (The Age of Liberty) **So: 1034**
Liberty, Personal *See* Personal liberty *in this index*
Liberty, Statue of *See* Statue of Liberty *in this index*
Liberty Bell [Philadelphia] **L: 232** *with picture*
Allentown **A: 373**
Pennsylvania *picture on* **P: 255**
Philadelphia (Downtown Philadelphia) **P: 359**
Liberty Bond
Statue of Liberty (Growth as a symbol) **So: 877**
United States, History of the (The United States in the war) **U: 188-189**
Liberty Enlightening the World **See** Statue of Liberty *in this index*
Liberty Island [island, New York City] **L: 233**
Statue of Liberty **So: 872** *with picture*
Liberty Lake
Nevada (Rivers and lakes) **N: 166-168**
Liberty Leading the People [painting by Delacroix]
Delacroix, Eugène **D: 95**
Liberty League [U.S. history] **L: 233**
Liberty of contract [law]
Labor movement (The early 1900's) **L: 11**
Lochner v. New York **L: 410**
Liberty Party [U.S. history] **L: 233**
Abolition movement **A: 13**
Liberty ship
Ship (Traditional general cargo ships) **S: 406-407**
Liberty State Park [New Jersey]
New Jersey (Places to visit) **N: 240**
Liberty Under Oath [poems by Paz]
Paz, Octavio **P: 205**
Libeskind, Daniel [American architect]
September 11 terrorist attacks (Moving forward) **S: 310b-310c**
Libido [psychology] **L: 233**
Libius Severus [Roman emperor]
Rome, Ancient (table) **R: 447**
Libra [astrology] **L: 233** *with picture*
Zodiac (The zodiac in astrology) **Z: 597** *with picture*
Librarian [career]
Library **L: 234** *with pictures*
Literature for children (The role of librarians) **L: 366**
Librarian of Congress [government official]
Library of Congress **L: 263**
Library L: 234 *with pictures*
See also the Libraries *sections in specific country, state, and province articles and the list of Related articles in the* Library *article*
Bookmobile **B: 474**
Dewey Decimal Classification **D: 177**
Franklin, Benjamin (Civic leader) **F: 487-488** *with picture*
Information science **I: 269**
Literature for children (The role of librarians) **L: 366**

New Hampshire (Interesting facts) **N: 209**
Newspaper (The editorial department) **N: 381-382**
Presidential libraries **P: 771**
Reading *picture on* **R: 160**
United States (Libraries) **U: 113**
Universities and colleges (Libraries) **U: 210**
White House *picture on* **W: 289**
A Guide to Research Skills **Research Guide: 26**
Library and Archives Canada
Library (Canadian government libraries) **L: 249**
Library and Information Center Committee, Federal
Library (United States government libraries) **L: 248-249**
Library and Museum of Performing Arts
Lincoln Center for the Performing Arts **L: 327**
Library Association, American *See* American Library Association *in this index*
Library Association, Canadian *See* Canadian Library Association *in this index*
Library Associations and Institutions, International Federation of
Library (International library programs) **L: 254**
Library board
Library (Administering a public library) **L: 242**
Library Company of Philadelphia
Library (Libraries in the United States) **L: 261**
Pennsylvania (Libraries) **P: 248**
Philadelphia (Libraries and museums) **P: 363**
Library Journal [magazine]
Dewey, Melvil **D: 177**
Library network
Library (The growth of information and technology) **L: 237-238** *with picture*
Library of Congress [Washington, D.C.] **L: 263** *with picture*
Book collecting **B: 469**
Hayes, Rutherford Birchard (Congressman) **H: 119-120**
Library (Research libraries) **L: 247**; (United States government libraries) **L: 248**; (Libraries in the United States) **L: 261**
Putnam, Herbert **P: 913**
Washington, D.C. *map on* **W: 76**; (Library of Congress) **W: 71**
Library of Congress Classification L: 264
A Guide to Research Skills **Research Guide: 29, Research Guide: 38**
Library of Congress James Madison Memorial Building [Washington, D.C.]
Washington, D.C. *map on* **W: 76**
Library of Congress Thomas Jefferson Building [Washington, D.C.]
Washington, D.C. *map on* **W: 76**
Library of Medicine, National [Bethesda, Maryland]
Library (United States government libraries) **L: 248**
Library of Parliament [Ottawa]
Library (Canadian government libraries) **L: 249**
Library of the Academy of Sciences of the U.S.S.R. [St. Petersburg] *See* Library of the Russian Academy of Sciences *in this index*
Library of the Russian Academy of Sciences [St. Petersburg]
Library (Eastern Europe and Russia) **L: 252**
Library school
Library (table) **L: 257**
Library science [education]
Library (Educational requirements) **L: 256**
Library Services Act [1956] *See* Library Services and Construction Act *in this index*
Library Services and Construction Act [1964]
Library (Supporting the public library) **L: 242-243**
Libration [astronomy]
Moon (Libration) **M: 785** *with diagrams*
Libretto [text]
Ballet (Kinds of ballet) **B: 48**
Musical comedy (The book) **M: 959**
Opera (The libretto) **O: 791**
Libreville [Gabon] **L: 264**
Gabon **G: 2**; (History) **G: 3**
Librium [drug]
Benzodiazepine **B: 256**
Libro de buen amor [book by Ruiz]
Ruiz, Juan **R: 519**
Libya L: 264 *with pictures and map*
Barbary States **B: 105** *with map*
Chad (History) **C: 367-368**
Flag *picture on* **F: 199**
Middle East **M: 530**
North Atlantic Treaty Organization (History) **N: 471**
Nuclear weapon (After the terrorist attacks of Sept. 11, 2001) **N: 602**
Obama, Barack (Foreign affairs) **O: 641**

Libyan Desert [region, Africa]
Egypt (The Western Desert) **E: 125** *with picture and map*
Libya (Land and climate) **L: 266**
Sahara **S: 20**
Lice *See* Louse *in this index*
License [document] **L: 268**
Automobile (Driving an automobile) **A: 954**
Medicine (A career as a doctor) **M: 370-371**
New York (Interesting facts) **N: 291**
Nursing (Licensing) **N: 619**
Sales (Regulation of selling) **S: 64**
License tax
Taxation (Taxes on transactions) **T: 53**
Licensed pilot
Airplane (Learning to fly) **A: 226**
Licensed practical nurse
Nursing (Licensed practical nurses) **N: 619**
Licensed vocational nurse
Nursing (Licensed practical nurses) **N: 617**
Licensing Act [1737]
Fielding, Henry (His life) **F: 94**
Lichen [plant] **L: 269** *with pictures*
Antarctica (Living things) **A: 534**
Earth *picture on* **E: 22**
Fungi (How a fungus lives) **F: 559**
Litmus **L: 391**
Symbiosis **So: 1065**
Licht, Frank [American political leader]
Rhode Island (table) **R: 311**
Lichtenstein, Roy [American artist] **L: 269**
Painting (Pop Art) **P: 86** *with picture*
Pop Art *picture on* **P: 659**
Licinius [East Roman emperor]
Constantine the Great **Ci: 993**
Rome, Ancient (table) **R: 447**
Lick Observatory [California] **L: 270**
Licorice [food]
Candy (Other candies) **C: 176**
Licorice [plant] **L: 270**
Lictor [ancient Rome]
Fasces **F: 49**
Lidar [instrument]
Radar (How radar works) **R: 68**
Tornado (Radar) **T: 336-337**
Liddell, Alice [British public figure]
Alice in Wonderland **A: 367**
Carroll, Lewis (The *Alice* books) **C: 249**
Liddy, G. Gordon [American public figure]
Watergate (The break-in and cover-up) **W: 144**
Lidice [Czechoslovakia] **L: 270**
Heydrich, Reinhard **H: 220**
Lido [resort]
Venice (The city) **V: 306-307** *with map*
Lidocaine [drug] **L: 270**
Lie [golf]
Golf (table) **G: 261**
Lie, Trygve [Norwegian statesman] **L: 270**
United Nations (The secretary-general) **U: 83** *with portrait*
Lie detector [instrument] **L: 271** *with pictures*
Reflex action (How reflex action occurs) **R: 195**
Liébeault, Ambroise-Auguste [French doctor]
Hypnosis (Scientific studies) **H: 480**
Lieber, Francis [German-American editor]
Encyclopedia (Encyclopedias of the 1800's and 1900's) **E: 268b**
Lieber, Stanley Martin [real name of]
Lee, Stan **L: 180**
Lieberman, Joseph Isadore [American political leader] **L: 271**
Gore, Al (Political career) **G: 274**
Liebig, Justus von [German chemist]
Chemistry (Development of organic chemistry) **C: 404**
Liechtenstein L: 272 *with picture and map*
Flag *picture on* **F: 206**
German language **G: 137**
Liechtenstein, Johann-Adam [prince of Liechtenstein]
Liechtenstein (History) **L: 273**
Lied von der Erde, Das [music by Mahler]
Mahler, Gustav **M: 65**
Lieder [music] **L: 273**
Classical music (The Romantic era) **Ci: 648**
Schubert, Franz Peter (His works) **S: 187**
Song **So: 592**
Liège [Belgium] **L: 273**
Liège, University of
Belgium (Education) **B: 229-230**
Liek, Harry J. [American mountain climber]
Mount McKinley **M: 886**
Liele, George [American religious leader]
African Americans (Free blacks) **A: 136g-136h**
Lien [law] **L: 273**
Lieutenant
Rank, Military (table) **R: 140**

Lieutenant colonel
Rank, Military (table) R: 140
Lieutenant commander
Rank, Military (table) R: 140
Lieutenant general
General G: 82
Rank, Military (table) R: 140
Lieutenant governor [office] L: 273
Canada, Government of (The 10 provinces)
C: 136
State government (Other officers) So: 863
Life L: 274 with pictures
See also Extraterrestrial life in this index
Biochemistry B: 310
Biodiversity B: 310
Biology B: 316
Carbon cycle C: 206
Death D: 61
Earth (The biosphere) E: 20
Environment E: 329
Evolution E: 426
Extinction E: 456
Extremophile E: 458
Gaia G: 5
Heredity H: 200
Intelligent design I: 320
Island (How life develops on islands) I: 473
Life cycle L: 280
Medical ethics M: 361
Nitrogen (Nitrogen and life) N: 425
Nitrogen cycle N: 426
Ocean picture on O: 651; (Life in the ocean)
O: 655 with pictures
Protoplasm P: 837
Soil (Effects of living things) So: 574
Water (Water in living things) W: 118
Life [magazine]
Bourke-White, Margaret B: 517
Eisenstaedt, Alfred E: 155
Luce, Henry Robinson L: 513
Life after death
See also Reincarnation in this index
Egypt, Ancient pictures on E: 140; (Painting and
sculpture) E: 139
Funeral customs F: 557
Immortality I: 86
Religion (A doctrine of salvation) R: 215-216
Resurrection R: 264
Roman Catholic Church (Life after death) R: 403
Tutankhamun T: 527
Life and Adventures of James P. Beckwourth
[book by Beckwourth]
Beckwourth, James Pierson B: 197
Life and Adventures of Joaquín Murieta, The
[book by Ridge]
Murieta, Joaquín M: 930
Life and Adventures of Nat Love, The [book by
Love]
Love, Nat L: 508
*Life and Extraordinary Adventures of Private Ivan
Chonkin, The* [book by Voinovich]
Russian literature (Modern Soviet literature)
R: 564-565
Life and Flowers [essay by Maeterlinck]
Maeterlinck, Maurice M: 41
*Life and Memorable Actions of George
Washington, The* [book by Weems]
Biography (The 1800's) B: 314
Lincoln, Abraham (Education) L: 312-313
Weems, Mason Locke W: 180
*Life and Opinions of Tristram Shandy, Gentleman,
The* See Tristram Shandy in this index
Life and Times of Michael K., The [book by
Coetzee]
Coetzee, J. M. Ci: 753
Life annuity with installments
Insurance (Annuities) I: 311
Life chances [sociology]
Social class (How people are categorized)
So: 550-551
Life cycle [biology] L: 280
Butterfly (The life cycle of butterflies) B: 739 with
pictures
Metamorphosis M: 428 with picture
Reproduction R: 242
Rust R: 567
Life estate [law]
Estate E: 360
Life expectancy L: 280
Medicine M: 363
Old age O: 738
World (table) W: 409
Life for the Tsar, A [opera by Glinka]
Glinka, Mikhail Ivanovich G: 231
Life history
Life cycle L: 280
Life in the Fields [short story collection]

Verga, Giovanni V: 317
Life insurance
Insurance (Life insurance) I: 309 with diagram;
(Insurance in the United States) I: 315
Investment (Life insurance policies) I: 369
Trust fund (Kinds of trusts) T: 474
Life Is a Dream [play by Calderón de la Barca]
Calderón de la Barca, Pedro C: 27
Spanish literature (The 1600's) So: 759-760
Life jacket L: 281
Life line [palmistry]
Palmistry P: 111 with diagram
Life of Dante [book by Boccaccio]
Biography (The Middle Ages) B: 313
Life of Émile Zola, The [film]
Motion picture (Best picture: 1937) M: 861
Life of George Washington [book by Weems]
See Life and Memorable Actions of George
Washington, The in this index
Life of Jesus [book by Renan]
Biography (The 1800's) B: 314
Life of Marianne, The [book by Marivaux]
Marivaux, Pierre M: 213
Life of Mr. Jonathan Wild the Great, The [book by
Fielding]
Fielding, Henry (His novels) F: 94-95
Life of Pi [book by Martel]
Martel, Yann M: 233
Life of Samuel Johnson, The [book by Boswell]
Biography (The 1700's) B: 313-314
English literature (The Johnson circle) E: 319
Life of the Bees, The [book by Maeterlinck]
Maeterlinck, Maurice M: 41
Life of the Swindler [book by Quevedo]
Quevedo, Francisco de Q: 41
Life of Sir William Osler, The [book by Cushing]
Cushing, Harvey Ci: 1200
Life on the Mississippi [book by Twain]
Mississippi River M: 646
Twain, Mark (Productive years in Hartford) T: 529
Life peer [title]
House of Lords H: 384
Nobility (The creation of peerages) N: 450
Parliament (The House of Lords) P: 173
United Kingdom (National government) U: 49-50
Life preserver
Boating (Boating regulations) B: 429
Life jacket L: 281
Life-Saving Service
Coast Guard, United States (New duties) Ci: 737
Life science
See also the list of Related articles in the Biology
article
Careers (Life, physical, and social sciences) C: 225
Science (The life sciences) S: 193
Life Scout [rank]
Boy Scouts (Star Scouts, Life Scouts, and Eagle
Scouts) B: 537
Life span
Aging (Why people age) A: 141
Animal (table: Length of life of animals) A: 473
Dog (The life of a dog) D: 266-277
Life expectancy L: 280
Life Studies [poems by Lowell]
Lowell, Robert L: 511
Life-support system
Space exploration (Meeting basic needs in space)
So: 703
Life vest
Life jacket L: 281
Life with Father [book by Day]
Day, Clarence D: 52
Life with Father [play by Lindsay and Crouse]
Lindsay, Howard L: 333
Life with Mother [book by Day]
Day, Clarence D: 52
Lifeline
Diving, Underwater picture on D: 246
Lifelong learning
Adult education A: 68
Life's Highway [poems by Guest]
Guest, Edgar Albert G: 421
Lifesaving
Drowning (Methods of rescue) D: 349
Trauma center T: 405
Lifesaving Medal
Medals, decorations, and orders (table) M: 357
Liffey [river, Ireland]
Dublin (The city) D: 371 with picture
Joyce, James J: 177
Lift [machine] L: 281
Elevator E: 234
Lift [physics]
Aerodynamics (Principles of aerodynamics) A: 85
with diagrams
Airplane A: 208; (Principles of flight) A: 220 with
diagrams

Airship (Lift) A: 250
Bernoulli's principle B: 271
Bird (In the air) B: 352 with diagrams
Helicopter (Lift) H: 171 with diagram
Kite (How kites fly) K: 339 with diagram
Lift-and-thrust aircraft
V/STOL V: 452
Lift bridge
Bridge (Moveable bridges) B: 602 with diagram
"Lift Every Voice and Sing" [song by Johnson]
Johnson, James Weldon J: 143
Lift-fan aircraft
V/STOL V: 452
Lift pump
Pump (Reciprocating pumps) P: 901
Lifting [meteorology]
Cloud (How clouds form) Ci: 708-711 with
pictures
Lifting [safety]
Safety (Safety on the job) S: 13 with picture
Liftoff
Rocket picture on R: 387
Ligament [anatomy] L: 281
Heart (Outer lining and muscle) H: 133
Human body (The skeletal system) H: 418 with
picture
Joint J: 155
Knee K: 345
Shell diagram on S: 385
Skeleton (The human skeleton) S: 479
Sprain So: 805
Ligan [law]
Flotsam, jetsam, and lagan F: 267
Ligase [enzyme]
Genetic engineering (How genes are
reintroduced into cells) G: 84b with diagram
Ligature [medicine] L: 281
"Ligeia" [story by Poe]
Poe, Edgar Allan (Fiction and theory of fiction)
P: 590
Liger [animal]
Lion (Cubs) L: 341
Tiger (The body of a tiger) T: 283-284
Liggett Group [company]
Tobacco (History) T: 307-308
Light [physics] L: 282 with pictures
See also the list of Related articles in the Light
article
Aberration A: 10
Alhazen A: 366
Astronomy (table: The electromagnetic
spectrum) A: 839; (Optical astronomy) A: 839
Black hole B: 388
Camera C: 80 with diagrams
Candle C: 175
Chlorophyll C: 517
Color (The relation between color and light)
Ci: 817; (The roles of the eyes and brain)
Ci: 818; (Characteristics of color) Ci: 824
Diffraction D: 201
Electromagnetic waves E: 201
Electronics (Electronics and light) E: 212
Eye (Adaptation to light and dark) E: 464
Fiber optics F: 88
Fire (Light) F: 122
Fluorescence F: 304
Foucault, Jean Bernard Léon F: 429
Gem (Index of refraction) G: 77
Gravitation (Predictions of general relativity)
G: 332
Huygens, Christiaan H: 460
Interference I: 323
Interior design (Elements of design) I: 327;
(Pattern and texture) I: 328
Laser L: 81 with pictures
Leaf (Obtaining the raw materials) L: 155 with
diagram
Maxwell, James Clerk M: 319
Metric system (Light) M: 440
Newton, Sir Isaac (Light and color) N: 389
Newton's rings N: 390
Optics O: 813
Painting (Light and shade) P: 35
Phosphorescence P: 402
Photochemistry P: 404
Photoelectric effect P: 405
Photography P: 406; (Light) P: 414 with pictures
Photon P: 430
Photoperiodism P: 430
Photosynthesis P: 430
Physics (Light) P: 437; (Newton) P: 439;
(Developments in the 1800's) P: 440; (Quantum
theory) P: 441
Prism P: 805 with picture
Quantum mechanics (Quanta of energy) Q: 6
Rainbow R: 127 with pictures
Raman, Sir Chandrasekhara Venkata R: 132

Redshift **R: 191**
Refraction **R: 199**
Relativity (The Michelson-Morley experiment) **R: 210**; (Distortions in space-time) **R: 212**
Sculpture (Form and treatment) **S: 230-231**
Spectrometer **So: 771**
Spectroscopy **So: 772**
Spectrum **So: 772** *with diagram*
Sun **So: 974**; (Energy output) **So: 976**
Telescope **T: 102**
Waves **W: 150**
Zeeman effect **Z: 588**
Light, Electric *See* Electric light *in this index*
Light, Polarized *See* Polarized light *in this index*
Light, Speed of
Foucault, Jean Bernard Léon **F: 429**
Light (The spectrum of light sources) **L: 284**; (Refraction) **L: 288**; (The speed of light) **L: 290**
Light-year **L: 294**
Michelson, Albert Abraham **M: 487**
Physics (Einstein and relativity) **P: 441**
Radiation (Electromagnetic radiation) **R: 75**
Relativity (The Michelson-Morley experiment) **R: 210**; (Special relativity) **R: 210**; (General relativity) **R: 211**
Star (Converting mass to energy) **So: 846**
Light, William [British surveyor]
Adelaide **A: 55**
Barossa Valley **B: 117**
Light airplane *See* Light plane *in this index*
Light amplification by stimulated emission of radiation [laser] *See* Laser *in this index*
Light antitank weapon
Bazooka **B: 178** *with picture*
Light beer [beverage]
Beer **B: 211**
Light bulb L: 293
Edison, Thomas Alva *picture on* **E: 81**; (The electric light) **E: 79**
Electric light **E: 174**, *picture on* **E: 176**; (The bulb) **E: 174**
Environmental pollution (Individual efforts) **E: 338**
Glass (Soda-lime glass) **G: 213**; (Etching) **G: 217**; (table) **G: 218**
Light (Incandescence) **L: 283**; (Energy and brightness) **L: 290**
Lighting (Quantity of light) **L: 297**; (Lighting problems) **L: 297-298**
Light crude [oil]
Petroleum (The composition of petroleum) **P: 331**
Light-emitting device
Electronics (Light-emitting devices) **E: 213**
Light-emitting diode [electronics] **L: 293** *with picture*
Clock (Electric clocks) **Ci: 682k**
Computer (Monitors) **Ci: 916**
Electric light (Other sources of electric light) **E: 175**
Electronics (Light-emitting devices) **E: 213**
Indium **I: 224**
Light (Light and energy efficiency) **L: 291**
Light flyweight [boxing]
Boxing (table) **B: 527**
Light heavyweight [boxing]
Boxing (table) **B: 527**
Light horse
Horse (Kinds of horses) **H: 343**; (Light horses) **H: 343** *with pictures*
Light-Horse Harry Lee [nickname]
Lee, Henry **L: 176**
Light hydrogen
Isotope (Separating isotopes) **I: 476**
Light in August [book by Faulkner]
Faulkner, William **F: 55**
Light in the Attic, A [book by Silverstein]
Silverstein, Shel **S: 465**
Light in the Piazza, The [musical]
Musical comedy (Musical comedy today) **M: 961**
Light infantry division
Infantry (Divisions) **I: 264**
Light list [publication]
Lighthouse (Identifying lighthouses) **L: 294**
Light meter [instrument] **L: 293**
See also Exposure meter *in this index*
Camera (Automatic exposure control) **C: 82** *with picture*
Light microscope *See* Optical microscope *in this index*
Light middleweight class
Boxing (table) **B: 527**
Light pen [electronic device]
Computer (A light pen) **Ci: 915**
Light plane
Airplane *picture on* **A: 209**; (General aviation planes) **A: 211** *with picture*

Aviation (General aviation activities) **A: 984** *with picture*
Light rail transit
Transit **T: 374**
Transportation (Urban public transportation) **T: 393**
Light rain
Rain (Characteristics of rain) **R: 122-123**
Light-sensing device [electronics] *See* Electric eye *in this index*
Light show
Laser *picture on* **L: 81**; (Scanning) **L: 82**
Light switch
Electric switch **E: 189** *with diagram*
Light That Failed, The [book by Kipling]
Kipling, Rudyard (Early literary success) **K: 334**
Light truck
Automobile (The 2000's) **A: 972**
Truck *pictures on* **T: 459**
Light water reactor
Nuclear energy (Power reactors) **N: 584-586**; (Advanced fission reactors) **N: 594**
Light welterweight class
Boxing (table) **B: 527**
Light-year [astronomy] **L: 294**
Astronomy (Units of distance) **A: 837**
Galaxy **G: 8**
Planet (Planets in other solar systems) **P: 512**
Star **So: 840**
Weights and measures (Miscellaneous weights and measures) **W: 184**
Lighter [boat]
Barge **B: 109**
Lighthouse L: 294 *with pictures*
Lighthouse of Alexandria *See* Pharos of Alexandria *in this index*
Lighthouse Route
Nova Scotia (Places to visit) **N: 560**
Lighthouse Service, Federal *See* Federal Lighthouse Service *in this index*
Lighting L: 296 *with pictures*
Animation (Lighting and rendering) **A: 513**
Fluorescent lamp **F: 305** *with diagram*
Invention *pictures on* **I: 356**
Lamp **L: 52** *with pictures*
Motion picture (Preparing to shoot) **M: 852** *with picture*
Opera (Rehearsing a production) **O: 796**
Photography (Light) **P: 412** *with pictures*
Road (Lighting) **R: 359**
Theater (Lighting and sound) **T: 240** *with pictures*
Lighting control board
Theater *picture on* **T: 241**
Lighting designer
Theater (Lighting methods) **T: 240**
Lighting fixture
Lighting (Lighting problems) **L: 297-298**; (Lighting devices) **L: 298**
Lighting ratio
Photography (Intensity) **P: 415**
Lightness
Color (Characteristics of color) **Ci: 824**
Lightning [meteorology] **L: 299** *with pictures*
Camping (Safety) **C: 96**
Electricity *picture on* **E: 190**; (Static electricity) **E: 192**; (Electrical dangers outdoors) **E: 196**; (Experiments with electric charge) **E: 196-197**
Franklin, Benjamin (The scientist) **F: 488**
Jupiter (Weather) **J: 200**
Life (Creating simple organic compounds) **L: 279**
Ozone **O: 894**
Plasma **P: 552**
Storm *picture on* **So: 913**
Thunder **T: 272** *with diagram*
Thunderstorm **T: 272**
Lightning [sailing]
Sailing (Catboats and sloops) **S: 24**
Lightning, Tampa Bay [team]
Hockey (table: National Hockey League) **H: 281**
Lightning bug *See* Firefly *in this index*
Lightning rod L: 302
Franklin, Benjamin *picture on* **F: 490**; (Experiments with electricity) **F: 488**
Lightning (Protection from lightning) **L: 301**
"Light's Golden Jubilee" [celebration]
Edison, Thomas Alva (Honors) **E: 82**
Lightship
Lighthouse **L: 294**
Lightweight
Boxing (table) **B: 527**
Lightweight concrete
Cement and concrete (Lightweight concrete) **C: 343**
Lignin [botany] **L: 302**
Forest products (Lignin products) **F: 402**
Termite **T: 171**
Wood (The composition of wood) **W: 390**

Lignite [coal] **L: 302**
Coal (Coal rank) **Ci: 718**; (The uses of coal) **Ci: 718-719**; (How coal was formed) **Ci: 720-721**; (Where coal is found) **Ci: 721**
Greece (Mining) **G: 361**
North Dakota (Interesting facts) **N: 497** *with picture*
Lignum-vitae [tree] **L: 302**
LIGO [instrument] *See* Laser Interferometer Gravitational-Wave Observatory *in this index*
Ligon, Thomas Watkins [American political leader]
Maryland (table) **M: 255**
Liguest, Pierre Laclède [French frontiersman] *See* Laclède Liguest, Pierre *in this index*
Ligule [botany]
Grass (The grass plant) **G: 324**
Liguori, Saint Alphonsus [Italian religious leader]
Alphonsus Liguori, Saint **A: 384**
Ligurian Sea [Mediterranean] **L: 302**
Liholiho [king of Hawaii]
Hawaii (The kingdom of Hawaii) **H: 106**
Lij Iyasu [emperor of Ethiopia]
Ethiopia (Menelik II) **E: 371**
Like a Virgin [recording]
Madonna **M: 37**
Rock music (Madonna and Michael Jackson) **R: 380c**
Like Water for Chocolate [book by Esquivel]
Latin American literature (The post-Boom) **L: 114**
Like Water for Chocolate [film]
Latin America (Motion pictures) **L: 101**
Likud [political party]
Israel (Politics) **I: 479**; (Unity government) **I: 489**
Kadima **K: 208**
Netanyahu, Benjamin **N: 137**
Olmert, Ehud **O: 745**
Peres, Shimon **P: 285**
Shamir, Yitzhak **S: 371**
Sharon, Ariel **S: 377**
"Li'l Abner" [comic strip]
Capp, Al **C: 198**
Lilac [color]
Lilac **L: 303**
Syringa **So: 1077**
Lilac [shrub] **L: 302** *with pictures*
Flower (Flowering shrubs) **F: 281** *with picture*
Leaf *pictures on* **L: 152**
Lilienblum, Moshe Leib [Hebrew author]
Hebrew literature (Modern Hebrew literature) **H: 162**
Lilienthal, David Eli [American government official] **L: 303**
Lilienthal, Otto [German engineer]
Airplane (First human flights) **A: 230** *with picture*
Glider (Early days) **G: 230** *with picture*
Lilies of the Field [film]
Poitier, Sidney **P: 602**
Liliom [play by Molnár]
Molnár, Ferenc **M: 696**
Lilith [sculpture by Smith]
Sculpture (From the mid-1900's to the early 2000's) **S: 259-260** *with picture*
Liliuokalani, Lydia Kamekeha [queen of Hawaii] **L: 303**
Harrison, Benjamin (International affairs) **H: 73**
Hawaii (The Republic of Hawaii) **H: 108**
Liljecrona's Home [book by Lagerlöf]
Lagerlöf, Selma **L: 30**
Lillard, Joseph [American religious leader]
Illinois (French and British control) **I: 72**
Lille [France] **L: 303**
Lilley, George L. [American political leader]
Connecticut (table) **Ci: 967**
Lillie, Beatrice [British actress] **L: 303** *with portrait*
Lillington, Alexander [American patriot]
North Carolina (Revolution and independence) **N: 492**
Lilliput [fictional place]
Gulliver's Travels **G: 440**
Lilliputians [fictional people]
Gulliver's Travels **G: 440**
Swift, Jonathan: (Gulliver's Travels) **So: 1040** *with picture*
Lillo, George [British dramatist]
Drama (England) **D: 334-335**
Lilly Endowment [foundation] **L: 303**
Foundation (table) **F: 430**
Lilongwe [Malawi] **L: 303**
Lily [plant] **L: 303** *with picture*
See also the list of Related articles in the Lily *article*
Cell *picture on* **C: 331**
Easter (Easter lilies) **E: 44**
Easter lily **E: 45**
Flower *pictures on* **F: 272**, **F: 291**; (Garden perennials grown from bulbs) **F: 280** *with picture*; (table) **F: 301** *with picture*
Lily, Water [plant] *See* Water lily *in this index*

Lily of the valley [plant] **L: 304** *with picture*
  Flower *picture on* **F: 278**
Lily tree
  Tree (Palm, pandanus, and lily trees) **T: 415**
Lim Fiord
  Denmark (Land regions) **D: 137-138**
Lima [Peru] **L: 304** *with picture*
  City *picture on* **Ci: 574**
  Peru **P: 306** *with picture*; (Housing) **P: 309** *with pictures*
Lima, Almeida [Portuguese physician]
  Lobotomy **L: 405**
Lima bean L: 305
  Bean (Kinds of beans) **B: 181** *with picture*
Limb [zoology]
  Animal (Adaptations for moving about) **A: 488**
  Arm **A: 717** *with diagram*
  Leg **L: 181** *with diagram*
  Mammal (Skeleton) **M: 118-119**
  Tetrapod **T: 182b**
  Vertebrate **V: 340**
Limb-girdle muscular dystrophy [disease]
  Muscular dystrophy (Facioscapulohumeral and limb-girdle muscular dystrophies) **M: 937**
Limb lengthening [surgery]
  Dwarfism (Causes) **D: 395**
Limber pine
  Pine (Western pines) **P: 469**
Limbo [dance]
  Trinidad and Tobago (People) **T: 446**
Limbo [religion] **L: 306**
Limbourg, Herman de [Dutch painter] *See Limbourg brothers in this index*
Limbourg, Jean de [Dutch painter] *See Limbourg brothers in this index*
Limbourg, Pol de [Dutch painter] *See Limbourg brothers in this index*
Limbourg brothers [Dutch painters] **L: 306**
  Europe *picture on* **E: 409**
  Jesus Christ *picture on* **J: 109**
  Middle Ages *picture on* **M: 522**
  Painting (Gothic painting) **P: 50-51**
  World, History of the *picture on* **W: 432**
Limburger
  Cheese (Semisoft cheese) **C: 392** *with picture*
Limbus infantium [religion]
  Limbo **L: 306**
Limbus patrum [religion]
  Limbo **L: 306**
Lime [chemical] **L: 306**
  Acid rain **A: 27**
  Calcite **C: 20**
  Water (Purifying and treating water) **W: 126**
Lime [fruit] **L: 306** *with pictures*
  Tree *picture on* **T: 426**
Lime chloride [chemical]
  Antiseptic (History) **A: 559**
Lime saltpeter [chemical]
  Saltpeter **S: 76a**
Lime soap deposit [chemical]
  Detergent and soap **D: 164**
Lime-soda process
  Water softening **W: 140**
Lime tree *See Linden in this index*
Limelight [film]
  Chaplin, Charlie **C: 376**
Limerick [Ireland] **L: 307**
Limerick [poetry] **L: 307**
  Poetry (table) **P: 594**
Limerick, Treaty of [1691]
  Boyne, Battle of the **B: 540**
Limes [fortification]
  Germany (Ancient times) **G: 162**
Limestone [rock] **L: 307** *with pictures*
  Building stone **B: 685** *with picture*
  Cave (How caves are formed) **C: 319**
  Chalk **C: 370**
  Coral (Stony corals) **Ci: 1048a**
  Coral reef **Ci: 1048b**
  Earth *picture on* **E: 21**
  Iron and steel (The blast furnace process) **I: 440** *with diagram*
  Lake (How lakes are formed) **L: 32**
  Marble (Properties) **M: 192**
  Protozoan (Importance) **P: 837**
  Rock (Organic sediments) **R: 372**; (table) **R: 373** *with picture*
  Sinkhole **S: 473**
  Slovenia (Land and climate) **S: 511**
  Travertine **T: 405**
Limewater
  Lime **L: 307**
Liminal period [sociology]
  Rite of passage **R: 350**
Limit [investment]
  Auction **A: 881**
Limit [mathematics]

Calculus (Limits) **C: 23**; (Finding areas) **C: 24**; (The definite integral) **C: 24-25**
  Series (Working with infinite series) **S: 317**
Limitation of armaments *See Arms control in this index*
Limitations, Statute of
  Debt (Time limits on collection of debts) **D: 66**
  Statute of limitations **So: 879**
Limited animation
  Animation (Animation in the mid-1900's) **A: 514b**
Limited company [economics] **L: 308**
Limited English proficient student [education]
  Hispanic Americans (Education) **H: 256-257**
Limited jurisdiction [law]
  Court (Types of courts) **Ci: 1101**; (State courts) **Ci: 1102**
Limited liability [law]
  Business (Corporations) **B: 726**
  Corporation (Business corporations) **Ci: 1069**
Limited monarchy
  Government (Monarchy) **G: 286**
  Monarchy **M: 700**
Limited partnership
  Partnership (Rights and responsibilities of partners) **P: 188**
Limited payment policy
  Insurance (Cash value life insurance) **I: 310**
Limited Test Ban Treaty [1963]
  Arms control (Arms control in the mid-1900's) **A: 721-722**
  Nuclear weapon (Arms control) **N: 600**
  Pauling, Linus Carl **P: 202**
Limited veto
  Veto **V: 346**
Limited warfare
  Air force (Air forces in limited wars) **A: 186**
  Cold War (The Korean War) **Ci: 764-765**
  International relations (Conducting international relations) **I: 344**
Limner [artist]
  Folk art (Painting) **F: 316** *with picture*
Limnology [ecology] **L: 308**
  Biology (table) **B: 317**
Limoges [France]
  Porcelain (French porcelain) **P: 677**
Limón, José [American choreographer] **L: 308**
Limón Bay
  Panama Canal (Entering the canal) **P: 122** *with map*
Limonite [mineral] **L: 308**
  Iron and steel (Kinds of iron ore) **I: 438**
Limousin [cattle]
  Cattle (Limousin) **C: 309** *with picture*; (table) **C: 312**
Limp [airship]
  Blimp **B: 400**
Limpet L: 308 *with picture*
  Animal *picture on* **A: 486**
  Mollusk (Gastropods) **M: 695**
  Shell *picture on* **S: 386**; (Gastropods) **S: 385**
Limpopo [province, South Africa]
  South Africa (Provincial government) **So: 609**
Limpopo National Park [Mozambique]
  Great Limpopo Transfrontier Park **G: 346**
Limpopo River [Africa] **L: 308**
  South Africa (Rivers) **So: 615** *with map*
Lin, Maya Ling [American architect]
  Vietnam Veterans Memorial **V: 372**
Lin Biao [Chinese political leader] **L: 309** *with portrait*
Lin Piao [Chinese political leader] *See Lin Biao in this index*
Lin Yutang [Chinese author] **L: 309**
Linberry [fruit]
  Lingonberry **L: 335** *with picture*
Lincoln [England] **L: 309**
Lincoln [Nebraska] **L: 309** *with picture*
Lincoln [automobile]
  Automobile *picture on* **A: 967**
Lincoln, Abraham [grandfather of]
  Lincoln, Abraham (Family background) **L: 311**
Lincoln, Abraham [U.S. president] **L: 310** *with pictures and maps*
  African Americans (The end of slavery) **A: 136i**
  Autograph *picture on* **A: 943**
  Booth, John Wilkes **B: 480**
  Buchanan, James (Prelude to war) **B: 661**
  Civil War, American *picture on* **Ci: 618**; (Developments in the political party system) **Ci: 616**; (Blacks and the war) **Ci: 621**; (In the North) **Ci: 622**; (Cavalry maneuvers) **Ci: 631**; (The South surrenders) **Ci: 633**
  Congress of the United States (Growth and conflict) **Ci: 948**
  Davis, David **D: 47**
  Douglas, Stephen Arnold **D: 312**
  Emancipation Proclamation **E: 253** *with pictures*

  Executive order **E: 436**
  Frémont, John Charles **F: 511**
  Gettysburg Address **G: 176**
  Ghost **G: 182**
  Hamlin, Hannibal **H: 33**
  Hampton Roads Conference **H: 37**
  Howells, William Dean **H: 401**
  Illinois (Places to visit) **I: 62** *with picture*
  Johnson, Andrew (Vice-President) **J: 139** *with picture*
  Lincoln, Mary Todd **L: 327**
  Lincoln, Robert Todd **L: 327**
  Lincoln Memorial *picture on* **L: 328**
  Lincoln's Birthday **L: 329**
  McClellan, George Brinton **M: 332c**
  Mount Rushmore National Memorial *picture on* **M: 887**
  National cemetery **N: 31**
  President of the United States *picture on* **P: 764**
  Presidents' Day **P: 772**
  Reconstruction (Lincoln's plan) **R: 177**
  Republican Party *picture on* **R: 256**
  Rutledge, Ann **R: 569**
  Seymour, Horatio **S: 341**
  Springfield [Illinois] **So: 807**
  Stanton, Edwin McMasters **So: 839**
  United States, History of the (The election of 1860) **U: 176-177**; (Abolition of slavery) **U: 178**
  Whitman, Walt (His work) **W: 294**
Lincoln, Benjamin [American general]
  Revolution, American (Savannah and Charleston) **R: 284**
Lincoln, Edward Baker [son of]
  Lincoln, Abraham (Lincoln's family) **L: 315**
Lincoln, Enoch [American political leader]
  Maine (table) **M: 87**
Lincoln, Levi [American political leader]
  Jefferson, Thomas (table) **J: 83**
  Justice, Department of (table) **J: 203**
  Massachusetts (table) **M: 288**
Lincoln, Mary Todd [wife of Abraham Lincoln] **L: 327**
  Civil War, American (How the states lined up) **Ci: 617-618**
  Lincoln, Abraham *picture on* **L: 316**; (Lincoln's family) **L: 315**; (Life in the White House) **L: 322** *with picture*
Lincoln, Mordecai [American pioneer]
  Lincoln, Abraham (Family background) **L: 311-312**
Lincoln, Nancy Hanks [mother of]
  Lincoln, Abraham (Family background) **L: 311-312**
Lincoln, Robert Todd [American government official] **L: 327** *with portrait*
  Garfield, James Abram (table) **G: 42**
  Lincoln, Abraham (Lincoln's family) **L: 315**; (Life in the White House) **L: 322** *with picture*
Lincoln, Samuel [American pioneer]
  Lincoln, Abraham (Family background) **L: 311-312**
Lincoln, Tad [son of Abraham Lincoln] *See Lincoln, Thomas in this index*
"Lincoln, the Man of the People" [poem by Markham]
  Markham, Edwin **M: 214**
Lincoln, Thomas [father of]
  Lincoln, Abraham (Family background) **L: 311**
Lincoln, Thomas [son of]
  Lincoln, Abraham (Lincoln's family) **L: 315**; (Life in the White House) **L: 322** *with picture*
Lincoln, William Wallace [son of]
  Lincoln, Abraham (Lincoln's family) **L: 315**; (Life in the White House) **L: 322** *with picture*
Lincoln: A Photobiography [book by Freedman]
  Freeman, Russell **F: 500**
Lincoln Bedroom [White House]
  White House (Rebuilding and redecorating) **W: 290**
Lincoln Boyhood National Memorial [Indiana]
  Indiana (Places to visit) **I: 206**
  National Park System (table: National memorials) **N: 54**
Lincoln Center for the Performing Arts [New York City] **L: 327**
  New York City (The arts) **N: 336** *with picture*
  Rockefeller, John Davison, III **R: 383**
Lincoln Center Jazz Orchestra
  Jazz *picture on* **J: 68**
Lincoln County War [1878]
  New Mexico (Territorial days) **N: 275**
Lincoln-Douglas debates [U.S. history]
  Debate (Forms of competitive debate) **D: 64**
  Douglas, Stephen Arnold **D: 312**
  Lincoln, Abraham (The debates with Douglas) **L: 317-318** *with pictures*
Lincoln Highway [road] **L: 327**

Lincoln Home National Historic Site [Illinois]
National Park System (table: National historic sites) **N:** 52-53
Springfield **So:** 807
Lincoln Memorial [Washington, D.C.] **L:** 328 *with pictures*
National Park System (table: National memorials) **N:** 54
Washington, D.C. *map on* **W:** 76; (Lincoln Memorial) **W:** 73
Lincoln Park [Michigan] **L:** 329
Lincoln Park [park, Illinois]
Chicago (The North Side) **C:** 423-424
Lincoln Park Zoo
Chicago *picture on* **C:** 430
Lincoln sheep
Sheep (Long-wooled sheep) **S:** 382
Lincoln Tunnel [New York-New Jersey] **L:** 329
Hudson River tunnels (The Lincoln Tunnel) **H:** 407
Lincoln University [Pennsylvania] **L:** 329 *with picture*
Lincoln's Birthday L: 329
Lincoln's Inn [London]
Inns of Court **I:** 275
Lincoln's New Salem State Historic Site
Illinois (Places to visit) **I:** 62 *with picture*
Lincoln's Tomb [Springfield, Illinois]
Lincoln, Abraham *picture on* **L:** 326
Lind, James [Scottish doctor]
Vitamin (History) **V:** 432
Lind, Jenny [Swedish singer] **L:** 329 *with picture*
Andersen, Hans Christian **A:** 451
Lind, John [American political leader]
Minnesota (table) **M:** 602
Linda [painting by Close]
Close, Chuck *picture on* **Ci:** 685
Lindane [insecticide]
Insecticide (Chlorinated hydrocarbon insecticides) **I:** 302
Lindbergh, Anne Morrow [American poet] **L:** 329
Lindbergh, Charles Augustus (Good-will ambassador) **L:** 330
Lindbergh, Charles Augustus [American aviator] **L:** 330 *with picture*
Airplane (Fliers of the golden age) **A:** 237
Kidnapping **K:** 311
Lindbergh, Anne Morrow **L:** 329
United States, History of the (The Roaring Twenties) **U:** 189; (Heroes) **U:** 190 *with picture*
Lindbergh, Charles Augustus, Jr. [son of]
Lindbergh, Charles Augustus (The Lindbergh kidnapping) **L:** 330
Lindbergh, Charles Augustus, Sr. [father of]
Lindbergh, Charles Augustus (Early life) **L:** 330
Lindbergh law [U.S. history]
Kidnapping **K:** 311
Lindbergh, Charles Augustus (The Lindbergh kidnapping) **L:** 330
Linde, Carl von [German chemist]
Liquid air (Making liquid air) **L:** 347
Refrigeration (Mechanical refrigeration) **R:** 201
Linde process
Liquid air (Making liquid air) **L:** 347
Linden [tree] **L:** 331 *with picture*
Tree *pictures on* **T:** 422
Linden looper moth
Moth *picture on* **M:** 841
Lindenmann, Jean [Swiss microbiologist]
Interferon **I:** 324
Lindenwald [estate]
Van Buren, Martin (Later years) **V:** 273
Linderhof Palace
Ludwig II **L:** 515
Lindgren, Astrid [Swedish author] **L:** 332
Lindley, Alfred D. [American mountain climber]
Mount McKinley **M:** 886
Lindner, Richard [American artist] **L:** 332 *with picture*
Painting (Mass) **P:** 35
Lindneux, Robert [American painter]
Indian, American *picture on* **I:** 178b
Lindsay, Howard [American dramatist] **L:** 333
Lindsay, John Vliet [American political leader] **L:** 333
Lindsay, Robert Burns [American political leader]
Alabama (table) **A:** 274
Lindsay, Vachel [American poet] **L:** 333
American literature (Realist poetry) **A:** 421
Lindsay plaid
Tartan *picture on* **T:** 47
Lindsey, Washington E. [American political leader]
New Mexico (table) **N:** 272
Lindstrom, Fred [American baseball player]
Baseball (table: Hall of Fame) **B:** 134a
Line [art]
Painting (The elements of painting) **P:** 34-35
Photography (Line) **P:** 409 *with pictures*

Line [fiber]
Linen (Preparing the fibers) **L:** 334-335
Line [fishing]
Fishing (Lines) **F:** 177
Line [mathematics]
Geometry (Terms) **G:** 102; (Properties of geometric figures) **G:** 102 *with diagram*; (Non-Euclidean geometry) **G:** 105
Line [measurement]
Weights and measures (table: Miscellaneous weights and measures) **W:** 184
Line [military]
Army (The rise of modern armies) **A:** 727
Line [palmistry]
Palmistry **P:** 111 *with diagram*
Line art
Printing (Preparing illustrations for reproduction) **P:** 797
Line camp
Cowboy (On the ranch) **Ci:** 1110
Line copy
Printing (Flat color printing) **P:** 802
Line graph
Graph (Line graphs) **G:** 321 *with picture*
Line-haul railroad
Railroad (Railroad systems) **R:** 113
Line Islands [Pacific] **L:** 333
Kiribati **K:** 335
Line-item veto [law]
Congress of the U.S. (Continued struggle for power) **Ci:** 948
Constitution of the United States (Article I, Section 7) **Ci:** 1006
Veto (Line-item veto) **V:** 346; (Presidents' use of the veto) **V:** 346
Line judge
Football (The officials) **F:** 362
Line level [tool]
Level **L:** 217 *with picture*
Line monitor [electronic device]
Television (The control room) **T:** 112-113
Line of Demarcation [Latin American history]
L: 333 *with map*
Brazil *map on* **B:** 584
Columbus, Christopher (Return to Spain) **Ci:** 861
Latin America (European discovery and exploration) **I:** 103
Spain (The Spanish Empire) **So:** 747
Line of longitude
Longitude **L:** 451
Line of position
Navigation (Piloting) **N:** 70-71
Line-of-sight [physics]
Radio (table) **R:** 84; (Transmitting FM band signals) **R:** 87 *with diagram*
Line officer [rank]
Navy, United States (Training an officer) **N:** 83
Line-out [sports]
Baseball (Outs by batters) **B:** 128-129
Rugby football *picture on* **R:** 512; (Rugby Union) **R:** 510-511
Line reproduction [printing]
Printing (Preparing illustrations for reproduction) **P:** 797
Line rider
Cowboy (On the ranch) **Ci:** 1110
Line segment [mathematics]
Geometry (Terms) **G:** 102 *with diagram*; (Bisecting a line segment) **G:** 103 *with diagrams*
Line-up dog
Police dog **P:** 626
Lineage [ancestry]
See also Genealogy *in this index*
Africa (Marriage and the family) **A:** 113
Family (Non-Western families) **F:** 24
Linear accelerator [machine]
Cancer (Radiation therapy) **C:** 172
Particle accelerator (How accelerators work) **P:** 184 *with diagram*
Linear alkylbenzene sulfonate [chemical]
Detergent and soap (The development of detergents) **D:** 165-166
Linear B [writing]
Greece, Ancient (History) **G:** 372
Ventris, Michael George Francis **V:** 309
Linear bearing [machine]
Bearing **B:** 188
Linear electric motor L: 334 *with diagram*
Air cushion vehicle (History) **A:** 181
Linear equation
Algebra (Solving linear equations in two variables) **A:** 357
Linear function
Algebra (Functions) **A:** 356-357
Linear induction motor
Linear electric motor **L:** 334
Magnetic levitation train (Maglev propulsion)

M: 56
Linear low density polyethylene
Polyethylene **P:** 650
Linear measure
Weights and measures (table: Length and distance) **W:** 185
Linear motion [physics]
Machine *diagram on* **M:** 13
Linear perspective [art]
Brunelleschi, Filippo **B:** 652
Leonardo da Vinci (Paintings) **L:** 200b
Painting (The Renaissance) **P:** 51-52
Perspective **P:** 304 *with pictures*
Renaissance (Arts of the 1300's and early 1400's) **R:** 236
Linear plan [aviation]
Airport (Terminal designs) **A:** 248 *with diagram*
Linear rhythm [art]
Sculpture (Indus Valley) **S:** 235-236 *with pictures*
Linear synchronous motor
Linear electric motor **L:** 334 *with diagram*
Magnetic levitation train (Maglev propulsion) **M:** 56
Linebacker
Football (The defensive team) **F:** 357 *with diagrams*
Linecaster [machine]
Linotype **L:** 338
Printing (Hot-metal typesetting) **P:** 797
Linen [fabric] **L:** 334 *with picture*
Colonial life in America (Clothing) **Ci:** 799
Flax **F:** 230
Textile (Natural fibers) **T:** 212
Liner [ship] *See* Ocean liner *in this index*
Linesman
Hockey (The officials) **H:** 278
Soccer (The officials) **So:** 545 *with diagram*
Lineup
Baseball (The game) **B:** 128
Linezolid [drug]
Antibiotic (History) **A:** 552-553
Ling [plant]
Heath **H:** 156
Lingberry [fruit]
Lingonberry **L:** 335 *with picture*
Lingenberry [fruit]
Lingonberry **L:** 335 *with picture*
Lingle, Linda [American political leader]
Hawaii (table) **H:** 105; (The early 2000's) **H:** 109
Lingonberry [fruit] **L:** 335 *with pictures*
Lingua franca [language]
Papua New Guinea (People) **P:** 140
Linguistic analysis [philosophy]
Philosophy (Philosophy in the 1900's) **P:** 380-391
Linguistic anthropology
Anthropology (Linguistic anthropology) **A:** 547
Linguistic competence
Linguistics (Descriptive linguistics) **L:** 335-336
Linguistic typology
Linguistics (Comparative and historical linguistics) **L:** 336
Linguistics [study] **L:** 335
Anthropology (Linguistic anthropology) **A:** 547
Communication (The study of communication) **Ci:** 887
Language (The science of language) **L:** 66
Mythology (Comparative approaches) **M:** 989
Philosophy (The philosophy of language) **P:** 385
Lingvo Internacia [book by Zamenhof]
Esperanto **E:** 358
Liniment [medication] **L:** 337
Lining
Sewing (Linings) **S:** 333
Lining paper
Paperwork (Lining papers) **P:** 138
Link [computing] *See* Hyperlink *in this index*
Link, Arthur A. [American political leader]
North Dakota (table) **N:** 513
Link, Edwin Albert [American inventor] **L:** 337
Link cent [money]
Cent *pictures on* **C:** 350
Link trainer [machine]
Link, Edwin Albert **L:** 337
Linkage [international relations]
Cold War (The Cold War after 1980) **Ci:** 770
Linked genes [genetics]
Heredity (Sex-linked genes) **H:** 202
Linkedin [website]
Internet (Social networking websites) **I:** 350b
Linking verb [grammar]
Verb (Linking, or copulative, verbs) **V:** 315
Linn [tree] *See* Linden *in this index*
Linnaea [plant]
Twinflower **T:** 531
Linnaeus, Carolus [Swedish botanist] **L:** 337 *with portrait*
Biology (The origins of scientific classification)

B: 318 *with picture*
Bird-of-paradise **B: 373**
Botany (The development of modern botany)
  B: 509
Classification, Scientific (Development of
  classification) **Ci: 656**
Museum (Museums of the 1700's) **M: 939**
Science *picture on* **S: 200**
Twinflower **T: 531**
Zoology (History) **Z: 606**
Linné, Carl von *See* Linnaeus, Carolus *in this index*
Linnet [bird] **L: 338** *with picture*
Linoleum L: 338
  Cork (Uses) **Ci: 1055**
Linoleum-block printing
  Block printing **B: 405** *with pictures*
Linotype [machine] **L: 338** *with pictures*
  Book (The 1800's) **B: 467**
  Communication *picture on* **Ci: 884**
  Mergenthaler, Ottmar **M: 417**
  Printing (Hot-metal typesetting) **P: 797**
Linseed oil L: 339
  Flax **F: 230**
  Linoleum **L: 338**
  Oil (Fixed oils) **O: 706**
Linsey-woolsey [fabric] **L: 339**
  Colonial life in America (Clothing) **Ci: 799**
  Pioneer life in America (Clothing) **P: 482**
Lint [fiber]
  Cotton (Uses of cotton) **Ci: 1086**
Lintel [construction]
  Building construction (Beams, girders, and
    columns) **B: 682-683**
  House *diagram on* **H: 383**
Linters
  Cotton (Uses of cotton) **Ci: 1086**
Linton, Ralph [American anthropologist] **L: 339**
Linus, Saint [pope]
  Pope (table) **P: 666**
Linux [operating system]
  Thorvalds, Linus **T: 345**
Linyphiid [spider]
  Spider (Linyphiids) **So: 789**
Lion [animal] **L: 340** *with pictures and map*
  Animal *pictures on* **A: 472**, **A: 477**; (Teeth and
    jaws) **A: 491** *with picture*
  Circus *picture on* **Ci: 562a**
  Giraffe (The life of a giraffe) **G: 194-195**
  Mammal *pictures on* **M: 124**, **M: 127**
Lion [astrology] *See* Leo *in this index*
Lion Country Safari [West Palm Beach]
  Florida (Places to visit) **F: 252**
Lion Fighting a Bull [sculpture]
  Sculpture (Middle Eastern) **S: 233** *with picture*
Lion King, The [musical]
  Musical comedy (During the late 1900's) **M: 960-
    961** *with picture*
Lion of Lucerne [sculpture]
  Lucerne **L: 513**
  Swiss Guard **So: 1049**
Lion of the Punjab [name for]
  Ranjit Singh **R: 139**
Lion tamarin [animal]
  Tamarin **T: 22** *with picture*
Lion taming
  Lion (Training lions) **L: 343**
Lioness
  Lion (The body of a lion) **L: 340** *with picture*
Lionfish
  Fish *picture on* **F: 144**
Lionhead [fish]
  Goldfish *picture on* **G: 258**
Lions, British Columbia [team] *See* British
  Columbia Lions *in this index*
Lions, Detroit [team] *See* Detroit Lions *in this index*
Lions Clubs International L: 344 *with picture*
Lions Gate Bridge
  Vancouver (Transportation) **V: 275-276**
Liopleurodon [extinct animal]
  Plesiosaur **P: 573**
Lip [anatomy]
  Cleft palate **Ci: 661**
  Mouth **M: 902** *with diagram*
  Races, Human (Alternatives to racial
    classification) **R: 55** *with pictures*
Lip [zoology]
  Shell *diagram on* **S: 385**
Lip reading L: 344
  Audiology **A: 882**
  Deafness (Special language techniques) **D: 58**
Lip-synching [cinematography]
  Animation (Making the model move) **A: 513**
Lipase [enzyme]
  Digestive system (In the small intestine) **D: 202**
  Enzyme **E: 340** *with diagram*
Lipchitz, Jacques [American sculptor] **L: 344** *with
  picture*

Sculpture (Cubism and futurism) **S: 257**
Liphistiid [spider]
  Spider **So: 782**
Lipid [nutrition] **L: 344**
  Cell (Inside a living cell) **C: 328**
  Cholesterol **C: 520**
  Ester **E: 360**
  Fat substitute **F: 53**
  Human body (Chemical elements and molecules)
    H: 417; (Cells and tissues) **H: 417-418**
  Life *diagram on* **L: 277**; (Lipids) **L: 278**;
    (Developing complexity) **L: 279**
  Lynen, Feodor **L: 536**
  Oil **O: 706**
Lipizzaner [horse]
  Horse (Saddle horses) **H: 343-345** *with picture*
  Slovenia **S: 510**
Lipmann, Fritz Albert [American biochemist]
  L: 345
Lipoma [disorder]
  Skin (Tumors) **S: 491**
  Tumor **T: 484**
Lipoprotein [biochemistry]
  Cholesterol **C: 520**
  Physical fitness (Cholesterol levels) **P: 434**
Liposuction [surgery]
  Plastic surgery (Cosmetic surgery) **P: 553**
Lippershey, Hans [Dutch optician]
  Telescope **T: 102**
Lippi, Filippino [Italian painter] **L: 345**
Lippi, Filippo [Italian painter] **L: 345** *with picture*
Lippitt, Charles W. [American political leader]
  Rhode Island (table) **R: 311**
Lippitt, Henry [American political leader]
  Rhode Island (table) **R: 311**
Lippizaner [horse] *See* Lipizzaner *in this index*
Lippmann, Gabriel [French physicist]
  Nobel Prizes (Physics: 1908) **N: 440**
Lippmann, Walter [American journalist] **L: 345**
Lippold, Richard [American sculptor] **L: 346**
Lipscomb, William Nunn, Jr. [American chemist]
  Nobel Prizes (Chemistry: 1976) **N: 444**
Lipstick
  Cosmetics (Kinds of cosmetics) **Ci: 1074**
Liptinite [geology]
  Coal (Analyzing coal composition) **Ci: 717-718**
Lipton, Sir Thomas Johnstone [British
  businessman] **L: 346**
Liquefaction [geology]
  Earthquake (Collapsing buildings) **E: 33**
Liquefaction [industrial process]
  Coal (Coal research) **Ci: 730-731**
  Gas [fuel] (Storing gas) **G: 55**
Liquefied gas extinguisher
  Fire extinguisher (Liquefied gas extinguishers)
    F: 130
Liquefied natural gas
  Petroleum (Transporting petroleum) **P: 342**
Liquefied natural gas carrier [ship]
  Tanker (Kinds of tankers) **T: 28**
Liquefied petroleum gas
  Butane and propane **B: 728**
  Fuel (Natural gas) **F: 551**
  Gas [fuel] (In the home) **G: 51**
  Heating (Gas) **H: 159**
  Petroleum (Petroleum as a fuel) **P: 332**
Liqueur [beverage]
  Alcoholic beverage (Other distilled drinks) **A: 337**
Liquid L: 346
  Boiling point **B: 439**
  Cohesion **Ci: 756**
  Condensation **Ci: 929**
  Gas [physics] **G: 47**
  Hydraulics **H: 463**
  Liquid crystal **L: 347**
  Matter (States of matter) **M: 311**
  Melting point **M: 389**
  Molecule (Molecules and matter) **M: 693**
  Solution (Liquid solutions) **So: 587**
  Superfluid **So: 993**
Liquid air L: 346 *with diagram*
  Nitrogen (Uses of nitrogen) **N: 425**
Liquid asset
  Bank (Bank services) **B: 88**
Liquid asset fund *See* Money market fund *in this
  index*
Liquid column chromatography
  Chromatography (Liquid column
    chromatography) **C: 537**
Liquid-cooled engine
  Gasoline engine (Cooling) **G: 63-64**
Liquid crystal [physics] **L: 347** *with pictures*
  Television (Flat-panel displays) **T: 126** *with picture*
Liquid crystal display [electronics]
  Liquid crystal **L: 347**
  Audio-visual materials (Projection devices)
    A: 882-883

Camera (Positioning the camera) **C: 80**
Clock (Electric clocks) **Ci: 682k**
Computer (Monitors) **Ci: 916**
Electronics (Liquid crystal displays) **E: 213**;
  (Electronics today) **E: 216-217**
Nintendo **N: 424**
Photography (Compact cameras) **P: 408**
Polarized light (Uses of polarized light) **P: 618**
Projector (Digital projectors) **P: 817**
Telephone (The display) **T: 95**
Television (Flat-panel displays) **T: 126** *with picture*
Thermometer (Liquid crystal thermometers)
  T: 255 *with picture*
Watch (Quartz watches) **W: 114**
Liquid-crystal polymer [plastic]
  Plastics (Recent developments) **P: 560**
Liquid fertilizer
  Fertilizer (Production and sale) **F: 80**
Liquid fuel
  Fuel (Liquid fuels) **F: 550**
Liquid gas
  Gas [physics] (How gases behave) **G: 48**; (History)
    G: 49
Liquid helium
  Helium (Properties) **H: 176**
Liquid hydrogen
  Cryogenics **Ci: 1165**
  Rocket (Nuclear rockets) **R: 389** *with diagram*
Liquid immersion freezing
  Food, Frozen (Commercial methods of quick-
    freezing) **F: 338**
Liquid measure
  Weights and measures (table: Volume and
    capacity) **W: 186**
Liquid metallic hydrogen
  Jupiter (Interior) **J: 200** *with diagram*
Liquid mirror
  Telescope (Reflecting telescopes) **T: 104-105**
Liquid natural gas
  Gas [fuel] (Storing gas) **G: 55**
Liquid nitrogen
  Nitrogen (Uses of nitrogen) **N: 425**
Liquid oxygen
  Liquid air **L: 346**
  Oxygen (Chemical properties) **O: 889**; (Other
    uses of oxygen) **O: 889**
  Rocket (Parts of a rocket) **R: 385**
Liquid propellant [fuel]
  Guided missile (The engine) **G: 424** *with diagram*
  Rocket (Liquid-propellant rockets) **R: 388** *with
    diagram*
  Space exploration (Getting into space and back)
    So: 698
Liquid-propellant rocket
  Rocket (Liquid-propellant rockets) **R: 388** *with
    diagram*
Liquid thermometer
  Thermometer (Thermal expansion
    thermometers) **T: 254** *with diagram*
Liquid waste
  Energy supply (Solid and liquid wastes) **E: 279**
  Waste disposal **W: 112**
Liquidation [economics]
  Bankruptcy (Features of bankruptcy) **B: 97**
  Stock (Kinds of stock) **So: 903**
Liquidity [economics]
  Investment (Direct investments) **I: 367**
Liquor *See* Alcoholic beverage *in this index*
Liquor laws
  Prohibition **P: 814**
Lira [money] **L: 348**
Lisa [computer]
  Apple Inc. **A: 573**
Lisa, Manuel [Spanish-American trader]
  Nebraska (American exploration and settlement)
    N: 111
Lisboa [Portugal] *See* Lisbon *in this index*
Lisboa, Antônio Francisco [Brazilian sculptor]
  Brazil (The arts) **B: 576** *with picture*
Lisbon [Portugal] **L: 348** *with picture*
  Portugal *picture on* **P: 689**; (Population and
    ancestry) **P: 687**
Lisbon, Treaty of [2009]
  European Union (Recent developments) **E: 420**
Lisbon Disaster, The [poem by Voltaire]
  Voltaire (Later years) **V: 447**
Lisbon Traviata, The [play by McNally]
  McNally, Terrence **M: 344**
Lisbon University
  Portugal (Education) **P: 689**
Lisgar, Baron [British administrator] **L: 349**
Lismer, Arthur [Canadian painter]
  Group of Seven **G: 402**
Lisping [speech] **L: 349**
Lissouba, Pascal [Congolese political leader]
  Congo, Republic of the (History) **Ci: 940e-940f**
List, Robert [American political leader]

Nevada (table) **N:** 173
List system [political science]
 Proportional representation (The List System)
 P: 828
Listed bond [economics]
 Stock exchange (How a stock exchange operates)
 So: 904
Listed stock [economics]
 Stock exchange (How a stock exchange operates)
 So: 904
Listening Woman [book by Hillerman]
 Hillerman, Tony **H:** 232
Lister, Ernest [American political leader]
 Washington (table) **W:** 65
Lister, Sir Joseph [British doctor] **L:** 349
 Antiseptic (History) **A:** 559
 Ligature **L:** 281
 Medicine (Antiseptic surgery) **M:** 375
 Sterilization **So:** 893
Listeria [bacteria] **L:** 349
Listeriosis [disease]
 Listeria **L:** 349
Liston, Sonny [American boxer]
 Boxing *picture on* **B:** 533; (The Ali era) **B:** 532a
Listserv [electronics]
 Internet (Communication) **I:** 350b
Liszt, Franz [Hungarian composer] **L:** 349
Litani River
 Lebanon (Land and climate) **L:** 172
Litchfield Law School
 Connecticut *picture on* **Ci:** 969; (Schools) **Ci:** 956
Litchi [tree] **L:** 350 *with picture*
Litchi nut
 Litchi **L:** 350
Liter [measurement] **L:** 350
 Metric system (The metric system at a glance)
 M: 438 *with picture*; (Non-SI metric units)
 M: 440
 Weights and measures (table: Volume and
 capacity) **W:** 186
Literacy [education] **L:** 350
 See also Illiteracy *in this index and the Education*
 sections of specific country articles, such as
 Argentina (Education)
 Africa (Education) **A:** 109, **A:** 114-115
 Education (Literacy programs) **E:** 106
 Latin America (Education) **L:** 99
 Reading (The importance of reading) **R:** 155-
 156; (Developing good readers) **R:** 159-160;
 (Reading and society) **R:** 162
Literacy test
 Voting Rights Act of 1965 **V:** 451
Literacy U.S., Project
 Literacy (Illiteracy in the United States) **L:** 351-
 352
Literacy Volunteers of America
 Literacy (Illiteracy in the United States) **L:** 351-
 352
Literary agent
 Writing (Free-lance markets) **W:** 511
Literary award
 Caldecott Medal **C:** 26
 Literature for children (Awards) **L:** 367
 Newbery Medal **N:** 358
 Pulitzer Prizes (Prizes in literature, drama, and
 music) **P:** 886b
 Regina Medal **R:** 206
Literary biography
 Biography (Forms of biography) **B:** 312
Literary character
 Literature (Characters) **L:** 353
Literary Chinese [language]
 Chinese language (Development) **C:** 510
Literary Club [British history]
 Johnson, Samuel **J:** 153
Literary criticism
 Criticism **Ci:** 1146
 Literature (Judging literature) **L:** 352-353
Literary Digest [magazine]
 Public opinion poll (History) **P:** 863
Literary Revolution [Chinese history]
 Chinese language (Development) **C:** 510
Literary tale
 Storytelling (Literary tales) **So:** 914
Literature L: 352 *with pictures*
 See also the list of Related articles in the Literature
 article and the Arts or Literature sections of
 specific country articles, such as Denmark (Arts)
 Bible (Literary contexts) **B:** 287
 Copyright (Works protected) **Ci:** 1046
 Criticism **Ci:** 1146
 Impressionism (Music, literature, and sculpture)
 I: 94
 Minimalism **M:** 573
 Modernism **M:** 685
 Mythology (Literary approaches) **M:** 990
 Rome, Ancient (Literature) **R:** 443

Literature for children L: 354 *with pictures*
 See also the list of Related articles in the Literature
 for children *article*
 Caldecott Medal **C:** 26
 Newbery Medal **N:** 358
 Regina Medal **R:** 206
 Writing (Literature for children) **W:** 512
Litharge [chemical] **L:** 386
Lithification [geology]
 Rock (Clastic sediments) **R:** 372
Lithium [element] **L:** 386
 Brown dwarf **B:** 644
 Nuclear weapon (Thermonuclear weapons)
 N: 597
Lithium 6 deuteride [compound]
 Nuclear weapon (Thermonuclear weapons)
 N: 597
Lithium battery [electricity]
 Battery (Types and uses of batteries) **B:** 171
Lithium carbonate [chemical]
 Mental illness (Somatic therapy) **M:** 407
Lithium-ion battery [electricity]
 Battery (Secondary batteries) **B:** 170; (Types and
 uses of batteries) **B:** 171; (History) **B:** 171
Lithography [printing] **L:** 387 *with pictures*
 Graphic arts **G:** 322
 Magazine (Editing and assembling an issue)
 M: 43-44
 Offset **O:** 677 *with diagram*
 Printing (Offset lithography) **P:** 798 *with picture;*
 (Printing in color) **P:** 801
 Printing press **P:** 804
 Senefelder, Alois **S:** 297
 United States, History of the (Cultural changes)
 U: 173
Lithopone [chemical]
 Barium **B:** 110
Lithosphere [geology]
 Earth (Earth's spheres) **E:** 18-20 *with picture*
 Earthquake (How an earthquake begins) **E:** 35
 Geophysics **G:** 106a
 Mantle **M:** 168
 Plate tectonics (Structure of tectonic plates)
 P: 561
Lithotripter [medical device]
 Gallbladder **G:** 15
 Kidney stone **K:** 313
 Ultrasound (Medical uses) **U:** 16
Lithuania L: 388 *with pictures and map*
 Belarus (History) **B:** 224b-224c
 Flag *picture on* **F:** 206
 Ukraine (Lithuanian and Polish rule) **U:** 12
 Union of Soviet Socialist Republics (World War II)
 U: 37; (Threats to unity) **U:** 40-41
 Vilnius **V:** 385
 World War II (The invasion of the Soviet Union)
 W: 477
Litmus [chemistry] **L:** 391
 Lichen (The importance of lichens) **L:** 269
Litoral, National University of the
 Santa Fe **S:** 114
Litre [measurement] *See* Liter *in this index*
Litter [garbage]
 Oregon (Interesting facts) **O:** 827
Litter [reproduction]
 Dog (The life of a dog) **D:** 266
Litter [soil]
 Forestry (Water) **F:** 406
Litter box
 Cat (Training) **C:** 294 *with picture*
 Pet (House training) **P:** 320-321
Little, John Sebastian [American political leader]
 Arkansas (table) **A:** 712
Little, Malcolm [birth name of]
 Malcolm X **M:** 103
Little Abaco Island
 Bahamas (Land and climate) **B:** 29 *with map*
Little America [region, Antarctica]
 Byrd, Richard Evelyn **B:** 746
 Exploration (The exploration of Antarctica) **E:** 450
Little Bear [constellation]
 Big and Little Dippers (The Little Dipper) **B:** 296
Little Belt Mountains
 Montana (Land regions) **M:** 752
Little Bighorn, Battle of the [1876] **L:** 391
 Crazy Horse **Ci:** 1123
 Custer, George Armstrong **Ci:** 1200
 Gall **G:** 15
 Indian wars (Little Bighorn) **I:** 193
 Little Bighorn Battlefield National Monument
 L: 391
 Montana (Indian fighting) **M:** 758 *with picture*
 Reno, Marcus Albert **R:** 240
 Sitting Bull **S:** 477
Little Bighorn Battlefield National Monument
 [Montana] **L:** 391
 Montana (Places to visit) **M:** 750

National Park System (table: National
 monuments) **N:** 51
Little Bookroom, The [book by Farjeon]
 Farjeon, Eleanor **F:** 28
"**Little Boy Blue**" [poem by Field]
 Field, Eugene **F:** 91
Little Caucasus Mountains [Asia]
 Azerbaijan (Land and climate) **A:** 996 *with map*
 Georgia (Land and climate) **G:** 110 *with map*
Little Cayman Island [Caribbean]
 Cayman Islands **C:** 323
Little chief hare [animal]
 Pika **P:** 461 *with picture*
Little Clay Cart, The [play by Kalidasa]
 Drama (India) **D:** 336
Little Corporal [nickname]
 Napoleon I **N:** 13
Little Diomede Island
 Alaska (Coastline) **A:** 294
Little Dipper [constellation]
 Big and Little Dippers (The Little Dipper) **B:** 296
Little Dorrit [book by Dickens]
 Dickens, Charles (Dickens's life) **D:** 187-188; (The
 second phase) **D:** 188-189
Little Egypt [former country]
 Roma (History) **R:** 402b
Little Eva [literary figure]
 Uncle Tom's Cabin **U:** 20
Little Eyolf [play by Ibsen]
 Ibsen, Henrik (His plays) **I:** 4
Little Foxes, The [play by Hellman]
 Blitzstein, Marc **B:** 403
 Hellman, Lillian **H:** 178
Little Friend, Little Friend [book by Jarrell]
 Jarrell, Randall **J:** 63
Little Giant [nickname]
 Douglas, Stephen Arnold **D:** 312
"**Little Gidding**" [poem by Eliot]
 Eliot, T. S. (His works) **E:** 237-238
Little Havana [Miami]
 Hispanic Americans (Cuban immigration)
 H: 254-255
"**Little House**" books [books by Wilder]
 Wilder, Laura Ingalls **W:** 302
Little Hunting Creek Plantation
 Mount Vernon (The buildings) **M:** 888
Little Ice Age [climatology]
 Climate (Activity on the sun's surface) **Ci:** 676d-
 677
Little Image series [paintings by Krasner]
 Krasner, Lee **K:** 386
Little Island, The [book by MacDonald]
 Weisgard, Leonard **W:** 188
Little Italy [district]
 New York City (Manhattan) **N:** 323-324
Little John [legendary figure]
 Robin Hood **R:** 367
Little League Baseball L: 391
 Baseball (Amateur leagues) **B:** 131
Little League World Series
 Little League Baseball **L:** 391
Little Learning, A [book by Waugh]
 Waugh, Evelyn **W:** 149
Little Lord Fauntleroy [book by Burnett]
 Burnett, Frances Hodgson **B:** 708
Little Manitou Lake [Sasketchewan]
 Saskatchewan (Interesting facts) **S:** 129
Little Mary [marionette]
 Puppet (Marionettes) **P:** 906
Little Master [book by Natsume Soseki]
 Natsume Soseki **N:** 64
Little Mermaid, The [sculpture]
 Copenhagen (The city) **Ci:** 1038
Little metalmark [butterfly]
 Butterfly *picture on* **B:** 735
Little Minister, The [book by Barrie]
 Barrie, J. M. **B:** 118
Little Nell [literary figure]
 Dickens, Charles (The first phase) **D:** 188
Little Nemo [film]
 Animation (Pioneers of American animation)
 A: 514a
"**Little Nemo in Slumberland**" [comic strip]
 Comics (Comic strips) **Ci:** 869
Little penguin
 Penguin (The body of a penguin) **P:** 238
Little People of America [organization]
 Dwarfism (Living with dwarfism) **D:** 395
Little Pretty Pocket-Book, A [book]
 Literature for children (The 1700's) **L:** 362
Little Prince, The [book by Saint-Exupéry]
 Saint-Exupéry, Antoine de **S:** 33
Little red book [Chinese history]
 Cultural Revolution **Ci:** 1185
"**Little Red Corvette**" [song]
 Rock music (Rock videos and MTV) **R:** 380c
"**Little Red Riding Hood**" [story]

Grimm's Fairy Tales G: 394
Little Red Spot [astronomy]
  Jupiter (Ovals) J: 199-200
Little Richard [American singer]
  Rock music (The first generation) R: 377
Little River [Alabama]
  Alabama (Interesting facts) A: 257
Little River Canyon National Preserve [Alabama]
  National Park System (table: National preserves)
  N: 58
Little Rock [Arkansas] L: 392
  Arkansas A: 694, *picture on* A: 695; (Average
    monthly weather) A: 708; (Statehood and the
    Civil War) A: 714
  Eisenhower, Dwight David (Civil rights) E: 153-
    154
  United States, History of the *picture on* U: 195
Little Rock Central High School
  African Americans (The civil rights movement)
    A: 136o *with picture*
  Eisenhower, Dwight David (Civil rights) E: 147-
    148
**Little Rock Central High School National Historic
Site**
  National Park System (table: National historic
    sites) N: 52-53
Little Rocky Mountains
  Montana (Land regions) M: 752
Little Sahara State Park [Oklahoma]
  Oklahoma *picture on* O: 723
Little Saint Bernard Pass [Switzerland]
  Saint Bernard Passes (Little St. Bernard) S: 32
Little skipper [dog] *See* Schipperke *in this index*
Little sparrowhawk [bird]
  Bird of prey *picture on* B: 374b
Little Sure Shot [nickname]
  Oakley, Annie O: 638
Little Traverse Bay [bay, Michigan]
  Lake Michigan (Surface features) L: 41
Little Turtle [American Indian chief] L: 392
  Indian wars (Conflicts in the Midwest) I: 191
  Miami Indians M: 482
  Ohio (Exploration and settlement) O: 700
Little War [1879-1880]
  Cuba (Struggle against Spain) Ci: 1176
Little White Bird, The [book by Barrie]
  Peter Pan P: 325
Little White House [Warm Springs]
  Georgia (Visitor's guide) G: 122 *with picture*
Little Women [book by Alcott]
  Alcott, Louisa May A: 338
  American literature (The sentimental novel)
    A: 415-418
  Literature for children (Masterpieces of fiction)
    L: 363
Littlefield, Alfred H. [American political leader]
  Rhode Island (table) R: 311
Littlepage Manuscripts, The [books by Cooper]
  Cooper, James Fenimore Ci: 1035
Liturgical church
  Christianity (Forms of worship) C: 522h
Liturgical drama
  Drama (Liturgical drama) D: 328
Liturgical year
  Christianity (Forms of worship) C: 522h-523
Liturgy [religion] L: 392
  Christianity (Forms of worship) C: 522h
  Protestantism (Worship) P: 834
  Roman Catholic Church (Worship) R: 403
  Vatican Council II (The Constitution on the
    Liturgy) V: 289
Liu Bang [emperor of China] L: 393
  Han dynasty H: 38
Liu Hui [Chinese mathematician]
  Mathematics (Chinese mathematics) M: 306
Liu Pang [emperor of China] *See* Liu Bang *in this
  index*
Liu Xiaobo [Chinese political leader]
  Nobel Prizes (Peace: 2010) N: 449
Live-bearer [zoology]
  Aquarium, Home (Choosing fish and plants)
    A: 578-578a
  Molly M: 696
  Tropical fish T: 451
Live donation [surgery]
  Organ donation O: 852
Live-forever [botany]
  Houseleek H: 389 *with picture*
  Sedum S: 280
Live oak L: 393 *with picture*
  Oak (Red oaks) O: 635-636; (Other oaks) O: 636
  Tree *pictures on* T: 423
Live sound
  Radio (From sound waves to electric waves) R: 86
Liver [anatomy] L: 393 *with diagram*
  Alcoholism (Effects of alcoholism) A: 338
  Bile B: 300

Blood (Transporting nutrients and wastes)
  B: 408-410 *with diagram*; (Destruction of worn-
    out blood components) B: 411
  Cancer *pictures on* C: 173
  Cell (Death of a cell) C: 332
  Circulatory system (In nutrition) Ci: 560
  Cirrhosis Ci: 566
  Frog *picture on* F: 537
  Gallbladder G: 14 *with diagram*
  Gland (table) G: 209
  Hepatitis H: 192
  Human body (The small intestine and large
    intestine) H: 420; (table) H: 422 *with diagram*
  Organ donation O: 853
  Transplant (Organ transplants) T: 379
Liver [food]
  Iron (How bodies use iron) I: 435
Liver spots *See* Age spots *in this index*
Liverleaf [plant]
  Hepatica H: 192
Liverpool [England] L: 395 *with picture*
  Rock music (The Beatles) R: 379
Liverpool, Earl of [British political leader]
  United Kingdom (table: British prime ministers)
    U: 72
Liverpool and Manchester Railway
  Railroad (Invention of the locomotive) R: 115
Liverwort [plant] L: 395 *with picture*
  Bryophyte B: 656
  Hepatica H: 192
  Plant *picture on* P: 522; (Nonvascular plants)
    P: 518; (Classification of plants) P: 546 *with
    picture*
Lives of Famous Men [book by Petrarch]
  Biography (The Middle Ages) B: 313
Lives of Girls and Women [book by Munro]
  Munro, Alice M: 928
Lives of the Caesars [book by Suetonius]
  Biography (Early biographies) B: 312-313
  Suetonius So: 957
Lives of the English Poets, The [book by Johnson]
  English literature (Samuel Johnson) E: 319
  Johnson, Samuel (Later years) J: 153
*Lives of the Most Eminent Painters, Sculptors, and
Architects* [book by Vasari]
  Biography (The Renaissance) B: 313
Livesay, Dorothy [Canadian poet]
  Canadian literature (Literature between the
    world wars) C: 158
Livestock [agriculture] L: 396 *with pictures*
  Agriculture (Agricultural products) A: 147 *with
    picture*; (Raising livestock) A: 150; (Reforming
    agricultural practices) A: 151; (History) A: 153-
    154
  Brucellosis B: 648
  Factory farming F: 5
  Farm and farming (Basic principles of livestock
    production) F: 39 *with pictures*
  Grain (Uses) G: 301
  Meat packing (Marketing of livestock and meat)
    M: 350
Living benefits provision
  Insurance (Riders) I: 311
Living Bible, The
  Bible (Modern English translations) B: 286
Living Buddha [king of Mongolia]
  Mongolia (History) M: 723
Living Desert, The [film]
  Disney, Walt (Full-length movies) D: 236-237
    with picture
Living Free [book by Adamson]
  Adamson, Joy A: 45
Living History Farms
  Iowa (Places to visit) I: 384 *with picture*
Living history museum
  Museum (History museums) M: 938
Living room
  Interior design *picture on* I: 326
Living Sea, The [book by Cousteau]
  Cousteau, Jacques-Yves Ci: 1106
Living standard *See* Standard of living *in this index*
Living Theater [organization]
  Drama (Experimental theater) D: 340
Living things *See* Life *in this index*
Living trust [economics]
  Trust fund (Kinds of trusts) T: 474
Living will [law] L: 398
  Death (The right to die) D: 61
  Euthanasia (Termination of life-sustaining
    treatment) E: 421
Livingston, Edward [American government
  official]
  Jackson, Andrew (table) J: 11
Livingston, H. Brockholst [American jurist]
  Supreme Court of the United States (table)
    So: 1000
Livingston, Henry [American land surveyor]

Santa Claus (Santa's appearance) S: 114
Livingston, Philip [American patriot] L: 399
Livingston, Robert R. [American political leader]
  L: 399
  Declaration of Independence *picture on* D: 77
  Jefferson, Thomas (The Louisiana Purchase) J: 85
  Louisiana Purchase (Trouble begins) L: 502
  State, Department of (Establishment) So: 860-
    861
  Washington, George (Inauguration Day) W: 101
Livingston, William [American political leader]
  L: 399
  New Jersey (table) N: 249
Livingstone, David [British explorer]
  Stanley and Livingstone So: 837 *with picture
    and map*
  Exploration (The exploration of Africa) E: 448-449
    with picture and map
  Malawi (History) M: 97-98
  Missionary (History) M: 621
  Victoria Falls V: 358
  Zambia (History) Z: 585
Livni, Tzipi [Israeli political leader]
  Israel (The early 2000's) I: 489-490
  Kadima K: 209
Livonia [region]
  Latvia (History) L: 119
Livy [Roman historian] L: 399
  History (The ancient Greeks and Romans)
    H: 261-262
  Latin literature (The Augustan Age) L: 116
Liza [fish]
  Mullet M: 915
Lizard L: 399 *with pictures*
  See also the list of Related articles in the Lizard
    article
  Animal *picture on* A: 492
  Brain *diagram on* B: 559
  Dinosaur (How dinosaurs lived) D: 211
  Iguana I: 50
  Reptile (Lizards, amphisbaenians, and snakes)
    R: 250 *with pictures*
  Skeleton *diagram on* S: 481
  Skink S: 494
Lizardite [mineral]
  Serpentine S: 318
Ljubljana [Slovenia] L: 401
Llama [animal] L: 401 *with picture*
  Alpaca A: 381
Llanero [ranch]
  Venezuela (The Llanos) V: 302 *with picture*
Llanfairpwllgwyngyll [Wales] L: 402
Llano Estacado [region, New Mexico-Texas]
  New Mexico (Land regions) N: 266 *with map*
  Texas (Land regions) T: 196
Llanos [region, Colombia-Venezuela]
  Colombia (The Eastern Plains) Ci: 782 *with picture*
  South America (The Central Plains) So: 628
  Venezuela (The Llanos) V: 302 *with picture*
Lloyd, Chris Evert [American tennis player] *See*
  Evert, Chris *in this index*
Lloyd, Edward [American political leader]
  Maryland (table) M: 255
Lloyd, Edward [English businessman]
  Insurance (The growth of insurance) I: 315
  Lloyd's L: 403
Lloyd, Frank [Scottish-American director]
  Motion picture (Best achievement in directing:
    1928-29, 1932-33) M: 862
Lloyd, Harold [American actor] L: 402 *with portrait*
Lloyd, Henry [American political leader]
  Maryland (table) M: 255
Lloyd, Henry Demarest [American author] L: 402
Lloyd, Pop [American baseball player]
  Baseball (table: Hall of Fame) B: 134a
Lloyd D. Jackson Square
  Hamilton (History) H: 31-32
Lloyd George, David [British political leader]
  L: 402 *with portrait*
  Law, Andrew Bonar L: 140
  United Kingdom (World War I) U: 70
  Versailles, Treaty of V: 339
  World War I (The Paris Peace Conference) W: 465
Lloyd Webber, Andrew [British composer] L: 403
  Musical comedy (During the late 1900's) M: 960
Lloyd's [insurance company] L: 403
  Insurance *picture on* I: 316; (Types of insurance
    companies) I: 315
Lloyd's List [newspaper]
  Lloyd's L: 403
Lloyd's of London *See* Lloyd's *in this index*
Lloyd's underwriter
  Lloyd's L: 403
Llywelyn II [Welsh political leader]
  Wales (Revolts against England) W: 12
Llywelyn ap Iorwerth [Welsh prince]
  Wales (Revolts against England) W: 12

Llywelyn the Great [Welsh prince] *See* Llywelyn ap Iorwerth *in this index*
LM [space exploration] *See* Lunar module *in this index*
LMNA [gene]
  Progeria **P:** 811
LNG [fuel]
  Gas [fuel] (Storing gas) **G:** 55
LNG carrier [ship]
  Tanker (Kinds of tankers) **T:** 28
LNM Group [steel company]
  Iron and steel (Recent developments) **I:** 452
Lo Spagnoletto [nickname]
  Ribera, Jusepe de **R:** 321
Loa River [river, Chile]
  Chile (The Northern Desert) **C:** 464
Loach [fish] **L:** 403
  Fish *picture on* **F:** 157
Load [geology]
  River (River systems) **R:** 351
Load [investment]
  Mutual fund **M:** 969
Load [measurement]
  Weights and measures (table: Miscellaneous weights and measures) **W:** 184
Load [physics]
  Building construction (Parts of a building) **B:** 682
Load arm
  Lever **L:** 217
Load dispatcher [job]
  Electric power (Providing reliable service) **E:** 185
Load fund
  Mutual fund **M:** 969
Load ring
  Balloon (Operation of a gas balloon) **B:** 60
Loading apron
  Airport (Loading aprons and taxiways) **A:** 245
Loadstone *See* Lodestone *in this index*
Loafer
  Shoe (Kinds of shoes) **S:** 431 *with picture*
Loafing barn
  Dairying (Housing) **D:** 7
Loam [earth] **L:** 403
  Soil (Texture) **So:** 575
Loan [economics]
  See also Mortgage *in this index*
  Bank (Making loans) **B:** 89
  Bond **B:** 454
  Credit **Ci:** 1124
  Credit union **Ci:** 1125
  Finance company **F:** 103
  Interest **I:** 321
  International Development Association **I:** 339
  International Monetary Fund **I:** 343
  Loan company **L:** 404
  Pawnbroker **P:** 202
  Savings and loan association **S:** 165
  Universities and colleges (Student loan debt) **U:** 211
  Usury **U:** 229
  Veterans Affairs, Department of (Benefits and other services) **V:** 343
Loan company L: 404
Loan contract [economics]
  Credit (Lending institutions) **Ci:** 1124
Loan-sharking
  Crime (Organized crime) **Ci:** 1136
  Loan company **L:** 404
  Usury **U:** 229
Lob [sports]
  Badminton (Playing) **B:** 24-25
  Tennis (The ball in play) **T:** 163
Lobachevskian geometry
  Geometry (Non-Euclidean geometry) **G:** 105
Lobachevsky, Nikolai [Russian mathematician] **L:** 404
  Geometry (Non-Euclidean geometry) **G:** 105; (Rise of non-Euclidean geometry) **G:** 106
  Mathematics (In the 1800's) **M:** 307
Lobamba [Swaziland]
  Swaziland **So:** 1017 *with map*
Lobbying [government] **L:** 404
  Congress of the United States (How Congress makes laws) **Ci:** 944
  Propaganda (Organizations) **P:** 824
  Public relations (Methods) **P:** 863-864
Lobe [anatomy]
  Brain (The parts of the brain) **B:** 550a-550b *with diagram*
  Lung (Parts of the lung) **L:** 523 *with diagram*
Lobe-fin [fish]
  Amphibian (The history of amphibians) **A:** 441
  Prehistoric animal (The first animals with backbones) **P:** 736-737
  Tetrapod (Early tetrapods) **T:** 182b
  Tiktaalik **T:** 286
Lobe pump

Pump (Rotary pumps) **P:** 900b
Lobed leaf
  Leaf (The blade) **L:** 153 *with picture*
Lobel, Arnold [American artist and author] **L:** 404
  Literature for children *picture on* **L:** 370
Lobelia [botany] **L:** 404
Lobengula [African ruler]
  Zimbabwe (History) **Z:** 592-593
Lobi [people]
  Burkina Faso (People) **B:** 706
Loblolly pine
  Pine *picture on* **P:** 470; (Southeastern pines) **P:** 468
  Tree *pictures on* **T:** 425
Lobo Sosa, Porfirio [Honduran political leader]
  Honduras (Recent developments) **H:** 313
Lobotomy [surgery] **L:** 405
  Brain (Making decisions) **B:** 555-556
Lobster L: 405 *with pictures*
  Animal *picture on* **A:** 494
  Crustacean *picture on* **Ci:** 1164
Lobster Fishermen, Corea, Maine [painting by Hartley]
  Hartley, Marsden *picture on* **H:** 79
Lobster pot [fishing]
  Lobster (Lobster fishing) **L:** 406
Lobule [anatomy]
  Liver *picture on* **L:** 394; (Structure of the liver) **L:** 393
  Lung (Parts of the lungs) **L:** 523
Lobworm [sea animal] *See* Lugworm *in this index*
Local anesthesia [medicine]
  Anesthesia (Local anesthesia) **A:** 458
  Benzocaine **B:** 255
  Dentistry (Modern dentistry) **D:** 144-145
  Drug (Anesthetics) **D:** 352
  Surgery (Anesthesia) **So:** 1004
Local area network [computing]
  Computer (Computer networks) **Ci:** 920; (Local area networks [LAN's]) **Ci:** 922
  Computer network **Ci:** 925
  Radio (Webcasting and podcasting) **R:** 87
Local color writing [literature]
  Cable, George Washington **C:** 7
  Harte, Bret **H:** 77
Local control [education]
  Education (Control and support of U.S. education) **E:** 94
Local exchange carrier
  Telephone (Traditional phone calls) **T:** 96 *with diagram*
Local food movement
  Agriculture (Local food movements) **A:** 151
Local government L: 406
  Civil service (State and local civil service) **Ci:** 612
  Colonial life in America (Local government) **Ci:** 795
  Government *picture on* **G:** 283
  Income tax (State and local income taxes) **I:** 105
  Metropolitan area (Problems of metropolitan areas) **M:** 442
  Property tax **P:** 827
  Taxation (Taxation in the United States) **T:** 54
  Town meeting **T:** 352
  Township **T:** 353
Local Government Act [1985]
  London (Dealing with problems) **L:** 442-443
Local Group [astronomy] **L:** 409
  Galaxy (Galaxy groups, clusters, and beyond) **G:** 9
  Maffei galaxies **M:** 41
  Triangulum Galaxy **T:** 439
  Universe **U:** 205
Local heating device
  Heating (Local heating devices) **H:** 160
Local magnitude scale [geology] *See* Richter magnitude *in this index*
Local migration
  Migration (Types of migration) **M:** 538
Local option [law]
  Prohibition (The movement toward prohibition) **P:** 815
Local race [anthropology]
  Races, Human (The geographical-race theory) **R:** 54-55 *with map*
Local road
  Road (Local and secondary roads) **R:** 357
Local Supercluster [astronomy]
  Galaxy (Galaxy groups, clusters, and beyond) **G:** 9
  Universe **U:** 205
Local time
  Time (Local and standard time) **T:** 292
Local universe [astronomy]
  Galaxy (Elliptical galaxies) **G:** 8b
Local wind
  Wind (Local winds) **W:** 329
Localization of function
  Nervous system (Disorders of the nervous

system) **N:** 136
Localized attack
  Corrosion **Ci:** 1072
Locard, Edmond [French doctor]
  Forensic science **F:** 388a
Locard exchange principle
  Forensic science **F:** 388b
Locarno Conference [1925] **L:** 409
  Germany (The Weimar Republic) **G:** 167
Location
  Industry (Production location) **I:** 259; (Product differentiation) **I:** 260
  Motion picture *picture on* **M:** 849; (Assembling the production team) **M:** 850; (Filming on location) **M:** 851 *with picture*
Loch [lake]
  Scotland (Rivers and lakes) **S:** 217
Loch Lomond [lake, Scotland] **L:** 409 *with map*
  United Kingdom (The land) **U:** 58-61 *with map*
Loch Ness monster **L:** 410 *with picture*
  Folklore (Legends) **F:** 324
  Scotland (Rivers and lakes) **S:** 217
Loch Tay [Scotland]
  Europe *picture on* **E:** 394
Lochner v. New York [U.S. history] **L:** 410
  Fourteenth Amendment **F:** 438
  Labor movement (The early 1900's) **L:** 11
  Peckham, Rufus W. **P:** 227
  Supreme Court of the United States (table) **So:** 1002
Loci Communes [book by Melanchthon]
  Melanchthon, Philipp **M:** 388
Lock L: 410 *with pictures*
  Yale, Linus, Jr. **Y:** 548
Lock [engineering]
  Canal (Canal locks) **C:** 163 *with diagram*
  Inland waterway **I:** 274
  Panama Canal **P:** 122, *picture on* **P:** 124
  Saint Lawrence Seaway *picture on* **S:** 44
Lock stitch
  Sewing machine (History) **S:** 333
Lock-up clutch [engine]
  Transmission (A torque converter) **T:** 376-377
Locke, Alain LeRoy [American educator] **L:** 412
  American literature (The Harlem Renaissance) **A:** 422
  Harlem Renaissance **H:** 61
Locke, Gary [American political leader]
  Commerce, Department of (table) **Ci:** 871
  Obama, Barack (table) **O:** 640h
  Washington (table) **W:** 65; (The late 1900's) **W:** 68-69
Locke, John [English philosopher] **L:** 413
  Civil rights (Natural rights) **Ci:** 611
  Declaration of Independence (The importance of the Declaration) **D:** 76
  Democracy (Democracy in England) **D:** 122
  Enlightenment **E:** 326a
  Freedom (During the Enlightenment) **F:** 503
  Government (The Enlightenment) **G:** 290
  Liberalism (History) **L:** 228
  Philosophy (Empiricism) **P:** 389; (The Enlightenment) **P:** 389
  Political science (Constitutionalism) **P:** 639
  Psychology (Beginnings) **P:** 849
  Sterne, Laurence **So:** 894
Locke, Joseph [American designer]
  Glass (Types of art glass) **G:** 220
Locke, Sylvanus D. [American inventor]
  Reaper **R:** 173
Locked-in syndrome [disease]
  Brain (From injury) **B:** 550d-551
Lockhart, Frank [American race driver]
  Automobile racing (table: Indianapolis 500 winners) **A:** 980
Lockheed Martin Corporation
  Aviation (Aircraft manufacturing) **A:** 984; (World War I [1914-1918]) **A:** 987-988
Lockjaw [disease]
  Tetanus **T:** 182b
Lockout [labor relations] **L:** 413
  Labor movement (Handling labor disputes) **L:** 6-7
  Strike (Kinds of strikes) **So:** 928
Lockwood, Belva Ann Bennett [American social reformer] **L:** 413 *with portrait*
Lockwood, Lorna [American jurist]
  Arizona (The mid-1900's) **A:** 691
Lockyer, Joseph Norman [British astronomer]
  Helium **H:** 176
  Sun (History of modern solar study) **So:** 986
Locofocos [U.S. history] **L:** 413
Locomotion [zoology]
  Ameba **A:** 406
  Insect (Wings) **I:** 288
Locomotive [train] **L:** 414 *with pictures*
  Baldwin, Matthias William **B:** 39 *with picture*
  Civil War, American (Raids) **Ci:** 629

Cooper, Peter Ci: 1035 *with picture*
Industrial Revolution (Railroads) I: 251
Railroad (Rolling stock) R: 107 *with pictures*;
(Invention of the locomotive) R: 115
Railroad, Model (Locomotives) R: 120
Stephenson, George So: 890
Transportation (The steam age) T: 389 *with pictures*
Trevithick, Richard T: 436
Locomotive, The [drawing by Hopper]
Drawing *picture on* D: 344
Locomotive Engineers, Brotherhood of
Railway brotherhoods R: 122
Locomotive Firemen and Enginemen, Brotherhood of
Railway brotherhoods R: 122
Locomotor system [anatomy] *See* Musculoskeletal system *in this index*
Locoweed [plant] L: 418
Locus [genetics]
Genetic testing (How genes carry information) G: 84d
Locus ceruleus [anatomy]
Brain (Attention and consciousness) B: 554-555
Locust [plant] L: 418 *with pictures*
Honey locust H: 315 *with picture*
Tree *pictures on* T: 422
Locust [insect] L: 418 *with pictures*
See also Cicada *in this index*
Grasshopper (Short-horned grasshoppers) G: 328
Insect *picture on* I: 281; (Wings) I: 288;
(Hibernation and migration) I: 296 *with picture*
Locust bird
Courser Ci: 1101
Locusts, Plague of
Locust L: 419
Lode deposit [earth]
Gold (Types of deposits) G: 252
Lodestone [rock] L: 419
See also Magnetite *in this index*
Electricity (Early discoveries) E: 196
Magnetism (Permanent magnets) M: 60 *with picture*; (Early discoveries) M: 60d
Lodge [animal home]
Beaver (Building lodges) B: 195 *with picture*
Lodge [dwelling]
Indian, American *pictures on* I: 138, I: 159
Lodge, David [British author]
Novel (The novel today) N: 575
Lodge, Henry Cabot [American political leader] L: 419
United Nations (table) U: 86
Wilson, Woodrow (Opposition to the League) W: 327
Lodge, Henry Cabot, Jr. [American political leader] L: 419
Kennedy, John Fitzgerald (Campaign for the Senate) K: 262; (Steps to the White House) K: 263
Lodge, John [American political leader]
Connecticut (table) Ci: 967
Lodge, Sir Oliver Joseph [British physicist] L: 420
Lodge Federal Elections Bill [1890]
Force bill F: 371
Lodgepole pine
Pine (Western pines) P: 469
Lodger, The [film]
Hitchcock, Alfred H: 263
Lodi, Ibrahim [sultan of Delhi]
India (The Mughal Empire) I: 129
Łódź [Poland] L: 420
Loe, Thomas [English religious leader]
Penn, William (Youthful rebel) P: 241-242
Loeb, Jacques [American physiologist] L: 420
Loeb, Richard A. [American public figure]
Darrow, Clarence Seward D: 38
Loeffler, Friedrich [German biologist]
Virus (Discovery) V: 427
Loess [earth] L: 420
China (The Inner Mongolian Border Uplands) C: 491
Dust (Dust deposits) D: 390
Ice age (Evidence of ice ages and their climates) I: 6-7
Minnesota (Natural resources) M: 599
Loesser, Frank [American composer] L: 420
Loewe, Frederick [American composer]
Lerner, Alan Jay L: 206
Musical comedy (The modern musical emerges) M: 960
Loewi, Otto [Austrian physiologist]
Nobel Prizes (Physiology or medicine: 1936) N: 445
Löffler, Friedrich August Johannes [German bacteriologist] L: 420
Lofoten Islands [Norway]
Norway (Coast and islands) N: 542 *with map*

Loft [sports]
Bowling (table) B: 521
Lofting, Hugh [British author] L: 420 *with picture*
Newbery Medal (table) N: 359
Log [book]
Logbook L: 425
Log [instrument] L: 421 *with pictures*
Knot K: 355
Log cabin [dwelling] L: 422 *with picture*
Colonial life in America (Houses) Ci: 796-797
Lincoln, Abraham *picture on* L: 311
Pioneer life in America (A pioneer settlement) P: 479 *with picture*
Westward movement in America (The Old West) W: 245
Log Cabin, The [newspaper]
Greeley, Horace (His publications) G: 379
Log chip and line [navigation]
Knot K: 355
Log debarker [machine]
Lumber (Sawing logs) L: 519
Log rule [logging]
Lumber (table) L: 518
Logan [American Indian chief] L: 422
Logan, George [American political leader]
Logan Act L: 423
Logan, John Alexander [Union general] L: 423
Memorial Day (History) M: 392
Logan, Joshua [American director] L: 423
Logan, Mount *See* Mount Logan *in this index*
Logan, Stephen Trigg [American lawyer]
Lincoln, Abraham (Early practice) L: 315
Logan, Sir William Edmond [Canadian geologist] L: 423
Mount Logan M: 885
Museum (Early Canadian museums) M: 940
Logan Act [1799] L: 423
Logan International Airport
Boston (Transportation) B: 502
Loganberry [fruit] L: 423 *with pictures*
Dewberry D: 176
Logarithms [mathematics] L: 423
Calculator C: 22
Mathematics (Mathematics and the scientific revolution) M: 306-307
Napier, John N: 12
Logbook [navigation] L: 425
Logger *See* Lumberjack *in this index*
Loggerhead shrike [bird]
Bird (Birds of brushy areas) B: 338 *with picture*
Shrike S: 439
Loggerhead turtle
Ocean *picture on* O: 656
Logging [industry]
Canada (Forestry) C: 125 *with picture*
Deforestation (Logging) D: 90
Elephant *picture on* E: 227
Lumber (From forest to sawmill) L: 518
Oregon *picture on* O: 844
Spotted owl So: 804
Logging on [computing]
Computer (Mainframes and supercomputers) Ci: 910
Logic L: 425
Aristotle (Logic) A: 663
Artificial intelligence (Knowledge representation and reasoning) A: 760
Deductive method D: 81
Fallacy F: 16
Geometry (The study of geometry) G: 101
Inductive method I: 240
Liberal arts L: 226
Mathematics (Branches of mathematics) M: 303
Philosophy (Logic) P: 384; (Philosophy and science) P: 385; (The philosophy of language) P: 385
Scholasticism (History) S: 179
Science (Mathematics and logic) S: 192; (Using logic) S: 194
Set theory (In logic) S: 322
Logic circuit
Electronics (Digital circuits) E: 213-214
Logic of Scientific Discovery, The [book by Popper]
Popper, Karl Raimund P: 668
Logical Positivism [philosophy]
Empiricism E: 263
Metaphysics (Opinions about metaphysics) M: 430
Philosophy (Philosophy in the 1900's) P: 390
Positivism (Logical positivism) P: 697
Wittgenstein, Ludwig W: 374
Logicism [philosophy]
Mathematics (Philosophies of mathematics) M: 307
Logistics [warfare] L: 426
Army (Armies in the two world wars) A: 728
Army, United States (Logistic units) A: 735

Logogram [word sign] *See* Logography *in this index*
Logography [communications]
Writing system (Logograms) W: 512; (Phonetization) W: 513
Logone River
Chad (Land and climate) C: 366-367 *with map*
Logopedics, Institute of
Wichita (Education and cultural life) W: 297
Logos [philosophy]
Heraclitus H: 194
Logperch [fish]
Darter D: 38
Logrolling [politics] L: 426
Congress of the United States (Legislative bargaining) Ci: 944-945
Logrolling [sport]
Birling B: 375
Logwood [wood] L: 426
Lohengrin [opera by Wagner]
Germany *picture on* G: 154
Wagner, Richard W: 3
Lohi [seamount, Hawaii]
Hot spot H: 374a
Lohit [river, Asia]
Brahmaputra River B: 548
Loihi [seamount]
Seamount S: 269
Loincloth
India (Clothing) I: 117-118
Loire River [France] L: 426
Lok Sabha [government]
India (Central government) I: 109
Loki [Norse mythology] L: 426
Balder B: 38
Mythology (Teutonic mythology) M: 285-986 *with picture*
Lola [opera character]
Opera: *(Cavalleria Rusticana)* O: 803
Lolita [book by Nabokov]
Nabokov, Vladimir N: 2
Novel (After World War II) N: 574
Lollards [European history] L: 426
Wycliffe, John W: 515
Lolo Trail [Idaho]
Lewis and Clark expedition (Crossing the mountains) L: 222c
Loman, Willy [literary figure]
Miller, Arthur M: 553
Lomax, Alan [American folklorist]
Morton, Jelly Roll M: 821
Lombard, Carole [American actress]
Gable, Clark G: 2
Lombard, Peter [Italian theologian] L: 427
Scholasticism (The Scholastic method) S: 179
Lombard League [Italian history]
Alexander III A: 341
Frederick I F: 497
Lombard Street
San Francisco *picture on* S: 96; (Downtown San Francisco) S: 92-93
Lombardi, Ernie [American baseball player]
Baseball (table: Hall of Fame) B: 134a
Lombardi, I [opera by Verdi]
Verdi, Giuseppe V: 316
Lombardi, Vince [American football coach] L: 427
Lombards [people] L: 427
Italy (The Middle Ages) I: 513
Lombardy [region, Italy] L: 427
Lombards L: 427
Lombardy poplar [tree]
Poplar P: 668
Lombroso, Cesare [Italian criminologist]
Criminology (History) Ci: 1145-1146
Lomé [Togo] L: 427
Togo T: 310 *with map, picture on* T: 310
Lomond, Loch [lake] *See* Loch Lomond *in this index*
Lomonosov, Mikhail [Russian poet]
Russian literature (Western influences) R: 559
Lomonosov Ridge [Arctic Ocean]
Arctic Ocean (The deep basin) A: 643 *with map*
Lon Nol [Cambodian political leader] L: 427
Cambodia (History) C: 72-73
Lon Po Po [book by Young]
Literature for children *picture on* L: 357
Londinium [historic name]
England (The Roman conquest) E: 303-304
London (History) L: 439
London [England] L: 428 *with pictures and maps*
See also the list of Related articles in the London article
Architecture *picture on* A: 624
Big Ben B: 297 *with picture*
Christmas *picture on* C: 530
City *picture on* Ci: 586; (The people) Ci: 582
Cockney Ci: 745
Coffee house Ci: 755
England E: 292 *with picture*; (Population) E: 294

Europe *picture on* E: 380
Fire department (Fire protection in Europe)
F: 127-128
Franklin, Benjamin (A delegate in London) F: 490
Map (Development of thematic and inventory
mapping) M: 185
Marx, Karl (Move to London) M: 237
Old Bailey O: 739
Shakespeare, William *picture on* S: 352; (Early
career in London) S: 347; (Shakespeare's
London) S: 349
Subway So: 949
Terrorism (Recent developments) T: 180 *with
picture*
Thames River T: 229
United Kingdom U: 48 *with picture*; (Population)
U: 54 *with picture*; (table: Average monthly
weather) U: 62; (Recent developments) U: 74
World War II *pictures on* W: 475; (The Battle of
Brtain) W: 476
London [Ontario] L: 444
London, Convention of [1818]
Lake of the Woods L: 43
London, Declaration of [1909]
Blockade B: 406
Right of search R: 340
London, Jack [American author] L: 444 *with
portrait*
London, Port of
London (Trade) L: 438
London, Tower of *See* Tower of London *in this index*
London, Treaties of L: 444
London, Treaty of [1839]
London, Treaties of (The Treaty of 1839) L: 444
London, Treaty of [1913]
Balkans (The First Balkan War) B: 42
London, Treaties of (The Treaty of 1913) L: 444
London, Treaty of [1915]
Benedict XV B: 247
London, Treaties of (The Treaty of 1915) L: 445
London, Treaty of [1930] *See* London Naval Treaty
in this index
London, Treaty of [1936]
London, Treaties of (The Treaty of 1936) L: 445
London, University of L: 445
London (Education) L: 433
London Blitz *See* Blitz, The *in this index*
London Bridge L: 445 *with picture*
Arizona (Places to visit) A: 678
London (The Middle Ages) L: 439-440 *with
picture*
London Bridge [painting by Derain]
Fauves *picture on* F: 57
London Company [U.S. history] L: 445
Colonial life in America (Early English
settlements) Ci: 789
Jamestown J: 28
Virginia (The Jamestown settlement) V: 418
London Conference [1909]
Right of search R: 340
London Fire [1666] *See* Great Fire of London
London Government Act [1963]
London (Rebuilding) L: 442
London Marathon [sports]
London (Recreation) L: 434
London Metropolitan Police
Scotland Yard S: 221
London Naval Treaty [1930]
Arms control (History of arms control) A: 721
Hoover, Herbert Clark (Foreign policy) H: 330
London, Treaties of (The Treaty of 1930) L: 445
London Penny Post
Postal services (The creation of the Penny Post)
P: 706
London plane [tree]
Tree *picture on* T: 427
London Prize Ring Rules
Boxing (The revival of boxing) B: 532
London Protocol [1830]
Greece (Independence) G: 362
London Shrinking [industrial process]
Wool (Making fabric) W: 401
London Stock Exchange
London (Finance and business) L: 438
London symphonies [music by Haydn]
Haydn, Joseph H: 117
London-type smog
Smog (London-type smog) S: 519
Londonderry [Northern Ireland] L: 445
Lone Eagle [nickname]
Lindbergh, Charles Augustus L: 330 *with picture*
Lone Scout
Boy Scouts (Boy Scouts of America) B: 534
Lone wolf
Wolf (The life of a wolf) W: 375
"Loneliness of the Long Distance Runner, The"
[story by Sillitoe]

Sillitoe, Alan S: 462
Lonely Crusade [book by Himes]
Himes, Chester H: 234
"Lonely Land, The" [poem by Smith]
Canadian literature (Literature between the
world wars) C: 158-159
Lones [scouting]
Girl Scouts (Lones) G: 199
Lonesome Dove [book by McMurtry]
McMurtry, Larry M: 343
Long [American political leaders] L: 445 *with
portrait*
Long, Crawford Williamson [American doctor]
L: 446
Anesthesia (History) A: 459
Ether E: 365
Hospital (The 1800's) H: 373
Medicine (The first anesthetic) M: 375
Morton, William Thomas Green M: 821
Long, Earl Kemp [American political leader]
Long (Earl Kemp Long) L: 446
Louisiana (table) L: 496
Long, George Shannon [American political leader]
Long (George Shannon Long) L: 446
Long, Huey Pierce [American political leader]
Long (Huey Pierce Long) L: 445 *with portrait*
Baton Rouge (Description) B: 166
Louisiana (table) L: 496; (Huey P. Long) L: 500
with picture
Long, James [husband of]
Long, Jane L: 446
Long, Jane [American pioneer] L: 446
Long, John D. [American political leader]
Massachusetts (table) M: 288
McKinley, William (table) M: 342
Roosevelt, Theodore (table) R: 466
Long, John Luther [American author]
Opera: (*Madama Butterfly*) O: 804
Long, Rose McConnell [wife of Huey Long]
Long (Huey Pierce Long) L: 445-446
Long, Russell Billiu [American political leader]
Long (Russell Billiu Long) L: 446
Long, Stephen Harriman [American explorer]
L: 446
Minnesota (The Louisiana Purchase) M: 603-604
Nebraska (American exploration and settlement)
N: 111-112
Pikes Peak P: 462
Westward movement in America (Exploration)
W: 248
Long Beach [California] L: 447
Long-beaked common dolphin [sea animal]
Dolphin (The common dolphins) D: 297
Long-billed curlew [bird]
Curlew Ci: 1195 *with picture*
Long boom [Australian history]
Australia (Economic changes) A: 923
Long Bridge [New Orleans]
Louisiana (Transportation) L: 495
"Long count" [boxing]
Boxing (Boxing's Golden Age) B: 532-532a
Dempsey, Jack D: 130 *with picture*
Long Count [calendar]
Calendar (The Maya) C: 31
Long dam [engineering]
Tennessee Valley Authority (The dams) T: 158
Long dash skipper [butterfly]
Butterfly *picture on* B: 734
Long-day plant
Plant (Environmental factors) P: 538
Long Day's Journey into Night [play by O'Neill]
American literature (Drama) A: 422-423
Drama (United States drama) D: 339
O'Neill, Eugene O: 762
Long distance carrier
Telephone (Traditional phone calls) T: 96 *with
diagram*; (In the United States) T: 99
Long division [mathematics]
Division (Long division) D: 249
Long-eared owl
Owl (Important owls) O: 884-886
Long-finned pilot whale
Dolphin (table) D: 298
Whale *picture on* W: 257
Long grain rice
Rice (Kinds of rice) R: 323-324
Long-haired cat
Cat *pictures on* C: 289; (Long-haired breeds)
C: 292
Long-haired chimpanzee
Chimpanzee C: 471
Long-horned beetle
Antennae *picture on* A: 544
Long house [structure] *See* Longhouse *in this index*
Long House religion
Indian, American (Prophets) I: 148
Long Island [New York] L: 447 *with map*

Levittown L: 219
Long Island, Battle of [1776]
Long Island (History) L: 447
Revolution, American (table) R: 276; (The
campaign in New York) R: 281 *with map*
Long Island City [district]
New York City (Queens) N: 329
Long Island Sound [waterway, Connecticut-New
York] L: 448
Long John Silver [literary figure]
Stevenson, Robert Louis (Novels) So: 898
Long jump [track and field] L: 448
Track and field (Jumping events) T: 357 *with
picture*
Long-lining [fishing]
Fishing industry (Hooks) F: 185 *with picture*
Long March [Chinese history]
China (Nationalist rule) C: 504 *with map*
Mao Zedong (His life) M: 174-175
Long March [spacecraft]
Rocket *picture on* R: 384; (Liquid-propellant
rockets) R: 388
Space exploration *picture on* So: 699
Long measure [poetry]
Poetry (Rhythm and meter) P: 591-592
Long Parliament [English history] L: 448
Charles I [of England] C: 380
England (table) E: 308
Parliament (Parliament gains strength) P: 174
Rump Parliament R: 519
Long-period comet [astronomy]
Comet *picture on* Ci: 868
Meteor (The parent comet) M: 431
Oort cloud O: 788
Long-playing record *See* LP record *in this index*
Long-range forecast [meteorology]
Weather (Mathematical models) W: 166
Long Range Mountains
Newfoundland and Labrador (Mountains) N: 370
with map
Long-range radar
Radar *picture on* R: 66
Long ship
Ship (Viking ships) *picture on* S: 419
Vikings (The Vikings as shipbuilders) V: 381
Warship *picture on* W: 42; (Early warships) W: 41
Long shot
Horse racing (Betting) H: 365
Long-staple cotton
Egypt (Agriculture) E: 128-129 *with picture*
Long swings [economics] *See* Kuznets cycles *in
this index*
Long sword
Sword So: 1062
Long-tailed chinchilla [animal]
Chinchilla C: 508
Long-tailed weasel [animal]
Weasel W: 155 *with pictures*
Long-term care insurance
Insurance (Other types of health insurance) I: 312
Long-term credit
Credit (Types of credit) Ci: 1124
Long-term loan
Interest (Length of a loan) I: 323
Long-term memory [psychology]
Memory (The memory system) M: 392
Long-term nonprogressor [medicine]
AIDS (Opportunistic illness) A: 164a-164b
Long Tom Coffin [literary figure]
Cooper, James Fenimore Ci: 1035
Long ton [measurement]
Ton T: 327
Long-track skating
Ice skating (Long-track skating) I: 14
Long View of London [engraving by Visscher]
Shakespeare, William *picture on* S: 352
"Long Walk" [American history]
Navajo Indians N: 70
Long-wooled sheep
Sheep (Long-wooled sheep) S: 382
Wool (Sources of wool) W: 399
Longarm squid [animal]
Squid (Kinds of squids) So: 814a *with picture*
Longboard
Surfing So: 1003
Longbow [weapon]
Archery (Bows) A: 601-602
Crossbow Ci: 1156
Weapon (Prehistoric weapons) W: 154a
Longevity *See* Life expectancy *in this index*
Longevity pay
Rank, Military (Rank and pay) R: 140
Longfellow, Frances Appleton [wife of]
Longfellow, Henry Wadsworth (Professor and
family man) L: 448-449 *with portrait*
Longfellow, Henry Wadsworth [American poet]
L: 448 *with pictures*

American literature (Poetry) **A: 418** *with portrait*
Hiawatha **H: 221**
Maine (Places to visit) **M: 78** *with picture*
Minneapolis (Parks) **M: 582**
Nova Scotia **N: 555**
Poe, Edgar Allan (Poe's life) **P: 589**
September (Quotations) **S: 309**
Longfellow, Mary Potter [wife of]
Longfellow, Henry Wadsworth (Professor and family man) **L: 448-449**
Longfellow National Historic Site [Massachusetts]
Longfellow, Henry Wadsworth (Professor and family man) *picture on* **L: 449-450**
National Park System (table: National historic sites) **N: 52-53**
Longfin inshore squid [animal]
Squid (Kinds of squids) **So: 814a**
Longfin mako [shark]
Mako shark (The longfin mako) **M: 94**
Longhi, Alessandro [Italian artist]
Casanova, Giacomo *picture on* **C: 271**
Longhorn
Cattle (Beginning of breeding) **C: 315**
Texas *picture on* **T: 205**; (Agriculture) **T: 202**
Longhorns, University of Texas [team]
Texas *picture on* **T: 189**
Longhouse
Cayuga Indians **C: 323**
Dayaks **D: 53**
Indian, American (Shelter) **I: 136d**; (Before European contact) **I: 154-155** *with picture*
Mahican Indians **M: 65**
Malaysia (Rural life) **M: 98c**
Seneca Indians **S: 297**
Longino, Andrew H. [American political leader]
Mississippi (table) **M: 640**
Longinus [Greek author] **L: 451**
Criticism (History of literary criticism) **Ci: 1146**
Longitude [geography] **L: 451** *with pictures*
Map (Geographic grids) **M: 178** *with diagram*
Moon (Libration) **M: 785** *with diagram*
Longitudinal chromatic aberration [optics]
Aberration (Chromatic aberration) **A: 11**
Longitudinal wave [physics]
Waves *diagram on* **W: 150**; (Types of waves) **W: 152**
Longleaf pine
Pine *picture on* **P: 470**; (Southeastern pines) **P: 468**
Longley, James B. [American political leader]
Maine (table) **M: 87**
Longmen Grottoes [caves]
Asia *picture on* **A: 771**
Longnose gar [fish]
Fish *picture on* **F: 158**
Gar **G: 28** *with picture*
Longs Peak [mountain, Colorado]
Long, Stephen Harriman **L: 446**
Rocky Mountain National Park **R: 394**
Longshan culture [Chinese history]
China (Beginnings of Chinese civilization) **C: 499**
Longshoremen's Association, International
Bridges, Harry **B: 607**
Labor movement (table) **L: 8**
Longsightedness *See* Farsightedness *in this index*
Longspine squirrelfish
Fish *picture on* **F: 154**
Longspur [bird]
Bird *picture on* **B: 337**
Longstocking, Pippi [fictional character]
Lindgren, Astrid **L: 332**
Longstreet, James [Confederate general] **L: 452**
Civil War, American (The commanding officers) **Ci: 618**; (Second Battle of Bull Run) **Ci: 627**
Longueuil, Sieur de [Canadian colonist] *See* Le Moyne, Charles, Sieur de Longueil et de Châteauguay *in this index*
Longus [Greek author]
Greek literature (The Greco-Roman Age) **G: 378**
Novel (Ancient Greek and Roman narratives) **N: 572**
Longwall mine
Coal (The longwall system) **Ci: 724** *with picture*
Mining (Caving) **M: 576**
Longway Planetarium [Michigan]
Flint *picture on* **F: 235**
Longworth, Alice Roosevelt [daughter of]
Roosevelt, Theodore (Life in the White House) **R: 465-466**
Longworth, Nicholas [American political leader]
Roosevelt, Theodore (Life in the White House) **R: 465-466**
Longworth House Office Building [Washington, D.C.]
Washington, D.C. *map on* **W: 76**
Longyi [clothing]
Myanmar (Way of life) **M: 970a**

Lonigan, Studs [literary figure]
Farrell, James T. **F: 48**
Lönnrot, Elias [Finnish doctor]
Finland (The arts) **F: 112**
Lonsdale Belt [award]
Boxing (Professional boxing) **B: 531**
Loofah [plant]
Gourd **G: 281** *with picture*
Look-and-say instruction
Reading (Sight words and look-and-say instruction) **R: 159**
Look Back in Anger [play by Osborne]
Drama (Later British drama) **D: 340**
English literature (Literature after World War II) **E: 322-323**
Osborne, John **O: 861**
Looker, Othneil [American political leader]
Ohio (table) **O: 699**
Looking Backward [book by Bellamy]
Bellamy, Edward **B: 242**
Looking Glass War, The [book by Le Carré]
Le Carré, John **L: 174**
Lookout Mountain [Tennessee]
Tennessee (Places to visit) **T: 144** *with picture*
Lookout Mountain, Battle of [1863]
Civil War, American (Battle of Chattanooga) **Ci: 630**
Loom [weaving]
Cartwright, Edmund **C: 268**
Indian, American *picture on* **I: 176**
Invention (Economic needs) **I: 355**
Jacquard, Joseph Marie **J: 20**
Weaving (Weaving on a loom) **W: 173** *with picture*
Wool *picture on* **W: 401**
Loon [bird] **L: 452**
Animal *picture on* **A: 485**
Bird (Birds of inland waters and marshes) **B: 340** *with picture*
Loop, The [district, Chicago]
Chicago (Downtown Chicago) **C: 420-421**
Looped stitch
Crochet **Ci: 1148d**
Embroidery (Embroidery stitches) **E: 257** *with picture*
Looper [insect] *See* Measuring worm *in this index*
Loophole [taxation]
Income tax (Defining taxable income) **I: 102-103**
Loos, Adolf [Austrian architect]
Architecture (Early modern architecture in Europe) **A: 627-629** *with picture*
Austria (Architecture) **A: 932-933**
Loose-fill insulation
Insulation (In buildings) **I: 306** *with picture*
Loose housing
Dairying (Housing) **D: 7** *with picture*
Loose housing [agriculture]
Dairying (Housing) **D: 7**
Loose packing [slavery]
African Americans (Beginning of the slave trade) **A: 136c-136d**
Loose pattern [manufacturing]
Cast and casting (Patterns for casting) **C: 278**
Loosestrife [plant] **L: 453**
Looting
Riot (Expressive riots) **R: 348**
Lop [rabbit]
Rabbit (Domestic rabbits) **R: 46** *with picture*
Lope de Vega [Spanish dramatist] *See* Vega, Lope de *in this index*
Lopez, Al [American baseball manager]
Baseball (table: Hall of Fame) **B: 134a**
López, Carlos Antonio [Paraguayan political leader]
Paraguay (Independence) **P: 149**
López, Francisco Solano [Paraguayan political leader]
Paraguay (Military ruin) **P: 149**
Lopez, Jennifer [American singer/actress] **L: 453** *with portrait*
Lopez, Nancy [American golfer] **L: 453**
López Arellano, Osvaldo [Honduran political leader]
Honduras (Revolutions and reforms) **H: 313**
López de Legazpi, Miguel [Spanish explorer] *See* Legazpi, Miguel López de *in this index*
López de Mendoza, Iñigo [Spanish author] *See* Santillana, Marquis of *in this index*
López de Santa Anna, Antonio [Mexican political leader] *See* Santa Anna, Antonio López de *in this index*
López Obrador, Andrés Manuel [Mexican political leader]
Calderón Hinojosa, Felipe **C: 27**
López Portillo, José [Mexican political leader] **L: 453**
Mexico (The 1late 1900's) **M: 474-475**
López Tijerina, Reies [American social reformer]

Hispanic Americans (The Chicano movement) **H: 256**
López y Fuentes, Gregorio [Mexican author]
Latin American literature (The early 1900's) **L: 113**
Lophira procera [tree]
Plant *picture on* **P: 527**
Lophophore [biology]
Bryozoan **B: 657**
Loquat [fruit] **L: 453**
Loran [navigation]
Log (Electronic navigation devices) **L: 421**
Navigation (Other radio navigation systems) **N: 73**
Lorandite [mineral]
Thallium **T: 229**
Lorazepam [drug]
Benzodiazepine **B: 256**
Lord [title] **L: 454**
Baron **B: 116**
Feudalism **F: 81**
Freedom (The Middle Ages) **F: 502**
Middle Ages (Barbarian Europe) **M: 523**; (The Carolingian Empire) **M: 524**; (Feudalism) **M: 524**; (Life of the people) **M: 526**
Nobility (Privileges of the peerage) **N: 450**
Lord, Bernard [Canadian political leader]
New Brunswick (table) **N: 195**
Lord, Betty Bao [American author]
Novel (The novel today) **N: 575**
Lord, William Paine [American political leader]
Oregon (table) **O: 845**
Lord chamberlain [title]
Royal Household of the United Kingdom **R: 498**
Lord Chamberlain's Men [theater group]
Shakespeare, William (His work in theater companies) **S: 347**; (The Globe Theatre) **S: 348**; (Acting companies) **S: 352-353**
Lord Dunmore's War [1774]
Cornstalk **Ci: 1066**
Indian wars (Lord Dunmore's War [1774]) **I: 191**
Virginia (Westward expansion) **V: 418-420**
Lord Durham's Report [document]
Canada, History of (Lord Durham's report) **C: 143**
Confederation of Canada (Lord Durham's Report) **Ci: 933**
Durham, Earl of **D: 389**
Lord God Made Them All, The [book by Herriot]
Herriot, James **H: 216**
Lord Haw-Haw [stage name]
Old Bailey **O: 740**
Lord High Admiral [rank]
Admiralty **A: 59**
Lord Jim [book by Conrad]
Conrad, Joseph **Ci: 973**
Lord mayor [title]
London (The Middle Ages) **L: 439-440**
Lord Mayor's Show
London (Ceremonies) **L: 437**
Lord of appeals [office]
Parliament (The House of Lords) **P: 173-74**
Lord of the Flies [book by Golding] **L: 454**
Golding, William **G: 258**
Lord of the Miracles [festival]
Peru *picture on* **P: 311**
Lord of the Rings, The [books by Tolkien]
Fairy (Fairies in literature) **F: 11**
Tolkien, J. R. R. **T: 321**
Lord of the Rings, The [film trilogy]
Jackson, Peter **J: 15**
Lord of the Rings: The Fellowship of the Ring, The [film]
Jackson, Peter **J: 15**
Lord of the Rings: The Return of the King, The [film]
Animation *pictures on* **A: 514**
Jackson, Peter **J: 15**
Motion picture *picture on* **M: 873**; (Best picture: 2003) **M: 861**
Lord of the Rings: The Two Towers, The [film]
Jackson, Peter **J: 15**
Lord proprietor [title]
South Carolina (Exploration and settlement) **So: 659**
Lord Protector [title]
Cromwell, Oliver (The Protectorate) **Ci: 1152**
England (The Civil War) **E: 308-309**
Lord spiritual [title]
House of Lords **H: 384**
Lord **L: 454**
Parliament (The House of Lords) **P: 173-174**
Lord steward [title]
Royal Household of the United Kingdom **R: 498**
Lord Temporal [title]
Lord **L: 454**
Lord Weary's Castle [poem by Lowell]
Lowell, Robert **L: 511**
Lordosis [disorder]

Spine **So:** 793
Lords, House of *See* House of Lords *in this index*
Lords Chamber [London]
Parliament *picture on* **P:** 173
Lord's Cricket Ground
London (Recreation) **L:** 434
Lord's Day
Sunday **So:** 989
Lord's Prayer L: 454
Lord's Resistance Army [political group]
Congo, Democratic Republic of the (New government) **Ci:** 940d
Uganda (History) **U:** 3-4
Lord's Supper *See* Communion *in this index*
Lorelei [legendary figure]
Rhine River (The course of the Rhine) **R:** 292
Lorelei [mountain, Germany] **L:** 454
Rhine River (The course of the Rhine) **R:** 292 *with picture*
"Lorelei, The" [poem by Heine]
Heine, Heinrich **H:** 166
Loren, Sophia [Italian actress]
Motion picture (Best performance by an actress: 1961) **M:** 862
Lorentz, Hendrik Antoon [Dutch physicist] **L:** 454
Physics (Einstein and relativity) **P:** 441
Relativity (Lorentz transformations) **R:** 211
Lorentz-Fitzgerald contraction [physics]
Relativity (Lorentz-Fitzgerald contraction) **R:** 211
Lorentz transformation [physics]
Lorentz, Hendrik Antoon **L:** 454
Relativity (Lorentz transformations) **R:** 211
Lorenz, Konrad Zacharias [Austrian naturalist] **L:** 454 *with portrait*
Lorenzini, Carlo [Italian author] *See* Collodi, Carlo *in this index*
Lorenzo the Magnificent [Florentine ruler] *See* Medici, Lorenzo de' *in this index*
Lorikeet [bird]
Bird (Birds of the Pacific Islands) **B:** 349 *with picture*
Parrot *picture on* **P:** 180; (Kinds of parrots) **P:** 179
Loris [animal] **L:** 455 *with picture*
Potto **P:** 719
Primate *diagram on* **P:** 778b; (Galagos and lorises) **P:** 778
Lorkipanidze, David [Georgian anthropologist]
Prehistoric people (table) **P:** 754
Lorne, Marquess of [Canadian statesman] **L:** 455
Lorrain, Claude [French artist] *See* Claude *in this index*
Lorraine [France] *See* Alsace-Lorraine *in this index*
Lorris, Guillaume de [French poet]
French literature (Narrative poetry) **F:** 518
Lory [bird]
Parrot (Kinds of parrots) **P:** 179
Los ...
Titles beginning Los *appear under their key words, as in* Pazos de Ulloa, Los. *Place names appear below*
Los Alamos National Laboratory [New Mexico] **L:** 455
Sandia National Laboratories **S:** 109
Los Alamos National Security, LLC [organization]
Los Alamos National Laboratory **L:** 455
Los Alamos Neutron Science Center
Los Alamos National Laboratory **L:** 455
Los Angeles [California] **L:** 456 *with pictures and maps*
Automobile (Air pollution) **A:** 964
California **C:** 36; (Population) **C:** 40; (table: Average monthly weather) **C:** 51; (The mid-1900's) **C:** 62-63
City *picture on* **Ci:** 589
Hollywood **H:** 293
Mosley, Walter **M:** 830
Olympic Games (Between the wars) **O:** 751; (Boycotts) **O:** 753
Riot (During the 1900's) **R:** 349
Los Angeles [airship]
Airship *picture on* **A:** 250
Los Angeles Angels of Anaheim [team]
Baseball (table) **B:** 130
Los Angeles Clippers [team]
Basketball (table) **B:** 150
Los Angeles County
Los Angeles **L:** 456, *map on* **L:** 458
Los Angeles County Museum of Art
Los Angeles (Museums) **L:** 466
Los Angeles Dodgers [team]
Baseball (table) **B:** 130
Los Angeles earthquake [1994]
California (The late 1900's) **C:** 63-64
Los Angeles International Airport
Airport *picture on* **A:** 242; (table) **A:** 245
Los Angeles Kings [team]
Hockey (table: National Hockey League) **H:** 281

Los Angeles Lakers [team]
Basketball (table) **B:** 150
Bryant, Kobe **B:** 655
Los Angeles Zoo
Los Angeles (Recreation) **L:** 467 *with picture*
Losantiville [former village]
Cincinnati **Ci:** 554; (Early days) **Ci:** 556
Los Chorros [park, El Salvador]
El Salvador (Recreation) **E:** 250
Los Dinos [band]
Selena **S:** 293
Los Glaciares National Park [Argentina]
National park (Argentina) **N:** 42b; (table) **N:** 42g
Loss pooling
Insurance **I:** 309
Losses [book by Jarrell]
Jarrell, Randall **J:** 63
Lossless compression [electronics]
Computer (Research and development) **Ci:** 924
Data compression **D:** 41
Photography (Storing digital images) **P:** 421
Lossy compression [electronics]
Computer (Research and development) **Ci:** 924
Data compression **D:** 41
Photography (Storing digital images) **P:** 421
Lost City Museum [Overton]
Nevada (Museums) **N:** 161
Lost Colony [U.S. history] **L:** 472
Colonial life in America (Early English settlements) **Ci:** 789
Lumbee Indians **L:** 516
North Carolina **N:** 473; (Visitor's guide) **N:** 482 *with picture*; (Exploration and settlement) **N:** 490 *with picture*
Raleigh, Sir Walter (His expeditions) **R:** 131
United States, History of the (The American Colonies (1607-1753)) **U:** 152
Lost Colony, The [play by Green]
Green, Paul Eliot **G:** 379
Lost Dauphin [king of France] *See* Louis XVII *in this index*
Lost Empires [book by Priestley]
Priestley, John Boynton **P:** 776
Lost Generation [literature] **L:** 472
American literature (The Lost Generation) **A:** 421
United States, History of the (The Lost Generation and Flaming Youth) **U:** 190
Lost Horizon [book by Hilton]
Hilton, James **H:** 233
Lost in the Funhouse [stories by Barth]
Barth, John **B:** 120
Lost in Yonkers [play by Simon]
Simon, Neil **S:** 466
Lost River Range [mountains, Idaho]
Idaho (Mountains) **I:** 36-38
Lost Steps, The [book by Carpentier]
Latin American literature (The mid-1900's) **L:** 114
Lost Weekend, The [film]
Motion picture (Best picture: 1945) **M:** 861
Lost World, The [book by Jarrell]
Jarrell, Randall **J:** 63
Lost years [English literature]
Shakespeare, William (The lost years) **S:** 347
Lot [Biblical figure] **L:** 472
Abraham **A:** 17
Dead Sea **D:** 56
Sodom and Gomorrah **So:** 569
Lot [real estate]
House (Building a house) **H:** 380
Lothair I [Holy Roman emperor]
Germany (The breakup of Charlemagne's empire) **G:** 162
Verdun, Treaty of **V:** 316
Lothar of Segni *See* Innocent III *in this index*
Lotharingia [European history]
Verdun, Treaty of **V:** 317
Lotophagi [Greek mythology]
Lotus-eaters **L:** 473
"Lotos-Eaters, The" [poem by Tennyson]
Lotus-eaters **L:** 473
Lot's wife [Biblical figure]
Lot **L:** 472
Lötschberg Base Tunnel [Switzerland]
Alps (Alpine travel) **A:** 386
Tunnel (table) **T:** 491
Lott, Trent [American political leader] **L:** 472
Lottery L: 473
Gambling (Types of gambling) **G:** 20
New Hampshire (The mid-1900's) **N:** 226-227
"Lottery, The" [story by Jackson]
Jackson, Shirley **J:** 16
Lotus [plant] **L:** 473 *with picture*
Flower **F:** 271 *with picture, picture on* **F:** 292
Lotus-eaters [Greek mythology] **L:** 473
Odyssey: (Odysseus describes his wanderings) **O:** 675
Lotus position [yoga]

Yoga **Y:** 567
Lotze, Rudolf Hermann [German philosopher] **L:** 473
Lou Gehrig's disease *See* Amyotrophic lateral sclerosis *in this index*
Louangphrabang [Laos]
Indochina (A new kingdom) **I:** 225; (French influence) **I:** 225
Loubet, Émile [French political leader]
Dreyfus, Alfred (Efforts to clear Dreyfus's name) **D:** 347-348
Loud, John H. [American inventor]
Pen (History) **P:** 234
Louderback, Harold [American jurist]
Impeachment (History) **I:** 91-92
Loudness [sound]
Sound (table) **So:** 599; (Intensity and loudness) **So:** 600-601
Loudspeaker
Computer (Speakers) **Ci:** 917
Radio (The speaker) **R:** 89 *with picture*
Speaker **So:** 767
Stereophonic sound system (Parts of a stereo system) **So:** 892
Lough [lake]
Northern Ireland (Lakes, rivers, and bays) **N:** 523
Lough Leane [lake, Ireland]
Lakes of Killarney **L:** 49 *with map*
Lough Neagh [lake, Northern Ireland] **L:** 474
United Kingdom (The land) **U:** 58-61 *with map*
Loughead, Allan [American businessman]
Aviation (World War I) **A:** 987-988
Loughead, Malcolm [American businessman]
Invention (The early and middle 1900's) **I:** 363
Loughead, James [Canadian political leader]
Bennett, Richard Bedford (Entry into politics) **B:** 252
Lougheed, Peter [Canadian political leader]
Alberta (table) **A:** 328
Clark, Joe (Political worker and student) **Ci:** 640-641
Loughner, Jared [American public figure]
Arizona (The early 2000's) **A:** 692
Louis I [king of Hungary]
Hungary (The Kingdom of Hungary) **H:** 445
Louis I [king of Spain]
Philip V **P:** 370
Louis I [king of the Franks] **L:** 474
Louis II [prince of Monaco]
Monaco (History) **M:** 700
Louis II, the German [king of Germany]
Germany (The breakup of Charlemagne's empire) **G:** 162
Verdun, Treaty of **V:** 316
Louis VI [king of France]
France (table) **F:** 471
Louis VII [king of France]
Crusades (The Second Crusade) **Ci:** 1160
Eleanor of Aquitaine **E:** 157
France (table) **F:** 471
Louis VIII [king of France]
France (table) **F:** 471
Louis IX, Saint [king of France] **L:** 474
Clothing *picture on* **Ci:** 702
Crusades (Other Crusades) **Ci:** 1161
Louis X [king of France]
France (table) **F:** 471
Louis XI [king of France] **L:** 474
Charles VIII **C:** 381
France (A period of wars) **F:** 473
Postal services (The growth of public mail systems) **P:** 703
Louis XII [king of France] **L:** 474
Louis XIII [king of France] **L:** 474
Estates-General **E:** 360
France (The age of absolutism) **F:** 473
Hairdressing (The 1600's) **H:** 12
Huguenots (Flight from France) **H:** 411
Marie de Médicis **M:** 200
Orchestra (Beginnings) **O:** 822
Richelieu, Cardinal **R:** 331
Swiss Guard **So:** 1049
Louis XIV [king of France] **L:** 474 *with portrait*
Anne of Austria **A:** 517
Ballet (The rise of professional ballet) **B:** 51
Canada, History of (The royal province) **C:** 140
Colbert, Jean Baptiste **Ci:** 760
Dance (Social dances) **D:** 26-27
Etiquette (The origins of etiquette) **E:** 374
France (The age of absolutism) **F:** 473
Huguenots (Flight from France) **H:** 411
Maintenon, Marquise de **M:** 93
Nantes, Edict of **N:** 11
Roman Catholic Church (Gallicanism) **R:** 408-409
Succession wars (The War of the Spanish Succession) **So:** 950
Versailles, Palace of **V:** 339

William III **W:** 308
Louis XIV style
Furniture (Louis XIV furniture) **F:** 575 *with picture*
Interior design (Style) **I:** 327
Louis XV [king of France] **L:** 475 *with portrait*
Pompadour, Marquise de **P:** 653
Louis XV style
Furniture (The Rococo style) **F:** 576-577 *with picture*
Louis XVI [king of France] **L:** 476 *with portrait*
Estates-General **E:** 360
France (The French Revolution) **F:** 474
French Revolution (Background) **F:** 524-525; (The revolution begins) **F:** 525; (The Legislative Assembly) **F:** 526; (The National Convention) **F:** 526
Marie Antoinette **M:** 200
Louis XVI style
Furniture (The neoclassical style) **F:** 577
Louis XVII [king of France] **L:** 476
Louis XVIII [king of France] **L:** 476 *with portrait*
Bourbon (In France) **B:** 516
Napoleon I (Exile to Elba) **N:** 16
Napoleonic Wars (The Hundred Days) **N:** 20
Ney, Michel **N:** 391
Louis, Joe [American boxer] **L:** 477
Boxing (Boxing's Golden Age) **B:** 532-532a *with picture*
Braddock, James J. **B:** 543
Marciano, Rocky **M:** 196
Louis, Morris [American artist]
Painting (Color-field painting) **P:** 85
Louis, Saint [king of France] *See* Louis IX, Saint, *in this index*
Louis Alexander of Battenberg [prince of Bulgaria]
Battenberg **B:** 167
Louis Napoleon [emperor of France] *See* Napoleon III *in this index*
Louis Philippe [king of France] **L:** 477
Caricature **C:** 238
Charles X [of France] **C:** 382
Foreign Legion (History) **F:** 386
France (The revolutions of 1830 and 1848) **F:** 474
July Revolution **J:** 190
Lafayette, Marquis de (Last years) **L:** 28
Louis S. St. Laurent National Historic Site [Quebec]: Canada (table: National historic sites) **C:** 115
Louis the Great [king of France] *See* Louis XIV *in this index*
Louis the Pious [king of the Franks] *See* Louis I *in this index*
Louisbourg [Nova Scotia] **L:** 477
Nova Scotia (The struggle in Acadia) **N:** 568
Louisbourg, Battle of [1745]
Louisbourg **L:** 477
Louisbourg, Battle of [1758]
Louisbourg **L:** 477
Quebec, Battle of **Q:** 37
Louisbourg, Fortress of [Nova Scotia]
Louisbourg **L:** 477
Nova Scotia (Places to visit) **N:** 560
Louise, Lake *See* Lake Louise *in this index*
Louise de Marillac, Saint [French religious leader]
Nun **N:** 608
Roman Catholic Church (Catholic revival in France) **R:** 408
Louise of Mecklenburg-Strelitz [queen of Prussia] **L:** 477
Louisiana **L:** 478 *with pictures and maps*
See also the list of Related articles in the Louisiana *article*
Cajuns **C:** 19
Creationism (The 1900's) **Ci:** 1123-1124
Exploration (The French and English in North America) **E:** 446-447
Hurricane Katrina **H:** 456 *with picture*
Long **L:** 445
Mississippi Scheme **M:** 649
New France (The British conquest) **N:** 205
Louisiana moss [plant] *See* Spanish moss *in this index*
Louisiana Purchase [U.S. history] **L:** 502 *with maps*
Iowa (Territorial days) **I:** 393
Jefferson, Thomas (The Louisiana Purchase) **J:** 85 *with picture*
Livingston, Robert R. **L:** 399
Louisiana (Territorial days) **L:** 498
Missouri (Settlement) **M:** 669
Nebraska (The Louisiana Purchase) **N:** 111
Oklahoma (American ownership) **O:** 731
Texas (The mission period) **T:** 204-206
United States, History of the *map on* **U:** 184; (The Louisiana Purchase) **U:** 164 *with picture and map*
Westward movement in America (The Louisiana

Purchase) **W:** 248
Louisiana Purchase Exposition [Saint Louis]
Missouri *picture on* **M:** 672; (Progress as a state) **M:** 671
World's fair **W:** 500
Louisiana State Museum
Louisiana (Museums) **L:** 483
Louisiana State University L: 503
Louisiana *picture on* **L:** 483
Louisiana Story [film]
Flaherty, Robert Joseph **F:** 225
Thomson, Virgil **T:** 265
Louisiana Superdome
New Orleans (Downtown New Orleans) **N:** 278-279 *with picture*; (The early 2000's) **N:** 285
Louisiana tanager [bird]
Tanager **T:** 24
Louisiana Territory [U.S. history]
Lewis and Clark expedition (Jefferson's plans) **L:** 222
Louisiana Purchase (Boundary disputes) **L:** 503
Westward movement in America (The Louisiana Purchase) **W:** 248
"Louisiana Trilogy" [music by Gottschalk]
Gottschalk, Louis Moreau **G:** 280
Louisiana waterthrush [bird]
Bird (Birds of inland waters and marshes) **B:** 340 *with picture*
Louisianian, The [newspaper]
Pinchback, P. B. S. **P:** 467
Louisville [Kentucky] **L:** 504 *with picture and map*
Kentucky *picture on* **K:** 273; (table: Average monthly weather) **K:** 286
Louisville, University of
Louisville (Cultural life) **L:** 505
Louisville/Jefferson County Metro Government
Louisville **L:** 504
Louisville Jockey Club [organization]
Louisville (History) **L:** 506
Loulé [Portugal]
Portugal *picture on* **P:** 689
Lounsbury, George E. [American political leader]
Connecticut (table) **Ci:** 967
Lounsbury, Phineas C. [American political leader]
Connecticut (table) **Ci:** 967
Lourdes [France] **L:** 507
Lourenço Marques [former name]
Maputo **M:** 189
Louse [insect] **L:** 507 *with picture*
Relapsing fever **R:** 209
Skin (Infections) **S:** 490
Louse, Plant [insect] *See* Aphid *in this index*
Lousewort [plant]
Figwort family **F:** 97
Flower (Flowers of the Arctic tundra) **F:** 283 *with picture*
Louverture, Toussaint [Haitian patriot] *See* Toussaint Louverture *in this index*
Louvre [museum, Paris] **L:** 507
Paris (Famous buildings) **P:** 163 *with picture and map*; (Museums and art galleries) **P:** 164 *with picture*
Lovastatin [drug]
Cholesterol (Treatment of high blood cholesterol) **C:** 520
Heart (Treatment) **H:** 138
Love [book by Morrison]
Morrison, Toni **M:** 817
Love [emotion]
Cupid **Ci:** 1193
Empedocles **E:** 261
Sexuality (Love and sex) **S:** 338b
Love [tennis]
Tennis (Scoring) **T:** 162-163
Love, Augustus E. H. [British physicist]
Earthquake (Surface waves) **E:** 38
Love, John A. [American political leader]
Colorado (table) **Ci:** 844
Love, Mike [American musician]
Beach Boys **B:** 179 *with picture*
Love, Nat [American frontiersman] **L:** 508 *with portrait*
Love apple
Tomato (History) **T:** 325
Love Canal [New York]
Environmental pollution (Hazardous waste) **E:** 334-335
New York (The late 1900's) **N:** 319-320
Love for Love [play by Congreve]
Congreve, William **Ci:** 949
Love for Three Oranges, The [opera by Prokofiev]
Prokofiev, Sergei Sergeyevich **P:** 817
Love-lies-bleeding [plant]
Amaranth **A:** 400 *with picture*
Love of Zion [book by Mapu]
Hebrew literature (Modern Hebrew literature) **H:** 162

Love potion
Mandrake **M:** 137
"Love Song of J. Alfred Prufrock, The" [poem by Eliot]
Eliot, T. S. (His works) **E:** 237
Love! Valour! Compassion! [play by McNally]
Drama (Later United States drama) **D:** 340-341
McNally, Terrence **M:** 344
Love wave [physics]
Earthquake *diagram on* **E:** 34; (Surface waves) **E:** 38
Lovebird [bird] **L:** 508 *with picture*
Parakeet **P:** 151
Parrot (Kinds of parrots) **P:** 179
Pet *picture on* **P:** 320
Lovebug [insect] **L:** 508
Lovecraft, H. P. [American author] **L:** 508
American literature (Popular forms) **A:** 422-423
Derleth, August D: 152
Loved and the Lost, The [book by Callaghan]
Callaghan, Morley **C:** 67
Lovejoy, Asa L. [American settler]
Portland [Oregon] **P:** 683
Lovejoy, Elijah Parish [American social reformer] **L:** 508
Abolition movement **A:** 13
Phillips, Wendell **P:** 382
Lovelace, Ada [British mathematician]
Computer (Punched-card devices) **Ci:** 924a-924b
Lovelace, Richard [English poet] **L:** 509
Loveless, Herschel C. [American political leader]
Iowa (table) **I:** 391
Lovell, Sir Bernard [British astronomer] **L:** 509
Lovell, James Arthur, Jr. [American astronaut] **L:** 509
Astronaut (Achievements in space) **A:** 829
Space exploration (Orbiting the moon) **So:** 715
Lovell, Robert [British social reformer]
Southey, Robert **So:** 688b
Lovell House [Los Angeles]
Neutra, Richard Joseph **N:** 153 *with picture*
Lovell Telescope
Jodrell Bank Observatory **J:** 130
Lovell, Sir Bernard **L:** 509
Lovelock [hair]
Hairdressing (The 1600's) **H:** 12
Lovelock, James E. [British chemist]
Gaia **G:** 6
Lovelock Cave
Nevada (Indian days) **N:** 173
Lover, The [novel by Yehoshua]
Hebrew literature (A new generation of Hebrew writers) **H:** 163
Lovers with Two Attendants [painting]
Painting *picture on* **P:** 45
Love's Labour's Lost [play by Shakespeare]
Shakespeare, William (The years of fame) **S:** 347; (Love's Labour's Lost) **S:** 357
Love's Martyr [book]
Shakespeare, William ("The Phoenix and the Turtle") **S:** 367
Loves of a Blonde [film]
Motion picture (Movies in the 1960's) **M:** 870-871
Lovesick [book by Mastretta]
Latin American literature (The post-Boom) **L:** 114
Lovett, Robert A. [American government official]
Defense, Department of (table) **D:** 87
Truman, Harry S. (table) **T:** 469
Low [meteorology]
Storm (Polar lows) **So:** 913
Weather (Air pressure) **W:** 157; (table: Weather terms) **W:** 157; (Synoptic-scale systems) **W:** 159-161
Wind (Synoptic-scale circulations) **W:** 329
Low, Frederick F. [American political leader]
California (table) **C:** 59
Low, Juliette Gordon [American public figure] **L:** 509
Girl Scouts (History) **G:** 200
Savannah **S:** 165
Low altitude orbit
Satellite, Artificial (Satellite orbits) **S:** 150d *with picture*
Low-compression engine
Gasoline engine (High and low compression) **G:** 63
Low Countries [region, Europe]
Belgium (Habsburg rule) **B:** 233
Netherlands (Early days) **N:** 148
Low Country [region]
South Carolina **So:** 640
Low-density lipoprotein [physiology]
Cholesterol **C:** 520
Physical fitness (Cholesterol levels) **P:** 434
Trans fats **T:** 369
Low density polyethylene [plastic]
Polyethylene **P:** 650

Low Earth orbit satellite
Communications satellite (Types of satellites)
Ci: 888a
Low-emissivity window [device]
Light (Light and energy efficiency) L: 291-292
Low energy density food
Weight control (Dieting) W: 181-182
Low explosive
Ammunition (The propellant) A: 435
Explosive (Low explosives) E: 454
Low-fat food
Nutrition (Evaluate claims about foods and
dietary supplements carefully) N: 630
Low-flow toilet
Plumbing (How toilets work) P: 579-580
Low gear
Transmission (How a manual transmission works)
T: 377-378 with diagram
Low German [language]
German language (Low German) G: 138
Germany (Language) G: 150
Low islands [geography]
Pacific Islands (The land and climate) P: 7 with
picture
Low-level language [computing] See Machine
language in this index
Low-mass star
Star (Low-mass stars) So: 852
Low-pressure sodium vapor lamp
Electric light (Low-pressure sodium lamps) E: 175
Lighting (Efficient use of lighting) L: 297
Low-pressure tire
Tire (History) T: 297-298
Low profile tire
Tire (Low profile tires) T: 297 with diagrams
Low-sulfur coal
Coal (Coal as a fuel) Ci: 718
Low tide
Tide T: 280 with diagram
Low townsendia [plant]
Flower picture on F: 287
Lowboy [furniture]
Colonial life in America (Furnishings) Ci: 797-798
Lowden, Frank O. [American political leader]
Harding, Warren Gamaliel (The smoke-filled
room) H: 57
Illinois (table) I: 71
Lowe, Annie [Australian political leader]
Woman suffrage (Australia) W: 381
Lowe, Enoch Louis [American political leader]
Maryland (table) M: 255
Lowe, Ralph P. [American political leader]
Iowa (table) I: 391
Lowe, Thaddeus [American balloonist]
Balloon (Balloons in war) B: 61
Lowell [Massachusetts] L: 509
Lowell, Amy [American poet] L: 509
Lowell, Francis Cabot [American businessman]
L: 510
Industrial Revolution (Spread of the Industrial
Revolution) I: 252-253
Massachusetts (Progress as a state) M: 292
Lowell, James Russell [American poet] L: 510
American literature (Poetry) A: 418
Holmes, Oliver Wendell (His life) H: 294
June (Quotations) J: 193
Launfal, Sir L: 121
Magazine (Magazines in the 1800's) M: 45
May (Quotations) M: 321
Lowell, Percival [American astronomer] L: 510
Mars (Observation from Earth) M: 226c
Pluto P: 581
Lowell, Robert [American poet] L: 510
American literature ("Confessional" poetry)
A: 423 with portrait
Lowell National Historical Park [Massachusetts]
National Park System (table: National historical
parks) N: 56-57
Lowell Observatory [Arizona]
Flagstaff picture on F: 225
Lowell, Percival L: 510
Lower, Louis [American founder]
DeMolay International D: 129
Lower animal See Invertebrate in this index
Lower Avon [river, England]
Avon, River A: 994
Lower California [region, Mexico]
Mexico (The Pacific Northwest) M: 460
Lower Canada [Canadian history]
Canada, History of (The United Empire Loyalists)
C: 142 with map; (The struggle for responsible
government [1816-1867]) C: 143
Confederation of Canada (Early colonies of
Canada) Ci: 933
Ontario (Political unrest) O: 786
Papineau, Louis Joseph P: 139
Quebec (The 1700's) Q: 36-37

Rebellions of 1837 (In Lower Canada) R: 173
Union, Act of U: 27
Lower-case letter
Alphabet (Small letters) A: 383
Lower class [sociology]
City (The people) Ci: 578-580
Colonial life in America (The structure of colonial
society) Ci: 794
Social class (Class structure) So: 550
Lower Depths, The [play by Gorki]
Gorki, Maxim G: 276
Russian literature (Late realism) R: 562-563 with
picture
Lower East Side [district]
New York City (Manhattan) N: 323-324
Lower Egypt [Egyptian history]
Egypt, Ancient map on E: 136; (Beginnings)
E: 142
World, History of the (The Nile Valley) W: 424
Lower esophageal sphincter [physiology]
Acid reflux A: 27
Esophagus E: 357
Lower Falls [waterfall]
Spokane picture on So: 798
Lower Fort Garry National Historic Site
[Manitoba]
Canada (table: National historic sites) C: 115
Manitoba (Places to visit) M: 152
Lower Geyser Basin
Yellowstone National Park (The Lower Loop)
Y: 558 with map
Lower House [government]
Parliament (The House of Commons) P: 173
Lower Loop [road]
Yellowstone National Park (Touring Yellowstone)
Y: 558 with map
Lower middle class [sociology]
City (The people) Ci: 589-590
Lower Paleolithic Period
Prehistoric people (The Stone Age) P: 751
Lower risk species See Rare species in this index
Lowery, Samuel [American educator]
African Americans (During the late 1800's)
A: 136k-136l
Lowfat milk
Milk (table) M: 547
Löwig, Carl J. [German chemist]
Bromine B: 636
Lowland rice
Grass (Rice) G: 326
Lowlands
Scotland (Land regions) S: 217
Lowndes, Lloyd [American political leader]
Maryland (table) M: 255
Lowry, Lois [American author] L: 511
Newbery Medal (table) N: 359
Regina Medal (table: 1994) R: 206
Lowry, Malcolm [British author] L: 511
Lowry, Mike [American political leader]
Washington (table) W: 65
Lowry, Robert [American political leader]
Mississippi (table) M: 640
LOX [industrial product] See Liquid oxygen in this
index
Loya jirga [council]
Afghanistan (Government) A: 92-92a; (Recent
developments) A: 96
Loyal opposition [political science]
Democracy (Political parties) D: 120-121
Loyal Order of Moose [organization]
Moose International, Inc. M: 799
Loyalist House [Saint John]
New Brunswick (Places to visit) N: 188
Loyalist Province [nickname]
New Brunswick N: 181
Loyalists [North American history]
See also United Empire Loyalists in this index
New Brunswick (British settlement) N: 196
Nova Scotia (Progress as a province) N: 568-570
Revolution, American (Progress of the war)
R: 278; (Patriot governments) R: 280
Washington, George (Symbol of independence)
W: 98
Loyalists [Spanish history] See Republicans in this
index
Loyalties [play by Galsworthy]
Galsworthy, John G: 17
Loyalty board [U.S. history]
McCarthyism M: 332c
Loyalty Islands [Pacific]
New Caledonia N: 200
Loyalty oath
Johnson, Andrew (Plans for Reconstruction)
J: 139-140
Naturalization N: 67 with picture
Un-American Activities Committee U: 19
Loyola, Saint Ignatius [Spanish religious leader]

L: 511
Canisius, Saint Peter C: 177
Jesuits (History) J: 103
Xavier, Saint Francis X: 543
Lozeau, Albert [Canadian poet]
Canadian literature (Poetry: 1850-1918) C: 157
Lozenge
Heraldry picture on H: 195
LP gas See Liquefied petroleum gas in this index
LP record
Phonograph (How phonographs work) P: 400;
(History) P: 401-402
Recording industry (History) R: 182
LPG [gas] See Liquefied petroleum gas in this index
LPGA [organization]
Golf (Tournaments) G: 264; (Women's golf)
G: 266
LPN [occupation] See Licensed practical nurse in
this index
Lr [symbol]
Lawrencium L: 147
LSD [drug] L: 511
Brain (How drugs affect brain chemistry) B: 556
Drug abuse (Hallucinogenic drugs) D: 362; (table:
Some commonly abused drugs) D: 363
Hallucinogenic drug H: 26
Ltd. [business]
Limited company L: 308
LTTE [terrorist group] See Liberation Tigers of Tamil
Eelam in this index
Lu [symbol]
Lutetium L: 527
Lu Xun [Chinese author]
Chinese literature (Modern Chinese literature)
C: 512
Lualaba River [Africa]
Congo River Ci: 940f
Luanda [Angola] L: 511
Angola picture on A: 466
Stanley and Livingstone (Livingstone's
discoveries) So: 837 with map
Luapula River [Zambia]
Lake Bangweulu L: 36
Luau [custom]
Hawaii (Food) H: 94
Luba [former kingdom]
Congo, Democratic Republic of the (Early days)
Ci: 940b
Luba [people] L: 512
Lubber grasshopper [insect]
Grasshopper pictures on G: 327; (Short-horned
grasshoppers) G: 328
Lubbock [Texas] L: 512
Lubbock, Francis R. [American political leader]
Texas (table) T: 203
Lube distillate [petroleum]
Gas oil G: 60
Lübeck [Germany] L: 513
City (The people) Ci: 582
Lübeck, Treaty of [1629]
Thirty Years' War (The Danish period) T: 260
Lubricant
Bearing (Plain bearings) B: 188
Petroleum (Other uses) P: 333
Lubrication system
Automobile (The lubrication system) A: 953
Gasoline engine (The lubrication system) G: 66
Invention picture on I: 361
Lubricator cup [device]
McCoy, Elijah M: 332f
Lubs, Herbert [American geneticist]
Fragile X syndrome F: 450
Lucan [Roman poet]
Latin literature (The Imperial Period) L: 116
Lucas, Anthony F. [American industrialist]
Beaumont B: 191
Lucas, Frank E. [American political leader]
Wyoming (table) W: 532
Lucas, George [American director] L: 513
Ford, Harrison Fo: 379
Motion picture (A new generation of filmmakers)
M: 871
Star Wars So: 855
Lucas, Louis [French chemist]
Glass (Glass) G: 218
Lucas, Robert [American political leader]
Iowa (Territorial days) I: 393-395; (Statehood)
I: 395
Ohio (table) O: 699
Lucas, Robert Emerson, Jr. [American economist]
Economics (Modern economics) E: 64-65
Nobel Prizes (Economics: 1995) N: 449
Lucas Oil Stadium
Indianapolis (History) I: 222-223
LucasArts Entertainment Company
Lucas, George L: 513
Lucayo Indians

Bahamas (History) **B:** 29
Lucca Madonna [painting by Van Eyck]
   Van Eyck, Jan *picture on* **V:** 282
Luce, Clare Boothe [American diplomat] **L:** 513
Luce, Cyrus G. [American political leader]
   Michigan (table) **M:** 507
Luce, Henry Robinson [American publisher] **L:** 513
   Journalism (The age of sensationalism) **J:** 175
Luce, Stephen B. [American military leader]
   Naval War College **N:** 70
Lucent Technologies, Inc.
   AT&T Inc. **A:** 852
Lucerne [Switzerland] **L:** 513
Lucerne [plant]
   Alfalfa **A:** 345 *with pictures*
Lucerne, Lake of [Switzerland]
   Lake of Lucerne **L:** 42
Lucerne, Lion of [sculpture by Thorvaldsen]
   Lucerne **L:** 513
   Swiss Guard **So:** 1049
Lucey, Patrick J. [American political leader]
   Wisconsin (table) **W:** 365
Lucha libre [wrestling] **L:** 513
Luchadore [wrestler]
   Lucha libre **L:** 513
Lucia di Lammermoor [opera by Donizetti]
   Donizetti, Gaetano **D:** 307
   Opera: *(Lucia di Lammermoor)* **O:** 804
Lucian of Samosata [Greek author]
   Greek literature (The Greco-Roman Age) **G:** 378
Lucid, Shannon Wells [American astronaut] **L:** 514
   with portrait
   Astronaut (table) **A:** 830
   Space exploration (Docking with Mir) **So:** 725
Lucid dream
   Dream (The content of dreams) **D:** 344
Lucier, Etienne [American settler]
   Portland [Oregon] (History) **P:** 684
Lucifer [Biblical figure] **L:** 514
Lucilius, Gaius [Roman author]
   Latin literature (Early Latin literature) **L:** 115-116
Lucius I, Saint [pope]
   Pope (table) **P:** 666
Lucius II [pope]
   Pope (table) **P:** 666
Lucius III [pope]
   Pope (table) **P:** 666
Lucius Tarquinius Priscus [legendary figure]
   Mythology (The seven kings) **M:** 983
Lucius Tarquinius Superbus [legendary figure]
   Mythology (The seven kings) **M:** 983
Lucius Verus [Roman emperor]
   Marcus Aurelius **M:** 197
   Rome, Ancient (table) **R:** 447
Luck
   Superstition **So:** 995
"Luck of Roaring Camp, The" [story by Harte]
   Harte, Bret **H:** 78
Lucknow [India] **L:** 514
Lucky Jim [book by Amis]
   Amis, Kingsley **A:** 432
Lucky Lindy [nickname]
   Lindbergh, Charles Augustus **L:** 330
Lucretius [Roman philosopher] **L:** 514
   Atomism **A:** 877
   Latin literature (The age of Cicero) **L:** 116
   Materialism **M:** 300b
Lucumo [king]
   Etruscans (Government and economy) **E:** 375
Lucy [hominid]
   Australopithecus **A:** 927
   Johanson, Donald Carl **J:** 131
   Prehistoric people (Types of australopithecines)
   P: 745; (table) **P:** 754
Lucy Stoner [U.S. history]
   Stone, Lucy **So:** 909
Luddites [British history]
   Industrial Revolution (The working class) **I:** 251-252
   Riot (Causes of riots) **R:** 348
Ludendorff, Erich Friedrich Wilhelm [German
   general] **L:** 514
   Hindenburg, Paul von **H:** 234
   World War I (The Eastern Front) **W:** 456; (The
   Battle of Verdun) **W:** 458; (The last campaigns)
   W: 463
Ludington, Harrison [American political leader]
   Wisconsin (table) **W:** 365
Ludington, Henry [American military leader]
   Ludington, Sybil **L:** 515
Ludington, Sybil [American patriot] **L:** 515
Ludlow, George C. [American political leader]
   New Jersey (table) **N:** 249
Ludus [teacher]
   Education (Ancient Roman education) **E:** 98
Ludwig [prince of Bavaria]
   Oktoberfest **O:** 738

Ludwig II [king of Bavaria] **L:** 515
Ludwig, Emil [German-Swiss author]
   Biography (Modern biography) **B:** 314
Luffa [plant]
   Gourd **G:** 281 *with picture*
Luffing [sailing]
   Sailing (Basic sailing maneuvers) **S:** 26
Luftwaffe [military] **L:** 515
   Air force (The German air force) **A:** 184; (World
   War II) **A:** 185
   World War II (The Battle of Britain) **W:** 476
Luganda [language]
   Ganda **G:** 24
Lugano [Switzerland]
   Lake Lugano **L:** 40
   Switzerland (table: Average monthly weather)
   So: 1056
Lugano, Lake [Switzerland]
   Lake Lugano **L:** 40
Lugbait [sea animal] *See* Lugworm *in this index*
Luge [sport] **L:** 515 *with picture*
   Olympic Games (Winter Olympic Games) **O:** 746d
Luger [gun]
   Handgun *picture on* **H:** 44
Luger, George [Austrian-born inventor]
   Handgun (Rapid-fire handguns) **H:** 45
Lugh [Celtic god]
   Cuchulainn **Ci:** 1182
Lugnasadh [holiday]
   Witchcraft (Witchcraft as a religion) **W:** 371-372
Lugo, Fernando [Paraguayan political leader]
   Mercosur **M:** 413
   Paraguay (Recent developments) **P:** 150 *with
   picture*
Lugosi, Bela [Hungarian-born actor] **L:** 515
Lugworm [sea animal] **L:** 516
Luisetti, Hank [American basketball player] **L:** 516
   Basketball *picture on* **B:** 153; (Changes in the
   game) **B:** 151-152
Lujack, Johnny [American football player]
   Football (table) **F:** 363
Lujan, Manuel, Jr. [American government official]
   Interior, Department of the (table) **I:** 325
Lukas, Paul [Hungarian actor]
   Motion picture (Best performance by an actor:
   1943) **M:** 862a
Lukashenko, Aleksandr [Belarusian political
   leader]
   Belarus (Recent developments) **B:** 224b-224c
Luke, Gospel of [New Testament]
   Bible (The Gospels) **B:** 283
   Gospels **G:** 278
   Jesus Christ (Sources of information about Jesus)
   J: 104; (Early life) **J:** 105; (Public life) **J:** 106; (The
   Passion) **J:** 108
   New Testament (Contents) **N:** 287; (Critical
   studies) **N:** 288
Luke, Saint [early Christian] **L:** 516
   See also Luke, Gospel of *in this index*
   Acts of the Apostles **A:** 31
   Gospels **G:** 278
Lukeman, Henry A. [American sculptor]
   Stone Mountain **So:** 910
Lukoil [company]
   Manufacturing (table) **M:** 170
Luks, George Benjamin [American artist] **L:** 516
   Ashcan School **A:** 768
Lukuga River [Congo]
   Lake Tanganyika **L:** 46 *with map*
Lula da Silva, Luiz Inácio [Brazilian political leader]
   Brazil (The early 2000's) **B:** 586
   Latin America (In the early 2000's) **L:** 111
LULAC [organization] *See* League of United Latin
   American Citizens *in this index*
Lulach [king of Scotland]
   Macbeth **M:** 5
Lullaby [music]
   Nursery rhyme (Lullabies) **N:** 615
Lully, Jean-Baptiste [French composer] **L:** 516
   Overture **O:** 882
Lulu [opera by Berg]
   Berg, Alban **B:** 257
Lumbar puncture [medicine] *See* Spinal tap *in
   this index*
Lumbar vertebra [anatomy]
   Skeleton (The axial skeleton) **S:** 479-480 *with
   diagram*
   Spine **So:** 792 *with diagram*
Lumbee Indians L: 516
   Lost Colony **L:** 472
Lumber L: 517 *with pictures*
   See also Logging; Wood *in this index*
   Colonial life in America (Lumbering and
   shipbuilding) **Ci:** 810 *with picture*
   Forest (Economic value) **F:** 391
   Forest products **F:** 400 *with pictures*
   House (Building materials) **H:** 380

Weyerhaeuser, Frederick W: 253
Lumberjack
   Birling **B:** 375
Lumen [measurement]
   Candela **C:** 175
   Electric light (Incandescent lamps) **E:** 174
   Lighting (Quantity of light) **L:** 297
   Metric system (Light) **M:** 440
Lumière, Auguste [French inventor]
   Lumière brothers **L:** 522
Lumière, Louis Jean [French inventor]
   Lumière brothers **L:** 522
Lumière brothers [French inventors] **L:** 522
   Motion picture (The invention of motion
   pictures) **M:** 863 *with picture*
   Photography (Dramatic changes) **P:** 425
Luminal [drug]
   Anticonvulsant **A:** 553
Luminance signal [electronics]
   Television (Encoding the color signals) **T:** 123
Luminescence [light] **L:** 522
   Bioluminescence **B:** 322
   Light (Luminescence and fluorescence) **L:** 283
   Phosphorescence **P:** 402
Luminol [chemical]
   Crime scene investigation (Collecting evidence)
   Ci: 1140-1141
Luminosity [astronomy]
   Star *diagram on* **So:** 844; (Characteristics of
   stars) **So:** 842; (Evolution of stars) **So:** 848 *with
   diagram*
Luminous flux
   Light (The brightness of light) **L:** 290-291
   Metric system (Light) **M:** 440
Luminous intensity [physics]
   Foot-candle **F:** 353
   Light (Energy and brightness) **L:** 290
   Metric system (Light) **M:** 440
Luminous Mysteries [religion]
   Rosary **R:** 474
Lummus, John N. [American businessman]
   Miami Beach **M:** 482
Lumpectomy [surgery]
   Breast cancer **B:** 591
   Cancer (Surgery) **C:** 172
   Mastectomy **M:** 297
Lumpfish [fish] **L:** 522 *with picture*
Lumpkin, Wilson [American political leader]
   Georgia (table) **G:** 130
Lumpy jaw [disease]
   Actinomycosis **A:** 30
Lumumba, Patrice [Congolese political leader]
   Cold War (Africa) **Ci:** 768
   Congo, Democratic Republic of the
   (Independence) **Ci:** 940b-940c
Lun Dayeh [people]
   Rain forest (Asia) **R:** 126b
Luna [mythology] **L:** 523
   See also Selene *in this index*
Luna [space probes]
   Moon (Apollo missions) **M:** 795
   Space exploration (Lunar probes) **So:** 708-709
   Luna 2
      Solar wind **So:** 582
   Luna 3
      Moon **M:** 783
   Luna 16
      Astronomy (Direct sampling) **A:** 846
Luna, Count di [opera character]
   Opera: *(Trovatore, Il)* **O:** 808
Luna moth
   Insect *picture on* **I:** 291
   Moth *picture on* **M:** 840
Luna y Arellano, Tristán de [Spanish frontiersman]
   Alabama (European exploration and settlement)
   A: 275
   Pensacola **P:** 272
Lunar caustic [chemical]
   Silver nitrate **S:** 465
Lunar Crater Observation and Sensing Satellite
   Moon (Recent exploration) **M:** 795
Lunar day
   Moon (Rotation and orbit) **M:** 783
Lunar eclipse
   Eclipse **E:** 51 *with diagram*
   Moon (Eclipses) **M:** 784
Lunar module [spacecraft]
   Space exploration (Apollo: Mission to the moon)
   So: 714-715 *with pictures*
Lunar month
   Calendar **C:** 29
Lunar orbit rendezvous
   Space exploration (Apollo: Mission to the moon)
   So: 714-715
Lunar Orbiter [space probes]
   Space exploration (Lunar probes) **So:** 708-709
Lunar probe

Space exploration (Lunar probes) So: 708 *with picture*
Lunar Prospector [space probe]
Moon (Recent exploration) M: 795
Space exploration (Lunar probes) So: 708-710
Lunar Reconnaissance Orbiter [spacecraft]
Moon (Recent exploration) M: 795
Space exploration (Lunar probes) So: 708-710
Lunar roving vehicle
Moon *picture on* M: 791
Space exploration *picture on* So: 720; (Other moon landings) So: 719
Lunar year
Calendar C: 29
Year (The calendar year) Y: 554
Lunate bone
Hand (Parts of the hand) H: 40
Wrist *diagram on* W: 510
Luncheon of the Boating Party, The [painting by Renoir]
Painting (Edouard Manet and the impressionists) P: 71-72
Renoir, Pierre Auguste *picture on* R: 241
Luncheon on the Grass [painting by Manet]
Manet, Édouard M: 138
Lunda [former kingdom]
Congo, Democratic Republic of the (Early days) Ci: 940b
Lunda L: 523
Lunda [people] L: 523
Lundstrom, John [Swedish manufacturer]
Match (The first safety matches) M: 300a
Lundy, Benjamin [American social reformer] L: 523
Garrison, William Lloyd G: 45
United States, History of the (The abolition movement) U: 173
Lundy's Lane, Battle of [1814]
War of 1812 (Lundy's Lane) W: 32
Lunéville, Treaty of [1801]
Napoleon I (Peacemaking) N: 15
Napoleonic Wars (A brief peace) N: 18
Lung [anatomy] L: 523 *with diagrams*
Amphibian (Breathing) A: 440
Animal (Adaptations for breathing) A: 491-492 *with picture*
Asthma A: 824b
Blood (Carrying oxygen and carbon dioxide) B: 408 *with diagram*
Bronchodilator B: 637
Chronic obstructive pulmonary disease C: 539
Cough Ci: 1095
Death (Defining death) D: 61
Emphysema (How emphysema affects breathing) E: 262 *with diagrams*
Frog *picture on* F: 537
Hantavirus H: 54
Heart (The work of the heart) H: 135 *with diagrams*
Human body (table) H: 422 *with diagram*
Hyperventilation H: 477
Lung cancer L: 525
Pneumonia P: 586
Silicosis S: 458
Tuberculosis T: 477 *with pictures*
Lung Association, American
American Lung Association A: 428
Lung cancer [disease] L: 525
Cancer (Classification by primary body site) C: 167-168 *with diagrams*; (table) C: 170
Cigarette C: 553
Radon (How radon affects health) R: 100
Smoking S: 520
Lung capacity
Spirometer So: 797
Lungfish [fish] L: 525
Coelacanth Ci: 752
Fish (Fleshy-finned fish) F: 148 *with picture*; (How fish rest) F: 166-167
Lungi [clothing]
Bangladesh (Way of life) B: 80-81
Pakistan (Clothing) P: 96
Lungwort [botany] L: 525
Lunt, Alfred [American actor] L: 526
Fontanne, Lynn F: 327
Lunula [anatomy]
Nail N: 4
Lunule [zoology]
Shell *diagram on* S: 385
Luoyang [China]
Han dynasty H: 38 *with map*
Lupercalia [history of Rome]
Valentine's Day (Beginnings) V: 261
Lupine [plant] L: 526
Flower (Garden perennials) F: 278 *with picture, picture on* F: 283
Prince Edward Island *picture on* P: 790a
Luppis, Giovanni [Austrian seaman]

Torpedo (History) T: 341
Lupus [disease] L: 526
Lupus erythematosus [disease]
Lupus L: 526
Lupus vulgaris [disease]
Lupus L: 526
Luray Caverns [Virginia] L: 526
Cave (table) C: 320
Stalactite So: 824 *with picture*
Lurçat, Jean [French artist]
Tapestry (History) T: 39-40
Lure [fishing]
Fishing *pictures on* F: 177
Luria, Salvador Edward [Italian-American biologist]
Nobel Prizes (Physiology or medicine: 1969) N: 446
Lurton, Horace H. [American jurist]
Supreme Court of the United States (table) So: 1000
Lusaka [Zambia] L: 526
Zambia Z: 584, *picture on* Z: 586
Lüshun [China] L: 526
Russo-Japanese War R: 566a
Lusíadas, Os [poem by Camões]
Portugal (The arts) P: 689-690
Lusignan, Guy de [French nobleman]
Cyprus (History) Ci: 1207
Lusitania [former country]
Portugal (Roman rule) P: 692
Lusitania [ship] L: 526
Submarine (World Wars I and II) So: 943
United States, History of the (The United States in the war) U: 188
Wilson, Woodrow (World War I begins) W: 324
World War I (The war at sea) W: 460; (The United States enters the war) W: 462
Lussac, Joseph Louis Gay- [French chemist] *See* Gay-Lussac, Joseph Louis *in this index*
Luster [physical property]
Mineral (Luster) M: 567
Wood (Wood figure) W: 390
Luster painting [art]
Islamic art *picture on* I: 468; (Pottery) I: 470
Lute [musical instrument] L: 527 *with picture*
Dowland, John D: 316
Music (Stringed instruments) M: 948-949 *with picture*
Lutefisk [food]
Christmas (Christmas feasting) C: 534-535
Luteinizing hormone
Hormone (Growth and sex hormones) H: 336
Menstruation (Ovulation) *diagram on* M: 403
Lutetia [name for Paris]
Lutetium L: 527
Paris (Early days) P: 166
Lutetium [element] L: 527
Luther [play by Osborne]
Osborne, John O: 861
Luther, Martin [German religious leader] L: 527 *with picture*
Augsburg Confession A: 885
Bible (Early English translations) B: 285
Christianity (The Reformation) C: 524 *with picture*
Classical music (The Reformation) Ci: 646
Eck, Johann E: 50
Evangelicalism E: 422
German literature (Between the golden ages [1250-1750]) G: 139
Germany (The Reformation) G: 164 *with picture*
Holocaust (Before the Holocaust) H: 296
Hymn (History) H: 475
Leo X L: 198
Lutherans L: 529
Melanchthon, Philipp M: 388
Peasants' War P: 224
Predestination P: 734
Protestantism (History) P: 834
Reformation (Martin Luther) R: 197
Roman Catholic Church (The Reformation) R: 408
Worms W: 501
Worms, Edict of W: 501
Zwingli, Huldreich (His ideas) Z: 610
Lutheran church *See* Lutherans *in this index*
Lutheran Church in America [religious group]
Evangelical Lutheran Church in America E: 421
Lutheran Church—Missouri Synod [religious group] L: 529
Lutherans [religious group] L: 529
Augsburg Confession A: 885
Christianity (Protestant churches) C: 522g; (The Reformation) C: 524
Luther, Martin (Building and defending the church) L: 528
Muhlenberg, Henry Melchior M: 911
Norway (Religion) N: 541
Protestantism (The conservative reform

movements) P: 834
Reformation (Martin Luther) R: 197
Religious life (Religious life in the 1700's and 1800's) R: 227
Sweden (Religion) So: 1024; (The beginnings of modern Sweden) So: 1033-1034; (Recent developments) So: 1035
Luthuli, Albert John [South African social reformer] L: 529
Lutine [ship]
Insurance *picture on* I: 316
Lutyens, Sir Edwin Landseer [British architect] L: 530
New Delhi (History) N: 203
Lützen, Battles of [German history]
Thirty Years' War (The Swedish period) T: 260
Luwian [language]
Hittites (Way of life) H: 269
Lux [measurement]
Foot-candle F: 353
Lux Mundi [book by Gore]
Oxford Movement O: 888
Luxembourg [country] L: 530 *with picture and map*
Benelux B: 248
Christmas (In The Netherlands, Belgium, and Luxembourg) C: 531
Euro E: 379
Flag *picture on* F: 206
World War II (The invasion of the Low Countries) W: 474
Luxembourg [city] L: 532
Luxembourg L: 530 *with picture*
Luxembourg Gardens
Paris (Gardens, squares, and parks) P: 162 *with picture and map*
Luxembourg Palace
Paris (Famous buildings) P: 163-164 *with picture and map*
Luxemburg, Rosa [German social reformer] L: 532
Luxor [Egypt]
Thebes T: 250
Luxor, Obelisk of
Paris (Gardens, squares, and parks) P: 162 *with picture*
Luyendyk, Arie [Dutch race driver]
Automobile racing (table: Indianapolis 500 winners) A: 980
Luzán, Ignacio [Spanish author]
Spanish literature (The 1700's) So: 760
Luzern [Switzerland]
Lucerne L: 513
Luzhniki Stadium
Moscow (Entertainment and recreation) M: 825
Luzon [island, Philippines]
Philippines (The main islands) P: 376 *with pictures and map*
LVAD [medicine] *See* Left-ventricular assist device *in this index*
Lviv [Ukraine] L: 532
Ukraine (Climate) U: 10
Lvov [Ukraine] *See* Lviv *in this index*
Lvov, George [Russian political leader]
Lenin, V. I. (The February Revolution) L: 193
Lwoff, André [French microbiologist]
Nobel Prizes (Physiology or medicine: 1965) N: 446
Lwów [Ukraine] *See* Lviv *in this index*
Ly [dynasty]
Vietnam (Independence) V: 370
Lycabettus [hill]
Athens (Landmarks) A: 854-855 *with map*
Lycaena orus [butterfly]
Butterfly *picture on* B: 734
Lycanthropy [psychology]
Werewolf W: 197
Lycaon [Greek mythology]
Werewolf W: 197
Lycée [school]
France (Education) F: 460-461
Lyceum [organization] L: 532
Adult education (History of adult education in the United States) A: 69
Lyceum [school, ancient Greece] L: 532
Aristotle (Aristotle's life) A: 663
Education (Ancient Greek education) E: 98
Library (Rome) L: 258
Lychee [tree]
Litchi L: 350 *with picture*
"Lycidas" [poem by Milton]
Idyl I: 47
Milton, John (His early life and works) M: 557
Lycophyte [plant]
Plant *pictures on* P: 522; (Vascular plants) P: 518; (Classification of plants) P: 546 *with pictures*
Lycurgus [Greek political leader] L: 532
Lycus, King [Greek mythology]
Farnese Bull F: 46

Lydia [ancient country] **L: 533** *with map*
Croesus **Ci: 1150**
Money (Early coins) **M: 705** *with picture*
Lye [chemical] *See* Sodium hydroxide *in this index*
Lyell, Sir Charles [British geologist] **L: 533**
Evolution (Darwin's theory) **E: 432**
Geology (Experimental geology) **G: 99**
Lyly, John [English author] **L: 533**
Drama (Elizabethan playwrights) **D: 331-332**
English literature (Elizabethan fiction) **E: 317**
Novel (Early novels) **N: 572**
Lyme disease L: 533
Deer tick **D: 86**
Tick **T: 279**
Lymph [physiology]
Lymphatic system **L: 533**
Cancer (How damaged genes cause cancer) **C: 169**
Human body (The lymphatic system) **H: 424**
Lymph node [anatomy]
Lymphatic system (Lymph nodes) **L: 534** *with diagram*; (Fighting infection) **L: 535**
Biopsy **B: 326**
Blood (Formation of new blood components) **B: 411-412**
Breast cancer **B: 591**
Cancer (Causes) **C: 170**; (Surgery) **C: 172**
Gland (Glandlike structures) **G: 208-209**
Hodgkin's disease **H: 283**
Human body (The lymphatic system) **H: 424**
Immune system (Parts of the immune system) **I: 87** *with diagram*
Lung cancer **L: 525**
Toxoplasmosis **T: 353**
Lymphatic filariasis [disease] *See* Elephantiasis *in this index*
Lymphatic system [physiology] **L: 533** *with diagrams*
Cancer (Classification by primary body site) **C: 167-168**
Edema **E: 75**
Human body (The lymphatic system) **H: 424**
Immune system (Parts of the immune system) **I: 87-88**
Lymphatic vessel [anatomy]
Human body (The lymphatic system) **H: 424**
Immune system *diagram on* **I: 88a**
Lymphatic system (Lymphatic vessels) **L: 534**; (Return of interstitial fluid) **L: 534-535** *with diagram*
Lymphedema [disorder]
Edema **E: 76**
Lymphocyte [physiology]
Blood (Protecting against disease) **B: 410**; (Formation of new blood components) **B: 411**
Immune system (Parts of the immune system) **I: 87**
Interferon **I: 324**
Lymphatic system (Lymphocytes) **L: 534**; (Fighting infection) **L: 535**
Thymus **T: 274**
Tonsil **T: 329**
Virus (Immune response) **V: 428a**
Lymphoid cell [physiology]
Leukemia **L: 215**
Lymphoid organ [physiology]
Immune system (Lymphocytes) **I: 87**
Lymphoid tissue [anatomy]
Lymphatic system (Lymphoid tissue) **L: 534**
Tonsil **T: 329**
Lymphokine [chemical]
Immune system (The cell-mediated immune response) **I: 88-88a**
Lymphoma [disease]
Cancer (Classification by primary body site) **C: 167-168**
Lynch, Charles [American military leader]
Lynching **L: 535**
Lynch, Charles [American political leader]
Mississippi (table) **M: 640**
Lynch, John [American political leader]
New Hampshire (table) **N: 223**
Lynch, John M. [Irish government official]
Ireland (table) **I: 428**
Lynch, Thomas, Jr. [American patriot] **L: 535**
Lynch v. Donnelly [U.S. history]
Supreme Court of the United States (table) **So: 1002**
Lynching [crime] **L: 535**
Wells-Barnett, Ida Bell **W: 195**
Lyndon B. Johnson National Historical Park [Texas]
National Park System (table: National historical parks) **N: 56-57**
Lyndon B. Johnson Space Center *See* Johnson Space Center *in this index*
Lyndon Baines Johnson Library and Museum

[Austin]
Austin (Description) **A: 892-893** *with picture*
Texas (Libraries) **T: 188-189**
Lyndon Baines Johnson Memorial Grove on the Potomac
National Park System (table: National memorials) **N: 54**
Lynen, Feodor [German chemist] **L: 536**
Lyng, Richard E. [American government official]
Agriculture, Department of (table) **A: 161**
Reagan, Ronald Wilson (table) **R: 169**
Lynn, Loretta [American singer]
Country music (Modern country music) **Ci: 1098c**
Lynx L: 536 *with picture*
Animal *picture on* **A: 472**
Caracal **C: 200** *with picture*
Fur (table) **F: 561**
Lynx-hare cycle [zoology]
Taiga **T: 14**
Lyon [France] **L: 536** *with picture*
France *picture on* **F: 459**
French literature (Lyon) **F: 520**
Lyon, John [English educator]
Harrow School **H: 77**
Lyon, Mary [American educator] **L: 537**
Lyon, Nathaniel [American general]
Missouri (The American Civil War) **M: 671**
Lyon, Richard [American educator]
Bay Psalm Book **B: 176**
Lyon, Sterling R. [Canadian political leader]
Manitoba (table) **M: 159**
Lyons, Joseph A. [Australian political leader]
Australia (table) **A: 923**
Menzies, Sir Robert Gordon **M: 410**
Lyons, Ted [American baseball player]
Baseball (table: Hall of Fame) **B: 134a**
Lyophilization [industrial process]
Freeze-drying **F: 510**
Lyra [constellation] **L: 537**
LYRASIS [network]
Library (The growth of information and technology) **L: 237-238**
Lyre [musical instrument] **L: 537** *with picture*
Lyre of Orpheus, The [book by Davies]
Davies, Robertson **D: 46**
Lyrebird L: 537 *with picture*
Bird (Birds of Australia and New Zealand) **B: 346** *with picture*
Lyric Opera Company [Chicago]
See also opera in the Opera *article*
Chicago (The arts) **C: 428**
Lyric Pieces [music by Grieg]
Grieg, Edvard **G: 392**
Lyric poetry
English literature (Elizabethan poetry) **E: 316**
French literature (Early French literature) **F: 518**
Greek literature (Lyric poetry) **G: 377**
Poetry (Lyric poetry) **P: 591**
Lyric soprano
Opera (The singers) **O: 792**
Lyric Suite [music by Berg]
Berg, Alban **B: 257**
Lyric tenor
Opera (The singers) **O: 792**
Lyrical Ballads [poems by Coleridge and Wordsworth]
Coleridge, Samuel Taylor (His life) **Ci: 771**
English literature (Romantic poetry) **E: 320**
Poetry (Romantic poetry) **P: 597**
Wordsworth, William **W: 404**
Lyrics [music]
Musical comedy (Elements of musical comedy) **M: 959**
Lyrics of Earth [poems by Lampman]
Lampman, Archibald **L: 54**
Lysander [literary figure]
Shakespeare, William (*A Midsummer Night's Dream*) **S: 357**
Lysander [Spartan general] **L: 538**
Lysenko, Trofim Denisovich [Soviet biologist] **L: 538**
Lysergic acid diethylamide *See* LSD *in this index*
Lysias [Greek orator] **L: 538**
Lysin [protein]
Virus (Infection) **V: 428**
Lysippus [Greek sculptor] **L: 538**
Sculpture (Classical sculpture) **S: 245-246**
Lysistrata [play by Aristophanes]
Aristophanes **A: 663**
Lysithea [satellite]
Jupiter (Outer satellites) **J: 200a**
Lysosome [biology]
Cell (The cytoplasm) **C: 329** *with diagram*
Lysozyme [biology]
Computer graphics *picture on* **Ci: 924h**
Fleming, Sir Alexander **F: 232**
Lyte, Henry Francis [British clergyman] **L: 538**

Lytton, Baron [British author] *See* Bulwer-Lytton, Edward George Earle Lytton *in this index*
LZ-1 [airship]
Airship (The zeppelins) **A: 252**
LZ-127 [airship]
Airship (Between world wars) **A: 252**

M

M [letter] **M: 1** *with pictures*
M [film]
Lang, Fritz **L: 60**
Motion picture (The movies talk) **M: 867**
M-1 [money]
Money (The money supply) **M: 715**
M-1 Abrams Main Battle tank
Army, United States (Armor) **A: 734**
M1 rifle
Garand rifle **G: 28**
M1A1 tank
Tank *diagram on* **T: 27**
M-2 [money]
Money (The money supply) **M: 715**
M3 submachine gun
Machine gun (Ground weapons) *picture on* **M: 16**
M16 rifle
Garand rifle **G: 28**
M16A2 rifle
Rifle (Automatic and semiautomatic rifles) **R: 339** *with picture*
M31 [galaxy] *See* Andromeda Galaxy *in this index*
M33 [galaxy] *See* Triangulum Galaxy *in this index*
M60 machine gun
Machine gun (Ground weapons) **M: 16**
M83 [galaxy]
Astronomy *picture on* **A: 839**
M87 [galaxy]
Galaxy *picture on* **G: 8a**
M100 [galaxy]
Galaxy *picture on* **G: 8a**
M240B machine gun
Machine gun *picture on* **M: 15**
Ma, Yo-Yo [Chinese-born cellist] **M: 2**
Ma Duanlin [Chinese scholar]
Encyclopedia (From the 1200's to the 1600's) **E: 268a**
Ma huang [herb] *See* Ephedra *in this index*
Ma Rainey's Black Bottom [play by Wilson]
Wilson, August **W: 316**
Ma Ying-jeou [Taiwanese political leader]
Taiwan (History) **T: 17-18**
Ma Yuan [Chinese painter] **M: 2**
Maas River [river, Europe] *See* Meuse River *in this index*
Maasai [people] **M: 2**
Africa *picture on* **A: 116**
Cattle (Nomadic cattle raising) **C: 315**
Kenya (Way of life) **K: 298-299**
Tanzania (Population and ancestry) **T: 31**
Maasai Mara Game Reserve [Kenya]
Africa *picture on* **A: 98**
National park (table) **N: 42f**
Maasai Steppe
Tanzania (The plateaus) **T: 33** *with map*
Maastricht Treaty [1992] *See* European Union, Treaty on *in this index*
Maathai, Wangari Muta [Kenyan conservationist]
Nobel Prizes (Peace: 2004) **N: 449**
Maazel, Lorin [American conductor] **M: 2**
Mab, Queen [legendary figure]
Fairy (Trooping fairies) **F: 10**
Mabey, Charles R. [American political leader]
Utah (table) **U: 245**
Mabillon, Jean [French monk]
Paleography **P: 103**
Mabinogion [stories]
Mythology (Celtic mythology) **M: 984**
Wales (The arts) **W: 9-10**
Mabo v. Queensland [court case]
Australia (Aboriginal land decisions) **A: 925**
Mabovitz, Golda *See* Meir, Golda *in this index*
Mabry, Thomas J. [American political leader]
New Mexico (table) **N: 272**
Mabus, Ray [American political leader]
Mississippi (table) **M: 640**
Mac [dynasty]
Vietnam (Independence) **V: 370**
Mac...
Names beginning Mac *are alphabetized as single words:* MacArthur, Charles, *appears after* Macaroni. *Names beginning* Mc *appear after headings beginning* Mb
Mac Bethad [name for]
Macbeth **M: 5**
Macadam [building material]
McAdam, John Loudon **M: 332**
Road (Paving) **R: 359**; (From the 500's to the 1800's) **R: 361**

Macadamia nut M: 2
  Nut (Kinds of nuts) N: 621 *with picture*
MacAlpin, Kenneth [king of Scotland] *See* Kenneth I MacAlpin *in this index*
Macao [region, China] *See* Macau *in this index*
Macapagal-Arroyo, Gloria [Filipino political leader]
  Philippines (Recent developments) P: 381
Macaque [animal] M: 2
  Barbary ape B: 105
  Primate (Old World monkeys) P: 778a *with pictures*
  Snow monkey S: 541
Macaroni [food]
  Pasta P: 192
Macaroni wheat
  Grass (Cereals) G: 326
MacArthur, Arthur [American general]
  MacArthur, Douglas (Early career) M: 3
MacArthur, Arthur [American political leader]
  Wisconsin (table) W: 365
MacArthur, Charles [American dramatist]
  Hayes, Helen H: 117
  Hecht, Ben H: 164
MacArthur, Douglas [American general] M: 3 *with picture*
  Autograph *picture on* A: 943
  Japan (Allied military occupation) J: 58
  Korean War (The Inchon landing) K: 381 *with picture*; (The Allies move north) K: 381; (The "Battle for the Hills") K: 382
  Philippines (Japanese control) P: 380
  Truman, Harry S. (The Korean War) T: 471
  World War II *picture on* W: 492; (Early Japanese victories) W: 487-488; (The South Pacific) W: 489; (Peace with Japan) W: 498
MacArthur, John D. [American philanthropist]
  MacArthur Foundation M: 5
MacArthur Fellows Program
  MacArthur Foundation M: 4
MacArthur Foundation M: 4
  Foundation (table) F: 430
MacArthur Lock
  Soo Canals (The American canals) So: 594-595 *with map*
MacArthur Park [Arkansas]
  Arkansas (Places to visit) A: 704
Macassar oil
  Hairdressing (The 1800's) H: 12
Macau [region, China] M: 4
  China (Hong Kong and Macau) C: 506
  Portugal P: 686; (End of the empire) P: 695
Macaulay, David [British-born author/illustrator] M: 4
  Caldecott Medal (table: 1991) C: 26
  Literature for children *picture on* L: 384
Macaulay, Thomas Babington [British historian] M: 5
  Biography (The 1800's) B: 314
  Fourth estate F: 438
Macaw [bird] M: 5
  Animal *picture on* A: 480
  Bird (Birds of Central and South America) B: 344a *with picture*
  Parrot *picture on* P: 180; (Kinds of parrots) P: 179
Macay, Spruce [American lawyer]
  Jackson, Andrew (Lawyer) J: 8
Macbeth [king of Scotland] M: 5
  Duncan I D: 383
Macbeth [play by Shakespeare]
  Macbeth M: 5
  Shakespeare, William *picture on* S: 351; (*Macbeth*) S: 363; (Imagery) S: 368
Macbeth, Lady [literary figure]
  Shakespeare, William: (*Macbeth*) S: 363
MacBride, Sean [Irish statesman]
  Nobel Prizes (Peace: 1974) N: 448b
Maccabee, Judah [Jewish leader] *See* Judah Maccabee *in this index*
Maccabees [books]
  Bible (The Christian Old Testament) B: 282
Maccabees [Jewish rulers]
  Palestine (Invasions and conquests) P: 104
MacCauley, Clay [American artist]
  Indian, American *picture on* I: 158
MacCool, Finn [legendary figure] *See* Finn MacCool *in this index*
MacCorkle, William A. [American political leader]
  West Virginia (table) W: 225
MacDermot, Galt [American musician]
  Rock music (Fresh directions) R: 380-380a
MacDiarmid, Alan Graham [American chemist]
  Nobel Prizes (Chemistry: 2000) N: 444
Macdonald, Andrew Archibald [Canadian political leader]
  Confederation of Canada (Fathers of Confederation) Ci: 935 *with picture*

Macdonald, Angus L. [Canadian political leader]
  Nova Scotia (table) N: 567
Macdonald, Brian [Canadian choreographer]
  Ballet (Ballet in Canada) B: 54
Macdonald, Hugh [father of]
  Macdonald, Sir John Alexander (Boyhood and education) M: 6
Macdonald, Hugh John [Canadian political leader]
  Macdonald, Sir John Alexander (Marriages) M: 7
  Manitoba (table) M: 159
Macdonald, Isabella [wife of]
  Macdonald, Sir John Alexander (Marriages) M: 7
MacDonald, J. E. H. [Canadian painter]
  Group of Seven G: 402 *with picture*
  Painting (Composition) P: 35
MacDonald, James Ramsay [British political leader] M: 5
  Labour Party (History) L: 16
  United Kingdom (The rise of the Labour Party) U: 70
Macdonald, Sir John Alexander [Canadian political leader] M: 6 *with pictures*
  Abbott, Sir John Joseph Caldwell (The Pacific Scandal) A: 6
  Canada, History of *picture on* C: 139; (Confederation) C: 144; (Growth of the Dominion [1868-1913]) C: 144
  Confederation of Canada (Moves toward confederation) Ci: 933; (Fathers of Confederation) Ci: 935 *with picture*
  Laurier, Sir Wilfrid (The execution of Louis Riel) L: 124-125
  Mackenzie, Alexander (Leader of the opposition) M: 22; (Economic difficulties and defeat) M: 22
  Ontario *picture on* O: 785
  Prime minister of Canada (History) P: 780 *with picture*
  Progressive Conservative Party P: 812
MacDonald, John D. [American author] M: 10
Macdonald, John Sandfield [Canadian political leader] M: 10 *with portrait*
  Ontario (table) O: 783; (Confederation) O: 786
MacDonald, Rodney [Canadian political leader]
  Nova Scotia (table) N: 567
MacDonald, Ross [American author] M: 11
MacDonnell Ranges [mountains, Australia]
  Australia (Mountains) A: 908 *with map*
Macdonough, Thomas [American military leader] M: 11
  War of 1812 (The war at sea) W: 31; (Lake Champlain) W: 32
MacDowell, Edward Alexander [American composer] M: 11
Macduff [literary figure]
  Shakespeare, William: (*Macbeth*) S: 363-364
Mace [spice] M: 11
  Nutmeg N: 623 *with picture*
Mace [symbol] M: 11
Mace [tear gas] M: 11
Macedonia [historic region, Europe] M: 11 *with map*
  Alexander the Great A: 342 *with map*
  Byzantine Empire (The middle period) B: 754
  Europe (Ancient Greece) E: 407
  Exploration (The Greeks) E: 441
  Greece (Macedonia) G: 357
  Greece, Ancient (The rivalry between Athens and Sparta) G: 373-374
  Macedonia (country) (History) M: 12a
  Philip II P: 369
  Rome, Ancient (The Roman Republic) R: 444-445
  Skopje S: 495
Macedonia [country, Europe] M: 12 *with picture and map*
  Berlin, Congress of B: 265
  Flag *picture on* F: 206
  North Atlantic Treaty Organization (History) N: 471
  Serbia (History) S: 314-316
  Yugoslavia Y: 576
Macedonian [language]
  Macedonia (country) (People) M: 12
Maceral [geology]
  Coal (Analyzing coal composition) Ci: 717-718
MacFlecknoe [poem by Dryden]
  Dryden, John D: 370
MacGillivray, William [Scottish naturalist]
  Audubon, John James (His works) A: 885
MacGregor, Robert [Scottish bandit] *See* Rob Roy *in this index*
MacGregor plaid
  Tartan *picture on* T: 47
Mach, Ernst [Austrian physicist] M: 12b
Mach number [measurement]
  Aerodynamics (Supersonic aerodynamics) A: 87
  Airplane (Supersonic airplanes) A: 238
  Mach, Ernst M: 12b

Machado, Gerardo [Cuban political leader]
  Cuba (The Platt Amendment) Ci: 1176-1177
Machado de Assis, Joaquim Maria [Brazilian author] M: 12b
  Brazil (The arts) B: 576-577
  Latin American literature (Realism) L: 113
Machaut, Guillaume de [French composer] M: 12b
  Classical music (Secular music) Ci: 646
Machel, Graca [Mozambican political leader]
  Mandela, Nelson (End of white rule) M: 137
Machiavelli, Niccolò [Italian philosopher] M: 12b *with portrait*
  Borgia, Cesare B: 487
  Italian literature (Humanism and the Renaissance) I: 494
  Political science (Secularism) P: 639
  Renaissance (Niccolò Machiavelli) R: 234
Machigonne [former name]
  Portland [Maine] P: 683
Machine [device] M: 13 *with pictures*
  See also the list of Related articles in the Machine article
  Automation A: 944
  Cybernetics Ci: 1203
  Efficiency E: 115
  Ergonomics E: 350
  Simple machines S: 467
  Treadmill T: 406
Machine [politics]
  City government (Influencing city government) Ci: 597
Machine age
  See also Industrial Revolution *in this index*
  Machine M: 13
Machine bolt
  Bolt B: 449 *with pictures*
Machine gun M: 15 *with pictures*
  Air force (World War I) A: 185
  Air Force, United States (World War I) A: 194
  Gatling, Richard Jordan G: 68
  Gun control (Approaches to gun control) G: 440-441
  Weapon *picture on* W: 154a
  World War I *picture on* W: 457; (A build-up of military might) W: 453-454
Machine Hall [Paris]
  Architecture *picture on* A: 625
Machine language [computing]
  Computer (Compiling or assembling a program) Ci: 923
  Computer language (Machine languages) Ci: 924h
Machine screw
  Screw (Uses) S: 225 *with pictures*
Machine tool M: 17 *with pictures*
  Aluminum (Machining) A: 396
  Die and diemaking D: 195
  Mass production M: 269
  Nasmyth, James N: 24
  Toolmaking T: 330
Machine vision system [manufacturing]
  Light (Light in manufacturing) L: 292
Machining [manufacturing]
  Automobile (Manufacturing) A: 958
  Machine tool M: 17
Machining center [manufacturing]
  Machine tool M: 17
Machinist [occupation]
  Careers (Production) C: 229
  Machine tool M: 17
Machinists and Aerospace Workers, International Association of [labor union] M: 20
  Labor movement (table) L: 8
Machinist's hammer
  Hammer H: 34 *with picture*
MACHO [physics] *See* Massive compact halo object *in this index*
Machpelah, Cave of
  Abraham A: 17
  Hebron H: 163
Machu Picchu [Peru] M: 20
  Architecture (Pre-Columbian architecture) A: 614
  Indian, American *picture on* I: 174
  Latin America *picture on* L: 91
  Peru *picture on* P: 315
Macias Nguema, Francisco [Equatorial Guinea political leader]
  Equatorial Guinea (History) E: 347
Macintosh [computer]
  Advertising *picture on* A: 78
  Apple Inc. A: 573
  Computer (Personal computers) Ci: 909-910; (The personal computer) Ci: 924c-924d
  Desktop publishing D: 158
Macintosh, Charles [British inventor] M: 20
  Rubber (The rubber industry begins) R: 501
  Waterproofing W: 146

Mack, Alexander [German religious leader]
Brethren, Church of the **B:** 594
Mack, Connie [American baseball manager] **M:** 20
Baseball (table: Hall of Fame) **B:** 134a
"Mack the Knife" [song]
Weill, Kurt **W:** 188
MacKay, Alice G. [Canadian secretary]
Vancouver Foundation **V:** 278
MacKay, Buddy [American political leader]
Florida (table) **F:** 260
Mackay, John William [American businessman]
M: 20
MacKay, Peter [Canadian political leader]
Conservative Party of Canada **Ci:** 992
Mackay, R. A. [Canadian diplomat]
United Nations (table) **U:** 86
Mackenzie, Alexander [Canadian political leader]
M: 21 with portrait
Canada, History of (The return of Macdonald) **C:** 145
Macdonald, Sir John Alexander (The Pacific Scandal) **M:** 9
Mackenzie, Sir Alexander [Canadian explorer]
M: 22
Alberta picture on **A:** 330; (The fur trade) **A:** 329
Canada, History of (Exploration of the West) **C:** 143
Exploration (Crossing North America) **E:** 447 with map
Fraser River **F:** 495
Northwest Territories (European exploration) **N:** 533
Mackenzie, George [Canadian lawyer]
Macdonald, Sir John Alexander (Boyhood and education) **M:** 6
Mackenzie, Helen Neil [wife of]
Mackenzie, Alexander (Emigration to Canada) **M:** 21
Mackenzie, Jane Sym [wife of]
Mackenzie, Alexander (Emigration to Canada) **M:** 21
MacKenzie, K. R. [American physicist]
Astatine **A:** 823
Mackenzie, Roderick [Canadian frontiersman]
M: 23
Alberta (The fur trade) **A:** 329
Mackenzie, William Lyon [Canadian political leader] **M:** 23 with portrait
Canada, History of (The uprisings of 1837) **C:** 143
King, William Lyon Mackenzie (Boyhood) **K:** 324-325
Macdonald, Sir John Alexander (Lawyer) **M:** 6
Ontario picture on **O:** 785; (Political unrest) **O:** 786
Rebellions of 1837 **R:** 173
Mackenzie Inuit [people] See Inuvialuit in this index
Mackenzie King Square [Kitchener]
Kitchener **K:** 338
Mackenzie Mountains [Canada]
Northwest Territories (Land) **N:** 530 with map
Rocky Mountains (Chief ranges of the Rockies) **R:** 394
Mackenzie River [Canada] **M:** 23 with map
British Columbia (Rivers, waterfalls, and lakes) **B:** 624
Canada (The Arctic Basin) **C:** 120
River (table) **R:** 352
Mackenzie Valley [region, Northwest Territories]
Northwest Territories (Land) **N:** 530
Mackerel [fish] **M:** 23 with picture
Fish picture on **F:** 153
Kingfish **K:** 329 with picture
Mackerel tabby
Cat (Coat) **C:** 287
Mackey, Biz [American baseball player]
Baseball (table: Hall of Fame) **B:** 134a
Mackinac, Straits of [Michigan] **M:** 24
Lake Huron **L:** 39 with map
Mackinac Bridge [Michigan]
Bridge (table: Suspension) **B:** 603
Mackinac, Straits of **M:** 24
Michigan (Interesting facts) **M:** 489 with picture
Mackinac Island [Michigan] **M:** 24
Lake Huron **L:** 39 with map
Mackinder, Sir Halford [British geographer]
Geopolitics **G:** 106b
MacKinnon, Roderick [American physicist]
Nobel Prizes (Chemistry: 2003) **N:** 444
Mackinnon, William [British businessman]
Emin Pasha **E:** 260
Mackintosh [clothing]
Macintosh, Charles **M:** 20
Rubber (The rubber industry begins) **R:** 501
Waterproofing **W:** 146
MacLachlan, Patricia [author]
Newbery Medal (table) **N:** 359
MacLaine, Shirley [American actress]
Dance picture on **D:** 30

Motion picture (Best performance by an actress: 1983) **M:** 862a
MacLean, J. Angus [Canadian political leader]
Prince Edward Island (table) **P:** 791
MacLean, John D. [Canadian political leader]
British Columbia (table) **B:** 628
MacLeish, Archibald [American poet] **M:** 24
MacLellan, Russell [Canadian political leader]
Nova Scotia (table) **N:** 567
MacLennan, Hugh [Canadian author] **M:** 25
Canadian literature (Modern English-Canadian fiction) **C:** 160
Macleod, John James Rickard [Scottish physiologist]
Banting, Sir Frederick Grant **B:** 99
Insulin (History) **I:** 308
Nobel Prizes (Physiology or medicine: 1923) **N:** 445
MacLeod of Lewis plaid
Tartan picture on **T:** 47
Maclure, William [American geologist]
New Harmony **N:** 228
MacMillan, A. Stirling [Canadian political leader]
Nova Scotia (table) **N:** 567
MacMillan, Donald Baxter [American explorer]
M: 25
Macmillan, Harold [British political leader] **M:** 25
United Kingdom (Economic recovery—and collapse) **U:** 72
Macmillan, Kirkpatrick [Scottish blacksmith]
Bicycle (Early bicycles) **B:** 291
MacMillan, W. J. P. [Canadian political leader]
Prince Edward Island (table) **P:** 791
Macmillan bicycle
Transportation picture on **T:** 389
Macmillan plaid
Tartan picture on **T:** 47
MacMillan Space Centre
Vancouver (Museums) **V:** 276
MacMurrough, Dermot [Irish king]
Ireland (The Norman invaders) **I:** 425
MacNab, Sir Allan [Canadian political leader]
Hamilton (Cultural life) **H:** 31
MacNelly, Jeff [American cartoonist]
Cartoon picture on **C:** 264
Macon [Georgia] **M:** 25
Macon [airship]
Airship (Between world wars) **A:** 252
Macon, Nathaniel [American political leader]
Macon **M:** 25
Macon Act [1810]
War of 1812 (American reaction) **W:** 29-30
Macoun, John [Canadian botanist]
Regina (History) **R:** 206
MacPhail, Agnes Campbell [Canadian political leader] **M:** 25
MacPhail, Larry [American baseball executive]
Baseball (table: Hall of Fame) **B:** 134a
MacPhail, Lee [American baseball executive]
Baseball (table: Hall of Fame) **B:** 134a
Macpherson, James [Scottish poet]
Finn MacCool **F:** 119
Macpherson dress plaid
Tartan picture on **T:** 47
Macquarie, Lachlan [Australian government official] **M:** 26
Australia (The New South Wales Corps) **A:** 920-921
Macquarie, Lake [Australia] See Lake Macquarie in this index
Macquarie Island [Pacific]
Tasmania (Land and climate) **T:** 48
Macramé [handicraft] **M:** 26 with picture
Macready, William Charles [English actor] **M:** 26
Macrinus [Roman emperor]
Rome, Ancient (table) **R:** 447
Macro-Algonquian [language group]
Indian, American (Language groups) **I:** 149-150
Macro-Chibchan [language group]
Indian, American (Language groups) **I:** 149-150
Macro lens
Camera (Single-lens reflex [SLR] cameras) **C:** 82-83
Photography (Types of lenses) **P:** 411
Macro-Otomanguean [language group]
Indian, American (Language groups) **I:** 149-150
Macro-Siouan [language group]
Indian, American (Language groups) **I:** 149-150
Macro virus [computer]
Computer virus **Ci:** 925
Macroeconomics
Economics (Fields of economics) **E:** 64
Keynes, John Maynard **K:** 308a
Macromolecule [biology]
Human body (Chemical elements and molecules) **H:** 417
Molecular biology (The beginning of molecular

biology) **M:** 691-692
Macron
Diacritical mark **D:** 180
Macronutrient
Nutrition (Kinds of nutrients) **N:** 625
Macrophage [physiology]
AIDS (How HIV affects the body) **A:** 164
Blood (Protecting against disease) **B:** 410 with pictures
Disease diagram on **D:** 232
Gaucher's disease **G:** 68
Immune system (Antigen-presenting cells) **I:** 88
Lung (Other jobs of the lungs) **L:** 524
Lymphatic system (Lymph nodes) **L:** 534; (Fighting infection) **L:** 535
Spleen **So:** 797
Macropod [mammal]
Kangaroo **K:** 213
Marsupial (Kinds of marsupials) **M:** 232
Wallaby **W:** 15
Macroscelidea [zoology]
Mammal (table) **M:** 128 with picture
Macrostructure
Materials **M:** 300b
Macrosystem [psychology]
Child (The influence of the child's environment) **C:** 452
Macrozamia [tree]
Australia (Native plants) **A:** 911-912
Mactan [island, Philippines]
Magellan, Ferdinand picture on **M:** 48
Mactaquac Provincial Park
New Brunswick (Places to visit) **N:** 188
MacTavish plaid
Tartan picture on **T:** 47
Macuahuitl [weapon]
Aztec (Warfare) **A:** 1002
Macula [anatomy]
Eye picture on **E:** 461; (The retina) **E:** 462; (Diseases of the retina) **E:** 467
Macular degeneration **M:** 26
Macular degeneration [disorder] **M:** 26
Angiogenesis **A:** 461
Blindness (Diseases) **B:** 401
Eye (Diseases of the retina) **E:** 467
Macumba [religion]
Brazil (Religion) **B:** 575
Magic (Africa and the Americas) **M:** 50
Rio de Janeiro (People) **R:** 345
MacVeagh, Franklin [American government official]
Garfield, James Abram (table) **G:** 42
Taft, William Howard (table) **T:** 11
MacVeagh, I. Wayne [American government official]
Justice, Department of (table) **J:** 203
MAD [policy] See Mutually assured destruction in this index
Mad Anthony Wayne [nickname] See Wayne, Anthony in this index
Mad cow disease M: 26
Cattle (Diseases) **C:** 312-314
Meat packing (Trends and changes in meat packing) **M:** 352
Prion **P:** 804
Mad Forest [play by Churchill]
Churchill, Caryl **C:** 543
Mad Ludwig [nickname]
Ludwig II **L:** 515
Mad Max [film]
Gibson, Mel **G:** 187
"Mad Scene"
Opera: (Lucia di Lammermoor) **O:** 804
Madagascar M: 27 with pictures and map
Flag picture on **F:** 199
Funeral customs (The funeral) **F:** 557
Madagascar leaf-nosed snake
Snake picture on **S:** 526
Madagascar palm
Palm (Products of palms) **P:** 109
Madam
Prostitution **P:** 830
Madam C. J. Walker Manufacturing Company
Walker, Madam C. J. **W:** 13
Madama Butterfly [opera by Puccini]
Opera: (Madama Butterfly) **O:** 804 with picture
Puccini, Giacomo **P:** 869
Madama Palace
Rome (Churches, palaces, and fountains) **R:** 429
Madame Bovary [book by Flaubert]
Flaubert, Gustave **F:** 230
French literature (Realism) **F:** 522
Novel (France) **N:** 573
Madame Roland [French political leader] See Roland de la Platière, Marie Jeanne in this index
Madame Tussaud's Exhibition [London]
Tussaud, Marie Gresholtz **T:** 525

Madden Dam
  Panama Canal (The canal since 1920) P: 126
Madden Lake
  Panama Canal (The canal since 1920) P: 126
Madder [plant] M: 29
  Dye (Natural dyes) D: 396
  Gardenia G: 29
  Lake L: 35
Maddock, Walter [American political leader]
  North Dakota (table) N: 513
Maddox [destroyer]
  Vietnam War (The Gulf of Tonkin incident) V: 375
Maddox, Lester G. [American political leader]
  Georgia (table) G: 130; (The mid-1900's) G: 134
Maddox, Richard L. [British doctor]
  Photography (Technical improvements) P: 423
Maddux, Greg [American baseball player] M: 29
Madeira Islands [Atlantic] M: 30
  Henry the Navigator H: 191
  Portugal P: 686
Madeira River [Brazil] M: 30
  Amazon River (The course of the Amazon) A: 403
Madeira wine
  Portugal (Agriculture and fishing) P: 691-692
Madeline's Rescue [book by Bemelmans]
  Bemelmans, Ludwig B: 246
Mademoiselle de Scudéry [book by Hoffmann]
  Hoffmann, Ernst Theodor Amadeus H: 284
Mademoiselle Modiste [operetta by Herbert]
  Herbert, Victor H: 197
Madero, Francisco Indalecio [Mexican political
  leader] M: 30
  Latin America (Political circumstances in the early
    to middle 1900's) L: 109
  Mexican Revolution of 1910 (The revolution)
    M: 445
  Mexico (The Revolution of 1910) M: 472
  Mexico City (Revolution and growth) M: 478
  Obregón, Álvaro O: 643
  Zapata, Emiliano Z: 586
Madhubuti, Haki [American author]
  African American literature (The 1900's) A: 136a
Madhya Pradesh [state, India]
  Asia (Languages) A: 773
Madigan, Edward R. [American government
  official]
  Agriculture, Department of (table) A: 161
Madikizela-Mandela, Winnie [South African
  political leader]
  Mandela, Nelson (Imprisonment) M: 136
Madisar [custom]
  Clothing (Identity) Ci: 687-688
Madison [Wisconsin] M: 30 *with picture*
  Wisconsin *pictures on* W: 350, W: 364
Madison, Dolley Payne [wife of James Madison]
  M: 31
  First ladies of the United States F: 143 *with picture*
  Jefferson, Thomas (Life in the White House) J: 83
  Madison, James (Congressman) M: 34 *with
    portrait*; (Life in the White House) M: 36
  White House hostesses W: 291
Madison, James [U.S. president] M: 32 *with pictures*
  Bill of rights (The Constitution of the United
    States) B: 301
  Constitution of the United States (The
    Constitutional Convention) Ci: 999-1000; (The
    Bill of Rights) Ci: 1001; (The development of
    the Constitution) Ci: 1001
  Federalist, The F: 66
  Hamilton, Alexander (Early political career) H: 32
  Jefferson, Thomas (National statesman) J: 81
  Louisiana Purchase (Trouble begins) L: 502
  Madison, Dolley Payne M: 31
  Marbury v. Madison M: 179
  United States, History of the (Establishing a
    government) U: 161-162; (The War of 1812)
    U: 165
  Virginia (The *Mother of Presidents*) V: 421
Madison, Mount
  New Hampshire (Mountains) N: 220 *with map*
Madison Mountains
  Montana (Land regions) M: 752
Madison Square Garden [New York City]
  New York City (Sports) N: 338
Madjapahit [former kingdom]
  Indonesia (Hindu and Buddhist kingdoms) I: 236;
    (The spread of Islam) I: 237
Mádl, Ferenc [Hungarian political leader]
  Hungary (Recent developments) H: 448
Madonna [American singer] M: 37
  Penn, Sean P: 241
  Rock music *picture on* R: 381; (Madonna and
    Michael Jackson) R: 380c
Madonna [painting by Baldovinetti]
  Madonna and Child (Types of Madonna
    paintings) M: 38
Madonna [painting by Massys]

Madonna and Child (Types of Madonna
    paintings) M: 38
Madonna and Child [art] M: 37 *with picture*
  Lippi, Filippo *picture on* L: 345
  Painting (Medieval painting) P: 48-49 *with
    picture*; (The Renaissance) P: 51 *with pictures*
  Raphael R: 142
  Renaissance *pictures on* R: 234; (Arts of the 1400's
    and early 1500's) R: 236
Madonna and Child [engraving by Mantegna]
  Engraving *picture on* E: 326
Madonna and Child [painting by Fra Filippo Lippi]
  Lippi, Filippo L: 345 *with picture*
Madonna and Child [sculpture by Stoss]
  Stoss, Veit *picture on* So: 916
Madonna and Child Enthroned [painting by
  Giotto]
  Giotto *picture on* G: 193
Madonna and Child Jesus [sculpture by Della
  Robbia]
  Della Robbia, Luca *picture on* D: 117
Madonna and Child with Chancellor Rolin, The
  [painting by van Eyck]
  Madonna and Child (Types of Madonna
    paintings) M: 38
  Painting (Religious subjects) P: 32
Madonna Enthroned with Angels, The [painting
  by Cimabue]
  Painting (The 1300's) P: 51
  Renaissance *picture on* R: 234
Madonna Enthroned with Saints [painting by
  Giotto]
  Giotto (Giotto's works) G: 193
Madonna lily [plant]
  Easter lily E: 45
  Flower (Garden perennials grown from bulbs)
    F: 280 *with picture*
  Lily L: 304
Madonna of Chancellor Rolin [painting by Van
  Eyck]
  Renaissance *picture on* R: 238
Madonna of the Goldfinch [painting by Raphael]
  Classicism (The qualities of Classicism) Ci: 653
  Madonna and Child (Types of Madonna
    paintings) M: 38
  Painting (The High Renaissance) P: 54-55 *with
    picture*
Madonna of the Meadow [painting by Raphael]
  Europe *picture on* E: 393
Madonna of the Rocks [painting by Leonardo]
  Leonardo da Vinci (Years in Milan) L: 199
  Painting (The 1400's) P: 52-53 *with picture*
Madonna of the Stars [painting by Fra Angelico]
  Madonna and Child (Types of Madonna
    paintings) M: 38
Madras [India] *See* Chennai *in this index*
Madras House, The [play by Granville-Barker]
  Granville-Barker, Harley G: 318
Madrasah [religious school]
  Architecture (Islamic architecture) A: 613-614
  Islamic art *picture on* I: 467; (Madrasahs) I: 468
  Mullah M: 914
  Pakistan (Education) P: 96 *with picture*
Madraspatam [former name]
  Chennai C: 408
Madre de Dios [ship]
  Newport, Christopher N: 379
Madrid [Spain] M: 38 *with pictures*
  Spain *pictures on* So: 731, So: 737; (table:
    Average monthly weather) So: 742; (Recent
    developments) So: 751
  Spanish Civil War (Progress of the war) So: 756a
Madrid, Treaty of [1750]
  Brazil (Independence) B: 583-584
Madrid-Barajas Airport
  Airport (table) A: 245
Madrid Hurtado, Miguel de la [Mexican political
  leader] *See* De la Madrid Hurtado, Miguel *in this
  index*
Madrid Protocol [1991]
  Antarctica (International agreements) A: 538-539
Madrid Zoo [Spain]
  Zoo (The first modern zoos) Z: 604-605
Madrigal [song] M: 40
  Classical music (The Renaissance) Ci: 646
  Morley, Thomas M: 805
  Poetry (Renaissance poetry) P: 596
Madrileños [people]
  Madrid (The people) M: 38
Madroña [tree] M: 40
Madrone [tree] *See* Madroña *in this index*
Madurese [people]
  Indonesia (People) I: 227
  Java J: 65
Maduro Joest, Ricardo [Honduran political leader]
  Honduras (Recent developments) H: 313
Maecenas [Roman patron]

  Horace H: 334
  Virgil (His life) V: 391
Maelstrom [current, Arctic] M: 40
  Norway (Coast and islands) N: 542
  Whirlpool W: 281
Maenad [Greek mythology]
  Dionysus D: 215
Maestà, The [painting by Duccio Di Buoninsegna]
  Duccio di Buoninsegna D: 373
  Pilate, Pontius *picture on* P: 462
Maestoso
  Music (table) M: 954
Maeterlinck, Maurice [Belgian author] M: 40
  Belgium (The arts) B: 230
  Drama (Symbolism) D: 339
Maeve, Queen [legendary figure] M: 41
  Irish literature (Heroic tales, romances, and sagas)
    I: 430
  Mythology (The Ulster cycle) M: 985
Maffei, Paolo [Italian astronomer]
  Maffei galaxies M: 41
Maffei galaxies [astronomy] M: 41
Mafia [organization] M: 41
  Italy (Social problems) I: 518
  Sicily (The people) S: 446
Magarac, Joe [legendary figure] M: 41
Magazine [journalism] M: 42 *with pictures*
  Advertising (Magazines) A: 74 *with picture*
  Journalism (Fields of journalism) J: 171
  Literature for children (Children's magazines)
    L: 365; (New children's magazines) L: 365
  Publishing (Scheduling, printing, and posting)
    P: 867; (Magazines and journals) P: 869
  Television (Other forms of entertainment) T: 121
  Trade publication T: 363
  Writing W: 511
Magazine [munitions] M: 46
  Handgun (Types of handguns) H: 43
  Machine gun M: 15
Magazine [photography]
  Motion picture (The camera) M: 856-857
Magazine [printing]
  Linotype (How the linotype works) L: 338
Magazine Mountain
  Arkansas (Land regions) A: 706
Magdalena River [river, Colombia]
  Colombia (The Andes Mountains) Ci: 782
  South America (Rivers) So: 628
Magdalene, Mary [Biblical figure] *See* Mary
  Magdalene *in this index*
Magdalenian culture [anthropology]
  Lascaux Cave L: 80
Magdeburg [Germany]
  Thirty Years' War (The Swedish period) T: 260
Magellan [space probe]
  Space exploration (Probes to Venus and Mercury)
    So: 710-711
  Venus (Flights to Venus) V: 313
Magellan, Ferdinand [Portuguese navigator]
  M: 46 *with pictures and map*
  Exploration *map on* E: 443; (Magellan's globe-
    circling expedition) E: 445
  Latin America *map on* L: 105 ; (European
    discovery and exploration) L: 103
  Mariana Islands M: 199
  Pacific Islands (European explorers) P: 12
  Pacific Ocean P: 194
  Patagonia P: 194
  Philippines (Spanish settlement and rule) P: 379
Magellan, Strait of [South America] M: 48 *with
  maps*
  Magellan, Ferdinand (The voyage begins) M: 47
Magellanic Clouds [astronomy] M: 48
  Leavitt, Henrietta Swan L: 170
  Supernova (Results of supernovae) So: 994
Magellanic penguin [bird]
  Zoo *picture on* Z: 600
Magen David Adom [organization]
  Red Cross R: 185
Magenta [color]
  Printing (Process color printing) P: 802 *with
    picture*
Magerit [ancient fortress]
  Madrid (History) M: 40
Maggie: A Girl of the Streets [book by Crane]
  Crane, Stephen Ci: 1120
  Novel (The United States) N: 573
Maggie L. Walker National Historic Site [Virginia]
  National Park System (table: National historic
    sites) N: 52-53
Maggiore, Lake [Italy-Switzerland]
  Lake Maggiore L: 40
Maggot [zoology] M: 48
  Apple (Pests and diseases) A: 572
  Bot fly B: 507
  Fly (table) F: 310; (Larva) F: 310 *with picture*
  Fruit fly F: 549

Insect (Complete metamorphosis) **I:** 293
Magi [religion] **M:** 48
 Christmas **C:** 528
 Epiphany **E:** 344
 Jesus Christ (Early life) **J:** 105
Magic [belief] **M:** 48 *with pictures*
 Alchemy **A:** 334
 Doll (Dolls in magic) **D:** 288 *with picture*
 Fairy **F:** 9
 Fetish **F:** 81
 Indian, American (Shamans) **I:** 147
 Mask **M:** 263
 Occultism **O:** 647
 Superstition (Kinds of superstitions) **So:** 995
 Witchcraft **W:** 371
Magic [illusion]
 Magic **M:** 49
 Magician **M:** 51 *with pictures*
Magic, Orlando [team]
 Basketball (table) **B:** 150
Magic Barrel, The [book by Malamud]
 Malamud, Bernard **M:** 95
Magic City [nickname]
 Birmingham (History) **B:** 376
Magic Flute, The [opera by Mozart]
 Mozart, Wolfgang Amadeus (Operas) **M:** 906-907; (His style) **M:** 907-908
 Opera: *(Magic Flute, The)* **O:** 805 *with picture*
 Puppet *picture on* **P:** 905
Magic Kingdom [theme park]
 Walt Disney Company **W:** 20
Magic Mountain, The [book by Mann]
 German literature (Impressionism, Neoromanticism, and Symbolism) **G:** 141
 Mann, Thomas **M:** 164
Magic realism [arts]
 Cuba (The arts) **Ci:** 1171-1172
 Ellison, Harlan **E:** 244
 Latin American literature (The "Boom") **L:** 114
 Magritte, René **M:** 63
 Novel (The novel today) **N:** 575
 Rushdie, Salman **R:** 522
Magician M: 51 *with pictures*
 Magic (Elements of magic) **M:** 49
Maginot Line [French history] **M:** 52
 France (Between World Wars) **F:** 475
 World War II (The Phony War) **W:** 473; (The fall of France) **W:** 475
Magistrate [office]
 Court (How courts work) **Ci:** 1101
 Etruscans (Government and economy) **E:** 375
Magistrate, The [play by Pinero]
 Pinero, Arthur Wing **P:** 473
Maglev train *See* Magnetic levitation train *in this index*
Magloire, Paul E. [Haitian political leader]
 Haiti (History) **H:** 15-16
Magma [geology]
 Earthquake (Why a quake begins) **E:** 36
 Geothermal energy **G:** 136
 Granite **G:** 311
 Hot spot **H:** 374a
 Igneous rock **I:** 49
 Metamorphic rock **M:** 428
 Moon (Origin and evolution of the moon) **M:** 788; (Mantle) **M:** 791
 Rock (Igneous rock) **R:** 371
 Seamount **S:** 268
 Volcano **V:** 438
Magma chamber
 Volcano **V:** 438, *diagram on* **V:** 442a
Magmatic water
 Mineral water **M:** 572
Magna Carta [English history] **M:** 52 *with picture*
 Civil rights (Natural law) **Ci:** 610
 Democracy (Democracy in England) **D:** 122
 Due process of law **D:** 377
 England (Magna Carta) **E:** 306
 Freedom (The Middle Ages) **F:** 502
 Government (The rise of monarchies and nation-states) **G:** 290
 Human rights (The development of human rights) **H:** 428
 John **J:** 131
 Runnymede **R:** 521
Magna Charta *See* Magna Carta *in this index*
Magna cum laude
 Degree, College (The bachelor's degree) **D:** 93
Magna Graecia [settlement]
 Greece, Ancient (The development of the Greek city-state) **G:** 372
Magnalia Christi Americana [book by Mather]
 American literature (New England) **A:** 414
 Mather, Cotton **M:** 309
Magnani, Anna [Italian actress]
 Motion picture (Best performance by an actress: 1955) **M:** 862

Magnesia [ancient country]
 Lodestone **L:** 419
Magnesia [chemical] **M:** 54
Magnesium [metal] **M:** 54
 Alloy (Alloys for strength and lightness) **A:** 378
 Aluminum (Properties of aluminum alloys) **A:** 391-392
 Anodizing **A:** 518
 Dolomite **D:** 296
 Nutrition (Minerals) **N:** 625-626
Magnesium diboride [chemical]
 Superconductivity **So:** 992
Magnesium hydroxide [chemical]
 Magnesia **M:** 54
Magnesium oxide [chemical] *See* Magnesia *in this index*
Magnesium sulfate [chemical]
 Epsom salt **E:** 345
Magnet [physics] *See* Magnetism *in this index*
Magnet school
 Alternative school **A:** 388
 Education (Who should choose a child's school?) **E:** 106
Magnetar [astronomy]
 Magnetism (Other astronomical bodies) **M:** 60d
 Neutron star **N:** 155
 Pulsar **P:** 900a
Magnetic amplifier M: 54
Magnetic arc-suppression circuit breaker
 Circuit breaker **Ci:** 558
Magnetic bottle [machine]
 Fusion **F:** 589
Magnetic compass [instrument]
 Compass **Ci:** 902b *with picture*
 Gyrocompass **G:** 452
 Invention (China) **I:** 359 *with picture*; (The Middle Ages) **I:** 359-360
Magnetic confinement [physics]
 Nuclear energy (Research on new types of reactors) **N:** 592-593
Magnetic dipole moment [astronomy]
 Jupiter (Magnetic field) **J:** 198
Magnetic domain [physics]
 Magnetism (In materials) **M:** 60c
Magnetic equator [geography] **M:** 55 *with map*
 Equator (The magnetic equator) **E:** 346
Magnetic field [physics]
 See also Field [physics] *in this index*
 Magnetism (Magnets and their properties) **M:** 59-60 *with diagram*; (How magnetism works) **M:** 60b
 Aurora **A:** 891
 Bird (How birds migrate) **B:** 361
 Celsius, Anders **C:** 342
 Cosmic rays (Primary cosmic rays) **Ci:** 1076 *with diagram*
 Electric generator (A simple generator) **E:** 170
 Electric motor (Basic principles) **E:** 179 *with diagram*
 Electricity (Electric and magnetic fields) **E:** 196
 Electromagnetism **E:** 202
 Force (The magnetic force) **F:** 371
 Hall effect **H:** 22
 Heliosphere (Magnetic field) **H:** 175
 Inductance **I:** 240
 Jupiter (Magnetic field) **J:** 198
 Lenz's law **L:** 197 *with diagram*
 Light (Electromagnetic waves) **L:** 286
 Magnetic equator **M:** 55 *with map*
 Magnetic resonance imaging **M:** 56
 Magnetic storm **M:** 57
 Magnetohydrodynamics **M:** 62
 Magnetometer **M:** 62
 Map (Advances in European cartography) **M:** 184
 Mars (Core) **M:** 225
 Materials (Magnetic properties) **M:** 300c
 Moon (Core) **M:** 791
 Particle accelerator (Uses of accelerators) **P:** 184
 Petroleum (Geophysical studies) **P:** 336
 Plate tectonics (Evidence of plate movement) **P:** 563
 Polarized light (Understanding polarized light) **P:** 617
 Pulsar **P:** 900a
 Quantum field theory **Q:** 5
 Radiation (Electromagnetic radiation) **R:** 75
 Range (Electric ranges) **R:** 137-138
 Relativity (The Michelson-Morley experiment) **R:** 210
 Seismograph **S:** 288
 Space exploration (The beginning of space) **So:** 696
 Sun **So:** 975; (Magnetic field) **So:** 977 *with pictures*
 Sunspot (How sunspots form) **So:** 991
 Superconductivity **So:** 992
 Tape recorder (Erasing and recording) **T:** 38

 Universe **U:** 205
 Uranus (Magnetic field) **U:** 219 *with diagram*
 Van Allen belts **V:** 269
 Voyager **V:** 451
 Weber **W:** 175
 Zeeman effect **Z:** 588
Magnetic flow meter
 Water meter **W:** 135
Magnetic flux [physics]
 Weber **W:** 175
Magnetic force [physics]
 Force (The magnetic force) **F:** 371
 Quantum field theory **Q:** 5
Magnetic Hill Complex
 New Brunswick (Places to visit) **N:** 188
Magnetic induction cooktop [appliance]
 Range (Electric ranges) **R:** 137-138
Magnetic lens
 Electron microscope (Transmission electron microscopes) **E:** 204 *with diagram*
Magnetic levitation train M: 55 *with pictures*
 Air cushion vehicle (History) **A:** 181
 Electric railroad **E:** 188
 Linear electric motor **L:** 334 *with diagram*
 Magnetism (In transportation) **M:** 60a
 Monorail **M:** 733
 Shanghai (History) **S:** 372
 Transportation *picture on* **T:** 398; (Transportation today) **T:** 392-394
Magnetic mine
 Mine warfare (Kinds of naval mines) **M:** 565
Magnetic pole
 See also North magnetic pole; South magnetic pole *in this index*
 Magnetism **M:** 58; (Magnetic poles) **M:** 59 *with diagram*; (The magnetism of astronomical bodies) **M:** 60d; (Magnetic monopoles) **M:** 61
 Boothia Peninsula **B:** 481
 Compass (Variation) **Ci:** 902b
 Magnetic equator **M:** 55
 North Pole **N:** 517
 Pole **P:** 618
 South Pole **So:** 685
Magnetic properties
 Materials (Magnetic properties) **M:** 300c
Magnetic resonance imaging M: 56 *with picture*
 Absolute zero **A:** 17
 Biophysics **B:** 326
 Brain (Imaging) **B:** 551; (Disorders of the brain) **B:** 557-558
 Cancer (Preliminary diagnosis) **C:** 171
 Computer (Medical visualization software) **Ci:** 920 *with picture*
 Cryogenics **Ci:** 1165
 Dyslexia **D:** 398
 Magnetism *picture on* **M:** 58; (In science and medicine) **M:** 60b; (Magnetic resonance) **M:** 61
 Medicine (Diagnosis) **M:** 364
 Mental illness (Recent developments) **M:** 409
 Multiple sclerosis **M:** 920
 Superconductivity **So:** 992
Magnetic storm [astronomy] **M:** 57
 Aurora **A:** 892
 Van Allen belts **V:** 269
Magnetic-stripe card
 Smart card **S:** 513
Magnetic susceptibility [engineering]
 Materials (Magnetic properties) **M:** 300c
Magnetic tape [electronics]
 See also Tape drive *in this index*
 Motion picture (The sound track) **M:** 857
 Tape recorder **T:** 36; (How tape recorders work) **T:** 37 *with picture*
Magnetic Telegraph Company
 Telegraph (Construction and growth) **T:** 90-91
Magnetism [physics] **M:** 58 *with pictures*
 See also Electromagnet; Electromagnetism *in this index*
 Electricity (Electric and magnetic fields) **E:** 195; (Electricity and magnetism) **E:** 196
 Electromagnetic waves **E:** 201
 Hypnosis (Mesmerism) **H:** 479
 Lodestone **L:** 419
 Permalloy **P:** 289
 Physics (Electricity and magnetism) **P:** 437; (Developments in the 1800's) **P:** 440
 Sun (Magnetic field) **So:** 977
 Tachometer **T:** 4
 Zeeman effect **Z:** 588
Magnetite [mineral]
 Electricity (Early discoveries) **E:** 196
 Iron and steel (Kinds of iron ore) **I:** 438
 Lodestone **L:** 419
 Magnetism (Permanent magnets) **M:** 60 *with picture*; (Magnets in living things) **M:** 61
 Mars (Possibility of life) **M:** 226c
 Mineral *picture on* **M:** 568

Taconite T: 5
Magnetization [physics]
  Magnetism (Magnetization) M: 59
Magneto [machine] M: 62
  Electric generator (Parts of a generator) E: 170-171
  Ignition I: 49
Magneto-optical recording
  Compact disc (Minidiscs) Ci: 902a
Magnetohydrodynamics [physics] M: 62
  Energy supply (Magnetohydrodynamic [MHD] generators) E: 279
Magnetometer [measuring device] M: 62
  Petroleum (Geophysical studies) P: 336
  Prospecting P: 829
Magnetophon
  Tape recorder (History) T: 38-39
Magnetosphere [physics]
  Aurora A: 891
  Cassini C: 276
  Jupiter J: 197
  Magnetism (Earth) M: 60d
  Saturn S: 150i
  Solar wind So: 582
  Space exploration (The beginning of space) So: 696
Magnetron [electronic device]
  Electronics (The vacuum tube era) E: 215
  Microwave oven M: 520
  Radar (Advances during World War II) R: 72
  Vacuum tube (Microwave tubes) V: 259
Magnificat [music by Johann Sebastian Bach]
  Bach, Johann Sebastian (His works) B: 16-17
Magnification
  See also Magnifying glass in this index
  Electron microscope E: 203
  Microscope M: 517
  Telescope T: 102; (Producing detailed images) T: 103
Magnificent Ambersons, The [film]
  Welles, Orson W: 194
Magnificent frigatebird [bird]
  Bird picture on B: 344
Magnificent Mile [area]
  Chicago (Downtown Chicago) C: 420-421
Magnifying glass M: 62
  See also Magnification in this index
Magnifying power [optics] See Magnification in this index
Magnitude [astronomy] M: 62
  Star (Characteristics of stars) So: 842
Magnolia [tree] M: 63 with picture
Magnolia State [nickname]
  Mississippi M: 622
Magnus I [king of Denmark and Norway]
  Harald III H: 55
Magnuson Clinical Center
  National Institutes of Health N: 39
Magoon, Charles E. [American government official]
  Cuba (The Platt Amendment) Ci: 1176
Magpie [bird] M: 63 with picture
Magritte, René [Belgian painter] M: 63
Maguey [plant] M: 63
Maguire, Matthew [American labor leader]
  Labor Day L: 2
Magyar [language]
  Hungary (Language) H: 439
Magyars [people] M: 63
  Hungary (Ancestry) H: 439; (History) H: 445
  Transylvania T: 402
Mah-jongg [Chinese game] M: 64 with picture
  Game (Tile games) G: 22
Mahabharata [Hindu poem] M: 64
  Bhagavad-Gita B: 276
  Dance (Asian theatrical dance) D: 28-29
  Hinduism (Sacred writings) H: 235
  India (Literature) I: 120
  Krishna K: 388
  Vishnu V: 429
Mahakam River
  Borneo (The land and its resources) B: 489 with map
Mahaleb cherry tree
  Cherry C: 410
Mahama, John Dramani [Ghanaian political leader]
  Ghana (History) G: 179-180
Mahan, Alfred Thayer [American historian] M: 64
Maharajah [title]
  Rajah R: 130
Maharashtra [state, India]
  Mumbai (History) M: 925
Mahathir bin Mohamad [Malaysian political leader] M: 65
  Malaysia (Recent developments) M: 102
Mahatma [title]

Gandhi, Mohandas Karamchand (Gandhi's beliefs) G: 25
Mahatma, The [nickname]
  Rickey, Branch R: 335
Mahavira [Indian religious leader] M: 65
  India (Jainism) I: 117
  Jainism J: 22
Mahayana [religion]
  Bodhisattva B: 434
  Buddhism (Buddhist schools) B: 669
  Religion (Buddhism) R: 220
Mahdi [Sudanese political leader] See Ahmad, Muhammad in this index
Mahdi, Sadiq al [Sudanese political leader]
  Sudan (Civil war) So: 953
Mahé [island]
  Seychelles S: 339
Mahendra [king of Nepal]
  Nepal (History) N: 126-127
Mahendra-Mala, Order of [Nepal]
  Medals, decorations, and orders (table) M: 359
Mahfouz, Naguib [Egyptian author] M: 65
  Arabic literature (Fiction) A: 583-584
  Egypt (The arts) E: 125
  Nobel Prizes (Literature: 1988) N: 448
Mahi mahi [fish] See Dolphinfish in this index
Mahican Indians M: 65
Mahler, Gustav [Bohemian-born Austrian composer] M: 65
  Austria (Music) A: 932
  Walter, Bruno W: 21
Mahmud of Ghazni [Afghan ruler]
  India (Period of invasions) I: 129
  Pakistan (The Islamic impact) P: 99
Mahogany [wood] M: 66
Mahomet [prophet] See Muhammad in this index
Mahony, Roger Michael [American religious leader] M: 66
Mahoré See Mayotte in this index
Mahuad, Jamil [Ecuadorean political leader]
  Ecuador (The 1900's) E: 73-74
Mai Idris Alooma [king of Kanem]
  Kanem K: 213
Maid Marian [literary figure]
  Robin Hood R: 367
Maid of honor
  Marriage (Wedding ceremonies) M: 220
Maid of Orléans See Joan of Arc, Saint in this index
Maid of the Mist, The [ship]
  Niagara Falls (Tourism) N: 392 with picture
Maida, Adam J. [American religious leader]
  Cardinal (table: American cardinals) C: 211
Maidan [park, Kolkata]
  Kolkata (The city) K: 362
Maiden of Kosovo [sculpture by Meštrović]
  Meštrović, Ivan M: 424
Maiden race
  Horse racing (Maiden races) H: 365
Maidenhair fern [plant]
  Tree (Ginkgo trees) T: 415
Maidenhair tree [tree]
  Ginkgo G: 192
  Tree (Ginkgo trees) T: 415
Maids of Honor, The [painting by Velázquez] See Meninas, Las in this index
Maidu Indians M: 66
  California (Early days) C: 60
  Folklore picture on F: 322
Maigret, Inspector Jules [literary figure]
  Detective story (The pattern) D: 162
  Simenon, Georges S: 466
Maigret and the Enigmatic Lett [book by Simenon]
  Simenon, Georges S: 466
Maijishan Tunnel [Japan]
  Tunnel (table) T: 491
Maikop culture
  Bronze Age B: 639
Mail See E-mail; Post office in this index
Mail [armor]
  Armor (During the Middle Ages) A: 719
  Knights and knighthood (Armor) K: 350
Mail carrier See Letter carrier in this index
Mail handler [occupation]
  Postal services (Sorting) P: 703
Mail-order business M: 66
  Advertising (Direct mail) A: 74
  United States, History of the (Improved sales methods) U: 180-181
Mail-order nursery [horticulture]
  Nursery N: 614
Mail services See Postal services in this index
Mailbox
  Postal services pictures on P: 704; (Collection) P: 702
Mailer, Norman [American author] M: 66
  Novel (The novel today) N: 575
Mailing list

Advertising (Direct mail) A: 74
Maillard, Louis Camille [French scientist]
  Cooking (Methods) Ci: 1029
Maillard reaction [chemistry]
  Cooking (Methods) Ci: 1029
Maillol, Aristide [French sculptor] M: 67
Maiman, Theodore [American physicist]
  Invention (Recent developments) I: 364
  Laser (History) L: 86
  Physics picture on P: 442
Maimed of Lepanto [name for]
  Cervantes, Miguel de (His early life) C: 363
Maimon, Solomon ben See Maimonides, Moses in this index
Maimonides, Moses [Jewish philosopher] M: 67
  Hebrew literature (Medieval works) H: 162
Main [plumbing]
  Gas [fuel] (Transmitting and distributing gas) G: 55
  Pipeline (Gas pipelines) P: 490
  Plumbing (The water supply system) P: 577
  Water (Distributing water) W: 127
Main battle tank
  Tank T: 27 with diagram
Main Belt [astronomy]
  Asteroid A: 823, diagram on A: 824a
  Ceres C: 362
  Satellite (Satellites of the terrestrial planets) S: 150; (Nonplanetary satellites) S: 150b
  Solar system (Asteroids) So: 581
Main clause [grammar]
  Clause C: 657
Main-Danube Canal [Germany]
  Canal (table) C: 164
  Danube River D: 34
Main deck
  Ship (Basic structure) S: 403-404
Main entry [mining]
  Coal (The room-and-pillar system) Ci: 723 with diagram
Main Line [area]
  Philadelphia (The metropolitan area) P: 362
Main line [tackle]
  Fishing industry (Hooks) F: 185 with picture
Main-line track
  Railroad (Tracks) R: 108
Main memory [computer] See Random-access memory in this index
Main ring [astronomy]
  Jupiter (Rings) J: 200a with picture
Main sequence [astronomy]
  Star (Intermediate-mass stars) So: 848
Main Street [book by Lewis]
  Lewis, Sinclair L: 221
  Roaring Twenties (Cultural trends) R: 364
Main Street of the United States [name for]
  Lincoln Highway L: 327
Main-Travelled Roads [stories by Garland]
  Garland, Hamlin G: 43
Maïnassara, Ibrahim Bare [Niger political leader]
  Niger (History) N: 409
Maine [ship] M: 67 with picture
  Cuba (Struggle against Spain) Ci: 1176 with picture
  McKinley, William (The Spanish-American War [1898]) M: 340-341
  Roosevelt, Theodore (The Rough Riders) R: 463
  Spanish-American War (Background to the war) So: 753
  United States, History of the (The Spanish-American War) U: 185
Maine [state] M: 68 with pictures and maps
  See also the list of Related articles in the Maine article
Maine, University of M: 93
  Maine picture on M: 73
Maine coon [cat]
  Cat picture on C: 289; (Long-haired breeds) C: 292
Maine Farmers' Almanac [magazine]
  Blue moon B: 421
Maine Historical Society
  Maine picture on M: 73
Maine Indian Claims Settlement Act
  Maine picture on M: 92
Maine Islands [painting by Marin]
  Marin, John picture on M: 203
Maine Lighthouse Museum [Rockland]
  Maine (Places to visit) M: 78 with picture
Maine Lobster Festival [Rockland]
  Maine picture on M: 79
Maine Maritime Museum [Bath]
  Maine (Places to visit) M: 78
Maine-Montparnasse Tower
  Paris (Renewal and new construction) P: 166-167
Maine Rx [program]
  Maine (The early 2000's) M: 92
Maine Yankee [power plant]

Maine (The late 1900's) **M:** 92
Mainframe computer [machine]
Computer (Mainframes and supercomputers) **Ci:** 910 *with picture*
United States, History of the (The Information Age) **U:** 196b *with picture*
Mainichi Shimbun [newspaper]
Newspaper (In Asia) **N:** 386
Mainland [island, Orkney Islands]
Orkney Islands **O:** 856
Mainland [island, Shetland Islands]
Shetland Islands **S:** 398
Mainline denomination [religion]
Christianity (Christianity today) **C:** 526-527
Mainlining [slang]
Heroin **H:** 213
Mainmast [part of ship]
Galleon **G:** 15
Sailing (Spars) **S:** 23
Ship (The full-rigged ship) **S:** 418-419
Maino, Sonia [Indian political leader] *See* Gandhi, Sonia *in this index*
Mainsail [part of ship]
Sailing (Sails) **S:** 24 *with diagram*
Mainspring [device]
Clock (Mechanical clocks) **Ci:** 682j
Watch (Mechanical watches) **W:** 114 *with picture*
Mainstreaming [education]
Deafness (Education) **D:** 59
Special education **So:** 770
Maintain the right [motto]
Royal Canadian Mounted Police *picture on* **R:** 495
Maintenance bilingual program
Bilingual education (Transitional bilingual education) **B:** 300
Maintenance-of-membership clause [labor]
Right-to-work law **R:** 340
Maintenance worker
Careers (Construction, maintenance, and repair) **C:** 221
Maintenon, Marquise de [wife of Louis XIV] **M:** 93
Louis XIV **L:** 475
Mainz [Germany] **M:** 93
Mouse Tower **M:** 902
Maio [island]
Cape Verde **C:** 189 *with map*
Maiolica [pottery] *See* Majolica *in this index*
Mair, Charles [Canadian author] **M:** 93
Maison de l'Art Nouveau [Paris]
Art Nouveau **A:** 749
Maisonneuve, Sieur de [French explorer]
Montreal **M:** 768; (French settlement) **M:** 777
Maitland, Frederic William [British historian] **M:** 93
Maitland, L. J. [American military leader]
Hawaii (The Territory of Hawaii) **H:** 108
Maius [month]
Calendar (The Romans) **C:** 31
Maize [food] *See* Corn *in this index*
Maize and Wheat, International Center for the Improvement of
Food supply (Research programs) **F:** 351
Maizière, Lothar de [German political leader]
Germany (East Germany) **G:** 170-171
Majardah River
Tunisia (Land) **T:** 488 *with map*
Majas [paintings by Goya]
Goya, Francisco **G:** 295
Majdanek [concentration camp]
Concentration camp (Nazi concentration camps) **Ci:** 926-927
Maji Maji rebellion [Tanzanian history]
Tanzania (Colonial rule) **T:** 35
Majlis [government]
Iran (National government) **I:** 399; (The Qajar dynasty) **I:** 406
Maldives (Government) **M:** 104
Majluta, Jacobo [Dominican Republic political leader]
Dominican Republic (History) **D:** 304-305
Majolica [pottery] **M:** 93
Pottery *picture on* **P:** 717; (Early pottery) **P:** 718
Major [education]
Curriculum (Curriculum content) **Ci:** 1197
Teaching (Teacher-training programs) **T:** 67-68
Major [rank]
Rank, Military (table) **R:** 140
Major, Elliott W. [American political leader]
Missouri (table) **M:** 668
Major, John [British political leader] **M:** 94
Heseltine, Michael Ray Dibdin **H:** 218
United Kingdom (Thatcher resigned) **U:** 73
Major airline
Airport (Commercial service airports) **A:** 243
Major axis [geometry]
Ellipse **E:** 243 *with diagram*
Major Barbara [play by Shaw]
Shaw, George Bernard (Mature period) **S:** 378

Major decision [wrestling]
Wrestling (High school and intercollegiate wrestling) **W:** 505
Major general [rank]
General **G:** 82
Rank, Military (table) **R:** 140
Major histocompatibility complex protein [genetics]
Immune system *diagram on* **I:** 88b; (The cell-mediated immune response) **I:** 88
Major interval [music]
Music (Harmony) **M:** 951
Major League Baseball Players Association
Labor movement (table) **L:** 8
Major League Soccer
Soccer (In North America) **So:** 548
Major leagues
Baseball (Major leagues) **B:** 130; (The early 1900's) **B:** 135
Major medical expense benefit
Insurance (Major medical expense benefits) **I:** 312
Major planet [astronomy]
Planet **P:** 507
Major scale
Music (Tone) **M:** 950 *with diagram*
Major tone
Tone **T:** 327
Majorca [island, Mediterranean] **M:** 94
Balearic Islands **B:** 40
Majorette
Baton twirling **B:** 167
Majorian [Roman emperor]
Rome, Ancient (table) **R:** 447
Majority, Age of
Minor **M:** 607
Majority leader [government]
Congress of the United States (The Senate) **Ci:** 942
Majority party [government]
Prime minister **P:** 778c
United States, Government of the (Party leadership) **U:** 138
Majority rule M: 94
Democracy (Features of democracy) **D:** 120
Parliamentary procedure (Electing officers) **P:** 175
Voting **V:** 449
Majuro [Marshall Islands] **M:** 94
Majuscule [writing]
Alphabet (Capital letters) **A:** 383
Mak yong [drama]
Malaysia (The arts) **M:** 99
Makah [people]
Nootka Indians **N:** 453
Makalu, Mount *See* Mount Makalu *in this index*
Makanin, Vladimir [Russian author]
Russian literature (Modern Russian literature) **R:** 565
Makara Sankranti [custom]
January **J:** 30
Makarezos, Nicholas [Greek political leader]
Greece (The revolt of 1967) **G:** 364; (The restoration of democracy) **G:** 365
Makarios III [Cypriot political leader]
Cyprus (History) **Ci:** 1207
Makarov Basin [geography]
Arctic Ocean (The deep basin) **A:** 643 *with map*
Makarova, Natalia [Soviet-born dancer]
Ballet (Ballet in Russia) **B:** 52-53
Makarska Riviera [region]
Croatia *picture on* **Ci:** 1148b
Makassar [Indonesia]
Indonesia (Sulawesi) **I:** 233
Make Way for Ducklings [book by McCloskey]
McCloskey, Robert **M:** 332d *with picture*
Makeba, Miriam [South African singer]
Masekela, Hugh **M:** 263
Makemake [dwarf planet]
Dwarf planet **D:** 394
Planet (The outer dwarf planets) **P:** 512
Makeready
Printing (Offset presses) **P:** 798-799
Makerere University
Uganda (People) **U:** 2-3
Makers and Finders [book by Brooks]
Brooks, Van Wyck **B:** 641
Makeup
See also Cosmetics *in this index*
Motion picture *picture on* **M:** 853
Theater (Makeup techniques) **T:** 243 *with pictures*
Thespis **T:** 257
Makhna [elephant]
Elephant (Asian elephants) **E:** 227-228
Makhosetive [prince of Swaziland]
Swaziland (History) **So:** 1019
Maki sushi [food]
Sushi **So:** 1012

Makkah Royal Clock Tower [Mecca]
Skyscraper (table) **S:** 498
Mako shark M: 94
Shark (Kinds of sharks) **S:** 375 *with picture*
Makoko [Batéké king]
Congo, Republic of the (History) **Ci:** 940e
Makonde [people]
Tanzania (Population and ancestry) **T:** 31
Makropoulos Secret, The [play by Čapek]
Čapek, Karel **C:** 191
Maksud al-Kashani [Islamic weaver]
Islamic art **I:** 469
Malabar [region, India]
Cardamom **C:** 209
Malabo [Equatorial Guinea] **M:** 94
Malacca [Malaysia] *See* Melaka *in this index*
Malachi, Book of [Bible] **M:** 95
Malachite [mineral] **M:** 95
Mineral *picture on* **M:** 569
Malachite kingfisher [bird]
Bird *picture on* **B:** 345
Malagasy [language]
Madagascar (People) **M:** 27
Malagasy Republic [former name]
Madagascar **M:** 27; (History) **M:** 29
Malagueta pepper
Liberia (Early days) **L:** 231
Malaita Eagle Force [political group]
Solomon Islands (History) **So:** 585
Malaita Island
Solomon Islands (History) **So:** 585
Malakula [island, Vanuatu]
Vanuatu **V:** 284
Malamud, Bernard [American author] **M:** 95
Novel (After World War II) **N:** 574
Malamute [dog] *See* Alaskan malamute *in this index*
Malan, Daniel François [South African political leader] **M:** 95
South Africa (Apartheid) **So:** 619
Malaprop, Mrs. [literary figure]
Sheridan, Richard Brinsley **S:** 396
Malaria [disease] **M:** 95 *with pictures*
Colonial life in America (Health and medicine) **Ci:** 809
Disease *picture on* **D:** 229
Evolution (Balancing or diversifying selection) **E:** 429
Laveran, Charles Louis Alphonse **L:** 129
Quinine **Q:** 42
Races, Human (Susceptibility to genetic diseases) **R:** 58
Malas, Spiro [American singer]
Opera *picture on* **O:** 792
Malaspina Glacier
Alaska (Glaciers) **A:** 295
Glacier (Famous glaciers) **G:** 204
Malathion [insecticide]
Insecticide (Organophosphate insecticides) **I:** 302
Malawi M: 96 *with picture and map*
Flag *picture on* **F:** 199
Malawi, Lake
Malawi **M:** 96 *with picture and map*
Malay language M: 98
Malays **M:** 98
Malaysia (People) **M:** 98b-98c
Malaya [former region, Malaysia] **M:** 98
Malaysia **M:** 98a
World War II (Early Japanese victories) **W:** 487
Malaya, Federation of
Malaysia (Independence) **M:** 102
Malayalam [language]
Dravidians **D:** 342
Malayan bear *See* Sun bear *in this index*
Malayan tapir [animal]
Tapir **T:** 41
Malayo-Polynesian language
Africa (Languages) **A:** 105
Language *map on* **L:** 65; (Other language families) **L:** 66
Malay language **M:** 98
Malays [people] **M:** 98
Indonesia (People) **I:** 227
Malaysia *picture on* **M:** 98d; (People) **M:** 98b-98c
Sri Lanka (People) **So:** 817
Sumatra **So:** 971
Malaysia M: 98a *with pictures and map*
Asia (The arts) **A:** 785
Borneo **B:** 489 *with map*
Dayaks **D:** 53
Flag *picture on* **F:** 203
Forest *picture on* **F:** 399
Indonesia (Indonesia under Sukarno) **I:** 238
Kuala Lumpur **K:** 390
Raffles, Sir Thomas Stamford **R:** 101
Rain forest *picture on* **R:** 126
Straits Settlements **So:** 918
Malaysia, Federation of [Malaysian history]

Malaysia (Building national unity) M: 102
Malcolm II [king of Scotland]
Duncan I D: 383
Scotland (Beginning of the Scottish kingdom) S: 219
Malcolm III [king of Scotland]
David (David I) D: 45
Henry I [king of England] H: 185
Macbeth M: 5
Scotland (Beginning of the Scottish kingdom) S: 219
Malcolm Canmore [king of Scotland] *See* Malcolm III *in this index*
Malcolm X [American social reformer] M: 103 *with portrait*
African Americans (Black militancy) A: 136q
Black Muslims B: 390
Farrakhan, Louis F: 48
Muhammad, Elijah M: 911
Malcolm X [film by Lee]
Lee, Spike L: 180
"Malcolm's Katie" [poem by Crawford]
Canadian literature (Poetry: 1850-1918) C: 157
Malden, Karl [American actor]
Motion picture (Best performance by an actor in a supporting role: 1951) M: 862a
Maldives M: 103 *with picture and map*
Flag *picture on* F: 203
Maldonado, Diego [Spanish explorer]
Pensacola P: 272
Male [Maldives] M: 105
Male [sexuality]
See also Boy; Man *in this index*
Animal (Sexual reproduction) A: 496
Ant A: 520
Fragile X syndrome F: 451
Growth (Growth rate) G: 405
Heredity (Chromosomes and sexual determination) H: 202; (Sex-linked genes) H: 202
Penis P: 241
Reproduction, Human (The human reproductive system) R: 244-245 *with diagram*
Sex ratio S: 336
Sexuality (Biological factors) S: 337
Steroid (The sex steroids) So: 894
Male pattern baldness
Baldness B: 38
Malebo Pool [lake]
Congo, Republic of the (Land) Ci: 940d-940e *with map*
Congo River Ci: 940f
Malecite Indians *See* Maliseet Indians *in this index*
Malecón [road]
Havana (The city) H: 86
Malemiuts [people]
Alaskan malamute A: 305
Malemute [dog] *See* Alaskan malamute *in this index*
Malenkov, Georgi Maximilianovich [Soviet political leader] M: 105
Cold War (To the brink and back) Ci: 765
Union of Soviet Socialist Republics (The rise of Khrushchev) U: 38
Malevich, Kasimir [Russian artist] M: 105 *with picture*
Painting (Nonobjective painting in Russia) P: 79 *with picture*
Malherbe, François de [French poet] M: 106
French literature (Classical poetry) F: 520
Mali M: 106 *with pictures and map*
Africa *picture on* A: 113
Clothing *picture on* Ci: 698
Exploration (The exploration of Africa) E: 448
Flag *picture on* F: 199
French West Africa F: 528 *with map*
Mask *picture on* M: 264
Mali, Federation of [African history]
French West Africa (History) F: 528
Mali (History) M: 108-109
Senegal (History) S: 299
Mali Empire [African history] M: 109 *with map*
Africa (The empires of west Africa) A: 131
African Americans (The cultural heritage) A: 136c
Exploration (Muslim exploration) E: 442
Guinea (History) G: 432
Mali (History) M: 108
Mandinka M: 137
Sundiata Keita So: 990
World, History of the (African civilizations) W: 437 *with picture*
Malice [law]
Libel L: 226
Murder M: 929
Malicious virus [software]
Computer virus Ci: 925
Malietoa Tanumafili II [Samoan government official]

Samoa (Government) S: 80
Malignancy [medicine] M: 110
Malignant melanoma [disease] *See* Melanoma *in this index*
Malignant tumor [disorder]
See also Cancer *in this index*
Biopsy B: 326
Malignancy M: 110
Skin (Tumors) S: 491
Tumor T: 484
Maligne Lake [Alberta]
Canada *picture on* C: 115
Maliki, Nouri Kamel al- [Iraqi political leader] M: 110
Iraq (A new government) I: 414a *with picture*
Malinche [American Indian]
Cortés, Hernán (Arrival in Mexico) Ci: 1072
Exploration (Spain's conquests in the New World) E: 445
Latin America (The conquest of the American Indians) L: 103
Malinke [people]
Guinea (People) G: 431
Mali (People) M: 106
Mandinka M: 137
Malinowski, Bronisław [British anthropologist] M: 110
Anthropology (The early 1900's) A: 548
Mythology (Anthropological approaches) M: 989-990
Malintzin [American Indian] *See* Malinche *in this index*
Maliseet Indians
Indian, American (The push for Indian rights) I: 179
Maine (The late 1900's) M: 92 *with picture*
New Brunswick (First Nations) N: 196
Saint John (Government and history) S: 35
Mall [business]
Shopping center S: 434
Mall [Washington, D.C.]
Washington, D.C. (The Mall) W: 71
Mall of America [Minneapolis]
Minneapolis (Recreation) M: 582
Minnesota (Places to visit) M: 594
Mallard [bird] M: 110 *with picture*
Duck *picture on* D: 375; (Dabbling ducks) D: 376
Mallarmé, Stéphane [French poet] M: 110
American literature (Poetry) A: 418-419
French literature (Symbolism) F: 522
Mallea, Eduardo [Argentine author]
Latin American literature (The mid-1900's) L: 114
Malleability [physical property]
Copper (Malleability) Ci: 1041
Ductility D: 377
Gold (Physical properties) G: 249
Metal (What metals are) M: 425
Mallee scrub [plant]
Australia (Native plants) A: 911-912
Mallein test [medicine]
Glanders G: 210
Mallet [instrument]
Cymbal Ci: 1204
Mallet, Paul [French explorer]
Nebraska (Exploration) N: 111
Mallet, Pierre [French explorer]
Nebraska (Exploration) N: 111
Mallet, Robert [Irish engineer]
Geology (Experimental geology) G: 99
Malleus [anatomy]
Ear *diagram on* E: 10; (The middle ear) E: 7-8 *with diagram*
Mallon, Mary [American public figure] *See* Typhoid Mary *in this index*
Mallophaga [entomology]
Insect (table) I: 300
Mallorca [island, Mediterranean] *See* Majorca *in this index*
Mallory, Stephen Russell [American political leader] M: 111
Malloum, Félix [Chadian political leader]
Chad (History) C: 367
Mallow [botany] M: 111
Flower *picture on* F: 291; (table) F: 300 *with picture*
Malloy, Dan [American political leader]
Connecticut (table) C: 967
Malmö [Sweden] M: 111
Malmöhus Castle
Malmö M: 111
Malnutrition [disorder] M: 111
Food (How the body uses food) F: 330
Food supply (Basic human food needs) F: 346
Nutrition (Deficiency diseases) N: 630
Malocclusion [disorder]
Dentistry (Orthodontics) D: 143
Orthodontics O: 860

Teeth (Malocclusion) T: 84 *with pictures*
Malodor
Deodorizer D: 148
Malone, Dorothy [American actress]
Motion picture (Best performance by an actress in a supporting role: 1956) M: 862b
Malone, Edmund [British scholar]
Boswell, James B: 506
Shakespeare, William (Editions of the 1700's and 1800's) S: 369
Malone, Karl [American basketball player] M: 111
Chamberlain, Wilt C: 371
Malone, Vivian [American public figure]
Alabama (The mid-1900's) A: 278
Malone Dies [book by Beckett]
Novel (After World War II) N: 574
Maloof, Sam [American designer]
Furniture (Post-modern design) F: 585-586
Malory, Sir Thomas [English author] M: 111
Arthur, King A: 757
English literature (The development of English romances) E: 315
Maloti Mountains
Lesotho (Land) L: 207
Malotte, Albert H. [American composer]
Lord's Prayer L: 454
Malpeque Bay
Prince Edward Island (Land and climate) P: 790
Malpighi, Marcello [Italian anatomist] M: 112
Biology (Early discoveries with the microscope) B: 318
Malpighian tube [entomology]
Insect (Digestive system) I: 289 *with diagram*
Malpractice insurance
Insurance (Product and professional liability insurance) II: 314
Malpractice suit M: 112
Medicine (Financing advanced medical care) M: 377-378
Malpractice suit [law] M: 112
Consumer protection (The right to be heard) Ci: 1018-1019
Medicine (Treatment) M: 364-365
Malraux, André [French author] M: 112
Malt [grain] M: 112
Barley (Uses of barley) B: 113
Beer B: 211
Brewing (Malting) B: 595
Grain (Other uses) G: 301
Malt liquor [beverage]
Alcoholic beverage (Beer) A: 336
Beer B: 211
Malt sugar [carbohydrate] *See* Maltose *in this index*
Malta [country] M: 113 *with picture and map*
Flag *picture on* F: 206
Knights Hospitallers K: 351
Malta [island, Mediterranean]
Malta M: 113 *with map*
Malta, Knights of *See* Knights Hospitallers *in this index*
Malta fever *See* Brucellosis *in this index*
Maltese [dog] M: 115
Dog *picture on* D: 274
Maltese [language]
Malta (People) M: 113
Maltese cross [symbol]
Cross *picture on* Ci: 1155
Medals, decorations, and orders (Orders) M: 355
Maltese Falcon, The [book by Hammett]
Hammett, Dashiell H: 35
Maltese Falcon, The [film]
Bogart, Humphrey B: 436
Huston, John H: 458
Maltese Labour Party [political party]
Malta (History) M: 113-114
Maltese Nationalist Party [political party]
Malta (History) M: 113-114
Malthus, Thomas Robert [British economist] M: 115
Birth control (The birth control movement) B: 378
Economics (The classical economists) E: 64
Evolution (Darwin's theory) E: 432
Food supply F: 345
Population (Effects) P: 674
Malting [industrial process]
Vinegar (Making vinegar) V: 386
Yeast (How yeast is used) Y: 554-555
Maltose [sugar]
Carbohydrate (Kinds of carbohydrates) C: 203 *with diagram*
Saliva S: 67
Starch (Use in foods) So: 855
Sugar (Kinds of sugar) So: 960
Malvinas, Islas [islands] *See* Falkland Islands *in this index*
Malvolio [literary figure]

Shakespeare, William: (*Twelfth Night)* S: 360-361
Malware [software]
Internet (Internet crime) I: 350f
Maly Theatre [Russia]
Theater (Russia) T: 248-249 *with picture*
Mälzel, Johann N. [German inventor]
Doll (Inventions) D: 291
Metronome M: 442
Mamba [snake] M: 115 *with picture*
Snake *picture on* S: 526
Mambo [dance]
Ballroom dancing B: 63
Puente, Tito P: 871
Mamelukes [people] *See* Mamluks *in this index*
Mamet, David [American playwright] M: 115
American literature (Drama) A: 426
Drama (Later United States drama) D: 340
Mamikonian, Vartan [Armenian military leader]
Armenia (History) A: 718b
Mamluks [people] M: 115
Cairo (History) C: 17-18
Egypt (Muslim rule) E: 130; (Ottoman and French control) E: 130
Palestine (Arab control) P: 104-105
Syria (The Mamluks and Ottomans) So: 1075
Mamma Mia! [musical]
Musical comedy (Musical comedy today) M: 961
Mammal [zoology] M: 116 *with pictures*
See also the list of Related articles in the Mammal *article*
Animal (table: Length of life of animals) A: 473; (How animals raise their young) A: 498
Brain (Among vertebrates) B: 560 *with diagram*
Circulatory system (Vertebrates) Ci: 561
Earth (The Mesozoic Era) E: 27
Emotion (The basic emotion approach) E: 261
Estrous cycle E: 363
Evolution *picture on* E: 429; (The fossil record) E: 430
Hair H: 9
Heart (Birds and mammals) H: 146
Lactation L: 25
Molting M: 697
Pleistocene Epoch P: 572
Prehistoric animal (Mammals) P: 739; (The Age of Mammals) P: 740 *with pictures*
Reproduction (Mammals) R: 243
Skin (Animal skin) S: 491
Teeth (Teeth of animals) T: 86 *with picture*
Tetrapod T: 182b *with diagram*
Mammalogy [science]
Zoology (What zoologists study) Z: 606-607
Mammals, Age of *See* Cenozoic Era *in this index*
Mammary glands [anatomy] M: 129
Breast B: 590
Gland (table) G: 209
Lactation L: 25
Mammal (Care of the young) M: 124
Mammogram [medicine]
Cancer (Cancer checkups) C: 171 *with picture*
Mammography M: 129
Mammography [medicine] M: 129
Breast B: 590
Cancer (Cancer checkups) C: 171 *with picture*
Medicine *picture on* M: 364
Mammoth [extinct animal] M: 130
Extinction *picture on* E: 456
Fossil *picture on* F: 427; (Other processes) F: 425 *with picture*
Nebraska (Interesting facts) N: 95 *with picture*
Mammoth Cave National Park [Kentucky] M: 130
Kentucky (Places to visit) K: 282 *with picture*
National Park System (table: National parks) N: 48
Mammoth-Flint Ridge Cave System [Kentucky]
Cave (table) C: 320
Kentucky (Interesting facts about Kentucky) K: 273
Mammoth Hot Springs
Yellowstone National Park (The Upper Loop) Y: 559 *with map*
Mammoth Spring
Arkansas A: 694; (Springs) A: 708
Man
See also Human being; Male *in this index*
Marriage M: 219
Man, Isle of [island, Irish Sea] M: 130
"Man Against the Sky, The" [poem by Robinson]
Robinson, Edwin Arlington R: 368
Man and Superman [play by Shaw]
Shaw, George Bernard (Mature period) S: 378
Man & Woman by a Hedge [print by Harunobu]
Japanese print *picture on* J: 63
Man Called White, A [book by White]
White, Walter Francis W: 285
Man for All Seasons, A [film]
Motion picture (Best picture: 1966) M: 861
Zinnemann, Fred Z: 595

Man Friday [literary figure]
Robinson Crusoe R: 369
Man from Glengarry, The [book by Gordon]
Canadian literature (Fiction: 1850-1918) C: 157-158
Man in a Red Cap [painting by Titian]
Titian *picture on* T: 301
Man in the High Castle, The [book by Dick]
Dick, Philip K. D: 187
Man Lay Dead, A [book by Marsh]
Marsh, Ngaio M: 228
Man Nobody Knows, The [book by Barton]
Roaring Twenties (Rising prosperity) R: 363
Man o' War [horse]
Horse racing (History) H: 366
Man of Aran [film]
Flaherty, Robert Joseph F: 225
Man of Honor, A [book by Fontane]
Fontane, Theodor F: 327
Man of Property, The [book by Galsworthy]
Galsworthy, John G: 16
Man of war bird *See* Frigatebird *in this index*
"Man That Corrupted Hadleyburg, The" [story by Twain]
Twain, Mark (Later works) T: 530
Man-to-man defense [sports]
Basketball (Defensive strategies) B: 147
Football (The defensive team) F: 357-358
Man Who Came to Dinner, The [play by Kaufman and Hart]
Hart, Moss H: 77
Man Who Died Twice, The [poems by Robinson]
Robinson, Edwin Arlington R: 368
Man Who Loved Children, The [book by Stead]
Australia (Literature) A: 904-905
Man with a Guitar [painting by Braque]
Braque, Georges B: 564
Cubism *picture on* Ci: 1181
Man With the Golden Arm, The [book by Algren]
Algren, Nelson A: 366
"Man with the Hoe, The" [poem by Markham]
Markham, Edwin M: 214
"Man Without a Country, The" [story by Hale]
Hale, Edward Everett H: 18
Mana [religion]
Mythology (Mana and taboo) M: 984
Manacles
Handcuffs H: 42
Managed care plans M: 131
Insurance (Managed care plans) I: 312
Medicine (The United States) M: 367-368; (Financing advanced medical care) M: 377-378
Managed floating [economics]
Balance of payments (Balance of payments and exchange rates) B: 36
Exchange rate E: 436
Management [business]
Business (Top management) B: 726
Careers (Management) C: 227
Farm and farming (Farm management) F: 41
Industrial relations I: 245
Industry (Management) I: 259 *with diagram*
Personnel management P: 303
Management accounting
Accounting (Fields of accounting) A: 23
Management analyst [career]
Careers (Management) C: 227-228
Management and Budget, Office of [U.S.] M: 131
Budget (Government budgets) B: 671
Budget, Bureau of the B: 672
National budget (Creating a budget) N: 30
President of the United States (The executive branch) P: 764
Management consultant [career]
Careers (Management) C: 227-228
Management consulting service
Accounting (Fields of accounting) A: 23
Management sectional center
Postal services (Sorting) P: 703
Manager [career]
Airport (Airline passenger services) A: 246
Baseball (Players) B: 125
Boxing (Boxing in the United States) B: 530
Careers (Management) C: 227 *with picture*
Office work O: 677
Managing editor [career]
Newspaper (The editorial department) N: 381-382
Managua [Nicaragua] M: 131
Nicaragua N: 396 *with picture*; (Manufacturing) N: 398
Managua, Lake
Lake Nicaragua L: 42
Manahoac Indians
Virginia (Early days) V: 418
Manakin [bird] M: 132 *with picture*
Manama [Bahrain] M: 132

Bahrain B: 29 *with map*
Manapouri, Lake [New Zealand] *See* Lake Manapouri *in this index*
Manas National Park [India]
National park (table) N: 42f
Manasarowar, Lake [Tibet]
Himalaya (Peaks) H: 233
Manassa Mauler [nickname]
Dempsey, Jack D: 130
Manassas, Battles of *See* Bull Run, Battle of *in this index*
Manassas National Battlefield Park [Virginia]
National Park System (table: National battlefields) N: 55
Manasseh [son of Joseph]
Joseph (Settling his family in Egypt) J: 168
Manasseh, Prayer of [Bible]
Bible (The Christian Old Testament) B: 282
Manatee [sea animal] M: 132 *with picture*
Animal *picture on* A: 486
Mammal (table) M: 129 *with picture*
Manaus [Brazil]
Brazil (The Amazon Region) B: 577; (table: Average monthly weather) B: 579
Manbo [priestess]
Vodou V: 436
Mancala [board game]
Game (Board games) G: 22
Manchester [England] M: 133
City (The people) Ci: 586
Manchester [New Hampshire] M: 133
New Hampshire *picture on* N: 209; (Population) N: 212
Manchester Ship Canal [England]
Canal (table) C: 164
Manchester M: 133
Manchester terrier M: 133
Dog *picture on* D: 272
Manchester United [team]
Beckham, David B: 197
Manchester Unity [organization]
Odd Fellows, Independent Order of O: 673
Manchester Valley [painting by Pickett]
Pickett, Joseph P: 451
Manchild in the Promised Land [book by Claude Brown]
American literature (Works by minority writers) A: 425
Manchin, Joe, III [American political leader]
West Virginia (table) W: 225
Manchukuo [Chinese history]
China (Nationalist rule) C: 504
Manchuria (History) M: 134
Pu Yi P: 855
Sino-Japanese War of 1937-1945 S: 473
Manchuria [region, China] M: 134 *with maps*
China (The land) C: 490
Japan (Imperialism) J: 57
League of Nations (The League's shortcomings) L: 160
Russo-Japanese War (Underlying causes) R: 566a
Sino-Japanese War of 1937-1945 S: 473
World War II (Aggression on the march) W: 470
Manchurian Incident [Chinese history]
Tojo, Hideki T: 311
Manchurian wapiti [animal]
Elk (The European elk) E: 242
Manchus [people] M: 135
Boxer Rebellion B: 525
China (The early rule of the Manchus) C: 502; (The fall of the Manchus) C: 503 *with map*
Korea, History of (The Choson dynasty) K: 366-367
Mongolia (History) M: 723
Nanjing (History) N: 10
Painting (Chinese painting) P: 44-46
Mandala [religion]
Meditation M: 380
Mandalay [Myanmar] M: 135
Mandamus [law] M: 135
Mandan Indians M: 135 *with picture*
Exploration (Crossing North America) E: 447
Indian, American *pictures on* I: 159, I: 161
North Dakota (Exploration and early settlement) N: 513, *picture on* N: 514
Mandarin [official] M: 135
Mandarin [fruit] M: 136
Tangerine T: 26
Mandarin dialect [language]
China (Languages) C: 481
Chinese language (Spoken Chinese) C: 510
Mandarin M: 135
Mandarin duck
Duck *picture on* D: 375
Mandate [program]
City government (Sources of revenue) Ci: 597
Mandated territory [political unit] M: 136

Arabs (Ottoman and European rule) **A:** 590
Palestine (World War I and the Balfour
Declaration) **P:** 105 *with map*
Mandatory eight-count
Boxing (Fight rules) **B:** 527
Mandatory injunction [law]
Injunction **I:** 272
Mande [language]
Mandinka **M:** 137
Mande [people]
Burkina Faso (People) **B:** 706
Mandel, Eli [Canadian poet]
Canadian literature (Modern Canadian poets)
C: 161
Mandel, Marvin [American political leader]
Maryland (table) **M:** 255
Mandela, Nelson [South African political leader]
M: 136 *with portrait*
African National Congress **A:** 137
De Klerk, Frederik Willem **D:** 94
South Africa (The dismantling of apartheid)
So: 620 *with picture*
Mandela, Winnie [South African political leader]
See Madikizela-Mandela, Winnie *in this index*
Mandelbrot, Benoît [French-American
mathematician]
Fractal **F:** 443
Mandelbrot set [geometry]
Fractal **F:** 443
Mandible [anatomy]
Face **F:** 3
Head *diagram on* **H:** 123
Human body (table) **H:** 422 *with diagram*
Tongue **T:** 329 *with picture*
Mandible [entomology]
Ant (The bodies of ants) **A:** 521 *with picture*
Beetle (The bodies of beetles) **B:** 215 *with picture*
Insect (Mouthparts) **I:** 286 *with diagrams*
Mandingo [people] *See* Mandinka *in this index*
Mandinka [people] **M:** 137
Gambia (People) **G:** 18
Mali (People) **M:** 106
Senegal (People) **S:** 297
Mandioca [shrub] *See* Cassava *in this index*
Mandolin [musical instrument] **M:** 137 *with picture*
Mandrake [plant] **M:** 137 *with picture*
Mayapple **M:** 327
Mandrake [sculpture by Roszak]
Roszak, Theodore *picture on* **R:** 485
Mandrel [machine]
Glass (Drawing) **G:** 215-216
Mandrill [animal] **M:** 137 *with picture*
Mandylion [cloth]
Shroud of Turin **S:** 440
Mane [zoology]
Lion (The body of a lion) **L:** 340 *with picture*
Mané, Ansumane [Guinea-Bissau political leader]
Guinea-Bissau (History) **G:** 434
Maned wolf [animal]
Fox (South American "foxes") **F:** 440
Manesse Song Manuscript
Folklore *picture on* **F:** 323
Manet, Édouard [French painter] **M:** 138 *with
pictures*
Alabama picture on **A:** 255
Impressionism (French Impressionism) **I:** 93-94
Morisot, Berthe **M:** 805
Painting (Édouard Manet and the Impressionists)
P: 71 *with picture*
Mangabey [animal]
Monkey *picture on* **M:** 727
Mangaia [island, Pacific]
Cook Islands **Ci:** 1026
Mangal [swamp] *See* Mangrove forest *in this index*
Mangan, James Clarence [Irish poet]
Irish literature (Early works in English) **I:** 431
Manganese [element] **M:** 139
Aluminum (Properties of aluminum alloys)
A: 391-392
Trace elements **T:** 355
Manganese dioxide [chemical]
Manganese (Industrial uses) **M:** 139
Manganese nodule
Pacific Ocean (Resources) **P:** 15
Manganese ore
Manganese (Sources) **M:** 139
Manganese steel
Manganese (Industrial uses) **M:** 139
Manganese sulfate [chemical]
Manganese (Industrial uses) **M:** 139
Mangas Coloradas [Apache leader]
Indian wars (Apache warfare) **I:** 195
Mange [disease] **M:** 139
Hog (Diseases) **H:** 287
Mangel-wurzel [plant]
Beet **B:** 212
Manger [barn]

Horse (Food) **H:** 355
Mango [tree] **M:** 140 *with picture*
Mangosteen [tree] **M:** 140 *with picture*
Mangrove [tree] **M:** 140 *with picture*
Evolution *picture on* **E:** 427
Mangrove forest
Cuba (The land) **Ci:** 1172-1173
Plant (Aquatic regions) **P:** 528
Swamp **So:** 1015
Mangu Khan [Mongol political leader]
Kublai Khan **K:** 391
Manhattan [ship]
Northwest Passage **N:** 530
Manhattan Bridge
New York City (Brooklyn) **N:** 326
Manhattan Company
JPMorgan Chase & Co. **J:** 177
Manhattan Island [New York City] **M:** 141
Minuit, Peter **M:** 613
New York *picture on* **N:** 317; (Exploration and
settlement) **N:** 314 *with picture*
New York City (The city) **N:** 323 *with picture and
map*; (Industry) **N:** 333; (Transportation) **N:** 334
Manhattan Project [U.S. history] **M:** 141
Nuclear energy (The development of nuclear
weapons) **N:** 590
Nuclear weapon (World War II) **N:** 601
Oppenheimer, J. Robert **O:** 812
Rotblat, Joseph **R:** 487
World War II (The atomic bomb) **W:** 493
Manhattan Transfer [book by Dos Passos]
Dos Passos, John **D:** 311
Mani [food] *See* Peanut *in this index*
Mani [Persian religious leader]
Manichaeism **M:** 141
Mani-Kongo [title]
Kongo **K:** 364
Mania [psychology]
Bipolar disorder **B:** 327
Mental illness (Mood disorders) **M:** 405
Maniac Magee [book by Spinelli]
Spinelli, Jerry **So:** 793
Manic-depressive illness *See* Bipolar disorder *in
this index*
Manic episode [psychology]
Bipolar disorder **B:** 327
Depression **D:** 151
Manichaeism [religion] **M:** 141
Manifest [shipping]
Bill (In transportation) **B:** 300-301
Manifest destiny [U.S. history] **M:** 141
Latin America (Early years of independence)
L: 107-108
Mexican War (Background of the war) **M:** 445-446
Polk, James Knox **P:** 640
United States, History of the (Manifest destiny)
U: 169
Westward movement in America (The
Southwest) **W:** 249
Manifesto of Futurism, The [book by Marinetti]
Italian literature (The 1900's) **I:** 495
Manifesto of Surrealism [book by Breton]
Breton, André **B:** 594
Manifesto of the Communist Party *See* Communist
Manifesto *in this index*
Manifold, Intake [engine]
Carburetor **C:** 208
Manihot [tree]
Rubber (The rubber tree) **R:** 502
Manila [Philippines] **M:** 141 *with picture and map*
Dewey, George **D:** 176
Philippines *pictures on* **P:** 372, **P:** 373, **P:** 374,
P: 379
Quezon City **Q:** 41
Spanish-American War (Manila Bay) **So:** 753-754
Manila Bay [Philippines] **M:** 143 *with picture*
China Sea **C:** 508 *with map*
Manila Bay, Battle of [1898]
Dewey, George **D:** 176
Spanish-American War (Manila Bay) **So:** 753
United States, History of the *picture on* **U:** 186
Manila hemp [fiber]
Abacá **A:** 3
Philippines *picture on* **P:** 379
Rope (Natural-fiber rope) **R:** 473 *with picture*
Manioc [plant] *See* Cassava *in this index*
Maniple [Roman Empire]
Army (Ancient armies) **A:** 726
Legion **L:** 183
Manipulation under anesthesia [medicine]
Chiropractic **C:** 514
Manipulator
Diving, Underwater (Diving in vehicles) **D:** 246
Manipur bush-quail [bird]
Quail **Q:** 4
Manipuri [dance]
Dance (Asian theatrical dance) **D:** 28-29

Manistee National Forest
Michigan (Places to visit) **M:** 498
Manito [religion]
Indian, American (Indians of the Northeast)
I: 154-155
Manitoba **M:** 145
Manitoba [province, Canada] **M:** 144 *with pictures
and maps*
See also the list of Related articles in the Manitoba
article
Canada, Government of *picture on* **C:** 131
Lake Agassiz **L:** 35
Métis **M:** 435
Prairie Provinces **P:** 733
Manitoba, Lake
Lake Manitoba **L:** 40 *with map*
Manitoba (Rivers and lakes) **M:** 154
Manitoba, University of M: 164
Manitoba Act [1870]
Macdonald, Sir John Alexander (Completing the
Dominion) **M:** 8
Manitoba (The Red River Rebellion) **M:** 160-162
Manitoba Centennial Centre
Winnipeg (Cultural life) **W:** 341
Manitoba lowland
Manitoba (Land regions) **M:** 154
Manitoba Schools Crisis [Canadian history]
Abbott, Sir John Joseph Caldwell (Prime minister)
A: 6
Bowell, Sir Mackenzie (The Manitoba Schools
Crisis) **B:** 519
Laurier, Sir Wilfrid (The Manitoba school issue)
L: 125; (Prime minister) **L:** 125
Manitou Island [Lake Michigan]
Michigan (Islands) **M:** 500
Manitoulin Island [Lake Huron] **M:** 164
Lake Huron **L:** 39
Ontario (Shoreline and coastline) **O:** 778
Mankiewicz, Joseph L. [American director]
Motion picture (Best achievement in directing:
1949, 1950) **M:** 862
Manley, Charles [American political leader]
North Carolina (table) **N:** 490
Manley, Effa [American baseball executive]
Baseball (table: Hall of Fame) **B:** 134a
Manley, Michael Norman [Jamaican political
leader]
Jamaica (History) **J:** 24
Mann, Delbert [American director]
Motion picture (Best achievement in directing:
1955) **M:** 862
Mann, Horace [American educator] **M:** 164
United States, History of the (Better education)
U: 173
Mann, Thomas [German author] **M:** 164
German literature (Impressionism,
Neoromanticism, and Symbolism) **G:** 141;
(Postwar German literature [1945-1990]) **G:** 142
Novel (New directions in the novel) **N:** 573-574
Mann, William Hodges [American political leader]
Virginia (table) **V:** 417
Mann Act [1913]
Johnson, Jack **J:** 143
Manna [religion] **M:** 164
Manned Spacecraft Center *See* Johnson Space
Center *in this index*
Manned underwater station
Diving, Underwater (History) **D:** 247
Mannerheim, Carl Gustaf Emil von [Finnish
general]
Finland (The new republic) **F:** 117; (World War II)
F: 117; (Postwar developments) **F:** 118
Mannerism [art] **M:** 165 *with picture*
Cellini, Benvenuto **C:** 339
Greco, El **G:** 351
Italian literature (Humanism and the
Renaissance) **I:** 494
Lippi, Filippino **L:** 345
Painting (Mannerism) **P:** 56 *with picture*
Sculpture (Michelangelo) **S:** 252-253 *with picture*
Manners *See* Etiquette *in this index*
Manners, Comedy of *See* Comedy of manners *in
this index*
Mannheim [Germany] **M:** 165
Manning, Daniel [American government official]
Cleveland, Grover (table) **Ci:** 671
Manning, Ernest Charles [Canadian political
leader]
Alberta (table) **A:** 328
Manning, Preston **M:** 166
Manning, Helen Herron Taft [daughter of]
Taft, William Howard (Taft's family) **T:** 9
Manning, Patrick [Trinidad political leader]
Trinidad and Tobago (History) **T:** 446-447
Manning, Peyton [American football player]
M: 165
Football *picture on* **F:** 368

Manning, Preston [Canadian political leader]
M: 165
Campbell, Kim (The 1993 election) C: 90d
Chrétien, Jean (The 1993 election) C: 522c
Reform Party R: 195
Manning, Timothy [American religious leader]
Cardinal (table: American cardinals) C: 211
Mannock, Edward [British aviator]
Ace A: 24
Mannogalactan [chemical]
Guar G: 411
Mano [people]
Liberia (Civil war) L: 232
Manoir Papineau National Historic Site [Nova Scotia]
Canada (table: National historic sites) C: 115
Manometer [measuring device] M: 166
Hydraulics (Use of hydrostatic principles) H: 463
Manon [opera by Massenet]
Massenet, Jules M: 296
Opera *picture on* O: 794
Manon Lescaut [book by Prévost]
French literature (The Enlightenment) F: 520-521
Manon Lescaut [opera by Puccini]
Puccini, Giacomo P: 870
Manor
Manorialism M: 166
Serf S: 316b
Manorialism [European history] M: 166
Agriculture (The Middle Ages) A: 156-157 *with picture*
City (Economy) Ci: 584
Europe (The Middle Ages) E: 409
Feudalism F: 81
Food (The Middle Ages) F: 336 *with picture*
Middle Ages (Barbarian Europe) M: 523
Revolution of 1848 R: 288
Serf S: 316b
Manouches [people]
Roma R: 402b
Manpower Development and Training Act [1962]
Vocational education (The 1900's and early 2000's) V: 435
Manrico [opera character]
Opera: *(Trovatore, Il)* O: 808
Manrique, Jorge [Spanish author]
Spanish literature (The 1400's) So: 758
Mansa Magha I [Mali ruler]
Mansa Musa M: 166
Mansa Musa [Mali ruler] M: 166
African Americans (The cultural heritage) A: 136c
Mali (History) M: 108-109
Mali Empire M: 109
Mansard roof
Roof R: 450c *with picture*
Mansell, Nigel [British race car driver]
Automobile racing (table: Formula One World Drivers' Championship) A: 980
Mansfield, Arabella Babb [American educator] M: 166
Mansfield, John Melvin [American educator]
Mansfield, Arabella Babb M: 166
Mansfield, Katherine [British author] M: 166 *with portrait*
New Zealand (The arts) N: 349
Mansfield, Mike [American political leader] M: 167
Mansfield, Mount
Green Mountains G: 381
Mansfield, Sir Peter [British physiologist]
Magnetism (Magnetic resonance) M: 61
Nobel Prizes (Physiology or medicine: 2003) N: 447
Mansfield, Richard [American actor] M: 167
Mansfield Park [book by Austen]
Austen, Jane A: 892
Mansion [theater]
Drama (Mystery plays) D: 328-329 *with picture*
Mansion, The [book by Faulkner]
Faulkner, William F: 55
Manslaughter [crime] M: 167
Homicide H: 305
Negligence N: 119
Manson, Sir Patrick [Scottish doctor] M: 167
Manta ray [fish]
Animal *picture on* A: 507
Fish *picture on* F: 152
Mantegna, Andrea [Italian painter] M: 167 *with picture*
Engraving *picture on* E: 326
Fresco *picture on* F: 529
Jesus Christ *picture on* J: 108a
Painting (The 1400's) P: 52-53 *with picture*
Renaissance *picture on* R: 232
Mantell, Gideon [British physician]
Dinosaur (Dinosaur discoveries) D: 213
Iguanodon I: 50
Mantell, Mary Ann [British naturalist]

Dinosaur (Dinosaur discoveries) D: 213
Iguanodon I: 50
Manticore, The [book by Davies]
Davies, Robertson D: 46
Mantid [insect] *See* Praying mantis *in this index*
Mantis [insect] *See* Praying mantis *in this index*
Mantissa [mathematics]
Logarithms (Common logarithms) L: 424
Mantle [zoology] M: 168
Clam (The body of a clam) Ci: 637
Mollusk M: 694
Octopus (The body of an octopus) O: 672 *with diagram*
Oyster (Shell) O: 890 *with diagram*
Pearl (How pearls are formed) P: 216 *with diagram*
Shell (How shells are formed) S: 385
Squid (The body of a squid) So: 814
Mantle [geology] M: 168
Earth *diagram on* E: 20; (Earth's interior) E: 23
Earthquake (How an earthquake begins) E: 35 *with diagram*
Hot spot H: 374a
Mars (Physical features of Mars) M: 225
Moon (The interior of the moon) M: 790
Ocean (How the sea floor was formed) O: 662
Plate tectonics (Structure of tectonic plates) P: 561
Uranus (Structure and composition) U: 218
Volcano (Where volcanoes form) V: 441
Mantle [lamp]
Lamp (Gas lamps) L: 53-54 *with picture*
Mantle, Mickey [American baseball player] M: 168
Baseball (table: Hall of Fame) B: 134a
Mantle plume [geology]
Plate tectonics (Evidence of plate movement) P: 563
Mantle scallop [sea animal]
Shell *picture on* S: 387
Mantling [cape]
Heraldry (Elements of a coat of arms) H: 196 *with picture*
Mantodea [entomology]
Insect (table) I: 299
Mantra [religion]
Buddhism (The Vajrayana) B: 669
Meditation M: 380
Mantrayana [religion]
Buddhism (The Vajrayana) B: 669
Mantua [garment]
Clothing (The 1600's) Ci: 703
Mantua, Duke of [opera character]
Opera: *(Rigoletto)* O: 806
Manu [religion] M: 168
Manu, Code of [Hinduism]
Manu M: 168
Manu National Park [Peru]
National park (table) N: 42g
South America *picture on* So: 623
Manu Smriti [Hinduism]
Manu M: 168
Manua Islands
American Samoa A: 429 *with map*
Manual [keyboard]
Harpsichord H: 66b *with picture*
Organ (Pipe organs) O: 851-852 *with picture*
Manual alphabet, American
Sign language S: 453 *with picture*
Manual arts
Industrial arts (Beginnings) I: 243
Manual communication [sign language]
Deafness (Special language techniques) D: 58
Manual of Botany [book by Gray]
Gray, Asa G: 334
Manual of Discipline [document]
Dead Sea Scrolls D: 56
Manual of Parliamentary Practice, A [book by Jefferson]
Jefferson, Thomas (Vice president) J: 82 *with picture*
Manual Training School [U.S. history]
Vocational education (Early vocational education in schools) V: 435
Manual transmission
Automobile (From power plant to wheels) A: 948-949
Transmission (How a manual transmission works) T: 377 *with diagram*
Manual typewriter
Typewriter (Kinds of typewriters) T: 538
Manuel I, the Fortunate [king of Portugal]
Da Gama, Vasco (Early life) D: 4
Magellan, Ferdinand (Planning the expedition) M: 46
Portugal (The arts) P: 689; (The age of exploration) P: 693
Manuel II [king of Portugal]

Portugal (The first Portuguese republic) P: 694
Manuel, Don Juan [Spanish author]
Spanish literature (Early medieval literature) So: 757-758
Manuel M. Torres Dam [Mexico]
Dam (table) D: 18
Mexico (Energy sources) M: 467
Manueline style [art]
Portugal (The arts) P: 689
Manuelito [American Indian chief] M: 168 *with portrait*
Manufactured fertilizer
Fertilizer (Production and sale) F: 80
Manufactured fiber
Textile (Sources of textile fibers) T: 212-213
Thread T: 269 *with diagram*
Manufactured gas
Coke oven gas Ci: 759
Fuel (Manufactured gas) F: 551
Gas [fuel] G: 50; (How gas is manufactured) G: 55; (First uses of manufactured gas) G: 57
Manufactured house
House (Building materials) H: 380
Mobile home M: 682
Manufacturing M: 169 *with pictures*
Automation (Uses of automation) A: 944
Careers (Production) C: 229
Clothing (The clothing industry) Ci: 705-706
Factory F: 5
Light (Light in manufacturing) L: 292
Mass production M: 269
Safety (In manufacturing plants) S: 13
Sales (Selling by manufacturers) S: 62
Space exploration (Expanding space activities) So: 728
United States, History of the (Economic growth) U: 169-170; (Industrialization and reform [1870-1916]) U: 179 *with picture*; (The economy--boom and bust) U: 191
World *picture on* W: 413
Manufacturing grade
Milk (At a dairy farm) M: 546-547
Manufacturing Heartland of Canada
Ontario O: 764
Manuka [tree] *See* Teatree *in this index*
Manumission [slavery]
Slavery (Ancient times) S: 501
Manure [agriculture] M: 172
Dairying (Housing) D: 7
Farm and farming (Special crop-growing methods) F: 37-38 *with picture*
Gardening (Fertilizing) G: 32
Manus Island [New Guinea]
Admiralty Islands A: 59 *with picture*
Bismarck Archipelago B: 382
Manus Islands [New Guinea] *See* Admiralty Islands *in this index*
Manuscript M: 172 *with pictures*
Biology *picture on* B: 318
Book (The Middle Ages) B: 466
Encyclopedia (Editing the manuscript) E: 267 *with picture*
Illuminated manuscript I: 78
Library (Medieval collections) L: 259 *with picture*
Publishing (Preparing content for publication) P: 866
Writing (Preparing and submitting a manuscript) W: 512
Manuscript editor [occupation]
Publishing (Editors and fact checkers) P: 867
Manuscript writing
Handwriting (Kinds of handwriting) H: 47; (Learning to write) H: 47 *with picture*
Manush, Heinie [American baseball player]
Baseball (table: Hall of Fame) B: 134a
Manutius, Aldus [Italian printer]
Book (The spread of printed books) B: 467 *with picture*
Italics I: 495
Punctuation P: 902
Manx [cat]
Cat *pictures on* C: 288, C: 289; (Short-haired breeds) C: 290-291
Manx language
Gaelic languages G: 5
Man, Isle of M: 130
Many Waters [book by L'Engle]
L'Engle, Madeleine L: 191
Many Young Men of Twenty [play by Keane]
Irish literature (Drama) I: 432
Manyatta [African homestead]
Maasai M: 2
Man'yoshu [poems]
Japanese literature (Beginnings) J: 61
Manzanar National Historic Site [California]
National Park System (table: National historic sites) N: 52-53

Manzanita [shrub] **M**: 174 *with picture*
Manzikert, Battle of [1071]
Turkey (The Seljuk Turks) **T**: 509
Manzoni, Alessandro [Italian author] **M**: 174
Italian literature (Romanticism) **I**: 495
Verdi, Giuseppe **V**: 316
Mao Tse-tung [Chinese political leader] *See* Mao Zedong *in this index*
Mao Zedong [Chinese political leader] **M**: 174 *with portrait*
Beijing (History) **B**: 223-224
China (History) **C**: 499-505 *with picture*
Chinese literature (Modern Chinese literature) **C**: 512
Cold War (Communist expansion in Asia) **Ci**: 764
Communism (World War II) **Ci**: 893-894 *with picture*; (China after Mao) **Ci**: 896
Cultural Revolution **Ci**: 1185
Deng Xiaoping (His life) **D**: 131
Guerrilla warfare (Types of guerrilla movements) **G**: 420
Jiang Qing **J**: 125
MAOI [drug] *See* Monoamine oxidase inhibitor *in this index*
Maoists [Nepalese history]
Nepal (History) **N**: 126-127
Maori [language]
New Zealand (People) **N**: 348
Maori [people] **M**: 175 *with picture*
Auckland **A**: 880
Mythology (Genetic relationships) **M**: 975; (Creation myths of the Pacific Islands) **M**: 983-984
National park (New Zealand) **N**: 42d; (The rights of original inhabitants) **N**: 42i
New Zealand **N**: 346; (People) **N**: 348 *with picture*; (History) **N**: 354 *with picture*
Sculpture (Pacific Islands sculpture) **S**: 241-242 *with picture*
Map [island, Pacific]
Yap Islands **Y**: 553
Map [document] **M**: 176 *with pictures and maps*
See also the list of Related articles in the Map *article*
Archaeology (Surveying sites) **A**: 596
Atlas **A**: 868
City planning *picture on* **Ci**: 600
Geographic information system **G**: 92
Geography **G**: 92 *with picture*; (Mapping) **G**: 95
Globe **G**: 233
Great-circle route **G**: 338
Isobar **I**: 474 *with map*
Isotherm **I**: 475 *with map*
Latitude **L**: 117
Longitude **L**: 451, *diagrams on* **L**: 452
Moon (Early observations with telescopes) **M**: 792 *with picture*
Navigation (Traditional navigation) **N**: 70
Photogrammetry **P**: 405 *with picture*
Races, Human (The clinal approach) **R**: 55-56 *with map*
Telescope (Adaptive optics systems) **T**: 106
Weather (Weather maps) **W**: 164 *with picture*
World, History of the *picture on* **W**: 441
Map of the British and French Dominions in America
Map (Mapping the Americas) **M**: 184-185
Map projection
Map **M**: 176; (Map projections) **M**: 180, **M**: 182 *with diagrams*
Mapai [political party]
Ben-Gurion, David **B**: 246
Eshkol, Levi **E**: 357
Maple [tree] **M**: 186 *with pictures*
Leaf *picture on* **L**: 151
Plant *picture on* **P**: 531, **P**: 541-542 *with picture*
Tree *pictures on* **T**: 420, **T**: 422
Wood *picture on* **W**: 389
Maple, Flowering [shrubs]
Flowering maple **F**: 303 *with picture*
Maple leaf [symbol]
Canada, History of (The return of the Liberals) **C**: 149-150
"Maple Leaf Rag" [song]
Dance *picture on* **D**: 30
Maple Leafs, Toronto [team] *See* Toronto Maple Leafs *in this index*
Maple sugar
Maple syrup **M**: 187
Maple syrup M: 187 *with pictures*
Vermont (Interesting facts) **V**: 319 *with picture*
Mapother, Thomas Cruise, IV [birth name of]
Cruise, Tom **Ci**: 1158
Mapp v. Ohio [U.S. history]
Supreme Court of the United States (Criminal law) **So**: 1001; (table) **So**: 1002
Mapping program
Map (Production and reproduction) **M**: 181

Mapping radar
Radar (In the military) **R**: 65-66
Mapplethorpe, Robert [American photographer] **M**: 188 *with picture*
Mapu, Abraham [Hebrew author]
Hebrew literature (Modern Hebrew literature) **H**: 162
Mapuche [American Indians] **M**: 189
Chile (Ancestry) **C**: 460; (Early days) **C**: 467
Maputo [Mozambique] **M**: 189 *with picture*
Mozambique **M**: 904 *with picture*
Mapuzugun [language]
Mapuche **M**: 189
Maqamah [literature]
Arabic literature (Fiction) **A**: 583
Maquette [art]
Animation (Modeling) **A**: 513
Sculpture (The sculptor at work) **S**: 232
Maquiladora [factory]
Baja California **B**: 31
Mexico (Manufacturing) **M**: 464-465
Maquis [organization] **M**: 189
France (World War II) **F**: 475
Maquoketa River
Iowa (Rivers and lakes) **I**: 386
Mar del Plata [Argentina] **M**: 189 *with picture*
Mara [animal]
Cavy **C**: 322
Mara, Ratu Sir Kamisese [Fijian political leader]
Fiji (History) **F**: 98
Marabou [bird] **M**: 190 *with picture*
Stork **So**: 913
Marabout [title]
Senegal (People) **S**: 297-298
Maracaibo [Venezuela] **M**: 190 *with picture*
Morgan, Sir Henry (Early career) **M**: 803
Maracaibo, Lake *See* Lake Maracaibo *in this index*
Maracaña Stadium
Brazil (Recreation) **B**: 575
Rio de Janeiro (People) **R**: 345-346
Maracanda [former city]
Samarqand **S**: 78
Maracas [musical instrument]
Venezuela (Recreation) **V**: 301
Marae [meeting places]
Maori **M**: 175
Marajó [island, Brazil] **M**: 190
Marañón River [river, Peru]
Amazon River (The course of the Amazon) **A**: 403
Maranville, Rabbit [American baseball player]
Baseball (table: Hall of Fame) **B**: 134a
Marasmus [disorder]
Famine (Death and disease) **F**: 26a
Malnutrition **M**: 111
Nutrition (Deficiency diseases) **N**: 630
Marat, Jean-Paul [French political leader] **M**: 190 *with portrait*
Corday, Charlotte **Ci**: 1051
French Revolution (The National Convention) **F**: 526 *with picture*
Marat/Sade [play by Weiss]
Drama (Later German-language drama) **D**: 340
Maratha War [1803-1805]
Wellington, Duke of (Young soldier) **W**: 194
Marathas [people]
India (The Mughal Empire) **I**: 129-130
Mughal Empire **M**: 910
Marathi [language]
India (Languages) **I**: 114
Mumbai (People) **M**: 924
Marathon [race] **M**: 191
Canoeing (Marathon racing) **C**: 181
Marathon, Battle of (The battle) **M**: 191
Running **R**: 521
United States *picture on* **U**: 115
Marathon, Battle of [490 B.C.] **M**: 191
Darius I **D**: 36
Miltiades **M**: 557
Marathon Oil Company
Manufacturing (table) **M**: 170
United States Steel Corporation **U**: 204
Maravich, Pete [American basketball player] **M**: 191
Marble [rock] **M**: 191 *with pictures*
Rock (table) **R**: 373 *with picture*
Marble [toy]
Marbles **M**: 192 *with pictures*
West Virginia (Interesting facts) **W**: 207 *with picture*
Marble, S. S. [American political leader]
Maine (table) **M**: 87
Marble bones [disorder]
Osteosclerosis **O**: 868
Marble Faun, The [book by Hawthorne]
Hawthorne, Nathaniel (His novels) **H**: 115
Marble House [estate]
Rhode Island (Places to visit) **R**: 304

Marbled godwit [bird]
Godwit **G**: 246
Marbled paper
Paperwork (End papers) **P**: 138
Marbled polecat [mammal]
Polecat **P**: 619
Marbled salamander
Amphibian *picture on* **A**: 439
Marbles [game] **M**: 192 *with pictures*
Marbling [fat]
Beef **B**: 209
Marbois, François de Barbé [French government official]
Louisiana Purchase (Napoleon's decision) **L**: 503
Marbury, William [American government official]
Jefferson, Thomas (The courts) **J**: 84
Marbury v. Madison **M**: 193
Marbury v. Madison [U.S. history] **M**: 193
Jefferson, Thomas (The courts) **J**: 84
Judicial review **J**: 184
Law (Beginnings of U.S. law) **L**: 136
Marshall, John (Chief justice) **M**: 230
Nullification **N**: 603
Supreme Court of the United States (Landmark decisions) **So**: 1000; (table) **So**: 1002
United States, Government of the (Authority of the courts) **U**: 141-144
United States, History of the (The power of the federal government) **U**: 164
Marc, Franz [German artist]
Germany *picture on* **G**: 155
Kandinsky, Wassily **K**: 213
Painting (Expressionism) **P**: 78-79
Marceau, Marcel [French mime] **M**: 193
Pantomime *picture on* **P**: 132
Marcel, Gabriel [French philosopher] **M**: 193
Marcel wave
Hairdressing (The 1800's) **H**: 12
Marcellinus, Ammianus [Roman historian]
Latin literature (Later periods) **L**: 117
Library (Libraries of the Middle Ages and the Renaissance) **L**: 259
Marcellinus, Saint [pope]
Pope (table) **P**: 666
Marcello [opera character]
Opera: (*Bohème, La*) **O**: 801
Marcellus [pen name]
Adams, John Quincy (Lawyer and writer) **A**: 40-41
Marcellus I, Saint [pope]
Pope (table) **P**: 666
Marcellus II [pope]
Pope (table) **P**: 666
March [music] **M**: 193
Sousa, John Philip **So**: 607
March [month] **M**: 194 *with pictures*
March, Fredric [American actor]
Motion picture (Best performance by an actor: 1931-32) **M**: 862a
March, Jo [literary figure]
Alcott, Louisa May **A**: 338
March, Peyton Conway [American military leader] **M**: 196
March equinox [astronomy]
Equinox **E**: 348 *with diagram*
March of Dimes Foundation M: 196
March on Washington [1963] **M**: 196
African Americans (The growing movement) **A**: 136o-136p *with picture*
King, Martin Luther, Jr. (The growing movement) **K**: 321 *with picture*
United States, History of the (The civil rights movement) **U**: 196a *with picture*
March Sand [painting by Kiefer] *See* Märkischer Sand *in this index*
Marchand, F.-Gabriel [Canadian political leader]
Quebec (table) **Q**: 29
Marchegiano, Rocco [birth name of]
Marciano, Rocky **M**: 196
Marcher lords [English history]
Wales (Revolts against England) **W**: 12
Marches [former region]
Wales (Revolts against England) **W**: 12
Marching band [music]
Band (Marching bands) **B**: 74 *with picture*
Baton twirling **B**: 167
Drum corps **D**: 368
Music *picture on* **M**: 947
Marching bugle tuba
Tuba **T**: 477
Marchioness [title]
Lady **L**: 25
Nobility (In the United Kingdom) **N**: 450
Marciano, Rocky [American boxer] **M**: 196
Boxing *picture on* **B**: 532b; (Boxing's Golden Age) **B**: 532-532a; (The 1950's) **B**: 532a
Marco Polo [Italian explorer] *See* Polo, Marco *in this index*

Marco Polo [ship]
  New Brunswick (Interesting facts) N: 181 *with picture*
Marco Polo sheep
  Animal *picture on* A: 475
  Sheep (Wild sheep) S: 380
Marconi, Guglielmo [Italian inventor] M: 196 *with picture*
  Communication (The development of electronics) Ci: 883 *with picture*
  Radio R: 83; (Early development) R: 91 *with picture*
  Radio, Amateur (History) R: 96
  Tesla, Nikola (Other inventions) T: 181
  Wireless communication (History) W: 345
Marconi National Historic Site [Nova Scotia]
  Canada (table: National historic sites) C: 115
Marcos, Ferdinand Edralin [Filipino political leader] M: 197
  Aquino, Corazon A: 580a
  Philippines (The Marcos era) P: 380
Marcos, Imelda [Filipino political figure]
  Marcos, Ferdinand Edralin M: 197
Marcos, Subcomandante [Mexican political leader]
  Tamaulipas T: 22
  Zapatista Army of National Liberation Z: 587
Marcus, Rudolph Arthur [American chemist]
  Nobel Prizes (Chemistry: 1992) N: 444
Marcus, Saint [pope]
  Pope (table) P: 666
Marcus Agrippa [Roman general] *See* Agrippa, Marcus *in this index*
Marcus Aurelius [Roman emperor] M: 197
  Rome, Ancient (The decline of the empire) R: 447
Marcuse, Herbert [American philosopher]
  Socialism (The New Left) So: 561
Marcy, Geoffrey [American astronomer]
  Planet (The first discoveries) P: 513
Marcy, Mount
  Adirondack Mountains A: 56
  New York (Land regions) N: 304 *with map*
Marcy, William L. [American political leader]
  New York (table) N: 313
  Pierce, Franklin (table) P: 456
  Polk, James Knox (table) P: 643
Mardalsfossen Falls [waterfalls, Norway]
  Waterfall (table: Famous waterfalls of the world) W: 143
Marden, Brice [American artist]
  Painting (Abstract artists) P: 88-89
Mardi [book by Melville]
  Melville, Herman (His literary career) M: 390
Mardi Gras [custom] M: 198
  Alabama (Visitor's guide) A: 266
  Easter (Carnivals) E: 44
  Louisiana L: 478, *picture on* L: 489; (Visitor's guide) L: 488
  Mask (Festive masks) M: 264
  New Orleans (Annual events) N: 282 *with picture*
  Shrove Tuesday S: 441
Marduk [Babylonian god] M: 198
  Assyria (Religion) A: 821
  Mythology *picture on* M: 976; (Babylonian mythology) M: 978
Marduk, Temple of [Babylon]
  Babylon (The Neo-Babylonian Empire) B: 12
Mare [horse]
  Horse (Life history) H: 351
  Horse racing (Thoroughbred horses) H: 363-364
  Mule M: 913
Mare Imbrium [lunar feature]
  Moon (Determining the origin of craters) M: 793-794
Mare Nostrum [name for]
  Mediterranean Sea (History of the Mediterranean) M: 382
Marechal, Leopoldo [Argentine author]
  Latin American literature (The mid-1900's) L: 114
Marek's disease
  Poultry (Raising poultry) P: 720-721
Marengo [horse]
  Horse (table: Famous horses in history and legend) H: 361
Maresha [plow]
  Ethiopia (Way of life) E: 368
Marfan syndrome [disorder] M: 198
Margai, Sir Milton [Sierra Leone political leader]
  Sierra Leone (History) S: 452
Margaret [daughter of Henry VII]
  Henry VII [of England] H: 188
  Scotland (The House of Stuart) S: 219
Margaret [queen of Denmark]
  Denmark *picture on* D: 140; (A great power) D: 139
  Norway (Union with Denmark) N: 545
  Sweden (Union with Norway and Denmark)

Margaret [queen of Scotland, 1283-1290]
  Scotland (Fight for independence) S: 219
Margaret [wife of Henry VI]
  Warwick, Earl of W: 44
Margaret, Princess [sister of]
  Elizabeth II (Early life) E: 239-240
Margaret Fleming [play by Herne]
  Herne, James A. H: 212
Margaret Hunt Hill Bridge
  Dallas (Recent developments) D: 15
Margaret Island [former city, Hungary]
  Budapest B: 666
Margaretta [ship]
  Maine (Places to visit) M: 78; (The Revolutionary War) M: 89
Margarine [food] M: 198
Margarita [island]
  Venezuela (European exploration and settlement) V: 304
Margay [wild cat] M: 198 *with picture*
Marggraf, Andreas Sigismund [German chemist]
  Zinc Z: 594
Marghera [Italy]
  Venice (The people) V: 307; (Economy) V: 307-308
Margherita Peak [Africa]
  Congo, Democratic Republic of the (The highland) Ci: 940a *with map*
  Uganda (Land) U: 3
Margin [botany]
  Plant (Leaves) P: 529
Margin [economics]
  Commodity exchange (Forward and futures contracts) C: 873
  Securities Exchange Act S: 279
  United States, History of the (The stock market crash of 1929) U: 191
Marginal sea
  Atlantic Ocean (Boundaries and size) A: 864
  Caribbean Sea C: 236
  Gulf G: 436
  Pacific Ocean (Boundaries) P: 14
Margrethe II [queen of Denmark]
  Denmark (Postwar years) D: 141
Marguerite [opera character]
  Opera: (*Faust*) O: 804
Marguerite of Navarre [French author]
  French literature (The Renaissance) F: 519
Margulis, Lynn Alexander [American microbiologist]
  Gaia G: 6
Mari-Diata [Malian king] *See* Sundiata Keita *in this index*
Maria [grand duchess of Russia]
  Nicholas II [czar] *picture on* N: 403
Maria [astronomy]
  Moon M: 783; (Maria) M: 789; (Describing lunar evolution) M: 794
María [book by Isaacs]
  Colombia (The arts) Ci: 781
  Latin American literature (Romanticism) L: 112-113
Maria Chapdelaine [book by Hémon]
  Canadian literature (Literature between the world wars) C: 158
María Cristina [mother of Alfonso XIII]
  Alfonso XIII A: 348
  Spain (The reign of Alfonso XIII) So: 749
Maria Island [Australia]
  Tasmania (Land and climate) T: 48
Maria Laach Abbey Church [Germany]
  Architecture *picture on* A: 619
Maria Theresa [Holy Roman empress] M: 199
  Austria (Wars in the 1700's and 1800's) A: 937-938 *with picture*
  Germany (The rise of Prussia) G: 164
  Habsburg, House of H: 3
  Pragmatic sanction P: 729
  Seven Years' War (In Europe) S: 328
  Succession wars (The War of the Austrian Succession) So: 950
Maria Theresa [wife of Louis XIV]
  Louis XIV L: 475
Mariachi band [music]
  Hispanic Americans (Entertainment and arts) H: 249
  Mexico (Music) M: 460
  Music *picture on* M: 947
Mariah Carey [recording]
  Carey, Mariah C: 236
Marian, Maid [literary figure]
  Robin Hood R: 367
Marian Exiles [European history]
  Knox, John (Later career) K: 358
Mariana Islands [Pacific] M: 199
  See also Northern Mariana Islands,

  Commonwealth of the *in this index*
  Pacific Islands, Trust Territory of the P: 13
  World War II (Island hopping in the Central Pacific) W: 489
Mariana Trench [oceanography]
  Deep D: 81
  Deep sea (The deep-sea floor) D: 82a
  Exploration (Deep-sea exploration) E: 450-451
  Ocean (Depth) O: 651-652
  Pacific Ocean (The ocean floor) P: 14; (Scientific research) P: 15
Mariánské Lázně [Czech Republic]
  Czech Republic (The Bohemian Mountains) Ci: 1211
Marias River [Montana]
  Lewis and Clark expedition (The homeward journey) L: 222d-223
Maric, Maria [wife of Albert Einstein] *See* Einstein, Mileva Maric *in this index*
Marichal, Juan [American baseball player]
  Baseball (table: Hall of Fame) B: 134a
Maricopa County [Arizona]
  Phoenix (Layout of Phoenix) P: 396
Maricopa Indians
  Indian, American *picture on* I: 167
Maricourt, Pierre de [French soldier] *See* Peregrinus, Peter *in this index*
Mariculture *See* Aquaculture *in this index*
Marie [opera character]
  Opera: (*Wozzeck*) O: 808
Marie Adélaïde [grand duchess of Luxembourg]
  Luxembourg (History) L: 531
Marie Antoinette [queen of France] M: 199 *with portrait*
  Lafayette, Marquis de (The revolution at home) L: 28
Marie Antoinette and Her Children [painting by Wertmüller]
  Marie Antoinette *picture on* M: 200
Marie Calumet [book by Girard]
  Canadian literature (Fiction: 1850-1918) C: 157
Marie de Médicis [wife of Henry IV] M: 200
  Henry IV [king of France] H: 186
  Louis XIII L: 474
  Medici M: 362
  Richelieu, Cardinal (Strengthening the monarchy) R: 331
  Rubens, Peter Paul (His art) R: 506-507
Marie Louise [wife of Napoleon I] M: 200
  Napoleon I (Divorce and remarriage) N: 15
  Napoleon II N: 17
Marie Thérèse of Spain [painting by Mignard]
  Clothing *picture on* Ci: 703
Marielitos [people]
  Hispanic Americans (Cuban immigration) H: 254
Marietta [Ohio]
  Northwest Territory (Settlement) N: 535 *with picture*
  Ohio Company (The second Ohio Company) O: 704-705
Marignac, Jean de [Swiss chemist]
  Gadolinium G: 4
  Ytterbium Y: 574
Marignano, Battle of [1515]
  Francis I F: 480
Marigold [plant] M: 201 *with picture*
  Flower *picture on* F: 285; (Garden annuals) F: 276 *with picture*; (Flowers of the desert) F: 290 *with picture*
  Gardening *picture on* G: 33
  Plant *picture on* P: 526
Marigold [ship]
  Drake, Sir Francis (Voyage around the world) D: 321
Marihuana [drug] *See* Marijuana *in this index*
Mariinsky Theater [Saint Petersburg]
  Saint Petersburg [Russia] (Education and cultural life) S: 55
Marijuana [drug] M: 201 *with picture*
  Drug abuse (Abuse of illegal drugs) D: 362; (table: Some commonly abused drugs) D: 363; (History) D: 365
  Hemp H: 183
Marijuana Tax Act [1937]
  Drug abuse (History) D: 365-366
Marília de Dirceu [poems by Gonzaga]
  Latin American literature (Colonial literature) L: 112
Marilyn Monroe Diptych [painting by Warhol]
  Painting (Pop Art) P: 86
  Warhol, Andy *picture on* W: 36
Marimba [musical instrument] M: 202 *with picture*
  Mexico (Music) M: 460
Marín, Don Francisco de Paula [Spanish settler]
  Hawaii (The kingdom of Hawaii) H: 106
Marin, John [American painter] M: 202 *with pictures*

Painting *picture on* P: 41
Marin County Civic Center
Wright, Frank Lloyd *picture on* W: 507; (Later career) W: 508
Marine [military] M: 203 *with picture*
See also Marine Corps, United States *in this index*
Navy N: 76
Marine animal [zoology]
Animal (Animals of the oceans) A: 486 *with pictures*
Aquarium, Public A: 578b *with picture*
Marine biology M: 204
Ocean (Life in the ocean) O: 655 *with pictures*
Marine Band, United States
Marine Corps, United States M: 206
Sousa, John Philip So: 607
Marine biology M: 204 *with pictures*
Biology (What biologists study) B: 316-317
Ocean *picture on* O: 665; (Careers in oceanography) O: 666
Marine chronometer [instrument]
Chronometer C: 539
Clock *picture on* Ci: 682j
Marine Corps, United States M: 206 *with pictures*
Flag *pictures on* F: 194, F: 211
Infantry (Divisions) I: 264
Navy, Department of the N: 81
Navy, United States (The Marine Corps) N: 85
Sandino, Augusto César S: 109
United States Naval Academy U: 203
Marine Corps Band
Marine Corps, United States M: 206
Marine Corps War Memorial [Arlington, Virginia]
Marine Corps, United States *picture on* M: 206
Washington, D.C. (Marine Corps War Memorial) W: 78 *with picture*
Marine division
Infantry (Divisions) I: 264
Marine dolphin [sea animal]
Dolphin D: 297 *with pictures*
Marine Drive
Nova Scotia (Places to visit) N: 560
Marine eelgrass
Eelgrass E: 115
Marine fish
Fish (Saltwater environments) F: 150 *with pictures*; (How fish adjust to change) F: 168
Marine geology
Ocean (Careers in oceanography) O: 666 *with picture*
Marine geophysics
Ocean (Careers in oceanography) O: 666
Marine Highway
Alaska (Places to visit) A: 290
Marine iguana [reptile]
Galapagos Islands G: 7 *with picture*
Iguana I: 50
Lizard (Food) L: 401
Marine insurance
Insurance (Other kinds of property and liability insurance) I: 313; (The growth of insurance) I: 315
Marine invasion [geology]
Jurassic Period J: 201
Marine park
National park (Canada) N: 42c
Marine plant
Ocean (The importance of the ocean) O: 654; (Life in the ocean) O: 655 *with pictures*
Marine propeller
Propeller (Ship propellers) P: 826 *with picture*
Marine snail
Snail (Where snails live) S: 522 *with picture*
Marine snow [biology]
Deep sea (Environment) D: 82-82a
Marine toad *See* Cane toad *in this index*
Marineland Dolphin Adventure
Aquarium, Public (History) A: 579
Florida (Places to visit) F: 252
Mariner 2 [space probe]
Space exploration (Probes to Venus and Mercury) So: 710
Venus (Flights to Venus) V: 313
Mariner 4 [space probe]
Mars (Observation by spacecraft) M: 226c
Space exploration (Probes to Mars) So: 710
Mariner 5 [space probe]
Venus (Flights to Venus) V: 313
Mariner 6 [space probe]
Mars (Observation by spacecraft) M: 226c
Mariner 7 [space probe]
Mars (Observation by spacecraft) M: 226c
Mariner 9 [space probe]
Mars (Observation by spacecraft) M: 226c-226d
Space exploration (Probes to Mars) So: 710
Mariner 10 [space probe]
Mercury (Flights to Mercury) M: 415 *with picture*

Mariners, Seattle [team] *See* Seattle Mariners *in this index*
Mariner's compass
Compass Ci: 902b
Mariners Harbor [district]
New York City (Staten Island) N: 330
"Marines' Hymn, The" [song]
Marine Corps, United States M: 206
Marinetti, Filippo Tommaso [Italian poet]
Futurism F: 589
Italian literature (The 1900's) I: 495
Marino, Dan [American football player] M: 211
Favre, Brett F: 56
Marino, Eugene Antonio [American religious leader] M: 211
Marino, Giambattista [Italian poet]
Italian literature (The Baroque period and the Enlightenment) I: 494
Marinol [drug]
Marijuana (History) M: 201-202
Marinsky, J. A. [American chemist]
Promethium P: 818
Marinus [founder of]
San Marino (History) S: 104
Marinus I [pope]
Pope (table) P: 666
Marinus II [pope]
Pope (table) P: 666
Mario [opera character]
Opera: (Tosca) O: 807
Marion, Francis [American general] M: 211
Guerrilla warfare (History) G: 420
Revolution, American (Savannah and Charleston) R: 284-285
South Carolina (The Revolutionary War) So: 659-660
Marion, Lake
South Carolina (Rivers, waterfalls, and lakes) So: 652-654 *with map*
Marion Democratic Mirror [newspaper]
Harding, Warren Gamaliel (Newspaper career) H: 56
Marion Star [newspaper]
Harding, Warren Gamaliel (Newspaper career) H: 56
Marionette [toy]
Puppet *picture on* P: 905; (Marionettes) P: 906
Mariotte, Edme [French chemist]
Gas [physics] (Gas laws) G: 48
Mariotte's Law [chemistry]
Gas [physics] (Gas laws) G: 48 *with pictures*
Mariposa Grove
Yosemite National Park Y: 569
Mariposa lily [flower] M: 212 *with picture*
Flower *picture on* F: 290
Maris, Roger [American baseball player] M: 212 *with portrait*
Baseball (Recent developments) B: 137
Marisol [American sculptor] M: 212
Maritain, Jacques [French philosopher] M: 212
Marital rape [crime]
Rape R: 141
Maritime academy
United States Merchant Marine Academy U: 200
Maritime Administration [U.S.] M: 212
Transportation, Department of (Agencies) T: 400
Maritime Aquarium [Norwalk]
Connecticut (Places to visit) Ci: 960
Maritime Commission, Federal [U.S.] *See* Federal Maritime Commission *in this index*
Maritime law [international law] M: 213
Admiralty A: 59
Flotsam, jetsam, and lagan F: 267
Maritimes [Canada] *See* Atlantic Provinces *in this index*
Marius, Gaius [Roman general] M: 213
Caesar, Julius (Early life) C: 13
Legion L: 183
Rome, Ancient (The later years of the republic) R: 445
Marius Hills complex [lunar feature]
Moon (Rilles) M: 790
Marius the Epicurean [book by Pater]
Pater, Walter P: 195
Marivaux, Pierre [French author] M: 213
Drama (France) D: 335
Marjoram [plant] M: 213 *with picture*
Oregano O: 825
Mark [money] M: 213
Mark, Gospel of [New Testament]
Bible (The Gospels) B: 283; (Historical contexts) B: 287
Gospels G: 278
Jesus Christ (Sources of information about Jesus) J: 104; (Public life) J: 106; (The Passion) J: 108
New Testament (Gospels) N: 287; (Critical studies)

N: 288
Mark, Saint [apostle] M: 213
See also Mark, Gospel of *in this index*
Gospels G: 278
Mark Antony [Roman military leader] *See* Antony, Mark *in this index*
Mark Clark Expressway Bridge [South Carolina]
Bridge (table: Continuous truss) B: 603
Mark of cadency [symbol]
Heraldry (Elements of a coat of arms) H: 196 *with pictures*
Mark I [computer]
Computer (The first electronic computers) Ci: 924b
Mark Twain [American author] *See* Twain, Mark *in this index*
Mark twain [navigation]
Twain, Mark (Newspaper work in the West) T: 529
Mark Twain Boyhood Home & Museum [Hannibal]
Missouri (Places to visit) M: 660 *with picture*
Mark Twain Cave [Hannibal]
Missouri (Places to visit) M: 660
Mark Twain House & Museum [Hartford]
Connecticut (Places to visit) Ci: 960 *with picture*
Mark Twain National Forest
Missouri (Places to visit) M: 660
Marka [people]
Burkina Faso (People) B: 706
Markarian's Chain [galaxies]
Astronomy *picture on* A: 839
Markell, Jack [American political leader]
Delaware (table) D: 109
Market [economics]
Capitalism (Capitalism in its ideal form) C: 194
Cartel C: 251
Commodity exchange Ci: 873
Economics E: 57
Market research M: 213
Marketing (Market research) M: 214
Price P: 774
Trade (The use of markets) T: 362
Market [shopping]
Africa *picture on* A: 110
Chile *picture on* C: 460
Hong Kong *picture on* H: 319
India *picture on* I: 116
La Paz *picture on* L: 73
London (Recreation) L: 434 *with picture*
Mexico (Rural life) M: 455
Russia *picture on* R: 534
Trading post T: 364
Market, Stock *See* Stock exchange *in this index*
Market Church in Halle, The [painting by Feininger]
Feininger, Lyonel *picture on* F: 67
Market economy *See* Capitalism *in this index*
Market Hall [Belgium]
Bruges B: 649
Market index [economics]
Mortgage M: 820
Market intervention [economics]
Price (Government intervention) P: 775
Market Place, The [book by Frederic]
Frederic, Harold F: 497
Market power [economics]
Capitalism (Ensuring competition) C: 195
Market price
Investment (table) I: 366
Price (How price is determined) P: 774
Market research M: 213
Advertising (Research) A: 76a
Automobile (Planning the car) A: 956
Marketing (Market research) M: 214
Public opinion poll (Business companies) P: 862
Sociology (Careers) So: 567
Market value
Appraisal A: 575
Marketing M: 214
Business (Specialized departments) B: 726
Farm and farming (Marketing farm products) F: 42
Food (Marketing) F: 335
Fruit (Marketing fruit) F: 548
Industry (Product differentiation) I: 260
Livestock (Marketing livestock) L: 398
Market research M: 213
Meat packing (Marketing livestock and meat) M: 350
Packaging P: 18
Publishing (Marketing) P: 867
Sales S: 62
Vegetable (Harvesting and marketing vegetables) V: 294
Marketing channel
Marketing (Distribution) M: 214
Marketing cooperative

Cooperative (Marketing cooperatives) **Ci: 1036**
Farm and farming (Marketing farm products) **F: 42**
Fishing industry (Marketing) **F: 187**
Food (Marketing) **F: 335**
Markets of Trajan [ruins]
Rome (Forums) **R: 433**
Markham, Sir Clements R. [British author]
Baffin, William **B: 25**
Markham, Edwin [American poet] **M: 214**
Markham, Henry H. [American political leader]
California (table) **C: 59**
Markham, Robert [pen name]
Amis, Kingsley **A: 433**
Markham, William [American colonial leader]
Pennsylvania (Colonial days) **P: 264**
Marking
Horse (Coat and skin) **H: 348-349**
Marking to market [economics]
Commodity exchange (Forward and futures contracts) **Ci: 873**
Märkischer Sand [painting by Kiefer]
Painting (Neoexpressionism) **P: 87** *with picture*
Markova, Alicia [British dancer] **M: 215**
Dolin, Anton **D: 285**
Markowitz, Harry Max [American economist]
Nobel Prizes (Economics: 1990) **N: 449**
Marks, Albert S. [American political leader]
Tennessee (table) **T: 152**
Marks, Lillian Alicia [birth name of]
Markova, Alicia **M: 215**
Marks and marking [education]
Grading **G: 296**
Markup [computing]
HyperText Markup Language **H: 477**
Markup [economics]
Marketing (Pricing) **M: 214**
Markup session [government]
Congress of the United States (Working in committees) **Ci: 944**
Marland, Ernest W. [American political leader]
Oklahoma (table) **O: 730**
Marland, William C. [American political leader]
West Virginia (table) **W: 225**
Marlatt, Daphne [Canadian author]
Canadian literature (Modern English-Canadian fiction) **C: 160**
Marlborough [book by Churchill]
Churchill, Sir Winston Leonard Spencer (Between wars) **C: 547**
Marlborough, Duke of [English general] **M: 215**
Blenheim, Battle of **B: 400**
Churchill River **C: 550**
England (War with France) **E: 309**
Marley, Bob [Jamaican musician] **M: 215**
Latin America (Music) **L: 100**
Reggae **R: 204**
Rock music (World music) **R: 380d**
Marley, David "Ziggy" [Jamaican musician]
Marley, Bob **M: 215**
Marlin [fish] **M: 215** *with picture*
Fish *picture on* **F: 152**
Marlins, Miami [team] *See* Miami Marlins *in this index*
Marlowe, Christopher [English author] **M: 216**
Blank verse **B: 398**
Drama (Elizabethan playwrights) **D: 331-332**
English literature (Elizabethan drama) **E: 317**
Poetry (Renaissance poetry) **P: 596**
Marlowe, Philip [literary figure]
Chandler, Raymond **C: 374**
Marmaduke, John S. [American political leader]
Missouri (table) **M: 668**
Marmaduke, Meredith M. [American political leader]
Missouri (table) **M: 668**
Marmara, Sea of [Turkey] **M: 216**
Marmion [poem by Scott]
Scott, Sir Walter (His life) **S: 222**
Mármol Domingo, José [Argentine author]
Latin American literature (Romanticism) **L: 112-113**
Marmoset [animal] **M: 216** *with picture*
Animal *picture on* **A: 480**
Primate (New World monkeys) **P: 778-778a**
Marmot [animal] **M: 216**
Marne, Battle of the [1914]
Paris (Paris in wartime) **P: 166**
World War I (The Western Front) *map on* **W: 455-456**
Marne, Second Battle of The [1918]
World War I (The last campaigns) **W: 463**
Marne River [France] **M: 216**
Marner, Silas [literary figure]
Eliot, George **E: 237**
Marois, Pauline [Canadian political leader]
Quebec (table) **Q: 29**; (Recent developments)

Q: 33
Maroni River
French Guiana (The land and climate) **F: 514** *with map*
Maronite Church [religious group]
Eastern Catholic Churches **E: 45**
Lebanon (Ethnic groups and religion) **L: 171**
Maroons [people] **M: 217**
Jamaica (History) **J: 24**
Marot, Clement [French poet] **M: 217**
Marot, Daniel [French cabinetmaker]
Furniture (The French influence spreads) **F: 575** *with picture*
Marouflage [art]
Mural **M: 929**
Marpesia marcella [butterfly]
Butterfly *picture on* **B: 735**
Marple, Miss [literary figure]
Christie, Agatha **C: 527**
Marquand, John Phillips [American author] **M: 217**
Marquard, Rube [American baseball player]
Baseball (table: Hall of Fame) **B: 134a**
Marque and reprisal [warfare]
Privateer **P: 808b**
Marquesas Islands [islands, Pacific] **M: 217** *with picture*
French Polynesia **F: 524**
Marquess [title]
Duke **D: 380**
Nobility (In the United Kingdom) **N: 450**
Marquess of O..., The [book by Kleist]
German literature (Other writers) **G: 140**
Marquetry [decoration]
Inlay **I: 274**
Marquette, Jacques [French explorer] **M: 217** *with map*
Arkansas **A: 713**
Chicago (Exploration and early settlement) **C: 434**
Exploration (The French and English in North America) **E: 446-447** *with map*
Illinois (French and British control) **I: 72**
Jolliet, Louis **J: 156**
Michigan (French exploration and settlement) **M: 508**
Missouri (Exploration) **M: 669**
Missouri River (History) **M: 675-676**
Peoria **P: 277**
Marquette University M: 218
McGuire, Al **M: 335**
Márquez, Gabriel García [Colombian author] *See* García Márquez, Gabriel José *in this index*
Marquis, Don [American author] **M: 218**
Marquis de Lafayette [painting by Morse]
Morse, Samuel Finley Breese (Morse as artist) **M: 818** *with picture*
Marquis of Queensberry rules [boxing]
Boxing (Bare knuckles to gloves) **B: 532**
Marquise [cut]
Gem (Types of gem cuts) *picture on* **G: 79**
Marr, Wilhelm [German author]
Anti-Semitism **A: 559**
Marrakech [Morocco] **M: 218**
Marranos [people]
Jews (Jews in Christian Europe) **J: 122-123**
Marriage M: 219 *with pictures*
See also Same-sex marriage; Same-sex union *in this index*
Africa (Marriage and family) **A: 108** *with picture*
Annulment **A: 518**
Anthropology **A: 546**
Bigamy **B: 298**
Breach of promise **B: 587**
Christianity (Sacraments) **C: 522h**
Civil union **Ci: 613**
Desertion **D: 157**
Divorce **D: 253**
Domestic violence **D: 300**
Dower **D: 316**
Eastern Orthodox Churches (Sacraments) **E: 46-47**
Family (Development of the family) **F: 21-22**
Gay rights movement **G: 73**
Homosexuality (Attitudes toward homosexuality) **H: 307**
Indian, American (Marriage) **I: 136c**
Latin America (Family life) **L: 96-97**
Mormons (Church doctrines and ordinances) **M: 806-807**; (The Mormons in Utah) **M: 809**
Oneida Community **O: 762**
Polygamy **P: 650**
Ring **R: 342** *with picture*
Roman Catholic Church (Worship) **R: 403-404**
Rome, Ancient (Family life) **R: 440**
Suttee **So: 1013**
Women's movement (From the Renaissance to

the 1800's) **W: 384**
Marriage à la Mode [paintings by Hogarth]
Hogarth, William **H: 288** *with picture*
Marriage à la Mode [play by Dryden]
Dryden, John **D: 370**
Marriage counselor
Divorce (No-fault divorce) **D: 253-254**
Marriage (Marriage problems) **M: 222**
Marriage license
Marriage (Laws concerning marriage) **M: 219**
Vital statistics (Collecting and publishing vital statistics) **V: 429**
Marriage of Figaro, The [opera by Mozart]
Beaumarchais, Pierre Augustin Caron de **B: 191**
Mozart, Wolfgang Amadeus (Operas) **M: 906-907**
Opera: *(Marriage of Figaro, The)* **O: 805**
Marriage of Figaro, The [play by Beaumarchais]
French literature (The Enlightenment) **F: 520-521**
Marriage of the Virgin [painting by Raphael]
Raphael (His works) **R: 143** *with picture*
Married [story by Strindberg]
Strindberg, August **So: 929**
"Married...with Children" [television program]
Television (The 1980's and 1990's) **T: 120**
Marrow [anatomy] *See* Bone marrow *in this index*
Marryat, Frederick [British author] **M: 222**
Mars [god] **M: 222**
Mythology (table) **M: 981**; (Roman divinities) **M: 982**; (Romulus and Remus) **M: 983**
Romulus and Remus **R: 450a**
Tuesday **T: 481**
Mars [planet] **M: 223** *with pictures and map*
Astrobiology **A: 826**
Astronomy (How the planets move) **A: 835**
Earthquake (Quakes elsewhere in the solar system) **E: 38b**
Kepler, Johannes (His life) **K: 305**
Life (In our solar system) **L: 280**
Mars Exploration Rover Mission **M: 227**
Meteor *picture on* **M: 432**
Mountain **M: 891**
Planet **P: 507** *with pictures*
Satellite **S: 149**; (Physical characteristics) **S: 149**; (Satellites of the terrestrial planets) **S: 149** *with picture*; (table: Major planets of the solar system) **S: 150b**
Space exploration *picture on* **So: 709**; (Probes to Mars) **So: 710**
Volcano (Volcanoes in the solar system) **V: 442b** *with picture*
Mars, Field of [Rome]
Mars **M: 222**
Mars Exploration Rover Mission M: 227
Mars (Observation by spacecraft) **M: 226c-226d** *with picture*
Space exploration *picture on* **So: 709**; (Probes to Mars) **So: 710**
Mars Express [space probe]
European Space Agency **E: 418**
Mars (Observation by spacecraft) **M: 226c-226d** *with picture*
Space exploration (Probes to Mars) **So: 710**
Mars Global Surveyor [space probe]
Mars *picture on* **M: 226a**; (Core) **M: 225**; (Observation by spacecraft) **M: 226c-226d** *with picture*
Space exploration (Probes to Mars) **So: 710**
Mars Observer [space probe]
Space exploration (Probes to Mars) **So: 710**
Mars Odyssey [space probe]
Astronomy *picture on* **A: 843**
Mars (Observation by spacecraft) **M: 226c-226d**
Space exploration (Probes to Mars) **So: 710**
Mars Pathfinder [space probe]
Mars (Observation by spacecraft) **M: 226c-226d**
Space exploration (Probes to Mars) **So: 710**
Mars Reconnaissance Orbiter [spacecraft]
Mars (Observation by spacecraft) **M: 226c-226d**
Space exploration (Probes to Mars) **So: 710**
Mars Science Laboratory [spacecraft]
Mars (Observation by spacecraft) **M: 226c-227**
Marsalis, Branford [American musician]
Jazz (Recent developments) **J: 73** *with picture*
Marsalis, Delfeayo [American trombonist]
Jazz *picture on* **J: 74**
Marsalis, Ellis [American pianist]
Jazz *picture on* **J: 74**
Marsalis, Jason [American drummer]
Jazz *picture on* **J: 74**
Marsalis, Wynton [American musician] **M: 227**
Jazz (Recent developments) **J: 73** *with picture*
Marschallin [opera character]
Opera: *(Rosenkavalier, Der)* **O: 807**
"Marseillaise" [song] **M: 227**
Marseille [France] **M: 227**
Marsh [fruit]
Grapefruit **G: 320**

Marsh [geography] M: 228
  Bird (Birds of inland waters and marshes) B: 340
    with pictures
  Wetland W: 252a; (Marshes and wet meadows)
    W: 252b with picture
Marsh, George Perkins [American naturalist]
  Conservation (Early conservation problems)
    Ci: 985
Marsh, Henry L., III [American political leader]
  Richmond (History) R: 333
Marsh, Ngaio [New Zealand author] M: 228
Marsh, Othniel C. [American paleontologist]
  Apatosaurus A: 563
  Camptosaurus C: 97
Marsh, Reginald [American artist] M: 228
  Realism picture on R: 172
Marsh Arabs [Iraqi history]
  Iraq (The Persian Gulf War of 1991) I: 414-414a
Marsh-Billings National Historical Park
  [Vermont]
  National Park System (table: National historical
    parks) N: 56-57
Marsh calla [plant]
  Calla C: 66
Marsh deer
  Deer (table) D: 85; (Central and South American
    deer) D: 85-86
Marsh gas See Methane in this index
Marsh hawk [bird] See Northern harrier in this index
Marsh hen [bird] See Coot in this index
Marsh marigold [plant]
  Cowslip Ci: 1113
  Flower picture on F: 285
Marsh wren [bird]
  Wren W: 504
Marshaling [symbol]
  Heraldry picture on H: 195
Marshaling yard [railroad] See Classification yard
  in this index
Marshall, Alfred [British economist] M: 228
  Economics (Modern economics) E: 64
Marshall, Barry James [American physician]
  Nobel Prizes (Physiology or medicine: 2005)
    N: 447
Marshall, E. G. [American actor]
  Drama picture on D: 340
Marshall, F. Ray [American government official]
  Labor, Department of (table) L: 2
Marshall, George Catlett [American statesman]
  M: 228
  China (Civil war) C: 504
  Cold War (The containment policy) Ci: 764
  Truman, Harry S. (table) T: 469
Marshall, James [American author]
  Laura Ingalls Wilder Award (table) L: 121
Marshall, James Wilson [American settler] M: 229
  California (The gold rush) C: 62
Marshall, John [American jurist] M: 229 with
  portrait
  Adams, John (table) A: 38; (Election of 1800)
    A: 39
  Judicial review J: 184
  Marbury v. Madison M: 193
  Supreme Court of the United States (Landmark
    decisions) So: 1000
  United States, History of the (The power of the
    federal government) U: 164
Marshall, John [British explorer]
  Marshall Islands (History) M: 231
Marshall, Ray [American government official]
  Carter, Jimmy (table) C: 257
Marshall, Thomas Riley [American political leader]
  M: 230
  Indiana (table) I: 214
  Vice president of the United States portrait on
    V: 349; (President of the Senate) V: 352
Marshall, Thurgood [American jurist] M: 230 with
  portrait
  African Americans (Political gains) A: 136p with
    picture
  Brown v. Board of Education of Topeka B: 645
  Johnson, Lyndon Baines (Other developments)
    J: 151
  National Association for the Advancement of
    Colored People N: 29
Marshall, William R. [American political leader]
  Minnesota (table) M: 602
Marshall Field and Company
  Field, Marshall, I F: 92
  Merchandise Mart M: 412
  Palmer, Potter P: 110
**Marshall Field and Company Wholesale
  Warehouse** [Chicago]
  Architecture (Early modern architecture in
    America) A: 629
Marshall Field Wholesale Store [building]
  Richardson, Henry Hobson R: 330

Marshall Islands [islands, Pacific] M: 231 with map
  Flag picture on F: 203
  Pacific Islands, Trust Territory of the P: 13
  World War II (Island hopping in the Central
    Pacific) W: 489
Marshall Plan [U.S. history] M: 231
  Acheson, Dean Gooderham A: 26
  Cold War (The containment policy) Ci: 764
  Europe (Postwar Europe) E: 414-415
  Marshall, George Catlett M: 228
  Organisation for Economic Co-operation and
    Development O: 853
  Truman, Harry S. (The Marshall Plan) T: 470
  World War II (New power struggles) W: 497
Marshall Research Library [Lexington, Virginia]
  Marshall, George Catlett (Statesman) M: 229
Marshall scholarship
  Oxford, University of (Educational program)
    O: 887
Marshall Space Flight Center [Alabama]
  Alabama (Population) A: 260; (The mid-1900's)
    A: 278
Marshall University
  West Virginia picture on W: 211
"Marshes of Glynn, The" [poem by Lanier]
  Lanier, Sidney L: 68
Marshmallow [food]
  Candy (Whipped candies) C: 176
Marsupial [zoology] M: 232 with pictures
  Australia (Native animals) A: 911
  Bandicoot B: 76
  Conservation (Australia) Ci: 989
  Cuscus Ci: 1200
  Glider [animal] G: 231
  Kangaroo K: 213
  Koala K: 359 with picture
  Mammal (Reproduction) M: 123-124 with picture;
    (table) M: 128 with pictures
  Prehistoric animal (Mammals) P: 739; (The
    distribution of mammals) P: 741
  Quoll Q: 44
  Reproduction (Mammals) R: 243
  Wallaby W: 15
Marsupial mole [animal]
  Mammal (table) M: 128 with picture
  Marsupial (Kinds of marsupials) M: 232-233 with
    picture
Marsupial mouse [animal] M: 233 with picture
Martel, Charles [Frankish ruler] See Charles Martel
  in this index
Martel, Yann [Canadian author] M: 233
Martelly, Michel [Haitian political leader]
  Haiti (History) H: 15-17
Marten [animal] M: 233 with picture
  Fur (table) F: 561
Martenot, Maurice [French inventor]
  Electronic music E: 205
Martha's Vineyard [island, Massachusetts] M: 233
  Massachusetts (Places to visit) M: 280
Martí, José Julián [Cuban patriot] M: 234
  Cuba (The arts) Ci: 1171-1172; (Struggle against
    Spain) Ci: 1176
  Latin American literature (Modernism) L: 113
Martial [Roman poet]
  Epigram E: 343
  Latin literature (The Imperial Period) L: 116-117
Martial arts [sport] M: 234 with picture
  Capoeira C: 197
  Karate K: 245 with picture
  Kickboxing K: 310 with picture
  Kung fu K: 392
  Motion picture (Motion pictures today) M: 872-
    873
  Tae kwon do T: 6
  T'ai chi chuan T: 14
Martial eagle
  Eagle (Other kinds of eagles) E: 5
Martial law M: 234a
Martin [bird] M: 234a with picture
  Bird pictures on B: 358, B: 367
Martin I, Saint [pope]
  Pope (table) P: 666
Martin IV [pope]
  Pope (table) P: 666
Martin V [pope]
  Pope (The troubles of the papacy) P: 664; (table)
    P: 666
  Roman Catholic Church (The Great Schism)
    R: 407
  Sigismund S: 453
Martin, Agnes [American artist]
  Painting (Abstract artists) P: 88-89
Martin, Alexander [American political leader]
  North Carolina (table) N: 490
Martin, Archer John Porter [British biochemist]
  Nobel Prizes (Chemistry: 1952) N: 443
Martin, Charles H. [American political leader]

  Oregon (table) O: 845
Martin, Christy [American boxer]
  Boxing (Women's boxing) B: 532b-533
Martin, Clarence D. [American political leader]
  Washington (table) W: 65
Martin, Daniel [American political leader]
  Maryland (table) M: 255
Martin, Dean [American entertainer]
  Sinatra, Frank S: 468
Martin, Edward [American political leader]
  Pennsylvania (table) P: 263
Martin, Eleanor Adams [mother of]
  Martin, Paul (Early life) M: 234b
Martin, Émile [French inventor]
  Iron and steel (The birth of modern steelmaking)
    I: 450-451
Martin, Glenn Luther [American engineer]
  Aviation (Beginnings) A: 986-987
Martin, James G. [American political leader]
  North Carolina (table) N: 490
Martin, James Purdon [British physician]
  Fragile X syndrome F: 450
Martin, John [American political leader]
  Georgia (table) G: 130
Martin, John Alexander [American political
  leader]
  Kansas (table) K: 234
Martin, John W. [American political leader]
  Florida (table) F: 260
Martin, Joseph [Canadian political leader]
  British Columbia (table) B: 628
Martin, Joseph William, Jr. [American political
  leader]
  MacArthur, Douglas (The Korean War) M: 3-4
Martin, Joshua Lanier [American political leader]
  Alabama (table) A: 274
Martin, Josiah [British colonial official]
  Revolution, American (Fighting in the
    Chesapeake and Southern colonies) R: 276-
    278
Martin, Lynn [American government official]
  Labor, Department of (table) L: 2
Martin, Noah [American political leader]
  New Hampshire (table) N: 223
Martin, Paul [Canadian political leader] M: 234b
  with pictures
  Canada, History of (Canada under Martin) C: 152
  Harper, Stephen Joseph (Member of Parliament)
    H: 66a
  Liberal Party of Canada L: 227
Martin, Paul, Sr. [Canadian political leader]
  Martin, Paul (Early life) M: 234b
Martin, Pierre [French inventor]
  Iron and steel (The birth of modern steelmaking)
    I: 450-451
Martin, Ricky [Puerto Rican musician]
  Latin America (Music) L: 100
Martin, T. Mower [Canadian painter]
  Indian, American picture on I: 163
Martin-Bell syndrome [former name]
  Fragile X syndrome F: 450
Martin Chuzzlewit [book by Dickens]
  Dickens, Charles (The first phase) D: 188
Martin Eden [book by London]
  London, Jack L: 444
Martín Fierro [poem by Hernández]
  Argentina (The arts) A: 651-652
  Latin American literature (Romanticism) L: 112-
    113
Martin House
  Buffalo (Other interesting places to visit) B: 678
Martin Luther King, Jr., Community Center
  Dallas (Commercial growth) D: 15
Martin Luther King, Jr., Day [U.S. holiday] M: 235
Martin Luther King, Jr., National Historic Site
  [Georgia] M: 235
  National Park System (table: National historic
    sites) N: 52-53
Martin Luther King, Jr. National Memorial
  [Washington, D.C.]
  King, Martin Luther, Jr. (King's death) K: 323
  National Park System (National memorials) N: 54
  Washington, D.C. map on W: 76; (The Tidal Basin)
    W: 73
Martin Luther King Memorial Library
  [Washington, D.C.]
  Washington, D.C. map on W: 76
Martin Marprelate controversy [English history]
  Nashe, Thomas N: 22
Martin of Tours, Saint [French religious leader]
  M: 235
Martin Van Buren National Historic Site [New
  York]
  National Park System (table: National historic
    sites) N: 52-53
  Van Buren, Martin (Later years) V: 273
Martineau, John Ellis [American political leader]

Arkansas (table) **A:** 712
Martinelli, Ricardo [Panamanian political leader]
Panama (Recent developments) **P:** 121
Martinez, Bob [American political leader]
Florida (table) **F:** 260
Martinez, Conchita [Spanish tennis player]
Tennis (table: Wimbledon) **T:** 166
Martinez, Maria [American artist]
Indian, American (Achievements in the arts)
I: 181
Martinez, Melquiades R. [American government official]
Bush, George Walker (table) **B:** 722h
Housing and Urban Development, Department of (table) **H:** 393
Martinez, Susana [American political leader]
New Mexico (table) **N:** 272; (Recent developments) **N:** 276
Martini, Simone [Italian painter] *See* Simone Martini *in this index*
Martinique [island, Caribbean Sea] **M:** 235
Martins, Peter [Danish-born dancer] **M:** 236
Martin's Head [mountain]
Maryland *picture on* **M:** 241
Martinson, Harry Edmund [Swedish author]
Nobel Prizes (Literature: 1974) **N:** 448
Martius [month]
Calendar (The Romans) **C:** 31
Martlet [symbol]
Heraldry *picture on* **H:** 195
Martorell, Joanot [Spanish author]
Spanish literature (The 1400's) **So:** 758
Marty [film]
Motion picture (Best picture: 1955) **M:** 861
Martyr [religion]
Jihad **J:** 126
Saint **S:** 29
Martyrdom of Saint Maurice [painting by El Greco]
Greco, El **G:** 351
Martyrdom of Savonarola [painting]
Perspective *picture on* **P:** 304
Martyrology, The [book by Nichol]
Canadian literature (Modern Canadian poets) **C:** 161
Martz, Judy [American political leader]
Montana (table) **M:** 757; (The early 2000's) **M:** 761
Maruki, Toshi [Japanese author]
Literature for children *picture on* **L:** 355
Marvel Cave
Missouri (Springs and caves) **M:** 664
Marvel-of-Peru [plant] *See* Four-o'clock *in this index*
Marvell, Andrew [English poet] **M:** 236
Marver [tool]
Glass (Glass terms) **G:** 222
Marvil, Joshua [American political leader]
Delaware (table) **D:** 109
Marvin, Lee [American actor]
Motion picture (Best performance by an actor: 1965) **M:** 862a
Marvin, William [American political leader]
Florida (table) **F:** 260
"Marvin Redpost" series [books by Sachar]
Sachar, Louis **S:** 5
Marwān ibn al-Hakam [Muslim ruler]
Muslims (The Muslim Empire) **M:** 964c
Marx, Chico [American comedian]
Marx Brothers **M:** 238 *with picture*
Marx, Groucho [American comedian]
Marx Brothers **M:** 238 *with picture*
Marx, Gummo [American comedian]
Marx Brothers **M:** 238
Marx, Harpo [American comedian]
Marx Brothers **M:** 238 *with picture*
Marx, Heinrich [father of]
Marx, Karl (Childhood) **M:** 236
Marx, Henrietta [mother of]
Marx, Karl (Childhood) **M:** 236
Marx, Herbert [American comedian]
Marx Brothers **M:** 238
Marx, Karl [German philosopher] **M:** 236 *with portrait*
See also Marxism *in this index*
Capitalism (Changing attitudes toward capitalism) **C:** 196
Caricature *picture on* **C:** 238
Christianity (The 1800's) **C:** 526
Communism **Ci:** 889; (The party state) **Ci:** 891
Economic determinism **E:** 57
Economics (Karl Marx and Communism) **E:** 64
Engels, Friedrich **E:** 283
Enlightenment (Criticism of the Enlightenment) **E:** 326b
Europe (The Industrial Revolution) **E:** 413
Feuerbach, Ludwig Andreas **F:** 83
Germany (Literature and philosophy) **G:** 153
Government (Communism) **G:** 286
Lenin, V. I. **L:** 191

Materialism **M:** 300b
Middle class **M:** 529
Philosophy (Philosophy in the 1800's) **P:** 390
Political science (Democracy and socialism) **P:** 639
Ricardo, David **R:** 321
Russia (Nicholas II) **R:** 551-552
Social change **So:** 550
Social class (How people are categorized) **So:** 550
Socialism (Karl Marx) **So:** 560
Union of Soviet Socialist Republics (Privileged classes) **U:** 32
Marx, Milton [American comedian]
Marx Brothers **M:** 238
Marx, Robert S. [founder of]
Disabled American Veterans **D:** 223
Marx, Zeppo [American comedian]
Marx Brothers **M:** 238
Marx Brothers [American comedians] **M:** 238 *with picture*
Marxism [philosophy]
See also Marx, Karl *in this index*
Allende Gossens, Salvador **A:** 373
Communism **Ci:** 889; (The ideas of Marx) **Ci:** 890
Economic determinism **E:** 57
Economics (Karl Marx and Communism) **E:** 64
Marx, Karl (Marx's ideas) **M:** 237
Plekhanov, Georgi Valentinovich **P:** 572
Political science (Democracy and socialism) **P:** 639
Russia (Nicholas II) **R:** 551-552
Russian Revolution of 1917 (Background to the revolution) **R:** 565
Sociology **So:** 566
Union of Soviet Socialist Republics (History) **U:** 35
Marxism-Leninism [philosophy]
Communism (Communism in theory) **Ci:** 890; (Communist influence in other areas) **Ci:** 894
Government (Communism) **G:** 286-288
Marx, Karl (Marx's influence) **M:** 238
Political science (Democracy and socialism) **P:** 639
Mary [mother of Jesus] **M:** 238
Annunciation **A:** 518
Assumption **A:** 820
Christianity (Origins) **C:** 523
Fátima, Our Lady of **F:** 55
Guadalupe Day **G:** 407
Immaculate Conception **I:** 79
Jesus Christ (The Nativity) **J:** 105 *with picture*
Joseph **J:** 167
Juan Diego, Saint **J:** 178
Madonna and Child **M:** 37 *with picture*
May Day **M:** 322
Sculpture (Later medieval sculpture) **S:** 250-251 *with picture*
Mary I [queen of England] **M:** 238 *with portrait*
Elizabeth I (Early years) **E:** 238
Grey, Lady Jane **G:** 391
Henry VIII (king of England) **H:** 188
Ireland (The conquest of Ireland) **I:** 426
Tudor, House of **T:** 481
Mary II [queen of England] **M:** 239
Pennsylvania (Colonial days) **P:** 264
William III **W:** 309
Mary, Queen of Scots [queen of Scotland] **M:** 239 *with portrait*
Bothwell, Earl of **B:** 510
Elizabeth I (Mary, Queen of Scots) **E:** 239
Scotland (History) **S:** 218-219
Mary, Queen of the World, Basilica of
Montreal (Churches) **M:** 773
Mary, Virgin *See* Mary *in this index*
Mary Barton [book by Gaskell]
Gaskell, Elizabeth **G:** 61
"Mary Had a Little Lamb" [poem by Hale]
Hale, Sarah Josepha **H:** 19
Mary Magdalene [Biblical figure] **M:** 239
Jesus Christ (The Resurrection) **J:** 108b
Mary McLeod Bethune Council House National Historic Site [Washington, D.C.]
National Park System (table: National historic sites) **N:** 52-53
Mary of Burgundy [wife of Maximilian I]
Maximilian I **M:** 319
Mary of Guise [mother of Mary, Queen of Scots]
Knox, John (Early years) **K:** 358
Mary, Queen of Scots **M:** 239
Mary of Teck [wife of George V]
Clothing *picture on* **Ci:** 704
Mary Poppins [book by Travers]
Travers, P. L. **T:** 405
Mary Poppins [film]
Andrews, Julie **A:** 456
Disney, Walt (Full-length movies) **D:** 236
Marye's Heights [hills, Virginia]
Civil War, American (Battle of Fredericksburg)

Ci: 627
Maryhill Museum
Washington (Places to visit) **W:** 56
Maryknoll [religious group]
Missionary (Organization) **M:** 621
Maryland M: 240 *with pictures and maps*
See also the list of Related articles in the Maryland article
Colonial life in America (Development of the Thirteen Colonies) **Ci:** 790 *with map*
United States, History of the *picture on* **U:** 155; (Virginia and Maryland) **U:** 153
Maryland, University System of M: 261 *with picture*
Baltimore (Education) **B:** 68
Maryland Gazette [newspaper]
Maryland (Communication) **M:** 255
Maryland Historical Society
Maryland (Museums) **M:** 244
Maryland Institute for Emergency Medical Services [Baltimore]
Trauma center **T:** 405
Maryland Journal, The [newspaper]
Goddard, Mary Katherine **G:** 244
Goddard, William **G:** 245
Marylebone Cricket Club
Cricket (History) **Ci:** 1134-1135
Marys Peak
Oregon (Land regions) **O:** 838 *with map*
Mary's Well
Nazareth **N:** 91
Marzipan [food]
Candy (Other candies) **C:** 176 *with picture*
Masaccio [Italian painter] **M:** 261 *with picture*
Painting (The 1400's) **P:** 52-53 *with picture*
Renaissance (Arts of the 1300's and early 1400's) **R:** 236
Masada [Jewish history] **M:** 262 *with picture*
Jews (Roman rule) **J:** 122
Masai [people] *See* Maasai *in this index*
Masanobu, Kano [Japanese artist]
Painting (Japanese painting) **P:** 47
Masaryk, Jan Garrigue [Czechoslovak political leader]
Masaryk, Tomáš Garrigue **M:** 262
Masaryk, Tomáš Garrigue [Czechoslovak political leader] **M:** 262
Czech Republic (The creation of Czechoslovakia) **Ci:** 1213
Czechoslovakia (The formation of Czechoslovakia) **Ci:** 1215
Masbate [island, Philippines]
Philippines (The main islands) **P:** 376-378 *with map*
Mascagni, Pietro [Italian composer] **M:** 262
Opera: (*Cavalleria Rusticana*) **O:** 803
Mascon [astronomy]
Space exploration (Lunar probes) **So:** 708-709
Masculine gender
Gender **G:** 80
Noun (Gender) **N:** 552-553
Masculinity
Sexuality (Sex and gender) **S:** 338; (Gender roles) **S:** 338a
Masefield, John [British author] **M:** 262
Masekela, Hugh [South African trumpeter] **M:** 263
Maser [electronics] **M:** 263
Laser (History) **L:** 86
Prokhorov, Alexander Mikhailovich **P:** 817
Maseru [Lesotho] **M:** 263
Lesotho **L:** 206 *with picture*
Mash [industrial product]
Alcoholic beverage (Beer) **A:** 336
Brewing (Mashing) **B:** 595
Corn (The fermentation and distilling industry) **Ci:** 1062
Distilling **D:** 239
Whiskey **W:** 282
Mashantucket Pequot Museum and Research Center [Mashantucket]
Connecticut (Places to visit) **Ci:** 960 *with picture*
Mashhad [Iran] **M:** 263
Mashona [people] *See* Shona *in this index*
Mashup map
Map (Mapmaking and modern technology) **M:** 185
Masina, Julietta [Italian actress]
Fellini, Federico **F:** 68
Masire, Quett Ketumile Joni [Botswanan political leader]
Botswana (History) **B:** 512
Masjid-e-Imam [mosque, Isfahan]
Isfahan **I:** 462
Mask [covering] **M:** 263 *with pictures*
Africa (Fine arts) **A:** 115 *with picture*
Baseball (Equipment) **B:** 125 *with picture*
Drama *picture on* **D:** 327

Egypt, Ancient *picture on* **E:** 141
Indian, American *pictures on* **I:** 138, **I:** 151, **I:** 156,
  I: 162; **I:** 167, **I:** 172
Sculpture (Royal and public sculpture) **S:** 240
  with picture; (The European impact) **S:** 244-245
  with picture
Tutankhamun *picture on* **T:** 526
Maskawa, Toshihide [Japanese physicist]
  Nobel Prizes (Physics: 2008) **N:** 442
Masked palm civet [animal]
  Civet **Ci:** 604
Maskin, Eric S. [American economist]
  Nobel Prizes (Economics: 2007) **N:** 449
Masking agent [drug]
  Doping **D:** 309
Masks, Temple of [Guatemala]
  Maya *picture on* **M:** 326
Masks of God, The [book by Campbell]
  Campbell, Joseph **C:** 90a
Maslow, Abraham Harold [American psychologist]
  M: 265
  Psychology (Modern psychology) **P:** 850
Mason [construction] *See* Bricklayer *in this index*
Mason [organization] *See* Masonry [organization]
  in this index
Mason, Charles [British astronomer]
  Mason-Dixon Line **M:** 266
Mason, Charles Harrison [American religious
  leader]
  Church of God in Christ, The **C:** 543
Mason, George [American patriot] **M:** 265 *with
  portrait*
  Constitution of the United States (The
    Constitutional Convention) **Ci:** 999-1000; (The
    Bill of Rights) **Ci:** 1001
  Virginia (Independence and statehood) **V:** 420
  Washington, George (The coming revolution)
    W: 96
Mason, James Murray [Confederate political
  leader] **M:** 266
  Lincoln, Abraham (Foreign relations) **L:** 322
  Slidell, James **S:** 508
  Trent Affair **T:** 435
  Wilkes, Charles **W:** 306
Mason, John [American settler]
  Maine (Ownership disputes) **M:** 89
Mason, John [English colonist]
  Connecticut (The Pequot War) **Ci:** 968
  New Hampshire (Settlement) **N:** 224
Mason, John Young [American government
  official]
  Justice, Department of (table) **J:** 203
  Ostend Manifesto **O:** 866
  Polk, James Knox (table) **P:** 643
  Tyler, John (table) **T:** 534
Mason, Lowell [American composer] **M:** 266
Mason, Perry [literary figure]
  Gardner, Erle Stanley **G:** 39
Mason, Stevens T. [American political leader]
  Madison (Government and history) **M:** 31
  Michigan (table) **M:** 507; (Territorial period)
    M: 509
Mason & Dixon [book by Pynchon]
  Pynchon, Thomas **P:** 915
Mason bee
  Bee (Solitary bees) **B:** 205-206 *with picture*
Mason-Dixon Line [U.S. history] **M:** 266 *with map*
  Maryland (Colonial days) **M:** 256-258
Mason Island
  Connecticut (Coastline) **Ci:** 962
Mason jar
  Glass (Early American glass) **G:** 219-222
Masonic Temple [Chicago]
  Root, John Wellborn **R:** 472
Masonry [construction]
  Cement and concrete (Concrete masonry) **C:** 343
Masonry [organization] **M:** 266 *with pictures*
  Eastern Star **E:** 47
  Hall, Prince **H:** 22
  Mozart, Wolfgang Amadeus (His style) **M:** 907
  Rainbow for Girls **R:** 129
  Shriners International **S:** 440
Masonry dam
  Dam (Masonry dams) **D:** 17 *with picture*
Mason's level [tool]
  Level **L:** 217
Masoretic Text [religious book]
  Bible (Literary contexts) **B:** 287
Maspeth [district]
  New York City (Queens) **N:** 329
Masqat [Oman] *See* Muscat *in this index*
Masque [drama] **M:** 268
  Ballet (The birth of ballet) **B:** 50-51
  Drama (Elizabethan playwrights) **D:** 331-332
    with picture
  Mask (Theatrical masks) **M:** 265
Masque of Judgment, The [play by Moody]
  Moody, William Vaughn **M:** 781
Masr [Egypt] *See* Cairo *in this index*
Mass [art]
  Painting (The elements of painting) **P:** 34-35
Mass [music]
  Classical music (The Middle Ages) **Ci:** 645-646
  Machaut, Guillaume de **M:** 12b
Mass [physics] **M:** 268
  See also Atomic mass number *in this index*
  Atom (The parts of an atom) **A:** 870-871
  Density **D:** 142
  Einstein, Albert (Famous theories) **E:** 146-146b
  $E=mc^2$ **E:** 3
  Energy (Weight and mass) **E:** 275
  Falling bodies, Law of **F:** 16
  Force (Acceleration) **F:** 369-370
  Gravitation **G:** 331; (Newton's theory of
    gravitation) **G:** 331
  Heat (Changes in temperature) **H:** 152
  Higgs, Peter Ware **H:** 227
  Higgs boson **H:** 227
  Inertia **I:** 262
  Kilogram **K:** 316
  Matter **M:** 310
  Metric system (Structure of the metric system)
    M: 437; (The metric system at a glance) **M:** 438-
    439 *with picture*
  Planet (Kepler's third law) **P:** 509-510
  Relativity (Mass-energy relationship) **R:** 211;
    (General relativity) **R:** 211-212
  Star (Mass) **So:** 845; (Converting mass to energy)
    So: 846; (Evolution of stars) **So:** 848
  Weight **W:** 181
Mass [religion] **M:** 268
  Holy Grail (The search for the Grail) **H:** 299
  Roman Catholic Church (Worship) **R:** 403-404
    with picture
  Transubstantiation **T:** 401
Mass, Center of [physics]
  Gravity, Center of **G:** 334
  Orbit **O:** 819
  Space exploration (Overcoming gravity) **So:** 699-
    701
Mass communication
  Advertising (Ways of advertising) **A:** 72
  Invention (Social needs) **I:** 355
Mass defect [physics]
  $E=mc^2$ **E:** 3
Mass extinction [zoology]
  Biodiversity (Protecting biodiversity) **B:** 311
  Extinction (Mass extinction) **E:** 456
  Prehistoric animal (Evolution and extinction)
    P: 742
Mass in B Minor [music by Bach]
  Bach, Johann Sebastian (His works) **B:** 16
Mass media *See* Media [communication] *in this
  index*
Mass noun
  Noun (Mass nouns and count nouns) **N:** 552
Mass number [physics] *See* Atomic mass number
  in this index
Mass of Life, A [music by Delius]
  Delius, Frederick **D:** 116
Mass production [manufacturing] **M:** 269
  Automobile (The birth of the automobile
    industry) **A:** 966
  City (Economy) **Ci:** 588
  Edison, Thomas Alva (Philosophy) **E:** 81
  Technology (The Industrial Revolution) **T:** 75
  Whitney, Eli (Arms manufacturer) **W:** 295
Mass spectrometer [instrument]
  Mass spectrometry **M:** 269 *with diagram*
  Molecule (Individual molecules) **M:** 692-693
Mass spectrometry [physics] **M:** 269 *with diagram*
  Isotope (Separating isotopes) **I:** 476-477
Mass spectrum [physics]
  Mass spectrometry **M:** 269
Mass stranding [biology]
  Dolphin (The life of dolphins) **D:** 298-299
Mass transfer [physics]
  Star (Binary stars) **So:** 852 *with picture*
Mass transportation *See* Public transportation *in
  this index*
Massachusetts M: 270 *with pictures and maps*
  See also the list of Related articles in the
    Massachusetts *article*
  Colonial life in America (Development of
    the Thirteen Colonies) **Ci:** 790 *with map;*
    (Education) **Ci:** 803; (Money) **Ci:** 811
  Education (Development of U.S. education)
    E: 102
  Juvenile court (In the United States) **J:** 205
  Same-sex marriage **S:** 78
  School (The development of U.S. schools) **S:** 183
Massachusetts, University of M: 294
Massachusetts Agricultural College
  Massachusetts, University of **M:** 295
Massachusetts Bay Colony [U.S. history] **M:** 295
  Colonial life in America (English expansion)
    Ci: 790
  Endecott, John **E:** 272
  Massachusetts (Massachusetts Bay Colony)
    M: 289; (Other colonies) **M:** 289
  Money (Paper money) **M:** 708-709; (History of
    United States currency) **M:** 710
  Pine-tree shilling **P:** 471 *with pictures*
  Post office (Postal service in the United States)
    P: 706
  United States, History of the (New England)
    U: 154
  Winthrop, John **W:** 342
Massachusetts Bay Transportation Authority
  Boston (Transportation) **B:** 502
Massachusetts Constitution [1780]
  Adams, John (Diplomat) **A:** 36
Massachusetts game
  Baseball (From rounders to baseball) **B:** 132
Massachusetts Government Act [law]
  Intolerable Acts **I:** 353
Massachusetts Institute of Technology M: 295
Massachusetts Provincial Congress [U.S. history]
  Hancock, John **H:** 39
Massachusetts Spy [newspaper]
  Thomas, Isaiah **T:** 261
  Worcester **W:** 403
"Massachusetts to Virginia" [poem by Whittier]
  Whittier, John Greenleaf **W:** 295
Massacre at Haun's Mill [1838]
  Mormons (Mormons in the Middle West) **M:** 808-
    809
Massacre in Korea [painting by Picasso]
  Picasso, Pablo (Later career) **P:** 449
Massacre of Saint Bartholomew's Day *See* Saint
  Bartholomew's Day, Massacre of *in this index*
Massacre of the Innocents, The [sculpture by
  Pisano]
  Sculpture (Italian Renaissance sculpture) **S:** 251
    with picture
Massage M: 295
Massalia [ancient colony]
  Marseille (History) **M:** 228
Massanutten [mountains, Virginia]
  Shenandoah Valley **S:** 394
  Virginia (Land regions) **V:** 410
Massasauga [snake]
  Snake *picture on* **S:** 534
Massasoit [American Indian chief] **M:** 295 *with
  picture*
  Indian wars (The Pequot War [1637]) **I:** 191
  Massachusetts (King Philip's War) **M:** 291
  Plymouth Colony (The first year) **P:** 583
  Samoset **S:** 81
  Squanto **So:** 811
Massecuite [by-product]
  Molasses **M:** 689
Massenet, Jules [French composer] **M:** 296
Massey, Vincent [Canadian statesman] **M:** 296
  Canada, Government of (The governor general)
    C: 129
  Saint Laurent, Louis Stephen (Prime minister
    [1948-1957]) **S:** 40
Massey Foundation
  Pearson, Lester Bowles (Education and war
    service) **P:** 220-221
Massey-Harris Company
  Massey, Vincent **M:** 296
Massi, Nick [American musician]
  Valli, Frankie **V:** 267 *with picture*
Massine, Léonide [Russian choreographer] **M:** 296
Massinger, Philip [English dramatist] **M:** 296
Massinissa [Berber chieftain]
  Algeria (History) **A:** 364
Massinissa [king of Numidia]
  Numidia **N:** 608
Massive compact halo object [physics]
  Dark matter **D:** 37
Massive open on-line course [education]
  Universities and colleges (Online learning) **U:** 211
Massive retaliation [warfare]
  Cold War (To the brink and back) **Ci:** 765
Massively multiplayer online role-playing game
  Electronic game *picture on* **E:** 204a; (Social
    gaming) **E:** 204e-204f
  Game (Internet games) **G:** 22
  Internet (Online communities) **I:** 350b
Masson, André [French artist] **M:** 296
  Painting (Surrealism) **P:** 81; (Europeans in
    America) **P:** 84
Massoud, Ahmad Shah [Afghan political leader]
  Afghanistan War **A:** 97
Mast [device]
  Crane **Ci:** 1120 *with picture*
  Sailing (Spars) **S:** 23 *with diagram*
  Ship (Sailing ships) **S:** 406

Mast cell [biology]
  Allergy (Allergic reactions) **A:** 373-374
  Immune system (Allergies) **I:** 88c
Mastaba [pyramid]
  Pyramids (Egyptian pyramids) **P:** 916
Mastectomy [surgery] **M:** 296
  Breast cancer **B:** 591
  Surgery (Some common surgical operations)
    So: 1006
Master [hunting]
  Fox hunting **F:** 442
Master [labor]
  Apprentice **A:** 575
  Guild (Craft guilds) **G:** 428
  Labor movement (Craft guilds) **L:** 9
Master [rank]
  Ship (Officers and crew) **S:** 410
Master Builder, The [play by Ibsen]
  Drama (Ibsen) **D:** 338
  Ibsen, Henrik (His plays) **I:** 4
Master Class [play by McNally]
  McNally, Terrence **M:** 344
Master contract
  Teaching (Employment practices) **T:** 68
Master cylinder
  Brake (Hydraulic brakes) **B:** 560
"Master Harold"...and the Boys [book by Fugard]
  Fugard, Athol **F:** 553
Master Mason
  Masonry (The lodges and degrees of Masonry)
    M: 267
Master of Ballantrae, The [book by Stevenson]
  Stevenson, Robert Louis (Novels) **So:** 898
Master of Flémalle [name for]
  Campin, Robert **C:** 91
Master of the horse [title]
  Royal Household of the United Kingdom **R:** 498
Master plan [city planning]
  City planning (City: 598; (The master plan) **Ci:** 599
Master-planned community [city planning]
  Houston (The city) **H:** 394-395
Master sergeant
  Rank, Military (table) **R:** 140
Master tape [recording]
  Phonograph (How phonograph records are
    made) **P:** 401
Master-teacher program
  Education (Who should teach?) **E:** 106-107
Mastering [industrial process]
  Recording industry (Mastering) **R:** 182
Masterpiece
  Guild (Craft guilds) **G:** 428
"Masterpiece" [television series]
  Television *picture on* **T:** 115
Masters, Edgar Lee [American author] **M:** 297
  American literature (Realist poetry) **A:** 421
Masters, William Howell [American doctor]
  Masters and Johnson **M:** 297
Masters and Johnson [American scientists] **M:** 297
Master's degree
  Degree, College (The master's degree) **D:** 92
  Education (Higher education) **E:** 92
  Universities and colleges (Degrees) **U:** 209
Masters of the fishing spear
  Dinka **D:** 205
Masters Tournament [contest]
  Georgia (Visitor's guide) **G:** 122 *with picture*
  Golf (Tournaments) **G:** 264; (Masters Tournament)
    G: 265
Mastersinger [German history] *See Meistersinger
  in this index*
Mastersingers of Nuremberg, The [opera by
  Wagner]
  Opera (The stage director) **O:** 794
  Wagner, Richard (Later career) **W:** 5
Masterson, Bat [American frontiersman] **M:** 297
Masterson, William Barclay [American
  frontiersman] *See Masterson, Bat in this index*
Masthead [journalism]
  Newspaper (table) **N:** 383
Mastic [resin] **M:** 297
Mastication [digestion] **M:** 298
  Ruminant **R:** 519
  Saliva **S:** 68 *with diagram*
Mastiche [gum]
  Chewing gum (History) **C:** 416
Mastiff [dog] **M:** 298
  Dog *picture on* **D:** 267
Mastitis [disease]
  Cattle (Diseases) **C:** 312-313
Mastodon [extinct animal] **M:** 298 *with picture*
Mastoid [anatomy] **M:** 298
Mastoid process [anatomy]
  Mastoid **M:** 298
Mastoid tumor [disorder]
  Tumor **T:** 484
Mastoiditis [disorder]

Mastoid **M:** 298
Mastretta, Angeles [Mexican author]
  Latin American literature (The post-Boom) **L:** 114
Mastro Don Gesualdo [book by Verga]
  Verga, Giovanni **V:** 317
Masturbation
  Adolescent (Dating and sex) **A:** 62
  Homosexuality **H:** 307
Masu salmon *See Cherry salmon in this index*
Masur, Kurt [German conductor] **M:** 298
Masurian lakes, Battle of [1914]
  World War I (The Eastern Front) **W:** 456
Masurium [former name]
  Technetium **T:** 73
Masvingo [Zimbabwe]
  Zimbabwe (History) **Z:** 592-593
Mat [printing]
  Linotype (How the linotype works) **L:** 338
  Stereotyping **So:** 893
Mat foundation [engineering]
  Building construction (Foundations) **B:** 682
Mat lodge [dwelling]
  British Columbia (Early days) **B:** 628
Mata Hari [German spy] **M:** 298 *with picture*
Matabele [people] *See Ndebele in this index*
Matador
  Bullfighting (Types of bullfights) **B:** 695 *with
    pictures*
Matagorda Bay [Texas]
  La Salle, René-Robert Cavelier, Sieur de
    (Expeditions to the Gulf of Mexico) **L:** 80 *with
    map*
Matai [family]
  Samoa (Government) **S:** 80
Matanuska Valley [region, Alaska] **M:** 299
  Alaska *picture on* **A:** 292
Mataram [former kingdom]
  Indonesia (Hindu and Buddhist kingdoms) **I:** 236;
    (The spread of Islam) **I:** 237
Match [sports]
  Tennis (Scoring) **T:** 162-163
Match [tool] **M:** 299 *with pictures*
  Fire (Methods of starting fires) **F:** 121
  Ohio (Interesting facts) **O:** 681
Match penalty [hockey]
  Hockey (Violations and penalties) **H:** 278
Match-plate pattern [manufacturing]
  Cast and casting (Patterns for casting) **C:** 278
Match play
  Golf (Match play) **G:** 262
Match sprint
  Bicycle racing (Track races) **B:** 292
Matchbook cover
  Match (Collecting matchbook covers) **M:** 299-300
    with pictures
Matching funds
  Election campaign (Campaign financing) **E:** 160
Matchlock [gun]
  Handgun (Early handguns) **H:** 45
  Harquebus **H:** 67
  Musket **M:** 962
Matchlock Gun, The [book by Edmonds]
  Edmonds, Walter Dumaux **E:** 83
Matchmaker, The [play by Wilder]
  Wilder, Thornton **W:** 303
Mate [rank] **M:** 300a
  Ship (Officers and crew) **S:** 410
Maté [drink] **M:** 300a *with picture*
  Argentina (Food and drink) **A:** 650
  Uruguay (Food and drink) **U:** 225
Matejko, Jan [Polish painter]
  Poland (The arts) **P:** 607
"Mateo Falcone" [story by Mérimée]
  Mérimée, Prosper **M:** 417
Mater et Magistra [encyclical, 1963]
  John XXIII [pope] **J:** 132
Material cause [philosophy]
  Aristotle (Philosophy of nature) **A:** 664
Material culture
  Culture (Forming patterns) **Ci:** 1187
Materialism [art]
  Abstract art **A:** 18
Materialism [philosophy] **M:** 300a
  Hobbes, Thomas **H:** 272
  Idealism **I:** 46
  Marx, Karl (Marx's ideas) **M:** 237
  Philosophy (Metaphysics) **P:** 383-384
Materialistic physiology
  Biology (Materialistic physiology and the cell
    theory) **B:** 319
Materials [physics] **M:** 300b *with pictures*
  *See also Strength of materials in this index and the
    list of Related articles in the* Materials *article*
  Composite materials **Ci:** 904
  Magnetism (Kinds of magnets) **M:** 60; (In
    materials) **M:** 60c
  Metallurgy (Careers in metallurgy) **M:** 427

Materials engineering
  Engineering (Materials engineering) **E:** 287 *with
    picture*
  Materials **M:** 300b
Maternity [play by Brieux]
  Brieux, Eugène **B:** 608
Maternity unit
  Hospital (Hospital units) **H:** 372
Matewan Massacre [1921]
  West Virginia (Labor developments) **W:** 229
Math co-processor [electronics]
  Computer (Personal computers) **Ci:** 909
Mathematical Composition [book by Ptolemy]
  Ptolemy **P:** 854
*Mathematical Foundations of Quantum
  Mechanics, The* [book by Von Neumann]
  Von Neumann, John **V:** 448
Mathematical model
  See also Computer modeling *in this index*
  Greenhouse effect (Studying the greenhouse
    effect) **G:** 383
  Science (Modeling with computers) **S:** 195
  Systems analysis **So:** 1077
  Weather (Mathematical models) **W:** 166
Mathematical symbol
  Algebra (Symbols in algebra) **A:** 354
  Set theory (History) **S:** 322
"Mathematical Theory of Communication, A"
  [paper by Shannon]
  Information theory **I:** 269
Mathematics M: 302 *with pictures*
  *See also the list of Related articles in the
    Mathematics article*
  Algebra **A:** 350
  Algorithm **A:** 366
  Careers (Technical and mathematical
    occupations) **C:** 232
  Egypt, Ancient (Sciences) **E:** 139
  Enlightenment (The worship of reason) **E:** 326a
  Geometry **G:** 101
  Infinity **I:** 266
  New mathematics **N:** 255
  Philosophy (Philosophy and science) **P:** 385;
    (Rationalism) **P:** 388-389
  Science (Mathematics and logic) **S:** 192;
    (Expressing findings mathematically) **S:** 195;
    (Ancient Greece) **S:** 196
  Social science **So:** 552
Mathematike Syntaxis [book by Ptolemy]
  Ptolemy **P:** 854
Mather, Cotton [American religious leader] **M:** 308
  American literature (New England) **A:** 414
Mather, Increase [American religious leader]
  M: 309
Mather, John Cromwell [American physicist]
  Nobel Prizes (Physics: 2006) **N:** 442
Mather, Richard [American religious leader]
  M: 309
Mather, Stephen T. [American government official]
  National Park System (History) **M:** 58
Matheson, Alexander W. [Canadian political
  leader]
  Prince Edward Island (table) **P:** 791
Matheson, Scott M. [American political leader]
  Utah (table) **U:** 245
Mathew [ship]
  Cabot, John **C:** 8
Mathews, Eddie [American baseball player]
  Baseball (table: Hall of Fame) **B:** 134a
Mathews, F. David [American government official]
  Ford, Gerald Rudolph (table) **F:** 378
Mathews, Forrest David [American government
  official]
  Health and Human Services, Department of
    (table) **H:** 128
Mathews, George [American political leader]
  Georgia (table) **G:** 130
Mathews, Henry M. [American political leader]
  West Virginia (table) **W:** 225
Mathews, William T. [American painter]
  Garfield, James Abram *picture on* **G:** 40
  McKinley, William *picture on* **M:** 338
Mathewson, Christy [American baseball player]
  M: 309
  Baseball (table: Hall of Fame) **B:** 134a; (The early
    1900's) **B:** 135 *with picture*
Mathieson, John A. [Canadian political leader]
  Prince Edward Island (table) **P:** 791
Mathieu, Albert [French engineer]
  English Channel **E:** 311
Mathiews, Franklin K. [American author]
  Book Week **B:** 470
Mathilde [asteroid]
  Asteroid (History of study) **A:** 824b
  Space exploration (Probes to asteroids) **So:** 711
Mathis der Maler [opera by Hindemith]
  Hindemith, Paul **H:** 234

Matilda [daughter of Henry I]
David (David I) **D:** 45
Plantagenet **P:** 550
Stephen **So:** 890
Matilda [wife of Henry I]
Henry I [king of England] **H:** 185
Mating [biology]
Animal (Sexual reproduction) **A:** 496
Frog (Mating) **F:** 538
Mammal (Mating) **M:** 122
Mating flight
Ant (Reproduction) **A:** 524
Bee (Mating flight) **B:** 203
Matins [religion]
Hour **H:** 379
Matisse, Henri [French artist] **M:** 309 *with pictures*
Fauves **F:** 56
Painting (The Fauves) **P:** 77 *with picture;*
(Expressionism) **P:** 78
Matlin, Marlee [American actress]
Motion picture (Best performance by an actress:
1986) **M:** 862a
Matoaka [name for]
Pocahontas **P:** 588
Matos, Gregório de [Brazilian author]
Latin American literature (Colonial literature)
L: 112
Matriarch [title]
Jews (Beginnings) **J:** 120
Matriarch [zoology]
Elephant (Intelligence) **E:** 229
Matrilineage
Family (Non-Western families) **F:** 24
Matrimonial offense [law]
Divorce (Grounds for divorce) **D:** 253
Matrix [anatomy]
Nail **N:** 4
Matrix [chemistry]
Composite materials **Ci:** 904
Materials **M:** 300b; (Composite materials)
M: 300d
Matrix [printing]
Linotype (How the linotype works) **L:** 338
Stereotyping **So:** 893
Matrix mechanics [physics]
Heisenberg, Werner **H:** 167
Matron [Roman history]
Women's movement (In ancient societies) **W:** 384
Matron of honor
Marriage (Wedding ceremonies) **M:** 220
Matryoshka [doll]
Doll (Traditional dolls) **D:** 287 *with picture*
Matsu [islands, Formosa Strait]
Cold War (To the brink and back) **Ci:** 765
Taiwan (History) **T:** 17-18
Matsuo Basho [Japanese poet]
Japanese literature (The Tokugawa period) **J:** 62
Matsuri [religion]
Shinto **S:** 401
Mattamuskeet, Lake
North Carolina (Rivers, waterfalls, and lakes)
N: 484 *with map*
Mattapan [district, Boston]
Boston (The south side) **B:** 500
Mattathias [Biblical figure]
Judah Maccabee **J:** 179
Matte screen
Projection screen **P:** 816
Matter [physics] **M:** 310
*See also the list of Related articles in the Matter
article*
Anaxagoras **A:** 448b
Antimatter **A:** 556
Atom **A:** 870
Berkeley, George **B:** 259
Dark matter **D:** 37
Energy (Energy and matter) **E:** 274
Interstellar medium **I:** 352
Mass **M:** 268
Materialism **M:** 300a
Mechanist philosophy **M:** 355
Molecule **M:** 692
Nuclear energy (The composition of matter)
N: 581
Physical change **P:** 431
Quantum mechanics **Q:** 6
Relativity (General relativity) **R:** 211-212
Spectroscopy **So:** 772
Subatomic particle **So:** 936
Universe (Changing views of the universe)
U: 205-206
Vacuum **V:** 256
Matter of fact [philosophy]
Hume, David (Hume's thought) **H:** 432
Matter wave [physics]
Radiation (Particle radiation) **R:** 76; (The quantum
theory) **R:** 81

Matterhorn [mountain, Italy-Switzerland] **M:** 312
Alps **A:** 384 *with picture*
Mountain (table) **M:** 896 *with diagram*
Matteson, Joel Aldrich [American political leader]
Illinois (table) **I:** 71
Matthau, Walter [American actor]
Motion picture (Best performance by an actor in
a supporting role: 1966) **M:** 862b
Matthew, Gospel of [New Testament]
Bible (The Gospels) **B:** 283
Gospels **G:** 278
Jesus Christ (Sources of information about Jesus)
J: 104; (Early life) **J:** 105; (Public life) **J:** 106; (The
Passion) **J:** 108
New Testament (Gospels) **N:** 287; (Critical studies)
N: 288
Matthew, Saint [apostle] **M:** 312
See also Matthew, Gospel of *in this index*
Gospels **G:** 278
Painting (Early medieval painting in the West)
P: 49-50 *with picture*
Matthews, Claude [American political leader]
Indiana (table) **I:** 214
Matthews, Joseph W. [American political leader]
Mississippi (table) **M:** 640
Matthews, Stanley [American jurist]
Supreme Court of the United States (table)
So: 1000
Matthias, Saint [apostle] **M:** 312
Matthias Corvinus [king of Hungary]
Hungary (The Kingdom of Hungary) **H:** 445
Matting
Television (Adding special effects) **T:** 112
Mattock [tool]
Colonial life in America (Farming) **Ci:** 809
Mattocks, John [American political leader]
Vermont (table) **V:** 333
Mattress
Bed **B:** 197
Maturation [biology]
Adolescent (The timing of puberty) **A:** 61
Sexuality (Biological factors) **S:** 337
Mature field
Petroleum (History) **P:** 332
Maturin, Charles [Irish author]
Gothic novel **G:** 279
Maturity [economics]
Bond **B:** 454
Credit (Lending institutions) **Ci:** 1124
Matzah [food] *See* Matzo *in this index*
Matzeliger, Jan Ernst [American inventor] **M:** 312
Shoe (History) **S:** 431-432
Matzo [food]
Bread *picture on* **B:** 588
Judaism *picture on* **J:** 179
Passover **P:** 192
Mau [Samoan history]
Samoa (History) **S:** 80a-80b
Mau Mau [Kenyan history] **M:** 312
Kenya (Opposition to the British) **K:** 303
Maua, Our Boatman [painting by La Farge]
La Farge, John *picture on* **L:** 26
Mauborgne, Joseph O. [American inventor]
Codes and ciphers (History) **Ci:** 751
Mauchly, John William [American engineer]
M: 312
Computer (The first electronic computers)
Ci: 924b *with picture*
Eckert, J. Presper, Jr. **E:** 50
Electronics *picture on* **E:** 216; (The vacuum tube
era) **E:** 215
Maud [daughter of Henry I] *See* Matilda *in this index*
Maud [poem by Tennyson]
Tennyson, Lord (His poems) **T:** 166f
Maudūdī, Abū al-A`lā' al- [Islamic leader]
Muslims (Reform and renewal) **M:** 964d-965
Maugham, W. Somerset [British author] **M:** 312
Maui [island, Hawaii]
Haleakala National Park **H:** 19 *with picture*
Hawaii (Maui) **H:** 100
Maui [legendary figure]
Mythology (Pacific Islands divinities) **M:** 984
Mauke [island, Pacific]
Cook Islands **Ci:** 1026
Maul [sports]
Rugby football (Rugby Union) **R:** 510-511
Mauldin, Bill [American cartoonist] **M:** 313 *with
picture*
Kennedy, John Fitzgerald *picture on* **K:** 268
Maule, Matthew [literary figure]
Hawthorne, Nathaniel (His novels) **H:** 115
Maull, Joseph O. [American political leader]
Delaware (table) **D:** 109
Mauna Kea [volcano, Hawaii] **M:** 313
Hawaii (Places to visit) **H:** 98; (Hawaii) **H:** 100
Mountain **M:** 891; (table) **M:** 896 *with diagram*
Observatory (Ground-based observatories)

O: 644-645 *with picture*
Mauna Loa [volcano, Hawaii] **M:** 313
Hawaii (Hawaii) **H:** 100
Hawai'i Volcanoes National Park **H:** 110
Kilauea **K:** 315
Mountain (table) **M:** 896 *with diagram*
Volcano (Shield volcanoes) **V:** 442; (table) **V:** 442b
Maunder, E. Walter [British astronomer]
Sunspot (Other findings) **So:** 992
Maunder minimum [astronomy]
Sunspot (Other findings) **So:** 992
Maundy Thursday [religion] **M:** 313
Easter (Holy Week) **E:** 42
Holy Week **H:** 300
Maupassant, Guy de [French author] *See* De
Maupassant, Guy *in this index*
Mauretania [ancient region]
Moors **M:** 797
Mauretania [ship]
Ship (Stronger, faster ships) **S:** 425-426 *with
picture*
Mauri [people]
Moors **M:** 797
Mauriac, Claude [French author]
Mauriac, François **M:** 314
Mauriac, François [French author] **M:** 313
Maurice, F. D. [British theologian]
Christianity (The 1800's) **C:** 526
Maurin, Peter [French-born philosopher]
Day, Dorothy **D:** 52
Mauritania **M:** 314 *with picture and map*
Flag *picture on* **F:** 199
French West Africa **F:** 528 *with map*
Morocco (Dispute over Western Sahara) **M:** 815
Western Sahara **W:** 241
Mauritian Militant Movement [political party]
Mauritius (History) **M:** 317
Mauritius **M:** 316 *with picture and map*
Dodo **D:** 261
Flag *picture on* **F:** 199
Mauro, Humberto [Brazilian director]
Latin America (Motion pictures) **L:** 101-102
Maurois, André [French author] **M:** 317
Biography (Modern biography) **B:** 314
Maury, James [American educator]
Jefferson, Thomas (Education) **J:** 77
Maury, Matthew Fontaine [American
meteorologist] **M:** 318
Mauryan Empire [history of India] **M:** 318
Ashoka **A:** 769
Bangladesh (Early history) **B:** 85
Chandragupta Maurya **C:** 374
India (The Mauryan Empire) **I:** 128 *with map*
Pakistan (Invasions and conquests) **P:** 98
World, History of the (The Mauryan Empire in
India) **W:** 430
Maus: A Survivor's Tale [book by Spiegelman]
Comics (The new comics) **Ci:** 870
Graphic novel **G:** 323 *with picture*
Spiegelman, Art **So:** 791
Maus II [book by Spiegelman]
Comics (The new comics) **Ci:** 870
Mauser [gun]
Rifle *picture on* **R:** 339
Mäuseturm, Der [building] *See* Mouse Tower *in
this index*
Mausoleum at Halicarnassus [Turkey]
Seven Wonders of the Ancient World *picture
on* **S:** 327; (The Mausoleum at Halicarnassus)
S: 325
Mausoleum of Augustus [Italy]
Rome (Other remains) **R:** 433
Mausoleum of Galla Placidia [Italy]
Ravenna **R:** 151
Mausolus [Persian government official]
Seven Wonders of the Ancient World (The
Mausoleum at Halicarnassus) **S:** 325
Mauvoisin Dam [Switzerland]
Dam (table) **D:** 18
Mave, Queen [legendary figure] *See* Maeve, Queen
in this index
Maverick [cattle]
Maverick, Samuel Augustus **M:** 318
Maverick, Samuel Augustus [American pioneer]
M: 318
Mavericks, Dallas [team] *See* Dallas Mavericks *in
this index*
Maw, Herbert B. [American political leader]
Utah (table) **U:** 245
Mawensi [mountain summit]
Kilimanjaro **K:** 315
Mawsil, Al- [Iraq] *See* Mosul *in this index*
**Max Planck Society for the Advancement of
Science** **M:** 318
Maxentius [West Roman emperor]
Constantine the Great **Ci:** 993
Maxillae [anatomy]

Ant (The head) **A: 521**
Face **F: 3**
Insect (Mouthparts) **I: 286** *with diagrams*
Maxillary bone [anatomy]
Head *diagram on* **H: 123**
Human body (table) **H: 422** *with diagram*
Maxillary sinus [anatomy]
Sinus **S: 474** *with diagram*
Maxim [saying]
French literature (Classical prose) **F: 520**
Maxim, Sir Hiram Stevens [American-British inventor] **M: 318**
Airplane (Powered flight) **A: 230-231**
Machine gun (History) **M: 17**
Maxim, Hudson [American inventor] **M: 318**
Maxim gun
Machine gun (History) **M: 16** *with picture*
Maxim, Sir Hiram Stevens **M: 318**
Maxim Gun Company
Maxim, Sir Hiram Stevens **M: 318**
Maximian [Roman emperor]
Diocletian **D: 214**
Rome, Ancient (table) **R: 447**; (The decline of the empire) **R: 447-448**
Maximilian [emperor of Mexico] **M: 319**
Latin America (Early years of independence) **L: 107-108**
Mexico (The French invasion) **M: 471-472**
Mexico City (Independence) **M: 478**
Querétaro **Q: 40**
Maximilian I [Holy Roman emperor] **M: 319**
Austria (The Habsburgs) **A: 937**
Habsburg, House of **H: 3**
Maximilian armor
Armor (During the Middle Ages) **A: 719-720**
Maximilian Joseph [elector of Bavaria]
Succession wars (The War of the Bavarian Succession) **So: 950**
Maximinus [Roman emperor]
Rome, Ancient (table) **R: 447**
Maximinus Thrax [Roman emperor]
Rome, Ancient (table) **R: 447**
Maximite [explosive]
Maxim, Hudson **M: 318**
Maxims [book by La Rochefoucauld]
La Rochefoucauld, Duc de **L: 77**
Maxims of the Saints [book by Fénelon]
Fénelon, François de Salignac de la Mothe- **F: 71**
Maximum family benefit [insurance]
Social security (How benefits are figured) **So: 554**
Maximum permissible dose [radiology]
Radiation (Dose) **R: 79-80**
Maximum security prison
Prison (Types of correctional institutions) **P: 805** *with picture*
San Quentin **S: 105**
Maximum speed [aviation]
Airplane (Measuring flying speed) **A: 225-226**
Maximus Poems, The [work by Olson]
American literature (Poetry) **A: 423**
Olson, Charles **O: 745**
Maxwell, James Clerk [Scottish physicist] **M: 319**
Antenna (History) **A: 544**
Communication (The development of electronics) **Ci: 883**
Electricity (Electricity and magnetism) **E: 197**
Electromagnetic waves (History) **E: 202**
Electromagnetism **E: 203**
Light (Electromagnetic waves) **L: 286**
Magnetism (Electricity and magnetism) **M: 60d**
Physics (Developments in the 1800's) **P: 440**
Quantum mechanics **Q: 6**
Radar (The development of radar) **R: 71**
Radiation (Electromagnetic waves) **R: 80**
Radio (Early development) **R: 91**
Relativity (The Michelson-Morley experiment) **R: 210**
Science *picture on* **S: 202**; (Scientific advances of the 1800's) **S: 200**
Maxwell-Gunter Air Force Base [Montgomery]
Montgomery (Description) **M: 766**
Maxwell Montes [mountain, Venus]
Mountain (On Venus) **M: 895**
Maxwell Motor Corporation
Chrysler, Walter Percy **C: 540**
Maxwell mountain range
Venus (Surface and atmosphere) **V: 311-312**
Maxwell Museum of Anthropology [Albuquerque]
New Mexico, University of **N: 277**
May [month] **M: 320** *with pictures*
Cinco de Mayo **Ci: 557**
May, Elaine [American actress]
Nichols, Mike **N: 404**
May apple [plant]
Plant *picture on* **P: 525**
May beetle *See* Junebug *in this index*

May bell [plant]
Lily of the valley **L: 304** *with picture*
May Day [custom] **M: 322**
May **M: 320**
Union of Soviet Socialist Republics *picture on* **U: 31**
May-Day [poems by Emerson]
Emerson, Ralph Waldo (His poetry) **E: 259**
May fly *See* Mayfly *in this index*
May Fourth Movement [Chinese history]
Beijing (History) **B: 223-224**
China (The war lord period) **C: 503**
May-pole of Merrymount, The [story by Hawthorne]
Hawthorne, Nathaniel (His stories and sketches) **H: 115**
May procession [custom]
May Day **M: 322**
Maya [people] **M: 322** *with pictures and maps*
Agriculture (In the Americas) **A: 157**
Architecture (Pre-Columbian architecture) **A: 614** *with picture*
Belize (History) **B: 238**
Calendar *picture on* **C: 29**; (The Maya) **C: 31**
Central America (Early history) **C: 355**
Chichén Itzá **C: 439**
Clothing (Maya and Aztec) **Ci: 700**
Copán **Ci: 1038**
Decimal system (Invention of the decimal system) **D: 73**
Exploration (Spain's conquests in the New World) **E: 445**
Guatemala (Indian period) **G: 416**
Hieroglyphics (Other hieroglyphic writing) **H: 227** *with picture*
Honduras *picture on* **H: 313**
Indian, American **I: 136**, *picture on* **I: 146**; (Empires and states) **I: 144**; (Ceremonies) **I: 148**; (Writing) **I: 150** *with picture*; (Indians of Middle America) **I: 169** *with pictures*
Jewelry (Pre-Columbian jewelry) **J: 118**
Latin America (Architecture) **L: 99**; (Early inhabitants) **L: 102**
Mexico (The Classic Period) **M: 468** *with picture*
Number (The Maya) **N: 607**
Quintana Roo **Q: 43**
Rain forest (The Americas) **R: 126b**
Sculpture (Later Indian sculpture) **S: 243** *with picture*
Stephens, John Lloyd **So: 890**
Tikal **T: 286**
Writing system (Phonetization) **W: 513**
Zapatista Army of National Liberation **Z: 587**
Maya Mountains [mountains, Belize]
Belize (Land and climate) **B: 237** *with map*
Mayagüez [ship]
Ford, Gerald Rudolph (Foreign affairs) **F: 378**
Mayakovsky, Vladimir [Russian poet] **M: 326**
Russian literature (Post-symbolism) **R: 563**
Mayall, John [British musician]
Rock music (Fresh directions) **R: 380**
Mayapán [ancient city]
Maya (The Postclassic Period) **M: 326**
Mayapple [plant] **M: 327**
Flower *picture on* **F: 285**
Maybach, Wilhelm [German engineer] **M: 327**
Automobile (The gasoline car) **A: 965-966**
Daimler, Gottlieb **D: 5**
Mayday [signal]
Signaling (Distress signals) **S: 455**
Mayer, Julius Robert von [German physicist] **M: 327**
Heat (Heat and energy) **H: 93**
Mayer, Maria Goeppert [American physicist] **M: 327**
Jensen, J. Hans **J: 92**
Mayer, Marianna [American author]
McDermott, Gerald **M: 332h**
Mayflower [plant]
Trailing arbutus **T: 368**
Mayflower [ship] **M: 327** *with picture*
See also Mayflower Compact *in this index*
Alden, John and Priscilla **A: 338**
Massachusetts (The Pilgrims and Plymouth Colony) **M: 289**
Pilgrims **P: 463** *with picture*
Plymouth Colony **P: 582**; (The honored ones) **P: 584**
Plymouth Rock **P: 585**
Mayflower Compact [U.S. history] **M: 328**
See also Mayflower [ship] *in this index*
Democracy (American democracy) **D: 123**
Massachusetts (The Pilgrims and Plymouth Colony) **M: 289**
Plymouth Colony (The founding of Plymouth Colony) **P: 582**
United States, History of the (New England)

U: 154
Mayflower II [ship]
Mayflower **M: 328** *with picture*
Plymouth **P: 582**
Mayflower in Plymouth Harbor, The [painting by Halsall]
Pilgrims *picture on* **P: 463**
Mayfly [insect] **M: 328** *with picture*
Animal *picture on* **A: 469**
Insect *picture on* **I: 279**; (The life cycle of insects) **I: 292**
Mayhem [law] **M: 328**
Maykov, Vasili Ivanovich [Russian author]
Russian literature (The classical movement) **R: 559-560**
Maym [letter]
M **M: 1** *with picture*
Mayne, Thom [American architect] **M: 328** *with picture*
Maynor, Dorothy [American singer] **M: 329**
Mayo, Charles Horace [American surgeon] **M: 329**
Mayo, Plaza de
Buenos Aires (The city) **B: 672**
Mayo, William James [American physician] **M: 329**
Mayo, William Worrall [American physician] **M: 329**
Mayo Clinic [Minnesota] **M: 329**
Mayo, William Worrall **M: 329**
Minnesota *picture on* **M: 605**; (Industrial development) **M: 604**
Mayo Foundation
Mayo, William James **M: 329**
Mayombé Escarpment [region]
Congo, Republic of the (Land) **Ci: 940d** *with map*
Mayon [volcano, Philippines]
Philippines *picture on* **P: 378**
Mayor [office] **M: 330**
Address, Forms of (Officials of the United States) **A: 53**; (Officials of the Commonwealth of Nations) **A: 53-54**
City government (The mayor-council form) **Ci: 595** *with diagrams*
Mayor, Michel [Swiss astronomer]
Planet (The first discoveries) **P: 513**
Mayor-council government
City government (The mayor-council form) **Ci: 595** *with diagrams*
Mayor of Casterbridge, The [book by Hardy]
Hardy, Thomas **H: 59**
Mayor of the palace [title]
Charles Martel **C: 383**
Mayotte [island, Comoros] **M: 330**
Comoros **Ci: 899**
Maypole [custom]
Dance (Folk dances) **D: 26**
May Day **M: 322**
Maypop [plant] *See* Passion-flower *in this index*
Mayr, Ernst [German-born American biologist] **M: 330**
Evolution (The synthetic theory) **E: 432**
Mays, Benjamin Elijah [American educator] **M: 330**
King, Martin Luther, Jr. (Early life) **K: 320-321**
Mays, Willie [American baseball player] **M: 330** *with portrait*
Baseball *picture on* **B: 138**; (table: Hall of Fame) **B: 134a**; (Recent developments) **B: 137**
Mayweather, Floyd, Jr. [American boxer]
Boxing (Boxing today) **B: 533**
Mazama, Mount [Oregon]
Crater Lake **Ci: 1121**
Mazar-e Sharif [Afghanistan]
Afghanistan *picture on* **A: 93**
Mazariegos, Diego de [Spanish explorer]
Chiapas **C: 419**
Mazarin, Jules [French statesman] **M: 331**
École des Beaux-Arts **E: 52**
Fronde **F: 541**
Library (France) **L: 260**
Louis XIV **L: 475**
Mazarin Bible
Gutenberg, Johannes **G: 444**
Mazarine Library [Paris]
Library (France) **L: 260**
Mazda [automobile]
Automobile *picture on* **A: 971**
Maze [puzzle]
Labyrinth **L: 19** *with picture*
Learning (Multiple-response learning) **L: 163**
Mazeroski, Bill [American baseball player]
Baseball (table: Hall of Fame) **B: 134a**
Mazovia [Polish history]
Warsaw (History) **W: 38**
Mazowiecki, Tadeusz [Polish political leader]
Poland (Free elections) **P: 614**
Mazzei, Philip [Italian merchant] **M: 331**
Mazzini, Giuseppe [Italian patriot] **M: 331**

Italy (The French Revolution and Napoleon)
I: 514-515
Mazzuoli, Dionisio [Italian sculptor]
Adonis *picture on* **A:** 65
Mba, Leon [Gabonese political leader]
Gabon (History) **G:** 3
Mbabane [Swaziland] **M:** 331
Swaziland **So:** 1017 *with picture and map*
Mbari [people]
Sculpture (Royal and public sculpture) **S:** 240
with picture
Mbeki, Thabo [South African political leader]
M: 331 *with portrait*
African National Congress **A:** 137
South Africa (Recent developments) **So:** 621
Mbemba, Nzinga [king of Kongo]
Kongo **K:** 364
Mbira [musical instrument]
Music (African music) **M:** 956
M'Bochi [people]
Congo, Republic of the (People) **Ci:** 940d
Mbuti [people]
Africa *picture on* **A:** 117; (Peoples of Africa) **A:** 104
Pygmies **P:** 914 *with picture*
McAdam, John Loudon [Scottish engineer] **M:** 332
Industrial Revolution (Roads) **I:** 251
Road (From the 500's to the 1800's) **R:** 361
McAdoo, William Gibbs [American government
official]
Hudson River tunnels (The PATH tunnels)
H: 406-407
McAfee, Mildred Helen [American educator]
M: 332
Navy, United States (World War II [1939-1945])
N: 89
McAleese, Mary [Irish political leader] **M:** 332
McAlister, Hill [American political leader]
Tennessee (table) **T:** 152
McArdle, H. A. [American painter]
Alamo *picture on* **A:** 281
McArthur, Duncan [American political leader]
Ohio (table) **O:** 699
McAuliffe, Christa [American educator] **M:** 332
with portrait
Astronaut (Accidents in space) **A:** 830-831
Challenger disaster **C:** 370
New Hampshire (Recent developments) **N:** 227
Space exploration (The Challenger disaster)
So: 725
McBain, Ed [American author] **M:** 332
McBride, Henry [American political leader]
Washington (table) **W:** 65
McBride, Richard [Canadian political leader]
British Columbia (table) **B:** 628; (Progress as a
province) **B:** 630
McCahon, Colin [New Zealand painter]
New Zealand (The arts) **N:** 349
McCain, John [American political leader] **M:** 332
with portrait
Bush, George Walker (Election as president)
B: 722f
Obama, Barack **O:** 640b; (The 2008 election)
O: 640f *with picture*
Palin, Sarah Heath **P:** 108
McCall, Jack [American public figure]
Hickok, Wild Bill **H:** 223
McCall, Samuel W. [American political leader]
Massachusetts (table) **M:** 288
McCall, Tom [American political leader]
Oregon (table) **O:** 845
McCallum, Scott [American political leader]
Wisconsin (table) **W:** 365
McCambridge, Mercedes [American actress]
Motion picture (Best performance by an actress
in a supporting role: 1949) **M:** 862b
McCardle, Eliza [wife of Andrew Johnson] *See*
Johnson, Eliza McCardle *in this index*
McCarey, Leo [American director]
Motion picture (Best achievement in directing:
1937, 1944) **M:** 862
McCarran, Patrick Anthony [American political
leader] **M:** 332a
McCarran International Airport
Airport (table) **A:** 245
Las Vegas (Economy) **L:** 89
McCarran-Walter Act [1952] *See* Immigration and
Nationality Act *in this index*
McCarrick, Theodore Edgar [American religious
leader]
Cardinal (table: American cardinals) **C:** 211
McCarthy, Charlie [dummy]
Ventriloquism *picture on* **V:** 309
McCarthy, Cormac [American author] **M:** 332a
with portrait
American literature (Fiction and other prose)
A: 424
McCarthy, Eugene Joseph [American political

leader] **M:** 332a
Johnson, Lyndon Baines (The widening Vietnam
War) **J:** 150-151
McCarthy, Joe [American baseball manager]
Baseball (table: Hall of Fame) **B:** 134a
McCarthy, John [American educator]
Artificial intelligence **A:** 760
McCarthy, Joseph Raymond [American political
leader] **M:** 332b *with picture*
Blacklist **B:** 393
Eisenhower, Dwight David (Challenges from the
Old Guard) **E:** 152
Kennedy, John Fitzgerald (Senator Kennedy)
K: 262
McCarthyism **M:** 332b
Patriotism (Abuses of patriotism) **P:** 198
Television (Early programs) **T:** 118 *with picture*
United States, History of the (McCarthyism)
U: 197
Wisconsin (Decline of La Follette Progressivism)
W: 368
McCarthy, Mary [American author] **M:** 332b
McCarthy, Tommy [American baseball player]
Baseball (table: Hall of Fame) **B:** 134a
McCarthyism [U.S. history] **M:** 332b
Communism (The Cold War) **Ci:** 895
McCarthy, Joseph Raymond **M:** 332b
United States, History of the (McCarthyism)
U: 197
McCartney, Paul [British musician] **M:** 332c *with
picture*
Beatles **B:** 189
Rock music *picture on* **R:** 380; (The Beatles) **R:** 379
McCarty, Dan [American political leader]
Florida (table) **F:** 260
McCarty, Henry [real name of]
Billy the Kid **B:** 306
McCauly, George [husband of]
Pitcher, Molly **P:** 499
McCauly, Mary [American patriot]
Pitcher, Molly **P:** 499
McCausland, John [Confederate general]
Pennsylvania (The Civil War) **P:** 267
McCay, Winsor [American cartoonist]
Animation (Pioneers of American animation)
A: 514a *with picture*
Comics (Comic strips) **Ci:** 869
McClellan, George Brinton [Union general]
M: 332c *with portrait*
Civil War, American (The drive to take Richmond)
Ci: 626
Lee, Robert E. (Opening campaigns) **L:** 178
Lincoln, Abraham (Building the army) **L:** 321 *with
picture*
New Jersey (table) **N:** 249
President of the United States *picture on* **P:** 764
**McClellan-Kerr Arkansas River Navigation
System**
Arkansas (Rivers and lakes) **A:** 706-708; (The late
1900's) **A:** 715
Canal (table) **C:** 164
Oklahoma (Recent developments) **O:** 734
Tulsa (History) **T:** 483-484
McClelland, Robert [American government
official]
Interior, Department of the (table) **I:** 325
Michigan (table) **M:** 507
Pierce, Franklin (table) **P:** 456
McClintock, Barbara [American geneticist]
M: 332d *with portrait*
Botany (Later developments) **B:** 509
McCloskey, John [American religious leader]
M: 332d
Cardinal (table: American cardinals) **C:** 211
McCloskey, Robert [American author/artist]
M: 332d *with picture*
Caldecott Medal (table: 1942, 1958) **C:** 26
Regina Medal (table: 1974) **R:** 206
McCloy, John J. [American government official]
Warren Report **W:** 37
McClung, Nellie [Canadian reformer] **M:** 332e
Famous Five **F:** 26b
McClure, Sir Robert John Le Mesurier [British
admiral] **M:** 332e
Exploration (Arctic exploration) **E:** 449 *with map*
Northwest Passage **N:** 529 *with picture*
McClure, Samuel Sidney [American publisher]
M: 332e
McClure Syndicate
McClure, Samuel Sidney **M:** 332e
McClure's Magazine
Cather, Willa **C:** 302
Magazine (Magazines in the 1800's) **M:** 45
McClure, Samuel Sidney **M:** 332e
McClurg, Joseph W. [American political leader]
Missouri (table) **M:** 668
McCollum, Andrew [American programmer]

Facebook (History) **F:** 4
McCollum, Elmer Verner [American biochemist]
Vitamin (History) **V:** 432
McConaughy, James L. [American political leader]
Connecticut (table) **C:** 967
McCone, Sharon [literary character]
Muller, Marcia **M:** 915
McConnell, John Wilson [Canadian financier]
McConnell Family Foundation **M:** 332e
McConnell, William J. [American political leader]
Idaho (table) **I:** 42
McConnell Family Foundation [organization]
M: 332e
Foundation (table) **F:** 430
McCool, William [American astronaut]
Columbia disaster **Ci:** 852
Space exploration (The Columbia disaster)
So: 725
McCord, David [American author] **M:** 332e
McCord, Jim [American political leader]
Tennessee (table) **T:** 152
McCormack, John [American singer] **M:** 332e
Ireland (The arts) **I:** 421-422
McCormack, John William [American political
leader] **M:** 332f
McCormick, Cyrus Hall [American inventor]
M: 332f
Reaper **R:** 173
Wheat (The mechanization of wheat farming)
W: 276
McCormick, John [American settler]
Indianapolis (History) **I:** 222
McCormick, Robert Rutherford [American
publisher] **M:** 332f
McCormick Place
Chicago (The South Side) **C:** 424-425
McCorvey, Norma [American public figure]
Roe v. Wade **R:** 399
McCovey, Willie [American baseball player]
M: 332f
Baseball (table: Hall of Fame) **B:** 134a
McCown, Theodore D. [American anthropologist]
Prehistoric people (table) **P:** 754
McCoy [American family]
Feud **F:** 81
McCoy, Elijah [American inventor] **M:** 332f *with
portrait*
Invention *picture on* **I:** 361
McCrae, John [Canadian poet] **M:** 332f
McCrary, George W. [American government
official]
Hayes, Rutherford Birchard (table) **H:** 121
McCray, Warren T. [American political leader]
Indiana (table) **I:** 214
McCreery, Joseph [American inventor]
Air conditioning (History) **A:** 180
McCreight, John Foster [Canadian political leader]
British Columbia (table) **B:** 628; (The colonial
period) **B:** 630
McCuish, John [American political leader]
Kansas (table) **K:** 234
McCullers, Carson [American author] **M:** 332g
with portrait
American literature (Southern fiction) **A:** 424
McCulloch, Hugh [American government official]
Arthur, Chester Alan (table) **A:** 756
Lincoln, Abraham (table) **L:** 323
McCulloch, James [American public figure]
McCulloch v. Maryland **M:** 332g
McCulloch v. Maryland [U.S. history] **M:** 332g
Marshall, John (Chief justice) **M:** 230
Supreme Court of the United States (table)
So: 1002
McCullough, Colleen [Australian author] **M:** 332g
McCullough, John G. [American political leader]
Vermont (table) **V:** 333
McCully, Emily Arnold [American author]
Caldecott Medal (table: 1993) **C:** 26
McCully, Jonathan [Canadian political leader]
Confederation of Canada (Fathers of
Confederation) **Ci:** 935 *with picture*
McCurdy, John A. D. [Canadian aviator]
Airplane (Other pioneer planes and fliers) **A:** 233
Nova Scotia (Interesting facts) **N:** 555 *with picture*
McDaniel, Hattie [American actress] **M:** 332g *with
picture*
Motion picture (Best performance by an actress
in a supporting role: 1939) **M:** 862b
McDaniel, Henry D. [American political leader]
Georgia (table) **G:** 130
McDermott, Gerald [American artist] **M:** 332h
Caldecott Medal (table: 1975) **C:** 26
McDonagh, Martin [Irish dramatist]
Irish literature (Drama) **I:** 432
McDonald, Charles J. [American political leader]
Georgia (table) **G:** 130
McDonald, Jesse F. [American political leader]

Colorado (Interesting facts) Ci: 829; (table)
Ci: 844
McDonald, John D. [American general]
Whiskey Ring W: 282
McDonald, Lake [Montana]
Glacier National Park (Lakes) G: 205
McDonald, Maurice [American businessman]
McDonald's Corporation M: 332h
McDonald, Richard [American businessman]
McDonald's Corporation M: 332h
McDonald, Ronald [corporate symbol]
McDonald's Corporation M: 332h
McDonald, William C. [American political leader]
New Mexico (table) N: 272; (Early statehood)
N: 275
McDonald's Corporation [company] M: 332h
McDonnell, Robert F. [American political leader]
Virginia (table) V: 417
McDonnell Douglas Corporation
Aviation (Aviation progress) A: 988
McDormand, Frances [American actress]
Motion picture (Best performance by an actress:
1996) M: 862a
McDougal, John [American political leader]
California (table) C: 59
McDougall, George [Canadian religious leader]
Alberta (Missionary activity) A: 329
McDougall, John [Canadian religious leader]
Alberta (Missionary activity) A: 329
McDougall, William [Canadian patriot]
Confederation of Canada (Fathers of
Confederation) Ci: 935 with picture
Red River Rebellion (The revolt) R: 189
McDowell, Ephraim [American doctor] M: 332h
with picture
Surgery (History) So: 1007
McDowell, Irvin [Union general] M: 333
Civil War, American (The commanding officers)
Ci: 618-619; (Fort Sumter) Ci: 624-625
Lincoln, Abraham (Building the army) L: 321
McDowell, James [American political leader]
Virginia (table) V: 417
McDowell, Jane [wife of]
Foster, Stephen Collins F: 428
McElderry, Margaret K. [American publisher]
Regina Medal (table: 2007) R: 206
McElroy, Mary Arthur [sister of]
Arthur, Chester Alan (Life in the White House)
A: 756 with portrait
White House hostesses W: 291
McElroy, Neil H. [American government official]
Defense, Department of (table) D: 87
Eisenhower, Dwight David (table) E: 152
McEnery, John [American political leader]
Louisiana (table) L: 496
McEnery, Samuel D. [American political leader]
Louisiana (table) L: 496
McEnroe, John [American tennis player] M: 333
with portrait
Tennis (Tennis today) T: 166d-166e with picture
McEntire, Reba [American singer] M: 333 with
portrait
Country music (Modern country music)
Ci: 1098c-1098d
McEwan, Ian [British author] M: 333
McEwen, Sir John [Australian political leader]
Australia (table) A: 923
McFadden, Daniel Little [American economist]
Economics (Modern economics) E: 64-65
Nobel Prizes (Economics: 2000) N: 449
McFarland, David Ford [American scientist]
Kansas (Interesting facts) K: 217
McFarland, Ernest W. [American political leader]
Arizona (table) A: 687
Goldwater, Barry Morris (Political career) G: 259
McFarlane, Robert C. [American government
official]
Iran-contra affair (Charges and court actions)
I: 407
McGahern, John [Irish author]
Irish literature (Fiction) I: 432
McGee, Thomas D'Arcy [Canadian political leader]
Confederation of Canada (Fathers of
Confederation) Ci: 935 with picture
McGill, Andrew R. [American political leader]
Minnesota (table) M: 602
McGill, James [Canadian businessman] M: 334
McGill University M: 334
Football (The history of football) F: 365
Hockey (Beginnings) H: 280-281
McGill, James M: 334
Quebec (Libraries) Q: 15 with picture
McGillicuddy, Cornelius [birth name of]
Mack, Connie M: 20
McGillivray, Alexander [American Indian chief]
M: 334
McGillivray, James [American journalist]

Bunyan, Paul B: 701
McGillivray, William [Canadian businessman]
M: 334
McGinley, Phyllis [American poet] M: 334
McGinnity, Joe [American baseball player]
Baseball picture on B: 135; (table: Hall of Fame)
B: 134a
McGivney, Michael J. [American religious leader]
Knights of Columbus K: 352
McGovern, Francis E. [American political leader]
Wisconsin (table) W: 365
McGovern, George Stanley [American political
leader] M: 334 with portrait
Democratic Party (Times of trouble) D: 127
Eagleton, Thomas Francis E: 6
Nixon, Richard Milhous (The 1972 election)
N: 435
McGowan, Bill [American baseball umpire]
Baseball (table: Hall of Fame) B: 134a
McGranery, James P. [American government
official]
Justice, Department of (table) J: 203
Truman, Harry S. (table) T: 469
McGrath, J. Howard [American government
official]
Justice, Department of (table) J: 203
Rhode Island (table) R: 311
Truman, Harry S. (table) T: 469
McGraw, John [American baseball player/
manager] M: 335
Baseball picture on B: 135; (table: Hall of Fame)
B: 134a
McGraw, John [American political leader]
Washington (table) W: 65
McGreevey, James E. [American political leader]
New Jersey (table) N: 249; (The early 2000's)
N: 254
McGuffey, William Holmes [American educator]
M: 335 with picture
Ohio (Schools) O: 684-685
McGuffey's Reader [book]
McGuffey, William Holmes M: 335 with picture
McGuigan, James Charles [Canadian religious
leader]
Cardinal (table: Canadian cardinals) C: 211
McGuinness, Frank [Irish dramatist]
Irish literature (Drama) I: 432
McGuinty, Dalton [Canadian political leader]
Ontario (table) O: 783; (Recent developments)
O: 787
McGuire, Al [American basketball coach] M: 335
McGuire, Peter J. [American labor leader]
Labor Day L: 2
McGuire Act [1952]
Fair-trade laws F: 8
McGwire, Mark [American baseball player] M: 336
with picture
Baseball (Recent developments) B: 137
McHale, Kevin [American basketball player] M: 336
McHenry, Donald F. [American government
official]
United Nations (table) U: 86
McHenry, Fort See Fort McHenry National
Monument and Historic Shrine in this index
McHenry, James [American patriot] M: 336
Adams, John (table) A: 38
Washington, George (table) W: 102
McIntire, Albert W. [American political leader]
Colorado (table) C: 844
McIntire-Stennis Act [1962]
Agricultural experiment station A: 145
McIntosh, Caroline Carmichael [wife of]
Fillmore, Millard (Later years) F: 102
McIntosh, Lachlan [American general]
Gwinnett, Button G: 447
McIntosh apple
Apple (Varieties of apples) A: 571 with picture
McIntyre, James Francis Aloysius [American
religious leader]
Cardinal (table: American cardinals) C: 211
McKay, Alexander [Canadian explorer] M: 336
McKay, Claude [American author] M: 337
American literature (The Harlem Renaissance)
A: 422
Harlem Renaissance H: 61
McKay, David S. [American geochemist]
Mars (Possibility of life) M: 226c
McKay, Donald [Canadian engineer] M: 337
Clipper ship Ci: 682i
Ship (Clipper ships) S: 422
McKay, Douglas [American government official]
Eisenhower, Dwight David (table) E: 152
Interior, Department of the (table) I: 325
Oregon (table) O: 845
McKay, Thomas [Canadian lumberman]
Ottawa (Rideau Hall) O: 872
McKean, Thomas [American patriot] M: 337

Delaware (table) D: 109
Pennsylvania (table) P: 263
McKechnie, Bill [American baseball manager]
Baseball (table: Hall of Fame) B: 134a
McKeithen, John J. [American political leader]
Louisiana (table) L: 496
McKeldin, Theodore R. [American political leader]
Maryland (table) M: 255
McKellen, Ian [British actor] M: 337
McKelvie, Samuel R. [American political leader]
Nebraska (table) N: 110
McKenna, Frank [Canadian political leader]
New Brunswick (table) N: 195
McKenna, Joseph [American jurist]
Justice, Department of (table) J: 203
McKinley, William (table) M: 342
Supreme Court of the United States (table)
So: 1000
McKenna, Siobhan [Irish actress] M: 337
McKennan, Thomas M. T. [American government
official]
Fillmore, Millard (table) F: 102
Interior, Department of the (table) I: 325
McKenzie, D. P. [British geologist]
Plate tectonics (History of tectonic theory)
P: 564-565
McKernan, John R., Jr. [American political leader]
Maine (table) M: 87
McKernan, Ron "Pigpen" [American singer]
Grateful Dead G: 329
McKiernan, John S. [American political leader]
Rhode Island (table) R: 311
McKinley, Ida Saxton [wife of William McKinley]
First ladies of the United States (table) F: 142
McKinley, William picture on M: 340; (McKinley's
family) M: 339
McKinley, John [American jurist]
Supreme Court of the United States (table)
So: 1000
McKinley, Mount See Mount McKinley in this index
McKinley, Robin [American author] M: 337
Newbery Medal (table) N: 359
McKinley, William [U.S. president] M: 338 with
pictures
Bryan, William Jennings (Democratic Party
leader) B: 654
Buffalo (Other interesting places to visit) B: 678
Cuba (Struggle against Spain) Ci: 1176
Hanna, Mark H: 52
Hawaii (The Territory of Hawaii) H: 108
Hobart, Garret Augustus H: 272
Ohio (table) O: 699
Roosevelt, Theodore (Vice president) R: 463
Spanish-American War (Background to the war)
So: 753
United States, History of the (The Spanish-
American War) U: 185
McKinley Monument [Buffalo, New York]
Buffalo (Other interesting places to visit) B: 678
McKinley National Memorial [Ohio]
Canton C: 184
McKinley Tariff Act [1890]
Harrison, Benjamin (Domestic affairs) H: 72
McKinly, John [American political leader]
Delaware (table) D: 109; (The American
Revolution) D: 110
McKinney, Louise [Canadian reformer]
Famous Five F: 26b
McKinney, Philip W. [American political leader]
Virginia (table) V: 417
McKissack, Fredrick L. [American author]
McKissack, Patricia M: 342
Regina Medal (table: 1998) R: 206
McKissack, Patricia [American author] M: 342
Regina Medal (table: 1998) R: 206
McKissick, Floyd Bixler [American social reformer]
M: 342
McKuen, Rod [American poet/composer] M: 342
McLachlin, Beverley Marian [Canadian jurist]
M: 43
Supreme Court of Canada (table) So: 997 with
portrait
McLaglen, Victor [British actor]
Motion picture (Best performance by an actor:
1935) M: 862a
McLane, John [American political leader]
New Hampshire (table) N: 223
McLane, Louis [American government official]
Jackson, Andrew (table) J: 11; (Jackson's second
Administration) J: 12
McLane, Robert M. [American political leader]
Maryland (table) M: 255
McLaren, Norman [American animator]
Animation (Animation in the mid-1900's)
A: 514b-514c
McLaughlin, Ann Dore [American government
official]

Labor, Department of (table) **L: 2**
McLaughlin, Audrey Marlene [Canadian political leader] **M: 343**
  Campbell, Kim (The 1993 election) **C: 90d**
McLaurin, Anselm J. [American political leader]
  Mississippi (table) **M: 640**
McLean, Angus Wilton [American political leader]
  North Carolina (table) **N: 490**
McLean, George P. [American political leader]
  Connecticut (table) **Ci: 967**
McLean, John [American jurist]
  Jackson, Andrew (table) **J: 11**
  Supreme Court of the United States (table)
    So: 1000
McLean House [Virginia]
  Appomattox Court House **A: 574**
McLeod, Neil [Canadian political leader]
  Prince Edward Island (table) **P: 791**
McLoughlin, John [Canadian pioneer] **M: 343**
  Oregon (Exploration and settlement) **O: 846**
  Washington (Settlement) **W: 66**
McLoughlin, Mount
  Oregon (Land regions) **O: 838** *with map*
McLoughlin House National Historic Site
  [Oregon]
  Oregon (Places to visit) **O: 836**
McLuhan, Marshall [Canadian author] **M: 343**
M'Clure, Sir Robert John le Mesurier [British admiral] *See* McClure, Sir Robert John le Mesurier *in this index*
McMahon, Sir William [Australian political leader]
  Australia (table) **A: 923**
McMaster, W. H. [American political leader]
  South Dakota (table) **So: 680**
McMaster University
  Hamilton (Education) **H: 31** *with map*
McMath, Sidney Sanders [American political leader]
  Arkansas (table) **A: 712**
McMath, Virginia Katherine [birth name of]
  Rogers, Ginger **R: 400**
McMath-Pierce solar telescope
  National Optical Astronomy Observatories **N: 42**
  Sun *pictures on* **So: 978**; (Earth-based studies)
    So: 987
McMillan, Edwin Mattison [American chemist]
  Neptunium **N: 130**
  Nobel Prizes (Chemistry: 1951) **N: 443**
  Plutonium **P: 581**
McMillan, Margaret [British educator]
  Preschool (History) **P: 756b-757**
McMillan, Rachel [British educator]
  Preschool (History) **P: 756b-757**
McMillin, Benton [American political leader]
  Tennessee (table) **T: 152**
McMinn, Joseph [American political leader]
  Tennessee (table) **T: 152**
McMullen, Adam [American political leader]
  Nebraska (table) **N: 110**
McMullen, Richard C. [American political leader]
  Delaware (table) **D: 109**; (The early 1900's) **D: 112**
McMurdo Station
  Antarctica (Scientific research) **A: 539** *with picture*
McMurtry, Larry [American novelist] **M: 343**
McNab, Sir Allan [Canadian political leader]
  Macdonald, Sir John Alexander (Early public career) **M: 7**
McNair, Alexander [American political leader]
  Missouri (table) **M: 668**
McNair, John B. [Canadian political leader]
  New Brunswick (table) **N: 195**
McNair, Lesley James [American general]
  Army, United States (World War II) **A: 739**
McNair, Ronald E. [American astronaut]
  Challenger disaster **C: 370**
  Space exploration (The Challenger disaster)
    So: 725
McNairy, John [American jurist]
  Jackson, Andrew (Lawyer) **J: 8**
McNally, Terrence [American playwright] **M: 344**
  Drama (Later United States drama) **D: 340-341**
McNamar, John [American settler]
  Rutledge, Ann **R: 569**
McNamara, James B. [American labor leader]
  Darrow, Clarence Seward **D: 38**
McNamara, John J. [American labor leader]
  Darrow, Clarence Seward **D: 38**
McNamara, Robert Strange [American government official] **M: 344**
  Kennedy, John Fitzgerald (table) **K: 266**
McNary, Charles Linza [American political leader]
  M: 344
McNaughton, Andrew George Latta [Canadian military leader] **M: 344**
  United Nations (table) **U: 86**
McNee, John [Canadian diplomat]
  United Nations (table) **U: 86**

McNeer, May [American author]
  Regina Medal (table: 1975) **R: 206**
McNichols, Stephen L. R. [American political leader]
  Colorado (table) **Ci: 844**
McNutt, Alexander G. [American political leader]
  Mississippi (table) **M: 640**
McNutt, Paul V. [American political leader]
  Indiana (table) **I: 214**
McPhee, Bid [American baseball player]
  Baseball (table: Hall of Fame) **B: 134a**
McPherson, Aimee Semple [American religious leader] **M: 344**
  Faith healing **F: 12**
McPherson, Conor [Irish dramatist]
  Irish literature (Drama) **I: 432**
McPherson, James B. [Union general]
  Fort McPherson **F: 414**
McQuigg, Esther [American social reformer]
  Morris, Esther Hobart **M: 816**
McRae, John J. [American political leader]
  Mississippi (table) **M: 640**
McRae, Thomas Chipman [American political leader]
  Arkansas (table) **A: 712**
McReynolds, James Clark [American jurist]
  Justice, Department of (table) **J: 203**
  Supreme Court of the United States (table)
    So: 1000
McTavish, Simon [Canadian businessman] **M: 344**
McTeer, Maureen [wife of]
  Clark, Joe (Member of Parliament) **Ci: 641** *with picture*
McVay, Hugh [American political leader]
  Alabama (table) **A: 274**
McVeigh, Timothy J. [American public figure]
  Oklahoma City bombing **O: 737**
McWherter, Ned Ray [American political leader]
  Tennessee (table) **T: 152**
McWillie, William [American political leader]
  Mississippi (table) **M: 640**
M.D. [degree]
  Medicine (A career as a doctor) **M: 370**
MD [disorder] *See* Macular degeneration *in this index*
MD [recording] *See* Minidisc *in this index*
Md [symbol]
  Mendelevium **M: 398**
MDA [organization]
  Red Cross **R: 185**
MDMA [drug] *See* Ecstasy *in this index*
Me [laws]
  Mythology (Sumerian mythology) **M: 976-977**
Me-163 Komet [airplane]
  Airplane *picture on* **A: 235**; (During World War II [1939-1945]) **A: 238**
Me-262 [airplane]
  Airplane (During World War II [1939-1945]) **A: 238**
Mea Shearim [area]
  Jerusalem *picture on* **J: 99**; (West Jerusalem) **J: 95** *with map*
Mead [drink]
  Alcoholic beverage (Other fermented beverages) **A: 336**
Mead, Albert E. [American political leader]
  Washington (table) **W: 65**
Mead, John A. [American political leader]
  Vermont (table) **V: 333**
Mead, Lake *See* Lake Mead *in this index*
Mead, Larkin G. [American architect]
  Springfield **So: 807**
Mead, Margaret [American anthropologist] **M: 344**
  Anthropology (Development of field research)
    A: 548 *with picture*
  Sexuality (Cultural influences) **S: 338a**
Mead, Matt [American political leader]
  Wyoming (table) **W: 532**
Meade, George Gordon [Union general] **M: 345**
  Civil War, American (Battle of Gettysburg) **Ci: 627**
  Gettysburg, Battle of **G: 176**
  Lee, Robert E. (Later battles) **L: 178**
  Lincoln, Abraham (The Gettysburg Address)
    L: 323
Meade, James Edward [British economist]
  Nobel Prizes (Economics: 1977) **N: 449**
Meades Ranch Triangulation Station [Kansas]
  Geodetic center of North America **G: 91**
Meadow
  Forest (Forest succession) **F: 397** *with picture*
Meadow lily [plant]
  Lily **L: 304**
Meadow mushroom *See* Field mushroom *in this index*
Meadow saffron [plant]
  Colchicum (table) **Ci: 760** *with picture*
Meadow-stream pond
  Pond (Kinds of ponds) **P: 656-657**

Meadow vole [animal]
  Vole **V: 443** *with picture*
Meadowlark [bird] **M: 345** *with picture*
  Bird *picture on* **B: 358**; (Birds of grasslands) **B: 336** *with picture*
Meadows, Clarence W. [American political leader]
  West Virginia (table) **W: 225**
Meal [agriculture]
  Soybean (Soy meal) **So: 690**
Meal [food]
  Cooking **Ci: 1027**
  Corn (The dry-milling industry) **Ci: 1061-1062**
  Food (Customs) **F: 332-333**
  Nutrition **N: 624**
Mealy Mountains
  Newfoundland and Labrador (Mountains) **N: 370** *with map*
Mean [mathematics] **M: 345**
  Average **A: 982**
  Median **M: 361**
  Statistics (Probability) **So: 868-869**
Mean [philosophy]
  Aristotle (Ethics and politics) **A: 664**
Mean Streets [film]
  Scorsese, Martin **S: 210**
Meander [geography]
  River (Flood plains) **R: 353** *with diagram*
Meaning [aesthetics]
  Art and the arts (The reasons for art) **A: 745**
Meaning analysis [psychology]
  Emotion (The appraisal approach) **E: 261**
Meaning of Meaning, The [book by Richards]
  Richards, I. A. **R: 329**
Meaning of Treason, The [book by West]
  West, Rebecca **W: 199**
Meaning of Witchcraft, The [book by Gardner]
  Witchcraft (Witchcraft in modern times) **W: 373**
Means, Abby Kent [American public figure]
  Pierce, Franklin (Life in the White House) **P: 456**
  White House hostesses **W: 291**
Means, Russell [American activist]
  American Indian Movement **A: 412**
Means of production [economics]
  Collectivism **Ci: 775**
  Communism **Ci: 889**
  Protestant ethic **P: 833**
  Socialism **So: 560**
Meany, George [American labor leader] **M: 345**
  Labor movement (Reunification of the AFL and the CIO) **L: 13** *with picture*
Mears, Rick [American race driver]
  Automobile racing (table: Indianapolis 500 winners) **A: 980**
Measles [disease] **M: 346**
  Colonial life in America (Health and medicine)
    Ci: 809
  Disease (table) **D: 226**
  Enders, John Franklin **E: 272**
  Rubella **R: 506**
Measure [music]
  Music (Indicating time values) **M: 953-954**
Measure for Measure [play by Shakespeare]
  Shakespeare, William: *(Measure for Measure)*
    S: 362
Measurement *See* Weights and measures *in this index*
Measurement standard
  Weights and measures **W: 184**
Measurement system
  Weights and measures (Measurement systems)
    W: 184
Measurement unit
  Weights and measures **W: 184**
Measuring worm [insect] **M: 346** *with picture*
  Animal *picture on* **A: 490**
  Moth (Measuringworm moths) **M: 841** *with picture*
Measuringworm moth
  Moth (Measuringworm moths) **M: 841** *with pictures*
Meat [food] **M: 346** *with pictures*
  See also the list of Related articles in the Meat *article*
  Cooking (Methods) **Ci: 1027**
  Food (Food from animals) **F: 330**
  Food, Frozen (Freezing food at home) **F: 338-339**
  Food supply (Livestock and fish) **F: 347**; (Reducing the demand for feed grain) **F: 350**
  Meat packing **M: 350** *with picture*
  Nutrition (Kinds of nutrients) **N: 625**; (Nutrition guidelines) **N: 626**
  Pemmican **P: 233**
  Pioneer life in America (Food) **P: 481**
  Vegetarianism **V: 294**
Meat carving
  Meat *pictures on* **M: 348**
Meat cut

Meat (How to select meat) **M:** 347
Pork **P:** 679
Meat extract [food] **M:** 350
Meat grades
Beef (Grades of beef) **B:** 209
Meat Inspection Act [1906]
Pure food and drug laws (History) **P:** 909
Roosevelt, Theodore (Domestic problems)
R: 466-467
Meat packing [industry] **M:** 350 *with picture*
See also the list of Related articles in the Meat
packing *article*
Colorado *picture on* **Ci:** 843
Food (Processing) **F:** 334
Muckrakers **M:** 908
Saskatchewan (Manufacturing) **S:** 143 *with
picture*
Swift, Gustavus Franklin **So:** 1039
United States, History of the (Theodore
Roosevelt) **U:** 187
Meat-type hog
Hog (Kinds of hogs) **H:** 285
Mecca [Saudi Arabia] **M:** 352 *with picture*
Hajj **H:** 17
Islam **I:** 463; (The Five Pillars of Islam) **I:** 463 *with
picture*
Jiddah **J:** 126
Malcolm X **M:** 103
Muhammad (The Hijrah) **M:** 911
Muslims (Muhammad) **M:** 964
Religion *picture on* **R:** 214; (Islam) **R:** 223
Saudi Arabia **S:** 155 *with picture*
Mecham, Evan [American political leader]
Arizona (table) **A:** 687; (The late 1900's) **A:** 691-
692
Mechanic [career]
Careers (Construction, maintenance, and repair)
C: 221-222
Mechanic, The [painting by Léger]
Léger, Fernand *picture on* **L:** 183
Mechanical advantage [physics]
Machine (Mechanical advantage) **M:** 14 *with
picture*
Block and tackle (Mechanical advantage) **B:** 404
Lever (Law of equilibrium) **L:** 217-218
Pulley **P:** 900 *with diagram*
Wheel and axle **W:** 278
Mechanical arts
Vocational education (Early vocational education
in schools) **V:** 435
Mechanical clock
Clock (Mechanical clocks) **Ci:** 682j *with diagram*;
(History) **Ci:** 682k *with pictures*
Mechanical drawing M: 353 *with pictures*
Blueprint **B:** 424
Mechanical efficiency [physics]
Machine (Efficiency) **M:** 14
Mechanical energy [physics]
Energy **E:** 273
Heat (Changing heat to motion) **H:** 153
Piezoelectricity **P:** 458
Mechanical engineering
Engineering *picture on* **E:** 288; (Mechanical
engineering) **E:** 287
Mechanical equivalent of heat
Heat (Heat and energy) **H:** 155
Mechanical lock
Lock (Mechanical locks) **L:** 411
Mechanical pencil
Pencil (Mechanical pencils) **P:** 236
Mechanical properties
Materials (Properties of materials) **M:** 300b
Mechanical reasoning aptitude
Careers (Aptitudes) **C:** 215
Mechanical refrigeration
Heat (Refrigeration) **H:** 154
Mechanical solidarity [sociology]
Durkheim, Émile **D:** 389
Mechanical top
Top (Kinds of tops) **T:** 331
Mechanical ventilation *See* Artificial respiration
in this index
Mechanical watch
Watch (Mechanical watches) **W:** 114 *with pictures*
Mechanics [physics] **M:** 354
Biomedical engineering (Biomechanics) **B:** 324
Galileo (Mature scientific career) **G:** 11-12
Leonardo da Vinci (Drawings and scientific
studies) **L:** 200-200a
Physics (Mechanics) **P:** 437
Mechanics' institute [school]
Adult education (History of adult education in
the United States) **A:** 69
Ontario (Libraries) **O:** 769
Mechanic's lien [law]
Lien **L:** 273
"Mechanism in Thought and Morals" [lecture by

Holmes]
Holmes, Oliver Wendell (His writings) **H:** 294-295
Mechanist philosophy M: 355
Philosophy (Metaphysics) **P:** 383-384;
(Rationalism) **P:** 388-389
Mechanistic materialistic physiology
Biology (Materialistic physiology and the cell
theory) **B:** 319
Mechanization
Automation (How automation works) **A:** 945
Clothing (Factory-made clothing) **Ci:** 691-695
Coal (Mineworkers) **Ci:** 728-729
Mechanized infantry division
Infantry (Divisions) **I:** 264
Mechem, Edwin L. [American political leader]
New Mexico (table) **N:** 272
Mechem, Merritt C. [American political leader]
New Mexico (table) **N:** 272
Meck, Nadezhda von [friend of]
Tchaikovsky, Peter Ilich (His life) **T:** 61
Mecoptera [entomology]
Insect (table) **I:** 300 *with picture*
MECP2 [gene]
Rett syndrome (Cause) **R:** 266
Medal *See* Medals, decorations, and orders *in this
index*
Medal, The [poem by Dryden]
Dryden, John **D:** 370
Medal of Freedom *See* Presidential Medal of
Freedom *in this index*
Medal of Honor
MacArthur, Douglas (World War II) **M:** 3
Medals, decorations, and orders (Military awards)
M: 355 *with pictures*
Walker, Mary Edwards **W:** 14
Medals, decorations, and orders M: 355 *with
pictures*
Olympic Games (Medals) **O:** 746c *with picture*
Medan Merdeka [public square]
Jakarta (The city) **J:** 22
Medawar, Sir Peter Brian [British zoologist]
Burnet, Sir Macfarlane **B:** 708
Nobel Prizes (Physiology or medicine: 1960)
N: 446
Medb [legendary figure] *See* Maeve, Queen *in this
index*
Medea [Greek mythology] **M:** 360
Theseus **T:** 257
Medea [play by Euripides]
Drama (Tragedy) **D:** 326-327
Médecins sans Frontières [organization] *See*
Doctors Without Borders *in this index*
Medeiros, Humberto Sousa [American religious
leader] **M:** 360
Medellín [Colombia] **M:** 360
Colombia (Civil war) **Ci:** 784
Medes [ancient people]
Media **M:** 360
Persia, Ancient (Early times) **P:** 297-298
World, History of the (Civilizations of southwest
Asia) **W:** 426
Medfly [insect] *See* Mediterranean fruit fly *in this
index*
Medford [Oregon]
Oregon (table: Average monthly weather) **O:** 841
Media [ancient country] **M:** 360 *with map*
Media [communications]
See also Communication; Magazine; Newspaper;
Radio; Television *in this index*
Advertising (Ways of advertising) **A:** 72
Communication *pictures on* **Ci:** 878
Election campaign (Developing support) **E:** 159
Journalism **J:** 170
Sexuality (Cultural influences) **S:** 338a
Media center
Library (School libraries) **L:** 244
A Guide to Research Skills **Research Guide: 26**
Media director
Election campaign (Campaign organizations)
E: 160
Media player, Portable *See* Portable media player
in this index
Media research
Advertising (Research) **A:** 76a
Media specialist
Library (School libraries) **L:** 244
Medial collateral ligament [anatomy]
Anterior cruciate ligament **A:** 544
Medial moraine [geology]
Glacier (How glaciers shape the land) **G:** 203 *with
diagram*
Moraine **M:** 799
Median [mathematics] **M:** 360
Average **A:** 982
Median nerve [anatomy]
Carpal tunnel syndrome **C:** 245 *with diagram*
Human body (table) **H:** 422 *with diagram*

Median strip
Automobile (Roads) **A:** 959
Road (Primary highways) **R:** 358
Mediastinal septum [anatomy]
Chest **C:** 414
Mediastinum [anatomy]
Chest **C:** 414
Mediation [labor]
Labor movement (Handling labor disputes) **L:** 6
National Mediation Board **N:** 40
Strike (Strike settlements) **So:** 928
Mediation Board, National [U.S.]
Labor movement (Handling labor disputes) **L:** 6
Railway Labor Act **R:** 122
Mediator [physiology]
Allergy (Allergic reactions) **A:** 373-374
Mediator Dei [encyclical, 1947]
Pius XII **P:** 503
Medic Alert [emblem] *See* MedicAlert *in this index*
Medicaid [federal program] **M:** 361
Abortion (Abortion in the United States) **A:** 15-16
Insurance (Health insurance) **I:** 311
Medicine (The United States) **M:** 367
Welfare (Medicaid) **W:** 190
Medical acoustics [science]
Acoustics **A:** 29
Medical anthropology
Anthropology (Cultural anthropology) **A:** 547
Medical Association, American *See* American
Medical Association *in this index*
Medical botany
Botany (Uses of plants) **B:** 508
Medical College of Louisiana
Tulane University **T:** 482
Medical College of Virginia [former name]
Virginia Commonwealth University **V:** 424
Medical costs
Medicine *diagrams on* **M:** 371; (Providing medical
care) **M:** 366
Medical ethics M: 361
Abortion (Abortion methods) **A:** 14-15
Birth control (Opposition to birth control) **B:** 379
Cloning (Ethical concerns) **Ci:** 683
Hippocrates **H:** 240
Medicine (The challenge of genetics) **M:** 378
World Medical Association **W:** 451
Medical examiner [public official] **M:** 361
Crime scene investigation (Beginning an
investigation) **Ci:** 1140
Forensic pathology **F:** 389a
Medical genetics
Genetic counseling (Techniques of genetic
counseling) **G:** 84a
Medicine (table) **M:** 369
Medical insurance
See also Health insurance *in this index*
Social security (Medicare) **So:** 555
Medical intensive care unit [medicine]
Intensive care unit **I:** 321
Medical payments coverage
Insurance (Automobile insurance) **I:** 313
Medical records
Hospital (Professional services departments)
H: 371-372
Medical savings account
Insurance (Other types of health insurance) **I:** 312
Medical school
Medicine (A career as a doctor) **M:** 370; (During
the Middle Ages) **M:** 373
Medical service plan
Insurance (Medical service plans) **I:** 312
Medical social worker
Medicine (Other careers in medicine) **M:** 371
Medical tag
First aid (Examine the victim) **F:** 136
Medical technician
Medicine *picture on* **M:** 366
Medical technologist
Medicine (Other careers in medicine) **M:** 371
Medical visualization software
Computer (Medical visualization software)
Ci: 919 *with picture*
Medical waste
Incinerator **I:** 100
MedicAlert [emblem] **M:** 361
Medicare [insurance, Canada]
Medicine (Canada) **M:** 367
Medicare [insurance, U.S.] **M:** 362
Bush, George Walker (Medicare overhaul) **B:** 722h
Insurance (Health insurance) **I:** 311; (Social
insurance) **I:** 314
Medicine (The United States) **M:** 367
Old age (Health care) **O:** 739
Social security (Social Security in the United
States) **So:** 553; (Medicare) **So:** 555
Medicare Advantage Plan
Insurance (Medicare) **I:** 314

Medication See Drug in this index
Medici [Italian history] M: 362
  Florence (History) F: 241
  Pawnbroker P: 203
  Renaissance (The Italian Renaissance) R: 233
    with picture
Medici, Catherine de' See Catherine de Médicis
  in this index
Medici, Cosimo de' [Florentine ruler] M: 362
Medici, Cosimo II de' [Italian nobleman]
  Galileo (Mature scientific career) G: 11
Medici, Giovanni Angelo de' [birth name of]
  Pius IV P: 502
Medici, Giuliano de' [brother of Lorenzo de'
  Medici]
  Sculpture (Michelangelo) S: 252-253
Medici, Giulio de' [birth name of]
  Clement VII Ci: 662a
Medici, Lorenzo de' [Florentine ruler] M: 362
  Italian literature (Humanism and the
    Renaissance) I: 494
  Italy picture on I: 514
  Michelangelo (Early life) M: 483
  Renaissance picture on R: 232
Medici, Marie de' See Marie de Médicis in this index
Medici, Piero de' [Florentine ruler]
  Medici, Lorenzo de' M: 362
Medici Chapel [Florence, Italy]
  Michelangelo (The Medici Chapel) M: 486 with
    picture
  Sculpture picture on S: 253
Medici Madonna [sculpture by Michelangelo]
  Madonna and Child M: 37
Medicinal flowers and plants
  Drug (Plants and molds) D: 355
  Herbal medicine H: 196
  Plant (Medicines) P: 517
Medicinal leech [animal]
  Leech L: 180
Medicine [drug] See Drug in this index
Medicine [profession] M: 363 with pictures
  See also the list of Related articles in the Medicine
    article
  Aerospace medicine A: 89
  Alternative medicine A: 388
  Blood (The significance of blood groups) B: 412;
    (Medical uses of blood) B: 413
  Disease (Medical treatment) D: 232
  Electricity (In medicine and science) E: 191
  Electronics (Medicine and research) E: 207
  First aid F: 136 with pictures
  Health (Medical and dental care) H: 126
  Incubator I: 106
  Internal medicine I: 336
  Light (Light in technology and industry) L: 291
    with picture
  Living will L: 398
  Marijuana (History) M: 201; (Medical marijuana)
    M: 202
  Neonatology N: 124
  New Age movement N: 178
  Obstetrics and gynecology O: 646
  Occupational medicine O: 647
  Palliative care P: 108
  Pediatrics P: 227
  Plastics (How plastics are used) P: 554-555
  Psychosomatic medicine P: 851
  Sports medicine So: 803
  Diagnosis and treatment
  Acupuncture A: 31 with picture
  Chemistry (Alchemy) C: 400-401
  Computer graphics (In medicine) Ci: 924h
  Fiber optics (Uses of optical fibers) F: 88-89
  Hypnosis H: 479
  Isotope (Uses of radioisotopes) I: 477
  Magnetic resonance imaging M: 56
  Photography (Scientific photographers) P: 428
  Positron emission tomography P: 697
  Radiation (Uses of radiation) R: 74 with picture
  Radiology R: 98
  Ultrasound (Ultrasound devices) U: 16 with
    picture
  X rays (In medicine) X: 540 with picture
  History
  Colonial life in America (Health and medicine)
    Ci: 809
  Egypt, Ancient (Sciences) E: 139
  Galen G: 10
  Hippocrates H: 239
  Pioneer life in America (Health) P: 483
  Sydenham, Thomas So: 1063
  Medicine and society
  Health insurance, National H: 129
  Malpractice suit M: 112
  Medical ethics M: 361
  Public health P: 855 with pictures
  Pure food and drug laws (Drugs and devices)

    P: 908
  Suicide (Types) So: 964
Medicine, Doctor of
  Degree, College (The doctor's degree) D: 93
  Medicine (A career as a doctor) M: 370
Medicine, Institute of
  National Academy of Sciences N: 27
Medicine, National Library of [Bethesda,
  Maryland]
  Library (United States government libraries)
    L: 248
Medicine ball cabinet [U.S. history]
  Hoover, Herbert Clark (Life in the White House)
    H: 330
Medicine bundle
  Indian, American (Indians of the Northeast)
    I: 154-156
Medicine Lake
  South Dakota (Rivers and lakes) So: 676
Medicine man or woman
  Indian, American (Shamans) I: 147
  Inuit (Religion) I: 354e
  Magic (The magician) M: 49
Medicine pipe
  Indian, American picture on I: 138
Medicine Rocks
  Montana (Places to visit) M: 750
Médicis, Catherine de [wife of Henry II] See
  Catherine de Médicis in this index
Médicis, Marie de [wife of Henry IV] See Marie de
  Médicis in this index
Medieval drama
  Drama (Medieval drama) D: 328
Medieval Latin
  Latin language (During the Middle Ages) L: 115
Medieval period See Middle Ages in this index
Medigap insurance
  Insurance (Medicare) I: 314
Medill, Joseph [American publisher] M: 379
  McCormick, Robert Rutherford M: 332f
Medill, William [American political leader]
  Ohio (table) O: 699
Medina [original settlement]
  Morocco (Way of life) M: 811
Medina [Saudi Arabia] M: 380
  Islam I: 463
  Muhammad (His teachings) M: 911; (The Hijrah)
    M: 911
  Muslims (Muhammad) M: 964a
  Religion (Islam) R: 223
  Saudi Arabia S: 155
Medina, Danilo [Dominican political leader]
  Dominican Republic (History) D: 304-305
Medina, Harold Raymond [American jurist]
  M: 380
Medina Sidonia, Duke of [Spanish military leader]
  Spanish Armada (The two fleets) So: 755; (The
    battle) So: 756
Mediolanum [former town]
  Milan (History) M: 541
Meditation M: 380
  Buddhism (Meditation) B: 669
  Mysticism M: 972
  New Age movement N: 178
  Religion (Religious rituals) R: 217
Meditations [book by Marcus Aurelius]
  Marcus Aurelius M: 197
Meditations on First Philosophy [book by
  Descartes]
  Descartes, René (His philosophy) D: 154
Meditations on Quixote [book by Ortega y Gasset]
  Ortega y Gasset, José O: 859
Mediterranean class [breeds]
  Chicken (Kinds of chickens) C: 441; (table) C: 443
Mediterranean climate See Subtropical dry
  summer climate in this index
Mediterranean fruit fly M: 380 with picture
  Fruit fly F: 549
Mediterranean pine [tree]
  Plant picture on P: 521
Mediterranean Sea M: 380 with map
  See also the list of Related articles in the
    Mediterranean Sea article
  France (The land) F: 464-466 with picture
Medium [biology]
  Culture Ci: 1190
Medium [physics]
  Waves W: 152
Medium [spiritualism]
  Ghost G: 182
  Spiritualism (The medium) So: 796
Medium density fiberboard
  Forest products (Fiber products) F: 402
Medium-format camera
  Photography (Other types of cameras) P: 409
Medium grain rice
  Rice (Kinds of rice) R: 323-324

Medium of exchange
  Money M: 704
Medium-range ballistic missile [weapon]
  Guided missile (Surface-to-surface missiles)
    G: 425-426
Medium red salmon [fish] See Coho in this index
Medium security prison
  Prison (Types of correctional institutions) P: 805
Medium-sulfur coal
  Coal (Coal as a fuel) Ci: 718
Medium truck
  Truck pictures on T: 459
Medium-wooled sheep
  Wool (Sources of wool) W: 399
Medulla [anatomy]
  Adrenal gland A: 67 with diagram
  Hair (The root and shaft) H: 9 with diagram
  Kidney (How the kidneys produce urine) K: 311
    with diagrams
Medullary cavity [anatomy]
  Bone (Structure of the bones) B: 456 with
    diagram
Medum [Egypt]
  Pyramids (The first pyramids) P: 916
Medusa [Greek mythology] M: 383
  Gorgons G: 274
  Pegasus P: 229
  Perseus P: 295
Medusa [sea animal] See Jellyfish in this index
Medvedev, Dmitry [Russian political leader]
  Putin, Vladimir Vladimirovich P: 913
  Russia (Recent developments) R: 555-556
Medwick, Joe [American baseball player]
  Baseball (table: Hall of Fame) B: 134a
Meeber, Carrie [literary figure]
  Dreiser, Theodore D: 346
Meech Lake accord [Canadian history]
  Bloc Québécois B: 404
  Campbell, Kim (The 1993 election) C: 90d
  Canada, History of (The constitutional crisis)
    C: 151
  Chrétien, Jean (Election as party leader) C: 522c
  Martin, Paul (First bid for party leadership)
    M: 234d
  Mulroney, Brian (Prime minister) M: 917
  Quebec (The late 1900's) Q: 32-33
  Trudeau, Pierre Elliott (Later years) T: 465
Meeker, Ezra [American author] M: 383
Meeker, Jotham [American settler]
  Kansas (Interesting facts) K: 217
Meeker, Nathan C. [American government official]
  Colorado (Territorial days) Ci: 845
Meeker Massacre [1879]
  Colorado (Territorial days) Ci: 845
Meerkat [animal] M: 383 with picture
  Animal picture on A: 502
Meerschaum [earth] M: 383
  Pipe P: 489 with picture
Meese, Edwin P., III [American government official]
  Justice, Department of (table) J: 203
  Reagan, Ronald Wilson (table) R: 169
Meet John Doe [film]
  Cooper, Gary Ci: 1034
Meet Me in the Green Glen [book by Warren]
  Warren, Robert Penn W: 37
"Meet the Press" [television program]
  Journalism (Television journalism) J: 175
Meeting
  Parliamentary procedure P: 175; (Holding
    meetings) P: 176
Meeting of the School Trustees, The [painting by
  Harris]
  Harris, Robert picture on H: 69
Meeting of the Waters [sculpture by Milles]
  Saint Louis (Places to visit) S: 49
Mefistofele [opera by Boito]
  Boito, Arrigo B: 440
Mefloquine [medication]
  Quinine Q: 42
Mega [prefix]
  Metric system (Metric prefixes) M: 439
Mega yacht [boat]
  Boating (Motorboats) B: 428
Megabyte [measurement]
  Computer (Computer code) Ci: 911
Megadose
  Vitamin V: 430
Megaera [Greek mythology]
  Furies F: 566
Megaflood
  Flood (Other floods) F: 237
Megagametophyte [botany]
  Plant diagram on P: 534; (Seeds) P: 531-532 with
    picture
  Seed (The parts of a seed) S: 281 with diagram;
    (How seeds develop) S: 281
Megahertz [measurement]

Radar (How radar works) **R:** 68
Radio (Broadcasting power and frequency)
  R: 87-88
  Short waves **S:** 435
Megakaryocyte [cell]
  Blood (Formation of new blood components)
  B: 411-412
Megalithic monuments [archaeology] **M:** 383
  Tomb **T:** 325
Megalopolis [region] **M:** 383 *with map*
  City (Future cities) **Ci:** 593
  Metropolitan area (Defining metropolitan areas)
  M: 442
Meganeura [insect]
  Prehistoric animal (The move onto land) **P:** 737
Megapixel [electronics]
  Charge-coupled device **C:** 378
  Photography (Capturing digital images) **P:** 420-421
Megapode [bird]
  Bird (Laying and hatching eggs) **B:** 357-359
Megara [ancient city]
  Greece, Ancient (Manufacturing) **G:** 368 *with map*
Megaron [building]
  Architecture (Mycenaean architecture) **A:** 615
Megasporangium [botany]
  Plant (Sexual reproduction) **P:** 532-533
Megaspore [botany]
  Spore (Plant spores) **So:** 801 *with diagram*
Megaton [measurement]
  Nuclear weapon (Effects of nuclear weapons)
  N: 598-599
Megavirus [biology]
  Virus (Structure) **V:** 427
Megawati Sukarnoputri [Indonesian political leader]
  Indonesia (Recent developments) **I:** 239
Megawatt [measurement]
  Watt **W:** 148
Mege-Mouries, Hippolyte [French chemist]
  Margarine (History) **M:** 198
Meghna River
  Bangladesh **B:** 78; (Rivers and streams) **B:** 83
Megiddo [ancient city]
  Armageddon **A:** 717
Megiddo, Battle of [1918]
  Allenby, Lord **A:** 372
Mehitabel [fictional character]
  Marquis, Don **M:** 218
Mehmed II [sultan of the Ottoman Empire] *See*
  Mehmet II *in this index*
Mehmet II [sultan of the Ottoman Empire] **M:** 384
  Ottoman Empire (Expansion and decline) **O:** 878
Mehmet V [Turkish ruler]
  Turkey (The Young Turks) **T:** 510
Mehta, Zubin [Indian conductor] **M:** 384 *with portrait*
Meidan-e-Imam [square]
  Isfahan **I:** 462
Meidani, Rexhep [Albanian political leader]
  Albania (End of Communist rule) **A:** 308-309
Meier, Julius L. [American political leader]
  Oregon (table) **O:** 845
Meier, Richard [American architect] **M:** 384 *with picture*
  Getty Center **G:** 176
Meier, Sidney K. [American game designer]
  Electronic game (The growth of computer gaming) **E:** 204e
Meier Helmbrecht [poem by Wernher the Gardener]
  German literature (Popular literature) **G:** 139
Meighen, Arthur [Canadian political leader]
  M: 385 *with portrait*
  King, William Lyon Mackenzie (First term as prime minister) **K:** 325
Meigs, Cornelia Lynde [American author]
  Newbery Medal (table) **N:** 359
Meigs, Return, Jr. [American political leader]
  Ohio (table) **O:** 699
Meiji, Emperor [Japanese history] **M:** 386
  Japan (Meiji era) **J:** 56
  Tokyo (Western influence) **T:** 318-319
Meiji era [Japanese history]
  Japan (Meiji era) **J:** 56
  Meiji, Emperor **M:** 386
Meiji Restoration [Japanese history]
  Japan (Meiji era) **J:** 56
Meiji Shrine [Tokyo]
  Tokyo (Shrines and temples) **T:** 316
Meiko Central Bridge [Tokyo]
  Bridge (table: Cable-stayed) **B:** 603
Meilhac, Henri [French librettist]
  Opera: (*Carmen*) **O:** 802
Mein Kampf [book by Hitler] **M:** 386
  Hitler, Adolf (Mein Kampf) **H:** 266
Meiosis [biology]

Cell (Meiosis) **C:** 331 *with pictures*
Heredity (Sex cells and reproduction) **H:** 201
Reproduction (Through sexual reproduction)
  R: 242
Reproduction, Human (How sex is determined)
  R: 246
Meir, Golda [Israeli political leader] **M:** 387 *with portrait*
  Israel (The Yom Kippur War) **I:** 488
Meirelles, Fernando [Brazilian director]
  Latin America (Motion pictures) **L:** 101-102
Meissen china
  Dresden china **D:** 346
  Germany *picture on* **G:** 154
Meissen porcelain
  Porcelain (German porcelain) **P:** 677 *with picture*
Meister, Joseph [patient of]
  Pasteur, Louis (His work in medicine) **P:** 193
Meistersinger [German history] **M:** 387
Meistersinger von Nürnberg, Die [opera by Wagner] *See* Mastersingers of Nuremberg, The, *in this index*
Meitner, Lise [Austrian physicist] **M:** 387
  Fermi, Enrico **F:** 74
  Hahn, Otto **H:** 7
  Meitnerium **M:** 387
  Nuclear energy (Artificial fission) **N:** 590
  Protactinium **P:** 831
  Strassmann, Fritz **So:** 918
Meitnerium [element] **M:** 387
  Transuranium element **T:** 401
Mejía Domínguez, Hipólito [Dominican political leader]
  Dominican Republic (History) **D:** 304-305
Mekong giant catfish
  Catfish **C:** 300
Mekong River [Asia] **M:** 387
  Cambodia (Land) **C:** 72
  Laos (Land and climate) **L:** 71
  River (table) **R:** 352
  Vietnam (Southern Vietnam) **V:** 368
Mekong River Delta
  Vietnam (Southern Vietnam) **V:** 368
Melaka [Malaysia] **M:** 388
  Indonesia (The spread of Islam) **I:** 237; (The coming of the Europeans) **I:** 237
  Magellan, Ferdinand (Early life) **M:** 45-46
  Malays **M:** 98
  Malaysia (History) **M:** 101
Melamine- and urea-formaldehyde
  Plastics (table) **P:** 556
Melancholic humor
  Personality (Personality types) **P:** 301
Melanchthon, Philipp [German religious leader] **M:** 388
  Augsburg Confession **A:** 885
  German literature (The Renaissance) **G:** 139
  Luther, Martin (Building and defending the church) **L:** 528
  Reformation (Martin Luther) **R:** 197
Melanesia [islands, Pacific]
  See also Melanesians *in this index*
  Pacific Islands **P:** 3 *with map*
  Sculpture (Pacific Islands sculpture) **S:** 241-242 *with pictures*
Melanesian race [theory]
  Races, Human (The geographical-race theory)
  R: 54
Melanesians [people]
  Bismarck Archipelago **B:** 382
  New Britain **N:** 179
  New Caledonia **N:** 200
  New Guinea (People) **N:** 206
  Pacific Islands (Melanesians) **P:** 4 *with picture*
  Papua New Guinea (People) **P:** 140
  Vanuatu (People) **V:** 284
Melanin [pigment]
  Eye (The uveal tract) **E:** 460
  Hair (Color and texture) **H:** 10
  Mole **M:** 691
  Races, Human (Alternatives to racial classification) **R:** 55; (Climatic adaptations) **R:** 58
  Skin (Epidermis) **S:** 489; (Skin color) **S:** 490 *with picture*
  Sunburn **So:** 989
  Vitiligo **V:** 432
Melanocyte [biology]
  Skin (Epidermis) **S:** 489; (Skin color) **S:** 490 *with picture*
  Skin cancer (Melanoma) **S:** 491
  Vitiligo **V:** 432
Melanocyte-stimulating hormone
  Hormone (Other hormones) **H:** 336
Melanoma [disease]
  Cancer *picture on* **C:** 173; (Classification by primary body site) **C:** 167-168

Eye (Diseases of the uveal tract) **E:** 467
Mole **M:** 691
Skin cancer **S:** 491 *with pictures*
Melanose [plant disease]
  Orange (Pests and diseases) **O:** 815
Melatonin [hormone]
  Pineal gland **P:** 471
Melba, Nellie [Australian singer] **M:** 388
Melbourne [Australia] **M:** 388 *with picture*
  Olympic Games (The postwar games) **O:** 751-752
  Victoria **V:** 356
Melbourne, Viscount [British political leader]
  United Kingdom (table: British prime ministers)
  U: 72
Melbourne-Cooper, Arthur [British inventor]
  Animation (Early animation) **A:** 514a
Melbourne Cup [horse race]
  Horse racing (Types of horse races) **H:** 364-365
Melcher, Frederic Gershom [American publisher]
  M: 389
  Book Week **B:** 470
  Caldecott Medal **C:** 26
  Literature for children (Awards) **L:** 367
  Regina Medal (table: 1962) **R:** 206
Melchiades, Saint [pope]
  Pope (table) **P:** 666
Melchior [Biblical figure]
  Magi **M:** 48
Melchizedek order
  Mormons (Church organization) **M:** 807
Meld [cards]
  Pinochle **P:** 474
Melekeok [state, Palau] **M:** 389
  Palau **P:** 101
Melgar Castro, Juan Alberto [Honduran political leader]
  Honduras (Revolutions and reforms) **H:** 313
Méliador [book by Froissart]
  Froissart, Jean **F:** 541
Melibea [literary figure]
  Spanish literature (The 1400's) **So:** 758
Melic poetry
  Greek literature (Lyric poetry) **G:** 377
Melkite Catholic Church [religious group]
  Eastern Catholic Churches **E:** 45
Mellette, Arthur Calvin [American political leader]
  South Dakota (table) **So:** 680; (Statehood)
  So: 683
Mello, Craig Cameron [American biologist]
  Nobel Prizes (Physiology or medicine: 2006)
  N: 447
Mellon [ship]
  Coast Guard, United States *picture on* **Ci:** 734
Mellon, Andrew William [American financier]
  M: 389
  Foundation (Arts and humanities) **F:** 431
  National Gallery of Art **N:** 36
Mellon, Paul [American philanthropist]
  Mellon Foundation **M:** 389
Mellon Foundation M: 389
  Foundation (table) **F:** 430
Melmouth the Wanderer [book by Maturin]
  Gothic novel **G:** 279
Melodic minor scale [music]
  Music (Tone) **M:** 950
Melodrama
  Drama (Melodrama) **D:** 325; (Romanticism)
  D: 337-338
  Soap opera **So:** 543
Melody [music]
  Counterpoint **Ci:** 1097
  Music (Melody) **M:** 951
  Variation **V:** 286
Melon [plant] **M:** 389
Melon [zoology]
  Beluga whale **B:** 246 *with picture*
  Dolphin (The bodies of dolphins) **D:** 297-298 *with picture*
Melon aphid [insect]
  Cucumber **Ci:** 1183
Melos [island, Greece] *See* Milos *in this index*
Melpomene [Greek mythology]
  Muses **M:** 937
  Mythology *picture on* **M:** 981
Melqart [Phoenician god]
  Phoenicia (Religion) **P:** 393
Meltdown
  Nuclear energy (Hazards and safeguards)
  N: 587-588
Melting point [physics] **M:** 389
  Freezing point **F:** 510
  Glacier (Kinds of glaciers) **G:** 202
  Heat (Changes in state) **H:** 153 *with diagram*
Melting pot
  Ethnic group **E:** 373
  Multiculturalism **M:** 918
  United States (Ancestry) **U:** 109-110

Meltwater [geology]
Glacier *diagrams on* G: 204; (Kinds of glaciers)
G: 202; (How glaciers form) G: 202
Meltzer, Milton [American author]
Laura Ingalls Wilder Award (table) L: 121
Regina Medal (table: 2000) R: 206
Melvill, Michael [American test pilot]
Astronaut (Achievements in space) A: 829-830
Space exploration (Private launch services)
So: 728
Melville, Herman [American author] M: 390 *with portrait*
American literature *picture on* A: 416; (The
romance) A: 418 *with portrait*
Novel (The United States) N: 573
Melville, Lake
Newfoundland and Labrador (Rivers and lakes)
N: 370 *with map*
Melville Island [Arctic Ocean] M: 391
Mem [letter]
M M: 1
Member of the equation [mathematics]
Algebra (Statements and equations) A: 351
Member of the Wedding, The [book by McCullers]
McCullers, Carson M: 332g
Membrane [biology] M: 391
Blood (Red blood cells) B: 408
Cell (The cytoplasm) C: 329 *with diagrams*
Mucus M: 909
Paramecium P: 152
Pleura P: 573
Membrane [chemistry]
Osmosis O: 865 *with diagrams*
Membrane roof [building construction]
House (The roof) H: 382
Membrane theory of nerve conduction
[physiology]
Nervous system (How neurons carry impulses)
N: 134-135
Membranous croup [disorder]
Croup Ci: 1157
Membranous labyrinth [anatomy]
Ear (The inner ear) E: 8
Meme [culture]
Dawkins, Richard D: 51
Internet (Spreading ideas) I: 350e
Memel [former name] *See* Klaipėda *in this index*
Memel River [Belarus] *See* Neman River *in this index*
Memling, Hans [Flemish painter]
Clothing *picture on* Ci: 702
Memoirs from Beyond the Grave [book by
Chateaubriand]
Chateaubriand, François-René de C: 387
Memoirs of a Dutiful Daughter [book by Beauvoir]
Beauvoir, Simone de B: 191
Memoirs of a Midget [book by De la Mare]
De la Mare, Walter D: 95
Memorial [architecture] M: 391
Sculpture (As monuments and memorials) S: 229
Memorial Day [holiday] M: 391
Grand Army of the Republic G: 305
Logan, John Alexander L: 423
May M: 320
Memorial reconstruction [literature]
Shakespeare, William (Quartos) S: 369
Memorial University of Newfoundland
Newfoundland and Labrador (Schools) N: 364
with picture
Memory [electronics]
See also Memory chip *in this index*
Calculator C: 22
Computer (Parts of computers) Ci: 911
Electronics (Digital circuits) E: 213
Memory [psychology] M: 392
Alzheimer's disease A: 398
Brain (Memory and imagination) B: 554
Hypnosis (Hypnotic phenomena) H: 478;
(Enhancing memory) H: 479
Learning disabilities (Types) L: 165
Senility S: 300
Memory, Immune *See* Immune memory *in this
index*
Memory B cell [physiology]
Disease (Immune responses) D: 231-232
Immune system (The humoral immune response)
I: 88
Memory chip [electronic device]
Computer (Parts of computers) Ci: 911
Computer chip Ci: 924e
Digital technology D: 203
Telephone (The circuit board) T: 95
Memory T cell [biology]
Disease (Immune responses) D: 231-232
Memphis [ancient city] M: 394
Cairo (History) C: 17
Cleopatra's Needles Ci: 662b
Egypt, Ancient (The land) E: 135-136 *with map*

Memphis [Tennessee] M: 394 *with pictures and
map*
Tennessee T: 134 *with picture*; (table: Average
monthly weather) T: 148; (Reconstruction)
T: 154 *with picture*
Memphis [designers]
Furniture *picture on* F: 586; (Postmodern design)
F: 585
Memphis Brooks Museum of Art
Memphis (Cultural life) M: 396
Memphis Grizzlies [team]
Basketball (table) B: 150
Memphis in May International Festival
Memphis (Recreation) M: 396
Tennessee (Visitor's guide) T: 144
Memphis Recording Service
Presley, Elvis P: 772
MEMS [machines] *See* Microelectromechanical
systems *in this index*
Men and Women [book by Browning]
Browning, Robert (Browning's poems) B: 646
Men-at-arms [army]
Army (Armies in the Middle Ages) A: 727
Men at Arms [book by Waugh]
Waugh, Evelyn W: 149
Men in Black [film]
Smith, Will So: 518
Men in White [play by Kingsley]
Kingsley, Sidney K: 331
Mena, Juan de [Spanish author]
Spanish literature (The 1400's) So: 758
Menaechmi [play by Plautus]
Plautus P: 570
Menagerie
Circus (History) Ci: 562b-563
Zoo (History) Z: 604
Menander [Greek dramatist] M: 397
Drama (New Comedy) D: 327 *with picture*
Greek literature (Drama) G: 377
Menaphon [book by Greene]
Greene, Robert G: 382
Ménard, René [French explorer]
Michigan (French exploration and settlement)
M: 508
Wisconsin (European exploration and settlement)
W: 365
Menasci, Guido [Italian librettist]
Opera: (*Cavalleria Rusticana*) O: 803
Menchú, Rigoberta [Guatemalan political leader]
M: 397
Mencius [Chinese philosopher] M: 397
Confucianism (Early Confucianism) Ci: 936
Mencken, H. L. [American author] M: 397
American literature (Satirists) A: 422
Essay (Personal essays) E: 359
Roaring Twenties (Cultural trends) R: 364
Mendaña, Álvaro de [Spanish explorer]
Marquesas Islands M: 217
Solomon Islands (History) So: 585
Mende [people]
Sierra Leone (People) S: 451
Mendel, Gregor Johann [Austrian botanist] M: 398
Agriculture (Agricultural genetics) A: 158
Botany (Later developments) B: 509
Cell (Before 1900) C: 337
Evolution (The synthetic theory) E: 432-433
Genetics (Transmission genetics) G: 87
Heredity H: 200; (Mendel's laws) H: 208
Science *picture on* S: 202
Mendel Art Gallery [Saskatoon]
Saskatchewan (Places to visit) S: 136
Mendele the Bookseller [Hebrew author] *See*
Abramovich, Shalom Jacob *in this index*
Mendeleev, Dmitri Ivanovich [Russian chemist]
M: 398
Chemistry (Formation of the periodic table)
C: 402
Mendelevium M: 398
Mendelevium [element] M: 398
Transuranium element T: 401
Mendeleyev Ridge [geography]
Arctic Ocean (The deep basin) A: 643 *with map*
Mendelian disease
Genetic testing (Genes associated with disease)
G: 84d
Mendel's laws [genetics]
Heredity (Mendel's laws) H: 208
Mendel, Gregor Johann (His work) M: 398
Mendelsohn, Eric [German architect] M: 399
Germany *picture on* G: 155
Mendelssohn, Felix [German composer] M: 399
Bach, Johann Sebastian (His works) B: 16
Germany (Music) G: 151
Hymn (Words and music) H: 475
Overture O: 882
Mendelssohn, Moses [German philosopher]
M: 399

Jews (Emergence into freedom) J: 123
Mendenhall Glacier
Alaska (Places to visit) A: 290; (Glaciers) A: 295
with picture
Menderes, Adnan [Turkish political leader]
Turkey (After World War II) T: 511
Mendes, Sam [American director]
Motion picture (Best achievement in directing:
1999) M: 862
Mendes, Sergio [Brazilian composer]
Brazil (The arts) B: 576-577
Mendez, Aparicio [Uruguayan government
official]
Uruguay (Military government) U: 228
Mendez, Diego [Spanish explorer]
Columbus, Christopher (The hard journey home)
Ci: 863
Méndez, José [Cuban baseball player]
Baseball (table: Hall of Fame) B: 134a
Méndez Montenegro, Julio César [Guatemalan
political leader]
Guatemala (The mid-1900's) G: 417
Mendicant orders [religion]
Friar F: 531
Monasticism (Non-Christian monasticism) M: 701
"Mending Wall" [poem by Frost]
Frost, Robert (His poems) F: 543
Mendota, Lake [Wisconsin]
Madison M: 30
Mendoza, Antonio de [Spanish colonial official]
Cabrillo, Juan Rodríguez C: 8
Coronado, Francisco Vásquez de Ci: 1067
Menehune [mythical creature]
Mythology (Pacific Islands divinities) M: 984
Menehune Fishpond [Hawaii]
Hawaii (Places to visit) H: 98
Menelaus [legendary figure]
Helen of Troy H: 168
Messenia M: 423
Mythology (Greek heroes) M: 982
Trojan War (The beginning of the war) T: 449
Troy (The legendary Troy) T: 454
Menelik I [emperor of Ethiopia]
Ethiopia E: 368
Menelik II [emperor of Ethiopia] M: 400
Djibouti (History) D: 257
Eritrea (History) E: 353-354
Ethiopia (Menelik II) E: 371
Menem, Carlos Saúl [Argentine political leader]
Argentina (The late 1900's) A: 658
Menéndez de Avilés, Pedro [Spanish explorer]
M: 400
Florida (Exploration and Spanish settlement)
F: 261
Georgia (Spanish control) G: 131
Hispanic Americans (Exploration and settlement)
H: 250
Menes [king of ancient Egypt]
Egypt, Ancient (Beginnings) E: 142 *with picture*
Memphis M: 394
World, History of the (The Nile Valley) W: 424
Meneses, Jorge de [Portuguese colonial official]
New Guinea (History) N: 207
Meng Ke [Chinese philosopher]
Mencius M: 397
Meng-tzu [book by Mencius]
Mencius M: 397
Mengele, Josef [Nazi war criminal] M: 400
Mengistu Haile-Mariam [Ethiopian political
leader]
Ethiopia (Military take-over) E: 372; (The late
1900's) E: 372
Mengzi [book by Mencius]
Mencius M: 397
Menhaden [fish] M: 400
Fish *picture on* F: 153
Menhir [archaeology]
Megalithic monuments M: 383
Ménière's disease
Deafness (Diseases) D: 57
Ear (Diseases) E: 12
Menilek II [emperor of Ethiopia] *See* Menelik II *in
this index*
Meninas, Las [painting by Velázquez]
Painting (Composition) P: 35; (The Spanish
masters) P: 64-65 *with picture*
Velázquez, Diego V: 295
Meninges [anatomy]
Brain (From injury) B: 550d
Meningitis M: 400
Meningitis [disease] M: 400
Brain (From injury) B: 550d; (Infectious diseases)
B: 558
Deafness (Diseases) D: 57
Encephalitis E: 265
Headache (Secondary headache) H: 124-125
Nervous system (Disorders of the nervous

system) N: 136
Meningoencephalitis [disease]
Encephalitis E: 265
Meningomyelocele [disorder]
Spina bifida So: 792
Meniscus cartilage [anatomy]
Cartilage C: 263
Menkaure [king of ancient Egypt]
Pyramids (The pyramids of Giza) P: 917
Menlo Park [New Jersey]
Edison, Thomas Alva (The Wizard of Menlo Park)
E: 78; (Honors) E: 82
Menninger, Charles Frederick [American psychiatrist]
Menninger Clinic M: 401
Menninger, Karl Augustus [American psychiatrist]
M: 401
Menninger, William Claire [American psychiatrist]
M: 401
Menninger Clinic M: 401
Mennonite Heritage Village [Manitoba]
Manitoba (Places to visit) M: 152
Mennonites [religious group] M: 401
Amish A: 433
Anabaptists A: 447
Kansas *picture on* K: 220; (The nation's breadbasket) K: 237
Pennsylvania Dutch P: 270
Meno [book by Plato]
Plato (The dialogues) P: 567; (Immortality of the soul) P: 568-569
Menocal, Armando [Cuban painter]
Cuba (The arts) Ci: 1171-1172
Menominee Indians M: 402
Indian, American *picture on* I: 155
Menopause [physiology] M: 402
DES D: 153
Estrogen E: 363
Hormone replacement therapy H: 338
Menstruation M: 404
Osteoporosis (Causes) O: 867-868
Ovary O: 881
Reproduction, Human (The human reproductive system) R: 244-245
Menorah [symbol]
B'nai B'rith *picture on* B: 426
Hanukkah H: 54
Menorca [island, Mediterranean] *See* Minorca *in this index*
Menotti, Gian Carlo [Italian-American composer] M: 402
Opera (American opera) O: 800
Men's magazine
Magazine (Consumer magazines) M: 42
Mensa International [organization] M: 402
Menses [biology]
Menstruation M: 404 *with diagram*
Mensheviks [Russian history] M: 403
Bolsheviks B: 449
Communism (Before 1917) Ci: 892
Lenin, V. I. (Beginnings of revolution) L: 192
Russia (Nicholas II) R: 551-552
Russian Revolution of 1917 (Background to the revolution) R: 565
Menstrual cycle *See* Menstruation *in this index*
Menstrual period
Menstruation M: 404 *with diagram*
Pregnancy (Confirming pregnancy) P: 734a
Premature birth P: 755
Premenstrual syndrome P: 755
Menstruation [physiology] M: 403 *with diagrams*
Breast B: 590
Endometriosis E: 272
Estrogen E: 363
Estrous cycle E: 364
Menopause M: 402
Pregnancy (Confirming pregnancy) P: 734a
Premenstrual syndrome P: 755
Reproduction, Human (The human reproductive system) R: 244-245
Sexuality (Biological factors) S: 337-338
Toxic shock syndrome T: 353
Mental ability test
Testing (Tests of learning ability) T: 182a
Mental age
Intelligence quotient (Calculating IQ) I: 320
Mental health
Beers, Clifford Whittingham B: 212
Health (Elements of mental health) H: 126
Mental illness M: 404
Social work (Mental health) So: 558
Mental Hygiene, American Foundation for
Beers, Clifford Whittingham B: 212
Mental illness M: 404 *with pictures*
See also the list of Related articles in the Mental Illness article
Abnormal psychology A: 11

Clinical psychology (Psychotherapy and consultation) Ci: 681
Disability (Mental illness and cognitive disabilities) D: 219
Dix, Dorothea Lynde D: 255
Homelessness (Causes and conditions) H: 302
Huntington's disease H: 451
Hypnosis (Hypnotic phenomena) H: 478; (Uses of hypnotism) H: 479
Insanity I: 277
Introvert I: 354
Mind (Alterations of the mind) M: 563
National Alliance on Mental Illness N: 28
Occupational therapy (Helping people with mental illness) O: 649
Psychiatry P: 845
Psychoanalysis P: 846
Senility S: 300
Special education (Children with emotional disturbances) So: 771
Mental imagery
Imagination I: 79
Mental retardation *See* Intellectual disability *in this index*
Mental state attribution
Mind (Parts of the mind) M: 562-563
Mental telepathy *See* Telepathy *in this index*
Mentalist
Magician (Mentalist magic) M: 52
Menteng [district]
Jakarta (The city) J: 22
Menthol [chemical] M: 410
Menthyl acetate
Ester E: 360
Mentor [Greek mythology] M: 410
Mentuhotep II [king of ancient Egypt]
Egypt, Ancient (The Middle Kingdom) E: 143
Menuhin, Yehudi [American violinist] M: 410
Menzel, Jiri [Czechoslovak director]
Motion picture (Movies in the 1960's) M: 870-871
Menzies, Sir Robert Gordon [Australian political leader] M: 410 *with portrait*
Australia (table) A: 923
Meperidine [medication]
Analgesic A: 448
Mephistopheles [literary figure] M: 411
Opera: (Faust) O: 804
Mer de Glace [glacier, France]
Glacier (Famous glaciers) G: 204
Mont Blanc M: 741
Mer-en-re [king of ancient Egypt]
Embalming (Ancient embalming) E: 255
Mera, Juan León [Ecuadorean author]
Latin American literature (Romanticism) L: 112-113
Merak [star]
North Star *picture on* N: 519
Meramec Caverns [Sullivan]
Missouri (Places to visit) M: 660 *with picture*
Mercado Común del Sur [organization] *See* Mercosur *in this index*
Mercalli, Giuseppe [Italian scientist]
Earthquake (The Modified Mercalli Intensity [MMI] scale) E: 38b
Mercantile gambling
Gambling (Types of gambling) G: 20
Mercantilism [economics] M: 411
Capitalism (History of capitalism) C: 195
Colonial life in America (Trade) Ci: 811
Colonialism (Colonial economic policies) Ci: 814
Economics (Early theories) E: 63
Physiocrats P: 444
Tariff (The first tariffs) T: 44
Mercaptan [chemical]
Fuel (Natural gas) F: 551
Gas [fuel] (Transmitting and distributing gas) G: 55
Mercaptopurine [drug]
Elion, Gertrude Belle E: 236
Mercator, Gerardus [Flemish geographer] M: 411
Atlas (History) A: 868
Map (Advances in European cartography) M: 184
Mercator projection [cartography]
Map M: 177; (Map projections) M: 182 *with diagram*; (Advances in European cartography) M: 1184
Mercator, Gerardus M: 411
Merced Canyon [region, California]
Yosemite National Park (Yosemite Valley) Y: 570
Merced River [California]
Ribbon Meadow R: 321
Yosemite National Park (Yosemite Valley) Y: 570
Mercedes [automobile]
Daimler, Gottlieb D: 5
Maybach, Wilhelm M: 327
Mercedes-Benz [automobile]
Automobile *pictures on* A: 967, A: 969

Daimler, Gottlieb D: 5
Daimler AG D: 5
Mercedinus [month]
Calendar (The Romans) C: 31
Mercenary [soldier] M: 411
Army (Armies in the Middle Ages) A: 727
Mercer, George [American colonist]
Washington, George (Washington the man) W: 90
Mercer, John Francis [American political leader]
Maryland (table) M: 255
Mercer, Johnny [American lyricist] M: 411
Mercer, Lucy [American public figure] *See* Rutherfurd, Lucy Mercer *in this index*
Mercerization [industrial process]
Cellulose (Industrial uses) C: 341
Cotton (Finishing) Ci: 1091
Sewing (Choosing the equipment, fabric, and pattern) S: 332
Textile (Finishing the fabric) T: 217
Thread T: 269
Mercês [church]
Belém B: 224d
Merchandise manager [career]
Clothing (The clothing industry) Ci: 705-706
Merchandise Mart [Chicago] M: 412
Chicago (Downtown Chicago) C: 420-421
Merchandising [economics]
Clothing (The clothing industry) Ci: 705-706
Retailing R: 264
Merchant [economics]
City (Economy) Ci: 580-581, Ci: 584-585 *with picture*
Trade (Early trade) T: 362-363
Merchant, Paul [pen name of]
Ellison, Harlan H: 244
Merchant flag
Flag (Flags of the sea) F: 208
Merchant guild [European history]
Guild (Merchant guilds) G: 428
Merchant marine M: 413
Maritime Administration M: 212
Ship (Flags and registration) S: 412
Merchant Marine Academy, United States *See* United States Merchant Marine Academy *in this index*
Merchant Marine Act [1936]
Ship (The United States merchant marine) S: 412
Merchant of Venice, The [play by Shakespeare]
Shakespeare, William: (The Merchant of Venice) S: 358
Merchiston, Laird of [Scottish mathematician] *See* Napier, John *in this index*
Merci Retriever [medicine]
Stroke (Treatment) So: 930
Mercia [ancient kingdom]
Egbert E: 115
Wales (Struggles against the Anglo-Saxons) W: 12
Mercier, Désiré Joseph [Belgian religious leader] M: 413
Mercier, Honoré [Canadian political leader]
Quebec (table) Q: 29
Mercosur [organization] M: 412
Common market Ci: 875
South America (International trade) So: 637
Mercurous sulfate [chemical]
Mercury (Compounds) M: 414
Mercury [element] M: 413 *with picture*
Cinnabar Ci: 557
Environmental pollution (Hazardous waste) E: 334-335
Thermometer (Thermal expansion thermometers) T: 254
Water pollution (Industrial wastes) W: 136
Mercury [planet] M: 414 *with pictures*
Astronomy (How the planets move) A: 835
Evening star E: 423
Gravitation (Newton's law of gravitation) G: 331; (Einstein's theory of gravitation) G: 331
Meteor (Other planets and moons) M: 432
Planet P: 507 *with pictures*
Satellite (Satellites of the terrestrial planets) S: 150
Space exploration *picture on* So: 709; (Probes to Venus and Mercury) So: 710
Transit T: 374
Mercury [Roman mythology] M: 415 *with picture*
See also Hermes *in this index*
Mythology (table) M: 981
Sculpture (European sculpture) S: 253-254 *with picture*
Mercury [sculpture by Coysevox]
Sculpture (Form and treatment) S: 230-231
Mercury [sculpture by Giambologna]
Mercury *picture on* M: 416
Mercury barometer

Barometer (Kinds of barometers) **B:** 115 *with diagram*
Torricelli, Evangelista **T:** 343
Mercury glass
Glass (Types of art glass) **G:** 220-221
Mercury program [space exploration]
Cooper, Gordon **Ci:** 1034
Glenn, John Herschel, Jr. (Early life) **G:** 226
Grissom, Virgil Ivan **G:** 396
Space exploration (Vostok and Mercury: The first human beings in space) **So:** 712 *with pictures*
Mercury-Redstone [rocket]
Space exploration *picture on* **So:** 698
Mercury Theatre
Citizen Kane **Ci:** 568
Mercury Theatre on the Air [radio program]
Radio (The Golden Age of Broadcasting) **R:** 92-93
Mercury vapor lamp
Electric light (High-pressure gaseous-discharge lamps) **E:** 175
Lighting (Efficient use of lighting) **L:** 297
Mercutio [literary figure]
Shakespeare, William: *(Romeo and Juliet)* **S:** 357-358
Mercy killing *See* Euthanasia *in this index*
Mercy of a Rude Stream [books by Roth]
Roth, Henry **R:** 487
Meredith, Edwin T. [American government official]
Agriculture, Department of (table) **A:** 161
Meredith, George [British author] **M:** 416
English literature (Later Victorian literature) **E:** 321
Meredith, James Howard [American activist] **M:** 416 *with portrait*
Kennedy, John Fitzgerald (Civil rights) **K:** 264-265
Mississippi *picture on* **M:** 643; (The mid-1900's) **M:** 644
Meredith, William M. [American government official]
Taylor, Zachary (table) **T:** 60
Meres, Francis [English author]
Shakespeare, William (The years of fame) **S:** 347
Merganser [bird] **M:** 416 *with picture*
Duck (Food) **D:** 375 *with picture*; (Sea ducks) **D:** 376
Mergenthaler, Ottmar [German-American inventor] **M:** 417
Linotype (History) **L:** 339
Merger [economics] **M:** 417
Antitrust laws **A:** 560
Bank (Diversification and mergers) **B:** 94
Business (Recent developments) **B:** 727
Conglomerate **Ci:** 938
Consumer protection (The right to choose) **Ci:** 1018
Insider trading **I:** 303
United States, History of the (The rise of "trusts") **U:** 181
Meriam Report [U.S. history]
Indian, American (In the United States) **I:** 179
Mérida [Mexico]
Yucatán Peninsula **Y:** 575 *with map*
Meridian [geography]
Greenwich meridian **G:** 386
International date line **I:** 339 *with map*
Longitude **L:** 451, *diagrams on* **L:** 452
Map (Geographic grids) **M:** 179 *with diagram*
Time (International time zones) **T:** 292a
Transit **T:** 374
Meridian [philosophy]
Acupuncture **A:** 31
Meridiani Planum [Mars]
Mars (Observation by spacecraft) **M:** 226c-226d
Mars Exploration Rover Mission **M:** 227
Space exploration (Probes to Mars) **So:** 710
Meridion [zoology]
Diatom *picture on* **D:** 186
Mérimée, Prosper [French author] **M:** 417
Opera: *(Carmen)* **O:** 802
Merina [kingdom]
Madagascar **M:** 27
Merina [people]
Madagascar (History) **M:** 29
Mering, Josef von [German physician]
Insulin (History) **I:** 308
Merino [animal]
Sheep (Fine-wooled sheep) **S:** 381
Wool (Sources of wool) **W:** 399; (History) **W:** 401
Merisi, Michelangelo [Italian painter] *See* Caravaggio, Michelangelo Merisi da *in this index*
Meristem [botany]
Root (The root tip) **R:** 470 *with diagram*
Meristematic cell [botany]
Plant (Germination) **P:** 535-537
Meristematic tissue [botany]
Tissue (Plant tissues) **T:** 299
Merit badge

Boy Scouts (Boy Scouting) **B:** 535-537
Merit pay
Education (Who should teach?) **E:** 106-107
Teaching (Rewards of teaching) **T:** 69
Merit system
Civil service **Ci:** 612
Merit Systems Protection Board
Civil service (Federal civil service) **Ci:** 612
Meritor Savings Bank v. Vinson [U.S. history]
Supreme Court of the United States (table) **So:** 1002
Merkel, Angela [German political leader] **M:** 417 *with portrait*
Germany (The early 2000's) **G:** 172
Merleau-Ponty, Maurice [French psychologist]
Phenomenology **P:** 357
Merlin [poem by Robinson]
Robinson, Edwin Arlington **R:** 368
Merlin [legendary figure] **M:** 417
Arthur, King **A:** 757
Round Table (Origin) **R:** 491
Merlin [bird]
Falcon *picture on* **F:** 13; (Other North American falcons) **F:** 14
Merlin [book by Boron]
Excalibur **E:** 435
MERLIN [telescope]
Jodrell Bank Observatory **J:** 130
Merlin, Joseph [Belgian inventor]
Roller skating **R:** 402
Merlon [architecture]
Castle (Structure) **C:** 280
Mermaid [legendary creature] **M:** 418
Mermaid [ship]
Brig *picture on* **B:** 608
Mermaids' purse [zoology]
Skate **S:** 478
Merman [legendary creature]
Mermaid **M:** 418
Merman, Ethel [American singer/actress] **M:** 418
Merodach-Baladan I [king of Babylonia]
Sennacherib **S:** 300
Merodach-Baladan II [king of Babylonia]
Chaldeans **C:** 370
Meroe [kingdom] *See* Kush *in this index*
Meron, Mount
Israel (The Judeo-Galilean Highlands) **I:** 482
Merope [Greek mythology]
Orion **O:** 856
Sisyphus **S:** 477
Meroplankton [biology]
Plankton **P:** 515
Merovingian dynasty [French history] **M:** 418
France (Victory of the Franks) **F:** 471
Franks **F:** 494
Merriam, Frank F. [American political leader]
California (table) **C:** 59
Merriam, William R. [American political leader]
Minnesota (table) **M:** 602
Merrick, Joseph [British public figure]
Neurofibromatosis **N:** 152
Merrifield, Robert Bruce [American chemist]
Nobel Prizes (Chemistry: 1984) **N:** 444
Merrill, Charles [American businessman] **M:** 418
Merrill, Frank [American general]
Merrill's Marauders **M:** 419
Merrill, James [American poet] **M:** 418
American literature (Variations on Modernist poetry) **A:** 423
Merrill, Robert [American singer] **M:** 419
Merrill, Samuel [American political leader]
Iowa (table) **I:** 391
Merrill, Steve [American political leader]
New Hampshire (table) **N:** 223
Merrill Lynch [company]
Bank of America **B:** 96
Merrill, Charles **M:** 418
Merrill's Marauders [U.S. history] **M:** 419
Merrimack [ship] *See* Monitor *and* Merrimack *in this index*
Merrimack River [New Hampshire-Massachusetts] **M:** 419
Massachusetts (Rivers and lakes) **M:** 284
New Hampshire (Rivers and lakes) **N:** 220 *with map*
Merrimack Valley [region, New England]
New Hampshire (Visitor's guide) **N:** 216; (Land regions) **N:** 218
Merriman, Brian [Irish poet]
Irish literature (Modern works in Gaelic) **I:** 431
Merritt, Ezekiel [American frontiersman]
California (The Mexican War) **C:** 60
Merritt, Lake [California]
Oakland (Description) **O:** 637 *with picture*
Merritt, Leonidas [American businessman]
Mesabi Range **M:** 421
Minnesota (Industrial development) **M:** 604

Merritt Island [Florida]
Kennedy Space Center **K:** 271 *with map*
Merry-go-round **M:** 419
Merry Monarch [nickname, Kalakaua]
Hawaii (Growth of constitutional government) **H:** 106-108
Merry Pranksters
Kesey, Ken **K:** 307
Merry Widow, The [operetta by Lehár]
Lehár, Franz **L:** 185
Merry Wives of Windsor, The [play by Shakespeare]
Shakespeare, William: *(The Merry Wives of Windsor)* **S:** 361
Mersenne, Marin [French mathematician]
Prime number (Special primes) **P:** 780-781
Sound (The study of waves) **So:** 605
Mersenne prime [mathematics]
Prime number (Special primes) **P:** 780-781
Mersey, River [England] **M:** 419
Liverpool **L:** 395
Mersey River [Nova Scotia]
Nova Scotia (Rivers and lakes) **N:** 562 *with map*
Merton, Robert Cox [American economist]
Merton, Robert King **M:** 419
Nobel Prizes (Economics: 1997) **N:** 449
Merton, Robert King [American sociologist] **M:** 419
Communication (The effects of media) **Ci:** 887
Merton, Thomas [Roman Catholic monk] **M:** 419
Merton College
Oxford, University of **O:** 887
Merv [region, Turkmenistan] **M:** 420
Merwin, John D. [American government official]
Virgin Islands, United States (United States rule) **V:** 397
Merwin, W. S. [American poet] **M:** 420
Poet laureate (table: Poets laureate of the United States) **P:** 590
Merychippus [extinct animal]
Horse (Origins of the horse) **H:** 360 *with picture*
Prehistoric animal *picture on* **P:** 740
Merz [art]
Schwitters, Kurt **S:** 190
Merz Drawing [collage by Schwitters]
Collage *picture on* **Ci:** 773
Painting (Dadaism) **P:** 80-81
Mesa [Arizona] **M:** 420
Mesa [geography] **M:** 420 *with picture*
Oklahoma *picture on* **O:** 724
South Dakota *picture on* **So:** 665
United States, History of the *picture on* **U:** 151
Mesa Central [region]
Mexico (The Mesa Central) **M:** 462 *with picture*
Mesa del Norte [region]
Mexico (The Mesa del Norte) **M:** 462
Mesa Falls
Idaho (Rivers, waterfalls, springs, and lakes) **I:** 38
Mesa Verde National Park [Colorado] **M:** 420
Anasazi (History) **A:** 448a
Colorado (Places to visit) **Ci:** 836 *with picture*
National Park System (table: National parks) **N:** 48
Mesabi Range [hills, Minnesota] **M:** 421
Hibbing **H:** 222
Minnesota (Industrial development) **M:** 604
Taconite **T:** 5
Mescal [drink]
Century plant **C:** 359
Mescaline [drug] **M:** 421
Drug abuse (Hallucinogenic drugs) **D:** 362; (table: Some commonly abused drugs) **D:** 363
Hallucinogenic drug **H:** 25
Meselson, Matthew S. [American geneticist]
Heredity (The chemistry of genes) **H:** 208-209
Mesencephalon [anatomy]
Yawning **Y:** 553
Meseta [region, Portugal-Spain]
Portugal (Land regions) **P:** 690
Spain *pictures on* **So:** 740, **So:** 743; (The Meseta) **So:** 739 *with picture*
Meseta Central [region]
Costa Rica (The Central Highlands) **Ci:** 1082 *with picture*
Mesha [king of the Moabites]
Jordan (Early days) **J:** 164
Moabite stone **M:** 681
Mesha inscription [monument]
Moabite stone **M:** 681
Mesha stele [monument]
Moabite stone **M:** 681
Meshach [Biblical figure]
Daniel, Book of **D:** 33
Meshrano Jirga [assembly]
Afghanistan (Government) **A:** 92-92a
Meskill, Thomas J. [American political leader]
Connecticut (table) **Ci:** 967
Mesmer, Franz Anton [Austrian physician] **M:** 421
Hypnosis (Mesmerism) **H:** 479

Mesmerism [theory]
Hypnosis (Mesmerism) **H:** 479
Mesmer, Franz Anton **M:** 421
Mesocarp [botany]
Fruit (Types of fruits in botany) **F:** 544
Mesocyclone
Tornado (How a tornado forms) **T:** 334 *with diagram*; (Forecasting tornadoes) **T:** 335-336
Mesoderm [biology]
Coelom **Ci:** 753
Mesogloea [zoology]
Jellyfish *picture on* **J:** 90
Mesohippus [extinct animal]
Horse (Origins of the horse) **H:** 360 *with picture*
Mesolithic people [anthropology]
Prehistoric people (The Stone Age) **P:** 751
Mesolithic Period [anthropology]
Stone Age **So:** 909
Meson [subatomic particle] **M:** 421
Hadron **H:** 5
Physics (Uncovering the secrets of the atom) **P:** 442
Quark **Q:** 7
Subatomic particle (Composite particles) **So:** 937
Yukawa, Hideki **Y:** 578
Mesonero Romanos, Ramón de [Spanish author]
Spanish literature (The 1800's) **So:** 761-762
Mesopause [atmosphere]
Air (The mesosphere) **A:** 173-174 *with diagram*
Mesosphere **M:** 422
Thermosphere **T:** 256
Mesopotamia [ancient region] **M:** 421 *with map*
Agriculture (Mesopotamia and Egypt) **A:** 156
Architecture (Mesopotamian architecture) **A:** 611
Biology *picture on* **B:** 318
Clothing (Mesopotamia) **Ci:** 696
Glass (Early times) **G:** 217-218
Invention (The first civilizations) **I:** 358
Iraq (Early days) **I:** 413
Library (Ancient libraries of clay) **L:** 257
Mythology (Middle Eastern mythology) **M:** 976
Sculpture (Middle Eastern) **S:** 233
Slavery (Ancient times) **S:** 501
Transportation (The first great civilizations) **T:** 385
Water (Water and civilization) **W:** 132
Mesopotamia [region, South America]
Argentina (Northern Argentina) **A:** 652-653 *with map*; (Agriculture) **A:** 654
Mesoscale convective system [meteorology]
Tornado (Winds) **T:** 334-335
Mesoscale system [weather]
Weather (Weather systems) **W:** 158; (Mesoscale and microscale systems) **W:** 162
Mesosphere [atmosphere] **M:** 422
Air (Structure of the atmosphere) **A:** 172 *with diagram*
Mesosystem [psychology]
Child (The influence of the child's environment) **C:** 452
Mesothelioma [disease]
Asbestos (Hazards of asbestos) **A:** 765
Mesozoic Era [geology]
Cretaceous Period **Ci:** 1127
Dinosaur **D:** 206a
Earth *pictures on* **E:** 29; (The Mesozoic Era) **E:** 27 *with pictures*; (table) **E:** 30
Forest (Later forests) **F:** 398
Jurassic Period **J:** 201
Plant (The evolution of plants) **P:** 544-545
Prehistoric animal (The world of prehistoric animals) **P:** 736; (The Age of Reptiles) **P:** 737 *with picture*; (The Age of Mammals) **P:** 740
Reptile (The evolution of reptiles) **R:** 252
Triassic Period **T:** 439
Mesplet, Fleury [French printer]
Quebec (Communication) **Q:** 29
Mesquite [shrub] **M:** 422 *with picture*
Plant *picture on* **P:** 526
Tree *pictures on* **T:** 422
Mesrop, Saint [Armenian monk]
Alphabet (Other alphabets) **A:** 383
"Message to Garcia, A" [essay by Hubbard]
García Iñiguez, Calixto **G:** 29
Messaggero, Il [newspaper]
Rome (Economy) **R:** 431
Messenger [horse]
Harness racing (Harness horses) **H:** 63
Messenger [occupation]
Mercury **M:** 416
Postal services (Ancient times) **P:** 703
Messenger [spacecraft]
Mercury (Flights to Mercury) **M:** 415
Planet (Mercury) **P:** 511
Space exploration *picture on* **So:** 709; (Probes to Venus and Mercury) **So:** 710-711
Messenger RNA [genetics]
Cell (Producing proteins) **C:** 333-334 *with diagram*
Heredity (How proteins are made) **H:** 206-208
RNA **R:** 357
Messenia [department, Greece] **M:** 423 *with map*
Messerschmitt [airplane]
Aircraft, Military (World War II [1939-1945]) **A:** 205 *with picture*
Airplane *picture on* **A:** 235; (During World War II [1939-1945]) **A:** 238
Aviation (World War II [1939-1945]) **A:** 989
World War II (The air war) **W:** 482-483
Messiaen, Olivier [French composer] **M:** 423
Classical music (Atonal music) **Ci:** 649-650
Messiah [music by Handel]
Classical music (Oratorios) **Ci:** 644
Handel, George Frideric (His work) **H:** 42
Oratorio **O:** 818
Messiah [religion] **M:** 423
Christianity (Origins) **C:** 523
David **D:** 44
Jesus Christ **J:** 104; (The early Christians) **J:** 108b
Judaism (The Messiah) **J:** 180
Malachi, Book of **M:** 95
New Testament (Historical Jesus research) **N:** 287
Messianic Age [Judaism]
Judaism (The Messiah) **J:** 180
Messiah **M:** 423
Messier, Charles [French astronomer] **M:** 423
Astronomy (Discovering other galaxies) **A:** 848
Messier, Mark [Canadian hockey player] **M:** 424
Messier catalog [book]
Astronomy (Discovering other galaxies) **A:** 848
Messina [Italy] **M:** 424
Messini [Greece]
Messenia **M:** 423
Mestizaje [people]
Latin America (Mestizaje) **L:** 106
Mestizos [people]
Argentina (Rural life) **A:** 650; (Settlement and colonial life) **A:** 655
Bolivia (Population and ancestry) **B:** 443; (Colonial rule) **B:** 447
Chile (Ancestry) **C:** 460
Colombia (Ancestry) **Ci:** 779
Ecuador (People) **E:** 69
El Salvador (Ancestry) **E:** 249
Hispanic Americans (Who Hispanic Americans are) **H:** 245-246
Honduras (Ancestry) **H:** 309
Indian, American (In Latin America) **I:** 178
Latin America (Ancestry) **L:** 92-94; (Mestizaje) **L:** 106
Mexico **M:** 448; (Ancestry) **M:** 451; (Spanish rule) **M:** 469-470
Mexico City (People) **M:** 476b
Peru (Ethnic groups) **P:** 307; (Ways of life) **P:** 309
Uruguay (Population) **U:** 223
Mestral, Georges de [Swiss engineer]
Velcro **V:** 296
Mestre [Italy]
Venice (The people) **V:** 307; (Economy) **V:** 307-308
Meštrović, Ivan [Croatian sculptor] **M:** 424
Meta tag [computing]
HyperText Markup Language **H:** 477
Metabolism [physiology] **M:** 424
Biochemistry (Biochemical research) **B:** 310
Cell (Metabolic diseases) **C:** 336
Disease (Metabolic diseases) **D:** 229
Fast **F:** 52
Goiter **G:** 248
Heat (Chemical reactions) **H:** 149
Hibernation (Warm-blooded hibernators) **H:** 222
Hormone (Metabolic hormones) **H:** 335
Krebs cycle **K:** 387
Life (Metabolism) **L:** 275
Potassium **P:** 711
Metacarpal bone [anatomy]
Frog *picture on* **F:** 537
Hand (Parts of the hand) **H:** 40 *with diagram*
Human body (table) **H:** 422 *with diagram*
Wrist *diagram on* **W:** 510
Metacomet [Amercan Indian chief] *See* Philip, King *in this index*
Metadihydroxybenzene [chemical]
Resorcinol **R:** 259
Metagenes [Greek architect]
Seven Wonders of the Ancient World (The Temple of Artemis at Ephesus) **S:** 325
Metal M: 425
See also Alloy *in this index; and the list of Related articles in the* Metal *article*
Composite materials **Ci:** 904
Ductility **D:** 377
Electricity (Conductors and insulators) **E:** 193 *with diagram*
Element, Chemical *diagram on* **E:** 221
Extrusion **E:** 459
Materials (Metals and alloys) **M:** 300d
Metalloid **M:** 426
Metallurgy **M:** 426
Plastics (To replace metals) **P:** 554
Prehistoric people (The end of prehistoric times) **P:** 753-754a
Metal dam [dam]
Dam (Other types of dams) **D:** 19
Metal deactivator [chemical]
Gasoline (Gasoline blends and additives) **G:** 61-62
Metal del Diablo [novel by Céspedes]
Bolivia (The arts) **B:** 444
Metal detector M: 425
Metal drill
Drill (Metal drills) **D:** 348
Metal forming operations
Machine tool (Metal forming operations) **M:** 19
Metal halide lamp
Electric light (High-pressure gaseous-discharge lamps) **E:** 175 *with picture*
Lighting (Efficient use of lighting) **L:** 297
Metal hydride battery [electricity]
Battery (Secondary batteries) **B:** 170; (Types and uses of batteries) **B:** 171
Metal inert gas welding
Welding (Arc welding) **W:** 189
Metal master [recording]
Phonograph (How phonograph records are made) **P:** 401
Metal oxide semiconductor field effect transistor
Transistor (How transistors work) **T:** 372 *with diagram*
Metal stamping [manufacturing]
Automobile (Manufacturing) **A:** 958
Metal sulfide [chemistry]
Hydrothermal vent **H:** 473
Metal type [printing]
Type **T:** 536 *with picture*
Metallic bond
Materials (Physical bonds) **M:** 301
Metallic fiber
Fiber (Synthetic fibers) **F:** 87-88
Textile (Manufactured fibers) **T:** 213-214
Metallic luster [physical property]
Mineral (Luster) **M:** 567
Metallography [metallurgy] **M:** 426
Metalloid [element] **M:** 426
Metallurgical coke
Coke **Ci:** 759
Metallurgical engineering
Metallurgy (Careers in metallurgy) **M:** 427
Mining (Mining careers) **M:** 577-578
Metallurgy M: 426
See also the list of Related articles in the Metallurgy *article*
Geology (The Renaissance) **G:** 98
Metallography **M:** 426
Mining (Mining careers) **M:** 577-578
Metalmark [butterfly]
Butterfly *pictures on* **B:** 735; (Metalmarks) **B:** 736
Metalworking
Antique (Metalwork) **A:** 558
Brass (Making brass) **B:** 565-566
Forging **F:** 409
Indian, American (Metalwork) **I:** 145 *with picture*
Industrial arts (Industrial arts courses) **I:** 242-243
Islamic art (Metalware) **I:** 469
Machine tool **M:** 17 *with pictures*
Sculpture (China) **S:** 238
Tool (Metalworking tools) **T:** 330
Metamorphic rock [geology] **M:** 427
Asbestos (Sources of asbestos) **A:** 765
Earth (Earth's rocks) **E:** 20-21 *with picture*
Gem (Sources of gems) **G:** 77-79
Gneiss **G:** 238
Marble **M:** 191
Mountain (Volcanic mountains) **M:** 892
Rock (Metamorphic rock) **R:** 373 *with pictures*; (The rock cycle) **R:** 373
Serpentine **S:** 318
Metamorphism [geology]
Rock (Metamorphic rock) **R:** 373
Metamorphoses [book by Apuleius]
Latin literature (The Imperial Period) **L:** 116-117
Novel (Ancient Greek and Roman narratives) **N:** 572
Metamorphoses [book by Ovid]
Latin literature (The Augustan Age) **L:** 116
Narcissus **N:** 20
Ovid **O:** 882
Pygmalion **P:** 914
Metamorphosis [biology] **M:** 428 *with pictures*
Amphibian (Reproduction) **A:** 440 *with pictures*
Bee **B:** 203 *with pictures*

Beetle (The life cycle of beetles) B: 216 *with picture*
Butterfly (The life cycle of butterflies) B: 739-740 *with pictures*
Chrysalis C: 539
Cocoon Ci: 747
Fly (The life of a fly) F: 310 *with pictures*
Frog (Tadpoles) F: 539 *with picture*
Insect (Incomplete metamorphosis) I: 293 *with pictures*; (Complete metamorphosis) I: 293 *with pictures*
Larva L: 78
Moth (The life cycle of moths) M: 838-839 *with pictures*
Pupa P: 904
Tadpole T: 6
Toad (The life of a toad) T: 304
Metamorphosis [sculpture by Noguchi]
Noguchi, Isamu *picture on* N: 451
Metaphase [biology]
Cell (Mitosis) C: 330
Metaphor [language] M: 429
Shakespeare, William (Rhetoric) S: 368
Slang (Figures of speech) S: 500
Metaphysical Journals [book by Marcel]
Marcel, Gabriel M: 193
Metaphysical poets [English literature] M: 429
Cowley, Abraham Ci: 1113
Donne, John D: 308
English literature (Metaphysical and Cavalier poets) E: 317
Herbert, George H: 197
Marvell, Andrew M: 236
Poetry (Renaissance poetry) P: 596
Metaphysics [book by Aristotle]
Aristotle (Metaphysics) A: 664
Metaphysics [philosophy] M: 429
Aristotle (Metaphysics) A: 664
Idealism I: 46
Philosophy (Metaphysics) P: 383; (Aristotle) P: 387
Metaphysis [anatomy]
Bone (Structure of the bones) B: 456 *with diagram*
Metaproterenol [drug]
Bronchodilator B: 637
Metastasio, Pietro [Italian author]
Italian literature (The Baroque period and the Enlightenment) I: 494-495
Metastasis [biology]
Cancer (How damaged genes cause cancer) C: 169 *with picture*
Metastatic breast cancer [disease]
Breast cancer B: 591
Metatarsal [anatomy]
Foot (The bones) F: 352 *with diagram*
Frog *picture on* F: 537
Metatarsal arch [anatomy]
Foot (The arches) F: 352
Metaxas, Joannes [Greek political leader]
Greece (Between world wars) G: 363
Metazoa [biology] *See* Animalia *in this index*
Metcalf, Ralph [American political leader]
New Hampshire N: 223
Metcalf, Victor H. [American government official]
Commerce, Department of (table) Ci: 871
Roosevelt, Theodore (table) R: 466
Metcalfe, Charles Theophilus [British statesman] M: 430
Metchnikoff, Élie [Russian biologist] M: 431
Meteor [astronomy] M: 430 *with pictures*
Cretaceous Period Ci: 1127
Fireball F: 133
Solar system (Meteoroids) So: 581
Meteor [ship]
Atlantic Ocean (The beginnings of scientific oceanography) A: 867
Meteor Crater [Arizona] M: 432
Arizona (Places to visit) A: 678
Meteor *picture on* M: 431; (Impact craters and basins) M: 432
Meteor shower
Meteor (Meteor showers) M: 431
Meteor storm
Meteor (Meteor showers) M: 431
Meteorite [astronomy]
Meteor (Meteorites) M: 432 *with picture*
Asteroid A: 824
Astronomy (Direct sampling) A: 846
Earth (Earth's interior) E: 23
Iron and steel (The Iron Age) I: 449
Life (Creating simple organic compounds) L: 279
Mars (Possibility of life) M: 226c
Tektite T: 88
Meteoroid [astronomy]
Mars (Craters and impact basins) M: 226
Meteor M: 431 *with picture*

Solar system (Meteoroids) So: 581
Meteorologica [book by Aristotle]
Meteorology M: 432
Meteorological Organization, International
World Meteorological Organization W: 451
Meteorological rocket
Rocket (Atmospheric research) R: 386
Meteorological Service of Canada
Weather (Reporting the weather) W: 166
Meteorologist
Meteorology M: 432
Careers (Life, physical, and social sciences) C: 225-226
Tornado (Forecasting tornadoes) T: 335; (Studying tornadoes) T: 336
Weather W: 156; (Mathematical models) W: 166; (Careers in weather) W: 170
Meteorology M: 432
See also Weather *in this index*
Balloon (Sounding balloons) B: 58
Chaos C: 376
Geophysics G: 106a
Lamarck, Chevalier de L: 50
Radiosonde R: 99
Rain gauge R: 127
Weather W: 156; (Measuring the weather) W: 162; (Weather forecasting) W: 164
Weather vane W: 172
Meter [measurement] M: 433
Light (The speed of light) L: 290
Metric system (Advantages of the metric system) M: 436-437; (Structure of the metric system) M: 437; (The metric system at a glance) M: 438 *with pictures*
Weights and measures (Measurement systems) W: 184; (Comparison of measurement systems) W: 185
Meter [music]
Music (table) M: 954
Meter [poetry] M: 433
Poetry (Rhythm and meter) P: 591-592; (table) P: 594
Meter, Electric
Electric meter E: 176 *with pictures*
Meter, Gas *See* Gas meter *in this index*
Meter, Treaty of the [1875]
Metric system (Evolution of the metric system) M: 441
Weights and measures (The metric system) W: 187
Metered-dose inhaler [medicine]
Bronchodilator B: 637
Metered postage
Postal Service, United States (Other services) P: 700
Metering pattern [photography]
Camera (Automatic exposure control) C: 82
Meth lab [illegal business]
Methamphetamine M: 434
Methadone [drug] M: 433
Drug abuse (Heroin) D: 362
Methamphetamine [drug] M: 433
Amphetamine A: 439
Drug abuse (Abuse of illegal drugs) D: 362
Ecstasy E: 66
Methane [gas] M: 434
Air pollution (Natural sources) A: 199
Coal (Mine safety) Ci: 729
Gas [fuel] (The composition of natural gas) G: 50
Greenhouse effect (The natural greenhouse effect) G: 382-383
Petroleum (The composition of petroleum) P: 331
Titan T: 299
Methane hydrate [chemical] *See* Gas hydrate *in this index*
Methanol [chemical] M: 434
Alcohol (Methanol) A: 335
Automobile racing (Indy and Champ car racing) A: 977
Methedrine [drug] *See* Methamphetamine *in this index*
Methemoglobin [physiology]
Hemoglobin H: 182
Methicillin-resistant *Staphylococcus aureus* [bacteria]
Staphylococcus So: 839
Methionine [amino acid]
Sulfur So: 966
Method acting M: 434
See also Stanislavski method *in this index*
Brando, Marlon B: 563
Moscow Art Theater M: 828
"Method of Reaching Extreme Altitudes, A" [paper by Goddard]
Goddard, Robert Hutchings G: 244
Methodist Episcopal Church [religious group]

Asbury, Francis A: 766
Methodists (Early history) M: 435
Wesley, John (Formation of the Methodist Church) M: 198
Methodist Protestant Church [religious group]
Methodists (Social change and division) M: 435
Methodists [religious group] M: 434
Asbury, Francis A: 766
Christianity (Protestant churches) C: 522g; (The 1600's and 1700's) C: 525-526
Protestantism (Pietism) P: 835
United Methodist Church U: 75
Wesley, Charles W: 197
Wesley, John W: 197
Methodius, Saint [Greek missionary]
Alphabet (Other alphabets) A: 383
"Methought I Saw My Late Espoused Saint" [poem by Milton]
Milton, John (Middle years) M: 557
Methoxychlor [insecticide]
Insecticide (Chlorinated hydrocarbon insecticides) I: 302
Methuen Treaty [1703]
Portugal (A brief revival) P: 694
Methuselah [Biblical figure] M: 435
Methuselah [tree]
Bristlecone pine B: 610 *with picture*
Methyl [compound]
Herzberg, Gerhard H: 217
Methyl alcohol [chemical] *See* Methanol *in this index*
Methyl isocyanate [chemical]
Bhopal disaster B: 276
Methyl mercury [chemical]
Mercury (Mercury in the environment) M: 413
Methyl salicylate [chemical]
Salicylic acid S: 66
Methyl-tert-amyl ether [chemical]
Gasoline (Gasoline blends and additives) G: 61-62
Methylbenzene [chemical] *See* Toluene *in this index*
Methylene [compound]
Herzberg, Gerhard H: 217
Methylmorphine [drug] *See* Codeine *in this index*
Methylphenidate [drug] *See* Ritalin *in this index*
Metis [Greek mythology]
Athena A: 853
Metis [satellite]
Jupiter (Inner satellites) J: 200a *with picture*
Planetary ring P: 514d
Métis [people] M: 435
Canada, History of (New provinces) C: 144; (The North West Rebellion) C: 145
Dumont, Gabriel D: 383
Indian, American (In Canada) I: 178
Macdonald, Sir John Alexander (Threats to Canadian unity) M: 10
North West Rebellion N: 519
Northwest Territories (People) N: 530
Red River Rebellion R: 189
Riel, Louis R: 336
Saskatchewan (Métis and American Indian troubles) S: 146
Métis National Council
Indian, American (In Canada) I: 178b
Metonymy [language]
Slang (Figures of speech) S: 500
Metoprolol [drug]
Beta-blocker B: 274
Metre [measurement] *See* Meter *in this index*
Metric Conversion Act [1975]
Weights and measures (The metric system) W: 187
Metric photogrammetry [cartography]
Photogrammetry P: 405
Metric system [measurement] M: 436 *with pictures*
See also the list of Related articles in the Metric System article
Fraction (History) F: 449-450
International Bureau of Weights and Measures I: 338
Light (Light and measurement) L: 290
Weights and measures (Measurement systems) W: 184; (Comparison of measurement systems) W: 185; (The metric system) W: 187
Metric ton [measurement]
Metric system (The metric system at a glance) M: 438-439 *with picture*; (Non-SI metric units) M: 440
Ton T: 327
Metrical modulations [music]
Carter, Elliott C: 251
Metro [transportation]
Moscow (Transportation) M: 826 *with picture*
Washington, D.C. (Transportation) W: 84
Métro [transportation]

Montreal *picture on* M: 770, *map on* M: 771; (Transportation) M: 775-776
Paris (Economy) P: 165
Metro-Goldwyn-Mayer [company]
Goldwyn, Samuel G: 259
Motion picture (Movies become big business) M: 865-866
Metrodome [sports stadium]
Minneapolis *picture on* M: 580
Metronome [instrument] M: 441 *with picture*
Metronome mark
Music (Indicating time values) M: 953-955
Metropolis [film]
Germany *picture on* G: 154
Lang, Fritz L: 60
Metropolitan area M: 442 *with map*
City (The 100 largest urban centers in the world) Ci: 576; (Metropolitan cities) Ci: 588; (Governmental problems) Ci: 592
Latin America (City life) L: 95
Local government (Conflicts in authority) L: 408
Megalopolis M: 383
Metropolitan Area Church Council
Columbus (People) Ci: 854-855
Metropolitan Assembly [government]
Tokyo (Government) T: 318
Metropolitan city
City (Metropolitan cities) Ci: 588
Metropolitan correctional center
Prison (Types of correctional institutions) P: 805
Metropolitan District Commission
Boston (Government) B: 502-503
Metropolitan division
Metropolitan area (Defining metropolitan areas) M: 442
Metropolitan Museum of Art [New York City] M: 444
New York (Museums) N: 297
New York City (Museums) N: 338 *with picture*
Metropolitan Opera [New York City]
Levine, James L: 219
Lincoln Center for the Performing Arts L: 327
New York *picture on* N: 302
Opera O: 791 *with picture*
Metropolitan statistical area
Metropolitan area (Defining metropolitan areas) M: 442 *with map*
Metropolitan Transit Authority
New York City (Transportation) N: 334
Metropolitan Water Reclamation District of Greater Chicago
Chicago Sanitary and Ship Canal C: 439
Metropolitana [subway]
Rome (Economy) R: 431
Metrozoo [Miami]
Florida (Places to visit) F: 252
Mets, New York [team] *See* New York Mets *in this index*
Metternich [Austrian statesman] M: 444
Aix-la-Chapelle, Congress of A: 253
Austria (Metternich and revolution) A: 938
German literature (The Young Germany) G: 140
Metz, Battle of [1870]
Franco-Prussian War (Progress of the war) F: 483
Metz, Christian [German religious leader]
Amanites A: 400
Metzinger, Jean [French painter]
Cubism Ci: 1181
Meung, Jean de [French poet]
French literature (Narrative poetry) F: 518
Meuse-Argonne Offensive [1918]
A.E.F. A: 81
World War I (The last campaigns) W: 463 *with picture*
Meuse River [Europe] M: 444
Belgium (The land) B: 230 *with map*
Netherlands (The land) N: 144 *with map*
MeV [measurement]
Particle accelerator (How accelerators work) P: 184
Mevacor [drug] *See* Lovastatin *in this index*
Mexica [people]
Aztec A: 999
Mexicali [Mexico] M: 444
Mexico (The Pacific Northwest) M: 460
Mexican American Political Association
Hispanic Americans (Effects of World War II) H: 253
Mexican Americans [people]
See also Hispanic Americans *in this index*
American GI Forum of the United States A: 411
Cinco de Mayo Ci: 557
Cortina, Juan Nepomuceno Ci: 1073
Día de los muertos D: 178
Great Depression (Human suffering) G: 340-341
Hispanic Americans H: 244 *with pictures*
Los Angeles (Ethnic groups) L: 463 *with picture*

Minority group (Hispanic Americans) M: 609
Sánchez, George Isidore S: 106
Texas (Population) T: 188
Mexican bean beetle *See* Bean beetle *in this index*
Mexican Bolero [book by Mastretta]
Latin American literature (The post-Boom) L: 114
Mexican Cession [1848]
Mexican War (The peace treaty) M: 447 *with map*
United States, History of the *map on* U: 184; (Manifest destiny) U: 169 *with map*
Mexican dipper [bird]
Dipper D: 217 *with picture*
Mexican eagle
Caracara C: 201
Mexican free-tailed bat [animal]
Bat (Brazilian free-tailed bats) B: 161
Mexican fruit fly
Fruit fly F: 549
Mexican hairless [dog] M: 444
Mexican hat dance
Mexico (Clothing) M: 456-457 *with picture*
Mexican onyx
Onyx O: 788
Mexican redknee tarantula [spider]
Spider *picture on* So: 788
Mexican Revolution of 1910 M: 444
Carranza, Venustiano C: 247
Hispanic Americans (The early 1900's) H: 252
Madero, Francisco Indalecio M: 30
Mexico *picture on* M: 459; (The Revolution of 1910) M: 472 *with map*
Mexico City (Revolution and growth) M: 478
Wilson, Woodrow (Crisis in Mexico) W: 323
Mexican territory [U.S. history]
United States, History of the (The Mexican War) U: 169 *with map*
Mexican turnip *See* Jicama *in this index*
Mexican War [1846-1848] M: 445 *with picture and map*
Arizona (Spanish exploration) A: 688
Army, United States (The Mexican War) A: 738
California (The Mexican War) C: 60
Carson, Kit (Rise to prominence) C: 250
Frémont, John Charles F: 511
Guadalupe Hidalgo, Treaty of G: 408
Hispanic Americans *picture on* H: 251; (Conflict) H: 252
Kearny, Stephen Watts K: 253
Latin America (Early years of independence) L: 107-108
Lee, Robert E. (The Mexican War) L: 177
Marine Corps, United States (The 1800's) M: 208-209
Mexico (Difficulties of the early republic) M: 471
New Mexico (The Mexican War) N: 275
Polk, James Knox (The Mexican War) P: 643
Taylor, Zachary (Mexican War) T: 58-59 *with picture*
Texas (Statehood and early progress) T: 207
United States, History of the (The Mexican War) U: 167
War (table) W: 25
Western frontier life in America (The shifting frontier) W: 232
Mexican zinnia [plant]
Zinnia *picture on* Z: 595
Mexico M: 448 *with pictures and maps*
See also the list of *Related articles* in the Mexico article
Adobe A: 59
Clothing *picture on* Ci: 695
North America *picture on* N: 458
Police *picture on* P: 623
Texas (The Texas revolution) T: 206
Agriculture
Mexico (Agriculture) M: 465
Migrant labor M: 538
Art and architecture
Mexico (Arts) M: 459 *with pictures*
Dance *picture on* D: 26
Music *picture on* M: 947
Painting (Modern Mexican painting) P: 83 *with picture*
Climate
Mexico (Climate) M: 463
Communications and mass media
Mexico (Communication) M: 467
Television (In Latin America) T: 117
Education
Mexico (Education) M: 459
Government
Mexico (Government) M: 449
North American Free Trade Agreement N: 470
History
Mexico (History) M: 468 *with pictures and maps*
Black Seminole B: 391
California (Mexican rule) C: 60

Cortés, Hernán Ci: 1072
Foreign Legion (History) F: 386
Immigration (The fourth wave) I: 83
Latin America (The movement toward independence) L: 106-107; (Early years of independence) L: 107-108; (Political circumstances in the early to middle 1900's) L: 109
Mexican Revolution of 1910 M: 444
Mexican War M: 445 *with map*
San Antonio (History) S: 86-87
Tenochtitlan T: 167
Teotihuacán T: 169
United States, History of the *map on* U: 184; (The Mexican War) U: 167
Language and literature
Mexico (Language) M: 451; (Literature) M: 460
Manufacturing
Mexico (Manufacturing) M: 464
Mining
Mexico (Mining) M: 466
People
See also Mexican Americans *in this index*
Mexico (People) M: 451
Aztec A: 999 *with pictures*
Hispanic Americans (In Mexico) H: 247; (In the Southwest) H: 251; (Conflict) H: 252; (Stricter immigration laws) H: 255
Indian, American (Indians of the Southwest) I: 166; (Indians of Middle America) I: 169; (In Latin America) I: 178
Maya M: 322
Olmec Indians O: 744
Toltec Indians T: 323
Zapotec Indians Z: 587
Religion
Mexico (Religion) M: 458 *with picture*
Social and cultural life
Mexico (Way of life) M: 451 *with pictures*
Christmas (In Latin America) C: 532 *with picture*
Cinco de Mayo Ci: 557
Transportation
Mexico (Transportation) M: 467
Railroad (In other countries) R: 113
México [state] M: 475
Mexico, Gulf of *See* Gulf of Mexico *in this index*
Mexico, National Autonomous University of M: 475
Latin America *picture on* L: 101
Mexico (Education) M: 459
Mexico City (Education) M: 476b-477
Mexico City [Mexico] M: 476 *with pictures and map*
Environmental pollution *picture on* E: 330
Mexico *pictures on* M: 456; (City life) M: 454; (The Mesa Central) M: 462; (table: Average monthly weather) M: 464
Olympic Games (The 1968 games) O: 752
Tenochtitlan T: 167
Teotihuacán T: 169
World *picture on* W: 418
Meyer, Adolf [German architect]
Gropius, Walter G: 397
Meyer, Albert Gregory [American religious leader]
Cardinal (table: American cardinals) C: 211
Meyer, Christian Erich Hermann von [German scientist]
Plateosaurus P: 565
Meyer, Eugene [American businessman]
Graham, Katharine G: 300
Meyer, George von Lengerke [American government official]
Roosevelt, Theodore (table) R: 466
Meyer, Josef [German publisher]
Encyclopedia (Encyclopedias of the 1800's and 1900's) E: 268b
Meyer, Julius Lothar [German chemist]
Chemistry (Formation of the periodic table) C: 402
Meyer, Louis [American race driver]
Automobile racing (table: Indianapolis 500 winners) A: 980
Meyer, Stephanie [American author] M: 479 *with portrait*
Meyerbeer, Giacomo [German composer] M: 479
Opera (Grand opera) O: 798
Meyerhof, Otto Fritz [German physiologist]
Nobel Prizes (Physiology or medicine: 1922) N: 445
Meyner, Robert B. [American political leader]
New Jersey (table) N: 249
Mezzo [adjective]
Music (table) M: 954
Mezzo-rilievo [art]
Relief R: 213
Mezzo-soprano
Opera (The singers) O: 792
Singing (Voice classification) S: 472

Mfecane [African history]
Africa (African societies in the 1800's) A: 133
South Africa (The Zulu and the Mfecane) So: 618
Mfengu [people]
Doll (Dolls in religion) D: 288
Mfume, Kweisi [American political leader] M: 479
with portrait
Mg [symbol]
Magnesium (Properties) M: 54
MGM [company] See Metro-Goldwyn-Mayer in this index
MGM Grand Hotel/Casino [Las Vegas]
Las Vegas (The city) L: 88
MHC protein [biochemistry] See Major histocompatibility complex protein in this index
MHD [abbreviation] See Magnetohydrodynamics in this index
Mia Hamm Foundation [organization]
Hamm, Mia H: 34
Miacis [extinct animal]
Cat (History) C: 296
Dog (History) D: 281
Prehistoric animal (The development of placentals) P: 741
Miami [Florida] M: 479 with picture and map
Florida (table: Average monthly weather) F: 256
Miami [book by Didion]
Didion, Joan D: 195
Miami and Erie Canal [waterway]
Cincinnati (The 1800's) Ci: 556
Ohio O: 702
Toledo (History) T: 321
Miami Beach [Florida] M: 481
Florida picture on F: 251
Miami Confederacy
Miami Indians M: 482
Miami-Dade County [Florida]
County (Duties) Ci: 1099
Election of 2000 (Court challenges) E: 161
Miami (The city) M: 479
Miami Dolphins [team]
Football (National Football League) F: 364
Shula, Don S: 442
Miami Heat [team]
Basketball (table) B: 150
James, LeBron J: 27
Miami Indians M: 482
Miami International Airport
Florida (Transportation) F: 260
Miami Marlins [team]
Baseball (table) B: 130
Miami River [river, Ohio]
Ohio (The early 1900's) O: 702 with picture
Miata [automobile]
Automobile picture on A: 971
Mica [mineral] M: 482
Mineral picture on M: 566
Mica Dam [Canada]
British Columbia (The mid-1900's) B: 630
Micah, Book of [Bible] M: 482
Micawber, Wilkins [literary figure]
Dickens, Charles (Dickens's life) D: 187
Mice See Mouse in this index
Micelle [chemistry]
Colloid Ci: 777
Michael [czar of Russia]
Romanov R: 426
Michael [king of Romania]
Romania (World War II) R: 424; (Communist control) R: 424-425
Michael VIII Palaeologus [Byzantine ruler]
Byzantine Empire (The late Byzantine period) B: 754
Michael, Saint [Biblical figure] M: 482
Michaelmas M: 482
"Michael Angelo" [poem by Longfellow]
Longfellow, Henry Wadsworth (Translations, lyric poems and dramatic poems) L: 451
Michael Cerularius [Byzantine religious leader]
Roman Catholic Church (Split with the East) R: 407
Michael Kohlhaas [book by Kleist]
German literature (Other writers) G: 140
Michael L. Printz Award
Literature for children (Awards) L: 367
Michaelmas [custom] M: 482
Michaelmas daisy [plant]
Aster A: 823
Michel, Hartmut [German chemist]
Nobel Prizes (Chemistry: 1988) N: 444
Michel, James [Seychellois political leader]
Seychelles (History) S: 340-341
Michelangelo [Italian artist] M: 483 with pictures
Architecture (Later Renaissance architecture) A: 621
David pictures on D: 45
Isaiah, Book of picture on I: 461

Italy picture on I: 505
Jeremiah, Book of picture on J: 92
Madonna and Child M: 37
New Testament picture on N: 287
Painting (Religious subjects) P: 32; (The High Renaissance) P: 54 with picture
Religion picture on R: 216
Renaissance (Arts of the 1400's and early 1500's) R: 236
Saint Peter's Basilica (History) S: 53-54
Sculpture (Michelangelo) S: 252 with picture
Sistine Chapel S: 477
Michelet, Jules [French historian]
History (History in the universities) H: 262-263
Micheletti, Roberto [Honduran political leader]
Honduras (Recent developments) H: 313
Michelson, Albert Abraham [American physicist] M: 487
Betelgeuse B: 274
Ether E: 365
Light (The speed of light) L: 290
Physics (Einstein and relativity) P: 441
Relativity (The Michelson-Morley experiment) R: 210
Michelson-Morley experiment
Physics (Einstein and relativity) P: 441
Relativity (The Michelson-Morley experiment) R: 210
Michener, James A. [American author] M: 487
Michener, Roland [Canadian statesman] M: 487
Michigan M: 488 with pictures and maps
See also the list of Related articles in the Michigan article
Michigan, Lake See Lake Michigan in this index
Michigan, University of M: 512
Michigan (Libraries) M: 492
Michigan Agricultural College
Michigan State University M: 513
Michigan Avenue [street]
Chicago picture on C: 427
Michigan State University M: 513
Michigan (Interesting facts) M: 489
Michilimackinac [former name]
Mackinac Island M: 24
Michipicoten [island, Ontario]
Lake Superior (Description) L: 45 with map
Michoud Assembly Facility [New Orleans]
New Orleans (Industry) N: 282-283
Mickelson, George S. [American political leader]
South Dakota (table) So: 680
Mickelson, George T. [American political leader]
South Dakota (table) So: 680
Mickelson, Phil [American golfer]
Golf picture on G: 267
Mickey, John H. [American political leader]
Nebraska (table) N: 110
Mickey Mouse [cartoon character]
Animation (Walt Disney) A: 514b
Disney, Walt (The first Disney cartoons) D: 235-236 with pictures
Mickiewicz, Adam [Polish poet]
Poland (The arts) P: 607
Micmac Indians See Mi'kmaq Indians in this index
Micombero, Michel [African political leader]
Burundi (History) B: 713-714
Micro [prefix]
Metric system (Metric prefixes) M: 439
Micro-mirror technology
Projector (Digital data projectors) P: 817
Micro-Tom [tomato]
Tomato (The tomato plant) T: 324-325
Microampere [measurement]
Ampere A: 438
Microbe See Microorganism in this index
Microbial insecticide
Insecticide (Microbial insecticides) I: 302
Microbiology M: 513
Biology (What biologists study) B: 316-317
Careers (Life, physical, and social sciences) C: 225
Microbiotheria [zoology]
Mammal (table) M: 128 with picture
Microburst [weather hazard]
Wind shear W: 332
Microchip [electronics] See Computer chip in this index
Microcline [mineral]
Feldspar F: 68
Microcomputer
See also Personal computer in this index
Remote control (The parts of a remote control system) R: 230
Microcrystalline wax [by-product]
Paraffin P: 143
Wax (Mineral wax) W: 153
Microeconomics
Economics (Fields of economics) E: 64
Microelectromechanical systems [technology]

M: 513
Microelectronics
Electronics E: 207
Microencapsulation [industrial process] M: 513
Microfarad [measurement]
Capacitor (Capacitance) C: 186
Farad F: 27
Microfiber [material] M: 514
Microfiche [photography]
Microfilm M: 514
Microfilm [lacquer]
Airplane, Model (Indoor models) A: 241
Microfilm [photography] M: 514
Microfilm reader [machine]
Microfilm M: 514
Microform
Microfilm M: 514
Microgametophyte [botany]
Seed (Seed development in angiosperms) S: 281
Micrographia [book by Hooke]
Biology (Early discoveries with the microscope) B: 318 with picture
Microgravity
Space exploration (Living in space) So: 701 with pictures
Microlight
Airplane (General aviation planes) A: 211-212
Micromégas [book by Voltaire]
Voltaire (Exile and return to France) V: 446
Micrometeoroid [astronomy]
Jupiter (Rings) J: 200a-200b
Moon (Origin and evolution of the moon) M: 788
Micrometer [measuring device] M: 514 with picture
Micrometer [measurement] M: 514
Weights and measures (Miscellaneous weights and measures) W: 184
Micromount
Rock (Displaying rocks) R: 375
Micron [metric unit] See Micrometer [metric unit] in this index
Micronesia [islands, Pacific]
See also Micronesia in this index
Pacific Islands P: 3 with map
Mariana Islands M: 199
Nauru N: 68
Northern Mariana Islands, Commonwealth of the N: 525
Palau P: 101
Sculpture (Pacific Islands sculpture) S: 241
Micronesia, Federated States of M: 515 with picture and map
Flag picture on F: 204
Pacific Islands, Trust Territory of the P: 13
Micronesian race [theory]
Races, Human (The geographical-race theory) R: 54
Micronesians [people]
Marshall Islands (People) M: 231
Pacific Islands (Micronesians) P: 5
Micronutrients [biochemistry]
Fertilizer (The importance of fertilizer) F: 78
Nutrition (Kinds of nutrients) N: 625
Microorganism
See also the list of Related articles in the Microbiology article
Antibiotic A: 550
Antiseptic A: 559
Deep sea (Deep-sea life) D: 82a
Disinfectant D: 235
Food poisoning F: 340
Food preservation (How food spoils) F: 341
Gargle G: 43
Gnotobiotics G: 239
Medicine (The beginnings of modern research) M: 374; (Scientific study of the effects of disease) M: 375 with picture
Microbiology M: 513
Sterilization So: 893
Microphone M: 516 with pictures
Computer (A microphone) Ci: 915
Hearing aid H: 130 with diagram
Radio (From sound waves to electric waves) R: 86
Telephone (The microphone) T: 95
Television (Microphones) T: 111; (Creating television signals) T: 121
Videophone V: 360
Microphotography [photography]
Microfilm M: 514
Micropolitan statistical area
Metropolitan area (Defining metropolitan areas) M: 442
Microprism [optics]
Photography (Types of lenses) P: 411
Microprocessor [electronics]
See also Computer chip in this index
Camera (Automatic controls) C: 80
Computer Ci: 909; (Parts of computers) Ci: 911

with picture
Computer chip **Ci: 924e** with picture
Digital technology **D: 203**
Electronics (Types of electronic circuits) **E: 209-210** with picture; (The solid-state revolution) **E: 215-216** with picture
Ignition (The direct-fire ignition system) **I: 49**
Invention (Recent developments) **I: 364**
Remote control (The parts of a remote control system) **R: 230**
Scale, Weighing (Electronic scales) **S: 169**
Smart card **S: 513**
Technology (The computer age) **T: 75**
Telephone (The circuit board) **T: 95**
Micropyle [botany]
Plant (Sexual reproduction) **P: 532-535**
Microrace [anthropology]
Races, Human (The geographical-race theory) **R: 55**
Microscale systems [weather]
Weather (Weather systems) **W: 158**; (Mesoscale and microscale systems) **W: 162**
Microscope M: 517 with pictures
See also Electron microscope in this index
Cell picture on **C: 338**; (Looking at a cell) **C: 327**
Eye picture on **E: 467**
Ion microscope **I: 372**
Leeuwenhoek, Anton van **L: 181**
Nanotechnology (Applications of nanotechnology) **N: 10**
Ultramicroscope **U: 15**
World, History of the picture on **W: 442**
Microscopic anatomy
Anatomy **A: 448b**
Microsecond [measurement]
Metric system (Space and time) **M: 437**
Microsoft Corporation M: 519
Antitrust laws **A: 560**
Computer (Manufacturing) **Ci: 924**; (The personal computer) **Ci: 924c-924d**
Electronic game (Competition for older players) **E: 204e**
Gates, Bill **G: 67**
Gates Foundation **G: 67**
NBC **N: 93**
Microsoft Disk Operating System [computer software] See MS-DOS in this index
Microsoft Encarta [software]
Encyclopedia (Today's encyclopedias) **E: 268b-269**
Microsoft PowerPoint [software]
Audio-visual materials **A: 882**
Presentation software **P: 757**
Microsporangium [botany]
Plant (Sexual reproduction) **P: 532-533**
Microspore [botany]
Spore (Plant spores) **So: 801-802** with diagram
Microstructure
Materials **M: 300b**
Microsurgery
Medicine (The medical revolution) **M: 376-377**
Surgery (Technique) **So: 1005**
Microsystem [psychology]
Child (The influence of the child's environment) **C: 452**
Microtome [instrument] **M: 520** with picture
Microtomy [process] **M: 520**
Microscope (The stage) **M: 518**
Microtone [music]
Music (Asian music) **M: 955-956**
Microtubule [biology]
Flagellum **F: 224**
Microwave [electronics] **M: 520**
Astronomy (Radio and microwave astronomy) **A: 843**
Burglar alarm **B: 704**
Cosmic microwave background (CMB) radiation **Ci: 1075**
Cosmology **Ci: 1077**
Marconi, Guglielmo (Short-wave radio) **M: 197**
Maser **M: 263**
Microwave oven **M: 520**
Prokhorov, Alexander Mikhailovich **P: 817**
Radar (Advances during World War II) **R: 72**
Radiation (Electromagnetic radiation) **R: 75-76** with picture
Telecommunications **T: 89**
Telephone (Traditional phone calls) **T: 96-97**
Telescope (Microwave telescopes) **T: 108**
Television (Microwaves) **T: 123**
Microwave astronomy
Astronomy (Radio and microwave astronomy) **A: 843**
Microwave Landing System
Airport (Air traffic control) **A: 246-247**
Microwave oven M: 520 with diagram
Cooking (Other cooking methods) **Ci: 1029**

Microwave telescope
Telescope (Microwave telescopes) **T: 108**
Microwave tube
Vacuum tube (Microwave tubes) **V: 259**
Microzoan [organism] See Protozoan in this index
Mictlan [legendary place]
Mythology (Aztec mythology) **M: 987**
Mictlancíhuatl [Aztec goddess]
Mythology (Aztec mythology) **M: 987**
Mictlantecuhtli [Aztec god]
Mythology (Aztec mythology) **M: 987**
Midas [Greek mythology] **M: 521**
Mid-Atlantic Ridge
Atlantic Ocean (The Atlantic seafloor) **A: 864** with map
Mountain **M: 891**; (At mid-ocean ridges) **M: 892**
Ocean (Deep-sea peaks, valleys, and plains) **O: 662** with map
Plate tectonics (Divergent plate boundaries) **P: 561-562**
Midbrain
Brain diagram on **B: 551**
Middle age M: 521
Middle Age of Mrs. Eliot, The [book by Wilson]
Wilson, Angus **W: 316**
Middle Ages [European history] **M: 522** with pictures and map
Aristotle (Aristotle's place in Western thought) **A: 664**
Cat (History) **C: 296**
City (Medieval cities) **Ci: 581** with pictures
Communication (During the Middle Ages) **Ci: 879** with picture
Dark Ages **D: 36**
Doll (The Middle Ages) **D: 288**
Map (Maps in the Middle Ages) **M: 183**
Name (Ancestors) **N: 6**; (The history of names) **N: 7**
Agriculture
Agriculture (The Middle Ages) **A: 156** with picture
Manorialism **M: 166**
Art and architecture
Middle Ages (Learning and the arts) **M: 527**
Architecture (Medieval architecture) **A: 617**
Carolingian art **C: 244**
Castle **C: 280** with pictures
Cathedral (Historical importance of cathedrals) **C: 301**
Classical music (The Middle Ages) **Ci: 645**
Europe (Medieval art) **E: 391** with picture
Furniture (The Middle Ages) **F: 571** with picture
Gargoyle **G: 43**
Glass (The Middle Ages) **G: 218**
Gothic art **G: 278**
Illuminated manuscript **I: 78**
Norman architecture **N: 455**
Painting (Medieval painting) **P: 48** with pictures
Sculpture (Medieval sculpture) **S: 248** with pictures
Shelter (The Middle Ages) **S: 393**
Stained glass (Early stained-glass windows) **So: 822** with picture
Tapestry (History) **T: 39-40**
Unicorn **U: 26**
Defense
Armor (During the Middle Ages) **A: 719** with pictures
Army (Armies in the Middle Ages) **A: 727**
Navy (Navies in the Middle Ages) **N: 79**
Sword **So: 1062**
Government
Middle Ages (Feudal government) **M: 524**
City-state **Ci: 603**
Curia regis **Ci: 1194**
Democracy (The Middle Ages) **D: 122**
Domesday Book **D: 300**
Estates-General **E: 360**
Feudalism **F: 81**
Free city **F: 498**
Freedom (The Middle Ages) **F: 502**
Government (Feudalism) **G: 290**
Law (History) **L: 134**
Magna Carta (Reasons for the charter) **M: 52**
Nationalism (The rise of nationalism) **N: 62-63**
Parliament (History) **P: 174**
Health and welfare
Bath (History) **B: 164**
Medicine (During the Middle Ages) **M: 373** with picture
Mental illness (Early attitudes) **M: 408**
History
Middle Ages (The fall of Rome) **M: 522**
Belgium (The Middle Ages) **B: 232**
Europe (The Middle Ages) **E: 409** with picture
Exploration (Medieval exploration) **E: 441**
France (History) **F: 471** with map

History (The Bible and post-Roman history) **H: 262**
Holy Roman Empire **H: 299**
Hundred Years' War **H: 437**
Italy (The Middle Ages) **I: 513**
Normans **N: 456**
Philosophy (Medieval philosophy) **P: 388**
Renaissance **R: 232**
Slavery (The Middle Ages) **S: 501**
Switzerland (The struggle for freedom) **So: 1059**
Vikings **V: 378**
World, History of the (The world from 500 to 1500) **W: 432** with pictures and map
Labor
Guild **G: 428**
Labor movement (Origins of the labor movement) **L: 9**
Language and literature
Biography (The Middle Ages) **B: 313**
Book (The Middle Ages) **B: 466**
Drama (Medieval drama) **D: 328** with pictures
Greek literature (Medieval literature) **G: 378**
Hebrew literature (Medieval works) **H: 162**
Holy Grail **H: 299**
Japanese literature (The medieval period) **J: 62**
Library (Libraries of the Middle Ages and the Renaissance) **L: 259**
Manuscript (European manuscripts of the Middle Ages) **M: 173**
Novel (Medieval narratives) **N: 572**
Poetry (Medieval poetry) **P: 596**
Storytelling (The Middle Ages) **So: 915**
People
Family (Development of the Western family) **F: 22**
Herald **H: 194**
Serf **S: 316b**
Villein **V: 384**
Yeoman **Y: 564**
Religion
Middle Ages (The Christian church) **M: 523**; (The power of the church) **M: 525**; (Troubles in the church) **M: 528**
Anti-Semitism **A: 559**
Christianity (The medieval church) **C: 524**
Freedom of religion (History) **F: 506**
Jews (The Talmudic period and the Middle Ages) **J: 122**
Pope (The early Middle Ages) **P: 663**; (The peak of papal power) **P: 663**
Reformation (Causes of the Reformation) **R: 196**
Religion (Christianity) **R: 222-223**
Roman Catholic Church (The early Middle Ages) **R: 406**
Social and cultural life
Middle Ages (Life of the people) **M: 526**
Bed (History) **B: 198**
Circus (History) **Ci: 562b**
City (The people) **Ci: 582** with picture
Clothing (The Middle Ages) **Ci: 700** with picture
Food (The Middle Ages) **F: 336** with picture
Hairdressing (The Middle Ages) **H: 11**
Homage **H: 300**
Knights and knighthood **K: 348**
Textile (During the Middle Ages) **T: 218**
Women's movement (During the Middle Ages) **W: 384**
Technology and science
Drug (Drugs in the Middle Ages) **D: 358**
Invention (The Middle Ages) **I: 359**
Physics (The Middle Ages) **P: 438**
Science (The Middle Ages) **S: 197**
Trade
Middle Ages (Economic recovery) **M: 526**
Hanseatic League **H: 53**
Transportation
Transportation (The Middle Ages) **T: 387**
Middle America M: 529
North America **N: 458**
Middle Assyrian Laws [text]
Assyria (Language and literature) **A: 821**
Middle Atlantic States [region, United States] **M: 529**
United States (Regions) **U: 99-101** with map
Middle Atlas Mountains [Africa]
Atlas Mountains **A: 869**
Middle childhood
Child (The school-age years) **C: 449**
Middle class [sociology] **M: 529**
City (Economy) **Ci: 584-585**
Colonial life in America (The structure of colonial society) **C: 793**
Communism (European reality in the early 1900's) **Ci: 890**
French Revolution (Background) **F: 524**; (The

revolution ends) **F: 527**
Gay Nineties (Middle-class prosperity) **G: 72**
German literature (Popular literature) **G: 139**
Industrial Revolution (The middle and upper classes) **I: 252**
Latin America *picture on* **L: 96**
Social class (Class structure) **So: 550**
United States, History of the (The rich and the poor) **U: 182**
World, History of the (The Industrial Revolution) **W: 444**
Middle Colonies [U.S. history]
Colonial life in America *picture on* **Ci: 792;** (Development of the Thirteen Colonies) **Ci: 790-791** *with map*
United States, History of the (The Middle Colonies) **U: 154**
Middle Congo [former name]
Congo, Republic of the (History) **Ci: 940e**
Middle ear [anatomy]
Deafness (Types of hearing loss) **D: 57**
Ear (The middle ear) **E: 7-8** *with diagrams*
Mastoid **M: 298**
Middle-earth [fictional place]
Tolkien, J. R. R. **T: 321**
Middle East M: 530 *with pictures and maps*
See also the list of Related articles in the Middle East *article*
Agriculture (Origins of agriculture) **A: 154**
Air force (Wars in the Middle East) **A: 187**
Arab-Israeli conflict **A: 582** *with map*
Arabs **A: 584**
Bank (Banks throughout the world) **B: 91-92**
Civilization (Development) **Ci: 635**
Clothing *pictures on* **Ci: 692;** (Clothing under Islam) **Ci: 697** *with pictures*
Cold War (The Suez crisis) **Ci: 766;** (The Eisenhower Doctrine) **Ci: 767**
Conservation (Asia) **Ci: 989**
Eisenhower, Dwight David (Crises in the Middle East and Asia) **E: 154**
Exploration (Muslim exploration) **E: 442**
Guerrilla warfare (History) **G: 420-421**
Library (The Middle East) **L: 252**
Mythology (Middle Eastern mythology) **M: 976** *with pictures*
Nationalization **N: 63**
Newspaper (In Africa and the middle East) **N: 386**
Petroleum *map on* **P: 336**
Television (In the Middle East) **T: 116**
Middle English [language]
English language (Middle English) **E: 313**
English literature (Middle English literature) **E: 315**
Language (Language change) **L: 64**
Middle Ground, The [book by Drabble]
Drabble, Margaret **D: 317**
Middle guard
Football (The defensive team) **F: 357** *with diagrams*
Middle Island [New Brunswick]
New Brunswick (Interesting facts) **N: 181** *with picture*
Middle Kingdom [Egyptian history]
Egypt, Ancient (The Middle Kingdom) **E: 143**
Painting (Egyptian painting) **P: 40-41**
Middle latitudes [geography]
Cyclone **Ci: 1203**
Middle linebacker
Football (The defensive team) **F: 357** *with diagrams*
Middle name
Name **N: 5**
Middle Paleolithic Period
Prehistoric people (The Stone Age) **P: 751**
Middle Rockies [U.S.]
Rocky Mountains (Chief ranges of the Rockies) **R: 394**
Middle school M: 535
Careers (Teaching) **S: 231**
China (Education) **C: 486**
Education (Intermediate education) **E: 91**
Junior high school **J: 196**
Library (Middle school and junior high school libraries) **L: 244**
School (Intermediate schools) **S: 181**
Middle Stone Age *See* Mesolithic Period *in this index*
Middle Temple [London]
Inns of Court **I: 275**
Middle Way [religion]
Buddhism (The dharma) **B: 668**
Dharma **D: 178**
Religion (Buddhism) **R: 220**
Middleman [economics]
Trade (The use of markets) **T: 362**
Middlemarch [book by Eliot]

Eliot, George **E: 237**
English literature (Later Victorian literature) **E: 321-322**
Middlesex Standard [newspaper]
Liberty Party **L: 233**
Middleton, Arthur [American patriot] **M: 535**
Middleton, Catherine Elizabeth [birth name of]
Catherine, Duchess of Cambridge **C: 302**
Middleton, Thomas [English dramatist]
Massinger, Philip **M: 296**
Shakespeare, William: (*Timon of Athens*) **S: 364**
Middleveld [region]
South Africa (The Plateau) **So: 614** *with map*
Middleweight [boxing]
Boxing (table) **B: 527**
Middlings [food]
Bran **B: 563**
Rye (Uses) **R: 573**
Midewiwin Society
Chippewa Indians **C: 514**
Indian, American (Shamans) **I: 147-148;** (Before European contact) **I: 154-155**
Pontiac **P: 657**
Midfielder [sports]
Soccer (The midfielders) **So: 545** *with diagram*
Midgard Serpent [Norse mythology]
Thor **T: 265**
Midge [insect] **M: 535** *with picture*
Antarctica (Living things) **A: 534**
Fly **F: 308**
Insect (Wings) **I: 288**
Sand fly **S: 107**
Midget
Stratton, Charles Sherwood **So: 921**
Midget car
Automobile racing (Other kinds of racing) **A: 978**
Midgut [biology]
Insect (Digestive system) **I: 289** *with diagram*
Mid-Indian Ridge [ocean ridge]
Ocean (Deep-sea peaks, valleys, and plains) **O: 662** *with map*
Midland Empire [region, Montana]
Billings **B: 306**
Midlands
England (The English Lowlands) **E: 300** *with map*
United Kingdom (The English Lowlands) **U: 59**
Midnight
Time (Time in today's world) **T: 292** *with diagram*
Midnight Court, The [poem by Merriman]
Irish literature (Modern works in Gaelic) **I: 431**
Midnight Cowboy [film]
Motion picture (Best picture: 1969) **M: 861**
Midnight Express [film]
Stone, Oliver **So: 909**
Midnight in Paris [film]
Allen, Woody **A: 372**
Midnight judges [U.S. history]
Jefferson, Thomas (The courts) **J: 84**
Midnight Ride of Paul Revere, The [painting by Wood]
Wood, Grant **W: 390**
Midnight sun [geography] **M: 535** *with diagrams*
Arctic (Land and climate) **A: 636**
Arctic Circle **A: 640**
Finland **F: 108;** (Climate) **F: 114**
Iceland **I: 20**
Inuit (The land of the Inuit) **I: 354-354a**
Norway **N: 536** *with picture;* (Climate) **N: 542-543**
Sweden **So: 1020**
Midnight's Children [book by Rushdie]
Rushdie, Salman **R: 522**
Mid-ocean ridge [geology]
Atlantic Ocean (The Mid-Atlantic Ridge) **A: 864**
Deep sea (The deep-sea floor) **D: 82a**
Earthquake (Interplate quakes) **E: 38**
Hydrothermal vent **H: 473**
Mountain (Volcanic mountains) **M: 892**
Ocean (Deep-sea peaks, valleys, plains) **O: 662**
Plate tectonics (Divergent plate boundaries) **P: 561-562**
Volcano (Mid-ocean ridges) **V: 442a** *with picture*
Midrib [botany]
Leaf (The blade) **L: 153-154** *with diagram*
Midshipman [rank]
United States Naval Academy **U: 203** *with picture*
Midsummer Dance [painting by Zorn]
Sweden *picture on* **So: 1027**
Midsummer Day [holiday]
June **J: 192**
Sweden *picture on* **So: 1025**
Midsummer Night's Dream, A [music by Mendelssohn]
Mendelssohn, Felix (His life) **M: 399**
Midsummer Night's Dream, A [play by Shakespeare]
Canada *picture on* **C: 111**
Fairy (Fairies in literature) **F: 11** *with picture*

Puck **P: 870**
Shakespeare, William *picture on* **S: 358;** (*A Midsummer Night's Dream*) **S: 357**
Midsummer's Eve [custom]
Sweden (Holidays) **So: 1026**
Midway, Battle of [1942] **M: 536**
Air force (World War II) **A: 185-186**
Midway Island **M: 536**
Spruance, Raymond Ames **So: 809**
World War II (The Battle of Midway) **W: 488**
Midway Airport
Chicago (Transportation) **C: 433**
Midway Geyser Basin
Yellowstone National Park (The Lower Loop) **Y: 558** *with map*
Midway Island [Pacific] **M: 536**
See also Midway, Battle of *in this index*
Midwest [region, United States] *See* Midwestern States *in this index*
Midwest Stock Exchange *See* Chicago Stock Exchange *in this index*
Midwestern States [region, U.S.] **M: 536**
New York City (The growing city) **N: 341**
United States *picture on* **U: 98;** (Regions) **U: 99-104** *with map*
Midwife M: 536
Nursing (History) **N: 619**
Pregnancy (Planning for pregnancy) **P: 734a**
Midwife toad **M: 536** *with picture*
Mielot, Jean [French artist]
World, History of the *picture on* **W: 434**
Miers, Harriet [American jurist]
Bush, George Walker (Supreme Court) **B: 722j**
Mies van der Rohe, Ludwig [German-American architect] **M: 537** *with picture*
Architecture *picture on* **A: 632;** (Early modern architecture in Europe) **A: 627-629;** (Ludwig Mies van der Rohe) **A: 631**
Bauhaus *picture on* **B: 173**
Chicago (Architecture) **C: 428**
Furniture (table: The Bauhaus) **F: 582-583** *with picture;* (Recent developments) **F: 584**
Johnson, Philip Cortelyou **J: 152**
Miescher, Friedrich [Swiss biochemist]
Cell (The 1900's) **C: 337-338**
Mieszko I [Polish prince]
Poland (The early Polish state) **P: 611**
Mifepristone [drug]
Abortion (Abortion methods) **A: 14;** (Abortion in the United States) **A: 16**
Birth control (Methods of birth control) **B: 378-379**
Mifflin, Thomas [American political leader] **M: 537**
Pennsylvania (table) **P: 263**
United States *picture on* **U: 116**
MiG-15 [airplane]
Korean War (The air war) **K: 382**
MiG-21 fighter
Aircraft, Military *picture on* **A: 205**
MiG-29 Fulcrum [aircraft]
Aircraft, Military (Fighters) **A: 203**
MiG-29K [aircraft]
Air force *picture on* **A: 183**
MiG Alley
Korean War (The air war) **K: 382**
Mighty Ducks, Anaheim [team]
Hockey (table: National Hockey League) **H: 281**
"Mighty Fortress Is Our God, A" [hymn]
Hymn (History) **H: 475**
Mignard, Pierre [French painter]
Clothing *picture on* **Ci: 703**
Mignonette [plant]
Henna **H: 185**
Migraine [disorder] **M: 537**
Migrant and seasonal farmworker
Migrant labor **M: 538**
Migrant Girl [photograph by Lange]
Photography *picture on* **P: 427**
Migrant labor [agriculture] **M: 538**
Farm and farming (Farm organizations) **F: 44**
Hispanic Americans (Effects of World War II) **H: 253**
Migration [biology] **M: 538**
Animal (Animal migration) **A: 502** *with picture*
Bird (Bird migration) **B: 360** *with pictures*
Bird of prey (Migration) **B: 374b**
Butterfly (Migration) **B: 742** *with picture*
Fish (Fish migration) **F: 151**
Goose (The life of a wild goose) **G: 271**
Gray whale **G: 335**
Insect (Hibernation and migration) **I: 296**
Mammal (Migration) **M: 125**
Moth (Migration) **M: 839**
Photoperiodism **P: 430**
Radar (In scientific research) **R: 68**
Seal (Seal rookeries) **S: 266**
Tree (How forests spread) **T: 429**

Whale (Migrations) **W:** 261
Migration [geology]
Petroleum (How petroleum deposits form) **P:** 333
Migration [sociology]
See also Immigration *in this index*
Famine (Effects of famine) **F:** 26a
Germany (East Germany) **G:** 170
Indian, American (In the United States) **I:** 178-178a *with picture*
Migrant labor **M:** 538
Population (Urban and rural population) **P:** 673
Prehistoric people (Migration from Africa) **P:** 747; (The spread of settlement) **P:** 752
Races, Human (Migration and gene flow) **R:** 59 *with picture*
Migration of the Negro, The [painting by Lawrence]
Literature for children *picture on* **L:** 359
Migratory Bird Treaty [1916]
Bird (Protective laws and treaties) **B:** 368
Migratory locust [insect]
Grasshopper (Short-horned grasshoppers) **G:** 328
Mihajlović, Draža [Yugoslav military leader]
Serbia (World War II) **S:** 315-316
Yugoslavia (World War II) **Y:** 576
Mihrab [architecture]
Islam *picture on* **I:** 465
Islamic art (Mosques) **I:** 468
Mosque **M:** 831 *with picture*
Mihura, Miguel [Spanish dramatist]
Spanish literature (Spanish literature today) **So:** 763
Mikado [Japanese history]
Chrysanthemum **C:** 540
Mikado, The [operetta by Gilbert and Sullivan]
Gilbert and Sullivan **G:** 190
Mikan, George [American basketball player]
M: 539
Basketball *picture on* **B:** 153
Mike [device] *See* Microphone *in this index*
Mike O'Callaghan-Pat Tillman Memorial Bridge [United States]
Bridge (table: Concrete arch) **B:** 603
Hoover Dam **H:** 302
Mikimoto, Kokichi [Japanese businessman]
Pearl (Cultured pearls) **P:** 217
Mi'kmaq Indians **M:** 540
Indian, American *picture on* **I:** 145
New Brunswick (Interesting facts) **N:** 181; (First Nations) **N:** 196
Newfoundland and Labrador (Early European exploration) **N:** 375
Nova Scotia (Early inhabitants) **N:** 567; (The struggle in Acadia) **N:** 568 *with picture*
Prince Edward Island **P:** 783
Mikonos [island, Greece]
Greece *picture on* **G:** 361
Mikrokosmos [music by Bartók]
Bartók, Béla **B:** 121
Milam, Benjamin [American military leader]
Texas (The Texas revolution) **T:** 206
Milam, J. W. [American public figure]
Emmett Till case **E:** 260
Milan [Italy] **M:** 540 *with picture*
Italy (table: Average monthly weather) **I:** 509
Leonardo da Vinci (Years in Milan) **L:** 199
Renaissance (The Italian Renaissance) **R:** 233 *with map*
Milan [Ohio]
Edison, Thomas Alva *picture on* **E:** 78; (Honors) **E:** 82
Milan Cathedral [Italy] **M:** 541 *with picture*
Milan Decree [1807] **M:** 541
Continental System **Ci:** 1022
Napoleon I (Fall from power) **N:** 15
Milankovitch, Milutin [Serbian mathematician]
Climate (Changes in the earth's orbit) **Ci:** 677 *with diagram*
Milano [name for]
Milan **M:** 540
Milbanke, Anne Isabella [wife of]
Byron, Lord (Byron's life) **B:** 748
Mild [coffee]
Coffee (Kinds of coffee) **Ci:** 755
Mild cognitive impairment [disorder]
Dementia **D:** 118
Mild porcelain
Porcelain (Hard-paste porcelain) **P:** 675-676
Mildew [fungus] **M:** 541 *with picture*
Barley (Diseases and insect pests) **B:** 113
Book (Caring for books) **B:** 465
Fungal disease (In plants) **F:** 558
Mile [measurement] **M:** 542 *with diagram*
Mile High City [nickname]
Butte **B:** 729
Denver **D:** 145
Mile Square

Indianapolis (The city) **I:** 220
Miles, John E. [American political leader]
New Mexico (table) **N:** 272
Miles, Nelson Appleton [American general]
M: 542
Montana (Indian fighting) **M:** 758-760
Milesians [legendary people]
Mythology (The mythological cycle) **M:** 985
Milestone, Lewis [American director]
Motion picture (Best achievement in directing: 1927-28, 1929-30) **M:** 862
Miletus [ancient city]
City planning (Ancient times) **Ci:** 602 *with diagram*
Milford [Utah]
Utah (table: Average monthly weather) **U:** 242
Milford Lake
Kansas (Rivers and lakes) **K:** 230
Milhaud, Darius [French composer] **M:** 543
Miliband, Ed [British political leader]
Labour Party (Recent developments) **L:** 17
Militant Islam
Arabs (Relations with Europe and the United States) **A:** 590a
Muslims (The Muslim world today) **M:** 965
Militant Socialist Movement [political party]
Mauritius (History) **M:** 317
Militarists [Japanese history]
Tojo, Hideki **T:** 311
Military Academy, United States *See* United States Military Academy *in this index*
Military aircraft *See* Aircraft, Military *in this index*
Military Appeals, Court of [law] *See* Court of Appeals for the Armed Forces, United States *in this index*
Military Armistice Commission
Korean War (The truce talks) **K:** 382-383
Military attaché [diplomat]
Attaché **A:** 878
Military band
Band (Military bands) **B:** 74
Military Commissions Act [2006]
Habeas corpus **H:** 2
Terrorism (Counterterrorism measures) **T:** 179-180
Military court
Court-martial **Ci:** 1104
Military discharge **M:** 543
Military draft *See* Draft, Military *in this index*
Military field cipher [cryptology]
Codes and ciphers (History) **Ci:** 751
Military flag
Flag (Military flags) **F:** 195 *with pictures*
Military fold
Flag (Caring for the flag) **F:** 222
Military induction *See* Draft, Military *in this index*
Military insignia [emblem]
Air Force, United States *pictures on* **A:** 189
Army, United States *pictures on* **A:** 732
Insignia **I:** 303
Marine Corps, United States *pictures on* **M:** 207
Navy, United States *pictures on* **N:** 86
Military Justice, Uniform Code of *See* Uniform Code of Military Justice *in this index*
Military law
Martial law **M:** 234a
Military League [organization]
Greece (George I) **G:** 362
Military march
March **M:** 193
Military oath [law]
Oath (Military oaths) **O:** 639
Military occupational specialty
Army, United States (Training a soldier) **A:** 730-731
Military operations other than war
Marine Corps, United States (Recent Marine operations) **M:** 210
Military pension
Pension (Federal pension plans) **P:** 272-273
Military plane *See* Aircraft, Military *in this index*
Military police **M:** 543
Military revolver
Handgun (Types of handguns) **H:** 43 *with picture*
Military rocket
Rocket (Military use) **R:** 386 *with picture*; (Solid-propellant rockets) **R:** 387
Military satellite
Satellite, Artificial (Types of artificial satellites) **S:** 150f-150g *with picture*
Military school **M:** 543
See also the list of Related articles in the Military School *article*
Military training **M:** 544
Military science [warfare] **M:** 544
Military training **M:** 544
Military service, Compulsory *See* Draft, Military

in this index
Military Service Act [1917]
Borden, Sir Robert Laird (Conscription crisis) **B:** 486
Military Staff Committee [United Nations]
United Nations (Meetings and committees) **U:** 82
Military Surface Deployment and Distribution Command
Army, United States (Army service component commands) **A:** 736-737
Military tank *See* Tank *in this index*
Military training **M:** 544
Air Force, United States (Recruit training) **A:** 188; (Officer training) **A:** 190
Army, United States (Training a soldier) **A:** 730 *with pictures*
Marine Corps, United States (Training a Marine) **M:** 206; (Training an officer) **M:** 208
Military school **M:** 543
National Guard **N:** 37
Navy, United States (Life in the Navy) **N:** 83
Reserve Officers Training Corps **R:** 258
Military Tribunal, International [international law]
Nuremberg Trials (The trials) **N:** 613
Military tribune [ancient Rome]
Legion **L:** 183
Tribune **T:** 440
Military unit
Brigade **B:** 608
Corps **Ci:** 1070
Division **D:** 247
Militia [military] **M:** 544
Army **A:** 724; (Armies in the Middle Ages) **A:** 727
Army, United States (The Continental Army) **A:** 737
Draft, Military (Military drafts throughout history) **D:** 318
Lebanon (Political struggle) **L:** 174
Pioneer life in America (Government) **P:** 484
Revolution, American (The beginning of the war) **R:** 274; (The fighting forces) **R:** 278
Second Amendment **S:** 278
Switzerland (Defense) **So:** 1051
Milk [food] **M:** 545 *with pictures*
See also Dairying *in this index and the list of Related articles in the* Milk *article*
Baby (The first month) **B:** 6
Breast **B:** 590
Cattle (Udder) **C:** 308; (Dairy cattle) **C:** 309; (Dual-purpose cattle) **C:** 311
Fallout (The fallout hazard) **F:** 19
Food (Food from animals) **F:** 330
Goat (Products) **G:** 239
Hormone (Agricultural uses) **H:** 337-338
Ice cream **I:** 8
Lactation **L:** 25
Mammal (Care of the young) **M:** 124
Mammary glands **M:** 129
Nutrition (Proteins) **N:** 625
Pasteurization **P:** 193
Sheep (Other types) **S:** 382
Vegetarianism **V:** 294
Yogurt **Y:** 567
Milk, Harvey [American political leader]
San Francisco (Political leaders murdered) **S:** 98
Milk chocolate
Chocolate (Milk chocolate) **C:** 519 *with picture*
Hershey, Milton Snavely **H:** 216
Milk for Babes [book by Cotton]
Cotton, John **Ci:** 1094
Milk glass
Glass (Types of art glass) **G:** 220-221
Milk Maid, The [painting by Vermeer]
Vermeer, Jan **V:** 317
Milk name
Name (The history of names) **N:** 7
Milk of lime
Lime **L:** 307
Milk of magnesia [medication]
Magnesia **M:** 54
Milk snake **M:** 550
Snake *picture on* **S:** 533
Milk sugar *See* Lactose *in this index*
Milk teeth
Teeth (Deciduous teeth) **T:** 79 *with picture*
Milking
Cattle (Udder) **C:** 307-308
Dairying (Milking) **D:** 6 *with picture*
Farm and farming *picture on* **F:** 32
Milking machine **M:** 550
Cattle (Udder) **C:** 308
Dairying (Milking) **D:** 6-7 *with picture*
Farm and farming *picture on* **F:** 32
Milk *picture on* **M:** 545; (At a dairy farm) **M:** 546
Milking parlor [dairying]
Barn **B:** 113
Cattle *picture on* **C:** 307

Dairying (Milking) D: 6-7 *with picture*
Milking Shorthorn [cattle]
Cattle (Other beef cattle) C: 309; (Milking Shorthorn) C: 311 *with picture*
Dairying (Dairy cattle) D: 6
Milko-tester [machine]
Milk (Separation or standardization) M: 548 *with picture*
Milkweed [plant] M: 550
Fruit (Simple fruits) F: 544 *with picture*
Milkweed butterfly
Butterfly *pictures on* B: 735; (Milkweed butterflies) B: 736; (The thorax) B: 738-739 *with picture*
Plant (How plants protect themselves) P: 540
Milkweed floss [botany]
Milkweed M: 551
Milky lactarius [fungus]
Mushroom (Nonpoisonous mushrooms) M: 943-945
Milky Way [astronomy] M: 550 *with picture*
Andromeda Galaxy A: 457
Astronomy (Observing the sky) A: 835
Black hole (Galactic black holes) B: 388; (Supermassive black holes) B: 388
Cosmology (The movement of galaxies) Ci: 1078
Earth (How Earth moves) E: 17
Extraterrestrial intelligence E: 458
Galaxy G: 8
Hubble, Edwin Powell H: 403
Interstellar medium I: 352
Local Group L: 409
Star cluster (Kinds of clusters) So: 853
Triangulum Galaxy T: 439
Mill [tool]
Paint (Grinding) P: 24 *with diagram*
Pioneer life in America (Tools) P: 483
Uranium (Refining and processing uranium ore) U: 215
Mill, Harriet Taylor [British author] M: 552
Mill, James [British author] M: 552
Utilitarianism U: 251
Mill, John Stuart [British philosopher] M: 552
Economics (The classical economists) E: 64
English literature (Early Victorian literature) E: 321
Ethics (Bentham and Mill) E: 367
Mill, Harriet Taylor M: 552
Philosophy (Philosophy in the 1800's) P: 390
Ricardo, David R: 321
Utilitarianism U: 251
Mill, The [painting by Beckmann]
Beckmann, Max *picture on* B: 197
Mill at Wijk, The [painting by Ruisdael]
Painting (The Dutch masters) P: 62-63
Mill City [Minnesota]
Minneapolis (Industrial development) M: 583
Minnesota (Industrial development) M: 604
Mill Ends Park
Oregon (Interesting facts) O: 827 *with picture*
Mill on the Floss, The [book by Eliot]
Eliot, George E: 237
Mill paste [chemical]
Paint (Grinding) P: 24
Mill Springs, Battle of [1862]
Kentucky (The Civil War) K: 293
Millais, Sir John Everett [British painter] M: 552
Carlyle, Thomas *picture on* C: 240
Painting (The Pre-Raphaelite Brotherhood) P: 71 *with picture*
Pizarro, Francisco *picture on* P: 504
Pre-Raphaelite Brotherhood P: 756
Milland, Ray [American actor]
Motion picture (Best performance by an actor: 1945) M: 862a
Millar, Kenneth [American author]
Macdonald, Ross M: 11
Millau Viaduct [France]
Bridge (table: Cable-stayed) B: 603
Millay, Edna St. Vincent [American poet] M: 552
Mille Lacs National Wildlife Refuge [Minnesota]
National Wildlife Refuge System N: 61
Milled soap
Detergent and soap (Bar soaps) D: 164
Milledge, John [American political leader]
Georgia (table) G: 130
Millefiori glass
Glass (Types of art glass) G: 220-221
Millefleurs design
Tapestry (History) T: 39-40 *with picture*
Millennial [demography] *See* Generation Y *in this index*
Millennials Rising [book by Howe and Strauss]
Generation Y G: 84
Millennium [time period] M: 552
Millennium [religion] M: 553
Millennium Assembly
United Nations (Meetings and voting) U: 81

Millennium bug [computing]
Folklore (Legends) F: 324
Millennium Democratic Party [political party]
Korea, South (Recent developments) K: 378d
Millennium Park [Chicago]
Chicago (Downtown Chicago) C: 420-421; (Places to visit) C: 430-431; (New construction) C: 437
Illinois (Places to visit) I: 62
"Millennium" trilogy [books by Larsson]
Detective story (History) D: 162-163
Millepede [animal] *See* Millipede *in this index*
Miller, Agatha Mary Clarissa [British author] *See* Christie, Agatha *in this index*
Miller, Alfred Jacob [American artist]
Indian, American *picture on* I: 165
United States, History of the *picture on* U: 167
Miller, Arthur [American dramatist] M: 553
American literature (Drama) A: 426
Drama (Later United States drama) D: 340
United States *picture on* U: 119
Miller, Benjamin Meek [American political leader]
Alabama (table) A: 274
Miller, Bertha Mahony [American editor]
Regina Medal (table: 1967) R: 206
Miller, Bob [American political leader]
Nevada (table) N: 173
Miller, Bode [American skier] M: 553
Miller, Charles R. [American political leader]
Delaware (table) D: 109
Miller, Dan [Canadian political leader]
British Columbia (table) B: 628
Miller, Delvin [American harness driver]
Harness racing (History) H: 64
Miller, Dorie [American sailor] M: 553 *with portrait*
Miller, Frank [American author]
Graphic novel G: 323
Miller, Frank S. [Canadian political leader]
Ontario (table) O: 783
Miller, G. William [American government official]
Carter, Jimmy (table) C: 257
Miller, Glenn [American musician] M: 553
Miller, Henry [American author] M: 554
Miller, Joaquin [American poet] M: 554
Miller, John [American political leader]
Missouri (table) M: 668
North Dakota (table) N: 513
Miller, Joseph [American astronomer]
Lick Observatory L: 270
Miller, Keith [American political leader]
Alaska (table) A: 300
Miller, Leslie A. [American political leader]
Wyoming (table) W: 532
Miller, Lewis [American businessman]
Chautauqua (The Chautauqua Institution) C: 389
Western frontier life in America (Improvements in farming) W: 233-234
Miller, Merton Howard [American economist]
Nobel Prizes (Economics: 1990) N: 449
Miller, Mina [wife of]
Edison, Thomas Alva (Family and friends) E: 81
Miller, Phineas [American businessman]
Whitney, Eli (The cotton gin) W: 295
Miller, Portia Simpson [Jamaican political leader]
Jamaica (History) J: 24-25
Miller, Samuel Freeman [American jurist] M: 554
Miller, Stanley L. [American chemist]
Life (Creating simple organic compounds) L: 279
Miller, Stephen [American political leader]
Minnesota (table) M: 602
Miller, Walter Dale [American political leader]
South Dakota (table) So: 680
Miller, William [American political leader]
North Carolina (table) N: 490
Miller, William [American religious leader]
Adventists A: 70
Miller, William Edward [American political leader] M: 554
Goldwater, Barry Morris G: 259
Johnson, Lyndon Baines (Full-term president) J: 149-150
Miller, William H. H. [American government official]
Justice, Department of (table) J: 203
Miller, William R. [American political leader]
Arkansas (table) A: 712
Miller, Zell Bryan [American political leader]
Georgia (table) G: 130
Miller-Tydings Act [1937]
Fair-trade laws F: 8
Miller v. California [U.S. history]
Obscenity and pornography (Legal history for obscenity) O: 644
Supreme Court of the United States (table) So: 1002
Millerites [religious group]
Adventists A: 70
Eggleston, Edward E: 118

Milles, Carl [Swedish-American sculptor] M: 554
Millesgården [park, Stockholm]
Milles, Carl M: 554
Millet [plant] M: 554 *with picture*
Grain G: 301
Millet [political group]
Ottoman Empire (People) O: 877
Millet, Jean François [French painter] M: 555
Barbizon School B: 108
Markham, Edwin M: 214
Millhone, Kinsey [literary character]
Grafton, Sue G: 299
Milli [prefix]
Metric system (Use of standard prefixes) M: 437; (Metric prefixes) M: 439
Milli Majlis [parliament]
Azerbaijan (Government) A: 996
Millibar [measurement]
Barometer B: 115
Isobar I: 474 *with map*
Milligan, Ex parte [U.S. history] *See* Ex parte Milligan *in this index*
Milligan, Keith [Canadian political leader]
Prince Edward Island (table) P: 791; (The late 1900's) P: 793
Milligan, Lambdin [American public figure]
Ex parte Milligan E: 435
Millikan, Robert Andrews [American physicist] M: 555
Electron E: 203
Physics (Uncovering the secrets of the atom) P: 442
Milliken, Carl E. [American political leader]
Maine (table) M: 87
Milliken, William G. [American political leader]
Michigan (table) M: 507
Millimeter [measurement]
Metric system (Kinds of metric units) M: 436; (The metric system at a glance) M: 438 *with picture*
Millimeter of mercury [measurement]
Metric system (Non-SI metric units) M: 440
Milling [food processing]
Bran B: 562
Bread (History) B: 589
Flour (How white flour is milled) F: 269 *with diagram*
Rice (Food) R: 323; (Removing the bran layers) R: 326
Milling [industrial process]
Copper (How copper metal is produced) Ci: 1041 *with diagrams*; (Milling) Ci: 1042
Gold *diagram on* G: 250; (Exposing the gold) G: 253
Leather *picture on* L: 168
Machine tool (Milling) M: 18 *with picture*
Million Acre Farm [nickname]
Prince Edward Island P: 783
Million Dollar Baby [film]
Motion picture (Best picture: 2004) M: 861
Million Man March [U.S. history]
African Americans (Politics) A: 136s
Farrakhan, Louis F: 48
Millions More Movement [U.S. history]
Farrakhan, Louis F: 48
Millipede [animal] M: 555 *with picture*
Arthropod A: 752 *with picture*
Millisecond pulsar [astronomy]
Pulsar P: 900a
Millisecond radio pulsar [astronomy]
Neutron star N: 155
Mills, Enos [American naturalist]
Rocky Mountain National Park R: 394
Mills, Heather [wife of]
McCartney, Paul M: 332c
Mills, John [British actor]
Motion picture (Best performance by an actor in a supporting role: 1970) M: 862b
Mills, John Atta [Ghanaian political leader]
Ghana (History) G: 179-180
Mills, Ogden L. [American government official]
Hoover, Herbert Clark (table) H: 330
Mills, Robert [American architect] M: 555
Baltimore (Other interesting places to visit) B: 69
Washington Monument W: 110
Mills of the Kavanaughs, The [book by Lowell]
Lowell, Robert L: 511
Millwork [building material]
Lumber (table) L: 518
Milne, A. A. [British author] M: 556
Literature for children *picture on* L: 363; (Poetry) L: 357
Milne, David Brown [Canadian painter] M: 556 *with picture*
Milnes, Sherrill [American singer] M: 556
Milo [plant]
Sorghum (Grain sorghums) So: 596
Milo of Kroton [Greek wrestler]

Olympic Games (The ancient games) O: 750
Milos [island, Greece] M: 556
  Venus de Milo V: 314
Milošević, Slobodan [Serbian political leader]
  M: 556
  Balkans (Recent developments) B: 42
  Croatia (History) Ci: 1148b
  Serbia (History) S: 314-316
  War crime (The United Nations and war crimes)
    W: 27
  Yugoslavia (The breakup of Yugoslavia) Y: 577;
    (The end of Yugoslavia) Y: 577
Miłosz, Czesław [Polish author]
  Nobel Prizes (Literature: 1980) N: 448
Milstein, César [Argentine physiologist]
  Immune system (Further breakthroughs) I: 88d
  Nobel Prizes (Physiology or medicine: 1984)
    N: 446
Milstein, Nathan [American violinist] M: 557
Milt [zoology]
  Fish (Reproductive system) F: 163
Miltiades [Greek general] M: 557
  Marathon, Battle of (The battle) M: 191
Miltiades, Saint [pope]
  Pope (table) P: 666
Milton, Elizabeth Minshull [wife of]
  Milton, John (Retirement) M: 557
Milton, John [American political leader]
  Florida (table) F: 260
Milton, John [English poet] M: 556
  Angel A: 459
  Doré, Gustave D: 310
  English literature (John Milton) E: 318
  Essay (Formal essays) E: 359
  Figure of speech F: 97
  Freedom of the press (History) F: 508
  Journalism (The first newspapers) J: 174
Milton, Katherine Woodcock [wife of]
  Milton, John (Middle years) M: 557
Milton, Mary Powell [wife of]
  Milton, John (Middle years) M: 557
Milton, Tommy [American race driver]
  Automobile racing (table: Indianapolis 500
    winners) A: 980
Milton Hershey School
  Hershey, Milton Snavely H: 216
Milvian Bridge [Italy]
  Constantine the Great Ci: 993
Milwaukee [Wisconsin] M: 558 with pictures and
  map
  Wisconsin (table: Average monthly weather)
    W: 360
Milwaukee Art Museum
  Milwaukee (Museums) M: 560 with picture
  Wisconsin picture on W: 347
Milwaukee Avenue
  Chicago (The North Side) C: 424
Milwaukee Brewers [team]
  Baseball (table) B: 130
Milwaukee Bucks [team]
  Basketball (table) B: 150
Milwaukee County Zoo [Wisconsin]
  Zoo picture on Z: 600
Milwaukee Public Museum
  Wisconsin (Museums) W: 351
Milwaukee River [river, Wisconsin]
  Milwaukee picture on M: 558
Mimas [satellite]
  Satellite (Mimas) S: 150c
  Saturn (Rings) S: 150j; (Satellites) S: 151-152
Mime [drama]
  Drama (Minor forms) D: 328
Mimetic criticism
  Criticism (Kinds of literary criticism) Ci: 1146
Mimi [opera character]
  Opera picture on O: 802; (Bohème, La) O: 801
Mimic-queen [butterfly]
  Butterfly picture on B: 735
Mimicry [humor]
  Humor (The types of humor) H: 435-436
Mimicry [zoology] M: 561
  Animal (Camouflage) A: 493-496 with pictures
  Bird (Calls and songs) B: 354
  Fish (Shape) F: 160
  Insect (Protection from enemies) I: 297 with
    picture
  Leaf insect L: 158 with picture
  Protective coloration P: 831
  Walkingstick W: 14
Mimosa [tree] M: 562 with picture
  See also Acacia in this index
Min [dialect]
  Chinese language (Spoken Chinese) C: 510
Minamoto [Japanese clan]
  Japan (Rise of the shogun) J: 54 with picture
  Shogun S: 433
  World, History of the (The rise of Japanese

civilization) W: 435-436 with picture
Minamoto Yoritomo [Japanese political leader]
  M: 562
  Japan (Rise of the shogun) J: 54
  Samurai S: 82
  Shogun S: 433
Minangkabau [people]
  Sumatra So: 971
Minaret [architecture] M: 562 with picture
  Cairo (The city) C: 16 with picture
  Islam (The Five Pillars of Islam) I: 463
  Islamic art picture on I: 467; (Mosques) I: 468
  Mosque M: 831
Minas Basin
  Bay of Fundy B: 175
  Nova Scotia (Land regions) N: 562 with map
Minbar [religion]
  Islam picture on I: 465
  Mosque M: 831 with picture
Mind [psychology] M: 562
  See also the list of Related articles in the Mind
    article
  Anaxagoras A: 448b
  Locke, John (His philosophy) L: 413
  Metaphysics (Mind and body) M: 430
Mind/body problem [philosophy]
  Mind (The mind/body problem) M: 563
Mind reading
  Clairvoyance Ci: 636
  Extrasensory perception E: 457
  Telepathy T: 93
Mind That Found Itself, A [book by Beers]
  Beers, Clifford Whittingham B: 212
Mindanao [island, Philippines]
  Philippines (The main islands) P: 376 with map
Mindaugas [Lithuanian ruler]
  Lithuania (History) L: 389
Mindel ice age [geology]
  Ice age (Evidence of ice ages and their climates)
    I: 6-7
Mindelo [Cape Verde]
  Cape Verde picture on C: 191
Mindoro [island, Philippines]
  Philippines (The main islands) P: 376 with map
Mindszenty, József [Hungarian religious leader]
  M: 563
  Hungary (Unsuccessful revolution) H: 447
Mine [explosive device]
  Mine warfare M: 563 with pictures
Mine [place] See Mining; Open-pit mine in this
  index
Mine detector
  Mine warfare (Detecting land mines) M: 564
Mine safety [industry]
  Coal (Mine safety) Ci: 729 with picture
  Damp D: 22
  Helmet picture on H: 178
  Safety (In mines) S: 14
  Safety lamp S: 16
Mine warfare M: 563 with pictures
  Navy (Wartime roles) N: 77
  Navy, United States (World War I [1914-1918])
    N: 88
Mine Workers of America, United See United
  Mine Workers of America in this index
Minefield [pattern]
  Mine warfare (Land mines) M: 564
Minehunter [ship]
  Mine warfare (Detecting naval mines) M: 565
Minelayer [ship]
  Mine warfare (Naval mines) M: 565
Miner [occupation]
  See also Mining in this index
  Coal Ci: 716, picture on Ci: 731; (Surface mining)
    Ci: 721-722; (Mineworkers) Ci: 728 with
    pictures
Miner, Jack [Canadian conservationist] M: 565
Miner, John Thomas
  Miner, Jack M: 565
Mineral [geology] M: 566 with pictures
  See also the list of Related articles in the Mineral
    article
  Berzelius, Jöns Jakob B: 273
  Coal (The composition of coal) Ci: 717
  Conservation (Mineral conservation) Ci: 982
  Drug (Minerals) D: 355
  Earth (The lithosphere) E: 20
  Gem G: 77; (Sources of gems) G: 77
  Hardness H: 59
  Mining M: 574
  Natural resources (Uses and importance) N: 64
  Ocean (Sediments) O: 654
  Prospecting P: 829
  Soil (Minerals) So: 573
Mineral [nutrition]
  Dietary supplement D: 200
  Food (Regulating body processes) F: 331

Food additive (Kinds of additives) F: 339
  Milk (Minerals) M: 546
  Nutrition (Kinds of nutrients) N: 625; (Deficiency
    diseases) N: 630-631
Mineral block
  Rabbit (Food) R: 48-49
Mineral conservation
  Conservation (Mineral conservation) Ci: 982
Mineral deficiency [disorder]
  Malnutrition M: 111
  Nutrition (Deficiency diseases) N: 630-631
Mineral deposit [geology]
  Mining (Mineral deposits) M: 574
Mineral dressing [industrial process]
  Metallurgy (Mineral dressing) M: 426
Mineral oil M: 572
  Laxative L: 147
Mineral spring [geology]
  Mineral water M: 572
  Spring So: 806
Mineral tanning [industrial process]
  Leather (Tanning) L: 167
Mineral water M: 572
Mineral well
  Well (Water wells) W: 193
Mineralization [process]
  Water pollution (Disruption of natural processes)
    W: 138
Mineralocorticoid [hormone]
  Adrenal gland A: 67
  Hormone (Blood composition hormones) H: 336
Mineralogy
  Mineral M: 566
Miner's lamp
  Helmet picture on H: 178
Minerva [Roman mythology] M: 572
  See also Athena in this index
  Mythology (table) M: 981; (Roman divinities)
    M: 982-983
  Venus V: 310
Minerva Club [organization]
  New Harmony N: 229
Minerva Park
  Guatemala City G: 418
Minerva Terrace
  Yellowstone National Park (The Upper Loop)
    Y: 559 with picture
Minesweeper [ship]
  Mine warfare (Detecting naval mines) M: 565
  Warship picture on W: 43; (Small combatants)
    W: 41
Mineta, Norman Yoshio [American political leader]
  M: 572
  Asian Americans (World War II and Japanese
    Americans) A: 812f
  Bush, George Walker (table) B: 722h
  Transportation, Department of (table) T: 400
Ming dynasty [Chinese history] M: 572
  Asia (Nomadic invasions) A: 805-806
  Beijing (History) B: 223-224
  China picture on C: 489; (The Ming dynasty)
    C: 502
  Great Wall of China (History) G: 350
  Korea, History of (Early years) K: 366
  Nanjing (History) N: 10
  Porcelain picture on P: 675; (Oriental porcelain)
    P: 676
  Zheng He Z: 591
Ming Huang [emperor of China]
  Tang dynasty (The middle years) T: 26
Mingan Archipelago National Park [Quebec]
  Canada (table: National parks and national park
    reserves) C: 113
Minghella, Anthony [British director]
  Motion picture (Best achievement in directing:
    1996) M: 862
Mingus, Charles [American musician] M: 573
Mini mill
  Iron and steel (The steel industry) I: 447-448
Mini stereo system
  Stereophonic sound system (Types of systems)
    So: 891-892
Miniature [art]
  Byzantine art (Other art forms) B: 751
  France picture on F: 463
  Illuminated manuscript I: 78
  Manuscript (Illustrated manuscripts) M: 174
Miniature bull terrier [dog] M: 573
Miniature pinscher M: 573
  Dog picture on D: 274
Miniature poodle [dog]
  Poodle P: 658
Miniature rose [plant]
  Rose (table) R: 474; (Types of roses) R: 474-475
Miniature schnauzer [dog] M: 573
  Dog picture on D: 273
Minibike

Motorcycle (Kinds of motorcycles) **M:** 878
Minicomputer
Computer (Mainframes and supercomputers)
Ci: 910
Minicycle
Motorcycle (Kinds of motorcycles) **M:** 878
Minidisc [recording medium]
Compact disc (Other formats) **Ci:** 902-902a
Recording industry (History) **R:** 182
Minidoka National Historic Site [Idaho]
National Park System (table: National historic
sites) **N:** 52-53
Minié bullet
Rifle (History) **R:** 339-340
Minifundio [property]
South America (Agriculture) **So:** 634
Minimalism [arts] **M:** 573
Carver, Raymond **C:** 269
Classical music (Minimalism) **Ci:** 651
Glass, Philip **G:** 224
Newman, Barnett **N:** 378
Opera (American opera) **O:** 800
Painting (Minimalism) **P:** 87
Sculpture (Varieties of abstraction) **S:** 258; (From
the mid-1900's to the early 2000's) **S:** 259-260
Serra, Richard **S:** 318
Stella, Frank **So:** 886 *with picture*
Minimata disease [mercury poisoning]
Mercury (Mercury in the environment) **M:** 413
Minimum competency [education]
Literacy (Illiteracy in the United States) **L:** 351-
352
Minimum dialect
Pidgin English **P:** 452
Minimum security prison
Prison (Minimum security prisons) **P:** 806
Minimum tillage [agriculture] *See* Conservation
tillage *in this index*
Minimum wage M: 573
Fair Labor Standards Act **F:** 8
Poverty (Measures to improve job opportunities)
P: 724
Minimumweight class [boxing]
Boxing (table) **B:** 527
Mining [industry] **M:** 574 *with pictures*
See also Mine safety *in this index*
Africa (Mining) **A:** 127 *with picture*
Australia (Mining) **A:** 915-916 *with picture*
Careers (Production) **C:** 229
Chile (Recent developments) **C:** 470
Coal **Ci:** 716; (Where coal is found) **Ci:** 721;
(Surface mining) **Ci:** 721 *with picture*
Conservation (Mineral conservation) **Ci:** 982
Copper (Sources of copper) **Ci:** 1042
Gas [fuel] (Producing gas) **G:** 55
Gold (Mining) **G:** 252
Gold rush (Gold rushes in the United States)
G: 254 *with picture*
Iron and steel (Mining and processing iron ore)
I: 438
Law of the Sea Convention **L:** 141
Louisiana *picture on* **L:** 495
Ocean (Sediments) **O:** 654
Quarrying **Q:** 7
Rome, Ancient (Mining) **R:** 443
Russia *picture on* **R:** 543
Safety (In mines) **S:** 14
Salt (Salt from the ground) **S:** 73-74 *with picture*;
(History of salt) **S:** 74-75 *with picture*
South Africa (Mining) **So:** 616 *with picture*
Uranium (Mining uranium) **U:** 215
Well **W:** 193
West Virginia (History) **W:** 226 *with picture*
Western frontier life in America (The shifting
frontier) **W:** 232; (Mining) **W:** 234 *with picture*
Westward movement in America (California)
W: 249 *with picture*
Mining bee
Bee (Solitary bees) **B:** 205-206 *with picture*
Mining engineering
Engineering (Other specialized fields) **E:** 287
Mining geologist
Geology (Areas of specialization) **G:** 100-101
Minion [ship]
Drake, Sir Francis (Early life) **D:** 321
Miniseries
Television (The 1970's) **T:** 119-120
Minister [diplomat] **M:** 578
Foreign Service (Beginnings) **F:** 388-388a
Government (Parliamentary democracy) **G:** 286
Minister [government official]
Minister **M:** 578
Parliament **P:** 172
Prime minister **P:** 778c
Prime minister of Canada (Roles of the prime
minister) **P:** 778c-778d
United Kingdom (National government) **U:** 49

Minister [religion] **M:** 578
Address, Forms of (Members of the clergy) **A:** 54
Minister-counselor [diplomat]
Diplomacy (Diplomatic representatives) **D:** 216
Minister of ...
Ministers appear under their key words, as in
Foreign affairs, Minister of
Minister plenipotentiary [diplomat]
Diplomacy (Diplomatic representatives) **D:** 216
Minister president [office]
Germany (State government) **G:** 147
Minister resident [diplomat]
Diplomacy (Diplomatic representatives) **D:** 216
Ministers, Council of
See also European Union, Council of the *in this*
index
Hungary (National government) **H:** 439
Russia (National government) **R:** 531
Union of Soviet Socialist Republics (National
government) **U:** 29
"Minister's Black Veil, The" [story by Hawthorne]
Hawthorne, Nathaniel (His stories and sketches)
H: 115
Minister's Wooing, The [book by Stowe]
Stowe, Harriet Beecher (Other works) **So:** 916
Ministry [government] **M:** 578
Ministry of Internal Affairs
Police (In other countries) **P:** 623
Minivan [vehicle]
Automobile *picture on* **A:** 971; (Challenges to the
Big Three) **A:** 972
Transportation *picture on* **T:** 391
"Miniver Cheevy" [poem by Robinson]
Robinson, Edwin Arlington **R:** 368
Mink [animal] **M:** 579 *with picture*
Fur *picture on* **F:** 562; (table) **F:** 561
Mink, Patsy K. [American political leader]
Asian Americans (Notable Asian American "firsts")
A: 812f
Mink ranch
Mink **M:** 579
Minke whale M: 579 *with picture*
Whale (Rorquals) **W:** 255-258 *with picture*
Minkowski, Hermann [German mathematician]
Fourth dimension **F:** 438
Minkowski, Oskar [German physician]
Insulin (History) **I:** 308
Minna von Barnhelm [play by Lessing]
Lessing, Gotthold Ephraim **L:** 209
Minneapolis [Minnesota] **M:** 580 *with pictures*
and maps
Architecture *picture on* **A:** 606
Minnesota **M:** 584; (Population) **M:** 588; (table:
Average monthly weather) **M:** 598
Minneapolis Institute of Arts [Minneapolis]
Minneapolis (Museums) **M:** 582
Minnehaha [literary figure]
Longfellow, Henry Wadsworth (Narrative poems)
L: 450
Minnehaha Falls [Minnesota] **M:** 583
Minneapolis (Parks) **M:** 582
Minnesota *picture on* **M:** 593; (Lakes, rivers, and
waterfalls) **M:** 598
Minnehaha Park
Minneapolis (Parks) **M:** 582
Minnelli, Liza [American actress]
Garland, Judy **G:** 44
Motion picture (Best performance by an actress:
1972) **M:** 862
Minnelli, Vincente [American director]
Motion picture (Best achievement in directing:
1958) **M:** 862
Minner, Ruth Ann [American political leader]
Delaware (table) **D:** 109; (The early 2000's) **D:** 113
Minnesinger [German history] **M:** 583
Classical music (Secular music) **Ci:** 646
German literature (Minnesingers) **G:** 138
Minstrel **M:** 611 *with picture*
Walther von der Vogelweide **W:** 21
Minnesota M: 584 *with pictures and maps*
See also the list of Related articles in the Minnesota
article
Minnesota, University of M: 607
Minnesota (Libraries) **M:** 589 *with picture*
Minnesota Discovery Center [Minnesota]
Minnesota (Places to visit) **M:** 594
Minnesota Pioneer [newspaper]
Minnesota (Communication) **M:** 601
Minnesota Point [sandbar]
Duluth **D:** 381
Minnesota River [Minnesota-South Dakota]
M: 607
Minnesota Timberwolves [team]
Basketball (table) **B:** 150
Minnesota Twins [team]
Baseball (table) **B:** 130
Minnesota *picture on* **M:** 588

Minnesota Vikings [team]
Football (National Football League) **F:** 364
Minnesota Wild [team]
Hockey (table: National Hockey League) **H:** 281
Minnesota Zoo
Minnesota (Places to visit) **M:** 594 *with picture*
Minnow [fish] **M:** 607 *with picture*
Minoan culture [ancient Greece]
Aegean civilization **A:** 82 *with picture*
Architecture (Minoan architecture) **A:** 615 *with*
picture
Atlantis **A:** 868
Clothing (Crete) **Ci:** 696 *with pictures*
Crete (History) **Ci:** 1128
Galley **G:** 15
Greece, Ancient (History) **G:** 372 *with picture*
Painting (Aegean painting) **P:** 41
Sculpture (Aegean) **S:** 234 *with picture*
Ship (Minoan and Mycenaean ships) **S:** 415
World, History of the (The Greeks) **W:** 428
Minolta Company
Planetarium (Modern planetariums)
P: 514b-514c
Minor [law] **M:** 607
Incompetence (Incompetence) **I:** 105
Minor [mathematics]
Determinant (Using higher order determinants)
D: 166-167
Minor, William T. [American political leader]
Connecticut (table) **Ci:** 967
Minor arts
Decorative arts **D:** 80
Minor axis [geometry]
Ellipse **E:** 243 *with diagram*
Minor interval [music]
Music (Harmony) **M:** 951
Minor leagues
Baseball (Minor leagues) **B:** 130
Hockey (Professional leagues) **H:** 278
Minor planet *See* Asteroid *in this index*
Minor scale
Music (Tone) **M:** 950 *with diagram*
Minor tone
Tone **T:** 327
Minorca [bird]
Chicken (Mediterranean class chickens) **C:** 441;
(table) **C:** 443
Minorca [island, Mediterranean] **M:** 608 *with*
picture
Minority group [sociology] **M:** 608
See also the list of Related articles in the Minority
group *article*
Affirmative action **A:** 91
Assimilation **A:** 818
Census (Controversy over census results) **C:** 349
Civil rights (Protecting the rights of minorities)
Ci: 609
Culture (Culture and society) **Ci:** 1188
Democracy (Majority rule and minority rights)
D: 120
Ghetto **G:** 181
National Medical Association **N:** 40
Poverty (Social factors) **P:** 723
Prejudice **P:** 754b
Riot (Causes of riots) **R:** 348
Segregation **S:** 285
United States, History of the (The civil rights
movement) **U:** 196a
Minority leader [government]
Congress of the United States (How Congress is
organized) **Ci:** 942
Minos [Greek mythology] **M:** 611
Aegean civilization (The Minoan culture) **A:** 83
Daedalus **D:** 3
Hades **H:** 4
Hercules (The twelve labors) **H:** 198-199
Labyrinth **L:** 19
Minos, Palace of [Crete]
Aegean civilization *picture on* **A:** 82
Architecture (Minoan architecture) **A:** 615 *with*
picture
Crete *picture on* **Ci:** 1128
Evans, Sir Arthur John **E:** 422
World, History of the (The Greeks) **W:** 428
Minot, George Richards [American doctor]
Nobel Prizes (Physiology or medicine: 1934)
N: 445
Minotaur [Greek mythology] **M:** 611 *with picture*
Daedalus **D:** 3
Labyrinth **L:** 19
Minoxidil [drug]
Baldness **B:** 39
Minshull, Elizabeth [wife of]
Milton, John (Retirement) **M:** 557
Minsi, Mount [Pennsylvania]
Delaware Water Gap **D:** 114
Minsk [Belarus] **M:** 611

Belarus **B: 224a** *with picture*
Minsky, Billy [American showman]
Burlesque **B: 707**
Minstrel [European history] **M: 611** *with picture*
Ballad **B: 43**
Minstrel show [U.S. history] **M: 611** *with picture*
Foster, Stephen Collins **F: 428**
Popular music (1840's to the Civil War) **P: 669**
Minstrelsy of the Scottish Border [book by Scott]
Scott, Sir Walter (His life) **S: 222**
Mint [money] **M: 612**
See also United States Mint *in this index*
Assaying (Wet assaying) **A: 817**
Coin collecting (Collecting United States coins)
Ci: 757
Money (Modern coins) **M: 707**; (Money in the
new United States) **M: 712**; (How money is
manufactured) **M: 714**
Pennsylvania *picture on* **P: 245**
Mint [plant] **M: 612** *with picture*
Mint mark [symbol]
Coin collecting (Collecting United States coins)
Ci: 757
Minthorn, Henry J. [uncle of]
Hoover, Herbert Clark (Education) **H: 326**
Minto, Earl of [British statesman] **M: 612**
Minton, Sherman [American jurist]
Supreme Court of the United States (table)
So: 1000
Minuend [mathematics]
Subtraction (Subtraction terms) **So: 944**
Minuet [dance] **M: 613**
Minuit, Peter [Dutch colonial leader] **M: 613**
Manhattan Island **M: 141**
New York *picture on* **N: 317**; (Exploration and
settlement) **N: 314**
Minus sign [arithmetic]
Subtraction (Writing subtraction) **So: 944**
Minuscule [writing]
Alphabet (Small letters) **A: 383**
Minute [geography]
Inertial guidance **I: 263**
Latitude **L: 117**
Minute [religion]
Quakers (Worship) **Q: 5**
Minute [time] **M: 613**
Minute Man, The [sculpture by French]
French, Daniel Chester **F: 511**
Minute Man National Historical Park
[Massachusetts]
Massachusetts *picture on* **M: 279**; (Places to visit)
M: 280
National Park System (table: National historical
parks) **N: 56-57**
Minuteman [weapon]
Air Force, United States (Missiles) **A: 191**
Guided missile *picture on* **G: 423**
Minuteman Missile National Historic Site [South
Dakota]
National Park System (table: National historic
sites) **N: 52-53**
Minutemen [U.S. history] **M: 613**
Flag *picture on* **F: 209**
Revolution, American (Lexington and Concord)
R: 274-275
Minutes
Parliamentary procedure (Minutes) **P: 176**
Minyan [religion]
Judaism (Worship) **J: 181**
Miocene Epoch [geology]
Earth (The Cenozoic Era) **E: 28-29**; (table) **E: 30**
Prehistoric animal (table) **P: 740** *with picture*
Snake (The evolution of snakes) **S: 534-535**
Miohippus [extinct animal]
Horse (Origins of the horse) **H: 360**
Miquelon [island, Atlantic] *See* Saint-Pierre and
Miquelon *in this index*
Mir [space station] **M: 613** *with picture*
Astronaut (Achievements in space) **A: 829-830**
International Space Station (History) **I: 346b**
Lucid, Shannon Wells **L: 514**
Space exploration *picture on* **So: 704**; (Mir)
So: 722 *with picture*; (Docking with Mir) **So: 725**
Mir 2 [proposed space station]
International Space Station (History) **I: 346b**
Mirabeau, Comte de [French political leader]
M: 614
Franklin, Benjamin **F: 487**
Lafayette, Marquis de (The revolution at home)
L: 28
Marie Antoinette (The revolution) **M: 200**
Miracle [religion] **M: 615**
Faith healing **F: 12**
Jesus Christ (The miracles) **J: 107** *with picture*
Saint **S: 29**
Miracle, The [play by Reinhardt]
Reinhardt, Max **R: 209**

Miracle play [European history] **M: 615**
Drama (Miracle plays and morality plays) **D: 329**
English literature (Early English drama) **E: 316**
French literature (Early drama) **F: 519**
Miracle Worker, The [film]
Keller, Helen (She helps others) **K: 255**
Sullivan, Anne Mansfield **So: 969**
Mirador Nacional [mountain, Uruguay]
Uruguay (The interior lowlands) **U: 225-226**
Miraflores Lake [Panama]
Panama Canal (The Pedro Miguel and Miraflores
locks) **P: 124**
Miraflores Locks [Panama]
Panama Canal *map on* **P: 123**; (The Pedro Miguel
and Miraflores locks) **P: 124** *with diagram*
Miraflores Palace
Caracas (The city) **C: 201**
Mirage [airplane]
Aircraft, Military (Fighters) **A: 203** *with picture*
Mirage [illusion] **M: 615** *with pictures*
Miramachi [New Brunswick]
New Brunswick (table: Average monthly weather)
N: 193
Miramax Films [company]
Walt Disney Company **W: 21**
Miramichi River [New Brunswick] **M: 615**
Miranda [literary figure]
Shakespeare, William: (*The Tempest*) **S: 365**
Miranda [satellite]
Satellite (The middle-sized icy satellites of Saturn
and Uranus) **S: 150b**
Uranus (Satellites) **U: 218** *with picture*
Miranda, Ernesto A. [American public figure]
Miranda v. Arizona **M: 616**
Miranda, Francisco de [Venezuelan patriot]
M: 616
Latin America (The movement toward
independence) **L: 106-107**
Miranda v. Arizona [U.S. history] **M: 616**
Confession **C: 936**
Criminal justice system (The police) **Ci: 1143**
Supreme Court of the United States (Criminal
law) **So: 1001**; (table) **So: 1002**
Mirèio [poem by Mistral]
Mistral, Frédéric **M: 676**
Miró, Gabriel [Spanish author]
Spanish literature (The Generation of 1898)
So: 762
Miró, Joan [Spanish painter] **M: 616**
Painting (Surrealism) **P: 81** *with picture*
Miron, Gaston [Canadian poet]
Canadian literature (Modern Canadian poets)
C: 161
Mirren, Helen [British actress]
Motion picture (Best performance by an actress:
2006) **M: 862a**
Mirrlees, James Alexander [British economist]
Nobel Prizes (Economics: 1996) **N: 449**
Mirror **M: 616** *with diagrams*
Aberration **A: 10**
Heliograph **H: 174**
Solar energy (Solar heating) **So: 579**
Southern African Large Telescope **So: 687**
Telescope *pictures on* **T: 108**, **T: 109**; (Optical
telescopes) **T: 103**
Mirror for Magistrates, A [biography]
Biography (The Renaissance) **B: 313**
Mirror of the World, The [book]
Encyclopedia (From the 1200's to the 1600's)
E: 268a
Mirror Shadow VIII [sculpture by Nevelson]
Sculpture (Assemblages) **S: 257-258** *with picture*
Mirrors [music by Ravel]
Ravel, Maurice **R: 150**
MIRV [warhead] *See* Multiple Independently
Targetable Reentry Vehicle *in this index*
Misas de Gallo [masses]
Christmas (In Asia) **C: 533**
Miscarriage **M: 617**
Abortion **A: 14**
DES **D: 153**
Infertility **I: 265**
Pregnancy (Miscarriage) **P: 735**
Mischief Night [custom]
Halloween (Mischief Night) **H: 24b**
Mischling [German history]
Holocaust (Before the Holocaust) **H: 296**
Misconduct penalty [hockey]
Hockey (Violations and penalties) **H: 278** *with
picture*
Misdemeanor [law] **M: 617**
Crime (Felonies and misdemeanors) **Ci: 1136**
Felony **F: 69**
Fine **F: 104**
Prison (Medium security prisons) **P: 806**
Misérables, Les [book by Hugo]
Hugo, Victor (His works) **H: 410**

Miserere [prints by Rouault]
Rouault, Georges **R: 490**
Miseries and Misfortunes of War, The [etchings
by Callot]
Callot, Jacques **C: 69**
Mishima, Yukio [Japanese author]
Japanese literature (The modern period) **J: 62**
Mishnah [Jewish law]
Akiva ben Joseph **A: 254**
Galilee **G: 11**
Hebrew literature (Early works) **H: 162**
Jews (The Talmudic period) **J: 122**
Judaism (The Talmud) **J: 180**
Maimonides, Moses **M: 67**
Rabbi **R: 46**
Talmud **T: 21**
Miskito Indians
Honduras (Ancestry) **H: 309**
Miskolc [Hungary] **M: 618**
Miss Julie [play by Strindberg]
Strindberg, August **So: 929**
Miss Lonelyhearts [book by West]
West, Nathanael **W: 198**
Missa brevis [music by Kodály]
Kodály, Zoltán **K: 360**
Missa Pro Defunctis [music by Thomson]
Thomson, Virgil **T: 266**
Missa solemnis [music by Beethoven]
Beethoven, Ludwig van (The third period) **B: 214**
Missence mutation [genetics]
Heredity (Mutation) **H: 203**
Missile, Guided *See* Guided missile *in this index*
Missile boat **M: 618** *with diagram*
Warship *picture on* **W: 43**; (Small combatants)
W: 41
Missile gap [world history]
Cold War (The missile gap) **Ci: 767**
Missing in action
Unknown soldier **U: 212**
Missing link [biology]
Dubois, Eugène **D: 372**
Mission
United Nations (Delegations) **U: 86**
Mission, Congregation of the [religious order]
Vincent de Paul, Saint **V: 386**
Mission ...
*Missions appear under their key words, as in San
José, Mission*
Mission control
Space exploration (Communicating with Earth)
So: 704 *with picture*
Mission Control Center
Johnson Space Center **J: 154**
Mission Exchange [organization]
Missionary (Organization) **M: 621**
Mission Indians [U.S. history]
Indian, American (After European contact) **I: 164**
Mission life in America **M: 618** *with pictures*
Hispanic Americans *picture on* **H: 247**; (In Mexico)
H: 248; (In the Southwest) **H: 251**
Indian, American (After European contact) **I: 164**
Los Angeles (Spanish missions) **L: 468** *with
picture*
Mission Mountains
Montana (Land regions) **M: 752**
Mission specialist
Astronaut **A: 828**; (Selecting the NASA
astronauts) **A: 831**
Space exploration (The shuttle era begins)
So: 723
Missionaries of Charity [religious group]
Teresa, Mother **T: 169**
Missionary [religion] **M: 620**
*See also the list of Related articles in the Missionary
article*
Africa (Education) **A: 114** *with picture*
Baptists (Early history) **B: 101**
Judson, Adoniram **J: 185**
Pacific Islands (Missionaries, traders, and settlers)
P: 12
Roman Catholic Church (The nature of the
church) **R: 403**
Treaty (Ecclesiastical treaties) **T: 409**
Women's movement (The beginnings of women's
movements) **W: 384-385**
Missionary Ridge, Battle of [1863]
Civil War, American (Battle of Chattanooga)
Ci: 630
Missionary Ridge Fire
Colorado (The early 2000's) **Ci: 847-848**
Missionary Sisters of the Sacred Heart [religious
group]
Cabrini, Saint Frances Xavier **C: 9**
Mississauga [Ontario] **M: 621**
Mississauga Indians
Indian, American *picture on* **I: 156**
Mississippi **M: 622** *with pictures and maps*

See also the list of Related articles in the Mississippi *article*
Mississippi, University of M: 646 *with picture*
Mississippi Alluvial Plain [region, U.S.]
Louisiana (Land regions) L: 490
Mississippi (Land regions) M: 634 *with picture*
Missouri (Land regions) M: 662
Mississippi Bubble [U.S. history]
Mississippi Scheme M: 649
Mississippi Company [U.S. history]
Mississippi Scheme M: 649
Mississippi Delta [geography]
Louisiana *picture on* L: 492
Mississippi Emergency Relief Fund
National Association for the Advancement of
Colored People (Activities) N: 29
Mississippi Flyway [route]
Bird (Where birds migrate) B: 360-361
Iowa *picture on* I: 388
Mississippi Freedom Democratic Party
Hamer, Fannie Lou H: 29
Mississippi National River and Recreation Area
[Minnesota]
National Park System (table: National parkways
and other national parklands) N: 56
Mississippi Plateau [region, Kentucky]
Kentucky (Land regions) K: 285
Mississippi Project [1964]
Student Nonviolent Coordinating Committee
So: 932
Mississippi River [U.S.] M: 646 *with pictures and maps*
See also the list of Related articles in the Mississippi River *article*
Delta D: 118 *with map*
De Soto, Hernando D: 160 *with picture and map*
Exploration (The French and English in North America) E: 446
Flood (River floods) F: 236; (Flood control) F: 238
Inland waterway I: 274
Jolliet, Louis J: 156
La Salle, René-Robert Cavelier, Sieur de L: 79 *with map*
Levee L: 216
Louisiana L: 478; (Rivers, bayous, and lakes) L: 490
Marquette, Jacques M: 217
Minnesota *picture on* M: 605; (Lakes, rivers, and waterfalls) M: 598
Mississippi *picture on* M: 631
New Orleans (The city) N: 278
River (table) R: 352
Mississippi River-Gulf Outlet
Louisiana (Transportation) L: 495; (The mid-1900's) L: 500
New Orleans (Transportation) N: 283
Mississippi River Logging Company
Weyerhaeuser, Frederick W: 253
Mississippi Scheme [U.S. history] M: 649
Law, John L: 141
Mississippi State University M: 649
Mississippi University for Women M: 649
Mississippian Epoch [geology]
Carboniferous Period C: 208
Earth (table) E: 30
Mississippian Indians
Mound builders (Mississippian Period) M: 883 *with pictures*
Missoula [Montana] M: 649
Missoula, Lake [Montana]
Flood (Other floods) F: 237
Missouri [state] M: 650 *with pictures and maps*
See also the list of Related articles in the Missouri *article*
United States, History of the (The Missouri crisis) U: 166
Missouri [ship]
Battleship *picture on* B: 173; (The modern battleship) B: 172 *with picture*
Pearl Harbor (The war memorials) P: 219 *with picture*
World War II (Victory in the Pacific) W: 493
Missouri, University of M: 673
Missouri (Interesting facts) M: 651
Missouri Botanical Garden
Botanical garden B: 507
Saint Louis (Parks) S: 48
Missouri Breaks [North Dakota]
North Dakota (Land regions) N: 506
Missouri Compromise [1820] M: 673
Clay, Henry (The Missouri Compromise) Ci: 658
Dred Scott Decision (The background of the case) D: 345
Maine (Statehood) M: 89
Missouri (Statehood and expansion) M: 669
Monroe, James (Beginnings of sectionalism) M: 737

Randolph, John R: 137
United States, History of the (The Missouri crisis) U: 166-167; (The Kansas-Nebraska Act) U: 175
Missouri Headwaters State Park
Montana *picture on* M: 743
Missouri National Recreational River [Nebraska-South Dakota]
National Park System (table: National parkways and other national parklands) N: 56
Missouri River [U.S.] M: 674 *with picture and map*
Dam *picture on* D: 18
Flood (River floods) F: 236
Kansas (Rivers and lakes) K: 230
Kansas City (Missouri) (The city) K: 241
Lewis and Clark expedition (Up the Missouri) L: 222a *with map*
North Dakota (Rivers and lakes) N: 508
River (table) R: 352
South Dakota (Rivers and lakes) So: 676; (Transportation) So: 679
Missouri River Basin Project [conservation]
Nebraska (The mid-1900's) N: 114
South Dakota (The mid-1900's) So: 684
Missouri Territory [U.S. history]
Missouri (Territorial days) M: 669
Missouri Compromise M: 673
Mist [weather]
Fog F: 314
Mistassini, Lake
Quebec (Rivers, waterfalls, and lakes) Q: 24 *with map*
Mister ...
See Mr. ... *in this index*
Mistletoe [plant] M: 676 *with picture*
Christmas (Christmas decorations) C: 535
Plant (Photosynthesis) P: 537-538 *with picture*
Poisonous plant (Some poisonous plants) P: 602
Mistral, Frédéric [French poet] M: 676
Mistral, Gabriela [Chilean poet] M: 676
Latin American literature (The early 1900's) L: 113
Mistress of the Inn, The [play by Goldoni]
Italian literature (The Baroque period and the Enlightenment) I: 494-495
Mistress of the robes [title]
Royal Household of the United Kingdom R: 498
Mistrial [law]
Trial (Presenting evidence) T: 436
MIT [school] *See* Massachusetts Institute of Technology *in this index*
Mitanni [ancient country] M: 676
Mitchell, Arthur [American choreographer] M: 677
Ballet (Ballet in the United States) B: 53-54
Mitchell, Billy [American general] M: 677
Air force (History) A: 184-185
Air Force, United States (Between world wars) A: 195
Aviation (table: Aviation speed records) A: 990
United States Air Force Academy (History) U: 198
Mitchell, David B. [American political leader]
Georgia (table) G: 130
Mitchell, Edgar Dean [American astronaut]
Space exploration (Other moon landings) So: 719
Mitchell, George [American Indian leader]
American Indian Movement A: 411
Mitchell, George John [American political leader] M: 677
Baseball (Recent developments) B: 137-139
Mitchell, Helen Porter [birth name of]
Melba, Nellie M: 388
Mitchell, Henry L. [American political leader]
Florida (table) F: 260
Mitchell, James [Canadian political leader]
New Brunswick (table) N: 195
Mitchell, James Paul [American government official]
Eisenhower, Dwight David (table) E: 152
Labor, Department of (table) L: 2
Mitchell, Joan [American artist] M: 677
Mitchell, John [British botanist]
Map (Mapping the Americas) M: 184-185
Mitchell, John Newton [American government official] M: 677
Watergate W: 144
Mitchell, Margaret [American author] M: 677
Gone with the Wind G: 268
Mitchell, Maria [American astronomer] M: 678
Mitchell, Mitch [British drummer]
Hendrix, Jimi H: 184
Mitchell, Mount *See* Mount Mitchell *in this index*
Mitchell, Nathaniel [American political leader]
Delaware (table) D: 109
Mitchell, Peter [Canadian political leader]
Confederation of Canada (Fathers of Confederation) Ci: 935
Mitchell, Peter Dennis [British chemist]
Nobel Prizes (Chemistry: 1978) N: 444
Mitchell, Thomas [Irish-American actor]

Motion picture (Best performance by an actor in a supporting role: 1939) M: 862a
Mitchell, Sir Thomas Livingstone [Australian explorer]
Australia *map on* A: 921
Mitchell, Wesley Clair [American economist]
Economics (Modern economics) E: 64
Mitchell, William D. [American government official]
Hoover, Herbert Clark (table) H: 330
Justice, Department of (table) J: 203
Mitchell, William Landrum [American general] *See* Mitchell, Billy *in this index*
Mitchell Park
Milwaukee (Parks) M: 560
Mite [animal] M: 678 *with picture*
Apple (Pests and diseases) A: 572
Bee (Enemies) B: 205
Cat (Veterinary care) C: 295
Chigger C: 447
Hog (Diseases) H: 287
Pear (Diseases and pests) P: 216
Tick T: 279
Miter box [tool]
Saw (Handsaws) S: 166
Mithra [Persian god] M: 678
Mysteries M: 972
Mithraism [religion]
Mithra M: 678
Mysteries M: 972
Mithridates VI [king of Pontus] M: 678
Sulla, Lucius Cornelius So: 968
Mitilini [island] *See* Lesbos *in this index*
Mitilini [Lesbos]
Lesbos L: 206
Mitnaggedim [religion]
Jews (Eastern European religious movements) J: 123
Mitochondria [biology] M: 679
Cell (The cytoplasm) C: 329 *with diagrams*; (Producing energy) C: 332 *with diagram*
Cloning (Differences among clones) Ci: 683
Mitochondrial DNA [biology]
Cloning (Differences among clones) Ci: 683
Mitosis [biology]
Cell (Mitosis) C: 330 *with pictures*
Evolution (Mutation) E: 427-428
Heredity (Sex cells and reproduction) H: 201
Protozoan (Reproduction) P: 837
Mitra [Hindu god]
Mithra M: 678
Mitral valve [anatomy]
Heart (Chambers, valves, and inner lining) H: 133-135 *with pictures*; (The work of the heart) H: 135; (Valve disease) H: 141
Mitral valve prolapse M: 679
Mitral valve prolapse [disorder] M: 679
Heart (Valve disease) H: 141
Mitre, Bartolomé [Argentine political leader]
Argentina (The Constitution of 1853) A: 656-657
Mitridate Eupatore, Il [opera by Scarlatti]
Scarlatti, Alessandro S: 173
Mitropoulos, Dimitri [Greek-American conductor] M: 679
Mitsotakis, Constantine [Greek political leader]
Greece (The restoration of democracy) G: 365
Mitsubishi [company]
Aviation (World War II [1939-1945]) A: 989-990
Mitsui O.S.K. Lines, Ltd. [shipping company]
Ship *picture on* S: 426
Mitte [district]
Berlin (Downtown Berlin) B: 260
Mitterrand, François Maurice [French political leader] M: 679
France (Socialists win power) F: 478
Miwok Indians M: 679
Mix, Tom [American actor] M: 680
Mixdown [recording]
Recording industry (The mixdown) R: 181
Mixed art
Theater T: 232
Mixed breed *See* Mongrel *in this index*
Mixed drink
Alcoholic beverage (Distilled drinks) A: 336
Mixed economy
Socialism (The New Left) So: 561-562
World (Economic systems) W: 412b
Mixed episode [psychology]
Bipolar disorder B: 327
Mixed farming
Farm and farming (Mixed farms) F: 32
United Kingdom (Agriculture) U: 65
Mixed-feed industry
Corn (Corn in industry) Ci: 1061
Mixed forest
Tree (Broadleaf forests) T: 428-429
Mixed martial arts [sports] M: 680

Boxing (Boxing today) **B: 533**
Martial arts (Mixed martial arts [MMA]) **M: 234a**
Mixed member proportional system
[government]
New Zealand (Political changes) **N: 356**
Mixed-motive game
Game theory **G: 23**
Mixed numbers [mathematics]
Fraction (Improper fractions) **F: 448**
Mixed-use development
City planning (Proposals of the plan) **Ci: 599**
Mixing [sound recording]
Motion picture (Mixing the sound) **M: 856** *with picture*
Recording industry (The mixdown) **R: 181**
Mixson, Wayne [American political leader]
Florida (table) **F: 260**
Mixtec Indians M: 680
Indian, American *picture on* **I: 172**
Oaxaca **O: 640a**
Mixture
Compound **Ci: 906**
Melting point **M: 389**
Mixture of Frailties, A [book by Davies]
Davies, Robertson **D: 46**
Miyako [former name]
Kyoto **K: 398**
Miyako Islands [islands, Pacific]
Ryukyu Islands **R: 574**
Miyamoto, Shigeru [Japanese game designer]
Electronic game (The Nintendo revolution) **E: 204d**; (Renewed interest in consoles) **E: 204e**
Nintendo **N: 423**
Mize, Johnny [American baseball player]
Baseball (table: Hall of Fame) **B: 134a**
Mizzenmast [part of ship]
Sailing (Spars) **S: 23**
Ship (The full-rigged ship) **S: 418-419**
Mjollnir [Norse mythology]
Thor **T: 265**
MK IV [tank]
World War I *picture on* **W: 457**
MK luminosity classification system
Star (The Hertzsprung-Russell diagram) **So: 845-846**
Mkapa, Benjamin [Tanzanian political leader]
Tanzania (After socialism) **T: 35**
MLA style
Footnote **F: 369**
Mladenov, Petar [Bulgarian political leader]
Bulgaria (Political changes) **B: 693**
Mladić, Ratko [Serbian military leader]
Srebrenica massacre **So: 816**
Mlle. ...
See Mademoiselle ... *in this index*
Mlolongo [election]
Kenya (Building the new nation) **K: 303-304**
MLS [aviation]
Airport (Air traffic control) **A: 246-247**
MMA [sports] *See* Mixed martial arts *in this index*
Mme. ...
See Madame ... *in this index*
M-Maybe [painting by Lichtenstein]
Pop Art *picture on* **P: 659**
MMORPG [electronic game] *See* Massively multiplayer online role-playing game *in this index*
Mn [symbol]
Manganese (Properties) **M: 139**
M'Naghten's Case [1843]
Insanity **I: 277**
MNC [business] *See* Multinational corporation *in this index*
Mnemonic device [memory aid]
Memory (Mnemonic devices) **M: 393**
Mnemosyne [Greek mythology]
Muses **M: 937**
Mo [symbol]
Molybdenum **M: 697**
M.O. [criminology]
Crime scene investigation (Reconstructing the crime) **Ci: 1142**
Mo Di [Chinese philosopher]
Photography (Early developments) **P: 422**
Moa [extinct bird] **M: 680** *with picture*
Bird *picture on* **B: 369**
Moabite stone [archaeology] **M: 681**
Moabites [people]
Jordan (Early days) **J: 164**
Moabite stone **M: 681**
Moai [statues]
Easter Island **E: 45** *with picture*
Moana [film]
Flaherty, Robert Joseph **F: 225**
Moat [defense]
Castle (Structure) **C: 280** *with picture*
Zoo *picture on* **Z: 600**; (Displaying animals) **Z: 601**
Mob [zoology]

Kangaroo (The life of a kangaroo) **K: 214**
Mob action
Lynching **L: 535**
Riot **R: 347**
Mobil Corporation
Exxon Mobil Corporation **E: 459**
Mobile [Alabama] **M: 681** *with picture*
Alabama *picture on* **A: 257**; (Average monthly weather) **A: 270**; (Territorial days) **A: 275**
Mobile [sculpture] **M: 682**
Calder, Alexander **C: 26** *with picture*
Sculpture (Form and treatment) **S: 230-231** *with picture*
Mobile Bay
Alabama *picture on* **A: 257**
Mobile Bay, Battle of [1864]
Alabama *picture on* **A: 277**; (The Civil War and Reconstruction) **A: 276**
Civil War, American (table) **Ci: 624**; (Battle of Mobile Bay) **Ci: 632**
Farragut, David Glasgow **F: 47**
Mobile (History) **M: 681-682**
Mobile crane [machine]
Building construction (Constructing a skyscraper) **B: 683-684**
Mobile Delta
Alabama (Land regions) **A: 268**
Mobile genetic element
McClintock, Barbara **M: 332d**
Mobile home [house] **M: 682**
Trailer **T: 367**
Mobile Intensive Care Unit
Paramedic (Duties) **P: 153**
Mobile library *See* Bookmobile *in this index*
Mobile phone *See* Cellular telephone *in this index*
Mobile Register, The
Alabama (Communication) **A: 273**
Mobile River [Alabama] **M: 683**
Alabama (Rivers and lakes) **A: 270**
Mobile starting gate [harness racing]
Harness racing (The race) **H: 63** *with picture*
Mobile switching center
Telephone (Cellular phone calls) **T: 97**
Mobile telephone switching office
Cellular telephone (How cellular telephones work) **C: 340**
Telephone (Cellular phone calls) **T: 97**
Mobility map *See* Navigation map *in this index*
Möbius, August Ferdinand [German mathematician]
Mathematics (In the 1800's) **M: 307**
Möbius strip [mathematics] **M: 683** *with diagram*
Mobutu, Joseph Désiré [Zairian political leader]
See Mobutu Sese Seko *in this index*
Mobutu Sese Seko [Congolese political leader]
Congo, Democratic Republic of the (Civil disorder) **Ci: 940c**; (The fall of Mobutu) **Ci: 940c**
Mobutu Sese Seko [Zairian political leader] **M: 683**
Moby [American electronic artist]
Rock music (Rock music today) **R: 381**
Moby-Dick [book by Melville]
American literature *picture on* **A: 416**; (The romance) **A: 418**
Melville, Herman **M: 390**
Novel (The United States) **N: 573**
Mocambo [settlement]
Palmares **P: 110**
Moccasin [clothing] **M: 683**
Indian, American *picture on* **I: 156**
Shoe (Kinds of shoes) **S: 431**
Moccasin flower
Lady's-slipper **L: 25**
Moccasin snake
Water moccasin **W: 135** *with picture*
Mocha [coffee]
Coffee (Kinds of coffee) **Ci: 755**
Moche [people] **M: 683** *with picture*
Indian, American (Indians of the Andes) **I: 173** *with picture*
Peru *picture on* **P: 311**
Pyramids (American pyramids) **P: 917**
Mochica [American Indians] *See* Moche *in this index*
Mock orange [shrub] **M: 684**
Syringa **So: 1077**
Mock-up
Airplane (Design and testing) **A: 228**
Astronaut (Advanced mission training) **A: 832-833**
Mocker swallowtail [butterfly]
Butterfly *picture on* **B: 737**
Mockernut hickory [tree]
Hickory **H: 224**
Plant *picture on* **P: 525**
Mockingbird M: 684
Bird *picture on* **B: 358**; (Birds of urban areas) **B: 333** *with picture*
Moco [animal]

Cavy **C: 322**
Moctezuma [Aztec emperors] *See under* Montezuma *in this index*
Modal auxiliary [grammar]
Mood (Verb phrases) **M: 781**
Modal verb [grammar]
Verb (Modal verbs) **V: 314**
Mode [grammar]
Mood **M: 780**
Mode [mathematics] **M: 684**
Average **A: 982**
Mode [music]
Classical music (Early music) **Ci: 645**
Modekngei [religion]
Palau (People) **P: 102**
Model [economics]
Econometrics **E: 57**
Model [geyser]
Geyser (How geysers form) **G: 177-178**
Model [occupation] *See* Modeling *in this index*
Model, Mathematical *See* Computer modeling; Mathematical model *in this index*
Model A [automobile]
Automobile (The rise of the Big Three) **A: 968-970**
Ford, Henry (Industrial accomplishments) **F: 380**
Model Aeronautics, Academy of
Airplane, Model **A: 240**
Model Aeronautics Association of Canada
Airplane, Model **A: 240**
Model agency
Modeling (Model agencies) **M: 685**
Model airplane *See* Airplane, Model *in this index*
Model car *See* Automobile, Model *in this index*
Model making
Airplane, Model **A: 240** *with pictures*
Automobile (Planning the car) **A: 956**
Automobile, Model **A: 974** *with pictures*
Cell *picture on* **C: 338**
City planning *picture on* **Ci: 598**
Hobby (Handicrafts) **H: 272-273**
Railroad, Model **R: 119** *with pictures*
Rocket, Model **R: 391** *with pictures*
Science projects (Kinds of science projects) **S: 206**
Theater *picture on* **T: 239**
Model Parliament [English history] **M: 684**
England (The beginnings of Parliament) **E: 306**
Model railroad *See* Railroad, Model *in this index*
Model Railroad Association, National
Railroad, Model (History) **R: 121**
Model rocket *See* Rocket, Model *in this index*
Model ship *See* Ship, Model *in this index*
Model T [automobile]
Automobile *picture on* **A: 965**; (Mass production) **A: 966**; (The rise of the Big Three) **A: 968**
Ford, Henry (Industrial accomplishments) **F: 380** *with picture*
Ford Motor Company **F: 382**
Modeling [art]
Sculpture (The sculptor at work) **S: 232** *with picture*
Modeling [career] **M: 684**
Careers (Sales) **C: 229-230**
Clothing *picture on* **Ci: 706**
Modem [electronic device] **M: 685**
Broadband communication **B: 635**
Computer (A modem or a network interface card) **Ci: 915**
Telephone (VoIP phone calls) **T: 97**
Moderate [political science]
Conservatism **Ci: 991**
Moderate clothing
Clothing (Marketing categories of fashion) **Ci: 705**
Moderate rain
Rain (Characteristics of rain) **R: 122-123**
Moderate Republican [U.S. history]
Reconstruction (The Radicals and the Moderates) **R: 178**
Moderato
Music (table) **M: 954**
Moderator
Nuclear energy (Nuclear fission) **N: 582-583**; (Power reactors) **N: 584-585**
Modern Comedy, A [book by Galsworthy]
Galsworthy, John **G: 16**
Modern dance
Dance (Modern dance) **D: 30** *with picture*
Graham, Martha **G: 300**
Modern Instance, A [book by Howells]
Howells, William Dean **H: 401**
Modern interior
Interior design (Style) **I: 327**
Modern Jazz Quartet
Jazz *picture on* **J: 68**
Lewis, John Aaron **L: 220**
Modern Love [poems by Meredith]

Meredith, George M: 416
Modern Maturity [magazine]
AARP A: 3
Modern Orthodoxy [religion]
Judaism (Orthodox Judaism) J: 180
Modern Painters [book by Ruskin]
Ruskin, John R: 523
Modern pentathlon [sports] *See* Pentathlon,
Modern *in this index*
Modern Republicanism [U.S. history]
Eisenhower, Dwight David ("Modern
Republicanism") E: 152
Modern rose
Rose (Types of roses) R: 474
Modern shrub
Rose (Types of roses) R: 474-475
Modern Standard Arabic [language]
Arabs (Language) A: 586
Modern Times [film]
Chaplin, Charlie C: 376
Modern Wing [building]
Art Institute of Chicago A: 749
Modernism [arts] M: 685
American literature (The world wars and
depression [1914-1945]) A: 420
Latin American literature (Modernism) L: 113
Postmodernism P: 709
Rodó, José Enrique R: 399
Spanish literature (Modernism) So: 762
Modernism [religion]
Roman Catholic Church (Pius X) R: 410
"Modest Proposal, A" [essay by Swift]
Swift, Jonathan (Swift's other works) So: 1040
Modiano, Patrick [French author]
French literature (Recent French literature) F: 523
Modified atmosphere package
Packaging P: 18
Modified free enterprise system [economics]
Capitalism (How capitalism differs from central
planning) C: 194
Modified Mercalli Intensity scale [seismology]
Earthquake (table) E: 38; (The Modified Mercalli
Intensity [MMI] scale) E: 38b
Modifier [grammar]
Adjective A: 56
Adverb (Sentence modifiers) A: 70
A Guide to Writing Skills **Research Guide:** 9
Modigliani, Amedeo [Italian artist] M: 686 *with
picture*
Modigliani, Franco [American economist]
Nobel Prizes (Economics: 1985) N: 449
Modoc Indians M: 686
Captain Jack C: 199
Indian wars (The Modoc War [1872-1873]) I: 194
Klamath Indians K: 343
Oregon (Indian treaties and conflicts) O: 846-848
Modoc War [1872-1873]
Captain Jack C: 199
Indian, American (After European contact) I: 166
Indian wars (The Modoc War [1872-1873]) I: 194
Oregon (Indian treaties and conflicts) O: 846-848
Modred, Sir [legendary figure]
Arthur, King A: 757
Lancelot, Sir L: 56
Round Table (The decline of the Round Table)
R: 491
Modrow, Hans [German political leader]
Germany (East Germany) G: 170-171
Modular construction
Building construction (Prefabricated
construction) B: 684
Modular unit
Furniture (The 1900's to the present) F: 582; (The
retro style) F: 584
Modulation [music]
Harmony H: 63
Music (Harmony) M: 951-952
Modulator [electronics]
Radar (The modulator) R: 71 *with diagram*
Module [agriculture]
Cotton (Harvesting) Ci: 1090-1091
Module [architecture]
Architecture (table) A: 608-609; (Classical Greek
architecture) A: 615-616
Module [construction]
Building construction (Prefabricated
construction) B: 684
Module [engineering]
Solar energy (Using photovoltaic cells) So: 578
Module [spacecraft]
International Space Station I: 346a
Space exploration (Space stations) So: 721
Modus operandi [criminology]
Crime scene investigation (Reconstructing the
crime) C: 1142
Modyford, Thomas [English colonial official]
Morgan, Sir Henry (Early career) M: 803

Moe, Jørgen [Norwegian author]
Asbjørnsen, Peter Christen A: 766
Storytelling (The 1800's) So: 915
Moebius strip *See* Möbius strip *in this index*
Moeur, Benjamin B. [American political leader]
Arizona (table) A: 687
Moffat, David Halliday [American businessman]
Moffat Tunnel M: 686
Moffat Tunnel [Colorado] M: 686
Rocky Mountains (History) R: 395-396
Mofford, Rose [American political leader]
Arizona (table) A: 687; (The late 1900's) A: 691-
692
Mogadiscio [Somalia] *See* Mogadishu *in this index*
Mogadishu [Somalia] M: 686
Somalia (History) So: 587
Mogae, Festus [Botswanan political leader]
Botswana (History) B: 512
Mogollon [American Indians] M: 687
Indian, American (Indians of the Southwest)
I: 166
New Mexico (Indian peoples) N: 272
Mogollon Rim
Arizona (Land regions) A: 680-682
Mogul [skiing]
Skiing (Freestyle skiing) S: 483
Mogul Empire [history of India] *See* Mughal Empire
in this index
Mohács, Battle of [1526]
Hungary (Ottoman Empire) H: 445
Turkey (The rise of the Ottoman Empire) T: 510
Mohair [fabric] M: 687
Angora A: 467
Goat (Domestic goats) G: 239
Mohamed, Mohamed Abdullahi [Somali political
leader]
Somalia (History) So: 589-590
Mohammad [prophet] *See* Muhammad *in this index*
Mohammad Reza Pahlavi [shah of Iran] M: 687
Carter, Jimmy (The Iranian crisis) C: 258
Iran I: 398; (Economy) I: 403; (The nationalist
movement) I: 406; (Reforms and growing
unrest) I: 406; (Revolution and the Islamic
Republic) I: 406a
Iran-Iraq War I: 407
Khomeini, Ruhollah K: 308b
Mohammed [prophet] *See* Muhammad *in this index*
Mohammed V [sultan of Morocco]
Morocco (Independence) M: 815
Mohammed VI [king of Morocco]
Hassan II H: 82
Mohammed, Khalid Shaikh [Pakistani-born public
figure]
September 11 terrorist attacks (Global war on
terrorism) S: 310a
Mohammed, Murtala Ramat [Nigerian political
leader]
Nigeria (Oil wealth) N: 418
Mohammed, Warith Deen [American religious
leader]
Black Muslims B: 390
Farrakhan, Louis F: 48
Nation of Islam N: 27
Mohave Desert [California] *See* Mojave Desert *in
this index*
Mohave Indians M: 687
Mohawk Indians M: 688
Indian, American (Indians of the Northeast)
I: 154; (Current issues) I: 182
Iroquois Indians I: 455
Mahican Indians M: 65
Mohawk River [New York] M: 688
Hudson River H: 406
New York (Rivers) N: 306
Mohawk Trail [U.S. history] M: 688
Pioneer life in America (Crossing the
Appalachians) P: 477-478 *with map*
Mohegan Bluffs
Rhode Island (Places to visit) R: 304
Mohegan Indians M: 688
Connecticut (Early days) Ci: 968
Mohel [religion]
Circumcision Ci: 561
Mohéli [island, Comoros]
Comoros Ci: 899
Mohenjo-Daro [ancient city]
Indus Valley civilization *picture on* I: 241
Pakistan (Early civilizations) P: 98
World, History of the (The Indus Valley) W: 425
with picture
Moher, Cliffs of [County Clare]
Ireland *picture on* I: 423
Mohican Indians [fictional tribe]
Mahican Indians M: 65
Mohegan Indians M: 688
Moholy-Nagy, László [Hungarian-American artist]
Photography (Dramatic changes) P: 425-426

Mohs, Friedrich [German mineralogist]
Mineral (Hardness) M: 567
Mohs scale [mineralogy]
Gem (Hardness) G: 77
Mineral (Hardness) M: 567 *with diagram*
Moi, Daniel Toroitich arap [Kenyan political
leader] M: 688 *with portrait*
Kenya (Building the new nation) K: 303-304
Moiety [group]
Indian, American (Family groups) I: 136c
Moil [glass]
Glass (Glass terms) G: 222
Moirai [Greek mythology]
Fates F: 54
Moiré pattern [design] M: 689 *with picture*
Moisiu, Alfred [Albanian political leader]
Albania (Recent developments) A: 309
Moissan, Henri [French chemist]
Fluorine F: 306
Nobel Prizes (Chemistry: 1906) N: 442
Moist gangrene [disease]
Gangrene G: 27
Moisture
Humidity H: 433
Tornado (How a tornado forms) T: 333
Weather (Humidity) W: 158
Moisture barrier [building construction]
House (The foundation) H: 380
Mojave Desert [California]
California (The Basin and Range Region) C: 50
with picture
Mojave desert star [plant]
Flower *picture on* F: 290
Mojave National Preserve [California]
National Park System (table: National preserves)
N: 58
Mojave Point
Grand Canyon *picture on* G: 306
Moke-ta-ra-to [name for]
Black Kettle B: 389
Moko disease
Banana (How bananas grow) B: 73
Moksha [religion]
Hinduism (Reincarnation and karma) H: 236
Manu M: 168
Yoga Y: 566
Mokuaweoweo [crater]
Mauna Loa M: 313
Mola [handicraft]
Latin America (Handicrafts) L: 102 *with picture*
Panama *picture on* P: 116
Mola, Emilio [Spanish military leader]
Fifth column F: 96
Molar [anatomy]
Dog (Body structure) D: 263-265
Elephant (Tusks and teeth) E: 228
Teeth (Deciduous teeth) T: 79; (Permanent teeth)
T: 79-80 *with pictures*
Molasses [food] M: 689
Molasses Act [1733] M: 689
Molay, Jacques de [French religious leader] *See* De
Molay, Jacques *in this index*
Mold [form]
Cast and casting C: 277 *with pictures*
Fossil (How fossils form) F: 425 *with picture*
Pottery *picture on* P: 718; (Shaping the clay)
P: 716-717
Mold [fungus] M: 689
Cancer (Genes damaged by substances in the
environment) C: 170
Fermentation F: 73
Food poisoning F: 340
Food preservation (How food spoils) F: 341
Fungi (The importance of fungi) F: 559-560
Hay fever (Causes and prevention) H: 116
Penicillin (Forms of penicillin) P: 240 *with picture*
Mold casting [industrial process]
Iron and steel (Shaping and finishing steel) I: 445
Moldaver, Michael [Canadian jurist]
Supreme Court of Canada (table) So: 997 *with
portrait*
Moldavia [region, Europe]
See also Moldova *in this index*
Bessarabia B: 273
Moldova M: 690
Roma (History) R: 402b
Romania (Land regions) R: 419-420 *with map*;
(Unification movement) R: 423; (Ottoman rule)
R: 423
Moldavian Soviet Socialist Republic
Moldova M: 690
Moldavians [people] *See* Moldovans *in this index*
Moldboard [tool]
Deere, John D: 87
Farm and farming (Preparing the soil) F: 35 *with
picture*
Plow (The moldboard plow bottom) P: 575 *with*

picture
Western frontier life in America (Improvements in farming) **W: 233-234**
Moldboard bottom
Plow (The moldboard plow bottom) **P: 575** *with picture*
Molding [industrial process]
Bottle **B: 513**
Plastics (Making plastic products) **P: 557**
Pottery (Shaping the clay) **P: 716-717**
Rubber (Shaping) **R: 505**
Moldova M: 690 *with picture and map*
Bessarabia **B: 273**
Flag *picture on* **F: 207**
Moldovan Communist Party
Moldova (Government) **M: 690**
Moldovans [people]
Moldova (People) **M: 690**
Union of Soviet Socialist Republics (People) **U: 31**
Moldoveanu, Mount
Romania (Surface features) **R: 419**
Mole [animal] **M: 690b** *with picture*
Fur (table) **F: 561**
Hand (Animal hands) **H: 40**
Mammal *picture on* **M: 116**; (Underground) **M: 122**
Mole [chemistry] **M: 690b**
Metric system (Structure of the metric system) **M: 437**; (Chemistry) **M: 440**
pH **P: 353**
Mole [dermatology] **M: 691**
Birthmark **B: 380**
Skin (Tumors) **S: 491**
Skin cancer (Melanoma) **S: 491**
Mole [food]
Mexico (Food and drink) **M: 456**
Mole Antonelliana [building]
Turin **T: 501** *with picture*
Mole cricket M: 691 *with picture*
Mole-rat [animal] **M: 691** *with picture*
Naked mole-rat **N: 4** *with picture*
Mole trap
Trapping *picture on* **T: 404**
Molecular biology M: 691
Biology (table) **B: 317**
Botany (How plants function) **B: 508**
Evolution (Contributions from other scientific fields) **E: 433**
Prehistoric people (The single origin theory) **P: 750-751**; (Analysis of the genetic materials) **P: 754b**
Zoology (What zoologists study) **Z: 606-607**; (History) **Z: 606-607**
Molecular flow [physics]
Vacuum (Properties) **V: 256**
Molecular gastronomy
Cooking (Other cooking methods) **Ci: 1028**
Molecular genetics
Genetics (Molecular genetics) **G: 86**
Heredity **H: 201**
Molecular hydrogen [element]
Hydrogen **H: 468**
Molecular mass
Molecule (Individual molecules) **M: 692-693**
Molecular medicine M: 692
Cancer (Molecular medicine) **C: 173**
Molecular-orbital theory
Mulliken, Robert Sanderson **M: 915**
Molecular physics
Physics (Atomic, molecular, and electron physics) **P: 437**
Molecular weight *See* Molecular mass *in this index*
Molecule [chemistry] **M: 692** *with pictures*
See also the list of Related articles in the Molecule article
Boiling point (Why boiling points differ) **B: 440**
Bond **B: 454**
Bragg, Sir William Henry **B: 547**
Bragg, Sir William Lawrence **B: 547**
Chemical reaction **C: 397**
Chemistry (Fundamental ideas of chemistry) **C: 398-399**
Computer graphics *picture on* **Ci: 924h**
Diffusion **D: 201**
Electricity (Molecules) **E: 192**
Evaporation (How evaporation occurs) **E: 422** *with diagram*
Expansion **E: 438**
Human body (Chemical elements and molecules) **H: 417**
Light (How light is produced) **L: 283**
Materials (The role of bonds) **M: 301**
Nanotechnology **N: 10**
Physics (Atomic, molecular, and electron physics) **P: 437**
Vacuum (Properties) **V: 256**
Moleskin [fur]

Mole **M: 690b**
Molesworth, Sir William [Australian government official]
Australia (End of transportation) **A: 921-922**
Molesworth Committee
Australia (End of transportation) **A: 921-922**
Molière [French dramatist] **M: 694**
Drama (Neoclassical playwrights) **D: 333-334**
French literature (Classical drama) **F: 520**
Molina, Mario José [American chemist]
Nobel Prizes (Chemistry: 1995) **N: 444**
Molina, Tirso de [Spanish dramatist] *See* Tirso de Molina *in this index*
Molino del Rey, Battle of [1847]
Mexican War (Scott's campaign) **M: 446-447**
Molitor, Paul [American baseball player]
Baseball (table: Hall of Fame) **B: 134a**
Moll Flanders [book by Defoe]
Defoe, Daniel (His writings) **D: 89**
English literature (The rise of the novel) **E: 318-319**
Novel (The first English novelists) **N: 572**
Mollisol [soil]
Indiana (Natural resources) **I: 211**
Soil *map on* **So: 575**; (How soils are classified) **So: 576**
Molloy [book by Beckett]
Beckett, Samuel **B: 196**
Moll's Gap [Ireland]
Ireland *picture on* **I: 416**
Mollusk [zoology] **M: 694** *with pictures*
See also the list of Related articles in the Mollusk article
Animal (A classification of the animal kingdom) **A: 506** *with picture*
Aquaculture **A: 578**
Clam **Ci: 636** *with pictures*
Heart (Hearts of animals) **H: 146**
Invertebrate **I: 366** *with picture*
Larva **L: 78**
Ocean *picture on* **O: 651**; (The nekton) **O: 655**
Pearl (How pearls are formed) **P: 216**
Prehistoric animal (Invertebrates) **P: 737**
Seafood **S: 264**
Shell **S: 384** *with picture*
Mollweide projection [cartography]
Map (Map projections) **M: 182** *with diagram*
Molly [fish] **M: 696**
Fish *picture on* **F: 157**
Molly Maguires [organization] **M: 696**
Molly on the Shore [song]
Grainger, Percy **G: 302**
Molnár, Ferenc [Hungarian dramatist] **M: 696**
Hungary (The arts) **H: 442**
Molokai [island, Hawaii]
Damien, Father **D: 21**
Hawaii (Molokai) **H: 100** *with picture*
Molotov, Vyacheslav Mikhailovich [Soviet political leader] **M: 696**
Stalin, Joseph *picture on* **So: 827**
Molting [zoology] **M: 696** *with picture*
Beetle (The life cycle of beetles) **B: 216**
Bird (Feathers) **B: 362**
Butterfly (The larva) **B: 741**
Camel (The body of a camel) **C: 77**
Crustacean (Growth and development) **Ci: 1163** *with picture*
Duck (Habits) **D: 376**
Insect *picture on* **I: 292**; (Skeleton) **I: 286**
Lobster (Growth) **L: 406**
Rabbit (Health) **R: 49**
Reptile (Skin) **R: 251** *with picture*
Snake (Scales and color) **S: 525**
Spider (Spiderlings) **So: 788**
Moltke, Helmuth Karl von [Prussian general] **M: 697**
Franco-Prussian War (Progress of the war) **F: 483**
Seven Weeks' War **S: 325**
World War I (The Western Front) **W: 455-456**
Molto [music]
Music (table) **M: 954**
Molucca Islands [Indonesia]
Indonesia (The Molucca Islands) **I: 234**
Netherlands (Immigration) **N: 150**
Moluccans [people]
Indonesia (The Molucca Islands) **I: 234**
Netherlands (Immigration) **N: 150**
Molybdenite [mineral]
Molybdenum **M: 697**
Rhenium **R: 290**
Molybdenum [element] **M: 697**
Alloy (Alloys of iron) **A: 377-378**
Colorado (Mining) **Ci: 843**
Leadville **L: 150**
Technetium **T: 73**
Momaday, N. Scott [American author]
American literature (Works by minority writers)

A: 425
Indian, American (Achievements in the arts) **I: 181**
Mombasa [Kenya] **M: 697**
Moment [physics]
Gravity, Center of **G: 333**
Lever (Law of equilibrium) **L: 217-218**
Moment in Peking [book by Lin Yutang]
Lin Yutang **L: 309**
Moment magnitude [seismology] **M: 697**
Earthquake (The moment magnitude scale) **E: 38b**
Richter magnitude **R: 334**
Moment of silence
School prayer **S: 186**
Momentum [physics] **M: 698** *with diagram*
Quantum mechanics (Wave-particle duality) **Q: 6**
Rocket (How rockets work) **R: 385**
Mommie Dearest [book by Crawford]
Crawford, Joan **Ci: 1122**
Mommsen, Theodor [German historian]
Nobel Prizes (Literature: 1902) **N: 447**
Rome, Ancient (Learning about ancient Rome) **R: 448**
MON [measurement] *See* Motor octane number *in this index*
Mon [people]
Myanmar (Early days) **M: 970d**
Thailand (History) **T: 226**
Mon-Khmer language
India (Languages) **I: 114**
Language *map on* **L: 65**; (Other language families) **L: 66**
Laos (People) **L: 70**
Mona Lisa [painting by Leonardo da Vinci] **M: 698**
Leonardo da Vinci **L: 199** *with picture*; (Paintings) **L: 200b-201**
Monacan Indians
Virginia (Early days) **V: 418**
Monaco [country] **M: 698** *with picture and map*
Flag *picture on* **F: 207**
Monte Carlo **M: 762**
Rainier III **R: 129**
Monaco [city, Monaco]
Monaco (Land) **M: 699**
Monad [philosophy]
Leibniz, Gottfried Wilhelm **L: 185**
Monadnock [geography]
New Hampshire (Visitor's guide) **N: 216**; (Mountains) **N: 220** *with map*
Monadnock, Mount
New Hampshire (Mountains) **N: 220** *with map*
Monadnock Building [Chicago]
Burnham, Daniel Hudson **B: 709**
Monal [bird]
Bird (Birds of Asia) **B: 344f** *with picture*
Monarch [ruler] *See* King; Queen *in this index*
Monarch butterfly [insect]
Animal (Animal migration) **A: 502-503**
Butterfly *pictures on* **B: 735, B: 739, B:740**; (Milkweed butterflies) **B: 736**; (Migration) **B: 742**
Insect (Hibernation and migration) **I: 296**
Plant (How plants protect themselves) **P: 540**
Monarchia, The [essay by Dante]
Dante Alighieri (His works) **D: 34**
Monarchy [political science] **M: 700**
Dictatorship **D: 191**
Divine right of kings **D: 242**
Government *picture on* **G: 288**; (Monarchy) **G: 286**; (The rise of monarchies and nation-states) **G: 290**
Petition of Right **P: 327**
United Kingdom (National government) **U: 49**
Monastery [religion]
Architecture (Carolingian architecture) **A: 618**
Bhutan *picture on* **B: 277**
Book (The Middle Ages) **B: 466**
Cloister **Ci: 682k**
Hermit **H: 211**
Irish literature (Early Irish literature) **I: 430**
Library (Medieval collections) **L: 259** *with picture*
Middle Ages (The Christian church) **M: 523-524**
Monasticism **M: 701**
Painting (Early medieval painting in the West) **P: 48-49**
Monastery of Kildare [Ireland]
Brigid, Saint **B: 609**
Monastic Brotherhood [religious group]
Religious life (table) **R: 227**
Monasticism [religion] **M: 701** *with picture*
Abbot **A: 4**
Anthony of Thebes, Saint **A: 545**
Athanasius, Saint **A: 853**
Benedict of Nursia, Saint **B: 247**
Benedictines **B: 248**
Christianity (The medieval church) **C: 524**

Copts Ci: 1045
Monk M: 725
Pachomius, Saint P: 2
Roman Catholic Church (The recognition of
   Christianity) R: 405-406
Trappists T: 404
Monastiraki Square
   Athens (Landmarks) A: 854 *with map*
Monaural recording *See* Monophonic recording
   in this index
Monazite [mineral]
   Holmium H: 296
   Ytterbium Y: 574
   Yttrium Y: 575
Mönch [mountain, Switzerland]
   Alps *picture on* A: 385
Monck, Charles Stanley [British political leader]
   See Monck, Viscount *in this index*
Monck, George [English general] M: 701
   England (The Restoration) E: 309
   Restoration R: 263
Monck, Viscount [British political leader] M: 702
   Ottawa (Rideau Hall) O: 872
Mönckeberg's arteriosclerosis [disease]
   Arteriosclerosis A: 750
Moncton [New Brunswick] M: 702
Mondale, Walter Frederick [American political
   leader] M: 702 *with portrait*
   Carter, Jimmy (Rise to prominence) C: 255-256
      with picture
   Democratic Party (The late 1900's) D: 127
   Ferraro, Geraldine Anne F: 76
   Minnesota (Politics) M: 602-603
   Reagan, Ronald Wilson *picture on* R: 169
   Vice president of the United States (Growth of
      the vice presidency) V: 353-354
Monday [day] M: 702
Mondrian, Piet [Dutch painter] M: 702
   Painting (Line) M: 35; (De Stijl) P: 80 *with picture*;
      (Europeans in America) P: 84
Monégasques [people]
   Monaco (People) M: 699
Monel metal M: 703
Moneran [biology] *See* Prokaryote *in this index*
Monestrous mammal [zoology]
   Mammal (Mating) M: 122-123
Monet, Claude [French painter] M: 703 *with picture*
   Derain, André D: 152
   Impressionism (French Impressionism) I: 93
   Painting (Light and shade) P: 35 *with picture*;
      (Edouard Manet and the Impressionists) P: 71
   Renoir, Pierre Auguste R: 241
Moneta, Ernesto Teodoro [Italian statesman]
   Nobel Prizes (Peace: 1907) N: 448
Monetarism [economics]
   Economics (Modern economics) E: 64-65
   Keynes, John Maynard K: 308a
Monetary Conference, International [1944]
   Bretton Woods B: 594
   Morgenthau, Henry, Jr. M: 805
   New Hampshire (The mid-1900's) N: 226-227
      with picture
Monetary History of the United States, A [book by
   Friedman]
   Friedman, Milton F: 533
Monetary policy
   Depression (Depressions since World War II)
      D: 150
   Economics (Government intervention) E: 59;
      (Modern economics) E: 64-65
   Federal Reserve System F: 65
   Government (Commerce) G: 283
   Inflation I: 267; (Weapons against inflation) I: 268
   Money (Monetary policy) M: 717
   Recession (Fighting recession) R: 175
   Unemployment (Programs and policies) U: 23
Money M: 704 *with pictures*
   See also the list of Related articles in the Money
      article
   Coin collecting Ci: 756 *with pictures*
   Colonial life in America (Money) Ci: 811
   Convertibility Ci: 1024
   Counterfeiting Ci: 1097
   Devaluation D: 173
   Economics (The world economy) E: 61
   Exchange rate E: 435
   Free silver F: 499
   Gold (Money) G: 251
   Gold standard G: 254
   Gresham's law G: 391
   Income I: 100
   Indian, American (Money) I: 149 *with picture*
   Industry (Capital) I: 258
   Inflation I: 266
   Investment I: 366
   Legal tender L: 182
   Money laundering M: 718

Trade (The use of money) T: 362
Money [book by Amis]
   Novel (The novel today) N: 575
Money [play by Bulwer-Lytton]
   Bulwer-Lytton, Edward George Earle Lytton
      B: 698
Money bill [law]
   Parliament (The House of Commons) P: 173
Money fund [economics] *See* Money market fund
   in this index
Money Honey [device]
   Slot machine S: 508a
Money laundering [crime] M: 718
Money market account
   Bank (Safeguarding deposits) B: 88-89
   Investment (Indirect investments) I: 367
Money market fund M: 718
   Bank (A boom in money market funds) B: 94
   Investment (Other kinds of indirect investments)
      I: 368
   Mutual fund M: 969
Money order M: 718 *with pictures*
   Postal Service, United States (Other services)
      P: 700
Money supply
   Federal Reserve System F: 65
   Inflation I: 267
   Money (The money supply) M: 715; (Monetary
      policy) M: 717
Money wages
   Wages and hours (Wages) W: 2-3
Moneylender
   Pawnbroker P: 202
Moneywort [plant]
   Loosestrife L: 453
Mongkut [king of Thailand] M: 718
   Thailand (Modernization) T: 227
Mongol Empire [Asian history] M: 719 *with pictures
   and map*
   Asia (Nomadic invasions) A: 805-806 *with map*
   China (Mongol rule) C: 501 *with map*
   Genghis Khan G: 88 *with map*
   Georgia (History) G: 111
   Hungary (The Kingdom of Hungary) H: 445
   Iran (The rise of Islam) I: 405
   Kublai Khan K: 391 *with map*
   Kyrgyzstan (History) K: 400
   Mongolia (History) M: 723
   Muslims (The fall of the Abbāsids) M: 964c
   Russia (Mongol rule) R: 548
   Timur T: 292d *with map*
   Uzbekistan (History) U: 254
Mongolia M: 721 *with picture and map*
   Asia (Way of life in Central Asia) A: 790 *with
      picture*
   Clothing *picture on* Ci: 693
   Communism (The Comintern) Ci: 893
   Exploration (Medieval European exploration)
      E: 442
   Family *picture on* F: 24
   Flag *picture on* F: 204
   Genghis Khan G: 88
   Kublai Khan K: 391 *with map*
Mongolia, Inner [region, China]
   China (The Inner Mongolian Border Uplands)
      C: 491
   Mongolia M: 721
Mongolian gerbil [animal]
   Gerbil G: 136
Mongolian jird [animal]
   Gerbil G: 136
Mongolian oak [tree]
   Oak (Other oaks) O: 636
Mongolian People's Party
   Mongolia (History) M: 723
Mongolian People's Revolutionary Party
   Mongolia (History) M: 723
Mongolians [people] *See* Mongols *in this index*
Mongolism [birth defect] *See* Down syndrome *in
   this index*
Mongoloids [people]
   Races, Human (The three-race theory) R: 53-54
      with picture
Mongols [people]
   China (Nationalities) C: 481 *with picture*
   Manchuria (People) M: 134
   Mongolia M: 722; (The people) M: 722
   Russia (Ancestry) R: 532
Mongoose [animal] M: 724 *with picture*
   Cobra Ci: 742
Mongrel [animal]
   Dog *picture on* D: 262; (Kinds of dogs) D: 265-
      266; (Choosing a dog) D: 277-278
   Pet (Choosing a pet) P: 320
Moniac [computer]
   Analog computer A: 448
Monier, Joseph [French inventor]

Cement and concrete (History) C: 345
Monilia [fungus]
   Vaginitis V: 260
Mo'Nique [American actress]
   Motion picture (Best performance by an actress
      in a supporting role: 2009) M: 862b
Monism [philosophy]
   Metaphysics (Mind and body) M: 430
Monito del monte [animal]
   Mammal (table) M: 128 *with picture*
   Marsupial (Kinds of marsupials) M: 232
Monitor [education]
   School (The development of British schools)
      S: 185
Monitor [electronic device]
   See also Computer monitor *in this index*
   Photography (How a camera works) P: 407-408
   Television (The control room) T: 112 *with picture*
   Video art V: 359
Monitor [reptile] M: 724
   Lizard *picture on* L: 400; (Sizes of lizards) L: 399
Monitor and Merrimack [ships] M: 724
   Battleship (Development of the battleship)
      B: 172
   Civil War, American (First battle between
      ironclads) Ci: 626 *with picture*
   Ericsson, John E: 350
   Navy, United States *picture on* N: 90; (The Civil
      War [1861-1865]) N: 88
Monitorial school
   Education (Development of British education)
      E: 101
Monitoring center
   Burglar alarm B: 704
Monitoring station [radio] M: 724
Moniz, Antônio Egas [Portuguese physician]
   Lobotomy L: 405
   Nobel Prizes (Physiology or medicine: 1949)
      N: 445
Monk [religion] M: 725
   Asia *picture on* A: 785
   Buddhism (The sangha) B: 668 *with picture*
   Friar F: 531
   Hermit H: 211
   Monasticism M: 701
   Religious life R: 226
   Trappists T: 404
   World, History of the *picture on* W: 434
Monk, George [English general] *See* Monck,
   George *in this index*
Monk, The [book by Lewis]
   Gothic novel G: 279
Monk, Thelonious [American musician] M: 725
   with portrait
Monk parakeet [bird]
   Parrot P: 179
Monkey M: 725 *with pictures and map*
   AIDS (History) A: 166
   Animal *pictures on* A: 481, A: 499, A: 507; (A table
      of animal intelligence) A: 493
   Ape (Differences between apes and monkeys)
      A: 563
   Capuchin C: 199 *with picture*
   Colobus Ci: 777
   Guenon G: 419
   Macaque M: 2
   Monkeypox M: 730
   Primate (Anthropoids) P: 778 *with picture*; (The
      evolution of primates) P: 778b *with diagram*
   Rhesus monkey R: 291 *with picture*
Monkey bread [fruit]
   Baobab B: 100
Monkey-faced owl *See* Barn owl *in this index*
Monkey flower [shrub] M: 729
   Flower *picture on* F: 288
Monkey pod [tree]
   Rain tree R: 127
Monkey puzzle tree M: 730 *with pictures*
   Tree (Needleleaf trees) T: 414-415
Monkeypox [disease] M: 730
   Smallpox S: 513
Monk's Mound [Illinois]
   Mound builders (Mississippian Period) M: 883
      with picture
Monkshood [plant]
   Aconite A: 28 *with picture*
Monmouth, Battle of [1778]
   Lee, Charles L: 176
   New Jersey (The American Revolution) N: 250
      with picture
   Pitcher, Molly P: 499
   Revolution, American (table) R: 276; (France's
      entry into the Revolutionary War) R: 283
Monmouth, Duke of [English public figure] M: 730
Monnet, Jean [French economist] M: 731
   European Union (History) E: 420
Monnet Plan [economics]

Monnet, Jean **M:** 731
Mono [disease] *See* Mononucleosis *in this index*
Mono gramático, El [book by Paz]
    Paz, Octavio **P:** 205
Monoalphabetic substitution [cryptology]
    Codes and ciphers (Substitution) **Ci:** 750
Monoamine oxidase inhibitor [drug]
    Antidepressant **A:** 553
Monoblock process [manufacturing]
    Artillery (The monoblock process) **A:** 763
Monocacy, Battle of [1864]
    Maryland (The Civil War) **M:** 258-259
Monocacy National Battlefield [Maryland]
    National Park System (table: National battlefields)
    N: 55
Monochromatic color scheme
    Color (Producing color harmony) **Ci:** 823-824
        with diagram
    Interior design (Using color) **I:** 331
    Malevich, Kasimir **M:** 105 *with picture*
Monochromatic light
    Laser (Characteristics of laser light) **L:** 84
Monochromatic vision
    Color blindness **Ci:** 827
Monochrome ink painting
    Painting (Japanese painting) **P:** 47
Monoclinic system [chemistry]
    Crystal (Classifying crystals) **Ci:** 1166-1167 *with picture*
    Pyroxene **P:** 920
Monoclonal antibody [physiology] **M:** 731
    Cancer (Biological response modifiers) **C:** 172-173
    Immune system (Further breakthroughs) **I:** 88d
Monocoque [engineering]
    Airplane *picture on* **A:** 232; (Other pioneer planes and fliers) **A:** 233-234
    Automobile racing (Formula One racing) **A:** 976-977
Monocot [botany] *See* Monocotyledon *in this index*
Monocotyledon [botany] **M:** 731
    Angiosperm **A:** 462
    Cotyledon **Ci:** 1095
    Flower (The classifying of flowers) **F:** 298; (The evolution of flowering plants) **F:** 299; (table) **F:** 301 *with pictures*
    Gardening (Pruning) **G:** 36
    Plant *picture on* **P:** 530; (Angiosperms) **P:** 520; (Classification of plants) **P:** 546-547 *with picture*
    Seed (The parts of a seed) **S:** 281 *with diagram*
    Stem *picture on* **So:** 888; (Herbaceous stems) **So:** 887
    Tree (Broadleaf trees) **T:** 414
Monocular vision [physiology]
    Bird (Sight) **B:** 364-365 *with diagram*
Monoculture [agriculture]
    Agriculture (Growing plant crops) **A:** 150; (Threats to biodiversity) **A:** 153
    Plant (Loss of biodiversity) **P:** 543
Monocyte [physiology]
    Blood (Protecting against disease) **B:** 410
    Immune system (Other white blood cells) **I:** 88
Monod, Jacques Lucien [French biochemist]
    Nobel Prizes (Physiology or medicine: 1965) **N:** 446
Monody [music]
    Classical music (The Baroque period) **Ci:** 647
    Song **So:** 592
Monoecious plant [botany]
    Flower (Variations in flower structure) **F:** 294
Monofilament [thread]
    Fishing (Lines) **F:** 177
Monogamy [marriage]
    Marriage (Laws concerning marriage) **M:** 219
Monogenean [animal]
    Flatworm **F:** 229
Monogenetic field [geology]
    Volcano (Monogenetic fields) **V:** 442a *with picture*
Monolithic idea [electronics]
    Kilby, Jack **K:** 315
Monologion [book by Anselm]
    Anselm, Saint **A:** 519
Monomer [chemistry] **M:** 731
    Plastics (The chemistry of plastics) **P:** 556
    Polyester **P:** 649
    Polyethylene **P:** 650
    Polymer **P:** 651
    Polypropylene **P:** 651 *with diagram*
    Polystyrene **P:** 651 *with diagram*
    Polyvinyl chloride **P:** 652 *with diagram*
    Rubber (The chemistry of rubber) **R:** 501
Monometer [poetry]
    Poetry (table) **P:** 594
Monomial [mathematics]
    Algebra (Other definitions) **A:** 354
Monomyth [story]
    Campbell, Joseph **C:** 90a

Mythology (Literary approaches) **M:** 990-991
Monona, Lake [Wisconsin]
    Madison **M:** 30
Monongahela National Forest
    West Virginia (Places to visit) **W:** 216
Monongahela River [Pennsylvania-West Virginia]
    M: 731
    Pittsburgh (The city) **P:** 500a *with picture*
Mononucleosis [disease] **M:** 731
    Disease (table) **D:** 226
    Epstein-Barr virus **E:** 345
Monophonic recording
    Stereophonic sound system (History) **So:** 892
Monophony [music]
    Classical music (Songs) **Ci:** 644; (The Middle Ages) **Ci:** 645
Monophysitism [religion]
    Roman Catholic Church (The recognition of Christianity) **R:** 405-406
Monoplacophora [zoology]
    Mollusk *picture on* **M:** 695; (Monoplacophora) **M:** 696
    Shell (Kinds of mollusk shells) **S:** 385
Monoplane [airplane]
    Aircraft, Military (World War I [1914-1918]) **A:** 204
    Airplane (Other pioneer planes and fliers) **A:** 233 *with pictures*
    Blériot, Louis **B:** 400
Monopod [device]
    Photography (Shutter speed) **P:** 412
Monopole [electronics]
    Antenna (Types of antennas) **A:** 543
    Magnetism (Magnetic monopoles) **M:** 61
Monopoly and competition [economics] **M:** 732
    See also Competition *in this index*
    Capitalism (Ensuring competition) **C:** 195
    Cartel **C:** 251
    Consumer protection (The right to choose) **Ci:** 1018; (Beginnings of modern consumerism) **Ci:** 1019
    Industry (Monopolies) **I:** 261
    Inflation (The cost-push theory) **I:** 268
    Price (How price is determined) **P:** 774
    Public utility **P:** 865
    Telephone (Competition in the U.S. telephone industry) **T:** 101
    United States, History of the (The rise of "trusts") **U:** 181
Monorail [railroad] **M:** 733 *with picture*
    Washington (Interesting facts about Washington) **W:** 47
Monosaccharide [sugar]
    Carbohydrate (Kinds of carbohydrates) **C:** 203 *with diagram*; (How the body uses carbohydrates) **C:** 204
    Glucose **G:** 236
    Saccharides **S:** 4
Monosodium glutamate [chemical] **M:** 733
    Migraine **M:** 537
    Wheat (Other uses) **W:** 267
Monotheism [religion]
    Mythology (The influence of Egyptian mythology) **M:** 980
    Polytheism **P:** 652
    Religion (Belief in a deity) **R:** 215; (Judaism) **R:** 219
    Theism **T:** 251
Monotreme [mammal]
    Echidna **E:** 49
    Mammal (Reproduction) **M:** 123-124 *with picture*; (table) **M:** 128 *with picture*
    Platypus **P:** 569
Monotype [printing]
    Printing (Hot-metal typesetting) **P:** 797
Monounsaturated fatty acid [chemical]
    Fat (Structure) **F:** 52
    Nutrition (Fats) **N:** 625
Monowitz [concentration camp]
    Auschwitz **A:** 892
Monozygotic twins *See* Identical twins *in this index*
Monroe [racing car]
    Chevrolet, Louis **C:** 415
Monroe, Bill [American musician] **M:** 733
    Country music (Bluegrass music) **Ci:** 1098a *with picture*
Monroe, Charlie [American musician]
    Monroe, Bill **M:** 733
Monroe, Elizabeth Jones [mother of]
    Monroe, James (Boyhood) **M:** 734
Monroe, Elizabeth Kortright [wife of James Monroe]
    First ladies of the United States (table) **F:** 142
    Monroe, James (Monroe's family) **M:** 735-736 *with portrait*; (Life in the White House) **M:** 737
Monroe, Harriet [American editor] **M:** 733
Monroe, James [U.S. president] **M:** 734 *with pictures*

Adams, John Quincy (Secretary of state) **A:** 42
Jefferson, Thomas (Governor) **J:** 80; (The Louisiana Purchase) **J:** 85
Louisiana Purchase (New Orleans closed to Americans) **L:** 503
Monroe Doctrine **M:** 739
Paine, Thomas (French revolutionary) **P:** 22-23
Virginia (table) **V:** 417; (The Mother of Presidents) **V:** 421
White House (A new building) **W:** 290
Monroe, Marilyn [American actress] **M:** 738 *with portrait*
    DiMaggio, Joe **D:** 204
    Miller, Arthur **M:** 553
    Warhol, Andy **W:** 36 *with picture*
Monroe, Mount
    New Hampshire (Mountains) **N:** 220 *with map*
Monroe, William Smith [American musician] *See* Monroe, Bill *in this index*
Monroe Doctrine [international relations] **M:** 739
    California (Spanish and Russian settlement) **C:** 60
    Maximilian **M:** 319
    Monroe, James (The Monroe Doctrine) **M:** 738 *with picture*
    Roosevelt, Theodore (Foreign policy) **R:** 465
    United States, History of the (The Monroe Doctrine) **U:** 169
Monrovia [Liberia] **M:** 740 *with picture*
    Liberia (Transportation and communication) **L:** 230-231 *with pictures*; (The Liberian settlement) **L:** 231 *with picture*
Monserrate [mountain, Colombia]
    Bogotá **B:** 437
Monsieur Verdoux [film]
    Chaplin, Charlie **C:** 376
Monsoon [weather] **M:** 740
    Asia (Climate) **A:** 796
    Bangladesh (Climate) **B:** 83
    China (Climate) **Ci:** 494
    India (The rainy season) **I:** 124 *with picture and map*
    Japan (Climate) **J:** 48
    Java **J:** 65
    Korea, North (Climate) **K:** 372
    Korea, South (Climate) **K:** 378a
    Rain (Rainfall distribution) **R:** 124
    Storm (Monsoonal storms) **So:** 913
    Vietnam (Climate) **V:** 368
    Wind (Local winds) **W:** 329
Monster [legendary creature]
    See also the list of Related articles in the Mythology *article*
    Bigfoot **B:** 298
    Frankenstein **F:** 484
    Loch Ness monster **L:** 410
    Yeti **Y:** 565
Monstera [plant] **M:** 741
Monster's Ball [film]
    Berry, Halle **B:** 272
Mont Blanc [mountain, Europe] **M:** 741
    Alps **A:** 384 *with picture*
    France (The land) **F:** 464-466 *with picture and map*
    Mountain (table) **M:** 896 *with diagram*
"Mont Blanc" [poem by Shelley]
    Shelley, Percy Bysshe (His writings) **S:** 391
Mont Blanc [ship]
    Halifax explosion **H:** 22
    Shipwreck (table: Major shipwrecks) **S:** 428
Mont Blanc Tunnel [France-Italy]
    Tunnel (table) **T:** 491
Mont D'Iberville [Canadian Shield]
    Quebec (Land regions) **Q:** 22 *with map*
Mont Kartala [volcano, Comoros]
    Comoros (Land and climate) **Ci:** 900 *with map*
Mont-Saint-Michel [island, France] **M:** 741
    France *picture on* **F:** 453
Mont-Saint-Michel and Chartres [book by Adams]
    Adams, Henry **A:** 33
Mont Sainte-Victoire [mountain, France]
    Cézanne, Paul **C:** 365 *with picture*
Mont Sainte-Victoire [painting by Cézanne]
    Cézanne, Paul *picture on* **C:** 365
Mont Tremblant Provincial Park
    Quebec (Land regions) **Q:** 22 *with map*
Montage [art]
    Eisenstein, Sergei Mikhailovich **E:** 155
    Motion picture (Filmmaking in Europe) **M:** 866
Montagnais Indians *See* Innu Indians *in this index*
Montagne d'Ambre National Park [Madagascar]
    National park (table) **N:** 42f
Montagnier, Luc [French biologist]
    Nobel Prizes (Physiology or medicine: 2008) **N:** 447
Montagu, Mary Wortley [English author]
    Jenner, Edward **J:** 91
Montagu-Chelmsford Reforms [1919]

India (Rise of Indian nationalism) I: 131
Montagu House [London]
British Museum B: 632
Montague [literary figures]
Shakespeare, William: (Romeo and Juliet) S: 357-358
Montague, Andrew Jackson [American political leader]
Virginia (table) V: 417
Montaigne, Michel Eyquem de [French author] M: 741
Essay (Personal essays) E: 359
French literature (Michel de Montaigne) F: 520
Montalbán, Manuel Vázquez [Spanish author]
Spanish literature (Spanish literature today) So: 763
Montale, Eugenio [Italian poet] M: 741
Italian literature (The 1900's) I: 495
Montalvo, Garci Ordóñez de [Spanish author]
Amadis of Gaul A: 399
Montana M: 742 with pictures and maps
See also the list of Related articles in the Montana article
Montana, Joe [American football player] M: 761
Montana, University of M: 761
Montana Historical Society [Helena]
Montana (Libraries) M: 746
Montana Power Company
Montana (The early 2000's) M: 761
Montana State University M: 762
Montanari doll
Doll (Wax dolls) D: 290
Montana's Museum [Helena]
Montana (Museums) M: 746
Montane forest
Forest (Mountain evergreen forests) F: 395
Montauk Block building [Chicago]
Root, John Wellborn R: 472
Montcalm, Marquis de [French general] M: 762 with portrait
French and Indian wars (The French and Indian War) F: 512-513
Quebec (The 1700's) Q: 36
Quebec, Battle of Q: 37
Wolfe, James W: 377
Montcalm-Gozon, Louis Joseph de See Montcalm, Marquis de in this index
Monte, Philippe de [Franco-Flemish composer]
Classical music (Instrumental music) Ci: 646
Monte Albán [ancient city] M: 762
Mexico (The Southern Uplands) M: 462; (The Classic Period) M: 468
Zapotec Indians Z: 587
Monte Carlo [Monaco] M: 762
Monaco M: 699 with picture
Monte Cassino [abbey, Italy] M: 762
Benedict of Nursia, Saint B: 248
Monte Cristo [island, Mediterranean] See Montecristo in this index
Monte Rosa [mountain, Europe]
Alps A: 384 with picture
Montecristo [island, Mediterranean] M: 762
Montejo, Francisco de, the Younger [Spanish colonial official]
Yucatán Peninsula Y: 575
Montemayor, Jorge de [Spanish author]
Spanish literature (The 1500's) So: 758-759
Montenegrins [people]
Montenegro (People) M: 763
Montenegro M: 763 with picture and map
Balkans (The First Balkan War) B: 42; (The Second Balkan War) B: 42
Croatia (History) Ci: 1148a-1148c
Flag picture on F: 207
Serbia (History) S: 314-316
Monteregians [hills]
Quebec (Land regions) Q: 22
Monterey [California] M: 764
Monterey [ship]
Ford, Gerald Rudolph (Naval officer) F: 374
Monterey Bay Aquarium [California]
Aquarium, Public (Conservation) A: 578b
Monterey Bay National Marine Sanctuary
California (Places to visit) C: 46
Monterey cypress
Cypress Ci: 1205
Tree pictures on T: 424
Monterey International Pop Festival
Rock music (Outdoor rock festivals) R: 380b
Monterey Jack [cheese]
Cheese (Kinds of cheese) C: 392
Monterey Peninsula [California]
California (Places to visit) C: 46
Monterey pine
Pine (Western pines) P: 469-470
Monterrey [Mexico] M: 764
Mexico (The Sierra Madre Oriental) M: 462; (table:

Average monthly weather) M: 464
Monterrey, Battle of [1846]
Mexican War (Taylor's campaign) M: 446
Montespan, Marquise de [mistress of Louis XIV]
Maintenon, Marquise de M: 93
Montesquieu [French author] M: 764
Democracy (French contributions to democracy) D: 122
Enlightenment (The orderliness of nature) E: 326a-326b
Freedom (During the Enlightenment) F: 503
French literature (The Enlightenment) F: 520-521
Political science (Liberalism) P: 639
Montessori, Maria [Italian educator] M: 764a with portrait
Education (Early childhood education) E: 91
Montessori method M: 764a
Preschool (Learning through play) P: 756b
Montessori method [education] M: 764a
Education (Early childhood education) E: 91
Montessori, Maria M: 764a
Preschool (Learning through play) P: 756b
Montessori Society, American
Montessori method M: 764a
Monteux, Pierre [French conductor] M: 764a
Monteverdi, Claudio [Italian composer] M: 764a with portrait
Italy (Music) I: 505
Opera (Early Baroque opera) O: 797
Montevideo [Uruguay] M: 764b with picture
Uruguay U: 222 with picture; (Way of life) U: 223; (Climate) U: 226
Montez, Pedro [Spanish slave trader]
Amistad Rebellion A: 433
Montezuma I [Aztec emperor]
Aztec (Middle American growth of the Aztec empire) A: 1003
Mexico City (City of the Aztec) M: 478
Montezuma II [Aztec emperor] M: 764b with picture
Aztec (The Spanish conquest) A: 1003
Cortés, Hernán (Victory over the Aztec) Ci: 1073
Indian, American (After European contact) I: 171
Mexico (The Spanish conquest) M: 469 with picture
Montezuma baldcypress
Tree (Interesting facts about trees) T: 411
Montezuma Castle National Monument [Arizona] M: 765 with picture
National Park System (table: National monuments) N: 51
Montezuma quail [bird]
Quail Q: 4
Montfort, Simon de [English political leader]
Henry III H: 186
Parliament (History) P: 174
Montgolfier, Jacques Étienne [French inventor]
Montgolfier brothers M: 765
Montgolfier, Joseph Michel [French inventor]
Montgolfier brothers M: 765
Montgolfier brothers [French inventors] M: 765
Airplane picture on A: 229; (First human flights) A: 230
Balloon (History) B: 60 with picture
Montgomery [Alabama] M: 765 with picture
Alabama (Interesting facts) A: 257; (The Civil War and Reconstruction) A: 276
Confederate States of America (Government) Ci: 931
King, Martin Luther, Jr. K: 320
Selma marches S: 290
Montgomery, Bernard Law [British general] M: 766 with portrait
World War II (The Western Desert Campaign) W: 476-477
Montgomery, Lucy Maud [Canadian author] M: 766
Canadian literature (Fiction: 1850-1918) C: 157
Montgomery, Richard [American general]
Arnold, Benedict (A courageous soldier) A: 741
Montgomery M: 766
Revolution, American (The invasion of Canada) R: 275-276
Montgomery bus boycott [U.S. history] M: 767
African Americans (The civil rights movement) A: 1360
Alabama (The mid-1900's) A: 278 with picture
King, Martin Luther, Jr. (The early civil rights movement) K: 321
Parks, Rosa Louise P: 171
Montgomery GI Bill
Veterans Affairs, Department of (Benefits and other services) V: 343
Montgomery Improvement Association
Montgomery bus boycott M: 767
Montgomery of Alamein, Viscount [British general] See Montgomery, Bernard Law in this

index
Montgomery Street
San Francisco (Downtown San Francisco) S: 92-93
Montgomery Ward and Company
Mail-order business M: 66
Ward, Aaron Montgomery W: 35
Month M: 767
Calendar C: 29
Month in the Country, A [play by Turgenev]
Drama (Russian drama and Chekhov) D: 338
Russian literature (Early realism) R: 562
Monti, Mario [Italian political leader]
Italy (Recent developments) I: 519
Monticello [estate] M: 767
Charlottesville C: 385
Jefferson, Thomas (Lawyer) J: 78 with picture; (The sage of Monticello) J: 87
Nickel N: 404 with picture
Montigny mitrailleuse [gun]
Machine gun (History) M: 16 with picture
Montini, Giovanni Battista [birth name of]
Paul VI P: 200
Montmartre [hill]
Paris (Famous buildings) P: 163-164 with map
Montmorency Falls [Quebec]
Quebec (Rivers, waterfalls, and lakes) Q: 24; (Parks) Q: 36
Montmorency River [Quebec]
Quebec (Rivers, waterfalls, and lakes) Q: 24
Montoya, Joseph [American political leader]
Hispanic Americans (Expanding influence) H: 256
Montoya, Juan [Colombian race driver]
Automobile racing (table: Indianapolis 500 winners) A: 980
Montpelier [Vermont] M: 767
Montreal [Quebec] M: 768 with pictures and maps
Architecture picture on A: 610
Cartier, Jacques (Exploration of Canada) C: 262
Olympic Games (Boycotts) O: 753
Quebec Q: 10, picture on Q: 11; (Population) Q: 14 with pictures; (table: Average monthly weather) Q: 25
Quebec, Battle of (The attack on Quebec) Q: 37-38
Montreal, Island of
Montreal (The city) M: 768-769
Montreal, School of [poetry]
Canadian literature (Poetry: 1850-1918) C: 157; (Literature between the world wars) C: 158
Montreal, University of M: 779
Montreal Alouettes [team]
Football (Canadian Football League) F: 364
Montreal (Sports) M: 775
Montreal Canadiens [team]
Hockey (table: National Hockey League) H: 281
Montreal Exchange [stock exchange]
Montreal (Trade and finance) M: 776-777
Montreal Harbour
Montreal (Transportation) M: 775-776
Montreal Museum of Fine Arts
Montreal (Museums) M: 773
Quebec (Museums) Q: 15
Montreal-Pierre Elliott Trudeau International Airport
Montreal (Transportation) M: 775-776
Montreal Protocol on Substances That Deplete the Ozone Layer [1987]
Antarctica (Scientific research) A: 539-540
United Nations (Important dates in UN history) U: 94
Montresor, Beni [Italian artist]
Caldecott Medal (table: 1965) C: 26
Montreux Convention [1936]
Bosporus B: 494
Dardanelles D: 35
Monts, Sieur de [French explorer] See Du Gua, Pierre, Sieur de Monts in this index
Montserrat [island, Caribbean Sea] M: 779
Montserrat [monastery, Spain] M: 780
Montserrat [mountain, Spain]
Montserrat M: 780
Montuno [clothing]
Panama (Clothing) P: 118
"Monty Python's Flying Circus" [television program] M: 780
Cleese, John Ci: 661 with picture
Monty Python's Spamalot [musical]
"Monty Python's Flying Circus" M: 780
Musical comedy (Musical comedy today) M: 961
Monument [architecture] M: 780
American Battle Monuments Commission A: 408
Sculpture (As monuments and memorials) S: 229
Monument Avenue [Richmond]
Richmond (The city) R: 332 with picture
Monument of African Renaissance [statue]
Dakar D: 9
Monument to Independence

Mexico City *picture on* M: 476
Monument to the Boy Heroes
Mexico (Difficulties of the early republic) M: 471
Mexico City (Independence) M: 478
Monument Valley
Arizona (Land regions) A: 680 *with picture*
Earth *picture on* E: 28
Utah *picture on* U: 230; (Places to visit) U: 238
Monument Valley Navajo Tribal Park
Arizona (Places to visit) A: 678
MOOC [education]
Universities and colleges (Online learning) U: 211
Mood [emotion] M: 780
Bipolar disorder B: 327
Depression D: 151
Mental illness M: 404
Seasonal affective disorder S: 272
Mood [grammar] M: 780
Conjugation Ci: 950
Mood disorder [psychology]
Fibromyalgia F: 90
Mental illness (Mood disorders) M: 405
Mood episode [psychology]
Bipolar disorder B: 327
Moodie, Susanna [Canadian author] M: 781
Canadian literature (Early English-Canadian literature) C: 157
Moodie, Thomas H. [American political leader]
North Dakota (table) N: 513
Moody, Dan [American political leader]
Texas (table) T: 203
Moody, Dwight Lyman [American religious leader] M: 781
Hymn (History) H: 475
Revivalism R: 269
Moody, Helen Wills [American tennis player] M: 781
Tennis (The spread of tennis) T: 165-166d *with picture*
Moody, Maryon Elspeth [wife of]
Pearson, Lester Bowles (Boyhood) P: 220
Moody, Paul [American inventor]
Lowell, Francis Cabot L: 510
Moody, William Henry [American jurist]
Justice, Department of (table) J: 203
Roosevelt, Theodore (table) R: 466
Supreme Court of the United States (table) So: 1000
Moody, William Vaughn [American author] M: 781
Moody, Z. F. [American political leader]
Oregon (table) O: 845
Moody Bible Institute [Chicago] M: 781 *with picture*
Moog, Robert A. [American physicist]
Synthesizer So: 1068
Moon M: 782 *with pictures and maps*
See also Satellite *in this index*
Armstrong, Neil Alden A: 723
Astronaut (Achievements in space) A: 829 *with picture*
Astronomy (How the moon moves) A: 835; (Direct sampling) A: 846
Blue moon B: 421
Calendar C: 29
Chinese New Year C: 512
Earth (Earth and its moon) E: 18
Earthquake (Quakes elsewhere in the solar system) E: 38b
Eclipse E: 51
Exploration (Human space travel) E: 452
Geology (Geology of the solar system) G: 100
Harvest moon H: 81
Laser (Measuring) L: 83 *with picture*
Magnetism (Other astronomical bodies) M: 60d
Month M: 767
Ocean (Tides) O: 659
Planetarium P: 514a
Selene S: 289
Space exploration So: 694 *with picture*; (Lunar probes) So: 708 *with picture*; (Apollo: Mission to the moon) So: 714 *with pictures*
Telescope *picture on* T: 107
Television *picture on* T: 110
Tidal forces T: 280
Tide T: 280 *with diagrams*
Volcano (Volcanoes in the solar system) V: 442b
Moon, Keith [British musician]
Who, The W: 296
Moon, Sun Myung [Korean religious leader]
Cult (Modern cults) Ci: 1185
Moon and Sixpence, The [book by Maugham]
Maugham, W. Somerset M: 312
Moon bear
Bear (Asiatic black bears) B: 185
Moon for the Misbegotten, A [play by O'Neill]
American literature (Drama) A: 422-423
O'Neill, Eugene (His plays) O: 762

Moon rock
Moon *picture on* M: 790
Mooney, Edward Francis [American religious leader]
Cardinal (table: American cardinals) C: 211
Mooney, William [American political leader]
Tammany, Society of T: 22
Moonflower M: 796 *with picture*
Morning-glory M: 809
Moonies [cult]
Cult (Modern cults) Ci: 1185
Moonlight [play by Pinter]
Pinter, Harold P: 475
Moonlit Street Scene in Edo [painting by Hiroshige]
Tokyo *picture on* T: 319
Moonquake [seismology]
Earthquake (Quakes elsewhere in the solar system) E: 38b
Moonshine [liquor]
Alcoholic beverage (History) A: 337
Moonstone [mineral] M: 796
Feldspar F: 68
Gem *picture on* G: 78
Moonstone, The [book by Collins]
Collins, Wilkie Ci: 776
Detective story (History) D: 162-163
Moor [geography] M: 796
Scotland (Land regions) S: 217
Moor [nautical term]
Ship (Nautical terms) S: 405
Moor [person] See Moors *in this index*
Moore, A. Harry [American political leader]
New Jersey (table) N: 249
Moore, Alfred [American jurist]
Supreme Court of the United States (table) So: 1000
Moore, Andrew Barry [American political leader]
Alabama (table) A: 274
Moore, Anne Carroll [American librarian]
Regina Medal (table: 1960) R: 206
Moore, Arch A., Jr. [American political leader]
West Virginia (table) W: 225
Moore, Archie [American boxer]
Boxing (The 1950's) B: 532a
Moore, Brian [Irish author]
Irish literature (Fiction) I: 432
Moore, Charles F. [American political leader]
Idaho (table) I: 42
Moore, Clement Clarke [American poet] M: 796
Christmas (Other customs) C: 536
Santa Claus (Santa's appearance) S: 114
Moore, Daniel K. [American political leader]
North Carolina (table) N: 490
Moore, Douglas Stuart [American composer] M: 796
Moore, G. E. [British philosopher] M: 796
Moore, Gabriel [American political leader]
Alabama (table) A: 274
Moore, George Edward [British philosopher] See Moore, G. E. *in this index*
Moore, Gerald [British pianist]
Fischer-Dieskau, Dietrich F: 143
Moore, Gordon [American engineer]
Noyce, Robert N: 518
Moore, Harriet Louise [wife of]
Bowell, Sir Mackenzie (Early life) B: 518
Moore, Henry [British sculptor] M: 797
Hirshhorn Museum and Sculpture Garden H: 243 *with picture*
Sculpture (Henry Moore) S: 258 *with picture*
Moore, Hiram [American inventor]
Combine Ci: 866
Moore, Marianne [American poet] M: 797 *with portrait*
Moore, Samuel B. [American political leader]
Alabama (table) A: 274
Moore, Sara Jane [American public figure]
Ford, Gerald Rudolph (Two attempted assassinations) F: 378
Moore, Stanford [American chemist]
Nobel Prizes (Chemistry: 1972) N: 444
Moore, Thomas [Irish poet] M: 797
Irish literature (Early works in English) I: 431
Popular music (Revolutionary War to 1840) P: 669
Moore, Thomas O. [American political leader]
Louisiana (table) L: 496
Moore, William [American political leader]
Pennsylvania (table) P: 263
Moore College of Art & Design
Philadelphia (Education) P: 362
Moorer, Thomas Hinman [American admiral]
Joint Chiefs of Staff (table) J: 156
Moore's Creek Bridge, Battle of [1776]
North Carolina (Revolution and independence) N: 492
Revolution, American (table) R: 276; (Fighting in the Chesapeake and Southern colonies)

R: 276-278
Moores Creek National Battlefield [North Carolina]
National Park System (table: National battlefields) N: 55
Moorhead [Minnesota]
Fargo F: 28
Moorhen [bird]
Bird *picture on* B: 344e
Gallinule G: 16
Mooring [oceanography]
Ocean (Research ships) O: 662-663
Mooring mast
Airship (Storage) A: 251
Moorish architecture
Alhambra A: 366 *with picture*
Islamic art I: 467 *with picture*
Moorish Empire See Moors *in this index*
Moorish idol [fish]
Fish *picture on* F: 154
Moorland-Spingarn Research Center
Howard University H: 400
Moors [people] M: 797 *with picture*
Alhambra A: 366
Boabdil B: 427
Granada G: 304, G: 304
Mali (People) M: 106
Mauritania (People) M: 314
Sri Lanka (People) So: 817
Moor's Indian Charity School
Dartmouth College D: 39
Moose M: 798 *with picture*
Animal *picture on* A: 478
Ecology (Ecosystems) E: 54-55
Maine (Plant and animal life) M: 82 *with picture*
Moose, Loyal Order of [organization]
Moose International, Inc. M: 799
Moose International, Inc. [organization] M: 799 *with picture*
Moose Jaw [Saskatchewan] M: 799
Moosehaven [Florida]
Moose International, Inc. M: 799
Moosehead Lake
Maine (Rivers and lakes) M: 82
Mooseheart [Illinois]
Moose International, Inc. M: 799
Moosilauke, Mount
New Hampshire (Mountains) N: 220 *with map*
Moot court
Law *picture on* L: 138
Moped [motorcycle]
Motorcycle (Motorbikes) M: 878
Transportation *picture on* T: 393
Mora, Juan Rafael [Costa Rican political leader] M: 799
Costa Rica (Independence) Ci: 1084
Moraine [geology] M: 799
Alps (How the Alps were formed) A: 384
Glacier (How glaciers shape the land) G: 203 *with pictures*
Ice age (Extent of the Pleistocene glaciers) I: 6
Island (Barrier islands) I: 473
Minnesota (Land regions) M: 596
Moraine Lake [Alberta]
Banff National Park B: 77
Moral development
Moral education (Methods of moral education) M: 799
Moral dilemma
Moral education (Moral development) M: 799
Moral education M: 799
Curriculum (Curriculum changes) Ci: 1197
Moral Essays [book by Pope]
Pope, Alexander P: 667
Moral philosophy
Philosophy (Philosophy and science) P: 385
Morale [psychology] M: 800
Fatigue F: 55
Morales, Evo [Bolivian political leader]
Bolivia (Recent developments) B: 447
Latin America (In the early 2000's) L: 111
Morales Bermúdez, Francisco [Peruvian political leader]
Peru (Socialist reforms) P: 316
Moralist literature
French literature (Classical prose) F: 520
Morality play M: 800
Drama (Miracle plays and morality plays) D: 329
English literature (Early English drama) E: 316
French literature (Early drama) F: 519
Morals See Ethics; Moral education *in this index*
Morals [book by Plutarch]
Plutarch P: 580
Moran [people]
Maasai M: 2
Moran, Edward [American artist]
Statue of Liberty *picture on* So: 877

Morane-Saulnier M.S. 760 [airplane]
Airplane *picture on* A: 236
Morant Bay Rebellion [Jamaican history]
Jamaica (History) J: 24
Moratín, Leandro Fernández de [Spanish author]
Spanish literature (The 1800's) So: 761
Moratorium [economics] M: 800
Whale (The future of whales) W: 264
Morava [region, Czech Republic] *See* Moravia *in this index*
Morava River [Czech Republic-Serbia]
Czech Republic (Land and climate) Ci: 1211 *with map*
Moravia M: 800
Serbia (Land and climate) S: 314 *with map*
Moravia [region, Czech Republic] M: 800 *with picture and map*
Czech Republic Ci: 1209; (Habsburg rule) Ci: 1213
Czechoslovakia Ci: 1215 *with maps*
Moravia, Alberto [Italian author]
Italian literature (The 1900's) I: 495
Moravian Church [religious group] M: 801
Brethren B: 593
Easter (Other customs) E: 44
Pennsylvania Dutch P: 270
Protestantism (History) P: 834
Moravian Empire [Czech history] *See* Great Moravian Empire *in this index*
Moravian Lowlands [region, Czech Republic]
Czech Republic (Land and climate) Ci: 1211 *with map*
Moraviantown, Battle of *See* Thames River, Battle of *in this index*
Moray [sea animal]
Eel E: 114
Fish *pictures on* F: 154, F: 155
Moray Firth [bay, Scotland]
Scotland (Rivers and lakes) S: 217 *with map*
Morazán, Francisco [Central American political leader]
Costa Rica (Independence) Ci: 1084
Mordan, Sampson [British engineer]
Pencil (History) P: 236
Mordant [chemistry] M: 801
Dye (How dyes work) D: 395
Lake L: 35
Mordecai [Biblical figure]
Esther, Book of E: 360
Mordvinoff, Nicolas [American author/artist]
Caldecott Medal (table: 1952) C: 26
More [sociology] *See* Mores *in this index*
More, Sir Thomas [English government official] M: 801 *with portrait*
Biography (The Renaissance) B: 313
Holbein, Hans, the Younger H: 289
Renaissance (Desiderius Erasmus and Saint Thomas More) R: 238
Science fiction (Forerunners of science fiction) S: 205
Utopia U: 252
More Bab Ballads [poems by Gilbert]
Gilbert, Sir William Schwenck G: 189
More Die of Heartbreak [book by Bellow]
Bellow, Saul B: 244
More New Arabian Nights [stories by Stevenson]
Stevenson, Robert Louis (Other writings) So: 898
More Than Human [book by Sturgeon]
Sturgeon, Theodore So: 934
Morea [region, Greece] *See* Peloponnesus *in this index*
Moreau, Gustave [French painter]
Prometheus *picture on* P: 818
Moreau River
South Dakota (Rivers and lakes) So: 676 *with map*
Morehead, John H. [American political leader]
Nebraska (table) N: 110
Morehead, John M. [American political leader]
North Carolina (table) N: 490
Morehead Planetarium and Science Center
North Carolina (Places to visit) N: 482
Morehouse, Albert P. [American political leader]
Missouri (table) M: 668
Morel
Mushroom (Mushroomlike fungi) M: 945
Morel, Carlos [Argentine painter]
Argentina (The arts) A: 651-652
Morelos [state, Mexico]
Mexico City (Metropolitan area) M: 476b
Morelos y Pavón, José María [Mexican patriot]
Latin America (The movement toward independence) L: 106-107
Mexico (Revolt against the Spaniards) M: 470
Moreno, Mario [Mexican actor]
Mexico (Motion pictures) M: 460
Moreno, Rita [Puerto Rican actress]
Motion picture (Best performance by an actress

in a supporting role: 1961) M: 862b
Moréri, Louis [French editor]
Encyclopedia (From the 1200's to the 1600's) E: 268a
Mores [sociology] M: 802
Custom Ci: 1201
Sumner, William Graham So: 973
Moresby, John [British explorer]
Port Moresby P: 681
Moresby Island
Queen Charlotte Islands Q: 39
Moreton Bay [Australia]
Queensland (History) Q: 40
Moreton Bay fig [tree]
Tree *picture on* T: 427
Morga, Antonio de [Spanish colonial official]
Rizal, José R: 357
Morgagni, Giovanni Battista [Italian anatomist] M: 802
Morgan, Barbara [American educator]
Space exploration (Completing the station) So: 726
Morgan, Daniel [American general] M: 802
Revolution, American (Cowpens and Guilford Courthouse) R: 285
Morgan, Edwin Denison [American political leader]
Arthur, Chester Alan (Political growth) A: 755
New York (table) N: 313
Morgan, Ephraim F. [American political leader]
West Virginia (table) W: 225; (Labor developments) W: 229
Morgan, Garrett Augustus [American inventor] M: 802 *with portrait*
Morgan, Sir Henry [English pirate] M: 803
Panama (The Spanish colonial period) P: 120
Panama City P: 128
Pirate (The Caribbean) P: 495
Morgan, J. P. [American banker] M: 803 *with portrait*
Carnegie, Andrew (Retirement) C: 242
Cleveland, Grover (Saving the gold standard) Ci: 673
JPMorgan Chase & Co. J: 177
Pierpont Morgan Library P: 458
Roosevelt, Theodore ("Trust buster") R: 464
United States Steel Corporation U: 204
Morgan, J. P., Jr. [American banker] M: 803
Pierpont Morgan Library P: 458
Morgan, Jason [American scientist]
Plate tectonics (History of tectonic theory) P: 564-565
Morgan, Joe [American baseball player]
Baseball (table: Hall of Fame) B: 134a
Morgan, John Hunt [Confederate general] M: 804
Civil War, American (Raids) Ci: 629
Indiana (The Civil War) I: 216
Morgan, John Pierpont [American banker] *See* Morgan, J. P. *in this index*
Morgan, John Pierpont, Jr. [American banker] *See* Morgan, J. P., Jr. *in this index*
Morgan, Julia [American architect] M: 804
Morgan, Junius Spencer [American banker] M: 804
Morgan, Justin [American farmer] M: 804
Morgan, Leon O. [American physicist]
Americium A: 432
Morgan, Lewis Henry [American anthropologist] M: 804
Anthropology (Early anthropological thought) A: 548
Morgan, Morgan [American settler]
West Virginia (White settlement) W: 226
Morgan, Sally [Australian author]
Australia (Literature) A: 904-905
Morgan, Thomas Hunt [American geneticist] M: 804
Biology (The growth of modern biology) B: 319-320
Cell (The 1900's) C: 337-338
Evolution (The synthetic theory) E: 432-433
Heredity (The birth of genetics) H: 208
Morgan, William [American public figure]
Anti-Masonic Party A: 556
Morgan, William G. [American educator]
Massachusetts (Interesting facts) M: 271
Volleyball V: 445
Young Men's Christian Association (History) Y: 573
Morgan, William W. [American astronomer]
Star (The Hertzsprung-Russell diagram) So: 845-846
Morgan horse
Horse *picture on* H: 344; (table: Some types and breeds of horses) H: 343; (Saddle horses) H: 343
Morgan, Justin M: 804

Morgan Library & Museum [New York City] *See* Pierpont Morgan Library *in this index*
Morganite [mineral]
Gem *picture on* G: 78
Morgan's Raiders [U.S. history]
Civil War, American (Raids) Ci: 629
Indiana (The Civil War) I: 216
Morgan, John Hunt M: 804
Ohio (The Civil War) O: 702
Morgantown [West Virginia] M: 805
Morgarten, Battle of [1315]
Switzerland (The struggle for freedom) So: 1059
Morgenstern, Oskar [Austrian economist]
Economics (Modern economics) E: 64-65
Game theory G: 23
Morgenthau, Henry, Jr. [American government official] M: 805
Truman, Harry S. (table) T: 469
Morgenthau Plan [World War II]
Morgenthau, Henry, Jr. M: 805
Morial, Ernest N. "Dutch" [American political leader]
Louisiana (The mid-1900's) L: 500-501
New Orleans (The late 1900's) N: 285
Morínigo, Higinio [Paraguayan political leader]
Paraguay (Political unrest) P: 149
Morison, Samuel Eliot [American historian] M: 805
Morisot, Berthe [French painter] M: 805 *with picture*
Impressionism (French Impressionism) I: 93-94
Painting (Edouard Manet and the Impressionists) P: 71; (Women artists) P: 73-75
Morita, Akio [Japanese businessman]
Sony Corporation So: 594
"Mork and Mindy" [television program]
Williams, Robin W: 310
Morley, Christopher [American author]
Doyle, Arthur Conan D: 316
Morley, Clarence J. [American political leader]
Colorado (table) Ci: 844
Morley, Edward W. [American physicist]
Ether E: 365
Michelson, Albert Abraham M: 487
Physics (Einstein and relativity) P: 441
Relativity (The Michelson-Morley experiment) R: 210
Morley, Thomas [English composer] M: 805
Morley-Minto Reforms [1909]
India (Rise of Indian nationalism) I: 131
Mormon [butterfly]
Butterfly *picture on* B: 737
Mormon cricket [insect] M: 806 *with picture*
Grasshopper (Long-horned grasshoppers) G: 328
Utah (The Mormons) U: 246
Mormon Tabernacle [Salt Lake City]
Mormons *picture on* M: 808
Salt Lake City (The city) S: 76
Mormon Tabernacle Choir
Mormons (Mormons today) M: 809 *with picture*
Mormon Temple [Salt Lake City]
Mormons *picture on* M: 808
Utah (Visitor's guide) U: 238 *with picture*
Mormon Trail [U.S. history]
Wyoming W: 517; (The great trails) W: 533
Mormon War *See* Utah War *in this index*
Mormons [religious group] M: 806 *with pictures*
Brigham Young University B: 608
Deseret D: 154
Genealogy G: 82
Idaho (Exploration and early settlement) I: 42
Las Vegas (Early days) L: 89
Marriage (Wedding ceremonies) M: 220
Nauvoo N: 69
Nevada (Early settlement) N: 174
Pioneer life in America (Crossing the Plains) P: 485-486
Salt Lake City S: 75
Smith, Joseph S: 517
Utah U: 230; (The Mormons) U: 246
Western frontier life in America (Newcomers) W: 234
Westward movement in America (Utah) W: 249
Young, Brigham Y: 571
Mormyrid, Elephant-nose [fish] *See* Elephant-nose mormyrid *in this index*
Morning-after pill
Birth control (Methods of birth control) B: 378
Morning-glory [flower] M: 809 *with picture*
Flower (Garden annuals) F: 276 *with picture*; (table) F: 300 *with picture*
Morning sickness
Pregnancy (Other common symptoms of pregnancy) P: 734b
Morning star [planet]
Evening star E: 423
Lucifer L: 514
Morningside Heights [district]

New York City (Manhattan) N: 323-326
Moro [people]
 Moors M: 797
 Pershing, John Joseph (Promotion) P: 296
Moro, Aldo [Italian political leader]
 Italy (Social problems) I: 518
Moro Islamic Liberation Front [political group]
 Philippines (Recovering democracy) P: 381;
  (Recent developments) P: 381
Moro Naba [title]
 Burkina Faso (People) B: 706
Moro National Liberation Front [political group]
 Philippines (Recovering democracy) P: 381
Moroccan Letters [play by Cadalso]
 Spanish literature (The 1700's) So: 760
Morocco M: 810 *with pictures and maps*
 Africa *picture on* A: 107
 Barbary States B: 105 *with map*
 Clothing *pictures on* Ci: 690, Ci: 692
 Flag *picture on* F: 199
 Middle East M: 530
 Tangier T: 27
 Western Sahara W: 241
Moroni [angel]
 Mormons (Church doctrines and ordinances)
  M: 806 *with picture*; (Revelations) M: 808
 Smith, Joseph (Early life) S: 517
Moroni [Comoros] M: 816
 Comoros *picture on* Ci: 900
Moronobu [Japanese printmaker]
 Japanese print (The master print artists) J: 63
Morphea [disease]
 Scleroderma S: 209
Morpheme [linguistics]
 Language (Words and morphemes) L: 62
Morpheus [Greek mythology] M: 816
 Hypnos H: 477
Morphine [drug] M: 816
 Analgesic A: 448
 Codeine Ci: 749
 Drug (Effect on the body) D: 354
 Drug abuse (Heroin) D: 362; (table: Some
  commonly abused drugs) D: 363; (History)
  D: 365
 Morpheus M: 816
 Opiate O: 810
 Opium O: 811
Morphological type [classification]
 Archaeology (Classification) A: 597
Morphology [science] M: 816
 Botany (Plant classification and form) B: 508
Morrill, Anson P. [American political leader]
 Maine (table) M: 87
Morrill, David L. [American political leader]
 New Hampshire (table) N: 223
Morrill, Edmund Needham [American political
 leader]
 Kansas (table) K: 234
Morrill, Justin Smith [American political leader]
 M: 816
 Land-grant university L: 56
Morrill, Lot M. [American government official]
 Maine (table) M: 87
Morrill Act [1862]
 Agricultural education (Colleges and universities)
  A: 144
 Civil War, American (Economy) Ci: 623
 Land-grant university L: 56
 Morrill, Justin Smith M: 816
 Public lands (Disposal of public lands) P: 858
 Universities and colleges (Governing boards)
  U: 208
 Vocational education (Early vocational education
  in schools) V: 435
Morrill Act [1890]
 Land-grant university L: 56
Morrill Tariff Act [1861]
 Morrill, Justin Smith M: 816
Morris, Desmond [British zoologist] M: 816
Morris, Esther Hobart [American social reformer]
 M: 816
 Wyoming W: 517; (Territorial progress) W: 534
Morris, Gouverneur [American patriot] M: 816
 Cent C: 350
 Constitution of the United States (The
  Constitutional Convention) Ci: 999-1000
 Erie Canal E: 351
Morris, Lewis [American jurist]
 New Jersey (Colonial days) N: 250
 Zenger, John Peter Z: 589
Morris, Lewis [American patriot] M: 817
Morris, Luzon B. [American political leader]
 Connecticut (table) Ci: 967
Morris, Mark [American choreographer]
 Ballet (Ballet in Europe) B: 54 *with picture*
 Dance (Modern dance) D: 30-31
Morris, Robert [American patriot] M: 817

Philadelphia (The Revolutionary War period)
 P: 366
 Washington, George (Recall to duty) W: 107
Morris, Steveland Judkins [birth name of]
 Wonder, Stevie W: 389
Morris, William [British designer] M: 817
 Architecture (Early modern architecture in
  Europe) A: 627
 Book (The 1800's) B: 467-468
 Tapestry (History) T: 39-40
Morris Canal
 Newark (History) N: 357-358
Morris chair
 Morris, William M: 817
Morris dance
 Dance (Folk dances) D: 26
Morrisania [district]
 New York City (The Bronx) N: 328-329
Morrison, Cameron [American political leader]
 North Carolina (table) N: 490
Morrison, deLesseps S. [American political leader]
 New Orleans (Civic improvements) N: 284
Morrison, Frank B. [American political leader]
 Nebraska (table) N: 110
Morrison, John T. [American political leader]
 Idaho (table) I: 42
Morrison, Marion Michael [American actor] *See*
 Wayne, John *in this index*
Morrison, Robert [British missionary]
 Missionary (History) M: 621
Morrison, Toni [American author] M: 817
 African Americans *picture on* A: 136r
 American literature (Works by minority writers)
  A: 425 *with portrait*
Morrison, William [American inventor]
 Automobile *picture on* A: 963; (The electric car)
  A: 965
Morrissey [ship]
 Bartlett, Robert Abram B: 121
Morristown [New Jersey]
 Washington, George (Shortage of supplies) W: 99
Morristown National Historical Park [New Jersey]
 National Park System (table: National historical
  parks) N: 56-57
 New Jersey (Places to visit) N: 240
Morro Castle [Cuba]
 Santiago de Cuba S: 116
Morrow, Anne [American poet] *See* Lindbergh,
 Anne Morrow *in this index*
Morrow, Dwight Whitney [American diplomat]
 Coolidge, Calvin (Foreign affairs) Ci: 1033
Morrow, Jeremiah [American political leader]
 Ohio (table) O: 699
Morse, Samuel Finley Breese [American inventor]
 M: 817 *with pictures*
 Cable (Telegraph cables) C: 5
 Communication (The 1800's) Ci: 881-882 *with
  picture*; (Famous first words) Ci: 884
 Morse code M: 819
 Telegraph (The Morse telegraph) T: 90 *with
  picture*
Morse code [communications] M: 819 *with pictures*
 Flag (Flags that talk) F: 208
 Heliograph H: 174
 Radio, Amateur R: 95
 Telegraph T: 90; (The Morse telegraph) T: 90 *with
  picture*
Morsi, Mohamed [Egyptian political leader]
 Egypt (Recent developments) E: 133
Mortal Kombat [electronic game]
 Electronic game (Fighting games) E: 204e
Mortality
 Life expectancy L: 280
Mortality, Infant *See* Infant mortality *in this index*
Mortality rate *See* Death rate *in this index*
Mortality table
 Insurance (How life insurance premiums are
  determined) I: 310
Mortar [building material]
 Brick (Mortar) B: 599
Mortar [weapon] M: 820 *with picture*
 Army *picture on* A: 725
 Artillery (Kinds of artillery) A: 762
 Civil War, American *picture on* Ci: 619
Mortarboard [clothing]
 Graduation G: 297
Morte Darthur, Le [book by Malory]
 Arthur, King A: 757
 English literature (The development of English
  romances) E: 315
 Galahad, Sir G: 7
 Gawain, Sir G: 71
 Lancelot, Sir L: 56
 Malory, Sir Thomas M: 111
Mortensen, Dale T. [American economist]
 Nobel Prizes (Economics: 2010) N: 450
Mortgage [economics] M: 820

African Americans (Housing and lending
 discrimination) A: 136s
Bank (Crisis in finance) B: 95
Bush, George Walker (Economy) B: 722j
Credit (Lending institutions) Ci: 1124
Equity E: 348
Federal Home Loan Mortgage Corporation F: 64
Federal National Mortgage Association F: 64
Government National Mortgage Association
 G: 292
Housing (Private housing) H: 390; (Housing since
 1900) H: 391
Interest I: 321
Savings and loan association S: 165
Mortgage bond
 Bond (Kinds of bonds) B: 454
Mortician
 Embalming (Modern embalming) E: 255
Mortise lock
 Lock (Types of locks) L: 410-411 *with picture*
Morton, Jelly Roll [American musician] M: 821
 Jazz (Early jazz) J: 70
Morton, John [American patriot] M: 821
Morton, Julius Sterling [American political leader]
 M: 821
 Arbor Day A: 592
 Cleveland, Grover (table) Ci: 672
 Nebraska (Places to visit) N: 102
Morton, Levi Parsons [American political leader]
 M: 821
 Harrison, Benjamin (Election of 1888) H: 71-72;
  (table) H: 72
 New York (table) N: 313
 Vice president of the United States V: 348 *with
  portrait*
Morton, Marcus [American political leader]
 Massachusetts (table) M: 288
Morton, Oliver Perry [American political leader]
 M: 821
 Harrison, Benjamin (Army commander) H: 70
 Indiana (table) I: 214
Morton, Paul [American government official]
 Roosevelt, Theodore (table) R: 466
Morton, Rogers Clark Ballard [American
 government official]
 Commerce, Department of (table) Ci: 871
 Interior, Department of the (table) I: 325
Morton, William Thomas Green [American
 dentist] M: 821
 Anesthesia (History) A: 459
 Dentistry (Modern dentistry) D: 144-145
 Ether E: 365
 Hospital (The 1800's) H: 373
 Long, Crawford Williamson L: 446
 Medicine *picture on* M: 374; (The first anesthetic)
  M: 375
Morton Arboretum [Illinois]
 Illinois (Places to visit) I: 62
Mortuary science
 Embalming (Modern embalming) E: 255
Morula [biology]
 Reproduction, Human (The first days of
  pregnancy) R: 246
Morumbi Stadium
 São Paulo (The city) S: 117-118
Mosaddeq, Mohammad [Iranian political leader]
 Iran (The nationalist movement) I: 406
 Mohammad Reza Pahlavi M: 687
Mosaic [art] M: 822 *with pictures*
 Architecture (Medieval architecture) A: 617
 Byzantine art (Frescoes and mosaics) *picture on*
  B: 749, B: 750
 Byzantine Empire *pictures on* B: 752, B: 754
 Europe (Medieval art) E: 391
 Indian, American *picture on* I: 146
 Mural M: 929
 Rome, Ancient *picture on* R: 439; (Sculpture,
  painting, and mosaics) R: 442
 Shell *picture on* S: 390
Mosaic Code [law]
 Law (Early developments in the East) L: 133
Mosaic disease M: 822
 Lily L: 304
 Raspberry (Diseases and pests) R: 145
Mosander, Carl [Swedish chemist]
 Erbium E: 349
 Lanthanum L: 69
 Terbium T: 169
 Yttrium Y: 575
Mosasaur [extinct reptile]
 Dinosaur (Plant and animal life) D: 206b
 Lizard (How lizards move) L: 399
 Prehistoric animal (Other reptiles) P: 737
Mosbacher, Robert A. [American government
 official]
 Commerce, Department of (table) Ci: 871
Mosby, John Singleton [Confederate military

leader] M: 822
Moscone, George [American political leader]
  San Francisco (Political leaders murdered) S: 98
Moscoso, Luis de [Spanish explorer]
  De Soto, Hernando (Journey to the Mississippi)
    D: 161 with map
Moscoso, Mireya [Panamanian political leader]
  Latin America (Family life) L: 96-97
  Panama (The 1990's) P: 121
Moscow [Russia] M: 823 with pictures and map
  Ivan IV, the Terrible I: 520
  Kremlin K: 387
  Lenin, V. I. picture on L: 194
  Olympic Games (Boycotts) O: 753
  Russia pictures on R: 525, R: 537; (City life) R: 533;
    (The rise of Moscow) R: 548; (Alexander I)
    R: 550; (Recent developments) R: 555
  Terrorism (Recent developments) T: 180
  Union of Soviet Socialist Republics pictures on
    U: 29, U: 31
  World War II (The invasion of the Soviet Union)
    W: 477
Moscow, Battle of [1812]
  Napoleonic Wars (The invasion of Russia) N: 19
    with map
Moscow, Peace of [1940]
  Russo-Finnish wars (The Winter War) R: 566a
Moscow, Treaty of [2002]
  Arms control (Arms control in the late 1900's and
    early 2000's) A: 722
  Bush, George Walker (Arms control) B: 722h-722i
Moscow Art Theater [Russia] M: 828
  Russian literature picture on R: 558
  Theater (Russia) T: 248-249
Moscow Canal [Russia]
  Canal (table) C: 164
Moscow Declaration on General Security [1943]
  United Nations (The Atlantic Charter) U: 94
Moscow State University
  Moscow (Education) M: 824
Moscow to the End of the Line [book by Erofeev]
  Russian literature (Modern Soviet literature)
    R: 564-565
Mosel River See Moselle River in this index
Moseley, Henry Gwyn-Jeffreys [British physicist]
  M: 828
Moseley, William D. [American political leader]
  Florida (table) F: 260
Moseley Braun, Carol [American political leader]
  M: 828 with portrait
  African Americans picture on A: 136q
Mosella [book by Ausonius]
  Latin literature (Later periods) L: 117
Moselle [wine]
  Moselle River M: 828
Moselle River [France-Germany] M: 828
  Luxembourg (Economy) L: 531
  Wine (Wines from Germany) W: 337
Moser-Pröll, Annemarie [Austrian skier]
  Skiing (The middle and late 1900's) S: 487-488
Moses [Biblical figure] M: 828 with picture
  Aaron A: 3
  Bible (The Law) B: 280 with picture
  Deuteronomy D: 172
  Exodus E: 438
  Jews (The Exodus) J: 121
  Judaism (The Hebrew Bible) J: 180
  Law (Early developments in the East) L: 133
  Pentateuch P: 274
  Qur'ān Q: 44
  Religion (Judaism) R: 219 with picture
  Ten Commandments T: 131
Moses [sculpture by Michelangelo]
  Italy picture on I: 505
Moses, Grandma [American painter] M: 830 with
    pictures
Moses, Horace A. [American businessman]
  Junior Achievement J: 196
Moses, John [American political leader]
  North Dakota (table) N: 513
Moses, Phoebe Ann [birth name of]
  Oakley, Annie O: 638
Moses, Thomas Salmon [husband of]
  Moses, Grandma M: 830
Moses de Leon [Spanish author]
  Hebrew literature (Medieval works) H: 162
  Kabbalah K: 208
Moses-Saunders Dam [Saint Lawrence River]
  Saint Lawrence Seaway (The hydroelectric power
    project) S: 44
MOSFET [electronics] See Metal oxide
  semiconductor field effect transistor in this index
Moshav [community]
  Asia (Country life) A: 779-780
  Israel (Rural life) I: 481 with picture
Moshoeshoe [African king]
  Lesotho (History) L: 208

Moshoeshoe II, Motlotlehi [king of Lesotho]
  Lesotho (History) L: 208
Mosi-oa-Tunya [waterfall] See Victoria Falls in this
  index
Mosi-oa-Tunya National Park [Zambia]
  National park (table) N: 42f; (Other interesting
    national parks) N: 42h
Moskovitz, Dustin [American programmer]
  Facebook (History) F: 4
Moslems [religious group] See Muslims in this index
Mosley, Walter [American author] M: 830
Mosque [architecture] M: 830 with picture
  Afghanistan picture on A: 93
  Africa pictures on A: 108, A: 116a
  Architecture diagram on A: 614; (Islamic
    architecture) A: 613
  Asia picture on A: 779
  Cairo (The city) C: 16 with picture
  Egypt picture on E: 125
  Iran picture on I: 398
  Islam picture on I: 465; (The Five Pillars of Islam)
    I: 463
  Islamic art picture on I: 467; (Mosques) I: 468
  Middle East picture on M: 530
  Minaret M: 562 with picture
  Ottoman Empire (Cultural life) O: 877
  Turkey picture on T: 503
  United Arab Emirates picture on U: 44
  World, History of the picture on W: 436
Mosquitia [region, Honduras-Nicaragua] See
  Mosquito Coast in this index
Mosquito M: 831 with pictures
  Antennae A: 544
  Disease (Spread of infectious diseases) D: 228
  Elephantiasis E: 233
  Finlay, Carlos Juan F: 118
  Fly (Head) F: 309; (Egg) F: 310; (table) F: 310
  Insect picture on I: 282; (Hearing) I: 290
  Larva picture on L: 78
  Malaria M: 95 with picture
  Reed, Walter R: 194
  West Nile virus W: 205
  Yellow fever Y: 556
Mosquito bite
  Malaria (Spread) M: 96
  Mosquito (How a mosquito "bites") M: 831 with
    diagram
  Parasite picture on P: 154
Mosquito boat
  PT boat P: 853
Mosquito Coast [region, Honduras-Nicaragua]
  M: 834
  Honduras (The Northeastern Plain) H: 310
Mosquito hawk See Nighthawk in this index
Moss [plant] M: 834 with pictures
  Bryophyte B: 656
  Plant picture on P: 522; (Nonvascular plants)
    P: 518; (Sexual reproduction) P: 532-533;
    (Classification of plants) P: 546 with picture
  Spore (Plant spores) So: 801 with diagram
Moss agate [mineral]
  Agate A: 139
Moss animal See Bryozoan in this index
Moss campion [plant]
  Flower picture on F: 289
  Plant picture on P: 524
Moss man [doll]
  Doll (Traditional dolls) D: 287
Moss rose
  Rose (Types of roses) R: 474-475
Mössbauer, Rudolf Ludwig [German physicist]
  M: 836
Mössbauer effect [physics]
  Mössbauer, Rudolf Ludwig M: 836
Mossbunker [fish] See Menhaden in this index
Mosses from an Old Manse [book by Hawthorne]
  Hawthorne, Nathaniel (His stories and sketches)
    H: 115
Mossi [people]
  Burkina Faso (History) B: 706; (People) B: 706
    with picture
Mossolov, Georgi [Soviet aviator]
  Aviation (Aviation speed records) A: 990
Mossyrock Dam [Washington]
  Dam (table) D: 18
Most-favored-nation clause [international
  relations]
  Reciprocal trade agreement R: 175
  Tariff T: 43
Most Holy Redeemer, Congregation of the
  [religious group]
  Alphonsus Liguori, Saint A: 384
**Most Venerable Order of the Hospital of Saint
  John of Jerusalem, The** [organization]
  Saint John, Order of S: 36
Mosul [Iraq] M: 836
Motagua River

Guatemala (The Highlands) G: 414 with map
Motecuhzoma [Aztec emperors] See under
  Montezuma in this index
Motel M: 836 with picture
  Automobile picture on A: 969
  Hotel H: 376
Motel chain
  Motel M: 836
Motet [music]
  Classical music (Church music) Ci: 645-646
  Desprez, Josquin D: 161
  Lasso, Orlando di L: 87
Moth M: 837 with pictures
  See also the list of Related articles in the Moth
    article
  Animal (Camouflage) A: 493
  Butterfly B: 732 with picture
  Caterpillar C: 299
  Flower (Cross-pollination) F: 295
  Insect pictures on I: 279, I: 282; (Smell) I: 291
  Jumping bean J: 190 with picture
  Metamorphosis M: 428
  Pea (Diseases and pests) P: 205
  Rain forest picture on R: 126c
Moth fly
  Sand fly S: 107
Moth orchid [plant]
  Orchid picture on O: 824
Mother See Parent in this index
Mother [sound recording]
  Phonograph (How phonograph records are
    made) P: 401
Mother, The [book by Gorki]
  Gorki, Maxim G: 277
Mother and Child, Divided [art by Hirst]
  Hirst, Damien H: 243 with picture
Mother and Sister of the Artist, The [painting by
  Morisot]
  Morisot, Berthe picture on M: 805
Mother Bickerdyke [name for]
  Bickerdyke, Mary Ann Ball B: 289
Mother Carey's chicken [bird]
  Petrel P: 328
Mother Earth [magazine]
  Goldman, Emma G: 258
Mother Frost [legendary figure]
  Jack Frost J: 2
Mother Goose [legendary figure] M: 842
  Fairy (Fairy tales) F: 11
  Literature for children pictures on L: 360, L: 370;
    (Mother Goose) L: 362
  Perrault, Charles P: 293
Mother Goose's Melody [book]
  Mother Goose (The history of Mother Goose
    literature) M: 842
  Nursery rhyme (History) N: 615-616
Mother Hubbard dress
  Pacific Islands (Clothing) P: 7
Mother-in-law
  Family (Family relationships) F: 21
Mother Jones [name for]
  Jones, Mary Harris M: 159
Mother of Canada [name for]
  Saint Lawrence River S: 41
Mother of Exiles [name for]
  Statue of Liberty (The statue as a symbol)
    So: 872-873
Mother of God [name for]
  Mary M: 238
Mother of Parliaments [name for]
  United Kingdom (National government) U: 49
Mother-of-pearl [zoology] M: 842
  Mussel M: 966
  Oyster (Shell) O: 890
  Pearl (Cultured pearls) P: 217
  Shell (How shells are formed) S: 385; (Uses of
    shells) S: 389-390 with picture
Mother of Presidents [name for]
  Ohio O: 680
  Virginia V: 398
Mother of States [name for]
  Virginia V: 398
Mother of the West [name for]
  Missouri M: 650
Mother Road [name for]
  Route 66 R: 493
Mother Seton [American religious leader] See
  Seton, Saint Elizabeth Ann in this index
Mother superior [title]
  Convent Ci: 1024
Mother Teresa [Indian religious leader] See Teresa,
  Mother in this index
Motherboard [electronics]
  Computer (Parts of computers) Ci: 911-912 with
    picture
  Computer chip picture on Ci: 924f
Mothering Sunday [custom]

Mother's Day M: 843
Motherland Party
Turkey (Political changes) T: 512
Mothers, National Congress of [organization]
Birney, Alice Josephine McLellan B: 377
Hearst, Phoebe Apperson H: 131
National Congress of Parents and Teachers N: 32
Mothers' Aid [program]
Welfare (History) W: 191
Mother's Day [custom] M: 843 *with picture*
Howe, Julia Ward H: 401
May M: 320
Mothers' Pension [program]
Welfare (History) W: 191
Motherwell, Robert [American painter] M: 843
with picture
Painting (Abstract painting) P: 34; (Composition)
P: 35
Motier, Marie Joseph Paul Yves Roch Gilbert du
[birth name of]
Lafayette, Marquis L: 27
Motion [parliamentary procedure]
Parliamentary procedure (Motions) P: 176
Motion [physics] M: 843 *with picture*
Coriolis effect Ci: 1053
Dynamics D: 397
Energy E: 273
Force (Characteristics of force) F: 369
Galileo (Mature scientific career) G: 11
Heat (Changing heat into motion) H: 154 *with
diagram*
Inertia I: 262
Machine *diagrams on* M: 13
Momentum M: 698
Newton, Sir Isaac (The theories of motion and
gravitation) N: 388
Perpetual motion machine P: 293
Relativity (Galilean relativity) R: 209; (Special
relativity) R: 210; (General relativity) R: 211
Time (Our understanding of time) T: 292a-292b
Velocity V: 297
Motion, Andrew [British poet] M: 845
Poet laureate (table: Poets laureate of the United
Kingdom) P: 590
Motion, Laws of *See* Newton's laws of motion *in
this index*
Motion capture [cinematography]
Animation (Making the model move) A: 513
Motion picture M: 846 *with pictures*
See also Film *in this index* and the list of Related
articles in the Motion picture article
Academy of Motion Picture Arts and Sciences
A: 20
Animation A: 511
Audio-visual materials (Video presentations)
A: 883
Australia (Theater and motion pictures) A: 906
with picture
Ballet (Preserving a ballet) B: 50
Blindness (Aids for blind people) B: 402
Camera (Motion-picture cameras) C: 84
Canada (Motion pictures) C: 111 *with picture*
Communication (The 1800's) Ci: 881-883 *with
picture*
Copyright (Works protected) Ci: 1046
Disney, Walt D: 235; (Full-length movies) D: 236
with picture
Doll (After the war) D: 292
DVD D: 393
Edison, Thomas Alva (Motion pictures) E: 80
Germany (Motion pictures) G: 156
India (Music and dance) I: 120; (Motion pictures)
I: 121 *with picture*
Italy I: 506
Latin America (Motion pictures) L: 101
Los Angeles (Industry) L: 464
Muybridge, Eadweard M: 969
New Jersey (The early 1900's) N: 253 *with picture*
Projection screen P: 816
Public opinion (The motion picture) P: 860
Sweden (Motion pictures) So: 1028
Television (VCR's and DVR's) T: 110c; (Other forms
of entertainment) T: 121
United States *pictures on* U: 118
United States, History of the (The Gilded Age)
U: 183 *with picture*
Walt Disney Company W: 21
Western frontier life in America (Entertainment)
W: 240
Westerns W: 242 *with picture*
Writing (Scriptwriting) W: 512
Motion Picture Arts and Sciences, Academy of
See Academy of Motion Picture Arts and Sciences
in this index
Motion Picture Association of America
Motion picture (Censorship and self-regulation)
M: 860-861

Motion-picture camera *See* Movie camera *in this
index*
Motion Picture Patents Company
Edison, Thomas Alva (Motion pictures) E: 80
**Motion Picture Producers and Distributors of
America**
Motion picture (Censorship and self-regulation)
M: 860
Motion-picture projector *See* Projector *in this
index*
Motion sickness [disorder] M: 874
Dramamine D: 342
Ear (Disturbances of the organs of balance) E: 11
Motivation [psychology] M: 875
Child (Motivating the child's behavior) C: 451
Developmental psychology (Constructivist
theory) D: 174
Industrial psychology (Organizational
psychologists) I: 245
Instinct (Motivation) I: 305
Learning (Motivation) L: 164
Literature (Characters) L: 353
Motivation M: 875
Perception (Learning, emotion, and motivation)
P: 283
Personality (Personality development) P: 302
Sales (Characteristics needed) S: 65
Motivation research [psychology] M: 875
Advertising (Research) A: 76a
Motive [music]
Counterpoint Ci: 1097
Music (Melody) M: 951
Motley, Constance Baker [American jurist]
Spingarn Medal (table: 2003) So: 794
Motmot [bird] M: 876 *with picture*
Bird *picture on* B: 344b
Moto Perpetuo [music by Paganini]
Paganini, Niccolò P: 20
Motocross [race]
Bicycle racing (Bicycle motocross races) B: 293
Motorcycle (Motorcycling as a sport) M: 879
Moton, Robert Russa [American educator] M: 876
Motonobu, Kano [Japanese artist]
Painting (Japanese painting) P: 47
Motor *See* Engine *in this index*
Motor, Electric *See* Electric motor *in this index*
Motor car *See* Automobile *in this index*
Motor Carrier Act [1980]
Public utility (History) P: 865-866
Motor City [nickname]
Detroit D: 167
Motor coach [vehicle]
Bus B: 714
Motor cortex
Brain (Controlling movement) B: 553 *with
diagram*
Motor fuel tax *See* Gasoline tax *in this index*
Motor home [vehicle]
Recreational vehicle *picture on* R: 183; (Motor
homes) R: 184
Motor hotel *See* Motel *in this index*
Motor inn *See* Motel *in this index*
Motor lodge *See* Motel *in this index*
Motor neuron
Amyotrophic lateral sclerosis A: 446
Brain (Controlling movement) B: 553
Human body (The peripheral nervous system)
H: 426
Nervous system *diagram on* N: 135; (How the
nervous system works) N: 132 *with diagram*
Motor octane number
Gasoline (Octane ratings) G: 61
Octane number O: 669
Motor paralysis *See* Paralysis *in this index*
Motor play
Play P: 570
Motor scooter
Motorcycle (Kinds of motorcycles) M: 878
Motor skills
Baby (From 1 to 6 months) B: 7 *with pictures*
Motor Vehicle Code [law]
Code Ci: 748
Motorbike
Motorcycle (Kinds of motorcycles) M: 878
Motorboat
Boating *pictures on* B: 430; (Motorboats) B: 428
with picture
Motorboat racing M: 876 *with pictures*
Motorboat racing M: 876 *with pictures*
Motorcade [ballet]
Ballet *picture on* B: 55
Motorcycle M: 877 *with pictures*
Maybach, Wilhelm M: 327
Motorcycle Operator Skills Test
Motorcycle M: 878
Motorcycle racing
Motorcycle (Motorcycling as a sport) M: 879

Motorcyclist Association, American
Motorcycle (Motorcycling as a sport) M: 879
Motorized rifle division
Infantry (Divisions) I: 264-265
Motorship
Ship (Engine-driven ships) S: 406; (Stronger,
faster ships) S: 425-426
Motorway [expressway]
England (Transportation and communication)
E: 302
Road (Primary highways) R: 358
Motorway 25 [road]
London (Dealing with problems) L: 442
Motown and Didi: A Love Story [book by Myers]
Myers, Walter Dean M: 970f
Motown Record Corporation
Gaye, Marvin G: 73
Gordy, Berry G: 273
Rock music (Independent producers) R: 379
Mott, Charles Stewart [American businessman]
Mott Foundation M: 880
Mott, John Raleigh [American religious leader]
Nobel Prizes (Peace: 1946) N: 448a
Mott, Lucretia Coffin [American social reformer]
M: 880 *with portrait*
Philadelphia (Industrial beginnings) P: 366
Stanton, Elizabeth Cady So: 839
Woman suffrage (Beginnings of the movement)
W: 380
Women's movement (The beginnings of women's
movements) W: 384-385
Mott, Sir Nevill [British physicist]
Nobel Prizes (Physics: 1977) N: 441
Mott Foundation M: 880
Motte [structure]
Castle (Structure) C: 280
Mottelson, Ben Roy [Danish physicist]
Nobel Prizes (Physics: 1975) N: 441
Mottled feather
Chicken (Kinds of chickens) C: 441
Motto [expression]
*For the mottoes of each of the states of the United
States, see the Facts in brief section of the specific
articles, such as* California (California in brief)
Motto [heraldry]
Heraldry (Elements of a coat of arms) H: 196 *with
picture*
Mottola, Tony [American recording executive]
Carey, Mariah C: 236
Motu [reef]
Pacific Islands (The low islands) P: 8
Mouawad, René [Lebanese political leader]
Lebanon (Political struggle) L: 174
Mouflon [animal]
Sheep (Wild sheep) S: 380-381 *with picture*
Moulting [zoology] *See* Molting *in this index*
Moultrie, William [American general] M: 880
Flag *picture on* F: 209
Fort Moultrie F: 415
South Carolina So: 640
Mound [baseball]
Baseball (The infield) B: 126 *with diagram*
Mound [entomology]
Termite (Kinds of termites) T: 171
Mound bird M: 880 *with picture*
Mound builders [American Indians] M: 881 *with
pictures*
Effigy Mounds National Monument E: 115
Indian, American (The first farmers) I: 152
Indiana (Indian days) I: 215
Iowa (Indian days) I: 393
Missouri (Early days) M: 669
Ohio (Places to visit) O: 690 *with picture*; (Indian
days) O: 700
Tennessee (Early days) T: 153
West Virginia (Indian days) W: 226
Mounds, Cave of the [Wisconsin]
Wisconsin (Places to visit) W: 356
Mount [palmistry]
Palmistry P: 111 *with diagram*
Mount [riding]
Horse (Mounting a horse) H: 353 *with pictures*
Mount, James A. [American political leader]
Indiana (table) I: 214
Mount Aconcagua [Argentina] *See* Aconcagua *in
this index*
Mount Adams [New Hampshire]
New Hampshire (Mountains) N: 220 *with map*
Mount Aetna [Sicily] *See* Mount Etna *in this index*
Mount Agel [Monaco]
Monaco (Land) M: 699
Mount Airy Forest
Cincinnati (Parks and playgrounds) Ci: 556
Mount Apo [Philippines]
Philippines (Land and climate) P: 376 *with map*
Mount Apo National Park [Philippines]
National park (table) N: 42f

Mount Aragats [Armenia]
Armenia (Land and climate) **A: 718a** *with map*
Mount Ararat [Turkey] **M: 883**
Ararat **A: 592**
Mountain (table) **M: 896** *with diagram*
Turkey *picture on* **T: 502;** (The land) **T: 507-508**
with map
Mount Arvon [Michigan]
Michigan (The Superior Upland) **M: 500** *with map*
Mount Assiniboine Provincial Park [British
Columbia]
British Columbia *picture on* **B: 612**
Mount Athos [religious community]
Greece (Macedonia) **G: 357**
Religious life (The Eastern Orthodox Churches)
R: 227
Mount Bagzane [Niger]
Niger (Land and climate) **N: 408**
Mount Bălănesti [Moldova]
Moldova (Land and climate) **M: 690-690a**
Mount Barbeau [Nunavut]
Nunavut (Land and resources) **N: 609** *with map*
Mount Bartle Frere [Australia]
Queensland (Land and climate) **Q: 39**
Mount Bia [Laos]
Laos (Land and climate) **L: 71** *with map*
Mount Cameroon [Cameroon]
Cameroon (Land and climate) **C: 86** *with map*
Mount Cardigan [New Hampshire]
New Hampshire *picture on* **N: 209;** (Mountains)
N: 220 *with map*
Mount Carleton [New Brunswick]
New Brunswick (Land regions) **N: 190** *with picture
and map*
Mount Caubvick [Canada]
Newfoundland and Labrador (Mountains) **N: 370**
with map
Quebec (Land regions) **Q: 22** *with map*
Mount Cenis Tunnel *See* Fréjus Tunnels *in this index*
Mount Chapman [North Carolina-Tennessee]
Great Smoky Mountains **G: 348**
Mount Clay [New Hampshire]
New Hampshire (Mountains) **N: 220**
Mount Cleveland [Montana]
Glacier National Park (Mountains) **G: 205**
Mount Collins [North Carolina-Tennessee]
Great Smoky Mountains **G: 348**
Mount Columbia [Alberta]
Alberta (The Rocky Mountains and Foothills)
A: 322 *with map*
Mount Cook [New Zealand] *See* Aoraki/Mount
Cook *in this index*
Mount Damavand [Iran]
Iran (The Mountains) **I: 402**
Mount Desert Island [Maine]
Maine (Mountains) **M: 82**
Mount Elbert [Colorado]
Rocky Mountains (Chief ranges of the Rockies)
R: 394 *with map*
Mount Elbrus [Russia] **M: 883**
Caucasus Mountains **C: 317**
Mountain (table) **M: 896** *with diagram*
Russia (The European Plain) **R: 539** *with map*
Mount Elgon [Uganda-Kenya]
Uganda (Land) **U: 3**
Mount Erebus [Antarctica]
Antarctica (Land) **A: 531** *with picture*
Exploration (The exploration of Antarctica) **E: 450**
Ross, Sir James Clark **R: 482**
Mount Etna [Sicily] **M: 883** *with picture*
Italy (Sicily) **I: 508**
Mountain (table) **M: 894** *with diagram*
Volcano (table) **V: 442b**
Mount Evans [Colorado]
Colorado (Transportation) **Ci: 843**
Mount Everest [Nepal-Tibet] **M: 884** *with picture*
Asia *picture on* **A: 791**
Hillary, Sir Edmund Percival **H: 231**
Mountain **M: 891;** (table) **M: 896** *with diagram*
National park (Other interesting national parks)
N: 42h
Seven natural wonders of the world (Mount
Everest) **S: 324b** *with picture*
Tenzing Norgay **T: 169**
Tibet **T: 276**
Yeti **Y: 565**
Mount Fairweather [Alaska-British Columbia] *See*
Fairweather Mountain *in this index*
Mount Frissell [Connecticut-Massachusetts]
Connecticut (Mountains) **Ci: 962**
Mount Fuji [Japan] **M: 884** *with picture*
Japan *picture on* **J: 32;** (Honshu) **J: 45** *with picture*
Mountain (table) **M: 896** *with diagram*
Mythology (Mythical places) **M: 975**
National park *picture on* **N: 42c;** (Japan) **N: 42d**
Tokyo (The city) **T: 313**
Mount Godwin Austen [Kashmir] *See* K2 *in this*

index
Mount Gréboun [Niger]
Niger (Land and climate) **N: 408**
Mount Greylock [Massachusetts]
Massachusetts *picture on* **M: 284;** (Land regions)
M: 282
Mount Gunnbjørn [Greenland]
Greenland (The land) **G: 385** *with map*
Mount Guyot [North Carolina-Tennessee]
Great Smoky Mountains **G: 348**
Mount Hamilton [California]
Lick Observatory **L: 270**
Mount Hermon [Lebanon-Syria]
Jordan River **J: 167**
Mount Hillaby [Barbados]
Barbados (Land) **B: 104**
Mount Hira [Saudi Arabia]
Religion (Islam) **R: 223**
Mount Holyoke College
Coeducation **Ci: 752**
Lyon, Mary **L: 537**
Mount Hood [Oregon] **M: 885**
Mountain (table) **M: 896** *with diagram*
Oregon (Land and climate) **O: 838** *with picture
and map*
Mount Horeb [Sinai Peninsula] *See* Mount Sinai *in
this index*
Mount Hoverla [Ukraine]
Ukraine (The Eastern Carpathian Mountains) **U: 9**
with map
Mount Ida [Crete]
Crete (Land and climate) **Ci: 1127**
Mount Inyangani [Zimbabwe]
Zimbabwe (Land and climate) **Z: 592** *with map*
Mount Jacques Cartier [Quebec]
Gaspé Peninsula **G: 66**
Mount Sir James MacBrien [Canada]
Northwest Territories (The Mackenzie Mountains)
N: 531
Mount Jefferson [New Hampshire]
New Hampshire (Mountains) **N: 220**
Mount Jefferson [Oregon]
Oregon *picture on* **O: 840;** (Land regions) **O: 838**
with map
Mount Kailas [Tibet]
Himalaya (Peaks) **H: 233**
Mount Kamet [Asia]
Himalaya (Peaks) **H: 233**
Mount Kanchenjunga [Nepal-Sikkim] **M: 885**
Mountain (table) **M: 896** *with diagram*
Mount Katahdin [Maine]
Maine (Mountains) **M: 82** *with picture*
Mount Katmai [Alaska]
Alaska (Land regions) **A: 292-294**
Mount Kearsarge [New Hampshire]
New Hampshire (Mountains) **N: 220** *with map*
Mount Kebnekaise [Sweden]
Sweden (The Mountain Range) **So: 1028** *with
map*
Mount Kékes [Hungary]
Hungary (The land) **H: 442** *with map*
Mount Kenya [Kenya] **M: 885**
Kenya *picture on* **K: 299;** (Land regions) **K: 301**
with map
Mountain (table) **M: 896** *with diagram*
Mount Kenya National Park [Kenya]
Mount Kenya **M: 885**
Mount Kephart [North Carolina-Tennessee]
Great Smoky Mountains **G: 348**
Mount Kilimanjaro [Tanzania] *See* Kilimanjaro *in
this index*
Mount Kinabalu [Borneo]
Borneo (The land and its resources) **B: 489** *with
map*
Malaysia (Land and climate) **M: 99** *with picture*
Mount Kinchinjunga [Nepal-Sikkim] *See* Mount
Kanchenjunga *in this index*
Mount Klyuchevskaya [Russia]
Russia (The East Siberian Uplands) **R: 541**
Siberia (The land and climate) **S: 443-444**
Mount Korab [Albania-Macedonia]
Albania (Land) **A: 306**
Mount Kosciuszko [Australia] **M: 885**
Australia *picture on* **A: 912;** (Mountains) **A: 908**
with map
Mountain (table) **M: 896** *with diagram*
Mount Le Conte [North Carolina-Tennessee]
Great Smoky Mountains **G: 348**
Mount Logan [Yukon] **M: 885**
Mountain (table) **M: 896** *with diagram*
Saint Elias Mountains **S: 33**
Yukon (Location, size, and description) **Y: 578**
with map
Mount Madison [New Hampshire]
New Hampshire (Mountains) **N: 220** *with map*
Mount Makalu [Nepal-Tibet] **M: 885**
Hillary, Sir Edmund Percival **H: 231**

Mountain (table) **M: 896** *with diagram*
Mount Mansfield [Vermont]
Green Mountains **G: 381**
Vermont (Land regions) **V: 328** *with map*
Mount Marcy [New York]
Adirondack Mountains **A: 56**
New York (Land regions) **N: 304** *with map*
Mount Mazama [Oregon]
Crater Lake **Ci: 1121**
Mount McKinley [Alaska] **M: 886**
Alaska **A: 282** *with picture*
Mountain (table) **M: 896** *with diagram*
Mount McKinley National Park [Alaska] *See* Denali
National Park *in this index*
Mount McLoughlin [Oregon]
Oregon (Land regions) **O: 838** *with map*
Mount Meron [Israel]
Israel (The Judeo-Galilean Highlands) **I: 482**
Mount Minsi [Pennsylvania]
Delaware Water Gap **D: 114**
Mount Mitchell [North Carolina]
Blue Ridge Mountains **B: 421**
North Carolina (Land regions) **N: 484** *with map*
Mount Moldoveanu [Romania]
Romania (Surface features) **R: 419**
Mount Monadnock [New Hampshire]
New Hampshire (Mountains) **N: 220** *with map*
Mount Monroe [New Hampshire]
New Hampshire (Mountains) **N: 220** *with map*
Mount Moosilauke [New Hampshire]
New Hampshire (Mountains) **N: 220** *with map*
Mount Moriah Cemetery [South Dakota]
South Dakota (Places to visit) **So: 672**
Mount Nebo [Bible]
Mount Pisgah **M: 886**
Mount Nebo [Utah]
Wasatch Range **W: 45**
Mount Nimba [Guinea]
Guinea (Land and climate) **G: 431** *with map*
Mount of Olives [hills, Israel] **M: 886**
Mount Olivet *See* Mount of Olives *in this index*
Mount Olympus [Cyprus]
Cyprus (Land and climate) **Ci: 1206**
Mount Olympus [Greece] **M: 886**
Mountain (table) **M: 896** *with diagram*
Mythology (Mythical places) **M: 975;** (The Greek
creation myth) **M: 980-981**
Zeus **Z: 590**
Mount Olympus [Washington]
Olympic Mountains **O: 755**
Mount Olympus National Monument
[Washington]
Olympic National Park **O: 756**
Mount Ossa [Australia]
Tasmania (Land and climate) **T: 48**
Mount Palomar Observatory *See* Palomar
Observatory *in this index*
Mount Parnassus [Greece]
Parnassus **P: 177**
Mount Pelée [Caribbean Sea] **M: 886**
Martinique **M: 235**
Volcano (Pyroclastic hazards) **V: 440;** (table)
V: 442b
West Indies (Land and climate) **W: 204**
Mount Pinatubo [Philippines] **M: 886**
Climate (Volcanic eruptions) **Ci: 676d**
Philippines (Recovering democracy) **P: 381** *with
picture*
Volcano (table) **V: 442b**
Mount Pisgah [mountain range, Jordan] **M: 886**
Mount Rainier [Washington] **M: 887**
Cascade Range **C: 271**
Mountain (table) **M: 896** *with diagram*
Seattle (Landmarks) **S: 273** *with picture*
Washington *pictures on* **W: 46, W: 55**
Mount Rainier National Park [Washington]
M: 887
National Park System (table: National parks) **N: 48**
Mount Revelstoke National Park [British
Columbia]
Canada (table: National parks and national park
reserves) **C: 113**
Mount Roberts Tramway
Alaska *picture on* **A: 296**
Mount Robson [mountain, Canada]
Canada (The Rocky Mountains) **C: 116** *with map*
Mount Rogers [Virginia]
Virginia (Land regions) **V: 410**
Mount Royal [Quebec]
Cartier, Jacques (Exploration of Canada) **C: 262**
Montreal (Parks) **M: 774**
Quebec (Land regions) **Q: 22**
Mount Royal Park [Quebec]
Montreal *picture on* **M: 774;** (Parks) **M: 774**
Quebec (Places to visit) **Q: 20**
Mount Rushmore National Memorial [South
Dakota] **M: 887** *with picture*

Borglum, Gutzon B: 488
National Park System (table: National memorials)
   N: 54
   South Dakota So: 664 *with picture, picture on*
   So: 682
Mount Rushmore State [nickname]
   South Dakota So: 665
Mount Sage [Tortola]
   Virgin Islands V: 392 *with map*
Mount Saint Elias [Alaska]
   Alaska (Land regions) A: 292
   Saint Elias Mountains S: 33
Mount Saint Helens [Washington] M: 888 *with picture*
   Cascade Range C: 271
   Mountain (table) M: 896 *with diagram*
   Volcano (table) V: 442b
   Washington (The late 1900's) W: 68 *with picture*
Mount Saint Helens National Volcanic Monument [Washington]
   Washington (Places to visit) W: 56
Mount Sir Sandford [British Columbia]
   Selkirk Mountains S: 290
Mount Shasta [California] M: 888
   California (Land regions) C: 48-50
   Cascade Range C: 271
   Mountain (table) M: 896 *with diagram*
Mount Shkhara [Georgia]
   Georgia (Land and climate) G: 110 *with map*
Mount Sinai [Sinai Peninsula] M: 888
   Moses (The covenant with God) M: 829
   Ten Commandments T: 131
Mount Soira [Eritrea]
   Eritrea (Land and climate) E: 353 *with map*
Mount Sokhondo [Russia]
   Yablonovyy Mountains Y: 548
Mount Somma [Italy]
   Vesuvius V: 342 *with picture*
Mount Soufrière [Saint Vincent]
   Saint Vincent and the Grenadines (Land and climate) S: 57 *with map*
Mount Suribachi [Japan]
   Iwo Jima, Battle of I: 365
   World War II (Closing in on Japan) W: 492-493
Mount Tabor [Israel]
   Deborah D: 65
Mount Tahat [Algeria]
   Algeria (The Sahara) A: 363
Mount Tambora [Indonesia]
   Volcano (table) V: 442b
Mount Tammany [New Jersey]
   Delaware Water Gap D: 114
Mount Terror [Antarctica]
   Exploration (The exploration of Antarctica) E: 450
Mount Titano [Italy]
   San Marino [city] S: 104
Mount Titano [San Marino]
   San Marino [country] (Land) S: 103
Mount Vernon [estate, Virginia] M: 888 *with pictures*
   Virginia (Visitor's guide) V: 408 *with picture*
   Washington, D.C. (Mount Vernon) W: 78
   Washington, George (Boyhood) W: 92; (Surrender of Fort Necessity) W: 94; (Farmer and landowner) W: 96 *with picture*
Mount Vernon [suburb, New York] M: 890
Mount Vernon Ladies' Association
   Mount Vernon (A national shrine) M: 890
Mount Vesuvius [Italy] *See* Vesuvius *in this index*
Mount Waddington [British Columbia]
   British Columbia (Land regions) B: 622 *with map*
Mount Waialeale [Hawaii]
   Hawaii (Kauai) H: 102
   Rain (Some rainfall records) R: 124 *with map*
   United States (Climate) U: 126-128
Mount Washington [hill, Pittsburgh]
   Pittsburgh (The city) P: 500a-500b
Mount Washington [New Hampshire] M: 890
   New Hampshire (Places to visit) N: 216; (Mountains) N: 220 *with map*
   White Mountains W: 291
Mount Washington Cog Railway
   New Hampshire (Places to visit) N: 216 *with picture*
Mount Washington Observatory
   New Hampshire (Land regions) *picture on* N: 218; (table: Average monthly weather) N: 220
   White Mountains W: 291
Mount Whitney [California] M: 890
   California (Land regions) C: 48
   Mountain (table) M: 896 *with diagram*
   Sequoia National Park S: 311
Mount Williamson, Sierra Nevada, from Manzanar, California 1944 [photograph by Adams]
   Adams, Ansel *picture on* A: 33
Mount Wilson Observatory [California] M: 890

Mount Woodroffe [Australia]
   South Australia (Land and climate) So: 639
Mountain M: 891 *with pictures and map*
   See also Volcano in this index and the list of Related articles in the Mountain *article*
   Animal (Animals of the mountains) A: 474 *with pictures and map*
   Climate (The role of topography) Ci: 676a; (Highland climates) Ci: 676d; (Mountain building) Ci: 678
   Deep sea (The deep-sea floor) D: 82a
   Earth (Mountain building) E: 24
   Ocean (The land at the bottom of the sea) O: 659 *with map*
   Pacific Ocean (The ocean floor) P: 14
   Plant *picture on* P: 524
   Plate tectonics (Convergent plate boundaries) P: 562 *with diagram*
   Railroad (The roadbed and route) R: 109
   Weather (Synoptic-scale systems) W: 159-160
   World (table) W: 417 *with map*
Mountain, The [French history]
   Danton, Georges-Jacques D: 34
   French Revolution (The National Convention) F: 526
Mountain ash [tree] M: 897
   Tree *pictures on* T: 422
Mountain avens [plant] M: 897
   Flower *picture on* F: 283
   Plant *picture on* P: 524
Mountain beaver [animal] M: 897
Mountain bicycle
   Bicycle (Kinds of bicycles) B: 289 *with picture;* (Bicycle riding today) B: 291-292
   Bicycle racing (Road races) B: 292-293
Mountain blue [butterfly]
   Butterfly *picture on* B: 737
Mountain bluebird
   Bluebird B: 423
Mountain climbing [sport] M: 897
   Alps (Climbing the Alps) A: 386
   Hiking H: 230
   Scotland (Recreation) S: 214-215
Mountain cranberry [fruit]
   Lingonberry L: 335 *with picture*
Mountain dulcimer
   Dulcimer D: 380 *with picture*
Mountain evergreen forest
   Forest (Mountain evergreen forests) F: 395 *with map*
Mountain goat M: 898 *with picture*
   Animal *picture on* A: 474
   Ibex I: 3
Mountain gorilla
   Fossey, Dian F: 421
   Gorilla G: 275
   Primate (Conservation) P: 778c
Mountain hemlock [tree]
   Hemlock H: 182
Mountain kingsnake
   Snake *picture on* S: 533
Mountain Language [play by Pinter]
   Pinter, Harold P: 475
Mountain laurel [plant] M: 898
   Laurel L: 121
   Poisonous plant (Some poisonous plants) P: 602
Mountain lion [animal] M: 898 *with pictures*
   Animal *pictures on* A: 472, A: 501
   Florida panther F: 266
Mountain Meadows Massacre [1857]
   Utah (Territorial days and statehood) U: 246-248
Mountain men [U.S. history]
   Fur trade (The 1800's) F: 565
   Westward movement in America (Exploration) W: 248-249
Mountain nestor [bird] *See* Kea *in this index*
Mountain pass [geography] M: 899
   Himalaya (Passes and glaciers) H: 233
Mountain plover [bird]
   Plover P: 574
Mountain quail [bird]
   Quail Q: 4 *with picture*
Mountain rosebay [shrub]
   Rhododendron R: 318
Mountain Sami [people]
   Sami S: 79 *with picture*
Mountain sheep *See* Bighorn *in this index*
Mountain silverbell [plant]
   Silverbell S: 465
Mountain State [nickname]
   West Virginia W: 206
Mountain State Forest Festival
   West Virginia (Visitor's guide) W: 216 *with picture*
Mountain top removal [mining]
   Coal (Strip mining) Ci: 722
Mountain View [Arkansas]
   Arkansas *picture on* A: 705

Mountain viscacha [rodent]
   Viscacha (Mountain viscachas) V: 428b
Mountain wave
   Glider (Soaring) G: 229
Mountain zebra
   Zebra Z: 587
Mountaineering [sport] *See* Mountain climbing *in this index*
Mountains and the Sea [painting by Frankenthaler]
   Painting (Abstract painting) P: 34 *with picture;* (Color-field painting) P: 85
Mountains of Antrim [Northern Ireland]
   Northern Ireland (Surface features) N: 523 *with map*
Mountains of California, The [book by Muir]
   American literature (Nonfiction writers) A: 420
Mountbatten, Louis [British admiral] M: 899
   Philip, Prince P: 371
   World War II (Burma) W: 492
Mountbatten, Philip [British prince] *See* Philip, Prince *in this index*
Mountbatten-Windsor [British history]
   Windsor W: 334
Mounted animal
   Taxidermy T: 55 *with pictures*
Mounted Police *See* Royal Canadian Mounted Police *in this index*
Mounties [police force] *See* Royal Canadian Mounted Police *in this index*
Mountolive [book by Durrell]
   Durrell, Lawrence D: 389
Mourne Mountains [Northern Ireland]
   Northern Ireland (Surface features) N: 523 *with map*
Mourning
   Flag (Raising and lowering the flag) F: 219
   Funeral customs (Mourning) F: 558
Mourning Becomes Electra [play by O'Neill]
   Naturalism (Naturalism in drama) N: 66
   O'Neill, Eugene (His plays) O: 762
Mourning Bride, The [play by Congreve]
   Congreve, William Ci: 949
Mourning cloak [butterfly]
   Butterfly (Brush-footed butterflies) B: 736
Mourning dove [bird] M: 900 *with picture*
   Dove D: 314 *with picture*
   Pigeon (Wild pigeons) P: 460
Mourning wheatear [bird]
   Desert *picture on* D: 155
Mouse [animal] M: 900 *with pictures*
   Dormouse D: 310
   Jumping mouse J: 190 *with pictures*
   Parasite (Influence on behavior) P: 155
   Skull *picture on* S: 495
Mouse [electronic device]
   Computer (Input devices) Ci: 912 *with picture*
   Electronic game (Personal computers) E: 204c-204d
   Word processing (Personal computers) W: 403
Mouse pad [device]
   Computer (A mouse) Ci: 914
Mouse Tower [Germany] M: 902
Mousetrap
   Trapping (Kinds of traps) T: 403 *with picture*
Mousetrap, The [play by Christie]
   Christie, Agatha C: 527
Moussaoui, Zacarias [French-born public figure]
   September 11 terrorist attacks (Global war on terrorism) S: 310a
Moussavi, Mir Hussein [Iranian political leader]
   Iran (Recent developments) I: 406b
Moussavi, Ruhollah [Iranian religious leader] *See* Khomeini, Ruhollah *in this index*
Mousseau, J.-Alfred [Canadian political leader]
   Quebec (table) Q: 29
Moutan peony [plant]
   Peony P: 276 *with picture*
Mouth [anatomy] M: 902 *with diagram*
   Cancer (table) C: 170
   Cleft palate C: 661
   Cosmetics (Kinds of cosmetics) Ci: 1074
   Human body (The digestive system) H: 419; (table) H: 422 *with diagram*
   Insect (Mouthparts) I: 286 *with diagrams*
   Reproduction, Human (Development of organs and organ systems) R: 248
   Trench mouth T: 434
Mouth brush [biology]
   Mosquito (Larva) M: 833
Mouth organ [musical instrument]
   Harmonica H: 61
Mouth puppet
   Puppet (Hand puppets) P: 906
Mouth-to-mouth resuscitation
   First aid (Giving artificial respiration) F: 138 *with pictures*
Mouthbreeder [fish]

Fish *picture on* F: 170
Mouthparts [zoology]
  Butterfly (The head) B: 738 *with diagram*
Mouthpiece [sports]
  Boxing (Equipment) B: 526
Mouton, Alexandre [American political leader]
  Louisiana (table) L: 496
Movable feast [religion]
  Calendar (The Christian church calendar) C: 29
Movable joint [anatomy]
  Human body (The skeletal system) H: 418
  Joint J: 155 *with diagrams*
Movable pulley
  Pulley P: 900 *with diagram*
Movable type [printing]
  Book (The development of printed books) B: 466
  Communication (The rise of printing) Ci: 879-880
    with picture
  Gutenberg, Johannes G: 444
  Printing (Printing P: 796; (The invention of movable type)
    P: 803
  Printing press P: 804
  Type (History) T: 537
MOVE [organization]
  Philadelphia (Continued growth) P: 367
Moveable bridge
  Bridge (Moveable bridges) B: 602 *with diagram*
Moveable Feast, A [book by Hemingway]
  Hemingway, Ernest (Later years) H: 180
Movement [art]
  Design (Rhythm and movement) D: 157
  Sculpture (Form and treatment) S: 230
Movement [biology]
  Life (The characteristics of living things) L: 275
Movement [mechanism]
  Clock (Kinds of clocks) Ci: 682i *with diagrams*
  Watch (Mechanical watches) W: 114
Movement [music]
  Classical music (Orchestral music) Ci: 644
  Symphony So: 1067
Movement education
  Physical education (Elementary school programs)
    P: 432
Movement for Democracy [political party]
  Cape Verde (Government) C: 189-190; (History)
    C: 190-191
Movement for Democracy and Justice in Chad
  [political group]
  Chad (History) C: 367-368
Movement for Democratic Change [political
  party]
  Zimbabwe (History) Z: 592-594
Movement for the Liberation of Congo [political
  party]
  Congo, Democratic Republic of the (Recent
    developments) Ci: 940c
**Movement for the Restoration of the Ten
  Commandments of God** [cult]
  Uganda (History) U: 3-4
Movement of Democratic Forces of Casamance
  [political group]
  Senegal (History) S: 299-300
Movement Toward Socialism [political party]
  Bolivia (Recent developments) B: 447
Movie *See* Motion picture *in this index*
Movie camera
  See also Camcorder *in this index*
  Camera (Motion-picture cameras) C: 84
  Communication *picture on* Ci: 885
Movin' Out [musical]
  Dance *picture on* D: 31
  Musical comedy (Musical comedy today) M: 961
  Tharp, Twyla T: 231 *with picture*
Moving-coil microphone
  Microphone (Moving-coil microphones) M: 516
    with diagram
Moving Picture Experts Group
  Portable media player P: 681
Moving sidewalk
  Conveyor belt (Uses) Ci: 1024 *with picture*
Moving Target, The [book by Macdonald]
  Macdonald, Ross M: 11
Movius, Hallam L. [American anthropologist]
  Prehistoric people (table) P: 754
Mowat, Farley [Canadian author] M: 903
Mowat, Sir Oliver [Canadian political leader]
  M: 903
  Confederation of Canada (Fathers of
    Confederation) Ci: 935
  Macdonald, Sir John Alexander (Lawyer) M: 6
  Ontario (table) O: 783
Mowgli [literary figure]
  Kipling, Rudyard (Kipling in America) K: 334
Mowing [process]
  Lawn (Lawns and the environment) L: 144
  Western frontier life in America (Improvements in
    farming) W: 233-234

Moynihan, Daniel Patrick [American government
  official] M: 903
  Clinton, Hillary Rodham Ci: 682h
  United Nations (table) U: 86
Mozambican National Resistance [political
  group] *See* Renamo *in this index*
Mozambique M: 904 *with pictures and map*
  Flag *picture on* F: 199
  Portugal (Empire and wealth) P: 693-694 *with
    map*
  Portuguese language P: 695
  Zimbabwe (History) Z: 592-593
Mozarabic [language]
  Spanish literature (Early medieval literature)
    So: 757-758
Mozart, Leopold [Austrian composer]
  Mozart, Wolfgang Amadeus (His life) M: 906 *with
    picture*
Mozart, Wolfgang Amadeus [Austrian composer]
  M: 906 *with picture*
  Austria (Music) A: 932
  Beethoven, Ludwig van (Beethoven's life) B: 213
  Brain (Myths about the human brain) B: 556
  Classical music (The Classical period) Ci: 647-648
    with picture
  Clementi, Muzio Ci: 662a
  Concerto Ci: 928
  Germany (Music) G: 153
  Haydn, Joseph H: 117
  Opera (Mozart) O: 798; (*Don Giovanni*) O: 803
    with picture; (*Magic Flute, The*) O: 805 *with
    picture*; (*Marriage of Figaro, The*) O: 805
  Overture O: 882
  Symphony So: 1067
Mozzarella [cheese]
  Cheese (Kinds of cheese) C: 392
Mozzetta [vestment]
  Pope (Titles, clothing, and symbols) P: 661-662
MP [police]
  Military police M: 543
MP3 [electronics]
  Portable media player P: 681
  Recording industry (History) R: 182
MPD [political party] *See* Movement for Democracy
  in this index
MPEG [electronics]
  Portable media player P: 681
MPLA [political party] *See* Popular Movement for
  the Liberation of Angola *in this index*
MPR [political party]
  Congo, Democratic Republic of the (Rebuilding
    the nation) Ci: 940c
Mpumalanga [province, South Africa]
  South Africa (Provincial government) So: 609
MQ-1 Predator drone [aircraft]
  Air Force, United States *picture on* A: 192
Mr. and Mrs. Andrews [painting by Gainsborough]
  Painting (People) P: 31 *with picture*; (Landscapes
    and seascapes) P: 32-33
Mr. Bones [minstrel character]
  Minstrel show M: 612 *with picture*
Mr. Civil Rights [name for]
  Wilkins, Roy W: 306
"Mr. Flood's Party" [poem by Robinson]
  Robinson, Edwin Arlington R: 368
Mr. H. [play by Lamb]
  Lamb, Charles (His essays) L: 50
Mr. Madison's War [U.S. history]
  Madison, James ("Mr. Madison's War") M: 35
  War of 1812 (Declaration of war) W: 30-31
Mr. Mani [book by Yehoshua]
  Hebrew literature (A new generation of Hebrew
    writers) H: 163
Mr. Moto [literary figure]
  Marquand, John Phillips M: 217
Mr. President [book by Asturias]
  Asturias, Miguel Angel A: 850
Mr. Sammler's Planet [book by Bellow]
  Bellow, Saul B: 244
Mr. Tambo [minstrel character]
  Minstrel show M: 612 *with picture*
Mr. Wilson's War [book by Dos Passos]
  Dos Passos, John D: 311
MRBM [weapon] *See* Medium-range ballistic
  missile *in this index*
MRI [medicine] *See* Magnetic resonance imaging
  in this index
mRNA [biology] *See* Messenger RNA *in this index*
Mrs. Frisby and the Rats of NIMH [book by O'Brien]
  O'Brien, Robert C. O: 643
Mrs. Miniver [film]
  Motion picture (Best picture: 1942) M: 861
Mrs. Silence Dogood [pen name]
  Franklin, Benjamin (Student and apprentice)
    F: 487
MS [disease] *See* Multiple sclerosis *in this index*
Ms. [magazine]

  Feminism F: 70
  Steinem, Gloria So: 885
M.S. 760 [airplane]
  Airplane *picture on* A: 236
MS-DOS [software]
  Computer (Operating system software) Ci: 917
  Gates, Bill G: 67
  Microsoft Corporation M: 520
MSA [insurance]
  Insurance (Other types of health insurance) I: 312
MSA [language] *See* Modern Standard Arabic *in
  this index*
MSC [electronic device]
  Telephone (Cellular phone calls) T: 94
MSF [organization] *See* Doctors Without Borders
  in this index
MSFW [economics]
  Migrant labor M: 538
MSG [chemical] *See* Monosodium glutamate *in
  this index*
MSH [hormone]
  Hormone (Other hormones) H: 336
MSNBC [news channel]
  NBC N: 93
Mt [symbol]
  Meitnerium M: 387
Mthethwa [people]
  Shaka S: 343
MTSO [communications] *See* Mobile telephone
  switching office *in this index*
MTV [television network] M: 908
  Rock music (The 1980's) R: 380c
M-type asteroid [astronomy]
  Asteroid (Composition) A: 824
Mu [letter]
  M M: 1 *with picture*
Mu-neutrino [atomic particle]
  Lepton L: 206
Mu'āwiya ibn Abī Sufyān [Muslim ruler]
  Muslims (Muhammad) M: 964a; (Ali) M: 964b;
    (The Muslim Empire) M: 964c
  Saudi Arabia (The rise of Islam) S: 160
Muay Thai [sport] *See* Kickboxing *in this index*
Mubarak, Hosni [Egyptian political leader] M: 908
  with portrait
  Egypt (Recent developments) E: 133
  Middle East (2011 protests) M: 534b
Much Ado About Nothing [play by Shakespeare]
  Shakespeare, William: (*Much Ado About Nothing*)
    S: 360 *with picture*
Mucha, Alphonse [Czech artist]
  Art Nouveau *picture on* A: 749
Mucilage [glue]
  Dextrin D: 178
Muckrakers [U.S. history] M: 908
  Consumer protection (Beginnings of modern
    consumerism) Ci: 1019
  Journalism (The age of sensationalism) J: 175
  Lloyd, Henry Demarest L: 402
  Magazine (Magazines in the 1800's) M: 45
  Progressive Era (Social reforms) P: 814
  Sinclair, Upton S: 468
  Steffens, Lincoln So: 883
  Tarbell, Ida Minerva T: 42
  United States, History of the (The Progressive
    Era) U: 186
Muckross Lake [Ireland]
  Lakes of Killarney L: 49 *with map*
Mucocutaneous leishmaniasis [disease]
  Leishmaniasis L: 187
Mucous colitis [disease]
  Colitis Ci: 772
Mucous gland
  Gland (table) G: 209
Mucous membrane [anatomy]
  See also Mucus *in this index*
  Biofilm B: 311
  Disease (Natural barriers) D: 231 *with diagram*
  Membrane M: 391
  Mouth M: 903
  Nose N: 548
  Nosebleed N: 549
Mucoviscidosis [disease] *See* Cystic fibrosis *in this
  index*
Mucus [physiology] M: 909
  Cystic fibrosis Ci: 1208
  Disease (Natural barriers) D: 231
  Esophagus E: 357
  Eye (The outer parts) E: 460
  Human body (The air passages) H: 420
  Lung (Other jobs of the lungs) L: 524
  Membrane (Mucous membranes) M: 391
MUD [electronics] *See* Multi-user domain *in this
  index*
Mud bath
  Bath (Bathing for relaxation or pleasure) B: 163
Mud-brick architecture

Arabs (Architecture) **A: 588**
Mud dauber [insect]
Wasp **W: 111**
Mud hen [bird]
Coot **Ci: 1038**
Mud log
Petroleum (Directional drilling) **P: 339-340**
Mud pickerel [fish]
Pickerel **P: 450**
Pike **P: 461**
Mud turtle
Turtle (Kinds of turtles) **T: 522**
Mudd, Samuel Alexander [American doctor]
M: 909
Lincoln, Abraham (The trial of the conspirators)
L: 326
Muddy Mountains [Nevada]
Las Vegas *with picture* **L: 89**
Muddy River [Nevada]
Nevada (Rivers and lakes) **N: 166**
Muddy shore [ocean]
Seashore (Life on muddy shores) **S: 270** *with picture*
Mudflat [geology]
Estuary **E: 364**
Mudflow [geology]
Volcano (Lahars) **V: 440** *with diagram*
Mudpot
Yellowstone National Park (The Lower Loop) **Y: 558**
Mudpuppy [amphibian] **M: 909** *with picture*
Mudra [gesture]
Dance (Asian theatrical dance) **D: 28-29**
Mudrock [geology]
Earth (Sedimentary rocks) **E: 21**
Mudskipper [fish]
Wetland (Animal life) **W: 252b**
Mudumalai National Park [India]
National park (table) **N: 42f**
Muelich, Hektor [German artist]
Germany *picture on* **G: 163**
Mueller, Frederick H. [American government official]
Commerce, Department of (table) **Ci: 871**
Eisenhower, Dwight David (table) **E: 152**
Mueller, Robert Swan, III [American political leader]
Federal Bureau of Investigation (History) **F: 62-63**
Muench, Aloisius Joseph [American religious leader]
Cardinal (table: American cardinals) **C: 211**
Muerto Canyon virus *See* Pulmonary syndrome hantavirus *in this index*
Muezzin [religion]
Cairo (The city) **C: 16**
Islam (The Five Pillars of Islam) **I: 463**
Minaret **M: 562**
Mufakat [government]
Indonesia (Rural life) **I: 229**
Muff [bird]
Chicken (Kinds of chickens) **C: 441**
Muffle furnace
Furnace (Sources of heat) **F: 567**
Muffler [mechanism] **M: 909** *with diagram*
Automobile (The exhaust system) **A: 953**
Gasoline engine (The exhaust system) **G: 65**
Mugabe, Robert Gabriel [Zimbabwe political leader] **M: 909**
Zimbabwe **Z: 592**; (History) **Z: 592-594**
Mugger crocodile
Crocodile (Kinds of crocodiles) **Ci: 1149-1150**
Muggeridge, Edward James [British-born photographer] *See* Muybridge, Eadweard *in this index*
Mughal Empire M: 910
Aurangzeb **A: 891**
Babur **B: 3**
Bangladesh (Mughal rule) **B: 85**
India (The Mughal Empire) **I: 129** *with map*; (The rise of the East India Company) **I: 130**
Mongol Empire (Breakup) **M: 721**
Muslims (The Mughal Empire) **M: 964d**
Painting (Indian painting) **P: 44** *with picture*
Pakistan (The Mughal Empire) **P: 99**
Punjab (History) **P: 903-904**
Sikhism (History) **S: 455**
World, History of the (The Islamic empires) **W: 441-442**
Mugwort [plant]
Wormwood **W: 502**
Mugwumps [U.S. history] **M: 910**
Cleveland, Grover (Election of 1884) **Ci: 670**
Muhajirs [people]
Pakistan (Cultural groups and languages) **P: 93**
Muhammad [prophet] **M: 910** *with picture*
Arabs (The rise and spread of Islam) **A: 589**
Biography (The Middle Ages) **B: 313**

Government (Asia and the Middle East) **G: 289-290**
Islam **I: 463**
Jerusalem (Islamic sites) **J: 96**
Jihad **J: 126**
Medina **M: 380**
Middle Ages (The rise of Islam) **M: 524**
Middle East (Religion) **M: 531**; (The spread of Islam) **M: 533**
Muslims **M: 964**
Qur'ān **Q: 44**
Ramadan **R: 132**
Religion (Islam) **R: 223**
Saudi Arabia **S: 155**; (The rise of Islam) **S: 160**
Shi`ites **S: 400**
Sufism **So: 959**
Sunnis **So: 961**
World, History of the (The Islamic world) **W: 434**
Muhammad II [sultan of the Ottoman Empire] *See* Mehmet II *in this index*
Muhammad VI [king of Morocco]
Morocco (Recent developments) **M: 815**
Muhammad, Elijah [American religious leader] **M: 911**
African Americans (Black militancy) **A: 136q**
Black Muslims **B: 390**
Malcolm X **M: 103**
Nation of Islam **N: 27**
Muhammad, Warith Deen [American religious leader] *See* Mohammed, Warith Deen *in this index*
Muhammad Ali [American boxer] *See* Ali, Muhammad *in this index*
Muhammad Ali [Ottoman military leader] **M: 911**
Africa (African societies in the 1800's) **A: 133**
Alexandria (History) **A: 344**
Egypt (Muhammad Ali and modernization) **E: 131**
Mamluks **M: 115**
Muhammad Ali Mosque
Cairo (The city) **C: 16**
Muhammad Daoud Khan [Afghan political leader] *See* Daoud Khan, Muhammad *in this index*
Muhammad of Ghor [king of the Turks]
Delhi Sultanate **D: 116**
Muhammadan art *See* Islamic art *in this index*
Muhammadanism *See* Islam *in this index*
Muhammadiyyah [political movement]
Muslims (Reform and renewal) **M: 964d-965**
Muharram [religion]
Calendar (The Islamic calendar) **C: 29**
Muhlenberg, Frederick Augustus Conrad [American political leader]
Muhlenberg, Henry Melchior **M: 912**
Muhlenberg, Henry Melchior [American religious leader] **M: 911**
Muhlenberg, John Peter Gabriel [American general] **M: 912**
Muhlenberg, Henry Melchior **M: 912**
Muhlenberg, William Augustus [American religious leader]
Muhlenberg, Henry Melchior **M: 912**
Muir, John [American conservationist] **M: 912**
American literature (Nonfiction writers) **A: 420**
Conservation *picture on* **Ci: 986**; (Early conservation problems) **Ci: 985**
Sierra Club **S: 450** *with picture*
Muir Woods National Monument [California] **M: 912** *with picture*
Muir, John **M: 912**
National Park System (table: National monuments) **N: 51**
Mujahideen [Afghan history]
Afghanistan (The Soviet invasion) **A: 96**
Bin Laden, Osama **B: 307**
Guerrilla warfare (History) **G: 420**
Middle East (The 1970's and 1980's) **M: 534a**
Qa`ida, Al- **Q: 2**
Mujibur Rahman [Bangladeshi political leader] **M: 912**
Bangladesh (East Pakistan) **B: 85-86** *with picture*
Mujica, José [Uruguayan political leader]
Uruguay (Recent developments) **U: 228**
Mukasey, Michael B. [American government official]
Bush, George Walker (table) **B: 722h**; (Other domestic issues) **B: 723**
Justice, Department of (table) **J: 203**
Mukden [China] *See* Shenyang *in this index*
Mukden, Battle of [1905]
Russo-Japanese War (Final battles) **R: 566b**
Mukerji, Dhan Gopal [Indian author]
Newbery Medal (table) **N: 359**
Mukoshima [island, Japan]
Bonin Islands **B: 460**
Mulatto [people] **M: 912**
Brazil (Ancestry) **B: 572**
Cuba (Ancestry and language) **Ci: 1170**
Haiti (People) **H: 14-15**

Hispanic Americans (Who Hispanic Americans are) **H: 245-246**
Indian, American (In Latin America) **I: 178**
Latin America (Ancestry) **L: 92-94**
Mulberry [tree] **M: 913** *with picture*
Fruit (Types of fruits in botany) **F: 544-546** *with picture*
Silk (Discovery of silk) **S: 460**
Tree *pictures on* **T: 422**
Mulberry Bend [U.S. history]
Riis, Jacob August **R: 341**
Mulch [agriculture] **M: 913**
Compost **Ci: 905**
Farm and farming (Preparing the soil) **F: 35**
Gardening (Mulching) **G: 35**
Mulct Law [1894]
Iowa (The temperance movement) **I: 395**
Muldoon, Paul [Irish poet]
Irish literature (The Irish literary revival) **I: 433**
Muldoon, Sir Robert David [New Zealand political leader] **M: 913**
Muldowney, Shirley [American race driver]
Automobile racing (Automobile racing today) **A: 980-981**
Mule [animal] **M: 913** *with pictures*
Evolution (Evolution of new species) **E: 429-430**
Mule [locomotive]
Panama Canal (The Gatun Locks) **P: 123**
Mule [machine]
Spinning (The mule) **So: 794**
Mule deer M: 914 *with picture*
Animal *picture on* **A: 483**
Balance of nature (Upsetting the balance) **B: 36**
Deer *picture on* **D: 84**; (North American deer) **D: 85**
Mule-Foot hog
Hog (Feet) **H: 287**
Muleta [cloth]
Bullfighting (The order of the bullfight) **B: 696-697** *with picture*
Mulhacén [mountain]
Spain (The Meseta) **So: 739** *with map*
Mullah [title] **M: 914**
Afghanistan (Religion) **A: 93-94**
Mullein [plant] **M: 914** *with picture*
Mullen [plant] *See* Mullein *in this index*
Mullen, Larry, Jr. [Irish musician]
Bono **B: 462**
U2 **U: 2**
Mullen, Michael G. [American government official]
Joint Chiefs of Staff (table) **J: 156**
Mullens, Priscilla [American colonist] *See* Alden, John and Priscilla *in this index*
Mullens, William [Pilgrim]
Alden, John and Priscilla **A: 339**
Müller, Erwin W. [German-American physicist]
Ion microscope **I: 372**
Müller, Friedrich Max [German linguist]
Mythology (Comparative approaches) **M: 989**
Religion (The origin of religion) **R: 218**
Müller, Heiner [German dramatist]
Drama (Later German-language drama) **D: 340**
Muller, Hermann Joseph [American geneticist]
Heredity (The birth of genetics) **H: 208**
Nobel Prizes (Physiology or medicine: 1946) **N: 445**
Müller, Herta [German author]
Nobel Prizes (Literature: 2009) **N: 448**
Müller, Herta [Romanian author]
German literature (Recent German literature) **G: 142**
Müller, Johannes P. [German physiologist]
Psychology (Psychology becomes a science) **P: 849**
Müller, Karl Alexander [Swiss physicist]
Nobel Prizes (Physics: 1987) **N: 442**
Muller, Marcia [American author] **M: 915**
Müller, Paul Hermann [Swiss chemist]
Agriculture (Chemical pesticides) **A: 159**
DDT **D: 55**
Müller, Walther [German physicist]
Geiger counter **G: 76**
Müllerian mimicry [biology]
Mimicry **M: 561**
Mullet [fish] **M: 915** *with picture*
Mullet [heraldry]
Heraldry *picture on* **H: 195**
Mulligan, Gerry [American saxophonist] **M: 915**
Jazz (Cool jazz) **J: 72**
Mulliken, Robert Sanderson [American chemist] **M: 915**
Mullion [construction]
Window **W: 334**
Mullis, Kary Banks [American chemist]
Nobel Prizes (Chemistry: 1993) **N: 444**
Mulock, Sir William [Canadian political leader]
King, William Lyon Mackenzie (Education) **K: 325**

Mulroney, Brian [Canadian political leader] **M: 916** *with pictures*
  Campbell, Kim **C: 90b**; (Member of parliament) **C: 90c-90d**
  Canada, History of (Constitutional changes) **C: 151**; (Canada under Mulroney) **C: 151**
  Chrétien, Jean (Political career) **C: 522b**
  Clark, Joe (Prime Minister) **Ci: 641**
  Progressive Conservative Party **P: 812**
  Quebec (The late 1900's) **Q: 32-33**
  Turner, John Napier (Political comeback) **T: 517**
Multatuli [Dutch author]
  Netherlands (Arts) **N: 142-144**
Multiband radio
  Radio (How radio programs are received) **R: 88**
Multicell cluster thunderstorm
  Thunderstorm **T: 272**
Multicellular organism
  Life (The structure of living things) **L: 276-277**
Multiconductor cable
  Cable (Cable construction) **C: 4** *with diagram*
Multicore microprocessor [electronic device]
  Computer (Microprocessors) **Ci: 912**
Multicultural education program
  African Americans (Developments since 1970) **A: 136r**
  Education (Education for whom?) **E: 107**
  Multiculturalism **M: 918**
  Teaching (Current issues in U.S. teaching) **T: 69**
Multiculturalism [sociology] **M: 918**
  Culture (Culture and society) **Ci: 1188**
Multi-infarct dementia [disease]
  Senility **S: 300**
Multilateral aid
  Foreign aid (Multilateral aid programs) **F: 385**
Multilateral development bank
  Bank (Kinds of banks) **B: 90-91**
Multilateral Investment Guarantee Agency [UN]
  World Bank **W: 450**
Multilateral treaty
  International relations (Treaties) **I: 344**
Multilateral well
  Petroleum (Directional drilling) **P: 339** *with diagram*
Multilevel well
  Petroleum (Directional drilling) **P: 339** *with diagram*
Multimedia [electronics]
  Audio-visual materials **A: 882**
  Compact disc (CD-ROM's) **Ci: 901**
  Information retrieval **I: 268b**
  Library *picture on* **L: 236**; (Library resources) **L: 235**
  Video art **V: 359**
  World Wide Web **W: 499**
Multimedia encyclopedia
  Encyclopedia (Today's encyclopedias) **E: 268b** *with pictures*
Multimedia Super Corridor [area, Malaysia]
  Putrajaya **P: 913**
Multimeter [instrument]
  Electric meter **E: 176**; (Digital meters) **E: 177** *with picture*
Multimodality therapy [treatment]
  Cancer (Multimodality therapy) **C: 172**
Multi-mode fiber
  Fiber optics (Kinds of optical fibers) **F: 88** *with diagram*
Multinational corporation M: 919
  Chemistry (The chemical industry) **C: 405**
  Corporation (Business corporations) **Ci: 1069**
  Globalization (Features of globalization) **G: 233**
Multiparty system
  Democracy (Political parties) **D: 120-121**
  Political party (Multiparty systems) **P: 634**
Multi-payer health care system
  Health insurance, National **H: 129**
Multiperil insurance
  Crop insurance **Ci: 1153**
Multiple [measurement]
  Metric system (Kinds of metric units) **M: 436**
Multiple birth M: 919 *with picture*
  Infertility (Treatment) **I: 265**
  Reproduction, Human (Multiple birth) **R: 246**
Multiple element antenna
  Antenna *picture on* **A: 543**
Multiple fracture
  Fracture **F: 450** *with diagram*
Multiple fruit
  Fruit (Types of fruit in botany) **F: 544-546** *with pictures*
Multiple Independently Targetable Reentry Vehicle [weapon]
  Guided missile *diagrams on* **G: 425**; (The warhead) **G: 423**
Multiple intelligences [psychology]
  Teaching (Guiding and assisting student learning) **T: 66**
Multiple-line insurance
  Insurance (Homeowners' insurance) **I: 313**
Multiple origins theory [anthropology]
  Prehistoric people (The multiple origins theory) **P: 749**
Multiple-party system *See* Multiparty system *in this index*
Multiple personality [psychology]
  Mental illness (Dissociative disorders) **M: 406**
Multiple-product forestry
  Forestry (Community forestry) **F: 406**
Multiple-response learning
  Education (How people learn) **E: 89**
  Learning (Multiple-response learning) **L: 163**
Multiple sclerosis [disease] **M: 920**
  Brain (Multiple sclerosis) **B: 559**
  Nervous system (Disorders of the nervous system) **N: 136**
  Occupational therapy (Helping people with physical disabilities) **O: 648**
Multiple tracks
  Railroad (Tracks) **R: 108**
Multiple-unit operation
  Locomotive (Kind of locomotives) **L: 414**
Multiple use forest management
  Conservation (Forest conservation) **Ci: 981**
  Forestry **F: 404**
Multiplex system
  Radio (Stereophonic receivers) **R: 89**
Multiplicand [arithmetic]
  Arithmetic (Multiplication) **A: 667**
  Multiplication (Writing multiplication) **M: 921**
Multiplication [mathematics] **M: 921** *with pictures*
  Algebra (Multiplication) **A: 355**
  Arithmetic (Multiplication) **A: 667** *with picture*; (Arithmetic of small fractions) **A: 668**; (Arithmetic of negative numbers) **A: 668-669**
  Binary number (In arithmetic) **B: 307**
  Decimal system (Multiplication) **D: 71** *with diagrams*
  Division (Checking by multiplication) **D: 251**
  Fraction *diagram on* **F: 449**; (Equivalent fractions) **F: 446** *with diagram*; (Calculations using fractions) **F: 446**
  Logarithms (Multiplication) **L: 424**
Multiplication table
  Multiplication (Multiplication facts) **M: 921** *with picture*
Multiplier [mathematics]
  Arithmetic (Multiplication) **A: 667**
  Multiplication (Writing multiplication) **M: 921**
Multipolar system [political science]
  Balance of power **B: 37**
Multiport fuel injection system
  Automobile (The fuel system) **A: 953**
  Fuel injection **F: 552**
Multisensory materials
  Audio-visual materials (Multisensory materials) **A: 883**
Multispindle machine
  Machine tool (Metal removal) **M: 17**
Multistage flash distillation
  Water *diagram on* **W: 128**; (Distillation) **W: 127**
Multistage rocket
  Rocket (Multistage rockets) **R: 386**
Multistop truck
  Truck *picture on* **T: 459**
Multitrack recorder [machine]
  Recording industry (Recording) **R: 181**
Multi-user domain [electronics]
  Electronic game (The growth of computer gaming) **E: 204e**
  Internet (Online communities) **I: 350b**
Multiwall bag [container]
  Paper bag **P: 138**
Multnomah Falls [waterfall, Oregon]
  Waterfall (table: Famous waterfalls of North America) **W: 142** *with picture*
Muluzi, Bakili [Malawi political leader]
  Malawi (History) **M: 97-98**
Mumbai [India] **M: 924** *with picture*
  India **I: 108**, *picture on* **I: 115**; (Service industries) **I: 126**; (Recent developments) **I: 134-135**
  Terrorism (Recent developments) **T: 180**
Mumbo Jumbo [book by Reed]
  American literature (Experimental styles) **A: 425**
Mummers [actors]
  Christmas *picture on* **C: 530**
Mummers Parade
  Pennsylvania *picture on* **P: 255**
  Philadelphia (The arts) **P: 363** *with picture*
Mummification
  Anubis **A: 562**
  Fossil (Other processes) **F: 425**
Mumming [custom]
  Halloween (Halloween customs and symbols) **H: 24a**
Mummy [archaeology] **M: 925** *with pictures*
  Egypt, Ancient (Religion) **E: 137**
  Embalming (Ancient embalming) **E: 255**
  Funeral customs (History) **F: 558**
  Pyramids (Egyptian pyramids) **P: 916**
Mummy bale
  Mummy *picture on* **M: 925**
Mumps [disease] **M: 926**
  Disease (table) **D: 226**
Mumtaz Mahal [wife of Shah Jahan]
  Taj Mahal **T: 18**
Munch, Edvard [Norwegian artist] **M: 926** *with picture*
  Expressionism **E: 455**
  Norway (Arts) **N: 541** *with picture*
  Painting (Symbolism) **P: 76**
Munchausen, Baron [literary figure] **M: 927**
München [Germany] *See* Munich *in this index*
Munchhausen, Karl Friedrich Hieronymus [German military officer]
  Munchausen, Baron **M: 927**
Munda, Battle of [45 B.C.]
  Caesar, Julius (Last victories) **C: 13**
Mundelein, George William [American religious leader]
  Cardinal (table: American cardinals) **C: 211**
Mundell, Robert Alexander [Canadian economist]
  Nobel Prizes (Economics: 1999) **N: 449**
Mundugumor [people]
  Sexuality (Cultural influences) **S: 338a**
Mundus Novus [letter by Vespucci]
  Vespucci, Amerigo (Life and expeditions) **V: 341-342**
Mundy Scheme, The [play by Friel]
  Friel, Brian **F: 533**
Mung bean
  Bean (Kinds of beans) **B: 181**
Muni, Paul [American actor]
  Motion picture (Best performance by an actor: 1936) **M: 862a**
Munich [Germany] **M: 927** *with picture*
  Bavaria **B: 174**
  Germany *picture on* **G: 151**
  Olympic Games (Terrorism in Munich) **O: 752**
Munich Agreement [1938] **M: 927**
  Czech Republic (The Munich Agreement) **Ci: 1213**
  Czechoslovakia (The Munich Agreement) **Ci: 1215**
  United Kingdom ("Peace in our time") **U: 70**
  World War II (The failure of appeasement) **W: 472**
Municipal Assistance Corporation [New York]
  New York City (Problems) **N: 342**
Municipal Auditorium and Theater
  Mobile (The city) **M: 681**
Municipal authority *See* Special district *in this index*
Municipal bond
  Bond (Kinds of bonds) **B: 454**
  Investment (Bonds) **I: 368**
Municipal Building
  Kansas City *picture on* **K: 240**
Municipal Civic Center
  New York City *picture on* **N: 340**; (Manhattan) **N: 323-324**
Municipal corporation
  Corporation (Other corporations) **Ci: 1070**
Municipal government *See* City government *in this index*
Municipal solid waste
  Environmental pollution (Solid waste) **E: 334**
  Landfill **L: 57**
  Waste disposal **W: 112**
Municipality
  City government **Ci: 594**
  Local government (Units of local government) **L: 407**
Municipality of Metropolitan Toronto
  Toronto (Growth and federation) **T: 340c**
Município [district]
  Brazil (Local government) **B: 569**
Munitions *See* Ammunition; Bomb; Weapon *in this index*
Munn v. Illinois [U.S. history]
  Granger cases **G: 311**
Muñoz Marín, Luis [Puerto Rican political leader] **M: 928**
  Puerto Rico (Building a democracy) **P: 883**
Munro, Alice [Canadian author] **M: 928**
  Canadian literature (Modern English-Canadian fiction) **C: 160** *with portrait*
Munro, Hector Hugh [British author] **M: 928**
Munsee Indians M: 928
  Delaware Indians **D: 113**
Munsell, Albert H. [American painter]
  Color (The Munsell Color System) **Ci: 824**

Munsell Color System
Color (The Munsell Color System) Ci: 824 *with diagrams*
Munster [cheese]
Cheese (Semisoft cheese) C: 392 *with picture*
Münter, Gabriele [German artist]
Painting (Expressionism) P: 78-79
Muntjac [animal]
Deer (Asian and European deer) D: 86
Muntz metal
Brass B: 565
Muon [subatomic particle] M: 928
Anderson, Carl David A: 451
Cosmic rays (Secondary cosmic rays) Ci: 1076
Lepton L: 205
Relativity (Time dilation) R: 211
Subatomic particle (Kinds of subatomic particles) So: 937
Muon-neutrino [subatomic particle]
Astronomy (Neutrino astronomy) A: 845-846
Neutrino N: 154
Muonio River
Finland (Rivers) F: 114
Muppets [puppets]
Henson, Jim H: 191
Muqaddimah [book by Ibn Khaldūn]
Ibn Khaldūn I: 3
Muqarnas vault [architecture]
Islamic art (Other buildings) I: 468-469
Muqdisho [Somalia] *See* Mogadishu *in this index*
Murad, Ferid [American pharmacologist]
Nobel Prizes (Physiology or medicine: 1998) N: 446
Murakami, Takashi [Japanese artist]
Painting (Postmodernism) P: 88
Mural [art] M: 928 *with picture*
See also Mosaic *in this index*
Benton, Thomas Hart B: 254
Hispanic Americans *picture on* H: 255
Latin America *picture on* L: 101
Mexico *picture on* M: 459; (Arts) M: 460
Orozco, José Clemente *picture on* O: 858
Painting (Modern Mexican painting) P: 83
Rivera, Diego R: 354 *with picture*
Siqueiros, David S: 475
Murano [Italy]
Glass (The Middle Ages) G: 218
Venice (Economy) V: 307-308
Murano glass
Italy *picture on* I: 505
Murasaki Shikibu [Japanese author] M: 929
Japanese literature (The Heian period) J: 61-62
Painting (Japanese painting) P: 47
Murchison Falls [Africa] *See* Kabalega Falls *in this index*
Murder [crime] M: 929
Euthanasia (Active euthanasia) E: 421
Homicide H: 305
Manslaughter M: 167
Murder in the Cathedral [play by Eliot]
Eliot, T. S. (His works) E: 237-238
Murder of Lidice, The [book by Millay]
Millay, Edna St. Vincent M: 552
Murder-suicide
Suicide (Types) So: 964
"Murders in the Rue Morgue, The" [story by Poe]
Detective story (History) D: 162
Poe, Edgar Allan P: 589; (Poe's life) P: 589
Murdoch, Iris [British author] M: 930
English literature (Recent English fiction) E: 323
Murdoch, Paul [American architect]
September 11 terrorist attacks (Pennsylvania) S: 310c
Murdoch, Peter [designer]
Furniture *picture on* F: 587
Murdoch, Rupert [Australian publisher] M: 930
Fox F: 441
Murdock, William [British inventor]
Gas [fuel] (First uses of manufactured gas) G: 57
Lamp (Gas lamps) L: 53
Murex sea snail
Shell *picture on* S: 386; (Uses of shells) S: 389-390
Murfreesboro, Battle of [1863]
Civil War, American (table) Ci: 624; (Battle of Stones River) Ci: 629
Muri [food]
Bangladesh *picture on* B: 80
Muriatic acid *See* Hydrochloric acid *in this index*
Murieta, Joaquín [legendary figure] M: 930
Murillo, Bartolomé Esteban [Spanish painter] M: 930
Murine typhus [disease]
Typhus (Murine typhus) T: 541
Muriqui [monkey]
Monkey (Kinds of monkeys) M: 725
Murkowski, Frank Hughes [American political leader]

Alaska (table) A: 300
Murmansk [Russia] M: 930
Murmur [disorder]
Heart murmur H: 147
Rheumatic fever R: 291
Murnau, Friedrich [German director]
Motion picture (Filmmaking in Europe) M: 866
Muroc Army Air Base
Edwards Air Force Base E: 114
Murphree, Dennis [American political leader]
Mississippi (table) M: 640
Murphy, Al [fictional character]
Paulsen, Gary P: 202
Murphy, Audie [American soldier] M: 931 *with portrait*
Texas (The mid-1900's) T: 208
Murphy, Charles Francis [American political leader]
Wilson, Woodrow (Presidential candidate) W: 322
Murphy, Eddie [American actor] M: 931 *with portrait*
Murphy, Emily Gowan [Canadian reformer] M: 931
Famous Five F: 26b
Murphy, Francis P. [American political leader]
New Hampshire (table) N: 223
Murphy, Frank [American jurist]
Michigan (table) M: 507
Roosevelt, Franklin Delano (table) R: 454
Supreme Court of the United States (table) So: 1000
Murphy, Franklin [American political leader]
New Jersey (table) N: 249
Murphy, Isaac [American political leader]
Arkansas (table) A: 712
Murphy, Jimmy [American race driver]
Automobile racing (table: Indianapolis 500 winners) A: 980
Murphy, John [American political leader]
Alabama (table) A: 274
Murphy, William Parry [American physician]
Nobel Prizes (Physiology or medicine: 1934) N: 445
Murphy bed
Bed (Types of beds) B: 198
Murrah, Pendleton [American political leader]
Texas (table) T: 203
Murrah Federal Building *See* Alfred P. Murrah Federal Building *in this index*
Murray, Alfalfa Bill [American political leader]
Oklahoma (The 1930's) O: 732
Murray, Andy [British tennis player]
Olympic Games *picture on* O: 749
Murray, Donald [British inventor]
Telegraph (Decline) T: 92
Murray, Eddie [American baseball player]
Baseball (table: Hall of Fame) B: 134a
Murray, George H. [Canadian political leader]
Nova Scotia (table) N: 567
Murray, James [British colonial official] M: 931
Canada, History of (The Quebec Act) C: 141-142
Murray, James A. [Canadian political leader]
New Brunswick (table) N: 195
Murray, John Courtney [American theologian]
Vatican Council II (Other documents) V: 290
Murray, Johnston [American political leader]
Oklahoma (The 1930's) O: 730; (The mid-1900's) O: 734
Murray, Joseph Edward [American physiologist]
Nobel Prizes (Physiology or medicine: 1990) N: 446
Murray, Margaret A. [British anthropologist]
Witchcraft (Witchcraft in modern times) W: 373
Murray, Philip [American labor leader] M: 931
Congress of Industrial Organizations Ci: 941
Labor movement (Reunification of the AFL and the CIO) L: 13
Murray, William H. [American political leader]
Oklahoma (table) O: 730; (The 1930's) O: 732
Murray River [Australia] M: 932
Australia (Rivers) A: 909 *with map*
Exploration (Exploring Australia's interior) E: 448
River (table) R: 352
South Australia (Land and climate) So: 639
Murre [bird] M: 932 *with picture*
Auk A: 890
Murrieta, Joaquín [legendary figure] *See* Murieta, Joaquín *in this index*
Murrow, Edward R. [American journalist] M: 932 *with portrait*
Murrumbidgee [river, Australia]
Australia (Rivers) A: 909 *with map*
Exploration (Exploring Australia's interior) E: 448
Murry and Leonie Guggenheim Foundation
Guggenheim, Meyer G: 421
Musa, Said [Belize political leader]
Belize (History) B: 238
Musala Peak
Bulgaria (The land) B: 691 *with map*

Musandam Peninsula
Oman (Land and climate) O: 758
Musashi [ship]
Battleship (The modern battleship) B: 172
Muscadine grape
Grape (North American grapes) G: 319
Muscat [Oman] M: 932
Arabs *picture on* A: 588
Oman O: 757
Muscat (History) O: 759
Muscat and Oman [former name]
Oman (History) O: 759
Muscat of Alexandria [raisin]
Raisin (Varieties) R: 129; (Preparation for market) R: 129-130
Muscle [anatomy] M: 933 *with diagrams*
Back B: 17
Cataplexy C: 298
Convulsions Ci: 1025
Cramp Ci: 1116
Curare Ci: 1193
Fish (Skeleton and muscles) F: 161
Hand (Parts of the hand) H: 40 *with diagram*
Heart (Outer lining and muscle) H: 133
Human body *diagram on* H: 416; (Cells and tissues) H: 417-418; (The muscular system) H: 418 *with picture*; (table) H: 422 *with diagram*
Incontinence I: 106
Insect (Muscular system) I: 289
Iron (How bodies use iron) I: 435
Knee K: 345
Nervous system *diagrams on* N: 134
Neurology N: 152
Paralysis P: 152
Physical fitness (Muscular strength) P: 433
Posture P: 710
Rheumatism R: 291
Rheumatology R: 291
Rotator cuff R: 486
Tendon T: 132 *with diagram*
Tissue (Animal tissues) T: 298-299
Muscle car
Automobile *picture on* A: 967; (The postwar years) A: 970-971
General Motors Company G: 83
Muscle Shoals [region, Alabama] M: 936
Goethals, George Washington (Early life) G: 246
Tennessee Valley Authority (Other activities) T: 160
Muscle Shoals [town, Alabama]
Rock music (Soul music) R: 380a-380b
Muscling [slang]
Heroin H: 213
Muscovite [mineral]
Mica M: 482
Mineral *picture on* M: 569
Muscovite literature
Russian literature (Muscovite literature) R: 559
Muscovites [people]
Moscow (People) M: 824
Muscovy Company [British history]
Hudson, Henry (Northern voyages) H: 404
Muscular Christianity
Kingsley, Charles K: 331
Muscular dystrophy M: 936
Heredity (table) H: 204
Paralysis (Paralysis of muscular origin) P: 152
Muscular system *See* Muscle *in this index*
Musculoskeletal system [anatomy]
Bone B: 456
Osteopathic medicine O: 867
Musée d'Art Contemporain [museum, Montreal]
Montreal *picture on* M: 775
Museé d'Orsay [museum, Paris]
Paris (Museums and art galleries) P: 164-165
Muses [Greek mythology] M: 937
Mythology *picture on* M: 981; (Greek divinities) M: 982
Musetta [opera character]
Opera: (*Bohème, La*) O: 801
"Musetta's Waltz" [aria]
Opera: (*Bohème, La*) O: 801
Museum M: 937 *with pictures*
See also the list of *Related articles in the Museum article*
Doll (Dolls in museums) D: 294
United States *picture on* U: 113; (Museums) U: 114
Museum and Library Services Act [1996]
Library (Supporting the public library) L: 242-243; (School library standards) L: 245
Museum at Warm Springs [Oregon]
Oregon (Places to visit) O: 836
Museum Island [island]
Berlin (Downtown Berlin) B: 260
Museum of African American History [Detroit] M: 940
United States *picture on* U: 113

Museum of African Art, National [Washington D.C.] *See* National Museum of African Art *in this index*
Museum of Anthropology [Mexico]
Library *picture on* L: 254
Museum of Contemporary Art [Brasília]
Brazil *picture on* B: 576
Museum of Decorative Art [Paris]
Paris (Museums and art galleries) P: 164-165
Museum of Fine Arts [Boston]
Boston (Cultural life and recreation) B: 501-502 *with picture*
Folk art (Folk art collections) F: 319
Museum of Fine Arts [Houston]
Houston (Museums and libraries) H: 397
Museum of History and Technology, National *See* National Museum of American History *in this index*
Museum of Modern Art [New York City] M: 940
New York City (A visitor's guide) N: 338
Photography (A diversity of styles) P: 426-427
Museum of Natural History [Providence]
Rhode Island (Museums) R: 301
Museum of Natural History, American *See* American Museum of Natural History *in this index*
Museum of Natural History, National *See* National Museum of Natural History *in this index*
Museum of New Mexico [Santa Fe]
New Mexico (Libraries and museums) N: 260
Museum of Science and Industry [Chicago] M: 940
Chicago (Museums) C: 428-429
Illinois (Museums) I: 56 *with picture*
Museum of the Confederacy [Richmond]
Richmond (Other interesting places to visit) R: 332
Virginia (Libraries and museums) V: 402-403 *with picture*
Museum of the Fur Trade [Chadron]
Nebraska (Places to visit) N: 102
Museum of the Plains Indian [Montana]
Montana (Museums) M: 746
Museum of the Rockies [Bozeman]
Montana (Museums) M: 746
Museums and Women [stories by Updike]
Updike, John U: 213
Museums of Old York [York, Maine]
Maine (Places to visit) M: 78
Museveni, Yoweri [Ugandan political leader]
Uganda (History) U: 3-4
Musgrave Ranges [mountain ranges]
Australia (Mountains) A: 908 *with map*
Musgrove, Ronnie [American political leader]
Mississippi (table) M: 640
Musharraf, Pervez [Pakistani political leader] M: 941
Pakistan (Musharraf) P: 100
Mushet, Robert Forester [British metallurgist]
Iron and steel (The birth of modern steelmaking) I: 450-451
Mushroom M: 941 *with pictures*
Mushroom anchor
Anchor A: 449 *with picture*
Mushroom coral
Coral *picture on* Ci: 1048a
Musial, Stan [American baseball player] M: 945
Baseball (table: Hall of Fame) B: 134a; (Depression and war) B: 136
Music M: 946 *with pictures*
See also the list of Related articles in the Music article
Arabs (Literature and the arts) A: 587-588
Ballet (Music) B: 50
Baroque (Baroque music) B: 117
Careers (Sports and entertainment) C: 230-231
China (Music) C: 490 *with picture*
Colonial life in America (Music) Ci: 808
Copyright (Works protected) Ci: 1046
Drama (Other parts of drama) D: 325
Electronic game (Sound) E: 204b
Folk music F: 321
Impressionism (Music, literature, and sculpture) I: 94
Indian, American (Music) I: 148
Minimalism M: 573
Motion picture (Adding music and sound effects) M: 856
Poe, Edgar Allan (Poetry and poetic theory) P: 589-590
Pulitzer Prizes (Prizes in literature, drama, and music) P: 886b; (table) P: 899
Radio (Entertainment) R: 85
Rhythm R: 319
Romanticism (Romanticism in music) R: 427
Television (Adding music and sound effects) T: 112
Western frontier life in America (Recreation)

W: 238
Music box M: 958 *with picture*
Music Box Revues [musicals]
Berlin, Irving B: 266
Music Center-Performing Arts Center of Los Angeles County
Los Angeles (The arts) L: 466 *with picture*
Music City, U.S.A. [nickname]
Nashville N: 23
Music Clubs, National Federation of M: 958
Music in the Tuileries Gardens [painting by Manet]
Painting (Edouard Manet and the Impressionists) P: 71 *with picture*
Music Television [network] *See* MTV *in this index*
Music therapy
Music (Careers in music) M: 957
Music video
Jackson, Michael J: 15
MTV M: 908
Popular music (New technologies) P: 671
Television *picture on* T: 119
Musical [entertainment] *See* Musical comedy *in this index*
Musical acoustics [science]
Acoustics A: 29
Musical chairs
Game *picture on* G: 21
Musical comedy M: 958 *with pictures*
Ballet *picture on* B: 54
Dance (Musical comedy) D: 31 *with picture*
Hammerstein, Oscar, II H: 35
Hart, Lorenz H: 77
Motion picture (Movies in the 1930's) M: 867 *with picture*
Popular music (Vaudeville and musical comedy) P: 670
Theater *picture on* T: 244
United States *picture on* U: 119
Musical glasses [musical instrument] *See* Glass harmonica *in this index*
Musical instrument
Music (Musical instruments) M: 948 *with pictures*
Catgut C: 301
Country music (The instruments) Ci: 1098
Orchestra O: 820 *with pictures*
Suzuki method So: 1013
Musical Offering [music by Bach]
Canon C: 183
Musical pause [poetry]
Poetry (Rhythm and meter) P: 591-593
Musical Ride [custom]
Royal Canadian Mounted Police *picture on* R: 495
Musical score
Opera (The elements of opera) O: 791
Orchestra (The conductor) O: 821
Musical top
Top (Kinds of tops) T: 331
Musician *See* Music *in this index*
Musicians, American Federation of [labor union] M: 961
Labor movement (table) L: 8
Petrillo, James Caesar P: 329
Musicians of the United States and Canada, American Federation of *See* Musicians, American Federation of *in this index*
Musique concrète [music]
Classical music (Electronic music) Ci: 650
Musk [animal product]
Civet Ci: 604
Deer (Asian and European deer) D: 86
Musk deer M: 962
Perfume (Animal substances) P: 286
Skunk S: 496
Weasel W: 155
Musk deer M: 962 *with picture*
Deer (Asian and European deer) D: 86
Musk hog
Peccary P: 226
Musk ox M: 962
Animal *picture on* A: 484
Arctic (Animal life) A: 637
Takin T: 18b
Musk turtle
Turtle (Kinds of turtles) T: 522 *with picture*
Muskellunge [fish] M: 962
Fish *picture on* F: 159
Pike F: 461
Musket [gun] M: 962
Army (The rise of modern armies) A: 727
Blunderbuss B: 425
Flintlock F: 236
Revolution, American (Weapons and tactics) R: 279 *with pictures*
Muskie, Edmund Sixtus [American political leader] M: 963
Humphrey, Hubert Horatio (Presidential candidate) H: 437

Maine (table) M: 87; (The mid-1900's) M: 91 *with picture*
Nixon, Richard Milhous (The 1968 election) N: 432
Muskingum River [Ohio]
Ohio River O: 705
Muskmelon [food] M: 963 *with picture*
Muskogee Indians
Creek Indians Ci: 1125
Muskoka Lakes [Ontario] M: 963
Muskrat [animal] M: 963 *with picture*
Animal *picture on* A: 479
Fur *picture on* F: 562; (table) F: 561
Wetland *picture on* W: 253
Musky [fish] *See* Muskellunge *in this index*
Muslim American Society
Black Muslims B: 390
Muslim art *See* Islamic art *in this index*
Muslim Brotherhood [political group] M: 964
Egypt (The 1940's) E: 132
Hamas H: 28
Muslims (Reform and renewal) M: 964d-965
Qutb, Sayyid Q: 44
Muslim Girls Training [organization]
Nation of Islam N: 27
Muslim League [history of India] M: 964
Bangladesh (British India) B: 85
India (Rise of Indian nationalism) I: 131; (New Constitution) I: 132; (World War II [1939-1945]) I: 132-133; (Independence and partition) I: 133
Jinnah, Mohammad Ali J: 127
Pakistan (The nationalist movement) P: 99
Muslims [religious group] M: 964 *with pictures*
See also Islam *in this index*
Africa (Religions) A: 106 *with picture*
Algeria (Religion) A: 362
Arab Americans (Who Arab Americans are) A: 580a
Arab-Israeli conflict A: 582
Arabs (Religion) A: 584 *with picture*; (Religion) A: 586
Asia (Religions) A: 779 *with picture*
Azerbaijan (People) A: 996
Bangladesh (Religion) B: 82
Black Muslims B: 389
Bosnia-Herzegovina (People) B: 492; (History) B: 492-493
Chechnya C: 390
China (Religion) C: 485-486
Christianity (The medieval church) C: 524; (Christianity today) C: 526-527
Columbus, Christopher (Years of waiting) Ci: 858
Crusades Ci: 1159
Egypt (Religion) E: 124 *with picture*; (Muslim rule) E: 130
Ethiopia (Religion) E: 369
Europe (Religions) E: 386
Exploration (Muslim exploration) E: 442; (The age of European exploration) E: 442
France (Recent developments) F: 478
Hausa H: 86
India (Islam) I: 117 *with picture*; (History) I: 129
Indonesia I: 226; (Religion) I: 232 *with picture*
Iran I: 398
Iraq (Religion) I: 411
Lebanon (Ethnic groups and religion) L: 171
Libya (Religion) L: 266 *with picture*
Malaysia (Religion) M: 98d
Marriage (Wedding ceremonies) M: 220
Middle Ages (The rise of Islam) M: 524
Middle East (Religion) M: 531
Moors M: 797
Muslim Brotherhood M: 964
Name (Black names) N: 5-6
Niger (People) N: 407-408
Nigeria (Religion) N: 413 *with picture*
Palestinians P: 107
Philippines (Recovering democracy) P: 381
Punjab (History) P: 903
Qur'ān Q: 44
Racial profiling R: 61
Radicalism (Around the world today) R: 82
Senegal (People) S: 297
Srebrenica massacre So: 816
Sunnis So: 991
Syria (Religion) So: 1071
Tajikistan (People) T: 18a
Turkey (Religion) T: 506
Turkmenistan (People) T: 514
Uzbekistan (People) U: 253
Women's movement (In developing nations) W: 387
History
Asia (The people) A: 781
Eastern Orthodox Churches (History) E: 45-46
Europe (Muslims in medieval Europe) E: 410; (Recent developments) E: 416
Exploration (Medieval exploration) E: 441-442;

(The age of European exploration) **E: 443**
Harūn al-Rashīd **H: 79**
Iran (The rise of Islam) **I: 405**
Jerusalem (Muslim rule) **J: 101**
Ottoman Empire **O: 877**
Palestine **P: 103**
Persia, Ancient (The Sasanian dynasty) **P: 299-300**
Portugal (Visigoths and Muslims) **P: 693**
Saracens **S: 123**
Seljuks **S: 290**
Slavery (The Middle Ages) **S: 501**
Spain (Muslim control) **So: 746**
World, History of the (The Islamic world) **W: 434-435** *with picture*; (The age of invasions of India) **W: 436**; (African civilizations) **W: 437**
Way of life
Circumcision **Ci: 561**
Fast **F: 52**
Food (Religious reasons) **F: 332**
Friday **F: 532**
Hajj **H: 17**
Harem **H: 60**
Islamic art (Characteristics) **I: 467**
Mecca **M: 352**
Medina **M: 380**
New Year's Day (The date of New Year's) **N: 289**
Saudi Arabia (Religion) **S: 158**
Sheik **S: 383**
Muslims, Black *See* Black Muslims *in this index*
Muslin [fabric] **M: 966**
Mosul **M: 836**
Muslin wheel [machine]
Spinning (The mule) **So: 794**
Muspellsheim [Norse mythology]
Mythology (Teutonic mythology) **M: 985**
Musquodoboit River
Nova Scotia (Rivers and lakes) **N: 562** *with map*
Mussel [sea animal] **M: 966**
Deep sea *picture on* **D: 82**; (Invertebrates) **D: 82a-82b**
Mollusk (Bivalves) **M: 695**
Pearl (How pearls are formed) **P: 216-217**
Shell *pictures on* **S: 387**
Musset, Alfred de [French author] **M: 966**
Drama (Romanticism) **D: 337-338**
French literature (Romantic poetry) **F: 521**; (Romantic drama) **F: 521**
Sand, George **S: 106**
Mussolini, Benito [Italian dictator] **M: 966** *with picture*
Fascism (Fascism in Italy) **F: 49**
Government (Fascism) **G: 288**
Hitler, Adolf (World War II) **H: 268**
Italo-Ethiopian War **I: 495**
Italy (Italy under Mussolini) **I: 517**; (World War II) **I: 517**
League of Nations (The League in action) **L: 160**
Rome (Period of construction) **R: 435**
World War II *picture on* **W: 471**; (The rise of dictatorships) **W: 469**; (The invasion of Italy) **W: 483**
Mussorgsky, Modest [Russian composer] **M: 967**
Opera: (*Boris Godunov*) **O: 801-802** *with picture*
Rimsky-Korsakov, Nikolai **R: 342**
Must [juice]
Wine (How wine is made) **W: 337-338**
Must [zoology]
Elephant (Musth) **E: 231**
Mustagh Range [mountains, India-Pakistan]
Himalaya **H: 233**
Mustang [automobile]
Automobile *picture on* **A: 969**; (The postwar years) **A: 970-971**
Mustang [horse] **M: 967** *with picture*
Cowboy (His horse) **Ci: 1109**
Horse (table: Horse terms) **H: 343**; (Wild horses) **H: 348**
Mustard [plant] **M: 968** *with picture*
Flower (table) **F: 300** *with picture*
Mustard gas
Chemical-biological-radiological warfare (Chemical) **C: 396**
Mustard plaster
Mustard **M: 968**
Mustard poultice
Mustard **M: 968**
Mustel, Auguste [French inventor]
Celesta **C: 325**
Musth [zoology]
Elephant (Musth) **E: 231**
Musyawarah [government]
Indonesia (Rural life) **I: 229**
Mut [Egyptian goddess]
Amun **A: 445**
Mutagen [genetics]

Heredity (Mutation) **H: 203**
Mutation **M: 968**
Mutant gene [genetics]
Evolution (How mutations change a species) **E: 428**
Mutation **M: 968**
Mutara III [Watusi king]
Rwanda (History) **R: 571**
Mutation [genetics] **M: 968**
Antibiotic (Resistance to antibiotics) **A: 551**
Brain (Genetics) **B: 551**
Cell (Metabolic diseases) **C: 336**
De Vries, Hugo **D: 176**
Dwarfism (Causes) **D: 394-395**
Evolution (Causes of evolutionary change) **E: 427**
Fragile X syndrome **F: 450**
Fruit (Developing new fruit cultivars) **F: 548**
Genetic testing (How genes carry information) **G: 84d**
Genetics (Molecular genetics) **G: 86**
Heredity (Sources of genetic variation) **H: 203**; (Heredity and natural selection) **H: 203**
Prion **P: 804**
Races, Human (Mutation) **R: 58**
Radiation (Effects of radiation) **R: 79**
Mutation Theory, The [book by De Vries]
De Vries, Hugo **D: 176**
Mutawwiin [Islam]
Saudi Arabia (Religion) **S: 158**
Mute swan
Swan (Kinds) **So: 1016** *with picture*
Mutebi II, Ronald Muwenda [Ugandan political leader]
Ganda **G: 24**
Mutesa II, Sir Edward [Ugandan political leader]
Ganda **G: 24**
Uganda (History) **U: 3-4**
Mutharika, Bingu wa [Malawian political leader]
Malawi (History) **M: 97-98**
Mutiny [law] **M: 969**
Mutiny on the Bounty [book by Nordhoff and Hall]
Nordhoff and Hall **N: 453**
Mutiny on the Bounty [film]
Motion picture (Best picture: 1935) **M: 861**
Mutis, Alvaro [Colombian author]
Colombia (The arts) **Ci: 781**
Mutiwa, Peter Nzube [Kenyan anthropologist]
Prehistoric people (table) **P: 754**
Mutsuhito [emperor of Japan] *See* Meiji, Emperor *in this index*
Mutt [dog] *See* Mongrel *in this index*
Mutt and Jeff [cartoon characters]
Comics (Comic strips) **Ci: 869**
Muttart Conservatory
Edmonton *picture on* **E: 84**
Mutton [food] **M: 969**
Lamb **L: 50**
Meat (Kinds of meat) **M: 347**
Mutton chops [hair]
Beard **B: 186**
Mutual Assistance, Council on
Cold War (The containment policy) **Ci: 764**
Mutual Fire Society
Fire department (The 1700's) **F: 128**
Mutual fund [investment] **M: 969**
Bank (Other services) **B: 89**
Investment (Other kinds of indirect investments) **I: 368**
Money market fund **M: 718**
Mutual inductance [electricity]
Inductance **I: 240**
Mutual insurance
Insurance (Types of insurance companies) **I: 315**
Mutual of Omaha [company]
Nebraska (Service industries) **N: 108**
Mutual savings bank *See* Savings bank *in this index*
Mutualism [biology]
Life (The biological environment) **L: 276**
Plant (How plants protect themselves) **P: 540**
Symbiosis **So: 1065**
Mutualist socialism
Proudhon, Pierre Joseph (Ideas) **P: 838**
Mutually assured destruction [policy]
Guided missile (Postwar developments) **G: 427**
Nuclear weapon (Nuclear strategy) **N: 600**
Mutwatallis [Hittite military leader]
Hittites (History) **H: 269**
Muumuu [clothing]
Hawaii (Clothing) **H: 94**
Pacific Islands (Clothing) **P: 7**
Muwashshaha [poetry]
Spanish literature (Early medieval literature) **So: 757**
Muybridge, Eadweard [British-born photographer] **M: 969**
Edison, Thomas Alva (Motion pictures) **E: 80**
Motion picture (The history of motion pictures)

M: 863 *with picture*
Muzaffar al-Din [shah of Iran]
Iran (The Qajar dynasty) **I: 406**
Muzdalifah [encampment]
Islam (The Five Pillars of Islam) **I: 463-464**
Muzorewa, Abel T. [Zimbabwe political leader]
Zimbabwe (History) **Z: 592-593**
Muzzle [gun]
Artillery (Parts of an artillery weapon) **A: 762**
Rifle (The parts of a rifle) **R: 338** *with diagram*
Muzzle velocity
Ballistics (Interior ballistics) **B: 56**
MVD [Russian government agency]
Police (In other countries) **P: 623**
MVP [disorder] *See* Mitral valve prolapse *in this index*
Mwanamutapa Empire [African history]
Zimbabwe (History) **Z: 592-593**
Mwanawasa, Levy [Zambian political leader]
Zambia (History) **Z: 585-586**
Mwinyi, Ali Hassan [Tanzanian political leader]
Tanzania (After socialism) **T: 35**
My Ántonia [book by Cather]
Cather, Willa **C: 302**
My Brilliant Career [film]
Australia *picture on* **A: 906**
"My Country Calls" [song]
Wyss, Johann Rudolph **W: 538**
My Egypt [painting by Demuth]
Painting (Precisionism) **P: 82-83** *with picture*
My Experiments with Truth [book by Gandhi]
Gandhi, Mohandas Karamchand (Gandhi's beliefs) **G: 25**
My Fair Lady [film]
Motion picture (Best picture: 1964) **M: 861**
My Fair Lady [musical]
Andrews, Julie **A: 456**
Lerner, Alan Jay **L: 206**
Musical comedy (The modern musical emerges) **M: 960**
Pygmalion **P: 914**
Shaw, George Bernard (Mature period) **S: 378**
My Fatherland [music by Smetana]
Smetana, Bedřich **S: 515**
My Friend Flicka [book by O'Hara]
O'Hara, Mary **O: 679**
My Friend's Book [book by France]
France, Anatole **F: 480**
"My Generation" [song by Townshend]
Rock music (The Who) **R: 380**
My Heart is Broken [book by Gallant]
Gallant, Mavis **G: 13**
My Lai Massacre [Vietnamese history] **M: 969**
Vietnam War (Growing protest) **V: 376**
War crime (The Vietnam War) **W: 27**
My Life [book by Clinton]
Clinton, Bill (Later years) **Ci: 682g**
My Little Chickadee [film]
Fields, W. C. F. **95** *with picture*
My Michael [novel by Oz]
Hebrew literature (A new generation of Hebrew writers) **H: 163**
My Movie Business: A Memoir [book by Irving]
Irving, John **I: 459**
My Name is Kofi [book by Asare]
Literature for children *picture on* **L: 355**
My Old Field Horse: Stable Scene [painting by Bingham]
Bingham, George Caleb *picture on* **B: 309**
My Old Kentucky Home [Bardstown]
Kentucky (Places to visit) **K: 282** *with picture*
My Past and Thoughts [book by Herzen]
Herzen, Alexander Ivanovich **H: 217**
My Twinn doll
Doll (The 1990's) **D: 293**
Myanmar M: 970
See also the list of Related articles in the Myanmar *article in this index*
Clothing *picture on* **Ci: 693**
Dance (Asian theatrical dance) **D: 28-29**
Flag *picture on* **F: 204**
India (British India) **I: 130-131**
World War II (Early Japanese victories) **W: 487**; (The China-Burma-India theater) **W: 491**
Myasthenia gravis [disease] **M: 970e**
Thymus **T: 274**
Mycelium [biology]
Fungi (Parts of a fungus) **F: 558**
Mushroom **M: 941**; (Fairy rings) **M: 943**
Mycena [mushroom]
Mushroom *picture on* **M: 944**
Mycenae [ancient city] **M: 970f**
Aegean civilization (The Mycenaean culture) **A: 83**
Architecture (Mycenaean architecture) **A: 615**
Galley **G: 15**
Greece, Ancient (History) **G: 372**

Mediterranean Sea (History of the
Mediterranean) **M:** 382
Mythology (Greek mythology) **M:** 980
Ship (Minoan and Mycenaean ships) **S:** 415
World, History of the (The Greeks) **W:** 428
Mycenaean culture [ancient Greece]
Aegean civilization **A:** 82
Painting (Aegean painting) **P:** 41
Mycenaean Greek
Greek language (Development of ancient Greek)
G: 376
Mycerinus [king of ancient Egypt]
Sculpture (Egyptian) **S:** 234 *with picture*
Mycobacterium bovis [bacteria]
Tuberculosis (How tuberculosis affects the body)
T: 477
Mycobacterium leprae [bacteria]
Leprosy (Causes) **L:** 204 *with picture*
Mycobacterium tuberculosis [bacteria]
Bacteriology (History) **B:** 22-23
Tuberculosis (How tuberculosis affects the body)
T: 477
Mycology [botany]
Fungi **F:** 558
Mushroom (Kinds of mushrooms) **M:** 943
Mycoplasma mycoides [bacterium]
Cell (The future) **C:** 329
Mycoplasma pneumoniae [microbe]
Pneumonia (How pneumonia develops) **P:** 586
Mycorrhiza [biology]
Fungi (How a fungus lives) **F:** 559
Mushroom (How a mushroom obtains food)
M: 942
Plant (Roots) **P:** 528
Mycotoxin [botany] **M:** 970f
Plant (Diseases) **P:** 539-540
Myelin [anatomy] **M:** 970f
Brain (The cerebrum) **B:** 550a-550b
Multiple sclerosis **M:** 920
Nervous system (The axon) **N:** 133-134 *with
diagram*
Myeloid cell [physiology]
Leukemia **L:** 215
Myers, Richard [American government official]
Joint Chiefs of Staff (table) **J:** 156
Myers, Walter Dean [American author] **M:** 970f
Myerson, Roger B. [American economist]
Nobel Prizes (Economics: 2007) **N:** 450
Mygalomorph [spider]
Spider **So:** 782
Myiasis [disorder]
Bot fly **B:** 507
Myna [bird] **M:** 970f *with picture*
Bird (Birds of Asia) **B:** 344f *with picture*
Mynyw [Wales]
David, Saint **D:** 46
Myocardial infarction [disorder]
Coronary thrombosis **Ci:** 1068
Myocarditis [disease] **M:** 971
Heart (Inflammatory heart disease) **H:** 142
Myocardium [anatomy]
Heart (Outer lining and muscle) **H:** 133;
(Inflammatory heart disease) **H:** 142
Myocarditis **M:** 971
Myoelectricity [physiology]
Artificial limb (Control of artificial limbs) **A:** 761
Myoglobin [physiology]
Iron (How bodies use iron) **I:** 435
Kendrew, Sir John Cowdery **K:** 259
Myomere [zoology]
Fish (Skeleton and muscles) **F:** 161
Myopathy [disease]
Muscle (Disorders of the muscles) **M:** 935-936
Myopia [disorder] **M:** 971
Contact lens **Ci:** 1020 *with picture*
Eye (Nearsightedness) **E:** 464 *with pictures*
Glasses (Prescription glasses) **G:** 224-225
Myosin cross-bridge [anatomy]
Muscle (How muscles work) **M:** 935
Myotonic muscular dystrophy
Muscular dystrophy (Myotonic muscular
dystrophy) **M:** 937
MyPlate [nutrition]
Nutrition (Nutrition guidelines) **N:** 626 *with
picture*
Obesity (Prevention of obesity) **O:** 642b
Myrdal, Alva Reimer [Swedish diplomat] **M:** 971
Myrdal, Gunnar [Swedish sociologist] **M:** 971
Myriad Gardens [Oklahoma City]
Oklahoma *picture on* **O:** 713
Myrick, Sue [American political leader]
Charlotte (Government and history) **C:** 385
Myriobiblion [book by Photius]
Photius **P:** 404
Myron [Greek sculptor]
Europe *picture on* **E:** 391
Myrrh [tree product] **M:** 971

Myrtle [shrub] **M:** 971
Myrtle Beach
South Carolina (Places to visit) **So:** 650 *with
picture*
Myrtlewood
Laurel **L:** 121
Mysophobia [psychology]
Phobia **P:** 392
Myst [electronic game]
Electronic game (The growth of computer
gaming) **E:** 204e
Mysteries [religion] **M:** 972
Christianity (Sacraments) **C:** 522h
Mysteries of Udolpho, The [book by Radcliffe]
Gothic novel **G:** 279
Mysterious Stranger, The [book by Twain]
Twain, Mark (Later works) **T:** 530
Mystery and Melancholy of a Street [painting by
Chirico]
Chirico, Giorgio de *picture on* **C:** 514
Mystery of Edwin Drood, The [book by Dickens]
Detective story (History) **D:** 162
Dickens, Charles (The second phase) **D:** 188-189
"Mystery of Marie Rogêt, The" [story by Poe]
Detective story (History) **D:** 162
Mystery play [drama] **M:** 972
Drama (Mystery plays) **D:** 328
English literature (Early English drama) **E:** 316
French literature (Early drama) **F:** 519
Miracle play **M:** 615
Morality play **M:** 800
Mystery story
Detective story **D:** 162
Literature for children (Mystery and detective
stories) **L:** 360
Mystic Aquarium and Institute for Exploration
Connecticut (Places to visit) **Ci:** 960
Mystic Marriage of Saint Catherine, The [painting
by Correggio]
Correggio *picture on* **Ci:** 1071
Mystic Seaport [Connecticut]
Connecticut (Places to visit) **Ci:** 960 *with picture*
Mysticism [belief] **M:** 972
Alcoholic beverage (History) **A:** 337
Kabbalah **K:** 208
Meditation **M:** 380
Spanish literature (The 1400's) **So:** 758-759
Myth [story]
Mythology **M:** 973
Campbell, Joseph **C:** 90a
Folklore (Myths) **F:** 323
Legend **L:** 182
Literature for children (Traditional literature)
L: 357-358
Religion (The use of sacred stories) **R:** 217
Storytelling (Myths, epics, and legends) **So:** 914
Myth of Sisyphus, The [book by Camus]
Camus, Albert **C:** 97
French literature (Existentialism) **F:** 523
Myth of the Twentieth Century [book by
Rosenberg]
Rosenberg, Alfred **R:** 479
Mytheme
Mythology (Structuralist approaches) **M:** 991
Mythological cycle
Irish literature (Heroic tales, romances, and sagas)
I: 430
Mythology (The Irish cycles) **M:** 985
Mythologiques [book by Lévi-Strauss]
Mythology (Structuralist approaches) **M:** 991
Mythology M: 973 *with pictures*
See also the list of Related articles in the Mythology
article
Campbell, Joseph **C:** 90a
Fire (Fire in legend and religion) **F:** 122
Greece, Ancient (Religion) **G:** 367
Lévi-Strauss, Claude **L:** 218
Painting (Mythology paintings) **P:** 34
Raven **R:** 151
Myths and Texts [book by Snyder]
American literature (Poetry) **A:** 423
Myxedema [disorder]
Thyroid gland (Underactive thyroid) **T:** 274-275
Myxomatosis [disease]
Australia (Introduced species) **A:** 913
Conservation (Australia) **Ci:** 989-990

N

N [letter] **N:** 1 *with pictures*
N [symbol]
Newton **N:** 388
Nitrogen **N:** 425
**N-channel metal oxide semiconductor field
effect transistor** [electronics]
Transistor (Metal oxide semiconductor field effect
transistors [MOSFET's]) **T:** 374
N-doped crystal [electronics]

Semiconductor (Doped crystals) **S:** 291; (Using
doped crystals) **S:** 292
N gauge [size]
Railroad, Model (Scale and size) **R:** 120 *with
picture*
N-type dopant
Solar energy (How a photovoltaic cell is made)
So: 577-578
N-type material
Solar energy (How a photovoltaic cell is made)
So: 577-578 *with diagram*
N-type semiconductor [physics]
Electronics (Active components) **E:** 210
Transistor (Transistor materials) **T:** 372
Na [symbol]
Sodium (Chemical properties) **So:** 569
Na-Dene [language group]
Indian, American (Language groups) **I:** 149-150
NAA
National Aeronautic Association **N:** 27
NAACP *See* National Association for the
Advancement of Colored People *in this index*
**NAACP Legal Defense and Educational Fund,
Inc.** [organization]
Marshall, Thurgood **M:** 231
National Association for the Advancement of
Colored People **N:** 29
Naam [religion]
Sikhism (Beliefs and practices) **S:** 455
Nááts'íhch'oh National Park [Northwest
Territories]
Canada (table: National parks and national park
reserves) **C:** 113
NAB
National Alliance of Business **N:** 28
Nabataeans [ancient people]
Arabs (The Arabs before Islam) **A:** 589
Jordan (Early days) **J:** 164
Petra **P:** 327
Saudi Arabia (History) **S:** 160
Nabis [art group]
Bonnard, Pierre **B:** 461
Nabiyev, Rakhman [Tajik political leader]
Tajikistan (Since independence) **T:** 18b
Nabokov, Vladimir [Russian-American author] **N:** 2
American literature (Experimental styles) **A:** 425
Novel (After World War II) **N:** 574
Nabopolassar [king of Babylonia]
Babylon (The Neo-Babylonian Empire) **B:** 12
Chaldeans **C:** 370
Nabrit, James Madison, Jr. [American educator]
N: 2
Nabu [Assyrian god]
Assyria (Religion) **A:** 821
Nabucco [opera by Verdi]
Verdi, Giuseppe **V:** 316
NACA [organization]
National Aeronautics and Space Administration
N: 27
Nacelle [airplane]
Airplane (The wing) **A:** 213-214
Nacimiento [custom]
Christmas (In Spain) **C:** 531
NaCl [formula]
Salt **S:** 72
Nacogdoches [Texas]
Bowie, James **B:** 520
Nacre [biology]
See also Mother-of-pearl *in this index*
Pearl (How pearls are formed) **P:** 216 *with
diagram*; (Cultured pearls) **P:** 217
Nacreous layer [zoology]
Shell (How shells are formed) **S:** 385
Nadal, Rafael [Spanish tennis player] **N:** 2
Nadar [French photographer]
Photography (Artistic advances) **P:** 424
Nader, Ralph [American lawyer] **N:** 2 *with portrait*
Arab Americans (Arab American
accomplishments) **A:** 580b
Automobile (The growth of government
regulation) **A:** 971
Consumer protection (Growth of the movement)
Ci: 1019
Green party **G:** 381
Nader's Raiders [organization]
Consumer protection (Growth of the movement)
Ci: 1019
Nadir Shah [king of Iran]
Iran (The rule of Nadir Shah) **I:** 406
Nadir Shah, Muhammad [king of Afghanistan]
Afghanistan (Independence) **A:** 95
Nadolol [drug]
Beta-blocker **B:** 274
NAEP [organization] *See* National Assessment of
Educational Progress *in this index*
Naevius, Gnaeus [Roman author]
Latin literature (Early Latin literature) **L:** 115

Nafcillin [drug]
Penicillin (Forms of penicillin) **P:** 240
NAFTA [trade agreement] *See* North American Free Trade Agreement *in this index*
Nagana [disease]
Tsetse fly **T:** 475
Nagananda [play by Harsha]
Harsha **H:** 77
Nagas [people]
India (Religious and ethnic unrest) **I:** 134
Sri Lanka (History) **So:** 819
Nagasaki [Japan] **N:** 2
Nuclear weapon **N:** 596, *picture on* **N:** 598; (World War II) **N:** 601
Truman, Harry S. (The end of World War II) **T:** 469
United States, History of the (World War II) **U:** 193-194 *with picture*
World, History of the *picture on* **W:** 446
World War II (The atomic bomb) **W:** 493
Nagche [people]
Mapuche **M:** 189
Nagel, Charles [American government official]
Commerce, Department of (table) **Ci:** 871
Taft, William Howard (table) **T:** 11
Nagewaza
Judo (Judo techniques) **J:** 185
Nagorno-Karabakh [region]
Armenia (History) **A:** 718b
Azerbaijan (Government) **A:** 996; (History) **A:** 997-998
Nagoya [Japan] **N:** 3
Naguib, Muhammad [Egyptian political leader]
Egypt (Republic) **E:** 132
Faruk I **F:** 48
Nagumo, Chuichi [Japanese admiral]
Pearl Harbor (The attack) **P:** 218
Nagy, Imre [Hungarian political leader]
Cold War (Unrest in Eastern Europe) **Ci:** 766
Hungary (Communist Hungary) **H:** 447; (Unsuccessful revolution) **H:** 447
Naha [Okinawa]
Okinawa **O:** 710 *with picture and map*
Nahanni National Park [Northwest Territories]
Canada (table: National parks and national park reserves) **C:** 113
Northwest Territories (National parklands) **N:** 531
Nahl, Charles [American artist]
Western frontier life in America (Art) **W:** 239
Nahr Ibrahim [river, Lebanon]
Lebanon (Land and climate) **L:** 172
Nahrawan, Battle of [A.D. 658]
Muslims (Ali) **M:** 964b-964c
Nahtwin [ceremony]
Myanmar (Way of life) **M:** 970a
Nahuatl [language]
Aztec (Language) **A:** 1002; (The Aztec heritage) **A:** 1003-1004
El Salvador (Ancestry) **E:** 249
Nahuel Huapi [park, Argentina]
National park (Argentina) **N:** 42b; (table) **N:** 42g
Nahum, Book of [Biblical figure] **N:** 3
Nahyssan Indians
Virginia (Early days) **V:** 418
NAIA [organization] *See* National Association of Intercollegiate Athletics *in this index*
Naiad [entomology]
Insect (Incomplete metamorphosis) **I:** 293
Larva **L:** 78
Naiad [mythology]
Nymph **N:** 633
NAICS [economics] *See* North American Industry Classification System *in this index*
Nail [hardware] **N:** 3 *with pictures*
Nail [anatomy] **N:** 3
Cosmetics (Kinds of cosmetics) **Ci:** 1074
Skin *picture on* **S:** 490; (Hair, nails, and glands) **S:** 489
Nailsea glass
Glass (Types of art glass) **G:** 220-221
Nailset [tool]
Nail (The parts of a nail) **N:** 3
Nain [Newfoundland and Labrador]
Newfoundland and Labrador (table: Average monthly weather) **N:** 372
Naipaul, V. S. [Trinidad-born author] **N:** 4
Nobel Prizes (Literature: 2001) **N:** 448
Novel (The novel today) **N:** 575
Nairobi [Kenya] **N:** 4
Kenya **K:** 297, *picture on* **K:** 299
Naismith, James [Canadian-American educator] **N:** 4
Basketball (Beginnings) **B:** 151
Young Men's Christian Association (History) **Y:** 573
Naismith Memorial Basketball Hall of Fame [Massachusetts]
Basketball (The history of college basketball)

B: 154a
Hall of fame (Sports halls of fame) **H:** 23
Massachusetts (Places to visit) **M:** 280
Springfield (Description) **So:** 807-808
Najd [region]
Saudi Arabia (The Central Plateau) **S:** 158 *with map*
Naked and the Dead, The [book by Mailer]
Mailer, Norman **M:** 67
Naked Ape, The [book by Morris]
Morris, Desmond **M:** 816
Naked flower
Flower (Variations in flower structure) **F:** 294
Naked mole-rat [animal] **N:** 4 *with picture*
Mole-rat **M:** 691 *with picture*
Naked seed [botany]
Plant (Gymnosperms) **P:** 520; (Seeds) **P:** 531 *with picture*
Seed (Kinds of seeds) **S:** 280
Nakota Indians
Sioux Indians **S:** 475
Nakotchtank Indians
Washington, D.C. (Early days) **W:** 85
Naktong River [South Korea]
Korea, South (The land) **K:** 378-378a *with map*
Naltrexone [drug]
Alcoholism (Treatment) **A:** 338
Nam Viet [Vietnamese history]
Indochina (The Viets) **I:** 224-225
Vietnam (History) **V:** 369
Nama [people]
Khoikhoi **K:** 308b
Namath, Joe [American football player] **N:** 5
Nambu, Yoichiro [American physicist]
Nobel Prizes (Physics: 2008) **N:** 442
Name N: 5
Capitalization (Names) **C:** 196
Iceland (People) **I:** 21
Pen name **P:** 234
Pseudonym **P:** 844
Name [underwriter]
Lloyd's **L:** 403
Name Above the Title, The [book by Capra]
Capra, Frank **C:** 198
Named perils policy
Insurance (Homeowners' insurance) **I:** 313
Nameless and Friendless [painting by Osborn]
Painting (Women artists) **P:** 73 *with picture*
Namgyal, Palden Thondup [king of Sikkim]
Sikkim (History) **S:** 456
Namgyal, Penchu [king of Sikkim]
Sikkim (History) **S:** 456
NAMI [organization] *See* National Alliance on Mental Illness *in this index*
Namib Desert [Africa]
South Africa (The Namib and Kalahari deserts) **So:** 615 *with map*
Namibia N: 7 *with picture and map*
Africa (Struggles for independence) **A:** 134-135
Flag *picture on* **F:** 199
Mandated territory **M:** 136
United Nations (Working for self-government) **U:** 93-94
Namingha, Dan [American painter]
Indian, American *picture on* **I:** 182
NAMMCO [organization] *See* North Atlantic Marine Mammal Commission *in this index*
Nammu [goddess]
Mythology (Sumerian mythology) **M:** 976-977
Namphy, Henri [Haitian political leader]
Haiti (History) **H:** 15-16
Namur [Belgium]
Wallonia **W:** 18 *with map*
Namyong-Ho [ship]
Shipwreck (table: Major shipwrecks) **S:** 428
Nan Ginen [afterworld]
Vodou **V:** 436
Nan Sdins National Historic Site [British Columbia]
Canada (table: National historic sites) **C:** 115
Nana [book by Zola]
Zola, Émile **Z:** 598
Nanak [Indian religious leader]
India (Sikhism) **I:** 117
Sikhism (History) **S:** 455
Nance, Albinus [American political leader]
Nebraska (table) **N:** 110
Nanching [China] *See* Nanjing *in this index*
Ñandutí [lace]
Paraguay (The arts) **P:** 147
Nang Klao [king of Thailand]
Mongkut **M:** 718
Nanga Parbat [mountain, Kashmir]
Himalaya (Peaks) **H:** 233
Nangnang [former territory]
Korea, History of (Early years) **K:** 366
Nanjing [China] **N:** 9

Nanjing, Treaty of [1842]
China (Clash with the Western powers) **C:** 502
Hong Kong (British control) **H:** 319
Nanking [China] *See* Nanjing *in this index*
Nanking, Rape of *See* Nanking Massacre *in this index*
Nanking Massacre [Chinese history] **N:** 10
Nanny [occupation]
Day care (Day care for children) **D:** 52
Nanny goat
Goat **G:** 239
Nano [prefix]
Metric system (Metric prefixes) **M:** 439
Nanocomposite [engineering]
Nanotechnology (Applications of nanotechnology) **N:** 10
Nanocrystal [engineering]
Nanotechnology (Applications of nanotechnology) **N:** 10
Nanodevice [engineering]
Nanotechnology (Applications of nanotechnology) **N:** 10
Nanometer [unit of measure]
Color *diagram on* **Ci:** 818
Electromagnetic waves (The electromagnetic spectrum) **E:** 202
Light (The spectrum of light sources) **L:** 284
Nanotechnology **N:** 10
Ultraviolet rays **U:** 17
Nanook of the North [film]
Flaherty, Robert Joseph **F:** 225
Nanoparticle [engineering]
Nanotechnology (Applications of nanotechnology) **N:** 10
Nanoscale [measurement]
Nanotechnology **N:** 10
Nanotechnology [engineering] **N:** 10
Nanotube [molecule]
Carbon (Fullerenes) **C:** 205 *with diagram*
Nanotechnology (Applications of nanotechnology) **N:** 10
Nansen, Fridtjof [Norwegian explorer] **N:** 11
Refugee (Efforts to help refugees) **R:** 203
Nansen Basin [geography]
Arctic Ocean (The deep basin) **A:** 643 *with map*
Nansen bottle [oceanography]
Nansen, Fridtjof **N:** 11
Nansen-Gakkel Ridge [geography]
Arctic Ocean (The deep basin) **A:** 643
Nansen International Office for Refugees [organization]
Nobel Prizes (Peace: 1938) **N:** 448a
Nansen passport [document]
Nansen, Fridtjof **N:** 11
Nansen sled [vehicle]
Sled **S:** 505
Nantahala Gorge [region]
North Carolina (Places to visit) **N:** 482
Nantes [France] **N:** 11
Nantes, Edict of [1598] **N:** 11
France (Religious wars) **F:** 473; (The age of absolutism) **F:** 473
Henry IV [of France] **H:** 186
Huguenots (The massacre) **H:** 410-411
La Rochelle **L:** 77
Louis XIV **L:** 475
Nantucket [Massachusetts] **N:** 11
Nantucket Island [Massachusetts]
Massachusetts (Places to visit) **M:** 280
Nanumanga [island, Pacific]
Tuvalu *map on* **T:** 527; (Land and climate) **T:** 528
Nanumea [island, Pacific]
Tuvalu *map on* **T:** 527; (Land and climate) **T:** 528
Naomi [Biblical figure]
Ruth, Book of **R:** 568
Nap
Sleep (Human sleep patterns) **S:** 506
Napa Valley [California]
California *picture on* **C:** 56
Napalm [weapon] **N:** 12
Bomb (Incendiary bombs) **B:** 451
Flame thrower **F:** 225
Naphtha [chemical]
Petroleum *diagram on* **P:** 344
Naphthalene [chemistry]
Hydrocarbon (Aromatics) **H:** 465
Napier, John [Scottish mathematician] **N:** 12
Logarithms (History) **L:** 424
Mathematics (Mathematics and the scientific revolution) **M:** 306-307
Naples [Italy] **N:** 12 *with picture*
Bourbon (In Naples and Sicily) **B:** 517
Italy *picture on* **I:** 503
Naples, Bay of
Naples (The city) **N:** 12 *with picture*
Naples, Kingdom of [Italian history]
Sicilies, Kingdom of the Two **S:** 446

Naples, University of [Italy]
Frederick II **F:** 497
Naples (Way of life) **N:** 12-13
Napoleon I [emperor of France] **N:** 13 *with picture*
Austria (Wars in the 1700's and 1800's) **A:** 937-938
Autograph *picture on* **A:** 943
Caricature *picture on* **C:** 238
Josephine **J:** 168
Marie Louise **M:** 200
Milan Decree **M:** 541
Muslims (Colonialism) **M:** 964d
Napoleonic Wars **N:** 17
Paris (The Napoleonic era) **P:** 166
Saint Helena **S:** 33 *with picture*
Domestic affairs
Arc de Triomphe **A:** 593
Code Napoléon **Ci:** 748
Continental System **Ci:** 1022
Fascism (History) **F:** 49
Fire department (Fire protection in Europe) **F:** 127-128
French Revolution (The revolution ends) **F:** 527
Government (The Enlightenment) **G:** 290-291
Lafayette, Marquis de (The revolution at home) **L:** 28
Law (The first modern law codes) **L:** 135-136
Medals, decorations, and orders (Europe) **M:** 358
Napoleon II **N:** 17
Painting (History paintings) **P:** 33
Talleyrand (Joins Napoleon) **T:** 20
Military leader
Alexander I [czar] **A:** 341
Antwerp (History) **A:** 561-562
Army (The rise of modern armies) **A:** 727-728 *with picture*
Artillery (History) **A:** 763
Belgium (The Brabant Revolution) **B:** 233
Egypt (Ottoman and French control) **E:** 130
Europe *map on* **E:** 409; (Revolution, democracy, and nationalism) **E:** 412
France (Napoleon) **F:** 474
Francis II [Holy Roman emperor] **F:** 481
Germany (Conflicts with France) **G:** 164-165
Italy (The French Revolution and Napoleon) **I:** 514-515
Latin America (The movement toward independence) **L:** 106
Minnesota (The Louisiana Purchase) **M:** 603
Moscow (Destruction and rebirth) **M:** 827
Ney, Michel **N:** 390
Rome (Under Napoleon) **R:** 434
Russia (Alexander I) **R:** 550
Toussaint Louverture **T:** 350
Trafalgar, Battle of **T:** 365
United Kingdom (The Napoleonic Wars) **U:** 68
Waterloo, Battle of **W:** 145
Wellington, Duke of (Victory at Waterloo) **W:** 194-195
Napoleon II [son of Napoleon I] **N:** 17
Marie Louise **M:** 200
Napoleon III [emperor of France] **N:** 17
France (The revolutions of 1830 and 1848) **F:** 474
Franco-Prussian War (Background to the war) **F:** 483
Maximilian **M:** 319
Mexico (The French invasion) **M:** 471-472
Paris (The Napoleonic era) **P:** 166
Revolution of 1848 **R:** 288
Napoleon of Notting Hill, The [book by Chesterton]
Chesterton, G. K. C. **B:** 415
Napoleon of the Stump [nickname]
Polk, James Knox (Lawyer and legislator) **P:** 641
Napoleon on the Battlefield at Eylau [painting by Gros]
Army *picture on* **A:** 727
Napoleonic Code *See* Code Napoléon *in this index*
Napoleonic Ideas [book by Napoleon III]
Napoleon III (Early life) **N:** 17
Napoleonic Wars [1796-1815] **N:** 17 *with map*
Austria (Wars in the 1700's and 1800's) **A:** 937-938
Europe (Revolution, democracy, and nationalism) **E:** 412
Jackson, Andrew (Foreign affairs) **J:** 13
Paris, Treaties of (The treaties of 1814 and 1815) **P:** 167
Sweden (The Napoleonic Wars) **So:** 1034
Napoleon's Tomb [Paris]
Napoleon I (The Hundred Days and Waterloo) **N:** 16
Napoli *See* Naples *in this index*
Napolitano, Janet [American political leader]
Arizona (table) **A:** 687
Homeland Security, Department of (table) **H:** 301
Obama, Barack (table) **O:** 640h

Napster [company]
Copyright (Users' rights) **Ci:** 1047-1048
Narayan, R. K. [Indian author]
India (Literature) **I:** 120
Narayan Shah, Prithwi [king of Nepal]
Nepal (History) **N:** 126
Narborough Island
Galapagos Islands **G:** 7 *with map*
Narcissa and Other Fables [stories by Auchincloss]
Auchincloss, Louis **A:** 880
Narcissus [plant] **N:** 20 *with picture*
Daffodil **D:** 3 *with picture*
Poisonous plant (Some poisonous plants) **P:** 602
Narcissus [Greek mythology] **N:** 20
Narcolepsy [disease] **N:** 20
Amphetamine (Medical uses) **A:** 439
Cataplexy **C:** 298
Narcotic [drug] **N:** 21
Analgesic **A:** 448
Drug (Analgesics) **D:** 352
Pain (Treatment) **P:** 22
Nares, George S. [British explorer]
Exploration (Deep-sea exploration) **E:** 450-451
Narita International Airport
Japan (Transportation) **J:** 51-52
Tokyo (Transportation) **T:** 318
Narragansett Indians **N:** 21
Indian, American (In the United States) **I:** 179
Indian wars (The Pequot War [1637]) **I:** 191
Rhode Island (Early days) **R:** 312
Narration [literature]
Novel **N:** 571
Narrative interpretation
Bible (Literary contexts) **B:** 287
Narrative of Arthur Gordon Pym, The [book by Poe]
Poe, Edgar Allan (Poe's life) **P:** 589; (Fiction and theory of fiction) **P:** 590
Narrative of the Life of Frederick Douglass [book by Douglass]
African American literature (The 1800's) **A:** 136a
Douglass, Frederick **D:** 314
Narrative poetry
English literature (Elizabethan poetry) **E:** 316-317
Fiction **F:** 90
French literature (Early French literature) **F:** 518
Narrow-angle glaucoma [disease]
Eye (Glaucoma) **E:** 466
"Narrow Fellow in the Grass, A" [poem by Dickinson]
Dickinson, Emily (Her poems) **D:** 190
Narrow-footed marsupial mouse *See* Dunnart *in this index*
Narrow-leafed zinnia [plant]
Zinnia *picture on* **Z:** 595
Narrow-mouthed toad
Frog (Other frogs) **F:** 540
Narrow spectrum antibiotic [drug]
Antibiotic (Antibacterial antibiotics) **A:** 550
Narrowcasting
Television (Cable television) **T:** 110c; (The 1980's and 1990's) **T:** 120
Narrowleaf sword fern [plant]
Evolution (Evolution of new species) **E:** 429-430
Narrowleaf tree
Leaf **L:** 151 *with pictures*
Narrows [channel]
Virgin Islands, British **V:** 393
Narthex [architecture]
Architecture (Medieval architecture) **A:** 617
Naruhito [Japanese prince]
Akihito **A:** 253
Narva River [Europe]
Estonia (Land and climate) **E:** 361 *with map*
Narváez, Pánfilo de [Spanish explorer] **N:** 21
Cortés, Hernán (Victory over the Aztec) **Ci:** 1073
Florida (Exploration and Spanish settlement) **F:** 261
Narwhal [sea animal] **N:** 21
Whale *picture on* **W:** 257; (Belugas and narwhals) **W:** 258
NAS [organization] *See* National Academy of Sciences *in this index*
NASA [organization] *See* National Aeronautics and Space Administration *in this index*
Nasal allergy [disorder]
Allergy **A:** 373
Nasal bone [anatomy]
Face **F:** 3
Head *diagram on* **H:** 123
Human body (table) **H:** 422 *with diagram*
Nasal duct [anatomy]
Tears **T:** 72
Nasal passage [anatomy]
Nose **N:** 548 *with diagram*
Nasal sac system [zoology]
Whale (Senses) **W:** 260

NASC [organization]
Student government **So:** 932
Nasca [people] *See* Nazca *in this index*
NASCAR [organization] **N:** 21
Automobile racing (Racing organizations) **A:** 976
Gordon, Jeff **G:** 273
Nevada *picture on* **N:** 165
Petty, Richard **P:** 351
NASCAR Craftsman Truck Race
NASCAR **N:** 21
NASCAR Hall of Fame
Charlotte (Government and history) **C:** 385
NASCAR **N:** 21
North Carolina (Places to visit) **N:** 482
Nascimento, Milton [Brazilian musician]
Brazil (The arts) **B:** 576-577
Latin America (Music) **L:** 100
Nasdaq [stock market] **N:** 21
Naseby, Battle of [1645]
Cromwell, Oliver (Rise to power) **Ci:** 1151
Nash, Abner [American political leader]
North Carolina (table) **N:** 490
Nash, Charles William [American businessman] **N:** 22
Nash, Francis [American general]
Nashville **N:** 23
Nash, George K. [American political leader]
Ohio (table) **O:** 699
Nash, J. Slade [American aviator]
Aviation (table: Aviation speed records) **A:** 990
Nash, John Forbes, Jr. [American economist] **N:** 22
Economics (Modern economics) **E:** 64-65
Nobel Prizes (Economics: 1994) **N:** 449
Nash, Ogden [American poet] **N:** 22
Nash, Steve [American basketball player] **N:** 22
Nash equilibrium [mathematics]
Nash, John Forbes, Jr. **N:** 22
Nash Motors Company
Nash, Charles William **N:** 22
Nasharo Council
Pawnee Indians **P:** 203
Nashe, Thomas [English author] **N:** 22
English literature (Elizabethan fiction) **E:** 317
Nashim [Talmud]
Talmud **T:** 21
Nashoba [community]
Wright, Frances **W:** 507
Nashua [New Hampshire] **N:** 22
Nashville [Tennessee] **N:** 23 *with picture*
Country music (History) **Ci:** 1098a-1098b
Tennessee (Places to visit) **T:** 144 *with pictures*; (table: Average monthly weather) **T:** 148
Nashville, Battle of [1864]
Civil War, American (table) **Ci:** 624; (North to Nashville) **Ci:** 632
Nashville Basin
Tennessee (Land regions) **T:** 146 *with map*
Nashville Predators [team]
Hockey (table: National Hockey League) **H:** 281
Nashville sound [music]
Atkins, Chet **A:** 858
Cline, Patsy **Ci:** 681
Country music (The Nashville sound) **Ci:** 1098a; (History) **Ci:** 1098a-1098c
Naskapi Indians *See* Innu Indians *in this index*
Nasmyth, James [Scottish engineer] **N:** 24
Nassau [Bahamas] **N:** 24
Bahamas **B:** 28 *with picture*
Nassau, House of
Luxembourg (Government) **L:** 530
Nassau County [New York]
New York City (Metropolitan area) **N:** 330
Nassau grouper [fish]
Fish *picture on* **F:** 154
Grouper **G:** 403
Nasser, Gamal Abdel [Egyptian political leader] **N:** 24
Arab-Israeli conflict (The Suez crisis of 1956) **A:** 582
Cold War (The Suez crisis) **Ci:** 766
Egypt (Republic) **E:** 132; (The United Arab Republic) **E:** 132; (Progress and conflict) **E:** 133
Israel (The Six-Day War) **I:** 488
Middle East (Cold War alliances) **M:** 534
Muslim Brotherhood **M:** 964
Suez Canal (History) **So:** 958
Suez crisis **So:** 959
United Arab Republic **U:** 46
Nasser, Lake *See* Lake Nasser *in this index*
Nast, Thomas [American cartoonist] **N:** 24 *with picture*
Caricature **C:** 238
Carpetbaggers *picture on* **C:** 247
Cartoon (Editorial cartoons) **C:** 263-265
Democratic Party *picture on* **D:** 125
New York City *picture on* **N:** 342
Republican Party *picture on* **R:** 254

Santa Claus (Santa's appearance) **S: 114**
Tammany, Society of **T: 23**
Tweed, William Marcy **T: 531**
Nasturtium [plant] **N: 25** *with picture*
Flower *picture on* **F: 276**; (table) **F: 300** *with picture*
Natal [province, South Africa] **N: 25**
Natation Amateur, Fédération Internationale de [organization]
Diving (Diving meets) **D: 243**
Natchez [Mississippi] **N: 26**
Mississippi *picture on* **M: 622**
Natchez Indians N: 26
Indian, American (Empires and states) **I: 144**; (Indians of the Southeast) **I: 157**
Natchez National Historic Park [Mississippi]
National Park System (table: National historical parks) **N: 56-57**
Natchez Trace [U.S. history] **N: 26**
Natchez Trace National Scenic Trail
National Park System (table: National parkways and other national parklands) **N: 56**
Natchez Trace Parkway
Alabama (Places to visit) **A: 266**
Mississippi (Places to visit) **M: 632** *with picture*
National Park System (table: National parkways and other national parklands) **N: 56**
Natchitoches [Louisiana]
Louisiana (Places to visit) **L: 488** *with picture*
Nathan [Biblical figure]
Parable **P: 141**
Nathan, George Jean [American newspaper editor]
Mencken, H. L. **M: 397**
Nathan the Wise
Toronto (Landmarks) **T: 338**
Nathan the Wise [play by Lessing]
German literature (The Enlightenment) **G: 139**
Nathanael [Biblical figure]
Bartholomew, Saint **B: 120**
Nazareth **N: 91**
Nathans, Daniel [American physiologist]
Nobel Prizes (Physiology or medicine: 1978) **N: 446**
Nation N: 26
Country **Ci: 1097**
Culture (The boundaries of cultures) **Ci: 1187**
Intervention **I: 352**
Nationalism **N: 62**
Tribe **T: 440**
World (Nations of the world) **W: 407**; (table) **W: 410**
Nation, Carry Amelia Moore [American social reformer] **N: 26** *with portrait*
Kansas (Spirit of reform) **K: 237**
Nation, The [magazine]
Godkin, Edward Lawrence **G: 245**
Nation of Islam [organization] **N: 26**
See also Black Muslims *in this index*
Ali, Muhammad (Early life) **A: 367**
Farrakhan, Louis **F: 47**
Nation-state [political science]
Government (The rise of monarchies and nation-states) **G: 290**
Middle Ages (The decline of feudalism) **M: 527**
Nationalism (The rise of nationalism) **N: 62**
Patriotism (Foundations of patriotism) **P: 198**
National [person]
Citizenship **Ci: 568**
National Academies N: 27
National Research Council **N: 60**
National Academy of Engineering
National Academies **N: 27**
National Academy of Sciences **N: 27**
National Academy of Recording Arts and Sciences
Recording industry (Recording industry awards) **R: 182**
National Academy of Santa Cecilia
Rome (Music and theater) **R: 429**
National Academy of Sciences N: 27
National Academies **N: 27**
National Research Council **N: 60**
Nutrition (Eat a balanced diet) **N: 626**
National Academy of Television Arts and Sciences
Television (Television awards) **T: 116**
National Action Charter
Bahrain (History) **B: 30-31**
National Action Committee on the Status of Women [organization]
Feminism **F: 70**
Women's movement (Women's organizations) **W: 386**
National Action Party
Baja California **B: 32**
Calderón Hinojosa, Felipe **C: 27**

Fox Quesada, Vicente **F: 442**
Mexico (Opposition to the PRI) **M: 474**; (Recent developments) **M: 474**
National Advertising Review Board
Advertising (Advertising associations) **A: 77**
National Advisory Commission on Civil Disorders *See* Kerner Commission Report *in this index*
National Advisory Committee for Aeronautics
National Aeronautics and Space Administration **N: 27**
National Aeronautic Association N: 27
National Aeronautics and Space Administration N: 27
See also Space exploration *in this index*
Astronaut **A: 828**
Electronics (Research and development) **E: 214**
Exploration (Space exploration) **E: 451-452**
Extraterrestrial intelligence **E: 458**
Galileo **G: 12**
Gravitation (Predictions of general relativity) **G: 332**
Houston (Population growth) **H: 398**
Hubble Space Telescope (How the telescope works) **H: 403**
International Space Station (History) **I: 346b-347**
Jet Propulsion Laboratory **J: 115**
Johnson, Lyndon Baines (Majority leader) **J: 147-148**
Kennedy Space Center **K: 270**
Mars Exploration Rover Mission **M: 227**
Medals, decorations, and orders (Civilian awards) **M: 355-357**; (table) **M: 357**
Observatory (Observatories with telescopes) **O: 644-645**
Space exploration (Organizing and managing space activities) **So: 708**
Texas **T: 184**, *picture on* **T: 205**; (The mid-1900's) **T: 208**
Virtual reality **V: 427**
Voyager **V: 451**
Washington, D.C. *map on* **W: 76**
National Aeronautics and Space Administration Launch Operations Center [Cape Canaveral]
Cape Canaveral **C: 187**
National Agricultural Library
Library (United States government libraries) **L: 248** *with picture*
National Air and Space Museum [Washington, D.C.] **N: 28** *with picture*
Smithsonian Institution (Museums) **S: 519**
Washington, D.C. *map on* **W: 76**; (Smithsonian museums) **W: 71-72**
National Air Transport
Aviation *picture on* **A: 989**
National airline
Airport (Commercial service airports) **A: 243**
National Alliance for Reconstruction [political party]
Trinidad and Tobago (History) **T: 446**
National Alliance of Business N: 28
National Alliance on Mental Illness N: 28
Mental illness (The mid-1990's) **M: 409**
National American Woman Suffrage Association
Anthony, Susan Brownell **A: 545**
National anthem N: 28
See also the Facts in brief *section of various country articles, such as* Italy (Italy in brief)
National Aquarium in Baltimore
Baltimore *picture on* **B: 68**
National Archaeological Museum [Naples]
Naples (Way of life) **N: 12**
National Archery Association
Archery (Target archery) **A: 602-603**
National Archives and Records Administration [Washington, D.C.] **N: 29**
Declaration of Independence *picture on* **D: 79**
Library (United States government libraries) **L: 248**
Presidential libraries **P: 771**
Washington, D.C. *picture on* **W: 72**, *map on* **W: 76**; (Executive branch buildings) **W: 75**
National Archives Building [Washington]
National Archives and Records Administration **N: 29**
National Arts Centre
Ottawa (The National Arts Centre) **O: 872** *with picture*
National Assembly [French history]
Estates-General **E: 360**
French Revolution (The National Assembly) **F: 525**; (The revolution begins) **F: 525**
National Assembly [government]
Canada, Government of (The 10 provinces) **C: 136**
Hungary (National government) **H: 439**
Laos (Government) **L: 70**

Mali (Government) **M: 106**
Poland (Government) **P: 604**
Quebec (Legislature) **Q: 29** *with picture*
South Africa (National government) **So: 608**
Thailand (Government) **T: 221**
National Assembly, Eidsvoll 1814, The [painting by Wergeland]
Norway *picture on* **N: 546**
National Assembly for Wales
Wales (The National Assembly for Wales) **W: 7**
National Assembly of People's Power
Cuba (National government) **Ci: 1168**
National Assessment of Educational Progress [U.S.] **N: 29**
Education (How can student performance be improved?) **E: 105**
National Association for Stock Car Auto Racing
See NASCAR *in this index*
National Association for the Advancement of Colored People N: 29
African Americans (The rise of new black leaders) **A: 136l-136m**; (The civil rights movement) **A: 136o**
Bond, Julian **B: 455**
Bridges, Ruby **B: 607**
Du Bois, W. E. B. **D: 372**
Evers-Williams, Myrlie **E: 425**
Marshall, Thurgood **M: 230**
Mfume, Kweisi **M: 479**
Niagara Movement **N: 394**
O'Reilly, Leonora **O: 851**
Spingarn Medal **So: 793**
Wells-Barnett, Ida Bell **W: 195**
Wichita (History) **W: 298**
Wilkins, Roy **W: 306**
National Association for the Education of Young Children
Kindergarten (Kindergartens today) **K: 319**
Preschool (Preschools in the United States) **P: 757**
National Association of Colored Women
Terrell, Mary Church **T: 173**
National Association of Government Employees
Labor movement (table) **L: 8**
National Association of Intercollegiate Athletics
Basketball (College competition) **B: 150-151**
Football (College competition) **F: 364**
National Association of Letter Carriers of the United States of America
Labor movement (table) **L: 8**
National Association of Realtors
Real estate **R: 171**
National Association of Rocketry
Rocket, Model (Model rocket clubs and competition) **R: 393**
National Association of Securities Dealers
Nasdaq **N: 21**
National Association of Securities Dealers Automated Quotation system *See* Nasdaq *in this index*
National Association of Social Workers *See* Social Workers, National Association of *in this index*
National Association of Student Councils
Student government **So: 932**
National Association of the Deaf
Deafness (Education) **D: 59**
National Audubon Society *See* Audubon Society, National *in this index*
National Ballet [Canada]
Ballet (Ballet in Canada) **B: 54**
Canada (Ballet and opera) **C: 111**
National Balloon Classic [Indianola]
Iowa *picture on* **I: 384**
National bank
Bank (Regulation of U.S. banks) **B: 92**
National Bank Acts [1863-1864]
Bank (The national banking system) **B: 93**
National Bank Note
Money (Money in the American Civil War) **M: 713**
National Baptist Convention, USA, Inc. [religious group] **N: 30**
Baptists (Baptists in America) **B: 101**
National Baptist Convention of America, Inc. [religious group] **N: 30**
Baptists (Baptists in America) **B: 101**
National Baseball Congress
Baseball (Amateur leagues) **B: 131-132**
National Baseball Hall of Fame and Museum *See* Baseball Hall of Fame *in this index*
National Baseball League *See* National League *in this index*
National Basketball Association N: 30
Basketball (Professional competition) **B: 151**
National Basketball League
National Basketball Association **N: 30**
National battlefield
National Park System *map on* **N: 45**; (table: National battlefields) **N: 55**

National Battlefields Park
Quebec (Parks) Q: 36
Quebec, Battle of (The attack on Quebec)
Q: 37-38
National Bell Telephone Company
Telephone (The Bell System) T: 100
National Bison Range [Montana]
Montana (Places to visit) M: 750
National Blindness Information Center
Blindness (Education and training) B: 403
National Blood Transfusion Service
Red Cross (Health services) R: 186
**National Board for Professional Teaching
Standards**
Teaching (Certification of teachers) T: 68
National Book Award for Children's Books
Literature for children (Awards) L: 367
**National Book Award for Young People's
Literature**
Literature for children (Awards) L: 367
National Broadcasting Company See NBC in this
index
National Broadcasting Company Symphony
[orchestra]
Toscanini, Arturo T: 346
National Brotherhood of Electrical Workers
Electrical Workers, International Brotherhood
of E: 189
National budget N: 30
Budget (Government budgets) B: 671
Budget, Bureau of the B: 672
Taft, William Howard (Legislative achievements)
T: 11
National Bureau of Economic Research N: 31
Recession R: 175
National Bureau of Standards See National
Institute of Standards and Technology in this
index
National Business Hall of Fame
Junior Achievement J: 195
National Capital Parks
National Park System (table: National parkways
and other national parklands) N: 56
National Catholic Educational Association N: 31
Teaching (Teachers organizations) T: 69
National Catholic Welfare Council
Benedict XV B: 247
National cemetery N: 31
**National Center for Complementary and
Alternative Medicine**
National Institutes of Health N: 39
National Center for Education Statistics
Literacy (Illiteracy in the United States) L: 351
National Center for Health Statistics
Vital statistics (Collecting and publishing vital
statistics) V: 429-430
National Center on Child Abuse and Neglect
Child abuse C: 455
**National Center on Minority Health and Health
Disparities**
National Institutes of Health N: 39
National Centers for Environmental Prediction
[Washington, D.C.]
Weather Service, National W: 172
National certification [program]
Education (Who should teach?) E: 106-107
National Civil Rights Museum [Memphis]
Memphis (The economy) M: 395
National Collegiate Athletic Association N: 32
Basketball (College competition) B: 150
Football (College competition) F: 364
Hockey (Amateur organization) H: 279-280;
(Amateur development) H: 281
Track and field (Organizations) T: 359
National Commission on Excellence in Education
Education (What should be taught?) E: 105
**National Commission on Terrorist Attacks Upon
the United States** See 9/11 Commission in this
index
**National Commission on the Causes and
Prevention of Violence**
Riot (During the 1900's) R: 349
National Committee for Mental Hygiene
Beers, Clifford Whittingham B: 212
**National Committee on the Cause and Cure of
War**
Catt, Carrie Chapman C: 305
National Computer Center
Income tax (Processing income tax returns) I: 105
National Conference for Community and Justice
[organization] N: 32
National Conference of Catholic Bishops
Benedict XV B: 247
National Conference of Christians and Jews
[organization] See National Conference for
Community and Justice in this index
National Congress [legislature]

Libya (Government) L: 264
National Congress [political party]
Sudan (Civil war) So: 953-954
National Congress of American Indians N: 32
Deloria, Vine, Jr. D: 117
National Congress of Mothers
Birney, Alice Josephine McLellan B: 377
Hearst, Phoebe Apperson H: 131
National Congress of Parents and Teachers N: 32
National Congress of Parents and Teachers N: 32
Birney, Alice Josephine McLellan B: 377
Hearst, Phoebe Apperson H: 131
Parent-teacher organizations (Parent-Teacher
Associations) P: 158
National Conservation Commission
Conservation (The rise of the conservation
movement) Ci: 985-986
National Consumer Council
Consumer protection (The right to be heard)
Ci: 1018
National Consumers League N: 32
Kelley, Florence K: 255
National Convention [French history]
Danton, Georges-Jacques D: 34
French Revolution (The National Convention)
F: 526; (Terror and anarchy) F: 526-527
**National Council for Accreditation of Teacher
Education**
Teaching (Teacher-training programs) T: 67
National Council of Churches N: 33
Bible (Modern English translations) B: 286
National Council of Government
Uruguay (National Council government) U: 228
National Council of Jewish Women
Jewish Women, National Council of J: 119
National Council of La Raza [organization] N: 33
National Council of Provinces
South Africa (National government) So: 608
National Council of Senior Citizens
Old age (Employment and other activities) O: 739
National Council of Teachers of English
Literature for children (Awards) L: 367
Teaching (Teachers organizations) T: 69
National Council on Disability
Americans with Disabilities Act A: 431
National Covenant [1638]
Covenanters Ci: 1106
Scotland (War with the king) S: 220
National Cowboy & Western Heritage Museum
[Oklahoma City]
Oklahoma (Places to visit) O: 722 with picture
National Credit Union Administration
Bank (Regulation of U.S. banks) B: 92
National Crime Information Center
Federal Bureau of Investigation (Other services)
F: 62
Police (Federal law enforcement agencies) P: 622
National culture
Culture (The boundaries of cultures) Ci: 1187
National Dairy Herd Information Association
Dairying (Improvements in dairy farming) D: 7
National Day [holiday]
Iceland picture on I: 1
National debt N: 33 with diagrams
Constitution of the United States (Article VI)
Ci: 1011
Obama, Barack (Debt limit battle) O: 640h
Treasury, Department of the (Department
functions) T: 407
National Defence Force
South Africa (Armed forces) So: 609
National Defense, Council of [U.S. history]
Civil defense (History of civil defense in the
United States) Ci: 606
National Defense Act [1916]
Reserve Officers Training Corps (History) R: 258
National Defense Education Act [1958] N: 34
**National Defense Program, Committee to
Investigate the**
Truman, Harry S. (The Truman Committee) T: 468
National Democratic Congress [political party]
Ghana (History) G: 179-180
National Democratic Party [Egypt]
Egypt (Politics) E: 121
National Doukhobor Heritage Village
[Saskatchewan]
Saskatchewan (Places to visit) S: 136
National Drug Control Policy, Office of
President of the United States (The executive
branch) P: 764
National Economic Council
President of the United States (The executive
branch) P: 764
National Economic Council [U.S.]
Rubin, Robert Edward R: 507
National economy
Gross domestic product G: 399

Inflation I: 266
National Education Association N: 34
Labor movement (table) L: 8
Teaching (Teachers organizations) T: 69
Utah (The mid-1900's) U: 249
National Endowment for the Arts
National Foundation on the Arts and the
Humanities N: 36
Orchestra (Modern orchestras) O: 822-823
National Endowment for the Humanities
National Foundation on the Arts and the
Humanities N: 36
National Enquirer [magazine]
Lundy, Benjamin L: 523
National Environmental Policy Act [1970]
Conservation (Renewed interest in conservation)
Ci: 986-987
Environmental impact statement E: 329
**National Environmental Satellite, Data and
Information Service**
National Oceanic and Atmospheric
Administration N: 42
National Equality March
Gay rights movement G: 73
National Farm Workers Association
Chavez, Cesar Estrada C: 389
Huerta, Dolores Fernandez H: 408
National Farmers' Bank [Owatonna, Minnesota]
Sullivan, Louis Henri picture on So: 970
National Farmers Organization
Farm and farming (Farm organizations) F: 44
National Farmers Union N: 34
National Fascist Party [Italian history]
Mussolini, Benito (Fascist dictator) M: 967
National Federation for Catholic Youth Ministry
Catholic Youth Organization C: 304
National Federation of Federal Employees
American Federation of Government Employees
A: 409
National Federation of Music Clubs
Music Clubs, National Federation of M: 958
**National Federation of State High School
Associations**
Football (High school competition) F: 364
National Federation of the Blind
Blindness (Education and training) B: 403
National Fertilizer Development Center
Tennessee Valley Authority (Other activities)
T: 160
National FFA Organization
FFA F: 84
National Field Archery Association
Archery (History) A: 603-604
National Film Board of Canada
Canada (Motion pictures) C: 111 with picture
National Fire Academy
Fire department (The 1900's) F: 129
**National Fire Prevention and Control
Administration** [U.S.]
Fire department (The 1900's) F: 129
National Fire Prevention Week
Fire prevention (In the community) F: 131-132;
(Fire prevention laws) F: 132
*National Five-Digit ZIP Code and Post Office
Directory* [publication]
Postal Service, United States (Other services)
P: 700
National flag
Flag F: 192 with picture
National Flood Insurance Program [U.S.]
Insurance (Other government insurance
programs) I: 314
National Football Conference
Football (Professional competition) F: 364
National Football League N: 35
National Football League N: 35
Football (Professional competition) F: 364; (table:
U.S. professional football champions) F: 365;
(The rise of professional football) F: 367
Shula, Don S: 442
Thorpe, Jim T: 267
National Forensic League
Debate (Academic debate) D: 64
National forest N: 35 with pictures
Forest Service F: 403
National Foundation Day [holiday]
February F: 61
October O: 670
National Foundation for Infantile Paralysis
March of Dimes Foundation M: 196
Roosevelt, Franklin Delano (Battle with polio)
R: 451
National Foundation— March of Dimes
[organization]
March of Dimes Foundation M: 196
**National Foundation on the Arts and the
Humanities** N: 36

National 4-H Conference
4-H (National, state, and county events) **F: 435**
National 4-H Conference Center
4-H (The National 4-H Council) **F: 434**
National 4-H Congress
4-H (National, state, and county events) **F: 435**
National 4-H Council
4-H (The National 4-H Council) **F: 434**
National 4-H Foundation
4-H (The National 4-H Council) **F: 434**
National 4-H Service Committee
4-H (The National 4-H Council) **F: 434**
National 4-H Service Foundation
4-H (The National 4-H Council) **F: 434**
National 4-H Youth Conference Center
4-H (The National 4-H Council) **F: 434**
National Fraternal Congress
Fraternal organization (History) **F: 495**
National Fraternal Congress of America
Fraternal organization (History) **F: 495**
National Front [France]
France (Politics) **F: 455**
National Front [Malaysia]
Malaysia (Political parties) **M: 98b**
National Front for the Liberation of Angola
[political group]
(History) **A: 465-466**
National Gallery of Art [Washington, D.C.] **N: 36**
with picture
Smithsonian Institution (Affiliated institutions)
S: 519
Washington, D.C. map on **W: 76**, picture on **W: 78**;
(Smithsonian museums) **W: 71-73**
National Gallery of Australia
Australia (Painting) **A: 905-906** with picture
National Gallery of Canada **N: 36**
National Geodetic Survey
Four Corners **F: 433**
National Geographic Kids [magazine]
National Geographic Society **N: 37**
National Geographic Magazine
National Geographic Society **N: 37**
National Geographic Society **N: 37**
National Geographic Traveler [magazine]
National Geographic Society **N: 37**
National Geospatial-Intelligence Agency [U.S.]
Map (Database development) **M: 180**
National Grange See Grange, National in this index
National guard [military]
Army **A: 724**
National Guard [U.S.] **N: 37** with picture
Air Force, United States (Air Force reserves)
A: 194
Army, United States (Organization of the Army)
A: 735
Militia **M: 544**
National Health Council
Health Council, National **H: 129**
National health insurance See Health insurance,
National in this index
National Health Service [United Kingdom]
Insurance (Health insurance) **I: 311**
National Health Service Act [United Kingdom]
Labour Party (History) **L: 16**
National Health Service Corps
Medicine (Providing medical care) **M: 366**
National Heart, Lung and Blood Institute
Framingham Heart Study **F: 451**
National Highway System
Interstate Highway System **I: 352**
Road (Modern roads) **R: 362**
National Highway Traffic Safety Administration
Consumer protection (The right to safety)
Ci: 1018
National Hispanic Heritage Month
Hispanic Americans (Holidays) **H: 250**
**National Historic Oregon Trail Interpretive
Center**
Oregon (Places to visit) **O: 836**
National historic site
National Park System map on **N: 45**; (table:
National historic sites) **N: 52**
National Historic Trails Interpretive Center
[Casper]
Wyoming (Places to visit) **W: 516**
National HIV/AIDS Strategy
AIDS (History) **A: 166-167**
National Hockey Association
Hockey (Professional hockey) **H: 281**
National Hockey League
Canada (Recreation and sports) **C: 108-109**
Hockey (How to play hockey) **H: 274**;
(Professional leagues) **H: 278**; (History of
hockey) **H: 280-281**
Stanley Cup **So: 838**
National holiday
Holiday (In the United States) **H: 291**

National Honor Society **N: 37**
National Horseshoe Pitchers' Association
Horseshoe pitching (History) **H: 369**
National Hot Rod Association
Automobile racing (Racing organizations) **A: 976**
National Housing Agency [U.S.]
Housing and Urban Development, Department
of (History) **H: 393**
National Ignition Facility
Laser (Solid-state lasers) **L: 85**
Lawrence Livermore National Laboratory **L: 147**
Nuclear energy (Experimental fusion devices)
N: 592-593
National income **N: 37** with diagram
Income (National income and gross domestic
product) **I: 101**
National Income and Its Composition, 1919-1938
[book by Kuznets]
Kuznets, Simon **K: 397**
National Indian Education Association
Indian, American (In the United States) **I: 179**
National Industrial Recovery Act [1933]
National Recovery Administration **N: 59**
New Deal (Helping industry and labor) **N: 201**
Schechter v. United States **S: 174**
**National Institute for Occupational Safety and
Health** [U.S.] **N: 39**
Centers for Disease Control and Prevention
C: 351
National Institute of Food and Agriculture [U.S.]
Cooperative Extension System **Ci: 1037**
National Institute of Justice [U.S.]
Police (Federal law enforcement agencies) **P: 622**
National Institute of Standards and Technology
N: 39
Weights and measures (Measurement systems)
W: 184
**National Institute on Alcohol Abuse and
Alcoholism** [U.S.]
Drug abuse (Causes and effects of drug abuse)
D: 364
National Institute on Drug Abuse [U.S.]
Drug abuse (Causes and effects of drug abuse)
D: 364; (History) **D: 365-366**
National Institutes of Health [U.S.] **N: 39**
Animal experimentation (Laws and regulations)
A: 510
Cloning (Ethical concerns) **Ci: 683-684**
Genetic engineering (Concerns about genetic
engineering) **G: 84c**
Health and Human Services, Department of
(Organization) **H: 128**
Heredity (History of the study of heredity)
H: 208-209
Hormone replacement therapy **H: 338**
Obesity (Treatment of obesity) **O: 642b**
Stem cell **So: 889**
National Insurance [government program]
Social security (Social security in other countries)
So: 556
National Insurance Act [1967]
Norway (Social welfare) **N: 541**; (Social and
economic changes) **N: 547**
National Interfraternity Conference
Fraternity (Organization) **F: 496**
National Invitation Tournament
Basketball (College competition) **B: 150-151**
National Islamic Front [political group]
Sudan (Civil war) **So: 953**
National Junior Honor Society
National Honor Society **N: 37**
National Labor Relations Act [1935] **N: 39**
Labor movement (The New Deal) **L: 12**
New Deal (The National Labor Relations Act)
N: 202
Taft-Hartley Act **T: 12**
National Labor Relations Board [U.S.] **N: 39**
Great Depression (The New Deal) **G: 341**
National Labor Relations Act **N: 39**
*National Labor Relations Board v. Jones and
Laughlin Steel Corporation* [U.S. history]
Interstate commerce (Interstate commerce
today) **I: 351**
Labor movement (The New Deal) **L: 12**
National labor union
Labor movement (The first nationwide labor
organizations) **L: 9-10**
National laboratory [U.S.] **N: 40**
Brookhaven National Laboratory **B: 639**
National League
Baseball (Players) **B: 125**; (Major leagues) **B: 130**;
(table) **B: 130**; (Professional baseball) **B: 133-
134b**
National League for Democracy [political party]
Aung San Suu Kyi **A: 890**
Myanmar (Military rule) **M: 970e**
National League of Cities **N: 40**

National Legal Aid and Defender Association
Legal aid **L: 182**
National Liberation Army
Colombia (Civil war) **Ci: 784**
National Liberation Forces [political group]
Burundi (History) **B: 713-714**
National Liberation Front [Albania]
Albania (World War II) **A: 307-308**
National Liberation Front [Algeria] See Front de
Libération Nationale in this index
National Liberation Front [Chad] See Frolinat in
this index
National Liberation Front [Vietnam]
Viet Cong **V: 363**
National Liberation Front [Yemen]
Yemen (Formation of South Yemen) **Y: 563**
National Library [Rio de Janeiro]
Brazil (Education) **B: 575-576**
National library [U.S.]
Library (United States government libraries)
L: 248
National Library of Australia [Canberra]
Canberra picture on **C: 166**
National Library of Medicine [Bethesda,
Maryland]
Library (United States government libraries)
L: 248
Medicine (Computers and electronic
communication) **M: 370**
National Mall [Washington, D.C.]
National Park System (table: National parkways
and other national parklands) **N: 56**
National Marine Fisheries Service
National Oceanic and Atmospheric
Administration **N: 42**
National Mediation Board [U.S.] **N: 40**
Labor movement (Handling labor disputes) **L: 6**
Railway Labor Act **R: 122**
National Medical Association **N: 40**
Medicine (Professional organizations and
medical reform) **M: 376**
National memorial
National Park System map on **N: 45**
National Memorial Cemetery of the Pacific
Hawaii (World War II) **H: 108**
National Merit Scholarship
College entrance examination (In the United
States) **Ci: 775**
Foundation (Education) **F: 430-431**
Scholarship (Merit scholarships) **S: 178**
National Military Establishment [U.S. history]
Defense, Department of (History) **D: 88**
National military park
National Park System (table: National military
parks) **N: 55**
National Mining Association
Coal (The coal industry) **Ci: 728**
National missile defense
Guided missile (Surface-to-air missiles) **G: 426**
National Model Railroad Association
Railroad, Model (History) **R: 121**
National monument
National Park System map on **N: 45**
National Motto, United States **N: 40**
National Movement for Simeon II [political party]
Bulgaria (Recent developments) **B: 693**
National Movement of the Development Society
[political party]
Niger (Government) **N: 407**
National Museum, United States
National Museum of American History **N: 41**
National Museum of African Art [Washington,
D.C.] **N: 40**
Smithsonian Institution (Museums) **S: 519**
Washington, D.C. map on **W: 76**
National Museum of American History
[Washington, D.C.] **N: 41**
Smithsonian Institution (Museums) **S: 519**
Washington, D.C. map on **W: 76**; (Smithsonian
museums) **W: 71-72**
National Museum of Anthropology
Mexico (Architecture) **M: 459-460**
Mexico City (Cultural life and recreation) **M: 476b**
with picture
National Museum of History and Technology
See National Museum of American History in
this index
National Museum of Iraq [Baghdad]
Baghdad (The city) **B: 26** with picture
National Museum of Modern Art [Paris]
Paris (Museums and art galleries) **P: 164**
National Museum of Natural History
[Washington, D.C.] **N: 41** with picture
Smithsonian Institution (Museums) **S: 519**
Washington, D.C. map on **W: 76**; (Smithsonian
museums) **W: 71-73**
National Museum of Painting and Sculpture See

Prado *in this index*
National Museum of the American Indian N: 41
　Washington, D.C. (Smithsonian museums)
　　W: 71-72
National Museum of the Building Arts
　[Washington, D.C.]
　Washington, D.C. *map on* W: 76
National Museum of the United States Air Force
　Ohio (Museums) O: 685
National Museum of Women in the Arts
　[Washington, D.C.]
　Washington, D.C. (Other Washington museums)
　　W: 75
National Music Museum [Vermillion]
　South Dakota *picture on* So: 672
National Naval Medical Center [Washington, D.C.]
　See Walter Reed National Military Medical Center
　Bethesda *in this index*
National Negro Business League
　Washington, Booker T. (Racial leader) W: 89
National Nurses United
　Labor movement L: 8
National Ocean Service [U.S.]
　National Oceanic and Atmospheric
　　Administration N: 42
**National Oceanic and Atmospheric
　Administration** [U.S.] N: 41
　Earle, Sylvia Alice E: 14
National Opposition Union [political group]
　Nicaragua (The late1900's) N: 400-401
National Optical Astronomy Observatories [U.S.]
　N: 42
National Organ Transplant Act [1984]
　Organ donation O: 853
National Organization for Women N: 42
　Equal Rights Amendment E: 346
　Feminism F: 70
　Friedan, Betty F: 532
　Women's movement (Women's organizations)
　　W: 386
National Organization for Women v. Scheidler
　[U.S. history]
　Abortion (Abortion in the United States) A: 15-16
National Origins Act [1924] *See* Immigration Act
　[1924] *in this index*
National origins policy [U.S. history]
　Immigration (Effects of immigration) I: 81
National Palace [Mexico City]
　Rivera, Diego *picture on* R: 355
National Panhellenic Conference
　Sorority So: 597
National Parent Teacher Association *See* National
　Congress of Parents and Teachers *in this index*
National park N: 42a *with pictures*
　Canada (Recreation and sports) C: 108; (table:
　　National Park System of Canada) C: 113
　National Park System N: 43
　Park (State, provincial, and national parks) P: 168;
　　(History) P: 168
　Wildlife conservation (History) W: 304-305
National Park of American Samoa *See* American
　Samoa, National Park of *in this index*
National Park Service [U.S.] N: 42j
　National Park System N: 43
　National Trails System N: 61
National Park System N: 43 *with pictures and map*
　Canada (table: National parks and national park
　　reserves) C: 113
　Wildlife conservation (History) W: 304-305
National Parliament Building [Dhaka,
　Bangladesh]
　Bangladesh *picture on* B: 79
National Party [Australia]
　Australia (Between the wars) A: 924
National Party [New Zealand]
　Bolger, Jim B: 441
　Key, John K: 308
　New Zealand (Political parties) N: 347
　Shipley, Jenny S: 428
National Party Congress
　China (The Communist Party) C: 477
National Patriotic Front of Liberia [political
　group]
　Liberia (Civil war) L: 232
National People's Congress
　China (National government) C: 477 *with picture*
National Philanthropist [newspaper]
　Garrison, William Lloyd G: 45
National Police Services [Canada]
　Royal Canadian Mounted Police (Duties) R: 495
National Policy [Canadian history]
　Canada, History of (The return of Macdonald)
　　C: 145
　Macdonald, Sir John Alexander (The national
　　policy) M: 9; (Threats to Canadian unity) M: 10
　Mackenzie, Alexander (Economic difficulties and
　　defeat) M: 22

National Portrait Gallery [Washington, D.C.]
　Smithsonian Institution (Museums) S: 519
　Washington, D.C. *map on* W: 76
National Postal Museum [Washington, D.C.]
　Washington, D.C. (Smithsonian museums)
　　W: 71-73
National PTA
　National Congress of Parents and Teachers N: 32
National Public Radio [radio network] N: 59
　Journalism (Radio) J: 171
"National Question and Social Democracy, The"
　[article by Stalin]
　Stalin, Joseph (Young revolutionist) So: 825-826
National Radio Astronomy Observatory N: 59
　with picture
　Green Bank Telescope G: 380
　West Virginia *picture on* W: 227; (Places to visit)
　　W: 216
National Railroad Adjustment Board [U.S.]
　Railway Labor Act R: 122
National Railroad Passenger Corporation *See*
　Amtrak *in this index*
National Rainbow Coalition [political group]
　Kenya (Building the new nation) K: 303-304
National Recovery Act *See* National Industrial
　Recovery Act *in this index*
National Recovery Administration [U.S. history]
　N: 59
　Great Depression (The New Deal) G: 341
　New Deal (Helping industry and labor) N: 201
National recreation area
　National Park System (table: National recreation
　　areas) N: 49
National Republican Movement [political party]
　France (Politics) F: 455
National Republican Party [U.S. history] N: 60
　Adams, John Quincy (Democratic-Republican
　　Party split) A: 42
　Clay, Henry (National leader) Ci: 658
National Research Council N: 60
　National Academies N: 27
　National Academy of Sciences N: 27
**National Research Council Canada Institute for
　Scientific and Technical Information**
　Library (Canadian government libraries) L: 249
National Resistance Movement [political
　organization]
　Mozambique (History) M: 905-906
　Uganda (History) U: 3-4
National Revolutionary Movement
　Bolivia (The Revolution of 1952) B: 447
National Revolutionary Party *See* Partido
　Nacional Revolucionario *in this index*
National Rifle Association of America N: 60
National Right to Life Committee N: 60
　Abortion (Abortion in the United States) A: 15
National Road [U.S. history] N: 60
　Baltimore (The 1800's) B: 69
　Indianapolis (History) I: 222
　Pioneer life in America (Crossing the
　　Appalachians) P: 477-478 *with map*
　Transportation (Development of inland
　　transport) T: 388-389
　United States, History of the (The American
　　System) U: 165-166 *with picture*
National Romanization
　Japanese language J: 61
National Safety Council N: 60
National Salvation Front [political organization]
　Romania (Protests and political change) R: 425
National School Lunch Program
　Agriculture, Department of A: 161
National Science Foundation [U.S.] N: 60
　Electronics (Research and development) E: 214
　Green Bank Telescope G: 380
　Lead L: 150
　National Radio Astronomy Observatory N: 59
National Science Foundation Network
　Internet (The early Internet) I: 350g
National Search and Rescue Secretariat
　Canadian Armed Forces (Organization) C: 154
National Security Act of 1947
　Central Intelligence Agency (History) C: 357
　Defense, Department of (History) D: 88
**National Security Agency/Central Security
　Service** [U.S.] N: 60
　Central Intelligence Agency (Functions) C: 356-
　　357
National Security Branch
　Federal Bureau of Investigation (History) F: 62-63
National Security Council [U.S.] N: 61
　Central Intelligence Agency (Functions) C: 356-
　　357
　Iran-contra affair (Administration actions) I: 407
　President of the United States (The executive
　　branch) P: 764
　State, Department of (Since World War II) So: 862

National Security Medal
　Medals, decorations, and orders (table) M: 357
National September 11 Memorial and Museum
　[New York City] N: 61
　New York City (A time of change) N: 343-344
　September 11 terrorist attacks (The World Trade
　　Center) S: 310c *with pictures*
National service *See* Draft, Military *in this index*
National Short Ballot Organization
　City government (The council-manager form)
　　Ci: 596
National Ski Hall of Fame
　Michigan (Places to visit) M: 498
National Socialist German Workers' Party *See*
　Nazism *in this index*
National Socialist Party *See* Nazism *in this index*
National Society for Hebrew Day Schools
　Parochial school P: 178
**National Society for the Study and Correction of
　Speech Disorders**
　Speech therapy (History) So: 774
National Society of Professional Engineers N: 61
**National Society of the Colonial Dames of
　America**
　Colonial Dames of America, National Society of
　　the Ci: 786
National Softball Hall of Fame
　Oklahoma (Places to visit) O: 720
National Solar Observatory
　National Optical Astronomy Observatories N: 42
　Sun (Earth-based studies) So: 986 *with picture*
National Spiritual Assembly [religion]
　Bahá'ís B: 27
National Stadium of Tokyo
　Japan *picture on* J: 44
　Tokyo (Recreation) T: 316
National Statistics [agency]
　Unemployment (Measuring unemployment)
　　U: 22-23
National Storytelling Association
　Storytelling (The 1900's) So: 915
National Storytelling Festival
　Storytelling (The 1900's) So: 915
　Tennessee *picture on* T: 138
National Symphony Orchestra
　Kennedy Center for the Performing Arts K: 270
National Synchrotron Light Source [machine]
　Brookhaven National Laboratory B: 639
National Teachers Association
　National Education Association N: 34
National Technical Institute for the Deaf
　Deafness (Education) D: 59
National Telegraphic Union [labor union]
　Telegraph (Uses for the telegraph) T: 91
National Theater [Munich]
　Munich (The city) M: 927
National Tom Sawyer Days
　Missouri *picture on* M: 654
National Toxicology Program
　Artificial sweetener A: 761
　Saccharin S: 4
National Traffic and Motor Vehicle Safety Act
　[1966]
　Nader, Ralph N: 2
　Tire (History) T: 297-298
National Trails System N: 61
National Transitional Council [legislature]
　Libya (Government) L: 264
National Union Catalog [U.S.]
　Library (Research libraries) L: 247
**National Union for the Total Independence of
　Angola** [political group]
　Angola (History) A: 465-466
National University of Ireland
　Ireland (Education) I: 420-421
National University of Nicaragua
　Nicaragua (People) N: 396-397
National University of the Litoral
　Santa Fe S: 114
National Urban League *See* Urban League *in this
　index*
National Vital Statistics Division
　Vital statistics (Collecting and publishing vital
　　statistics) V: 429-430
National War Memorial
　Ottawa (The National War Memorial) O: 872
National Water Carrier [water system]
　Israel (The Negev Desert) I: 484
　Negev N: 119
National Weather Service *See* Weather Service,
　National *in this index*
National Wildlife Federation N: 61
National Wildlife Refuge System [U.S.] N: 61 *with
　picture*
　Alaska (Federally protected lands) A: 294
　Wildlife conservation (History) W: 304-305
National Woman Suffrage Association

Davis, Paulina Wright **D:** 49
United States, History of the (The drive for woman suffrage) **U:** 186
Woman suffrage (Growth of the movement) **W:** 380
Women's movement (The right to vote) **W:** 385
National Woman's Party [political party]
Equal Rights Amendment **E:** 345
Paul, Alice **P:** 200
National Woman's Relief Corps *See* Woman's Relief Corps, National *in this index*
National Woman's Rights Convention [1850]
Massachusetts (Interesting facts) **M:** 271
National Women's Political Caucus
Abzug, Bella Savitzky **A:** 19
Friedan, Betty **F:** 532
Steinem, Gloria **So:** 886
Women's movement (Women's organizations) **W:** 386
National Women's Trade Union League of America
O'Reilly, Leonora **O:** 851
National World War II Memorial [Washington, D.C.] **N:** 62 *with picture*
National Park System (table: National memorials) **N:** 54
Washington, D.C. (The National World War II Memorial) **W:** 73 *with picture*
National Wrestling Hall of Fame [Stillwater]
Oklahoma (Places to visit) **O:** 722
National Youth Administration [U.S. history]
Johnson, Lyndon Baines (Youth administrator) **J:** 146
New Deal (table) **N:** 201
National Zoological Park [Washington, D.C.] **N:** 62
Smithsonian Institution (Other facilities) **S:** 519
Washington, D.C. (Smithsonian museums) **W:** 71-73
Zoo (The first modern zoos) **Z:** 604-605
Nationalism N: 62
Arabs (Arab nationalism) **A:** 590
Christianity (The 1800's) **C:** 526
Classical music (The Romantic era) **Ci:** 648-649
Clothing (Regional traditional costumes) **Ci:** 696
Education (The rise of universal public schools) **E:** 101
Europe (Revolution, democracy, and nationalism) **E:** 412; (The new nationalism) **E:** 416
German literature (Romanticism) **G:** 140
Imperialism (Motives) **I:** 93
Italian literature (Romanticism) **I:** 495
Latvia (History) **L:** 119-120
Middle East (Struggles for independence) **M:** 534
Nation **N:** 26
Nazism (The birth of Nazism) **N:** 92
Opera (Nationalism) **O:** 799
Patriotism (Foundations of patriotism) **P:** 198
Prejudice **P:** 755
Revolution of 1848 **R:** 288
Roman Catholic Church (The decline of church influence) **R:** 410
United States, History of the (The Era of Good Feeling) **U:** 165
Westward movement in America (The frontier influence) **W:** 252
World, History of the (The rise of democracy and nationalism) **W:** 443; (Imperialism) **W:** 445; (The birth of new nations) **W:** 448
World War I (The rise of nationalism) **W:** 452
World War II (Nationalism) **W:** 469
Nationalist China *See* Taiwan *in this index*
Nationalist Party [China] *See* Kuomintang Party *in this index*
Nationalist Republican Alliance [political party]
El Salvador (Government) **E:** 248-249; (The 1900's) **E:** 252
Nationalists [Northern Ireland]
Bloody Sunday (In Northern Ireland) **B:** 418
Troubles **T:** 452
Nationalists [political party, Spain]
Franco, Francisco (His early life) **F:** 483
Spanish Civil War **So:** 756 *with picture*
Nationality N: 63
See also Citizenship *in this index*
Nationality mark
Aviation (table) **A:** 986
Nationalization [government] **N:** 63
See also Government ownership *in this index*
Communism (The centrally planned economy) **Ci:** 891
Labour Party (History) **L:** 16
Lenin, V. I. (Lenin the dictator) **L:** 194
Privatization **P:** 808b
United Kingdom (The welfare state) **U:** 71
Nationalrat [council]
Austria (Government) **A:** 929
Nationals [political party]

Australia (Political parties) **A:** 897
Nationals, Washington [team]
Baseball (table) **B:** 130
Nations, Battle of the [1813]
Napoleon I (The enemy alliance) **N:** 16
Napoleonic Wars (Napoleon's downfall) **N:** 19-20 *with map*
Nations, Law of [Roman Empire]
Law (Ancient Roman law) **L:** 133-134
Nations Cup [contest]
Horse (Jumping) **H:** 357
Nation's Report Card [nickname]
National Assessment of Educational Progress **N:** 29
NationsBank
Bank of America **B:** 96
Nationwide Series [racing]
NASCAR **N:** 21
Nationwide Tour [golf]
Golf (Golf today) **G:** 267
Native American Graves Protection and Repatriation Act [1990]
Archaeology (Archaeology today) **A:** 600
Indian, American (Current issues) **I:** 182-183
Native American Rights Fund
Indian, American (In the United States) **I:** 179
Native Americans
See also Indian, American *in this index*
Indian, American **I:** 136; (American Indians or Native Americans?) **I:** 136c
Native bear *See* Koala *in this index*
Native Council of Canada
Indian, American (In Canada) **I:** 178b
Native Land Court [New Zealand history]
New Zealand (The New Zealand Wars) **N:** 355
Native metal
Ore **O:** 825
Native school
Alberta (Schools) **A:** 317
Native Son [book by Wright]
African American literature (The 1900's) **A:** 136a
Wright, Richard **W:** 508
Native states [government] *See* Princely states *in this index*
Native Tribal Act [1993]
Australia (Aboriginal land decisions) **A:** 925
Nativism [philosophy]
Latin American literature (Romanticism) **L:** 112-113
Morse, Samuel Finley Breese (Morse as artist) **M:** 818
Psychology (Beginnings) **P:** 849
Roaring Twenties **R:** 363
Roman Catholic Church (In the United States) **R:** 412
Nativity [religion]
Christmas **C:** 528 *with picture*
Jesus Christ (The Nativity) **J:** 105 *with picture*
Nativity, The [painting by Dürer]
Dürer, Albrecht *picture on* **D:** 388
NATO [organization] *See* North Atlantic Treaty Organization *in this index*
Natron [mineral]
Mummy (Egyptian mummies) **M:** 925-926
Natsume Soseki [Japanese author] **N:** 64
Japanese literature (The modern period) **J:** 62
Natta, Giulio [Italian chemist]
Nobel Prizes (Chemistry: 1963) **N:** 443
Polypropylene **P:** 651
Natty Bumppo [literary figure]
Cooper, James Fenimore **Ci:** 1034
Natural
Music (Indicating pitch) **M:** 952-953
Natural, The [book by Malamud]
Malamud, Bernard **M:** 95
Natural areas
National Park System (Areas preserved for natural features) **N:** 43
Natural bridge [geology]
Rainbow Bridge National Monument **R:** 128
Virginia (Places to visit) **V:** 408 *with picture*
Natural Bridges National Monument [Utah]
National Park System (table: National monuments) **N:** 51
Natural cereal
Cereal **C:** 361
Natural childbirth
Childbirth (Methods of childbirth) **C:** 456-457
Natural Chimneys [formations]
Virginia (Places to visit) **V:** 408
Natural dye
Lake **L:** 35
Natural fiber
Clothing (Clothing materials) **Ci:** 695
Rope (Natural-fiber rope) **R:** 473
Textile (Sources of textile fibers) **T:** 212
Thread **T:** 269 *with diagram*

Natural food
Food preservation (Modern food preservation) **F:** 344
Health food **H:** 129
Organic food (Standards) **O:** 853
Natural fur
Fur (Kinds of fur) **F:** 561 *with pictures*
Natural gas [fuel]
Alberta **A:** 312
Bolivia (Energy sources) **B:** 446 *with picture*
Brunei (Economy) **B:** 651
Energy supply (Fossil fuels) **E:** 277-278; (Depletion of fuel reserves) **E:** 281
Fossil fuel **F:** 427
Fuel (Natural gas) **F:** 551
Gas [fuel] **G:** 50; (The composition of natural gas) **G:** 50; (How natural gas was formed) **G:** 52 *with diagrams*; (Early uses of natural gas) **G:** 56; (Development of the natural gas industry) **G:** 57
Heating (Gas) **H:** 159
Helium (Production) **H:** 176
Netherlands (Mining) **N:** 147
Ocean (Sources of energy) **O:** 654
Oklahoma (Mining) **O:** 729
Persian Gulf **P:** 300
Pipeline **P:** 490
Russia *picture on* **R:** 545
Texas (Mining) **T:** 201
West Virginia (Early industries) **W:** 226
Natural gas hydrate
Petroleum (The future of petroleum) **P:** 349
Natural gas liquids N: 64
Gas [fuel] (Gas as a raw material) **G:** 52
Natural gasoline
Gasoline (Gasoline production) **G:** 61
Natural glass
Pumice **P:** 900a
Natural guide-star system [astronomy]
Telescope (Adaptive optics systems) **T:** 106
Natural habitat [ecology] *See* Habitat *in this index*
Natural History [book by Pliny the Elder]
Botany (The history of botany) **B:** 509
Pliny the Elder **P:** 573
Science (Ancient Rome) **S:** 197
Natural History, National Museum of *See* National Museum of Natural History *in this index*
Natural history museum
Museum (Science museums) **M:** 938
Natural increase
Population **P:** 672
Natural killer cell [physiology]
Disease (Immune responses) **D:** 231-232
Immune system (The cell-mediated immune response) **I:** 88-88a
Natural language processing
Artificial intelligence (Speech and natural language processing) **A:** 760
Information retrieval (Research) **I:** 268-269
Natural law [philosophy]
Civil rights (Development of civil rights) **Ci:** 610
Law (Ancient Roman law) **L:** 133-134; (Beginnings of U.S. law) **L:** 136
Natural light
Light (Sources of light) **L:** 283
Photography (Light) **P:** 414
Natural logarithms [mathematics]
Euler, Leonhard **E:** 378
Logarithms (Natural logarithms) **L:** 424
Natural materials
Materials (Natural materials) **M:** 300c
Natural minor scale [music]
Music (Tone) **M:** 950 *with diagram*
Natural number [mathematics]
Gauss, Carl Friedrich **G:** 70
Infinity **I:** 266
Integer **I:** 317
Number (Kinds of numbers) **N:** 605
Number theory **N:** 607
Natural pest control [agriculture]
Environmental pollution (Agriculture) **E:** 337
Pest control **P:** 318
Natural philosophy
Philosophy (Philosophy and science) **P:** 385
Natural Questions [work by Seneca]
Latin literature (The Imperial Period) **L:** 116
Natural raisin
Raisin (Preparation for market) **R:** 129-130
Natural resource and environmental economics
Economics (Fields of economics) **E:** 64
Natural resources N: 64
Conservation **C:** 974
Economics (Economic growth) **E:** 62
Industry (Natural resources) **I:** 257 *with diagram*; (The needs of industry) **I:** 257
Interior, Department of the **I:** 324
Mountain (As a wealth of natural resources)

M: 892
National park (Development of park resources)
  N: 42h
Technology (Using technology safely) T: 77
United States, History of the (Industrialization
  and reform [1870-1916]) U: 179-180
Water pollution (Reduced use of natural
  resources) W: 138
World (Threats to the environment) W: 418
Natural rights [philosophy]
Civil rights (Development of civil rights) Ci: 610-
  611
Democracy (Origins of democracy) D: 122
Freedom (During the Enlightenment) F: 503
Locke, John (His philosophy) L: 413
Natural satellite *See* Satellite [astronomy] *in this
  index*
Natural science
Liberal arts L: 226
Social science So: 552
Natural selection [biology] N: 65
Adaptation A: 45
Agriculture (Origins of agriculture) A: 154
Animal (How species change) A: 503
Darwin, Charles Robert (Darwin's theories) D: 40
Dawkins, Richard D: 51
Evolution (Main ideas of evolutionary theory)
  E: 426; (Natural selection) E: 428
Genetics (Population genetics) G: 87
Heredity (Heredity and natural selection) H: 203
Life (Adaptation) L: 275
Protective coloration P: 832
Races, Human (Evolutionary theory) R: 53;
  (Natural selection) R: 57
Social Darwinism So: 551
Wallace, Alfred Russel W: 15
Natural State, The [nickname]
Arkansas A: 694
Natural Tunnel
Virginia (Places to visit) V: 408
Naturalism [literature] N: 65
American literature (Naturalists) A: 419
Drama (Early realism) D: 338
Dreiser, Theodore D: 346
French literature (Naturalism) F: 522
German literature (Naturalism) G: 141
Latin American literature (Realism) L: 113
Novel (France) N: 573
Realism (In fiction) R: 171-172
Naturalistic exhibit
Zoo (Exhibits) Z: 601
Naturalization [law] N: 66 *with picture*
Citizenship (Naturalization) Ci: 570 *with picture*;
  (U.S. citizenship laws) Ci: 571
Citizenship and Immigration Services, United
  States Ci: 572
Immigration and Naturalization Service I: 86
Naturalization Act [1798]
Alien and Sedition Acts A: 368
Nature [book by Emerson]
Emerson, Ralph Waldo (His prose works) E: 259
Nature [journal]
Jefferson, Thomas (Jefferson and Sally Hemings)
  J: 79
Nature [philosophy]
See also Balance of nature *in this index*
Aristotle (Philosophy of nature) A: 664
Balance of nature B: 34
Behavior (The nature/nurture debate) B: 221
Civil rights (Development of civil rights) Ci: 610
Enlightenment (The orderliness of nature)
  E: 326a
God G: 243
Lotze, Rudolf Hermann L: 473
Nature study N: 67
Nature worship N: 68
Painting (What painters paint) P: 28-32
Science (The importance of science) S: 191-192
Spinoza, Baruch So: 795
Wordsworth, William W: 404
Nature Conservancy [organization] N: 67
Nature reserve
National park N: 42a
Nature School
Mythology (Comparative approaches) M: 989
Nature study N: 67
Nature versus nurture
Heredity (Heredity and environment) H: 205
Nature worship [religion] N: 68
Religion (Religion today) R: 223-224
Naturopathy [medicine]
Alternative medicine A: 388
Naturwissenschaften, Die [publication]
Max Planck Society for the Advancement of
  Science M: 318
Natyasastra [essay by Bharata]
Drama (India) D: 336

Naudé, Gabriel [French librarian]
Library (France) L: 260
Naughty Marietta [operetta by Herbert]
Herbert, Victor H: 197
Naulahka, The [book by Kipling and Balestier]
Kipling, Rudyard (Kipling in America) K: 334
Nauplius [zoology]
Barnacle B: 114
Larva L: 78
Nauru N: 68 *with maps*
Flag *picture on* F: 204
Pacific Islands (Pacific alliances and
  independence movements) P: 12
Nauruans [people]
Nauru (People) N: 68
Nausea [book by Sartre]
French literature (Existentialism) F: 523
Sartre, Jean-Paul S: 127
Nausea [disorder] N: 68
Vomiting V: 447
Nautical chart [map]
Map (Navigation maps) M: 178
Nautical league [unit of measure]
League L: 159
Nautical mile [unit of measure]
Inertial guidance I: 263
Knot K: 355
Latitude L: 117
League L: 159
Mile M: 542
Nautilus [nuclear submarine]
Connecticut (Places to visit) Ci: 960; (The mid-
  1900's) Ci: 971 *with picture*
Exploration (The North Pole) E: 450 *with map*
Navy, United States (The nuclear age Navy) N: 89-
  90 *with picture*
Nuclear energy (The first peaceful uses) N: 591
Rickover, Hyman George R: 335
Ship (Nuclear power and automation) S: 426
Submarine (Nuclear submarines) So: 943
Warship (Warships in the nuclear age) W: 42
Nautilus [sea animal] N: 69 *with picture*
Mollusk (Octopuses and squids) M: 695
Shell *pictures on* S: 387; (Octopuses and squids)
  S: 388
Nautilus [submarine]
Fulton, Robert (The inventor) F: 555
Submarine (Early submarines) So: 942
Nautilus, Paper [sea animal] *See* Argonaut [sea
  animal] *in this index*
Nauvoo [Illinois] N: 69
Illinois (Places to visit) I: 62 *with picture*
Mormons (Mormons in the Middle West) M: 808-
  809
Smith, Joseph (Life at Nauvoo) S: 517
Nauvoo Legion [U.S. history]
Smith, Joseph (Life at Nauvoo) S: 517
Nauvoo Temple
Nauvoo N: 69
Navaho Indians *See* Navajo Indians *in this index*
Navaho Weavers [painting by Begay]
Indian, American *picture on* I: 168
Navajo Community College
Arizona (Schools) A: 674; (The mid-1900's) A: 691
Navajo Indians N: 69
Navajo Indians N: 69
Arizona (Population) A: 674
Code talkers Ci: 749
Hogan H: 356
Indian, American *picture on* I: 136a; (Shelter)
  I: 136d; (Weaving) I: 146; (Indians of the
  Southwest) I: 166-168 *with picture*
Indian reservation (Description) I: 188
Indian wars (Navajo conflicts) I: 195
Manuelito M: 168
Sand painting S: 107
Navajo National Monument [Arizona]
National Park System (table: National
  monuments) N: 57
Naval Academy, United States *See* United States
Naval Academy *in this index*
Naval Air Basic Training Command [Florida]
Pensacola Naval Air Station P: 272
Naval Air Station Corpus Christi [Texas]
Corpus Christi (History) Ci: 1070-1071
Naval Air Station Pensacola [Florida]
Pensacola Naval Air Station P: 272 *with picture*
Naval Air Training Command, United States
[Florida]
Pensacola Naval Air Station P: 272
Naval architect
Ship S: 402; (Building a ship) S: 413
Naval attaché [military officer]
Attaché A: 878
Naval Aviation Museum [Florida]
Pensacola Naval Air Station P: 272
Naval base

Navy, United States (The Shore Establishment)
  N: 85
Naval Consulting Board
Edison, Thomas Alva (Final work) E: 81
Naval Forces Central Command
Navy, United States (The Operating Forces) N: 85
Naval Forces Europe
Navy, United States (The Operating Forces) N: 85
Naval mine
Mine warfare (Naval mines) M: 565
Navy (Wartime roles) N: 77
Naval Observatory, United States [Washington,
  D.C.] N: 70
*Naval Officer, or Scenes and Adventures in the Life
  of Frank Mildmay, The* [book by Marryat]
Marryat, Frederick M: 222
Naval Reserve
Navy, United States (The active-duty Navy and
  reserves) N: 85
Naval Reserve Officers Training Corps
Navy, United States (Training an officer) N: 83
Reserve Officers Training Corps (Navy ROTC)
  R: 258
Naval School of Aviation Medicine [Florida]
Pensacola Naval Air Station P: 272
Naval Service Bill [1910]
Borden, Sir Robert Laird (A new Conservative
  program) B: 485
Naval Special Warfare Command
Navy, United States (The Operating Forces) N: 85
Naval Station Norfolk [Virginia]
Norfolk (Economy) N: 454
Virginia *picture on* V: 417
Naval stores [industry]
Forest products (Naval stores) F: 402
Lumber (History) L: 521-522
Naval Surface Weapons Center [Dahlgren,
  Virginia]
Ballistics B: 56
Naval War College [Rhode Island] N: 70
Navy, United States (Training an officer) N: 83
Rhode Island (The Gilded Age) R: 313-315
Naval War of 1812, The [book by Roosevelt]
Roosevelt, Theodore (State legislator) R: 462
Navarino, Battle of [1827]
Greece (Independence) G: 362
Navarino Island [Chile]
Tierra del Fuego T: 283
Navarre, Henry of [king of France] *See* Henry IV *in
  this index*
Nave [architecture]
Architecture (table) A: 608-609 *with picture*;
  (Medieval architecture) A: 617
Basilica B: 140
Byzantine art (Architecture) B: 749
Cathedral (The plan of a cathedral) C: 301 *with
  diagram*
Romanesque architecture R: 415
Navel [anatomy]
Baby (Birth) B: 6 *with picture*; (Bathing the baby)
  B: 10
Umbilical cord U: 18
Navel orange [tree]
Orange (Sweet oranges) O: 815
Navicular [disease]
Horse (Medical care) H: 356
Navicular bone [anatomy]
Wrist W: 510 *with diagram*
Navigation N: 70 *with pictures*
See also the list of Related articles in the Navigation
  article
Airplane (Air navigation) A: 226 *with picture*
Bird (How birds migrate) B: 361
Chronometer C: 539
Global Positioning System G: 231
Great-circle route G: 338
Gyrocompass G: 452
Laser (Guiding) L: 83
Migration (How migrating animals find their
  way) M: 539
Radar (In ship navigation) R: 65 *with diagram*
Radio (Navigation) R: 85
Ship (Navigation) S: 410
Shoran S: 434
Space exploration (Navigation, guidance, and
  control) So: 704
Vikings (The Vikings as navigators) V: 381
Navigation Acts [English history] N: 75
Colonial life in America (Trade) Ci: 811
Virginia (Westward expansion) V: 418
Navigation canal
Canal C: 162 *with pictures*
Navigation light
Airplane (The wing) A: 213-214
Navigation map
Map (Types of maps) M: 177 *with picture*
Navigation Rules, International-Inland

Boating (Boating regulations) **B:** 429
Navigation satellite
  Rocket (Launching probes and satellites) **R:** 386
  Satellite, Artificial (table) **S:** 150e; (Types of artificial satellites) **S:** 150f
Navigators Islands
  Samoa Islands **S:** 80b
Navistar International Corporation
  McCormick, Cyrus Hall **M:** 332l
Navona, Piazza [Rome]
  Rome *picture on* **R:** 430
Navratilova, Martina [American tennis player] **N:** 75
  Tennis (Tennis today) **T:** 166d-166e *with picture*
Navstar Global Positioning System *See* Global Positioning System *in this index*
Navy N: 76 *with pictures*
  See also the list of Related articles in the Navy *article*
  Flag (Military flags) **F:** 195-208
  Mine warfare (Naval mines) **M:** 565
Navy, Canadian *See* Royal Canadian Navy *in this index*
Navy, Department of the [U.S.] **N:** 81
  Defense, Department of (History) **D:** 88
  Navy, United States (Organization of the Navy) **N:** 85
Navy, Secretary of the [office]
  Navy, Department of the **N:** 81
  Navy, United States (Organization of the Navy) **N:** 85
Navy, United States N: 82 *with pictures*
  See also the list of Related articles in the Navy, United States *article*
  Admiral **A:** 58
  Coast Guard, United States (National defense) **Ci:** 735; (History) **Ci:** 737
  Defense, Department of **D:** 87
  Flag *pictures on* **F:** 197; (Military flags) **F:** 195-208 *with pictures*
  Hydrofoil (Modern hydrofoil development) **H:** 468
  Jones, John Paul **J:** 158
  Medals, decorations, and orders (Military awards) **M:** 355 *with pictures*
  Navy (Major navies of the world) **N:** 78
  Navy, Department of the **N:** 81
  Pensacola Naval Air Station **P:** 272
  Puerto Rico (Puerto Rico today) **P:** 884
  Rank, Military **R:** 139
  Reserve Officers Training Corps (Navy ROTC) **R:** 258
  Shore Patrol **S:** 434
  United States Naval Academy **U:** 203
  Warship (Kinds of warships) **W:** 39
Navy and Marine Corps Medal
  Medals, decorations and orders (table) **M:** 357
Navy bean [plant]
  Bean (Kinds of beans) **B:** 181
Navy College Program for Afloat College Education
  Navy, United States (A typical day) **N:** 83-84
Navy commission pennant [U.S.]
  Flag *picture on* **F:** 194
Navy Cross
  Medals, decorations, and orders (table) **M:** 357 *with picture*
Navy Jack [flag]
  Flag *picture on* **F:** 194; (Flags of the United States and Canada) **F:** 208
Navy Pier
  Chicago (New construction) **C:** 437
Navy ROTC
  Navy, United States (Training an officer) **N:** 83
  Reserve Officers Training Corps (Navy ROTC) **R:** 258
Navy SEALs, United States N: 91
  Bin Laden, Osama **B:** 307
  Navy, United States (Wars in Iraq and Afghanistan) **N:** 89
Nawab [office]
  Bangladesh (Mughal rule) **B:** 85
Nawruz [holiday]
  Islam (Holidays and celebrations) **I:** 465
Naxçivan Autonomous Republic [region]
  Azerbaijan **A:** 996
Naylor, Phyllis Reynolds [American author] **N:** 91
  Newbery Medal (table) **N:** 359
Naypyidaw [Myanmar] **N:** 91
  Myanmar (Recent developments) **M:** 970e
  Yangon **Y:** 551
Nazarbayev, Nursultan [Kazakh political leader]
  Kazakhstan (History) **K:** 251-252
Nazareth [Israel] **N:** 91
Nazca [people] **N:** 91
  Indian, American (Indians of the Andes) **I:** 173
Nazca line [etching]

Nazca **N:** 92
Peru *picture on* **P:** 314
Nazi Party [Germany] *See* Nazism *in this index*
Nazi Party [U.S.]
  Nazism (Neo-Nazism) **N:** 92-93
Nazism [European history] **N:** 92
  See also the list of Related articles in the Nazism *article*
  Anti-Semitism **A:** 559
  Aryans **A:** 764
  Babi Yar **B:** 3
  Beckmann, Max **B:** 197
  Concentration camp **Ci:** 926
  Fascism (Fascism in Germany) **F:** 49
  Flag *picture on* **F:** 217
  German literature (Literature under the Nazis) **G:** 142
  Germany (Nazi Germany) **G:** 167 *with picture*
  Gestapo **G:** 175
  Göring, Hermann Wilhelm **G:** 276
  Government (Fascism) **G:** 288
  Hess, Rudolf **H:** 218
  Hindenburg, Paul von **H:** 234
  Hitler, Adolf **H:** 264; (Birth of the Nazi Party) **H:** 265
  Hitler Youth **H:** 268
  Holocaust **H:** 296
  Jews (Beginnings of Nazi persecution) **J:** 124; (The Holocaust) **J:** 124
  Kristallnacht **K:** 388
  Mein Kampf **M:** 386
  Nationalism (The effects of nationalism) **N:** 62
  Nietzsche, Friedrich (His life) **N:** 407
  Nuremberg **N:** 613
  Nuremberg Trials **N:** 613
  Pius XII **P:** 503
  Propaganda (Between the wars) **P:** 825
  Races, Human (Race and discrimination) **R:** 59
  Rosenberg, Alfred **R:** 479
  Swastika **So:** 1017 *with picture*
  War (Changes in the rules of war) **W:** 24
  Warsaw (History) **W:** 38
  Wiesenthal, Simon **W:** 299
  World War II *picture on* **W:** 470; (Nationalism) **W:** 469; (Peace with Germany) **W:** 498
Nb [symbol]
  Niobium **N:** 424
NBA [organization] *See* National Basketball Association *in this index*
NBA Development League
  National Basketball Association **N:** 30
NBC [network] **N:** 93
  ABC **A:** 7
  New York City (Rockefeller Center) **N:** 338
  Radio (The start of broadcasting) **R:** 92
  Television (The national networks) **T:** 113; (History of U.S. television broadcasting) **T:** 117
NBC Universal, Inc.
  General electric Company **G:** 83
NBCNews.com [website]
  NBC **N:** 93
NC-17 [rating]
  Motion picture (Censorship and self-regulation) **M:** 860-861
NCAA *See* National Collegiate Athletic Association *in this index*
NCAI [organization] *See* National Congress of American Indians *in this index*
NCCJ [organization] *See* National Conference for Community and Justice *in this index*
NCJW [organization] *See* Jewish Women, National Council of *in this index*
NCLB [law] *See* No Child Left Behind Act *in this index*
NCM [organization] *See* National Congress of Mothers *in this index*
NCR Corporation
  AT&T Inc. **A:** 851
Nd [symbol]
  Neodymium **N:** 123
Ndadaye, Melchior [African political leader]
  Burundi (History) **B:** 713-714
Ndayizeye, Domitien [Burundi political leader]
  Burundi (History) **B:** 713-714
NDEA [law] *See* National Defense Education Act *in this index*
Ndebele [people]
  Africa *picture on* **A:** 116a
  Bulawayo **B:** 686
  Rhodes, Cecil John (Gains Rhodesia) **R:** 317
  Zimbabwe (People) **Z:** 592; (History) **Z:** 592-593
Nd:glass laser [machine]
  Laser (Solid-state lasers) **L:** 85
N'Djamena [Chad] **N:** 93 *with picture*
  Chad **C:** 365
Ndlovukazi [title]
  Swaziland (Government) **So:** 1017

NDP *See* New Democratic Party *in this index*
Ndyuka Maroons [people]
  Maroons **M:** 217
Ne [symbol]
  Neon **N:** 124
Ne Win, U [Burmese political leader]
  Myanmar (History) **M:** 970d
NEA [organization] *See* National Education Association *in this index*
Neagh, Lough [lake, Northern Ireland] *See* Lough Neagh *in this index*
Neal, Patricia [American actress]
  Dahl, Roald **D:** 5
  Motion picture (Best performance by an actress: 1963) **M:** 862
Neale, Thomas [English colonial official]
  Postal Service, United States (Colonial times) **P:** 700
  Postal services (Postal service in the United States) **P:** 706
Neandertals [anthropology] **N:** 93
  Cave dwellers **C:** 321
  Clothing (Protection) **Ci:** 686
  Europe (Prehistoric times) **E:** 406
  Evolution (Contributions from other scientific fields) **E:** 433
  Funeral customs (History) **F:** 558
  Germany (Ancient times) **G:** 162
  Prehistoric people (The origin of *Homo sapiens*) **P:** 748-750 *with pictures*; (How the Neandertals lived) **P:** 751; (table) **P:** 754 *with map*; (Analysis of the genetic materials) **P:** 754b *with picture*
Neap tide
  Ocean (Tides) **O:** 659
  Tide *diagram on* **T:** 281; (The actual tide) **T:** 282
Neapolis [former name]
  Naples **N:** 12
Neapolitan pizza [food]
  Pizza **P:** 504
Neapolitans [people]
  Naples **N:** 12
Near-complementary color
  Color (Producing color harmony) **Ci:** 823-824 *with diagram*
Near-Earth asteroid [astronomy]
  Asteroid (Orbital groups) **A:** 824 *with diagram*
Near Earth Asteroid Rendezvous-Shoemaker [space probe]
  Asteroid (History of study) **A:** 824b
  Eros **E:** 355
  Space exploration (Probes to asteroids) **So:** 711
Near money [economics]
  Money (The money supply) **M:** 715
Near Oceania [region]
  Pacific Islands (Peoples of the Pacific Islands) **P:** 4
Near rhyme
  Rhyme **R:** 319
NEAR-Shoemaker [space probe] *See* Near Earth Asteroid Rendezvous-Shoemaker *in this index*
Near side
  Moon *map on* **M:** 786; (Rotation and orbit) **M:** 783
Nearchus [Greek explorer]
  Exploration (The Greeks) **E:** 441
"Nearer My God to Thee" [hymn]
  Mason, Lowell **M:** 266
Nearsightedness [disorder] *See* Myopia *in this index*
Neat [drink]
  Alcoholic beverage (Distilled drinks) **A:** 336
Neat soap
  Detergent and soap (The kettle method) **D:** 164
Nebi'im [Bible] *See* Prophets, The *in this index*
Neblina, Pico da [mountain]
  Brazil (The Amazon Region) **B:** 577 *with map*
Nebraska N: 94 *with pictures and maps*
  See also the list of Related articles in the Nebraska *article*
  Abortion (Abortion in the United States) **A:** 15-16
  Farm and farming *picture on* **F:** 33
  Kansas-Nebraska Act **K:** 243
Nebraska, University of N: 115
  Lincoln **L:** 309
  Nebraska (Museums) **N:** 98
Nebraska Education Television Act [1963]
  Nebraska (The mid-1900's) **N:** 114
Nebraska marble
  Nebraska (Territorial days) **N:** 112
Nebraska National Forest
  Nebraska (Interesting facts) **N:** 95
Nebraska Palladium and Platte Valley Advocate [newspaper]
  Nebraska (Communication) **N:** 109
Nebraska State Historical Society [Lincoln]
  Nebraska (Museums) **N:** 98
Nebraska Territory
  Nebraska (Territorial days) **N:** 112
Nebraskaland Days

Nebraska (Visitor's guide) N: 102
Nebraskan ice age [geology]
  Ice age (Evidence of ice ages and their climates) I: 6-7
Nebrija, Antonio de [Spanish author]
  Spanish literature (The 1400's) So: 758
Nebuchadnezzar II [king of Babylonia] N: 116
  Babylon (The Neo-Babylonian Empire) B: 12
  Babylonia (The dynasties of Babylon) B: 14
  World, History of the (Civilizations of southwest Asia) W: 426
Nebula [astronomy] N: 116 *with picture*
  Astronomy (Discovering other galaxies) A: 848
  Galaxy (Spiral galaxies) G: 8a
  Nebular hypothesis N: 116
  Universe (Changing views of the universe) U: 205
Nebular hypothesis [astronomy] N: 116
  Laplace, Marquis de L: 73
NEC Corporation
  Computer (Manufacturing) Ci: 924
Nečas, Peter [Czech political leader]
  Czech Republic (Recent developments) Ci: 1214
Necessity [philosophy]
  Metaphysics (Possibility and necessity) M: 430
Neck [anatomy]
  Shaken baby syndrome S: 343
  Skeleton (The axial skeleton) S: 479 *with diagrams*
  Throat T: 270
  Whiplash W: 281
Neck [harp]
  Harp H: 65 *with picture*
Necker, Anne Louise Germaine [French author]
  Staël, Madame de So: 820
Necker, Jacques [French government official]
  Louis XVI L: 476
Neckerchief
  Cowboy (His clothing) Ci: 1108-1109
Necklace
  Africa *picture on* A: 116
  Jewelry J: 117 *with pictures*
  Pearl (Matching pearls) P: 217 *with picture*
Necktie N: 117
Necrology [list] N: 117
Necropolis [archaeology] N: 117
Necropsy [law] *See* Autopsy *in this index*
Necrosis [disorder]
  Death (Medical aspects of death) D: 61
  Match (The first matches) M: 300-300a
Necrotizing fasciitis [infection]
  Streptococcus S: 926
Necrotizing ulcerative gingivitis [disease] *See* Trench mouth *in this index*
Nectar [botany] N: 117
  Bee (Life of the honey bee) B: 202-204
  Honey H: 314
  Honeyeater H: 315
Nectar [Greek mythology]
  Ambrosia A: 405
Nectar corridor [conservation]
  Butterfly (Butterfly conservation) B: 743
Nectaries [botany]
  Bee (Making honey) B: 204
Nectarine [fruit] N: 117 *with picture*
Nedda [opera character]
  Opera: (*Pagliacci*) O: 806
Neddermeyer, Seth H. [American physicist]
  Muon M: 928
Nederlanders [people]
  Netherlands N: 138
Nednais [American Indians]
  Geronimo G: 173
Need [psychology]
  Child (Understanding the child's basic needs) C: 451
  Culture (Satisfying basic needs) Ci: 1187
  Human relations (The study of human relations) H: 428
Needham, James [English explorer]
  Tennessee (Exploration) T: 153
Needle [botany] *See* Needleleaf tree *in this index*
Needle [tool] N: 117 *with pictures*
  Acupuncture A: 31
  Sewing S: 332
Needle bar
  Rugs and carpets (Tufting) R: 515
Needle-clawed galago [animal]
  Galago G: 7
Needle-exchange program
  AIDS (Education) A: 165
Needle-leaved cedar [tree]
  Cedar (Needle-leaved cedars) C: 324 *with picture*
Needle-punched fabric
  Rugs and carpets (Other methods) R: 516
  Textile (Other textiles) T: 215
Needlefish
  Gar G: 28

Needleleaf tree
  Cell *picture on* C: 327
  Flower (Flowers of woodlands and forests) F: 284 *with pictures*
  Leaf L: 151 *with pictures*
  Pine P: 468 *with pictures*
  Tree *pictures on* T: 413, T: 424, T: 425; (Needleleaf trees) T: 414; (Leaves) T: 417 *with diagram*; (Needleleaf forests) T: 429 *with picture*
Needlepoint [handicraft] N: 118 *with pictures*
  Petit point P: 326 *with picture*
Needlepoint lace [fabric]
  Lace L: 20 *with pictures*
Needle's Eye, The [book by Drabble]
  Drabble, Margaret D: 317
Needlework [handicraft]
  Colonial life in America (Decorative arts) Ci: 807-808 *with picture*
  Crochet Ci: 1148c *with pictures*
  Embroidery E: 256 *with picture*
  Knitting K: 353 *with diagrams*
  Needlepoint N: 118 *with picture*
  Petit point P: 326 *with picture*
  Quilt Q: 41 *with picture*
  Sampler S: 81 *with picture*
  Sewing S: 332 *with diagrams*
Needs-based education
  Education (What should be taught?) E: 105
Néel, Louis Eugène Félix [French physicist]
  Nobel Prizes (Physics: 1970) N: 441
Néel temperature [physics]
  Magnetism (In materials) M: 60c
Neely, Matthew M. [American political leader]
  West Virginia (table) W: 225
Neem tree [tree] N: 118 *with picture*
Ne'eman, Yuval [Israeli physicist]
  Gell-Mann, Murray G: 77
Nefertari [wife of Ramses II]
  Abu Simbel, Temples of A: 19
Nefertiti [queen of ancient Egypt] N: 119 *with portrait*
Neff, Pat M. [American political leader]
  Texas (table) T: 203; (The early 1900's) T: 207-208
Negative [photography]
  Photography (Developing the film) P: 419 *with picture*; (Making prints) P: 419 *with picture*
  Talbotype T: 19
  Technicolor T: 73
Negative acceleration [physics]
  Velocity (Acceleration) V: 297
Negative angle [geometry]
  Angle A: 462
Negative charge [electricity]
  Electricity (Electric charge) E: 191
  Vacuum tube (How a vacuum tube works) V: 258
Negative eugenics [genetics]
  Eugenics E: 377
Negative-expectation game
  Gambling (Types of gambling) G: 20
Negative externality [economics]
  Industry (Social costs) I: 261
Negative income tax [welfare]
  Friedman, Milton F: 533
Negative ion [chemistry]
  Bond (An ionic bond) B: 454
Negative lens
  Lens (Lens shapes) L: 196; (Viewed through a negative lens) L: 196b
Negative number
  Algebra (Positive and negative numbers) A: 352
  Arithmetic (Arithmetic of negative numbers) A: 668
  Mathematics (Branches of mathematics) M: 303
  Scientific notation S: 207
  Square root So: 812
Negative-pressure respirator [machine]
  Respirator R: 262
Negative reinforcement [psychology]
  Behavior (Learning) B: 220-221
Negative theology
  Neoplatonism N: 124
Negative transfer [psychology]
  Learning (Transfer of training) L: 164
Negative tropism [botany]
  Plant (Environmental factors) P: 538
Negative-working offset plate [printing]
  Printing (Offset printing plates) P: 798
Negev [region, Israel] N: 119
  Irrigation (Other sources) I: 456
  Israel (The Negev Desert) I: 484 *with picture*
Negishi, Ei-ichi [Japanese chemist]
  Nobel Prizes (Chemistry: 2010) N: 444
Neglect [law]
  Child abuse C: 454
  Juvenile court J: 205
Negligence [law] N: 119
  Homicide H: 305

  Insurance (Property and liability insurance) I: 312
  Medicine (Treatment) M: 364-365
  Product liability suit P: 810
Negligent homicide [crime]
  Negligence N: 119
Negotiable instrument [law] N: 119
  Note (Liability of the maker) N: 550
Negotiable order of withdrawal account
  Bank (A boom in money market funds) B: 94
  Check (Checks and the economy) C: 391
Negotiation
  International relations (Diplomacy) I: 344
Negret, Edgar [Colombian sculptor]
  Colombia (The arts) Ci: 781
Negrín, Juan [Spanish political leader]
  Spanish Civil War (Progress of the war) So: 756a-756b
Negrito [botany]
  Ivory palm I: 522
Negritos [people] N: 120
  Philippines (Ancestry) P: 373-374; (Early days) P: 379
  Pygmies P: 914
Negro Business League, National
  Washington, Booker T. (Racial leader) W: 89
Negro Digest [magazine]
  Magazine (Magazines in the 1900's) M: 45
Negro Family in the United States, The [book by Frazier]
  Frazier, Edward Franklin F: 497
Negro History Week
  Black History Month B: 388
Negro in Our History [book by Woodson]
  Woodson, Carter Godwin W: 395
Negro league
  Baseball (Postwar baseball) B: 136
Negroes [people] *See* African Americans; Blacks *in this index*
Negroids [people]
  Races, Human (The three-race theory) R: 53-54 *with picture*
Negroponte, John [American political leader]
  United Nations (table) U: 86
Negros [island, Philippines]
  Philippines (The main islands) P: 376-378 *with map*
Nehemiah, Book of [Bible] N: 120
Neher, Erwin [German physiologist]
  Nobel Prizes (Physiology or medicine: 1991) N: 446
Nehru [Indian family] N: 120 *with picture*
Nehru, Indira Priyadarshini [birth name of]
  Gandhi, Indira G: 24
Nehru, Jawaharlal [Indian political leader]
  Nehru N: 120 *with picture*
  India (Independence and partition) I: 133 *with picture*; (India in the 1950's and early 1960's) I: 133
  Indian National Congress I: 185
Nehru, Motilal [Indian political leader]
  Nehru N: 120
Nehru Report [book by Nehru]
  Nehru (Motilal Nehru) N: 120
Neige noire [book by Aquin]
  Canadian literature (Modern literature: 1945 to the present) C: 159-160
Neighborhood [sociology]
  City (Cultural variety in cities) Ci: 593
  New York City (Social problems) N: 332-333
Neighborhood center [social work]
  Addams, Jane A: 46
Neighborhood committee
  China (Urban life) C: 483
Neighborhood health clinic
  Hospital (Recent developments) H: 374
Neighborhood Watch program
  Police (In the United States since the mid-1900's) P: 624
Neihardt, John [American author] N: 121
Neil, Helen [wife of]
  Mackenzie, Alexander (Emigration to Canada) M: 21
Neill, Sam [Australian actor]
  Australia *picture on* A: 906
Neisseria gonorrhoeae [bacteria]
  Gonorrhea G: 268
  Pelvic inflammatory disease P: 233
Nekton [biology]
  Ocean *pictures on* O: 656, O: 657; (The nekton) O: 655
Nelligan, Émile [Canadian poet]
  Canadian literature (Poetry: 1850-1918) C: 157
Nelmes, Sarah [patient of]
  Jenner, Edward (Jenner's work) J: 91
Nelson, C. William [American political leader]
  Astronaut (A look at the astronauts) A: 831
Nelson, E. Benjamin [American political leader]

Nebraska (table) N: 110
Nelson, Gaylord A. [American political leader]
Earth Day E: 32
Wisconsin (table) W: 365; (Decline of LaFollette Progressivism) W: 368
Nelson, Horatio [British admiral] N: 121 with pictures
London picture on L: 428
Trafalgar, Battle of T: 365
United Kingdom (The Napoleonic Wars) U: 68
Nelson, John [American government official]
Justice, Department of (table) J: 203
Tyler, John (table) T: 534
Nelson, Knute [American political leader]
Minnesota (table) M: 602
Nelson, S. D. [American illustrator]
Literature for children picture on L: 360
Nelson, Samuel [American jurist]
Supreme Court of the United States (table) So: 1000
Nelson, Thomas, Jr. [American patriot] N: 122
Virginia (table) V: 417
Nelson, Viscount See Nelson, Horatio in this index
Nelson, William Rockhill [American editor] N: 122
Nelson, Willie [American composer/singer] N: 122
Country music (Modern country music) Ci: 1098c-1098d with picture
Nelson-Atkins Museum of Art [Kansas City, Missouri]
Kansas City [Missouri] (Cultural life) K: 241
Missouri (Museums) M: 655 with picture
Nelson Pillar [Dublin]
Ireland picture on I: 428
Nelson River [Manitoba] N: 123
Canada (The Hudson Bay and Hudson Strait Basin) C: 120
Nelson's Column [London]
London picture on L: 428; (Squares) L: 435
Nelson, Horatio (Nelson monument) N: 122
NEM [Hungarian history] See New Economic Mechanism in this index
Neman River [Belarus-Lithuania] N: 123
Lithuania (Land and climate) L: 388-389
Nemanja, Stefan [king of Serbia]
Serbia (History) S: 314
Nematocyst [zoology]
Ribbon worm R: 321
Nematode [worm] See Roundworm
Nembutal [medication]
Barbiturate (Medical uses) B: 107
Drug abuse (table: Some commonly abused drugs) D: 363
Nemean Games [ancient Greece]
Olympic Games (The ancient games) O: 750
Nemean lion [Greek mythology]
Hercules (The twelve labors) H: 198-199
Nemerov, Howard [American poet]
Poet laureate (table: Poets laureate of the United States) P: 590
Nemertea [zoology]
Animal (A classification of the animal kingdom) A: 506 with picture
Nemesis [Greek mythology]
Helen of Troy H: 168
Németh, Miklós [Hungarian political leader]
Hungary (Beginnings of change) H: 448
Nemi [ancient Rome]
Mythology (Anthropological approaches) M: 989
Nemi, Lake [Italy] See Lake Nemi in this index
Nemirovich-Danchenko, Vladimir [Russian businessman]
Moscow Art Theater M: 828
Nemo, Captain [literary figure]
Verne, Jules V: 337
Nemours, Pierre Samuel du Pont de See Du Pont de Nemours, Pierre Samuel in this index
Nemov, Alexei [Russian gymnast]
Olympic Games (The recent games) O: 753-754
Nemunas River [Belarus] See Neman River in this index
Nene [bird] N: 123
Bird (Birds of the Pacific Islands) B: 349 with picture
Neo-Babylonian Empire [Asian history]
Babylon (The Neo-Babylonian Empire) B: 12
Chaldeans map on C: 370
World, History of the (Civilizations of southwest Asia) W: 426
Neoclassicism [arts]
Architecture (Neoclassical architecture) A: 623 with pictures
Classical music (Neoclassicism) Ci: 649
Drama (Italian Renaissance drama) D: 330; (The French theater) D: 333
English literature (The Augustan Age) E: 318
Furniture (The neoclassical style) F: 577
Ingres, Jean Auguste Dominique I: 271

Italian literature (The Baroque period and the Enlightenment) I: 494-495
Latrobe, Benjamin Henry L: 118
Painting (Neoclassicism) P: 66 with picture; (Later neoclassicism) P: 67
Picasso, Pablo (The 1920's and 1930's) P: 448b-449
Poetry (Neoclassical poetry) P: 596
Sculpture (European sculpture) S: 253-254 with picture
Spanish literature (The 1700's) So: 760
Stravinsky, Igor (Neoclassical works) So: 922
Neocolonialism [political science]
Colonialism (Decolonization) Ci: 814
Neo-Confucianism [religion]
China (The Song dynasty) C: 501
Confucianism (Later Confucianism) Ci: 937
Painting (Chinese painting) P: 44-45
Philosophy (Eastern philosophy) P: 386
Religion (Confucianism) R: 220-221
Song dynasty So: 592
Neo-Darwinism [biology]
Darwin, Charles Robert (The influence of Darwin's ideas) D: 40
Neo-Destour Party [political party]
Tunisia (History) T: 489
Neodymium [element] N: 123
Neoexpressionism [art]
Painting (Recent painting) P: 87 with picture
Schnabel, Julian S: 177 with picture
Neogenic Period [geology]
Earth (table) E: 30
Forest picture on F: 398
Neoimpressionism [art]
Painting (Postimpressionism) P: 75-76 with picture
Seurat, Georges S: 324
Neoliberalism [political science]
Latin America (Neoliberalism) L: 111
Neolithic Period [anthropology]
City (How cities began and developed) Ci: 575-577 with pictures
Lake dwelling L: 37
Prehistoric people (The Stone Age) P: 751; (Changes in lifestyle) P: 753
Stone Age So: 909
Neomycin [medication]
Antibiotic (table) A: 551
Neon [element] N: 123 with pictures
Atom diagram on A: 872
Neon goby [fish]
Fish picture on F: 154
Neon light
Electric light (Neon lamps) E: 174 with picture
Invention picture on I: 356
Plasma P: 552
Neon sign
Color picture on Ci: 817
Neon picture on N: 124
Neon tetra [fish]
Aquarium, Home picture on A: 578a
Fish picture on F: 157
Neon Vernacular [book by Komunyakaa]
African American literature (The 1900's) A: 136a
Neonatal death
Infant mortality I: 264
Neonatal period [medicine]
Neonatology N: 124
Neonaticide [homicide]
Infanticide I: 264
Neonatology [medicine] N: 124
Neo-Nazism [political science]
Germany (The unification of East and West Germany) G: 171
Nazism (Neo-Nazism) N: 92
Neo-Orthodoxy [religion]
Christianity (The 1900's) C: 526
Neophonic Orchestra [music]
Kenton, Stan K: 271
Neoplasia [disorder]
Cervical cancer C: 364
Neoplasm [disorder] See Tumor in this index
Neoplasticism [art]
Mondrian, Piet M: 703
Neoplatonism [philosophy] N: 124
Augustine, Saint (His life) A: 888
Humanism (Work of the humanists) H: 431
Hypatia H: 475
Philosophy (Neoplatonism) P: 388
Plato (Plato's place in Western thought) P: 569
Plotinus P: 574
Neoprene [material]
Rubber (Special-purpose rubbers) R: 504
Neopterygian [animal]
Fish (The first modern fish) F: 171
Neoptolemus [legendary figure]
Odyssey picture on O: 675

Priam P: 774
Neorealism [art]
Italian literature (The 1900's) I: 495
Italy I: 506
Motion picture (Postwar Realism) M: 869 with picture
Neoromanticism [literature]
German literature (Impressionism, Neoromanticism, and Symbolism) G: 141
Neotropical rattlesnake
Snake picture on S: 528
Neo-Volcanic Range [region of Mexico]
Mexico (The Plateau of Mexico) M: 461
NEP See New Economic Policy in this index
Nepal N: 124 with pictures and maps
Flag picture on F: 204
Food picture on F: 333
Food supply picture on F: 345
Gurkhas G: 443
Marriage (Same-sex unions and marriages) M: 220
Nepalese [people]
Sikkim (People) S: 456
Nepali [language]
Nepal (People) N: 125
Nepenthe [legend]
Douglas, Norman D: 312
Nephele [legendary figure]
Golden Fleece G: 255
Nephrectomy
Surgery (Some common surgical operations) So: 1006
Nephridium [zoology]
Earthworm picture on E: 39
Nephrite [mineral]
Jade (Nephrite) J: 20
Nephritis [disease] N: 127
Bright, Richard B: 609
Nephroblastoma [disease]
Cancer (Cancer in children) C: 169
Nephron [anatomy]
Human body (The urinary system) H: 424
Kidney (How the kidneys produce urine) K: 311 with diagrams
Nephthys [Egyptian goddess]
Mythology picture on M: 977; (The Great Ennead) M: 979; (The Osiris myth) M: 979
Nepotism [politics] N: 128
Neptune [Roman mythology] N: 128 with picture
See also Poseidon in this index
Mythology (table) M: 981
Neptune [planet] N: 128 with picture
Astronomy (Finding new objects) A: 848
Kuiper belt K: 392
Planet P: 507 with pictures
Planetary ring P: 514d with picture
Pluto P: 581
Satellite S: 149; (Satellites of the gas giants) S: 150; (table: Major satellites of the solar system) S: 150b
Science (Forming a hypothesis) S: 195
Space exploration (Probes to Jupiter and beyond) So: 711
Triton T: 448
Volcano (Volcanoes in the solar system) V: 442b-443
Voyager V: 451
Neptune [ship]
Shipwreck (table: Major shipwrecks) S: 428
Neptunist
Geology (The rock dispute) G: 98-99
Neptunium [element] N: 128
Transuranium element T: 401
Nereid [satellite]
Neptune (Satellites and rings) N: 129
Satellite (Nereid) S: 150b
Nereids [Greek mythology] N: 130
Mythology (Greek divinities) M: 982
Nymph N: 633
Nereus [Greek mythology] N: 130
Nereids N: 130
Neri, Saint Philip [Italian religious leader] N: 130
Neris River [Lithuania]
Lithuania picture on L: 388
Nernst, Walther Hermann [German chemist]
Nobel Prizes (Chemistry: 1920) N: 443
Nero [Roman emperor] N: 130 with portrait
Agrippina the Younger A: 162
Claudius Ci: 657
Petronius P: 351
Seneca, Lucius Annaeus S: 296
Vatican City (History) V: 288
Nero, Tiberius Claudius [Roman emperor] See Claudius in this index
Nerone [opera by Boito]
Boito, Arrigo B: 440
Neruda, Pablo [Chilean poet] N: 131

Chile (The arts) C: 463
Latin American literature (The early 1900's) L: 113
Nerva [Roman emperor]
Rome, Ancient (The Roman Empire) R: 446; (table) R: 447
Trajan T: 368
Nerval, Gérard de [French poet] N: 131
French literature (Gautier and Nerval) F: 521
Nerve [anatomy]
See also Nervous system *in this index*
Human body (table) H: 422 *with diagram*; (The nervous system) H: 425
Marine biology (What marine biologists do) M: 204-205
Nervous system N: 132 *with diagrams, diagrams on* N: 134
Neuralgia N: 152
Neuritis N: 152
Nerve agent
Chemical-biological-radiological warfare (Chemical) C: 396
Nerve cell [anatomy]
See also Neuron *in this index*
Cell (Shapes of cells) C: 328 *with picture*; (Death of a cell) C: 332
Myelin M: 970f
Nerve fiber *See* Axon; Dendrite *in this index*
Nerve impulse *See* Impulse *in this index*
Nerve membrane [anatomy]
Nervous system (Parts of a neuron) N: 133
Nerve net [zoology]
Nervous system (In invertebrates) N: 136
Nervi, Pier Luigi [Italian architect] N: 131
Nervous breakdown N: 131
Mental illness M: 404
Nervous system [biology] N: 132 *with diagrams*
See also the list of Related articles in the Nervous system *article*
Bird (The circulatory system) B: 366
Brain B: 550a
Butterfly (The internal organs) B: 739 *with diagram*
Depressant D: 149
Fish (Nervous system) F: 163
Heart H: 132; (Regulating the heart rate) H: 135-136
Human body (table) H: 422 *with diagram*; (The nervous system) H: 425
Insect (Nervous system) I: 289 *with diagram*
Learning disabilities (Causes) L: 165
Leprosy L: 204
Mammal (Internal organ systems) M: 119-120
Neurofibromatosis N: 152
Neurology N: 152
Reflex action (How reflex action occurs) R: 195
Tissue (Animal tissues) T: 298-299
Nervous tissue [anatomy]
Human body (Cells and tissues) H: 417-418
Tissue (Animal tissues) T: 298-299
Nesians [people]
Pacific Islands (Recent developments) P: 13
Neskhi [writing]
Islamic art (Calligraphy) I: 468
Ness, Eliot [American crime fighter] N: 136 *with portrait*
Ness, Evaline [American artist]
Caldecott Medal (table: 1967) C: 26
Nessie [name for]
Loch Ness monster L: 410 *with picture*
Nessler, Charles L. [German-American inventor]
Hairdressing (The 1900's) H: 12
Nessus [Greek mythology]
Hercules (The death of Hercules) H: 199
Nest [zoology] N: 137
Animal (Animal homes and communities) A: 501
Ant (Nests) A: 523 *with picture*
Bird (Building a nest) B: 356 *with pictures*
Bird of prey (Reproduction and growth) B: 374a
Chipmunk *picture on* C: 513
Hornet H: 340
Hummingbird (Habits) H: 435 *with picture*
Rhea R: 290
Spider (How spiders use silk) So: 786 *with picture*
Squirrel (Obtaining shelter) So: 815
Stork *picture on* So: 912
Termite (Kinds of termites) T: 171
Wasp (Nests) W: 112 *with pictures*
Weaver *picture on* W: 172
Nest-egg gourd
Gourd G: 281 *with picture*
Nestlé [company]
Manufacturing (table) M: 170
Nestor [legendary figure]
Messenia M: 423
Nestor Company
Hollywood H: 294
Nestorius [early Christian]

Cyril of Alexandria, Saint Ci: 1208
Roman Catholic Church (Conflict with the East) R: 406
Nestos, R. A. [American political leader]
North Dakota (table) N: 513
Nestroy, Johann [Austrian dramatist]
Austria (Literature) A: 933
Net [computing] *See* Internet *in this index*
Net [fabric] N: 137 *with pictures*
See also Net, Fishing *in this index*
Textile (Other textiles) T: 215
Net [sports]
Tennis (The court and equipment) T: 161 *with diagram*
Net, Fishing
Fishing industry (Nets) F: 183 *with pictures*
Oyster (Oyster harvesting) O: 892
Net asset value
Mutual fund M: 969
Net ball
Tennis (The serve) T: 163
Net blotch [plant disease]
Barley (Diseases and insect pests) B: 113
Net-casting spider *See* Ogre-faced spider *in this index*
Net force [physics] *See* Resultant force *in this index*
Net income
Income (Gross and net income) I: 100
Net national product
National income (Determining national income) N: 37-38
Net neutrality [communications]
Internet (Net neutrality) I: 350g
Net tonnage
Ship (Nautical measurements) S: 406
Net worth [economics]
Taxation (Other taxes) T: 54
Netanyahu, Benjamin [Israeli political leader] N: 137 *with portrait*
Israel (The 1990's) I: 489; (The early 2000's) I: 489-490
Netball [game]
Australia (Recreation) A: 903
Netbook [computer]
Laptop computer (Types) L: 74
Netflix [company]
Internet (Changing industries) I: 350e
Netherlands N: 138 *with pictures and maps*
See also the list of Related articles in the Netherlands *article, and* Dutch... *in this index*
Aruba A: 764
Euro E: 379
Agriculture
Tulip T: 482
Art and architecture
Painting (The Dutch masters) P: 62 *with pictures*
Communications and mass media
Postal services (Competition and privatization) P: 707
Education
Education (Control) E: 96-97
History
Netherlands (History) N: 148 *with pictures*
Asia (The Western conquest of Asia) A: 806
Belgium (Habsburg rule) B: 233
Brazil (Portuguese rule) B: 583
Colonialism (Early European colonialism) Ci: 813
Dutch East India Company D: 392
Indonesia I: 226; (Dutch rule) I: 237; (Independence) I: 237; (Indonesia under Sukarno) I: 238
Luxembourg (History) L: 531
Marine (History) M: 204
Navy (The beginning of modern navies) N: 79
Palmares P: 110
South Africa (History) So: 617
World War II (The invasion of the Low Countries) W: 474
People
Netherlands (People) N: 139
Christmas (In the Netherlands, Belgium, and Luxembourg) C: 531 *with picture*
Clothing *picture on* Ci: 694
Ice skating (History) I: 16
Trade
Benelux B: 248
Netherlands, Kingdom of the [European history]
Belgium *map on* B: 234; (The Brabant Revolution) B: 233
Netherlands (The Kingdom of the Netherlands) N: 139
Netherlands Antilles [islands, Caribbean] N: 151
Aruba A: 764
Netherlands (Political changes) N: 150
Netherlands Indies [former name, Indonesia]

Indonesia (Dutch rule) I: 237
Netherlands New Guinea [former name, New Guinea]
New Guinea (History) N: 207
Netherlands West Indies *See* Netherlands Antilles *in this index*
Netleaf hackberry [shrub]
Hackberry H: 3
NetLibrary [electronic library]
Library (The growth of information and technology) L: 237-238
NetPost Mailing Online [service]
Postal Service, United States (Electronic services) P: 700
Nets, New Jersey [team]
Basketball (table) B: 150
Netsuke [ornament]
Ivory (Ivory carving) I: 521 *with picture*
Netted garment
Clothing (Handmade clothing) Ci: 691
Nettle [plant] N: 151
Nettle rash [disorder]
Hives H: 270
Network [communications]
See also Computer network *in this index*
Radio (Stations and networks) R: 90; (The start of broadcasting) R: 92
Television (The national networks) T: 113
Network, Computer *See* Computer network *in this index*
Network effect [economics]
Industry (Network effects) I: 260
Network externality [economics]
Industry (Network effects) I: 260
Network interface card [electronic device]
Computer (A modem or a network interface card) Ci: 915
Network time
Advertising (Television) A: 73
Networking
Careers (Finding job opportunities) C: 217
Netzahualcóyotl [Mexico] N: 151
Neuber, Caroline [German actress]
Drama (Germany) D: 336
Neuberger, Richard Lewis [American political leader]
Peace Corps (History) P: 208
Neue Rheinische Zeitung [magazine]
Marx, Karl (Marriage and move to Paris) M: 236-237
Neues Schloss [castle]
Stuttgart So: 935 *with picture*
Neuilly, Treaty of [1919]
World War I (The Paris Peace Conference) W: 465
Neumann, Balthasar [German architect]
Architecture (Baroque architecture) A: 622
Neumann, Frank [American seismologist]
Earthquake (The Modified Mercalli Intensity [MMI] scale) E: 38b
Neumann, Saint John Nepomucene [American religious leader] N: 152
Neume [symbol]
Classical music (The Middle Ages) Ci: 645-646
Neumeier, John [American choreographer]
Ballet (Ballet in Europe) B: 54
Neural circuit [physiology]
Nervous system (Simple pathways) N: 134
Neural network
Artificial intelligence (Knowledge representation and reasoning) A: 760
Neural tube [central nervous system]
Reproduction, Human (Development of organs and organ systems) R: 248
Neural tube defect [disorder]
Folic acid F: 315
Neuralgia [disorder] N: 152
Neuritis [disorder] N: 152
Neuralgia N: 152
Neurobiology
Biology (table) B: 317; (The growth of modern biology) B: 319-320
Brain B: 550b
Zoology (History) Z: 606-607
Neuroblastoma [disease]
Cancer (Cancer in children) C: 169
Neurodermatitis [disorder]
Eczema E: 74
Neurofibrillary tangle [physiology]
Alzheimer's disease (Diagnosis) A: 398-399
Neurofibroma [disorder]
Neurofibromatosis N: 152
Neurofibromatosis [disorder] N: 152
Neurofibromin [protein]
Neurofibromatosis N: 152
Neurogenic shock [disorder]
Shock S: 429
Neuroleptic drug

Psychiatry (Somatic therapy) P: 845
Neurological surgery
Medicine (table) M: 369
Neurologist [career]
Neurology N: 152
Neurology N: 152
Medicine (table) M: 369
Neuromancer [book by Gibson]
Science fiction (Recent developments) S: 206
Neuromuscular junction [anatomy]
Myasthenia gravis M: 970e
Neuron [anatomy]
Nervous system *diagrams on* N: 134; (How the
nervous system works) N: 132 *with diagram*;
(Parts of a neuron) N: 133
Brain B: 550a; (How neurons work) B: 557 *with
diagram*
Human body (The nervous system) H: 425
Neuropathology [medicine] N: 153
Neurophysiology [science]
Galvani, Luigi G: 17
Neuroptera [entomology]
Insect *picture on* I: 281; (table) I: 300
Neuroscience
Brain B: 550a
Psychology (Modern psychology) P: 850
Neurosis [psychology] N: 153
Clinical psychology (Psychotherapy and
consultation) Ci: 681
Introvert I: 354
Mental illness M: 404
Psychiatry (Psychiatric disorders) P: 845
Neurosurgery
Cushing, Harvey Ci: 1200
Medicine (table) M: 369
Neurotoxin [poison]
Snake (Fangs and venom glands) S: 528
Neurotransmitter [physiology]
Alcoholism (Causes of alcoholism) A: 337-338
Antidepressant A: 553
Brain (How neurons work) B: 55 *with diagram*
Depression D: 151
Dopamine D: 309
Mental illness (Chemical imbalances in the brain)
M: 406
Nervous system (Transmission across synapses)
N: 135
Ritalin R: 350
Schizophrenia S: 176
Serotonin S: 318
Smoking S: 520
Neuschwanstein Castle [Bavaria]
Germany *picture on* G: 145
Ludwig II L: 515
Neuse River
North Carolina (Rivers, waterfalls, and lakes)
N: 484 *with map*
Neusiedler Lake [Austria]
Austria (Land and climate) A: 933 *with map*
Neustria [former region]
Charlemagne *map on* C: 379
Neuter gender
Gender G: 80
Noun (Gender) N: 552-553
Neutering
Cat (Birth control) C: 295
Pet (Birth control) P: 322
Rabbit (Health) R: 49
Neutra, Richard Joseph [Austrian-American
architect] N: 153 *with picture*
Neutral [mechanics]
Transmission T: 375; (How a manual transmission
works) T: 377-378
Neutral Buoyancy Laboratory
Astronaut (Basic mission training) A: 832
Neutral corner
Boxing (Fight rules) B: 527
Neutral nation
Cold War Ci: 762
Neutrality N: 153
Third World T: 258
Neutral Nations' Repatriation Commission
Korean War (The end of the war) K: 382-383
Neutral trait [biology]
Races, Human (Evolutionary theory) R: 53-54
Neutralino [atomic particle]
Dark matter D: 37
Neutrality [political science] N: 153
Austria (After World War II) A: 939-940
International law (The laws of neutrality) I: 341
Switzerland (Neutrality in the world wars)
So: 1060
Neutrality, Principle of [economics]
Taxation (Other principles of taxation) T: 54
Neutrality Proclamation [1793]
Washington, George (Neutrality proclamation)
W: 105

Neutralization [chemistry] N: 154
Neutralization [political science]
Neutrality N: 153
Neutrino [atomic particle] N: 154 *with picture*
Astronomy (Neutrino astronomy) A: 845
Dark matter D: 37
Lepton L: 205
Nuclear physics N: 596
Observatory (Neutrino observatories) O: 645
Pauli, Wolfgang P: 201
Physics (Physics today) P: 442-443
Radiation (Beta particles) R: 76
Star (Hydrogen fusion) So: 846-847
Subatomic particle (Kinds of subatomic particles)
So: 937
Sun (Analyzing neutrinos) So: 984
Neutrino astronomy
Astronomy (Neutrino astronomy) A: 845
Neutrino detector [machine]
Neutrino N: 154 *with picture*
Neutrino observatory
Observatory (Neutrino observatories) O: 645
Neutron [atomic particle] N: 155
Alpha particle A: 381
Atom (The parts of an atom) A: 870 *with
diagrams*; (The properties of atoms) A: 871
with diagrams; (Forces in the nucleus) A: 873
Baryon B: 122
Chadwick, Sir James C: 368
Cosmic rays (Galactic cosmic rays) Ci: 1076
Electricity (Electric charge) E: 191
Element, Chemical (The periodic table of the
elements) E: 219
Fermi, Enrico F: 73
Force (Kinds of force) F: 370
Gluon G: 237
Kendall, Henry Way K: 258
Magnetism (How magnetism works) M: 60b
Matter (Structure of matter) M: 310
Neutron star N: 155
Nuclear energy (Atoms and nuclei) N: 581 *with
diagram*; (Nuclear fission) N: 582; (Artificial
fission) N: 590
Nuclear physics N: 595
Nuclear weapon (How nuclear weapons work)
N: 596
Physics (Uncovering the secrets of the atom)
P: 442
Quark Q: 7
Radiation (In science) R: 75; (Radiation and
radioactivity) R: 75; (Particle radiation) R: 76
Star (Fusion in stars) So: 846; (Supernovae)
So: 850
Subatomic particle So: 936
Neutron activation analysis
Radiation (In science) R: 75
Radiochemistry R: 98
Neutron bomb [weapon]
Nuclear weapon (Thermonuclear weapons)
N: 597
Neutron capture [physics]
Isotope (Artificial radioisotopes) I: 477
Neutron diffraction [physics]
Molecule (Studying molecules) M: 694
Neutron star [astronomy] N: 155
Astronomy (Finding pulsars) A: 849
Bell Burnell, Jocelyn B: 242
Black hole (Galactic black holes) B: 388
Cosmic rays (Galactic cosmic rays) Ci: 1076
Gravitational wave G: 333
Magnetism (Other astronomical bodies) M: 60d
Pulsar P: 900a
Relativity (Gravitational waves) R: 212
Star (Neutron stars) So: 851
Supernova (Results of supernovae) So: 994
Telescope (X-ray telescopes) T: 109
X rays (In outer space) X: 543
Neutropenia [disorder]
Blood (White-cell abnormalities) B: 414
Neutrophil [physiology]
Blood *diagram on* B: 409; (Protecting against
disease) B: 410
Immune system (Other white blood cells) I: 88
Neuville, René [French anthropologist]
Prehistoric people (table) P: 754
Neva River [Russia]
Russia *picture on* R: 533
Nevada N: 156 *with pictures and maps*
See also the list of Related articles in the Nevada
article
United States *picture on* U: 124
Nevada, University of *See* Nevada System of
Higher Education *in this index*
Nevada Falls [falls, California]
Yosemite National Park (Waterfalls) Y: 570
Nevada Historical Society
Nevada (Museums) N: 161

Nevada National Security Site
Nevada (Service industries) N: 169-171
Nevada State Museum [Carson City]
Nevada (Museums) N: 161
Nevada System of Higher Education N: 178
Nevada (Schools) N: 160-161 *with picture*;
(Libraries) N: 161
Nevado del Ruiz [volcano, Colombia]
Colombia (The Andes Mountains) Ci: 782
Volcano (Lahars) V: 440; (table) V: 442b
Neve, Felipe de [Spanish colonial official]
Los Angeles (Settlement) L: 469
Nevelson, Louise [American sculptor] N: 178 *with
picture*
Sculpture (Assemblages) S: 257-258 *with picture*
Never Cry Wolf [book by Mowat]
Mowat, Farley M: 903
Never-Never Land [fictional place]
Peter Pan P: 325
Nevermind [recording]
Nirvana N: 424
Rock music (Alternative rock) R: 381
Neves, Tancredo de Almeida [Brazilian political
leader]
Brazil (Return to civilian government) B: 586
Neville, Emily Cheney [American author]
Newbery Medal (table) N: 359
Neville, Keith [American political leader]
Nebraska (table) N: 110
Neville, Richard [English political leader]
Warwick, Earl of W: 44
Nevins, Allan [American historian] N: 178
Nevis [island, Caribbean Sea]
Saint Kitts and Nevis S: 38
Nevis, Ben [mountain] *See* Ben Nevis *in this index*
New, Harry S. [American government official]
Hoover, Herbert Clark (table) H: 330
New Age movement [cultural movement] N: 178
New Albion [U.S. history]
California (Spanish and English exploration) C: 60
New American Practical Navigator, The [book by
Bowditch]
Bowditch, Nathaniel B: 517
New American Standard Bible
Bible (Modern English translations) B: 286
New Amsterdam [former name]
Buffalo B: 676
New Amsterdam [U.S. history]
Manhattan Island M: 141
Minuit, Peter M: 613
Netherlands (Prosperity and power) N: 148-149
New York (Exploration and settlement) N: 314
with picture
New York City (People) N: 331; (English rule)
N: 341; (Settlement) N: 341 *with picture*
Stuyvesant, Peter So: 935
United States, History of the (The Middle
Colonies) U: 154-155
New and Collected Poems [poems by Wilbur]
Wilbur, Richard W: 300
New Arabian Nights [stories by Stevenson]
Stevenson, Robert Louis (Other writings) So: 898
New Art of Writing Plays, The [book by Vega]
Vega, Lope de V: 292
New Atlantis, The [book by Bacon]
Science (The scientific revolution) S: 198-199
New Babylonian Empire [Asian history] *See* Neo-
Babylonian Empire *in this index*
New Bedford [Massachusetts] N: 179
New Bedford Whaling National Historical Park
National Park System (table: National historical
parks) N: 57
New Bedford N: 179
New Beetle [automobile]
Volkswagen AG V: 444
New Bern [North Carolina] N: 179
North Carolina (Colonial days) N: 492
New Britain [island, Papua New Guinea] N: 179
Bismarck Archipelago B: 382
New Britain [city, Connecticut] N: 179
New Brunswick [city, New Jersey] N: 179
New Brunswick [province, Canada] N: 180 *with
pictures and maps*
See also the list of Related articles in the New
Brunswick *article*
Acadia A: 21
Atlantic Provinces A: 867
Canada, Government of *picture on* C: 131
New Brunswick, University of N: 199
New Brunswick *picture on* N: 185
New Brunswick Aquarium and Marine Centre
New Brunswick (Places to visit) N: 188
New Brunswick Museum [Saint John]
New Brunswick (Museums) N: 185 *with picture*
New Bullards Bar Dam [California]
Dam (table) D: 18
New Caledonia [islands, Pacific] N: 200 *with picture*

New Caledonian crow [bird]
Crow (Kinds of crows) **Ci: 1157**
New Castle [Delaware]
Delaware (Places to visit) **D: 102**
New Castle and Frenchtown Railroad
Delaware (Transportation) **D: 108**
New Cathedral [Cuenca]
Ecuador **E: 69**
New Church
Amsterdam (The city) **A: 443-444**
New city
City (Future cities) **Ci: 593**
City planning (Building new communities)
Ci: 601
New City Hall [Munich]
Munich *picture on* **M: 927**
"New Colossus, The" [poem by Lazarus]
Statue of Liberty (The statue as a symbol)
So: 872-873
New Columbia [proposed U.S. state]
Washington, D.C. (Government changes)
W: 87-88
New comedy
Drama (New Comedy) **D: 327**
Greek literature (Drama) **G: 377**
New Connecticut [former name]
Vermont (Independent republic) **V: 334**
New Criticism [literature]
Criticism (History of literary criticism) **Ci: 1146-1147**
Ransom, John Crowe **R: 140**
New Deal [Canadian history]
Bennett, Richard Bedford (Economic reforms)
B: 253
New Deal [U.S. history] **N: 200** *with picture*
African Americans (The Great Depression)
A: 136n
Democratic Party (The New Deal) **D: 126**
Fair Labor Standards Act **F: 8**
Government regulation **G: 293**
Great Depression (The New Deal) **G: 341**
Great Society (Development) **G: 349**
Hopkins, Harry Lloyd **H: 333**
Hughes, Charles Evans **H: 408**
Jackson, Robert Houghwout **J: 16**
Johnson, Lyndon Baines (Election to the House)
J: 146
La Guardia, Fiorello Henry **L: 31**
Republican Party (After the Great Depression)
R: 256
Roosevelt, Franklin Delano **R: 450d**; (The
Hundred Days) **R: 453**; (The Supreme Court)
R: 454
Securities Exchange Act **I: 352**
United States, History of the (Recovery and
reform) **U: 193**
Wallace, Henry Agard **W: 16**
Works Progress Administration **W: 405**
New Delhi [India] **N: 202** *with picture*
Delhi **D: 115**
India **I: 108**, *picture on* **I: 111**
New Democracy Party [Greece]
Greece (Politics) **G: 353**
New Democratic Party [Canada] **N: 203**
British Columbia (Politics) **B: 628**
Canada, Government of (Political parties) **C: 136**
McLaughlin, Audrey Marlene **M: 343**
Ontario (Politics) **O: 784**
Political party (Other parties) **P: 636-637**
Saskatchewan (Politics) **S: 144**; (Economic
changes) **S: 147**; (Political changes) **S: 147**
Woodsworth, James Shaver **W: 396**
New Development Policy [Malaysian history]
Malaysia (Recent developments) **M: 102**
New drug
Drug (The new drug application) **D: 358**
Pure food and drug laws (Drugs and devices)
P: 908
New Economic Mechanism [Hungarian history]
Hungary (Beginnings of change) **H: 448**
New Economic Policy [Malaysian history]
Malaysia (Building national unity) **M: 102**
New Economic Policy [Russian history]
Communism (Under Lenin) **Ci: 892**
Lenin, V. I. (Civil war) **L: 194-195**
Russia (Civil war and the formation of the U.S.S.R.)
R: 553
Union of Soviet Socialist Republics (The New
Economic Policy) **U: 36**
New England [region, U.S.] **N: 203**
American literature (Colonial literature [1608-
1764]) **A: 414**
Colonial life in America (Economic reasons)
Ci: 788; (Geographic divisions) **Ci: 791** *with
map*; (Government and law enforcement)
Ci: 795
Cotton (American colonists) **Ci: 1092**

Dialect **D: 180**
Puritans (History) **P: 910**
United States (Regions) **U: 99** *with picture and
map*
United States, History of the (New England)
U: 154
New England, Council for [U.S. history]
Plymouth Colony (Life in Plymouth Colony)
P: 583
Plymouth Company **P: 585**
New England, Dominion of [U.S. history] **N: 203**
Plymouth Colony (Later years) **P: 584**
New England, United Colonies of [U.S. history]
New England Confederation **N: 204** *with map*
New England Air Museum [Windsor Locks]
Connecticut (Places to visit) **Ci: 960** *with picture*
New England Anti-Slavery Society [U.S. history]
Massachusetts (Progress as a state) **M: 292**
New England aster [plant]
Aster **A: 823**
New England Confederation [U.S. history] **N: 204**
with map
New England Council [1620] *See* New England,
Council for *in this index*
New England Patriots [team]
Brady, Tom **B: 547**
Football (National Football League) **F: 364**
New England Primer [textbook]
Colonial life in America (Education) **Ci: 803-804**
Literature for children (The Puritans) **L: 362**
"New England Reformers" [essay by Emerson]
Emerson, Ralph Waldo (His prose works) **E: 259**
New England Telephone Company
Telephone (The Bell System) **T: 100**
New English Bible
Bible (Modern English translations) **B: 286**
New English Dictionary on Historical Principles, A
Dictionary (Modern dictionaries) **D: 194**
New evangelization [religion]
Roman Catholic Church (John Paul II) **R: 411**
New Federalism
Nixon, Richard Milhous (The national scene)
N: 433
New Fire Ceremony
Aztec (Religion) **A: 1000-1001**
New France [Canadian history] **N: 204** *with picture
and map*
Canada, History of (The development of New
France [1604-1688]) **C: 139** *with picture and
map*
Quebec **Q: 34**; (The beginning of European rule)
Q: 30
Tennessee (Exploration) **T: 153**
New Freedom, The [book by Wilson]
Wilson, Woodrow (Presidential candidate) **W: 322**
New French Revue, The [newspaper]
French literature (The early years) **F: 522**
Gide, André **G: 188**
New Frontier [U.S. history]
Democratic Party (The New Frontier) **D: 127**
Kennedy, John Fitzgerald **K: 260**; (The 1960
campaign) **K: 263-264**; (The New Frontier)
K: 264
New Frontier Party [political party]
Japan (Recent developments) **J: 59**
New Granada [Colombian history] *See* New
Kingdom of Granada *in this index*
New Guinea [island, Pacific] **N: 206** *with pictures
and maps*
See also the list of Related articles in the New
Guinea *article*
Agriculture (Centers of domestication) **A: 154-
155**
Indonesia (Papua) **I: 234**
Mead, Margaret **M: 344**
Pacific Islands **P: 3**
Rain forest *picture on* **R: 126a**
Ship (Sailing ships in the 1900's) **S: 423** *with
picture*
World War II (The Battle of the Coral Sea) **W: 488**;
(The South Pacific) **W: 489**
New Guinea, Trust Territory of [UN]
New Guinea (History) **N: 207**
Pacific Islands (Pacific alliances and
independence movements) **P: 12-13**
New Hampshire **N: 208** *with pictures and maps*
See also the list of Related articles in the New
Hampshire *article*
Colonial life in America (Development of the
Thirteen Colonies) **Ci: 790** *with map*
United States, History of the (New England)
U: 154
Vermont (Independent republic) **V: 334**
New Hampshire, University of **N: 228** *with picture*
New Hampshire chicken
Chicken (American class chickens) **C: 441**; (table)
C: 443

**New Hampshire College of Agriculture and
Mechanic Arts**
New Hampshire, University of **N: 228**
New Hampshire Gazette [newspaper]
New Hampshire (Communication) **N: 223**
New Hampshire Grants [U.S. history]
Vermont (Land disputes) **V: 334**
New Harmony [Indiana] **N: 228** *with pictures*
Indiana (Schools) **I: 200-201**; (Places to visit)
I: 206; (Early statehood) **I: 216**
Owen, Robert (New Harmony) **O: 882**
New Harmony Gazette [magazine]
Owen, Robert Dale **O: 883**
Wright, Frances **W: 507**
New Haven [Connecticut] **N: 229** *with picture*
Blue laws **B: 420**
Eaton, Theophilus **E: 48**
New Haven Colony [U.S. history]
Connecticut (Expanding the colony) **Ci: 968**
New Hebrides Islands [islands, Pacific]
See also Vanuatu *in this index*
Mythology (Pacific Islands divinities) **M: 984**
New Heloise, The [book by Rousseau]
French literature (The Enlightenment) **F: 520-521**
Rousseau, Jean-Jacques (His ideas) **R: 493**
New historicism [literature]
Criticism (History of literary criticism) **Ci: 1146-
1147**
New Horizons [space probe]
Jupiter (History of Jupiter study) **J: 200b**
Kuiper belt **K: 392**
Pluto **P: 581**
Satellite (Exploration by spacecraft) **S: 150c**
Space exploration (Probes to Jupiter and beyond)
So: 711
New Image movement [art]
Painting (New image painting) **P: 87** *with picture*
New immigration
Immigration (The third wave) **I: 82**
New Industrial State, The [book by Galbraith]
Galbraith, John Kenneth **G: 9**
New International Version
Bible (Modern English translations) **B: 286**
New Ireland [island, Papua New Guinea] **N: 229**
Bismarck Archipelago **B: 382**
Sculpture (Pacific Islands sculpture) **S: 241-242**
with picture
New Jersey [state] **N: 230** *with pictures and maps*
See also the list of Related articles in the New
Jersey *article*
Boy Scouts (Organization) **B: 538**
Colonial life in America (Development of the
Thirteen Colonies) **Ci: 790** *with map*
Ellis Island **E: 244**
New York City (Metropolitan area) **N: 330-331**;
(Trade) **N: 333-334**
United States, History of the (The Middle
Colonies) **U: 154**
New Jersey [ship]
Battleship (The modern battleship) **B: 172**
New Jersey, College of
Princeton University (History) **P: 795**
New Jersey Devils [team]
Hockey (table: National Hockey League) **H: 281**
New Jersey Nets [team]
Basketball (table) **B: 150**
New Jersey Plan [U.S. history]
Constitution of the United States (The
compromises) **Ci: 1000**
New Jersey (The American Revolution) **N: 250-
251**
Paterson, William **P: 196**
New Jersey State Museum [Trenton]
New Jersey (Museums) **N: 235**
New Jersey Turnpike
New Jersey (Transportation) **N: 248**
New Jerusalem, The [religious group]
Swedenborgians **So: 1035**
New Journalism
Wolfe, Tom **W: 378**
New Kingdom [Egyptian history]
Egypt, Ancient (The people) **E: 136**; (The New
Kingdom) **E: 143**
Painting (Egyptian painting) **P: 40-41**
New Kingdom of Granada
Bogotá **B: 437**
Colombia (History) **Ci: 783**
New Left [political science] **N: 255**
Socialism (The New Left) **So: 561**
New Life [poems by Dante]
Dante Alighieri (His works) **D: 34**
New Line Cinema [company]
Time Warner Inc. **T: 292d**
New Living Translation [Bible]
Bible (Modern English translations) **B: 286-287**
New London [Connecticut] **N: 255**
New Look [fashion]

Dior, Christian **D:** 215
New Madrid Fault Zone
Earthquake (Intraplate quakes) **E:** 38a
Missouri (Settlement) **M:** 669
New Market [race track]
Horse racing (History) **H:** 366
New Market, Battle of [1864]
Virginia Military Institute **V:** 425
New mathematics N: 255
Mathematics (Trends in teaching mathematics)
M: 308
Set theory (History) **S:** 322
New Meaning of Treason, The [book by West]
West, Rebecca **W:** 199
New Mecklenburg
West Virginia (White settlement) **W:** 226
New Medina [district]
Casablanca **C:** 270
New Melones Dam [California]
Dam (table) **D:** 18
New Mexico N: 256 *with pictures and maps*
See also the list of *Related articles in the* New
Mexico *article*
Hispanic Americans (In the Southwest) **H:** 251
Mission life in America (Western missions)
M: 618-619
Peonage **P:** 276
United States, History of the *picture on* **U:** 151
New Mexico, University of N: 277
New Mexico *picture on* **N:** 260
New Mexico State University N: 277
New Mexico Territorial Library [Santa Fe]
New Mexico (Libraries and museums) **N:** 260
New moon
Moon (Phases) **M:** 783-784
New Mosque [Turkey]
Turkey *picture on* **T:** 503
New National Party [South Africa]
Hertzog, James Barry Munnik **H:** 217
South Africa (The rise of Afrikaner nationalism)
So: 619
New Nationalism [U.S. history]
Roosevelt, Theodore ("Bull Moose" Candidate)
R: 468
Taft, William Howard (Election of 1912) **T:** 12
New Negro: An Interpretation, The [book by
Locke]
Harlem Renaissance **H:** 61
Locke, Alain LeRoy **L:** 412
New Negro movement *See* Harlem Renaissance
in this index
New Netherland [U.S. history] **N:** 277
Dutch West India Company **D:** 393
Fire department (Early fire services) **F:** 128
Minuit, Peter **M:** 613
Netherlands (Prosperity and power) **N:** 148-149
New York **N:** 290; (Exploration and settlement)
N: 314
Stuyvesant, Peter **So:** 935
United States, History of the (The Middle
Colonies) **U:** 154
New Novel movement
French literature (The middle and late 1900's)
F: 523
Novel (After World War II) **N:** 574
New Objectivity [artistic style]
Beckmann, Max **B:** 197
New Order [German history]
Hitler, Adolf (The New Order) **H:** 266
New Order [musical group]
Rock music (New wave and mainstream rock)
R: 380c
New Orleans [Louisiana] **N:** 278 *with pictures and
maps*
Bechet, Sidney **B:** 196
Bridges, Ruby **B:** 607
Civil War, American (Capture of New Orleans)
Ci: 629
Hurricane Katrina **H:** 456 *with picture*
Ironwork, Decorative *picture on* **I:** 454
Jazz (Early jazz) **J:** 70
Louisiana **L:** 478 *with picture*; (Places to visit)
L: 488 *with picture*; (table: Average monthly
weather) **L:** 492
Louisiana Purchase **L:** 502
Mardi Gras **M:** 198
Mississippi River *picture on* **M:** 648
New Orleans, Battle of **N:** 286
New Orleans [boat]
Louisiana (Statehood) **L:** 485
New Orleans (The early 1800's) **N:** 283
Roosevelt, Nicholas J. **R:** 459
New Orleans, Battle of [1815] **N:** 285
Jackson, Andrew *picture on* **J:** 10; (Glory at New
Orleans) **J:** 9
Louisiana *picture on* **L:** 499; (Statehood) **L:** 498
War of 1812 ("The needless battle") **W:** 31 *with*

picture; (New Orleans) **W:** 33
New Orleans, University of
New Orleans (Education) **N:** 281
New Orleans Hornets [basketball team]
Basketball (table) **B:** 150
New Orleans (Recreation) **N:** 282
New Orleans Jazz National Historical Park
[Louisiana]
National Park System (table: National historical
parks) **N:** 56-57
New Orleans Saints [team]
Football (National Football League) **F:** 364;
(Violence issues) **F:** 368
New Orleans Union [newspaper]
Louisiana (Communication) **L:** 495
New Panama Canal Company [French history]
Panama Canal (The French failure) **P:** 125
New Philadelphia [former city]
Montgomery (Government and history) **M:** 766
New Play, A [play by Tamayo y Baus]
Spanish literature (The 1800's) **So:** 761
New process system
Corn (The dry-milling industry) **Ci:** 1061
New Providence Island
Bahamas **B:** 28 *with map*
New Purchase [U.S. history]
Indiana (Early statehood) **I:** 216
New Religions [religious groups]
Japan (Religion) **J:** 40-41
Shinto **S:** 401
New religious movement *See* Cult *in this index*
New Religious Right [religious movement]
Christianity (Christianity today) **C:** 526-527
Fundamentalism (Development of Protestant
fundamentalism) **F:** 556-557
New Republic [magazine]
Lippmann, Walter **L:** 346
New Revised Standard Version
Bible (The Christian Old Testament) **B:** 282;
(Modern English translations) **B:** 286
New Right [U.S. history]
United States, History of the (The revival of
conservatism) **U:** 196b
New River [aqueduct, London]
Aqueduct (Later aqueducts) **A:** 580
New River [U.S.]
Kanawha River **K:** 212
Virginia (Rivers and lakes) **V:** 412 *with map*
West Virginia *picture on* **W:** 217
New River Gorge Bridge [West Virginia]
Bridge (table: Steel arch) **B:** 603
West Virginia *picture on* **W:** 220; (Places to visit)
W: 216
New River Gorge National River [West Virginia]
National Park System (table: National parkways
and other national parklands) **N:** 56
New Salem [Illinois]
Lincoln, Abraham (Youth on the frontier) **L:** 313
New Salem State Historic Site [Illinois]
Illinois (Places to visit) **I:** 62 *with picture*
Springfield **So:** 807
New School
New York City (Education) **N:** 332
New Scotland [former name]
Nova Scotia **N:** 554
New Scotland Yard [London]
Police (In other countries) **P:** 623
New South Wales [state, Australia] **N:** 285 *with
picture and map*
Queensland (History) **Q:** 40
New South Wales Corps [Australian history]
Australia (The New South Wales Corps) **A:** 920
New Spain [Mexican history]
Mexico City (Spanish rule) **M:** 478
New Spirit [arts]
Le Corbusier **L:** 175
New Stone Age *See* Neolithic Period *in this index*
New Strategic Arms Reduction Treaty [2010]
Nuclear weapon (Arms control) **N:** 600
New Sweden [U.S. history] **N:** 287
Delaware (Exploration and early settlement)
D: 110
Stuyvesant, Peter **So:** 935
United States, History of the (The Middle
Colonies) **U:** 154-155
New Symphony Orchestra
Varèse, Edgard **V:** 285
New Taiwan dollar [money]
Yuan **Y:** 575
New Territories [region, Hong Kong]
Hong Kong **H:** 316
New Testament N: 287 *with picture*
See also the list of *Related articles in the* New
Testament *article*
Bible **B:** 279; (table) **B:** 281; (The New Testament)
B: 282 *with pictures*; (Formation of the New
Testament) **B:** 284

Christianity (The Bible) **C:** 522g-522h
Four Horsemen of the Apocalypse **F:** 437 *with
picture*
Gospels **G:** 278
Jesus Christ (Sources of information about Jesus)
J: 104
Simon, Saint **S:** 467
New Tokyo International Airport *See* Narita
International Airport *in this index*
New topographics [art]
Photography (A diversity of styles) **P:** 426-427
New town
City (Future cities) **Ci:** 593
City planning (Building new communities)
Ci: 601 *with picture*
Housing (New towns) **H:** 390
Singapore (The city of Singapore) **S:** 470
Washington, D.C. (Metropolitan area) **W:** 80-81
New Town [Chicago]
Chicago (The North Side) **C:** 423-424
New traditionalist [music]
Country music (Modern country music)
Ci: 1098c-1098d
New Valley
Egypt (Recent developments) **E:** 133-134
New Variorum Edition [book by Furness]
Shakespeare, William (Editions of the 1700's and
1800's) **S:** 369
New Voyage Around the World, A [book by
Dampier]
Dampier, William **D:** 22
New Wave [arts]
France (Motion pictures) **F:** 464
Motion picture (The New Wave in France) **M:** 870
with picture
Popular music (New forms of rock) **P:** 671
Punk rock **P:** 904
Rock music (New wave) **R:** 380c; (New wave and
mainstream rock) **R:** 380c
Science fiction (The New Wave) **S:** 206
New Way to Pay Old Debts, A [play by Massinger]
Massinger, Philip **M:** 296
New Westminster [British Columbia] **N:** 288
New Wind in a Dry Land [book by Laurence]
Laurence, Margaret **L:** 122
New wool
Wool (Types of wool) **W:** 399
New World [geography] **N:** 289
Exploration (Exploring the New World) **E:** 444
Hemisphere **H:** 181
Indian, American **I:** 136
United States, History of the (European
discoveries) **U:** 150; (Exploration and early
settlement) **U:** 151
World (How nations are grouped) **W:** 407
New World coral snake
Coral snake **Ci:** 1050
New World cotton
Cotton (New World cotton) **Ci:** 1087
New World monkey
Monkey (Kinds of monkeys) **M:** 725 *with pictures*
Primate *diagram on* **P:** 778b; (Anthropoids)
P: 778
New World porcupine [animal]
Porcupine **P:** 678
New World Symphony [music by Dvořák]
Dvořák, Antonín **D:** 393
New World vulture
Bird of prey **B:** 374a
Vulture (New World vultures) **V:** 454 *with pictures*
New World warbler [bird]
Warbler **W:** 34 *with picture*
New Year's Day N: 289 *with picture*
April Fools' Day **A:** 578
Chinese New Year **C:** 512
Islam (Holidays and celebrations) **I:** 465
New York [state] **N:** 290 *with pictures and maps*
See also the list of *Related articles in the* New York
article
Colonial life in America (Development of the
Thirteen Colonies) **Ci:** 790 *with map*
Ellis Island **E:** 244
New York City (Trade) **N:** 333-334
United States, History of the (The Middle
Colonies) **U:** 154
Vermont (Independent republic) **V:** 334
New York, City University of N: 321
New York, Port Authority of *See* Port Authority of
New York and New Jersey *in this index*
New York, State University of N: 321
Buffalo (Education) **B:** 677
New York (Schools) **N:** 294
**New York and Mississippi Valley Printing
Telegraph Company**
Western Union **W:** 241
New York aster [plant]
Flower *picture on* **F:** 278

New York Athletic Club
Track and field (Revival in the 1800's) T: 359-360
New York Botanical Garden
New York City (The Bronx) N: 328; (Parks) N: 338
New York Central Railroad
Railroad (Expansion in the United States) R: 115
New York City [New York] N: 322 *with pictures and maps*
See also the list of Related articles in the New York City *article*
Ballet (Ballet in the United States) B: 53
City Ci: 574
Colonial life in America (Commercial expansion) Ci: 792
Hall of fame (The Hall of Fame for Great Americans) H: 22
Hispanic Americans (Where Hispanic Americans live) H: 246; (Puerto Rican migration) H: 253
New York N: 290 *with pictures*; (table: Average monthly weather) N: 307
Painting (Europeans in America) P: 84
Police (Law and order in America) P: 624
Revolution, American (The campaign in New York) R: 281
September 11 terrorist attacks S: 310 *with picture*
Subway So: 949
Theater (Theater in the United States) T: 244
Triangle Shirtwaist Factory Fire T: 438
United Nations (Building UN Headquarters) U: 95
United States, History of the (The Middle Colonies) U: 154-155
United States capitals U: 199
New York City Ballet
Balanchine, George B: 37
Ballet (Ballet in the United States) B: 53
Lincoln Center for the Performing Arts L: 327
New York City Center of Music and Drama
New York City (The arts) N: 336
New York City Marathon
Running R: 521
New York City Opera
Lincoln Center for the Performing Arts L: 327
New York Cotton Exchange
Cotton (Selling) Ci: 1091
New York Curb Market [organization]
American Stock Exchange A: 430
New York fern [plant]
Plant *picture on* P: 522
New-York Gazette [newspaper]
New York (Communication) N: 312
New York Giants [team]
Football (National Football League) F: 364
McGraw, John M: 335
New York City (Sports) N: 338
New York Harbor
New York City (Trade) N: 333; (The growing city) N: 341
New York Herald [newspaper]
Journalism (The growth of U.S. newspapers) J: 174
New York Islanders
Hockey (table: National Hockey League) H: 281
New York City (Sports) N: 338
New York Jets [team]
Football (National Football League) F: 364
Namath, Joe N: 5
New York City (Sports) N: 338
New York Journal [newspaper]
Hearst, William Randolph H: 131
Outcault, Richard Felton O: 879
New York Knickerbockers [team]
Basketball (table) B: 150
Ewing, Patrick E: 435
New York City (Sports) N: 338
New York Mercantile Exchange
Commodity exchange Ci: 873
New York Mets [team]
Baseball (table) B: 130
New York City (Sports) N: 338
New York Military Band
Goldman, Edwin Franko G: 258
New York Nine [team]
Baseball *picture on* B: 133
New York Online Virtual Electronic Library
New York (Libraries) N: 294-296
New York Peace Society [organization]
Peace (The 1800's and early 1900's) P: 206
New York Philharmonic [orchestra]
Bernstein, Leonard B: 271
Lincoln Center for the Performing Arts L: 327
Masur, Kurt M: 298
New York City (The arts) N: 336
New York Port Authority *See* Port Authority of New York and New Jersey *in this index*
New York Public Library [New York City] N: 344
Lincoln Center for the Performing Arts L: 327
New York *picture on* N: 297

New York City (Libraries) N: 337
New York Rangers [team]
Hockey (table: National Hockey League) H: 281
New York City (Sports) N: 338
New York Renaissance Big Five
Basketball (The history of professional basketball) B: 154a-155
New York School of Philanthropy
Social work (History) So: 559
New York State Canal System N: 345 *with map*
Erie Canal E: 351
Great Lakes (Water routes to the sea) G: 344
New York (Waterways) N: 311
New York State Museum [Albany]
New York *picture on* N: 296; (Museums) N: 297
New York State Theater
Lincoln Center for the Performing Arts L: 327
New York Stock Exchange N: 345
American Stock Exchange A: 430
Dow Jones averages D: 315
Great Depression (The stock market crash) G: 340
New York *picture on* N: 310
New York City (Finance) N: 334; (Financial District) N: 338
New York style pizza [food]
Pizza P: 504
New York Sun [newspaper]
Dana, Charles Anderson D: 22
Journalism (The growth of U.S. newspapers) J: 174
New York Symphony Society
Damrosch, Walter Johannes D: 22
New York Times, The [newspaper]
New York (Communication) N: 312
New York City *picture on* N: 333; (Communications) N: 335
Ochs, Adolph Simon O: 668
Raymond, Henry Jarvis R: 153
Sulzberger, Arthur Hays So: 971
New York Times Co. v. Sullivan [U.S. history]
Supreme Court of the United States (Freedom of speech) So: 1001; (table) So: 1002
New York Times Index, The [reference]
A Guide to Research Skills **Research Guide:** 30
New York Tribune [newspaper]
Dana, Charles Anderson D: 22
Greeley, Horace G: 379
Journalism (The growth of U.S. newspapers) J: 174
Linotype (History) L: 339
New York University N: 345
New-York Weekly Journal [newspaper]
Journalism (Early American journalism) J: 174
New York (Under English rule) N: 314-315
Zenger, John Peter Z: 589
New York World, The [newspaper]
Crossword puzzle Ci: 1156
Journalism (The age of sensationalism) J: 175
Outcault, Richard Felton O: 879
Pulitzer, Joseph (His career) P: 886a
New York World's Fair [1939-1940]
New York City (Queens) N: 329
New York Yankees [team]
Baseball (table) B: 130; (The Babe Ruth Era) B: 135; (Postwar baseball) B: 136
Jeter, Derek B: 116
New York City (Sports) N: 338
New Yorker, The [magazine]
Addams, Charles A: 46
Cartoon (Single panel cartoons) C: 265-266
Magazine (Magazines in the 1900's) M: 45
Ross, Harold Wallace R: 482
Steinberg, Saul So: 885 *with picture*
Updike, John U: 212
New-Yorker, The [newspaper]
Greeley, Horace (His publications) G: 379
New Youth [journal]
China (The war lord period) C: 503
New Zealand N: 346 *with pictures and maps*
See also the list of Related articles in the New Zealand *article*
Bank (Australia and New Zealand) B: 92
Bird (Birds of Australia and New Zealand) B: 346 *with pictures*
Boxing (Boxing in Australia and New Zealand) B: 531
Cook, James (First Pacific voyage) Ci: 1025
Exploration (Exploring the Pacific) E: 447-448 *with map*
Girl Scouts (New Zealand) G: 199
Gold rush (Gold rushes in other countries) G: 254
Immigration (Australia and New Zealand) I: 85
Maori M: 175
Money (History of the pound) M: 709-710
National park (New Zealand) N: 42d; (table) N: 42f; (The rights of original inhabitants) N: 42i

Newspaper (In Australia and New Zealand) N: 386
Pacific Islands P: 3; (Pacific alliances and independence movements) P: 12
Parliament (Parliaments in other countries) P: 174
Railroad (In Australia and New Zealand) R: 114
Remembrance Day R: 229
Samoa (History) S: 80a-80b
Tasman, Abel Janszoon T: 48
Television (In Australia and New Zealand) T: 117
Textile (In Australia and New Zealand) T: 218
Welfare (Welfare throughout the world) W: 190
Woman suffrage (New Zealand) W: 381
Women's movement (The right to vote) W: 385
New Zealand bellbird [bird]
Bird *picture on* B: 348
New Zealand Company [British history]
New Zealand (European colonization) N: 355
New Zealand Defence Force
New Zealand (Armed forces) N: 348
New Zealand fantail [bird]
Bird *picture on* B: 348
New Zealand kaka [bird]
Bird *picture on* B: 348
New Zealand pigeon [bird]
Bird *picture on* B: 348
New Zealand Professional Boxing Association
Boxing (Boxing in Australia and New Zealand) B: 531
Newark [Delaware] N: 357
Newark [New Jersey] N: 357 *with picture*
New Jersey (table: Average monthly weather) N: 244
Riot (During the 1900's) R: 349
Newark Airport [Newark]
New Jersey (The late 1900's) N: 253
Newark Earthworks
Ohio (Places to visit) O: 690
Newark Museum [Newark]
New Jersey (Museums) N: 235
Newberry, Truman H. [American government official]
Roosevelt, Theodore (table) R: 466
Newberry Library [Chicago]
Chicago (Libraries) C: 430
Library (Research libraries) L: 247
Newbery, John [British publisher] N: 358
Literature for children (The 1700's) L: 362
Newbery Medal N: 358
Newbery Medal [award] N: 358 *with picture*
Literature for children (Awards) L: 367
Melcher, Frederic Gershom M: 389
Newbold, Joshua G. [American political leader]
Iowa (table) I: 391
Newborn center
Hospital (Recent developments) H: 374
Newcastle [Australia] N: 358
Newcastle, Duke of [British political leader]
Pitt, William P: 500
United Kingdom (table: British prime ministers) U: 72
Newcastle disease
Poultry (Raising poultry) P: 720-721
Newcastle upon Tyne [England] N: 359
Newcomen, Thomas [English inventor] N: 359
Industrial Revolution (The steam engine) I: 249
Steam engine (The first steam engines) So: 881
Newcomes, The [book by Thackeray]
Thackeray, William Makepeace (Later career) T: 220
Newell, William A. [American political leader]
New Jersey (table) N: 249
Newfoundland and Labrador N: 360 *with pictures and maps*
See also the list of Related articles in the Newfoundland and Labrador *article*
Atlantic Provinces A: 867
Bowell, Sir Mackenzie (The Newfoundland question) B: 519
Canada, Government of *picture on* C: 131
Leif Erikkson L: 186
Newfoundland dog N: 378
Dog *picture on* D: 267
Newgate Prison [London] N: 378
Fry, Elizabeth Gurney F: 549
Newhouser, Hal [American baseball player]
Baseball (table: Hall of Fame) B: 134a
Newkirk, Ingrid [American activist]
People for the Ethical Treatment of Animals P: 277
Newlands Irrigation Project
Nevada N: 156; (Natural resources) N: 169; (Mine failure and recovery) N: 176
Newman, Barnett [American painter] N: 378
Painting (Abstract Expressionism) P: 84-85
Newman, I. DeQuincey [American public official]
South Carolina (The late 1900's) So: 662-663

Newman, John Henry [British religious leader]
N: 378
Oxford Movement O: 888
Newman, Larry [American balloonist]
Balloon (Long-distance balloon flights) B: 62
Newman, Paul [American actor] N: 379 with
portrait
Motion picture (Best performance by an actor:
1986) M: 862a
Newman, Robert [American patriot]
Old North Church O: 740
Newman's Own [company]
Newman, Paul N: 379
Newport [Rhode Island] N: 379
Colonial life in America (Commercial expansion)
Ci: 792
Jazz (The spread of jazz) J: 72-73
Rhode Island pictures on R: 296, R: 297, R: 303,
R: 304; (The Gilded Age) R: 313-315
Newport, Christopher [English sea captain] N: 379
Jamestown J: 28
Newport News N: 379
Richmond (History) R: 333
Newport Bridge
Rhode Island picture on R: 303
Newport Casino
Rhode Island picture on R: 301
Newport Folk Festival
Rock music (Bob Dylan) R: 380 with picture
Newport Music Festival
Rhode Island R: 304
Newport News [Virginia] N: 379
Virginia (Manufacturing) V: 413-415 with picture
News and Observer, The [newspaper]
North Carolina (Communication) N: 489
News Corporation Limited
Murdoch, Rupert M: 930
"News Item" [poem by Parker]
Parker, Dorothy P: 169
News magazine See Newsmagazine in this index
News media See Media in this index
News photography See Photojournalism in this
index
News service [communications]
Journalism (Fields of journalism) J: 170
Newspaper (News services) N: 383 with picture
News syndicate
Journalism (News services) J: 171
Newsboard
Cardboard C: 209
Newscast
Journalism (Radio) J: 171; (Television) J: 172 with
picture
Radio (Information) R: 85
Television (Commercial television) T: 110a-110b;
(Planning and preparation) T: 110c-110d with
picture
Newseum [Washington, D.C.]
Washington, D.C. map on W: 76
Newsgroup [computing]
Computer (The Internet) Ci: 920-921
Newsmagazine
Journalism (Magazines) J: 171
Magazine (Consumer magazines) M: 42
Television (Commercial television) T: 110a-110b
Newspaper N: 380 with pictures
See also the list of Related articles in the
Newspaper article; the Communication section
of specific state, province, and country articles;
and Journalism in this index
Advertising (Newspapers) A: 74 with picture
Colonial life in America (Communication) Ci: 806
Communication (The 1800's) Ci: 881; (The digital
age) Ci: 885
Employment agency E: 263
Fourth estate F: 438
Franklin, Benjamin (Publisher) F: 487
Journalism (Fields of journalism) J: 170 with
picture; (History) J: 174
Magazine M: 42
Public opinion (The press) P: 860
Publishing (Scheduling, printing, and posting)
P: 867; (Newspapers) P: 868
Spanish-American War So: 753
Telegraph (Uses for the telegraph) T: 91
Writing W: 511
Newspaper Rock [anthropology]
Arizona picture on A: 688
Newspaper syndicate [communications]
Newspaper (News services) N: 383
Newsprint [paper]
Newspaper (Kinds of newspapers) N: 380
Paper (Special kinds of paper) P: 136
Newsroom
Newspaper picture on N: 380
Newsstand
Magazine (Sales) M: 44

Newt [animal] N: 388 with picture
Amphibian pictures on A: 441
Newton [unit of measure] N: 388
Force (Characteristics of force) F: 369
Metric system (Mechanics) M: 437-440
Power P: 727
Weight W: 180
Newton, Cam [American football player]
Football (table) F: 363
Newton, Eddie [American entertainer]
Jones, Casey J: 157
Newton, Huey P. [American social reformer]
African Americans (Black militancy) A: 136q-136r
Black Panther Party B: 390
Newton, Sir Isaac [English physicist] N: 388 with
pictures
Astronomy (Developing the modern view) A: 847
Calculus (History) C: 25
Châtelet, Marquise Du C: 388
Color (Newton and Goethe) Ci: 826
Dynamics D: 397
Energy (Calculating quantities of energy) E: 274
Force (Overcoming inertia) F: 369; (Gravitation)
F: 370
Gravitation (Newton's law of gravitation) G: 331
Inertia I: 262
Light (Modern study) L: 285
Mathematics (Mathematics and the scientific
revolution) M: 306-307
Momentum M: 698
Motion (Newton's laws of motion) M: 844
Newton's rings N: 390
Physics picture on P: 441; (Newton) P: 439
Planet (Kepler's third law) P: 509-510
Quantum mechanics Q: 6
Radiation (Electromagnetic waves) R: 80
Relativity (Inertial frames) R: 210-211; (General
relativity) R: 211
Science (Expressing findings mathematically)
S: 195; (The scientific revolution) S: 198
Space exploration (The dawn of the space age)
So: 706
Spectroscopy So: 772
Telescope (Reflecting telescopes) T: 104
Tide (The study of the tides) T: 282
Time (Time in classical physics) T: 292a
Newton, Wayne [American singer] N: 390
Newtonian equation [physics]
Energy (Calculating quantities of energy) E: 274
Newton's constant [physics] See Gravitational
constant in this index
Newton's laws of motion [physics]
Aerodynamics (Lift) A: 85-86
Airplane (Gravity and lift) A: 220-221
Force (Acceleration) F: 369-370
Jet propulsion (The principle of jet propulsion)
J: 110
Mass M: 268
Motion (Newton's laws of motion) M: 844
Newton, Sir Isaac (The theories of motion and
gravitation) N: 388
Physics (Newton) P: 439
Relativity (Inertial frames) R: 210-211; (General
relativity) R: 211
Rocket (How rockets work) R: 385
Space exploration (The dawn of the space age)
So: 706
Newton's rings [physics] N: 390 with picture
Newton's theory of gravitation [physics]
Force (Gravitation) F: 370
G G: 2
Gravitation (Newton's theory of gravitation)
G: 331
Mass (Mass and weight) M: 268
Newton, Sir Isaac (The theories of motion and
gravitation) N: 388
Newtowne [former name]
Cambridge C: 75
NEXRAD [network]
Weather (Weather radar) W: 162-163
Next of kin [law] N: 390
Nexus One [phone]
Google Inc. G: 270
Ney, Michel [French general] N: 390
Napoleon (Exile to Elba) N: 16
Neyman, Jerzy [English statistician]
Statistics (History) So: 869-870
Nez Perce Indians N: 391
Indian, American picture on I: 166
Indian wars (The Nez Perce War [1877]) I: 194
Lewis and Clark expedition (The homeward
journey) L: 222d
Nez Perce National Historical Park [Idaho]
National Park System (table: National historical
parks) N: 57
Nez Perce War [1877]
Idaho (Indian fighting) I: 44

Indian, American (After European contact) I: 166
Indian wars (The Nez Perce War [1877]) I: 194
with picture
Joseph, Chief J: 168
Montana (Indian fighting) M: 758 with picture
Oregon (Indian treaties and conflicts) O: 846-848
NF [disorder] See Neurofibromatosis in this index
NFB [organization]
Blindness (Education and training) B: 403
NFFE [organization]
American Federation of Government Employees
A: 409
NFL [organization] See National Football League
in this index
NFL Europa [organization]
Football (New professional leagues) F: 368
NFL Europe [organization]
Football (New professional leagues) F: 368
Ngalops [people]
Bhutan (People) B: 277
Ngami, Lake [Botswana]
Stanley and Livingstone (Livingstone's
discoveries) So: 837 with map
Ngardok, Lake [Palau]
Melekeok M: 389
NGC 598 [galaxy] See Triangulum Galaxy in this
index
NGC 1365 [galaxy]
Galaxy picture on G: 8a
NGC 6093 [star cluster]
Star cluster picture on So: 853
Ngendandumwe, Pierre [African political leader]
Burundi (History) B: 713-714
Ngeneo, Bernard [Kenyan anthropologist]
Prehistoric people (table) P: 754
Ngewo [religion]
Sierra Leone (People) S: 451
NGL [chemical] See Natural gas liquids in this index
Ngo Dinh Diem [Vietnamese political leader]
N: 391
Geneva Accords G: 87
Viet Cong V: 363
Vietnam (The Vietnam War) V: 371
Vietnam War (The divided country) V: 373-374;
(The Buddhist crisis) V: 374
Ngo Dinh Nhu [Vietnamese political leader]
Ngo Dinh Diem N: 391
Vietnam War (The Buddhist crisis) V: 374
Ngo Quyen [Vietnamese ruler]
Vietnam (Nam Viet) V: 369
Ngor, Haing S. [Cambodian-American actor]
Asian Americans (Notable Asian American "firsts")
A: 812f
Motion picture (Best performance by an actor in
a supporting role: 1984) M: 862b
Ngorongoro National Park [Tanzania]
National park (table) N: 42f
Nguyen [dynasty]
Vietnam (Independence) V: 370
Nguyen Ai Quoc [pseudonym]
Ho Chi Minh N: 270
Nguyen Anh [Vietnamese ruler]
Vietnam (Independence) V: 370
Nguyen Du [Vietnamese poet]
Vietnam (The arts) V: 366-368
Nguyen Huy Thiep [Vietnamese author]
Vietnam (The arts) V: 367-368
Nguyen Sang [Vietnamese artist]
Vietnam (The arts) V: 366
Nguyen Trai [Vietnamese author]
Vietnam (The arts) V: 366-368
Nguyen Tu Nghiem [Vietnamese artist]
Vietnam (The arts) V: 366
Ngwane II [Swazi chief]
Swaziland (History) So: 1019
Ngwenyama [title]
Swaziland (Government) So: 1017
Nhialic [African god]
Dinka D: 205
NHL [organization] See National Hockey League in
this index
NHRA [organization]
Automobile racing (Racing organizations) A: 976
NHS [medicine] See National Health Service Corps
in this index
NHS [transportation] See National Highway System
in this index
Nhu, Ngo Dinh [Vietnamese political leader] See
Ngo Dinh Nhu in this index
Ni [symbol]
Nickel N: 404
Ni-Cad [electricity] See Nickel-cadmium battery in
this index
Ni Chonaill, Eibhlin Dubh [Irish poet]
Irish literature (Modern works in Gaelic) I: 431
Ni Tsan [Chinese artist]
Painting (Chinese painting) P: 44-46

Niacin [vitamin]
Vitamin (Niacin) **V: 431**; (table) **V: 431**
Cholesterol (Treatment of high blood cholesterol) **C: 520**
Goldberger, Joseph **G: 255**
Nutrition (Vitamins) **N: 626**
Pellagra **P: 232**
Niagara [ship]
Erie **E: 351**
Pennsylvania (Places to visit) **P: 254** *with picture*
Perry, Oliver Hazard **P: 294** *with picture*
Niagara Escarpment [region, Canada]
Hamilton (The city) **H: 30**
Niagara Falls (History) **N: 392**
Ontario (Land regions) **O: 776**
Niagara Falls [painting by Church]
Church, Frederic Edwin **C: 542** *with picture*
Niagara Falls [waterfall, Canada-U.S.] **N: 391** *with pictures and map*
Buffalo (Economy) **B: 677**
New York (Places to visit) **N: 302** *with picture*; (Waterfalls) **N: 306**
Niagara River **N: 394**
Ontario (Places to visit) **O: 774** *with picture*
Tesla, Nikola (The alternating-current system) **T: 181**
Waterfall (table: Famous waterfalls of North America) **W: 142** *with picture*
Niagara Falls Park [park, U.S.]
Niagara Falls (History) **N: 392-393**
Niagara Movement [U.S. history] **N: 394**
African Americans (The rise of new black leaders) **A: 136l**
Du Bois, W. E. B. **D: 372**
Niagara River [Canada-U.S.] **N: 394**
Lake Ontario **L: 43** *with map*
Niagara Falls **N: 391** *with picture*
River (table) **R: 352**
Niamey [Niger] **N: 395**
Niger (People) **N: 407-408**
Nian gao [food]
Chinese New Year **C: 512**
Niari Valley [Congo]
Congo, Republic of the (Land) **Ci: 940d-940e**
Nib [device]
Pen (Fountain pens) **P: 233**
Nib [food product]
Chocolate (Manufacturing chocolate) **C: 518**
Nibelung [mythology]
Nibelungenlied **N: 395**
Nibelungenlied [poem] **N: 395**
Brunhild **B: 652**
German literature (The Germanic epic) **G: 138**
Mythology (Teutonic heroes) **M: 9874**
Siegfried **S: 449**
NIC [electronic device] *See* Network interface card *in this index*
Nicaea, Councils of *See* Nicene Council *in this index*
Nicaragua **N: 396** *with pictures and maps*
See also Central America *in this index; and the list of Related articles in the* Nicaragua *article*
Central America (Attempts at unification) **C: 355-356**
Hispanic Americans (Central American migration) **H: 255**
Iran-contra affair (Background) **I: 406b**
Latin America (Return to civilian government) **L: 111**
United Nations *picture on* **U: 91**
Walker, William **W: 14**
Nicaragua, Lake *See* Lake Nicaragua *in this index*
Nicaragua, National University of
León **L: 198**
Nicaragua Canal [U.S. history]
Nicaragua (The United States and Nicaragua) **N: 400**
Nicarao Indians
Nicaragua **N: 396**; (The colonial period) **N: 398**
Nice [France] **N: 401**
Nice, Harry W. [American political leader]
Maryland (table) **M: 255**
Nicene-Constantinopolitan Creed [religion]
Eastern Orthodox Churches (Doctrines) **E: 46**
Nicene Council [325]
Arianism **A: 661**
Arius **A: 669**
Athanasius, Saint **A: 853**
Constantine the Great **Ci: 993**
Nicene Councils **N: 402**
Roman Catholic Church (The recognition of Christianity) **R: 405**
Trinity **T: 447**
Nicene Council [787]
Nicene Councils **N: 402**
Nicene Councils [religious history] **N: 402**
Eastern Orthodox Churches (History) **E: 45**
Nicene Creed [religion]

Christianity (Creeds and catechisms) **C: 522h**; (Constantine) **C: 523-524**
Constantine the Great **Ci: 993**
Nicene Councils **N: 402**
Roman Catholic Church (Roman Catholic beliefs) **R: 403**
Niche [ecology] *See* Ecological niche *in this index*
Niche media
Journalism (Fields of journalism) **J: 170**
Magazine (Magazines in the 1900's) **M: 45**
Niche product [commerce]
Internet (Connected customers) **I: 350e**
Nichol, Barrie Phillip [Canadian poet]
Canadian literature (Modern Canadian poets) **C: 161**
Nicholas I, Saint [pope]
Pope (table) **P: 666**
Nicholas I [czar of Russia] **N: 402**
Russia (table: Czars and empresses) **R: 549**; (Nicholas I) **R: 551**
Nicholas II [pope] **N: 402**
Pope (The early Middle Ages) **P: 663**
Nicholas II [czar of Russia] **N: 402** *with picture*
Duma (The early Duma) **D: 381**
Finland (Control by Russia) **F: 116-117**
Hague Conventions **H: 7**
Lenin, V. I. (Young revolutionist) **L: 192**
Peace (The 1800's and early 1900's) **P: 206**
Rasputin, Grigori Efimovich **R: 145**
Romanov **R: 426**
Russia (table: Czars and empresses) **R: 549**; (Nicholas II) **R: 551**; (The Revolution of 1905) **R: 552**; (The February Revolution) **R: 553**
Russian Revolution of 1917 **R: 565**
Saint Petersburg [Russia] (History) **S: 55**
Stalin, Joseph (Boyhood and education) **So: 825**
Union of Soviet Socialist Republics (The February Revolution) **U: 35**
World War I (The Russian Revolution) **W: 461-462**
Nicholas III [pope]
Pope (table) **P: 666**
Nicholas IV [pope]
Pope (table) **P: 666**
Nicholas V [antipope]
Pope (table) **P: 666**
Nicholas V [pope] **N: 403**
Pope (table) **P: 666**
Nicholas, Saint [early Christian] **N: 403**
Christmas (In The Netherlands, Belgium, and Luxembourg) **C: 531** *with picture*; (Gift giving) **C: 534**
Netherlands (Holidays and recreation) **N: 141**
Santa Claus **S: 113**
Nicholas, Wilson Cary [American political leader]
Virginia (table) **V: 417**
Nicholas Nickleby [book by Dickens]
Dickens, Charles (The first phase) **D: 188**
Nicholas of Cusa [German religious leader] **N: 403**
Nicholls, Francis T. [American political leader]
Louisiana (table) **L: 496**
Nichols, Kid [American baseball player]
Baseball (table: Hall of Fame) **B: 134a**
Nichols, Mike [American director] **N: 403**
Motion picture (Best achievement in directing: 1967) **M: 862**
Nichols, Terry L. [American public figure]
Oklahoma City bombing **O: 737**
Nichols Arboretum [Ann Arbor]
Michigan (Places to visit) **M: 498**
Nicholson, Ben [British artist] **N: 404**
Nicholson, Jack [American actor] **N: 404** *with portrait*
Motion picture (Best performance by an actor: 1975, 1997) **M: 862a**; (Best performance by an actor in a supporting role: 1983) **M: 862b**
Nicholson, Jim [American government official]
Veterans Affairs, Department of (table) **V: 343**
Nicias [Greek political leader]
Peloponnesian War **P: 232**
Nicias, Peace of [ancient Greece]
Peloponnesian War **P: 232**
Nickajack Dam [Tennessee River]
Tennessee River **T: 158**
Nickel [element] **N: 404**
Brass **B: 565**
Greater Sudbury **G: 350**
Manitoba (The mid-1900's) **M: 162-163**
Monel metal **M: 703**
Thompson **T: 262**
Nickel [money] **N: 404** *with pictures*
Money (Nickels) **M: 714**
Nickel-cadmium battery
Battery (Types and uses of batteries) **B: 171**
Nickel Capital of the World [nickname]
Greater Sudbury **G: 350**
Nickel metal hydride battery [electricity]
Battery (Metal hydride batteries) **B: 170**

Nickelodeon [theater]
Motion picture (The nickelodeon) **M: 863** *with picture*
Nicklaus, Jack [American golfer] **N: 405**
Golf (British Open) **G: 264**
Nickname
Name (Nicknames) **N: 7**
Nicks [English bandit]
Turpin, Dick **T: 519**
Nicobar Islands [India]
Bay of Bengal **B: 175**
Nicodemus National Historic Site [Kansas]
National Park System (table: National historic sites) **N: 52-53**
Nicol, Mary Douglas [British anthropologist] *See* Leakey, Mary Douglas *in this index*
Nicola, Lewis [American military leader]
Washington, George (Turning down a crown) **W: 100**
Nicolet, Jean [French explorer] **N: 405**
Michigan (French exploration and settlement) **M: 508**
Wisconsin (European exploration and settlement) **W: 365**
Nicolle, Charles Jules Henri [French physiologist]
Nobel Prizes (Physiology or medicine: 1928) **N: 445**
Nicollet Mall
Minneapolis (Downtown redevelopment) **M: 583** *with picture*
Nicomachean Ethics [book by Aristotle]
Aristotle (Ethics and politics) **A: 664**
Nicosia [Cyprus] **N: 405**
Cyprus **Ci: 1205**, *picture on* **Ci: 1207**
Nicotine [chemical] **N: 405**
Cigarette **C: 553**
Drug abuse (Tobacco) **D: 361**
Insecticide (Botanical insecticides) **I: 302**
Smoking **S: 520**; (Smoking regulations) **S: 521**
Tobacco **T: 305**
Nicotine patch [drug]
Drug abuse (Treatment of substance use disorders) **D: 364**
Nictitating membrane [zoology]
Bird (Smell, taste, and touch) **B: 365**
Eye (Eyes of animals) **E: 469** *with picture*
Nidhoggr [legendary creature]
Mythology (The construction of the world) **M: 986**
Niebuhr, H. Richard [American theologian] **N: 405**
Christianity (Neo-Orthodoxy) **C: 526**
Niebuhr, Reinhold [American theologian] **N: 405**
Christianity (Neo-Orthodoxy) **C: 526**
Niekro, Phil [American baseball player]
Baseball (table: Hall of Fame) **B: 134a**
Niello [art]
Islamic art (Metalware) **I: 469-470**
Nielsen, Carl August [Danish composer] **N: 406**
Nielsen Media Research
Television (Measuring a program's success) **T: 113**
Niemen River [Belarus] *See* Neman River *in this index*
Niemeyer, Oscar [Brazilian architect] **N: 406** *with picture*
Brasília (History) **B: 565**
Brazil (The arts) **B: 576-577** *with picture*
Niépce, Joseph Nicéphore [French inventor] **N: 406**
Communication (The 1800's) **Ci: 881**
Photography (The invention of photography) **P: 422** *with picture*
Nietzsche, Elisabeth [sister of]
Nietzsche, Friedrich (His life) **N: 407**
Nietzsche, Friedrich [German philosopher] **N: 406**
Ethics (Nietzsche) **E: 367**
Existentialism **E: 437**
Philosophy (Philosophy in the 1800's) **P: 390**
Nieuwe Kerk [church, Netherlands]
Amsterdam (The city) **A: 443-444**
Delft **D: 115**
Nieuwe Maas [river, Netherlands]
Rotterdam **R: 489**
Nifedipine [drug]
Calcium channel blocker **C: 21**
Niflheim [Norse mythology]
Mythology (Teutonic mythology) **M: 985**
Niger **N: 407** *with picture and map*
Flag *picture on* **F: 199**
French West Africa **F: 528** *with map*
Hausa **H: 86**
Niger-Congo [language]
Language *map on* **L: 65**; (Other language families) **L: 66**
Niger-Kordofanian language
Africa (Languages) **A: 105**
Niger River [Africa] **N: 409**
Exploration (The exploration of Africa) **E: 448**

Mali (Land and climate) **M:** 107 *with map*
Niger (Land and climate) **N:** 408-409
Nigeria (Niger Delta) **N:** 415 *with picture and map*
Park, Mungo **P:** 168
River (table) **R:** 352
Nigeria N: 410 *with pictures and maps*
　See also the list of Related articles in the Nigeria
　article
Benin **B:** 250
Clothing *picture on* **Ci:** 692
Flag *picture on* **F:** 199
Hausa **H:** 86
Igbo **I:** 47
Oil spill (Responses) **O:** 707-708
Sculpture (African sculpture) **S:** 239
Nigeriens [people]
Niger (People) **N:** 407
Nigger of the "Narcissus," The [book by Conrad]
Conrad, Joseph **Ci:** 735
Nigh, George [American political leader]
Oklahoma (table) **O:** 730
Night *See* Day and night *in this index*
Night [book by Wiesel]
Wiesel, Elie **W:** 299
Night [sculpture by Michelangelo]
Sculpture (Michelangelo) **S:** 252-253 *with picture*
Night After Night [film]
West, Mae **W:** 199
"Night and Day" [song by Porter]
Porter, Cole **P:** 682
Night blindness
Blindness **B:** 401
Eye (Diseases of the retina) **E:** 467
Night-blooming cereus
Flower *picture on* **F:** 272
Night Café, The [painting by Van Gogh]
Van Gogh, Vincent **V:** 282
Night crawler *See* Earthworm *in this index*
Night eating syndrome [eating disorder]
Eating disorder **E:** 48
Night game
Baseball (Depression and war) **B:** 136
Night in Acadie, A [book by Chopin]
Chopin, Kate **C:** 521
Night in Lisbon, The [book by Remarque]
Remarque, Erich Maria **R:** 228
Night monkey
Monkey *picture on* **M:** 728; (Kinds of monkeys)
　M: 725
'night Mother [play by Norman]
Norman, Marsha **N:** 455
Night Must Fall [book by Williams]
Williams, Emlyn **W:** 310
Night of Broken Glass [German history] *See*
Kristallnacht *in this index*
Night on Bald Mountain, A [music by Mussorgsky]
Mussorgsky, Modest **M:** 967
Night school [education]
School (Other kinds of schools) **S:** 182
Night shade [plant] *See* Nightshade *in this index*
Night sweat [disorder]
Hormone replacement therapy **H:** 338
Menopause **M:** 402
Night vision systems [electronic devices] **N:** 419
　with picture
Night Watch, The [painting by Rembrandt]
Netherlands *picture on* **N:** 144
Rembrandt (The last years: 1640-1669) **R:** 229
Nightglow [astronomy]
Venus (Flights to Venus) **V:** 313-314
Nighthawk [bird] **N:** 419 *with picture*
Bird *picture on* **B:** 363
Nighthawks [painting by Hopper]
Hopper, Edward **H:** 334
Nightingale [bird] **N:** 419 *with picture*
Bird *picture on* **B:** 344d; (Birds of Europe) **B:** 344c
Thrush **T:** 271
Nightingale, Florence [British nurse] **N:** 420 *with*
　portrait
Medicine *picture on* **M:** 374
Nursing (History) **N:** 619
Nightingale, William [father of]
Nightingale, Florence (Early years) **N:** 420
Nightingale Training School for Nurses [London]
Nightingale, Florence (Return to England) **N:** 420
Nursing (History) **N:** 619
Nightjar [bird]
Goatsucker **G:** 242 *with picture*
"Nightline" [television program]
Koppel, Ted **K:** 365
Nightmare N: 420
Nights [poem by Musset]
French literature (Romantic poetry) **F:** 521
Nights of Cabiria [film]
Fellini, Federico **F:** 68
Nightshade [botany] **N:** 421 *with pictures*
　See also the Related articles in the Nightshade

article
Flower (table) **F:** 301 *with picture*
Poisonous plant **P:** 602
NIH [organization] *See* National Institutes of Health
in this index
Nihilism [philosophy] **N:** 421
Russian literature (Early realism) **R:** 562
Turgenev, Ivan **T:** 500
Nihon Sumo Kyokai [organization]
Sumo **So:** 973
Nihongi [book]
Jimmu **J:** 127
Shinto **S:** 401
Niihau [island]
Hawaii (Niihau) **H:** 102
Niinistö, Sauli [Finnish political leader]
Finland (Recent developments) **F:** 118
Nijinsky, Vaslav [Russian dancer] **N:** 421 *with*
　picture
Ballet (Ballet in Russia) **B:** 52 *with picture*
Nikau palm [tree]
Tree *picture on* **T:** 427
Nike [Greek mythology]
Winged Victory **W:** 339
Nike, Temple of [Athens]
Acropolis **A:** 30
Nikkei Index [economics]
Stock exchange (Stock prices and indexes)
　So: 904
Nikko National Park [Japan]
National park (table) **N:** 42f
Nikoli [company]
Sudoku **So:** 957
Nikolić, Tomislav [Serbian political leader]
Serbia (Recent developments) **S:** 316a
Nile, Battle of the [1798]
Nelson, Horatio (Battle of the Nile) **N:** 122
Nile crocodile
Crocodile (Kinds of crocodiles) **Ci:** 1149-1150
Reptile **R:** 250 *with picture*
Nile Delta [region, Egypt]
Arabs (Land of the Arabs) **A:** 585-586
Delta **D:** 118 *with map*
Egypt (The land) **E:** 125 *with map*
Nile River (The Nile Valley and Nile Delta) **N:** 423
　with map
Nile monitor [reptile]
Lizard *picture on* **L:** 400
Nile River [Africa] **N:** 422 *with pictures and map*
Bruce, James **B:** 647
Egypt (The land) **E:** 125; (Agriculture) **E:** 128
Egypt, Ancient (The land) **E:** 135-136 *with picture*
　and map
Exploration (The exploration of Africa) **E:** 448
Flood (River floods) **F:** 236-237
Inland waterway **I:** 274
Irrigation (History) **I:** 459
Lake Victoria **L:** 48
Mythology (Egyptian mythology) **M:** 978
River (table) **R:** 352
Sudan (Land and climate) **So:** 951; (Way of life)
　So: 951
Nile Valley [region, Egypt]
Africa *picture on* **A:** 107
Arabs (Land of the Arabs) **A:** 585-586
Egypt (The land) **E:** 125 *with picture*
Nile River (The Nile Valley and Nile Delta) **N:** 423
　with map
World, History of the (The Nile Valley) **W:** 424
Niles, John M. [American government official]
Van Buren, Martin (table) **V:** 273
Nilgai [animal]
Antelope (Kinds of antelope) **A:** 542
Nilo-Saharan [language]
Africa (Languages) **A:** 105
Language on **L:** 65; (Other language
　families) **L:** 66
Nilson, Lars [Swedish chemist]
Scandium **S:** 171
Nilsson, Birgit [Swedish singer]
Opera *picture on* **O:** 807
Nilsson, Leopoldo Torre [Argentina director]
Latin America (Motion pictures) **L:** 101-102
Nimba Mountains
Liberia (Land and climate) **L:** 230
Nimbostratus cloud
Cloud (Middle clouds) **Ci:** 707
Nimeiri, Gaafar [Sudanese political leader]
Juba **J:** 178
Sudan (Independence) **So:** 953
Nîmes [France]
World, History of the *picture on* **W:** 429
Nimitz [ship]
Aircraft carrier (The United States carrier fleet)
　A: 206
Nimitz, Chester William [American admiral] **N:** 423
World War II (The Battle of Midway) **W:** 488;

(Island hopping in the Central Pacific) **W:** 489;
　(The South Pacific) **W:** 489
Niña [ship]
Caravel **C:** 202
Columbus, Christopher (First voyage westward)
　Ci: 858-859 *with picture*
Exploration (Columbus reaches America) **E:** 444
Nine-ball [game]
Billiards (Pool) **B:** 305
Nine-banded armadillo [animal]
Armadillo **A:** 717 *with picture*
Nine-day queen *See* Grey, Lady Jane *in this index*
9/11 [U.S. history] *See* September 11 terrorist
attacks *in this index*
9/11 Commission
Bush, George Walker (Homeland security)
　B: 722g; (Commission report) **B:** 722j
September 11 terrorist attacks (Investigations)
　S: 310b
9/11 Memorial [New York City] *See* National
September 11 Memorial and Museum *in this*
index
Nine Inch Nails [rock group]
Rock music (Alternative rock) **R:** 381
Nine-Power Treaty [1921-1922]
Washington Conference **W:** 109
Nine-spotted ladybug
Beetle *picture on* **B:** 218
9-volt battery
Battery *diagram on* **B:** 170
Nine-wicket croquet [game]
Croquet **Ci:** 1154
Ninepins [game]
Bowling (Other kinds of bowling) **B:** 524b
1984 [book by Orwell]
English literature (Literature after World War II)
　E: 322-323
Orwell, George **O:** 860
1919 [book by Dos Passos]
Dos Passos, John **D:** 311
Nineteenth Amendment
Civil rights (The struggle for women's rights)
　Ci: 609
Constitution of the United States (Amendment
　19) **Ci:** 1015
Sex discrimination (Sex-based laws) **S:** 335
Stanton, Elizabeth Cady **So:** 839
United States, History of the (The Roaring
　Twenties) **U:** 189
Woman suffrage (The 19th Amendment) **W:** 381
Women's movement (The right to vote) **W:** 385
19th Century Village [New York]
New York (Places to visit) **N:** 302
98th meridian [geography]
Western frontier life in America **W:** 232
Ninety-Five Theses [religion]
Luther, Martin (The Ninety-Five Theses) **L:** 527
Reformation (Martin Luther) **R:** 197
Tetzel, Johann **T:** 183
94th Pursuit Squadron
Air Force, United States (World War I) **A:** 194
Ninety-Nines [organization]
Earhart, Amelia (Flights) **E:** 14
Ninety Six National Historic Site [South Carolina]
National Park System (table: National historic
　sites) **N:** 52-53
Ninety-Three [book by Hugo]
Hugo, Victor (His works) **H:** 410
Nineveh [ancient city] **N:** 423
Nahum, Book of **N:** 3
World, History of the (Civilizations of southwest
　Asia) **W:** 426
Ninfale Fiesolano [poem by Boccaccio]
Boccaccio, Giovanni **B:** 433
Ningaui [animal]
Marsupial mouse **M:** 233 *with picture*
Ningbo [China]
Treaty port **T:** 409
Ninhursag [goddess]
Mythology (The influence of Sumerian
　mythology) **M:** 977
Ninja [Japanese history]
Martial arts (Japanese martial arts) **M:** 234
Terrorism (Early terrorism) **T:** 178
Ninjas [political group]
Congo, Republic of the (History) **Ci:** 940e-940f
Ninjutsu [sport]
Martial arts (Japanese martial arts) **M:** 234
Niños envueltos [food]
Christmas (In Latin America) **C:** 532
Nintendo [manufacturer] **N:** 423
Electronic game (History) **E:** 204d
Nintendo Entertainment System
Electronic game (The Nintendo revolution)
　E: 204d
Nintendo **N:** 424
Nintendo 64 [machine]

Electronic game (Renewed interest in consoles)
E: 204e
Ninth Amendment
Constitution of the United States Ci: 1013
Ninurta [Assyrian god]
Assyria (Religion) A: 821
Ninus [mythology]
Semiramis S: 293
Niobe [Greek mythology] N: 424
Niobium [element] N: 424
Niobrara National Scenic Riverway [Nebraska-
South Dakota]
National Park System (table: National parkways
and other national parklands) N: 56
Niobrara River [Nebraska-Wyoming]
Nebraska (Rivers and lakes) N: 106
Niokolo-Koba National Park [Senegal]
National park (table) N: 42f
NIOSH [organization]
National Institute for Occupational Safety and
Health N: 39
Nipkow, Paul Gottlieb [German physicist]
Television (Early development) T: 127
Nipple [anatomy]
Breast B: 590 with diagram
Mammal (Care of the young) M: 124 with picture
Nippon Oil [company]
Manufacturing (table) M: 170
Nirenberg, Marshall Warren [American
biochemist]
Cell (The 1900's) C: 337-338
Heredity (The chemistry of genes) H: 208-209
Nobel Prizes (Physiology or medicine: 1968)
N: 446
Nirvana [religion] N: 424
Bodhisattva B: 434
Buddha (The search for enlightenment) B: 667
Buddhism (Buddha) B: 667
Dharma D: 178
Religion (Buddhism) R: 220
Nirvana [rock group] N: 424 with picture
Rock music (Alternative rock) R: 381
Nisan [month]
Calendar (The Hebrew calendar) C: 29
Nisga'a Treaty
British Columbia (Recent developments) B: 631
Nishani, Bujar [Albanian political leader]
Albania (Recent developments) A: 309
Nishizawa, Hiroyoshi [Japanese aviator]
Ace A: 24
Niska, Maralin [American singer]
Opera picture on O: 808
Nisqually Indians
Salish Indians (The Coast Salish) S: 67
Nissan Motor Company
Automobile picture on A: 971
Manufacturing (table) M: 170
Sports car So: 802
Nit [entomology]
Head lice H: 123
Louse L: 507
NIT [sports]
Basketball (The history of college basketball)
B: 154a
Nit-picking
Head lice H: 124
Niter [mineral] See Saltpeter in this index
Nitrate [chemistry] N: 425
Eutrophication (Eutrophication and water
pollution) E: 421
Nitrate bacteria
Nitrogen cycle N: 426 with diagram
Nitrate of silver See Silver nitrate in this index
Nitric acid [chemical] N: 425
Acid rain A: 27
Lithography (How lithography works) L: 387
Nitrogen (Nitrogen and life) N: 425
Nitric oxide [chemistry]
Catalysis C: 297
Nitrifying bacteria
Nitrogen cycle N: 426
Nitrile [chemistry]
Saturn (Satellites) S: 151
Nitrite [chemistry] N: 425
Bacon B: 18
Sausage S: 163
Nitrite bacteria
Nitrogen cycle N: 426 with diagram
Nitrocarbonitrate [chemical]
Dynamite (History) D: 397
Nitrocellulose
Guncotton G: 441
Gunpowder (Kinds of gunpowder) G: 441
Nitrogen [element] N: 425
Air (Gases of the air) A: 169 with diagram
Bends B: 247
Diving, Underwater (Dangers of underwater

diving) D: 246-247
Fertilizer (Inorganic fertilizers) F: 79
Haber process H: 2
Life (The chemical basis of life) L: 277 with
diagram
Liquid air L: 346
Nitrogen cycle N: 426 with diagram
Star (Hydrogen fusion) So: 846-847
Triton T: 448
Weather (What causes weather) W: 157
Nitrogen cycle [biology] N: 426 with diagram
Bacteria (Helpful bacteria) B: 19
Nitrogen (Nitrogen and life) N: 425
Root (The importance of roots) R: 471
Nitrogen deposition
Soil pollution So: 576
Nitrogen fixation [chemistry]
Cropping system Ci: 1153
Nitrogen (Nitrogen and life) N: 425
Nitrogen cycle N: 426
Nitrogen-fixing bacteria
Nitrogen cycle N: 426 with diagram
Nitrogen freezing
Cryobiology Ci: 1165
Food, Frozen (Cryogenic freezing) F: 338
Nitrogen monoxide [gas] See Nitrous oxide in
this index
Nitrogen narcosis [disorder]
Diving, Underwater (Dangers of underwater
diving) D: 246-247
Helium (Uses) H: 176 with picture
Nitrogen oxides [gas]
Acid rain A: 27
Catalytic converter C: 298
Nitrogen (Nitrogen and pollution) N: 426
Nitroglycerin N: 426
Angina pectoris A: 461
Dynamite D: 397
Glycerol (Uses) G: 237
Heart (Treatment) H: 138
Peanut (In industry) P: 214
Nitrosamine [chemical]
Bacon B: 18
Food preservation (Curing) F: 341
Nitrite N: 425
Nitrous oxide [gas] N: 427
Dentistry (Modern dentistry) D: 144-145
Niue [Pacific island]
Pacific Islands (table) P: 9
Niulakita [island, Pacific]
Tuvalu map on T: 527; (Land and climate) T: 528
Niutao [island, Pacific]
Tuvalu map on T: 527; (Land and climate) T: 528
Nivelle, Robert [French general]
World War I (Allied failures) W: 461
Niven, David [British actor]
Motion picture (Best performance by an actor:
1958) M: 862a
Nix [satellite]
Planet (Pluto) P: 512
Pluto P: 581
Nix [spirit]
Lorelei L: 454
Nixon, Harry C. [Canadian political leader]
Ontario (table) O: 783
Nixon, Jay [American political leader]
Missouri (table) M: 668
Nixon, Julie [daughter of] See Eisenhower, Julie
Nixon in this index
Nixon, Pat [wife of Richard M. Nixon]
First ladies of the United States (table) F: 142
Nixon, Richard Milhous (Nixon's family) N: 430;
(Life in the White House) N: 435 with picture
Nixon, Patricia [daughter of]
Nixon, Richard Milhous picture on N: 435
with pictures
Nixon, Richard Milhous [U.S. president] N: 428
with pictures
Agnew, Spiro Theodore A: 142
Blackmun, Harry Andrew B: 394
Bush, George Herbert Walker (Appointive
positions) B: 718; (Early political career) B: 718
Chemical-biological-radiological-warfare
(Biological) C: 396
China (Improved relations with the West) C: 505
Cold War (The spirit of Camp David) Ci: 767; (The
Cold War in the 1970's) Ci: 770
Congress of the United States (Continued
struggle for power) Ci: 948
Debate (Political debate) D: 63
Democratic Party (Times of trouble) D: 127
Eisenhower, Dwight David picture on E: 153;
(Election of 1952) E: 151
Ford, Gerald Rudolph F: 372; (The resignation
of Nixon) F: 375; (The Nixon pardon) F: 377
with picture
Impeachment (In the United States) I: 90-91
Journalism (Television journalism) J: 175

Kissinger, Henry Alfred K: 337
Postal Service, United States (Establishment of
the Postal Service) P: 701
President of the United States (The Watergate
scandal) P: 769
Republican Party (Defeat, then victory) R: 256;
(The Watergate scandal) R: 257
Richardson, Elliot Lee R: 330
Television (The 1960's) T: 119
Un-American Activities Committee U: 19
Union of Soviet Socialist Republics picture on
U: 39
United States, History of the (The Vietnam War)
U: 196a; (Political scandals) U: 196b; (The end
of the Cold War) U: 196d
Vietnam War (The U.S. withdrawal begins) V: 376
Watergate W: 144
Nixon, Thelma Ryan [wife of Richard M. Nixon] See
Nixon, Pat in this index
Nixon, Walter L., Jr. [American jurist]
Impeachment (History) I: 91-92
Nixon in China [opera by Adams]
Opera (American opera) O: 800
Niyama [religion]
Yoga Y: 567
Niyazov, Saparmurad A. [Turkmen political
leader]
Turkmenistan (History) T: 514b
Niza, Marcos de [Spanish explorer]
Arizona (Spanish exploration) A: 688
New Mexico (Exploration, conquest, and
settlement) N: 273
Nizāris [sect]
Islam (Divisions of Islam) I: 466
Nizhniy Novgorod [Russia] N: 438
Njal's Saga [story]
Saga S: 1
Scandinavian literature (Beginnings) S: 171
Njord [Norse mythology]
Frey F: 531
Freyja F: 531
NK cell [biology] See Natural killer cell in this index
Nkisi [sculpture]
Sculpture (Royal and public sculpture) S: 240
with picture
Nkomo, Joshua [Zimbabwe political leader]
Zimbabwe (History) Z: 592-594
Nkrumah, Kwame [Ghanaian political leader]
N: 438
Ghana (History) G: 179-180
Nkurunziza, Pierre [Burundi political leader]
Burundi (History) B: 713-714
Nkuwu, Nzinga [king of Kongo] See Nzinga Nkuwu
in this index
NLD [political party] See National League for
Democracy in this index
NLF [political groups] See under National Liberation
Front in this index
NLRB See National Labor Relations Board in this
index
NMA [organization] See National Medical
Association in this index
NMAI [museum] See National Museum of the
American Indian in this index
NMR [medicine] See Nuclear magnetic resonance
in this index
No [drama] See Noh in this index
No [symbol]
Nobelium N: 450
No ball
Cricket (Scoring) Ci: 1132
No Child Left Behind Act [2001] N: 438
Education (Recent developments) E: 105;
(Accountability testing) E: 106
Elementary and Secondary Education Act E: 224
Hispanic Americans (Education) H: 256-257
School (Growth and reform) S: 184
No contest [boxing]
Boxing (A knockout) B: 528
No Country for Old Men [film]
Motion picture (Best picture: 2007) M: 861
No Cross, No Crown [book by Penn]
Penn, William (Persecution) P: 242
No Doubt [rock group]
Rock music (Alternative rock) R: 381
No Exit [play by Sartre]
French literature (Existentialism) F: 523
No fault [law]
Law (Law since 1900) L: 136-137
No-fault divorce
Abandonment A: 4
Divorce (No-fault divorce) D: 253
No-fault insurance N: 438
Insurance (Automobile insurance) I: 313
No-fly zone
Iraq (The Persian Gulf War of 1991) I: 414-414a
No-hitter

Baseball (Baseball terms) **B:** 124
No Laughing Matter [book by Heller]
Heller, Joseph **H:** 177
No-load fund
Mutual fund **M:** 969
No man's land
World War I (Trench warfare) **W:** 457
No Man's Land [play by Pinter]
Pinter, Harold **P:** 475
No Name in the Street [book by Baldwin]
Baldwin, James **B:** 39
No-par stock [economics]
Stock (Kinds of stock) **So:** 903
No Place to Be: Voices of Homeless Children [book by Berck]
Literature for children (Information books) **L:** 361
No-see-um [insect]
Gnat **G:** 238
Midge **M:** 535
No-till [agriculture]
Conservation (Soil conservation) **Ci:** 979-980
Farm and farming (Preparing the soil) **F:** 35
NOAA [organization] *See* National Oceanic and Atmospheric Administration *in this index*
NOAA-H [satellite]
Satellite, Artificial (A sun-synchronous, polar orbit) **S:** 150e
Noachian Period
Mars (Periods of evolution) **M:** 226b-226c
Noah [Biblical figure] **N:** 439
Ark **A:** 693
Deluge **D:** 118
Mount Ararat **M:** 883
Noailles, Adrienne de [wife of]
Lafayette, Marquis de **L:** 27
NOAO [observatory] *See* National Optical Astronomy Observatories *in this index*
Noatak National Preserve [Alaska]
National Park System (table: National preserves) **N:** 58
Nob Hill [area]
San Francisco **S:** 92
Nobel, Alfred Bernhard [Swedish chemist] **N:** 439 *with portrait*
Dynamite (History) **D:** 397
Gunpowder (History) **G:** 441
Nitroglycerin **N:** 427
Nobel Prizes *picture on* **N:** 440
Peace (The 1800's and early 1900's) **P:** 206
Nobel, Ludwig [Swedish shipbuilder]
Ship (Tankers) **S:** 408
Nobel Foundation
Foundation (table) **F:** 430
Nobel Institute for Physics
Nobelium **N:** 450
Nobel Prizes N: 439 *with pictures*
Nobel, Alfred Bernhard **N:** 439
Obama, Barack **O:** 640b
Nobelium [element] **N:** 450
Transuranium element **T:** 401
Nobile, Umberto [Italian explorer]
Amundsen, Roald (Other achievements) **A:** 446
Exploration (The North Pole) **E:** 450
Nobility N: 450
Heraldry (The development of heraldry) **H:** 194
Noble, John W. [American government official]
Harrison, Benjamin (table) **H:** 72
Interior, Department of the (table) **I:** 325
Noble, Noah [American political leader]
Indiana (table) **I:** 214
Noble Eightfold Path [religion]
Buddhism (The dharma) **B:** 668
Dharma **D:** 178
Nirvana **N:** 424
Religion (A doctrine of salvation) **R:** 215-216
Noble fir [tree]
Fir **F:** 119
Noble gas [chemistry] **N:** 451
Element, Chemical *diagram on* **E:** 221; (Classes) **E:** 224
Helium **H:** 175
Radon **R:** 100
Noble metal [chemistry]
Catalytic converter **C:** 298
Noble Order of the Knights of Labor *See* Knights of Labor *in this index*
Noble savage
Latin American literature (Romanticism) **L:** 112-113
Romanticism (Romanticism and society) **R:** 427
Nobody Knows My Name [book by Baldwin]
Baldwin, James **B:** 39
Nobunaga, Oda [Japanese military leader]
Hideyoshi **H:** 225
Japan (Warring states period) **J:** 54
Noces, Les [ballet]
Robbins, Jerome **R:** 365

Noche triste, La [battle]
Mexico (The Spanish conquest) **M:** 469
Nociceptor [anatomy]
Pain (How the body feels pain) **P:** 21
Nock
Archery (Arrows) **A:** 602 *with diagram*
Nocking point
Archery (Bows) **A:** 601-602
Noctural animal
Zoo (Exhibits) **Z:** 601
Noda, Yoshihiko [Japanese political leader]
Japan (Recent developments) **J:** 59
Noddack, Walter [German chemist]
Rhenium **R:** 290
Node [botany]
Fruit (Fruit production) **F:** 546
Plant (Stems) **P:** 529 *with picture*
Node of Ranvier [anatomy]
Myelin **M:** 970f
Nervous system (Conduction along the axon) **N:** 135 *with diagrams*
Nodule [botany]
Alfalfa *picture on* **A:** 345
Legume **L:** 185
Nodule [oceanography]
Ocean (Sediments) **O:** 654
Nodule [physiology]
Leprosy (Symptoms) **L:** 204
Silicosis **S:** 458
Thyroid gland (Overactive thyroid) **T:** 275
Noe, James A. [American political leader]
Louisiana (table) **L:** 496
Noel, Edmond F. [American political leader]
Mississippi (table) **M:** 640
Noel, Philip W. [American political leader]
Rhode Island (table) **R:** 311
Noel-Baker, Philip John [British statesman]
Nobel Prizes (Peace: 1959) **N:** 448b
Noel Kempff Mercado National Park [Bolivia]
National park (table) **N:** 42g
Nofukuji, Temple of [Japan]
Kobe **K:** 360
Noguchi, Isamu [American sculptor] **N:** 451 *with picture*
Noh [drama]
Dance (Asian theatrical dance) **D:** 28-29
Drama (Japan) **D:** 336
Japan (Theater) **J:** 43
Japanese literature (The medieval period) **J:** 62
Mask (Theatrical masks) **M:** 265
Music (Japanese music) **M:** 956
Tokyo *picture on* **T:** 316
Noise [communications]
Information theory **I:** 269
Photography (Capturing digital images) **P:** 420-421
Noise [sound] **N:** 451
Acoustics **A:** 29
Deafness (Environmental factors) **D:** 57
Sound (Noises) **So:** 599
Noise pollution
Environmental pollution (Noise pollution) **E:** 335
Acoustics **A:** 29
Airport (Airport noise) **A:** 249
Disease (Environmental and occupational diseases) **D:** 230
Road (Noise control) **R:** 360
Sound (Controlling sound) **So:** 604
Nok [ancient civilization] **N:** 451
Nigeria (The arts) **N:** 414
Nok [village, Nigeria]
Nok **N:** 452
Nokia Corporation
Finland (Communication) **F:** 116
Manufacturing (table) **M:** 170
Nolan, Philip [literary figure]
Hale, Edward Everett **H:** 18
Nolan, Sir Sidney [Australian painter]
Australia (Painting) **A:** 905-906
Noland, Kenneth [American artist]
Painting (Color-field painting) **P:** 85
Nolde, Emil [German painter]
Painting (Expressionism) **P:** 78
Noli Me Tangere [book by Rizal]
Rizal, José **R:** 357
Nom de plume [name] *See* Pen name *in this index*
Nomad [sociology] **N:** 452
Africa (Rural life) **A:** 110-112
Arabs (Life in the Arab world) **A:** 586
Asia (Country life) **A:** 779
Iran *picture on* **I:** 404
Mali *picture on* **M:** 108; (People) **M:** 106-107
Middle East (Ways of life) **M:** 530
Niger (People) **N:** 407-408
Oman **O:** 757-758
Roma (Language and culture) **R:** 402b
Sahara (People) **S:** 21

Sami **S:** 78
Nomadic cattle raising
Cattle (Nomadic cattle raising) **C:** 315
Nomadic forager [person]
Nomad **N:** 452
Nomarch [office]
Crete (Government) **Ci:** 1128
Nombre de Díos Mission
Mission life in America (A visitor's guide) **M:** 620
Nome [Alaska] **N:** 452
Nome [political division]
Egypt, Ancient (Government) **E:** 139-142
Nome sledge [vehicle]
Sled **S:** 505
Nomenclature, Binomial [biology]
Classification, Scientific (The language of classification) **C:** 655
Nomex [fiber] *See* Aramid *in this index*
Nominal [grammar]
Noun (Nominals) **N:** 552
Nominal account
Bookkeeping (Accounts) **B:** 472
Nominal damages [law]
Damages **D:** 20
Nominal income
Income (Nominal and real income) **I:** 100
Nominal interest rate [economics]
Interest (Inflation) **I:** 322
Nominalistic theory [philosophy]
Metaphysics (Universals and particulars) **M:** 430
Nominating convention *See* Political convention *in this index*
Nominating election *See* Primary election *in this index*
Nominating speech
Political convention (Making nominations) **P:** 629
Nomination [voting]
Election campaign (Winning the nomination) **E:** 159
Parliamentary procedure (Electing officers) **P:** 175
Political convention (Convention activities) **P:** 629
Nominative case [grammar]
Case (Cases in Latin) **C:** 271-272; (Pronouns) **C:** 272
Declension **D:** 80
Nomoli [religion]
Sierra Leone (People) **S:** 451
Nomothetic study
Abnormal psychology (Studies in abnormal psychology) **A:** 12
Non la [hat]
Vietnam (Clothing) **V:** 366
Nonadaptive trait [biology]
Races, Human (Evolutionary theory) **R:** 53-54
Nonaggression pact [international relations] **N:** 452
Communism (World War II) **Ci:** 893
Russia (World War II) **R:** 554
Union of Soviet Socialist Republics (Stalin's policies) **U:** 36-37
Nonaligned nation *See* Neutral nation *in this index*
Nonballistic missile
Guided missile (Nonballistic missiles) **G:** 425
Nonbearing wall [construction]
Building construction (Types of construction) **B:** 683
Noncanonical writings *See* Apocrypha *in this index*
Noncitizen national
Citizenship **Ci:** 568; (The rights of citizens) **Ci:** 569
Noncommissioned officer
Army, United States (Training a soldier) **A:** 730-731
Rank, Military **R:** 139
Nonconnected committee
Political action committee **P:** 627
Noncooperative game
Game theory **G:** 23
Nondegerming system
Corn (The dry-milling industry) **Ci:** 1061-1062
Nondiscrimination [trade policy]
General Agreement on Tariffs and Trade **G:** 83
Nondispersive wave
Waves (How waves move) **W:** 152
Nondrying oil
Oil (Fixed oils) **O:** 706
Nondurable goods
Gross domestic product (Measuring GDP) **G:** 399
Industry (By the way goods are used) **I:** 257
Manufacturing (Kinds of manufacturing) **M:** 169
Nonelectrolyte [chemistry]
Electrolyte **E:** 201
Nones [Roman calendar]
Month **M:** 767
Nonessential amino acid
Protein (The structure of proteins) **P:** 832
Non-Euclidean geometry
Geometry (Types of geometry) **G:** 103 *with*

diagrams; (Rise of non-Euclidean geometry)
G: 106
Lobachevsky, Nikolai L: 404
Mathematics (Branches of mathematics) M: 303
Riemann, Georg Friedrich Bernhard R: 337
Nonexecutive president
President P: 757
Nonexpandable clay
Clay Ci: 658
Nonfiction [literature]
Literature L: 352
Literature for children (Children's nonfiction)
L: 365
Novel (The novel today) N: 575
Writing (Nonfiction) W: 511
Nonfiction novel [literature]
Novel (The novel today) N: 575
Nonfigurative art See Abstract art *in this index*
Nonfinite verb
Verb (Finite and nonfinite verbs) V: 315
Nongovernmental organization
Food for Peace F: 340
UNESCO U: 24
Nongraded school
Education (Elementary education) E: 91
Elementary school (Kinds of elementary schools)
E: 224
School (Elementary schools) S: 181
Teaching (Checking student progress) T: 67
Non-Hodgkin's lymphoma [disease]
Cancer (Classification by primary body site)
C: 167-168
Non-Importation Act [1806]
War of 1812 (American reaction) W: 29
Nonimportation association [U.S. history]
Jefferson, Thomas (Revolutionary leader) J: 79
Nonindigenous species
Conservation (Biodiversity conservation) Ci: 976-977
Noninfectious disease
Disease *picture on* D: 225; (Noninfectious diseases) D: 228
Non-Intercourse Act [1809]
Embargo Act E: 256
United States, History of the (Jefferson's foreign policy) U: 164
War of 1812 (American reaction) W: 29-30
Nonionizing radiation [physics]
Radiation (Ionizing ability) R: 79
Nonlinear editing system
Motion picture (Editing the film) M: 855
Nonmaterial culture
Culture (Forming patterns) Ci: 1187
Nonmetal [chemistry]
Element, Chemical *diagram on* E: 221
Nonmetallic luster [physical property]
Mineral (Luster) M: 567
Nonmilitary sanction
International relations (Nonmilitary sanctions)
I: 345
Nonobjective art See Abstract art *in this index*
Nonofficial cover
Central Intelligence Agency (Functions) C: 356-357
Nonparasitic lamprey [sea animal]
Lamprey (Habits) L: 55
Nonparticipating policy
Insurance (Dividends) I: 310
Nonpartisan election
City government (Administering city government) Ci: 596
Primary election (Nonpartisan primaries) P: 777
Nonpoint source pollution
Environmental pollution E: 330
Water pollution W: 136; (Nonpoint sources)
W: 138; (Nonpoint control) W: 138
Nonprofit corporation
Corporation (Other corporations) Ci: 1070
Foundation F: 429
Nonprofit voluntary hospital
Hospital (Type of ownership) H: 371
Non-Proliferation of Nuclear Weapons, Treaty on the See Nuclear Nonproliferation Treaty [1968]
in this index
NonREM sleep
Sleep (The structure of sleep) S: 506
Sleepwalking S: 508
Nonrenewable resource
Conservation Ci: 974
Fossil fuel (Concerns) F: 428
Industry (Natural resources) I: 257-258
Natural resources (Conservation and development) N: 64-65
Nonresistance [philosophy]
Pacifism P: 18
Nonscheduled flight
Aviation (Airline operations) A: 984-985

Nonseminoma [disease]
Testicular cancer T: 182
Nonsense verse
Literature for children (Poetry) L: 357
Nursery rhyme (Nonsense rhymes) N: 615
Nonsporting dog
Dog *pictures on* D: 275; (Nonsporting dogs)
D: 266
Nonsteroidal anti-inflammatory drug
Aspirin (How aspirin works) A: 816
Pain (Treatment) P: 22
Nonstore retailing
Retailing (Nonstore retailing) R: 265
Nonstriker
Cricket Ci: 1131
Nonsyncytium inducing protein [biology]
Evolution (Direct observation of evolution) E: 431
Nonvascular plant
Plant *pictures on* P: 522; (Kinds of plants) P: 518;
(Classification of plants) P: 546 *with pictures*
Nonverbal behavior
Kinesics K: 319
Nonverbal communication
Body language B: 435
Communication (The study of communication)
Ci: 887
Fashion (Why people follow fashion) F: 50
Nonverbal learning disability
Learning disabilities (Types) L: 165-166
Nonviolent action
Pacifism P: 18
Nonviolent resistance
Gandhi, Mohandas Karamchand G: 25
India (Rise of Indian nationalism) I: 131
King, Martin Luther, Jr. (The early civil rights movement) K: 321
Pacifism P: 18
Nonvolatile memory [electronics]
Computer chip (Memory chips) Ci: 924f
Nonvolatile RAM [memory]
Electronics (Digital circuits) E: 213-214
Nonwoven fabric
Textile (Other textiles) T: 215
Nonzero-sum game
Game theory G: 23
Noodle [food]
Pasta P: 192
Noon
Day and night D: 52
Time (Solar time) T: 288; (Units of time) T: 292
with diagram
Noonan, Frederick J. [American aviator]
Earhart, Amelia (Disappearance) E: 14
Nooning [custom]
Pioneer life in America (Life on the trail) P: 486-487
Nootka Convention [1790]
British Columbia (The Nootka Sound controversy)
B: 628
Nootka Indians N: 453 *with picture*
Nootka Sound Controversy [Canadian history]
British Columbia (The Nootka Sound controversy)
B: 628
Nopal See Prickly pear *in this index*
NORAD [defense] N: 453
Air Force, United States (Defense and deterrence)
A: 190
Colorado (The mid-1900's) Ci: 847
North Warning System N: 519
Noradrenalin See Norepinephrine *in this index*
Norbeck, Peter [American political leader]
South Dakota (table) So: 680
Norblad, A. W. [American political leader]
Oregon (table) O: 845
Nord-Ostsee-Kanal [waterway, Germany] See Kiel
Canal *in this index*
Nordberg, Martin [American chemist]
Glass (table) G: 218
Norden [region, Europe]
Scandinavia S: 170
Nordenskjöld, Nils Adolf Erik [Swedish explorer]
N: 453
Exploration (Arctic exploration) E: 449
Nordestinos [people, Brazil]
Brazil (The Northeast Region) B: 579-580
Nordhoff, Charles Bernard [American author]
Nordhoff and Hall N: 453
Nordhoff and Hall [American authors] N: 453
Nordic combined [sports]
Olympic Games (Winter Olympic Games)
O: 746d-746e
Skiing (Nordic competitions) S: 487
Nordic Council [alliance]
Finland (Postwar developments) F: 118
Nordic skiing
Skiing *diagrams on* S: 484; (Nordic skiing) S: 482
with pictures; (Ski equipment and clothing)

S: 483; (Nordic competitions) S: 487
Nördlingen, Battle of [1634]
Thirty Years' War (The Swedish period) T: 260
Nordraak, Rikard [Norwegian composer]
Grieg, Edvard G: 392
Norepinephrine [hormone]
Adrenal gland A: 67
Fibromyalgia F: 90
Hormone (Stress hormones) H: 336
Mental illness (Chemical imbalances in the brain)
M: 406
Ritalin R: 350
Norfolk [Virginia] N: 453
Virginia (table: Average monthly weather) V: 412
Norfolk International Terminals
Norfolk (Economy) N: 454
Norfolk Island [island, Pacific] N: 454
Norfolk National Fish Hatchery
Arkansas (Interesting facts about Arkansas)
A: 695
Norfolk Southern Corporation
Railroad (Railroad systems) R: 112
Norfolk terrier [dog] N: 454 *with picture*
Norgay, Tenzing [Nepalese mountain climber] See
Tenzing Norgay *in this index*
Norge [airship]
Airship (Between world wars) A: 252
Amundsen, Roald (Other achievements) A: 445-446
Exploration (The North Pole) E: 450
Norheim, Sondre [Norwegian skier]
Skiing (The development of modern skiing)
S: 487
Nori [food]
Algae (Kinds of algae) A: 349
Noriega, Manuel Antonio [Panamanian political leader] N: 454
Bush, George Herbert Walker (International affairs) B: 721
Panama (The Noriega years) P: 120-121 *with picture*; (The 1990's) P: 121
Norm [sociology]
Human relations (Human relations skills) H: 428
Norma [opera by Bellini]
Bellini, Vincenzo B: 244
Normal [optics]
Light (Reflection and absorption) L: 287
Mirror (Plane mirrors) M: 616
Normal distribution
Statistics (Probability) So: 868-869 *with diagram*
Normal fault [geology]
Earthquake *diagram on* E: 37; (Tsunamis) E: 34
Mountain (Fault-block mountains) M: 893
Normal heptane [chemistry]
Gasoline (Octane ratings) G: 61
Octane number O: 669
Normal school [teacher training school]
Education (Advances in public education) E: 103
Mann, Horace M: 164
Teaching (The effectiveness of teacher training)
T: 70
Normal School Association, American
National Education Association N: 34
Normalcy [U.S. history]
United States, History of the (Looking backward)
U: 191
Norman, E. Herbert [Canadian diplomat]
United Nations (table) U: 86
Norman, Marsha [American dramatist] N: 455
Norman architecture N: 455 *with picture*
England (The arts) E: 298
Norman Conquest [English history] N: 455 *with
picture*
Bayeux Tapestry B: 176 *with picture*
England (The Norman Conquest) E: 305
English language (Middle English) E: 313
Hastings, Battle of H: 83
Scotland (Struggles with England) S: 219
Norman Conquests, The [play by Ayckbourn]
Ayckbourn, Alan A: 995
Norman Wells [Northwest Territories]
Northwest Territories (Mining) N: 532 *with picture*
Normand, Mable [American actress]
Sennett, Mack *picture on* S: 301
Normandie [ship]
Ship (Passenger vessels) S: 426
Normandy [region, France] N: 456
France (The land) F: 464 *with picture and map*;
(The Capetian dynasty) F: 471-472
Normandy, Duke of [father of]
William I, the Conqueror W: 308
Normandy Bridge [Le Havre, France]
Bridge (table: Cable-stayed) B: 603
Normandy Invasion [1944]
Canada, History of *picture on* C: 149
D-day D: 2
Eisenhower, Dwight David (Operation Overlord)

E: 150
World War II (D-Day) W: 483-484 *with picture and map*
Normans [people] N: 456
Ireland (The Norman invaders) I: 425
Norns [Norse mythology] N: 456
Mythology (The construction of the world) M: 986
Norodom Ranariddh [Cambodian political leader]
Cambodia (History) C: 72-74
Hun Sen H: 437
Norodom Sihamoni [king of Cambodia]
Cambodia (History) C: 72-74
Norodom Sihanouk N: 457
Norodom Sihanouk [king of Cambodia] N: 457
Indochina (World War II) I: 225
Lon Nol L: 427
Norquay, John [Canadian political leader]
Manitoba (table) M: 159
Norris, Clarence [American public figure]
Scottsboro case S: 223
Norris, Edwin L. [American political leader]
Montana (table) M: 757
Norris, Frank [American author] N: 457
American literature (Naturalists) A: 419
Dreiser, Theodore D: 346
Novel (The United States) N: 573
Norris, George William [American political leader] N: 457
Nebraska (Economic depression) N: 114
Norris-La Guardia Act N: 457
Taft, William Howard (Legislative defeats) T: 10
Norris, Tobias C. [Canadian political leader]
Manitoba (table) M: 159; (Political developments) M: 162
Norris Dam [Clinch River]
Tennessee Valley Authority *picture on* T: 158
Norris Geyser Basin
Yellowstone National Park (The Upper Loop) Y: 559 *with map*
Norris-La Guardia Act [1932] N: 457
La Guardia, Fiorello Henry L: 31
Labor movement (The Great Depression) L: 12
Norrish, Ronald George Wreyford [British chemist]
Nobel Prizes (Chemistry: 1967) N: 443
Norse mythology
Mythology (Teutonic mythology) M: 985
Raven R: 151
Norsemen *See* Vikings *in this index*
Norte Chico [region]
Chile (The Northern Desert) C: 464
Peru (History) P: 314
North, Andrew [pen name]
Norton, Andre N: 535
North, Douglass Cecil [American economist]
Nobel Prizes (Economics: 1993) N: 449
North, Idea of [literature]
Canadian literature (Characteristics of Canadian literature) C: 156
North, Lord [British political leader] N: 457
Revolution, American (The Tea Act) R: 273
North, Oliver L. [American public figure]
Iran-contra affair (Administration actions) I: 407
Reagan, Ronald Wilson (The Iran-contra affair) R: 170
North, Sir Thomas [English scholar]
Plutarch P: 580
North Against South [book by Verne]
Verne, Jules V: 338
North America N: 458 *with pictures and maps*
See also the list of Related articles in the North America *article*
Bird (Birds of North America) B: 332 *with pictures*
Clothing *pictures on* Ci: 695
Continent Ci: 1021
Exploration (Linking the globe) E: 446 *with map*
Monsoon M: 740
National park (table) N: 42g
Prehistoric animal (The distribution of mammals) P: 741
Prehistoric people (The spread of settlement) P: 752
Wheat (North America) W: 272 *with map*
North American Aerospace Defense Command
See NORAD *in this index*
North American Aviation [company]
Aviation (The industry comes of age) A: 989
North American beaver
Beaver (The body of a beaver) B: 192 *with pictures*
North American Free Trade Agreement [1992] N: 470
Bush, George Herbert Walker (International trade) B: 722
Campbell, Kim (The 1993 election) C: 90d
Canada, Government of (Relations with the United States) C: 137

Canada, History of (Foreign affairs) C: 151
Chrétien, Jean (The 1993 election) C: 522c
Clinton, Bill (International affairs) Ci: 682e
Common market Ci: 875
Copyright (International agreements) Ci: 1048
Globalization (Features of globalization) G: 233
International trade (Government trade policies) I: 348-349
Latin America (Neoliberalism) L: 111
Mexico (Opposition to the PRI) M: 474
Mulroney, Brian (Other economic developments) M: 917-918
Ontario (The late 1900's) O: 787
United States, History of the (Economic changes) U: 196b-196c
North American hognose snake
Snake *picture on* S: 526; (Protection against predators) S: 531
North American Indian Days
Montana *picture on* M: 751
North American Industry Classification System
Industry (The North American Industry Classification System [NAICS]) I: 257; (Sectors of industry) I: 258
North American Plate [geology]
Plate tectonics (Transform plate boundaries) P: 563
San Andreas Fault S: 84 *with map*
North American porcupine [animal]
Porcupine P: 678 *with picture*
North American river otter
Otter *picture on* O: 876
North American Soccer League
Soccer (In North America) So: 548
North American turkey
Turkey T: 513 *with picture*
North and South [book by Gaskell]
Gaskell, Elizabeth G: 61
North arrow [cartography]
Map (Reading a map) M: 178
North Asia [region, Asia]
Asia *picture on* A: 773; (Way of life in North Asia) A: 789 *with pictures*; (The land) A: 792
North Atlantic Council
North Atlantic Treaty Organization (Organization) N: 471
North Atlantic Current
Arctic Ocean *map on* A: 642; (Currents) A: 643
North Atlantic Deep Water
Atlantic Ocean (Subsurface currents) A: 866
North Atlantic Marine Mammal Commission [organization]
Whale (The future of whales) W: 264
North Atlantic Ocean
Atlantic Ocean (Boundaries and size) A: 864
North Atlantic Oscillation [meteorology]
Atlantic Ocean (Climate) A: 864
North Atlantic Treaty [1949]
Cold War (The West rearms) Ci: 764
International relations (Treaties) I: 344
Nonaggression pact N: 452
North Atlantic Treaty Organization (History) N: 471
North Atlantic Treaty Organization [alliance] N: 470
Afghanistan (Recent developments) A: 96
Air Force, United States (The Balkans) A: 196
Balkans (Recent developments) B: 42
Bosnia-Herzegovina (History) B: 492-494
Cold War (The West rearms) Ci: 764; (The great blocs split) Ci: 769
Communism (The Cold War) Ci: 895
Czech Republic (Recent developments) Ci: 1214
Eisenhower, Dwight David (NATO commander) E: 150-151
Estonia (Independence regained) E: 363
Europe (The Cold War) E: 415
European Union (Relations with other countries) E: 419
Flag *picture on* F: 216
Foreign aid (Economic development and mutual security) F: 383-384
Foreign policy (Alliances) F: 387
France (France under de Gaulle) F: 476-477
Germany (Armed forces) G: 147
Greece (Politics) G: 353
Hungary (Multiparty elections) H: 448
International relations (The Cold War begins) I: 345
Kosovo (History) K: 384b
Latvia (Recent developments) L: 120-121
Organization for Security and Co-operation in Europe O: 854
Putin, Vladimir Vladimirovich P: 912
Serbia (Kosovo crisis) S: 316-316a
Stalin, Joseph (The Cold War) So: 827
Truman, Harry S. (Foreign affairs) T: 471

United States, History of the (The Cold War) U: 195-196; (The Balkan conflicts) U: 196d
Warsaw Pact W: 39
Yugoslavia (Kosovo crisis) Y: 577
North Beach [district]
San Francisco (Other neighborhoods) S: 93 *with map*
North Borneo [Malaysia history]
Malaysia (Coming of the Europeans) M: 101
North Bridge [Concord]
Massachusetts *picture on* M: 279
Revolution, American (Lexington and Concord) R: 274-275 *with map*
North Canal
Soo Canals (The American canals) So: 594 *with map*
North Carolina N: 472 *with pictures and maps*
See also the list of Related articles in the North Carolina *article*
Colonial life in America (Development of the Thirteen Colonies) C: 790 *with picture*
United States, History of the (North Carolina, South Carolina, and Georgia) U: 156
North Carolina, University of N: 495 *with picture*
Lumbee Indians L: 516
North Carolina (The mid-1900's) N: 493
North Carolina Agricultural and Technical State University [Greensboro]
North Carolina, University of N: 495
North Carolina Battleship Memorial [Wilmington]
North Carolina (Places to visit) N: 482
North Carolina Central University [Durham]
North Carolina, University of N: 495
North Carolina Gazette [newspaper]
North Carolina (Communication) N: 489
North Carolina Museum of Art
North Carolina (Museums) N: 477
North Carolina Research Triangle
North Carolina (The mid-1900's) N: 493
North Carolina School of Science and Mathematics [Durham]
North Carolina, University of N: 495
North Carolina School of the Arts [Winston-Salem]
North Carolina, University of N: 495
North Carolina State University [Raleigh]
North Carolina, University of N: 495
North Carolina Zoological Park [Asheboro]
North Carolina (Places to visit) N: 482 *with picture*
North Cascades National Park [Washington] N: 495 *with picture*
National Park System (table: National parks) N: 48
North Central States [region, U.S.] N: 495
North Channel [waterway, Canada-U.S.]
Lake Huron L: 39 *with map*
North Charleston [South Carolina]
South Carolina (Population) So: 644
North Coast Harbor
Cleveland (Comeback City) Ci: 667
North Dakota N: 496 *with pictures and maps*
See also the list of Related articles in the North Dakota *article*
North Dakota, University of N: 517
North Dakota Heritage Center [Bismarck]
North Dakota (Libraries and museums) N: 500
North Dakota State University N: 517
North-East Greenland National Park [Greenland]
National park (table) N: 42g
North East Land [island, Arctic]
Svalbard So: 1014
North End [district, Boston]
Boston (The North End) B: 497
North Equatorial Current [Atlantic]
Atlantic Ocean (Moving ocean waters) A: 866
Caribbean Sea (Currents) C: 237
Gulf Stream G: 437
Ocean (Circulation) O: 658
Pacific Ocean (Currents) P: 14-15
North geographic pole
North Pole N: 517
North German Confederation [German history]
Germany (The unification of Germany) G: 165
Prussia (German empire) P: 843
North Island
New Zealand (The North Island) N: 351 *with map*
North Korea *See* Korea, North *in this index*
North Korean Workers' Party [Korean political party]
Pyongyang P: 915
North magnetic pole
Magnetic equator M: 55
North Pole N: 517
North Mountain
Nova Scotia (Land regions) N: 562
North of 36 [book by Hough]
Hough, Emerson H: 378
North Pacific Current [oceanography]

Pacific Ocean (Currents) P: 14-15
North Pacific giant octopus
Octopus O: 672 *with picture*
North Philadelphia [district, Philadelphia]
Philadelphia (Residential districts) P: 360-362
North Platte [Nebraska] N: 517
North Platte River [U.S.]
Platte River P: 569
North Pole [geography] N: 517
Amundsen, Roald (Other achievements) A: 445-446 *with map*
Arctic Ocean A: 640
Cook, Frederick Albert Ci: 1025
Earth (How Earth moves) E: 17
Exploration (The North Pole) E: 450
Henson, Matthew Alexander H: 191
Midnight sun M: 535
North Star N: 518
Peary, Robert Edwin P: 224
Season (The four seasons) S: 270-272
North pole [physics] *See* Magnetic pole *in this index*
North pole of balance [geography]
North Pole N: 517
North Portico
White House *picture on* W: 286
North Sami [dialect]
Sami (Language and culture) S: 79
North Saskatchewan River
Alberta (Rivers and lakes) A: 322 *with map*
North Sea N: 517 *with picture and map*
England (The land) E: 299
Great Britain G: 337
Scotland (Energy sources) S: 218 *with map*
United Kingdom (Energy sources) U: 65-66 *with picture*
North Sea Canal [waterway, Netherlands]
Canal (table) C: 164
Netherlands (Transportation) N: 147
North Ship, The [poems by Larkin]
Larkin, Philip L: 77
North Shore [Minnesota]
Minnesota (Places to visit) M: 594
North-South Ministerial Council [organization] N: 518
Ireland (Recent developments) I: 428
Northern Ireland (Government) N: 521; (The Good Friday Agreement) N: 525
United Kingdom (Regional government) U: 50
North Star [newspaper]
Douglass, Frederick D: 314
North Star [star] N: 518 *with pictures*
Astronomy (How the stars move) A: 835
Big and Little Dippers (The Big Dipper) B: 296; (The Little Dipper) B: 296
Equator E: 346
Navigation (Keeping time) N: 71
Pole P: 618
North Vietnam
Vietnam V: 364; (History) V: 369-371
Cold War (To the brink and back) Ci: 765; (The Vietnam War) Ci: 769
Geneva Accords G: 87
Ho Chi Minh H: 270
Indochina (The Geneva Accords) I: 225
Tet Offensive T: 182a
Viet Cong V: 363
Vietnam War V: 372 *with map*
North Warning System [defense] N: 519
Radar *picture on* R: 66; (In the military) R: 65
North West Company [Canadian history] N: 519
Canada, History of (Exploration of the West) C: 143
Fur trade (The early fur trade) F: 564
Grand Portage National Monument G: 309
Hudson's Bay Company (Growth and problems) H: 407
Manitoba (History) M: 160 *with picture*
McTavish, Simon M: 344
Minnesota (Struggle for control) M: 603
Saskatchewan (The coming of the fur traders) S: 146
Winnipeg (History) W: 341
North-West Mounted Police
Alberta *picture on* A: 330
Royal Canadian Mounted Police (History) R: 497 *with picture*
North West Rebellion [1885] N: 519
Canada, History of (The North West Rebellion) C: 145
Crowfoot Ci: 1158
Dumont, Gabriel D: 383
Laurier, Sir Wilfrid (The execution of Louis Riel) L: 124-125
Macdonald, Sir John Alexander (Threats to Canadian unity) M: 10
Métis M: 435
Poundmaker P: 722

Quebec (Early years as a province) Q: 30
Riel, Louis R: 337
Royal Canadian Mounted Police (History) R: 497
Saskatchewan (Métis and American Indian troubles) S: 146
North-West Territories [former name]
Northwest Territories (European exploration) N: 533
Nunavut (Arrival of the Europeans) N: 612
North Yemen [former country]
Yemen Y: 561
Northampton, Battle of [1460]
Warwick, Earl of W: 44
Northanger Abbey [book by Austen]
Austen, Jane A: 892
Gothic novel G: 258
Northcliffe, Viscount [British publisher] N: 520
Northeast Division
Hockey (table: National Hockey League) H: 281
Northeast Passage [Arctic Ocean]
Amundsen, Roald (Other achievements) A: 445-446
Exploration (The search for a northern passage) E: 446
Northen, William J. [American political leader]
Georgia (table) G: 130
Norther [weather] N: 520
Northern Alliance [Afghan history]
Afghanistan (Recent developments) A: 96
September 11 terrorist attacks (Global war on terrorism) S: 310a
Northern Argentina [region]
Argentina (Northern Argentina) A: 652 *with map*
Northern Baptist Convention [former name]
American Baptist Churches in the U.S.A. A: 408
Northern bobwhite [bird]
Bird *picture on* B: 338
Quail Q: 4
Northern cardinal [bird]
Bird *pictures on* B: 333, B: 358
Cardinal C: 211 *with picture*
Northern catalpa [tree]
Tree *pictures on* T: 421
Northern Caucasus [region]
Caucasus C: 317
Northern Chinese [dialect] *See* Mandarin *in this index*
Northern crested caracara [bird]
Caracara C: 201 *with picture*
Northern deciduous-evergreen forest
Forest (Forests of the United States and Canada) F: 394 *with map*
Northern diver [bird]
Loon L: 453
Northern elephant seal [sea animal]
Elephant seal E: 232 *with picture*
Northern flicker [bird]
Yellowhammer Y: 557
Northern fulmar [bird]
Fulmar F: 555
Northern goshawk [bird]
Hawk *picture on* H: 112; (Kinds of hawks) H: 111
Northern hairy-nosed wombat [animal]
Wombat W: 382
Northern harrier [bird] N: 520 *with picture*
Harrier H: 67
Hawk *picture on* H: 112
Northern Hemisphere [geography]
Astronomy (The stars and constellations of the Northern Hemisphere) *map on* A: 836
Hemisphere H: 181 *with diagram*
Ocean (Circulation) O: 658
Season (The four seasons) S: 270 *with diagram*
Northern Ireland N: 521 *with pictures and map*
See also Ireland *in this index*
Adams, Gerry A: 33
Bloody Sunday B: 418
Heaney, Seamus H: 130
Ireland I: 416; (Religious persecution) I: 426; (The Irish Free State) I: 427; (The Republic of Ireland) I: 427-428
Irish literature (Poetry) I: 433
Irish Republican Army I: 433
North-South Ministerial Council N: 518
Orange Order O: 817
Parliament (The House of Commons) P: 173
Terrorism (Terrorist groups and movements) T: 178
Trimble, David T: 445
Troubles T: 452
Ulster Unionist Party U: 15
United Kingdom U: 48 *with picture*; (Regional government) U: 50; (Local government) U: 54; (The land) U: 58-61 *with map*; (Postwar problems) U: 70; (Political changes) U: 74
Northern Ireland Assembly
Ireland (Recent developments) I: 428

Northern Ireland (Government) N: 521
United Kingdom (Regional government) U: 50
Northern Ireland Civil Rights Association
Bloody Sunday (In Northern Ireland) B: 418
Northern Ireland Office
Northern Ireland (Government) N: 521
Northern jacana [bird]
Jacana J: 2 *with picture*
Northern jezebel [butterfly]
Butterfly *picture on* B: 737
Northern lapwing [bird]
Lapwing L: 75
Northern lights *See* Aurora *in this index*
Northern Lights [book by Pullman]
Pullman, Philip P: 900
Northern Limestone Alps [mountains, Austria]
Austria (Land regions) A: 933-934 *with map*
Northern Mariana Islands, Commonwealth of the N: 525 *with picture and map*
Flag *picture on* F: 213
Pacific Islands, Trust Territory of the P: 13
Northern mockingbird
Bird *pictures on* B: 333, B: 358
Mockingbird M: 684
Northern Nigeria, Protectorate of [former colony]
Nigeria (British rule) N: 417
Northern oriole [bird] *See* Baltimore oriole *in this index*
Northern Pacific Railroad
North Dakota *picture on* N: 515
Northern Pacific rattlesnake
Rattlesnake R: 149 *with picture*
Northern pike [fish]
Fish *picture on* F: 159
Pike P: 461 *with picture*
Northern red oak
Oak (Red oaks) O: 635
Tree *pictures on* T: 423
Northern Rhodesia [former name]
Zambia Z: 584; (History) Z: 585
Zimbabwe (History) Z: 592-593
Northern Rockies [U.S.]
Rocky Mountains (Chief ranges of the Rockies) R: 394
Northern Rugby Union [organization]
Rugby football (History) R: 513
Northern School [literary group]
Irish literature (Poetry) I: 433
Northern Securities Company
Morgan, J. P. M: 803
Roosevelt, Theodore ("Trust buster") R: 464
Northern shoveler [duck]
Shoveler S: 437
Northern shrike [bird]
Shrike S: 439
Northern spotted owl [bird]
Spotted owl So: 804
Northern Territory [Australia] N: 526 *with pictures*
Northern water snake
Snake *picture on* S: 533
Northern white-cedar
Cedar (Scale-leaved cedars) C: 324
Plant *picture on* P: 530
Tree *pictures on* T: 424
Northern wild rice [plant]
Wild rice W: 301
Northfield [Minnesota] N: 528
Northmen *See* Vikings *in this index*
Northrop, John Howard [American biochemist] N: 528
Northrop Grumman Newport News [shipyard]
Virginia (Interesting facts) V: 399
Northumberland Strait [Canada]
New Brunswick (Economic developments) N: 199
Northumbria [ancient kingdom]
English literature (Old English poetry) E: 314-315
Northwest Atlantic Fisheries Organization
(The late 1900's) N: 377
Northwest Coast Indians
Indian, American (Indians of the Northwest Coast) I: 161-162 *with pictures and map*
Kwakiutl Indians K: 397
Mask M: 263
Sculpture (The European impact) S: 244-245
Totem T: 347 *with picture*
Northwest Defense Proects [Canadian history]
Northwest Territories (The early and middle 1900's) N: 533
Northwest Division
Hockey (table: National Hockey League) H: 281
Northwest Highlands [mountains, Scotland]
Scotland (Land regions) S: 217
Northwest Ordinance [1787] N: 528 *with pictures and map*
Fugitive slave laws F: 553
Illinois (Early national period) I: 72-74
Jefferson, Thomas (Delegate to the Congress)

J: 80-81
King, Rufus **K:** 323
Northwest Territory (Early history) **N:** 534-535
Ohio (Exploration and settlement) **O:** 700
Ohio Company (The second Ohio Company) **O:** 704
Pioneer life in America (Government) **P:** 484
Territory (Territories in the United States) **T:** 174
Westward movement in America (The Northwest Ordinance) **W:** 247
Northwest Passage [Arctic Ocean] **N:** 528 *with picture and map*
Amundsen, Roald (Other achievements) **A:** 445-446 *with map*
Arctic (Search for the Northwest Passage) **A:** 638
Cabot, Sebastian **C:** 8
Coast Guard, United States (The Coast Guard since World War II) **Ci:** 738
Davis, John **D:** 48
Exploration (The search for a northern passage) **E:** 446; (Exploring the Pacific) **E:** 447-448; (Arctic exploration) **E:** 449
Frobisher, Sir Martin **F:** 535
Hudson, Henry **H:** 404 *with map*
Mackenzie, Sir Alexander **M:** 22
McClure, Sir Robert John Le Mesurier **M:** 332e
Northwest Territories N: 530 *with pictures and map*
See also the list of Related articles in the Northwest Territories *article*
Nunavut **N:** 608; (Arrival of the Europeans) **N:** 612
Ohio (Exploration and settlement) **O:** 700
Saskatchewan (North-West Territories) **S:** 146
Northwest Territory [U.S. history] **N:** 534 *with picture*
Clark, George Rogers **Ci:** 639
Jefferson, Thomas (Delegate to the Congress) **J:** 80-81; (Exploration and expansion) **J:** 85
Northwest Ordinance **N:** 528
Pioneer life in America (Government) **P:** 484
Territory (In the United States) **T:** 174
Westward movement in America (The Northwest Ordinance) **W:** 247
Northwestern crow [bird]
Crow (Kinds of crows) **Ci:** 1157
NorthWestern Energy [company]
Montana (The early 2000's) **M:** 761
Northwestern Hawaiian Islands Marine National Monument [Hawaii]
Bush, George Walker (Other domestic issues) **B:** 723
Hawaii (The early 2000's) **H:** 109
Northwestern University N: 535
Chicago (Education) **C:** 427
Willard, Frances Elizabeth Caroline **W:** 307
Norton, Andre [American author] **N:** 535
Norton, Gale A. [American government official]
Bush, George Walker (table) **B:** 722h
Interior, Department of the (table) **I:** 325
Norwalk Islands
Connecticut (Coastline) **Ci:** 962
Norway N: 536 *with pictures and maps*
See also the list of Related articles in the Norway *article*
Christmas (In Denmark, Norway, and Sweden) **C:** 531
Clothing *picture on* **Ci:** 694
Greenland (History) **G:** 385
Lapland **L:** 74
Newspaper (Newspapers in other countries) **N:** 385
Races, Human *picture on* **R:** 56
Sami **S:** 78
Scandinavia **S:** 170 *with map*
Sweden (History) **So:** 1032-1033
Terrorism (Recent developments) **T:** 180
Vikings (The Norwegian Vikings) **V:** 382
Welfare state **W:** 192
Whale (The future of whales) **W:** 264
World War II (The conquest of Denmark and Norway) **W:** 473
Norway lemming [animal]
Lemming **L:** 188
Norway maple [tree]
Maple (Other maples) **M:** 187 *with picture*
Norway pine [tree]
Tree *pictures on* **T:** 413
Norway spruce [tree]
Tree *picture on* **T:** 427
Norwegian Broadcasting Corporation
Norway (Communication) **N:** 544
Norwegian elkhound [dog] **N:** 548
Dog *picture on* **D:** 270
Norwegian Folk Tales [book by Asbjørnsen and Moe]
Asbjørnsen, Peter Christen **A:** 766
Norwegian forest cat

Cat (Long-haired breeds) **C:** 292
Norwegian saltpeter
Saltpeter **S:** 76a
Norwich terrier [dog] **N:** 548 *with picture*
Norfolk terrier **N:** 454
Nose [anatomy] **N:** 548 *with diagrams*
See also index entries under Nasal *in this index*
Cocaine **C:** 742
Smell (How odors are detected) **S:** 514
Nose [astronomy]
Heliosphere **H:** 174
Nose [torpedo]
Torpedo (How a torpedo works) **T:** 340d *with diagram*
Nose clip [ornament]
Indian, American *picture on* **I:** 140
Nose guard
Football (The defensive team) **F:** 357 *with diagrams*
Nose leather
Cat (Head) **C:** 286-287
Nose ring [ornament]
Ring **R:** 342
Nosebleed N: 549 *with pictures*
Bleeding (First aid for bleeding) **B:** 399
First aid (Nosebleed) **F:** 141
Nosepiece
Microscope (Tube and lenses) **M:** 517-518 *with pictures*
Nosferatu [film]
Motion picture (Filmmaking in Europe) **M:** 866
Noshi [craft]
Origami **O:** 855
Nostradamus [French astrologer] **N:** 549 *with portrait*
Nostril
Nose **N:** 548 *with diagram*
Nostromo [book by Conrad]
Conrad, Joseph **Ci:** 973
Novel (New directions in the novel) **N:** 573-574
NOT-gate [electronics]
Electronics (Digital circuits) **E:** 213-214
Not Honour More [book by Cary]
Cary, Joyce **C:** 270
Notary public [office] **N:** 549 *with picture*
Notater [occupation]
Ballet (A dancer's life) **B:** 47-48
Notation [symbols] **N:** 550
Classical music (The Middle Ages) **Ci:** 645-646
Music (Musical notation) **M:** 952 *with diagrams*
Note [banking] **N:** 550
See also Bank note *in this index*
Draft **D:** 318
Note [music]
Music (The elements of music) **M:** 950 *with pictures*; (Musical notation) **M:** 952 *with pictures*
Note [odor]
Perfume **P:** 286
Note of hand [economics]
Note **N:** 550
Notebook computer
Computer (Personal computers) **Ci:** 909-910
Laptop computer (Types) **L:** 74
Notebooks [books by Leonardo]
Leonardo da Vinci (Drawings and scientific studies) **L:** 200-200a
Notebooks of Malte Laurids Brigge, The [book by Rilke]
Rilke, Rainer Maria **R:** 341
Notebooks of Thomas Wolfe, The [book by Wolfe]
Wolfe, Thomas **W:** 378
Notes from the House of the Dead [book by Dostoevsky]
Dostoevsky, Fyodor **D:** 311
Notes from Underground [book by Dostoevsky]
Dostoevsky, Fyodor **D:** 311
Notes of a Native Son [book by Baldwin]
Baldwin, James **B:** 39
Notes on the State of Virginia [book by Jefferson]
Jefferson, Thomas (Delegate to the Congress) **J:** 80
Nothing But the Truth [book by Avi]
Avi **A:** 982
Notice of allowance [law]
Patent (How to get a U.S. patent) **P:** 194-195
Notochord [zoology]
Amphioxus **A:** 443
Animal (Invertebrates and vertebrates) **A:** 488 *with diagram*
Chordate **C:** 522
Notorious Byrd Brothers, The [recording]
Rock music (Fresh directions) **R:** 380
Notoryctemorphia [zoology]
Mammal (table) **M:** 128 *with picture*
Notre Dame, Cathedral of [Antwerp, Belgium]
Belgium *picture on* **B:** 226
Notre Dame, Cathedral of [Chartres, France] *See*

Chartres Cathedral *in this index*
Notre Dame, Cathedral of [Paris, France] **N:** 551 *with picture*
Paris *picture on* **P:** 160; (Famous buildings) **P:** 163-164 *with map*
Notre Dame, Cathedral of [Reims, France]
City *picture on* **Ci:** 582
Reims **R:** 208 *with picture*
Sculpture (The peak of architectural sculpture) **S:** 249-250 *with picture*
Notre Dame, University of [Indiana] **N:** 551 *with picture*
Indiana *picture on* **I:** 201
Notre-Dame Basilica *See* Basilique Notre-Dame *in this index*
Notre-Dame-de-Bon-Secours Church
Montreal (Churches) **M:** 773
Notre-Dame-de-la-Garde [church, France]
Marseille (The city) **M:** 227-228
Notre-Dame-la-Grande [church, Poitiers]
Romanesque architecture *picture on* **R:** 415
Notre Dame Mass [music by Machaut]
Classical music (Secular music) **Ci:** 646
Notre-Dame Mountains
Quebec (Land regions) **Q:** 22
Notte, John A., Jr. [American political leader]
Rhode Island (table) **R:** 311
Notte, La [film]
Antonioni, Michelangelo **A:** 561
Nottingham [England] **N:** 552
Nottoway Indians
Virginia (Early days) **V:** 418
Nouabalé-Ndoki National Park [Republic of the Congo]
National park (table) **N:** 42f
Nouadhibou [Mauritania]
Mauritania (Land) **M:** 314 *with map*
Nouakchott [Mauritania] **N:** 552
Mauritania **M:** 314 *with picture*
Nougat
Candy (Whipped candies) **C:** 176
Nouméa [New Caledonia]
New Caledonia **N:** 200 *with picture*
Noun [grammar] **N:** 552
Antecedent **A:** 581
Capitalization (Proper nouns) **C:** 196
Case (Nouns) **C:** 272
Gender (Nouns) **G:** 81
Grammar **G:** 303
Number **N:** 604
Participle **P:** 184
Sentence (Subject and predicate) **S:** 303
Nouveau roman [literature]
Novel (After World War II) **N:** 574
Nova [astronomy] **N:** 553 *with pictures*
See also Supernova *in this index*
Star (Binary stars) **So:** 852
Nova Colonia do Sacramento
Uruguay (Colonial years) **U:** 227
Nova Scotia N: 554 *with pictures and maps*
See also the list of Related articles in the Nova Scotia *article*
Acadia **A:** 21
Atlantic Provinces **A:** 867
Canada, Government of *picture on* **C:** 131
Tupper, Sir Charles **T:** 493
Nova Scotia [magazine]
Magazine (Early magazines) **M:** 44-45
Nova Scotia duck tolling retriever [dog] **N:** 571
Dog *picture on* **D:** 267
Nova Scotia Power Corporation
Nova Scotia (The early to middle 1900's) **N:** 570
Novalis [German poet] **N:** 571
German literature (Romanticism) **G:** 140
Novascotian [newspaper]
Howe, Joseph **N:** 400
Novatian [antipope]
Pope (table) **P:** 666
Novaya Zemlya [islands, Arctic] **N:** 571
Barents, Willem **B:** 109
Novel [literature] **N:** 571
See also the list of Related articles in the Literature *article*
American literature (The sentimental novel) **A:** 415
English literature (The rise of the novel) **E:** 318; (Fiction between the wars) **E:** 322
Fiction **F:** 90
Fielding, Henry **F:** 94
French literature (Classical prose) **F:** 520; (The middle and late 1900's) **F:** 523
Graphic novel **G:** 322 *with picture*
Literature for children (Realistic young adult novels) **L:** 365
Romance **R:** 414
Writing (Fiction) **W:** 511
Novel of manners

American literature (Mark Twain and Henry James) **A: 420**
Novel (Britain) **N: 573**
Novel of the soil
Canadian literature (Early Québécois literature) **C: 157**
Novelas ejemplares [stories by Cervantes]
Cervantes, Miguel de (His literary career) **C: 363**
Novelty
Advertising (Other ways of advertising) **A: 75** *with picture*
November [month] **N: 576** *with pictures*
Calendar (The Romans) **C: 31**
Noverre, Jean Georges [French dancer]
Ballet *picture on* **B: 52**; (Ballet d'action) **B: 51**
Novgorod [Russia] *See* Velikiy Novgorod *in this index*
Novi Sad [Serbia] **N: 578**
Novial [language]
Universal language **U: 205**
Novice [religion]
Religious life **R: 226**
Novillada [bullfighting]
Bullfighting (Types of bullfights) **B: 695**
Novillero [bullfighting]
Bullfighting (Types of bullfights) **B: 695-696**
Novísimos [literature]
Spanish literature (Spanish literature today) **So: 763**
Novitiate [religion]
Nun **N: 608**
Novo-Kholmogory [former name]
Arkhangelsk **A: 716**
Novocain [medication] *See* Procaine *in this index*
Novoselic, Krist [American bassist]
Nirvana **N: 424**
Novoselov, Konstantin [British/Russian physicist]
Nobel Prizes (Physics: 2010) **N: 442**
Novosibirsk [Russia] **N: 578**
Russia *picture on* **R: 534**
Siberia (The people) **S: 444**
Novotný, Antonín [Czechoslovak political leader]
Czechoslovakia (Communist rule) **Ci: 1216**
Novum Organum [book by Bacon]
Philosophy (Modern philosophy) **P: 388**
Novus ordo seclorum [motto]
Great Seal of the United States (The reverse side) **G: 348**
NOW [organization] *See* National Organization for Women *in this index*
NOW account *See* Negotiable order of withdrawal account *in this index*
Now and Then [poems by Warren]
Warren, Robert Penn **W: 37**
Now Is Your Time [book by Myers]
Myers, Walter Dean **M: 970f**
Nowruz [holiday]
Iran (Recreation) **I: 402**
Noyce, Robert [American physicist] **N: 578**
Computer chip (History) **Ci: 924f**
Electronics (The solid-state revolution) **E: 215-216**
Invention (Recent developments) **I: 364**
Kilby, Jack **K: 315**
Noyes, Alfred [British poet] **N: 578**
Noyes, Edward F. [American political leader]
Ohio (table) **O: 699**
Noyes, John Humphrey [American social reformer]
Oneida Community **O: 762**
Noye's Fludde [play by Britten]
Britten, Benjamin **B: 634**
Noyori, Ryoji [Japanese chemist]
Nobel Prizes (Chemistry: 2001) **N: 444**
Nozze di Figaro, Le [opera] *See* Marriage of Figaro, The *in this index*
Nozzle [mechanics]
Guided missile (The engine) **G: 424** *with diagrams*
Rocket (Parts of a rocket) **R: 385**
Turbine (How turbines work) **T: 495-496**
Np [symbol]
Neptunium **N: 130**
NPN transistor
Transistor (How transistors work) **T: 372-373** *with picture*
NPR [radio system] *See* National Public Radio *in this index*
NRA [organization]
National Rifle Association of America **N: 60**
NRA [U.S. agency] *See* National Recovery Administration *in this index*
NRAO [observatory] *See* National Radio Astronomy Observatory *in this index*
NRC [organization] *See* Nuclear Regulatory Commission *in this index*
NROTC [military] *See* Naval Reserve Officers Training Corps *in this index*
NSA/CSS *See* National Security Agency/Central

Security Service *in this index*
NSAID [drug] *See* Nonsteroidal anti-inflammatory drug *in this index*
NSC [organization] *See* National Security Council *in this index*
NSF [organization] *See* National Science Foundation *in this index*
NSPE [organization] *See* National Society of Professional Engineers *in this index*
Ntaryamira, Cyprien [African political leader]
Burundi (History) **B: 713-714**
Ntibantunganya, Sylvestre [African political leader]
Burundi (History) **B: 713-714**
NTSC system [electronics]
Television (Camera scanning patterns) **T: 122**
Nu [letter]
N **N: 1** *with picture*
Nu, U [Burmese political leader]
Myanmar (Independence) **M: 970d**
Nubia [ancient region, Sudan] **N: 578** *with map*
Nubian goat *See* Anglo-Nubian goat *in this index*
Nubians [people]
Egypt (People) **E: 123**
Nuclear bomb
See also Atomic bomb; Hydrogen bomb; Nuclear weapon *in this index*
Bikini Atoll **B: 299**
Nuclear depth bomb
Depth charge **D: 151**
Nuclear deterrence
Nuclear weapon (Nuclear strategy) **N: 600**
War (The Cold War era) **W: 26**
Nuclear disarmament *See* Arms control *in this index*
Nuclear division [biology]
Cell (Cell division) **C: 330** *with diagram*
Nuclear energy **N: 579** *with pictures*
See also the list of Related articles in the Nuclear energy *article*
Einstein, Albert (Famous theories) **E: 146-146b**
E=mc[2] **E: 3**
Environmental pollution (Hazardous waste) **E: 334-335**; (Weighing benefits and risks) **E: 339**
Fermi, Enrico **F: 73**
Fission **F: 189**
Fusion **F: 589**
International Atomic Energy Agency **I: 337**
Invention (The early and middle 1900's) **I: 363**
Physics (Uncovering the secrets of the atom) **P: 442**
Uranium **U: 214**
Uses
Electric power (Nuclear power plants) **E: 184**
Energy supply (Nuclear energy) **E: 278**
Engineering (Nuclear engineering) **E: 287**
Furnace (Sources of heat) **F: 567**
Heat (Sources of heat) **H: 149**
Laser (Heating) **L: 82-83**
Perpetual motion machine **P: 293**
Ship (Nuclear power and automation) **S: 426**
Submarine (The power plant) **So: 941**
United Nations (Peaceful uses of nuclear energy) **U: 89**
Uranium (History of the use of uranium) **U: 216-217**
Nuclear engineering
Engineering *picture on* **E: 288**; (Nuclear engineering) **E: 287**
Nuclear family [sociology]
Family (Varieties of families) **F: 20** *with picture*
Nuclear fission *See* Fission *in this index*
Nuclear forces [physics] *See* Strong interaction *in this index*
Nuclear fuel
Fuel (Nuclear fuels) **F: 551**
Nuclear fusion *See* Fusion *in this index*
Nuclear magnetic resonance
Magnetic resonance imaging **M: 56**
Magnetism (Magnetic resonance) **M: 61**
Spectroscopy **So: 772**
Nuclear magnetic resonance spectroscopy [physics]
Magnetic resonance imaging **M: 57**
Nuclear medicine
Isotope (Uses of radioisotopes) **I: 477**
Medicine (table) **M: 369**
Nuclear membrane [biology]
Cell (The nucleus) **C: 328** *with diagram*
Nuclear nonproliferation [strategy]
Cold War (Soviet-American relations) **Ci: 769**
Nuclear weapon (Controlling nuclear weapons) **N: 600**
Nuclear Nonproliferation Regime [agreements]
Nuclear weapon (Treaties) **N: 601**
Nuclear Nonproliferation Treaty [1968] **N: 595**

Arms control (Arms control in the mid-1900's) **A: 721-722**
Cold War (Soviet-American relations) **Ci: 769**
International Atomic Energy Agency **I: 337**
Nuclear energy (The spread of nuclear capability) **N: 591**
Nuclear weapon (Treaties) **N: 601**
Peace (Arms control) **P: 207**
Ukraine (Independence) **U: 13-14**
United Nations (Arms control) **U: 92**
Nuclear physics **N: 595**
Atom (Studying the nucleus) **A: 876**
Physics (Nuclear physics) **P: 437**
Science (Achievements of the mid-1900's) **S: 202**
Nuclear power *See* Nuclear energy *in this index*
Nuclear power plant
See also Nuclear reactor *in this index*
Glass (Modern glassmaking) **G: 222-223**
Nuclear energy (The role of nuclear energy in power production) **N: 580** *with pictures*
Nuclear physics **N: 596**
Pennsylvania (Economic decline) **P: 268** *with picture*
Technology (Using technology safely) **T: 77**
Nuclear radiation
Nuclear energy **N: 579**; (Radioactive decay) **N: 582**
Nuclear weapon (Effects of nuclear weapons) **N: 598-599**
Radiation **R: 74**; (Particle radiation) **R: 76**
Nuclear reaction
Isotope (Artificial radioisotopes) **I: 477**
Nuclear weapon (How nuclear weapons work) **N: 597**
Transmutation of elements **T: 378**
Nuclear reactor **N: 596**
Chernobyl disaster **Ci: 408**
Electric power (Nuclear power plants) **E: 184**
Energy supply *picture on* **E: 277**
Fallout (History) **F: 19**
Graphite **G: 323**
Idaho National Laboratory **I: 46**
Nuclear energy **N: 579** *with pictures*; (How nuclear energy is produced) **N: 584** *with pictures*; (Research on new types of reactors) **N: 592** *with pictures*
Nuclear weapon (Arms control) **N: 600**
Radiation (Artificial radioactive substances) **R: 77**; (Dose) **R: 79-80** *with picture*
Rocket (Nuclear rockets) **R: 389** *with diagram*
Transmutation of elements **T: 379**
Nuclear Regulatory Commission [U.S.] **N: 596**
Hazardous wastes **H: 122**
Nuclear energy (Government regulation) **N: 589**; (The spread of nuclear capability) **N: 591**
Nuclear rocket
Rocket **R: 384**; (Nuclear rockets) **R: 389** *with diagram*
Space exploration (Developing more efficient rockets) **So: 728**
Nuclear shell model [physics]
Atom (Forces in the nucleus) **A: 873-874**
Radiation (Causes of radiation) **R: 78**
Nuclear ship
Navy (Navies during the Cold War) **N: 80**
Ship (Nuclear power and automation) **S: 426**
Warship (Warships in the nuclear age) **W: 42** *with pictures*
Nuclear submarine
Connecticut (The mid-1900's) **Ci: 971** *with picture*
Navy (Navies during the Cold War) **N: 80**
Submarine (The power plant) **So: 941**; (Nuclear submarines) **So: 943**
Warship (Warships in the nuclear age) **W: 42** *with picture*
Nuclear superiority
Nuclear weapon (Mutually assured destruction) **N: 600**
Nuclear theory *See* Atomic theory *in this index*
Nuclear transfer [biology]
Cloning (Cloning animals) **Ci: 682l** *with picture*
Nuclear umbrella [arms control]
Nuclear weapon (Inducements) **N: 601**
Nuclear war
Nuclear weapon **N: 596**
Nuclear winter **N: 602**
War (The Cold War era) **W: 26**
Nuclear War, International Physicians for the Prevention of
Nobel Prizes (Peace: 1985) **N: 448b**
Nuclear waste
Nevada (The early 2000's) **N: 177**
Nuclear energy (Wastes and waste disposal) **N: 588**
Radiation (Artificial radioactive substances) **R: 77-78**
Nuclear weapon **N: 596** *with pictures*

See also the list of Related articles in the Nuclear weapon article
Air force (Air forces in the nuclear age) A: 186
Arms control (The current arms-control debate) A: 721; (History of arms control) A: 721-722
Army (Prevention of war) A: 725; (Armies in the nuclear age) A: 728
Canada, History of (The return of the Liberals) C: 149
Chemical-biological-radiological warfare (Radiological) C: 396
Civil defense (History of civil defense in the United States) Ci: 606
Clinton, Bill (International affairs) Ci: 682f
Cold War (To the brink and back) Ci: 765; (The missile gap) Ci: 767 with picture; (The shifting Cold War background) Ci: 769; (Easing Cold War tensions) Ci: 769
Diefenbaker, John George (Nuclear controversy) D: 198
Fallout F: 18; (History) F: 19
Guided missile (The warhead) G: 423
International relations (The Cold War begins) I: 345
Iran (Recent developments) I: 406b
Iraq (The Persian Gulf War of 1991) I: 414-414a
Korea, North (Nuclear tensions) K: 374
Los Alamos National Laboratory L: 455
Navy (Navies during the Cold War) N: 80
Nevada picture on N: 175
New Zealand (International tensions) N: 355-356
North Atlantic Treaty Organization (History) N: 471
Nuclear energy (The development of nuclear weapons) N: 590
Nuclear Nonproliferation Treaty N: 595
Pacific Islands (Nuclear testing) P: 12
Pakistan (Struggle for democracy) P: 100
Pauling, Linus Carl P: 202
Strategic Arms Limitation Talks So: 919
Strategic Arms Reduction Treaty So: 919
Strategic Defense Initiative So: 919
Technology (Challenges of technology) T: 77
Terrorism (Nuclear attacks) T: 176
United Nations (Arms control) U: 92
War (The history of warfare) W: 25-26
Weapon (World War II) W: 154b
Nuclear winter N: 602
Nuclear weapon (Thermal radiation) N: 599
Nucleic acid [biology]
Human body (Chemical elements and molecules) H: 417
Life (Nucleic acids) L: 278
Nucleoid [biology]
Bacteria (The structure of bacteria) B: 20 with diagram
Nucleolus [biology]
Cell (The nucleus) C: 328 with diagrams
Nucleon [subatomic particle]
Baryon B: 122
Nucleotide [biology]
DNA D: 258
Heredity (The flow of genetic information) H: 205
Life (Nucleic acids) L: 278
RNA R: 357
Nucleus [astronomy]
Comet Ci: 867
Halley's Comet H: 24
Nucleus [biology]
Ameba A: 406
Blood (Red blood cells) B: 408
Cell C: 326; (The nucleus) C: 328 with diagrams
Cloning (Cloning animals) Ci: 682l
Heredity (Chromosomes and genes) H: 201
Life (Cells) L: 277
Nucleus [physics]
Atom (The parts of an atom) A: 870-871 with diagrams; (Forces in the nucleus) A: 873; (Studying the nucleus) A: 876
Bacteria (The structure of bacteria) B: 20
Cosmic rays (Galactic cosmic rays) Ci: 1076
Electricity (Atoms) E: 191-192
Electron E: 203
Fusion F: 589
Heisenberg, Werner H: 167
Magnetic resonance imaging M: 56
Magnetism M: 56; (Magnetic resonance) M: 61
Neutron N: 155
Nuclear energy (Atoms and nuclei) N: 581 with diagram
Nuclear physics N: 595
Particle accelerator (Uses of accelerators) P: 184
Physics (Nuclear physics) P: 437; (Uncovering the secrets of the atom) P: 442
Radiation (Radiation and radioactivity) R: 75; (Particle radiation) R: 76; (Sources of radiation) R: 77 with diagrams

Rutherford, Ernest R: 569
Star (Fusion in stars) So: 846
Nucleus accumbens [anatomy]
Brain (Regulating body processes) B: 554
Nude Descending a Staircase, No. 2 [painting by Duchamp]
Duchamp, Marcel D: 373 with picture
Nueces River [Texas]
Mexican War (Background of the war) M: 445 with map; (Events leading up to the war) M: 446
Nuer [people] N: 602
Africa picture on A: 116a
Anthropology (Linguistic anthropology) A: 547
Nuer, The [book by Evans-Pritchard]
Ethnography E: 373
Nuestra Señora del Monte Carmelo
Mission life in America (A visitor's guide) M: 620
Nueva Isabela [Latin American history]
Santo Domingo S: 117
Nuevo Cine Mexicano [movement]
Mexico (Motion pictures) M: 460
Nuevo Laredo [Mexico] N: 603 with picture
Laredo L: 76
Nuffield Radio Astronomy Laboratories, Jodrell Bank
Jodrell Bank Observatory J: 130
Nuggets, Denver [team]
Basketball (table) B: 150
Nui [island, Pacific]
Tuvalu map on T: 527; (Land and climate) T: 528
Nujoma, Sam [Namibian political leader]
Namibia (History) N: 9
Nuku Hiva [island, Pacific]
Marquesas Islands M: 217 with picture
Nuku'alofa [Tonga]
Tonga T: 327 with map; (Economy) T: 328
Nukufetau [island, Pacific]
Tuvalu map on T: 527; (Land and climate) T: 528
Nukulaelae [island, Pacific]
Tuvalu map on T: 527; (Land and climate) T: 528
Null and void [law]
Nullification N: 603
Null set [mathematics]
Set theory (Empty sets) S: 321
Nullarbor Plain [Australia]
Australia (Land regions) A: 907 with map
Nullification [U.S. history] N: 603
Calhoun, John Caldwell C: 35
Force bill F: 371
Hayne, Robert Young H: 122
Jackson, Andrew (Split with Calhoun) J: 11
South Carolina (Nullification) So: 660
States' rights (Early history) So: 866
United States, History of the (Jackson as president) U: 171
Webster, Daniel (The U.S. senator) W: 177
Nullification, Ordinance of [1832]
South Carolina (Nullification) So: 660
Numa Pompilius [legendary figure]
Calendar (The Romans) C: 31
February F: 60
Mythology (The seven kings) M: 983
Rome, Ancient (The regal period) R: 444
Numbat [animal] N: 603 with picture
Number [cards]
Bridge (Bidding) B: 604
Number [grammar] N: 604
Noun (Number and case) N: 552
Number [mathematics] N: 604 with pictures
Arabic numerals A: 584
Arithmetic A: 665
Flag pictures on F: 197
Integer I: 317
Maya (Communication and learning) M: 324
Roman numerals R: 413
Scientific notation S: 207
Number, Denominate [mathematics] See Denominate number in this index
Number 8 [painting by Rothko]
Rothko, Mark picture on R: 488
Number line [mathematics]
Addition (Regrouping) A: 49
Number 9: In Praise of Gertrude Stein [painting by Tomlin]
Tomlin, Bradley Walker picture on T: 326
Number 10 Downing Street
London (Central London) L: 429-430
Number the Stars [book by Lowry]
Lowry, Lois L: 511
Number theory [mathematics] N: 607
Fermat, Pierre de F: 73
Numbers, Book of [Bible] N: 607
Pentateuch P: 274
Numeral [mathematics]
See also Numeral system in this index
Number N: 605

Numeral flag
Flag pictures on F: 197
Numeral system [mathematics]
Decimal system D: 70
Duodecimal system D: 386
Gupta dynasty (Cultural life under the guptas) G: 442-443
Number N: 605; (History) N: 607
Zero Z: 590
Numerator [mathematics]
Fraction (In symbols) F: 444
Numerianus [Roman emperor]
Rome, Ancient (table) R: 447
Numerical control
Machine tool (History) M: 20
Numerical reasoning aptitude
Careers (Aptitudes) C: 215
Numerical weather prediction model
Meteorology (Computer modeling) M: 433
Numerology [belief] N: 607
Fortunetelling (Methods of fortunetelling) F: 420
Numidia [ancient region] N: 608
Numismatics See Coin collecting in this index
Numitor [legendary figure]
Romulus and Remus R: 450a
Nummulite [extinct organism] N: 608 with picture
Nun [Egyptian god]
Mythology (The Great Ennead) M: 979
Nun [letter]
N N: 1 with picture
Nun [religion] N: 608
Address, Forms of (Members of the clergy) A: 54
Convent N: 1024
Monasticism M: 701
Religious life R: 226
Nun buoy [navigation]
Buoy B: 701
Nunatsiavut Government
Newfoundland and Labrador (Aboriginal government) N: 375
Nunavut [territory, Canada] N: 608 with pictures and map
Boothia Peninsula B: 481
Canada, History of (Canada under Chrétien) C: 152
Ellesmere Island E: 242
Flag picture on F: 214
Indian, American (Current issues) I: 182-183
Inuit (History) I: 354i
Northwest Territories (The late 1900's) N: 534, N: 534
Nunavut Act [1999]
Nunavut (Establishment of Nunavut) N: 612
Nunavut Land Claims Agreement Act [1993]
Nunavut (Establishment of Nunavut) N: 612
Nuncio [diplomat]
Pope (The powers of the pope) P: 661
Vatican City (Diplomatic corps) V: 288
Nunes, Pedro [Portuguese navigator]
Great-circle route G: 338
Núñez de Arce, Gaspar [Spanish author]
Spanish literature (The 1800's) So: 761
Núñez del Prado, Marina [Bolivian artist]
Bolivia (The arts) B: 444
Nunivak Island
Alaska (Coastline) A: 294
Nuoc mam [food]
Vietnam (Food and drink) V: 366
Nuqrashi, Mahmud [Egyptian political leader]
Muslim Brotherhood M: 964
Nur Adde [Somali political leader]
Somalia (History) So: 589-590
Nūr al-Dīn [Muslim political leader]
Fātimid dynasty F: 55
Nur Hassan Hussein [Somali political leader]
Somalia (History) So: 589-590
Nurek Dam [Vakhsh River, Tajikistan]
Dam (table) D: 18
Nuremberg [Germany] N: 612
Bavaria B: 174
Clock picture on Ci: 682k
Doll (The Renaissance) D: 288
Germany picture on G: 169
Nuremberg Chronicle [book]
Library picture on L: 239
Nuremberg Laws [German history]
Holocaust (Before the Holocaust) H: 296
Nuremberg N: 613
Nuremberg Trials [1945-1949] N: 613
Germany (Occupied Germany) G: 169
Gestapo G: 175
Holocaust (The Nuremberg Trials) H: 297
Human rights (The development of human rights) H: 428-428a
International law (Punishment) I: 341
Jackson, Robert Houghwout J: 16
War crime (World War II) W: 27

World War II *picture on* **W:** 497
Nureyev, Rudolf [Russian dancer] **N:** 613 *with picture*
Ballet (Ballet in Russia) **B:** 52-53
Fonteyn, Margot **F:** 327 *with picture*
Nurmi, Paavo [Finnish athlete] **N:** 613
Olympic Games (Between the wars) **O:** 751
Track and field (The early and middle 1900's) **T:** 360
Nürnberg *See* Nuremberg *in this index*
Nurse *See* Nursing *in this index*
Nurse [entomology]
Insect (Family life) **I:** 294-295
Nurse, Sir Paul [British biologist]
Nobel Prizes (Physiology or medicine: 2001) **N:** 447
Nurse manager
Nursing (Nurse managers) **N:** 617
Nurse-midwife
Midwife **M:** 536
Pregnancy (Planning for pregnancy) **P:** 734a
Nurse practitioner
Medicine (Other health-care professionals) **M:** 366
Nursing (Nurse practitioners) **N:** 617
Nurse researcher
Nursing (Other nursing careers) **N:** 618
Nurse shark [fish] **N:** 614
Shark (Nurse sharks) **S:** 375 *with picture*
Zoo *picture on* **Z:** 602
Nursery [agriculture] **N:** 614 *with picture*
Conservation *picture on* **Ci:** 980
Nursery name
Name (Nicknames) **N:** 7
Nursery rhyme N: 614 *with picture*
Literature for children *picture on* **L:** 370; (Poetry) **L:** 357
Nursery Rhymes of England, The [book by Halliwell]
Nursery rhyme (History) **N:** 615-616
Nursery school *See* Preschool *in this index*
Nursery-web spider
Spider *picture on* **So:** 787; (Nursery-web spiders) **So:** 790
Nurse's aide N: 616
Hospital (The professional services staff) **H:** 371
Nurses' Settlement [New York City]
Wald, Lillian D. **W:** 6
Nursing [career] **N:** 616 *with pictures*
Barton, Clara **B:** 121
Careers (Health care) **C:** 223-224
Emergency room **E:** 258
Hospital (The professional services staff) **H:** 371; (The 1800's) **H:** 373
Medicine **M:** 365, *pictures on* **M:** 365
Nightingale, Florence **N:** 420
Nurse's aide **N:** 616
Nutting, Mary Adelaide **N:** 632
Wald, Lillian D. **W:** 6
Nursing [feeding]
See also Breast-feeding *in this index*
Baby (Feeding procedures) **B:** 9
Cat (Growth and development) **C:** 293 *with picture*
Dog (Life history) **D:** 266-277 *with picture*
Mammal **M:** 117, *pictures on* **M:** 119; (Care of the young) **M:** 124 *with picture*
Mammary glands **M:** 129
Nursing home N: 619 *with picture*
Foster care **F:** 429
Nursing sister [occupation]
Nursing (Nurse managers) **N:** 617
Nurture [psychology]
Behavior (The nature/nurture debate) **B:** 221
Nurturing and protecting response [physiology]
Stress (How stress affects the body) **So:** 926-927
Nüsslein-Volhard, Christiane [German physiologist]
Nobel Prizes (Physiology or medicine: 1995) **N:** 446
Nut [Egyptian goddess]
Mythology *picture on* **M:** 974; (The Great Ennead) **M:** 979; (The Osiris myth) **M:** 979
Nut [food] **N:** 620 *with pictures*
See also the list of Related articles in the Nut *article*
Halloween (Fortunetelling) **H:** 24b
Horticulture (Pomology) **H:** 369
Nutrition (Kinds of nutrients) **N:** 625
Tree (Food products) **T:** 412
Nut [hardware]
Bolt **B:** 449
Nutcrack Night [custom]
Halloween (Fortunetelling) **H:** 24b
Nutcracker [bird] **N:** 622 *with picture*
Nutcracker, The [ballet] **N:** 622 *with picture*
Ballet (Kinds of ballet) **B:** 48
Baryshnikov, Mikhail *picture on* **B:** 123

"Nutcracker and the Mouse King" [story by Hoffmann]
Nutcracker, The **N:** 622
Nuthatch [bird] **N:** 622 *with picture*
Bird (Birds of forests and woodlands) **B:** 334 *with picture*
Nutmeg [spice] **N:** 623 *with picture*
Mace **M:** 11
Nutmeg State [nickname]
Connecticut (Colonial life) **Ci:** 968-970
Nutria [animal] **N:** 623 *with picture*
Fur (table) **F:** 561
Invasive species (Managing invasive species) **I:** 354k
Nutriculture [agriculture] *See* Hydroponics *in this index*
Nutrient [biology]
Blood (Transporting nutrients and wastes) **B:** 408 *with diagram*
Ecology **E:** 53
Environmental pollution (Water pollution) **E:** 334
Fertilizer **F:** 78
Food (How the body uses food) **F:** 330
Food additive (Kinds of additives) **F:** 339
Milk **M:** 545
Nutrition (Kinds of nutrients) **N:** 625
Ocean (The food cycle) **O:** 655-658
Plant (Environmental factors) **P:** 538-539
Rain forest (Climate and soil) **R:** 126
Soil **So:** 573
Starvation **So:** 859
Vegetable **V:** 292
Vitamin **V:** 430
Water pollution *diagram on* **W:** 137; (Disruption of natural processes) **W:** 138
Nutrition N: 624 *with pictures*
See also the list of Related articles in the Nutrition *article*
Cancer (Reducing the risk of cancer) **C:** 171
Carbohydrate **C:** 202
Center for Science in the Public Interest **C:** 351
Circulatory system (In nutrition) **Ci:** 560 *with picture*
Disease (Metabolic diseases) **D:** 229
Family and consumer sciences (Nutrition, dietetics, and food science) **F:** 26
Fat (Biological and nutritional importance) **F:** 52-53
Fiber, Dietary **F:** 88
Flour **F:** 268
Food (How the body uses food) **F:** 330
Food supply (Basic human food needs) **F:** 346 *with pictures*
Health (Nutrition) **H:** 125
Health food **H:** 129
Malnutrition **M:** 111
Milk **M:** 545
Mushroom (The importance of mushrooms) **M:** 945
Obesity (Causes of obesity) **O:** 642a
Physical fitness (Developing physical fitness) **P:** 435
Protein (Proteins in the diet) **P:** 832
Seafood **S:** 265
Teeth (A good diet) **T:** 81
Trace elements **T:** 355
Trans fats **T:** 369
Vegetarianism **V:** 294
Weight control (Maintaining a healthy body weight) **W:** 181
Nutrition Labeling and Education Act [1990]
Center for Science in the Public Interest **C:** 351
Nutrition (Eat a balanced diet) **N:** 626
Nutritionist
Nutrition (Careers in nutrition) **N:** 631 *with picture*
Nutter, Donald G. [American political leader]
Montana (table) **M:** 757
Nutting, Mary Adelaide [Canadian-American nurse] **N:** 632
Nuu-chah-nulth [people]
Nootka Indians **N:** 453
Nuuanu Pali [cliff]
Hawaii (Places to visit) **H:** 98
Nuuanu Pali, Battle of [1795]
Kamehameha I **K:** 212
Nuuk [Greenland] **N:** 632
Greenland (People) **G:** 384-385 *with picture*
Nuwas, Abu [Arab poet]
Arabic literature (Poetry) **A:** 583
Nuyoricans [people]
Hispanic Americans **H:** 244
NVM [electronics]
Computer chip (Memory chips) **Ci:** 924f
NYA [U.S. history] *See* National Youth Administration *in this index*
Nyamwezi [people]
Tanzania (The development of trade) **T:** 34-35

Nyasa, Lake [Africa] *See* Lake Nyasa *in this index*
Nyasaland [former name]
Malawi **M:** 96
Nyaya [philosophy]
Hinduism (The six schools of philosophy) **H:** 236
Nye, Bill [American author] **N:** 632
Nye, Edgar Wilson
Nye, Bill **N:** 632
Nye, James Warren [American political leader]
Nevada (Nevada becomes a territory) **N:** 174
Nye and Riley's Railway Guide [book by Nye and Riley]
Nye, Bill **N:** 632
Nyerere, Julius Kambarage [Tanzanian political leader] **N:** 632
Tanzania (Independence) **T:** 35; (The united republic and socialism) **T:** 35
Nyhan, William [American physician]
Lesch-Nyhan syndrome **L:** 206
Nyhavn Canal [Copenhagen]
Denmark *picture on* **D:** 132
Nyiragongo [volcano, Congo]
Lava *picture on* **L:** 127
Nyíregyháza Zoo [Hungary]
Zoo *picture on* **N:** 603
Nylon [synthetic] **N:** 632
Air conditioning (In business and industry) **A:** 176-177
Aramid **A:** 591
Fiber *picture on* **F:** 87
Interior design (Choosing patterns and textures) **I:** 332
Plastics (table) **P:** 556; (Growth of the plastics industry) **P:** 560
Rope (Synthetic-fiber rope) **R:** 473 *with picture*
Rugs and carpets (Materials used in rugs and carpets) **R:** 514
Sailing (Sails) **S:** 24
Textile (Manufactured fibers) **T:** 213
Nylon salt
Nylon (How nylon is made) **N:** 633
Nylon 6
Nylon (History) **N:** 633
Nylon 66
Nylon (History) **N:** 633
Nymph [entomology]
Cicada (Development) **Ci:** 551
Insect (Incomplete metamorphosis) **I:** 293
Larva **L:** 78
Nymph [mythology] **N:** 633
Dionysus **D:** 215
Mythology (Greek divinities) **M:** 982
Nymph of Fontainebleau [sculpture by Cellini]
Cellini, Benvenuto **C:** 339
Nymphidia [poem by Drayton]
Drayton, Michael **D:** 344
Nynorsk
Norway (Language) **N:** 539
Nyoman River [Belarus] *See* Neman River *in this index*
NYSE [stock exchange] *See* New York Stock Exchange *in this index*
NYSE Alternext [name for]
American Stock Exchange **A:** 430
NYSE Euronext [company]
American Stock Exchange **A:** 430
New York Stock Exchange **N:** 345
NYSE Euronext [stock exchange]
New York Stock Exchange **N:** 345
NYSE Group Inc.
New York Stock Exchange **N:** 345
Nystagmus [disorder] **N:** 633
Nystatin [medication]
Antibiotic (Disruption of the cell membrane) **A:** 550-551
Nyswander, Marie [American doctor]
Methadone **M:** 433
NYU [university] *See* New York University *in this index*
Nyx [Greek mythology]
Hypnos **H:** 477
Nzinga Mbemba [king of Kongo]
Kongo **K:** 364
Nzinga Nkuwu [king of Kongo] **N:** 633
Kongo **K:** 364

O

O [letter] **O:** 634 *with pictures*
O [symbol]
Oxygen (Chemical properties) **O:** 889
"O" [water show]
Swimming (Synchronized swimming) **So:** 1047
O. Henry *See* Henry, O. *in this index*
O-16 [isotope]
Ice age (Evidence from oceans) **I:** 7
O-18 [isotope]
Ice age (Evidence from oceans) **I:** 7

Ó Cadhain, Máirtin [Irish author]
  Irish literature (Modern works in Gaelic) I: 431
"O Canada" [song] O: 635
"O Captain! My Captain!" [poem by Whitman]
  Whitman, Walt (His work) W: 294
O gauge [size]
  Railroad, Model (Scale and size) R: 120 *with picture*
"O God, Our Help in Ages Past" [hymn]
  Hymn (Words and music) H: 475
O Guarani [book by Alencar]
  Latin American literature (Romanticism) L: 112-113
Ó Rathaille, Aodhagán [Irish poet]
  Irish literature (Modern works in Gaelic) I: 431
O ring
  Challenger disaster C: 370
  Space exploration (The Challenger disaster) So: 725
"O soave fanciulla" [aria]
  Opera: (*Bohème, La*) O: 801
Ó Súilleabháin, Eoghan Rua [Irish poet]
  Irish literature (Modern works in Gaelic) I: 431
OAAU [organization]
  Malcolm X M: 103
Oahe, Lake
  South Dakota (Rivers and lakes) So: 676 *with map*
Oahu [island, Hawaii]
  Hawaii H: 88; (Oahu) H: 102
  Honolulu H: 320
Oak [tree] O: 635 *with pictures*
  Acorn A: 28
  Forest (Forest succession) F: 397
  Live oak L: 393 *with picture*
  Plant *pictures on* P: 525; (How plants protect themselves) P: 540-541
  Tree *pictures on* T: 423, T: 427
  Wood *picture on* W: 389
Oak Creek Canyon [Arizona]
  Arizona (Places to visit) A: 678
Oak-deer-maple biome [biology] *See* Temperate deciduous forest *in this index*
Oak Hammock Marsh [Manitoba]
  Manitoba (Places to visit) M: 152
Oak Hill [estate]
  Monroe, James (Later years) M: 738
Oak Park [Illinois]
  Architecture *picture on* A: 631
Oak Ridge Cemetery [Illinois]
  Lincoln, Abraham (Assassination) L: 326 *with picture*
  Springfield So: 807
Oak Ridge National Laboratory [Tennessee] O: 636
Oak titmouse [bird]
  Titmouse T: 302 *with picture*
Oak-tree shilling [money]
  Colonial life in America (Money) Ci: 811-812
  Money *picture on* M: 707; (Tree shillings) M: 710
Oakblue [butterfly]
  Butterfly *picture on* B: 734
Oakland [California] O: 637 *with picture*
  California (The late 1900's) C: 63
Oakland Athletics [team]
  Baseball (table) B: 130
Oakland Raiders [team]
  Football (National Football League) F: 364
Oaklawn Park [Arkansas]
  Arkansas *picture on* A: 705
Oakley, Annie [American entertainer] O: 638 *with picture*
Oakmoss [lichen]
  Lichen (The importance of lichens) L: 269
Oar
  Rowing R: 493
Oarfish [fish] O: 638
  Fish *picture on* F: 156
OAS [Algerian history] *See* Secret Army Organization *in this index*
OAS [organization] *See* Organization of American States *in this index*
OASDI [government program] *See* Old-age, survivors, and disability insurance *in this index*
OASHDI [government program] *See* Social Security *in this index*
Oasis O: 638 *with picture*
  Africa *picture on* A: 117
  Merv M: 420
Oasis mirage
  Mirage M: 615
Oates, Joyce Carol [American author] O: 639 *with portrait*
  American literature (Fiction and other prose) A: 424 *with portrait*
Oates, William Calvin [American political leader]
  Alabama (table) A: 274
Oath [law] O: 639

Perjury P: 288
  Witness W: 374
Oath of allegiance [Canada]
  Citizenship (The Canadian oath of citizenship) Ci: 572
Oath of allegiance [U.S.]
  Citizenship (The United States oath of allegiance) Ci: 570
  Oath (Oath of office) O: 639
Oath of Hippocrates *See* Hippocratic oath *in this index*
Oath of office [law]
  Oath (Oath of office) O: 639
Oath of the Horatii, The [painting by David]
  David, Jacques Louis D: 46
  Painting (History paintings) P: 33-34; (Neoclassicism) P: 66-67 *with picture*
Oaths of Strasbourg [842]
  French language (Old French) F: 517
Oatmeal [food] O: 640 *with pictures*
  Scotland (Food and drink) S: 214
Oats [plant] O: 640 *with pictures*
  Grain G: 301
  Grass (Cereals) G: 326
  Horse (Food) H: 355
  Leaf *picture on* L: 151
OAU [organization] *See* Organization of African Unity *in this index*
Oaxaca [state, Mexico]
  Mixtec Indians M: 680
Oaxaca [city, Mexico] O: 640a
Oaxaca Plateau
  Mexico (The Southern Uplands) M: 462
Ob River [Russia] O: 640a
  Russia (The West Siberian Plain) R: 540-541
Oba [king]
  Yoruba Y: 569
Obadiah, Book of [Bible] O: 640a
Obama, Barack [U.S. president] O: 640b *with pictures*
  African Americans *picture on* A: 136s; (Race relations) A: 136t *with picture*
  Biden, Joe B: 294
  Clinton, Hillary Rodham Ci: 682h
  Cuba (Recent developments) Ci: 1179
  Democratic Party (The early 2000's) D: 128
  Exploration (Human space travel) E: 452
  Gulf oil spill of 2010 G: 437
  Illinois (Corruption cases) I: 71
  McCain, John M: 332
  Nebraska (The early 2000's) N: 115
  No Child Left Behind Act N: 438
  Nobel Prizes (Peace: 2009) N: 449
  Obama, Michelle Robinson O: 642
  Political convention *picture on* P: 628
  Romney, Mitt R: 450
  United States, History of the (Historic selection) U: 196f
Obama, Barack Hussein, Sr. [father of]
  Obama, Barack (Early life) O: 640b
Obama, Malia [daughter of]
  Obama, Barack (Obama's family) O: 640d *with picture*
Obama, Michelle Robinson [American lawyer] O: 642
  First ladies of the United States (table) F: 142
  Obama, Barack (Obama's family) O: 640d *with picture*
Obama, Sasha [daughter of]
  Obama, Barack (Obama's family) O: 640d *with picture*
Obamacare [law] *See* Patient Protection and Affordable Care Act *in this index*
O'Bannon, Frank L. [American political leader]
  Indiana (table) I: 214
Obasan [book by Kogawa]
  Canadian literature (Modern English-Canadian fiction) C: 160
Obasanjo, Olusegun [Nigerian political leader]
  Nigeria (Changes in government) N: 418
Obeah [religion]
  Virgin Islands, United States (Religion) V: 394
Obed Wild and Scenic River [Tennessee]
  National Park System (table: National parkways and other national parklands) N: 56
Obedience training
  Dog (Obedience training) D: 280 *with picture*
Obedience trial
  Dog (Dog competitions) D: 280-281
Obelisk [architecture] O: 642
  Cleopatra's Needles *picture on* Ci: 662b
  Time (Solar time) T: 288
  Washington Monument W: 109
Obelisk of Luxor
  Obelisk O: 642
  Paris (Gardens, squares, and parks) P: 162 *with picture*

Oberammergau [Germany]
  Passion play P: 192
Oberlin College
  Coeducation Ci: 752
  United States, History of the (Women's rights) U: 173
  Women's movement (The beginnings of women's movements) W: 384-385
Oberon [legendary figure]
  Fairy (Fairies in literature) F: 11 *with picture*
  Shakespeare, William: (*A Midsummer Night's Dream*) S: 357
Oberon [satellite]
  Uranus *picture on* U: 219
Oberth, Hermann [German physicist]
  Rocket (Rockets of the early 1900's) R: 390
  Space exploration (Early dreams of space flight) So: 706
Oberto [opera by Verdi]
  Verdi, Giuseppe V: 316
Obesity [disorder] O: 642 *with diagram*
  See also Weight control *in this index*
  Binge eating B: 308
  Child (Physical disabilities and challenges) C: 453
  Diabetes (Type 2 diabetes) D: 179
  Fat (Fats and disease) F: 53
  Food (Recent developments) F: 337
  Health (Nutrition) H: 125
  Nutrition (Do not overeat) N: 630 *with picture*
Obiang Nguema Mbasogo, Teodoro [Equatorial Guinea political leader]
  Equatorial Guinea (History) E: 347
Object [computing]
  Computer (Using programming languages) Ci: 923
Object [grammar]
  Case (Pronouns) C: 272
  Grammar G: 303
Object ball
  Billiards B: 304
Object marble
  Marbles M: 193
Object-oriented programming [computing]
  Computer (Using programming languages) Ci: 923
Objective case [grammar]
  Case (Pronouns) C: 272
  Declension D: 80
Objective lens
  Binoculars B: 309 *with diagram*
  Microscope (Tube and lenses) M: 517-518 *with pictures*
  Telescope (Refracting telescopes) T: 103 *with diagram*
Objectivism [philosophy]
  Philosophy (Ethics and political philosophy) P: 385
  Rand, Ayn R: 136
Oblast [political unit]
  Russia (Local government) R: 531
  Ukraine (Local government) U: 6
Oblate spheroid [geometry]
  Spheroid So: 780
Obligation [philosophy]
  Ethics (Modern ethics) E: 366
Oblique circular cylinder [geometry]
  Cylinder Ci: 1204
Oblique fault [geology]
  Earthquake *diagram on* E: 37
Oblique prism
  Prism P: 805
Obliquity [astronomy]
  Mars (Orbit and rotation) M: 225
Oblomov [book by Goncharov]
  Russian literature (Early realism) R: 562
OBO [ship] *See* Ore/bulk/oil carrier *in this index*
Obock [Djibouti]
  Djibouti (History) D: 257
Oboe [musical instrument] O: 643 *with pictures*
  Music (Wind instruments) M: 949 *with picture*
Obote, Milton [Ugandan political leader]
  Ganda G: 24
  Uganda (History) U: 3-4
O'Boyle, Patrick Aloysius [American religious leader]
  Cardinal (table: American cardinals) C: 211
Obrecht, Jacob [Flemish composer]
  Classical music (Franco-Flemish music) Ci: 646
Obregón, Alejandro [Colombian painter]
  Colombia (The arts) Ci: 781
Obregón, Álvaro [Mexican political leader] O: 643
  Mexico (Reforms of the early 1900's) M: 472; (The Revolution of 1910) M: 472
  Villa, Pancho V: 384 *with picture*
Obrenović, Miloš [Serbian political leader]
  Serbia (Ottoman rule) S: 314
O'Brien, Davey [American football player]

Football (table) **F:** 363
O'Brien, Edmond [British actor]
Motion picture (Best performance by an actor in a supporting role: 1954) **M:** 862a
O'Brien, Edwin [American religious leader]
Cardinal (table: American cardinals) **C:** 211
O'Brien, Flann [Irish author]
Irish literature (Fiction) **I:** 432
O'Brien, Joseph C. [American harness driver]
Harness racing (History) **H:** 64
O'Brien, Lawrence Francis [American political leader]
Johnson, Lyndon Baines (table) **J:** 151
O'Brien, Parry [American track athlete]
Track and field (The early and middle 1900's) **T:** 360
O'Brien, Robert C. [American author] **O:** 643
Newbery Medal (table) **N:** 359
Obscene Bird of the Night, The [book by Donoso]
Latin American literature (The "Boom") **L:** 114
Obscenity and pornography O: 643
Censorship (Moral censorship) **C:** 345
Freedom of the press **F:** 507
Observation [psychology]
Pestalozzi, Johann Heinrich **P:** 318
Psychology (Naturalistic observation) **P:** 847
Observation balloon
Balloon (Balloons in war) **B:** 61
Observation elevator
Elevator (Special kinds of elevators) **E:** 235
Observational study
Statistics (Collecting the data) **So:** 868
Observatory [astronomy] **O:** 644 *with picture*
See also the list of Related articles in the Observatory *article*
National Radio Astronomy Observatory **N:** 59
Telescope *picture on* **T:** 102
Observed trial [race]
Bicycle racing (Road races) **B:** 292-293
Observer mission [UN]
United Nations (Peacekeeping operations) **U:** 90
Obsession [psychology]
Mental illness (Anxiety disorders) **M:** 405
Obsessive-compulsive disorder **O:** 646
Obsessive-compulsive disorder [psychology] **O:** 646
Anxiety disorder **A:** 562
Hoarding **H:** 271
Mental illness (Anxiety disorders) **M:** 405
Obsidian [rock] **O:** 646
Glass (Early times) **G:** 217-218
Igneous rock **I:** 49
Rock (Extrusive rock) **R:** 371; (table) **R:** 373 *with picture*
Tula **T:** 482
Obsidian Cliff
Yellowstone National Park (The Upper Loop) **Y:** 559 *with map*
Obstetrical toad *See* Midwife toad *in this index*
Obstetrics and gynecology O: 646
Medicine (table) **M:** 369
Surgery (Obstetrics and gynecology) **So:** 1007
Obstructive jaundice [disorder]
Jaundice **J:** 65
Obstructive lung disease
Lung (Diseases of the lungs) **L:** 524
Obstructive sleep apnea [disorder]
Sleep apnea **S:** 507
Obtuse angle [mathematics]
Angle **A:** 462 *with diagram*
Obtuse triangle [geometry]
Triangle (Kinds of triangles) **T:** 437 *with diagram*
Óbuda [former city, Hungary]
Budapest **B:** 666
Öcalan, Abdullah [Kurdish military leader]
Turkey (Recent developments) **T:** 512
O'Callaghan, Mike [American political leader]
Nevada (table) **N:** 173
Ocarina [musical instrument] **O:** 646 *with picture*
O'Casey, Sean [Irish dramatist] **O:** 646
Irish literature (The Irish literary revival) **I:** 431-432
Realism (In drama) **R:** 172
Occam, William of [English theologian] *See* William of Ockham *in this index*
Occaneechi Indians
Virginia (Early days) **V:** 418
Occasional Offices [religion]
Eastern Orthodox Churches (Services) **E:** 46
Occasions, The [book by Montale]
Montale, Eugenio **M:** 741
Occipital bone [anatomy]
Head **H:** 123 *with diagram*
Human body (table) **H:** 422 *with diagram*
Skull **S:** 495
Occipital lobe [anatomy]
Brain (The cerebrum) **B:** 550a-550b *with diagram*

Occluded front
Weather (Synoptic-scale systems) **W:** 159-161
Occult
New Age movement **N:** 178
Witchcraft (Witchcraft as a religion) **W:** 371
Occultation [astronomy]
Eclipse **E:** 51
Occultism O: 647
See also the list of Related articles in the Occultism *article*
Religion (Religion today) **R:** 223-224
Occupancy [law] **O:** 647
Occupation
For a list of articles on career opportunities, see the Related articles in the Careers *article*
Career education **C:** 213
Careers **C:** 214 *with pictures*
Name (Occupations) **N:** 6
Occupation zone [German history]
Cold War (The alliance breaks up) **Ci:** 763
Germany (Occupied Germany) **G:** 169 *with map*
Occupational disease
Disease (Environmental and occupational diseases) **D:** 230
Health (Occupational health hazards) **H:** 127
Occupational medicine **O:** 647
Occupational health nurse
Nursing (Occupational and industrial health nursing) **N:** 617
Occupational medicine O: 647
Occupational Safety and Health Act [1970]
Personnel management (Development of personnel management) **P:** 303
Occupational Safety and Health Administration [U.S.] **O:** 647
Asbestos (Hazards of asbestos) **A:** 765
Labor, Department of (Functions) **L:** 2
National Institute for Occupational Safety and Health **N:** 39
Occupational therapist
Occupational therapy **O:** 648 *with pictures*; (Careers) **O:** 649
Occupational therapy O: 648 *with pictures*
Hospital (Professional services departments) **H:** 371
Occupational therapy assistant
Occupational therapy **O:** 648; (Careers) **O:** 649
Occupational Therapy Association, American
Occupational therapy (Careers) **O:** 649
OCD [disorder] *See* Obsessive-compulsive disorder *in this index*
Ocean O: 650 *with pictures and maps*
See also the list of Related articles in the Ocean *article*
Animal (Animals of the oceans) **A:** 486 *with pictures*
Bird (Birds of the ocean and the Antarctic) **B:** 344 *with pictures*
Climate (Oceans and large lakes) **Ci:** 676a; (Changes in ocean circulation) **Ci:** 676d
Conservation (Ocean conservation) **Ci:** 978 *with picture*
Deep **D:** 81
Deep sea **D:** 82
Estuary **E:** 364
Exploration (Deep-sea exploration) **E:** 450
Fish (Saltwater environments) **F:** 150 *with pictures*
Fishing industry (Ocean fisheries) **F:** 181 *with pictures*
Global warming (Harm to ocean life) **G:** 232a
Ice age (Evidence from oceans) **I:** 7
Law of the Sea Convention **L:** 141
Oceanography **O:** 667
Plate tectonics (Plate interactions) **P:** 561 *with diagram*
Rain **R:** 122
Salt (Salt from the sea) **S:** 72
Seamount **S:** 268
Seashore **S:** 269
Seaweed **S:** 276 *with pictures*
Tide **T:** 280 *with diagrams*
Tsunami **T:** 475
United Nations (Peaceful uses of outer space and the seabed) **U:** 93
World *map on* **W:** 408; (Water) **W:** 415
Ocean basin [geography]
Earth (The shaping of the continents) **E:** 24
Ocean conservation
Conservation (Ocean conservation) **Ci:** 978 *with picture*
Ocean current *See* Current, Ocean *in this index*
Ocean Drilling Program
Ocean drilling programs **O:** 667
Ocean drilling programs O: 667 *with diagrams*
Indian Ocean (Exploration) **I:** 187
Ocean engineering
Engineering (Other specialized fields) **E:** 287

Ocean (Careers in oceanography) **O:** 666
Ocean floor *See* Seafloor *in this index*
Ocean Island [Pacific] *See* Banaba *in this index*
Ocean liner [ship]
Cruise ship **Ci:** 1159
Ship (Passenger vessels) **S:** 426
Transportation *picture on* **T:** 390; (Overseas public transportation) **T:** 395
Ocean marine insurance
Insurance (Marine insurance) **I:** 313
Ocean ridge [geology]
Plate tectonics (Divergent plate boundaries) **P:** 561-562
Ocean Springs [Mississippi]
Le Moyne, Pierre, Sieur d'Iberville **L:** 189
Ocean State, The [nickname]
Rhode Island **R:** 296
Ocean sunfish
Fish *picture on* **F:** 153
Ocean to Ocean [book by Grant]
Grant, George Monro **G:** 311
Oceanarium
Aquarium, Public **A:** 578b; (History) **A:** 579
Oceania [region]
Pacific Islands **P:** 3
Oceanic and Atmospheric Administration, National *See* National Oceanic and Atmospheric Administration *in this index*
Oceanic island [geography]
Evolution (Geographic distribution of species) **E:** 430
Seamount **S:** 269
Oceanic whitetip shark [fish]
Shark *picture on* **S:** 374
Oceanid [mythology]
Nymph **N:** 633
Oceanography O: 667
Exploration (Deep-sea exploration) **E:** 450
Geography *picture on* **G:** 92; (Physical geography) **G:** 94
Geophysics **G:** 106a
Marine biology (Biological oceanographers) **M:** 205
Ocean **O:** 650; (Exploring the ocean) **O:** 662; (Careers in oceanography) **O:** 666 *with pictures*
Pacific Ocean (Scientific research) **P:** 15
Scripps Institution of Oceanography **S:** 227
Woods Hole Oceanographic Institution **W:** 395
Ocellated turkey
Turkey **T:** 513
Ocelli [entomology]
Ant (Sense organs) **A:** 522
Insect (Sight) **I:** 290
Ocelot [animal] **O:** 668
Animal *pictures on* **A:** 472, **A:** 480
Ocher [mineral]
Limonite **L:** 308
Ochoa, Ellen [American astronaut]
Astronaut (table) **A:** 830
Ochoa, Severo [Spanish-American biochemist]
Nobel Prizes (Physiology or medicine: 1959) **N:** 446
Ochs, Adolph Simon [American publisher] **O:** 668
Sulzberger, Arthur Hays **So:** 971
Ochs, Baron [opera character]
Opera: (*Rosenkavalier, Der*) **O:** 807
Ocicat [animal]
Cat (Short-haired breeds) **C:** 290-291
Ockeghem, Johannes [Flemish composer]
Classical music (Franco-Flemish music) **Ci:** 646
Ockham, William of [English theologian] *See* William of Ockham *in this index*
Ockham's Razor
William of Ockham **W:** 309
OCLC [library network]
Library (The growth of information and technology) **L:** 237-238 *with picture*
Ocmulgee National Monument [Georgia] **O:** 668
Georgia (Museums) **G:** 117
National Park System (table: National monuments) **N:** 51
O'Connell, Daniel [Irish political leader] **O:** 668
Ireland (Union with Britain) **I:** 426
Peel, Sir Robert **P:** 229
O'Connell, William H. [American religious leader]
Cardinal (table: American cardinals) **C:** 211
O'Connell Bridge
Dublin *picture on* **D:** 371
O'Connell Street
Dublin (The city) **D:** 371
Ireland *picture on* **I:** 427
O'Connor, Flannery [American author] **O:** 668
American literature (Southern fiction) **A:** 424
Novel (After World War II) **N:** 574
O'Connor, Frank [Irish author]
Irish literature (Fiction) **I:** 432
O'Connor, John Joseph [American religious

leader]
Cardinal (table: American cardinals) C: 211
O'Connor, Sandra Day [American jurist] O: 668
with portrait
Arizona (The late 1900's) A: 691-692
Bush, George Walker (Supreme Court) B: 722j
Reagan, Ronald Wilson *picture on* R: 165; (Events at home) R: 167-168
O'Connor, Turlough [king of the Irish]
Ireland (The Norman invaders) I: 425
O'Conor, Herbert R. [American political leader]
Maryland (table) M: 255
Ocotillo [shrub] O: 669 *with picture*
Plant *picture on* P: 526
Ocracoke Island [North Carolina]
North Carolina (Places to visit) N: 482
Octadecanoic acid *See* Stearic acid *in this index*
Octagon [geometry] O: 669 *with diagram*
Octagon House [U.S. history]
Madison, James (Life in the White House) M: 36
Octahedron [geometry] O: 669 *with diagram*
Polyhedron P: 651 *with diagram*
Topology (Algebraic topology) T: 332 *with picture*
Octameter [poetry]
Poetry (table) P: 594
Octane [petroleum] O: 669
Octane number [petroleum] O: 669
Gasoline *picture on* G: 62; (Octane ratings) G: 61
Petroleum (Cracking processes) P: 344
Octave [music]
Music (Tone) M: 950
Octave [poetry]
Poetry (table) P: 594
Sonnet So: 593
Octavia [wife of Mark Antony] O: 669
Antony, Mark A: 561
Cleopatra (Cleopatra and Mark Antony) Ci: 662a-662b
Octavia [wife of Nero]
Nero N: 130
Octavian [opera character]
Opera: (Rosenkavalier, Der) O: 807 *with picture*
Octavian [Roman emperor] *See* Augustus *in this index*
Octavian Library [Rome]
Library (Rome) L: 258
Octavianus, Gaius Julius Caesar *See* Augustus *in this index*
Octavius [literary figure]
Shakespeare, William: (Antony and Cleopatra) S: 364
Octavo [publishing]
Folio F: 315
October [month] O: 670 *with pictures*
Calendar (The Romans) C: 31
October Revolution [1917]
Russian Revolution of 1917 R: 565
Communism (Before 1917) Ci: 892
Lenin, V. I. (The October Revolution) L: 193
Mayakovsky, Vladimir M: 326
Russia (The October Revolution) R: 553
Russian Revolution of 1917 (The October Revolution) R: 566
Stalin, Joseph (Young revolutionist) So: 825-826
Union of Soviet Socialist Republics (The October Revolution) U: 35
October War [1973]
Arab-Israeli conflict (The 1973 war) A: 582a
Octofoil [symbol]
Heraldry *picture on* H: 195
Octopod [animal]
Deep sea *picture on* D: 82; (Invertebrates) D: 82a-82b
Octopus [sea animal] O: 672 *with pictures*
Animal *picture on* A: 486
Brain (Invertebrates) B: 559
Deep sea *picture on* D: 82; (Invertebrates) D: 82a-82b
Mollusk (Octopuses and squids) M: 695 *with picture*
Shell (Octopuses and squids) S: 388
Octopus, The [book by Norris]
Novel (The United States) N: 573
Ocular [lens]
Microscope (Tube and lenses) M: 517-518 *with pictures*
Oculist [career]
Eye (Receiving regular eye examinations) E: 469
Oculus [architecture]
Pantheon P: 131
O.D. [degree]
Optometry O: 814
O'Daniel, W. Lee [American political leader]
Texas (table) T: 203
Odd Couple, The [play by Simon]
Simon, Neil S: 466
Odd Fellows, Independent Order of

[organization] O: 673
Odd number [mathematics]
Series (Working with odd numbers) S: 317
Oddi, Sphincter of [anatomy]
Gallbladder G: 14
Oddie, Tasker L. [American political leader]
Nevada (table) N: 173
Ode [poetry] O: 673
Greek literature (Lyric poetry) G: 377
Pindar P: 468
Poetry (Lyric poetry) P: 591
"Ode: Intimations of Immortality" [poem by Wordsworth]
Wordsworth, William (Later career) W: 404
"Ode on a Distant Prospect of Eton College" [poem by Gray]
Gray, Thomas G: 334
"Ode to Evening" [poem by Collins]
Ode O: 673
"Ode to Felitsa" [poem by Derzhavin]
Russian literature (The classical movement) R: 559-560
Ode to the Agriculture of the Torrid Zone [poem by Bello]
Latin American literature (Romanticism) L: 112-113
"Ode to the West Wind" [poem by Shelley]
Shelley, Percy Bysshe (His writings) S: 391
Odell, Benjamin B., Jr. [American political leader]
New York (table) N: 313
Odell, Jonathan [Canadian author]
Canadian literature (Early English-Canadian literature) C: 157
O'Dell, Scott [American author] O: 673
Newbery Medal (table) N: 359
Regina Medal (table: 1978) R: 206
Odelsting [government]
Norway (National government) N: 537-539
Odenathus, Septimius [Palmyrene military leader]
Palmyra P: 111
Odeon [theater]
Athens *picture on* A: 854; (Other buildings) A: 856
Oder-Neisse boundary [Germany-Poland]
Oder River O: 674
Oder River [Europe] O: 674
Odes [poems by Horace]
Horace H: 334
Latin literature (The Augustan Age) L: 116
Odes and Various Poems [work by Hugo]
French literature (Romantic poetry) F: 521
Hugo, Victor (Early life) H: 409
Odessa [Ukraine] O: 674
Odets, Clifford [American dramatist] O: 674
American literature (Drama) A: 422-423
Odin [Norse god] O: 674
Balder B: 38
Brunhild B: 652
Mythology (Teutonic mythology) M: 985-986
Raven R: 151
Vikings (Religion) V: 380
Odinga, Raila [Kenyan political leader]
Kenya (Recent developments) K: 304
Odoacer [Ostrogoth ruler] O: 674
Europe (Germanic invasions) E: 408
Italy (History) I: 512-513
Ravenna R: 151
Rome, Ancient (The decline of the empire) R: 447-448
Romulus Augustulus R: 450a
Theodoric T: 252
Odometer [measuring device]
Speedometer So: 775 *with diagram*
Odonata [entomology]
Insect *picture on* I: 280; (table) I: 299 *with picture*
Odor
Deodorizer D: 148
Flower (The corolla) F: 293
Perfume P: 286
Smell S: 514
Odorant
Perfume P: 286
Odría, Manuel [Peruvian political leader]
Peru (The rise of APRA) P: 316
Odysseus [legend] *See* Ulysses *in this index*
Odyssey [poem by Homer] O: 674 *with pictures*
Argus A: 661
Art and the arts (The aesthetic experience) A: 745
Epic E: 342
Greek language (Development of ancient Greek) G: 376
Greek literature (Epic poetry) G: 377
Homer H: 303
Literature for children (Epics) L: 358
Lotus-eaters L: 473
Mythology (Greek mythology) M: 980
Penelope P: 238

Poetry (Narrative poetry) P: 591; (Ancient poetry) P: 595
Poseidon P: 697
Sirens S: 476
Ulysses U: 17
Odyssey: A Modern Sequel, The [poem by Kazantzakis]
Kazantzakis, Nikos K: 252
Oe, Kenzaburo [Japanese author] O: 676
Oea [Libya]
Tripoli T: 448
Oeconomicus [book by Xenophon]
Economics (Early theories) E: 63
O.E.D. [dictionary]
Dictionary (Modern dictionaries) D: 194
Oedema *See* Edema *in this index*
Oedipe [play by Voltaire]
Voltaire (Imprisonment and early success) V: 446
Oedipus [Greek mythology] O: 676 *with picture*
Antigone A: 554
Mythology (Greek heroes) M: 982
Oedipus complex [psychology] O: 676
Psychoanalysis (Psychoanalytic theory) P: 846
Oedipus Rex [play by Sophocles]
Aristotle (Literary criticism) A: 664
Drama (Tragedy) D: 326-327
Irony I: 455
Oedipus O: 676
OEEC [organization]
Marshall Plan M: 232
Oenone [Greek mythology]
Paris P: 159
OER [education]
Universities and colleges (Online learning) U: 211
Öeresund Fixed Link
Bridge (table: Cable-stayed) B: 603
Oerlikon gun
Machine gun (Antiaircraft weapons) M: 16
Oersted, Hans Christian [Danish physicist] O: 676
Aluminum (The first aluminum) A: 397
Electric meter (History) E: 177
Electric motor (History) E: 181
Electricity (Electricity and magnetism) E: 197
Electromagnet E: 201
Electromagnetism E: 203
Magnetism (Electricity and magnetism) M: 60d
Physics (Developments in the 1800's) P: 440
Telegraph (Development of the telegraph) T: 90
Oerter, Al [American track athlete]
Track and field (The early and middle 1900's) T: 360
Oesophagus [anatomy] *See* Esophagus *in this index*
"Of Friendship" [essay by Montaigne]
Montaigne, Michel Eyquem de M: 741
Of Human Bondage [book by Maugham]
Maugham, W. Somerset M: 312
Of Pandas and People [book]
Intelligent design I: 321
Of Plimoth Plantation [book by Bradford]
Bradford, William [1590-1657] B: 544
Of Reformation in England [pamphlet by Milton]
Milton, John (Middle years) M: 557
Of Thee I Sing [musical]
Gershwin, George G: 174
Musical comedy (Musical comedy matures) M: 960
Of Time and the River [book by Wolfe]
Wolfe, Thomas W: 377
O'Faolain, Sean [Irish author]
Irish literature (Fiction) I: 432
Ofcom [agency]
Radio (Government regulation of radio) R: 90-91
O'Feeney, Sean Aloysius [birth name of]
Ford, John F: 381
O'Ferrall, Charles T. [American political leader]
Virginia (table) V: 417
Off-Broadway theater
Broadway B: 635
Drama (Later United States drama) D: 340
New York City (The arts) N: 336
Theater (New York City) T: 244-245
Off-campus experience
Cooperative education Ci: 1037
Off-highway truck [vehicle]
Truck (Off-highway trucks) T: 458
Off-off-Broadway theater
Broadway B: 635
Off-road race
Automobile racing (Other kinds of racing) A: 978
Off Stonington [painting by Marin]
Painting *picture on* P: 41
Off-track betting
Horse racing (Betting) H: 365
Offa [king of Mercia]
Money (History of the pound) M: 709
Wales (Struggles against the Anglo-Saxons) W: 12

Offa's Dyke [English history]
Wales (Struggles against the Anglo-Saxons)
W: 12
Offenbach, Jacques [German-French composer]
O: 676
Operetta O: 809
Offhand grinding
Grinding and polishing (Grinding methods)
G: 395
Office [business]
Furniture *picture on* F: 569
Interior design *pictures on* I: 327, I: 335
Lighting (In offices, stores, and factories) L: 296
Office work O: 677
Office and Professional Employees International Union
Labor movement (table) L: 8
Office-block ballot
Ballot (In the United States) B: 63
Office Girls [painting by Soyer]
Soyer brothers So: 693 *with picture*
Office of ...
*Government offices appear under their key words,
as in* Management and Budget, Office of
Office work O: 677
See also the list of Related articles in the Office
work *article*
Careers (Administrative support) C: 219
Safety (In offices) S: 14
Secretarial work S: 278
Officer
Parliamentary procedure (Officers) P: 175
Rank, Military R: 139
Reserve Officers Training Corps R: 258
Ship (Officers and crew) S: 410
Officer and Laughing Girl [painting by Vermeer]
Vermeer, Jan *picture on* V: 317
Officer-Candidate School
Navy, United States (Training an officer) N: 83
Officer Candidate Training Progam
Canadian Armed Forces (Recruitment and
training) C: 155
Officers and Gentlemen [book by Waugh]
Waugh, Evelyn W: 149
Officers Reserve Corps [military]
Reserve Officers Training Corps (History) R: 258
Official [sports]
Basketball *diagrams on* B: 149
Official IRA [political group]
Irish Republican Army (Violence and peace)
I: 433-434
Official Languages Act [1969]
Canada (Languages) C: 106
Canada, History of (The separatist threat) C: 150
New Brunswick (The middle and late 1900's)
N: 198-199
Trudeau, Pierre Elliott (The national scene) T: 464
Official Test [sports]
Cricket (History) Ci: 1134-1135
Offset [printing] O: 677 *with diagram*
Book (Modern books) B: 468
Magazine (Editing and assembling an issue)
M: 43-44
Newspaper (Printing the newspaper) N: 385 *with
picture*
Printing (Offset lithography) P: 798 *with diagram*
Printing press P: 804
Offset press
Offset O: 677
Offshore banking unit
Bank (Asia and the Middle East) B: 91-92
Offshore racing
Motorboat racing (Types of racing) M: 877
Offshore well
Energy supply *picture on* E: 277
Gas [fuel] *picture on* G: 51; (Producing gas) G: 55
Nigeria *picture on* N: 416
Ocean (Sources of energy) O: 654
Petroleum *pictures on* P: 333, P:340; (table) P: 332
with picture
Offshoring [business]
Outsourcing O: 880
Offside [sports]
Football (Violations and penalties) F: 363
Hockey (Playing the game) H: 277
Lacrosse (Men's lacrosse) L: 23
Soccer (Fouls) So: 546
Offutt, Denton [American businessman]
Lincoln, Abraham (Youth on the frontier) L: 313
Offutt, Jarvis J. [American airman]
Offutt Air Force Base O: 678
Offutt Air Force Base [Nebraska] O: 678
Nebraska (The mid-1900's) N: 114 *with picture*
O'Flaherty, Liam [Irish author] O: 678
Irish literature (Fiction) I: 432
Ofrenda [altar]
Día de los muertos D: 178

Og [Biblical figure]
Giant G: 183
Ogaden [region, Ethiopia]
Ethiopia (Haile Selassie) E: 371
Somalia (History) So: 589
Ogallala Aquifer
Kansas (Agriculture) K: 231-233
Ogam [writing]
Celts C: 343
Ogasawara-gunto [former name]
Bonin Islands B: 460
Ogbu, John [Nigerian anthropologist]
Anthropology (The middle and late 1900's)
A: 549
Ogden [Utah] O: 679
Ogden, Aaron [American businessman]
Gibbons v. Ogden G: 186
New Jersey (table) N: 249
Ogden, Peter Skene [American settler]
Nevada (Exploration) N: 173
Ogden O: 679
Ogeechee-lime [tree]
Tupelo T: 492
Ogeechee tupelo [tree]
Tupelo T: 492
Ogilvie, Richard B. [American political leader]
Illinois (table) I: 71
Oglala Indians
Crazy Horse Ci: 1123
Red Cloud R: 185
Sioux Indians S: 475
Sun dance So: 987
Wounded Knee (The 1973 incident) W: 502
Oglasa [former name]
Montecristo M: 762
Ogle, Benjamin [American political leader]
Maryland (table) M: 255
Oglebay Park
Wheeling W: 279
Oglesby, Richard J. [American political leader]
Illinois (table) I: 71
Oglethorpe, James Edward [British colonial
official] O: 679
Fort Frederica National Monument F: 413
Georgia *picture on* G: 133
Savannah S: 165
United States, History of the (North Carolina,
South Carolina, and Georgia) U: 156
Ogooué River [river, Gabon]
Gabon (History) G: 3; (Land) G: 3 *with map*
Ogotai [Mongol leader]
Mongol Empire (Invasions) M: 720
Ogre-faced spider
Spider *pictures on* So: 783, So: 785; (Ogre-faced
spiders) So: 789
Ogygia [legendary place]
Odyssey: (The *Odyssey* begins) O: 675
Oh, Lady! Lady! [musical]
Kern, Jerome K: 305
Oh, Sadaharu [Japanese baseball player] O: 679
Ohain, Hans von [German physicist]
Jet propulsion (Development of jet propulsion)
J: 114
O'Hara, Frank [American poet]
American literature (Poetry) A: 423
O'Hara, John [American author] O: 679
O'Hara, John Francis [American religious leader]
Cardinal (table: American cardinals) C: 211
O'Hara, Mary [American author] O: 679
O'Hara, Scarlett [literary figure]
Gone with the Wind G: 268
Mitchell, Margaret M: 678
O'Hare International Airport
Airport (table) A: 245
Chicago (The North Side) C: 423-424;
(Transportation) C: 433
Illinois (Transportation) I: 70
O'Higgins, Bernardo [Chilean political leader]
O: 679
Argentina *picture on* A: 657
Chile (Building the nation) C: 468;
(Independence) C: 468 *with picture*
Latin America (The movement toward
independence) L: 106-107
San Martín, José de S: 105
Ohio O: 680 *with pictures and maps*
See also the list of Related articles in the Ohio
article
Ohio [nuclear submarine]
Navy, United States (The nuclear age Navy)
N: 89-90
Submarine (Nuclear submarines) So: 943
Ohio Company [U.S. history] O: 704 *with picture*
Northwest Territory (Settlement) N: 535
Ohio (Exploration and settlement) O: 700
Putnam, Rufus P: 913
Ohio Company of Associates [U.S. history]

Ohio Company (The second Ohio Company)
O: 704
Ohio Company of Virginia [U.S. history]
Ohio Company (The first Ohio Company) O: 704
Ohio gang [U.S. history]
Harding, Warren Gamaliel (Government scandals)
H: 58
Ohio River [river, U.S.] O: 705 *with map*
Ohio *picture on* O: 694; (Rivers and lakes) O: 692
with map
West Virginia (Rivers and lakes) W: 218
Ohio State University O: 705
Columbus (Education) Ci: 855
Ohio *picture on* O: 684
Ohio University O: 706
Ohio Valley Indians
Indian wars (Conflicts in the Midwest) I: 191
Ohlin, Bertil Gotthard [Swedish economist]
Nobel Prizes (Economics: 1977) N: 449
Ohlmann, Klaus [German pilot]
Glider (table) G: 230
Ohm [unit of measure] O: 706
Ohm, Georg Simon O: 706
Ohm, Georg Simon [German physicist] O: 706
Electricity (Experiments with electric charge)
E: 196-197
Ohm's law O: 706
Ohman, Olof [Swedish farmer]
Kensington rune stone K: 271
Ohmmeter [instrument]
Electric meter E: 176
Ohm O: 706
Ohm's law [physics] O: 706
Electric circuit (Circuit mathematics) E: 167
Electricity (Experiments with electric charge)
E: 196-197
Ohnaka, Keiichi [astronomer]
Betelgeuse B: 274
Ohno, Apolo Anton [American skater]
Asian Americans (Notable Asian American "firsts")
A: 812f
Ohrid, Lake See Lake Ohrid *in this index*
OIC [organization]
Sullivan, Leon Howard So: 969
Oil [mineral product] See Petroleum *in this index*
Oil [organic product] O: 706
See also Vegetable oil *in this index, and the list of
Related articles in the* Oil *article*
Fat F: 52
Fat substitute F: 53
Lipid L: 344
Nutrition (Nutrition guidelines) N: 626
Perfume (How perfumes are made) P: 286
Oil-based paint
Paint (Household paints) P: 23-24
**Oil, Chemical and Atomic Workers International
Union**
United Steelworkers U: 204
Oil circuit breaker [electricity]
Circuit breaker Ci: 558
Oil derrick
Petroleum (table) P: 332 *with picture;* (A rotary
drilling rig) P: 338 *with diagram*
Oil filter
Gasoline engine *picture on* G: 63
Oil-for-food program
Iraq (The Persian Gulf War of 1991) I: 414-414a
United Nations (Policy disagreements) U: 96
Oil gas
Gas [fuel] (Other manufactured gases) G: 56
Oil gland [anatomy] See Sebaceous gland *in this
index*
Oil immersion lens
Microscope (Tube and lenses) M: 517-518
Oil lamp
Invention *picture on* I: 356
Lamp (Fat or oil lamps) L: 52 *with pictures*
Oil of bergamot [tree product]
Bergamot B: 257
Oil of ginger [spice]
Ginger G: 191
Oil of tansy [poison]
Tansy T: 29
Oil painting [art]
Painting (Materials and techniques) P: 36; (Oil
painting) P: 39 *with picture;* (The northern
Renaissance) P: 57
Oil palm [tree]
Palm oil P: 109
Oil priming
Painting (Grounds) P: 36
Oil refinery
Indiana *picture on* I: 197
Petroleum P: 330 *with picture*
Oil roasting [process]
Peanut (Processing peanuts) P: 214
Oil sands See Bituminous sands *in this index*

Oil shale [geology] O: 707 *with diagram*
Colorado (Mining) Ci: 843
Energy supply (Fossil fuels) E: 277-278
Fuel (Synthetic liquid fuels) F: 550
Petroleum *picture on* P: 331
Oil spill O: 707 *with picture*
Alabama (The 2000's) A: 279
Alaska (Recent developments) A: 304
Coast Guard, United States (The Coast Guard since World War II) Ci: 738-739 *with picture*
Environmental pollution *picture on* E: 332
Exxon Valdez oil spill E: 459
Gulf oil spill of 2010 G: 437
Nigeria (Oil pollution) N: 418
Ocean (Oil pollution) O: 665 *with picture*
Persian Gulf War of 1991 (Consequences of the war) P: 300d
Royal Dutch pcl R: 498
Ship (Pollution) S: 413-414 *with picture*
Tanker (Oil spills) T: 28
Oil tanker [ship]
Tanker (Kinds of tankers) T: 28 *with picture*
Oil tanning [industrial process]
Leather (Tanning) L: 167-168
Oil well
Persian Gulf War of 1991 (Consequences of the war) P: 300d *with picture*
Petroleum (Drilling for petroleum) P: 337 *with diagrams*; (Completing the well) P: 340 *with diagram*
Well (Oil and natural gas wells) W: 193
Oilbird O: 708 *with picture*
Oiler [occupation]
Ship (Officers and crew) S: 410
Oilers, Edmonton [team]
Edmonton (Culture and recreation) E: 84-85
Hockey (table: National Hockey League) H: 281
Oilseed crops
Food supply (Developing new sources of food) F: 350
Oireachtas [government, Ireland]
Ireland (Parliament) I: 417
Oise River [France]
Aisne River A: 253
Oisin [legendary figure]
Finn MacCool F: 119
Ojeda, Alonso de [Spanish explorer]
Aruba A: 764
Exploration *map on* E: 443
Latin America *map on* L: 105
Vespucci, Amerigo (Life and expeditions) V: 342
Ojibwa Indians *See* Chippewa Indians *in this index*
Ojukwu, Odumegwu [Nigerian military leader]
Nigeria (Civil war) N: 418
O.K. Corral [U.S. history]
Earp, Wyatt E: 15
Tombstone T: 326
Oka [river, Russia]
Volga River V: 444
Okanagan [river]
British Columbia (Rivers, waterfalls, and lakes) B: 624
Okanagan Lake
British Columbia (Rivers, waterfalls, and lakes) B: 624
Okapi [animal] O: 709 *with picture*
Okavango [river, Africa]
Botswana (Land and climate) B: 511-512
Okavango Swamps [Botswana]
Botswana (Land and climate) B: 511
Okeechobee, Lake *See* Lake Okeechobee *in this index*
O'Keeffe, Georgia [American painter] O: 709 *with picture*
Painting (Georgia O'Keeffe) P: 83 *with picture*
Stieglitz, Alfred So: 900
Okefenokee National Wildlife Refuge [Florida-Georgia]
Okefenokee Swamp O: 710 *with picture*
Okefenokee Swamp [region, Florida-Georgia] O: 709 *with picture*
Georgia (Places to visit) G: 122 *with picture*
Okello, Tito [Ugandan political leader]
Uganda (History) U: 3-4
Okhrana [Russian history]
Secret police S: 278
Okies [people]
Dust Bowl D: 391
Okinawa [island, Pacific] O: 710 *with pictures and map*
Japan (The Ryukyu and Bonin islands) J: 48
Karate K: 245
Ryukyu Islands R: 574
World War II (Closing in on Japan) W: 492
Oklahoma O: 712 *with pictures and maps*
See also the list of Related articles in the Oklahoma *article*

Chickasaw Indians C: 439
Indian Territory I: 189 *with map*
Riot (During the 1900's) R: 349
Trail of Tears T: 367
Oklahoma! [musical]
Ballet *picture on* B: 54
De Mille, Agnes D: 119
Hammerstein, Oscar, II H: 35
Musical comedy (The modern musical emerges) M: 960 *with picture*
Oklahoma O: 712
Rodgers, Richard R: 398
Oklahoma, University of O: 735
Oklahoma City [Oklahoma] O: 735 *with picture*
Oklahoma O: 712 *with picture*; (table: Average monthly weather) O: 726
Oklahoma City bombing [U.S. history] O: 737 *with picture*
Clinton, Bill *picture on* Ci: 682a
Crime scene investigation (Collecting evidence) Ci: 1140
Oklahoma City Museum of Art [Oklahoma City]
Oklahoma (Places to visit) O: 722
Oklahoma City National Memorial [Oklahoma]
National Park System *picture on* N: 52; (table: National memorials) N: 54
Oklahoma (Places to visit) O: 722; (The 2000's) O: 722
Oklahoma City Thunder [team]
Oklahoma *picture on* O: 723
Oklahoma History Center [Oklahoma City]
Oklahoma (Places to visit) O: 722
Oklahoma land rush [U.S. history]
Oklahoma (Great land rushes) O: 732
Oklahoma State University O: 737
Oklahoma *picture on* O: 717
Oklahoma Territory [U.S. history]
Oklahoma (Progress toward statehood) O: 732
Okra [plant] O: 737 *with picture*
Hibiscus H: 223
Oktoberfest [festival] O: 738
Germany *picture on* G: 151
Ol' Man Adam an' His Chillun [book by Bradford]
Bradford, Roark B: 544
Olaf [Norwegian kings] *See under* Olav *in this index*
Olaf, Saint *See* Olav II *in this index*
Olah, George Andrew [Hungarian-born chemist]
Nobel Prizes (Chemistry: 1994) N: 444
Olajuwon, Hakeem [Nigerian-American basketball player] O: 738
Öland [island]
Sweden (The land) So: 1028 *with map*
Olav I Tryggvason [king of Norway]
Norway (The Viking period) N: 545
Olav II [king of Norway]
Norway (The Viking period) N: 545
Olav V [king of Norway]
Norway (Postwar developments) N: 546-547
Olbers, Heinrich [German astronomer]
Cosmology (The dark sky) Ci: 1077-1078
Olbers's paradox [astronomy]
Cosmology (The dark sky) Ci: 1077-1078
Olbrich, Josef [Austrian architect]
Architecture (Early modern architecture in Europe) A: 627-628 *with picture*
Olcott, Ben W. [American political leader]
Oregon (table) O: 845
Old age O: 738
See also Geriatrics *in this index*
Aging A: 141
Alzheimer's disease A: 398
Day care (Day care for the elderly) D: 53
Death (Attitudes about death) D: 62
Gray Panthers G: 335
Growth (When people stop growing) G: 406
Incontinence I: 106
Library (Services for special groups) L: 241
Medicaid M: 361
Medicare M: 362
Nursing home N: 619
Senility S: 300
Old Age Security program [Canada]
Retirement R: 265
Social security (Social security in Canada) So: 556
Old-age, survivors, and disability insurance
Insurance (Social insurance) I: 314
Social security (Social Security in the United States) So: 553
Old-age, survivors, disability, and hospital insurance *See* Social Security *in this index*
Old Bailey [London] O: 739
Old Barracks Museum [Trenton]
Colonial life in America (Places to visit) Ci: 800
Old Believers [religious group]
Russia (The early Romanovs) R: 549
Old Biloxi [U.S. history]
Le Moyne, Pierre, Sieur d'Iberville L: 189

Old Blood and Guts [nickname]
Patton, George Smith, Jr. P: 199
Old Bullion [nickname]
Benton, Thomas Hart B: 254
Old Capitol Museum [Jackson]
Mississippi (Museums) M: 627 *with picture*
Old Cathedral Library [Vincennes]
Indiana (Libraries) I: 201
Old Catholic Church of the Netherlands
Old Catholic churches O: 740
Old Catholic churches [religious group] O: 740
Old Christmas [book by Irving]
Caldecott, Randolph C: 25
Old Church Slavonic [language]
Alphabet (Other alphabets) A: 383-384
Russian language (History) R: 557
Russian literature (Religious literature) R: 558
Old City [district]
Jerusalem (The Old City) J: 95 *with picture*
Old comedy [Greek drama]
Drama (Old Comedy) D: 327
Greek literature (Drama) G: 377
Old Constitution House [Windsor]
Vermont (Places to visit) V: 326
Old Course [golf courset]
United Kingdom *picture on* U: 57
Old Courthouse [St. Louis]
Missouri *picture on* M: 651
Old Curiosity Shop, The [book by Dickens]
Dickens, Charles (The first phase) D: 188
Old Dominion [nickname]
Virginia V: 398
Old Dominion Foundation
Mellon Foundation M: 389
Old English [language]
Beowulf B: 256
English language (Old English) E: 313
English literature *picture on* E: 316; (Old English literature) E: 314
Language (Language change) L: 64
Old English black-breasted red game rooster
Chicken *picture on* C: 442
Old English mastiff [dog]
Mastiff M: 298
Old English sheepdog O: 740
Dog *picture on* D: 276
Old Faithful [geyser]
Geyser G: 177
Wyoming *picture on* W: 525
Yellowstone National Park (The Lower Loop) Y: 558-559 *with map*
Old Farmer's Almanac [book]
Almanac A: 379
Old Field schools
Virginia (Schools) V: 402
"Old Folks at Home" [song]
Suwannee River So: 1013
Old Fort Niagara [New York] *See* Fort Niagara *in this index*
Old Fort Western [Augusta]
Maine (Places to visit) M: 78 *with picture*
Old French [language]
French language (Old French) F: 517
Old Fuss and Feathers [nickname]
Scott, Winfield S: 222
Old Gaol Museum [York, Maine]
Colonial life in America (Places to visit) Ci: 801
Old garden rose
Rose (Types of roses) R: 474
Old Glory [flag] *See* United States flag *in this index*
Old Glory, The [plays by Lowell]
Lowell, Robert L: 511
Old Gringo, The [book by Fuentes]
Fuentes, Carlos F: 553
Old Guard [U.S. politics]
Eisenhower, Dwight David (Presidential candidate) E: 151; (Challenges from the Old Guard) E: 152
Old Guitarist, The [painting by Picasso]
Color *picture on* Ci: 817
Painting (Color) P: 35; (Cubism) P: 77
Picasso, Pablo (The Blue Period) P: 448a
Old Harbor
Marseille (The city) M: 227
Old Hickory [nickname]
Jackson, Andrew J: 6
Old immigration
Immigration (The third wave) I: 82
Old Ironsides [locomotive]
Baldwin, Matthias William B: 39 *with picture*
Railroad (Developments in the United States) R: 115
"Old Ironsides" [poem by Holmes]
Constitution Ci: 995
Holmes, Oliver Wendell (His life) H: 294
Old Ironsides [ship] *See* Constitution [ship] *in this index*

Old King, The [painting by Rouault]
  Rouault, Georges *picture on* R: 489
Old Kingdom [Egyptian history]
  Egypt, Ancient (The Old Kingdom) E: 142
Old Line State [nickname]
  Maryland M: 240
Old Main [building]
  Pennsylvania State University *picture on* P: 271
Old Man and the Sea, The [book by Hemingway]
  American literature *picture on* A: 417
  Hemingway, Ernest (Later years) H: 180
Old man cactus
  Cactus (Kinds of cactuses) C: 11 *with picture*
Old Man Eloquent [name for]
  Adams, John Quincy A: 40
Old Man in the Corner [literary figure]
  Detective story (History) D: 162-163
Old Man of the Mountain [formation]
  New Hampshire (Places to visit) N: 216; (The early
    2000's) N: 227 *with pictures*
  White Mountains W: 291
Old Man of the Sea [Greek mythology]
  Nereus N: 130
Old man of the woods [fungus]
  Mushroom (Nonpoisonous mushrooms) M: 943-
    945 *with picture*
Old Man River [nickname]
  Mississippi River M: 646
Old man's beard [lichen]
  Lichen *picture on* L: 269
Old Manse [estate]
  Hawthorne, Nathaniel (Life) H: 114
Old Market [Omaha]
  Nebraska (Places to visit) N: 102
Old Market Square [Winnipeg]
  Manitoba *picture on* M: 148
Old Medina [district]
  Casablanca C: 270
Old Montreal [district]
  Montreal *picture on* M: 778; (The city) M: 768-769
    with picture; (Old Montreal) M: 770
Old Mother Frost [legendary figure]
  Jack Frost J: 2
Old Narragansett Church [North Kingstown,
    Rhode Island]
  Colonial life in America (Places to visit) Ci: 801
Old Norse
  Norway (Language) N: 539
Old North Church [Boston] O: 740 *with picture*
Old Northwest
  Westward movement in America (Reaching the
    Mississippi River) W: 246
Old Orchard Beach
  Maine (Land regions) M: 80
Old Order Amish Church [religious group] *See*
  Amish *in this index*
Old Osawatomie Brown [nickname]
  Brown, John (The abolitionist) B: 643
Old Persian [language]
  Persia, Ancient (Literature and language) P: 297
Old Post Office Building [Washington, D.C.]
  Washington, D.C. *map on* W: 76
Old Pretender [Scottish history] *See* Stuart, James
  Francis Edward *in this index*
Old process system
  Corn (The dry-milling industry) Ci: 1061-1062
Old Quarter [district]
  Hanoi H: 53
Old Religion
  Witchcraft W: 371
Old Rough and Ready [nickname]
  Taylor, Zachary T: 58
Old Saint Peter's Church [Rome]
  Architecture (Medieval architecture) A: 617 *with
    picture*
Old Salamander [nickname]
  Farragut, David Glasgow F: 47
Old Salem [Winston-Salem]
  Colonial life in America (Places to visit) Ci: 801
  North Carolina (Places to visit) N: 482
Old Shepherd's Chief Mourner, The [painting by
    Landseer]
  Painting (Art for a new public) P: 70 *with picture*
Old shrub
  Rose (Types of roses) R: 474-475
Old Silk Trade Route
  Road (The first roads) R: 361
Old South Meeting House
  Boston (Downtown Boston) B: 496
Old Southwest
  Westward movement in America (Reaching the
    Mississippi River) W: 246
Old Spanish Days Fiesta [Santa Barbara]
  California *picture on* C: 47
Old Spanish Fort [Pascagoula]
  Mississippi (Places to visit) M: 632
Old Spanish Trail [U.S. history]

Nevada (Exploration) N: 173
Pioneer life in America (Routes to the West)
  P: 486
Old squaw duck [bird]
  Duck (Sea ducks) D: 376
Old State House [Philadelphia]
  Independence Hall I: 107
Old State House [Providence]
  Providence (Description) P: 839-840
Old Stone Age *See* Paleolithic Period *in this index*
Old Stone House [Richmond]
  Richmond (Other interesting places to visit)
    R: 332
Old Sturbridge Village
  Folk art (Folk art collections) F: 319
Old Testament O: 740
  See also Bible; Hebrew Bible *in this index*
  Bible B: 279; (table) B: 281; (The Christian Old
    Testament) B: 282
  Christianity (The Bible) C: 522g
  Dead Sea Scrolls D: 56
  Judaism J: 179
  Pentateuch P: 274
  Poetry (Ancient poetry) P: 595-596
  Psalms, Book of P: 844
  Septuagint S: 310d
Old-time music
  Country music (Varieties of country music)
    Ci: 1098
Old Times [play by Pinter]
  Pinter, Harold P: 475
Old Town [district]
  Chicago (The North Side) C: 423
  Montevideo M: 764b
Old Town Lunenburg [Nova Scotia]
  Nova Scotia *picture on* N: 561
Old Town square [district]
  Prague (The city) P: 730 *with picture*
Old Vic company [theater group]
  Theater (Britain) T: 247-248
Old Water Tower
  Chicago (Downtown Chicago) C: 420-421
Old West [U.S. history] *See* West, The *in this index*
Old Wives Lake
  Saskatchewan (Rivers and lakes) S: 138
Old Wives' Summer
  Indian summer I: 189
Old Wives' Tale, The [book by Bennett]
  Bennett, Arnold B: 251
  English literature (Literature before World War
    I) E: 322
Old World [geography] O: 741
  World (How nations are grouped) W: 407
Old World badger [animal]
  Badger B: 23
Old World common cuckoo [bird]
  Cuckoo Ci: 1182
Old World cotton
  Cotton (Old World cotton) Ci: 1089
Old World monkey
  Monkey (Kinds of monkeys) M: 725 *with pictures*
  Primate *diagram on* P: 778b; (Anthropoids) P: 778
Old World porcupine [animal]
  Porcupine P: 678
Old World vulture
  Bird of prey B: 374a
  Vulture (Old World vultures) V: 454 *with picture*
Old World Wisconsin
  Wisconsin (Places to visit) W: 356
Old York Road
  Pennsylvania (Transportation) P: 262
Olden, Charles S. [American political leader]
  New Jersey (table) N: 249
Oldenburg, Claes [American sculptor] O: 741 *with
    picture*
  Performance art P: 285
Oldfield, Barney [American race driver] O: 742
  Aviation *picture on* A: 988
Olds, Ransom Eli [American businessman] O: 742
  Michigan (The early 1900's) M: 509
Olds Motor Works
  Michigan (The early 1900's) M: 509
  Olds, Ransom Eli O: 742
Oldsmobile [automobile]
  Automobile *picture on* A: 965; (Mass production)
    A: 966
  Olds, Ransom Eli O: 742
Oldtown Folks [book by Stowe]
  Stowe, Harriet Beecher (Other works) So: 916
Olduvai Gorge [Africa] O: 742
  Homo habilis H: 306
  Leakey, Louis Seymour Bazett L: 161
  Prehistoric people (The first human beings)
    P: 746
Oleander [shrub] O: 742
  Poisonous plant (Some poisonous plants) P: 602
O'Leary, Catherine [American public figure]

Chicago (The Great Chicago Fire) C: 435
Chicago Fire C: 438
O'Leary, Hazel Rollins [American government
    official] O: 742
O'Leary, Patrick [American public figure]
  Chicago Fire C: 438
OLED [electronics]
  Light-emitting diode L: 293
Olefin [chemistry]
  Fiber (Synthetic fibers) F: 87
  Hydrocarbon (Aliphatic hydrocarbons) H: 465
  Petrochemicals P: 329
  Rugs and carpets (Materials used in rugs and
    carpets) R: 514
Oleg [Varangian ruler]
  Russia (The state of Kievan Rus) R: 547
  Ukraine (Kievan Rus) U: 12
Olein [chemical]
  Lard L: 75
Oleomargarine [food] *See* Margarine *in this index*
Oleoresin [tree product]
  Resin (Natural resins) R: 259
Oleoresinous varnish
  Varnish (Types of varnish) V: 286
Olericulture [horticulture]
  Horticulture (The horticulture industry) H: 369
Olestra [fat substitute]
  Fat substitute F: 54
Oleum [chemical]
  Sulfuric acid (Uses and properties) So: 968
Oleuropein [chemical]
  Olive (Appearance of the fruit and tree) O: 743
Olfaction [term for]
  Smell S: 514
Olfactory bulb [anatomy]
  Nose N: 549 *with picture*
  Smell (How odors are detected) S: 514 *with
    diagram*
Olfactory nerve [anatomy]
  Nose N: 548
Olfactory system
  Smell S: 514 *with diagram*
Olga [grand duchess of Russia]
  Nicholas II [czar] *picture on* N: 403
Olibanum [tree product]
  Frankincense F: 485
Oligarchs [Russian history]
  Russia (Recent developments) R: 555-556
Oligarchy [government] O: 742
  Greece, Ancient (Government) G: 372
Oligocene Epoch [geology]
  Earth (The Cenozoic Era) E: 28-29; (table) E: 30
  Prehistoric animal (table) P: 740
Oligochaete worm
  Worm (Segmented worms) W: 501
Oligodendrocyte [anatomy]
  Myelin M: 970f
  Nervous system (Parts of a neuron) N: 133-134
Oligopoly [economics]
  Inflation (The cost-push theory) I: 268
  Monopoly and competition (Kinds of monopoly
    and competition) M: 732
Oliphant, Patrick Bruce [American cartoonist]
  O: 743
Olitski, Jules [American artist]
  Painting (Color-field painting) P: 85
Olivares, Antonio [Spanish missionary]
  Alamo (Early days) A: 280
  San Antonio (History) S: 86-87
Olive [tree] O: 743 *with picture*
  Fruit (Subtropical fruits) F: 546 *with picture*
Olive Branch Petition [U.S. history]
  Revolution, American (The Declaration of
    Independence) R: 278
Olive foots
  Olive oil O: 744
Olive fruit fly
  Fly (table) F: 310
Olive oil O: 744
  Invention (Ancient Greece) I: 359
  Olive O: 743
  Vegetable oil V: 294
Olive orchard
  Spain *picture on* So: 743
Olive Tree [alliance]
  Prodi, Romano P: 810
Olive warbler [bird]
  Warbler W: 34
Oliver! [film]
  Motion picture (Best picture: 1968) M: 861
Oliver, Jack E. [American geologist]
  Plate tectonics (History of tectonic theory)
    P: 564-565
Oliver, James [American inventor]
  Indiana (Early statehood) I: 216
Oliver, James H. [American government official]
  Virgin Islands, United States (Direct U.S. rule)

V: 397
Oliver, John [Canadian political leader]
British Columbia (table) B: 628
Oliver Cromwell's Letters and Speeches [book by Carlyle]
Carlyle, Thomas (Later career) C: 240
Oliver Hazard Perry class
Frigate F: 534
Oliver Twist [book by Dickens]
Child labor C: 455
Dickens, Charles (The first phase) D: 188 *with picture*
English literature (Early Victorian literature) E: 321 *with picture*
Olives, Mount of [hills, Jerusalem]
Mount of Olives M: 886
Olivet, Mount
Mount of Olives M: 886
Olivia [literary figure]
Shakespeare, William: *(Twelfth Night)* S: 360-361
Olivia [pig]
Falconer, Ian F: 14
Olivier, Laurence [British actor] O: 744 *with picture*
Motion picture (Best performance by an actor: 1948) M: 862a
Shakespeare, William *picture on* S: 359
Olivine [mineral] O: 744
Mantle M: 168
Peridot P: 287
Ollie Matson's House Is Just a Square Red Cloud [painting by Milne]
Milne, David Brown *picture on* M: 556
Olmec Indians O: 744
Indian, American (Before European contact) I: 169
Latin America (Early inhabitants) L: 102
Maya (The Preclassic Period) M: 325
Mexico (The growth of villages) M: 467
Sculpture (Early sculpture) S: 242 *with picture*
Olmedo, José Joaquín [Ecuadorian poet]
Latin American literature (The 1800's) L: 112
Olmert, Ehud [Israeli political leader] O: 745
Israel (The early 2000's) I: 489-490
Kadima K: 208
Olmstead v. United States [U.S. history]
Wiretapping (Laws concerning wiretapping) W: 345
Olmsted, Frederick Law [American landscape architect] O: 745
Landscape architecture (History) L: 59
Montreal (Parks) M: 774
Park (History) P: 168
Olmsted, Frederick Law, Jr. [American landscape architect]
Olmsted, Frederick Law O: 745
Olmütz, Bishop of [German religious leader]
Pied Piper of Hamelin P: 453
Olney, Richard [American government official]
Cleveland, Grover (Foreign affairs) Ci: 673
Justice, Department of (table) J: 203
Olney Hymns [hymns]
Cowper, William Ci: 1113
Olof Skötkonung [king of Sweden]
Sweden (The early kingdom) So: 1032-1033
Olson, Allen I. [American political leader]
North Dakota (table) N: 513
Olson, Charles [American poet] O: 745
American literature (Poetry) A: 423
Olson, Culbert L. [American political leader]
California (table) C: 59
Olson, Floyd B. [American political leader]
Farmer-Labor Party F: 46
Minnesota (table) M: 602; (The early 1900's) M: 604-606
Olson, Ole H. [American political leader]
North Dakota (table) N: 513
Olson, Regina [friend of]
Kierkegaard, Søren Aabye (His life) K: 314
Olustee, Battle of [1864]
Florida (The Civil War and Reconstruction) F: 262 *with picture*
Olvera Street
Los Angeles *picture on* L: 462; (Downtown Los Angeles) L: 458-460
Olvidados, Los [film]
Latin America (Motion pictures) L: 101
Motion picture (Postwar Realism) M: 869
Olybrius [Roman emperor]
Rome, Ancient (table) R: 447
Olympia [region, Greece] O: 745
Olympic Games (Olympic ceremonies and symbols) O: 746-746a; (The ancient games) O: 750 *with picture*
Olympia [Washington] O: 746
Olympia [painting by Manet]
Manet, Édouard M: 138
Olympia [ship]

Dewey, George D: 176
Navy, United States *picture on* N: 90; (The Spanish-American War [1898]) N: 88
Olympiad [time] O: 746
Olympian Zeus, Temple of
Athens (Other buildings) A: 856
Olympians [mythology]
Mount Olympus M: 886
Mythology (Greek mythology) M: 980-981; (The construction of the world) M: 986
Olympias [mother of Alexander the Great] O: 746
Alexander the Great (His youth) A: 342
Olympic flag
Flag *picture on* F: 216
Olympic flame
Olympic Games (Olympic ceremonies and symbols) O: 746-746a
Olympic Games O: 746 *with pictures*
Ali, Muhammad (Later years) A: 367
Basketball (Basketball today) B: 155
Beijing (History) B: 223-224
Blood doping B: 415
British Columbia (Recent developments) B: 631
Calgary (History) C: 34
Canada *picture on* C: 108
China (Recent developments) C: 506-507
Decathlon D: 66
Discus throw D: 224
Greece, Ancient *pictures on* G: 371; (Recreation) G: 367-368
Hockey (Amateur development) H: 281
Homing pigeon (History) H: 305
Horse racing (History) H: 366
Ice skating (History) I: 16
International Olympic Committee I: 343
London (Recent developments) L: 443
Marathon M: 191
Moscow (The early 1900's) M: 827
Olympia O: 745
Owens, Jesse O: 883
Peace (Ancient Greece and Rome) P: 206
Pentathlon, Modern P: 275
Phelps, Michael P: 356
Romney, Mitt R: 450
Television (Commercial television) T: 110-110a *with picture*
Track and field (History) T: 359
Vancouver (Recent events) V: 277
Olympic Mountains [Washington] O: 755
Olympic National Park [Washington] O: 755
National Park System (table: National parks) N: 48
Washington *pictures on* W: 47, W: 57; (Land regions) W: 58 *with map*
Olympic Ocean Strip [region, Washington]
Olympic National Park O: 756
Olympic Stadium [Berlin]
Berlin (Recreation) B: 262
Olympic Village
Olympic Games (The International Olympic Committee) O: 746a-746b; (Between the wars) O: 751
Olympics See Olympic Games *in this index*
Olympio, Sylvanus [Togolese political leader]
Togo (History) T: 310-311
Olympus, Mount [mountain, Cyprus]
Cyprus (Land and climate) Ci: 1206
Olympus, Mount [mountain, Greece] See Mount Olympus *in this index*
Olympus, Mount [mountain, Washington]
Olympic Mountains O: 755
Olympus Mons [volcano, Mars]
Mars (Volcanoes) M: 226
Mountain M: 891
Volcano (Volcanoes in the solar system) V: 442b *with picture*
Om [religion]
Hinduism *picture on* H: 237
Omaha [Nebraska] O: 756 *with picture*
Curfew Ci: 1194
Nebraska *picture on* N: 95; (table: Average monthly weather) N: 106
Omaha [horse]
Kentucky Derby (table) K: 296
Omaha Indians O: 757
Neihardt, John G. N: 344
O'Malley, Martin [American political leader]
Maryland (table) M: 255
O'Malley, Séan P. [American religious leader]
Cardinal (table: American cardinals) C: 211
Oman O: 757 *with pictures and map*
Arabs *picture on* A: 588
Flag *picture on* F: 204
Middle East M: 530
Oman, Gulf of
Persian Gulf P: 300 *with map*
Omar Khayyám [Persian poet] O: 759
Algebra (History) A: 359

FitzGerald, Edward F: 190
Mathematics (Arab mathematics) M: 306
Rubaiyat R: 499
Omasum [zoology]
Cattle (Stomach) C: 307 *with diagram*
Ruminant R: 519 *with diagram*
Omayyad, Order of the [Syria]
Medals, decorations, and orders (table) M: 359
Omayyad dynasty See Umayyad dynasty *in this index*
OMB [organization] See Management and Budget, Office of *in this index*
Ombú [tree]
Tree (Interesting facts about trees) T: 411 *with picture*
Ombudsman [government official] O: 760
Denmark (Government) D: 132-133
New Zealand (Ombudsman) N: 347
Norway (Government) N: 537
Sweden (Ombudsmen and ombudswomen) So: 1023
Omdurman [Sudan] O: 760
Omdurman, Battle of [1898]
Sudan (Egyptian and British control) So: 953
Omega-minus [particle]
Gell-Mann, Murray G: 77
Omega navigation system
Navigation (Other radio navigation systems) N: 73
Omen [belief] O: 760
Omeros [poem by Walcott]
Walcott, Derek W: 6
Omertà [custom]
Sicily (The people) S: 446
Ometepe [island, Nicaragua]
Lake Nicaragua L: 42
Omicron [letter]
O O: 634 *with picture*
Omineca Mountains
British Columbia (Land regions) B: 622
Ommatidium [zoology]
Compound eye Ci: 906 *with diagram*
OMNI Study
Framingham Heart Study F: 451
Omnibus [vehicle]
Bus (History) B: 715
Omnibus bill [political science] O: 760
Omnibus Crime Control and Safe Streets Act [1968]
Wiretapping (Laws concerning wiretapping) W: 345
Omnicom Group [company]
Advertising (The advertising industry) A: 77
Omnidirectional microphone
Microphone M: 516
Omnirange navigation system
Navigation (Omnirange) N: 73
Omnivore [zoology]
Mammal (What mammals eat) M: 121
Omomyid [animal]
Primate (The evolution of primates) P: 778b
Omonoia Square
Athens (Landmarks) A: 854 *with map*
Omoo [book by Melville]
Melville, Herman (His early life) M: 390
Omri [king of ancient Israel]
Samaria S: 77
Omsk [Russia] O: 760
Omyéné [people]
Gabon (History) G: 3; (People) G: 3
"On a Grecian Urn" [poem by Keats]
Keats, John (His work) K: 253-254
"On a Piece of Chalk" [essay by Huxley]
Huxley, Thomas Henry H: 459
On Agriculture [book by Cato the Elder]
Latin literature (Early Latin literature) L: 115-116
On Architecture [book by Alberti]
Architecture (Early Renaissance architecture) A: 620-621
On Becoming a Person [book by Rogers]
Rogers, Carl Ransom R: 400
On Civility in Children [book by Erasmus]
Etiquette (Books on etiquette) E: 375
On Coming-to-be and Passing-away [book by Aristotle]
Aristotle (Philosophy of nature) A: 664
On Crimes and Punishments [book by Beccaria]
Criminology (History) Ci: 1145
On-deck circle
Baseball (Foul territory) B: 127
On Eloquence in the Vernacular [essay by Dante]
Dante Alighieri (His works) D: 34
On Eternal Peace [book by Kant]
Political science (Liberalism) P: 639
"On First Looking into Chapman's Homer" [poem by Keats]
Chapman, George C: 377

Keats, John (His work) K: 253
On Germany [book by Staël]
  Staël, Madame de So: 820
On guard [fencing]
  Fencing *picture on* F: 70
On Heroes, Hero-Worship, and the Heroic in History [book by Carlyle]
  Carlyle, Thomas (Early career) C: 240
On-highway truck [vehicle]
  Truck (On-highway trucks) T: 457
"On His Being Arrived at the Age of Twenty-Three" [poem by Milton]
  Figure of speech F: 97
On Laws [book by Suárez]
  Suárez, Francisco So: 936
On Learned Ignorance [work by Nicholas]
  Nicholas of Cusa N: 403
On Liberty [essay by Mill]
  English literature (Early Victorian literature) E: 321
  Mill, Harriet Taylor M: 552
  Mill, John Stuart M: 552
On-line ... *See* Online ... *in this index*
On Literature [book by Staël]
  French literature (The Preromantics) F: 521
On Nature [poem by Parmenides]
  Parmenides P: 177
On Painting [book by Alberti]
  Perspective P: 305
On spec [publishing]
  Publishing (Proposals) P: 866
On Temporal Authority, To What Extent It Should Be Obeyed [book by Luther]
  Luther, Martin (Reformation leader) L: 528
On the 6 [recording]
  Lopez, Jennifer L: 453
On the Aesthetic Education of Man in a Series of Letters [essay by Schiller]
  German literature (The second golden age [1750-1830]) G: 139
"On the Banks of the Wabash, Far Away" [song by Dreiser]
  Dreiser, Theodore D: 346
"On the Beautiful, Blue Danube" [music by Strauss]
  Strauss, Johann, Jr. So: 922
On the Church [book by Hus]
  Hus, John H: 457
"On the Crown" [speech by Demosthenes]
  Demosthenes D: 130
"On the Electrodynamics of Moving Bodies" [paper by Einstein]
  Einstein, Albert (Famous theories) E: 146-146a
On the Fabric of the Human Body [book by Vesalius] *See* On the Structure of the Human Body *in this index*
On the Heavens [book by Aristotle]
  Aristotle (Philosophy of nature) A: 664
"On the Hypotheses Which Lie at the Foundation of Geometry" [lecture by Riemann]
  Riemann, Georg Friedrich Bernhard R: 337
On-the-job training
  Careers (On-the-job training) C: 217
  Vocational education (Other sources) V: 434
On the Law of War and Peace [book by Grotius]
  Peace (From the 1400's to the 1700's) P: 206
On the Magnet, Magnetic Bodies, and the Great Magnet of the Earth [book by Gilbert]
  Gilbert, William G: 189
On the Magnitudes and Distances of the Sun and Moon [essay by Aristarchus]
  Aristarchus A: 662
On the Mall [music by Goldman]
  Goldman, Edwin Franko G: 258
On the Nature of Things [poem by Lucretius]
  Atomism A: 877
  Latin literature (The age of Cicero) L: 116
  Lucretius L: 514
On the Origin of Species [book by Darwin] *See* Origin of Species, The *in this index*
"On the Principles of Geometry" [paper by Lobachevsky]
  Lobachevsky, Nikolai L: 404
On the Pyramid of Choula [poem by Heredia]
  Latin American literature (Romanticism) L: 112
On the Revolutions of the Heavenly Spheres [book by Copernicus]
  Copernicus, Nicolaus (Theories of heavenly motion) Ci: 1039; (Life) Ci: 1039-1040
  Geology (The Renaissance) G: 98
  Science (The rebirth of science) S: 197
On the Road [book by Kerouac]
  American literature (Fiction and other prose) A: 424
  Beat movement B: 189
  Kerouac, Jack K: 306
On the rocks [drink]
  Alcoholic beverage (Distilled drinks) A: 336

On the Seats and Causes of Diseases [book by Morgagni]
  Morgagni, Giovanni Battista M: 802
On the Shores of the River Sar [poem by Castro]
  Spanish literature (The 1800's) So: 761
On the Soul [book by Aristotle]
  Aristotle (Philosophy of nature) A: 664
On the Southern Plains [painting by Remington]
  Cavalry *picture on* C: 318
On the Sphere and Cylinder [book by Archimedes]
  Archimedes A: 604
On the Structure of the Human Body [book by Vesalius]
  Biology (The Renaissance) B: 318 *with picture*
  Science (The rebirth of science) S: 197-198
  Vesalius, Andreas V: 341
On the Sublime [essay by Longinus]
  Longinus L: 451
On the Town [musical]
  Bernstein, Leonard B: 271
"On the Trail" [music by Grofé]
  Grofé, Ferde G: 397
On the Waterfront [film]
  Brando, Marlon B: 563
  Motion picture (Best picture: 1954) M: 861
On the Wing of Occasions [stories by Harris]
  Harris, Joel Chandler H: 68
On to Ottawa Trek [Canadian history]
  Saskatchewan (The Great Depression) S: 147
On War [book by Clausewitz]
  Clausewitz, Karl von Ci: 657
On World-Government [essay by Dante]
  Dante Alighieri (His works) D: 34
Ona Indians
  Indian, American *pictures on* I: 140; (Indians of the Marginal Regions) I: 176-177
Onager [animal] O: 760 *with picture*
Onassis, Aristotle Socrates [Greek businessman]
  Kennedy, John Fitzgerald (Kennedy's family) K: 262
  Onassis, Jacqueline Kennedy O: 761
Onassis, Jacqueline Kennedy [American public figure] O: 761 *with portrait*
  Johnson, Lyndon Baines *picture on* J: 149
  Kennedy, John Fitzgerald (Kennedy's family) K: 262; (Life in the White House) K: 265 *with picture*
  President of the United States *picture on* P: 767
  White House (Rebuilding and redecorating) W: 290
Oñate, Juan de [Spanish explorer] O: 761
  El Paso E: 247
  New Mexico (Exploration, conquest, and settlement) N: 273
Once in a Lifetime [play by Kaufman and Hart]
  Hart, Moss H: 67
Once Upon a Time in the North [book by Pullman]
  Pullman, Philip P: 900
Oncenter Complex
  Syracuse So: 1069
Oncogene [genetics]
  Cancer (How damaged genes cause cancer) C: 169
Oncology [medicine] O: 761
  Cancer C: 167
  Medicine (Specialty care physicians) M: 365-366; (table) M: 369
Oncosphere [biology]
  Tapeworm T: 40
Ondaatje, Michael [Canadian author]
  Canadian literature (Modern English-Canadian fiction) C: 160 *with portrait*
One, The [philosophy]
  Neoplatonism N: 124
  Plotinus P: 574
One-and-one
  Basketball (Fouls) B: 147-148
One-celled organism [biology]
  Protist P: 836
  Protozoan P: 837 *with pictures*
  Reproduction (Through asexual reproduction) R: 242 *with picture*
One Day in the Life of Ivan Denisovich [book by Solzhenitsyn]
  Russian literature (Modern Soviet literature) R: 564
  Solzhenitsyn, Alexander So: 587
One-design class [racing]
  Boating *picture on* B: 431
One Earth, Four or Five Worlds [book by Paz]
  Paz, Octavio P: 205
One Flew over the Cuckoo's Nest [book by Kesey]
  American literature (Experimental styles) A: 425
  Kesey, Ken K: 307
One Flew Over the Cuckoo's Nest [film]
  Motion picture (Best picture: 1975) M: 861
  Nicholson, Jack N: 404

One for the Road [play by Pinter]
  Pinter, Harold P: 475
158-Pound Marriage, The [book by Irving]
  Irving, John I: 459
100 Mile House [British Columbia]
  British Columbia (Interesting facts about British Columbia) B: 613
101 Ranch Wild West Show
  Pickett, Bill P: 451
100-year flood
  Flood (River floods) F: 236
One Hundred Years of Solitude [book by García Márquez]
  García Márquez, Gabriel José G: 29
  Latin American literature (The "Boom") L: 114
One Laptop per Child [program]
  Computer *picture on* Ci: 921
  Laptop computer (History) L: 74
One-party system
  Political party (One-party systems) P: 633
One-time pad [cryptology]
  Codes and ciphers (Unbreakable ciphers) Ci: 751
One-way clutch [engine]
  Transmission (Clutches) T: 377
One Way to Heaven [book by Cullen]
  Cullen, Countee Ci: 1184
One World [book by Willkie]
  Willkie, Wendell Lewis (His public career) W: 314
One World Trade Center [building]
  New York City (A time of change) N: 343-344
  September 11 terrorist attacks (Moving forward) S: 310b-310c
O'Neal, Edward Asbury [American political leader]
  Alabama (table) A: 274
O'Neal, Emmett [American political leader]
  Alabama (table) A: 274
O'Neal, Shaquille [American basketball player] O: 761
  Basketball *picture on* B: 154b
O'Neal, Tatum [American actress]
  Motion picture (Best performance by an actress in a supporting role: 1973) M: 862b
O'Neale, Peggy [American public figure] O: 761
  Jackson, Andrew (Split with Calhoun) J: 11
Onega, Lake [Russia]
  Lake Onega L: 43
Onegin, Eugene [literary figure]
  Russian literature (Early Romanticism) R: 560-561
Oneida Community [U.S. history] O: 761
  Family (Varieties of families) F: 20-21
Oneida Indians
  Indian, American (Indians of the Northeast) I: 154
  Iroquois Indians I: 455
Oneida Ltd. [company]
  Oneida Community O: 762
O'Neill, C. William [American political leader]
  Ohio (table) O: 699
O'Neill, Danny [literary figure]
  Farrell, James T. F: 48
O'Neill, Eugene [American dramatist] O: 762
  American literature (Drama) A: 423 *with portrait*
  Drama (United States drama) D: 339
  Naturalism (Naturalism in drama) N: 66
  Realism (In drama) R: 172
O'Neill, Hugh [Irish nobleman]
  Ireland (The conquest of Ireland) I: 426
O'Neill, Paul Henry [American government official]
  Bush, George Walker (table) B: 722h
  Treasury, Department of the (table) T: 407
O'Neill, Rose [American artist]
  Doll (Before World War I) D: 291 *with picture*
O'Neill, Shane [Irish nobleman]
  Ireland (The conquest of Ireland) I: 426
O'Neill, Thomas Philip [American political leader] O: 762
O'Neill, William A. [American political leader]
  Connecticut (table) Ci: 967
Oneness churches [religion]
  Pentecostal churches (Major Pentecostal churches) P: 275-276
Onion [plant] O: 763 *with pictures*
  Gardening (Planting and transplanting) G: 34
  Vegetable (Bulbs) V: 292 *with picture*
Onizuka, Ellison Shoji [American astronaut] O: 763
  Astronaut (table) A: 830
  Challenger disaster C: 370
  Space exploration (The Challenger disaster) So: 725
Online auction
  Auction A: 881
  E-commerce (Business-to-consumer transactions) E: 2
Online bill pay
  Internet (Commerce) I: 350b
Online catalog [information storage]

Database D: 42
Library (Other features) L: 237
Online Computer Library Center
Library (The growth of information and technology) L: 237-238
Online database [information system]
Library (The growth of information and technology) L: 237-238
Online electronic encyclopedia
Encyclopedia (Today's encyclopedias) E: 268b
Online investing
Investment (How investors buy stocks) I: 369
Online journalism
Journalism (Fields of journalism) J: 170
Online magazine
Magazine (Other magazines) M: 42-43; (Online versions) M: 44
Online newspaper
Newspaper (Online newspapers) N: 381; (Recent trends) N: 386-387
Online public access catalog
Library (Information science and technology) L: 251
Online service provider [company] *See* Internet service provider *in this index*
Only Opal [book by Whiteley]
Literature for children *picture on* L: 379
Only True Mother Goose Melodies, The [book by Newbery]
Mother Goose (The history of Mother Goose literature) M: 842
Onnes, Heike Kamerlingh [Dutch physicist] *See* Kamerlingh Onnes, Heike *in this index*
Ono, Yoko [American musician]
Lennon, John L: 196
Ono Waterfall [print by Hokusai]
Hokusai *picture on* H: 289
Onomatopoeia [language]
Poetry (table) P: 594
Onondaga Indians
Indian, American (Indians of the Northeast) I: 154
Iroquois Indians I: 455
Onorata Società [criminal organization]
Mafia M: 41
Onsager, Lars [American chemist]
Nobel Prizes (Chemistry: 1968) N: 443
Onside kick
Football (The kickoff) F: 359-360
Ontario O: 764 *with pictures and maps*
See also the list of Related articles in the Ontario *article*
Canada (Ontario) C: 101
Canada, Government of *picture on* C: 131
Flag *picture on* F: 218
Ontario O: 764
Ontario, Lake *See* Lake Ontario *in this index*
Ontario Health Insurance Plan
Ontario (The late 1900's) O: 787
Ontario Place
Toronto (Landmarks) T: 338-339
Ontario Science Centre
Toronto (Museums and libraries) T: 340a
Ontogeny [biology]
Biogenesis B: 312
Ontology [philosophy]
Philosophy (Metaphysics) P: 383
Onyx [gem] O: 788
Gem *picture on* G: 78
Oocyte [cell]
Reproduction, Human (The human reproductive system) R: 244-245
Oolong tea
Tea (Processing tea) T: 62
Oöphorectomy
Surgery (Some common surgical operations) So: 1006
Ooqueah [Inuit explorer]
Exploration (The North Pole) E: 450
Oort, Jan H. [Dutch astronomer]
Oort cloud O: 788
Oort cloud [astronomy] O: 788
Comet (The life of a comet) Ci: 867-868 *with diagram*
Solar system (Comets) So: 581
Oostende *See* Ostend *in this index*
Oosterhoff, William [Canadian artist]
Canada, Government of *pictures on* C: 131
Ootah [Inuit explorer]
Exploration (The North Pole) E: 450
Op art
Moiré pattern M: 689
Opacity [physical property]
Light (Scattering) L: 288
Opal [gem] O: 788 *with picture*
Gem *picture on* G: 78; (Value of gems) G: 79
Opal glass
Glass (Specialty glasses) G: 212; (Types of art

glass) G: 220-221
Opal Terrace
Yellowstone National Park (The Upper Loop) Y: 559
Opaque material *See* Opacity *in this index*
Opaque projector
Audio-visual materials (Projection devices) A: 882
Projector (Projector operation) P: 816
Oparin, Alexander Ivanovich [Soviet biochemist] O: 789
Life (Modern explanations) L: 278-279
OPEC [organization] *See* Organization of the Petroleum Exporting Countries *in this index*
OPEC Fund for International Development
Foreign aid (Regional development programs) F: 385
Opechancanough [American Indian chief]
Indian wars (Jamestown) I: 190-191
Powhatan Indians P: 728
Opelousas [Louisiana]
Baton Rouge (Government and history) B: 166
Open adoption
Adoption (Rights of adoptive parents and adoptees) A: 66-67
Open-angle glaucoma [disease]
Eye (Glaucoma) E: 466
Open area excavation
Archaeology (Excavating sites) A: 597
"Open Boat, The" [story by Crane]
Crane, Stephen Ci: 1120
Open caisson [construction]
Caisson C: 18
Open circuit
Electric circuit E: 166
Open circuit scuba
Diving, Underwater (Ambient diving) D: 245
Open City [film]
Motion picture (Postwar Realism) M: 869
Open city [warfare]
Athens (War and decline) A: 857-858
International law (The laws of war) I: 341
Paris (Paris in wartime) P: 166
Open classroom
Alternative school (Features of alternative schools) A: 388-389
Elementary school (Elementary school instruction) E: 224-225
Open cluster [astronomy]
Milky Way (Shape of the galaxy) M: 550
Star cluster (Kinds of clusters) So: 853
Open cockpit
Automobile racing (Safety measures) A: 975-976
Open couplet [literature]
Couplet Ci: 1100
Open dating
Consumer protection (The right to information) Ci: 1018
Open-door admission policy [education]
Community college (Importance to students) Ci: 899
Open-Door Policy [international relations] O: 789
China (The Open-Door Policy) C: 503
Hay, John Milton H: 116
McKinley, William (America becomes a world power) M: 341
Open dump
Waste disposal (Land disposal) W: 113
Open education resources movement
Universities and colleges (Online learning) U: 211
Open-end investment company
Investment (Other kinds of indirect investments) I: 368
Mutual fund M: 969
Open enrollment [public school]
Education (Who should choose a child's school?) E: 106
Open fracture [injury]
Fracture F: 450 *with diagram*
OPEN Government Act [2007]
Freedom of Information Act F: 505
Open-heart surgery
Heart (Development of heart surgery) H: 144 *with picture*
Hypothermia H: 481
Open-hearth furnace
Iron and steel (The open-hearth process) I: 443 *with diagram*
Open-hearth process
Iron and steel (The open-hearth process) I: 443 *with diagram*; (The birth of modern steelmaking) I: 450-451
Open housing [law] O: 789
Housing (Housing since 1900) H: 391-392
Open market operations [economics]
Federal Reserve System (Monetary policy) F: 65
Interest (Government policy) I: 322
Open-mesh fabric

Textile (Other textiles) T: 215
Open nutrient cycle [agriculture]
Agriculture (Artificial fertilizers) A: 158-159
Open occupancy law [U.S.]
Open housing O: 789
Open perils policy
Insurance (Homeowners' insurance) I: 313
Open-pit method
Aluminum (Sources of aluminum) A: 392-393
Open-pit mine
Asbestos (How asbestos is mined and processed) A: 765
Bauxite (Mining and processing bauxite) B: 174
Brazil *picture on* B: 582
Copper (Sources of copper) Ci: 1042
Gold (Mining) G: 252
Iron and steel (Mining and processing iron ore) I: 438 *with picture*
Mining (Open-pit mining) M: 575 *with picture*
Newfoundland and Labrador *picture on* N: 361
Uranium (Mining uranium) U: 215
Open primary
Election (Nomination of candidates) E: 158
Primary election (Open and closed) P: 776-777
Open range
Ranching R: 134; (History) R: 136
Wyoming (Territorial progress) W: 534-536
Open-reel tape recorder
Tape recorder T: 37 *with diagram*; (Kinds of tape recorders) T: 38
Open shop [labor] O: 789
Labor movements (Organizing workers) L: 4
Open Society and Its Enemies, The [book by Popper]
Popper, Karl Raimund P: 668
Open Society Institute
Foundation (International affairs) F: 431
Open source agreement [law]
Thorvalds, Linus T: 345
Open space classroom [education]
Alternative school (Features of alternative schools) A: 389
Open-stack system
Library (Other features) L: 237
Open stage
Theater (Modern theater architecture) T: 233-234 *with picture*
Open Theater [organization]
Drama (Experimental theater) D: 340
Open tournament
Golf (Tournaments) G: 264
Tennis (Tennis tournaments) T: 165
Open turn
Swimming (Starts and turns) So: 1046
Open University [Netherlands]
Netherlands (Education) N: 142
Open University [United Kingdom]
Distance learning D: 238
United Kingdom (Education) U: 56-57
Opencast method
Aluminum (Sources of aluminum) A: 392-393
Opening night
Opera *picture on* O: 791
Opening of Japan, The [painting by Gassan]
Japan *picture on* Ji: 55
Opening of the Field, The [poems by Duncan]
Duncan, Robert D: 384
Opening of the West
See also Westward movement in America *in this index; and the Related articles in the* Westward movement in America *article*
Gold rush (Gold rushes in the United States) G: 254
Homestead Act (Effects of the law) H: 304
Squatter's rights So: 814
Westward movement in America W: 244 *with pictures*
Opening to the left [Italian history]
Italy (The Italian republic) I: 517-518
Opera O: 790 *with pictures*
See also the list of Related articles in the Opera *article*
Classical music (Operas) Ci: 644; (The Romantic era) Ci: 648
Drama (Intermezzi and operas) D: 330
Intermezzo I: 336
Italy *picture on* I: 505
Operetta O: 809
Overture O: 882
Opera buffa [music]
Opera (table) O: 791; (Opera seria and opera buffa) O: 797; *(Barber of Seville, The)* O: 801
Opera Company of Boston
Caldwell, Sarah C: 28
Opéra de la Bastille [Paris]
Paris (Arts) P: 164
Opera house

Opera O: 790
Opera seria
Opera (table) O: 791; (Opera seria and opera buffa) O: 797 *with picture*
Operant conditioning [psychology]
Behavior (Learning) B: 220
Education (How people learn) E: 89
Learning (Instrumental conditioning) L: 163
Mouse *picture on* M: 902
Skinner, B. F. S: 495
Operating Engineers, International Union of
Engineers, International Union of Operating E: 291
Operating Forces
Navy, Department of the N: 81
Navy, United States (The Operating Forces) N: 85
Operating foundation
Foundation (Kinds of foundations) F: 430
Operating room [hospital]
Medicine *picture on* M: 365
Nursing *picture on* N: 618
Surgery *picture on* So: 1005
Operating system [electronics]
Cellular telephone (Features) C: 341
Computer (Operating system software) Ci: 917
Microsoft Corporation M: 519
Software (Kinds of software) So: 572
Operation [medicine] *See* Surgery *in this index*
Operation Barbarossa [World War II]
World War II (The invasion of the Soviet Union) W: 477
Operation Blue [World War II]
World War II (The Battle of Stalingrad) W: 481
Operation Bootstrap [Puerto Rican history]
Puerto Rico (Building a democracy) P: 883
Operation Desert Storm [1991]
Army (Armies in the nuclear age) A: 728-729
Persian Gulf War of 1991 P: 300a
Operation Enduring Freedom
Afghanistan War A: 97
Operation Harvest
Irish Republican Army (Division in the IRA) I: 433
Operation Highjump
Antarctica (Exploration by air) A: 537-538
Byrd, Richard Evelyn B: 746
Operation Iceberg [World War II]
World War II (Operation Iceberg) W: 493
Operation Iraqi Freedom
Iraq War I: 414c
Operation New Dawn
Iraq War I: 414c
Operation Overlord [World War II]
Eisenhower, Dwight David (Operation Overlord) E: 150
World War II (D-Day) W: 483
Operation PUSH [organization]
Jackson, Jesse Louis J: 15
Operation Rescue [organization]
Abortion (Abortion in the United States) A: 15
Operational audit [business]
Audit A: 884
Operational Test and Evaluation Force
Navy, United States (The Operating Forces) N: 85
Operator [career]
Telephone (Operator services) T: 98 *with picture*
Operculum [botany]
Moss (How mosses live) M: 834-835
Operculum [zoology]
Conch Ci: 928
Mollusk (Gastropods) M: 695
Shell (Gastropods) S: 385 *with diagram*
Snail (Where snails live) S: 522 *with diagram*
Whelk W: 279
Operetta O: 809
See also the list of Related articles in the Operetta *article*
Musical comedy (The first musicals) M: 959
Ophelia [literary figure]
Shakespeare, William: (*Hamlet*) S: 361-362
Ophelia [painting by Millais]
Painting (The Pre-Raphaelite Brotherhood) P: 71 *with picture*
Ophiderpeton [animal]
Prehistoric animal (The move onto land) P: 737
Ophidiophobia [psychology]
Phobia P: 392
Ophthalmia [disease] O: 810
Ophthalmia neonatorum [disease]
Blindness (Diseases) B: 401-402
Ophthalmia O: 810
Ophthalmologist [career]
Eye (Receiving regular eye examinations) E: 469
Ophthalmology O: 810
Ophthalmology [medicine] O: 810
Glasses (How glasses are prescribed and made) G: 225
Medicine (table) M: 369

Surgery (Ophthalmology) So: 1007
Ophthalmoscope [instrument] O: 810 *with picture*
Helmholtz, Hermann Ludwig Ferdinand von H: 179
Medicine *picture on* M: 364
Opiate [drug] O: 810
Drug (Analgesics) D: 352
Drug abuse (Heroin) D: 362
Tasmania (Economy) T: 49
Opinion
Public opinion P: 858
Public opinion poll P: 861
Opinion [law]
Supreme Court of the United States (Written opinions) So: 999
Opinion poll
Public opinion poll P: 861
Opioid [drug]
Brain (Regulating body processes) B: 554
Endorphin E: 272
Oxycodone O: 889
Opium [drug] O: 811 *with picture*
Afghanistan (Agriculture) A: 94
China (Clash with the Western powers) C: 502
Codeine Ci: 749
De Quincey, Thomas D: 151
Drug (Plants and molds) D: 355 *with picture*
Drug abuse (Heroin) D: 362; (History) D: 365
Morphine M: 816
Oxycodone O: 889
Poppy P: 668
Opium poppy [plant]
Opium O: 811 *with picture*
Opium wars *See* Anglo-Chinese War, First; Anglo-Chinese War, Second *in this index*
Opłatek [food]
Christmas (In Poland) C: 531
OPM [government agency]
Civil service (Federal civil service) Ci: 612
Oporto [Portugal] *See* Porto *in this index*
Opossum [animal] O: 811 *with pictures*
Animal *picture on* A: 479
Fur (table) F: 561
Mammal (Reproduction) M: 123-124 *with picture*; (Methods of attack and defense) M: 126; (table) M: 128 *with picture*
Marsupial (Kinds of marsupials) M: 232
Oppel, Kenneth [Canadian author]
Literature for children *picture on* L: 377
Oppenheimer, J. Robert [American physicist] O: 812
Manhattan Project M: 141
Oppidan [student]
Eton College E: 375
Opponent color theory
Color (The opponent color theory) Ci: 826
Opportunistic infection
AIDS (Opportunistic illness) A: 164a
Immune system (Immune deficiency diseases) I: 88c
Pneumonia (How pneumonia develops) P: 586
Opportunities Industrialization Center [Philadelphia]
Sullivan, Leon Howard So: 969
Opportunity [spacecraft]
Mars (Observation by spacecraft) M: 226c-226d *with picture*
Mars Exploration Rover Mission M: 227
Space exploration *picture on* So: 709; (Probes to Mars) So: 710
Opposable thumb
Hand H: 39
Monkey (Hands and feet) M: 726
Opposition [astronomy] O: 812
Opposition [politics]
Democracy (Political parties) D: 120-121
Parliament (How the House of Commons works) P: 173
Political party (Providing opposition) P: 633
United Kingdom *picture on* U: 50; (National government) U: 49
"Oprah Winfrey Show, The" [TV program]
Winfrey, Oprah W: 338
"Opry" [radio program] *See* "Grand Ole Opry" *in this index*
Opryland [Tennessee]
"Grand Ole Opry" G: 308
Ops [Roman mythology]
Mythology (table) M: 981
Saturn S: 150h
Opštini [districts]
Macedonia (Government) M: 12
Opt-out privacy policy
Internet (Ongoing controversies) I: 350h
Optacon [device]
Blindness (Aids for blind people) B: 402
Optic chiasm [anatomy]

Eye (Depth perception) E: 463 *with picture*
Optic lobe
Brain (Invertebrates) B: 559
Optic nerve [anatomy]
Blind spot B: 401
Brain (Sensing the environment) B: 552
Eye *picture on* E: 461; (The retina) E: 462 *with picture*; (Diseases of the optic nerve) E: 468
Optic neuritis [disease]
Eye (Diseases of the optic nerve) E: 468
Optical absorption [physics]
Materials (Optical properties) M: 300c
Optical astronomy
Astronomy (Optical astronomy) A: 839
Optical axis [optics]
Aberration (Point aberration) A: 10
Lens (Creating an image) L: 196
Optical cavity
Laser (Parts of a laser) L: 83 *with diagram*
Optical character reader [machine]
Postal services *picture on* P: 704; (Sorting) P: 703
Optical character recognition [electronics]
Census (Processing the results) C: 348-349
Computer (A scanner) Ci: 915
Optical disc [electronics]
Electronic game (Gaming platforms) E: 204c
Optical fiber [physics] *See* Fiber optics *in this index*
Optical glass
Glass *picture on* G: 211; (Kinds of glass) G: 212
Quartz (Uses) Q: 8
Optical illusion O: 812 *with pictures*
Color (Surprising color-vision effects) Ci: 819 *with pictures*
Mirage M: 615 *with pictures*
Perception (Principles of perception) P: 284 *with pictures*
Optical mark recognition [electronics]
Census (Processing the results) C: 348-349
Optical microscope
Cell (Looking at a cell) C: 327
Microscope (Optical microscopes) M: 517 *with pictures*
Optical mouse [electronic device]
Computer (A mouse) Ci: 914
Optical properties
Materials (Optical properties) M: 300c
Optical radar
Radar (How radar works) R: 68; (Continued progress) R: 72-73 *with picture*
Optical scanner
See also Scanner *in this index*
Automobile *diagram on* A: 957
Bar coding B: 102
Blindness (Aids for blind people) B: 402
Voting (Methods of voting) V: 449-450
Voting machine (Kinds of electoral voting machines) V: 450
Optical telescope
Astronomy (Optical astronomy) A: 839
Observatory (Observatories with telescopes) O: 644
Palomar Observatory P: 112
Telescope T: 102; (Optical telescopes) T: 103 *with pictures*
Optical viewfinder
Photography (Compact cameras) P: 408
Optically scanned paper ballot
Voting machine (Kinds of electoral voting machines) V: 450
Optician [career]
Eye (Receiving regular eye examinations) E: 469
Glasses (How glasses are prescribed and made) G: 225
Ophthalmology O: 810
Opticks [book by Newton]
Newton, Sir Isaac (Light and color) N: 389
Optics [book by Ptolemy]
Ptolemy P: 854
Optics [physics] O: 813
Kepler, Johannes (His life) K: 305
Lens L: 196 *with diagrams*
Leonardo da Vinci (Paintings) L: 200b
Light (Early ideas) L: 285; (Studying light) L: 292
Physics (Light) P: 437
Prism P: 805
Optimist Childhood Cancer Campaign
Optimist International O: 813
Optimist International [organization] O: 813
Option [feature]
Automobile (Manufacturing) A: 958
Option [football]
Football (table) F: 356
Option [investment]
American Stock Exchange A: 430
Commodity exchange (Options contracts) Ci: 874
Stock exchange (Trading) So: 904
Option [law]

Motion picture (Developing the story)
M: 848-849
Optional referendum [government]
Initiative and referendum (The referendum)
I: 272
Optoelectronic device
Electronics (Electronics and light) E: 212
Optometrist [career]
Eye (Receiving regular eye examinations) E: 469
Glasses (How glasses are prescribed and made)
G: 225
Optometry O: 814
Optometry [medicine] O: 814
Opus maius [book by Bacon]
Bacon, Roger (His life) B: 19; (His work) B: 19
Or [color]
Heraldry (Expansion) H: 194 *with picture*
OR-gate [electronics]
Electronics (Digital circuits) E: 213-214
Or Shall We Die [music by Berkeley]
McEwan, Ian M: 334
Oracle [mythology] O: 814
Delphi D: 117
Greece, Ancient (Religion) G: 367
Mythology (Greek divinities) M: 982
Parnassus P: 177
Riddle R: 335
Oracle bones [religion]
China (Literature) C: 487
World, History of the (The Huang He Valley)
W: 425
Oraibi [Arizona]
Arizona *picture on* A: 689
Hopi Indians H: 333
Oral arm [zoology]
Jellyfish J: 90
Oral cavity [anatomy]
Mouth M: 903
Oral contraceptive
Birth control (Methods of birth control) B: 378
Oral formulaic [literature]
Epic E: 342
Oral groove [biology]
Paramecium P: 152 *with picture*
Oral hygiene
Teeth (Cleaning the teeth) T: 81
Oral Law [religion]
Talmud T: 21
Oral literature
Africa (Literature) A: 116b
Scandinavian literature (Beginnings) S: 171
Oral message [literature]
Ferlinghetti, Lawrence F: 73
Oral pathology
Dentistry (Oral pathology) D: 144
Oral phase [psychology]
Libido L: 233
Psychoanalysis (Psychoanalytic theory) P: 846
Oral surgery
Dentistry (Oral surgery) D: 144
Oral tradition
Folklore F: 322
Oralist method [education]
Deafness (Education) D: 59
Oran [Algeria] O: 814
Orang Asli [people]
Malaysia (People) M: 98b; (Early days) M: 101
Orang Laut [people]
Malaysia (People) M: 98b; (Early days) M: 101
Orang Ulu [people]
Dayaks D: 53
Orange [color]
Color *diagram on* Ci: 821
Orange [tree] O: 814 *with pictures*
Belize *picture on* B: 238
Citrange Ci: 572 *with picture*
Florida *picture on* F: 259
Fruit (Simple fruits) F: 544 *with picture*
Mandarin M: 136
Spain (Agriculture) So: 743 *with picture*
Tangor T: 27
Wood *picture on* W: 389
Orange, House of [English history]
Mary II M: 239
William III W: 308
Orange Book [standard]
Compact disc (CD-R) Ci: 902; (CD-RW) Ci: 902
Orange Bowl Parade
Florida *picture on* F: 246
Orange County
Los Angeles (Metropolitan area) L: 462 *with picture*
Orange Free State [province, South Africa] O: 817
Anglo-Boer Wars A: 463
Orange gourd
Gourd G: 281 *with picture*
Orange hawkweed [plant]

Devil's paintbrush D: 175
Orange juice
Food, Frozen *picture on* F: 338
Orange O: 814; (Harvesting and processing)
O: 815
Orange Order [organization] O: 817
Northern Ireland (Religion) N: 522
Orange Revolution [Ukrainian history]
Ukraine *picture on* U: 13; (Political changes) U: 14
Orange River [South Africa] O: 817
Namibia (Land and climate) N: 8
South Africa (Rivers) So: 615 *with map*
Orange roughy [fish]
Roughy R: 490 *with picture*
Orange sulphur [insect]
Butterfly *picture on* B: 737
Orangemen [Irish history]
Northern Ireland (Religion) N: 522
Orange Order O: 817
Orangerie [museum]
Paris (Museums and art galleries) P: 164-165
Orangetip [butterfly]
Butterfly *picture on* B: 737
Orangutan [animal] O: 817 *with picture*
Animal *picture on* A: 481
Ape A: 563 *with picture*
Conservation *picture on* Ci: 975
Endangered species (table) E: 270
Galdikas, Biruté G: 10
Primate (Great apes) P: 778a
Orangutan Foundation International
Galdikas, Biruté G: 10
Oranjestad [Aruba]
Aruba A: 764
Oranmiyan [king of Benin]
Benin B: 251
Oration
Oratory O: 818
Orator
Oratory O: 818
Oratorians [religious group]
Neri, Saint Philip N: 130
Oratorio [music] O: 818
Classical music (Oratorios) Ci: 644
Handel, George Frideric (His work) H: 42
Opera O: 790
Oratory [architecture]
Cloister Ci: 682l
Oratory [speech] O: 818
See also the list of Related articles in the Oratory
article
Greek literature (Philosophical literature) G: 377-
378
Orb [symbol]
Coronation (The British coronation) Ci: 1068
Orb weaver [spider]
Spider *pictures on* So: 786, So: 788; (Orb weavers)
So: 789
Orbán, Viktor [Hungarian political leader]
Hungary (Recent developments) H: 448
Orbis Pictus Award
Literature for children (Awards) L: 367
Orbis Sensualium Pictus [book by Comenius]
Literature for children (Early children's literature)
L: 361-362
Orbit [anatomy]
Eye (Parts of the eye) E: 460
Orbit [astronomy] O: 819 *with diagram*
Asteroid (Orbital groups) A: 824a *with diagrams*
Climate (Changes in the earth's orbit) Ci: 677 *with
diagram*
Comet C: 867
Copernicus, Nicolaus (Theories of heavenly
motion) Ci: 1039
Earth (Earth as a planet) E: 16-17 *with diagram*
Halley's Comet H: 24 *with diagram*
Jupiter (Orbit and rotation) J: 198
Kepler, Johannes (Kepler's laws) K: 305
Mercury (Orbit) M: 414
Moon (The movements of the moon) M: 783 *with
diagram*
Planet (How planets move) P: 508 *with diagrams*
Satellite, Artificial (Satellite orbits) S: 150d;
(Falling from orbit) S: 150g
Solar system So: 580
Space exploration *diagrams on* So: 697
Orbital magnetic field [physics]
Magnetism (In atoms) M: 60b
Orbital plane [astronomy]
Earth (How Earth moves) E: 17
Jupiter (Orbit and rotation) J: 198
Orbital resonance [astronomy]
Saturn (Rings) S: 150j
Orbital velocity [physics]
Space exploration (Getting into space and back)
So: 698
Orbiter [spacecraft]

Space exploration *picture on* So: 700; (Space
shuttles) So: 723
Orca [sea mammal] *See* Killer whale *in this index*
Orchard [agriculture]
Tree (Food products) T: 412
Orchard, Harry [American public figure]
Idaho (Early statehood) I: 44
Orchard oriole [bird]
Oriole O: 856
Orchardgrass
Grass *picture on* G: 325
Orchestra [music] O: 820 *with pictures*
See also the list of Related articles in the Orchestra
article
Classical music (Orchestral music) Ci: 644
Opera (The orchestra) O: 793 *with picture*
Orchestra [theater]
Drama (Greek drama) D: 326
Orchestra bells O: 823
Bell *picture on* B: 239
Glockenspiel G: 234
Orchestration
Music (Tone color) M: 952
Orchid [plant] O: 823 *with pictures*
Flower *pictures on* F: 272, F: 292; (table) F: 301
with picture
Plant (Interesting facts about plants) P: 519 *with
picture*
Rain forest *picture on* R: 126c
Root (Kinds of roots) R: 469-470 *with diagram*
Orcus [Roman mythology]
Pluto P: 581
Orczy, Baroness [British author] O: 825
Detective story (History) D: 162-163
Ordeal, Trial by *See* Trial by ordeal *in this index*
Ordeal of Richard Feverel, The [book by Meredith]
Meredith, George M: 416
Ordeal of the Union, The [book by Nevins]
Nevins, Allan N: 178
Ordeal of Woodrow Wilson, The [book by Hoover]
Hoover, Herbert Clark (Elder statesman) H: 330-
331
Order [architecture]
Architecture A: 609 *with diagrams*
Order [biology] O: 825
Classification, Scientific (Groups in classification)
Ci: 655
Order [geology]
Soil (How soils are classified) So: 576
Order [organization]
Knighthood, Orders of K: 346
Medals, decorations, and orders M: 355
Order in Council [British history] O: 825
Jefferson, Thomas (The struggle for neutrality)
J: 86-87
Order of ...
Orders appear under their key words, as in Bath,
Order of the
Order of business
Parliamentary procedure (Order of business)
P: 176
Order of protection [law]
Restraining order R: 263
Order of Things, The [book by Foucault]
Foucault, Michel F: 429
Ordered pair [mathematics]
Algebra (Functions) A: 356-357
Orders, Religious
Religious life R: 226
Roman Catholic Church (Church organization)
R: 404; (Innocent III) R: 407
Ordinance [law]
Code Ci: 748
Ordinance [religion]
Christianity (Sacraments) C: 522h
Mormons (Church doctrines and ordinances)
M: 806
Ordinance of 1784 [U.S. history]
Jefferson, Thomas (Delegate to the Congress)
J: 80
Ordinance of 1785 [U.S. history]
Jefferson, Thomas (Delegate to the Congress)
J: 80
Northwest Territory (Early history) N: 534-535
Pioneer life in America (How the pioneers
obtained land) P: 479
Public lands (Disposal of public lands) P: 858
Westward movement in America (The Ordinance
of 1785) W: 246 *with diagrams*
Ordinance of 1787 *See* Northwest Ordinance *in
this index*
Ordinance of Secession [U.S. history]
Lincoln, Abraham (The South secedes) L: 320
Ordinary [bicycle]
Bicycle (Early bicycles) B: 291
Ordinary [tavern]
Colonial life in America (Recreation) Ci: 802-803

Ordinary construction
Building construction (Classification of buildings) B: 683
Ordinary People [film]
Motion picture (Best picture: 1980) M: 861
Ordinary seaman
Ship (Officers and crew) S: 410
Ordinate [mathematics]
Geometry (Analytic geometry) G: 105 *with diagrams*
Ordination [religion]
See also Holy orders *in this index*
Christianity (Sacraments) C: 522h
Religion (Religious rituals) R: 217
Ordóñez de Montalvo, Garci [Spanish author]
Amadís of Gaul A: 399
Spanish literature (The 1400's) So: 758
Ordovician Period [geology] O: 825
Earth (The Paleozoic Era) E: 27; (table) E: 30
Extinction (The Ordovician extinction) E: 456
Prehistoric animal (table) P: 738
Ore [mineral] O: 825
Gold (Types of deposits) G: 252
Iron and steel (Sources of iron ore) I: 437 *with picture*; (Mining and processing iron ore) I: 438
Mining (Mineral deposits) M: 574 *with picture*
Rock R: 371
Ore/bulk/oil carrier [ship]
Ship (Tankers) S: 408 *with picture*
Tanker (Combination carriers) T: 28
Ore Mountains [Czech Republic]
Czech Republic (Land and climate) Ci: 1211 *with map*
Ore-oil carrier
Tanker (Kinds of tankers) T: 28
Oread [mythology]
Nymph N: 633
Oregano [seasoning] O: 825
Marjoram M: 213
Oregon O: 826 *with pictures and maps*
See also the list of Related articles in the Oregon *article*
Euthanasia (Physician-assisted suicide) E: 421
Freedom of assembly (In the United States) F: 504
McLoughlin, John M: 343
Polk, James Knox ("Oregon fever") P: 643
Same-sex marriage S: 78
Westward movement in America (The Oregon Trail) W: 249
Oregon [ship]
Panama Canal (The United States and the canal) P: 125
Oregon, University of O: 849
Oregon *picture on* O: 831
Oregon Beach Bill [1967]
Oregon (The late 1900's) O: 849
Oregon Boundary Treaty *See* Oregon Treaty *in this index*
Oregon Caves National Monument [Oregon]
National Park System (table: National monuments) N: 51
Oregon (Places to visit) O: 836
Oregon Country [U.S. history]
Oregon Territory O: 850
Ross, Alexander R: 480
United States, History of the *map on* U: 184; (Manifest destiny) U: 169
Washington (Settlement) W: 66
Oregon grape [plant] O: 849
Oregon holly grape [plant]
Oregon grape O: 849
Oregon junco [bird]
Junco J: 191 *with picture*
Oregon laurel [tree] *See* California laurel *in this index*
Oregon region
Lewis and Clark expedition L: 222 *with map*
Pioneer life in America (Crossing the Plains) P: 485-486
Oregon Spectator [newspaper]
Oregon (Communication) O: 844
Oregon State University O: 850
Oregon Statesman [newspaper]
Oregon (Communication) O: 844
Oregon System [political science]
Oregon (The early 1900's) O: 848
Oregon Territory [U.S. history] O: 850
Fifty-Four Forty or Fight F: 96
Gray, Robert G: 334
Oregon (Provisional and territorial governments) O: 848
Polk, James Knox ("Oregon fever") P: 643
Washington (Territorial days) W: 66
Oregon Trail [U.S. history] O: 850 *with map*
Meeker, Ezra M: 383
Nebraska (American exploration and settlement)

N: 111
Oregon (Exploration and settlement) O: 846 *with picture*
Palmer, Joel P: 110
Parkman, Francis P: 171
Pioneer life in America (Routes to the West) P: 486 *with picture*
Westward movement in America (The Oregon Trail) W: 249
Wyoming W: 517; (The great trails) W: 533
Oregon Trail, The [book by Parkman]
Parkman, Francis P: 171
Oregon Trail, The [painting by Bierstadt]
Painting (Light and shade) P: 35
Pioneer life in America *picture on* P: 486
Oregon Treaty [1846]
Oregon Territory O: 850
Polk, James Knox ("Oregon fever") P: 643
Oregon white oak
Oak (White oaks) O: 635
Oregonian, The [newspaper]
Oregon (Communication) O: 844
O'Reilly, Edward [American journalist]
Pecos Bill P: 227
O'Reilly, Leonora [American labor leader] O: 851
Orellana, Francisco de [Spanish explorer] O: 851
Amazon River (History) A: 404
Exploration *on* E: 443; (Spain's conquests in the New World) E: 445
Latin America *map on* L: 105
Orenda [religion]
Indian, American (Beliefs) I: 147
Oresme, Nicole [French mathematician]
Physics (The Renaissance) P: 438-439
Oresteia [plays by Aeschylus]
Aeschylus A: 90
Drama (Tragedy) D: 326
Orestes [father of]
Romulus Augustulus R: 450a
Orestes [legendary figure]
Electra E: 165
Iphigenia I: 397
Orestes [Roman political leader]
Hypatia H: 475
Öresund Link [bridge/tunnel, Sweden-Denmark]
Malmö M: 111
Sweden (Transportation) So: 1032
Orfeo [opera by Gluck]
Gluck, Christoph Willibald G: 235
Orfeo [opera by Monteverdi]
Monteverdi, Claudio M: 764a
Opera (Early Baroque opera) O: 797
Orff, Carl [German composer] O: 851
Organ [anatomy]
Cell C: 326
Evolution (Vestigial organs) E: 431
Frog *picture on* F: 537
Human body (Organs and organ systems) H: 418; (table) *diagrams on* H: 422
Life (Tissues, organs, and organ systems) L: 277 *with diagram*
Organ donation O: 852
Reproduction, Human (Origin of tissues and organs) R: 247; (Development of organs and organ systems) R: 248
Stem cell So: 889
Transplant T: 379
Xenotransplant X: 544
Organ [musical instrument] O: 851 *with diagram*
Harmonium H: 62
Organ donation [medicine] O: 852
Transplant (Sources of donor organs) T: 380
Organ of Corti [anatomy]
Deafness (Sensorineural hearing loss) D: 57; (Environmental factors) D: 57
Ear *diagram on* E: 10; (The inner ear) E: 8-9 *with diagram*
Organ-pipe cactus
Cactus (Kinds of cactuses) C: 11 *with picture*
Plant *picture on* P: 526
Organ Pipe Cactus National Monument [Arizona]
Arizona *picture on* A: 670
National Park System (table: National monuments) N: 51
Organ Procurement Organization
Transplant (Sources of donor organs) T: 380
Organ specific autoimmune disease
Immune system (Autoimmune disorders) I: 88c
Organ system [biology]
Human body (Organs and organ systems) H: 418; (table) *diagrams on* H: 422
Life (Tissues, organs, and organ systems) L: 277 *with diagram*
Organ transplant *See* Transplant *in this index*
Organelle [biology]
Cell (The cytoplasm) C: 329
Life (Cells) L: 277

Prokaryote P: 817
Organic Act [1884]
Alaska (American purchase) A: 301
Organic Act [1900]
Puerto Rico (United States rule) P: 883
Organic Act [1912]
Alaska (The early 1900's) A: 301
Organic Act [1917]
Puerto Rico (United States rule) P: 883
Organic chemistry O: 853
Carbon (Carbon compounds) C: 204
Chemistry (Development of organic chemistry) C: 404
Hydrocarbon H: 465
Wöhler, Friedrich W: 374
Organic compound [chemistry]
Compound Ci: 906
Hydrogen (Compounds) H: 469
Inorganic chemistry I: 276
Life (Carbon) L: 278; (Creating simple organic compounds) L: 279
Organic chemistry O: 853
Organic design
Furniture (Organic design) F: 583 *with picture*
Organic evolution *See* Evolution *in this index*
Organic farming
Agriculture (Organic agriculture) A: 151
Alfalfa (Organic alfalfa) A: 348
Cotton (Recent developments) Ci: 1093
Farm and farming (Special crop-growing methods) F: 37
Plant (Disease and pest control) P: 541
Vegetable (Pest control) V: 293
Organic fertilizer
Fertilizer (Organic fertilizers) F: 79
Organic food O: 853
Dairying (Organic dairying) D: 7
Health food H: 129
Organic hypoglycemia [disorder]
Hypoglycemia H: 481
Organic light-emitting diode [electronics]
Light-emitting diode L: 293
Organic matter
Gardening (Analyzing the soil) G: 31
Soil So: 573 *with diagram*
Topsoil T: 333
Wetland (Water and soil) W: 252a
Organic psychosis
Psychosis P: 851
Organic sediment [geology]
Rock (Organic sediments) R: 372
Organic solidarity [sociology]
Durkheim, Émile D: 389
Organic Statutes [1834]
Romania (Russian control) R: 423
Organic waste
Sewage S: 329
Organisation for Economic Co-operation and Development O: 853
Foreign aid (Other countries' aid programs) F: 384-385
International trade (Government trade policies) I: 348-349
Marshall Plan M: 232
Organism [biology]
Cloning Ci: 682l
Life L: 274
Organization
Parliamentary procedure (Forming an organization) P: 175
Organization for Economic Cooperation and Development *See* Organisation for Economic Co-operation and Development *in this index*
Organization for European Economic Cooperation
Marshall Plan M: 232
Organization for Popular Democracy-Labor Movement [political party]
Burkina Faso (History) B: 706-707
Organization for Security and Co-operation in Europe O: 853
Helsinki Accords H: 179
Organization of African Unity
Africa (Africa since independence) A: 135
African Union A: 137
Chad (History) C: 367-368
Organization of Afro-American Unity
Malcolm X M: 103
Organization of American States O: 854
Flag *picture on* F: 216
Haiti (History) H: 15-17
Pan-American conferences (Stronger ties) P: 113
Organization of the Petroleum Exporting Countries O: 854
Cartel C: 251
Iraq (The Persian Gulf War of 1991) I: 414
Kuwait (Economy) K: 395-396

Middle East (The 1970's and the 1980's) **M: 534a**
Persian Gulf War of 1991 (Background to the war)
  P: 300b
Petroleum (The postwar period) **P: 349**
Saudi Arabia (The oil industry) **S: 159**
Organizational psychology
  Industrial psychology **I: 245**
Organized crime
  Capone, Al **C: 198**
  Crime (Organized crime) **Ci: 1136**
  Italy (Social problems) **I: 518**
  Racketeering **R: 63**
Organized Crime Control Act [1970]
  Racketeering **R: 63**
Organized labor *See* Labor movement; Labor
  union *in this index*
**Organized Trades and Labor Unions of the
  United States and Canada, Federation of**
  American Federation of Labor and Congress of
    Industrial Organizations (History) **A: 410**
Organizer [labor]
  Labor movement (Organizing workers) **L: 4**
Organochlorine [insecticide]
  Insecticide (Chlorinated hydrocarbon
    insecticides) **I: 302**
Organometallic catalyst [chemistry]
  Rubber (General-purpose synthetic rubbers)
    R: 504
Organon [book by Aristotle]
  Aristotle (Logic) **A: 663**
Organophosphate insecticide
  Insecticide (Organophosphate insecticides) **I: 302**
Organum [music]
  Classical music (The Middle Ages) **Ci: 645**
Orhan [Ottoman sultan]
  Osman I **O: 865**
Oriana [literary figure]
  Amadís of Gaul **A: 399**
Oribe, Manuel [Uruguayan political leader]
  Uruguay (Civil war) **U: 227**
Oriel window
  Window **W: 334**
Orient [region, Asia] **O: 855**
Orient Express
  Railroad (Worldwide development) **R: 116**
Oriental alabaster [mineral]
  Alabaster **A: 280**
Oriental amethyst [gem]
  Amethyst **A: 432**
Oriental cat
  Cat (Short-haired breeds) **C: 290-291**
Oriental coral snake
  Coral snake **Ci: 1050**
Oriental fruit fly
  Fruit fly **F: 549**
Oriental furniture
  Furniture (Oriental furniture) **F: 571** *with pictures*
Oriental Institute
  Breasted, James Henry **B: 591**
  Chicago, University of (Research program) **C: 438**
Oriental Jews
  Israel (Jews) **I: 480**
Oriental Magazine: or, Calcutta Amusement
  [magazine]
  Magazine (Early magazines) **M: 44-45**
Oriental Mask [collage by Janco]
  Dadaism *picture on* **D: 3**
Oriental pear
  Pear (Varieties) **P: 215**
Oriental pearl
  Pearl (Color) **P: 217**
Oriental poppy
  Flower *picture on* **F: 279**
  Poppy **P: 668**
Oriental rug
  Asia *picture on* **A: 780**
  Rugs and carpets (Oriental rugs) **R: 516** *with
    pictures*
  Turkey *picture on* **T: 506**
Oriental tobacco
  Tobacco (Sun-cured tobacco) **T: 306**
Orientale Basin [lunar feature]
  Moon (Basins) **M: 789**
Orientation-related disability
  Learning disabilities (Types) **L: 165**
Oriente [region]
  Bolivia (The Oriente) **B: 445**
  Ecuador **E: 67**; (The Eastern Lowland) **E: 70**
Oriente tree snail
  Shell *picture on* **S: 386**
Orienteering [sport]
  Hiking **H: 230**

Orifice meter
  Water meter **W: 135**
Origami [Japanese art] **O: 855** *with picture*
  Paperwork (Paper handicrafts) **P: 138**
Origin of Life on Earth, The [book by Oparin]
  Oparin, Alexander Ivanovich **O: 789**
Origin of Species, The [book by Darwin]
  Christianity (The 1800's) **C: 526**
  Darwin, Charles Robert **D: 40**
  English literature (Victorian literature) **E: 320**
  Evolution (Darwin's theory) **E: 432**
  Races, Human (Evolutionary theory) **R: 53-54**
  Science (Scientific advances of the 1800's) **S: 200**
  Zoology (History) **Z: 606**
Original Celtics [team]
  Basketball (The history of professional basketball)
    B: 154a
Original dance
  Ice skating (Ice dancing) **I: 13**
Original Dixieland Jass Band
  Jazz (Early jazz) **J: 70**
Original jurisdiction [law]
  Court (Types of courts) **Ci: 1101**; (Federal courts)
    Ci: 1102
  Supreme Court of the United States (Original and
    appellate jurisdiction) **So: 998**
Original Poems for Infant Minds [book by Taylor]
  Literature for children (Masterpieces of poetry)
    L: 364
Original sin
  Christianity (Sin and salvation) **C: 522g**
  Roman Catholic Church (Sin, the Incarnation, and
    salvation) **R: 403**
Originating post office
  Postal services (Sorting) **P: 703**
Origins of Totalitarianism [book by Arendt]
  Arendt, Hannah **A: 645**
Orinoco crocodile
  Crocodile (Kinds of crocodiles) **Ci: 1149-1150**
Orinoco River [Colombia-Venezuela] **O: 855**
  South America (Rivers) **So: 628**
  Venezuela (The Llanos) **V: 302**
Oriole [bird] **O: 856**
  Bird (Bird as B: 358**; (Birds of forests and
    woodlands) **B: 334** *with picture*
Orioles [pop group]
  Rock music (A variety of styles) **R: 378**
Orioles, Baltimore [team] *See* Baltimore Orioles
  in this index
Orion [spacecraft] *See* Crew Exploration Vehicle *in
  this index*
Orion [Greek mythology] **O: 856**
Orion [constellation] **O: 856**
  Betelgeuse **B: 274**
  Nebula *picture on* **N: 116**
  Star (Names of stars) **So: 842** *with picture*
Orion and Other Poems [book by Roberts]
  Roberts, Charles G. D. **R: 365**
Oriskany, Battle of [1777]
  Revolution, American (Victory at Saratoga) **R: 282**
  Saint Leger, Barry **S: 45**
Orizaba [Mexico]
  Orizaba, Pico de **O: 856**
Orizaba, Pico de [mountain, Mexico] **O: 856**
  Mexico (The Plateau of Mexico) **M: 461** *with map*
  Mountain (table) **M: 896** *with diagram*
Orkney and Shetland, Duke of [Scottish
  nobleman]
  Bothwell, Earl of **B: 510**
Orkney Islands [Scotland] **O: 856**
Orlando [opera by Handel]
  Handel, George Frideric (His work) **H: 42-43**
Orlando [Florida] **O: 856**
Orlando [book by Woolf]
  Woolf, Virginia **W: 401**
Orlando, Vittorio Emanuele [Italian political
  leader] **O: 857**
  Versailles, Treaty of **V: 339**
  Wilson, Woodrow *picture on* **W: 326**
  World War I (The Paris Peace Conference) **W: 465**
Orlando Furioso [poem by Ariosto]
  Ariosto, Ludovico **A: 662**
  Italian literature (Humanism and the
    Renaissance) **I: 494**
Orlando innamorato [poem by Boiardo]
  Italian literature (Humanism and the
    Renaissance) **I: 494**
Orlando Magic [team]
  Basketball (table) **B: 150**
Orléans [France] **O: 857**
Orléans, Battle of [1429]
  England (The Hundred Years' War) **E: 306**
  Joan of Arc, Saint (Joan's military career) **J: 129**
Orléans, Île d' [island, Quebec]
  Quebec, Battle of (Bombardment of Quebec)
    Q: 37
Orléans, Maid of *See* Joan of Arc, Saint *in this index*

Orloff, Prince [Russian nobleman]
  Diamond (Famous diamonds) **D: 182**
Orloff diamond
  Diamond *picture on* **D: 181**; (Famous diamonds)
    D: 182
Orly Airport
  Paris (Economy) **P: 165**
Orman, James B. [American political leader]
  Colorado (table) **Ci: 844**
Ormandy, Eugene [American conductor] **O: 857**
Ormer [animal] *See* Abalone *in this index*
Ormond [book by Brown]
  Brown, Charles Brockden **B: 642**
Ormond-Daytona Beach
  Florida (Places to visit) **F: 252**
Ormsbee, Ebenezer J. [American political leader]
  Vermont (table) **V: 333**
Ornament *See* Art and the arts; Clothing; Gem;
  Jewelry *in this index*
Ornamental crop
  Crop **Ci: 1153**
Ornamental garden
  Gardening (Ornamental gardens) **G: 30** *with
    picture*
Ornamental grass
  Grass (Ornamental grasses) **G: 326**
Ornithischian [extinct animal]
  Dinosaur (Kinds of dinosaurs) **D: 206b** *with
    pictures*
Ornitholestes [dinosaur] **O: 857**
  Dinosaur *picture on* **D: 207**
Ornithological Biography [book by Audubon and
  MacGillivray]
  Audubon, John James (His works) **A: 885**
Ornithology [zoology] **O: 857**
  Biology (What biologists study) **B: 316-317**
  Bird (Bird study and protection) **B: 367**
Ornithomimus [dinosaur] **O: 858**
  Dinosaur *pictures on* **D: 206a, D: 207**; (True
    dinosaurs) **D: 206b-211**
Ornithopod [dinosaur]
  Camptosaurus **C: 97**
  Dinosaur (True dinosaurs) **D: 206b-206c**
Ornithopter [aircraft] **O: 858**
  Airplane (Early experiments and ideas) **A: 229-
    230** *with picture*
Ornithosis [disease] *See* Psittacosis *in this index*
Orogeny [geology]
  Earth (Mountain building) **E: 24**
Oromiffa [language]
  Ethiopia (People) **E: 368**
Oromo [people]
  Ethiopia (People) **E: 368**
Orontes River
  Lebanon (Land and climate) **L: 172**
  Syria (The valleys and plains) **So: 1073**
Oroonoko [book by Behn]
  Behn, Aphra **B: 221**
O'Rourke, Jim [American baseball player]
  Baseball (table: Hall of Fame) **B: 134a**
Oroville Dam [Feather River, California] **O: 858**
  California (Water) **C: 54-55**
  Dam (table) **D: 18**
Orozco, José Clemente [Mexican painter] **O: 858**
  with picture
  Fresco **F: 529**
  Mexico *picture on* **M: 470**
  Painting (Modern Mexican painting) **P: 83**
Orphan drug
  Drug (U.S. drug laws) **D: 357-358**
Orphanage *See* Children's home *in this index*
Orphans of the Storm [film]
  Gish, Dorothy **G: 201** *with picture*
Orpheus [Greek mythology] **O: 858**
  Eurydice **E: 420**
  Mythology (Greek divinities) **M: 982**
Orpheus [play by Cocteau]
  Cocteau, Jean **Ci: 747**
Orpheus [sculpture by Rodin]
  Sculpture (Form and treatment) **S: 230-231**;
    (Sculpture from 1600 to 1900) **S: 253-255**
Orpheus and Eurydice [opera by Gluck]
  Gluck, Christoph Willibald **G: 235**
Orpheus in the Underworld [opera by Offenbach]
  Offenbach, Jacques **O: 676**
Orpington [chicken]
  Chicken (table) **C: 443**
Orr, Bobby [Canadian hockey player] **O: 859**
Orr, Gustavus J. [American educator]
  Georgia (Schools) **G: 116**
Orr, Kay A. [American political leader]
  Nebraska (table) **N: 110**; (The late 1900's) **N: 115**
Orr, Robert D. [American political leader]
  Indiana (table) **I: 214**
Orrefors glass
  Glass (Types of art glass) **G: 220-221**
Orrery [machine]

Planetarium (Early planetariums) P: 514a *with picture*
Orrisroot [botany] O: 859
Iris I: 430
Orrorin turgenensis [hominid]
Human being (Prehuman ancestors) H: 414
Prehistoric people *picture on* P: 748; (The earliest hominids) P: 744; (table) P: 754 *with map*
Orsay Museum [Paris]
France (Museums and libraries) F: 461 *with picture*
Orsino [literary figure]
Shakespeare, William: (*Twelfth Night*) S: 360-361
Ortega, Daniel [Nicaraguan political leader] O: 859 *with portrait*
Latin America (Return to civilian government) L: 111
Nicaragua (The late1900's) N: 400-401; (Recent developments) N: 401
Ortega, José Francisco de [Spanish explorer]
Santa Barbara S: 113
Ortega y Gasset, José [Spanish philosopher] O: 859
Spanish literature (The Generation of 1898) So: 762
Orteig, Raymond [American businessman]
Lindbergh, Charles Augustus (His historic flight) L: 330
Ortelius, Abraham [Flemish cartographer]
Atlas (History) A: 868
Map (Advances in European cartography) M: 184
Orthoclase [mineral]
Feldspar F: 68
Orthocone nautiloid [animal]
Ordovician Period O: 825
Orthodontics [dentistry] O: 859
Dentistry (Orthodontics) D: 143 *with picture*
Teeth (Malocclusion) T: 84-85
Orthodox Churches, Eastern *See* Eastern Orthodox Churches *in this index*
Orthodox Judaism [religion]
Jerusalem (The people of Jerusalem) J: 96-98 *with picture*
Judaism (Orthodox Judaism) J: 180; (Worship) J: 181
Religion (Judaism) R: 219-220
Orthodox Muslims *See* Sunnis *in this index*
Orthogneiss [rock]
Gneiss G: 238
Orthographic projection
Mechanical drawing (Information in the drawing) M: 353 *with picture*
Orthography [language]
Spelling So: 775
Orthopaedics *See* Orthopedics *in this index*
Orthopedics [medicine] O: 860
Medicine (table) M: 369
Orthophosphoric acid [chemical]
Phosphoric acid P: 403
Orthoptera [entomology]
Insect *pictures on* I: 280; (table) I: 299
Orthopyroxene [mineral]
Pyroxene P: 920
Orthorhombic sulfur
Sulfur (Forms) So: 966
Orthorhombic system
Crystal (Classifying crystals) Ci: 1166-1167 *with picture*
Pyroxene P: 920
Orwell, George [British author] O: 860 *with portrait*
English literature (Literature after World War II) E: 322-323
Novel (After World War II) N: 574
Orwell Corner Historic Village [Orwell]
Prince Edward Island (Places to visit) P: 788
Oryx [animal]
Addax A: 46
Antelope (Kinds of antelope) A: 542-543 *with picture*
Gemsbok G: 80
Oryx and Crake [book by Atwood]
Atwood, Margaret A: 880
OS [electronics] *See* Operating system *in this index*
Os [symbol]
Osmium O: 865
Os ...
Titles beginning Os appear under their key words, as in Lusíadas, Os
Osage Indians O: 860
Chouteau, Jean Pierre C: 522
Osage orange [tree] O: 860 *with picture*
Osage Plains
Missouri (Land regions) M: 662; (Natural resources) M: 665
Osage River [Missouri]
Lake of the Ozarks L: 42 *with map*
Osaka [Japan] O: 861 *with picture*

Japan *pictures on* J: 35, J: 38
Osaka Port Bridge [Japan]
Bridge (table: Cantilever) B: 603
Osborn, Chase S. [American political leader]
Michigan (table) M: 507
Osborn, Emily [British artist]
Painting (Women artists) P: 73 *with picture*
Osborn, Henry Fairfield [American paleontologist] O: 861
Osborn, Sidney P. [American political leader]
Arizona (table) A: 687
Osborn, Thomas A. [American political leader]
Kansas (table) K: 234
Osborne, Henry [British government official]
Newfoundland and Labrador (War with France) N: 375
Osborne, John [British dramatist] O: 861
Drama (Later British drama) D: 340
English literature (Literature after World War II) E: 322-323 *with picture*
Osborne, John E. [American political leader]
Wyoming (table) W: 532
Osborne, Thomas Mott [American social reformer] O: 862
Osborne 1 [computer]
Laptop computer (History) L: 74
Osbourne, Fanny [wife of]
Stevenson, Robert Louis (Marriage) So: 897
Osbourne, Lloyd [stepson of]
Stevenson, Robert Louis (Novels) So: 898 *with picture*
Oscan [language] O: 862
Oscar [award] *See* Academy Awards *in this index*
Oscar [satellite]
Radio, Amateur (Uses of amateur radio) R: 95; (History) R: 96
Oscar Peterson Trio
Peterson, Oscar P: 325
OSCE [organization] *See* Organization for Security and Co-operation in Europe *in this index*
Osceola [American Indian chief] O: 862 *with portrait*
Fort Moultrie F: 415
Indian wars (Conflicts in the South) I: 192
Seminole Indians S: 293
Oschin Telescope
Palomar Observatory P: 112
Oscillation [physics]
Electromagnetic waves E: 201
Electronics (Transistors) E: 212
Light (The properties of waves) L: 285; (Light and measurement) L: 290
Oscilloscope O: 862
Polarized light (Understanding polarized light) P: 617 *with diagram*
Oscillation, Period of [physics]
Pendulum (The oscillator) P: 236 *with diagram*
Oscillator [device]
Electronics (Transistors) E: 212
Radar (The oscillator) R: 70 *with diagram*
Radio (The tuner) R: 88-89
Vacuum tube (Triodes) V: 258-259
Watch (How watches work) W: 114
Oscilloscope [instrument] O: 862 *with picture*
Electroscope E: 218
Osculum
Sponge (Body openings) So: 799 *with diagram*
Osei Tutu [Ashanti leader]
Ashanti A: 767
OSHA [U.S.] *See* Occupational Safety and Health Administration *in this index*
O'Shaughnessy, Margaret Mary [American government official]
Heckler, Margaret Mary H: 164
Oshawa [Ontario] O: 862
O'Shea, William [Irish political leader]
Parnell, Charles Stewart P: 177
Osheroff, Douglas Dean [American physicist]
Nobel Prizes (Physics: 1996) N: 442
Osier [tree] O: 863
Osiris [Egyptian god] O: 863 *with picture*
Anubis A: 562
Egypt, Ancient *picture on* E: 140; (Religion) E: 137
Horus H: 370
Isis I: 462
Mythology *picture on* M: 977; (The Great Ennead) M: 979; (The Osiris myth) M: 979 *with picture*
Serapis S: 312
Seth S: 323
Osler, Sir William [Canadian doctor] O: 863 *with portrait*
Oslo [Norway] O: 864 *with pictures*
Norway *picture on* N: 537
Terrorism (Recent developments) T: 180
Oslo, University of
Norway (Education) N: 541
Oslo O: 864

Oslo accords [peace treaty]
Intifada I: 353
Middle East (The 1990's) M: 534a-534b
Norway (Political changes) N: 547
Sharon, Ariel S: 377
Osman I [Ottoman sultan] O: 865
Muslims (The Ottoman Empire) M: 964d
Ottoman Empire O: 877
Osmium [element] O: 865
Osmosis [biology] O: 865 *with diagrams*
Fish (How fish adjust to change) F: 168
Plant (Movement of water) P: 537
Water (Reverse osmosis) W: 128
Osmotic pressure
Osmosis O: 865
Osprey [bird] O: 866 *with picture*
Bird *picture on* B: 363
OSS [organization] *See* Strategic Services, Office of *in this index*
Ossa, Mount [mountain] *See* Mount Ossa *in this index*
Osservatore Romano, L' [newspaper]
Rome (Economy) R: 431
Vatican City (Communications) V: 288
Ossetians [people]
Georgia (History) G: 111
Ossian [legendary figure]
Finn MacCool F: 119
Ossicle [anatomy]
Deafness (Types of hearing loss) D: 57
Ear (The middle ear) E: 7-8 *with diagram*; (Diseases) E: 12
Ossietzky, Carl von [German journalist]
Nobel Prizes (Peace: 1935) N: 448a
Ossining Correctional Facility [New York]
Sing Sing S: 469
Ossoli, Angelo [Italian public figure]
Fuller, Margaret F: 554
Östberg, Ragnar [Swedish architect]
Sweden (Fine arts) So: 1027
Osteichthyes [zoology]
Fish (table) F: 172 *with pictures*
Osteitis fibrosa [disease]
Bone (Bone disorders) B: 457
Ostend [Belgium] O: 866
Ostend Manifesto [U.S. history] O: 866
Buchanan, James (Minister to the United Kingdom) B: 660
Ostenso, Martha [Canadian author]
Canadian literature (Literature between the world wars) C: 158-159
Osteoarthritis [disorder]
Arthritis (Osteoarthritis) A: 751 *with diagram*
Disease (Diseases associated with aging) D: 230
Osteoblast [physiology]
Bone (Composition of bone) B: 456
Osteoclast [physiology]
Bone (Composition of bone) B: 456
Osteocyte [physiology]
Bone (Composition of bone) B: 456
Osteoderm [zoology]
Reptile (Skin) R: 251
Osteomalacia [disease]
Bone (Bone disorders) B: 457
Rickets R: 335
Osteomyelitis [disease] O: 866
Osteon [physiology]
Haversian canals H: 87
Osteopathic Association, American
Osteopathic medicine (Careers in osteopathic medicine) O: 867
Osteopathic manipulation
Osteopathic medicine O: 867
Osteopathic medicine O: 866
Medicine (A career as a doctor) M: 370
Osteopathy, Doctor of
Medicine (A career as a doctor) M: 370
Osteopathic medicine (Careers in osteopathic medicine) O: 867
Osteopetrosis [disease]
Osteosclerosis O: 868
Osteoporosis [disease] O: 867 *with pictures*
Bone (Bone disorders) B: 457
Hormone replacement therapy H: 338
Menopause M: 402
Nutrition (Other diseases) N: 631
Osteosclerosis [disease] O: 868
Osterley Park House [London]
Adam [family] A: 32
Architecture (Neoclassical architecture) A: 623-624
Österreich *See* Austria *in this index*
Ostia [zoology]
Insect (Circulatory system) I: 288
Sponge (Body openings) So: 799 *with diagram*
Ostracod [animal]
Deep sea (Invertebrates) D: 82a-82b

Ostracoderm [extinct animal]
Fish (The first fish) F: 171
Ostrakon [artifact]
Government *picture on* G: 290
Ostrava [Czech Republic] O: 868
Ostrich [bird] O: 868 *with pictures*
Animal *pictures on* A: 476, A: 488
Bird *picture on* B: 329; (On land) B: 353 *with picture*
Cell (Sizes of cells) C: 328
Rhea R: 290
Ostrogoths [people]
Goths G: 280
Italy (The Middle Ages) I: 513
Theodoric T: 252
Ostrom, Elinor [American economist]
Nobel Prizes (Economics: 2009) N: 450
Ostrovsky, Alexander N. [Russian dramatist]
Drama (Russian drama and Chekhov) D: 338
Russian literature (Early realism) R: 562
Ostwald, Wilhelm [German chemist] O: 869
Chemistry (Development of physical chemistry) C: 404-405
Ostwald process [chemistry]
Nitric acid N: 425
O'Sullivan, John L. [American author]
Manifest destiny M: 141
O'Sullivan, Timothy [American photographer]
Photography (Artistic advances) P: 424-425
Osumi Islands [islands, Pacific]
Ryukyu Islands R: 574
Oswald, Lee Harvey [American public figure] O: 869
Kennedy, John Fitzgerald *picture on* K: 268; (The death of Oswald) K: 267
Texas (The mid-1900's) T: 208-209
Warren Report W: 37
Oswald, Richard [British diplomat]
Revolution, American (The Treaty of Paris) R: 286
Oswego [New York] O: 870
Oswego Canal
New York State Canal System N: 345 *with map*
Oświęcim [Poland] *See* Auschwitz *in this index*
OTA [organization]
Technology Assessment, Office of T: 78
Ota Dokan [Japanese war lord]
Tokyo (Early development) T: 318
Otago, University of [New Zealand]
Universities and colleges (Governing boards) U: 208L
Otago Plateaus
New Zealand (The South Island) N: 351-352
Otchipwe Indians *See* Chippewa Indians *in this index*
Otello [opera by Verdi]
Boito, Arrigo B: 440
Opera (Giuseppe Verdi) O: 798
Verdi, Giuseppe V: 316
Othello [play by Shakespeare]
Shakespeare, William: (Othello) S: 363 *with picture*
Other Paris, The [book by Gallant]
Gallant, Mavis G: 13
Other Voice, The [book by Paz]
Paz, Octavio P: 205
Other Worlds [book by Cyrano de Bergerac]
Science fiction (Forerunners of science fiction) S: 205
Otherwise Engaged [play by Gray]
Gray, Simon G: 334
Othman [Ottoman sultan] *See* Osman I *in this index*
Otho [Roman emperor]
Rome, Ancient (table) R: 447
Otis, Elisha Graves [American inventor] O: 870
Elevator (History) E: 235 *with picture*
Otis, James [American patriot] O: 870 *with portrait*
Writ of assistance W: 510
Otis Elevator Company
New York (Interesting facts) N: 291
Otitis media [disorder]
Deafness (Diseases) D: 57
Ear (Diseases) E: 12
Otolaryngology
Medicine (table) M: 369
Otolith [zoology]
Ear (The response to gravity) E: 11
Fish (Other senses) F: 164
Otomi Indians
Querétaro Q: 40
Otosclerosis [disease]
Deafness (Diseases) D: 57
Ear (Diseases) E: 12
Otoscope [instrument] O: 870 *with picture*
Medicine *picture on* M: 364
Ototoxic drug
Deafness (Environmental factors) D: 57
Otranto, Strait of
Adriatic Sea A: 68 *with map*

Otrepiev, Gregory [czar of Russia]
Russia (The Time of Troubles) R: 549
Ott, Mel [American baseball player]
Baseball (table: Hall of Fame) B: 134a
Ottar [Norwegian explorer]
White Sea W: 292
Ottawa [Ontario] O: 871 *with pictures and map*
Ontario O: 764, *picture on* O: 773; (table: Average monthly weather) O: 778
Ottawa, University of O: 875
Ottawa (Schools) O: 874
Ottawa Indians
Potawatomi Indians P: 714
Ottawa National Forest
Michigan (Places to visit) M: 498
Ottawa River [Quebec] O: 875
Ontario (Rivers, waterfalls, and lakes) O: 778
Quebec (Rivers, waterfalls, and lakes) Q: 24 *with map*
Saint Lawrence River (The course of the St. Lawrence) S: 41
Ottawa Senators [team]
Hockey (table: National Hockey League) H: 281
Otter [animal] O: 875 *with pictures*
Animal *picture on* A: 478
Fur (table) F: 561
Sea otter S: 262a *with picture*
Otter [ship]
California (American settlement) C: 60
Otter, C. L. "Butch" [American political leader]
Idaho (table) I: 42
Otter board
Fishing industry (Nets) F: 183 *with diagram*
Otter Island [Bering Sea]
Pribilof Islands P: 774
Otter Tail River [Minnesota]
Red River of the North R: 188
Otter trawl
Fishing industry (Nets) F: 183 *with diagram*
Otterbein United Methodist Church
Baltimore (The people) B: 68
Otterhound [dog] O: 876 *with picture*
Otto I, the Great [Holy Roman emperor] O: 877
Austria (Early years) A: 936
Germany (The breakup of Charlemagne's empire) G: 162 *with picture*
Holy Roman Empire H: 299
Italy (The Middle Ages) I: 513
Middle Ages (Feudal government) M: 524-525
Otto I [king of Greece] O: 876
George I G: 106b
Greece (Otto I) G: 362
Otto II [Holy Roman emperor] O: 877
Austria (Early years) A: 936
Otto, Nikolaus August [German engineer]
Automobile (The gasoline car) A: 965-966
Gasoline engine (Development of the gasoline engine) G: 56
Otto, Rudolf [German theologian]
Religion (The origin of religion) R: 218
Otto the Child [duke of Brunswick]
Brunswick B: 652
Ottokar [king of Bohemia]
Austria (The Habsburgs) A: 937
Ottoman Empire O: 877 *with maps*
Albania (Ottoman rule) A: 307
Algeria (Ottoman rule) A: 364
Arabs (Ottoman and European rule) A: 590
Armenia (History) A: 718b
Armenian Genocide A: 719
Army (Armies in the Middle Ages) A: 727
Baghdad (History) B: 26
Balkans (Early history) B: 42
Belgrade (History) B: 236
Berlin, Congress of B: 265
Bosnia-Herzegovina (History) B: 492
Bulgaria (Ottoman rule) B: 692
Clothing (Clothing under Islam) Ci: 697
Columbus, Christopher (The world of Columbus) Ci: 857
Croatia (History) Ci: 1148a-1148b
Cyprus (History) Ci: 1207
Edirne E: 77
Egypt (Ottoman and French control) E: 130; (Muhammad Ali and modernization) E: 131
Europe *map on* E: 408; (Muslims in medieval Europe) E: 410
Greece (Ottoman rule) G: 361
Hungary (Ottoman Empire) H: 445
Iraq (Ottoman control) I: 413
Istanbul (History) I: 491
Janissaries J: 29
Jerusalem (Muslim rule) J: 101
John III Sobieski J: 132
Jordan (Arab and Ottoman rule) J: 164
Macedonia M: 12
Magyars M: 64

Mamluks M: 115
Middle East (The Ottoman Empire) M: 534
Moldova (History) M: 690a
Montenegro (History) M: 763
Muslims (The spread of Islam) M: 964d
Navy (The beginning of modern navies) N: 79
Nicholas I N: 402
Osman I O: 865
Palestine (World War I and the Balfour Declaration) P: 105
Peter I, the Great (Early life) P: 323
Romania (Ottoman rule) R: 423
Russia (Nicholas I) R: 551
Russo-Turkish wars R: 566b
Safavid dynasty S: 8
Serbia (Ottoman rule) S: 314
Süleyman I So: 965
Syria (The Mamluks and Ottomans) So: 1075
Turkey (The Ottoman decline) T: 510 *with map*; (The rise of the Ottoman Empire) T: 510 *with map*
World, History of the (The Islamic world) W: 434-435; (The Islamic empires) W: 441
World War I (The rise of nationalism) W: 452-453; (Fighting elsewhere) W: 457; (The fighting ends) W: 463; (Political consequences) W: 464
Ottoman Turkish [language]
Turkey (Languages) T: 505
Ottomans [people]
Egypt (Ottoman and French control) E: 130
Turks T: 514b
Otway, Thomas [English dramatist]
Drama (England) D: 334-335
Ouabain [medication]
Poison P: 600
Ouachita, Lake [Arkansas]
Lake Ouachita L: 44 *with map*
Ouachita Mountains
Arkansas (Land regions) A: 706
Oklahoma (Land regions) O: 724 *with map*
Ouachita River [Arkansas-Louisiana] O: 878
Arkansas (Land regions) A: 706
Ouaddai [former kingdom]
Chad (History) C: 367
Ouagadougou [Burkina Faso] O: 878
Burkina Faso B: 706
Ouattara, Alassane [Ivorian political leader]
Côte d'Ivoire (History) Ci: 1084b-1085
Oubangui River *See* Ubangi River *in this index*
Oud [musical instrument]
Music (Arab music) M: 956
Ouellet, Marc [Canadian religious leader]
Cardinal (table: Canadian cardinals) C: 211
Ouémé River
Benin (Land and climate) B: 249-250 *with map*
Ouezzin Coulibaly, Daniel [African political leader]
Burkina Faso (History) B: 706-707
Oughtred, William [English mathematician]
Calculator C: 22
Ouija board O: 878
Ouimet, Gédéon [Canadian political leader]
Quebec (table) Q: 29
Ould Daddah, Mokhtar [Mauritanian political leader]
Mauritania (History) M: 315
Oulujoki [river, Finland]
Finland (Rivers) F: 114
Ounasjoki [river, Finland]
Finland (Rivers) F: 114
Ounce [unit of measure] O: 879
Apothecaries' weight A: 567
Ounce [wild cat] *See* Snow leopard *in this index*
Oungan [priest]
Vodou V: 436
Ounsi [assistant]
Vodou V: 436
Our American Cousin [play]
Lincoln, Abraham (Assassination) L: 326
Our Cabaña [home]
Girl Scouts (In other countries) G: 199
Our Chalet [home]
Girl Scouts (In other countries) G: 199
"Our country, right or wrong" [quotation]
Decatur, Stephen D: 67
Our Father [prayer] *See* Lord's Prayer *in this index*
Our Home Is Russia [political party]
Russia (Politics) R: 531
Our Lady, Cathedral of [Antwerp, Belgium]
Antwerp (Chief buildings) A: 561
Our Lady, Church of [Nuremberg]
Clock *picture on* Ci: 682k
Our Lady of Fátima [religion] *See* Fátima, Our Lady of *in this index*
Our Lady of Guadalupe [religion]
Guadalupe Day G: 408
Juan Diego, Saint J: 178
Our Lady of Mercy [church, Antigua]

Guatemala *picture on* G: 414
Our Lady of Mount Carmel, Order of [religious group]
Carmelites C: 241
Our Lady of Peace [church]
Côte d'Ivoire *picture on* Ci: 1084b
Yamoussoukro Y: 550
Our Lady of the Assumption, Cathedral of
Cuba *picture on* Ci: 1171
Our Land and Land Policy [book by George]
George, Henry G: 108
Our Mr. Wrenn [book by Lewis]
Lewis, Sinclair L: 221
Our Mutual Friend [book by Dickens]
Dickens, Charles (The second phase) D: 188-189
Our Nig [book by Wilson]
African American literature (The 1800's) A: 136a
Our Penal Machinery and Its Victims [book by Altgeld]
Altgeld, John Peter A: 389
Our Town [play by Wilder]
American literature (Drama) A: 422-423
Wilder, Thornton W: 303
Our Ukraine-People's Self-Defense [political group]
Ukraine (Politics) U: 6
Ouray [American Indian chief]
Colorado (Territorial days) Ci: 845
Ute Indians U: 251
Ouro Prêto [Brazil]
Brazil B: 575
Ousmane, Mahamane [Niger political leader]
Niger (History) N: 409
Out [sports]
Baseball (Outs by batters) B: 128; (Base runners—advancing and outs) B: 129
Cricket (Outs) Ci: 1132
Out-apiary
Bee (As an industry) B: 206-207
Out for Christmas Trees [painting by Moses]
Moses, Grandma *picture on* M: 830
Out of Africa [book by Dinesen]
Dinesen, Isak D: 205
Out of Africa [film]
Motion picture (Best picture: 1985) M: 861
Out-of-pocket maximum [insurance]
Insurance (Major medical expense benefits) I: 312
"Out of the Cradle Endlessly Rocking" [poem by Whitman]
Whitman, Walt (His work) W: 294
Out of the Dust [book by Hesse]
Hesse, Karen H: 219
Out of the Silent Planet [book by Lewis]
Lewis, C. S. L: 220
Outback [region, Australia] O: 879 *with map*
Australia A: 894 *with picture*; (Country life) A: 902
Outboard cruiser [boat]
Boating *picture on* B: 430
Outboard motor
Boating (Motorboats) B: 428; (Boating today) B: 432
Motorboat racing (Hull designs) M: 876
Outboard runabout [boat]
Boating *picture on* B: 430
Outbreeding [animal husbandry]
Livestock (Outbreeding) L: 398
Outcast [sociology]
See also Untouchable *in this index*
City (The people) Ci: 578-580
Outcast of the Islands, An [book by Conrad]
Conrad, Joseph Ci: 973
"Outcasts of Poker Flat, The" [story by Harte]
Harte, Bret H: 78
Outcault, Richard Felton [American cartoonist] O: 879
Comics (Comic strips) Ci: 869 *with picture*
Outcrop [mining]
Coal (Strip mining) Ci: 722
Mining (Mining terms) M: 577
Outcrossing [animal husbandry]
Livestock (Outbreeding) L: 398
Outdoor air pollution
Environmental pollution (Air pollution) E: 331
Outdoor relief
Welfare (History) W: 191
Outdoor sign
Advertising (Outdoor signs) A: 75
Outer bark [botany]
Tree (Trunk and branches) T: 416-417 *with diagram*
Outer core [geology]
Earth *diagram on* E: 20; (Earth's interior) E: 23
Outer ear [anatomy]
Deafness (Types of hearing loss) D: 57
Ear *diagram on* E: 8; (The outer ear) E: 7 *with diagram*

Outer Hebrides [islands, Scotland]
Hebrides H: 163
Outer Mongolia [former name] *See* Mongolia *in this index*
Outer space *See* Space [astronomy] *in this index*
Outer Space Treaty [1967]
Arms control (Arms control in the mid-1900's) A: 721-722
Outerbridge, Mary Ewing [American sportswoman]
Tennis (The spread of tennis) T: 165
Outerbridge Crossing
New York City (Transportation) N: 334
Outfield
Baseball (The outfield) B: 126 *with diagram*
Outfielder
Baseball (Player positions) B: 127
Outfitting pier
Ship (Launching and outfitting) S: 413
Outlaw [criminal]
Bandit B: 76
Outlaw [music]
Country music (Modern country music) Ci: 1098c-1098d *with picture*
Nelson, Willie N: 123
Outlaw strike
Labor movement (Handling labor disputes) L: 6-7
Outlet glacier [geology]
Glacier (Kinds of glaciers) G: 202
Outline O: 880
Composition (Organizing your thinking) Ci: 905
Public speaking (Outline) P: 865
A Guide to Writing Skills **Research Guide: 11, Research Guide: 16**
Outline of History, The [book by Wells]
Wells, H. G. W: 195
Outpatient clinic
Hospital (Recent developments) H: 374
Outpatient expense benefit
Insurance (Outpatient expense benefits) I: 312
Output [automation]
Automation (How automation works) A: 945
Output [economics]
Business (Productive resources) B: 725
Industry (The needs of industry) I: 257
Inflation (Severe inflation) I: 267
Output device [electronics]
Computer (Output devices) Ci: 916
Output equipment [electronics]
Electronics (How an electronic system works) E: 208
Output per worker-hour [measurement]
Wages and hours (Wages) W: 2-3
Output shaft
Transmission *diagram on* T: 376; (The gears) T: 378 *with diagram*
Outram, John [British architect]
Architecture (Architecture today) A: 632-633
Outre-Mer [book by Longfellow]
Longfellow, Henry Wadsworth (Professor and family man) L: 449
Outrigger [boat] O: 880
Crane (Types of cranes) C: 1120
Outside insider [business]
Insider trading I: 303
Outside linebacker [sports]
Football (The defensive team) F: 357 *with diagrams*
Outsiders, The [book by Hinton]
Hinton, S. E. H: 237
Outsourcing [business] O: 880
Tennessee (The early 2000's) T: 157
Outward Bound [educational organization] O: 880
Outwash plain [geography]
Glacier (How glaciers shape the land) G: 203-204 *with diagram*
Ova [biology] *See* Egg [reproduction] *in this index*
Oval cut
Gem (Types of gem cuts) *picture on* G: 79
Oval Office
President of the United States (The White House) P: 766 *with picture*
Oval track [racing]
Automobile racing A: 975 *with picture, diagram on* A: 976
Oval window [anatomy]
Ear *diagram on* E: 10; (The middle ear) E: 7-8 *with diagrams*
Ovalbumin [chemical]
Albumin A: 333
Ovambo [people]
Namibia (People) N: 8
Ovamboland [region]
Namibia (People) N: 8
Ovando, Nicolás de [Spanish colonial official]
Columbus, Christopher (Columbus in disgrace) Ci: 862-863; (Fourth voyage westward) Ci: 863

Ovarian cancer [disease] O: 880
Cancer (table) C: 170
Ovariohysterectomy [surgery]
Dog (Social and moral responsibilities) D: 279-280
Ovary [anatomy] O: 881
Cancer (table) C: 170
Chicken (Producing eggs) C: 443
Endometriosis E: 272
Gland (table) G: 208
Human body (table) H: 422 *with diagram*; (The reproductive system) H: 425
Hysterectomy H: 482
Insect (Reproductive system) I: 289 *with diagram*
Menstruation (The menstrual cycle) M: 404 *with pictures*
Ovarian cancer O: 880
Reproduction, Human (The human reproductive system) R: 244-245 *with diagram*
Sexuality (Biological factors) S: 337
Taxol T: 56
Ovary [botany]
Flower F: 271, *picture on* F: 293; (The carpels) F: 294; (Fertilization) F: 296
Fruit (Types of fruits in botany) F: 544
Plant (Flowers) P: 531 *with picture*; (Seeds) P: 531; (Sexual reproduction) P: 532-533 *with diagram*
Pollen (Fertilization) P: 645
Seed (Kinds of seeds) S: 280-281
Vegetable (Fruits) V: 292
Oven
Baking (The baking process) B: 33
Bread (How yeast bread is made) B: 588-589 *with picture*
Cooking (Cooking with dry heat) Ci: 1028
Indian, American (Food) I: 136d
Microwave oven M: 520
Range R: 137 *with pictures*
Ovenbird [bird] O: 881 *with picture*
Animal *picture on* A: 479
Warbler W: 35
Over [sports]
Cricket (The fielding side) Ci: 1134
Over Prairie Trails [book by Grove]
Grove, Frederick Philip G: 404
"Over-Soul, The" [essay by Emerson]
Emerson, Ralph Waldo (His prose works) E: 259
Over-the-counter drug
Drug (Nonprescription drugs) D: 356
Drug abuse (Abuse of legal drugs) D: 361
Pure food and drug laws (Over-the-counter drugs) P: 908
Over-the-counter trading
Nasdaq N: 22
Stock exchange (How a stock exchange operates) So: 904
Over-the-horizon radar
Radar (In the military) R: 65
"Over the Rainbow" [song]
Garland, Judy G: 43
Wizard of Oz, The W: 374
Over-the-Rhine [district]
Cincinnati (The 1800's) Ci: 556
Over-the-road bus
Bus B: 714
"Over There" [song]
Cohan, George M. Ci: 756
Overall operating budget
Budget (Business budgets) B: 670
Overbey, John [American businessman]
Bush, George Herbert Walker (Independent oilman) B: 718
Overbite
Teeth (Malocclusion) T: 84 *with picture*
Overburden [mining]
Aluminum (Sources of aluminum) A: 392-393
Bauxite (Mining and processing bauxite) B: 174
Coal (Surface mining) Ci: 721
Iron and steel (Open-pit mining) I: 438
Mining *diagram on* M: 575; *picture on* M: 574
Overcast stitch
Sewing (Hand stitches) S: 332
"Overcoat, The" [story by Gogol]
Russian literature (Late Romanticism) R: 561-562
Overcup oak [tree]
Oak (White oaks) O: 635
Overdrive [gear]
Transmission (Gears) T: 375-376
Overdubbing [recording]
Recording studio (Recording) R: 181
Overeaters Anonymous [organization] O: 881
Overflow tube
Plumbing (How toilets work) P: 579 *with diagram*
Overgrazing [farming]
Conservation (Conservation of grazing lands) Ci: 981
Desert (How deserts develop and change)

D: 156-157
Overhand knot
Knots, hitches, and splices (The language of knots) K: 356 *with diagram*
Overhand loop
Knots, hitches, and splices (The language of knots) K: 356
Overhaul
Fire department (Firefighting) F: 123-124
Overhead engine
Gasoline engine (Valve arrangement) G: 64
Overhead projector
Audio-visual materials (Projection devices) A: 882
Projector (Types of projectors) P: 816-817
Overhead smash [sports]
Tennis (The ball in play) T: 163
Overland Campaign [1864]
Lee, Robert E. (Final engagements) L: 179
Overland Monthly [magazine]
Harte, Bret H: 77
Overland Trail [Wyoming]
Wyoming (The great trails) W: 533-534
Overlapping set [mathematics]
Set theory (Kinds of sets) S: 321 *with diagrams*
Overpopulation
Birth control (The birth control movement) B: 378
Population (Effects) P: 674
Overpressure [physics]
Nuclear weapon (Blast wave) N: 599
Overreach, Sir Giles [literary figure]
Massinger, Philip M: 296
Overrunning clutch
Starter (Automobile starters) So: 858 *with diagram*
Overshot water wheel
Water wheel W: 141 *with picture*
Overstrung scale
Steinway, Henry Engelhard So: 886
Overthrust Belt [region]
Wyoming (Minerals) W: 529
Overtime [employment]
Fair Labor Standards Act F: 8
Overton, John [American jurist]
Memphis (History) M: 396
Overton Park
Memphis (Recreation) M: 396
Overtone [music]
Harmonics H: 62 *with diagrams*
Pitch P: 498
Sound (Sound quality) So: 601
Overtrick [bridge]
Bridge (Scoring) B: 605
Overture [music] O: 881
Classical music (Orchestral music) Ci: 644
Opera (The orchestra) O: 793
Overuse injury
Rotator cuff R: 486
Overvote
Voting machine (Advantages and disadvantages) V: 450
Overweight
See also Obesity; Weight control *in this index*
Obesity O: 642 *with diagram*
Ovid [Roman poet] O: 882
Latin literature (The Augustan Age) L: 116
Narcissus N: 20
Oviduct [zoology]
See also Fallopian tube *in this index*
Bird (The reproductive system) B: 366
Chicken (Producing eggs) C: 443
Egg (Development of the bird's egg) E: 117
Fallopian tube F: 17
Insect *diagram on* I: 286; (Abdomen) I: 288
Oviedo, Lino [Paraguayan political leader]
Paraguay (Stroessner's rule and overthrow) P: 149-150
Ovington, Earle [American aviator]
Airmail A: 207
Postal Service, United States (Technological advancements) P: 701
Oviparous animal [zoology] O: 882
Reptile (Reproduction) R: 252
Ovipositor [zoology]
Fly (Egg) F: 310
Grasshopper (The body) G: 327-328 *with diagrams*
Ichneumon wasp I: 24 *with picture*
Insect *diagram on* I: 286; (Abdomen) I: 288
Oviraptor [dinosaur] O: 882
Ovoid [astronomy]
Uranus (Satellites) U: 218
Ovoviviparity [zoology]
Reptile (Reproduction) R: 252
Ovulation [physiology]
Menstruation (The menstrual cycle) M: 404 *with picture*

Ovary O: 881
Progesterone P: 811
Reproduction, Human (The human reproductive system) R: 244-245
Ovule [botany]
Angiosperm A: 462
Flower (Fertilization) F: 296
Plant (Flowers) P: 531; (Sexual reproduction) P: 532-533 *with diagrams*
Pollen (Fertilization) P: 645
Seed (Kinds of seeds) S: 280
Ovum [biology] *See* Egg [reproduction] *in this index*
Owen, John [American political leader]
North Carolina (table) N: 490
Owen, Lemuel C. [Canadian political leader]
Prince Edward Island (table) P: 791
Owen, Sir Richard [British scientist]
Dinosaur (Dinosaur discoveries) D: 213
Owen, Robert [British social reformer] O: 882
Collectivism Ci: 775
Indiana (Early statehood) I: 216
Kindergarten (Early kindergartens) K: 319
New Harmony N: 228
Socialism (Early socialist ideas) So: 560
Wright, Frances W: 507
Owen, Robert Dale [American political leader] O: 883
Wright, Frances W: 507
Owen, Ruth Bryan [American diplomat] O: 883
Owen, Wilfred [British poet]
Britten, Benjamin B: 634
Owen Falls Dam [Nile River, Uganda]
Lake Victoria L: 48
Owenites [social reformers]
New Harmony N: 229
Owens, Bill [American political leader]
Colorado (table) Ci: 844
Owens, Jesse [American athlete] O: 883
Olympic Games *picture on* O: 753; (Between the wars) O: 751
Track and field (The early and middle 1900's) T: 360
Owens, Mary [American settler]
Lincoln, Abraham (Search for a career) L: 314
Owens, Michael Joseph [American inventor]
Toledo (History) T: 321
Owens, Steve [American football player]
Football (table) F: 363
Owens-Illinois, Inc.
Fiberglass (History) F: 89
Owensboro [Kentucky] O: 883
Owenson, Sydney [Irish poet]
Irish literature (Early works in English) I: 431
Owl [bird] O: 883 *with pictures*
Animal *pictures on* A: 478, A: 483, A: 494
Bird (In nature) B: 330 *with picture*; (Birds of grasslands) B: 336 *with picture*; (Birds of the desert) B: 339 *with picture*; (Sight) B: 364-365 *with picture*
Bird of prey B: 374
Brain (Among vertebrates) B: 560
Minerva M: 572
Owl [magazine]
Literature for children (New children's magazines) L: 365-366
"**Owl and the Pussy-Cat, The**" [poem by Lear]
Lear, Edward L: 162
Owl monkey *See* Night monkey *in this index*
Owl parrot
Parrot (Kinds of parrots) P: 179
Owlet moth
Moth (Owlet moths and underwingmoths) M: 840 *with pictures*
Owl's clover
Flower *picture on* F: 288
Owl's Head, Penobscot Bay, Maine [painting by Lane]
Painting (Landscapes and seascapes) P: 32-33 *with picture*
Own-rooting [botany]
Rose (Reproducing and growing roses) R: 475
Owners [play by Churchill]
Churchill, Caryl C: 543
Ownership
Business (Types of business ownership) B: 725
Marx, Karl (Marx's ideas) M: 237
Property P: 826
Title T: 302
Owyhee Dam [Owyhee River, Oregon] O: 886
Oregon (The early 1900's) O: 848
Owyhee River
Nevada (Rivers and lakes) N: 166 *with map*
Ox O: 886
Aurochs A: 891
Cell *picture on* C: 327
Transportation *picture on* T: 387
Oxalic acid [chemical] O: 886

Oxalis O: 887
Rhubarb R: 319
Oxalis [botany] O: 886 *with picture*
Oxaloacetic acid [chemistry]
Krebs cycle K: 387
Oxbow lake [geography] O: 887 *with picture*
Arkansas (Rivers and lakes) A: 706-708
Kentucky (Land regions) K: 285-286
Louisiana (Rivers, bayous, and lakes) L: 490-492
River (Flood plains) R: 353 *with diagram*
Oxen *See* Ox *in this index*
Oxeye daisy [plant]
Daisy D: 8 *with picture*
Oxford [England] O: 887
England (The beginnings of Parliament) E: 306
Oxford, University of O: 887
Oxford [Mississippi]
Faulkner, William F: 55
Kennedy, John Fitzgerald (Civil rights) K: 264-265
Oxford [shoe]
Shoe (Kinds of shoes) S: 431 *with picture*
Oxford, University of [England] O: 887 *with picture*
Architecture *picture on* A: 626
Bodleian Library B: 434
England (Education) E: 297; (The beginnings of Parliament) E: 306
Europe *picture on* E: 390
History (History in the universities) H: 262-263
Penn, William (Youthful rebel) P: 241-242
Rhodes Scholarship R: 317
Oxford and Asquith, Earl of *See* Asquith, Herbert Henry *in this index*
Oxford Dictionary of Nursery Rhymes, The
Nursery rhyme (History) N: 615-616
Oxford English Dictionary
Dictionary (Modern dictionaries) D: 194
Oxford Movement [religion] O: 888
Newman, John Henry N: 378
Oxford University *See* Oxford, University of *in this index*
Oxford Work [book by Duns Scotus]
Duns Scotus, John D: 386
Oxidation [chemistry] O: 888 *with pictures*
Antioxidant A: 557
Battery (Half-cell reactions) B: 170 *with diagram*
Catalytic converter C: 298
Corrosion Ci: 1071
Deodorizer D: 148
Electrolysis (How electrolysis works) E: 200
Fire (What is fire?) F: 120
Forest (The cycling of chemicals) F: 396
Fuel cell (How a fuel cell works) F: 551
Heat (Chemical reactions) H: 149
Hydrogen peroxide H: 470
Ink (Printing inks) I: 273
Paint (Household paints) P: 23-24
Reduction R: 192
Rust R: 567
Vitamin (Vitamin E) V: 432
Oxidation catalyst [chemistry]
Catalytic converter C: 298
Oxide [chemistry] O: 888
Anodizing A: 518
Ore O: 825
Oxygen (Chemical properties) O: 889
Oxidizer [fuel]
Fuel cell F: 551
Guided missile (The engine) G: 424 *with diagram*
Rocket R: 384 *with diagram*; (Propellants) R: 385; (Liquid-propellant rockets) R: 388 *with diagram*
Space exploration (Getting into space and back) So: 698
Oxisol [soil]
Soil *map on* So: 575; (How soils are classified) So: 576
Oxley, John [Australian political leader]
Brisbane B: 609
Oxyacetylene
Acetylene A: 25
Oxycodone [drug] O: 889
Drug abuse (table: Some commonly abused drugs) D: 363
OxyContin [drug]
Oxycodone O: 889
Oxygen [element] O: 889
See also the list of Related articles in the Oxygen *article*
Air (Gases of the air) A: 169 *with diagram*
Altitude sickness A: 390
Animal (Adaptations for breathing) A: 491
Blood B: 407; (What blood does in the body) B: 408 *with diagram*
Brain B: 550a
Chemistry (Lavoisier's contributions) C: 401
Drug abuse (Inhalants) D: 361
Earth (The lithosphere) E: 20
Electrolysis (How electrolysis works) E: 200

Fire (Kinds of fire) F: 120; (Gases) F: 122
Forest (Environmental value) F: 391
Heart (Coronary artery disease) H: 137
Human body (The exchange of carbon dioxide
 and oxygen) H: 421 *with picture*
Hyperbaric oxygen therapy H: 475
Ice age (Evidence of ice ages and their climates)
 I: 6-7
Iron (How bodies use iron) I: 435
Life (The chemical basis of life) L: 277 *with
 diagram*
Liquid air L: 346
Lung (Gas exchange in the lungs) L: 523
Oxidation O: 888
Ozone O: 893
Photosynthesis P: 430
Plant (In ecosystems) P: 518
Priestley, Joseph P: 776
Respiration R: 260
Weather (What causes weather) W: 157
Oxygen lance [industry]
Iron and steel (The basic oxygen process [BOP])
 I: 441-442 *with diagram*; (The open-hearth
 process) I: 443-444 *with diagram*
Oxygen poisoning
Diving, Underwater (Dangers of underwater
 diving) D: 246-247
Oxygen sensor
Gasoline engine (Air pollution controls) G: 66
Oxygen tank
Oxygen (Making oxygen) O: 889
Oxygen tent O: 890
Oxygenate [chemical]
Gasoline (Gasoline additives) G: 61; (Pollution
 control) G: 62
Oxyhemoglobin [physiology]
Hemoglobin H: 182
Oxytocin [hormone]
Hormone (Other hormones) H: 336
Hypothalamus H: 481
Pituitary gland P: 502
Oyapock River
French Guiana (The land and climate) F: 514
 with map
Oyashio Current [Pacific]
Japan (Climate) J: 48
Oyo [African history]
Nigeria (Early kingdoms) N: 417
Oyster [sea animal] O: 890 *with pictures*
Egg (Other kinds of eggs) E: 116
Fossil *picture on* F: 424
Louisiana *picture on* L: 479
Mollusk (Bivalves) M: 695
Pearl P: 216 *with pictures*; (Cultured pearls) P: 217
 with picture
Shell *picture on* S: 387
Oyster farming
Oyster (Oyster farming) O: 892
Oyster mushroom
Mushroom (Nonpoisonous mushrooms) M: 943-
 945 *with picture*
Oyster plant *See* Salsify *in this index*
Oystercatcher [bird] O: 893 *with picture*
Bird (Birds of the seacoasts) B: 342 *with picture*
Oz, Amos [Israeli author]
Hebrew literature (A new generation of Hebrew
 writers) H: 163
Ozaki, Takashi [Japanese mountain climber]
Mount Everest M: 884
Ozark Folk Center
Arkansas (Places to visit) A: 704
Ozark Mountains [U.S.] O: 893
Arkansas (Land regions) A: 706
Ozark National Scenic Riverways [Missouri]
National Park System (table: National parkways
 and other national parklands) N: 56
Ozark-Ouachita Highlands [region, U.S.]
United States *map on* U: 123; (The Ozark-
 Ouachita Highlands) U: 124
Ozark Plateau
Missouri *picture on* M: 650; (Land regions) M: 662
 with picture
Ozarks, Lake of the *See* Lake of the Ozarks *in this
 index*
Ozawa, Seiji [Japanese conductor] O: 893
Ozenfant, Amedée [French painter]
Le Corbusier L: 175
Ozick, Cynthia [American author] O: 893
Ozone [gas] O: 893
See also Ozone hole *in this index*
Catalysis C: 297
Earth (The atmosphere) E: 18-19
Environmental pollution (Air pollution) E: 331
Greenhouse effect (The natural greenhouse
 effect) G: 382-383
Mesosphere M: 422
Oxygen (Chemical properties) O: 889

Smog (Photochemical smog) S: 519
Ultraviolet rays (Harmful effects) U: 17
Ozone hole [meteorology] O: 894 *with pictures*
Air (Changes in the atmosphere) A: 175
Antarctica (Scientific research) A: 539-540
Chlorofluorocarbon C: 517
Fire extinguisher (Liquefied gas extinguishers)
 F: 130
Nitrogen (Nitrogen and pollution) N: 426
Ozone O: 893
Southern Ocean (Scientific research) So: 688b

P

P [letter] P: 1 *with pictures*
P [symbol]
Phosphorus P: 403
P-Celtic [language]
Celts C: 343
**P-channel metal oxide semiconductor field
 effect transistor** [electronics]
Transistor (Metal oxide semiconductor field effect
 transistors [MOSFET's]) T: 374
P-doped crystal [electronics]
Semiconductor (Doped crystals) S: 291; (Using
 doped crystals) S: 292
P-N junction [electronics]
Electronics (Active components) E: 210 *with
 diagram*
P-p chain [physics] *See* Proton-proton chain *in
 this index*
P2P networking *See* Peer-to-peer networking *in
 this index*
P-type dopant
Solar energy (How a photovoltaic cell is made)
 So: 577
P-type material
Solar energy (How a photovoltaic cell is made)
 So: 577 *with diagram*
P-type semiconductor [physics]
Electronics (Active components) E: 210 *with
 diagram*
Transistor (Transistor materials) T: 372
P wave [geology] *See* Primary wave *in this index*
PA [organization] *See* Palestinian Authority *in this
 index*
Pa [symbol]
Pascal P: 189
Protactinium P: 831
Paasikivi, Juho K. [Finnish political leader]
Finland (Postwar developments) F: 118
PABA [chemical]
Sulfa drug (How sulfa drugs work) So: 965
Pablos, Juan [Italian printer]
Printing (Early printing in North America) P: 803
PAC [government] *See* Political action committee
 in this index
PAC [political group] *See* Pan-Africanist Congress
 in this index
Pac-Man [electronic game]
Electronic game (History) E: 204d
Paca [animal] P: 2 *with picture*
Paca, William [American patriot] P: 2
Annapolis A: 516
Maryland (table) M: 255
Pacaembu Stadium
São Paulo (The city) S: 117-118
Paccard, Michel G. [French mountain climber]
Alps (Climbing the Alps) A: 386
Mont Blanc M: 741
Pace [gait]
Horse (Gaits) H: 353-354
Mammal (On land) M: 121-122
PACE [labor union] *See* Paper, Allied-Industrial,
 Chemical and Energy Workers International
 Union *in this index*
Pacelli, Eugenio [pope] *See* Pius XII *in this index*
Pacemaker [medicine]
Arrhythmia A: 743
Electronics (Transistors) E: 212
Heart (Abnormal heart rhythms) H: 142
Medicine *picture on* M: 376
Spastic paralysis So: 767
Pacer [horse]
Harness racing H: 63
Pacers, Indiana [team]
Basketball (table) B: 150
Pachacuti [Inca emperor]
Inca (The empire) I: 98
Machu Picchu M: 20
Pacheco, Alex [American activist]
People for the Ethical Treatment of Animals
 P: 277
Pacheco, Francisco [Spanish artist]
Velázquez, Diego V: 296
Pacheco, Romualdo [American political leader]
California (table) C: 59
Pachelbel, Johann [German composer] P: 2

Pachomius, Saint [early Christian] P: 2
Monasticism (Christian monasticism) M: 701
Religious life (Religious life in early Christianity)
 R: 226
Pachuca [city, Mexico]
Hidalgo H: 224
Pachycephalosaur [dinosaur]
Dinosaur (True dinosaurs) D: 206b-208
Pachycephalosaurus [dinosaur] P: 2
Pachyderm [zoology]
Elephant (The body of an elephant) E: 228
Pacific, The U.S. Army
Army, United States (Army service component
 commands) A: 736-737
Pacific Air Forces
Air Force, United States (Combat commands)
 A: 193
Pacific Aviation Museum
Honolulu (Cultural life) H: 321-322 *with picture*
Pacific barracuda [fish]
Barracuda *picture on* B: 117
Pacific blockade [international relations]
Blockade (Pacific blockade) B: 406
Pacific bonito [fish]
Bonito B: 460 *with picture*
Pacific Bottom Water
Pacific Ocean (Water masses) P: 15
Pacific cable [Australia-Canada]
Fleming, Sir Sandford F: 233
Pacific Coast States [region, U.S.]
United States (Regions) U: 99-108 *with map*
Pacific coastal forest
Forest (Pacific coastal forests) F: 396 *with map*
Pacific cod [fish]
Cod (Appearance and habits) Ci: 748 *with picture*
Pacific Command, United States [military]
Camp H. M. Smith C: 90
Pacific Deep Water
Pacific Ocean (Water masses) P: 15
Pacific Division
Hockey (table: National Hockey League) H: 281
Pacific dogwood [plant]
Dogwood D: 284
Pacific Fleet
Navy, United States (The Operating Forces) N: 85
Pacific Flyway [route]
Bird (Where birds migrate) B: 360-361
Pacific Fur Company
North West Company N: 519
Pacific Great Eastern Railway
British Columbia (The mid-1900's) B: 630
Pacific halibut [fish]
Fish *picture on* F: 153
Halibut H: 20
Pacific herring [fish]
Herring H: 215 *with picture*
Pacific Islands P: 3 *with pictures and maps*
Bird (Birds of the Pacific Islands) B: 349 *with
 pictures*
Heyerdahl, Thor H: 220
Mythology (Mythology of the Pacific Islands)
 M: 983 *with picture*
Prehistoric people (The spread of settlement)
 P: 752
Rain forest (Australia and the Pacific Islands)
 R: 126c *with map*
Sculpture (Pacific Islands sculpture) S: 241 *with
 pictures*
Stevenson, Robert Louis (The South Seas) So: 897
 with picture
Pacific Islands, Trust Territory of the [UN] P: 13
Pacific Islands (Pacific alliances and
 independence movements) P: 12-13
Palau P: 101
Territory (Territories in the United States) T: 174
Pacific Islands Forum [organization]
Pacific Islands (Pacific alliances and
 independence movements) P: 12
Pacific mackerel *See* Chub mackerel *in this index*
Pacific Mountain System
Alaska (Land regions) A: 292
Mountain M: 891; (The Pacific Mountain System)
 M: 895
Pacific National Exhibition
Vancouver (Parks) V: 276
Pacific Northwest [region, U.S.] P: 13
Pacific Ocean P: 13 *with map*
Arctic Ocean (Waters) A: 643
Balance of nature (Upsetting the balance) B: 36
Balboa, Vasco Núñez de B: 37
Climate (Changes in ocean circulation) Ci: 676d
Columbus, Christopher (Further explorations)
 Ci: 863
Cook, James Ci: 1025
Deep sea (The deep-sea floor) D: 82a
El Niño E: 245
Exploration (The first explorers) E: 439-440;

(Magellan's globe-circling expedition) E: 445; (Exploring the Pacific) E: 447
Fishing industry (Where fish are caught) F: 181-182
Hurricane H: 452
Magellan, Ferdinand (Sailing across the Pacific) M: 47
Ocean (The world ocean) O: 651; (Discoveries) O: 664
Pacific Islands P: 3
Plate tectonics (Plate movement) P: 563
Seamount S: 268
Pacific pearl oyster [sea animal]
Oyster *picture on* O: 891
Pacific Plate [geology]
Plate tectonics (Transform plate boundaries) P: 563
San Andreas Fault S: 84 *with map*
Pacific Railroad Act [1862]
Civil War, American (Economy) Ci: 623
Railroad (The first transcontinental rail lines) R: 116
Transcontinental railroad (The United States) T: 370-371
Western frontier life in America (Improvements in transportation) W: 233
Pacific Railway Dispute [Canadian history]
Mackenzie, Alexander (The Pacific Railway dispute) M: 22
Pacific Ranges and Lowlands [region, North America]
Canada (The Pacific Ranges and Lowlands) C: 115
North America (Land regions) N: 462
United States *map on* U: 122; (The Pacific Ranges and Lowlands) U: 125 *with picture*
Pacific Rim National Park [British Columbia]
Canada (table: National parks and national park reserves) C: 113
National park (table) N: 42g
Pacific salmon
Salmon S: 69
Pacific Scandal [Canadian history]
Abbott, Sir John Joseph Caldwell (The Pacific Scandal) A: 6
Canada, History of (The Pacific Scandal) C: 145
Macdonald, Sir John Alexander (The Pacific Scandal) M: 9
Mackenzie, Alexander (Leader of the opposition) M: 22
Pacific Science Center [Seattle]
Washington *picture on* W: 50
Pacific silver fir [tree]
Fir F: 120
Pacific thorny oyster [sea animal]
Shell *picture on* S: 387
Pacific Wonderland [name for]
Oregon O: 826
Pacific yew [tree]
Taxol T: 56
Pacifism [philosophy] P: 17
Conscientious objector Ci: 974
Pacino, Al [American actor] P: 18
Motion picture (Best performance by an actor: 1992) M: 862a
Pacioli, Fra Luca [Italian mathematician]
Accounting (The history of accounting) A: 23
Bookkeeping (History) B: 473
Pack [scouting]
Boy Scouts (Cub Scouting) B: 535
Pack, Law of the [scouting]
Boy Scouts (Cub Scouting) B: 535
Pack, Wolf
Wolf (The life of a wolf) W: 375 *with pictures*
Pack animal
Transportation *picture on* T: 387
Pack ice [geology]
Antarctica (Ocean) A: 532-534
Ice formation I: 9
Pack rat *See* Woodrat *in this index*
Pack skating
Ice skating *picture on* I: 16; (Pack skating) I: 14
Package [electronics]
Computer chip (External connections) Ci: 924f *with picture*
Package [motion pictures]
Motion picture (Acquiring financing) M: 849
Package dyeing
Wool (Making fabric) W: 401
Package ice
Food, Frozen (Packaging) F: 339
Package policy [insurance]
Insurance (Homeowners' insurance) I: 313
Package services
Postal Service, United States (Classes of mail) P: 699
Packaging P: 18
Brewing *picture on* B: 595

Cellophane C: 340
Environmental pollution (Business and industry) E: 336-337 *with picture*; (Individual efforts) E: 338
Food (Packaging) F: 335
Food, Frozen (Packaging) F: 339 *with pictures*
Food preservation (Aseptic packaging) F: 343
Milk (Packaging) M: 549 *with diagram*
Paperwork (Wrapping paper) P: 138
Plastics (To replace paper) P: 555 *with picture*; (Plastics and the environment) P: 560
Packard, Vance [American author]
Consumer protection (Growth of the movement) Ci: 1019
Packard Foundation, David and Lucille
Foundation (table) F: 430; (Science and technology) F: 431
Packer, William Fisher [American political leader]
Pennsylvania (table) P: 263
Packers, Green Bay *See* Green Bay Packers *in this index*
Packet [electronics] *See* Packet switching *in this index*
Packet ship
Ship (Packet ships) S: 421 *with picture*
Packet sniffer [program]
Computer (Computer security) Ci: 924
Packet switching [electronics]
Communication (The development of the Internet) Ci: 886
Internet (Software) I: 350c *with diagram*
Telephone (How a telephone call travels) T: 95-96
Packing house [food processing] *See* Meat packing *in this index*
Pacquiao, Manny [Philippine boxer] P: 19
Boxing *picture on* B: 526; (Boxing today) B: 533
Pact of Paris *See* Kellogg-Briand Pact *in this index*
Pacu [fish] P: 19 *with picture*
Pacuvius, Marcus [Roman poet]
Latin literature (Early Latin literature) L: 115-116
P.A.D. pedigree
United Kennel Club U: 47
Paddle *See* Racket *in this index*
Paddle [oar]
Canoeing (Paddles) C: 180 *with picture*
Indian, American *picture on* I: 140
Paddle doll
Doll (Ancient times) D: 288
Paddlefish [fish] P: 19
Fish *picture on* F: 159; (Bony fish) F: 147-148
Paddling
Canoeing (Paddling and steering) C: 181
Paddock
Horse racing ("They're off!") H: 365
Paddy [agriculture]
Agriculture *picture on* A: 146
Rice (Kinds of rice) R: 323-324 *with picture*
Vietnam *picture on* V: 364; (Economy) V: 369
Paddy Clarke Ha Ha Ha [book by Doyle]
Novel (The novel today) N: 575
Paddy rice
Rice (How rice is processed) R: 326
Padelford, Seth [American political leader]
Rhode Island (table) R: 311
Pademelon [animal]
Wallaby (Kinds of wallabies) W: 15
Paderewski, Ignace Jan [Polish pianist] P: 19
Padjelanta National Park [Sweden]
National park (table) N: 42g
Padlock
Lock (Mechanical locks) L: 411
Padma River *See* Ganges river *in this index*
Padre Island [island, Texas] P: 20
Texas (Coastline) T: 196
Padre Island National Seashore [Texas]
National Park System (Areas preserved for recreational use) N: 46; (table: National seashores) N: 57
Texas (Places to visit) T: 194 *with picture*
Padres, San Diego [team] *See* San Diego Padres *in this index*
Padua [Italy] P: 20 *with picture*
Paducah [Kentucky]
Kentucky *picture on* K: 276
Paekche [former region]
Korea, History of (Early years) K: 366 *with map*
Paektu-san [mountain, North Korea]
Korea, North (The land) K: 371 *with map*
Paella [food]
Spain (Food and drink) So: 733
Páez, José Antonio [Venezuelan political leader]
Venezuela (The struggle for independence) V: 304
Pagan [ancient city]
Myanmar (Early days) M: 970d
Pagan Papers [book by Grahame]
Grahame, Kenneth G: 301

Paganica [game]
Golf (Beginnings) G: 264
Paganini, Niccolò [Italian violinist] P: 20
Liszt, Franz (His life) L: 349
Pagans [religion]
Theodosius I T: 252
Page [computing] *See* Web page *in this index*
Page [European history]
Knights and knighthood (The page) K: 348 *with pictures*
Page [occupation] *See* Congressional page *in this index*
Page, Carroll S. [American political leader]
Vermont (table) V: 333
Page, Earle [Australian political leader]
Australia (table) A: 923
Page, Geraldine [American actress]
Motion picture (Best performance by an actress: 1985) M: 862a
Page, Jimmy [British guitarist]
Led Zeppelin L: 175
Page, John [New Hampshire political leader]
New Hampshire (table) N: 223
Page, John [Virginian political leader]
Virginia (table) V: 417
Page, John B. [American political leader]
Vermont (table) V: 333
Page, Larry [American businessman]
Google Inc. G: 270
Page, P. K. [Canadian poet]
Canadian literature (Modern Canadian poets) C: 161
Page, Walter [American musician]
Basie, Count B: 140
Page, William Tyler [American government employee]
American's Creed A: 431
Page layout program [software]
Magazine (Editing and assembling an issue) M: 43
Page makeup [printing]
Newspaper *picture on* N: 384; (Making up the pages) N: 383
Printing (Electronic imagesetting) P: 797; (Page makeup) P: 797
Pageant wagon
Drama (Mystery plays) D: 328-329 *with picture*
Mystery play M: 972
Pager [electronics] P: 20
Etiquette (Telephone etiquette) E: 374
Pagliacci [opera by Leoncavallo]
Leoncavallo, Ruggiero L: 202
Opera (table on O: 805; (Verismo opera) O: 794; (Cavalleria Rusticana) O: 803; (Pagliacci) O: 806
Pago Pago [American Samoa]
American Samoa A: 429 *with picture and map*
Pagoda [architecture] P: 20 *with picture*
Architecture (Chinese architecture) A: 612
China (Architecture) C: 490
Myanmar *picture on* M: 970; (The arts) M: 970c
Nepal *picture on* N: 126
Pahlavi *See* Mohammad Reza Pahlavi; Reza Shah Pahlavi *in this index*
Pahoehoe [geology]
Volcano (Lava) V: 439
Paid-up insurance
Insurance (Cash value life insurance) I: 310
PAIGC [political party]
Guinea-Bissau (Government) G: 433; (History) G: 434
Paige, Roderick R. [American government official]
Bush, George Walker (table) B: 722h
Education, Department of (table) E: 110
Paige, Satchel [American baseball player] P: 21
Baseball (table: Hall of Fame) B: 134a; (Postwar baseball) B: 136 *with picture*
Paik, Nam June [Korean-American artist]
Video art V: 359
Pain P: 21
Analgesic A: 448
Brain (Controlling movement) B: 553
Drug (Analgesics) D: 352
Endorphin E: 272
Morphine M: 816
Oxycodone O: 889
Placebo P: 505
Pain medicine [medical specialty]
Pain P: 21
Pain pathway [physiology]
Pain (How the body feels pain) P: 21-22
Paine, Charles [American political leader]
Vermont (table) V: 333
Paine, Lewis [American public figure]
Lincoln, Abraham (The trial of the conspirators) L: 326
Paine, Robert Treat [American statesman] P: 22
Paine, Thomas [American patriot] P: 22

American literature (The revolutionary period [1765-1787]) **A:** 415
Declaration of Independence (The Continental Congress) **D:** 74
Revolution, American (The Declaration of Independence) **R:** 278; (Results of the revolution) **R:** 287
United States, History of the (The Revolutionary War begins) **U:** 159-160

Paint P: 23 with pictures
Acrylic **A:** 30
Automobile picture on **A:** 957
Illuminated manuscript **I:** 78
Lead **L:** 148
Painting (Materials and techniques) **P:** 36 with picture

Paint [horse]
Horse (Coat and skin) **H:** 348-349 with picture

Paint brush [tool]
Paint pictures on **P:** 26; (Applying the paint) **P:** 25
Painting (Materials and techniques) **P:** 36 with picture; (Water-color painting) **P:** 39; (Chinese painting) **P:** 44

Paint pad [tool]
Paint (Applying the paint) **P:** 25-26 with picture

Painted Bronze [sculpture by Johns]
Johns, Jasper **J:** 135 with picture

Painted bulletin
Advertising (Outdoor signs) **A:** 75

Painted bunting [bird]
Bird (Birds of brushy areas) **B:** 338 with picture
Bunting **B:** 700

Painted cup [plant] See Indian paintbrush in this index

Painted daisy [plant]
Pyrethrum **P:** 920

Painted Desert [region, Arizona] **P:** 26 with picture
Arizona (Places to visit) **A:** 678

"Painted Dreams" [soap opera]
Soap opera **So:** 543

Painted House, A [book by Grisham]
Grisham, John **G:** 396

Painted lady [butterfly]
Butterfly picture on **B:** 735

Painted lady [plant]
Pyrethrum **P:** 920

Painted redstart [bird]
Redstart **R:** 192

Painted-tongue [plant] **P:** 27 with picture

Painted trillium [plant]
Plant picture on **P:** 525
Trillium **T:** 445

Painted turtle
Turtle picture on **T:** 520

Painter [artist]
See also the list of painters in the Related articles of the Painting article
Painting **P:** 28

Painter [workman] **P:** 27
Building trade (Career opportunities) **B:** 686

"Painter of Modern Life, The" [essay by Baudelaire]
Baudelaire, Charles **B:** 173

Painters and Allied Trades, International Union of
Labor movement (table) **L:** 8

Painter's colic [disorder] **P:** 27
Lead poisoning **L:** 150

Painting [art] **P:** 28 with pictures
See also the list of Related articles in the Painting article and Cave painting in this index
Barbizon School **B:** 107
Baroque (Baroque painting) **B:** 117
Byzantine art **B:** 749 with pictures
China (Painting) **C:** 487 with picture
Classicism (The qualities of Classicism) **Ci:** 653
Colonial life in America (Painting) **Ci:** 807 with picture
Cubism **Ci:** 1181 with pictures
Egypt, Ancient (Painting and sculpture) **E:** 139
Expressionism (Expressionist painting) **E:** 455
Fauves **F:** 56 with picture
Finger painting **F:** 105 with pictures
Folk art (Painting) **F:** 316 with pictures
Fresco **F:** 529
Gothic art (Gothic sculpture and painting) **G:** 279 with picture
Impressionism **I:** 93 with pictures
Indian, American (Painting) **I:** 146
Islamic art picture on **I:** 469
Minimalism **M:** 573
Modernism **M:** 685
Netherlands picture on **N:** 144; (Arts) **N:** 142
Porcelain (Painting) **P:** 676
Postimpressionism **P:** 708 with picture
Prehistoric people (The appearance of art) **P:** 752 with picture

Realism (In painting) **R:** 172 with picture
Renaissance (The fine arts) **R:** 236 with pictures
Romanticism (Romanticism in painting) **R:** 427
Rome, Ancient picture on **R:** 439; (Sculpture, painting, and mosaics) **R:** 442
Surrealism **So:** 1010 with picture

Painting, Bark See Bark painting in this index

Paintpot [geology]
Yellowstone National Park (Touring Yellowstone) **Y:** 558

Pair [skating]
Ice skating (Long-track skating) **I:** 14

Pair annihilation [physics]
Antimatter **A:** 556
Radiation (Beta particles) **R:** 76

Pair bond [zoology]
Bird (Courtship and mating) **B:** 356

Pairs play [bridge]
Bridge (Duplicate bridge) **B:** 605

Pairs skating
Ice skating (Pairs skating) **I:** 12 with picture
Roller skating (Artistic skating) **R:** 402a with picture

Paisan [film]
Motion picture (Postwar Realism) **M:** 869

Paise [money]
Rupee **R:** 521

Paisiello, Giovanni [Italian composer]
Opera: (Marriage of Figaro, The) **O:** 805

Paisley [Scotland] **P:** 91

Paisley, Ian [Irish political leader] **P:** 91
Adams, Gerry **A:** 33
Ulster Unionist Party **U:** 15

Paiute Indians P: 91
Indian, American picture on **I:** 139; (Shelter) **I:** 136d
Klamath Indians **K:** 343

Pajama [clothing]
India (Clothing) **I:** 117-118

Pak choi [vegetable]
Chinese cabbage **C:** 509

Pakehas [people]
New Zealand (People) **N:** 348; (Maori-Pakeha relations) **N:** 356

Pakenham, Sir Edward Michael [British general]
New Orleans, Battle of **N:** 285
War of 1812 ("The needless battle") **W:** 31

Pakhto [language] See Pashto in this index

Pakhtuns [people] See Pashtuns in this index

Pakicetus [whale]
Prehistoric animal (The development of placentals) **P:** 741

Pakistan P: 92 with pictures and maps
Army picture on **A:** 725
Asia (Way of living in South Asia) **A:** 781; (Other struggles) **A:** 810
Bangladesh (British India) **B:** 85
Bin Laden, Osama **B:** 307
Clinton, Bill (International affairs) **Ci:** 682f
Cold War (The great blocs split) **Ci:** 769
Immigration (Asia) **I:** 85
India (New Constitution) **I:** 132; (Independence and partition) **I:** 133 with map; (Recent developments) **I:** 134-135
Iqbal, Sir Muhammad **I:** 397
Jinnah, Mohammad Ali **J:** 127
Kashmir **K:** 247
Khyber Pass **K:** 309 with map
Middle East **M:** 530
Musharraf, Pervez **M:** 941
Muslim League **M:** 964
Muslims picture on **M:** 966; (Reform and renewal) **M:** 964d-965
Nuclear weapon (The end of the Cold War) **N:** 601-602
Pashtuns **P:** 190
United Nations (Arms control) **U:** 92-93
Urdu language **U:** 220

Pakistan Muslim League [political party]
Muslim League **M:** 964
Pakistan (Politics) **P:** 93

Pakistan People's Party
Bhutto, Benazir **B:** 278
Pakistan (Politics) **P:** 93

Pakistani dwarf goat
Goat (The bodies of goats) **G:** 240

PAL [electronics]
Television (Camera scanning patterns) **T:** 122

Pal Joey [musical]
Musical comedy (Musical comedy matures) **M:** 960

Palace [architecture] **P:** 101
See also the list of Related articles in the Palace article

Palace at 4 A.M., The [sculpture by Giacometti]
Giacometti, Alberto **G:** 183
Sculpture (Assemblages) **S:** 257-258 with picture

Palace of ...
Palaces appear under their key words, as in Versailles, Palace of

Palace of Desire [book by Mahfouz]
Mahfouz, Naguib **M:** 65

Palace School [European history]
Charlemagne (Administration and influence) **C:** 379

Palace Walk [book by Mahfouz]
Mahfouz, Naguib **M:** 65

Palacio Municipal [Quito]
Ecuador picture on **E:** 68

Palacio Valdés, Armando [Spanish author]
Spanish literature (The 1800's) **So:** 761-762

Palade, George Emil [American physiologist]
Nobel Prizes (Physiology or medicine: 1974) **N:** 446

Palaestra [school]
Olympia **O:** 745

Palais de la Nation [building, Brussels]
Belgium picture on **B:** 227

Palais de Luxembourg [France]
Museum (Museums of the 1700's) **M:** 939

Palais Garnier [building]
Architecture (Combined styles) **A:** 626 with picture
Paris (Arts) **P:** 164

Palais Stoclet [Brussels]
Architecture (Early modern architecture in Europe) **A:** 627-628 with picture

Palamas, Kostis [Greek poet]
Greek literature (Modern Greek literature) **G:** 378

Palamedes [legendary figure]
Ulysses (The Trojan War) **U:** 17-18

Palamon [literary figure]
Shakespeare, William: (The Two Noble Kinsmen) **S:** 366

Palance, Jack [American actor]
Motion picture (Best performance by an actor in a supporting role: 1991) **M:** 862b

Palaquium gutta [tree]
Gutta-percha **G:** 445

Palate [anatomy] **P:** 101 with diagram
Cleft palate **Ci:** 661
Throat **T:** 270

Palatine bone [anatomy]
Face **F:** 3

Palatine Hill
Rome **R:** 429

Palatine tonsil [anatomy]
Tonsil **T:** 329 with diagram
Tonsillitis **T:** 329

Palau P: 101 with map
Flag picture on **F:** 204
Pacific Islands picture on **P:** 7; (Pacific alliances and independence movements) **P:** 12-13
Pacific Islands, Trust Territory of the **P:** 13

Palau Islands [Pacific]
Caroline Islands **C:** 244
Pacific Islands (Pacific alliances and independence movements) **P:** 12-13
World War II (Island hopping in the Central Pacific) **W:** 489-490

Palawan [island, Philippines]
Philippines (The main islands) **P:** 376-378 with map

Palazzo Vecchio
Florence (The city) **F:** 239-240

Pale [region, Ireland]
Ireland (The Norman invaders) **I:** 425-426

Pale of Settlement [Russian history]
Jews (The growth of anti-Semitism) **J:** 123
Sholem Aleichem **S:** 433

Pale-winged trumpeter [bird]
Bird picture on **B:** 344b

Palenque [Maya ruins]
Maya (The Maya heritage) **M:** 326

Paleo-Indians P: 102
Clothing (Indians of North America) **Ci:** 700
Nova Scotia (Early inhabitants) **N:** 567

Paleoanthropology
Anthropology (Physical anthropology) **A:** 546 with picture
Prehistoric people **P:** 744

Paleobotany [science] **P:** 102
Paleontology **P:** 103

Paleocene Epoch [geology]
Earth (table) **E:** 30 with map
Prehistoric animal (table) **P:** 740

Paleogenic Period [geology]
Earth (table) **E:** 30
Forest picture on **F:** 398

Paleogeography
Paleontology **P:** 103

Paleography [writing] **P:** 102

Paleolithic Period [anthropology]
Lascaux Cave **L:** 80

Painting (Prehistoric painting) **P: 40**
Prehistoric people *picture on* **P: 754a**; (The Stone Age) **P: 751**
Stone Age **So: 909**
Paleomagnetism [geology]
Plate tectonics (Evidence of plate movement) **P: 563**; (History of tectonic theory) **P: 564-565**
Paleontology [geology] **P: 103**
Biology (table) **B: 317**; (The origins of scientific classification) **B: 318-319**
Dinosaur (Working with dinosaur fossils) **D: 210** *with pictures*
Earth (Life on Earth) **E: 27**
Evolution (The fossil record) **E: 430**; (Contributions from other scientific fields) **E: 433**
Fossil (How fossils reveal the past) **F: 422-423**
Geology (Areas of specialization) **G: 100-101** *with picture*
Lamarck, Chevalier de **L: 50**
Paleobotany **P: 102**
Prehistoric animal **P: 736**
Zoology (What zoologists study) **Z: 606-607**
Paleotide [geology]
Tide (The study of the tides) **T: 282**
Paleozoic Era [geology]
Cambrian Period **C: 74**
Earth *pictures on* **E: 28**; (The Paleozoic Era) **E: 27**; (table) **E: 30**
Prehistoric animal (The world of prehistoric animals) **P: 736**; (Early forms of animal life) **P: 736**; (The Age of Reptiles) **P: 737** *with picture*
Palermo [district]
Buenos Aires (The city) **B: 672**
Palermo [Italy] **P: 103**
Italy *picture on* **I: 508**
Sicily **S: 446**
Palestine P: 103 *with picture and maps*
See also Canaanites; Israel, Ancient; Israelites; Judah; Judea; Philistines *in this index*
Arab Americans **A: 580a**
Arab-Israeli conflict **A: 582**
Arab League **A: 582b**
Arabs (Land of the Arabs) **A: 585**; (The Arab-Israeli conflict) **A: 590a**
Balfour Declaration **B: 40**
Fatah **F: 54**
Hamas **H: 28**
Holocaust (After the Holocaust) **H: 296b**
Israel **I: 478**; (Beginnings of a new state) **I: 486**
Jerusalem (British rule) **J: 101**
Jews *map on* **J: 121**; (The Zionist movement) **J: 123**; (The rebirth of Israel) **J: 124**
Jordan (History) **J: 164**
Joshua **J: 169**
Middle East (History) **M: 533-534**
Palestine Liberation Organization **P: 106**
Palestinians **P: 107**
Philistines **P: 382**
United Nations (Working for self-government) **U: 93-94**
Zionism **Z: 595**
Palestine Liberation Organization P: 106
Abbas, Mahmoud **A: 4**
Arab-Israeli conflict **A: 582**
Arabs (The search for unity) **A: 590-590a**
Arafat, Yasir **A: 590**
Barak, Ehud **B: 102**
Fatah **F: 54**
Gaza Strip **G: 74**
Israel (History) **I: 486-488**
Jericho **J: 93**
Jordan (History) **J: 164-165**
Lebanon (Internal conflicts) **L: 173**; (War and terrorism) **L: 173**; (Political struggle) **L: 174**
Libya (Independence) **L: 267-268**
Middle East (History) **M: 533-534a**
Netanyahu, Benjamin **N: 137**
Palestine (The continuing conflict and peace efforts) **P: 106**
Palestinian Authority (History) **P: 107**
Rabin, Yitzhak **R: 50**
West Bank (History and government) **W: 200**
Palestine National Council
Palestine Liberation Organization (Organization) **P: 106**
Palestinian Authority [government] **P: 107**
Abbas, Mahmoud **A: 4**
Arafat, Yasir **A: 590b**
Hamas **H: 28**
Palestine Liberation Organization (History) **P: 106**
Palestinians **P: 107**
Palestinian National Authority [government] *See* Palestinian Authority *in this index*
Palestinians [people] **P: 107**
Arab-Israeli conflict **A: 582**
Arabs (The Arab-Israeli conflict) **A: 590a**

Arafat, Yasir **A: 591**
Asia (Arab-Israeli conflicts) **A: 810** *with picture*
Gaza Strip **G: 73**
Hamas **H: 28**
Hezbollah **H: 221**
Intifada **I: 353**
Jerusalem (The people of Jerusalem) **J: 96**
Jordan (Ancestry) **J: 162**; (History) **J: 164** *with picture*
Lebanon (Ethnic groups and religion) **L: 171**; (Internal conflicts) **L: 173**
Olympic Games (Terrorism in Munich) **O: 752**
Palestine Liberation Organization **P: 106**
Palestinian Authority **P: 107**
Sharon, Ariel **S: 377**
Terrorism (Terrorist groups and movements) **T: 178**
United Nations (Aid to refugees) **U: 88**; (Working for self-government) **U: 93-94**
West Bank **W: 199**
Palestrina, Giovanni [Italian composer]
Classical music (Italian music) **Ci: 646**
Classicism (The qualities of Classicism) **Ci: 653**
Palette [tool]
Painting (Other materials) **P: 36** *with picture*
Palette knife [tool]
Knife **K: 345**
Painting (Other materials) **P: 36** *with diagram*
Paley, William [British theologian]
Intelligent design **I: 320**
Paley, William S. [American businessman]
CBS **C: 323**
Palikir [Federated States of Micronesia] **P: 108**
Micronesia, Federated States of **M: 515**
Palin, Michael [British actor]
Cleese, John **Ci: 661** *with picture*
"Monty Python's Flying Circus" **M: 780**
Palin, Sarah Heath [American political leader] **P: 108** *with portrait*
Alaska (table) **A: 300**; (Recent developments) **A: 304**
Obama, Barack (The 2008 election) **O: 640e**
Palin, Todd [American businessman]
Palin, Sarah Heath (Early life and family) **P: 108**
Palisade [fence]
Castle (Structure) **C: 280**
Indian, American *picture on* **I: 156**; (Before European contact) **I: 154-155**
Palisade tissue [botany]
Leaf (Photosynthesis) **L: 155** *with diagram*
Palisades, The [cliffs, New Jersey-New York]
Hudson River **H: 406**
Palla [clothing]
Clothing (Rome) **Ci: 697**
Rome, Ancient (Clothing) **R: 440**
Tunic **T: 487**
Palladian revival [architecture]
Architecture (The Palladian Revival) **A: 623** *with picture*
Palladian style
Furniture (The Palladian style) **F: 578**
Palladio, Andrea [Italian architect] **P: 108**
Architecture (Later Renaissance architecture) **A: 621** *with picture*; (The Palladian Revival) **A: 623**
Furniture (The Palladian style) **F: 578**
Georgian architecture **G: 136**
Monticello **M: 752**
Palladis Tamia: Wit's Treasury [book by Meres]
Shakespeare, William (The years of fame) **S: 347**
Palladium [element] **P: 108**
Palladius [Irish religious leader]
Patrick, Saint (Life) **P: 197**
Pallas [asteroid]
Asteroid (Sizes and shapes) **A: 824**; (History of study) **A: 824b**
Pallas [Roman mythology]
Aeneid **A: 84**
Pallavas dynasty
India (Southern India) **I: 129**
Pallet [mattress]
Bed (History) **B: 198**
Pallet [mechanism]
Clock (Mechanical clocks) **Ci: 682j**
Organ (Pipe organs) **O: 851-852**
Watch (Mechanical watches) **W: 114**
Palliative care [medicine] **P: 108**
Pallid bat
Animal *picture on* **A: 483**
Pallidotomy [medicine]
Parkinson disease (Other treatments) **P: 171**
Palliser, John [Irish explorer]
Saskatchewan (North-West Territories) **S: 146**
Pallium [clothing]
Pope (Titles, clothing, and symbols) **P: 661-662** *with picture*
Palm [anatomy]

Hand (Parts of the hand) **H: 40**
Palm [tree] **P: 109**
Date palm **D: 42** *with picture*
Ivory palm **I: 522** *with pictures*
Manuscript (Palm leaf manuscripts) **M: 173**
Tree *pictures on* **T: 413**, **T: 426**, **T: 427**; (Palm, pandanus, and lily trees) **T: 415**
Palm and needle method
Knots, hitches, and splices (Preparing rope for knots) **K: 356**
Palm Beach County [Florida]
Election of 2000 (Court challenges) **E: 161**
Palm civet [animal]
Civet **Ci: 604**
Palm cockatoo [bird]
Parrot (Kinds of parrots) **P: 179**
Palm oil P: 109
Palm reading *See* Palmistry *in this index*
Palm Springs [California] **P: 110**
Palm Sunday [religion] **P: 110**
Ash Wednesday **A: 767**
Easter **E: 42** *with picture*; (Holy Week) **E: 42** *with picture*
Holy Week **H: 300**
Mexico *picture on* **M: 458**
Palma [Majorca]
Balearic Islands **B: 40**
Majorca **M: 94**
Palma, Ricardo [Peruvian author]
Latin American literature (Romanticism) **L: 112-113**
Peru (The arts) **P: 311**
Palmach [military]
Rabin, Yitzhak **R: 50**
Palmares [Brazilian history] **P: 110**
Maroons **M: 217**
Palmate leaf [botany]
Leaf (The blade) **L: 153-154** *with picture*
Palme, Olof [Swedish public official]
Sweden (Political changes) **So: 1035**
Palmer [Alaska]
Alaska *picture on* **A: 291**
Palmer, A. Mitchell [American political leader] **P: 110**
Palmer, Arnold [American golfer] **P: 110**
Golf *picture on* **G: 266**; (British Open) **G: 264**; (Masters Tournament) **G: 265**
Palmer, Carson [American football player]
Football (table) **F: 363**
Palmer, Daniel David [American chiropractor]
Chiropractic **C: 515**
Palmer, Edward [Canadian political leader]
Confederation of Canada (Fathers of Confederation) **Ci: 935** *with picture*
Palmer, Herbert J. [Canadian political leader]
Prince Edward Island (table) **P: 791**
Palmer, Jim [American baseball player]
Baseball (table: Hall of Fame) **B: 134a**
Palmer, Joel [American government official] **P: 110**
Illinois (table) **I: 71**
Palmer, John M. [American political leader]
Illinois (table) **I: 71**
Palmer, Nathaniel Brown [American sea captain]
Antarctica (Early exploration) **A: 536**
Exploration (The exploration of Antarctica) **E: 450**
Palmer, Olive Freeman [wife of]
Diefenbaker, John George (Young lawyer) **D: 197**
Palmer, Potter [American businessman] **P: 110**
Palmer, Volney B. [American businessman]
Advertising (The development of advertising agencies) **A: 79**
Palmer, William A. [American political leader]
Vermont (table) **V: 333**
Palmer Land
Antarctica (Early exploration) **A: 536**
Palmer Raids [U.S. history]
Palmer, A. Mitchell **P: 110**
Palmer Station
Antarctica (Scientific research) **A: 540**
Palmer System
Palmer, Potter **P: 110**
Palmerston, Viscount [British political leader] **P: 111**
United Kingdom (Political confusion) **U: 69**
Palmetto [tree] **P: 111**
Palmetto State [nickname]
South Carolina **So: 640**
Palmistry P: 111 *with diagram*
Fortunetelling (Methods of fortunetelling) **F: 420**
Palmitic acid [chemical]
Lard **L: 75**
Palmitin [chemical]
Lard **L: 75**
Palmito Ranch, Battle of [1865]
Texas (The Civil War and Reconstruction) **T: 207**
Palmtop computer
Computer (Personal computers) **Ci: 909-910**
Handheld computer **H: 45**

Palmyra [ancient city] **P: 111**
  Arabs (The Arabs before Islam) **A: 589**
  Syria *picture on* **So: 1074**
Palmyra [New York]
  Mormons (Revelations) **M: 808**
Palmyra palm [tree] **P: 112**
  Palm (Products of palms) **P: 109**
Palo Alto [California] **P: 112**
Palo Alto, Battle of [1846]
  Mexican War (Taylor's campaign) **M: 446** *with picture*; (Principal battles) **M: 447**
Palo Alto Battlefield National Historical Park [Texas]
  National Park System (table: National historical parks) **N: 56-57**
Palomar Observatory [California] **P: 112**
  Halley's Comet **H: 24a**
  Quasar **Q: 8**
  San Diego (Recreation) **S: 90a**
Palometa [fish]
  Pompano **P: 653**
Palomino [horse]
  Horse (table: Some types and breeds of horses) **H: 343**; (Color types) **H: 345** *with picture*
Paloverde [tree] **P: 112**
  Plant *picture on* **P: 526**
Palpi [entomology]
  Grasshopper (The body) **G: 327**
Palpitations *See* Tachycardia *in this index*
Palsy [disorder]
  Bell's palsy **B: 244**
  Parkinson disease **P: 170**
Paltrow, Gwyneth [American actress]
  Motion picture (Best performance by an actress: 1998) **M: 862a**
Paludamentum [garment]
  Clothing (The Middle Ages) **Ci: 700**
Paly [symbol]
  Heraldry *picture on* **H: 195**
Pamela [book by Richardson]
  Fielding, Henry (His novels) **F: 94**
  Novel (The first English novelists) **N: 572**
  Richardson, Samuel **R: 330**
Pamina [opera character]
  Opera: (*Magic Flute, The*) **O: 805**
Pamirs [region, Asia] **P: 112**
  Asia (Mountains) **A: 792-794**
  Tajikistan *picture on* **T: 18b**; (Land and climate) **T: 18a** *with map*
Pampas [region, Argentina] **P: 113**
  Argentina (The Pampas) **A: 653** *with map*; (Agriculture) **A: 654** *with picture*
  Prairie **P: 731**
  South America (The Central Plains) **So: 628**
Pampas deer
  Deer (Central and South American deer) **D: 85-86**
Pamplona [Spain]
  Spain *picture on* **So: 738**; (Holidays) **So: 736-737**
Pamuk, Orhan [Turkish author]
  Nobel Prizes (Literature: 2006) **N: 448**
PAN [chemical]
  Smog (Photochemical smog) **S: 519-520**
Pan [Greek mythology] **P: 113** *with picture*
  Faun **F: 56**
  Midas **M: 521**
  Mythology (Greek divinities) **M: 982**
Pan [gun]
  Harquebus **H: 67**
Pan [satellite]
  Saturn (Satellites) **S: 151**
Pan, Peter *See* Peter Pan *in this index*
Pan-Africanism [international relations]
  Africa (Africa since independence) **A: 135**
  Du Bois, W. E. B. **D: 372**
  Kenyatta, Jomo **K: 304**
Pan-Africanist Congress
  South Africa (History) **So: 617-619**
Pan-American conferences **P: 113**
  Harrison, Benjamin (International affairs) **H: 73**
Pan American Exposition [1901]
  McKinley, William (McKinley's second Administration [1901]) **M: 341**
  New York **N: 317**; (The early 1900's) **N: 318**
Pan American Games [sports] **P: 114**
Pan American Highway [road] **P: 114** *with map*
  Monterrey **M: 764**
  Panama City **P: 128**
  Peru (Transportation) **P: 314**
Pan American Highway Congress
  Pan American Highway (Development) **P: 114**
Pan American Union [alliance]
  Organization of American States **O: 854**
  Pan-American conferences (The "new" Pan Americanism) **P: 113**
Pan American World Airways
  Aviation (The industry comes of age) **A: 989** *with picture*

Pan-Arabism [political movement]
  Arabs (Arab nationalism) **A: 590**
  Iraq (The 1950's) **I: 413-414**
Pan bread [food]
  Bread (Kinds of bread) **B: 588**
Pan frying
  Cooking (Pan-frying) **Ci: 1028**
Pan-Islamism [political movement]
  Muslims (Reform and renewal) **M: 964d**
Panama **P: 115** *with pictures and maps*
  Bush, George Herbert Walker (International affairs) **B: 721**
  Columbus, Christopher (Further explorations) **Ci: 863**
  Flag *picture on* **F: 201**
  Herrera, Tomás **H: 214**
  Merchant marine (Merchant fleets) **M: 413**
  Noriega, Manuel Antonio **N: 454**
  Panama Canal **P: 122** *with map*
  Panama Canal Zone **P: 127**
Panama, Free State of [Panamanian history]
  Herrera, Tomás **H: 214**
Panama, Isthmus of [region, Central America]
  Panama **P: 115**; (Land and climate) **P: 118**
  Panama Canal **P: 122** *with map*
Panama-California Exposition [1915-1916]
  California (Progress as a state) **C: 62**
  San Diego (Growth) **S: 91**
Panama Canal [waterway] **P: 122** *with pictures and maps*
  Canal (table) **C: 164**; (The Panama and Suez canals) **C: 164**
  Carter, Jimmy (Foreign affairs) **C: 257**
  De Lesseps, Ferdinand Marie **D: 114**
  Goethals, George Washington **G: 246**
  Gorgas, William Crawford **G: 274**
  Hay-Pauncefote Treaty **H: 116**
  North America (Transportation and communication) **N: 469**
  Panama **P: 115**; (Economy) **P: 119**; (History) **P: 120**
  Roosevelt, Theodore *picture on* **R: 466**; (Foreign policy) **R: 465**
Panama Canal Authority
  Panama Canal (Administration) **P: 124-125**
Panama Canal Commission [U.S.]
  Panama Canal (Administration and defense) **P: 124**
Panama Canal Company
  Panama Canal Zone **P: 127**
Panama Canal treaties [1977]
  Carter, Jimmy (Foreign affairs) **C: 257-258** *with picture*
  Panama **P: 115**; (Relations with the United States) **P: 120**
Panama Canal Zone [U.S.] **P: 127** *with map*
  Panama **P: 115**; (Progress as a nation) **P: 120**
  Panama Canal **P: 122**; (The canal since 1920) **P: 126-127**
  Taft, William Howard (Secretary of war) **T: 10**
Panama City [Panama] **P: 127**
  Morgan, Sir Henry (Attack on Panama) **M: 804**
  Panama *pictures on* **P: 115**, **P: 118**; (Way of life) **P: 116**
Panama disease
  Banana (How bananas grow) **B: 73**
Panama hat [clothing]
  Panama (Clothing) **P: 118**
Panama-Pacific International Exposition [1915]
  California (Progress as a state) **C: 62**
Panama Railroad
  Panama Canal (The Panama Railroad) **P: 125**
Panama Tolls Act [1912]
  Wilson, Woodrow (Foreign affairs) **W: 323**
Panamanian Revolution [1903]
  Panama (Colombian rule) **P: 120**
  Panama Canal (The United States and the canal) **P: 125-126**
Panamera [car]
  Porsche AG *picture on* **P: 680**
Panamint Mountains [California]
  Death Valley **D: 62** *with picture*
Panasonic Corporation
  Manufacturing (table) **M: 170**
Panay [island, Philippines]
  Philippines (The main islands) **P: 376-378** *with map*
Pancake [food]
  Food (Interesting facts about food) **F: 329**
Pancake Day [custom]
  Mardi Gras **M: 198**
  Shrove Tuesday **S: 441**
Pancake Tuesday *See* Pancake Day *in this index*
Pancasila [government]
  Indonesia (Government) **I: 226**
Panchama *See* Untouchable *in this index*
Panchatantra [stories]

Fable **F: 3**
  India (Literature) **I: 120**
Panchayat [government]
  India (Village life) **I: 114-115**
Panchen Lama [Tibetan religious leader]
  Tibet (History and government) **T: 277**; (Religion and culture) **T: 277**
Panchromatic film
  Photography (Color sensitivity) **P: 417**
Pancoast, Thomas J. [American businessman]
  Miami Beach **M: 482**
Pancratium [ancient sport]
  Olympic Games (The ancient games) **O: 750**
Pancratium [sport]
  Mixed martial arts **M: 680**
Pancreas [anatomy] **P: 128** *with diagram*
  Cancer (table) **C: 170**
  Diabetes (Type 1 diabetes) **D: 179**
  Gland (table) **G: 208**
  Hormone (Metabolic hormones) **H: 335**
  Human body (The small intestine and large intestine) **H: 420**; (table) **H: 422** *with diagram*
  Insulin **I: 308**
  Pancreatitis **P: 128**
Pancreatic juice [physiology]
  Digestive system (In the small intestine) **D: 202**
Pancreatitis [disorder] **P: 128**
Panda [animal] **P: 129** *with pictures*
  Animal *picture on* **A: 475**
  Ecology (Energy flow) **E: 54**
  Endangered species (table) **E: 270**
  Evolution (Contributions from other scientific fields) **E: 433**
  National park *picture on* **N: 42g**
Pandanus
  Tree *picture on* **T: 427**; (Palm, pandanus, and lily trees) **T: 415**
Pandavas [literary figures]
  Mahabharata **M: 64**
Panday, Basdeo [Trinidad political leader]
  Trinidad and Tobago (History) **T: 446**
Pandemic [disease]
  Black Death **B: 386**
  Disease (Spread of infectious diseases) **D: 228**
  Epidemic **E: 343**
  Influenza (Flu epidemics) **I: 268b**
  Plague (History of plague) **P: 506**
  Swine flu **So: 1048**
Pandemos [Greek mythology]
  Aphrodite **A: 565**
Pandit, Vijaya Lakshmi [Indian political figure] **P: 130**
Pandora [Greek mythology] **P: 130**
  Hesiod **H: 218**
Pandora's box [Greek mythology]
  Pandora **P: 130**
Pandosto [stories by Greene]
  Greene, Robert **G: 382**
Pane [window]
  Window **W: 334**
Panel
  Cartoon (Kinds of cartoons) **C: 263**
Panel truck
  Truck *picture on* **T: 459**
Paneling [building material]
  Lumber (table) **L: 518**
Panetta, Leon E. [American government official]
  Defense, Department of (table) **D: 87**
  Obama, Barack (table) **O: 640h**
Panettone [food]
  Christmas (In Italy) **C: 531**
Panfish *See* Sunfish *in this index*
Panfrying *See* Sautéing *in this index*
Pangaea [geology] **P: 130**
  Carboniferous Period **C: 208**
  Earth *map on* **E: 31**; (The shaping of the continents) **E: 24**
  Jurassic Period **J: 201**
  Mediterranean Sea (Formation) **M: 382**
  Permian Period **P: 289**
  Plate tectonics *map on* **P: 564**; (Plate movement) **P: 563**
  Prehistoric animal (The distribution of mammals) **P: 741**
  Triassic Period **T: 440**
Pangborn, Clyde [American aviator]
  Airplane (Fliers of the golden age) **A: 237**
Pangolin [animal] **P: 130** *with picture*
  Anteater **A: 541**
  Mammal (table) **M: 128** *with picture*
Panhandle [land region]
  Alaska (Land regions) **A: 292**
  Florida **F: 242**
  Idaho (Land regions) **I: 36**
  Jefferson, State of **J: 75**
  Oklahoma (Land regions) **O: 724-726** *with picture*; (Great land rushes) **O: 732**

Texas (Land regions) **T:** 196; (Mining) **T:** 201
West Virginia (Land regions) **W:** 218
Panhard et Levassor [car]
Automobile *picture on* **A:** 963
Panhard et Levassor [company]
Automobile *picture on* **A:** 963
Panhellenic Socialist Movement [political party]
Greece (Politics) **G:** 353; (The restoration of democracy) **G:** 365
Panic [economics]
Depression **D:** 150
Panic attack
Anxiety disorder **A:** 562
Panic disorder **P:** 130
Panic disorder P: 130
Anxiety disorder **A:** 562
Fatigue **F:** 55
Mental illness (Anxiety disorders) **M:** 405
Panic of 1837 [U.S. history]
United States, History of the (Politics after Jackson) **U:** 171
Van Buren, Martin (The Panic of 1837) **V:** 272
Wildcat bank **W:** 301
Panic of 1873 [U.S. history]
Black Friday **B:** 387
Depression (U.S. depressions) **D:** 150
Grant, Ulysses S. (The Panic of 1873) **G:** 317
Greenback Party **G:** 381
Panic of 1893 [U.S. history]
Cleveland, Grover (Saving the gold standard) **Ci:** 673
Panicle [botany]
Inflorescence **I:** 268a
Rice (Structure) **R:** 323
Panini [Indian grammarian]
Language (The science of language) **L:** 66
Sanskrit literature (The Classical period) **S:** 112
Panipat, Battles of [1526, 1556]
India (The Mughal Empire) **I:** 129
Pankhurst, Emmeline Goulden [British social reformer] **P:** 131
Woman suffrage (United Kingdom) **W:** 381
Pankration [sports]
Olympic Games (The ancient games) **O:** 750
Pankration [sport]
Mixed martial arts **M:** 680
Panleukopenia [disease]
Cat (Veterinary care) **C:** 295
Distemper **D:** 238
Panmunjom [Korea] **P:** 131
Korean War (The truce talks) **K:** 382
Panned candy
Candy (Other candies) **C:** 176
Pannier [device]
Clothing (The 1700's) **Ci:** 703
Panning [mining]
Gold (Mining) **G:** 252
Mining (Placer mining) **M:** 575
Western frontier life in America (A typical mining camp) **W:** 235
Pannonian Plains [region, Europe]
Croatia (Land and climate) **Ci:** 1148a
Serbia (Land and climate) **S:** 314 *with map*
Panpipes [musical instrument]
Indian, American *picture on* **I:** 175
Latin America (Music) **L:** 100
Pan **P:** 113
Panama *picture on* **P:** 116
Panspermia [theory]
Life (Panspermia) **L:** 279
Pansy [plant] **P:** 131
Flower (Garden annuals) **F:** 276 *with picture*
Gardening *picture on* **G:** 33
Violet **V:** 388
Pantagruel [book by Rabelais]
Rabelais, François **R:** 49
Pantaloon [clown]
Drama (Commedia dell' arte) **D:** 331 *with picture*
Pantomime **P:** 131
Pantaloon Serenading His Mistress [painting]
Drama *picture on* **D:** 330
Pantanal [region]
Brazil (The Central and Southern Plateaus) **B:** 580
Pantanal National Park [Brazil]
National park (table) **N:** 42g
Panthalassa [geology]
Earth (The shaping of the continents) **E:** 24
Plate tectonics (The overall pattern) **P:** 563
Pantheism [religion] **P:** 131
Pantheon [Rome] **P:** 131
Architecture *picture on* **A:** 616
Rome (Other remains) **R:** 433 *with picture*
Panthéon [Paris]
Architecture (Neoclassical architecture) **A:** 623-624
Paris (Famous buildings) **P:** 163-164
Panther [animal] **P:** 131

Leopard **L:** 202
Mountain lion **M:** 898
Panthera [zoology]
Animal (The scientific classification of animals) **A:** 472-473
Panthers, Carolina [team]
Football (National Football League) **F:** 364
Panthers, Florida [team]
Hockey (table: National Hockey League) **H:** 281
Pantin doll
Doll (The 1600's and 1700's) **D:** 289
Panting [physiology]
Dog (Why dogs do the things they do) **D:** 263 *with picture*
Perspiration **P:** 305
Pantograph [instrument] **P:** 131
Pantograph [railroad]
Electric railroad *picture on* **E:** 187; (Kinds of electric railroads) **E:** 188
Locomotive (Electric locomotives) **L:** 416
Pantomime [drama] **P:** 130 *with picture*
Drama (Minor forms) **D:** 328; (England) **D:** 334-335
Marceau, Marcel **M:** 193
Pantothenic acid [vitamin]
Vitamin (Vitamin B₆, pantothenic acid, and biotin) **V:** 431; (table) **V:** 431
Nutrition (Vitamins) **N:** 626
Pantothere [extinct animal]
Mammal (The first mammals) **M:** 126-127
Pants [clothing]
Jeans **J:** 75
Panza, Sancho [literary figure]
Don Quixote **D:** 306
Paoli, Giovanni [Italian printer]
Printing (Early printing in North America) **P:** 803
Paoli, Pasquale [Corsican patriot]
Boswell, James **B:** 506
Napoleon I (Early military career) **N:** 14
Paoli Massacre [1777]
Pennsylvania (The Revolutionary War) **P:** 265
Paolini, Christopher [American author] **P:** 132
Pap test [medicine] **P:** 132
Cancer (Cancer checkups) **C:** 171
Cervical cancer **C:** 364
Human papillomavirus **H:** 427
Papa [legendary figure]
Mythology (Creation myths of the Pacific Islands) **M:** 983-984
Papacy *See* Pope *in this index*
Papademos, Lucas [Greek political leader]
Greece (Recent developments) **G:** 365
Papadopoulos, George [Greek political leader]
Greece (The revolt of 1967) **G:** 364; (The restoration of democracy) **G:** 365
Papago Indians See Tohono O'odham Indians *in this index*
Papagos, Alexander [Greek political leader]
Greece (The 1950's) **G:** 364
Papahanaumokuakea Marine National Monument [Hawaii]
Bush, George Walker (Other domestic issues) **B:** 723
Hawaii (The early 2000's) **H:** 109
Papain [enzyme]
Papaya **P:** 133
Papal infallibility [religion]
Acton, Lord **A:** 31
Christianity (The Roman Catholic Church) **C:** 522g
Old Catholic churches **O:** 740
Pope (The powers of the pope) **P:** 661
Roman Catholic Church (Vatican Council I) **R:** 410
Vatican Council I **V:** 289
Papal Palace
Avignon **A:** 993 *with picture*
Papal Schism *See* Great Schism *in this index*
Papal States [Italian history] **P:** 132 *with map*
Christianity (The 1800's) **C:** 526
Ghetto (Early ghettos) **G:** 181
Italy (The Middle Ages) **I:** 513 *with map*
Pope (The powers of the pope) **P:** 661
Rome (Early days) **R:** 434; (Under Napoleon) **R:** 434
Vatican City (History) **V:** 288-289
Papandreou, Andreas [Greek political leader]
Greece (The restoration of democracy) **G:** 365
Papandreou, George [1888-1968, Greek political leader]
Greece (The revolt of 1967) **G:** 364
Papandreou, George [1952- , Greek political leader]
Greece (Recent developments) **G:** 365
Papanicolaou, George [American doctor]
Pap test **P:** 132
Papanicolaou Smear Test [medicine] *See* Pap test *in this index*

Papaw [tree]
Pawpaw **P:** 204
Papaya [fruit] **P:** 133 *with picture*
Pawpaw **P:** 204
Papeete [Tahiti]
Tahiti **T:** 13
Papen, Franz von [German political leader] **P:** 133
Paper P: 134 *with pictures*
Cardboard **C:** 209
Forest products (Paper and paperboard) **F:** 401
Hornbook **H:** 339
Library (Paper, printing, and libraries) **L:** 260
Lignin **L:** 302
Maine (Manufacturing) **M:** 84 *with picture*
Manuscript (Paper manuscripts) **M:** 173
Money (Printing paper money) **M:** 715
New Brunswick *picture on* **N:** 193
Painting (Supports) **P:** 36; (Water-color painting) **P:** 39
Papyrus **P:** 141
Parchment **P:** 155
Photography (Making prints) **P:** 419-420
Plastics (To replace paper) **P:** 555
Uruguay (Forestry) **U:** 226 *with picture*
Wasp (Nests) **W:** 112
Watermark **W:** 145
Wisconsin (Manufacturing) **W:** 361-363
Paper, Allied-Industrial, Chemical and Energy Workers International Union [labor union]
Labor movement (table) **L:** 8
United Steelworkers **U:** 204
Paper bag P: 138
Paper (Special kinds of paper) **P:** 136
Paper birch [tree]
Birch (Paper birch) **B:** 327 *with pictures*
Leaf *picture on* **L:** 153
Tree *pictures on* **T:** 420
Paper blockade [warfare]
Blockade (Paper blockade) **B:** 406
Paper folding See Origami *in this index*
Paper gold [economics]
Special Drawing Rights **So:** 770
Paper money
Engraving and Printing, Bureau of **E:** 326a
Greenback **G:** 381
Money **M:** 704 *with pictures*; (Paper money) **M:** 708 *with pictures*; (History of United States currency) **M:** 710 *with pictures*; (U.S. paper money) **M:** 714; (Printing paper money) **M:** 715
Paper nautilus [sea animal] *See* Argonaut *in this index*
Paper wasp
Insect *pictures on* **I:** 283
Paper weaving
Weaving (Weaving without a loom) **W:** 174
Paper Wheat [drama]
Canadian literature (Modern Canadian drama) **C:** 161
Paperback book
Book (Inside a book) **B:** 464; (The 1800's) **B:** 467-468 *with picture*; (Modern books) **B:** 468
Paperbark [tree]
Invasive species (How invasive species affect habitats) **I:** 354j-354k
Paperboard
Cardboard **C:** 209
Paperless design [engineering]
Computer (Computer-aided design [CAD] programs) **Ci:** 919
Paperwhite narcissus [plant]
Narcissus **N:** 20
Paperwork [decorative art] **P:** 138
Origami **O:** 855 *with picture*
Papiamento [language]
West Indies (Languages) **W:** 201-202
Papier-mâché [art] **P:** 138 *with pictures*
Doll (The 1800's) **D:** 289 *with picture*
Papilionoideae [botany]
Legume **L:** 185
Papilla [anatomy]
Cat *picture on* **C:** 285; (Head) **C:** 286
Frog (Skin) **F:** 536
Hair (The root and shaft) **H:** 9 *with diagram*
Skin (Dermis) **S:** 489
Taste **T:** 50 *with diagrams*
Tongue **T:** 329 *with picture*
Papilloma virus
Cancer (Viruses) **C:** 171
Papillon [dog] **P:** 138 *with picture*
Papin, Denis [French physicist]
Pump (History) **P:** 901
Papineau, Louis Joseph [Canadian political leader] **P:** 139
Canada, History of (The uprisings of 1837) **C:** 143
Rebellions of 1837 **R:** 173
Paprika [seasoning] **P:** 139
Hungary (Food and drink) **H:** 441

Papua [region, Indonesia]
  Indonesia (Papua) **I:** 234; (Independence) **I:** 237; (Indonesia under Sukarno) **I:** 238; (Indonesia under Suharto) **I:** 238-239; (Recent developments) **I:** 239
  Netherlands (Political changes) **N:** 150
  New Guinea (Political units) **N:** 206 *with picture and map*; (History) **N:** 207
Papua, Territory of [former territory]
  Papua New Guinea (History) **P:** 141
Papua New Guinea P: 139 *with picture and map*
  Flag *picture on* **F:** 204
  Indonesia (Indonesia under Suharto) **I:** 238-239
  Mask *picture on* **M:** 264
  New Guinea (Political units) **N:** 206 *with pictures and map*
  Pacific Islands (Pacific alliances and independence movements) **P:** 12-13
  Sculpture (Pacific Islands sculpture) **S:** 241-242 *with picture*
  Shelter *picture on* **S:** 394
Papuans [people]
  Indonesia (Papua) **I:** 234
Papyrus [plant] **P:** 141 *with picture*
  Book (Early books) **B:** 465
  Egypt, Ancient (Education) **E:** 136-137
  Hieroglyphics (Development of hieroglyphic writing) **H:** 225-226
  Library (Ancient libraries of papyrus) **L:** 257
  Manuscript (Papyrus manuscripts) **M:** 172; (Illustrated manuscripts) **M:** 174
  Mythology *picture on* **M:** 978
  Paper (History) **P:** 136 *with picture*
  Parchment (History) **P:** 155
  Scroll **S:** 227
Paquin, Anna [New Zealand actress]
  Motion picture (Best performance by an actress in a supporting role: 1993) **M:** 862b
Par
  Golf (The course) **G:** 260
Par value [economics]
  Investment (table) **I:** 366
  Stock (Kinds of stock) **So:** 903
Para-aminobenzoic acid
  Sulfa drug (How sulfa drugs work) **So:** 965
Para nut [nut]
  Brazil nut **B:** 587 *with picture*
Parable [literature] **P:** 141
  Jesus Christ (His teaching) **J:** 107
Parabola [geometry] **P:** 141 *with diagram*
  Calculus (Finding areas) **C:** 24 *with diagram*
  Mathematics (Branches of mathematics) **M:** 303
  Orbit **O:** 819 *with diagram*
Parabolic dish system
  Solar energy (Parabolic dish systems) **So:** 579
Parabolic mirror [optics]
  Telescope (Reflecting telescopes) **T:** 104
Parabolic trough system
  Solar energy (Solar thermal conversion) **So:** 578
Paracas [ancient city]
  Necropolis **N:** 117
Paracelsus, Philippus Aureolus [Swiss doctor] **P:** 142
  Alchemy **A:** 334
  Gnome **G:** 238
  Medicine (The Renaissance) **M:** 373-374
Parachute P: 142 *with pictures*
  Air *diagram on* **A:** 172
  Airborne troops **A:** 201 *with picture*
  Missouri (Interesting facts) **M:** 651 *with picture*
  Skydiving **S:** 496
Parachute flare
  Fireworks (Other uses of fireworks) **F:** 135
Parachute top [balloon part]
  Balloon (Operation of hot-air balloon) **B:** 60
Parade P: 143
  Circus (At the circus) **Ci:** 562 *with picture*; (The Greatest Show on Earth) **Ci:** 563 *with picture*
  Flag (Carrying the flag) **F:** 219
Parade [ballet]
  Picasso, Pablo (Picasso as a designer) **P:** 448b
Parade [music by Satie]
  Satie, Erik **S:** 150h
Parade's End [books by Ford]
  English literature (Fiction between the wars) **E:** 322
  Ford, Ford Madox **F:** 371
Paradise [book by Morrison]
  Morrison, Toni **M:** 817
Paradise [religion] **P:** 143
  Divine Comedy **D:** 242
Paradise Lost [opera by Penderecki]
  Penderecki, Krzysztof **P:** 236
Paradise Lost [poem by Milton]
  Angel **A:** 459
  Beelzebub **B:** 211
  Doré, Gustave **D:** 310

  English literature (John Milton) **E:** 318
  Milton, John **M:** 557
Paradise Regained [poem by Milton]
  Milton, John **M:** 557
Paradise tanager [bird]
  Bird *picture on* **B:** 344b; (Birds of Central and South America) **B:** 344a
Paradise tree snake
  Snake *picture on* **S:** 533
Paradise Valley [region, Washington]
  Mount Rainier **M:** 887
Paradiso [work by Dante]
  Divine Comedy **D:** 242
Paraffin [wax] **P:** 143
  Candle **C:** 175
  Hydrocarbon (Aliphatic hydrocarbons) **H:** 465
  Wax (Mineral wax) **W:** 153
Paraffin oil
  Mineral oil **M:** 572
Parafoil [kite]
  Kite (The flexible kite) **K:** 340 *with picture*
Paragneiss [rock]
  Gneiss **G:** 238
Paragraph [grammar] **P:** 143
Paraguay P: 144 *with pictures and maps*
  See also the Related articles in the Paraguay *article*
  Flag *picture on* **F:** 201
  Latin America (Early years of independence) **L:** 107-108
Paraguay River [Brazil-Paraguay] **P:** 150
  Asunción **A:** 850
  Exploration (Spain's conquests in the New World) **E:** 445
  Paraguay (The land and climate) **P:** 147 *with map*
  Paraná River **P:** 153
Paraguay tea *See* Maté *in this index*
Paraguayan War *See* Triple Alliance, War of the *in this index*
Parakeet [bird] **P:** 150 *with pictures*
  Bird (As pets) **B:** 331 *with picture*
  Parrot **P:** 179
  Pet (Pets for the home) **P:** 319-320
Parakramabahu VI [Ceylonese king]
  Sri Jayewardenepura Kotte **So:** 817
Paralegal work [career]
  Careers (Law) **C:** 225
  Law (The practice of law) **L:** 139
Parallax [measurement] **P:** 151 *with diagram*
  Astronomy *picture on* **A:** 844; (Units of distance) **A:** 837-838
  Rangefinder **R:** 139
Parallax error [optics]
  Photography (Compact cameras) **P:** 408
Parallel [geography]
  Latitude **L:** 117
  Map (Geographic grids) **M:** 179 *with diagram*
Parallel [mathematics]
  Geometry (Non-Euclidean geometry) **G:** 105
Parallel axiom [geometry]
  Axiom **A:** 994
  Geometry (Euclidean geometry) **G:** 104-105
  Lobachevsky, Nikolai **L:** 404
  Riemann, Georg Friedrich Bernhard **R:** 337
Parallel bars
  Gymnastics (Men's events) **G:** 448 *with picture*; (Women's events) **G:** 449 *with picture*
Parallel circuit
  Electric circuit (Parallel circuits) **E:** 167 *with diagram*
  Electricity (Series and parallel circuits) **E:** 194
Parallel computer
  Computer (Mainframes and supercomputers) **Ci:** 910
Parallel hybrid vehicle
  Automobile (Hybrid power systems) **A:** 954
Parallel Lives of Illustrious Greeks and Romans
  See Plutarch's *Lives in this index*
Parallel motion linkage [mechanics]
  Watt, James **W:** 148
Parallel postulate [geometry] *See* Parallel axiom *in this index*
Parallel slalom [skiing]
  Skiing (Alpine competitions) **S:** 486-487
Parallelism [poetry]
  Whitman, Walt (His work) **W:** 294
Parallels Between the Ancients and the Moderns [book by Perrault]
  Perrault, Charles **P:** 293
Paralysis [disorder] **P:** 152
  Narcolepsy **N:** 20
  Poliomyelitis **P:** 626
  Spastic paralysis **So:** 767
Paramagnetic material [physics]
  Magnetism (In materials) **M:** 60c
Paramaribo [Suriname] **P:** 152
  Suriname **So:** 1008 *with picture and map*
Paramecium [microorganism] **P:** 152 *with picture*

  Heredity *picture on* **H:** 200
  Protozoan (Structure) **P:** 837
  Reproduction *picture on* **R:** 243
Paramedic P: 153
  Ambulance *picture on* **A:** 406
  Careers (Health care) **C:** 223-225 *with picture*
  Emergency Medical Services **E:** 258
  Fire department (Emergency medical operations) **F:** 124 *with picture*
  Medicine (Other careers in medicine) **M:** 371
Parameswara [Sumatran prince]
  Singapore (History) **S:** 471
Paramount Pictures Corporation [company]
  Motion picture (Movies become big business) **M:** 865-866
  Viacom Inc. **V:** 347
Paraná [Argentina] **P:** 153
Paraná pine [tree]
  Brazil (Forestry) **B:** 581
Paraná Plateau [Paraguay]
  Paraguay (Land and climate) **P:** 147
Paraná River [South America] **P:** 153
  Brazil *picture on* **B:** 583; (The Central and Southern Plateaus) **B:** 580; (Energy sources) **B:** 581
  Exploration (Spain's conquests in the New World) **E:** 445
  Inland waterway **I:** 274
  Paraguay (The land and climate) **P:** 147 *with map*
  Paraguay River **P:** 150
Paranasal sinuses [anatomy]
  Sinus **S:** 474
Paranoia [disorder]
  Mental illness (Schizophrenia) **M:** 405; (Personality disorders) **M:** 406
Paranormal powers
  Occultism **O:** 647
Paranthropus [hominid]
  Prehistoric people (Types of australopithecines) **P:** 745
Parapithecid [animal]
  Primate (The evolution of primates) **P:** 778b
Paraplegia [disorder]
  Paralysis (Paralysis of central nervous system origin) **P:** 152
Paraprofessional
  Teaching (Certification of teachers) **T:** 68
Parapsychology P: 153
  Extrasensory perception **E:** 457
  Psychical research **P:** 846
  Telepathy **T:** 93
Parasaurolophus [dinosaur]
  Dinosaur (True dinosaurs) **D:** 206b-208
Parasite [biology] **P:** 153 *with pictures*
  See also the list of Related articles in the Parasite *article*
  Balance of nature (Disease and parasites) **B:** 35
  Cat (Veterinary care) **C:** 295
  Cattle (Diseases) **C:** 312-314
  Flatworm **F:** 229 *with diagram*
  Food poisoning **F:** 340
  Fungal disease **F:** 558
  Fungi **F:** 558
  Gall **G:** 13
  Insect (Beneficial insects) **I:** 284
  Life (The biological environment) **L:** 276 *with picture*
  Mushroom (How a mushroom obtains food) **M:** 942
  Plant (Photosynthesis) **P:** 537-538
  Symbiosis **So:** 1065
  Tick **T:** 279
Parasitic jaeger [bird]
  Bird (Birds of the Arctic) **B:** 343 *with picture*
Parasitic lamprey [sea animal]
  Lamprey (Habits) **L:** 55 *with picture*
Parasitic leech [animal]
  Leech **L:** 180 *with picture*
Parasitoid [insect]
  Butterfly (Butterflies and ecosystems) **B:** 742-743
Paraskenia [theater]
  Drama (Greek drama) **D:** 326
Parasol
  Umbrella **U:** 18
Parasol ant [insect]
  Animal *picture on* **A:** 480
  Ant (Fungus-growing ants) **A:** 527
Parasol mushroom [fungus]
  Mushroom (Nonpoisonous mushrooms) **M:** 943-945 *with picture*
Parasympathetic nervous system [anatomy]
  Nervous system (The autonomic nervous system) **N:** 133 *with diagram*
Parathion [insecticide]
  Insecticide (Organophosphate insecticides) **I:** 302
Parathormone [hormone] *See* Parathyroid hormone *in this index*

Parathyroid gland [anatomy] **P:** 155
Gland (Endocrine glands) **G:** 207 *with diagram;*
(table) **G:** 208
Parathyroid hormone
Gland (Endocrine glands) **G:** 207
Hormone (Blood composition hormones) **H:** 336
Parathyroid gland **P:** 155
Paratroops [military]
Air force *picture on* **A:** 183
Airborne troops **A:** 201
Army (Armies in the two world wars) **A:** 728
Parachute (Uses of parachutes) **P:** 142
Paratyphoid fever [disease]
Typhoid fever (Paratyphoid fever) **T:** 539
Parboiling [cooking]
Rice (Food) **R:** 323
Parc nationaux
Quebec (Places to visit) **Q:** 20
Parcae [Roman mythology]
Fates **F:** 54
Parcel delivery truck
Truck (Kinds of trucks) **T:** 457
Parcel post [mail] **P:** 155
Postal Service, United States (Package services)
P: 699
Parchment P: 155
Book (Early books) **B:** 465
Library (Ancient libraries of animal skin) **L:** 258-
259
Manuscript (Parchment manuscripts) **M:** 172
Pardalote [bird]
Bird (Birds of Australia and New Zealand) **B:** 346
with picture
Pardee, George C. [American political leader]
California (table) **C:** 59
Pardo Bazán, Emilia [Spanish author]
Spanish literature (The 1800's) **So:** 761-762
Pardon [law] **P:** 155
Amnesty **A:** 437
Paré, Ambroise [French doctor] **P:** 156
Medicine *picture on* **M:** 373; (The Renaissance)
M: 373-374
Surgery (History) **So:** 1007
Paregoric [medication]
Opium (Medical uses) **O:** 811
Parenchyma [botany]
Potato (The potato plant) **P:** 712
Stem (Herbaceous stems) **So:** 887
Parenchyma [zoology]
Flatworm **F:** 229
Parent P: 156
Adolescent (Family relationships) **A:** 62;
(Independence and responsibility) **A:** 62
Adoption **A:** 66
Child (The role of the family) **C:** 451 *with picture*
Child abuse **C:** 454
Family (Varieties of families) **F:** 20; (Family
relationships) **F:** 21
Guardian **G:** 411
Home schooling **H:** 301
Parent education **P:** 156
Planned Parenthood Federation of America
P: 515
Reading (Learning in the home) **R:** 160
Parent, S.-Napoléon [Canadian political leader]
Quebec (table) **Q:** 29
Parent advisory committee
Parent-teacher organizations (Local parent
advisory committees) **P:** 158
Parent comet
Meteor (The parent comet) **M:** 431
Parent-cooperative school
Preschool **P:** 756a
Parent education P: 156
Parent material
Soil (How soil is formed) **So:** 573 *with diagram*
Parent-Teacher Association
National Congress of Parents and Teachers **N:** 32
Parent-teacher organizations (Parent-Teacher
Associations) **P:** 158
Parent-teacher organizations P: 157
Parent-Teacher-Student Association
Parent-teacher organizations (Parent-Teacher-
Student Associations) **P:** 158
Parental leave
Women's movement (Legal gains) **W:** 386-387;
(On attitudes and values) **W:** 388
Parenthesis [grammar]
Punctuation (Parentheses) **P:** 903
Parents and Teachers, National Congress of *See*
National Congress of Parents and Teachers *in
this index*
Parents Without Partners [organization] **P:** 158
Pareto, Vilfredo [Italian economist] **P:** 158
Paretsky, Sara [American author] **P:** 159
American literature (Popular genres) **A:** 425
Parfleche [container]

Indian, American *picture on* **I:** 161
Parham, Charles Fox [American religious leader]
Pentecostal churches (Major Pentecostal
churches) **P:** 275
Pari-mutuel betting
Harness racing (Betting) **H:** 64
Horse racing (Betting) **H:** 365
Paricutín [volcano, Mexico] **P:** 159 *with picture*
Seven natural wonders of the world (Paricutín)
S: 324b *with picture*
Volcano (Monogenetic fields) **V:** 442a; (table)
V: 442b
Parietal bones [anatomy]
Head *diagram on* **H:** 123
Human body (table) **H:** 422 *with diagram*
Skull **S:** 495
Parietal lobe [anatomy]
Brain (The cerebrum) **B:** 550a-550b *with diagram*
Parietal pleura [anatomy]
Pleura **P:** 573
Parigi, Alfonso [Italian designer]
Opera *picture on* **O:** 797
Parini, Giuseppe [Italian poet]
Italian literature (The Baroque period and the
Enlightenment) **I:** 494-495
Paris [legendary figure] **P:** 159
Helen of Troy **H:** 168
Iliad **I:** 51
Mythology (Greek heroes) **M:** 982
Trojan War (The beginning of the war) **T:** 449
Troy (The legendary Troy) **T:** 454
Paris [France] **P:** 160 *with pictures and maps*
Atget, Eugène **A:** 852 *with picture*
Ballet (History) **B:** 50-51
City (The people) (table) **C:** 582; (Description) **Ci:** 589
City planning (The Renaissance) **Ci:** 602
France *pictures on* **F:** 452, **F:** 461, **F:** 468, **F:** 474,
F: 476
Franco-Prussian War (The siege and Commune
of Paris) **F:** 483
July Revolution *picture on* **J:** 190
Marx, Karl (Marriage and move to Paris) **M:** 236
Painting (Rococo painting) **P:** 65; (The 1800's)
P: 67
Paris, Treaties of **P:** 167
World War II *picture on* **W:** 484; (The fall of
France) **W:** 475
Paris, Congress of [1856]
Congress **Ci:** 941
Paris, Declaration of [1856]
Blockade **B:** 406
Paris, Pact of *See* Kellogg-Briand Pact *in this index*
Paris, Peace Of [1919] *See* Paris, Treaties of, *in this
index*
Paris, Treaties of P: 167
1763
Paris, Treaties of (The treaty of 1763) **P:** 167
French and Indian wars (The French and Indian
War) **F:** 512-513
Maine (Indian wars) **M:** 89
Montreal (British settlement) **M:** 777
New York (Under English rule) **N:** 314-315
Newfoundland and Labrador (War with France)
N: 375-377
Prince Edward Island (Exploration and early
history) **P:** 791
Quebec (The beginning of European rule)
Q: 30; (The 1700's) **Q:** 36
Quebec, Battle of **Q:** 37; (The attack on
Quebec) **Q:** 37-38
Seven Years' War (In North America and India)
S: 328
United States, History of the (The French and
Indian War) **U:** 158
Wisconsin (Struggle for control) **W:** 366
1783
Paris, Treaties of (The treaty of 1783) **P:** 167
Franklin, Benjamin (Serving in France) **F:** 491
Gálvez, Bernardo de **G:** 18
Jay, John **J:** 67
Mississippi (Exploration and early settlement)
M: 641
Revolution, American (The Treaty of Paris)
R: 286
Spain (Conflict with Great Britain) **So:** 748
United States, History of the (Forming a new
nation [1784-1819]) **U:** 160 *with map*
Wisconsin (Struggle for control) **W:** 366
1814 and 1815
Paris, Treaties of (The treaties of 1814 and
1815) **P:** 167, **P:** 167
Napoleonic Wars (Napoleon's downfall)
N: 19-20
1856
Paris, Treaties of (The treaty of 1856) **P:** 167
Privateer **P:** 808b
1898

Paris, Treaties of (The treaty of 1898) **P:** 167
Cuba (Struggle against Spain) **Ci:** 1176
Puerto Rico (United States rule) **P:** 883
Spanish-American War (Results of the war)
So: 754
United States, History of the (The Spanish-
American War) **U:** 185
1919
Paris, Treaties of (The treaties of 1919) **P:** 167
1947
Paris, Treaties of (The Paris treaties of 1947)
P: 168
1951
European Union (History) **E:** 420
1973
Paris, Treaties of (The treaties of 1973) **P:** 168
Paris, University of P: 168
Education (The rise of the universities) **E:** 99-100
with picture
Paris (Schools and libraries) **P:** 165
Sorbonne **So:** 596
Universities and colleges (European universities)
U: 210
Paris and Helen [opera by Gluck]
Gluck, Christoph Willibald **G:** 235
Paris Basin
France (The land) **F:** 464
Gypsum **G:** 452
Paris (The city) **P:** 161
Paris Commune [French history]
Franco-Prussian War (The siege and Commune
of Paris) **F:** 483
Paris Gun
Artillery (History) **A:** 763
Paris of America [nickname]
New Orleans (The *Paris of America*) **N:** 284
Paris Opéra
Ballet (The rise of professional ballet) **B:** 51
Paris Peace Accords [1973]
Paris, Treaties of (The treaties of 1973) **P:** 168
Paris Peace Conference [1919]
Foch, Ferdinand **F:** 313
Fourteen Points **F:** 438
Lloyd George, David (Prime minister) **L:** 403
Paris, Treaties of (The treaties of 1919) **P:** 167
United States, History of the (The peace treaty)
U: 189
Versailles, Treaty of (Provisions) **V:** 340
World War I (The peace settlement) **W:** 465
World War II (The Peace of Paris) **W:** 468
Paris Peace Talks
Nixon, Richard Milhous (Foreign policy) **N:** 432-
433
Vietnam War (The Tet Offensive) **V:** 375-376
Paris Spleen [poems by Baudelaire]
Baudelaire, Charles **B:** 173
Paris Zoo [France]
Zoo (The first modern zoos) **Z:** 604-605
Parish [political unit]
Colonial life in America (Local government)
Ci: 795
County (Importance) **Ci:** 1099
Local government (Units of local government)
L: 407
Louisiana (Local government) **L:** 496
Roman Catholic Church (Pastor and parish)
R: 404
Parisian chanson [music]
Classical music (Music in other countries) **Ci:** 646
Parisii [ancient people]
Paris (Early years) **P:** 166
Parison [material]
Plastics (Making plastic products) **P:** 557
Parity [physics]
Wu, Chien-shiung **W:** 513
Parizeau, Jacques [Canadian political leader]
Quebec (The late 1900's) **Q:** 32-33
Park P: 168 *with picture*
National park **N:** 42a
National Park System **N:** 43 *with pictures*
Playground **P:** 571
State government (Recreation) **So:** 864
Park, Guy B. [American political leader]
Missouri (table) **M:** 668
Park, J. K. [American inventor]
Envelope **E:** 328
Park, Linda Sue [American author]
Newbery Medal (table) **N:** 359
Park, Maud Wood [American social reformer]
Woman suffrage (Growth of the movement)
W: 380
Park, Mungo [Scottish explorer] **P:** 168
Exploration (The exploration of Africa) **E:** 448
with map
Niger River **N:** 409
Park, National *See* National park *in this index*
Park, Robert E. [American sociologist]

Collective behavior **Ci:** 774
Park Center Plaza
  San Jose (History) **S:** 101-102
Park Chung Hee [Korean political leader] **P:** 169
  Korea, South (History) **K:** 378c
  Seoul (History) **S:** 306-307
Park City [Utah]
  Utah picture on **U:** 239
Park, Parkway, and Recreation Area Study Act
  [1936]
  National Park System (History) **N:** 58
Park Range
  Colorado (Land regions) **Ci:** 838 with map
Park trailer [vehicle]
  Recreational vehicle (Park trailers) **R:** 184
Parka [clothing]
  Indian, American (Peoples of the Arctic) **I:** 152-
  153
  Inuit (Clothing) **I:** 354b-354c
Parkchester
  New York City (The Bronx) **N:** 328-329
Parke County
  Indiana (Places to visit) **I:** 206
Parker, Alton Brooks [American political leader]
  P: 169
Parker, Annise [American political leader]
  Houston (The early 2000's) **H:** 398
Parker, B. [Australian author]
  Literature for children picture on **L:** 354
Parker, Charlie [American saxophonist] **P:** 169
  Davis, Miles **D:** 49
  Hines, Earl **H:** 237
Parker, Claire [American artist]
  Animation (Animation in Europe) **A:** 514a
Parker, Dorothy [American author] **P:** 169 with
  portrait
Parker, Ely Samuel [American government official]
  P: 170
Parker, Francis Wayland [American educator]
  Education (New theories of education) **E:** 104
  Progressive education (Progressive educators)
  P: 813
Parker, Sir Hyde [British admiral]
  Nelson, Horatio (Battle of Copenhagen) **N:** 122
Parker, Isaac C. [American jurist]
  Arkansas (Interesting facts about Arkansas)
  A: 695
  Western frontier life in America (Law and order)
  W: 238
Parker, Joel [American political leader]
  New Jersey (table) **N:** 249
Parker, John [British military leader]
  Lexington and Concord, Battles of (Lexington)
  L: 224
Parker, John M. [American political leader]
  Louisiana (table) **L:** 496
Parker, N. [Australian illustrator]
  Literature for children picture on **L:** 354
Parker, Peter Benjamin [fictional character]
  Spider-Man **So:** 791 with picture
Parker, Quanah [American Indian chief]
  Quanah **Q:** 5
Parker, Robert B. [American author] **P:** 170
Parker, Samuel [American inventor]
  Leather (History) **L:** 169
Parker, Theodore [American religious leader]
  Unitarians (History) **U:** 42
Parker, Tom [American businessman]
  Presley, Elvis **P:** 772
Parker Bowles, Camilla [wife of Prince Charles]
  Charles, Prince **C:** 383
Parkes process
  Silver (Extracting and refining silver) **S:** 464
Parkhurst, Frederic H. [American political leader]
  Maine (table) **M:** 87
Parking
  Airport (Ground transportation and parking)
  A: 245
  Traffic (Traffic problems) **T:** 365-366
Parking brake
  Brake (Mechanical brakes) **B:** 560
Parking meter
  Traffic (Parking meters) **T:** 366
Parkinson, James [British doctor]
  Parkinson disease **P:** 170
Parkinson, Mark [American political leader]
  Kansas (table) **K:** 234
Parkinson disease P: 170
  Brain (Making decisions) **B:** 555; (Parkinson
  disease) **B:** 559
  Dopamine **D:** 309
Parkinsonism [disease]
  Parkinson disease (Causes) **P:** 170
Parkinson's disease See Parkinson disease in this
  index
Parkland
  National Park System **N:** 43

Parklands [region, Alberta]
  Alberta (The Alberta Plain) **A:** 322
Parkman, Francis [American historian] **P:** 171
Parks, Gordon [American photographer/director]
  P: 171
Parks, Rosa Louise [American civil rights activist]
  P: 171 with portrait
  African Americans (The civil rights movement)
  A: 136o with picture
  King, Martin Luther, Jr. (The early civil rights
  movement) **K:** 321
  Montgomery bus boycott **M:** 767
Parks, Suzan-Lori [American playwright] **P:** 172
  African American literature (Recent
  developments) **A:** 136a
  American literature (Drama) **A:** 426
Parks, William [American printer]
  Virginia (Communication) **V:** 416
Parkway
  Road (Primary highways) **R:** 358
Parlby, Irene [Canadian reformer]
  Famous Five **F:** 26b
Parliament [Australia]
  Australia (The federal government) **A:** 895
Parliament [Canada]
  Canada, Government of picture on **C:** 128; (The
  Parliament) **C:** 130; (The prime minister) **C:** 130
  Prime minister of Canada **P:** 778c
Parliament [lawmaking body] **P:** 172 with pictures
  See also specific parliaments, such as Parliament
  (United Kingdom) in this index
  Government (Parliamentary democracy) **G:** 286
Parliament [Russia]
  Russia (National government) **R:** 531 with picture
Parliament [United Kingdom]
  Parliament (The Parliament of the United
  Kingdom) **P:** 172
  Democracy (Democracy in England) **D:** 122
  England (Government) **E:** 292-293; (The
  beginnings of Parliament) **E:** 306
  Government picture on **G:** 282; (The
  Enlightenment) **G:** 290
  Grattan, Henry **G:** 329
  House of Commons **H:** 384
  House of Lords **H:** 384
  Industrial Revolution (The working class) **I:** 251-
  252
  Nobility (Privileges of the peerage) **N:** 450
  Northern Ireland (Government) **N:** 521
  Rump Parliament **R:** 519
  United Kingdom (Government) **U:** 49 with picture;
  (The era of reform) **U:** 68
Parliament, Houses of [London]
  London picture on **L:** 431; (The Houses of
  Parliament) **L:** 435
Parliament, Palace of [Bucharest]
  Bucharest **B:** 662
Parliament Buildings [Ottawa]
  Ontario (Places to visit) **O:** 774
  Ottawa **O:** 871 with picture; (The Parliament
  Buildings) **O:** 872
Parliament Buildings [Victoria]
  British Columbia picture on **B:** 614
Parliament House [Canberra]
  Australia picture on **A:** 897
Parliament House [New Delhi]
  India picture on **I:** 111
Parliament of Fowls, The [poem by Chaucer]
  Chaucer, Geoffrey (Poetry) **C:** 388
Parliamentarian [office]
  Parliamentary procedure (Officers) **P:** 175
Parliamentary Act [1911]
  Asquith, Herbert Henry **A:** 816
  Parliament (The decline of the House of Lords)
  P: 174
Parliamentary Act [1949]
  Parliament (The decline of the House of Lords)
  P: 174
Parliamentary procedure P: 175
Parliamentary system [government]
  Cabinet (The cabinet system of government) **C:** 4
  Election (Elections in a democracy) **E:** 158
  Government diagrams on **G:** 287; (Parliamentary
  democracy) **G:** 286
  Political party (Organizing the government)
  P: 632
Parlor organ [musical instrument]
  Harmonium **H:** 62
Parma [Italy] **P:** 177
Parma, University of [Italy]
  Parma **P:** 177
Parmenides [Greek philosopher] **P:** 177
  Pre-Socratic philosophy (The teachings of
  Parmenides) **P:** 772
  Zeno of Elea **Z:** 589
Parmenides [book by Plato]
  Plato (The dialogues) **P:** 567

Parmenion [Macedonian general]
  Alexander the Great (Central Asia and the Indus)
  A: 343
Parmesan [cheese]
  Cheese (Very hard, or grating, cheese) **C:** 392
  with picture
Parnaíba River [Brazil]
  Brazil (The Northeast Region) **B:** 579-580 with
  map
Parnassian [butterfly]
  Butterfly picture on **B:** 736; (Swallowtails) **B:** 738
Parnassus [mountain, Greece] **P:** 177
  Deucalion **D:** 172
Parnell, Charles Stewart [Irish political leader]
  P: 177 with portrait
Parnell, Harvey [American political leader]
  Arkansas (table) **A:** 712
  Caraway, Hattie Ophelia Wyatt **C:** 202
Parnell, Sean [American political leader]
  Alaska (table) **A:** 300
Parochial school P: 177
  Education (Control and support of U.S.
  education) **E:** 94
  Elementary school (Kinds of elementary schools)
  E: 224
  Montreal (Education) **M:** 772
  Parent-teacher organizations (Home and School
  Associations) **P:** 158
  Private school **P:** 808b
  Religious education (Private education) **R:** 225
  School (Private schools) **S:** 183
Parody [humor] **P:** 178
  Humor (The types of humor) **H:** 435-436
Parole [law] **P:** 178
  Sentence **S:** 304
Paroles [poems by Prévert]
  Prévert, Jacques **P:** 774
Paromomycin [drug]
  Antibiotic (Other kinds of antibiotics) **A:** 550
Paroquet See Parakeet in this index
Parotid gland [anatomy]
  Mumps **M:** 926
  Saliva **S:** 68 with diagram
Parotitis See Mumps in this index
Parotoid gland [gland]
  Cane toad **C:** 177
  Toad **T:** 303
Parquet floor
  Flooring **F:** 239
Parr, Catherine [wife of]
  Henry VIII [of England] **H:** 188
Parr, Martin [British photographer]
  Photography picture on **P:** 429; (A diversity of
  styles) **P:** 426-427
Parra, Nicanor [Chilean poet]
  Latin American literature (The mid-1900's) **L:** 114
Parrain [European history]
  Knights and knighthood (Knighting) **K:** 348
Parrakeet See Parakeet in this index
Parrillada criollo
  Uruguay (Food and drink) **U:** 225
Parris, Albion K. [American political leader]
  Maine (table) **M:** 87
Parris, Samuel [American religious leader]
  Salem witchcraft trials **S:** 61
Parrish, Maxfield [American artist] **P:** 179
  Pied Piper of Hamelin picture on **P:** 453
  Pyle, Howard **P:** 915
Parrot [bird] **P:** 179 with pictures
  Animal picture on **A:** 507
  Bird (As pets) **B:** 331
  Endangered species (table) **E:** 270
  Macaw **M:** 5
Parrot fever See Psittacosis in this index
Parrot fish See Parrotfish in this index
Parrotfinch [bird]
  Bird (Birds of the Pacific Islands) **B:** 349 with
  picture
Parrotfish P: 181 with picture
Parrs Ridge
  Maryland (Land regions) **M:** 250
Parry [sports]
  Boxing picture on **B:** 529
  Fencing (The foil) **F:** 70-71 with picture
Parry, Milman [American scholar]
  Homer (The Homeric question today) **H:** 304
Parry, Sir William Edward [British explorer] **P:** 181
  Arctic (Search for the Northwest Passage)
  A: 638-639
  Exploration map on **E:** 451; (Arctic exploration)
  E: 449
  Melville Island **M:** 391
  Ross, Sir James Clark **R:** 482
Parsec [unit of measure]
  Astronomy (Units of distance) **A:** 837-838
Parsis [religious group]
  Funeral customs (Burial) **F:** 557-558

India (Other religions) **I:** 117
Zoroastrianism (History) **Z:** 607
Parsley [plant] **P:** 181 *with picture*
Flower (table) **F:** 301 *with picture*
Parsnip [plant] **P:** 182 *with picture*
Parson Capen House [Massachusetts]
Architecture *picture on* **A:** 624
Parson Russell terrier [dog] **P:** 182 *with picture*
Parson Weems [name for]
Weems, Mason Locke **W:** 180
Parsons, Andrew [American political leader]
Michigan (table) **M:** 507
Parsons, Benny [American race driver]
Automobile racing (table: NASCAR Sprint Cup
champions) **A:** 981
Parsons, Charles A. [British inventor]
Invention (The Industrial Revolution) **I:** 361
Ship (Stronger, faster ships) **S:** 425
Turbine (History) **T:** 498-499
Parsons, Elsie Clews [American anthropologist]
P: 182
Parsons, Estelle [American actress]
Motion picture (Best performance by an actress
in a supporting role: 1967) **M:** 862b
Parsons, Johnny [American race driver]
Automobile racing (table: Indianapolis 500
winners) **A:** 980
Parsons, Lewis E. [American political leader]
Alabama (table) **A:** 274
Parsons, Samuel [American settler]
Ohio Company (The second Ohio Company)
O: 704
Parsons, Talcott [American sociologist] **P:** 183
Sociology (Development of social research)
So: 566
Parson's Cause [U.S. history]
Henry, Patrick (Early life) **H:** 189-190
Part of Speech, A [poetry by Brodsky]
Brodsky, Joseph **B:** 636
Part-score [bridge]
Bridge (Scoring) **B:** 605
Part song
Classical music (Songs) **Ci:** 644
Parthenogenesis [biology]
Aphid **A:** 565
Rotifer **R:** 489
Shark (The body of a shark) **S:** 374
Parthenon [Athens] **P:** 183
Acropolis **A:** 29 *with picture*
Elgin Marbles **E:** 236
Greece *picture on* **G:** 352
Greece, Ancient *pictures on* **G:** 370
Phidias **P:** 357
Relief (Low relief) **R:** 212
Parthenon [Tennessee]
Nashville (Cultural life and recreation) **N:** 23
Parthenope [former name]
Naples **N:** 12
Parthenos *See* Athena *in this index*
Parthia [ancient country] **P:** 183 *with map*
Hadrian **H:** 4
Persia, Ancient (The Parthians) **P:** 298
Parti Démocratique de Guinée [political party]
Guinea (History) **G:** 432
Parti Québécois [political party] **P:** 183
Bloc Québécois **B:** 404
Canada, History of (The separatist threat) **C:** 150
Lévesque, René **L:** 218
Quebec (Politics) **Q:** 30; (The late 1900's) **Q:** 32-33
Partial [music]
Harmonics **H:** 62
Partial-birth abortion
Abortion (Abortion in the United States) **A:** 15-16
Partial blindness
Blindness **B:** 401
Partial eclipse
Eclipse (Lunar eclipses) **E:** 51; (Solar eclipses)
E: 51
Partial parasite [biology]
Plant (Photosynthesis) **P:** 537-538 *with picture*
Partial product
Multiplication (Multiplying by large numbers)
M: 923
Participant observation
Anthropology (How anthropologists work)
A: 547
Participating policy
Insurance (Dividends) **I:** 310
Participatory caucus [meeting]
Caucus **C:** 317
Political convention (Delegate selection) **P:** 628-
629
Participle [grammar] **P:** 184
Verb (Formal characteristics) **V:** 314
Particle, Subatomic *See* Subatomic particle *in
this index*
Particle accelerator [machine] **P:** 184 *with*

diagrams
Atom (How scientists study atoms) **A:** 874 *with
picture*
CERN **C:** 363
Electricity *picture on* **E:** 198
Element, Chemical (Groups) **E:** 223
Fermi National Accelerator Laboratory **F:** 74
Fusion **F:** 589
Lawrence, Ernest Orlando **L:** 145
Magnetism *picture on* **M:** 60a; (In science and
medicine) **M:** 60b
Matter (Antimatter) **M:** 311; (Quark-gluon
plasmas) **M:** 311
Neutrino **N:** 154
Particle detector **P:** 186
Physics (Particle physics) **P:** 438
Quark **Q:** 7
Radiation (Artificial radioactive substances)
R: 77-78
Radiocarbon (Radiocarbon dating) **R:** 97-98 *with
diagram*
Radiochemistry **R:** 98
Superconductivity **So:** 993
Supersymmetry **So:** 995
Transmutation of elements **T:** 379
Transuranium element **T:** 401
Walton, Ernest Thomas Sinton **W:** 21
Particle detector [machine] **P:** 186 *with picture*
Particle physics
Physics (Particle physics) **P:** 438
Particle radiation [physics]
Radiation **R:** 74; (Particle radiation) **R:** 76
Particleboard [building material]
Forest products (Particleboard) **F:** 401 *with
picture*
Particular truth *See* Contingent truth *in this index*
Particulate [chemistry] *See* Fiber *in this index*
Particulate [pollution]
Environmental pollution (Air pollution) **E:** 331
Particulate filter
Gas mask **G:** 60
Particulate radiation [physics] *See* Particle
radiation *in this index*
Partido Comunista de Cuba [political party]
Cuba (Government) **Ci:** 1169
Partido Nacional Revolucionario [political party]
Mexico (Politics) **M:** 451; (Reforms of the early
1900's) **M:** 473
Querétaro **Q:** 40
Partido Popular [political party]
Spain (Poltical parties) **So:** 733; (Poltical changes)
So: 751
Partido Revolucionario Institucional [political
party]
Mexico (Politics) **M:** 451; (Reforms of the early
1900's) **M:** 472; (Opposition to the PRI) **M:** 474
Zedillo Ponce de León, Ernesto **Z:** 588
Partido Socialista Obrero Español [political party]
Spain (Poltical parties) **So:** 733; (Political changes)
So: 751
Partisans [warfare] **P:** 187
Guerrilla warfare (Types of guerrilla movements)
G: 420
Partisans [Yugoslav history]
Serbia (World War II) **S:** 315-316
Yugoslavia (World War II) **Y:** 576
Partition [construction]
House (Interior construction) **H:** 382 *with diagram*
Partitions of Poland [Polish history]
Poland (The partitions) **P:** 612 *with maps*
Partner [business]
Partnership **P:** 188
Partnering
Ballet (A ballet class) **B:** 46-47 *with picture*
Partnership [business] **P:** 188
Business (Partnerships) **B:** 725
Partnership for Peace [program]
North Atlantic Treaty Organization (History)
N: 471
Parton, Dolly [American singer] **P:** 188 *with portrait*
Country music (Modern country music)
Ci: 1098c-1098d *with picture*
Tennessee (Places to visit) **T:** 144
Partridge [bird] **P:** 188 *with picture*
Bird *pictures on* **B:** 344e, **B:** 351
Grouse **G:** 403
Partridgeberry [fruit]
Lingonberry **L:** 335 *with picture*
Parts of speech [grammar] **P:** 189
Dictionary (What a dictionary tells you) **D:** 193
English language (Grammar) **E:** 312
Grammar **G:** 303
Parturition [biology] *See* Labor *in this index*
Party, Political *See* Political party *in this index*
Party caucus [meeting]
Caucus **C:** 317
Political convention (Delegate selection) **P:** 628-

629
Party column ballot
Ballot (In the United States) **B:** 63
Party congress [Soviet history]
Union of Soviet Socialist Republics (The
Communist Party) **U:** 29
Party convention system [politics]
Caucus **C:** 317
Party line [political policy]
Communism (The role of the party) **Ci:** 891
Party of Democratic Socialism
Germany (Politics) **G:** 147; (East Germany)
G: 170-171
Party of Regions [political party]
Ukraine (Politics) **U:** 6
Party of the Mexican Revolution
Mexico (Reforms of the early 1900's) **M:** 472
Party politics
Political party (Organizing the government)
P: 632-633
Party state [political theory]
Communism (The party state) **Ci:** 891
Parvanov, Georgi [Bulgarian political leader]
Bulgaria (Recent developments) **B:** 693
Parvati [Hindu goddess]
Hinduism (Deities) **H:** 236
Parzival [poem by Wolfram von Eschenbach]
German literature (The romance) **G:** 138
Wolfram von Eschenbach **W:** 378
Pas de deux [dance]
Ballet *picture on* **B:** 46; (table) **B:** 45; (Kinds of
ballet) **B:** 48
Dance *picture on* **D:** 29
Pasadena [California] **P:** 189
Pasadena Freeway
California (Transportation) **C:** 58
Pascagoula River
Mississippi **M:** 623
Pascal [computer language]
Computer (Using programming languages)
Ci: 923
Pascal [measurement]
Isobar **I:** 474
Pascal [unit of measure] **P:** 189
Metric system (Mechanics) **M:** 437-440
Pressure **P:** 773
Vacuum **V:** 256
Pascal, Blaise [French philosopher] **P:** 189
Computer (History) **Ci:** 924a
French literature (Classical prose) **F:** 520
Hydraulics (Laws of hydrostatics) **H:** 463-464
Insurance (The growth of insurance) **I:** 315
Permutations and combinations (History) **P:** 291
Pressure **P:** 773
Roman Catholic Church (Jansenism) **R:** 409
Pascal Triangle [mathematics]
Binomial theorem **B:** 310
Permutations and combinations (History) **P:** 291
with diagram
Pascal's law [physics] **P:** 190
Hydraulics (Laws of hydrostatics) **H:** 463-464
Pascal, Blaise **P:** 189
Pressure **P:** 773
Pasch, Gustave E. [Swedish chemist]
Match (The first safety matches) **M:** 300a
Pascha [name for]
Easter **E:** 42
Paschal [antipope]
Pope (table) **P:** 666
Paschal I, Saint [pope]
Pope (table) **P:** 666
Paschal II [pope] **P:** 190
Pope (table) **P:** 666
Paschal III [antipope]
Pope (table) **P:** 666
Pascoli, Giovanni [Italian poet]
Italian literature (Romanticism) **I:** 495
Pascua Florida [former name]
Florida **F:** 243
Paseo [custom]
Bullfighting (The order of the bullfight) **B:** 696
with picture
Paseo de la Reforma [street]
Mexico City (Residential and commercial centers)
M: 476a *with picture*
Paseo del Rio [district]
Texas *picture on* **T:** 185
Pashto [language]
Afghanistan (Ethnic groups and languages)
A: 92a
Pakistan (Cultural groups and languages) **P:** 93
Pashtuns **P:** 190
Pashtuns [people] **P:** 190
Afghanistan (Ethnic groups and languages)
A: 92a; (Way of life) **A:** 92a-93

Pakistan (Cultural groups and languages) P: 93
Pasig River [Philippines]
Manila (Description) M: 142 *with picture*
Pasiphae [satellite]
Jupiter (Outer satellites) J: 200a
Paso [literature]
Spanish literature (The 1500's) So: 758-759
Paso doble [dance]
Ballroom dancing B: 63
PASOK [political party] *See* Panhellenic Socialist
Movement *in this index*
Pasolini, Pier Paolo [Italian poet]
Italian literature (The 1900's) I: 495
Pasqueflower [plant] P: 190
Anemone A: 458
Crocus Ci: 1150
Flower (Flowers of prairies and dry plains) F: 286
with picture
Pass [geography]
Mountain pass M: 899
Pass [sports]
Football *diagram on* F: 359; (Advancing the ball)
F: 360-361 *with pictures*
Hockey (Hockey skills) H: 276
Soccer (Passing) So: 547
Pass axis [optics]
Polarized light (Polarizing filters) P: 618
Passacaglia [music]
Counterpoint Ci: 1097
Passage [geography]
Strait So: 917
Passage [movement]
Horse (Dressage) H: 357
"Passage to India" [poem by Whitman]
Whitman, Walt (His work) W: 294
Passage to India, A [book by Forster]
Forster, E. M. F: 410
Passaic River
New Jersey (Rivers and lakes) N: 244
Paterson P: 195
Passamaquoddy Bay [Canada-U.S.] P: 190
Passamaquoddy Indians
Indian, American (In the United States) I: 179
Maine (The late 1900's) M: 92 *with picture*
Passau, Treaty of [1552]
Schmalkaldic League S: 177
Passbook account
Savings bank S: 165
Passchendaele, Battle of [1917]
World War I (Allied failures) W: 461
Passeggiata [custom]
Italy (Recreation) I: 503
Passel, Charles F. [American explorer]
Wind chill W: 331
Passenger compartment
Automobile (The passenger compartment)
A: 950
Passenger elevator
Elevator E: 234
Passenger facility charge [fee]
Airport (Airport operations) A: 246
Passenger locomotive
Locomotive (Kinds of locomotives) L: 414
Passenger pigeon [extinct bird] P: 190
Audubon, John James *picture on* A: 884
Bird (Extinct birds) B: 369-370 *with picture*
Pigeon (Wild pigeons) P: 460
Passenger ship
Ship S: 407, *picture on* S: 410; (Passenger ships)
S: 409; (Officers and crew) S: 410; (Passenger
vessels) S: 426
Passenger train
Railroad (Passenger service) R: 105 *with map*;
(Rolling stock) R: 107 *with picture*; (Leading
countries in railroad transportation) R: 114
Passing [book by Larsen]
African American literature (The 1900's) A: 136a
Passion, The [religion]
Jesus Christ (The Passion) J: 108
Lent L: 196b
Passion According to Saint John, The [music by
Bach]
Bach, Johann Sebastian (His works) B: 16
Passion According to Saint Matthew, The [music
by Bach]
Bach, Johann Sebastian (His works) B: 16
Passion music P: 191
Passion-flower [plant] P: 191 *with picture*
Passion Flower, The [play by Benavente]
Spanish literature (Drama) So: 763
Passion fruit
Passion-flower P: 191
Passion music P: 191
Classical music (Oratorios) Ci: 644
Passion of Joan of Arc, The [film]
Motion picture (The movies talk) M: 867
Passion of Sacco and Vanzetti, The [painting by

Shahn]
Shahn, Ben *picture on* S: 342
Passion play [drama] P: 191 *with picture*
Easter (Easter customs) E: 44
Passionate Pilgrim, The [book by Jaggard]
Shakespeare, William (Composition and
publication) S: 367
"Passionate Shepherd to His Love, The" [poem
by Marlowe]
Marlowe, Christopher M: 216
Passionflower [plant] *See* Passion-flower *in this
index*
Passive autofocus [photography]
Camera (Automatic focusing) C: 82
Photography (Types of lenses) P: 411
Passive component
Electronics (Passive components) E: 212
Passive euthanasia
Death (The right to die) D: 61
Euthanasia (Active euthanasia) E: 421
Passive immunity
Immune system (Passive immunity) I: 88b
Passive resistance
Thoreau, Henry David (His beliefs and works)
T: 266
Passive safety system
Nuclear energy (Advanced fission reactors)
N: 594
Passive smoking [cigarette] *See* Secondhand
smoke *in this index*
Passive sonar system
Sonar (How sonar works) So: 591
Passive voice [grammar]
Conjugation Ci: 951
Voice V: 437
Passively safe reactor
Nuclear energy (Safety concern) N: 592
Passover [religion] P: 192
Easter E: 42
Jesus Christ (Childhood) J: 106 *with picture*; (The
Passion) J: 108
Judaism (The pilgrimage festivals) J: 181 *with
picture*
Moses (The covenant with God) M: 829
Religion *picture on* R: 217
Passport P: 192
Visa V: 428b
Passy, Frédéric [French statesman]
Nobel Prizes (Peace: 1901) N: 448
Past and Present [book by Carlyle]
Carlyle, Thomas (Later career) C: 240
Past participle [grammar]
Participle P: 184
Verb (Regular or irregular verbs) V: 315
Past perfect tense [grammar]
Tense T: 168
Past Recaptured, The [book by Proust]
Proust, Marcel P: 838
Past tense [grammar]
Tense T: 168
Past Through Tomorrow, The [book by Heinlein]
Heinlein, Robert A. H: 167
Pasta [food] P: 192
Italy (Food and drink) I: 502
Nutrition (Carbohydrates) N: 625
Wheat (Food for people) W: 266-267
Paste [glass]
Gem (Imitation and synthetic gems) G: 79
Paste-up [printing]
Newspaper (Making up the pages) N: 383
Pastel [art]
Crayon Ci: 1122
Painting (Pastel) P: 39
Pastel de choclo [food]
Chile (Food and drink) C: 462
Pasterka [religion]
Christmas (In Poland) C: 531
Pasternak, Boris [Soviet author] P: 192
Russian literature (Post-symbolism) R: 563-564;
(Modern Soviet literature) R: 564
Pasteur, Louis [French biochemist] P: 193 *with
portrait*
Bacteria (History) B: 22
Bacteriology (History) B: 22
Fermentation F: 73
Immune system (The study of the immune
system) I: 88d *with picture*
Life (Spontaneous generation) L: 278
Medicine (Scientific study of the effects of
disease) M: 375
Pasteurization P: 193
Spontaneous generation So: 801
Yeast Y: 554
Pasteur Institute [Paris]
Pasteur, Louis (His life) P: 193
Pasteurization [food processing] P: 193
Butter (Pasteurization) B: 730

Food preservation (Other methods) F: 344
Milk (Pasteurization) M: 548 *with picture*
Pasteur, Louis (His work in industry) P: 193
Scrofula S: 227
Pastiche [art]
Postmodernism P: 709
Pastor, Tony [American producer]
Vaudeville V: 290
Pastor Aeternus [Roman Catholic constitution]
Vatican Council I V: 289
**Pastoral Constitution on the Church in the
Modern World, The**
Vatican Council II (The Pastoral Constitution on
the Church in the Modern World) V: 290
Pastoral literature
Drama (Italian Renaissance drama) D: 330
English literature (Elizabethan fiction) E: 317
Greek literature (The Hellenistic Age) G: 378
Italian literature (Humanism and the
Renaissance) I: 494
Novel (Ancient Greek and Roman narratives)
N: 572
Poetry (Renaissance poetry) P: 596
Spanish literature (The 1500's) So: 758-759
Theocritus T: 251
Pastoral nomad [sociology]
Nomad N: 452
Pastoralism [agriculture]
Africa (The development of agriculture) A: 129-
130
Agriculture (Subsistence agriculture) A: 149
Kenya *picture on* K: 301; (Way of life) K: 298-299
Pastore, John Orlando [American political leader]
Rhode Island (table) R: 311
Pastorius, Francis Daniel [American settler] P: 193
Pastrana Arango, Andrés [Colombian political
leader]
Colombia (Civil war) Ci: 784-785
Pastry [food] P: 194
Baking B: 32 *with picture*
Pasture [agriculture]
Cattle *picture on* C: 306
Pastures of Heaven, The [book by Steinbeck]
Steinbeck, John So: 885
Patagonia [region, South America] P: 194
Argentina (Patagonia) A: 653 *with picture and
map*
Chile *picture on* C: 462
Patagonian hare [animal]
Cavy C: 322
Pataki, George E. [American political leader]
New York (table) N: 313
Pataliputra [ancient city]
Mauryan Empire M: 318
Patapsco River [Maryland]
Baltimore B: 66 *with map*
United States, History of the *picture on* U: 155
Patas monkey
Monkey *picture on* M: 728
Patassé, Ange-Félix [Central African political
leader]
Central African Republic (History) C: 353
Patch, Transdermal *See* Transdermal patch *in this
index*
Patch antenna [device]
Antenna (Types of antennas) A: 543
Patchouli [oil] P: 194
Patella [anatomy]
Human body (table) H: 422 *with diagram*
Knee K: 345
Leg (The knee joint) L: 182 *with diagram*
Patellar reflex [physiology]
Reflex action R: 194
Patent [law] P: 194
Agriculture (Genetic engineering) A: 161
Copyright Ci: 1046
Edison, Thomas Alva E: 77
Genetic engineering (History) G: 84c
Intellectual property I: 318
Manufacturing (How governments help
manufacturing) M: 172
Piracy P: 493
Public domain P: 855
Vermont (Interesting facts) V: 319
Patent and Trademark Office [U.S.]
Commerce, Department of (History) Ci: 871-872
Edison, Thomas Alva E: 77
Patent P: 194; (How to get a U.S. patent) P: 194-
195
Patent Cooperation Treaty [1978]
Patent (International patent agreements) P: 195
Patent ductus arteriosus [disorder]
Heart (Abnormal openings in the heart) H: 141
Patent fingerprint
Fingerprinting (Types of fingerprints) F: 106
Patent law
Patent (Patent laws of other countries) P: 195

Patent leather
  Leather *picture on* **L:** 167; (Final processing)
    L: 168-169
Pater, Walter [British author] **P:** 195
Pater Noster [prayer] *See* Lord's Prayer *in this index*
Paterfamilias [person]
  Family (Ancient families) **F:** 21-22
  Rome, Ancient (Family life) **R:** 440
Paternity test
  Blood (The significance of blood groups) **B:** 412
  DNA fingerprinting **D:** 258
Paterno, Joe [American football coach]
  Robinson, Eddie **R:** 368
Paterson [New Jersey] **P:** 195
Paterson [poem by Williams]
  Williams, William Carlos **W:** 312
Paterson, Andrew Barton [Australian poet] *See*
  Paterson, Banjo *in this index*
Paterson, Banjo [Australian poet]
  Australia (Literature) **A:** 904-905
Paterson, David A. [American political leader]
  New York (table) **N:** 313; (The early 2000's) **N:** 320
Paterson, Katherine [American author] **P:** 195
  Newbery Medal (table) **N:** 359
  Regina Medal (table: 1988) **R:** 206
Paterson, William [American jurist] **P:** 196
  New Jersey (table) **N:** 249
Paterson Great Falls National Historical Park
  [New Jersey]
  National Park System (table: National historical
    parks) **N:** 56-57
Path of totality [astronomy]
  Eclipse (Solar eclipses) **E:** 51
Path to Rome, The [book by Belloc]
  Belloc, Hilaire **B:** 244
PATH tunnels [New Jersey-New York]
  Hudson River tunnels (The PATH tunnels) **H:** 406
Pathans [people] *See* Pashtuns *in this index*
Pather Panchali [film]
  Ray, Satyajit **R:** 152
Pathet Lao [political group]
  Laos (History) **L:** 71-72
Pathétique Symphony [music by Tchaikovsky]
  Tchaikovsky, Peter Ilich **T:** 61
Pathfinder, The [book by Cooper]
  Cooper, James Fenimore **C:** 1035
Pathfinder of the Seas [nickname]
  Maury, Matthew Fontaine **M:** 318
Pathfinders [scouting]
  Girl Scouts (Pathfinders) **G:** 199
Pathogen [medicine]
  Disease (Infectious diseases) **D:** 227
  Immune system **I:** 87
Pathology [medicine] **P:** 196
  Biology (table) **B:** 317
  Crime scene investigation (Beginning an
    investigation) **Ci:** 1140
  Medicine (table) **M:** 369; (Scientific study of the
    effects of disease) **M:** 375
  Virchow, Rudolf **V:** 391
Pathways program
  Girl Scouts (Girls Scouts of the USA) **G:** 196
Patience [card game] *See* Solitaire *in this index*
Patient care assistant *See* Nurse's aide *in this index*
Patient Protection and Affordable Care Act
  [2010]
  Insurance (Health care reform) **I:** 316
  Obama, Barack (Health insurance reform)
    O: 640g-640h; (Health care law upheld) **O:** 641
Patients' Bill of Rights [congressional bill]
  Edwards, John **E:** 114
Patina [chemistry]
  Copper (Resistance to corrosion) **Ci:** 1041-1042
  Corrosion **Ci:** 1072
Patio
  Mexico (City life) **M:** 454
Patmos [island, Greece] **P:** 196
Patois [language]
  Calypso (Development) **C:** 71
  West Indies (Languages) **W:** 201-202
Paton, Alan [South African author] **P:** 196
Patriarch [title] **P:** 196
  Abraham **A:** 16
  Jews (Beginnings) **J:** 120
  Mormons (Church organization) **M:** 807
Patriarch Militant [title]
  Odd Fellows, Independent Order of (Purpose and
    organization) **O:** 673
Patriarch of the West [title]
  Patriarch **P:** 196
Patriarchal cross [symbol]
  Cross *picture on* **Ci:** 1155
Patriarchal history
  Genesis **G:** 84
Patricians [ancient Rome] **P:** 196
  Plebeians **P:** 571
  Rome, Ancient (The Roman Republic) **R:** 438

Patrick, Danica [American race driver]
  Automobile racing (Automobile racing today)
    A: 980-981
Patrick, Deval L. [American political leader]
  Massachusetts (table) **M:** 288; (The early 2000's)
    M: 293
Patrick, Mason M. [American general]
  Patrick Air Force Base **P:** 197
Patrick, Saint [Irish religious leader] **P:** 197
  Ireland (Saint Patrick) **I:** 425
  Irish literature (Heroic tales, romances, and sagas)
    I: 430
Patrick Air Force Base [Florida] **P:** 197
Patrick Henry Before the Virginia House of
Burgesses [painting by Rothermel]
  Henry, Patrick *picture on* **H:** 190
Patrilineage
  Family (Non-Western families) **F:** 24
Patrimony [book by Roth]
  Roth, Philip **R:** 487
Patriot [missile]
  Guided missile (Surface-to-air missiles) **G:** 426
  Rocket *picture on* **R:** 386
Patriot Act [2001] **P:** 197
  Civil rights (The war on terrorism) **Ci:** 610
  September 11 terrorist attacks (Protecting the
    homeland) **S:** 310b
  United States, History of the (September 11
    terrorist attacks) **U:** 196d
  Wiretapping (Laws concerning wiretapping)
    W: 345
Patriotic Salvation Movement [Chadian rebel
  group]
  Chad (History) **C:** 367-368
Patriotism **P:** 197
  See also Nationalism *in this index*
Patriots, The [play by Kingsley]
  Kingsley, Sidney **K:** 331
Patroclus [legendary figure]
  Hector **H:** 164
  Iliad **I:** 51
Patrol [scouting]
  Boy Scouts (Boy Scouting) **B:** 535
  Girl Scouts (Guides) **G:** 199
Patrol boat
  Warship (Small combatants) **W:** 41
Patrol dog
  Police dog **P:** 626
Patrol Hydrofoil Missileship
  Hydrofoil *picture on* **H:** 466; (Modern hydrofoil
    development) **H:** 468
Patrol officer
  Police (Police activities) **P:** 620 *with pictures*
Patron [arts]
  Painting **P:** 28
Patron, Susan [American author]
  Newbery Medal (table) **N:** 359
Patronage [politics] **P:** 198
  City government (Administering city
    government) **Ci:** 596
  Graft **G:** 298
  Political party (National conventions and
    committees) **P:** 634-635
  President of the United States (Party head) **P:** 766
  Spoils system **So:** 798
Patrons of Husbandry *See* Grange, National *in*
  this index
Patroon system [U.S. history] **P:** 199
  New York (Exploration and settlement) **N:** 314
  Van Rensselaer, Kiliaen **V:** 284
Patsayev, Victor I. [Russian cosmonaut]
  Astronaut (table) **A:** 830; (Accidents in space)
    A: 830-831
  Space exploration (Salyut and Skylab) **So:** 721
Pattakos, Stylianos [Greek general]
  Greece (The restoration of democracy) **G:** 365
Pattern [design]
  Cast and casting (Patterns for casting) **C:** 278
  Interior design (Pattern and texture) **I:** 328 *with*
    picture; (Choosing patterns and textures) **I:** 332
    with picture
  Sewing (Preparing for a sewing project) **S:** 332
Pattern [psychology]
  Gestalt psychology **G:** 175
Pattern, Cultural
  Culture (Forming patterns) **Ci:** 1187
Patterson, Anne W. [American diplomat]
  United Nations (table) **U:** 86
Patterson, Haywood P. [American public figure]
  Scottsboro case **S:** 223
Patterson, I. L. [American political leader]
  Oregon (table) **O:** 845
Patterson, John M. [American political leader]
  Alabama (table) **A:** 274
Patterson, Malcolm R. [American political leader]
  Tennessee (table) **T:** 152
Patterson, Martha Johnson [daughter of]

  Johnson, Andrew (Life in the White House) **J:** 141
  White House hostesses **W:** 291
Patterson, Paul L. [American political leader]
  Oregon (table) **O:** 845
Patterson, Robert P. [American government
  official]
  Truman, Harry S. (table) **T:** 469
Patterson, Tom [Canadian journalist]
  Stratford Shakespeare Festival **So:** 920
Patteson, Okey L. [American political leader]
  West Virginia (table) **W:** 225
Pattison, Edward [American businessman]
  Connecticut (Colonial life) **Ci:** 968-970
Pattison, John M. [American political leader]
  Ohio (table) **O:** 699
Pattison, Robert Emory [American political leader]
  Pennsylvania (table) **P:** 263
Pattison, William [American businessman]
  Connecticut (Colonial life) **Ci:** 968-970
Patton [film]
  Motion picture (Best picture: 1970) **M:** 861
Patton, Elizabeth [wife of]
  Crockett, Davy (Early life) **Ci:** 1148d
Patton, George Smith, Jr. [American general]
  P: 199 *with portrait*
  Bradley, Omar Nelson **B:** 545
  World War II (D-Day) **W:** 483-484
Patton, John Mercer [American political leader]
  Virginia (table) **V:** 417
Patton, Robert Miller [American political leader]
  Alabama (table) **A:** 274
Pattullo, Thomas D. [Canadian political leader]
  British Columbia (table) **B:** 628
Patuxet Indians
  Thanksgiving Day (Plymouth Colony) **T:** 230
Paucituberculata [zoology]
  Mammal (table) **M:** 128 *with picture*
Paul [czar of Russia]
  Russia (table: Czars and empresses) **R:** 549;
    (Catherine the Great) **R:** 550
Paul [Yugoslav prince]
  Peter II **P:** 324
  Serbia (A new country) **S:** 314-315
  Yugoslavia (A new country) **Y:** 576
Paul I [king of Greece] **P:** 199
  Greece (World War II) **G:** 363-364
Paul III [pope] **P:** 199
  Pope (Renaissance and Reformation) **P:** 664 *with*
    picture
Paul IV [pope] **P:** 199
  Ghetto (Early ghettos) **G:** 181
  Index of Forbidden Books **I:** 107
Paul V [pope]
  Vatican City (Vatican Palace) **V:** 287
Paul VI [pope] **P:** 200 *with portrait*
  Birth control (Opposition to birth control) **B:** 379
  Eastern Orthodox Churches (History) **E:** 45-46
  Pope *picture on* **P:** 661; (The 1900's and 2000's)
    P: 665-667 *with picture*; (table) **P:** 666
  Protestantism (The ecumenical movement)
    P: 835-836
  Roman Catholic Church *picture on* **R:** 413; (Paul
    VI) **R:** 411
  Vatican Council II (The work of the council) **V:** 289
  Vulgate **V:** 453
Paul, Alice [American activist] **P:** 200 *with portrait*
  Equal Rights Amendment **E:** 345
  Woman suffrage (Growth of the movement)
    W: 380-381
Paul, Epistles of [New Testament]
  Jesus Christ (Other writings) **J:** 105
  Paul, Saint (Paul's letters and ideas) **P:** 201
Paul, Johnny [American magician]
  Magician (Close-up magic) **M:** 51
Paul, Les [American guitarist]
  Electric guitar **E:** 174
Paul, Lewis [British inventor]
  Industrial Revolution (Spinning machines)
    I: 248-249
Paul, Saint [Christian religious leader] **P:** 200 *with*
  map
  Acts of the Apostles **A:** 31
  Barnabas **B:** 113
  Bible (The Letters) **B:** 284
  Carolingian art *picture on* **C:** 245
  Colossians, Epistle to the **Ci:** 850
  Corinthians, Epistles to the **Ci:** 1053
  Galatians, Epistle to the **G:** 8
  Gamaliel **G:** 18
  Malta (History) **M:** 113
  Mark, Saint **M:** 213
  New Testament (Letters) **N:** 287 *with picture*;
    (Authorship) **N:** 288
  Philemon, Epistle to **P:** 368
  Roman Catholic Church (The first 300 years)
    R: 405
  Romans, Epistle to the **R:** 426

Timothy T: 292d
Titus T: 303
Paul, Samuel [American insurance agent]
Insurance (Greater regulation) I: 316
Paul, Wolfgang [German physicist]
Nobel Prizes (Physics: 1989) N: 442
Paul Bunyan See Bunyan, Paul *in this index*
Paul Clifford [book by Bulwer-Lytton]
Bulwer-Lytton, Edward George Earle Lytton
B: 698
Paul Revere and the World He Lived In [book by Forbes]
Forbes, Esther F: 369
"**Paul Revere's Ride**" [poem by Longfellow]
Longfellow, Henry Wadsworth (Narrative poems)
L: 450-451
Revere, Paul R: 268
Paul Taylor Dance Company
Taylor, Paul T: 57
Paul v. Virginia [1868]
Insurance (Greater regulation) I: 316
Paulding, James K. [American author]
Irving, Washington (Early career) I: 460
Van Buren, Martin (table) V: 273
Pauldron [armor]
Knights and knighthood (Armor) K: 350
Paulen, Ben S. [American political leader]
Kansas (table) K: 234
Pauli, Wolfgang [Austrian physicist] P: 201
Pauli exclusion principle [physics]
Pauli, Wolfgang P: 201
Pauline [poem by Browning]
Browning, Robert (Browning's poems) B: 646-647
Pauline letters [New Testament]
Bible (The Letters) B: 284
New Testament (Authorship) N: 288
Paul, Saint (Paul's letters and ideas) P: 201
Pauling, Linus Carl [American chemist] P: 202
Paulinus, Suetonius [Roman general]
Boudicca B: 515
Paulistanos [people]
São Paulo (People) S: 118
Paulists [religious group] P: 202
Paulos, Abune [Ethiopian religious leader]
Africa *picture on* A: 106
Paulsen, Gary [American author] P: 202
Regina Medal (table: 1995) R: 206
Paulson, Henry M., Jr. [American government official]
Treasury, Department of the (table) T: 407
Paulus, Friedrich von [German general]
Stalingrad, Battle of So: 828
World War II (The Battle of Stalingrad) W: 481
Paulus Hook [former name]
Jersey City (Government and history) J: 94
Pauncefote, Julian [British statesman]
Hay-Pauncefote Treaty H: 117
Paunch [zoology]
Ruminant R: 519 *with diagram*
Pauper children [British history]
Child labor (Early child labor laws) C: 455
Pausanias [Greek author]
Greek literature (The Greco-Roman Age) G: 378
Pausanias [king of Sparta]
Thirty Tyrants T: 259
Pausinystalia [tree]
Plant *picture on* P: 527
Pavarotti, Luciano [Italian singer] P: 202
Opera *picture on* O: 802
Pavelić, Ante [Croatian leader]
Yugoslavia (World War II) Y: 576
Pavement [building material]
Road (Paving) R: 359 *with picture*
Pavese, Cesare [Italian author]
Italian literature (The 1900's) I: 495
Pavillon d'Armide, Le [ballet]
Ballet *picture on* B: 53
Pavise [shield]
Shield S: 400
Pavlov, Ivan Petrovich [Russian physiologist]
P: 202
Behavior (Learning) B: 220
Education (How people learn) E: 86
Learning (Classical conditioning) L: 163
Nobel Prizes (Physiology or medicine: 1904)
N: 444 *with picture*
Psychology (Behaviorism) P: 849-850
Reflex action (Conditioned reflex) R: 195
Pavlova [food]
New Zealand (Food and drink) N: 348
Pavlova, Anna [Russian dancer] P: 202 *with picture*
Ballet (Ballet in Russia) B: 52 *with picture*
Paw [zoology]
Cat (Body size and structure) C: 286 *with picture*
Pawl [machine]
Ratchet R: 147
Pawlenty, Tim [American political leader]

Minnesota (table) M: 602
Pawley, Howard R. [Canadian political leader]
Manitoba (table) M: 159
Pawn
Chess (The board and the men) C: 411-412 *with diagram*
Pawnbroker [career] P: 202
Pawnee Indians P: 203
Nebraska (Early days) N: 111
Pawnee Tribal Business Council
Pawnee Indians P: 203
Pawpaw [tree] P: 203 *with picture*
Papaya P: 133
Pawtucket [Rhode Island] P: 204
Pax Lodge
Girl Scouts (In other countries) G: 199
Pax Romana [Roman Empire]
Peace (Ancient Greece and Rome) P: 206
Rome, Ancient (The Roman Empire) R: 446
Paxinou, Katina [Greek actress]
Motion picture (Best performance by an actress in a supporting role: 1943) M: 862b
Paxoi [island, Greece]
Ionian Islands I: 373 *with map*
Paxton, Sir Joseph [British architect]
Architecture (The Industrial Revolution) A: 625 *with picture*
Paxton Boys [U.S. history]
Westward movement in America (Regional conflict) W: 245
Pay-per-view television
Television (Cable and satellite systems) T: 115
Payens, Hugh [French knight]
Knights Templars K: 353
Payload
Balloon (Hot-air balloons) B: 57
Bomber B: 453
Rocket (Parts of a rocket) R: 385
Space exploration (table) So: 696
Payload specialist [astronaut]
Astronaut A: 828
Space exploration (The shuttle era begins) So: 723
Payment-in-kind
Wheat (Controlling wheat production) W: 274-275
Payne, David [American settler]
Oklahoma (Great land rushes) O: 732
Payne, Dolley [wife of James Madison] See Madison, Dolley Payne *in this index*
Payne, Frederick G. [American political leader]
Maine (table) M: 87
Payne, Henry C. [American government official]
Roosevelt, Theodore (table) R: 466
Payne, John B. [American government official]
Interior, Department of the (table) I: 325
Payne, John Howard [American author] P: 204
Payne-Aldrich Tariff Act [1909]
Taft, William Howard (Legislative defeats)
T: 10-11
Payne-Gaposchkin, Cecilia Helena [English astronomer] P: 204
Paynter, Samuel [American political leader]
Delaware (table) D: 109
Payola [bribery]
Rock music (Setbacks) R: 379
Payout rate [law]
Foundation F: 429
Payroll tax
Obama, Barack (Tax deal) O: 640h
Pension (Federal pension plans) P: 272-273
Social security (Financing Social Security) So: 555
Taxation (Income taxes) T: 53
Pays de la Sagouine, Le [village]
New Brunswick *picture on* N: 184
Payton, Walter [American football player] P: 204 *with picture*
Football *picture on* F: 367
Paz, Octavio [Mexican author] P: 205
Latin American literature (The mid-1900's) L: 114
Paz Estenssoro, Víctor [Bolivian political leader]
Bolivia (The Revolution of 1952) B: 447
Pazyryk rug
Rugs and carpets (History) R: 517
Pazzi Chapel [Florence, Italy]
Brunelleschi, Filippo B: 651
Renaissance *picture on* R: 235; (Arts of the 1300's and early 1400's) R: 236
PB [drug] See Pyridostigmine bromide *in this index*
PBA Tournament of Champions
Bowling (table) B: 524a
PBA World Championship
Bowling (table) B: 524a
PBGC [agency] See Pension Benefit Guaranty Corporation *in this index*
PBGV [dog] See Petit basset griffon vendéen *in this index*

PbO [chemistry]
Litharge L: 386
PBS [organization] See Public Broadcasting Service *in this index*
PBX [service]
Telephone (Business services) T: 98
PBX [switch] See Private branch exchange *in this index*
P.C. [abbreviation]
Privy Council P: 808b
PC [personal computer] See Personal computer *in this index*
PCB [chemical] See Polychlorinated biphenyl *in this index*
PCC [political party] See Partido Comunista de Cuba *in this index*
PCI [economics] See Per capita income *in this index*
PCP [drug]
Drug abuse (Hallucinogenic drugs) D: 362; (table: Some commonly abused drugs) D: 363
Hallucinogenic drug H: 26
PDA [computer] See Personal digital assistant *in this index*
PDA [disorder] See Patent ductus arteriosus *in this index*
PDG [political party]
Guinea (History) G: 432
Pe [letter]
P P: 1 *with picture*
Pea [plant] P: 205 *with pictures*
Flower (table) F: 301 *with picture*
Heredity (Patterns of heredity) H: 202
Leaf *picture on* L: 157
Lupine L: 526
Nutrition (Carbohydrates) N: 625
Vegetable (Seeds) V: 292 *with picture*
Pea comb [zoology]
Chicken (Kinds of chickens) C: 441 *with picture*
Pea crab [sea animal]
Crab *picture on* Ci: 1115
Pea Ridge, Battle of [1862]
Civil War, American (Battles of Fort Henry and Fort Donelson) Ci: 628-629
Pea Ridge National Military Park [Arkansas]
Arkansas (Places to visit) A: 704
National Park System (table: National military parks) N: 55
Peabody, Elizabeth P. [American educator]
Kindergarten (Early kindergartens) K: 319
Peabody, Endicott [American political leader]
Massachusetts (table) M: 288
Peabody, George [American philanthropist]
Foundation (History) F: 431
Museum (Early United States museums) M: 940
Peabody, James H. [American political leader]
Colorado (Interesting facts) Ci: 829; (table)
Ci: 844
Peabody, Sophia [wife of]
Hawthorne, Nathaniel (Life) H: 114
Peabody Fund
Foundation (History) F: 431
Peabody Museum of Natural History [New Haven, Connecticut]
Connecticut (Museums) Ci: 956
Yale University (The Yale campus) Y: 548-549
Peace P: 206
Balance of power B: 36
Human rights (Peacekeeping) H: 428a
International law (The laws of peace) I: 341
United Nations (Working for peace and security)
U: 89
War (How wars end) W: 24; (Preventing war)
W: 25
Peace, Breach of the [law]
Breach of the peace B: 587
Peace, Palace of
Hague, The H: 6
Peace and Plenty [painting by Inness]
Inness, George I: 274 *with picture*
Peace bond
Breach of the peace B: 587
Peace Bridge [New York-Ontario] P: 207
Buffalo (Economy) B: 677
Peace church, Historic [religious organization]
Brethren B: 593
Peace conferences
Hague, The (History) H: 7
International law (History) I: 342
International relations (International conferences and organizations) I: 344
Israel (The 1990's) I: 489 *with picture*
Palestine Liberation Organization (History)
P: 106-107
Peace (The 1800's and early 1900's) P: 206
Peace Corps [U.S.] P: 207 *with pictures*
Foreign aid (Economic development and mutual security) F: 383-384

Kennedy, John Fitzgerald (The New Frontier)
K: 264
Shriver, Sargent S: 440
USA Freedom Corps U: 229
Peace Democrats [U.S. history]
Civil War, American (Government and politics)
Ci: 622
Peace dollar [money]
Dollar *picture on* D: 295
Peace Garden, International [Manitoba-North
Dakota]
International Peace Garden I: 343
Manitoba (Places to visit) M: 152 *with picture*
Peace Garden State [nickname]
North Dakota N: 496
Peace Memorial Park
Hiroshima H: 243
Peace Mission Movement
Divine, Father D: 241
Peace of ...
*Peace agreements appear under their key words, as
in* Utrecht, Peace of
Peace of God [European history]
Peace (The Middle Ages) P: 206
Peace Palace
Hague, The H: 6
Peace pipe P: 209
Peace River [Canada] P: 209
British Columbia (The mid-1900's) B: 630
Mackenzie River M: 23
Peace River District [region, British Columbia]
British Columbia (Land regions) *picture on* B: 622
Peace Society, New York [organization]
Peace (The 1800's and early 1900's) P: 206
Peace Tower [memorial]
Ottawa (Metropolitan Ottawa) O: 871; (The
Parliament Buildings) O: 872
Peace treaty
Treaty (Kinds of treaties) T: 408-409
Peaceable Kingdom, The [paintings by Hicks]
Folk art *picture on* F: 316
Hicks, Edward H: 224
Peaceful coexistence [international relations]
Cold War (New challenges) Ci: 766; (The spirit of
Geneva) Ci: 766; (Easing Cold War tensions)
Ci: 769
Union of Soviet Socialist Republics (Khrushchev's
policies) U: 38
Peacekeeping forces [UN]
United Nations (Peacekeeping operations) U: 90
with pictures
Peach [fruit] P: 210 *with pictures*
Fruit (Simple fruits) F: 544 *with picture*
Nectarine N: 117
Peach leaf curl [fungus]
Peach (Diseases) P: 211
Peach moth [insect] P: 211 *with picture*
Peach State [nickname]
Georgia G: 112
Peach twig borer [insect]
Peach (Insects) P: 211
Peachtree Center
Atlanta (The city) A: 859 *with picture*
Peacock [bird] P: 211 *with picture*
Evolution *picture on* E: 428
Peacock fly [insect]
Fruit fly F: 549
Peacock Throne [Iranian history]
Iran (The rule of Nadir Shah) I: 406
Peafowl [bird] *See* Peacock *in this index*
Peahen [bird]
Peacock P: 211
Peak flow meter [instrument]
Asthma A: 825
Peake, James B. [American government official]
Bush, George Walker (table) B: 722h
Veterans Affairs, Department of (table) V: 343
Peale [American painters] P: 212 *with picture*
Peale, Charles Willson [American painter]
Peale P: 212 *with picture*
Lafayette, Marquis de *picture on* L: 27
Lewis and Clark expedition *pictures on* L: 222a
Museum (Early United States museums) M: 939
Peale, James [American painter]
Peale P: 212
Peale, Norman Vincent [American religious leader]
P: 213
Peale, Raphaelle [American painter]
Peale P: 212
Peale, Rembrandt [American painter]
Peale P: 212
Peale, Sarah Miriam [American painter]
Peale P: 212
Peale, Titian [American naturalist]
Wake Island W: 6
Peale Islet [Pacific Ocean]
Wake Island W: 5

Peanut P: 213 *with pictures*
Carver, George Washington C: 268
Nigeria *picture on* N: 410
Nut (Kinds of nuts) N: 621
Peanut bread
Peanut (As food) P: 214
Peanut butter
Peanut (As food) P: 213
Peanut oil
Peanut (As food) P: 213-214; (Processing
peanuts) P: 214-215
Vegetable oil V: 294
"Peanuts" [comic strip]
Schulz, Charles Monroe S: 187 *with picture*
Pear [fruit] P: 215 *with picture*
Fruit (Simple fruits) F: 544 *with picture*
Pear cut
Gem (Types of gem cuts) *picture on* G: 79
Pear-leaf blister mite [insect]
Pear (Diseases and pests) P: 216
Pear psylla [insect]
Pear (Diseases and pests) P: 216
Pearl [gem] P: 216 *with pictures*
Gem *picture on* G: 78; (Value of gems) G: 79
Oyster (Shell) O: 890 *with picture*
Pearl [poem]
English literature (The age of Chaucer) E: 316
Pearl essence [animal product]
Pearl (Imitation pearls) P: 218
Pearl Fishers, The [opera by Bizet]
Bizet, Georges B: 385
Pearl Harbor [Hawaii] P: 218 *with picture*
Hawaii (Places to visit) H: 98; (Oahu) H: 102;
(Growth of constitutional government)
H: 106-108
Honolulu (History) H: 322
Roosevelt, Franklin Delano (Pearl Harbor) R: 456
World War II *picture on* W: 493; (Japan attacks)
W: 479 *with picture*
Yamamoto, Isoroku Y: 550
Pearl Harbor Naval Complex
Pearl Harbor (Pearl Harbor as a naval base) P: 219
Pearl Jam [rock group]
Rock music (Alternative rock) R: 381
Pearl millet [grain]
Millet M: 555
Pearl of Great Price [book by Smith]
Mormons (Church doctrines and ordinances)
M: 806
Pearl of the Orient [nickname]
Manila M: 141
Pearl popcorn
Corn (Popcorn) Ci: 1059
Pearleaf blister mite [animal]
Mite M: 678 *with picture*
Pearled barley [food]
Barley (Uses of barley) B: 113
Pearly eye [butterfly]
Butterfly *picture on* B: 735
Pearly-eyed thrasher [bird]
Thrasher T: 269
Pearly nautilus [sea animal]
Nautilus N: 69 *with picture*
Shell (Octopuses and squids) S: 388
Pearse, Patrick H. [Irish political leader]
Ireland (The Easter Rising) I: 427
Pearson, Annie Sarah [mother of]
Pearson, Lester Bowles (Boyhood) P: 220
Pearson, David [American race driver]
Automobile racing (table: NASCAR Sprint Cup
champions) A: 981
Pearson, Edwin Arthur [father of]
Pearson, Lester Bowles (Boyhood) P: 220
Pearson, Egon [English statistician]
Statistics (History) So: 869-870
Pearson, Geoffrey Arthur Holland [son of]
Pearson, Lester Bowles (Education and war
service) P: 220-221
Pearson, Grant [American mountain climber]
Mount McKinley M: 886
Pearson, Karl [British geneticist] P: 219
Pearson, Lester Bowles [Canadian political leader]
P: 220 *with picture*
Canada, History of (Increasing foreign
involvement) C: 149
Chrétien, Jean (Early posts) C: 522b
Diefenbaker, John George D: 196 *with portrait*;
(Nuclear controversy) D: 198
Nobel Prizes (Peace: 1957) N: 448b *with portrait*
Trudeau, Pierre Elliott (Parliamentary secretary)
T: 463
Pearson, Marmaduke [brother of]
Pearson, Lester Bowles (Boyhood) P: 220
Pearson, Maryon Moody [wife of]
Pearson, Lester Bowles *picture on* P: 223;
(Education and war service) P: 220-221
Pearson, Patricia Lillian [daughter of]

Pearson, Lester Bowles (Education and war
service) P: 220-221
Pearson, Vaughan [brother of]
Pearson, Lester Bowles (Boyhood) P: 220
Pearson, Vera [American pioneer]
Western frontier life in America (Education)
W: 239
Peary, Robert Edwin [American explorer] P: 224
with picture
Arctic (Race to the pole) A: 639
Bartlett, Robert Abram B: 121
Cape York C: 191
Exploration (The North Pole) E: 450 *with map*
Henson, Matthew Alexander H: 191
North Pole N: 517
Peary Arctic Club
Peary, Robert Edwin (Arctic expeditions) P: 224
Peasant [people]
See also Serf *in this index*
Middle Ages (Life of the people) M: 526
Russia (Ivan the Terrible) R: 548; (Alexander III)
R: 551
Union of Soviet Socialist Republics (History) U: 35
Peasant Unity Committee
Menchú, Rigoberta M: 397
Peasants' Crusade
Crusades (The First Crusade) Ci: 1160
Peasants' Revolt [English history] *See* Wat Tyler's
Rebellion *in this index*
Peasants' War [1524-1525] P: 224
Germany (The Reformation) G: 164
Pease, Elisha M. [American political leader]
Texas (table) T: 203
Pease, Howard [American author] P: 225
Peasecod [fashion]
Clothing (The Renaissance) Ci: 702 *with picture*
Peat [fuel] P: 225 *with picture*
Coal (How coal was formed) Ci: 720 *with
diagrams*
Fuel (Solid fuels) F: 550
Heath H: 157
Peat bog
Ireland (Surface features) I: 422
Mummy (Other mummies) M: 926
Peat P: 225 *with picture*
"Peat Bog Soldiers" [song]
Folk music (Kinds of folk music) F: 321
Peat moss [plant] P: 225 *with picture*
Bog B: 436 *with diagram*
Moss M: 834 *with picture*; (The importance of
mosses) M: 835
Peatland [area]
Wetland (Water and soil) W: 252a; (Marshes and
wet meadows) W: 252b
Peattie, Donald Culross [American author] P: 225
Peay, Austin [American political leader]
Tennessee (table) T: 152
Pebble Jackstones [game]
Jacks J: 4
Pebble mill [machine]
Paint (Grinding) P: 24-25
Pebrine [disease]
Pasteur, Louis (His work in industry) P: 193
Pecan [tree] P: 225 *with pictures*
Hickory H: 224
Nut (Kinds of nuts) N: 621 *with picture*
Tree *pictures on* T: 423
Peccary [animal] P: 226 *with picture*
Hog (Wild hogs) H: 286
Péchés de vieillesse [music by Rossini]
Rossini, Gioacchino Antonio R: 484
Pechorin [literary figure]
Russian literature (Late Romanticism) R: 561-562
Peck [unit of measure] P: 226
Peck, Asahel [American political leader]
Vermont (table) V: 333
Peck, George W. [American political leader]
Wisconsin (table) W: 365
Peck, Gregory [American actor]
Motion picture (Best performance by an actor:
1962) M: 862a
Peck, James [American jurist]
Impeachment (History) I: 91
Peck, Richard [American author] P: 226
Newbery Medal (table) N: 359
Peckham, Rufus W. [American jurist] P: 227
Pecking order [psychology] *See* Dominance *in
this index*
Pecksniff [literary figure]
Dickens, Charles (The first phase) D: 188
Pecos Bill [legendary figure] P: 227
Pecos National Historical Park [New Mexico]
P: 227
National Park System (table: National historical
parks) N: 56-57
New Mexico (Places to visit) N: 264
Pecos River [river, New Mexico-Texas] P: 227

New Mexico (Land regions) N: 266-268
Pécs [Hungary] P: 227
Pectin [carbohydrate] P: 227
Fat substitute F: 53
Jelly and jam J: 89
Pectoral fin [zoology]
Fish (Fins) F: 160-161 *with picture*
Pectoral girdle [zoology]
Frog *picture on* F: 537
Peculiar galaxy [astronomy]
Galaxy (Other types of galaxies) G: 8b
Peculiar Penguins [cartoon by Disney]
Disney, Walt *picture on* D: 236
Ped [soil]
Soil (Structure) So: 575
Pedal
Organ (Pipe organs) O: 851-852 *with picture*
Piano (The pedals) P: 446-447 *with picture*
Peddler
Sales (The Industrial Revolution) S: 64 *with picture*
Salesmanship (Early sales efforts) S: 64 *with picture*
Pedersen, Charles John [American chemist]
Nobel Prizes (Chemistry: 1987) N: 444
Pedestal
Harp H: 65 *with picture*
Pedestrian [traffic]
Safety (Pedestrian safety) S: 14
Pediatric cancer [disease]
Cancer (Cancer in children) C: 169
Pediatric dentistry
Dentistry (Pediatric dentistry) D: 144
Pediatric intensive care unit [medicine]
Intensive care unit I: 321
Pediatrician [career]
Pediatrics P: 227
Pediatrics [medicine] P: 227
Baby B: 4
Hospital (Hospital units) H: 372
Medicine (table) M: 369
Pedicab [vehicle] P: 228 *with picture*
Asia (Transportation) A: 803
Bangladesh *picture on* B: 80
Pedicel [biology]
See also Waist *in this index*
Raceme R: 51
Spider (The spider's body) So: 783-784 *with picture*
Pedigree [ancestry] P: 228
Pedigree chart [ancestry]
Genealogy G: 82
Pedigree line [agriculture]
Pedigree P: 228
Pediment [architecture]
Architecture (table) A: 608-609 *with picture*
Pedipalp [zoology]
Spider (Pedipalpi) So: 785 *with pictures*
Pediveliger [zoology]
Oyster (Youn) O: 891
Pedodontics
Dentistry (Pediatric dentistry) D: 144
Pedometer [instrument] P: 228
Pedophilia [disorder]
Child abuse C: 454
Pedrarias Dávila [Spanish colonial official]
Balboa, Vasco Núñez de (Later exploration) B: 38
Latin America (The conquest of the American Indians) L: 103
Pedro I [emperor of Brazil] P: 228
Andrada e Silva, José Bonifácio de A: 455
Brazil (Independence) B: 584 *with picture*
Latin America (The movement toward independence) L: 106-107
Lisbon *picture on* L: 348
Pedro II [emperor of Brazil] P: 228
Andrada e Silva, José Bonifácio de A: 455
Bell, Alexander Graham (The telephone) B: 241
Brazil (The reign of Pedro II) B: 584
Pedro IV [king of Portugal] *See* Pedro I *in this index*
Pedro, Felix [American prospector]
Fairbanks F: 9
Pedro Miguel Locks [Panama Canal]
Panama Canal *map on* P: 123; (The Pedro Miguel and Miraflores locks) P: 124 *with diagram*
Pedro Páramo [book by Rulfo]
Latin American literature (The mid-1900's) L: 114
Peduncle [botany]
Raceme R: 51
Pee Dee River [United States]
South Carolina (Rivers, waterfalls, and lakes) So: 652-654 *with map*
Peel, Lady [British actress]
Lillie, Beatrice L: 303 *with portrait*
Peel, Sir Robert [British political leader] P: 228 *with portrait*
Conservative Party Ci: 992

Police (Early law enforcement in England) P: 624
Scotland Yard S: 221
United Kingdom (Establishment of free trade) U: 69
Wellington, Duke of (Political career) W: 195
Peele, George [English dramatist]
Shakespeare, William: (*Titus Andronicus*) S: 356
Peeler [British history]
Peel, Sir Robert P: 229
Peeling the Onion [book by Grass]
Grass, Günter G: 326
Peelites [British history]
United Kingdom (Political confusion) U: 69
Peeping Tom [legend]
Godiva, Lady D: 245
Peer, Ralph [American record producer]
Country music (Early commercial success) Ci: 1098b
Rodgers, Jimmie R: 398
Peer group [sociology]
Adolescent (The "invention" of adolescence) A: 60 *with pictures*; (Relationships with peers) A: 62
Child (The preteen-age years) C: 450
Sexuality (Peer groups) S: 338a
Peer Gynt [music by Grieg]
Grieg, Edvard G: 392
Peer Gynt [play by Ibsen]
Grieg, Edvard G: 392
Ibsen, Henrik (His plays) I: 4
Theater *picture on* T: 247
Peer pressure [sociology]
Adolescent (The "invention" of adolescence) A: 60; (Independence and responsibility) A: 62
Peer review organization
Hospital H: 371
Peer-to-peer network
Computer (Personal computers) Ci: 909
Internet (File sharing) I: 350a
Peerage [nobility]
House of Lords H: 384
Nobility (In the United Kingdom) N: 450
Parliament (The House of Lords) P: 173
United Kingdom (National government) U: 49-50
Peerce, Jan [American singer] P: 229
Peeress [nobility]
Nobility (In the United Kingdom) N: 450
Peery, George C. [American political leader]
Virginia (table) V: 417
Peewit [bird]
Lapwing L: 75
Peg [botany]
Peanut (The peanut plant) P: 213-214
Pegasus [Greek mythology] P: 229 *with picture*
Chimera C: 471
Horse (table: Famous horses in history and legend) H: 361
Medusa M: 383
Pegasus [ship]
Missile boat M: 618
Pegging [economics]
Exchange rate E: 436
Peggy Stewart [ship]
Maryland (The Revolutionary War) M: 258
Peggy's Cove [Nova Scotia]
Nova Scotia *picture on* N: 554
Pegmatite [rock]
Feldspar F: 68
Gem (Sources of gems) G: 77-79
Rock (Intrusive rocks) R: 371-372
Tourmaline T: 350
Pegnitz Junction, The [book by Gallant]
Gallant, Mavis G: 14
Pégoud, Adolphe [French aviator]
Airplane (Other pioneer planes and fliers) A: 233-234
Pegwooden doll
Doll (Wooden dolls) D: 289
Pehm, Joseph [birth name of]
Mindszenty, József M: 563
Pei, I. M. [American architect] P: 230 *with picture*
National Gallery of Art N: 36 *with picture*
Paris *picture on* P: 164
Rock and Roll Hall of Fame and Museum R: 375
P.E.I. Preserve Company
Prince Edward Island (Places to visit) P: 788
Peipus, Lake [Estonia-Russia]
Estonia (Land and climate) E: 361 *with map*
Lake Peipus L: 44
Peirce, Charles Sanders [American philosopher] P: 230
James, William J: 27
Pragmatism P: 729
Peking [China] *See* Beijing *in this index*
Peking fossils [anthropology] P: 230
Black, Davidson B: 385
Prehistoric people (table) P: 754
Teilhard de Chardin, Pierre T: 88

Peking opera *See* Beijing opera *in this index*
Pekingese [dog] P: 230
Dog *picture on* D: 274
Pekoe [tea]
Tea (Grades of tea) T: 62-63
Pelagic fish
Fishing industry (Nets) F: 183
Pelagius I [pope]
Pope (table) P: 666
Pelagius II [pope]
Pope (table) P: 666
Pele [Polynesian goddess]
Mythology *picture on* M: 983
Pelé [Brazilian soccer player] P: 231
Pelée, Mount *See* Mount Pelée *in this index*
Peleliu [island, Pacific]
World War II (Island hopping in the Central Pacific) W: 489-490
Peleus [Greek mythology]
Achilles A: 26
Pelham [book by Bulwer-Lytton]
Bulwer-Lytton, Edward George Earle Lytton B: 698
Pelham, Henry [British political leader]
United Kingdom (table: British prime ministers) U: 72
Pelham bridle [riding equipment]
Horse (The bridle) H: 352
Pelias [Greek mythology]
Jason J: 64
Pelican [bird] P: 231 *with picture*
Bird *picture on* B: 328; (Birds of the seacoasts) B: 342 *with picture*
Pelican [ship]
Drake, Sir Francis (Voyage around the world) D: 321
Pelican Brief, The [book by Grisham]
Grisham, John G: 396
Pelican eel
Fish *picture on* F: 156
Pelican eel [fish]
Deep sea (Fish) D: 82b-82c *with picture*
Pelican flower [plant] P: 232
Pelican Island [Florida]
Florida (Interesting facts about Florida) F: 243
Pelican (Pelicans and people) P: 231
Wildlife conservation (History) W: 304-305
Pelican State [nickname]
Louisiana L: 478
Péligot, Eugène [French chemist]
Uranium U: 214
Pellagra [disease] P: 232
Goldberger, Joseph G: 255
Nutrition (Deficiency diseases) N: 630-631
Vitamin (Niacin) V: 431
Pelléas and Mélisande [opera by Debussy]
Debussy, Claude D: 66
Pelléas and Mélisande [play by Maeterlinck]
Maeterlinck, Maurice M: 41
Pellegrina, La
Gem (Some famous gems) G: 79
Pelles [English legend]
Holy Grail (Early history of the Grail) H: 299; (The search for the Grail) H: 299
Pellet [zoology]
Hawk H: 111
Pelletier, David [Canadian athlete]
Olympic Games (The recent games) O: 753-754
Pelletier, Gerard [Canadian diplomat]
United Nations (table) U: 86
Pellier, Louis [French farmer]
Prune P: 841
Pelly River [Yukon Territory]
Yukon River (The course of the Yukon) Y: 581 *with map*
Pelopidas [Greek general] P: 232
Boeotia B: 436
Pelopion [ancient Greece]
Olympia O: 745
Peloponnesian League [ancient Greece]
Arcadia A: 593
Peloponnesian War P: 232
Sparta (History) So: 766
Peloponnesian War [431-404 B.C.] P: 232
Alcibiades A: 334
Greece, Ancient (The rivalry between Athens and Sparta) G: 373 *with maps*
Pericles (War with Sparta) P: 287
Sparta (History) So: 766
Thebes T: 251
Thucydides T: 271
War (Struggles over power) W: 23-24
Peloponnesus [region, Greece] P: 232
Achaeans A: 25
Arcadia A: 593
Greece (The Peloponnesus) G: 358 *with map*
Messenia M: 423 *with map*

Pelops [Greek mythology]
Tantalus **T: 29**
Pelorus [instrument]
Navigation (Piloting) **N: 70-71**
Pelos [hat]
Hat (History) **H: 84**
Pelosi, Nancy [American political leader] **P: 232** *with portrait*
Democratic Party (The early 2000's) **D: 128** *with picture*
Pelosi, Paul F. [American businessman]
Pelosi, Nancy **P: 232**
Pelota [ball]
Jai alai **J: 21** *with picture*
Pel's fishing-owl [bird]
Owl (Important owls) **O: 884-886**
Pelt
Fur **F: 561**, *pictures on* **F: 563**
Fur trade **F: 564**
Peltier, J. C. A. [French physicist]
Thermocouple **T: 253**
Pelton, Lester A. [English inventor]
Turbine (History) **T: 498-499**
Pelton wheel
Turbine (Water turbines) **T: 496** *with pictures*
Pelvic fin [zoology]
Fish (Fins) **F: 160-161** *with picture*
Pelvic girdle [anatomy]
Skeleton (The appendicular skeleton) **S: 480** *with diagram*
Pelvic inflammatory disease P: 232
Chlamydia **C: 516**
Gonorrhea **G: 268**
Pelvic peritoneum [anatomy]
Pelvic inflammatory disease **P: 232**
Pelvis [anatomy] **P: 233** *with diagram*
Skeleton (The axial skeleton) **S: 479-480** *with diagrams*
Pelvis layer [anatomy]
Kidney (How the kidneys produce urine) **K: 311** *with diagram*
PEM fuel cell [device]
Fuel cell (A common fuel cell) **F: 551**
Pemadumcook Lake [Maine]
Penobscot River **P: 271**
Pemaquid Indians
Samoset **S: 80b**
Pemba Island [Tanzania]
Tanzania (The coastal lowlands and islands) **T: 32-33** *with map*
Zanzibar **Z: 586**
Pemberton, John Stith [American pharmacist]
Coca-Cola Company **Ci: 742**
Pembina
North Dakota (Exploration and early settlement) **N: 513-514**
Pembina Hills [North Dakota]
North Dakota (Land regions) **N: 506**
Pembroke Welsh corgi [dog] **P: 233**
Dog *picture on* **D: 276**
Pemigewasset River
New Hampshire (Rivers and lakes) **N: 220** *with map*
Pemmican [food] **P: 233**
Indian, American (Food) **I: 136d**
Pemmican Proclamation [Canadian history]
Manitoba (The Red River Colony) **M: 160**
Pen [bird]
Swan **So: 1016**
Pen [tool] **P: 233** *with pictures*
Ink (Writing inks) **I: 273**
Pen and ink drawing
Drawing *picture on* **D: 344**
Pen-based computer
Computer (A touch screen) **Ci: 914-915**
Handheld computer **H: 45**
Pen housing [agriculture]
Dairying (Housing) **D: 7**
Pen name P: 234
Name (Pseudonyms) **N: 7**
Pen pal
Letter writing (Other personal letters) **L: 213**
Peña, Federico Fabian [American government official] **P: 235**
Peña Nieto, Enqique [Mexican political leader]
Mexico (Recent developments) **M: 474-475**
Penacook [former name]
Concord [New Hampshire] **Ci: 929**
Penaeid [shrimp]
Shrimp (The life of a shrimp) **S: 440**
Penal colony [punishment] **P: 235**
Australia (History) **A: 919-920**
French Guiana **F: 514**
Queensland (History) **Q: 40**
Sydney (History) **So: 1064**
Penal Laws [British history]
Great Irish Famine **G: 343**

Penalty [sports]
Basketball (Fouls) **B: 147-148**
Football *pictures on* **F: 361**; (Violations and penalties) **F: 363**
Hockey (Violations and penalties) **H: 278** *with pictures*
Penalty area [sports]
Soccer (The field) **So: 544**
Penalty box [hockey]
Hockey (The rink) **H: 274-275**
Penalty goal
Rugby football (Scoring) **R: 510**
Penalty kick [sports]
Rugby football (Rugby Union) **R: 510**; (Rugby League) **R: 512**
Soccer (How soccer is played) **So: 545**; (Fouls) **So: 546**
Penalty killer [hockey]
Hockey (Defensive play) **H: 278**
Penalty privilege [mail]
Franking and penalty privileges **F: 485**
Penalty shot [hockey]
Hockey (Violations and penalties) **H: 278**
Penalty signal [football]
Football *pictures on* **F: 361**
Penalty spot [soccer]
Soccer (Fouls) **So: 546**
Penalty throw [water polo]
Water polo **W: 139**
Penan [people]
Rain forest (Asia) **R: 126b**
Penance [religion]
Christianity (Sacraments) **C: 522h**
Easter (Religious observances of Easter) **E: 42**
Eastern Orthodox Churches (Sacraments) **E: 46-47**
Roman Catholic Church (Worship) **R: 403-404**
Penang [state, Malaysia]
George Town **G: 109**
Malaysia (Coming of the Europeans) **M: 101**
Penates [Roman mythology] *See* Lares and penates *in this index*
Pencak silat [sport]
Indonesia (Recreation) **I: 232**
Malaysia (Recreation) **M: 98d**
Martial arts (Martial arts in other countries) **M: 234a**
Pence [money]
Money (History of the pound) **M: 709**
Penny **P: 271**
Pencil P: 235 *with pictures*
Eraser **E: 349**
Faber, Eberhard **F: 2**
Graphite **G: 323**
Pencil of Nature, The [book by Talbot]
Talbotype **T: 19**
Pend Oreille Lake [Idaho]
Idaho (Rivers, waterfalls, springs, and lakes) **I: 38**
Pendarvis [house]
Wisconsin (Places to visit) **W: 356**
Pendennis [book by Thackeray]
Thackeray, William Makepeace (Later career) **T: 220**
Pendentive [architecture]
Architecture (table) **A: 608-609** *with picture*; (Byzantine architecture) **A: 617**
Penderecki, Krzysztof [Polish composer] **P: 236**
Pendergast, James [American political leader]
Pendergast, Thomas Joseph **P: 236**
Pendergast, Thomas Joseph [American political leader] **P: 236**
Kansas City [Missouri] (History) **K: 242-243**
Truman, Harry S. (Political career) **T: 467-468**
Pendleton, George Hunt [American political leader] **P: 237**
Civil service (History) **Ci: 613**
Lincoln, Abraham (Election of 1864) **L: 323-324**
Pendleton, Joseph H. [American general]
Camp Pendleton **C: 90**
Pendleton Civil Service Act *See* Civil Service Act [1883] *in this index*
Pendulum P: 237 *with diagrams*
Clock (Mechanical clocks) **Ci: 682j** *with pictures*
Foucault, Jean Bernard Léon **F: 429**
Galileo (Mature scientific career) **G: 11**
Metronome **M: 442** *with picture*
Science *picture on* **S: 199**
Time (Clocks that count repeated actions) **T: 289**
Pendulum dial scale
Scale, Weighing (Mechanical scales) **S: 169**
Penelope [legendary figure] **P: 238**
Odyssey: (Odysseus returns home) **O: 675**
Ulysses (The Trojan War) **U: 17-18**; (Return to Ithaca) **U: 18**
Penetrator [ammunition]
Ammunition **A: 435**
Penetrator [space probe]

Space exploration (Space probes) **So: 708**
P'eng-hu [islands] *See* Pescadores *in this index*
Pengrowth Saddledome [arena]
Calgary (History) **C: 34**
Penguin [bird] **P: 238** *with pictures*
See also Emperor penguin; King penguin *in this index*
Animal *pictures on* **A: 484, A: 499**
Antarctica (Living things) **A: 534-535** *with picture*
Auk **A: 890**
Bird (Birds of the ocean and the Antarctic) **B: 344** *with picture*
Penguin [boat]
Sailing (Catboats and sloops) **S: 24**
Penguin Books
Book (Modern books) **B: 468**
Penguin Island [book by France]
France, Anatole **F: 480**
Penguins, Pittsburgh [team]
Hockey (table: National Hockey League) **H: 281**
Penicillin [drug] **P: 240** *with pictures*
Ampicillin **A: 443**
Antibiotic (Prevention of cell wall formation) **A: 550**; (Allergic reactions) **A: 551**; (History) **A: 552** *with picture*
Cephalosporin **C: 359**
Chemotherapy **C: 407**
Erythromycin **E: 356**
Fleming, Sir Alexander **F: 232**
Fungi (The importance of fungi) **F: 559-560**
Medicine (The medical revolution) **M: 376** *with picture*
Tyndall, John **T: 536**
Penicillin G [drug]
Antibiotic (table) **A: 551**
Penicillin (Early history) **P: 240**; (Forms of penicillin) **P: 240**
Penicillin V [drug]
Penicillin (Forms of penicillin) **P: 240**
Penicillium [mold]
Fungi (The importance of fungi) **F: 559-560** *with picture*
Medicine (The medical revolution) **M: 376** *with picture*
Penicillin (Forms of penicillin) **P: 240** *with picture*
Penicillium notatum [mold]
Fleming, Sir Alexander **F: 232**
Peninsula [geography] **P: 241** *with map*
Peninsula brown bear
Bear (Brown bears) **B: 184**
Peninsular Campaign [1862]
Civil War, American (The peninsular campaign) **Ci: 626**
McClellan, George Brinton (Military career) **M: 332c**
Peninsular Malaysia [region]
Malaysia **M: 98a** *with pictures and map*; (Land and climate) **M: 99**
Peninsular Ranges [mountains, Mexico-U.S.]
California (The Peninsular Ranges) **C: 50**
Peninsular War [1808-1814]
Continental System **Ci: 1023**
Guerrilla warfare **G: 419**
Napoleon I (The Peninsular War) **N: 15**
Napoleonic Wars (The Peninsular War) **N: 18** *with map*
Spain (French conquest) **So: 748**
Wellington, Duke of (Peninsular War) **W: 194**
Peninsulares [Mexican history]
Mexico (Spanish rule) **M: 469-470**
Penis [anatomy] **P: 241**
Circumcision **Ci: 561**
Condom **Ci: 929**
Erectile dysfunction **E: 349**
Human body (The reproductive system) **H: 425**
Reproduction, Human (The human reproductive system) **R: 244-245** *with diagram*
Sexuality (Biological factors) **S: 337**
Penitentiary
Prison (Types of correctional institutions) **P: 805**; (Early prison reform) **P: 807**
Penmanship
Handwriting **H: 46** *with pictures*; (The 1900's) **H: 50**
Penn, John [American patriot] **P: 241**
Penn, Sean [American actor/director] **P: 241**
Motion picture (Best performance by an actor: 2003, 2008) **M: 862a**
Penn, Sir William [father of]
Penn, William (Youthful rebel) **P: 241-242**
Penn, William [American colonial leader] **P: 241** *with pictures*
Delaware (English rule) **D: 110**
Peace (From the 1400's to the 1700's) **P: 206**
Pennsylvania *picture on* **P: 266**; (Colonial days) **P: 264**; (Exploration and settlement) **P: 264**
Philadelphia **P: 358**; (Early colonial days) **P: 365**

with picture
Quakers (History) **Q**: 5
Treaty *picture on* **T**: 408
United States, History of the (The Middle
 Colonies) **U**: 154-155 *with picture*
Penn Hills [suburb]
 Pittsburgh (The metropolitan area) **P**: 500b
Penn State *See* Pennsylvania State University *in
 this index*
Penn Station
 New York City (Transportation) **N**: 334-335
Pennant [baseball]
 Baseball (Play-offs) **B**: 130
Pennant [flag]
 Flag (table) **F**: 193
Pennell, Joseph [American artist] **P**: 243
Pennewill, Simeon S. [American political leader]
 Delaware (table) **D**: 109
Penney, James Cash [American businessman]
 P: 243
Penney Foundation
 Penney, James Cash **P**: 243
Pennine Alps [mountains, Switzerland]
 Switzerland (The Swiss Alps) **So**: 1055-1056
Pennine Chain [uplands, England] *See* Pennines
 in this index
Pennine Hills [uplands, England] *See* Pennines *in
 this index*
Pennines [uplands, England] **P**: 243
 England (The Pennines) **E**: 300 *with picture and
 map*
 United Kingdom (The Pennines) **U**: 59 *with map*
Pennington, William [American political leader]
 New Jersey (table) **N**: 249
Pennington, William S. [American political leader]
 New Jersey (table) **N**: 249
Pennock, Herb [American baseball player]
 Baseball (Hall of Fame) **B**: 134a
Pennoyer, Sylvester [American political leader]
 Oregon (table) **O**: 845
Penn's Treaty with the Indians [painting by West]
 United States, History of the *picture on* **U**: 154
 West, Benjamin **W**: 198
Pennsylvania P: 244 *with pictures and maps*
 Coal *picture on* **Ci**: 731
 Colonial life in America (Development of the
 Thirteen Colonies) **Ci**: 790 *with map*
 Penn, William **P**: 241
 Pennsylvania Dutch **P**: 270
 Quakers (History) **Q**: 5
 September 11 terrorist attacks **S**: 310
 United States, History of the (The Middle
 Colonies) **U**: 154-155
 Whiskey rebellion **W**: 282
Pennsylvania, Bank of [Philadelphia]
 Latrobe, Benjamin Henry **L**: 118
Pennsylvania, University of P: 269 *with picture*
 Franklin, Benjamin (Civic leader) **F**: 487-488
 Pennsylvania *picture on* **P**: 248
 Universities and colleges (The oldest U.S.
 universities and colleges) **U**: 210
Pennsylvania Academy of the Fine Arts
 [Philadelphia]
 Pennsylvania (Museums) **P**: 248
 Philadelphia (Education) **P**: 362; (Libraries and
 museums) **P**: 363-364
Pennsylvania Avenue
 Pennsylvania Avenue National Historic Site **P**: 270
 Washington, D.C. *pictures on* **W**: 84, **W**: 87; (North
 of the Mall) **W**: 74
Pennsylvania Avenue National Historic Site
 [Washington, D. C.] **P**: 270
 National Park System (table: National historic
 sites) **N**: 52-53
Pennsylvania Canal
 Pennsylvania (Industrial growth) **P**: 267
Pennsylvania Chronicle, The [newspaper]
 Goddard, Mary Katherine **G**: 244
 Goddard, William **G**: 245
Pennsylvania Dutch [people] **P**: 270 *with picture*
 Amish **A**: 433
 Folk art (Folk art collections) **F**: 319
 Folklore *picture on* **F**: 323
 Lancaster **L**: 55
 Mennonites **M**: 401
 Pennsylvania **P**: 244; (People) **P**: 248
Pennsylvania firefly [insect]
 Beetle *picture on* **B**: 218
Pennsylvania Fiscal Agency
 Credit Mobilier of America **Ci**: 1125
Pennsylvania Gazette [newspaper]
 Franklin, Benjamin (Printer) **F**: 487
 Philadelphia (Communication) **P**: 365
Pennsylvania Hospital [Philadelphia]
 Franklin, Benjamin (Civic leader) **F**: 487-488
 Hospital (Early hospitals) **H**: 373
Pennsylvania Journal [newspaper]

Bradford, William, III **B**: 544
Pennsylvania Prison Society
 Prison (Early prison reform) **P**: 807
Pennsylvania Railroad
 Railroad (Expansion in the United States) **R**: 115
Pennsylvania rifle [gun]
 Pennsylvania Dutch **P**: 270
Pennsylvania State University P: 271 *with picture*
Pennsylvania Station [New York City]
 New York City (Transportation) **N**: 334-335
Pennsylvania System
 Prison (Early prison reform) **P**: 807
Pennsylvania Turnpike [road] **P**: 271
 Pennsylvania (Transportation) **P**: 262
Pennsylvanian Epoch [geology]
 Carboniferous Period **C**: 208
 Earth (table) **E**: 30
 Reptile (The evolution of reptiles) **R**: 252
Penny [money] **P**: 271 *with pictures*
 Cent **C**: 350
 Money (History of the pound) **M**: 709; (Pennies)
 M: 714
Penny [unit of measure]
 Nail (Sizes of nails) **N**: 3
Penny Black [stamp]
 Postal services *picture on* **P**: 706
Penny dreadful [card]
 Valentine's Day (Commercial valentines) **V**: 264
Penny-farthing [bicycle]
 Bicycle (Early bicycles) **B**: 291
Penny icecap
 Icecap **I**: 19
Penny paper
 Journalism (The growth of U.S. newspapers)
 J: 174
Penny Post
 Postal services (The creation of the Penny Post)
 P: 706
"Penny saved is a penny earned, A" [quotation]
 Poor Richard's Almanac **P**: 659
Pennypacker, Samuel Whitaker [American
 political leader]
 Pennsylvania (table) **P**: 263
Pennyroyal [plant] **P**: 271
Pennyroyal Region
 Kentucky (Land regions) **K**: 285
Penobscot Expedition [U.S. history]
 Revere, Paul (Revolutionary soldier) **R**: 268
Penobscot Indians
 Indian, American (In the United States) **I**: 179
 Maine (The late 1900's) **M**: 92 *with picture*
Penobscot Marine Museum [Searsport]
 Maine (Places to visit) **M**: 78
Penobscot River [Maine] **P**: 271
 Maine (Rivers and lakes) **M**: 82
Penology
 Criminology (What criminologists study) **Ci**: 1145
Pensacola [Florida] **P**: 271 *with picture*
 Florida (The second Spanish period) **F**: 262
Pensacola Bay [Florida]
 Pensacola **P**: 271
Pensacola Dam [Neosho River, Oklahoma] **P**: 272
Pensées [book by Pascal]
 French literature (Classical prose) **F**: 520
 Pascal, Blaise **P**: 190
"Penseroso, Il" [poem by Milton]
 Milton, John (His early life and works) **M**: 557
Pension [income] **P**: 272
 See also the list of Related articles in the Pension
 article
 Pension Benefit Guaranty Corporation **P**: 274
 Poverty (Social welfare programs) **P**: 725
 Retirement **R**: 265
 Veterans Affairs, Department of (Benefits and
 other services) **V**: 343
Pension Benefit Guaranty Corporation P: 274
 Pension (Private pension plans) **P**: 273
Penstock [pipeline]
 Turbine (Water turbines) **T**: 496 *with diagram*
Pentaceratops [dinosaur]
 Dinosaur *picture on* **D**: 207; (True dinosaurs)
 D: 206b-208
Pentaerythritol tetranitrate [explosive]
 PETN **P**: 327
Pentagon [geometry] **P**: 274 *with diagram*
 Geometry (Solid geometry) **G**: 104-105
 Pyramid **P**: 916 *with diagram*
Pentagon Building [Arlington, Virginia] **P**: 274
 with picture
 See also September 11 terrorist attacks *in this
 index*
 Bush, George Walker (Terrorist attacks and
 military action) **B**: 722g
 Hijacking **H**: 230
 National September 11 Memorial and Museum
 N: 61
 September 11 terrorist attacks **S**: 310 *with picture*

United States, History of the (September 11
 terrorist attacks) **U**: 196d
 Washington, D.C. (The Pentagon) **W**: 78; (The
 2000's) **W**: 88
Pentagon Papers, The
 Freedom of the press (In the United States)
 F: 507-508
 Vietnam War (Growing protest) **V**: 376
Pentameter [poetry]
 Greek literature (Lyric poetry) **G**: 377
 Poetry (table) **P**: 594
Pentane
 Natural gas liquids **N**: 64
Pentateuch [Bible] **P**: 274
 See also Torah *in this index*
 Bible (The Hebrew Bible) **B**: 279 *with picture*; (The
 Christian Old Testament) **B**: 282; (Translations
 of the Bible) **B**: 284; (The Bible in worship)
 B: 286
 Deuteronomy **D**: 172
 Jews (The kingdom of Israel) **J**: 121
 Judaism **J**: 179 *with picture*; (The Hebrew Bible)
 J: 180
 Moses **M**: 828
 Old Testament **O**: 740; (Contents) **O**: 741
 Paul, Saint (Paul's letters and ideas) **P**: 201
 Religion (Judaism) **R**: 219
 Scroll *picture on* **S**: 227
 Septuagint **S**: 310d
Pentathlon [sports]
 Olympic Games (The ancient games) **O**: 750
Pentathlon, Modern [sports] **P**: 275
 Olympic Games (Summer Olympic Games)
 O: 746e-747
 Track and field (The decathlon, heptathlon, and
 pentathlon) **T**: 359
Pentavalent antimony salts [chemical]
 Leishmaniasis **L**: 187
Pentecost [religion] **P**: 275
 Christianity (The Trinity) **C**: 522g; (Forms of
 worship) **C**: 522h-523
 Easter (Religious observances of Easter) **E**: 42;
 (The end of the Easter season) **E**: 43
Pentecostal churches P: 275
 Assemblies of God **A**: 817
 Christianity (Protestant churches) **C**: 522g
 Churches of God **C**: 543
 Evangelicalism **E**: 422
 Faith healing **F**: 12
 Gospel music **G**: 277
 Protestantism *picture on* **P**: 833; (The modern
 evangelical and Pentecostal movements)
 P: 835
 Religion (Religion today) **R**: 223
Pentelic marble
 Parthenon **P**: 183
Penthesilea [legendary figure]
 Amazons **A**: 404
Pentjak silat [sport] *See* Pencak silat *in this index*
Pentland Firth [strait, Scotland]
 Orkney Islands **O**: 856
Pentlandite [mineral]
 Nickel (Mining nickel) **N**: 404
Pentode [electronics]
 Vacuum tube (History) **V**: 259
Pentolite [explosive]
 Ammunition (Artillery ammunition) **A**: 435-436
 Explosive (High explosives) **E**: 453
 PETN **P**: 327
Pentothal [drug]
 Thiopental **T**: 258
Penumbra [optics] **P**: 276 *with diagram*
 Shadow **S**: 341 *with diagram*
 Sunspot **So**: 991
Penutian [language group]
 Indian, American (Language groups) **I**: 150
Penwork [decoration]
 Furniture (The Regency style) **F**: 580
Penzias, Arno Allan [American physicist]
 Astronomy (Advances in astrophysics) **A**: 848
 Big bang **B**: 297
 Cosmic microwave background (CMB) radiation
 Ci: 1075
 Nobel Prizes (Physics: 1978) **N**: 441
 Telescope (Microwave telescopes) **T**: 108
Peonage [labor] **P**: 276
 Plantation ("Free"-labor plantations) **P**: 550
Peony [plant] **P**: 276 *with picture*
 Flower (Garden perennials) **F**: 278 *with picture*
People *See* Human being *in this index*
People, Yes, The [poems by Sandburg]
 Sandburg, Carl (His poetry) **S**: 108
People Behave Like Ballads [poem by Coffin]
 Coffin, Robert Peter Tristram **Ci**: 756
People Could Fly, The [book by Hamilton]
 Literature for children *picture on* **L**: 374
People for the Ethical Treatment of Animals

[organization] P: 277
Animal rights movement A: 510
People Go to the University—the University Goes to the People, The [mural by Siqueiros]
Latin America *picture on* L: 101
People Meter [machine]
Television (Measuring a program's success) T: 113-114
People mover [vehicle]
Airport (Terminal designs) A: 248-249
Transportation (Urban public transportation) T: 393
People of Seldwyla, The [stories by Keller]
Keller, Gottfried K: 254
People of the Abyss, The [essays by London]
London, Jack L: 444
People of the Deer [book by Mowat]
Mowat, Farley M: 903
People of the Goddess Danu [Irish clan]
Mythology (The Irish cycles) M: 985
People United to Save Humanity [organization]
Jackson, Jesse Louis J: 15
People's Action Party
Singapore (Government) S: 469-470; (History) S: 471
People's Assembly [legislature]
Egypt (National government) E: 121
People's Budget [British history]
Lloyd George, David (Early career) L: 402
People's committee [government]
Vietnam (Local level) V: 365
People's Consultative Assembly [government]
Indonesia (Government) I: 226 *with picture*
People's Council [government]
Vietnam (Local level) V: 365
People's courts
Russia (Courts) R: 532
Vietnam (Courts) V: 365
People's Democratic Party
Uzbekistan (Government) U: 253
People's Democratic Republic of Yemen *See South Yemen in this index*
People's Front [political party] *See Popular Front in this index*
People's Front for Democracy and Justice [political party]
Eritrea (Government) E: 352; (History) E: 353-354
People's Liberation Armed Forces
Viet Cong V: 363
People's Liberation Army
China (The armed forces) C: 481
People's National Movement [political party]
Trinidad and Tobago (Government) T: 445; (History) T: 446
People's Organs of Control [government]
Vietnam (Courts) V: 365
People's Partnership [political party]
Trinidad and Tobago (History) T: 446-447
People's Party [U.S. history]
Populism (The People's Party) P: 675
People's Republic of China *See China in this index*
People's Supreme Court
Cuba (Courts) Ci: 1170
People's Temple [cult]
Cult (Modern cults) Ci: 1185
Guyana (History) G: 446-447
People's United Party [political party]
Belize (History) B: 238
People's War [theory]
Guerrilla warfare (Types of guerrilla movements) G: 420
People's Will [Russian history]
Russia (Alexander II) R: 551
Peoria [Illinois] P: 277
Pep pill *See Amphetamine in this index*
Pepin of Herstal [Frankish nobleman]
France (The Carolingian dynasty) F: 471
Pepin the Short [king of the Franks] P: 277
Charlemagne (Military conquests) C: 379
France (The Carolingian dynasty) F: 471
Italy (The Middle Ages) I: 513
Merovingian dynasty M: 418
Middle Ages (The Carolingian Empire) M: 524
Papal States P: 132
Peplos [garment]
Clothing (Greece) Ci: 697
Pepper [spice] P: 277 *with pictures*
Pepper [plant] P: 278 *with picture*
Pepper tree *See Peppertree in this index*
Pepperdine University P: 278
Peppered moth
Heredity (Heredity and natural selection) H: 203
Pepperell, William [American general]
Maine (Indian wars) M: 89
Peppergrass [plant]
Cress Ci: 1127
Pepperidge [plant]

Tupelo T: 492
Peppermint [plant] P: 278 *with picture*
Menthol M: 410
Peppertree P: 279
Pepsi-Cola [beverage]
PepsiCo, Inc. P: 279
PepsiCo, Inc. [company] P: 279
Pepsin [enzyme] P: 279
Digestive system (From mouth to stomach) D: 202
Stomach (The stomach's work) So: 908
Ulcer U: 15
Peptic ulcer [disorder]
Antacid A: 529
Stomach (Peptic ulcers) So: 908
Ulcer U: 15 *with picture*
Peptide [physiology]
Endorphin E: 272
Protein (The structure of proteins) P: 832
Pepys, Samuel [English author] P: 279
Diary D: 184
English literature (Restoration prose) E: 318
Pequod [ship]
Melville, Herman (His literary career) M: 390
Pequonnock River [Connecticut]
Bridgeport B: 606
Pequot Indians
Connecticut (Early days) Ci: 968; (The Pequot War) Ci: 968
Indian wars (The Pequot War [1637]) I: 191
Mohegan Indians M: 688
Pequot War [1637]
Connecticut (The Pequot War) Ci: 968
Indian wars (The Pequot War [1637]) I: 191
Mohegan Indians M: 688
Per capita income [economics]
Developing country D: 173
Income (Income inequality) I: 101
Third World (The economic Third World) T: 258-259
Per cent [mathematics] *See Percentage in this index*
Per-Ramses [ancient city]
Ramses II R: 134
Peralta, Luis Maria [Spanish soldier]
Oakland (Government and history) O: 637
Peralta, Pedro de [Spanish colonial leader]
New Mexico (Exploration, conquest, and settlement) N: 273
Peramelemorphia [zoology]
Mammal (table) M: 128 *with picture*
Percale [fabric] P: 279
Percé Rock [island, Quebec]
Quebec *picture on* Q: 10; (Places to visit) Q: 20
Percentage [mathematics] P: 280 *with pictures*
Ratio R: 147
Percentile rank
College entrance examination (In the United States) Ci: 775
Perception [psychology] P: 282 *with pictures*
See also Senses in this index; and the list of Related articles in the Perception article
Color (How we see color) Ci: 818 *with pictures*
Ear (The sense of hearing) E: 9 *with pictures*
Eye (How we see) E: 462 *with pictures*
Hume, David (Hume's thought) H: 432
Learning disabilities (Types) L: 165
Leibniz, Gottfried Wilhelm L: 185
Optical illusion O: 812 *with pictures*
Pestalozzi, Johann Heinrich P: 318
Psychology (Major fields of psychology) P: 848
Reading (How we read) R: 156
Perceptual context
Perception (Understanding perception) P: 283-284 *with picture*
Perceptual disorder
Learning disabilities (Types) L: 165
Perceval [legendary figure]
Holy Grail (The search for the Grail) H: 299
Knights and knighthood *picture on* K: 348
Perceval, Spencer [British political leader]
United Kingdom (table: British prime ministers) U: 72
Perch [fish] P: 284
Climbing perch Ci: 680 *with picture*
Fish *picture on* F: 158, *diagrams on* F: 163
Skeleton *diagram on* S: 481
Percheron [horse]
Horse *picture on* H: 347; (table: Some types and breeds of horses) H: 343
Perching duck
Duck *picture on* D: 375; (Perching ducks) D: 376
Percussion [movement]
Massage M: 295
Percussion instrument [music]
Drum D: 367
Music *pictures on* M: 949; (Percussion instruments) M: 950

Orchestra O: 820 *with pictures*
Rhythm band R: 320
Percussion section [music]
Orchestra (The musicians) O: 820
Percussive martial arts
Martial arts M: 234
Percy, Thomas [British scholar]
Ballad (Ballads and literature) B: 43
Percy, Walker [American author]
American literature (Southern fiction) A: 424-425
Perdita [literary figure]
Shakespeare, William: (*The Winter's Tale*) S: 365
Perdix [Greek mythology]
Daedalus D: 3
Perdue, Beverly [American political leader]
North Carolina (table) N: 490; (Recent developments) N: 494
Perdue, Sonny [American political leader]
Georgia (table) G: 130; (The early 2000's) G: 134-135
Père David's deer
Deer (table) D: 85; (Asian and European deer) D: 86
Père Noël [legend]
Christmas (In France) C: 530
Pereda, José María de [Spanish author]
Spanish literature (The 1800's) So: 761-762
Peregrine falcon [bird] P: 284
Animal *pictures on* A: 489, A: 505
Bird *picture on* B: 329
Bird of prey (Physical appearance) B: 374a
Falcon *picture on* F: 14; (The peregrine falcon) F: 14
Peregrine Fund World Center for Birds of Prey
Idaho (Places to visit) I: 34
Peregrine-gyrfalcon hybrid [bird]
Falcon *picture on* F: 14
Peregrinus, Peter [French physicist]
Magnetism (Early discoveries) M: 60d
Pereira, Aristides [Guinea-Bissau political leader]
Guinea-Bissau (History) G: 434
Pereira, Raimundo [Guinea-Bissau political leader]
Guinea-Bissau (History) G: 434
Pereira da Sousa, Washington Luís [Brazilian political leader]
Brazil (Birth of the republic) B: 585
Perekop, Isthmus of [region, Ukraine]
Crimea Ci: 1142 *with map*
Perelman, Grigori [Russian mathematician]
Topology (History) T: 333
Perelman, S. J. [American author] P: 284
Perelmuth, Jacob Pincus [American singer] *See Peerce, Jan in this index*
Peremptory challenge [law]
Jury (Petit juries) J: 202
Perennial [botany] P: 285
Flower (Garden flowers) F: 274; (Garden perennials) F: 278 *with pictures*; (Garden perennials grown from bulbs) F: 280 *with pictures*
Fruit F: 544
Gardening (Planning an informal flower garden) G: 32-34
Grass (The grass plant) G: 324
Plant (Germination) P: 535-537
Vegetable V: 292
Weed (How weeds grow) W: 179
Perennial allergic rhinitis [disorder]
Hay fever (Treatment) H: 116
Perennial ragweed [plant]
Ragweed R: 103
Peres, Shimon [Israeli political leader] P: 285 *with portrait*
Israel (Unity government) I: 489
Perestrello Moniz, Felipa [wife of]
Columbus, Christopher (Young adulthood) Ci: 857-858
Perestroika [Soviet history]
Communism (The Soviet Union under Gorbachev) Ci: 895-896
Gorbachev, Mikhail Sergeyevich (Domestic policies) G: 272
Union of Soviet Socialist Republics (Economy) U: 33; (Gorbachev's reforms) U: 40
Peretz, Isaac Leib [Polish author]
Yiddish literature Y: 566
Perey, Marguerite [French chemist]
Francium F: 482
Pérez, Carlos Andrés [Venezuelan political leader]
Venezuela (The late 1900's) V: 305
Pérez, Juan [Spanish explorer]
British Columbia (European contact) B: 628
Vancouver Island (History) V: 278
Pérez, Tony [American baseball player]
Baseball (table: Hall of Fame) B: 134a
Pérez Balladares, Ernesto [Panamanian political leader]

Panama (The 1990's) P: 121
Pérez de Ayala, Ramón [Spanish author]
Spanish literature (The Generation of 1898)
So: 762
Pérez de Cuéllar, Javier [Peruvian diplomat] P: 285
United Nations (The secretary-general) U: 83
with portrait
Pérez Esquivel, Adolfo [Argentine activist]
Nobel Prizes (Peace: 1980) N: 448b
Pérez Jiménez, Marcos [Venezuelan political
leader]
Venezuela (The road to democracy) V: 305
Pérez Molina, Otto [Guatemalan political leader]
Guatemala (Political developments) G: 417
Perfect competition See Pure competition in this
index
"Perfect Day, A" [song by Bond]
Bond, Carrie Jacobs B: 455
Perfect flower
Plant pictures on P: 530, P: 534
Perfect game
Baseball (Baseball terms) B: 124
Perfect participle [grammar]
Participle P: 184
Perfect square [mathematics]
Series (Working with odd numbers) S: 317
Perfect tense [grammar]
Tense T: 168
Perfecting press
Printing (Offset presses) P: 798-799
Perfectionism [doctrine]
Oneida Community O: 762
Perforator [device]
Petroleum (Completing the well) P: 340-341 with
diagram
Performance art P: 285
Art and the arts picture on A: 746
Video art V: 359
Performance bond [economics]
Bonding B: 455
Commodity exchange (Forward and futures
contracts) Ci: 873
Performance competition
Horse (Horse shows) H: 356
Performance-enhancing drug
Doping D: 309
Performance report
Accounting (Management accounting) A: 23
Performing arts
Careers (Sports and entertainment) C: 230-231
Fine arts F: 104
Perfume P: 286
Ambergris A: 405
Civet Ci: 604
Flower (Other uses) F: 273-274
Frankincense F: 485
Herb H: 196
Patchouli P: 194
Pergamum [ancient city]
Library (Ancient libraries of animal skin) L: 258-
259
Pergolesi, Giovanni Battista [Italian composer]
P: 287
Classical music (Neoclassicism) Ci: 649
Opera (Opera seria and opera buffa) O: 797-798
Perham, Sidney [American political leader]
Maine (table) M: 87
Peri, Jacopo [Italian composer]
Opera (The development of opera) O: 797
Pericarditis [disorder]
Heart (Inflammatory heart disease) H: 142
Pericardium [anatomy]
Heart (Outer lining and muscle) H: 133;
(Inflammatory heart disease) H: 142
Membrane (Serous membranes) M: 391
Pericarp [botany]
Fruit (Types of fruits in botany) F: 544
Pericles [Greek military leader] P: 287
Athens (The Golden Age) A: 857
Greece, Ancient picture on G: 370
Oratory (Classical orators) O: 819
Pericles [play by Shakespeare]
Shakespeare, William: (Pericles) S: 364
Pericles, Age of See Golden Age of Athens in this
index
Pericycle [botany]
Root (The core) R: 471 with diagram
Periderm [botany]
Potato (The potato plant) P: 712 with picture
Peridot [gem] P: 287
Gem picture on G: 78
Olivine O: 744
Peridotite [rock]
Mantle M: 168
Mars (Physical features of Mars) M: 225
Rock (table) R: 373 with picture
Peridural anesthesia

Anesthesia (Local anesthesia) A: 458
Perigee [astronomy]
Month M: 767
Moon (Rotation and orbit) M: 783
Orbit O: 819
Space exploration (Kinds of earth orbits) diagram
on So: 697
Perihelion [astronomy]
Orbit O: 819
Peril [insurance]
Insurance I: 309
Perimeter [mathematics]
Algebra (Writing formulas) A: 353
Triangle (Perimeter and area) T: 437
Period [astronomy]
Comet Ci: 867
Hogg, Helen Sawyer H: 288
Kepler, Johannes (Kepler's laws) K: 305
Planet (How planets move) P: 508-509
Period [geology]
Earth (Age of Earth) E: 26
Extinction (Mass extinction) E: 456
Prehistoric animal (The world of prehistoric
animals) P: 736
Period [punctuation]
Punctuation (The period) P: 902
Period, Menstrual See Menstrual period in this
index
Period interior
Interior design (Style) I: 327
Period-luminosity relation [astronomy]
Leavitt, Henrietta Swan L: 170
Period of oscillation [physics]
Pendulum P: 236 with diagram
Periodic kiln [industry]
Brick (Firing bricks) B: 598
Periodic law
Mendeleev, Dmitri Ivanovich M: 398
Periodic table [chemistry]
Chemistry (Formation of the periodic table)
C: 402
Element, Chemical (The periodic table of the
elements) E: 219 with diagram
Mendeleev, Dmitri Ivanovich M: 398
Moseley, Henry Gwyn-Jeffreys M: 828
Science (Classifying data) S: 194
Periodic tenancy [law]
Tenant T: 132
Periodical [magazine]
Postal Service, United States (Classes of mail)
P: 699
Trade publication T: 363
Periodical cicada [insect]
Cicada (Types of cicadas) Ci: 551
Insect picture on I: 281
Periodontal disease
Teeth (Periodontal diseases) T: 85 with picture
Periodontal ligament
Teeth (Parts of a tooth) T: 80; (Periodontal
ligament) T: 81 with diagram
Periodontics
Dentistry (Periodontics) D: 144
Periodontitis [disease] P: 287
Teeth (Periodontal diseases) T: 85 with picture
Perioeci [people]
Sparta (The people) So: 766
Periosteum [anatomy]
Bone (Structure of the bones) B: 456 with
diagram
Membrane (Fibrous membranes) M: 391
Periostracum [biology]
Shell (How shells are formed) S: 385
Peripatetic philosophy P: 288
Aristotle (Aristotle's life) A: 663
Lyceum L: 532
Peripatologist [occupation]
Blindness (Education and training) B: 403
Peripatric speciation [biology]
Mayr, Ernst M: 330
Peripheral [machine]
Computer (Parts of computers) Ci: 911-912 with
picture
Peripheral nervous system [physiology]
Human body (The peripheral nervous system)
H: 426
Leprosy L: 204
Myelin M: 970f
Nervous system (The peripheral nervous system)
N: 133 with diagram
Pain (How the body feels pain) P: 21-22
Paralysis (Paralysis of peripheral nervous system
origin) P: 152
Peripheral vision
Eye (The retina) E: 462
Periscope [instrument] P: 288
Prism P: 805
Perissodactyla [zoology]

Mammal (table) M: 128 with picture
Peristalsis [physiology]
Alimentary canal A: 368
Stomach (The stomach's work) So: 908
Peristaltic waves See Peristalsis in this index
Peristome [botany]
Moss (How mosses live) M: 834-835
Peristyle [architecture]
Architecture picture on A: 616
Rome, Ancient (City life) R: 438 with picture
Perito Moreno Glacier
South America picture on So: 630
Perito Moreno National Park [Argentina]
Argentina picture on A: 653
Peritoneum [anatomy]
Abdomen A: 8
Membrane (Serous membranes) M: 391
Pelvic inflammatory disease P: 232
Peritonitis P: 288
Peritonitis [disorder] P: 288
Diverticulitis D: 241
Periwig
Clothing picture on Ci: 703
Hairdressing picture on H: 11; (The 1600's) H: 12
Wig W: 299
Periwinkle [plant]
Myrtle M: 972
Periwinkle [sea animal] P: 288
Perjury [crime] P: 288
Clinton, Bill (Domestic events) Ci: 682f
Oath O: 639
United States, History of the (The Clinton
impeachment) U: 196d
Witness W: 374
Perkin, Sir William Henry [British chemist]
Chemistry (Growth of industrial chemistry) C: 405
with picture
Coal tar Ci: 733
Dye (History) D: 396
Perkins, Edward J. [American diplomat]
United Nations (table) U: 86
Perkins, Frances [American political leader] P: 288
Truman, Harry S. (table) T: 469
Women's movement (Decline after 1920) W: 385
Perkins, George C. [American political leader]
California (table) C: 59
Perkins, Jacob [American engineer]
Refrigeration (Mechanical refrigeration) R: 201
Perkins, Lynne Rae [American author/illustrator]
Newbery Medal (table) N: 359
Perkins, Maxwell E. [American editor]
Wolfe, Thomas W: 377
Perkins, Simon [American banker]
Akron (History) A: 254
Perkins School for the Blind [Boston]
Howe, Samuel Gridley H: 401
Perl, Martin Lewis [American physicist]
Nobel Prizes (Physics: 1995) N: 442
Perlite [rock]
Lava (Properties of lava) L: 127-128
Plaster P: 552
Perlman, Itzhak [Israeli violinist] P: 289
Perlmutter, Saul [American physicist]
Nobel Prizes (Physics: 2011) N: 442
Perls, Frederick S. [German psychiatrist]
Psychotherapy (Humanistic-experiential
psychotherapy) P: 852
Permafrost P: 289 with map
Alaska (The Arctic Coastal Plain) A: 294
Arctic (Soil conditions) A: 636
Russia (Land regions) R: 539
Tundra T: 485
Permalloy [metal] P: 289
Permanent committee See Standing committee
in this index
Permanent Court of Arbitration [world history]
International Court of Justice I: 338
Peace (The 1800's and early 1900's) P: 206
Permanent Court of International Justice [world
history]
International Court of Justice I: 338
International law (Courts and arbitration) I: 341
Root, Elihu R: 471
Permanent magnet
Cobalt (Uses) Ci: 741
Magnetism (Kinds of magnets) M: 59
Permanent mold
Cast and casting (Types of molds) C: 278
Permanent resident [biology]
Bird (The distribution of birds) B: 331-332
Permanent teeth
Teeth (Permanent teeth) T: 79 with pictures
Permanent tissue [botany]
Tissue (Plant tissues) T: 299
Permanent wave [grooming]
Hairdressing (The 1900's) H: 12
Permeable rock [geology]

Petroleum (Migration) P: 333-334
Permian extinction [paleontology]
Earth (The Paleozoic Era) E: 27
Extinction (Mass extinction) E: 456
Permian Period P: 289
Triassic Period T: 439
Permian Period [geology] P: 289
Earth (The Paleozoic Era) E: 27; (table) E: 30 *with map*
Prehistoric animal (table) P: 738 *with picture*
Permineralization [geology]
Fossil (The action of minerals) F: 425
Permissible explosive
Dynamite (Kinds of dynamite) D: 397
Permit [fish]
Pompano P: 653
Permutations and combinations [mathematics] P: 290
Pernambuco [tree] *See* Brazilwood *in this index*
Pernicious anemia [disorder]
See also Anemia *in this index*
Anemia (Insufficient production of red blood cells) A: 457
Hodgkin, Dorothy Crowfoot H: 283
Pernštejn Castle
Moravia *picture on* M: 800
Perón, Eva Duarte de [Argentine political leader] P: 292 *with portrait*
Argentina (Argentina under Perón) A: 657 *with picture*
Perón, Juan Domingo P: 292
Perón, Isabel Martinez de [Argentine political leader]
Argentina (Argentina under Perón) A: 657-658
Perón, Juan Domingo P: 292
Perón, Juan Domingo [Argentine political leader] P: 292 *with portrait*
Argentina (History) A: 655-657 *with picture*
Latin America (Political circumstances in the early to middle 1900's) L: 109
Perón, Eva Duarte de P: 292
Peronistas [political group]
Argentina (Argentina under Perón) A: 657-658
Perot, Ross [American businessman] P: 292 *with portrait*
Bush, George Herbert Walker (The 1992 election) B: 722a
Clinton, Bill (The 1992 election) Ci: 682d; (The 1996 election) Ci: 682f
Reform Party R: 195
Pérotin [French composer]
Classical music (Church music) Ci: 645
Peroxide of hydrogen [chemical]
Bleach B: 399
Peroxyacetyl nitrate [chemical]
Smog (Photochemical smog) S: 519-520
Perpendicular line [mathematics]
Geometry (Some basic geometric constructions) G: 103 *with diagrams*
Perpendicular style [architecture]
Gothic art (Gothic architecture in England) G: 279
Tracery T: 355
Perpetrator [criminology]
Crime scene investigation Ci: 1140
Perpetual calendar
Calendar C: 30
Perpetual canon [music]
Canon C: 182
Perpetual Covenant [Swiss history]
Switzerland (The struggle for freedom) So: 1059
Perpetual Emigrating Fund [U.S. history]
Utah (The Mormons) U: 246
Perpetual Motion [music by Paganini]
Paganini, Niccolò P: 20
Perpetual motion machine P: 293 *with diagrams*
Machine (Efficiency) M: 14
Thermodynamics T: 253
Perpetual rose
Rose (Types of roses) R: 475
Perpetuity [law]
Foundation F: 429
Perpich, Rudy [American political leader]
Minnesota (table) M: 602
Perrault, Charles [French author] P: 293
Fairy (Fairy tales) F: 11
Literature for children (Mother Goose) L: 362
Mother Goose (The history of Mother Goose literature) M: 842
Perrault, Claude [French architect]
Louvre L: 507
Perrault, Charles P: 293
Perrier, Carlo [Italian physicist]
Technetium T: 73
Perrin, Jean Baptiste [French physicist]
Nobel Prizes (Physics: 1926) N: 440
Perrot, Jules [French choreographer]
Ballet (Romantic ballet) B: 51

Perrot, Nicholas [French explorer]
Iowa (Exploration and early settlement) I: 393
Perry, Edward A. [American political leader]
Florida (table) F: 260
Perry, Gaylord [American baseball player]
Baseball (table: Hall of Fame) B: 134a
Perry, Madison S. [American political leader]
Florida (table) F: 260
Perry, Matthew Calbraith [American military leader] P: 294
Asia (The age of colonialism) A: 806
Fillmore, Millard (Accomplishments) F: 102
Japan *picture on* J: 55; (Renewed relations with the West) J: 56
Tokyo (Western influence) T: 318-319
Yokohama Y: 567
Perry, Oliver Hazard [American military leader] P: 294 *with picture*
Flag *picture on* F: 210
Ohio *picture on* O: 700, O: 702
Pennsylvania *picture on* P: 254
War of 1812 (Lake Erie) W: 32
Perry, Rick [American political leader]
Texas (table) T: 203
Perry, William James [American government official] P: 295
Perryman, George [American rancher]
Tulsa (History) T: 483
Perryman, Lewis [American businessman]
Tulsa (History) T: 483
Perry's Victory and International Peace Memorial [Ohio]
National Park System (table: National memorials) N: 54
Ohio (Places to visit) O: 690
Perryville, Battle of [1862]
Civil War, American (table) Ci: 624; (Battle of Perryville) Ci: 629
Kentucky (The Civil War) K: 293 *with picture*
Persad-Bissessar, Kamla [Trinidad political leader]
Trinidad and Tobago (History) T: 446-447
Persephone P: 295
Adonis A: 65
Ceres C: 362
Demeter D: 118
Orpheus O: 858
Pomegranate P: 652
Persepolis [ancient city] P: 295
Alexander the Great (Victory over Darius) A: 343
Architecture (Mesopotamian architecture) A: 611
Persia, Ancient *picture on* P: 297
Sculpture (India) S: 236
Perseus [sculpture by Canova]
Canova, Antonio C: 183
Perseus [sculpture by Cellini]
Cellini, Benvenuto C: 339
Sculpture (Michelangelo) S: 252-253 *with picture*
Perseus [Greek mythology] P: 295
Andromeda A: 457
Gorgons G: 274
Medusa M: 383
Sculpture *picture on* S: 253
Perseus [constellation] P: 295
Perseveration [disorder]
Learning disabilities (Types) L: 165
Pershing, John Joseph [American general] P: 295 *with picture*
A.E.F. A: 81
Mexico (The Constitution of 1917) M: 472
Missouri (Progress as a state) M: 671
Villa, Pancho V: 384
World War I (American troops in Europe) W: 463
Pershing missile
Rocket (High-altitude rockets) R: 390-391
Persia *See* Iran *in this index*
Persia, Ancient P: 296 *with pictures and map*
See also the list of Related articles in the Persia, Ancient, *article*
Afghanistan (Early invasions) A: 95
Alexander the Great A: 342
Architecture (Mesopotamian architecture) A: 611
Armenia (History) A: 718b
Asia (The Tigris-Euphrates Valley) A: 804-805
Azerbaijan (History) A: 997
Cuneiform C: 1192
Fire (Fire in legend and religion) F: 122
Greece, Ancient (The Persian wars) G: 372
Islamic art (Pottery) I: 470
Marathon, Battle of M: 191
Painting (Islamic painting) P: 48
Postal services (Ancient times) P: 703
Sculpture (Middle Eastern) S: 233
Tajikistan (History) T: 18b
Themistocles T: 251
Thermopylae T: 255
Turkey (History) T: 509
World, History of the (Civilizations of southwest

Asia) W: 426-428; (The Islamic empires) W: 441-442
Persian cat
Cat *picture on* C: 289; (Long-haired breeds) C: 292
Persian Gulf [Arabian peninsula] P: 300 *with map*
Persian Gulf War of 1991 (Consequences of the war) P: 300d
Reagan, Ronald Wilson (Persian Gulf conflicts) R: 170
Persian Gulf War of 1991 P: 300a *with pictures and maps*
Air force (In the Persian Gulf War of 1991) A: 187
Air Force, United States (The Persian Gulf War of 1991) A: 196
Arabs (Economic inequality) A: 590a
Army *picture on* A: 724; (Armies in the nuclear age) A: 728-729
Army, United States (The Persian Gulf War of 1991) A: 739
Baghdad (History) B: 26
Bahrain (History) B: 30-31
Basra B: 156
Bush, George Herbert Walker (International affairs) B: 721
Camouflage *picture on* C: 87
Canada, History of (Foreign affairs) C: 151
Egypt (Recent developments) E: 133-134
Fahd F: 6
Gas mask G: 60
Guided missile (Postwar developments) G: 427-428
Gulf War syndrome G: 438
Hussein, Saddam H: 457
International law (After World War II) I: 342
International relations (The Persian Gulf War of 1991) I: 346
Iraq (The Persian Gulf War of 1991) I: 414
Iraq War (Background to the war) I: 414c
Kurds K: 393
Kuwait (History) K: 396-397 *with picture*
Middle East (The 1990's) M: 534a-534b
Mulroney, Brian (The Persian Gulf War of 1991) M: 918
Navy, United States (The Persian Gulf War of 1991) N: 89
Ocean (Marine pollution) O: 664-665
Oil spill (Notable spills) O: 708
Oman (History) O: 759
Petroleum (Petroleum and war) P: 346; (Perisan Gulf wars) P: 349
Prisoner of war P: 808
Red Cross (In the United States) R: 187-188
Saudi Arabia (The Persian Gulf War of 1991) S: 162
Schwarzkopf, H. Norman S: 189
Syria (Other conflicts) So: 1076
Tank (History) T: 27-28
United Arab Emirates (History) U: 45
United Nations (Military actions) U: 91-92
United States, History of the (The Persian Gulf War) U: 196d
War (Conflicts over resources) W: 23; (table) W: 25
War crime (Wars in Iraq) W: 27
Persian Gulf War of 2003- *See* Iraq War *in this index*
Persian knot
Rugs and carpets (Oriental rugs) R: 516 *with diagram*
Persian lamb
Fur (table) F: 561
Karakul K: 245
Persian language
Iran (Language) I: 401
Middle East (Identity and language) M: 530
Persian Letters [book by Montesquieu]
French literature (The Enlightenment) F: 520-521
Montesquieu M: 764a
Persian rug
Iran (The arts) I: 402
Islamic art (Rugs) I: 469 *with picture*
Rugs and carpets (Oriental rugs) R: 516-517 *with pictures*
Persian walnut *See* English walnut *in this index*
Persian Wars [ancient Greece]
Greece, Ancient (The Persian wars) G: 373
Herodotus H: 213
Phoenicia (Decline) P: 395
Themistocles T: 251
Persiles and Sigismunda [book by Cervantes]
Cervantes, Miguel de (His literary career) C: 363
Persimmon [tree] P: 300e *with picture*
Ebony E: 49
Tree *pictures on* T: 423
Persis [ancient region]
Iran (Early days) I: 405
Persistence of Memory [painting by Dalí]
Dalí, Salvador D: 10
Painting (Surrealism) P: 81-82 *with picture*

Persistence of vision [physiology]
Motion picture (How motion pictures work)
M: 856
Persistent infection [medicine]
Virus (Infection) V: 428-428a
Persistent organic pollutant
Environmental pollution (Government action)
E: 335-336
Persistent train [astronomy]
Meteor M: 431
Persistent vegetative state [disorder] P: 300f
Person [grammar] P: 300f
Person-centered therapy See Client-centered
therapy *in this index*
Person, Place and Thing [book by Shapiro]
Shapiro, Karl Jay S: 372
"Person to Person" [television show]
Murrow, Edward R. M: 932
Personal computer [machine] P: 300f
See also Computer *in this index*
Apple Inc. A: 573
Computer (Kinds of computers) Ci: 909; (The
personal computer) Ci: 924c *with pictures*
Desktop publishing D: 158
Electronic game (Gaming platforms) E: 204c;
(The growth of computer gaming) E: 204e
International Business Machines Corporation
I: 338
Map M: 177
Microsoft Corporation M: 519
United States, History of the (The Information
Age) U: 196b
Word processing W: 403
Personal digital assistant [computer]
Computer (Personal computers) Ci: 909-910
Personal essay [literature]
Essay E: 359
Personal finance company [economics]
Loan company L: 404
Personal flotation device
Life jacket (Boating regulations) L: 281
Personal foul [sports]
Basketball (Fouls) B: 147 *with diagram*
Lacrosse (Men's lacrosse) L: 23
Personal identification number
Automated teller machine A: 944
Bank (Electronic banking) B: 89-90
Personal identity [psychology] See Identity *in
this index*
Personal income
Income I: 100
Personal letter
Letter writing (Personal letters) L: 212
Personal liberty
Civil rights Ci: 607
Communism (Restrictions on personal freedom)
Ci: 891-892
Habeas corpus H: 2
Personal liberty law [U.S. history]
Fugitive slave laws F: 553
Personal pension plan See Individual pension plan
in this index
Personal pronoun [grammar]
Antecedent A: 541
Gender (Personal pronouns) G: 80
Pronoun P: 819
Personal property [law] P: 300f
Property P: 827
Property tax P: 827
Real estate R: 171
Personal radio
Radio (Radio since the 1950's) R: 94
Personal Recollections of Joan of Arc [book by
Twain]
Twain, Mark (Later works) T: 530
Personal reference
Careers (Writing a résumé) C: 217
**Personal Responsibility and Work Opportunity
Reconciliation Act** [1996]
Welfare (Welfare reform in the United States)
W: 191-192
Personal selling See Sales *in this index*
Personal services
Careers (Personal services) C: 228 *with picture*
Personal-social guidance
Guidance (Personal-social guidance) G: 422
Personal umbrella liability insurance
Insurance (Other types of property and liability
insurance) I: 313
Personal video recorder [device] See Digital video
recorder *in this index*
Personal year number
Numerology N: 608
Personality [psychology] P: 300f *with pictures*
See also Behavior *in this index*
Aggression A: 141
Baby (Growth and development) B: 6

Careers (Interests) C: 215
Graphology G: 323
Linton, Ralph L: 339
Mental illness (Personality disorders) M: 406
Psychology (Major fields of psychology) P: 848
Sexuality (Psychological factors) S: 338
Testing (Personality tests) T: 182a
Personality test
Testing (Personality tests) T: 182a
Personhood
Abortion (Arguments for abortion) A: 15
Personification [language]
Capitalization (Personification) C: 197
Figure of speech F: 97
Personnel management [business] P: 303
See also Industrial relations *in this index*
Careers (Management) C: 227-228
Personnel Management, Office of [U.S.]
Civil service (Federal civil service) Ci: 612
Washington, D.C. *map on* W: 76
Personnel psychology See Industrial psychology
in this index
Persons, Gordon [American political leader]
Alabama (table) A: 274
Persons Case [Canadian history]
Famous Five F: 26b
Perspective [art] P: 303 *with pictures*
Alberti, Leon Battista A: 332
Drama (The Italian stage) D: 330 *with picture*
Leonardo da Vinci (Paintings) L: 200b
Painting (Roman painting) P: 42-43; (The
Renaissance) P: 51-52
Perspective control lens
Photography (Types of lenses) P: 411
Perspiration P: 305
Elimination E: 236
Skin (Hair, nails, and glands) S: 489
Persuasion
Sales (Persuasion) S: 63
Persuasion [book by Austen]
Austen, Jane A: 892
Perth [Australia] P: 305 *with picture*
Australia *map on* A: 901
Western Australia W: 230
Perthite [mineral]
Feldspar F: 68
Pertinax [Roman emperor]
Rome, Ancient (table) R: 447
Pertussis [disease]
Whooping cough W: 296
Peru P: 306 *with pictures and maps*
See also the list of Related articles in the Peru *article*
Andean Community A: 450
Bolívar, Simón B: 441
Crown *picture on* Ci: 1158
Ecuador (The 1900's) E: 73
El Niño E: 245
Flag *picture on* F: 201
Indian, American (Indians of the Andes) I: 173;
(Indians of the Tropical forest) I: 175
Latin America (Early years of independence)
L: 107-108
Moche M: 683
Mummy *picture on* M: 925
Sculpture (Early sculpture) S: 242 *with picture*
Peru Current [Pacific] P: 317
Ocean (Circulation) O: 658
Pacific Ocean (Currents) P: 14-15
Peru (Climate) P: 313
South America (Climate) So: 629-631
Perugino [Italian painter]
Raphael (Life) R: 142
Perutz, Max Ferdinand [British biologist]
Kendrew, Sir John Cowdery K: 259
Peruvian Traditions [book by Palma]
Latin American literature (Romanticism) L: 112-
113
Pervasive developmental disorder
Autism A: 941
Pesah [religion] See Passover *in this index*
Pescadores [islands, Taiwan] P: 317
Pesci, Joe [American actor]
Motion picture (Best performance by an actor in
a supporting role: 1990) M: 862b
Pescovegetarianism
Vegetarianism V: 294
Peseta [money] P: 317 *with pictures*
Pesharim [commentaries]
Dead Sea Scrolls D: 56
Peshkov, Alexey Maximovich [Russian author] See
Gorki, Maxim *in this index*
Peshtigo fire [1871]
Wisconsin (Statehood) W: 366 *with picture*
Peso [money] P: 317 *with pictures*
Argentina (The economic crisis of 2001) A: 659
Dollar D: 294
Pest [former city, Hungary]

Budapest B: 666
Pest control [agriculture] P: 317
Environmental pollution (Agriculture) E: 337
Farm and farming (Pest control) F: 34
Fumigation F: 556
Gardening (Pests) G: 35
Insect (Insect control) I: 284
Insecticide I: 301 *with picture*
Plant (Plant diseases and pests) P: 539 *with
picture*
Rat (Rats and people) R: 147
Vegetable (Pest control) V: 293
Pestalozzi, Johann Heinrich [Swiss educator]
P: 318
Herbart, Johann Friedrich H: 197
Pesticide
Agriculture (Growing plant crops) A: 150;
(Chemical pesticides) A: 159
Cancer (Genes damaged by substances in the
environment) C: 170
Environmental pollution *picture on* E: 332; (Soil
pollution) E: 334; (Hazardous waste) E: 334-
335; (Agriculture) E: 337
Farm and farming (Pest control) F: 34
Fruit (Caring for the crop) F: 546-547
Gulf War syndrome G: 438
Insecticide I: 301
Invasive species (Managing invasive species)
I: 354k
Neem tree N: 118
Peregrine falcon P: 284
Pest control P: 318
Plant (Disease and pest control) P: 541
Pure food and drug laws (Food additives)
P: 907-908
Soil pollution So: 576
Vegetable (Pest control) V: 293
Pet P: 319 *with pictures*
See also the list of Related articles in the Pet *article*
PET [medicine] See Positron emission tomography
in this index
PET [plastic] See Polyethylene terephthalate *in
this index*
Pet name
Name (Nicknames) N: 7
PET scan [medicine]
Positron emission tomography P: 698 *with
pictures*
Pet Sounds [recording]
Rock music (Independent producers) R: 379
PETA [organization] See People for the Ethical
Treatment of Animals *in this index*
Peta [prefix]
Metric system (Metric prefixes) M: 439
Pétain, Henri Philippe [French general] P: 323
with portrait
De Gaulle, Charles André Joseph Marie (Leader of
the Free French) D: 91
France (World War II) F: 475
World War I (The Battle of Verdun) W: 458; (Allied
failures) W: 461
World War II (The fall of France) W: 475
Petal [botany]
Flower (The corolla) F: 293 *with picture*
Plant (Flowers) P: 531 *with picture*
Petar I [king of Serbia] See Peter I *in this index*
Petasus [hat]
Hat *picture on* H: 84
Peter I [king of Serbia] P: 323
Yugoslavia (A new country) Y: 576
Peter I, the Great [czar of Russia] P: 323 *with
portrait*
Moscow (History) M: 826-827
Romanov R: 426
Russia (Architecture) R: 536; (Peter the
Great) R: 549 *with picture*; (table: Czars and
empresses) R: 549
Russian literature (Western influences) R: 559
Russo-Turkish wars R: 566b
Saint Petersburg [Russia] S: 54; (History) S: 55
Peter II [czar of Russia]
Russia (table: Czars and empresses) R: 549
Peter II [king of Yugoslavia] P: 324
Serbia (History) S: 314-315
Yugoslavia (A new country) Y: 576
Peter III [czar of Russia]
Russia (table: Czars and empresses) R: 549
Seven Years' War (In Europe) S: 328
Peter, Daniel [Swiss businessman]
Chocolate (History) C: 519
Peter, Epistles of [New Testament] P: 324
Bible (The Letters) B: 284
Peter, Saint (Later years) P: 325
Peter, Gospel of [document]
Jesus Christ (Other gospels) J: 105
"Peter, Peter, Pumpkin Eater" [nursery rhyme]
Nursery rhyme *picture on* N: 615

Peter, Saint [apostle] **P:** 324
  Leo I, Saint **L:** 197
  Pope **P:** 660, *picture on* **P:** 663; *(table)* **P:** 666
  Roman Catholic Church (The first 300 years)
    R: 405
  Vatican City (History) **V:** 288-289
Peter and John [book by De Maupassant]
  De Maupassant, Guy **D:** 118
Peter Pan [literary figure] **P:** 325
  Barrie, J. M. **B:** 118
  London *picture on* **L:** 429; (Parks) **L:** 435-436
Peter Pan [play by Barrie]
  Barrie, J. M. **B:** 118
  Peter Pan **P:** 325
"Peter Piper"
  Nursery rhyme (Tongue twisters) **N:** 615
Peter Rabbit, The Tale of [book by Potter]
  Literature for children *picture on* **L:** 362
  Potter, Beatrix **P:** 715
Peter the First [book by Tolstoy]
  Tolstoy, Alexei **T:** 322
Peter the Great *See* Peter I, the Great *in this index*
Peter the Hermit [French religious leader] **P:** 325
  Crusades (The First Crusade) **Ci:** 1160
Peterborough [New Hampshire]
  Library (Libraries in the United States) **L:** 261
Peterhof [palace]
  Saint Petersburg [Russia] (The city) **S:** 54-55
Petermann Glacier
  Iceberg (Northern Hemisphere icebergs) **I:** 17-18
Peters, Arthur [Canadian political leader]
  Prince Edward Island (table) **P:** 791
Peters, Frederick [Canadian political leader]
  Prince Edward Island (table) **P:** 791
Peters, John S. [American political leader]
  Connecticut (table) **Ci:** 967
Peters, Mary E. [American government official]
  Transportation, Department of (table) **T:** 400
Peters, Samuel [British author]
  Blue laws **B:** 420
Petersburg [Virginia] **P:** 325
Petersburg, Saint [Russia] *See* Saint Petersburg *in this index*
Petersburg, Siege of [1864-1865]
  Civil War, American (table) **Ci:** 624; (Siege of Petersburg) **Ci:** 631
  Lee, Robert E. (Final engagements) **L:** 179
Petersburg National Battlefield [Virginia]
  National Park System (table: National battlefields) **N:** 55
Petersen, Hjalmar [American political leader]
  Minnesota (table) **M:** 602
Petersen House [Washington, D.C.]
  Washington, D.C. (Ford's Theatre) **W:** 75
Petersham, Maud Fuller [American artist]
  Caldecott Medal (table: 1946) **C:** 26
Petersham, Miska [American artist]
  Caldecott Medal (table: 1946) **C:** 26
Peterson, David [Canadian political leader]
  Ontario (table) **O:** 783
Peterson, Oscar [American musician] **P:** 325
Peterson, Peter G. [American government official]
  Commerce, Department of (table) **Ci:** 871
Peterson, Roger Tory [American artist] **P:** 325
Peterson, Russell W. [American political leader]
  Delaware (table) **D:** 109
Peterson, Val [American political leader]
  Nebraska (table) **N:** 110
Peterson, Walter R., Jr. [American political leader]
  New Hampshire (table) **N:** 223
Peterson Air Force Base [Colorado]
  NORAD **N:** 453
Peterson Field Guide Series [books by Peterson]
  Peterson, Roger Tory **P:** 325
Petillo, Kelly [American race driver]
  Automobile racing (table: Indianapolis 500 winners) **A:** 980
Petiole [botany]
  Celery **C:** 325 *with picture*
  Leaf *picture on* **L:** 153; (The petiole) **L:** 154
  Plant (Leaves) **P:** 529-531 *with picture*
  Vegetable (Leaves) **V:** 292
Petiole [entomology]
  Ant (The abdomen) **A:** 522 *with picture*
Pétion, Alexandre [Haitian general]
  Haiti (History) **H:** 15-16
Petipa, Marius [French choreographer] **P:** 326
  Ballet (Ballet in Russia) **B:** 52
  Nutcracker, The **N:** 622
Petit, Roland [French dancer] **P:** 326
Petit basset griffon vendéen [dog] **P:** 326 *with picture*
Petit Caporal, Le [name for]
  Napoleon I **N:** 13
Petit Gulf [cotton]
  Mississippi (Statehood) **M:** 642
Petit jury [law]

Jury (Petit juries) **J:** 202
Petit larceny [crime]
  Larceny **L:** 75
Petit mal seizure [disease]
  Epilepsy **E:** 343
Petit point [handicraft] **P:** 326 *with picture*
  Needlepoint **N:** 118
Petit Testament, Le [poem by Villon]
  Villon, François **V:** 385
Petit Trianon [palace, Versailles]
  Marie Antoinette **M:** 200
  Versailles, Palace of **V:** 339
Petitcodiac River [Canada]
  Moncton **M:** 702
Petitgrain bigarade [oil]
  Petitgrain oil **P:** 327
Petitgrain oil P: 327
Petition [law] **P:** 327
  Freedom of assembly (History) **F:** 504
Petition of Right [English history] **P:** 327
  Democracy (Democracy in England) **D:** 122
  England (The first Stuarts) **E:** 308
Petits Poèmes en prose [poems by Baudelaire]
  Baudelaire, Charles **B:** 173
Petits Violons, Les [string ensemble]
  Lully, Jean-Baptiste **L:** 516
PETN [explosive] **P:** 327
  Ammunition (Artillery ammunition) **A:** 435-436
  Bomb (The explosive material) **B:** 450
Peto [fish]
  Wahoo **W:** 5 *with picture*
Petőfi, Sándor [Hungarian poet]
  Hungary (The arts) **H:** 442
Petoskey stone [mineral] **P:** 327
  Gem *picture on* **G:** 78
Petra [ancient city] **P:** 327
  Arabs (The Arabs before Islam) **A:** 589
  Jordan **J:** 160 *with picture*; (Early days) **J:** 164
Petrarch [Italian poet] **P:** 327
  Humanism (The development of humanism) **H:** 430
  Italian literature (Humanism and the Renaissance) **I:** 494
  Renaissance (Petrarch and Giovanni Boccaccio) **R:** 234
Petrarchan sonnet
  Poetry (Forms) **P:** 595
Petrel [bird] **P:** 328
  Antarctica (Living things) **A:** 535 *with picture*
  Bird (Birds of the ocean and the Antarctic) **B:** 344 *with picture*
Petrie, Sir Flinders [British archaeologist]
  Alphabet (Semitic scripts) **A:** 381
  Archaeology (The 1800's) **A:** 599
Petrifaction [geology]
  Fossil *picture on* **F:** 426; (The action of minerals) **F:** 425 *with picture*
  Petrified forest **P:** 328 *with picture*
Petrified forest [geology] **P:** 328 *with picture*
  Tree (Fossil trees) **T:** 415
Petrified Forest [Mississippi]
  Mississippi (Places to visit) **M:** 632
Petrified Forest, The [film]
  Bogart, Humphrey **B:** 436
Petrified Forest, The [play by Sherwood]
  Sherwood, Robert Emmet **S:** 398
Petrified Forest National Park [Arizona] **P:** 328 *with picture*
  Arizona (Visitor's guide) **A:** 678
  National Park System (table: National parks) **N:** 48
Petrified peat [geology]
  Coal (The composition of coal) **Ci:** 717
Petrified wood [rock]
  Fossil *picture on* **F:** 426
  Petrified forest **P:** 328 *with picture*
  Quartz (Types) **Q:** 8
Petrillo, James Caesar [American labor leader] **P:** 329
Petrine theory [religion]
  Leo I, Saint **L:** 197
Petrissage [movement]
  Massage **M:** 240
Petrobras [company]
  Manufacturing (table) **M:** 170
Petrochemicals P: 329
  Gas [fuel] (Gas as a raw material) **G:** 52
  Hydrocarbon **H:** 465
  Natural gas liquids **N:** 64
  Petroleum (Petroleum as a raw material) **P:** 333
  Textile (Manufactured fibers) **T:** 213
PetroChina [company]
  Manufacturing (table) **M:** 170
Petroglyph [carving]
  Labyrinth *picture on* **L:** 19
  Nova Scotia *picture on* **N:** 568
Petroglyph National Monument [New Mexico]
  National Park System (table: National

monuments) **N:** 51
Petrograd [former name]
  Saint Petersburg [Russia] **S:** 54; (History) **S:** 55
Petrographer [career]
  Geology (Areas of specialization) **G:** 100-101
Petrography [geology]
  Coal (Analyzing coal composition) **Ci:** 717
Petrol [fuel]
  Gasoline **G:** 61
Petrol engine *See* Gasoline engine *in this index*
Petrolatum [medication] **P:** 329
  Mineral oil **M:** 572
  Wax (Mineral wax) **W:** 153
Petroleum P: 330 *with pictures*
  See also Gasoline; Oil spill *in this index; and the list of Related articles in the* Petroleum *article*
  Fossil fuel **F:** 427
  International aspects
    Arabs **A:** 585; (Economy) **A:** 589 *with picture*; (Arabs today) **A:** 590
    Bush, George Herbert Walker (Persian Gulf crisis) **B:** 721
    International Energy Agency **I:** 340
    Iraq (Economy) **I:** 412; (The Persian Gulf War of 1991) **I:** 414
    Libya (Strained relations with the United States) **L:** 268 *with picture*
    Mexico (The late 1900's) **M:** 473
    Middle East (The 1970's and the 1980's) **M:** 534a
    Nationalization **N:** 63
    Organization of the Petroleum Exporting Countries **O:** 854
    Persian Gulf War of 1991 **P:** 300a
    Saudi Arabia (Continued progress) **S:** 161-162
    Strategic Petroleum Reserve **So:** 920
    United States, History of the (Environmental and energy concerns) **U:** 196a
  Production
    Argentina (Mining) **A:** 654 *with picture*
    Atlantic Ocean (Ocean resources) **A:** 867
    Canada *picture on* **C:** 123
    Distillation (Rectification) **D:** 239
    Exxon Valdez oil spill **E:** 459
    Grand Banks **G:** 306
    Gulf oil spill of 2010 **G:** 437
    Indonesia (Mining) **I:** 235
    Industry *picture in* **I:** 256
    Iran (Mining) **I:** 404
    Kansas (Mining) **K:** 233 *with picture*
    Malaysia *picture on* **M:** 100
    Middle East (Economy) **M:** 531 *with picture*
    Montana *picture on* **M:** 471
    Netherlands *picture on* **N:** 147
    North Dakota *picture on* **N:** 497
    Northwest Territories (Mining) **N:** 532 *with picture*
    Ocean (Sources of energy) **O:** 654; (Marine pollution) **O:** 664 *with picture*
    Oil shale **O:** 707
    Oklahoma (Mining) **O:** 729 *with picture*
    Paleontology **P:** 103
    Persian Gulf **P:** 300
    Saudi Arabia (Economy) **S:** 159
    Seismograph (Searching for oil) **S:** 288
    South America (Mining) **So:** 636 *with picture*
    Texas (Natural resources) **T:** 199; (Mining) **T:** 201 *with picture*
    Tower **T:** 351
    United Arab Emirates **U:** 43; (Economy) **U:** 44 *with picture*; (History) **U:** 45
    United Kingdom *picture on* **U:** 66
    Venezuela (International trade) **V:** 303
    Western frontier life in America (Mining) **W:** 234-235
    Wyoming *picture on* **W:** 531; (History) **W:** 534
  Transportation
    Pipeline **P:** 490
    Ship (Tankers) **S:** 408
    Transportation (Declining fule reserves) **T:** 397; (Related industries) **T:** 397
  Uses
    Asphalt (Asphalt production) **A:** 815
    Automobile (Demand for petroleum) **A:** 961
    Energy supply (Fossil fuels) **E:** 277; (Depletion of fuel reserves) **E:** 281
    Fuel (Petroleum) **F:** 550
    Gasoline **G:** 61
    Heating (Oil) **H:** 159
    Petroleum coke **P:** 350
    Saccharin **S:** 4
    Wax (Mineral wax) **W:** 153
Petroleum coke [fuel] **P:** 350
Petroleum engineering [career]
  Engineering (Other specialized fields) **E:** 287
Petroleum Exporting Countries, Organization of the *See* Organization of the Petroleum Exporting

Countries *in this index*
Petroleum field
Petroleum (table) **P: 332**
Petroleum fraction [chemistry]
Paraffin **P: 143**
Petroleum geologist [career]
Geology (Areas of specialization) **G: 100**
Petroleum jelly
Petrolatum **P: 329**
Wax (Mineral wax) **W: 153**
Petroleum trap
Petroleum (Uses of petroleum) **P: 333-334**
Petrolia [Ontario]
London **L: 444**
Petrology [geology] **P: 350**
Petronas [company]
Petronas Towers **P: 350**
Petronas Towers [Kuala Lumpur, Malaysia] **P: 350**
Asia *picture on* **A: 812**
Malaysia *picture on* **M: 98a**; (City life) **M: 98c-98d**
Skyscraper (table) **S: 498** *with picture*
Petronius [Roman author] **P: 351**
Latin literature (The Imperial Period) **L: 116**
Novel (Ancient Greek and Roman narratives)
N: 572
Petronius Maximus [Roman emperor]
Rome, Ancient (table) **R: 447**
Petropavlovsk-Kamchatskiy [Russia]
Kamchatka Peninsula **K: 212**
Petrosian, Tigran [Russian chess player]
Chess (World chess champions) **C: 414**
Petrouchka [ballet]
Stravinsky, Igor (Early works) **So: 922**
Petrovac [town, Montenegro]
Montenegro *picture on* **M: 764**
Petrović, Djordge [Serbian political leader]
Serbia (Ottoman rule) **S: 314**
Petrozavodsk [Russia]
Karelia **K: 246**
Petruchio [literary figure]
Shakespeare, William: (*The Taming of the Shrew*)
S: 356
Petticoat [clothing]
Clothing (The 1600's) **Ci: 703**
Pettoruti, Emilio [Argentine painter]
Argentina (The arts) **A: 651-652**
Pettus, John J. [American political leader]
Mississippi (table) **M: 640**
Petty, Adam [American race driver]
Petty, Richard **P: 351**
Petty, Kyle [American race driver]
Petty, Richard **P: 351**
Petty, Lee [American race driver]
Automobile racing (table: NASCAR Sprint Cup
champions) **A: 981**
Petty, Richard [American race driver] **P: 351**
Automobile racing (table: NASCAR Sprint Cup
champions) **A: 981**
Petty, Sir William [English economist]
Econometrics **E: 57**
Petty-Fitzmaurice, Henry Charles Keith
[Canadian statesman] *See* Lansdowne, Marquess
of *in this index*
Petty jury *See* Petit jury *in this index*
Petty larceny [crime]
Larceny **L: 75**
Petty officer [rank]
Navy, United States (Training a sailor) **N: 83**
Rank, Military (table) **R: 140**
Pettygrove, Francis W. [American settler]
Portland [Oregon] **P: 683**
Petunia [plant] **P: 351**
Flower (Garden annuals) **F: 276** *with picture*
Nightshade **N: 421**
Petuntse [earth]
Porcelain **P: 675**
Petzval, Josef M. [Hungarian mathematician]
Photography (The invention of photography)
P: 422-423
Peugeot [company]
Automobile (The birth of the automobile
industry) **A: 966**
Manufacturing (table) **M: 170**
Peul [people] *See* Fulani *in this index*
Pevsner, Antoine [Russian-French artist] **P: 351**
with picture
Pew [literary figure]
Stevenson, Robert Louis (Novels) **So: 898**
Pew, Joseph N. [American businessman]
Pew Charitable Trusts **P: 351**
Pew Charitable Trusts P: 351
Pewee [bird] **P: 352** *with picture*
Pewenche [people]
Mapuche **M: 189**
Pewter [metal] **P: 352** *with picture*
Alloy (Costly and ornamental alloys) **A: 378**
Antique (Metalwork) **A: 558**

Colonial life in America (Furnishings) **Ci: 797**;
(Decorative arts) **Ci: 807** *with picture*
Peyote [plant]
Mescaline **M: 421**
Peyrony, Denis [French anthropologist]
Prehistoric people (table) **P: 754**
Peyto Lake [Alberta]
Banff National Park **B: 77**
Peytral
Armor *picture on* **A: 720**
Pfaff, Judy [American sculptor]
Sculpture *picture on* **S: 260**
PFD
Life jacket **L: 281**
Pfiesteria [organism] **P: 353**
PG [rating]
Motion picture (Censorship and self-regulation)
M: 860-861
PG-13 [rating]
Motion picture (Censorship and self-regulation)
M: 860-861
PGA [organization] *See* Professional Golfers'
Association *in this index*
PGA Tour [organization]
Golf (Tournaments) **G: 264**; (The rise of
professional golf) **G: 266**
pH [chemistry] **P: 353**
Phacelia [flower]
Flower *picture on* **F: 289**
Phädon [book by Mendelssohn]
Mendelssohn, Moses **M: 399**
Phaeacians [legendary people]
Odyssey: (The *Odyssey* begins) **O: 675**
Phaedo [book by Plato]
Plato (The dialogues) **P: 567**
Socrates (Socrates's life) **So: 567-568**
Phaedrus [Greek scholar]
Aesop's fables **A: 90**
Phaedrus [book by Plato]
Plato (The dialogues) **P: 567**
Phagocyte [physiology]
Blood (Protecting against disease) **B: 410**
Disease (Immune responses) **D: 231-232**
Echinacea **E: 49**
Immune system (Other white blood cells) **I: 88**
Interleukin **I: 335**
Metchnikoff, Élie **M: 431**
Phagocytosis [physiology]
Blood *diagram on* **B: 409**; (Protecting against
disease) **B: 410**
Immune system (Antigen-presenting cells) **I: 88**
Phalange [anatomy]
Foot (The bones) **F: 352** *with diagram*
Hand (Parts of the hand) **H: 40** *with diagram*
Human body (table) **H: 422** *with diagram*
Wrist *diagram on* **W: 510**
Phalanx [anatomy]
Frog *picture on* **F: 537**
Phalanx [warfare]
Army (Ancient armies) **A: 726**
Greece, Ancient (Military forces) **G: 372**
Philip II **P: 369**
Phalarope [bird] **P: 353**
Bird (Birds of the Arctic) **B: 343** *with picture*
Phalera [decoration]
Medals, decorations, and orders (History) **M: 359**
Phallic phase [human development]
Psychoanalysis (Psychoanalytic theory) **P: 846**
Phan Si Pan [mountain] *See* Fan Si Pan *in this index*
Phanariots [Romanian history]
Romania (Ottoman rule) **R: 423**
Phanerozoic Eon [geology]
Earth (Age of Earth) **E: 26**
Prehistoric animal (The world of prehistoric
animals) **P: 736**
Phantom color
Color (Surprising color-vision effects) **Ci: 819** *with
diagram*
Phantom of the Opera, The [musical by Lloyd
Webber]
Lloyd Webber, Andrew **L: 403**
Musical comedy (During the late 1900's) **M: 960-
961**
Phantom Ranch [Arizona]
Grand Canyon National Park (Recreational
activities) **G: 307-308**
Pharaoh [title] **P: 353**
Valley of the Kings **V: 266**
Pharaoh hound [dog] **P: 353** *with picture*
Pharaoh's ant
Ant (The importance of ants) **A: 528**
Phares [Biblical figure]
Judah **J: 179**
Pharisees [religious group] **P: 354**
Jews (The Hellenistic period) **J: 121-122**
Sadducees **S: 8**
Sanhedrin **S: 110**

Pharmaceutical aerosol
Aerosol **A: 89**
Pharmaceutics
Pharmacy (Training and careers in pharmacy)
P: 354
Pharmacist [career]
Medicine (Other health-care professionals)
M: 366
Pharmacy **P: 354**
World, History of the *picture on* **W: 435**
Pharmacodynamics [science]
Pharmacology **P: 354**
Pharmacokinetics [science]
Pharmacology **P: 354**
Pharmacology [chemistry] **P: 354**
Pharmacy (Training and careers in pharmacy)
P: 354
Pharmacy P: 354
Hospital (Professional services departments)
H: 371
Pharnaces II [king of Pontus]
Caesar, Julius (Last victories) **C: 13**
Mithridates VI **M: 679**
Pharos of Alexandria [lighthouse]
Lighthouse (Notable lighthouses) **L: 295**
Seven Wonders of the Ancient World *picture on*
S: 327; (The Lighthouse of Alexandria) **S: 325**
Pharsalia [poem by Lucan]
Latin literature (The Imperial Period) **L: 116**
Pharsalus, Battle of [48 B.C.]
Caesar, Julius (Civil war) **C: 13**
Pharynx [anatomy] **P: 355**
Alimentary canal **A: 368** *with diagram*
Cancer (table) **C: 170**
Diphtheria (Cause, symptoms, and
complications) **D: 216**
Human body (The air passages) **H: 420-421**;
(table) **H: 422** *with diagram*
Mouth **M: 903** *with diagram*
Respiration (Structures of breathing) **R: 260**
Throat **T: 270**
Phase [astronomy]
Astronomy (How the moon moves) **A: 835**
Mercury (Phases) **M: 414**
Moon (Phases) **M: 783**; (Simulating the phases of
the moon) **M: 793** *with pictures*
Venus (Phases) **V: 310**
Phase [botany]
Plant (Sexual reproduction) **P: 532**
Phase [physics]
See also Interference *in this index*
Waves (Interference) **W: 153**
Phase, of matter [physics]
Heat (What heat does) **H: 152** *with diagram*
Matter (States of matter) **M: 311**
Phase-change recording [electronics]
Compact disc (CD-RW) **Ci: 902**
Phase contrast microscope
Microscope (Phase contrast microscopes) **M: 519**
Phase modulation [electronics]
Antenna **A: 543**
Wireless communication (How wireless
communication works) **W: 344**
Phase rule
Chemistry (Development of physical chemistry)
C: 404
Phase shifter
Radar (Continued progress) **R: 72**
Phased array radar
Radar (Continued progress) **R: 72**
Phasmatodea [entomology]
Insect (table) **I: 300**
Ph.D. [degree]
Degree, College (table) **D: 92**
Pheasant [bird] **P: 355** *with pictures*
Bird *pictures on* **B: 353, B: 363**
Poultry **P: 720**
Pheasant-tailed jacana
Jacana **J: 2**
Pheasant's-eye [plant]
Adonis **A: 66** *with picture*
Phèdre [play by Racine]
Romanticism (The qualities of Romanticism)
R: 427
Pheidippides [Greek runner]
Marathon, Battle of (The battle) **M: 191**
Phelloderm [botany]
Bark (Inner bark) **B: 110** *with diagram*
Stem (Woody stems) **So: 887**
Phellogen [botany] *See* Phloem *in this index*
Phelps, Edmund Strother [American economist]
Nobel Prizes (Economics: 2006) **N: 449**
Phelps, John S. [American political leader]
Missouri (table) **M: 668**
Phelps, Michael [American swimmer] **P: 356**
Olympic Games *picture on* **O: 748**; (The recent
games) **O: 753-754** *with picture*

Swimming (History) So: 1047
Phenacetin [medication]
Acetaminophen A: 25
Phenakistoscope [device]
Animation (Early animation) A: 514a
Phenobarbital [drug]
Anticonvulsant A: 553
Barbiturate (Medical uses) B: 107
Phenol [chemical]
Disinfectant D: 235
Phenolic P: 356
Phenolic P: 356
Plastics (table) P: 556
Phenolic resin
Plastics (The invention of Bakelite) P: 559-560
Phenology [biology] P: 356
Phenolphthalein [chemical] P: 356
Laxative L: 147
Phenomena [philosophy]
Phenomenology P: 356
Phenomena of Life Common to Animals and Plants [book by Bernard]
Bernard, Claude B: 270
Phenomenology [philosophy] P: 356
Existentialism E: 437
Personality (Ratings and self-reports) P: 301
Philosophy (Philosophy in the 1900's) P: 390
Phenomenology of Spirit [book by Hegel]
Hegel, G. W. F. (Hegel's writings) H: 165
Phenotype [genetics]
Heredity (Heredity and environment) H: 205
Races, Human (How human populations develop and change) R: 57
Phenylalanine [amino acid]
Brain (Genetic disorders) B: 558
Phenylketonuria P: 357
Phenylglycine [chemical]
Indigo I: 223
Phenylketonuria [birth defect] P: 357
Brain (Genetic disorders) B: 558
Cell (Metabolic diseases) C: 336
Heredity (table) H: 204
Intellectual disability (Causes) I: 318
Phenylthiocarbamide [chemical]
Heredity (Patterns of heredity) H: 202
Phenytoin [drug]
Anticonvulsant A: 553
Pheromone [zoology] P: 357
Ant (Communication) A: 525
Butterfly (The life cycle of butterflies) B: 739-740
Codling moth Ci: 752
Gland (Exocrine glands) G: 207-208
Moth (The head) M: 837-838
Phi Beta Kappa P: 357
Fraternity F: 495
Virginia (Interesting facts) V: 399
William and Mary, College of W: 309
Phibun Songkhram [Thai political leader]
Thailand (Changes in government) T: 227
Phidias [Greek sculptor] P: 357
Classicism (Greece) Ci: 653
Greece, Ancient on G: 371
Seven Wonders of the Ancient World (The statue of Zeus) S: 325
Philadelphia [film]
Hanks, Tom H: 51
Philadelphia [Pennsylvania] P: 358 *with pictures and maps*
See also the list of Related articles in the Philadelphia article
American literature (Colonial literature [1608-1764]) A: 414-415
City planning pictures on Ci: 600
Colonial life in America (Geographic divisions) Ci: 791
Franklin, Benjamin (Civic leader) F: 487
Pennsylvania picture on P: 248; (Places to visit) P: 254; (table: Average monthly weather) P: 259
United States, History of the (The Middle Colonies) U: 154-155
United States capitals U: 199
Philadelphia [ancient Greece] P: 368
Philadelphia [frigate]
Decatur, Stephen D: 67
Philadelphia, Here I Come! [play by Friel]
Friel, Brian F: 533
Philadelphia Eagles [team]
Football (National Football League) F: 364
Philadelphia Evening Post and Daily Advertiser
Philadelphia (Communication) P: 365
Philadelphia Female Anti-Slavery Society
Mott, Lucretia Coffin M: 880
Philadelphia Flyers
Hockey (table: National Hockey League) H: 281
Philadelphia History Museum
Philadelphia (Libraries and museums) P: 363-364

Philadelphia Museum of Art
Philadelphia (Libraries and museums) P: 363-364
Philadelphia Orchestra
Philadelphia (The arts) P: 363
Philadelphia Phillies [baseball team]
Baseball (table) B: 130
Philadelphia 76ers [team]
Basketball (table) B: 150
Iverson, Allen I: 520
Philadelphia Society for Alleviating the Miseries of Public Prisons
Prison (Early prison reform) P: 807
Philadelphia Story, The [play by Barry]
Barry, Philip B: 119
Philadelphia style ice cream
Ice cream (The composition of ice cream) I: 8
Philadelphia Zoo [Pennsylvania]
Philadelphia (Recreation) P: 364
Zoo (The evolution of zoos) Z: 605
Philanthropist [newspaper]
Ohio (Communication) O: 698
Philanthropy P: 368
For a list of famous philanthropists, see the list of Related articles in the Philanthropy article
Foundation F: 429
Philanthropy UK [organization]
Foundation F: 430
Philately [hobby]
Stamp collecting So: 829
Philbrook Museum of Art
Oklahoma (Museums) O: 717 *with picture*
Philemon, Epistle to [New Testament] P: 368
Bible (The Letters) B: 284
Philidor [French chess player]
Chess (History) C: 414
Philike Hetairia [organization]
Greece (Ottoman rule) G: 361
Philip [antipope]
Pope (table) P: 666
Philip [archduke of Austria]
Maximilian I M: 319
Philip I [king of France]
France (table) F: 471
Philip II [king of France] P: 368 *with portrait*
Crusades (The Third Crusade) Ci: 1160 *with map*
France (Growth of royal power) F: 472-473
John J: 132
Louvre L: 507
Paris (Early years) P: 166
Philip II [king of Macedonia] P: 369 *with portrait*
Alexander the Great (His youth) A: 342
Demosthenes D: 129
Greece, Ancient (The rivalry between Athens and Sparta) G: 373-374
Macedonia M: 12
Olympias O: 746
Thebes T: 251
Philip II [king of Spain] P: 369
Austria (The Habsburgs) A: 937
Belgium (Habsburg rule) B: 233
Drake, Sir Francis (Voyage around the world) D: 321-322; (Expeditions against Spain) D: 322
Elizabeth I (Problems at home and abroad) E: 238-239
Escorial E: 357
Henry IV [of France] H: 186
Madrid (History) M: 40
Mary I M: 239
Netherlands (Eighty Years' War) N: 148
Spain (The Spanish Empire) So: 747
Spanish Armada (Background to battle) So: 755; (The two fleets) So: 755
William I, Prince of Orange W: 308
Philip III [king of France]
France (table) F: 471
Philip III Arrhidaeus [king of Macedonia]
Alexander the Great (His death) A: 344
Philip IV [king of France] P: 370 *with picture*
France (Growth of royal power) F: 472-473
Knights Templars K: 353
Salic law S: 66
Philip IV [king of Spain]
Painting (The Spanish masters) P: 64 *with picture*
Velázquez, Diego V: 296
Philip V [king of France]
France (table) F: 471
Philip V [king of Macedonia]
Antigonid dynasty A: 555
Philip V [king of Spain] P: 370 *with picture*
Spain (The Spanish decline) So: 747
Succession wars (The War of the Spanish Succession) So: 950
Utrecht, Peace of U: 252
Philip VI [king of France] P: 370
Crécy, Battle of Ci: 1124
Dauphin D: 44
Philip, Danny [Solomon Islands political leader]

Solomon Islands (History) So: 585-586
Philip, King [American Indian chief] P: 370
Indian wars (King Philip's War [1675-1676]) I: 191
Maine (Indian wars) M: 89
Massachusetts (King Philip's War) M: 291
Massasoit M: 296
Plymouth Colony (Later years) P: 584
Rhode Island (King Philip's War) R: 312
Philip, Prince [husband of Elizabeth II] P: 371 *with picture*
Battenberg B: 167
Charles, Prince C: 382
Elizabeth II (Marriage and succession to the throne) E: 240
Philip Augustus See Philip II [king of France] *in this index*
Philip Morris [company]
Manufacturing (table) M: 170
Philip of Anjou See Philip V [king of Spain] *in this index*
Philip of Bethsaida, Saint [apostle] P: 371
Philip the Evangelist [Biblical figure] P: 371
Philip the Fair See Philip IV [of France] *in this index*
Philipp, Emanuel L. [American political leader]
Wisconsin (table) W: 365
Philippeion [ancient Greece]
Olympia O: 745
Philippi [ancient city] P: 371
Philippi, Battle of [42 B.C.]
Philippi P: 371
Philippi, Battle of [1861]
West Virginia (The Civil War and statehood) W: 227-228
Philippians, Epistle to the [New Testament] P: 371
Bible (The Letters) B: 284
Philippics [speeches]
Cicero, Marcus Tullius (His works) Ci: 552
Demosthenes D: 129
Philippine eagle [bird]
Eagle (Other kinds of eagles) E: 5
Philippine mahogany [wood]
Mahogany M: 66
Philippine Republic [Philippine history]
Aguinaldo, Emilio A: 163
Philippine Sea, Battle of the [1944]
Spruance, Raymond Ames So: 809
World War II (Island hopping in the Central Pacific) W: 489-490
Philippine Trench [Pacific Ocean]
Philippines (Land and climate) P: 376
Philippines P: 372 *with pictures and maps*
Asian Americans (History of Asian immigration) A: 812d *with picture*
Bataan Death March B: 162
Christmas (In Asia) C: 533
Clothing picture on C: 693
Corregidor Ci: 1071
Exploration (Magellan's globe-circling expedition) E: 445
Flag picture on F: 204
Independence Day I: 107
Line of Demarcation L: 333
MacArthur, Douglas (World War II) M: 3
Magellan, Ferdinand (Sailing across the Pacific) M: 47
Martial law M: 234a
McKinley, William (America becomes a world power) M: 341
Rizal, José R: 357
Spanish-American War (Chief events) So: 753-754; (Results of the war) So: 754
Taft, William Howard (Governor of the Philippines) T: 10
World War II picture on W: 486; (Early Japanese victories) W: 487-488; (Island hopping in the Central Pacific) W: 489-490; (The liberation of the Philippines) W: 491
Philippines, University of the
Manila (Education and cultural life) M: 142
Philippus [Roman emperor]
Rome, Ancient (table) R: 447
Philips Electronics See Royal Philips Electronics *in this index*
Philipse, Frederick [Dutch businessman]
Yonkers Y: 583
Philistia [ancient region]
Palestine (Early history and settlement) P: 104
Philistines [ancient people] P: 382
Ark of the Covenant A: 693 *with picture*
David (Early life) D: 44-45
Palestine (Early history and settlement) P: 104
Palestinians P: 107
Samson S: 82
Philles Records [company]
Rock music (Independent producers) R: 379
Phillies, Philadelphia See Philadelphia Phillies *in this index*

Phillip, Arthur [British colonial leader]
Australia (British settlement) A: 920
New South Wales (History) N: 286
Phillips, Alonzo Dwight [American inventor]
Match (The first matches) M: 300-300a
Phillips, Caryl [Caribbean-born author]
English literature (Recent English fiction) E: 323
Phillips, Jeanne [American journalist]
Van Buren, Abigail V: 269
Phillips, John C. [American political leader]
Arizona (table) A: 687
Phillips, Leon C. [American political leader]
Oklahoma (table) O: 730
Phillips, Pauline Esther Friedman [American journalist] See Van Buren, Abigail in this index
Phillips, Sam [American businessman]
Presley, Elvis P: 772
Rock music (Elvis Presley) R: 376; (Sun Records) R: 376
Phillips, Simon [British musician]
Who, The W: 296
Phillips, Thomas [British painter]
Byron, Lord picture on B: 748
Phillips, Wendell [American social reformer] P: 382
Phillips, William Daniel [American physicist]
Nobel Prizes (Physics: 1997) N: 442
Phillips Collection
Washington, D.C. (Other Washington museums) W: 75
Phillips Economics Computer
Analog computer A: 448
Philo [Jewish philosopher]
Plato (Plato's place in Western thought) P: 569
Philoctetes [legendary figure]
Paris P: 159
Philodendron [botany] P: 382 with picture
Gardening picture on G: 37
Philography [hobby]
Autograph (Collecting autographs) A: 943
Philology
Linguistics L: 335
Renaissance (Humanism) R: 233-234
Philosopher's stone
Alchemy A: 334
Philosophes [philosophy] P: 382
Enlightenment (Influence of the Enlightenment) E: 326b
French literature (The Enlightenment) F: 520
French Revolution (Background) F: 524-525
History (Antiquarian research and the philosophes) H: 262
Pope (The 1700's and 1800's) P: 665
Philosophiae naturalis principia mathematica [book by Newton] See Principia mathematica in this index
Philosophical Enquiry into the Origin of Our Ideas of the Sublime and Beautiful [essay by Burke]
English literature (The Johnson circle) E: 319
Philosophical Letters [book by Voltaire]
Voltaire (Exile and return to France) V: 446
Philosophical rationalism [philosophy]
Rationalism R: 148
Philosophical Society, American See American Philosophical Society in this index
Philosophy P: 383 with pictures
See also the list of Related articles in the Philosophy article
Enlightenment E: 326a
Ethics E: 365
Greece, Ancient (Philosophy) G: 368
Greek literature (Philosophical literature) G: 377-378
Human being H: 413
Idealism I: 46
Mathematics (Philosophies of mathematics) M: 307
Political science (Political theory and philosophy) P: 638
Pre-Socratic philosophy P: 772
Psychology (Beginnings) P: 849
Romanticism (Romanticism and society) R: 427
Science (To philosophical thought) S: 192
Philosophy, Doctor of
Degree, College (The doctor's degree) D: 93
Philosophy in the Bedroom [book by Sade]
Enlightenment (The orderliness of nature) E: 326a-326b
"Philosophy of Composition, The" [essay by Poe]
Poe, Edgar Allan (Poe's life) P: 589; (Poetry and poetic theory) P: 589
Philosophy of Right [book by Hegel]
Hegel, G. W. F. (Hegel's writings) H: 165
Phimosis [disorder]
Circumcision Ci: 561
Phineus [legendary figure]
Harpy H: 67
Phipps, James [patient of]

Jenner, Edward (Jenner's work) J: 91
Phipps Conservatory and Botanical Gardens
Pittsburgh (Recreation) P: 500d
Phips, Sir William [British colonial official]
Massachusetts (Troubles with England) M: 291
Nova Scotia (The struggle in Acadia) N: 568
Quebec (Early days) Q: 36
Phishing [computing]
Internet (Glossary of Internet terms) I: 350a; (Internet crime) I: 350f
Phlebitis [disease]
Vein V: 295
Phlebotomy [medicine]
Bloodletting B: 417
Phlegethon [Greek mythology]
Tartarus T: 48
Phloem [botany]
Bark (Inner bark) B: 110 with diagram
Plant (Parts of plants) P: 528
Root (The core) R: 471 with diagrams
Sap (Vascular sap) S: 121 with diagram
Stem (Herbaceous stems) So: 887
Tree (Trunk and branches) T: 416 with diagram
Phloem necrosis [plant disease]
Elm (Diseases) E: 245
Phlogiston theory
Chemistry (The phlogiston theory) C: 401
Phlogopite [mineral]
Mica M: 482
Phlox [plant] P: 391
Flower (Garden perennials) picture on F: 279; (table) F: 301 with picture
Plant picture on P: 524
PHM [boat] See Patrol Hydrofoil Missileship in this index
Phnom Penh [Cambodia] P: 391
Cambodia C: 71; (Economy) C: 72
Khmer Rouge K: 308b
Pho [soup]
Vietnam (Food and drink) V: 366
Phobia [psychology] P: 392
Anxiety disorder A: 562
Mental illness (Anxiety disorders) M: 405-406
Personality (Emotional reactions) P: 302
Phobos [moon]
Mars (Satellites) M: 226b
Satellite (Satellites of the terrestrial planets) S: 150 with picture
Phocomelia [disorder]
Thalidomide T: 229
Phoebe [bird] P: 392 with picture
Phoebe [satellite]
Iapetus I: 2
Satellite (Phoebe) S: 150c
Phoebus Apollo [Greek mythology]
Apollo A: 566
Phoenicia [ancient country] P: 392 with pictures and map
Alphabet (Proto-Canaanite and Phoenician) A: 383 with pictures; (The Greeks) A: 383
Canaanites C: 97
Carthage (History) C: 260
Colonialism (Ancient colonialism) Ci: 813
David (King of Israel) D: 45
Exploration (The Phoenicians) E: 441 with map
Mediterranean Sea (History of the Mediterranean) M: 382
Ship (Phoenician and Greek ships) S: 415 with picture
Transportation (The first great civilizations) T: 385
Tyre T: 541
Utica U: 251
World, History of the (Civilizations of southwest Asia) W: 426-428
Phoenician [ancient language]
Alphabet (Proto-Canaanite and Phoenician) A: 383 with pictures
Phoenicians [people]
Phoenix (The people) P: 396
Phoenix [Arizona] P: 395 with pictures and map
Arizona A: 671 with picture; (Population) A: 674; (table: Average monthly weather) A: 682
Phoenix [Greek mythology] P: 399
Phoenix P: 395
Phoenix [ship]
Ship (Oceangoing steamships) S: 424
Stevens, John So: 896
Phoenix [weapon]
Guided missile picture on G: 425
"Phoenix and the Turtle, The" [poem by Shakespeare]
Shakespeare, William ("The Phoenix and the Turtle") S: 367
Phoenix Coyotes [hockey team]
Hockey (table: National Hockey League) H: 281
Phoenix Islands [Pacific]
Kiribati K: 335

Phoenix Mars Lander [spacecraft]
Mars (Observation by spacecraft) M: 226c-226d
Space exploration (Probes to Mars) So: 710
Vacuum picture on V: 256
Phoenix Sky Harbor International Airport [Phoenix]
Phoenix (Transportation and communication) P: 398
Phoenix South Mountain Park [Phoenix]
Phoenix (Recreation) P: 397
Phoenix Suns [team]
Basketball (table) B: 150
Phoenix Too Frequent, A [play by Fry]
Fry, Christopher F: 549
Pholidota [zoology]
Mammal (table) M: 128 with picture
Phon [unit of measure]
Sound (Intensity and loudness) So: 600-601
Phonation [sound]
Dolphin (Social life) D: 299
Whale (Group life) W: 261
Phone See Telephone in this index
Phone card
Telephone (Other services) T: 98
Phoneme [linguistics]
Animation (Making the model move) A: 513
Language (The sounds of language) L: 62
Reading (Phonics instruction) R: 159
Spelling So: 775
Phonetic alphabet
Hindi language (Alphabet and grammar) H: 235
Linguistics L: 335
Phonetics (An international phonetic alphabet) P: 400
Phonetic compound [writing]
Chinese language (Written Chinese) C: 509-510 with picture
Phonetic ideal
Phonetics (Phonetics and spelling) P: 400
Phonetic sign
Chinese language (Development) C: 510
Phonetics [speech] P: 399
Phonetization [language]
Writing system (Phonetization) W: 513
Phonics [language] P: 400
Reading (Comprehending what is perceived) R: 157; (Phonics instruction) R: 159
Phonogram [language]
Hieroglyphics (Development of hieroglyphic writing) H: 225-226
Phonograph P: 400 with pictures
Communication (The 1800's) Ci: 881-883 with picture
Edison, Thomas Alva picture on E: 77; (The Wizard of Menlo Park) E: 78; (Phonograph developments) E: 80 with picture
Invention picture on I: 360
Popular music (The recording era) P: 671
Stereophonic sound system (Parts of a stereo system) So: 892; (History) So: 892
Phonograph needle See Stylus in this index
Phonograph record
Berliner, Emile B: 267
Edison, Thomas Alva (Phonograph developments) E: 80
Phonograph P: 400 with pictures
Phonology [grammar]
Dyslexia D: 398
Linguistics (The components of a grammar) L: 336
Phony War
World War II (The Phony War) W: 473
Phorcys [Greek mythology]
Gorgons G: 274
Phosphate [chemistry] P: 402
Baking powder B: 33
Battery (Lithium-ion batteries) B: 170-171
Cell (DNA--the wondrous molecule) C: 334-335 with diagram
Detergent and soap (The development of detergents) D: 165-166
DNA D: 258
Fertilizer (Inorganic fertilizers) F: 79
Heredity (The structure of DNA) H: 205
Nauru (History) N: 68
Phosphorus P: 403
RNA R: 357
Tennessee Valley Authority (The valley) T: 158
Phosphate rock [mineral] P: 403
Phosphate P: 402
Phosphorus P: 403
Phospholipid [biology]
Cell (Inside a living cell) C: 328
Life (Lipids) L: 278
Lipid (Kinds of lipids) L: 345
Phosphor [chemical]
Electric light (Fluorescent lamps) E: 174

Fluorescent lamp F: 305 *with diagram*
Phosphorescence P: 402 *with picture*
Television (Cathode-ray tube screens) T: 125
Tungsten T: 486
Phosphorescence [light] P: 402 *with picture*
Light (Luminescence and fluorescence) L: 283
Luminescence L: 522
Phosphorus P: 403
Phosphorescent light
Phosphorescence P: 402
Phosphoric acid [chemical] P: 403
Phosphoric candle
Match (Early fire-making devices) M: 300
Phosphorite [mineral]
Phosphorus P: 403
Phosphorus [astronomy]
Venus V: 310
Phosphorus [element] P: 403
Fertilizer (Inorganic fertilizers) F: 79
Isotope *diagram on* I: 477
Match (The first matches) M: 300-300a
Nutrition (Minerals) N: 625-626
Phosphorus cycle P: 403
Semiconductor (Doped crystals) S: 291
Transistor (Transistor materials) T: 372
Phosphorus cycle [biology] P: 403 *with diagram*
Ecology (Cycling of materials) E: 55
Phossy jaw [disorder]
Match (The first matches) M: 300a
Photic zone [oceanography]
Ocean (Life in the ocean) O: 655
Photius [Byzantine scholar] P: 404
Eastern Orthodox Churches (History) E: 45-46
Roman Catholic Church (Split with the East) R: 407
Photo dectector [Digital audio]
Compact disc *picture on* Ci: 902
Photo editor [publishing]
Encyclopedia *picture on* E: 268
Photo-Secession [art]
Painting (Steiglitz and "291") P: 82
Photography (Artistic advances) P: 424-425
Photocatalyst [chemistry]
Nanotechnology (Applications of nanotechnology) N: 10
Photocathode [electronics]
Image orthicon I: 79
Photomultiplier tube P: 430
Photocell [electricity]
Electric eye (How electric eyes work) E: 169 *with diagram*
Smoke alarm S: 520
Photochemical glass
Glass (Specialty glasses) G: 212-213; (table) G: 218
Photochemical smog
Ozone O: 894
Smog (Photochemical smog) S: 519
Photochemistry P: 404
Light (Photochemistry) L: 291
Photochromic glass
Glass (Specialty glasses) G: 212-213; (table) G: 218; (Modern glassmaking) G: 222-223
Photocomposition [printing] P: 404 *with pictures*
Communication (The digital age) Ci: 885
Linotype L: 338
Newspaper (Making up the pages) N: 383
Printing (Typesetting) P: 797
Type T: 536
Photoconductive cell [device]
Electric eye (How electric eyes work) E: 169 *with diagram*
Photoelectric effect P: 405
Photocopying *See* Copying machine *in this index*
Photodegradable plastics
Plastics (Plastics and the environment) P: 560-561
Photodetector [electronic device]
Microscope (Scanning optical microscopes) M: 518
Photodiode [electronic component]
Electronics (Light-sensing devices) E: 213
Photoelectric cell [electronics]
Electric eye (How electric eyes work) E: 169 *with diagram*
Electronics (The vacuum tube era) E: 215
Photoelectric effect P: 405
Photoelectric detection
Smoke alarm S: 520
Photoelectric effect [physics] P: 405
Einstein, Albert (Famous theories) E: 146-146a
Light (Photoelectric effect) L: 291
Photon P: 404
Radiation (The quantum theory) R: 81
Photoelectrochemical cell
Solar energy (Other solar cells) So: 578
Photoelectrochemistry

Electrochemistry E: 200
Photoelectrolysis
Electrolysis (Uses of electrolysis) E: 200-201
Photoemissive cell [electronics]
Photoelectric effect P: 405
Photoengraving [printing]
Printing (History) P: 803-804
Photoflash bomb [weapon]
Bomb (Other bombs) B: 451
Photoflood lamp
Photography (Artificial lighting devices) P: 416
Photogram [art]
Photography (Dramatic changes) P: 425-426
Photogrammetry [cartography] P: 405 *with pictures*
Mountain (Measuring mountains) M: 896b
Photographic film *See* Film *in this index*
Photographic memory
Memory (Exceptionally good memory) M: 393
Photographic model [occupation]
Modeling (Physical requirements for modeling) M: 684-685
Photographic type [printing] *See* Cold type *in this index*
Photography P: 406 *with pictures*
See also the list of Related articles in the Photography *article*
Baekeland, Leo Hendrik B: 25
Communication (The 1800's) Ci: 881 *with picture*
Eastman, George E: 47
Industrial arts (Industrial arts courses) I: 242-243
Pulitzer Prizes (table) P: 893
Applications
Astronomy (Optical astronomy) A: 839-840
Ballistics (Terminal ballistics) B: 56 *with picture*
Blueprint B: 424
Compact disc (CD-ROM's) Ci: 901
Copying machine (Projection copying) Ci: 1045
Encyclopedia (Basic steps in the preparation of a World Book article) E: 268 *with picture*
Modeling M: 684
Newspaper (Making up the pages) N: 383
Painting (New visual sources) P: 72
Particle detector (Photographic films and plates) P: 186
Photochemistry P: 404
Photocomposition P: 404 *with diagram*
Photogrammetry P: 405 *with pictures*
Police (Investigations of crimes) P: 621
Telescope (Detecting faint objects) T: 103
Type T: 536
Equipment and processes
Camera C: 80
Daguerreotype D: 5
Kirlian photography K: 336 *with picture*
Light meter L: 294
Photography (Cameras) P: 407 *with pictures*
Polarized light (Uses of polarized light) P: 618
Silver nitrate S: 465
Stereoscope So: 893
Talbotype T: 19
Photography, Director of
Motion picture (Assembling the production team) M: 850 *with picture*; (Shooting the movie) M: 852-853
Photoimagesetter [machine]
Printing (Electronic imagesetting) P: 797
Photoimagesetting *See* Photocomposition *in this index*
Photojournalism
Photography (Artistic advances) P: 424-425; (Photojournalism) P: 428
Riis, Jacob August R: 340
Photolithography [technique]
Light (Light in manufacturing) L: 292
Printing (History) P: 803-804
Photomicrography [photography]
Cell *pictures on* C: 326
Photomontage [art]
Photography (Dramatic changes) P: 425-426
Photomultiplier tube [electronics] P: 430
Spectrometer So: 772 *with diagram*
Photon [atomic particle] P: 430
Astronomy (Energy) A: 839
Atom (Electron energy levels) A: 873 *with diagram*
Boson B: 494
Charge-coupled device C: 378
Electromagnetic waves (History) E: 202
Laser (Producing laser light) L: 84 *with diagram*
Light (How light is produced) L: 283; (Photons) L: 286 *with diagram*
Photochemistry P: 404
Photoelectric effect P: 405
Physics (Quantum theory) P: 441
Quantum field theory Q: 6
Quantum mechanics (Quantum nature of light)

Q: 6
Radiation (Electromagnetic radiation) R: 75; (Causes of radiation) R: 78-79; (The quantum theory) R: 81
Spectrum So: 772
Subatomic particle (Elementary particles) So: 937
Photonics [engineering]
Electronics (Electronics today) E: 216
Light (Photonics) L: 291
Photoperiodism [biology] P: 430
Photophobia [disorder]
Iritis I: 434
Photophore [anatomy]
Lanternfish L: 69
Squid (The life of a squid) So: 814
Photoresist [film]
Compact disc (Manufacturing) Ci: 901
Photosensitive glass
Glass (Specialty glasses) G: 212-213; (table) G: 218
Photosite [electronics]
Photography (Capturing digital images) P: 420
Photosphere
Sun (Sun terms) So: 976; (Zones of the sun) So: 979-980 *with diagram*
Photostat machine
Copying machine (Projection copying) Ci: 1045
Photosynthesis [botany] P: 430
Agriculture (Food from plants) A: 147
Air (Origin of the atmosphere) A: 174
Algae (Structure of algae) A: 349
Archaea A: 593
Biochemistry (Biochemical research) B: 310
Biomass B: 322
Biophysics B: 326
Botany (The importance of botany) B: 508
Carbohydrate C: 202
Carbon cycle C: 206
Cell (Producing energy) C: 332-333
Cellulose (Biological importance) C: 341
Chlorophyll C: 517
Coral (Stony corals) Ci: 1048a
Coral reef (Where coral reefs exist) Ci: 1048b
Deep sea (Environment) D: 82
Ecology (Energy flow) E: 54
Forest (The flow of energy) F: 396
Global warming (Causes of global warming) G: 232; (Carbon sequestration) G: 232c
Hydrothermal vent H: 473
Leaf (Photosynthesis) L: 155 *with diagram*
Lichen (How lichens grow) L: 269
Manganese M: 139
Ocean (Life in the ocean) O: 655
Plankton P: 515
Plant (Photosynthesis) P: 537
Protist P: 836
Respiration (Respiration in plants) R: 261
Sap (Vascular sap) S: 121
Starch So: 855
Photosynthetic bacteria
Bacteria (How bacteria obtain food) B: 21
Photosynthesis P: 430
Phototropism [botany]
Plant (Environmental factors) P: 538 *with picture*
Tropism T: 451
Phototube [electronics]
Electric eye (How electric eyes work) E: 169
Phototypesetting *See* Photocomposition *in this index*
Photovoltaic cell [electronics]
Energy supply (Solar energy) E: 278
Photoelectric effect P: 405
Photovoltaic conversion
Solar energy So: 577 *with pictures*
Photovoltaic effect [physics]
Light (Photoelectric effect) L: 291
Solar energy (Photovoltaic conversion) So: 577
Phou Bia [mountain, Laos]
Laos (Land and climate) L: 71 *with map*
Phra Chom Klao [king of Thailand] *See* Mongkut *in this index*
Phrase [grammar]
Grammar G: 303; (Subordination) G: 304
Preposition P: 756
Phratry [ancient Greece]
Athens (Democracy) A: 857
Phrenic nerve [anatomy]
Diaphragm D: 184
Phrenology [pseudoscience] P: 430
Phronesis [philosophy]
Ethics (Aristotle) E: 366
Phrygia [ancient country] P: 431
Hittites (History) H: 269
Phthalocyanine [pigment]
Ink I: 272
Phumiphon Adunyadet [king of Siam] *See* Bhumibol Adulyadej *in this index*

Phyfe, Duncan [American furniture designer]
P: 431
Furniture *picture on* F: 569
Phylloxera [insect] P: 431 *with picture*
PhyloCode [biology]
Classification, Scientific (Development of
classification) Ci: 656
Phylogenetic system
Botany (Later developments) B: 509
Phylogeny [biology]
Biogenesis B: 312
Phylum [biology]
Animal (A classification of the animal kingdom)
A: 506
Classification, Scientific (Groups in classification)
Ci: 655
Physiatrics
Medicine (table) M: 369
Physical anthropology
Anthropology (Physical anthropology) A: 546
with picture
Races, Human R: 53
Physical bond
Materials (The role of bonds) M: 301
Physical capital
Capital C: 192
Physical change [chemistry] P: 431
Physical chemistry P: 431
Chemistry (Development of physical chemistry)
C: 404
Physical culture
Physical education (During the 1800's) P: 433
Physical cycle
Biorhythm B: 326
Physical disability
See also Disability *in this index*
Occupational therapy (Helping people with
physical disabilities) O: 648
Reading (Reading problems) R: 161-162
Physical disintegration [geology]
Soil *diagram on* So: 574; (How soil forms) So: 573
Physical education P: 431 *with picture*
Gymnasium G: 447
Physical fitness (Developing physical fitness)
P: 435 *with pictures*
Physical environment
Life (The physical environment) L: 275
Physical evidence
Forensic science F: 388b
Physical examination
Medicine (Diagnosis) M: 364
Physical fitness P: 433 *with pictures*
Bicycle (Bicycle riding today) B: 291
Education *picture on* E: 96
Health (Exercise) H: 125
Jogging J: 131
Physical geography
Geography (Physical geography) G: 94
Physical geology
Geology G: 97
***Physical Impossibility of Death in the Mind of
Someone Living, The*** [art by Hirst]
Hirst, Damien H: 243
Physical metallurgy
Metallurgy (Physical metallurgy) M: 427
Physical meteorologist
Weather (Careers in weather) W: 170
Physical oceanography
Ocean (Careers in oceanography) O: 666
Oceanography O: 667
Physical optics [Physics]
Optics O: 813
Physics (Light) P: 437
Physical quantity
Metric system (Kinds of metric units) M: 436
Physical science
Careers (Life, physical, and social sciences) C: 225
Science (The physical sciences) S: 193 *with
picture*; (Scientific advances of the 1800's)
S: 200
Physical therapy [medicine] P: 435
Careers *picture on* C: 224
Cerebral palsy (Treatment) C: 361-362
Disability (Health care and assistive devices)
D: 221 *with picture*
Hospital (Professional services departments)
H: 371
Hydrotherapy H: 472 *with picture*
Medicine (Other careers in medicine) M: 371
Poliomyelitis (Treatment of poliomyelitis) P: 627
Stroke (Rehabilitation) So: 930
Physical training
Physical education (During the 1800's) P: 433
Physician [medicine]
See also Medicine *in this index*
Address, Forms of (Other forms) A: 54
Boxing (Officials) B: 527

Careers (Health care) C: 223
Colonial life in America (Health and medicine)
Ci: 809
Emergency room E: 258
Euthanasia E: 421
Hospital (The professional services staff) H: 371
Insurance (How private health insurance is
provided) I: 311-312
Managed care plans (In other countries) M: 131;
(In the United States) M: 131
Medicine M: 363 *with pictures*
Suicide (Types) So: 964
Physician assistant
Careers (Health care) C: 223-224
Medicine (Other careers in medicine) M: 371
Physician-assisted suicide
Death (The right to die) D: 61
Euthanasia (Physician-assisted suicide) E: 421
Palliative care P: 109
Suicide (Types) So: 964
**Physicians for the Prevention of Nuclear War,
International**
Nobel Prizes (Peace: 1985) N: 448b
Physics P: 436 *with pictures*
See also the list of Related articles in the Physics
article
Astrophysics A: 850
Atom (The forces within an atom) A: 873
Careers (Life, physical, and social sciences)
C: 225-226
Electronics E: 206
Energy E: 273
Quantum mechanics Q: 6
Relativity R: 209
Science (The physical sciences) S: 193 *with
picture*; (Science in the early 1900's) S: 201
with picture
Physics [book by Aristotle]
Aristotle (Philosophy of nature) A: 664
Physiocrats [economics] P: 444
Capitalism (The development of capitalism)
C: 196
Du Pont de Nemours, Pierre Samuel D: 387
Economics (Early theories) E: 63
Laissez faire L: 31
Quesnay, François Q: 40
Physiologic jaundice [disorder]
Jaundice J: 65
Physiological acoustics [science]
Acoustics A: 29
Physiological Researches on Life and Death [book
by Bichat]
Bichat, Marie François Xavier B: 289
Physiological theory [learning]
Education (How people learn) E: 89-90
Physiology P: 445
Anatomy A: 448b
Biology B: 316; (Materialistic physiology and the
cell theory) B: 319
Botany (How plants function) B: 508
Education (Theories of learning) E: 89-90
Science (The life sciences) S: 193
Zoology (What zoologists study) Z: 606-607
Physiosorption [physics]
Absorption and adsorption (Adsorption) A: 18
Physiotherapy [medicine] *See* Physical therapy *in
this index*
Physostigmine [drug]
Julian, Percy Lavon J: 187
Phytochemical [biology]
Cancer (Nutrition) C: 171
Vegetarianism V: 295
Phytogeography [botany]
Geography (Physical geography) G: 94
Phytohormone [botany]
Gall G: 13
Phytomedicinal *See* Herbal medicine *in this index*
Phytonutrient [botany]
Vegetable V: 292
Phytoplankton [botany]
Arctic Ocean (Ocean life) A: 643
Atlantic Ocean (Ocean life) A: 866; (Pollution)
A: 867
Global warming (Geoengineering) G: 232c
Indian Ocean I: 185
Marine biology (Biological oceanographers)
M: 205
Ocean (The food cycle) O: 655 *with pictures*; (The
plankton) O: 655
Pacific Ocean (Ocean life) P: 15
Plankton P: 515
Pi [letter]
P P: 1 *with picture*
Pi [mathematics] P: 445
Archimedes (His mathematics) A: 605
Circle (The use of pi) Ci: 558
Decimal system (Decimals and fractions) D: 72

Euler, Leonhard E: 378
Mathematics (The Greeks) M: 306
Number (Irrational numbers) N: 606
Proportion P: 828
Rational number R: 148
Series (Working with infinite series) S: 317
Pi meson [atomic particle] *See* Pion *in this index*
Pi Sheng *See* Bi Sheng *in this index*
Pia mater [anatomy]
Brain (From injury) B: 550d
Piaf, Edith [French singer] P: 445 *with portrait*
Piaffe
Horse (Dressage) H: 357
Piaget, Jean [Swiss psychologist] P: 445
Child (The stages of childhood) C: 448
Developmental psychology (Constructivist
theory) D: 174
Pianissimo
Music (table) M: 954; (Indicating expression)
M: 955
Piankashaw Indians
Miami Indians M: 482
Piano [music term]
Music (table) M: 954
Piano [musical instrument] P: 445 *with pictures*
See also the list of Related articles in the Piano
article
Classical music (The Classical period) Ci: 647-648
Clavichord Ci: 657
Jazz (The piano) J: 69 *with picture*
Tone T: 327
Piano Lesson, The [play by Wilson]
Wilson, August W: 316
Piano organ [musical instrument]
Hand organ H: 41
Piano quintet
Classical music (Chamber music) Ci: 644
Piano rag [music]
Ragtime R: 103
Pianoforte
Piano *picture on* P: 448; (History) P: 447
Piast dynasty [Polish history]
Poland (The early Polish state) P: 611
Piatigorsky, Gregor [Russian-American cellist]
P: 448
Piave, Francesco Maria [Italian librettist]
Opera: (Rigoletto) O: 806; (Traviata, La) O: 807-
808
Traviata, La T: 406
Piazza Colonna
Rome R: 429
Piazza del Campo
Europe *picture on* E: 390
Piazza della Signoria
Florence (The city) F: 239 *with picture*
Piazza Navona [Rome]
Rome *picture on* R: 430
Piazzi, Giuseppe [Italian astronomer]
Asteroid (History of study) A: 824b
Ceres C: 362
Piazzolla, Astor [Argentine musician]
Argentina (The arts) A: 651
Pibroch [music]
Scotland (The arts) S: 215-217
Pica [unit of measure]
Type (Sizes of type) T: 537
Picabia, Francis [French painter]
Dadaism D: 2
Picadillo [food]
Cuba (Food and drink) Ci: 1170
Picador
Bullfighting (The order of the bullfight) B: 696
with picture
Picaresque novel
Novel (Early novels) N: 572
Spanish literature (The 1500's) So: 758-759; (The
1600's) So: 759
Picasso, Pablo [Spanish artist] P: 448 *with pictures*
Chicago (Places to visit) C: 430-431 *with picture*
Color *picture on* Ci: 817
Cubism Ci: 1181 *with picture*
Matisse, Henri M: 310
Painting (Color) P: 35; (Cubism) P: 77
Sculpture (Cubism and futurism) S: 257 *with
picture*
Spanish Civil War (Progress of the war) So: 756a
Picasso Museum [France]
Paris (Museums and art galleries) P: 164-165
Piccadilly Circus [London]
London (Central London) L: 429-430 *with map*
Piccard, Auguste [Swiss physicist] P: 450
Balloon *picture on* B: 61; (Balloon explorations)
B: 62
Diving, Underwater (History) D: 247
Exploration (Deep-sea exploration) E: 450-451
Piccard, Bertrand [Swiss balloonist]
Airplane (table: Notable airplane flights) A: 236

Balloon (Long-distance balloon flights) B: 62
Piccard, Jacques [Swiss oceanographer] P: 450
Exploration (Deep-sea exploration) E: 450-451
Pacific Ocean (Scientific research) P: 15
Piccard, Jean [Swiss engineer] P: 450
Piccard, Jeannette [American balloonist]
Piccard, Jean P: 450
Piccolo [musical instrument] P: 450 with pictures
Flute F: 307
Music (Wind instruments) M: 949 with picture
Pichincha [volcano, Ecuador] P: 450
Pichincha, Battle of [1822]
Ecuador (Spanish rule) E: 73
Pichincha P: 450
Sucre, Antonio José de So: 951
Pichon, Louis [French diplomat]
Louisiana Purchase (Trouble begins) L: 502
Pick
Basketball (Offensive strategies) B: 146
Pick-off play
Baseball (Baseball terms) B: 124
Pick-Sloan Missouri Basin Program
Missouri River (History) M: 675-676
Nebraska (The mid-1900's) N: 114
South Dakota (The mid-1900's) So: 684
Pick up [electronic device]
Animation (Making the model move) A: 513
Pickens, Andrew [American general]
Revolution, American (Savannah and Charleston)
R: 284-285
South Carolina (The Revolutionary War) So: 659-
660
Pickens, Israel [American political leader]
Alabama (table) A: 274
Pickerel [fish] P: 450 with picture
Pike P: 461
Pickering, John [American jurist]
Impeachment (History) I: 91
Jefferson, Thomas (The courts) J: 84
Pickering, Thomas R. [American diplomat]
United Nations (table) U: 86
Pickering, Timothy [American political leader]
P: 451
Adams, John (table) A: 38
Washington, George (table) W: 102
Pickersgill, Mary [American public figure]
Baltimore (Other interesting places to visit) B: 69
Picket [labor]
Labor movement (Handling labor disputes) L: 6-7
with picture
Strike (Strike tactics) So: 928
Pickett, Bill [American cowboy] P: 451
Pickett, George Edward [Confederate general]
P: 451 with portrait
Civil War, American (Battle of Gettysburg)
Ci: 627-628
Gettysburg, Battle of G: 176
Pickett, Joseph [American painter] P: 451
Pickett's charge [1863]
Civil War, American (Battle of Gettysburg)
Ci: 627-628
Gettysburg, Battle of G: 176
Pickett, George Edward P: 451
Pickford, Martin [British anthropologist]
Prehistoric people (table) P: 754
Pickford, Mary [American actress] P: 451 with
portrait
Fairbanks, Douglas, Sr. F: 9 with picture
Motion picture (Best performance by an actress:
1928-29) M: 862
New Jersey (The early 1900's) N: 253 with picture
Picking machine [cotton] See Cotton picker in
this index
Pickle [food] P: 451
Cucumber Ci: 1183
Pickling [food processing]
Fishing industry (Methods of processing) F: 186
Vinegar (Uses of vinegar) V: 386-387
Pickling [industrial process]
Iron and steel (Rolling) I: 445-447
Pickling spices [food]
Pickle P: 452
Pickmore, Sir Francis [British colonial official]
Newfoundland and Labrador (Representation
and independence) N: 377
Pick's disease
Alzheimer's disease (Causes) A: 399
Pickup [electronics]
Electric guitar E: 173
Pickup arm
Phonograph (Parts of a phonograph) P: 400-401
Pickup cover
Recreational vehicle picture on R: 183
Pickup truck
Automobile picture on A: 969
Truck T: 456, picture on T: 459; (Kinds of trucks)
T: 457

Pickwick Papers, The [book by Dickens]
Dickens, Charles (Literary success) D: 188
Picnic [play by Inge]
Inge, William I: 270
Pico [prefix]
Metric system (Metric prefixes) M: 439
Pico, Pío [Californian patriot]
California (Mexican rule) C: 60
Pico Bonito National Park [Honduras]
Honduras picture on H: 310
Pico da Neblina [mountain, Brazil]
Brazil (The Amazon Region) B: 577 with map
Pico de Aneto [mountain, Spain]
Pyrenees P: 920
Pico de Orizaba [mountain, Mexico] See Orizaba,
Pico de in this index
Pico de Teide [mountain, Canary Islands]
Canary Islands C: 166 with map
Pico Mogotón [mountain, Nicaragua]
Nicaragua (The Central Highlands) N: 397
Pico Ruivo [mountain, Madeira]
Madeira Islands (The island of Madeira) M: 30
Pico Turquino [mountain, Cuba]
Cuba (The land) Ci: 1172 with map
Picofarad [unit of measure]
Capacitor (Capacitance) C: 186
Farad F: 27
Picot stitch
Crochet Ci: 1148d
Picotte, Susan La Flesche [American doctor]
P: 452
Picquart, Georges [French military leader]
Dreyfus, Alfred (Efforts to clear Dreyfus's name)
D: 347
Picralima umbellata [tree]
Plant picture on P: 527
Pictogram [communication] P: 452
Alphabet (Semitic scripts) A: 381
Asia (The Huang He and Yangtze valleys) A: 805
Aztec (Language) A: 1002 with picture
Chinese language (Written Chinese) C: 509-510
with picture
Communication (Prehistoric times) Ci: 879
Cuneiform Ci: 1192
Handwriting (Early forms of writing) H: 49-50
Hieroglyphics (Development of hieroglyphic
writing) H: 225-226
Indian, American (Writing) I: 150
Pictography [communication]
Pictogram P: 452
Pictorialism [photography]
Photography (Artistic advances) P: 424-425
Picts [ancient people] P: 452
Caledonia C: 28
England (The Germanic invasions) E: 304
Rome, Ancient (The decline of the empire)
R: 447-448
Scotland (The Roman invasion) S: 219
Picture book
Literature for children (Picture books) L: 356 ;
(The early 1900's) L: 365
Picture Builder [painting by Salle]
Painting (Postmodernism) P: 89 with picture
Picture button
Button (History) B: 745
Picture compact disc [recording medium]
Compact disc (CD-ROM's) Ci: 901
Picture editor [occupation]
Publishing (Picture editors) P: 867
Picture element [electronics] See Pixel in this index
Picture graph
Graph (Picture graphs) G: 321 with picture
Picture of Dorian Gray [book by Wilde]
Wilde, Oscar W: 301
Picture Province [nickname]
New Brunswick N: 181
Picture stone
Vikings (Cultural life and recreation) V: 381 with
picture
Picture This [book by Heller]
Heller, Joseph H: 177
Picture tube See Cathode-ray tube in this index
Picture writing See Pictogram in this index
Pictured Rocks National Lakeshore [Michigan]
Lake Superior (Description) L: 45
Michigan (Places to visit) M: 498 with picture
National Park System (table: National lakeshores)
N: 58
Picturephone [machine]
Videophone V: 360
Pictures at an Exhibition [music by Mussorgsky]
Mussorgsky, Modest M: 967
Ravel, Maurice M: 151
PID [disease] See Pelvic inflammatory disease in
this index
Pidal, Ramón Menéndez [Spanish author]
Spanish literature (The Generation of 1898)

So: 762
Pidgeon process [chemistry]
Magnesium (How magnesium is obtained) M: 54
Pidgin [language]
Pacific Islands (Languages) P: 5
Pidgin English [dialect] P: 452
Papua New Guinea (People) P: 140
Pie [food] P: 452
Pastry P: 194
PIE [language] See Proto-Indo-European in this
index
Pie chart
Graph (Circle graphs) G: 322 with picture
Piece
Chess (The board and the men) C: 411-412 with
diagram; (The moves) C: 412
Piece dyeing
Dye (Dyeing textiles) D: 396
Wool (Making fabric) W: 401
Piece-mold method
Sculpture (China) S: 238
Piece of eight [money] P: 452 with pictures
Money picture on M: 708; (A scarcity of money)
M: 710
Pied avocet [bird]
Avocet A: 994
Bird picture on B: 344e
"Pied Beauty" [poem by Hopkins]
Poetry (Sounds) P: 594
Pied Piper of Hamelin [legendary figure] P: 453
with picture
Piedmont [region, Argentina]
Argentina (The Andean Region) A: 653 with map
Piedmont [region, Italy] P: 453
Piedmont glacier [geology]
Glacier (Kinds of glaciers) G: 202
Ice formation I: 9
Piedmont Plateau [U.S.]
Virginia (Land regions) V: 410
Piedmont Region [U.S.] P: 453 with map
Alabama (Land and climate) A: 268 with map
Charlotte (Economy) C: 385
Georgia (Land regions) G: 124
Maryland (Land regions) M: 250
North Carolina (Land regions) N: 484 with map
Pennsylvania (Land regions) P: 256
South Carolina (Land regions) So: 652 with map
United States (The Coastal Lowlands) U: 121
Pieplant [plant]
Rhubarb R: 319 with picture
Pier [engineering]
Architecture (table) A: 608-609; (Romanesque
architecture) A: 618
Building construction (Foundations) B: 682
Romanesque architecture R: 415
Pier plan [aviation]
Airport (Terminal designs) A: 248 with diagram
Pierce, Barbara [wife of George W. Bush] See Bush,
Barbara Pierce in this index
Pierce, Benjamin [American political leader]
New Hampshire (table) N: 223
Pierce, Franklin (Early life) P: 454
Pierce, E. D. [American prospector]
Idaho (Exploration and early settlement) I: 42
Pierce, Franklin [U.S. president] P: 454 with pictures
Kansas-Nebraska Act K: 243
Pierce, Jane Appleton [wife of Franklin Pierce]
First ladies of the United States (table) F: 142
Pierce, Franklin (Pierce's family) P: 455; (Life in the
White House) P: 456 with picture
Pierce, Samuel Riley, Jr. [American government
official] P: 457
Pierce, Walter M. [American political leader]
Oregon (table) O: 845
Pierce, William [American political leader]
Madison, James (Constitutional Convention)
M: 33-34
Pierced Hemisphere (Telstar) [sculpture by
Hepworth]
Hepworth, Barbara picture on H: 193
Piercing [decoration]
Body art B: 434
Piero da Vinci, Ser [father of]
Leonardo da Vinci (Early career) L: 199
Piero della Francesca [Italian painter] P: 457
Easter picture on E: 43
Jesus Christ picture on J: 106
Painting (Composition) P: 35
Piérola, Nicolás de [Peruvian political leader]
Peru (The early 1900's) P: 315
Pierpont, Francis Harrison [American political
leader] P: 457
Virginia (table) V: 417
Pierpont Morgan Library [New York City] P: 458
Morgan, J. P., Jr. M: 804
Pierre [South Dakota] P: 458
South Dakota picture on So: 673; (Statehood)

So: 683
Pierre Auger Observatory
  Cosmic rays (Cosmic ray research) **Ci: 1077**
Pierre-Louis, Michèle [Haitian political leader]
  Haiti (History) **H: 15-17**
Pierrepont, Edwards [American government
  official]
  Justice, Department of (table) **J: 203**
Piers Plowman See Vision of Piers Plowman, The
  in this index
Pierson, Abraham [American educator]
  Yale University (History) **Y: 549**
Pietà [sculpture by Meštrović]
  Meštrović, Ivan **M: 424**
Pietà [sculpture by Michelangelo]
  Michelangelo picture on **M: 486**; (Early life)
  M: 483-484
  Saint Peter's Basilica (The interior) **S: 53**
Pietermaritzburg [South Africa] **P: 458**
Pietists [religious group]
  Brethren **B: 593**
  Christianity (The 1600's and 1700's) **C: 525**
  Moravian Church **M: 801**
  Pennsylvania Dutch **P: 270**
  Protestantism (Pietism) **P: 835**
Pietrain [hog]
  Hog (Other breeds) **H: 286**; (table) **H: 286**
Pietri, Dorando [Italian athlete]
  Olympic Games (The modern games) **O: 750-751**
Piezoelectric crystal [physics]
  Electricity (Sources of current) **E: 194**
  Microphone (Crystal microphones and ceramic
  microphones) **M: 516** with diagram
  Piezoelectricity **P: 458**
  Tourmaline **T: 350**
Piezoelectric effect [physics] See Piezoelectricity
  in this index
Piezoelectricity [physics] **P: 458**
  Materials (Smart materials) **M: 301**
  Quartz (Uses) **Q: 8**
Piezophile [biology]
  Extremophile **E: 458**
Pig [animal] See Hog in this index
Pig iron
  Iron and steel (Kinds of iron and steel) **I: 436-437**
  with picture; (Making iron products) **I: 441**
  Smelting **S: 515**
Pig-nosed turtle
  Turtle (Other kinds of turtles) **T: 524**
Pigafetta, Antonio [Italian sailor]
  Magellan, Ferdinand (Results of the voyage)
  M: 48
Pigeon [bird] **P: 458** with pictures
  Bird pictures on **B: 348**, **P: 362**, **P: 364**, **P: 366**; (In
  nature) **B: 330**
  Passenger pigeon **P: 190**
  Poultry **P: 720**
Pigeon Feathers [book by Updike]
  Updike, John **U: 213**
Pigeon guillemot [bird]
  Guillemot **G: 429**
Pigeon racing [sport]
  Homing pigeon (Pigeon racing) **H: 305**
Pigeonberry [plant]
  Pokeweed **P: 603** with picture
Pigeon's blood [color]
  Ruby **R: 508**
Pigeon's milk [zoology]
  Dove **D: 314**
  Pigeon (Life history) **P: 460**
Pigfish [fish]
  Grunt **G: 407** with picture
Piggott, Lester [British jockey]
  Horse racing (History) **H: 366**
Piggyback service [shipping]
  Railroad (Freight service) **R: 106**; (Rolling stock)
  R: 107-108 with picture
Piglet [literary figure]
  Milne, A. A. **M: 556**
Pigment [color] **P: 461**
  Albino **A: 332**
  Color (Mixing colorants) **Ci: 819-820** with
  diagrams
  Fish (Skin and color) **F: 160**
  Hair (Color and texture) **H: 10**
  Ink **I: 272**
  Paint **P: 23**
  Painting (Materials and techniques) **P: 36** with
  picture
  Plastics (Making synthetic resins) **P: 556-557**
  Skin (Epidermis) **S: 489**
  Wald, George **W: 6**
Pigment figure
  Wood (Wood figure) **W: 390**
Pignut hickory [tree]
  Hickory **H: 224** with pictures
Pigskin

Hog (Other uses) **H: 286**
Pigweed [plant]
  Lamb's-quarters **L: 51**
Piikani Indians
  Blackfeet Indians **B: 392**
Pijper, Willem [Dutch composer]
  Netherlands (Arts) **N: 142-144**
Pika [animal] **P: 461** with picture
  Animal picture on **A: 474**
Pike [fish] **P: 461** with picture
Pike [weapon]
  Army (Armies in the Middle Ages) **A: 727**
  Spear So: **768**
Pike, Albert [Confederate military leader]
  Oklahoma (The American Civil War) **O: 731**
Pike, James Albert [American religious leader]
  P: 461
Pike, Zebulon Montgomery [American explorer]
  P: 461
  Colorado (Exploration and settlement) **Ci: 845**
  Iowa (Territorial days) **I: 393**
  Minnesota (The Louisiana Purchase) **M: 603**
  Pikes Peak **P: 462**
  Rocky Mountains (History) **R: 395-396**
  Westward movement in America (Exploration)
  W: 248
Pike perch See Walleye in this index
Pike pole [tool]
  Fire department picture on **F: 127**
Pike position
  Diving picture on **D: 244**; (Kinds of dives) **D: 243**
Pikes Peak [mountain, Colorado] **P: 462**
  Colorado (Places to visit) **Ci: 836**; (Exploration
  and settlement) **Ci: 845** with picture
  Gold rush (Gold rushes of the United States)
  G: 254
  Mountain (table) **M: 896** with diagram
  Pike, Zebulon Montgomery **P: 461**
  Rocky Mountains (History) **R: 395-396**
"Pikes Peak or bust" [slogan]
  Colorado (The gold rush) **Ci: 845**
Pikuni Indians
  Blackfeet Indians **B: 393**
Pilate, Pontius [Roman government official] **P: 462**
  with picture
  Barabbas **B: 102**
  Jesus Christ (The trial) **J: 108** with picture
Pilâtre de Rozier, Jean François [French
  balloonist]
  Airplane (First human flights) **A: 230**
  Balloon (History) **B: 60-61**
  Montgolfier brothers **M: 765**
Pilau [food]
  Pakistan (Food and drink) **P: 96**
Pilchard [fish]
  Sardine **S: 124** with picture
Pilcher, Percy S. [British aviator]
  Airplane (First human flights) **A: 230**
  Glider (Early days) **G: 230**
Pilcomayo River
  Paraguay (The land and climate) **P: 147** with map
Pile [construction] **P: 462**
  Breakwater **B: 589**
  Building construction (Foundations) **B: 682**
Pile [electrical device]
  Battery (History) **B: 171**
  Electricity (Experiments with electric charge)
  E: 196-197 with picture
Pile [weaving]
  Rugs and carpets (Materials used in rugs and
  carpets) **R: 514**
  Velvet **V: 297**
Pile, Atomic See Nuclear reactor in this index
Pile driver [machines]
  Building construction (Foundations) **B: 682**
Pile o' Bones
  Saskatchewan (Interesting facts) **S: 129** with
  picture
Pile weave
  Weaving (Fancy weaves) **W: 173**
Pileated woodpecker [bird]
  Woodpecker (Kinds) **W: 394** with picture
Piles [disorder] See Hemorrhoids in this index
Pilgrim Holiness Church [religious group]
  Wesleyan Church **W: 198**
Pilgrimage
  Architecture (Romanesque architecture) **A: 618**
  Islam (The Five Pillars of Islam) **I: 463-464** with
  picture
  Judaism (The pilgrimage festivals) **J: 181**
  Religion (Religious rituals) **R: 217**
Pilgrims [U.S. history] **P: 462** with pictures
  Bradford, William [1590-1657] **B: 541**
  Colonial life in America (Religious and political
  reasons) **Ci: 788**; (Plymouth Colony) **Ci: 789**
  Congregationalists **Ci: 940f**
  Indian, American (After European contact) **I: 156**

Indian wars (The Pequot War [1637]) **I: 191**
  Massachusetts (The Pilgrims and Plymouth
  Colony) **M: 289**
Mayflower **M: 327**
  Mayflower Compact **M: 328**
  Plymouth Colony **P: 582** with picture
  Thanksgiving Day (Plymouth Colony) **T: 230**
  United States, History of the picture on **U: 152**;
  (New England) **U: 154**
Pilgrims Going to Church [painting by Boughton]
  Pilgrims picture on **P: 463**
Pilgrim's Progress, The [book by Bunyan]
  Bunyan, John **B: 700**
  English literature (Restoration prose) **E: 318**
  Literature for children (The Puritans) **L: 362**
Pili [biology]
  Bacteria (How bacteria move) **B: 21**
Pilipino [language] See Filipino in this index
Pilkey, Dav [American author/illustrator] **P: 464**
Pill [medication]
  Drug pictures on **D: 350**
Pill bug [animal] **P: 464**
Pillar [architecture]
  Column **Ci: 865**
Pillar [harp]
  Harp **H: 65** with picture
Pillar [mining]
  Mining (Mining terms) **M: 577**
Pillar of Fire [ballet]
  Ballet (Ballet in the United States) **B: 53-54**
Pillars of Faith [Islam]
  Ramadan **R: 132**
Pillars of Hercules
  Gibraltar, Strait of **G: 187**
Pillbug [animal] See Pill bug in this index
Pillory [punishment] **P: 464**
  Colonial life in America (Crime and punishment)
  Ci: 796 with picture
Pillow lava [geology]
  Basalt **B: 123**
Pillsbury, John Sargent [American political leader]
  Minnesota (table) **M: 602**
Pilosa [zoology]
  Mammal (table) **M: 129** with picture
Pilot [career]
  See also Astronaut; Piloting in this index
  Air Force, United States (History) **A: 194**
  Airplane (Principles of flight) **A: 220-221**; (Flying
  an airplane) **A: 222**; (Air navigation) **A: 226**;
  (History) **A: 229-231**
  Aviation (Careers in aviation) **A: 992**
  Balloon **B: 57**
  Careers (Transportation) **C: 235**
  Glider **G: 228**; (Flying a glider) **G: 229**
  Helicopter (Piloting a helicopter) **H: 171**
  Radio (Navigation) **R: 85** with picture
  Ship (Navigation) **S: 410**
  Women's movement picture on **W: 388**
Pilot, The [book by Cooper]
  Cooper, James Fenimore **Ci: 1035**
Pilot astronaut
  Astronaut **A: 828**; (Selecting the NASA
  astronauts) **A: 831**
Pilot certificate
  Airplane (Learning to fly) **A: 226**
Pilot episode
  Television (Choosing new programs) **T: 113**
Pilot flag
  Flag (Flags of the sea) **F: 208**
Pilot light
  Range (Gas ranges) **R: 138**
Pilot whale [sea animal] **P: 464** with picture
  Dolphin on **D: 298**; (Other species) **D: 297**
  Whale picture on **W: 257**
Pilotage See Piloting in this index
Pilotfish **P: 465** with picture
Piloting [navigation]
  Airplane (Flying an airplane) **A: 222**; (Air
  navigation) **A: 226**
  Flag (Flags of the sea) **F: 208**
  Navigation (Piloting) **N: 70**
  Ship (Navigation) **S: 410**
Pilotis [architecture]
  Architecture picture on **A: 632**; (Le Corbusier)
  A: 631
Pilotweed [plant]
  Compass plant **Ci: 903** with picture
Pilsen [Czech Republic] See Plzeň in this index
Pilsner beer [drink]
  Beer **B: 211**
Piłsudski, Józef [Polish patriot] **P: 465**
  Poland (The struggle against foreign rule) **P: 612**
Piltdown hoax [anthropology] **P: 465**
Pima cotton
  Cotton (Kinds of cotton) **Ci: 1087**
Pima Indians **P: 465**
  Indian, American (Indians of the Southwest)

I: 166-167
Pimento [spice]
 Pimento P: 465
Pimento [tree] P: 465 *with picture*
Pimento pepper
 Pepper P: 278
 Pimento P: 465
Pimp
 Prostitution P: 830
Pimpernel [plant] *See* Scarlet pimpernel *in this index*
Pimple P: 466
 Abscess A: 17
 Acne A: 28 *with diagram*
PIN [banking] *See* Personal identification number *in this index*
Pin [bowling]
 Bowling (Aiming) B: 522; (The pins) B: 523 *with pictures*; (Canadian fivepins) B: 524
Pin [fastener] P: 466 *with pictures*
Pin [wrestling]
 Wrestling W: 504 *with picture*
Pin-back button
 Button B: 744-745 *with picture*
Pin grid array [electronics]
 Computer chip (External connections) Ci: 924f
Pin money
 New Year's Day (Early customs) N: 289
Pin screen animation [photography]
 Animation (Pin screen animation) A: 514a
Pin-tumbler lock
 Lock (Mechanical locks) L: 411 *with picture*
Pin-wale corduroy [fabric]
 Corduroy Ci: 1052
Piña cloth [fabric]
 Pineapple (Cultivation and production) P: 472-473
Pinacoteca [museum, Italy]
 Bologna B: 448
Piñata [custom]
 Christmas (In Latin America) C: 532 *with picture*
 Mexico (Holidays) M: 457-458
Pinatubo, Mount [volcano] *See* Mount Pinatubo *in this index*
Pinch hitter [Baseball]
 Baseball (Baseball terms) B: 124
Pinch pot [pottery]
 Pottery (Shaping the clay) P: 716
Pinch runner
 Baseball (Baseball terms) B: 124
Pinchback, P. B. S. [American political leader] P: 466
 Louisiana (table) L: 496
Pinchingbug [insect]
 Stag beetle So: 821
Pinchot, Gifford [American political leader] P: 467
 Conservation Ci: 975; (The rise of the conservation movement) Ci: 985
 Pennsylvania (table) P: 263
 Taft, William Howard (Legislative defeats) T: 10-11
Pinckney, Charles [American political leader] P: 467
 Monroe, James (Diplomat under Jefferson) M: 736
Pinckney, Charles [husband of]
 Pinckney, Eliza Lucas P: 467
Pinckney, Charles Cotesworth [1746-1825, American political leader] P: 467
 Pinckney, Eliza Lucas P: 467
 XYZ Affair X: 546
Pinckney, Eliza Lucas [American colonial leader] P: 467
Pinckney, Thomas [American political leader] P: 467
 Pinckney, Eliza Lucas P: 467
 United States, History of the (Problems in foreign affairs) U: 163
Pinckney Treaty [1795] P: 467
 Alabama (Territorial days) A: 275
 Pinckney, Thomas P: 467
 United States, History of the (Problems in foreign affairs) U: 163
 Westward movement in America (The Northwest Ordinance) W: 247
Pindar [Greek poet] P: 468
 Greek literature (Lyric poetry) G: 377
 Poetry (Ancient poetry) P: 595
Pindaric ode [poetry]
 Ode O: 673
 Pindar P: 468
 Poetry (Lyric poetry) P: 591
Pinder [food] *See* Peanut *in this index*
Pindling, Lynden O. [Bahamian political leader]
 Bahamas (History) B: 29
Pindus Mountains
 Greece *picture on* G: 358; (The land) G: 357

Pine [tree] P: 468 *with pictures*
 See also Bristlecone pine *in this index;* and *the list of Related articles in the* Pine *article*
 Cell *picture on* C: 327
 Conifer Ci: 950
 Forest (Forest succession) F: 397 *with picture*
 Leaf *picture on* L: 151
 Maine (Natural resources) M: 84
 Plant (*pictures on* P: 521, P: 525, P: 547
 Tree (*pictures on* T: 417, T: 425, T: 427; (Needleleaf trees) T: 414-415
 Turpentine T: 519
Pine, Robert Edge [American painter]
 United States, History of the *picture on* U: 159
Pine, Theodore [American painter]
 Lee, Robert E. *picture on* L: 177
Pine cone
 Gymnosperm *picture on* G: 451
 Pine P: 468 *with pictures*
Pine crab
 Crab *picture on* Ci: 1115
Pine grosbeak [bird]
 Grosbeak G: 398
Pine marten [animal]
 Marten M: 233
Pine needle
 Cell *picture on* C: 327
 Pine P: 468 *with pictures*
Pine nut [food]
 Piñon P: 474
Pine oil disinfectant
 Disinfectant D: 235
Pine Ridge
 Nebraska (Land regions) N: 104-106 *with picture*
Pine Ridge Indian Reservation [South Dakota]
 Wounded Knee W: 502
Pine siskin [bird] P: 471 *with picture*
Pine Tree Ceremonial Dance [painting by Toledo]
 Indian, American *picture on* I: 147
Pine tree dance [custom]
 Indian, American *picture on* I: 147
Pine-tree shilling [money] P: 471 *with pictures*
 Coin collecting *picture on* Ci: 758
 Money (Tree shillings) M: 710
Pine Tree State
 Maine M: 68
Pineal gland [anatomy] P: 471 *with picture*
 Gland (table) P: 208
 Psychology (Beginnings) P: 849
Pineapple [plant] P: 472 *with picture*
 Fruit (Types of fruits in botany) F: 544-546 *with picture*
 Hawaii (Agriculture) H: 104
 Puerto Rico (Agriculture) P: 882 *with picture*
Pineda, Alonso Álvarez de [Spanish explorer]
 Alabama (European exploration and settlement) A: 275
 Texas (Spanish exploration) T: 204
Pinel, Philippe [French physician]
 Mental illness (Humane treatment) M: 408 *with picture*
Piñera, Sebastián [Chilean political leader]
 Chile (Recent developments) C: 470
Pinero, Arthur Wing [British dramatist] P: 473
Piñero, Jesús Toribio [Puerto Rican political leader]
 Puerto Rico (Building a democracy) P: 883
Pines, Cathedral of the [memorial]
 New Hampshire (Places to visit) N: 216
Pines of Rome, The [music by Respighi]
 Respighi, Ottorino R: 259
Pinewood Derby
 Automobile, Model A: 974
Piney Woods
 Mississippi *picture on* M: 636
Ping-pong *See* Table tennis *in this index*
Pingo [geology]
 Tundra T: 485
Pingree, Hazen S. [American political leader]
 Michigan (table) M: 507
Pingree, Samuel E. [American political leader]
 Vermont (table) V: 333
Pinheiros River [Brazil]
 São Paulo (The city) S: 117
Pinhole aperture [photography]
 Camera *diagram on* C: 81
Pinhole projector
 Eclipse (Solar eclipses) E: 51
Pinion gear [mechanics]
 Gear G: 75
 Starter (Automobile starters) So: 858 *with diagram*
Pink [plant] P: 473
 Carnation C: 241
 Flower (table) F: 301 *with picture*
Pink bollworm [insect] P: 473 *with picture*
Pink conch
 Conch Ci: 928

Pink dolphin *See* Amazon River dolphin *in this index*
Pink fairy armadillo [animal]
 Armadillo A: 717
Pink flamingo [plant]
 Anthurium A: 550
Pink Floyd [musical group]
 Rock music (Progressive rock) R: 380b
Pink-headed fruit-dove [bird]
 Bird *picture on* B: 344g
Pink lady's-slipper [plant]
 Lady's-slipper L: 26
Pink Marsh [grapefruit]
 Grapefruit G: 320
Pink Palace Museum
 Memphis (Cultural life) M: 396
Pink salmon [fish]
 Salmon *picture on* S: 69; (Kinds of salmon) S: 70
Pinkerton [opera character]
 Opera: (*Madama Butterfly*) O: 804
Pinkerton, Allan [American detective] P: 473
 Espionage (History) E: 358
Pinkerton man [detective]
 Pinkerton, Allan P: 474
Pinkeye [disorder]
 Conjunctivitis Ci: 951
 Eye (Diseases of the outer parts) E: 468
Pinking shears
 Scissors S: 208
 Sewing (Seams) S: 332
Pinkney, Andrea [American author]
 Literature for children (The early 2000's) L: 366
Pinkney, Gloria Jean [American author]
 Literature for children *picture on* L: 370
Pinkney, Jerry [American artist]
 Caldecott Medal (table: 2010) C: 26
 Literature for children *picture on* L: 370
 Regina Medal (table: 2005) R: 206
Pinkney, William [American government official]
 Justice, Department of (table) J: 203
Pinnacles National Monument [California]
 National Park System (table: National monuments) N: 51
Pinnate leaf [botany]
 Leaf (The blade) L: 153-154 *with picture*
Pinnipedia [zoology]
 Seal S: 265
Pinocchio [film]
 Disney, Walt (Full-length movies) D: 236
Pinocchio [literary figure]
 Collodi, Carlo Ci: 776
 Fairy (Fairy tales) F: 11
Pinochet Ugarte, Augusto [Chilean military leader] P: 474
 Chile (Crisis and democracy) C: 470; (Marxism and military rule) C: 470; (Recent developments) C: 470
 Latin America (The rise of military regimes) L: 110
Pinochle [game] P: 474
Piñon [tree] P: 474
Piñones [seeds]
 Monkey puzzle tree M: 730
Pinscher [dog]
 Doberman pinscher D: 259
 Dog *pictures on* D: 267, D: 274
 German pinscher G: 143
 Miniature pinscher M: 573
Pinsky, Robert [American poet]
 Poet laureate (table: Poets laureate of the United States) P: 590
Pint [unit of measure] P: 475
Pinta [ship]
 Caravel C: 202
 Columbus, Christopher (First voyage westward) Ci: 858-859 *with picture*
 Exploration (Columbus reaches America) E: 444
Pintail [bird] P: 475 *with picture*
Pinter, Harold [British dramatist] P: 475
 Drama (Later British drama) D: 340
 English literature (Literature after World War II) E: 322-323
Pinto [horse]
 Horse (Coat and skin) H: 348-349 *with picture*
Pinwheel Galaxy *See* Triangulum Galaxy *in this index*
Pinworm [animal] P: 475
Pinyin [linguistics]
 Chinese language (Development) C: 510
Pinyon [tree]
 Piñon P: 474
Pinyon jay [bird]
 Jay J: 66
Pinzón, Martín Alonso [Spanish explorer]
 Columbus, Christopher (Ships and crews) Ci: 858-859
 Latin America *map on* L: 105
Pinzón, Vicente Yáñez [Spanish explorer]

Amazon River (History) **A:** 404
Columbus, Christopher (Ships and crews) **Ci:** 858-859
Exploration (Exploring the New World) **E:** 444
Pioche [Nevada]
Nevada (Places to visit) **N:** 164
Pion [atomic particle]
Hadron **H:** 5
Meson **M:** 421
Pioneer [railroad car]
Pullman, George Mortimer **P:** 900
Pioneer [space probes]
Space exploration (Solar probes) **So:** 710
Venus (Surface and atmosphere) **V:** 311
Pioneer 10
Jupiter (History of Jupiter study) **J:** 200b
Space exploration (Probes to Jupiter and beyond) **So:** 711
Pioneer 11
Saturn (History of study) **S:** 153
Space exploration (Probes to Jupiter and beyond) **So:** 711
Pioneer, The [magazine]
Lowell, James Russell (Early career) **L:** 510
Pioneer Center [community]
Brasilia (The city) **B:** 565
Pioneer Clubs [organization] **P:** 475
Pioneer life in America **P:** 476 *with pictures and map*
See also Western frontier life in America; Westward movement in America *in this index; and the list of Related articles in the* Pioneer life in America *article*
Family (Early Western families in America) **F:** 22
Lincoln, Abraham (Boyhood) **L:** 312 *with picture*
Log cabin **L:** 422 *with picture*
United States, History of the (Expansion [1820-1849]) **U:** 167 *with pictures*
Pioneer Mother [sculpture]
Oregon *picture on* **O:** 831
Pioneer-Saturn [space probe]
Jupiter (History of Jupiter study) **J:** 200b
Pioneer Venus 1 [space probe]
Space exploration (Probes to Venus and Mercury) **So:** 710
Venus (Flights to Venus) **V:** 313 *with picture*
Pioneer Venus 2 [space probe]
Space exploration (Probes to Venus and Mercury) **So:** 710
Venus (Flights to Venus) **V:** 313
Pioneer Village [Minden]
Nebraska (Places to visit) **N:** 102
Pioneers, The [book by Cooper]
Cooper, James Fenimore **Ci:** 1035
Pip [literary figure]
Dickens, Charles (The second phase) **D:** 188-189
Pipa [musical instrument]
Music (Chinese music) **M:** 956
Pipe [musical instrument] **P:** 488
Pipe [plumbing] **P:** 488
Plumbing **P:** 577
Pipe [tobacco] **P:** 489 *with picture*
Brier **B:** 608
Indian, American *pictures on* **I:** 138, **I:** 160
Meerschaum **M:** 383
Peace pipe **P:** 209
Sculpture (The European impact) **S:** 244
Smoking **S:** 520
Pipe of peace *See* Peace pipe *in this index*
Pipe organ [musical instrument]
Mormons *picture on* **M:** 808
Organ (Pipe organs) **O:** 851 *with diagram*
Pipe snake
Snake (Other snake families) **S:** 535
Pipe Spring National Monument [Arizona] **P:** 489
National Park System (table: National monuments) **N:** 51
Pipe tobacco
Tobacco **T:** 305
Pipe tomahawk [weapon]
Tomahawk **T:** 324 *with picture*
Pipefish [fish] **P:** 489 *with picture*
Pipeline **P:** 490 *with pictures*
Coal (Shipping coal) **Ci:** 727
Gas [fuel] **G:** 50; (Transmitting and distributing gas) **G:** 55 *with picture;* (Development of the natural gas industry) **G:** 57-58
Petroleum (Transporting petroleum) **P:** 342 *with diagram*
Russia *picture on* **R:** 545
Transportation (Land transportation) **T:** 383
Piper bellflower [plant]
Plant *picture on* **P:** 524
Piper Cherokee [airplane]
Airplane *picture on* **A:** 214
Piper Cub [airplane]
Airplane *picture on* **A:** 234

Piperacillin [drug]
Penicillin (Forms of penicillin) **P:** 240
Piperine [substance]
Pepper **P:** 278
Pipes, William T. [Canadian political leader]
Nova Scotia (table) **N:** 567
Pipestone National Monument [Minnesota]
Minnesota (Places to visit) **M:** 594
National Park System (table: National monuments) **N:** 51
Pipil Indians [people]
El Salvador (Ancestry) **E:** 249; (History) **E:** 252
Piping plover [bird]
Plover **P:** 574
Pipistrelle bat [animal]
Bat *picture on* **B:** 159
Pipit [bird] **P:** 492 *with picture*
Pippa Passes [play by Browning]
Browning, Robert **B:** 646
Pippi Longstocking [fictional character]
Lindgren, Astrid **L:** 332
Pippin, Horace [American artist] **P:** 492 *with picture*
Piqua, Battle of [1780]
Ohio (Exploration and settlement) **O:** 700
Piquet, Nelson [Brazilian race driver]
Automobile racing (table: Formula One World Drivers' Championship) **A:** 980
Piracy [seafaring] *See* Pirate *in this index*
Piracy [theft of ideas] **P:** 493
Internet (Changing industries) **I:** 350e
Piraeus [Greece] **P:** 493
Pirandello, Luigi [Italian author] **P:** 493 *with portrait*
Drama (Italian drama) **D:** 339
Italian literature (The 1900's) **I:** 495
Piranesi, Giovanni Battista [Italian artist] **P:** 493 *with picture*
Piranha [fish] **P:** 494 *with picture*
Fish *picture on* **F:** 157; (Harmful fish) **F:** 147
Pacu **P:** 19
Pirarucú [fish] *See* Arapaima *in this index*
Pirate **P:** 494 *with pictures*
Barbarossa **B:** 105
Barbary States **B:** 105
Blackbeard **B:** 391
Bonnet, Stede **B:** 461
Caribbean Sea (Economic importance) **C:** 237
Drake, Sir Francis **D:** 320
Haiti (History) **H:** 15-16
Kidd, William **K:** 311
Laffite, Jean **L:** 28
Morgan, Sir Henry **M:** 803
Privateer **P:** 808b
Somalia (History) **So:** 589-590
Vikings **V:** 378
Pirate spider
Spider (Enemies) **So:** 788
Pirated recording
Recording industry (Releasing the recording) **R:** 182
Pirates, Pittsburgh [team] *See* Pittsburgh Pirates *in this index*
Pirates of Penzance, The [operetta by Gilbert and Sullivan]
Gilbert and Sullivan **G:** 190
Pirating [crime]
Counterfeiting **Ci:** 1097
Pire, Dominique Georges [Belgian religious leader]
Nobel Prizes (Peace: 1958) **N:** 448b
Pirelli Building [Milan]
Milan (The city) **M:** 540
Pirouette
Ballet **B:** 45 *with picture*
Horse (Dressage) **H:** 357
Pisa [Italy] **P:** 496
Pisa, Council of [1409]
Pope (The troubles of the papacy) **P:** 664
Pisa, Leaning Tower of *See* Leaning Tower of Pisa *in this index*
Pisano, Giovanni [Italian sculptor] **P:** 496
Sculpture (Italian Renaissance sculpture) **S:** 251 *with picture*
Pisano, Nicola [Italian sculptor] **P:** 496
Relief *picture on* **R:** 213
Sculpture (Italian Renaissance sculpture) **S:** 251
Piscataqua River
New Hampshire (Rivers and lakes) **N:** 220 *with map*
Piscataway Park [Maryland]
National Park System (table: National parkways and other national parklands) **N:** 56
Piscator [literary figure]
Walton, Izaak **W:** 21
Pisces [astrology] **P:** 496 *with picture*
Zodiac (The zodiac in astrology) **Z:** 597 *with picture*

Pisgah, Mount *See* Mount Pisgah *in this index*
Pishon River [Bible]
Eden **E:** 76
Pishpek [former name] *See* Bishkek *in this index*
Pisiform bone
Hand (Parts of the hand) **H:** 40
Wrist *diagram on* **W:** 510
Pisistratus [Greek ruler] **P:** 496
Athens (Earliest times) **A:** 857
Library (Greece) **L:** 258
Solon **So:** 586
Pissarides, Christopher A. [Cypriot British economist]
Nobel Prizes (Economics: 2010) **N:** 450
Pissarro, Camille [French painter] **P:** 496 *with picture*
Cézanne, Paul **C:** 364
Impressionism (French Impressionism) **I:** 93
Painting (Edouard Manet and the Impressionists) **P:** 71
Pissis [mountain, Argentina]
Andes Mountains (Physical features) **A:** 452
Pistachio nut **P:** 497 *with picture*
Nut (Kinds of nuts) **N:** 621
Pistil [botany]
Flower (The carpels) **F:** 294
Plant (Flowers) **P:** 531
Pollen **P:** 644
Seed (Seed development in angiosperms) **S:** 281
Pistillate flower
Flower (Variations in flower structure) **F:** 294
Pistol [gun]
Duel **D:** 378
Handgun (Types of handguns) **H:** 43
Pistole [money]
Doubloon **D:** 312
Piston [machine]
Automobile (The engine block) **A:** 951 *with diagram*
Gasoline engine (Kinds of gasoline engines) **G:** 63 *with picture;* (The pistons and connecting rods) **G:** 64 *with diagrams*
Machine *diagram on* **M:** 13
Steam engine (Reciprocating steam engines) **So:** 880 *with diagrams*
Stirling engine **So:** 902 *with diagrams*
Piston, Walter [American composer] **P:** 497
Piston engine
Airplane (Reciprocating engines) **A:** 220
Pistons, Detroit
Basketball (table) **B:** 150
Detroit (Sports) **D:** 170
Pit [automobile racing]
Automobile racing **A:** 975
Pit [botany]
Fruit (Simple fruits) **F:** 544 *with pictures*
Pit [theater]
Drama (England) **D:** 334
Shakespeare, William (Theater buildings) **S:** 351
Pit bull [dog] **P:** 497
American Staffordshire terrier **A:** 430
Dogfighting **D:** 282
Pit house [dwelling]
Anasazi (History) **A:** 448a
Indian, American (Before European contact) **I:** 163-164
Pit organ [zoology]
Snake (Sense organs) **S:** 527-528
Pit trap
Trapping *picture on* **T:** 404
Pit viper [snake]
Bushmaster **B:** 723
Snake (Vipers) **S:** 535
Viper **V:** 390
Pita bread
Bread (Kinds of bread) **B:** 588
Pitcairn, John [British soldier]
Salem, Peter **S:** 61
Pitcairn Island [Pacific] **P:** 498
Norfolk Island **N:** 454
Pitcairn Islands Group [Pacific]
Pacific Islands (table) **P:** 9
Pitch [building material] **P:** 498
Pitch [measurement]
Airplane (Basic movements and controls) **A:** 222 *with diagrams*
Helicopter (Piloting a helicopter) **H:** 171 *with diagrams*
Propeller (Airplane propellers) **P:** 826
Pitch [sound] **P:** 498
Doppler effect **D:** 310
Music (Indicating pitch) **M:** 952-953 *with diagrams*
Singing (How people sing) **S:** 472
Sound (Frequency and pitch) **So:** 599 *with diagram;* (table) **So:** 599
Tuning fork **T:** 487

Pitch [sports]
Climbing (Technical climbing) **Ci:** 680
Cricket (The field) **Ci:** 1131
Pitch Lake [Trinidad]
Asphalt (Asphalt production) **A:** 815
Trinidad and Tobago (Economy) **T:** 446
Pitch pine [tree]
Pine (Eastern pines) **P:** 468
Pitchblende [mineral] **P:** 498
Curie, Marie Skłodowska **Ci:** 1194
Great Bear Lake **G:** 337
Uranium (Sources of uranium) **U:** 214
Pitcher [container]
Brass *picture on* **B:** 566
Pewter *pictures on* **P:** 352
Pitcher [sports]
Baseball (Pitching) **B:** 127; (Player positions)
B: 127; (Rule changes) **B:** 133; (table: Modern
major league records) **B:** 138
Softball (Types of softball) **So:** 571 *with diagram*
Pitcher, Molly [American patriot] **P:** 498
Pitcher, Nathaniel [American political leader]
New York (table) **N:** 313
Pitcher plant [plant] **P:** 499
Carnivorous plant **C:** 243
Endangered species (table) **E:** 270
Plant (Environmental factors) **P:** 538-539
Pitcher's rubber
Baseball (The infield) **B:** 126 *with diagram*
Pitching wedge
Golf (Golf clubs) **G:** 262 *with picture*
Pitchout [sports]
Football *picture on* **F:** 360
Pith [botany]
Potato (The potato plant) **P:** 712 *with picture*
Stem (Herbaceous stems) **So:** 887
Pith helmet
Helmet **H:** 178
Pithecanthropus erectus [hominid]
Dubois, Eugène **D:** 372
Pithecanthropus Erectus [recording]
Mingus, Charles **M:** 573
Pithias [wife of]
Aristotle (Aristotle's life) **A:** 663
Pitikwahanapiwiyin [Indian name of]
Poundmaker **P:** 722
Pitkin, Frederick W. [American political leader]
Colorado (table) **Ci:** 844
Pitman, Sir Isaac [British educator]
Shorthand **S:** 435
Pitney, Mahlon [American jurist]
Supreme Court of the United States (table)
So: 1000
Pitohui [bird] **P:** 499 *with picture*
Animal *picture on* **A:** 469
Pitot tube [measuring device]
Log (The pitot-static log) **L:** 421
Pitt, William [British political leader] **P:** 499 *with
portrait*
Franklin, Benjamin (Other studies) **F:** 489
Seven Years' War (In Europe) **S:** 328
Pitt, William, the Younger [British political leader]
P: 500 *with portrait*
Ireland (Union with Britain) **I:** 426
Pitt diamond [gem]
Diamond (Famous diamonds) **D:** 182
Pitta [bird]
Bird (Birds of Asia) **B:** 344f *with picture*
Pittman, Vail M. [American political leader]
Nevada (table) **N:** 173
Pitts, Hiram [American inventor]
Threshing machine **T:** 270
Pitts, John [American inventor]
Threshing machine **T:** 270
Wheat (The mechanization of wheat farming)
W: 276
Pittsburg Landing, Battle of *See* Shiloh, Battle of
in this index
Pittsburgh [Pennsylvania] **P:** 500a *with pictures
and map*
City *picture on* **Ci:** 587
Pennsylvania *picture on* **P:** 245; (Places to visit)
P: 254; (table: Average monthly weather)
P: 259
Pittsburgh, University of P: 502
Pittsburgh Penguins [team]
Hockey (table: National Hockey League) **H:** 281
Pittsburgh Pirates [baseball team]
Baseball (table) **B:** 130
Pittsburgh Reduction Company
Alcoa Inc. **A:** 334
Aluminum (Growth of the aluminum industry)
A: 397
Pittsburgh Renaissance [program]
Pittsburgh (Urban renewal) **P:** 501
Pittsburgh Steelers [football team]
Bradshaw, Terry **B:** 545

Football (National Football League) **F:** 364
Pituitary dwarfism [disorder]
Dwarfism (Causes) **D:** 394-395
Pituitary gland [anatomy] **P:** 502 *with diagram*
Brain (Regulating body processes) **B:** 553
Dwarfism (Causes) **D:** 394
Egg (Development of the bird's egg) **E:** 117
Giant **G:** 183
Gland (Endocrine glands) **G:** 207 *with diagram*;
(table) **G:** 208
Human body (table) **H:** 422 *with diagram*; (The
endocrine system) **H:** 425
Human growth hormone **H:** 427
Hypothalamus **H:** 481
Stress (How stress affects the body) **So:** 926-927
Più [music]
Music (table) **M:** 954
Pius IV [pope] **P:** 502
Pius V, Saint [pope] **P:** 502
Pius VII [pope]
Rome (Under Napoleon) **R:** 434-435
Pius IX [pope] **P:** 502
Immaculate Conception **I:** 79
Papal States **P:** 132
Rome (Republic of Rome) **R:** 435
Vatican City (History) **V:** 288-289
Vatican Council I **V:** 289
Pius X, Saint [pope] **P:** 503
Roman Catholic Church (Pius X) **R:** 410
Pius XI [pope] **P:** 503
Pius XII [pope] **P:** 503
Roman Catholic Church (Facing opposition)
R: 410
Vatican City (History) **V:** 288-289
Vulgate **V:** 453
Pius, Order of
Medals, decorations, and orders (table) **M:** 359
Pivot joint [anatomy]
Joint **J:** 155 *with diagram*
Pivot Rock [Arkansas]
Arkansas (Interesting facts about Arkansas)
A: 695 *with picture*
Pixar Animation Studios P: 503
Animation (The computer revolution) **A:** 514c
Walt Disney Company **W:** 21
Pixel [electronics]
Charge-coupled device **C:** 378
Computer graphics (How a computer creates
images) **Ci:** 924h
Liquid crystal *picture on* **L:** 347
Photography (Capturing digital images) **P:** 420-
421
Polarized light (Uses of polarized light) **P:** 618
Television (Solid-state cameras) **T:** 122
Pixie [imaginary creature]
Fairy **F:** 9
Pixii, Hippolyte [French inventor]
Electric motor (History) **E:** 181
Invention (The Industrial Revolution) **I:** 361-362
Pixilation [photography]
Animation (Pixilation) **A:** 514a
Pizarro [play by Sheridan]
Sheridan, Richard Brinsley **S:** 397
Pizarro, Francisco [Spanish explorer] **P:** 504 *with
pictures*
Conquistadors **Ci:** 973
Exploration *map on* **E:** 443; (Spain's conquests in
the New World) **E:** 445
Inca (The Spanish conquest) **I:** 99
Indian, American *picture on* **I:** 143; (After
European contact) **I:** 175
Latin America *map on* **L:** 105 ; (The conquest of
the American Indians) **L:** 103-104 *with map*
Panama (The Spanish colonial period) **P:** 120
Peru (Spanish conquest and rule) **P:** 314
Pizza [food] **P:** 504
Food (Interesting facts about food) **F:** 329
Naples (Way of life) **N:** 12
Pizzicato [music]
Music (Stringed instruments) **M:** 948-949
Violin (Playing the violin) **V:** 389-390
PKD [disease] *See* Polycystic kidney disease *in this
index*
PKU [disease] *See* Phenylketonuria *in this index*
PLA [military]
China (The armed forces) **C:** 481
Place [gambling]
Horse racing (Betting) **H:** 365
Place, Francis [English artist]
Penn, William *picture on* **P:** 242
Place Bonaventure
Montreal (Trade and finance) **M:** 776-777
Place Charles de Gaulle [Paris]
Paris (Gardens, squares, and parks) **P:** 162
Place de la Concorde
Paris (Gardens, squares, and parks) **P:** 162 *with
picture and map*

Place de l'Étoile [Paris]
Paris (Gardens, squares, and parks) **P:** 162
Place des Arts
Montreal *picture on* **M:** 774; (The arts) **M:** 773
Place hitting
Baseball (Batting) **B:** 128
Place kick
Football *picture on* **F:** 362; (The kickoff) **F:** 359-
360 *with picture*
Rugby football (Rugby Union) **R:** 510
Place Quebec
Quebec (Recent developments) **Q:** 37
Place Royale [Quebec]
New France *picture on* **N:** 205
Place-value system [mathematics]
Decimal system **D:** 70
Number (Numeral systems) **N:** 605
Placebo [medicine] **P:** 505
Placement counselor [career]
Employment agency **E:** 263
Placement office
Careers (Finding job opportunities) **C:** 217-218
Placenta [anatomy] **P:** 505
Baby (The developing baby) **B:** 4-5 *with diagram*
Childbirth (The birth process) **C:** 456
Gland (table) **G:** 209
Human body (The reproductive system) **H:** 425
Mammal (Reproduction) **M:** 123-124
Ovary **O:** 881
Preeclampsia **P:** 734
Pregnancy (Confirming pregnancy) **P:** 734a
Prehistoric animal (Mammals) **P:** 739-740
Reproduction, Human (The first days of
pregnancy) **R:** 246-247 *with diagram*
Umbilical cord **U:** 18
Uterus **U:** 251
Placental barrier [pregnancy]
Reproduction, Human (Nourishing the embryo)
R: 247
Placental malaria [disease]
Malaria (Symptoms) **M:** 95
Placental mammal
Mammal (Reproduction) **M:** 123 *with picture*
Prehistoric animal (Mammals) **P:** 739; (The
development of placentals) **P:** 741; (The
distribution of mammals) **P:** 741
Placentia [Newfoundland and Labrador] **P:** 505
Newfoundland and Labrador (Places to visit)
N: 368; (War with France) **N:** 375
Placer [geology]
Gold (Types of deposits) **G:** 252
Mining (Mining terms) **M:** 577
Sand **S:** 106
Placer mining
Mining (Surface mining methods) **M:** 575
Placid, Lake
Lake Placid **L:** 44
Placidia, Mausoleum of [Ravenna, Italy]
Ravenna **R:** 151
Placoderm [zoology]
Fish (The first fish) **F:** 171
Placoid scale [zoology]
Fish (Scales) **F:** 160 *with picture*
Shark (Teeth and scales) **S:** 374-375 *with picture*
Placuna oyster [sea animal]
Shell (Uses of shells) **S:** 389-390
Plagal cadence [music]
Music (Harmony) **M:** 951-952 *with diagram*
Plagiarism P: 505
Publishing (Fact checkers) **P:** 867
Plagioclase [mineralogy]
Basalt **B:** 123
Feldspar **F:** 68
Granite **G:** 311
Plague [disease] **P:** 505
Black Death **B:** 386
Cat (History) **C:** 296
Disease (Spread of infectious diseases) **D:** 228
London (War, plague, and fire) **L:** 441
Medicine (During the Middle Ages) **M:** 373
Middle Ages (A halt in progress) **M:** 528
Races, Human (The clinal approach) **R:** 55-56
Rat **R:** 146
Plague, Bubonic *See* Bubonic plague *in this index*
Plague, The [book by Camus]
Camus, Albert **C:** 97
French literature (Existentialism) **F:** 523
Plague of Ashdod [European history]
Plague (History of plague) **P:** 506
Plague of locusts
Joel, Book of **J:** 130
Locust **L:** 419
Plagues of Egypt
Moses (The Exodus) **M:** 828-829
Plaice [fish]
Flounder **F:** 267
Plaid [design]

Tartan **T:** 47
Plain [natural feature] **P: 506** *with picture*
Great Plains **G:** 346
Mars (Surface features) **M:** 225
Ocean (The land at the bottom of the sea) **O:** 659
with map
Plain, The [French history]
French Revolution (The National Convention)
F: 526
Plain bearing [machine]
Bearing (Plain bearings) **B:** 188 *with diagram*
Plain Dealer, The [play by Wycherley]
Wycherley, William **W:** 514
Plain of Esdraelon [region, Israel]
Israel (The Coastal Plain) **I:** 482
Plain of Jars [region, Laos]
Laos (History) **L:** 71
Plain of Sharon [region, Israel]
Israel (The Coastal Plain) **I:** 482
Plain People
Pennsylvania **P:** 244
Pennsylvania Dutch **P:** 270
Plain Tales from the Hills [book by Kipling]
Kipling, Rudyard (Early literary success) **K:** 334
Plain weave
Basket making (Methods) **B:** 141 *with pictures*
Textile (Woven fabrics) **T:** 214
Weaving (The plain weave) **W:** 173 *with picture*
Plainchant [music] *See* Gregorian chant *in this
index*
Plainclothes officer
Police (Investigations of crimes) **P:** 621
Plains Cree Indians
Cree Indians **Ci:** 1125
Manitoba (Precontact era) **M:** 160
Plains Indians
Indian, American (Indians of the Plains) **I:** 158
with pictures and map
Indian wars (Wars on the Plains) **I:** 192
Iowa (Indian days) **I:** 393
Pioneer life in America (Indians on the Plains)
P: 487
Sun dance **So:** 987
Tipi **T:** 169
Wyoming (History) **W:** 533-534
Plains of Abraham [plateau]
Quebec, Battle of (Bombardment of Quebec)
Q: 37
Plains prickly pear cactus
Flower *picture on* **F:** 287
Plains spadefoot toad
Amphibian *picture on* **A:** 439
Plains viscacha [rodent]
Viscacha (The plains viscacha) **V:** 428b
Plainsawing
Wood (Wood figure) **W:** 390 *with picture*
Plainsong [music] *See* Gregorian chant *in this index*
Plaintext
Codes and ciphers **Ci:** 749; (Communications
security) **Ci:** 749
Plaintiff [law]
Class action **Ci:** 642
Court (How civil courts work) **Ci:** 1102
Libel **L:** 226
Trial **T:** 436
Plaisted, Frederick W. [American political leader]
Maine (table) **M:** 87
Plaisted, Harris M. [American political leader]
Maine (table) **M:** 87
Plaiting [weaving]
Basket making (Plaiting) **B:** 141 *with pictures*
Plaka [district]
Athens (Landmarks) **A:** 854-855 *with map*
Plan de Ayala [Mexican history]
Zapata, Emiliano **Z:** 587
Plan of Iguala [Mexican history]
Iturbide, Agustín de **I:** 520
Plan of San Luis Potosí [Mexican history]
Madero, Francisco Indalecio **M:** 30
Plan of Union [1775]
Franklin, Benjamin (Organizing the new nation)
F: 490
Plan of Union [U.S. history] *See* Albany Plan of
Union *in this index*
Plan of Union, Albany [U.S. history] *See* Albany
Plan of Union *in this index*
Plan Position Indicator [radar]
Radar (The display) **R:** 71
Planar crystal
Snow (How snow forms) **S:** 539 *with picture*
Planarian [animal] **P:** 506 *with picture*
Animal *pictures on* **A:** 497, **A:** 506
Heredity (Sex cells and reproduction) **H:** 201
Worm (Flatworms) **W:** 500 *with picture*
Planchette [device]
Ouija board **O:** 879
Planck [space probe]

Astronomy (Radio and microwave astronomy)
A: 843
European Space Agency **E:** 418
Planck, Max Karl Ernst Ludwig [German physicist]
P: 507
Bohr, Niels **B:** 438
Light (Photons) **L:** 286
Photon **P:** 430
Physics (Quantum theory) **P:** 441
Quantum mechanics (Emission of quanta) **Q:** 6
Radiation (The quantum theory) **R:** 81
Science (Science in the early 1900's) **S:** 201
Planck's constant [physics]
Planck, Max Karl Ernst Ludwig **P:** 507
Plane *See* Airplane *in this index*
Plane [geometry]
Geometry **G:** 101; (Terms) **G:** 102; (Non-Euclidean
geometry) **G:** 105
Plane [tool]
Woodworking (Cutting) **W:** 397 *with picture*
Plane [tree]
Tree *picture on* **T:** 427
Plane geometry [mathematics]
Geometry (Euclidean geometry) **G:** 104
Mathematics (Branches of mathematics) **M:** 303
Plane mirror [optics]
Mirror (Plane mirrors) **M:** 616 *with diagram*
Plane of symmetry
Symmetry (A plane of symmetry) **So:** 1066
Plane survey [measurement]
Surveying (Types of surveys) **So:** 1011
Plane table [surveying]
Surveying (Early tools) **So:** 1011-1012
Plane trigonometry
Trigonometry **T:** 442
Planer [machine]
Industrial Revolution (The steam engine) **I:** 249
Planer, Minna [wife of]
Wagner, Richard (Early career) **W:** 3
Planet P: 507 *with pictures*
See also the list of Related articles in the Planet
article
Astrobiology **A:** 826
Astrology (The planets) **A:** 826
Astronomy (How the planets move) **A:** 835;
(Finding new objects) **A:** 848
Bode's law **B:** 434
Copernicus, Nicolaus **Ci:** 1039
Earth (Earth as a planet) **E:** 16; (Earth's size and
shape) **E:** 18
Galileo (Early scientific interests) **G:** 11
Geology (Geology of the solar system) **G:** 100
Horoscope (Parts of a horoscope) **H:** 341
Hydrogen (Occurrence) **H:** 469
Magnetism (Other astronomical bodies) **M:** 60d
Meteor (Other planets and moons) **M:** 432 *with
picture*
Mountain (Mountains on other planets) **M:** 895
with picture
Planetarium **P:** 514a
Planetary ring **P:** 514d
Relativity (General relativity) **R:** 211
Satellite **S:** 149
Solar system (Planets) **So:** 580 *with diagram*
Space exploration (Space between the planets)
So: 696; (Space probes) **So:** 708
Storm (Extraterrestrial storms) **So:** 913
Tidal forces **T:** 280
Transit **T:** 374
Volcano (Volcanoes in the solar system) **V:** 442b
with picture
Planet gear [mechanics]
Transmission (Planetary gears) **T:** 377 *with
diagrams*
Planetarium [machine] **P:** 514a *with pictures*
Astronomy (Careers) **A:** 849
Planetary exploration
Geophysics **G:** 106b
Planetary gears
Gear **G:** 75
Transmission (Planetary gears) **T:** 377 *with
diagrams*
Planetary geology
Geology (Geology of the solar system) **G:** 100
Planetary motion, Laws of *See* Kepler's laws *in
this index*
Planetary nebula [astronomy]
Nebula (Planetary nebulae) **N:** 116
Star *picture on* **So:** 841; (White dwarf phase)
So: 849
Planetary ring [astronomy] **P:** 514d *with picture*
Cassini **C:** 276
Cassini, Giovanni Domenico **C:** 277
Jupiter (Satellites and rings) **J:** 200a *with picture*
Neptune (Satellites and rings) **N:** 129
Planet (The planets of our solar system) **P:** 511
with picture

Saturn **S:** 150h *with picture*; (Rings) **S:** 150j *with
diagram*
Tidal forces **T:** 280
Uranus *picture on* **U:** 217; (Rings) **U:** 218 *with
pictures*
Planetary-scale systems
Weather (Weather systems) **W:** 158
Planetesimal [geology]
Jupiter (Formation of Jupiter) **J:** 200b
Planet (How the planets formed) **P:** 514
Solar system (Formation of our solar system)
So: 581
Planetoid [astronomy] *See* Asteroid *in this index*
Planets, The [music by Holst]
Holst, Gustav **H:** 298
Plangman, Mary Patricia [birth name of]
Highsmith, Patricia **H:** 229
Planing [manufacturing]
Machine tool (Planing, shaping, and broaching)
M: 18
Planing hull
Motorboat racing (Hull designs) **M:** 876
Planing mill
Lumber (Planing) **L:** 519
Plank [construction]
Lumber (table) **L:** 518
Plank, Ed [American baseball player]
Baseball (table: Hall of Fame) **B:** 134a
Plank sled
Inuit *picture on* **I:** 354d; (Transportation) **I:** 354c
Plankton [biology] **P:** 515 *with picture*
Algae **A:** 349
Animal (Filtering mechanisms) **A:** 490
Arctic Ocean (Ocean life) **A:** 643
Atlantic Ocean (Ocean life) **A:** 866
Copepod **Ci:** 1039
Diatom **D:** 185
Dinoflagellate **D:** 205
Fish (Fish in the balance of nature) **F:** 147
Gas [fuel] (How natural gas was formed) **G:** 52
Grand Banks **G:** 306
Ocean **O:** 656 *with pictures*; (The plankton) **O:** 655
Oyster (Young) **O:** 891
Pacific Ocean (El Niño) **P:** 14
Seashore **S:** 269
Planned community
Housing (New towns) **H:** 390
Planned economy [economics]
Capitalism **C:** 194
Communism (Communism in practice) **Ci:** 890;
(Under Stalin) **Ci:** 892; (The decline of
Communism) **Ci:** 895
Economics (The organization of economies)
E: 58; (Distribution of income) **E:** 63
Price **P:** 774
Union of Soviet Socialist Republics (Economy)
U: 33
Planned obsolescence [marketing]
Automobile (The rise of the Big Three) **A:** 968
Planned parenthood
See also Birth control *in this index*
Birth control **B:** 378
Planned Parenthood Federation of America
P: 515
Planned Parenthood Federation of America
[organization] **P:** 515
Sanger, Margaret **S:** 110
*Planned Parenthood of Eastern Pennsylvania v.
Casey* [U.S. history]
Abortion (Abortion in the United States) **A:** 15-16
Planning, City *See* City planning *in this index*
Planographic printing
Stamp collecting (Printing) **So:** 830
Plant [botany] **P:** 516 *with pictures and map*
See also Botany; Flower; Gardening;
Photosynthesis *in this index; and the list of
Related articles in the* Plant *article*
Agriculture (Agricultural products) **A:** 147 *with
picture*
Animal **A:** 468; (Importance of animals) **A:** 470
Biodiversity **B:** 310
Breeding (Plant breeding) **B:** 592
Carbon cycle **C:** 206 *with diagram*
Cell *diagram on* **C:** 329; (Mitosis) **C:** 330-331
Chlorophyll **C:** 517
Classification, Scientific (Groups in classification)
Ci: 655 *with pictures*
Cloning (Clones in nature) **Ci:** 684
Conservation (Biodiversity conservation) **Ci:** 976
Drainage **D:** 320
Drug (Plants and molds) **D:** 355
Ecology **E:** 53
Embryo **E:** 257
Endangered species **E:** 269
Evolution **E:** 426
Fossil **F:** 422 *with pictures*
Fruit **F:** 544

Fungi (How a fungus lives) F: 559
Gardening G: 30 *with pictures*
Genetic engineering (Concerns about genetic engineering) G: 84c
Global warming (Impact of global warming) G: 232a; (Sequestration in living plants) G: 232c
Grassland G: 329 *with picture*
Herbicide H: 198
Hormone (Plant hormones) H: 337
Horticulture H: 369
Invasive species I: 354j
Life L: 274 *with picture*
Marine biology M: 204
Materials (Biological materials) M: 300d
Mendel, Gregor Johann (His work) M: 398
Mountain (As a home for plants and animals) M: 892
Nitrogen (Nitrogen and life) N: 425
Nitrogen cycle N: 426
Nursery N: 614
Ocean (Life in the ocean) O: 655 *with pictures*
Paleobotany P: 102
Perfume (Plant substances) P: 286
Photoperiodism P: 430
Photosynthesis P: 430
Rain forest R: 126 *with pictures*
Reproduction R: 242; (How reproduction has evolved) R: 243
Respiration (Respiration in plants) R: 261
Silurian Period S: 463
Soil (Effects of living things) So: 573
Soil pollution So: 576
Tropism T: 451
Wetland W: 252a *with pictures*
Wildlife conservation W: 303
Plant, Aquatic *See* Water plant *in this index*
Plant, Henry B. [American businessman]
Tampa (History) T: 23-24
Plant, Robert [British singer]
Led Zeppelin L: 175
Plant breeding [botany]
See also the list of Related articles on Plant growing *in the* Plant *article*
Breeding (Plant breeding) B: 592
Fruit (Developing new fruit cultivars) F: 548
Grafting (Uses of grafting) G: 298
Hybrid (Producing hybrid plants) H: 461
Plant disease
See also the Plant Diseases and Pests *section of the* Related articles *in the* Plant *article*
Plant (Plant diseases and pests) P: 539 *with picture*
Botany (The importance of botany) B: 508-509
Cotton (Care during growth) Ci: 1090
Famine (Plant diseases and pests) F: 26a
Fungicide F: 560
Gardening (Disorders and diseases) G: 35
Insect (Harmful insects) I: 284 *with picture*
Potato (Potato pests) P: 713
Tree surgery T: 433
Plant ecology
Botany (Plant habitats) B: 508
Plant geography
Botany (Plant habitats) B: 508; (Later developments) B: 509
Geography (Physical geography) G: 94
Plant louse [insect]
See also Aphid *in this index*
Aphid A: 565
Phylloxera P: 431 *with picture*
Plant nema [worm] *See* Eelworm *in this index*
Plant patent [law]
Patent P: 194
Plant protein
Food supply (Protein) F: 346
Plant quarantine [law] P: 550
Quarantine Q: 7
Plantae [biology]
Kingdom K: 328
Plantagenet [English history] P: 550
England (table) E: 308
Plantagenet, Geoffrey [French nobleman] *See* Geoffrey, Count of Anjou *in this index*
Plantagenet, Henry *See* Henry II [of England] *in this index*
Plantain [plant] P: 550 *with picture*
Banana B: 73
Lawn *picture on* L: 143
Plantain family [botany]
Flower (table) F: 301 *with picture*
Plantar arch [anatomy]
Foot (The arches) F: 352 *with diagram*
Plantar wart
Skin (Tumors) S: 491
Plantation [agriculture] P: 550
Agriculture (Colonial agriculture) A: 157

Brazil *picture on* B: 584
Colonial life in America (Houses) Ci: 796-797
Latin America (Rural life) L: 96
Mississippi *picture on* M: 641
Slavery (Modern times) S: 502; (Slavery in the United States) S: 502
United States, History of the *pictures on* U: 155, U: 170
Plantation [political unit]
Maine (Local government) M: 88
Plantation of Ireland [Irish history]
Great Irish Famine G: 343
Ireland (The conquest of Ireland) I: 426
Planté, Gaston [French physicist]
Battery (History) B: 171
Planter [machine]
Farm and farming F: 36
Planter [ship]
Smalls, Robert S: 513
Planter [U.S. history]
London Company L: 445
Planthopper [insect]
Coconut palm (Growing coconut palms) Ci: 747
Planting [agriculture]
Cotton (Planting) Ci: 1090
Farm and farming (Planting) F: 35 *with picture*
Fruit (Planting) F: 546
Gardening (Cultivating an outdoor garden) G: 34
Transplanting T: 381 *with pictures*
Tree (Planting the tree) T: 431 *with pictures*
Vegetable (Planting) V: 293
Planting gun [tool]
Forestry *picture on* F: 404
Plantlet [botany]
Fruit (Fruit production) F: 546
Plant (Asexual reproduction) P: 535
Planula [zoology]
Jellyfish J: 90
Plaque [physiology]
Alzheimer's disease (Diagnosis) A: 398
Angioplasty A: 461 *with diagram*
Arteriosclerosis (Causes) A: 750
Biofilm B: 311
C-reactive protein C: 2
Fat (Fats and disease) F: 53
Heart *diagram on* H: 140; (Causes) H: 137 *with picture*
Multiple sclerosis M: 920
Teeth (Cleaning the teeth) T: 81; (Periodontal diseases) T: 85
Plasma [physiology] P: 551 *with pictures*
Blood (The composition of blood) B: 407; (How the body maintains its blood supply) B: 410
Blood transfusion B: 416
Circulatory system (The blood) Ci: 559
Drew, Charles Richard D: 347
Gamma globulin G: 23
Globulin G: 23
Human body (The blood) H: 421-424 *with picture*
Lymphatic system (Lymph) L: 534
Serum S: 319
Plasma [physics] P: 552
Electricity (Conductors) E: 193
Gas [physics] G: 48
Hydrogen (Uses) H: 469-470
Ion (Ions in gases) I: 371
Magnetism (In science and medicine) M: 60b
Magnetohydrodynamics M: 62
Matter (States of matter) M: 311
Nuclear energy (Nuclear fusion) N: 583
Petroleum (The future of petroleum) P: 349-350
Physics (Fluid and plasma physics) P: 438
Spitzer, Lyman, Jr. So: 797
Sun (Composition) So: 975
Plasma arc welding
Welding (Gas tungsten arc welding) W: 189
Plasma cell [physiology]
Immune system (Parts of the immune system) I: 87
Plasma display [electronics]
Electronics (Electronics today) E: 216-217
Television (Flat-panel displays) T: 126
Plasma membrane [biology]
Cell (Inside a living cell) C: 328
Life (Cells) L: 277
Plasmapheresis [medicine]
Myasthenia gravis M: 970f
Plasma (Uses in medicine) P: 551-552
Plasmid DNA [biology]
Cloning (Gene and cell cloning) Ci: 684
Plasmodium [botany]
Slime mold S: 508
Plasmodium [protozoan]
Malaria M: 95 *with pictures*
Parasite (An ectoparasite) P: 154
Plasmodium falciparum [protozoan]
Malaria M: 95

Plasmodium malariae [protozoan]
Malaria M: 95
Plasmodium ovale [protozoan]
Malaria M: 95
Plasmodium vivax [protozoan]
Malaria M: 95
Plassey, Battle of [1757]
Clive, Robert Ci: 682i
India (The rise of the East India Company) I: 130
Plaster [building material] P: 552 *with pictures*
House (Interior construction) H: 382
Islamic art (Carved and molded plaster) I: 470
Painting (Fresco painting) P: 38
Plaster of Paris P: 553
Gypsum G: 451
Plasterboard
Wallboard W: 17
Plastering [construction]
Building trade (Career opportunities) B: 686
Plastic [material] *See* Plastics *in this index*
Plastic explosive P: 553
Explosive (High explosives) E: 453
Plastic fingerprint
Fingerprinting (Types of fingerprints) F: 106
Plastic foam
Plastics (Foaming) P: 558
Plastic surgery [medicine] P: 553
Medicine (table) M: 369
Skin grafting S: 494
Surgery (Plastic surgery) So: 1007
Plastic worm [lure]
Fishing *picture on* F: 177
Plastic wrap
Plastics (To replace paper) P: 555
Plasticity [physical property]
Mechanics M: 354
Plasticization [industrial process]
Rubber (Plasticization) R: 504
Plasticizer
Alcohol (Other alcohols) A: 335
Explosive (High explosives) E: 453
Plastics (Making synthetic resins) P: 556-557
Plastics P: 554 *with pictures*
See also the list of Related articles in the Plastics *article*
Acrylic A: 29
Composite materials Ci: 904
Doll (Modern dolls) D: 292; (The doll industry today) D: 294
Extrusion E: 459
Forest products (Cellulose products) F: 402
Industrial arts (Industrial arts courses) I: 242-243
Manufacturing (How science helps manufacturing) M: 171
Materials (Plastics) M: 300d
Ocean (Marine pollution) O: 664
Phonograph (How phonograph records are made) P: 401
Recycling R: 184
Resin (Synthetic resins) R: 259
Sculpture (Modern International sculpture) S: 256-257
Plastid [biology]
Chloroplast C: 518
Plastron [zoology]
Turtle (Shell) T: 521 *with diagram*
Plat [map]
Map (General reference maps) M: 177-178
Plata, Río de la *See* Río de la Plata *in this index*
Plataea [ancient city]
Thebes T: 251
Plataea, Battle of [ancient Greece]
Thebes T: 251
Xerxes I X: 544
Plate [building construction]
House (The frame) H: 382 *with diagram*
Plate [geology] *See* Plate tectonics *in this index*
Plate [industry]
Iron and steel (Rolling) I: 445-447
Plate [printing]
Etching E: 364 *with pictures*
Newspaper (Making up the pages) N: 383 *with picture*; (Printing the newspaper) N: 385
Printing (Electronic imagesetting) P: 797; (Offset lithography) P: 798; (Platemaking) P: 798 *with diagram*; (Relief printing) P: 799
Printing press P: 804
Plate [zoology]
Reptile (Skin) R: 251 *with picture*
Plate armor
Armor (During the Middle Ages) A: 719-720
Plate block
Stamp collecting *picture on* So: 832
Plate clutch [engine]
Transmission (Clutches) T: 377
Plate cylinder [printing]
Printing (Offset presses) P: 798 *with diagram*

Plate flexing [geology]
Mountain (Forces that shape mountains) **M: 894**
Plate freezing
Food, Frozen (Indirect-contact freezing) **F: 338**
Food preservation (Freezing) **F: 342**
Plate girder bridge
Bridge (Girder bridges) **B: 600-601**
Plate tectonics [geology] **P: 561** *with diagrams*
Atlantic Ocean (The Mid-Atlantic Ridge) **A: 864**
Caribbean Sea (Climate and geology) **C: 237**
Earth (Earth's crust) **E: 23**; (The shaping of the continents) **E: 24** *with diagrams*
Earthquake (How an earthquake begins) **E: 35** *with map*; (Where earthquakes occur) **E: 38**
Fossil (Recording Earth's changes) **F: 424**
Geology (Experimental geology) **G: 99-100**
Geomorphology **G: 106a**
Geophysics **G: 106a**
Great Rift Valley **G: 347**
Hot spot **H: 374a**
Hydrothermal vent **H: 473**
Indian Ocean (Ocean floor) **I: 186-187**
Island *picture on* **I: 471**; (Tectonically formed islands) **I: 472**
Mantle **M: 168**
Mediterranean Sea (The seabed) **M: 381**
Mountain (How different types of mountains form) **M: 892**; (Forces that shape mountains) **M: 894**
Ocean (How the sea floor was formed) **O: 662**
Ocean drilling programs **O: 667**
Petroleum (Shifting of Earth's surface) **P: 334**
Ring of Fire **R: 342**
South America (The Andes Mountains) **So: 626**
Volcano (Where volcanoes form) **V: 441** *with map*
Plate tracery [architecture]
Tracery **T: 355**
Plateau [geography] **P: 565**
See also specific plateaus, such as Columbia Plateau, *in this index*
Mesa **M: 420**
Plateau, Joseph Antoine [Belgian scientist]
Animation (Early animation) **A: 514a**
Plateau basalt [geology]
Volcano (Flood basalts) **V: 442a** *with picture*
Plateau Indians
Indian, American (Indians of the Plateau) **I: 165** *with picture and map*
Platelet [physiology]
Blood (The composition of blood) **B: 407-408** *with picture*; (How the body maintains its blood supply) **B: 410-411**; (Bleeding disorders) **B: 414**
Blood transfusion **B: 416**
Human body (The blood) **H: 421-424** *with picture*
Osler, Sir William **O: 863**
Smoking (Why smoking is dangerous) **S: 520**
Plateletpheresis [medical procedure]
Blood transfusion (How blood is collected) **B: 416-417**
Platelike snow crystals
Snow (How snow forms) **S: 539** *with picture*
Platen
Typewriter (How a typewriter works) **T: 538**
Platen press [machine]
Printing (Letterpress printing) **P: 799-800**
Plateosaurus [dinosaur] **P: 565**
Dinosaur *picture on* **D: 206d**; (True dinosaurs) **D: 206b-208**
Plater, George [American political leader]
Maryland (table) **M: 255**
Plateresque style [sculpture]
Latin America (Sculpture) **L: 100**
Platero and I [book by Jiménez]
Jiménez, Juan Ramón **J: 127**
Platform [device]
Inertial guidance (Gyroscopic systems) **I: 263**
Platform [format]
Electronic game (Gaming platforms) **E: 204c**
Platform, Political
Political convention **P: 628**
Platform distribution
Motion picture (Distribution) **M: 860**
Platform diving
Diving (Types of diving) **D: 242**
Platform tennis [sport] **P: 565** *with picture*
Platform truck
Truck *picture on* **T: 459**; (On-highway trucks) **T: 457**
Plath, Sylvia [American poet] **P: 566**
American literature ("Confessional" poetry) **A: 423**
Hughes, Ted **H: 409**
Plating [industrial process]
Electroplating **E: 218** *with diagram*
Platinum [metal] **P: 566**
Palladium **P: 108**
Platinum group metal

Platinum **P: 566**
Platinum record
Recording industry (Recording industry awards) **R: 182**
Platinum resistance thermometer
Liquid air (Properties) **L: 346**
Plato [Greek philosopher] **P: 567** *with picture*
Aristotle **A: 663**
Atlantis **A: 868**
Communism (Early communism) **Ci: 890**
Ethics (Ancient ethics) **E: 366**
Geometry (Greek geometry) **G: 106**
Government (Ancient Greece) **G: 289**; (Legitimacy) **G: 289**
Greece, Ancient (Philosophy, science, and the arts) **G: 368-369**
Humanism (Work of the humanists) **H: 431**
Neoplatonism **N: 124**
Peripatetic philosophy **P: 288**
Philosophy (Ancient philosophy) **P: 386**
Plotinus **P: 574**
Political science (The development of political science) **P: 639**
Renaissance (The revival of Platonism) **R: 234**
Socrates (The Socratic problem) **So: 567**
Sophists **So: 595**
Writing system (The importance of writing) **W: 513**
Platonic Academy [Italy]
Plato (Plato's place in Western thought) **P: 569**
Platonic love
Neoplatonism **N: 124**
Renaissance (The ideal courtier) **R: 235-236**
Platonic solid [geometry]
Geometry (Solid geometry) **G: 104-105**
Polyhedron **P: 651** *with diagrams*
Platonism [philosophy]
Renaissance (The revival of Platonism) **R: 234**
Platoon [film]
Motion picture (Best picture: 1986) **M: 861**
Stone, Oliver **So: 909**
Platoon [military]
Army, United States (table) **A: 737**
Platoon school [education]
Indiana (Schools) **I: 200-201**
Platt, Thomas C. [American political leader]
Arthur, Chester Alan (Opposition to Garfield) **A: 756**
Roosevelt, Theodore (Governor of New York) **R: 463**
Platt Amendment [1901]
Cuba (The Platt Amendment) **Ci: 1176**
McKinley, William (McKinley's second Administration (1901]) **M: 341**
Roosevelt, Franklin Delano (Foreign policy) **R: 454**
Root, Elihu **R: 472**
Plattdeutsch *See* Low German *in this index*
Platte Bridge Station [Wyoming]
Casper **C: 274**
Platte River [Nebraska] **P: 569**
Nebraska (Rivers and lakes) **N: 106**
Platter [electronic device]
Computer (Hard drives) **Ci: 915**
Platters, The [singing group]
Rock music (A variety of styles) **R: 378** *with picture*
Platyhelminth *See* Flatworm *in this index*
Platypus [animal] **P: 569** *with picture*
Animal *picture on* **A: 469**
Australia *picture on* **A: 915**; (Native animals) **A: 911**
Mammal *picture on* **M: 119**; (Reproduction) **M: 123-124** *with picture*
Plautus [Roman dramatist] **P: 570**
Drama (Comedy) **D: 328**; (Medieval drama) **D: 328**
Latin literature (Early Latin literature) **L: 115-116**
Play [behavior] **P: 570**
Play [bridge]
Bridge **B: 604**; (The play) **B: 604** *with diagram*
Play [drama]
Drama **D: 324**
Theater **T: 232**
Writing (Scriptwriting) **W: 512**
Play [recreation] **P: 570**
See also the list of Related articles in the Play *article*
Animal (Learning and play) **A: 500**
Dog (Exercise and play) **D: 279**
Kindergarten (Equipment) **K: 318**
Playground **P: 570**
Preschool (Learning through play) **P: 756b**
Play bow
Dog (Exercise and play) **D: 279**
Play of color
Opal **O: 788**
Play of the Wise Men, The [play]
Spain (Literature) **So: 738**
Play-offs

Baseball (Play-offs) **B: 130**
Play on words
Humor (Puns) **H: 435**
Play therapy [psychology]
Mental illness (Psychotherapy) **M: 407-408**
Psychiatry (Psychotherapy) **P: 845**
Playa [geology]
Australia (Lakes) **A: 909-910**
Basin **B: 141**
Desert (Desert climate and land) **D: 155-156**
Playboy of the Western World, The [play by Synge]
Irish literature (The Irish literary revival) **I: 431**
Synge, John Millington **So: 1067**
Player
Game theory **G: 23**
Player, Gary [South African golfer]
Golf *picture on* **G: 266**; (U.S. PGA Championship) **G: 265**
Player piano
Piano (Player pianos) **P: 447** *with picture*
Player Piano [book by Vonnegut]
Vonnegut, Kurt **V: 448**
Playfair, John [Scottish mathematician]
Geology (The rock dispute) **G: 98-99**
Playfair algorithm [cryptology]
Codes and ciphers (Substitution) **Ci: 750**
Playground **P: 570** *with picture*
Playhouse Square Center [Cleveland]
Cleveland (The arts) **Ci: 665-666**
Playing cards
Card game (Playing cards) **C: 209** *with pictures*
Communication (The rise of printing) **Ci: 879**
Money *picture on* **M: 706**
PlayStation [machine]
Electronic game (Renewed interest in consoles) **E: 204e**; (Competition for older players) **E: 204e**; (Bigger games) **E: 204f**; (Handheld games) **E: 204f**
Sony Corporation **So: 594**
Playtester [career]
Electronic game (Game design) **E: 204b**
Playwright *See* Dramatist *in this index*
Playwrights Theater [theater company]
Glaspell, Susan **G: 210**
Plaza [public square]
Latin America (Rural life) **L: 96**
Mexico (City life) **M: 454**
Plaza de la Independencia [Quito]
Ecuador *picture on* **E: 68**
Plaza de Mayo
Argentina *picture on* **A: 647**
Buenos Aires (The city) **B: 672**
Plaza de toros
Bullfighting **B: 695**
Plaza Lasso, Galo [Ecuadorean political leader]
Ecuador (The 1900's) **E: 73**
Plaza Mayor [Peru]
Lima (The city) **L: 305** *with picture*
Plaza Murillo [La Paz]
La Paz **L: 72**
Plaza of the Republic [Brazil]
São Paulo (The city) **S: 117-118** *with picture*
Plaza San Martín
Lima (The city) **L: 305**
Plaza—State of Puebla [photograph by Strand]
Strand, Paul *picture on* **So: 918**
Plea bargaining [law] **P: 571**
Criminal justice system (Pretrial procedures) **Ci: 1143**; (Problems in the courts) **Ci: 1144**
Law enforcement (Trial) **L: 141**
Trial (The criminal defendant's rights) **T: 436-437**
Pleadings [law]
Court (How civil courts work) **Ci: 1102**
Pleasant, Ruffin G. [American political leader]
Louisiana (table) **L: 496**
Pleasants, James [American political leader]
Virginia (table) **V: 417**
Pleasure
Bentham, Jeremy **B: 254**
Epicurus **E: 342**
Hedonism **H: 165**
Locke, John (His philosophy) **L: 413**
Utilitarianism **U: 251**
Pleasure boating
Boating **B: 428** *with pictures*; (The development of pleasure boating) **B: 431**
Pleasure Steamers [book by Motion]
Motion, Andrew **M: 845**
Plebeians [ancient Rome] **P: 571**
Patricians **P: 196**
Rome, Ancient (The Roman Republic) **R: 438**
Plecoptera [entomology]
Insect (table) **I: 299**
Plectrum [music]
Banjo **B: 87** *with picture*
Guitar **G: 436**
Harpsichord **H: 66b**

Mandolin M: 137
Pledge [fraternity]
Fraternity (Membership) F: 495-496
Pledge [promise]
Oath O: 639
Pledge of Allegiance P: 572
Flag (Saluting the flag) F: 219-222
Pléiade [French literature]
Du Bellay, Joachim D: 370
French literature (The Renaissance) F: 519
Ronsard, Pierre de R: 450b
Pleiades [star cluster]
Star cluster So: 853
Pleistocene Epoch [geology] P: 572
See also Ice age *in this index*
Climate (Changes in the earth's orbit) Ci: 677-678
Earth (The Cenozoic Era) E: 28-29; (table) E: 30
Glacier (How glaciers form) G: 202-203
Ice age I: 6
Plant (The evolution of plants) P: 544-545
Prehistoric animal (table) P: 740; (The ice ages)
P: 741
River (Estuaries) R: 352
Plekhanov, Georgi Valentinovich [Russian philosopher] P: 572
Plenipotentiary [diplomat]
Diplomacy (Diplomatic representatives) D: 216
Plesiadapiform [animal]
Primate (The evolution of primates) P: 778b
Plesianthropus [anthropology]
Broom, Robert B: 641
Plesiosaur [extinct animal] P: 572 *with picture*
Anning, Mary A: 517
Prehistoric animal (Other reptiles) P: 737
Plessis, Armand Jean du *See* Richelieu, Cardinal *in this index*
Plessy, Homer A. [American public figure]
Plessy v. Ferguson P: 573
Plessy v. Ferguson [U.S. history] P: 573
African Americans (During the late 1800's)
A: 136k
Brown v. Board of Education of Topeka B: 645
Gay Nineties (Social developments) G: 72
National Association for the Advancement of
Colored People (History) N: 29
Segregation (Jim Crow laws) S: 285
Supreme Court of the United States (Civil rights)
So: 1001; (table) So: 1002
Pleura [anatomy] P: 573
Lung (Parts of the lungs) L: 523
Membrane (Serous membranes) M: 391
Pleurisy P: 573
Pneumothorax P: 587
Pleural effusion [disorder]
Pleurisy P: 573
Pleurisy [disorder] P: 573
Pleura P: 573
Plexus [anatomy] P: 573
Plié
Ballet (table) B: 45 *with picture*; (A ballet class)
B: 46
Plimoth Plantation
Colonial life in America (Places to visit) Ci: 801
with picture
Massachusetts (Places to visit) M: 280 *with picture*
Plimoth Plantation, Inc. [organization]
Plymouth Colony P: 582
Plimoth Colony *See* Plymouth Colony *in this index*
Plinian eruption [geology]
Volcano (Describing eruptions) V: 442b
Pliny the Elder [Roman author] P: 573
Biology (Beginnings) B: 317-318
Botany (The history of botany) B: 509
Encyclopedia (The first reference works) E: 268a
Geology (The Romans) G: 98
Pompeii (The eruption of Mount Vesuvius) P: 654
Science (Ancient Rome) S: 197
Pliny the Younger [Roman author] P: 574
Latin literature (The Imperial Period) L: 116-117
Pompeii (The eruption of Mount Vesuvius) P: 654
Pliocene Epoch [geology]
Earth (The Cenozoic Era) E: 28-29; (table) E: 30
Prehistoric animal (table) P: 740
Pliosaur [extinct animal]
Plesiosaur P: 572
Plique-à-jour [art]
Enamel (Techniques) E: 264
PLO *See* Palestine Liberation Organization *in this index*
Plomin, Robert [American psychologist]
Intelligence (The roles of heredity and environment) I: 319
Plot [literature]
Drama (The structure of drama) D: 325
Literature (Plot) L: 353
Plot Against America, The [book by Roth]
Roth, Philip R: 487

Plotinus [Greek philosopher] P: 574
Neoplatonism N: 124
Philosophy (Neoplatonism) P: 388
Plato (Plato's place in Western thought) P: 569
Plotter [electronic device]
Computer (Plotters) Ci: 917
Mechanical drawing (Creating a drawing) M: 354
with picture
Plough and the Stars, The [play by O'Casey]
Irish literature (Drama) I: 432
O'Casey, Sean O: 646
Plovdiv [Bulgaria] P: 574
Bulgaria *pictures on* B: 691, B: 692
Plover [bird] P: 574 *with picture*
Animal *picture on* A: 485
Bird (Birds of the seacoasts) B: 342 *with pictures*;
(Birds of the Arctic) B: 343 *with picture*
Killdeer K: 316
Upland sandpiper U: 213 *with picture*
Plow [tool] P: 574 *with pictures*
Agriculture (Mesopotamia and Egypt) A: 156
Colonial life in America (Farming) Ci: 809
Deere, John D: 87
Farm and farming (Preparing the soil) F: 35 *with pictures*
Indian, American *picture on* I: 139
Plowshare
Plow (The moldboard plow bottom) P: 575
PLP [political party]
Bahamas (History) B: 29
Plug [lock]
Lock (Mechanical locks) L: 411 *with picture*
Plug [lure]
Fishing *pictures on* F: 177; (Bait) F: 178
Plug fuse
Fuse F: 589 *with diagram*
Plugging [sports]
Baseball (Rounders) B: 132
Plum [tree] P: 576 *with pictures*
Fruit (Simple fruits) F: 544 *with picture*
Prune P: 841
Plum curculio [insect]
Weevil W: 180
Plumb line [tool]
Surveying (Early tools) So: 1011
Plumbago [plant] P: 577
Plumbeous forest-falcon [bird]
Bird of prey *picture on* B: 374b
Plumbing P: 577 *with diagrams*
Building trade (Career opportunities) B: 686
House (Plumbing) H: 382
Skyscraper (Service areas) S: 497
Plume [feather]
Bird (Feathers) B: 362
Plume [geology]
Hot spot H: 374a
Plumed Knight [nickname]
Blaine, James Gillespie B: 396
Plumed Serpent, The [book by Lawrence]
Lawrence, D. H. L: 145
Plumer, William [American political leader]
Monroe, James (Reelection) M: 738
New Hampshire (table) N: 223
Plummer, Christopher [Canadian actor]
Motion picture (Best performance by an actor in
a supporting role: 2011) M: 862b
Plummer, Henry [American settler]
Montana (The gold rush) M: 758
Plumule [botany]
Cotyledon Ci: 1095
Plant (Germination) P: 535-537 *with picture*
Seed (How seeds sprout) S: 282-283
PLUNA [airline]
Uruguay (Transportation and communication)
U: 227
Plunge-EDM [manufacturing]
Machine tool (Electrical discharge machining
[EDM]) M: 19
Plunket Shield [award]
Cricket (History) Ci: 1134-1135
Plunkett, Edward John Moreton Drax [Irish
author] *See* Dunsany, Lord *in this index*
Plunkett, Jim [American football player]
Football (table) F: 363
Plunkett, Roy J. [American chemist]
Teflon T: 87
Plurabelle, Anna Livia [literary figure]
Joyce, James J: 177
Plural [grammar]
Case (Nouns) C: 272
Number N: 604
Pluralism [sociology]
Immigration (Effects of immigration) I: 81
Plurality
Democracy D: 119
Electoral College E: 161
Majority rule M: 94

Parliamentary procedure (Electing officers) P: 175
Voting V: 449
Plurality opinion [law]
Supreme Court of the United States (Written
opinions) So: 999
Plus sign
Addition (Writing addition) A: 49
Plush rug
Rugs and carpets (Kinds of rugs and carpets)
R: 514-515 *with picture*
Plutarch [Greek author] P: 580
Biography (Early biographies) B: 312-313
Moon (Ancient ideas) M: 791-792
Plutarch's Lives [book by Plutarch]
Biography (Early biographies) B: 312-313
Greek literature (The Greco-Roman Age) G: 378
Plutarch P: 580
Pluto [dwarf planet] P: 580 *with pictures*
Astronomy (Finding new objects) A: 848
Dwarf planet D: 394
Eris E: 352
Kuiper belt K: 392
Planet P: 507; (The outer dwarf planets) P: 512
Satellite (Physical characteristics) S: 149; (table:
Major satellites of the solar system) S: 150b;
(Nonplanetary satellites) S: 150c
Space exploration (Probes to Jupiter and beyond)
So: 711
Pluto [god] P: 581
See also Hades *in this index*
Ceres C: 362
Mythology (table) M: 981
Pluto [nymph]
Tantalus T: 29
Plutoid [astronomy]
Eris E: 352
Kuiper belt K: 392
Planet (The dwarf planets) P: 512
Pluto P: 580
Solar system (Dwarf planets) So: 580
Plutonic rock
Earth (Igneous rocks) E: 21
Plutonist
Geology (The rock dispute) G: 98-99
Plutonium [element] P: 581
Actinide A: 30
Atom A: 870
Nuclear energy (Advanced fission reactors)
N: 594
Nuclear weapon (Fission weapons) N: 596-597
Transuranium element T: 401
Ply
Textile (Making the yarn) T: 215-216
Thread T: 269 *with picture*
Tire T: 295 *with pictures*
Plymouth [England] P: 582
Plymouth [Massachusetts] P: 582
Pilgrims P: 462
Plymouth Colony (The landing at Plymouth)
P: 582
Plymouth [Montserrat]
Montserrat M: 780
Plymouth Colony [U.S. history] P: 582 *with picture
and map*
See also the list of Related articles in the Plymouth
Colony *article*
Bradford, William [1590-1657] B: 544
Colonial life in America (Plymouth Colony)
Ci: 789
Massachusetts (The Pilgrims and Plymouth
Colony) M: 289
Mayflower Compact M: 328
Pilgrims P: 462 *with pictures*
Samoset S: 80b
Squanto So: 811
Thanksgiving Day (Plymouth Colony) T: 230
United States, History of the *picture on* U: 152;
(New England) U: 154
Plymouth Company [U.S. history] P: 584
Colonial life in America (Early English
settlements) Ci: 789
Plymouth Notch Historic District [Vermont]
Vermont (Places to visit) V: 326
Plymouth Plantation, History of [book by
Bradford]
Bradford, William [1590-1657] B: 544
Plymouth Rock [U.S. history] P: 585 *with picture*
Plymouth Rock chicken
Chicken *picture on* C: 442; (table) C: 443
Plywood [building material] P: 585 *with picture*
Forest products *picture on* F: 403; (Plywood)
F: 401
Laminating L: 51
Lumber (Engineered lumber) L: 518
Woodworking (Wood for woodworking) W: 398
Plzeň [Czech Republic]
Czech Republic (The Bohemian-Moravian

Highlands) **Ci:** 1211
PM [electronics] *See* Phase modulation *in this index*
Pm [symbol]
Promethium **P:** 818
P.M. [time]
Hour **H:** 379
PMC [military group]
Mercenary **M:** 411
PMP [device] *See* Portable media player *in this index*
PMS *See* Premenstrual syndrome *in this index*
Pneuma [physiology]
Galen **G:** 10
Pneumatic caisson [construction]
Air lock **A:** 197 *with diagram*
Caisson **C:** 18 *with diagram*
Pneumatic tire
Dunlop, John Boyd **D:** 386
Tire **T:** 295 *with pictures*; (History) **T:** 297
Pneumatic tool [tool] **P:** 586
Riveting **R:** 356
Pneumatic tube system [communication]
Pentagon Building **P:** 274
Pneumatophore [botany]
Wetland (Plant life) **W:** 252a
Pneumoconiosis [disease] *See* Black lung *in this index*
Pneumocystis carinii pneumonia [disease]
AIDS (Opportunistic illness) **A:** 164a
Pneumonia (How pneumonia develops) **P:** 586-587
Pneumonectomy [surgery]
Surgery (Some common surgical operations) **So:** 1006
Pneumonia [disease] **P:** 586
AIDS (Opportunistic illness) **A:** 164a
Disease (Death rates from diseases in the United States) **D:** 233
Pneumonic plague [disease]
Plague (Forms of plague) **P:** 506
Pneumonitis [disorder] *See* Pneumonia *in this index*
Pneumothorax [disorder] **P:** 587
Pleura **P:** 573
PNP transistor
Transistor (How transistors work) **T:** 372-373
Po [symbol]
Polonium **P:** 649
Po River [Italy] **P:** 587
Po Valley [Italy]
Italy (The Po Valley) **I:** 506-507 *with map*
Poaching [cooking]
Cooking (Simmering) **Ci:** 1029
Poaching [law] **P:** 587 *with picture*
Adamson, Joy **A:** 45
Africa (Native animals) **A:** 122-123
Conservation (Africa) **C:** 990
Endangered species (Wildlife trade) **E:** 269
Hunting (Laws and conservation) **H:** 450
Kenya (Animal life) **E:** 301-302
National park (Development of park resources) **N:** 42h *with picture*
Rhinoceros (Protecting the rhinoceros) **R:** 295
Poás Volcano [volcano, Costa Rica]
Lake *picture on* **L:** 33
Poás Volcano National Park [Costa Rica]
National park (Costa Rica) **N:** 42c
Pocahontas [American Indian] **P:** 588 *with portrait*
Colonial life in America (Jamestown) **Ci:** 789
Jamestown **J:** 29
Powhatan **P:** 728
Rolfe, John **R:** 402
Smith, John **S:** 516
Pocasset [former name, Portsmouth]
Rhode Island (Settlement) **R:** 312
Pocatello [Idaho] **P:** 588
Pochard duck
Duck (Food) **D:** 375 *with picture*; (Kinds of ducks) **D:** 376
Pochteca [merchant]
Aztec (Trade and transportation) **A:** 1002
Pocket beach
Beach **B:** 178
Pocket Books [publisher]
Book (Modern books) **B:** 468
Pocket borough [government]
Borough **B:** 491
Pocket compass
Compass *picture on* **Ci:** 902b
Pocket gopher [animal]
Gopher **G:** 272 *with picture*
Pocket mouse [animal]
Animal *picture on* **A:** 482
Kangaroo rat **K:** 215
Pocket veto
Congress of the U.S. (From bill to law) **Ci:** 945-946
Constitution of the United States (Article I, Section 7) **Ci:** 1006
United States, Government of the (Action by the

President) **U:** 144
Veto (Vetoing a bill) **V:** 346
Pocket watch
Watch (History) **W:** 115 *with picture*
Pocomoke River
Maryland *picture on* **M:** 250
Pocomoke Swamp
Maryland (Land regions) **M:** 250
Pod [botany]
Cacao *picture on* **C:** 9
Ivory palm *picture on* **I:** 522
Milkweed **M:** 551
Pod [entomology]
Grasshopper (Young) **G:** 328
Pod [zoology]
Dolphin (Social life) **D:** 299
Killer whale **K:** 316
Whale (Group life) **W:** 261
Podcast [recording]
Radio (Webcasting and podcasting) **R:** 87
Podgorica [Montenegro] **P:** 588
Montenegro **M:** 763
Podiatric Medical Association, American
Podiatry **P:** 588
Podiatry [medicine] **P:** 588
Podocarpus [botany]
Tree (Needleleaf trees) **T:** 414-415
Podophyllum resin [drug]
Mayapple **M:** 327
Poe, Edgar Allan [American author] **P:** 589
American literature (The romance) **A:** 418 *with portrait*; (Poetry) **A:** 418-419
Baudelaire, Charles **B:** 173
Detective story (History) **D:** 162
Fort Moultrie **F:** 415
Short story **S:** 434
Poe Lock
Soo Canals (The American canals) **So:** 594-595 *with map*
Poe Museum
Richmond (Other interesting places to visit) **R:** 332 *with picture*
Poem *See* Poetry *in this index*
Poem of the Cid, The [poem]
Spain (Literature) **So:** 738
Spanish literature (Early medieval literature) **So:** 757-758
Poem on Natural Law [poem by Voltaire]
Voltaire (Later years) **V:** 447
Poems [book by Emerson]
Emerson, Ralph Waldo (His poetry) **E:** 259
Poems on Various Subjects, Religious and Moral [book by Wheatley]
Colonial life in America (Literature) **Ci:** 806-807
Wheatley, Phillis **W:** 278
"Poet, The" [essay by Emerson]
Emerson, Ralph Waldo (His prose works) **E:** 259
Poet laureate [title] **P:** 590
Poetic Edda [poems]
Edda **E:** 74
Scandinavian literature (Beginnings) **S:** 171
Poetic Meditations [poems by Lamartine]
French literature (Romantic poetry) **F:** 521
Lamartine, Alphonse de **L:** 50
"Poetic Principle, The" [essay by Poe]
Poe, Edgar Allan (Poetry and poetic theory) **P:** 589-590
Poetic realism [literature]
German literature (Realism) **G:** 141
Poetical Sketches [poems by Blake]
Blake, William **B:** 397
Poetics [book by Aristotle]
Aristotle (Literary criticism) **A:** 664
Drama (The structure of drama) **D:** 325
Italian literature (Humanism and the Renaissance) **I:** 494
Poetry **P:** 591 *with pictures*
See also the list of Related articles in the Poetry *article*
American literature (Colonial literature [1608-1764]) **A:** 414; (The Era of Expansion [1831-1870]) **A:** 415-418; (The world wars and depression [1914-1945]) **A:** 420-421; (Literature from 1945 to the early 2000's) **A:** 423
Arabic literature (Poetry) **A:** 583
Arabs (Literature and the arts) **A:** 587
Canadian literature (Poetry: 1850-1918) **C:** 157; (Modern Canadian poets) **C:** 161
China (Literature) **C:** 487
Chinese literature (Poetry) **C:** 511
Colonial life in America (Literature) **Ci:** 806-807
English literature (Old English poetry) **E:** 314; (Elizabethan poetry) **E:** 316; (Metaphysical and Cavalier poets) **E:** 317; (Romantic poetry) **E:** 320; (Poetry between the wars) **E:** 322
French literature **F:** 518
Greek literature **G:** 377

Haiku **H:** 8
Irish literature **I:** 430
Literature for children (Poetry) **L:** 357; (Masterpieces of poetry) **L:** 364
Meter **M:** 433
Prose **P:** 828
Pulitzer Prizes (table) **P:** 897
Rhyme **R:** 319
Rubaiyat **R:** 499
Symbolism **So:** 1066
Writing (Fiction) **W:** 511-512
Poetry [magazine]
Magazine (Magazines in the 1900's) **M:** 45
Poetry: A Magazine of Verse [magazine]
Monroe, Harriet **M:** 733
Poetry and Experience [book by MacLeish]
MacLeish, Archibald **M:** 24
Poetry of Moonlight, The [painting by Blakelock]
Blakelock, Ralph Albert *picture on* **B:** 397
Poets' Corner [London]
Westminster Abbey **W:** 243
Poet's narcissus [plant]
Narcissus **N:** 20 *with picture*
Poggenpuhl Family, The [book by Fontane]
Fontane, Theodor **F:** 327
Pogo [aircraft] *See* XFY-1 *in this index*
Pogrom [persecution]
Anti-Semitism **A:** 559
Genocide **G:** 90
Holocaust (Before the Holocaust) **H:** 296
Jews (The growth of anti-Semitism) **J:** 123
Zionism (Movement to Palestine) **Z:** 595
Pogue, George [American settler]
Indianapolis (History) **I:** 222
Pogy [fish]
Menhaden **M:** 400
Pohamba, Hifikpunye [Namibian political leader]
Namibia (History) **N:** 9
Pohnpei [island, Pacific]
Caroline Islands **C:** 244
Micronesia, Federated States of (Government) **M:** 515
Pacific Islands, Trust Territory of the **P:** 13
Pohutukawa [tree]
Tree *picture on* **T:** 427
Poi [food]
Hawaii (Food) **H:** 94
Poikilothermic animal
Cold-blooded animal **Ci:** 761
Poincaré, Henri [French scientist]
Mathematics (In the 1800's) **M:** 307
Topology (History) **T:** 333
Poincaré, Raymond [French political leader] **P:** 599
Poincaré conjecture [mathematics]
Topology (History) **T:** 333
Poinciana [tree] **P:** 599
Poindexter, George [American political leader]
Mississippi (table) **M:** 640
Poindexter, John M. [American government official]
Iran-contra affair (Charges and court actions) **I:** 407
Reagan, Ronald Wilson (The Iran-contra affair) **R:** 170
Poinsett, Joel R. [American diplomat]
Poinsettia **P:** 600
Van Buren, Martin (table) **V:** 273
Poinsettia [plant] **P:** 599
Leaf *picture on* **L:** 157
Point [archery]
Archery (Arrows) **A:** 602 *with diagrams*
Indian, American (The first Americans) **I:** 151
Point [geography]
Cape **C:** 186
Point [geometry]
Geometry (Terms) **G:** 102 *with diagram*
Point [hunting]
Setter **S:** 323
Point [navigation]
Compass **Ci:** 902b
Point [printing]
Type (Sizes of type) **T:** 537 *with picture*
Weights and measures (Miscellaneous weights and measures) **W:** 184
Point [region]
Pittsburgh (The city) **P:** 500a-500b *with picture*
Point aberration [optics]
Aberration **A:** 10 *with diagram*
Point-and-shoot camera
Camera (Point-and-shoot cameras) **C:** 82 *with picture*
Photography (Compact cameras) **P:** 408
Point at infinity [geometry]
Infinity **I:** 266
Point Barrow
Alaska **A:** 282
Point Clark Lighthouse [Ontario]

Canada (table: National historic sites) **C:** 115
Point count method
Bridge (Evaluating the hand) **B:** 604
Point Counter Point [book by Huxley]
Huxley, Aldous Leonard **H:** 459
Point Defiance Park [Tacoma]
Washington (Places to visit) **W:** 56 *with picture*
Point Four Program [U.S. history]
Foreign aid (Economic development and mutual security) **F:** 383
Truman, Harry S. (Foreign affairs) **T:** 471
Point guard [sports]
Basketball (The players) **B:** 144
Point Lepreau Generating Station
New Brunswick *picture on* **N:** 197
Point mutation [genetics]
Heredity (Mutation) **H:** 203
Point of intersection [mathematics]
Geometry (Bisecting an angle) **G:** 103 *with diagram*
Point of No Return [book by Marquand]
Marquand, John Phillips **M:** 217
Point of order
Parliamentary procedure (table) **P:** 176
Point-of-purchase display
Advertising *picture on* **A:** 73; (Other ways of advertising) **A:** 75
Point-of-sale system [electronics]
Bank (Electronic banking) **B:** 89-90
Cash register **C:** 273
Point of view
Literature (Style) **L:** 353
Novel **N:** 571
Point Pelee National Park [Ontario]
Canada (table: National parks and national park reserves) **C:** 113
Point Pleasant, Battle of [1774]
Cornstalk **Ci:** 1066
Point rationing
Rationing **R:** 148
Point Reyes National Seashore [California]
National Park System (table: National seashores) **N:** 57
Point source pollution
Environmental pollution **E:** 330
Water pollution **W:** 136
Point State Park
Pittsburgh (The city) **P:** 500a-500b *with picture*
Point system [sports]
Boxing (Scoring a fight) **B:** 528
Pointe-au-Père Lighthouse [Ontario]
Canada (table: National historic sites) **C:** 115
Pointe work [dancing]
Ballet (table) **B:** 45 *with picture*; (Pointe work) **B:** 47
Pointer [computing]
Computer (A keyboard) **Ci:** 912
Pointer [dog] **P:** 600
Dog (Sporting dogs) **D:** 268 *with pictures*
Pointers, The [painting by Thomson]
Canada *picture on* **C:** 110
Pointillism [art]
Gauguin, Paul (Early career) **G:** 69
Painting (Postimpressionism) **P:** 75-76 *with picture*
Postimpressionism *picture on* **P:** 709
Seurat, Georges **S:** 324
Vermeer, Jan **V:** 317
Pointing stick [electronic device]
Computer (A pointing stick) **Ci:** 914
Poirot, Hercule [literary figure]
Christie, Agatha **C:** 527
Poison P: 600
See also the list of Related articles in the Poison *article*
Amphibian (Amphibians and people) **A:** 442
First aid (Treatment for poisoning) **F:** 137; (Snakebite) **F:** 141
Fish (Harmful fish) **F:** 147
Forensic science (What a forensic scientist analyzes) **F:** 389
Frog (Skin) **F:** 536
Insecticide (Dangers of insecticides) **I:** 302
Pharmacology **P:** 354
Pitohui **P:** 499
Plant (Environmental factors) **P:** 538-539; (How plants protect themselves) **P:** 540
Snakebite **S:** 536
Poison dart frog [animal] **P:** 601 *with picture*
Poison elder [shrub] *See* Poison sumac *in this index*
Poison gas
Chemical-biological-radiological warfare (Chemical) **C:** 396
Fumigation **F:** 556
Gas mask **G:** 60
Iraq (War with Iran) **I:** 414
Poison (Kinds of poisons) **P:** 600

World War I (Trench warfare) **W:** 457-458 *with picture*
Poison hemlock [plant]
Hemlock **H:** 181 *with pictures*
Poison ivy [plant] **P:** 601 *with picture*
Eczema **E:** 74
Ivy **I:** 522
Plant *picture on* **P:** 541
Poison oak **P:** 601
Poison oak [plant] **P:** 601 *with picture*
Eczema **E:** 74
Poison ivy **P:** 601
Poison sumac [shrub]
Elder **E:** 157
Poison ivy **P:** 601
Sumac **So:** 971
Poisoning *See* Poison *in this index*
Poisonous lizard [reptile]
Lizard (Defenses) **L:** 400
Poisonous plant P: 602
See the list of Related articles in the Poisonous plant *article*
Poisson, Jeanne-Antoinette *See* Pompadour, Marquise de *in this index*
Poitevin, Alphonse Louis [French inventor]
Printing (Developments in platemaking) **P:** 803-804
Poitier, Sidney [American actor] **P:** 602 *with portrait*
Motion picture (Best performance by an actor: 1973) **M:** 862a
Poitiers, Battle of [1356] **P:** 603
England (The Hundred Years' War) **E:** 306
Feudalism (The decline of feudalism) **F:** 83
Hundred Years' War **H:** 437
Poke bonnet [hat]
Hat *picture on* **H:** 84
Poker [game] **P:** 603
Gambling (Poker) **G:** 21
Pokeweed [plant] **P:** 603 *with picture*
Pol Pot [Cambodian political leader] **P:** 603
Cambodian (History) **C:** 72-73
Khmer Rouge **K:** 308b
Polacco, Patricia [American author]
Regina Medal (table: 2012) **R:** 206
Poland P: 604 *with pictures and maps*
Belarus (History) **B:** 224b-224c
Bielski partisans **B:** 295
Christmas (In Poland) **C:** 531
Cold War (Unrest in Eastern Europe) **Ci:** 766; (The Cold War in the 1970's) **Ci:** 770
Communism (In Eastern Europe) **Ci:** 896
Cossacks **Ci:** 1079
Curzon Line **Ci:** 1199
Flag *picture on* **F:** 207
Hitler, Adolf (The road to war) **H:** 267-268
Jews (Eastern European religious movements) **J:** 123
Katyn Massacre **K:** 249
Lithuania (History) **L:** 389
North Atlantic Treaty Organization (History) **N:** 471
Prussia (Decline of Prussia) **P:** 843
Russia (World War II) **R:** 554
Ukraine (Lithuanian and Polish rule) **U:** 12
Union of Soviet Socialist Republics (Civil war) **U:** 36
Wałęsa, Lech **W:** 13
Warsaw Pact **W:** 39
World War II (The invasion of Poland) **W:** 472 *with picture*; (The Soviet advance) **W:** 486
Poland China [hog]
Hog (Kinds of hogs) **H:** 285 *with picture*; (table) **H:** 286
Polanie [people]
Poland **P:** 604
Polanski, Roman [Polish director]
Motion picture (Best achievement in directing: 2002) **M:** 862; (Movies in the 1960's) **M:** 870-871
Polanyi, John Charles [Canadian chemist]
Nobel Prizes (Chemistry: 1986) **N:** 444
Polar air mass [meteorology]
Weather (Synoptic-scale systems) **W:** 159 *with diagram*
Polar anticyclone [weather]
Calms, Regions of (Subpolar regions) **C:** 69
Polar bear [animal] **P:** 616 *with pictures*
Animal *picture on* **A:** 484
Bear *picture on* **B:** 186; (Polar bears) **B:** 185
Inuit (Hunting and fishing) **I:** 354d-354e
Manitoba (Interesting facts) **M:** 145 *with picture*
Nunavut *picture on* **N:** 612
Zoo (Interesting facts about zoo animals) **Z:** 601
Polar cap
Mars (Polar deposits) **M:** 226a
Polar covalent bond [chemistry]

Bond (A covalent bond) **B:** 454
Polar desert
Arctic (Land regions) **A:** 636
Desert **D:** 155
Polar easterly [weather]
Weather (Planetary-scale systems) **W:** 158-159
Wind (General circulation) **W:** 329 *with diagram*
Polar Express, The [book by Van Allsburg]
Van Allsburg, Chris **V:** 269
Polar Express, The [film]
Animation (Making the model move) **A:** 513
Polar front [meteorology]
Climate (Atmospheric circulation) **Ci:** 676a
Southern Ocean **So:** 688
Weather (Planetary-scale systems) **W:** 158-159
Polar glacier [geology]
Glacier (Kinds of glaciers) **G:** 202
Polar jet [wind]
Jet stream **J:** 115 *with map*
Ozone hole **O:** 894
Polar low [air mass]
Storm (Polar lows) **So:** 913
Polar molecule [chemistry]
Ion (Ions in liquids) **I:** 371
Polar night jet [wind]
Jet stream **J:** 115
Polar nucleus [botany]
Plant (Sexual reproduction) **P:** 532-535
Pollen (Fertilization) **P:** 645
Seed (Seed development in angiosperms) **S:** 281
Polar orbit
Space exploration *diagrams on* **So:** 697
Polar-orbiting weather satellite
Weather (Weather satellites) **W:** 163-164
Polar plume [astronomy]
Corona **Ci:** 1067
Polar regions
Animal (Animals of the polar regions) **A:** 484 *with pictures and maps*
Rain (Rainfall distribution) **R:** 124-125
Polarimetric radar
Radar (Radar in the future) **R:** 73
Polaris [star] *See* North Star *in this index*
Polaris [weapon]
Rocket (High-altitude rockets) **R:** 390-391
Polarization [physics]
Acoustics **A:** 29
Cosmic microwave background (CMB) radiation **Ci:** 1075
Inflation theory **I:** 268a
Light (The properties of waves) **L:** 285-286; (Electromagnetic waves) **L:** 286
Nervous system (The beginning of an impulse) **N:** 135 *with diagram*
Polarized light **P:** 617
Polarized glass
Glass (table) **G:** 218
Polarized light [physics] **P:** 617 *with pictures*
Polarizer [filter] *See* Polarizing filter *in this index*
Polarizing filter
Land, Edwin Herbert **L:** 56
Light (Electromagnetic waves) **L:** 286
Photography (Filters) **P:** 416
Polarized light *picture on* **P:** 617; (Polarizing filters) **P:** 618
Polaroid Land camera
Land, Edwin Herbert **L:** 56
Photography (Dramatic changes) **P:** 425-426
Polder [geography]
Belgium (The Coastal and Interior Lowlands) **B:** 230
Netherlands **N:** 138; (The land) **N:** 144 *with picture and map*
Pole [biology]
Cell (Mitosis) **C:** 330
Pole [electricity] *See* Electrode *in this index*
Pole [geography] **P:** 618
Climate (The role of latitude) **Ci:** 676
Earth (Earth's size and shape) **E:** 18
Latitude **L:** 117
North Pole **N:** 517
South Pole **So:** 685
Pole [magnetism] *See* Magnetic pole *in this index*
Pole spear
Spearfishing **So:** 768 *with picture*
Pole Star *See* North Star *in this index*
Pole vault [sport] **P:** 618 *with diagram*
Track and field (Jumping events) **T:** 357-358
Polecat [animal] **P:** 619
Ferret **F:** 76
Polemonium
Flower *picture on* **F:** 289
Poles [people]
Holocaust **H:** 296
Poland (History) **P:** 605 *with pictures*
Russia (The Time of Troubles) **R:** 549
Polestar *See* North Star *in this index*

Poletti, Charles [American political leader]
New York (table) **N: 313**
Police P: 620 *with pictures*
See also the list of Related articles in the Police *article*
Crime scene investigation (Beginning an investigation) **Ci: 1140** *with picture*
Criminal justice system **Ci: 1143;** (Problems of the police) **Ci: 1144**
Law enforcement **L: 141**
Radio (In public safety) **R: 84** *with picture*
Royal Canadian Mounted Police **R: 495** *with pictures*
Texas Rangers **T: 211** *with picture*
Police, International
Interpol **I: 350h**
Police, The [musical group]
Rock music (New wave and mainstream rock) **R: 380c**
Police action
International law (After World War II) **I: 342**
Police Associations, International Union of
Labor movement (table) **L: 8**
Police brutality
Police (In the United States since the mid-1900's) **P: 624**
Police dog [dog] **P: 625**
Doberman pinscher **D: 259**
German shepherd dog **G: 143**
Police jury [law]
Louisiana (Local government) **L: 496**
Police Motu [language]
Papua New Guinea (People) **P: 140**
Police patrol [law]
Criminal justice system (Problems of the police) **Ci: 1144**
Police revolver [gun]
Handgun (Double-action revolvers) **H: 43** *with picture*
Police state [political science] **P: 626**
Communism (Restrictions on personal freedom) **Ci: 891-892**
Policy
Insurance **I: 309**
Policy committee [government]
Senate (The leaders of the senate) **S: 294-295**
Policy debate
Debate (Forms of competitive debate) **D: 64**
Policy Development, Office of [U.S.]
President of the United States (The executive branch) **P: 764**
Policy resolution
Debate (Types of resolutions) **D: 64**
Policyholder
Insurance **I: 309**
Poling [industrial process]
Copper (Smelting) **Ci: 1043**
Poling [sport]
Canoeing (Poling and sailing) **C: 182**
Polio *See* Poliomyelitis *in this index*
Poliomyelitis [disease] **P: 626** *with picture*
Disease (table) **D: 226**
Enders, John Franklin **E: 272**
Iron lung **I: 453**
Kenny, Elizabeth **K: 271**
Nervous system (Disorders of the nervous system) **N: 136**
Roosevelt, Franklin Delano (Battle with polio) **R: 451**
Sabin, Albert Bruce **S: 3**
Salk, Jonas Edward **S: 68**
Virus (Structure) **V: 427-428** *with picture;* (Infection) **V: 428-428a**
Polisario Front [political group]
Hassan II **H: 82**
Mauritania (History) **M: 315**
Morocco (Dispute over Western Sahara) **M: 815**
Western Sahara **W: 241**
Polish [breed]
Chicken (Other classes) **C: 441**
Polish Corridor [region, Poland] **P: 627** *with map*
Prussia (Decline of Prussia) **P: 843**
Polish lowland sheepdog
Dog *picture on* **D: 276**
Polish People's Party [political party]
Poland (Politics) **P: 605;** (Free elections) **P: 614-615**
Polish Succession, War of the *See* Succession wars *in this index*
Polishing [industrial process]
Diamond (How diamonds are cut to make jewels) **D: 182**
Gem (Cutting and polishing) **G: 79**
Grinding and polishing (Polishing) **G: 395**
Polistes wasp
Wasp (Nests) **W: 112** *with picture*
Politburo [organization] **P: 627**

China (The Communist Party) **C: 477**
Communism (Communist party structures) **Ci: 891**
Khrushchev, Nikita Sergeyevich (Rise as a Communist) **K: 309**
Union of Soviet Socialist Republics (Government) **U: 29**
Politeness
Etiquette **E: 374**
Politi, Leo [American artist]
Regina Medal (table: 1966) **R: 206**
Political action committee P: 627
Congress of Industrial Organizations **Ci: 941**
Congress of the United States (Congressional ethics) **Ci: 948**
Election campaign (Campaign financing) **E: 160**
Political party (Raising funds) **P: 633**
Political anthropology
Anthropology (Social anthropology) **A: 547**
Political behavior
Political science (Political behavior) **P: 638**
Political campaign *See* Election campaign *in this index*
Political candidate *See* Candidate *in this index*
Political cartoon
Cartoon (Editorial cartoons) **C: 263-265** *with picture*
Political conservatism
Conservatism **Ci: 991**
Political convention P: 628 *with picture*
Election (Nomination of candidates) **E: 158**
Election campaign (Winning the nomination) **E: 159**
Political party (Selecting candidates) **P: 631;** (National conventions and committees) **P: 634**
Vice president of the United States (Nomination) **V: 350**
Political crime
Crime (Political crime) **Ci: 1137**
Political culture
City (Political culture) **Ci: 593**
Political debate
Debate (Political debate) **D: 63**
Political economy
See also Economics *in this index*
Communication (Communication and politics) **Ci: 888**
Political Fictions [book by Didion]
Didion, Joan **D: 195**
Political freedom [law]
Freedom (Kinds of freedom) **F: 501;** (Limits on political freedom) **F: 502**
Political geography
Geography (Human geography) **G: 94**
Political machine
Graft **G: 298**
United States, History of the (Government and the people) **U: 185**
Political map
Map (General reference maps) **M: 177-178**
Political party P: 631 *with picture*
See also the list of Related articles in the Political party *article*
Caucus **C: 317**
City government (Influencing city government) **Ci: 597**
Coalition **Ci: 733**
Conservatism **Ci: 991**
Constitution of the United States (Ratifying the Constitution) **Ci: 1001**
Democracy (Political parties) **D: 120**
Government (Political parties) **G: 285**
Political convention **P: 628**
United States, Government of the (Representative democracy) **U: 137-138;** (Party leadership) **U: 138**
United States, History of the (Establishing political parties) **U: 163**
Washington, George (Rise of political parties) **W: 104**
Political philosophy
Philosophy (Ethics and political philosophy) **P: 385**
Political prisoner P: 637
Political science P: 638
See also Government; International relations *in this index*
Aristotle (Ethics and politics) **A: 664**
Careers (Life, physical, and social sciences) **C: 225-226**
Plato (Psychology and politics) **P: 568**
Science (The social sciences) **S: 194**
Political theory
Geopolitics **G: 106b**
Political science (Political theory and philosophy) **P: 638**
Radicalism **R: 82**

Politically disempowered group [sociology]
Minority group **M: 608**
"Politics" [essay by Emerson]
Emerson, Ralph Waldo (His prose works) **E: 259**
Politics of God [book by Quevedo]
Quevedo, Francisco de **Q: 41**
Politzer, H. David [American physicist]
Gluon **G: 237**
Nobel Prizes (Physics: 2004) **N: 442**
Subatomic particle (The Standard Model) **So: 938**
Poliziano, Angelo [Italian author]
Italian literature (Humanism and the Renaissance) **I: 494**
Polk, Charles [American political leader]
Delaware (table) **D: 109**
Polk, James Knox [U.S. president] **P: 640** *with pictures*
Dallas, George Mifflin **D: 16**
McDowell, Ephraim **M: 332h**
Mexican War (Background of the war) **M: 445**
Oregon (Exploration and settlement) **O: 846**
Taylor, Zachary (Mexican War) **T: 58-59**
Tennessee (Places to visit) **T: 144;** (table) **T: 152;** (Building the state) **T: 153**
United States, History of the (The Mexican War) **U: 169**
Washington (Settlement) **W: 66**
Polk, Jane Knox [mother of]
Polk, James Knox (Childhood) **P: 640**
Polk, Leonidas [Confederate general] **P: 644**
Polk, Samuel [father of]
Polk, James Knox (Childhood) **P: 640**
Polk, Sarah Childress [wife of James Knox Polk]
First ladies of the United States (table) **F: 142**
Polk, James Knox (Polk's family) **P: 641;** (Life in the White House) **P: 642** *with picture*
Polk, Trusten [American political leader]
Missouri (table) **M: 668**
Polk Doctrine [U.S. history]
Polk, James Knox ("The Polk Doctrine") **P: 643**
Polk Place [estate]
Polk, James Knox (Retirement) **P: 643**
Poll [statistics] *See* Public opinion poll *in this index*
Poll [voting]
Election (Election procedures) **E: 158**
Poll book [voting]
Political party (Local organizations) **P: 635**
Poll tax [U.S. history] **P: 644**
Constitution of the United States (Amendment 24) **Ci: 1016**
Hispanic Americans (Political developments) **H: 256**
Reconstruction (Effects of Reconstruction) **R: 179-180**
Voting (Who may vote) **V: 449**
Voting Rights Act of 1965 **V: 451**
Poll watcher
Election (Election procedures) **E: 158**
Pollack [fish] *See* Pollock *in this index*
Pollack, Sydney [American director]
Motion picture (Best achievement in directing: 1985) **M: 862**
Pollaiuolo, Antonio del [Italian artist] **P: 644**
Renaissance *picture on* **R: 237**
Sculpture (Early Renaissance) **S: 252**
Pollard, John Garland [American political leader]
Virginia (table) **V: 417**
Polled cattle
Cattle (Horns) **C: 307**
Polled Hereford [animal]
Cattle (Hereford) **C: 309**
Polled Shorthorn [animal]
Cattle (Other beef cattle) **C: 309**
Pollen [botany] **P: 644** *with pictures*
Bee (Finding food) **B: 204**
Bumble bee (Importance of bumble bees) **B: 699**
Butterfly **B: 733** *with picture;* (Butterflies and ecosystems) **B: 742-743**
Climate (Pollen) **Ci: 679**
Corn (How the plant reproduces) **Ci: 1058**
Electron microscope *picture on* **E: 204**
Flower **F: 271;** (The role of flowers in reproduction) **F: 294;** (The evolution of flowering plants) **F: 299**
Hay fever **H: 116**
Honeyeater **H: 315**
Insect (Beneficial insects) **I: 284** *with picture*
Plant (Flowers) **P: 531;** (Sexual reproduction) **P: 532-533** *with pictures*
Ragweed **R: 103**
Seed (How seeds develop) **S: 281**
Tree (How trees reproduce) **T: 419** *with pictures*
Pollen basket [entomology]
Bee (Legs) **B: 201-202** *with picture*
Pollen cone [botany]
Plant (Sexual reproduction) **P: 532-535** *with diagrams*

Seed (Seed development in gymnosperms)
S: 281-282
Pollen index
Hay fever (Causes and prevention) H: 116
Pollen tube [botany]
Flower (Fertilization) F: 296
Plant (Sexual reproduction) P: 532-533 with picture
Seed (Seed development in angiosperms) S: 281
Pollination See Pollen in this index
Polling place [voting]
Flag (Displaying the flag) F: 218
Voting (Voting districts) V: 449
Pollinosis See Hay fever in this index
Polliwog See Tadpole in this index
Pollock [fish] P: 646
Pollock, Jackson [American painter] P: 646
Abstract Expressionism A: 19
Krasner, Lee K: 386
Painting (Abstract Expressionism) P: 84-85
United States picture on U: 116
Pollock, James [American political leader]
Pennsylvania (table) P: 263
Pollock, Sharon [Canadian dramatist]
Canadian literature (Modern Canadian drama) C: 161
Pollster
Public opinion poll P: 861 with picture
Pollution See Environmental pollution in this index
Pollux [Greek mythology]
Castor and Pollux C: 282
Pollux [star]
Gemini G: 80
Polo [sport] P: 646 with pictures
Polo, Maffeo [Italian explorer]
Polo, Marco (Early life) P: 648 with map
Polo, Marco [Italian explorer] P: 647 with map
China (Mongol rule) C: 501
Exploration (Medieval European exploration) E: 442-443
Geography (Era of exploration) G: 95
Glasses G: 224
Money (Paper money) M: 708
Mongol Empire (European contacts) M: 720
Polo, Nicolò [Italian explorer]
Polo, Marco (Early life) P: 648 with map
Polo, Water [sport] See Water polo in this index
Polo pony
Polo (The horses) P: 646 with picture
Polonium [element] P: 649
Curie, Marie Skłodowska Ci: 1194
Metalloid M: 426
Polonius [literary figure]
Shakespeare, William: (Hamlet) S: 361-362
Polotsky, Simeon [Russian author]
Russian literature (Western influences) R: 559
"Polovtsian Dances" [ballet]
Borodin, Alexander B: 490
Polovtsians [people]
Russian literature (Nonreligious literature) R: 559
Poltava, Battle of [1709]
Charles XII C: 382
Poltoratsk [former name]
Ashgabat A: 769
Poly-Olbion [poem by Drayton]
Drayton, Michael D: 344
Polyakov, Valery [Russian cosmonaut]
Astronaut (Achievements in space) A: 829-830; (table) A: 830
Space exploration (Mir) So: 722
Polyalphabetic substitution
Codes and ciphers (Substitution) Ci: 750
Polyamid [fiber] See Nylon in this index
Polyandry [marriage]
Family (Varieties of families) F: 20-21
Marriage (Other marriage laws and practices) M: 220
Nepal (People) N: 125
Polygamy P: 650
Polyanthus primrose [plant]
Flower picture on F: 278
Polybus [Greek mythology]
Oedipus O: 676
Polycarbonate [plastics]
Plastics (table) P: 556
Polychaete worm
Worm (Segmented worms) W: 501
Polychlorinated biphenyl [chemical] P: 649
Great Lakes (Water quality) G: 345
Water pollution (Human illness) W: 138
Polyculture [agriculture]
Agriculture (Shifting cultivation) A: 149
Polycyclic aromatic hydrocarbon [chemical]
Smoking (Why smoking is dangerous) S: 520
Polycystic kidney disease P: 649
Polycystin [protein]
Polycystic kidney disease P: 649

Polycythemia [disorder]
Bloodletting B: 417
Polydectes [Greek mythology]
Perseus P: 295
Polydeuces [satellite]
Saturn (Satellites) S: 151-152
Polyester P: 649
Ester E: 360
Fiber (Synthetic fibers) F: 87
Interior design (Choosing patterns and textures) I: 332
Plastics picture on P: 554; (Growth of the plastics industry) P: 560
Rope (Synthetic-fiber rope) R: 473
Rugs and carpets (Materials used in rugs and carpets) R: 514
Textile (The age of modern textiles) T: 219
Polyestrous mammal [zoology]
Mammal (Mating) M: 122
Polyetheretherketone [plastic]
Plastics (Recent developments) P: 560
Polyetherimide [plastic]
Plastics (Recent developments) P: 560
Polyethylene [plastics] P: 650
Plastics diagram on P: 557; (table) P: 556; (Growth of the plastics industry) P: 560
Polymer P: 651
Polyethylene terephthalate [plastics]
Bottle B: 513
Plastics (table) P: 556
Polyester P: 649
Polygamy [marriage] P: 650
See also Polygyny in this index
Family (Varieties of families) F: 20-21
Freedom of religion (In the United States) F: 505
Marriage (Other marriage laws and practices) M: 220 with picture
Oneida Community O: 762
Smith, Joseph (Life at Nauvoo) S: 517-518
Polygenic trait [genetics]
Heredity (Patterns of heredity) H: 202
Polygon [geometry] P: 650 with diagram
Geometry (Euclidean geometry) G: 104 with diagram
Octagon O: 669 with diagram
Pyramid P: 916
Polygraph See Lie detector in this index
Polygraph [copier]
Jefferson, Thomas (The sage of Monticello) J: 87
Polygraph Association, American
Lie detector L: 271
Polygraphic substitution
Codes and ciphers (Substitution) Ci: 750
Polygyny [marriage]
See also Polygamy in this index
Africa (Marriage and the family) A: 108, A: 113
Family (Varieties of families) F: 20-21; (Development of the family) F: 21-22
Marriage (Other marriage laws and practices) M: 220
Mormons (The Mormons in Utah) M: 809
Nepal (People) N: 125
Polygamy P: 650
Xhosa X: 544
Zulu Z: 608
Polyhedron [geometry] P: 651 with diagrams
Archimedean solid A: 604
Geometry (Solid geometry) G: 104 with pictures
Octahedron O: 669 with diagram
Polyhymnia [Greek mythology]
Muses M: 937
Polymer [chemistry] P: 651
Cellulose (Biological importance) C: 341
Cement and concrete (Polymer concrete) C: 343
Composite materials (Polymer composites) Ci: 904
Fuel cell (A common fuel cell) F: 551
Hydrocarbon (Aliphatic hydrocarbons) H: 465
Monomer M: 731
Phenolic P: 356
Plastics P: 554; (The chemistry of plastics) P: 556
Polyethylene P: 650
Polypropylene P: 651 with diagram
Polystyrene P: 651 with diagram
Polyvinyl chloride P: 652 with diagram
Resin (Synthetic resins) R: 259
Rubber (The chemistry of rubber) R: 501
Teflon T: 87
Viscosity V: 428b
Polymer concrete
Cement and concrete (Polymer concrete) C: 343
Polymer electrolyte membrane fuel cell [device]
Fuel cell (A common fuel cell) F: 551
Polymer gesso
Painting (Grounds) P: 36
Polymerase chain reaction [technique]
DNA fingerprinting D: 258

Polymeric alloy
Plastics (The chemistry of plastics) P: 556
Polymerization [chemistry]
Nylon (How nylon is made) N: 633
Petroleum (Conversion) P: 344-345
Plastics (Making synthetic resins) P: 556
Polymer P: 651
Polyvinyl chloride P: 652
Synthetics So: 1068
Polymorphic mineral
Mineral (Mineral composition and structure) M: 570-571
Polymorphism [biology] P: 651
Polynesia [islands, Pacific]
See also Polynesians in this index
Pacific Islands P: 3 with map
Mythology (Pacific Islands divinities) M: 984
Sculpture (Pacific Islands sculpture) S: 241 with picture
Tattooing T: 51
Polynesian Cultural Center
Hawaii (Places to visit) H: 98 with picture
Honolulu (Cultural life) H: 321
Polynesian race [theory]
Races, Human (The geographical-race theory) R: 54
Polynesians [people]
Hawaii (Early days) H: 106 with picture
New Zealand (History) N: 354
Pacific Islands (Polynesians) P: 4 with picture
Samoa picture on S: 80b; (People) S: 80a
Polynia [area]
Arctic Ocean (Sea ice) A: 641
Polynices [literary figure]
Antigone A: 554
Polynomial [mathematics]
Algebra (Other definitions) A: 354
Gauss, Carl Friedrich G: 70
Polynucleotide [chemistry]
DNA D: 258
RNA R: 357
Polyp [disorder]
Colon cancer Ci: 786
Colonoscopy Ci: 815
Hay fever (Symptoms) H: 116
Polyp [sea animal]
Cnidarian Ci: 715
Coral Ci: 1048
Coral reef (How coral reefs form) Ci: 1048b
Jellyfish J: 90
Sea anemone S: 262
Sea fan S: 262a
Polypeptide [chemical]
Cell (Producing proteins) C: 333
Heredity (The flow of genetic information) H: 205
Protein (The structure of proteins) P: 832
Polyphase alloy
Alloy (Characteristics of alloys) A: 377
Polyphase current
Electric current (Direct and alternating current) E: 168
Polyphase motor
Tesla, Nikola (The alternating-current system) T: 181
Polyphemus [legendary figure]
Cyclops C: 1204
Poseidon P: 697
Ulysses (Return to Ithaca) U: 18
Polyphemus moth [insect]
Moth picture on M: 840
Polyphenylene sulfide [plastic]
Plastics (Recent developments) P: 560
Polyphony [music]
Classical music (Songs) Ci: 644; (Church music) Ci: 645
Counterpoint Ci: 1097
Music (table) M: 954
Song So: 592
Polyploidy [genetics]
Colchicum Ci: 760
Evolution (Evolution of new species) E: 429-430
Polypropylene [plastic] P: 651 with diagram
Plastics (table) P: 556
Rope (Synthetic-fiber rope) R: 473
Polysaccharide [chemistry] See Complex carbohydrate in this index
Polysemy [semantic relation]
Semantics S: 291
Polystyrene [plastic] P: 651 with diagram
Plastics (Making synthetic resins) P: 556; (table) P: 556; (Growth of the plastics industry) P: 560
Polystyrene foam
Polystyrene P: 652
Polysulfone [plastic]
Plastics (Recent developments) P: 560
Polytetrafluoroethylene [polymer]
Plastics (table) P: 556

Teflon **T: 87**
Polytheism [religion] **P: 652**
  Egypt, Ancient (Religion) **E: 137**
  Pantheism **P: 131**
  Rammohun Roy **R: 133**
  Religion (Belief in a deity) **R: 215**
Polyunsaturated fats
  Fat (Structure) **F: 52**
  Margarine **M: 198**
  Nutrition (Fats) **N: 625**
Polyunsaturated fatty acid [chemical]
  Vitamin (Vitamin E) **V: 430**
Polyurethane
  Plastics (table) **P: 556**
  Rubber (Special-purpose rubbers) **R: 504**
  Spandex **So: 753**
Polyvinyl acetate [paint]
  Paint (Household paints) **P: 23**
Polyvinyl chloride [plastic] **P: 652** *with diagram*
  Pipe (Kinds of pipe) **P: 489**
  Plastics (table) **P: 556**; (Growth of the plastics
    industry) **P: 560**
Polyvinylidene chloride [plastic]
  Plastics (table) **P: 556**
Pölzl, Klara [mother of]
  Hitler, Adolf (Boyhood) **H: 264-265**
Pomace fly [insect]
  Fruit fly **F: 549**
Pome [botany]
  Fruit (Simple fruits) **F: 544** *with pictures*
  Loquat **L: 453**
Pomegranate [tree] **P: 652** *with picture*
Pomelo [tree]
  Tangelo **T: 26**
Pomeranian [dog] **P: 652**
  Dog *picture on* **D: 274**
Pommel [riding equipment]
  Saddle **S: 8** *with picture*
Pommel horse [event]
  Gymnastics (Men's events) **G: 448** *with picture*
Pomo Indians P: 653
  California (Early days) **C: 60**
  Indian, American (Shelter) **I: 136d**; (Basketry)
    I: 145 *with picture*
Pomology [agriculture]
  Fruit (Fruit production) **F: 546**
  Horticulture (The horticulture industry) **H: 369**
Pomona [Roman mythology]
  Mythology (Roman divinities) **M: 982-983**
Pomona [ship]
  Shipwreck (table: Major shipwrecks) **S: 428**
Pomona glass
  Glass (Types of art glass) **G: 220-221**
Pomp and Circumstance March No. 1 [music by
  Elgar]
  Elgar, Sir Edward **E: 235**
Pompadour, Marquise de [French public figure]
  P: 653
  Louis XV **L: 476**
Pompano [fish] **P: 653**
  Fish *picture on* **F: 153**
Pompeii [ancient city] **P: 653** *with picture*
  Architecture *picture on* **A: 616**; (Neoclassical
    architecture) **A: 623**
  Atrium *picture on* **A: 877**
  Painting (Roman painting) **P: 42-43**;
    (Neoclassicism) **P: 66**
Pompeian style [art]
  Painting (Roman painting) **P: 42-43** *with picture*
Pompey, Sextus [Roman military leader]
  Augustus (Rise to power) **A: 889**
Pompey the Great [Roman political leader] **P: 655**
  Caesar, Julius (Alliance with Pompey) **C: 13**; (Civil
    war) **C: 13**; (Last victories) **C: 13**
  Cato, Marcus Porcius, the Younger **C: 305**
  Mithridates VI **M: 678**
  Rome, Ancient (The later years of the republic)
    R: 445
Pompez, Alex [American baseball owner/
  executive]
  Baseball (table: Hall of Fame) **B: 134a**
Pompidou, Georges Jean Raymond [French
  political leader]
  France (France after de Gaulle) **F: 477**
Pompidou Center [Paris]
  Paris (Museums and art galleries) **P: 164** *with
    picture*
Ponape [island, Pacific] *See* Pohnpei *in this index*
Ponce Art Museum [Puerto Rico]
  Puerto Rico (Places to visit) **P: 877**
Ponce de León, Juan [Spanish explorer] **P: 655**
  with picture and map
  Dry Tortugas National Park **D: 369**
  Exploration *map on* **E: 443**; (Spain's conquests in
    the New World) **E: 445**
  Florida *picture on* **F: 263**; (Exploration and
    Spanish settlement) **F: 261**

Puerto Rico (Spanish rule) **P: 883** *with picture*
Ponce Enríquez, Camilo [Ecuadorean political
  leader]
  Ecuador (The 1900's) **E: 73**
Ponchatoula Strawberry Festival
  Louisiana *picture on* **L: 489**
Poncho [clothing]
  Camping (Clothing) **C: 94**
  Inca *picture on* **I: 98**
  Latin America (Clothing) **L: 97**
  Mexico (Clothing) **M: 456**
Pond [geography] **P: 656** *with diagrams*
  Lake **L: 32**
Pond, Charles H. [American political leader]
  Connecticut (table) **Ci: 967**
Pond, Peter [American frontiersman]
  Alberta (The fur trade) **A: 329**
Pond lily *See* Water lily *in this index*
Pond pine [tree]
  Pine (Southeastern pines) **P: 468-469**
Pond turtle
  Turtle (Pond, box, and water turtles) **T: 522**
Ponder, James [American political leader]
  Delaware (table) **D: 109**
Ponderosa [tomato]
  Tomato (The tomato plant) **T: 324-325**
Ponderosa pine [tree]
  Oregon (Natural resources) **O: 841**
  Pine *picture on* **P: 470**; (Western pines) **P: 469**
    with picture
  Tree *pictures on* **T: 425**
Pong [electronic game]
  Electronic game (Arcade games) **E: 204d**
Ponomariov, Ruslan [Ukrainian chess player]
  Chess (World chess champions) **C: 414**
Pons [anatomy]
  Human body (table) **H: 422** *with diagram*
Ponsonby, Vere Brabazon [British statesman] *See*
  Bessborough, Earl of *in this index*
Pont-Aven school [art]
  Gauguin, Paul (Early career) **G: 69**
Pont du Gard [aqueduct]
  World, History of the *picture on* **W: 429**
Ponta Delgada [city, Azores]
  Azores **A: 998**
Pontalba Buildings
  New Orleans (Downtown New Orleans) **N: 278**
Pontchartrain [locomotive]
  Railroad (Developments in the United States)
    R: 115
Pontchartrain, Lake [Louisiana] *See* Lake
  Pontchartrain *in this index*
Pontchartrain Railroad
  Louisiana (Transportation) **L: 495**
Ponte, Lorenzo da [Italian librettist]
  Opera: (*Don Giovanni*) **O: 803**; (*Marriage of Figaro,
    The*) **O: 805-806**
Ponte Vecchio [bridge]
  Florence (The city) **F: 239-240** *with picture*
Pontiac [American Indian chief] **P: 657** *with portrait*
  Illinois (French and British control) **I: 72**
  Indian wars (Pontiac's War [1763]) **I: 191**
  Michigan (British control) **M: 508**
  Pennsylvania (Colonial wars) **P: 264-265**
Pontiac [automobile]
  Automobile *picture on* **A: 967**; (The postwar
    years) **A: 970-971**
Pontiac's War [1763]
  Indian wars (Pontiac's War [1763]) **I: 191**
  Michigan (British control) **M: 508**
  Pontiac **P: 657**
  United States, History of the (Policy changes)
    U: 158
Pontianus, Saint [pope]
  Pope (table) **P: 666**
Pontifex maximus [title]
  Rome, Ancient (Religion) **R: 441**
Pontiff [title]
  See also Pope *in this index*
  Rome, Ancient (Religion) **R: 441**
Pontifical College Josephinum
  Columbus (Education) **Ci: 855**
Pontifical North American College [Italy]
  Rome (Schools) **R: 430**
Pontifical Swiss Guard
  Swiss Guard **So: 1049**
Pontil [tool]
  Glass (Glass terms) **G: 222**
Pontius Pilate *See* Pilate, Pontius *in this index*
Pontoon bridge P: 657
Pontoon bridge [bridge]
  Ford **F: 371**
  Washington (Transportation) **W: 64**
Pontoppidan, Henrik [Danish author]
  Denmark (Arts) **D: 136**
  Nobel Prizes (Literature: 1917) **N: 447**
Pontormo, Jacopo [Italian painter]
  Mannerism *picture on* **M: 165**

Painting (Space) **P: 35**
Pontus [ancient region]
  Mithridates VI **M: 678**
Pony [horse]
  Horse (Kinds of horses) **H: 343**; (table: Some
    types and breeds of horses) **H: 343**; (Ponies)
    H: 347 *with pictures*
  Shetland pony **S: 398**
Pony express [U.S. history] **P: 657** *with picture*
  Postal Service, United States (During the 1800's
    and early 1900's) **P: 700-701** *with picture*
  Western frontier life in America (New forms of
    communication) **W: 233**
Pony Express Stables [Saint Joseph]
  Missouri (Places to visit) **M: 660**
Pony of the Americas
  Horse (table: Some types and breeds of horses)
    H: 343
Pony Penning
  Virginia (Visitor's guide) **V: 408** *with picture*
Pony Tracks [book by Remington]
  Remington, Frederic **R: 230**
Poodle [dog] **P: 658** *with picture*
  Dog *picture on* **D: 275**
Pooh [literary figure] *See* Winnie-the-Pooh *in this
  index*
Pool [game]
  Billiards (Pool) **B: 305** *with picture*
Pool, Swimming *See* Swimming pool *in this index*
Poole, Elijah *See* Muhammad, Elijah *in this index*
Poona [game]
  Badminton **B: 24**
Poop deck
  Galleon **G: 15**
Poopó, Lake [Bolivia]
  Andes Mountains (Glaciers, lakes, and rivers)
    A: 453
Poor Bitos [play by Anouilh]
  Anouilh, Jean **A: 519**
Poor Clares, Order of [religious group]
  Franciscans **F: 482**
Poor Folk [book by Dostoevsky]
  Dostoevsky, Fyodor **D: 311**
Poor Henry [poem by Hartmann von Aue]
  Hartmann von Aue **H: 79**
Poor Little Rich Girl [film]
  New Jersey *picture on* **N: 253**
"Poor Liza" [story by Karamzin]
  Russian literature (Sentimentalism) **R: 560**
Poor-man's-weatherglass [plant]
  Scarlet pimpernel **S: 173**
Poor men of Lyon [religious group]
  Waldenses **W: 7**
Poor People's March [U.S. history]
  Abernathy, Ralph David **A: 10**
Poor Richard's Almanac [book by Franklin] **P: 658**
  with picture
  Almanac **A: 379**
  Franklin, Benjamin **F: 487**, *picture on* **F: 488**;
    (Publisher) **F: 487**
  Proverb **P: 839**
Poor Robin's Almanac [book]
  April (Quotations) **A: 577**
Poorhouse
  Welfare (History) **W: 191**
Poorwill [bird] *See* Whip-poor-will *in this index*
Pop [drink] *See* Soft drink *in this index*
POP [electonics]
  Internet (Software) **I: 350c-350d**
POP [pollutant] *See* Persistent organic pollutant *in
  this index*
Pop Art P: 659 *with picture*
  Dine, Jim **D: 204**
  Furniture *picture on* **F: 587**
  Lichtenstein, Roy **L: 269**
  Lindner, Richard **L: 332**
  Painting (Pop Art) **P: 86** *with picture*
  Rivers, Larry **R: 356**
  Rosenquist, James Albert **R: 479**
  Warhol, Andy **W: 36** *with picture*
Pop culture
  Collectibles **Ci: 774**
  Culture **Ci: 1186**
Pop music *See* Popular music *in this index*
Pop safety valve
  Safety valve **S: 17** *with diagram*
Pop-up
  Baseball (Outs by batters) **B: 128-129**
Pop-up ad
  Internet (Advertising) **I: 350b**
Pop-up book
  Literature for children *picture on* **L: 370**
Pop Warner League
  Football (Football competition) **F: 364**
Po'Pay [American Indian leader] *See* Popé *in this
  index*
Popcorn [food] **P: 659**

Corn (Kinds of corn) **Ci:** 1058-1059
Popé [American Indian leader] **P:** 659
  Indian, American (Prophets) **I:** 148
  Indian wars (The Pueblo revolt [1680-1692])
    I: 191
Pope [title] **P:** 660 *with pictures*
  Bull **B:** 694
  Cardinal **C:** 210
  Christianity (The Roman Catholic Church)
    C: 522g; (History) **C:** 523-524
  Gelasius I, Saint **G:** 76
  Lombards **L:** 427
  Middle Ages (The Carolingian Empire) **M:** 524;
    (Troubles in the church) **M:** 528
  Nicholas II [pope] **N:** 402
  Peter, Saint **P:** 324
  Ring **R:** 342 *with picture*
  Roman Catholic Church (The pope) **R:** 404
  Swiss Guard **So:** 1049
Pope, Alexander [English poet] **P:** 667
  English literature (Swift and Pope) **E:** 318
  Enlightenment (The orderliness of nature)
    E: 326a-326b
  Epistle **E:** 344
  Essay (Formal essays) **E:** 359
  Poetry (Stress meters) **P:** 593-594; (Neoclassical
    poetry) **P:** 596-597
Pope, James C. [Canadian statesman]
  Prince Edward Island (Member of the union)
    P: 791; (table) **P:** 791
Pope, John [Union general]
  Civil War, American (The commanding officers)
    Ci: 618-619; (The peninsular campaign)
    Ci: 626; (Second Battle of Bull Run) **Ci:** 627
  Lincoln, Abraham (Building the army) **L:** 321
  Porter, Fitz-John **P:** 682
Pope, John Russell [American architect]
  Jefferson Memorial **J:** 88
Pope, Nathaniel [American political leader]
  Illinois (Early statehood) **I:** 74
Pope, William Henry [Canadian political leader]
  Confederation of Canada (Fathers of
    Confederation) **Ci:** 935 *with picture*
Pope's Creek Farm
  Washington, George (Boyhood) **W:** 92 *with
    picture*
Popeye [fish]
  Goldfish *picture on* **G:** 258
Popham, Sir John [English jurist]
  Maine (Exploration and settlements) **M:** 89
Poplar [tree] **P:** 667 *with picture*
  Plant *picture on* **P:** 525
  Tree *pictures on* **T:** 424
Pople, John Anthony [British chemist]
  Nobel Prizes (Chemistry: 1998) **N:** 444
Popliteal artery [anatomy]
  Leg (Blood and nerve supply) **L:** 182
Popocatépetl [volcano, Mexico] **P:** 668
  Mountain (table) **M:** 896 *with diagram*
Popolo d'Italia, Il [newspaper]
  Mussolini, Benito (Early life) **M:** 966
Popova, Liubov [Russian artist]
  Painting (Nonobjective painting in Russia) **P:** 79
Popper, Karl Raimund [Austrian-born
  philosopher] **P:** 668
Poppet valve
  Gasoline engine (The valves) **G:** 64 *with diagrams*
Popping crease [sports]
  Cricket (The field) **Ci:** 1131
Poppy [plant] **P:** 668
  Flower *pictures on* **F:** 277, **F:** 291; (Garden
    perennials) **F:** 278 *with picture*; (Flowers of the
    Arctic tundra) **F:** 283 *with picture*; (Flowers
    of summer-dry regions) **F:** 288 *with pictures*;
    (table) **F:** 301 *with picture*
  Opium **O:** 811 *with picture*
Poppy Day [custom]
  Memorial Day (Observance) **M:** 392
Poppy seed
  Poppy **P:** 668
Popular biography
  Biography (Forms of biography) **B:** 312
Popular culture *See* Pop culture *in this index*
Popular Front [Latvian political party]
  Latvia (History) **L:** 119-120
Popular Front [Spanish history]
  Spanish Civil War (Background to the war)
    So: 756-756a
Popular Movement for the Liberation of Angola
  [political party]
  Angola (History) **A:** 465
Popular music P: 669
  See also the list of Related articles in the Popular
    music *article*
  Country music **Ci:** 1098
  Music (Western music) **M:** 955
  Rap music **R:** 141

Popular National Congress [political party]
  Sudan (Civil war) **So:** 953-954
Popular Party [Italy]
  Italy (Political changes) **I:** 519
Popular Party [Spain] *See* Partido Popular *in this
  index*
Popular Rhymes and Nursery Tales [book by
  Halliwell]
  Nursery rhyme (History) **N:** 615-616
Popular sovereignty [U.S. history] **P:** 672
  Buchanan, James (The struggle over slavery)
    B: 660
  Douglas, Stephen Arnold **D:** 313
  Government (Sovereignty) **G:** 288-289
  Kansas (The struggle over slavery) **K:** 235
  Kansas-Nebraska Act **K:** 243
  Lincoln, Abraham (The debates with Douglas)
    L: 317
  Mexican War (Results of the war) **M:** 447
  United States, History of the (The nation divided
    [1850-1869]) **U:** 174
Population P: 672
  For population figures, see the World *article, and
    the* Facts in brief *table and map index in each
    continent, country, state or province, and large
    city article*
  Animal (Human population growth) **A:** 505
  Baby boom generation **B:** 11
  Birth and death rates **B:** 377
  Birth control **B:** 378
  Census **C:** 346
  City **Ci:** 574; (The 100 largest urban centers in the
    world) **Ci:** 576; (Population growth) **Ci:** 578;
    (Future cities) **Ci:** 593
  Colonial life in America (Population growth)
    Ci: 791
  Conservation (To meet demands for resources)
    Ci: 975
  Demography **D:** 129
  Environmental pollution (Effect of population
    growth) **E:** 339
  Famine (Fighting famine) **F:** 26a-26b
  Food supply (Increased demand for food) **F:** 348
  Genetics (Population genetics) **G:** 87
  Hispanic Americans (A rapidly growing minority)
    H: 258
  Immigration (Effects of immigration) **I:** 81
  Industrial Revolution (The middle and upper
    classes) **I:** 252
  Local government (Population changes) **L:** 407
  Malthus, Thomas Robert **M:** 115
  Natural resources (Conservation and
    development) **N:** 64-65
  Races, Human (The population approach) **R:** 57
    with map
  Sociology (Population characteristics) **So:** 564
  Vital statistics **V:** 429
  War (Waging war) **W:** 24
  World (People of the world) **W:** 412b *with map*
  World, History of the (The world since 1900)
    W: 445
Population [biology]
  Balance of nature **B:** 34
  Ecology (Populations) **E:** 53
  Elephant (Elephant families) **E:** 229
  Evolution (Causes of evolutionary change) **E:** 427
  Heredity (Heredity and natural selection) **H:** 203
Population [statistics]
  Public opinion poll (Defining the goals) **P:** 862
  Statistics (Collecting the data) **So:** 868
Population, Census of
  Census (Kinds of censuses) **C:** 346-347
Population, Center of [geography]
  United States *map on* **U:** 109
Population I star [astronomy]
  Star (Supernovae) **So:** 850-851
  Sun (Comparison with other stars) **So:** 978-979
Population II star [astronomy]
  Star (Supernovae) **So:** 850-851
  Sun (Comparison with other stars) **So:** 978-979
Population III star [astronomy]
  Star (Supernovae) **So:** 850-851
  Sun (Comparison with other stars) **So:** 978-979
Population Bomb, The [book by Ehrlich]
  Ehrlich, Paul Ralph **E:** 145
Population density
  Population (table: Population density of the
    continents) **P:** 673
  World (table) **W:** 409; (Population) **W:** 412b *with
    map*
Population density map
  Map *picture on* **M:** 177; (Thematic maps) **M:** 178
Population displosion [sociology]
  City (Social problems) **Ci:** 591
Population explosion [sociology]
  City (Population growth) **Ci:** 578; (Metropolitan
    cities) **Ci:** 588

  India (City life) **I:** 115-116
  Population (The population explosion) **P:** 673
Population genetics
  Genetics (Population genetics) **G:** 87
Population geography
  Geography (Human geography) **G:** 94
Population inversion [physics]
  Laser (Producing laser light) **L:** 84
Population of the Valley of Teotihuacán, The
  [book by Gamio]
  Gamio, Manuel **G:** 23
Populism [U.S. history] **P:** 674
  Donnelly, Ignatius **D:** 308
  Free silver **F:** 499
  Gay Nineties (Industrial growth) **G:** 72
  Harrison, Benjamin (Bid for reelection) **H:** 73
  Kansas (Spirit of reform) **K:** 237
  Nebraska (Growth of agriculture) **N:** 112-114
  Political parties (Third parties) **P:** 636
  United States, History of the (Early reform efforts)
    U: 185
  Watson, Thomas Edward **W:** 148
Populist Party [U.S. history]
  Populism (The People's Party) **P:** 675
Poquelin, Jean Baptiste [French author] *See*
  Molière *in this index*
Porcelain P: 675 *with pictures*
  Antique (Ceramic antiques) **A:** 558
  Böttger, Johann Friedrich **B:** 512
  China (Sculpture and pottery) **C:** 488 *with picture*
  Doll (Porcelain dolls) **D:** 290; (Rivalry in the doll
    industry) **D:** 291
  Dresden china **D:** 346 *with picture*
  Germany *picture on* **G:** 154
  Invention (China) **I:** 359
  Kaolin **K:** 244
  Ming dynasty **M:** 573
  Pottery (Porcelain) **P:** 716 *with pictures*
  Wedgwood ware **W:** 179 *with picture*
Porcelain enamel
  Ceramics (Kinds of ceramic products) **C:** 359
Porcupine [animal] **P:** 677 *with picture*
  Animal *pictures on* **A:** 479, **A:** 494
  Mammal *picture on* **M:** 119
Porcupine Mountains
  Michigan *picture on* **M:** 488; (Land regions)
    M: 500 *with map*
Porcupinefish P: 678 *with picture*
  Fish *picture on* **F:** 145
Pore [anatomy] **P:** 678
  Acne **A:** 27
  Pimple **P:** 466
Pore [astronomy]
  Sunspot **So:** 991
Pore space
  Soil (Composition) **So:** 573
Porgy [book by Heyward]
  Heyward, DuBose **H:** 221
  Opera: *(Porgy and Bess)* **O:** 806
Porgy [fish] **P:** 678 *with picture*
Porgy and Bess [opera by Gershwin]
  Gershwin, George **G:** 174
  Gershwin, Ira **G:** 175
  Heyward, DuBose **H:** 221
  Opera (American opera) **O:** 800; *(Porgy and Bess)*
    O: 806
Porifera [zoology] *See* Sponge *in this index*
Pork [food] **P:** 679
  Hog (Food) **H:** 286
  Meat (Kinds of meat) **M:** 347 *with pictures*
  Meat packing **M:** 350
  Trichina **T:** 441
Pork barrel [government]
  Congress of the United States (Legislative
    bargaining) **C:** 944
Pork producer [farmer]
  Hog **H:** 284
Porkfish [fish]
  Fish *picture on* **F:** 155
Pornography
  Comstock Law **Ci:** 926
  Obscenity and pornography **O:** 643
Porosity [physical property] **P:** 679
Porous-pointed pen
  Pen (Soft-tip pens) **P:** 234 *with picture*
Porphyria [disorder]
  George III **G:** 107
Porphyry [Greek philosopher]
  Neoplatonism **N:** 124
Porpoise [sea animal] **P:** 679 *with picture*
  Dolphin **D:** 296
  Whale (Dolphins and porpoises) **W:** 258
Porsche, Ferdinand [Austrian engineer]
  Porsche AG **P:** 680
  Volkswagen AG **V:** 444
Porsche, Ferry [Austrian engineer]
  Porsche AG **P:** 680

Porsche AG [company] **P:** 679
  Sports car (History) **So:** 803 *with picture*
  Volkswagen AG **V:** 444
Port [electronics]
  Computer (Parts of computers) **Ci:** 911-912 *with picture*
Port [nautical term]
  Boating (Boating regulations) **B:** 429
  Ship **S:** 403; (Nautical terms) **S:** 405
Port [shipping] **P:** 680
  International trade *picture on* **I:** 348
  New York City (Trade) **N:** 333
  Ship (Kinds of ships) **S:** 406
Port [valve]
  Gasoline engine (The valves) **G:** 64
Port [wine]
  Portugal (Agriculture and fishing) **P:** 691
  Wine (Fortified wines) **W:** 336; (Wine styles from other countries) **W:** 337
Port Arthur [China]
  Lüshun **L:** 526
Port Arthur [Ontario]
  Thunder Bay **T:** 272
Port au Choix National Historic Park [Newfoundland and Labrador]
  Canada (table: National historic sites) **C:** 115
Port-au-Prince [Haiti] **P:** 680
  Haiti **H:** 14 *with picture and map, picture on* **H:** 16
Port Authority of New York and New Jersey **P:** 680
  New York City (Trade) **N:** 333
Port Chicago Naval Magazine National Memorial [California]
  National Park System (National memorials) **N:** 54
Port Clarence [former name]
  Malabo **M:** 95
Port Colborne [Ontario]
  Welland Ship Canal **W:** 193 *with map*
Port Dalhousie [Ontario]
  Welland Ship Canal **W:** 193 *with map*
Port de bras [movement]
  Ballet (table) **B:** 45; (A ballet class) **B:** 46-47
Port de Grave [region, Newfoundland and Labrador]
  Newfoundland and Labrador (Places to visit) **N:** 368 *with picture*
Port du Salut [cheese]
  Cheese (Semisoft cheese) **C:** 392 *with picture*
Port Elizabeth [South Africa] **P:** 681
Port Gibson [Mississippi]
  Mississippi (Libraries) **M:** 627
Port Hawkesbury [Nova Scotia]
  Nova Scotia *picture on* **N:** 565
Port Hudson [Louisiana]
  African Americans (The American Civil War) **A:** 136i-136j
Port Jackson [harbor]
  Sydney **So:** 1063
Port-La-Joye—Fort Amherst National Historic Site [Prince Edward Island]
  Canada (table: National historic sites) **C:** 115
  Prince Edward Island (Places to visit) **P:** 788
Port Lawrence [former settlement]
  Toledo (History) **T:** 321
Port Louis [Mauritius] **P:** 681
  Mauritius **M:** 316
Port Macquarie [town, Australia]
  Australia *picture on* **A:** 902
Port Mann Bridge [British Columbia]
  Bridge (table: Steel arch) **B:** 603
Port Moresby [Papua New Guinea] **P:** 681
  New Guinea (Political units) **N:** 206 *with picture and map*
  Papua New Guinea *picture on* **P:** 140
  World War II (The Battle of the Coral Sea) **W:** 488
Port Newark [New Jersey]
  Newark (Economy) **N:** 357; (History) **N:** 357-358
Port of Boston
  Boston (Trade) **B:** 502
Port of entry [shipping]
  Customs Service, United States **Ci:** 1201
  Free trade zone **F:** 501
Port of Houston
  Houston (Commercial city) **H:** 398
Port of London
  London (Trade) **L:** 438
Port of Los Angeles
  Los Angeles (The Port of Los Angeles) **L:** 461; (Trade) **L:** 464 *with picture*
Port-of-Spain [Trinidad] **P:** 681
  Trinidad and Tobago **T:** 445 *with picture and map*
Port of Yokohama
  Tokyo (Trade) **T:** 317-318
Port-Orford-cedar [tree]
  Cedar (Scale-leaved cedars) **C:** 324 *with picture*
Port Phillip Bay [Australia]
  Victoria (Land and climate) **V:** 356

Port Republicain [former name]
  Port-au-Prince **P:** 680
Port Richmond [district]
  New York City (Staten Island) **N:** 330
Port Robinson [Ontario]
  Welland Ship Canal **W:** 193 *with map*
Port-Royal [Canadian history]
  Annapolis Royal **A:** 516
  Champlain, Samuel de (Early life) **C:** 373
  Nova Scotia (Exploration and settlement) **N:** 567-568 *with picture*; (The struggle in Acadia) **N:** 568
  Poutrincourt, Jean de Biencourt de **P:** 722
Port Royal [Jamaica]
  Kingston **K:** 332
Port-Royal National Historic Site [Nova Scotia]
  Canada (table: National historic sites) **C:** 115
Port Said [Egypt] **P:** 681 *with picture*
Port-Vila [Vanuatu]
  Vanuatu **V:** 284
Port Walter [Alaska]
  Alaska (Climate) **A:** 296
Port Weller [Ontario]
  Welland Ship Canal **W:** 193 *with map*
Port-wine stain
  Birthmark **B:** 380
Porta, Giacomo della *See* Della Porta, Giacomo *in this index*
Portability [electronics]
  Computer (Compiling or assembling a program) **Ci:** 923
Portable media player **P:** 681
  Computer (Personal computers) **Ci:** 909-910
  Stereophonic sound system (Parts of a stereo system) **So:** 892
  United States, History of the *picture on* **U:** 196c
Portable radio
  Radio *picture on* **R:** 93; (Radio since the 1950's) **R:** 94
Portage [travel]
  Canoeing (Portaging a canoe) **C:** 181
Portal [computing]
  Internet (Search engines) **I:** 350a
Portal vein [anatomy]
  Liver (Structure of the liver) **L:** 393
Portales Palazuelos, Diego [Chilean political leader]
  Chile (Building the nation) **C:** 468
Portcullis [defense]
  Castle (Structure) **C:** 280
Porteños [people]
  Buenos Aires (The people) **B:** 673
Porteous, G. Thomas [American jurist]
  Impeachment (History) **I:** 91-92
Porter [drink]
  Beer **B:** 211
Porter, Albert G. [American political leader]
  Indiana (table) **I:** 214
Porter, Cole [American composer] **P:** 682
Porter, David [American naval officer] **P:** 682
  Farragut, David Glasgow **F:** 47
Porter, David Dixon [American naval officer] **P:** 682
  Farragut, David Glasgow **F:** 47
Porter, David Rittenhouse [American political leader]
  Pennsylvania (table) **P:** 263
Porter, Edwin S. [American director]
  Great Train Robbery, The **G:** 349
  Motion picture (Early motion pictures) **M:** 863 *with picture*
Porter, Fitz-John [American soldier] **P:** 682
Porter, Sir George [British chemist]
  Nobel Prizes (Chemistry: 1967) **N:** 443
Porter, James D. [American political leader]
  Tennessee (table) **T:** 152
Porter, James Madison [American government official]
  Tyler, John (table) **T:** 534
Porter, Katherine Anne [American author] **P:** 682
Porter, Peter B. [American government official]
  Adams, John Quincy (table) **A:** 43
Porter, Rodney Robert [British physiologist]
  Nobel Prizes (Physiology or medicine: 1972) **N:** 446
Porter, William Sydney *See* Henry, O. *in this index*
Portfolio
  Modeling (Careers) **M:** 685
Portia [literary figure]
  Shakespeare, William: (*The Merchant of Venice*) **S:** 358
Portia [satellite]
  Uranus *picture on* **U:** 219
Portico
  Architecture (Classical Greek architecture) **A:** 615-616
Portillo [Chile]

Chile (Recreation) **C:** 462 *with picture*
Portillo Cabrera, Alfonso [Guatemalan political leader]
  Guatemala (Political developments) **G:** 417
Portinari, Beatrice [Italian public figure]
  Dante Alighieri (His life) **D:** 33
  Divine Comedy **D:** 242
Portinari, Cândido [Brazilian painter]
  Brazil (The arts) **B:** 576-577 *with picture*
Portland [Maine] **P:** 682
  Maine **M:** 68 *with picture*; (table: Average monthly weather) **M:** 83
Portland [Oregon] **P:** 683 *with pictures*
  Oregon *pictures on* **O:** 827, **O:** 830, **O:** 831; (table: Average monthly weather) **O:** 841
Portland, Duke of [British political leader]
  United Kingdom (table: British prime ministers) **U:** 72
Portland Art Museum
  Oregon (Museums) **O:** 831
Portland Building
  Architecture *picture on* **A:** 633
  Graves, Michael **G:** 330
Portland Canal [waterway, Kentucky]
  Louisville (History) **L:** 506
Portland cement [building material]
  Cement and concrete **C:** 343; (Raw materials) **C:** 344; (History) **C:** 345
  Edison, Thomas Alva (Ore milling and cement) **E:** 81
Portland Cement Association
  Cement and concrete (History) **C:** 345
Portland cement concrete [material]
  Road (Paving) **R:** 359
Portland Head Light [lighthouse]
  Maine *picture on* **M:** 68; (Places to visit) **M:** 78
  Portland (Maine) **P:** 683
Portland Museum of Art
  Maine (Museums) **M:** 73 *with picture*
Portland Rose Festival
  Oregon (Visitor's guide) **O:** 836
Portland Trail Blazers [team]
  Basketball (table) **B:** 150
Portland Vase
  Glass **G:** 219
Portman, Natalie [American actress]
  Motion picture (Best performance by an actress: 2010) **M:** 862a
Portnoy's Complaint [book by Roth]
  Roth, Philip **R:** 487
Porto [Portugal] **P:** 685
  Portugal (Population and ancestry) **P:** 687
Pôrto Alegre [Brazil] **P:** 685
Porto-Novo [Benin] **P:** 685
Porto Santo Island
  Madeira Islands **M:** 30
Portobelo [Panama]
  Morgan, Sir Henry (Early career) **M:** 803
Portocarrero, René [Cuban painter]
  Cuba (The arts) **Ci:** 1171-1172
Portoferraio [Italy]
  Elba **E:** 156
Portolá, Gaspar de [Spanish explorer]
  California (Spanish and Russian settlement) **C:** 60
  Los Angeles (Exploration) **L:** 469
Portolan chart
  Map (Maps in the Middle Ages) **M:** 183-184
Portrait button
  Button (History) **B:** 745
Portrait doll
  Doll (After the war) **D:** 292
Portrait Gallery, National [Washington, D.C.]
  Washington, D.C. *map on* **W:** 76; (Smithsonian museums) **W:** 71-73
Portrait in Sepia [book by Allende]
  Allende, Isabel **A:** 372
Portrait of a Killer [book by Cornwell]
  Cornwell, Patricia **Ci:** 1066
Portrait of a Lady, The [book by James]
  American literature (Mark Twain and Henry James) **A:** 420
  James, Henry (His works) **J:** 26
Portrait of Charles I Hunting [painting by Van Dyck]
  Painting (Baroque) **P:** 58-61 *with picture*
  Van Dyck, Sir Anthony **V:** 281
Portrait of Isaac Royall and His Family [painting by Feke]
  Colonial life in America *picture on* **Ci:** 807
  Feke, Robert **F:** 68
Portrait of Isabella Brant [drawing by Rubens]
  Drawing *picture on* **D:** 343
Portrait of Lady Guilford [painting by Holbein]
  Clothing *picture on* **Ci:** 702
Portrait of Madame Matisse [painting by Matisse]
  Matisse, Henri *picture on* **M:** 310
Portrait of Madame Récamier [painting by David]

David, Jacques Louis *picture on* **D: 46**
Portrait of Madame Seriziat [painting by David]
   Clothing *picture on* **Ci: 704**
Portrait of Marchesa Doria [painting by Van Dyck]
   Clothing *picture on* **Ci: 702**
Portrait of Pope Clement VII [painting by
   Sebastiano del Piombo]
   Painting (The Renaissance in Venice) **P: 55-56**
      with picture
Portrait of the Artist [painting by Largillière]
   Clothing *picture on* **Ci: 703**
Portrait of the Artist, As an Old Man [book by
   Heller]
   Heller, Joseph **H: 177**
Portrait of the Artist as a Young Dog [book by
   Thomas]
   Thomas, Dylan **T: 261**
Portrait of the Artist as a Young Man, A [book by
   Joyce]
   Irish literature (Fiction) **I: 432**
   Joyce, James **J: 176**
   Novel (New directions in the novel) **N: 573-574**
Portrait of the Assassin [book by Ford and Stiles]
   Ford, Gerald Rudolph (Rise to power) **F: 375**
Portraiture [art]
   Painting (People) **P: 31** *with picture*; (Baroque)
      P: 58-61
   Photography (Portrait photographers) **P: 428**
Portrule [device]
   Telegraph (The Morse telegraph) **T: 90**
Ports and Waterways Safety Act [1972]
   Coast Guard, United States (The Coast Guard
      since World War II) **Ci: 738**
Ports of Call [music by Ibert]
   Ibert, Jacques **I: 3**
Portsmouth [England] **P: 685**
Portsmouth [New Hampshire] **P: 685**
   New Hampshire (Places to visit) **N: 216** *with
      picture*
Portsmouth [Rhode Island]
   Rhode Island (Settlement) **R: 312**
Portsmouth, Treaty of [1905]
   Russo-Japanese War (Treaty of Portsmouth)
      R: 566b
Portsmouth Area Project [U.S.]
   Ohio (The mid-1900's) **O: 703**
Portsmouth Naval Shipyard [New Hampshire]
   P: 685
   New Hampshire *picture on* **N: 225**
Portugal P: 686 *with pictures and maps*
   See also the list of Related articles in the Portugal
      article
   Africa (The Atlantic slave trade) **A: 132**
   Angola (History) **A: 465**
   Brazil (History) **B: 583**
   Colonialism (Early European colonialism) **Ci: 813**;
      (Later colonialism) **Ci: 813-814**
   Columbus, Christopher (Early years) **Ci: 857**; (The
      plan to sail westward) **Ci: 858**; (Return to Spain)
      Ci: 861
   East Timor **E: 40**; (History) **E: 41**
   Euro **E: 379**
   Europe (Recent developments) **E: 416**
   Exploration (The great age of European
      exploration) **E: 443** *with map*
   Flag *picture on* **F: 207**
   India (India in the 1950's and early 1960's) **I: 133**
   Indonesia (The coming of the Europeans) **I: 237**
   Line of Demarcation **L: 333** *with map*
   Macau **M: 4**
   Palmares **P: 110**
   Portuguese language **P: 695**
   Rio de Janeiro (History) **R: 346**
   São Tomé and Príncipe (History) **S: 120**
   United States, History of the (The Spanish and
      Portuguese) **U: 151**
Portuguese East Africa
   Mozambique (History) **M: 905**
Portuguese East India Company
   East India Company **E: 40**
Portuguese Guinea *See* Guinea-Bissau *in this index*
Portuguese language P: 695
   Portugal (Language) **P: 689**
Portuguese man-of-war [sea animal] **P: 696** *with
   picture*
Portuguese Timor
   Portugal (End of the empire) **P: 695**
Portuguese water dog [dog] **P: 696** *with picture*
Portulaca [plant] **P: 696** *with picture*
Portus Cale
   Portugal (Roman rule) **P: 692**
POS system [electronics] *See* Point-of-sale system
   in this index
Posadas, Las [custom]
   Christmas (In Latin America) **C: 532**
   Hispanic Americans (In Mexico) **H: 248** *with
      picture*; (Holidays) **H: 250**

Mexico (Holidays) **M: 457-458**
Poseidon [Greek mythology] **P: 697**
   See also Neptune *in this index*
   Andromeda **A: 457**
   Isthmian Games **I: 492**
   Mythology (Greek mythology) **M: 980**; (table)
      M: 981
   Sculpture (The importance of sculpture) **S: 228**
      with picture
   Ulysses (Return to Ithaca) **U: 18**
Poseidon, Temple of [Italy]
   World, History of the *picture on* **W: 426**
Posey, Cum [American baseball player/mamager]
   Baseball (table: Hall of Fame) **B: 134a**
Posey ring
   Ring **R: 342**
Positano [Italy]
   Italy *picture on* **I: 497**
Position [ballet]
   Ballet *pictures on* **B: 48**
Position light
   Airplane (The wing) **A: 213-214**
Position paper
   Election campaign (Planning campaign strategy)
      E: 159
Positional system [mathematics] *See* Place-value
   system *in this index*
Positive [photography]
   Photography (Color reversal film) **P: 419**; (Making
      prints) **P: 419**
Positive acceleration [physics]
   Velocity (Acceleration) **V: 297**
Positive angle [geometry]
   Angle **A: 462**
Positive charge
   Electricity (Electric charge) **E: 191**
   Vacuum tube (How a vacuum tube works) **V: 258**
Positive degree [grammar]
   Adjective (Comparison of adjectives) **A: 57**
   Comparison (The three degrees of comparison)
      Ci: 902b
Positive displacement pump
   Pump **P: 900b**
Positive feedback loop [meteorology]
   Hurricane (How a hurricane forms) **H: 453**
Positive integer [mathematics] *See* Natural
   number *in this index*
Positive ion [physics]
   Bond (An ionic bond) **B: 454**
   Radiation (Effects of radiation) **R: 79**
Positive lens [optics]
   Lens (Lens shapes) **L: 196**; (Viewed through a
      positive lens) **L: 196b** *with diagram*
Positive method [philosophy]
   Positivism (Comte's positivism) **P: 697**
Positive number
   Algebra (Positive and negative numbers) **A: 352**
   Square root **So: 812**
Positive-pressure respirator [machine]
   Respirator **R: 262**
Positive reinforcement [psychology]
   Behavior (Learning) **B: 220-221**
Positive train control
   Railroad (Other train controls) **R: 112**
Positive transfer [psychology]
   Learning (Transfer of training) **L: 164**
Positive tropism [botany]
   Auxin **A: 981**
   Plant (Environmental factors) **P: 538**
Positive-working offset plate [printing]
   Printing (Offset printing plates) **P: 798**
Positivism [philosophy] **P: 697**
   Comte, Auguste **Ci: 926**
   Empiricism **E: 263**
   Metaphysics (Opinions about metaphysics)
      M: 430
Positron [atomic particle]
   Anderson, Carl David **A: 451**
   Antimatter **A: 556**
   Cosmic rays (Galactic cosmic rays) **Ci: 1076**
   Gamma rays **G: 24**
   Joliot-Curie, Irène **J: 156**
   Matter (Unusual forms of matter) **M: 311**
   Nuclear physics **N: 596**
   Particle accelerator (How accelerators work)
      P: 184-185
   Positron emission tomography **P: 698**
   Radiation (Beta particles) **R: 76**
   Star (Hydrogen fusion) **So: 846-847**
   Subatomic particle **So: 936**
   Transmutation of elements **T: 379**
Positron emission tomography [medicine] **P: 697**
   with pictures
   Alzheimer's disease (Diagnosis) **A: 398-399**
   Antimatter **A: 557**
   Brain (Imaging) **B: 551**
   Mental illness (Recent developments) **M: 409**

Possessed, The [book by Dostoevsky]
   Dostoevsky, Fyodor **D: 311**
Possession [law]
   Title **T: 302**
Possession, Demonic
   Exorcism **E: 438**
Possessive case [grammar]
   Case (Nouns) **C: 272**; (Pronouns) **C: 272**
   Declension **D: 80**
   Grammar (Inflection) **G: 303**
   Noun (Number and case) **N: 552**
Possum [animal] **P: 698** *with picture*
   See also Opossum *in this index*
   Cuscus **Ci: 1199** *with picture*
   Glider (animal) **G: 231** *with picture*
   Marsupial (Kinds of marsupials) **M: 232**
Post, Charles W. [American businessman]
   Michigan (Interesting facts) **M: 489**
Post, Emily [American author] **P: 698**
   Etiquette (Books on etiquette) **E: 375**
Post, Wiley [American aviator] **P: 698** *with portrait*
   Airplane (Fliers of the golden age) **A: 237**
   Automatic flight control system (History) **A: 944**
Post-...
   Headings beginning with the prefix Post- *are
   alphabetized as single words:* Post-mortem
   appears after Postmodernism
Post and lintel
   Architecture (table) **A: 608-609** *with picture*
Post-chariot [vehicle]
   Chariot **C: 378**
Post Electronic Courier Service
   Postal Service, United States (Electronic services)
      P: 700
Post exchange [store] **P: 699**
Post flag [U.S. Army]
   Flag (table) **F: 193**
Post oak [tree]
   Oak (White oaks) **O: 635**
Post office
   See also the list of Related articles in the Postal
      services *article*
   Colonial life in America (Communication) **Ci: 806**
   Communication (The 1700's) **Ci: 880-881** *with
      picture*
   Franklin, Benjamin (Civic leader) **F: 487**;
      (Organizing the new nation) **F: 490**
   Massachusetts (Interesting facts) **M: 271**
   Parcel post **P: 155**
   Pony express **P: 657**
   Postal services **P: 702** *with pictures*
Post-office box
   Postal Service, United States (Other services)
      P: 700
Post Office Department *See* Postal Service, United
   States *in this index*
Post Office Protocol [electonics]
   Internet (Software) **I: 350c-350d**
Post Office Reform [pamphlet by Hill]
   Postal services (The creation of the Penny Post)
      P: 706
Post Office Tower
   London (Rebuilding) **L: 442**
Post rider [occupation]
   Colonial life in America (Communication) **Ci: 806**
Post road [route]
   Colonial life in America (Communication) **Ci: 806**
Postage meter [machine]
   Postal Service, United States (Other services)
      P: 700
Postage stamp
   Doll (Doll collecting) **D: 294**
   Postal Service, United States *pictures on* **P: 701**;
      (Stamps and other mailing materials) **P: 699**
   Postal services (Collection) **P: 702**; (The creation
      of the Penny Post) **P: 706** *with picture*
   Stamp collecting **So: 829** *with pictures*
Postal card [mail]
   Postal Service, United States (Stamps and other
      mailing materials) **P: 699**
Postal clerk
   Postal services (Sorting) **P: 703**
Postal money order
   Money order **M: 718** *with picture*
   Postal Service, United States (Other services)
      P: 700
Postal Rate Commission [U.S.]
   Postal Service, United States (Organization)
      P: 700
Postal Service, United States P: 699 *with pictures*
   Civil service (Federal civil service) **Ci: 612**
   Comstock Law **Ci: 926**
   Nixon, Richard Milhous (The national scene)
      N: 433-434
   Postal services **P: 702**
   Washington, D.C. *map on* **W: 76**
   ZIP Code **Z: 596**

Postal services P: 702 *with pictures*
  Rome, Ancient (Transportation and
    communication) R: 443-444
Postal Telegraph Company
  Mackay, John William M: 20
Postal service, Universal [UN] P: 708
  Postal services (The creation of the Penny Post)
    P: 706
  Treaty (Kinds of treaties) T: 408-409
Postal Workers Union, American
  Labor movement (table) L: 8
Poster [communications] P: 708
  Advertising (Outdoor signs) A: 75
  China (Communication) C: 498-499
  Poland *picture on* P: 609
Poster board
  Cardboard C: 209
Posterior cruciate ligament [anatomy]
  Anterior cruciate ligament A: 544
Posterior vena cava [zoology]
  Frog *picture on* F: 537
Post-hallucinogenic perceptual disorder
  Hallucinogenic drug H: 26
Posthouse
  Postal services (Ancient times) P: 703
Posthumous [literary figure]
  Shakespeare, William: (*Cymbeline*) S: 365
Posthumous Papers of the Pickwick Club, The *See*
  Pickwick Papers, The *in this index*
Postimpressionism [art] P: 708 *with picture*
  Cézanne, Paul C: 364
  France (Painting) F: 462
  Painting (Postimpressionism) P: 75 *with pictures*
Posting [communication]
  Publishing (Scheduling, printing, and posting)
    P: 867
Posting [riding]
  Horse (Gaits) H: 353-354
Postman Always Rings Twice, The [book by Cain]
  Cain, James M. C: 15
Postmaster general [office]
  Postal Service, United States (Organization)
    P: 700
Postmillennialism [religion]
  Millennium M: 553
Postmodernism [arts] P: 709
  Architecture (Architecture today) A: 632-633
    with picture
  Furniture (Postmodern design) F: 585 *with
    pictures*
  Graves, Michael G: 330
  Jahn, Helmut J: 21 *with picture*
  Johnson, Philip Cortelyou J: 152
  McLuhan, Marshall M: 343
  Modernism M: 685
  Painting (Postmodernism) P: 88 *with picture*
  Venturi, Robert V: 310 *with picture*
Postmodernism [social theory]
  Postmodernism P: 709
Postmortem [book by Cornwell]
  Cornwell, Patricia C: 1066
Post-mortem examination *See* Autopsy *in this
  index*
Post-mortem inspection
  Meat packing (Slaughtering and dressing)
    M: 351-352
Postneonatal death
  Infant mortality I: 264
Post-9/11 GI Bill [2009]
  Veterans Affairs, Department of (Benefits and
    other services) V: 343
Postpartum blues [disorder]
  Postpartum depression P: 709
Postpartum depression [disorder] P: 709
Postpartum psychosis [disorder]
  Postpartum depression P: 709
Postpetiole [entomology]
  Ant (The abdomen) A: 522 *with picture*
Post-polio syndrome [disorder]
  Poliomyelitis (Kinds of poliomyelitis) P: 626
Post-production
  Motion picture (Post-production) M: 854 *with
    pictures*
  Television (Post-production) T: 111
Postsale service
  Sales (Persuasion) S: 63-64
PostScript [programming language]
  Desktop publishing D: 158
Post-soul literature
  African American literature (Recent
    developments) A: 136a
Postsynaptic potential [physiology]
  Nervous system (Transmission across synapses)
    N: 135
Post-traumatic stress disorder [psychology]
  P: 710
  Anxiety disorder A: 562

  Hypnosis (Scientific studies) H: 480
Postulant [religion]
  Religious life R: 226
Postulate *See* Axiom *in this index*
Posture P: 710
Post-visualization [photography]
  Photography (A diversity of styles) P: 426-427
Pot [drug] *See* Marijuana *in this index*
Pot [fishing]
  Lobster (Lobster fishing) L: 406
Pot barley
  Barley (Uses of barley) B: 113
Pot roast
  Meat *pictures on* M: 349
Pot still
  Distilling D: 239
Potable water
  Plumbing P: 577
Potala Palace [Tibet]
  Tibet *picture on* T: 278; (Cities) T: 277
Potash [chemical] P: 710
  Detergent and soap (Early soap) D: 165
  Israel (Mining) I: 486 *with picture*
  Potassium P: 711
  Saskatchewan (Mining) S: 141 *with picture*
Potassium [element] P: 710
  Fertilizer (Inorganic fertilizers) F: 79
  Glauconite G: 226
Potassium-argon dating [archaeology]
  Archaeology (Dating) A: 598
  Prehistoric people (Placing prehistoric people in
    time) P: 754a-754b
Potassium carbonate [chemical] *See* Potash *in
  this index*
Potassium chloride [chemical]
  Fertilizer (Raw materials) F: 80
  Potash P: 710
  Potassium P: 711
Potassium cyanide [chemical]
  Cyanide Ci: 1202
  Prussic acid P: 843
Potassium feldspar [mineral]
  Mineral *picture on* M: 569
Potassium ferrocyanide [chemical]
  Invisible ink I: 369
Potassium hydroxide [chemical]
  Detergent and soap (How soap is made) D: 164
Potassium iodide [chemical]
  Iodine (Uses of iodine) I: 370 *with picture*
Potassium nitrate *See* Saltpeter *in this index*
Potassium oxide equivalent
  Potash P: 710
Potassium permanganate [chemical]
  Deodorizer D: 148
  Manganese (Industrial uses) M: 139
Potato [plant] P: 711 *with pictures*
  Great Irish Famine G: 343
  Idaho (Agriculture) I: 41 *with picture*
  Maine (Agriculture) M: 86 *with picture*
  Nightshade N: 421 *with picture*
  Nutrition (Carbohydrates) N: 625
  Plant (Asexual reproduction) P: 535
  Poisonous plant (Some poisonous plants) P: 602
  Potato beetle P: 714
  Vegetable (Tubers) V: 293 *with picture*
Potato beetle [insect] P: 714 *with pictures*
  Beetle (Leaf beetles) B: 217
Potato Famine [1845-1848] *See* Great Irish Famine
  in this index
Potato flea beetle [insect]
  Beetle *picture on* B: 218
Potato late blight [plant disease]
  Rot R: 485
Potato War [European history]
  Succession wars (The War of the Bavarian
    Succession) So: 950
Potawatomi Indians P: 714
  Chicago (History) C: 433
  Indiana (Indian days) I: 215
Potch [gem]
  Opal O: 788
Potemkin [film]
  Motion picture *picture on* M: 847; (Filmmaking in
    Europe) M: 866
Potemkin Steps [stairway]
  Odessa O: 674
Potential energy [physics]
  Energy E: 273; (Potential energy of a raised
    object) E: 275 *with diagram*
Potential hydrogen *See* pH *in this index*
Potentiometer [instrument] P: 714
Pothier, Aram J. [American political leader]
  Rhode Island (table) R: 311
Potion
  Witchcraft (Witchcraft as sorcery) W: 371
Potiphar [Biblical figure]
  Joseph (A slave in Egypt) J: 167

Potlatch [custom]
  Haida Indians H: 7
  Indian, American (Before European contact)
    I: 162 *with picture*
  Kwakiutl Indians K: 397
  Totem T: 347
Potline [device]
  Aluminum (Smelting the alumina) A: 393
Potomac Heritage National Scenic Trail
  National Park System (table: National parkways
    and other national parklands) N: 56
Potomac River [U.S.] P: 714 *with picture*
  Maryland (Rivers and lakes) M: 252
  Virginia (Rivers and lakes) V: 412 *with map*
  Washington, D.C. (The city) W: 78
Potowmak Guardian and Berkeley Advertiser
  [newspaper]
  West Virginia (Communication) W: 224
Potowski, Ernestine [American social reformer]
  See Rose, Ernestine Potowski *in this index*
Potsdam [Germany] P: 715
Potsdam Conference [1945] P: 715
  Cold War (The alliance breaks up) Ci: 763
  Germany (Occupied Germany) G: 169
  World War II (Peace with Germany) W: 498
Potsdam Declaration [1945]
  Potsdam Conference P: 715
Potsherd [artifact]
  Archaeology (Recording and preserving
    evidence) A: 597 *with picture*
Pott, Johann Heinrich [Prussian chemist]
  Aluminum (History) A: 397
Potted plant
  Gardening (Container gardens) G: 31; (Cultivating
    an indoor garden) G: 36 *with pictures*;
    (Repotting) G: 37 *with pictures*
Potter [career]
  Pottery P: 715
Potter, Beatrix [British author] P: 715
  Literature for children *picture on* L: 362; (Picture
    books) L: 365
Potter, Harry [literary figure] P: 715
  Fairy (Fairies in literature) F: 11
  Literature for children *picture on* L: 377; (Fantasy
    and science fiction) L: 361; (The early 2000's)
    L: 366
  Motion picture (Motion pictures today) M: 872-
    873
  Rowling, J. K. R: 494
Potter, Mary [wife of]
  Longfellow, Henry Wadsworth (Professor and
    family man) L: 449
Potter's field [cemetery] P: 715
Potter's wheel [machine]
  Handicraft *picture on* H: 45
  Pottery *pictures on* P: 719; (Shaping the clay)
    P: 716-717
Pottery P: 715 *with pictures*
  See also Ceramics; Porcelain *in this index; and the
    list of Related articles in the* Pottery *article*
  Anasazi (Way of life) A: 448a-448b
  Antique (Ceramic antiques) A: 558
  Ceramics (History) C: 360
  China (The arts) C: 487 *with pictures*
  Inca (Arts and architecture) I: 98 *with picture*
  Indian, American *pictures on* I: 167, I: 172, I: 173,
    I: 175, I: 176; (Pottery) I: 145 *with pictures*
  Islamic art *picture on* I: 468; (Pottery) I: 470
  Majolica M: 93
  Painting (Greek painting) P: 42 *with picture*
  Prehistoric people (The end of prehistoric times)
    P: 753
  Pueblo Indians *picture on* P: 871
  Stoneware So: 912
  Tang dynasty *picture on* T: 26
Pottinger, Charlotte [mother of]
  Thompson, Sir John Sparrow David (Early life)
    T: 263
Potto [animal] P: 719 *with picture*
Pouched mammal *See* Marsupial *in this index*
Pouke [literary figure]
  Puck P: 870
Poulenc, Francis [French composer] P: 720
Poulsen, Valdemar [Danish engineer]
  Tape recorder (History) T: 38
Poult [bird]
  Turkey T: 513
Poulter's Measure [poetry]
  Limerick L: 307
Poultry P: 720 *with picture*
  See also the list of Related articles in the Poultry
    article
  Bird (As a source of food and raw materials)
    B: 330 *with picture*
  Farm and farming (Specialized livestock farms)
    F: 31-32 *with picture*
  Food (Food from animals) F: 330

Food, Frozen (Freezing food at home) F: 338-339
Livestock L: 396 *with picture*
Vegetarianism V: 294
Poultry feed
Poultry (Raising poultry) P: 720-721
Pound [money] P: 721 *with pictures*
Money (History of the pound) M: 709
Pound [unit of measure] P: 721
Apothecaries' weight A: 567
Avoirdupois A: 994
Mass M: 268
Pound, Ezra [American poet] P: 721
American literature (Modernist poetry) A: 421
Eliot, T. S. (His life) E: 237
Lost Generation L: 472
Pound, Roscoe [American jurist] P: 722
Pound cake
Cake C: 19
Pound sterling [money]
Money (History of the pound) M: 709
Pound P: 721
Poundage [English history]
Tariff (The first tariffs) T: 44
Poundmaker [American Indian chief] P: 722 *with portrait*
Poupée [dolls]
Doll (Porcelain dolls) D: 290
Poussin, Nicolas [French painter] P: 722 *with picture*
Classicism (The qualities of Classicism) Ci: 653
Painting (Classicism) P: 61 *with picture*; (Rococo painting) P: 65; (Neoclassicism) P: 66
Poussinists [art history]
Painting (Rococo painting) P: 65
Poutrincourt, Jean de Biencourt de [French colonist] P: 722
Du Gua, Pierre, Sieur de Monts D: 379
Poverty P: 723 *with pictures*
See also the list of Related articles in the Poverty article
Brazil (City life) B: 573
City (The people) Ci: 589; (Economic problems) Ci: 592
Crime (Social conditions and crime) Ci: 1138-1139
Developing country D: 173
Economics (Distribution of income) E: 63
Ford Foundation (Programs) F: 382
Gay Nineties (The despair of poverty) G: 72
Ghetto G: 181
Great Society G: 349
Hispanic Americans H: 244; (Employment) H: 258
Homelessness (Causes and conditions) H: 302
Industrial Revolution (The working class) I: 251
Juvenile delinquency (What causes delinquency?) J: 206
Liberation theology L: 228
Mexico *picture on* M: 456
United States, History of the (The rich and the poor) U: 182 *with picture*; (The United States in the Great Depression) U: 192; (Poverty and discrimination) U: 195
Welfare W: 190
Women's movement (In developing nations) W: 387
World, History of the (A turbulent and interdependent world) W: 448a-448b
Poverty Is No Crime [play by Ostrovsky]
Russian literature (Early realism) R: 562
Poverty level See Poverty line *in this index*
Poverty line [income]
Poverty (Poverty standards) P: 723
Welfare (Welfare in the United States) W: 190
Poverty Point mound [Louisiana]
Mound builders (Archaic Period) M: 881
Poverty Point National Monument [Louisiana]
National Park System (table: National monuments) N: 51
Poverty rate [economics]
Economics (Distribution of income) E: 63
Poverty (Poverty rates) P: 723
POW See Prisoner of war *in this index*
Powder horn [ammunition] P: 725
Powder Keg of Europe [nickname]
Balkans B: 41
World War I (The rise of nationalism) W: 452-453
Powder metallurgy [industrial process] P: 725
Aluminum (Other shaping processes) A: 396
Powderly, Terence V. [American labor leader]
Knights of Labor K: 352
Labor movement (The first nationwide labor organizations) L: 9-10
Powderpuff Chinese crested [dog]
Chinese crested C: 509
Powdery mildew [fungus]
Mildew M: 541
Powell, Adam Clayton, Jr. [American political

leader] P: 725 *with portrait*
Powell, Anthony [British author] P: 726
English literature (Literature after World War II) E: 322-323
Powell, Cecil Frank [British physicist]
Meson M: 421
Nobel Prizes (Physics: 1950) N: 441
Powell, Clifford R. [American political leader]
New Jersey (table) N: 249
Powell, Colin Luther [American government official] P: 726 *with portrait*
African Americans *picture on* A: 136r
Bush, George Walker (table) B: 722h
Powell, James R. [American engineer]
Magnetic levitation train (Electrodynamic maglev) M: 55
Powell, John Wesley [American geologist] P: 726
Grand Canyon (History) G: 307
Powell, Lake See Lake Powell *in this index*
Powell, Lewis Franklin, Jr. [American jurist] P: 726
Bakke case B: 33
Nixon, Richard Milhous (The national scene) N: 433-434
Powell, Mary [wife of]
Milton, John (Middle years) M: 557
Powell, Wesley [American political leader]
New Hampshire (table) N: 223
Powell, William H. [American painter]
De Soto, Hernando *picture on* D: 161
Powell v. Alabama [U.S. history]
Scottsboro case S: 223
Power [physics] P: 726 *with diagrams*
Energy (Energy and power) E: 275
Horsepower H: 367
Jupiter (Temperature) J: 198
Light (Energy and brightness) L: 290 *with diagram*
Metric system (Mechanics) M: 437-440
Power plant P: 728
Star (Magnitude and luminosity) So: 842-843
Transmission T: 375
Water power W: 139
Work W: 405
Power [social sciences] P: 727
Balance of power B: 36
War (Struggles over power) W: 23
Power [arithmetic] P: 728
Binary number (Places) B: 307
Binomial theorem B: 309
Logarithms (Raising a number to a power) L: 424
Number (The decimal system) N: 605
Scientific notation S: 207
Power, Henry [English chemist]
Gas [physics] (Gas laws) G: 48
Power and the Glory, The [book by Greene]
English literature (Fiction between the wars) E: 322
Power and the Glory, The [film]
Tracy, Spencer T: 362
Power-assisted brake
Brake (Hydraulic brakes) B: 560-562
Power Authority of the State of New York
Saint Lawrence Seaway (The hydroelectric power project) S: 44
Power brake
Automobile (The brake system) A: 950
Power Corporation of Canada
Martin, Paul (College years and early career) M: 234b-234c
Power district
Electric power (In the United States) E: 186
Power drill [tool]
Drill D: 348
Power elite [sociology]
Power (Systems of power) P: 727-728
Power failure See Blackout *in this index*
Power function [mathematics]
Calculus (Derivatives) C: 23
Power grid
Automobile (Other infrastructure) A: 960
Electric power (Transmitting and distributing electric power) E: 184
Power loom [machine]
Cartwright, Edmund C: 268
Weaving (Kinds of looms) W: 174
Wool *picture on* W: 401
Power of attorney [law] P: 728
See also Durable power of attorney *in this index*
Power outage See Blackout *in this index*
Power pack
Railroad, Model (Locomotives) R: 120
Power plant P: 728
Automobile (Power systems) A: 947
Coal (Electric power production) Ci: 718-719
Edison, Thomas Alva (Electric utilities and manufacturing) E: 79
Electric power E: 182 *with pictures*

Solar energy *picture on* So: 579
Power play
Hockey (Offensive play) H: 277
Power pool [network]
Electric power (Providing reliable service) E: 185
Power saw [tool]
Fire department (Rescue trucks) F: 126 *with picture*
Saw (Power saws) S: 167 *with pictures*
Power series [mathematics]
Series S: 316b
Power station
Power plant P: 728
Power steering
Automobile (The steering system) A: 949-950 *with diagram*
Power stroke
Automobile (The engine cycle) A: 953
Power structure [sociology]
Power (Systems of power) P: 727-728
Power take-off
Tractor (Parts of a tractor) T: 360
Power tool
Tool (History of tools) T: 330
Woodworking (Steps in woodworking) W: 396-397 *with pictures*
Power train [device]
Automobile *diagrams on* A: 948, A: 949; (Automobile systems) A: 947
Transmission T: 375
Power tumbling [sport]
Gymnastics (Trampoline and tumbling) G: 449
Powerade Drag Racing Championship
Automobile racing (Drag racing) A: 978
Powered balloon
Balloon B: 57
Powerlifting [sport]
Weightlifting W: 183
Powers, Abigail [wife of Millard Fillmore] See Fillmore, Abigail Powers *in this index*
Powers, Francis Gary [American pilot]
Cold War (The U-2 incident) Ci: 767
Powers, Hiram [American sculptor] P: 728
Powers, Llewellyn [American political leader]
Maine (table) M: 87
Powers, Ridgley C. [American political leader]
Mississippi (table) M: 640
Powhatan [American Indian chief] P: 728
Colonial life in America (Jamestown) Ci: 789
Indian wars (Jamestown) I: 190
Jamestown J: 28
Pocahontas P: 588
Powhatan Confederacy [American Indians]
Powhatan P: 728
Powhatan Indians P: 728
Richmond (History) R: 333
Powhatan Indians P: 728
Powwow [meeting]
Indian, American *picture on* I: 136a; (Bands) I: 143
North Dakota *picture on* N: 505
Pox [disease] See Smallpox *in this index*
Poynter, Sir Edward [British artist]
Painting (Later neoclassicism) P: 67-68
Poynter, William A. [American political leader]
Nebraska (table) N: 110
Poznań [Poland] P: 728
Pozzuolana [building material]
Cement and concrete (History) C: 345
PPD [disorder] See Postpartum depression *in this index*
PPFA [organization] See Planned Parenthood Federation of America *in this index*
PPI radar
Radar (The display) R: 71
PPO [health care] See Preferred provider organization *in this index*
PQ [organization] See Parti Québécois *in this index*
PR [abbreviation] See Public relations *in this index*
Pr [symbol]
Praseodymium P: 733
Prachanda [Nepalese political leader]
Nepal (History) N: 126-127
Practical nurse
Hospital (The professional services staff) H: 371
Prader-Willi syndrome [disorder]
Obesity (Causes of obesity) O: 642a
Prado [museum]
Madrid (Education and cultural life) M: 39
Spain (Museums and libraries) So: 737
Prado, Diego de [Spanish explorer]
Torres, Luis Vaez de T: 342
Prado, Manuel [Peruvian political leader]
Peru (The rise of APRA) P: 316
Praetor [Ancient Rome] P: 729
Law (Ancient Roman law) L: 133
Praetorian Guard [Roman Empire] P: 729

Augustus (Emperor of Rome) A: 889
Rome, Ancient *picture on* R: 445; (The army) R: 438
Pragmatic sanction [European history] P: 729
Austria (Wars in the 1700's and 1800's) A: 937-938
Maria Theresa M: 199
Pragmatism [philosophy] P: 729
Dewey, John D: 177
James, William J: 27
Peirce, Charles Sanders P: 230
Philosophy (Epistemology) P: 384; (Philosophy in the 1900's) P: 390
Prague [Czech Republic] P: 729 *with picture*
Czech Republic Ci: 1209 *with picture*
Prague, Treaty of [1866]
Seven Weeks' War S: 325
Prague Castle [Czechoslovakia]
Prague (The city) P: 730
Prague Spring [Czech history]
Communism (In Eastern Europe) Ci: 896
Czech Republic (The 1960's) Ci: 1214
Czechoslovakia (The 1960's) Ci: 1216
Prague (History) P: 730
Praha [Czech Republic] *See* Prague *in this index*
Prahlad [legendary figure]
Holi H: 290
Praia [Cape Verde]
Cape Verde C: 189 *with map*
Prairie [geography] P: 730 *with picture and map*
Flower (Flowers of prairies and dry plains) F: 286 *with pictures*
Grassland G: 329 *with picture*
Plant (Grasslands) P: 527
Prairie, The [book by Cooper]
Cooper, James Fenimore Ci: 1035
Prairie buttercup [plant]
Flower *picture on* F: 287
Prairie-chicken [bird] P: 731
Bird (Birds of grasslands) B: 336 *with picture*
Prairie coneflower [plant]
Flower *picture on* F: 287
Prairie cordgrass [plant]
Plant *picture on* P: 526
Prairie crocus [plant] *See* Eastern pasqueflower *in this index*
Prairie dog [animal] P: 732 *with pictures*
Animal *picture on* A: 477
Monkeypox (Outbreaks) M: 730
Prairie falcon [bird]
Falcon (Other North American falcons) F: 14
Prairie Hills
South Dakota (Land regions) So: 674
"Prairie Home Companion, A" [radio show]
Keillor, Garrison K: 254
Prairie pothole [wetland]
Conservation (Canada) Ci: 988
Prairie Provinces [region, Canada] P: 733
Canada (The Prairies) C: 104
Prairie rose [plant]
Flower *picture on* F: 287
Prairie Scene: Mirage [painting by Miller]
United States, History of the *picture on* U: 167
Prairie schooner [vehicle]
Pioneer life in America (The wagon train) P: 486
Wagon W: 5
Prairie State [nickname]
Illinois I: 52
Prairie States Forestry Project [U.S. history]
Windbreak W: 333
Prairie style [architecture]
Architecture *picture on* A: 631; (Frank Lloyd Wright) A: 629
Chicago (Architecture) C: 428
House *picture on* H: 381
United States *picture on* U: 117
Wright, Frank Lloyd (Early career) W: 507
Prairie sunflower [plant]
Evolution (Direct observation of evolution) E: 431-432
Prairie View A&M University
Texas A&M University T: 210
Prairie wolf
Coyote Ci: 1114 *with picture*
"Prairies, The" [poem by Bryant]
Bryant, William Cullen (His early works) B: 655-656
Praise of Folly [book by Erasmus]
Humanism (The spread of humanism) H: 431
Praise of Folly, The [book by Erasmus]
Erasmus, Desiderius E: 349
Renaissance (Desiderius Erasmus and Saint Thomas More) R: 238
Prajna [religion]
Yoga Y: 566
Prakrti [religion]

Yoga Y: 566
Prall, Horace G. [American political leader]
New Jersey (table) N: 249
Pram [boat]
Sailing S: 23
Prambanan [temples, Indonesia]
Indonesia (The arts) I: 232-233
Pramoedya Ananta Toer [Indonesian author]
Indonesia (The arts) I: 232-233
Prang, Louis [American artist]
Valentine's Day *picture on* V: 262
Praseodymium [element] P: 733
Praslin [island]
Seychelles S: 339
Prasutagus [king of the Iceni]
Boudicca B: 515
Prater [park, Vienna]
Vienna (The city) V: 361-362
Pratt, E. J. [Canadian poet] P: 733
Pratt, Enoch [American businessman]
Maryland (Libraries) M: 244
Pratt, Thomas G. [American political leader]
Maryland (table) M: 255
Pratt, William Henry [birth name of]
Karloff, Boris K: 246
Pratt and Whitney Company
Aviation (Aviation progress) A: 988-989
Pravda [newspaper]
Lenin, V. I. (Outcast) L: 193
Prawn [sea animal]
Crustacean *picture on* Ci: 1164
Shrimp S: 439
Praxiteles [Greek sculptor] P: 733 *with picture*
Classicism (Greece) Ci: 653
Prayer [religion] P: 734
Africa *picture on* A: 106
Faith healing F: 12
Islam (The Five Pillars of Islam) I: 463
Lord's Prayer L: 454
Meditation M: 380
Religion (Religious rituals) R: 217
School prayer S: 185
Prayer for Owen Meany, A [book by Irving]
Irving, John I: 459
Prayer rug
Rugs and carpets (Oriental rugs) R: 516-517
Prayer wheel [religion]
Meditation M: 380
Praying Hands [painting by Dürer]
Dürer, Albrecht D: 388
Praying mantis [insect] P: 734
Animal *picture on* A: 495
Eye *picture on* E: 468
Insect *picture on* I: 280
Pre-...
Headings beginning Pre- are alphabetized as single words: Pre-emption *appears after* Preeclampsia
Preacher bird *See* Red-eyed vireo *in this index*
Preachers, Order of *See* Dominicans *in this index*
Preaching Friars *See* Dominicans *in this index*
Preadolescence [psychology] *See* Preteen-age years *in this index*
Preakness Stakes
Maryland (Visitor's guide) M: 248 *with picture*
Preamble [document]
Constitution of the United States (Preamble) Ci: 1004
Preamplifier [electronics]
Microphone (Condenser microphones) M: 517
Precambrian Time [geology]
Earth *pictures on* E: 28; (Life on Earth) E: 27; (table) E: 27
Precast concrete
Cement and concrete (Precast concrete) C: 343
Precaution [book by Cooper]
Cooper, James Fenimore Ci: 1035
"Precaution" [poem by Frost]
Frost, Robert (His poems) F: 543
Precedent [law]
Law (Common law systems) L: 132
Preceptor training
Dental hygiene (Education) D: 143
Preceptorial system [education]
Princeton University (Educational program) P: 795
Wilson, Woodrow (University president) W: 321
Precession [physics]
Ballistics (Exterior ballistics) B: 56
Gravitation (Newton's law of gravitation) G: 331
Gyroscope (Gyroscopic properties) G: 453-454 *with diagram*
Precession of the equinoxes [astronomy]
Climate (Changes in the earth's orbit) Ci: 677 *with diagram*
Equinox E: 348
Hipparchus H: 239

North Star N: 518
Prechamber engine
Diesel engine (How a diesel engine works) D: 199
Precinct [voting]
Election (Election procedures) E: 158
Voting (Voting districts) V: 449
Precinct captain [office]
Political party (Local organizations) P: 635
Precious coral
Coral (Other kinds of corals) Ci: 1048a
Precious stone *See* Gem *in this index*
Precipitation [weather]
See also Rain *in this index*
Climate (Kinds of climates) Ci: 676a
Cloud seeding C: 711
Hail H: 8 *with pictures*
Ocean (Composition) O: 654
Rain gauge R: 127
Sleet S: 508
Snow S: 539
Water (Precipitation) W: 120 *with diagram*
Weather (table: Weather terms) W: 157; (Synoptic-scale systems) W: 159-160
Precipitator [device]
Air cleaner (Types of air cleaners) A: 175
Aluminum (How aluminum is produced) A: 393 *with diagram*
Mining (Pumping methods) M: 577
Precision [measurement]
Weights and measures (Conversion factors) W: 184-185
Precision bombing
World War II (The air war) W: 482
Precision casting [manufacturing]
Cast and casting (Other types of casting) C: 278 *with pictures*
Precisionism [art]
Painting (Precisionism) P: 82 *with picture*
Preclinical training
Medicine (A career as a doctor) M: 370
Pre-Clovis culture
Paleo-Indians P: 102
Precocial bird
Bird (Caring for the young) B: 359
Precognition [telepathy]
Clairvoyance Ci: 636
Extrasensory perception (What parapsychologists study) E: 457
Pre-Columbian jewelry
Jewelry (Pre-Columbian jewelry) J: 118
Precursor cell [biology]
Blood (Formation of new blood components) B: 411
Stem cell So: 889
Predation [biology]
Animal (How animals protect themselves) A: 493 *with picture*
Balance of nature (Predators) B: 35 *with picture*; (Upsetting the balance) B: 36
Insect (Beneficial insects) I: 284 *with picture*
Life (The biological environment) L: 276
Mammal (Group life) M: 125; (Methods of attack and defense) M: 126
Protective coloration P: 831
Predator [zoology] *See* Predation *in this index*
Predators, Nashville [team]
Hockey (table: National Hockey League) H: 281
Predestination [religion] P: 734
Calvin, John (Calvinism) C: 71
Christianity (The Reformed tradition) C: 525
Edwards, Jonathan E: 114
Fatalism F: 54
Presbyterians (Teaching and worship) P: 756a
Predicate [grammar]
Sentence (Subject and predicate) S: 303
Predicate adjective [grammar]
Adjective (The position of adjectives) A: 57
Prednisone [drug]
Transplant (Preventing rejection) T: 380-381
Preeclampsia [disorder] P: 734
Pregnancy (Complications) P: 735
Pre-emption [U.S. history] P: 734a
Tyler, John (Tyler's accomplishments) T: 534
Pre-emption Act [1841]
Western frontier life in America (Newcomers) W: 234
Preen gland [bird]
Bird (Feather care) B: 354
Preening [bird]
Bird (Feather care) B: 354
Preexisting condition
Insurance (Greater regulation) I: 316
Prefabrication [construction]
Arctic (Modernization) A: 640
Building construction (Prefabricated construction) B: 684 *with picture*
House (Building materials) H: 380

Shelter (Building methods and materials) S: 392-393

Preface
Book (Inside a book) B: 464-465

Prefaces to Shakespeare [book by Granville-Barker]
Granville-Barker, Harley G: 318

Prefecture [political unit]
Japan (Local government) J: 35
Rome, Ancient map on R: 447

Preferential tariff
Tariff T: 43

Preferred provider organization
Insurance (Managed care plans) I: 312
Managed care plans (In the United States) M: 131
Medicine (The United States) M: 367-368

Preferred stock [economics]
Investment (Stocks) I: 368
Stock (Kinds of stock) So: 903

Prefix [language]
Metric system (Metric prefixes) M: 439
Spelling (Spelling rules) So: 776-777

Pre-Flight School [Florida]
Pensacola Naval Air Station P: 272

Prefrontal cortex [anatomy]
Brain (Regulating body processes) B: 554; (Making decisions) B: 555-556

Prefrontal lobotomy [surgery]
Brain (Making decisions) B: 555-556

Pregl, Fritz [Austrian chemist]
Nobel Prizes (Chemistry: 1923) N: 443

Pregnancy P: 734a
See also Reproduction, Human *in this index*
Abortion A: 14
Adolescent (Pregnancy) A: 63
AIDS (How HIV is transmitted) A: 164b; (Prevention) A: 165
Amniocentesis A: 438
Baby (The expectant mother) B: 5
Birth control B: 378
Birth defect B: 380
Cerebral palsy (Causes) C: 361
Chlamydia C: 516
DES D: 153
Diabetes (Symptoms) D: 179
Disease (Environmental and occupational diseases) D: 230
Fetal alcohol syndrome F: 80
Growth (Early development) G: 404-405
Heart (Birth defects) H: 140
Infertility (Treatment) I: 265
Lactation L: 25
Listeria L: 349
Miscarriage M: 617
Nutrition (Eat a balanced diet) N: 626-628
Obstetrics and gynecology O: 646
Pelvic inflammatory disease P: 233
Placenta P: 505
Preeclampsia P: 734
Premature birth P: 755
Progesterone P: 811
Reproduction, Human R: 244; (Fertilization) R: 246; (The first days of pregnancy) R: 246 with pictures
Rubella R: 506
Smoking (Why smoking is dangerous) S: 520
Syphilis So: 1069
Thalidomide T: 229
Toxoplasmosis T: 353
Ultrasound (Medical uses) U: 16 with picture

Preheat fluorescent lamp
Fluorescent lamp F: 305 with diagram

Prehensile tail
Mammal (In trees) M: 122
Primate (Anthropoids) P: 778

Prehistoric animal P: 736 with pictures
See also the list of Related articles in the Prehistoric animal *article*
Evolution (The fossil record) E: 430
Extinction E: 457
Fossil F: 422 with pictures

Prehistoric art
See also Cave painting in this index
Painting (Prehistoric painting) P: 40
Petrified Forest National Park picture on P: 329
Prehistoric people picture on P: 754a; (The appearance of art) P: 752 with picture
Sculpture (Prehistoric sculpture) S: 233 with pictures

Prehistoric people P: 743 with pictures and map
Archaeology A: 594
Arrowhead A: 744 with pictures
Cave dwellers C: 321
Civilization (Development) Ci: 635
Clothing (Handmade clothing) Ci: 691
England (History) E: 303
Europe (Prehistoric times) E: 406

Evolution (Contributions from other scientific fields) E: 433
Food (Prehistoric times) F: 336
Fossil (Understanding ancient plants and animals) F: 423
Hairdressing (Hairdressing through the ages) H: 11
Human being (Early human beings) H: 415
Invention (Prehistoric times) I: 358
Kenya (Early days) K: 303
Laetoli fossil site L: 26
Lascaux Cave L: 80
Leakey, Louis Seymour Bazett L: 161
Leakey, Mary Douglas L: 161
Leakey, Meave Gillian L: 161
Leakey, Richard Erskine Frere L: 161
Medicine (History) M: 371
Neandertals N: 93
Olduvai Gorge O: 742
Paint (The history of paint) P: 26
Painting (Prehistoric painting) P: 40
Pleistocene Epoch P: 572
Races, Human R: 52
Religion (The origin of religion) R: 218 with picture
Sculpture S: 228
Stone Age S: 909
Tool (History of tools) T: 330
Transportation (Prehistoric times) T: 385
Weapon (Prehistoric weapons) W: 154a
World, History of the W: 420

Prehistory
Prehistoric people P: 743

Prehypertension [disorder]
Blood pressure B: 416
Hypertension H: 476

Preignition [engine]
Gasoline (Engine requirements) G: 61

Preinvasive neoplasia [disorder]
Cervical cancer C: 364

Prejudice P: 754b
Ethnocentrism E: 373
Hate crime H: 85
Latin America (Attitudes toward race) L: 94
Races, Human (Race and discrimination) R: 59
Racism R: 62
Stereotyping So: 893

Prejudices [essays by Mencken]
American literature (Satirists) A: 422
Mencken, H. L. M: 398

Prekindergarten program See Preschool in this index

Preliminary hearing [law]
Law enforcement (Trial) L: 141

Preliminary injunction [law] See Temporary injunction in this index

Preliminary SAT/National Merit Scholarship Qualifying Test
College entrance examination (In the United States) Ci: 775
Scholarship (Merit scholarships) S: 178

Preliterary Latin
Latin language (Development) L: 115

Prelog, Vladimir [Swiss chemist]
Nobel Prizes (Chemistry: 1975) N: 444

Prelude [music]
Classical music (Free form) Ci: 645
Overture O: 882

Prelude, The [poem by Wordsworth]
Wordsworth, William W: 404; (Later career) W: 404

Prelude to "The Afternoon of a Faun" [music by Debussy]
Debussy, Claude D: 66

Prem Tinsulanonda [Thai political leader]
Thailand (Democracy gains strength) T: 227

Premadasa, Ranasinghe [Sri Lankan political leader]
Sri Lanka (History) So: 819

Premature birth P: 755
Baby (The developing baby) B: 4-5
Cerebral palsy (Causes) C: 361; (Prevention) C: 362
Eye (Diseases of the retina) E: 467
Hospital picture on H: 373
Incubator (Incubators for babies) I: 106
Multiple birth (Complications of multiple birth) M: 920
Neonatology N: 124
Pregnancy (Premature birth) P: 735
Respiratory distress syndrome R: 262

Premedical education
Medicine (A career as a doctor) M: 370

Premeditation [law]
Murder M: 930

Premenstrual syndrome [physiology] P: 755
Menstruation (Effects of menstruation) M: 404

Premier [office]
See also Prime minister in this index
Address, Forms of (Officials of the Commonwealth of Nations) A: 53
Australia (State government) A: 895
Canada, Government of (The three territories) C: 136

Premier Mine [South Africa]
Diamond (Famous diamonds) D: 182

Premillennialism [religion]
Millennium M: 553

Premise
Deductive method D: 81
Logic L: 425
Philosophy (Logic) P: 384

Premium [economics]
Insurance I: 309; (How life insurance premiums are dtermined) I: 310
Investment (table) I: 366

Premium channel
Television (Cable and satellite systems) T: 115

Premium score [cards]
Bridge (Scoring) B: 605

Premolar [anatomy]
Dog (Body structure) D: 263-265
Teeth (Permanent teeth) T: 79-80 with pictures

Premutation carrier [genetics]
Fragile X syndrome F: 451

Přemyslid dynasty [Bohemian history]
Czech Republic (The rise of Bohemia) Ci: 1213

Prenatal care
Baby (The expectant mother) B: 5-6
Pregnancy (Prenatal care) P: 734b

Prendergast, Maurice Brazil [American painter] P: 755 with picture
Ashcan School A: 768

Preoperational period [pyschology]
Child (The stages of childhood) C: 448
Piaget, Jean P: 445

Preparation plant
Coal (Cleaning coal) Ci: 726

Preparator [career]
Museum (Exhibition and care of materials) M: 939

Preparatory school [education]
School (High schools) S: 181

Prepared piano [musical instrument]
Cage, John C: 14
Classical music (Experimental music) Ci: 650

Preposition [grammar] P: 756
Grammar G: 303

Prepositional phrase [grammar]
Preposition P: 756

Preproduction
Motion picture (Preproduction) M: 849

Prepuce [anatomy]
Circumcision Ci: 561
Penis P: 241

Pre-Raphaelite Brotherhood [art] P: 756 with picture
Burne-Jones, Sir Edward B: 708
Millais, Sir John Everett M: 552
Painting (The Pre-Raphaelite Brotherhood) P: 71 with picture
Rossetti, Dante Gabriel R: 482

Prerecorded sound
Radio (From sound waves to electric waves) R: 86

Preromanticism
French literature (The Preromantics) F: 521
Russian literature (Preromanticism) R: 560

Presa Canario [dog] See Dogo Canario in this index

Présages, Les [ballet]
Massine, Léonide M: 296

Presbycusis [disorder]
Deafness (Aging) D: 57
Ear (Diseases) E: 12

Presbyopia [disorder]
Eye (Farsightedness) E: 464
Glasses (Prescription glasses) G: 224-225

Presbyter [religion]
Presbyterians P: 756a

Presbytère [museum]
New Orleans (Downtown New Orleans) N: 278

Presbyterian Church (U.S.A.) [religious group] P: 756

Presbyterian Ministers' Fund
Insurance (Insurance in the United States) I: 315

Presbyterians [religious group] P: 756a
Calvin, John (Calvinism) C: 71
Covenanters Ci: 1106
Presbyterian Church (U.S.A.) P: 756
Protestantism (The conservative reform movements) P: 834
Scotland (Religion) S: 215

Presbytery [religion]
Presbyterian Church (U.S.A.) P: 756
Presbyterians P: 756a

Preschool [education] **P:** 756a *with picture*
 Early childhood education (Formal education
  programs) **E:** 15
 Education (Early childhood education) **E:** 91
 Montessori method **M:** 764a
 School (Kinds of schools) **S:** 181
Preschooler
 Child (The preschool years) **C:** 449
Prescott, Benjamin F. [American political leader]
 New Hampshire (table) **N:** 223
Prescott, Edward C. [American economist]
 Nobel Prizes (Economics: 2004) **N:** 449
Prescott, Samuel [American patriot] **P:** 757
 Dawes, William **D:** 51
 Revere, Paul (Paul Revere's ride) **R:** 268
 Revolution, American (Lexington and Concord)
  R: 274-275
Prescott, William [American military leader] **P:** 757
 Bunker Hill, Battle of **B:** 700
Prescribed fire
 Conservation (Conservation of grazing lands)
  Ci: 981 *with picture*; (Forest conservation)
  Ci: 981
 Fire (How fires behave) **F:** 121
 Forestry (Fire and forests) **F:** 407
Prescription [European history]
 Villein **V:** 385
Prescription [medicine]
 Drug (Prescription drugs) **D:** 356
 Drug abuse (Prescription drugs) **D:** 361
 Herbal medicine **H:** 196
 Pharmacy (Duties of a pharmacist) **P:** 354
 Pure food and drug laws (Drugs and devices)
  P: 908
 ℞ **R:** 46
Prescription drug coverage
 Insurance (Medicare) **I:** 314
Presence and Immortality [book by Marcel]
 Marcel, Gabriel **M:** 193
Presenilin [protein]
 Alzheimer's disease (Causes) **A:** 399
Present at the Creation [book by Acheson]
 Acheson, Dean Gooderham **A:** 26
Present participle [grammar]
 Participle **P:** 184
Present perfect tense [grammar]
 Tense **T:** 168
Present tense [grammar]
 Tense **T:** 168
Presentation
 Sales (Presentation) **S:** 63
Presentation software [electronics] **P:** 757
 Computer (Graphics programs) **Ci:** 918-919
Presentation tool [electronics]
 Computer (Spreadsheet programs) **Ci:** 917-918
Presepio [Nativity]
 Christmas (In Italy) **C:** 531
Preservation, Food See Food preservation *in this
  index*
**Preservation and Perpetuation of Storytelling,
 National Association for the** [organization]
 Storytelling (The 1900's) **So:** 915
Preservation Hall
 Louisiana *picture on* **L:** 489
 New Orleans (The arts) **N:** 281
Preservative
 Food additive (Kinds of additives) **F:** 339
 Food preservation (Additives) **F:** 343
 Health food (Types of health foods) **H:** 129
Preserves See Jelly and jam *in this index*
Preset guidance
 Guided missile (Preset guidance) **G:** 426 *with
  diagram*
Preshrinking
 Wool (Making fabric) **W:** 401
Presidency [Yugoslav government]
 Serbia (Communist rule) **S:** 316
 Yugoslavia (Communist rule) **Y:** 576-577
President [ship]
 Decatur, Stephen **D:** 67
President [title] **P:** 757
 Address, Forms of (Officials of the
  Commonwealth of Nations) **A:** 53-54
 Foreign policy (The executive) **F:** 387
 Government *diagrams on* **G:** 287; (Presidential
  democracy) **G:** 285
 Parliamentary government (Officers) **P:** 175
 Universities and colleges (Administration) **U:** 208
President Benjamin Harrison Memorial Home
 Indianapolis (Cultural sites) **I:** 221-222 *with map*
President of the Senate [title]
 Congress of the United States (The Senate)
  Ci: 942
 Vice president of the United States **V:** 349;
  (President of the Senate) **V:** 352
**President of the Union of Soviet Socialist
 Republics** [office]

 Union of Soviet Socialist Republics (Gorbachev's
  reforms) **U:** 40
President of the United States P: 758 *with pictures*
 See also the list of Related articles in the President
  of the United States *article*
 Address, Forms of (Officials of the United States)
  A: 53
 Air Force One **A:** 196
 Alien and Sedition Acts **A:** 368
 Atchison, David Rice **A:** 853
 Checks and balances **C:** 391
 Congress of the United States (From bill to law)
  Ci: 945-946; (Handling presidential election
  results) **Ci:** 946; (History of Congress) **Ci:** 947
 Constitution of the United States (Article
  II) **Ci:** 1008; (Amendment 12) **Ci:** 1013;
  (Amendment 22) **Ci:** 1015
 Election campaign **E:** 159
 Electoral College **E:** 161
 Executive order **E:** 436
 First ladies of the United States **F:** 142
 Flag *picture on* **F:** 211
 Government (Presidential democracy) **G:** 285
 "Hail to the Chief" **H:** 8
 Political convention **P:** 628
 Political party (Organizing the government)
  P: 632
 Presidential libraries **P:** 771
 Presidential succession **P:** 771
 Republican Party **R:** 253
 Secret Service, United States **S:** 278
 State, Department of (Relationship with the
  president and Congress) **So:** 860
 Supreme Court of the United States (table)
  So: 1002
 Treaty (Negotiation) **T:** 409
 United States, Government of the (The
  presidency) **U:** 140; (Action by the President)
  U: 144; (Current issues in U.S. government)
  U: 146
 Veto **V:** 346
 Woodhull, Victoria Claflin **W:** 393
President pro tempore [title]
 Congress of the United States (The Senate)
  Ci: 942
 Senate (Organization of the U.S. Senate) **S:** 294
Presidente [official]
 Bullfighting (The order of the bullfight) **B:** 696
Presidential assistant [government official] **P:** 770
Presidential Citizens Medal
 Medals, decorations, and orders (Civilian awards)
  M: 355-357; (table) **M:** 357
Presidential dollar
 Money *picture on* **M:** 709; (Dollar coins) **M:** 714
Presidential election
 President of the United States (The presidential
  election) **P:** 762 *with diagram*
 Advertising (Political effects) **A:** 78 *with picture*
 Bush v. Gore **B:** 724
 Constitution of the United States (Amendment
  12) **Ci:** 1013
 Election Day **E:** 161
 Election of 2000 **E:** 161
 Political convention **P:** 628
 Primary election (The presidential primary)
  P: 777
Presidential government
 Government *diagrams on* **G:** 287; (Presidential
  democracy) **G:** 285
Presidential libraries P: 771
Presidential Medal of Freedom [award]
 Medals, decorations, and orders (Civilian awards)
  M: 355-358; (table) **M:** 357 *with picture*
Presidential press secretary
 Presidential assistant **P:** 770
Presidential Problems [book by Cleveland]
 Cleveland, Grover (Later years) **Ci:** 673
Presidential Range [mountains, New Hampshire]
 Mount Washington **M:** 890
 New Hampshire (Mountains) **N:** 220 *with map*
 White Mountains **W:** 291
Presidential signing statement
 President of the United States (Legislative leader)
  P: 765
Presidential succession [U.S.] **P:** 771
 Constitution of the United States (Amendment
  20) **Ci:** 1015; (Amendment 25) **Ci:** 1016
 President of the United States *diagram on* **P:** 762;
  (Other roads to the White House) **P:** 763
Presidential Succession Act [1947]
 Presidential succession **P:** 771
Presidential unit citation pennant [U.S.]
 Flag *picture on* **F:** 194
**President's Award for Distinguished Federal
 Civilian Service**
 Medals, decorations, and orders (table) **M:** 357
President's Cottage [building]

 White Sulphur Springs **W:** 292
**President's Council on Physical Fitness, Sports
 and Nutrition**
 Physical fitness (Developing physical fitness)
  P: 435
Presidents Cup [tournament]
 Golf (Tournaments) **G:** 264
Presidents' Day [holiday] **P:** 771
 Washington's Birthday **W:** 110
Presiding Bishopric
 Mormons (Church organization) **M:** 807
Presidio [fort, California]
 Monterey **M:** 764
Presidio of San Francisco [California]
 San Francisco (Other neighborhoods) **S:** 93-94
  with map
Presidium See Politburo *in this index*
Presidium of the Supreme Soviet
 Union of Soviet Socialist Republics (National
  government) **U:** 29
Presley, Elvis [American singer] **P:** 772 *with portrait*
 Graceland **G:** 296
 Memphis (The city) **M:** 394
 Mississippi (Places to visit) **M:** 632 *with picture*
 Rock music (Elvis Presley) **R:** 376 *with picture*;
  (Rock 'n' roll gains popularity) **R:** 377
 Tennessee (Places to visit) **T:** 144 *with picture*
 United States *picture on* **U:** 118
Presley, Lisa Marie [American singer]
 Jackson, Michael **J:** 16
Presley, Priscilla [wife of Elvis Presley]
 Graceland **G:** 296
Pre-Socratic philosophy P: 772
 See also the list of Related articles in the Pre-
  Socratic philosophy *article*
 Philosophy (Ancient philosophy) **P:** 386
Presorting [service]
 Postal services (Competition and privatization)
  P: 707
Press [journalism] See Journalism *in this index*
Press [printing] See Printing press *in this index*
Press [sports]
 Basketball (Defensive strategies) **B:** 147
Press, Freedom of the See Freedom of the press
  in this index
Press agent [career]
 Public relations (Methods) **P:** 863-864
Press brake
 Machine tool *picture on* **M:** 17; (Metal forming
  operations) **M:** 19
Press cake [food product]
 Chocolate (Cocoa) **C:** 518
Press pool [journalism]
 War correspondent **W:** 26
Press secretary, Presidential
 Presidential assistant **P:** 770
Pressburg [Slovakia] See Bratislava *in this index*
Pressburg, Treaty of [1805]
 Austerlitz, Battle of **A:** 892
Pressed glass
 Antique (Glass) **A:** 558
Pressing [industrial process]
 Ceramics (Making ceramics) **C:** 360
 Glass (Pressing) **G:** 215 *with diagram*
 Pottery (The mold method) **P:** 717
Pressure [physics] **P:** 773
 Aerodynamics (Principles of aerodynamics) **A:** 85
 Boiling point **B:** 439
 Gas (physics) (How gases behave) **G:** 48
 Metric system (Mechanics) **M:** 437-440
 Pascal's law **P:** 190
Pressure altimeter [instrument]
 Altimeter **A:** 389
Pressure cycled respirator [machine]
 Respirator **R:** 262
Pressure gauge [instrument]
 Gauge (Pressure gauges) **G:** 69
Pressure group [political science]
 Propaganda (Organizations) **P:** 824
Pressure hull
 Submarine **So:** 939
Pressure mine
 Mine warfare (Kinds of naval mines) **M:** 565
Pressure plate [mechanical device]
 Transmission (The clutch) **T:** 378
Pressure point [anatomy]
 Bleeding (First aid for bleeding) **B:** 399
Pressure sensor [device]
 Tsunami **T:** 476
Pressure sore
 Bedsore **B:** 199
Pressure wave [geology] See Compressional wave
  in this index
Pressurized cabin
 Airplane (Engineering improvements) **A:** 237-238
Pressurized Mating Adapter [device]
 International Space Station (History) **I:** 346b

Pressurized Mating Adapter [machine]
  International Space Station (History) I: 346b
Pressurized water reactor
  Nuclear energy (Steam production) N: 587 *with diagram*
Prester John [legendary figure] P: 773
Prestes, Júlio [Brazilian political leader]
  Brazil (Birth of the republic) B: 585
Prestes, Luis Carlos [Brazilian military leader]
  Brazil (Birth of the republic) B: 585
Prestidigitation [magic]
  Magician (Sleight of hand) M: 51
Prestissimo
  Music (table) M: 954
Presto
  Music (table) M: 954
Preston, James Patton [American political leader]
  Virginia (table) V: 417
Preston, Steven C. [American government official]
  Bush, George Walker (table) B: 722h
  Housing and Urban Development, Department of (table) H: 393
Preston, Thomas [British military leader]
  Adams, John (In New England) A: 35-36
  Boston Massacre B: 505
Preston, Thomas J., Jr. [American educator]
  Cleveland, Grover (Cleveland's family) Ci: 671
Preston, William B. [American government official]
  Taylor, Zachary (table) T: 60
Prestressed concrete
  Cement and concrete (Prestressed concrete) C: 343
Presumed consent
  Organ donation O: 852
  Transplant (Sources of donor organs) T: 380
Presumption [law]
  Evidence (Presumptions) E: 426
Presumption [logic]
  Fallacy F: 16
Presupposition [semantic relation]
  Semantics S: 291
Pretax fund
  Insurance (How private health insurance is provided) I: 311
Preteenage years
  Child (The school-age years) C: 449 *with picture*
Pretest [education]
  Differentiated instruction D: 200
Pretoria [South Africa] P: 773
Pretreatment of waste
  Water pollution (Pretreatment and reduction of wastes) W: 138
Pretrial intervention [law]
  Criminal justice system (Problems in the courts) Ci: 1144
"Pretty Girl Is Like a Melody, A" [song by Berlin]
  Berlin, Irving B: 266
Pretzel [food] P: 773
  Easter (Other foods) E: 44
  Food (Interesting facts about food) F: 329
Preus, Jacob A. O. [American political leader]
  Minnesota (table) M: 602
Preussen [ship]
  Ship (Sailing ships in the 1900's) S: 423
Prevailing westerly [weather] P: 773
  Atlantic Ocean (Winds) A: 866
  Cyclone Ci: 1204
  Pacific Ocean (Winds) P: 14
  Southern Ocean (Winds) So: 688a
  Wind (General circulation) W: 329 *with diagram*
Prevailing wind [weather]
  Wind (General circulation) W: 329 *with diagram*
Préval, René [Haitian political leader]
  Haiti (History) H: 15-17
Prevent defense [sports]
  Football (table) F: 356
Prevention of Cruelty to Animals, Society for the *See* Society for the Prevention of Cruelty to Animals *in this index*
Preventive detention
  Bail B: 31
Preventive medicine
  Disease (Preventing disease) D: 233
  Holistic medicine H: 292
  Medicine (Prevention) M: 364; (table) M: 369
  Occupational medicine O: 647
  Prophylaxis P: 827
  Public health (Providing preventive health care services) P: 856 *with picture*
Prévert, Jacques [French poet] P: 774
Preview
  Motion picture (Distribution) M: 860
Previn, André [American musician] P: 774
Prévost, Abbé [French author]
  French literature (The Enlightenment) F: 520-521
Prevost, Sir George [British general]
  War of 1812 (Lake Champlain) W: 32

Prez [nickname]
  Young, Lester Willis Y: 572
PRI [political party] *See* Partido Revolucionario Institucional *in this index*
Priam [legendary figure] P: 774
  Hector H: 164
  Iliad I: 51
  Paris P: 159
Pribilof, Gerasim Loginovich [Russian explorer]
  Pribilof Islands P: 774
Pribilof Islands [Bering Sea] P: 774
  Alaska (Coastline) A: 294
  Bering Sea controversy B: 258
  Seal (Hunting of seals) S: 267
Price [economics] P: 774
  See also Price control *in this index*
  Deflation D: 88
  Industry (Industrial organization) I: 260
  Inflation I: 266
  Marketing (Pricing) M: 214
  Supply and demand So: 996
  Tariff (Higher prices) T: 43
  Trade (The use of money) T: 362
Price, George C. [Belize political leader]
  Belize (History) B: 238
Price, Hugh Bernard [American social reformer] P: 775
Price, James H. [American political leader]
  Virginia (table) V: 417
Price, Leontyne [American singer] P: 775
Price, Nick [South African golfer]
  Golf (British Open) G: 264; (U.S. PGA Championship) G: 265
Price, Rodman M. [American political leader]
  New Jersey (table) N: 249
Price, Sterling [Confederate general]
  Missouri (table) M: 668; (The American Civil War) M: 671
Price Building [Quebec]
  Canada *picture on* C: 99
Price ceiling [economics]
  Agriculture (Economic controls) A: 152
  Price (Government intervention) P: 775
Price control [economics] P: 775
  Inflation (Wage and price controls) I: 268
  Nixon, Richard Milhous (The national scene) N: 433-434
  Price (Government intervention) P: 775
  Rationing R: 148
Price fixing [economics]
  Antitrust laws A: 560
  Consumer protection (The right to choose) Ci: 1018
  Fair-trade laws F: 8
Price floor [economics]
  Agriculture (Economic controls) A: 152
  Price (Government intervention) P: 775
Price freeze [economics]
  Price (Government intervention) P: 775
Price index [economics]
  Economic indicator E: 57
Price support [economics]
  Farm and farming (Federal farm programs) F: 44
  Milk (Marketing) M: 547
  Price (Government intervention) P: 775
  Wheat (Controlling wheat production) W: 274-275
Prickle [botany]
  Leaf (Protective leaves) L: 156
  Plant (How plants protect themselves) P: 540
Prickly-ash [tree] P: 775
Prickly heat [disorder] P: 776
Prickly pear [plant] P: 776
  Cactus (Kinds of cactuses) C: 11 *with picture*
  Flower (Flowers of prairies and dry plains) F: 286 *with picture*
  Plant *pictures on* P: 521, P: 526
Pride [zoology]
  Lion (The life of a lion) L: 341 *with picture*
Pride, Thomas [English military leader]
  Long Parliament L: 448
  Rump Parliament R: 520
Pride and Prejudice [book by Austen]
  Austen, Jane A: 892
  English literature (Romantic prose) E: 320
  Literature (Judging literature) L: 352-353
  Novel (Britain) N: 573
Pride's Purge [English history]
  Long Parliament L: 448
  Rump Parliament R: 520
Pridi Phanomyong [Thai political leader]
  Thailand (Changes in government) T: 227
Priene [ancient city]
  City *picture on* Ci: 579
Priest [religion] P: 776
  Address, Forms of (Members of the clergy) A: 54
  Augur A: 885

  Careers *picture on* C: 221
  Druids D: 367
  Eastern Orthodox Churches (Clergy) E: 46
  Egypt, Ancient (Religion) E: 137
  Indian, American (Priests) I: 148
  Taoism T: 36
Priestley, John Boynton [British author] P: 776
Priestley, Joseph [British chemist] P: 776
  Air (The study of air) A: 175
  Chemistry (The phlogiston theory) C: 401
  Electricity (Experiments with electric charge) E: 196-197
  Nitrous oxide N: 427
  Oxygen (History) O: 890
  Rubber (First uses) R: 500-501
Prigioner superbo, Il [opera by Pergolesi]
  Pergolesi, Giovanni Battista P: 287
Prigogine, Ilya [Belgian chemist]
  Nobel Prizes (Chemistry: 1977) N: 444
Primacy [religion]
  Gregory I, Saint G: 387
  Roman Catholic Church (The recognition of Christianity) R: 405-406; (Vatican Council I) R: 410
Primakov, Yevgeny Maksimovich [Russian political leader]
  Russia (The new nation) R: 555
Primaquine [medication]
  Malaria (Treatment and prevention) M: 96
  Quinine Q: 42
Primary [device] *See* Stator *in this index*
Primary aluminum industry
  Aluminum (The aluminum industry) A: 396
Primary Association [organization]
  Mormons (Church organization) M: 807-808
Primary battery
  Battery B: 168 *with diagram*
Primary body site [medicine]
  Cancer (Major types of cancer) C: 167
Primary boycott
  Boycott B: 539
Primary care
  Medicine *picture on* M: 363; (Primary care) M: 366
Primary Chronicle [book]
  Russia (Early days) R: 547
Primary color
  Color (Mixing colorants) Ci: 819-821 *with diagram*; (Mixing colored lights) Ci: 821-822 *with diagram*
  Photography (Exposing the film) P: 416
  Television *diagram on* T: 124; (Capturing the image) T: 122
Primary consumer [ecology]
  Ecology (Energy flow) E: 54
  Forest (The flow of energy) F: 396
Primary cosmic rays
  Astronomy (Cosmic-ray astronomy) A: 846
  Cosmic rays (Primary cosmic rays) Ci: 1076 *with diagram*
Primary data
  Market research M: 214
Primary election [voting] P: 776
  Election (Nomination of candidates) E: 158
  Election campaign (Winning the nomination) E: 159
  Political convention (Delegate selection) P: 628-629
  Political party (Selecting candidates) P: 631
Primary explosive
  Improvised explosive device I: 95
Primary flight feather [bird]
  Bird (Feathers) B: 362 *with diagram*
Primary footprint [measurement]
  Carbon footprint C: 207
Primary headache
  Headache H: 124
Primary highway
  Road (Primary highways) R: 358
Primary industry
  Industry (By stage of production) I: 256
Primary lead [metal]
  Lead L: 149
Primary lymphoid organ [physiology]
  Immune system (Lymphocytes) I: 87
Primary mineral [geology]
  Soil (Minerals) So: 573
Primary mirror [optics]
  Telescope (Reflecting telescopes) T: 104
Primary party organization [Soviet history]
  Union of Soviet Socialist Republics (The Communist Party) U: 29
Primary processor [electronics]
  Computer (Personal computers) Ci: 909
Primary producer [ecology]
  Ecology (Energy flow) E: 54
  Forest (The flow of energy) F: 396
Primary rainbow

Rainbow (How to find a rainbow) R: 127 *with picture*
Primary recovery
Petroleum (Recovering petroleum) P: 341 *with diagram*
Primary response [physiology]
Virus (Immune response) V: 428a
Primary root [botany]
Plant (Roots) P: 528 *with pictures*
Root (Kinds of roots) R: 469 *with diagram*
Seed (The parts of a seed) S: 281
Primary school [education] *See* Elementary school *in this index*
Primary sewage treatment
Sewage (Urban sewerage systems) S: 329
Water pollution (Sewage treatment) W: 138
Primary source
History (The evidence) H: 260
Primary succession [biology]
Ecology (Changes in communities) E: 54
Primary teeth
Teeth (Deciduous teeth) T: 79 *with picture*
Primary tissue [botany]
Root (Secondary tissues) R: 471
Stem (Herbaceous stems) So: 887
Primary wave [physics]
Earthquake (Body waves) E: 35
Primary winding [electricity]
Transformer T: 371 *with diagram*
Primate [zoology] P: 777 *with pictures*
Anthropology (Physical anthropology) A: 546
Human being (Scientific classification) H: 413
Mammal (table) M: 129 *with picture*
Primate of All England [title]
Archbishop of Canterbury A: 601
Church of England (Organization) C: 542
Primates Meetings
Anglican Communion (Organization) A: 463
Primatology [science]
Primate (The study of nonhuman primates) P: 778a
Primavera, La [painting by Botticelli]
Botticelli, Sandro *picture on* B: 513
Graces G: 296 *with picture*
Prime factor [mathematics]
Factor (Prime factors) F: 4
Prime meat
Beef (Grades of beef) B: 209
Meat packing (Quality grading) M: 351
Prime meridian *See* Greenwich meridian *in this index*
Prime minister [title] P: 778c
Address, Forms of (Officials of the Commonwealth of Nations) A: 53
Australia (Government) A: 894-895
Cabinet (The cabinet system of government) C: 4
England (Government) E: 292-293
Foreign policy (The executive) F: 387
Government (Parliamentary democracy) G: 286
Parliament P: 172
United Kingdom *picture on* U: 50; (Government) U: 49
Prime Minister, Office of
Prime minister of Canada (Roles of the prime minister) P: 778c-778d; (History) P: 780
Prime minister of Canada P: 778c *with pictures*
Canada, Government of (The prime minister) C: 130
Prime mover [engineering]
Electric generator (Basic principles) E: 170
Prime number [mathematics] P: 780
Codes and ciphers (Public-key systems) Ci: 750
Factor F: 4
Gauss, Carl Friedrich G: 70
Number theory N: 607
Sieve of Eratosthenes S: 452
Prime of Life, The [book by Beauvoir]
Beauvoir, Simone de B: 191
Prime of Miss Jean Brodie, The [book by Spark]
Spark, Muriel So: 764
Prime rate
Interest (The prime rate) I: 323
Prime time [television]
Advertising (Television) A: 73
Television (Measuring a program's success) T: 113
Primer [ammunition]
Ammunition (Small-arms ammunition) A: 435 *with diagrams*; (The primer) A: 435 *with diagrams*
Artillery (Parts of an artillery weapon) A: 762
Firearm (Mechanism) F: 132-133
Rifle (How a rifle works) R: 338
Primer [paint]
Automobile *diagram on* A: 957
Paint (Household paints) P: 23-24; (Industrial paints) P: 24
Primeval history

Genesis G: 84
Priming [agriculture]
Tobacco (Harvesting) T: 306
Priming charge [explosives]
Detonator D: 167
Primitive blind snake
Snake (Early blind snakes) S: 535
Primo de Rivera, José Antonio [Spanish political leader]
Falange Española F: 12
Primo de Rivera, Miguel [Spanish political leader]
Alfonso XIII A: 348
Falange Española F: 12
Spain (The reign of Alfonso XIII) So: 749
Spanish Civil War (Background to the war) So: 756
Primogeniture [law] P: 781
Feudalism (The principles of feudalism) F: 82
Jefferson, Thomas (Virginia lawmaker) J: 80
Primordial black hole [astronomy]
Hawking, Stephen William H: 113
Primordial dwarfism [disorder]
Dwarfism (Causes) D: 394-395
Primordial fireball [astronomy]
Universe (Changing views of the universe) U: 205-206
Primrose [plant] P: 781 *with pictures*
Flower *picture on* F: 286; (Garden perennials) F: 278 *with picture*; (Flowers of the desert) F: 290 *with picture*; (table) F: 301 *with picture*
Prince [American singer]
Rock music (Rock videos and MTV) R: 380c
Prince [title] P: 781
Address, Forms of (Officials of the Commonwealth of Nations) A: 53
Prince, Morton H. [American doctor]
Hypnosis (Scientific studies) H: 480
Prince, The [book by Machiavelli]
Borgia, Cesare B: 487
Italian literature (Humanism and the Renaissance) I: 494
Machiavelli, Niccolò M: 13
Renaissance (Niccolò Machiavelli) R: 234-235
Prince Albert [Saskatchewan] P: 781
Prince Albert National Park [Saskatchewan]
Canada (table: National parks and national park reserves) C: 113
Saskatchewan (Places to visit) S: 136 *with picture*
Prince and the Pauper, The [book by Twain]
Twain, Mark (Productive years in Hartford) T: 529
Prince Arthur's Landing [former name]
Thunder Bay T: 272
Prince Charles [prince of Wales] *See* Charles, Prince *in this index*
Prince Charles [dog]
English toy spaniel E: 325
Prince Charles Foreland [island, Arctic]
Svalbard So: 1014
Prince consort [title] P: 781
Albert, Prince A: 311
Philip, Prince P: 371
Prince Edward Island P: 782 *with pictures and maps*
See also the list of Related articles in the Prince Edward Island *article*
Acadia A: 21
Atlantic Provinces A: 867
Canada, Government of *picture on* C: 131
Nova Scotia (The struggle in Acadia) N: 568
Prince Edward Island, University of
Prince Edward Island (Schools) P: 786
Prince Edward Island National Park
Canada (table: National parks and national park reserves) C: 113
Prince Friedrich von Homburg [play by Kleist]
German literature (Other writers) G: 140
Prince George [British Columbia] P: 793 *with picture*
Prince Hall Freemasonry
Masonry (Prince Hall Freemasonry) M: 267; (History) M: 267-268
Prince Igor [opera by Borodin]
Borodin, Alexander B: 490
Prince of the United Kingdom [title]
Philip, Prince P: 371
Prince of Wales [title] P: 794
Charles, Prince C: 382
Edward II E: 112
England (The beginnings of Parliament) E: 306
Prince P: 781
Prince of Wales College
Prince Edward Island (Schools) P: 786
Prince of Wales Fort [Manitoba]
Canada (table: National historic sites) C: 115
Prince of Wales Island [Alaska]
Alaska (Coastline) A: 294
Torres Strait Islands T: 343

Prince Rupert [British Columbia] P: 794 *with picture*
Prince William Forest Park [Virginia]
National Park System (table: National parkways and other national parklands) N: 56
Prince William Henry [ship]
Wake Island W: 6
Prince William Sound
Alaska (Coastline) A: 294
Coast Guard, United States (The Coast Guard since World War II) Ci: 738-739
Exxon Valdez oil spill E: 459
Princely Pleasures at Kenilworth Castle, The [work by Gascoigne]
Gascoigne, George G: 60
Princely states [government]
India (British India) I: 130
Princes Street
Edinburgh E: 77
Scotland *picture on* S: 212
Princess [title]
Address, Forms of (Officials of the Commonwealth of Nations) A: 53
Prince P: 781
Princess Alice [ship]
Shipwreck (table: Major shipwrecks) S: 428
Princess of Clèves, The [book by La Fayette]
French literature (Classical prose) F: 520
La Fayette, Madame de L: 27
Princess of Mars, A [book by Burroughs]
Burroughs, Edgar Rice B: 711
Princess Royal [title]
Prince P: 781
Princess shows [musicals]
Kern, Jerome K: 305
Musical comedy (Musical comedy matures) M: 960
Princeton [New Jersey]
New Jersey (The American Revolution) N: 250-251
United States capitals U: 199
Princeton [ship]
Ericsson, John E: 350
Tyler, John (Life in the White House) T: 534
Princeton, Battle of [1777]
Princeton University (Campus buildings) P: 795
Revolution, American *picture on* R: 281; (table) R: 276; (Trenton and Princeton) R: 282
Princeton University P: 794 *with picture*
Football (The history of football) F: 365
New Jersey *picture on* N: 235
Universities and colleges (The oldest U.S. universities and colleges) U: 210
Wilson, Woodrow (University president) W: 321
Princip, Gavrilo [Serbian assassin]
Austria-Hungary A: 941
Franz Ferdinand F: 494
World War I (The assassination of an archduke) W: 455
Principal [economics]
Bond B: 454
Interest (Types of interest) I: 321
Mortgage M: 820
Principal [law]
See also Trust fund *in this index*
Agent A: 140
Guaranty G: 411
Principal, School
High school (High schools in the United States) H: 228
School (Public schools) S: 182
Principal meridian [surveying]
Public lands (Management of public lands) P: 858
Principal part [grammar]
Verb (Regular and irregular verbs) V: 315
Príncipe Island [island, Gulf of Guinea]
São Tomé and Príncipe S: 119 *with map*
Principi, Anthony J. [American government official]
Bush, George Walker (table) B: 722h
Veterans Affairs, Department of (table) V: 343
Principia Ethica [book by Moore]
Moore, G. E. M: 796
Principia mathematica [book by Newton]
Châtelet, Marquise Du C: 388
Energy (Calculating quantities of energy) E: 274
Gravitation (Newton's law of gravitation) G: 331
Newton, Sir Isaac (The *Principia*) N: 388
Physics (Newton) P: 439
Relativity (Inertial frames) R: 210-211; (General relativity) R: 211
Principia mathematica [book by Russell and Whitehead]
Mathematics (Philosophies of mathematics) M: 307
Russell, Bertrand R: 523
Whitehead, Alfred North W: 293
Principle of ...

Principles appear under their key words, as in Equivalence, Principle of
Principles and Practice of Medicine [book by Osler]
  Osler, Sir William (His writings) O: 863
Principles of Economics [book by Marshall]
  Marshall, Alfred M: 228
Principles of Geology [book by Lyell]
  Evolution (Darwin's theory) E: 432
  Geology (Experimental geology) G: 99
  Lyell, Sir Charles L: 533
Principles of Literary Criticism [book by Richards]
  Richards, I. A. R: 329
Principles of Mathematics [book by Russell]
  Russell, Bertrand R: 523
Principles of Orchestration [book by Rimsky-Korsakov]
  Rimsky-Korsakov, Nikolai R: 342
Principles of Philosophy [book by Descartes]
  Descartes, René D: 154
Principles of Political Economy [book by Mill]
  Mill, Harriet Taylor M: 552
  Mill, John Stuart M: 552
Principles of Political Economy and Taxation [book by Ricardo]
  Ricardo, David R: 321
Principles of Psychology, The [book by James]
  American literature (Nonfiction writers) A: 420
  James, William (Early career) J: 27
  Psychology (Psychology becomes a science) P: 849
Prins Alexander Polder
  Netherlands (The Polders) N: 144
Prins Johan Willem Friso [ship]
  Saint Lawrence Seaway (Construction of the seaway) S: 45
Prinsenhof [museum, Netherlands]
  Delft D: 115
Print [art]
  Intaglio I: 317
  Japanese print J: 62 *with pictures*
  World, History of the *picture on* W: 435
Print [butter]
  Butter (Packaging) B: 730
Print [outline]
  Fossil (Formation of impressions, molds, and casts) F: 425
Print [photography]
  Photography (Making prints) P: 419 *with pictures*; (Printing digital images) P: 422; (Technical improvements) P: 423
Print on demand
  Publishing (Going out of print) P: 869
Print server [computer]
  Computer (Local area networks [LAN's]) Ci: 922
Printed circuit [electronics]
  Electronics (Types of electronic circuits) E: 209-210 *with picture*
Printer [electronic device] P: 795
  Computer (Printers) Ci: 916 *with picture*
  Desktop publishing D: 158
  Ink (Printing inks) I: 273
  Inkjet printer I: 273
  Mechanical drawing (Creating a drawing) M: 354
  Photography (Printing digital images) P: 422
  Printing (Digital printing) P: 801
Printing [industry] P: 796 *with pictures*
  See also the list of Related articles in the Printing [industry] *article*
  Advertising (The impact of printing) A: 79
  Block printing B: 405 *with pictures*
  Book (The development of printed books) B: 466
  Careers (Production) C: 229
  Caxton, William C: 322
  Communication *picture on* Ci: 884; (The rise of printing) Ci: 879-880; (The 1700's) Ci: 880-881 *with picture*; (The 1800's) Ci: 881
  Desktop publishing D: 158
  Education (The invention of printing) E: 100
  Encyclopedia E: 268 *with picture*
  English literature (The beginning of Modern English [1485-1603]) E: 316
  Engraving (Printing the engraving) E: 325
  Europe (The Renaissance) E: 410 *with picture*
  Graphic arts G: 322
  Invention (The Renaissance) I: 360-361
  Library (Paper, printing, and libraries) L: 260
  Linotype L: 338
  Lithography (How lithography works) L: 387 *with pictures*
  Magazine (Editing and assembling an issue) M: 43-44 *with picture*
  Money (Printing paper money) M: 715
  New York (Manufacturing) N: 310-311
  New York City (Industry) N: 333
  Newspaper (Printing the newspaper) N: 385 *with picture*
  Publishing P: 866

Textile (Finishing the fabric) T: 217 *with picture*
Type T: 536 *with picture*
World, History of the (China) W: 435 *with picture*
Printing [photography]
  Motion picture (Shooting the movie) M: 852-853
Printing [writing]
  Handwriting (Learning manuscript writing) H: 47; (Manuscript writing) H: 47
Printing, Bureau of Engraving and *See* Engraving and Printing, Bureau of *in this index*
Printing calculator
  Calculator C: 22
Printing press P: 804
  English literature (The beginning of Modern English [1485-1603]) E: 316
  Gutenberg, Johannes G: 444
  Money *picture on* M: 712; (Printing paper money) M: 715
  Newspaper (Printing the newspaper) N: 385 *with picture*
  Printing (Methods of printing) P: 798 *with diagrams*; (Process color printing) P: 802
  Publishing (Kinds of publishing) P: 868
  Technology (Technological advances) T: 75
Prío Socarrás, Carlos [Cuban political leader]
  Batista y Zaldívar, Fulgencio B: 165
  Cuba (The Batista era) Ci: 1177
Prion [particle] P: 804
  Creutzfeldt-Jakob disease Ci: 1128
  Mad cow disease M: 26
  Prion P: 804
Prion protein
  Prion P: 804
Prior, Edward C. [Canadian political leader]
  British Columbia (table) B: 628
Prior restraint [law]
  Journalism (Restrictions on freedom of the press) J: 173
Priority debt [law]
  Bankruptcy (Features of bankruptcy) B: 97
Priority Mail
  Postal Service, United States (First-Class Mail service) P: 699
Pripyat Marshes [swamp]
  Belarus (Land) B: 224b
Priroda earth observatory [space exploration]
  Mir M: 614 *with picture*
Prishtina [Kosovo] *See* Priština *in this index*
Prism [optics] P: 805 *with picture*
  Binoculars B: 309 *with diagram*
  Color (The relation between color and light) Ci: 817
  Light *picture on* L: 282, *diagram on* L: 287; (The spectrum of light sources) L: 284 *with diagram*
  Lighthouse (Development of the lighthouse) L: 294-295
  Rainbow (How rainbows appear) R: 128
  Science *picture on* S: 200
  Spectrometer So: 772 *with diagram*
Prismatic layer [zoology]
  Shell (How shells are formed) S: 385
Prison P: 805 *with pictures*
  See also the list of Related articles in the Prison *article*
  African Americans (Social struggles) A: 136s-136t
  Criminal justice system (Problems in the correctional system) Ci: 1144
  Fry, Elizabeth Gurney F: 549
  Howard, John H: 399
  Law enforcement (Imprisonment) L: 141
  Parole P: 178
  Prisons, Federal Bureau of P: 808
  Probation P: 809
  State government (Issues confronting state governments) So: 865
Prison camp *See* Concentration camp *in this index*
Prison guard
  Prison (The prison staff) P: 806
Prison of Love, The [book by San Pedro]
  Spanish literature (The 1400's) So: 758
Prisoner for God [book by Bonhoeffer]
  Bonhoeffer, Dietrich B: 459
Prisoner of Grace [book by Cary]
  Cary, Joyce C: 270
Prisoner of war P: 808
  Geneva Conventions G: 88
  Hague Conventions H: 7
  International law (The laws of war) I: 341
  Korean War (The truce talks) K: 382; (Prisoner exchange) K: 383
  Slavery (The Middle Ages) S: 501
  War (The basic rules of warfare) W: 24
Prisoner's Dilemma
  Game theory G: 23
Prisons [etchings by Piranesi]
  Piranesi, Giovanni Battista P: 493 *with picture*
Prisons, Federal Bureau of [U.S.] P: 808

Prison P: 805
Priština [Kosovo] P: 808a
  Kosovo K: 384a *with picture*
Pritzker Pavilion [Chicago]
  Chicago (Places to visit) C: 430-431
Prius [automobile]
  Automobile *picture on* A: 973
  Hybrid car H: 461
  Toyota Motor Corporation T: 355
Privacy, Right of [law] P: 808a
  Abortion (Abortion in the United States) A: 15
  Computer (Computer security) Ci: 924
  Internet (Identity and privacy) I: 350f; (Ongoing controversies) I: 350h
  Roe v. Wade R: 399
Privacy Act [1974]
  Freedom of Information Act F: 505
  Privacy, Right of P: 808a
Private [rank]
  Rank, Military (table) R: 140
Private adoption
  Adoption (The adoption process) A: 66
Private bill [legislation]
  Congress of the United States (Proposing new laws) Ci: 944
Private carrier [transportation]
  Truck (Industrial uses) T: 456
Private corporation
  Corporation (Business corporations) Ci: 1069-1070
Private course [golf]
  Golf G: 260
Private duty nurse
  Nursing (Private duty nurses) N: 617
Private education *See* Private school *in this index*
Private enterprise [economics] *See* Capitalism; Free enterprise system *in this index*
Private eye [fiction]
  Detective story (History) D: 162-163
Private government
  Government G: 282
Private health insurance
  Health insurance, National H: 129
  Insurance (Health insurance) I: 311
Private-label merchandise
  Retailing R: 264
Private land mobile radio service
  Walkie-talkie W: 14
Private law
  Law (Branches of law) L: 130; (Law since 1900) L: 136
  Supreme Court of Canada (Authority) So: 996-997
  United States, Government of the (Functions) U: 138
Private line service
  Telephone (Business services) T: 98
Private Lives [play by Coward]
  Coward, Noël Ci: 1107
Private military company
  Mercenary M: 411
Private school [education] P: 808a
  Education (Control and support of U.S. education) E: 94; (Who should choose a child's school?) E: 106
  Elementary school (Kinds of elementary schools) E: 224
  Parochial school P: 177
  Religious education (Private education) R: 225
  School (Kinds of schools) S: 181; (Private schools) S: 183
Private theater [English history]
  Shakespeare, William (Theater buildings) S: 351
Privateer [sea raider]
  Caribbean Sea (Economic importance) C: 237
  Pirate P: 494
Privateer [ship] P: 808b
  Revolution, American (Maritime forces) R: 280
Privately supported foundation
  Foundation (Kinds of foundations) F: 430
Privatization [economics] P: 808b
  Education (How should schools be run?) E: 108
  Nationalization N: 63
  Postal services (Competition and privatization) P: 707
  Prison (Reforms in the 1900's) P: 807-808
Privet [shrub]
  Henna H: 185
Privilege [law]
  Evidence (Privilege) E: 426
Privileges, Charter of [1701]
  Pennsylvania (Colonial days) P: 264
Privy Council [British government] P: 808b
Privy Council Office
  Prime minister of Canada (Roles of the prime minister) P: 778c-778d; (History) P: 780
Priyadarsika [play by Harsha]

Harsha H: 77

Prize Stock [book by Oe]
Oe, Kenzaburo O: 676
Prizefighting [sport] *See* Boxing *in this index*
PRO [organization]
Hospital H: 371
Pro-...
Headings beginning Pro- are alphabetized as single words: Pro-nuncio *appears after* Pronunciation
Pro Football Hall of Fame [Ohio]
Canton C: 184
Hall of fame (Sports halls of fame) H: 23
Ohio (Places to visit) O: 690 *with picture*
Pro-rally [race]
Automobile racing (Other kinds of racing) A: 978-979
Pro Stock car
Automobile racing (Drag racing) A: 978
Pro wrestling *See* Wrestling, Professional *in this index*
Proactive interference [psychology]
Memory (Interference) M: 393
Proapoptotic gene [biology]
Apoptosis A: 566
Probability [mathematics] P: 808b
Artificial intelligence (Knowledge representation and reasoning) A: 760
Fermat, Pierre de F: 73
Inductive method I: 240
Insurance I: 309; (The growth of insurance) I: 315
Mathematics (Branches of mathematics) M: 303
Pascal, Blaise P: 189
Permutations and combinations P: 290
Ratio R: 148
Statistics (Analyzing the data) So: 868; (Probability) So: 868-869 *with diagrams*
Probability histogram [mathematics]
Statistics (Probability) So: 868-869 *with diagram*
Probable cause [law]
Court (How courts work) Ci: 1101
Probainognathus [extinct animal]
Evolution *picture on* E: 429
Probate [law] P: 809
Executor E: 436
Probate court [law]
Probate P: 809
Probation [law] P: 809
Criminal justice system (The trial) Ci: 1143-1144
Law enforcement (Imprisonment) L: 141
Parole P: 178
Probation officer [official]
Probation P: 809
Probe [instrument]
Thermometer (Resistance thermometers) T: 255 *with diagram*
Probe [tool]
Inuit (Hunting and fishing) I: 354d
Probe, Space *See* Space probe *in this index*
Probenecid [drug]
Gout G: 281
"Problem, The" [poem by Emerson]
Emerson, Ralph Waldo (His poetry) E: 259
Problem play [drama]
French literature (Realism) F: 522
Problem solving
Artificial intelligence (Planning and problem solving) A: 760
Dewey, John D: 177
Education (How people learn) E: 89-90
Statistics (Using statistics to study problems) So: 868
Thorndike, Edward Lee T: 267
Problems of Lasting Peace, The [book by Hoover]
Hoover, Herbert Clark (Elder statesman) H: 330
Proboscidea [zoology]
Elephant (Protecting elephants) E: 231
Mammal (table) M: 129 *with picture*
Proboscis [zoology]
Butterfly (The head) B: 738 *with diagram*
Fly (Head) F: 309 *with diagram*
Gnat G: 237
Insect (Mouthparts) I: 286-287 *with diagram*
Mosquito (The body of a mosquito) M: 831 *with diagram*
Moth (The head) M: 837-838 *with diagram*
Ribbon worm R: 321
Proboscis monkey [animal] P: 809 *with picture*
Monkey *picture on* M: 728
Proboscis worm *See* Ribbon worm *in this index*
Probus [Roman emperor]
Rome, Ancient (table) R: 447
Procaine [medication]
Benzocaine B: 255
Procardia [drug]
Calcium channel blocker C: 21
Procedural due process [law]
Due process of law D: 378

Process [equipment]
Automation (How automation works) A: 945
Process and Reality [book by Whitehead]
Whitehead, Alfred North W: 293
Process cheese
Cheese (Process cheese) C: 393
Process color printing
Printing (Process color printing) P: 802 *with pictures*
Process of National Reorganization [Argentine history]
Argentina (The "dirty war") A: 658
Processed meats
Pork P: 679
Processed vegetable
Vegetable V: 292
Processing-catcher vessel [ship]
Fishing industry (How fish are caught) F: 183
Procession of Boats with Distant Smoke, Venice [painting by Turner]
Turner, J. M. W. *picture on* T: 515
Processional Street [Babylon]
Babylon (The Neo-Babylonian Empire) B: 12
Processor [electronics]
See also Microprocessor *in this index*
Computer (Parts of computers) Ci: 911
Electronics (Digital circuits) E: 213-214
Prochain épisode [book by Aquin]
Canadian literature (Modern literature: 1945 to the present) C: 159-160
Pro-choice movement
Abortion (Abortion methods) A: 14-15
Proclamation of 1763 [U.S. history]
Colonial life in America (The struggle for land) Ci: 793
Indian wars (Pontiac's War [1763]) I: 191
Pioneer life in America (Pioneers and Indians) P: 485
Revolution, American (The Proclamation of 1763) R: 272
Westward movement in America (The Proclamation of 1763) W: 246
Proclamation of Amnesty and Reconstruction [1865]
Lee, Robert E. (Last years) L: 179
Proclus [Greek philosopher]
Euclid E: 377
Neoplatonism N: 124
Procompsognathus [extinct animal]
Dinosaur *picture on* D: 206d
Procter, Henry [British general]
War of 1812 (Thames River) W: 33
Procter & Gamble Company
Manufacturing (table) M: 170
Proctor, A. Phimister [Canadian-born sculptor]
Oregon *picture on* O: 831
Proctor, Fletcher D. [American political leader]
Vermont (table) V: 333
Proctor, Mortimer R. [American political leader]
Vermont (table) V: 333
Proctor, Redfield [American political leader]
Harrison, Benjamin (table) H: 72
Vermont (table) V: 333
Proctor, Richard A. [British astronomer]
Moon (Determining the origin of craters) M: 793-794
Procynosuchus [extinct animal]
Evolution *picture on* E: 429
Procyon [star]
Star (table: The 10 brightest stars as seen from Earth) So: 842
Prodi, Romano [Italian political leader] P: 810
Italy (Recent developments) I: 519
Prodigal Son, The [parable]
Jesus Christ (His teaching) J: 107
Prodigy, The [rock group]
Rock music (Alternative rock) R: 381
Produce [agriculture]
Truck farming T: 458
Producer [career]
Electronic game (Game design) E: 204b
Motion picture (How motion pictures are made) M: 847-848
Recording industry (In a recording studio) R: 181
Television (Production and preparation) T: 110c
Theater (The producer) T: 235
Producer gas [fuel]
Carbon monoxide C: 207
Gas (fuel) (Other manufactured gases) G: 56
Producer goods *See* Capital goods *in this index*
Producer Price Index [economics]
Inflation (Measuring inflation) I: 267
Producers, The [musical]
Musical comedy (Musical comedy today) M: 961
Product [arithmetic]
Algebra (Multiplication) A: 355
Arithmetic (Multiplication) A: 667

Multiplication (Writing multiplication) M: 921
Product [chemistry]
Chemical reaction C: 397
Product character [symbol]
Advertising (Product characters) A: 76
Product development
Marketing (Product development) M: 214
Product differentiation [economics]
Industry (Product differentiation) I: 260
Product liability insurance
Insurance (Product and professional liability insurance) I: 314
Product liability suit [law] P: 810
Consumer protection (The right to be heard) Ci: 1018-1019
Product pipeline
Pipeline (Liquid pipelines) P: 490-491
Product placement
Advertising (Other ways of advertising) A: 75
Product recall [merchandising]
Consumer protection (The right to safety) Ci: 1018
Pure food and drug laws (Enforcement) P: 908-909
Production [economics] P: 810
Business (Specialized departments) B: 726
Communism (The centrally planned economy) Ci: 891
Economics E: 58
Food (Production) F: 334
Manufacturing (Kinds of manufacturing) M: 169
Marx, Karl: *(Das Kapital)* M: 237
Production, Mass *See* Mass production *in this index*
Production, Means of [economics] *See* Means of production *in this index*
Production brigade [work unit]
China (Rural life) C: 482
Production car
Automobile racing A: 975 *with picture*
Production control [industry]
Manufacturing (Making products) M: 170-171
Production coordinator *See* Production manager *in this index*
Production garden
Gardening (Kinds of outdoor gardens) G: 30 *with picture*
Production line [industry] *See* Assembly line *in this index*
Production manager [career]
Motion picture (Assembling the production team) M: 850
Television (Production specialists) T: 110d
Production team [work unit]
China (Rural life) C: 482
Production test pilot [aviation]
Test pilot P: 182
Production well
Well (Oil and natural gas wells) W: 193
Production worker
Careers (Production) C: 229 *with picture*
Productive bound morpheme [linguistics]
Language (Words and morphemes) L: 62
Productive resources *See* Input *in this index*
Productivity [economics] P: 810
Economics (Economic growth) E: 62
Industry (Labor) I: 259
Taxation (Productivity) T: 54
Profane Prose [book by Darío]
Darío, Rubén D: 36
Profession [religion]
Religious life R: 226
Profession, Choice of *See* Careers *in this index*
Professional and Technical Engineers, International Federation of
Labor movement (table) L: 8
Professional Bowlers Association
Bowling (Professional bowling) B: 524
Professional Chess Association
Chess (History) C: 414
Kasparov, Garry K: 248
Professional fraternity [organization]
Fraternity (Professional fraternities) F: 496
Professional Golfers' Association
Golf (Tournaments) G: 264; (U.S. PGA Championship) G: 265; (The rise of professional golf) G: 266
Professional leave
Teaching (Rewards of teaching) T: 69
Professional liability insurance
Insurance (Product and professional liability insurance) I: 314
Professional prophet [religion]
Prophet P: 827
Professional school
Careers (Professional and graduate schools) C: 217
Professional Ski Instructors of America

Skiing (Ski instruction) S: 486
Professional standards review organizations
Hospital H: 371
Professional theater
Theater (Theater in the United States) T: 244 *with pictures*
Professional Women's Bowling Association
Bowling (Professional bowling) B: 524
Professional wrestling See Wrestling, Professional *in this index*
Professor
Address, Forms of (Other forms) A: 54
Universities and colleges (Faculty) U: 208
Professor, The [book by Brontë]
Brontë sisters (Their works) B: 637
Proficiency pay
Rank, Military (Rank and pay) R: 140
Profile [computing]
Facebook (Uses) F: 4
Internet (Social networking websites) I: 350b
Profile Mountain
New Hampshire (Places to visit) N: 216; (Mountains) N: 220
White Mountains W: 291
Profiles in Courage [book by Kennedy]
Kennedy, John Fitzgerald (Senator Kennedy) K: 262-263
Profit [economics] P: 810
Business (Profits) B: 725
Capitalism (Capitalism in its ideal form) C: 194
Economics (The free market) E: 59; (Distribution of income) E: 63
Income tax (Effects of inflation) I: 103
Investment (Kinds of investments) I: 366
Percentage (Profits) P: 282
Profit motive
Business (Profits) B: 725
Profit sharing [economics] P: 811
Pension (Private pension plans) P: 273
Proganochelys [turtle]
Turtle T: 520
Progeria [disease] P: 811
Progesterone [hormone] P: 811
Hormone (Growth and sex hormones) H: 336
Hormone replacement therapy H: 338
Julian, Percy Lavon J: 187
Menopause M: 402
Menstruation (Luteal phase) *diagram on* M: 403; (The menstrual cycle) M: 404
Miscarriage M: 617
Ovary O: 881
Pregnancy (How pregnancy affects women) P: 734b
Reproduction, Human (The human reproductive system) R: 244-245
Steroid (The sex steroids) So: 894
Prograde motion [astronomy]
Planet (How planets move) P: 508-509
Program [computer software]
Calculator C: 22
Computer Ci: 909; (Programming a computer) Ci: 923
Database D: 41
Desktop publishing D: 158
Software So: 572
Program director [career]
Radio (Careers) R: 90
Program mode [photography]
Camera (Automatic exposure control) C: 82
Program music
Berlioz, Hector B: 267
Classical music (The Romantic era) Ci: 648-649
Program signal
Radio (From electric waves to radio waves) R: 86
Program symphony [music]
Classical music (The Romantic era) Ci: 648-649
Programmable calculator
Calculator C: 22
Programmed cell death [biology] See Apoptosis *in this index*
Programmed instruction [education]
Skinner, B. F. S: 495
Programmer [occupation]
Careers (Technical and mathematical occupations) C: 232 *with picture*
Computer (Programming a computer) Ci: 923; (Careers) Ci: 924a
Programming [computer]
Computer (Programming a computer) Ci: 923
Hopper, Grace Murray H: 334
Personal computer P: 300f
Programming [television]
Television (Producing television programs) T: 110c
Programming language See Computer language *in this index*
Programming service

Television (Cable and satellite systems) T: 115
Progress [space station]
Mir M: 613 *with picture*
Space exploration (Salyut and Skylab) So: 721
Progress and Poverty [book by George]
George, Henry G: 108
Progress of Love, The [painting by Fragonard]
Fragonard, Jean Honoré F: 451
"Progress of Poesy, The" [poem by Gray]
Gray, Thomas G: 335
Progression [mathematics] P: 812
Progressive Conservative Party [political party] P: 812
Campbell, Kim C: 90b
Canada, Government of (Political parties) C: 136
Charest, Jean C: 378
Clark, Joe Ci: 639
Conservative Party of Canada Ci: 992
Diefenbaker, John George (Member of Parliament) D: 197
Mulroney, Brian M: 916
Ontario (Politics) O: 784
Saskatchewan (Economic changes) S: 147
Progressive derecho [storm]
Derecho D: 152
Progressive education P: 813
Education (New theories of education) E: 104 *with picture*
Progressive Era [U.S. history] P: 813 *with picture*
United States, History of the (The Progressive Era) U: 186 *with picture*
Progressive form [grammar]
Conjugation C: 951
Tense T: 168
Progressive income tax
Income tax (Types of income taxes) I: 102; (Current issues) I: 102
Taxation (Equity) T: 54
Progressive Labour Party [political party]
Bermuda (History) B: 268-269
Progressive Liberal Party [political party]
Bahamas (History) B: 29
Progressive Party [Canada]
Political party (Other parties) P: 636-637
Progressive Party [U.S. history] P: 814
Political party (Third parties) P: 636
Bull Moose Party
Progressive Party (The "Bull Moose" Party) P: 814
Republican Party (The party splits) R: 255
Roosevelt, Theodore ("Bull Moose" candidate) R: 468
Taft, William Howard (Election of 1912) T: 12
United States, History of the (Taft and Wilson) U: 187
La Follette Progressives
La Follette (Robert Marion La Follette, Sr.) L: 29; (Robert Marion La Follette, Jr.) L: 29
Coolidge, Calvin ("Keep Cool with Coolidge") Ci: 1033
Progressive Party (The La Follette Progressives) P: 814
Progressive Party of 1948
Progressive Party (The Progressive Party of 1948) P: 814
Truman, Harry S. (Election of 1948) T: 470
Wallace, Henry Agard W: 16
Progressive Republicans [U.S. history]
Kansas (Spirit of reform) K: 237
Progressive rock [music]
Rock music (The 1970's) R: 380b
Progressive scanning [electronics]
Television (Camera scanning patterns) T: 122-123; (High-definitionl television) T: 128
Progressive wave
Waves (How waves move) W: 152
Progressivism [political science]
La Follette (Robert Marion La Follette, Sr.) L: 29
Liberalism L: 228
Progressive Era P: 813
Wisconsin W: 346; (History) W: 365-366
Prohibition [U.S. history] P: 814 *with picture*
Alcoholic beverage (History) A: 337
Chicago (The Roaring Twenties) C: 436
Constitution of the United States (Amendment 18) Ci: 1014; (Amendment 21) Ci: 1015
Hoover, Herbert Clark (Election of 1928) H: 329
Illinois (Prohibition and the Great Depression) I: 75 *with picture*
Maryland (The early 1900's) M: 259
Nassau N: 24
Nation, Carry Amelia Moore N: 26
Ness, Eliot N: 136
Roaring Twenties (Changing attitudes) R: 363-364 *with picture*
Roosevelt, Franklin Delano (The Hundred Days) R: 453

United States, History of the (Social reform) U: 173; (Prohibition) U: 189
Volstead Act V: 445
Woman's Christian Temperance Union W: 382
Prohibition Party [political party] P: 816
Political party (Third parties) P: 636
Prohibition (Prohibition in the United States) P: 815
Prohibitory injunction [law]
Injunction I: 272
Project, Science See Science projects *in this index*
Project for Perpetual Peace [book by Saint-Pierre]
Peace (From the 1400's to the 1700's) P: 206
Project LINK
Klein, Lawrence Robert K: 343
Projectile [physics]
Ammunition A: 434
Ballistics (Interior ballistics) B: 56 *with picture*
Rocket R: 384
Torpedo T: 340d *with diagram*
Projectile weapon
Weapon W: 154a
Projection [cartography] See Map projection *in this index*
Projection copying
Copying machine (Projection copying) Ci: 1045
Projection screen P: 816
Projection television system
Projector (Types of projectors) P: 816-817
Television (Display devices) T: 125; (Technological advances) T: 127-128
Projective test [psychology]
Personality (Projective tests) P: 301
Psychology (Systematic assessment) P: 848
Projector [machine] P: 816
Audio-visual materials (Projection devices) A: 882
Edison, Thomas Alva (Motion pictures) E: 80
Motion picture (The projector) M: 858 *with pictures*
Planetarium (Modern planetariums) P: 514b *with picture*
Prokaryote [biology] P: 817
Animal A: 468
Bacteria B: 19
Classification, Scientific (Groups in classification) Ci: 655
Domain D: 300
Flagellum F: 224
Kingdom K: 328
Prokaryotic cell [biology]
Archaea A: 593
Cell (table) C: 327
Classification, Scientific (Groups in classification) Ci: 655
Cyanobacteria Ci: 1202
Domain D: 300
Kingdom K: 328
Life (Cells) L: 277
Prokaryote P: 817
Prokhorov, Alexander Mikhailovich [Russian physicist] P: 817
Laser (History) L: 86
Prokofiev, Sergei Sergeyevich [Russian composer] P: 817
Prolactin [hormone]
Hormone (Endocrine control hormones) H: 336
Prolate spheroid [geometry]
Spheroid So: 780
Proleg [zoology]
Butterfly (The larva) B: 740 *with diagram*
Caterpillar (Appearance) C: 300
Proletarian literature
Russian literature (From 1917 to 1920) R: 564
Proletariat [sociology]
Communism (The ideas of Marx) Ci: 890
Lenin, V. I. (Beginnings of revolution) L: 192
Marx, Karl (*Das Kapital*) M: 237
Social class (How people are categorized) So: 550
Pro-life movement
Abortion (Abortion methods) A: 14-15
Prometheus [Greek mythology] P: 817 *with picture*
Deucalion D: 171
Hercules (Other adventures) H: 199
Mythology (Comparative approaches) M: 989
Pandora P: 130
Prometheus Unbound [poem by Shelley]
English literature (Romantic poetry) E: 320
Shelley, Percy Bysshe (His writings) S: 391
Promethium [element] P: 818
Prominence [astronomy]
Sun *pictures on* So: 985; (Solar activity) So: 980-981 *with picture*
Promise, Breach of [law]
Breach of promise B: 587
Promise, Scout See Scout Promise *in this index*
Promissory note [economics]
Bill (In bookkeeping) B: 300

Commercial paper Ci: 872
Negotiable instrument (Forms) N: 119
Note N: 550
Promontory [geography]
Cape C: 186
Promontory [Utah]
Railroad (The first transcontinental rail lines)
R: 116 with picture
Promoter
Boxing (Boxing in the United States) B: 530
Promotion [chess]
Chess (The moves) C: 412-413
Promotion [employment]
Careers (Chances for advancement) C: 216
Rank, Military (Promotion) R: 140
Promotion [selling]
Marketing (Promotion) M: 214
Sales S: 62
Promotion of Equality and Prevention of Unfair
Discrimination Act [South Africa, 2000]
Disability (The 1900's) D: 221-222
Prompt nuclear radiation
Nuclear weapon (Prompt nuclear radiation)
N: 599
Promptbook
Shakespeare, William (Folios) S: 369
Prompter [occupation]
Opera picture on O: 796
Pronghorn [animal] P: 818 with picture
Animal picture on A: 476
Horn H: 338
Pronoun [grammar] P: 819
Antecedent A: 541
Case (Pronouns) C: 272
Declension D: 80
Gender (Personal pronouns) G: 80
Person P: 300f
A Guide to Writing Skills **Research Guide:** 9
Prontosil [medication]
Domagk, Gerhard D: 300
Drug (The drug revolution) D: 359
Sulfa drug (Development of sulfa drugs) So: 966
Pronunciation [speech] P: 820
Accent A: 22
Dictionary (What a dictionary tells you) D: 193
English language (Pronunciation and spelling)
E: 312
Lisping L: 349
Phonics P: 400
Pro-nuncio [diplomat]
Vatican City (Diplomatic corps) V: 288
Pronzini, Bill [American author]
Muller, Marcia M: 915
Proof [alcohol]
Alcoholic beverage (Distilled drinks) A: 336
Proof [mathematics]
Geometry (Axiomatic system) G: 102
Mathematics (The Greeks) M: 306
Proof [printing]
Magazine (Editing and assembling an issue)
M: 43-44
Printing (Typesetting) P: 797
Proofreading P: 822
Proof coin
Coin collecting (Collecting United States coins)
Ci: 757
Proofreaders' marks [printing]
Proofreading P: 822 with pictures
Proofreading [printing] P: 822
Encyclopedia picture on E: 268
Printing (Typesetting) P: 797
Prop [theater]
Theater (Properties and set dressing) T: 240
Prop root [botany]
Corn (How the plant develops) Ci: 1057-1058
with picture
Root (Kinds of roots) R: 469-470 with diagram
Propaganda P: 823 with pictures
Central Intelligence Agency (Functions) C: 356-
357
Communication (Communications and politics)
Ci: 888
Guerrilla warfare (Guerrilla warfare techniques)
G: 419
Psychological warfare P: 846
Public opinion (Public opinion and government)
P: 860-861
World War II picture on W: 493; (Propaganda)
W: 494
Propagation [biology]
See also Breeding in this index
Fruit (Fruit production) F: 546
Gardening (Obtaining new plants from cuttings)
G: 38
Propagation of the Faith, Congregation for the
[organization]
Missionary (Organization) M: 621

Propaganda (History) P: 824
Propagation of the Faith, Society for the
[organization]
Sheen, Fulton John S: 380
Propane [fuel]
Balloon (Hot-air balloons) B: 57
Butane and propane B: 728
Gas [fuel] (In the home) G: 51
Natural gas liquids N: 64
Propanol [chemical]
Alcohol (Propanol) A: 335
Propecia [drug] See Finasteride in this index
Propellant [ammunition]
Ammunition A: 435 with diagrams; (Small-arms
ammunition) A: 435 with diagrams
Propellant [fuel]
Aerosol A: 89
Guided missile (The engine) G: 424 with diagrams
Rocket R: 384; (Parts of a rocket) R: 385; (Kinds of
rocket engines) R: 387 with diagrams
Space exploration (Getting into space and back)
So: 698
Propeller P: 826 with pictures
See also Airplane propeller in this index
Ducted propeller D: 377
Motorboat racing (Engine designs) M: 876
Ship diagram on S: 405; (Engine-driven ships)
S: 406; (The first propeller-driven ships) S: 425
Proper adjective [grammar]
Adjective (Classifying adjectives) A: 57
Proper fraction [mathematics]
Fraction (Improper fractions) F: 448
Proper lunar month
Month M: 767
Proper noun [grammar]
Capitalization (Proper nouns) C: 196
Noun (Proper and common nouns) N: 552
Propertius [Roman author]
Latin literature (The Augustan Age) L: 116
Property [film]
Motion picture (Developing the story) M: 848-
849
Property [law] P: 826
See also Real estate in this index; and the list of
Related articles in the Property article
Abandonment A: 4
Colonial life in America (Economic reasons)
Ci: 788; (The struggle for land) Ci: 793; (Voting
and other rights) Ci: 795
Davis, Paulina Wright D: 49
Divorce (Divorce provisions) D: 254
Economics (The organization of economies)
E: 58; (Government intervention) E: 59
Eminent domain E: 260
Government (Communism) G: 286
Law (Private law) L: 130; (Beginnings of U.S. law)
L: 136
Lease L: 166
Marx, Karl M: 236
Torrens system T: 342
Trespass T: 436
Vandalism V: 278
Women's movement (The beginnings of women's
movements) W: 384-385
Property [mathematics]
Geometry (Properties of geometric figures)
G: 102
Property, Personal See Personal property in this
index
Property insurance
Insurance diagram on I: 310; (Property and
liability insurance) I: 312
Property interest [law]
Property P: 827
Property manager [career]
Television (Production specialists) T: 110d
Property tax P: 827
California (The late 1900's) C: 63
Education (Control and support of U.S.
education) E: 94; (How should education be
financed?) E: 108
Government (Taxation) G: 283
Metropolitan area (Finances and taxation) M: 443
Taxation (Property taxes) T: 53
Prophase [biology]
Cell (Mitosis) C: 330
Prophet [religion] P: 827
Indian, American (Prophets) I: 148
Islam (Teachings and practices) I: 463
Jews (The divided kingdom) J: 121
Prophet, The [book by Gibran]
Gibran, Kahlil G: 187
Prophète, Le [opera by Meyerbeer]
Meyerbeer, Giacomo M: 479
Prophets, The [Bible]
Bible (The Hebrew Bible) B: 279; (table) B: 281
Old Testament O: 740

Prophet's Camel Bell, The [book by Laurence]
Laurence, Margaret L: 122
Prophylaxis [medicine] P: 827
Propionibacterium acnes [bacteria]
Acne A: 28
Propitious Garden of Plane Image, Second
Version, The [painting by Marden]
Painting (Abstract artists) P: 88-89
Propliopithecid [animal]
Primate (The evolution of primates) P: 778b
Propontis [name for]
Marmara, Sea of M: 216
Proportion [mathematics] P: 827
Geometry (Similarity) G: 103
Proportional control thermostat
Thermostat (How thermostats work) T: 256
Proportional divider [instrument]
Divider D: 241
Proportional representation [government] P: 828
Democracy D: 119
Duma (The modern Duma) D: 382
Voting V: 449
Proportional spacing
Typewriter (How a typewriter works) T: 538-539
Proportional tax
Income tax (Types of income taxes) I: 102
Proposal [debating]
Debate (Types of resolutions) D: 64
Proposal [document]
Publishing (Preparing content for publication)
P: 866
Proposition [logic]
Debate (Types of resolutions) D: 64
Proposition 13
California (The late 1900's) C: 63
Proposition 209
Affirmative action A: 91
Propranolol [drug]
Beta-blocker B: 274
Proprietary colony [U.S. history]
Colonial life in America (Changes in colonial
control) Ci: 791
South Carolina (Colonial days) So: 659
United States, History of the (The American
colonies [1607-1753]) U: 152-153
Proprietary hospital
Hospital (Type of ownership) H: 371
Proprietary material
Public domain P: 855
Proprietary school
Vocational education (Proprietary schools) V: 434
Proprietorship
Business (Single proprietorships) B: 725
Propyl alcohol See Propanol in this index
Propylaea [building, Athens]
Athens (The Acropolis and its buildings) A: 856
Propylene [chemical]
Glycerol (Production) G: 237
Pro-rally [race]
Automobile racing (Other kinds of racing)
A: 978-979
Prosaurolophus [dinosaur]
Dinosaur (True dinosaurs) D: 206b-206c
Prosauropod [dinosaur]
Dinosaur (Saurischians) D: 208
Proscenium [theater]
Drama (The Italian stage) D: 330-331
Theater (The stage) T: 233 with picture
Prose [literature] P: 828
See also the list of Related articles in the Prose
article
English literature (Prose writings) E: 317;
(Restoration prose) E: 318; (Romantic prose)
E: 320
Greek literature (Historical literature) G: 377; (The
Greco-Roman Age) G: 378
Irish literature I: 430
Prose Edda [book by Snorri]
Edda E: 74
Prose poem [literary form]
Baudelaire, Charles B: 173
Prosecuting attorney
Court (How courts work) Ci: 1101
District attorney D: 240
Law enforcement (Trial) L: 141
Prosecutor-general [office]
Russia (Courts) R: 532
Proserpina [mythology] See Persephone in this
index
Prosimian [zoology]
Primate P: 777; (Kinds of primates) P: 777 with
pictures
Proslavery movement [U.S. history] P: 828
Slavery (Views of slavery) S: 502-503
Proslogion [book by Anselm]
Anselm, Saint A: 519
Proso millet [grain]

Millet **M: 555**
Prosoma [biology]
Horseshoe crab **H: 368**
Prosopopéia [book by Texeira Pinto]
Latin American literature (Colonial literature)
L: 112
Prospect Creek [Alaska]
United States (Climate) **U: 126** *with picture*
Prospect Park [park]
New York City (Brooklyn) **N: 326-328**
Prospecting P: 829
Gas [fuel] (Exploring for gas) **G: 53**
Gold (Gold deposits) **G: 252**
Gold rush **G: 254** *with picture*
Western frontier life in America (Mining) **W: 234**
Westward movement in America (California)
W: 249 *with picture*
Prospecting [sales]
Sales (Prospecting) **S: 62**
Prospectus [report]
Initial public offering **I: 271**
Prospero [literary figure]
Shakespeare, William: *(The Tempest)* **S: 365**
Prosser, Gabriel [American slave revolt leader] *See*
Gabriel *in this index*
Prost, Alain [French race driver]
Automobile racing (table: Formula One World
Drivers' Championship) **A: 980**
Prostaglandin [physiology] **P: 829**
Abortion (Abortion methods) **A: 14-15**
Aspirin (How aspirin works) **A: 816**
Fever **F: 83**
Ulcer **U: 15**
Prostate cancer [disorder] **P: 829**
Cancer (Classification by primary body site)
C: 167-168; (table) **C: 170**
Prostate gland [anatomy] **P: 830**
Gland (table) **G: 209**
Human body (table) **H: 422** *with diagram*
Incontinence **I: 106**
Prostate cancer **P: 829**
Reproduction, Human (The human reproductive
system) **R: 244-245** *with diagram*
Vasectomy **V: 287**
Prostate-specific antigen [protein]
Prostate cancer **P: 829**
Prosthesis [medicine]
Artificial limb **A: 760** *with picture*
Prosthetics **P: 830** *with picture*
Prosthetic eye
Artificial eye **A: 759**
Prosthetic group [physiology]
Enzyme (Structure) **E: 341**
Prosthetics [medicine] **P: 830** *with picture*
Disability *picture on* **D: 218**
Prosthodontics [medicine]
Dentistry (Prosthodontics) **D: 144**
Prostitution P: 830
Bath (History) **B: 164**
Prostrate spurge [plant]
Spurge **So: 810**
Protactinium [element] **P: 831**
Protagoras [book by Plato]
Plato (The dialogues) **P: 567**
Protagoras [Greek philosopher]
Oratory (Beginnings) **O: 818**
Sophists **S: 595**
Protea [tree] **P: 831** *with picture*
Protease [enzyme]
AIDS (Treatment) **A: 164b-165**
Protease inhibitor [drug]
AIDS (Treatment) **A: 164b-165**
Protecting exposures [method]
Fire department (Firefighting) **F: 123-124**
Protection
See also Conservation; Protective coloration *in
this index*
Animal (How animals protect themselves) **A: 493**
with pictures; (Providing protection) **A: 500;**
(How human beings protect animals) **A: 505**
with picture
Clothing (Protection) **Ci: 686**
Free trade **F: 499**
Protection from abuse order [law]
Restraining order **R: 263**
Protection piece
Climbing (Technical climbing) **Ci: 680**
Protectionism [policy]
Economics (The world economy) **E: 61**
International trade (Government trade policies)
I: 348
Protectionists [Australian history]
Australia (Building a nation) **A: 923**
Protective coloration [biology] **P: 831** *with picture*
See also Mimicry *in this index*
Animal (Camouflage) **A: 493** *with pictures*
Bird (Protection against enemies) **B: 355** *with

picture*
Butterfly (How butterflies protect themselves)
B: 742
Fish (Skin and color) **F: 160;** (How fish protect
themselves) **F: 165-166** *with picture*
Flounder **F: 267** *with picture*
Grasshopper *picture on* **G: 327**
Insect (Protection from enemies) **I: 297** *with
picture*
Lizard (Defenses) **L: 400**
Mammal (Methods of attack and defense) **M: 126**
with picture
Moth *picture on* **M: 837**
Reptile (Protection) **R: 252**
Protective order [law]
Restraining order **R: 263**
Protective resemblance *See* Mimicry *in this index*
Protective tariff [economics]
Republican Party (Political inactivity) **R: 255**
Tariff (Main kinds of tariffs) **T: 43**
Protectorate, The [English history]
England (table) **E: 308;** (The Civil War) **E: 308-309**
Protein [biology] **P: 832**
Amino acid **A: 432**
Cell (The nucleus) **C: 328;** (Producing proteins)
C: 333 *with diagrams*
Decay **D: 67**
Enzyme **E: 340**
Fat substitute **F: 53**
Flour (Types of flour) **F: 268**
Food (Building and repairing tissues) **F: 331**
Food supply (Protein) **F: 346**
Genomics **G: 90**
Heredity **H: 200;** (The flow of genetic
information) **H: 205**
Human body (Chemical elements and molecules)
H: 417
Kwashiorkor **K: 398**
Life (Proteins) **L: 278**
Lymphatic system (Absorption of fats) **L: 535**
Metabolism (Anabolism) **M: 424**
Milk (Proteins) **M: 546**
Molecular biology (The beginning of molecular
biology) **M: 691-692**
Nitrogen (Nitrogen and life) **N: 425**
Nutrition (Kinds of nutrients) **N: 625;** (Deficiency
diseases) **N: 630**
Pellagra **P: 232**
Prion **P: 804**
Proteomics **P: 833**
RNA **R: 357**
Soybean **So: 689;** (Soy meal) **So: 690**
Vegetarianism **V: 294**
Protein-calorie malnutrition *See* Protein-energy
malnutrition *in this index*
Protein-energy malnutrition
Food supply (Basic human food needs) **F: 346**
Malnutrition **M: 111**
Nutrition (Deficiency diseases) **N: 630**
Proteome [biology]
Genomics **G: 90**
Proteomics **P: 833**
Proteomics [science] **P: 833**
Proterozoic Eon [geology]
Earth (Age of Earth) **E: 26**
Ice age **I: 6;** (The Proterozoic ice ages) **I: 7**
Protest *See* Social protest *in this index*
Protest [legal document]
Note (Liability of the maker) **N: 550-551**
Protestant ethic [sociology] **P: 833**
Reformation (Political and social influences)
R: 198
Weber, Max **W: 176**
Protestant Ethic and the Spirit of Capitalism, The
[book by Weber]
Protestant ethic **P: 833**
Weber, Max **W: 176**
Protestant Old Order Amish [sect]
Evolution (Genetic drift) **E: 429**
Protestant Reformation *See* Reformation *in this
index*
Protestantism [religion] **P: 833**
*See also the list of Related articles in the
Protestantism article*
Augsburg Confession **A: 885**
Bible (table) **B: 281;** (The Christian Old Testament)
B: 282; (The Bible in worship) **B: 286**
Calvin, John **C: 70**
Christianity (Organization) **C: 522g;** (The
Reformation) **C: 524;** (Christianity today)
C: 526-527
Congregationalists **Ci: 940f**
Counter Reformation (Counteracting
Protestantism) **Ci: 1096**
Divorce (The divorce rate) **D: 254-255**
England (The English Reformation) **E: 307**
Europe (Religions) **E: 386-387**

Evangelicalism **E: 422**
Family (Development of the Western family) **F: 22**
Fundamentalism (Development of Protestant
fundamentalism) **F: 556**
Grace **G: 295**
Hus, John **H: 457**
Knox, John **K: 358**
Latin America (Religion) **L: 98-99**
Luther, Martin **L: 527**
Melanchthon, Philipp **M: 388**
Minister **M: 578**
Missionary (Organization) **M: 621**
National Council of Churches **N: 33**
Northern Ireland **N: 521;** (Protestant settlement)
N: 524
Old Testament (Contents) **O: 741**
Orange Order **O: 817**
Parochial school **P: 178**
Protestant ethic **P: 833**
Reformation **R: 195**
Religion (How the major religions are organized)
R: 218; (Christianity) **R: 222-223**
Religious life (Religious life in the 1500's and
1600's) **R: 227;** (Religious life in the 1700's and
1800's) **R: 227**
Sacrament **S: 5**
School (The development of Canadian schools)
S: 184
Wesley, John **W: 197**
Women's movement (From the Renaissance to
the 1800's) **W: 384**
Wycliffe, John **W: 515**
Zwingli, Huldreich **Z: 610**
Proteus [Greek mythology]
Helen of Troy **H: 168**
Poseidon **P: 697**
Proteus [literary figure]
Shakespeare, William: *(The Two Gentlemen of
Verona)* **S: 356**
Proteus syndrome [disorder]
Neurofibromatosis **N: 152**
Prothallium [botany]
Fern (Life cycle of a fern) **F: 75**
Prothrombin
Anticoagulant **A: 553**
Protist [biology] **P: 836**
Algae (Structure of algae) **A: 349**
Animal **A: 468**
Classification, Scientific (Groups in classification)
Ci: 655
Kingdom **K: 328**
Protista [biology]
Kingdom **K: 328**
Protist **P: 836**
Protium [isotope]
Atom (The atomic mass number) **A: 871-872**
Hydrogen (Isotopes) **H: 469**
Proto-Canaanite [alphabet]
Alphabet (Proto-Canaanite and Phoenician)
A: 383
Protoceratops [dinosaur]
Dinosaur (True dinosaurs) **D: 206b-208**
Protocol [computing]
Computer (Internet software) **Ci: 922**
Internet **I: 350**
Protocol [document] **P: 836**
Protocol [etiquette]
Etiquette **E: 374**
Protoctista [biology] *See* Protista *in this index*
Proto-Indo-European [language]
English language (Origins) **E: 313**
Etymology (Etymons and cognates) **E: 376**
Linguistics (Comparative and historical research)
L: 337
Mythology (Comparative approaches) **M: 989**
Proto-language
Language (Language families) **L: 65**
Linguistics (Comparative reconstruction) **L: 336**
Proton [physics] **P: 836**
Alpha particle **A: 381**
Atom (The parts of an atom) **A: 870** *with
diagrams;* (The properties of atoms) **A: 871**
with diagrams; (Forces in the nucleus) **A: 873**
Baryon **B: 122**
Battery (How batteries work) **B: 168**
Cosmic rays (Galactic cosmic rays) **Ci: 1076**
Electricity (Electric charge) **E: 191** *with diagram*
Electron **E: 203**
Electronics (How a circuit works) **E: 208**
Element, Chemical (The periodic table of the
elements) **E: 219**
Force (Kinds of force) **F: 370**
Gluon **G: 237**
Kendall, Henry Way **K: 258**
Magnetism (How magnetism works) **M: 60b**
Matter (Structure of matter) **M: 310**
Nuclear energy (Atoms and nuclei) **N: 581** *with

diagram; (Nuclear fission) N: 582
Nuclear physics N: 595
Nuclear weapon (How nuclear weapons work)
  N: 597
Particle accelerator (Uses of accelerators) P: 184
Physics (Uncovering the secrets of the atom)
  P: 442
Quark Q: 7
Radiation (Radiation and radioactivity) R: 75;
  (Particle radiation) R: 76
Relativity (General relativity) R: 211
Rutherford, Ernest R: 569
Star (Fusion in stars) So: 846
Subatomic particle So: 936
Proton [spacecraft]
Space exploration *picture on* So: 699
Proton donor [chemistry]
Acid A: 26
Proton exchange membrane fuel cell [device]
Fuel cell (A common fuel cell) F: 551
Proton-proton chain [physics]
Astronomy (Advances in astrophysics) A: 848
Star (Hydrogen fusion) So: 846
Sun (Nuclear fusion) So: 978
Protonema [botany]
Moss (How mosses live) M: 834-835
Proto-oncogene [gene]
Cancer (How damaged genes cause cancer)
  C: 169
Protoplanetary disk [astronomy]
Planet (How the planets formed) P: 514
Protoplasm [biology] P: 837
Proto-Sinaitic [alphabet]
Alphabet (Semitic scripts) A: 381 *with pictures*
Protostar [astronomy]
Star (Fusion in stars) So: 846; (Evolution of stars)
  So: 848
Protostellar wind
Star (Intermediate-mass stars) So: 848
Prototype [engineering]
Airplane (Design and testing) A: 228
Automobile (Testing the car) A: 956
Industrial design (How an industrial designer
  works) I: 244
Manufacturing (Design and engineering) M: 170
Protozoan [organism] P: 837 *with pictures*
Ameba A: 406 *with diagrams*
Antibiotic (Other kinds of antibiotics) A: 550
Disease *picture on* D: 229; (Other infectious
  diseases) D: 227
Flagellum F: 224
Heredity *picture on* H: 200
Malaria M: 95 *with pictures*
Paramecium P: 152 *with picture*
Parasite (Types) P: 154
Protist P: 836
Spore (Protozoan spores) So: 802 *with diagram*
Protractor [measuring device] P: 838 *with picture*
Angle A: 462
Protura [entomology]
Insect (table) I: 299
Proudhon, Pierre Joseph [French author] P: 838
Anarchism A: 448
Government (Anarchism) G: 288
Marx, Karl (Early development) M: 237
Socialism (Early socialist ideas) So: 560
Proust, Joseph Louis [French chemist] P: 838
Proust, Marcel [French author] P: 838
French literature (The early years) F: 522
Merrill, James M: 418
Novel (New directions in the novel) N: 573-574
Prouty, George H. [American political leader]
Vermont (table) V: 333
Proved area [mining]
Gas [fuel] (Exploring for gas) G: 53
Proved recoverable reserves [mining]
Coal (World coal reserves) Ci: 721
Provençal [language]
French language (Old French) F: 517
Mistral, Frédéric M: 676
Romance languages R: 415
Spanish literature (Early medieval literature)
  So: 757-758
Troubadour T: 452
Provence [region, France]
Gaul G: 70
Provence, Count of *See* Louis XVIII *in this index*
Provensen, Alice [American author]
Caldecott Medal (table: 1984) C: 26
Literature for children *picture on* L: 382
Provensen, Martin [American author]
Caldecott Medal (table: 1984) C: 26
Literature for children *picture on* L: 382
Proverb [expression] P: 839
Fable F: 2
Folklore (Characteristics of folklore) F: 323
Proverbs, Book of [Bible] P: 839

Bible (The Writings) B: 281-282
Proverb P: 839
Proverbs of Solomon [Bible]
Proverbs, Book of P: 839
Providence [Rhode Island] P: 839 *with picture*
Rhode Island *picture on* R: 297; (table: Average
  monthly weather) R: 308; (Settlement) R: 312
Williams, Roger (In Massachusetts) W: 311
Providence Canyon State Park
Georgia *picture on* G: 124
Providence Gazette, The [newspaper]
Goddard, Mary Katherine G: 244
Goddard, William G: 245
Providence Plantations [U.S. history]
Rhode Island R: 296
Providence Public Library
Rhode Island (Libraries) R: 300
Providence River
Rhode Island (Rivers and lakes) R: 306 *with map*
Provident Hospital [Chicago]
Williams, Daniel Hale W: 310
Province [political unit] P: 840
Canada, Government of (The constitution)
  C: 129; (The 10 provinces) C: 136
South Africa (Provincial government) So: 609
Province House National Historic Site [Prince
  Edward Island]
Canada (table: National historic sites) C: 115
Prince Edward Island (Places to visit) P: 788
Province of the Heart, The [essays by McGinley]
McGinley, Phyllis M: 334
Provincetown [Massachusetts]
Cape Cod C: 188 *with map*
Massachusetts *picture on* M: 271
Provincetown Players [theater company]
Glaspell, Susan G: 210
Provincial Academy of Arts and Sciences
New Brunswick, University of N: 199
Provincial court
Canada, Government of (The courts) C: 136
Provincial Letters [book by Pascal]
Pascal, Blaise P: 189
**Provincial Museum of Newfoundland and
  Labrador** [St. John's]
Newfoundland and Labrador (Libraries and
  museums) N: 364
Provincial park
Park (State, provincial, and national parks) P: 168
Provincial Seamen's Museum [Grand Bank]
Newfoundland and Labrador (Libraries and
  museums) N: 364
Proving [remedy]
Homeopathy H: 303
Provisional government P: 840
Provisional IRA [Irish history]
Irish Republican Army (Violence and peace)
  I: 433-434
Provisions of Oxford [English history]
Henry III H: 186
Provitamin A
Vitamin (Vitamin A) V: 430
Provo [Utah] P: 840 *with picture*
Prow [ship device]
Vikings (Shipbuilding and navigation) V: 381
Proxemics [study]
Communication (The study of communication)
  Ci: 887
Proxima Centauri [star]
Alpha Centauri A: 381
Star So: 840; (table: The 10 known stars nearest
  Earth) So: 843
Proximate analysis [geology]
Coal (Analyzing coal composition) Ci: 717
Proximity fuse [device]
Ammunition (How shells explode) A: 436
Bomb (How bombs work) B: 450
Warship (Warships in the two world wars)
  W: 41-42
Proximity fuze [device]
Guided missile (The warhead) G: 423-424
Proxmire, William [American political leader]
P: 841
Proxy [document]
Business (Stockholders) B: 726
Voting (Methods of voting) V: 449-450
Proxy appointment [document]
Living will L: 399
Prozac [drug] *See* Fluoxetine *in this index*
Prudence [philosophy]
Ethics (Aristotle) E: 366
Prudential Building
Buffalo (The city) B: 676
Prudential Center [Boston]
Boston (Back Bay) B: 497
Prudhoe Bay [Alaska]
Alaska (Mining) A: 298; (The discovery of oil)
  A: 304 *with picture*

Prudhomme, Manuel [American frontiersman]
Hot Springs H: 374b
Prune [fruit] P: 841
Plum (Kinds of plums) P: 577
Prune plum [fruit]
Prune P: 841
Pruning [gardening] P: 841 *with pictures*
Fruit (Caring for the crop) F: 546-547
Gardening *pictures on* G: 35; (Pruning) G: 36
Tree (Caring for the tree) T: 431
Tree surgery T: 433
Prusiner, Stanley Ben [American physiologist]
Nobel Prizes (Physiology or medicine: 1997)
  N: 446
Prussia [former country] P: 842 *with map*
See also the list of Related articles in the Prussia
  article
Army (The rise of modern armies) A: 727-728
Berlin (Prussian capital) B: 264
Draft, Military (Military drafts throughout history)
  D: 318
Education (The rise of universal public schools)
  E: 101
Franco-Prussian War F: 483
Germany (The rise of Prussia) G: 164
Marx, Karl (Marx's life) M: 236
Poland (The partitions) P: 612 *with maps*
Seven Weeks' War S: 324b
Seven Years' War S: 328
Warsaw (History) W: 38
Prussian blue [chemical] P: 843
Prussic acid [chemical] P: 843
Almond A: 380
Tapioca T: 41
"Prydain Chronicles" [books by Alexander]
Alexander, Lloyd A: 342
Prynne, Hester [literary figure]
Hawthorne, Nathaniel (His novels) H: 115
Pryor, David H. [American political leader]
Arkansas (table) A: 712
Przewalski, Nikolai M. [Russian explorer]
Przewalski's horse P: 844
Przewalski's horse P: 844
Horse *picture on* H: 360; (Wild horses) H: 348
  with picture
PSA test [medicine]
Prostate cancer P: 829
Psalm 23 [Bible]
Metaphor M: 429
Psalms, Book of [Bible] P: 844
Bible (The Writings) B: 281; (The Bible in worship)
  B: 286
Illuminated manuscript I: 78
Psalter *See* Psalms, Book of *in this index*
PSAT/NMSQT [test] *See* Preliminary SAT/National
  Merit Scholarship Qualifying Test *in this index*
Pseudepigrapha [documents]
Dead Sea Scrolls D: 56
Pseudocoelomate [biology]
Coelom Ci: 753
Pseudomonas [bacteria]
Antibiotic (Resistance to antibiotics) A: 551
Pseudomonas mallei [bacteria]
Glanders G: 210
Pseudonym [name] P: 844
Name (Pseudonyms) N: 7
Pen name P: 234
Pseudonymous Letters
New Testament (Letters) N: 287
Pseudopod [biology]
Ameba A: 406
Pseudoscience
Alchemy A: 334
Graphology G: 323
Numerology N: 607
Palmistry P: 111
Phrenology P: 430
Psi particle [nuclear particle] P: 844
Physics (Advances in the mid-1900's) P: 442
Psittacosaurus [dinosaur]
Dinosaur (True dinosaurs) D: 206b-208
Psittacosis [disease] P: 844
Parrot (Parrots and people) P: 179-181
Veterinary medicine V: 345
Psocoptera [entomology]
Insect (table) I: 300
PSOE [political party] *See* Partido Socialista Obrero
  Español
Psoralen [drug]
Vitiligo V: 432
Psoriasis [disorder] P: 844
PSR 1913+16 [astronomy]
Gravitation (Gravitational waves) G: 332
PSR B1257+12 [astronomy]
Planet (The first discoveries) P: 513
Pulsar P: 900a
PSRO [organization]

Hospital H: 371
PSTN [electronics] *See* Public Switched Telephone Network *in this index*
Psyche [mythology] **P: 845**
  Butterfly **B: 732**
  Cupid **Ci: 1193**
Psyche [philosophy]
  Psychology (Beginnings) **P: 849**
Psychedelic drug
  Hallucinogenic drug **H: 25**
Psychedelic rock
  Rock music (Psychedelic rock) **R: 380a**
Psychiatric illness *See* Mental illness *in this index*
Psychiatric social worker
  Psychotherapy **P: 851**
Psychiatric unit
  Hospital (Hospital units) **H: 372**
Psychiatrist [career]
  Psychoanalysis **P: 846**
  Psychotherapy **P: 851**
Psychiatry P: 845
  Barbiturate (Medical uses) **B: 107**
  Medicine (table) **M: 369**
  Mental illness (Treatment of mental illness) **M: 407**
  Psychology (Psychology and other sciences) **P: 847**
Psychic
  Fortunetelling **F: 419**
Psychical research [psychology] **P: 846**
  See also Extrasensory perception *in this index*
Psychoanalysis [psychiatry] **P: 846**
  See also Freudian theory *in this index; and the list of Related articles in the* Psychoanalysis *article*
  Biography (Modern biography) **B: 314**
  Catharsis **C: 301**
  Freud, Sigmund (His life) **F: 530**
  Jung, Carl Gustav **J: 194**
  Libido **L: 233**
  Mental illness (Psychotherapy) **M: 407**
  Personality (Personality change) **P: 302-303**
  Psychiatry (Psychotherapy) **P: 845**
  Psychology (Psychoanalysis) **P: 850**
  Psychotherapy (Psychodynamic-interpersonal psychotherapy) **P: 852**
  Unconscious **U: 20**
Psychoanalyst [career]
  Psychoanalysis **P: 846**
Psychodrama [psychology]
  Role playing **R: 402**
Psychodynamic theory [psychiatry]
  Abnormal psychology (Theories of abnormal psychology) **A: 12**
Psychogenic amnesia [psychology]
  Memory (Memory disorders) **M: 394**
Psychogenic fugue [disorder]
  Amnesia **A: 437**
  Mental illness (Dissociative disorders) **M: 406**
Psychographics [sociology]
  Magazine **M: 42**
Psychokinesis [psychology]
  Extrasensory perception (What parapsychologists study) **E: 457**
  Parapsychology **P: 153**
Psycholinguistic disability
  Learning disabilities (Types) **L: 165-166**
Psychological acoustics [science]
  Acoustics **A: 29**
Psychological anthropology
  Anthropology (Cultural anthropology) **A: 547**
Psychological stress evaluator
  Lie detector **L: 271**
Psychological warfare P: 846
  Propaganda **P: 823**
  World War II (Propaganda) **W: 494-495**
Psychologist [career]
  Careers (Life, physical, and social sciences) **C: 225-226**
  Psychology (Careers in psychology) **P: 850**
  Psychotherapy **P: 851**
Psychology P: 847 *with pictures*
  See also the list of Related articles in the Psychology *article*
  Clinical psychology **Ci: 681**
  Comparative psychology **Ci: 902a**
  Ego **E: 119**
  Evolutionary psychology **E: 434**
  Gestalt psychology **G: 175**
  Habit (How we learn habits) **H: 2**
  Learning **L: 162**
  Mental illness (Treatment of mental illness) **M: 407**
  Motivation **M: 875**
  Mythology (Psychological approaches) **M: 990**
  Personality **P: 300f**
  Phobia **P: 392**
  Plato (Psychology and politics) **P: 568**

Psychiatry **P: 845**
Psychoanalysis **P: 846**
Psychosomatic medicine **P: 851**
Science (The social sciences) **S: 194**
Unconscious **U: 20**
Wundt, Wilhelm **W: 514**
Psychomotor epilepsy
  Epilepsy **E: 343**
Psychopathology *See* Abnormal psychology *in this index*
Psychosexual development
  Psychoanalysis (Psychoanalytic theory) **P: 846**
Psychosis [psychiatry] **P: 851**
  Clinical psychology (Psychotherapy and consultation) **Ci: 681**
  Cocaine (Physical and psychological effects) **Ci: 742-743**
  Mental illness **M: 404**
  Postpartum depression **P: 709**
  Psychiatry (Psychiatric disorders) **P: 845**
  Tranquilizer **T: 369**
Psychosomatic medicine [psychology] **P: 851**
Psychotherapy [psychiatry] **P: 851**
  Catharsis **C: 301**
  Clinical psychology (Psychotherapy and consultation) **Ci: 681**
  Depression **D: 151**
  Disease (Medical treatment) **D: 232-233**
  Hypnosis (Uses of hypnosis) **H: 479**
  Mental illness (Psychotherapy) **M: 407**
  Psychiatry (Treatment) **P: 845**
  Psychoanalysis **P: 846**
  Social work (Mental health) **So: 558**
Psychrometer [instrument]
  Hygrometer (The psychrometer) **H: 474**
Psychrophile [biology]
  Extremophile **E: 458**
Psyllium [plant] **P: 852** *with picture*
Pt [symbol]
  Platinum **P: 566**
PT boat P: 853 *with picture*
PTA [organization] *See* Parent-Teacher Association *in this index*
Ptah [Egyptian god]
  Egypt, Ancient *picture on* **E: 140**; (Religion) **E: 137**
  Mythology *picture on* **M: 977**; (Other Egyptian divinities) **M: 980**
Ptarmigan [bird] **P: 853**
  Animal *pictures on* **A: 484, A: 485**
  Bird *pictures on* **B: 355**; (Birds of the Arctic) **B: 343** *with picture*
  Protective coloration *picture on* **P: 831**
PTC [chemical] *See* Phenylthiocarbamide *in this index*
Pteranodon [extinct animal]
  Pterosaur **P: 854** *with picture*
Pterodactyl [extinct animal]
  Fossil *picture on* **F: 423**
  Pterosaur **P: 854** *with picture*
Pterosaur [extinct animal] **P: 853** *with picture*
  Anning, Mary **A: 517**
  Dinosaur **D: 206a**
  Fossil (Understanding ancient plants and animals) **F: 423** *with picture*
  Prehistoric animal (Other reptiles) **P: 737**
Pteryla [zoology]
  Feather (Kinds and parts of feathers) **F: 59**
PTF boat
  PT boat **P: 853**
Ptolemaic dynasty [Egyptian]
  Egypt, Ancient (The Ptolemies) **E: 144** *with picture*
Ptolemy [Greek astronomer] **P: 854**
  Antarctica (Exploration) **A: 535**
  Astronomy (Earth-centered theories) **A: 835**; (History) **A: 846-847** *with diagram*
  Atlas (History) **A: 868**
  Circle (History) **Ci: 558**
  Columbus, Christopher (The plan to sail westward) **Ci: 858**
  Copernicus, Nicolaus (Theories of heavenly motion) **Ci: 1039**
  Galileo (Early scientific interests) **G: 11**
  Geography (Early study) **G: 95**
  Map *picture on* **M: 176**; (Ancient maps) **M: 182-183**; (Advances in European cartography) **M: 184**
  Mathematics (The Greeks) **M: 306**
  Moon (Ancient ideas) **M: 791-792**
  Physics (The Greeks) **P: 438**
  Planet (How planets move) **P: 508-509**
Ptolemy I [king of ancient Egypt] **P: 854**
  Alexandria (History) **A: 344**
  Bible (The first translations) **B: 284**
  Library (Egypt) **L: 258**
Ptolemy II [king of ancient Egypt]
  Library (Egypt) **L: 258**
Ptolemy V [king of ancient Egypt]

Rosetta stone **R: 479**
Ptolemy XII [king of ancient Egypt]
  Cleopatra (Cleopatra and Caesar) **Ci: 662a**
Ptolemy XIII [king of ancient Egypt]
  Cleopatra (Cleopatra and Caesar) **Ci: 662a**
Ptolemy XIV [king of ancient Egypt]
  Cleopatra (Cleopatra and Caesar) **Ci: 662a**
Ptolemy XV [king of ancient Egypt] *See* Caesarion *in this index*
Ptolemy Philadelphos [son of]
  Cleopatra (Cleopatra and Mark Antony) **Ci: 662a-662b**
PTSA [organization]
  Parent-teacher organizations (Parent-Teacher-Student Associations) **P: 158**
PTSD [psychology] *See* Post-traumatic stress disorder *in this index*
Ptyalin [enzyme]
  Mastication **M: 298**
  Saliva **S: 67**
Pu [symbol]
  Plutonium **P: 581**
Pu-239 [isotope]
  Nuclear energy (Wastes and waste disposal) **N: 588**
Pu Yi [emperor of China] **P: 855**
Pub
  England (Recreation) *picture on* **E: 294-296**
  Ireland (Way of life) **I: 420**
  London (Recreation) **L: 434** *with picture*
Puberty [human development]
  Adolescent **A: 60**
  Child (The preteen-age years) **C: 450**
  Hormone (Growth and sex hormones) **H: 336**
  Middle school **M: 535**
  Reproduction, Human (The human reproductive system) **R: 244**
  Sex education (How sex education is taught) **S: 336**
  Sexuality (Biological factors) **S: 337**
  Testosterone **T: 182a**
Pubis [anatomy]
  Dinosaur *picture on* **D: 206c**
  Human body (table) **H: 422** *with diagram*
  Pelvis **P: 233** *with diagram*
Pubis Angelical [book by Puig]
  Latin American literature (The post-Boom) **L: 114**
Public [people]
  Public relations **P: 864**
Public accountant [career]
  Accounting (Fields of accounting) **A: 23**
Public administration [government]
  Political science (Public administration) **P: 638**
Public administrator [law]
  Administrator **A: 58**
Public advocate [office]
  New York City (Government) **N: 339-340**
Public Against Violence [political party]
  Czechoslovakia (The Velvet Revolution) **Ci: 1216**
Public and society benefit [program]
  Foundation (Public and society benefits) **F: 431**
Public aquarium *See* Aquarium, Public *in this index*
Public assistance
  See also Welfare *in this index*
  Insurance (Social insurance) **I: 313**
  Poverty (Social welfare programs) **P: 725**
  Welfare **W: 190**
Public bath
  Bath (History) **B: 164** *with picture*
  Rome (Baths) **R: 433**
Public bill [legislation]
  Congress of the United States (Proposing new laws) **Ci: 944**
Public Broadcasting, Corporation for *See* Corporation for Public Broadcasting *in this index*
Public Broadcasting Service P: 855
  Burns, Ken **B: 709**
  Television (Public stations) **T: 114-115** *with picture*
Public choice [economics]
  Economics (Fields of economics) **E: 64**
Public Citizen, Inc. [organization]
  Nader, Ralph **N: 2**
Public corporation
  Corporation (Business corporations) **Ci: 1069**
  Nationalization (Forms of nationalization) **N: 63**
Public defender [law] **P: 855**
  Court (How courts work) **Ci: 1101**
Public domain [law] **P: 855**
  Copyright **Ci: 1046**
  Publishing (Picture editors) **P: 867**
Public-domain land
  Public lands **P: 857**
Public economics
  Economics (Fields of economics) **E: 64**
Public education
  Charter school **C: 386**

Colonial life in America (Education) **Ci: 803**
Creationism (The 1900's) **Ci: 1123**
Education (Control and support of U.S. education) **E: 94**; (Education in Canada) **E: 95**
Elementary school (Kinds of elementary schools) **E: 224**
Germany (Education) **G: 151** *with picture*
High school (High schools in the United States) **H: 228**
Local government (Functions of local government) **L: 407**
No Child Left Behind Act **N: 438**
Reconstruction (New state programs and policies) **R: 179**
Religious education (Public schools) **R: 225**
School (Kinds of schools) **S: 181**; (Public schools) **S: 182**; (The development of U.S. schools) **S: 183**; (The development of Canadian schools) **S: 184**
Teaching (Employment practices) **T: 68**
United States, History of the (Better education) **U: 173**
Public enemy [law]
Common carrier **Ci: 874**
Public Enemy [rap group]
Rock music (Rap) **R: 380d**
Public Enemy, The [film]
Cagney, James **C: 14**
Motion picture (Movies in the 1930's) **M: 867**
Public figure [law]
Libel **L: 226**
Public forum debate
Debate (A public forum debate) **D: 65**
Public Garden [Boston]
Boston (Downtown Boston) **B: 496-497**
Public goods [economics]
Capitalism (Protecting the public interest) **C: 195**
Public government
Government **G: 282**
Public health P: 855 *with pictures*
See also the list of Related articles in the Public Health *article*
Disease (Governments) **D: 234**
Epidemic **E: 343**
Global warming (Threats to human health) **G: 232b**
Health (Public health) **H: 127**
Immunization (Immunization and public health) **I: 90**
Local government (Functions of local government) **L: 407**
Medical ethics **M: 361**
Medicine (Prevention) **M: 364**
Nursing (Community health nurses) **N: 617**
Prophylaxis **P: 827**
Sanitation **S: 111**
State government (Health) **So: 864**
Public Health Agency of Canada
Quarantine **Q: 7**
Public Health Service [U.S.]
Health (Public health) **H: 127**
Health, Board of **H: 127**
Health and Human Services, Department of (Organization) **H: 128**
Public health **P: 855**
Surgeon general of the United States **So: 1004**
Public house *See* Pub *in this index*
Public housing
England (City life) **E: 296**
Housing (Affordable housing) **H: 391**
Housing and Urban Development, Department of (Functions) **H: 393**
Welfare (Other public assistance programs) **W: 191**
Public Information, Committee on [U.S. history]
Propaganda (During World War I) **P: 825**
Public Information, Department of
United Nations (Publications and information services) **U: 86-87**
Public instruction, Superintendent of [office]
State government (Other officers) **So: 863**
Public-key system [computing]
Codes and ciphers **Ci: 749**; (Public-key systems) **Ci: 750**; (Later developments) **Ci: 751**
Computer (Computer security) **Ci: 924**
Public lands P: 857
Conservation (The rise of the conservation movement) **C: 985**
Homestead Act **H: 304**
Public domain **P: 855**
Public law
Law (Branches of law) **L: 130**; (Law since 1900) **L: 136-137**
United States, Government of the (Functions) **U: 138**
Public Law 600 [1950]
Puerto Rico (Building a democracy) **P: 883**

Public Libraries Act [1850]
Library (Britain) **L: 260**
Public library
Library (Active community service) **L: 236-237**; (Public libraries) **L: 240** *with pictures*; (Western Europe) **L: 252**; (Libraries in the United States) **L: 261**
Public official bond
Bonding **B: 455**
Public-only health care system
Health insurance, National **H: 129**
Public opinion P: 858 *with picture*
Foreign policy (Public opinion) **F: 388**
Journalism (Influencing public opinion) **J: 173**
Public opinion poll **P: 861**
Public Opinion, American Institute of
Gallup, George Horace **G: 16**
Public opinion poll P: 861 *with picture*
Political convention (Measuring convention success) **P: 630**
Psychology (Systematic assessment) **P: 848**
Sociology (Surveys) **So: 565**
Public option [insurance]
Obama, Barack (Domestic issues) **O: 640g**
Public ownership *See* Government ownership *in this index*
Public policy medical ethics
Medical ethics **M: 361**
Public printer [office]
Government Printing Office **G: 292**
Public-private partnership
Urban renewal (The role of government) **U: 220**
Public relations P: 863
Public Safety, Committee of [French history] *See* Committee of Public Safety *in this index*
Public school [England]
Education (The rise of universal public schools) **E: 101**; (Who should choose a child's school?) **E: 106**
England (Education) **E: 297**
London (Education) **L: 433**
Private school **P: 808a**
United Kingdom (Education) **U: 56-57**
Public school [United States] *See* Public education *in this index*
Public service
Careers (Community and social services) **C: 221** *with picture*
Government (Public services and other functions) **G: 283**
Public service announcement
Radio (Information) **R: 85**
Public Service Commission of Canada
Civil service (Civil service in other lands) **Ci: 613**
Public speaking P: 864
See also Debate *in this index*
Oratory **O: 818**
A Guide to Speaking Skills **Research Guide: 20**
Public Square
Cleveland (Downtown Cleveland) **Ci: 663**
Ohio *picture on* **O: 681**
Public Switched Telephone Network
Telephone (How a telephone call travels) **T: 95**
Public television
Corporation for Public Broadcasting **Ci: 1070**
Public Broadcasting Service **P: 855**
Television (Public television) **T: 110b**; (Public stations) **T: 114** *with picture*
Public theater [English history]
Shakespeare, William (Theater buildings) **S: 351** *with picture*
Public transportation
Disability *picture on* **D: 219**
Safety (Safety in transportation) **S: 14**
Transit **T: 374**
Transportation (Urban public transportation) **T: 393** *with picture*; (Inadequate public transportation facilities) **T: 398**
Public utility P: 865
Economics (Government intervention) **E: 59**
Electric power (The electric power industry) **E: 186**
Franchise (Public franchises) **F: 480**
Industry (Monopolies) **I: 261**
Monopoly and competition (Kinds of monopoly and competition) **M: 732**
Poverty (Social welfare programs) **P: 725**
Public works
State government (State services) **So: 864**
United States, History of the (Recovery and reform) **U: 193**
Public Works Administration [U.S. history]
Great Depression (The New Deal) **G: 341**
Housing (Housing since 1900) **H: 391**
New Deal (Helping the needy) **N: 201** *with picture*; (table) **N: 201**
Publicis Groupe [company]

Advertising (The advertising industry) **A: 77**
Publicity
Political convention (Attracting publicity) **P: 630**
Public relations (Methods) **P: 863-864**
Publick Occurrences Both Forreign and Domestick [newspaper]
Harris, Benjamin **H: 68**
Journalism (Early American journalism) **J: 174**
Newspaper (Development of U.S. newspapers) **N: 386**
Publicly supported foundation
Foundation (Kinds of foundations) **F: 430**
Publicola [pen name]
Adams, John Quincy (Lawyer and writer) **A: 40-41**
Publisher [occupation]
Newspaper (The staff of a newspaper) **N: 381**
Publishing **P: 868**
Publishing [communications] **P: 868** *with picture*
Book **B: 464**
Communication (The digital age) **Ci: 885**
Computer (Publishing programs) **Ci: 919**
Copyright (How to obtain a copyright) **Ci: 1048**
Desktop publishing **D: 158** *with picture*
Magazine **M: 42**
New York (Manufacturing) **N: 310-311**
New York City (Industry) **N: 333**
Newspaper **N: 380**
Printing **P: 796**
Writing (Free-lance markets) **W: 511**
Publius [pen name]
Federalist, The **F: 66**
Puccini, Giacomo [Italian composer] **P: 869**
Belasco, David **B: 224d**
Opera *picture on* **O: 802**; (Giacomo Puccini) **O: 799**; *(Bohème, La)* **O: 801**; *(Madama Butterfly)* **O: 804** *with picture*; *(Tosca)* **O: 807**
Puccoon [plant]
Bloodroot **B: 417**
Puchero [food]
Paraguay (Food and drink) **P: 146**
Puck [electronic device]
Computer (A digitizing tablet) **Ci: 914**
Puck [hockey]
Hockey **H: 274**
Puck [legendary figure] **P: 870**
Fairy (Fairies in literature) **F: 11**
Shakespeare, William: *(A Midsummer Night's Dream)* **S: 357**
Puck [magazine]
Republican Party *picture on* **R: 256**
Puck [satellite]
Uranus *picture on* **U: 219**
Puckett, Kirby [American baseball player]
Baseball (table: Hall of Fame) **B: 134a**
Puddling [agriculture]
Rice (Preparing the ground) **R: 325** *with pictures*
Puddling furnace
Industrial Revolution (The revolution in ironmaking) **I: 249-250**
Pudong area [district]
Shanghai (History) **S: 372** *with picture*
Pudong International Airport
Airport (table) **A: 245**
Pudu [animal]
Deer *picture on* **D: 84**; (Central and South American deer) **D: 85**; (table) **D: 85**
Puebla [city, Mexico] **P: 870**
Puebla [state, Mexico] **P: 870**
Mixtec Indians **M: 680**
Puebla, Battle of [1862]
Cinco de Mayo **Ci: 557**
Pueblo [Colorado] **P: 870**
Pueblo [dwelling]
Anasazi (History) **A: 448a**
New Mexico *picture on* **N: 257**
Pueblo Indians **P: 870**
Pueblo [ship]
Korea, North (North-South relations) **K: 373**
Pueblo Bonito
Chaco Culture National Historical Park **C: 365**
New Mexico *picture on* **N: 274**; (Indian peoples) **N: 272**
Pueblo de Los Ángeles [area]
Los Angeles (Downtown Los Angeles) **L: 458**
Pueblo Indians P: 870 *with pictures*
Anasazi **A: 448a**
Hopi Indians **H: 333**
Indian, American *pictures on* **I: 147**, **I: 180**; (Weaving) **I: 146**; (Ceremonies) **I: 148**; (Indians of the Southwest) **I: 166**
Indian wars (The Pueblo revolt [1680-1692]) **I: 191**
Mission life in America (Western missions) **M: 618-619**
Nevada (Indian days) **N: 173**
Pueblo jóven [town]
Peru (Housing) **P: 309-310**

Pueblo Revolt [1680-1692]
Indian wars (The Pueblo revolt [1680-1692])
I: 191
Puelche [people]
Mapuche M: 189
Puente, Tito [American musician] P: 871
Puerperal fever [disease]
Holmes, Oliver Wendell (His life) H: 294
Puerta de Europa [Madrid]
Spain picture on So: 731
Puerta del Sol [plaza]
Madrid (The city) M: 38
Puerto Cortés [Honduras]
Honduras (The Northern Coast) H: 309 with map
Puerto del Buceo [Montevideo]
Uruguay picture on U: 222
Puerto Montt [Chile]
Chile (Climate) C: 465
Puerto Rican cherry [fruit]
Acerola A: 24 with picture
Puerto Rican Day Parade [New York City]
Hispanic Americans picture on H: 244
Puerto Rican parrot [bird]
Parrot (Kinds of parrots) P: 179
Puerto Ricans [people]
See also Hispanic Americans in this index
Hispanic Americans H: 244 with pictures
Minority group (Hispanic Americans) M: 609
New York City (Ethnic groups) N: 331-332
Puerto Rico [U.S. commonwealth] P: 872 with
pictures and maps
See also the list of Related articles in the Puerto
Rico article
Coquí Ci: 1048
Flag picture on F: 213
Hispanic Americans (In Puerto Rico and Cuba)
H: 247
Naturalization N: 67
Spanish-American War (Land battles) So: 754
Puerto Rico, University of P: 885
Puerto Rico picture on P: 876
Puerto Rico Trench [oceanography]
Atlantic Ocean (The Mid-Atlantic Ridge) A: 864
Deep D: 81
Ocean (Depth) O: 651-652
West Indies (Land and climate) W: 204
Pueyrredón, Prilidiano [Argentine painter]
Argentina (The arts) A: 651-652
Puff adder [snake]
Adder A: 47
Viper V: 391
Puff port [device]
Air cushion vehicle (How an ACV works) A: 181
with diagram
Puffball [fungus] P: 885
Mushroom (Mushroomlike fungi) M: 945
Puffer [fish] P: 885 with picture
Fish (Other useful fish) F: 146-147
Puffin [bird] P: 885 with picture
Auk A: 890
Newfoundland and Labrador picture on N: 369
Pug [dog] P: 886
Dog picture on D: 274
Pugachev, Emelian Ivanovich [Russian soldier]
Russia (Catherine the Great) R: 550
Puget, Peter [British admiral] P: 886
Washington (Discovery and exploration) W: 66
Puget Island [Washington]
Puget, Peter P: 886
Puget Sound [Washington] P: 886 with map
Washington (Land regions) W: 58 with map
Pugin, A. W. N. [British architect]
Architecture (The Gothic Revival) A: 626
Pugmill mixer [machine]
Asphalt (Paving with asphalt) A: 815
Pugsley, William [Canadian political leader]
New Brunswick (table) N: 195
**Pugwash Conferences on Science and World
Affairs** P: 886
Nobel Prizes (Peace: 1995) N: 448b
Rotblat, Joseph R: 486
Pugwash Organization
Pugwash Conferences on Science and World
Affairs P: 886a
Puig, Manuel [Argentine author]
Latin American literature (The "Boom") L: 114
Novel (The novel today) N: 575
Puisne judge [office]
Supreme Court of Canada (Organization) So: 996
with pictures
Puissance [competition]
Horse (Jumping) H: 357
Pujols, Albert [Dominican-born American baseball
player] P: 886a
Pujols Family Foundation
Pujols, Albert P: 886a
Pukaskwa National Park [Ontario]

Canada (table: National parks and national park
reserves) C: 113
Pukhtu [language] See Pashto in this index
Pukhtuns [people] See Pashtuns in this index
Pulaski, Casimir [Polish general] P: 886
Pulaski's Legion [U.S. history]
Pulaski, Casimir P: 886
Pulau Penang [city, Malaysia] See George Town in
this index
Pulci, Luigi [Italian poet]
Italian literature (Humanism and the
Renaissance) I: 494
Pulcinella [ballet by Stravinsky]
Classical music (Neoclassicism) Ci: 649
Pulcinella [literary figure]
Punch and Judy P: 902
Pulenu'u [government official]
Samoa (Government) S: 80-80a
Puli [dog] P: 886
Dog picture on D: 262
Pulitzer, Joseph [American publisher] P: 886
Hearst, William Randolph H: 131
Pulitzer Prizes P: 886a
Spanish-American War (Background to the war)
So: 753
Statue of Liberty (Construction and dedication)
So: 876-877
Pulitzer Prizes [awards] P: 886a
Pulitzer, Joseph P: 886
Pulitzer Trophy race
Airplane (The golden age) A: 235-237
Pulled wool
Wool (Types of wool) W: 399
Pulley [machine] P: 900 with diagram
Archimedes (His discoveries) A: 605
Block and tackle B: 404
Machine (Pulley) M: 15 with pictures
Simple machines S: 467
Pulling Down the Statue of George III [picture by
McCrae]
Declaration of Independence picture on D: 78
Pulling the goalie
Hockey (Hockey terms) H: 275
Pullman [former town]
Pullman, George Mortimer P: 900
Pullman, George Mortimer [American
businessman] P: 900
Railroad (Engineering improvements) R: 117
Pullman, Philip [British author] P: 900
Pullman Company
See also Pullman Strike in this index
Pullman, George Mortimer P: 900
Pullman Palace Car Company
Pullman, George Mortimer P: 900
Railroad (Engineering improvements) R: 117
Pullman sleeping car See Sleeping car in this index
Pullman Strike [1894] P: 900
Cleveland, Grover (Labor unrest) Ci: 672
Darrow, Clarence Seward D: 38
Debs, Eugene Victor D: 65
Labor movement (Opposition to unions) L: 10
with picture
Pulmonary artery [anatomy]
Artery (Principal arteries) A: 751
Circulatory system (In respiration) Ci: 559-560
Heart (Blood vessels) H: 135 with picture; (The
work of the heart) H: 135
Human body (The blood vessels) H: 421; (table)
H: 422 with diagram
Lung (Gas exchange in the lungs) L: 523-524
with diagram
Pulmonary capillary [anatomy]
Emphysema (How emphysema affects breathing)
E: 262
Lung (Parts of the lungs) L: 523
Pulmonary circulation [physiology]
Circulatory system (In respiration) Ci: 559 with
picture
Lung (Parts of the lungs) L: 523
Pulmonary edema [disorder]
Altitude sickness A: 390
Edema E: 75
Pulmonary pleura [anatomy]
Pleura P: 573
Pulmonary surfactant [physiology]
Respiratory distress syndrome R: 262
Pulmonary syndrome hantavirus [virus]
Hantavirus H: 54
Pulmonary tuberculosis [disease]
Tuberculosis (The disease) T: 478
Pulmonary vascular disease
Lung (Diseases of the lungs) L: 524-525
Pulmonary vein [anatomy]
Circulatory system (In respiration) Ci: 559-560
Heart (Blood vessels) H: 135 with picture
Human body (The blood vessels) H: 421; (table)
H: 422 with diagram

Lung (Gas exchange in the lungs) L: 523-524
with diagram
Pulmonic circulation [physiology]
Heart (Birds and mammals) H: 146
Pulmonic valve [anatomy]
Heart (Chambers, valves, and inner lining) H: 133-
135; (Blockage of blood flow) H: 141
Pulp [material]
Paper (Raw materials) P: 134 with diagram
Pulp, Dental See Dental pulp in this index
Pulp, Wood See Wood pulp in this index
Pulp chamber [dentistry]
Teeth (Pulp) T: 80 with picture
Pulp magazine
Science fiction (The early 1900's) S: 205
Pulper [machine]
Paper (How paper is made) P: 134
Pulping [industrial process]
Coffee (Preparation for market) Ci: 754
Pulping [publishing]
Publishing (Going out of print) P: 869
Pulpwood
Paper (How paper is made) P: 134 with picture
Pulque [drink]
Century plant C: 359
Maguey M: 63
Pulque agave [plant]
Maguey M: 63
Pulsar [astronomy] P: 900a
Arecibo Observatory A: 645
Astronomy (Finding pulsars) A: 849
Bell Burnell, Jocelyn Bell B: 242
Binary star B: 308
Gravitation (Gravitational waves) G: 332
Lick Observatory L: 270
Neutron star N: 155
Planet (The first discoveries) P: 513
Star (Names of stars) So: 842; (Neutron stars)
So: 851
Supernova (Results of supernovae) So: 994
Telescope (Radio and microwave telescopes)
T: 106
Pulse [agriculture]
Agriculture (Pulses) A: 147
Pulse [physiology] P: 900a
Pulse-combustion drying
Food preservation (Drying) F: 342-343
Pulse induction [electronics]
Metal detector M: 425
Pulse radar
Radar diagram on R: 70; (Pulse radar) R: 69
Pulsed laser
Laser (Kinds of lasers) L: 85
Pulverized coal
Coke Ci: 759
Pulvillus [entomology]
Fly (Thorax) F: 309 with diagram
Puma [wild cat]
Mountain lion M: 898 with pictures
Pumice [rock] P: 900a
Rock (Extrusive rock) R: 371; (table) R: 373 with
picture
Volcano (Pyroclasts) V: 439
Pummelo [tree]
Grapefruit (History) G: 321
Pump P: 900a with diagrams
Fire department (Trucks and vehicles) F: 126;
(Fire protection in North America) F: 128
Invention (Ancient Greece) I: 359
Pump [shoe]
Shoe (Kinds of shoes) S: 431 with picture
Pump, Implantable [medicine]
Drug (Entrance into the body) D: 353
Pump-action rifle [gun]
Rifle (Slide-action rifles) R: 339
Pump-generator [machine]
Grand Coulee Dam G: 308
Pumper [truck]
Fire department picture on F: 129
Pumping [industrial process]
Gas [fuel] (Transmitting and distributing gas)
G: 55
Mining (Pumping methods) M: 577
Petroleum (Primary recovery) P: 332-333
Pumping [lasers]
Laser (Parts of a laser) L: 83
Pumping centers [physiology]
Circulatory system (Invertebrates) Ci: 561
Pumpkin [plant] P: 901 with picture
Jack-o'-lantern J: 3
United States picture on U: 112
Pumpkin hose [fashion]
Clothing (The Renaissance) Ci: 702-703
Pumpkinseed [fish]
Fish picture on F: 159
Sunfish So: 990
Pun [humor]

Humor (The humor of words) H: 435
Riddle R: 335
Shakespeare, William (Rhetoric) S: 368
Puna [region, Argentina]
Argentina (The Andean Region) A: 653 *with map*
Punahou School
Obama, Barack (Boyhood) O: 640c
Puncak Jaya [mountain, New Guinea]
Indonesia (Papua) I: 234
New Guinea (Land and climate) N: 206
Punch [sports]
Boxing (Boxing skills) B: 529
Punch and Judy [puppets] P: 902
Puppet (Hand puppets) P: 906
Punch-card ballot
Ballot (In the United States) B: 63
Voting (Methods of voting) V: 449-450
Voting machine (Kinds of electoral voting
machines) V: 450
Punch press
Machine tool *picture on* M: 17; (Metal forming
operations) M: 19
Punched-card computer
Computer (Punched-card devices) Ci: 924a *with
picture*
Puncheon [construction]
Pioneer life in America (A pioneer settlement)
P: 479-480
Punctuated equilibrium [biology]
Biology (Current research and issues) B: 320
Evolution (Main ideas of evolutionary theory)
E: 426-427
Gould, Stephen Jay G: 281
Punctuation [grammar] P: 902
Sentence S: 302
Punic [language]
Phoenicia (Language) P: 393
Punic Wars [European history] P: 903
Carthage (History) C: 260-261
Fabius Maximus, Quintus F: 2
Hamilcar Barca H: 29
Hannibal (His early life) H: 52 *with picture*
Numidia N: 608
Regulus, Marcus Atilius R: 206
Rome, Ancient (The Roman Republic) R: 444-445
Utica U: 251
War (Superior force and resources) W: 24
Punishment
Behavior (Operant conditioning) B: 220-221
Capital punishment C: 193
Child (Motivating the child's behavior) C: 451
Child abuse C: 454
Colonial life in America (Crime and punishment)
Ci: 796
Crime (Crime prevention) Ci: 1139
Criminal justice system (The trial) Ci: 1143
Criminology (What criminologists study) Ci: 1145
Learning (Motivation) L: 164
Penal colony P: 235
Punitive damages [law]
Damages D: 20
Punjab [province, Pakistan]
Lahore L: 31
Pakistan (Provincial and local government) P: 93;
(Land and climate) P: 96 *with map*; (History)
P: 98
Punjab P: 903
Punjab [region, India-Pakistan] P: 903
India (India under Indira Gandhi) I: 133-134
Ranjit Singh R: 139
Sikhism S: 455
Punjab [state, India]
Punjab P: 903
Punjabi [language]
India (Languages) I: 114
Pakistan (Cultural groups and languages) P: 93
Punjabis [people]
Pakistan (Cultural groups and languages) P: 93
Punk rock [music] P: 904
Clothing (Political influences) Ci: 690-691 *with
picture*
Popular music (New forms of rock) P: 671
Rock music (Punk rock) R: 380b
Punk the Penguin [cartoon character]
Oliphant, Patrick Bruce O: 743
Punkie [insect]
Gnat G: 238
Punt [ancient history]
Exploration (Ancient exploration) E: 440
Puntland P: 904
Punt [sports]
Football (Advancing the ball) F: 360-362 *with
picture*
Punta del Este [resort area]
Uruguay *picture on* U: 225
Punta del Este, Charter of [1961]
Alliance for Progress A: 375

Puntland [region, Africa] P: 904
Somalia (History) So: 589
Punty [tool]
Glass (Glass terms) G: 222
Pup [animal]
Dog (The life of a dog) D: 266 *with picture*
Fox (Young) F: 439 *with picture*
Rat (The life of a rat) R: 146-147
Seal (Birth) S: 266 *with picture*
Wolf (Young) W: 376
Pupa [entomology] P: 904 *with picture*
Ant (Reproduction) A: 524 *with picture*
Beetle (The life cycle of beetles) B: 216 *with
diagram*
Butterfly (The pupa) B: 741 *with picture*
Chrysalis C: 539
Cocoon C: 747
Fly (Pupa) F: 310 *with picture*
Insect (Complete metamorphosis) I: 293 *with
picture*
Metamorphosis (The pupa) M: 428-429 *with
picture*
Moth (The life cycle of moths) M: 838-839 *with
pictures*
Puparium [entomology]
Fly (Pupa) F: 310
Pupa P: 904
Pupfish [fish] P: 905 *with pictures*
Endangered species (table) E: 270
Pupienus [Roman emperor]
Rome, Ancient (table) R: 447
Pupil [anatomy]
Eye (The uveal tract) E: 460-461 *with picture*
Reptile (Sense organs) R: 251 *with pictures*
Pupin, Michael Idvorsky [Serbian-American
engineer] P: 905
Puppen Reform [art movement]
Doll (Before World War I) D: 291
Puppet P: 905 *with pictures*
See also Doll *in this index*
Drama (Japan) D: 336-337
Indonesia (The arts) I: 232
Japan (Theater) J: 43
Punch and Judy P: 902
Ventriloquism V: 309 *with picture*
Puppet animation
Animation (Stop-motion animation) A: 514a
with picture
Puppet show
Puppet P: 905
Puppeteer
Henson, Jim H: 191
Puppet P: 905
Puppeteers of America
Puppet (Organizations for puppeteers) P: 907
Puppy
Dog (The life of a dog) D: 266 *with picture*
Pet (Training your pet) P: 320
Pupusa [food]
El Salvador (Food) E: 249
Puranas [stories]
Hinduism (Sacred writings) H: 235
Holi H: 290
Purcell, Edward Mills [American physicist]
Magnetism (Magnetic resonance) M: 61
Nobel Prizes (Physics: 1952) N: 440-441
Purcell, Henry [English composer]
Classical music (The Baroque period) Ci: 647
Purchasing [manufacturing]
Manufacturing (The main steps in
manufacturing) M: 170
Purchasing cooperative [economics]
Cooperative (Supply, or purchasing,
cooperatives) Ci: 1036
Farm and farming (Managing production costs)
F: 42
Purchasing power [economics]
Depreciation D: 149
Income (Nominal and real income) I: 100
Inflation I: 266
Standard of living (Measuring standard of living)
I:So: 833-834
Purdue, John [American philanthropist]
Purdue University P: 907
Purdue University P: 907
Indiana University I: 220
Purdy, Al [Canadian poet]
Canadian literature (Modern Canadian poets)
C: 161
Pure competition [economics]
Capitalism (Private choices) C: 194
Monopoly and competition (Kinds of monopoly
and competition) M: 732
Pure democracy [political science] *See* Direct
democracy *in this index*
Pure-dye silk
Silk (Boiling off and weighting) S: 460

Pure food and drug laws P: 907 *with picture*
Pure mathematics
Mathematics (The importance of mathematics)
M: 302; (The Greeks) M: 306; (The Renaissance)
M: 306
Pure Monday
Lent L: 196b
Pure risk
Insurance I: 309
Pure substance
Melting point M: 389
Purebred
American Kennel Club A: 412
Cat (Breeds of cats) C: 290
Cattle C: 306
Dairying (Dairy cattle) D: 6
Dog (Kinds of dogs) D: 265; (Choosing a dog)
D: 277-278
Horse (table: Horse terms) H: 343; (Breeding
horses) H: 358
Pet (Choosing a pet) P: 320
United Kennel Club U: 47
Purebred Dairy Cattle Association
Dairying (Improvements in dairy farming) D: 7-8
Purgatorio [work by Dante]
Divine Comedy D: 242
Purgatorius [animal]
Primate (The evolution of primates) P: 778b
Purgatory [religion] P: 909
Divine Comedy D: 242
Purge [Soviet history] *See* Great Purge *in this index*
Purging [physiology]
Bulimia B: 694
Puri [India]
Juggernaut *picture on* J: 185
Purim [religion] P: 909
Dance *picture on* D: 25
Esther, Book of E: 360
Judaism (Other holidays) J: 182
March M: 195
Purine [compound]
Gout G: 281
Purísima Concepción, La [mission]
Mission life in America (A visitor's guide) M: 620
Puritan Revolution [English history]
Puritans (History) P: 910
Puritani, I [opera by Bellini]
Bellini, Vincenzo B: 244
Puritans [English history] P: 909 *with picture*
American literature (New England) A: 414
Bath (History) B: 164
Calvin, John (Calvinism) C: 71
Christianity (The 1600's and 1700's) C: 525
Colonial life in America (Religion) Ci: 804
Congregationalists Ci: 940f
Defoe, Daniel (His writings) D: 89
English literature (The early and middle 1600's)
E: 317
Hairdressing (The 1600's) H: 12
Indian wars (The Pequot War [1637]) I: 191
James (James I) J: 25
Laud, William L: 121
Literature for children (The Puritans) L: 362
Massachusetts (Massachusetts Bay Colony)
M: 289
Massachusetts Bay Colony M: 295
Milton, John (Middle years) M: 557
Pilgrims P: 462 *with picture*
Protestantism (The conservative reform
movements) P: 834-835; (The radical reform
and free church movements) P: 835
Restoration R: 263
Theocracy T: 251
United States, History of the (New England)
U: 154
Purkinje, Johannes [Czechoslovak physiologist]
Protoplasm P: 837
Purkinje cell [physiology]
Autism (Causes) A: 942
Purl [stitch]
Knitting (Knitting the fabric) K: 354
Purlin [construction]
Building construction (Beams, girders, and
columns) B: 682-683
"Purloined Letter, The" [story by Poe]
Detective story (History) D: 162
Purple [color]
Color *diagram on* C: 821
Purple amaranth [plant]
Amaranth A: 400
Purple Balloon, The [book by Raschka]
Raschka, Chris R: 144
Purple coneflower
Echinacea E: 49
Purple finch [bird]
Bird *picture on* B: 335
Purple gallinule [bird]

Gallinule G: 16
Purple Heart
Medals, decorations, and orders (Military awards) M: 355 *with picture*
Purple heron [bird]
Heron (Kinds of herons) H: 214
Purple Land, The [book by Hudson]
Hudson, William Henry H: 405
Purple loosestrife [plant]
Loosestrife L: 453
Purple martin [bird]
Bird *pictures on* B: 358, B: 367
Martin M: 234a *with picture*
Swallow So: 1015
Purple mountain saxifrage [plant]
Flower *picture on* F: 283
Purple of Cassius [material]
Gold (Other uses) G: 251-252
Purple owl's clover
Flower *picture on* F: 288
Purple prairie clover [plant]
Flower *picture on* F: 287
Purple saxifrage [plant]
Flower *picture on* F: 283
Purple-throated sunbird [bird]
Bird (Birds of Asia) B: 344f *with picture*
Purple tube [sea animal]
Sponge *picture on* So: 799
Purpure [purple]
Heraldry *picture on* H: 195
Purse [prize]
Horse racing (Types of horse races) H: 364
Purse line [tackle]
Fishing industry (Nets) F: 183 *with diagram*
Purse seine [net]
Fishing industry (Nets) F: 183 *with diagram*
Tuna T: 485
Purslane [plant] P: 911 *with picture*
Pursuit
Bicycle racing (Track races) B: 292
"Pursuit of Diarmuid and Grainne, The" [story]
Mythology (The Fionn cycle) M: 985
Purús River [Brazil-Peru]
Amazon River (The course of the Amazon) A: 403
Purusha [religion]
Yoga Y: 566
Purva-mimamsa [philosophy]
Hinduism (The six schools of philosophy) H: 236
Purvis, Robert [American abolitionist]
Philadelphia (Industrial beginnings) P: 366-367
Pus [physiology]
Abscess A: 17
Acne A: 28 *with pictures*
Boil B: 438 *with pictures*
Pusan [South Korea] P: 911
Asia *picture on* A: 787
Pusan Perimeter
Korean War (The Pusan Perimeter) K: 381 *with map*
Pusey, Edward Bouverie [British religious leader]
Oxford Movement O: 888
Pusey, Joshua [American lawyer]
Match (The invention of book matches) M: 300a
PUSH, Operation [organization]
Jackson, Jesse Louis J: 15
Pusher [transportation]
City *picture on* Ci: 591
Pusher unit
Locomotive (Diesel locomotives) L: 414-415
Pushkin, Alexander [Russian poet] P: 911
Glinka, Mikhail Ivanovich G: 231
Russian literature (Early Romanticism) R: 560-561
Pushmataha [Indian chief]
Mississippi (Territorial days) M: 641-642
Pushmi-Pullyu [fictional animal]
Lofting, Hugh *picture on* L: 420
Pushtu [language] See Pashto *in this index*
Pushtuns [people] See Pashtuns *in this index*
Pussy See Cat *in this index*
Pussy willow [tree] P: 912 *with picture*
Insect *picture on* I: 284
Willow W: 315
Pustule
Monkeypox M: 730
Smallpox S: 513
Soybean (Diseases and pests) So: 692
Put option [investment]
Commodity exchange (Options contracts) Ci: 874
Putin, Vladimir Vladimirovich [Russian political leader] P: 912 *with portrait*
Russia (Politics) R: 531-532; (The rise of Putin) R: 555
Yeltsin, Boris Nikolayevich Y: 561
Putnam, George Palmer [American publisher]
Earhart, Amelia (Flights) E: 14
Putnam, Grace Storey [American sculptor]
Doll (After the war) D: 292 *with picture*

Putnam, Herbert [American librarian] P: 913
Putnam, Israel [American general] P: 913
Putnam, James [American lawyer]
Adams, John (Education) A: 34
Putnam, Rufus [American general] P: 913
Ohio (Exploration and settlement) O: 700
Ohio Company (The second Ohio Company) O: 704
Putonghua [language]
China (Languages) C: 481
Chinese language (Spoken Chinese) C: 510
Hong Kong (Languages) H: 317
Mandarin M: 135
Putrajaya [Malaysia] P: 913
Malaysia M: 98a; (Recent developments) M: 102-103
Putrefaction [decay]
Decay D: 67
Decomposition D: 80
Putrid Lake
Azov, Sea of A: 998
Putsch [German history]
Hitler, Adolf (The Beer Hall Putsch) H: 266
Putt [sports]
Golf (The green) G: 261
Putty [building material] P: 913
Pu'uhonua o Honaunau National Historical Park [Hawaii]
Hawaii (Places to visit) H: 98
National Park System (table: National historical parks) N: 56-57
Puukohola Heiau National Historic Site [Hawaii]
National Park System (table: National historic sites) N: 52-53
Puységur, Marquis de [French hypnotist]
Hypnosis (Mesmerism) H: 479-480
Puzo, Mario [American author] P: 913
Puzzle
Crossworld puzzle Ci: 1156 *with picture*
Sudoku So: 957
PVC [plastics] See Polyvinyl chloride *in this index*
PVR [device] See Digital video recorder *in this index*
PVS [disorder] See Persistent vegetative state *in this index*
PWA [U.S. history] See Public Works Administration *in this index*
Pwe [drama]
Myanmar (Recreation) M: 970a
PX [store] See Post exchange *in this index*
Pye, Henry James [British poet]
Poet laureate (table: Poets laureate of the United Kingdom) P: 590
Pyelonephritis [disease]
Kidney (Kidney diseases) K: 312
Pygmalion [legendary figure] P: 914
Dido D: 195
Pygmalion [play by Shaw]
Campbell, Mrs. Patrick C: 91
Pygmalion P: 914
Shaw, George Bernard (Mature period) S: 378
Pygmies [people] P: 914 *with picture*
Africa (Peoples of Africa) A: 104
Burundi (People) B: 713
Congo, Democratic Republic of the (Ancestry) Ci: 938
Dwarfism D: 394
Gabon (People) G: 3
Rain forest (Africa) R: 126b-126c
Rwanda (People) R: 570
Pygmy blue [butterfly]
Butterfly B: 732 *with picture*
Pygmy chimpanzee [animal] See Bonobo *in this index*
Pygmy glider [animal]
Glider (animal) G: 231
Pygmy goat
Goat (Domestic goats) G: 239
Pygmy hippopotamus [animal]
Hippopotamus (The pygmy hippopotamus) H: 241 *with picture*
Pygmy killer whale [sea animal]
Killer whale K: 316
Pygmy marmoset [animal]
Marmoset M: 216 *with picture*
Pygmy mouse lemur [animal]
Lemur L: 189
Pygmy nuthatch [bird]
Nuthatch N: 623
Pygmy parrot [bird]
Parrot (Kinds of parrots) P: 179
Pygmy possum [possum]
Possum P: 698
Pygmy python [snake]
Python P: 922
Pygmy rattlesnake
Rattlesnake R: 149
Pygmy right whale [sea animal]

Whale (Right whales) W: 255
Pygmy tree mouse
Mouse (Unusual mice) M: 902
Pyhä Falls
Finland (Rivers) F: 114
Pyle, Ernie [American journalist] P: 914
Foreign correspondent F: 386
War correspondent W: 26
Pyle, Howard [American artist] P: 914
Witchcraft *picture on* W: 373
Pyle, J. Howard [American political leader]
Arizona (table) A: 687
Pylon [architecture]
Architecture (Egyptian architecture) A: 612
Pylon [aviation]
Bomber B: 453
Pyloric sphincter [anatomy]
Stomach (The stomach's work) So: 908 *with diagram*
Pym, John [English political leader] P: 915
Pynchon, Thomas [American author] P: 915
American literature (Experimental styles) A: 425
Novel (The novel today) N: 575
Pynchon, William [American businessman]
Springfield (Government and history) So: 808
Pyongyang [North Korea] P: 915 *with picture*
Korea (City life) K: 370
Korea, North K: 368 *with pictures*
Pyorrhea [disease]
Periodontitis P: 287
Teeth (Periodontal diseases) T: 85
Pyralis firefly [insect]
Firefly F: 134 *with picture*
Pyramid [geometry] P: 916 *with diagrams*
Geometry *picture on* G: 104
Pyramid Age
Egypt, Ancient (The Old Kingdom) E: 142
Pyramid Lake [Nevada]
Nevada (Rivers and lakes) N: 166-168 *with map*
Paiute Indians P: 91
Pyramid of biomass [ecology]
Ecology (Energy flow) E: 54-55
Pyramid of energy [ecology]
Ecology (Energy flow) E: 54-55
Pyramid of numbers [ecology]
Elton, Charles Sutherland E: 253
Pyramid of the Sun [Mexico]
Aztec *picture on* A: 999
Pyramids (American pyramids) P: 917 *with picture*
Pyramiding [crime]
Tax evasion T: 52
Pyramiding [economics]
Holding company H: 290
Pyramids [architecture] P: 916 *with pictures*
Architecture (Egyptian architecture) A: 612; (Pre-Columbian architecture) A: 614 *with picture*
Aztec *picture on* A: 999
Egypt (Tourism) E: 129 *with picture*
Egypt, Ancient *picture on* E: 140; (Arts and sciences) E: 139
Maya (Religion) M: 322-323
Memphis M: 394
Mythology (The Great Ennead) M: 979
Seven Wonders of the Ancient World *picture on* S: 326; (The pyramids of Egypt) S: 325
Pyramids, Battle of the [1798]
Egypt (Ottoman and French control) E: 130
Napoleon I (Egypt invaded) N: 14
Pyramus and Thisbe [Roman legend] P: 919
Pyrenean oak [tree]
Oak (Other oaks) O: 636
Pyrenean shepherd [dog] P: 919
Pyrenees [mountains, France-Spain] P: 919
France (The land) F: 464-466 *with map*
Spain *picture on* So: 740
Pyrethrum [insecticide]
Insecticide (Botanical insecticides) I: 302
Pyrethrum P: 920
Pyrethrum [medication]
Pyrethrum P: 920
Pyrethrum [plant] P: 920
Pyrex [glass]
Glass (Borosilicate glass) G: 213; (table) G: 218
Pyridostigmine bromide [drug]
Gulf War syndrome G: 438
Pyridoxine
Nutrition (Vitamins) N: 626
Pyrilampes [stepfather of]
Plato (Plato's life) P: 567
Pyrite [mineral] P: 920
Crystal (Classifying crystals) Ci: 1166 *with picture*
Iron and steel (Kinds of iron ore) I: 438
Mineral *picture on* M: 568
Pyroceram [glass]
Glass (table) G: 218
Pyroclast [geology]
Volcano (Products of eruption) V: 439 *with*

picture; (Pyroclastic hazards) **V: 440** *with diagram*; (Stratovolcanoes) **V: 442** *with diagram*
Pyroclastic [geology] *See* Pyroclast *in this index*
Pyroclastic flow or surge [geology]
Volcano (Pyroclastic hazards) **V: 440** *with diagram*
Pyrolysis [chemistry]
Combustion **Ci: 867**
Varnish (Making varnish) **V: 286**
Pyromania [psychology] **P: 920**
Pyrometer [thermometer]
Thermometer (Radiation thermometers) **T: 255**
Pyrope [gem]
Garnet **G: 45**
Pyrosis [disorder]
Heartburn **H: 147**
Pyrotechnics P: 920
Fireworks **F: 135**
Pyroxene [geology] **P: 920**
Basalt **B: 123**
Pyroxylin [chemical]
Painting (Synthetic resins) **P: 40**
Plastics (The invention of Celluloid) **P: 559**
Pyrrha [Greek mythology]
Deucalion **D: 171**
Pyrrhic victory
Pyrrhus **P: 920**
Pyrrho of Elis [Greek philosopher] **P: 920**
Philosophy (Skepticism) **P: 387-388**
Skepticism **S: 481**
Pyrrhonian Skepticism [philosophy]
Skepticism **S: 481**
Pyrrhotite [mineral]
Mineral *picture* on **M: 568**
Pyrrhus [Greek general] **P: 920**
Pyruvic acid [biochemistry]
Cell (Producing energy) **C: 332-333** *with diagram*
Metabolism (Catabolism) **M: 424**
Respiration (Cellular respiration) **R: 261**
Pysanka [folk art]
Alberta (Interesting facts) **A: 313** *with picture*
Ukraine (The arts) **U: 8** *with picture*
Pythagoras [Greek mathematician] **P: 921**
Geometry (Greek geometry) **G: 106**
Mathematics (The Greeks) **M: 306**
Number (The Greeks) **N: 606**
Pre-Socratic philosophy (The first pre-Socratics) **P: 772**
Series (Working with odd numbers) **S: 317**
Sound (Early ideas about sound) **So: 605**
Triangle (Right triangles and the Pythagorean theorem) **T: 437-438**
Pythagorean theorem [geometry] **P: 921** *with diagrams*
Mathematics (Chinese mathematics) **M: 306**
Pythagoras **P: 921**
Triangle (Right triangles and the Pythagorean theorem) **T: 437**
Pytheas [Greek explorer] **P: 922**
Arctic (Arctic exploration) **A: 638**
Arctic Ocean **A: 641**
Exploration (The Greeks) **E: 441** *with map*
Thule **T: 271**
Pythia [Greek prophetess]
Apollo **A: 566**
Delphi **D: 117**
Oracle **O: 814**
Pythian games [ancient Greece]
Delphi **D: 117**
Olympic Games (The ancient games) **O: 750**
Pythian Sisters [organization]
Knights of Pythias **K: 352**
Pythias [legendary figure]
Damon and Pythias **D: 21**
Pythias, Knights of [organization]
Knights of Pythias **K: 352**
Pythios [Greek architect]
Seven Wonders of the Ancient World (The Mausoleum at Halicarnassus) **S: 325**
Python [snake] **P: 922** *with picture*
Animal (Incubation) **A: 498-500**
Reptile **R: 250** *with picture*
Snake *picture* on **S: 526**; (Protection against predators) **S: 531**; (Snakes as invasive species) **S: 532**; (Snakes as pets) **S: 532** *with picture*; (Pythons) **S: 535**
Pyu [people]
Myanmar (Early days) **M: 970d**

Q

Q [letter] **Q: 1** *with pictures*
Q [Biblical studies]
Bible (The Gospels) **B: 283**; (Historical contexts) **B: 287**
New Testament (Critical studies) **N: 288**
Q-BOP [industrial process]
Iron and steel (The basic oxygen process [BOP]) **I: 441-442** *with diagram*

Q-Celtic [language]
Celts **C: 343**
Q fever [disease]
Rickettsia **R: 335**
Q signal [communications]
Radio, Amateur **R: 95**
Qaboos bin Said [sultan of Oman]
Oman (History) **O: 759**
Qadhāfī, Muʿammar Muhammad al- [Libyan political leader] **Q: 2**
Chad (History) **C: 367**
Libya (Government) **L: 264**; (Independence) **L: 267-268**
Middle East (2011 protests) **M: 534b**
Obama, Barack (Libya) **O: 641**
Qaʿeda, Al- [organization] *See* Qaʿida, Al- *in this index*
Qafzeh [archaeological site]
Prehistoric people (The single origin theory) **P: 750**; (The Stone Age) **P: 751**; (table) **P: 754**
Qaʿida, Al- [organization] **Q: 2**
Afghanistan (Recent developments) **A: 96**
Afghanistan War **A: 97**
Air Force, United States (The war in Afghanistan) **A: 196**
Arabs (Relations with Europe and the United States) **A: 590a**
Bin Laden, Osama **B: 307**
Bush, George Walker **B: 722b**
Guantánamo **G: 411**
Guerrilla warfare (History) **G: 420-421**
Iraq War (Illegal weapons) **I: 414c**; (Resistance to the coalition) **I: 414e**; (Disagreements over the war) **I: 414f-415**
Middle East (The 2000's) **M: 534b**
Saudi Arabia (Recent developments) **S: 162**
September 11 terrorist attacks **S: 310**
Terrorism (Terrorist organizations) **T: 176**; (The changing face of terrorism) **T: 179**; (The September 11 terrorist attacks) **T: 179**
Yemen (Unification) **Y: 564**
Qajar dynasty
Iran (The Qajar dynasty) **I: 406**
Qalʿat al-Bahrain [ruins]
Manama **M: 132**
Qanat [agriculture]
Persia, Ancient (Economy) **P: 297**
Qandahar [Afghanistan] *See* Kandahar *in this index*
Qanun [musical instrument]
Music (Arab music) **M: 956**
Qasim, Abdul Karim [Iraqi political leader] *See* Kassem, Abdul Karim *in this index*
Qat [plant] *See* Khat *in this index*
Qatar Q: 2 *with picture and map*
Flag *picture* on **F: 204**
Middle East **M: 530**
Qatsi [films]
Glass, Philip **G: 224**
Qattara Depression [region, Egypt]
Desert (Desert climate and land) **D: 155-156**
Qayt Bey Mosque
Cairo (The city) **C: 16**
QCD [physics] *See* Quantum chromodynamics *in this index*
QED [physics] *See* Quantum electrodynamics *in this index*
Qi [force]
Confucianism (Later Confucianism) **Ci: 937**
Qiana [fiber]
Nylon (History) **N: 633**
Qin [musical instrument]
Music (Chinese music) **M: 956**
Qin dynasty [Chinese history] **Q: 4**
Asia (The Huang He and Yangtze valleys) **A: 805** *with map*
China **C: 474**; (The Qin dynasty) **C: 500** *with map*
Great Wall of China (History) **G: 350**
Terra-cotta army of Xi'an **T: 172**
World, History of the (The unification of China) **W: 431**
Qin Ling Mountains
China (The Central Uplands) **C: 493** *with map*
Qing dynasty [Chinese history]
China *map* on **C: 504**; (The early rule of the Manchus) **C: 502**
Manchus **M: 135**
Painting (Chinese painting) **P: 44-46**
Porcelain (Oriental porcelain) **P: 676**
Qingdao [China]
Yellow Sea **Y: 557**
Qinghai [province, China]
Asia (Way of life in Central Asia) **A: 790**
Qishon River
Israel (The Coastal Plain) **I: 482**
Qizilbash [Turkic warriors]
Abbas I **A: 4**
Safavid dynasty **S: 8**

Qom [Iran] **Q: 4**
Qop [letter]
Q **Q: 1** *with picture*
Qoppa [letter]
Q **Q: 1** *with picture*
QR code [electronics]
Bar coding **B: 102**
Qu Yuan [Chinese poet]
Chinese literature (Beginnings) **C: 511**
Quabbin Reservoir
Massachusetts (Rivers and lakes) **M: 284-285**
Quad [vehicle] *See* All-terrain vehicle *in this index*
Quad-Cities [Illinois-Iowa]
Davenport **D: 44**
Quad Plan [education]
Wilson, Woodrow (University president) **W: 321**
Quad skate
Roller skating (Roller skates) **R: 402** *with picture*
Quadrant [instrument]
Exploration (The age of European exploration) **E: 443**
Navigation (Early instruments) **N: 74**
Quadratic equation [mathematics]
Algebra (Quadratic equations in one unknown) **A: 358**
Al-Khwārizmī **A: 370**
Quadriceps femoris [anatomy]
Leg (The thigh) **L: 181-182**
Quadrilateral [geometry]
Geometry (Deductive reasoning) **G: 101**; (Euclidean geometry) **G: 104** *with diagram*
Quadriplegia [disorder]
Paralysis (Paralysis of central nervous system origin) **P: 152**
Quadrivium [European history]
Education (Christian education in the Middle Ages) **E: 99**
Quadroon [people]
Mulatto **M: 912**
Quadros, Jânio [Brazilian political leader]
Brazil (Return to constitutional government) **B: 585-586**
Quadruped [zoology]
Skeleton (Animal skeletons) **S: 480**
Quadruple Alliance [European history]
Holy Alliance **H: 298**
Quadruplets
Multiple birth **M: 919**
Quadruplex telegraphy
Edison, Thomas Alva (Inventor and businessman) **E: 78**
Telegraph (Service expansion and improvement) **T: 91-92**
Quaestiones Naturales [book by Seneca]
Geology (The Romans) **G: 98**
Quagga [animal]
Zebra **Z: 587**
Quail [bird] **Q: 4** *with picture*
Bird (Birds of the desert) **B: 339** *with picture*
Partridge **P: 188**
Quaker City [nickname]
Philadelphia **P: 358**
Quaker Oats Company
PepsiCo, Inc. **P: 279**
Quaker Poet [nickname]
Whittier, John Greenleaf **W: 295**
Quaker State [nickname]
Pennsylvania **P: 245**
Quakers [religious group] **Q: 5**
American Friends Service Committee **A: 411**
Conscientious objector **Ci: 974**
Dyer, Mary **D: 397**
Fox, George **F: 441**
Hicks, Edward **H: 224**
Marriage (Wedding ceremonies) **M: 220**
Murder **M: 930**
New Jersey (English control) **N: 250**
Oath (Affirmation) **O: 639**
Pacifism **P: 18**
Pastorius, Francis Daniel **P: 193**
Peace (From the 1400's to the 1700's) **P: 206**
Penn, William **P: 241**
Pennsylvania *picture* on **P: 265**; (Colonial days) **P: 264**
Philadelphia (Ethnic groups) **P: 362**
Prison (Early prison reform) **P: 807**
United States, History of the (The Middle Colonies) **U: 154-155**
Quaking aspen [tree]
Aspen **A: 815**
Tree *pictures* on **T: 420**
Quaking bog [geography]
Bog *diagram* on **B: 436**
Quality control
Deming, W. Edwards **D: 119**
Manufacturing (Making products) **M: 170-171**
Quality grade

Beef (Grades of beef) **B:** 209
  Meat packing (Quality grading) **M:** 351
Quality of life
  Conservation (To maintain the quality of life)
    Ci: 976
Quanah [American Indian chief] **Q:** 5
Quantity demanded [economics]
  Economics (table) **E:** 60
Quantity supplied [economics]
  Economics (table) **E:** 60
Quantity theory [economics]
  Inflation (Theories about the causes of inflation)
    I: 268
Quantrill, William Clarke [Confederate military
  leader] **Q:** 5
  Kansas (Statehood) **K:** 237 *with picture*
Quantum [physics]
  Light (Photons) **L:** 286
  Quantum mechanics **Q:** 6
  String theory **So:** 929
Quantum chromodynamics [science]
  Gluon **G:** 237
  Subatomic particle (The Standard Model) **So:** 938
Quantum computing [technology]
  Atom (Recent discoveries) **A:** 876
  Electronics (Electronics today) **E:** 216
Quantum electrodynamics [physics]
  Feynman, Richard Phillips **F:** 84
  Subatomic particle (The Standard Model) **So:** 938
Quantum field theory [physics] **Q:** 5
Quantum mechanics [physics] **Q:** 6
  Atom (The forces within an atom) **A:** 873
  Bohr, Niels **B:** 438
  Born, Max **B:** 489
  Einstein, Albert (Famous theories) **E:** 146-146a;
    (Further scientific work) **E:** 146b
  Hawking, Stephen William **H:** 113
  Heisenberg, Werner **H:** 167
  Light (Photons) **L:** 286-287
  Magnetism (Magnetic properties of materials)
    M: 60d-61
  Motion (The motion of subatomic particles)
    M: 845
  Photon **P:** 430
  Physics (Quantum theory) **P:** 441
  Planck, Max Karl Ernst Ludwig **P:** 507
  Quantum field theory **Q:** 5
  Radiation (The quantum theory) **R:** 81
  Schrödinger, Erwin **S:** 186
  Science (Science in the early 1900's) **S:** 201
  Solid-state physics **So:** 583
  String theory **So:** 929
  Subatomic particle **So:** 936
  Vacuum (In particle physics) **V:** 256
Quantum optics [physics]
  Optics **O:** 813
Quantum state [physics] *See* Energy level *in this
  index*
Quantum theory [physics] *See* Quantum
  mechanics *in this index*
Quanzhen Tao [religion]
  Taoism **T:** 36
Quaoar [space object]
  Kuiper belt **K:** 392
  Planet (The outer dwarf planets) **P:** 511
Qu'Appelle River
  Saskatchewan (Rivers and lakes) **S:** 138 *with map*
Quarantine Q: 7
  Insect (Insect control) **I:** 284-285
  Plant quarantine **P:** 550
  Public health (History) **P:** 856
  Zoo (Medical care) **Z:** 603
Quare Fellow, The [play by Behan]
  Behan, Brendan **B:** 220
  Irish literature (Drama) **I:** 432
Quark [physics] **Q:** 7
  Atom (The nucleus) **A:** 871; (Recent discoveries)
    A: 876
  Baryon **B:** 122
  Big bang **B:** 296
  Electricity (Electric charge) **E:** 191
  Fermion **F:** 74
  Gluon **G:** 237
  Hadron **H:** 5
  Kendall, Henry Way **K:** 258
  Matter (Structure of matter) **M:** 310; (Quark-
    gluon plasmas) **M:** 311
  Meson **M:** 421
  Motion (The motion of subatomic particles)
    M: 845
  Neutron **N:** 155
  Neutron star **N:** 155
  Physics (Advances in the mid-1900's) **P:** 442;
    (Physics today) **P:** 442-443
  Proton **P:** 836
  Psi particle **P:** 844
  Subatomic particle (Kinds of subatomic particles)

So: 937; (Theories of forces) **So:** 937-938
Quark-gluon plasma [physics]
  Matter (States of matter) **M:** 311
Quarles, Benjamin Arthur [American historian]
  Q: 7
Quarrel of the Ancients and the Moderns, The
  [literature]
  Perrault, Charles **P:** 293
Quarry
  Marble *picture on* **M:** 192
  Quarrying **Q:** 7
Quarrying [industry] **Q:** 7
  Mining (Quarrying) **M:** 575
  Vermont (Places to visit) **V:** 326; (Mining) **V:** 332
    with picture
Quart [measurement] **Q:** 7
  Liter **L:** 350
  Weights and measures (Comparison of
    measurement systems) **W:** 185
Quarter [district]
  City (The people) **Ci:** 582
Quarter [money] **Q:** 8
  Money (Quarters) **M:** 714
Quarter horse
  Horse (Kinds of horses) **H:** 343; (Saddle horses)
    H: 343 *with picture*; (table: Some types and
    breeds of horses) **H:** 343
Quarter midget [automobile]
  Automobile racing (Other kinds of racing) **A:** 978
Quarter of coverage [measurement]
  Social security (Old-age, survivors, and disability
    insurance) **So:** 553
Quarter system [education]
  Universities and colleges (The academic
    calendar) **U:** 209-210
Quarterback [sports]
  Football (The offensive team) **F:** 356 *with
    diagrams*
Quarterdeck [sailing]
  Galleon **G:** 15
Quartering Act [1765]
  Revolution, American (The Quartering and
    Stamp acts) **R:** 272
  United States, History of the (Policy changes)
    U: 158
Quartering Act [1774]
  Intolerable Acts **I:** 353
Quartermaine's Terms [play by Gray]
  Gray, Simon **G:** 334
Quartermaster [military]
  Army (Armies in the Middle Ages) **A:** 727
Quartersawing
  Wood (Wood figure) **W:** 390 *with picture*
Quartet [music]
  Barbershop quartet singing **B:** 107
  Jazz *picture on* **J:** 8
Quartet for the End of Time [music by Messiaen]
  Messiaen, Olivier **M:** 423
Quartier Schuetzenstrasse [housing project]
  Rossi, Aldo *picture on* **R:** 483
Quarto [publishing]
  Folio **F:** 315
  Shakespeare, William (Publishing history) **S:** 368
Quartz [mineral] **Q:** 8
  Crystal (Classifying crystals) **Ci:** 1166-1167 *with
    picture*
  Electricity (Sources of current) **E:** 194
  Gem (Hardness) **G:** 77
  Granite **G:** 311
  Mineral *pictures on* **M:** 566, **M:** 569
  Silica **S:** 457
Quartz-based clock
  Clock (Electric clocks) **Ci:** 682k
  Watch (Quartz watches) **W:** 114 *with pictures*
Quartz heater
  Heating (Room heaters) **H:** 160
Quartz Mountain State Park [Oklahoma]
  Oklahoma *picture on* **O:** 712
Quartzite [mineral] **Q:** 8
  Rock (table) **R:** 373 *with picture*
Quasar [astronomy] **Q:** 8
  Astronomy (Radio quasars) **A:** 849
  Galaxy (Galaxy evolution) **G:** 9
  Telescope (Radio and microwave telescopes)
    T: 106
  Universe (Size of the universe) **U:** 205
Quasi-public corportion
  Corporation (Other corporations) **Ci:** 1070
Quasi-stellar object *See* Quasar *in this index*
Quasi-stellar radio source [astronomy] *See* Quasar
  in this index
Quasicrystal [solid] **Q:** 9 *with picture*
Quasimodo [literary figure]
  Hugo, Victor (His works) **H:** 410
Quasimodo, Salvatore [Italian poet]
  Italian literature (The 1900's) **I:** 495
  Nobel Prizes (Literature: 1959) **N:** 447

Quaternary ammonium compound [chemical]
  Disinfectant **D:** 235
Quaternary Period [geology]
  Earth (table) **E:** 30
  Pleistocene Epoch **P:** 572
Quatrain [verse]
  Poetry (table) **P:** 594
Quatrefoil [design]
  Ghiberti, Lorenzo **G:** 182
Quattro Pezzi Sacri [music by Verdi]
  Verdi, Giuseppe **V:** 316
Quattrocento [history]
  Painting (The 1400's) **P:** 52
Quayle, Ben [American political leader]
  Quayle, Dan (Political career) **Q:** 9
Quayle, Dan [American political leader] **Q:** 9 *with
  portrait*
  Bush, George Herbert Walker *picture on* **B:** 720;
    (Election as president) **B:** 719
  Vice president of the United States (Growth of
    the vice presidency) **V:** 353-354
Quebec [province] **Q:** 10 *with pictures and maps*
  See also the list of Related articles in the Quebec
  article
  Canada *picture on* **C:** 108; (Quebec) **C:** 101
  Parti Québécois **P:** 183
  Quebec **Q:** 10
  School (The development of Canadian schools)
    S: 184
  Trudeau, Pierre Elliott (Later years) **T:** 465
  Wisconsin (Struggle for control) **W:** 366
  Government
    Canada, Government of *picture on* **C:** 131
    Chrétien, Jean (Political career) **C:** 522b
    Law (The development of Canadian law) **L:** 136
    Mulroney, Brian **M:** 916; (The constitutional
      crisis) **M:** 918
  History
    Acadia **A:** 21
    Canada, History of (The United Empire
      Loyalists) **C:** 142 *with map*
    Lévesque, René **L:** 218
    Trudeau, Pierre Elliott (Entry into public life)
      T: 462
Quebec [city, Quebec] **Q:** 34 *with picture and map*
  Canada *picture on* **C:** 99
  Champlain, Samuel de (The founding of Quebec)
    C: 373
  Exploration (The French and English in North
    America) **E:** 446
  French and Indian wars (The French and Indian
    War) **F:** 512-513
  Fur trade (The early fur trade) **F:** 564
  New France (Colonial life) **N:** 204-205 *with picture*
  Quebec **Q:** 10; (Places to visit) **Q:** 20 *with picture*;
    (table: Average monthly weather) **Q:** 25
  Quebec, Battle of **Q:** 37
Quebec, Battle of [1759] **Q:** 37
  Canada, History of *picture on* **C:** 142
  French and Indian wars (The French and Indian
    War) **F:** 512-513 *with picture*
  Montcalm, Marquis de **M:** 762
  Murray, James **M:** 931
  Quebec (The 1700's) **Q:** 36
  Wolfe, James **W:** 377
Quebec, Battle of [1775]
  Revolution, American (The invasion of Canada)
    R: 275-276; (table) **R:** 276
Quebec, School of [poetry]
  Canadian literature (Poetry: 1850-1918) **C:** 157
Quebec, University of Q: 38
Quebec Act [1774] **Q:** 38
  Canada, History of (The Quebec Act) **C:** 141; (The
    United Empire Loyalists) **C:** 142
  Law (The development of Canadian law) **L:** 136
  Wisconsin (Struggle for control) **W:** 366
Quebec Bridge [St. Lawrence River]
  Bridge (table: Cantilever) **B:** 603
Quebec Conference [1864] **Q:** 38
  Canada, History of (Confederation) **C:** 144
  Confederation of Canada (Moves toward
    confederation) **Ci:** 933-934
  Macdonald, Sir John Alexander (Forming the
    Dominion) **M:** 7 *with picture*
  Taché, Sir Étienne-Paschal **T:** 4
  Tupper, Sir Charles (Confederation) **T:** 494
Quebec Gazette [newspaper]
  Quebec (Communication) **Q:** 29
Quebec Party *See* Parti Québécois *in this index*
Quebec Pension Plan
  Social security (The Canada Pension Plan) **So:** 556
Quebec Resolutions [1864]
  Confederation of Canada (Moves toward
    confederation) **Ci:** 933-934
Quebec separatist movement
  Bloc Québécois **B:** 404
  Canada, History of (The Quebec separatist

movement) C: 149; (The separatist threat)
  C: 150
Canadian literature (Modern Canadian poets)
  C: 161
Lévesque, René L: 218
Martin, Paul (The 1995 Quebec referendum)
  M: 234d
Montreal (The separatist movement) M: 779
Quebec (Postwar Quebec) Q: 32; (The late 1900's)
  Q: 32
Trudeau, Pierre Elliott (Entry into public life)
  T: 462; (The national scene) T: 464
Quebec Urban Community
  Quebec (Recent developments) Q: 37
Quebec Winter Carnival [Quebec City]
  Quebec picture on Q: 21
Québécois [people]
  Canada (Languages) C: 106
Québécois, Bloc See Bloc Québécois in this index
Québécois literature
  Canadian literature C: 156
Quebracho [tree]
  Argentina (Northern Argentina) A: 652
  Paraguay (The land and climate) P: 147;
    (Agriculture and forestry) P: 148
Quechan Indians Q: 38
  California (Early days) C: 60
  Indian, American (Indians of the Southwest)
    I: 166-167
  Yuma Y: 582
Quechua [language]
  Inca (Communication and learning) I: 97; (The
    Inca heritage) I: 99
  Indian, American (After European contact) I: 175
  Peru (Languages) P: 309
Quechua Indians
  Races, Human (Evolutionary theory) R: 53-54
Queen [cat]
  Cat (Reproduction) C: 293
Queen [chess]
  Chess (The board and the men) C: 411-412 with
    diagram; (The moves) C: 412
Queen [insect]
  Ant A: 520 with pictures
  Bee (The honey bee colony) B: 201 with picture;
    (Life of the honey bee) B: 202 with picture;
    (Sting) B: 202
  Bumble bee B: 698 with picture
  Hornet H: 340
  Insect (Family life) I: 294-295 with picture
  Termite (The termite colony) T: 171 with picture
  Wasp (Group life) W: 112
Queen [mole-rat]
  Naked mole-rat N: 5
Queen [title] Q: 38
  See also individual queens in this index, such as
    Elizabeth II
  Address, Forms of (Officials of the
    Commonwealth of Nations) A: 53
  Parliament (The Parliament of the United
    Kingdom) P: 172
Queen, Ellery [pen name] Q: 39
Queen Alexandra's birdwing [butterfly]
  Butterfly B: 732 with picture
Queen angelfish
  Fish picture on F: 154
Queen Anne style
  Furniture picture on F: 577; (The Queen Anne
    style) F: 579
  House picture on H: 381
Queen Anne's lace [plant]
  Wild carrot W: 300 with picture
Queen Anne's Revenge [ship]
  Blackbeard B: 391
Queen Anne's War [1702-1713]
  Canada, History of (The colonial wars) C: 141
  French and Indian wars (Queen Anne's War)
    F: 512
  South Carolina (Colonial days) So: 659
  Succession wars (The War of the Spanish
    Succession) So: 950
Queen Charlotte Islands [Pacific] Q: 39
  British Columbia (Land regions) B: 622 with map
Queen City Ex [festival]
  Regina (Education and cultural life) R: 205
Queen City of the Plains
  Regina R: 204
Queen City of the West [nickname]
  Cincinnati Ci: 554
Queen conch
  Conch Ci: 928 with picture
Queen consort [title]
  Queen Q: 38
Queen dowager [title]
  Queen Q: 38
Queen Elizabeth [ship]
  Ship (Passenger vessels) S: 426

Queen Elizabeth Park
  Park picture on P: 168
Queen Emma's Summer Palace [Honolulu]
  Honolulu (Cultural life) H: 321
Queen Guenevere See Guenevere in this index
Queen Mab [legendary figure]
  Fairy (Trooping fairies) F: 10
Queen Mab [poem by Shelley]
  Shelley, Percy Bysshe (His life) S: 391
Queen Mary [ship]
  Long Beach (Economy) L: 447
  Ship (Passenger vessels) S: 426
Queen Mary 2 [ship]
  Ship picture on S: 404-405
Queen Mave [legendary figure] See Maeve, Queen
  in this index
Queen mother [title]
  Queen Q: 38
Queen of Hearts [literary figure]
  Carroll, Lewis (The Alice books) C: 249 with picture
  Nursery rhyme (Verse stories) N: 615
Queen of Sheba [Biblical figure] See Sheba, Queen
  of in this index
Queen of Soul [nickname]
  Franklin, Aretha F: 485
Queen of Spades, The [opera by Tchaikovsky]
  Tchaikovsky, Peter Ilich (His music) T: 61-62
"Queen of Spades, The" [story by Pushkin]
  Russian literature (Early Romanticism) R: 560-561
Queen of the Adriatic [nickname]
  Venice V: 306
Queen of the Night [opera character]
  Opera: (Magic Flute, The) O: 805
Queen parrotfish [fish]
  Parrotfish P: 181 with picture
Queen regnant [title]
  Queen Q: 38
Queen Street [Cardiff]
  Wales picture on W: 11
Queen Victoria Park
  Niagara Falls (History) N: 392-393
Queening the pawn
  Chess (The moves) C: 412-413
Queens [borough, New York City]
  New York City (The city) N: 323; (Queens) N: 329
    with picture
Queen's College [former name]
  Rutgers, The State University of New Jersey
    R: 567
Queen's County [Irish history]
  Ireland (The conquest of Ireland) I: 426
Queen's Day [holiday]
  Netherlands (Holidays and recreation) N: 141
    with picture
Queen's Gallery
  Buckingham Palace B: 664
Queen's House [Greenwich, England]
  England (The arts) E: 298-299
Queen's Plate [race]
  Horse racing (Stakes races) H: 364-365
Queen's Road
  Pennsylvania (Transportation) P: 262
Queen's standard [flag]
  Flag (Flags of individuals) F: 195 with picture
Queen's Theatre [London]
  Vanbrugh, Sir John V: 269
Queen's University at Kingston
  Grant, George Monro G: 311
Queen's University of Belfast
  Northern Ireland (Education) N: 522
Queen's Ware [china]
  Wedgwood ware W: 179 with picture
Queensberry, Marquess of [British sportsman]
  Boxing (Bare knuckles to gloves) B: 532
Queensberry Rules [boxing]
  Boxing (Bare knuckles to gloves) B: 532
Queensland [state, Australia] Q: 39 with picture
  and map
Queensland, University of
  Queensland (People) Q: 39
Queensland blue heeler [dog]
  Australian cattle dog A: 927
Queensland heeler [dog]
  Australian cattle dog A: 927
Queensland nut See Macadamia nut in this index
Queenston Heights, Battle of [1812]
  War of 1812 (Queenston Heights) W: 33
Queenston Heights National Historic Site
  [Ontario]
  Canada (table: National historic sites) C: 115
Queets Corridor [region, Washington]
  Olympic National Park O: 756
Queirós, Pedro Fernandes de [Portuguese
  explorer] See Quirós, Pedro Fernandez de in this
  index
Queloz, Didier [Swiss astronomer]
  Planet (The first discoveries) P: 513

Quemoy [islands, Formosa Strait] Q: 40
  Cold War (To the brink and back) Ci: 765
  Taiwan (History) T: 17-18
Quentin McAdam [painting by Raeburn]
  Raeburn, Sir Henry picture on R: 101
Querétaro [city, Mexico]
  Querétaro Q: 40
Querétaro [state, Mexico] Q: 40
  Maximilian M: 319
Querétaro, Protocol of [U.S. history]
  Hispanic Americans (Conflict) H: 252
Quern [tool]
  Pioneer life in America (Tools) P: 483
Query [computing]
  Information retrieval (How information retrieval
    works) I: 268b
  Search engine S: 268
Query letter [publishing]
  Writing (Preparing and submitting a manuscript)
    W: 512
Quesnay, François [French economist] Q: 40
  Physiocrats P: 445
Question answering
  Information retrieval (Research) I: 268-269
Question mark
  Punctuation (The question mark) P: 902
Question time
  Parliament (How the House of Commons works)
    P: 173
Questioned document examination [law
  enforcement]
  Graphology G: 323
Questionnaire
  Census C: 346
  Public opinion poll (Designing the questionnaire)
    P: 862
Questions of Travel [poetry by Bishop]
  American literature (Poetry) A: 423
Quetico Provincial Park [Atikokan]
  Ontario picture on O: 778
Quetzal [bird] Q: 40
  Bird (Birds of Central and South America) B: 344a
    with picture
Quetzalcoatl [Aztec god]
  Aztec picture on A: 1002; (Religion) A: 1000; (The
    Spanish conquest) A: 1003
  Chichén Itzá C: 439
  Montezuma II M: 764b
  Mythology (Aztec mythology) M: 987 with picture
  Orozco, José Clemente picture on O: 858
  Toltec Indians T: 323
Quetzalcoatlus [extinct animal]
  Pterosaur P: 854
Quevedo, Francisco de [Spanish philosopher]
  Q: 41
  Spanish literature (The 1600's) So: 759
Quezon City [Philippines] Q: 41
Quezon y Molina, Manuel Luis [Filipino political
  leader]
  Philippines (American rule) P: 380
  Quezon City Q: 41
Quick bread [food]
  Bread (Kinds of bread) B: 588 with pictures
Quick-cooking rice
  Rice (Food) R: 323
Quick-freezing [food processing]
  Food, Frozen F: 338
Quick-kill trap See Conibear in this index
Quick printing
  Printing (The electronic age) P: 804
Quickening [pregnancy]
  Abortion (Abortion in the United States) A: 15
Quickie strike
  Labor movement (Handling labor disputes) L: 6-7
Quicklime [chemical]
  Lime L: 306
Quicksand Q: 41
Quicksand [book by Larsen]
  African American literature (The 1900's) A: 136a
Quicksilver See Mercury in this index
Quickstep [dance]
  Ballroom dancing B: 63
Quid pro quo [law]
  Sexual harassment (Types of sexual harassment)
    S: 337
Quidde, Ludwig [German statesman]
  Nobel Prizes (Peace: 1927) N: 448a
Quie, Albert H. [American political leader]
  Minnesota (table) M: 602
Quiescent prominence [astronomy]
  Sun (Prominences) So: 981 with picture
Quiet Don, The [book by Sholokhov]
  Russian literature (The period of socialist realism)
    R: 564
  Sholokhov, Mikhail S: 433
Quiet Man, The [film]
  Ford, John F: 382

Quiet Revolution [political movement]
Canada, History of (The Quebec separatist movement) C: 149
Canadian literature (Modern Canadian poets) C: 161
Martin, Paul (College years and early career) M: 234b-234c
Quebec (Postwar Quebec) Q: 32
Quietism [philosophy]
Fénelon, François de Salignac de la Mothe- F: 71
Quill
Animal *picture on* A: 494
Feather (Kinds and parts of feathers) F: 59 *with diagram*
Hair H: 9
Pen (History) P: 234
Porcupine P: 677 *with picture*
Quill Lake
Saskatchewan (Rivers and lakes) S: 138
Quillwork [handicraft]
Indian, American *pictures on* I: 145, I: 156
Quillwort [plant]
Club moss Ci: 714
Plant *picture on* P: 522; (Lycophytes) P: 518; (Classification of plants) P: 546
Quilt [handicraft] Q: 41 *with picture*
Quilting bee
Quilt Q: 41
Quimby, Phineas [American religious leader]
Eddy, Mary Baker E: 75
Quinby, Henry B. [American political leader]
New Hampshire (table) N: 223
Quince [tree] Q: 41 *with picture*
Quinceañera [celebration] Q: 42
Doll (Dolls in celebrations) D: 287-288
Hispanic Americans *picture on* H: 249
Quincy, Josiah [American lawyer]
Boston Massacre B: 505
Quincy Grammar School [Boston]
School (Improvements in school design) S: 184
Quinidine [medication]
Quinine Q: 42
Quinine [medication] Q: 42
Colonial life in America (Health and medicine) Ci: 809
Malaria (Treatment and prevention) M: 96
Tree (Other tree products) T: 412
Quinn, Anthony [American actor]
Motion picture (Best performance by an actor in a supporting role: 1952, 1956) M: 862a
Quinn, Patrick J. [American political leader]
Illinois (table) I: 71; (The death penalty) I: 76
Quinn, Robert E. [American political leader]
Rhode Island (table) R: 311
Quinn, William F. [American political leader]
Hawaii (table) H: 105
Quinnat *See* Chinook salmon *in this index*
Quinoa [grain] Q: 42
Bolivia (Food) B: 443
Quinsigamond
Worcester W: 403
Quintain [sport]
Knights and knighthood *picture on* K: 349
Quintana Roo [state, Mexico] Q: 43
Quintana Roo, Andrés [Mexican statesman]
Quintana Roo Q: 43
Quintilian [Roman educator] Q: 43
Latin literature (The Imperial Period) L: 116-117
Oratory (Classical orators) O: 819
Quintilianus, Marcus Fabius *See* Quintilian *in this index*
Quintilis [Roman calendar]
July J: 188
Quintuplets
Multiple birth M: 919
Quipu [communications]
Inca (Communication and learning) I: 97
Indian, American *picture on* I: 140; (Writing) I: 150
Quirinal Hill [Rome] Q: 43
Rome R: 429
Quirinal Palace [Rome]
Rome (Churches, palaces, and fountains) R: 429
Quirinus [Roman mythology]
Mythology (Roman divinities) M: 982
Quirinal Hill Q: 43
Quiroga, Horacio [Uruguayan author]
Uruguay (The arts) U: 225
Quirós, Pedro Fernandez de [Portuguese explorer]
Torres, Luis Vaez de T: 342
Tuamotu Islands T: 476
Vanuatu (History) V: 284
Quisling [traitor]
Quisling, Vidkun Q: 43
Quisling, Vidkun [Norwegian traitor] Q: 43
Norway (World War II) N: 546
Quit India Movement [history of India]

India (World War II [1939-1945]) I: 132
Quitclaim deed [real estate]
Deed D: 81
Quite [bullfighting]
Bullfighting (The order of the bullfight) B: 696
Quitman, John A. [American political leader]
Mississippi (table) M: 640
Quito [Ecuador] Q: 43 *with picture*
Ecuador E: 67 *with picture, picture on* E: 68
Equator (The equatorial climate) E: 346
Latin America *picture on* L: 100
Quitus [people]
Quito Q: 43
Quiver
Archery (Arrows) A: 602 *with diagram*
Quivira [legendary city]
Coronado, Francisco Vásquez de Ci: 1068
Quixote, Don *See* Don Quixote *in this index*
Quiz show
Television (Early programs) T: 118 *with picture*
Qum [Iran] *See* Qom *in this index*
Qumran [region, Israel]
Dead Sea Scrolls D: 56
Quo Vadis? [book by Sienkiewicz]
Sienkiewicz, Henryk S: 450
Quoll [animal] Q: 44 *with picture*
Quonset hut [dwelling]
Rhode Island (Interesting facts) R: 297 *with picture*
Quonset Point Naval Air Station [Rhode Island]
Rhode Island (Interesting facts) R: 297 *with picture*
Quorum [parliamentary procedure]
Parliamentary procedure (Holding meetings) P: 176
Quota
See also Import quota *in this index*
Affirmative action A: 91
Arab Americans (History of Arab immigration) A: 581
Canada (Communication) C: 126-127
Immigration (A temporary decline) I: 83; (The fourth wave) I: 83
Quota sample [statistics]
Public opinion poll (History) P: 863
Quotation
Dictionary (What a dictionary tells you) D: 193
Quotation mark
Punctuation (Quotation marks) P: 902
Quotations from Chairman Mao [book]
Cultural Revolution Ci: 1185
Quotient [mathematics]
Arithmetic (Division) A: 668
Division (Writing division) D: 248
Quqon, Khanate of [Asian history]
Kyrgyzstan (History) K: 400
Qur'ān [religious book] Q: 44
Arabic literature A: 583
Arabs (Literature and the arts) A: 587
`Īd al-Ad-hā I: 25
Islam I: 463
Islamic art (Calligraphy) I: 468
Jihad J: 126
Jinni J: 127
Mullah M: 914
Muslims (Muhammad) M: 964a
Ottoman Empire (People) O: 877
Painting (Islamic painting) P: 48
Ramadan R: 82
Shari`ah S: 373
Wahhābis W: 5
Qur'ānic school
Niger (People) N: 407-408
Quraysh [people]
Muslims (Muhammad) M: 964
Qurei, Ahmed [Palestinian political leader]
Palestinian Authority P: 107
Qurnat as Sawda [mountain, Lebanon]
Lebanon (Land and climate) L: 172
Qutb, Sayyid [Egyptian religious leader] Q: 44
Muslim Brotherhood M: 964
Qutb ub-din Aybak [Muslim general]
India (Period of invasions) I: 129
Quttinirpaaq National Park [Nunavut]
Canada (table: National parks and national park reserves) C: 113
Nunavut (Economy) N: 610
q.v. [abbreviation]
Cross-reference Ci: 1155
QWERTY keyboard
Keyboard K: 308 *with picture*
Typewriter (History) T: 539
Qwest Communications International Inc.
Telephone (In the United States) T: 99

R

R [letter] R: 45 *with pictures*

R [mathematics]
Division (Short division) D: 251
R [rating]
Motion picture (Censorship and self-regulation) M: 860-861
R. Caldecott's Picture Book No. 1 [book]
Literature for children *picture on* L: 362
R-34 [airship]
Airship (Between world wars) A: 252
R & B [music] *See* Rhythm and blues *in this index*
R and R: A Story About Two Alphabets [book by Raschka]
Raschka, Chris R: 144
R-value [construction]
Insulation (In buildings) I: 306
R [symbol] R: 46
Ra [Egyptian god] *See* Re *in this index*
Ra [symbol]
Radium (Properties) R: 100
Ra-II [boat]
Heyerdahl, Thor H: 221
Rabat [Morocco] R: 46
Morocco M: 810 *with picture*
Rabaul [New Britain]
Bismarck Archipelago B: 383
New Britain N: 179
World War II (The South Pacific) W: 489
Rabbath Ammon [ancient city]
Amman A: 433
Rabbi [religion] R: 46
Address, Forms of (Members of the clergy) A: 54
Judaism (The rabbi) J: 181
Rabbit [animal] R: 46 *with pictures*
Animal *picture on* A: 483; (Introduction of new species) A: 505
Australia (Introduced species) A: 913
Balance of nature *picture on* B: 35
Conservation (Australia) Ci: 989
Easter (Easter symbols) E: 43-44
Fur (table) F: 561
Hare H: 59
Tularemia T: 482
Rabbit, Run [book by Updike]
Updike, John U: 213
Rabbit at Rest [book by Updike]
Updike, John U: 213
Rabbit Creek [Yukon]
Klondike K: 344
Rabbit deer *See* Pudu *in this index*
Rabbit-eye blueberry
Blueberry B: 422
Rabbit fever *See* Tularemia *in this index*
Rabbit Hill [book by Lawson]
Lawson, Robert L: 147
Rabbitry
Rabbit (Domestic rabbits) R: 46
Rabe, David [American dramatist]
Drama (Later United States drama) D: 340-341
Rabelais, François [French author] R: 49
French literature (The Renaissance) F: 519
Humanism (The spread of humanism) H: 431
Rabi I [month]
Calendar (The Islamic calendar) C: 29
Rabi II [month]
Calendar (The Islamic calendar) C: 29
Rabi, Isidor Isaac [American physicist]
Nobel Prizes (Physics: 1944) N: 440
Rabi`a of Basra [Muslim religious leader]
Sufism So: 959
Rabies [disease] R: 49
Bat (Bats and people) B: 162
Cat (Veterinary care) C: 295
Dog (Medical care) D: 279
Immune system *picture on* I: 88d
Pasteur, Louis (His work in medicine) P: 193
Veterinary medicine V: 345
Rabin, Jean [birth name of]
Audubon, John James (His life) A: 884
Rabin, Yitzhak [Israeli political leader] R: 50 *with portrait*
Israel (The Yom Kippur War) I: 488; (The 1990's) I: 489 *with picture*
Rabinowitz, David L. [American astronomer]
Eris E: 352
Planet (Haumea) P: 512
Rabinowitz, Sholem [Yiddish author] *See* Sholem Aleichem *in this index*
Rabuka, Sitiveni [Fijian political leader]
Fiji (History) F: 98-99
Rabun, William [American political leader]
Georgia (table) G: 130
Rabushka, Alvin [American economist]
Flat tax F: 228
Raccoon [animal] R: 50 *with pictures*
Animal *picture on* A: 479
Fur (table) F: 561
Panda (Classifying pandas) P: 129

Raccoon butterflyfish [fish]
Animal *picture on* **A: 487**
Raccoon coat
Roaring Twenties *picture on* **R: 363**
Raccoon dog
Fox (Raccoon dogs) **F: 440**
Race *See* Race relations; Races, Human *in this index*
Race [botany]
Corn (The corn plant) **Ci: 1057**
Race [marking]
Horse (Coat and skin) **H: 348-349**
Race horse
Horse racing **H: 363** *with pictures*
Kentucky *picture on* **K: 276**
Race record [recording]
Rhythm and blues **R: 320**
Race relations
See also Discrimination; Segregation *in this index*
Affirmative action **A: 91**
African Americans **A: 136b**
Los Angeles (Recent developments) **L: 470**
Minority group **M: 608**
Races, Human (The social significance of race) **R: 59**
Riot (Major riots in the United States) **R: 348**
Segregation **S: 284**
South Africa **So: 608**
United States, History of the (Poverty and discrimination) **U: 195**
Race runner [lizard]
Lizard *picture on* **L: 400**
Race track
Hippodrome **H: 240**
Horse racing (At the races) **H: 365**
Race Track or Death on a Pale Horse, The [painting by Ryder]
Ryder, Albert Pinkham *picture on* **R: 573**
Race-walking
Walking **W: 14**
Raceme [botany] **R: 51**
Inflorescence **I: 268a**
Racer [snake] **R: 51**
Snake *picture on* **S: 533**
Races, Human R: 52 *with pictures and map*
See also the list of Related articles in the Races, Human *article and* Race relations *in this index*
Adoption (Transracial adoptions) **A: 66**
Blood (The significance of blood groups) **B: 412**
Minority group **M: 608**
Prehistoric people (The origin of *Homo sapiens*) **P: 748**
Racism **R: 62**
World **W: 407**
Rachel [Biblical figure] **R: 60**
Jacob **J: 19**
Joseph (The prime minister) **J: 168**
Rachis [biology]
Feather (Kinds and parts of feathers) **F: 59** *with diagram*
Leaf (The blade) **L: 153-154**
Rachmaninoff, Sergei Vassilievich [Russian composer] **R: 60**
Racial discrimination *See* Discrimination [sociology] *in this index*
Racial minority [sociology]
Minority group **M: 608**
Racial profiling [law enforcement] **R: 61**
African Americans (Race relations) **A: 136t**
Racism (Types of racism) **R: 62**
Racial segregation *See* Segregation *in this index*
Racial stratification
Minority group (Relationships between groups) **M: 609**
Racicot, Marc [American political leader]
Montana (table) **M: 757**
Racine, Jean [French dramatist] **R: 61**
Drama (Neoclassical playwrights) **D: 333-334**
French literature (Classical drama) **F: 520**
Racine Art Museum [Racine]
Wisconsin *picture on* **W: 351**
Racing [sport] **R: 61**
Airplane (The golden age) **A: 235-236**
Canoeing (Canoe racing) **C: 181** *with picture*
Swimming *picture on* **So: 1042**
Racing bike
Bicycle (Road bikes) **B: 289**
Racing car
Automobile racing **A: 975**
Racing spur
Horse (Spurs) **H: 351**
Racism R: 62
See also Discrimination *in this index*
Hate crime **H: 85**
Indian, American (Current issues) **I: 182-183**
Stereotyping **So: 893**
Rack [barn]
Horse (Food) **H: 355**

Rack [gait]
Horse (Gaits) **H: 353-354**
Rack-and-pinion gear
Automobile *diagram on* **A: 950**
Gear **G: 75**
Rack car
Railroad *picture on* **R: 108**
Rack gear
Gear **G: 75**
Racket [sports]
Badminton (Playing) **B: 24** *with picture*
Squash **So: 813** *with picture*
Table tennis **T: 3** *with picture*
Tennis (Tennis rackets) **T: 162** *with picture*
Racket toss
Tennis (How tennis is played) **T: 162**
Racketeer Influenced and Corrupt Organizations Act [1970]
Racketeering **R: 63**
Racketeering [crime] **R: 63**
Rackham, Arthur [British artist] **R: 63** *with picture*
Literature for children *picture on* **L: 359**
Rackham, "Calico Jack" [English pirate]
Pirate (Other regions) **P: 495** *with picture*
Racking room [brewing]
Brewing *picture on* **B: 595**
Racquet [sports] *See* Racket *in this index*
Racquetball [sport] **R: 63** *with diagram*
Rad [unit of measure]
Ion (Producing ions) **I: 372**
Radiation (Dose) **R: 79**
Radama I [king of Madagascar]
Madagascar (History) **M: 29**
Radames [opera character]
Opera: (*Aida*) **O: 801**
Radar [electronics] **R: 64** *with pictures and map*
Airplane (Safety) **A: 227-228**
Antenna **A: 543**
Guided missile (Beam-riding guidance) **G: 426**
Navigation (Electronic navigation) **N: 72** *with picture*
Radio (Navigation) **R: 85**
Rain (Measuring rainfall) **R: 125**
Rangefinder **R: 139**
Remote sensing **R: 231**
Ship (Navigation) **S: 410-411**
Tornado (Field studies) **T: 336**
Warship (Aircraft carriers) **W: 39**
Watson-Watt, Sir Robert Alexander **W: 148**
Weather (Weather radar) **W: 162** *with pictures*
Radar altimeter [instrument]
Altimeter **A: 389**
Radar (In aviation) **R: 64-65**
Radar astronomy
Radar (In scientific research) **R: 68**
Radar echo
Weather (Weather radar) **W: 162** *with picture*
Radar map
Radar (In scientific research) **R: 68** *with picture*; (Pulse radar) **R: 69** *with picture*
Weather *picture on* **W: 166**
Radar transponder [navigation]
Airplane (Safety) **A: 227**
Radbourn, Charlie [American baseball player]
Baseball (table: Hall of Fame) **B: 134a**; (Early strategy and stars) **B: 134b**
Radcliffe, Ann [British author]
Gothic novel **G: 279**
Radcliffe-Brown, A. R. [British anthropologist] **R: 73**
Radcliffe College R: 73
Harvard University (History) **H: 80-81**
Radcliffe Institute for Advanced Study
Harvard University (History) **H: 80-81**
Radcliffe College **R: 73**
Radford, Arthur William [American admiral] **R: 73**
Radial [signal]
Airplane *diagram on* **A: 226**
Radial artery [anatomy]
Human body (table) **H: 422** *with diagram*
Pulse **P: 900a**
Radial design prison
Prison (Prison buildings) **P: 806**
Radial engine
Gasoline engine (Cylinder arrangement) **G: 64** *with diagram*
Radial nerve [anatomy]
Human body (table) **H: 422** *with diagram*
Radial symmetry [biology]
Echinoderm **E: 49**
Flower (The parts of a flower) **F: 293**
Radial tire
Tire (Types of tires and tread patterns) **T: 297**
Radian [unit of measure] **R: 73** *with diagram*
Radiant [astronomy]
Meteor (Meteor showers) **M: 431**
Radiant heating

Heating (Steam and hot-water heating systems) **H: 159** *with diagrams*; (Room heaters) **H: 160**
Radiant intensity [physics]
Light (Energy and brightness) **L: 290**
Radiant Way, The [book by Drabble]
Drabble, Margaret **D: 317**
Radiation [physics] **R: 74** *with pictures*
See also Irradiation, Radioactivity, *and* X rays *in this index and the list of Related articles in the* Radiation *article*
Effects
Aerospace medicine (Space medicine) **A: 89**
Cancer (Genes damaged by substances in the environment) **C: 170**; (Radiation therapy) **C: 172**
Cosmic rays (Effects of cosmic rays) **Ci: 1077**
Dew **D: 176**
Environmental pollution (Hazardous waste) **E: 334-335**
Extremophile **E: 458**
Fallout **F: 18** *with picture and map*
Lead (Uses) **L: 149**
Nuclear weapon (Thermal radiation) **N: 599**
Radiation sickness **R: 81**
History
Pauling, Linus Carl **P: 202**
Planck, Max Karl Ernst Ludwig **P: 507**
Universe (Changing views of the universe) **U: 205-206**
Sources
Heat *diagram on* **H: 151**; (How heat travels) **H: 152**
Nuclear energy (Hazards and safeguards) **N: 587**
Quasar **Q: 8**
Sun (Energy output) **So: 976**
Uses
Food preservation (Irradiation) **F: 343**
Heating (Steam and hot-water heating systems) **H: 159**
Insulation (Insulation to control heat flow) **I: 306**
Technology (Emerging technologies) **T: 76**
Thallium **T: 229**
Radiation-absorbing glass
Glass (Specialty glasses) **G: 212-213**
Radiation belt [astronomy]
Uranus (Magnetic field) **U: 219**
Radiation budget [meteorology]
Weather satellite **W: 171**
Radiation counter [instrument]
Radiocarbon (Radiocarbon dating) **R: 97-98** *with diagram*
Radiation detector
Geiger counter **G: 76** *with pictures*
Radiation fog
Fog **F: 314** *with diagram*
Radiation sickness R: 81
Fallout (The fallout hazard) **F: 19**
Ion (Producing ions) **I: 372**
Nuclear weapon (Effects of nuclear weapons) **N: 599-600**
Radiation (Dose) **R: 79-80**
Radiation therapy *See* Radiotherapy *in this index*
Radiation-transmitting glass
Glass (Specialty glasses) **G: 212-213**
Radiation weighting factor [radiology]
Radiation (Dose) **R: 79-80**
Radiator [device] **R: 82**
Automobile (The cooling system) **A: 953**
Heating (Room heaters) **H: 160**
Radical [chemistry] **R: 82**
Radical [mathematics]
Root **R: 469**
Square root **So: 812**
Radical Chic & Mau Mauing the Flak Catchers [book by Wolfe]
Wolfe, Tom **W: 378**
Radical Civic Union [political party]
Argentina (Reform movements) **A: 657**
Radical hysterectomy [surgery]
Cervical cancer **C: 364**
Hysterectomy **H: 482**
Radical Islam *See* Militant Islam *in this index*
Radical mastectomy [surgery]
Mastectomy **M: 296**
Radical modern design
Furniture (Radical modern design) **F: 585**
Radical Party [political party]
Spain (The Spanish republic) **So: 750**
Radical Reformation [religion]
Christianity (The Reformation) **C: 524**
Radical Republicans [U.S. history]
African Americans (Temporary gains) **A: 136k**
Civil War, American (Government and politics) **Ci: 622-623**
Grant, Ulysses S. (National hero) **G: 315**

Reconstruction (The Radicals and the Moderates) R: 178
Republican Party (The Radical Republicans and Reconstruction) R: 254
Tennessee (Reconstruction) T: 154
Radicalism [political science] R: 82
Left wing L: 181
Roaring Twenties (Changing attitudes) R: 363
Radicals [Chinese history]
China (The Great Leap Forward) C: 505
Radicals [Texas history]
Texas (The Civil War and Reconstruction) T: 207
Radicle [botany]
Germination G: 173
Radičová, Iveta [Slovak political leader]
Slovakia (Recent developments) S: 509
Radiculopathy [disorder]
Neuralgia N: 152
Radio [communications] R: 83 with pictures
See also the list of Related articles in the Radio article
Advertising (Radio) A: 74; (The rise of radio and television) A: 79
Cellular telephone C: 340
Citizens band radio Ci: 568
Communication (The development of electronics) Ci: 883 with picture
Country music (History) Ci: 1098a-1098b
De Forest, Lee D: 89
Electronics (The development of electronics) E: 215
Federal Communications Commission F: 63
Frequency modulation F: 528
Global Positioning System G: 231
Ionosphere I: 373
Journalism (Fields of journalism) J: 170; (Radio journalism) J: 175
Marconi, Guglielmo M: 196
Navigation (Radio navigation) N: 72 with picture
Pager P: 20
Public opinion (Radio and television) P: 860
Radio, Amateur R: 95 with picture
Railroad (Other train controls) R: 112
Remote control (The parts of a remote control system) R: 230
Roaring Twenties (Rising prosperity) R: 363
Soap opera So: 543
Space exploration (Communicating with Earth) So: 704
Telephone (Types of telephones) T: 94
Television (Other forms of entertainment) T: 121; (Early development) T: 127
Tesla, Nikola (Other inventions) T: 181
Voice of America V: 437
Walkie-talkie W: 14
Radio, Amateur R: 95 with picture
Radio announcer
Radio (Careers) R: 90
Radio beacon [navigation]
Beacon B: 179
Radio City Music Hall [New York City]
New York (Interesting facts) N: 291 with picture
New York City (Manhattan) N: 323-325; (Rockefeller Center) N: 338
Radio control
Airplane, Model (Radio control models) A: 241 with picture
Automobile, Model A: 974 with pictures
Remote control (The parts of a remote control system) R: 230
Watch (Quartz watches) W: 114-115
Radio Corporation of America
Communication (The development of electronics) Ci: 883-884
Radio (The start of broadcasting) R: 92
Sarnoff, David S: 126
Television (The start of broadcasting) T: 117
Radio data system
Radio (Radio data system [RDS] receivers) R: 90
Radio detection and ranging
Radar R: 64
Radio direction finding
Navigation (Radio direction finding) N: 73
Radio Free Europe/Radio Liberty R: 96
Propaganda (After World War II) P: 825
Radio-frequency catheter ablation [medicine]
Heart (Progress in treatment and prevention) H: 145
Radio frequency identification
Library (Security) L: 238-239
Radio-frequency wave
Radio (From electric waves to radio waves) R: 86
Radio Golf [play by Wilson]
Wilson, August W: 316
Radio interferometer [astronomy]
Telescope (Types of radio telescopes) T: 106-107 with picture

Radio Liberty [organization] See Radio Free Europe/Radio Liberty in this index
Radio Marti [radio station]
Voice of America V: 437
Radio modem [electronics]
Radio, Amateur (Uses of amateur radio) R: 95
Radio pulsar See Pulsar in this index
Radio Relay League, American
Radio, Amateur (Amateur radio organizations) R: 96
Radio remote control units
Locomotive (Diesel locomotives) L: 414-415
Radio station
Radio (Broadcasting) R: 83; (Radio stations) R: 86; (Stations and networks) R: 90
Radio telescope
Arecibo Observatory A: 645
Astronomy (Radio and microwave astronomy) A: 843
Extraterrestrial intelligence E: 458
Green Bank Telescope G: 380
Jansky, Karl Guthe J: 29
Jodrell Bank Observatory J: 130
Lovell, Sir Bernard L: 509
National Radio Astronomy Observatory N: 59
Observatory (Ground-based observatories) O: 644-645
Telescope (Radio and microwave telescopes) T: 106 with pictures
Radio tube [device]
Vacuum tube (History) V: 259
Radio-ulna [zoology]
Frog picture on F: 537
Radio wave [zoology]
Astronomy (table: The electromagnetic spectrum) A: 839; (Radio and microwave astronomy) A: 843
Communications satellite Ci: 888a
Electromagnetic waves (The electromagnetic spectrum) E: 202 with diagram
Gravitation (Bending and slowing of radio waves) G: 332
Jupiter (Radio emissions) J: 199
Magnetic resonance imaging M: 56
Microwave M: 520
Physics (Developments in the 1800's) P: 440
Pulsar P: 900a
Radar R: 64
Radiation (In communication) R: 74; (Electromagnetic radiation) R: 75-76 with picture
Radio R: 83; (Transmitting radio waves) R: 86 with diagrams
Spectroscopy So: 772
Sun (Energy output) So: 976
Telecommunications T: 89
Telescope (Radio and microwave telescopes) T: 106
Waves W: 152
Wireless communication W: 344
Radioactive decay [physics]
Alpha particle A: 381
Element, Chemical (The periodic table of the elements) E: 219
Isotope (Radioactive isotopes) I: 476
Plate tectonics (Maintaining tectonic activity) P: 564
Radiation (Radiation and radioactivity) R: 75
Radium (How radium forms and breaks down) R: 100
Time (Natural processes) T: 292
Transmutation of elements T: 378
Transuranium element T: 401
Radioactive decay series [physics]
Radiation diagram on R: 79; (Naturally radioactive substances) R: 77
Radioactive fallout See Fallout in this index
Radioactive isotope [physics]
Atom (Radioactivity) A: 873
Biochemistry (Investigative methods) B: 310
Fallout F: 18
Fossil (Dating fossils) F: 427
Isotope (Radioactive isotopes) I: 476 with diagrams
Lawrencium L: 147
Prehistoric people (Placing prehistoric people in time) P: 754a-754b
Satellite (Formation) S: 150
Radioactive tracer [medicine]
Radiation (Refining the uses of radiation) R: 81
Radioactive waste
Electric power (Nuclear power plants) E: 184
Environmental pollution (Hazardous waste) E: 334-335
Hazardous wastes H: 122
Nuclear energy (Wastes and waste disposal) N: 588

Technology (Using technology safely) T: 77
Radioactivity [physics]
Atom (Radioactivity) A: 873
Curie Ci: 1194
Curie, Marie Skłodowska Ci: 1194
Curie, Pierre Ci: 1194
Fallout F: 18
Geiger counter G: 76
Isotope I: 476
Mars (Mantle) M: 225
Nuclear energy (Radioactive decay) N: 582; (Hazards and safeguards) N: 587
Nuclear physics N: 595
Physics (The beginning of modern physics) P: 440-441; (Physics today) P: 442-443
Radiation (Radiation and radioactivity) R: 75; (Sources of radiation) R: 77; (Discovery of radioactivity) R: 81
Radiocarbon R: 97
Radiochemistry R: 98
Radiogeology R: 98
Radium R: 99
Relativity (Time dilation) R: 211
Transuranium element T: 401
Uranium (Properties of uranium) U: 214
RadioAstron mission
Telescope (Types of radio telescopes) T: 106-108
Radiocarbon [isotope] R: 97 with diagrams
Archaeology (Dating) A: 598
Cosmic rays (Effects of cosmic rays) Ci: 1077
Radiogeology R: 98
Time (Radioactive decay) T: 292
Radiocarbon dating [archaeology]
Archaeology (Dating) A: 598
Fossil (Dating fossils) F: 427
Nuclear physics N: 595
Prehistoric people (Placing prehistoric people in time) P: 754a-754b
Radioactivity (In science) R: 75
Radiocarbon (Radiocarbon dating) R: 97 with diagrams
Radiogeology R: 98
Radiochemistry R: 98
Radiogeology R: 98
Earth (Age of Earth) E: 26
Radiograph [medicine]
Radiology R: 98
X rays (Uses of X rays) X: 540 with pictures
Radiography [medicine]
Ballistics (Terminal ballistics) B: 56
Radiohead [rock band]
Rock music (Rock music today) R: 381
Radioisotope [physics]
Fallout F: 18
Isotope (Radioactive isotopes) I: 476
Nuclear physics N: 595
Radiochemistry R: 98
Radiogeology R: 98
Radiolaria [zoology]
Protozoan (Sarcodines) P: 837-838
Radiologic technologist [medicine]
Medicine (Other careers in medicine) M: 371
Radiological dispersion device [weapon] See Dirty bomb in this index
Radiological warfare
Chemical-biological-radiological warfare (Radiological) C: 396
Radiologist [occupation]
Radiology R: 98 with picture
Radiology [medicine] R: 98 with picture
Dentistry (Radiology) D: 144
Hospital picture on H: 372; (Professional services departments) H: 371
Medicine (table) M: 369
X rays X: 540 with pictures
Radiometer [instrument]
Crookes, Sir William Ci: 1153
Radionuclide [physics] See Radioisotope in this index
Radionuclide imaging [medicine]
Heart (Symptoms and diagnosis) H: 137
Radioresistant [biology]
Extremophile E: 458
Radiosonde [instrument] R: 99
Balloon (Sounding balloons) B: 58
Weather (Weather balloons, airplanes, and ships) W: 163 with picture
Radiotherapy [medicine]
Cancer (Radiation therapy) C: 172
Cervical cancer C: 364
Disease (Medical treatment) D: 232-233
Mastectomy M: 297
Radiation (Refining the uses of radiation) R: 81
Radish R: 99 with pictures
Gardening (Planning a kitchen garden) G: 34
Radisson, Pierre Esprit [French explorer] R: 99
Groseilliers, Médard Chouart, Sieur des G: 398

Minnesota (Exploration) M: 603
Wisconsin (European exploration and settlement) W: 365
Radium [element] R: 99
Curie, Marie Skłodowska Ci: 1194
Pitchblende P: 498
Radon R: 100
Radius [anatomy]
Arm A: 717 *with diagram*
Bird (Skeleton and muscles) B: 364 *with diagram*
Elbow E: 157 *with diagrams*
Human body (table) H: 422 *with diagram*
Wrist W: 510 *with diagram*
Radius [geometry]
Circle (Parts of a circle) Ci: 558 *with diagram*
Diameter D: 180
Polygon P: 650 *with diagram*
Sphere So: 779 *with diagram*
Radnitzky, Emmanuel [birth name of]
Ray, Man R: 152
Rado, James [American musician]
Rock music (Fresh directions) R: 380-380a
Radon [element] R: 100
Air pollution (Indoor air pollution) A: 199
Environmental pollution (Air pollution) E: 331-334
Radon Abatement Act, Indoor [1988]
Radon (Protection against radon) R: 100
Radon daughter [physics]
Radon (Radon decay) R: 100
Radula [zoology]
Limpet L: 308
Mollusk (Gastropods) M: 695
Squid (The body of a squid) So: 814
Rae, Bob [Canadian political leader]
Ontario (table) O: 783
Rae, Saul [Canadian diplomat]
United Nations (table) U: 86
Raeburn, Sir Henry [Scottish painter] R: 101 *with picture*
RAF [organization] *See* Royal Air force *in this index*
Raffaellino del Garbo [Italian artist]
Christianity: *picture on* C: 522f
Raffarin, Jean-Pierre [French political leader]
France (Recent developments) F: 478
Raffia [fiber] R: 101
Raffia palm [tree]
Leaf L: 151
Palm (The leaves) P: 109
Raffles, Sir Thomas Stamford [British merchant] R: 101
Singapore (History) S: 471
Rafflesia [plant] R: 101 *with picture*
Flower *picture on* F: 272
Plant (Photosynthesis) P: 537-538
Rain forest (Asia) R: 126b *with picture*
Rafsanjani, Ali Akbar Hashemi [Iranian political leader] R: 102 *with portrait*
Iran (After Khomeini) I: 406a
Raft [boat] R: 102 *with picture*
Rafting R: 102 *with picture*
Ship *picture on* S: 416; (Early watercraft) S: 414-415
Raft foundation [engineering]
Building construction (Foundations) B: 682
Raft of El Dorado, The [sculpture]
Colombia *picture on* Ci: 781
Raft of the Medusa, The [painting by Géricault]
Géricault, Théodore G: 137
Painting (Romanticism) P: 68-69 *with picture*
Rafter [construction]
House (The roof) H: 382 *with diagram*
Rafting R: 102 *with picture*
Rag doll
Doll (The 1970's) D: 293 *with picture*
Rag paper
Paper (Raw materials) P: 134
Rag rug
Rugs and carpets (History) R: 517
Raga [music]
India (Music and dance) I: 120
Music (Indian music) M: 956
Sitar S: 477
Ragamala [art]
Painting (Indian painting) P: 44 *with picture*
Ragdoll cat
Cat (Long-haired breeds) C: 292
Ragged Dick [books by Alger]
Alger, Horatio A: 359
Raggedy Andy [doll]
Doll (Before World War I) D: 291-292
Raggedy Ann [doll]
Doll (Before World War I) D: 291
Raggedy Ann Stories [book by Gruelle]
Doll (Before World War I) D: 291-292
Raging Bull [film]
De Niro, Robert D: 131

Scorsese, Martin S: 210
Ragnarok [Norse mythology]
Balder B: 38
Mythology (The end of the world) M: 987
Odin O: 674
Thor T: 266
Ragni, Gerome [American musician]
Rock music (Fresh directions) R: 380-380a
Ragtime [book by Doctorow]
Doctorow, E. L. D: 260
Ragtime [musical]
United States *picture on* U: 119
Ragtime [music] R: 102
Jazz (The roots of jazz) J: 70
Johnson, James P. J: 143
Joplin, Scott J: 160
Popular music (Ragtime, jazz, and blues) P: 670
Ragweed [plant] R: 103 *with picture*
Hay fever (Causes and prevention) H: 116
Rahal, Bobby [race driver]
Automobile racing (table: Indianapolis 500 winners) A: 980
Rahman, Mujibur [Bangladeshi political leader]
See Mujibur Rahman *in this index*
Rahmonov, Emomali [Tajik political leader]
Tajikistan (Since independence) T: 18b
Rahula [son of]
Buddha (Early life) B: 667
Raï [music]
Arab Americans (Arab American accomplishments) A: 580b-581
Raider [business]
Business (Recent developments) B: 727
Merger M: 417
Raiders, Oakland *See* Oakland Raiders *in this index*
Raiders of the Lost Ark [film]
Ford, Harrison F: 379
Lucas, George L: 513
Raikes, Robert [British educator] R: 103
Räikkönen, Kimi [Finnish race driver]
Automobile racing (table: Formula One World Drivers' Championship) A: 980
Rail [bird] R: 103 *with picture*
Rail [transportation]
Freight F: 510
Locomotive (Electric locomotives) L: 416
Railroad (What makes up a railroad) R: 106-107
Railcar [train]
Railroad (Railroad cars with built-in power units) R: 108
Railroad [sports]
Bowling (table) B: 521
Railroad [transportation] R: 104 *with pictures and map*
See also Monorail *in this index; and the list of Related articles in the* Railroad *article and the Transportation sections of the country, state, and province articles*
Air conditioning (Air conditioners for vehicles) A: 179
Careers (Transportation) C: 235
Channel Tunnel C: 375
Chicago (Growth as a city) C: 435
Coal (Shipping coal) Ci: 727 *with picture*
Electric railroad E: 187 *with pictures*
Europe *picture on* E: 411
Industrial Revolution *pictures on* I: 253; (Railroads) I: 251
Interstate commerce (The Interstate Commerce Act) I: 351
Locomotive L: 414 *with pictures*
Magnetic levitation train M: 55 *with picture*
Postal Service, United States *picture on* P: 701
Russia (Transportation and communication) R: 546 *with picture*
Seattle (Railroads and growth) S: 276
Telegraph (Uses for the telegraph) T: 91
Time (Local and standard time) T: 292
Transcontinental railroad T: 370
Transit T: 374
Transportation *pictures on* T: 389, T: 390, T: 394; (Land transportation) T: 383
Truck farming (History) T: 460
Tunnel (Railroad tunnels) T: 491
United States, History of the (Advances in transportation and communications) U: 170 *with picture*; (Railroads) U: 180 *with picture*
Western frontier life in America (Improvements in transportation) W: 233
Westward movement in America (Cattle frontiers) W: 251
Railroad, Elevated *See* Elevated railroad *in this index*
Railroad, Model R: 119 *with pictures*
Railroad rail
Iron and steel (Rolling) I: 445-447 *with diagram*
Railroad Reorganization Act [1973]

Railroad (Economic recovery-and decline) R: 118
Railroad retirement
Pension (Federal pension plans) P: 272-273
Railroad Retirement Board R: 121
Railroad Retirement Act [1935]
Railroad Retirement Board R: 122
Railroad Retirement Board [U.S.] R: 121
Railroad Safety Appliance Act [1893]
Railroad (Engineering improvements) R: 117
Railroad Trainmen, Brotherhood of
Railway brotherhoods R: 122
Railroad worm [beetle]
Insect *picture on* I: 279
Railroad worm [fly] *See* Apple maggot *in this index*
Railroads, Association of American
Railroad (Cooperation among railroads) R: 113
Railsplitter [name for]
Lincoln, Abraham (Election of 1860) L: 318 *with picture*
Railway *See* Railroad *in this index*
Railway brotherhoods [labor unions] R: 122
Railway Conductors and Brakemen, Order of
Railway brotherhoods R: 122
Railway Exchange Building [Chicago]
Burnham, Daniel Hudson *picture on* B: 709
Railway Labor Act [1926] R: 122
National Mediation Board N: 40
Railroad (Railroad unions) R: 113; (The 1920's and the Great Depression) R: 118
Railway Union, American
Debs, Eugene Victor D: 65
Raimund, Ferdinand [Austrian dramatist]
Austria (Literature) A: 933
Rain R: 122 *with pictures and map*
See also See also the list of Related articles in the Rain *article in this index*
Acid rain A: 27
Climate (Kinds of climates) Ci: 676a
Cloud seeding C: 711
Cloudburst C: 712
Drought D: 349
Famine (Too much rainfall) F: 26a
Flash flood F: 227
India (The rainy season) I: 124 *with picture and map*
Irrigation I: 456
Monsoon M: 740
Rain forest (Environmental value) R: 126c
Rain gauge R: 127
Thunderstorm T: 272
Tornado (The life of a tornado) T: 335
Water (World distribution of water) W: 122 *with picture and map*
Weather (Synoptic-scale systems) W: 159-160
Rain [book by Stojic]
Literature for children *picture on* L: 367
Rain dance R: 125
Indian, American (Ceremonies) I: 148
Rain Dance [play by Wilson]
Wilson, Lanford W: 317
Rain forest R: 126 *with pictures and map*
Amazon rain forest A: 401
Animal (Animals of the tropical forests) A: 480 *with pictures and map*; (Destruction of habitat) A: 504 *with picture*
Biome B: 324; (table) B: 323 *with map*
Brazil (The Amazon Region) B: 577
Climate (Tropical wet climates) Ci: 676a *with picture*
Congo, Democratic Republic of the (The tropical rain forest) Ci: 940
Conservation (Latin America) Ci: 988
Deforestation *picture on* D: 89
Endangered species (Loss of habitat) E: 269
Forest *picture on* F: 390, *map on* F: 395; (Kinds of forests) F: 392 *with map*
Gaia G: 6
Indian, American (Indians of the Tropical Forest) I: 175
Indonesia (Papua) I: 234 *with picture*
Malaysia *picture on* M: 99
Mexico *picture on* M: 463
Olympic National Park O: 756
Plant *map on* P: 523; (Tropical rain forests) P: 527 *with pictures*
South America *picture on* So: 623; (Tropical rain forests) So: 629
Tropics T: 452
Zoo *picture on* Z: 603
Rain gauge [measuring device] R: 127
Rain (Measuring rainfall) R: 125
Weather (Land-based observation stations) W: 162
Rain Man [film]
Motion picture (Best picture: 1988) M: 861
Rain shadow [weather]
Climate (The role of topography) Ci: 676a

Rain Shower on Ohashi Bridge [print by Hiroshige]
Hiroshige *picture on* H: 242
Rain tree R: 127
Rainband [meteorology]
Hurricane (Hurricane) H: 454 *with diagram*
Rainbow R: 127 *with pictures*
Spectrum So: 772
Rainbow [ship]
Clipper ship Ci: 682h
Rainbow, The [book by Lawrence]
Lawrence, D. H. L: 145
Rainbow Bridge National Monument [Utah]
R: 128
National Park System (table: National
monuments) N: 51
Utah *picture on* U: 239; (Interesting facts) U: 231
Rainbow Coalition [organization]
Jackson, Jesse Louis J: 15
Rainbow darter [fish]
Darter D: 38
Fish *picture on* F: 158
Rainbow Falls [Valley Head]
Alabama *picture on* A: 267
Rainbow for Girls [organization] R: 128
Rainbow lorikeet [bird]
Parrot *picture on* P: 180
Rainbow PUSH Coalition [organization]
Jackson, Jesse Louis J: 15
Rainbow smelt [fish]
Smelt S: 514 *with picture*
Rainbow trout [trout]
Fish *picture on* F: 159
Invasive species (How invasive species affect
habitats) I: 354j
Trout (True trout) T: 453 *with picture*
Rainbow Warrior [ship]
Greenpeace G: 386
New Zealand (International tensions) N: 355-356
Raincoat
Rubber (The rubber industry begins) R: 501
Raindrop
Rain (Characteristics of rain) R: 122
Rainbow (How rainbows appear) R: 128 *with
diagram*
Raindrop horse *See* Appaloosa *in this index*
Rainer, Luise [Austrian actress]
Motion picture (Best performance by an actress:
1936, 1937) M: 862
Rainfall *See* Rain *in this index*
Rainier III [prince of Monaco] R: 129
Kelly, Grace K: 256
Monaco (History) M: 700
Rainmaking [meteorology] *See* Cloud seeding *in
this index*
Rainwater, James [American physicist]
Nobel Prizes (Physics: 1975) N: 441
Rainy Lake [Minnesota-Ontario] R: 129
Rainy Night [painting by Burchfield]
Burchfield, Charles Ephraim *picture on* B: 702
Raisa, Rosa [Polish singer] R: 129
Raise [mining]
Mining (Mining terms) M: 577
Raised atoll [geology]
Pacific Islands (The low islands) P: 8
Raised relief map
Map (Production and reproduction) M: 181
Raisin [food] R: 129
Fresno F: 529
Grape (European grapes) G: 318
Raisin in the Sun, A [play by Hansberry]
African American literature (The 1900's) A: 136a
American literature (Drama) A: 426
Drama (Later United States drama) D: 340
Hansberry, Lorraine H: 53
Raisin River National Battlefield Park [Michigan]
National Park System (table: National battlefields)
N: 55
Rajab [month]
Calendar (The Islamic calendar) C: 29
Rajah [title] R: 130
Rajang River
Borneo (The land and its resources) B: 489
Rajapakse, Mahinda [Sri Lankan political leader]
Sri Lanka (History) So: 819-820
Rajghat [shrine]
Delhi (The city) D: 115
Rajoelina, Andry [Madagascar political leader]
Madagascar (History) M: 29
Rajoy, Mariano [Spanish political leader]
Spain (The early 2000's) So: 751
Rajput courts [Indian history]
Painting (Indian painting) P: 44
Rajya Sabha [Indian government]
India (Central government) I: 109
Raka [religion]
Islam (The Five Pillars of Islam) I: 463-464
Rake [tool] R: 130

Gardening (Cultivating an outdoor garden) G: 34
Rake's Progress, A [paintings by Hogarth]
Hogarth, William H: 288
Rake's Progress, The [opera by Stravinsky]
Auden, W. H. A: 881
Stravinsky, Igor (Neoclassical works) So: 922
Raketa [boat]
Hydrofoil (Modern hydrofoil development)
H: 468
Rákóczi, Francis II [Hungarian nobleman]
Hungary (Habsburg rule) H: 445
Rákosi, Matthias [Hungarian political leader]
Hungary (Communist Hungary) H: 447
Ralegh, Sir Walter [English explorer] *See* Raleigh,
Sir Walter *in this index*
Raleigh [North Carolina] R: 130 *with picture*
Raleigh, Sir Walter [English explorer] R: 131 *with
portrait*
Gilbert, Sir Humphrey G: 189
Lost Colony L: 472
Virginia V: 398; (Early days) V: 418
Raleighvallen-Voltzberg National Park
[Suriname]
National park (table) N: 42g
Rallentando [music]
Music (table) M: 954
Rallis, George [Greek political leader]
Greece (The restoration of democracy) G: 365
Rally [race]
Automobile racing (Other kinds of racing) A: 978
Balloon *picture on* B: 57
Rally [tennis]
Tennis (The ball in play) T: 163
Rally for the Republic [political party]
Chirac, Jacques René C: 514
France (Socialists win power) F: 478
Rally of the French People [French political party]
De Gaulle, Charles André Joseph Marie
(Peacetime leader) D: 91
Rally point system
Volleyball (The game) V: 445
Rally scoring [sports]
Beach volleyball B: 179
Raloxifene [hormone]
Hormone replacement therapy H: 338
Ralston, Alexander [American architect]
Indianapolis (The city) I: 220
Ralston, Samuel M. [American political leader]
Indiana (table) I: 214
Ram [animal]
Sheep (The body of the sheep) S: 380
RAM [computing] *See* Random-access memory *in
this index*
Ram [tool]
Extrusion E: 459 *with diagram*
Ram [weapon]
Battering ram B: 167 *with picture*
Galley G: 15
Ship (Phoenician and Greek ships) S: 415
Ram, Hydraulic [device]
Elevator (How elevators work) E: 234 *with
diagram*
Rama [Hindu god] R: 131
Diwali D: 255
India (Hinduism) I: 116; (Religious and ethnic
unrest) I: 134
Ramayana R: 132
Vishnu V: 429
Rama I [king of Thailand]
Bangkok (History) B: 77
Rama III [king of Thailand]
Mongkut M: 718
Rama IV [king of Thailand] *See* Mongkut *in this
index*
Rama IX [king of Thailand] *See* Bhumibol Adulyadej
in this index
Rama Road
Nicaragua (The Somoza period) N: 400
Ramacharitmanas [poem by Tuslidas]
Hindi language (Hindi literature) H: 235
Ramadan [month] R: 132 *with picture*
Calendar (The Islamic calendar) C: 29
Fast F: 52
Feasts and festivals (In Islam) F: 58
Food (Religious reasons) F: 332
`Id al-Fitr I: 25
Islam (The Five Pillars of Islam) I: 463-464
Religion *on* R: 214
Ramadan War [1973]
Arab-Israeli conflict (The 1973 war) A: 582a
Ramakrishna Mission [religious group]
Monasticism (The influence of monasticism
today) M: 701
Ramakrishnan, Venkatraman [American chemist]
Nobel Prizes (Chemistry: 2009) N: 444
Raman, Sir Chandrasekhara Venkata [Indian
physicist] R: 132

Raman effect [physics]
Raman, Sir Chandrasekhara Venkata R: 132
Ramat Polin [housing development]
Jerusalem *picture on* J: 99
Ramathibodi [king of Ayutthaya]
Thailand (Early kingdoms) T: 226
Ramayana [religious book] R: 132
Dance (Asian theatrical dance) D: 28-29
Hinduism (Sacred writings) H: 235
India (Literature) I: 120
Rama R: 131
Vishnu V: 429
Ramayana Ballet
Indonesia *picture on* I: 233
Ramble [bird sanctuary]
New York City (Parks) N: 338
Rambler, The [essays by Johnson]
Johnson, Samuel (Later years) J: 153
Rambler rose
Rose (Types of roses) R: 474
Rambouillet [sheep]
Sheep (Fine-wooled sheep) S: 381-382
Rameau, Jean-Philippe [French composer] R: 133
Rameau's Nephew [book by Diderot]
Diderot, Denis D: 195
Rameses II *See* Ramses II *in this index*
Ramezay, Claude de [Canadian political leader]
Quebec (Museums) Q: 15
Ramezay, Jean-Baptiste [French general]
Quebec, Battle of (The attack on Quebec) Q: 37
Ramgoolam, Navinchandra [Mauritian political
leader]
Mauritius (History) M: 317
Ramie [plant] R: 133
Ramjet [engine]
Jet propulsion J: 112 *with diagram*; (Ramjet)
J: 114
Ramkhamhaeng [Sukothai king]
Thailand (Early kingdoms) T: 226
Ramlee, P. [Malaysian actor]
Malaysia (The arts) M: 99
Rammohun Roy [Indian religious leader] R: 133
Ramna [district]
Dhaka D: 178
Ramon, Ilan [Israeli astronaut]
Columbia disaster Ci: 852
Space exploration (The Columbia disaster)
So: 725
Ramón y Cajal, Santiago [Spanish physiologist]
Nobel Prizes (Physiology or medicine: 1906)
N: 445
Ramos, Fidel Valdez [Filipino political leader]
Philippines (Recovering democracy) P: 381
Ramos, Graciliano [Brazilian author]
Brazil (The arts) B: 576-577
Latin American literature (The early 1900's) L: 113
Ramos-Horta, José [Timorese political leader]
East Timor (History) E: 41
Nobel Prizes (Peace: 1996) N: 448b
Ramotar, Donald [Guyana political leader]
Guyana (History) G: 446-447
Ramoth-Gilead [ancient city]
Cities of refuge Ci: 568
Ramp [highway]
Road (Primary highways) R: 358
Ramp [plant] R: 133
Ramp agent [occupation]
Airport (Airline passenger services) A: 246
Ramparts [region, Alaska]
Yukon River (Upper Yukon) Y: 582 *with map*
Rampolla del Tindaro, Mariano [Italian religious
leader] R: 133
Rampton, Calvin L. [American political leader]
Utah (table) U: 245
Rams, Saint Louis *See* Saint Louis Rams *in this
index*
Ramsar Convention [1971]
Bird (Protective laws and treaties) B: 368
Wetland (Conservation) W: 253
Ramsay, Allan [Scottish painter]
Scotland (The arts) S: 215-217
Ramsay, Sir William [British chemist] R: 133
Helium H: 176
Krypton K: 389
Neon N: 123
Noble gas N: 451
Ramsdell, George A. [American political leader]
New Hampshire (table) N: 223
Ramses II [king of ancient Egypt] R: 134 *with
picture*
Abu Simbel, Temples of A: 19
Embalming (Ancient embalming) E: 255
Hittites (History) H: 269
Sculpture (Egyptian) S: 234
Ramses III [king of ancient Egypt]
Hieroglyphics *pictures on* H: 225
Ramsey, Alec [fictional character]

Farley, Walter **F: 28**
Ramsey, Alexander [American political leader]
Hayes, Rutherford Birchard (table) **H: 121**
Minnesota (table) **M: 602**; (Territorial days)
M: 604
Ramsey, Norman Foster [American physicist]
Nobel Prizes (Physics: 1989) **N: 442**
Rana [Nepalese history]
Nepal (History) **N: 126**
Ranavalona I [queen of Madagascar]
Madagascar (History) **M: 29**
Rance River [France]
Electric power (Growth of the electric power
industry) **E: 186**
Ranch See Ranching in this index
Ranch house
House picture on **H: 381**
Ranchero [title]
California (The California missions) **C: 60**
Ranching R: 134 with pictures
Cattle **C: 306**
Farm and farming (Specialized livestock farms)
F: 31 with picture
Western frontier life in America (Ranching)
W: 236 with picture
Rancho
California (The California missions) **C: 60**
Paraguay (Rural life) **P: 145**
Venezuela (Ways of life) **V: 299** with picture
Ranchos de Taos [district]
Taos **T: 36**
Ranchu [fish]
Goldfish picture on **G: 258**
Rand, Ayn [American author] **R: 136** with portrait
RAND Corporation R: 136
Rand McNally building [Chicago]
Root, John Wellborn **R: 472**
Randall, Alexander W. [American political leader]
Wisconsin (table) **W: 365**
Randalls Island [New York]
New York City (Small islands) **N: 330**
Randolph, A. Philip [American labor leader] **R: 136**
with portrait
African Americans (World War II [1939-1945])
A: 136n-136o
March on Washington **M: 196**
Randolph, Beverley [American political leader]
Virginia (table) **V: 417**
Randolph, Edmund [American political leader]
R: 137
Constitution of the United States (The
Constitutional Convention) **Ci: 999-1000**
United States, History of the picture on **U: 162**
Virginia (table) **V: 417**; (The Mother of Presidents)
V: 421
Washington, George (Cabinet) **W: 102** with
picture; (Cabinet scandal) **W: 106**
Randolph, Edward [English colonial official] **R: 137**
Randolph, John [American political leader] **R: 137**
Duel **D: 378**
Randolph, Martha Jefferson [daughter of]
Jefferson, Thomas (Life in the White House) **J: 83**
with picture
White House hostesses **W: 291**
Randolph, Peyton [American political leader]
R: 137 with portrait
Continental Congress (The First Continental
Congress) **Ci: 1021**; (Second Continental
Congress) **Ci: 1022**
Virginia (table) **V: 417**
Randolph, Theodore F. [American political leader]
New Jersey (table) **N: 249**
Randolph, Thomas Mann [American political
leader]
Virginia (table) **V: 417**
Randolph Institute [organization]
Rustin, Bayard **R: 567**
Randolph of Roanoke, John [American political
leader] See Randolph, John in this index
Random-access memory [electronics]
Computer (Memory chips) **Ci: 912** with picture
Computer chip (Memory chips) **Ci: 924f**
Electronics (Digital circuits) **E: 213**
Random digit dialing
Public opinion poll (Selecting the sample) **P: 862**
Random fractal [geometry]
Fractal **F: 443**
Random House Book of Mother Goose, The [book
by Lobel]
Literature for children picture on **L: 370**
Random motion [physics]
Ion (Behavior of ions) **I: 371-372**
Random sample [statistics]
Public opinion poll (History) **P: 863**
Statistics (Sampling) **So: 869**
Random sound
Noise **N: 451**

Randomized controlled experiment
Statistics (Collecting the data) **So: 868**
Randomness
Entropy **E: 328**
Randori [competition]
Judo (Judo contests) **J: 185**
Raney nickel [metal]
Hydrogenation **H: 470**
Range [appliance] **R: 137** with pictures
Range [distance]
Ballistics (Exterior ballistics) **B: 56**
Radar **R: 64**
Range [mathematics]
Algebra (Working with equations) **A: 356**
Range [music]
Singing (Training the voice) **S: 472**
Range [surveying]
Public lands (Management of public lands) **P: 858**
Range [zoology]
Bird (The distribution of birds) **B: 331**
Forestry (Rangeland) **F: 407**
Range finder [instrument] See Rangefinder in this
index
Range instrumentation radar
Radar (In the military) **R: 65-66**
Range war [U.S. history]
Ranching (History) **R: 136**
Rangefinder [instrument] **R: 138**
Laser (Measuring) **L: 83**
Photography (Compact cameras) **P: 408-409**
Rangel, Charles Bernard [American political
leader] **R: 139**
Ranger [aircraft carrier]
Aircraft carrier (History) **A: 207**
Ranger [ship]
Flag (First United States flags) **F: 208-210**
Rangers [military] **R: 139**
Army, United States (Special units) **A: 735**
Commando **Ci: 871**
Hale, Nathan (The Revolutionary War) **H: 18**
Rogers's Rangers **R: 401**
Rangers [scouting]
Girl Scouts (Rangers) **G: 199**
Rangers, New York [team] See New York Rangers
Rangers, Texas See Texas Rangers in this index
Rangi [legendary figure]
Mythology (Creation myths of the Pacific Islands)
M: 983-984
Rangoon [Myanmar] See Yangon in this index
Ranibizumab [drug]
Macular degeneration **M: 26**
Ranji Trophy
Cricket (History) **Ci: 1134-1135**
Ranjit Singh [Indian ruler] **R: 139**
Rank [chess]
Chess (The board and the men) **C: 411-412** with
diagram
Rank [coal]
Coal (Coal rank) **Ci: 718**
Rank [sociology]
Nobility **N: 450**
Rank, Military R: 139
Admiral **A: 58**
Commission, Military **Ci: 872**
General **G: 82**
Ranke, Leopold von [German historian] **R: 140**
History (History in the universities) **H: 262**
Rankin, Jeannette [American political leader]
R: 140 with portrait
Montana picture on **M: 759**; (Progress as a state)
M: 760
Ranking
Information retrieval (How information retrieval
works) **I: 268b**
Ranomafana National Park [Madagascar]
National park (table) **N: 42f**
Ransom
Kidnapping **K: 311**
Ransom, Epaphroditus [American political leader]
Michigan (table) **M: 507**
Ransom, John Crowe [American author] **R: 140**
American literature (Modernist poetry) **A: 421**
Ransome, Arthur [British author] **R: 141**
Ranthambhore National Park [India]
National park (Other interesting national parks)
N: 42h
Rantisi, Abdel Aziz al- [Palestinian political leader]
Hamas **H: 28**
Ranula [disorder]
Cyst **Ci: 1208**
Ranvier, Node of [anatomy] See Node of Ranvier
in this index
Rao, P. V. Narasimha [Indian political leader] **R: 141**
India (Religious and ethnic unrest) **I: 134**
Indian National Congress **I: 185**
Rao, Pamulaparti Venkata Narasimha See Rao, P.
V. Narasimha in this index

Rap music R: 141
Hip-hop **H: 238**
Music (Western music) **M: 955**
Popular music (The rise of rap) **P: 671**
Rock music (Rap) **R: 380d** with picture; (Rock
music today) **R: 381**
Rapa Nui National Park [Easter Island]
National park (table) **N: 42g**
Rapanui [language]
Easter Island **E: 44**
Rape [crime] **R: 141**
Abortion (Arguments for abortion) **A: 15**
Rape [plant] **R: 142** with picture
Canola oil **C: 182**
Rape of Europa, The [painting by Reni]
Europa picture on **E: 379**
Rape of Europa II [sculpture by Lipchitz]
Lipchitz, Jacques picture on **L: 344**
Rape of Ganymede [painting by Rembrandt]
Rembrandt (Early Amsterdam years) **R: 229**
Rape of Lucrece, The [poem by Shakespeare]
Shakespeare, William (His first poems) **S: 347**;
(Shakespeare's poems) **S: 366**
Rape of the Lock, The [poem by Pope]
English literature (Swift and Pope) **E: 318**
Pope, Alexander **P: 667**
Rape shield [law]
Rape **R: 142**
Rapeseed [plant]
Rape [plant] **R: 142**
Raphael [Italian painter] **R: 142** with pictures
Classicism (The qualities of Classicism) **Ci: 653**
Europe picture on **E: 393**
Madonna and Child (Painters of the Madonna)
M: 37-38 with picture
Painting (The High Renaissance) **P: 54-55** with
picture
Plato picture on **P: 567**
Pre-Raphaelite Brotherhood **P: 756**
Renaissance picture on **R: 234**; (Arts of the 1400's
and early 1500's) **R: 236** with picture
Tapestry (History) **T: 39-40**
Raphia ruffia [tree]
Raffia **R: 101**
Raphia taedigera [tree]
Raffia **R: 101**
Rapid City [South Dakota] **R: 143**
South Dakota (table: Average monthly weather)
So: 676
Rapid Creek [South Dakota]
Rapid City **R: 144**
Rapid eye movement [sleep] See REM sleep in
this index
Rapid-start lamp
Fluorescent lamp **F: 305**
Rapide Blanc [falls]
Quebec (Rivers, waterfalls, and lakes) **Q: 24**
Rapide des Quinze [falls]
Quebec (Rivers, waterfalls, and lakes) **Q: 24**
Rapids [geography]
River (Waterfalls and rapids) **R: 352** with diagram
Waterfall **W: 141**
Rapier [weapon]
Sword **So: 1061** with picture
Rapp, George [American religious leader]
New Harmony **N: 228** with picture
"Rappaccini's Daughter" [story by Hawthorne]
Hawthorne, Nathaniel (His stories and sketches)
H: 115
Rappahannock River [Virginia] **R: 144**
Virginia (Rivers and lakes) **V: 412** with picture
and map
Rappelling [technique]
Climbing (Technical climbing) **Ci: 680**
Mountain climbing (Basic mountaineering
equipment and methods) **M: 897**
"Rapper's Delight" [song]
Rap music **R: 141**
Rock music (Rap) **R: 380d**
Raptor [bird] See Bird of prey in this index
Raptors, Toronto See Toronto Raptors in this index
Rare book
Book collecting (Specimen collections) **B: 469**
Rare earth [chemistry] **R: 144**
See also Lanthanide in this index
Rare species
Animal (How human beings protect animals)
A: 505
Endangered species **E: 269**
Wildlife conservation (Classifications of scarce
wildlife) **W: 304**
Rarefaction [physics]
Anaximenes **A: 449**
Sound (table) **So: 599**; (The nature of sound)
So: 599 with diagram; (Beats) **So: 604** with
diagram
Raritan River [New Jersey]

New Jersey (Rivers and lakes) **N:** 244
Rarotonga [island, Pacific]
  Cook Islands **Ci:** 1026
Ras al Khaymah [state]
  United Arab Emirates **U:** 43; (History) **U:** 45
Ras Dashen [mountain]
  Ethiopia (The Ethiopian Plateau) **E:** 369-370
Ras Tafari [title]
  Haile Selassie **H:** 8
  Jamaica (People) **J:** 23
  Rastafarians **R:** 146
Ras Tanura [Saudi Arabia]
  Saudi Arabia (Transportation and communication) **S:** 160 *with picture*
Rasa [Sanskrit literature]
  Drama (India) **D:** 336
Raschka, Chris [American illustrator/author] **R:** 144 *with picture*
  Caldecott Medal (table: 2006, 2012) **C:** 26
Rash [disorder]
  Lupus **L:** 526
  Measles **M:** 346
  Syphilis **So:** 1069
Rashi [French Jewish scholar] **R:** 144
Rashomon [film]
  Kurosawa, Akira **K:** 393
  Motion picture *picture on* **M:** 847
Raskin, Ellen [American author] **R:** 145
Raskob, John J. [American businessman]
  Roaring Twenties (Rising prosperity) **R:** 363
Rasle, Sebastian [American religious leader]
  Maine (Schools) **M:** 72
Raspberry [plant] **R:** 145 *with picture*
  Fruit (Types of fruits in botany) **F:** 544-546 *with picture*
Raspberry tongue
  Scarlet fever (Symptoms) **S:** 173
Raspe, Rudolph Erich [German author]
  Munchausen, Baron **M:** 927
Rasputin, Grigori Efimovich [Russian public figure] **R:** 145 *with portrait*
  Russia (The February Revolution) **R:** 553
  Russian Revolution of 1917 (World War I [1914-1918]) **R:** 566
Rasputin, Valentin [Russian author]
  Russian literature (Modern Soviet literature) **R:** 564-565
Rasselas, Prince of Abyssinia [book by Johnson]
  English literature (Samuel Johnson) **E:** 319
  Johnson, Samuel (Later years) **J:** 153
Rassemblement, Le [organization]
  Trudeau, Pierre Elliott (Entry into public life) **T:** 462
Rassemblement pour l'Indépendance Nationale [organization]
  Montreal (The separatist movement) **M:** 779
Rastafarians [religious group] **R:** 145
  Jamaica (People) **J:** 23
Rastatt, Treaty of [1714]
  Succession wars (The War of the Spanish Succession) **So:** 950
Raster [electronics]
  Type **T:** 536
Raster image processor [machine]
  Type **T:** 536
Rasterization [electronics]
  Computer graphics (How a computer creates images) **C:** 924h
Rasūl [religion]
  Islam (Prophets) **I:** 463
Rat [animal] **R:** 146 *with pictures*
  Cell *picture on* **C:** 327
Rat-kangaroo [animal]
  Kangaroo **K:** 213
Rat Pack [entertainers]
  Sinatra, Frank **S:** 468
Rat snake
  Snake *picture on* **S:** 527
Ratapoil [sculpture by Daumier]
  Bronze *picture on* **B:** 638
  Daumier, Honoré **D:** 44
Ratchet [tool] **R:** 147
Rate [mathematics]
  Fraction **F:** 444
  Vital statistics (Using vital statistics) **V:** 429
Rate of change [mathematics]
  Calculus (Rate of change of a function) **C:** 23
Rate of exchange *See* Exchange rate *in this index*
Rate of interest *See* Interest *in this index*
Rate of labor productivity [economics]
  Industry (Labor) **I:** 259
Ratel [animal] **R:** 147 *with picture*
Rathbone, Justus Henry [American founder]
  Knights of Pythias **K:** 352
Rather, Dan [American newscaster]
  Journalism *picture on* **J:** 172
Rathman, Peggy [American artist]

Caldecott Medal (table: 1996) **C:** 26
Rathmann, Jim [American race driver]
  Automobile racing (table: Indianapolis 500 winners) **A:** 980
Ratification [law]
  Constitution of the United States (Ratifying the Constitution) **Ci:** 1001; (Article V) **Ci:** 1010
  Treaty **T:** 408
  United States, History of the (Adopting the Constitution) **U:** 162
Rating [television]
  Television (Measuring a program's success) **T:** 113; (Self-regulation) **T:** 116
Ratio [mathematics] **R:** 147
  Fraction **F:** 444
  Proportion **P:** 827
  Trigonometry (Right triangles) **T:** 443
Ration *See* Rationing *in this index*
Ration stamp
  Stamp **So:** 829
Rational expectations theory [economics]
  Economics (Modern economics) **E:** 64-65
Rational number **R:** 148
  Decimal system (Decimals and fractions) **D:** 72
  Fraction **F:** 444
  Number (Rational numbers) **N:** 605
  Square root (Square roots of positive numbers) **So:** 812
"Rationale of Verse, The" [essay by Poe]
  Poe, Edgar Allan (Poetry and poetic theory) **P:** 589-590
Rationalism [philosophy] **R:** 148
  Philosophy (Rationalism) **P:** 388
Rationalism, Age of *See* Enlightenment *in this index*
Rationing [economics] **R:** 148
  Black market **B:** 389
  World War II *picture on* **W:** 494; (Government controls) **W:** 495-496
Ratkiller, The [etching by Rembrandt]
  Rembrandt *picture on* **R:** 229
Ratner, Payne [American political leader]
  Kansas (table) **K:** 234
RATO [aviation]
  Airplane (Rocket engines) **A:** 220
Ratsiraka, Didier [Madagascar military leader]
  Madagascar (History) **M:** 29
Rattail [fish]
  Deep sea (Fish) **D:** 82b-82c
  Fish *picture on* **F:** 156
Rattan [tree product] **R:** 148
  Rain forest (Economic value) **R:** 126c
Rattan palm
  Palm (Products of palms) **P:** 109
Ratti, Ambrogio Damiano Achille
  Pius XI **P:** 503
Rattle [musical instrument]
  Indian, American *pictures on* **I:** 156, **I:** 167
Rattle [zoology]
  Rattlesnake **R:** 149 *with picture*
Rattle watch
  Fire department (Early fire services) **F:** 128
Rattler *See* Rattlesnake *in this index*
Rattlesnake **R:** 149 *with pictures*
  Animal *picture on* **A:** 494; (Adaptations for sensing the environment) **A:** 492-493
  Snake **S:** 528 *with picture, picture on* **S:** 534
  Viper **V:** 391
Rattlesnake master [plant]
  Flower (Flowers of prairies and dry plains) **F:** 286 *with picture*
Rattner, Abraham [American painter] **R:** 150 *with picture*
Ratzinger, Joseph Alois [German cardinal] *See* Benedict XVI *in this index*
Rauschenberg, Robert [American artist] **R:** 150 *with picture*
  Painting *picture on* **P:** 85; (The revival of subject matter) **P:** 86
Rauschenberg Overseas Cultural Exchange [program]
  Rauschenberg, Robert **R:** 150
Rauschenbusch, Walter [American clergyman]
  Christianity (The 1800's) **C:** 526
Ravalomanana, Marc [Madagascar political leader]
  Madagascar (History) **M:** 29
Ravana [legendary figure]
  Rama **R:** 131
  Ramayana **R:** 132
Rave [party]
  Ecstasy **E:** 66
  Hallucinogenic drug **H:** 26
Ravel, Maurice [French composer] **R:** 150
  Bolero **B:** 440
  Impressionism (Music, literature, and sculpture) **I:** 94
Ravelstein [book by Bellow]

Bellow, Saul **B:** 244
Raven **R:** 151 *with picture*
  Animal *picture on* **A:** 501
"Raven, The" [poem by Poe]
  Poe, Edgar Allan (Poe's life) **P:** 589; (Poetry and poetic theory) **P:** 589-590
Ravenna [Italy] **R:** 151
  Architecture *picture on* **A:** 617
Ravens, Baltimore
  Football (National Football League) **F:** 364
Ravensbrück [concentration camp]
  Concentration camp *picture on* **C:** 927
Ravenscroft, George [English glassmaker]
  Glass (The Middle Ages) **G:** 218-219
Ravenswood, Edgardo di [opera character]
  Opera: (Lucia di Lammermoor) **O:** 804
Ravine [geology]
  Canyon **C:** 185
Ravinia Music Festival
  Illinois *picture on* **I:** 63
Ravioli [food]
  Pasta **P:** 192
Raw format [photography]
  Photography (Storing digital images) **P:** 421-422
Raw materials
  Agriculture (Raw materials) **A:** 148
  Factory **F:** 5
  Industry (Classification of industries) **I:** 257
  Natural resources **N:** 64
  Plant (As raw materials) **P:** 517
  Recycling **R:** 184
Raw milk
  Milk (At a dairy farm) **M:** 546-547
Raw sugar
  Sugar (Making cane sugar) **So:** 961 *with diagram*
Rawinsonde [instrument]
  Weather (Weather balloons, airplanes, and ships) **W:** 163
Rawlings, Jerry John [Ghanaian political leader] **R:** 151
  Ghana (History) **G:** 179-180
Rawlings, Marjorie Kinnan [American author] **R:** 152
Rawlings-Blake, Stephanie [American political leader]
  Baltimore (The early 2000's) **B:** 70
Rawlins, Ezekiel "Easy" [fictional character]
  Mosley, Walter **M:** 830
Rawlins, John A. [American government official]
  Grant, Ulysses S. (Return to the Army) **G:** 314; (table) **G:** 316
Rawlinson, Sir Henry [British archaeologist]
  Cuneiform **Ci:** 1192
Ray [fish] **R:** 152
  Animal *picture on* **A:** 507
  Electric ray **E:** 189
  Fish (Sharks, rays, and chimaeras) **F:** 148 *with picture*
  Skate **S:** 478
  Stingray **So:** 901
Ray [moon]
  Moon **M:** 789
Ray [physics]
  Light (Early ideas) **L:** 285
Ray [zoology]
  Fish (Fins) **F:** 160
Ray, Dixy Lee [American political leader] **R:** 152
  Washington (table) **W:** 65
Ray, James B. [American political leader]
  Indiana (table) **I:** 214
Ray, James Earl [American assassin]
  King, Martin Luther, Jr. (King's death) **K:** 323
  Memphis (The people) **M:** 394-395
  Tennessee (The mid-1900's) **T:** 156-157
Ray, John [English biologist]
  August **A:** 887
Ray, Man [American artist] **R:** 152 *with picture*
Ray, Robert D. [American political leader]
  Iowa (table) **I:** 391
Ray, Robert W. [American attorney]
  Clinton, Bill (Domestic events) **Ci:** 682f-682g
Ray, Satyajit [Indian director] **R:** 152
  India (Motion pictures) **I:** 121
Ray-finned fish
  Prehistoric animal (The first animals with backbones) **P:** 736-737
Ray flower [botany]
  Composite family **Ci:** 904
Ray tracing
  Computer graphics (How a computer creates images) **C:** 924h
Rayburn, Sam [American political leader] **R:** 152 *with portrait*
Rayburn House Office Building [Washington, D.C.]
  Washington, D.C. *map on* **W:** 76
Rayleigh, Baron [British physicist] *See* Rayleigh,

Lord *in this index*
Rayleigh, Lord [British physicist]
Argon A: 660
Earthquake (Surface waves) E: 38
Nobel Prizes (Physics: 1904) N: 440
Noble gas N: 451
Rayleigh wave [physics]
Earthquake *diagram on* E: 34
Rayman: Origins [electronic game]
Electronic game *picture on* E: 204c
Raymond, Henry Jarvis [American journalist]
R: 153
Raymond of Toulouse [Christian crusader]
Crusades (The First Crusade) Ci: 1160 *with map*
Rayograph [art]
Ray, Man R: 152 *with picture*
Rayon [fiber] R: 153 *with pictures*
Air conditioning (In business and industry)
A: 176-177
Clothing (Clothing materials) Ci: 695
Fiber (Regenerated fibers) F: 87
Textile (The age of modern textiles) T: 219
Rayonism [art]
Painting (Nonobjective painting in Russia) P: 79
Rayonnant [architecture]
Gothic art (High Gothic architecture) G: 279
Rays, Tampa Bay [team] *See* Tampa Bay Rays *in this index*
Raza Unida, La [political party]
Gutiérrez, José Angel G: 445
Hispanic Americans (The Chicano movement)
H: 256
Razaf, Andy [American lyricist]
Waller, Fats W: 17
Razak, Najib [Malaysian political leader]
Malaysia (Recent developments) M: 102-103
Razor [tool] R: 153
Barber B: 106
Razor fish
Animal *picture on* A: 495
Razorback
Hog (Wild hogs) H: 286
Razorbill [bird]
Bird *picture on* B: 358
Rb [symbol]
Rubidium R: 507
RBC transfusion
Blood transfusion (Types of transfusion) B: 417
RBI [baseball] *See* Runs batted in *in this index*
RCA [company] *See* Radio Corporation of America *in this index*
RCA Building
New York City (Manhattan) N: 323-325;
(Rockefeller Center) N: 338
RCA Victor Records
Atkins, Chet A: 858
Presley, Elvis P: 772
RCAF *See* Royal Canadian Air Force *in this index*
RCC [political organization] *See* Revolutionary Command Council *in this index*
RCM [government] *See* Regional county municipality *in this index*
RCMP [police] *See* Royal Canadian Mounted Police *in this index*
RDA [nutrition] *See* Recommended Dietary Allowances *in this index*
RDS [electronics] *See* Radio data system *in this index*
RDX [explosive] R: 154
Ammunition (Artillery ammunition) A: 435-436
Bomb (The explosive material) B: 450
Plastic explosive P: 553
Re [Egyptian god] R: 154
Egypt, Ancient *picture on* E: 140; (Religion) E: 137;
(The New Kingdom) E: 143
Mythology *picture on* M: 977; (The Great Ennead)
M: 979; (Other Egyptian divinities) M: 980
Re [symbol]
Rhenium R: 290
Re-Harakhte [Egyptian god]
Egypt, Ancient (Painting and sculpture) E: 139
REA [agency] *See* Rural Electrification Administration *in this index*
Reach [marketing]
Advertising (Media selection) A: 76a
Reaching [sailing]
Sailing (Basic sailing maneuvers) S: 26 *with diagram*
Reactant [chemistry]
Chemical reaction C: 397
Reaction [physics]
Motion (The third law) M: 844
Rocket (How rockets work) R: 385
Reaction center
Biophysics B: 326
Reaction turbine
Turbine (Kinds of turbines) T: 496 *with picture*

Reactionary [philosophy]
Conservatism Ci: 991
Reactive hypoglycemia [disorder]
Hypoglycemia H: 481
Reactor, Nuclear *See* Nuclear reactor *in this index*
Reactor vessel
Nuclear energy (Power reactors) N: 584 *with picture*
Read, Albert C. [American aviator]
Curtiss, Glenn Hammond Ci: 1199
Read, Deborah [wife of]
Franklin, Benjamin (Printer) F: 487
Read, George [American patriot] R: 154
Delaware (table) D: 109
Read, Mary [English pirate]
Pirate (Other regions) P: 495
Read-only memory [electronics]
Compact disc (CD-ROM's) Ci: 901
Computer (Memory chips) Ci: 912
Computer chip (Memory chips) Ci: 924f
Electronics (Digital circuits) E: 213
Read/write head [electronic device]
Computer (Hard drives) Ci: 915
Readability
Reading (Readability) R: 157
Reader
Fortunetelling F: 419
Reader [device]
E-book E: 2
Reader [religion]
Eastern Orthodox Churches (Clergy) E: 46
Reader-printer [machine]
Microfilm M: 514
Reader-response theory [literature]
Criticism (History of literary criticism) Ci: 1146-1147
Readers' Guide to Periodical Literature [reference]
A Guide to Research Skills **Research Guide:** 30-31
Readiness
Differentiated instruction D: 200
Handwriting (Writing readiness) H: 47
Learning (Readiness to learn) L: 164
Reading (Developing good readers) R: 159
Reading [Pennsylvania] R: 154
Reading [skill] R: 155 *with pictures*
See also the list of Related articles in the Reading article
Child *picture on* C: 449
Dyslexia D: 398
Literacy L: 350
Phonics P: 400
Speed reading So: 774
Storytelling So: 914
A Guide to Writing Skills **Research Guide:** 12-13
Reading disability
Dyslexia D: 398
Reading (Reading problems) R: 161
Reading Is Fundamental [organization]
Reading *picture on* R: 162
Reading readiness
Reading (Developing good readers) R: 159
Readjuster Party [American political party]
Virginia (The Civil War and Reconstruction)
V: 421-422
Ready and Easy Way to Establish a Free Commonwealth, The [pamphlet by Milton]
Milton, John (Middle years) M: 557
Ready-made [art]
Duchamp, Marcel D: 373
Ray, Man R: 152
Ready Reserve [military]
Air Force, United States (Air Force reserves)
A: 194
Marine Corps, United States (Reserves) M: 208
Navy, United States (The active-duty Navy and reserves) N: 85
Ready-to-eat cereal
Cereal C: 360
Ready-to-wear [industry]
Clothing (The 1800's) Ci: 702; (The 1900's)
Ci: 703; (Marketing categories of fashion)
Ci: 706
Fashion (The fashion industry) F: 51
Reagan, John E. [father of]
Reagan, Ronald Wilson (Boyhood) R: 164
Reagan, John Neil [brother of]
Reagan, Ronald Wilson (Boyhood) R: 164
Reagan, Nancy Davis [wife of Ronald Reagan]
Bush, George Herbert Walker *picture on* B: 719
First ladies of the United States F: 143 *with picture*; (table) F: 142
Reagan, Ronald Wilson *picture on* R: 170; (Family life) R: 166
Reagan, Nelle Wilson [mother of]
Reagan, Ronald Wilson (Boyhood) R: 164
Reagan, Ronald Wilson [U.S. president] R: 164 *with pictures*

Autograph *picture on* A: 943
Baker, James Addison, III B: 32
Brady, Nicholas Frederick B: 546
Bush, George Herbert Walker (Vice president)
B: 719 *with picture*
California (table) C: 59
Cold War (The Cold War after 1980) Ci: 770
Ford, Gerald Rudolph (The 1976 election) F: 378
Grenada (History and government) G: 389-390
Hispanic Americans (Cuban immigration) H: 254
Iran-contra affair (Background) I: 406b
Kirkpatrick, Jeane Jordan K: 336
Republican Party (Victories in the 1980's) R: 257
with picture
Union of Soviet Socialist Republics (The collapse of détente) U: 40
United States, History of the (The revival of conservatism) U: 196b; (The end of the Cold War) U: 196d
Reaganomics [economic policy]
Reagan, Ronald Wilson (Events at home) R: 167
Real estate R: 171
See also Property *in this index*
Appraisal A: 575
Deed D: 81
Dower D: 316
Indian, American (The destruction of Indian America) I: 177-178
Investment (Direct investments) I: 367
Property tax P: 827
Torrens system T: 342
Real estate agent
Careers (Sales) C: 229 *with picture*
Sales (Other types of selling) S: 62; (Steps in selling) S: 62-63
Real estate broker
Real estate R: 171
Real Gabinete Português de Leitura [library]
Library *picture on* L: 254
Real image
Lens (Creating an image) L: 196 *with diagram*
Magnifying glass M: 62
Mirror (Concave mirrors) M: 617
Real income
Income (Nominal and real income) I: 100
Real interest rate [economics]
Interest (Inflation) I: 322
Real IRA [group]
Irish Republican Army (Violence and peace)
I: 433-434
Real line
Photography (Line) P: 409
Real McCoy [expression]
McCoy, Elijah M: 332f
Real national income
National income (Determining national income)
N: 37-38
Real number
Cube root Ci: 1180
Number (Real numbers) N: 606
Square root (Square roots of negative numbers)
So: 812
Real property
Personal property P: 300f
Property P: 827
Real wages
Wages and hours (Wages) W: 2-3
Reales Staats-und-Zeitungs-Lexicon [book]
Encyclopedia (An age of experiment) E: 268a
Realia [education]
Library (School libraries) L: 244 *with picture*
Realism [arts] R: 171
American literature (The Age of Realism [1871-1913]) A: 419; (Realist poetry) A: 421; (Realist fiction) A: 422
Beethoven, Ludwig van (Beethoven's place in music history) B: 214
Caravaggio, Michelangelo Merisi da C: 201
Courbet, Gustave Ci: 1100
Drama (Early realism) D: 338
Europe (From 1600 to 1900) E: 392
France (Literature) F: 461-462
French literature (Realism) F: 522
German literature (Realism) G: 141
Italian literature (Romanticism) I: 495
Latin American literature (Realism) L: 113
Literature for children (Realistic fiction) L: 361
Motion picture (Postwar Realism) M: 869 *with picture*
Naturalism (Theory of naturalism) N: 65
Novel N: 571; (The 1800's) N: 572-573
O'Neill, Eugene (His plays) O: 762
Painting (The Renaissance) P: 51-52; (Realism)
P: 70 *with picture*; (Painting outside France)
P: 72
Realism (In painting) R: 172 *with picture*
Russian literature (The age of realism) R: 562

Scandinavian literature (The Golden Age) **S: 171**
Spanish literature (The 1800's) **So: 761-762**
Realism [philosophy]
 Idealism **I: 46**
 Metaphysics (Universals and particulars) **M: 430**
Reality [philosophy]
 Christian Scientists (Beliefs) **C: 522e**
 Parmenides **P: 177**
 Philosophy **P: 383**
Reality, Virtual [computer graphics] *See Virtual reality in this index*
Reality show [television program]
 Television *pictures on* **T: 110, T: 119**; (The 1980's and 1990's) **T: 120**
Realtor [occupation]
 Real estate **R: 171**
Realtors, National Association of
 Real estate **R: 171**
Ream, Vinnie [American artist]
 Wisconsin (Interesting facts) **W: 347**
Reaming [industrial process]
 Machine tool (Metal removal) **M: 17-18**
Reaney, James [Canadian poet] **R: 173**
Reaper [machine] **R: 173**
 McCormick, Cyrus Hall **M: 332f**
Reapportionment [political science]
 Apportionment **A: 574**
 House of Representatives (Size) **H: 385**
 Illinois (The mid-1900's) **I: 75-76**
Rear admiral [rank]
 Admiral **A: 58**
 Rank, Military (table) **R: 140**
Rear-fanged water snake
 Snake (Homalopsids) **S: 535**
Rear-projection TV *See Projection television system in this index*
Rear swing arm [device]
 Motorcycle (The parts of a motorcycle) **M: 878-879** *with picture*
Rear-wheel drive
 Automobile (The drive system) **A: 949**
 Transmission (Transmissions and drives) **T: 375**
Rearrangement [biology]
 Chromosome **C: 538**
Rearview mirror
 Automobile (Operaring a car) **A: 954-955**
Reason [psychology] **R: 173**
 Artificial intelligence (Knowledge representation) **A: 760**
 Enlightenment **E: 326a**
 Fallacy **F: 16**
 Hume, David (Hume's thought) **H: 432**
 Metaphysics **M: 429**
 Philosophy (Logic) **P: 384**; (Rationalism) **P: 388**
 Rationalism **R: 148**
 Scholasticism **S: 179**
Reason, Age of *See Enlightenment in this index*
Reasonable and customary charge
 Insurance (Surgical expense benefits) **I: 312**
Reasonable Doubt [recording]
 Jay-Z **J: 67**
Reb [soldier]
 Civil War, American **Ci: 614**
Rebab [musical instrument]
 Indonesia (The arts) **I: 232-233**
Rebate [economics] **R: 173**
 Roosevelt, Theodore (Domestic problems) **R: 466**
Rebbe [spiritual leader]
 Hasidism **H: 82**
Rebecca [Biblical figure]
 Isaac **I: 461**
Rebecca [book by Du Maurier]
 Du Maurier, Daphne **D: 382**
Rebecca [film]
 Hitchcock, Alfred **H: 263**
 Motion picture (Best picture: 1940) **M: 861**
 Olivier, Laurence **O: 744** *with picture*
Rebecca of Sunnybrook Farm [book by Wiggin]
 Wiggin, Kate Douglas **W: 299**
Rebekah lodges [organization]
 Odd Fellows, Independent Order of (Purpose and organization) **O: 673**
Rebel, The [essay by Camus]
 Camus, Albert **C: 97**
Rebel Angels, The [book by Davies]
 Davies, Robertson **D: 46**
Rebel Without a Cause [motion picture]
 Dean, James **D: 60**
Rebellion [political science]
 Revolution **R: 269**
Rebellion in the Backlands [book by Cunha]
 Latin American literature (The early 1900's) **L: 113**
Rebellions of 1837 [Canadian history] **R: 173**
 Canada, History of (The uprisings of 1837) **C: 143**
 Cartier, Sir George Étienne **C: 261**
 Macdonal, SirJohn Alexander (Lawyer) **M: 6**
 Mackenzie, William Lyon **M: 23**

Ontario (Political unrest) **O: 786**
 Papineau, Louis Joseph **P: 139**
Reber, Grote [American inventor]
 Radio, Amateur (History) **R: 96**
 Radio wave **R: 97**
Rebirth [religion] *See Reincarnation in this index*
Rebound [sports]
 Basketball (Basketball terms) **B: 145**; (Playing the game) **B: 146** *with picture*
Rebound headache
 Headache (Primary headache) **H: 124**
Rebozo [clothing]
 Mexico (Clothing) **M: 456**
Rebreather
 Diving, Underwater (Ambient diving) **D: 245**
Rebus [game] **R: 174** *with picture*
 Writing system (Phonetization) **W: 513**
Rebuttal
 Debate (Framework of a round) **D: 64**
Recall [political science] **R: 174**
 California (The beginning of the 2000's) **C: 64**
 Initiative and referendum (History) **I: 272**
 Progressive Era (Political reforms) **P: 814**
 Voting **V: 449**
Recall [psychology]
 Memory (Measuring memory) **M: 392**
Recall, Product *See Product recall in this index*
Recapitulation [biology]
 Evolution (Embryology) **E: 431**
Recapitulation [music]
 Classical music (Sonata) **Ci: 645**
Recapitulation of Christ [religion]
 Irenaeus, Saint **I: 429**
Recapitulation theory [biology]
 Biogenesis **B: 312**
 Haeckel, Ernst Heinrich **H: 5**
Recapping
 Tire (Retreading tires) **T: 297**
Receipt [economics] **R: 174**
Receiver [communications]
 Hearing aid **H: 130** *with diagram*
 Navigation (Radio navigation) **N: 72**
 Radar (The receiver) **R: 71** *with diagram*
 Radio **R: 83**; (How radio programs are received) **R: 88**
 Telephone (Parts of a telephone) **T: 95**
 Television (Receiving television signals) **T: 124** *with diagram*
 Wireless communication (How wireless communication works) **W: 344**
Receiver [law] **R: 174**
 Bankruptcy (Features of bankruptcy) **B: 97**
Receiver [parapsychology]
 Extrasensory perception (Early ESP research) **E: 457**
Receiving tube [electronics]
 Vacuum tube (Kinds of vacuum tubes) **V: 258**
Receptacle [botany]
 Blackberry **B: 392**
 Plant *picture on* **P: 530**
Receptor [anatomy]
 Antidepressant **A: 553**
 Hormone (How hormones work) **H: 337**
 Human body (The peripheral nervous system) **H: 426**
 Nervous system (How the nervous system works) **N: 132** *with diagram*
 Perception (Factors affecting perception) **P: 283**
 Reflex action (How reflex action occurs) **R: 195**
 Senses **S: 301** *with diagrams*
 Smell (How odors are detected) **S: 514**
 Taste **T: 50** *with diagram*
 Virus (Infection) **V: 428**
Receptor theory
 Drug (Action in the body) **D: 353-354** *with diagram*
Recess printing
 Printing **P: 800** *with diagram*; (Printing in color) **P: 801**
Recession [economics] **R: 175**
 See also Contraction *in this index*
 Automobile (Economic impact) **A: 959**; (The 2000's) **A: 972**
 Capitalism (Stabilizing the economy) **C: 195**
 Deflation **D: 88**
 Depression **D: 150**
 Economics (Economic growth) **E: 62**
 Ford, Gerald Rudolph (The economy) **F: 377**
 Income (National income and gross domestic product) **I: 101**
 Money (Monetary policy) **M: 717**
 National budget (Deficits and surpluses) **N: 31**
 Nationalization (Advantages and disadvantages) **N: 63**
 Reagan, Ronald Wilson (Events at home) **R: 167**
 Roosevelt, Franklin Delano (Recession of 1937) **R: 455**

September 11 terrorist attacks (Weakened economy) **S: 310b**
Recessional moraine [geology]
 Glacier (How glaciers shape the land) **G: 203-204** *with diagram*
Recessive disease
 Genetic testing (Genes associated with disease) **G: 84d**
Recessive gene
 Heredity (Patterns of heredity) **H: 202**
Recessive gene abnormality
 Muscular dystrophy **M: 936**
Rechargeable battery
 See also Secondary battery *in this index*
 Battery (Secondary batteries) **B: 170**; (Types and uses of batteries) **B: 171**
 Electricity (Batteries) **E: 194**
Recherche du temps perdu, À la [book by Proust]
 See Remembrance of Things Past in this index
Recife [Brazil] **R: 175**
Reciprocal Beneficiaries Act [1997]
 Civil union **Ci: 613**
Reciprocal beneficiary relationship [law]
 Civil union **Ci: 613**
Reciprocal inhibition [physiology]
 Brain (Making decisions) **B: 555**
Reciprocal trade agreement [international relations] **R: 175**
 Foreign policy (Economic factors) **F: 387**
 McKinley, William (Revised policies) **M: 341**
Reciprocal Trade Agreements Act [1934]
 Reciprocal trade agreement **R: 176**
 Tariff (The 1900's) **T: 45**
Reciprocating engine
 Airplane (Reciprocating engines) **A: 220**
 Gasoline engine (Kinds of gasoline engines) **G: 63**
 Hydraulic engine **H: 463**
 Steam engine (Reciprocating steam engines) **So: 880**
 Stirling engine **So: 902** *with diagrams*
Reciprocating motion [mechanics]
 Pneumatic tool **P: 586**
Reciprocating pump
 Pump (Reciprocating pumps) **P: 901** *with diagrams*
Récit [French literature]
 Gide, André **G: 188**
Recitative [music]
 Handel, George Frideric (His work) **H: 42**
 Opera (table) **O: 791**; (Recitative and arias) **O: 792**; (Early Baroque opera) **O: 797**
Reckless [horse]
 Horse (table: Famous horses in history and legend) **H: 361**
Reclamation [industry]
 Mining (Surface mining methods) **M: 575**
Reclamation, Bureau of [U.S.] **R: 176**
 Grand Coulee Dam **G: 308**
 Irrigation (History) **I: 459**
Reclamation Act [1902]
 Irrigation (History) **I: 459**
 Roosevelt, Theodore (Conservation) **R: 465**
Reclamation of land [conservation]
 Coal *picture on* **C: 730**; (Strip mining) **Ci: 722**
Reclining Figure [sculpture by Moore]
 Moore, Henry **M: 797**
 Sculpture (Henry Moore) **S: 258** *with picture*
Recluse spider
 Spider (Dangerous spiders) **So: 790**
Recognition [political science]
 Nation **N: 26**
Recognition [psychology]
 Memory (Measuring memory) **M: 392**
 Perception (Types of perception) **P: 283**
Recognition society
 Fraternity (Honor and recognition societies) **F: 496**
Recognizance [law]
 Bail **B: 31**
Recoil system
 Machine gun (Operation) **M: 15-16**
Recoilless rifle
 Artillery (Kinds of artillery) **A: 762**
Recoleta [district]
 Buenos Aires (The city) **B: 672**
Recollections of Geoffry Hamlyn, The [book by Kingsley]
 Australia (Literature) **A: 904-905**
Recollections of Solferino [book by Dunant]
 Dunant, Jean Henri **D: 383**
Recombinant DNA [genetics]
 Bacteria (How bacteria reproduce) **B: 21-22**
 Cell (The 1900's) **C: 337-338**
 Cloning (Gene and cell cloning) **Ci: 684**
 Drug (The drug revolution) **D: 359**
 Genetic engineering (How genes are reintroduced into cells) **G: 84b** *with diagram*

Heredity (The era of genetic engineering) **H: 209**
Recombination [genetics]
Evolution (Mutation) **E: 427-428**
Heredity (Genetic recombination) **H: 203**
Recommended Dietary Allowances
Health (Nutrition) **H: 125**
Nutrition (Eat a balanced diet) **N: 626**; (table)
N: 628
Protein **P: 832**
Vitamin **V: 430**
Recompression chamber
Diving, Underwater (Dangers of underwater
diving) **D: 246-247**
Reconciliation [politics]
Aborigines, Australian (Aboriginal life today)
A: 14
Reconciliation [religion] *See* Penance *in this index*
Reconnaissance [defense]
Air force (The role of air forces) **A: 182**
Aircraft, Military (Reconnaissance aircraft) **A: 203**
with picture
Reconnaissance aircraft
Air force (Aircraft and missiles) **A: 183**
Air Force, United States (Other aircraft) **A: 191**
Reconstituted tobacco sheet
Tobacco (Cigar leaf tobacco) **T: 306**
Reconstruction [U.S. history] **R: 176** *with pictures*
African Americans (The first years of freedom)
A: 136j *with picture*; (Temporary gains) **A: 136k**
Carpetbaggers **C: 246**
Civil rights (The struggle for the rights of African
Americans) **Ci: 609**
Democratic Party (After the Civil War) **D: 125**
Grant, Ulysses S. (Reconstruction policies) **G: 315**
Hayes, Rutherford Birchard (The election dispute)
H: 120; (The end of Reconstruction) **H: 120**
Johnson, Andrew (Johnson's Administration)
J: 139
Ku Klux Klan (Birth of the Klan) **K: 390**
Mississippi (After the war) **M: 642**
Republican Party (The Radical Republicans and
Reconstruction) **R: 254**
Scalawags **S: 169**
Stevens, Thaddeus **So: 896**
United States, History of the (Reconstruction)
U: 178 *with picture*
Virginia (The Civil War and Reconstruction) **V: 421**
Reconstruction Acts [1867]
Reconstruction (The Reconstruction Acts) **R: 178**
Reconstruction Finance Corporation [U.S. history]
Great Depression (Hoover's policies) **G: 341**
Hoover, Herbert Clark (Recovery efforts) **H: 329**
Reconstructionist Judaism
Judaism (Reconstructionist Judaism) **J: 180**;
(Worship) **J: 181**
Reconstructive surgery
Plastic surgery **P: 553**
Record [information]
Database **D: 42** *with picture*
Record, Phonograph *See* Phonograph record *in
this index*
Record of Rites [text]
China (Music) **C: 490**
Record player *See* Phonograph *in this index*
Recordable DVD [electronics]
DVD **D: 393**
Recorder [musical instrument] **R: 180** *with picture*
Recording industry R: 180 *with picture*
Country music (History) **Ci: 1098a-1098b**
Popular music (The recording era) **P: 671**
Recording Industry Association of America
Recording industry (Recording industry awards)
R: 182
Recording secretary
Parliamentary procedure (Officers) **P: 175**
Recording studio
Recording industry (In a recording studio) **R: 181**
with picture
Recount
Voting (Methods of voting) **V: 449-450**
Recovery unit
Hospital (Hospital units) **H: 372**
Recreation R: 182
See also the list of Related articles in the Recreation
article and the Way of life *or* People *sections of
the various country articles, such as* Argentina
(Way of life)
Camping **C: 92** *with pictures*
Colonial life in America (Recreation) **Ci: 802** *with
picture*
Dance (Recreational reasons) **D: 24**
Forestry (Recreation areas) **F: 407** *with picture*
Game **G: 21** *with picture*
Greece, Ancient (Recreation) **G: 367**
Indian, American (Recreation) **I: 142** *with picture*
Park **P: 168**
Pioneer life in America (Social activities) **P: 485**

Play **P: 570**
Radio (The Golden Age of Broadcasting) **R: 92**
Reading (Recreational reading) **R: 156**
Rome, Ancient (Recreation) **R: 440**
Safety (Safety in recreation) **S: 12**
Space exploration (Meeting basic needs in space)
So: 703 *with picture*
State government (State services) **So: 864**
United States (Recreation) **U: 114** *with pictures*
Western frontier life in America (Life on the
ranches) **W: 237**; (Recreation) **W: 238**
Recreation trail
National Trails System **N: 61**
Recreational therapist [medicine]
Medicine (Other careers in medicine) **M: 371**
Recreational vehicle R: 183 *with pictures*
Camping (Recreational vehicle camping) **C: 92**
with picture
Recruit [military]
Rank, Military (table) **R: 140**
Recruiting Officer, The [play by Farquhar]
Farquhar, George **F: 47**
Theater *picture on* **T: 242**
Recrystallization [process]
Forging **F: 409**
Marble (Properties) **M: 192**
Metamorphic rock **M: 428**
Rectangle [geometry]
Geometry (Euclidean geometry) **G: 104** *with
diagram*
Golden section **G: 256**
Rectangular system [mathematics]
Geometry (Analytic geometry) **G: 105** *with
diagram*
Rectification [process]
Distillation **D: 238**
Rectifier [electronics]
Electric current (Direct and alternating current)
E: 168
Electric generator (Uses of DC generators)
E: 173-174
Electronics (Diodes) **E: 210-212**
Locomotive (Diesel locomotives) **L: 414-415**
Radio (How radio programs are received) **R: 88**
Vacuum tube (Kinds of vacuum tubes) **V: 258-
259**
Rectilinear motion
Amphisbaenian **A: 443**
Recto [printing]
Book (Inside a book) **B: 464-465**
Rector, Henry Massey [American political leader]
Arkansas (table) **A: 712**
Rector of Justin, The [book by Auchincloss]
Auchincloss, Louis **A: 880**
Rectum [anatomy]
Alimentary canal **A: 368** *with diagram*
Cancer (Classification by primary body site)
C: 167-168; (table) **C: 170**
Colon **Ci: 786**
Colon cancer **Ci: 786**
Colonoscopy **Ci: 815**
Colostomy **Ci: 850**
Frog *picture on* **F: 537**
Hemorrhoids **H: 183**
Human body (table) **H: 422** *with diagram*
Inflammatory bowel disease **I: 266**
Intestine (The large intestine) **I: 353** *with
diagrams*
Prostate cancer **P: 829**
Recumbent bicycle
Bicycle (Specialty bicycles) **B: 290**
Recurrence interval [geology]
Flood (River floods) **F: 236**
Recurrent nova [astronomy]
Nova **N: 553**
Recurve bow
Archery (Archery equipment) **A: 601** *with picture*
Recuyell of the Historyes of Troye, The [book]
Book (The spread of printed books) **B: 467**
Caxton, William **C: 322**
Recyclable resource
Conservation **Ci: 974**
Recycled wool
Wool (Types of wool) **W: 399**
Recycling R: 184
Aluminum *picture on* **A: 391**; (Recycling) **A: 397**
Conservation (Minerals recycled in the United
States) **Ci: 982**; (Mineral conservation) **Ci: 982-
983** *with picture*
Environmental pollution (Business and industry)
E: 336-337 *with picture*; (Individual efforts)
E: 338
Glass (Modern glassmaking) **G: 222-223** *with
picture*
Plastics (Plastics and the environment) **P: 560**
Polyester **P: 649**
Technology (Using technology safely) **T: 77** *with*

picture
Waste disposal (Recycling and waste reduction)
W: 113
Red [color]
Color *diagrams on* **Ci: 821**; (The relation between
color and light) **Ci: 817-818** *with diagram*
Symbol (Symbols with different meanings)
So: 1066
Red admiral [butterfly]
Butterfly *picture on* **B: 735**
Red alder [tree]
Alder **A: 339**
Red algae [plant]
Algae (Kinds of algae) **A: 349**
Ocean (Medicines) **O: 654**
Seaweed (Kinds) **S: 276** *with picture*
Red and the Black, The [book by Stendhal]
French literature (Romantic fiction) **F: 521**
Novel (France) **N: 573**
Stendhal **So: 889**
Red Army
Leningrad, Siege of **L: 195**
Union of Soviet Socialist Republics (History)
U: 35-36
Red ash [tree]
Ash **A: 767**
Red-backed salamander
Animal *picture on* **A: 478**
Red-backed shrike [bird]
Bird *picture on* **B: 351**
Red Badge of Courage, The [book by Crane]
Crane, Stephen **Ci: 1120**
Red Baron [name for]
Richthofen, Baron Manfred von **R: 334**
Red bat [animal]
Bat (Red bats and hoary bats) **B: 161**
Red Beard [name for]
Frederick I **F: 497**
Red Beds Plains [Oklahoma]
Oklahoma (Land regions) **O: 724-726** *with map*
Red-bellied piranha [fish]
Piranha **P: 494**
Red birch [tree]
Birch (River birch) **B: 327**
Red blood cell [biology]
Anemia **A: 457**
Blood (The composition of blood) **B: 407-408**
with picture; (How the body maintains its blood
supply) **B: 410**; (Blood groups) **B: 412**
Blood doping **B: 415**
Blood transfusion (Types of transfusion) **B: 417**
Cell (Death of a cell) **C: 332**
Hemoglobin **H: 182**
Human body (The blood) **H: 421-424** *with picture*
Leeuwenhoek, Anton van **L: 181**
Respiration (Gas transport between the lungs
and tissues) **R: 261**
Rh factor **R: 289**
Sickle cell anemia **S: 447**
Red bone marrow
Bone (Structure of the bones) **B: 456**
Red Book [Jung]
Jung, Carl Gustav (His theories) **J: 195**
Red Book [recording standard]
Compact disc (Audio CD's) **Ci: 901**
Red-breasted merganser [bird]
Duck *picture on* **D: 375**
Merganser **M: 416**
Red-breasted nuthatch [bird]
Nuthatch **N: 622** *with picture*
Red Brigades [terrorist organization]
Italy (Social problems) **I: 518**
Red bug [animal]
Mite **M: 678**
Red cabbage [plant]
Cabbage (Kinds of cabbage) **C: 2**
Red Carpet for the Sun, A [poems by Layton]
Layton, Irving **L: 148**
Red Cavalry [book by Babel]
Russian literature (The period of rebirth) **R: 564**
Red cedar [tree] *See* Redcedar *in this index*
Red China *See* China *in this index*
Red Cloud [American Indian chief] **R: 185** *with
portrait*
Indian wars (Red Cloud's War [1866-1868]) **I: 193**
South Dakota (Territorial days) **So: 681**
Red Cloud's War [1866-1868]
Indian wars (Red Cloud's War [1866-1868]) **I: 193**
South Dakota (Territorial days) **So: 681**
Red clover [plant]
Clover (Red clover) **Ci: 713** *with picture*
Shamrock **S: 371**
Red colobus [monkey]
Monkey *picture on* **M: 728**
Red Crescent [organization]
Flag *picture on* **F: 216**
Red Cross **R: 185**

Red-crested turaco [bird]
Turaco *picture on* T: 495
Red Cross [organization] R: 185 *with picture*
Barton, Clara (The Red Cross) B: 121
Dunant, Jean Henri D: 383
Flag *picture on* F: 216
Food supply *picture on* F: 351
Nobel Prizes (Peace: 1917, 1944) N: 448; (Peace: 1963) N: 448a
Red Cross Train [painting by Severini]
Futurism *picture on* F: 590
Red crossbill [bird]
Crossbill Ci: 1155 *with picture*
Red Crystal
Flag *picture on* F: 216
Red Data Book
Conservation (International problems) Ci: 990
Wildlife conservation (International cooperation) W: 305
Red deer R: 188
Animal *picture on* A: 479
Deer *picture on* D: 84; (Asian and European deer) D: 86
Red Deer River
Alberta (The Alberta Plain) A: 322 *with map*
Red Desert
Wyoming (Land regions) W: 526
Red Dog Mine
Alaska *picture on* A: 298
Red drum [fish]
Drum D: 367
Redfish R: 191
Red dwarf [star]
Brown dwarf B: 644
Red Eagle [American Indian chief]
Alabama (Territorial days) A: 275
Red Ensign [flag]
Canada, History of (The return of the Liberals) C: 149-150
Flag *picture on* F: 195; (History of the Canadian flag) F: 215 *with picture*
Red-eyed tree frog
Tree frog *picture on* T: 433
Red-Eyed Tree Frog [book by Cowley]
Literature for children *picture on* L: 380
Red-eyed vireo [bird]
Bird (Birds of forests and woodlands) B: 334 *with picture*
Vireo V: 391
Red-figure style
Painting (Greek painting) P: 42
Red Flag Law [1865]
Automobile (The steam car) A: 965
Red-footed booby
Bird *picture on* B: 344
Red Fork [Oklahoma]
Tulsa (History) T: 483
Red Fort [India]
Delhi (The city) D: 115
Red fox [animal]
Fox F: 438 *with pictures*
Fox hunting F: 442
Mammal *diagram on* M: 121
Red giant star
Star (Red-giant phase) So: 848
Sun So: 975; (Evolution of the sun) So: 982
White dwarf W: 285
Red Globe onion
Onion *picture on* O: 763
Red-green defect [disorder]
Color blindness Ci: 827
Red grouper [fish]
Grouper G: 403 *with picture*
Red Guard [Chinese history]
Beijing B: 223-224
China (The Cultural Revolution) C: 505
Cultural Revolution Ci: 1185
Red Guard [Finnish history]
Finland (The new republic) F: 117
Red gum [tree]
Sweet gum So: 1036 *with picture*
Tree *pictures on* T: 423
Wood *picture on* W: 389
Red Hat Order of Lamas [religious group]
Bhutan (People) B: 277
Red haw [tree] *See* Hawthorn *in this index*
Red Heart, The [book by Reaney]
Reaney, James R: 173
Red Horse [American Indian chief]
Western frontier life in America (Settlers and Native Americans) W: 239
Red hot [food]
Sausage S: 163
Red Hot Peppers [jazz band]
Morton, Jelly Roll M: 821
Red-hot poker [flower]
Flower *picture on* F: 272

Red imported fire ant [insect]
Fire ant F: 122
Red Jacket [American Indian leader] R: 188 *with portrait*
Red Jacket [tent colony]
West Virginia *picture on* W: 228
Red Jacket Monument
Buffalo (Other interesting places to visit) B: 678
Red Jamaica [banana]
Banana B: 72
Red juniper [tree]
Tree *pictures on* T: 425
Red kangaroo
Australia *picture on* A: 915
Kangaroo (Kinds of kangaroos) K: 213
Red king crab
Crab Ci: 1155
Horseshoe crab H: 368
Red Knight [German aviator]
Ace A: 24
Red Lake [Minnesota]
Minnesota (Lakes, rivers, and waterfalls) M: 598
Red-legged kittiwake [bird]
Gull (Kinds of gulls) G: 439
Red-legged partridge [bird]
Bird *pictures on* B: 344e, B: 351
Red line speed [aviation]
Airplane (Measuring flying speed) A: 225-226
Red maple [tree]
Maple (Red maple) M: 186
Tree *pictures on* T: 422
Red meat
Meat M: 346
Red mulberry [plant]
Mulberry M: 913
Tree *pictures on* T: 422
Red mullet [fish]
Mullet M: 915
Red-necked wallaby [animal]
Wallaby (Kinds of wallabies) W: 15
Red Norland [potato]
Potato *picture on* P: 711
Red oak [tree]
Oak (Red oaks) O: 635
Tree *pictures on* T: 423
Red ocher [mineral]
Hematite H: 180
Red-osier dogwood [tree]
Osier O: 863
Red panda [animal]
Panda P: 128 *with picture*
Red pepper [seasoning] *See* Cayenne pepper *in this index*
Red Petals [sculpture by Calder]
Sculpture (Form and treatment) S: 230-231 *with picture*
Red phalarope [bird]
Bird (Birds of the Arctic) B: 343 *with picture*
Red phosphorus
Phosphorus P: 403
Red pine [tree]
Pine (Eastern pines) P: 468
Tree *pictures on* T: 413
Red Poll [cattle]
Cattle (Dual-purpose cattle) C: 311
Red puccoon [plant]
Bloodroot B: 417 *with picture*
Red Queen, The [book by Drabble]
Drabble, Margaret D: 317
"Red, Red Rose, A" [song]
Burns, Robert (Burns's works) B: 710
Red River [U.S.] R: 188
Oklahoma (Rivers and lakes) O: 727
Ross, Alexander R: 481
United States, History of the *map on* U: 184
Red River [Vietnam]
Vietnam (Northern Vietnam) V: 368
Red River Colony [Canadian history]
Canada, History of (Exploration of the West) C: 143
Manitoba (The Red River Colony) M: 160
Métis M: 435
Red River of the North [Canada-U.S.] R: 188 *with map*
Flood (Flood control) F: 238
Lake Agassiz L: 35
Red River Rebellion [1869-1870] R: 189
Canada, History of (New provinces) C: 144-145
Macdonald, Sir John Alexander (Completing the Dominion) M: 8
Manitoba (The Red River Rebellion) M: 160
Métis M: 435
Riel, Louis R: 337
Red River Valley
North Dakota (Land regions) N: 506 *with picture*
Red River of the North R: 188
Red River Rebellion R: 189

Red Robe, The [play by Brieux]
Brieux, Eugène B: 608
Red robin [plant]
Geranium G: 136
Red Rock Canyon
Nevada *picture on* N: 156
Red Rocks Amphitheater [Colorado]
Colorado (Places to visit) Ci: 836
Red Room
White House *picture on* W: 288; (Public rooms) W: 286 *with picture*
Red Rose [photograph by Haas]
Photography *picture on* P: 428
Red salamander
Salamander *picture on* S: 59
Red salmon *See* Sockeye salmon *in this index*
Red Scare [U.S. history]
Roaring Twenties (Changing attitudes) R: 363
Red Sea R: 189 *with map*
Plate tectonics (The rifting of continents) P: 562
Red sea anemone [animal]
Ocean *picture on* O: 656
Red-shafted flicker [bird]
Flicker F: 234 *with picture*
Red shift [physics] *See* Redshift *in this index*
Red Shirts [Italian history]
Garibaldi, Giuseppe G: 43
Italy (Italy united) I: 515-516 *with picture*
Red-shouldered hawk [bird]
Buzzard B: 745
Red-sided garter snake [reptile]
Garter snake G: 46
Red Sindhi [breed]
Cattle (Other dairy cattle) C: 311
Red snapper [fish]
Snapper *picture on* S: 537
Red Sokoto [animal]
Goat (Domestic goats) G: 239
Red Sox, Boston [team] *See* Boston Red Sox *in this index*
Red-spotted newt [animal]
Newt N: 388 *with picture*
Red sprite [meteorology]
Lightning (Jets, sprites, and elves) L: 301
Red Square [Moscow]
Cold War *picture on* Ci: 762
Lenin, V. I. (Death) L: 195 *with picture*
Moscow *picture on* M: 823; (Famous landmarks) M: 823-824 *with picture and map*
Russia *pictures on* R: 525, R: 533
Union of Soviet Socialist Republics *picture on* U: 31
Red squirrel
Classification, Scientific *picture on* Ci: 654
Invasive species (How invasive species affect habitats) I: 354j
Squirrel (Tree squirrels) So: 814b *with pictures*
Red-stem filaree [plant]
Geranium G: 136
Red-stemmed storksbill [plant]
Flower *picture on* F: 288
Red Sticks [American Indians]
Alabama (Territorial days) A: 275
Creek Indians Ci: 1126
Indian wars (The Red Sticks) I: 192
Red Stockings, Cincinnati [team]
Baseball (Professional baseball) B: 133
Ohio *picture on* O: 701
Red supergiant star
Betelgeuse B: 274
Star (High-mass stars) So: 849-850
Red-tailed hawk [bird]
Buzzard B: 745
Eye *picture on* E: 468
Hawk H: 111, *picture on* H: 112
Red-Tailed Hawk [painting by Namingha]
Indian, American *picture on* I: 182
Red tape [expression] R: 190
Red tide [oceanography] R: 190
Ocean (Phytoplankton) O: 655
Pacific Ocean (Offshore pollution) P: 17
Red uakari [animal]
Monkey *picture on* M: 728
Red Volta [river, Burkina Faso]
Burkina Faso (Land) B: 706
Red ware [china]
Wedgwood ware W: 179
Red Wheel, The [books by Solzhenitsyn]
Solzhenitsyn, Alexander So: 587
Red wine
Alcoholic beverage (Wine) A: 336
Wine (Types of wine) W: 336; (How wine is made) W: 337-338
Red-winged blackbird
Bird *picture on* B: 358
Blackbird B: 392 *with picture*
Wetland *picture on* W: 253

Red Wings, Detroit [team]
Detroit (Sports) **D:** 170
Hockey (table: National Hockey League) **H:** 281
Red wolf [animal]
Endangered species (table) **E:** 270
Wolf **W:** 375
Redaction criticism
Bible (Historical contexts) **B:** 287
New Testament (Critical studies) **N:** 288
Redback spider
Spider *picture on* **So:** 789; (Dangerous spiders) **So:** 790
Redbelly dace [fish]
Fish *picture on* **F:** 158
Redbird R: 190
Cardinal **C:** 211 *with picture*
Redbud [tree] **R:** 190 *with pictures*
Tree *pictures on* **T:** 423
Redburn [book by Melville]
Melville, Herman (His early life) **M:** 390
Redbush [grapefruit]
Grapefruit **G:** 320
Redcap [chicken]
Chicken (English class chickens) **C:** 441; (table) **C:** 443
Redcap [railroad]
Townsend, Willard Saxby **T:** 352
Redcedar [tree]
Juniper **J:** 196 *with picture*
Plant *picture on* **P:** 524
Tree *picture on* **T:** 425
Redcoat [U.S. history]
Lexington and Concord, Battles of (Lexington) **L:** 224
Revolution, American *picture on* **R:** 279; (The beginning of the war) **R:** 274
Redd [nest]
Trout (The life of a trout) **T:** 454
Redding, Noel [British bassist]
Hendrix, Jimi **H:** 184
Reddish egret [bird]
Egret (Kinds) **E:** 119 *with picture*
Redeemer, Feast of the [custom]
Venice (The people) **V:** 307
Redeemer, Order of the [award]
Medals, decorations, and orders (table) **M:** 359
Redemptioner [U.S. history]
Colonial life in America (The lower class) **Ci:** 794
Redemptorists [religious group]
Alphonsus Liguori, Saint **A:** 384
Religious life (table) **R:** 227
Redeye bass [fish]
Bass (Black bass) **B:** 156
Redfield, William C. [American government official]
Commerce, Department of (table) **Ci:** 871
Redfin pickerel [fish]
Pike **P:** 461
Redfish R: 191
Redford, Alison [Canadian political leader]
Alberta (table) **A:** 328; (Recent developments) **A:** 331, a: 351
Redford, Robert [American actor] **R:** 191 *with portrait*
Motion picture (Best achievement in directing: 1980) **M:** 862
Redgrave, Michael [British actor] **R:** 191
Redgrave, Vanessa [British actress]
Motion picture (Best performance by an actress in a supporting role: 1977) **M:** 862b
Redhead [bird]
Canvasback **C:** 185
Redheaded woodpecker
Woodpecker (Kinds) **W:** 394-395
Redi, Francesco [Italian scientist]
Life (Spontaneous generation) **L:** 278
Spontaneous generation **So:** 801
Redistricting
Apportionment **A:** 574
Voting (Voting districts) **V:** 449
Redonda [island, Caribbean Sea]
Antigua and Barbuda **A:** 555
Redoubling [cards]
Bridge (Bidding) **B:** 604
Redox process [chemistry]
Oxidation **O:** 888
Reduction **R:** 192
Redpoll [bird] **R:** 191 *with picture*
Reds [Soviet history]
Lenin, V. I. (Civil war) **L:** 194
Russian Revolution of 1917 (The October Revolution) **R:** 566-566a
Union of Soviet Socialist Republics (History) **U:** 35-36
Reds, Cincinnati [team] *See* Cincinnati Reds *in this index*
Redshift [physics] **R:** 191 *with picture*

Astronomy (Spectroscopy) **A:** 840-841; (Radio and microwave astronomy) **A:** 843 *with picture*
Cosmology (The movement of galaxies) **Ci:** 1078
Quasar **Q:** 8
Telescope (Analyzing spectra) **T:** 105-106
Universe (Size of the universe) **U:** 205
Redskins, Washington [team] *See* Washington Redskins *in this index*
Redstart [bird] **R:** 192
Animal *picture on* **A:** 478
Bird (Birds of forests and woodlands) **B:** 334 *with picture*
Warbler **W:** 35
Redstone [rocket]
Rocket (The space age) **R:** 391
Redstone Arsenal [Alabama]
Alabama (Population) **A:** 260; (The mid-1900's) **A:** 278
Huntsville **H:** 451
Redtop [grass]
Bentgrass **B:** 254
Reduccione [settlement]
Paraguay (Jesuit missionaries) **P:** 149
Reduced-fat milk
Milk (table) **M:** 547
Reduced hemoglobin [physiology]
Cyanosis **Ci:** 1202
Reduced tillage [agriculture]
Farm and farming (Preparing the soil) **F:** 35
Reducing agent [chemistry]
Hydrogen (Uses) **H:** 469
Iron and steel (How iron is made) **I:** 439
Reducing fractions [mathematics]
Fraction (Equivalent fractions) **F:** 446 *with diagram*
Reducing lathe [machine]
Money *picture on* **M:** 711; (Minting coins) **M:** 714-715
Reductio ad absurdum [philosophy]
Zeno of Elea **Z:** 589
Reduction [chemistry] **R:** 192
Battery (Half-cell reactions) **B:** 170 *with diagram*
Catalytic converter **C:** 298
Corrosion **C:** 1071
Electrolysis (How electrolysis works) **E:** 200
Fuel cell (How a fuel cell works) **F:** 551
Magnesium (Properties) **M:** 54
Oxidation **O:** 888
Reduction [mechanics]
Transmission (Gears) **T:** 375
Reduction gear [mechanics]
Elevator (How elevators work) **E:** 234
Redwall series [books by Jacques]
Jacques, Brian **J:** 20
Redwood [tree] **R:** 192 *with picture*
Bark (Outer bark) **B:** 110-111
California (Visitor's guide) **C:** 46 *with picture*; (Forests) **C:** 54
Conifer **Ci:** 950
Sequoia **S:** 310d
Tree *pictures on* **T:** 425; (Interesting facts about trees) **T:** 411
Redwood Highway
California (Places to visit) **C:** 46
Redwood Library [Newport]
Rhode Island (Libraries) **R:** 300
Redwood National Park [California] **R:** 193
National Park System *picture on* **N:** 47; (table: National parks) **N:** 48
Reed [plant] **R:** 194
Reed [weaving]
Weaving (How a loom works) **W:** 173-174
Reed, Carol [British director]
Motion picture (Best achievement in directing: 1968) **M:** 862
Reed, Clyde M. [American political leader]
Kansas (table) **K:** 234
Reed, D. E. [American publisher]
Nebraska (Communication) **N:** 109
Reed, Donna [American actress]
Motion picture (Best performance by an actress in a supporting role: 1953) **M:** 862b
Reed, Esther De Berdt [American civic leader]
Revolution, American (The home front) **R:** 280
Reed, Harrison [American political leader]
Florida (table) **F:** 260
Reed, John [American journalist] **R:** 194
Reed, John H. [American political leader]
Maine (table) **M:** 87
Reed, Joseph [American political leader]
Pennsylvania (table) **P:** 263
Reed, Kasim [American political leader]
Atlanta (Recent developments) **A:** 861
Reed, Ralph [American social reformer]
Christian Coalition of America **C:** 522e
Reed, Stanley F. [American jurist]
Supreme Court of the United States (table)

So: 1000
Reed, Thomas Brackett [American political leader] **R:** 194
Reed, Walter [American doctor] **R:** 194 *with portrait*
Yellow fever (History) **Y:** 556
Reed boat
Canoeing *picture on* **C:** 182
Ship *picture on* **S:** 416
Reed instrument
Jazz (The reeds) **J:** 69
Music (Wind instruments) **M:** 949 *with pictures*
Reed **R:** 194
Reed Medical Center *See* Walter Reed National Military Medical Center Bethesda *in this index*
Reed organ [musical instrument]
Harmonium **H:** 62
Reed pipe [musical instrument]
Organ (Pipe organs) **O:** 851-852
Pipe **P:** 488
Reed-Sternberg cell [physiology]
Hodgkin's disease **H:** 283
Reed's Rules [U.S. history]
Reed, Thomas Brackett **R:** 194
Reef
See also Coral reef *in this index*
Oyster (Oysters and ecosystems) **O:** 891
Reef-building coral
Coral *picture on* **Ci:** 1048a
Reel [fishing]
Fishing (Reels) **F:** 176 *with pictures*
Reel-to-reel tape recorder *See* Open-reel tape recorder *in this index*
Reeling [process]
Silk (Reeling) **S:** 460
Reese, Pee Wee [American baseball player]
Baseball (table: Hall of Fame) **B:** 134a
Reeve
Flag (table) **F:** 193
Reeve [bird]
Ruff **R:** 509
Reeve [English history]
Police (Early law enforcement in England) **P:** 624
Sheriff **S:** 397
Reeve, Christopher [American actor]
Superman *picture on* **So:** 993
Reeve, Tapping [American jurist]
Connecticut (Schools) **Ci:** 956
Reeves, Orlando [American settler]
Orlando **O:** 857
Reeves pheasant
Pheasant (Kinds of pheasants) **P:** 355
Referee [sports]
Basketball (The officials) **B:** 145
Boxing *picture on* **B:** 530; (Officials) **B:** 527
Football (The officials) **F:** 362
Hockey (The officials) **H:** 278
Rugby football (Rugby Union) **R:** 510
Soccer (The officials) **So:** 545 *with diagram*
Referee's position
Wrestling *picture on* **W:** 506
Reference [business]
Careers (Writing a résumé) **C:** 217
Reference beam [holography]
Holography **H:** 298
Reference biography
Biography (Forms of biography) **B:** 312
Reference book
See also specific types of reference books, such as Encyclopedia, *in this index*
A Guide to Research Skills **Research Guide:** 30, **Research Guide:** 36
Reference fuel
Octane number **O:** 669
Reference service
Library (Assisting patrons) **L:** 236; (The work of librarians) **L:** 255
Referendum [government]
Initiative and referendum **I:** 271
Law (By direct action of the people) **L:** 132
Progressive Era (Political reforms) **P:** 814
Voting **V:** 449
Referendum by petition [government]
Initiative and referendum (The referendum) **I:** 272
Refill valve
Plumbing (How toilets work) **P:** 579 *with diagram*
Refinery *See* Oil refinery *in this index*
Refining [industrial process]
Gold *diagram on* **G:** 250; (Refining) **G:** 253
Iron and steel (Special refining processes) **I:** 444
Lead (Production) **L:** 149-150
Metallurgy (Extractive metallurgy) **M:** 426
Petroleum (Refining petroleum) **P:** 344 *with diagram*
Reflected light meter
Photography (Exposure meters) **P:** 413
"Reflecting Absence" [memorial]

National September 11 Memorial and Museum
N: 61
September 11 terrorist attacks (Moving forward)
S: 310b-310c *with pictures*
Reflecting Pool [Washington, D.C.]
Washington, D.C. *map on* W: 76
Reflecting telescope
Hubble Space Telescope H: 403
Keck Observatory K: 254
Palomar Observatory P: 112
Telescope (Reflecting telescopes) T: 104 *with diagrams*
Reflection [physics] R: 194
Echo E: 50
Light *diagram on* L: 289; (Reflection and absorption) L: 287; (Refraction) L: 288
Mirror M: 616 *with diagrams*
Polarized light (Polarizing filters) P: 618 *with diagram*
Prism P: 805 *with picture*
Rainbow (How rainbows appear) R: 128
Sound (Reflection) So: 602
Waves *diagram on* W: 151; (Refraction and reflection) W: 152
Reflection Lake [California]
Lassen Volcanic National Park L: 87
Reflection nebula [astronomy]
Nebula (Diffuse nebulae) N: 116
Reflection seismology
Gas [fuel] (Exploring for gas) G: 53
Reflectional symmetry [geometry]
Symmetry (A plane of symmetry) So: 1066
Reflections [book by La Rochefoucauld]
French literature (Classical prose) F: 520
Reflections in a Golden Eye [book by McCullers]
McCullers, Carson M: 332g
Reflections on the Revolution in France [book by Burke]
Burke, Edmund B: 705
Reflective insulation
Insulation (In buildings) I: 306
Reflectivity mode
Weather (Weather radar) W: 162
Reflector [device]
Lamp (Fat or oil lamps) L: 52-53 *with picture*
Lighthouse (Development of the lighthouse) L: 294
Reflector [electronics]
Antenna *pictures on* A: 543
Radar (The antenna) R: 71
Reflector [telescope] *See* Reflecting telescope *in this index*
Reflex action [physiology] R: 194 *with diagram*
Anesthesia (General anesthesia) A: 458
Behavior (Learning) B: 220
Brain (Controlling movement) B: 553
Instinct I: 304
Nervous system (Simple pathways) N: 134
Yawning Y: 553
Reflex camera
Camera (Single-lens [SLR] cameras) C: 83 *with picture*
Photography *pictures on* P: 420; (Single-lens [SLR] reflex cameras) P: 409
Reflexive pronoun [grammar]
Pronoun P: 819
Reform Act [1832]
Industrial Revolution (The working class) I: 251-252
United Kingdom (The era of reform) U: 68
William IV W: 309
Reform Act [1867]
Conservative Party Ci: 992
Disraeli, Benjamin D: 237
Gladstone, William Ewart G: 206
Industrial Revolution (The working class) I: 251-252
Parliament (Parliament gains strength) P: 174
Reform Act [1884]
Parliament (Parliament gains strength) P: 174
United Kingdom (Gladstone and Disraeli) U: 69
Reform Judaism [religion]
Judaism (Reform Judaism) J: 180; (Worship) J: 181
Religion (Judaism) R: 219-220
Wise, Isaac Mayer W: 370
Reform Laws [1859]
Mexico (Reform) M: 471
Reform Party [Canada] R: 195
Alberta (The late 1900's) A: 331
Campbell, Kim (The 1993 election) C: 90d
Chrétien, Jean (The 1993 election) C: 522c; (Prime minister) C: 522c-522d
Harper, Stephen Joseph (Reform Party pioneer) H: 66a
Manning, Preston M: 165
Political party (Other parties) P: 636-637

Reform Party [United States] R: 195
Minnesota (The early 2000's) M: 606
Perot, Ross P: 292
Reform school
Reformatory R: 199
Reformation [European history] R: 195 *with pictures*
See also the list of Related articles in the Reformation *article*
Christianity (The Reformation) C: 524
Church and state (History) C: 542
Classical music (The Reformation) Ci: 646
Communication (The rise of printing) Ci: 879-880
Counter Reformation Ci: 1096
Cromwell, Thomas Ci: 1152
Democracy (The Renaissance and the Reformation) D: 122
Education (The Reformation) E: 100
Europe (The Reformation) E: 410
Freedom (The Renaissance and the Reformation) F: 503
Freedom of religion (History) F: 506
German literature (The Reformation) G: 139
Germany (The Reformation) G: 164
Hymn (History) H: 475
Luther, Martin L: 527
Melanchthon, Philipp M: 388
Netherlands (Eighty Years' War) N: 148
Painting (Baroque) P: 58
Pope (Renaissance and Reformation) P: 664
Protestantism P: 833; (History) P: 834
Religion (Christianity) R: 222-223
Religious life (Religious life in the 1500's and 1600's) R: 227
Roman Catholic Church (The Reformation) R: 408
Saint (Christian saints) S: 29
Tetzel, Johann T: 183
Thirty-Nine Articles T: 259
Trent, Council of T: 434
Women's movement (From the Renaissance to the 1800's) W: 384
Reformatory [prison] R: 199
Reformed church [religion]
Christianity (Protestant churches) C: 522g; (The Reformation) C: 524
Presbyterians P: 756a
Protestantism (The conservative reform movements) P: 834
Reformed Church in America [religious group] R: 199
Reformed spelling [language]
Phonetics (Phonetics and spelling) P: 398-400
Reforming [industrial process]
Petroleum (Conversion) P: 344-345
Refoulement [law]
Refugee (The rights of refugees) R: 203
Refracting telescope
Galileo G: 11 *with picture*
Telescope (Refracting telescopes) T: 103 *with diagram*
Refraction [physics] R: 199 *with pictures*
Astronomy (Optical astronomy) A: 839-840
Eye (Focusing) E: 462
Gem (Index of refraction) G: 77
Lens (Creating an image) L: 196
Light (Refraction) L: 288 *with diagram*
Mirage M: 615 *with pictures*
Prism P: 805
Rainbow (How rainbows appear) R: 128
Sound (Refraction) So: 602 *with diagrams*
Waves (Refraction and reflection) W: 152
Refraction, Index of [physics]
Gem (Index of refraction) G: 77
Materials (Optical properties) M: 300c
Refractive errors [vision]
LASIK surgery L: 86
Refractive index [physics]
Gem (Index of refraction) G: 77
Light (Refraction) L: 288
Refraction R: 199
Refractor [telescope] *See* Refracting telescope *in this index*
Refractory R: 200
Brick (Refractory bricks) B: 597
Ceramics (Kinds of ceramic products) C: 359
Furnace F: 567
Refractory pot
Glass (Melting) G: 215
Refrigerant
Ammonia (Properties of ammonia) A: 434
Heat (Refrigeration) H: 154
Heat pump H: 156
Refrigerator-control device
Refrigeration *diagram on* R: 202; (The electric refrigerator) R: 201 *with diagram*
Refrigeration R: 200 *with pictures*
Air conditioning (Controlling the temperature)

A: 178
Ammonia (Properties of ammonia) A: 434
Cold storage Ci: 761
Dry ice D: 369
Food (Transportation) F: 335
Food, Frozen F: 338
Food preservation (Cold storage) F: 342
Heat (Refrigeration) H: 154
Heat pump H: 156
Meat packing M: 350
Refrigerator *See* Refrigeration *in this index*
Refrigerator car [railroad]
Railroad *pictures on* R: 105, R: 108
Refuge [conservation] *See* Wildlife refuge *in this index*
Refuge, Cities of
Cities of refuge Ci: 568
Refugee [person] R: 203
Berlin (The Berlin Wall) B: 264
Ford, Gerald Rudolph (The Vietnam War) F: 378
Germany (East Germany) G: 170; (West Germany) G: 170; (The unification of East and West Germany) G: 171-172
Haiti (History) H: 15-17
Hispanic Americans (Cuban immigration) H: 254; (Central Americans immigration) H: 255
Immigration I: 80; (The fourth wave) I: 83
India (Independence and partition) I: 133; (India under Indira Gandhi) I: 133-134
Iraq (The Persian Gulf War of 1991) I: 414-414a
Kosovo (History) K: 384b
Palestine (World War II and the division of Palestine) P: 105
Rwanda (History) R: 571-572
Serbia (Kosovo crisis) S: 316-316a
United Nations (Aid to refugees) U: 88
Vietnam (Postwar Vietnam) V: 371 *with picture*
War (Refugees) W: 25
World War II (Displaced persons) W: 497
Refugee Act [1980]
Immigration (The fourth wave) I: 83
Refugee camp
Jordan *picture on* J: 165
Refugees, Freedmen, and Abandoned Lands, Bureau of *See* Freedmen's Bureau *in this index*
Refugees, International Office for
Nobel Prizes (Peace: 1981) N: 448b
Refus global [text]
Canadian literature (Modern Canadian poets) C: 161
Refusal [sports]
Horse (Jumping) H: 357
Refuse
Sanitation (Solid waste disposal) S: 111
Waste disposal W: 112
Reg [geography]
Sahara (Land and climate) S: 20
Regal murex [shell]
Shell *picture on* S: 386
Regalia [ornament]
Coronation (The British coronation) Ci: 1068
Tower of London T: 351
Regan [literary figure]
Shakespeare, William: *(King Lear)* S: 363
Regan, Donald T. [American government official]
Reagan, Ronald Wilson (table) R: 169
Regan, Gerald [Canadian political leader]
Nova Scotia (table) N: 567
Regatta [race]
Rowing (Competition) R: 494
Régence style
Furniture (French styles) F: 576
Regency Act of 1937 [British history]
Regent R: 204
Regency period
Furniture (The Regency style) F: 580
Heyer, Georgette H: 220
Regenerated fiber
Fiber (Regenerated fibers) F: 87
Regeneration [biology] R: 203
Animal (Regeneration) A: 498
Crustacean (Growth and development) Ci: 1163-1164 *with picture*
Liver L: 393
Lizard (Defenses) L: 400
Planarian P: 507
Plant (Asexual reproduction) P: 535
Sponge (Regeneration) So: 800
Starfish (The life of a starfish) So: 856
Regeneration [book by Loeb]
Loeb, Jacques L: 420
Regenerative braking
Automobile (Batteries and braking) A: 954
Electric car (How electric cars work) E: 165
Hybrid car H: 461
Regenerative gas furnace
Iron and steel (The birth of modern steelmaking)

I: 450-451

Regenerative nodule [disorder]
Cirrhosis **Ci: 566**
Regenerator [device]
Stirling engine **So: 902** *with diagrams*
Turbine (Gas turbines) **T: 497-498**
Regent [office] **R: 204**
Regent diamond
Diamond *picture on* **D: 181**; (Famous diamonds)
D: 182
Regents, Board of
Universities and colleges (Governing boards)
U: 208
*Regents of the University of California v. Allan
Bakke* [U.S. history] *See* Bakke case *in this index*
Reggae [music] **R: 204**
Rastafarians **R: 146**
Rock music (World music) **R: 380d**
Regin [legendary figure]
Fafnir **F: 6**
Mythology *picture on* **M: 986**
Regina [Saskatchewan] **R: 204** *with picture and map*
Saskatchewan *pictures on* **S: 129, S: 141**; (table:
Average monthly weather) **S: 140**
Regina [opera by Blitzstein]
Blitzstein, Marc **B: 403**
Regina Manifesto [Canadian history]
Regina (History) **R: 206**
Regina Medal R: 206
Literature for children (Awards) **L: 67**
Regiomontanus [German mathematician]
Mathematics (The Renaissance) **M: 306**
Trigonometry **T: 442**
Region
Geography (Regional characteristics) **G: 93**;
(Regional geography) **G: 94**
Region of elongation [botany]
Root (The root tip) **R: 470** *with diagram*
Regional airline
Airport (Commercial service airports) **A: 243**
Regional county municipality
Quebec (Local government) **Q: 30**
Regional enteritis [disorder] *See* Crohn's disease
in this index
Regional fair
Fair (Agricultural fairs) **F: 7**
Regional forecaster
Weather (Careers in weather) **W: 170**
Regional holding company [business]
Telephone (Competition in the U.S. telephone
industry) **T: 101**
Regional metamorphism [geology]
Metamorphic rock **M: 428**
Regional nerve block [medicine]
Anesthesia (Local anesthesia) **A: 458**
Regional railroad
Railroad (Railroad systems) **R: 112-113**
Regional Seas Programme
Water pollution (Laws) **W: 138**
Regional traditional costume
Clothing (Regional traditional costumes) **Ci: 696**
Regional Transportation Authority [Illinois]
Chicago (Transportation) **C: 433**
Regionalism [art]
Benton, Thomas Hart **B: 254**
Curry, John Steuart **Ci: 1198**
Painting (Regionalism) **P: 83** *with picture*
Wood, Grant **W: 390**
Regionalists [literature]
Spanish literature (The 1800's) **So: 761-762**
Register [computer]
Computer (The digital logic unit) **C: 912**
Electronics (Digital circuits) **E: 213-214**
Register pin [device]
Motion picture *diagram on* **M: 858**; (The camera)
M: 856-857
Registered animal
Dairying (Dairy cattle) **D: 6**
Registered horse
Horse (Breeding horses) **H: 358-359**
Registered insider [business]
Insider trading **I: 303**
Registered mail
Postal Service, United States (Extra protection)
P: 700
Registered nurse
Hospital (The professional services staff) **H: 371**
Nursing (Nursing careers) **N: 616**
Registered partnership [law]
Civil union **Ci: 613**
Marriage (Laws concerning marriage) **M: 219-220**
Registered Partnership Law [1989]
Civil union **Ci: 613**
Registered retirement savings plan
Pension (Pensions in other countries) **P: 273**
Registrar [museum]
Museum (Acquisition of materials) **M: 938-939**

Registration [computing]
Website **W: 176**
Registration [printing]
Lithography (Color lithography) **L: 387**
Registration of voters
Voting (Registration) **V: 449**
Registry, Breed
Horse (Breeding horses) **H: 358**
Rego, José Lins do [Brazilian author]
Latin American literature (The early 1900's) **L: 113**
Regolith [astronomy]
Moon (Origin and evolution of the moon) **M: 788**
Regression [psychology] **R: 206**
Regression [reading]
Reading (How we read) **R: 156-157**
Speed reading **So: 774**
Regret [horse]
Kentucky Derby **K: 297**
Regrets [poems by Bellay]
Du Bellay, Joachim **D: 370**
Regrouping [mathematics]
Addition (Regrouping) **A: 49**
Regular army
Army **A: 724**
Regular Army [U.S.]
Army, United States (Organization of the Army)
A: 735
Regular flower [botany]
Rose (The rose family) **R: 476**
Regular fractal [geometry]
Fractal **F: 443** *with diagram*
Regular hexagon [geometry]
Hexagon **H: 220** *with diagram*
Regular octagon [geometry]
Octagon **O: 669** *with diagram*
Regular octahedron [geometry]
Octahedron **O: 669** *with diagram*
Regular Officer Training Program
Canadian Armed Forces (Recruitment and
training) **C: 155**
Regular polygon [geometry]
Polygon **P: 650** *with diagram*
Polyhedron **P: 651**
Regular polyhedron [geometry]
Geometry (Solid geometry) **G: 104-105**
Polyhedron **P: 651** *with diagrams*
Regular pyramid [geometry]
Pyramid **P: 916** *with diagram*
Regular satellite [astronomy]
Satellite **S: 149**; (Satellites of the gas giants)
S: 150
Regular verb [grammar]
Verb (Regular and irregular verbs) **V: 314**
Regulator [clock]
Pendulum (Clock pendulums) **P: 237-238**
Regulators [U.S. history]
North Carolina (Revolution and independence)
N: 492
Westward movement in America (Regional
conflict) **W: 245**
Regulatory agency
President of the United States (The independent
agencies) **P: 764**
United States, Government of the (Executive
departments and agencies) **U: 140**
Regulatory commission
United States, Government of the (Executive
departments and agencies) **U: 140**
Regulatory T cell [physiology]
Immune system (The cell-mediated immune
response) **I: 88-88a**
Regulus, Marcus Atilius [Roman general] **R: 206**
Regurgitation [biology]
Ant *picture on* **A: 521**; (Internal organs) **A: 522**
Regurgitation [medicine]
Heart (Other heart disorders) **H: 141**
Reh pinscher [dog]
Miniature pinscher **M: 573**
Rehabilitation [medicine]
Hospital (Professional services departments)
H: 371
Insurance (Wokers' compensation) **I: 314**
Mental illness (Psychotherapy) **M: 407-408** *with
picture*
Physical therapy **P: 435**
Stroke (Rehabilitation) **So: 930**
Vocational rehabilitation **V: 435**
Rehabilitation [social reform]
Crime (Crime prevention) **Ci: 1139**
Criminal justice system (The correctional system)
Ci: 1144
Criminology (What criminologists study) **Ci: 1145**
Prison (How prisons operate) **P: 806** *with picture*;
(Reforms in the 1900's) **P: 807**
Sentence **S: 304**
Rehabilitation Act [1973]
Disability (The 1900's) **D: 221-222**

Rehabilitation engineering
Biomedical engineering (Specialty areas of
biomedical engineering) **B: 324-325**
Rehabilitation therapy
Disease (Medical treatment) **D: 232-233**
Rehearsal
Memory (Other ways to improve memory)
M: 393
Motion picture (Holding rehearsals) **M: 851**
Opera *picture on* **O: 795**; (Rehearsing a
production) **O: 796**
Orchestra (The conductor) **O: 821**
Television (Rehearsals) **T: 111**
Theater *picture on* **T: 240**; (Rehearsing) **T: 236**
with picture
Rehnquist, William Hubbs [American jurist] **R: 207**
Nixon, Richard Milhous (The national scene)
N: 434
Roberts, John Glover, Jr. **R: 365**
Rehoboam [Biblical figure]
Solomon **So: 584**
Rehoboth Beach
Delaware (Interesting facts about Delaware)
D: 97 *with picture*
Reich [German history] **R: 207**
Reich, Ferdinand [German chemist]
Indium **I: 224**
Reich, Robert B. [American government official]
Clinton, Bill (table) **Ci: 682d**
Labor, Department of (table) **L: 2**
Reich, Steve [American composer]
Classical music (Minimalism) **Ci: 651**
Reichenstein, Franz Müller von [Austrian chemist]
Tellurium **T: 129**
Reichsmark [money]
Mark **M: 213**
Reichstadt, Duke of [son of Napoleon I]
Napoleon II **N: 17**
Reichstag [German history]
Berlin (Recent developments) **B: 265**
Germany (The German Empire) **G: 166**; (The
Weimar Republic) **G: 167**
Hitler, Adolf (The New Order) **H: 266-**
Reichstein, Tadeus [Swiss chemist]
Nobel Prizes (Physiology or medicine: 1950)
N: 445
Reid, Bill [Canadian sculptor]
Canada (Painting and sculpture) **C: 109**
Reid, D. S. [American political leader]
North Carolina (table) **N: 490**
Reid, David B. [British inventor]
Air conditioning (History) **A: 180**
Reid, George Houston [Australian political leader]
Australia (table) **A: 923**
Reid, Harry [American political leader] **R: 207**
Democratic Party *picture on* **D: 128**
Reid, Richard G. [Canadian political leader]
Alberta (table) **A: 328**
Reid, Whitelaw [American political leader] **R: 207**
Reid, William F. [American political leader]
Virginia (Political changes) **V: 422**
Reifel, Benjamin [American political leader]
Indian, American (Political gains) **I: 182**
Reigen [play by Schnitzler]
Schnitzler, Arthur **S: 178**
Reign of Terror [French history] **R: 207**
Danton, Georges-Jacques **D: 34**
French Revolution (Terror and equality) **F: 526**;
(The revolution ends) **F: 527**
Jacobins **J: 20**
Robespierre **R: 366**
Terrorism (The beginnings of modern terrorism)
T: 178 *with picture*
Reims [France] **R: 207** *with picture*
City *picture on* **Ci: 582**
Joan of Arc, Saint (Joan sees the king) **J: 128**
Vulgate **V: 453**
Reina Regenta [ship]
Shipwreck (table: Major shipwrecks) **S: 428**
Reincarnation R: 208
Buddhism (The dharma) **B: 668**
Hinduism (Reincarnation and karma) **H: 236**
India (Hinduism) **I: 116**
Plato (Immortality of the soul) **P: 568**
Pythagoras **P: 921**
Sikhism (Beliefs and practices) **S: 455**
Theosophy **T: 253**
Reindeer [animal] **R: 208** *with picture*
Inuit (New ways of life) **I: 354g-354h**
Lapland **L: 74**
Sami **S: 78** *with picture*
Reindeer Island [Canada]
Lake Winnipeg **L: 48** *with map*
Reindeer Lake [Canada] **R: 209**
Reindeer moss R: 209
Lichen (The importance of lichens) **L: 269**
Reines, Frederick [American physicist]

Neutrino N: 154
Nobel Prizes (Physics: 1995) N: 442
Reinfeldt, Fredrik [Swedish political leader]
Sweden (Recent developments) So: 1035
Reinforced concrete
Cement and concrete (Reinforced concrete)
C: 343
Reinforced plastics
Plastics (Making sythetic resins) P: 556-557
Reinforcement [chemistry]
Composite materials Ci: 904
Reinforcement [psychology]
Behavior (Learning) B: 220-221
Developmental psychology (Learning theory)
D: 174
Habit (How we learn habits) H: 2
Learning (Classical conditioning) L: 163;
(Instrumental conditioning) L: 163
Psychiatry (Psychotherapy) P: 845
Reinhardt, Django [Belgian guitarist]
Jazz (The spread of jazz) J: 72-73
Reinhardt, Max [Austrian director] R: 209
Reiniger, Lotte [German filmmaker]
Animation (Animation in Europe) A: 514b
Reins
Harness H: 63 with diagram
Horse (table: Riding equipment) H: 351; (The
bridle) H: 352 with pictures
Reivers, The [book by Faulkner]
Faulkner, William F: 55
Reizenstein, Elmer Leopold [birth name of]
Rice, Elmer R: 328
Rej, Mikołaj [Polish poet]
Poland (The arts) P: 607
Rejection [medicine]
Transplant (Preventing rejection) T: 380
Xenotransplant X: 544
Rejewski, Marian [Polish mathematician]
Codes and ciphers (Later developments) Ci: 751
Rejlander, Oscar [British inventor]
Photography (Artistic advances) P: 424
Rekindle [fire]
Fire department (Firefighting) F: 123-124
Relapse, The [play by Vanbrugh]
Vanbrugh, Sir John V: 269
Relapsing
Drug abuse (Treatment of substance use
disorders) D: 364
Relapsing fever R: 209
Related color scheme [art]
Interior design (Using color) I: 331
Relation [mathematics]
Algebra (Working with equations) A: 356
Relation of ideas [philosophy]
Hume, David (Hume's thought) H: 432
Relational database [software]
Database D: 42
Relationship-oriented sales
Sales (Current trends in sales) S: 65
Relative
Family (Family relationships) F: 21
Relative atomic mass [physics]
Atom (Relative atomic mass) A: 872
Carbon (Chemical properties) C: 203-204
Element, Chemical (The periodic table of the
elements) E: 219; (Relative atomic mass) E: 223
Hydrogen (Properties) H: 468
Metric system (Chemistry) M: 440
Molecule (Individual molecules) M: 692-693
Relative dating [archaeology]
Archaeology (Dating) A: 598
Relative humidity
Air (Moisture in the air) A: 170
Heat index H: 156
Heating H: 157
Humidity H: 433
Hygrometer H: 474
Weather (Humidity) W: 158; (Synoptic-scale
systems) W: 159-160
Relative molecular mass [chemistry]
Metric system (Chemistry) M: 440
Molecule (Individual molecules) M: 692-693
Relative prime [mathematics]
Factor (Relative primes) F: 5
Relative pronoun [grammar]
Pronoun P: 819
Relativism [philosophy]
Metaphysics (Space and time) M: 429
Philosophy (Epistemology) P: 384; (Ethics and
political philosophy) P: 385
Pope (The 1900's and 2000's) P: 665-667
Relativistic equation [physics]
Energy (Calculating quantities of energy) E: 274
Relativistic Heavy Ion Collider [machine]
Brookhaven National Laboratory B: 639
Particle accelerator (How accelerators work)
P: 184-186

Relativity [physics] R: 209
See also the list of Related articles in the Relativity
article
Black hole B: 388
Dark energy D: 36
Dark matter D: 37
De Sitter, Willem D: 158
Eddington, Sir Arthur Stanley E: 75
Einstein, Albert E: 146
Energy (Calculating quantities of energy) E: 274;
(Energy and matter) E: 274
Force (Einstein's theory of general relativity)
F: 370
Fourth dimension F: 438
Geometry (Non-Euclidean geometry) G: 105
Gravitation (Einstein's theory of gravitation)
G: 331; (Predictions of general relativity) G: 332
Gravitational wave G: 333
Light (The speed of light) L: 290
Motion (Motion is relative) M: 845
Physics (Einstein and relativity) P: 441
Riemann, Georg Friedrich Bernhard R: 337
String theory So: 929
Subatomic particle (Theories of forces) So: 937-
938
Time (Our understanding of time) T: 292a-292b
with diagram
Universe (The future of the universe) U: 206
Relaxation
See also Rest in this index
Meditation M: 380
New Age movement N: 178
Recreation R: 182
Sleep (The structure of sleep) S: 506
Stress (Managing stress) So: 927
Relaxin [hormone]
Hormone (Other hormones) H: 336
Relay race
Ice skating (Short-track skating) I: 15-16
Skiing (Nordic competitions) S: 487
Swimming (Kinds of races) So: 1044-1046
Track and field (Relays) T: 357 with picture
Relay services [telecommunications]
Deafness (Assistive technology) D: 58-59
Relay system
Postal services (Ancient times) P: 703
Relearning [psychology]
Memory (Measuring memory) M: 392
Release-time instruction
Religious education (Public schools) R: 225
Releaser [psychology] See Stimulus in this index
Releasing hormone [physiology]
Hormone (Endocrine control hormones) H: 336
Hypothalamus H: 481
Relenza [drug]
Virus (Antiviral drugs) V: 428a
Relevance, Fallacy of
Fallacy F: 16
Reliability
Statistics (Sampling) So: 869
Reliance Building [Chicago]
Architecture picture on A: 629
Burnham, Daniel Hudson B: 709
Chicago picture on C: 421
Root, John Wellborn R: 472
Relic
Saint S: 29
Relief [art] R: 212 with pictures
Drama picture on D: 327
Ivory (Ivory carving) I: 521 with picture
Persia, Ancient picture on P: 299
Sculpture picture on S: 247; (Kinds of sculpture)
S: 230
Relief [geology]
Mountain M: 891
Relief [welfare] See Welfare in this index
Relief Corps, National Woman's
Woman's Relief Corps, National W: 382
Relief map
Map (Production and reproduction) M: 181
Relief of the Poor, Act for the [1601]
Welfare (History) W: 191
Relief printing
Printing (Relief printing) P: 799 with diagram;
(Printing in color) P: 801
Stamp collecting (Printing) So: 830
Religio Laici [poem by Dryden]
Dryden, John D: 370
Religio Medici [book by Browne]
English literature (Prose writings) E: 317
Religion R: 214 with pictures
See also the list of Related articles in the Religion
article and the Way of life or People sections of
the various country articles, such as Argentina
(Way of life)
Animism A: 514d
Aztec (Religion) A: 1000 with pictures

Celibacy C: 325
Censorship (Religious censorship) C: 346
City (The people) Ci: 578-580
Colonial life in America (Religious and political
reasons) Ci: 788; (Religion) Ci: 804 with picture;
(Literature) Ci: 806
Communism (Restrictions on personal freedom)
Ci: 891-892
Conservatism (Features of political conservatism)
Ci: 991
Creationism Ci: 1123
Dance (Why people dance) D: 24 with picture
Doll (Dolls in religion) D: 288
Evolution (Acceptance of evolution) E: 433
Existentialism (The influence of existentialism)
E: 437
Fire (Fire in legend and religion) F: 122
Flag picture on F: 216
Food (Religious reasons) F: 332
God G: 243
Greece, Ancient (Religion) G: 367
Hermit H: 211
Human being H: 413
Hume, David (Hume's thought) H: 432
Indian, American (Religion) I: 146 with pictures
Inuit (Religion) I: 354e
Kant, Immanuel (Kant's ideas) K: 244
Kierkegaard, Søren Aabye (His philosophy) K: 313
Knights and knighthood (Knighting) K: 348 with
picture
Magic M: 49
Meditation M: 380
Missionary M: 620
Mythology M: 973
New Age movement N: 178
New Year's Day (The date of New Year's) N: 289
Philosophy (Philosophy and religion) P: 386
Pioneer life in America (Religion) P: 484
Prejudice P: 754b
Radio (The Golden Age of Broadcasting) R: 92-93
Reformation R: 195
Rome, Ancient (Religion) R: 441
Sacrifice S: 6
Saint S: 29
Santayana, George S: 115
Sculpture (Personal sculpture) S: 241
Sex discrimination (Views on sex discrimination)
S: 335
Spiritualism (Spiritualism and religion) So: 796
Terrorism (Terrorist groups and movements)
T: 178-179
Theism T: 251
Union of Soviet Socialist Republics (Personal
freedom) U: 31
United States (Religion) U: 114 with picture
Witchcraft W: 371
World (Religion) W: 414
Religion, Freedom of See Freedom of religion in
this index
Religions of the Book
Religion R: 215
Religious art
See also Islamic art in this index
Cathedral C: 301 with pictures
Germany (Painting and sculpture) G: 155 with
pictures
Icon I: 24
Madonna and Child M: 37 with picture
Middle Ages (Learning and the arts) M: 527
Painting (Religious subjects) P: 32; (Indian
painting) P: 44
Russia (Painting and sculpture) R: 537 with picture
Sculpture (The 1000's) S: 249 with pictures
Stained glass So: 821 with pictures
Religious court
Israel (Courts) I: 480
Religious discrimination See Discrimination in
this index
Religious drama
Drama (Liturgical drama) D: 328; (Religious plays)
D: 333
Religious education R: 225
School prayer S: 185
Religious festivals
See also the list of Related articles in the Feasts and
Festivals article
Feasts and festivals F: 58
Religious freedom See Freedom of Religion in
this index
Religious Freedom, Statute of [1786]
Jefferson, Thomas (Virginia lawmaker) J: 80
Madison, James (Virginia assemblyman) M: 33
Religious institute [organization]
See also Orders, Religious in this index
Roman Catholic Church (Religious institutes)
R: 404
Religious life R: 226

See also the list of Related articles in the Religious life *article*
Religious music
See also Sacred music *in this index*
Music (In ceremonies) M: 947
Religious orders See Orders, Religious *in this index*
Religious Right [movement]
Evangelicalism E: 422
Religious Settlement [1559]
Elizabeth I (Problems at home and abroad) E: 238
Religious Society of Friends See Quakers *in this index*
Religious tolerance See Freedom of religion *in this index*
Reliquary [religion]
Byzantine art (Other art forms) B: 751
Reliques of Ancient English Poetry [book by Percy]
Ballad (Ballads and literature) B: 43
Relish [food]
Pickle P: 451
Rell, M. Jodi [American political leader]
Connecticut (table) Ci: 967; (The early 2000's) Ci: 971
"Reluctant Dragon, The" [story by Grahame]
Grahame, Kenneth G: 301
R.E.M. [musical group]
Rock music (New wave and mainstream rock) R: 380c
Rem [unit of measure]
Radiation (Dose) R: 79-80
Radiation sickness R: 81
REM sleep
Dream (The biology of dreams) D: 344; (The meaning and function of dreams) D: 344
Narcolepsy N: 20
Nightmare N: 421
Sleep (The structure of sleep) S: 506
Sleepwalking S: 508
Remainder [mathematics]
Arithmetic (Division) A: 668
Division (table) D: 248; (Remainders in division) D: 250
Remaindering [publishing]
Publishing (Going out of print) P: 869
Remains of the Day, The [book by Ishiguro]
Novel (The novel today) N: 575
Remand centre
Prison (Juvenile correctional institutions) P: 806
Remarque, Erich Maria [German-American author] R: 228
Rembrandt [Dutch artist] R: 228 *with pictures*
Aristotle *picture on* A: 663
Baroque (Baroque painting) B: 117
Etching (History) E: 364
Netherlands *picture on* N: 144
Painting (The Dutch masters) P: 62-63 *with picture*
World, History of the *picture on* W: 440
Remek, Vladimir [Czechoslovak astronaut]
Astronaut (table) A: 830
"Remember Goliad!" [slogan]
Texas (The Texas revolution) T: 206
"Remember Pearl Harbor!" [slogan]
Pearl Harbor R: 218
"Remember the Alamo!" [slogan]
Alamo (The siege) A: 280-281
Texas (The Texas revolution) T: 206
"Remember the *Maine***"** [slogan]
Maine M: 67
Spanish-American War (Background to the war) So: 753
Remembrance Day [holiday] R: 229
Veterans Day V: 344
Remembrance of Things Past [books by Proust]
French literature (The early years) F: 522
Novel (New directions in the novel) N: 573-574
Proust, Marcel P: 838
Remington, Frederic [American artist] R: 229 *with picture*
Cavalry *picture on* C: 318
Pony express *picture on* P: 658
Sculpture (American sculpture) S: 255-256 *with picture*
Spanish-American War *picture on* So: 754
Western frontier life in America (Art) W: 239
Remington and Sons [company]
Typewriter (History) T: 539
Reminiscences [book by MacArthur]
MacArthur, Douglas (Last years) M: 4
Remission [medicine]
Leukemia (Acute leukemias) L: 215
Remittance [money]
Latin America (People) L: 92
Mexico (Economy) M: 463-464
Remodeling [medicine]
Osteoporosis (Causes) O: 867
Remonstrance [book]

Arminianiam A: 719
Remora [fish] R: 230
Fish *picture on* F: 168
Remote control R: 230 *with picture*
Locomotive (Diesel locomotives) L: 414-415
Radio (Remote control) R: 85
Surgery *picture on* So: 1007
Remote sensing [electronics] R: 231 *with picture*
Archaeology (Locating sites) A: 595-596
Geography (Mapping) G: 95; (Scientific instruments) G: 95
Map (Mapmaking and modern technology) M: 185
Photogrammetry P: 405
Remote telecast
Television (Live telecasts) T: 112
Remote truck [vehicle]
Television (Live telecasts) T: 112
Remote video encoding
Postal services (Sorting) P: 703
Remotely operated aircraft See Unmanned aerial vehicle *in this index*
Remotely operated vehicle [machine]
Marine biology (Biological oceanographers) M: 205
Ocean (Submersibles) O: 663
Remotely piloted vehicle See Unmanned aerial vehicle *in this index*
Remus [legendary figure]
Romulus and Remus R: 450a
Remus, Uncle [literary figure] See Uncle Remus *in this index*
Renaissance [European history] R: 232 *with pictures and map*
See also the list of Related articles in the Renaissance *article*
Architecture (Renaissance architecture) A: 620 *with pictures*
Baroque B: 116
Biography (The Renaissance) B: 313
Black Death B: 386
City planning (The Renaissance) Ci: 602
Classical music *picture on* Ci: 648; (Renaissance) Ci: 646
Clothing (The Renaissance) Ci: 702 *with pictures*
Communication (The rise of printing) Ci: 879
Democracy (The Renaissance and the Reformation) D: 122
Doll (The Renaissance) D: 288
Drama (Italian Renaissance drama) D: 330
Education (The Renaissance) E: 100
Europe (Renaissance art) E: 392 *with picture*; (The Renaissance) E: 410 *with picture*
Freedom (The Renaissance and the Reformation) F: 503
French literature (The Renaissance) F: 519
Fresco F: 529
Geology (The Renaissance) G: 98
German literature (The Renaissance) G: 139
Hairdressing (The Renaissance) H: 11
History (The Humanist movement) H: 262
Humanism H: 430
Illuminated manuscript I: 78
Invention (The Renaissance) I: 360
Italian literature (Humanism and the Renaissance) I: 494
Italy (Arts) I: 504; (Rise of the city-states) I: 513-514
Library (Renaissance collections) L: 259
Medicine (The Renaissance) M: 373
Middle Ages (The late Middle Ages) M: 527
Painting (The Renaissance) P: 51 *with pictures*
Philosophy (Modern philosophy) P: 388
Physics (The Renaissance) P: 438
Poetry (Renaissance poetry) P: 596
Pope (Renaissance and Reformation) P: 664
Roman Catholic Church (The close of the Middle Ages) R: 407
Rome, Ancient (Learning about ancient Rome) R: 448
Sculpture (Italian Renaissance sculpture) S: 251 *with pictures*
Women's movement (From the Renaissance to the 1800's) W: 384
World, History of the (The Renaissance) W: 438
Renaissance Big Five, New York [team]
Basketball (The history of professional basketball) B: 154a-155
Renaissance Center
Detroit (The late 1900's) D: 171
Michigan *picture on* M: 489
Renaissance Festival [Minnesota]
Minnesota (Places to visit) *picture on* M: 594-595
Renal artery [anatomy]
Human body (table) H: 422 *with diagram*
Kidney (How the kidneys produce urine) K: 311 *with diagrams*

Renal disease
Anemia (Anemia of renal disease) A: 458
Hantavirus H: 54
Renal vein [anatomy]
Human body (table) H: 422 *with diagram*
Kidney (How the kidneys produce urine) K: 311-312 *with diagrams*
Renamo [political organization]
Mozambique (Government) M: 904; (History) M: 905-906
Renan, Ernest [French historian]
Biography (The 1800's) B: 314
Renard, Charles [French engineer]
Airship (The first airships) A: 251
Renard, Jean-Claude [French poet]
French literature (Recent French literature) F: 523
"Renascence" [poem by Millay]
Millay, Edna St. Vincent M: 552
Renaud, Madeleine [French actress]
Barrault, Jean-Louis B: 118
Renault [company]
Automobile (The birth of the automobile industry) A: 966
Manufacturing (table) M: 170
Renault, Louis [French statesman]
Nobel Prizes (Peace: 1907) N: 448
Rendell, Ed [American political leader]
Pennsylvania (table) P: 263
Rendering [art]
Animation (Lighting and rendering) A: 513
Computer graphics Ci: 924g
Rendezvous [fur trade]
Fur trade (The 1800's) F: 565
Rendezvous site [zoology]
Wolf (Young) W: 376
René, France Albert [Seychellois political leader]
Seychelles (History) S: 340
Renewable resource
Biofuel B: 312
Conservation Ci: 974
Forest products (Wood products) F: 400
Industry (Natural resources) I: 257-258
Petroleum (The future of petroleum) P: 349
Renga [poetry]
Japanese literature (The medieval period) J: 62
Reni, Guido [Italian artist]
Europa *picture on* E: 379
Renin [hormone]
Adrenal gland A: 67
Hypertension (Causes) H: 476
Renmin Ribao [newspaper]
Newspaper (In Asia) N: 386
Renminbi [money]
Yuan Y: 575
Rennebohm, Oscar [American political leader]
Wisconsin (table) W: 365
Rennet [animal product]
Cheese (Separating the curd) C: 392-393
Rennin [enzyme]
Casein C: 272
Genetic engineering (In industry) G: 84c
Rennutet [Egyptian goddess]
Egypt, Ancient (Religion) E: 137
Reno [Nevada] R: 239
Nevada (Population) N: 160 *with picture*; (Visitor's guide) N: 164
Reno, Janet [American government official] R: 240 *with portrait*
Justice, Department of (table) J: 203
Reno, Jesse W. [American inventor]
Escalator E: 356
Reno, Marcus Albert [American military leader] R: 240
Custer, George Armstrong (The battle) Ci: 1200
Little Bighorn, Battle of the L: 391
Renoir, Jean [French director] R: 240
Motion picture (Movies in the 1930's) M: 867-868 *with picture*
Renoir, Pierre Auguste [French painter] R: 240 *with pictures*
Impressionism (French Impressionism) I: 93 *with picture*
Painting (Edouard Manet and the Impressionists) P: 71
Renoir, Jean R: 240
Rensselaerswyck [U.S. history]
Patroon system P: 199
Van Rensselaer, Kiliaen V: 284
Rent [economics]
Economics (Distribution of income) E: 63
Lease L: 166
Rental
Motion picture (Exhibition) M: 860
Renter's insurance
Insurance (Homeowners' insurance) I: 313
Renwick, James [American architect]
Saint Patrick's Cathedral S: 51

Renwick Gallery [Washington, D.C.]
Washington, D.C. *map on* W: 76; (Smithsonian museums) W: 71-73
Reo [automobile]
Olds, Ransom Eli O: 742
Reo Motor Car Company
Olds, Ransom Eli O: 742
Reorganization [law]
Bankruptcy (In the United States) B: 97
Reorganization Objectives, Army Division
Army, United States (The atomic age Army) A: 739
Reorganized Church of Jesus Christ of Latter Day Saints *See* Community of Christ *in this index*
Rep [occupation] *See* Sales representative *in this index*
Repair worker
Careers (Construction, maintenance, and repair) C: 221
Reparations [policy] R: 241
Dawes Plan D: 51
Germany (World War I) G: 166-167
Versailles, Treaty of (Provisions) V: 340
World War I (Economic consequences) W: 464
World War II (Causes of the war) W: 468
Repatriation program [U.S. history]
Hispanic Americans (Immigration restrictions and growing discrimination) H: 252
Repeal [law] R: 241
Repeating decimal fraction
Decimal system (Decimals and fractions) D: 72 *with diagram*
Rational number R: 148
Repeating pistol
Colt, Samuel C: 850
Repertory theater
Opera O: 790
Repetition
Advertising (Repetition) A: 76a
Classical music (Classical music forms) Ci: 644
Design (Repetition) D: 157 *with picture*
Propaganda (Simplicity and repetition) P: 824
Repetitive factory
Factory (Kinds of factories) F: 5
Repetitive strain injury R: 242
Disease (Environmental and occupational diseases) D: 230
Repin, Ilya [Russian artist]
Painting (Painting outside France) P: 72
Replacement [reaction]
Fossil (The action of minerals) F: 425
Replete [entomology]
Ant (Honey ants) A: 527
Replication [genetics]
Genetics (Molecular genetics) G: 86
Heredity (Replication) H: 206
Life (The puzzle of replication) L: 279
Report of the Exploring Expedition to the Rocky Mountains [book by Frémont]
Frémont, John Charles F: 511
Report on the Affairs of British North America
Durham, Earl of D: 389
Report on the Geology of Canada, A [book by Logan]
Logan, Sir William Edmond L: 423
Reporting [journalism]
Journalism J: 170 *with pictures*
Newspaper (Gathering information) N: 382 *with picture*; (Writing and editing stories) N: 383
Pulitzer Prizes (Prizes in journalism) P: 886b; (table) P: 887
War correspondent W: 26
Reports of Medical Cases [book by Bright]
Bright, Richard B: 609
Repotting
Gardening (Repotting) G: 37 *with pictures*
Repoussé [decoration]
Embossing E: 256
Representation [philosophy]
Schopenhauer, Arthur S: 186
Representative [office] R: 242
Congress of the United States (table) Ci: 943; (Members of Congress at work) Ci: 946
House of Representatives H: 385
Representative, The [play by Hochhuth] *See* Deputy, The *in this index*
Representative democracy
Democracy D: 119
Government (Democracy) G: 285
Representative fraction [cartography]
Map (Scale) M: 178
Representative government
Apportionment A: 574
Democracy D: 119
Republic R: 253
United States, Government of the (Representative democracy) U: 137

Representative Men [book by Emerson]
Emerson, Ralph Waldo (His prose works) E: 259
Representatives, House of *See* House of Representatives *in this index*
Repression [psychology]
Memory (Motivated forgetting) M: 393
Psychology (Psychoanalysis) P: 850
Psychotherapy (Psychodynamic-interpersonal psychotherapy) P: 852
Reprieve [law] R: 242
Reprocessing plan
Nuclear energy (Wastes and waste disposal) N: 588-589
Reproduction [biology] R: 242 *with pictures*
See also Reproduction, Human *in this index; and the list of Related articles in the* Reproduction *article*
Alternation of generations A: 388
Animal (How animals reproduce) A: 496 *with pictures*
Bacteria (How bacteria reproduce) B: 21 *with picture*
Bird (The reproductive system) B: 366
Butterfly (The internal organs) B: 739 *with diagram*; (The life cycle of butterflies) B: 739 *with pictures*
Cell (Cell division) Ci: 330 *with diagram*
Estrous cycle E: 363
Evolution (Evolution of new species) E: 429
Fertilization F: 78
Flower (The role of flowers in reproduction) F: 294
Fruit (Developing new fruit cultivars) F: 548
Fungi (How a fungus lives) F: 559
Heredity (Sex cells and reproduction) H: 201
Insect (Reproduction) I: 292
Life (Reproduction) L: 275
Life cycle L: 280
Mammal (How mammals reproduce) M: 122 *with pictures*
Migration (Why animals migrate) M: 539
Plant (The reproduction of plants) P: 532 *with pictures*
Reptile (Reproduction) R: 252
Reproduction, Human R: 244 *with pictures*
See also the list of Related articles in the Reproduction, Human *article*
Baby (The developing baby) B: 4 *with diagrams*
Cancer (Classification by primary body site) C: 167-168
Fertilization F: 78
Human body (table) H: 422 *with diagram*; (The reproductive system) H: 425 *with picture*
In vitro fertilization I: 95
Infertility I: 265
Medical ethics M: 361
Pregnancy P: 734a
Prostaglandin P: 829
Sexuality (Before birth) S: 338
Uterus U: 251
Vagina V: 259
Reproductive Biology Research Foundation
Masters and Johnson M: 297
Reproductive caste [entomology]
Termite (The termite colony) T: 171
Reproductive isolating factor [biology]
Evolution (Evolution of new species) E: 429
Reproductive part [botany]
Plant (Parts of plants) P: 528
Reproductive system *See* Reproduction, Human *in this index*
Reprogramming [biology]
Cloning (Nuclear transfer) Ci: 682l-683
Repsol YPF [company]
Manufacturing (table) M: 170
Reptile [zoology] R: 250 *with pictures*
See also the list of Related articles in the Reptile *article*
Animal (table: Length of life of animals) A: 473; (A table of animal intelligence) A: 493
Brain (Among vertebrates) B: 560 *with diagram*
Carboniferous Period C: 208
Dinosaur D: 206
Evolution (The fossil record) E: 430
Heart (Amphibians and reptiles) H: 146
Prehistoric animal (The Age of Reptiles) P: 737 *with pictures*
Reproduction (How reproduction has evolved) R: 243
Tetrapod T: 182b *with diagram*
Triassic Period T: 439
Reptiles, Age of [geology] *See* Mesozoic Era *in this index*
Repubblica, La [newspaper]
Italy (Communication) I: 512
Repubblica Italiana *See* Italy *in this index*
Republic [political science] R: 253

Democracy D: 119
Government (Democracy) G: 285
Republic [ship]
Radio (Early development) R: 91-92
Republic, Roman *See* Roman Republic *in this index*
Republic, The [book by Plato]
Communism (Early communism) Ci: 890
Plato (The dialogues) P: 567; (Plato's philosophy) P: 568
Republic Day [holiday]
India (Independence and partition) I: 133
Republic of China *See* Taiwan *in this index*
Republic of Cyprus
Cyprus Ci: 1205
Republic of Ireland *See* Ireland *in this index*
Republic of Texas [Texas history]
Houston, Sam H: 399
Texas (The Republic of Texas) T: 206
Republic of the Congo *See* Congo, Republic of the *in this index*
Republic of the Fiji Islands *See* Fiji *in this index*
Republic of Yemen *See* Yemen *in this index*
Republica de Cabo Verde *See* Cape Verde *in this index*
Republican government *See* Republic *in this index*
Republican Guard [military]
Iraq War (Battle in Baghdad) I: 414d
Republican Party [Irish political party] *See* Fianna Fáil *in this index*
Republican Party [U.S. political party] R: 253 *with pictures*
See also the list of Related articles in the Republican Party *article*
Bush, George Herbert Walker (Republican Party chairman) B: 718
Civil War, American (Developments in the political party system) Ci: 616
Congress of the United States (How Congress is organized) Ci: 942
Democratic Party D: 124
Democratic-Republican Party D: 129
Garfield, James Abram (Congressman) G: 41-42
Hamlin, Hannibal H: 33
Medill, Joseph M: 380
Political convention P: 628
Political party (The Republican Party) P: 636
President of the United States (The presidential election) P: 762-763
Reconstruction (The struggle over Reconstruction) R: 178; (The Reconstruction governments) R: 179; (The end of Reconstruction) R: 179
Scalawags S: 169
Republican Party of Minnesota
Minnesota (The mid-1900's) M: 606
Republicanism [government]
Renaissance (The Italian Renaissance) R: 233
Republicans [Spanish history]
Franco, Francisco F: 483
Spain (Civil war) So: 750
Spanish Civil War So: 756 *with picture*
Requiem [music by Fauré]
Fauré, Gabriel Urbain F: 56
Requiem [music by Mozart]
Mozart, Wolfgang Amadeus (Church music) M: 907
"Requiem" [poem by Stevenson]
Stevenson, Robert Louis (The South Seas) So: 897-898
Requiem for a Nun [book by Faulkner]
Faulkner, William F: 55
Requiem Mass [music by Verdi]
Verdi, Giuseppe V: 316
Rerum natura, De [book by Lucretius] *See* On the Nature of Things *in this index*
Rerum Novarum [papal encyclical, 1891]
Christianity (The 1800's) C: 526
Leo XIII L: 198
Resaca de la Palma, Battle of [1846]
Mexican War (Taylor's campaign) M: 446; (Principal battles) M: 447
Resale price maintenance laws *See* Fair-trade laws *in this index*
Resaw [machine]
Lumber *picture on* L: 520
Rescinding Act [1796]
Yazoo Fraud Y: 554
Rescue
Coast Guard, United States (Safety) Ci: 734 *with pictures*
Drowning (Methods of rescue) D: 349
Fire department F: 123 *with pictures*
Helicopter *picture on* H: 170; (For rescue missions) H: 169
Ice skating (Skating safety) I: 10-11
Rescue breathing *See* Artificial respiration *in this index*

Rescue truck
Fire department (Trucks and vehicles) F: 126
with picture
Research
A Guide to Research Skills **Research Guide: 26**
Biological research
Disease (Research) D: 234
Guinea pig G: 434
Rhesus monkey R: 291
Institutions
Battelle Memorial Institute B: 167
Institute for Advanced Study I: 305
National Academy of Sciences N: 27
National Bureau of Economic Research N: 30
National laboratory N: 40
National Research Council N: 60
National Science Foundation N: 60
RAND Corporation R: 136
United Nations University U: 97
Universities and colleges (Research and
laboratory work) U: 210
Research and development
Computer (Research and development) Ci: 924
Drug (Research and development) D: 355
Edison, Thomas Alva (The Wizard of Menlo
Park) E: 78
Electronics (The electronics industry) E: 214
Sources of research
Laboratory L: 16
Library (Research libraries) L: 247
Radar (In scientific research) R: 68
Rocket (Atmospheric research) R: 386
Universities and colleges (Faculty) U: 208
Types of research
Advertising (Research) A: 76a
Anthropology (How anthropologists work)
A: 547
Clinical psychology (Research) Ci: 681
Food (Food research) F: 335
Food supply (Research programs) F: 351 *with
picture*
History (History in the universities) H: 262
Invention (Research laboratories) I: 357 *with
picture*
Manufacturing (How science helps
manufacturing) M: 171
Market research M: 213
Medicine (Medical researchers) M: 369
Motivation research M: 875
Psychology (Methods of psychological
research) P: 847
Public relations (Methods) P: 863
Science (How scientists work) S: 194; (Recent
developments) S: 203
Space exploration (Conducting scientific
observations and research) So: 704
Water (Fresh water from the sea) W: 127
Research Council, National [U.S.]
National Academy of Sciences N: 27
National Research Council N: 60
Research fellow
Universities and colleges (Faculty) U: 208
Research Libraries, Association of
Library (Research libraries) L: 247
Research library
Library (Research libraries) L: 247 *with pictures;*
(Special libraries) L: 250
Research octane number
Gasoline (Octane ratings) G: 61
Octane number O: 669
Research paper
A Guide to Writing Skills **Research Guide: 14**
Research ship
Ocean (Research ships) O: 662
Ocean drilling programs O: 667 *with diagram*
Research Triangle Park [North Carolina]
North Carolina (The mid-1900's) N: 493
Researcher [publishing]
Encyclopedia (Editing the manuscript) E: 267
with picture
Réseau Jean Bernard [cave, France]
Cave (table) C: 320
Reservation See Indian reservation *in this index*
Reserve [banking]
Federal Reserve System (Reserve requirements)
F: 66
Inflation (Monetary policy) I: 268
Reserve [geology]
Coal (Where coal is found) Ci: 721
Reserve [investment]
Auction A: 881
Reserve [military] See Reserves *in this index*
Reserve [park]
Elephant (Protecting elephants) E: 231-232
Lion L: 340
Reserve, Indian See Indian reservation *in this index*
Reserve Mining Company [Minnesota]

Minnesota (The late 1900's) M: 606
Reserve Officers Training Corps [military] R: 258
Military training (Military training for civilians)
M: 544
Reserved powers
Constitution of the United States (The supreme
law of the land) Ci: 998
Reserves [military]
Air Force, United States (Air Force reserves)
A: 194
Army A: 724
Coast Guard, United States (Active-duty and
reserves) Ci: 736
Marine Corps, United States (Reserves) M: 208
Military training (Military training for civilians)
M: 544
Navy, United States (The active-duty Navy and
reserves) N: 85
Reserve Officers Training Corps R: 258
Reservoir [conservation] R: 258
Dam (The effects of dams) D: 17; (Planning) D: 19
Irrigation (Surface water) I: 456
Lake (How lakes are formed) L: 32 *with picture*
Reservoir [industry]
Petroleum (Uses of petroleum) P: 333-334
Reservoir rock
Gas [fuel] (From well to user) G: 52
Resh [letter]
R R: 45 *with picture*
Residence hall
Universities and colleges (Residence) U: 209
Residence of the Elector [Mannheim]
Mannheim M: 165
Residency [law]
Divorce (No-fault divorce) D: 253
Resident [biology]
Killer whale K: 316
Resident [government official]
India (British India) I: 130-131
Resident [medicine]
Hospital (The professional services staff) H: 371
Resident alien [law]
Alien A: 367
Resident bacteria
Disease (Bacterial diseases) D: 227; (Natural
barriers) D: 231
Residential hotel
Hotel (Kinds of hotels) H: 376
Residential school
Canada, History of (The return of the
Conservatives) C: 152
Children's home C: 457
Nunavut (Development of the modern Canadian
north) N: 612
Residential treatment center
Foster care F: 428
Residual fuel oil
Fuel (Petroleum) F: 550
Petroleum (Petroleum as a fuel) P: 332
Residual magnetism
Electric generator (Kinds of DC generators) E: 173
Residual nuclear radiation
Nuclear weapon (Residual nuclear radiation)
N: 599
Resilient floor
Interior design (Choosing patterns and textures)
I: 332
Resin [material] R: 259
Acrylic A: 29
Amber A: 404
Cement and concrete (Air-entrained concrete)
C: 343
Fir F: 119
Furfural F: 566
Ink I: 272
Lacquer L: 22
Paint P: 23
Painting (Synthetic resins) P: 40 *with picture*
Pine P: 468
Plastics (How plastics are made) P: 556 *with
diagrams;* (The invention of Bakelite) P: 559-
560
Rain forest (Asia) R: 126b
Rosin R: 480
Sap (Other saps) S: 121
Tree (Other tree products) T: 412
Varnish (Making varnish) V: 286; (Types of
varnish) V: 286; (Making varnish) V: 286
Resin bead
Antibiotic *diagram on* A: 552
Resist dying [craft]
Clothing (Clothing of Africa) Ci: 698
Resistance [electricity]
Electric circuit (Circuit mathematics) E: 167
Electric current (Conductors and insulators)
E: 168
Electricity (Resistance) E: 193

Electronics (How a circuit works) E: 208-209
Ohm's law O: 706
Thermometer (Resistance thermometers) T: 255
Resistance [medicine]
Antibiotic (Resistance to antibiotics) A: 551;
(History) A: 552
Penicillin (Resistance) P: 241
Stress (How stress affects the body) So: 926-927
Tuberculosis (Treatment of tuberculosis) T: 479
Resistance [warfare]
France (World War II) F: 475
Guerrilla warfare (Types of guerrilla movements)
G: 420
Italy (World War II) I: 517
Maquis M: 189
Underground U: 20
World War II (Resistance groups) W: 494
Resistance heating
Heating (Electric power) H: 159; (Electric radiant
heating) H: 159
Resistance thermometer
Thermometer (Resistance thermometers) T: 255
Resistance welding
Welding (Resistance welding) W: 189
Resistor [electrical component]
Electricity (Controlling electric current) E: 195
Electronics (Passive components) E: 212
Resnik, Judith A. [American astronaut]
Astronaut (A look at the astronauts) A: 831
Challenger disaster C: 370
Space exploration (The Challenger disaster)
So: 725
Resnik, Regina [American singer]
Opera *picture on* O: 792
Resolution
Debate D: 63; (Types of resolutions) D: 64
Resolution [literature]
Drama (The structure of drama) D: 325
Resolution [optics]
Microscope (Optical microscopes) M: 517
Motion picture (The film) M: 857
Telescope (Producing detailed images) T: 102-
103
Type T: 536
Resolution [ship]
Cook, James (Final voyage) Ci: 1026; (Second
Pacific voyage) Ci: 1026
Resolution Trust Corporation [banking]
Bank (The savings and loan crisis) B: 94
Resolving power [optics] See Resolution *in this
index*
Resonance [physics]
Acoustics A: 29
Sound (table) So: 599; (Resonance) So: 603 *with
diagram*
Resonance condition [physics]
Magnetic resonance imaging M: 56
Resonant antenna [device]
Antenna (Types of antennas) A: 543
Resonator [device]
Marimba M: 202
Resonator [physics] See Optical cavity *in this index*
Resorcinol [chemical] R: 259
Resort hotel
Hawaii *picture on* H: 104
Hotel (Kinds of hotels) H: 376 *with picture*
Resource board [government]
Northwest Territories (Government) N: 532-533
Resource center
Library (Variety of information) L: 235; (High
school libraries) L: 245
Resource Conservation and Recovery Act [1976]
Hazardous wastes H: 122
Resources
Economics E: 58
War (Conflicts over resources) W: 23; (Waging
war) W: 24
Resources, Natural See Natural resources *in this
index*
"Respect" [song]
Franklin, Aretha F: 485
Respighi, Ottorino [Italian composer] R: 259
Respiration [biology] R: 260
See also Breathing *in this index*
Animal (Adaptations for breathing) A: 491
Asphyxiation A: 816
Bird (The respiratory system) B: 365
Butterfly (The internal organs) B: 739 *with
diagram*
Cancer (Classification by primary body site)
C: 167-168
Circulatory system (In respiration) Ci: 559 *with
picture*
Cold, Common Ci: 760
Fish (Respiratory system) F: 161
Helium (Uses) H: 176
Human body (The respiratory system) H: 420

with diagram; (table) **H: 422** *with diagram*
Insect (Respiratory system) **I: 289** *with diagram*
Mammal (Internal organ systems) **M: 119-120**
Oxygen (How oxygen supports life) **O: 889**
Photosynthesis **P: 430**
Plant (Respiration) **P: 538**
Respirator **R: 261**
Rib **R: 321**
Spider (Respiratory system) **So: 785** *with diagram*
Respirator [machine] **R: 261**
Intensive care unit **I: 321**
Iron lung **I: 453** *with picture*
Oxygen tent **O: 890**
Poliomyelitis (Treatment of poliomyelitis) **P: 627**
Respiratory center
Respiration (Control of breathing) **R: 261**
Respiratory disease
Air pollution (Health) **A: 199**
Respiratory distress syndrome R: 262
Premature birth **P: 755**
Respiratory system *See* Respiration *in this index*
Respiratory therapist [medicine]
Medicine (Other careers in medicine) **M: 371**
Respiratory unit [anatomy]
Lung *diagram on* **L: 524**
Resplendent quetzal [bird]
Bird (Birds of Central and South America) **B: 344a**
with picture
Respondent
Public opinion poll (Interviewing the sample)
P: 862
Respondent learning
Education (How people learn) **E: 89**
Learning (Classical conditioning) **L: 163**
Response [psychology]
Behavior (Learning) **B: 220**
Learning (Classical conditioning) **L: 163**
Psychology (Behaviorism) **P: 849-850**
Response cost [Psychology]
Behavior (Learning) **B: 220-221**
Response to Sor Filotea de la Cruz [book by Juana
Inés de la Cruz]
Juana Inés de la Cruz **J: 178**
Responsibility
Adolescent (Independence and responsibility)
A: 62
Responsible government [Canadian history]
Baldwin, Robert **B: 40**
Canada, History of (The struggle for responsible
government [1816-1867]) **C: 143**
Confederation of Canada (Lord Durham's Report)
Ci: 933
Responsiveness [biology]
Life (Responsiveness) **L: 275**
Rest [music]
Music (Indicating time values) **M: 953**
Rest [physiology]
See also Relaxation *in this index*
Fatigue **F: 54**
Health (Rest and sleep) **H: 125**
Resta, Dario [American race driver]
Automobile racing (table: Indianapolis 500
winners) **A: 980**
Restaurant R: 262
Automobile (Other infrastructure) **A: 960**
Careers (Tourism and hospitality) **C: 233-234**
with picture
Interior design *picture on* **I: 334**
Restaurant chain
Restaurant (Chains and franchises) **R: 262**
Restauration style
Furniture (The Biedermeier and Restauration
styles) **F: 580** *with picture*
Restigouche River [Quebec-New Brunswick]
New Brunswick (Rivers and lakes) **N: 192**
Resting electrocardiogram [medicine]
Electrocardiograph **E: 199**
Resting energy expenditure [measurement]
Weight control (Energy expenditure) **W: 181**
Resting potential
Nervous system (The beginning of an impulse)
N: 135
Restitution, Edict of [1629]
Thirty Years' War (The Danish period) **T: 260**
Reston [Virginia]
City planning *picture on* **Ci: 601**
Washington, D.C. (Metropolitan area) **W: 80-81**
with map
Restoration [English history] **R: 263**
Charles II [of England] **C: 380**
Cromwell, Richard **Ci: 1152**
England (The Restoration) **E: 309**
English literature (Restoration literature) **E: 318**
Monck, George **M: 701**
Restoration Colonies [U.S. history]
Colonial life in America (English expansion)
Ci: 790

Restoration drama
English literature (Restoration drama) **E: 318**
Restorative dentistry
Dentistry **D: 143**
Restored cereal
Cereal **C: 361**
Restored Government of Virginia [U.S. history]
Pierpont, Francis Harrison **P: 457**
Restraining order [law] **R: 263**
Domestic violence **D: 301**
Restricted use pesticide
Pest control (Effects of pesticide use) **P: 318**
Restriction enzyme
Gene mapping **G: 81**
Genetic engineering (How genes are
reintroduced into cells) **G: 84b** *with diagram*
Genomics **G: 90**
Heredity (The era of genetic engineering) **H: 209**
Restrictive appositive [grammar]
Apposition **A: 575**
Restrictive endorsement
Negotiable instrument (Endorsement) **N: 119**
Restrictive lung disease
Lung (Diseases of the lungs) **L: 524-525**
Resultant force [physics]
Force (Concurrent forces) **F: 370**
Momentum **M: 698**
Résumé [document]
Careers *pictures on* **C: 218**; (Getting a job) **C: 217**
Letter writing (Letters of application) **L: 211**
Resurfacing [industry]
Road (How roads and highways are maintained)
R: 360
Resurgent caldera [geology]
Volcano (Silicic caldera complexes) **V: 442** *with
picture*
Resurrection [religion] **R: 263** *with picture*
Christianity (Sin and salvation) **C: 522g** *with
picture*
Easter **E: 42** *with picture*
Jesus Christ (The Resurrection) **J: 108b** *with
picture*
Mormons (Church doctrines and ordinances)
M: 806-807
Peter, Saint (Life as an apostle) **P: 324**
Religion (Christianity) **R: 222**
Resurrection, The [painting by El Greco]
Resurrection *picture on* **R: 263**
Resurrection, The [painting by Raffaellino]
Christianity *picture on* **C: 522f**
Resurrection Egg, The
Fabergé, Peter Carl *picture on* **F: 2**
Resurrection of Lazarus, The [painting by
Tintoretto]
Tintoretto *picture on* **T: 295**
Resurrection plant R: 264 *with pictures*
Retablo [handicraft]
Latin America (Handicrafts) **L: 102**
Retail Clerks International Union
United Food and Commercial Workers
International Union **U: 47**
Retail nursery [horticulture]
Nursery **N: 614**
Retail, Wholesale and Department Store Union
Labor movement (table) **L: 8**
Retailing [business] **R: 264** *with picture*
Bar coding **B: 102**
Food (Marketing) **F: 335**
Sales (Retail selling) **S: 62**
Trade (The use of markets) **T: 362**
Retained earnings statement
Bookkeeping (Bookkeeping and financial
statements) **B: 473**
Retainer [law] **R: 265**
Retake [cinematography]
Television (Editing) **T: 111**
Retardation *See* Intellectual disability *in this index*
Retarder [mechanism]
Railroad (At classification yards) **R: 110**
Truck (Common features of trucks) **T: 458**
Retching
Vomiting **V: 447**
Rétes [food]
Hungary (Food and drink) **H: 441**
Reticular formation [anatomy]
Brain (The brain stem) **B: 550c**
Reticular tissue [physiology]
Connective tissue **Ci: 972**
Reticulated python
Python (In Europe) **P: 922**
Reptile *picture on* **R: 250**
Reticulum [zoology]
Cattle (Stomach) **C: 307** *with diagram*
Ruminant **R: 519** *with diagram*
Retina [anatomy]
Color (The roles of the eyes and brain) **Ci: 818**
Eye (The retina) **E: 462** *with picture*; (Diseases of

the retina) **E: 467**
Light (Light in medicine) **L: 292**
Macular degeneration **M: 26**
Myopia **M: 971**
Ophthalmology **O: 810**
Wald, George **W: 6**
Retinal detachment [disorder]
Eye (Diseases of the retina) **E: 467**
Laser (Heating) **L: 82-83**
Retinal pigmented epithelium [anatomy]
Eye (Adaptation to light and dark) **E: 464**
Retinene [chemical]
Wald, George **W: 6**
Retinitis pigmentosa [disease]
Blindness (Diseases) **B: 401-402**
Eye (Diseases of the retina) **E: 467**
Retinoblastoma [disease]
Blindness (Diseases) **B: 401-402**
Cancer (Cancer in children) **C: 169**
Eye (Diseases of the retina) **E: 467**
Heredity (table) **H: 204**
Retinol [vitamin] *See* Vitamin A *in this index*
Retinopathy, Diabetic [disorder]
Blindness (Diseases) **B: 401**
Retinopathy of prematurity [disease]
Eye (Diseases of the retina) **E: 467**
Retired Reserve
Marine Corps, United States (Reserves) **M: 208**
Navy, United States (The active-duty Navy and
reserves) **N: 85**
Retired Senior Volunteer Program [U.S.]
Old age (Employment and other activities) **O: 739**
Retirement R: 265
Old age **O: 738**
Retirement Act [1920]
Civil service (History) **Ci: 613**
Retirement age
Baby boom generation (Effects of the baby
boom) **B: 11**
Old age **O: 738**
Retirement **R: 265**
Social security (Benefits) **So: 553**
Retirement community
Old age (Housing) **O: 739**
Retirement **R: 265**
Retirement hotel
Hotel (Kinds of hotels) **H: 376**
Retirement income *See* Pension; Social security
in this index
Retirement pension *See* Pension *in this index*
Retiro, The [park]
Madrid (The city) **M: 38**
Retort method
Food preservation (Canning) **F: 341-342**
Retorting [industrial process]
Oil shale **O: 707** *with diagram*
Retractable landing gear
Airplane (The landing gear) **A: 216-217**
Retreading [process]
Tire (Retreading tires) **T: 297**
Retreating longwall system [mining]
Coal (The longwall system) **Ci: 724-726**
Retribution
Prison (How prisons operate) **P: 806**
Retrieval failure [psychology]
Memory (Retrieval failure) **M: 393**
Retrieval system *See* Information retrieval *in this
index*
Retriever [dog] **R: 266** *with picture*
Dog (Sporting dogs) **D: 268** *with pictures*
Nova Scotia duck tolling retriever **N: 571**
Retro style [design]
Furniture (The retro style) **F: 584**
Retroactive interference [psychology]
Memory (Interference) **M: 393**
Retrograde amnesia [psychology]
Brain (Memory and imagination) **B: 554**
Memory (Memory disorders) **M: 394**
Retrograde motion [astronomy]
Astronomy *diagram on* **A: 847**; (How the planets
move) **A: 835**
Planet (How planets move) **P: 508-509**
Retrovirus [organism] **R: 266**
Rett, Andreas [Austrian physician]
Rett syndrome **R: 266**
Rett syndrome [disorder] **R: 266**
Retting [industrial process]
Flax (Growing and processing fiber flax) **F: 230**
Hemp **H: 183**
Linen (Preparing the fibers) **L: 334-335**
Return [economics] *See* Profit *in this index*l
Return, Law of [Israel]
Citizenship (Naturalization) **Ci: 570**
Immigration (Asia) **I: 85**
Return crease [sports]
Cricket (The field) **Ci: 1131**
Return of Christopher Columbus from the New

World, The [painting by Delacroix]
 Columbus, Christopher *picture on* Ci: 861
Return of the Ambassadors, The [painting by
   Carpaccio]
 World, History of the *picture on* W: 438
Return of the Jedi [film] *See* Star Wars: Episode VI—
   Return of the Jedi *in this index*
Return of the King, The [book by Tolkien]
 Tolkien, J. R. R. T: 321
Return of the Native, The [book by Hardy]
 Hardy, Thomas H: 59
Return of the Prodigal Son, The [painting by
   Rembrandt]
 Painting (The Dutch masters) P: 62-63 *with
   picture*
 Rembrandt (The last years: 1640-1669) R: 229
Return of the Soldier, The [book by West]
 West, Rebecca W: 199
Return of the Sphinx [book by MacLennan]
 MacLennan, Hugh M: 25
Return of Ulysses, The [opera by Monteverdi]
 Monteverdi, Claudio M: 764a
Return stroke [lightning]
 Lightning (Lightning strokes) L: 300
Reuben James [ship]
 Navy, United States (World War II [1939-1945])
   N: 89
Reuchlin, Johannes [German author]
 German literature (The Renaissance) G: 139
Reunion [painting by Guerin]
 Lincoln Memorial L: 328
Réunion [island, Indian Ocean] R: 267
Reusable launch vehicle
 Airplane (Future developments) A: 239
 Space exploration (Plans for the future) So: 727
Reuss, Henry S. [American political leader]
 Peace Corps (History) P: 208
Reuter, Baron de [German journalist] R: 267
 Thomson Reuters T: 265
Reuter, Paul Julius *See* Reuter, Baron de *in this
   index*
Reuters [news agency] *See* Thomson Reuters *in
   this index*
Reuther, Walter Philip [American labor leader]
 Labor movement (Reunification of the AFL and
   the CIO) L: 13 *with picture*
Revaluation [book by Leavis]
 Leavis, F. R. L: 170
Réveillon, Le [custom]
 Christmas (In France) C: 530
Revelation [Roman Catholic Church]
 Roman Catholic Church (Roman Catholic beliefs)
   R: 403
 Vatican Council II (The Constitution of Divine
   Revelation) V: 289
Revelation, Book of [New Testament] R: 267
 Bible (table) B: 281; (Revelation) B: 284
 Four Horsemen of the Apocalypse F: 437 *with
   picture*
 New Testament (Revelation) N: 287
 Patmos P: 195
Revelry [book by Adams]
 Adams, Samuel Hopkins A: 44
Revels, Hiram Rhodes [American political leader]
 R: 267 *with portrait*
Revenge [ship]
 Bonnet, Stede B: 461
 Perry, Oliver Hazard P: 295
"Revenge of Hamish, The" [poem by Lanier]
 Lanier, Sidney L: 68
Revenue [economics]
 Income tax I: 102
 Inland revenue I: 273
 Local government (Financial difficulties) L: 408
 National debt N: 33
 State government (State finances) So: 865
 Taxation T: 52
Revenue Act [1764]
 Revolution, American (The Sugar Act) R: 272
Revenue Act [1971]
 Election campaign (Campaign financing) E: 160
Revenue Cutter Service
 Coast Guard, United States (History) Ci: 737
Revenue stamp
 Stamp So: 829
Revenue tariff
 Tariff (Main kinds of tariffs) T: 43
Reverberation [sound]
 Acoustics A: 29
 Echo E: 50
 Sound (Controlling sound) So: 604-605
Reverberatory furnace
 Smelting S: 515
Revere, Anne [American actress]
 Motion picture (Best performance by an actress
   in a supporting role: 1945) M: 862b
Revere, Paul [American patriot] R: 267 *with pictures*

Boston Massacre *picture on* B: 505
 Dawes, William D: 51
 Lexington and Concord, Battles of (Background)
   L: 224
 Prescott, Samuel P: 757
 Revolution, American *picture on* R: 273;
   (Lexington and Concord) R: 274-275
Révérence [movement]
 Ballet (table) B: 45; (A ballet class) B: 46-47
Reverse bias [electronics]
 Electronics (Diodes) E: 210-211 *with diagram*
Reverse discrimination [sociology]
 Civil rights (Major changes in the field of civil
   rights) Ci: 609-610
Reverse fault [geology]
 Earthquake *diagram on* E: 37; (Tsunamis) E: 34;
   (Convergent boundaries) E: 38
Reverse gear
 Transmission *picture on* T: 377; (The gears) T: 378
   with diagram
Reverse osmosis [chemistry]
 Osmosis (Reverse osmosis) O: 866
 Water (Reverse osmosis) W: 128
Reverse piezoelectric effect [physics]
 Piezoelectricity P: 458
Reverse transcriptase [enzyme]
 AIDS (Treatment) A: 164b
 Heredity (The era of genetic engineering) H: 209
 Retrovirus R: 266
Reverse transcriptase inhibitor [drug]
 AIDS (Treatment) A: 164b
Reversible-pitch propeller
 Propeller (Airplane propellers) P: 826
Reversing Falls of Saint John [falls, New
   Brunswick]
 New Brunswick (Places to visit) N: 188; (Rivers
   and lakes) N: 192
 Saint John (Description) S: 35
Reversing mill [machine]
 Iron and steel (Rolling) I: 445-447
Revia [drug]
 Alcoholism (Treatment) A: 338
Review [law] *See* Judicial review *in this index*
Review, The [magazine]
 Defoe, Daniel (His life) D: 88
Reviewing [journalism]
 Book report B: 469
 Book review B: 470
 Criticism Ci: 1146
 Theater (New York City) T: 244-245
Revised Organic Act of the Virgin Islands [1954]
 Virgin Islands, United States (Government) V: 393
Revised Standard Version [Bible]
 Bible (Modern English translations) B: 286
Revisionists [Chinese history]
 China (The Great Leap Forward) C: 505
Revivalism [religion] R: 269
 Camp meeting C: 90
 Christianity (Growth in the United States) C: 526
 Colonial life in America (Religious diversity and
   tolerance) Ci: 805 *with picture*
 Great Awakening G: 335
 Missionary (History) M: 621
 United States, History of the (Looking backward)
   U: 191 *with picture*
Revocable trust [economics]
 Trust fund (Kinds of trusts) T: 474
Revolt in the Desert [book by Lawrence]
 Lawrence, T. E. L: 146
Revolt of the Angels, The [book by France]
 France, Anatole F: 480
Revolt of the Masses, The [book by Ortega y
   Gasset]
 Ortega y Gasset, José O: 859
Revolution [political science] R: 269
 Communism (Communism in theory) Ci: 890
 Europe (Revolution, democracy, and nationalism)
   E: 412
 Guerrilla warfare (Types of guerrilla movements)
   G: 420
 Lenin, V. I. L: 191
 Marx, Karl M: 236
 Russian literature (Literary revival) R: 563
Revolution, American [1775-1783] R: 270 *with
   pictures and maps*
  *See also the lists of military leaders in the Related
   articles in the Revolution, American article*
 African Americans (Colonial times) A: 136d-136f
   with picture
 American literature (The revolutionary period
   [1765-1787]) A: 415
 Brother Jonathan B: 642
 Cabal C: 3
 Canada, History of (The Quebec Act) C: 141-142
 Dawes, William D: 51
 Declaration of Independence D: 73
 Flag (First United States flags) F: 208 *with pictures*

Galloway, Joseph G: 16
 Gálvez, Bernardo de G: 18
 Gates, Horatio G: 67
 Government (The Enlightenment) G: 290-291
 Guerrilla warfare (History) G: 420
 Henry, Patrick (Career as governor) H: 190
 Indian, American (After European contact)
   I: 156-157
 Indian wars (The new nation) I: 191
 Jay Treaty J: 67
 Lafayette, Marquis de (Service to the United
   States) L: 28
 Lee, Richard Henry L: 176
 Ludington, Sybil L: 515
 Marion, Francis M: 211
 Mazzei, Philip M: 331
 North, Lord N: 457
 Paris, Treaties of (The treaty of 1783) P: 167
 Philadelphia (The Revolutionary War period)
   P: 366
 Prescott, Samuel P: 757
 Revere, Paul R: 267
 Sampson, Deborah S: 81
 Trumbull, John T: 472
 United Empire Loyalists U: 47
 United Kingdom (The Revolutionary War in
   America) U: 67
 War (table) W: 25
 Women's movement (Forces of change) W: 384
 World, History of the (The rise of democracy and
   nationalism) W: 443
 "Yankee Doodle" Y: 552
 Armed forces
  Revolution, American (Progress of the war)
    R: 278; (War losses) R: 287
  Army, United States (The Continental Army)
    A: 737
  Charles III [king of Spain] C: 381
  Espionage (History) E: 358
  Hessians R: 219 *with picture*
  Marine Corps, United States *picture on* M: 207;
    (The early Marine Corps) M: 208
  Militia M: 544
  Minutemen M: 613
  Navy, United States (The earliest colonial
    warships) N: 85-88
  Privateer P: 808b
  Weapon (Firearms) W: 154b
 Background and causes
  Adams, John (In New England) A: 36; (National
    politics) A: 36
  Adams, Samuel (The patriot) A: 44
  Boston Massacre B: 505
  Boston Port Act B: 505
  Boston Tea Party B: 506
  Committees of correspondence Ci: 872
  Committees of safety Ci: 873
  Hancock, John H: 39
  Intolerable Acts I: 353
  Jefferson, Thomas (Colonial statesman) J: 79
  Paine, Thomas (American revolutionary) P: 22
 Diplomacy
  Revolution, American (The campaign in New
    York) R: 281
  Adams, John (Diplomat) A: 36
  Franklin, Benjamin (The statesman) F: 490
  State, Department of (Establishment) So: 860
 Military campaigns
  Revolution, American (The beginning of the
    war) R: 274 *with pictures and maps*; (The war
    in the North) R: 281 *with pictures and map*;
    (The war in the West) R: 283 *with pictures*;
    (The war in the South) R: 284 *with pictures*;
    (Surrender at Yorktown) R: 286
  Bunker Hill, Battle of B: 700
  Camden, Battle of C: 76
  Fort Ticonderoga F: 416
  Lexington and Concord, Battles of L: 224
  Montreal (British settlement) M: 777
  Princeton University (Campus buildings) P: 795
  Saratoga, Battle of S: 123
  Trenton, Battle of T: 435
  United States, History of the (The movement
    for independence [1754-1783]) U: 158 *with
    picture*
  Valley Forge V: 266 *with picture*
  Westward movement in America (The
    Revolutionary War) W: 246
  Wyoming Valley Massacre W: 538
  Yorktown, Siege of Y: 569
 The colonies and the war
  Revolution, American (Background and causes
    of the revolution) R: 271
  Connecticut (The Revolutionary War) Ci: 970
  Georgia (The Revolutionary War) G: 132
  Massachusetts (The Revolutionary War) M: 291
  New Hampshire (The Revolutionary War in

America) N: 226
New Jersey (The American Revolution) N: 250
New York (The Revolutionary War) N: 315
North Carolina (Revolution and independence)
  N: 492
Pennsylvania (The Revolutionary War) P: 265
Rhode Island (The Revolutionary War) R: 313
South Carolina (The Revolutionary War)
  So: 659-660
United States, History of the (The movement
  for independence [1754-1783]) U: 158
Virginia (Independence and statehood) V: 420;
  (The course toward independence) V: 420
Revolution, French See French Revolution in this
index
Revolution, Russian See Russian Revolution of
1917 in this index
Revolution of 1830 [French history] See July
Revolution in this index
Revolution of 1848 [European history] R: 288
Austria (Metternich and revolution) A: 938
France (The revolutions of 1830 and 1848) F: 474
Germany (The Revolution of 1848) G: 165
Italy (Italy united) I: 515
Revolution of 1905 [Russian history]
Duma (The early Duma) D: 381
Lenin, V. I. (Revolt) L: 192-193
Russia (The Revolution of 1905) R: 552
Revolution of rising expectations
Revolution (Causes of revolution) R: 269
Revolutionary Alliance [Chinese history]
China (The fall of the Manchus) C: 503
Revolutionary Armed Forces of Colombia
Colombia (Civil war) Ci: 784
Revolutionary Command Council [Egypt]
Egypt (Republic) E: 132
Revolutionary Command Council [Libya]
Libya (Independence) L: 267-268
**Revolutionary Front for an Independent East
Timor**
East Timor (History) E: 41
Revolutionary Guards [military]
Iran (National government) I: 399
Revolutionary United Front [military group]
Sierra Leone (History) S: 452
Revolutionary war
War W: 23
Revolutionary War in America See Revolution,
American in this index
Revolutions per minute [measurement]
Tachometer T: 4
Revolver [gun]
Handgun (Types of handguns) H: 43
Weapon (Firearms) W: 154b
Revolving stage
Theater (Changing scenery) T: 240
Reward [psychology]
Aggression A: 141
Behavior (Learning) B: 220-221
Child (Motivating the child's behavior) C: 451
Habit (How we learn habits) H: 2
Learning (Motivation) L: 164
Motivation research M: 875
Rewards and Fairies [book by Kipling]
Puck P: 870
Rewritable DVD [electronics]
DVD D: 393
Rex cat
Cat picture on C: 288; (Short-haired breeds)
  C: 290-291
Rexford, Bill [American race driver]
Automobile racing (table: NASCAR Sprint Cup
  champions) A: 981
Reye, R. D. K. [Australian pathologist]
Reye's syndrome R: 288
Reyes, Neftalí [birth name of]
Neruda, Pablo N: 131
Reye's syndrome [disease] R: 288
Aspirin A: 816
Chickenpox C: 446
Reykjavík [Iceland] R: 288 with picture
Iceland (The lowlands) I: 22 with picture
Reymont, Władysław [Polish author]
Nobel Prizes (Literature: 1924) N: 447
Poland (The arts) P: 607-608
Reynaud, Paul [French political leader]
World War II (The fall of France) W: 475
Reynolds, Albert [Irish political leader]
Ireland (table) I: 428
Reynolds, John [American political leader]
Illinois (table) I: 71
Reynolds, John W. [American political leader]
Wisconsin (table) W: 365; (Decline of LaFollette
  Progressivism) W: 368
Reynolds, Sir Joshua [British painter] R: 289 with
picture
Boswell, James picture on B: 506

Reynolds, Robert J. [American political leader]
Delaware (table) D: 109
Reynolds, Thomas [American political leader]
Missouri (table) M: 668
Reynolds v. Sims [U.S. history]
Gerrymander G: 174
Supreme Court of the United States (Election
  issues) So: 1001; (table) So: 1002
Reza Khan [birth name of]
Reza Shah Pahlavi R: 289
Reza Shah Pahlavi [shah of Iran] R: 289
Iran I: 398; (World War I and Reza Shah) I: 406;
  (The nationalist movement) I: 406
Mohammad Reza Pahlavi M: 687
R.F.D. [mail] See Rural delivery in this index
RFE/RL [radio] See Radio Free Europe/Radio Liberty
in this index
Rh [symbol]
Rhodium R: 318
Rh factor [physiology] R: 289
Blood (Rh blood types) B: 413
Ear (Birth defects) E: 11
Rhabdomyolysis [disorder]
Statin So: 267
Rhabdomyosarcoma [disease]
Cancer (Cancer in children) C: 169
Rhabdovirus [virus]
Rabies (Cause) R: 49
Rhaeto-Romanic dialect
Romance languages R: 415
Rhamphorhynchoid [extinct animal]
Pterosaur P: 853 with picture
Rhapsody [music]
Classical music (Free form) Ci: 645
Liszt, Franz (His works) L: 350
Rhapsody in Blue [music by Gershwin]
Gershwin, George G: 174
Grofé, Ferde G: 397
Rhazes [Persian physician]
Medicine (During the Middle Ages) M: 373
RHC [business] See Regional holding company in
this index
Rhea [bird] R: 290 with picture
Rhea [Greek mythology] R: 290
Cronus Ci: 1152
Mythology (The Greek creation myth) M: 980-
  981; (table) M: 981
Titans T: 300
Rhea [satellite]
Saturn (Satellites) S: 151-153
Rhea Silvia [legendary figure]
Romulus and Remus R: 450a
Rhee, Syngman [Korean political leader] R: 290
Korea, South (History) K: 378c
Rheims [France] See Reims in this index
Rhein-Main Air Force Base
Frankfurt F: 485
Rheingold, Das [opera by Wagner]
Opera: (Ring of the Nibelung, The) O: 806-807
Rheinische Zeitung [newspaper]
Marx, Karl (Marx's life) M: 236
Rheita, Anton M. S. de [Italian astronomer]
Moon (Early observations with telescopes)
  M: 792
Rhenium [element] R: 290
Rhesus mcaque See Rhesus monkey in this index
Rhesus monkey R: 291 with picture
Macaque M: 2
Monkey picture on M: 729; (Communication)
  M: 729 with picture
Rh factor R: 289
Rhetoric [language]
Greek literature (Philosophical literature) G: 377-
  378
Latin literature (Characteristics of Latin literature)
  L: 115
Liberal arts L: 226
Oratory O: 818
Rome, Ancient (Education) R: 442
Shakespeare, William (Rhetoric) S: 368
Rhetorica ad Herennium [book]
Oratory (Classical orators) O: 819
Rhetorical criticism
Criticism (Kinds of literary criticism) Ci: 1146
Rheumatic disease
Rheumatology R: 291
Rheumatic fever [disease] R: 291
Chorea C: 522
Heart (Valve disease) H: 141
Scarlet fever (Complications) S: 173
Rheumatic heart disease
Heart (Valve disease) H: 141
Rheumatic fever R: 291
Rheumatism R: 291
Rheumatic fever R: 291
Rheumatoid arthritis
Arthritis (Rheumatoid arthritis) A: 752 with

diagram
Disease (Diseases associated with aging) D: 230
Rheumatologist [occupation]
Rheumatology R: 291
Rheumatology [medicine] R: 291
Rhine, Confederation of the [German history]
Napoleon I (Dominates Europe) N: 15
Rhine Gold, The [Wagner] See Rheingold, Das in
this index
Rhine-Main-Danube Canal [Germany] See Main-
Danube Canal in this index
Rhine River [Europe] R: 292 with pictures and map
Danube River D: 34
France (The land) F: 464 with map
Germany picture on G: 144; (The land) G: 156
Netherlands (The Polders) N: 144 with map
River (table) R: 352
Wine (Where wine comes from) W: 336-337
Rhineland [region, Europe] R: 293
Hitler, Adolf (The road to war) H: 267
Locarno Conference L: 409
Rhine River (The Rhine in history) R: 293
World War II (Allies) W: 470-472
Rhineland Security Pact [1925]
France (Between World Wars) F: 475
Locarno Conference L: 409
Rhinitis [disorder] R: 293
Allergy A: 373
Rhinoceros [animal] R: 293 with pictures
Animal picture on A: 477
Endangered species (table) E: 270
Mammal picture on M: 117
Rhinoceros [play by Ionesco]
Ionesco, Eugène I: 372
Rhinoceros beetle
Beetle picture on B: 218
Rhinoceros hornbill [bird]
Bird (Birds of Asia) B: 344f with picture
Rhinoplasty [operation]
Plastic surgery (Cosmetic surgery) P: 553
Rhinovirus [virus]
Cold, Common C: 760
Rhizobium [bacteria]
Gall G: 13
Legume L: 185
Rhizoid [botany]
Fungi (Parts of a fungus) F: 558-559 with diagram
Hornwort H: 341
Liverwort L: 395
Mold M: 690
Moss (The structure of mosses) M: 834
Plant (Nonvascular plants) P: 518
Rhizome [botany] R: 295
Fern (Kinds of ferns) F: 75
Grass (The grass plant) G: 324
Larkspur L: 77
Licorice L: 270
Rhizomorph [botany]
Mushroom (Parts of a mushroom) M: 942 with
picture
Rho [letter]
R R: 45 with picture
Rhode Island R: 296 with pictures and maps
See also the list of Related articles in the Rhode
  Island article
Colonial life in America (Development of the
  Thirteen Colonies) Ci: 790 with map
Dorr Rebellion D: 311
Narragansett Indians N: 21
Williams, Roger (In Rhode Island) W: 311
Rhode Island, University of R: 316
Rhode Island (A changing economy) R: 315 with
picture
**Rhode Island and Providence Plantations,
Charter of** [1663]
Rhode Island (Settlement) R: 312
Rhode Island Flag [U.S. history]
Flag picture on F: 210
Rhode Island Gazette [newspaper]
Rhode Island (Communication) R: 310
Rhode Island Red [chicken] R: 316
Chicken picture on C: 442; (table) C: 443
Rhode Island (Interesting facts) R: 297 with
picture
Rhode Island School of Design
Providence (Description) P: 839
Rhode Island White [chicken]
Chicken (table) C: 443
Rhodes [island, Aegean Sea] R: 316
Knights Hospitallers K: 351
Rhodes, Cecil John [British colonial leader] R: 317
with portrait
Rhodes Scholarship R: 317
South Africa (Discovery of diamonds and gold)
  So: 618
Zambia (History) Z: 585
Zimbabwe (History) Z: 592-593

Rhodes, Colossus of [ancient Greece]
Rhodes R: 317
Seven Wonders of the Ancient World *picture on* S: 327; (The Colossus of Rhodes) S: 325
Rhodes, Edgar N. [Canadian political leader]
Nova Scotia (table) N: 567
Rhodes, James A. [American political leader]
Ohio (table) O: 699
Rhodes, Knights of [religious and military order]
See Knights Hospitallers *in this index*
Rhodes, W. L. [American cowboy]
Western frontier life in America (The cattle drive) W: 237
Rhodes Scholarship R: 317
Oxford, University of (Educational program) O: 887
Scholarship (International scholarships) S: 179
Rhodes Trust
Foundation (table) F: 430
Rhodesia [African history]
Rhodes, Cecil John (Gains Rhodesia) R: 317
United Kingdom (Decline of the empire) U: 71
Zambia (History) Z: 585
Zimbabwe (History) Z: 592-593
Rhodesia and Nyasaland, Federation of [British history]
Zambia (History) Z: 585-586
Zimbabwe (History) Z: 592-593
Rhodesian ridgeback [dog] R: 317 *with picture*
Dog *picture on* D: 270
Rhodium [element] R: 318
Rhododendron [plant] R: 318 *with pictures*
Rhodope Mountains
Bulgaria (The land) B: 691 *with map*
Rhodopsin [anatomy]
Eye (The retina) E: 462; (Adaptation to light and dark) E: 464
"Rhodora, The" [poem by Emerson]
Emerson, Ralph Waldo (His poetry) E: 259
Rhombohedral system [chemistry]
Calcite C: 20
Crystal (Classifying crystals) Ci: 1166-1167 *with picture*
Rhombus [geometry] R: 318 *with diagram*
Geometry (Euclidean geometry) G: 104
Rhône glacier [Switzerland]
Rhône River R: 318
Rhône River [Switzerland-France] R: 318 *with map*
Lake Geneva L: 38
Lyon L: 536 *with picture*
River R: 351 *with picture*
Rhubarb [plant] R: 319 *with picture*
Rhuddlan, Statute of [English history]
Wales (Revolts against England) W: 12
Rhumb line [navigation]
Great-circle route G: 338
Rhumba [dance] See Rumba *in this index*
Rhyme [poetry] R: 319
Slang (Rhyming slang) S: 500
Rhyme scheme
Poetry (Sounds) P: 594; (table) P: 594
Rhyniophyte [plant]
Plant (The evolution of plants) P: 544
Rhyolite [rock]
Granite G: 311
Rhythm R: 319
Design (Rhythm and movement) D: 157 *with picture*
Jazz J: 68
Music (Rhythm) M: 951
Poetry (Rhythm and meter) P: 591
Rhythm [birth control]
Birth control (Methods of birth control) B: 378-379
Rhythm and blues [music] R: 320
Popular music (Other new styles of popular music) P: 671
Rock music (Beginnings of rock music) R: 376
Rhythm band [music] R: 320
Rhythm section [music]
Jazz (The sound of jazz) J: 68 *with picture*
Rhythmic gymnastics [sport]
Gymnastics *picture on* G: 450; (Rhythmic gymnastics) G: 449; (Judging) G: 450
Olympic Games (Summer Olympic Games) O: 746e-747
Rhytidectomy [surgery]
Plastic surgery (Cosmetic surgery) P: 553
Rial [money] R: 320
Rib [anatomy] R: 320 *with diagram*
Diaphragm D: 184 *with diagram*
Human body (table) H: 422 *with diagram*
Skeleton (The axial skeleton) S: 479-480 *with diagrams*
Rib [mining]
Coal (The room-and-pillar system) Ci: 723
Rib grass [plant]

Plantain P: 550
Rib stitch
Knitting (Knitting the fabric) K: 354
Ribaut, Jean [French colonial leader] R: 321
United States, History of the *picture on* U: 150
Ribbed smoke sheet [rubber]
Rubber (Processing crude rubber) R: 503
Ribbed vault [architecture]
Architecture (Gothic architecture) A: 618-619 *with picture*
Gothic art (Early Gothic architecture) G: 278
Vault V: 291
Ribbentrop, Joachim von [Nazi official] R: 321
Nuremberg Trials (The trials) N: 613
Stalin, Joseph *picture on* So: 827
World War II *picture on* W: 497
Ribbon
Typewriter (How a typewriter works) T: 538
Ribbon cable [electronics]
Cable (Cable construction) C: 4 *with diagram*
Ribbon Falls [falls, California] R: 321
California (Rivers, waterfalls, and lakes) C: 50-51
Waterfall (table: Famous waterfalls of North America) W: 142 *with picture*
Ribbon lightning
Lightning (Appearance) L: 300
Ribbon microphone
Microphone (Ribbon microphones) M: 517
Ribbon snake [reptile]
Garter snake G: 46
Ribbon worm R: 321
Animal (A classification of the animal kingdom) A: 506 *with picture*
Worm (Ribbon worms) W: 501 *with pictures*
Ribera, Jusepe de [Spanish painter] R: 321
Painting (The Spanish masters) P: 64
Ribicoff, Abraham A. [American political leader] R: 321
Connecticut (table) Ci: 967
Kennedy, John Fitzgerald (table) K: 266
Ribnica [former name]
Podgorica P: 588
Riboflavin [vitamin]
Nutrition (Vitamins) N: 626
Vitamin (Riboflavin) V: 431; (table) V: 431
Ribonuclease [enzyme]
Enzyme E: 341
Ribonucleic acid See RNA *in this index*
Ribose [sugar]
Cell (RNA—the master copy) C: 335-336 *with diagram*
RNA R: 357
Ribosomal RNA [biochemistry]
RNA R: 357
Ribosome [biology]
Cell (table) C: 327; (The cytoplasm) C: 329 *with diagrams*
Heredity (How proteins are made) H: 206-208
RNA R: 357
Ricardo, David [British economist] R: 321
Economics (The classical economists) E: 64
Marx, Karl (Early development) M: 237
Riccio, David [Italian musician]
Mary, Queen of Scotts (Her reign) M: 239
Riccioli, Giovanni Battista [Italian astronomer]
Moon (Early observations with telescopes) M: 792
Rice R: 322 *with pictures*
Arkansas *picture on* A: 695
Asia *pictures on* A: 784, A: 800
Food supply (Making farmland more productive) F: 349
Grain G: 301
Grass (Cereals) G: 326
India *picture on* I: 126
Indonesia (Food and drink) I: 229; (Agriculture) I: 235 *with picture*
Korea, North *picture on* K: 372
Korea, South *picture on* K: 378a
Malaysia (Agriculture) M: 100 *with picture*
Philippines (Agriculture) P: 378 *with picture*
Sushi So: 1012
Vietnam V: 364 *with picture*; (Economy) V: 369
Wild rice W: 301
Rice, Alexander H. [American political leader]
Massachusetts (table) M: 288
Rice, Buddy [American race driver]
Automobile racing (table: Indianapolis 500 winners) A: 980
Rice, Condoleezza [American government official] R: 327 *with portrait*
African Americans *picture on* A: 136s
Rice, Elmer [American dramatist] R: 328
American literature (Drama) A: 422-423
Rice, Grantland [American journalist] R: 328
Rice, Jerry [American football player] R: 328
Rice, Jim [American baseball player]

Baseball (table: Hall of Fame) B: 134a
Rice, Sam [American baseball player]
Baseball (table: Hall of Fame) B: 134a
Rice, Susan E. [American diplomat]
United Nations (table) U: 86
Rice, Tim [British lyricist]
Lloyd Webber, Andrew L: 403
Rice popcorn
Corn (Popcorn) Ci: 1059
Rice weevil [insect]
Grain weevil G: 302
Weevil W: 180
Ricebird See Bobolink *in this index*
Ricercare [music]
Classical music (Instrumental music) Ci: 646
Rich, Adrienne [American poet] R: 328
American literature (Diverse voices) A: 424
Rich, John T. [American political leader]
Michigan (table) M: 507
Rich, Robert [English colonial official]
Van Dyck, Sir Anthony *picture on* V: 281
Richard I [king of England] R: 328 *with portrait*
Crusades (The Third Crusade) Ci: 1160 *with map*
England (Magna Carta) E: 306
Flag *picture on* F: 216
Henry VI [of Germany] H: 187
Philip II [king of France] P: 369
Richard II [king of England] R: 328 *with portrait*
Wat Tyler's Rebellion W: 113
Richard II [play by Shakespeare]
Shakespeare, William: (*Richard II*) S: 357; (Imagery) S: 368
Richard III [king of England] R: 329 *with portrait*
Heraldry (Heraldry today) H: 196
Richard III [play by Shakespeare]
Olivier, Laurence O: 744
Shakespeare, William: (*Richard III*) S: 356; (Rhetoric) S: 368
Richard, Duke of Gloucester [former name] See Richard III *in this index*
Richard, Duke of York [English noble, 1411-1460]
York Y: 568
Richard, Duke of York [English noble, 1473-?]
Richard III R: 329
Tower of London T: 351
Richard, Sir Edward [Bermudian political leader]
Bermuda (History) B: 268-269
Richard, Eugene C. [American engineer]
Buick, David Dunbar B: 681
Richard, Henri [Canadian hockey player]
Richard, Maurice R: 329
Richard, Maurice [Canadian hockey player] R: 329
Richard Coeur de Lion See Richard I *in this index*
"Richard Corey" [poem by Robinson]
Robinson, Edwin Arlington R: 368
Richard J. Daley Plaza
Chicago (Places to visit) C: 430-431 *with picture*
Richard Nixon Library and Birthplace [Yorba Linda]
Nixon, Richard Milhous (Later years) N: 437
Richard the Lion-Hearted [king of England] See Richard I *in this index*
Richards, Ann [American political leader]
Bush, George Walker (Governor of Texas) B: 722e
Texas (table) T: 203
Richards, Charles D. [Canadian political leader]
New Brunswick (table) N: 195
Richards, DeForest [American political leader]
Wyoming (table) W: 532
Richards, Dickinson Woodruff [American physician]
Nobel Prizes (Physiology or medicine: 1956) N: 446
Richards, Ellen [American chemist]
Family and consumer sciences (History) F: 26
Richards, Sir Gordon [British jockey]
Horse racing (History) H: 366
Richards, I. A. [British author] R: 329
Richards, Keith [British musician]
Rock music (The Rolling Stones) R: 380
Rolling Stones R: 402a
Richards, Theodore William [American chemist]
Nobel Prizes (Chemistry: 1914) N: 443
Richards, William A. [American political leader]
Wyoming (table) W: 532
Richards, Sir William Buell [Canadian jurist] R: 329
Richardson, Bill [American government official] R: 330
Clinton, Bill (Domestic events) Ci: 682f
Hispanic Americans (Political gains) H: 256 *with picture*
New Mexico (table) N: 272
United Nations (table) U: 86
Richardson, Elliot Lee [American government official] R: 330
Watergate (The tape controversy) W: 144
Richardson, Friend William [American political

leader]
California (table) **C:** 59
Richardson, Henry Hobson [American architect]
R: 330 with picture
Architecture (Early modern architecture in
America) **A:** 629
Richardson, J. P. [American singer]
Rock music (Setbacks) **R:** 379
Richardson, John [Canadian author]
Canadian literature picture on **C:** 159; (Early
English-Canadian literature) **C:** 157
Richardson, Sir Owen Willans [British physicist]
Nobel Prizes (Physics: 1928) **N:** 440
Richardson, Robert Coleman [American physicist]
Nobel Prizes (Physics: 1996) **N:** 442
Richardson, Samuel [English author] **R:** 330
English literature (The rise of the novel) **E:** 318-
319
Novel (The first English novelists) **N:** 572
Richardson, Tony [British director]
Motion picture (Best achievement in directing:
1963) **M:** 862
Richardson, William Blaine [American
government official] See Richardson, Bill in this
index
Richardsonian Romanesque [architecture]
Richardson, Henry Hobson **R:** 330 with picture
Richelieu [play by Bulwer-Lytton]
Bulwer-Lytton, Edward George Earle Lytton
B: 698
Richelieu, Cardinal [French statesman] **R:** 331
Diplomacy (History) **D:** 217
France (The age of absolutism) **F:** 473
Louis XIII **L:** 474
Marie de Médicis **M:** 200
Thirty Years' War (The Swedish-French period)
T: 260
Richelieu, Duc de [French political leader]
Aix-la-Chapelle, Congress of **A:** 253
Richelieu River [Canada]
Quebec (Rivers, waterfalls, and lakes) **Q:** 24
Richet, Charles Robert [French physiologist]
Nobel Prizes (Physiology or medicine: 1913)
N: 445
Richler, Mordecai [Canadian author] **R:** 331
Richmond [former name] See Staten Island in this
index
Richmond [Virginia] **R:** 332 with pictures
Virginia picture on **V:** 399; (The Civil War and
Reconstruction) **V:** 421 with picture
Richmond, Mary E. [American social worker]
Social work (History) **So:** 559
Richmond National Battlefield Park [Virginia]
National Park System (table: National battlefields)
N: 55
Richmond Professional Institute [former name]
Virginia Commonwealth University **V:** 424
Richmond-San Rafael Bridge
California (Transportation) **C:** 58
Richmond Town [New York City] **R:** 333
Richter, Burton [American physicist]
Nobel Prizes (Physics: 1976) **N:** 441
Physics (Advances in the mid-1900's) **P:** 442
Richter, Charles F. [American seismologist]
Earthquake (The Richter scale) **E:** 38-38b
Moment magnitude **M:** 697
Richter magnitude **R:** 334
Richter, Conrad [American author] **R:** 333
Richter, Gerhard [German artist]
Painting (Recent painting) **P:** 87-88
Richter, Hieronymus Theodor [German chemist]
Indium **I:** 224
Richter magnitude [measurement] **R:** 334
Earthquake (Measuring earthquakes) **E:** 38a
Moment magnitude **M:** 697
Richter scale See Richter magnitude in this index
Richthofen, Baron Manfred von [German aviator]
R: 334
Ace **A:** 24
World War I (The war in the air) **W:** 460-461
Ricin [poison]
Castor oil **C:** 282
Rickard, George L. (Tex) [American businessman]
Boxing (Boxing's Golden Age) **B:** 532
Rickards, John E. [American political leader]
Montana (table) **M:** 757
Rickenbacker, Eddie [American aviator] **R:** 334
Ace **A:** 24
Air Force, United States (World War I) **A:** 194-195
Rickets [disease] **R:** 334 with picture
Bone (Bone disorders) **B:** 457
Nutrition (Deficiency diseases) **N:** 630-631
Ricketts, Howard Taylor [American pathologist]
Rickettsia **R:** 335
Rickett's circus
Circus (History) **Ci:** 562b
Rickettsia [microorganism] **R:** 335

Psittacosis **P:** 844
Rocky Mountain spotted fever **R:** 394
Typhus **T:** 540
Rickey, Branch [American baseball manager]
R: 335
Baseball (table: Hall of Fame) **B:** 134b
Rickover, Hyman George [American admiral]
R: 335
Carter, Jimmy (Naval career) **C:** 253
"Ricky Ricotta" series [books by Pilkey]
Pilkey, Dav **P:** 464
RICO [law] See Racketeer Influenced and Corrupt
Organizations Act in this index
Riddarholm Church [Sweden]
Stockholm picture on **So:** 905
Riddell, R. G. [Canadian diplomat]
United Nations (table) **U:** 86
Riddle [humor] **R:** 335
Nursery rhyme (Rhyming riddles) **N:** 615
Riddle of the Sphinx [Greek mythology]
Sphinx (The Greek sphinx) **So:** 781
Riddle of the Universe, The [book by Haeckel]
Haeckel, Ernst Heinrich **H:** 5
Riddleberger Act [1882]
Virginia (The Civil War and Reconstruction)
V: 421-422
Ride [sports]
Wrestling picture on **W:** 506
Ride, Sally Kristen [American astronaut] **R:** 335
with portrait
Astronaut (Achievements in space) **A:** 829; (table)
A: 830
Space exploration picture on **So:** 724
Ride to the Vistula [drawing by Kiefer]
Kiefer, Anselm picture on **K:** 313
Rideau Canal [waterway, Ontario] **R:** 336
Ottawa River **O:** 875
Rideau Falls [Ontario]
Ottawa (Metropolitan Ottawa) **O:** 871
Rideau Hall
Ottawa (Rideau Hall) **O:** 872
Rideau River [Ontario]
Ottawa (Metropolitan Ottawa) **O:** 871
Rider [insurance]
Insurance (Riders) **I:** 311
Riders of the Purple Sage [book by Grey]
Grey, Zane **G:** 391
Riders to the Sea [play by Synge]
Irish literature (The Irish literary revival) **I:** 431
Synge, John Millington **So:** 1068
Ridge, John Rollin [American author]
Murieta, Joaquín **M:** 930
Ridge, Mid-ocean See Mid-ocean ridge in this index
Ridge, Tom [American government official] **R:** 336
Bush, George Walker (Homeland security)
B: 722g
Homeland Security, Department of (History)
H: 301; (table) **H:** 301
Pennsylvania (table) **P:** 263
Ridge-and-Valley Province [region]
Appalachian Mountains (Physical features) **A:** 568
Ridge and Valley Region
United States (The Appalachian Highlands)
U: 120-121
Ridge beam [building construction]
House (The roof) **H:** 382
Ridge-nosed rattlesnake
Rattlesnake **R:** 149 with picture
Ridge-push [geology]
Plate tectonics (Causes of plate movement)
P: 564
Ridgeboard [construction]
House (The roof) **H:** 382 with diagram
Ridgely, Charles Carnan [American political
leader]
Maryland (table) **M:** 255
Ridgway, Matthew Bunker [American general]
R: 336
Korean War (The Allies retreat) **K:** 382; (The
"Battle for the Hills") **K:** 382; (The truce talks)
K: 382
Riding, Horseback See Horseback riding in this
index
Riding crop [instrument]
Horse (The whip) **H:** 351
Riding equipment
Horse (Riding equipment) **H:** 351 with pictures
Riding Mountain National Park [Manitoba]
Canada (table: National parks and national park
reserves) **C:** 113
Riding to hounds [sport] See Fox hunting in this
index
Ridley, Nicholas [English religious leader] **R:** 336
Ridley sea turtle See Kemp's ridley sea turtle in
this index
Riel, Louis [Canadian rebel] **R:** 336 with portrait
Canada, History of (Growth of the Dominion

[1868-1913]) **C:** 144
Dumont, Gabriel **D:** 383
Macdonald, Sir John Alexander picture on **M:** 9;
(Threats to Canadian unity) **M:** 10
Manitoba (The Red River Rebellion) **M:** 160-162
North West Rebellion **N:** 520
Quebec (Early years as a province) **Q:** 30
Red River Rebellion (The revolt) **R:** 189
Saskatchewan picture on **S:** 145
Riel House [Manitoba]
Canada (table: National historic sites) **C:** 115
Riel Rebellions See North West Rebellion; Red
River Rebellion in this index
Riemann, Georg Friedrich Bernhard [German
mathematician] **R:** 337
Geometry (Non-Euclidean geometry) **G:** 105;
(Rise of non-Euclidean geometry) **G:** 106
Mathematics (In the 1800's) **M:** 307
Topology (History) **T:** 333
Riemannian geometry
Geometry (Non-Euclidean geometry) **G:** 105
Riemann, Georg Friedrich Bernhard **R:** 337
Riemenschneider, Tilman [German sculptor]
R: 337 with picture
Germany (Painting and sculpture) **G:** 155 with
picture
Rienzi [opera by Wagner]
Wagner, Richard (Early career) **W:** 3
Rienzi, Cola di [Italian political leader] See Cola di
Rienzo in this index
Riess, Adam G. [American physicist]
Nobel Prizes (Physics: 2011) **N:** 442
Rietveld, Gerrit [Dutch architect]
Furniture (De Stijl) **F:** 582 with picture
Rif [mountains]
Morocco (Land regions) **M:** 813
Rifampin [drug]
Antibiotic (table) **A:** 551
Leprosy (Treatment) **L:** 205
Riffle box [tool]
Mining (Placer mining) **M:** 575
Rifle R: 338 with pictures
See also the list of Related articles in the Rifle article
Ballistics (Interior ballistics) **B:** 56
Civil War, American (The enlisted men) **Ci:** 619-
620 with picture
Firearm (History) **F:** 133 with picture
Hunting (Kinds of hunting) **H:** 450
Revolution, American (Weapons and tactics)
R: 279 with picture
Weapon (Firearms) **W:** 154b
Rifling [gun]
Artillery (Parts of an artillery weapon) **A:** 762;
(Rifling) **A:** 763
Gun **G:** 440
Rifle (How a rifle works) **R:** 338; (History) **R:** 339
Rift Valley See Great Rift Valley in this index
Rift valley [geography]
Valley (How valleys are formed) **V:** 266
Rifting [geology]
Mountain (Fault-block mountains) **M:** 893
Plate tectonics (Plate interactions) **P:** 561
Rig [derrick]
Petroleum (Preparatory measures) **P:** 337-338
with diagram
Rig [ship part]
Boating (Sailboats) **B:** 429
Ship (History) **S:** 414
Rig-Veda [religious book] See Rigveda in this index
Riga [Latvia] **R:** 340
Latvia **L:** 118 with pictures and map
Riga, Gulf of
Estonia (Land and climate) **E:** 361 with map
Riga, Treaty of [1921]
Curzon Line **Ci:** 1199
Poland (World War I and independence) **P:** 612
Rigali, Justin [American religious leader]
Cardinal (table: American cardinals) **C:** 211
Rigel [star]
Orion **O:** 856
Star (Brightness of stars) **So:** 840; (table: The 10
brightest stars as seen from Earth) **So:** 842 with
picture; (Characteristics of stars) **So:** 842-843
with picture
Rigger [artist]
Animation (Making the model move) **A:** 513
Rigging
Sailing (Rigging) **S:** 24
Ship (Sailing ships) **S:** 406
Rigging department [cinematography]
Animation (Making the model move) **A:** 513
Riggs, Bobby [American tennis player]
King, Billie Jean **K:** 320
Tennis (Tennis today) **T:** 166d-166e
Right angle
Angle **A:** 462 with diagram
Right ascension [measurement]

Astronomy *diagrams on* **A:** 842; (Locating objects in space) **A:** 838
Right Bank [district, Paris]
Paris (The city) **P:** 161-162 *with map*
Right circular cylinder [geometry]
Cylinder **Ci:** 1204
Right-hand rule [physics]
Electric motor (Basic principles) **E:** 179
Right Honourable [title]
Privy Council **P:** 808b
Right lymphatic duct
Human body (The lymphatic system) **H:** 424
Lymphatic system (Lymphatic vessels) **L:** 534 *with diagram*
Right of assembly *See* Freedom of assembly *in this index*
Right of attribution [law]
Copyright (Owners' rights) **Ci:** 1047
Right of blood [law]
Nationality **N:** 63
Right of deposit [U.S. history]
Louisiana Purchase (Reasons for the purchase) **L:** 502; (New Orleans closed to Americans) **L:** 503
Right of dissent
Civil disobedience (Is civil disobedience ever justified?) **Ci:** 607
Right of possession *See* Title *in this index*
Right of privacy *See* Privacy, Right of *in this index*
Right of search [international law] **R:** 340
Right of the place of one's birth [law]
Nationality **N:** 63
Right of way
Railroad (Tracks) **R:** 108-109
Road (Planning) **R:** 358
Right prism
Prism **P:** 805
Right to die
Death (The right to die) **D:** 61
Right to life
Abortion (Abortion methods) **A:** 14-15
Declaration of Independence (The Declaration of Rights) **D:** 76
Right to Read [project]
Literacy (Illiteracy in the United States) **L:** 351-352
Right-to-work law R: 340
Right triangle
Mathematics (Branches of mathematics) **M:** 303
Triangle (Kinds of triangles) **T:** 437 *with diagram*; (Right triangles and the Pythagorean theorem) **T:** 437
Trigonometry (Right triangles) **T:** 443 *with diagrams*
Right whale
Whale *pictures on* **W:** 256; (Right whales) **W:** 255 *with picture*; (The early days of whaling) **W:** 262
Right wing [political science] **R:** 340
See also Conservatism *in this index*
Left wing **L:** 181
Liberalism **L:** 228
Right You Are (If You Think You Are) [play by Pirandello]
Pirandello, Luigi **P:** 493
Rights, Bill of *See* Bill of rights *in this index*
Rights, Charter of [French history]
Jefferson, Thomas (Minister to France) **J:** 81
Rights, Civil *See* Civil rights *in this index*
Rights, Consumer's *See* Consumer protection *in this index*
Rights, Declaration of [1774]
Continental Congress (The First Continental Congress) **Ci:** 1021
Rights, Declaration of [1776]
Mason, George **M:** 265
Virginia (Independence and statehood) **V:** 420
Rights and Freedoms, Canadian Charter of [1982]
Bill of rights (Canada's Constitution) **B:** 301
Civil rights (Civil rights in other countries) **Ci:** 610
Rights of Man, Declaration of the [French history] **R:** 340
Bill of rights (French Bill of Rights) **B:** 301
French Revolution (The National Assembly) **F:** 525
Rights of Man, The [book by Paine]
Paine, Thomas (French revolutionary) **P:** 22
Rights of personal integrity
Human rights (Types of human rights) **H:** 428
Rigid insulation
Insulation (In buildings) **I:** 306
Rigid truck [vehicle] *See* Straight truck *in this index*
Rigoletto [opera by Verdi]
Opera: (*Rigoletto*) **O:** 806
Rigor mortis [physiology]
Crime scene investigation (Beginning an investigation) **Ci:** 1140

Death (Medical aspects of death) **D:** 61
Rigveda [religious book]
Brahman **B:** 548
Hinduism (The Vedas) **H:** 235
Vedas **V:** 291
Rihla [book by Ibn Battūta]
Exploration (Muslim exploration) **E:** 442
Ibn Battūta **I:** 3
Riis, Jacob August [American journalist] **R:** 340
Photography (Artistic advances) **P:** 424-425
Playground **P:** 571
United States, History of the *picture on* **U:** 183
Urban renewal (History) **U:** 220
Rijksmuseum [museum]
Netherlands *picture on* **N:** 144
Rikers Island [New York]
New York City (Small islands) **N:** 330
Rikishi [wrestler]
Sumo **So:** 973
Riksdag [Swedish government]
Sweden (National government) **So:** 1021; (The beginnings of modern Sweden) **So:** 1033; (The Age of Liberty) **So:** 1034
Riksmål [language]
Norway (Language) **N:** 539
Rikugien Garden [Tokyo]
Tokyo (Parks and gardens) **T:** 316
Riley, Bennett [American general]
Fort Riley **F:** 415
Riley, Bob [American political leader]
Alabama (table) **A:** 274; (The 2000's) **A:** 279
Riley, James Whitcomb [American poet] **R:** 341
Indiana (Places to visit) **I:** 206
June (Quotations) **J:** 193
Nye, Bill **N:** 632
Riley, Richard W. [American political leader]
Clinton, Bill (table) **Ci:** 682d
Education, Department of (table) **E:** 110
Rilke, Rainer Maria [German poet] **R:** 341
German literature (Impressionism, Neoromanticism, and Symbolism) **G:** 141
Rill [geography]
River *diagram on* **R:** 353; (Tributaries) **R:** 351
"Rill from the Town Pump, A" [story by Hawthorne]
Hawthorne, Nathaniel (His stories and sketches) **H:** 115
Rille [astronomy]
Moon (Rilles) **M:** 790
Rillieux, Norbert [American engineer] **R:** 341
Rim lock
Lock (Types of locks) **L:** 410-411 *with picture*
Rimbaud, Arthur [French poet] **R:** 341
French literature (Symbolism) **F:** 522
Verlaine, Paul **V:** 317
Rime *See* Rhyme *in this index*
"Rime of the Ancient Mariner, The" [poem by Coleridge]
Coleridge, Samuel Taylor **Ci:** 771
Rimes, LeAnn [American singer]
United States *picture on* **U:** 118
Rimland [geopolitics]
Geopolitics **G:** 106b
Rimmer, William [American sculptor]
Sculpture (American sculpture) **S:** 255
Rimsky-Korsakov, Nikolai [Russian composer] **R:** 341 *with portrait*
Mussorgsky, Modest **M:** 967
Opera: (*Boris Godunov*) **O:** 801-802
Rin [money]
Yen **Y:** 564
Rind [cheese]
Cheese (Separating the curd) **C:** 393
Rinderpest [disease] **R:** 342
Rindisbacher, Peter [American painter]
Indian, American *picture on* **I:** 141
Rindt, Jochen [Austrian race driver]
Automobile racing (table: Formula One World Drivers' Championship) **A:** 980
Rinehart, Mary Roberts [American author] **R:** 342
Ring [astronomy] *See* Planetary ring *in this index*
Ring [jewelry] **R:** 342 *with pictures*
Jewelry **J:** 117
Marriage (Wedding ceremonies) **M:** 220
Ring, Boxing
Boxing (The ring) **B:** 526 *with picture*
Ring, Circus
Circus (At the circus) **Ci:** 562; (The birth of the circus) **Ci:** 562b
Ring, The [magazine]
Boxing (Boxing today) **B:** 533
"Ring-a-Ring O'Roses"
Nursery rhyme (Singing game rhymes) **N:** 615
Ring and the Book, The [book by Browning]
Browning, Robert (Browning's poems) **B:** 646
English literature (Later Victorian literature) **E:** 321

Ring-billed gull [bird]
Gull (Kinds of gulls) **G:** 439 *with picture*
Ring laser gyro [device]
Inertial guidance (Strap-down systems) **I:** 263
Ring Nebula [astronomy]
Lyra **L:** 537
Ring-necked pheasant [bird]
Bird *picture on* **B:** 353
Pheasant (Kinds of pheasants) **P:** 355 *with picture*
Ring-necked plover [bird]
Plover **P:** 574 *with picture*
Ring of Fire [region, Pacific Ocean] **R:** 342 *with picture*
Mountain (The Andes Mountains) **M:** 895
Pacific Islands (The high islands) **P:** 7
Volcano (Subduction zones) **V:** 441
Ring of the Löwenskölds, The [books by Lagerlöf]
Lagerlöf, Selma **L:** 30
Ring of the Nibelung, The [operas by Wagner]
Brunhild **B:** 652
Classical music *picture on* **Ci:** 650
Nibelungenlied **N:** 395
Opera: (*Ring of the Nibelung, The*) **O:** 806-807
Siegfried **S:** 449
Wagner, Richard (Later career) **W:** 4
Ring Round the Moon [play by Anouilh]
Anouilh, Jean **A:** 519
Ring silicate [mineral]
Silicate **S:** 458
Ring system [astronomy]
Planetary ring **P:** 514d
Ring-tailed lemur [animal]
Lemur **L:** 189, *picture on* **L:** 190
Zoo *picture on* **Z:** 603
Ringe in Julen [custom]
Christmas (In Denmark, Norway, and Sweden) **C:** 531-532
Ringer [games]
Horseshoe pitching (Scoring) **H:** 368
Marbles **M:** 193
Ringette [sport] **R:** 343
Ringlet [astronomy]
Planetary ring **P:** 514d
Ringling brothers [American circus family] **R:** 343 *with picture*
Barnum, P. T. **B:** 115
Ringling Brothers and Barnum & Bailey Circus
Barnum, P. T. **B:** 115
Circus (The Ringling Brothers) **Ci:** 564
Ringling brothers **R:** 344
Ringneck snake
Snake *picture on* **S:** 533
Rings [gymnastics]
Gymnastics (Men's events) **G:** 448 *with picture*
Ringstrassen [roads]
Vienna (The city) **V:** 361-362
Ringtail [animal] **R:** 344
Ringuet [Canadian author]
Canadian literature (Literature between the world wars) **C:** 158
Ringwood, Gwen Pharis [Canadian author]
Canadian literature (Literature between the world wars) **C:** 158-159
Ringworm [disease] **R:** 344
Athlete's foot **A:** 858
Cat (Veterinary care) **C:** 295
Fungicide **F:** 560
Hair (Disorders of the hair and scalp) **H:** 10
Skin (Infections) **S:** 490
Rini, Snyder [Solomon Islands political leader]
Solomon Islands (History) **So:** 585-586
Rink [sports team]
Curling **Ci:** 1195
Rink [sports]
Curling (The rink) **Ci:** 1196 *with pictures*
Hockey (The rink) **H:** 274 *with picture*
Lawn bowling **L:** 144
Rinzai [religion]
Zen **Z:** 589
Rio [Brazil] *See* Rio de Janeiro *in this index*
Río Bravo [river] *See* Rio Grande *in this index*
Río Camuy Cave Park [Puerto Rico]
Puerto Rico (Places to visit) **P:** 877
Rio de Janeiro [Brazil] **R:** 344 *with picture and map*
Brazil **B:** 567, *picture on* **B:** 575; (City life) **B:** 573; (table: Average monthly weather) **B:** 579
Latin America *picture on* **L:** 97
Seven natural wonders of the world (The Harbor of Rio de Janeiro) **S:** 324b *with picture*
South America *picture on* **So:** 622
Río de la Plata [bay, Argentina-Uruguay] **R:** 346
Exploration (Spain's conquests in the New World) **E:** 445
South America (Rivers) **So:** 628
Río Dorado [river, Peru]
Peru *picture on* **P:** 312
Rio Grande [river, North America] **R:** 346 *with*

picture and map
Mexican War (Background of the war) **M: 445**
with map
New Mexico (Land regions) **N: 266-268**
Rio Grande Project **R: 347**
River (table) **R: 352**
Texas picture on **T: 184**; (Rivers and lakes) **T: 198**
Rio Grande Project [U.S.] **R: 347**
Rio Grande Wild and Scenic River [Texas]
National Park System (table: National parkways
and other national parklands) **N: 56**
Río Muni [territory, Equatorial Guinea]
Equatorial Guinea **E: 346** with map
Rio Negro [river, Brazil-Colombia]
Amazon River (The course of the Amazon) **A: 403**
with picture
Uruguay (The interior lowlands) **U: 225**
Rio-Niterói Bridge [Brazil]
Bridge (table: Plate and box girder) **B: 603**
Rio São Francisco [river, Brazil]
São Francisco, River **S: 117**
Rio Teodoro [river, Brazil]
Madeira River **M: 30**
Rio Tinto [company]
Alcan Inc. **A: 333**
Rio Treaty [1947] See Inter-American Treaty of
Reciprocal Assistance in this index
Rioni Valley [Caucasus Mountains]
Georgia (Land and climate) **G: 110**
Riordan, Richard J. [American political figure]
Los Angeles (Recent developments) **L: 470**
Ríos, Juan Antonio [Chilean political leader]
Chile (Years of progress) **C: 469**
Ríos Montt, Efrain [Guatemalan political leader]
Guatemala (Political developments) **G: 417**
Riot R: 347 with picture
African Americans (The rise of new black leaders)
A: 136l-136m; (The black migration to the
North) **A: 136m**; (Unrest in the cities) **A: 136q**;
(Race relations) **A: 136t**
Ammunition (Riot control ammunition) **A: 435**
Bush, George Herbert Walker (National affairs)
B: 720-721
California (The mid-1900's) **C: 62-63**
Cleveland (Social problems) **Ci: 665**
Detroit (The mid-1900's) **D: 171**
France (Recent developments) **F: 478**
Haymarket Riot **H: 121**
Los Angeles (Recent developments) **L: 470**
Newark (History) **N: 357-358**
Police (In the United States since the mid-1900's)
P: 624
Prison (Current problems) **P: 808**
Reconstruction (Violence against blacks) **R: 177**
Russia (The new nation) **R: 555**
Segregation (De facto segregation) **S: 285-286**
South Africa (The dismantling of apartheid)
So: 620
Tulsa (History) **T: 483-484**
Union of Soviet Socialist Republics (The February
Revolution) **U: 35**
United States, History of the (The civil rights
movement) **U: 196a**
Riot Act [England]
Freedom of assembly (History) **F: 504-505**
Rip panel
Balloon picture on **B: 58**; (Operation of hot-air
balloon) **B: 60**
Rip Van Winkle [play by Boucicault]
Boucicault, Dion **B: 515**
Jefferson, Joseph **J: 75**
"Rip Van Winkle" [story by Irving] **R: 349**
American literature (Literature of a young nation
[1788-1830]) **A: 415**
Irving, Washington **I: 460**
Ripcord
Parachute (Parts of a parachute) **P: 142-143** with
picture
Ripening [food processing]
Butter (Churning) **B: 730**
Cheese (Ripening) **C: 393**
Fruit (Harvesting) **F: 547**
Ripken, Cal, Jr. [American baseball player] **R: 350**
Baseball (table: Hall of Fame) **B: 134a**; (table:
Modern major league records) **B: 138**
Ripley, George [American author]
American literature (Nonfiction prose) **A: 418**
Brook Farm **B: 639**
Ripley, Robert LeRoy [American cartoonist] **R: 350**
Ripley, Tom [fictional character]
Highsmith, Patricia **H: 229**
Riposte [movement]
Fencing (The foil) **F: 70-71**
Ripple effect [ecology]
Balance of nature (Upsetting the balance) **B: 36**
Riprap [engineering]
Dam (Embankment dams) **D: 18**

Ripsaw [tool]
Saw (Handsaws) **S: 166** with picture
Woodworking (Cutting) **W: 397**
Ripuarians [people]
Franks **F: 494**
Riqueti, Honoré Gabriel Victor [birth name of]
Mirabeau, Comte de **M: 614**
Risch, Jim [American political leader]
Idaho (table) **I: 42**
Rise of Silas Lapham, The [book by Howells]
Howells, William Dean **H: 401**
Novel (The United States) **N: 573**
**Risen Christ Between Saint Andrew and Saint
Longinus, The** [engraving by Mantegna]
Mantegna, Andrea picture on **M: 167**
Riser [device]
Parachute (Parts of a parachute) **P: 142-143** with
picture
Rishchynski, Guillermo [Canadian diplomat]
United Nations (table) **U: 86**
Rising, The [recording by Springsteen]
Springsteen, Bruce So: **809**
Rising action [literature]
Literature (Plot) **L: 353**
Rising from the committee [parliamentary
procedure]
Committee of the whole **Ci: 872**
Rising Village, The [poem by Goldsmith]
Canadian literature (Early English-Canadian
literature) **C: 157**
Risk [economics]
Insurance **I: 309**
Interest (Degree of risk) **I: 323**
Investment (Kinds of investments) **I: 366**
Risk factor [medicine]
Framingham Heart Study **F: 451**
Heart (Progress in treatment and prevention)
H: 145-146
Risorgimento [Italian history]
Italian literature (Romanticism) **I: 495**
Risotto [food]
Italy (Food and drink) **I: 502-503**
Riss ice age [geology]
Ice age (Evidence of ice ages and their climates)
I: 6-7
Risso's dolphin [sea animal]
Dolphin (Other species) **D: 297**
Ritalin [drug] **R: 350**
Attention deficit disorder **A: 879**
Ritardando [music]
Music (table) **M: 954**
Ritchie, Albert C. [American political leader]
Maryland (table) **M: 255**
Ritchie, C. S. A. [Canadian diplomat]
United Nations (table) **U: 86**
Rite [religion]
Liturgy **L: 392**
Rite of passage R: 350
Funeral customs **F: 557**
Religion (Religious rituals) **R: 217-218**
Rite of Spring, The [ballet]
Classical music (Igor Stravinsky) **Ci: 649**
Stravinsky, Igor (Early works) So: **922**
Ritner, Joseph [American political leader]
Pennsylvania (table) **P: 263**
Ritonavir [drug]
AIDS (Treatments) **A: 164b-165**
Ritsos, Yannis [Greek poet]
Greek literature (Modern Greek literature)
G: 378-379
Ritter, Bill [American political leader]
Colorado (table) **Ci: 844**
Ritter, Halsted L. [American jurist]
Impeachment (History) **I: 91-92**
Ritter, John [American actor]
Ritter, Tex **R: 351**
Ritter, Joseph Elmer [American religious leader]
Cardinal (table: American cardinals) **C: 211**
Ritter, Karl [German geographer]
Geography (The growth of geography) **G: 96**
Ritter, Maurice [American musician]
Ritter, Tex **R: 350**
Ritter, Tex [American musician] **R: 350**
Ritty, James [American inventor] **R: 351**
Cash register **C: 273**
Ritty, John [American inventor]
Ritty, James **R: 351**
Ritual [magic]
Dance (Ritual ethnic dances) **D: 25**
Magic (Elements of magic) **M: 49**; (Modern
magic) **M: 51**
Mythology (Anthropological approaches) **M: 989**
Ritual [religion]
Education (History) **E: 97**
Liturgy **L: 392**
Religion (Religious rituals) **R: 217**
Sculpture (Early medieval sculpture) **S: 248**

Ritual ethnic dance
Dance (Ritual ethnic dances) **D: 25** with picture
Ritz, The [play by McNally]
McNally, Terrence **M: 344**
Rivadavia, Bernardino [Argentine political leader]
Argentina (Early independence) **A: 656**
Rivals, The [play by Sheridan]
Sheridan, Richard Brinsley **S: 396**
River R: 351 with pictures
Estuary **E: 364**
Flood **F: 236** with pictures
Ice age (Evidence of ice ages and their climates)
I: 6-7
Levee **L: 216**
World (Water) **W: 415**; (table) **W: 416** with map
River birch [tree]
Birch (River birch) **B: 327**
River dolphin R: 354 with picture
Dolphin **D: 297**
Whale (River dolphins) **W: 258**
River Glimpse, A [painting by Doughty]
Hudson River School picture on **H: 406**
River hippopotamus [animal]
Hippopotamus **H: 240** with pictures
River Leet [aqueduct, England]
Aqueduct (Later aqueducts) **A: 580**
River Moldau [music by Smetana]
Smetana, Bedřich **S: 515**
River of Canada [name for]
Saint Lawrence River (History) **S: 42**
River of No Return [nickname, Salmon River]
Idaho (Rivers, waterfalls, springs, and lakes) **I: 38**
River Queen [ship]
Hampton Roads Conference **H: 37**
River Raisin, Battle of [1813]
War of 1812 (Raisin River) **W: 33**
River system
River **R: 351**
River War, The [book by Churchill]
Churchill, Sir Winston Leonard Spencer (Soldier
and reporter) **C: 546**
Rivera, Diego [Mexican artist] **R: 354** with picture
Aztec picture on **A: 1004**
Indian, American picture on **I: 136**
Kahlo, Frida **K: 209**
Latin America (Painting) **L: 99-100**
Mexico (Painting) **M: 460**
Michigan picture on **M: 493**
Painting (Modern Mexican painting) **P: 83**
Rivera, Fructuoso [Uruguayan political leader]
Uruguay (Independence) **U: 227**
Rivera, José Eustacio [Colombian author]
Latin American literature (The early 1900's) **L: 113**
Riverboat
Mississippi picture on **M: 642**
Ship picture on **S: 416**
Tennessee picture on **T: 135**
Riverboat gambling
Iowa (Places to visit) **I: 384**; (The late 1900's) **I: 396**
Riverdale [district]
New York City (The Bronx) **N: 328**
Riverfront Plaza
Louisville (The city) **L: 504**
Riverine pond
Pond (Kinds of ponds) **P: 656-657**
Rivers, Eurith D. [American political leader]
Georgia (table) **G: 130**
Rivers, Larry [American painter] **R: 355** with picture
Rivers, William H. R. [British anthropologist]
Anthropology (Development of field research)
A: 548
Riverside Church
Bell (Famous bells) **B: 239-240**
New York City (Architecture) **N: 336-337**
Riverside wren [bird]
Wren picture on **W: 503**
Riverwalk [area]
Delaware picture on **D: 97**
Rivest, Ronald L. [American computer scientist]
Codes and ciphers (Public-key systems) **Ci: 750**
Rivet [fastener]
Riveting **R: 356**
Riveting [construction] **R: 356**
Riveting hammer
Hammer picture on **H: 34**
Riveting machine
Riveting **R: 356**
Riviera [region, France-Italy] **R: 356** with map
France (The land) **F: 464-466** with picture and
map
Riviera Maya [area, Mexico]
Quintana Roo **Q: 43**
Rivière, Marquis de [French diplomat]
Venus de Milo **V: 314**
Rixey, Eppa [American baseball player]
Baseball (table: Hall of Fame) **B: 134a**
Riyadh [Saudi Arabia] **R: 356** with picture

Saudi Arabia **S:** 154 *with picture*
Rizal, José [Filipino patriot] **R:** 357
  Philippines (The arts) **P:** 375-376; (Revolt against the Spaniards) **P:** 379-380
Rizal Park [Manila]
  Manila (Description) **M:** 142
Rizzuto, Phil [American baseball player]
  Baseball (table: Hall of Fame) **B:** 134a
RKO [company]
  Motion picture (Movies become big business) **M:** 865-866
RLG [navigation] *See* Ring laser gyro *in this index*
RLV [aircraft] *See* Reusable launch vehicle *in this index*
RN [occupation] *See* Registered nurse *in this index*
Rn [symbol]
  Radon (Chemical properties) **R:** 100
RNA [genetics] **R:** 357
  Cell (The nucleus) **C:** 328-329; (Producing proteins) **C:** 333-334 *with diagrams*; (RNA—the master copy) **C:** 335 *with diagrams*
  Enzyme **E:** 340
  Gene **G:** 81
  Heredity (How proteins are made) **H:** 206
  Human body (Chemical elements and molecules) **H:** 417
  Life (Nucleic acids) **L:** 278; (The puzzle of replication) **L:** 279 *with diagram*
  Molecular biology (The beginning of molecular biology) **M:** 691-692
  Retrovirus **R:** 266
  Viroid **V:** 426
  Virus (Structure) **V:** 427
Ro-ro ship *See* Roll-on/roll-off ship *in this index*
Roach [fish] **R:** 357
Roach [insect] *See* Cockroach *in this index*
ROAD [military]
  Army, United States (The atomic age Army) **A:** 739
Road [transportation] **R:** 357 *with pictures and map*
  See also the list of Related articles in the *Road* article
  Asphalt (Paving with asphalt) **A:** 815
  Automobile (Demand for services and facilities) **A:** 959
  Colonial life in America (Transportation) **Ci:** 805 *with picture*
  Industrial Revolution (Roads) **I:** 251
  Lighting (On streets and highways) **L:** 297
  McAdam, John Loudon **M:** 332
  Rome, Ancient (Transportation and communication) **R:** 443
  Traffic **T:** 365
  Transportation **T:** 383 *with picture*; (Ancient Rome) **T:** 387; (Private transportation) **T:** 392
Road, The [book by McCarthy]
  McCarthy, Cormac **M:** 332a
Road, The [play by Soyinka]
  Soyinka, Wole **So:** 693
Road Back, The [book by Remarque]
  Remarque, Erich Maria **R:** 228
Road bicycle
  Bicycle (Kinds of bikes) **B:** 289
Road locomotive [train]
  Locomotive (Kind of locomotives) **L:** 414
  Railroad (Rolling stock) **R:** 107 *with picture*
Road map
  Map (Types of maps) **M:** 177-178 *with picture*
Road of a Naturalist, The [book by Peattie]
  Peattie, Donald Culross **P:** 225
Road race
  Automobile racing **A:** 975, *pictures on* **A:** 976
  Bicycle racing (Road races) **B:** 292 *with picture*
  Kart racing **K:** 247
Road racer [bicycle] *See* Racing bike *in this index*
Road rally [race]
  Automobile racing (Other kinds of racing) **A:** 978-979
Road/sport bicycle
  Bicycle (Road bikes) **B:** 289
Road to Calvary [book by Tolstoy]
  Russian literature (The period of rebirth) **R:** 564
  Tolstoy, Alexei **T:** 322
Road to Perdition, The [book by Collins]
  Graphic novel **G:** 323
Road to Rome, The [play by Sherwood]
  Sherwood, Robert Emmet **S:** 398
Road to Versailles [painting by Sisley]
  Impressionism *picture on* **I:** 94
Road to Wigan Pier, The [book by Orwell]
  Orwell, George **O:** 860
Road Town [Virgin Islands]
  Virgin Islands, British **V:** 393
Road train [truck]
  Western Australia *picture on* **W:** 231
Roadbed
  Railroad (Tracks) **R:** 108 *with picture*

Roadmenders' Camp, The [paintings by Curry]
  Curry, John Steuart *picture on* **Ci:** 1198
Roadrunner [bird] **R:** 362
  Animal *picture on* **A:** 482
  Bird (Birds of the desert) **B:** 339 *with picture*
Roadside bomb *See* Improvised explosive device *in this index*
Roadside skipper [butterfly]
  Butterfly (Skippers) **B:** 734 *with picture*
Roadster horse
  Horse (Light harness horses) **H:** 345
Roadway
  Railroad (Tracks) **R:** 108
Roaming [communications]
  Cellular telephone (How ceullular telephones work) **C:** 340-341
  Telephone (Cellular phone calls) **T:** 97
Roan [horse]
  Horse (Coat and skin) **H:** 348-349
Roan antelope
  Antelope (Kinds of antelope) **A:** 542
Roane, Archibald [American political leader]
  Tennessee (table) **T:** 152
Roane, John Seldon [American political leader]
  Arkansas (table) **A:** 712
Roanoke [Virginia] **R:** 362
  Virginia (table: Average monthly weather) **V:** 412
Roanoke Island [North Carolina]
  Colonial life in America (Early English settlements) **Ci:** 789
  Lost Colony **L:** 472
  Raleigh, Sir Walter (His expeditions) **R:** 131
Roanoke River [North Carolina-Virginia]
  North Carolina (Rivers, waterfalls, and lakes) **N:** 484 *with map*
  Virginia (Rivers and lakes) **V:** 412 *with map*
Roaring forties [region, Pacific]
  Prevailing westerly **P:** 773
Roaring Twenties [U.S. history] **R:** 363 *with pictures*
  American literature (The Lost Generation) **A:** 421
  Chicago (The Roaring Twenties) **C:** 436
  Coolidge, Calvin **Ci:** 1030
  Fitzgerald, F. Scott **F:** 190
  Harding, Warren Gamaliel **H:** 56
  Held, John, Jr. **H:** 167 *with picture*
  Jazz (The 1920's) **J:** 70
  United States, History of the (The Roaring Twenties) **U:** 189 *with picture*
Roasted-in-shell peanut
  Peanut (As food) **P:** 214
Roaster [chicken]
  Chicken (Producing meat) **C:** 445
Roasting [cooking]
  Cooking (Roasting) **Ci:** 1028
Roasting [industrial process]
  Manganese (Sources) **M:** 139
  Metallurgy (Roasting) **M:** 426
Rob Roy [Scottish bandit] **R:** 364
Robards, Jason [American actor]
  Motion picture (Best performance by an actor in a supporting role: 1976, 1977) **M:** 862b
Robards, Rachel Donelson [wife of Andrew Jackson] *See* Jackson, Rachel Robards *in this index*
Robarts, Emma [British social reformer]
  Young Women's Christian Association (History) **Y:** 573
Robarts, John P. [Canadian political leader]
  Ontario (table) **O:** 783
Robarts Research Library [Toronto]
  Library *picture on* **L:** 247
Robb, Charles Spittal [American political leader]
  Virginia (table) **V:** 417
Robb, Lynda Bird Johnson [daughter of]
  Johnson, Lyndon Baines (Marriage) **J:** 146
Robbe-Grillet, Alain [French author]
  French literature (Recent French literature) **F:** 523; (The middle and late 1900's) **F:** 523
  Novel (After World War II) **N:** 574
Robber baron [U.S. history]
  United States, History of the (The rich and the poor) **U:** 182
Robber crab
  Hermit crab **H:** 212
Robbers, The [play by Schiller]
  German literature (German Preromanticism) **G:** 139
Robbery [crime] **R:** 365
  Bandit **B:** 76
  Burglary **B:** 704
  Crime (Types of crimes) **Ci:** 1136
Robbery Under Arms [book by Boldrewood]
  Australia (Literature) **A:** 904-905
Robbia, Della [Italian sculptor] *See* Della Robbia, Luca *in this index*
Robbins, Frederick Chapman [American physician]
  Nobel Prizes (Physiology or medicine: 1954)

N: 446
Robbins, Jerome [American choreographer] **R:** 365
  Ballet (Ballet in the United States) **B:** 53-54
  Dance (Musical comedy) **D:** 31
  Motion picture (Best achievement in directing: 1961) **M:** 862
  Musical comedy (The modern musical emerges) **M:** 960
Robbins, Ruth [American art director]
  Sidjakov, Nicolas **S:** 448 *with picture*
Robbins, Tim [American actor]
  Motion picture (Best performance by an actor in a supporting role: 2003) **M:** 862b
Rober, Lewis [American sportsman]
  Softball (History) **So:** 572
Robert [brother of William, the Conqueror]
  William II **W:** 308
Robert I [king of Scotland] *See* Bruce, Robert *in this index*
Robert I [duke of Normandy]
  William I, the Conqueror **W:** 308
Robert II [king of France]
  France (table) **F:** 471
Robert II [king of Scotland]
  Scotland (The House of Stuart) **S:** 219
Robert, Anne-Jean [French inventor]
  Balloon (The hydrogen balloon) **B:** 61
Robert, Marie-Noel [French inventor]
  Airplane (First human flights) **A:** 230
Robert, Nicholas Louis [French inventor]
  Paper (History) **P:** 136-137
Robert, Nicolas [French inventor]
  Balloon (The hydrogen balloon) **B:** 61
Robert C. Byrd Green Bank Telescope *See* Green Bank Telescope *in this index*
Robert E. Lee Memorial [Virginia]
  Arlington National Cemetery **A:** 717
  Lee, Robert E. *picture on* **L:** 179
Robert F. Sibert Informational Book Medal
  Literature for children (Awards) **L:** 367
Robert-Houdin, Jean Eugène [French magician]
  Houdini, Harry **H:** 377
  Magician (Illusions) **M:** 51-52 *with picture*
Robert Joffrey Ballet *See* Joffrey Ballet of Chicago *in this index*
Robert-le-Diable [opera by Meyerbeer]
  Meyerbeer, Giacomo **M:** 479
Robert Moses power plant [New York]
  Niagara River (Water power) **N:** 394-395
Robert of Flanders [French crusader]
  Crusades (The First Crusade) **Ci:** 1160 *with map*
Robert of Geneva [antipope] *See* Clement VII *in this index*
Robert of Molesme, Saint [French religious leader]
  Cistercians **Ci:** 567
Robert of Sorbon [French religious leader]
  Sorbonne **So:** 596
Robert Taylor Homes [Chicago]
  Chicago (The South Side) **C:** 424
Robert Trent Jones Golf Trail
  Alabama (Places to visit) **A:** 266
Roberts, A. H. [American political leader]
  Tennessee (table) **T:** 152
Roberts, Barbara [American political leader]
  Oregon (table) **O:** 845
Roberts, Bartholomew [British pirate]
  Pirate *picture on* **P:** 495
Roberts, Charles G. D. [Canadian author] **R:** 365
  Canadian literature (Poetry: 1850-1918) **C:** 157
Roberts, Dennis J. [American political leader]
  Rhode Island (table) **R:** 311
Roberts, Edward [American activist]
  Disability (The 1900's) **D:** 221
Roberts, Floyd [American race driver]
  Automobile racing (table: Indianapolis 500 winners) **A:** 980
Roberts, Frederick Sleigh [British military leader]
  Anglo-Boer War **A:** 463
  Kitchener, Horatio Herbert **K:** 338
Roberts, Henry [American political leader]
  Connecticut (table) **Ci:** 967
Roberts, John Glover, Jr. [American jurist] **R:** 365
  Bush, George Walker (Supreme Court) **B:** 722j
  Supreme Court of the United States *picture on* **So:** 999
Roberts, Joseph Jenkins [Liberian political leader]
  Liberia (The Liberian settlement) **L:** 231
Roberts, Julia [American actress]
  Motion picture (Best performance by an actress: 2000) **M:** 862a
Roberts, Marcus [American musician]
  Jazz *picture on* **J:** 68
Roberts, Oral [American clergyman]
  Faith healing **F:** 12
Roberts, Oran M. [American political leader]
  Texas (table) **T:** 203
Roberts, Owen Josephus [American jurist] **R:** 365

Roberts, Richard John [British-born physiologist]
Nobel Prizes (Physiology or medicine: 1993)
N: 446
Roberts, Robin [American baseball player]
Baseball (table: Hall of Fame) B: 134b
Robert's Rules of Order [book]
Parliamentary procedure P: 175
Robertson, Anna Mary [birth name of]
Moses, Grandma M: 830
Robertson, Cliff [American actor]
Motion picture (Best performance by an actor: 1968) M: 862a
Robertson, Donald [American educator]
Madison, James (Early life) M: 32-33
Robertson, Eck [American musician]
Country music (Early commercial success)
Ci: 1098b
Robertson, James [American pioneer]
Tennessee (Territorial years) T: 153
Westward movement in America (Crossing the Appalachians) W: 246
Robertson, James B. A. [American political leader]
Oklahoma (table) O: 730; (The 1920's) O: 732
Robertson, Oscar [American basketball player]
R: 365
Basketball *picture on* B: 154; (The history of professional basketball) B: 154a-155
Robertson, Pat [American religious leader]
Christian Coalition of America C: 522e
Evangelicalism E: 422
Robertson, Thomas B. [American political leader]
Louisiana (table) L: 496
Robertson, Wyndham [American political leader]
Virginia (table) V: 417
Robertson plaid [cloth]
Tartan *picture on* T: 47
Roberval, Jean François de La Roque, Sieur de [French explorer] R: 365
Robes, Mistress of the
Royal Household of the United Kingdom R: 498
Robeson, George M. [American government official]
Grant, Ulysses S. (table) G: 316
Robeson, Paul [American actor] R: 366 *with portrait*
Shakespeare, William *picture on* S: 363
Robespierre [French political leader] R: 366
Danton, Georges-Jacques D: 34
French Revolution (Terror and equality) F: 526-527; (The revolution ends) F: 527
Reign of Terror R: 207
Robichaud, Louis J. [Canadian political leader]
New Brunswick (table) N: 195; (The middle and late 1900's) N: 198-199
Robie, Frederick [American political leader]
Maine (table) M: 87
Robie house [Chicago]
Architecture (Frank Lloyd Wright) A: 629-630
Wright, Frank Lloyd *picture on* W: 508; (Early career) W: 507
Robin [bird] R: 366 *with picture*
Bird *pictures on* B: 344d, B: 358, B: 359, B: 363, B: 367; (Birds of urban areas) B: 333 *with picture*
Robin [fictional character]
Batman B: 165 *with picture*
Robin Goodfellow [legendary figure]
Puck P: 870
Robin Hood [legendary figure] R: 367 *with picture*
Literature for children (Ballads) L: 358
Robins, C. A. [American political leader]
Idaho (table) I: 42
Robinson, Bill [American entertainer] R: 367
Temple, Shirley *picture on* T: 131
Robinson, Brooks [American baseball player]
Baseball (table: Hall of Fame) B: 134b
Robinson, Charles [American political leader]
Kansas (table) K: 234
Robinson, Clifford W. [Canadian political leader]
New Brunswick (table) N: 195
Robinson, Craig [brother of]
Obama, Michelle Robinson O: 642
Robinson, Eddie [American football coach] R: 368 *with portrait*
Robinson, Edwin Arlington [American poet]
R: 368
American literature (Realist poetry) A: 421
Maine (Interesting facts) M: 69
Robinson, Frank [American baseball player] R: 368
Baseball (table: Hall of Fame) B: 134b; (Recent developments) B: 137
Robinson, George D. [American political leader]
Massachusetts (table) M: 288
Robinson, Henry Peach [British inventor]
Photography (Artistic advances) P: 424
Robinson, Jackie [American baseball player]
R: 368 *with picture*
African Americans *picture on* A: 136m; (Economic

and social progress) A: 136p-136q
Baseball (table: Hall of Fame) B: 134b; (Postwar baseball) B: 136 *with picture*
Robinson, Joan Violet [British economist] R: 369
Robinson, John S. [American political leader]
Vermont (table) V: 333
Robinson, Joseph Taylor [American political leader] R: 369
Arkansas (table) A: 712
Robinson, Lucius [American political leader]
New York (table) N: 313
Robinson, Mary [Irish political leader] R: 369
Ireland (The Republic of Ireland) I: 427-428
Robinson, Michelle [wife of Barack Obama] *See* Obama, Michelle Robinson *in this index*
Robinson, Moses [American political leader]
Vermont (table) V: 333
Robinson, Ray [American boxer] *See* Robinson, Sugar Ray *in this index*
Robinson, Ray Charles *See* Charles, Ray *in this index*
Robinson, Sir Robert [British chemist]
Nobel Prizes (Chemistry: 1947) N: 443
Robinson, Robert B. [American aviator]
Aviation (table: Aviation speed records) A: 990
Robinson, Robert P. [American political leader]
Delaware (table) D: 109
Robinson, Sugar Ray [American boxer] R: 369 *with portrait*
Boxing *picture on* B: 532b; (The 1950's) B: 532a
Robinson, Wilbert [American baseball player]
Baseball (table: Hall of Fame) B: 134b
Robinson, William [American inventor]
Railroad (Engineering improvements) R: 117
Robinson Crusoe [book by Defoe] R: 369
Defoe, Daniel D: 88
English literature (The rise of the novel) E: 318-319
Literature for children (The 1700's) L: 362
Novel (The first English novelists) N: 572
Robinson projection [cartography]
Map (Map projections) M: 182 *with diagram*
Roblin, Duff [Canadian political leader]
Manitoba (table) M: 159
Roblin, Sir Rodmond P. [Canadian political leader]
Manitoba (table) M: 159; (Political developments)
M: 162
Robot [machine] R: 369 *with picture*
Artificial intelligence (Robotics) A: 760
Automation (Uses of automation) A: 944; (History of automation) A: 945
Čapek, Karel C: 191
Electronics (Automation) E: 207
Factory (Location and design) F: 5
Remote control (History) R: 231
Robotic surgical device [medicine]
Surgery *picture on* So: 1007; (Instruments)
So: 1005
Robotics
Artificial intelligence (Robotics) A: 760
Robot R: 369
Robotnik [newspaper]
Piłsudski, Józef P: 465
Robson, George [American race driver]
Automobile racing (table: Indianapolis 500 winners) A: 980
Robson, John [Canadian political leader]
British Columbia (table) B: 628
Robust australopithecine [hominid]
Australopithecus A: 927
Prehistoric people (Types of australopithecines)
P: 745 *with picture*
Robusta coffee *See* Coffea robusta *in this index*
Roc [legendary creature]
Elephant bird E: 232
Rocard, Michel [French political leader]
France (Socialists win power) F: 478
Rochambeau, Comte de [French general] R: 370
Lafayette, Marquis de (Service to the United States) L: 28
Revolution, American (Surrender at Yorktown)
R: 286
Yorktown, Siege of Y: 569
Rochas, Beau de [French inventor]
Gasoline engine (Development of the gasoline engine) G: 66
Roche, Édouard [French astronomer]
Planetary ring P: 514d
Roche, Mazo de la [Canadian author] *See* De la Roche, Mazo *in this index*
Roche limit [astronomy]
Planetary ring P: 514d
Tidal forces T: 280
Roche moutonnée [geology]
Glacier *diagram on* G: 204
Rochelle salt [chemical]
Tartaric acid T: 48

Rochester [New York] R: 370
Douglass, Frederick D: 314
Rochester, Nathaniel [American settler]
Rochester R: 370
Rochesterville [former city]
Rochester (Government and history) R: 370
Rocinante [fictional animal]
Don Quixote D: 306
Rock [geology] R: 371 *with pictures and map*
See also the list of Related articles in the Rock article
Earth (Earth's rocks) E: 20 *with pictures*
Mantle M: 168
Metamorphic rock M: 427
Pyroxene P: 920
Quarrying Q: 7
Quartz Q: 8
Sand S: 106
Soil *diagram on* So: 574; (How soil forms) So: 573
Time (The formation of rock) T: 292
Rock, Allan [Canadian diplomat]
United Nations (table) U: 86
Rock, Johann [German religious leader]
Amanites A: 400
"Rock-a-bye Baby"
Nursery rhyme (Lullabies) N: 615
Rock and roll *See* Rock music *in this index*
Rock and Roll Hall of Fame and Museum [Cleveland] R: 375
Cleveland (Cultural life and recreation) Ci: 665-666 *with picture*
Rock and Roll Hall of Fame Foundation
Rock and Roll Hall of Fame and Museum R: 375
"Rock Around the Clock" [song]
Rock music (A variety of styles) R: 378 *with picture*
Rock Band [electronic game]
Electronic game (Broadening audiences) E: 204f *with picture*
Rock barnacle [sea animal]
Barnacle *picture on* B: 114
Rock cleavage [property of rock]
Metamorphic rock M: 428
Schist S: 176
Rock climbing *See* Climbing *in this index*
Rock club [organization]
Rock R: 371
Rock collecting
Rock R: 371; (Rocks as a hobby) R: 373 *with picture*
Rock cranberry [fruit]
Lingonberry L: 335 *with picture*
Rock Creek Park [Washington, D.C.]
National Park System (table: National parkways and other national parklands) N: 56
Rock crystal
Quartz (Types) Q: 8
Rock cycle
Earth (Cycles on and in Earth) E: 22
Rock (The rock cycle) R: 373
Rock dancing
Dance D: 23; (Social dances) D: 26-28 *with picture*
Rock drill [tool]
Drill (Rock drills) D: 348
Rock elm
Elm (Kinds) E: 244-245
Rock-fill dam
Dam (Embankment dams) D: 18
Rock garden
Gardening (Specialty gardens) G: 31
Rock hammer [tool]
Rock (Tools) R: 374
Rock magnetism [geology] *See* Paleomagnetism *in this index*
Rock music R: 376 *with pictures*
Country music (Rockabilly music) Ci: 1098a; (Emergence of the country music industry)
Ci: 1098b-1098c
Croatia (People) Ci: 1148-1148a
Dance D: 23; (Social dances) D: 28
Electric guitar E: 173
Music (Western music) M: 955
Popular music (Rock'n'roll) P: 671
Punk rock P: 904
Radio (Radio since the 1950's) R: 94
Rhythm and blues R: 320
Rock and Roll Hall of Fame and Museum R: 375
Rolling Stones R: 402a
United States *picture on* U: 118
Who, The W: 296
Woodstock festival W: 395
Rock 'n' roll *See* Rock music *in this index*
Rock of Gibraltar *See* Gibraltar, Rock of *in this index*
Rock painting [art]
Africa *picture on* A: 130
Australia (Painting) A: 905
Leakey, Mary Douglas L: 161
Rock phosphate [chemical]

Fertilizer (Inorganic fertilizers) F: 79
Rock pigeon [bird]
Pigeon (The life of a pigeon) P: 459; (Kinds of pigeons) P: 460
Rock ptarmigan [bird]
Animal picture on A: 484
Ptarmigan P: 853
Rock quarry
Mining (Open-pit mining) M: 575
Rock salt [mineral]
Salt (Salt from the ground) S: 73
Rock steady [music]
Reggae R: 204
Rock tunnel
Tunnel (Rock tunnels) T: 490
Rock video
Popular music (New technologies) P: 671
Rock music (The 1980's) R: 380c
Rock wallaby [animal]
Wallaby (Kinds of wallabies) W: 15
Rock wren [bird]
Wren W: 504
Rockabilly [music]
Country music (Rockabilly music) Ci: 1098a
Rock music (A variety of styles) R: 378
Rockaway [district]
New York City (Queens) N: 329-330
Rockaway [vehicle]
Carriage C: 248
Rockdusting [mining]
Coal (Mine safety) Ci: 729
Rockefeller, David [American banker]
Rockefeller, John Davison (Rockefeller's descendants) R: 382 with picture
Rockefeller, John Davison [American financier] R: 382 with picture
Standard Oil Company So: 834
Rockefeller, John Davison, Jr. [American philanthropist] R: 383
Rockefeller, John Davison (Rockefeller's descendants) R: 382 with picture
United Nations (Building UN Headquarters) U: 95
Williamsburg (Restoration) W: 313
Rockefeller, John Davison, III [American philanthropist] R: 383
Rockefeller, John Davison (Rockefeller's descendants) R: 382 with picture
Rockefeller, John Davison, IV [American political leader] R: 383
West Virginia (History) W: 225
Rockefeller, Laurance Spelman [American philanthropist]
Rockefeller, John Davison (Rockefeller's descendants) R: 382 with picture
Virgin Islands National Park V: 397
Rockefeller, Margaretta "Happy" [wife of]
Rockefeller, Nelson Aldrich (Early life) R: 383
Rockefeller, Mary Todhunter Clark [wife of]
Rockefeller, Nelson Aldrich (Early life) R: 383
Rockefeller, Nelson Aldrich [American political leader] R: 383 with portrait
Central Intelligence Agency (History) C: 357
New York (table) N: 313
Rockefeller, John Davison (Rockefeller's descendants) R: 382 with picture
Rockefeller, Winthrop [American political leader]
Arkansas (table) A: 712
Rockefeller, John Davison (Rockefeller's descendants) R: 382 with picture
Rockefeller Center [New York City]
New York City (Manhattan) N: 323-325; (A visitor's guide) N: 338 with picture
Rockefeller Foundation R: 383
Food supply (Food supply programs) F: 350-351
Foundation (The work of foundations) F: 430; (table) F: 430
Rockefeller Park
Cleveland (Recreation) Ci: 666
Rocket R: 384 with pictures
See also Guided missile in this index
Army, United States (Missiles) A: 735
Ballistics B: 56
Communications satellite (Types of satellites) Ci: 888a-888b
Congreve, Sir William Ci: 950
Fireworks F: 135
Fuel (Chemical fuels) F: 551
Goddard, Robert Hutchings G: 244
Helium (Uses) H: 176
Korolev, Sergei Pavlovich K: 384
Plasma P: 552
Satellite, Artificial (Launching the satellite) S: 150g
Space exploration (Getting into space and back) So: 698; (The dawn of the space age) So: 706 with pictures; (Developing more efficient rockets) So: 728

Technology (The computer age) T: 75
Utah picture on U: 249
Rocket [locomotive] R: 391
Locomotive picture on L: 414
Stephenson, George So: 891
Stephenson, Robert So: 891
Rocket, Model R: 391 with pictures
Rocket, The [nickname]
Laver, Rod L: 129
Rocket booster [space exploration] See Booster rocket in this index
Rocket City, U.S.A. [nickname]
Huntsville H: 451
"Rocket '88" [song]
Rock music (Sun Records) R: 376
Rocket engine
Airplane (Rocket engines) A: 220
Guided missile (The engine) G: 424 with diagrams
Rocket into Interplanetary Space, The [book by Oberth]
Space exploration (Early dreams of space flight) So: 706
Rocket launcher
Artillery (Kinds of artillery) A: 762
Ballistics (Interior ballistics) B: 56
Bazooka B: 177 with picture
Rocket picture on R: 387
Rocket Roger [nickname]
Clemens, Roger Ci: 662
Rocket Society, American
American Institute of Aeronautics and Astronautics A: 412
Rockets, Houston [team]
Basketball (table) B: 150
Rockfish
Fish picture on F: 156
Rockford [Illinois] R: 393
Rockhopper penguin [bird]
Antarctica (Living things) A: 534-535 with picture
Rockies, Colorado [team] See Colorado Rockies in this index
Rocking chair
Antique picture on A: 558
Rocking Chair, The [book by Klein]
Klein, A. M. K: 343
Rocking Chair and Other Poems, The [book by Klein]
Canadian literature (Literature between the world wars) C: 158-159
Rockingham, Marquess of [British political leader]
United Kingdom (table: British prime ministers) U: 72
Rockland County [New York]
New York City (Metropolitan area) N: 330
Rockne, Knute [American football coach] R: 393 with portrait
Football (Changes in the game) F: 366-367
Rockwell, Norman [American artist] R: 393 with picture
Rocky [film]
Motion picture (Best picture: 1976) M: 861
Rocky Mount [log house]
Tennessee (Places to visit) T: 144
Rocky Mountain bristlecone pine [tree]
Bristlecone pine B: 610
Rocky Mountain Fur Company
Fur trade (The 1800's) F: 565
Rocky Mountain goat
Animal picture on A: 474
Rocky Mountain House [Alberta]
Canada (table: National historic sites) C: 115
Rocky Mountain National Park [Colorado] R: 394
Colorado (Places to visit) Ci: 836 with picture
National Park System (table: National parks) N: 48
Rocky Mountain News
Colorado (Communication) Ci: 843
Rocky Mountain pika [animal]
Animal picture on A: 474
Rocky Mountain spotted fever [disease] R: 394
Rickettsia R: 335
Tick T: 279
Typhus T: 540
Rocky Mountain States [region, U.S.]
R: 394
United States (Regions) U: 99-105 with map
Rocky Mountain Trench [region, North America]
British Columbia (Land regions) B: 622
Rocky Mountain wood tick [animal]
Rocky Mountain spotted fever R: 394
Rocky Mountains [mountains, North America]
R: 394 with map and map
Alberta picture on A: 312
Canada picture on C: 115; (The Rocky Mountains) C: 116
Chinook C: 512
Colorado picture on Ci: 828; (Land regions) Ci: 838 with map
Lewis and Clark expedition L: 222 with picture

and map
Mountain (The Rocky Mountains) M: 895 with picture
Rocky Mountain National Park R: 394
United States map on U: 122; (The Rocky Mountains) U: 125 with picture
Rocky Mountains, The [painting by Bierstadt]
Bierstadt, Albert picture on B: 296
Rocky shore [ocean]
Seashore (Life on rocky shores) S: 270 with picture
Rococo [art] R: 396
Architecture (Rococo architecture) A: 623 with picture
Furniture (The Rococo style) F: 576 with picture
Germany picture on G: 154
Painting (Rococo painting) P: 65 with pictures
Sculpture (European sculpture) S: 253-254
Rococo revival [style]
Furniture (Historical revivals) F: 581 with picture
Rocque, Jean François de La [birth name of]
Roberval, Jean François de La Roque, Sieur de R: 366
Rod [anatomy]
Color (The roles of the eyes and brain) Ci: 818
Color blindness Ci: 827
Eye (The retina) E: 462 with picture
Perception (Receptors) P: 283
Wald, George W: 6
Rod [engine] See Connecting rod in this index
Rod [fishing]
Fishing (Rods) F: 176 with pictures
Rod [tool]
Plaster (Plastering) P: 552
Rod [unit of measure] R: 396
Rod puppet
Puppet (Rod puppets) P: 906 with picture
Roda [audience]
Capoeira C: 197
Rodbell, Martin [American physiologist]
Nobel Prizes (Physiology or medicine: 1994) N: 446
Roddick, Andy [American tennis player] R: 396
Rodent [zoology] R: 396 with picture
See also the list of Related articles in the Rodent article
Animal (A table of animal intelligence) A: 493
Hantavirus H: 54
Mammal (table) M: 129 with picture
Rodenticide [poison]
Pest control (Pesticides) P: 318
Rodeo R: 397 with picture
Arizona picture on A: 678; (Interesting facts about Arizona) A: 671
Cheyenne (Description) C: 417
Nebraska picture on N: 103
Oklahoma picture on O: 723
Uruguay (Recreation) U: 225
Western frontier life in America (Entertainment) W: 240
Rodeo [ballet]
Ballet (Ballet in the United States) B: 53-54
Copland, Aaron Ci: 1040
De Mille, Agnes D: 119
Rodeo Drive [Los Angeles]
Los Angeles picture on L: 460
Roderick Hudson [book by James]
James, Henry (His works) J: 26
Rodgers, Calbraith P. [American aviator]
Airplane (Other pioneer planes and fliers) A: 233-234
Rodgers, Jimmie [American singer] R: 398
Country music (The roots of country music) Ci: 1098a-1098b
Rodgers, Johnny [American football player]
Football (table) F: 363
Rodgers, Richard [American composer] R: 398
Hammerstein, Oscar, II H: 35
Hart, Lorenz H: 77
Musical comedy (Musical comedy matures) M: 960
Rodham, Hillary [American political leader] See Clinton, Hillary Rodham in this index
Ródhos [island, Aegean Sea]
Rhodes R: 316
Rodin, Auguste [French sculptor] R: 398
France picture on F: 463
Impressionism (Music, literature, and sculpture) I: 94
Philadelphia picture on P: 364
Sculpture (European sculpture) S: 253-255 with picture
Rodin Museum
Philadelphia (Libraries and museums) P: 363-364 with picture
Rodinia [landmass]
Cambrian Period C: 74
Earth (The shaping of the continents) E: 24

Rodney, Caesar [American political leader] **R:** 399
Delaware (table) **D:** 109
Rodney, Caesar A. [American government official]
Jefferson, Thomas (table) **J:** 83
Justice, Department of (table) **J:** 203
Rodney, Caleb [American political leader]
Delaware (table) **D:** 109
Rodney, Daniel [American political leader]
Delaware (table) **D:** 109
Rodó, José Enrique [Uruguayan philosopher]
R: 399
Latin American literature (Modernism) **L:** 113
Uruguay (The arts) **U:** 225
Rodrigo Díaz [Spanish hero] *See* Cid, The *in this index*
Rodriguez, Alex [American baseball player] **R:** 399
Rodríguez, Agustín [Spanish explorer]
New Mexico (Exploration, conquest, and settlement) **N:** 273
Rodriguez Bermejo [Spanish sailor]
Columbus, Christopher (Sailing west) **Ci:** 860
Rodríguez Lara, Guillermo [Ecuadorean political leader]
Ecuador (The 1900's) **E:** 73-74
Rodríguez Pedotti, Andrés [Paraguayan political leader]
Paraguay (Stroessner's rule and overthrow) **P:** 149-150
Roe [zoology]
Fish (Reproductive system) **F:** 163
Shad **S:** 341
Roe deer
Animal *picture on* **A:** 495
Deer (Habits) **D:** 85; (table) **D:** 85
Roe v. Wade [U.S. history] **R:** 399
Abortion (Abortion in the United States) **A:** 15
National Right to Life Committee **N:** 60
Stevens, John Paul **So:** 896
Supreme Court of the United States (Civil rights) **So:** 1001
Women's movement (In Western societies) **W:** 386
Roebling, Emily Warren [American engineer]
Brooklyn Bridge *picture on* **B:** 640
Roebling, John Augustus [American engineer]
Brooklyn Bridge *picture on* **B:** 640
Roebling, Washington Augustus [American engineer]
Brooklyn Bridge *picture on* **B:** 640
Roebling opal [gem]
Opal **O:** 789
Roebuck, Alvah C. [American businessman]
Sears, Roebuck and Co. **S:** 269
Roemer, Buddy [American political leader]
Louisiana (table) **L:** 496
Roemer, Olaus [Danish astronomer]
Eclipse (The study of eclipses) **E:** 52
Light (The speed of light) **L:** 290
Roentgen, Wilhelm Conrad [German physicist] **R:** 400
Electronics (Early experiments) **E:** 215
Invention (The late 1800's) **I:** 362
Physics (The beginning of modern physics) **P:** 440-441 *with picture*
Radiation (History) **R:** 80
X rays **X:** 540
Roentgen ray [radiation]
Roentgen, Wilhelm Conrad **R:** 400
Roentgenium [element] **R:** 400
Transuranium element **T:** 401
Roethke, Theodore [American poet] **R:** 400
American literature ("Confessional" poetry) **A:** 423
Rogaine [drug] *See* Minoxidil *in this index*
Rogan, Joe [American baseball player]
Baseball (table: Hall of Fame) **B:** 134b
Roger II [king of Sicily]
Exploration (Muslim exploration) **E:** 442
Roger II [duke of Apulia]
Ducat **D:** 373
Roger Williams National Memorial [Rhode Island]
National Park System (table: National memorials) **N:** 54
Roger Williams Park
Providence (Description) **P:** 839-840
Rogers, C. J. [American political leader]
Wyoming (table) **W:** 532
Rogers, Carl Ransom [American psychologist] **R:** 400
Personality (Ratings and self-reports) **P:** 301
Psychology (Modern psychology) **P:** 850
Psychotherapy (Humanistic-experiential psychotherapy) **P:** 852
Rogers, Daniel [American political leader]
Delaware (table) **D:** 109
Rogers, George [American football player]
Football (table) **F:** 363

Rogers, Ginger [American actress] **R:** 400
Astaire, Fred **A:** 822 *with picture*
Motion picture (Best performance by an actress: 1940) **M:** 862
Rogers, John [American political leader]
Washington (table) **W:** 65
Rogers, John [American sculptor]
Sculpture (American sculpture) **S:** 255-256
Rogers, John Jacob [American political leader]
Foreign Service (The Rogers Act) **F:** 388a
Rogers, Joseph W. [American aviator]
Aviation (table: Aviation speed records) **A:** 990
Rogers, Kenny [American singer]
Country music (Modern country music) **Ci:** 1098c-1098d
Rogers, Robert [colonial military leader]
Rogers's Rangers **R:** 401
Rogers, Roy [American actor] **R:** 401
Western frontier life in America (Entertainment) **W:** 240
Rogers, Will [American humorist] **R:** 401 *with portrait*
Oklahoma (Visitor's guide) **O:** 722
Rogers, William Pierce [American government official]
Eisenhower, Dwight David (table) **E:** 152
Justice, Department of (table) **J:** 203
Rogers Act [1924]
Foreign Service (The Rogers Act) **F:** 388a
Rogers Centre [stadium]
Toronto (Landmarks) **T:** 338-339 *with picture*
Rogers's Rangers [U.S. history] **R:** 401
Rangers **R:** 51
Roget, Peter Mark [British scholar] **R:** 401
Roget's Thesaurus of English Words and Phrases [book]
Roget, Peter Mark **R:** 401
Roggeveen, Jacob [Dutch admiral]
Easter Island **E:** 45
Samoa (History) **S:** 80a-80b
Rogue River Wars [1850's]
Oregon (Indian treaties and conflicts) **O:** 846-848
Roh Moo-hyun [Korean political leader]
Korea, South (Recent developments) **K:** 378d
Roh Tae Woo [Korean political leader]
Korea, South (A new constitution) **K:** 378c-378d
Roha [ancient city]
Ethiopia (The Zagwé dynasty) **E:** 371
Rohan, Chevalier de [French political figure]
Voltaire (Imprisonment and early success) **V:** 446
Rohmann, Eric [American illustrator]
Caldecott Medal (table: 2003) **C:** 26
Rohrer, Heinrich [Swiss physicist]
Nobel Prizes (Physics: 1986) **N:** 441
Rohypnol [drug]
Drug abuse (Club drugs) **D:** 363; (table: Some commonly abused drugs) **D:** 363
Roi s'amuse, Le [play by Hugo]
Opera: (Rigoletto) **O:** 806
Roi-soleil, Le [name for]
Louis XIV **L:** 474
Rojankovsky, Feodor [Russian-American artist]
Caldecott Medal (table: 1956) **C:** 26
Rojas, Fernando de [Spanish dramatist]
Spanish literature (The 1400's) **So:** 758
Rojas, Manuel [Chilean author]
Latin American literature (The mid-1900's) **L:** 114
Rokko tunnels [Japan]
Tunnel (table) **T:** 491
Rokossovsky, Konstantin K. [Soviet general]
Poland (Communist rule) **P:** 613
Roland [literary figure]
Roland de la Platière, Marie Jeanne **R:** 401
Roland de la Platière, Marie Jeanne [French political leader] **R:** 401
Roldán, Francisco [Spanish jurist]
Columbus, Christopher (Problems in Hispaniola) **Ci:** 862
Role [drama]
Theater (Creating a role) **T:** 238
Role, Social [social psychology] *See* Social role *in this index*
Role conflict
Social role **So:** 552
Role model [psychology]
Child (Serving as models of appropriate behavior) **C:** 451
Role playing [psychology] **R:** 402
Sexuality (In childhood) **S:** 338
Role-playing game
Electronic game (The growth of computer gaming) **E:** 204e
Game (Board games) **G:** 22
Internet (Online communities) **I:** 350b
Rolfe, John [English colonist] **R:** 402
Colonial life in America (Jamestown) **Ci:** 789
Jamestown **J:** 29
Pocahontas **P:** 588

Powhatan **P:** 728
Virginia (Progress of the colony) **V:** 418
Rolfe, Thomas [son of]
Pocahontas **P:** 588
Roll [archaeology]
Scroll **S:** 227
Roll [aviation]
Airplane (Basic movements and controls) **A:** 222 *with diagrams*
Ship (The chief parts of a ship) **S:** 424
Roll bar
Automobile racing (Safety measures) **A:** 975-976
Roll cage
Automobile racing (Safety measures) **A:** 975-976
Roll-call vote
Congress of the United States (Passing a bill) **Ci:** 945
Parliamentary procedure (Voting on motions) **P:** 177
Political convention (Making nominations) **P:** 629
Roll casting [process]
Aluminum (Thin slabs) **A:** 395
Roll-on/roll-off ship
Ship *picture on* **S:** 420; (Roll-on/roll-off ships) **S:** 408 *with picture*
Roll-out [sports]
Football (table) **F:** 356
Rolland, Romain [French author] **R:** 402
Rolled oats [food]
Oatmeal **O:** 640
Roller [bird] **R:** 402
Bird (Birds of Europe) **B:** 344c *with picture*; (Birds of Africa) **B:** 344h *with picture*
Roller [tool]
Paint (Applying the paint) **P:** 25 *with pictures*
Roller ball pen
Pen (Roller ball pens) **P:** 234
Roller bandage
Bandage **B:** 75
Roller bearing
Bearing (Rolling element bearings) **B:** 189 *with diagram*
Roller coaster [amusement] **R:** 402
Roller dam
Dam (Other types of dams) **D:** 19
Roller gin [machine]
Cotton (Ginning and baling) **Ci:** 1091
Roller hockey
Roller skating (Competitive roller skating) **R:** 402-402a
Roller mill [paint]
Paint *diagram on* **P:** 24
Roller printing
Textile (Finishing the fabric) **T:** 217
Roller skate
Roller skating (Roller skates) **R:** 402 *with picture*
Roller Skates [book by Sawyer]
Sawyer, Ruth **S:** 168
Roller skating [sport] **R:** 402 *with pictures*
Nebraska (Interesting facts) **N:** 95
Roller-spinning machine
Industrial Revolution (Spinning machines) **I:** 248-249
Rollerblades
Roller skating (Roller skates) **R:** 402 *with picture*
Rolling [industrial process]
Aluminum (Rolling) **A:** 395
Iron and steel (Rolling) **I:** 445 *with diagrams*
Rolling blackout
California (The beginning of the 2000's) **C:** 64
Rolling friction
Friction (Kinds of friction) **F:** 532
Rolling ingot
Aluminum (Casting the molten aluminum) **A:** 394
Rolling mill
Industrial Revolution (Coal and iron) **I:** 249
Iron and steel (Rolling) **I:** 445 *with diagrams*
Rolling stock
Railroad (Rolling stock) **R:** 107
Rolling Stones [musical group] **R:** 402a
Rock music (The Rolling Stones) **R:** 380; (Rock music today) **R:** 381 *with picture*
Rollins, Frank W. [American political leader]
New Hampshire (table) **N:** 223
Rollins, Sonny [American saxophonist] **R:** 402a
Davis, Miles *picture on* **D:** 49
Rollo [duke of Normandy]
Normandy **N:** 456
Normans **N:** 456
Vikings (The Danish Vikings) **V:** 383
Rolph, James, Jr. [American political leader]
California (table) **C:** 59
Rolvaag, Karl F. [American political leader]
Minnesota (table) **M:** 602
Rölvaag, Ole Edvart [Norwegian-American author]
American literature (Realist fiction) **A:** 422
Roly poly [animal] *See* Pill bug *in this index*

ROM [electronics] See Read-only memory in this index
Roma [people] R: 402a
  Flag picture on F: 218
  Flamenco F: 225
  Holocaust H: 296
  Romania R: 416
Romaine lettuce
  Lettuce (Kinds of lettuce) L: 214 with picture
Roman, Andre B. [American political leader]
  Louisiana (table) L: 496
Roman alphabet
  Alphabet (The Roman alphabet) A: 383 with pictures
Roman bath
  Rome (Baths) R: 433
Roman calendar
  Calendar (The Romans) C: 31; (The Julian calendar) C: 31
  Month M: 767
Roman candle
  Fireworks (How fireworks work) F: 135
Roman Catholic Church R: 402b with pictures
  See also the list of Related articles in the Roman Catholic Church article
  Bible (table) B: 281; (The Christian Old Testament) B: 282; (Translations of the Bible) B: 284-285; (The Bible in worship) B: 286
  Christianity (Organization) C: 522g; (The medieval church) C: 524; (Christianity today) C: 526-527
  Ireland (Way of life) I: 420
  Missionary (Organization) M: 621
  Monasticism (Christian monasticism) M: 701
  Pope P: 660
  Private school P: 808b
  Religion (How the major religions are organized) R: 218
  Religious life R: 226
  Riot (During the 1800's) R: 348-349
  School (The development of Canadian schools) S: 184
  Vodou V: 436
  Ceremonies, sacraments, and prayers
    Roman Catholic Church (Worship) R: 403
    Anointing of the sick A: 518
    Family (Development of the Western family) F: 22
    Marriage (Wedding ceremonies) M: 220
    Mass M: 269
    Meditation M: 380
    Rosary R: 473
    Sacrament S: 5
  Current issues
    Abortion (Arguments against abortion) A: 15; (Abortion history) A: 15
    Birth control (Opposition to birth control) B: 379
    Divorce (The divorce rate) D: 254-255
    In vitro fertilization I: 95
    Liberation theology L: 228
    Parochial school P: 177
  Doctrines and beliefs
    Roman Catholic Church (Roman Catholic beliefs) R: 403
    Apostles' Creed A: 567
    Bible (The Christian Old Testament) B: 282; (Modern English translations) B: 286; (The Bible in worship) B: 286
    Canonization C: 183
    Christianity (Beliefs) C: 522g
    Grace G: 295
    Immaculate Conception I: 79
    Limbo L: 306
    Mary M: 238
    Old Testament O: 740
    Philosophy (Medieval philosophy) P: 388
    Purgatory P: 909
    Saint (Roman Catholic saints) S: 30
    Transubstantiation T: 401
    Trinity T: 447
    Vulgate V: 453
  History
    Architecture (Baroque architecture) A: 622
    Counter Reformation Ci: 1096
    Eastern Catholic Churches E: 45
    Exploration (Spain's conquests in the New World) E: 445
    Galileo (Galileo and the Roman Catholic Church) G: 12
    Government (Feudalism) G: 290
    Hispanic Americans (Who Hispanic Americans are) H: 245; (In Mexico) H: 248
    Index of Forbidden Books I: 107
    Indulgence I: 240
    Inquisition I: 277
    Latin America (Colonial rule) L: 104; (The rise of

military regimes) L: 110
    Law (The Middle Ages) L: 134
    Mexico (Religion) M: 458
    Middle Ages (The Christian church) M: 523; (The power of the church) M: 525; (Troubles in the church) M: 528
    Mission life in America M: 618 with picture
    Painting (Baroque) P: 58
    Papal States P: 132
    Protestantism P: 833
    Quebec Act Q: 38
    Reformation R: 195
    Religion (Christianity) R: 222-223
    Rome, Ancient (The Roman heritage) R: 448
    Thirty-Nine Articles T: 259
    Trent, Council of T: 434
    Vatican City V: 287
    Vatican Council I V: 289
    Vatican Council II V: 289
    Western Church W: 231
    World, History of the (The Byzantine Empire) W: 434 with pictures
  Ways of life
    Argentina (Religion) A: 651 with picture
    Bolivia (Religion) B: 444
    Brazil (Religion) B: 575
    Italy (Religion) I: 503 with picture; (Social problems) I: 518
    Latin America (Religion) L: 98
    Mexico (Education) M: 459
    Northern Ireland N: 521; (Protestant settlement) N: 524
    Poland (Religion) P: 605
    Spain (Religion) So: 736
Roman Circus
  Circus Maximus
Roman Doric column
  Column (The Roman orders) Ci: 866 with picture
Roman Empire [ancient history]
  See also Byzantine Empire; Rome, Ancient in this index
  Rome, Ancient R: 436; (Government) R: 438; (The Roman heritage) R: 448
  Architecture (Roman architecture) A: 616 with pictures
  Christianity (History) C: 523 with picture
  Europe (The Roman Empire) E: 407 with picture and map
  Flag pictures on F: 216
  Middle Ages (The fall of Rome) M: 522
  Armed forces
    Archaeology picture on A: 596
    Armor picture on A: 720; (In early times) A: 719-720
    Galley G: 15
    Praetorian Guard P: 729
  Emperors See the Emperors of Rome table in the Rome, Ancient article
  Governments and law
    Caesar C: 12
    Citizenship (History) Ci: 572
    Government (Ancient Rome) G: 289
    Justinian Code J: 204
    Law (Ancient Roman law) L: 133
    Peace (Ancient Greece and Rome) P: 206
    Postal services (Ancient times) P: 703
    Torture T: 345
  Provinces
    Bonn (History) B: 461
    Bulgaria (Early history) B: 692
    Colonialism (Ancient colonialism) Ci: 813
    Egypt, Ancient (Later ancient Egypt) E: 144
    England (The Roman conquest) E: 303-304
    France (Early days) F: 471
    Gaul G: 70
    Greece, Ancient (Roman rule) G: 374 with picture
    Jerusalem (Roman rule) J: 101
    Jews (Roman rule) J: 122
    Middle East (Early civilizations) M: 533
    Palestine (Roman rule) P: 104
    Pompeii (Early days) P: 653
    Portugal (Roman rule) P: 692
    Romania (Ancestry) R: 417; (Early days) R: 423
    Spain picture on So: 746; (Roman conquest) So: 745
    Wales (History) W: 11-12
  Republic to empire
    Actium, Battle of A: 30
    Augustus A: 889 with map
    Rome, Ancient (The Roman Empire) R: 446
  The last years
    Rome, Ancient (The decline of the empire) R: 447
    Alaric A: 281
    Attila A: 879 with map
    Barbarian B: 104

    Goths G: 279
    Italy (End of the Roman Empire) I: 512-513
    Odoacer O: 674
  Transportation and trade
    Appian Way A: 569 with picture and map
    Exploration (The Romans) E: 441
Roman-fleuve [literature]
  Rolland, Romain R: 402
Roman Forum See Forum, Roman in this index
Roman gods See Rome, Ancient in this index
Roman Hat Mystery, The [book by Queen]
  Queen, Ellery Q: 39
Roman Holiday [film]
  Hepburn, Audrey H: 192
Roman-Kosh [mountain, Ukraine]
  Ukraine (The Crimean Mountains) U: 10 with map
Roman law
  Justinian Code J: 204
  Law (Civil law systems) L: 132; (Ancient Roman law) L: 133
  Rome, Ancient (The law) R: 438; (The Roman heritage) R: 448
  Twelve Tables, Laws of the T: 531
Roman mile [unit of measure]
  Mile M: 542
Roman mythology See Rome, Ancient in this index
Roman numerals R: 413
  Number (Roman numerals) N: 605; (The Romans) N: 607
Roman question [Italian history]
  Benedict XV B: 247
  Pius XI P: 503
Roman Republic
  See also Rome, Ancient in this index; and the Government and History sections in the Related articles of the Rome, Ancient article
  Rome, Ancient (The Roman Republic) R: 438; (History) R: 444
Roman type [printing]
  Handwriting (Early forms of writing) H: 49-50
  Type (Classes of type) T: 537 with picture
Roman walls [fortifications] R: 414 with picture
Romance [literature] R: 414
  American literature (The romance) A: 418
  English literature (The development of English romances) E: 315
  Fiction (History) F: 90
  French literature (Narrative poetry) F: 518
  German literature (The romance) G: 138
  Poetry (Medieval poetry) P: 596
  Romance languages R: 415
  Shakespeare, William (Shakespeare's plays) S: 354-355
  Spanish literature (The 1400's) So: 758
Romance [play by Mamet]
  Mamet, David M: 115
Romance languages R: 415
  Italian language I: 492
  Language (Indo-European) L: 65-66
  Romance R: 414
Romance of Renard [poem]
  French literature (Narrative poetry) F: 518-519
Romance of the Rose [poem]
  French literature (Narrative poetry) F: 518
Romance of the Three Kingdoms [book by Luo Guanzhong]
  Chinese literature (Drama and fiction) C: 511
Romanesque architecture R: 415 with picture
  Architecture (Romanesque architecture) A: 618 with picture; (Early modern architecture in America) A: 629
  Europe (Medieval art) E: 391
  Leaning Tower of Pisa L: 162 with picture
  Richardson, Henry Hobson R: 330 with picture
Romanesque art
  Painting (Romanesque painting) P: 50 with picture
Romanesques, Les [play by Rostand]
  Rostand, Edmond R: 484
Romani [language]
  Roma (Language and culture) R: 402b
Romani, Felice [Italian author]
  Bellini, Vincenzo B: 244
Romania R: 416 with pictures and maps
  See also the list of Related articles in the Romania article
  Communism (In Eastern Europe) Ci: 896-897
  Moldova M: 690
  Transylvania T: 402
  Warsaw Pact W: 39
  World War I (Eastern Europe) W: 459-460 with map
Romanian Athenaeum
  Bucharest B: 662
Romanian Rhapsodies [music by Enesco]
  Romania (The arts) R: 419
Romanies [people]

Roma R: 402a
Romano [cheese]
　Cheese (Very hard, or grating, cheese) C: 392
　　with picture
Romanos the Melode [Greek poet]
　Greek literature (Medieval literature) G: 378
Romanov [Russian history] R: 426
Romanov, Anastasia [czarina of Russia] *See*
　Anastasia, Grand Duchess *in this index*
Romanov, Michael [czar of Russia]
　Russia (table: Czars and empresses) R: 549; (The
　　early Romanovs) R: 549
Romanow, Roy [Canadian political leader]
　Saskatchewan (table) S: 144
Romans, Epistle to the [New Testament] R: 426
　Bible (The Letters) B: 284
Romans antiques [literature]
　French literature (Narrative poetry) F: 518
Romans bretons [literature]
　French literature (Narrative poetry) F: 518
Romansh [language]
　Switzerland (Language) So: 1053
Romantic comedy
　Comedy Ci: 867
Romantic hero [literature]
　Romanticism (The qualities of Romanticism)
　　R: 427
Romantic movement *See* Romanticism *in this index*
Romantic tutu [costume]
　Ballet (Sets and costumes) B: 49-50
Romanticism [arts] R: 426
　Ballet (Romantic ballet) B: 51
　Beethoven, Ludwig van (Beethoven's place in
　　music history) B: 214
　Classical music (The Romantic era) Ci: 648
　Classicism (The qualities of Classicism) Ci: 653
　Criticism (History of literary criticism) Ci: 1146
　Drama (Romanticism) D: 337
　English literature (Romantic literature) E: 319
　Europe (From 1600 to 1900) E: 392
　France (Literature) F: 461-462
　French literature (Romanticism) F: 521
　German literature (Romanticism) G: 140
　Italian literature (Romanticism) I: 495
　Latin American literature (Romanticism) L: 112
　Novel R: 571; (The 1800's) N: 572
　Opera (Romanticism) O: 798
　Painting (Romanticism) P: 68 *with pictures*
　Philosophy (Philosophy in the 1800's) P: 390
　Poetry (Romantic poetry) P: 597
　Realism R: 171
　Rousseau, Jean-Jacques (His literary influence)
　　R: 493
　Russian literature (The age of Romanticism)
　　R: 560
　Scandinavian literature (The Golden Age) S: 171
　Sculpture (European sculpture) S: 253-254 *with
　　picture*
　Spanish literature (The 1800's) So: 761
Romanus [pope]
　Pope (table) P: 666
Romberg, Sigmund [American composer] R: 427
　Musical comedy (The first musicals) M: 959
Rome [Italy] R: 428 *with pictures and maps*
　See also Rome, Ancient *in this index; and the list of
　　Related articles in the* Rome *article*
　City picture on Ci: 580
　Italy *pictures on* I: 497; (table: Average monthly
　　weather) I: 509
　Vatican City V: 287
Rome [New York] R: 435
Rome, Ancient R: 436 *with pictures and map*
　See also Roman Empire *in this index; the* Emperors
　　of Rome *table in the* Rome, Ancient *article*
　February F: 60
　Name (The history of names) N: 7
　Postal services (Ancient times) P: 703
　Rome R: 433 *with pictures and map*
　Art and architecture
　　Rome, Ancient (Way of life) R: 438 *with pictures;*
　　　(Arts and sciences) R: 442
　　Alphabet (The Roman alphabet) A: 383 *with
　　　pictures*
　　Arch A: 593
　　Architecture (Roman architecture) A: 616 *with
　　　pictures*
　　Classical music (Early music) Ci: 645
　　Classicism (Rome) Ci: 653
　　Colosseum Ci: 849 *with picture*
　　Column (The Roman orders) Ci: 866 *with
　　　pictures*
　　Drama (Roman drama) D: 328
　　Europe (The arts) E: 391
　　Hippodrome H: 240
　　Latin language L: 114
　　Latin literature L: 115
　　Novel (Ancient Greek and Roman narratives)

　　　N: 572
　　Painting (Egyptian painting) P: 40-41; (Roman
　　　painting) P: 42 *with picture*
　　Pantheon P: 131
　　Poetry (Ancient poetry) P: 595-596
　　Sculpture (Roman sculpture) S: 247 *with
　　　pictures*
　Defense
　　Rome, Ancient (The army) R: 438
　　Army (Ancient armies) A: 726
　　Germany (Ancient times) G: 162
　　Helmet H: 178 *with pictures*
　　Navy (Ancient navies) N: 79
　Education
　　Rome, Ancient (Education) R: 442
　　Education (Ancient Roman education) E: 98
　　Library (Rome) L: 258
　Government
　　Rome, Ancient (Government) R: 438
　　Augur A: 885
　　Ballot (Older customs) B: 63
　　Census (Early censuses) C: 349
　　Consul Ci: 1017
　　Democracy (Origins of democracy) D: 122
　　Dictatorship D: 191
　　Equestrian order E: 347
　　Fasces F: 48
　　Forum, Roman F: 420 *with picture*
　　Freedom (In ancient Greece and Rome) F: 502
　　Government (Ancient Rome) G: 289
　　Law (Ancient Roman law) L: 133
　　Patricians P: 196
　　Plebeians P: 571
　　Tribune T: 440
　　Triumvirate T: 448
　　Twelve Tables, Laws of the T: 531
　Health and welfare
　　Bath (History) B: 164 *with picture*
　　Fire department (History) F: 127
　History
　　Rome, Ancient (History) R: 444
　　England (The Roman conquest) E: 303
　　Etruscans E: 375
　　Europe (Ancient Rome) E: 407 *with map*
　　Exploration (The Romans) E: 441
　　Gaul G: 70
　　History (The ancient Greeks and Romans)
　　　H: 261
　　Lyon L: 537
　　Medicine (Greece and Rome) M: 372-373
　　Punic Wars P: 903
　　Romulus and Remus R: 450a
　　Sibyl S: 445
　　Slavery S: 501 *with picture*
　　Turkey (History) T: 509
　　Utica U: 251
　　World, History of the (The Romans) W: 429
　People
　　Rome, Ancient (The people) R: 437
　　City (Ancient cities) Ci: 578 *with picture*
　　Clothing (Rome) Ci: 697 *with picture*
　　Cork Ci: 1054
　　Family (Ancient families) F: 21-22
　　Fire prevention (Fire prevention laws) F: 132
　　Food (Ancient times) F: 336
　　Furniture (Ancient Rome) F: 570 *with picture*
　　Hairdressing (Ancient times) H: 11 *with picture*
　　Installment plan I: 304
　　Races, Human (Race and discrimination) R: 59
　　Ring *picture on* R: 342
　　Sabines S: 3
　　Shelter (Ancient times) S: 393
　Recreation and sports
　　Boxing (Ancient history) B: 531
　　Rome, Ancient (Recreation) R: 440 *with picture*
　Religion and mythology
　　Rome, Ancient (Religion) R: 441
　　Bell (History) B: 239
　　Galilee G: 11
　　Lares and penates L: 76
　　Mythology (table) M: 981; (Roman mythology)
　　　M: 982 *with picture*
　　New Year's Day (Early customs) N: 289
　　Rome, Ancient (Religion) R: 441
　　Saturnalia S: 153
　　Vesta V: 342
　Social and cultural life
　　Circus (History) Ci: 562b
　　Cremation Ci: 1126
　　Gladiator G: 206
　　Marriage (Origins of some wedding customs)
　　　M: 221
　　Tomb T: 326
　　Women's movement (In ancient societies)
　　　W: 384
　Technology and science
　　Rome, Ancient (Science) R: 443

　　Agriculture (Rome) A: 156
　　Aqueduct (Ancient aqueducts) A: 580
　　Astrology (History) A: 827
　　Calendar (The Romans) C: 31
　　Drug (Drugs in ancient times) D: 358
　　Geography (Early study) G: 95
　　Geology (The Romans) G: 98
　　Number (The Romans) N: 607
　　Paint (The history of paint) P: 26
　　Pipe (History) P: 489
　　Road (The first roads) R: 361
　　Roman numeral R: 413
　　Science (Ancient Rome) S: 197
　　Ship *pictures on* S: 418; (Roman ships) S: 416
　　Transportation (Ancient Rome) T: 387
　　Warship *picture on* W: 42
　Trade
　　Rome, Ancient (Trade) R: 443
　　Trade (Early trade) T: 362-363
　　Trade route (Early trade routes) T: 363
Rome, King of [son of Napoleon I]
　Napoleon II N: 17
Rome, Treaties of [1957]
　European Union (Formation of the European
　　Community) E: 420
Rome, University of [Italy] R: 449
　Rome (Schools) R: 430 *with picture*; (Period of
　　construction) R: 435
Rome Auditorium [Italy]
　Rome (Recent developments) R: 435
Rome Beauty [apple]
　Apple (table) A: 571 *with picture*
Rome-Berlin Axis [World War II]
　Axis A: 994
　Italy (World War II) I: 517
　World War II (Aggression on the march) W: 470-
　　472
Romé de l'Isle [French mineralogist]
　Mineral (The scientific study of mineral crystals)
　　M: 571
**Rome Statute of the International Criminal
　Court** [1998]
　International Criminal Court I: 339
Romeo and Juliet [opera by Gounod]
　Gounod, Charles G: 281
Romeo and Juliet [play by Shakespeare] R: 449
　Shakespeare, William: *(Romeo and Juliet)* S: 357
Romer, Roy [American political leader]
　Colorado (table) Ci: 844
Romer v. Evans [U.S. history]
　Homosexuality (Attitudes toward homosexuality)
　　H: 307
Romero, Carlos Humberto [Salvadoran political
　leader]
　El Salvador (The 1900's) E: 252
Romero, Oscar Arnulfo [Salvadoran archbishop]
　R: 450
　El Salvador (The 1900's) E: 252
Romero Barceló, Carlos [Puerto Rican political
　leader]
　Puerto Rico (Puerto Rico today) P: 884
Rommel, Erwin [German general] R: 450
　Montgomery, Bernard Law M: 766
　World War II (The Western Desert Campaign)
　　W: 476-477; (The Tunisia Campaign) W: 481-
　　482; (D-Day) W: 483-484
Romney [West Virginia]
　West Virginia (Interesting facts) W: 207
Romney, Ann Davies [wife of Mitt Romney]
　Romney, Mitt (Early life and family) R: 450
Romney, George Wilcken [American government
　official]
　Housing and Urban Development, Department
　　of (table) H: 393
　Michigan (table) M: 507; (The mid-1900's) M: 511
Romney, Mitt [American political leader] R: 450
　with portrait
　Massachusetts (table) M: 288
　Obama, Barack (The 2012 election) O: 642
　Ryan, Paul R: 572
Romney sheep
　Sheep *picture on* S: 381; (Long-wooled sheep)
　　S: 382
Romulus and Remus [legendary figures] R: 450a
　Calendar (The Romans) C: 31
　Mars M: 222
　Mythology (Romulus and Remus) M: 983 *with
　　picture*
　Rome, Ancient (The regal period) R: 444 *with
　　picture*
　Sabines S: 3
Romulus Augustulus [Roman emperor] R: 450a
　Rome, Ancient (table) R: 447
RON [measurement] *See* Research octane number
　in this index
Ronald Reagan [ship]
　Aircraft carrier (The United States carrier fleet)

A: 206
Ronald Reagan Building [Washington, D.C.]
Washington, D.C. *map on* W: 76
Ronald Reagan Washington National Airport
Washington, D.C. (Transportation) W: 84-85
Ronaldinho [Brazilian-born soccer player] R: 450a
Ronaldo [Brazilian soccer player] R: 450b *with picture*
Ronaldo, Cristiano [Portuguese soccer player]
R: 450b
Roncaglia, Diet of [meeting]
Adrian IV A: 67
Roncalli, Angelo Giuseppe [birth name of]
John XXIII J: 132
Rond de jambe [movement]
Ballet (table) B: 45
Rond-Point [landmark]
Paris (Gardens, squares, and parks) P: 162
Rondanini Pietà [sculpture by Michelangelo]
Michelangelo (Later years) M: 487
Rondel [poetry]
Poetry (table) P: 594
Rondine, La [opera by Puccini]
Puccini, Giacomo P: 870
Rondo [music]
Classical music (Rondo) Ci: 644
Ronne, Edith [American explorer]
Antarctica (Exploration by air) A: 537-538
Ronne, Finn [American explorer]
Antarctica (Exploration by air) A: 537-538
Ronsard, Pierre de [French poet] R: 450b
French literature (The Pléiade) F: 519-520
Roof R: 450b *with pictures*
Coal (Mine safety) Ci: 729
House (The roof) H: 382 *with diagram*
Pioneer life in America (A pioneer settlement)
P: 479-480
Shelter *picture on* S: 392
Roof comb [architecture]
Maya (Arts and crafts) M: 325
Roof of the World [nickname]
Pamirs P: 112
Tibet T: 276
Roof rat
Rat (The body of a rat) R: 146 *with picture*
Rook [bird] R: 450c
Rook [chess]
Chess (The board and the men) C: 411-412 *with diagram*; (The moves) C: 412
Rookery [zoology]
Penguin *picture on* P: 239
Rook R: 450c
Seal (Seal rookeries) S: 266
Rookery building [Chicago]
Root, John Wellborn R: 472
Rookwood [book by Ainsworth]
Turpin, Dick T: 519
Rookwood pottery
Pottery (Pottery of the 1700's and 1800's)
P: 718-719
Room
Interior design I: 326 *with pictures*
Room air conditioner
Air conditioning (Kinds of air conditioners)
A: 179; (Choosing a window air conditioner)
A: 179-180
Room-and-pillar mining
Coal (The room-and-pillar system) Ci: 723 *with diagram*
Mining (Self-supported mining) M: 576
Salt (Salt from the ground) S: 73-74
Room at the Top [book by Braine]
English literature (Literature after World War II)
E: 322-323
Room entry [mining]
Coal (The room-and-pillar syste) Ci: 723-724 *with diagram*
Room of One's Own, A [essay by Woolf]
Woolf, Virginia W: 401
Room service
Hotel H: 376
Rooms, The [Grand Bank]
Newfoundland and Labrador (Libraries and museums) N: 364
Rooney, Wayne [English soccer player] R: 450c
Roosevelt [ship] *See* Theodore Roosevelt *in this index*
Roosevelt, Alice [daughter of]
Roosevelt, Theodore (Life in the White House)
R: 465-466
Roosevelt, Alice Hathaway Lee [wife of]
Roosevelt, Theodore (First marriage) R: 462 *with picture*
Roosevelt, Anna Eleanor [daughter of]
Roosevelt, Franklin Delano (Roosevelt's family)
R: 450f *with picture*
Roosevelt, Edith Carow [wife of Theodore

Roosevelt]
First ladies of the United States (table) F: 142
Roosevelt, Theodore (Second marriage) R: 463 *with picture*; (Life in the White House) R: 465-466
Roosevelt, Eleanor [American stateswoman]
R: 450c *with portrait*
African Americans (The Great Depression)
A: 136n
First ladies of the United States F: 143 *with picture*
Franklin Delano Roosevelt Memorial F: 493
Roosevelt, Franklin Delano (Roosevelt's family)
R: 450f *with picture*; (Family crisis) R: 451; (Foreign policy) R: 454
Truman, Harry S. (First administration [1945-1949]) T: 468
Roosevelt, Elliott [son of]
Roosevelt, Franklin Delano (Roosevelt's family)
R: 450f *with picture*
Roosevelt, Franklin Delano [U.S. president]
R: 450d *with pictures*
African Americans (The Great Depression)
A: 136n
Asian Americans (Japanese internment) A: 812f
Atlantic Charter A: 862 *with picture*
Bank (The crisis of 1933) B: 93-94
Bennett, Richard Bedford *picture on* B: 253
Churchill, Sir Winston Leonard Spencer (Meetings with Roosevelt) C: 548 *with picture*
Cold War (The alliance breaks up) C: 763
Congress of the United States (Continued struggle for power) C: 948
Conservation (The rise of the conservation movement) Ci: 985-986
Democracy (Famous quotations about democracy) D: 120
Democratic Party D: 124; (The New Deal) D: 126 *with picture*
Einstein, Albert (Letter to President Roosevelt)
E: 147
Franklin Delano Roosevelt Memorial F: 493 *with picture*
Freedom (The 1900's) F: 503
Garner, John Nance G: 44
Great Depression G: 338
Hoover, Herbert Clark (Election of 1932) H: 330
Hopkins, Harry Lloyd H: 333
Jackson, Robert Houghwout J: 16
Japanese American internment J: 60
Johnson, Lyndon Baines (Election to the House)
J: 146
Knox, Frank K: 357
Monroe Doctrine (The Good Neighbor Policy)
M: 740
New Deal N: 200
New York (Places to visit) N: 302 *with picture*; (table) N: 313
Pearl Harbor (The attack) P: 218-219
President of the United States *picture on* P: 765; (The rebirth of presidential leadership)
P: 768-769
Presidential assistant P: 770
Public opinion poll (History) P: 863
Radio (The Golden Age of Broadcasting) R: 92-93 *with picture*
Roosevelt, Eleanor R: 450c
Saint Lawrence Seaway (Agreements of 1941 and 1954) S: 45
Stalin, Joseph (World War II) So: 827
Tehran Conference T: 88
Union of Soviet Socialist Republics (Results of the war) U: 37
United States, History of the (Recovery and reform) U: 193
Wallace, Henry Agard W: 16
White House (A new building) W: 290
Willkie, Wendell Lewis W: 314
Works Progress Administration W: 405
World War II (The United States enters the war)
W: 478 *with picture*; (The war in Europe and North Africa) W: 480
Roosevelt, Franklin Delano, Jr. [son of]
Roosevelt, Franklin Delano (Roosevelt's family)
R: 450f *with picture*
Roosevelt, James [father of]
Roosevelt, Franklin Delano (Boyhood) R: 450e
Roosevelt, James [son of]
Roosevelt, Franklin Delano (Roosevelt's family)
R: 450f *with picture*
Roosevelt, John [son of]
Roosevelt, Franklin Delano (Roosevelt's family)
R: 450f *with picture*
Roosevelt, Martha Bulloch [mother of]
Roosevelt, Theodore (Boyhood and education)
R: 460
Roosevelt, Nicholas J. [American inventor] R: 459
Roosevelt, Sara Delano [mother of]

Roosevelt, Franklin Delano (Boyhood) R: 450e
Roosevelt, Theodore [father of]
Roosevelt, Theodore (Boyhood and education)
R: 460
Roosevelt, Theodore [U.S. president] R: 460 *with pictures*
Cleveland, Grover (Governor of New York) Ci: 670
Congress of the United States (Continued struggle for power) Ci: 948
Conservation (The rise of the conservation movement) Ci: 985 *with picture*
Fairbanks, Charles Warren F: 9
Football (Changes in the game) F: 366
Hague Conventions H: 7
Madeira River M: 30
McKinley, William ("President of the whole people") M: 341; (Assassination) M: 341-342
Monroe Doctrine (The Roosevelt Corollary)
M: 739
Mount Rushmore National Memorial *picture on*
M: 887
Muckrakers M: 908
New York (table) N: 313; (The early 1900's) N: 318
Panama Canal (The United States and the canal)
P: 125-126 *with picture*
President of the United States *picture on* P: 765; (The rebirth of presidential leadership)
P: 768-769
Progressive Party (The "Bull Moose" Party) P: 814
Republican Party *picture on* R: 256; (The party splits) R: 255
Roosevelt, Franklin Delano R: 450d
Rough Riders R: 490
Russo-Japanese War (Treaty of Portsmouth)
R: 566b
Sierra Club *picture on* S: 450
Spanish-American War (Land battles) So: 754 *with picture*
Taft, William Howard (Secretary of war) T: 10; (Election of 1912) T: 12
Tyler, John T: 532
United States, History of the (Theodore Roosevelt) U: 187
Western frontier life in America (Literature)
W: 239
White House (A new building) W: 290
White House conference W: 291
Wilson, Woodrow (Presidential candidate) W: 322
Roosevelt, Theodore, Jr. [American government official] R: 469
American Legion (History) A: 413
Roosevelt and Hopkins: An Intimate History [book by Sherwood]
Sherwood, Robert Emmet S: 398
Roosevelt Campobello International Park [New Brunswick] R: 469
New Brunswick (Places to visit) N: 188 *with picture*
Roosevelt Corollary [American history]
Monroe Doctrine (The Roosevelt Corollary)
M: 739
Roosevelt, Theodore (Foreign policy) R: 465
Roosevelt Cottage
New Brunswick *picture on* N: 189
Roosevelt Dam [Salt River, Arizona] R: 469
Phoenix (History) P: 398-399
Roosevelt Island [New York]
New York City (Small islands) N: 330
Roosevelt Memorial [Washington, D.C.] *See*
Franklin Delano Roosevelt Memorial *in this index*
Roost [zoology]
Bird (Sleeping and resting) B: 355
Bird of prey (Roosting) B: 374b
Root [anatomy]
Hair (The root and shaft) H: 9 *with diagram*
Teeth (Kinds of teeth) T: 79; (Pulp) T: 80 *with diagram*
Root [arithmetic] R: 469
Algebra (Statements and equations) A: 351
Logarithms (Finding a root) L: 424
Root [aviation]
Airplane (The wing) A: 213
Root [botany] R: 469 *with diagrams*
Agriculture (Root crops) A: 147
Corn (How the plant develops) Ci: 1057-1058 *with picture*
Mangrove M: 140 *with picture*
Plant (Roots) P: 527 *with pictures*; (Germination) P: 535 *with pictures*; (Movement of water) P: 537; (Environmental factors) P: 538-539
Tree (Roots) T: 417 *with diagram*
Vegetable (Roots) V: 292 *with picture*
Root [spelling]
Spelling (Adding new words) So: 777
Root, Elihu [American statesman] R: 471
United States Army War College U: 198
Root, John Wellborn [American architect] R: 472

Architecture (Early modern architecture in America) A: 629
Burnham, Daniel Hudson B: 709
Root canal [anatomy]
Teeth (Pulp) T: 80 *with diagram*
Root canal therapy
Dentistry (Endodontics) D: 144
Teeth (Dental decay) T: 82-83
Root cap [botany]
Plant (Roots) P: 528 *with picture*
Root (The root tip) R: 470 *with diagram*
Root hair [botany]
Plant (Roots) P: 528 *with picture*
Root *diagram on* R: 470; (The outer tissues) R: 470
Tree (Roots) T: 417
Root-Takahira Agreement [1908]
Roosevelt, Theodore (Friction with Japan) R: 467
Rootling [agriculture]
Grape (Planting and cultivating) G: 319-320
Roots [book by Haley] R: 472
American literature (Works by minority writers) A: 425
Haley, Alex H: 19
"Roots" [television program]
Roots R: 472
Television (The 1970's) T: 119-120
Rootstock [botany]
Apple (Planting and caring for apple trees) A: 571
Fruit (Fruit production) F: 546
Grafting G: 298 *with picture*
Lemon (Growing lemons) L: 189
Pear (Planting and care) P: 215-216
Rose (Reproducing and growing roses) R: 475
Rope R: 472 *with pictures*
Cowboy (His rope) Ci: 1109 *with picture*
Knots, hitches, and splices K: 355
Macramé M: 26
Pulley P: 900 *with diagram*
Rope and Faggot [book by White]
White, Walter Francis W: 285
Roper, Daniel C. [American government official]
Commerce, Department of (table) Ci: 871
Roosevelt, Franklin Delano (table) R: 454
Roper, Elmo [American statistician]
Public opinion poll (History) P: 863
Roper, Sylvester H. [American inventor]
Automobile (The steam car) A: 965
Ropin' the Wind [recording]
Brooks, Garth B: 641
Roquefort [cheese]
Cheese (Semisoft cheese) C: 392 *with picture*
Mold M: 690
Rorqual [animal]
Whale (Rorquals) W: 255; (Skin and blubber) W: 259
Rorschach test [psychology]
Personality (Projective tests) P: 301-302
Rosa, Henrique [Guinea-Bissau political leader]
Guinea-Bissau (History) G: 434
Rosa, João Guimarães [Brazilian author]
Brazil (The arts) B: 576-577
Rosalie [mansion]
Mississippi picture on M: 622
Rosario [Argentina] R: 473
Rosary [religion] R: 473
Meditation M: 380
Rosary pea [seed]
Poisonous plant R: 602
Rosas, Juan Manuel de [Argentine political leader]
Argentina (Early independence) A: 656
Latin America (Early years of independence) L: 107-108
Pedro II P: 228
Rosat [satellite]
Telescope pictures on T: 107
Rosberg, Keke [Finnish race car driver]
Automobile racing (table: Formula One World Drivers' Championship) A: 980
Roscius, Quintus [Roman actor] R: 474
Rose [plant] R: 474 *with pictures*
Attar A: 878
Eglantine E: 119
Flower *picture on* F: 287; (Flowering shrubs) F: 281 *with picture*; (table) F: 301 *with picture*
Heraldry *picture on* H: 195
Oregon *picture on* O: 830
Rose water R: 478
Rosé [wine]
Alcoholic beverage (Wine) A: 336
Wine (Types of wine) W: 336
Rose, Derrick [American basketball player] R: 476
Basketball B: 154b
Rose, Ernestine Potowski [American social reformer] R: 476
Rose, Fred [American songwriter]
Country music (Emergence of the country music

industry) Ci: 1098b-1098c
Rose, Irwin [American chemist]
Nobel Prizes (Chemistry: 2004) N: 444
Rose, Sir John [Canadian political leader] R: 476
Rose, Mauri [American race driver]
Automobile racing (table: Indianapolis 500 winners) A: 980
Rose, Murray [Australian swimmer]
Swimming (History) So: 1047
Rose, Pete [American baseball player] R: 476 *with picture*
Baseball (Recent developments) B: 137-138 *with picture*; (table: Modern major league records) B: 138
Rose, Uriah Milton [American lawyer] R: 477
Rose Bowl
California (Visitor's guide) C: 46
Pasadena P: 189
Rose-breasted grosbeak
Bird picture on B: 358
Grosbeak G: 398 *with picture*
Rose bug [insect]
Rose chafer R: 477 *with picture*
Rose Center for Earth and Space [New York City]
Planetarium picture on P: 514a; (Modern planetariums) P: 514b-514c
Rose chafer [insect] R: 477 *with picture*
Rose comb [physiology]
Chicken (Kinds of chickens) C: 441 *with picture*
Rose-cut [gem]
Gem pictures on G: 79
Rose Fitzgerald Kennedy Greenway [parkland]
Boston (Building boom) B: 504
Rose Garden [book by Saadi]
Saadi S: 2
Rose geranium [plant]
Geranium G: 136
Rose-Marie [operetta by Friml]
Friml, Rudolf R: 534
Rose moss [plant]
Portulaca P: 696
Rose of Dutcher's Coolly [book by Garland]
Garland, Hamlin G: 43
Rose of Jericho [plant]
Resurrection plant R: 264
Rose of Lima, Saint [Peruvian religious figure] R: 477
Rose of Sharon [plant] R: 477 *with picture*
Flower (Flowering shrubs) picture on F: 281
Hibiscus H: 223
Rose Parade [Pasadena]
California picture on C: 47
Rose Period
Picasso, Pablo (The Rose Period) P: 448a *with picture*
Rose quartz [mineral]
Gem picture on G: 78
Quartz (Types) Q: 8
Rose Revolution [Georgian history]
Georgia (History) G: 111
Rose-ringed parakeet [bird]
Parrot (Kinds of parrots) P: 179
Rose water R: 478
Rose window
Stained glass (Technical improvements) So: 823
Window W: 334
Roseate spoonbill
Florida picture on F: 256
Spoonbill So: 801 *with picture*
Roseau [Dominica] R: 478 *with picture*
Dominica D: 302
Rosebay [shrub]
Flower picture on F: 283
Rhododendron R: 318 *with picture*
Rosebery, Earl of [British political leader]
United Kingdom (table: British prime ministers) U: 72
Rosecrans, William Starke [Union general] R: 478
Civil War, American (Battle of Stones River) Ci: 629; (Battle of Chickamauga) Ci: 629-630
Rosella [bird]
Parrot (Kinds of parrots) P: 179
Rosemary [shrub] R: 478 *with picture*
Rosenberg, Alfred [Nazi war criminal] R: 479
Hitler, Adolf (Rise of the Nazis) H: 266
Rosenberg, Julius and Ethel [American public figures] R: 479
Rosenberger v. University of Virginia [U.S. history]
Supreme Court of the United States (Church and state) So: 1001
Rosenborg Palace [Copenhagen]
Christian IV C: 522d
Rosencrantz and Guildenstern Are Dead [play by Stoppard]
Stoppard, Tom So: 912
Rosenkavalier, Der [opera by Strauss]
Opera (Richard Strauss) O: 799; (*Rosenkavalier,*

Der) O: 807 *with picture*
Rosenquist, James Albert [American painter] R: 479
Painting (Pop Art) P: 86
Pop Art P: 659
Rosenthal, Joe [American photographer]
Iwo Jima, Battle of picture on I: 523
Roses, Tournament of
California (Visitor's guide) C: 46
Roses, Wars of the See Wars of the Roses *in this index*
Rosetta [spacecraft]
Comet (Studying comets) Ci: 868-869
Space exploration (Probes to comets) So: 711
Rosetta stone R: 479 *with picture*
Egypt, Ancient (Learning about ancient Egypt) E: 144
Hieroglyphics (Deciphering hieroglyphic writing) H: 226
Rosette [zoology]
Jaguar J: 21
Rosewood [tree product] R: 480
Wood picture on W: 389
Rosh Ha-Shanah [religion] R: 480 *with picture*
Feasts and festivals (In Judaism) F: 58
Judaism (The High Holidays) J: 181
September S: 308
Rosicrucian Order [organization] R: 480
Rosie the Riveter [U.S. history]
United States, History of the (World War II) U: 193
World War II picture on W: 494
Rosie the Riveter National Historical Park [California]
National Park System (table: National historical parks) N: 57
Rosin [material] R: 480
Resin (Natural resins) R: 259
Rosina [opera character]
Opera: (Barber of Seville, The) O: 801 *with picture*
Rosini, Paul [American magician]
Magician (Sleight of hand) M: 51
Roskilde, Treaty of [1658]
Sweden (The age of expansion) So: 1034
Rospigliosi Cup
Shell picture on S: 390
Ross, Alexander [Scottish-born explorer] R: 480
Ross, Betsy [American public figure] R: 481 *with picture*
Flag (First United States flags) F: 208-210
United States flag (The first American flags) U: 200
Ross, C. Ben [American political leader]
Idaho (table) I: 42
Ross, Diana [American singer] R: 481 *with picture*
Gordy, Berry, Jr. G: 273
Ross, Edmund Gibson [American political leader] R: 482
Ross, George [American patriot] R: 482
Ross, George W. [Canadian political leader]
Ontario (table) O: 783
Ross, Harold Wallace [American editor] R: 482
Ross, J. H. [pseudonym of]
Lawrence, T. E. L: 146
Ross, Sir James Clark [British explorer] R: 482
Antarctica map on A: 538; (Early exploration) A: 536
Boothia Peninsula B: 481
Exploration (The exploration of Antarctica) E: 450 *with map*
Ross, John [American Indian chief] R: 482
Ross, John [husband of]
Ross, Betsy R: 481
Ross, Sir John [Scottish explorer]
Boothia Peninsula B: 481
Northwest Passage N: 528
Ross, John Jones [Canadian political leader]
Quebec (table) Q: 29
Ross, Lawrence S. [American political leader]
Texas (table) T: 203
Ross, Malcolm [American balloonist]
Balloon (Balloon explorations) B: 62 *with picture*
Ross, Nellie Tayloe [American political leader] R: 482
Wyoming W: 517, picture on W: 535; (table) W: 532; (The early 1900's) W: 536
Ross, Robert [British general]
Maryland (The War of 1812 and industrial development) M: 258
War of 1812 (Campaigns of 1814) W: 31
Ross, Shapley P. [American settler]
Waco W: 2
Ross, Sinclair [Canadian author]
Canadian literature (Literature between the world wars) C: 158-159
Ross, William B. [American political leader]
Ross, Nellie Tayloe R: 482
Wyoming (table) W: 532

Ross, William H. [American political leader]
Delaware (table) D: 109
Ross Dam [Skagit River, Washington] R: 482
Ross Dependency [region, Antarctica] R: 482
Ross House [post office]
Winnipeg (Cultural life) W: 341
Ross Ice Shelf [region, Antarctica]
Amundsen, Roald (The race to the South Pole)
A: 445
Antarctica (Ocean) A: 533-534 with map; (Early
exploration) A: 536
Exploration (The exploration of Antarctica) E: 450
Iceberg (Antarctic icebergs) I: 17
Ross Lake National Recreation Area
[Washington]
National Park System (table: National recreation
areas) N: 49
Ross Sea [bay]
Antarctica (Ocean) A: 532-534 with map
Exploration (The exploration of Antarctica) E: 450
Southern Ocean (Boundaries) So: 688
Ross seal
Antarctica (Living things) A: 534-535 with picture
Ross Trophy
Hockey (Professional leagues) H: 278-279
Rossbach, Battle of [1757]
Seven Years' War (In Europe) S: 328
Rossby, Carl-Gustaf [Swedish-American
meteorologist]
Meteorology (History) M: 433
Rosse, Lord [Irish astronomer]
Astronomy (Discovering other galaxies) A: 848
Rosseau Lake [Ontario]
Muskoka Lakes M: 963
Rossellini, Albert D. [American political leader]
Washington (table) W: 65
Rossellini, Roberto [Italian director]
Motion picture (Postwar Realism) M: 869
Rossellino, Antonio [Renaissance sculptor]
Sculpture (Early Renaissance) S: 252
Rosselló, Pedro J. [Puerto Rican political leader]
Puerto Rico (Puerto Rico today) P: 884
Rossetti, Christina Georgina [British poet] R: 482
March (Quotations) M: 195
Rossetti, Dante Gabriel [British artist] R: 483 with
picture
Ballade B: 43
Painting (The Pre-Raphaelite Brotherhood) P: 71
Pre-Raphaelite Brotherhood P: 756
Rossi, Aldo [Italian architect] R: 483 with picture
Rossi, Carlo [Italian architect]
Saint Petersburg [Russia] (The city) S: 54
Rossi, Dino [American political leader]
Washington (The late 2000's) W: 69
Rossignol, Lake
Nova Scotia (Rivers and lakes) N: 562 with map
Rossini, Gioacchino Antonio [Italian composer]
R: 484 with portrait
Opera: (Barber of Seville, The) O: 801 with picture
Rossio [structure]
Lisbon picture on L: 348
Rosso antico [china]
Wedgwood ware W: 179
Ross's Landing
Chattanooga C: 388
Rostand, Edmond [French author] R: 484
Rostenkowski, Dan [American political leader]
Congress of the United States (Congressional
ethics) Ci: 948
Rostock [Germany] R: 484
Rostov-on-Don [Russia] R: 484
Rostropovich, Mstislav [Russian musician] R: 484
Rostrum [biology]
Sawfish S: 167 [with picture]
Roswell [New Mexico] R: 484
Area 51 A: 645
New Mexico (table: Average monthly weather)
N: 268
Rosy boa [snake]
Boa B: 426
Rosy wolf snail [animal]
Invasive species (Managing invasive species)
I: 354k
Roszak, Theodore [American sculptor] R: 485 with
picture
Rot [plant disease] R: 485
Alfalfa (Diseases and pests) A: 347
Cotton (Diseases) Ci: 1090
Rotary club [organization]
Rotary International R: 486
Rotary drilling
Drill (Rock drills) D: 348
Gas [fuel] (Producing gas) G: 55
Petroleum (Methods of drilling) P: 338 with
diagram
Rotary engine R: 485 with diagrams
Gasoline engine (Kinds of gasoline engines) G: 63

Rotary International [organization] R: 486 with
picture
Rotary kiln
Furnace (Heating the charge) F: 567
Rotary motion [physics]
Gear G: 75
Machine diagram on M: 13
Pneumatic tool P: 586
Rotary plow
Plow (Other types of plow bottoms) P: 576 with
picture
Road (Clearing ice and snow) R: 360
Rotary press
Newspaper (Printing the newspaper) N: 385 with
picture
Printing (Offset presses) P: 798; (Letterpress
printing) P: 799-800; (Gravure presses) P: 800
with diagram
Rotary pump
Pump (Rotary pumps) P: 900b
Rotary screen printing
Textile (Finishing the fabric) T: 217 with picture
Rotary wing aircraft
Autogiro A: 942 with picture
Helicopter (Lift) H: 171 with diagram
Rotating gun turret
Warship (Warships of the 1800's) W: 41
Rotating reference frame [physics]
Centrifugal force C: 357
Rotating shutter [photography]
Motion picture (The projector) M: 858 with
diagram
Rotation [astronomy]
Coriolis effect Ci: 1053
Earth (How Earth moves) E: 17 with diagram
Jupiter (Orbit and rotation) J: 198
Moon (Rotation and orbit) M: 783
Planet (Rotation) P: 510
Tidal forces T: 280
Time diagram on T: 292; (Sidereal time) T: 288
Weather (Planetary-scale systems) W: 158
Rotation [game]
Billiards (Pool) B: 305
Rotation of crops See Crop rotation in this index
Rotational axis See Axis, of Earth; Axis [mechanics]
in this index
Rotational grazing
Alfalfa (Uses of alfalfa) A: 346-347
Rotational molding
Doll (The doll industry today) D: 294
Plastics (Molding) P: 557
Rotator cuff [anatomy] R: 486
Rotator cuff tendinitis [disorder]
Rotator cuff R: 486
Rotavirus [virus] R: 486
Disease D: 227
Rotblat, Joseph [Polish-born British physicist]
R: 486
Nobel Prizes (Peace: 1995) N: 448b
Pugwash Conferences on Science and World
Affairs P: 886
ROTC See Reserve Officers Training Corps in this
index
Rotenone [insecticide]
Insecticide (Botanical insecticides) I: 302
Jicama J: 126
Roth, Henry [American author] R: 487
Roth, Mark [American bowler] R: 487
Roth, Philip [American author] R: 487
American literature (Fiction and other prose)
A: 424
Novel (The middle and late 1900's) N: 575
Roth IRA [retirement plan]
Pension (Individual pension plans) P: 273
Roth v. United States [U.S. history]
Obscenity and pornography (Legal history for
obscenity) O: 644
Supreme Court of the United States (table)
So: 1002
Rothenberg, Susan [American artist]
Painting (New image painting) P: 87 with picture
Rothermel, Peter Frederick [American painter]
Henry, Patrick picture on H: 190
Rothko, Mark [American painter] R: 487 with
picture
Painting (Abstract Expressionism) P: 84-85
Rothschild [European bankers] R: 488
Rothschild, Amschel Mayer [German banker]
Rothschild (Mayer Amschel Rothschild) R: 488
Rothschild, Carl Mayer [German banker]
Rothschild (Mayer Amschel Rothschild) R: 488
Rothschild, David de [German banker]
Rothschild (David de Rothschild) R: 488
Rothschild, Evelyn de [British banker]
Rothschild (Guy de Rothschild) R: 488
Rothschild, Guy de [German banker]
Rothschild (Guy de Rothschild) R: 488

Rothschild, House of [company]
Rothschild R: 488
Rothschild, James Mayer [German banker]
Rothschild (Mayer Amschel Rothschild) R: 488
Rothschild, Lionel [British political leader]
Rothschild (Lionel Rothschild) R: 488
Rothschild, Mayer Amschel [German banker]
Rothschild (Mayer Amschel Rothschild) R: 488
Rothschild, Nathan Mayer [1777-1836, German
banker]
Rothschild (Nathan Mayer Rothschild) R: 488
Rothschild, Nathan Mayer [1840-1915, British
political leader]
Rothschild (Lionel Rothschild) R: 488
Rothschild, Salomon Mayer [German banker]
Rothschild (Mayer Amschel Rothschild) R: 488
Rothstein, Arthur [American photographer]
Photography (Dramatic changes) P: 425-426
Rothstein, Marshall [Canadian jurist]
Supreme Court of Canada (table) So: 997 with
portrait
Rotifer [microorganism] R: 488 with pictures
Animal (A classification of the animal kingdom)
A: 506 with picture
Rotogravure [printing]
Offset O: 678
Printing (Gravure cylinders) P: 800 with diagram
Rotor [aviation]
Helicopter (Types of helicopters) H: 170-171 with
diagrams
Rotor [motor part]
Automobile (Electric motors) A: 954
Electric generator (Parts of a generator) E: 170-
171
Electric motor (AC motors) E: 181 with picture
Electric power (Sources of electric power) E: 182
with diagram
Ignition (The conventional electronic ignition
system) I: 49
Linear electric motor L: 334 with diagram
Pneumatic tool P: 586
Rotten borough [English history]
Borough B: 491
Rotterdam [Netherlands] R: 489
Europe picture on E: 406
Netherlands picture on N: 147; (World War II)
N: 149 with picture
Rotting [industrial process]
Hemp H: 183
Rottweiler [dog] R: 489 with picture
Rotunda [U.S. Capitol]
Capitol, United States C: 197
Rouault, Georges [French artist] R: 489 with picture
Stained glass (Decline and revival) So: 823
Rouble [money]
Ruble R: 508
Roue, William J. [marine architect]
Bluenose B: 424
Rouen [France] R: 490 with picture
Rouen, Cathedral of
Rouen R: 490 with picture
Rouen Cathedral, Full Sunlight [painting by
Monet]
Painting picture on P: 35
Rouge [abrasive]
Grinding and polishing (Polishing) G: 395
Rouge Manufacturing Complex
Ford Motor Company F: 382
Rouget de Lisle, Claude Joseph [French
composer]
"Marseillaise" M: 227
Rough
Golf (The fairway) G: 261 with picture
Rough carpentry
Carpentry C: 246
Rough cut
Motion picture (The rough and final cuts) M: 855
Rough green snake
Snake picture on S: 533
Rough hardwood dimension
Lumber (Hardwood lumber) L: 517
Rough lumber
Lumber (Kinds of lumber) L: 517; (Grading
lumber) L: 519
Rough rice
Rice (How rice is processed) R: 326
Rough Riders [U.S. history] R: 490
Roosevelt, Theodore picture on R: 464; (The
Rough Riders) R: 463
Spanish-American War (Land battles) So: 754
with picture
Wood, Leonard W: 390
Rough stock event
Rodeo R: 397
Roughage [diet] See Fiber, Dietary in this index
Roughage feed
Beef (Food value) B: 211

Feed F: 67
Roughing [football]
Football (Violations and penalties) F: 363
Roughing It [book by Twain]
Twain, Mark (Newspaper work in the West) T: 529
Roughing It in the Bush [book by Moodie]
Moodie, Susanna M: 781
Roughing mill [machine]
Iron and steel (Ingot casting) I: 445 *with diagram*
Roughneck [job]
Petroleum (table) P: 332
Roughriders, Saskatchewan
Football (Canadian Football League) F: 364
Roughtail stingray [fish]
Stingray *picture on* So: 902
Roughy [fish] R: 490 *with picture*
Rougon-Macquart, The [books by Zola]
French literature (Naturalism) F: 522
Zola, Émile Z: 598
Rouleau, Félix R. [Canadian religious leader]
Cardinal (table: Canadian cardinals) C: 211
Roulette [gambling] R: 490
Gambling (Roulette) G: 21
Roulette [stamp collecting]
Stamp collecting (Separations) So: 830
Round [ammunition]
Ammunition (Small-arms ammunition) A: 435
Round [debating]
Debate (Framework of a round) D: 64
Round [food]
Cheese (Packaging) C: 393
Round [meeting]
General Agreement on Tariffs and Trade G: 83
Round [music]
Canon C: 182
Round [sports]
Boxing (Rounds) B: 527
Golf (The course) G: 260
Round brilliant cut
Diamond (How diamonds are cut to make jewels) D: 182
Gem (Cutting and polishing) G: 79 *with pictures*
Round dance [ceremony]
Indian, American (Indians of the Great Basin) I: 164-165
Round herring [food]
Herring (Uses) H: 216
Round Hill School [Northampton, Massachusetts]
Bancroft, George B: 74
Round-lobed hepatica [plant]
Flower *picture on* F: 285
Round Midnight [music by Monk]
Monk, Thelonious M: 725
Round Table [English legend] R: 491
Arthur, King A: 757
English literature (The development of English romances) E: 315
Holy Grail (The search for the Grail) H: 299 *with picture*
Lancelot, Sir L: 56
Launfal, Sir L: 121
Merlin M: 418
Round timber
Forest products (Round timbers) F: 400 *with picture*
Round whitefish
Whitefish W: 292
Round window [anatomy]
Ear (The inner ear) E: 8 *with diagrams*
Rounders [sport]
Baseball (Rounders) B: 132
Roundheads [English history]
England (The Civil War) E: 308
Hairdressing (The 1600's) H: 12
Rounds, Mike [American political leader]
South Dakota (table) So: 680
Roundup
Cowboy (The roundup) Ci: 1111
North Dakota *picture on* N: 497
Western frontier life in America (Ranching) W: 236
Roundworm R: 491
Alfalfa (Diseases and pests) A: 348
Animal (A classification of the animal kingdom) A: 506 *with picture*
Cat (Veterinary care) C: 295
Disease (Other infectious diseases) D: 227-228
Dog (Medical care) D: 279
Fumigation F: 556
Grape (Diseases and pests) G: 320
Human Genome Project H: 427
Plant (Diseases) P: 539
Worm (Roundworms) W: 501 *with pictures*
Rous, Francis Peyton [American physiologist] R: 492
Roush, Edd [American baseball player]
Baseball (table: Hall of Fame) B: 134b

Rousseau, Henri [French painter] R: 492
Rousseau, Jean-Jacques [French philosopher] R: 492
Democracy (French contributions to democracy) D: 122
Enlightenment E: 326a
French literature (The Enlightenment) F: 520; (The Preromantics) F: 521
Philosophes P: 382
Political science (Democracy and socialism) P: 639; (Liberalism) P: 639
Romanticism (Romanticism and society) R: 427
Rousseau, Judge of Jean Jacques [book by Rousseau]
Rousseau, Jean-Jacques (Later life) R: 492
Rousseau, Théodore [French painter]
Barbizon School B: 108 *with picture*
Rousseff, Dilma [Brazilian political leader]
Brazil (The early 2000's) B: 586
Roustabout [career]
Circus (Behind the scenes) Ci: 562
"Route of Evanescence, A" [poem by Dickinson]
Dickinson, Emily (Her life) D: 190
Route 66 [highway] R: 493
Automobile (Roads) A: 959
Router [electronic device]
Internet *diagram on* I: 350c
Telephone (VoIP phone calls) T: 97-98
Router [tool]
Woodworking (Cutting) W: 397
Routes of trade *See* Trade route *in this index*
Routhier, Sir Adolphe Basile [Canadian judge]
"O Canada" O: 635
Routt, John L. [American political leader]
Colorado (table) Ci: 844; (Statehood) Ci: 845
ROV [vehicle] *See* Remotely operated vehicle *in this index*
Rove beetle [insect]
Beetle *picture on* B: 218; (Rove beetles) B: 217
Rover Scout [rank]
Scouts Canada (Age groups) S: 224
Rovere, Francesco della *See* Sixtus IV *in this index*
Rovere, Giuliano della *See* Julius II *in this index*
Roving [yarn]
Cotton *picture on* Ci: 1092; (Spinning) Ci: 1091
Wool (Making yarn) W: 400
Row house
Housing (Kinds of housing) H: 389-390 *with picture*
New York City (Brooklyn) N: 326 *with picture*
Philadelphia (Housing) P: 363 *with picture*
San Francisco (Housing) S: 94
Wales (Way of life) W: 9
Washington, D.C. *picture on* W: 80
Row planter [agriculture]
Corn *picture on* Ci: 1062
Rowan, Carl Thomas [American journalist] R: 493
Rowan tree
Mountain ash M: 897
Rowboat
Boating *picture on* B: 430; (Types of boats) B: 428
Rowing R: 493
Transportation (Water transportation) T: 384
Rowe, Debbie [wife of]
Jackson, Michael J: 16
Rowe, Nicholas [English poet]
Poet laureate (table: Poets laureate of the United Kingdom) P: 590
Shakespeare, William (Editions of the 1700's and 1800's) S: 369
Rowel
Cowboy (His clothing) Ci: 1108-1109
Horse (Spurs) H: 351
Rowing [sport] R: 493 *with picture*
Olympic Games (Summer Olympic Games) O: 746e-747
Rowland, Frank Sherwood [American chemist]
Nobel Prizes (Chemistry: 1995) N: 444
Rowland, John G. [American political leader]
Connecticut (table) Ci: 967; (The early 2000's) Ci: 971
Rowlandson, Mary [American colonist]
Colonial life in America (Literature) Ci: 806
Rowlatt bills [1919]
Gandhi, Mohandas Karamchand (Gandhi's independence campaigns) G: 25
Rowling, J. K. [British author] R: 494
Fairy (Fairies in literature) F: 11
Literature for children *picture on* L: 377; (Fantasy and science fiction) L: 361
Potter, Harry P: 715
Publishing *picture on* P: 868
Roxane [wife of]
Alexander the Great (Central Asia and the Indus) A: 343
Roxas y Acuña, Manuel [Filipino political leader] R: 494

Philippines (Independence) P: 380
Roxbury [district, Boston]
Boston (The south side) B: 500
Roy, Arundhati [Indian author]
Novel (The novel today) N: 575
Roy, Gabrielle [Canadian author] R: 494
Canadian literature (Modern literature: 1945 to the present) C: 159
Roy, Louis [Canadian publisher]
Ontario (Communication) O: 782
Roy, Maurice [Canadian religious leader]
Cardinal (table: Canadian cardinals) C: 211
Roy, Patrick [Canadian ice hockey player] R: 494
Roy, Rammohun [Indian religious leader] *See* Rammohun Roy *in this index*
Roy, Rob [Scottish bandit] *See* Rob Roy *in this index*
Royal, Mount [Quebec]
Cartier, Jacques (Exploration of Canada) C: 262
Montreal M: 768; (Parks) M: 774
Quebec (Land regions) Q: 22
Royal, Ségolène [French political leader]
France (Recent developments) F: 478
Royal Academy of Arts
Gainsborough, Thomas G: 6
Reynolds, Sir Joshua R: 289
Royal Academy of Dancing [French history]
Ballet (The rise of professional ballet) B: 51
Royal Academy of Music [French history]
Ballet (The rise of professional ballet) B: 51
Royal Academy of Painting and Sculpture [France]
Painting (Classicism) P: 61
Royal Air Force
Air force (The British air force) A: 184; (History) A: 184-185
Flag *picture on* F: 195
World War II (The Battle of Britain) W: 476
Royal and Ancient Golf Club [Scotland]
Golf (Beginnings) G: 264
Scotland (Recreation) S: 214 *with picture*
Royal and Pontifical University
Mexico, National Autonomous University of M: 475
Royal Ascot [horse race]
Horse racing (Types of horse races) H: 364
United Kingdom *picture on* U: 57
Royal Ballet [United Kingdom]
Ballet *picture on* B: 44
De Valois, Ninette D: 173
Dolin, Anton D: 285
Fonteyn, Margot F: 327
Royal Bank [French history]
Law, John L: 141
Royal Botanic Gardens [London]
London (Parks) L: 435-436
Royal Botanical Gardens [Canada]
Hamilton (The city) H: 30 *with map*; (Cultural life) H: 31
Ontario (Places to visit) O: 774
Royal British Columbia Museum [Victoria]
British Columbia (Places to visit) B: 620
Royal Canadian Air Force
Canadian Armed Forces (Organization) C: 154 *with pictures*; (Weapons and equipment) C: 154-155
Royal Canadian Legion R: 495
Veterans' organizations (In Canada) V: 345
Royal Canadian Mint [Ottawa]
Canada, Government of (Money and taxation) C: 136
Royal Canadian Mounted Police R: 495 *with pictures*
Alberta (Early settlement) A: 329
Police (In Canada) P: 623 *with picture*
Saskatchewan (Places to visit) S: 136 *with picture*
Royal Canadian Navy
Canadian Armed Forces (Organization) C: 154 *with pictures*; (Weapons and equipment) C: 154-155
Royal Chitwan National Park [Nepal]
National park (table) N: 42f
Royal colony [U.S. history]
Colonial life in America (Changes in colonial control) Ci: 791
Royal comb venus [sea animal]
Shell *picture on* S: 387
Royal Commentaries [book by de la Vega]
Latin American literature (Colonial literature) L: 112
Royal crown
Crown Ci: 1158 *with pictures*
Royal Dutch Shell plc [company] R: 498
Manufacturing (table) M: 170
Royal family of the United Kingdom
Elizabeth II (The royal family) E: 240
Royal fern [plant]
Fern (Kinds of ferns) F: 75

Royal Festival Hall
London (The arts) **L:** 433
Royal Fireworks Music [music by Handel]
Handel, George Frideric (His work) **H:** 42-43
Royal flush
Poker **P:** 603
Royal Flying Corps
World War I *picture on* **W:** 461
Royal Flying Doctor Service of Australia
Australia (Transportation) **A:** 918 *with picture*
Aviation (General aviation activities) **A:** 984
Outback **O:** 879
Royal Geographical Society R: 498
Royal Gorge [canyon, Colorado] **R:** 498
Colorado (Places to visit) **Ci:** 836; (Rivers and lakes) **Ci:** 840
Royal Greenwich Observatory *See* Greenwich Observatory, Royal *in this index*
Royal Guipuzcoana Company
Venezuela (European exploration and settlement) **V:** 304
Royal Hibernian Academy
Ireland (The arts) **I:** 421
Royal Highway *See* El Camino Real *in this index*
Royal Household of the United Kingdom R: 498
Royal Humane Society
Medals, decorations, and orders (Europe) **M:** 358
Royal Hunt of the Sun, The [play by Shaffer]
Shaffer, Peter **S:** 342
Royal Institution [organization] **R:** 498
Royal jelly
Bee (From egg to adult) **B:** 202
Royal Liver Building
Liverpool **L:** 395 *with picture*
Royal Manas National Park [Bhutan]
National park (table) **N:** 42f
Royal Marines [Britain]
Marine (Marine forces of the world) **M:** 203-204 *with picture*
Royal Mile [road]
Edinburgh **E:** 77
Royal Military College of Canada R: 498
Royal Mint [London]
Mint **M:** 612
Royal Montreal Golf Club
Golf (Beginnings) **G:** 264
Royal moth
Moth (Giant silkworm moths and royal moths) **M:** 841-842 *with picture*
Royal National Eisteddfod [festival]
Wales (The arts) **W:** 9-10
Royal National Institute for the Blind
Disability (Early beliefs) **D:** 221
Royal National Park [Australia]
National park (Australia) **N:** 42b
Royal National Theatre
London (The arts) **L:** 433
Royal Navy
Navy *picture on* **N:** 76; (The United Kingdom) **N:** 79
Royal Niger Company [African history]
Nigeria (British rule) **N:** 417
Royal North-West Mounted Police
Royal Canadian Mounted Police (History) **R:** 497
Royal Ontario Museum
Ontario (Museums) **O:** 769
Toronto (Museums and libraries) **T:** 340a
Royal Opera House [Covent Garden]
London (The arts) **L:** 433
Royal Palace
Budapest (City) **B:** 666
Royal palm [tree] **R:** 498
Tree *pictures on* **T:** 413
Royal Pavilion
Brighton and Hove **B:** 609
Royal Philips Electronics
Netherlands (Manufacturing) **N:** 146
Royal Plowing Ceremony
May **M:** 320
Royal poinciana [tree]
Poinciana **P:** 599
Royal Portal [structure]
Chartres Cathedral **C:** 386
Royal Road [highway]
Persia, Ancient (Economy) **P:** 297
Royal Shakespeare Company [theater group]
Dench, Judi **D:** 130
Shakespeare, William *picture on* **S:** 358
Stratford-upon-Avon **So:** 920
Theater (Britain) **T:** 247-248
Royal Society [organization] **R:** 498
Winthrop, John, Jr. **W:** 343
Royal Society for the Protection of Birds
Bird (Bird study and protection) **B:** 367
Royal Society of Canada [organization] **R:** 499
Royal Society of London for Improving Natural Knowledge

Royal Society R: 498
Royal Standard [Britain]
Flag (Flags of individuals) **F:** 195 *with picture*
Royal Stewart plaid
Tartan *picture on* **T:** 47
Royal Swedish Academy of Sciences [Stockholm]
Nobel Prizes **N:** 439
Royal Toxophilite Society
Archery (History) **A:** 603-604
Royal Tyrrell Museum of Paleontology
Alberta (Interesting facts) **A:** 313
Royal Victorian Order
Knighthood, Orders of (Honorary orders) **K:** 347 *with picture*
Royal walnut moth
Moth *picture on* **M:** 840
Royal Winnipeg Ballet
Canada (Ballet and opera) **C:** 111
Royalists [English history]
England (The Civil War) **E:** 308
Royall, Anne Newport [American journalist] **R:** 499
Royall, Kenneth C. [American government official]
Truman, Harry S. (table) **T:** 469
Royals, Kansas City [team] *See* Kansas City Royals *in this index*
Royalty [income]
Copyright (Users' rights) **Ci:** 1047
Publishing (Contracts and advances) **P:** 866
Recording industry (Releasing the recording) **R:** 182
Writing (Nonfiction) **W:** 511; (Scriptwriting) **W:** 512
Roybal, Edward R. [American political leader]
Hispanic Americans (Political developments) **H:** 256
Royce, Josiah [American philosopher] **R:** 499
Lotze, Rudolf Hermann **L:** 473
Royce, Stephen [American political leader]
Vermont (table) **V:** 333
Rozelle, Pete [American football commissioner]
Football (The rise of professional football) **F:** 366
National Football League **N:** 35
Rozier, Ferdinand [American businessman]
Audubon, John James (His life) **A:** 884
Rozier, Mike [American football player]
Football (table) **F:** 363
Rozwi [people]
Zimbabwe (History) **Z:** 592-593
RPE [anatomy]
Eye (Adaptation to light and dark) **E:** 464
Rpm [measurement]
Tachometer **T:** 4
RQ [publication]
American Library Association **A:** 413
RRB [organization]
Railroad Retirement Board **R:** 121
rRNA [biochemistry] *See* Ribosomal RNA *in this index*
RS [disorder] *See* Rett syndrome *in this index*
RSA algorithm [cryptology]
Codes and ciphers (Public-key systems) **Ci:** 750; (Later developments) **Ci:** 751
RSA Battle House Tower [Mobile]
Mobile *picture on* **M:** 682
RSI [injury] *See* Repetitive strain injury *in this index*
R.S.V.P. [notation]
Letter writing (Formal invitations) **L:** 212-213; (Informal invitations) **L:** 213
RTT [disorder] *See* Rett syndrome *in this index*
Ru [symbol]
Ruthenium **R:** 569
RU-486 [drug] *See* Mifepristone *in this index*
Ruana [clothing]
Colombia (Clothing) **Ci:** 781
Ruanda-Urundi [African history] **R:** 499
Burundi **B:** 712; (History) **B:** 713
Rwanda (History) **R:** 571
Rub al Khali [region, Arabia]
Arabian Desert **A:** 582b
Middle East (The land) **M:** 531
Saudi Arabia (The Rub al Khali) **S:** 158 *with map*
Rubaiyat [poem by Omar Khayyam] **R:** 499
FitzGerald, Edward **F:** 190
Omar Khayyam **O:** 760
Rubber R: 500 *with pictures and map*
Doll (Rubber dolls) **D:** 290
Edison, Thomas Alva (Final work) **E:** 81
Guayule **G:** 418
Invention (The inventive process) **I:** 355-357
Latex **L:** 90
Malaysia (British rule) **M:** 101
Materials (Rubber) **M:** 300d *with picture*
Silicone (Uses) **S:** 458
Tire **T:** 295 *with pictures*
Rubber ball [toy]
Rubber (First uses) **R:** 500
Rubber boa [snake]

Boa **B:** 426
Rubber bridge [cards]
Bridge **B:** 604
Rubber bullet
Ammunition (Riot control ammunition) **A:** 435
Rubber cement
Rubber (Uses of rubber) **R:** 500
Rubber plant R: 506 *with picture*
Gardening on **G:** 37
Leaf *picture on* **L:** 153
Rubber plantation
Rubber (The first plantations) **R:** 501
Rubber tree
Liberia *picture on* **L:** 231
Rubber *picture on* **R:** 500; (The rubber tree) **R:** 502 *with diagram*
Rubbia, Carlo [Italian physicist]
Nobel Prizes (Physics: 1984) **N:** 442
Physics (Physics today) **P:** 442-443
Rubel, Ira [American printer]
Printing (Developments in platemaking) **P:** 803-804
Printing press **P:** 804
Rubella [disease] **R:** 506
See also Measles *in this index*
Autism (Causes) **A:** 942
Cerebral palsy (Causes) **C:** 361
Deafness (Birth defects) **D:** 57-58
Disease (table) **D:** 226
Intellectual disability (Causes) **I:** 318
Ruben, Samuel [American chemist]
Radiocarbon (Radiocarbon in biology) **R:** 98
Rubenists [art history]
Painting (Rococo painting) **P:** 65
Rubens, Peter Paul [Flemish painter] **R:** 506 *with picture*
Antwerp (Chief buildings) **A:** 561
Baroque (Baroque painting) **B:** 117
Daniel, Book of *picture on* **D:** 33
Drawing *picture on* **D:** 343
Jesus Christ *picture on* **J:** 108b
Marie de Médicis **M:** 200
Painting (Baroque) **P:** 58-59 *with picture*; (Rococo painting) **P:** 65
Rubeola *See* Measles *in this index*
Rubicon [river, Italy] **R:** 507
Rubidium [element] **R:** 507
Rubin, Robert Edward [American government official] **R:** 507
Rubin, Vera C. [American astrophysicist]
Dark matter **D:** 37
Rubinstein, Anton Gregor [Russian pianist] **R:** 507
Rubinstein, Arthur [American pianist] **R:** 508
Ruble [money] **R:** 508
Ruby [dog]
English toy spaniel **E:** 325
Ruby [fruit]
Grapefruit **G:** 320
Ruby [gem] **R:** 508 *with picture*
Gem *picture on* **G:** 78; (Cutting and polishing) **G:** 79
Laser (History) **L:** 86 *with picture*
Sapphire **S:** 122
Ruby, Jack [American assassin]
Kennedy, John Fitzgerald *picture on* **K:** 268; (The death of Oswald) **K:** 267
Oswald, Lee Harvey **O:** 869
Texas (The mid-1900's) **T:** 208-209
Warren Report **W:** 37
Ruby Beach [Washington]
Washington *picture on* **W:** 57
Ruby-crowned kinglet [bird]
Bird (Birds of forests and woodlands) **B:** 334 *with picture*
Kinglet **K:** 330
Ruby Lake
Nevada (Rivers and lakes) **N:** 166-168 *with map*
Ruby Mountains [Nevada]
Nevada (Places to visit) **N:** 164
Ruby-spot damselfly
Insect *picture on* **I:** 280
Ruby-throated hummingbird
Bird *picture on* **B:** 358
Hummingbird (Size) **H:** 433
Rucellai Palace [Florence, Italy]
Alberti, Leon Battista **A:** 332
Ruck [sports]
Rugby football (Rugby Union) **R:** 510-511
Ruckelshaus, William D. [American government official]
Environmental Protection Agency **E:** 340
Watergate (The tape controversy) **W:** 144
Rucker, Edmund W. [Confederate army leader]
Fort Rucker **F:** 416
Rudbeck, Olaus [Swedish scholar]
Sweden (Literature) **So:** 1026
Rudd, Kevin Michael [Australian political leader]

R: 508 *with portrait*
Australia (table) A: 923; (Recent developments) A: 926
Gillard, Julia G: 190
Rudder [device]
Airplane *picture on* A: 218; (The tail) A: 214 *with picture*; (The controls and instruments) A: 217; (Basic movements and controls) A: 222-223 *with diagram*
Airship (Control) A: 251
Glider (The tail) G: 229
Helicopter (Piloting a helicopter) H: 171-172 *with diagram*
Invention (The Middle Ages) I: 359-360
Sailing (Hull) S: 23 *with diagram*
Ship *diagram on* S: 405; (Propulsion and steering) S: 406; (The chief parts of a ship) S: 424-425
Transportation (The Middle Ages) T: 387-388
Rudder Grange [book by Stockton]
Stockton, Frank Richard So: 906
Ruddy duck
Duck *picture on* D: 375; (Stiff-tailed ducks) D: 376-377
Rude, François [French sculptor]
Arc de Triomphe A: 593
Rudin [book by Turgenev]
Russian literature (Early realism) R: 562
Rudolf I [Holy Roman emperor]
Austria (The Habsburgs) A: 937
Germany (The Holy Roman Empire) G: 162-163
Habsburg, House of H: 3
Rudolf IV [archduke of Austria]
Austria (The Habsburgs) A: 937
Rudolf, Lake *See* Lake Turkana *in this index*
Rudolph [son of]
Franz Joseph F: 494
Rudolph, Lucretia [wife of James A. Garfield] *See* Garfield, Lucretia Rudolph *in this index*
Rudolph, Paul [American architect] R: 508 *with picture*
Architecture (Architecture today) A: 632-633
Rudolph, Wilma R: 509 *with portrait*
Rue Petit-Champlain [Quebec]
Quebec *picture on* Q: 21
Rue Saint-Denis [street, Montreal]
Quebec *picture on* Q: 14
Rueda, Lope de [Spanish dramatist]
Drama (Secular drama) D: 333
Spanish literature (The 1500's) So: 758-759
Ruehl, Mercedes [American actress]
Motion picture (Best performance by an actress in a supporting role: 1991) M: 862b
Ruff [bird] R: 509
Ruff [collar]
Clothing (The Renaissance) Ci: 702-703 *with picture*
Ruffe [fish] R: 509 *with picture*
Ruffed grouse [bird] R: 509 *with picture*
Bird (Other means of communication) B: 354
Grouse G: 403
Partridge P: 189
Ruffed lemur [animal]
Lemur L: 189
Primate *picture on* P: 778
Ruffin, Edmund [Confederate soldier] R: 510
Ruffing, Red [American baseball player]
Baseball (table: Hall of Fame) B: 134b
Ruffner Pamphlet [document]
West Virginia (The Civil War and statehood) W: 226
Rufiji River
Tanzania (Rivers and lakes) T: 33 *with map*
Rufous hare-wallaby [animal]
Wallaby (Kinds of wallabies) W: 15
Rufous hummingbird
Hummingbird *picture on* H: 434
Rufus [name for]
William II W: 308
Rug *See* Rugs and carpets *in this index*
Rugby [North Dakota]
Geographic center of North America G: 92
Rugby football [sport] R: 510 *with pictures*
England (Recreation) E: 296-297
Football (The history of football) F: 365
Ireland (Recreation) I: 420
London (Recreation) L: 434
Pacific Islands (Recreation) P: 7 *with picture*
Wales (Recreation) W: 9
Rugby Football League
Rugby football (History) R: 513
Rugby league
Australia (Recreation) A: 903
Rugby football R: 510 *with pictures*
Rugby School [Rugby, England] R: 513
Rugby football (History) R: 513
Rugby union
Australia (Recreation) A: 903

New Zealand (Recreation) N: 348 *with picture*
Rugby football R: 510 *with pictures*
Ruger, Thomas H. [American general]
Georgia (table) G: 130
Rugger [sport] *See* Rugby football *in this index*
Rugs and carpets R: 513 *with pictures*
Insulation (Insulation against sound) I: 307
Interior design (Planning on paper) I: 330-331; (Choosing patterns and textures) I: 332 *with pictures*
Islamic art (Rugs) I: 469 *with picture*
Weaving *picture on* W: 174
Ruhr [region, Germany] R: 517 *with maps*
Europe (Manufacturing) E: 401
Germany (Manufacturing) G: 160 *with picture*
Ruhr River [Germany] R: 518
Ruhuna National Park [Sri Lanka]
National park (table) N: 42f
Ruisdael, Jacob van [Dutch painter] R: 518 *with picture*
Ruivo, Pico [mountain]
Madeira Islands (The island of Madeira) M: 30
Ruiz, José [Spanish slave trader]
Amistad Rebellion A: 433
Ruiz, Juan [Spanish poet] R: 519
Spanish literature (Early medieval literature) So: 757-758
Ruiz Cortines, Adolfo [Mexican political leader] R: 519
Ruíz-Tagle, Eduardo Frei [Chilean political leader]
Chile (Recent developments) C: 470
Rule [measurement]
Woodworking (Planning and design) W: 396 *with picture*
Rule [religion]
Christianity (The medieval church) C: 524
Monasticism (Christian monasticism) M: 701
Roman Catholic Church (Religious institutes) R: 404
Rule of cloister
Cloister Ci: 682l
Rule of Saint Benedict [religion]
Monasticism (Christian monasticism) M: 701
Rule of the Community [document]
Dead Sea Scrolls D: 56
Ruler on Horseback Leading an Army Across a Battlefield, A [painting]
Painting (Indian painting) P: 44 *with picture*
Rules Committee [government]
House of Representatives (Committees) H: 387; (Considering legislation) H: 387
United States, Government of the (How a bill moves through Congress) U: 142-143
Rules of order
Parliamentary procedure P: 175
Rules of the Game, The [film]
Renoir, Jean R: 240
Rules of the road
Automobile (Rules of the road) A: 955
Rules of the Road, International
Ship (Safety) S: 411
Rulfo, Juan [Mexican author]
Latin American literature (The mid-1900's) L: 114
Rum
Alcoholic beverage (Rum) A: 336; (History) A: 337
Puerto Rico *picture on* P: 882
"Rum, Romanism, and rebellion" [quotation]
Cleveland, Grover (Election of 1884) Ci: 670
Rumaila [oil field]
Persian Gulf War of 1991 (Disputes between Iraq and Kuwait) P: 300b
Rumania *See* Romania *in this index*
Rumba [dance] R: 519
Ballroom dancing B: 63
Latin America (Dance) L: 101
Rumble Fish [book by Hinton]
Hinton, S. E. H: 237
Rumble seat
Roaring Twenties *picture on* R: 363
Rumen [zoology]
Cattle (Stomach) C: 307 *with diagram*
Ruminant R: 519 *with diagram*
Rumford [former name]
Concord [New Hampshire] Ci: 929
Rumford, Count [American-British physicist] *See* Thompson, Benjamin *in this index*
Ruminant [zoology] R: 519 *with diagram*
Camel (Food) C: 79
Cattle (Stomach) C: 307
Deer (Food) D: 84-85
Goat (Digestive system) G: 240
Rump [anatomy]
Human being (Physical characteristics) H: 413
Rump cut [meat]
Ham (Kinds of ham) H: 28 *with pictures*
Rump Parliament [English history] R: 519
Long Parliament L: 448

"Rumpelstiltskin" [story]
Fairy (Fairy tales) F: 11 *with picture*
Grimm's Fairy Tales G: 394
Rumsfeld, Donald Henry [American government official] R: 520
Bush, George Walker (table) B: 722h
Cheney, Richard Bruce (Career) C: 407
Defense, Department of (table) D: 87
Rumung [island, Pacific]
Yap Islands Y: 553
Run [banking]
Bank (Making loans) B: 89
Federal Reserve System (History) F: 66
Run [sports]
Baseball (The game) B: 128; (table: Modern major league records) B: 138
Football *diagram on* F: 359
Run-D.M.C. [rap group]
Rock music (Rap) R: 380d
Run-of-mine coal
Coal (Cleaning and shipping coal) Ci: 726
Run-through train
Railroad (Cooperation among railroads) R: 113
Runabout [boat]
Boating *picture on* B: 430; (Motorboats) B: 428
Motorboat racing (Hull designs) M: 876 *with picture*
Rundle, Robert T. [Canadian religious leader]
Alberta (Missionary activity) A: 329
Rune [alphabet] R: 520 *with pictures*
Rune [Norse mythology]
Odin O: 674
Rune stone
Kensington rune stone K: 271
Runeberg, Johan Ludvig [Finnish poet]
Finland (The arts) F: 112
Rungis [France]
Paris (Renewal and new construction) P: 166-167
Runkle, John D. [American educator]
Vocational education (Early vocational education in schools) V: 435
Runnels, Hardin R. [American political leader]
Texas (table) T: 203
Runnels, Hiram G. [American political leader]
Mississippi (table) M: 640
Runner [botany]
Fruit (Fruit production) F: 546
Peanut (The peanut plant) P: 213-214
Plant (Asexual reproduction) P: 535
Watermelon W: 146
Running [sailing]
Sailing (Basic sailing maneuvers) S: 26 *with diagram*
Running [sport] R: 520
Cross-country Ci: 1155
Indian, American (Recreation) I: 142
Jogging J: 131
Marathon M: 191
Oregon *picture on* O: 830
Physical fitness *picture on* P: 434
Track and field (Track events) T: 356
Weight control (table) W: 182
Running back
Football (The offensive team) F: 356-357 *with diagrams*
Running bond
Brick (Bonds) B: 599 *with picture*
Running buffalo clover [plant]
Endangered species (table) E: 270
Running key
Codes and ciphers (Substitution) Ci: 750
Running of the bulls [custom] *See* San Fermin, Fiesta of *in this index*
Running rigging
Sailing (Rigging) S: 24
Running stitch
Sewing (Hand stitches) S: 332
Runnymede [meadow, England] R: 521
Kennedy, John Fitzgerald (The world mourns) K: 268
Magna Carta M: 52
Runoff election
Election (Nomination of candidates) E: 158
Runs batted in
Baseball (Baseball terms) B: 124; (table: Modern major league records) B: 138
Runway
Airport (Runways) A: 245
Runyon, Damon [American author] R: 521
Runyon, William N. [American political leader]
New Jersey (table) N: 249
Rupee [money] R: 521 *with picture*
Rupert's Land [region, Canada]
Canada, History of (New provinces) C: 144
Manitoba (Newcomers) M: 160; (The Red River Rebellion) M: 160
Rupp, Adolph [American coach] R: 521

Rupture
Hernia H: 212
R.U.R. [play by Čapek]
Čapek, Karel C: 191
Rural delivery [mail] R: 521
Postal Service, United States *picture on* P: 701
West Virginia (Interesting facts) W: 207
Rural Electrification Act [1936]
Housing (Farm housing) H: 390-391
Rural Electrification Administration [U.S.] R: 521
Rurik [Norse explorer]
Russia (Early days) R: 547
Rus [ancient people]
Ukraine (Kievan Rus) U: 12
Vikings V: 378; (The Swedish Vikings) V: 383
Ruse [Bulgaria]
Bulgaria *picture on* B: 691
Rush [botany] R: 522
Rush [fraternity]
Fraternity (Membership) F: 495
Rush, Benjamin [American doctor] R: 522
Mental illness (Humane treatment) M: 408
Rush, Geoffrey [Australian actor]
Motion picture (Best performance by an actor: 1996) M: 862a
Rush, Richard [American government official]
Adams, John Quincy (table) A: 43
Jackson, Andrew (Election of 1828) J: 10
Justice, Department of (table) J: 203
Rush-Bagot Agreement [1817]
Arms control (History of arms control) A: 721
Ghent, Treaty of G: 181
Monroe, James (Diplomacy) M: 738
Rushdie, Salman [Indian-born author] R: 522
English literature (Recent English fiction) E: 323
Novel (The novel today) N: 575
Rushes
Motion picture (Preliminary steps) M: 854-855
Rushlight [candle]
Rush R: 522
Rushmore, Mount *See* Mount Rushmore National Memorial *in this index*
Rusie, Amos [American baseball player]
Baseball (table: Hall of Fame) B: 134b
Rusizi River [Africa]
Lake Tanganyika L: 46 *with map*
Rusk, Dean [American statesman] R: 522
Kennedy, John Fitzgerald (table) K: 266
Rusk, Jeremiah McLain [American political leader]
Agriculture, Department of (table) A: 161
Wisconsin (table) W: 365
Ruska, Ernst [German physicist]
Electron microscope E: 204
Nobel Prizes (Physics: 1986) N: 442
Ruskin, John [British author] R: 523
Hill, Octavia H: 231
Whistler, James Abbott McNeill W: 283
Ruslan and Lyudmila [opera by Glinka]
Glinka, Mikhail Ivanovich G: 231
Russell, Bertrand [British philosopher] R: 523
Logic (Modern logic) L: 425
Mathematics (Philosophies of mathematics) M: 307
Philosophy (Philosophy in the 1900's) P: 390
Pugwash Conferences on Science and World Affairs P: 886
Russell, Bill [American basketball player] R: 523
Basketball *picture on* B: 153; (The history of professional basketball) B: 154a-155
Russell, Charles H. [American political leader]
Nevada (table) N: 173
Russell, Charles Marion [American artist] R: 523
Cowboy *picture on* Ci: 1109
Dodge City *picture on* D: 261
Western frontier life in America (The West in American culture) W: 239
Russell, Charles Taze [American religious leader]
Jehovah's Witnesses J: 89
Russell, D. L. [American political leader]
North Carolina (table) N: 490
Russell, Earl [British philosopher] *See* Russell, Bertrand; Russell, Lord John *in this index*
Russell, Francis [English political leader]
Russell family R: 524
Russell, George William [Irish author] R: 524
Russell, Harold [American actor]
Motion picture (Best performance by an actor in a supporting role: 1946) M: 862a
Russell, Hastings William Sackville [British nobleman]
Russell family R: 524
Russell, Henry Norris [American astronomer] R: 524
Russell, James E. [American educator]
Teachers College, Columbia University (History) T: 64
Russell, John [English clergyman]

Parson Russell terrier P: 182
Russell, John [English political leader]
Russell family R: 524
Russell, Lord John [British political leader] R: 524
Russell, John Robert [South African journalist]
Russell family R: 524
Russell, Lee M. [American political leader]
Mississippi (table) M: 640
Russell, Lillian [American actress] R: 524 *with portrait*
Russell, Majors, and Waddell [U.S. history]
Pony express P: 657
Russell, Richard Brevard [American political leader] R: 524
Georgia (table) G: 130
Russell, Steve [American programmer]
Electronic game (Early computer games) E: 204d
Russell, William [English political leader]
Russell family R: 524
Russell, William E. [American political leader]
Massachusetts (table) M: 288
Russell, William F. [American educator]
Teachers College, Columbia University (History) T: 64
Russell Cave National Monument [Alabama]
Alabama *picture on* A: 277; (Places to visit) A: 266
National Park System (table: National monuments) N: 51
Russell family R: 524
Russell Senate Office Building [Washington, D.C.]
Washington, D.C. *map on* W: 76
Russell's viper
Viper V: 391 *with picture*
Russet Burbank [potato]
Potato *picture on* P: 711, *picture on* P: 712
Russia R: 525 *with pictures and maps*
See also Union of Soviet Socialist Republics *in this index; and the list of Related articles in the* Russia *article*
Asia A: 770
Flag *pictures on* F: 207, F: 217
Lapland L: 74
Art and architecture
Russia (The arts) R: 536 *with pictures*
Ballet (Ballet in Russia) B: 52
Doll (Traditional dolls) D: 287 *with picture*
Painting (Painting outside France) P: 72; (Nonobjective painting in Russia) P: 79
Theater (Russia) T: 248 *with picture*
Communications and mass media
Russia (Transportation and communication) R: 546
Newspaper (In Europe) N: 386
Television (In Europe) T: 117
Defense
Russia (Armed forces) R: 532
Air force *picture on* A: 183; (The Russian Air Force) A: 184
Army (The Russian Army) A: 726
Hot line H: 374a
Navy (Major navies of the world) N: 78
Nuclear weapon (Controlling nuclear weapons) N: 600
Strategic Arms Reduction Treaty So: 919
Education
Russia (Education) R: 535
Library (Eastern Europe and Russia) L: 252 *with picture*; (Russia) L: 261
Government
Russia (National government) R: 531
Police (In other countries) P: 623
Ruble R: 508
Health and welfare
Abortion (In other countries) A: 16
History
Russia (History) R: 547
Abkhazia A: 11
Afghanistan (The Anglo-Afghan wars) A: 95
Armenia (History) A: 718b
Armenian Genocide A: 719
Azerbaijan (History) A: 997
Belarus (History) B: 224b-224c
Berlin, Congress of B: 265
Bloody Sunday B: 418
California (Spanish and Russian settlement) C: 60
Chechnya C: 390
Cold War (The Cold War after 1980) Ci: 770
Communism (Before 1917) Ci: 892
Cossacks Ci: 1079
Curzon Line Ci: 1199
Eastern Orthodox Church E: 45
Estonia (History) E: 362
Exploration (The Russians in Siberia) E: 447
Finland F: 108; (Control by Russia) F: 116
Georgia (History) G: 111
Inuit (New ways of life) I: 354g-354h; (The Inuit

today) I: 354h
Jews (The growth of anti-Semitism) J: 123
Kazakhstan (History) K: 251
Kyrgyzstan (History) K: 400
Latvia (History) L: 119
Lithuania (History) L: 389-390
Manchuria (History) M: 134
Moldova (History) M: 690a
Moscow M: 823
North Atlantic Treaty Organization (History) N: 471
Organization for Security and Co-operation in Europe O: 853
Poland (The partitions) P: 612 *with maps*
Romania (Russian control) R: 423
Russian Revolution of 1917 R: 565
Russo-Japanese War R: 566a
Russo-Turkish wars R: 566b
Seven Years' War S: 328
Tajikistan (History) T: 18b
Terrorism (Recent developments) T: 180
Turkestan (History) T: 501
Turkmenistan (History) T: 514b
Ukraine (Russian rule) U: 12
Union of Soviet Socialist Republics (History) U: 35
Uzbekistan (History) U: 254
Warsaw (History) W: 38
World War I W: 452; (The Russian Revolution) W: 461
Language and literature See Russian language; Russian literature *in this index*
Natural resources
Russia (The economy) R: 543 *with pictures and map*
Aluminum (The aluminum industry) A: 396
Conservation (Russia) Ci: 989
Nickel (Mining nickel) N: 404
People
Russia (People) R: 532; (Population density) *map on* R: 532
Family *picture on* F: 20
Sami S: 78
Social and cultural life
Russia (Way of life) R: 533 *with pictures*
Clothing *picture on* Ci: 694
Technology and science
Astronaut A: 828; (The cosmonauts) A: 833
Aviation (Aircraft manufacturing) A: 984
International Space Station I: 346a
Space exploration (Mir) So: 722; (Docking with Mir) So: 725
Transcontinental railroad (Around the world) T: 371
Russian Album, The [book by Ignatieff]
Ignatieff, Michael I: 48
Russian alphabet
Russian language (Alphabet) R: 557 *with pictures*
Russian-American Company [U.S. history]
Alaska (The Russian era) A: 301
Flag *picture on* F: 209
Russian bath
Bath (Bathing for cleanliness) B: 163
Turkish bath T: 514
Russian blue
Cat *picture on* C: 288; (Short-haired breeds) C: 290-291
Russian Catholic Church [religious group]
Eastern Catholic Churches E: 45
Russian Communist Party [Soviet history]
Russian Revolution of 1917 (The October Revolution) R: 566
Union of Soviet Socialist Republics (The October Revolution) U: 35-36
Russian desman [animal]
Mole (Kinds of moles) M: 690b
Russian Hill
San Francisco S: 92
Russian Imperial Ballet
Ballet (The rise of professional ballet) B: 51; (Ballet in Russia) B: 52
Russia (Catherine the Great) R: 550
Russian language R: 557
Russia (Language) R: 533
Ukraine (Language) U: 28
Union of Soviet Socialist Republics (People) U: 31
Russian literature R: 558 *with picture*
See also the list of Related articles in the Russian Literature *article*
Drama (Russian drama and Chekhov) D: 338
Nihilism N: 421
Novel (Russia) N: 573
Russian language (History) R: 557
Russian mulberry [plant]
Mulberry M: 913
Russian Orthodox Church [religious group]
Eastern Orthodox Churches E: 45

Ivan III, the Great I: 520
Moscow (Religion) M: 824
Russia (Religion) R: 535; (The early Romanovs)
  R: 549
Tolstoy, Leo (His conversion) T: 323
Russian Revolution of 1905
Bloody Sunday (In Russia) B: 418
Russia (The Revolution of 1905) R: 552
Russian Revolution of 1917 (The 1905
  Revolution) R: 566
Russian Revolution of 1917 R: 565
Communism (Before 1917) Ci: 892
Kerensky, Alexander Feodorovich K: 305
Lenin, V. I. (The road to power) L: 193
Reed, John R: 194
Russia (The February Revolution) R: 552-553;
  (The October Revolution) R: 553; (Civil war and
  the formation of the U.S.S.R.) R: 553
Stalin, Joseph (The Bolshevik revolution) So: 826
Trotsky, Leon T: 452
Union of Soviet Socialist Republics (History) U: 35
World War I (The Russian Revolution) W: 461
Russian Social Democratic Labor Party [political
party]
Communism (Before 1917) Ci: 892
Lenin, V. I. (Beginnings of revolution) L: 192
Mensheviks M: 403
Russian Revolution of 1917 (Background to the
  revolution) R: 565
Union of Soviet Socialist Republics (Background
  of the revolution) U: 35
Russian Soviet Federative Socialist Republic
Russia (Civil war and the formation of the U.S.S.R.)
  R: 553
Russian State Library [Moscow]
Library (Eastern Europe and Russia) L: 252 with
  picture
Moscow (Museums and libraries) M: 825
Russia (Museums and libraries) R: 536
Russian sturgeon [fish] See Beluga sturgeon in
this index
Russian thistle [plant]
Thistle T: 261
Tumbleweed T: 484
Russian turnip
Rutabaga R: 567
Russian wheat aphid [insect]
Invasive species (Managing invasive species)
  I: 354k
Russian wolfhound See Borzoi in this index
Russians [people]
Russia R: 525
Ukraine (People) U: 6
Union of Soviet Socialist Republics (People) U: 31
Uzbekistan (People) U: 253
Russia's Choice [political party] See Russia's
Democratic Choice in this index
Russia's Democratic Choice [political party]
Russia (Politics) R: 531
Russification [Russian history]
Belarus (History) B: 224b-224c
Stalin, Joseph (The five-year plan) So: 826
Ukraine (Language) U: 8
Russo-Finnish wars [1939-1944] R: 566a
Russo-Japanese War [1904-1905] R: 566a
Japan (Imperialism) J: 57
Manchuria (History) M: 134
New Hampshire (Interesting facts) N: 209
Nicholas II [czar] N: 402
President of the United States picture on P: 765
Russia (The Revolution of 1905) R: 552
Russo-Polish War [1919-1921]
Curzon Line Ci: 1199
Russo-Turkish wars [European history] R: 566b
See also Crimean War in this index
Berlin, Congress of B: 265
Russia (Nicholas I) R: 551
Russolo, Luigi [Italian painter]
Futurism F: 589
Russwurm, John Brown [American social
reformer] R: 566b
Rust [fungus] R: 566b
Barberry B: 107
Currant Ci: 1196
Fungal disease (In plants) F: 558
Lawn picture on L: 143
Wheat (Care during growth) W: 271 with pictures
Rust [chemistry] R: 567
Corrosion Ci: 1071
Iron (Properties) I: 435
Oxidation O: 888 with picture
Rustic capital [writing]
Paleography P: 103
Rustichello [Italian writer]
Polo, Marco (Later life) P: 648
Rustin, Bayard [American social reformer] R: 567
Rustproofing

Paint picture on P: 23; (Industrial paints) P: 24
Rutabaga [plant] R: 567
Rape [plant] R: 142
Rutgers, The State University of New Jersey
R: 567
Football (The history of football) F: 365
Universities and colleges (The oldest U.S.
  universities and colleges) U: 210
Ruth [Biblical figure]
Ruth, Book of R: 568
Ruth, Babe [American baseball player] R: 568 with
picture
Autograph picture on A: 943
Baltimore (Other interesting places to visit) B: 69
Baseball (table: Hall of Fame) B: 134b; (The Babe
  Ruth Era) B: 135 with picture; (table: Modern
  major league records) B: 138
United States, History of the (Heroes) U: 190 with
  picture
Ruth, Book of [Bible] R: 568
Bible (The Writings) B: 281-282
Shavuot S: 377
Ruth, George Herman See Ruth, Babe in this index
Ruth and Harold D. Uris Center for Education
Metropolitan Museum of Art (The Ruth and
  Harold D. Uris Center for Education) M: 444
Ruthenia [region, Europe] R: 568
Ruthenian Catholic Church [religious group]
Eastern Catholic Churches E: 45
Ruthenium [element] R: 568
Rutherford, Alexander C. [Canadian political
leader]
Alberta (table) A: 328
Rutherford, Daniel [Scottish doctor]
Nitrogen N: 425
Rutherford, Ernest [British physicist] R: 569
Atom (The first descriptions of atomic structure)
  A: 875-876 with diagram
Geology (Experimental geology) G: 99
Nuclear energy (The beginning of nuclear
  physics) N: 590
Physics (Uncovering the secrets of the atom)
  P: 442
Radiation (Discovery of radioactivity) R: 81
Rutherford, John [American political leader]
Virginia (table) V: 417
Rutherford, Johnny [American race driver]
Automobile racing (table: Indianapolis 500
  winners) A: 980
Rutherford, Margaret [British actress]
Motion picture (Best performance by an actress
  in a supporting role: 1963) M: 862b
Rutherford B. Hayes Library [Fremont]
Ohio (Libraries) O: 685; (Places to visit) O: 690
Rutherfordium [element] R: 569
Transuranium element T: 401
Rutherfurd, Lucy Mercer [American public figure]
Roosevelt, Franklin Delano (Family crisis) R: 451;
  (Death) R: 459
Rutile [mineral]
Crystal (Classifying crystals) Ci: 1166 with picture
Mineral picture on M: 568
Titanium T: 300
Rutland [Vermont] R: 569
Rutland Herald [newspaper]
Vermont (Communication) V: 332
Rutledge, Ann [American settler] R: 569
Lincoln, Abraham (Search for a career) L: 314
Rutledge, Edward [American patriot] R: 569
Rutledge, John [American political leader] R: 569
Rutledge, Wiley B. [American jurist]
Supreme Court of the United States (table)
  So: 1000
Rutskoi, Alexander Vladimirovich [Russian
political leader]
Russia (The new nation) R: 555
Rutte, Mark [Dutch political leader]
Netherlands (Recent developments) N: 150
Rutting season [zoology]
Mammal (Mating) M: 122-123
Ruttman, Troy [American race driver]
Automobile racing (table: Indianapolis 500
  winners) A: 980
Ruttmann, Walter [German filmmaker]
Animation (Animation in Europe) A: 514b
Ruwanweliseya [monument]
Sri Lanka picture on So: 818
Ruwenzori National Park [Uganda]
National park (table) N: 42f
Ruwenzori Range [mountains, Africa]
Africa (Mountains) A: 119
Ruysdael, Jacob van See Ruisdael, Jacob van in
this index
Ruz, Fidel Castro [Cuban political leader] See
Castro, Fidel in this index
Ruzhen [people]
Manchus M: 135

Ružička, Leopold [Swiss chemist]
Nobel Prizes (Chemistry: 1939) N: 443
RV See Recreational vehicle in this index
Rwanda R: 570 with picture and map
Burundi (History) B: 713
Flag picture on F: 199
Genocide G: 90
Ruanda-Urundi R: 499
Rwandan Patriotic Front
Rwanda (Government) R: 570; (History) R: 571-
  572
RWE [company]
Manufacturing (table) M: 170
Ryan, Claude [American businessman]
United Parcel Service, Inc. U: 97
Ryan, George [American political leader]
Illinois (table) I: 71; (The death penalty) I: 76;
  (Corruption cases) I: 76
Ryan, Janna Little [wife of]
Ryan, Paul (Early life and family) R: 572
Ryan, Kay [American poet]
Poet laureate (table: Poets laureate of the United
  States) P: 590
Ryan, Nolan [American baseball player] R: 572
Baseball picture on B: 139; (table: Hall of Fame)
  B: 134b; (Recent developments) B: 137; (table:
  Modern major league records) B: 138
Ryan, Paddy [Irish boxer]
Sullivan, John L. So: 969
Ryan, Paul [American political leader] R: 572 with
portrait
Ryan, Thelma Catharine "Pat" [wife of Richard
Nixon] See Nixon, Pat in this index
Ryder, Albert Pinkham [American painter] R: 573
with picture
Ryder, Samuel A. [British businessman]
Ryder Cup R: 573
Ryder Cup [golf] R: 573
Golf (Tournaments) G: 264
Rye [plant] R: 573 with picture
Ergot E: 350
Grain G: 301
Leaf picture on L: 153
Plant picture on P: 526
Triticale T: 448
Rye, Tom C. [American political leader]
Tennessee (table) T: 152
Rye bread
Rye (Uses) R: 573
Rye Patch Dam [Humboldt River, Nevada]
Nevada (Natural resources) N: 169
Rye whiskey
Whiskey W: 282
Ryegrass
Lawn (Types of lawns) L: 142
Ryerson, G. S. [Canadian military leader]
Red Cross (In Canada) R: 188
Ryga, George [Canadian dramatist]
Canadian literature (Modern Canadian drama)
  C: 161
Rylant, Cynthia [American author]
Newbery Medal (table) N: 359
Ryle, Sir Martin [British physicist]
Nobel Prizes (Physics: 1974) N: 441
Ryokan [hotel]
Tokyo (Visitor's guide) T: 316
Ryswick, Treaty of [1697]
French and Indian wars (King William's War)
  F: 512
Nova Scotia (The struggle in Acadia) N: 568
Ryukyu Islands [islands, Pacific] R: 574 with map
Japan (The Ryukyu and Bonin islands) J: 48
Okinawa O: 710

S

S [letter] S: 1 with pictures
S [symbol]
Sulfur (Properties) So: 966
S-A node [anatomy] See Sinoatrial node in this
index
S quark [physics] See Strange quark in this index
S. S. Klondike National Historic Site [Yukon]
Canada (table: National historic sites) C: 115
S-type asteroid [astronomy]
Asteroid (Composition) A: 824
S wave [geology] See Secondary wave in this index
Saá, Adolfo Rodríguez [Argentine political leader]
Argentina (The economic crisis of 2001) A: 659
Saadi [Persian author] S: 2
Saadians [ruling family]
Morocco (Corsairs and sharifs) M: 814
Saakashvili, Mikheil [Georgian political leader]
Georgia (The Rose Revolution) G: 111
Saanen [Switzerland]
Europe picture on E: 381
Saanen goat
Goat picture on G: 241; (Domestic goats) G: 239

Saar [state, Germany] *See* Saarland *in this index*
Saarinen, Eero [American architect] **S:** 2
　Architecture *picture on* **A:** 607
　Furniture *picture on* **F:** 583; (The retro style) **F:** 584
　Gateway Arch **G:** 67
　Saint Louis *picture on* **S:** 46
Saarinen, Eliel [Finnish-American architect]
　Finland (The arts) **F:** 112
Saarland [state, Germany] **S:** 2
Saavedra, Alvaro de [Spanish navigator]
　Bismarck Archipelago **B:** 383
Saavedra, Ángel de [Spanish author]
　Spanish literature (The 1800's) **So:** 761
Saavedra Lamas, Carlos [Argentine statesman]
　Nobel Prizes (Peace: 1936) **N:** 448a
Sab [people]
　Somalia (People) **So:** 588
Saba [island, Caribbean]
　Netherlands Antilles **N:** 151
Sabaeans [people]
　Saudi Arabia (History) **S:** 160
Sabah [state, Malaysia]
　Borneo (History) **B:** 490
　Malaysia **M:** 98a
Sabah I [Kuwaiti ruler]
　Kuwait (History) **K:** 396
Sabal palmetto [tree] **S:** 2
Sabatier, Paul [French chemist]
　Hydrogenation **H:** 470
　Nobel Prizes (Chemistry: 1912) **N:** 443
Sabbat [holiday]
　Witchcraft (Witchcraft as a religion) **W:** 371-372
Sabbath [religion] **S:** 2
　Jerusalem **J:** 94a
　Judaism (The Sabbath) **J:** 181
　Sunday **So:** 989
Sabbatical
　Teaching (Rewards of teaching) **T:** 69
Saber [weapon]
　Sword **So:** 1061 *with picture*
Saber saw [tool]
　Saw (Power saws) **S:** 167 *with picture*
　Woodworking (Cutting) **W:** 397-398 *with picture*
Saber-toothed cat [extinct animal] **S:** 2 *with picture*
Saber-toothed tiger [extinct animal] *See* Saber-toothed cat *in this index*
Sabin, Albert Bruce [American biochemist] **S:** 3
　Poliomyelitis (Prevention of poliomyelitis) **P:** 626
Sabin, Florence Rena [American biologist] **S:** 3
Sabin Convention Center
　Cincinnati (The city) **Ci:** 554 *with map*
Sabin Lock
　Soo Canals (The American canals) **So:** 594 *with map*
Sabin polio vaccine
　Sabin, Albert Bruce **S:** 3
Sabines [ancient people] **S:** 3
　Romulus and Remus **R:** 450a
Sabinian [pope]
　Pope (table) **P:** 666
Sable [animal] **S:** 3 *with picture*
　Fur *picture on* **F:** 562; (table) **F:** 561
Sable [color]
　Heraldry (Expansion) **H:** 194 *with picture*
Sable, Jean Baptiste Point du [American pioneer]
　See Du Sable, Jean Baptiste Point *in this index*
Sable antelope
　Antelope (Kinds of antelope) **A:** 542
Sable Island [Atlantic] **S:** 3 *with map*
Sable Island National Park [Nova Scotia]
　Canada (table: National parks and national park reserves) **C:** 113
Sabor [parliament]
　Croatia (History) **Ci:** 1148a-1148b
Sabotage [crime] **S:** 3
Sabots [clothing]
　Sabotage **S:** 4
Sabre [weapon]
　Fencing **F:** 70 *with picture*
Sabres, Buffalo
　Hockey (table: National Hockey League) **H:** 281
SAC [organization] *See* Strategic Air Command *in this index*
Sac Indians *See* Sauk Indians *in this index*
Saca, Elías Antonio [Salvadoran political leader]
　El Salvador (Recent developments) **E:** 253
Sacagawea [American Indian guide] **S:** 4
　Dollar (The United States dollar) **D:** 295 *with picture*
　Exploration (Crossing North America) **E:** 447
　Lewis and Clark expedition *picture on* **L:** 222d; (Up the Missouri) **L:** 222a-222b; (West to the Rockies) **L:** 222b
　Money (Dollar coins) **M:** 714
Sacajawea *See* Sacagawea *in this index*
Sacasa, Juan Batista [Nicaraguan political leader]
　Nicaragua (The Somoza period) **N:** 400

Somoza García, Anastasio So: 590
Saccadic movements [physiology]
　Reading (Perceiving reading matter) **R:** 156
Saccharides [chemistry] **S:** 4
　Carbohydrate (Kinds of carbohydrates) **C:** 203 *with diagram*
Saccharin [chemical] **S:** 4
　Artificial sweetener **A:** 761
Sacco, Nicola [American public figure]
　Sacco-Vanzetti case **S:** 4
Sacco and Vanzetti [opera by Blitzstein]
　Blitzstein, Marc **B:** 403
Sacco chair *See* Beanbag chair *in this index*
Sacco-Vanzetti case [U.S. history] **S:** 4
　Anderson, Maxwell **A:** 452
　Shahn, Ben **S:** 342 *with picture*
Saccomani, Lorenzo [Italian singer]
　Opera *picture on* **O:** 803
Saccule [anatomy]
　Ear (The inner ear) **E:** 8 *with diagram*
SACD [recording]
　Compact disc (Other formats) **Ci:** 902
Sachar, Louis [American author] **S:** 5
　Newbery Medal (table) **N:** 359
Sachem [leader]
　Indian, American (Indians of the Northeast) **I:** 154-155
　Indian wars (The Pequot War [1637]) **I:** 191
Sachs, Bernard [American physician]
　Tay-Sachs disease **T:** 56
Sachs, Nelly [German-Jewish author] **S:** 5
Sack [football]
　Football (table) **F:** 356
Sackler Gallery *See* Arthur M. Sackler Gallery *in this index*
Sackville-West, V. [British author] **S:** 5
Saco River
　Maine (Rivers and lakes) **M:** 82
　New Hampshire (Rivers and lakes) **N:** 220 *with map*
Sacra conversazione [painting]
　Bellini, Giovanni **B:** 243
Sacral vertebra [anatomy]
　Spine **So:** 792 *with diagram*
Sacrament [religion] **S:** 5
　Augustine, Saint (His beliefs) **A:** 888
　Christianity (Practices) **C:** 522h *with picture*
　Communion **C:** 889
　Eastern Orthodox Churches (Sacraments) **E:** 46
　Luther, Martin (The break with the Roman Catholic Church) **L:** 528
　Lutherans (Doctrine) **L:** 529
　Marriage (Wedding ceremonies) **M:** 220
　Protestantism (Celebration of the sacraments) **P:** 834
　Roman Catholic Church (Worship) **R:** 403-404
　Trent, Council of **T:** 434
Sacrament of the Altar [religion]
　Lutherans (Doctrine) **L:** 529
Sacramento [California] **S:** 5
　California **C:** 36
Sacramento Kings [team]
　Basketball (table) **B:** 150
Sacramento River [California] **S:** 6
　California (Rivers, waterfalls, and lakes) **C:** 50
Sacramento Valley
　California (Agriculture) **C:** 56
　Wintun Indians **W:** 343
Sacré Coeur, Basilique du
　Paris (Famous buildings) **P:** 163-164 *with map*
Sacré Coeur de Montmartre [painting by Utrillo]
　Utrillo, Maurice *picture on* **U:** 252
Sacre du Printemps, Le [music by Stravinsky] *See* Rite of Spring, The *in this index*
Sacred Band [ancient Greece]
　Pelopidas **P:** 232
Sacred bark [plant product]
　Cinchona **Ci:** 553
Sacred bundle
　Indian, American (Indians of the Northeast) **I:** 154-156
Sacred College of Cardinals [religion]
　Benedict XVI **B:** 247
　Cardinal **C:** 210
　Pope **P:** 660; (Present procedures) **P:** 662
Sacred fire [religion]
　Fire (Fire in legend and religion) **F:** 122
Sacred History [book by Euhemerus]
　Mythology (Allegorical approaches) **M:** 988
Sacred Hymns [book by Manzoni]
　Manzoni, Alessandro **M:** 174
Sacred ibis [bird]
　Ibis **I:** 3
Sacred music
　Classical music (Church music) **Ci:** 645
　Hymn **H:** 475
　Oratorio **O:** 818

Sacred Way [ancient Rome]
　Rome (Forums) **R:** 433
Sacrifice [religion] **S:** 6
　See also Human sacrifice *in this index*
　Abraham **A:** 17
　Aztec (Religion) **A:** 1000 *with picture*
　ʻĪd al-Ad-há **I:** 25
　Inca (Religion) **I:** 96-97
　Indian, American *pictures on* **I:** 171, **I:** 173; (Ceremonies) **I:** 148 *with picture*
　Mythology (Aztec mythology) **M:** 987
Sacrifice [sports]
　Baseball (Baseball terms) **B:** 124
Sacrifice fly
　Baseball (Baseball terms) **B:** 124
Sacroiliac joint [anatomy]
　Skeleton (The axial skeleton) **S:** 479-480
Sacrum [anatomy]
　Human body (table) **H:** 422 *with diagram*
　Pelvis **P:** 233 *with diagram*
　Skeleton (The axial skeleton) **S:** 479-480 *with diagram*
Sacsayhuaman [ancient fortress]
　Inca *picture on* **I:** 98
SAD [disorder] *See* Seasonal affective disorder *in this index*
Sad White Roses, The [photograph by Cameron]
　Photography *picture on* **P:** 425
Sadaqah [religion]
　Islam (The Five Pillars of Islam) **I:** 463-464
Sadarghat [district]
　Dhaka **D:** 178
Sadat, Anwar el- [Egyptian political leader] **S:** 7
　Arab-Israeli conflict (The Camp David Accords) **A:** 582a
　Begin, Menachem **B:** 219
　Carter, Jimmy (Foreign affairs) **C:** 257-258 *with picture*
　Egypt (Renewed warfare and peace) **E:** 133 *with picture*
　Israel (The Camp David Accords) **I:** 488
　Mubarak, Hosni **M:** 908
Saddle [riding equipment] **S:** 7 *with diagrams*
　Cowboy (His saddle) **Ci:** 1109
　Horse (The saddle) **H:** 351 *with pictures*
　Indian, American *picture on* **I:** 161
Saddle bronc riding
　Rodeo (Saddle bronc riding) **R:** 397
Saddle horse
　Horse (Saddle horses) **H:** 343; (table: Some types and breeds of horses) **H:** 343
Saddleback butterflyfish
　Fish *picture on* **F:** 155
Saddleback caterpillar
　Insect *picture on* **I:** 297
Sadducees [religious group] **S:** 8
　Jews (The Hellenistic period) **J:** 121-122
　Pharisees **P:** 354
　Sanhedrin **S:** 110
Sade, Marquis de [French author] **S:** 8
　Enlightenment (The orderliness of nature) **E:** 326a-326b
Sadhus [religion]
　Jainism **J:** 22
Sadhvis [religion]
　Jainism **J:** 22
Sadism [psychology]
　Sade, Marquis de **S:** 8
Sadko [opera by Rimsky-Korsakov]
　Rimsky-Korsakov, Nikolai **R:** 341
Sadler, Reinhold [American political leader]
　Nevada (table) **N:** 173
Sadler's Wells Ballet
　De Valois, Ninette **D:** 173
Sadness [emotion]
　Emotion (The basic emotion approach) **E:** 261
Sadowa, Battle of [1866]
　Seven Weeks' War **S:** 325
Sadr, Muqtada al- [Iraqi cleric]
　Iraq (The Iraq War) **I:** 414a-414b
　Iraq War (Resistance to the coalition) **I:** 414e-414f
Sadr City [Iraqi history]
　Iraq War (Resistance to the coalition) **I:** 414e-414f
SAE [program] *See* Supervised agricultural experience program *in this index*
SAE horsepower [measurement]
　Horsepower (SAE horsepower) **H:** 367
Sáenz Peña, Roque [Argentine political leader]
　Argentina (Reform movements) **A:** 657
Safari S: 8
　Africa (Native animals) **A:** 122-123
Safavid dynasty [Iranian history] **S:** 8
　Abbas I **A:** 4
　Iran (The Safavid dynasty) **I:** 405
　Muslims (The Safavid dynasty) **M:** 964d
Safdie, Moshe [Canadian architect] **S:** 8
　Canada (Architecture) **C:** 112

National Gallery of Canada **N:** 37 *with picture*
Safe area [Bosnian history]
Srebrenica massacre **So:** 816
Safe Drinking Water Act [1974]
Water pollution (Laws) **W:** 138
Safed Koh [mountain range]
Khyber Pass **K:** 309 *with map*
Safeguard [weapon]
Nixon, Richard Milhous (The national scene)
N: 433-434
SAFER barrier
Automobile racing (Safety measures) **A:** 975
Safety S: 9 *with pictures*
See also the list of Related articles in the Safety
article
Camping (Safety) **C:** 96
Canoeing (Other equipment) **C:** 180
Consumer protection (The right to safety)
Ci: 1018
Cooking (Preparation of ingredients) **Ci:** 1027
Dam (Dam safety) **D:** 19
Electricity (Electrical safety) **E:** 195 *with pictures*
Elevator (Safety features) **E:** 235
Fire department (Fire prevention and fire safety)
F: 125
Fire drill **F:** 129
Fire prevention **F:** 130
Halloween (Halloween customs and symbols)
H: 24a
Herbal medicine **H:** 197
Ice skating (Skating safety) **I:** 10
Kite (Flying a kite) **K:** 340
Lightning (Protection from lightning) **L:** 301
Local government (Health and safety functions)
L: 407
Mountain climbing (Mountain climbing safety)
M: 897
Red Cross (Health and safety training) **R:** 185
Shark (Shark attacks) **S:** 376
State government (State services) **So:** 864
Swimming (Water safety) **So:** 1042 *with picture*
Tornado (Air pressure) **T:** 335; (Forecasting
tornadoes) **T:** 335-336
Woodworking (Tool care and safety) **W:** 398
Home
Knife (Knife safety) **K:** 346
Match (Matches can be dangerous) **M:** 299
Poison **P:** 600
Industry
Safety (Safety on the job) **S:** 13
Business (Health and safety regulations) **B:** 727
Coal (Mine safety) **Ci:** 729 *with picture*
Health (Occupational health hazards) **H:** 127
Nuclear energy (Hazards and safeguards)
N: 587; (Safety concerns) **N:** 591
Transportation
Safety (Safety in transportation) **S:** 14
Airbag **A:** 200
Airplane (Safety) **A:** 227
Automobile (The passenger compartment)
A: 950-951; (Driving an automobile) **A:** 954;
(Safety problems) **A:** 961; (The growth of
government regulation) **A:** 971
Automobile (Automobile safety measures) **A:** 975
Aviation (Airline safety concerns) **A:** 991
Bicycle *picture on* **B:** 292; (Steering and
stopping) **B:** 290
Coast Guard, United States (Coast Guard
activities) **Ci:** 734
Motorcycle (Motorcycle safety) **M:** 879
Ship (Safety) **S:** 411
Transportation (Challenges of modern
transportation) **T:** 397
Safety [device]
Firearm (Mechanism) **F:** 132-133
Safety [football]
Football (The defensive team) **F:** 357-358 *with
diagrams*; (Scoring) **F:** 362
Safety, Committees of [U.S. history]
Committees of safety **Ci:** 873
Madison, James **M:** 32
Safety belt *See* Seatbelt *in this index*
Safety bicycle
Bicycle *picture on* **B:** 293; (Early bicycles) **B:** 291
with picture
Safety Council, National
National Safety Council **N:** 60
Safety engineering
Safety (In manufacturing plants) **S:** 13
Safety fuse [explosives]
Fuse **F:** 588
Safety glass
Glass *picture on* **G:** 211; (Specialty glasses) **G:** 212
Safety glasses
Glasses (Nonprescription glasses) **G:** 225
Safety lamp S: 16 *with picture*
Safety match

Match (Safety matches) **M:** 299; (The first safety
matches) **M:** 300a
Safety net of assistance [program] *See* Welfare
state *in this index*
Safety pin
Pin **P:** 466
Safety razor
Razor **R:** 153
Safety squeeze [baseball]
Baseball (Baseball terms) **B:** 124
Safety valve S: 17 *with diagram*
Boiler **B:** 439
Saffir, Herbert S. [American engineer]
Hurricane (Hurricane damage) **H:** 455
Saffir-Simpson scale [meteorology]
Hurricane (Hurricane damage) **H:** 455; (table)
H: 456
Safflower [plant] **S:** 17 *with picture*
Safflower oil [food]
Safflower **S:** 17
Vegetable oil **V:** 294
Saffron [seasoning] **S:** 17
Crocus **Ci:** 1150
Saffron crocus [plant]
Flower *picture on* **F:** 274
Plant (Interesting facts about plants) **P:** 519 *with
picture*
Safi al-Din, Sheik [Persian religious leader]
Safavid dynasty **S:** 8
SAG [organization] *See* Screen Actors Guild-
American Federation of Television and Radio
Artists *in this index*
Saga [literature] **S:** 17
Scandinavian literature (Beginnings) **S:** 171
Saga of Egill Skallagrimsson, The [book by Snorri
Sturluson]
Snorri Sturluson **S:** 538
Saga of Erik the Red, The [story]
Erik the Red **E:** 351
Saga of the Greenlanders, The [story]
Erik the Red **E:** 351
Saga of the Volsungs [book]
Sigurd **S:** 455
Sagamore [American Indians]
Mi'kmaq Indians **M:** 513
Sagamore Hill [house]
Roosevelt, Theodore *picture on* **R:** 467
Sagamore Hill National Historic Site [New York]
National Park System (table: National historic
sites) **N:** 52-53
Sagan, Carl [American astronomer] **S:** 18 *with
portrait*
Sagarmatha [name for]
Mount Everest **M:** 884
Sagarmatha National Park [Nepal]
National park (table) **N:** 42f; (Other interesting
national parks) **N:** 42h
Sage [plant] **S:** 18 *with picture*
Plant *pictures on* **P:** 525, **P:** 526
Pollen *picture on* **P:** 645
Sage, Anna [American public figure]
Dillinger, John Herbert **D:** 204
Sage, Margaret Olivia Slocum [American
philanthropist] **S:** 18
Sage, Mount [mountain, Tortola]
Virgin Islands **V:** 392 *with map*
Sagebrush [plant] **S:** 18 *with picture*
Wormwood **W:** 502
Sagebrush State
Nevada **N:** 156
Saginaw [Michigan] **S:** 19
Sagittal crest [anatomy]
Gorilla *diagram on* **G:** 276
Sagittarius [astrology] **S:** 19 *with picture*
Zodiac (The zodiac in astrology) **Z:** 597 *with
picture*
Sagittarius [astronomy]
Milky Way (The center of the galaxy) **M:** 551
Sagittarius A* [astronomy]
Black hole (Supermassive black holes) **B:** 388
Milky Way (The center of the galaxy) **M:** 551
Sago [tree product] **S:** 19
Palm (Products of palms) **P:** 109
Sagoyewatha [American Indian leader]
Red Jacket **R:** 188
Sagrada Familia, Church of the [Barcelona]
Gaudí, Antonio **G:** 69
Saguaro [plant] **S:** 19 *with picture*
Arizona (Plant and animal life) **A:** 683 *with picture*
Cactus (Cactus) **C:** 9 *with picture*; (Kinds of cactuses) **C:** 11
Plant *picture on* **P:** 526
Tree *picture on* **T:** 415
Saguaro National Park [Arizona] **S:** 20
Arizona *picture on* **A:** 683
National Park System (table: National parks) **N:** 48
Saguenay River [Quebec] **S:** 20 *with picture*
Saguenay-Saint Lawrence Marine Park

Canada (table: National marine conservation
areas) **C:** 114
Sahara [desert, Africa] **S:** 20 *with pictures and map*
Africa *picture on* **A:** 117
Algeria (The Sahara) **A:** 363 *with picture*
Desert **D:** 155
Egypt (The Western Desert) **E:** 125 *with picture
and map*
Harmattan **H:** 61
Libya (Land and climate) **L:** 266 *with picture*
Plant (Deserts) **P:** 523-525
Saharan Atlas Mountains [Africa]
Atlas Mountains **A:** 869
Sahel [region, Africa] **S:** 22
Famine (Drought) **F:** 26-26a
Sahelanthropus tchadensis [hominid]
Human being (Prehuman ancestors) **H:** 414
Prehistoric people *picture on* **P:** 748; (The earliest
hominids) **P:** 744 *with picture*; (table) **P:** 754
with map
Sai Gon River [Vietnam]
Mekong River **M:** 388
Said bin Taimur [sultan of Oman]
Oman (History) **O:** 759
Said Pasha [Egyptian political leader]
De Lesseps, Ferdinand Marie **D:** 114
Egypt (Muhammad Ali and modernization)
E: 131
Suez Canal (History) **So:** 958
Saiga [animal]
Animal *picture on* **A:** 483
Saigon [Vietnam] *See* Ho Chi Minh City *in this index*
Saikaku, Ihara [Japanese author]
Higuchi Ichiyo **H:** 229
Sail [boat]
Sailing **S:** 23 *with pictures*
Ship (Propulsion and steering) **S:** 406
Windsurfing **W:** 335 *with picture*
Sail [submarine]
Submarine **So:** 939
Sailboarding [sport]
Windsurfing **W:** 335 *with picture*
Sailboat
Aerodynamics (Lift and drag in a sailboat) **A:** 86
with diagram
Boating *pictures on* **B:** 431; (Types of boats)
B: 428-429 *with picture*
Sailing **S:** 23 *with pictures*
Transportation (Water transportation) **T:** 384
Sailendras [Indonesian rulers]
Indonesia (Hindu and Buddhist kingdoms) **I:** 236
with picture
Sailer, Toni [Austrian skier]
Skiing (The middle and late 1900's) **S:** 487
Sailfin molly [fish]
Molly **M:** 696
Sailfish [fish] **S:** 23
Fish *pictures on* **F:** 152
Sailing [sport] **S:** 23 *with pictures*
See also the list of Related articles in the Sailing
article
America's Cup **A:** 431
Canoeing (Poling and sailing) **C:** 182
Catamaran **C:** 298
Flag *pictures on* **F:** 197
Knots, hitches, and splices (Uses of knots) **K:** 355
Olympic Games (Summer Olympic Games)
O: 746e-746f
Transportation (The first great civilizations) **T:** 385
Sailing canoe
Canoeing (Canoes) **C:** 180
Sailing ship
Ship **S:** 402 *with picture*; (Propulsion and steering)
S: 406; (History) **S:** 414 *with pictures*
Sailor
See also Seaman *in this index*
Navy, United States (Training a sailor) **N:** 83
Sailor King [English history] *See* William IV *in this
index*
Sailors' Church, The
Montreal (Churches) **M:** 773
Sailplane [aircraft]
Airplane, Model *picture on* **A:** 241
Glider **G:** 228 *with pictures*
Sailsurfing [sport]
Windsurfing **W:** 335
Saimaa Lake System
Finland (Land regions) **F:** 113
Saint [title] **S:** 29
See also the list of Related articles in the Saint
article
All Saints' Day **A:** 370
Biography (The Middle Ages) **B:** 313
Canonization **C:** 153
Saint, Eva Marie [American actress]
Motion picture (Best performance by an actress
in a supporting role: 1954) **M:** 862b

Saint, Thomas [British inventor]
Sewing machine (History) S: 333
Saint ...
Individual saints appear under their names, as in Paul, Saint. Other entries, such as Saint Louis [Missouri], appear below
Saint Albans [Vermont]
Vermont V: 336
Saint Albans, Battle of [1455]
Wars of the Roses W: 38
York Y: 568
Saint Andrew, Order of
Knighthood, Orders of (Honorary orders) K: 347
Saint Andrews [Scotland] S: 30
United Kingdom U: 57
Saint Andrews [New Brunswick] S: 30
Saint Andrew's Blockhouse National Historic Site [New Brunswick]
Canada (table: National historic sites) C: 115
Saint Andrews-by-the-Sea
Saint Andrews S: 30
Saint Andrew's cross
Andrew, Saint A: 456
Cross picture on Ci: 1155
Flag picture on F: 217
Saint Andrews Golf Club [New York]
Golf (Beginnings) G: 264
Saint Anthony [former village]
Minneapolis (Industrial development) M: 583
Saint Anthony's cross
Cross picture on Ci: 1155
Saint-Augustin-de-Desmaures [Quebec]
Quebec (Recent developments) Q: 37
Saint Augustine [Florida] S: 30 with picture
Florida (Places to visit) F: 252 with picture; (Exploration and Spanish settlement) F: 261-262
Hispanic Americans (Exploration and settlement) H: 250 with picture
Menéndez de Avilés, Pedro M: 400
United States, History of the (The Spanish and Portuguese) U: 151
Saint Augustine grass
Lawn (Types of lawns) L: 142
Saint-Barthélemy [island, Caribbean]
Guadeloupe G: 408 with map
Saint Bartholomew's Day, Massacre of [1572] S: 31
France (Religious wars) F: 473
Huguenots (The massacre) H: 410 with picture
Saint Basil's Cathedral [Moscow]
Architecture (Byzantine architecture) A: 617
Europe picture on E: 387
Moscow picture on M: 823; (Famous landmarks) M: 823-824 with picture and map
Russia picture on R: 525; (Architecture) R: 536 with picture
Saint Benedict, Rule of [religion]
Monasticism (Christian monasticism) M: 701
Saint Bernard [dog] S: 31 with picture
Dog picture on D: 265
Saint Bernard monastery [Switzerland]
Saint Bernard S: 31
Saint Bernard Passes [Switzerland] S: 31
Saint Boniface, Cathedral of [Manitoba]
Manitoba (Visitor's guide) M: 152 with picture
Saint Catherine's Day
Holiday (In other countries) H: 291
Saint Cecilia [painting by Raphael]
Bologna B: 448
Saint Charles River
Quebec Q: 34
Saint Christopher [island, Caribbean Sea]
Saint Kitts and Nevis S: 38
Saint Clair, Arthur [American general] S: 32
Cincinnati Ci: 554
Indian wars (Conflicts in the Midwest) I: 191
Northwest Territory (Settlement) N: 535
Ohio Company (The second Ohio Company) O: 704-705
Saint Clair, Lake [Michigan-Ontario]
Lake Saint Clair L: 45
Saint Clair-sur-Epte, Treaty of [A.D. 911]
Vikings (The Danish Vikings) V: 383
Saint Clare, Augustine [literary figure]
Uncle Tom's Cabin U: 20
Saint Clemens, Cathedral of [Århus]
Århus A: 661
Saint Cloud [Minnesota] S: 32
Saint Crispin, Knights of
Labor movement (The first nationwide labor organizations) L: 9
Saint Croix
Virgin Islands V: 392 with map; (Recent developments) V: 397
Virgin Islands, United States V: 393
Saint Croix Island International Historic Site

[Maine] S: 32
National Park System (table: National parkways and other national parklands) N: 56
Saint Croix National Scenic Riverway [Minnesota-Wisconsin]
National Park System (table: National parkways and other national parklands) N: 56
Saint Croix River
Maine (Rivers and lakes) M: 82
New Brunswick picture on N: 180
Saint Croix Valley [Minnesota]
Minnesota (The Louisiana Purchase) M: 603-604
Saint David's monastery [Mynyw, Wales]
David, Saint D: 46
Saint-Denis [city]
Réunion R: 267
Saint Denis, Louis Juchereau de [French frontiersman]
Louisiana (French Louisiana) L: 497-498
Saint Denis, Ruth [American choreographer] S: 32 with picture
Dance (Modern dance) D: 30-31
Shawn, Ted S: 378
Saint-Domingue [colony]
Haiti (History) H: 15-16
Slavery (Modern times) S: 502
Toussaint Louverture T: 350
Saint Dunstan's University
Prince Edward Island (Schools) P: 786
Saint Elias Mountains [Alaska-Yukon] S: 33
Alaska (Land regions) A: 292
Yukon (Location, size, and description) Y: 578 with map
Saint Elmo's fire [electricity] S: 33
Saint Emmanuel Bueno, Martyr [book by Unamuno]
Unamuno, Miguel de U: 19
Saint Eustatius [island, Caribbean]
Netherlands Antilles N: 151
Saint-Exupéry, Antoine de [French author] S: 33
Saint Florian, Friedrich [American architect]
National World War II Memorial N: 62
Saint Francis, Lake [Canada]
Saint Lawrence River (The course of the St. Lawrence) S: 41
Saint Francis in Ecstasy [painting by Bellini]
Francis of Assisi, Saint picture on F: 481
Saint Francis River
Quebec (Rivers, waterfalls, and lakes) Q: 24
Saint Francis Xavier, University of
Bolivia (Education) B: 444
Saint-Gaudens, Augustus [American sculptor] S: 33 with picture
Saint-Gaudens National Historic Site [New Hampshire]
National Park System (table: National historic sites) N: 52-53 with picture
Saint George [Bermuda]
Bermuda (History) B: 268
Saint George [district]
New York City (Staten Island) N: 330
Saint George [sculpture by Donatello]
Donatello D: 307 with picture
Saint George, Order of [award]
Garter, Order of the G: 46
Saint George and the Dragon [painting by Crivelli]
Painting picture on P: 38
Saint George Island [Bering Sea]
Pribilof Islands P: 774
Saint George Slaying the Dragon [sculpture by Donatello]
Dragon picture on D: 319
Saint George's [Grenada] S: 34
Grenada G: 388 with picture and map
Saint George's Cathedral [Georgetown, Guyana]
Georgetown G: 109
Saint George's Chapel [England]
Windsor Castle W: 335
Saint George's cross
Flag picture on F: 217
George, Saint G: 108
Saint Germain, Ferdinand J. [American political leader]
Bank (A boom in money market funds) B: 94
Saint-Germain, Treaty of [1919] S: 34
World War I (The peace settlement) W: 465
Saint-Germain-en-Laye, Treaty of [1632]
Quebec (Early days) Q: 36
Saint-Germaine-la-Rivière [France]
Tomb T: 325
Saint Gilgen [town, Austria]
Austria picture on A: 932
Saint Gotthard Pass [Switzerland] S: 34
Saint Gotthard Road Tunnel [Switzerland]
Alps picture on A: 385; (Alpine travel) A: 386
Saint Gotthard tunnels S: 34
Switzerland (Transportation) So: 1058

Tunnel (table) T: 491 with picture
Saint Gotthard tunnels [Switzerland] S: 34
Tunnel (table) T: 491
Saint Helena [island, Atlantic] S: 34 with picture
Napoleon I (The Hundred Days and Waterloo) N: 16
Saint Helens, Mount [mountain] See Mount Saint Helens in this index
Saint Ignace [island, Ontario]
Lake Superior (Description) L: 45 with map
Saint Isaac of Dalmatia, Cathedral of
Saint Petersburg [Russia] (The city) S: 54
Saint James the Greater [carving by Riemenscher]
Germany picture on G: 154
Saint James's Palace [London] S: 35
London (Palaces) L: 435
Saint Jean, Cathedral of [France]
Lyon L: 536
Saint Jean Baptiste Day [holiday]
Canada picture on C: 108
Saint Joan [play by Shaw]
Joan of Arc, Saint (The memory of Joan of Arc) J: 129
McKenna, Siobhan M: 337
Shaw, George Bernard (Mature period) S: 378
Saint Joe River [Idaho]
Idaho (Interesting facts about Idaho) I: 27
Saint John [island]
Virgin Islands V: 392
Virgin Islands, United States V: 393
Virgin Islands National Park V: 397
Saint John [New Brunswick] S: 35
New Brunswick N: 180 with picture, picture on N: 198; (Population) N: 184 with pictures; (table: Average monthly weather) N: 193; (Transportation) N: 195; (Economic developments) N: 199
Saint John, J. Hector [French author]
Crèvecoeur, Michel-Guillaume Jean de Ci: 1129
Saint John, John Pierce [American political leader]
Kansas (table) K: 234
Saint John, Order of [organization] S: 36
Saint John Ambulance [foundation]
Saint John, Order of S: 36
Saint John Lateran [church, Rome]
Vatican City (St. Peter's Basilica) V: 287
Saint John Ophthalmic Hospital
Saint John, Order of S: 36
Saint John River [Maine]
Maine (Rivers and lakes) M: 82
Saint John River [New Brunswick] S: 36
New Brunswick (Places to visit) N: 188 with picture; (Rivers and lakes) N: 192
Reversing Falls of Saint John R: 269
Saint John the Baptist Day [holiday]
June J: 192
Saint John the Divine, Cathedral of [New York City]
Morgan, J. P. M: 803
Saint John's [Antigua and Barbuda]
Antigua and Barbuda A: 555
St. John's [Newfoundland and Labrador] S: 36 with picture
Newfoundland and Labrador N: 360 with pictures; (Population) N: 364; (table: Average monthly weather) N: 372
Saint John's Church [Richmond]
Richmond (Other interesting places to visit) R: 332
Virginia (Places to visit) V: 408 with picture
Saint John's College [Maryland]
Maryland (Schools) M: 244
Saint John's College at Rose Hill [former name]
Fordham University F: 383
Saint John's Island
Prince Edward Island (Exploration and early history) P: 791
Saint-John's-wort [shrub] S: 37 with picture
Herbal medicine H: 196
Saint Joseph [Missouri] S: 37
Saint Joseph's Oratory
Montreal (Churches) M: 773 with picture
Saint Julien, Cathedral of [France]
Le Mans L: 187
Saint Just, Baron de
Poutrincourt, Jean de Biencourt de P: 722
Saint Katherine's Dock [London]
Architecture (The Industrial Revolution) A: 625
Saint Kilda National Park [United Kingdom]
National park (table) N: 42g
Saint Kitts [island, Caribbean Sea]
Saint Kitts and Nevis S: 38
Saint Kitts and Nevis S: 38 with picture and map
Flag picture on F: 201
West Indies (Abolition and independence movements) W: 205
Saint-Lambert Lock [Montreal]

Quebec *picture on* Q: 28
Saint Laurens Church
 Rotterdam R: 489
Saint Laurent, Jean Paul [Canadian political
 leader]
 Saint Laurent, Louis Stephen (Marriage) S: 39
Saint Laurent, Louis Stephen [Canadian political
 leader] S: 39 *with pictures*
 Canada, History of (Increasing foreign
  involvement) C: 149
 King, William Lyon Mackenzie (Third term as
  prime minister) K: 327
 Liberal Party of Canada L: 227
Saint Laurent, Yves [French fashion designer] S: 40
Saint Lawrence, Gulf of [Canada]
 Gulf of Saint Lawrence G: 437
Saint Lawrence, Lake [New York]
 Saint Lawrence Seaway (The seaway system)
  S: 43; (The hydroelectric power project) S: 44;
  (Construction of the seaway) S: 45
"Saint Lawrence and the Saguenay, The" [poem
 by Sangster]
 Canadian literature (Poetry: 1850-1918) C: 157
Saint Lawrence Church
 Rotterdam R: 489
Saint Lawrence Deep Waterway Treaty [1932]
 Saint Lawrence Seaway (First construction plans)
  S: 44-45
Saint Lawrence Islands National Park [Ontario]
 Canada (table: National parks and national park
  reserves) C: 113
 Thousand Islands T: 268
Saint Lawrence Lowlands
 Canada (The St. Lawrence Lowlands) C: 118 *with
  picture*
 Ontario (Land regions) O: 776 *with picture and
  map*
 Quebec (Land regions) Q: 22 *with map*
Saint Lawrence River [Canada-U.S.] S: 41 *with map*
 Canada (Rivers, waterfalls, and lakes) C: 118-119
 Exploration (The search for a northern passage)
  E: 446
 Great Lakes (Drainage) G: 344
 Gulf of Saint Lawrence G: 437
 Montreal (The city) M: 768-769
 Ontario (Rivers, waterfalls, and lakes) O: 778
 Quebec Q: 11, Q: 34; (Rivers, waterfalls, and
  lakes) Q: 24 *with map*
 River (table) R: 352
 Saint Lawrence Seaway S: 42 *with picture and
  map*
 Thousand Islands T: 268 *with picture*
Saint Lawrence River Valley
 Quebec *picture on* Q: 24; (Land regions) Q: 22
Saint Lawrence Seaway [waterway, Canada-U.S.]
 S: 42 *with pictures and maps*
 Canada (Waterways and ports) C: 126 *with picture*
 Canal (Major canals in the United States and
  Canada) C: 164; (table) C: 164
 Chicago (Trade) C: 432
 Great Lakes (Water routes to the sea) G: 344
 Gulf of Saint Lawrence G: 437
 Inland waterway I: 274
 Lake Michigan (Routes) L: 41
 Lake Ontario L: 43
 Montreal (Transportation) M: 775
 North America (Transportation and
  communication) N: 469
 Ontario (Shoreline and coastline) O: 778;
  (Transportation) O: 782
 Quebec (Rivers, waterfalls, and lakes) Q: 24
 Saint Lawrence River S: 41
 Saint Lawrence Seaway Development
  Corporation S: 45
 Welland Ship Canal W: 193
**Saint Lawrence Seaway Development
 Corporation** [U.S.] S: 45
 Saint Lawrence Seaway (Canals and locks) S: 43
**Saint Lawrence Seaway Management
 Corporation** [Canada]
 Saint Lawrence Seaway (Canals and locks) S: 43
Saint Lazarus, Order of [religious group] S: 45
Saint Leger, Barry [British general] S: 45
 Revolution, American (Victory at Saratoga) R: 282
Saint Leger Stakes [race]
 Horse racing (Types of horse races) H: 364
Saint Louis [Missouri] S: 46 *with pictures and maps*
 Chouteau, René Auguste C: 522
 Climate (Oceans and large lakes) Ci: 676-676a
 Lewis and Clark expedition (Return to St. Louis)
  L: 222d
 Missouri *picture on* M: 651; (table: Average
  monthly weather) M: 664; (Settlement) M: 669
 United States *picture on* U: 110
Saint-Louis [Senegal]
 French West Africa (History) F: 528
Saint Louis, Lake [Canada]

Saint Lawrence River (The course of the St.
 Lawrence) S: 41
Saint Louis Blues [hockey team]
 Hockey (table: National Hockey League) H: 281
Saint Louis Cardinals [baseball team]
 Baseball (table) B: 130
 Pujols, Albert P: 886a
 Rickey, Branch R: 335
Saint Louis Cathedral
 New Orleans (Downtown New Orleans) N: 278
Saint Louis encephalitis virus
 Mosquito (Mosquitoes and people) M: 834
Saint Louis Post-Dispatch [newspaper]
 Pulitzer, Joseph (His career) P: 886a
Saint Louis Public Library
 Missouri (Libraries) M: 655
Saint Louis Rams [team]
 Football (National Football League) F: 364
Saint Louis River [Minnesota]
 Lake Superior (Description) L: 45 *with map*
 Saint Lawrence River (The course of the St.
  Lawrence) S: 41
Saint Louis Symphony
 Saint Louis (The arts) S: 48
Saint Louis World's Fair [1904] *See* Louisiana
 Purchase Exposition *in this index*
Saint Lucia S: 50 *with picture and map*
 Flag *picture on* F: 201
Saint Lucia Day [custom]
 Christmas (In Denmark, Norway, and Sweden)
  C: 531 *with picture*
 Sweden (Holidays) So: 1026
Saint Luke's Church [Smithfield]
 Virginia (Places to visit) V: 408
Saint Maarten Island *See* Saint Martin *in this index*
Saint Margaret, Chapel of
 Edinburgh E: 77
Saint Mark, Basilica of [Venice] S: 51
 Architecture (Byzantine architecture) A: 617
 Campanile C: 90a
 World, History of the *picture on* W: 434
Saint Mark's Square
 Venice (The city) V: 306 *with picture and map*
Saint Martin [island, Caribbean]
 Guadeloupe G: 408 *with map*
 Netherlands (The Kingdom of the Netherlands)
  N: 139
 Netherlands Antilles N: 151
Saint Martin d'Ainay, Church of [France]
 Lyon L: 536
Saint Martin's summer [weather]
 Indian summer I: 189
Saint Mary Lake [lake, Montana]
 Glacier National Park (Lakes) G: 205
Saint Mary-le-Bow Church [London]
 London (Ancestry) L: 435
Saint Mary Magdalene [painting by Van der
 Weyden]
 Van der Weyden, Rogier *picture on* V: 280
Saint Mary's City [Maryland]
 Colonial life in America (Places to visit) Ci: 800
 Maryland (Places to visit) M: 248 *with picture*
Saint Marys Falls Canal and Locks
 Soo Canals S: 594
Saint Mary's Hospital [Rochester, Minnesota]
 Mayo, William Worrall M: 329
Saint Marys River [Michigan-Ontario] S: 51
 Lake Huron L: 39 *with map*
 Soo Canals S: 594
Saint Mary's River [Nova Scotia]
 Nova Scotia (Rivers and lakes) N: 562 *with map*
Saint Matthew and the Angel [painting by Poussin]
 Poussin, Nicolas *picture on* P: 722
Saint Michael and Saint George, Order of [award]
 Knighthood, Orders of (Honorary orders) K: 347
 with picture
Saint Michael's Cathedral [Sitka]
 Alaska *picture on* A: 291
Saint-Mihiel, Battle of [1918]
 A.E.F. A: 81
 World War I (The last campaigns) W: 463
Saint Moritz [Switzerland] S: 51
Saint Nicholas [magazine]
 Dodge, Mary Elizabeth Mapes D: 260
 Literature for children (Children's magazines)
  L: 365
Saint Nicholas, Feast of [custom] S: 51
 Netherlands (Holidays and recreation) N: 141
Saint Nicholas Church [Leipzig]
 Leipzig (The city) L: 186
Saint Olaf, Order of [award]
 Knighthood, Orders of (Honorary orders) K: 347
Saint Patrick's Cathedral [Dublin]
 Dublin (History) D: 371
Saint Patrick's Cathedral [New York City] S: 51
 New York City (A visitor's guide) N: 338-339 *with
  picture*

Saint Patrick's cross
 Flag *picture on* F: 217
Saint Patrick's Day [custom] S: 51
 Ireland (Saint Patrick) I: 425
 March M: 194
Saint Paul [Minnesota] S: 52
 Minneapolis (The metropolitan area) M: 581
  with map
 Minnesota M: 584 *with pictures*; (Population)
  M: 588; (table: Average monthly weather)
  M: 598
Saint Paul Chamber Orchestra
 Orchestra *picture on* O: 821
Saint Paul-Illaire, Walter von [German
 government official]
 African violet A: 138
Saint Paul Island [Bering Sea]
 Pribilof Islands P: 774
Saint Paul University
 Ottawa, University of O: 875
Saint Paul Winter Carnival
 Minnesota (Visitor's guide) M: 594
Saint Paul's Cathedral [London]
 Architecture (Baroque architecture) A: 622 *with
  picture*
 London (Churches) L: 435 *with picture*; (The
  Middle Ages) L: 439-440 *with picture*
Saint Paul's Church [Norfolk]
 Virginia (Places to visit) V: 408
Saint Paul's Church National Historic Site [New
 York]
 National Park System (table: National historic
  sites) N: 52-53
Saint Paul's Episcopal Church [Richmond]
 Virginia (Places to visit) V: 408
Saint Peter, Collegiate Church of [London] *See*
 Westminster Abbey *in this index*
Saint Peter and Paul Association
 Vatican City (Armed forces) V: 288
Saint Peter's Basilica [Vatican City] S: 53 *with
 picture*
 Architecture (Later Renaissance architecture)
  A: 621 *with picture*; (Baroque architecture)
  A: 622
 Bernini, Gian Lorenzo B: 271
 Borromini, Francesco B: 491
 Bramante, Dono B: 562
 Peter, Saint (Later years) P: 325
 Rome (Churches, palaces, and fountains) R: 429
 Sculpture *picture on* S: 254
 Vatican City (St. Peter's Basilica) V: 287 *with
  picture*; (History) V: 288-289
Saint Peter's Church *See* Saint Peter's Basilica *in
 this index*
Saint Peter's Church, Old [Rome]
 Architecture (Medieval architecture) A: 617 *with
  picture*
Saint Peter's Square
 Pope *picture on* P: 660; (The daily life of the pope)
  P: 662
Saint Petersburg [Russia] S: 54 *with picture*
 Ballet (Ballet in Russia) B: 52
 Leningrad, Siege of L: 195
 Peter I, the Great (Policies within Russia) P: 324
 Russia (City life) R: 533 *with picture*
Saint Petersburg [Florida] S: 55
Saint Petersburg [poem by Bely]
 Russian literature (Symbolism) R: 563
Saint Petersburg State Conservatory
 Saint Petersburg [Russia] (Education and cultural
  life) S: 55
Saint Philibert [ship]
 Shipwreck (table: Major shipwrecks) S: 428
Saint-Pierre [Martinique]
 Martinique M: 235
Saint-Pierre, Charles Irénée Castel de [French
 author]
 Peace (From the 1400's to the 1700's) P: 206
Saint-Pierre and Miquelon [islands, Atlantic] S: 56
 Quebec, Battle of (The attack on Quebec)
  Q: 37-38
Saint Roch [ship]
 Northwest Passage N: 529
 Vancouver (Museums) V: 276
Saint-Saëns, Camille [French composer] S: 56
Saint Sava, Temple of [church]
 Belgrade (The city) B: 236 *with picture*
Saint Sebastian [painting by Mantegna]
 Painting (The 1400's) P: 52-53 *with picture*
Saint Serapion [painting by Zurbarán]
 Painting (The Spanish masters) P: 64 *with picture*
Saint Sernin [church, Toulouse]
 Architecture (Romanesque architecture) A: 618
Saint-Simon, Comte de [French philosopher] S: 56
 Avant-garde A: 982
Saint Simons Island [Georgia]
 Fort Frederica National Monument F: 413

Saint Stephen's Cathedral [Vienna]
Vienna (The city) **V:** 361-362
Saint Stephen's Cathedral [Zagreb]
Croatia *picture on* **Ci:** 1148a
Saint Stephen's Day [custom]
Stephen, Saint **So:** 890
Saint Sulpice Seminary
Montreal (Old Montreal) **M:** 770
Saint Thomas [island]
Virgin Islands **V:** 392 *with map*
Virgin Islands, United States **V:** 393, *picture on*
V: 394
Virgin Islands National Park **V:** 397
Saint Thomas African Episcopal Church
Jones, Absalom **J:** 157
Saint Thomas Aquinas, University of
Santo Domingo, Autonomous University of
S: 117
Saint Thomas' School [Leipzig, Germany]
Bach, Johann Sebastian (His life) **B:** 15-16
Saint Urbain's Horseman [book by Richler]
Richler, Mordecai **R:** 331
Saint Ursula's Convent [book by Hart]
New Brunswick (Interesting facts) **N:** 181
Saint Valentine's Day [custom]
Valentine's Day **V:** 263 *with pictures*
Saint Valentine's Day Massacre [1929]
Capone, Al **C:** 198
Chicago (The Roaring Twenties) **C:** 436
Saint Vincent [island, Caribbean Sea]
Grenadines **G:** 390
Saint Vincent and the Grenadines S: 56 *with
picture and map*
Flag *picture on* **F:** 201
Saint Vitus' Cathedral
Prague (The city) **P:** 730
Saint Vitus's dance [disease]
Chorea **C:** 522
Sainte-Anne-de-Beaupré [church, Quebec] **S:** 57
with picture
Quebec (Places to visit) **Q:** 20 *with picture*
Sainte-Beuve, Charles Augustin [French author]
S: 58
Sainte Chapelle [church, Paris]
Stained glass (Technical improvements) **So:** 823
Sainte-Famille [Quebec]
Quebec *picture on* **Q:** 20
Sainte Foy [Quebec]
Quebec, Battle of (The attack on Quebec)
Q: 37-38
Sainte Genevieve [Missouri]
Missouri *picture on* **M:** 661
Sainte Geneviève Library [Paris]
Architecture (The Industrial Revolution) **A:** 625
Sainte-Marie Among the Hurons [mission]
Ontario (Places to visit) **O:** 774
Saintpaulia [plant] *See African violet in this index*
Saints, New Orleans *See New Orleans Saints in
this index*
Saints Peter and Paul, Cathedral of *See
Washington National Cathedral in this index*
Saipan [island, Pacific] **S:** 58
Northern Mariana Islands, Commonwealth of the
N: 525 *with map*
World War II (Island hopping in the Central
Pacific) **W:** 489-490
Sairy Gamp [literary figure]
Dickens, Charles (The first phase) **D:** 188
Saison en enfer, Une [book by Rimbaud]
Rimbaud, Arthur **R:** 341
Sajama [mountain, Bolivia]
Andes Mountains (Physical features) **A:** 452
Sajudis [political movement]
Lithuania (History) **L:** 389-390
Saka Era [calendar]
Kanishka **K:** 215
Sakakawea *See Sacagawea in this index*
Sakakawea, Lake [North Dakota]
North Dakota (Places to visit) **N:** 504; (Rivers and
lakes) **N:** 508 *with picture*
Sake [drink]
See also Ch'ongju in this index
Alcoholic beverage (Other fermented beverages)
A: 336
Sakhalin [island, Russia] **S:** 58
Sakharov, Andrei Dmitriyevich [Soviet physicist]
S: 59 *with portrait*
Saki [pen name]
Munro, Hector Hugh **M:** 928
Saki [monkey]
Monkey (Kinds of monkeys) **M:** 725
Sakmann, Bert [German physiologist]
Nobel Prizes (Physiology or medicine: 1991)
N: 446
Sakoku [Japanese history]
Tokyo (Western influence) **T:** 318
Sakonnet River

Rhode Island (Rivers and lakes) **R:** 306 *with map*
Sakyamuni [Buddhist title] *See Buddha in this index*
Sal [island]
Cape Verde **C:** 189 *with map*
Sal soda
Soda **So:** 568
Salaam, Rashaan [American football player]
Football (table) **F:** 363
Salad bowl model [sociology]
Multiculturalism **M:** 919
Salad onion
Onion (Cultivation) **O:** 763 *with picture*
Saladin [Muslim warrior] **S:** 59
Cairo (History) **C:** 17-18
Crusades (The Third Crusade) **Ci:** 1160
Egypt (Muslim rule) **E:** 130
Fātimid dynasty **F:** 55
Palestine (Arab control) **P:** 104-105
Syria (Christian crusaders) **So:** 1075
Salafiyyah [political movement]
Muslims (Reform and renewal) **M:** 964d
Salam, Abdus [Pakistani physicist]
Nobel Prizes (Physics: 1979) **N:** 441
Subatomic particle (The Standard Model) **So:** 938
Salamanca [literary school]
Spanish literature (The 1500's) **So:** 758-759
Salamanca Place [Hobart]
Australia *picture on* **A:** 901
Salamander [animal] **S:** 59 *with pictures*
Amphibian (Kinds of amphibians) **A:** 440 *with
pictures*
Animal *picture on* **A:** 478; (Sexual reproduction)
A: 496-497; (Regeneration) **A:** 498
Lizard **L:** 399
Mudpuppy **M:** 909 *with picture*
Salamasina [Samoan political leader]
Samoa (History) **S:** 80a
Salamis [island, Greece] **S:** 60
Salammbô [book by Flaubert]
Flaubert, Gustave **F:** 230
Salary *See Wages and hours in this index*
Salary Grab Act [1873]
Wheeler, William Almon **W:** 279
Salary schedule
Teaching (Rewards of teaching) **T:** 69
Salāt [religion]
`Īd al-Ad-hâ **I:** 25
Islam (The Five Pillars of Islam) **I:** 463
Salât al-id [religion]
`Īd al-Fitr **I:** 25
Salaula [market]
Clothing (Geography and economics) **Ci:** 689-
690
Salazar, António de Oliveira [Portuguese political
leader] **S:** 60
Portugal (The Salazar dictatorship) **P:** 694
Salazar, Kenneth L. [American government
official]
Interior, Department of the (table) **I:** 325
Obama, Barack (table) **O:** 640h
Salazar y Espinoza, Juan de [Spanish explorer]
Paraguay (Early days) **P:** 148-149
Saldivar, Yolanda [American public figure]
Selena **S:** 289
Salé [Morocco]
Rabat **R:** 46
Sale, Jamie [Canadian athlete]
Olympic Games (The recent games) **O:** 753-754
Sale barn
Meat packing (Marketing livestock and meat)
M: 350
Salem [former city]
Winston-Salem **W:** 342
Salem [Massachusetts] **S:** 60 *with picture*
Massachusetts (Places to visit) **M:** 280;
(Massachusetts Bay Colony) **M:** 289
Salem [Oregon] **S:** 61
Salem, Peter [American soldier] **S:** 61
Salem Express [ship]
Shipwreck (table: Major shipwrecks) **S:** 428
Salem Maritime National Historic Site
[Massachusetts]
National Park System (table: National historic
sites) **N:** 52-53
Salem (Location and description) **S:** 60-61
Salem witchcraft trials [U.S. history] **S:** 61
Colonial life in America (Religion) **Ci:** 804-805
Massachusetts *picture on* **M:** 291
Mather, Cotton **M:** 309
Salem **S:** 61
Sewall, Samuel **S:** 331
Witchcraft (Middle Ages through the 1700's)
W: 372 *with picture*
Sales [economics] **S:** 61
Advertising **A:** 72
Careers (Sales) **C:** 229 *with picture*
Manufacturing (Distribution and sales) **M:** 171

Marketing **M:** 214
Sales tax **S:** 66
United States, History of the (Improved sales
methods) **U:** 180
Sales, Saint Francis de [French religious leader]
See Francis de Sales, Saint in this index
Sales agreement [document]
Sales (Persuasion) **S:** 63-64
Sales representative
Careers (Sales) **C:** 229
Publishing (Marketing) **P:** 867
Sales tax S: 66
Taxation (Taxes on transactions) **T:** 53
West Virginia (Interesting facts) **W:** 207
Salesians [religious group]
Aristide, Jean-Bertrand **A:** 662
Religious life (table) **R:** 227
Salesperson
Sales **S:** 61
Salian dynasty [German history]
Germany (The Holy Roman Empire) **G:** 162
Salians [people]
Franks **F:** 494
Salic law [European history] **S:** 66
Valois **V:** 267
Salicylate [compound]
Aspirin **A:** 816
Salicylic acid [chemical] **S:** 66
Salientia [zoology]
Frog (Kinds of frogs) **F:** 539
Salih, Al-Tayyib [Sudanese author]
Sudan (The arts) **S:** 951
Salih, Ali Abdullah [Yemeni political leader]
Middle East (2011 protests) **M:** 534b
Yemen (Formation of North Yemen) **Y:** 563;
(Unification) **Y:** 564
Salinas de Gortari, Carlos [Mexican political
leader] **S:** 66 *with portrait*
Mexico (Opposition to the PRI) **M:** 474
Salinas Pueblo Missions National Monument
[New Mexico]
National Park System (table: National
monuments) **N:** 51
Salinas Valley [region, California]
Lettuce (Growing lettuce) **L:** 214
Saline shooting star [plant]
Flower *picture on* **F:** 287
Salinger, J. D. [American author] **S:** 66
American literature (Fiction and other prose)
A: 424
Novel (After World War II) **N:** 574
Salinity [measurement]
Estuary **E:** 364
Salinometer [measuring device]
Hydrometer **H:** 471
Salisbury [England] **S:** 67 *with picture*
Salisbury [Zimbabwe] *See Harare in this index*
Salisbury, Marquess of [British political leader]
S: 67
Salisbury Cathedral
Salisbury **S:** 67 *with picture*
Salisbury Convention [1945]
House of Lords **H:** 384
Salish Indians S: 67
British Columbia (Early days) **B:** 628
Indian, American *picture on* **I:** 162
Saliva [physiology] **S:** 67 *with diagram*
See also Ptyalin in this index
Digestive system (From mouth to stomach)
D: 202
Human body (The mouth, esophagus, and
stomach) **H:** 419
Mastication **M:** 298
Salivary glands [anatomy]
Gland (table) **G:** 209
Human body (table) **H:** 422 *with diagram*
Mouth **M:** 903 *with diagram*
Mumps **M:** 926
Saliva **S:** 68 *with diagram*
Saljuqs [ancient people] *See Seljuks in this index*
Salk, Jonas Edward [American biochemist] **S:** 68
with picture
Poliomyelitis (Prevention of poliomyelitis) **P:** 626
Sabin, Albert Bruce **S:** 3
Salk Institute for Biological Sciences [La Jolla,
California]
Kahn, Louis Isadore *picture on* **K:** 210
Salka Valka [book by Laxness]
Scandinavian literature (The modern period in
Scandinavian literature) **S:** 171
Sall, Macky [Senegalese political leader]
Senegal (History) **S:** 299-300
Salle, David [American artist]
Painting (Postmodernism) **P:** 88 *with picture*
Sallé, Marie [French dancer]
Ballet (The rise of professional ballet) **B:** 51
Salley, John Peter [American explorer] *See Salling,*

John Peter *in this index*
Sallier, Charles [American pioneer]
  Lake Charles **L:** 36
Salling, John Peter [American explorer]
  West Virginia (Early settlement) **W:** 226
Sallust [Roman historian]
  History (The ancient Greeks and Romans)
    H: 261-262
  Latin literature (The age of Cicero) **L:** 116
"Sally Lockhart" trilogy [books by Pullman]
  Pullman, Philip **P:** 900
Salmagundi [magazine]
  Irving, Washington (Early career) **I:** 460
Salmon [fish] **S:** 69 *with pictures*
  Alaska *picture on* **A:** 299; (American purchase)
    A: 301
  Animal (Animal migration) **A:** 502-503
  Canada (Fishing industry) **C:** 125 *with picture*
  Fish *pictures on* **F:** 146
  Maine (Plant and animal life) **M:** 82-83
  Scotland (Food and drink) **S:** 214
  Seal (Seals and fishing crews) **S:** 267
  Washington (The late 1900's) **W:** 68-69
Salmon, Thomas P. [American political leader]
  Vermont (table) **V:** 333
Salmon Falls River
  New Hampshire (Rivers and lakes) **N:** 220 *with map*
Salmon River
  Idaho (Rivers, waterfalls, springs, and lakes) **I:** 38
  Nevada (Rivers and lakes) **N:** 166
Salmon River Mountains
  Idaho (Mountains) **I:** 36
Salmon Ruins
  New Mexico (Places to visit) **N:** 264
Salmon spear [weapon]
  Indian, American *picture on* **I:** 139
Salmonella [bacteria]
  Ampicillin **A:** 443
  Cattle (Diseases) **C:** 312-313
  Dysentery **D:** 398
  Food poisoning **F:** 340
  Salmonellosis **S:** 71
  Turtle (Turtles and human beings) **T:** 524
Salmonella typhi [bacteria]
  Typhoid fever (Cause and spread) **T:** 539
Salmonellosis [disease] **S:** 71
Salome [Biblical figure] **S:** 71
Salome [opera by Strauss]
  Opera: (*Salome*) **O:** 807 *with picture*
  Strauss, Richard **So:** 922
Salomé [play by Wilde]
  Opera: (*Salome*) **O:** 807
Salomon, Edward [American political leader]
  Wisconsin (table) **W:** 365
Salomon, Haym [American patriot] **S:** 71
Salon [French history]
  Salon **S:** 71
  Women's movement (From the Renaissance to
    the 1800's) **W:** 384
Salon [room] **S:** 71
Salon Carré [Paris]
  Salon **S:** 71
Salon des Refusés [Paris]
  Salon **S:** 71
Salonika [Greece] *See* Thessaloniki *in this index*
Salote Tupou III [queen of Tonga]
  Tonga (History) **T:** 328
Saloth Sar [Cambodian political leader] *See* Pol Pot
  in this index
Salsa [music]
  Cruz, Celia **Ci:** 1165
  Music (Western music) **M:** 955
  Puente, Tito **P:** 871
Salsify [plant] **S:** 71 *with picture*
  Goatsbeard **G:** 242
Salt S: 72 *with pictures*
  See also Salt, Chemical *in this index*
  Drainage **D:** 320
  Electricity (Ions) **E:** 192
  Food preservation (Curing) **F:** 341
  Horse (Food) **H:** 355
  Louisiana *picture on* **L:** 493
  Nutrition (Limit intake of sodium and sugar)
    N: 628
  Ocean (Composition) **O:** 654; (Sediments) **O:** 654
  Rock (Chemical sediments) **R:** 372
  Sodium (Where sodium is found) **So:** 569
  Thirst **T:** 259
SALT [meetings] *See* Strategic Arms Limitation Talks
  in this index
SALT [telescope] *See* Southern African Large
  Telescope *in this index*
Salt, Chemical S: 75
  Neutralization **N:** 154
Salt Acts [history of India]
  Gandhi, Mohandas Karamchand (Gandhi's

independence campaigns) **G:** 25
  India (New Constitution) **I:** 132
Salt Creek pupfish [fish]
  Pupfish *picture on* **P:** 905
Salt-cured meat
  Fishing industry (Methods of processing) **F:** 186
  Food preservation (Early methods) **F:** 344
Salt dome [geology]
  Louisiana (Land regions) **L:** 490
  Petroleum *diagram on* **P:** 337; (Migration)
    P: 333-334
  Salt (Salt from the ground) **S:** 73-74
Salt Eaters, The [book by Bambara]
  Novel (The novel today) **N:** 575
Salt Lake, Great *See* Great Salt Lake *in this index*
Salt Lake City [Utah] **S:** 75 *with picture*
  Mormons (Mormons today) **M:** 809 *with picture*
  Utah **U:** 230 *with picture*; (table: Average monthly
    weather) **U:** 242
Salt Lake Temple *See* Mormon Temple *in this index*
Salt lick
  Pioneer life in America (Food) **P:** 481-482
  Rabbit (Food) **R:** 48-49
  Salt *picture on* **S:** 73
Salt marsh [wetland]
  Marsh **M:** 228
Salt mine
  Salt (Salt from the ground) **S:** 73-74 *with picture*;
    (History of salt) **S:** 75
Salt River [Arizona] **S:** 76a
  Phoenix (The city) **P:** 395 *with map*; (Early
    developments) **P:** 399
Salt River Bay National Historical Park [U.S. Virgin
  Islands]
  National Park System (table: National historical
    parks) **N:** 56-57
Salt Sea
  Dead Sea **D:** 56
Salt water *See* Brine; Seawater *in this index*
Saltatory conduction [physiology]
  Myelin **M:** 970f
Saltbush [shrub]
  Australia (Native plants) **A:** 911-912
Saltcellar of Francis I [sculpture by Cellini]
  Cellini, Benvenuto **C:** 339 *with picture*
Salter, Susanna Madora [American political
  leader] **S:** 76a *with portrait*
  Kansas (Interesting facts) **K:** 217
Salto [Uruguay] **S:** 76a
Salton Sea [lake, California] **S:** 76a
  California (Rivers, waterfalls, and lakes) **C:** 50-51
Saltonstall, Leverett [American political leader]
  Massachusetts (table) **M:** 288
Saltpeter [mineral] **S:** 76a
  Mammoth Cave National Park **M:** 130
Saltwater crocodile
  Animal *picture on* **A:** 486
  Crocodile (Kinds of crocodiles) **Ci:** 1149-1150
Saltwater eel
  Eel **E:** 114
Saltwater fish
  Fish (Saltwater environments) **F:** 150 *with pictures*
Saluda River, Battle of [1769]
  Westward movement in America (Regional
    conflict) **W:** 245-246
Saluki [dog] **S:** 76a *with picture*
  Dog *picture on* **D:** 271; (History) **D:** 281
Salutation
  Letter writing (The salutation) **L:** 210 *with picture*
Salutatorian [education]
  Graduation **G:** 297
Salute [custom]
  Flag (Saluting the flag) **F:** 219
Salutin, Rick [Canadian dramatist]
  Canadian literature (Modern Canadian drama)
    C: 161
Salvador [Brazil] **S:** 76b
  Brazil *pictures on* **B:** 567, **B:** 573
Salvador, El *See* El Salvador *in this index*
Salvage [Newfoundland and Labrador]
  Newfoundland and Labrador *picture on* **N:** 364
Salvage [law] **S:** 76b
Salvage [process]
  Fire department (Firefighting) **F:** 123-124
Salvage service
  Salvage **S:** 76b
Salvarsan [medication]
  Ehrlich, Paul **E:** 145
Salvation [religion]
  Christianity (Sin and salvation) **C:** 522g; (The
    Reformation) **C:** 524-525
  Predestination **P:** 734
  Protestantism (Faith and grace) **P:** 834
  Religion (A doctrine of salvation) **R:** 215
  Roman Catholic Church (Sin, the Incarnation, and
    salvation) **R:** 403
Salvation Army [religious group] **S:** 76b *with*

pictures
  Booth, Evangeline Cory **B:** 480
  Booth, William **B:** 480
Salvayre, Lydie [French author]
  French literature (Recent French literature) **F:** 523
Salvia [plant] **S:** 77 *with picture*
Salvo Palace
  Montevideo **M:** 764b *with picture*
Salvor [person]
  Salvage **S:** 76b
Salyut [space station]
  Astronaut (Achievements in space) **A:** 829-830
  International Space Station (History) **I:** 346b
  Space exploration (Salyut and Skylab) **So:** 721
Salzburg [Austria] **S:** 77
  Austria *picture on* **A:** 931
  Reinhardt, Max **R:** 209
SAM [weapon]
  Guided missile (Surface-to-air missiles) **G:** 426
Sam Lawson's Oldtown Fireside Stories [book by
  Stowe]
  Stowe, Harriet Beecher (Other works) **So:** 916
Sama-Veda [religious book] *See* Samaveda *in this
  index*
Samaal [people]
  Somalia (People) **So:** 588
Samadhi [religion]
  Yoga **Y:** 567
Samak Sundaravej [Thai political leader]
  Thailand (Recent developments) **T:** 228
Samar [island, Philippines]
  Philippines (The main islands) **P:** 376-378 *with
    map*
Samara [Russia] **S:** 77
Samaras, Antonis [Greek political leader]
  Greece (Recent developments) **G:** 365
Samaria [ancient city] **S:** 77
Samaritans [ancient people] **S:** 78
Samarium [element] **S:** 78
Samarkand [Uzbekistan] *See* Samarqand *in this
  index*
Samarqand [Uzbekistan] **S:** 78
  Timur **T:** 292d
Samarra [Iraq]
  Iraq *picture on* **I:** 412
Samaveda [religious book]
  Vedas **V:** 291
Samba [dance]
  Ballroom dancing **B:** 63
  Latin America (Dance) **L:** 101 *with picture*
Sambar [food]
  India (Food and drink) **I:** 118
Samber, Robert [British author]
  Mother Goose (The history of Mother Goose
    literature) **M:** 842
Sambi, Ahmed Abdallah Mohamed [Comoran
  political leader]
  Comoros (History) **Ci:** 900-901
Sambo [sport]
  Wrestling (Chief forms of wrestling) **W:** 505
Sambre River [Belgium]
  Belgium (The land) **B:** 230 *with map*
Sambuke [musical instrument]
  Elder **E:** 157
Samburu [people]
  Kenya *picture on* **K:** 301
Same-sex marriage S: 78
  California (The beginning of the 2000's) **C:** 64
  Connecticut (The early 2000's) **Ci:** 971
  Evangelical Lutheran Church in America **E:** 422
  Gay rights movement **G:** 73
  Liberalism (Features of liberalism) **L:** 228
  Maine (The early 2000's) **M:** 92
  Marriage (Same-sex unions and marriages)
    M: 220
  Massachusetts (The early 2000's) **M:** 293
  Vermont (Recent developments) **V:** 337
  Washington (The late 2000's) **W:** 69
Same-sex union
  See also Civil union; Same-sex marriage *in this
    index*
  Evangelical Lutheran Church in America **E:** 422
  Family (Varieties of families) **F:** 20
  Gay rights movement **G:** 73
  Lutherans (Lutheranism in America) **L:** 529
  Marriage (Same-sex unions and marriages)
    M: 220
Samford, William James [American political
  leader]
  Alabama (table) **A:** 274
Samhain [custom]
  Halloween **H:** 24a; (History) **H:** 25
  October **O:** 670
  Witchcraft (Witchcraft as a religion) **W:** 371-372
Samhitas [religious books]
  Hinduism (The Vedas) **H:** 235
  Vedas **V:** 291

Sami [language]
  Sami (Language and culture) **S:** 79
Sami [people] **S:** 78 *with pictures*
  Arctic (Groups) **A:** 638
  Clothing *picture on* **Ci:** 690
  Europe *picture on* **E:** 401
  Finland *picture on* **F:** 113; (People) **F:** 111;
    (History) **F:** 116
  Lapland **L:** 74
  Norway (Ancestry) **N:** 539
  Reindeer **R:** 209
Samisen [musical instrument]
  Music (Japanese music) **M:** 956
Samizdat [publishing]
  Publishing (The power of published ideas) **P:** 869
Samlog scoring system
  Ice skating (Long-track skating) **I:** 14
Samnites [ancient people]
  Pompeii (Early days) **P:** 653
Samo [people]
  Burkina Faso (People) **B:** 706
Samoa S: 80 *with pictures and map*
  Flag *picture on* **F:** 204
Samoa Islands [Pacific] **S:** 80b
  Samoa **S:** 80
Samoan [language]
  Samoa (People) **S:** 80a
Samoset [American Indian chief] **S:** 80b
  Plymouth Colony (The first year) **P:** 583
Samothrace [island, Greece] **S:** 81
Samothraki [island, Greece]
  Samothrace **S:** 81
Samotlor [oil field]
  Siberia *picture on* **S:** 445
Samoyed [dog] **S:** 81
  Dog *picture on* **D:** 267
  Sled dog **S:** 505
Sampaio, Jorge [Portuguese political leader]
  Portugal (Recent developments) **P:** 695
Sampan [boat] **S:** 81
  Houseboat **H:** 389
  Transportation (Water transportation) **T:** 384
Sample [electronics]
  Compact disc (Recording) **Ci:** 901
  Tape recorder (Erasing and recording) **T:** 38
Sample [statistics]
  Census (Conducting censuses) **C:** 347-348
  Psychology (Naturalistic observation) **P:** 847-848
  Public opinion poll (Selecting the sample) **P:** 862
  Sociology (Surveys) **So:** 565
  Statistics (Collecting the data) **So:** 868;
    (Sampling) **So:** 869
Sampler [handicraft] **S:** 81 *with picture*
Sampling calorimeter [machine]
  Particle detector (Sampling calorimeters) **P:** 187
Sampling error [statistics]
  Public opinion poll (Evaluating a poll) **P:** 863
Sampras, Pete [American tennis player] **S:** 81
  Tennis (Tennis today) **T:** 166e-166e *with picture*
Sampson, Deborah [American patriot] **S:** 81
Sampson, William Thomas [American admiral]
  S: 81
Sam's Art [drawing by Steinberg]
  Steinberg, Saul *picture on* **So:** 885
Sam's Club [business]
  Wal-Mart Stores, Inc. **W:** 6
Samsara [religion]
  Buddhism (Buddha) **B:** 667
  Yoga **Y:** 567
Samson [Biblical figure] **S:** 82
  Delilah **D:** 116
Samson Agonistes [poem by Milton]
  Milton, John **M:** 557
Samsung Electronics
  Manufacturing (table) **M:** 170
Samudragupta [emperor of India]
  Gupta dynasty (Rise and fall of the dynasty)
    G: 442
Samuel [Biblical figure]
  Jews *picture on* **J:** 122
  Samuel, Books of **S:** 82
Samuel, Books of [Bible] **S:** 82
  Bible (The Prophets) **B:** 280
Samuelson, Don [American political leader]
  Idaho (table) **I:** 42
Samuelson, Paul Anthony [American economist]
  S: 82
  Economics (Modern economics) **E:** 64-65
Samuelsson, Bengt Ingemar [Swedish
  biochemist]
  Nobel Prizes (Physiology or medicine: 1982)
    N: 446
Samurai [Japanese history] **S:** 82 *with picture*
  Hara-kiri **H:** 55
  Japan (Creation of private estates) **J:** 53; (Meiji
    era) **J:** 56
  Sword **So:** 1062 *with picture*

San [letter]
  S **S:** 1 *with picture*
San [people] **S:** 83
  Africa (Peoples of Africa) **A:** 104-105
  Botswana (People) **B:** 511
  Drakensberg **D:** 323
  Family *picture on* **F:** 24
  Kalahari Desert **K:** 211
  South Africa (History) **So:** 617
  Zimbabwe (History) **Z:** 592
San Andreas Fault [California] **S:** 83 *with picture
  and map*
  California (Land regions) **C:** 48
  Earthquake *picture on* **E:** 37
  Plate tectonics (Transform plate boundaries)
    P: 563
  San Francisco earthquake of 1906 **S:** 99
  United States (The Pacific Ranges and Lowlands)
    U: 125-126
San Antonio [Texas] **S:** 84 *with pictures and map*
  Texas (The mission period) **T:** 204
San Antonio [ship]
  Magellan, Ferdinand (The voyage begins) **M:** 47
San Antonio de Béxar, Fort
  Texas (The mission period) **T:** 204
San Antonio de Valero, Mission
  Alamo (Early days) **A:** 280
  Mission life in America (A visitor's guide) **M:** 620
  Texas (The mission period) **T:** 204-206
San Antonio Missions National Historical Park
  [Texas]
  National Park System (table: National historical
    parks) **N:** 56-57
  San Antonio (Cultural life) **S:** 85-86
San Antonio Spurs [team]
  Basketball (table) **B:** 150
San Bernardino [California] **S:** 87 *with picture*
San Bernardino County [California]
  California (Land and climate) **C:** 48
San Blas Indians
  Panama (Way of life) **P:** 116-117 *with picture*;
    (Clothing) **P:** 118
San Blas Islands [Atlantic]
  Panama *picture on* **P:** 118
San Callisto, Catacomb of [Rome]
  Bible *picture on* **B:** 281
San Carlos, University of
  Guatemala (Education) **G:** 414
San Carlos Borromeo de Carmelo, Mission
  Mission life in America *picture on* **M:** 619
San Carlos Reservation [Arizona]
  Geronimo **G:** 173
  Indian wars (Apache warfare) **I:** 195
San Cristóbal Island
  Galapagos Islands **G:** 7 *with map*
San Diego [California] **S:** 88 *with pictures and maps*
San Diego Bay
  California (Coastline) **C:** 50
  San Diego **S:** 88 *with pictures*
San Diego Chargers [football team]
  Football (National Football League) **F:** 364
  Tomlinson, LaDainian **T:** 326
San Diego de Alcalá, Mission
  California *picture on* **C:** 61; (The California
    missions) **C:** 60
  Hispanic Americans *picture on* **H:** 247
  Mission life in America (Western missions)
    M: 618-619
San Diego Padres [baseball team]
  Baseball (table) **B:** 130
San Diego Ranges [mountains, Mexico-U.S.]
  California (Land regions) **C:** 48-50
San Diego Track Club [athletics]
  Triathlon **T:** 440
San Diego Zoo
  California (Places to visit) **C:** 46 *with picture*
  San Diego (Recreation) **So:** 90a *with picture*
San Diego Zoo Safari Park
  Zoo (Cageless zoos) **Z:** 602
San Domingo *See* Santo Domingo *in this index*
San Esteban Rey de Acoma
  Mission life in America (A visitor's guide) **M:** 620
San Felipe de Austin [former city]
  Texas (American settlement) **T:** 206
San Felipe de Neri [church]
  Albuquerque (Description) **A:** 333
San Fermin, Fiesta of [custom]
  Spain *picture on* **So:** 738; (Holidays) **So:** 736-737
San Fernando Rey de España, Mission [Los
  Angeles]
  Los Angeles *picture on* **L:** 468
San Fernando Valley [region, California]
  Automobile (Air pollution) **A:** 964
  Los Angeles (The San Fernando Valley) **L:** 460
    with picture; (Housing) **L:** 463; (Recent
    developments) **L:** 470-471
San Francesco di Paola [church, Naples]

  Architecture (Neoclassical architecture) **A:** 623-
    624
San Francisco [California] **S:** 92 *with pictures and
  maps*
  California **C:** 36; (table: Average monthly
    weather) **C:** 51
  Climate (Oceans and large lakes) **Ci:** 676-676a
  Gold rush (Gold rushes in the United States)
    G: 254
  Golden Gate Bridge **G:** 255
  Rock music *picture on* **R:** 380b; (The San Francisco
    scene) **R:** 380a
  San Francisco earthquake of 1906 **S:** 99
  United States *picture on* **U:** 98
  Western frontier life in America *pictures on*
    W: 232, W: 233
San Francisco, Rio [river, Brazil]
  São Francisco, River **S:** 117
San Francisco Bay [California]
  California (Coastline) **C:** 50
  San Francisco (Downtown San Francisco) **S:** 92-
    93 *with picture and map*
San Francisco Conference [1945]
  Truman, Harry S. (The end of World War II) **T:** 469
    with picture
  United Nations (The San Francisco Conference)
    U: 95
San Francisco de los Tejas
  Texas (French exploration) **T:** 204
San Francisco earthquake of 1906 S: 99
  California *picture on* **C:** 63; (Early statehood) **C:** 62
  San Francisco (Earthquake and fire) **S:** 98 *with
    picture*
San Francisco Examiner [newspaper]
  Hearst, William Randolph **H:** 131
San Francisco 49ers [team]
  Football (National Football League) **F:** 364
San Francisco Giants [team]
  Baseball (table) **B:** 130
San Francisco International Airport
  Airport (table) **A:** 245
  Aviation *picture on* **A:** 985
San Francisco Maritime National Historic Park
  [California]
  National Park System (table: National historical
    parks) **N:** 56-57
San Francisco Mountains [mountains, Arizona]
  Arizona *picture on* **A:** 671
San Francisco-Oakland Bay Bridge [California]
  S: 99
  Bridge (table: Combination) **B:** 603
  California (Transportation) **C:** 58
  San Francisco *picture on* **S:** 92
San Francisco Renaissance
  Duncan, Robert **D:** 384
San Gabriel Arcángel, Mission
  Los Angeles (Settlement) **L:** 469
San Isabel National Forest
  Colorado *picture on* **Ci:** 828
San Jacinto [ship]
  Trent Affair **T:** 435
San Jacinto, Battle of [1836] **S:** 99
  Mexico (Difficulties of the early republic) **M:** 471
  Santa Anna, Antonio López de (War with Texas)
    S: 113
  Texas (The Texas revolution) **T:** 206
  Westward movement in America (Texas) **W:** 249
San Jacinto Battleground State Historical Park
  [Texas]
  Houston (Landmarks) **H:** 395
San Jacinto Monument and Museum [Houston]
  Texas (Places to visit) **T:** 194
San Joaquin River [California] **S:** 100
  California (Rivers, waterfalls, and lakes) **C:** 50
San Joaquin Valley [region, California]
  California (Agriculture) **C:** 56
  San Joaquin River **S:** 100
San Jose [California] **S:** 100 *with pictures and map*
San José [Costa Rica] **S:** 102
  Costa Rica *picture on* **Ci:** 1084
San José, Mission
  Mission life in America (A visitor's guide) **M:** 620
    with picture
  San Antonio (Cultural life) **S:** 85-86
  Texas (Places to visit) **T:** 194
San José Mine [Chile]
  Chile (Recent developments) **C:** 470
San Jose scale [insect] **S:** 102 *with pictures*
  Insect *picture on* **I:** 281
  Scale insect **S:** 170
San Jose Sharks [team]
  Hockey (table: National Hockey League) **H:** 281
San Juan [Puerto Rico] **S:** 102
  Puerto Rico *pictures on* **P:** 872, P: 876; (People)
    P: 874-875 *with picture*; (table: Average
    monthly weather) **P:** 880
San Juan Capistrano [California] **S:** 103

San Juan Capistrano, Mission
Mission life in America (A visitor's guide) **M: 620**
San Juan-Chama project
New Mexico (The mid-1900's) **N: 275-276** *with picture*
San Juan de Los Caballeros [U.S. history]
New Mexico (Exploration, conquest, and settlement) **N: 273**
San Juan Hill, Battle of [1898]
Roosevelt, Theodore (The Rough Riders) **R: 463**
Rough Riders **R: 490**
Spanish-American War (Land battles) **So: 754**
San Juan Island National Historical Park [Washington]
National Park System (table: National historical parks) **N: 56-57**
San Juan Islands [islands, Washington]
Washington *picture on* **W: 47**
San Juan Mountains
Colorado (Land regions) **Ci: 838** *with map*
San Juan National Historic Site [Puerto Rico]
National Park System (table: National historic sites) **N: 52-53**
San Juan **S: 103**
San Lorenzo [settlement]
Olmec Indians **O: 744**
San Lorenzo, Church of
Architecture (Early Renaissance architecture) **A: 620**; (Baroque architecture) **A: 622**
Florence (The city) **F: 239-240**
San Lorenzo, Treaty of *See* Pinckney Treaty *in this index*
San Luis Potosí [city, Mexico] **S: 103**
San Marcos, Major National University of [Lima] **S: 103**
San Marino [country] **S: 103** *with picture and map*
Flag *picture on* **F: 207**
Italy **I: 496**
San Marino [city, San Marino] **S: 104** *with picture*
San Martín, José de [Argentine general] **S: 104** *with portrait*
Argentina (Road to becoming a nation) **A: 656** *with picture*
Chile (Independence) **C: 468**
Flag *picture on* **F: 217**
Latin America (The movement toward independence) **L: 106-107**
Peru (The war of independence) **P: 315**
San Martín, Plaza
Lima (The city) **L: 305**
San Miguel de Allende [Mexico]
Mexico *picture on* **M: 466**
San Miguel de Gualdape [settlement]
Hispanic Americans (Exploration and settlement) **H: 250**
South Carolina (Exploration and settlement) **So: 659**
United States, History of the (The Spanish and the Portuguese) **U: 151**
San Miguel Mission
New Mexico (Places to visit) **N: 264** *with picture*
San Pedrico [ship]
Torres, Luis Vaez de **T: 342**
San Pedro, Diego de [Spanish author]
Spanish literature (The 1400's) **So: 758**
San Pedro fig [fruit]
Fig **F: 96**
San Pedro Sula [Honduras] **S: 105**
Honduras (The Northern Coast) **H: 309** *with map*
San Quentin [prison, California] **S: 105**
San Salvador [El Salvador] **S: 105**
El Salvador **E: 248** *with picture*
San Salvador [island, Pacific]
Galapagos Islands **G: 7** *with map*
San Salvador Island [Atlantic]
Bahamas **B: 28** *with map*
Columbus, Christopher *map on* **Ci: 859**; (The first landing) **Ci: 860**
San Salvador Volcano [El Salvador]
El Salvador *picture on* **E: 248**
San Simeon [estate]
Hearst, William Randolph **H: 131**
Morgan, Julia **M: 804**
San Souci, Emery J. [American political leader]
Rhode Island (table) **R: 311**
San Stefano, Treaty of [1878]
Berlin, Congress of **B: 265**
Bulgaria (Ottoman rule) **B: 692**
San Vitale [church, Ravenna]
Architecture *picture on* **A: 617**
Byzantine art *picture on* **B: 749**
San Xavier del Bac Mission
Arizona (Places to visit) **A: 678** *with picture*
Kino, Eusebio Francisco **K: 332**
Mission life in America (A visitor's guide) **M: 620**
Sanaa [Yemen] **S: 105**
Yemen **Y: 561** *with picture*

Sanatorium [medicine]
Sanitarium **S: 111**
Sanchez, Florencio [Argentine dramatist]
Latin American literature (Realism) **L: 113**
Sánchez, George Isidore [American educator] **S: 105**
Sánchez, Oscar Arias [Costa Rican political leader]
See Arias Sánchez, Oscar *in this index*
Sanchez, Sonia [American poet]
African American literature (The 1900's) **A: 136a**
Sánchez Cerro, Luis [Peruvian political leader]
Peru (The realy 1900's) **P: 315-316**
Sánchez Vilella, Roberto [Puerto Rican political leader]
Puerto Rico (Puerto Rico today) **P: 884**
Sancho II [king of Castile]
Cid, The **Ci: 552**
Sancho, Ignatius [British author]
English literature (The Johnson circle) **E: 319**
Sancho Panza [literary figure]
Don Quixote **D: 306**
Sanctions, Economic [political science] **S: 106**
Human rights (Trade and diplomatic measures) **H: 428a**
League of Nations (The League's greatest failure) **L: 160**
Libya (United Nations sanctions) **L: 268**
Nuclear weapon (Sanctions) **N: 601**
Peace (International organizations) **P: 207**
Terrorism (Diplomatic, economic, and military pressure) **T: 177**
Sanctuary [book by Faulkner]
Faulkner, William **F: 56**
Sand S: 106
Desert (Desert climate and land) **D: 155-156**
Glass (Soda-lime glass) **G: 213**; (Early times) **G: 217-218**
Gravel **G: 329**
Loam **L: 403**
Ocean (Sediments) **O: 654**
Quicksand **Q: 41**
Seashore (Life on sandy shores) **S: 270**
Soil (Minerals) **So: 573**
Sand, George [French author] **S: 106** *with portrait*
Chopin, Frédéric François (His life) **C: 521**
French literature (Romantic fiction) **F: 521**
Liszt, Franz (His life) **L: 349-350**
Sand boa [snake]
Boa **B: 426**
Sand casting [industrial process]
Cast and casting (How castings are made) **C: 278** *with pictures*
Sand cherry [shrub]
Beach plum **B: 179**
Sand Creek Massacre [1864]
Cheyenne Indians **C: 417**
Colorado (Territorial days) **Ci: 845**
Indian wars (Sand Creek) **I: 192-193**
Sand Creek Massacre National Historic Site [Colorado]
National Park System (table: National historic sites) **N: 53**
Sand dollar [sea animal] **S: 107** *with picture*
Sand dune *See* Dune *in this index*
Sand fly [insect] **S: 107**
Fly (table) **F: 310**
Leishmaniasis **L: 187**
Sand Hills [Nebraska]
Nebraska (Land regions) **N: 104** *with picture*; (Rivers and lakes) **N: 106**
Sand mill [machine]
Paint (Grinding) **P: 24-25**
Sand painting [handicraft] **S: 107**
Indian, American (Painting) **I: 146**; (After European contact) **I: 168**
Sand pear
Pear (Varieties) **P: 215**
Sand Plains [Netherlands]
Netherlands (The land) **N: 144**
Sand sea [geology]
Desert (Desert climate and land) **D: 155-156**
Dune **D: 384**
Sand tiger [fish]
Nurse shark **N: 614**
Sand trap
Golf (Hazards) **G: 261** *with picture*
Sand verbena [plant] **S: 107**
Flower (Flowers of the desert) **F: 290** *with picture*
Sand wedge
Golf (Golf clubs) **G: 262** *with picture*
Sandal [clothing]
Shoe *pictures on* **S: 430, S: 432**
Sandalwood [wood] **S: 107**
Sandalwood oil
Sandalwood **S: 107**
Sandawe [people]
Religion *picture on* **R: 219**

Sandbagging [flood control]
Flood *picture on* **F: 238**
Sandberg, Ryne [American baseball player]
Baseball (table: Hall of Fame) **B: 134b**
Sandblasting [industrial process] **S: 107**
Glass (Sandblasting) **G: 217**
Sandbox tree
Plant (Interesting facts about plants) **P: 519**
Sandbur [plant] **S: 107**
Plant *picture on* **P: 531**
Sandburg, Carl [American author] **S: 107** *with portrait*
American literature (Realist poetry) **A: 421** *with portrait*
Sandburg Village
Chicago (The North Side) **C: 423**
Sande, Earl [American jockey] **S: 108**
Sander [tool]
Woodworking (Sanding and finishing) **W: 398** *with pictures*
Sanderling [bird] **S: 108**
Sanders, Barry [American football player] **S: 108**
Football (table) **F: 363**
Sanders, Billy [literary figure]
Harris, Joel Chandler **H: 68**
Sanders, Carl E. [American political leader]
Carter, Jimmy (Steps to the governorship) **C: 254**
Georgia (table) **G: 130**
Sanders, Deion [American football player/baseball player] **S: 109**
Sanders, George [British actor]
Motion picture (Best performance by an actor in a supporting role: 1950) **M: 862a**
Sanders, Jared Y. [American political leader]
Louisiana (table) **L: 496**
Sanders, Thomas [American businessman]
Telephone (The Bell System) **T: 100**
Sanderson, James [American composer]
"Hail to the Chief" **H: 8**
Sandglass [measuring device]
Hourglass **H: 379** *with picture*
Sandgrouse [bird] **S: 109**
Sandhill crane [bird]
Animal *picture on* **A: 485**
Crane (Kinds) **Ci: 1117** *with picture*
Sandia National Laboratories S: 109
New Mexico (Recent developments) **N: 276**
Sandiford, Erskine [Barbadian political leader]
Barbados (History) **B: 104**
Sanding
Woodworking (Sanding and finishing) **W: 398**
Sandinista National Liberation Front *See* Sandinistas *in this index*
Sandinistas [political group]
Communism (Communist influence in other areas) **Ci: 894**
Honduras (Recent developments) **H: 313**
Iran-contra affair (Background) **I: 406b**
Latin America (Return to civilian government) **L: 111**
Nicaragua (History) **N: 398-400** *with picture*
Ortega, Daniel **O: 859**
Sandino, Augusto César **S: 109**
Sandino, Augusto César [Nicaraguan revolutionary] **S: 109**
Nicaragua (Rebel victory) **N: 400**; (The United States and Nicaragua) **N: 400**
Somoza García, Anastasio **So: 590**
Sandoval, Brian [American political leader]
Nevada (table) **N: 173**
Sandoy [island]
Faroe Islands **F: 47**
Sandpaper
Woodworking (Sanding and finishing) **W: 398**
Sandpiper [bird] **S: 109**
Bird (Birds of inland waters and marshes) **B: 340** *with picture*
Ruff **R: 509**
Upland sandpiper **U: 213** *with picture*
Sandstone [rock] **S: 110**
Building stone **B: 685**
Quartz **Q: 8**
Rock (Clastic sediments) **R: 372**; (table) **R: 373** *with picture*
Sandstone Hills [region, Oklahoma]
Oklahoma (Land regions) **O: 724** *with map*
Sandstorm [weather] **S: 110**
Sandwich
Food (Interesting facts about food) **F: 329**
Sandwich, Earl of [English nobleman]
Food (Interesting facts about food) **F: 329**
Sandwich glass
Glass (Types of art glass) **G: 220-221**; (Early American glass) **G: 222**
Sandwich Islands
Hawaii (European exploration) **H: 106**
Sanford, Edward T. [American jurist]

Supreme Court of the United States (table)
So: 1000
Sanford, John F. A. [American public figure]
Dred Scott Decision (The background of the
case) D: 345
Sanford, Maria L. [American educator] S: 110
Sanford, Mark [American political leader]
South Carolina (table) So: 658
Sanford, Terry [American political leader]
North Carolina (table) N: 490
Sanford Underground Laboratory
Lead L: 150
Sanforizing [industrial process]
Textile (Finishing the fabric) T: 217
Sangam [center, India]
Girl Scouts (In other countries) G: 199
Sanger, Frederick [British chemist] S: 110
Sanger, Margaret [American social reformer]
S: 110 with portrait
Birth control (The birth control movement)
B: 378
Feminism F: 70
Planned Parenthood Federation of America
(History) P: 515
Women's movement (Birth control) W: 385
Sangha [people]
Congo, Republic of the (People) Ci: 940d
Sangha [religion]
Buddhism (The sangha) B: 668 with picture
Religion (How the major religions are organized)
R: 218
Sango [language]
Central African Republic (People) C: 352
Sangre de Cristo Mountains [Colorado-New
Mexico]
Colorado (Land regions) Ci: 838 with map
Sangster, Charles [Canadian poet] S: 110
Canadian literature (Poetry: 1850-1918) C: 157
Sanguine humor [psychology]
Personality (Personality types) P: 301
Sanguinetti, Julio Maria [Uruguayan political
leader]
Uruguay (The late 1900's) U: 228
Sanhá, Malam Bacai [Guinea-Bissau political
leader]
Guinea-Bissau (History) G: 434
Sanhedrin [ancient Israel] S: 110
Hillel I H: 232
Sanibel Island [Florida]
Florida (Places to visit) F: 252
Sanidine [mineral]
Feldspar F: 68
Sanitarium [medicine] S: 111
Tuberculosis (Treatment of tuberculosis) T: 479
Sanitary Commission, United States
Civil War, American (Hospitals) Ci: 630
Sanitary landfill
Landfill L: 57 with diagram
Waste disposal (Land disposal) W: 113
Sanitary napkin
Menstruation (Effects of menstruation) M: 404
Sanitary sewerage system
Sewage S: 329
Sanitation S: 111
City (Description) Ci: 578
Garbage disposal G: 28
Sewage S: 329 with diagrams
Waste disposal W: 112
Water (City water systems) W: 124
Sanity [law]
Insanity I: 277
Sankara [Hindu religious leader]
Monasticism (Non-Christian monasticism) M: 701
Sankara, Thomas [African political leader]
Burkina Faso (History) B: 707
Sankey, Ira D. [American singer]
Hymn (History) H: 475
Moody, Dwight Lyman M: 781
Sankhya [philosophy]
Hinduism (The six schools of philosophy) H: 236
Upanishads U: 212
Sankore Mosque [Timbuktu, Mali]
World, History of the picture on W: 436
Sannazaro, Jacopo [Italian poet]
Italian literature (Humanism and the
Renaissance) I: 494
Sannyasi [Hinduism]
Manu M: 168
Sans-serif type [printing]
Type (Classes of type) T: 537 with picture
Sansa [musical instrument]
Music (African music) M: 956
Sanskrit language S: 111 with picture
Aryans A: 764
Hindi language (History) H: 235
India (Languages) I: 114; (The Aryans) I: 128
Urdu language U: 220

Sanskrit literature S: 112
Drama (India) D: 336
India (Literature) I: 120; (The Aryans) I: 128
Sansovino, Jacopo [Italian sculptor]
Sculpture (Michelangelo) S: 252-253
Sant' Andrea, Church of [Mantua]
Architecture (Early Renaissance architecture)
A: 620-621 with picture
Santa Ana [El Salvador] S: 112
Santa Anna, Antonio López de [Mexican political
leader] S: 112 with portrait
Alamo (Early days) A: 280
Houston, Sam H: 399
Mexican War (Taylor's campaign) M: 446
Mexico (Reform) M: 471; (Difficulties of the early
republic) M: 471
Texas (American settlement) T: 206; (The Texas
revolution) T: 206 with picture
Santa Barbara [California] S: 113
Santa Bárbara, Mission
Mission life in America (A visitor's guide) M: 620
Santa Barbara Island [island, California]
Channel Islands National Park C: 375
Santa Catalina, Palace of
San Juan S: 103
Santa Cecilia, National Academy of
Rome (Music and theater) R: 429
Santa Claus [legendary figure] S: 113 with picture
Christmas (In the United States and Canada)
C: 529
Nicholas, Saint N: 403
Saint Nicholas, Feast of S: 51
Santa Claus [Indiana] S: 114
Indiana (Interesting facts) I: 197 with picture
Santa Croce, Church of [Florence, Italy]
Giotto (Giotto's works) G: 193
Santa Cruz [Bolivia] S: 114
Santa Cruz [island]
Galapagos Islands G: 7 with map
Santa Cruz, Andrés [Bolivian general]
Bolivia (Independence) B: 447
Santa Cruz de Tenerife [province, Spain]
Canary Islands C: 165 with map
Santa Fe [Argentina] S: 114
Santa Fe [New Mexico] S: 114
Hispanic Americans (In the Southwest) H: 251
New Mexico (Interesting facts) N: 257 with picture
Santa Fe Independent School District v. Doe [U.S.
history]
School prayer S: 185
Santa Fe Railroad
Los Angeles (Development and growth) L: 470
Santa Fe Republican [newspaper]
New Mexico (Communication) N: 271
Santa Fe Trail [U.S. history] S: 115
New Mexico picture on N: 274
Pioneer life in America (Routes to the West)
P: 486
Westward movement in America (The Santa Fe
Trail) W: 249
Santa Getrudis [cattle]
Cattle (Other beef cattle) C: 309
Santa Isabel [Equatorial Guinea]
Malabo M: 95
Santa Luzia [island]
Cape Verde S: 189 with map
Santa María [ship]
Caravel C: 203
Columbus, Christopher (First voyage westward)
Ci: 858-859 with picture
Exploration (Columbus reaches America) E: 444
Santa Maria delle Grazie, Monastery of
Milan (The city) M: 540
Santa Maria Island
Galapagos Islands G: 7 with map
Santa Maria Novella, Church of [Florence, Italy]
Alberti, Leon Battista A: 332
Architecture (Early Renaissance architecture)
A: 620-621
Santa Marta [Colombia] S: 115
**Santa Monica Mountains National Recreation
Area** [California]
National Park System (table: National recreation
areas) N: 49
Santangel, Luis de [Spanish government official]
Columbus, Christopher (Success in Spain) Ci: 858
Santayana, George [American philosopher] S: 115
Santee-Cooper Project [Santee River, South
Carolina]
South Carolina (The mid-1900's) So: 662
Santee Indians
Indian wars (The Great Sioux Uprising [1862])
I: 192
Sioux Indians S: 475
Santee River
South Carolina (Rivers, waterfalls, and lakes)
So: 652 with map

Santería [religion]
Cuba (Religion) Ci: 1171
Latin America (Religion) L: 98-99
Magic (Africa and the Americas) M: 50
Santero [craftworker]
Puerto Rico picture on P: 876
Santiago [Chile] S: 115 with picture
Chile C: 458 with picture; (City life) C: 460
Santiago [Dominican Republic] S: 116
Santiago [ship]
Magellan, Ferdinand (The voyage begins) M: 47
Santiago, Battle of [1898]
Sampson, William Thomas S: 81
Spanish-American War (Chief events) So: 753-
754
Santiago, Cathedral of
Santiago picture on S: 116
Santiago de Cuba [Cuba] S: 116
Cuba picture on Ci: 1171
Spanish-American War (Chief events) So: 753
Santiago de los Caballeros [Dominican Republic]
Santiago S: 116
Santillana, Marquis of [Spanish author]
Spanish literature (The 1400's) So: 758
Santo [handicraft]
Puerto Rico picture on P: 876
Santo, El [Mexican wrestler/actor]
Lucha libre L: 514
Mexico (Motion pictures) M: 460 with picture
Santo, Ron [American baseball player]
Baseball (table: Hall of Fame) B: 134b
Santo Amaro Lake
São Paulo (The city) S: 117-118
Santo Antão [island]
Cape Verde S: 189 with map
Santo Domingo [Dominican Republic] S: 117
Dominican Republic D: 303, picture on D: 304
Santo Domingo, Autonomous University of
[Dominican Republic] S: 117
Santo Domingo, Cathedral of
Mahogany M: 66
Santo Domingo S: 117
Santo Spirito, Church of [Florence]
Architecture (Early Renaissance architecture)
A: 620
Brunelleschi, Filippo picture on B: 652
Santo Tomás, University of [Philippines]
Manila (Education and cultural life) M: 142
Santon
Christmas (In France) C: 530 with picture
Santop, Louis [American baseball player]
Baseball (table: Hall of Fame) B: 134b
Santos [Brazil] S: 117
Santos, Juan Manuel [Colombian political leader]
Colombia (Recent developments) Ci: 785
Santos-Dumont, Alberto [Brazilian aviator] S: 117
Airplane (Other pioneer planes and fliers) A: 233
with picture
Airship (The first airships) A: 251
Sanusi, Muhammad Idris al Mahdi as- [Libyan
political leader] See Idris I in this index
Sanusi brotherhood [political organization]
Libya (Italian control) L: 267
Sanzio, Raffaello See Raphael in this index
São Francisco Church [Salvador, Brazil]
Brazil picture on B: 576
São Francisco River [Brazil] S: 117
South America (Rivers) So: 628
São Nicolau [island]
Cape Verde S: 189 with map
São Paulo [city, Brazil] S: 117 with pictures
Brazil B: 567, picture on B: 573
São Paulo, University of
Brazil (Education) B: 575-576
São Paulo (Education and cultural life) S: 118
São Tiago [island]
Cape Verde S: 189 with map
São Tomé [city, São Tomé and Príncipe] S: 119
São Tomé and Príncipe S: 119
São Tomé and Príncipe S: 119 with maps
Flag picture on F: 199
São Vicente [island]
Cape Verde S: 189 with picture and map
Saône River [France] S: 120
Lyon L: 536 with picture
Rhône River R: 319 with map
Sap [tree product] S: 120 with diagram
Maple syrup M: 187
Tree (Trunk and branches) T: 416
Sapa Inca [title]
Inca (Government) I: 97
Sapajou [animal] See Capuchin in this index
Sapas Mons [mountain, Venus]
Mountain picture on M: 896b
Sapeurs-Pompiers [firefighters]
Fire department (Fire protection in Europe)
F: 127-128

Saphenous vein [anatomy]
  Human body (table) **H: 422** *with diagram*
Sapienza University of Rome [Italy] *See* Rome,
  University of *in this index*
Sapir, Edward [American anthropologist]
  Linguistics (Structuralism) **L: 337**
Sapitwa [mountain, Malawi]
  Malawi (Land) **M: 97** *with map*
Sapling [botany]
  Tree (How a tree grows) **T: 418**
Sapmi [region, Europe]
  Lapland **L: 74**
  Sami (Land and climate) **S: 79**
Sapodilla [tree] **S: 121** *with picture*
  Chicle **C: 446**
  Gum tree **G: 440**
  Latex **L: 90**
Saponin [tree product]
  Soapberry **So: 543**
  Yam **Y: 549**
Sapphire [gem] **S: 122**
  Gem *picture on* **G: 78**
Sappho [Greek poet] **S: 122**
  Greek literature (Lyric poetry) **G: 377**
  Poetry (Ancient poetry) **P: 595**
Sapporo [Japan] **S: 122**
  Japan (Climate) **J: 48**
Saprobe [biology] *See* Saprophyte *in this index*
Saprophyte [biology] **S: 122**
  Fungi (How a fungus lives) **F: 559**
  Mushroom (How a mushroom obtains food)
    M: 942
Saprotroph [biology] *See* Saprophyte *in this index*
Sapsago [cheese]
  Cheese (Very hard, or grating, cheese) **C: 392**
    with picture
Sapsucker [bird] **S: 122** *with picture*
  Bird (Kinds of food) **B: 350** *with picture*
Sapwood [botany]
  Sap (Vascular sap) **S: 121**
  Tree (How trunks and branches grow thicker)
    T: 418 *with diagram*
Saqqarah [ancient city]
  Pyramids (The first pyramids) **P: 916**
Saquinavir [drug]
  AIDS (Treatments) **A: 164b-165**
Sar [vehicle]
  Ocean (Submersibles) **O: 663**
Sara [people]
  Chad (People) **C: 366**; (History) **C: 367**
Sara orangetip [butterfly]
  Butterfly *picture on* **B: 737**
Saracens [ancient people] **S: 123**
Sarafina! [musical]
  Masekela, Hugh **M: 263**
Saragossa [Spain] **S: 123**
Saragossa, Treaty of [1529]
  Line of Demarcation **L: 333** *with map*
Sarah [Biblical figure]
  Abraham **A: 16**
  Isaac **I: 461**
  Ishmael **I: 462**
  Muslims (Before Muhammad) **M: 964**
  Old Testament (Origins) **O: 740**
Sarai [ancient city]
  Russia (Mongol rule) **R: 548**
Sarajevo [Bosnia-Herzegovina] **S: 123**
  Bosnia-Herzegovina **B: 491**; (History) **B: 492-493**
    with picture
  Franz Ferdinand **F: 494**
Saramago, José [Portuguese author]
  Nobel Prizes (Literature: 1998) **N: 448**
Saramaka Maroons [people]
  Maroons **M: 217**
Saranac Laboratory [Saranac Lake, New York]
  Trudeau, Edward Livingston **T: 460**
Sarandon, Susan [American actress]
  Motion picture (Best performance by an actress:
    1995) **M: 862a**
Sarasota [Florida] **S: 123**
Saratoga [carrier]
  Aircraft carrier (History) **A: 207**
Saratoga [ship]
  War of 1812 (Lake Champlain) **W: 32**
Saratoga, Battle of [1777] **S: 123**
  Arnold, Benedict (A disappointed officer) **A: 741**
  Burgoyne, John **B: 705** *with picture*
  Franklin, Benjamin (Serving in France) **F: 491**
  New York (The Revolutionary War) **N: 315** *with*
    picture
  Revolution, American (table) **R: 276**; (Victory at
    Saratoga) **R: 282** *with picture*
Saratoga National Historical Park [New York]
  National Park System (table: National historical
    parks) **N: 56-57**
  New York (Places to visit) **N: 302**
Saratoga Springs [New York]

  New York (Places to visit) **N: 302**
Sarawak [state, Malaysia]
  Borneo (History) **B: 490**
  Malaysia **M: 98a**
Sarbanes-Oxley Act [2002]
  Accounting (The history of accounting) **A: 23**
  Business (Recent developments) **B: 727**
Sarcasm
  Humor (The types of humor) **H: 435-436**
  Satire **S: 150h**
Sarcodine [zoology]
  Protozoan (Sarcodines) **P: 837** *with picture*
Sarcoidosis [disease] **S: 123**
Sarcoma [disease]
  Cancer (Classification by tissue) **C: 168-169**
  Tumor **T: 484**
Sarcophagus [funeral] **S: 124**
Sarcopterygian [zoology]
  Coelacanth **C: 752**
  Fish (The Age of Fishes) **F: 171**
Sardegna *See* Sardinia *in this index*
Sardine [fish] **S: 124** *with picture*
  Fish *picture on* **F: 168**
Sardinia [island, Mediterranean] **S: 124**
  Austria (Metternich and revolution) **A: 938**
  Italy (Sardinia) **I: 509**
Sardinia, Kingdom of [Italian history] **S: 125**
  Italy (Italy united) **I: 515** *with map*
Sardinian dialect
  Romance languages **R: 415**
Sardonyx [gem] **S: 125**
  Gem *picture on* **G: 78**
  Onyx **O: 788**
Sardou, Victorien [French dramatist]
  Opera (*Tosca*) **O: 807**
Sarek National Park [Sweden]
  National park (table) **N: 42g**
  Sweden *picture on* **So: 1026**
Sargasso Sea [region, Atlantic] **S: 125** *with map*
  Atlantic Ocean (Ocean life) **A: 866**
  Seaweed (Kinds) **S: 276**
Sargassum [plant]
  Sargasso Sea (Origin of the seaweed) **S: 125**
Sargassum fish
  Fish *picture on* **F: 144**
  Sargasso Sea (Origin of the seaweed) **S: 125-126**
Sargassum weed [seaweed]
  Atlantic Ocean (Ocean life) **A: 866**
Sargent, Francis [American political leader]
  Massachusetts (table) **M: 288**
Sargent, John G. [American government official]
  Coolidge, Calvin (table) **Ci: 1032**
  Hoover, Herbert Clark (table) **H: 330**
  Justice, Department of (table) **J: 203**
Sargent, John Singer [American painter] **S: 126**
    with picture
  Impressionism (American Impressionism) **I: 94**
Sargent, Thomas J. [American economist]
  Nobel Prizes (Economics: 2011) **N: 450**
Sargent, Winthrop [American political leader]
  Mississippi (Territorial days) **M: 641**
Sargon II [king of Assyria]
  Architecture (Mesopotamian architecture) **A: 611**
  Sennacherib **S: 300**
Sargon of Akkad [king of Sumer] **S: 126**
  Babylonia (The Akkadian and Neo-Sumerian
    periods) **B: 14**
  World, History of the (The Tigris-Euphrates Valley)
    W: 422-424
Sargsyan, Serzh [Armenian political leader]
  Armenia (Recent developments) **A: 719**
Sargsyan, Vazgen [Armenian political leader]
  Armenia (Recent developments) **A: 719**
Sari [clothing]
  Asia (Country life) **A: 782**
  Clothing *picture on* **Ci: 689**; (Identity) **Ci: 687**;
    (India) **Ci: 699**
  India (Clothing) **I: 117**
Sarin [chemical agent]
  Terrorism (Chemical attacks) **T: 176** *with picture*;
    (Terrorist groups and movements) **T: 178-179**
Sark [island, English Channel] **S: 126**
  Channel Islands **C: 375** *with map*
Sarkisyan, Vazgen [Armenian political leader]
  Armenia (Recent developments) **A: 719**
Sarkozy, Nicolas [French political leader] **S: 126**
  France (Recent developments) **F: 478**
Sarles, E. Y. [American political leader]
  North Dakota (table) **N: 513**
Sarmatians [ancient people]
  Amazons **A: 404**
  Russia (Early days) **R: 547**
Sarmiento, Domingo Faustino [Argentine political
  leader]
  Argentina (The Constitution of 1853) **A: 656-657**
  Latin American literature (Romanticism) **L: 112-
    113**

Särna [Sweden]
  Sweden (table: Average monthly weather)
    So: 1030
Sarney, José [Brazilian political leader]
  Brazil (Return to civilian government) **B: 586**
Sarno River [Italy]
  Pompeii (Excavations) **P: 654**; (The eruption of
    Mount Vesuvius) **P: 654**
Sarnoff, David [American businessman] **S: 126**
Sarong [clothing]
  Indonesia (Clothing) **I: 229**
Saronic Gulf [Aegean Sea]
  Corinth Canal **Ci: 1053**
Saroyan, William [American author] **S: 127**
  American literature (Realist fiction) **A: 422**
Sarraute, Nathalie [French author]
  French literature (The middle and late 1900's)
    F: 523
SARS [disease] **S: 127**
Sarto, Giuseppe Melchiorre
  Pius X, Saint **P: 503**
Sartor Resartus [book by Carlyle]
  Carlyle, Thomas (Early career) **C: 240**
  English literature (Early Victorian literature) **E: 321**
Sartoris [book by Faulkner]
  Faulkner, William **F: 55**
Sartre, Jean-Paul [French philosopher] **S: 127**
  French literature (Existentialism) **F: 523**
  Novel (Existentialism) **N: 574**
  Philosophy *picture on* **P: 389**; (Philosophy in the
    1900's) **P: 390**
Sarus crane [bird]
  Crane (Kinds) **Ci: 1117** *with picture*
Sasanian dynasty
  Iran (The Sasanian dynasty) **I: 405**
  Iraq (Early days) **I: 413**
  Persia, Ancient *picture on* **P: 298**; (The Sasanian
    dynasty) **P: 299**
Sasanqua [plant]
  Camellia **C: 79**
Sash [construction]
  House (Interior construction) **H: 382**
  Window **W: 334**
Sashimi [food]
  Food (Interesting facts about food) **F: 329**
  Sushi **So: 1012**
Saskatchewan S: 128 *with pictures and maps*
  See also the list of Related articles in the
    Saskatchewan *article*
  Canada, Government of *picture on* **C: 131**
  Prairie Provinces **P: 733**
Saskatchewan Herald [newspaper]
  Saskatchewan (Communication) **S: 143**
Saskatchewan Party [political party]
  Saskatchewan (Politics) **S: 144**
Saskatchewan Plain
  Alberta (Land regions) **A: 322**
  Manitoba (Land regions) **M: 154**
Saskatchewan Rebellion [1885] *See* North West
  Rebellion *in this index*
Saskatchewan River [Canada] **S: 148**
  Saskatchewan (Rivers and lakes) **S: 138** *with map*
Saskatchewan Roughriders
  Football (Canadian Football League) **F: 364**
Saskatchewan Science Centre [Regina]
  Saskatchewan (Places to visit) **S: 136**
Saskatchewan Wheat Pool
  Regina (Economy) **R: 205**
  Saskatchewan (Territorial progress) **S: 147**
Saskatoon [Saskatchewan] **S: 148** *with picture*
  Saskatchewan (table: Average monthly weather)
    S: 140
Sasquatch [legendary creature]
  Bigfoot **B: 298**
Sassafras [tree] **S: 149** *with picture*
  Tree *pictures on* **T: 423**
Sassafras Mountain
  South Carolina (The Blue Ridge) **So: 652** *with map*
Sasseen, Mary Towles [American educator]
  Mother's Day **M: 843**
Sassou-Nguesso, Denis [Congolese political
  leader]
  Congo, Republic of the (History) **Ci: 940e-940f**
Sastruga [geography]
  Antarctica (Climate) **A: 532**
SAT [test]
  College entrance examination (In the United
    States) **Ci: 775**
Sata, Michael [Zambian political leader]
  Zambia (History) **Z: 585-586**
Satan *See* Devil *in this index*
Satanic Verses, The [book by Rushdie]
  Rushdie, Salman **R: 522**
Satanism
  Devil worship **D: 175**
Satan's Flight Through Chaos [engraving by Doré]
  Doré, Gustave *picture on* **D: 310**

Satavahanas dynasty *See* Andhras dynasty *in this index*
Satchmo [nickname]
　Armstrong, Louis **A:** 723
Satellite [astronomy] **S:** 149 *with pictures*
　Astrobiology **A:** 826
　Earth (Earth and its moon) **E:** 18
　Europa **E:** 379
　Ganymede **G:** 27 *with picture*
　Jupiter (Satellites and rings) **J:** 200a *with picture*
　Mars (Satellites) **M:** 226b
　Meteor (Other planets and moons) **M:** 432
　Moon **M:** 782
　Mountain (Mountains on other planets) **M:** 895
　Neptune (Satellites and rings) **N:** 129 *with picture*
　Planet **P:** 507
　Saturn (Satellites) **S:** 151 *with pictures*
　Solar system (Moons) **So:** 580
　Titan **T:** 299
　Volcano (Volcanoes in the solar system) **V:** 442b
　Voyager **V:** 451
Satellite [international relations]
　Cold War (The Iron Curtain descends) **Ci:** 763-764; (The great blocs split) **Ci:** 769
　Communism (World War II) **Ci:** 893-894
　Russia (The Cold War) **R:** 554
　Union of Soviet Socialist Republics (Beginnings of the Cold War) **U:** 38
Satellite, Artificial **S:** 150d *with pictures*
　See also Communications satellite; Weather satellite *in this index*
　Airport (Air traffic control) **A:** 246-247
　Altimeter **A:** 390
　Communications satellite **Ci:** 888a
　International Space Station **I:** 346a
　Map (How maps are made) **M:** 180
　Observatory (Satellite observatories) **O:** 645
　Ocean (Satellites) **O:** 663
　Perpetual motion machine **P:** 293
　Phenology **P:** 356
　Radar (In the military) **R:** 65
　Remote sensing **R:** 231 *with picture*
　Rocket (Launching probes and satellites) **R:** 386
　Space exploration (The dawn of the space age) **So:** 706-707; (Types of shuttle missions) **So:** 723; (Expanding space activities) **So:** 728
　Surveying (Surveying tools) **So:** 1011
　Telecommunications **T:** 89
　Telescope *picture on* **T:** 102; (Gamma-ray telescopes) **T:** 109
Satellite, Natural *See* Satellite [astronomy] *in this index*
Satellite galaxy [astronomy]
　Andromeda Galaxy **A:** 457
　Local Group **L:** 409
Satellite navigation system
　Airplane (Electronic navigation) **A:** 227
　Global Positioning System **G:** 231
　Navigation (Satellite navigation) **N:** 73; (Electronic navigation) **N:** 74
Satellite operations control center
　Communications satellite *picture on* **Ci:** 888b
Satellite plan [aviation]
　Airport (Terminal designs) **A:** 248-249 *with diagram*
Satellite radio
　Radio (Digital audio broadcasting [DAB]) **R:** 87; (Radio since the 1950's) **R:** 94
Satellite telephone
　Telephone (Types of telephones) **T:** 94-95
Satellite television
　Television (Satellite television) **T:** 110c; (Cable and satellite systems) **T:** 115; (Satellites) **T:** 123; (Tuner) **T:** 124; (The development of television technology) **T:** 127
Satellite terminal
　Airport (Terminal designs) **A:** 248-249 *with diagram*
Satherley, Arthur E. [American record producer]
　Country music (Early commercial success) **Ci:** 1098b
Sati [custom] *See* Suttee *in this index*
Satie, Erik [French composer] **S:** 150h
Satiety center [physiology]
　Weight control (How body weight is determined) **W:** 181
Satin [fabric] **S:** 150h
Satin glass
　Glass (Types of art glass) **G:** 220-221
Satin weave
　Textile (Woven fabrics) **T:** 214
　Weaving (The satin weave) **W:** 173; (Types of weaves) **W:** 173 *with picture*
Satire [literature] **S:** 150h
　Black humor **B:** 389
　Drama (England) **D:** 334
　English literature (Jacobean drama) **E:** 317; (Swift

and Pope) **E:** 318
　Humor (The types of humor) **H:** 435-436
Satires [book by Horace]
　Horace **H:** 334
　Latin literature (The Augustan Age) **L:** 116
Satires [poems by Donne]
　Donne, John (His poetry) **D:** 308
Sato, Eisaku [Japanese political leader]
　Nobel Prizes (Peace: 1974) **N:** 448b
Satori [religion]
　Buddhism (Meditation) **B:** 669
　Zen **Z:** 588
Satrap [title]
　India (Persian and Greek invasions) **I:** 128
　Persia, Ancient (The Achaemenid Empire) **P:** 298
Sattar, Abdus [Bangladeshi political leader]
　Bangladesh (The new nation) **B:** 86
Saturable reactor [electronics]
　Magnetic amplifier **M:** 54
Saturated fat
　Cholesterol (Factors that cause high cholesterol levels) **C:** 520
　Fat (Structure) **F:** 52
　Nutrition (Fats) **N:** 625; (Limit intake of saturated fats, trans fats, and cholesterol) **N:** 628
　Trans fats **T:** 369
Saturation **S:** 150h
　Humidity **H:** 433
　Hydrogenation **H:** 470
　Weather (Humidity) **W:** 158
Saturation bombing
　World War II (The air war) **W:** 482
Saturation habitat
　Diving, Underwater (History) **D:** 247
Saturation temperature *See* Dew point *in this index*
Saturday [day] **S:** 150h
Saturday Night and Sunday Morning [book by Sillitoe]
　Sillitoe, Alan **S:** 462
Saturday Night Fever [film]
　Disco music **D:** 224
　Rock music (Disco) **R:** 380c
　Travolta, John **T:** 406
"Saturday Night Live" [TV program]
　Murphy, Eddie **M:** 931
Saturday Review [newspaper]
　Beerbohm, Max **B:** 212
Saturn [Roman mythology] **S:** 150h
　See also Cronus *in this index*
　Jupiter **J:** 201
　Mythology (table) **M:** 981
　Saturnalia **S:** 153
Saturn [planet] **S:** 150h *with pictures*
　Astronomy (How the planets move) **A:** 835
　Cassini **C:** 276
　Cassini, Giovanni Domenico **C:** 277
　Enceladus **E:** 265
　Herschel, Sir William **H:** 216
　Iapetus **I:** 2
　Mountain (On Titan) **M:** 895
　Planet **P:** 507 *with pictures*
　Planetary ring **P:** 514d
　Satellite **S:** 149; (Satellites of the gas giants) **S:** 150 *with picture*; (table: Major satellites of the solar system) **S:** 150b
　Space exploration (Probes to Jupiter and beyond) **So:** 711
　Titan **T:** 299
　Voyager **V:** 451
Saturn 5 [rocket]
　Rocket (Space travel) **R:** 387
　Space exploration *picture on* **So:** 698; (Apollo: Mission to the moon) **So:** 714-715
Saturn system [astronomy]
　Saturn **S:** 150i
Saturnalia [ancient festival] **S:** 153
　Saturn **S:** 150h
Satyagraha [opera by Glass]
　Glass, Philip **G:** 224
Satyagraha [social reform] *See* Nonviolent resistance *in this index*
Satyr [butterfly]
　Butterfly (Satyrs and wood nymphs) **B:** 736
Satyr [Greek mythology] **S:** 153
　Dionysus **D:** 215
　Faun **F:** 56
Satyr play
　Drama (Satyr plays) **D:** 327
　Euripides **E:** 378
Satyricon [book by Petronius]
　Latin literature (The Imperial Period) **L:** 116
　Novel (Ancient Greek and Roman narratives) **N:** 572
　Petronius **P:** 351
Satyros [Greek architect]
　Seven Wonders of the Ancient World (The

Mausoleum at Halicarnassus) **S:** 325
Saucer, Flying *See* Unidentified flying object *in this index*
Saucer magnolia
　Magnolia **M:** 63
Saud [king of Saudi Arabia]
　Saudi Arabia (The new kingdom) **S:** 161
Saud dynasty
　Saudi Arabia (The Saud dynasty) **S:** 160
Saudades do Brasil [music by Milhaud]
　Milhaud, Darius **M:** 543
Saudi Arabia **S:** 154 *with pictures and maps*
　See also the list of Related articles in the Saudi Arabia *article*
　Bin Laden, Osama **B:** 307
　Bush, George Herbert Walker (Persian Gulf crisis) **B:** 721
　Clothing *picture on* **Ci:** 692
　Food *picture on* **F:** 328
　Ibn Saud **I:** 3
　Iraq (The Persian Gulf War of 1991) **I:** 414
　Kuwait (History) **K:** 396
　Mecca (History) **M:** 358-353
　Middle East **M:** 530
　Organization of the Petroleum Exporting Countries **O:** 854
　Persian Gulf War of 1991 **P:** 300a
　Riyadh **R:** 356
　United States, History of the (The Persian Gulf War) **U:** 196d
　Wahhābis **W:** 5
Sauer, Carl O. [American geographer]
　Geography (The growth of geography) **G:** 96
Sauerbraten [food]
　Germany (Food and drink) **G:** 150
Sauerkraut [food]
　Germany (Food and drink) **G:** 150
Sauger [fish]
　Perch **P:** 284
Saugus Iron Works National Historic Site [Massachusetts]
　Colonial life in America (Places to visit) **Ci:** 801 *with picture*
　Massachusetts (Places to visit) **M:** 280
　National Park System (table: National historic sites) **N:** 52-53
Sauk Indians **S:** 163
　Indian wars (Black Hawk) **I:** 192
　Iowa (Indian days) **I:** 393
　Wisconsin (Territorial days) **W:** 366
Saul [king of ancient Israel] **S:** 163
　Amalekites **A:** 400
　David **D:** 44
　Jews (The kingdom of Israel) **J:** 121
　Palestine (Early history and settlement) **P:** 104
Saul [music by Handel]
　Handel, George Frideric (His work) **H:** 42
Saul, John Ralston [Canadian political leader]
　Martin, Paul *picture on* **M:** 235
Saul of Tarsus [religious leader] *See* Paul, Saint *in this index*
Saulsbury, Gove [American political leader]
　Delaware (table) **D:** 109
Sault Sainte Marie [Ontario] **S:** 163
Sault Sainte Marie Canal *See* Soo Canals *in this index*
Sault Sainte Marie Canal National Historic Site [Ontario]
　Canada (table: National historic sites) **C:** 115
Sauna [bath] **S:** 163
　Bath *picture on* **B:** 164; (Bathing for cleanliness) **B:** 163
　Finland (Way of life) **F:** 111 *with picture*
Saund, Dalip Singh [American political leader]
　Asian Americans (Notable Asian American "firsts") **A:** 812f
Saunders, Albert C. [Canadian political leader]
　Prince Edward Island (table) **P:** 791
Saunders, Cicely [English physician]
　Hospice **H:** 370
Saunders, Richard [pen name of Franklin]
　Poor Richard's Almanac **P:** 658
Saunders, Wallace [American songwriter]
　Jones, Casey **J:** 157
Sauria, Charles [French physician]
　Match (The first matches) **M:** 300-300a
Saurischian [dinosaur]
　Dinosaur (Kinds of dinosaurs) **D:** 206b *with pictures*
　Eoraptor **E:** 341
Sauropod [dinosaur]
　Brachiosaurus **B:** 542
　Diplodocus **D:** 216
　Seismosaurus **S:** 288
　Supersaurus **So:** 994
Sauropodomorph [dinosaur]
　Dinosaur (True dinosaurs) **D:** 206b-208

Sauropsid [reptile]
Mammal (The ancestors of mammals) M: 126
Prehistoric animal (The Age of Reptiles) P: 737
Reptile R: 252
Sausage [food] S: 163
Meat packing *picture on* M: 351; (Sausage making) M: 352
Saussure, Ferdinand de [Swiss linguist]
Language (The science of language) L: 66-67
Linguistics (Structuralism) L: 337
Sautéing [cooking]
Cooking (Sautéing) Ci: 1028
Meat (How meat is cooked) M: 350
Vegetable oil (Uses) V: 294
Sauvé, J.-Paul [Canadian political leader]
Quebec (table) Q: 29
Sauvé, Jeanne Mathilde [Canadian political leader] S: 164
Sava I Bridge [Serbia]
Bridge (table: Plate and box girder) B: 603
Sava River [river, Croatia]
Croatia (Land and climate) Ci: 1148a *with map*
Savage, Edward [American painter]
United States, History of the *picture on* U: 159
Washington, George *picture on* W: 107
Savage, Eugene [American artist]
Bowie, James *picture on* B: 520
Savage, Ezra P. [American political leader]
Nebraska (table) N: 110
Savage, John [Canadian political leader]
Nova Scotia (table) N: 567
Savai'i [island, Pacific]
Samoa S: 80 *with map*
SAVAK [Iranian history]
Iran (Reforms and growing unrest) I: 406
Savane, La [music by Gottschalk]
Gottschalk, Louis Moreau G: 280
Savanna [geography] S: 164 *with picture*
Africa (Deserts, grasslands, and forests) A: 117
Biome B: 324; (table) B: 323 *with map*
Climate (Tropical wet and dry climates) Ci: 676a-676b
Ecology *picture on* E: 53
Forest *picture on* F: 390; (Kinds of forests) F: 392 *with map*; (Temperate savannas) F: 395 *with map*
Grassland G: 329
Great Limpopo Transfrontier Park G: 346
Plant *map on* P: 523; (Savannas) P: 527
Prairie (Climate and soil) P: 731
Savannah [Georgia] S: 164
Savannah [geography] *See* Savanna *in this index*
Savannah [nuclear ship]
Ship (Nuclear power and automation) S: 426
Savannah [steamship] S: 164 *with picture*
Ship (Oceangoing steamships) S: 424
Savannah, Battle of [1778]
Revolution, American (Savannah and Charleston) R: 284
Savannah, Siege of [1779]
Pulaski, Casimir P: 886
Savannah River [Georgia-South Carolina] S: 165
Georgia *picture on* G: 113
South Carolina (Rivers, waterfalls, and lakes) So: 652-654 *with map*
Savant syndrome [psychology]
Memory (Exceptionally good memory) M: 393-394
Save the Children [organization] S: 165
Saverin, Eduardo [American programmer]
Facebook (History) F: 4
Savery, Thomas [English inventor]
Industrial Revolution (The steam engine) I: 249
Newcomen, Thomas N: 359
Steam engine (The first steam engines) So: 881
Saville, Jenny [British artist]
Painting (Fresh approaches) P: 89
Savimbi, Jonas Malheiro [Angolan political leader]
Angola (History) A: 465-466
Saving Private Ryan [film]
Spielberg, Steven So: 792
Savings [economics]
Economics (Economic growth) E: 62
Investment I: 366; (Indirect investments) I: 367
Savings account
Bank (Safeguarding deposits) B: 88-89
Certificate of deposit C: 363
Investment (Indirect investments) I: 367
Savings and loan association S: 165
Bank (Savings and loan associations) B: 90; (Regulation of U.S. banks) B: 92; (The savings and loan crisis) B: 94
Bush, George Herbert Walker (National affairs) B: 720
Federal Deposit Insurance Corporation F: 63
Savings bank S: 165
Bank (Savings banks) B: 91

Savings bond S: 166
Investment (Bonds) I: 368
Savings plan *See* Thrift plan *in this index*
Savior Tower [Moscow]
Moscow *picture on* M: 823
Savi's pygmy shrew [animal]
Shrew S: 439
Savonarola, Girolamo [Italian religious leader] S: 166
Botticelli, Sandro B: 513
Perspective *picture on* P: 304
Savonnerie rug
Rugs and carpets (History) R: 517
Savoy [Italian history] S: 166
Savoy, Duchy of [former region]
Sardinia, Kingdom of S: 125
Savoy cabbage
Cabbage (Kinds of cabbage) C: 2
Savoy operas
D'Oyly Carte, Richard D: 317
Savoyards [drama]
D'Oyly Carte, Richard D: 317
Saw [tool] S: 166 *with pictures*
Forestry *picture on* F: 404
Woodworking (Cutting) W: 397 *with pictures*
Saw gin [machine]
Cotton (Ginning and baling) Ci: 11091
Saw-scaled viper [snake]
Snake (Vipers) S: 535 *with picture*
Saw set
Saw S: 166
Saw-whet [bird]
Animal *picture on* A: 494
Sawatch Range
Colorado (Land regions) Ci: 838 *with map*
Sawbill [bird]
Merganser M: 416 *with picture*
Sawdust
Lumber L: 517
Sawfish [fish] S: 167 *with picture*
Sawfly [insect] S: 167
Sawgrass Mills [mall]
Fort Lauderdale (Government and history) F: 414
Sawing [industrial process]
Machine tool (Sawing) M: 18 *with picture*
Sawmill [industry]
Lumber (From sawmill to lumberyard) L: 518
Tree (Wood products) T: 412 *with picture*
Sawpit [tool]
Lumber (History) L: 521
Sawtimber [trees]
Lumber (table) L: 518
Sawtooth Mountain Range [mountains]
Idaho *picture on* I: 26; (Mountains) I: 36-38
Sawyer, Charles [American government official]
Commerce, Department of (table) Ci: 871
Truman, Harry S. (table) T: 469
Sawyer, Charles H. [American political leader]
New Hampshire (table) N: 223
Sawyer, Eugene [American political leader]
Chicago (Political developments in the late 1900's) C: 436-437
Sawyer, Grant [American political leader]
Nevada (table) N: 173
Sawyer, Helen Battles [birth name of]
Hogg, Helen Sawyer H: 288
Sawyer, Ruth [American author] S: 168
Newbery Medal N: 359
Regina Medal (table: 1965) R: 206
Storytelling (The Middle Ages) So: 915
Sax, Adolphe [Belgian inventor]
Saxophone S: 168
Saxbe, William Bart [American government official]
Ford, Gerald Rudolph (table) F: 378
Justice, Department of (table) J: 203
Nixon, Richard Milhous (table) N: 433
Saxe-Coburg-Gotha [British history]
Windsor W: 334
Saxe-Weimar, Duke of [German nobleman]
Bach, Johann Sebastian (His life) B: 15
Saxifrage [plant] S: 168 *with picture*
Flower *pictures on* F: 283, F: 289; (table) F: 301 *with picture*
Plant *picture on* P: 524
Saxon dynasty [German history]
Germany (The breakup of Charlemagne's empire) G: 162
Saxons [ancient people] S: 168
Alfred the Great A: 348
Anglo-Saxons A: 464 *with map*
Charlemagne (Military conquests) C: 379
England (The Anglo-Saxon period) E: 304; (The Germanic invasions) E: 304
Rome, Ancient (The decline of the empire) R: 447-448
Trial (History) T: 437

Saxony [region, Germany]
Charlemagne *map on* C: 379
Germany (The breakup of Charlemagne's empire) G: 162
Saxons S: 168
Saxony rug
Rugs and carpets (Kinds of rugs and carpets) R: 514-515 *with picture*
Saxony wheel [machine]
Spinning (Early spinning wheels) So: 794 *with picture*
Saxophone [musical instrument] S: 168 *with pictures*
Jazz (The reeds) J: 69
Saxton, Ida [wife of William McKinley] *See* McKinley, Ida Saxton *in this index*
Say, Allen [American author/artist]
Caldecott Medal (table: 1994) C: 26
Literature for children *picture on* L: 378
Say, Thomas [American geologist]
New Harmony N: 228
Saya San [Burmese political leader]
Myanmar (British conquest and rule) M: 970d
Sayers, Dorothy L. [British author] S: 168
Sayers, Frances Clarke [American author]
Regina Medal (table: 1973) R: 206
Sayers, Joseph D. [American political leader]
Texas (table) T: 203
Sayers, Thomas [British boxer]
Boxing *picture on* B: 531
Saying Grace [painting by Rockwell]
Rockwell, Norman *picture on* R: 394
Sayings gospel
Gospels S: 278
Sayings of the High One, The [poem]
Edda E: 74
Sayles Belton, Sharon [American political leader]
Minneapolis (Recent developments) M: 583
Saylor, David O. [American businessman]
Cement and concrete (History) C: 345
Sb [symbol]
Antimony A: 557
SBA [U.S.]
Small Business Administration S: 512
SBC Communications Inc.
AT&T Inc. A: 851
SBR [synthetic]
Rubber (General-purpose synthetic rubbers) R: 504
Sc [symbol]
Scandium S: 171
Scab [labor]
Labor movement (Handling labor disputes) L: 6-7
Scab [physiology]
Blood (Controlling bleeding) B: 411
Scab [plant disease]
Apple (Pests and diseases) A: 572
Barley (Diseases and insect pests) B: 113
Fungicide F: 560
Scabies [disease] S: 169
Scabland [geography]
Washington (The Columbia Plateau) W: 58
Scafell Pike [mountain, England]
England (The Pennines) E: 300 *with map*
Scalawags [U.S. history] S: 169
Reconstruction (The Republicans in the South) R: 179
Scald [injury] *See* Burn *in this index*
Scale [biology] S: 169
Bud B: 665
Butterfly (The thorax) B: 738-739 *with picture*
Fish (Scales) F: 160 *with pictures*
Pangolin P: 130
Reptile (Skin) R: 251 *with picture*
Snake (Scales and color) S: 525
Scale [deposit]
Boiler B: 439
Scale [measurement]
Interior design (Scale) I: 328
Map (Scale) M: 178 *with pictures*
Railroad, Model (Scale and size) R: 120
Scale [music]
Key K: 307
Music (Tone) M: 950 *with diagrams*
Scale, Weighing S: 169
Scale insect S: 170
Insect *picture on* I: 281
Orange (Pests and diseases) O: 815
San Jose scale S: 102
Scale-leaved cedar [tree]
Cedar (Scale-leaved cedars) C: 324 *with picture*
Scaled Composites [company]
Space exploration (Private launch services) So: 728
Scalene triangle [geometry]
Triangle (Kinds of triangles) T: 437 *with diagram*
Scales, A. M. [American political leader]

North Carolina (table) N: 490
Scali, John A. [American diplomat]
United Nations (table) U: 86
Scalia, Antonin [American jurist] S: 170
Supreme Court of the United States *picture on*
So: 999
Scaliger, Julius [Italian scientist]
Platinum (History) P: 567
Scaling laws [engineering]
Nanotechnology N: 10
Scallop [sea animal] S: 170 *with pictures*
Mollusk (Bivalves) M: 695 *with picture*
Shell *picture on* S: 387
Scalp [anatomy]
Baldness B: 38
Dandruff D: 32
Hair H: 9
Head H: 123
Scalpel
Surgery (Instruments) So: 1004
Scalping
Indian, American (Why the Indians fought) I: 144
Scaly-breasted thrasher [bird]
Thrasher T: 269
Scandentia [zoology]
Mammal (table) M: 129 *with picture*
Scanderbeg [Albanian patriot]
Albania *picture on* A: 309; (Ottoman rule) A: 307
Scandinavia [region, Europe] S: 170 *with map*
Cooperative (In other countries) Ci: 1036
Vikings V: 378
Welfare (Welfare throughout the world) W: 191
Scandinavian design [style]
Furniture *pictures on* F: 569, F: 584; (Modern
Scandinavian design) F: 583
Scandinavian literature S: 171
See also the list of Related articles in the
Scandinavian literature article
Detective story (History) D: 162-163
Mythology (Teutonic mythology) M: 985
Theater *picture on* T: 247; (Scandinavia) T: 248
Scandinavian Peninsula
Scandinavia S: 170
Scandium [element] S: 171
Scania [region, Sweden]
Scandinavia S: 171
Scanner [electronic device]
See also Optical scanner *in this index*
Animation (Traditional animation) A: 512-513
Computer (A scanner) Ci: 915
Copying machine (Electrostatic copying) Ci: 1045
Desktop publishing D: 158
Electronics E: 206
Laser *picture on* L: 81; (Scanning) L: 82
Light (Lasers) L: 291
Photography (Processing digital images) P: 422
Printing (Preparing illustrations for reproduction)
P: 797; (Process color printing) P: 802
Scanning [electronics]
Television (Creating television signals) T: 121;
(High-definition television) T: 128
Scanning electron microscope
Electron microscope (Scanning electron
microscopes) E: 204 *with diagram*
Atom (How scientists study atoms) A: 874
Cell (Structure) C: 337-338
Microscope (Electron microscopes) M: 519
Mineral (Determining the structure of crystals)
M: 571
Scanning optical microscope
Microscope (Specialized optical microscopes and
techniques) M: 518
Scanning probe microscope S: 172 *with picture*
Microscope (Scanning probe microscopes)
M: 519
Scanning transmission electron microscope
Electron microscope (Scanning transmission
electron microscopes) E: 204
Scanning tunneling microscope
Atom (How scientists study atoms) A: 874
Cell (The 1900's) C: 337-338
Chemistry *picture on* C: 405
Microscopes (Scanning probe microscopes)
M: 519
Scanning probe microscope S: 172
Scaphoid bone [anatomy]
Hand (Parts of the hand) H: 40
Scaphopoda [zoology] *See* Tooth shell *in this index*
Scapula [anatomy]
Back B: 17
Collarbone Ci: 773 *with diagram*
Human body (table) H: 422 *with diagram*
Rotator cuff R: 486
Shoulder S: 437 *with picture*
Skeleton *diagrams on* S: 480
Scar S: 172
Keloid K: 257

Scarab [insect] S: 172
Beetle *picture on* B: 218; (Scarabs) B: 217
Scarcity
Economics E: 58
Value (Value and scarcity) V: 267
Scarface [film]
Hawks, Howard H: 114
Motion picture (Movies in the 1930's) M: 867
Scarface [nickname]
Capone, Al C: 198
Scarification [body art]
Africa *picture on* A: 116a; (Fine arts) A: 115
Body art B: 434
Scarlatti, Alessandro [Italian composer] S: 173
Classical music (The Baroque period) Ci: 647
Overture O: 882
Scarlatti, Domenico [Italian composer] S: 173
Scarlet fever [disease] S: 173
Scarlet globe mallow [plant]
Flower *picture on* F: 286
Scarlet haw [tree] *See* Hawthorn *in this index*
Scarlet ibis [bird]
Bird (Birds of Central and South America) B: 344a
with picture
Ibis I: 3
Scarlet Letter, The [book by Hawthorne]
Hawthorne, Nathaniel (His novels) H: 115
Novel (The United States) N: 573
Scarlet macaw [bird]
Bird *picture on* B: 344b; (Birds of Central and
South America) B: 344a
Parrot *picture on* P: 180
Scarlet oak [tree]
Oak (Red oaks) O: 635
Scarlet pimpernel [plant] S: 173
Scarlet Pimpernel, The [book by Orczy]
Orczy, Baroness O: 825
Scarlet runner bean [plant]
Bean (Kinds of beans) B: 181
Scarlet sage [plant]
Salvia S: 77 *with picture*
Scarlet tanager [bird]
Bird *picture on* B: 358; (Birds of forests and
woodlands) B: 334 *with picture*
Tanager T: 24
Scarp [astronomy]
Moon (Rilles) M: 790
Scarpetta, Kay [literary character]
Cornwell, Patricia Ci: 1066
Scarpia [opera character]
Opera: (Tosca) O: 807
Scarpland [region]
England (The English Lowlands) E: 300-301
Scarron, Paul [husband of]
Maintenon, Marquise de M: 93
Scat singing
Armstrong, Louis A: 723
Fitzgerald, Ella F: 190
Jazz (The 1920's) J: 70-71
Scatter package
Advertising (Television) A: 73
Scattering [optics]
Light (Scattering) L: 288
Scaup [bird]
Duck *picture on* D: 375
Scavenger beetle [insect]
Beetle *picture on* B: 218
SCCA [organization]
Automobile racing (Racing organizations) A: 976
Scelidosaurus [extinct animal]
Dinosaur *picture on* D: 206d
*Scene at the Signing of the Constitution of the
United States* [painting by Christy]
Constitution of the United States *picture on*
Ci: 996
Scene design
Theater (Scene design) T: 239 *with pictures*
Scenery
Ballet (Sets and costumes) B: 49 *with pictures*
Theater (Scene design) T: 239 *with pictures*
Scenic trail
National Trails System N: 61
Scent [zoology]
Territoriality T: 174
Scent hound [dog]
Dog (Hounds) D: 270 *with pictures*
Hound H: 378
Scent station [zoology]
Fox (The life of a fox) F: 439
Scepter [staff]
Coronation (The British coronation) Ci: 1068
Scève, Maurice [French poet]
French literature (Lyon) F: 520
Schachter, Stanley [American psychologist]
Emotion (The constructivist approach) E: 261
Schaefer, William D. [American political leader]
Maryland (table) M: 255

Schaeffer, Pierre [French composer]
Classical music (Electronic music) Ci: 650
Electronic music E: 205
Schafer, Edward T. [American political leader]
Agriculture, Department of (table) A: 161
Bush, George Walker (table) B: 722h
North Dakota (table) N: 513
Schaffner, Franklin J. [American director]
Motion picture (Best achievement in directing:
1970) M: 862
Schalk, Ray [American baseball player]
Baseball (table: Hall of Fame) B: 134b
Schaller, George Beals [American zoologist] S: 173
Schally, Andrew Victor [American physiologist]
Nobel Prizes (Physiology or medicine: 1977)
N: 446
Scharnhorst, Gerhard von [Prussian general]
Army (The rise of modern armies) A: 727-728
Schaumburg Palace [Germany]
Bonn (The city) B: 460
Schawlow, Arthur Leonard [American physicist]
Laser (History) L: 86
Nobel Prizes (Physics: 1981) N: 441
Schechter Poultry Corporation
Schechter v. United States S: 174
Schechter v. United States [U.S. history] S: 174
Interstate commerce (Interstate commerce
today) I: 351
Labor movement (The New Deal) L: 12
Supreme Court of the United States (table)
So: 1002
Scheckter, Jody [South African race driver]
Automobile racing (table: Formula One World
Drivers' Championship) A: 980
Scheduled airliner
Airport (General aviation airports) A: 243
Scheduled flight
Aviation (Airline operations) A: 984-985
Scheele, Carl Wilhelm [Swedish chemist]
Air (The study of air) A: 175
Chemistry (The phlogiston theory) C: 401
Chlorine C: 516
Citric acid C: 573
Glycerol G: 237
Lactic acid L: 24
Molybdenum M: 697
Oxygen (History) O: 890
Photography (Early developments) P: 422
Tungsten T: 487
Scheelite [mineral]
Tungsten T: 487
Scheer, Reinhard [German admiral]
Jutland, Battle of J: 485
World War I (The war at sea) W: 460
Scheherazade [ballet]
Ballet (Ballet in Russia) B: 52
Fokine, Michel F: 315
Scheherazade [legendary figure]
Aladdin A: 280
Arabian Nights A: 582b
Scheherazade [music by Rimsky-Korsakov]
Rimsky-Korsakov, Nikolai R: 341
Schelde River [Europe]
Belgium (The land) B: 230 *with map*
Netherlands (The land) N: 144 *with map*
Schell, Maximilian [Austrian actor]
Motion picture (Best performance by an actor:
1961) M: 862a
Schellenberg [former region]
Liechtenstein (History) L: 273
Schelling, Friedrich Wilhelm Joseph von [German
philosopher] S: 174
Schelling, Thomas Crombie [American economist]
Nobel Prizes (Economics: 2005) N: 449
Schelomo [music by Bloch]
Bloch, Ernest B: 404
Scheme [language]
Shakespeare, William (Rhetoric) S: 368
Schenck, Charles T. [American activist]
Schenck v. United States S: 174
Schenck v. United States [U.S. history] S: 174
Supreme Court of the United States (table)
So: 1002
Schenectady [New York] S: 174
Schenley Park
Pittsburgh (Recreation) P: 500d
Scherbius, Arthur [German electrical engineer]
Codes and ciphers (History) Ci: 751
Schertel, Hanns von [German engineer]
Hydrofoil (Modern hydrofoil developments)
H: 468
Scherzo [music]
Sonata So: 591
Scheveningen [Netherlands]
Hague, The (The city) H: 6
Schiaparelli, Giovanni V. [Italian astronomer]
Mars (Observation from Earth) M: 226c

Schichi-Go-San [holiday]
November N: 576
Schicklgruber, Anna [grandmother of]
Hitler, Adolf (Boyhood) H: 264-265
Schieffelin, Ed [American frontiersman]
Tombstone T: 326
Schiele, Egon [Austrian artist] S: 174 *with picture*
Schikaneder, Emanuel [German librettist]
Opera: *(Magic Flute, The)* O: 805
Schildkraut, Joseph [Austrian actor]
Motion picture (Best performance by an actor in
a supporting role: 1937) M: 862a
Schiller, Johann Christoph Friedrich von
[German author] S: 174
Beethoven, Ludwig van (Beethoven's place in
music history) B: 214
German literature (The second golden age [1750-
1830]) G: 139
Goethe, Johann Wolfgang von (Middle years)
G: 247
Schimmel, Wilhelm [American craftsman]
Folk art (Folk artists) F: 319
Woodcarving W: 391
Schimper, F. W. [German botanist]
Rain forest R: 126
Schindel, Morton [American author]
Regina Medal (table: 1979) R: 206
Schindler, Oskar [German businessman] S: 175
Schindler's Ark [book by Keneally]
Keneally, Thomas K: 259
Schindler's List [book by Keneally]
Keneally, Thomas K: 259
Schindler's List [film]
Motion picture (Best picture: 1993) M: 861
Spielberg, Steven So: 792
Schinkel, Friedrich [German architect]
Germany (Architecture) G: 156
Schiphol Airport
Airport (table) A: 245
Netherlands (Transportation) N: 147-148
Schipperke [dog] S: 175
Dog *picture on* D: 275
Schirra, Walter Marty, Jr. [American astronaut]
S: 175
Lovell, James Arthur Jr. L: 509
Space exploration (Vostok and Mercury: The
first human beings in space) So: 712-713 *with
pictures*
Schirrmann, Richard [German educator]
Youth hostel Y: 574
Schism [religious history]
See also Great Schism *in this index*
Eastern Orthodox Churches (History) E: 45-46
Roman Catholic Church (Split with the East)
R: 407
Schist [rock] S: 176
Earth *picture on* E: 21
Rock (Metamorphic rock) R: 373; (table) R: 373
with picture
Schistosity [geology]
Schist S: 176
Schistosome [animal]
Flatworm F: 229
Fluke F: 304
Schistosomiasis S: 176
Schistosomiasis [disease] S: 176
Aswan High Dam A: 851
Snail (Snails and people) S: 523
Schizophrenia [psychiatry] S: 176
Brain (Genetic disorders) B: 558
Catalepsy C: 297
Mental illness (Schizophrenia) M: 405
Shock treatment S: 429
Tranquilizer T: 369
Schlafly, Phyllis Stewart [American social critic]
S: 176
Schlegel, Friedrich [German author]
German literature (Romanticism) G: 140
Language (The science of language) L: 66
Linguistics (Comparative and historical research)
L: 337
Schleicher, August [German linguist]
Linguistics (Comparative and historical research)
L: 337
Schleiden, Matthias [German botanist]
Biology (Materialistic physiology and the cell
theory) B: 319
Cell (Before 1900) C: 337
Schlesinger, Arthur Meier, Jr. [American historian]
S: 177
Schlesinger, Bruno Walter [birth name of]
Walter, Bruno B: 21
Schlesinger, Frank [American astronomer]
Yerkes Observatory Y: 565
Schlesinger, James Rodney [American
government official]
Defense, Department of (table) D: 87

Energy, Department of (table) E: 276
Ford, Gerald Rudolph (table) F: 378
Schlesinger, John [British director]
Motion picture (Best achievement in directing:
1969) M: 862
Schleswig-Holstein [European history]
Denmark (The Schleswig wars) D: 140
Germany (The unification of Germany) G: 165
with map
Schley, William [American political leader]
Georgia (table) G: 130
Schley, Winfield Scott [American military leader]
Navy, United States (The Spanish-American War
[1898]) N: 88
Sampson, William Thomas S: 82
Schleyer, Johann Martin [German religious leader]
Universal language U: 205
Schlick, Moritz [German philosopher]
Positivism (Logical positivism) P: 697
Schlieffen, Alfred von [German general]
World War I (The Western Front) W: 455
Schliemann, Heinrich [German archaeologist]
S: 177
Aegean civilization A: 82
Mycenae M: 970f
Troy (The archaeological Troy) T: 455
Schliemann, Sophia [German archaeologist]
Schliemann, Heinrich S: 177
Schlitz, Laura Amy [American author]
Newbery Medal (table) N: 359
Schlossberg [castle ruins]
Graz G: 335
Schlossberg, Caroline Kennedy [daughter of]
Kennedy, John Fitzgerald *picture on* K: 265;
(Kennedy's family) K: 262
Kennedy, Joseph Patrick (His family) K: 269-270
Onassis, Jacqueline Kennedy O: 761
Schmalkaldic League [German history] S: 177
Schmedeman, Albert G. [American political
leader]
Wisconsin (table) W: 365
Schmeling, Max [German boxer]
Boxing (Boxing's Golden Age) B: 532-532a *with
picture*
Louis, Joe L: 477
Schmidt, Brian P. [Australian physicist]
Nobel Prizes (Physics: 2011) N: 442
Schmidt, Helmut [German political leader]
Germany (West Germany) G: 170
Schmidt, Maarten [Dutch-born physicist]
Astronomy (Finding quasars) A: 849
Schmidt, Mike [American baseball player]
Baseball (table: Hall of Fame) B: 134b
Schmidt-Rottluff, Karl [German painter]
Painting (Expressionism) P: 78
Schmidt telescope
Palomar Observatory P: 112
Schmitt, Harrison Hagan [American astronaut]
S: 177
Schmitt, Pál [Hungarian political leader]
Hungary (Recent developments) H: 448
Schnabel, Julian [American artist/filmmaker]
S: 177 *with picture*
Painting (Recent painting) P: 87
Schnauzer [dog]
Dog *picture on* D: 273
Giant schnauzer G: 184
Miniature schnauzer M: 573
Standard schnauzer So: 835 *with picture*
Schneider, Hannes [Austrian skier]
Skiing (The development of modern skiing)
S: 487
Schneider, Herman [American educator]
Cooperative education Ci: 744
Schneider, Louis [American race driver]
Automobile racing (table: Indianapolis 500
winners) A: 980
Schneider Trophy race
Airplane (The golden age) A: 235-237
Schnitzer, Eduard Karl Oskar Theodor [birth
name of]
Emin Pasha E: 259
Schnitzler, Arthur [Austrian author] S: 178
German literature (Impressionism,
Neoromanticism, and Symbolism) G: 141
Schoenberg, Arnold [Austrian composer] S: 178
Austria (Music) A: 933
Berg, Alban B: 256
Classical music (Atonal music) Ci: 649
Webern, Anton W: 176
Schoenbrunn Village [Ohio]
Ohio (Places to visit) O: 690
Schoendienst, Red [American baseball player]
Baseball (table: Hall of Fame) B: 134b
Schoenherr, John [American artist]
Caldecott Medal (table: 1988) C: 26
Schoenhut, Albert [German toymaker]

Doll (Before World War I) D: 291
Schoeppel, Andrew Frank [American political
leader]
Kansas (table) K: 234
Schöffer, Peter [German printer]
Gutenberg, Johannes G: 444
Schofield, John McAllister [American military
leader]
Civil War, American (North to Nashville) Ci: 632
Johnson, Andrew (table: Johnson's Cabinet)
J: 140
Scholarship [award] S: 178
Foundation (Education) F: 430-431
Scholastic aptitude
Careers (Aptitudes) C: 215
Scholastic aptitude test
See also SAT *in this index*
Testing (Tests of learning ability) T: 182a
Scholasticism [philosophy] S: 179
Humanism (The development of humanism)
H: 430
Middle Ages (Learning and the arts) M: 527
Philosophy (Medieval philosophy) P: 388
Political science (Scholasticism) P: 639
Roman Catholic Church (Scholasticism) R: 407
Scholes, Myron Samuel [American economist]
Nobel Prizes (Economics: 1997) N: 449
Scholten, Peter von [Dutch government official]
Virgin Islands, United States (Danish rule)
V: 396-397
Schomburg Center for Research in Black Culture
[New York]
New York Public Library N: 344
Schönbein, Christian Friedrich [German chemist]
Guncotton G: 441
Schönberg, Arnold [Austrian composer] *See*
Schoenberg, Arnold *in this index*
Schönbrunn, Treaty of [1809]
Napoleonic Wars (The Austrian war) N: 18-19
Schönbrunn Palace [Vienna]
Botanical garden *picture on* B: 507
Vienna (The city) V: 361-362
Schönbrunn Zoo [Vienna]
Zoo (The first modern zoos) Z: 604-605
Schongauer, Martin [German artist] S: 179
School [education] S: 180 *with pictures*
See also Education *in this index; and the list of
Related articles in the School article*
Africa (Education) A: 114 *with picture*
Alternative school A: 388
Charter school C: 386
Child (Obstacles to learning) C: 453
Children's home C: 457
Colonial life in America (Education) Ci: 803 *with
picture*
EdisonLearning, Inc. E: 82
India *picture on* I: 118
Pet (Pets in school) P: 320
Physical fitness (Developing physical fitness)
P: 435
Playground P: 571
Reading (Working with the school) R: 160
Reconstruction (New state programs and
policies) R: 179
Safety (Safety at school) S: 11
Sexuality (Cultural influences) S: 338a
Teaching T: 65 *with pictures*
Voucher V: 451
Western frontier life in America (Education)
W: 239
School [zoology]
Fish *picture on* F: 168; (How fish live together)
F: 167
Herring (Commercial fishing) H: 215
Whale (Group life) W: 261
School Act [1864]
Tupper, Sir Charles (Premier) T: 494
School-age years
Child (The school-age years) C: 449 *with picture*
School board *See* Education, Board of *in this index*
School bus
Bus (Kinds of bus service) B: 714-715
School busing *See* Busing *in this index*
School camp
Camping (Organized camping) C: 96-97
School Daze [film by Lee]
Lee, Spike L: 179
"School Daze" series [books by Spinelli]
Spinelli, Jerry So: 793
School district
Education (Control and support of U.S.
education) E: 94
Local government (Units of local government)
L: 407
School (Public schools) S: 182
*School District of Abington Township,
Pennsylvania, v. Schempp* [U.S. history]

Religious education (Public schools) R: 225
School prayer S: 185
School Employees, American Association of Classified
Labor movement (table) L: 8
School for Lifelong Learning
New Hampshire, University of N: 228
School for Scandal, The [play by Sheridan]
Drama *picture on* D: 335
Sheridan, Richard Brinsley S: 396
School for the Deaf [Japan]
Deafness (Education) D: 59
School for Wives, The [play by Molière]
Molière M: 694
School integration See Segregation *in this index*
School library
Library (Types of libraries) L: 235 *with picture*;
(Active community service) L: 236-237; (School libraries) L: 244 *with pictures*
School of ...
Proper names of schools appear under their key words, as in Montreal, School of
School of Athens [painting by Raphael]
Painting (The High Renaissance) P: 54-55
Raphael (His works) R: 143 *with picture*
Renaissance (Arts of the 1400's and early 1500's) R: 236 *with picture*
School of the air
Australia (Education) A: 903-904 *with picture*
School prayer S: 185
Religious education (Public schools) R: 225
Supreme Court of the United States (Church and state) So: 1001
School reform
Education (How should schools be run?) E: 108
School-site management
Education (How should schools be run?) E: 108
School Superintendents, Association of
National Education Association N: 34
School-to-work program
Careers (Preparing for a career) C: 216
School without walls
Alternative school (Features of alternative schools) A: 388-389
Schoolboy match [wrestling]
Wrestling (Internaational competition) W: 505
Schoolcraft, Henry Rowe [American author]
Minnesota *picture on* M: 605; (The Louisiana Purchase) M: 603-604
Schoolroom Poets
American literature (Poetry) A: 418
Schooner [ship]
Sailing (Yawls, ketches, and schooners) S: 24 *with picture*
Schopenhauer, Arthur [German philosopher] S: 186
Schorl [mineral]
Tourmaline T: 349
Schouten, Willem [Dutch navigator]
Admiralty Islands A: 59
Cape Horn C: 188
Tonga (History) T: 328
Schramm, Wilbur L. [American political analyst]
Communication (Communication and politics) Ci: 888
Schrank, John N. [American assassin]
Roosevelt, Theodore ("Bull Moose" candidate) R: 468
Schreiber, Martin J. [American political leader]
Wisconsin (table) W: 365
Schreyer, Edward Richard [Canadian government official] S: 186
Manitoba (table) M: 159
Schreyvogel, Charles [American artist]
Indian wars *picture on* I: 194
Schricker, Henry Frederick [American political leader]
Indiana (table) I: 214
Schrieffer, John Robert [American physicist]
Bardeen, John B: 109
Nobel Prizes (Physics: 1972) N: 441
Superconductivity So: 992
Schrock, Richard Royce [American chemist]
Nobel Prizes (Chemistry: 2005) N: 444
Schröder, Gerhard [German political leader] S: 186
Germany (Political changes) G: 171
Schrödinger, Erwin [Austrian physicist] S: 186
Born, Max B: 489
Physics (Quantum theory) P: 441
Schrödinger equation [physics]
Schrödinger, Erwin S: 186
Schubert, Franz Peter [Austrian composer] S: 187
Classical music (The Romantic era) Ci: 648 *with picture*
Schuler, Max [German engineer]
Inertial guidance (History) I: 264
Schuller, Gunther [American composer]

Classical music (Third-stream music) Ci: 650-651
Jazz (New directions) J: 73
Schultz, Augustus [American inventor]
Leather (History) L: 169
Schultz, Theodore William [American economist]
Nobel Prizes (Economics: 1979) N: 449
Schulz, Charles Monroe [American cartoonist] S: 187 *with picture*
Schulze, Johann H. [German physicist]
Photography (Early developments) P: 422
Schulze, John Andrew [American political leader]
Pennsylvania (table) P: 263
Schumacher, Michael [German race driver]
Automobile (table: Formula One World Drivers' Championship) A: 980
Schuman, William [American composer] S: 188
Schumann, Clara [German pianist] S: 188
Brahms, Johannes (His life) B: 548
Schumann, Robert (His life) S: 188
Schumann, Robert [German composer] S: 188
Brahms, Johannes (His life) B: 548
Classical music (The Romantic era) Ci: 648
Schumann, Clara S: 188
Schumpeter, Joseph Alois [Czechoslovak-American economist] S: 188
Economics (Modern economics) E: 64-65
Schurz, Carl [American political leader] S: 189 *with portrait*
Grant, Ulysses S. (Election of 1872) G: 316
Schurz, Margaretha Meyer [American educator]
Education (New theories of education) E: 104
Kindergarten (Early kindergartens) K: 319
Schussing [sports]
Skiing *diagram on* S: 484; (Alpine skiing) S: 482
Schütz, Heinrich [German composer]
Classical music (The Baroque period) Ci: 647
Schütz, Sinold von [German author]
Encyclopedia (An age of experiment) E: 268a
Schutzstaffel [German history] See SS *in this index*
Schuyler, Philip John [American general] S: 189
Schuylkill Canal [waterway, Pennsylvania]
Pennsylvania (Industrial growth) P: 267
Schuylkill River [Pennsylvania] S: 189
Philadelphia (The city) P: 358-359
Schwa [language]
Phonetics (An international phonetic alphabet) P: 400
Schwab, Charles Michael [American businessman]
United States Steel Corporation U: 204
Schwalbe [airplane]
World War II (The air war) W: 482-483
Schwaner Range [mountains, Borneo]
Borneo (The land and its resources) B: 489 *with map*
Schwann, Theodor [German physiologist]
Biology *picture on* B: 321; (Materialistic physiology and the cell theory) B: 319
Cell (Before 1900) C: 337 *with picture*
Science (Scientific advances in the 1800's) S: 200 *with picture*
Schwann cell [anatomy]
Myelin M: 970f
Nervous system (Parts of a neuron) N: 133-134
Schwartz, Barry K. [American fashion designer]
Klein, Calvin K: 343
Schwartz, Delmore [American poet] S: 189
Schwartz, Melvin [American physicist]
Neutrino N: 154
Nobel Prizes (Physics: 1988) N: 442
Schwarz, David [Austrian engineer]
Airship (The first airships) A: 251-252
Schwarzenegger, Arnold [American actor/political leader] S: 189 *with portrait*
California (table) C: 59; (The beginning of the 2000's) C: 64
Schwarzkopf, H. Norman [U.S. military leader] S: 189
Schwarzwald See Black Forest *in this index*
Schweigger, Johann Salomo Christoph [German physicist]
Electric meter (History) E: 177
Schweiker, Mark S. [American political leader]
Pennsylvania (table) P: 263
Schweiker, Richard S. [American government official]
Health and Human Services, Department of (table) H: 128
Reagan, Ronald Wilson (table) R: 169
Schweitzer, Albert [German-born humanitarian] S: 190 *with portrait*
Gabon G: 2
Nobel Prizes (Peace: 1952) N: 448a *with picture*
Organ (History) O: 852
Schweitzer, Brian [American political leader]
Montana (table) M: 742
Schwellenbach, Lewis B. [American government official]

Labor, Department of (table) L: 2
Truman, Harry S. (table) T: 469
Schwenkfeld, Caspar von Ossig [German religious leader]
Schwenkfelders S: 190
Schwenkfelders [religious group] S: 190
Schwinden, Ted [American political leader]
Montana (table) M: 757
Schwinger, Julian Seymour [American physicist]
Feynman, Richard Phillips F: 84
Nobel Prizes (Physics: 1965) N: 441
Subatomic particle (The Standard Model) So: 938
Schwitters, Kurt [German artist] S: 190
Avant-garde A: 982
Collage *picture on* Ci: 773
Painting (Dadaism) P: 80-81
Schwyz [canton, Switzerland]
Switzerland (The struggle for freedom) So: 1059
Schwyzerdütsch [language]
Switzerland (Language) So: 1053
Sciatic nerve [anatomy]
Human body (table) H: 422 *with diagram*
Leg (Blood and nerve supply) L: 182
Sciatica S: 190
Sciatica [disorder] S: 190
SCID [disease] See Severe combined immunodeficiency disease *in this index*
Science S: 191 *with pictures*
See also the list of Related articles in the Science *article*
Alchemy A: 334
Arabs (Science) A: 588
Christianity (The 1800's) C: 526
Colonial life in America (Science) Ci: 808
Electricity (In medicine and science) E: 191
Empiricism E: 263
Enlightenment E: 326a
Environmental pollution (Scientific efforts) E: 336
Europe (The scientific revolution and the Enlightenment) E: 412
Existentialism (What is existentialism?) E: 437
Foundation (Science and technology) F: 431
Galileo G: 11
Greece, Ancient (Science) G: 368
Mathematics (In science) M: 302; (Mathematics and the scientific revolution) M: 306
Radiation (In science) R: 75
Rome, Ancient (Science) R: 443
Science projects S: 206
Social science (Relationship to natural sciences) So: 552
Technology T: 74
World, History of the (Scientific and technological achievements) W: 448a
Science, American Association for the Advancement of
American Association for the Advancement of Science A: 408
Science, Bachelor of See Bachelor's degree *in this index*
Science, International Council for See International Council for Science *in this index*
Science, Master of See Master's degree *in this index*
Science, Philosophy of
Philosophy (Philosophy and science) P: 385
Popper, Karl Raimund P: 668
Science and Health with Key to the Scriptures [book by Eddy]
Christian Scientists (Beliefs) C: 522e
Science and Industry, Museum of See Museum of Science and Industry *in this index*
Science and Technology Policy, Office of [U.S.]
President of the United States (The executive branch) P: 764
Science fair
Science projects S: 206
Science fiction [literature] S: 205
American literature (Popular genres) A: 425
Literature for children (Fantasy and science fiction) L: 361; (The middle and late 1900's) L: 365 *with picture*
Novel N: 571; (The middle and late 1900's) N: 575
Science Foundation, National See National Science Foundation *in this index*
Science, Industry and Business Library [New York]
New York Public Library N: 344
Science museum
Museum (Science museums) M: 938
Science Museum [Richmond]
Planetarium (Digital projectors) P: 514c
Science Museum of Franklin Institute [Philadelphia] See Franklin Institute Science Museum *in this index*
Science Museum of Minnesota
Minnesota (Museums) M: 589 *with picture*; (Places to visit) M: 594

Science Museum Oklahoma
Oklahoma City (Education and cultural life) O: 736
Science of Judaism [study area]
Zunz, Leopold Z: 609
Science of Logic [book by Hegel]
Hegel, G. W. F. (Hegel's writings) H: 165
Science projects S: 206
Chemistry (A simple chemical experiment) C: 403 with pictures
Heredity (Studying heredity) H: 207 with pictures
Moon (Simulating the phases of the moon) M: 793 with pictures
Water (How detergents reduce the surface tension of water) W: 130 with pictures
Waves (Wave patterns in a ripple tank) W: 151 with pictures
Weather (A cloud in a bottle) W: 168 with pictures
Science, Technology and Society in Seventeenth Century England [book by Merton]
Merton, Robert King M: 419
Sciences, Academy of [France]
Institute of France I: 305
Sciences, National Academy of See National Academy of Sciences in this index
Scientific Affairs, Council on
Hypnosis (Enhancing memory) H: 479
Scientific and Technical Information, Canada Institute for
Library (Canadian government libraries) L: 249
Scientific classification See Classification, Scientific in this index
Scientific creationism [doctrine] See Creationism in this index
Scientific Management [work by Taylor]
Taylor, Frederick Winslow T: 57
Scientific method
Education (The Enlightenment) E: 101
Enlightenment E: 326a
Inductive method I: 240
Philosophy (Modern philosophy) P: 388
Psychology (Methods of psychological research) P: 847
Science (How scientists work) S: 194
World, History of the (The Renaissance) W: 438-440
Scientific notation [mathematics] S: 207
Scientific photography
Photography (Scientific photographers) P: 428
Scientific research satellite
Satellite, Artificial (table) S: 150e; (Types of artificial satellites) S: 150f
Scientific revolution
Magic (Europe) M: 50
Science (The scientific revolution) S: 198
Scientific visualization software
Computer (Scientific visualization software) Ci: 919
Computer graphics (In science) Ci: 924f-924g
Scientist astronaut
Astronaut (A look at the astronauts) A: 831
Scientology S: 208
Scieszka, Jon [American author] S: 208
Scintillator [instrument]
Particle detector (Scintillators) P: 187
Telescope (Gamma-ray telescopes) T: 109
Scion [botany]
Forestry (Tree improvement) F: 405
Grafting G: 298 with pictures
Scioto River [Ohio]
Columbus (The city) Ci: 854 with picture
Ohio (Rivers and lakes) O: 692 with map
Scipio Africanus, Publius Cornelius [Roman general]
Hannibal (The turning point) H: 52 with picture
Numidia N: 608
Rome, Ancient (The Roman Republic) R: 444-445
Scipio Africanus, Publius Cornelius [Roman military leader] S: 208
Scissor-tailed flycatcher [bird]
Bird picture on B: 358; (Birds of grasslands) B: 336 with picture
Flycatcher F: 311
Scissorbill [bird]
Skimmer S: 488
Scissors [tool] S: 208
Scissors kick
Swimming (The basic kicks) So: 1043
Scituate Reservoir
Rhode Island (Rivers and lakes) R: 306-308 with map
SCLC [organization] See Southern Christian Leadership Conference in this index
Sclera [anatomy]
Eye (The sclera and the cornea) E: 460 with picture; (Diseases of the sclera) E: 466
Scleritis [disease]

Eye (Diseases of the sclera) E: 466
Scleroderma [disease] S: 209
Sclerometer [instrument]
Hardness H: 59
Sclerosis [disorder]
See also Arteriosclerosis in this index
Multiple sclerosis M: 920
Sclerotherapy [medicine]
Varicose vein V: 286
Sclerotia [botany]
Ergot E: 350
Sclerotium rot [plant disease]
Larkspur L: 77
Scobee, Francis R. "Dick" [American astronaut]
Challenger disaster C: 370
Space exploration (The Challenger disaster) So: 725
Scofield, Edward [American political leader]
Wisconsin (table) W: 365
Scofield, Paul [British actor]
Motion picture (Best performance by an actor: 1966) M: 862a
Scoke [plant]
Pokeweed P: 603 with picture
Scolex [biology]
Tapeworm T: 40 with picture
Scoliosis [disorder] S: 209
Marfan syndrome M: 198
Scone, Stone of [British history] S: 209
Coronation (The British coronation) Ci: 1068
Edward I E: 112
Scotland (Fight for independence) S: 219
Scoon, Sir Paul Godwin [Grenada political leader]
Grenada (History and government) G: 389-390
Scooter, Motor
Motorcycle (Kinds of motorcycles) M: 878
Scopas [Greek sculptor]
Seven Wonders of the Ancient World (The Mausoleum at Halicarnassus) S: 325
Scopes, John T. [American educator]
Bryan, William Jennings (Later years) B: 655
Darrow, Clarence Seward D: 38
Evolution (Acceptance of evolution) E: 433
Scopes trial S: 209
Tennessee (The early 1900's) T: 154-156
Scopes trial [U.S. history] S: 209 with picture
Bryan, William Jennings (Later years) B: 655
Creationism (The 1900's) C: 1123
Darrow, Clarence Seward D: 38
Evolution (Acceptance of evolution) E: 433
Tennessee (The early 1900's) T: 154-156
Scopula [zoology]
Spider (Legs) So: 785
Scorched-earth policy
Indian wars (Navajo conflicts) I: 195
World War II (Civilian life) W: 496
SCORE [organization]
Old age (Employment and other activities) O: 739
Score [satellite]
Communications satellite (History) Ci: 888b-889
Scorekeeper
Basketball (The officials) B: 145
Scoria [geology]
Volcano (Pyroclasts) V: 439
Scoria [rock]
North Dakota (Land regions) N: 506-508
Rock (Extrusive rock) R: 371
Scoria cone [geology]
Paricutín P: 159 with picture
Scorpio [astrology] S: 210 with picture
Zodiac (The zodiac in astrology) Z: 597 with picture
Scorpion [animal] S: 210 with picture
Animal picture on A: 482
Scorpion orchid [plant]
Orchid picture on O: 824
Scorpionfly [insect] S: 210
Scorsese, Martin [American film director] S: 210
De Niro, Robert D: 131
Motion picture (Best achievement in directing: 2006) M: 862
Scotch [whisky] See Scotch whisky in this index
Scotch broom [shrub]
Broom B: 641
Scotch heather [plant]
Heath H: 156
Scotch-Irish [people]
Colonial life in America (Why the colonists came to America) Ci: 788
Scotch laburnum [tree]
Laburnum L: 19
Scotch pine [tree]
Pine (Other pines) P: 470 with picture
Tree picture on T: 427
Scotch whisky [drink]
Alcoholic beverage (Whiskey) A: 337
Scotland (Food and drink) S: 214

Whiskey W: 282
Scotia Square [Nova Scotia]
Halifax (Government and history) H: 21 with picture
Scotiabank Saddledome [arena]
Calgary picture on C: 33; (History) C: 34
Scotland S: 211 with pictures and maps
See also the list of Related articles in the Scotland article
Caledonia C: 28
Christmas (In England, Ireland, Scotland, and Wales) C: 530
Clan Ci: 638
Clothing picture on Ci: 694
Colonial life in America (Why the colonists came to America) Ci: 788
Edward I E: 112
England (The beginnings of Parliament) E: 306
Fox hunting F: 442
Gaelic languages G: 5
Gaels G: 5
Golf (History) G: 264
Halloween (Halloween symbols) H: 24b
Highland Clearances H: 229
Parliament (The House of Commons) P: 173
Picts P: 452
Scone, Stone of S: 209
United Kingdom U: 48 with picture; (Regional government) U: 50; (Politics) U: 54; (The land) U: 58-59; (Long-standing conflicts) U: 73
Scotland, Kingdom of [Scottish history]
Scotland (Beginning of the Scottish kingdom) S: 219
Scotland Yard [London] S: 221
Scots [people]
Caledonia C: 28
England (The Germanic invasions) E: 304
Rome, Ancient (The decline of the empire) R: 447-448
Scotland (Beginning of the Scottish kingdom) S: 219
Scott, Abram M. [American political leader]
Mississippi (table) M: 640
Scott, Adam Sherriff [Canadian artist]
Canada, History of picture on C: 138
Scott, Barbara Ann [Canadian skater] S: 221
Olympic Games (The postwar games) O: 751-752
Scott, Caroline Lavinia [wife of Benjamin Harrison]
See Harrison, Caroline Scott in this index
Scott, Coretta See King, Coretta Scott in this index
Scott, David Randolph [American astronaut]
Armstrong, Neil Alden A: 723
Moon picture on M: 791
Space exploration picture on So: 720; (Other moon landings) So: 719
Scott, Doug [British mountain climber]
Mount Everest M: 884
Scott, Dred [American public figure]
Dred Scott Decision (The background of the case) D: 345 with portrait
Scott, Duncan Campbell [Canadian author] S: 221
Canadian literature (Poetry: 1850-1918) C: 157
Scott, F. R. [Canadian poet] S: 221
Scott, George C. [American actor]
Motion picture (Best performance by an actor: 1970) M: 862a
Scott, James [English public figure]
Monmouth, Duke of M: 730
Scott, John W. [American educator]
Harrison, Benjamin (Education) H: 70
Scott, Rick [American political leader]
Florida (table) F: 260
Scott, Robert Falcon [British explorer] S: 222
Amundsen, Roald (The race to the South Pole) A: 445
Antarctica (Exploration) A: 535-536 with picture and map
Exploration (The exploration of Antarctica) E: 450
Scott, Robert W. [American political leader]
North Carolina (table) N: 490
Scott, Thomas [American businessman]
Carnegie, Andrew (Early life) C: 241-242
Scott, W. Kerr [American political leader]
North Carolina (table) N: 490
Scott, Sir Walter [Scottish author] S: 222
Bruce, Robert B: 648
December (Quotations) D: 69
English literature (Romantic prose) E: 320
Hail to the Chief H: 8
Irving, Washington (Years in Europe) I: 460
Novel (Britain) N: 573
Scotland (The arts) S: 215
Scott, Winfield [American army chaplain]
Scottsdale S: 224
Scott, Winfield [American general] S: 222
Lee, Robert E. (The Mexican War) L: 177
Mexican War (Scott's campaign) M: 446

Mexico (Difficulties of the early republic) M: 471
New Brunswick (The Aroostook War) N: 198
Pierce, Franklin (Election of 1852) P: 456
Taylor, Zachary (Mexican War) T: 58-59
War of 1812 (Campaigns of 1814) W: 31; (Lundy's Lane) W: 32-33
Whig Party (Decline of the Whigs) W: 280
Scott Air Force Base [military base] S: 223
Scott O'Dell Award for Historical Fiction
Literature for children (Awards) L: 367
Scottellia kamerunensis [tree]
Plant *picture on* P: 527
Scotti [people]
Gaels G: 5
Scottie [dog]
Scottish terrier S: 223
Scottish deerhound [dog] S: 223 *with picture*
Wolfhound W: 378
Scottish fold cat
Cat (Short-haired breeds) C: 290-291 *with picture*
Scottish Gaelic language
Gaelic languages G: 5
Scottish Highland pipe [musical instrument]
Bagpipe B: 26 *with pictures*
Scottish Rite
Masonry (Organization) M: 267; (The lodges and degrees of Masonry) M: 267
Scottish Symphony [music by Mendelssohn]
Mendelssohn, Felix (His music) M: 399
Scottish terrier [dog] S: 223
Dog *picture on* D: 273
Scotts Bluff National Monument [Nebraska]
National Park System (table: National monuments) N: 51
Scottsbluff [Nebraska]
Nebraska (table: Average monthly weather) N: 106
Scottsboro case [U.S. history] S: 223
Scottsdale [Arizona] S: 224
Scotus, John Duns *See* Duns Scotus, John *in this index*
Scouine, La [book by Laberge]
Canadian literature (Fiction: 1850-1918) C: 157
Scouring [industrial process]
Cotton (Finishing) Ci: 1091
Scouring rush [plant] *See* Horsetail *in this index*
Scouse [accent]
Liverpool L: 395
Scout [frontiersman] S: 224
Scout [rank]
See also Boy Scouts; Girl Scouts *in this index*
Scouts Canada (Age groups) S: 224
Scout, The [memorial]
Kansas City *picture on* K: 241
Scout bee [insect]
Bee (Swarming) B: 204 *with picture*
Scout Law
Boy Scouts (Boy Scouting) B: 535
Girl Scouts G: 196
Scout Motto
Boy Scouts (Boy Scouts of America) B: 535-536
Girl Scouts G: 196
Scout Oath
Boy Scouts (Boy Scouting) B: 535
Scout Promise
Boy Scouts (Boy Scouts of America) B: 535-536
Girl Scouts G: 196
Scouts [organization] *See* Boy Scouts; Girl Scouts *in this index*
Scouts Canada [organization] S: 224
Scouts of the Prairies [play]
Buffalo Bill B: 679
Western frontier life in America (Entertainment) W: 240
Scout's Rest Ranch
Nebraska (Places to visit) N: 102 *with picture*
Scoville heat unit [chemistry]
Chili pepper C: 471
Scow [boat]
Barge B: 109
Sailing (Hull) S: 23; (Catboats and sloops) S: 24
Scrambler [plant]
Liana L: 226
Scramjet [engine] *See* Supersonic combination ramjet *in this index*
Scramming
Nuclear energy (Hazards and safeguards) N: 587-588
Scranton [Pennsylvania] S: 224
Scranton, William Warren [American political leader]
Pennsylvania (table) P: 263
United Nations (table) U: 86
Scrap metal
Aluminum (Recycling) A: 397
Iron and steel (How steel is made) I: 441 *with diagrams*; (The electric furnace process)

I: 442-443
Sculpture (Movement) S: 230-231
Smelting S: 515
Scraper [tool]
Prehistoric people *picture on* P: 752
Scrapie [disease]
Mad cow disease M: 26
Prion P: 804
Scratching post
Cat (Training) C: 294 *with picture*
Scrawled filefish
Fish *picture on* F: 155
Scream, The [painting by Munch]
Expressionism E: 442
Munch, Edvard *picture on* M: 926
Painting (Symbolism) P: 76
Screech-owl
Owl (Important owls) O: 884
Screed [tool]
Plaster (Plastering) P: 552
Screen, Projection
Motion picture (The screen) M: 859 *with diagram*
Projection screen P: 816
Screen Actors Guild-American Federation of Television and Radio Artists
Labor movement (table) L: 8
Reagan, Ronald Wilson (Union leader) R: 166
Screen pass [football]
Football (table) F: 356
Screen printing [art]
Graphic arts G: 322
Painting (Pop Art) P: 86
Printing (Screen printing) P: 801
Textile (Finishing the fabric) T: 217
Screen printing [technique] S: 225 *with diagrams*
Screen shot [hockey]
Hockey (Hockey terms) H: 275
Screening mammography [medicine]
Mammography M: 130
Screening test
Blood (Blood tests) B: 413
Cancer (Cancer checkups) C: 171
Screenplay
Motion picture (Developing the story) M: 848
Screenwriter
Motion picture (Developing the story) M: 848
Screw [hardware] S: 225 *with pictures*
Brass *picture on* B: 566
Machine (Screw) M: 15 *with pictures*
Simple machines S: 467
Screw [propeller]
Propeller P: 826
Screw (Uses) S: 225-226
Ship (Engine-driven ships) S: 406
Screw, Archimedean [device] *See* Archimedean screw *in this index*
Screw-cutting lathe
Screw (History) S: 226
Screw pine [tree] *See* Pandanus *in this index*
Screw press [tool]
Invention (Ancient Greece) I: 359
Screw (History) S: 226
Screwball [baseball]
Baseball (Pitching) B: 127
Screwball comedy
Hawks, Howard H: 114
Motion picture (Movies in the 1930's) M: 867-868 *with picture*
Screwdriver [tool]
Woodworking (Fastening) W: 398 *with pictures*
Screwtape Letters, The [book by Lewis]
Lewis, C. S. L: 220
Screwworm [insect]
Insect (Insect control) I: 284-285 *with picture*
Scriabin, Alexander [Russian composer] S: 226
Scribe [occupation] S: 226
Accounting (The history of accounting) A: 23
Book (The Middle Ages) B: 466
Communication (During the Middle Ages) Ci: 879
Egypt, Ancient (Education) E: 136
Manuscript (European manuscripts of the Middle Ages) M: 173
New Testament (Textual criticism) N: 288
Scribe, Augustin Eugène [French dramatist] S: 226
French literature (Realism) F: 522
Scrim [scenery]
Theater (Kinds of scenery) T: 239
Scrimmage, Line of
Football (The players and coaches) F: 356 *with diagrams*
Scrimshaw [engraving]
Folk art (Scrimshaw) F: 318 *with picture*
Ivory (Ivory carving) I: 521
Scripps, Edward Wyllis [American publisher]
S: 227
Journalism (The age of sensationalism) J: 175
Newspaper (Development of U.S. newspapers)

N: 386-387
Scripps, Robert P. [American publisher]
Scripps, Edward Wyllis S: 227
Scripps-Howard Newspapers, Inc.
Scripps, Edward Wyllis S: 227
Scripps Institution of Oceanography [California]
S: 227
Marine biology (What marine biologists do) M: 204-205
Script [drama]
See also Screenplay *in this index*
Motion picture (Developing the story) M: 848-849 *with picture*; (Reviewing the script) M: 849; (Holding rehearsals) M: 851
Television (Planning and preparation) T: 110c
Theater (Acquiring a script) T: 235; (Interpreting the script) T: 235
Writing (Scriptwriting) W: 512
Script [writing]
Handwriting (Cursive writing) H: 47; (Learning cursive writing) H: 48
Script type [printing]
Type (Classes of type) T: 537 *with picture*
Scriptorium [room]
Illuminated manuscript I: 78
Library (Medieval collections) L: 259 *with picture*
Manuscript (European manuscripts of the Middle Ages) M: 173
Scriptures *See the Sacred writings section of the list of Related articles in the Religion article*
Scriptwriter News [magazine]
Writing (Scriptwriting) W: 512
Scrivener, Charles R. [Australian surveyor]
Australian Capital Territory A: 926
Canberra (History) C: 166
Scrofula [disease] S: 227
Scroll [art]
Painting (Egyptian painting) P: 40; (Japanese painting) P: 47 *with picture*
Scroll [book] S: 227 *with picture*
Book (Early books) B: 465
Mythology *picture on* M: 978
Scroll ball [electronic device]
Computer (A mouse) C: 914
Scroll wheel [electronic device]
Computer (A mouse) C: 914
Scrolls from the Dead Sea [book by Wilson]
Wilson, Edmund W: 316
Scrollwork [design]
Scroll S: 227
Scrooby [England]
Pilgrims P: 462
Scrophularia [plant]
Figwort family F: 97
Scrotum [anatomy]
Human body (The reproductive system) H: 425
Reproduction, Human (The human reproductive system) R: 244-245 *with diagram*
Testicle T: 182
Scrovegni frescoes [art]
Giotto (Giotto's works) G: 193
Mural *picture on* M: 929
Scrub jay [bird]
Jay J: 66 *with picture*
Scrub oak [plant]
Plant *picture on* P: 525
Scrub typhus [disease]
Rickettsia R: 335
Scrubber [device]
Air cleaner (Other types of air cleaners) A: 1176
Air pollution (Control of air pollution) A: 199
Coal (The uses of coal) Ci: 718
Deodorizer D: 148
Incinerator I: 100
Scruggs, Earl [American musician]
Country music (Bluegrass music) Ci: 1098a *with picture*
Scrugham, James G. [American political leader]
Nevada (table) N: 173
Scrum [rugby]
Rugby football (Rugby Union) R: 510-511; (Rugby League) R: 512-513 *with picture*
Scrummage [rugby]
Rugby football (The scrum) R: 513
Scruple [unit of measure]
Apothecaries' weight A: 567
Scrutiny [journal]
Leavis, F. R. L: 170
Scuba diving
Diving, Underwater (Ambient diving) D: 245
Skin diving S: 492 *with pictures*; (Scuba diving) S: 493
Scud [missile]
Persian Gulf War of 1991 (Iraq's response) P: 300d
Scudder, John [American physician]
Drew, Charles Richard D: 347
Scudéry, Madeleine de [French author]

Novel (Early novels) N: 572
Scull [boat]
　Rowing (Types of rowing) R: 493
Scullin, James [Australian political leader]
　Australia (table) A: 923
Sculling [sport]
　Rowing (Types of rowing) R: 493
Scully-Power, Paul D. [Australian-born astronaut]
　Astronaut (table) A: 830
Sculpin [fish] S: 227
Sculpture [art] S: 228 *with pictures*
　See also the list of Related articles in the Sculpture
　　article
　Africa (Ancient art) A: 115 *with pictures*
　Alabaster *picture on* A: 280
　Baroque (Baroque sculpture) B: 117
　China (Sculpture and pottery) C: 488 *with pictures*
　Classicism (Greece) Ci: 653
　Egypt, Ancient *picture on* E: 141
　Folk art (Sculpture) F: 317 *with pictures*
　Gargoyle G: 43
　Gothic art (Gothic sculpture and painting) G: 279
　Ife I: 47
　Impressionism (Music, literature, and sculpture)
　　I: 94
　Inca *picture on* I: 98
　Latin America (Sculpture) L: 100
　Marble (Uses) M: 192
　Maya (Arts and crafts) M: 325 *with pictures*
　Minimalism M: 573
　Mobile M: 682
　Nok N: 451
　Olmec Indians O: 744
　Relief R: 212
　Renaissance *picture on* R: 235; (The fine arts)
　　R: 236
　Rome, Ancient (Sculpture, painting, and mosaics)
　　R: 442
Sculpture coral [animal]
　Ocean *picture on* O: 656
Sculpture in the round [art]
　Sculpture (Kinds of sculpture) S: 230
Scum [biology]
　Euglena E: 377
Scurvy [disease] S: 261
　Cook, James (First Pacific voyage) Ci: 1025-1026
　Cranberry Ci: 1116
　Exploration (Exploring the Pacific) E: 447
　Nutrition (Deficiency diseases) N: 630-631
Scutari, Lake *See* Lake Scutari *in this index*
Scutching [industrial process]
　Flax (Growing and processing fiber flax) F: 230-
　　231
Scute [zoology]
　Turtle (Shell) T: 521
Scylla [Greek mythology] S: 261
Scyllac [fusion device]
　Energy supply *picture on* E: 282
Scyphozoan [zoology]
　Jellyfish J: 90
Scythe [tool]
　Wheat (The mechanization of wheat farming)
　　W: 276
Scythians [ancient people] S: 261
　Amazons A: 404
　Guerrilla warfare (History) G: 420
　Russia (Early days) R: 547
　Ukraine (Early days) U: 11-12
SDI [plan] *See* Strategic Defense Initiative *in this*
　index
SDS [organization] *See* Students for a Democratic
　Society *in this index*
Se [symbol]
　Selenium S: 289
Sea *See* Ocean *in this index*
Sea, Law of the [treaty, 1982] *See* Law of the Sea
　Convention *in this index*
Sea Adventure [ship] *See* Sea Venture *in this index*
Sea anemone [sea animal] S: 262 *with picture*
　Animal *pictures on* A: 486, A: 506
　Clownfish Ci: 714 *with picture*
　Ocean *picture on* O: 656
Sea Around Us, The [book by Carson]
　Carson, Rachel C: 250
Sea bass [fish]
　Bass (Sea bass) B: 156 *with picture*
Sea bird
　Bird (Birds of the seacoasts) B: 342 *with pictures;*
　　(Birds of the ocean) B: 344 *with pictures*
Sea bream [fish]
　Bream B: 590
Sea canary [name for]
　Beluga whale B: 247
Sea cave
　Cave (How caves are formed) C: 319
Sea Convention, Law of the [treaty] *See* Law of the
　Sea Convention *in this index*

Sea cow [sea animal] S: 262
　See also Manatee *in this index*
Sea cucumber [sea animal] S: 262 *with picture*
　Deep sea *picture on* D: 82; (Invertebrates)
　　D: 82a-82b
　Trepang T: 435
Sea dog [pirate]
　Pirate (The Caribbean) P: 495
Sea dragon [animal] *See* Seadragon *in this index*
Sea Drift [music by Delius]
　Delius, Frederick D: 116
Sea duck
　Duck *picture on* D: 375; (Kinds of ducks) D: 376
Sea elephant *See* Elephant seal *in this index*
Sea fan [sea animal] S: 262a
　Animal *picture on* A: 468
　Coral *picture on* Ci: 1048a
Sea floor *See* Seafloor *in this index*
Sea fog
　Fog F: 314
Sea grass [plant]
　Coral reef (Life on coral reefs) Ci: 1049
　Plant (Aquatic regions) P: 528
Sea gull [bird] *See* Gull *in this index*
Sea Gull, The [play by Chekhov]
　Chekhov, Anton C: 395
Sea ice
　Antarctica (Ocean) A: 532-534
　Arctic Ocean (Ice) A: 641 *with picture*
　Ice formation I: 9
Sea Island cotton
　Cotton (Pima cotton) Ci: 1088
Sea kayak [boat]
　Kayaking K: 250a
Sea krait [snake]
　Sea snake S: 262b
Sea lamprey [sea animal]
　Lamprey (Body) L: 54
Sea Launch Company
　Space exploration (Private launch services)
　　So: 728
Sea-Launched Missile Defense [program]
　Radar (In the military) R: 65
Sea lavender [plant]
　Statice So: 867 *with picture*
Sea Legs [boat]
　Hydrofoil (Modern hydrofoil development)
　　H: 468
Sea lettuce [plant]
　Seaweed *picture on* S: 277
Sea level S: 262a
　Cretaceous Period Ci: 1127
　Global warming (Rise in sea level) G: 232a
Sea Life Park
　Hawaii (Places to visit) H: 98 *with picture*
Sea lily [animal] S: 262a *with picture*
　Deep sea *picture on* D: 82; (Invertebrates)
　　D: 82a-82b
Sea Lion [code name]
　World War II (The Battle of Britain) W: 476
Sea lion [sea animal]
　Balance of nature (Upsetting the balance) B: 36
　Mammal *picture on* M: 126
　Ocean *picture on* O: 656
　Seal S: 265; (Birth) S: 266 *with picture*; (Seals and
　　fishing crews) S: 267; (Seals in captivity) S: 267
Sea Lion Caves [Florence]
　Oregon (Places to visit) O: 836 *with picture*
Sea loch [geography]
　Fiord F: 119
　Scotland (Rivers and lakes) S: 217
Sea mile [unit of measure]
　Mile M: 542
Sea mount [oceanography] *See* Seamount *in this*
　index
Sea nettle [sea animal]
　Jellyfish J: 90
Sea of Azov [Russia] *See* Azov, Sea of *in this index*
Sea of Chinnereth [name for]
　Galilee, Sea of G: 11
Sea of Cortés
　Gulf of California G: 436
Sea of Crete [Greece]
　Aegean Sea A: 83
Sea of Galilee *See* Galilee, Sea of *in this index*
Sea of Japan *See* Japan, Sea of *in this index*
Sea of Japan, Battle of the [1905]
　Russo-Japanese War (Final battles) R: 566b
Sea of Marmara [Turkey]
　Marmara, Sea of M: 216
Sea of Okhotsk [Russia]
　Exploration (The Russians in Siberia) E: 447
Sea onion [name for]
　Squill So: 814a
Sea otter [animal] S: 262a *with picture*
　Balance of nature (Upsetting the balance) B: 36
Sea parrot [bird] *See* Puffin *in this index*

Sea pen [sea animal]
　Animal *picture on* A: 486
Sea Peoples
　Philistines P: 382
Sea pigeon [bird]
　Guillemot G: 429
Sea power
　Navy N: 76 *with pictures*
Sea rover *See* Pirate *in this index*
Sea Scouting [program]
　Boy Scouts (Venturing) B: 538
Sea serpent [legendary creature] S: 262b
Sea shell
　Shell S: 384 *with pictures*
Sea slug [animal]
　Invertebrate *picture on* I: 366
Sea smoke [fog]
　Atlantic Ocean (Climate) A: 864
Sea snake [reptile] S: 262b
　Snake *picture on* S: 529
Sea squirt [sea animal] S: 262b
Sea star *See* Starfish *in this index*
Sea swallow [bird]
　Tern T: 172
Sea trout [fish] *See* Weakfish *in this index*
Sea turtle S: 262b *with pictures*
　Turtle T: 520 *with picture*; (Sea turtles) T: 522
　Animal (Animal travelers) A: 502-503
　Endangered species (table) E: 270
　Shell *picture on* S: 384
Sea urchin [sea animal] S: 263 *with picture*
　Animal *picture on* A: 486; (Sexual reproduction)
　　A: 496; (Providing food) A: 498
　Balance of nature (Upsetting the balance) B: 36
　Egg (How embryos develop) E: 117
　Marine biology (What marine biologists do)
　　M: 204-205
Sea Venture [ship]
　Bermuda (History) B: 268
　Newport, Christopher N: 379
Sea walnut [sea animal] *See* Ctenophore *in this*
　index
Sea wasp [animal] S: 264
　Jellyfish J: 90 *with picture*
Sea water *See* Seawater *in this index*
Sea whip [animal]
　Deep sea *picture on* D: 82
Sea Wolf, The [book by London]
　London, Jack L: 444
Seabed
　United Nations (Peaceful uses of outer space and
　　the seabed) U: 93
Seabed Arms Control Treaty [1972]
　Arms control (Arms control in the mid-1900's)
　　A: 721-722
　United Nations (Peaceful uses of outer space and
　　the seabed) U: 93
Seaborg, Glenn Theodore [American chemist]
　S: 264
　Americium A: 432
　Californium C: 66
　Curium Ci: 1195
　Plutonium P: 581
Seaborgium [element] S: 264
　Transuranium element T: 401
Seadragon [animal] S: 264
Seadragon [submarine]
　Northwest Passage N: 529
　Submarine (Nuclear submarines) So: 943
Seafloor
　Climate (Sea-floor sediments) Ci: 679
　Deep sea (The deep-sea floor) D: 82a
　Ocean (Sediments) O: 654; (The land at the
　　bottom of the sea) O: 659 *with picture*
　Ocean drilling programs O: 667
　Pacific Ocean (The ocean floor) P: 14
　Southern Ocean (The ocean floor) So: 688a
Seafloor spreading [geology]
　Atlantic Ocean (The Mid-Atlantic Ridge) A: 864
　Ocean *picture on* O: 651; (How the sea floor was
　　formed) O: 662
　Plate tectonics (Divergent plate boundaries)
　　P: 561
Seafood S: 264
　See also the list of Related articles in the Fishing
　　industry *article*
　Fish (The importance of fish) F: 146
　Fishing industry (How fish are processed and
　　marketed) F: 186 *with pictures*
Seaga, Edward [Jamaican political leader]
　Jamaica (History) J: 24-25
Seagram Building [New York City]
　Architecture (Ludwig Mies van der Rohe)
　　A: 631-632
　Mies van der Rohe, Ludwig M: 537
Seagull, The [book by Caballero]
　Spanish literature (The 1800's) So: 761-762

Seagull Monument [Salt Lake City]
　Salt Lake City (The city) S: 76
　Utah (Interesting facts) U: 231 *with picture*
Seahawks, Seattle [team] *See* Seattle Seahawks
　in this index
Seahorse [fish] S: 265 *with picture*
　Fish *picture on* F: 154
　Seadragon S: 264
Seal [sea animal] S: 265 *with pictures and map*
　Animal *pictures on* A: 500, A: 507
　Antarctica (Living things) A: 534-535 *with picture*
　Balance of nature (Upsetting the balance) B: 36
　Bering Sea controversy B: 258
　Elephant seal E: 232 *with picture*
　Fur (table) F: 561
　Hand (Animal hands) H: 40
　Inuit (Hunting and fishing) I: 354d; (Language)
　　I: 354f
　Mammal *picture on* M: 116
　Polar bear (Habits) P: 616
　Pribilof Islands P: 774
Seal [emblem] S: 268
　Persia, Ancient *picture on* P: 299
　World, History of the *picture on* W: 424
Seal Island [film]
　Disney, Walt (Full-length movies) D: 236
Seal of the President of the United States
　President of the United States *picture on* P: 758
Seal of the United States *See* Great Seal of the
　United States *in this index*
Sealant
　Acrylic A: 30
Seale, Bobby [American social reformer]
　African Americans (Black militancy) A: 136q-136r
　Black Panther Party B: 390
Sealer [paint]
　Paint (Household paints) P: 23-24
Sealift ship
　Navy, United States (Auxiliary ships) N: 84
SEALs [U.S. Navy] *See* Navy SEALs, United States *in*
　this index
Sealyham terrier [dog] S: 268
　Dog *picture on* D: 273
Seam [geology]
　Coal (How coal was formed) Ci: 720-721
Seam [sewing]
　Sewing (Seams) S: 332
Seaman [rank]
　Navy, United States (Training a sailor) N: 83
　Rank, Military (table) R: 140
　Ship (Officers and crew) S: 410
Seaman, Elizabeth Cochrane [real name of]
　Bly, Nellie B: 426
Seamanship
　Merchant marine (Careers in the merchant
　　marine) M: 413
　Sailing (Sailing a boat) S: 25 *with pictures*
Seamount [oceanography] S: 268 *with picture*
　Hot spot H: 374a
　Ocean (Deep-sea peaks, valleys, and plains)
　　O: 662
　Pacific Ocean (The ocean floor) P: 14
Seanad Éireann [Irish government]
　Ireland (Parliament) I: 417
Séance [spiritualism]
　Spiritualism (The medium) So: 796
Seaplane
　Airplane (Seaplanes) A: 212 *with picture*;
　　(Engineering improvements) A: 237
Seaplane base
　Airport (General aviation airports) A: 243
Seaport
　Harbor H: 55
　New York City (Trade) N: 333
　Port P: 680
Sear [device]
　Firearm (Mechanism) F: 132-133
Search, Right of
　Right of search R: 340
Search and rescue team
　Police (Other activities) P: 621
Search cost [economics]
　Industry (Search and switching costs) I: 260
Search engine [electronics] S: 268 *with picture*
　Google Inc. G: 270
　Internet (Search engines) I: 350a
　Yahoo! Inc. Y: 548
Search for Extraterrestrial Intelligence *See* SETI
　Institute *in this index*
Search term
　Search engine S: 268
Search warrant [law] S: 269
　Constitution of the United States (Amendment
　　4) Ci: 1012
　Warrant W: 37
Sears, Richard [American businessman]
　Sears, Roebuck and Co. S: 269

Sears Canada, Inc.
　Eaton, Timothy E: 48
Sears Holding Corp.
　Sears, Roebuck and Co. S: 269
Sears, Roebuck and Co. [U.S. company] S: 269
Sears Tower [Chicago] *See* Willis Tower *in this index*
Seascape [play by Albee]
　Albee, Edward A: 310
Seascape painting
　Painting (Landscapes and seascapes) P: 32
Seashore S: 269 *with pictures*
Seashore Trolley Museum [Kennebunkport]
　Maine (Places to visit) M: 78
Seasickness *See* Motion sickness *in this index*
Seaside and the Fireside, The [poems by
　Longfellow]
　Longfellow, Henry Wadsworth (Author and world
　　celebrity) L: 450
Seaside Park [Connecticut]
　Bridgeport B: 606
Seaside plantain [plant]
　Plantain P: 550
Season S: 270 *with diagram*
　Earth (How Earth moves) E: 17
　Weather (Air temperature) W: 157
Season [sports]
　Baseball (Regular season) B: 130
Season [tile]
　Mah-jongg M: 64 *with picture*
Season in Hell, A [book by Rimbaud]
　French literature (Symbolism) F: 522
　Rimbaud, Arthur R: 341
Seasonal affective disorder [psychology] S: 272
Seasonal migration
　Migration (Types of migration) M: 538
Seasonal unemployment
　Unemployment (Types of unemployment) U: 22
Seasonally dry tropical forest *See* Tropical dry
　forest *in this index*
Seasoning [cooking]
　Spice So: 781
Seasoning [industrial process]
　Leather *picture on* L: 168
　Lumber (Seasoning) L: 519
Seasons, The [book by Thomson]
　Thomson, James T: 264
Seatbelt
　Automobile *picture on* A: 970; (The passenger
　　compartment) A: 950-951
Seated Lincoln [sculpture by French]
　Lincoln Memorial *picture on* L: 328
SEATO [organization] *See* Southeast Asia Treaty
　Organization *in this index*
Seaton, Frederick A. [American government
　official]
　Eisenhower, Dwight David (table) E: 152
　Interior, Department of the (table) I: 325
Seattle [Washington] S: 272 *with pictures and maps*
　Washington W: 46 *with picture*; (Average monthly
　　weather) W: 61
Seattle Art Museum
　Seattle (Museums and libraries) S: 275
　Venturi, Robert *picture on* V: 310
Seattle Asian Art Museum
　Seattle (Museums and libraries) S: 275
Seattle Center
　Washington (Places to visit) W: 56
Seattle Mariners [team]
　Baseball (table) B: 130
　Griffey, Ken, Jr. G: 393
　Suzuki, Ichiro So: 1013
Seattle Public Library
　Seattle (Museums and libraries) S: 275 *with*
　　picture
Seattle Seahawks [team]
　Football (National Football League) F: 364
Seattle Slew [horse]
　Kentucky Derby K: 297
Seattle SuperSonics [team]
　Basketball (table) B: 150
Seaver, Tom [American baseball player]
　Baseball (table: Hall of Fame) B: 134b
Seawater
　Marine biology (What marine biologists do)
　　M: 204-205
　Ocean (Composition) O: 654
　Salt (Salt from the sea) S: 72
　Water (Fresh water from the sea) W: 127
Seawater, Purification of
　Water *diagrams on* W: 129; (Fresh water from the
　　sea) W: 127
Seaweed [plant] S: 276 *with pictures*
　Aquaculture A: 578
　Food *picture on* F: 332
　Sargasso Sea (Origin of the seaweed) S: 125
Seawise Giant [ship]
　Tanker (Kinds of tankers) T: 28

SeaWorld Orlando [Florida]
　Florida (Places to visit) F: 252 *with picture*
Seay, Thomas [American political leader]
　Alabama (table) A: 274
Sebaceous cyst [disorder]
　Wen W: 196
Sebaceous gland [anatomy]
　Acne A: 27 *with diagram*
　Gland (Exocrine glands) G: 207; (table) G: 209
　Hair *diagram on* H: 9; (Glands and muscles) H: 10
　Skin (Hair, nails, and glands) S: 489
Sebaste [ancient city]
　Samaria S: 77
Sebastian [literary figure]
　Shakespeare, William: (*Twelfth Night*) S: 360-361
Sebastian, Saint [Christian martyr] S: 277
Sebastiano del Piombo [Italian artist]
　Painting (The Renaissance in Venice) P: 55-56
　　with picture
Sebastopol [city, Ukraine] *See* Sevastopol *in this*
　index
Sebastopol [goose]
　Goose (Kinds of geese) G: 270-271
Sebelius, Kathleen [American political leader]
　Health and Human Services, Department of
　　(table) H: 128
　Kansas (table) K: 234
　Obama, Barack (table) O: 640h
Seberg, Jean [American actress]
　Motion picture *picture on* M: 871
Seborrheic dermatitis [disease]
　Dandruff D: 32
Sebum [physiology]
　Skin (Hair, nails, and glands) S: 489
SEC [organization] *See* Securities and Exchange
　Commission *in this index*
SECAM [electronics]
　Television (Camera scanning patterns) T: 122
Secant [geometry]
　Circle (Parts of a circle) Ci: 558
　Sphere So: 780
　Trigonometry (Right triangles) T: 443
Secession [U.S. history]
　Buchanan, James (Prelude to war) B: 661
　Confederate States of America Ci: 931
　Lincoln, Abraham (The South secedes) L: 320
　Nullification N: 603
　United States, History of the (The Secession) U: 177
Secession Building [Vienna]
　Architecture (Early modern architecture in
　　Europe) A: 627-628 *with picture*
Seclusion edicts [Japanese history]
　Japan (Tokugawa period) J: 55
Seconal [medication]
　Barbiturate (Medical uses) B: 107
　Drug abuse (table: Some commonly abused
　　drugs) D: 363
Second [combat]
　Duel D: 378
Second [time] S: 277
　Metric system (Structure of the metric system)
　　M: 437
　Minute M: 613
　Time (Units of time) T: 292
Second [unit of measure]
　Latitude L: 117
　Second S: 277
Second Amendment [U.S. Constitution] S: 278
　Constitution of the United States Ci: 1012
　Gun control (Opposition to gun control) G: 441
Second Balkan War *See* Balkan Wars *in this index*
Second Bank of the United States *See* Bank of the
　United States *in this index*
Second baseman
　Baseball (Player positions) B: 127
Second blessing [religion]
　Pentecostal churches (Major Pentecostal
　　churches) P: 275
Second British-Afghan War [1878-1881]
　India (British India) I: 130-131
Second Church [Boston]
　Mather, Increase M: 309
Second-class citizen
　Citizenship Ci: 569
Second-class lever
　Lever *picture on* L: 218; (Classes of levers) L: 217
　Machine (Lever) M: 14
Second Class Scout
　Boy Scouts (Second Class Scout) B: 537
Second Coming [religion]
　Adventists A: 70
　Pentecostal churches (Beliefs and practices)
　　P: 275
　Thessalonians, Epistles to the T: 257
　Wandering Jew W: 22
Second Continental Congress *See* Continental
　Congress *in this index*

Second cousin
Cousin Ci: 1105
Family (Family relationships) F: 21
Second-degree burn
Burn (Classification of burns) B: 708
First aid (Burns) F: 138
Nuclear weapon (Thermal radiation) N: 599
Skin (Burns) S: 490
Second-degree murder
Murder M: 930
Second Empire [French history]
France (The revolutions of 1830 and 1848) F: 474
Napoleon III (Becomes emperor) N: 17
Second estate [French history]
Estates-General E: 360
Second front [World War II]
Churchill, Sir Winston Leonard Spencer (Meetings with Roosevelt) C: 548
Second gear
Transmission (How a manual transmission works) T: 377-378 with diagram
Second hand smoke See Secondhand smoke in this index
Second Hittite Empire [Asian history] See Hittites in this index
Second Hundred Days [U.S. history]
New Deal (The Second Hundred Days) N: 201
Second Indochina War See Vietnam War in this index
Second International [organization]
Socialism (Moderate socialism) So: 561
Second intifada [uprising]
Israel (The early 2000's) I: 489
Second law of motion [physics]
Force (Acceleration) F: 369-370
Mass M: 268
Motion (Newton's laws of motion) M: 844
Second Mrs. Tanqueray, The [play by Pinero]
Pinero, Arthur Wing P: 473
Second Navigation Act [1663]
Navigation Acts N: 75
Second New Deal [U.S. history]
New Deal (The Second Hundred Days) N: 201
Roosevelt, Franklin Delano (Second New Deal) R: 453
Second of arc [measurement unit]
Surveying (Surveying tools) So: 1011
Second Punic War [218-201 B.C.] See Punic Wars in this index
Second Quorum of the Seventy
Mormons (Church organization) M: 807
Second Republic [French history]
France (The revolutions of 1830 and 1848) F: 474
Napoleon III (Becomes emperor) N: 17
Revolution of 1848 R: 288
Second Riel Rebellion See North West Rebellion in this index
Second Scroll, The [book by Klein]
Klein, A. M. K: 343
Second Seminole War See Seminole Wars in this index
Second Sex, The [book by Beauvoir]
Beauvoir, Simone de B: 191
French literature (The middle and late 1900's) F: 523
Second Sophistic Movement [literary movement]
Greek literature G: 378
Second strike capability
Nuclear weapon (Mutually assured destruction) N: 600
Second summer [weather]
Indian summer I: 189
Second Temple See Temple in Jerusalem in this index
Second Triumvirate See Triumvirate in this index
Second Vatican Council See Vatican Council II in this index
Second violin [music]
Orchestra (The musicians) O: 820
Second Virginia Convention [1775]
Jefferson, Thomas (Revolutionary leader) J: 79
Virginia (The course toward independence) V: 420
Second World
Third World (The political Third World) T: 258
Second World War See World War II in this index
Second World War [book by Churchill]
Churchill, Sir Winston Leonard Spencer (Leader of the opposition) C: 549
Secondary [device] See Rotor in this index
Secondary [football]
Football (The defensive team) F: 357-358 with diagrams
Secondary aluminum industry
Aluminum (The aluminum industry) A: 396
Secondary battery [electricity]
Battery B: 170 with diagram

Secondary boycott [labor]
Labor movement (Handling labor disputes) L: 6-7
Taft-Hartley Act T: 13
Secondary color
Color (Mixing colorants) Ci: 819-821 with diagram; (Producing color harmony) Ci: 823 with diagram
Secondary consumer
Ecology (Energy flow) E: 54
Forest (The flow of energy) F: 396
Secondary cosmic rays
Astronomy (Cosmic-ray astronomy) A: 846
Cosmic rays (Secondary cosmic rays) Ci: 1076 with diagram
Secondary crater [astronomy]
Moon (Craters) M: 789
Secondary data
Market research M: 214
Secondary education
See also High school in this index
Education (The organization of U.S. education) E: 90-92; (Education in other countries) E: 95
Junior high school J: 196
Language arts L: 67
Secondary electron [physics]
Electron microscope (Scanning electron microscopes) E: 204 with diagram
Secondary explosive
Improvised explosive device I: 95
Secondary fermentation [industrial process]
Champagne C: 373
Secondary fiber
Paper (How paper is made) P: 134
Secondary flight feather [bird]
Bird (Feathers) B: 362 with diagram
Secondary footprint [measurement]
Carbon footprint C: 207
Secondary headache
Headache H: 124
Secondary hypertension [disorder]
Blood pressure B: 416
Secondary industry
Industry (By stage of production) I: 256-257
Secondary infection [illness]
Influenza (Prevention and treatment) I: 268b
Secondary lymphoid organ [physiology]
Immune system (Lymphocytes) I: 87
Secondary market
Clothing (Marketing categories of fashion) Ci: 705
Secondary-modern school
England (Education) E: 297
Secondary mortgage market
Government National Mortgage Association G: 292
Secondary rainbow
Rainbow (How to find a rainbow) R: 127-128 with picture
Secondary recovery [industrial process]
Petroleum diagram on P: 341; (Secondary and tertiary recovery) P: 342
Secondary road
Road (Local and secondary roads) R: 357
Secondary root [botany]
Plant (Roots) P: 528 with pictures
Root (Kinds of roots) R: 469 with diagram
Secondary school
See also High school in this index
Education (The Renaissance) E: 100
School (High schools) S: 181
Secondary sewage treatment
Sewage (Urban sewerage systems) S: 329
Water pollution (Sewage treatment) W: 138
Secondary sexual characteristics [anatomy]
Adolescent (Sexual development) A: 61
Secondary source
History (The evidence) H: 260
Secondary strike
Strike (Kinds of strikes) So: 928
Secondary succession [biology]
Ecology (Changes in communities) E: 54
Secondary tissue [botany]
Root (Secondary tissues) R: 471 with diagram
Secondary wave [physics]
Earthquake (Body waves) E: 35
Secondary winding [electricity]
Transformer T: 371 with diagram
Secondat, Charles de [birth name of]
Montesquieu M: 764a
Secondhand smoke
Smoking (Secondhand smoke) S: 520
Secord, Laura Ingersoll [Canadian patriot] S: 278
Secret Army Organization [Algerian history]
France (France under de Gaulle) F: 476
Plastic explosive P: 553
Secret ballot [voting]
Ballot (In the United States) B: 63

Secret Diary [book by Byrd]
Byrd, William, II B: 747
Secret Garden
Seoul (The city) S: 304
Secret Garden, The [musical]
Norman, Marsha N: 455
Secret-key system [cryptology]
Codes and ciphers Ci: 749
"Secret Life of Walter Mitty, The" [story by Thurber]
Thurber, James T: 273
Secret police S: 278
Communism (The party state) Ci: 891
Gestapo G: 175
KGB K: 308a
Secret Service, United States S: 278
President of the United States (Guarding the president) P: 767
"Secret Sharer, The" [story by Conrad]
Conrad, Joseph Ci: 973
Secret writing See Codes and ciphers in this index
Secretarial work S: 278
Secretariat [government]
League of Nations (Powers and organization) L: 159
United Nations (The six major UN organs) U: 78 with diagram; (The Secretariat) U: 83
Secretariat [horse]
Horse racing (History) H: 366
Kentucky Derby K: 297
Secretariat [organization]
China (The Communist Party) C: 477
Communism (Communist party structures) Ci: 891
Union of Soviet Socialist Republics (Government) U: 29
Secretariat Building [New York City]
United Nations picture on U: 80
Secretariat of State [office]
Roman Catholic Church (The pope) R: 404
Secretary [office]
Parliamentary procedure (Officers) P: 175; (Minutes) P: 176
Secretary-bird [bird] S: 279
Animal picture on A: 477
Bird (Birds of Africa) B: 344h with picture
Bird of prey B: 374a
Secretary-general [office]
Address, Forms of (Foreign officials in the United States) A: 53
United Nations (The secretary-general) U: 83
Secretary hand [writing]
Handwriting picture on H: 50
Islamic art (Calligraphy) I: 468 with picture
Painting (Chinese painting) P: 44; (Islamic painting) P: 48
Secretary of ...
Secretaries of executive departments appear under their key words, as in State, Secretary of
Secretory cell [biology]
Fallopian tube F: 18
Sectarian Shinto
Religion (Shinto) R: 221-222
Section [unit of measure]
Public lands (Management of public lands) P: 858
Sectional form [music]
Classical music (Sectional form) Ci: 644
Sectionalism [U.S. history]
Civil War, American (The sectional division) Ci: 615
Sector [economics]
Industry (The North American Industry Classification System [NAICS]) I: 257; (Sectors of industry) I: 258
Secular humanism
Humanism (Later influence) H: 431
Secular institutes [religion]
Dominicans D: 305
Secularism [philosophy]
Christianity (Christianity today) C: 526-527
Liberalism (Features of liberalism) L: 228
Political science (Secularism) P: 639
Turkey (Religion) T: 506
Secularization Act [1833]
Mission life in America (Western missions) M: 618-619
Secure transaction [business]
E-commerce (Business-to-consumer transactions) E: 2
Secured debt
Bankruptcy (Features of bankruptcy) B: 97
Debt D: 65
Secured loan See Secured debt in this index
Securing the crime scene [criminology]
Crime scene investigation (Beginning an investigation) Ci: 1140 with picture
Forensic science (Crime scene investigations)

F: 388b
Securities [banking] *See* Security *in this index*
Securities and Exchange Commission [U.S.]
S: 279
Great Depression (The New Deal) G: 341-342
Industry (Lack of information) I: 261
Insider trading I: 303
New Deal (Helping savers and investors) N: 200-201
New York Stock Exchange N: 345
Securities Exchange Act S: 279
Stock exchange (Regulation) So: 904
Securities Exchange Act [1934] S: 279
Investment banking I: 369
Security [investment]
See also Bond; Stock *in this index*
Accounting (The history of accounting) A: 23
Engraving and Printing, Bureau of E: 326a
Investment (Indirect investments) I: 367-368
Mortgage M: 820
National debt (Budget deficit financing and the national debt) N: 33
Securities and Exchange Commission S: 279
Securities Exchange Act S: 279
Security [safety]
See also Computer security *in this index*
Airport (Airport security) A: 247 *with picture*
Homeland Security, Department of H: 301
Library (Security) L: 238
Terrorism (Security measures) T: 177
Transportation (Transportation security) T: 398
Security Police [Air Force]
Military police M: 543
Sedan, Battle of [1870]
Franco-Prussian War (Progress of the war) F: 483
Napoleon III (His defeat) N: 17
Sedative [medication] S: 279
Barbiturate B: 107
Drug (Antianxiety and hypnotic drugs) D: 352
Seddon, James Alexander [Confederate government official] S: 279
Seddon, Margaret R. [American astronaut]
Astronaut (A look at the astronauts) A: 831
Seder [religion]
Judaism *picture on* J: 179
Passover P: 192
Religion *picture on* R: 217
Sedge [plant] S: 279
Sedge wren [bird]
Wren W: 504
Sedgemoor, Battle of [1685]
Monmouth, Duke of M: 730
Sedges, John [pen name]
Buck, Pearl S. B: 663
Sediment [geology]
Climate (Determining past climates) Ci: 678-679
Dam (The effects of dams) D: 17
Earth (History of Earth) E: 25
Estuary E: 364
Flood (River floods) F: 236-237
Fossil F: 422
Ice age (Evidence of ice ages and their climates) I: 6
Ocean (Sediments) O: 654; (Deep-sea peaks, valleys, and plains) O: 662
Rock (Sedimentary rock) R: 372
Silt S: 463
Taconite T: 5
Sediment core [climatology]
Climate (Pollen) Ci: 679
Sedimentary basin [geology]
Coal (Where coal is found) Ci: 721
Sedimentary beach
Beach B: 178
Sedimentary breccia [rock]
Rock (Clastic sediments) R: 372
Sedimentary rock [geology] S: 280
Coal (The composition of coal) Ci: 717; (How coal was formed) Ci: 720 *with pictures*
Earth (Earth's rocks) E: 20-21 *with picture*
Fossil F: 422 *with diagram*
Gem (Sources of gems) G: 77-79
Mountain (Volcanic mountains) M: 892; (Tectonic mountains) M: 893
Paleobotany P: 102
Paleontology P: 103
Petroleum (How petroleum deposits form) P: 333
Rock (Sedimentary rock) R: 372 *with pictures*; (The rock cycle) R: 373
Sedimentation tank
Sewage (Primary treatment) S: 329; (Secondary treatment) S: 330
Sedition [law] S: 280
Alien and Sedition Acts A: 368
Freedom of the press F: 507
Sedition Act [1918]
Flynn, Elizabeth Gurley F: 313

Freedom of speech (In the United States) F: 506
Sedition S: 280
Sedition Acts [1798] *See* Alien and Sedition Acts *in this index*
Sedley, Amelia [literary figure]
Thackeray, William Makepeace (Later career) T: 220
Sedna [Inuit goddess]
Inuit (Religion) I: 354e
Sedna [space object]
Planet (The outer dwarf planets) P: 512
Sedum [botany] S: 280
Plant *picture on* P: 524
See, Holy [religion]
Pope P: 660
"See It Now" [television show]
Journalism (Television journalism) J: 175
Murrow, Edward R. M: 932
Seebeck, Thomas Johann [German physicist]
Thermocouple T: 253
Seed [botany] S: 280 *with pictures*
Agriculture (Food from plants) A: 147
Angiosperm A: 462 *with picture*
Cotyledon Ci: 1095
Flower F: 271; (Fertilization) F: 296
Fruit F: 544
Gardening (Planting and transplanting) G: 34
Germination G: 172
Gymnosperm G: 451 *with pictures*
Plant (Vascular plants) P: 518-520 *with picture*; (Seeds) P: 531 *with pictures*; (Sexual reproduction) P: 532-533 *with diagrams*; (The growth of plants) P: 535 *with picture*; (How plants protect themselves) P: 540-541
Reproduction (Plants) R: 243
Tree (Seeds) T: 417 *with pictures*; (How seeds sprout into trees) T: 418
Vegetable (Seeds) V: 292 *with picture*
Seed [glassmaking]
Glass (Glass terms) G: 222
Seed [medicine]
Cancer (Radiation therapy) C: 172
Seed, The [sculpture by Noguchi]
Noguchi, Isamu *picture on* N: 451
Seed bank [agriculture]
Agriculture (Preserving genetic diversity) A: 160
Plant *pictures on* P: 543; (Conservation efforts) P: 544
Seed coat [botany]
Corn (How the plant develops) Ci: 1057 *with diagram*
Cotton (Cottonseeds) Ci: 1086
Plant (Seeds) P: 532 *with pictures*; (Germination) P: 535-536 *with picture*
Seed (The parts of a seed) S: 281 *with diagrams*
Seed cone [botany]
Plant (Gymnosperms) P: 520; (Sexual reproduction) P: 532-535 *with diagram*
Seed (Seed development in gymnosperms) S: 281-282
Seed cotton [fiber]
Cotton *picture on* Ci: 1088; (Harvesting) Ci: 1090-1091
Seed drill [farm machine] *See* Drill *in this index*
Seed flax [plant]
Flax (Growing and processing seed flax) F: 231 *with picture*
Seed head [botany]
Switchgrass So: 1049 *with picture*
Seed hemp [plant]
Hemp H: 183
Seed lac [zoology]
Lac L: 19
Seed piece [botany]
Potato (The potato plant) P: 712
Seed plant
Plant (Kinds of plants) P: 518-520 *with pictures*; (Sexual reproduction) P: 532-533
Seed potato
Potato (Planting and cultivating) P: 712
Seed spike [botany]
Rye R: 573 *with picture*
Seed tree cutting
Forestry (Harvesting) F: 404 *with picture*
Seed tuber [botany]
Potato (The potato plant) P: 712
Seedball [botany]
Potato (The potato plant) P: 712
Seedbed [agriculture]
Farm and farming (Preparing the soil) F: 35
Seeding [gardening]
Lawn (Growing and maintaining a lawn) L: 144
Vegetable (Planting) V: 293
Seeding [tennis]
Tennis (Tennis tournaments) T: 165
Seeding agent [meteorology]
Cloud seeding C: 711

Seedless raisin
Raisin (Varieties) R: 129
Seedling [botany]
Transplanting T: 381
Tree (How a tree grows) T: 418
Seedling disease
Cotton (Diseases) Ci: 1090
Seeger, Pete [American musician] S: 283
Seegloo [Inuit explorer]
Exploration (The North Pole) E: 450
Seeing Eye, Incorporated [organization]
Guide dog G: 422
Seeing eye dog *See* Guide dog *in this index*
Seeiso [Lesotho prince]
Lesotho (History) L: 208
Seekonk River
Rhode Island (Rivers and lakes) R: 306 *with map*
Seeley, Elias P. [American political leader]
New Jersey (table) N: 249
Seelisberg Tunnel [Switzerland]
Tunnel (table) T: 491
Seepage [geology]
Irrigation (Bringing irrigation water to farms) I: 457
Seesaw [playground equipment]
Gravity, Center of G: 333
Sefer ha-Kuzari [book by Halevi]
Halevi, Judah H: 19
Seferis, George [Greek poet]
Greek literature (Modern Greek literature) G: 378
Nobel Prizes (Literature: 1963) N: 447
Sefström, Nils [Swedish chemist]
Vanadium V: 268
Sefuwa [African rulers]
Kanem K: 213
Sega Genesis console
Electronic game (The Nintendo revolution) E: 204d-204e
Segal, George [American sculptor] S: 284 *with picture*
Segmented mirror
Telescope (Reflecting telescopes) T: 104-105
Segmented worm
Animal (A classification of the animal kingdom) A: 506 *with picture*
Earthworm E: 39 *with pictures*
Invertebrate I: 366
Worm (Segmented worms) W: 501 *with pictures*
Sego lily [plant]
Mariposa lily M: 212
Segovia [Spain]
Castle *picture on* C: 281
Segovia, Andrés [Spanish guitarist] S: 284
Segrè, Emilio Gino [American physicist]
Astatine A: 823
Nobel Prizes (Physics: 1959) N: 441
Physics (Advances in the mid-1900's) P: 442
Technetium T: 73
Segregation [sociology] S: 284 *with picture*
See also Apartheid; Discrimination *in this index*
African Americans (The growth of discrimination) A: 136k; (The civil rights movement) A: 136o
Apartheid A: 563
Bridges, Ruby B: 607
Freedom riders F: 508
Ghetto G: 181
Jim Crow J: 126
Plessy v. Ferguson P: 573
Reconstruction (New state programs and policies) R: 179
South Africa So: 608
Tennessee (The mid-1900's) T: 156
Desegregation and integration
Boycott B: 539
Civil rights (The struggle for the rights of African Americans) Ci: 609
Jazz (The swing era) J: 71
King, Martin Luther, Jr. (The early civil rights movement) K: 321
Massachusetts (The mid-1900's) M: 293
Montgomery bus boycott M: 767
New York City (Social problems) N: 332-333
Parks, Rosa Louise P: 171
School integration
Alabama (The mid-1900's) A: 278
Arkansas (The mid-1900's) A: 714
Brown v. Board of Education of Topeka B: 645
Education (Education for whom?) E: 107
Eisenhower, Dwight David (Civil rights) E: 153-154
Louisiana (The mid-1900's) L: 500
Meredith, James Howard M: 416
Nixon, Richard Milhous (The national scene) N: 433-434
States' rights (Later developments) So: 866
Virginia (School integration) V: 422
Wallace, George Corley W: 16

Segregation, Law of [genetics]
Heredity (Mendel's laws) **H: 208**
Mendel, Gregor Johann (His work) **M: 398**
Segregation cell [construction]
Prison (Prison cells) **P: 806**
Sehna knot
Rugs and carpets (Oriental rugs) **R: 516** *with diagram*
Sei Shonagon [Japanese author]
Japanese literature (The Heian period) **J: 61-62**
Sei whale [sea animal] **S: 286**
Whale (Rorquals) **W: 255-258** *with picture*
Seibert, T. Laurence [American entertainer]
Jones, Casey **J: 157**
Seiche [wave] **S: 287** *with diagrams*
Flood (Other floods) **F: 237-238**
Seidel, Emil [American political leader]
Milwaukee (The 1900's) **M: 561**
Seif dune [geology]
Desert (Desert climate and land) **D: 155-156**
Seifert, Jaroslav [Czech author]
Nobel Prizes (Literature: 1984) **N: 448**
Seigneur [title]
Seigneurial system **S: 287**
Seigneurial system [Canadian history] **S: 287**
Canada, History of (The royal province) **C: 140**
Seigneury [land]
Seigneurial system **S: 287**
Seigniorial system *See* Seigneurial system *in this index*
Seikan Tunnel [Japan]
Japan (Transportation) **J: 51**
Tunnel (table) **T: 491**
Seine [net]
Fishing industry (Nets) **F: 183**
Seine River [France] **S: 287** *with picture*
Paris *picture on* **P: 160**; (The city) **P: 161-162** *with map*
River (table) **R: 352**
Seiner [boat]
Fishing industry (Nets) **F: 183** *with diagram*
Seinfeld, Jerry [American comedian]
Television (The 1980's and 1990's) **T: 120**
Seismic prospecting
Prospecting **P: 829**
Seismic station
Earthquake (Measuring earthquakes) **E: 38a**
Seismic studies
Petroleum (Geophysical studies) **P: 336**
Seismic tomography [measurement]
Earthquake (Using earthquakes to study Earth's interior) **E: 38b**
Seismic wave [geology]
Earthquake *diagrams on* **E: 34**; (How an earthquake spreads) **E: 37**; (Using earthquakes to study Earth's interior) **E: 38b**
Oscilloscope **O: 862**
Seismology **S: 288**
Tsunami **T: 476**
Seismograph [instrument] **S: 287** *with picture*
Earthquake (Measuring earthquakes) **E: 38a** *with picture*
Gas [fuel] (Exploring for gas) **G: 53**
Moment magnitude **M: 698**
Petroleum **P: 338** *with diagram*
Richter magnitude **R: 334**
Seismology **S: 288**
Tsunami **T: 476**
Seismologist [scientist]
Earthquake *picture on* **E: 38a**
Seismograph **S: 287**
Seismology **S: 288**
Seismology [geology] **S: 288**
See also Earthquake *in this index*
Moment magnitude **M: 697**
Seismograph **S: 287**
Seismometer [instrument]
Earthquake **E: 33**; (Measuring earthquakes) **E: 38a**
Mars (Interior) **M: 225**
Seismosaurus [dinosaur] **S: 288**
Dinosaur *picture on* **D: 206a**; (True dinosaurs) **D: 206b-209**
Prehistoric animal (Dinosaurs) **P: 737**
SEIU [organization] *See* Service Employees International Union *in this index*
Seizure [disorder]
Anticonvulsant **A: 553**
Epilepsy **E: 343**
Sejm [government]
Poland (National government) **P: 604**; (Free elections) **P: 614**
Sejong [king of Korea]
Alphabet (Other alphabets) **A: 383-384**
Sekeletu [African king]
Stanley and Livingstone (Livingstone's discoveries) **So: 837**

Selaginella [plant]
Plant *picture on* **P: 522**; (Lycophytes) **P: 518**; (Classification of plants) **P: 546**
Selassie, Haile [Ethiopian emperor] *See* Haile Selassie I *in this index*
Selby, Douglas [literary figure]
Gardner, Erle Stanley **G: 39**
Select committee
House of Representatives (Committees) **H: 387**
United States, Government of the (Committee system) **U: 138**
Select grade [agriculture]
Beef (Grades of beef) **B: 209**
Meat packing (Quality grading) **M: 351**
Selected Poems [book by Dove]
Dove, Rita **D: 315**
Selected Poems [book by Eberhart]
Eberhart, Richard **E: 48**
Selected reservist [occupation]
Navy, United States (The active-duty Navy and reserves) **N: 85**
Selected United States Government Publications [reference]
A Guide to Research Skills **Research Guide: 34**
Selection [biology] *See* Artificial selection; Natural selection *in this index*
Selection acts [Australian history]
Australia (Land reform) **A: 922-923**
Selection cutting
Forestry (Harvesting) **F: 404** *with picture*
Selection trial
Olympic Games (Selection of the athletes) **O: 746c**
Selective breeding *See* Breeding *in this index*
Selective estrogen receptor modulator [hormone]
Hormone replacement therapy **H: 338**
Selective herbicide
Vegetable (Pest control) **V: 293**
Selective posterior rhizotomy [surgery]
Cerebral palsy (Treatment) **C: 361-362**
Selective serotonin reuptake inhibitor [drug]
Antidepressant **A: 553**
Mental illness (Somatic therapy) **M: 407**
Selective Service Act [1917]
Army, United States (World War I) **A: 738-739**
Selective Service Act [1940]
Army, United States (World War II) **A: 739**
Selective Service System [U.S.] **S: 289**
Selective toxicity
Chemotherapy **C: 407**
Selectivity [electronics]
Radio (The tuner) **R: 88-89**
Selectman [office]
Maine (Local government) **M: 88**
Selector [device]
Transmission (How an automatic transmission works) **T: 376**
Selee, Frank [American baseball manager]
Baseball (table: Hall of Fame) **B: 134b**
Selegiline [drug]
Parkinson disease (Treatment with drugs) **P: 170-171**
Selena [American singer] **S: 289**
Selene [Greek mythology] **S: 289**
Endymion **E: 273**
SELENE [spacecraft]
Moon (Recent exploration) **M: 795**
Selenite [mineral]
Gypsum **G: 451**
Selenium [element] **S: 289**
Seles, Monica [American tennis player] **S: 289**
Seleucia [ancient city]
Babylon (The fall of Babylon) **B: 13**
Seleucid dynasty [Asian history] **S: 289**
Jews (The Hellenistic period) **J: 121** *with map*
Judah Maccabee **J: 179**
Palestine (Invasions and conquests) **P: 104**
Persia, Ancient (The Seleucid dynasty) **P: 298**
Seleucus I [Seleucid king]
Babylon (The fall of Babylon) **B: 13**
Persia, Ancient (The Seleucid dynasty) **P: 298**
Seleucid dynasty **S: 289**
Self [book by Martel]
Martel, Yann **M: 233**
Self [philosophy]
Hume, David (Hume's thought) **H: 432**
Self-acting principle [engineering]
Nasmyth, James **N: 24**
Self-actualization [psychology]
Maslow, Abraham Harold **M: 265**
Personality (Ratings and self-reports) **P: 301**
Self-assembly [process]
Nanotechnology (Making nanoscale objects) **N: 11**
Self coat
Cat (Coat) **C: 287** *with picture*

Self-contained classroom
Education (Elementary education) **E: 91**
Elementary school (Elementary school instruction) **E: 224-225**
Self-contained underwater breathing apparatus
See Scuba diving *in this index*
Self-deception
Existentialism (What is Existentialism?) **E: 437**
Sartre, Jean-Paul **S: 127**
Self-defense
Homicide **H: 305**
Judo **J: 184**
Karate **K: 245**
Martial arts **M: 234**
Self-determination [policy]
Indian Affairs, Bureau of **I: 185**
Indian reservation (History) **I: 189**
Nationalism (The rise of nationalism) **N: 62**
Self-directed education
Adult education (Informal adult education) **A: 69**
Universities and colleges (Instruction) **U: 209-210L**
Self-enumerated census
Census (Conducting censuses) **C: 347-348**
Self-esteem
Adolescent (Identity and self-esteem) **A: 62**
Child (The school-age years) **C: 449-450**
Self-excited generator
Electric generator (Kinds of DC generators) **E: 173**
Self-fertilization [zoology]
Hermaphrodite **H: 211**
Self-fruitful tree
Cherry **C: 410**
Self-governing area
Commonwealth of Nations (Dependencies) **Ci: 876**
Self Government Committee of St. Croix
Virgin Islands, United States (Recent developments) **V: 397**
Self-help magazine [publication]
Magazine (Consumer magazines) **M: 42**
Self-hypnosis
Hypnosis (Modifying thoughts and behaviors) **H: 479**
Self-image [psychology]
Child (The early school years) **C: 449-450**
Self-incrimination [law]
Evidence (Privilege) **E: 426**
Self-inductance [electricity]
Inductance **I: 240**
Self-insured plan
Insurance (Self-insured plans) **I: 312**
Self-pollination [botany]
Flower (Self-pollination) **F: 296**
Plant (Sexual reproduction) **P: 532-533**
Pollen (Methods of pollination) **P: 644**
Self-Portrait [painting by Dürer]
Painting (Albrecht Dürer) **P: 58** *with picture*
Self-Portrait [painting by Van Gogh]
Van Gogh, Vincent **V: 282** *with picture*
"Self-Portrait in a Convex Mirror" [poem by Ashbery]
Ashbery, John **A: 767**
Self-Portrait with Thorn Necklace and Hummingbird [painting by Kahlo]
Painting (Modern Mexican painting) **P: 83** *with picture*
Self-publishing
Publishing (Self-publishing) **P: 869**; (The power of published ideas) **P: 869**
Self-rake reaper [machine]
Reaper **R: 173**
Self-reflexive fiction
American literature (Experimental styles) **A: 425**
"Self-Reliance" [essay by Emerson]
Emerson, Ralph Waldo **E: 258**
Self-reliance course
Camp Fire USA (Self-reliance courses) **C: 89**
Self-similarity [geometry]
Fractal **F: 443**
Self-supported mining
Mining (Underground mining methods) **M: 576**
Self-unfruitful tree [botany]
Cherry **C: 410**
Plum (Growing plums) **P: 577**
Self-winding watch
Watch (Mechanical watches) **W: 114**
Selfish gene theory [biology]
Dawkins, Richard **D: 51**
Selfridge, Thomas [American military leader]
Airplane (Other pioneer planes and fliers) **A: 233-234**
Wright brothers (Exhibitions and accident) **W: 509-510**
Seligman, Arthur [American political leader]
New Mexico (table) **N: 272**
Selinger, Greg [Canadian political leader]

Manitoba (table) **M:** 159
Seljuks [ancient people] **S:** 290
  Iran (The rise of Islam) **I:** 405
  Osman I **O:** 865
  Palestine (Arab control) **P:** 104-105
  Turkey (The Seljuk Turks) **T:** 509
  Turks **T:** 514b
Selkirk, Alexander [Scottish sailor]
  Robinson Crusoe **R:** 369
Selkirk, Earl of [British philanthropist] **S:** 290
  Assiniboia **A:** 818
  Manitoba (The Red River Colony) **M:** 160
Selkirk Mountains [British Columbia] **S:** 290
  British Columbia (Land regions) **B:** 622
Selkirk rex cat
  Cat (Short-haired breeds) **C:** 290-291
Sellers, Peter [British actor]
  Motion picture *picture on* **M:** 871
Selling *See* Sales *in this index*
Selling price [economics]
  Percentage (Profits) **P:** 282
Selling short [economics]
  Cornering the market **Ci:** 1065
Sells Brothers Circus
  Circus *picture on* **Ci:** 563
Selma [Alabama]
  African Americans *picture on* **A:** 136t
  Alabama *picture on* **A:** 267
  Selma marches **S:** 290
Selma marches [U.S. history] **S:** 290 *with picture*
  African Americans (Political gains) **A:** 136p
  Bloody Sunday (In the United States) **B:** 418
  Voting Rights Act of 1965 **V:** 451
Selous Game Reserve [Tanzania]
  National park (table) **N:** 42f
  Tanzania (Animal life) **T:** 33 *with map*
Selsam, Millicent Ellis [American author] **S:** 291
Selten, Reinhard [German economist]
  Nobel Prizes (Economics: 1994) **N:** 449
Selva [region]
  Brazil (The Amazon Region) **B:** 577
  Peru (Indigenous people) **P:** 309 *with picture*;
    (Food) **P:** 310; (The Selva) **P:** 311-313 *with*
    picture and map
  South America (The Central Plains) **So:** 628
Selvagens [islands, Madeira]
  Madeira Islands **M:** 30
Selwyn Mountains [Canada]
  Rocky Mountains (Chief ranges of the Rockies)
    R: 394
Selye, Hans [Canadian physiologist]
  Stress (How stress affects the body) **So:** 926
Selznick, Brian [American author/illustrator]
  Caldecott Medal (table: 2008) **C:** 26
Semantic clue
  Reading (Comprehending what is perceived)
    R: 157
Semantics [language] **S:** 291
  Linguistics (The components of a grammar)
    L: 336
Semaphore [signal] **S:** 291
  Flag *picture on* **F:** 197; (Flags that talk) **F:** 208
  Signaling (Visual and sound signals) **S:** 454
  Telegraph (Development of the telegraph) **T:** 90
Semele [Greek mythology]
  Dionysus **D:** 215
Semen [physiology]
  Penis **P:** 241
  Pregnancy (Becoming pregnant) **P:** 734a
  Prostate gland **P:** 830
  Reproduction, Human (The human reproductive
    system) **R:** 244-246
  Vasectomy **V:** 287
Semenov, Nikolai N. [Soviet chemist]
  Nobel Prizes (Chemistry: 1956) **N:** 443
Semester [education]
  Universities and colleges (The academic
    calendar) **U:** 209
Semi [truck] *See* Tractor-semitrailer *in this index*
Semiarid climate
  Climate (Semiarid and desert climates) **Ci:** 676b
Semiautomatic gun
  Gun control (Approaches to gun control) **G:** 440-
    441
  Handgun (Types of handguns) **H:** 43
  Rifle (Kinds of rifles) **R:** 338 *with picture*
Semiblock form
  Letter writing (The form) **L:** 211 *with picture*
Semicircle
  Circle (Parts of a circle) **Ci:** 558
Semicircular canal [anatomy]
  Ear (The inner ear) **E:** 8 *with diagram*; (The sense
    of balance) **E:** 11 *with diagrams*
Semicolon
  Punctuation (The semicolon) **P:** 902
Semiconductor [electronics] **S:** 291 *with diagrams*
  Computer chip (Structure) **Ci:** 924e

Diamond (Synthetic diamonds) **D:** 183
Electric current (Conductors and insulators)
  E: 168
Electricity (Conductors and insulators) **E:** 193;
  (Semiconductors) **E:** 193
Electronics (Types of electronic circuits) **E:** 209-
  210; (Active components) **E:** 210 *with diagram*;
  (The solid-state revolution) **E:** 216
Germanium **G:** 143
Insulator, Electric **I:** 308
Laser (Semiconductor lasers) **L:** 85
Light (Refraction) **L:** 288; (Photoelectric effect)
  L: 291
Light-emitting diode **L:** 293
Materials (Semiconductors) **M:** 301
Physics (Solid-state physics) **P:** 438
Transistor (Transistor materials) **T:** 372
Semiconductor laser [physics]
  Electronics (Light-emitting devices) **E:** 213
  Laser (Semiconductor lasers) **L:** 85 *with diagram*
Semidiurnal tide
  Tide (The equilibrium tide) **T:** 280-282
Semidrying oil
  Oil (Fixed oils) **O:** 706
Semifixed ammunition
  Ammunition (Artillery ammunition) **A:** 435-436
Semilunar valve [anatomy]
  Heart (Chambers, valves, and inner lining) **H:** 133-
    135 *with picture*
Semimetal *See* Metalloid *in this index*
Seminal vesicle [anatomy]
  Gland (table) **G:** 209
  Human body (table) **H:** 422 *with diagram*
  Prostate gland **P:** 830
  Reproduction, Human (The human reproductive
    system) **R:** 244-245 *with diagram*
Seminar
  Universities and colleges (Instruction) **U:** 209
Seminary [education] **S:** 292
Seminary of Quebec
  Laval de Montmorency, François Xavier de **L:** 128
  Laval University **L:** 128
Seminiferous tubule [anatomy]
  Reproduction, Human (The human reproductive
    system) **R:** 244-245
  Testicle **T:** 182
Seminole Indians **S:** 292 *with picture*
  Black Seminole **B:** 391
  Creek Indians **Ci:** 1125
  Florida (Territorial days) **F:** 262
  Indian, American *pictures on* **I:** 156, **I:** 158, **I:** 180;
    (Indians of the Southeast) **I:** 157
  Indian Territory **I:** 189 *with map*
  Indian wars (Conflicts in the South) **I:** 192
Seminole Wars [U.S. history]
  Indian wars (The Seminole) **I:** 192
  Seminole Indians **S:** 292
  First Seminole War
    Florida (The second Spanish period) **F:** 262
    Monroe, James (War with the Seminole) **M:** 737
  Second Seminole War
    Florida (Territorial days) **F:** 262
    Osceola **O:** 862
Seminoma [disease]
  Testicular cancer **T:** 182
Semiotics [literature]
  Criticism (History of literary criticism) **Ci:** 1146-
    1147
Semipalmated plover [bird]
  Plover **P:** 574 *with picture*
Semipermeable membrane [biology]
  Osmosis **O:** 865 *with diagrams*
Semipostal [stamp]
  Stamp collecting (Special stamps) **So:** 830
Semiprofessional videotape recorder
  Videotape recorder (Types of videotape
    recorders) **V:** 360
Semiramis [legendary figure] **S:** 293
Semiregular convex polyhedron
  Archimedean solid **A:** 604 *with diagram*
Semisubmersible rig [device]
  Petroleum *picture on* **P:** 333, *diagram on* **P:** 340
Semi-subsistence agriculture
  Agriculture (Agricultural practices) **A:** 148-149
Semisweet chocolate
  Chocolate (Dark chocolate) **C:** 519
Semisynthetic penicillin [medication]
  Ampicillin **A:** 443
  Penicillin (Forms of penicillin) **P:** 240
Semi-terete hybrid orchid [plant]
  Orchid *picture on* **O:** 824
Semites [people] **S:** 293
  See also the list of Related articles in the Semites
    article
  Asia (The people) **A:** 778
  Babylonia (Language and literature) **B:** 13; (The
    Akkadian and Neo-Sumerian periods) **B:** 14

Ebla **E:** 49
Mesopotamia **M:** 422
Sargon of Akkad **S:** 126
World, History of the (The Tigris-Euphrates Valley)
  W: 422-424
Semitic languages **S:** 293
  Alphabet (Semitic scripts) **A:** 381 *with pictures*
  Egypt, Ancient (The people) **E:** 136
  Hebrew language **H:** 161
Semivegetarianism
  Vegetarianism **V:** 294
Semliki River [Africa]
  Lake Edward **L:** 37
Semlin, Charles A. [Canadian political leader]
  British Columbia (table) **B:** 628
Semmelweis, Ignaz Philipp [Hungarian doctor]
  Antiseptic (History) **A:** 559
  Medicine (Antiseptic surgery) **M:** 375
Semmes, Raphael [Confederate admiral] **S:** 293
  Alabama **A:** 255
Semolina [flour]
  Pasta **P:** 192
Sempach, Battle of [1386]
  Switzerland *picture on* **So:** 1059
  Winkelried, Arnold von **W:** 339
Semper Fidelis [motto]
  Marine Corps, United States **M:** 206
"**Semper Fidelis**" [music by Sousa]
  Marine Corps, United States **M:** 206
Sempervivum [plant]
  Succulent *picture on* **So:** 951
Semple, Ellen Churchill [American geographer]
  Geography (The growth of geography) **G:** 96
Semple, Jesse B. [fictional character]
  Hughes, Langston **H:** 409
Semple, Letitia Tyler [daughter of]
  Tyler, John (Life in the White House) **T:** 534
  White House hostesses **W:** 291
Semple, Robert [British colonial official]
  Manitoba (The Red River Colony) **M:** 160
Sen [money]
  Yen **Y:** 564
Senanayake, D. S. [Sri Lankan political leader]
  Sri Lanka (History) **So:** 819
Senanayake, Dudley [Sri Lankan political leader]
  Sri Lanka (History) **So:** 819
Senate [government] **S:** 294 *with pictures*
  Australia (The federal government) **A:** 895
  Canada, Government of (The Senate) **C:** 130;
    (How a bill becomes law in Canada) **C:** 132-133
    with diagrams
  Poland (Government) **P:** 604; (Free elections)
    P: 614
  Rome, Ancient (Government) **R:** 438
  State government (Organization) **So:** 863
Senate, President of the
  Vice president of the United States (President of
    the Senate) **V:** 352
Senate, United States
  Congress of the United States (The Senate)
    Ci: 942; (table) **Ci:** 943; (Passing a bill) **Ci:** 945
  Address, Forms of (Officials of the United States)
    A: 53
  Capitol, United States **C:** 197
  Constitution of the United States (Article
    I) **Ci:** 1004; (Amendment 12) **Ci:** 1013;
    (Amendment 17) **Ci:** 1014
  Impeachment (Procedure) **I:** 90
  Senate **S:** 294 *with pictures*
  United States, Government of the (The legislative
    branch) **U:** 138; (How a bill becomes law in the
    United States) **U:** 141
  Washington, D.C. *map on* **W:** 76
Senate Chamber [Washington, D.C.]
  Capitol, United States **C:** 197
  Senate *picture on* **S:** 294
Senate *Journal* [publication]
  Constitution of the United States (Article I,
    Section 5) **Ci:** 1006
Senate Square [Finland]
  Helsinki **H:** 179
Senator [office]
  See also Senate; Senate, United States *in this index*
  Address, Forms of (Officials of the
    Commonwealth of Nations) **A:** 53; (Officials of
    the United States) **A:** 53
  Congress of the United States (table) **Ci:** 943;
    (Members of Congress at work) **Ci:** 946
  Senate (Membership of the U.S. Senate) **S:** 294
Senatorial courtesy
  Senate (Other powers and duties) **S:** 295
Senators, Ottawa
  Hockey (table: National Hockey League) **H:** 281
Senatus Populusque Romanus [motto]
  Rome, Ancient (The Roman Republic) **R:** 444
Send Bygraves [book by Grimes]
  Grimes, Martha **G:** 393

Sendak, Maurice [American author] **S:** 296
  Literature for children *picture on* **L:** 356
Sender [parapsychology]
  Extrasensory perception (Early ESP research)
  E: 457
Sending [spell]
  Witchcraft (Witchcraft as sorcery) **W:** 371
Seneca, Lucius Annaeus [Roman author] **S:** 296
  Drama (Tragedy) **D:** 328; (Elizabethan
    playwrights) **D:** 331
  Geology (The Romans) **G:** 98
  Latin literature (The Imperial Period) **L:** 116
Seneca Chief [ship]
  Erie Canal **E:** 351
Seneca Indians S: 296
  Girty, Simon **G:** 201
  Handsome Lake **H:** 46
  Indian, American (Indians of the Northeast) **I:** 154
  Iroquois Indians **I:** 455
Seneca Lake [New York]
  Finger Lakes **F:** 104
Seneca Nation of Indians [political group]
  Seneca Indians **S:** 297
Senefelder, Alois [German inventor] **S:** 297
  Printing (Offset lithography) **P:** 798
  Printing press **P:** 804
Senegal S: 297 *with pictures and map*
  Clothing *picture on* **Ci:** 692
  Flag *picture on* **F:** 199
  Food *picture on* **F:** 328
  French West Africa **F:** 527 *with map*
  Gorée **G:** 274
  Government *picture on* **G:** 283
  Magic *picture on* **M:** 49
  Mali (History) **M:** 108-109
Sénégal River [Senegal]
  Mali (Land and climate) **M:** 107 *with map*
Senegambia [African history]
  Gambia (History) **G:** 19-20
  Gorée **G:** 274
  Senegal (History) **S:** 299-300
Senescence [biology]
  Geriatrics **G:** 137
Senet [game]
  Egypt, Ancient (Recreation) **E:** 137
Senghor, Léopold Sédar [Senegalese political
  leader] **S:** 300
  Senegal (History) **S:** 299-300
Sengstacke, John H. [American publisher]
  Abbott, Robert Sengstacke **A:** 6
Senile cataract [disease]
  Blindness (Diseases) **B:** 401
Senile osteoporosis [disease]
  Bone (Bone disorders) **B:** 457
Senility [disorder] **S:** 300
  Alzheimer's disease **A:** 398
Senior [education]
  Universities and colleges (The student body)
    U: 208
Senior citizen *See* Geriatrics; Old age *in this index*
Senior Citizens, National Council of
  Old age (Employment and other activities) **O:** 739
Senior Corps [organization]
  USA Freedom Corps **U:** 229
Senior day care
  Day care (Day care for the elderly) **D:** 53
Senior League
  Little League Baseball **L:** 391
Senior PGA Tour
  Golf (Golf today) **G:** 267
Seniority
  Labor movement (Arranging contracts) **L:** 4-6
Seniority principle
  Senate (Senate committees) **S:** 295
Seniors, Girl Scout
  Girl Scouts (Girl Scouts of the USA) **G:** 197 *with*
    picture
Senlac [English history]
  Hastings, Battle of **H:** 83
Senna [tree product]
  Cassia **C:** 276
Senna, Ayrton [Brazilian race driver]
  Automobile racing (table: Formula One World
    Drivers' Championship) **A:** 980
Senna, Danzy [American author]
  African American literature (Recent
    developments) **A:** 136a
Sennacherib [king of Assyria] **S:** 300
  Babylon (The Old Babylonian period) **B:** 11-12
  Hezekiah **H:** 221
  Library (Ancient libraries of clay) **L:** 257
Sennar [former city]
  Funj Sultanate **F:** 560
Sennett, Mack [Canadian director] **S:** 300 *with*
  picture
Senones [people]
  Gaul **G:** 70

Señor Presidente, El [book by Asturias]
  Latin American literature (The mid-1900's) **L:** 114
Sensation *See* Perception *in this index*
Sensationalism
  Journalism (The age of sensationalism) **J:** 175
Sense and Sensibility [book by Austen]
  Austen, Jane **A:** 892
Sensenbrenner, Maynard E. [American political
  leader]
  Columbus (History) **Ci:** 856
Senses S: 301 *with diagrams*
  See also Hearing; Perception; Smell; Taste; Touch;
    Vision *in this index, and the list of Related articles*
    in the Senses article
  Amphibian (Sense organs) **A:** 440
  Animal (Adaptations for sensing the
    environment) **A:** 492
  Baby (The first month) **B:** 6
  Bird (Senses) **B:** 364 *with pictures*
  Cat (Senses) **C:** 287
  Ear (The sense of hearing) **E:** 9; (The sense of
    balance) **E:** 11
  Mammal (Senses) **M:** 120
  Perception **P:** 282
Sensible horizon
  Horizon **H:** 335
Sensible perspiration
  Perspiration **P:** 305
Sensitive plant [plant] **S:** 302 *with pictures*
  Plant (Environmental factors) **P:** 538-539
Sensitivity training [psychology] **S:** 302
  Lewin, Kurt **L:** 220
Sensor [electronics]
  Airbag (How airbags work) **A:** 200
  Automation (Uses of automation) **A:** 944; (How
    automation works) **A:** 945 *with diagram*
  Burglar alarm **B:** 704
  Ignition (The direct-fire ignition system) **I:** 49
  Light meter **L:** 294
  Photography (How a camera works) **P:** 407
  Remote sensing **R:** 231
  Tachometer **T:** 4
  Television (Creating the video signals) **T:** 122
Sensorimotor period [psychology]
  Child (The stages of childhood) **C:** 448
  Piaget, Jean **P:** 445
Sensorineural hearing loss
  Deafness (Types of hearing loss) **D:** 57; (Medical
    treatment) **D:** 58
Sensory memory [psychology]
  Memory (The memory system) **M:** 392
Sensory neuron [anatomy]
  Human body (The peripheral nervous system)
    H: 426
  Nervous system (How the nervous system works)
    N: 132 *with diagram*
Sensory perception
  Brain (Sensing the environment) **B:** 552
  Perception **P:** 282
Sensory play [recreation]
  Play **P:** 570
Sensory receptor [anatomy] *See* Receptor *in this*
  index
Sentebale [organization]
  Lesotho **L:** 208
Sentence [grammar] **S:** 302
  Capitalization (The first word) **C:** 196
  Clause **Ci:** 657
  Conjunction **Ci:** 951
  English language (Grammar) **E:** 312
  Grammar **G:** 303
  Semantics **S:** 291
  A Guide to Writing Skills **Research Guide: 9**
Sentence [law] **S:** 304
  Criminal justice system (The trial) **Ci:** 1143;
    (Problems in the courts) **Ci:** 1144
  Parole **P:** 178
Sentence bargaining [law]
  Plea bargaining **P:** 571
Sentence modifier [grammar]
  Adverb (Simple adverbs) **A:** 70
Sentence outline
  Outline **O:** 890
Senter, DeWitt Clinton [American political leader]
  Tennessee (table) **T:** 152
Sentimental comedy
  Drama (England) **D:** 334-335
Sentimental novel
  American literature (The Era of Expansion [1831-
    1870]) **A:** 415
Sentimental Tommy [book by Barrie]
  Barrie, J. M. **B:** 118
Sentimentalism [literature]
  Literature (Theme) **L:** 353
  Russian literature (Sentimentalism) **R:** 560
Sentinel Falls
  Yosemite National Park (Waterfalls) **Y:** 570

Senufo [people]
  Burkina Faso (People) **B:** 706
Senut, Brigitte [French anthropologist]
  Prehistoric people (table) **P:** 754
Seoul [South Korea] **S:** 304 *with pictures and map*
  Korea, South **K:** 375 *with picture*
  Olympic Games (Charges of steroid use) **O:** 753
Seoul National University
  Seoul (The city) **S:** 304-306
Sepak takraw [game]
  Malaysia (Recreation) **M:** 98d *with picture*
Sepal [botany]
  Flower (The calyx) **F:** 293 *with picture*
  Plant (Flowers) **P:** 531 *with picture*
Separate but equal [U.S. history]
  African Americans (The growth of discrimination)
    A: 136k-136l
  Brown v. Board of Education of Topeka **B:** 645
  Civil rights (The struggle for the rights of African
    Americans) **Ci:** 609
Separate condenser [machine]
  Watt, James **W:** 148
Separate loading ammunition
  Ammunition (Artillery ammunition) **A:** 435-436
Separate school
  Alberta (Schools) **A:** 317
Separate segregated fund [committee]
  Political action committee **P:** 627
Separate spheres doctrine
  Sex discrimination (Origins of sex discrimination)
    S: 335
Separation [process]
  Milk (Separation or standardization) **M:** 548 *with*
    picture
Separation [sociology]
  Rite of passage **R:** 350
Separation, Legal
  Alimony **A:** 369
  Divorce **D:** 253
Separation negative [photography]
  Printing (Process color printing) **P:** 802
Separation of church and state *See* Church and
  state *in this index*
Separation of powers *See* Checks and balances
  in this index
Separatists [literature]
  Homer (Early scholarship) **H:** 303
Separatists [religious group]
  Congregationalists **Ci:** 940f
  Massachusetts (The Pilgrims and Plymouth
    Colony) **M:** 289
  Pilgrims **P:** 462
  Plymouth Colony (The founding of Plymouth
    Colony) **P:** 582
  Protestantism (The radical reform and free
    church movements) **P:** 835
  Puritans (History) **P:** 910-911
Separator [electrical device]
  Battery (Battery structure) **B:** 168 *with diagram*
Separator [machine]
  Butter (History) **B:** 731
  Centrifuge **C:** 358
  Refrigeration (The gas refrigerator) **R:** 202 *with*
    diagram
  Rubber (Processing latex) **R:** 503
Separator [television]
  Television (Amplifiers and separators) **T:** 125
Sephardic [language]
  Hebrew language **H:** 162
Sephardim [people] **S:** 307
  Israel (Jews) **I:** 480
  Jews **J:** 120
Sepia [pigment]
  Cuttlefish **Ci:** 1202
Sepik River [New Guinea]
  Rain forest *picture on* **R:** 126a
Sepiolite [earth]
  Meerschaum **M:** 383
Sepoy Rebellion [1857-1859] *See* Indian Rebellion
  in this index
Sepoys [people]
  Indian Rebellion **I:** 187
Seppuku [custom]
  Hara-kiri **H:** 55
Septal defect [birth defect]
  Heart (Abnormal openings in the heart) **H:** 141
September [month] **S:** 308 *with pictures*
  Calendar (The Romans) **C:** 31
September 11 terrorist attacks [U.S. history]
  S: 310 *with pictures*
  Afghanistan (Recent developments) **K:** 247
  Afghanistan War **A:** 97
  Airport (Airport security) **A:** 247
  Arab Americans (Arab Americans today) **A:** 581
  Arabs (Relations with Europe and the United
    States) **A:** 590a
  Ashcroft, John David **A:** 768

Aviation (Recent developments) **A:** 991
Bin Laden, Osama **B:** 307
Blair, Tony **B:** 396
Bush, George Walker **B:** 722b *with picture;* (Terrorist attacks and military action) **B:** 722g
Central Intelligence Agency (History) **C:** 357
Civil defense (Focus on terrorism) **Ci:** 606
Civil rights (The war on terrorism) **Ci:** 610
Federal Bureau of Investigation (History) **F:** 62-63
Fire department (Recent developments) **F:** 129
Giuliani, Rudolph William **G:** 201
Hijacking **H:** 230
Homeland Security, Department of (History) **H:** 301
International relations (The war against terrorism) **I:** 346
Middle East (The 2000's) **M:** 534b
National September 11 Memorial and Museum **N:** 61
New Jersey (The early 2000's) **N:** 254
New York (The early 2000's) **N:** 320
New York City (Recent developments) **N:** 321-322 *with picture;* (A time of change) **N:** 343 *with picture*
North Atlantic Treaty Organization (History) **N:** 471
Nuclear weapon (Post-Cold War strategy) **N:** 600; (Security) **N:** 601; (After the terrorist attacks of Sept. 11, 2001) **N:** 602
Patriot Act **P:** 197
Pentagon Building **P:** 274
Petroleum (Petroleum and security) **P:** 346-347
Qa`ida, Al- **Q:** 2
Ridge, Tom **R:** 336
Rumsfeld, Donald Henry **R:** 520
Statue of Liberty (The early 2000's) **So:** 878
Taliban **T:** 19
Terrorism *picture on* **T:** 175; (The September 11 terrorist attacks) **T:** 179
Transportation Security Administration **T:** 400
United Kingdom (Recent developments) **U:** 74
United Nations (Fighting terrorism) **U:** 93
United States, History of the (September 11 terrorist attacks) **U:** 196d *with picture*
War (The war against terrorism) **W:** 26
Washington, D.C. (The 2000's) **W:** 88
World, History of the (The war on terrorism) **W:** 448b
World Trade Center **W:** 451
September elm [tree]
Elm (Kinds) **E:** 244-245
September equinox
Equinox **E:** 348 *with diagram*
September Massacres [French history]
French Revolution (The Legislative Assembly) **F:** 526
Marat, Jean-Paul **M:** 190
Septic arthritis [disease]
Arthritis (Other forms of arthritis) **A:** 752
Septic shock [disorder]
Blood poisoning **B:** 416
Septic sore throat [disease] *See* Strep throat *in this index*
Septic tank [sanitation]
Garbage disposal **G:** 28
House (Plumbing) **H:** 382
Plumbing (History) **P:** 580
Sewage (Rural sewerage systems) **S:** 330
Water pollution (Sewage) **W:** 136
Septicemia *See* Blood poisoning *in this index*
Septicemic plague [disease]
Plague (Forms of plague) **P:** 506
Septimius Severus, Arch of [ruins]
Forum, Roman **F:** 421 *with picture*
Septuagint [Bible] **S:** 310d
Bible (The first translations) **B:** 284
Dead Sea Scrolls **D:** 56
Library (Egypt) **L:** 258
Old Testament (Ancient translations) **O:** 741
Septum [anatomy]
Heart *picture on* **H:** 134; (Outer lining and muscle) **H:** 133; (Abnormal openings in the heart) **H:** 141; (Cardiomyopathy) **H:** 142-143
Nose **N:** 548 *with diagram*
Nosebleed **N:** 549
Sepulchers, The [poem by Foscolo]
Foscolo, Ugo **F:** 421
Sequence [mathematics]
Series **S:** 316b
Sequencing [genetics]
Human Genome Project (The structure and importance of genomes) **H:** 427
Sequestered jury
Trial (Reaching a verdict) **T:** 436
Sequestrant [chemical]
Food additive (Kinds of additives) **F:** 339
Food preservation (Additives) **F:** 343

Sequoia [tree] **S:** 310d *with pictures*
California (Forests) **C:** 54
Conifer **Ci:** 950
Plant **P:** 516 *with picture*
Redwood **R:** 193
Tree *picture on* **T:** 410
Sequoia National Park [California] **S:** 311
Muir, John **M:** 912
National Park System (table: National parks) **N:** 48
Sequoya *See* Sequoyah *in this index*
Sequoyah [American Indian educator] **S:** 311 *with portrait*
Cherokee Indians **C:** 409
Indian, American (Writing) **I:** 150
Sequoyah Caverns
Alabama *picture on* **A:** 267
Serabit el-Khadim [ancient Egypt]
Alphabet (Semitic scripts) **A:** 381
Serahuli [people]
Gambia (People) **G:** 18
Serape [clothing]
Mexico (Clothing) **M:** 456
Seraphim [award]
Knighthood, Orders of (Honorary orders) **K:** 347
Seraphim, Order of the [award]
Medals, decorations, and orders (table) **M:** 359 *with picture*
Serapis [Egyptian god] **S:** 312
Serapis [ship]
Jones, John Paul (Defeat of the *Serapis*) **J:** 158
Revolution, American *picture on* **R:** 280
Serbia **S:** 312 *with pictures and map*
Austria-Hungary **A:** 941
Balkans (Recent developments) **B:** 42; (The First Balkan War) **B:** 42; (The Second Balkan War) **B:** 42
Bosnia-Herzegovina (History) **B:** 492
Croatia (History) **Ci:** 1148a-1148b
Flag *picture on* **F:** 207
Kosovo **K:** 384a
Montenegro **M:** 763
Priština **P:** 808a
United Nations, History of the (The Balkan conflicts) **U:** 196d
War crime (The United Nations and war crimes) **W:** 27
World War I **W:** 452
Serbia and Montenegro [former country]
See also Yugoslavia *in this index*
Berlin, Congress of **B:** 265
Montenegro **M:** 763
Serbia **S:** 312
Yugoslavia **Y:** 576
Serbs [people]
Bosnia-Herzegovina (People) **B:** 492
Croatia (People) **Ci:** 1148; (History) **Ci:** 1148a-1148b
Sarajevo **S:** 123
Serbia (People) **S:** 313
Srebrenica massacre **So:** 816
Serbs, Croats, and Slovenes, Kingdom of the
Belgrade (History) **B:** 236
Bosnia-Herzegovina (History) **B:** 492-493
Croatia (History) **Ci:** 1148a-1148b
Ljubljana **L:** 401
Montenegro **M:** 763
Serbia (A new country) **S:** 314-315
Slovenia (History) **S:** 512
Yugoslavia (A new country) **Y:** 576
Seredy, Kate [American author]
Newbery Medal (table) **N:** 359
Serenade [music] **S:** 316a
Serengeti National Park [Tanzania]
National park (table) **N:** 42f
Tanzania (Animal life) **T:** 33 *with map*
Serer [people]
Senegal (People) **S:** 297
Serf [Aztec class]
Aztec **A:** 999
Serf [European history] **S:** 316b
See also Peasant *in this index*
Germany (Serfdom in Germany) **G:** 163
Greece, Ancient (The people) **G:** 367
Peter I, the Great (Policies within Russia) **P:** 324
Russia (Ivan the Terrible) **R:** 548
Slavery (The Middle Ages) **S:** 501
Sergeant
Rank, Military (table) **R:** 140
Sergeant at arms [office]
Parliamentary procedure (Officers) **P:** 175
Sergeant Floyd Monument
Sioux City **S:** 474
Sergeant major
Rank, Military (table) **R:** 140
Sergeant major damselfish
Fish *picture on* **F:** 155
Sergeant Pepper's Lonely Hearts Club Band

[recording]
Rock music (Fresh directions) **R:** 380
Sergeant York [American soldier] *See* York, Alvin Cullum *in this index*
Sergeant York [film]
Hawks, Howard **H:** 114
Serger [machine]
Sewing (Seams) **S:** 333
Sergius I, Saint [pope]
Pope (table) **P:** 666
Serial bond
Bond (Kinds of bonds) **B:** 454
Serial derecho [storm]
Derecho **D:** 152
Serial extraction [dentistry]
Orthodontics **O:** 860
Serialism [music]
Classical music (Atonal music) **Ci:** 649-650
Schoenberg, Arnold **S:** 178
Sericin [gum]
Silk (Spinning the cocoon) **S:** 459
Series [mathematics] **S:** 316b
Series circuit [electricity]
Electric circuit (Series circuits) **E:** 166 *with diagram*
Electricity (Series and parallel circuits) **E:** 194
Series E bond
Savings bond **S:** 166
Series EE bond
Savings bond **S:** 166
Series HH bond
Savings bond **S:** 166
Series hybrid vehicle
Automobile (Hybrid power systems) **A:** 954
Series I bond
Savings bond **S:** 166
Series motor
Electric motor (DC motors) **E:** 181
Series of Unfortunate Events, A [books by Snicket]
Literature for children *picture on* **L:** 374
Snicket, Lemony **S:** 538
Serif [decoration]
Alphabet (Capital letters) **A:** 383
Serigraphy [art]
Printing (Screen printing) **P:** 801
Screen printing **S:** 225
Serious Money [play by Churchill]
Churchill, Caryl **C:** 543
Serious Proposal to the Ladies, A [book by Astell]
Feminism **F:** 69
Serling, Rod [American dramatist] **S:** 318
Serlio, Sebastiano [Italian set designer]
Drama (The Italian stage) **D:** 330 *with picture*
SERM [hormone]
Hormone replacement therapy **H:** 338
Sermersuaq [ice]
Greenland (The land) **G:** 385
Sermon on the Mount [New Testament]
Beatitudes **B:** 189
Golden rule **G:** 255
Jesus Christ (His teaching) **J:** 107
Serologic test [medicine]
Serum **S:** 319
Serotonin [biochemistry] **S:** 318
Alcoholism (Causes of alcoholism) **A:** 337-338
Drug abuse (Methamphetamine) **D:** 362
Fibromyalgia **F:** 90
Mental illness (Chemical imbalances in the brain) **M:** 406
Migraine **M:** 538
Obsessive-compulsive disorder **O:** 646
Schizophrenia **S:** 176
Serotonin receptor [anatomy]
Serotonin **S:** 318
Serous membrane [anatomy]
Membrane **M:** 391
Serous otitis media [disorder]
Ear (Diseases) **E:** 12
Serpent [animal]
See also Snake *in this index*
Adam and Eve **A:** 32
Mythology (Symbols) **M:** 975
Sea serpent **S:** 263
Serpent-eagle [bird]
Eagle (Other kinds of eagles) **E:** 5
Serpent Mound [Hillsboro]
Ohio (Places to visit) **O:** 690 *with picture*
Serpent star [sea animal]
Brittle star **B:** 634 *with picture*
Serpentary [plant]
Snakeroot **S:** 536
Serpentine [mineral] **S:** 318
Asbestos (Types of asbestos) **A:** 765
Plant (Environmental factors) **P:** 538-539
Serpentine [weapon]
Handgun (Early handguns) **H:** 45
Harquebus **H:** 67

Serpentine marble [stone]
  Serpentine S: 318
Serpentinization [chemistry]
  Hydrothermal vent H: 473
Serra, Junípero [Spanish missionary] S: 318
  California (The California missions) C: 60
  Mission life in America (Western missions)
    M: 618-619
  San Diego S: 88
  Santa Barbara S: 113
Serra, Richard [American artist] S: 318 with picture
  Sculpture (From the mid-1900's to the early
    2000's) S: 259-260
Serra da Estrela [mountain range]
  Portugal (Land regions) P: 690
Serrano Elias, Jorge [Guatemalan political leader]
  Guatemala (Political developments) G: 417
Serrão, Francisco [Portuguese sailor]
  Magellan, Ferdinand (Early life) M: 45-46
Sertão [region, Brazil]
  Brazil picture on B: 577; (The Northeast Region)
    B: 579
Sertões, Os [book by Cunha]
  Brazil (The arts) B: 576-577
  Cunha, Euclides da Ci: 1192
Sertorius [Roman general]
  Pompey the Great P: 655
Serum [physiology] S: 319
  Immune system (The humoral immune response)
    I: 88; (Passive immunity) I: 88b
  Immunization (Passive immunization) I: 89
Serum albumin [chemical]
  Albumin A: 333
Serva padrona, La [opera by Pergolesi]
  Opera (Opera seria and opera buffa) O: 797-798
  Pergolesi, Giovanni Battista P: 287
Serval [wildcat] S: 319 with picture
Servant [labor]
  Indentured servant I: 106
Serve [sports]
  Handball H: 41
  Table tennis (How the game is played) T: 3
  Tennis pictures on T: 164; (The serve) T: 163
Server [electronics]
  Computer (Personal computers) Ci: 909;
    (Dedicated computers) Ci: 911
  Dell, Michael D: 116
  Internet picture on I: 350d; (Hardware) I: 350c
Servetus, Michael [Spanish physiologist]
  Heart (Discovery of circulation) H: 144
Service [economics] See Goods and services in
  this index
Service [religion]
  Classical music (The Reformation) Ci: 646-647
Service [tennis]
  Tennis (The serve) T: 163
Service, Robert William [Canadian poet] S: 319
Service benefit
  Insurance (Medical service plans) I: 312
Service box [sports]
  Handball H: 41 with diagrams
Service cooperative [economics]
  Cooperative (Service cooperatives) Ci: 1036
Service Corps of Retired Executives [U.S.]
  Old age (Employment and other activities) O: 739
Service dog
  Pet (For work) P: 321
Service Employees International Union S: 319
  American Federation of Labor and Congress of
    Industrial Organizations (History) A: 410
  Labor movement (table) L: 8
Service gentry [Russian history]
  Russia (Ivan the Terrible) R: 548
Service industries S: 320
  See also the Economy sections of the various state
    and country articles.
  Retailing R: 264
  United States picture on U: 131
  United States, History of the (Economic changes)
    U: 196b
Service learning
  Camp Fire USA (Service learning programs) C: 89
  Character education C: 377
Service line
  Gas [fuel] (Transmitting and distributing gas)
    G: 55
  Pipeline (Gas pipelines) P: 490
  Plumbing (The water supply system) P: 577 with
    diagram
Service magazine
  Magazine (Consumer magazines) M: 42
Service mark [law]
  Trademark T: 364
Service module
  Space exploration (Vostok and Mercury: The first
    human beings in space) So: 712
Service Organizations, United See United Service

Organizations in this index
Servicemen's Readjustment Act [1944]
  Roosevelt, Franklin Delano (The home front)
    R: 457-458
  Veterans Affairs, Department of (Benefits and
    other services) V: 343
Servius Tullius [legendary figure]
  Mythology (The seven kings) M: 983
Servo [motor]
  Airplane, Model (Radio control models) A: 241
Servomechanism [electronics] S: 320
  Automatic flight control system (How an AFCS
    works) A: 944
SES [machine]
  Air cushion vehicle (How an ACV works) A: 181
Sesame [plant] S: 320 with picture
Sesenheimer Lieder [poems by Goethe]
  Goethe, Johann Wolfgang von (Early years)
    G: 247
Sesotho [language]
  Lesotho (People) L: 207
Sesquisulfide of phosphorus [chemical]
  Match (Strike-anywhere matches) M: 299; (The
    first matches) M: 300-300a
Sesshu [Japanese painter] S: 320
  Painting (Japanese painting) P: 47
Sessile oak [tree]
  Oak (Other oaks) O: 636
Session [religion]
  Presbyterians P: 756a
Session musician
  Country music (Emergence of the country music
    industry) Ci: 1098b-1098c
Sessions, Roger [American composer] S: 320
Sessions, William S. [American government
  official]
  Federal Bureau of Investigation (History) F: 62
Sestet [poetry]
  Poetry (table) P: 594
  Sonnet So: 593
Set [botany]
  Onion (Cultivation) O: 763
Set [Egyptian god] See Seth in this index
Set [mathematics] See Set theory in this index
Set [sports]
  Tennis (Scoring) T: 162-163
Set [theater]
  See also Scenery in this index
  Ballet (Sets and costumes) B: 49 with picture
  Drama (The Italian stage) D: 330 with picture;
    (England) D: 334 with picture; (Early realism)
    D: 338
  Motion picture (Filming on a sound stage) M: 851
    with picture
  Theater (Scene design) T: 239 with pictures
Set dressing
  Theater (Properties and set dressing) T: 240
Set point [psychology]
  Mood M: 780
Set prop
  Theater (Properties and set dressing) T: 240
Set rendering
  Theater (The scene designer) T: 239
Set theory [mathematics] S: 321 with diagrams
  Addition A: 350
  Algebra (Sets and variables) A: 350
  Boolean algebra B: 474 with diagrams
  Infinity I: 266
  Mathematics (Branches of mathematics) M: 303
Set-top box [device]
  Television (VCR's and DVR's) T: 110c; (Tuner)
    T: 124
Seta [botany]
  Moss (How mosses live) M: 834-835
Setae [zoology]
  Crustacean (Senses) Ci: 1163 with diagram
  Earthworm E: 39 with pictures
Seth [Egyptian god] S: 322
  Mythology picture on M: 977; (The Osiris myth)
    M: 979
Seth's Brother's Wife [book by Frederic]
  Frederic, Harold F: 497
Seti I [king of ancient Egypt] S: 323
  Ramses II R: 134
  Valley of the Kings V: 266
SETI Institute S: 323
  Extraterrestrial intelligence E: 458
Seton, Ernest Thompson [Canadian naturalist]
  S: 323
Seton, Saint Elizabeth Ann [American religious
  leader] S: 323 with portrait
Seton, William Magee [husband of]
  Seton, Saint Elizabeth Ann S: 323
Setsubun [holiday]
  February F: 61
Sett [design]
  Tartan T: 46

Setter [dog] S: 323
  Dog (Sporting dogs) D: 268 with pictures
Settignano, Desiderio da [Italian sculptor]
  Sculpture (Early Renaissance) S: 252
Setting [drama]
  Literature (Characters) L: 353
  Shakespeare, William (Scenic effects) S: 352
Setting Free the Bears [book by Irving]
  Irving, John I: 459
Settlement area [government]
  Northwest Territories (Government) N: 532-533
Settlement house S: 324
  Addams, Jane A: 46
  Gay Nineties (Social developments) G: 72
  Hull House H: 412
  Progressive Era (Social reforms) P: 814 with
    picture
  Social work (History) So: 559
  Toynbee, Arnold T: 354
Settlers of the Marsh [book by Grove]
  Canadian literature (Literature between the
    world wars) C: 158-159
Settling basin
  Water (Purifying and treating water) W: 126
Settlor [law]
  Trust fund (How a trust fund works) T: 473
Seurat, Georges [French painter] S: 324
  Painting (What do painters paint?) P: 28;
    (Postimpressionism) P: 75 with picture
  Postimpressionism P: 709 with picture
Seuss, Dr. [American author] S: 324
  Literature for children picture on L: 363; (Books
    for beginning readers) L: 365
  Regina Medal (table: 1982) R: 206
Sevan, Lake [Armenia] See Lake Sevan in this index
Sevastopol [Ukraine] S: 324
  Black Sea B: 391 with map
Seven Against Thebes [Greek mythology]
  Antigone A: 554
Seven Brothers [book by Kivi]
  Scandinavian literature (The Golden Age) S: 171
Seven-card stud [game]
  Poker P: 603
Seven Cities of Cíbola See Cíbola, Seven Cities of
  in this index
Seven Days, Battles of the [1862]
  Civil War, American (table) Ci: 624; (The
    peninsular campaign) Ci: 626
  Lee, Robert E. (Opening campaigns) L: 178
Seven Guitars [play by Wilson]
  Wilson, August W: 316
Seven Legends [book by Keller]
  Keller, Gottfried K: 254
Seven natural wonders of the world S: 324 with
  pictures
Seven Oaks, Battle of [1816]
  Manitoba (The Red River Colony) M: 160
Seven Pillars of Wisdom, The [book by Lawrence]
  Lawrence, T. E. L: 146
Seven Pines, Battle of [1862]
  Civil War, American (table) Ci: 624; (The
    peninsular campaign) Ci: 626
  Lee, Robert E. (Opening campaigns) L: 178
Seven Poor Men of Sydney [book by Stead]
  Australia (Literature) A: 904-905
Seven seas [mythology] S: 324b
Seven Sisters, The [book by Drabble]
  Drabble, Margaret D: 317
Seven Storey Mountain, The [book by Merton]
  Merton, Thomas M: 419
Seven Weeks' War [1866] S: 324b
  Bismarck, Otto von (Bismarck's wars) B: 382
  Franz Joseph F: 494
  Germany (The unification of Germany) G: 165
Seven Wonders of the Ancient World S: 325 with
  pictures and map
Seven Years' War [1756-1763] S: 328
  See also French and Indian War in this index
  Frederick II F: 497
  French and Indian wars (The French and Indian
    War) F: 512
  George II G: 106b
  Germany (The rise of Prussia) G: 164
  Louisbourg L: 477
  Newfoundland and Labrador (War with France)
    N: 375-377 with picture
  Nova Scotia (The struggle in Acadia) N: 568
  Paris, Treaties of (The treaty of 1763) P: 167
  Pitt, William P: 499
  Quebec, Battle of Q: 37
  United Kingdom (The growing empire) U: 67
  Washington, George (Messenger to the French)
    W: 93-94
Seveners [religious group]
  Fātimid dynasty F: 55
Seventeen-year locust [insect]
  Cicada (Types of cicadas) Ci: 551 with picture

Insect *picture on* I: 281
17D [vaccine]
Yellow fever (Prevention) Y: 556
Seventeenth Amendment
Constitution of the United States Ci: 1014
Progressive Era (Political reforms) P: 814
United States, History of the (Taft and Wilson)
U: 187-188
Seventh Amendment
Constitution of the United States Ci: 1012
Seventh Crusade [1248-1254]
Louis IX L: 474
Seventh-day Adventists [religious group] S: 328
Adventists A: 70
Battle Creek B: 172
Seventh Seal, The [film]
Motion picture (The art film revival) M: 870 *with picture*
77 Dream Songs [book by Berryman]
Berryman, John B: 272
76ers, Philadelphia [team] *See* Philadelphia 76ers *in this index*
Seventy years' captivity [religion]
Reformation (Religious causes) R: 196
Several Poems [book by Bradstreet]
American literature (Poetry) A: 414
Severance tax
Taxation (Taxes on transactions) T: 53
Severe acute respiratory syndrome *See* SARS *in this index*
Severe combined immunodeficiency disease
Heredity (The era of genetic engineering) H: 209
Immune system (Other disorders of the immune system) I: 88c
Severe cyclonic storm
Cyclone Ci: 1204
Hurricane H: 452
Severe porcelain
Porcelain (Hard-paste porcelain) P: 675-676
Severe tropical cyclone
Hurricane H: 452
Severe tropical storm
Cyclone Ci: 1204
Severed Head, A [book by Murdoch]
Murdoch, Iris M: 930
Severini, Gino [Italian painter]
Futurism F: 589 *with picture*
Italy *picture on* I: 505
Severinus [pope]
Pope (table) P: 666
Severn, River [United Kingdom] S: 328
England (Rivers and lakes) E: 300-301
United Kingdom (Rivers and lakes) U: 61 *with map*
Wales (Rivers and coastline) W: 11 *with map*
Seversky, Alexander Procofieff de [Russian-American engineer]
De Seversky, Alexander Procofieff D: 157
Severus [Roman emperor]
Rome, Ancient (table) R: 447
Severus, Lucius Septimius [Roman emperor]
Praetorian Guard P: 729
Rome, Ancient (table) R: 447
Severus Alexander [Roman emperor]
Rome, Ancient (table) R: 447
Seviche [food]
Food (Interesting facts about food) F: 329
Sevier, John [American political leader] S: 328
Franklin, State of F: 493
Tennessee (table) T: 152; (Territorial years) T: 153
Westward movement in America (Crossing the Appalachians) W: 246
Sevier Desert
Utah (Deserts) U: 242 *with map*
Sevier River
Utah (Rivers and lakes) U: 242 *with map*
Sevilla [Spain] *See* Seville *in this index*
Seville [Spain] S: 329
Spain (Architecture) So: 738-739; (table: Average monthly weather) So: 742
Seville [literary school]
Spanish literature (The 1500's) So: 758-759
Seville Cathedral [Spain]
Seville S: 329
Spain (Architecture) So: 738-739
Sèvres, Treaty of [1920] S: 329
Turkey (After World War I) T: 511
World War I (The peace settlement) W: 465-466
Sèvres porcelain
Porcelain (French porcelain) P: 677 *with picture*
Sewage S: 329 *with diagrams*
Environmental pollution *picture on* E: 332; (Water pollution) E: 334
Garbage disposal G: 28
House (Plumbing) H: 382
Incinerator I: 100
Ocean (Marine pollution) O: 664

Plumbing (The drain-waste-vent system) P: 578-579
Sanitation (Sewage treatment) S: 111
Water (Water management and conservation) W: 122; (Disposing of used water) W: 127
Water pollution (Sewage) W: 136; (Sewage treatment) W: 138
Sewage treatment plant
Plumbing (The drain-waste-vent system) P: 578-579
Sewage (Urban sewerage systems) S: 329 *with diagrams*
Sewall, Arthur [American political leader] S: 331
Sewall, Samuel [American jurist] S: 331
Sewall, Sumner [American political leader]
Maine (table) M: 87
Seward, William Henry [American political leader] S: 331
Alaska A: 283; (American purchase) A: 301
Civil War, American (The conflict over slavery) Ci: 615-616
Emancipation Proclamation *picture on* E: 254
Hampton Roads Conference H: 37
Johnson, Andrew (Foreign relations) J: 141
Lincoln, Abraham (Election of 1860) L: 318; (Foreign relations) L: 322; (table) L: 323
New York (table) N: 313
State, Department of *picture on* So: 862
United States, History of the (The nation divided [1850-1869]) U: 174-175
Seward Peninsula
Alaska (The Central Uplands and Lowlands) A: 294
"Seward's Folly" [U.S. history]
Alaska A: 283; (American purchase) A: 301
Seward, William Henry S: 331
"Seward's Icebox" *See* "Seward's Folly" *in this index*
Sewell, Anna [British author] S: 331
Literature for children (Masterpieces of fiction) L: 363
Sewell, Joe [American baseball player]
Baseball (table: Hall of Fame) B: 134b
Sewellel [animal]
Mountain beaver M: 897
Sewer [water system]
Sewage S: 329
Sewerage system
Garbage disposal G: 28
Sewage S: 329
Sewing S: 331 *with diagrams*
Beadwork B: 179 *with picture*
Bookbinding (Sewing) B: 471
Clothing (The 1900's) Ci: 703; (Ready-to-wear clothes) Ci: 704-705
Fur (Cutting and sewing) F: 563
Needle N: 117 *with picture*
Sewing machine S: 333 *with pictures*
Howe, Elias H: 400
Needle N: 117 *with picture*
Sewing S: 331
Singer, Isaac Merrit S: 472
Sex *See* Sexuality *in this index*
Sex cell [reproduction]
Cell (Meiosis) C: 231
Heredity (Chromosomes and genes) H: 201
Sex chromosome [genetics]
Hemophilia (How hemophilia is inherited) H: 182 *with diagram*
Heredity (Chromosomes and sexual determination) H: 202
Sex discrimination S: 334
Affirmative action A: 91
Civil rights (The struggle for women's rights) Ci: 609
Education (Nonsexist education) E: 107
Equal Rights Amendment E: 345
Sexual harassment (Sexual harassment law) S: 337
Woman suffrage W: 380
Women's movement (Contemporary women's movements) W: 386
Sex drive [psychology]
Sexuality (Psychological factors) S: 338
Sex education S: 336
Adolescent (Pregnancy) A: 63
Calderone, Mary Steichen C: 27
Sex hormone
Adrenal gland A: 67
DES D: 153
Hormone (Growth and sex hormones) H: 336
Lipid (Kinds of lipids) L: 345
Sex Information and Education Council of the United States
Calderone, Mary Steichen C: 27
Sex-linked gene
Heredity (Patterns of heredity) H: 202
Morgan, Thomas Hunt M: 804

Sex object [psychology]
Obscenity and pornography (Regulating pornography) O: 644
Sex organs *See* Genital organs *in this index*
Sex Pistols [rock band]
Punk rock P: 904
Rock music (Punk rock) R: 380b
Sex ratio [population] S: 336
Sex reversal [biology]
Goby G: 243
Sex role *See* Gender role *in this index*
Sexagesimal system [mathematics]
Mathematics (Early civilization) M: 303
Sexes Throughout Nature, The [book by Blackwell]
Blackwell, Antoinette Brown B: 394
Sexing the Cherry [book by Winterson]
Novel (The novel today) N: 575
Sexism [sociology]
See also Sex discrimination *in this index*
Education (Nonsexist education) E: 107
Equal Rights Amendment E: 345
Sex discrimination S: 335
Women's movement (Contemporary women's movements) W: 386; (Impact of women's movements) W: 387
Sexson, W. Mark [American clergyman]
Rainbow for Girls R: 129
Sextans A [galaxy]
Galaxy *picture on* G: 8a
Sextant [instrument] S: 336 *with picture*
Navigation *pictures on* N: 72; (Measuring angles) N: 71; (Early instruments) N: 74
Sextilis [month]
Calendar (The Romans) C: 31
Sexton, Anne [American poet] S: 337 *with portrait*
American literature ("Confessional" poetry) A: 423-424
Sexton beetle *See* Burying beetle *in this index*
Sextus Empiricus [Roman doctor]
Skepticism S: 481
Sexual abuse
Child abuse C: 454
Roman Catholic Church (Today) R: 412
Sexual Behavior in the Human Female [book by Kinsey]
Kinsey, Alfred Charles K: 332
Sexual Behavior in the Human Male [book by Kinsey]
Kinsey, Alfred Charles K: 332
Sexual dimorphism [biology]
Australopithecus A: 927
Homo habilis H: 306
Prehistoric people (The first human beings) P: 746
Sexual equality [sociology]
Women's movement W: 383
Sexual harassment [law] S: 337
Thomas, Clarence T: 261
Women's movement (Legal gains) W: 386
Sexual intercourse
Adolescent (Dating and sex) A: 62
AIDS (How HIV is transmitted) A: 164b; (Prevention) A: 165
Birth control (Methods of birth control) B: 378
Condom Ci: 929
Penis P: 241
Pregnancy (Becoming pregnant) P: 734a
Rape [crime] R: 141
Reproduction, Human (Fertilization) R: 246
Sexuality (Gender identity) S: 338; (Expressing sexuality) S: 338b
Sexually transmitted disease (Factors in the spread of STD's) S: 338b
Vagina V: 259
Sexual orientation [psychology]
Adolescent (Establishing a sexual identity) A: 63
Homosexuality H: 302
Sexuality (Sexual orientation) S: 338b
Sexual reassignment surgery
Transsexualism T: 401
Sexual reproduction [biology]
Animal (Sexual reproduction) A: 496 *with diagram*
Cloning (Nuclear transfer) Ci: 682l
Estrous cycle E: 363
Heredity (Sex cells and reproduction) H: 201
Life (Reproduction) L: 275
Plant (The reproduction of plants) P: 532 *with pictures*
Reproduction (Through sexual reproduction) R: 242; (How reproduction has evolved) R: 243
Reproduction, Human R: 244
Sexual Research, Institute for
Kinsey, Alfred Charles K: 332
Sexual selection [biology]
Evolution (Natural selection) E: 428-429 *with picture*

Sexuality S: 337
Adolescent (Sexual development) A: 61; (Dating and sex) A: 62; (Establishing a sexual identity) A: 63
Birth control B: 378
Brain (Between the sexes) B: 550d
Child (The preteen-age years) C: 450
Freud, Sigmund (On behavior) F: 530
Gay rights movement G: 73
Heredity (Chromosomes and sexual determination) H: 202
Homosexuality H: 307
Kinsey, Alfred Charles K: 332
Masters and Johnson M: 297
Prostitution P: 830
Reproduction, Human R: 244
Sex education S: 336
Sexually transmitted disease (Factors in the spread of STD's) S: 338b
Transsexualism T: 401
Sexually explicit materials
Obscenity and pornography O: 644
Sexually transmitted disease S: 338b
Adolescent (Risk taking) A: 64
AIDS (How HIV is transmitted) A: 164b
Chlamydia C: 516
Circumcision C: 561
Gonorrhea G: 268
Herpes, Genital H: 214
Human papillomavirus H: 427
Infertility (Causes) I: 265
Pelvic inflammatory disease P: 233
Prostitution P: 830
Syphilis So: 1069
Tabes T: 2
Seychelles S: 339 *with picture and map*
Flag *picture on* F: 199
Seyfert galaxy [astronomy]
Quasar Q: 9
Seymour, Edward [uncle of]
Edward VI E: 113
Seymour, Horatio [American political leader] S: 341
Grant, Ulysses S. (Election of 1868) G: 315
New York (table) N: 313
Seymour, Jane [wife of Henry VIII]
Edward VI E: 113
Henry VIII [of England] H: 188
Seymour, Thomas H. [American political leader]
Connecticut (table) Ci: 967
Seymouria [animal]
Prehistoric animal P: 738
Sforza, Ludovico [Italian nobleman]
Leonardo da Vinci (Years in Milan) L: 199
Sforzando [music]
Music (table) M: 954
Sfumato [art]
Leonardo da Vinci (Paintings) L: 200b
Mona Lisa M: 698
Painting (The 1400's) P: 52-53
SgrA* [astronomy] *See* Sagittarius A* *in this index*
Sgraffito [art]
Pottery (Decorating and glazing) P: 718
's Gravenhage *See* Hague, The *in this index*
Shaanxi [province, China]
Mao Zedong (His life) M: 174-175
Shabalala, Joseph [South African singer]
Ladysmith Black Mombazo L: 26
Shaban [month]
Calendar (The Islamic calendar) C: 29
Shabbazz, El-Hajj Malik El- [American social reformer] *See* Malcolm X *in this index*
Shabuot *See* Shavuot *in this index*
Shackamaxon, Treaty of [1682]
Pennsylvania (Colonial days) P: 264
Shackles
Handcuffs H: 42
Shackleton, Sir Ernest Henry [Irish explorer] S: 341
Antarctica (The "Heroic Era") A: 536
Exploration *picture on* E: 450
Shad [fish] S: 341 *with picture*
Menhaden M: 400
Shad fly *See* Mayfly *in this index*
Shaddock [tree]
Grapefruit (History) G: 321
Shade
Color *diagram on* Ci: 822
Painting (Light and shade) P: 35
Shade garden
Gardening (Specialty gardens) G: 31
Shade tree
Pruning S: 841
Shaded coat
Cat (Coat) C: 287 *with picture*
Shader [artist]
Animation (Lighting and rendering) A: 513

Shadoof [device]
Agriculture *picture on* A: 156
Shadow S: 341 *with diagrams*
Penumbra P: 276
Sculpture (Form and treatment) S: 230-231
Shadow Cabinet [government]
United Kingdom (National government) U: 49
Shadow clock [device]
Time (Solar time) T: 288
Shadow Line, The [book by Conrad]
Conrad, Joseph Ci: 973
Shadow matter [physics] S: 341
Shadow of a Gunman, The [play by O'Casey]
Irish literature (Drama) I: 432
O'Casey, Sean O: 646
Shadow of Night, The [poem by Chapman]
Chapman, George C: 377
Shadow of Paradise [book by Aleixandre]
Aleixandre, Vicente A: 340
Shadow of Sirius, The [book by Merwin]
Merwin, W. S. M: 420
Shadow price [economics]
Cost-benefit analysis Ci: 1079
Shadow puppet
Puppet (Shadow puppets) P: 907 *with picture*
Shadows on the Grass [book by Dinesen]
Dinesen, Isak D: 205
Shadrach [Biblical figure]
Daniel, Book of D: 33
Shadwell [estate]
Jefferson, Thomas (Boyhood) J: 76 *with picture*
Shadwell, Thomas [English poet]
Dryden, John D: 370
Poet laureate (table: Poets laureate of the United Kingdom) P: 590
Shafer, George F. [American political leader]
North Dakota (table) N: 513
Shafer, Raymond P. [American political leader]
Pennsylvania (table) P: 263
Shaffer, Peter [British dramatist] S: 342
English literature (Recent English drama) E: 323
Shafii [Muslim sect]
Yemen (People) Y: 562; (History) Y: 563
Shafroth, John F. [American political leader]
Colorado (table) Ci: 844
Shaft [anatomy]
Bone (Structure of the bones) B: 456 *with diagram*
Hair *picture on* H: 10; (The root and shaft) H: 9 *with diagrams*
Shaft [architecture]
Architecture (table) A: 608-609 *with picture*
Shaft [arrow]
Archery (Arrows) A: 602 *with diagram*
Shaft [biology]
Bird (Feathers) B: 362
Shaft [mining]
Mining (Mining terms) M: 577
Shaft furnace
Iron and steel (The Iron Age) I: 449-450
Shaft Graves
Mycenae M: 970f
Shaft mine
Coal (Underground mining) Ci: 723 *with diagram*
Iron and steel (Mining and processing iron ore) I: 438
Mining (Underground mining methods) M: 576 *with diagram*
Shaft tug
Harness *diagram on* H: 63
Shafter, William Rufus [American general]
Fort Shafter F: 416
Shagari, Shehu [Nigerian political leader]
Nigeria (Oil wealth) N: 418
Shagbark hickory [tree]
Hickory H: 224
Plant *picture on* P: 525
Tree *pictures on* T: 421
Shaggy mane [fungus]
Mushroom *picture on* M: 944
Shah [title] S: 342
Mohammad Reza Pahlavi M: 687
Reza Shah Pahlavi R: 289
Shah Jahan [Mughal emperor] S: 342
Delhi (History) D: 115
India (Architecture and sculpture) I: 119; (The Mughal Empire) I: 129
Mongol Empire (Breakup) M: 721
Mughal Empire M: 910
Taj Mahal T: 18
Shah-Namah [book by Firdausi]
Painting (Islamic painting) P: 48
Shahadah [religion]
Islam (The Five Pillars of Islam) I: 463
Shaheed Dibash [holiday]
February F: 61
Shaheen, Jeanne [American political leader]

New Hampshire (table) N: 223
Shahjahan [Mughal emperor] *See* Shah Jahan *in this index*
Shahn, Ben [American painter] S: 342 *with picture*
Painting (Tempera) P: 38-39
Shahriyar, King [legendary figure]
Arabian Nights A: 582b
Shaka [king of the Zulu] S: 342
Zulu Z: 608
"Shake, Rattle and Roll" [song]
Rock music (Musical roots) R: 376
Shaken baby syndrome S: 343
Shaker Festival [South Union]
Kentucky *picture on* K: 283
Shaker Village [Pleasant Hill]
Kentucky (Places to visit) K: 282 *with picture*
Shakers [religious group] S: 343 *with picture*
Antique *picture on* A: 558
Kentucky (Places to visit) K: 282 *with picture*
Shakespeare, Hamnet [son of]
Shakespeare, William (Marriage) S: 346-347; (His last years) S: 348
Shakespeare, John [father of]
Shakespeare, William (His life in Stratford) S: 345; (The years of fame) S: 347-348
Shakespeare, Judith [daughter of]
Shakespeare, William (Marriage) S: 346-347; (His last years) S: 348
Shakespeare, Mary Arden [mother of]
Shakespeare, William (His life in Stratford) S: 345-346
Shakespeare, Susanna [daughter of]
Shakespeare, William (Marriage) S: 346-347; (His last years) S: 348
Shakespeare, William [English author] S: 344 *with pictures*
See also the list of Related articles in the Shakespeare, William *article*
April (Quotations) A: 577
Blank verse B: 398
Dench, Judi D: 130
Drama (Elizabethan playwrights) D: 331-332
English literature (Elizabethan drama) E: 316-317; (Elizabethan drama) E: 317
Fairy (Fairies in literature) F: 11 *with picture*
Folger Shakespeare Library F: 315
Folklore (Folk tales) F: 323-324
Gielgud, John G: 181
Globe Theatre G: 233
Granville-Barker, Harley G: 318
Holinshed's Chronicles H: 292
January (Quotations) J: 31
Kean, Edmund K: 252
Language (Language change) L: 64
Olivier, Laurence O: 744
Plagiarism P: 505
Poetry (Forms) P: 595
Romeo and Juliet R: 449
Sonnet So: 593
Stratford Shakespeare Festival So: 920
Tragedy T: 366
Shakespeare Center
Stratford-upon-Avon So: 920
Shakespeare Festival
See also Stratford Shakespeare Festival *in this index*
Oregon *picture on* O: 837
Shakespeare in Love [film]
Dench, Judi D: 130
Motion picture (Best picture: 1998) M: 861
Shakespeare School
Stratford Shakespeare Festival So: 920
Shakespearean sonnet
Poetry (Forms) P: 595
Shakespeare's Birthplace [Stratford]
Shakespeare, William *pictures on* S: 346
Shakespeare's Sonnets [book]
Shakespeare, William (The sonnets) S: 348
Shaking palsy *See* Parkinson disease *in this index*
Shakir al-Sayyab, Badr [Iraqi author]
Arabic literature (Poetry) A: 583
Shakira [Colombian musician]
Latin America (Music) L: 100
Shakti [Hindu god]
Hinduism (Deities) H: 236
Shakuhachi [musical instrument]
Music (Japanese music) M: 956
Shakur, Tupac [American rapper] S: 370
Shalako [custom]
Zuni Indians Z: 609
Shalala, Donna E. [American government official]
Arab Americans (Arab American accomplishments) A: 580b
Clinton, Bill (table) Ci: 682d
Health and Human Services, Department of (table) H: 128
Shale [rock] S: 370

Earth (Sedimentary rocks) E: 21
Oil shale O: 707
Rock (table) R: 373 *with picture*
Sedimentary rock S: 280
Shalikashvili, John [American military leader]
Joint Chiefs of Staff (table) J: 156
Shallenberger, Ashton C. [American political leader]
Nebraska N: 110
Shallenberger, Oliver B. [American inventor]
Electric meter E: 178
Shallot [plant]
Gardening (Planting and transplanting) G: 34
Shallow cultivation
Dryland farming D: 370
Shallow draft hydrofoil [boat]
Hydrofoil (Fully submerged hydrofoils) H: 467-468 *with picture*
Shalmaneser III [king of Assyria]
Assyria (History) A: 822
Shalom Tower
Tel Aviv T: 88
Shalwar [clothing]
India (Clothing) I: 117
Shalwar-qamiz [clothing]
Pakistan (Clothing) P: 96
Sham Chun [river, China]
Hong Kong (The land) H: 318 *with map*
Shamal [wind]
Saudi Arabia (Climate) S: 158-159
Shamal Darfur [state]
Darfur D: 35
Shaman [religion] S: 370
Arctic (Traditional ways of life) A: 638
Exorcism E: 438
Indian, American (Shamans) I: 147
Inuit (Religion) I: 354e
Magic (The magician) M: 49
Mongolia (The people) M: 722
Religion *picture on* R: 219; (Religious rituals) R: 217; (Religion today) R: 223-224
Sami (Religion) S: 79
Shamash [Babylonian god]
Hammurabi *picture on* H: 36
Shamash [Judaism]
Hanukkah H: 54
Shambaugh, Jessie Field [American educator]
4-H (The first 4-H program) F: 436
Shame [book by Rushdie]
Rushdie, Salman R: 522
Shame of the Cities, The [book by Steffens]
Muckrakers M: 908
Shamela [book by Fielding] *See* Apology for the Life of Mrs. Shamela Andrews, An *in this index*
Shaming [punishment]
Colonial life in America (Crime and punishment) Ci: 796
Shamir, Adi [Israeli computer scientist]
Codes and ciphers (Public-key systems) Ci: 750
Shamir, Yitzhak [Israeli political leader] S: 371
Israel (Unity government) I: 489
Peres, Shimon P: 285
Shamma [clothing]
Ethiopia (Way of life) E: 368-369
Shammai [Jewish scholar]
Hillel I H: 232
Shamrock [plant] S: 371 *with picture*
Patrick, Saint (Legends of Saint Patrick) P: 197
Saint Patrick's Day S: 51
Shamshi-Adad [king of Assyria]
Assyria (History) A: 822
Shamsu'd-din Mohammad [Persian poet]
Hafiz H: 5
Shan [people]
Myanmar (Early days) M: 970d
Shandong Peninsula [China]
China (The Eastern Highlands) C: 492 *with map*
Shang dynasty [Chinese history] S: 371
Asia (The Huang He and Yangtze valleys) A: 805
China *map on* C: 501; (The arts) C: 487 *with pictures*; (The first dynasties) C: 499
Chinese language (Development) C: 510
Sculpture (China) S: 238
World, History of the (The Huang He Valley) W: 425 *with picture*
Shanghai [China] S: 371 *with picture*
China C: 474 *with picture*
Treaty port T: 409
Shanghai Communiqué
China (Improved relations with the West) C: 505
Shanghai Stock Exchange
China *picture on* C: 498
Shanghai World Financial Center
Shanghai (History) S: 372
Skyscraper (table) S: 498 *with picture*
Shangri-La [fictional place]
Hilton, James H: 233

Shangri-La [U.S. history]
Camp David C: 88
Shank [chicken]
Chicken (The body of a chicken) C: 440 *with picture*
Shank [cut]
Ham (Kinds of ham) H: 28 *with pictures*
Shankar, Ravi [Indian musician]
Sitar *picture on* S: 477
Shannon, Claude [American scientist]
Information theory I: 269
Shannon, James C. [American political leader]
Connecticut (table) Ci: 967
Shannon, Monica [American author]
Newbery Medal (table) N: 359
Shannon, River [Ireland] S: 372
Ireland (Rivers and lakes) I: 422
Shannon, Wilson [American political leader]
Ohio (table) O: 699
Shannon Airport [Ireland]
Limerick L: 307
Shanshui [art]
China *picture on* C: 488
Shantung [fabric]
Silk (Douppioni) S: 460
Shantytown [area]
Argentina (City life) A: 648-650
Shaolin [martial art]
Kung fu K: 392
Martial arts (Chinese martial arts) M: 234
Shape [aesthetics]
Photography (Shape) P: 409
Shape-memory materials [engineering]
Materials (Smart materials) M: 301
Shape of Things to Come, The [book by Wells]
Wells, H. G. W: 195
Shape-shifting
Witchcraft (Witchcraft as sorcery) W: 371
Shapes *See the list of Related articles in the* Geometry *article*
Shaping [industrial process]
Iron and steel (Shaping and finishing steel) I: 445 *with diagrams*
Machine tool (Planing, shaping, and broaching) M: 18
Shapiro, Karl Jay [American poet] S: 372
Shapiro, Samuel H. [American political leader]
Illinois (table) I: 71
Shapley, Harlow [American astronomer] S: 373
Shapp, Milton J. [American political leader]
Pennsylvania (table) P: 263
Shar-pei [dog] *See* Chinese shar-pei *in this index*
Sharaku [Japanese artist] S: 373 *with picture*
Japanese print (The master print artists) J: 63
Sharapova, Maria [Russian tennis player] S: 373 *with portrait*
Sharchops [people]
Bhutan (People) B: 277
Share [economics]
Investment (table) I: 366; (Stocks) I: 368
Stock So: 903
Share [television]
Television (Measuring a program's success) T: 113
Share [tool]
Plow (The moldboard plow bottom) P: 575
Share draft [banking]
Check (Checks and the economy) C: 391
Share lease [rent]
Plantation (Skilled-labor plantations) P: 551
Tenant farming T: 132
Share-the-Wealth Society
Long (Huey Pierce Long) L: 445-446
Sharecropper [agriculture]
Bangladesh (Agriculture) B: 84
Plantation ("Free"-labor plantations) P: 550
South America (Agriculture) So: 634
Shari'ah [religion] S: 373
Government (Asia and the Middle East) G: 289-290
Islam (The Shari'ah) I: 465
Muslims (Muhammad) M: 964a
Nigeria (Courts) N: 411; (Internal conflict) N: 418
Pakistan (Musharraf) P: 100
Saudi Arabia (National government) S: 155
Sharif, Mohammad Nawaz [Pakistani political leader]
Musharraf, Pervez M: 941
Pakistan (Struggle for democracy) P: 100
Sharif Sheik Ahmed [Somali political leader]
Somalia (History) So: 589-590
Sharifs [people]
Morocco (Corsairs and sharifs) M: 814
Shark [fish] S: 374 *with pictures*
See also the list of Related articles in the Shark *article*
Animal *pictures on* A: 471, A: 487
Brain *diagram on* B: 559

Dogfish D: 283
Fish *pictures on* F: 168, F: 170; (Harmful fish) F: 147; (Sharks, rays, and chimaeras) F: 148 *with picture*; (The Age of Fishes) F: 171 *with picture*
Sharkey, Tom [American boxer]
Bellows, George Wesley B: 244
Sharkey, William L. [American political leader]
Mississippi (table) M: 640
Sharks, San Jose
Hockey (table: National Hockey League) H: 281
Sharmarke, Omar Abdirashid Ali [Somali political leader]
Somalia (History) So: 589-590
Sharon, Ariel [Israeli political leader] S: 377
Israel (The early 2000's) I: 489
Kadima K: 208
Olmert, Ehud O: 745
Sharon, Plain of [region, Israel]
Israel (The Coastal Plain) I: 482
Sharp [music]
Music (Tone) M: 950; (Indicating pitch) M: 952-953
Sharp, Becky [literary figure]
Thackeray, William Makepeace (Later career) T: 220
Sharp, Granville [British social reformer]
Sierra Leone (History) S: 452
Sharp, Phillip Allen [American physiologist]
Nobel Prizes (Physiology or medicine: 1993) N: 446
Sharpe, Lake
South Dakota (Rivers and lakes) So: 676 *with map*
Sharpe, M. Q. [American political leader]
South Dakota (table) So: 680
Sharpe, William Forsyth [American economist]
Nobel Prizes (Economics: 1990) N: 449
Sharpless, K. Barry [American chemist]
Nobel Prizes (Chemistry: 2001) N: 444
"Sharps and Flats" [column by Field]
Field, Eugene F: 91
Sharps buffalo rifle
Rifle *picture on* R: 339
Sharpsburg, Battle of *See* Antietam, Battle of *in this index*
Sharptooth lemon shark
Lemon shark L: 189
Shasta, Mount [California]
Cascade Range C: 271
Mount Shasta M: 888
Shasta daisy [plant]
Burbank, Luther (His achievements and methods) B: 702
Shasta Dam [Sacramento River, California] S: 377
Dam *picture on* D: 17; (table) D: 18
Lake *picture on* L: 32
Shastina [volcano, California]
Mount Shasta M: 888
Shastri, Lal Bahadur [Indian political leader]
India (India under Indira Gandhi) I: 133
Shatt al Arab [river, Iran-Iraq]
Iraq (The southern plain) I: 411 *with map*
Middle East (The land) M: 531
Shaving [grooming]
Clothing (Ancient times) Ci: 696-697
Razor (Safety razors) R: 153
Shavuot [custom] S: 377
Judaism (The pilgrimage festivals) J: 181
May M: 320
Pentecost P: 275
Shaw, Anna Howard [American social reformer] S: 377
Shaw, George Bernard [Irish author] S: 378
Campbell, Mrs. Patrick C: 91
Drama (British drama) D: 338-339
English literature (Later Victorian literature) E: 321-322; (Literature before World War I) E: 322
Granville-Barker, Harley G: 318
Irish literature (Drama) I: 432
Realism (In drama) R: 172
Shaw, Irwin [American author] S: 378
Shaw, Leslie M. [American political leader]
Iowa (table) I: 391
Roosevelt, Theodore (table) R: 466
Shaw, Louis A. [American inventor]
Iron lung I: 453
Shaw, T. E. [name for]
Lawrence, T. E. L: 146
Shaw, Walter R. [Canadian political leader]
Prince Edward Island (table) P: 791
Shaw, Wilbur [American race driver]
Automobile racing (table: Indianapolis 500 winners) A: 980
Shaw Festival [Ontario]
Theater *picture on* T: 249
Shaw Memorial [sculpture by Saint-Gaudens]
Saint-Gaudens, Augustus S: 33

Shawe, Isabella [wife of]
Thackeray, William Makepeace (Early career)
T: 220
Shawinigan Falls
Quebec (Rivers, waterfalls, and lakes) Q: 24
Shawm [musical instrument]
Oboe O: 643
Shawmut Peninsula
Boston (The city) B: 495
Shawn, Edwin M. *See* Shawn, Ted *in this index*
Shawn, Ted [American dancer] S: 378
Saint Denis, Ruth S: 33 *with picture*
Shawnee Hills [region, Illinois]
Illinois (Land regions) I: 64 *with picture*
Shawnee Indians S: 379
Boone, Daniel (Indian captivity) B: 478
Indian wars (Lord Dunmore's War [1774]) I: 191;
(Conflicts in the Midwest) I: 191-192
Shawnee Prophet S: 379
Shawnee Prophet [American Indian chief] S: 379
Creek Indians Ci: 1126
Harrison, William Henry (Entry into politics)
H: 74-75
Indian, American (Prophets) I: 148
Indian wars (The Shawnee Prophet) I: 192
Shawnee Indians S: 379
Tecumseh T: 78
Shawnee Sun [newspaper]
Kansas (Interesting facts) K: 217
Shawwal [month]
Calendar (The Islamic calendar) C: 29
`Īd al-Fitr I: 25
Shaykh [title] *See* Sheik *in this index*
Shaykh Lutfullah Mosque [Isfahan]
Isfahan I: 462
Shays, Daniel [American settler]
Massachusetts (The Revolutionary War) M: 291-
292
Shays's Rebellion S: 379
Shays's Rebellion [U.S. history] S: 379
Constitution of the United States (The need for
the Constitution) Ci: 998-999
Massachusetts (The Revolutionary War) M: 291-
292
Springfield (Government and history) So: 808
United States, History of the (The Articles of
Confederation) U: 161
She [book by Haggard]
Haggard, H. Rider H: 6
She Done Him Wrong [film]
Grant, Cary G: 311
West, Mae W: 199
She Stoops to Conquer [play by Goldsmith]
English literature (The Johnson circle) E: 319
Goldsmith, Oliver G: 259
Shea, Ambrose [Canadian political leader]
Confederation of Canada (Fathers of
Confederation) Ci: 935
Shea Stadium
New York City (Sports) N: 338
Shear core [building construction]
Earthquake (Building design) E: 34 *with diagram*
Shear line
Glider (Soaring) G: 229-230
Shear stress [physics]
Aerodynamics (Principles of aerodynamics) A: 85
Shear wall [building construction]
Building construction (Types of construction)
B: 683
Earthquake (Building design) E: 34 *with diagram*
Shear wave [physics]
Earthquake *diagram on* E: 34
Shearer, Norma [American actress]
Motion picture (Best performance by an actress:
1929-30) M: 862
Shearing
Colonial life in America *picture on* Ci: 802
Scotland *picture on* S: 215
Wool (Processing of wool) W: 400 *with picture*
Shearing, George [British-American pianist]
Jazz (The spread of jazz) J: 72-73
Shears [machine tool]
Machine tool (Metal forming operations) M: 19
Shears [tool]
Scissors S: 208
Shearwater [bird] S: 379
Sheath [botany]
Grass (The grass plant) G: 324 *with picture*
Rice (Growth and reproduction) R: 323
Sheath dress
Clothing (The 1900's) Ci: 703
Sheathbill [bird]
Antarctica (Living things) A: 534-535 *with picture*
Sheathing [building material]
House (The frame) H: 382 *with diagram*; (The
roof) H: 382 *with diagram*
Sheave [mechanics]

Elevator (How elevators work) E: 234 *with
diagram*
Sheba, Queen of [Biblical figure]
Ethiopia E: 368
Mother Goose (Who was Mother Goose?) M: 842
Yemen (History) Y: 563
Shebat [month]
Calendar (The Hebrew calendar) C: 29
Shechem [ancient city]
Cities of refuge Ci: 568
Shechtman, Daniel [Israeli chemist]
Nobel Prizes (Chemistry: 2011) N: 444
Shedd Aquarium [Chicago]
Chicago (Museums) Ci: 428-429 *with picture*
Illinois (Museums) I: 56
Shedlock, Marie [British storyteller]
Storytelling (The 1900's) So: 915
Sheeler, Charles [American artist] S: 379
Painting (Precisionism) P: 82
Sheen, Fulton John [American religious leader]
S: 379
Sheep [animal] S: 380 *with pictures*
Agriculture *picture on* A: 147
Animal *pictures on* A: 474, 475
Biology (Current research and issues) B: 320-321
Cloning (Successes) Ci: 683 *with picture*
Conservation (Australia) Ci: 989
Heredity (The era of genetic engineering) H: 209
Mad cow disease M: 26
Mammal *diagram on* M: 121
Meat packing M: 350
Mutton M: 969
New Zealand *picture on* N: 354; (Agriculture)
N: 353
Prion P: 804
Ranching R: 134
Wool W: 399 *with picture*
Sheep bot fly
Bot fly B: 507
Sheep laurel [plant]
Plant *picture on* P: 524
Sheep shearing *See* Shearing *in this index*
Sheep tick [animal]
Tick T: 279 *with picture*
Sheepdog S: 383
See also the list of Related articles in the Sheepdog
article
Dog *pictures on* D: 276
Sheepdog [hairstyle]
Hairdressing (The 1900's) H: 12
Sheepshearing *See* Shearing *in this index*
Sheepswool [sea animal]
Sponge *picture on* So: 799
Sheet [boat]
Sailing (Rigging) S: 24
Sheet bend
Knots, hitches, and splices *diagram on* K: 356
Sheet-fed press
Printing (Methods of printing) P: 798
Sheet-fed scanner [electronic device]
Computer (A scanner) Ci: 915
Sheet lightning
Lightning (Appearance) L: 300
Sheet Metal Workers' International Association
Labor movement (table) L: 8
Sheet pile [construction]
Breakwater B: 589
Sheet silicate [mineral]
Silicate S: 458
Sheet steel
Iron and steel (Rolling) I: 445 *with diagram*
Sheet-web weaver [spider]
Spider (Linyphiids) So: 789
Sheeting [fabric]
Muslin M: 966
Sheetrock [material]
Wallboard W: 17
Sheffield [England] S: 383
Conservation *picture on* Ci: 985
Sheffield, Bill [American political leader]
Alaska (table) A: 300
Sheffield Shield [award]
Cricket (History) Ci: 1134-1135
Shehan, Lawrence Joseph [American religious
leader] S: 383
Shehitah [religion]
Judaism (Dietary laws) J: 182
Kosher K: 384a
Sheik [title] S: 383
Asia (Country life) A: 779
United Arab Emirates (Government) U: 44
Shekel [money] S: 383
Coin collecting *picture on* Ci: 758
Talent T: 20
Shel-tow-ee [Indian name of]
Boone, Daniel (Indian captivity) B: 478
Shelburne, Earl of [British political leader]

United Kingdom (table: British prime ministers)
U: 72
Shelburne Museum [Shelburne, Vermont]
Folk art (Folk art collections) F: 319
Vermont (Places to visit) V: 326
Shelby, George [literary figure]
Uncle Tom's Cabin U: 20
Shelby, Isaac [American political leader]
Kentucky (Statehood) K: 291
Sheldon, Charles H. [American political leader]
South Dakota (table) So: 680
Sheldon, George L. [American political leader]
Nebraska (table) N: 110
Sheldon, William [American psychiatrist]
Personality (Personality types) P: 301
Sheldon Museum of Art [Lincoln]
Nebraska (Museums) N: 98
Shelduck [bird]
Bird *picture on* B: 344e
Duck *picture on* D: 375; (Shelducks) D: 376
Shelf-life improver
Bread (How yeast bread is made) B: 588
Shell [ammunition]
Ammunition (Artillery ammunition) A: 435 *with
pictures*
Shrapnel S: 438
Shell [biology] S: 384 *with pictures*
Animal *picture on* A: 501
Carbon cycle C: 206
Diatom D: 185
Egg (The shell) E: 116 *with diagram*
Mollusk M: 694
Nautilus N: 69 *with picture*
Oyster (Shell) O: 890 *with pictures*
Pearl (How pearls are formed) P: 216 *with picture*
Scallop S: 170 *with picture*
Snail S: 522 *with pictures*
Turtle T: 520 *with pictures*
Wampum W: 22
Shell [boat]
Outrigger O: 880
Rowing (Types of rowing) R: 493-494
Shell [company] *See* Royal Dutch Shell plc *in this
index*
Shell, Electron [physics] *See* Electron shell *in this
index*
Shell, Joseph C. [American political leader]
Nixon, Richard Milhous (Defeat in California)
N: 432
Shell cameo [coloring]
Cat (Coat) C: 287
Shell molding [industrial process]
Candy (Chocolate candies) C: 176
Shell Oil Company
Nigeria (Oil pollution) N: 418
Shell Series [award]
Cricket (History) Ci: 1134-1135
Shell shock [psychology] *See* Post-traumatic stress
disorder *in this index*
Shellac [tree product] S: 391
Lac L: 19
Lacquerware L: 22
Paint (Industrial paints) P: 24
Varnish (Types of varnish) V: 286
Sheller [machine]
Rice (Cleaning and hulling) R: 326 *with picture*
Shelley, Mary Wollstonecraft [British author]
S: 391
Frankenstein F: 484
Godwin, William G: 246
Science fiction (The first science fiction) S: 205
Shelley, Percy Bysshe (His life) S: 391
Shelley, Percy Bysshe [British poet] S: 391 *with
portrait*
English literature (Romantic poetry) E: 320
Shelley, Mary Wollstonecraft S: 391
Shelley v. Kraemer [U.S. history]
Supreme Court of the United States (table)
So: 1002
Shellfish [animal]
Crustacean Ci: 1162 *with pictures*
Fishing industry (Where fish are caught) F: 181-
182
Seafood S: 264
Shelter S: 392 *with pictures*
See also Housing *in this index; and the list of
Related articles in the* Shelter *article*
Animal (Providing shelter) A: 500 *with pictures*
Civil defense (Shelter) Ci: 605
Domestic violence D: 301
Egypt, Ancient *picture on* E: 138; (Food, clothing,
and shelter) E: 137
Homelessness H: 302
House H: 380 *with pictures*
Indian, American *pictures on* I: 138; (Shelter)
I: 136d
Inuit (Shelter) I: 354c

Pioneer life in America (A pioneer settlement)
P: 479; (Establishing a homestead) P: 479
Shelter Belt Project [U.S. history]
Windbreak W: 333
Shelterbelt [structure] See Windbreak in this index
Sheltered workshop
Intellectual disability (Treatment) I: 318
Shelterwood cutting
Forestry (Harvesting) F: 404 with picture
Sheltie [dog] See Shetland sheepdog in this index
Shelton, H. Hugh [American military leader]
Joint Chiefs of Staff (table) J: 156
Shelton, Sarah Elmira Royster [fiancée of]
Poe, Edgar Allan (Poe's life) P: 589
Shem [Biblical figure]
Noah N: 439
Shemini Atzeret [custom]
Sukkot So: 965
Shenandoah National Park [Virginia] S: 394
National Park System (table: National parks) N: 48
Virginia picture on V: 398
Shenandoah River [Virginia] S: 394
Shenandoah Valley [region, Virginia] S: 394
Luray Caverns L: 526
Virginia (Land regions) V: 410 with picture
Shenyang [China] S: 394
Shenzhen [river]
Hong Kong (The land) H: 318 with map
Shenzhou [spacecraft]
Astronaut A: 829
Rocket picture on R: 384
Space exploration (China) So: 727
Sheol [religion]
Hell H: 176
Shepard, Alan Bartlett, Jr. [American astronaut]
S: 395 with portrait
Astronaut (Achievements in space) A: 829; (table)
A: 830
New Hampshire picture on N: 225; (The mid-
1900's) N: 226-227
Rocket (The space age) R: 391
Space exploration (Vostok and Mercury: The
first human beings in space) So: 712-713 with
picture
United States, History of the (The space race)
U: 196
Shepard, Ernest Howard [British artist] S: 395
Literature for children picture on L: 363
Shepard, Sam [American playwright] S: 395
Shephard, Esther [American author]
Bunyan, Paul B: 701
Shepheardes Calender, The [poem by Spenser]
Spenser, Edmund (Spenser's other poems)
So: 778
Shepherd, Alexander "Boss" [American political
leader]
Washington, D.C. (Territorial government
abolished) W: 86
Shepherd, William M. [American astronaut]
International Space Station (History) I: 346b with
picture
Shepherd Boy, A [sculpture by Thorvaldsen]
Sculpture (European sculpture) S: 253-254 with
picture
Shepherd dog
Anatolian shepherd A: 448b with picture
German shepherd dog G: 143
Pyrenean shepherd P: 919
Sheepdog S: 383
Shepherd kings
Hyksos H: 475
Shepherd life
Bedouins B: 199
Nomad N: 452
Shepherd moon [astronomy]
Planetary ring P: 514d
Saturn (Rings) S: 151j-151
Shepherd of the Hills, The [book by Wright]
Branson B: 564
Shepherd's pie [food]
England (Food and drink) E: 295-296
Shepherdstown [West Virginia]
West Virginia (White settlement) W: 226
Shepp, Carol [wife of]
McCain, John (Early life) M: 332-332a
Sher-Gil, Amrita [Indian painter]
India (Painting) I: 119-120
Sheraton, Thomas [British furniture designer]
S: 395
Sheraton style [furniture]
Sheraton, Thomas S: 395
Sherbet [food]
Ice cream (The composition of ice cream) I: 8
Sherbrooke [Quebec] S: 395
Sherbrooke, Lord [Canadian statesman]
Sherbrooke S: 396
Sheridan [Wyoming]

Wyoming (table: Average monthly weather)
W: 528
Sheridan, Philip Henry [Union general] S: 396
Civil War, American (Cavalry maneuvers) Ci: 631
Early, Jubal Anderson E: 15
Sheridan, Richard Brinsley [Irish dramatist] S: 396
Drama (England) D: 334-335 with picture
English literature (The Johnson circle) E: 319
Hastings, Warren H: 83
Irish literature (Early works in English) I: 431
Sheriff [office] S: 397
Police (Early law enforcement in England) P: 624
Sherlock Holmes See Holmes, Sherlock in this index
Sherman, Buren R. [American political leader]
Iowa (table) I: 391
Sherman, Cindy [American photographer] S: 396
with picture
Photography (A diversity of styles) P: 426-427
Postmodernism P: 709
Sherman, James Schoolcraft [American political
leader] S: 397
Taft, William Howard (Election of 1908) T: 10
Vice president of the United States portrait on
V: 348
Sherman, John [American political leader] S: 397
Sherman, John Ames [American inventor]
Envelope E: 328
Sherman, Roger [American patriot] S: 397 with
portrait
New Haven (History) N: 229
Sherman, William Tecumseh [Union general]
S: 397 with portrait
See also Sherman's March in this index
Atlanta (Destruction and redevelopment) A: 861
Civil War, American (The commanding officers)
Ci: 618-619 with picture; (Grant in command)
Ci: 631; (Closing in) Ci: 632 with picture; (The
Atlanta campaign) Ci: 632
South Carolina (The Civil War) So: 660
Sherman Antitrust Act [1890]
Antitrust laws A: 560
Capitalism (Ensuring competition) C: 195
Consumer protection (The right to choose)
Ci: 1018
Harrison, Benjamin (Domestic affairs) H: 72
Interstate commerce (Other regulatory
commissions) I: 351
Labor movement (Opposition to unions) L: 10
Monopoly and competition (History) M: 732
Standard Oil Company So: 835
United States, History of the (Government and
business reforms) U: 186
Sherman Silver Purchase Act [1890]
Cleveland, Grover (Saving the gold standard)
Ci: 673
Harrison, Benjamin (Domestic affairs) H: 72
Sherman's March [U.S. history]
Civil War, American (Sherman's march through
Georgia) Ci: 633 with picture; (The beginning of
modern warfare) Ci: 634
Georgia (The Civil War) G: 132
Sherman, William Tecumseh S: 397
Sherpas [people] S: 398
Nepal (People) N: 125
Races, Human (Evolutionary theory) R: 53-54
Tenzing Norgay T: 169
Sherrington, Sir Charles Scott [British
physiologist]
Nobel Prizes (Physiology or medicine: 1932)
N: 445
Sherry [wine]
Wine (Fortified wines) W: 336; (Wine styles from
other countries) W: 337
Sherwood, Robert Emmet [American author]
S: 398
Sherwood Forest [England]
Robin Hood R: 367
Shetland Islands [islands, Atlantic] S: 398
City picture on Ci: 577
Shetland pony S: 398
Horse (table: Some types and breeds of horses)
H: 343; (Ponies) H: 347 with picture
Shetland sheepdog S: 398 with picture
Shevardnadze, Eduard A. [Georgian political
leader]
Georgia [country] (History) G: 111
Shevardnadze, Eduard Amvrosiyevich [Georgian
political leader] S: 399
Shevchenko, Taras [Ukrainian poet] S: 399
Ukraine (The arts) U: 9
Shevell, Nancy [wife of]
McCartney, Paul M: 332c
Shevout [custom] See Shavuot in this index
Shi Huangdi [emperor of China] S: 399
Archaeology picture on A: 595
Asia picture on A: 804
China (The Qin dynasty) C: 500

Great Wall of China (History) G: 350
Qin dynasty Q: 4
Sculpture (China) S: 238 with picture
Terra-cotta army of Xi'an T: 172
World, History of the (The unification of China)
W: 431 with picture
Xi'an X: 545
**Shi`ah** [religious group] See Shi`ites in this index
Shiba inu [dog] S: 399 with picture
Shickellamy [American Indian leader]
Logan L: 423
Shield [armor] S: 399 with pictures
Armor picture on A: 720
Indian, American pictures on I: 138, I: 144; (Before
European contact) I: 162 with picture
Knights and knighthood (Armor) K: 350
Vikings (Weapons and armor) V: 382 with picture
Shield [heraldry]
Heraldry (The development of heraldry) H: 194
with pictures; (Elements of a coat of arms)
H: 196 with pictures
Shield [nuclear energy]
Nuclear energy (Hazards and safeguards) N: 587
Shield of David [emblem]
Judaism picture on J: 180
Star of David So: 854 with picture
Shield system [construction]
Tunnel (Earth tunnels) T: 490
Shield-tailed snake
Snake (Shield-tailed snakes) S: 535
Shield volcano
Mars (Volcanoes) M: 226
Volcano (Shield volcanoes) V: 442 with picture
Shielded metal arc welding
Welding (Arc welding) W: 189
Shields, Carol [American-born author]
Canadian literature (Modern English-Canadian
fiction) C: 160
Shift lens
Photography (Types of lenses) P: 411
Shifting cultivation [agriculture]
See also Slash-and-burn agriculture in this index
Africa (Rural life) A: 110-111
Agriculture (Subsistence agriculture) A: 149 with
picture
Shifting gears [engine]
Transmission (Gears) T: 375-376
Shiga, Naoya [Japanese author]
Japanese literature (The modern period) J: 62
Shigehiro, Tsuneo [Japanese mountain climber]
Mount Everest M: 884
Shigellosis [disease]
Dysentery D: 398
Shih Huang-ti [emperor of China] See Shi Huangdi
in this index
Shih Tzu [dog] S: 400 with picture
Shiitake mushroom
Mushroom (Nonpoisonous mushrooms) M: 943-
945 with picture
Shi`ites [religious group] S: 400
Arabs (Religion) A: 586
Egypt (Muslim rule) E: 130
Fatimid dynasty F: 55
Flag picture on F: 216
Hezbollah H: 221
Iran (Religion) I: 401
Iran-Iraq War I: 407
Iraq (Religion) I: 411; (History) I: 413-414
Iraq War (Resistance to the coalition) I: 414e
Islam (Divisions of Islam) I: 466
Lebanon (Ethnic groups and religion) L: 171;
(War and terrorism) L: 173
Middle East (Religion) M: 531
Muslims (Ali) M: 964b
Persian Gulf War of 1991 (Consequences of the
war) P: 300d
Qom Q: 4
Safavid dynasty S: 8
Shari`ah S: 374
Sunnis So: 991
Shiki, Masaoka [Japanese poet]
Haiku H: 8
Shikoku [island, Japan]
Japan (The land) J: 45-48 with map
Shikra [bird]
Hawk (Kinds of hawks) H: 111-112
Shilling [money] S: 401
Money picture on M: 707; (History of the pound)
M: 709; (Tree shillings) M: 710
Shiloh [book by Naylor]
Naylor, Phyllis Reynolds N: 91
Shiloh, Battle of [1862]
Civil War, American (table) Ci: 624; (Battle of
Shiloh) Ci: 629
Grant, Ulysses S. ("Unconditional Surrender"
Grant) G: 314
Johnston, Albert Sidney J: 154

Tennessee (The American Civil War) **T:** 154
Shiloh National Military Park [Tennessee]
National Park System (table: National military parks) **N:** 55
Shimogamo shrine [Kyoto]
Religion *picture on* **R:** 222
Shimomura, Osamu [American chemist]
Nobel Prizes (Chemistry: 2008) **N:** 444
Shimonoseki, Treaty of [1895]
Sino-Japanese War of 1894-1895 **S:** 473
Shin [anatomy]
Human body (table) **H:** 422 *with diagram*
Skeleton *diagrams on* **S:** 480
Shin guard
Baseball (Equipment) **B:** 125-126 *with picture*
Shin-pyu [ceremony]
Myanmar (Way of life) **M:** 970a
Shiner [fish]
Fish *picture on* **F:** 158
Shingle [building material]
House (The roof) **H:** 382 *with diagram*
Shingle style
House *picture on* **H:** 381
Shingles [disease] **S:** 401
Chickenpox **C:** 446
Shingon [religion]
Buddhism (The Vajrayana) **B:** 669
Shining Path [Peruvian political group]
Peru (Return to civilian government) **P:** 316
Shining Prince [literary figure]
Murasaki Shikibu **M:** 929
Shinjuku commuter station [Tokyo]
Japan *picture on* **J:** 33
Shinkansen [train] *See* Bullet train *in this index*
Shinn, Everett [American artist] **S:** 401
Ashcan School **A:** 768
Shinny [game]
Indian, American (Recreation) **I:** 142 *with picture*
Shinseki, Eric K. [American government official]
Asian Americans (Notable Asian American "firsts") **A:** 812f
Obama, Barack (table) **O:** 640h
Veterans Affairs, Department of (table) **V:** 343
Shinto [religion] **S:** 401 *with picture*
Architecture (Japanese architecture) **A:** 613
Asia (Life in Japan) **A:** 788
God (Gods of nature) **G:** 243
Japan *picture on* **J:** 42; (Religion) **J:** 40; (Architecture) **J:** 44
Religion **R:** 215; (Shinto) **R:** 221 *with picture*
Sumo **So:** 973
Tokyo (Ethnic groups and religion) **T:** 314
Shinty [game]
Indian, American (Recreation) **I:** 142 *with picture*
Ship S: 402 *with pictures*
See also Shipping, Boating, *and* Warship *in this index and the list of Related articles in the* Ship *article*
Air conditioning (Air conditioners for vehicles) **A:** 179
Brig **B:** 608 *with picture*
Colonial life in America (Transportation) **Ci:** 805
Cruise ship **Ci:** 1159
Flag *picture on* **F:** 197
Invention (The Middle Ages) **I:** 359-360
Log **L:** 421
Navy **N:** 76 *with pictures*
Norman Conquest *picture on* **N:** 456
Ocean (Exploring the ocean) **O:** 662
Ocean drilling programs **O:** 667 *with diagram*
Plastics (To replace wood and stone) **P:** 555
Propeller (Ship propellers) **P:** 826 *with picture*
Radar (In ship navigation) **R:** 65 *with pictures*
Salute (Military hand salutes) **S:** 76b
Signaling (Marine signaling) **s:** 454
Transportation *pictures on* **T:** 383, **T:** 390; (Water transportation) **T:** 384; (International freight) **T:** 396
Vikings (The Vikings as shipbuilders) **V:** 381 *with picture*
Weather (Weather balloons, airplanes, and ships) **W:** 163
Ship, Model S: 427 *with picture*
Ship of Fools [book by Porter]
Porter, Katherine Anne **P:** 682
Ship of the line
Battleship (Development of the battleship) **B:** 172
Warship *picture on* **W:** 42; (The age of sailing ships) **W:** 41
Ship rat [animal]
Rat (The body of a rat) **R:** 146 *with picture*
Ship repair
Dry dock **D:** 369
Ship Rock [hill, New Mexico]
New Mexico (Land regions) **N:** 266 *with map*
Ship-to-ship radio

Radio (Early development) **R:** 91-92
Ship-to-shore radio
Radio (Early development) **R:** 91-92
Shipbuilding [industry]
Colonial life in America (Lumbering and shipbuilding) **Ci:** 810
New Orleans (Industry) **N:** 282-283 *with picture*
Ship (Building a ship) **S:** 413 *with picture*
Vikings (Shipbuilding and navigation) **V:** 381 *with picture*
Shipibo [people]
Rain forest (The Americas) **R:** 126b
Shipley, Jenny [New Zealand political leader] **S:** 428
Clark, Helen Elizabeth **Ci:** 639
New Zealand (Political changes) **N:** 356
Shippen, Margaret [wife of]
Arnold, Benedict (A disappointed officer) **A:** 741-742
Shipping
See also Ship *in this index*
Careers (Transportation) **C:** 235
Freight **F:** 510
Great Lakes (Commerce) **G:** 344-345
Inland waterway **I:** 274
International Maritime Organization **I:** 342
Maritime Administration **M:** 212
New York City (Trade) **N:** 333
Port **P:** 680
Rome, Ancient (Transportation and communication) **R:** 443-444
Weights and measures (table: Volume and capacity) **W:** 186
Shipping bag
Paper bag **P:** 138
Shipping Board [U.S. history]
Merchant marine (Merchant fleets) **M:** 413
Ship's log [record]
Logbook **L:** 425
Ship's store
Post exchange **P:** 699
Shipton, Eric [British explorer]
Yeti **Y:** 565
Shipway
Ship (Construction) **S:** 413
Shipworm [sea animal] **S:** 428
Mollusk (Bivalves) **M:** 695
Shipwreck S: 428
Coast Guard, United States (History) **Ci:** 737
Disaster (table) **D:** 223
Shipyard
Ship (Construction) **S:** 413 *with picture*
Virginia (Manufacturing) **V:** 413-415 *with picture*
Shirakawa, Hideki [Japanese chemist]
Nobel Prizes (Chemistry: 2000) **N:** 444
Shiras, George, Jr. [American jurist]
Supreme Court of the United States (table) **So:** 1000
Shire [horse]
Horse (table: Some types and breeds of horses) **H:** 343; (Draft horses) **H:** 346 *with picture*
Shire [political unit] **S:** 429
Shire River [Africa]
Lake Nyasa **L:** 42 *with map*
Shirley [book by Brontë]
Brontë sisters (Their works) **B:** 637
Shirley, George [American singer]
Opera *picture on* **O:** 808
Shirley, William [British colonial official] **S:** 429
Shirley poppy [plant]
Poppy **P:** 668
Shirtwaist dress
Clothing (The 1800's) **Ci:** 702
Shisha [drink]
Egypt (Recreation) **E:** 124
Shishaldin Volcano [mountain, Alaska]
Aleutian Islands **A:** 340
Shiva [custom]
Judaism (Special occasions) **J:** 182
Shiva [Hindu god] **S:** 429
Hinduism (Deities) **H:** 236
India (Hinduism) **I:** 116; (Architecture and sculpture) **I:** 119
Sculpture (India) **S:** 236-237 *with picture*
Shivaji Bhonsle [Hindu prince]
India (The Mughal Empire) **I:** 129-130
Shivers, Allan [American political leader]
Texas (table) **T:** 203
Shives
Flax (Growing and processing fiber flax) **F:** 230-231
Shkhara, Mount [mountain, Georgia]
Georgia (Land and climate) **G:** 110 *with map*
Shkolnik, Levi [birth name of]
Eshkol, Levi **E:** 357
Shoals, Isles of [islands]
New Hampshire (Coastline) **N:** 220

Shoals, The [area] *See* Muscle Shoals *in this index*
Shoat [animal]
Hog (table) **H:** 284
Shock [disorder] **S:** 429
Anaphylactic shock **A:** 448
Bleeding (Effects of bleeding) **B:** 399
Burn (First-aid care) **B:** 708
First aid (Treat for shock) **F:** 136
Toxic shock syndrome **T:** 353
Shock, Electric *See* Electric shock *in this index*
Shock absorber S: 429
Automobile (Supporting the car) **A:** 950
Shock syndrome [disorder]
Dengue **D:** 131
Shock treatment [medicine] **S:** 429
Mental illness (Somatic therapy) **M:** 407
Shock wave [physics] **S:** 429
Aerodynamics (Shock waves) **A:** 87 *with diagram*
Crater **Ci:** 1121
Heliosphere (Shock waves) **H:** 175
Improvised explosive device **I:** 95
Nuclear weapon (Blast wave) **N:** 599
Shockley, William [American physicist] **S:** 430
Electricity (The electronic age) **E:** 198
Electronics (The solid-state revolution) **E:** 215 *with picture*
Transistor **T:** 372
Shoda, Michiko [Japanese empress]
Akihito **A:** 253
Shoddy [fabric]
Civil War, American (The enlisted men) **Ci:** 619-620
Wool (Types of wool) **W:** 399-400
Shoe [clothing] **S:** 430 *with pictures*
Ballet (Point work) **B:** 47 *with picture*
Clothing (The 1600's) **Ci:** 701 *with picture*
Matzeliger, Jan Ernst **M:** 312
Pioneer life in America (Clothing) **P:** 482-483
Rubber (First uses) **R:** 500
Shoe board
Cardboard **C:** 209
Shoe leather
Leather (Kinds of leather) **L:** 167 *with picture*
Shoebill [bird] **S:** 432 *with picture*
Bird (Birds of Africa) **B:** 344h *with picture*
Shoemaker, Bill [American jockey] **S:** 433
Arkansas (Interesting facts about Arkansas) **A:** 695
Horse racing (History) **H:** 366
Shoemaker, Carolyn [American astronomer]
Jupiter (History of Jupiter study) **J:** 200b
Shoemaker, Eugene Merle **S:** 433
Shoemaker, Eugene Merle [American geologist/astronomer] **S:** 433
Jupiter (History of Jupiter study) **J:** 200b
Moon (Describing lunar evolution) **M:** 794
Shoemaker, Willie *See* Shoemaker, Bill *in this index*
Shoemaker-Levy 9, Comet [astronomy]
Comet (table) **Ci:** 868; (Studying comets) **Ci:** 868-869
Jupiter (History of Jupiter study) **J:** 200b
Shoemaker's Holiday, The [play by Dekker]
Dekker, Thomas **D:** 94
Shoen [estate]
Japan (Creation of private estates) **J:** 53
Shoepack
Pioneer life in America (Clothing) **P:** 482-483
Shoeshine [film]
De Sica, Vittorio **D:** 157
Shoeshine Stand, Southeastern U.S. [photograph by Evans]
Photography *picture on* **P:** 426
Shofar [religion]
Horn **H:** 339
Rosh Ha-Shanah **R:** 480 *with picture*
Shofet [government official]
Phoenicia (Government) **P:** 394
Shogun [title] **S:** 433
Japan (Rise of the shogun) **J:** 54
Kamakura period **K:** 212
Meiji, Emperor **M:** 386
Minamoto Yoritomo **M:** 562
Painting (Japanese painting) **P:** 47
Shogunate [government]
Samurai **S:** 83
Sholem Aleichem [Jewish author] **S:** 433
Yiddish literature **Y:** 566
Sholes, Christopher Latham [American inventor] **S:** 433
Glidden, Carlos **G:** 227
Keyboard **K:** 308
Typewriter (History) **T:** 539
Sholokhov, Mikhail [Soviet author] **S:** 433
Russian literature (The period of socialist realism) **R:** 564
Sholtz, Dave [American political leader]
Florida (table) **F:** 260

Shona [people]
Great Zimbabwe **G: 350**
Zimbabwe (People) **Z: 592**; (History) **Z: 592-593**
Shookum Jim [Canadian prospector]
Yukon (History) **Y: 581**
Shooter
Marbles **M: 193**
Shooting [photography]
Motion picture (Developing the shooting
schedule) **M: 850**; (Shooting the movie) **M: 852**
Shooting [sports]
Biathlon **B: 278**
Hockey (Hockey skills) **H: 276-277**
Hunting (Kinds of hunting) **H: 450**
Olympic Games (Summer Olympic Games)
O: 746e-747
Skeet **S: 479**
Trapshooting **T: 404**
Shooting guard
Basketball (The players) **B: 144**
Shooting star [astronomy] See Meteor in this index
Shooting star [plant]
Cowslip **Ci: 1113**
Flower picture on **F: 287**
Shootout [sports]
Hockey (Playing time) **H: 277**
Shop
Safety (In other school areas) **S: 12**
Shop Around [recording]
Gordy, Berry **G: 273**
Shop-house
Singapore (The city of Singapore) **S: 470**
Shop steward [office]
Labor movement (Local unions) **L: 8**
Shoplifting S: 433
Shopping
Department store **D: 148**
Shopping center **S: 434**
Shopping bag
Paper bag **P: 138**
Shopping center S: 434
Shoran [navigation] **S: 434**
Shore
See also Beach in this index
Ocean (Waves) **O: 659**
Seashore **S: 269** with pictures
Shore, John [British musician]
Tuning fork **T: 487**
Shore, Stephen [American photographer]
Photography (A diversity of styles) **P: 426-427**
Shore Establishment
Navy, Department of the **N: 81**
Navy, United States (The Shore Establishment)
N: 85
Shore Patrol [U.S. Navy] **S: 434**
Military police **S: 543**
Short, Nigel [British chess player]
Kasparov, Garry **K: 248**
Short ballot [voting]
Ballot (In the United States) **B: 63**
Short-beaked common dolphin [sea animal]
Dolphin pictures on **D: 298, D: 299**; (The common
dolphins) **D: 297**
Short-day plant
Plant (Environmental factors) **P: 538**
Short division [mathematics]
Division (Short division) **D: 251**
Short-eared owl [bird]
Owl (Important owls) **O: 884-886**
Short grain rice
Rice (Kinds of rice) **R: 323-324**
Short-haired cat
Cat pictures on **C: 288**; (Short-haired breeds)
C: 290 with pictures
Short-horned grasshopper [insect]
Locust **L: 418**
Short line [sports]
Handball **H: 41** with diagrams
Short line railroad
Railroad (Railroad systems) **R: 112-113**
Short messaging service
Text messaging **T: 211**
Short-period comet [astronomy]
Comet picture on **Ci: 868**
Meteor (The parent comet) **M: 431**
Oort cloud **O: 788**
Short-range ballistic missile
Guided missile (Surface-to-surface missiles)
G: 425-426
Short-range forecast
Weather (Mathematical models) **W: 166**
Short splice
Knots, hitches, and splices diagram on **K: 357**
Short stop [chemical]
Photography (Black-and-white negative film)
P: 419
Short story [literature] **S: 434**

Fiction **F: 90**
Writing (Fiction) **W: 511**
Short-tailed chinchilla [animal]
Chinchilla **C: 508**
Short-tailed weasel [animal] See Ermine in this
index
Short-term credit [economics]
Credit (Types of credit) **Ci: 1124**
Short-term loan
Interest (Length of a loan) **I: 323**
Short-term memory [psychology]
Memory (The memory system) **M: 392**
Short ton [unit of measure]
Ton **T: 327**
Short-track skating
Ice skating (Short-track skating) **I: 15**
Olympic Games (Winter Olympic Games)
O: 746d-746e with picture
Short Treatise on the Game of Whist, A [book by
Hoyle]
Hoyle, Edmond **H: 402**
Short waves [radio] **S: 434**
Marconi, Guglielmo (Short-wave radio) **M: 197**
Radio (Transmitting short-wave signals) **R: 87**
Radio, Amateur **R: 95**
Shortboard
Surfing **So: 1003** with picture
Shortening [food]
Tallow **T: 21**
Shorter, John Gill [American political leader]
Alabama (table) **A: 274**
Shorter, Wayne [American saxophonist] **S: 435**
Shortfin mako [shark]
Mako shark (The shortfin mako) **M: 94**
Shark (Kinds of sharks) **S: 375** with picture
Shortfin molly [fish]
Fish picture on **F: 157**
Molly **M: 696**
Shorthand [writing] **S: 435**
Shorthand machine S: 435
Shorthorn [animal]
Cattle (Other beef cattle) **C: 309**; (table) **C: 312-313**
Shortleaf pine [tree]
Pine (Southeastern pines) **P: 468**
Shortnose gar [fish]
Gar **G: 28**
Shortridge, Eli C. D. [American political leader]
North Dakota (table) **N: 513**
Shorts [food product]
Bran **B: 563**
Shortsightedness See Myopia in this index
Shortstop [baseball]
Baseball (Player positions) **B: 127**
Shortwall mine
Coal (The longwall system) **Ci: 724-726**
Shoshone Falls
Idaho (Rivers, waterfalls, springs, and lakes) **I: 38**
with picture
Shoshone Indian Preparing His Meal [painting
by Miller]
Indian, American picture on **I: 165**
Shoshone Indians S: 435
Lewis and Clark expedition (West to the Rockies)
L: 222b-222c
Washakie **W: 45**
Wyoming (History) **W: 533-534** with picture
Shoshone National Forest [Wyoming]
Wyoming (Places to visit) **W: 524**
Shostakovich, Dimitri [Russian composer] **S: 436**
Shot [ammunition]
Ammunition (Shotgun cartridges) **A: 435** with
picture
Shotgun **S: 436**
Shot [sports]
Track and field (Throwing events) **T: 358** with
picture
"Shot heard round the world"
Revolution, American **R: 270**
Shot huckleberry [shrub]
Huckleberry **H: 404**
Shot on goal
Hockey (Hockey terms) **H: 275**
Shot-put [sport] **S: 436** with pictures
Track and field (Throwing events) **T: 358** with
picture
Shote [animal]
Hog (table) **H: 284**
Shotgun S: 436 with diagram
Ammunition (Small-arms ammunition) **A: 435**
with picture
Firearm diagram on **F: 133**
Hunting (Kinds of hunting) **H: 450**
Skeet **S: 479**
Trapshooting **T: 404**
Shotgun [house]
New Orleans (Residential districts) **N: 279**

Shoulder [anatomy] **S: 437** with pictures
Bursitis **B: 711**
Rotator cuff **R: 486**
Skeleton (The appendicular skeleton) **S: 480** with
diagrams
Shoulder blade [anatomy] See Scapula in this index
Shoulder pads
Football (Protective equipment) **F: 355-356** with
picture
Shoumatoff, Elizabeth [American painter]
Roosevelt, Franklin Delano (Death) **R: 459**
Shoup, George Laird [American political leader]
S: 437
Idaho (table) **I: 42**; (Early statehood) **I: 44**
Shoup, Oliver H. [American political leader]
Colorado (table) **Ci: 844**
Shovel-nosed snake
Animal picture on **A: 483**
Shoveler [bird] **S: 437**
Bird (Birds of inland waters and marshes) **B: 340**
with picture
Show [entertainment]
Circus **Ci: 562** with pictures
Motion picture **M: 846**
Theater **T: 232**
Show [gambling]
Horse racing (Betting) **H: 365**
Show Boat [book by Ferber]
Ferber, Edna **F: 72**
Show Boat **S: 438**
Show Boat [musical] **S: 438**
Hammerstein, Oscar, II **H: 35**
Kern, Jerome **K: 305**
Musical comedy (Musical comedy matures)
M: 960 with picture
Show jumping [sport] **S: 438**
Show Me State [nickname]
Missouri **M: 651**
Showa [title]
Hirohito **H: 242**
Shower [hygiene]
Bath (History) **B: 164-165** with picture
Showy baby's-breath [plant]
Baby's-breath **B: 14**
Showy gaillardia [plant]
Flower picture on **F: 287**
Showy lady's-slipper [plant]
Lady's-slipper **L: 25**
Shrapnel [ammunition] **S: 438**
Shrapnel, Henry [British military leader]
Shrapnel **S: 438**
Shrek [film]
Animation picture on **A: 511**
Shreve, Henry Miller [American navigator]
Louisiana (Statehood) **L: 498**
Shreveport **S: 438**
Shreveport [Louisiana] **S: 438**
Louisiana picture on **L: 487**; (Places to visit) **L: 488**;
(table: Average monthly weather) **L: 492**
Shrew [animal] **S: 438** with picture
Shrew opossum [animal]
Mammal (table) picture on **M: 128**
Shrew tenrec [animal]
Tenrec **T: 167**
Shrike [bird] **S: 439**
Bird picture on **B: 351**; (Birds of brushy areas)
B: 338 with picture; (Birds of Central and South
America) **B: 344a** with picture
Shrimp [sea animal] **S: 439** with picture
Crustacean (Outer body) **Ci: 1162** with diagram
Deep sea (Invertebrates) **D: 82a-82b**
Shrimp boat
Fishing industry picture on **F: 184**
Shrimp Festival
Mississippi (Visitor's guide) **M: 632** with picture
Shrine [religion] **S: 440**
Shrine of Democracy
South Dakota **So: 664**
Shriners International [organization] **S: 440**
Masonry (Organization) **M: 267**
Shrinkage stoping [mining]
Mining (Self-supported mining) **M: 576**
Shriver, Eunice Kennedy [sister of John F.
Kennedy]
Kennedy, John Fitzgerald (Boyhood) **K: 260-261**
Kennedy, Joseph Patrick (His family) **K: 269**
Shriver, Sargent **S: 440**
Special Olympics **So: 771**
Shriver, Maria [American journalist]
Schwarzenegger, Arnold **S: 189**
Shriver, Sargent **S: 440**
Shriver, Pam [American tennis player]
Navratilova, Martina **N: 75**
Shriver, Sargent [American political leader] **S: 440**
Nixon, Richard Milhous (The 1972 election)
N: 435
Peace Corps (History) **P: 208-209**

Shropshire [county, England]
United Kingdom *picture on* U: 61
Shropshire Lad, A [poems by Housman]
Housman, A. E. H: 393
Shropshire sheep
Sheep (Medium-wooled sheep) S: 382
Shroud [device]
Sailing (Rigging) S: 24
Shroud of Turin [religion] S: 440 *with pictures*
Shrove Tuesday [custom] S: 441
Mardi Gras M: 198
Tuesday T: 481
Shrub S: 441
Flower (Flowering shrubs) F: 281 *with pictures*
Pruning P: 841
Rose (table) R: 474; (Types of roses) R: 474-475
Tree T: 411
Shrub layer [forest]
Forest (The shrub layer) F: 392 *with picture*
Shrub live oak
Oak (Red oaks) O: 635-636
Shrubby cinquefoil [plant]
Flower *picture on* F: 283
Shtetl [town]
Yiddish literature Y: 566
Shtetl, A [book by Asch]
Asch, Sholem A: 766
Shu [Egyptian god]
Mythology *picture on* M: 974; (The Great Ennead)
M: 979
Shubenacadie River
Nova Scotia (Rivers and lakes) N: 562 *with map*
Shubun, Tensho [Japanese artist]
Painting (Japanese painting) P: 47
Shuck Faces
Mask (Ceremonial masks) M: 264
Shudra [caste]
Caste C: 279
Hinduism (Caste) H: 236
Shuffleboard [game] S: 441 *with diagram*
Shuisky, Basil [czar of Russia]
Russia (table: Czars and empresses) R: 549; (The
Time of Troubles) R: 549
Shula, Don [American football coach] S: 442 *with
portrait*
Shulevitz, Uri [Polish-American artist] S: 442 *with
picture*
Caldecott Medal (table: 1969) C: 26
Shull, Clifford Glenwood [American physicist]
Nobel Prizes (Physics: 1994) N: 442
Shull, George H. [American geneticist]
Corn (Development of hybrids) Ci: 1063
Shultz, George Pratt [American government
official] S: 442
Nixon, Richard Milhous (table) N: 433
Reagan, Ronald Wilson (table) R: 169
Shumlin, Peter [American political leader]
Vermont (table) V: 333
Shumway, Norman Edward [American doctor]
S: 443
Heart (The first heart transplants and artificial
hearts) H: 145
Shunk, Francis Rawn [American political leader]
Pennsylvania (table) P: 263
Shunt motor
Electric motor (DC motors) E: 181
Shura Council
Egypt (National government) E: 121
Shurtleff, Robert [pseudonym]
Sampson, Deborah S: 81
Shush [ancient city] *See* Susa *in this index*
Shushan [ancient city] *See* Susa *in this index*
Shuster, Joe [American cartoonist]
Comics (Comic books) Ci: 869
Superman So: 993
Shuswap Lake
British Columbia (Rivers, waterfalls, and lakes)
B: 624
Shut-off valve
Plumbing (The water supply system) P: 577 *with
diagram*
Shutout [baseball]
Baseball (Baseball terms) B: 124; (table: Modern
major league records) B: 138
Shutter [photography]
Camera (Controlling the exposure) C: 80
Motion picture *diagram on* M: 858; (The camera)
M: 856-857; (The projector) M: 858 *with
diagram*
Photography (How a camera works) P: 407
Shutter-priority mode [photography]
Camera (Automatic exposure control) C: 82
Shutter speed [photography]
Camera (Controlling the exposure) C: 80
Photography (Shutter speed) P: 412 *with pictures*
Shuttle [sports]
Badminton B: 24 *with picture*

Shuttle [tool]
Cotton (In England) Ci: 1092
Weaving (How a loom works) W: 173-174 *with
picture*
Shuttle bus
Bus (Special buses) B: 715
Shuttle diplomacy
Diplomacy (History) D: 217
Shuttle Mission Simulator
Astronaut (Advanced mission training) A: 832
Shuttle Training Aircraft
Astronaut (Flight training) A: 831
Shuttleless loom [machine]
Textile (Woven fabrics) T: 214
Shuttlesworth, Fred [American activist]
Alabama (The mid-1900's) A: 278
Shuttleworth, Mark [South African businessman]
International Space Station (History) I: 346-347
Shwe Dagon pagoda [Myanmar]
Myanmar *picture on* M: 970; (The arts) M: 970c
Shylock [literary figure]
Shakespeare, William: *(The Merchant of Venice)*
S: 358
Shyness
Introvert I: 354
SI [measurement] *See* Metric system *in this index*
Si [symbol]
Silicon S: 458
Siam *See* Thailand *in this index*
Siamang [ape] S: 443
Gibbon G: 185
Primate (Lesser apes) P: 778a
Siamese cat
Cat *picture on* C: 288; (Short-haired breeds)
C: 290-291
Siamese crocodile
Crocodile (Kinds of crocodiles) Ci: 1149-1150
Siamese fightingfish
Fightingfish F: 96 *with picture*
Fish *picture on* F: 157; (Hatching and care of the
young) F: 170 *with picture*
Siamese twins *See* Conjoined twins *in this index*
Sian [China] *See* Xi'an *in this index*
Sian Ka'an National Park [Mexico]
National park (table) N: 42g
Sibelius, Jean [Finnish composer] S: 443
Siberia [region, Asia] S: 443 *with pictures and map*
Arctic (Arctic peoples) A: 638
Asia *picture on* A: 773; (Way of life in North Asia)
A: 789-790
Exploration (The Russians in Siberia) E: 447
Hat *picture on* H: 85
Russia *picture on* R: 526; (Land regions) R: 539-
541 *with pictures and maps*
Trans-Siberian Railroad T: 401
Siberian cat
Cat (Long-haired breeds) C: 292
Siberian elm
Elm (Diseases) E: 245
Siberian husky [dog] S: 445 *with picture*
Dog *picture on* D: 278
Sled dog S: 505
Siberian pine [tree]
Pine (Other pines) P: 470
Sibley, Henry Hastings [American political leader]
Minnesota (table) M: 602; (Statehood) M: 604
Sibling
Child C: 448; (The influence of siblings) C: 452
Family (Family relationships) F: 21
Sibyl [legendary figure] S: 445
Sibylline Books [Roman legend]
Rome, Ancient (Religion) R: 441
Sibyl S: 445
Sic et Non [book by Abelard]
Abelard, Peter A: 10
"Sic semper tyrannis" [quotation]
Lincoln, Abraham (Assassination) L: 326
Sichuan Basin [region, China]
China (The Sichuan Basin) C: 493 *with map*
Sichuan Province [China]
Chengdu C: 408
Sichuan Ribao [newspaper]
China (Communication) C: 498-499
Sicilian dialect
Italian literature (The Middle Ages) I: 494
Sicilian pizza [food]
Pizza P: 504
Sicilian School
Italian literature (The Middle Ages) I: 494
Sicilian Vespers [Italian history]
Sicilies, Kingdom of the Two S: 446
Sicily (History) S: 447
Sicilians [people]
Sicily (The people) S: 446
Sicilies, Kingdom of the Two [Italian history]
S: 446
Garibaldi, Giuseppe G: 43

Italy (The French Revolution and Napoleon)
I: 514-515
Sicily [island, Italy] S: 446 *with picture*
Bourbon (In Naples and Sicily) B: 517
Dionysius the Elder D: 214
Italy (Sicily) I: 508 *with picture*
Mafia M: 41
Patton, George Smith, Jr. (African invasion) P: 199
World War II (The invasion of Italy) W: 483
Sick building syndrome
Environmental pollution (Air pollution) E: 331-
334
Sickle [tool]
Wheat (The mechanization of wheat farming)
W: 276
Sickle beta thalassemia [disorder]
Thalassemia T: 228
Sickle cell anemia [disorder] S: 447 *with pictures*
Anemia (Excessive destruction of red blood cells)
A: 458
Cell (Metabolic diseases) C: 336-337
Eugenics E: 357
Evolution (Balancing or diversifying selection)
E: 429
Eye (Diseases of the retina) E: 467
Genetic testing (How genes carry information)
G: 84d
Heredity (table) H: 204
Mutation M: 968
Races, Human (Susceptibility to genetic diseases)
R: 58
Thalassemia T: 228
Sickle cell retinopathy [disorder]
Eye (Diseases of the retina) E: 467
Sickle cell trait [physiology]
Sickle cell anemia S: 448 *with diagram*
Sickle hemoglobin [physiology]
Sickle cell anemia S: 447 *with picture*
Sicklefin lemon shark
Lemon shark L: 189
Sickness *See* Disease *in this index*
Sid Meier's Civilization [electronic game]
Electronic game (The growth of computer
gaming) E: 204e
Siddal, Elizabeth [wife of]
Rossetti, Dante Gabriel R: 483
Siddhartha Gautama [Indian religious leader] *See*
Buddha *in this index*
Siddons, Sarah Kemble [British actress] S: 448
with portrait
Siddons, William [British actor]
Siddons, Sarah Kemble S: 448
Side [geometry]
Angle A: 462
Polygon P: 650 *with diagram*
Side-angle-side axiom
Geometry (Congruence) G: 102
Side check
Harness *diagram on* H: 63
Side-delivery rake [machine]
Rake (The side-delivery rake) R: 130
Side effect [medicine]
Drug (Effect on the body) D: 354
Herbal medicine H: 197
Side judge [sports]
Football (The officials) F: 362
Side lighting
Photography (Direction) P: 415-416 *with picture*
Side-necked turtle
Turtle (Side-necked turtles) T: 523 *with picture*
Side out scoring
Volleyball (The game) V: 445
Side-out scoring [sports]
Beach volleyball B: 179
Side pod [device]
Automobile racing (Indy and Champ car racing)
A: 977
Side sewing [printing]
Bookbinding (Sewing) B: 471
Side show
Circus (The Greatest Show on Earth) Ci: 563
Side wall
Tire T: 295 *with diagram*
Sideburns
Burnside, Ambrose Everett B: 710 *with picture*
Sideline
Football (The field) F: 354-355
Sidelocks [grooming]
Clothing (Ancient times) Ci: 696-697
Sidepod [device]
Automobile racing (Indy and Champ car racing)
A: 977
Sidereal day [time]
Day and night D: 52
Earth (How Earth moves) E: 17
Sidereal time S: 448
Sidereal month [time]

Month M: 767
Moon (Rotation and orbit) M: 783
Sidereal time S: 448
Earth (How Earth moves) E: 17
Time (Astronomical cycles) T: 288
Sidereal year [time]
Earth (How Earth moves) E: 17
Year Y: 554
Siderite [mineral]
Iron and steel (Kinds of iron ore) I: 438
Sidesaddle flower [plant]
Pitcher plant P: 499
Sidestroke
Swimming (The basic strokes) So: 1043-1044
Sidewalk, Moving
Conveyor belt (Uses) Ci: 1024 *with picture*
Sidewinder [snake]
Animal *picture on* A: 482
Rattlesnake R: 149 *with picture*
Snake (Sidewinding) S: 529 *with picture*
Sidewinder [weapon]
Guided missile (Air-to-air missiles) G: 426;
(Postwar developments) G: 427
Siding [building material]
House (Building materials) H: 380; (The frame)
H: 382 *with diagram*
Siding [railroad]
Railroad (Tracks) R: 108
Sidjakov, Nicolas [American artist] S: 448 *with
picture*
Caldecott Medal (table: 1961) C: 26
Sidney, Sir Philip [English author] S: 449
English literature (Elizabethan fiction) E: 317
Sidon [ancient city] S: 449
Phoenicia (Way of life) P: 392
SIDS *See* Sudden infant death syndrome *in this
index*
Siebe, Augustus [German engineer]
Diving, Underwater (History) D: 247
SIECUS [organization]
Calderone, Mary Steichen C: 27
Siegbahn, Kai Manne Boerje [Swedish physicist]
Nobel Prizes (Physics: 1981) N: 441
Siegbahn, Karl Manne Georg S: 449
Siegbahn, Karl Manne Georg [Swedish physicist]
S: 449
Siege [warfare]
Castle (Uses) C: 280-281
Weapon (Siege weapons) W: 154b
Siege of Leningrad [Soviet history] *See* Leningrad,
Siege of *in this index*
Siege of Rhodes, The [opera by Davenant]
Davenant, Sir William D: 44
Siege Perilous [English legend]
Galahad, Sir G: 7
Round Table (Origin) R: 491
Siegel, Jerry [American cartoonist]
Comics (Comic books) Ci: 869
Superman So: 993
Siegelman, Donald [American political leader]
Alabama (table) A: 274; (The 2000's) A: 279
Siegfried [legendary figure] S: 449
See also Sigurd *in this index*
Mythology (Teutonic heroes) M: 987
Nibelungenlied N: 395
Opera: (*Ring of the Nibelung, The*) O: 806-807
Siegfried [opera by Wagner]
Fafnir F: 6
Opera *pictures on* O: 799; (*Ring of the Nibelung,
The*) O: 806-807
Wagner, Richard (Later career) W: 4
Siegfried Line [German history] S: 449
Haig, Douglas H: 8
Hindenburg, Paul von H: 234
World War I (Allied fighting) W: 461
World War II (The Phony War) W: 473
Siegfried of Ardennes [Luxembourg nobleman]
Luxembourg (History) L: 531
Sieglinde [opera character]
Opera: (*Ring of the Nibelung, The*) O: 807
Siegmund [opera character]
Opera: (*Ring of the Nibelung, The*) O: 806-807
Siemens, Sir Charles William [German inventor]
S: 449
Iron and steel (The birth of modern steelmaking)
I: 450-451
Siemens, Ernst Werner von [German inventor]
S: 450
Siemens, Friedrich [German inventor]
Iron and steel (The birth of modern steelmaking)
I: 450-451
Siemens AG [company]
Computer (Manufacturing) Ci: 924
Manufacturing (table) M: 170
Siena [Italy]
Europe *picture on* E: 390
Siena Cathedral [Italy]

Campanile *picture on* C: 90a
Sienkiewicz, Henryk [Polish author] S: 450
Poland (The arts) P: 607
Sierra Club S: 450 *with picture*
Muir, John M: 912
Sierra de Escambray [mountains, Cuba]
Cuba (The land) Ci: 1172
Sierra de los Órganos [mountains, Cuba]
Cuba (The land) Ci: 1172 *with map*
Sierra de Sancti Spíritus [mountains, Cuba]
Cuba (The land) Ci: 1172
Sierra de Trinidad [mountains, Cuba]
Cuba (The land) Ci: 1172
Sierra del Rosario [mountains, Cuba]
Cuba (The land) Ci: 1172 *with map*
Sierra Leone S: 450 *with picture and map*
Flag *picture on* F: 199
Medicine *picture on* M: 368
Sierra lily [plant]
Lily L: 304
Sierra Madre [mountains, Mexico] S: 452
Mexico (The Plateau of Mexico) M: 461-462 *with
picture and map*
Sierra Madre del Sur [mountains, Mexico]
Mexico *picture on* M: 449; (The Southern
Uplands) M: 462
Sierra Madre S: 452
Sierra Madre Occidental [mountains, Mexico]
Mexico (The Plateau of Mexico) M: 461-462 *with
picture and map*
Sierra Madre S: 452
Sierra Madre Oriental [mountains, Mexico]
Mexico (The Plateau of Mexico) M: 461-462 *with
map*
Sierra Madre S: 452
Sierra Maestra [mountains, Cuba]
Cuba (The land) Ci: 1172 *with picture and map*
Sierra Nevada [mountains, California] S: 452
California *picture on* C: 50; (Land regions) C: 48
Donner party D: 308
United States (The Pacific Ranges and Lowlands)
U: 125
Sierra Nevada [mountains, Spain]
Spain (The Meseta) So: 739 *with map*
Sierra Nevada de Santa Marta [mountains,
Colombia]
Colombia (The Andes Mountains) Ci: 782
Sierra redwood [tree]
Redwood R: 193
Sequoia S: 310d
Sieve of Eratosthenes [mathematics] S: 452
Sieve tube [botany]
Bark (Inner bark) B: 110
Sievert [unit of measure]
Radiation (Dose) R: 79-80
Radiation sickness R: 81
Sievert, Rolf M. [Swedish radiologist]
Radiation (Dose) R: 79-80
Sieyès, Abbé *See* Sieyès, Emmanuel Joseph *in this
index*
Sieyès, Emmanuel Joseph [French political leader]
S: 453
Sifaka [animal]
Lemur L: 190
Madagascar *picture on* M: 28
Siffin, Battle of [A.D. 657]
Muslims (Ali) M: 964b
Sifton, Arthur L. [Canadian political leader]
Alberta (table) A: 328
Sigatoka disease
Banana (How bananas grow) B: 73
Sight *See* Vision *in this index*
Sight [gun]
Handgun (Parts of a handgun) H: 43
Rifle (The parts of a rifle) R: 338 *with diagram*
Sight hound [dog]
Dog (Hounds) D: 270 *with pictures*
Hound H: 379
Sight word
Reading (Sight words and look-and-say
instruction) R: 159
Sightseeing bus
Bus (Special buses) B: 715
Sigismund [Holy Roman emperor] S: 453
Sigismund III [Polish king]
Warsaw (History) W: 38
Sigler, Kim [American political leader]
Michigan (table) M: 507
Sigma [letter]
S S: 1 *with picture*
Sigma 7 [spacecraft]
Schirra, Walter Marty, Jr. S: 176
Sigma Xi [organization] S: 453
Sigmoid colon [anatomy]
Colon Ci: 786
Intestine (The large intestine) I: 353 *with diagram*
Sign [astrology]

Astrology (The zodiac) A: 827 *with picture*
Horoscope (Parts of a horoscope) H: 341
Zodiac (The zodiac in astrology) Z: 597 *with
picture*
Sign [superstition]
Superstition (Kinds of superstitions) So: 995
Sign, Traffic *See* Traffic sign *in this index*
Sign communication
Deafness (Education) D: 59
Sign in Sidney Brustein's Window, The [play by
Hansberry]
Hansberry, Lorraine H: 53
Sign language S: 453 *with pictures*
Chimpanzee (Chimpanzees and people) C: 473
Deafness (Special language techniques) D: 58;
(Education) D: 59
Disability (Hearing disabilities) D: 219 *with picture*
Indian, American *pictures on* I: 161; (Other
communication) I: 151
Language (Signed languages) L: 63
Sign of the Beaver, The [book by Speare]
Speare, Elizabeth George So: 768
Signal [communication]
Baseball (Player positions) B: 127
Basketball *diagrams on* B: 149
Cricket *pictures on* Ci: 1135
Electronics E: 206
Football *pictures on* F: 361
Hockey *pictures on* H: 279
Language L: 62
Railroad (Traffic control) R: 110 *with pictures*
Television (Creating television signals) T: 121
Signal Corps, United States
Homing pigeon (History) H: 305
Signal dog *See* Hearing ear dog *in this index*
Signal Hill [district]
Long Beach (History) L: 447
Signal Hill National Historic Site [Newfoundland]
Canada (table: National historic sites) C: 115
Signal loss [electronics]
Cable (Fiber-optic cables) C: 5
Signal processor [electronics]
Radar (The signal processor) R: 71 *with diagram*
Signal transduction [medicine]
Cancer (Molecular medicine) C: 173-174
Signaling [communications] S: 454
See also the list of Related articles in the Signaling
article
Signals intelligence
National Security Agency/Central Security
Service N: 60
Signature [printing]
Bookbinding (Forming a book) B: 470
Printing (Offset presses) P: 798-799
Signature [writing]
Autograph A: 943
Letter writing (The signature) L: 211 *with picture*
Signed English
Deafness (Special language techniques) D: 58
Signed language *See* Sign language *in this index*
Signed number
Algebra (Positive and negative numbers)
A: 352-353
Signet ring
Ring R: 342 *with picture*
Significance of Sections in American History, The
[book by Turner]
Turner, Frederick Jackson T: 515
**"Significance of the Frontier in American
History, The"** [paper by Turner]
Turner, Frederick Jackson T: 515
Significant figures [mathematics]
Scientific notation (Significant figures) S: 207
Weights and measures (Conversion factors)
W: 184-185
Signing the Constitution [painting by Rossiter]
United States, History of the *picture on* U: 160
Signing the Marriage Contract [painting by
Hogarth]
Hogarth, William *picture on* H: 288
Signore [official]
Renaissance (The Italian Renaissance) R: 233
Signoret, Simone [French actress]
Motion picture (Best performance by an actress:
1959) M: 862
Signoria [government]
Renaissance (The Italian Renaissance) R: 233
Signoria, Piazza della
Florence (The city) F: 239-240 *with picture*
Signs of aggregation
Algebra (Symbols in algebra) A: 354
Sigurd [legendary figure] S: 455
See also Siegfried *in this index*
Brunhild B: 652
Edda E: 74
Fafnir F: 6
Mythology (Teutonic heroes) M: 987 *with picture*

Sigurdsson, Harald [king of Norway] *See* Harald III *in this index*
Sigyn [Norse mythology]
Loki L: 426
Sihanouk, Norodom [Cambodian political leader]
See Norodom Sihanouk *in this index*
Sikatuna, Ancient Order of [Philippines]
Medals, decorations, and orders (table) M: 359
Sikharulidze, Anton [Russian athlete]
Olympic Games (The recent games) O: 753-754
Sikhism [religion] S: 455 *with pictures*
India (Sikhism) I: 117; (India under Indira Gandhi)
I: 133-134
Lahore L: 31
Pakistan (The Mughal Empire) P: 99
Punjab (History) P: 903-904
Ranjit Singh R: 139
Religion R: 215
Sikhs *See* Sikhism *in this index*
Sikkim [state, India] S: 456
Sikorsky, Igor Ivanovich [American businessman]
S: 456 *with picture*
Airplane *picture on* A: 232; (Other pioneer planes
and fliers) A: 233-234
Helicopter *picture on* H: 174; (The first practical
helicopters) H: 173
Sikula, Derek [Solomon Islands political leader]
Solomon Islands (History) So: 585-586
Silage [feed]
Alfalfa (As livestock feed) A: 346
Corn (Livestock feed) Ci: 1057; (Harvesting)
Ci: 1061
Dairying (Feeding) D: 7
Feed F: 67
Grass (Grazing and forage grasses) G: 324
Silo S: 462
Silas Marner [book by Eliot]
Eliot, George E: 237
Sildenafil citrate [drug] *See* Viagra *in this index*
Silence Dogood [pseudonym]
Franklin, Benjamin (Student and apprentice)
F: 487
Silence of the Lambs, The [film]
Hopkins, Anthony H: 333
Motion picture (Best picture: 1991) M: 861
Silent assumption
Fallacy F: 16
Silent film
Motion picture (Early motion pictures) M: 863
Silent letter
Spelling (Spelling demons) So: 777
"Silent Night" [song]
Christmas (Christmas carols) C: 535-536
Silent Spring [book by Carson]
Carson, Rachel C: 250
Conservation (Renewed interest in conservation)
Ci: 986
DDT D: 55
Pest control (Effects of pesticide use) P: 318
Silent World, The [book by Cousteau]
Cousteau, Jacques-Yves Ci: 1106
Silenus [Greek mythology]
Midas M: 521
Siles Zuazo, Hernán [Bolivian political leader]
Bolivia (The Revolution of 1952) B: 447; (The late
1900's) B: 447
Silesia [region, Europe] S: 457
Maria Theresa M: 199
Silica [mineral] S: 457
Bauxite (How bauxite forms) B: 174
Earth (The lithosphere) E: 20
Glass (96 per cent silica glass) G: 213
Opal O: 788
Plant (How plants protect themselves) P: 540
Silica gel S: 457
Silicosis S: 458
Silica gel [chemical] S: 457
Silicate [mineral] S: 457 *with picture*
Ceramics (Properties of ceramics) C: 359
Interstellar medium I: 352
Materials (Ceramics) M: 300d
Mercury (Surface and atmosphere) M: 414
Satellite (Physical characteristics) S: 149
Silica S: 457
Silicon S: 458
Silicate slag
Iron and steel (Making iron products) I: 441
Silicic caldera complex [geology]
Volcano (Silicic caldera complexes) V: 442 *with
picture*
Silicon [element] S: 458
Aluminum (Properties of aluminum alloys)
A: 391-392
Carbon (Diamond) C: 204-205
Charge-coupled device C: 378
Computer chip (Structure) Ci: 924e
Earth (The lithosphere) E: 20

Electricity (Sources of current) E: 194
Electronics (Types of electronic circuits) E: 209-
210
Metalloid M: 426
Semiconductor S: 291
Silica S: 457
Silicone S: 458
Solar energy (The development of photovoltaic
cells) So: 577
Transistor (Transistor materials) T: 372
Silicon bronze [metal]
Bronze (Silicon and aluminum bronze) B: 638
Silicon carbide [chemical]
Grinding and polishing (Grinding wheels) G: 395
Silicon S: 458
Silicon dioxide [mineral] *See* Silica *in this index*
Silicon-oxygen tetrahedron
Silicate S: 457 *with picture*
Silicon photodiode [electronics]
Light meter L: 294
Photography (Capturing digital images) P: 420
Silicon Valley [California]
California (Manufacturing) C: 56; (The late 1900's)
C: 63
San Francisco (Industry) S: 97
San Jose (Economy) S: 100
Silicone [synthetic] S: 458
Inorganic chemistry I: 276
Plastics (table) P: 556; (Growth of the plastics
industry) P: 560
Waterproofing W: 146
Silicone gel [material]
Mastectomy M: 297
Silicone rubber
Silicone (Uses) S: 458
Silicosis [disease] S: 458
Dust (Influence on human health) D: 390
Silk [botany]
Corn (How the plant reproduces) Ci: 1058 *with
picture*
Silk [fiber] S: 459 *with pictures*
Clothing (China) Ci: 699; (The Middle Ages)
Ci: 700
Fiber (Animal fibers) F: 87
Materials (Biological materials) M: 300d
Moth (The importance of moths) M: 839 *with
picture*
Mulberry M: 913
Painting (Chinese painting) P: 44
Pasteur, Louis (His work in industry) P: 193
Silk Road S: 462
Spider (The spider's silk) So: 786 *with pictures;*
(Spiders and people) So: 790
Textile (Natural fibers) T: 212-213; (History) T: 218
Silk gland
Spider *diagram on* So: 784; (How spiders make
silk) So: 786
Silk Road [trade route] S: 461 *with map*
Han dynasty H: 38 *with map*
Kushan Empire K: 394
Trade route (Early trade routes) T: 363
Uzbekistan (History) U: 254
Silk-screen printing *See* Screen printing *in this
index*
Silko, Leslie Marmon [American author]
American literature (Works by minority writers)
A: 425
Indian, American (Achievements in the arts)
I: 181
Silks [clothing]
Horse racing (Jockeys) H: 364 *with picture*
Silkworm [insect]
Larva *picture on* L: 78
Silk (Raising silkworms) S: 459 *with pictures;*
(Sources of silk) S: 459; (Discovery of silk)
S: 460 *with pictures*
Silkworm mulberry [plant]
Mulberry M: 913
Silky anteater [animal]
Anteater A: 541
Silky oak [tree] S: 462
Silky terrier [dog] S: 462
Dog *picture on* D: 274
Sill [construction]
House (The frame) H: 382 *with diagram*
Sill [geology]
Rock (Intrusive rock) R: 371
Sill, Joshua W. [American general]
Fort Sill F: 416
Silla [former region]
Korea, History of (Early years) K: 366 *with picture
and map*
Sillanpää, Frans Eemil [Finnish author]
Nobel Prizes (Literature: 1939) N: 447
Silliman, Benjamin [American chemist]
Morse, Samuel Finley Breese (Early years) M: 817
Sillimanite [mineral] S: 462

Sillitoe, Alan [British author] S: 462
Sills, Beverly [American singer] S: 462
Silly Symphonies [cartoon]
Disney, Walt (The first Disney cartoons) D: 235-
236 *with picture*
Silmarillion, The [book by Tolkien]
Tolkien, J. R. R. T: 322
Silo [agriculture] S: 462
Farm and farming (Processing and storage) F: 37
Silo [warfare]
Guided missile (Launching equipment) G: 424
Silsbee, Joseph Lyman [American architect]
Wright, Frank Lloyd (Early career) W: 507
Silt [material] S: 463
Aswan High Dam A: 851
Dam (The effects of dams) D: 17
Loam L: 403
Soil (Texture) So: 575
Silty clay
Soil (Texture) So: 575
Silurian Period [geology] S: 463
Earth (The Paleozoic Era) E: 27; (table) E: 30
Prehistoric animal (table) P: 738
Silva y Velázquez, Diego Rodriguez de [Spanish
painter] *See* Velázquez, Diego *in this index*
Silver [element] S: 463 *with pictures*
See also Silverware *in this index*
Alloy (Costly and ornamental alloys) A: 378
Colorado (Interesting facts) Ci: 829 *with picture*
Free silver F: 499
Gresham's law G: 391
Mercantilism M: 411
Metal (Metals through the ages) M: 425
Mineral *picture on* M: 568
Teeth (Dental decay) T: 82-83
Western frontier life in America (Mining) W: 234-
235
Silver, Long John [literary figure]
Stevenson, Robert Louis (Novels) So: 898
Silver Age
Russian literature (Literary revival) R: 563
Silver Beach [district]
New York City (The Bronx) N: 328-329
Silver birch [tree]
Birch (Yellow birch) B: 327
Tree *picture on* T: 426
Silver Box, The [play by Galsworthy]
Galsworthy, John G: 17
Silver buffaloberry [shrub]
Buffaloberry B: 680 *with picture*
Silver certificate
Money *picture on* M: 709; (Money in the
American Civil War) M: 713
Silver chloride [chemical]
Chloride C: 516
Silver Cord, The [play by Howard]
Howard, Sidney M: 400
Silver Dart [airplane]
Airplane (Other pioneer planes and fliers) A: 233
Nova Scotia (Interesting facts) N: 555 *with picture*
Silver dollar [money]
Dollar (The United States dollar) D: 295 *with
pictures*
Free silver F: 499
Money *picture on* M: 709
Silver Dollar City [Branson]
Missouri (Places to visit) M: 660 *with picture*
Silver eel [fish]
Eel (Life cycle) E: 114-115
Silver fox [animal]
Fox (Kinds of foxes) F: 440
Silver hatchet fish
Fish *picture on* F: 157
Silver iodide [chemical]
Cloud seeding (Cloud-seeding methods) C: 711
Rain (The ice-crystal process) R: 124
Weather (How people affect the weather) W: 170
Silver King [nickname of H. A. W. Tabor]
Colorado (Statehood) Ci: 845-847
Silver maple [tree]
Maple (Silver maple) M: 186 *with pictures*
Tree *pictures on* T: 413
Silver nitrate [chemical] S: 465
Blindness (Diseases) B: 401-402
Silver plate
Brass B: 565
Electroplating E: 218 *with diagram*
Silver salmon *See* Coho *in this index*
Silver salt [chemical]
Photography (Exposing the film) P: 416;
(Developing the film) P: 419
Silver-Spangled Hamburg [breed]
Chicken *picture on* C: 442
Silver Spoon, The [book by Galsworthy]
Galsworthy, John G: 17
Silver-spotted skipper [butterfly]
Butterfly (Skippers) B: 734

Silver Springs [lake, Florida]
Lake (How lakes are formed) **L: 32**
Silver Star
Medals, decorations, and orders (table) **M: 357** with picture
Silver State [name for]
Nevada **N: 156**
Silver Strand Falls [California]
Yosemite National Park (Waterfalls) **Y: 570**
Silver Tassie, The [play by O'Casey]
O'Casey, Sean **O: 646**
Silver Valley [Idaho]
Idaho (Places to visit) **I: 34**
Silver wattle [shrub]
Mimosa **M: 562**
Silverado Squatters, The [book by Stevenson]
Stevenson, Robert Louis (Marriage) **So: 897**
Silverback [gorilla]
Ape (Way of life) **A: 563-564**
Silverbell [plant] **S: 465**
Silvered glass
Glass (Types of art glass) **G: 220-221**
Silverfish [insect] **S: 465**
Insect picture on **I: 280**; (Growth and development) **I: 292-293** with pictures
Silverleaf whitefly [insect]
Whitefly **W: 292**
Silverpoint drawing
Drawing (Materials and techniques) **D: 342**
Silverside salmon See Coho in this index
Silversmith
See also Silver in this index
Colonial life in America picture on **Ci: 811**
Silver (Uses of silver) pictures on **S: 464**
Silverstein, Shel [American author] **S: 465**
Silvertip bear
Bear (Brown bears) **B: 184**
Grizzly bear **G: 397**
Silverware
Colonial life in America (Decorative arts) **Ci: 807** with picture
Mexico picture on **M: 466**
Revere, Paul (Craftsman and industrialist) **R: 268** with picture
Silvery blue [butterfly]
Butterfly picture on **B: 734**
Silvia [literary figure]
Shakespeare, William: (*The Two Gentlemen of Verona*) **S: 356**
Silviculture
Forestry (Managing timber resources) **F: 404**; (Diseases and pests) **F: 407**
Silvio [opera character]
Opera: (*Pagliacci*) **O: 806**
Silzer, George S. [American political leader]
New Jersey (table) **N: 249**
Simbo [ritual]
Religion picture on **R: 219**
SimCity [electronic game]
Electronic game (The growth of computer gaming) **E: 204e**
Simcoe, John Graves [British military leader] **S: 465**
Ontario (Upper Canada) **O: 784**
Toronto **T: 338**; (Early settlement) **T: 340b-340c**
Simenon, Georges [French author] **S: 465**
Detective story (The pattern) **D: 162**
Simeon [Biblical figure]
Joseph (The prime minister) **J: 168**
Simeon I [king of Bulgaria]
Bulgaria (The first Bulgarian kingdom) **B: 692**
Simeon II [Bulgarian political leader]
Bulgaria (Recent developments) **B: 693**
Simhat Torah [religion] **S: 466**
Bible (The Bible in worship) **B: 286**
Dance (Why people dance) **D: 24**
Judaism (The pilgrimage festivals) **J: 181**
Simian immunodeficiency virus
Chimpanzee (Chimpanzees and people) **C: 473**
Simic, Charles [American poet]
Poet laureate (table: Poets laureate of the United States) **P: 590**
Similarity [geometry]
Geometry (Properties of geometric figures) **G: 102**
Triangle (Similarity) **T: 438**
Similarity, Law of [psychology]
Association **A: 819**
Simile [language] **S: 466**
Simitis, Costas [Greek political leader]
Greece (Recent developments) **G: 365**
Simmental
Cattle (Simmental) **C: 309** with picture; (table) **C: 312**
Simmering [cooking]
Cooking (Simmering) **Ci: 1029**
Simmons, Al [American baseball player]
Baseball (table: Hall of Fame) **B: 134b**

Simmons, Amelia [American author]
Connecticut (Interesting facts) **Ci: 953**
Simmons, William J. [American public figure]
Ku Klux Klan (Early 1900's) **K: 390**
Simms, John F. [American political leader]
New Mexico (table) **N: 272**
Simon, Claude [French author]
French literature (The middle and late 1900's) **F: 523**
Nobel Prizes (Literature: 1985) **N: 448**
Simon, Herbert Alexander [American economist] **S: 466**
Simon, Neil [American dramatist] **S: 466**
Simon, Paul [American singer] **S: 466**
Rock music (World music) **R: 380d**
Simon, Saint [apostle] **S: 467**
Simon, Theodore [French psychologist]
Intelligence (Theories of intelligence) **I: 319**
Simón Bolívar [volcano, Colombia]
Andes Mountains (Physical features) **A: 452-453**
Simon Fraser University
Architecture picture on **A: 607**
Erickson, Arthur Charles **E: 350**
Simon of Cyrene [Biblical figure]
Jesus Christ (The Crucifixion) **J: 108b**
Simon Peter See Peter, Saint in this index
Simone Martini [Italian painter] **S: 467**
Jesus Christ picture on **J: 108b**
Simonov, Konstantin [Russian author]
Russian literature (World War II) **R: 564**
Simons, Menno [Dutch religious leader]
Mennonites **M: 401**
Simont, Marc [American artist]
Caldecott Medal (table: 1957) **C: 26**
Simony [religion]
Gregory VII, Saint **G: 387**
Leo IX, Saint **L: 198**
Nicholas II [pope] **N: 402**
Pope (The early Middle Ages) **P: 663**
Simple [fictional character]
Hughes, Langston **H: 409**
Simple adverb [grammar]
Adverb (Simple adverbs) **A: 70**
Simple carbohydrate
Carbohydrate (Kinds of carbohydrates) **C: 203** with diagrams
Nutrition (Carbohydrates) **N: 625**
Simple distillation [chemistry]
Distillation (Simple distillation) **D: 238** with diagram
Simple eye [entomology]
Eye (Eyes of animals) **E: 469** with picture
Insect diagram on **I: 286**; (Sight) **I: 290**
Simple fracture [injury]
Fracture **F: 450** with diagram
Simple fruit
Fruit (Simple fruits) **F: 544** with pictures
Simple graph [character]
Chinese language (Written Chinese) **C: 509-510** with picture
Simple harmonic wave
Waves (How waves move) **W: 152**
Simple interest
Interest (Simple interest) **I: 321** with diagram
Simple leaf
Leaf (The blade) **L: 153-154** with picture
Plant (Leaves) **P: 529-531** with pictures
Simple machines [physics] **S: 467**
Machine (Six simple machines) **M: 14** with pictures
Simple mastectomy [surgery]
Mastectomy **M: 297**
Simple motor act [psychology]
Habit (Kinds of habits) **H: 3**
Simple recitative [music]
Opera (Early Baroque opera) **O: 797**
Simple salt [chemistry]
Salt, Chemical **S: 75**
Simple sentence
Sentence (Sentence classifications) **S: 303**
Simple Verses [poems by Martí]
Martí, José Julián **M: 234**
Simplex Linotype
Linotype (History) **L: 339**
Simplicissimus [book by Grimmelshausen]
German literature (Baroque literature) **G: 139**
Simplicius, Saint [pope]
Pope (table) **P: 666**
Simplon Pass and Tunnel [Switzerland]
Alps (Alpine travel) **A: 386**
Tunnel (The tunnel) **T: 491**
Simpson, Alan Kooi [American political leader] **S: 467**
Simpson, Sir George [Scottish businessman] **S: 467**
Hudson's Bay Company (Growth and problems) **H: 407**

Simpson, George Gaylord [American paleontologist]
Evolution (The synthetic theory) **E: 432**
Simpson, Sir James Young [Scottish physician]
Anesthesia (History) **A: 459**
Chloroform **C: 517**
Simpson, Milward L. [American political leader]
Wyoming (table) **W: 532**
Simpson, Nicole Brown [American public figure]
Simpson, O. J. **S: 468**
Simpson, O. J. [American football player] **S: 467** with picture
Football (table) **F: 363**
Simpson, Oramel H. [American political leader]
Louisiana (table) **L: 496**
Simpson, Robert H. [American meteorologist]
Hurricane (Hurricane damage) **H: 455**
Simpson, Wallis Warfield [British public figure]
Edward VIII **E: 113**
United Kingdom ("Peace in our time") **U: 70**
Simpson Desert [Australia]
Australia (Deserts) **A: 908** with map
Simpson Miller, Portia [Jamaican political leader]
Jamaica (History) **J: 24-25**
"Simpsons, The" [television program]
Fox **F: 441**
Television picture on **T: 110**
Sims, Billy [American football player]
Football (table) **F: 363**
Sims, Christopher A. [American economist]
Nobel Prizes (Economics: 2011) **N: 450**
Sims, The [electronic game]
(Social gaming) **E: 204e**
Sims, William S. [American admiral]
Navy, United States (World War I [1914-1918]) **N: 88**
Simulation
See also Computer simulation in this index
Astronaut (Training the astronauts) **A: 831-832** with picture
Simulcast betting
Horse racing (Betting) **H: 365**
Simultaneous contrast [vision]
Color (Surprising color-vision effects) **Ci: 819**
Sin [religion]
Augustine, Saint (His beliefs) **A: 888**
Christianity (Sin and salvation) **C: 522g**
Religion (A doctrine of salvation) **R: 215-216**
Sin City [book by Miller]
Graphic novel **G: 323**
Sin Nombre virus See Pulmonary syndrome hantavirus in this index
Sinai [mountain, Sinai Peninsula] See Mount Sinai in this index
Sinai Peninsula [region, Middle East] **S: 468**
Arab-Israeli conflict (The Suez crisis of 1956) **A: 582**
Egypt (The Sinai Peninsula) **E: 126** with picture and map; (Republic) **E: 132**; (Renewed warfare and peace) **E: 133**
Israel (History) **I: 486-487**
Middle East (Cold War alliances) **M: 534-534a**
Sinaloa [state, Mexico] **S: 468**
Sinan [Turkish architect]
Istanbul (The city) **I: 490-491**
Turkey (The arts) **T: 507**
Sinanthropus pekinensis [anthropology]
Peking fossils **P: 230**
Sinatra, Frank [American singer] **S: 468** with portrait
Motion picture (Best performance by an actor in a supporting role: 1953) **M: 862a**
Sinbad [literary figure]
Arabian Nights **A: 582b**
Sinclair, Elizabeth [British public figure]
Hawaii (Niihau) **H: 102**
Sinclair, Harry Ford [American businessman]
Teapot Dome **T: 72**
Sinclair, Upton [American author] **S: 468**
American literature (Naturalists) **A: 419**
Consumer protection (Beginnings of modern consumerism) **Ci: 1019**
Novel (The United States) **N: 573**
Publishing (The power of published ideas) **P: 869**
Roosevelt, Theodore (Domestic problems) **R: 466**
United States, History of the (Theodore Roosevelt) **U: 187**
Sinclair plaid
Tartan picture on **T: 47**
Sindh [region, Pakistan]
Pakistan (Provincial and local government) **P: 93**; (Land and climate) **P: 96** with map; (History) **P: 98**
Sindhis [people]
Pakistan (Cultural groups and languages) **P: 93**
Sine [mathematics]
Refraction **R: 199**

Trigonometry (Right triangles) T: 443
Sines, Law of
Trigonometry (The law of sines) T: 443
Sinew See Tendon *in this index*
Sinfonia [music]
Overture O: 882
Sinfonia [music by Berio]
Berio, Luciano B: 259
Sing-sing [custom]
Mask *picture on* M: 264
Sing Sing [prison, New York] S: 469
Sing to the Sun [book by Bryan]
Literature for children *picture on* L: 356
Singapore [country] S: 469 *with picture and map*
Flag *picture on* F: 204
Malaysia M: 98a; (Coming of the Europeans)
M: 101
Raffles, Sir Thomas Stamford R: 101
UNESCO (History) U: 25
World War II (Early Japanese victories) W: 487
Singapore [city] S: 471
Singapore S: 469 *with picture*; (The city of
Singapore) S: 470
Singapore Changi Airport
Airport (table) A: 245
Singapura cat
Cat (Short-haired breeds) C: 290-292
Singer See Singing *in this index*
Singer, Isaac Bashevis [Polish-born author] S: 471
Nobel Prizes (Literature: 1978) N: 448
Yiddish literature Y: 566
Singer, Isaac Merrit [American businessman]
S: 472
Clothing (The 1800's) Ci: 705
Sewing machine (History) S: 333-334
Singer, Israel Joshua [Yiddish author]
Yiddish literature Y: 566
Singer, Jerome [American psychologist]
Emotion (The constructivist approach) E: 261
Singer Sewing Company
Sewing machine (History) S: 333-334
Singh, Manmohan [Indian political leader]
Gandhi, Sonia G: 26
India (Recent developments) I: 134-135
Singh, Vijay [Fijian golfer]
Golf *picture on* G: 267
Singidunum [ancient city]
Belgrade (History) B: 236
Singing S: 472
See also the list of Related articles in the Singing
article
Careers (Sports and entertainment) C: 230-231
with picture
Opera (The singers) O: 792
Singing Bone, The [story by Freeman]
Detective story (History) D: 162-163
Singing Brakeman [name for]
Rodgers, Jimmie R: 398
Singing Gallery [sculpture by Della Robbia]
Della Robbia, Luca B: 116
Singing River
Mississippi M: 623
Singing Tower [Florida]
Bell (Uses of bells) B: 239
Single [sports]
Baseball (Reaching base) B: 129
Football (Canadian football) F: 364
Single-action revolver
Handgun (Types of handguns) H: 43
Single-action semiautomatic pistol
Handgun (Types of handguns) H: 43
Single cell protein [dietetics]
Yeast (How yeast is used) Y: 554-555
Single-cross seed [genetics]
Corn (Hybrid corn) Ci: 1059; (Development of
hybrids) Ci: 1063
Single-degree-of-freedom gyroscope
Gyroscope (Mechanical gyroscopes) G: 454
Single element set [mathematics]
Set theory (Kinds of sets) S: 321
Single European Act [1987]
Europe (Toward European unity) E: 415-416
European Union (Increasing cooperation) E: 420
Single-family home
Housing (Kinds of housing) H: 389-390
Single field laboratory
Industrial arts (Industrial arts courses) I: 242
Single-lens reflex camera
Camera (Single-lens (SLR) cameras) C: 83 *with
picture*
Photography *pictures on* P: 420; (Single-lens [SLR]
reflex cameras) P: 409
Single-mode fiber
Fiber optics (Kinds of optical fibers) F: 88 *with
diagram*
Single-mode school
Distance learning D: 238

Single nucleotide polymorphism [genetics]
Molecular medicine M: 692
Single-origin theory [anthropology]
Prehistoric people (The single origin theory)
P: 750
Single Parent, The [magazine]
Parents Without Partners P: 158
Single-parent family
Family (Varieties of families) F: 20 *with picture*
Single-payer health care system
Health insurance, National H: 129
Single-person corporation
Corporation (Other corporations) Ci: 1070
Single phase alloy
Alloy (Characteristics of alloys) A: 377
Single-phase generator
Electric generator (Kinds of AC generators) E: 173
Single point fuel injection system
Automobile (The fuel system) A: 953
Fuel injection F: 552
Single premium immediate annuity
Insurance (Annuities) I: 311
Single rhyme
Rhyme R: 319
Single-rotor helicopter
Helicopter (Types of helicopters) H: 170 *with
diagrams*
Single-shot pistol
Handgun (Single-shot pistols) H: 44
Single-stage rocket
Rocket (Multistage rockets) R: 386
Single-stage-to-orbit craft
Space exploration (Plans for the future) So: 727
Single stitch
Crochet Ci: 1148d *with diagrams*
Single tax [U.S. history] S: 472
George, Henry G: 108
Single-unit truck [vehicle] See Straight truck *in
this index*
Single-use camera
Camera (Fixed-focus cameras) C: 82
Photography (Compact cameras) P: 408-409
Single-wattled cassowary [bird]
Cassowary C: 277
Singles skating
Ice skating (Singles skating) I: 12 *with picture*
Roller skating (Artistic skating) R: 402a
Singleton, Angelica [daughter-in-law of Martin
Van Buren] See Van Buren, Angelica Singleton *in
this index*
Singleton, Benjamin "Pap" [American pioneer]
Western frontier life in America (Newcomers)
W: 234
Singspiel
Opera (table) O: 791; (Mozart) O: 798
Singular [grammar]
Number N: 604
Singularity [physics]
Black hole (Characteristics of black holes) B: 388
Star (Black holes) So: 851-852
Sinhala [language]
Sri Lanka (History) So: 819
Sinhalese [people]
Maldives (People) M: 104
Sri Lanka (People) So: 817; (History) So: 819
Sinister side
Heraldry (Expansion) H: 194
Sink [geology] See Sinkhole *in this index*
Sinker [botany]
Root (Kinds of roots) R: 469-470 *with diagram*
Sinker [pitch]
Baseball (Pitching) B: 127-128
Sinker [weight]
Fishing *pictures on* F: 178; (Sinkers) F: 177
Sinkhole [geology] S: 473
Cave (How caves are formed) C: 319 *with diagram*
Great Basin G: 336
Lake (How lakes are formed) L: 32
Sinkhole pond
Pond (Kinds of ponds) P: 656-657
Sinkiang [region, China] See Xinjiang *in this index*
Sinkwich, Frank [American football player]
Football (History) F: 363
Sinn Féin [Irish history] S: 473
Adams, Gerry A: 33
De Valera, Eamon D: 173
Griffith, Arthur G: 393
Ireland (The Easter Rising) I: 427; (The Irish Free
State) I: 427
Irish Republican Army I: 433
Sinner, George A. [American political leader]
North Dakota (table) N: 513
Sino-Japanese War of 1894-1895 S: 473
Sino-Japanese War of 1937-1945 S: 473
Nanking Massacre N: 10
Sino-Tibetan languages
India (Languages) I: 114

Language *map on* L: 65; (Other language
families) L: 66
Sinoatrial node [anatomy]
Heart (Regulating the heart rate) H: 135-136
Muscle (Cardiac muscle) M: 935
Sinope [satellite]
Jupiter (Outer satellites) J: 200a
Sinowatz, Fred [Austrian political leader]
Austria (After World War II) A: 939-940
Sinte [people]
Roma R: 402b
Sinte Gleska [real name of]
Spotted Tail So: 805
Sintering [industrial process]
Lead (Production) L: 149-150
Metallurgy (Sintering) M: 426
Powder metallurgy P: 725
Sinterklaas [legendary figure]
Netherlands (Holidays and recreation) N: 141-
142
Nicholas, Saint N: 403
Santa Claus (How the Santa Claus legend began)
S: 113-114
Sinti [people]
Roma R: 402b
Sinus [anatomy] S: 474 *with diagrams*
Blood (Formation of new blood components)
B: 411
Bone (Structure of the bones) B: 456
Hay fever (Symptoms) H: 116
Nose N: 549
Sinus headache
Headache (Secondary headache) H: 124
Sinus venosus [anatomy]
Heart (Fish) H: 146
Sinusitis [disorder]
Sinus S: 474
Sinusoid [anatomy]
Liver *picture on* L: 394; (Structure of the liver)
L: 393
Spleen So: 797
Sinyavsky, Andrey [Russian author]
Russian literature (Modern Soviet literature)
R: 564
Sioux City [Iowa] S: 474
Iowa (table: Average monthly weather) I: 388
Sioux Falls [South Dakota] S: 474
South Dakota *picture on* So: 665; (Population)
So: 668; (table: Average monthly weather)
So: 676
Sioux Indians S: 475 *with picture*
See also Oglala Indians; Sioux wars *in this index*
De Smet, Pierre Jean D: 159
Doll (Traditional dolls) D: 287
Funeral customs (Burial) F: 557-558
Indian, American *pictures on* I: 138, I: 143, I: 160;
(Indians of the Plains) I: 158-159; (In the United
States) I: 179
Indian wars (Wars on the Plains) I: 192
Iowa (Statehood) I: 395
Lewis and Clark expedition (Up the Missouri)
L: 222a-222b
Minnesota (Early days) M: 603 *with picture*;
(Territorial days) M: 604
North Dakota N: 496; (History) N: 513
Red Cloud R: 185
Sitting Bull So: 477
South Dakota (Early days) So: 681; (The late
1900's) So: 684-685
Sun dance S: 987
Western frontier life in America (Settlers and
Native Americans) W: 239
Westward movement in America (The last Indian
wars) W: 250-251
Wounded Knee W: 502
Sioux Sun Dance [painting by Howe]
Indian, American *picture on* I: 161
Sioux wars [1854-1890]
See also Sioux Indians *in this index*
Crazy Horse Ci: 1123
Indian wars (Wars on the Plains) I: 192
Minnesota (Statehood) M: 604
Wyoming (Indian and settler conflicts) W: 534
Sipe [groove]
Tire T: 295 *with diagram*
Siphon [physics] S: 475 *with diagram*
Siphon [zoology]
Clam (The body of a clam) Ci: 637
Mollusk (Bivalves) M: 695
Octopus (The body of an octopus) O: 672 *with
diagram*
Sea squirt S: 262b
Siphonaptera [entomology]
Insect *picture on* I: 282; (table) I: 300
Siphonophore [animal]
Deep sea (Invertebrates) D: 82a-82b
Siphuncle [zoology]

Nautilus N: 69
Siple, Paul Allman [American explorer]
Wind chill W: 331
Siqueiros, David [Mexican painter] S: 475
Latin America *picture on* L: 101
Mexico *picture on* M: 459; (Painting) M: 460
Painting (Synthetic resins) P: 40 *with picture*;
(Modern Mexican painting) P: 83
Pollock, Jackson P: 646
Sir [title]
Knighthood, Orders of (Honorary orders) K: 347
Sir ...
Knights appear under their names, as in Galahad,
Sir
Sir Charles Grandison [book by Richardson]
Richardson, Samuel R: 330
Sir Gawain and the Green Knight [poem]
Gawain, Sir G: 71
Poetry (Medieval poetry) P: 596
Sir George-Étienne Cartier [Quebec]
Canada (table: National historic sites) C: 115
Sir James MacBrien, Mount [Canada]
Northwest Territories (The Mackenzie Mountains)
N: 531
Sir Sanford, Mount [British Columbia]
Selkirk Mountains S: 290
Sir Wilfred Grenfell College [Corner Brook]
Newfoundland and Labrador (Schools) N: 364
Siracusa [Sicily]
Syracuse (ancient city) So: 1069
Sire [animal]
Cattle C: 306
Dog (Kinds of dogs) D: 265
Horse (table: Horse terms) H: 343
Siren [device]
Civil defense (Warning) Ci: 605
Sirenia [zoology] S: 476
Mammal (table) M: 128 *with picture*
Sirens [Greek mythology] S: 476
Capri C: 198
Odyssey: (Odysseus describes his wanderings)
O: 675 *with picture*
Sirhan, Sirhan Bishara [Jordanian-born assassin]
Kennedy, Robert Francis K: 270
Sirica, John J. [American judge]
Nixon, Richard Milhous (Events at home) N: 435-
436
Watergate (The tape controversy) W: 144
Siricius, Saint [pope]
Pope (table) P: 666
Siringo, Charlie [American cowboy]
Western frontier life in America (The cattle drive)
W: 237
Sirius [ship]
Ship (Oceangoing steamships) S: 424 *with picture*
Sirius [star] S: 476
Calendar (The Egyptians) C: 30
Star (table: The 10 brightest stars as seen from
Earth) So: 842; (table: The 10 known stars
nearest Earth) So: 843
Sirius B [star]
Sirius S: 476
Star (table: The 10 known stars nearest Earth)
So: 843
Sirius Satellite Radio Inc.
Radio (Radio since the 1950's) R: 94
Sirmilik National Park [Nunavut]
Canada (table: National parks and national park
reserves) C: 110-113
Nunavut (Economy) N: 610
Sirocco [weather] S: 476
Algeria (The Sahara) A: 363
Sicily (Land and climate) S: 447
Sisal [fiber]
Rope (Natural-fiber rope) R: 473
Sisal S: 476
Sisal [plant] S: 476
Sisal hemp [plant] *See* Sisal *in this index*
Sisavang Vong [King of Louangphrabang]
Indochina (Independence) I: 225; (World War
II) I: 225
Sisera [Biblical figure]
Deborah D: 65
Sisinnius [pope]
Pope (table) P: 666
Siskin, Pine [bird]
Pine siskin P: 471 *with picture*
Siskind, Aaron [American photographer]
Photography (A diversity of styles) P: 426
Siskiwit, Lake [Michigan]
Isle Royale National Park I: 474
Sisler, George [American baseball player]
Baseball (table: Hall of Fame) B: 134b
Sisley, Alfred [British painter] S: 476
Impressionism (French Impressionism) I: 93-94
with picture
Painting (Edouard Manet and the Impressionists)

P: 71
Sisowath Sirik Matak [Cambodian political leader]
Cambodia (History) C: 72-73
Sissinghurst Castle [England]
Gardening *picture on* G: 38
Sister [religion]
Address, Forms of (Members of the clergy) A: 54
Nun N: 608
Sister Carrie [book by Dreiser]
American literature (Naturalists) A: 419-420
Dreiser, Theodore D: 346
Novel (The United States) N: 573
Sister chromatid [biology]
Cell (Mitosis) C: 330 *with picture*
Sister Kenny [Australian nurse] *See* Kenny,
Elizabeth *in this index*
Sisters in Crime [organization]
Paretsky, Sara P: 159
Sisters of Charity [religious group]
Nun N: 608
Religious life (table) R: 227
Seton, Saint Elizabeth Ann S: 323
Vincent de Paul, Saint V: 386
Sisters of the Blessed Sacrament [religious order]
Drexel, Saint Katharine D: 347
Sisters Rosensweig, The [play by Wasserstein]
Wasserstein, Wendy W: 112
Sistine Chapel [Vatican City] S: 476
David *picture on* D: 45
Jeremiah, Book of *picture on* J: 92
Michelangelo *picture on* M: 483; (The Sistine
Chapel) M: 484
Painting (The High Renaissance) P: 54 *with
picture*
Religion *picture on* R: 216
Sistine Madonna [painting by Raphael]
Madonna and Child (Painters of the Madonna)
M: 37-38
Sistine Madonna, The [painting by Raphael]
Madonna and Child (Types of Madonna
paintings) M: 38
SiSwati [language]
Swaziland (People) So: 1017
Sisyphus [Greek mythology] S: 477
Ulysses (The Trojan War) U: 17-18
Sit-down strike
Labor movement (Handling labor disputes) L: 6-7
Strike (Kinds of strikes) So: 928
Sita [legendary figure]
Diwali D: 255
Rama R: 131
Ramayana R: 132
Sitar [musical instrument] S: 477 *with picture*
India (Music and dance) I: 120
Music *picture on* M: 947; (Indian music) M: 956
Sitatunga [animal]
Antelope A: 542
Site, Archaeological
Archaeology (What archaeologists study) A: 595
with picture
Prehistoric people (Examining prehistoric sites)
P: 754a *with picture*
"Site Unseen" [performance]
Art and the arts *picture on* A: 746
Sitka [Alaska] S: 477
Alaska (Places to visit) A: 290 *with picture*
Sitka National Historical Park [Alaska]
National Park System (table: National historical
parks) N: 56-57
Sitka spruce [tree]
Plant *picture on* P: 524
Sitka Times [newspaper]
Alaska (Communication) A: 299
Sitrah [island, Bahrain]
Bahrain (Land and climate) B: 30 *with map*
Sittang River [Myanmar]
Myanmar (Land regions) M: 970c *with map*
Sitter [occupation]
Day care (Day care for children) D: 52
Sitter, Willem de [Dutch astronomer] *See* De Sitter,
Willem *in this index*
Sitting Bull [American Indian leader] S: 477 *with
picture*
De Smet, Pierre Jean D: 159
Indian wars (Little Bighorn) I: 193; (Wounded
Knee) I: 194
South Dakota (Territorial days) So: 681-683
Western frontier life in America (Settlers and
Native Americans) W: 239
Westward movement in America *picture on*
W: 251
Situation and Crisis Center [Moscow]
Hot line H: 374a
Situation comedy
Comedy Ci: 867
Sitwell, Edith [British author] S: 478
Siva [Hindu god] *See* Shiva *in this index*

Sivan [month]
Calendar (The Hebrew calendar) C: 29
Sivapithecus [extinct animal]
Gigantopithecus G: 189
Sivash [area]
Azov, Sea of A: 998
Siwinowe Kesibwi [newspaper]
Kansas (Interesting facts) K: 217
Six, Les [music]
Honegger, Arthur H: 314
Milhaud, Darius M: 543
Poulenc, Francis P: 720
Six Characters in Search of an Author [play by
Pirandello]
Pirandello, Luigi P: 493
Six-Day War *See* Arab-Israeli conflict *in this index*
Six Flags Theme Parks
Texas (Places to visit) T: 194
Six Nations [U.S. history] *See* Iroquois League *in
this index*
606 [medication]
Ehrlich, Paul E: 145
Six-shooter [gun]
Colt, Samuel Ci: 850
Cowboy (His firearm) Ci: 1109
Sixpence in Her Shoe [essays by McGinley]
McGinley, Phyllis M: 334
16 Cygni B [planet]
Planet (The first discoveries) P: 513-514
16-millimeter film
Motion picture (The film) M: 857
Sixteenth Amendment
Constitution of the United States Ci: 1014
Income tax (History of U.S. income taxes) I: 105
United States, History of the (Taft and Wilson)
U: 187-188
Sixth Amendment
Constitution of the United States Ci: 1012
Escobedo v. Illinois E: 357
Gideon v. Wainwright G: 188
Trial (The criminal defendant's rights) T: 436-437
Sixtus I, Saint [pope]
Pope (table) P: 666
Sixtus II, Saint [pope]
Pope (table) P: 666
Sixtus III, Saint [pope]
Pope (table) P: 666
Sixtus IV [pope] S: 478
Pope (Renaissance and Reformation) P: 664;
(table) P: 666
Sixtus V [pope] S: 478
Pope (table) P: 666
"$64,000 Question, The" [television program]
Television *picture on* T: 118
Size [solution]
Painting (Other materials) P: 36
Sizing [material]
Cotton (Spinning) Ci: 1091
Dextrin D: 178
Glue (Uses of glue) G: 236
Paper (Special kinds of paper) P: 136
Sizwe Banzi Is Dead [book by Fugard]
Fugard, Athol F: 553
Sjælland [island, Denmark]
Copenhagen (The city) C: 1038
Denmark (Land regions) D: 137-138
SK [company]
Manufacturing (table) M: 170
Ska [music]
Reggae R: 204
Rock music (Alternative rock) R: 381
Skadi [Norse mythology]
Frey F: 531
Freyja F: 531
Skald [Icelandic literature] S: 478
Vikings (Cultural life and recreation) V: 381
Skaldic poetry
Skald S: 478
Skandagupta [emperor of India]
Gupta dynasty (Rise and fall of the dynasty)
G: 442
Skanderbeg [Albanian patriot] *See* Scanderbeg *in
this index*
Skåne [region, Sweden]
Scandinavia S: 171
Sweden (The Swedish Lowland) So: 1028-1029
Skármeta, Antonio [Chilean author]
Latin American literature (The post-Boom) L: 114
Skarnsundet Bridge [Norway]
Bridge (table: Cable-stayed) B: 603
Skate [fish] S: 478
Skate stride
Skiing *diagram on* S: 484; (Nordic skiing) S: 482-
483
Skateboarding [sport] S: 479 *with picture*
Hawk, Tony H: 113 *with picture*
Skater, The [painting by Stuart]

Stuart, Gilbert Charles **So: 931**
Skates, Hockey
  Hockey (Equipment) **H: 276** *with picture*
  Ice skating *picture on* **I: 11**
Skating [sport] *See* Ice skating; Roller skating *in this index*
Skeena River [British Columbia] **S: 479**
  British Columbia (Rivers, waterfalls, and lakes) **B: 624**
Skeet [sport] **S: 479**
Skeeter [iceboat]
  Iceboating (History) **I: 19**
Skein [unit of measure]
  Weights and measures (table: Miscellaneous weights and measures) **W: 184**
Skein dyeing
  Dye (Dyeing textiles) **D: 396**
  Wool (Making fabric) **W: 401**
Skeklet [custom]
  Halloween (Costumes) **H: 24a**
Skeletal age [physiology]
  Growth (Skeletal age) **G: 406**
Skeletal muscle [anatomy]
  Human body (Skeletal muscles) **H: 419** *with picture*
  Muscle (Skeletal muscles) **M: 933-934** *with diagrams*
  Muscular dystrophy **M: 936**
  Paralysis **P: 152**
  Tongue **T: 329**
Skeleton [sled]
  Skeleton **S: 479**
Skeleton [sport] **S: 479**
  Bobsledding **B: 433**
  Olympic Games (Winter Olympic Games) **O: 746d-746e**
Skeleton [anatomy] **S: 479** *with pictures*
  See also Bone; Exoskeleton; Joint *in this index; and the list of Related articles in the* Skeleton *article*
  Biology *picture on* **B: 320**
  Bird (Skeleton and muscles) **B: 364** *with diagram*
  Cat *picture on* **C: 285**; (Body size and structure) **C: 286**
  Dinosaur *picture on* **D: 210**
  Fish *diagram on* **F: 162**; (Kinds of fish) **F: 147**; (Skeleton and muscles) **F: 161**
  Fossil **F: 422** *with picture*; (Working with fragments) **F: 426**
  Frog *pictures on* **F: 537**
  Giraffe *diagram on* **G: 195**
  Gorilla *diagram on* **G: 276**
  Human body *diagram on* **H: 416**; (The skeletal system) **H: 418**; (table) **H: 422** *with diagram*
  Mammal *diagrams on* **M: 122**; (Skeleton) **M: 118** *with picture*
  Marfan syndrome **M: 198**
  Marsupial (Characteristics of marsupials) **M: 232**
  Rat *diagram on* **R: 146**
  Rattlesnake *picture on* **R: 149**
Skeleton construction
  Building construction (Types of construction) **B: 683** *with picture*
Skelton, John [English poet] **S: 481**
Skelton, Martha Wayles [wife of]
  Jefferson, Thomas (Jefferson's family) **J: 78**
Skeltonic meter [poetry]
  Skelton, John **S: 481**
Skene [theater]
  Drama (Greek drama) **D: 326**
Skep [enclosure]
  Bee (Beekeeping) **B: 206**
Skepticism [philosophy] **S: 481**
  Nihilism **N: 421**
  Philosophy (Epistemology) **P: 384**; (Skepticism) **P: 387**
  Pyrrho of Elis **P: 920**
Skerrett [book by O'Flaherty]
  O'Flaherty, Liam **O: 678**
Skerry [geography]
  Norway (Coast and islands) **N: 542**
Sketch Book of Geoffrey Crayon, Gent., The [book by Irving]
  American literature (Literature of a young nation [1788-1830]) **A: 415**
  Irving, Washington (Years in Europe) **I: 460**
  Rip Van Winkle **R: 349**
Sketch for a Historical Picture of the Progress of the Human Mind [book by Condorcet]
  Condorcet, Marquis de **Ci: 930**
  Enlightenment (Influence of the Enlightenment) **E: 326b**
Sketches by Boz [book by Dickens]
  Dickens, Charles (Dickens's life) **D: 187-188**
Sketches of Eighteenth Century America [book by Crèvecoeur]
  Crèvecoeur, Michel-Guillaume Jean de **Ci: 1129**
Sketching [art]

Drawing **D: 343** *with picture*
Skew line [mathematics] **S: 481**
Skhul [archaeological site]
  Prehistoric people (The single origin theory) **P: 750**; (The Stone Age) **P: 751**; (table) **P: 754**
Ski
  Skiing (Ski equipment and clothing) **S: 483**
  Water-skiing **W: 140** *with picture*
Ski boot
  Skiing (Ski boots) **S: 485** *with diagram*
Ski jumping
  Olympic Games (Winter Olympic Games) **O: 746d-746e**
  Skiing (Nordic skiing) **S: 482-483** *with picture*; (Nordic competitions) **S: 487**
Ski lift
  Skiing (Ski trails) **S: 486**
Ski pole
  Skiing (Ski poles) **S: 485** *with diagram*
Ski trail
  Skiing (Ski trails) **S: 486**
Skid [aviation]
  Airplane (Proper use of the controls) **A: 225**
Skid road [road]
  Lumber (table) **L: 518**
Skidding [logging]
  Lumber (table) **L: 518**
Skiff [boat]
  Fishing industry (Nets) **F: 183** *with diagram*
Skiing [sport] **S: 482** *with pictures*
  Biathlon **B: 278**
  Canada (Recreation and sports) **C: 108** *with picture*
  Chile *picture on* **C: 463**
  Norway (Recreation) **N: 540** *with picture*
  Olympic Games (Winter Olympic Games) **O: 746d**
  Safety (In winter sports) **S: 12**
  Snowboarding **S: 541**
  Switzerland (Tourism) **So: 1057** *with picture*
  Vermont (Visitor's guide) **V: 326** *with picture*
  West Virginia *picture on* **W: 210**
Skill
  Education **E: 86** *with pictures*
  Learning (Skill learning and verbal learning) **L: 164**
Skilled nursing care home
  Nursing home (Skilled nursing care homes) **N: 619**
Skilling, Jeffrey [American businessman]
  Enron Corporation **E: 327**
Skim milk
  Milk (Milk in the human diet) **M: 546**; (table) **M: 547**; (Separation or standardization) **M: 548**
Skimmer [bird] **S: 488**
  Bird *pictures on* **B: 351, B: 363**; (Birds of the seacoasts) **B: 342** *with picture*
Skimmer [device]
  Oil spill (Responses) **O: 707**
Skin [anatomy] **S: 488** *with pictures*
  See also the list of Related articles in the Skin *article*
  Acne **A: 27** *with diagram*
  Allergy **A: 373**
  Cell *picture on* **C: 328**
  Cosmetics (Kinds of cosmetics) **Ci: 1074**
  Dermatitis **D: 153**
  Dermatology **D: 153**
  Disease (Natural barriers) **D: 231** *with diagram*
  Erysipelas **E: 355**
  First aid (Other first-aid procedures) **F: 138**; (Poisons on the skin) **F: 138**
  Frostbite **F: 543**
  Human body *picture on* **H: 417**; (The skin) **H: 418**
  Keratin **K: 305**
  Leprosy **L: 204**
  Lupus **L: 526**
  Neurofibromatosis **N: 152**
  Psoriasis **P: 844**
  Races, Human **R: 52** *with picture, pictures on* **R: 54**; (Alternatives to racial classification) **R: 55**; (The problem of skin color in racial classification) **R: 56** *with pictures*; (Climatic adaptations) **R: 58**
  Scar **S: 172**
  Scleroderma **S: 209**
  Skin (Skin disorders) **S: 490**
  Skin cancer **S: 491**
  Sun lamp **So: 988**
  Sunburn **So: 989**
  Vitiligo **V: 432**
  Wart **W: 44**
Skin [zoology]
  See also Hide *in this index*
  Amphibian (Skin) **A: 440**
  Elephant (Kinds of elephants) **E: 227** *with picture*
  Frog (Skin) **F: 536** *with pictures*
  Hair **H: 9**
  Mammal (Skin and hair) **M: 118**
  Parchment **P: 155**

Reptile (Skin) **R: 251** *with pictures*
  Taxidermy (Process of mounting) **T: 56** *with picture*
Skin cancer [disease] **S: 491** *with pictures*
  Cancer (Classification by primary body site) **C: 167**; (table) **C: 170**
Skin cyst [disorder]
  Ear (Diseases) **E: 12**
Skin diving [sport] **S: 492** *with pictures*
  Diving, Underwater (Ambient diving) **D: 245**
Skin gelatin
  Gelatin **G: 76**
Skin grafting [medicine] **S: 494**
  Burn (Advanced medical care) **B: 708**
  Plastic surgery (Reconstructive plastic surgery) **P: 553**
  Transplant (Tissue transplants) **T: 379**
Skin Lodge of an Assiniboin Chief, A [painting by Bodmer]
  Indian, American *picture on* **I: 158**
Skin of Our Teeth, The [play by Wilder]
  Wilder, Thornton **W: 303**
Skin popping [slang]
  Heroin **H: 213**
Skin test [medicine]
  Allergy (Diagnosis) **A: 374**
  Tuberculosis (Diagnosis of tuberculosis) **T: 479**
Skin wool
  Wool (Types of wool) **W: 399**
Skink [reptile] **S: 494** *with picture*
  Lizard (How lizards move) **L: 399-400**
Skinner, B. F. [American psychologist] **S: 495**
  Behavior (Learning) **B: 220-221**
  Education (How people learn) **E: 86**
  Learning (Instrumental conditioning) **L: 163**
  Psychology (Behaviorism) **P: 849-850**
Skinner, Eugene [American settler]
  Eugene **E: 377**
Skinner, John S. [American government agent]
  "Star-Spangled Banner" (How the song came to be written) **So: 854**
Skinner, Richard [American political leader]
  Vermont (table) **V: 333**
Skinner, Samuel K. [American government official]
  Transportation, Department of (table) **T: 400**
Skinning
  Fur (Skinning) **F: 562**
Skip [mining]
  Mining (Mining terms) **M: 577**
Skip [sports]
  Curling (The rink) **Ci: 1196**
  Lawn bowling **L: 145**
Skip hoist
  Iron and steel (The blast furnace process) **I: 440**
Skipper [butterfly]
  Butterfly (Skippers) **B: 734** *with pictures*; (The thorax) **B: 738-739**
"Skipper Ireson's Ride" [poem by Whittier]
  Whittier, John Greenleaf **W: 295**
Skirt [clothing]
  Clothing *picture on* **Ci: 696**
Skirt [riding equipment]
  Saddle *diagrams on* **S: 7**
Skłodowska, Marie [Polish-French physicist] *See* Curie, Marie Skłodowska *in this index*
Skolt Sami [people]
  Sami **S: 79**
Skopje [Macedonia] **S: 495**
  Macedonia [country] **M: 12** *with picture*
Skou, Jens Christian [Danish chemist]
  Nobel Prizes (Chemistry: 1997) **N: 444**
Skriker, The [play by Churchill]
  Churchill, Caryl **C: 543**
Skua [bird] **S: 495**
  Antarctica (Living things) **A: 534-535** *with picture*
  Bird (Birds of the ocean and the Antarctic) **B: 344** *with picture*
Skuld [Norse mythology]
  Norns **N: 456**
Skuli Magnusson [Icelandic industrialist]
  Reykjavík **R: 288**
Skull [anatomy] **S: 495** *with pictures*
  Brain (From injury) **B: 550d**
  Frog *picture on* **F: 537**
  Head **H: 123** *with diagram*
  Mammal (Skeleton) **M: 118**
  Phrenology **P: 430**
  Prehistoric people (Prehuman ancestors) **P: 744** *with pictures*; (The first human beings) **P: 746** *with pictures*; (The origin of* Homo sapiens) **P: 748** *with pictures*
Skull and crossbones
  Pirate (A pirate's life) **P: 494-495** *with picture*
Skullcap
  Judaism (Orthodox Judaism) **J: 180**
Skunk [animal] **S: 495** *with picture*
  Animal *picture on* **A: 479**

Fur (table) F: 561
Skunk cabbage [plant] S: 496
  Flower *picture on* F: 294
Sky S: 496
  Astronomy (Observing the sky) A: 835
  Cosmology (The dark sky) Ci: 1077
  Planetarium P: 514a
Sky & Telescope [magazine]
  Blue moon B: 421
Sky Cathedral [sculpture by Nevelson]
  Nevelson, Louise *picture on* N: 178
Sky Harbor Airport
  Airport (table) A: 245
Sky lark [bird]
  Bird *picture on* B: 344d; (Birds of Europe) B: 344c
  Lark L: 76
Sky Pond [Colorado]
  Colorado *picture on* Ci: 837
Sky soldier *See* Airborne troops *in this index*
Sky wave
  Radio (Transmitting AM band signals) R: 87 *with diagram*
Skydiving [sport] S: 496
  Parachute (Uses of parachutes) P: 142
SkyDome [stadium] *See* Rogers Centre *in this index*
Skye, Isle of [island, Scotland]
  Hebrides H: 163
Skye terrier [dog] S: 496
  Dog *picture on* D: 272
Skyjacking [crime] *See* Hijacking *in this index*
Skylab [space station]
  Astronaut (Achievements in space) A: 829-830
  International Space Station (History) I: 346b
  Space exploration (Skylab) So: 721
  Sun (History of modern solar study) So: 986
Skylark *See* Sky lark *in this index*
Skyline [logging]
  Lumber (Transporting logs) L: 518
Skyline Project
  Denver (History) D: 147-148
Skyrocket
  Fireworks (How fireworks work) F: 135
Skyscraper [architecture] S: 497 *with pictures*
  Building construction (Constructing a skyscraper)
    B: 683 *with pictures*; (Types of construction)
    B: 683
  Burnham, Daniel Hudson B: 709 *with picture*
  Chicago (Architecture) C: 428
  New York City N: 322 *with picture*; (Architecture)
    N: 336
SLA [organization]
  Hearst, William Randolph H: 131
Slab [by-product]
  Lumber (table) L: 518
Slab [construction]
  Building construction (Beams, girders, and
    columns) B: 682-683
  House (The foundation) H: 380
  Iron and steel (Ingot casting) I: 445 *with diagram*
Slab [pottery]
  Pottery *picture on* P: 718; (Shaping the clay)
    P: 716-717
Slab avalanche
  Avalanche A: 982
Slab-pull [geology]
  Plate tectonics (Causes of plate movement)
    P: 564
Slab table
  Furniture (Ancient Rome) F: 570-571
SLAC [particle accelerator] *See* Stanford Linear
  Accelerator Center *in this index*
Slacking off
  Sailing (Trimming and tacking) S: 26
Slade, William [American political leader]
  Vermont (table) V: 333
Slag [by-product] S: 499
  Copper (Smelting) Ci: 1043
  Iron and steel (The blast furnace process) I: 440
    with diagram
  Lead (Production) L: 149-150
  Metallurgy (Smelting) M: 426
Slag ladle
  Iron and steel (The blast furnace process) I: 440-
    441 *with diagram*
Slaked lime [chemical]
  Lime L: 306
Slaking [industrial process]
  Lime L: 307
Slalom [race]
  Skiing (Alpine competitions) S: 486-487
  Snowboarding S: 541
Slam! [book by Myers]
  Myers, Walter Dean M: 970f
Slam [cards]
  Bridge (Bidding) B: 604
Slander [law] S: 499
  Damages D: 20

Freedom of speech (Limitations) F: 506
  Libel L: 226
Slang [language] S: 499
  Grammar (Grammar and usage) G: 304
Slant height [geometry]
  Pyramid P: 916 *with diagram*
Slant rhyme *See* Near rhyme *in this index*
Slap shot
  Hockey (Shooting) H: 277
Slapstick comedy
  Humor (The types of humor) H: 435-436
  Sennett, Mack S: 301
Slash-and-burn agriculture
  See also Shifting cultivation *in this index*
  Agriculture (Shifting cultivation) A: 149 *with
    picture*
  Aztec (Agriculture) A: 1002
  Deforestation (Agriculture) D: 90
  Indian, American (Farming) I: 141
  Indonesia (Agriculture) I: 235
  Mozambique (People) M: 904
Slash pine [tree]
  Pine (Southeastern pines) P: 468-469
Slashing machine
  Cotton (Spinning) Ci: 1091
Slat [airplane]
  Aerodynamics (Creating extra lift) A: 86
  Airplane (The wing) A: 213-214
Slate [rock] S: 500
  Building stone B: 685
  Rock (Metamorphic rock) R: 373; (table) R: 373
    with picture
Slater, John Fox [American businessman]
  Foundation (History) F: 431
Slater, Rodney E. [American government official]
  Clinton, Bill (table) Ci: 682d
  Transportation, Department of (table) T: 400
Slater, Samuel [American businessman] S: 501
  Industrial Revolution (Spread of the Industrial
    Revolution) I: 252
  Pawtucket P: 204
  Rhode Island *picture on* R: 314; (Industrial
    expansion) R: 313
Slater Mill [Pawtucket, Rhode Island]
  Rhode Island *picture on* R: 314
Slater Mill Historic Site [Rhode Island]
  Rhode Island (Places to visit) R: 304 *with picture*
Slaton, John M. [American political leader]
  Georgia (table) G: 130
Slatyheaded parakeet [bird]
  Parakeet P: 151 *with picture*
Slaughter, Enos [American baseball player]
  Baseball (table: Hall of Fame) B: 134b
Slaughter cattle
  Ranching (Life on a cattle ranch) R: 134
Slaughterhouse Cases [U.S. history]
  Miller, Samuel Freeman M: 554
Slaughterhouse-Five [book by Vonnegut]
  Vonnegut, Kurt V: 448
Slaughtering
  Meat packing (Meat-packing processes) M: 351
Slave, The [play by Baraka]
  Baraka, Amiri B: 103
Slave codes [law]
  African Americans (Colonial times) A: 136d-136f
  Colonial life in America (The lower class) Ci: 794
  United States, History of the (Why the colonists
    came) U: 157
Slave Dancer, The [book by Fox]
  Fox, Paula F: 441
Slave Lake, Great [Northwest Territories] *See* Great
  Slave Lake *in this index*
Slave-making ant
  Ant (Slave-making ants) A: 526 *with picture*
Slave River [Canada]
  Great Slave Lake G: 348
Slave Ship [play by Baraka]
  Baraka, Amiri B: 103
Slave Songs of the United States [book]
  Spiritual So: 796
Slavery S: 501 *with pictures and map*
  See also Abolition movement *in this index*
  Africa (The Atlantic slave trade) A: 132
  Amistad Rebellion A: 433
  Aztec (The Aztec empire) A: 999
  Berlin Conference B: 266
  Brazil (History) B: 583
  Calypso (Development) C: 71
  Concentration camp (Nazi concentration camps)
    Ci: 926-927
  Cuba (History) Ci: 1175
  Drake, Sir Francis (Early life) D: 321
  Ghana (History) G: 179
  Henry the Navigator H: 191
  Hispanic Americans (In Puerto Rico and Cuba)
    H: 247
  Kongo K: 364

Latin America (Colonial rule) L: 104
Law (The influence of ancient Greece) L: 133;
  (Ancient Roman law) L: 133-134
Mauritius (History) M: 317
Nigeria (The coming of the Europeans) N: 417
Pacific Islands (Missionaries, traders, and settlers)
  P: 12
Palmares P: 110
Rome, Ancient (The people) R: 437
São Tomé and Príncipe (History) S: 120
Serf S: 316b
Tanzania (The development of trade) T: 34-35
Togo (History) T: 310
Vodou V: 436
United States
  Abolition movement A: 12
  Adams, John Quincy (Back to Congress) A: 43
  African American literature (Early works)
    A: 136-136a; (The 1800's) A: 136a
  African Americans A: 136b; (Beginning of the
    slave trade) A: 136c *with pictures*, A: 136c
    with picture and map; (The years of slavery)
    A: 136d; (The end of slavery) A: 136i
  Black Seminole B: 391
  Brown, John B: 643
  Buchanan, James B: 658; (The struggle over
    slavery) B: 660
  Civil War, American (The conflict over slavery)
    Ci: 615 *with map*; (The end of slavery) Ci: 634
  Colonial life in America (Population growth)
    Ci: 791-792; (The lower class) Ci: 794 *with
    picture*; (Houses) Ci: 796-797; (Clothing)
    Ci: 799-802
  Compromise of 1850 Ci: 906
  Constitution of the United States (The
    compromises) Ci: 1000-1001; (Amendment
    13) Ci: 1013; (Amendment 14) Ci: 1014
  Cotton (In the U.S. South) Ci: 1092-1093
  Crittenden Compromise Ci: 1147
  Democratic Party (The slavery issue) D: 124
  Douglass, Frederick D: 313
  Dred Scott Decision D: 345
  Emancipation Proclamation E: 253
  Family (Early Western families in America)
    F: 22-23
  Folk music (American folk music) F: 321-322
  Franklin, Benjamin (The twilight years) F: 491
  Freedom Day, National F: 503
  Frémont, John Charles F: 511
  Gabriel G: 4
  Garrison, William Lloyd G: 45
  Gorée G: 274
  Gospel music G: 277
  Gullah G: 439
  Immigration (The first wave) I: 82
  Indian, American (In Latin America) I: 178
  Jackson, Andrew (Slavery and Texas) J: 14
  Jefferson, Thomas (Jefferson's family) J: 78;
    (Slave ownership) J: 78; (Jefferson and Sally
    Hemings) J: 79; (Later years) J: 87
  Kansas (The struggle over slavery) K: 235
  Kansas-Nebraska Act K: 243
  Liberia (History) L: 231
  Maroons M: 217
  Mason, George (His constitutional views)
    M: 265-266
  Mexican War (Results of the war) M: 447
  Missouri Compromise M: 673
  Pioneer life in America (Why the pioneers
    headed west) P: 476-477
  Plantation (Slave-labor plantations) P: 550
  Popular sovereignty P: 672
  Proslavery movement P: 828
  Taney, Roger Brooke T: 24
  Turner, Nat T: 517
  Uncle Tom's Cabin U: 19
  Underground railroad U: 20
  United States, History of the *picture on* U: 175;
    (Life in colonial America) U: 156; (The
    Jeffersonian triumph) U: 163; (Cotton and
    slavery) U: 166; (The Missouri crisis) U: 166;
    (The abolition movement) U: 173; (The
    nation divided [1850-1869]) U: 174 *with
    picture*; (Reconstruction) U: 178-179
  Vermont (Interesting facts) V: 319
  Virginia: (The Mother of Presidents) V: 421
  Walker, David W: 13
  Washington, D.C. (The issue of slavery) W: 86
  Whig Party (Decline of the Whigs) W: 280
  Wilberforce, William W: 300
  Wilmot Proviso W: 315
Slavey Indians
  Great Slave Lake G: 348
Slavic countries S: 504
  Slavs S: 505
Slavic language
  Language (Indo-European) L: 65-66

Russian language R: 557
Russian literature (Religious literature) R: 558
World, History of the (The Byzantine Empire) W: 434
Slavonic Dances [music by Dvořák]
Dvořák, Antonín D: 394
Slavs [people] S: 505
Alphabet (Other alphabets) A: 383
Bulgaria (People) B: 689
Croatia (History) Ci: 1148a
Czech Republic (Early days) Ci: 1213
Holocaust H: 296
Macedonia (People) M: 12
Russia (Ancestry) R: 532; (Early days) R: 547
Ukraine (Ancestry) U: 6
Union of Soviet Socialist Republics (People) U: 31
Slayton, Donald Kent [American astronaut] S: 505
Astronaut (Achievements in space) A: 829-830
Space exploration *pictures on* So: 713, So: 720
SLBM [weapon] *See* Submarine-launched ballistic missile *in this index*
SLE [disease] *See* Systemic lupus erythematosus *in this index*
Sled S: 505
Bobsledding B: 433 *with picture*
Inuit *pictures on* I: 354d; (Transportation) I: 354c
Luge L: 515
Skeleton S: 479
Sled dog S: 505
Snowmobiling S: 542 *with picture*
Tobogganing T: 308
Transportation (Prehistoric times) T: 385
Yukon *picture on* Y: 581
Sled [equipment]
Mine warfare *picture on* M: 565
Sled dog S: 505
Iditarod I: 47
Sled Dog Derby [Laconia]
New Hampshire *picture on* N: 217
Sledge [transportation]
Invention (Prehistoric times) I: 358
Sled S: 505
Transportation *picture on* T: 386; (Prehistoric times) T: 385
Sledge hammer
Fire department (Rescue trucks) F: 126 *with picture*
Sleep S: 506
Bird (Sleeping and resting) B: 355
Brain (Attention and consciousness) B: 554-555
Dream D: 344
Fibromyalgia F: 90
Fish (How fish rest) F: 166
Health (Rest and sleep) H: 125
Hibernation H: 222
Insomnia I: 303
Narcolepsy N: 20
Nightmare N: 420
Sleeping sickness S: 507
Sleepwalking S: 508
Snoring S: 538
Space exploration (Meeting basic needs in space) So: 703 *with picture*
Sleep apnea [disorder] S: 507
Sleep movement [biology]
Biological clock (Daily rhythms) B: 315
Sleep paralysis
Narcolepsy N: 20
Sleeper, Albert E. [American political leader]
Michigan (table) M: 507
"Sleeper, The" [poem by Poe]
Poe, Edgar Allan (Poetry and poetic theory) P: 589-590
Sleeping bag
Camping (Sleeping bags) C: 93
Sleeping Bear Dunes National Lakeshore [Michigan]
Michigan (Places to visit) M: 498
National Park System (table: National lakeshores) N: 58
"Sleeping Beauty" [story]
Grimm's Fairy Tales G: 394
Sleeping Beauty, The [ballet]
Art and the arts *picture on* A: 748
Ballet *picture on* B: 44
Sleeping Beauty Castle [Disneyland]
California *picture on* C: 46
Sleeping car [railroad]
Pullman, George Mortimer P: 900
Railroad (Engineering improvements) R: 117
Sleeping Car Porters, Brotherhood of [union]
Randolph, A. Philip R: 136
Sleeping pill
Barbiturate B: 107
Sleeping sickness [disease] S: 507 *with picture*
Bruce, Sir David B: 647
Laveran, Charles Louis Alphonse L: 129

Trypanosome T: 474
Tsetse fly T: 474
Sleeplessness *See* Insomnia *in this index*
Sleepwalking S: 508
Sleet [weather] S: 508
Sleeve Pekingese [dog]
Pekingese P: 231
Sleigh *See* Sled *in this index*
Sleight of hand [magic]
Magician (Sleight of hand) M: 51
Sleipnir [Norse mythology]
Horse (table: Famous horses in history and legend) H: 361
Slemmer, Adam J. [Union military leader]
Fort Pickens F: 415
Slender blind snake
Snake (Slender blind snakes) S: 535
Slender-horned gazelle
Gazelle G: 74
Slender loris [animal]
Loris L: 455
Slide [gun]
Handgun (Types of handguns) H: 43 *with picture*
Slide [microscope]
Microtomy M: 520
Slide [photography]
Audio-visual materials (Projection devices) A: 882
Projection screen P: 816
Slide-action rifle
Rifle (Kinds of rifles) R: 338-339
Slide Mountain [mountain, New York]
New York (Mountains) N: 306
Slide Mountain [New York]
Catskill Mountains C: 305
Slide projector
Projector (Types of projectors) P: 816-817
Slide rule
Calculator C: 22
Slide trombone [musical instrument] *See* Trombone *in this index*
Slidell, John [Confederate political leader] S: 508
Lincoln, Abraham (Foreign relations) L: 322
Mason, James Murray M: 266
Mexican War (Events leading up to the war) M: 446
Trent Affair T: 435
Wilkes, Charles W: 306
Slider
Baseball (Pitching) B: 127
Sliding
Baseball *picture on* B: 129
Sliding filament theory
Muscle (How muscles work) M: 935
Sliding tackle
Soccer (Tackling) So: 548
Sliding vane pump
Pump (Rotary pumps) P: 900b *with diagram*
Slieve Donard [mountain, Ireland]
Northern Ireland (Surface features) N: 523 *with map*
Slight Ache, A [play by Pinter]
Pinter, Harold P: 475
Slime mold [plant] S: 508
Sling [bandage]
Bandage B: 75
Sling [weapon] S: 508 *with picture*
Indian, American *picture on* I: 175
Sling club [weapon]
Indian, American *picture on* I: 144
Slingshot [weapon]
Sling S: 508
Slip [botany] *See* Cutting *in this index*
Slip [clay]
Ceramics (Making ceramics) C: 360
Doll (Rivalry in the doll industry) D: 291
Pottery (Shaping the clay) P: 716-717
Slip casting
Ceramics (Making ceramics) C: 360
Slip ring
Electric generator (Alternating-current generators) E: 171 *with diagrams*
Slip stitch
Crochet Ci: 1148d
Slipe wool
Wool (Types of wool) W: 399
Slipknot
Knots, hitches, and splices *diagram on* K: 357
Slipper
Shoe *pictures on* S: 432
Slipper bath [bathtub]
Bath (History) B: 164
Slipper lobster [sea animal]
Lobster L: 405
Slipperwort [plant] S: 508a
Slippery elm [tree]
Elm (Kinds) E: 244-245
Slippery Jack [fungus]

Mushroom (Nonpoisonous mushrooms) M: 943-945 *with picture*
Slippery When Wet [recording]
Rock music (New wave and mainstream rock) R: 380c-380d
Slipping
Boxing *picture on* B: 529
Slipstitch
Sewing (Hand stitches) S: 332
Sliver [textiles]
Cotton *picture on* Ci: 1092; (Making cotton into cloth) Ci: 1091
Spinning (The mule) So: 794-795
Textile *picture on* T: 216
Wool (Making yarn) W: 400 *with picture*
Sloan, Alfred Pritchard, Jr. [American businessman]
Automobile (The rise of the Big Three) A: 968
Sloan, John [American artist] S: 508a
Ashcan School A: 768 *with picture*
Sloane, Sir Hans [English biologist]
British Museum B: 632
Sloat, John D. [American military leader]
Mexican War (The occupation of New Mexico and California) M: 446
Slobodkin, Louis [American artist]
Caldecott Medal (table: 1944) C: 26
Sloe [shrub] S: 508a
Slogan
Advertising (Slogans) A: 76
Sloop [boat]
Boating *picture on* B: 431; (Sailboats) B: 429
Sailing (Catboats and sloops) S: 24 *with picture*
Slope mine
Coal (Underground mining) Ci: 723
Mining (Underground mining methods) M: 576
Slope wind
Glider (Soaring) G: 229
SLORC [organization] *See* State Law and Order Restoration Council *in this index*
Slot machine S: 508a *with picture*
Gambling (Casino gambling) G: 20
Sloth [animal] S: 508a
Animal *picture on* A: 480
Mammal *picture on* M: 117
Sloth bear [animal] S: 508c
Bear (Sloth bears) B: 186 *with picture*
Slouching Towards Bethlehem [book by Didion]
Didion, Joan D: 195
Slovak [language]
Slovakia (Ethnic groups and languages) S: 508c
Slovakia S: 508b *with pictures and maps*
Czech Republic Ci: 1209
Czechoslovakia Ci: 1215
Flag *picture on* F: 207
Hungary (Multiparty elections) H: 448
Slovaks [people]
Czech Republic Ci: 1209
Czechoslovakia Ci: 1215
Slovakia S: 508b
Slovenes [people]
Slovenia (People) S: 511
Slovenia S: 510 *with pictures and map*
Euro E: 379
Flag *picture on* F: 207
Serbia (History) S: 314-316
Yugoslavia Y: 576
Slovenian [language]
Italy (Language) I: 502
Slow earthquake
Earthquake (Why a quake begins) E: 36
Slow gait
Horse (Gaits) H: 353-354
Slow Learner [book by Pynchon]
Pynchon, Thomas P: 915
Slow loris [animal]
Loris L: 455 *with picture*
Slow nova [astronomy]
Nova N: 553
Slow-pitch softball
Softball (Types of softball) So: 571
Slow-release fertilizer
Fertilizer (Production and sale) F: 80
Slowdown
Labor movement (Handling labor disputes) L: 6
Slowworm [animal]
Blindworm B: 403
SLR [camera] *See* Single-lens reflex camera *in this index*
Sludge
Copper (Electrolytic refining) Ci: 1043
Sewage (Primary treatment) S: 329; (Secondary treatment) S: 330
Silver (Extracting and refining silver) S: 464
Sludge digestion tank
Sewage (Secondary treatment) S: 330
Slug [animal] S: 512 *with picture*

Gardening (Mulching) G: 35
Mollusk (Gastropods) M: 695
Slug [measurement]
  Mass M: 268
Slug [printing]
  Linotype (How the linotype works) L: 338-339
    with picture
Slug [projectile]
  Shotgun S: 436
Slugging average
  Baseball (Baseball terms) B: 124
Sluice box [mining]
  Mining (Mining terms) M: 577
Sluicing [mining]
  Mining (Placer mining) M: 575
  Western frontier life in America *picture on* W: 236;
    (A typical mining camp) W: 235
Slum
  Colombia (Way of life) Ci: 779-781
  Conservation (Urban conservation) Ci: 984
  Housing H: 389 *with picture*
  Latin America (City life) L: 95-96 *with picture*
  Tenement T: 133
  Urban renewal (History) U: 220
Slumdog Millionaire [film]
  Boyle, Danny B: 539
  Motion picture (Best picture: 2008) M: 861
Slurry [material]
  Bituminous sands B: 384
  Cement and concrete (Crushing and grinding)
    C: 344
  Coal (Shipping coal) Ci: 727
  Copper (Milling) Ci: 1042
  Food preservation (Drying) F: 342-343
  Iron and steel (Processing) I: 439
  Lime L: 307
  Pipeline (Solids pipelines) P: 491
  Plastics *diagram on* P: 557
Slurry explosive
  Dynamite (History) D: 397
Slye, Leonard Franklin [birth name of]
  Rogers, Roy R: 401
Sm [symbol]
  Samarium S: 78
Smack [slang]
  Heroin H: 213
Small, Albion W. [American sociologist]
  Chicago, University of (Research program) C: 438
Small, David [American artist]
  Caldecott Medal (table: 2001) C: 26
Small, Len [American political leader]
  Illinois (table) I: 71
Small, William [American educator]
  Jefferson, Thomas (Education) J: 77
Small arms
  Ammunition (Small-arms ammunition) A: 435
    with pictures
  Firearm F: 132
Small Business Administration [U.S.] S: 512
Small Catechism of 1529 [book by Luther]
  Luther, Martin (Building and defending the
    church) L: 528
Small-claims court S: 512
Small-clawed otter [animal]
  Otter (Body) O: 876
Small combatant [ship]
  Navy N: 76; (Small combatants) N: 78
  Warship (Small combatants) W: 41
Small corporation
  Business (Corporations) B: 726
Small Cowper Madonna, The [painting by Raphael]
  Renaissance *picture on* R: 234
Small craft advisory
  Boating (Buoys and other safety aids) B: 430 *with
    picture*
  Flag *picture on* F: 197
Small Crucifixion, The [painting by Grünewald]
  Grünewald, Matthias *picture on* G: 407
Small game [hunting]
  Hunting (Kinds of hunting) H: 450
Small House at Allington, The [book by Trollope]
  Trollope, Anthony T: 449
Small intestine [anatomy]
  Intestine (The small intestine) I: 353 *with diagram*
  Bariatric surgery B: 110 *with diagram*
  Blood (Transporting nutrients and wastes) B: 408
    with diagram
  Celiac disease C: 325
  Digestive system (In the small intestine) D: 202
    with diagrams
  Frog *picture on* F: 537
  Gland (table) G: 209
  Human body (The small intestine and large
    intestine) H: 420 *with picture*; (table) H: 422
    with diagram
Small Magellanic Cloud [astronomy]
  Magellanic Clouds M: 48

Small-scale map
  Map (Scale) M: 178
Small slam
  Bridge (Bidding) B: 604
Small white lady's-slipper [plant]
  Lady's-slipper L: 26
Small World [book by Lodge]
  Novel (The novel today) N: 575
Smaller festival [Islam] *See* `Íd al-Fitr *in this index*
Smalley, Richard Errett [American chemist]
  Carbon (Fullerenes) C: 205
  Nobel Prizes (Chemistry: 1996) N: 444
Smallholder Party [Hungarian history]
  Hungary (History) H: 445-447
Smallmouth bass [fish]
  Bass (Black bass) B: 156 *with picture*
  Fish *picture on* F: 158
Smallmouth buffalo fish
  Fish *picture on* F: 159
Smallpox [disease] S: 513
  Australia (Aborigines) A: 922
  Colonial life in America (Health and medicine)
    Ci: 809
  Disease D: 225
  Electron microscope *picture on* E: 204
  Exploration (Spain's conquests in the New World)
    E: 445; (The French and English in North
    America) E: 446
  Jenner, Edward J: 91
  Medicine (The development of immunology)
    M: 374
  Monkeypox (Prevention) M: 730
  Virus (Vaccines) V: 428a
Smalls, Robert [American political leader] S: 513
  African Americans (The American Civil War)
    A: 136i-136j
Smalltooth sawfish
  Fish *picture on* F: 152
Smallwood, Joseph R. [Canadian political leader]
  Newfoundland and Labrador (Confederation
    with Canada) N: 377
Smallwood, William [American political leader]
  Maryland (table) M: 255
Smart [automobile]
  Daimler AG D: 5
SMART-1 [lunar probe]
  European Space Agency E: 418
  Moon (Recent exploration) M: 795
  Rocket (Ion rockets) R: 389
  Space exploration (Lunar probes) So: 708-710
Smart bomb *See* Guided bomb *in this index*
Smart card [electronic device] S: 513
  Bank (Electronic banking) B: 89-90
Smart dust [engineering]
  Nanotechnology (Applications of
    nanotechnology) N: 10
Smart materials [engineering]
  Materials M: 300b; (Smart materials) M: 301
Smart mine
  Mine warfare (Kinds of land mines) M: 564
Smart phone *See* Smartphone *in this index*
Smart Set [magazine]
  Mencken, H. L. M: 397
Smart shell [ammunition]
  Ammunition (Guided ammunition) A: 436
Smartphone
  Cellular telephone C: 340
  Computer (Personal computers) Ci: 909-910
    with picture
  Electronics *picture on* E: 217
  Handheld computer H: 45
  Internet *diagram on* I: 350c; (The World Wide
    Web) I: 350d; (The evolving Internet) I: 350g
  Telephone *picture on* T: 97; (Types of telephones)
    T: 94-95
Smash [sports]
  Badminton (Playing) B: 24-25
SMD [program]
  Radar (In the military) R: 65
Smear
  Microtomy M: 520
Smeaton, John [British engineer]
  Cement and concrete (History) C: 345
Smell [sense] S: 514 *with diagram*
  Animal (Adaptations for sensing the
    environment) A: 492-493 *with picture*
  Dog (Senses) D: 265
  Fish (Smell and taste) F: 164
  Insect (Smell) I: 291
  Mammal (Senses) M: 120
  Nose N: 548
  Reptile (Sense organs) R: 251-252
  Senses S: 301
  Taste T: 50
Smelling salts [medication] S: 514
"Smells Like Teen Spirit" [song]
  Nirvana N: 424

Smelt [fish] S: 514 *with picture*
Smelter [industry]
  Indian, American *picture on* I: 140
Smelting [industrial process] S: 515
  Aluminum (Smelting the alumina) A: 393
  Copper (How copper metal is produced) Ci: 1041
    with diagrams; (Smelting) Ci: 1043
  Gold *diagram on* G: 250; (Smelting) G: 253
  Industrial Revolution (Early ironmaking) I: 249
  Metallurgy (Smelting) M: 426
  Slag S: 499
Smetana, Bedřich [Czech composer] S: 515
  Czech Republic (The arts) Ci: 1211
Smetona, Antanas [Lithuanian political leader]
  Lithuania (History) L: 389-390
Smiley, George [literary figure]
  Le Carré, John L: 174
Smirke, Sir Robert [British architect]
  Architecture (The Greek Revival) A: 625-626
Smit, Erik [Danish government official]
  Virgin Islands, United States (Danish rule) V: 396
Smith, Abigail [wife of John Adams] *See* Adams,
  Abigail Smith *in this index*
Smith, Abigail Adams [daughter of]
  Adams, John (Adams's family) A: 34-35
Smith, Adam [Scottish economist] S: 515
  Capital C: 192
  Capitalism (Capitalism in its ideal form) C: 194;
    (The development of capitalism) C: 196
  Economics (The free market) E: 59; (The classical
    economists) E: 64 *with picture*
  Laissez faire L: 31
  Liberalism (Features of liberalism) L: 228
  Marx, Karl (Early development) M: 237
Smith, Alfred Emanuel [American political leader]
  S: 515
  Democratic Party (During the 1920's) D: 126
  Hoover, Herbert Clark (Election of 1928) H: 329
  Liberty League L: 233
  New York (table) N: 313
  Roosevelt, Franklin Delano (Return to politics)
    R: 451 *with picture*
Smith, Benjamin [American political leader]
  North Carolina (table) N: 490
Smith, Bessie [American singer] S: 516
  Blues B: 425
Smith, Bruce [American football player]
  Football (table) F: 363
Smith, Caleb B. [American government official]
  Emancipation Proclamation *picture on* E: 254
  Interior, Department of the (table) I: 325
  Lincoln, Abraham (table) L: 323
Smith, Celia and Charity [American dollmakers]
  Doll (Cloth dolls) D: 289
Smith, Charles E. [American government official]
  McKinley, William (table) M: 342
  Roosevelt, Theodore (table) R: 466
Smith, Charles Kingsford [American aviator]
  Airplane (Notable airplane flights) A: 236
Smith, Charles M. [American political leader]
  Vermont (table) V: 333
Smith, Cyrus R. [American government official]
  Commerce, Department of (table) Ci: 871
  Johnson, Lyndon Baines (table) J: 151
Smith, David [American sculptor] S: 516
  Sculpture (Varieties of abstraction) S: 258 *with
    picture*
Smith, Dean [American basketball coach] S: 516
  Basketball *picture on* B: 154
Smith, Donald Alexander [Canadian
  businessman]
  Strathcona and Mount Royal, Baron of So: 920
Smith, Edmund Kirby [Confederate general]
  S: 516
Smith, Edward C. [American political leader]
  Vermont (table) V: 333
Smith, Edward J. [British captain]
  Titanic T: 300
Smith, Elmo [American political leader]
  Oregon (table) O: 845
Smith, Emmitt [American football player] S: 516
Smith, Forrest [American political leader]
  Missouri (table) M: 668
Smith, Francis [British military leader]
  Revere, Paul (Paul Revere's ride) R: 268
Smith, Francis Pettit [British inventor]
  Ship (The first propeller-driven ships) S: 425
Smith, George E. [American physicist]
  Nobel Prizes (Physics: 2009) N: 442
Smith, George I. [Canadian political leader]
  Nova Scotia (table) N: 567
Smith, George William [American political leader]
  Virginia (table) V: 417
Smith, Gladys Marie *See* Pickford, Mary *in this
  index*
Smith, Hamilton Othanel [American physiologist]
  Nobel Prizes (Physiology or medicine: 1978)

N: 446

Smith, Henry [American political leader]
Rhode Island (table) R: 311
Smith, Hilton [American baseball player]
Baseball (table: Hall of Fame) B: 134b
Smith, Hoke [American political leader]
Cleveland, Grover (table) Ci: 672
Georgia (table) G: 130
Interior, Department of the (table) I: 325
Smith, Holland McTyeire [American general]
Marine Corps, United States (The 1900's) M: 209
Smith, Hulett C. [American political leader]
West Virginia (table) W: 225
Smith, Hyrum [American religious leader]
Mormons (Mormons in the Middle West) M: 808-809
Nauvoo N: 69
Smith, Joseph (Life at Nauvoo) S: 517-518
Smith, Ian Douglas [Rhodesian political leader]
Zimbabwe (History) Z: 592-593
Smith, Isabel [American educator]
Youth hostel Y: 574
Smith, Israel [American political leader]
Vermont (table) V: 333
Smith, J. Gregory [American political leader]
Vermont (table) V: 333
Smith, James [American patriot] S: 516
Smith, James [American political leader]
Illinois (French and British control) I: 72
Smith, James, Jr. [American political leader]
Wilson, Woodrow (Governor of New Jersey)
W: 321
Smith, James M. [American political leader]
Georgia (table) G: 130
Smith, James Y. [American political leader]
Rhode Island (table) R: 311
Smith, Jean Kennedy [sister of John F. Kennedy]
Kennedy, John Fitzgerald (Boyhood) K: 260-261
Kennedy, Joseph Patrick (His family) K: 269
Smith, Jedediah Strong [American explorer]
S: 516
California (American settlement) C: 60
Nevada (Exploration) N: 173
Smith, Jeremiah [American political leader]
New Hampshire (table) N: 223
Smith, Jesse W. [American public figure]
Harding, Warren Gamaliel (Government scandals)
H: 58
Smith, Jessie Willcox [American artist]
Book Week B: 470
Smith, John [English colonial leader] S: 516
American literature (Virginia) A: 414
Jamestown J: 28
Map (Mapping the Americas) M: 184
Maryland (Exploration and settlement) M: 256
Newport, Christopher N: 379
Pocahontas P: 588
Powhatan P: 728
United States, History of the (Virginia and
Maryland) U: 153
Virginia (The Jamestown settlement) V: 418
Washington, D.C. (Early days) W: 85
Smith, John B. [American political leader]
New Hampshire (table) N: 223
Smith, John Cotton [American political leader]
Connecticut (table) Ci: 967
Smith, John Stafford [British musician]
National anthem N: 29
"Star-Spangled Banner" So: 854
Smith, John Walter [American political leader]
Maryland (table) M: 255
Smith, Joseph [American religious leader] S: 517
with portrait
Community of Christ Ci: 899
Illinois (Places to visit) I: 62
Mormons M: 806 with picture; (Revelations)
M: 808; (Mormons in the Middle West) M: 808-809
Nauvoo N: 69
Utah (The Mormons) U: 246
Young, Brigham Y: 571
Smith, Joseph, III [American religious leader]
Community of Christ Ci: 899
Smith, Kiki [American sculptor]
Sculpture (From the mid-1900's to the early
2000's) S: 259 with picture
Smith, Maggie [British actress]
Motion picture (Best performance by an actress:
1969) M: 862; (Best performance by an actress
in a supporting role: 1978) M: 862b
Smith, Mamie [American singer]
Jazz (Early jazz) J: 70
Smith, Margaret Chase [American political leader]
S: 518
Maine (The mid-1900's) M: 91 with picture
Smith, Margaret Jean [American tennis player] See
Court, Margaret Smith in this index

Smith, Margaret Mackall [wife of Zachary Taylor]
See Taylor, Margaret Smith in this index
Smith, Michael [Canadian chemist]
Nobel Prizes (Chemistry: 1993) N: 444
Smith, Michael J. [American astronaut]
Challenger disaster C: 370
Space exploration (The Challenger disaster)
So: 725
Smith, Monroe [American educator]
Youth hostel Y: 574
Smith, Nels H. [American political leader]
Wyoming (table) W: 532
Smith, Ozzie [American baseball player]
Baseball (table: Hall of Fame) B: 134b
Smith, Preston [American political leader]
Texas (table) T: 203
Smith, Robert [American government official]
Jefferson, Thomas (table) J: 83
Madison, James (table) M: 35
Smith, Robert Burns [American political leader]
Montana (table) M: 757
Smith, Rosalynn [wife of Jimmy Carter] See Carter,
Rosalynn Smith in this index
Smith, Rosamond [pseudonym]
Oates, Joyce Carol O: 639
Smith, Samuel E. [American political leader]
Maine (table) M: 87
Smith, Samuel Francis [American religious leader]
America A: 407
Smith, Thomas A. [American general]
Fort Smith F: 416
Smith, Tommie [American runner]
Olympic Games picture on O: 754; (The 1968
games) O: 752
Smith, Tony [American sculptor]
Sculpture (Varieties of abstraction) S: 258 with
picture
Smith, Troy [American football player]
Football (table) F: 363
Smith, Vernon Lomax [American economist]
Nobel Prizes (Economics: 2002) N: 449
Smith, Walker, Jr. [American boxer]
Robinson, Sugar Ray R: 369
Smith, Will [American actor] So: 518
Smith, William [American political leader]
Virginia (table) V: 417
Smith, William [British geologist]
Geology (Experimental geology) G: 99
Smith, William Alexander [Scottish merchant]
Boys' Brigade B: 540
Smith, William E. [American political leader]
Wisconsin (table) W: 365
Smith, William French [American government
official]
Justice, Department of (table) J: 203
Reagan, Ronald Wilson (table) R: 169
Smith, William Hugh [American political leader]
Alabama (table) A: 274
Smith, William Stephens [American government
official]
Adams, John (Adams's family) A: 34-35
Smith Act [1940] S: 518
Flynn, Elizabeth Gurley F: 313
Freedom of speech (In the United States) F: 506
Smith and Wesson [gun]
Gun control (Approaches to gun control) G: 440-441
Handgun (Types of handguns) H: 43; (Rapid-fire
handguns) H: 45
Smith College S: 518
Smith-Hughes Act [1917]
Agricultural education (History) A: 145
Education (Increased government support)
E: 104
FFA (History) F: 86
Smith-Lever Act [1914]
Agricultural education (History) A: 145
4-H (The first 4-H program) F: 436
Parent education (History) P: 157
Smith Robertson Museum and Cultural Center
[Jackson]
Mississippi (Places to visit) M: 632
Smithies, Oliver [American biologist]
Nobel Prizes (Physiology or medicine: 2007)
N: 447
Smithson, James [British chemist] S: 518
Foundation (History) F: 431
Smithsonian Institution S: 519
Smithsonian American Art Museum
[Washington, D.C.] S: 518
Washington, D.C. (Smithsonian museums)
W: 71-73
Smithsonian Astrophysical Observatory
[Cambridge]
Smithsonian Institution (Other facilities) S: 519
Smithsonian Institution [Washington, D.C.] S: 519
Hirshhorn Museum and Sculpture Garden H: 243

with picture
Library (United States government libraries)
L: 248; (Libraries in the United States) L: 261
National Air and Space Museum N: 28
National Museum of African Art N: 40
National Museum of American History N: 41
National Museum of Natural History N: 41
Smithson, James S: 518
Smithsonian American Art Museum S: 518
Washington, D.C. map on W: 76; (Smithsonian
museums) W: 71
Smithsonite [mineral]
Smithson, James S: 519
Zinc Z: 594
Smits, Jimmy [American actor]
Hispanic Americans picture on H: 248
Smog [pollution] S: 519
Aerosol A: 89
Air pollution picture on A: 197; (Forms of
transportation) A: 198; (Health) A: 199
Automobile (Air pollution) A: 964
Environmental pollution (Air pollution) E: 331
Lawn (Lawns and the environment) L: 144
Los Angeles (Recent developments) L: 470
Ozone O: 894
Weather (How people affect the weather) W: 170
Smoke S: 520
Fire (Gases) F: 122
Soot So: 595
Smoke alarm S: 520
Fire department (Public education programs)
F: 125
Safety (Safety from fire) S: 11 with picture
Smoke coat
Cat (Coat) C: 287 with picture
Smoke detector [device] See Smoke alarm in this
index
Smoke-filled room [U.S. history]
Harding, Warren Gamaliel (The smoke-filled
room) H: 57
Smoke generator
Ham (Curing and smoking) H: 28
Smoke jumper [firefighter]
Fire department (Additional operations) F: 124
with picture
Forestry (Fire and forests) F: 407
Smoke signal
Communication picture on Ci: 880
Indian, American (Other communication) I: 151
Smoked food
Bacon B: 18
Fishing industry (Methods of processing) F: 186
Food preservation (Curing) F: 341
Ham (Curing and smoking) H: 28
Hickory H: 224
Meat packing (Curing and smoking) M: 352
Smokehouse
Food preservation (Curing) F: 341
Ham (Curing and smoking) H: 28
Smokeless powder
Gunpowder (Kinds of gunpowder) G: 441
Smokey Bear Historical State Park [Capitan, N.M.]
New Mexico (Interesting facts) N: 257
Smokey Joe's Café [musical]
Musical comedy (Musical comedy today) M: 961
Smoking [practice] S: 520
Bronchitis B: 636
Cancer (Genes damaged by substances in the
environment) C: 170; (Avoiding carcinogens)
C: 171
Chronic obstructive pulmonary disease C: 539
Cigar Ci: 552
Cigarette Ci: 552
Disease (Environmental and occupational
diseases) D: 230
Drug abuse (Tobacco) D: 361
Health (Health hazards) H: 126
Heart (Coronary artery disease) H: 137; (Progress
in treatment and prevention) H: 145-146
Lung cancer L: 525
Pipe P: 489
Tobacco T: 305
Smoking [process] See Smoked food in this index
Smoky Mountains, Great See Great Smoky
Mountains in this index
Smoky Night [book by Bunting]
Diaz, David D: 186
Smoky quartz [mineral]
Quartz (Types) Q: 8
Smolenskin, Peretz [Hebrew author]
Hebrew literature (Modern Hebrew literature)
H: 162
Smollett, Tobias George [British author] S: 521
English literature (The rise of the novel) E: 318-319
Novel (The first English novelists) N: 572
Smoot, George Fitzgerald, III [American physicist]

Nobel Prizes (Physics: 2006) N: 442
Smoot-Hawley Tariff Act [1930]
Great Depression (Economic breakdown) G: 340
Hoover, Herbert Clark (Champion of prosperity)
H: 329
Smooth brome [plant]
Grass *picture on* G: 325
Smooth cayenne [fruit]
Pineapple (The pineapple plant) P: 472
Smooth fleabane [plant]
Flower *picture on* F: 286
Smooth fox terrier [dog] S: 521
Dog *picture on* D: 273
Wire fox terrier W: 344
Smooth meadow grass [plant] *See* Kentucky
bluegrass *in this index*
Smooth muscle [anatomy]
Human body (Smooth muscles) H: 419
Muscle *diagram on* M: 933; (Smooth muscles)
M: 934
Smooth newt [animal]
Amphibian *picture on* A: 441
Smooth softshell turtle
Turtle (Softshell turtles) T: 523
Smoothbore [gun]
Artillery (Parts of an artillery weapon) A: 762
Rifle (History) R: 339
Shotgun S: 436
Smörgåsbord [food]
Food (Customs) F: 332-333
Sweden (Food and drink) So: 1024
Smørrebrød [food]
Denmark (Food and drink) D: 135
Smouse Opportunity School [Des Moines]
Iowa (Schools) I: 378
Smuggler's Notch
Vermont (Places to visit) V: 326
Smuggling [crime] S: 521
Coast Guard, United States (Maritime security)
Ci: 735; (History) Ci: 737
Colombia (Trade) C: 783
Prohibition (Life during prohibition) P: 815
Right of search R: 340
Smut [fungus] S: 522
Barley (Diseases and insect pests) B: 113
Fungal disease (In plants) F: 558
Fungi *picture on* F: 559
Wheat (Care during growth) W: 271
Smuts, Jan Christiaan [South African general]
S: 522
South Africa (The Union of South Africa) So: 618-
619
United Nations (The preamble to the Charter of
the United Nations) U: 78
Smylie, Robert E. [American political leader]
Idaho (table) I: 42
Smyrna [Turkey] *See* İzmir *in this index*
Smyrna fig [fruit]
Fig F: 96
Smyslov, Vassily [Russian chess player]
Chess (World chess champions) C: 414
Smyth, Alexander [American general]
War of 1812 (Queenston Heights) W: 33
Smyth, Coke [Canadian painter]
Indian, American *picture on* I: 149
Smyth, Frederick [American political leader]
New Hampshire (table) N: 223
Smyth, John [English religious leader]
Baptists (Early history) B: 101
Protestantism (The radical reform and free
church movements) P: 835
Smyth sewing [printing]
Bookbinding (Sewing) B: 471 *with picture*
Smythe, William [Canadian political leader]
British Columbia (table) B: 628
Sn [symbol]
Tin T: 293
Snaefell [mountain]
Man, Isle of M: 130
Snaffle bit [riding equipment]
Horse (The bridle) H: 352 *with picture*
Snaffle bridle [riding equipment]
Horse (The bridle) H: 352
Snail [animal] S: 522 *with pictures*
Animal *pictures on* A: 501, A: 506
Hermit crab H: 211
Mollusk (Gastropods) M: 695
Parasite (Life cycle) P: 154 *with diagram*
Shell *pictures on* S: 384, S: 386; (Gastropods)
S: 385 *with diagram*
Snail darter [fish]
Conservation (Water conservation) Ci: 977-978
Darter D: 38
Snail kite [bird]
Kite K: 338 *with picture*
Snake [instrument]
Mine warfare (Detecting land mines) M: 564

Snake [reptile] S: 524 *with pictures*
See also the list of Related articles in the Snake
article
Animal *pictures on* A: 482, A: 491, A: 494
Herpetology H: 214
Molting *picture on* M: 697
Reptile (Lizards, amphisbaenians, and snakes)
R: 250 *with picture*
Teeth (Teeth of animals) T: 86 *with picture*
Tetrapod (Modern tetrapods) T: 183
Zoo (Interesting facts about zoo animals) Z: 601
Snake [sculpture by Serra]
Sculpture (From the mid-1900's to the early
2000's) S: 259-260
Snake [tool]
Plumbing (The drain-waste-vent system) P: 578
Snake charming S: 536
Cobra Ci: 742
Snake dance [custom] S: 536
Indian, American (Ceremonies) I: 148
Snake Indians *See* Shoshone Indians *in this index*
Snake-necked turtle
Turtle *picture on* T: 523
Snake Range [mountains]
Nevada (Land regions) N: 166 *with map*
Snake River [U.S.] S: 536
Idaho (Places to visit) I: 34 *with picture*; (Rivers,
waterfalls, springs, and lakes) I: 38 *with picture*
Inland waterway I: 274
Utah (Rivers and lakes) U: 242
Wyoming (Rivers and lakes) W: 528
Snake River Canyon [Idaho]
Spring So: 806
Snake River Plains [region, Idaho]
Snake River S: 536
Snake Society [Hopi Indians]
Snake dance S: 536
Snakebird [bird]
Anhinga A: 467
Wryneck W: 513
Snakebite S: 536
First aid (Snakebite) F: 141
Snake (Fangs and venom glands) S: 528;
(Protection against predators) S: 531;
(Snakebite) S: 533
Snakeroot S: 536
Snakeroot [plant] S: 536 *with picture*
Endangered species (table) E: 270
Poisonous plant (Some poisonous plants) P: 602
Snakes-head [plant]
Fritillary F: 535
SNAP [program] *See* Supplemental Nutrition
Assistance Program *in this index*
Snap Apple Night [custom]
Halloween (Fortunetelling) H: 24b
Snap bean [plant]
Bean (Kinds of beans) B: 181
Snap link [tool]
Mountain climbing (Basic mountaineering
equipment and methods) M: 897
Snapdragon [plant] S: 537 *with picture*
Flower *picture on* F: 276; (table) F: 301 *with
picture*
Snaphance [gun]
Handgun (Early handguns) H: 45
Snapper [fish] S: 537 *with picture*
Fish *picture on* F: 155
Snapping turtle [animal] S: 537
Animal *picture on* A: 479
Mimicry M: 562
Turtle (Snapping turtles) T: 523 *with picture*
Snapshot
Photography (Compact cameras) P: 408
Snapshot aesthetic [photography]
Photography *picture on* P: 429; (A diversity of
styles) P: 426-427
Snapweed [plant]
Impatiens I: 90
Snare [trap]
Trapping *picture on* T: 404
Snare drum
Drum D: 367
Snark [fictional animal]
Carroll, Lewis (Other works) C: 249
Snatch
Weightlifting W: 183
SNCC [organization] *See* Student Nonviolent
Coordinating Committee *in this index*
Snead, Sam [American golfer] S: 537
Golf *picture on* G: 266; (British Open) G: 264
Sneak preview
Motion picture (Distribution) M: 860
Sneezing S: 538
Allergy A: 373
Disease (Spread of infectious diseases) D: 228
with picture
Snell, Earl [American political leader]

Oregon (table) O: 845
Snell, George Davis [American immunologist]
Nobel Prizes (Physiology or medicine: 1980)
N: 446
Snell Lock
Saint Lawrence Seaway *picture on* S: 44
Snell van Roijen, Willebrord [Dutch
mathematician]
Refraction R: 199
Snelling, Josiah [American military leader]
Minneapolis (Early days) M: 582-583
Snelling, Richard A. [American political leader]
Vermont (table) V: 333
Snell's Law [mathematics]
Refraction R: 199
Sneva, Tom [American race driver]
Automobile racing (table: Indianapolis 500
winners) A: 980
Snicket, Lemony [American author] S: 538
Literature for children *picture on* L: 374
Snider, Duke [American baseball player]
Baseball (table: Hall of Fame) B: 134b
Snider, Stacey [American businesswoman]
Spielberg, Steven So: 792
Snip [marking]
Horse (Coat and skin) H: 348-349
Snipe [bird] S: 538 *with picture*
Snipe [boat]
Sailing (Catboats and sloops) S: 24
Snipe eel [fish]
Eel E: 114
Snipe fly [insect]
Deer fly D: 86
Snively, Cornelia Ellis [wife of]
Wallace, George Corley W: 16
Snook, Neta [American aviator]
Earhart, Amelia (Early life) E: 14
Snooker [game]
Billiards (Snooker) B: 305 *with picture*
Snoopy [cartoon character]
Schulz, Charles Monroe S: 187 *with picture*
Snoring S: 538
Snorkel [breathing device]
Diving, Underwater (Ambient diving) D: 245
Skin diving (Kinds of skin diving) S: 493 *with
pictures*
Submarine (The power plant) So: 941
Snorri Sturluson [Icelandic author] S: 538
Edda E: 74
Iceland (Early days) I: 23
Saga S: 17
Snorting [slang]
Heroin H: 213
Snout [biology]
Hog (Snout) H: 286
Snout beetle [insect]
Beetle (Weevils) B: 217
Boll weevil B: 448
Grain weevil G: 302
Snout butterfly
Butterfly (Snout butterflies) B: 736 *with pictures*
Snow S: 539 *with pictures*
Avalanche A: 982
Climate (Kinds of climates) Ci: 676a-676c
Cloud (How clouds form) Ci: 708-709
Glacier G: 202
Ice storm I: 16
Road (Clearing ice and snow) R: 360
Snow blindness S: 540
Snow line S: 540
Weather (Synoptic-scale systems) W: 159-160
Snow, C. P. [British author] S: 539
Snow, John [English physician]
Epidemic E: 343
Map (Development of thematic and inventory
mapping) M: 185
Public health (History) P: 857
Snow, John William [American government
official]
Treasury, Department of the (table) T: 407
Snow, Wilbert [American political leader]
Connecticut (table) Ci: 967
Snow blindness [disorder] S: 540
Blindness B: 401
"Snow-Bound" [poem by Whittier]
Whittier, John Greenleaf W: 296
Snow bunting [bird] S: 540 *with picture*
Snow crab [sea animal]
Crab Ci: 1115
Snow crystal
Snow S: 539 *with pictures*
Snow eater [wind] *See* Chinook *in this index*
Snow fence
Road (Clearing ice and snow) R: 360
Snow goose [bird]
Goose (Kinds of geese) G: 270 *with picture*
Snow Image and Other Twice-Told Tales, The

[book by Hawthorne]
Hawthorne, Nathaniel (His stories and sketches)
H: 115
Snow knife [tool]
Inuit (Shelter) I: 354c
Snow leopard [animal] S: 540 *with picture*
Animal *pictures on* A: 472, A: 475
Endangered species (table) E: 270
Snow line [geography] S: 540
Snow Maiden, The [opera by Rimsky-Korsakov]
Rimsky-Korsakov, Nikolai R: 341
Snow monkey [animal] S: 541
Macaque M: 2
Primate *picture on* P: 778
Snow petrel [bird]
Antarctica *picture on* A: 535
Snow snake [game]
Indian, American (Recreation) I: 142-143 *with picture*
"Snow-Storm, The" [poem by Emerson]
Emerson, Ralph Waldo (His poetry) E: 259
Snow tire
Tire (Tire tread patterns) T: 297
"Snow-White" [story]
Grimm's Fairy Tales G: 394
Snow White and the Seven Dwarfs [film]
Animation (Walt Disney) A: 514b *with picture*
Disney, Walt (Full-length movies) D: 236 *with picture*
United States *picture on* U: 118
Snowball [plant] S: 541 *with picture*
Snowball Earth [theory]
Earth (The ice ages) E: 24
Snowboard
Snowboarding S: 541 *with picture*
Snowboarding [sport] S: 541 *with picture*
Olympic Games (Winter Olympic Games)
O: 746d-746e
Snowdon [mountain, Wales]
Wales *picture on* W: 8; (Surface features) W: 11 *with map*
Snowdonia National Park [Wales]
United Kingdom *picture on* U: 58
Snowdrop [plant] S: 541 *with picture*
Snowflake [bird] *See* Snow bunting *in this index*
Snowflake [weather]
Cloud seeding (Cloud-seeding methods) C: 711
Heat (Disorder) H: 151 *with diagram*
Rain (The ice-crystal process) R: 124
Snow S: 539 *with pictures*
Snowhouse [dwelling]
Inuit *picture on* I: 354a; (Shelter) I: 354c
Snowmaking machine
Skiing (Ski area facilities) S: 486
Snowmobile [vehicle]
Safety (In winter sports) S: 12
Snowmobiling S: 542 *with picture*
Transportation (Land transportation) T: 383
Snowmobiling S: 542 *with picture*
Snowplow [machine]
Road (Clearing ice and snow) R: 360
Snowplow [skiing]
Skiing *diagram on* S: 484; (Alpine skiing) S: 482
Snowshoe
Indian, American *pictures on* I: 138, I: 141, I: 156
Snowshoe hare [animal] S: 542 *with picture*
Taiga T: 14
Snowstorm
Blizzard B: 404
Snow (Amounts of snowfall) S: 539
Weather *picture on* W: 167
Snowstorm: Steamboat off a Harbour's Mouth
[painting by Turner]
Painting (Romanticism) P: 68 *with picture*
Snowy Day, The [book by Keats]
Literature for children *picture on* L: 369
Snowy egret [bird]
Egret (Kinds) E: 119 *with picture*
Snowy Mountains Scheme [dams]
Australia *picture on* A: 918; (Rivers) A: 909
Snowy owl [bird]
Animal *picture on* A: 484
Owl (Important owls) O: 884-886 *with picture*
Snowy plover [bird]
Plover P: 574
Snowy tree cricket
Insect *picture on* I: 280
SNP [genetics]
Molecular medicine M: 692
Snuff [tobacco] S: 542
Tobacco T: 305
Snyder, Dianne [American author]
Literature for children *picture on* L: 378
Snyder, Gary [American poet]
American literature (Poetry) A: 423
Snyder, John W. [American government official]
Truman, Harry S. (table) T: 469

Snyder, Rick [American political leader]
Michigan (table) M: 507
Snyder, Simon [American political leader]
Pennsylvania (table) P: 263
So Big [book by Ferber]
Ferber, Edna F: 72
Soak-stain technique [painting]
Frankenthaler, Helen F: 484
Soaking [sports]
Baseball (Rounders) B: 132
Soaking pit
Iron and steel (Ingot casting) I: 445 *with diagram*
Soap
Bath (Bathing for cleanliness) B: 163
Detergent and soap D: 163 *with pictures*
Perfume P: 286
Soap Box Derby [race] So: 543
Soap curd [chemical]
Detergent and soap D: 164
Soap flakes
Detergent and soap (Granules and flakes) D: 164
Soap granules
Detergent and soap (Granules and flakes) D: 164
Soap opera So: 543
Radio (The Golden Age of Broadcasting) R: 92
Soap plant [plant] So: 543
Soapberry [tree] So: 543
Tree *pictures on* T: 423
Soapstone [rock] So: 543
Inuit (Food) I: 354b; (Canada) I: 354i *with picture*
Talc T: 19
Soapstone carving [art]
Nunavut (Economy) N: 610
Soapweed [plant]
Flower *picture on* F: 291
Yucca Y: 575
Soaring hawk [bird]
Hawk H: 111
Soaring Society of America
Glider G: 228; (Gliding today) G: 231
Sobhuza II [king of Swaziland]
Swaziland (History) So: 1019
Sobibor [concentration camp]
Concentration camp (Nazi concentration camps)
Ci: 926-927
Sobieski, John [king of Poland] *See* John III
Sobieski *in this index*
Sobrero, Ascanio [Italian chemist]
Nitroglycerin N: 426
Soccer [sport] So: 544 *with pictures*
Africa *picture on* A: 112
Argentina (Recreation) A: 650 *with picture*
Australia (Recreation) A: 903
Brazil *picture on* B: 574; (Recreation) B: 575
Culture *picture on* Ci: 1188
Europe (Recreation) E: 389
Germany *picture on* G: 153
Latin America (Recreation) L: 98 *with picture*
London (Recreation) L: 434
Northern Ireland (Recreation) N: 522
Pelé P: 231
Peru (Recreation) P: 310
Scotland (Recreation) S: 214
South Africa (Recreation) So: 611-613 *with picture*
United Kingdom *picture on* U: 58; (Recreation) U: 55
World Cup W: 450
Sociable weaver [bird]
Weaver W: 172
Social and Liberal Democratic Party [political party]
Labour Party (History) L: 16-17
Liberal Democrats L: 226
Social anthropology *See* Cultural anthropology *in this index*
Social anxiety disorder [psychology]
Anxiety disorder A: 562
Social assistance *See* Welfare *in this index*
Social change [sociology] So: 550
Conservatism Ci: 991
Culture (How cultures change) Ci: 1189
Marriage (Changing attitudes about marriage) M: 222
Sociology (Social change) So: 565
Social Christian Unity Party [political party]
Costa Rica (The late 1900's) Ci: 1084
Social class [sociology] So: 550 *with picture*
City (The people) Ci: 578-580
Colonial life in America (The structure of colonial society) Ci: 793
Communism (The ideas of Marx) Ci: 890
Egypt, Ancient (The people) E: 136
Fashion (The origins of fashion) F: 50
French Revolution (Background) F: 524-525
Gay Nineties (Life during the Gay Nineties) G: 71
Middle class M: 529

Peru (Ways of life) P: 309
Union of Soviet Socialist Republics (Privileged classes) U: 32
World War I (Social consequences) W: 465
Social Contract, The [book by Rousseau]
Democracy (French contributions to democracy) D: 122-123
Rousseau, Jean-Jacques (His ideas) R: 493
Social Contract Theory
Philosophy (Ethics and political philosophy) P: 385
Social Credit Party [political party]
Alberta (A new province) A: 329
Campbell, Kim (Provincial legislator) C: 90c
Diefenbaker, John George D: 196
Political party (Other parties) P: 636-637
Social dancing
Dance (Why people dance) D: 24; (Social dances) D: 26 *with picture*
Social Darwinism [philosophy] So: 551
Darwin, Charles Robert (The influence of Darwin's ideas) D: 40-41
Social Democratic Party [Austria]
Austria (Political parties) A: 930-931
Social Democratic Party [Denmark]
Denmark (Politics) D: 133
Social Democratic Party [Germany]
Bebel, August B: 196
Germany (Politics) G: 147
Luxemburg, Rosa L: 532
Schröder, Gerhard S: 186
Social Democratic Party [Japan]
Japan (Political changes) J: 59
Social Democratic Party [Portugal]
Portugal (Political changes) P: 695
Social Democratic Party [Sweden]
Sweden (Politics) So: 1023; (Political changes) So: 1035
Social Democratic Party [United Kingdom]
Liberal Democrats (Coalition government) L: 227
Social Democratic Party [United States]
Debs, Eugene Victor D: 65
Social Democratic Party of Romania [political party]
Romania (Protests and political change) R: 425-426
Social forestry
Forestry (Community forestry) F: 406
Social fraternal society
Fraternal organization F: 495
Social freedom
Freedom (Kinds of freedom) F: 501; (Limits on social freedom) F: 502
Social gambling
Gambling (Types of gambling) G: 20
Social geography
Geography (Human geography) G: 94
Social Gospel [religion]
Christianity (The 1800's) C: 526
Social group [zoology]
See also Group *in this index*
Mammal (Group life) M: 125 *with picture*
Social history
History (Approaches to history) H: 261
Social insect
Animal (Group living) A: 502
Ant A: 520
Bee B: 200 *with pictures*; (Social bees) B: 205
Beetle B: 215
Insect (Family life) I: 294-295
Wasp W: 111
Wilson, Edward Osborne W: 316
Social insurance [government program]
See also Social security *in this index*
Insurance (Social insurance) I: 314; (Insurance today) I: 316-317
Poverty (Social welfare programs) P: 725
Social security So: 553
Welfare W: 190
Social interest [psychology]
Adler, Alfred A: 58
Social learning
Aggression A: 141
Social legislation
Child abuse C: 455
Child labor (Early child labor laws) C: 455
Women's movement (Contemporary women's movements) W: 386-387
Social media marketing
Advertising (The Internet) A: 74
Social Network, The [film]
Zuckerberg, Mark Z: 608
Social networking website [computing]
Facebook F: 4
Freedom of assembly (In other countries) F: 504
Internet (Social networking websites) I: 350b; (The evolving Internet) I: 350g-350h

Zuckerberg, Mark **Z:** 608
Social organism [biology]
　Life (Other interactions) **L:** 276
Social parent
　Parent **P:** 156
Social protest
　Academic freedom (The 1900's) **A:** 20
　Civil disobedience **Ci:** 606
　Indian, American (In the United States) **I:** 179
　Painting (Social expression) **P:** 34; (Symbolism)
　　P: 76
　Riot **R:** 347
Social psychology So: 552
　Psychology (Major fields of psychology) **P:** 848
　Sociology (Social behavior) **So:** 564
Social realists [art history]
　Painting (Painting outside France) **P:** 72
Social rights
　Human rights (Types of human rights) **H:** 428
Social role [sociology] **So:** 552
　Linton, Ralph **L:** 339
　Sex discrimination (Views on sex discrimination)
　　S: 335
　Sexuality (In childhood) **S:** 338
　Social change **So:** 550
　Socialization **So:** 562
　Women's movement (Women's status through
　　the ages) **W:** 383
Social science So: 552
　See also the list of Related articles in the Social
　　Science article
　Careers (Life, physical, and social sciences) **C:** 225
　　with picture
　Culture **Ci:** 1186
　Liberal arts **L:** 226
　Science (The social sciences) **S:** 194
　Social studies **So:** 557
Social security [government program] **So:** 553
　with pictures
　See also Social insurance in this index
　Pension **P:** 272
　Retirement **R:** 265
　Taxation (Income taxes) **T:** 53
　Welfare **W:** 190
Social Security [U.S. program]
　Social security (Social Security in the United
　　States) **So:** 553 with pictures
　Baby boom generation (Effects of the baby
　　boom) **B:** 11
　Income tax (Federal income taxes in the United
　　States) **I:** 104
　Medicare **M:** 362
　National budget (Government spending) **N:** 30
　Old age (Finances) **O:** 739
　Pension (Federal pension plans) **P:** 272
　Retirement **R:** 265
Social Security Act [1935]
　Insurance (Greater regulation) **I:** 316
　Personnel management (Development of
　　personnel management) **P:** 303
　Retirement **R:** 265
　Roosevelt, Franklin Delano (Second New Deal)
　　R: 453
　Social security (History) **So:** 556-557
　Unemployment insurance **U:** 24
　Welfare (National welfare systems) **W:** 191
Social Security Administration [U.S.] **So:** 557
　Health and Human Services, Department of
　　(History) **H:** 128
　Social security (Social Security in the United
　　States) **So:** 553
Social Security card
　Social security (Social Security in the United
　　States) **So:** 553 with picture
Social services worker
　Careers (Community and social services) **C:** 221
Social settlement See Settlement house in this
　index
Social Sources of Denominationalism, The [book
　by Niebuhr]
　Niebuhr, H. Richard **N:** 405
Social stomach [entomology]
　Ant (Internal organs) **A:** 522 with diagram
Social stratification
　Social class **So:** 550
Social studies So: 557
　See also the list of Related articles in the Social
　　studies article
Social Theory and Social Structure [book by
　Merton]
　Merton, Robert King **M:** 419
Social welfare See Welfare in this index
Social work So: 557 with picture
　Child welfare **C:** 456
　Hospital (Nonmedical services) **H:** 373
　Medicine (Other careers in medicine) **M:** 371
　Psychotherapy **P:** 851

Settlement house **S:** 324
　Travelers Aid International **T:** 405
Social Workers, National Association of So: 559
Socialism [economics] **So:** 560 with picture
　See also the list of Related articles in the Socialism
　　article
　Capitalism **C:** 194
　Christianity (The 1800's) **C:** 526
　Collectivism **C:** 775
　Communism **Ci:** 889
　Debs, Eugene Victor **D:** 65
　Fabian Society **F:** 2
　Marx, Karl **M:** 236; (Marx's ideas) **M:** 237; (Marx's
　　influence) **M:** 238
　May Day **M:** 322
　Nationalization **N:** 63
　Political science (Democracy and socialism)
　　P: 639
　Radicalism (In Europe) **R:** 82
　World, History of the (The Industrial Revolution)
　　W: 444-445
Socialist Labor, Order of [China]
　Medals, decorations, and orders (table) **M:** 359
Socialist Party [France]
　France (Politics) **F:** 455; (Socialists win power)
　　F: 478
Socialist Party [U.S.]
　Debs, Eugene Victor **D:** 65
　Political party (Third parties) **P:** 636
　Socialism (Moderate socialism) **So:** 561
Socialist realism [Soviet history]
　Gorki, Maxim **G:** 277
　Russian literature (The period of socialist realism)
　　R: 564
　Union of Soviet Socialist Republics (The arts)
　　U: 33
Socialist revolutionaries [Russian history]
　Russia (Nicholas II) **R:** 551-552
Socialist Unity Party [political party]
　Germany (East Germany) **G:** 170
Socialization [sociology] **So:** 562
　Parent (The role of parents) **P:** 156
　Sociology (Social behavior) **So:** 564
Société des Bains de Mer [company]
　Monaco (Economy) **M:** 700
Société Radio-Canada [communications]
　Canadian Broadcasting Corporation **C:** 156
Society
　Culture **Ci:** 1186
　Durkheim, Émile **D:** 389
　Ethnocentrism **E:** 373
　Law **L:** 130
　Mythology **M:** 973
　Philosophy (The importance of philosophy)
　　P: 383
　Social change **So:** 550
　Social psychology **So:** 552
　Sociology **So:** 564
　Technology (Sharing the benefits of technology)
　　T: 78
Society [religion]
　Vodou **V:** 436
Society for Jewish Culture and Science
　Zunz, Leopold **Z:** 609
Society for Promoting Christian Knowledge
　Wales (Union with England) **W:** 12
**Society for the Advancement of Education
　So:** 563
**Society for the Preservation and
　Encouragement of Barber Shop Quartet
　Singing in America**
　Barbershop quartet singing **B:** 107
**Society for the Prevention of Cruelty to Animals
　So:** 563 with picture
　Humane society **H:** 430
Society Hill [district, Philadelphia]
　Philadelphia (Residential districts) **P:** 360 with
　　picture; (Urban renewal) **P:** 367
Society Islands [Pacific] **So:** 563
　French Polynesia **F:** 524
Society of American Magicians
　Magician (Becoming a magician) **M:** 52
Society of Friends See Quakers in this index
Society of German Maidens
　Hitler, Adolf (The New Order) **H:** 266-267-
Society of Jesus See Jesuits in this index
**Society of Missionary Priests of Saint Paul the
　Apostle** See Paulists in this index
Society of Tammany See Tammany, Society of in
　this index
Society of the Cincinnati See Cincinnati, Society of
　the in this index
Society of Women Engineers
　Engineering (table) **E:** 289
Socinus, Faustus [Polish religious leader]
　Unitarians (History) **U:** 42
Sociobiology So: 563

Biology (table) **B:** 317
　Wilson, Edward Osborne **W:** 316
Sociocultural theory [psychology]
　Developmental psychology (Sociocultural
　　theory) **D:** 174
　Psychology (Modern psychology) **P:** 850
Sociodrama [psychology]
　Role playing **R:** 402
Socioeconomic status [sociology]
　Social class **So:** 550
Sociological jurisprudence [law]
　Pound, Roscoe **P:** 722
Sociology So: 564 with pictures
　Careers (Life, physical, and social sciences)
　　C: 225-226
　Caste **C:** 279
　Collective behavior **Ci:** 774
　Comte, Auguste **Ci:** 926
　Criminology **Ci:** 1145
　Psychology (Psychology and other sciences)
　　P: 847
　Races, Human (The social significance of race)
　　R: 59
　Science (The social sciences) **S:** 194
　Stereotyping **So:** 893
Sociology of science
　Merton, Robert King **M:** 419
Sock [anatomy]
　Horse (Coats and skin) **H:** 348-349
Sockeye salmon
　Endangered species picture on **E:** 271
　Salmon picture on **S:** 69; (Kinds of salmon) **S:** 70
Socks
　Stockings **So:** 906
Socrates [Greek philosopher] **So:** 567 with picture
　Ethics (Plato) **E:** 366
　Euripides **E:** 378
　Greece, Ancient picture on **G:** 371; (Philosophy,
　　science, and the arts) **G:** 368-369
　Greek literature (Philosophical literature) **G:** 377-
　　378
　Law (The influence of ancient Greece) **L:** 133
　Philosophy (Ancient philosophy) **P:** 386 with
　　picture
　Plato (Plato's life) **P:** 567; (The early dialogues)
　　P: 568
Sócrates, José [Portuguese political leader]
　Portugal (The early 2000's) **P:** 695
Socratic method [philosophy]
　Philosophy (Ancient philosophy) **P:** 386-387
　Socrates (The Socratic method) **So:** 568
Socratic problem [philosophy]
　Socrates (The Socratic problem) **So:** 567
Sod [gardening]
　Lawn picture on **L:** 142; (Growing and
　　maintaining a lawn) **L:** 144
Sod house So: 568
　Nebraska (Territorial days) **N:** 112 with picture
Sod webworm [insect]
　Lawn picture on **L:** 143
Soda [chemical] **So:** 568
Soda ash
　Soda **So:** 568
Soda-lead glass
　Glass (Soda-lead glass) **G:** 213
Soda-lime glass
　Glass (Soda-lime glass) **G:** 213
Soda pop See Soft drink in this index
Soda Springs
　Idaho (Rivers, waterfalls, springs, and lakes) **I:** 38
Soda water
　Soft drink (History) **So:** 571
Soddy [house]
　Western frontier life in America (Shelter) **W:** 238
Soddy, Frederick [British chemist] **So:** 568
　Protactinium **P:** 831
Soderbergh, Steven [American director]
　Motion picture (Best achievement in directing:
　　2000) **M:** 862
Söderblom, Nathan [Swedish religious leader]
　Nobel Prizes (Peace: 1930) **N:** 448a
Sodium [element] **So:** 568
　Atom diagram on **A:** 872
　Electrolysis (Uses of electrolysis) **E:** 200
　Food (Recent developments) **F:** 337
　Isotope (Artificial radioisotopes) **I:** 477
　Monosodium glutamate **M:** 733
　Nutrition (Limit intake of sodium and sugar)
　　N: 628
　Soda **So:** 568
Sodium aluminate [chemical]
　Aluminum (How aluminum is produced) **A:** 393
　　with diagram
Sodium bicarbonate [chemical] See Bicarbonate
　of soda in this index
Sodium bisulfate [chemical]
　Salt, Chemical **S:** 75

Sodium borate [chemical] See Borax in this index
Sodium carbonate [chemical]
Carbonate C: 208
Hydrolysis H: 471
Soda So: 568
Sodium (Uses) So: 569
Sodium chloride [chemical]
Chloride C: 516
Salt S: 72 with picture
Salt, Chemical S: 75
Sodium (Where sodium is found) So: 569
Sodium cyanide [chemical]
Cyanide Ci: 1202
Prussic acid P: 843
Sodium hydroxide [chemical] S: 569
Aluminum (How aluminum is produced) A: 393
Detergent and soap (How soap is made) D: 164
Olive (Harvesting and preparation for market) O: 743
Textile (Finishing the fabric) T: 217
Sodium lamp See Sodium vapor lamp in this index
Sodium nitrate [mineral]
Chile (Mining) C: 466
Food preservation (Curing) F: 341
Saltpeter S: 76a
Sodium (Uses) So: 569
Sodium nitrite [chemical]
Food preservation (Curing) F: 341
Nitrite N: 425
Sodium oxide [chemical]
Glass (Soda-lime glass) G: 213
Sodium Pentothal [drug]
Thiopental T: 258
Sodium silicate [chemical]
Grinding and polishing (Grinding wheels) G: 395
Sodium sulfate [chemical]
Salt, Chemical S: 75
Sodium tetraborate [chemical] See Borax in this index
Sodium thiosulfate [chemical]
Sodium (Uses) So: 569
Sodium vapor lamp
Electric light (Gaseous-discharge lamps) E: 174-175
Lighting (Efficient use of lighting) L: 297
Sodom and Gomorrah [ancient cities] So: 569
Abraham A: 16
Lot L: 472
Soeharto [Indonesian political leader] See Suharto in this index
Soekarno [Indonesian political leader] See Sukarno in this index
Soetoro, Lolo [stepfather of]
Obama, Barack (Boyhood) O: 640c
Sofia [Bulgaria] So: 569 with picture
Bulgaria B: 688 with picture
Sofkee [food]
Indian, American (Indians of the Southeast) I: 157
Sofonisba [play by Trissino]
Drama (Italian Renaissance drama) D: 330
Soft-coated wheaten terrier [dog] So: 570 with picture
Soft consonant
Russian language (Pronunciation) R: 557
Soft contact lens
Contact lens Ci: 1020 with picture
Soft drink So: 570
Coca-Cola Company Ci: 742
Industry (Production location): I: 259
PepsiCo, Inc. P: 279
Soft good [merchandising]
Discount store D: 224
Retailing (Department stores) R: 265
Soft lander [space probe]
Space exploration (Space probes) So: 708
Soft money
Bush, George Walker (Campaign finance reform) B: 722h
Election campaign (Campaign financing) E: 161
Soft-mud process
Brick (Forming bricks) B: 597-598
Soft palate [anatomy]
Cleft palate C: 661
Mouth M: 903 with diagram
Palate P: 101 with diagram
Snoring S: 538
Throat T: 270
Soft-paste porcelain
Porcelain (Kinds of porcelain) P: 675-676;
(European porcelain) P: 677
Soft point bullet
Ammunition picture on A: 434
Soft rock [music]
Rock music (Rock music today) R: 381
Soft rot [plant disease]
Bacteria (Harmful bacteria) B: 20
Soft-shell clam

Clam (Types of clams) Ci: 637 with picture
Soft-shelled crab
Blue crab B: 420
Soft-shelled turtle See Softshell turtle in this index
Soft-stemmed plant
Leaf (A leaf begins its life) L: 152
Soft target [military science]
Bomb (Fragmentation bombs) B: 451
Soft-tip pen
Pen P: 234 with picture
Soft x ray
X rays (Wavelength) X: 541
Softball So: 571 with pictures
Little League Baseball L: 391
Softshell turtle
Turtle (Shell) T: 521; (Softshell turtles) T: 523 with picture
Software [electronics] So: 572
Computer Ci: 909; (Computer software) Ci: 917; (Internet software) Ci: 922
Copyright (Works protected) Ci: 1046-1047
Internet I: 350; (How the Internet works) I: 350b
Microsoft Corporation M: 519
Personal computer P: 300f
Word processing W: 403
Software piracy
Internet (Changing industries) I: 350e
Software publisher
Computer (Careers) Ci: 924a
Software suite
Computer (Software suites) Ci: 920
Softwood
Forest products (Lumber) F: 400
Lumber (Softwood lumber) L: 517
Plywood (Kinds of plywood) P: 585
Tree (Needleleaf trees) T: 414-415; (Needleleaf forests) T: 429 with picture
Wood (Kinds of wood) W: 389
Woodworking (Wood for woodworking) W: 398
Softwood dimension lumber
Lumber (table) L: 518
Sogavare, Mannasseh [Solomon Islands political leader]
Solomon Islands (History) So: 585-586
Sogdiana [ancient city]
Alexander the Great (Central Asia and the Indus) A: 343
Soglo, Nicephore [Benin political leader]
Benin (History) B: 250
Sogne Fiord [Norway]
Norway (Coast and islands) N: 542 with map
Soham [mineral]
Malachite M: 95
Soho [district]
London (Central London) L: 429-430 with map; (People) L: 430
SoHo [New York City]
New York City (Manhattan) N: 323-324; (Greenwich Village) N: 338
SOHO [spacecraft] See Solar and Heliospheric Observatory in this index
Soil [geology] So: 573 with pictures and map
See also Conservation in this index; the list of Related articles in the Soil article
Agronomy A: 162
Clay Ci: 657
Compost Ci: 905
Conservation (Soil conservation) Ci: 979 with pictures
Drainage D: 320
Dust D: 390
Dust storm D: 392
Earthworm E: 39
Environmental pollution (Soil pollution) E: 334
Erosion (Controlling erosion) E: 355
Fertilizer F: 78
Forestry (Water) F: 406
Gardening (Preparing an outdoor garden) G: 31; (Cultivating an outdoor garden) G: 34
Humus H: 437
Irrigation (Providing artificial drainage) I: 459
Lawn (Growing and maintaining a lawn) L: 142
Loam L: 403
Loess L: 420
Manure M: 172
Rock R: 371
Soil pollution So: 576
Topsoil T: 333
Wetland (Water and soil) W: 252a
Soil aggregate [geology]
Soil (Organic matter) So: 573
Soil Association
Organic food (History) O: 853
Soil Conservation Service [U.S.]
Dust Bowl D: 391
Soil horizon [geology]
Soil (Characteristics of soils) So: 574 with

diagrams
Soil management
Farm and farming (Soil management) F: 33
Soil particle
Soil (Composition) So: 573
Soil pollution So: 576
Environmental pollution (Soil pollution) E: 334
Soil solution [geology]
Soil (Organic matter) So: 573
Soil stack [device]
Plumbing (The drain-waste-vent system) P: 578 with diagram
Soil sterilant [chemical]
Herbicide H: 198
Soil taxonomy
Soil (How soils are classified) So: 576
Soilless agriculture See Hydroponics in this index
Soira, Mount [Eritrea]
Eritrea (Land and climate) E: 353 with map
Soja bean [plant] See Soybean in this index
Sojourner [U.S. history]
Immigration (The second wave) I: 82
Sojourner Rover [spacecraft]
Mars (Observation by spacecraft) M: 226c-226d
Space exploration (Probes to Mars) So: 710
Sokhondo, Mount [Russia]
Yablonovyy Mountains Y: 548
Sokol [organization] So: 576
Sokoto Caliphate [African history]
Africa (African societies in the 1800's) A: 133
Nigeria (Early kingdoms) N: 417
Sol [calendar]
Calendar (Calendar reform) C: 32
Sol [chemistry]
Colloid Ci: 777
Sol-Gel glass
Glass (Specialty glasses) G: 212-213
Solanaceae [botany]
Nightshade N: 421
Solar activity
Sun (Solar activity) So: 980
Solar and Heliospheric Observatory [spacecraft]
Astronomy (Ultraviolet astronomy) A: 844
Corona Ci: 1067
Sun (History of modern solar study) So: 986
Sunspot (Other findings) So: 992
Solar cell [electricity]
Electric eye (How electric eyes work) E: 169
Electric power (Other sources of electric power) E: 184
Electricity (Sources of current) E: 194
Electronics (Light-sensing devices) E: 213
Energy supply (Solar energy) E: 278
Environmental pollution (Scientific efforts) E: 336
Global warming (Alternative energy sources) G: 232b
Invention (The early and middle 1900's) I: 363-364
Materials picture on M: 300c
Semiconductor (Using doped crystals) S: 292 with diagrams
Solar energy (Photovoltaic conversion) So: 577
Solar collector [physics]
Greenhouse G: 382
Solar concentrator [device]
Solar energy (Solar thermal conversion) So: 578
Solar cosmic rays
Cosmic rays (Solar cosmic rays) Ci: 1076
Sun (Energy output) So: 977
Solar day
Day and night D: 52
Earth (How Earth moves) E: 17
Time (Solar time) T: 288
Solar Dynamics Observatory
Astronomy (Ultraviolet astronomy) A: 844
Sun picture on So: 979
Solar eclipse [astronomy]
Corona Ci: 1066
Eclipse E: 51 with pictures
Moon (Eclipses) M: 784
Relativity (Distortions in space-time) R: 212
Sun (History of modern solar study) So: 986 with picture
Solar energy So: 576 with pictures
Conservation picture on Ci: 983
Energy E: 273
Energy supply (Solar energy) E: 278
Environmental pollution (Scientific efforts) E: 336
Heat pipe H: 156
International Space Station I: 346a with picture
Photochemistry P: 404
Sun (Energy output) So: 976-977
Solar flare [astronomy]
Aurora A: 892
Heliosphere (Shock waves) H: 175
Magnetic storm M: 57
Magnetism (The sun) M: 60d with picture

Radiation (The sun and other stars) R: 77
Sun So: 975, *pictures on* So: 985, So: 986; (Solar activity) So: 980-981
Van Allen belts V: 269
Solar furnace
Energy supply *picture on* E: 277
Furnace (Sources of heat) F: 567
Heat (The sun) H: 149
Solar energy (Solar heating) So: 579
Solar halo
Halo *picture on* H: 26
Solar heating
Heating (Solar heating) H: 159
Solar energy (Solar heating) So: 579
Solar Hypothesis
Mythology (Comparative approaches) M: 989
Solar magnetism [astronomy]
Sun (Magnetic field) So: 977
Solar maximum [astronomy]
Aurora A: 892
Solar Maximum Mission satellite
Space exploration (Repair missions) So: 724
Sun (History of modern solar study) So: 986
Sunspot (Other findings) So: 992
Solar month
Month M: 767
Solar nebula [astronomy]
Jupiter (Formation of Jupiter) J: 200b
Planet (How the planets formed) P: 514
Solar system (Formation of our solar system) So: 581
Solar neutrino problem
Sun (Analyzing neutrinos) So: 984
Solar plexus [anatomy]
Solar energy So: 579
Solar power plant
Solar energy *picture on* So: 579
Solar radiation
Sun (Energy output) So: 976
Thermosphere T: 256
Weather (Air temperature) W: 157
Solar salt
Salt (Salt from the sea) S: 72
Solar Set [tomato]
Tomato (The tomato plant) T: 324-325
Solar system [astronomy] So: 580 *with picture*
See also the list of Related articles in the Solar system *article*
Earth (How Earth moves) E: 17
Galaxy (Spiral galaxies) G: 8a-8b
Geology (Geology of the solar system) G: 100
Life (The search for life on other worlds) L: 280
Milky Way M: 550
Planet P: 507 *with pictures*
Radar (In scientific research) R: 68
Sun So: 974
Volcano (Volcanoes in the solar system) V: 442b
Solar telescope
Sun (Earth-based studies) So: 986
Solar Terrestrial Relations Observatory [satellites]
Astronomy (Ultraviolet astronomy) A: 844
Solar thermal conversion
Solar energy So: 577 *with picture*
Solar time
Sidereal time S: 448
Time (Astronomical cycles) T: 288 *with picture*
Solar Two [power plant]
Solar energy (Central receiver systems) So: 579
Solar wind [astronomy] So: 581
Astronomy (Direct sampling) A: 846
Aurora A: 892
Comet (Parts of a comet) Ci: 867
Corona Ci: 1067
Cosmic rays (Galactic cosmic rays) Ci: 1076
Heliosphere (Solar wind) H: 175
Jupiter (Magnetic field) J: 198-199
Magnetic storm M: 57
Moon (The exosphere of the moon) M: 788
Planet (How the planets formed) P: 514
Solar system (The sun) So: 580; (Formation of our solar system) So: 581
Sun (Sun terms) So: 976; (Energy output) So: 977; (Zones of the sun) So: 979-980
Van Allen belts V: 269
Solar year
Calendar C: 29
Leap year L: 162
Year Y: 554
Solaris [book by Lem]
Science fiction (Growing popularity) S: 205
Solder [metal]
Alloy (Other alloys) A: 378
Lead (Uses) L: 149
Tin (Uses) T: 293
Solder, Glass
Glass (table) G: 218
Soldier

Army A: 724 *with pictures*
Army, United States (Life in the Army) A: 730 *with pictures*
GI G: 182
Mercenary M: 411
Rank, Military R: 139
United Nations (Peacekeeping operations) U: 90-91 *with pictures*
Soldier [entomology]
Ant (The bodies of ants) A: 521 *with picture*; (Castes) A: 523
Insect (Family life) I: 294-295
Termite (The termite colony) T: 171 *with picture*
Soldiers [play by Hochhuth]
Hochhuth, Rolf H: 273
Soldiers and Sailors Monument
Indianapolis (The city) I: 220
Soldiers' bonus
Hoover, Herbert Clark (The "Bonus Army") H: 330
"Soldiers' Chorus" [music by Gounod]
Opera: (*Faust*) O: 804
Soldier's Medal
Medals, decorations, and orders (table) M: 357
Soldier's Tale, The [ballet]
Stravinsky, Igor (Early works) So: 922
Soldiers Three [book by Kipling]
Kipling, Rudyard (Early literary success) K: 334
Sole [anatomy]
Foot (Ligaments and muscles) F: 352
Sole [fish] So: 582 *with picture*
Solemn League and Covenant, The [1643]
Covenanters Ci: 1106
Solenodon [animal] So: 582 *with picture*
Mammal (table) M: 129 *with picture*
Solenoid [electric current]
Magnetism (Electromagnets) M: 60a
Starter (Automobile starters) So: 857 *with diagram*
Soleri, Paolo [Italian architect] So: 583 *with picture*
Solfatara [geology]
Fumarole F: 556
Solicitor [name for]
Lawyer L: 147
Solicitor general [office]
Supreme Court of the United States (The court in action) So: 999
Solid [geometry] So: 583
Geometry G: 101; (Euclidean geometry) G: 104 *with pictures*
Solid [physics]
Aerogel A: 88
Cohesion Ci: 756
Density D: 142 *with diagram*
Gas [physics] G: 47
Matter (States of matter) M: 311
Melting point M: 389
Molecule (Molecules and matter) M: 693
Physics (Solid-state physics) P: 438
Solid So: 583
Solution (Solid solutions) So: 587
Solid coat
Cat (Coat) C: 287 *with picture*
Solid fuel
See also Solid propellant *in this index*
Fuel (Solid fuels) F: 550
Solid geometry
Geometry (Euclidean geometry) G: 104
Mathematics (Branches of mathematics) M: 303
Solid mechanics
Mechanics M: 354
Solid propellant [fuel]
Rocket (Solid-propellant rockets) R: 387
Space exploration (Getting into space and back) So: 698
Solid-propellant rocket
Guided missile (The engine) G: 424 *with diagram*
Rocket (Solid-propellant rockets) R: 387 *with diagram*
Solid South [U.S. history]
Reconstruction (Effects of Reconstruction) R: 179-180
Solid-state device [physics]
Electronics (Active components) E: 210 *with diagrams*; (The solid-state revolution) E: 215
Solid-state drive [electronic device]
Computer (Flash drives) Ci: 916
Solid-state electrometer [instrument]
Electroscope E: 218
Solid-state laser
Glass (Specialty glasses) G: 212-213
Laser (Kinds of lasers) L: 85
Solid-state physics So: 583
Physics (Solid-state physics) P: 438
Solid waste
Energy supply (Solid and liquid wastes) E: 279
Environmental pollution *picture on* E: 332; (Solid waste) E: 334

Landfill L: 57
Sanitation (Solid waste disposal) S: 111
Waste disposal W: 112
Solidarity [labor organization]
Communism (In Eastern Europe) Ci: 896
Gdańsk G: 74
Poland (History) P: 611-614 *with picture*
Wałęsa, Lech W: 13
Solidification [process]
Ink (Printing inks) I: 273
Soliloquy [drama]
Shakespeare, William (Dramatic conventions) S: 354
Soliman [Manilan ruler]
Manila (History) M: 143
Solis, Hilda [American government official]
Labor, Department of (table) L: 2
Obama, Barack (table) O: 640h
Solís, Juan Díaz de [Spanish explorer]
Argentina (Arrival of the Spanish) A: 655
Río de la Plata R: 346
Uruguay (Early days) U: 227
Solitaire [bird]
Dodo D: 261
Solitaire [game] So: 584
Card game C: 209
Solitaire [painting by Balthus]
Balthus *picture on* B: 65
Solitary [witch]
Witchcraft (Witchcraft as a religion) W: 371-372
Solitary confinement
Prison (Prison cells) P: 806
Solitary insect
Bee (Solitary bees) B: 205 *with pictures*
Beetle B: 215
Wasp W: 111 *with pictures*
Solitary mammal
Mammal (Group life) M: 125
Solitary oak leafminer [moth]
Moth *picture on* M: 837
Solitary wave
Waves *diagram on* W: 150; (How waves move) W: 152
Soliton [physics] See Solitary wave *in this index*
Solitudes [poem by Góngora]
Góngora, Luis de G: 268
Spanish literature (The 1600's) So: 759-760
Solleret [shoe]
Armor *picture on* A: 720
Solo, Jay [pen name of]
Ellison, Harlan H: 244
Solo flight
Airplane (Learning to fly) A: 226
Solo music
Classical music (Solo music) Ci: 643
Solomon [Biblical figure] So: 584
Ecclesiastes E: 49
Ethiopia E: 368
Jerusalem (Ancient times) J: 100
Jews (The kingdom of Israel) J: 121
Phoenicia (The spread of Phoenician influence) P: 394-395
Religion (Judaism) R: 219
Solomon, Temple of
Knights Templars K: 353
Solomon Gursky Was Here [book by Richler]
Richler, Mordecai R: 331
Solomon Islands [country] So: 584 *with picture and map*
Exploration (Exploring the Pacific) E: 447-448 *with map*
Flag *picture on* F: 204
Solomon Islands [islands, Pacific] So: 586
Amphibious warfare (History of amphibious warfare) A: 442
Solomon's-seal [plant] So: 586 *with picture*
Plant *picture on* P: 525
Solomos, Dionysios [Greek poet]
Greek literature (Modern Greek literature) G: 378
Solon [Greek political leader] So: 586
Athens (Earliest times) A: 857
Greece, Ancient (New forms of government) G: 372-373
Law (The influence of ancient Greece) L: 133
Solow, Robert [American economist]
Nobel Prizes (Economics: 1987) N: 449
Solstice [astronomy] So: 586
Season (The four seasons) S: 270-271
Stonehenge So: 912
Solti, Sir Georg [Hungarian-born British conductor] So: 586
Solubility [chemistry]
Solution (Liquid solutions) So: 587
Solute [chemistry]
Solvent So: 587
Solution [chemistry] So: 586
Osmosis O: 865 *with diagrams*

Suspension **So:** 1012
Solution cave [geology]
  Cave (How caves are formed) **C:** 319 *with diagram*
Solution mining
  Mining (Pumping methods) **M:** 577
  Salt (Salt from the ground) **S:** 73-74
Solution set [mathematics]
  Algebra (Statements and equations) **A:** 351
  Set theory (In algebra) **S:** 322
Solvated ion [chemistry]
  Ion (Ions in liquids) **I:** 371
Solvent [chemistry] **So:** 587
  Dry cleaning **D:** 368
  Ink **I:** 272
  Lipid (Importance of lipids) **L:** 344
  Paint **P:** 23
  Water (The properties of water) **W:** 129-130
Solvent extraction [industrial process]
  Corn oil **Ci:** 1064
  Cottonseed oil **Ci:** 1094
  Perfume (Plant substances) **P:** 286
  Soybean *diagram on* **So:** 692; (Soybean products)
    So: 690
  Vegetable oil (Production) **V:** 294
Sólyom, László [Hungarian political leader]
  Hungary (Recent developments) **H:** 448
Solzhenitsyn, Alexander [Russian author] **So:** 587
  Russian literature (Modern Soviet literature)
    R: 564
Somali [people]
  Ethiopia (People) **E:** 368
Somali cat
  Cat *picture on* **C:** 289; (Long-haired breeds) **C:** 292
Somali National Movement
  Somalia (History) **So:** 589
Somali Star, Order of the [Somalia]
  Medals, decorations, and orders (table) **M:** 359
Somalia So: 587 *with picture and map*
  Bush, George Herbert Walker (U.S. troops in
    Somalia) **B:** 722a
  Clothing *picture on* **Ci:** 692
  Ethiopia (Haile Selassie) **E:** 371; (Recent
    developments) **E:** 372
  Flag *picture on* **F:** 199
  Militia **M:** 544
  Pirate (Other regions) **P:** 495-496
  Puntland **P:** 904
  Somaliland **So:** 590
Somaliland [region, Africa] **So:** 590
  Djibouti (History) **D:** 257
  Somalia (History) **So:** 589
Somaliland, French
  Djibouti **D:** 256
Somaliland Republic *See* Somaliland *in this index*
Somatic cell [biology]
  Cell (table) **C:** 327
  Gene therapy **G:** 82
  Heredity (Chromosomes and genes) **H:** 201;
    (Sources of genetic variation) **H:** 203
Somatic death
  Death (Medical aspects of death) **D:** 61
Somatic mutation
  Heredity (Mutation) **H:** 203
  Mutation **M:** 968
Somatic therapy
  Psychiatry (Somatic therapy) **P:** 845
Somatoform disorder [illness]
  Mental illness (Somatoform disorders) **M:** 406
Somatosensory cortex [anatomy]
  Brain (Sensing the environment) **B:** 552 *with
    diagram*
Somatostatin [hormone]
  Hypothalamus **H:** 481
Somatotropin [hormone]
  Dwarfism (Causes) **D:** 394
  Human growth hormone **H:** 427
Sombo [sport]
  Wrestling (Chief forms of wrestling) **W:** 505
Sombrero [hat]
  Mexico (Clothing) **M:** 456
Somchai Wongsawat [Thai political leader]
  Thailand (Recent developments) **T:** 228
Some Fruits of Solitude [book by Penn]
  Penn, William (Arrested again) **P:** 242
Somers [New York]
  Circus (The circus grows) **Ci:** 562b
Somers, Sir George [British admiral]
  Bermuda (History) **B:** 268
Somers, Will [English jester]
  Jester **J:** 103
Somers Islands
  Bermuda (History) **B:** 268
Somersault
  Gymnastics (Power tumbling) **G:** 449
  Swimming (Starts and turns) **So:** 1046
Somerset, Duke of [English regent]
  Edward VI **E:** 113

Somerset House [London]
  Architecture (Neoclassical architecture) **A:** 623
Something Happened [book by Heller]
  Heller, Joseph **H:** 177
Something of Myself [book by Kipling]
  Kipling, Rudyard (Later career) **K:** 334
Something Wicked This Way Comes [book by
    Bradbury]
  Bradbury, Ray **B:** 542
Sometimes a Great Notion [book by Kesey]
  Kesey, Ken **K:** 307
Somma, Mount [Italy]
  Vesuvius **V:** 342 *with picture*
Somme, Battle of the [1916]
  Tank (History) **T:** 27
  World War I (The Battle of the Somme) **W:** 458
Somnambulism *See* Sleepwalking *in this index*
Somnus [Roman mythology]
  See also Hypnos *in this index*
  Mythology (table) **M:** 981
Somoza Debayle, Anastasio [Nicaraguan political
    leader]
  Nicaragua (The Somoza period) **N:** 400
  Ortega, Daniel **O:** 859
  Somoza García, Anastasio **So:** 590
Somoza Debayle, Luis [Nicaraguan political
    leader]
  Nicaragua (The Somoza period) **N:** 400
  Somoza García, Anastasio **So:** 590
Somoza García, Anastasio [Nicaraguan political
    leader] **So:** 590
  Nicaragua (The Somoza period) **N:** 400
Son of a Smaller Hero [book by Richler]
  Richler, Mordecai **R:** 331
Son of God [religion]
  Jesus Christ **J:** 104
  Trinity **T:** 447
Son of the Circus, A [book by Irving]
  Irving, John **I:** 459
Son of the Middle Border, A [book by Garland]
  Garland, Hamlin **G:** 43
Son of the Wolf, The [book by London]
  London, Jack **L:** 444
Sonar [navigation] **So:** 590 *with diagrams*
  Archaeology (Working underwater) **A:** 597
  Atlantic Ocean (New techniques) **A:** 867
  Bragg, Sir William Henry **B:** 547
  Echo **E:** 50
  Ultrasound (Other uses) **U:** 16
Sonar transducer [device]
  Geology *picture on* **G:** 100
  Transducer **T:** 371
Sonata [music] **So:** 591
  Classical music (Sonata) **Ci:** 645
Sonata Mulattica [book by Dove]
  Dove, Rita **D:** 315
Sonatas and Interludes for Prepared Piano [music
    by Cage]
  Cage, John **C:** 14
Sondergaard, Gale [American actress]
  Motion picture (Best performance by an actress
    in a supporting role: 1936) **M:** 862b
Sondheim, Stephen [American composer] **So:** 591
  Musical comedy (During the late 1900's) **M:** 960
Sones, F. Mason, Jr. [American physician]
  Heart (Development of heart surgery) **H:** 144-145
Song [biology]
  Bird (Calls and songs) **B:** 354; (Sleeping and
    resting) **B:** 355; (Bird watching) **B:** 367
  Humpback whale **H:** 436
  Whale (Group life) **W:** 261
Song [music] **So:** 591
  See also the list of Related articles in the Song
    article
  Classical music (Songs) **Ci:** 644
  Folk music **F:** 321
  Lieder **L:** 273
  Madrigal **M:** 40
  National anthem **N:** 28
Song cycle
  Classical music (The Romantic era) **Ci:** 648
Song dynasty [Chinese history] **So:** 592
  China (The arts) **C:** 487 *with picture*; (The Song
    dynasty) **C:** 501
  Lacquerware *picture on* **L:** 22
  Painting (Chinese painting) **P:** 44-45
  Porcelain (Oriental porcelain) **P:** 676
  Pottery *picture on* **P:** 716
  Tang dynasty (The fall of the dynasty) **T:** 26
  World, History of the (China) **W:** 435
"Song for St. Cecilia's Day, 1687, A" [poem by
    Dryden]
  Cecilia, Saint **C:** 324
"Song of Deborah" [Bible]
  Deborah **D:** 65
  Hebrew literature (Early works) **H:** 162
Song of Esther [painting by Rattner]

  Rattner, Abraham *picture on* **R:** 150
Song of Hiawatha, The [poem by Longfellow]
  Chippewa Indians **C:** 514
  Finland (The arts) **F:** 112
  Hiawatha **H:** 221
  Longfellow, Henry Wadsworth **L:** 450
  Minnehaha Falls **M:** 583
  Minnesota (Lakes, rivers, and waterfalls) **M:** 598
  Remington, Frederic **R:** 230
"Song of India" [music by Rimsky-Korsakov]
  Rimsky-Korsakov, Nikolai **R:** 342
"Song of Myself" [poem by Whitman]
  Whitman, Walt (His work) **W:** 294
Song of Roland, The [poem]
  Charlemagne (Military conquests) **C:** 379
  French literature (Narrative poetry) **F:** 518
  Roland **R:** 401
Song of Solomon [Bible] **So:** 592
  Bible (The Writings) **B:** 281
  Solomon **So:** 584
Song of Solomon [book by Morrison]
  Morrison, Toni **M:** 817
Song of Songs [Bible] *See* Song of Solomon *in
    this index*
Song of the Earth, The [music by Mahler]
  Mahler, Gustav **M:** 65
Song of the Lark [painting by Breton]
  Breton, Jules Adolphe **B:** 594 *with picture*
Song of the Nibelungs [poem] *See* Nibelungenlied
    in this index
"Song of the Rhine Army" [former name]
  "Marseillaise" **M:** 227
Song sparrow
  Bird *picture on* **B:** 358
  Sparrow **So:** 764 *with picture*
"Song to Bolívar" [poem by Olmedo]
  Latin American literature (The 1800's) **L:** 112
Songbird
  Bird (Calls and songs) **B:** 354
Songe [people]
  Africa *pictures on* **A:** 116
Songhai Empire [African history] **So:** 592 *with map*
  Africa (The empires of west Africa) **A:** 131
  African Americans (The cultural heritage) **A:** 136c
  Askia Muhammad **A:** 814
  French West Africa (History) **F:** 528
  Mali (History) **M:** 108
  Mali Empire **M:** 110
  Niger (History) **N:** 409
  Nigeria (Early kingdoms) **N:** 417
  World, History of the (African civilizations) **W:** 437
Songs [poems by Leopardi]
  Italian literature (Romanticism) **I:** 495
Songs and Sonnets [poems by Donne]
  Donne, John (His poetry) **D:** 308
Songs for the Nursery [book by Fleet]
  Mother Goose (Who was Mother Goose?) **M:** 842
Songs from Vagabondia [book by Carman and
    Hovey]
  Carman, Bliss **C:** 240
Songs of a Semite [book by Lazarus]
  Lazarus, Emma **L:** 148
Songs of Chu [poems]
  Chinese literature (Beginnings) **C:** 511
Songs of Experience [poems by Blake]
  Blake, William **B:** 397
Songs of Innocence [poems by Blake]
  Blake, William **B:** 397
Songs of Life and Hope [book by Darío]
  Darío, Rubén **D:** 36
Songs of the Common Day [book by Roberts]
  Roberts, Charles G. D. **R:** 365
Songs of the Sabbath Sacrifice [document]
  Dead Sea Scrolls **D:** 56
Songs of Zion [book by Halevi]
  Hebrew literature (Medieval works) **H:** 162
Songs on the Death of Children [music by Mahler]
  Mahler, Gustav **M:** 65
Songs Without Words [music by Mendelssohn]
  Mendelssohn, Felix (His music) **M:** 399
Songs Without Words [poem by Verlaine]
  French literature (Symbolism) **F:** 522
  Verlaine, Paul **V:** 317
Songster [song book]
  Popular music (Revolutionary War to 1840) **P:** 669
Sonic boom So: 593
  Aerodynamics (Supersonic aerodynamics) **A:** 87
    with diagram
  Shock wave **S:** 430
Soninke [people]
  Ghana Empire **G:** 180
  Mali (People) **M:** 106
Sonnambula, La [opera by Bellini]
  Bellini, Vincenzo **B:** 244
Sonnet [poetry] **So:** 593
  English literature (Elizabethan poetry) **E:** 316
  Poetry (Lyric poetry) **P:** 591; (table) **P:** 594;

(Forms) P: 595
Shakespeare, William (The sonnets) S: 348; (Shakespeare's poems) S: 366
Sonnet 138 [poem by Shakespeare]
Shakespeare, William (Themes) S: 366-367
Sonnet sequence
English literature (Elizabethan poetry) E: 316-317
Poetry (table) P: 594
"Sonnet—To Science" [poem by Poe]
Poe, Edgar Allan (Poetry and poetic theory) P: 589-590
Sonnets [poems by Shakespeare]
Shakespeare, William (The sonnets) S: 348
Sonnet So: 593
Sonnets for Hélène [poems by Ronsard]
Ronsard, Pierre de R: 450b
Sonnets from the Portuguese [poems by Browning]
Browning, Elizabeth Barrett B: 646
Sonnets to Orpheus [book by Rilke]
Rilke, Rainer Maria R: 341
Sonora Matancera, La [band]
Cruz, Celia Ci: 1165
Sonoran Desert [Mexico-United States] So: 593
Sonoran Mountain kingsnake
Snake *picture on* S: 533
Sons and Lovers [book by Lawrence]
Lawrence, D. H. L: 145
Sons of Liberty [Canadian history]
Rebellions of 1837 (In Lower Canada) R: 173
Sons of Liberty [U.S. history] So: 594
Declaration of Independence *picture on* D: 78
North Carolina (Revolution and independence) N: 492
Putnam, Israel P: 913
United States, History of the (Colonial reaction) U: 158
Sons of Mil [legendary people]
Mythology (The Irish cycles) M: 985
Sons of the American Revolution [organization] So: 594
Sons of thunder [religion]
James the Greater, Saint J: 28
John, Saint J: 133
Sontag, Susan [American author] So: 594
American literature (Essays) A: 426
Essay (Formal essays) E: 359
Sony Building [New York City]
Architecture (Architecture today) A: 632-633
Sony Corporation So: 594
E-book E: 2
Electronic game (Renewed interest in consoles) E: 204e
Manufacturing (table) M: 170
Portable media player P: 681
Soo Canals [waterways, Michigan-Ontario] So: 594 *with map*
Canal *picture on* C: 162; (Major canals in the United States and Canada) C: 164; (table) C: 164
Great Lakes (Water routes to the sea) G: 344
Lake Huron L: 39
Soochow [China] *See* Suzhou *in this index*
Sooner [U.S. history]
Oklahoma (Great land rushes) O: 732
Sooner State [nickname]
Oklahoma O: 712
Soong Mei-ling, Chiang [Chinese public figure] *See* Chiang Soong Mei-ling *in this index*
Soot So: 595
Fire (What fire produces) F: 121
Sooty-owl [bird]
Owl (Important owls) O: 884
Sooty oystercatcher [bird]
Oystercatcher O: 893
Sooty tern [bird]
Tern T: 172
Sophia [queen of Spain]
Juan Carlos I J: 177
Sophia [sister of]
Peter I, the Great (Early life) P: 323
Russia (Peter the Great) R: 549
Sophie [opera character]
Opera: (Rosenkavalier, Der) O: 807 *with picture*
Sophie [wife of]
Franz Ferdinand F: 494
Sophie's Choice [book by Styron]
Styron, William So: 936
Sophist, The [book by Plato]
Plato (The dialogues) P: 567; (The later dialogues) P: 568
Sophists So: 595
Greek literature (Philosophical literature) G: 377; (The Greco-Roman Age) G: 378
Socrates (Socrates's life) So: 567-568
Sophists' Banquet [book by Athenaeus of Naucratis]

Greek literature (The Greco-Roman Age) G: 378
Sophocles [Greek dramatist] So: 595
Drama (Tragedy) D: 326-327
Greek literature (Drama) G: 377
Sophomore [education]
Universities and colleges (The student body) U: 208
Soprano [music]
Singing (Voice classification) S: 472
Treble T: 409
Sopwith Camel [airplane]
Aircraft, Military *picture on* A: 204
Sor Juana [Mexican poet] *See* Juana Inés de la Cruz *in this index*
Sora [bird]
Rail R: 103
Sorak National Park [South Korea]
National park (table) N: 42f
Soraya [queen of Iran]
Mohammad Reza Pahlavi M: 687
Sorber, Diane Claire [American artist] *See* Dillon, Leo and Diane *in this index*
Sorbonne [college, France] So: 596
Paris, University of P: 168
Rabelais, François R: 49
Sorcerer's Apprentice, The [music by Dukas]
Dukas, Paul Abraham D: 380
Sorcery
Magic (The magician) M: 49
Witchcraft W: 371
Sore mouth [disease]
Goat (Disease) G: 241
Soredia [biology]
Lichen (How lichens grow) L: 269
Sorel, Julien [literary figure]
Stendhal So: 889
Sørensen, Søren [Danish biochemist]
pH P: 353
Sorensen, Virginia [American author]
Newbery Medal (table) N: 359
Sorenstam, Annika [Swedish golfer] So: 596
Golf *picture on* G: 267
Soret, J. Louis [Swiss chemist]
Holmium H: 296
Sorghum [botany] So: 596 *with picture*
Grain G: 301
Sorghum [syrup]
Sorghum (Sweet sorghums) So: 596
Sorgo [plant]
Sorghum (Sweet sorghums) So: 596
Soricomorph [mammal]
Mammal (table) M: 129 *with picture*
Sorlie, A. G. [American political leader]
North Dakota (table) N: 513
Soro, Guillaume [Ivorian political leader]
Côte d'Ivoire (History) Ci: 1084b-1085
Soroban [calculator]
Abacus A: 3
Sorokin, Peter [American physicist]
Laser (History) L: 86
Sorority [organization] So: 596
Universities and colleges (Fraternities and sororities) U: 209
Soros, George [American financier] So: 597
Foundation (International affairs) F: 431
Sorrel [plant] *See* Sourwood; Wood sorrel *in this index*
Sorrentino, Gilbert [American author]
American literature (Experimental styles) A: 425
Sorrows of Young Werther, The [book by Goethe]
German literature (German Preromanticism) G: 139
Goethe, Johann Wolfgang von (Early years) G: 247
Sortie [warfare]
Air Force, United States (Offense) A: 190
Sorting [unit of measure]
Barter B: 120
Sorting yard [railroad] *See* Classification yard *in this index*
Sortland, Bjorn [Norwegian author]
Literature for children *picture on* L: 354
Sorus [botany]
Fern (Parts of a fern) F: 74-75
Plant (Sexual reproduction) P: 532-533 *with picture*
Sorvino, Mira [American actress]
Motion picture (Best performance by an actress in a supporting role: 1995) M: 862b
SOS [signal] So: 597
Sosa, Sammy [Dominican baseball player] So: 597
Baseball (Recent developments) B: 137
Soseki, Natsume [Japanese author] *See* Natsume Soseki *in this index*
Sosigenes [Greek astronomer]
Calendar (The Julian calendar) C: 31
Soso [kingdom]

Sundiata Keita So: 990
Sosso [people]
Ghana Empire G: 181 *with map*
Sostenuto [music]
Piano (The pedals) P: 446-447
Sostratos [Greek architect]
Seven Wonders of the Ancient World (The Lighthouse of Alexandria) S: 325
Sot-Weed Factor, The [book by Barth]
Barth, John B: 120
Soter, Saint [pope]
Pope (table) P: 666
Sotho [people]
South Africa (People) So: 609
Soto [religion]
Zen Z: 589
Soto, Hernando de [Spanish explorer] *See* De Soto, Hernando *in this index*
Sotomayor, Sonia [American jurist] So: 597 *with portrait*
Hispanic Americans (Political gains) H: 256 *with picture*
Obama, Barack (Court milestone) O: 640g
Supreme Court of the United States *picture on* So: 999
Soubeiran, Eugene [French chemist]
Chloroform C: 517
Souders, George [American race driver]
Automobile racing (table: Indianapolis 500 winners) A: 980
Soufflot, Jacques [French architect]
Architecture (Neoclassical architecture) A: 623-624
Soufrière [mountain, Saint Vincent]
Saint Vincent and the Grenadines (Land and climate) S: 57 *with map*
West Indies (Land and climate) W: 204
Soufrière [village, Dominica]
Dominica *picture on* D: 302
Soufrière Hills [region, Caribbean Sea]
Montserrat M: 780
Souk Waqif [market]
City *picture on* Ci: 575
Soul
Augustine, Saint (His beliefs) A: 888
Hinduism (Reincarnation and karma) H: 236
Immortality I: 86
Mythology (Anthropological approaches) M: 989
Plato (Immortality of the soul) P: 568
Religion (A doctrine of salvation) R: 215-216
Spiritualism (Beliefs) So: 796
Soul cake [custom]
Halloween (Halloween customs and symbols) H: 24a
Soul City [North Carolina]
McKissick, Floyd Bixler M: 343
Soul music
Cooke, Sam Ci: 1027
Popular music (Soul music) P: 671
Rock music (Soul music) R: 380a
Soul on Fire [book by Cleaver]
Cleaver, Eldridge Ci: 660
Soul on Ice [book by Cleaver]
Cleaver, Eldridge Ci: 660
Soul patch [hair]
Beard B: 187
Soule, John [American journalist]
Greeley, Horace (His publications) G: 379
Soulé, Pierre [American government official]
Ostend Manifesto O: 866
Soulé, Samuel W. [American inventor]
Sholes, Christopher Latham S: 433
Typewriter (History) T: 539
Souling [custom]
Halloween (Halloween customs and symbols) H: 24a
Souls of Black Folk, The [book by Du Bois]
American literature (Nonfiction writers) A: 420
Du Bois, W. E. B. D: 372
Sound [physics] So: 598 *with pictures*
Acoustics A: 28
Decibel D: 70
Ear (The sense of hearing) E: 9; (How sounds reach the brain) E: 10 *with diagram*
Echo E: 50
Interference I: 323
Language (The sounds of language) L: 62
Physics (Sound) P: 437
Shock wave S: 430
Theater (Sound production) T: 242
Vibration V: 347
Waves W: 150
Sound, Speed of
Aerodynamics (Supersonic aerodynamics) A: 87
Airplane (Supersonic airplanes) A: 238
Mach, Ernst M: 12b
Sound (The speed of sound) So: 601

Wind tunnel **W: 333**
Yeager, Charles Elwood **Y: 554**
Sound and the Fury, The [book by Faulkner]
American literature (Modernist fiction) **A: 421-422**
Faulkner, William **F: 55**
Novel (New directions in the novel) **N: 573-574**
Sound barrier
Sonic boom **So: 593**
Sound bite [communications]
Debate (Political debate) **D: 63-64**
Sound bite [communication]
Television (Effects on society) **T: 121**
Sound card [electronic device]
Computer (A microphone) **Ci: 915**
Sound co-processor [electronics]
Computer (Personal computers) **Ci: 909**
Sound effect
Motion picture (Adding music and sound effects) **M: 856**
Radio *picture on* **R: 93**
Shakespeare, William (Costumes and sound effects) **S: 352**
Television (Adding music and sound effects) **T: 112**
Sound mixer
Motion picture (Shooting the movie) **M: 852**
Sound of Music, The [film]
Motion picture (Best picture: 1965) **M: 861**
Sound of Music, The [musical]
Rodgers, Richard **R: 398**
Sound-post
Violin (Parts of the violin) **V: 389**
Sound quality
Sound (table) **So: 599**; (Sound quality) **So: 601**
Sound ranging [warfare]
Bragg, Sir William Lawrence **B: 548**
Sound recording
Animation (Preliminary steps in animation) **A: 511**
Compact disc **Ci: 901**
Electronic game (Sound) **E: 204b** *with picture*
Motion picture (The sound track) **M: 857** *with pictures*; (The movies talk) **M: 867**
Phonograph **P: 400** *with pictures*
Recording industry **R: 180**
Tape recorder **T: 36** *with pictures*
Videotape recorder **V: 360** *with picture*
Sound shift
Linguistics (Internal reconstruction) **L: 336**
Sound stage
Motion picture *picture on* **M: 848**; (Assembling the production team) **M: 850**; (Filming on a sound stage) **M: 851**
Sound track
Motion picture (Preliminary steps) **M: 854**; (The sound track) **M: 857** *with diagram*
Sound wave [physics]
Sound (The nature of sound) **So: 599** *with diagram*; (How sound behaves) **So: 601-602** *with diagrams*
Microphone **M: 516** *with diagrams*
Music (Musical instruments) **M: 948**
Radio (From sound waves to electric waves) **R: 86**
Sonar (How sonar works) **So: 591** *with diagram*
Soundboard
Piano (The soundboard) **P: 447** *with picture*
Soundbox
Harp **H: 65** *with picture*
Sounder [telegraph]
Telegraph (The Morse telegraph) **T: 90** *with picture*
Soundgarden [rock group]
Rock music (Alternative rock) **R: 381**
Sounding [meteorology]
Radiosonde **R: 99**
Sounding [navigation]
Fathometer **F: 54**
Sounding balloon
Balloon (Gas balloons) **B: 58**
Sounding rocket
Rocket (Atmospheric research) **R: 386**
Space exploration (Early unmanned explorations) **So: 708**
Soundproofing
Insulation (Insulation against sound) **I: 307**
Souphanouvong [Laotian prince]
Laos (History) **L: 71-72**
Sour cherry [tree]
Cherry **C: 410** *with picture*
Sour cream
Milk (table) **M: 547**
Sour natural buttermilk
Buttermilk **B: 744**
Sour orange [tree]
Orange (Sour or bitter oranges) **O: 815**
Source [geography]

River (Sources of river water) **R: 351** *with picture*
Source terminal [transistor]
Electronics (Transistors) **E: 212**
Sourgum [tree]
Tupelo **T: 492**
Sourwood [tree] So: 606 *with pictures*
Sous-vide [cooking]
Cooking (vacuum cooking) **Ci: 1028**
Sousa, John Philip [American composer] **So: 607** *with portrait*
Marine Corps, United States **M: 206**
Yankee Doodle **Y: 552**
Sousaphone [musical instrument]
Music *picture on* **M: 949**; (Wind instruments) **M: 949-950**
Tuba **T: 477**
Sousa's Band [ensemble]
Sousa, John Philip **So: 607**
Sousley, Franklin R. [American soldier]
Iwo Jima, Battle of *picture on* **I: 523**
Souster, Raymond [Canadian poet] **So: 607**
Soutache braid
Braiding **B: 549**
Souter, David Hackett [American jurist] **So: 607**
South [region, U.S.] *See* Southern States *in this index*
South, The U.S. Army
Army, United States (Army service component commands) **A: 736-737**
South Africa So: 608 *with pictures and maps*
See also the list of Related articles in the South Africa *article*
Africa *picture on* **A: 136**; (Struggles for independence) **A: 134-135**
African National Congress **A: 137**
Afrikaners **A: 138**
Anglo-Boer Wars **A: 463**
Angola (History) **A: 465-466**
Apartheid **A: 563**
Botswana (History) **B: 512**
Clothing *picture on* **Ci: 692**
Concentration camp (Other concentration camps) **Ci: 927**
Diamond (Where natural diamonds are found) **D: 181**
Disability (The 1900's) **D: 221-222**
Girl Scouts (South Africa) **G: 199**
Gold (World gold production) **G: 253**
Human rights (Trade and diplomatic measures) **H: 428a**
Inkatha Freedom Party **I: 273**
Library (Africa) **L: 252-253**
Minority group (Minority groups in other countries) **M: 610**
Namibia **N: 7**; (History) **N: 9**
National park (South Africa) **N: 42e** *with picture*
Olympic Games (Boycotts) **O: 753**; (The recent games) **O: 753**
Parliament (Parliaments in other countries) **P: 174**
Racism (History) **R: 62**
Railroad (In Africa) **R: 114**
Segregation (Segregation in other countries) **S: 286**
Sullivan, Leon Howard **So: 969**
Tennis (Tennis today) **T: 166d-166e**
Truth commission **T: 474**
UNESCO (History) **U: 25**
United Kingdom (Gladstone and Disraeli) **U: 69**; (Decline of the empire) **U: 71**
United Nations (Working for self-government) **U: 93-94**
South African cycad [tree]
Tree *pictures on* **T: 413**
South African Native National Congress [political party]
South Africa (The Union of South Africa) **So: 618-619**
South African Republic [former name]
Anglo-Boer Wars **A: 463**
Cape Colony **C: 188**
South Africa (Discovery of diamonds and gold) **So: 618**
South African Students' Organization
Biko, Steve **B: 299**
South African War *See* Anglo-Boer Wars *in this index*
South America So: 622 *with pictures and maps*
See also the list of Related articles in the South America *article*
Andean Community **A: 450**
Clothing *pictures on* **Ci: 695**
Continent **Ci: 1021**
Continental divide **Ci: 1022**
Inca **I: 95**
Indian, American (Indians of the Andes) **I: 173** *with pictures*; (Indians of the Tropical Forest) **I: 175**; (Indians of the South American Marginal Regions) **I: 176** *with pictures and map*

Latin America (The movement toward independence) **L: 106-107**; (Political circumstances in the early to middle 1900's) **L: 109**
Line of Demarcation **L: 333** *with map*
Marsupial (History of marsupials) **M: 233**
Monroe Doctrine **M: 739**
Monsoon **M: 740**
National park (table) **N: 42g**
Prehistoric animal (The distribution of mammals) **P: 741**
Prehistoric people (The spread of settlement) **P: 752**
Rain forest (The Americas) **R: 126b** *with map*
Wheat (South America) **W: 273** *with map*
South American coral snake
Coral snake **Ci: 1050**
South American discus fish
Fish *picture on* **F: 157**
South American ostrich
Rhea **R: 290** *with picture*
South American trypanosomiasis [disorder] *See* Chagas disease *in this index*
South Arabia, Federation of
Yemen (Formation of South Yemen) **Y: 563**
South Asia
Asia (Way of life in South Asia) **A: 781** *with pictures*; (The land) **A: 792**
Martial arts (Central and South Asian martial arts) **M: 234a**
South Atlantic Ocean
Atlantic Ocean (Boundaries and size) **A: 864**
South Australia [state, Australia] So: 639 *with picture and map*
Adelaide **A: 51**
South Bank [district]
London (Central London) **L: 429-430**
South Bay [Los Angeles]
Los Angeles (South Bay) **L: 461**
South Bend [Indiana] So: 639
South Boston [Massachusetts]
Boston (South Boston) **B: 498**
South Canal
Soo Canals (The American canals) **So: 594** *with map*
South Carolina So: 640 *with pictures and maps*
See also the list of Related articles in the South Carolina *article*
Calhoun, John Caldwell **C: 35**
Colonial life in America (Development of the Thirteen Colonies) **Ci: 790** *with map*
United States, History of the (North Carolina, South Carolina, and Georgia) **U: 156**; (Jackson as president) **U: 171**
South Carolina, University of So: 663
South Carolina (Libraries) **So: 645** *with picture*
South Carolina Botanical Garden [Clemson]
South Carolina *picture on* **So: 645**
South Carolina Canal and Railroad Company
Railroad (Developments in the United States) **R: 115**
South Carolina Exposition [U.S. history]
Jackson, Andrew (Split with Calhoun) **J: 11**
Nullification **N: 603**
South Carolina (Nullification) **So: 660**
South Carolina Weekly Journal
South Carolina (Communication) **So: 657**
South China Sea
China Sea **C: 508** *with map*
South Dakota So: 664 *with pictures and maps*
See also the list of Related articles in the South Dakota *article*
South Dakota, University of So: 685
South Dakota (Libraries) **So: 668** *with picture*
South Dakota State University So: 685
South End [district, Boston]
Boston (The south side) **B: 500**
South Equatorial Current
Atlantic Ocean (Moving ocean waters) **A: 866**
Ocean (Circulation) **O: 658**
Pacific Ocean (Currents) **P: 14-15**
South European Pipeline
Pipeline (In other countries) **P: 491-492**
South Foreland Lighthouse [England]
Electric power (Early developments) **E: 186**
South Fork Dam [Pennsylvania]
Johnstown Flood **J: 155**
South Fork Fishing and Hunting Club
Johnstown Flood **J: 155**
South Gate [gate, Seoul]
Seoul *picture on* **S: 305**
South geographic pole
South Pole **So: 685**
South Georgia [island, Atlantic]
Penguin *picture on* **P: 239**
South Island [island]
New Zealand (European colonization) **N: 355**

New Zealand (The South Island) **N: 351** *with picture and map*
South Island kiwi [bird]
  Bird *picture on* **B: 348**
South Jersey glass
  Glass (Types of art glass) **G: 220-221**
South Korea *See* Korea, South *in this index*
South lawn [park]
  White House (The south lawn) **W: 286**
South Luangwa National Park [Zambia]
  National park (table) **N: 42f**
South magnetic pole [geography]
  Antarctica *map on* **A: 531**, *picture on* **A: 531**
  Magnetic equator **M: 55**
  South Pole **So: 685**
South Ossetia [region]
  Georgia (History) **G: 111**
South Pacific [musical]
  Michener, James A. **M: 487**
  Rodgers, Richard **R: 398**
South Pacific Forum [organization]
  Pacific Islands (Pacific alliances and independence movements) **P: 12**
South Pass [Wyoming]
  Wyoming (The great trails) **W: 533**
South Philadelphia [district, Philadelphia]
  Philadelphia (Residential districts) **P: 360**
South Platte River [Colorado-Nebraska]
  Platte River **P: 569**
South polar skua [bird]
  Bird (Birds of the ocean and the Antarctic) **B: 344** *with picture*
South Pole [geography] **So: 685**
  Amundsen, Roald **A: 445** *with map*
  Antarctica **A: 530**; (Exploration) **A: 535-536** *with pictures*; (Scientific research) **A: 539**
  Balchen, Bernt **B: 38**
  Byrd, Richard Evelyn **B: 746**
  Earth (How Earth moves) **E: 17**
  Exploration (The exploration of Antarctica) **E: 450**
  Midnight sun **M: 535**
  Season (The four seasons) **S: 270-272**
  Shackleton, Sir Ernest Henry **S: 341**
South pole [physics] *See* Magnetic pole *in this index*
South Pole-Aitken Basin [lunar feature]
  Moon (Origin and evolution of the moon) **M: 788**
South pole of balance [geography]
  South Pole **So: 685**
South Pole Telescope
  Antarctica *picture on* **A: 540**
South Sea [former name, Pacific]
  Balboa, Vasco Núñez de **B: 37**
South Sea Bubble [English history]
  George I **G: 106b**
South Shore Canal [waterway]
  Quebec (Transportation) **Q: 28**
South Slavs [people]
  Slavs (South Slavs) **S: 505**
  Yugoslavia (Land of the South Slavs) **Y: 576**
South Sudan *See* Sudan, South *in this index*
South Vietnam
  Vietnam **V: 364**; (History) **V: 369-371**
  Cold War (To the brink and back) **Ci: 765**; (The Vietnam War) **Ci: 769**
  Geneva Accords **G: 87**
  Indochina (The Geneva Accords) **I: 225**
  Tet Offensive **T: 182a**
  Viet Cong **V: 363**
  Vietnam War **V: 372** *with map*
South Vietnamese Army
  Vietnam War **V: 373**
South West Africa [former name] *See* Namibia *in this index*
South West Africa People's Organization
  Namibia (Government) **N: 8**; (History) **N: 9**
  United Nations (Working for self-government) **U: 93-94**
South Wind [book by Douglas]
  Douglas, Norman **D: 312**
South Yemen [former country]
  Yemen **Y: 561**
Southampton [England] **So: 686** *with picture*
Southampton, Earl of [English nobleman]
  Shakespeare, William (His first poems) **S: 347**
Southampton Island [Hudson Bay]
  Nunavut (Land and resources) **N: 609** *with map*
Southard, Samuel L. [American political leader]
  Adams, John Quincy (table) **A: 43**
  New Jersey (table) **N: 249**
Southdown sheep
  Sheep (Medium-wooled sheep) **S: 382**
Southeast Asia [region, Asia] **So: 686** *with map*
  Asia (Way of life in Southeast Asia) **A: 783** *with pictures*; (The land) **A: 792**; (Climate) **A: 796-797** *with maps*; (Plants) **A: 799** *with map*; (The spread of Communism) **A: 807**
  Asian Americans (Arrivals of the late 1900's)

A: 813
  Association of Southeast Asian Nations **A: 820**
  Colombo Plan **Ci: 785**
  East Indies **E: 40**
  Library (South and Southeast Asia) **L: 253**
  Vietnam War **V: 374** *with map*
Southeast Asia Treaty Organization [alliance] **So: 687**
  Cold War (To the brink and back) **Ci: 765**
Southeast Division [hockey]
  Hockey (table: National Hockey League) **H: 281**
Southeast Lighthouse
  Rhode Island (Places to visit) **R: 304**
Southeastern Pennsylvania Transportation Authority
  Philadelphia (Transportation) **P: 365**
Southern African Development Community
  Africa (Africa since independence) **A: 135**
Southern African Large Telescope A: 687
Southern Alps [mountains, New Zealand]
  New Zealand (The South Island) **N: 351** *with picture and map*
Southern Baptist Convention [religious group] **So: 687**
  Baptists (Baptists in America) **B: 101**
Southern black widow [spider]
  Black widow **B: 391** *with picture*
Southern bottlenose whale
  Antarctica (Living things) **A: 534-535** *with picture*
Southern California, University of So: 688
Southern Christian Leadership Conference [organization] **So: 688**
  Abernathy, Ralph David **A: 10**
  African Americans (The growing movement) **A: 136o**
  King, Martin Luther, Jr. (The early civil rights movement) **K: 321**
  Rustin, Bayard **R: 567**
Southern Colonies
  Colonial life in America *picture on* **Ci: 792**; (Geographic divisions) **Ci: 791** *with map*
  Revolution, American (Fighting in the Chesapeake and Southern colonies) **R: 276**
Southern Cross [constellation] **So: 688**
Southern Cross, National Order of the [Brazil]
  Medals, decorations, and orders (table) **M: 359**
Southern deciduous-evergreen forest
  Forest (Southern deciduous-evergreen forests) **F: 394** *with map*
Southern elephant seal [sea animal]
  Antarctica (Living things) **A: 534-535** *with picture*
  Elephant seal **E: 232**
Southern fulmar [bird]
  Fulmar **F: 555**
Southern hairy-nosed wombat [animal]
  Wombat **W: 382**
Southern Hemisphere
  Astronomy (The stars and constellations of the Southern Hemisphere) *map on* **A: 837**
  Hemisphere **H: 181** *with diagram*
  Ocean (Circulation) **O: 658**
  Season (The four seasons) **S: 270** *with diagram*
Southern leopard frog
  Amphibian *picture on* **A: 441**
  Leopard frog *picture on* **L: 203**
Southern lights *See* Aurora *in this index*
Southern Limestone Alps [mountains, Austria]
  Austria (Land regions) **A: 933-934** *with map*
Southern Methodist University So: 688
  Dallas (Education) **D: 12-13**
Southern Mississippi, University of
  Mississippi *picture on* **M: 627**
Southern Nigeria, Colony and Protectorate of [former colony]
  Nigeria (British rule) **N: 417**
Southern Ocean So: 688 *with map*
  Antarctica (Ocean) **A: 532** *with map*
  Atlantic Ocean (Boundaries and size) **A: 864**
  Iceberg (Antarctic icebergs) **O: 651**
  Ocean (The world ocean) **O: 651** *with picture*
Southern Ocean Whale Sanctuary
  Whale (The future of whales) **W: 264**
Southern Oscillation
  El Niño **E: 245**
  Ocean (Discoveries) **O: 664**
  Pacific Ocean (El Niño) **P: 14**
Southern Pacific Railroad
  California (Early statehood) **C: 62**
  Los Angeles (Development and growth) **L: 470**
Southern Poverty Law Center
  Bond, Julian **B: 455**
Southern red lily
  Lily **L: 304**
Southern Rhodesia
  Zambia (History) **Z: 585-586**
  Zimbabwe (History) **Z: 592-593**
Southern Ring Nebula

Star *picture on* **So: 841**
Southern Rockies [U.S.]
  Rocky Mountains (Chief ranges of the Rockies) **R: 394**
Southern snout [butterfly]
  Butterfly *picture on* **B: 737**
Southern Song Academy [Chinese history]
  Painting (Chinese painting) **P: 44-46**
Southern States [region, U.S.] **So: 688b**
  African Americans (The growth of slavery) **A: 136f** *with pictures*; (The antislavery movement) **A: 136h**; (Temporary gains) **A: 136k**; (The growth of discrimination) **A: 136k**; (During the early 1900's) **A: 136l**
  Civil rights (The struggle for the rights of African Americans) **Ci: 609**
  Civil War, American **Ci: 614**
  Dixie **D: 255**
  Reconstruction **R: 176**
  United States *picture on* **U: 108**; (Regions) **U: 99-104** *with map*
  United States, History of the (The abolition movement) **U: 173**; (The nation divided [1850-1869]) **U: 174**; (The South and white supremacy) **U: 183**
Southey, Robert [British poet] **So: 688b**
  Coleridge, Samuel Taylor (His life) **Ci: 771**
  Inchcape Rock **I: 99**
  Lake Poets **L: 44**
  Nelson, Horatio (Victory at Trafalgar) **N: 122**
Southwark [district, Philadelphia]
  Philadelphia (Residential districts) **P: 360**
Southwark [England]
  Shakespeare, William *picture on* **S: 352**; (The Globe Theatre) **S: 348**
Southwest Asia
  Asia (Way of life in Southwest Asia) **A: 774** *with pictures*; (The land) **A: 792**; (Wild animals) **A: 798** *with map*
Southwest Indians
  Indian, American (Indians of the Southwest) **I: 166** *with picture and map*
Southwest Pass
  Mississippi River *picture on* **M: 649**
Southwestern Indian Polytechnic Institute
  Albuquerque (Description) **A: 333**
Southwestern States [region, U.S.] **So: 688b**
  United States (Regions) **U: 99-105** *with picture and map*
Southworth, Billy [American baseball manager]
  Baseball (table: Hall of Fame) **B: 134b**
Souvanna Phouma [Laotian prince]
  Laos (History) **L: 71-72**
Souvenir de Solferino, Un [book by Dunant]
  Red Cross (Beginnings) **R: 187**
Souvenir sheet
  Stamp collecting *picture on* **So: 832**
Souvlaki [food]
  Cyprus (People) **Ci: 1205**
Sovereign [money]
  Money (History of the pound) **M: 709-710** *with picture*
  Pound **P: 721**
Sovereign Grand Inspector General [degree]
  Masonry (The lodges and degrees of Masonry) **M: 267**
Sovereignty [political science] **So: 688b**
  Government (Common elements of government) **G: 288**
  Human rights (The development of human rights) **H: 428-428a**
  International relations **I: 344**
  Territorial waters **T: 173**
  Treaty **T: 408**
Sovereignty association [government]
  Parti Québécois **P: 183**
Soviet [Russian history] **So: 689**
  Lenin, V. I. (The February Revolution) **L: 193**
  Union of Soviet Socialist Republics (National government) **U: 29**; (History) **U: 35**
Soviet literature
  Russian literature (Soviet literature) **R: 564**
Soviet of Nationalities [Soviet history]
  Union of Soviet Socialist Republics (National government) **U: 29**
Soviet of the Union [Soviet history]
  Union of Soviet Socialist Republics (National government) **U: 29**
Soviet of Workers' and Soldiers' Deputies [Russian history]
  Lenin, V. I. (The February Revolution) **L: 193**
  Russian Revolution of 1917 (The February Revolution) **R: 566**
  Union of Soviet Socialist Republics (The February Revolution) **U: 35**
Soviet of Workers' Deputies [Russian history]
  Russia (The Revolution of 1905) **R: 552**

Soviet satellite *See* Satellite [international relations] *in this index*
Soviet Union *See* Union of Soviet Socialist Republics *in this index*
Sovkhozy [agriculture] *See* State farm *in this index*
Sow [animal]
  Hog (table) H: 284
Sow bug [insect]
  Pill bug P: 464
  Wood louse W: 391
Soweto [community, South Africa] So: 689
Sowthistle [plant] So: 689 *with picture*
Soy derivative
  Soybean (Soy meal) So: 690
Soy meal
  Soybean (Soy meal) So: 690
Soy milk [food]
  Asian Americans (Asian influences on American culture) A: 812c
Soy oil
  Soybean (Soy oil) So: 690
  Vegetable oil V: 294
Soy protein concentrate
  Soybean (Soy meal) So: 690
Soya bean [plant] *See* Soybean *in this index*
Soybean [plant] So: 689 *with pictures and map*
  Bean B: 180
  Food supply (Other major food sources) F: 348; (Developing new sources of food) F: 350
  Genetically modified food (Production and consumption) G: 85
  Iowa (Agriculture) I: 389
  Julian, Percy Lavon J: 187
  Missouri (Agriculture) M: 665
  Tofu T: 308
  Vegetable oil V: 294
Soybean curd
  Tofu T: 308
Soybean meal
  Soybean (Soy meal) So: 690
Soyer, Moses [American artist]
  Soyer brothers So: 693
Soyer, Raphael [American artist]
  Soyer brothers So: 693 *with picture*
Soyer brothers [American artists] So: 693 *with picture*
Soyinka, Wole [Nigerian author] So: 693
  Drama (Drama in other countries) D: 341
  Nobel Prizes (Literature: 1986) N: 448
Soyuz missions [space exploration]
  Astronaut (Achievements in space) A: 829
  Rocket (Liquid-propellant rockets) R: 388
  Space exploration (Making ready) So: 715; (Soviet attempts to reach the moon) So: 720 *with picture*; (The Apollo-Soyuz Test Project) So: 721; (Salyut and Skylab) So: 721
Soyuz-TM [spacecraft]
  Mir M: 613 *with picture*
Soyuz-U [spacecraft]
  Space exploration *picture on* So: 699
Spa [resort]
  Bath (Medical bathing) B: 163
  Hungary (Recreation) H: 441
  Hydrotherapy H: 473
  Mineral water M: 572
Spaak, Paul-Henri [Belgian statesman] So: 693
Spaatz, Carl [American general] So: 693
Space [aesthetics]
  Painting (The elements of painting) P: 34-35
  Photography (Space) P: 410
Space [game]
  Division (Fun with division) D: 252
Space [philosophy]
  Metaphysics (Space and time) M: 429
Space [physics]
  Relativity (Lorentz transformations) R: 211
  Sky S: 496
  Space exploration (What is space?) So: 696; (Living in space) So: 701
  United Nations (Peaceful uses of outer space and the seabed) U: 93
  Vacuum V: 256
Space adaptation syndrome [disorder]
  Motion sickness M: 874
  Space exploration (Microgravity) So: 701-702
Space age
  Eisenhower, Dwight David (The space age) E: 154
  Science (Achievements of the mid-1900's) S: 202 *with picture*
  Space exploration (The dawn of the space age) So: 706
  Technology (The computer age) T: 75
  World, History of the (The world since 1900) W: 445 *with picture*
Space and Missile Defense Command/Army Forces Strategic Command
  Army, United States (Army service component

  commands) A: 736-737
Space and Rocket Center, U.S. [Huntsville]
  Alabama (Places to visit) A: 266 *with picture*
  Huntsville H: 451
Space band [printing]
  Linotype (How the linotype works) L: 338
Space exploration So: 694 *with pictures*
  See also the list of Related articles in the Space exploration *article*
  Exploration (Space exploration) E: 451
  International Space Station I: 346a
  Life (In our solar system) L: 280
  Map (Mapmaking and modern technology) M: 185
  Mars (Observation by spacecraft) M: 226c *with picture*
  Mercury (Flights to Mercury) M: 415
  Mir M: 613 *with picture*
  Moon (Apollo missions) M: 795
  Radar (In space travel) R: 67 *with picture*
  Rocket (Space travel) R: 387 *with picture*; (The space age) R: 391
  Satellite (Exploration by spacecraft) S: 150c
  Telemetry T: 93
  Union of Soviet Socialist Republics (Khrushchev's policies) U: 38-39
  United Nations (Peaceful uses of outer space and the seabed) U: 93
  United States, History of the (The space race) U: 196
  Von Braun, Wernher V: 448
  Voyager V: 451
  World, History of the (The world since 1900) W: 445 *with picture*
Space Exploration Technologies [company]
  Rocket (The space age) R: 391
  Space exploration (Developing new spacecraft) So: 728
Space measurement
  Metric system (Space and time) M: 437
Space medicine
  Aerospace medicine A: 89
  Space exploration (Living in space) So: 701 *with pictures*
Space Needle [building]
  Seattle (Landmarks) S: 273 *with picture*
  Washington *picture on* W: 67; (Places to visit) W: 56
Space probe
  Astronomy *picture on* A: 843; (Space probes) A: 846
  Geology (Geology of the solar system) G: 100
  Heliosphere (Probing the heliosphere) H: 175
  Mountain (Measuring mountains) M: 896b
  Rocket (Launching probes and satellites) R: 386
  Satellite (Exploration by spacecraft) S: 150c
  Space exploration So: 694 *with picture*; (Space probes) So: 708 *with pictures*
  Sun (History of modern solar study) So: 986
  Voyager V: 451
Space race [international relations]
  Cold War (The space race) Ci: 768
  Space exploration So: 695; (The space race begins) So: 707
  United States, History of the (The space race) U: 196
Space shuttle
  Astronaut (Achievements in space) A: 829-830
  Challenger disaster C: 370
  Florida (The early 2000's) F: 265 *(with picture)*
  National Aeronautics and Space Administration N: 28
  Rocket (Liquid-propellant rockets) R: 388
  Space exploration *pictures on* So: 695, So: 699, So: 700; (Getting into space and back) So: 698-700 *with diagrams*; (Space shuttles) So: 723 *with pictures*
Space station
  See also International Space Station; Mir *in this index*
  Astronaut (Achievements in space) A: 829-830
  Space exploration (Assembling space stations) So: 704 *with picture*; (Space stations) So: 721 *with pictures*
Space Station Seventh Grade [book by Spinelli]
  Spinelli, Jerry So: 793
Space suit
  Astronaut *picture on* A: 828
  Helmet *picture on* H: 178
  Space exploration (Leaving the spacecraft) So: 704-705 *with pictures*
Space surveillance [defense]
  Radar (In the military) R: 65
Space Surveillance Network
  Radar (In the military) R: 65
Space telescope
  See also Hubble Space Telescope *in this index*

  Spitzer, Lyman, Jr. So: 797
Space-time [mathematics]
  Einstein, Albert E: 146
  Fourth dimension F: 438
  Gravitation (Space-time) G: 331
  Gravitational wave G: 333
  Relativity (Lorentz transformations) R: 211; (General relativity) R: 211-212
  Time (Our understanding of time) T: 292a-292b *with diagram*
Space travel *See* Space exploration *in this index*
Space tug
  Rocket (Space travel) R: 387
Space walk *See* Extravehicular activity *in this index*
Spacecraft
  Engineering (Aerospace engineering) E: 284
  Radar (In space travel) R: 67
  Space exploration So: 694 *with pictures*
Spacek, Sissy [American actress]
  Motion picture (Best performance by an actress: 1980) M: 862
Spacelab [spacecraft]
  Astronaut (Achievements in space) A: 829-830
  Careers *picture on* C: 227
  European Space Agency E: 418
  Space exploration (Spacelab missions) So: 724 *with picture*
Spaceplane [aircraft]
  Airplane (Future developments) A: 239
Spaceport America
  New Mexico (Recent developments) N: 276
SpaceShipOne [rocket]
  Astronaut (Achievements in space) A: 829-830
  Rocket (Hybrid rockets) R: 388-389
  Space exploration *picture on* So: 727; (Private launch services) So: 728
Spacewar! [electronic game]
  Electronic game (Early computer games) E: 204d *with picture*
SpaceX [company] *See* Space Exploration Technologies *in this index*
Spacey, Kevin [American actor]
  Motion picture (Best performance by an actor: 1999) M: 862a; (Best performance by an actor in a supporting role: 1995) M: 862b
S.P.A.D. 13 [airplane]
  Aircraft, Military *picture on* A: 204
Spade [suit]
  Card game (History) C: 209
Spade [tool]
  Gardening (Cultivating an outdoor garden) G: 34
Spade, Sam [literary figure]
  Hammett, Dashiell H: 35
Spade bit [drill]
  Drill (Metal drills) D: 348
Spadefoot toad
  Amphibian *picture on* A: 439
  Frog (Other frogs) F: 540
Spadix [botany]
  Anthurium A: 550
  Jack-in-the-pulpit J: 3
Spadolini, Giovanni [Italian political leader]
  Italy (Political changes) I: 519
Spaghetti
  Pasta P: 192
Spagnoletto, Lo [nickname]
  Ribera, Jusepe de R: 321
Spahn, Warren [American baseball player] So: 729
  Baseball (table: Hall of Fame) B: 134b
Spaight, R. D., Jr. [American political leader]
  North Carolina (table) N: 490
Spaight, Richard Dobbs [American political leader] So: 729
  North Carolina (table) N: 490
Spain So: 730 *with pictures and maps*
  See also the list of Related articles in the Spain *article*
  Flag *pictures on* F: 207, F: 209, F: 217
  Art and architecture
    Spain (The arts) So: 738 *with pictures*
    Furniture (Spain) F: 573 *with picture*
    Painting (The Spanish masters) P: 64 *with pictures*
  Finance and banking
    Euro E: 379
  History
    Spain (History) So: 746 *with pictures*
    Argentina (Settlement and colonial life) A: 655
    Aztec (The Spanish conquest) A: 1003 *with picture*
    Belgium (Habsburg rule) B: 233
    Bolivia (Colonial rule) B: 447
    Bourbon (In Spain) B: 517
    Buenos Aires (History) B: 673
    California (Spanish and Russian settlement) C: 60
    Central America (The colonial period) C: 355

Chile (Colonial period) **C:** 468; (Spanish conquest) **C:** 468
Colombia (History) **Ci:** 783
Colonialism **Ci:** 813; (Early European colonialism) **Ci:** 813; (Later colonialism) **Ci:** 813-814
Columbus, Christopher (Years of waiting) **Ci:** 858
Cuba **Ci:** 1168; (History) **Ci:** 1175
Drake, Sir Francis (Expeditions against Spain) **D:** 322
Ecuador (Spanish rule) **E:** 73
Exploration (The age of European exploration) **E:** 443 with picture
Fascism (Fascism in other countries) **F:** 50
Gibraltar **G:** 186
Haiti (History) **H:** 15-16
Hispanic Americans (Cultural backgrounds) **H:** 247; (History) **H:** 250
Indian, American (In Latin America) **I:** 178
Indian wars (The Pueblo revolt [1680-1692]) **I:** 191
Jews (The Jews under Islam) **J:** 122; (Jews in Christian Europe) **J:** 122-123
Latin America (Colonial discontent) **L:** 106 with diagram
Line of Demarcation **L:** 333
Louisiana Purchase **L:** 502
Mexico (History) **M:** 468-469
Mission life in America **M:** 618 with picture
Monroe Doctrine (Origins) **M:** 739
Netherlands (History) **N:** 148
Pacific Islands (Colonial rule) **P:** 12
Panama (The Spanish colonial period) **P:** 120
Paraguay (History) **P:** 148-149
Peru (History) **P:** 314
Philippines (History) **P:** 379
Pueblo Indians **P:** 870
Renaissance (The Renaissance outside Italy) **R:** 237
Spanish Armada **So:** 755
Spanish Civil War **So:** 756 with map
Tenochtitlan **T:** 167
United States, History of the (The Spanish and Portuguese) **U:** 151
Uruguay (Colonial years) **U:** 227; (Independence) **U:** 227
Virginius Affair **V:** 425
Western Sahara **W:** 241
World War II (The Spanish Civil War) **W:** 472
Language and literature See Spanish language; Spanish literature *in this index*
People
Spain (People) **So:** 733
Sephardim **S:** 307
Social and cultural life
Christmas (In Spain) **C:** 531
Clothing *picture on* **Ci:** 694
Flamenco **F:** 225 with picture
Spalding, Albert G. [American baseball player]
Baseball (table: Hall of Fame) **B:** 134b
Spalding, Eliza [American missionary]
Idaho (Exploration and early settlement) **I:** 42
Spalding, Henry H. [American missionary]
Idaho (Exploration and early settlement) **I:** 42 with picture
Whitman, Marcus **W:** 293
Spallanzani, Lazzaro [Italian biologist] **So:** 753
Food preservation (Modern food preservation) **F:** 344
Spam [advertising]
Advertising (Recent developments) **A:** 80
E-mail **E:** 2
Internet (Glossary of Internet terms) **I:** 350a; (Internet crime) **I:** 350f
Span [engineering]
Bridge **B:** 600
Spandex [fiber] **So:** 753
Spandrel column [construction]
Bridge (Arch bridges) **B:** 601 with diagram
Spangled feather
Chicken (Kinds of chickens) **C:** 441
Spangler, Edward [American public figure]
Lincoln, Abraham (The trial of the conspirators) **L:** 326
Spaniel [dog] **So:** 753
Cavalier King Charles spaniel **C:** 318
Dog (Sporting dogs) **D:** 268 with pictures
Field spaniel **F:** 94 with picture
Sussex spaniel **So:** 1012
Spanish America [Latin America] **So:** 753
Hispanic Americans (Cultural backgrounds) **H:** 247
Spanish-American War [1898] **So:** 753 with picture and map
See also the list of Related articles in the Spanish-American War *article*

Army, United States (The Spanish-American War [1898]) **A:** 738
Buffalo Soldiers **B:** 680
Cuba (Struggle against Spain) **Ci:** 1176
Dewey, George **D:** 176
Gay Nineties (A growing world power) **G:** 72
Latin America (The movement toward independence) **L:** 106-107
Manila Bay **M:** 143
Marine Corps, United States *picture on* **M:** 207; (The 1800's) **M:** 208-209
McKinley, William (The Spanish-American War [1898]) **M:** 340
Navy, United States (The Spanish-American War [1898]) **N:** 88
Paris, Treaties of (The treaty of 1898) **P:** 167
Philippines (The Spanish-American War) **P:** 380
Roosevelt, Theodore (The Rough Riders) **R:** 463
Spain (The reign of Alfonso XIII) **So:** 749
Spanish literature (The 1900's) **So:** 762
United States, History of the *picture on* **U:** 186; (The Spanish-American War) **U:** 185
War (table) **W:** 25
Spanish Armada [European history] **So:** 755 with picture
Bay of Biscay **B:** 176
Drake, Sir Francis (Expeditions against Spain) **D:** 322
Navy (The beginning of modern navies) **N:** 79
Philip II [of Spain] **P:** 369
Ship (The galleon) **S:** 419-420
Spain *picture on* **So:** 749; (The Spanish decline) **So:** 747
Spanish bayonet [tree] **So:** 756
Spanish black [paint]
Cork (Uses) **Ci:** 1055
Spanish chicken
Chicken (table) **C:** 443
Spanish Civil War [1936-1939] **So:** 756 with picture and map
Falange Española **F:** 12
Fifth column **F:** 96
Franco, Francisco (His early life) **F:** 483
Madrid (History) **M:** 40
Picasso, Pablo (The 1920's and 1930's) **P:** 448b-449
Spain (Civil war) **So:** 750
Spanish literature (Spanish literature today) **So:** 763
World War II (The Spanish Civil War) **W:** 472
Spanish Confederation of Autonomous Rightist Parties [political party]
Spain (The Spanish republic) **So:** 750
Spanish-Cuban-American War [1895-1898]
Cuba (Struggle against Spain) **Ci:** 1176
Spanish dollar *See* Piece of eight *in this index*
Spanish flu [disease]
Influenza (Flu epidemics) **I:** 268b
Spanish Hour, The [music by Ravel]
Ravel, Maurice **R:** 151
Spanish Inquisition *See* Inquisition *in this index*
Spanish language So: 756b
Closed captioning **Ci:** 685
Hispanic Americans (Who Hispanic Americans are) **H:** 244; (A rapidly growing minority) **H:** 258
Inflection **I:** 268a
Name (Hispanic names) **N:** 6; (Other family names) **N:** 7
Phonetics (Phonetics and spelling) **P:** 400
Spain (Language) **So:** 733
United States (Language) **U:** 110
Spanish literature So: 757 with pictures
See also the list of Related articles in the Spanish literature *article*
Drama (The Golden Age of Spanish drama) **D:** 332
Hebrew literature (Medieval works) **H:** 162
Spain (Literature) **So:** 738
Spanish lynx [animal] *See* Iberian lynx *in this index*
Spanish mackerel [fish]
Kingfish **K:** 329
Mackerel **M:** 24
Spanish Main [Latin American history] **So:** 764
Pirate (The Caribbean) **P:** 495
Spanish milled dollar
Piece of eight *pictures on* **P:** 452
Spanish moss [plant] **So:** 764
Epiphyte **E:** 344 with picture
Spanish onion
Onion (Cultivation) **O:** 763
Spanish Phalanx [political party] *See* Falange Española *in this index*
Spanish process
Olive (Harvesting and preparation for market) **O:** 743
Spanish Sahara *See* Western Sahara *in this index*

Spanish Socialist Workers' Party *See* Partido Socialista Obrero Español
Spanish Succession, War of the *See* Succession wars *in this index*
Spanish Tragedy, The [play by Kyd]
Drama (Elizabethan playwrights) **D:** 331
English literature (Elizabethan drama) **E:** 317
Kyd, Thomas **K:** 398
Spanish War Veterans, United [organization]
Veterans' organizations (In the United States) **V:** 344
Spanishfly [insect] **So:** 764
Spanworm [caterpillar]
Measuring worm **M:** 346
Spar [pole]
Sailing (Spars) **S:** 23
Spar [ship]
Northwest Passage **N:** 529
Spare [bowling]
Bowling *picture on* **B:** 523; (Scoring) **B:** 521; (table) **B:** 521; (Bowling for spares) **B:** 522
Spark, Muriel [Scottish author] **So:** 764
English literature (Recent English fiction) **E:** 323
Spark chamber [physics]
Particle detector (Spark chambers) **P:** 186
Spark-ignition engine
Diesel engine (How a diesel engine works) **D:** 199
Ignition **I:** 49
Spark of Life [book by Remarque]
Remarque, Erich Maria **R:** 228
Spark plug [device]
Automobile (The engine cycle) **A:** 953 with diagram
Gasoline engine *picture on* **G:** 63; (The ignition system) **G:** 65 with diagram
Ignition (Parts of an ignition system) **I:** 49
Sparkle Plenty doll
Doll (Modern dolls) **D:** 292
Sparkling wine
Champagne **C:** 373
Grape (European grapes) **G:** 318
Wine (Types of wine) **W:** 336; (Clarifying and aging the wine) **W:** 338
Sparkman, John Jackson [American political leader] **So:** 764
Eisenhower, Dwight David (Election of 1952) **E:** 151
Nixon, Richard Milhous (The 1952 campaign) **N:** 430-431
Sparks [rank]
Girl Scouts (Sparks) **G:** 198
Sparks, Chauncey [American political leader]
Alabama (table) **A:** 274
Sparks, John [American political leader]
Nevada (table) **N:** 173
Sparks Street Mall [Ottawa]
Ottawa *picture on* **O:** 874
Sparring partner
Boxing (Boxing skills) **B:** 529
Sparrow [bird] **So:** 764 with pictures
See also House sparrow *in this index*
Bird *pictures on* **B:** 358; (Birds of grasslands) **B:** 336 with picture; (Birds of Asia) **B:** 344f with picture
Sparrowhawk So: 765 with picture
Bird of prey *picture on* **B:** 374b
Hawk **H:** 111
SPARS [U.S.]
Coast Guard, United States (World War II) **Ci:** 737-738; (The Coast Guard since World War II) **Ci:** 738
Sparta [ancient city] **So:** 766 with maps
Education (Ancient Greek education) **E:** 98
Greece, Ancient (Government) **G:** 372 with map; (History) **G:** 372
Lycurgus **L:** 532
Messenia **M:** 423 with map
Peloponnesian War **P:** 232
Pericles (War with Sparta) **P:** 287
Police state **P:** 626
Thirty Tyrants **T:** 259
Women's movement (In ancient societies) **W:** 384
Sparta [modern Greece]
Otto I **O:** 876
Spartacus [Roman gladiator] **So:** 767
Crassus, Marcus Licinius **Ci:** 1121
Spartacus Party [political party]
Luxemburg, Rosa **L:** 532
Spartanburg [South Carolina]
South Carolina (table: Average monthly weather) **So:** 654
Spartans [people]
Greece, Ancient (Education) **G:** 367
Sparta (The people) **So:** 766
Spasm [disorder]
Asthma **A:** 825
Cramp **Ci:** 1116

Tetanus **T: 182b**
Tetany **T: 182b**
Spassky, Boris [Russian chess player]
　Chess (World chess champions) **C: 414**
　Fischer, Bobby **F: 143**
Spastic colon
　Colitis **Ci: 773**
Spastic paralysis So: 767
　Cerebral palsy (Types) **C: 361-362**
　Paralysis (Paralysis of central nervous system origin) **P: 152**
Spathe [botany]
　Anthurium **A: 550**
　Flower *picture on* **F: 294**
　Jack-in-the-pulpit **J: 3**
　Skunk cabbage **S: 496**
Spatial relations aptitude
　Careers (Aptitudes) **C: 215**
Spatter [geology]
　Volcano (Pyroclasts) **V: 439**
Spatter cone [geology]
　Volcano (Pyroclasts) **V: 439**
Spatter rampart [geology]
　Volcano (Spatter) **V: 439**
Spaulding, Huntley N. [American political leader]
　New Hampshire (table) **N: 223**
Spaulding, Rolland H. [American political leader]
　New Hampshire (table) **N: 223**
Spavin [disease] **So: 767**
Spawn [zoology] **So: 767**
　Fish (Reproductive system) **F: 163;** (How fish reproduce) **F: 169**
　Salmon (The life of a salmon) **S: 69** *with picture;* (Salmon conservation) **S: 70**
Spawning [zoology]
　Fish (How fish reproduce) **F: 169** *with pictures*
Spaying
　Cat (Birth control) **C: 295-296**
　Dog (Social and moral responsibilities) **D: 279-280**
　Pet (Birth control) **P: 322**
　Rabbit (Health) **R: 49**
SPCA [organization] *See* Society for the Prevention of Cruelty to Animals *in this index*
"Speak softly and carry a big stick" [quotation]
　Roosevelt, Theodore (Governor of New York) **R: 463**
Speakeasy [bar]
　Prohibition (Life during prohibition) **P: 815**
　Roaring Twenties (Changing attitudes) **R: 363-364**
　United States, History of the (The Lost Generation and Flaming Youth) **U: 190**
Speaker [electronics] **So: 767**
　Computer (Speakers) **Ci: 917**
　Headphones **H: 125**
　Radio (The speaker) **R: 89** *with picture*
　Stereophonic sound system (Parts of a stereo system) **So: 892**
　Telephone (The speaker) **T: 95**
Speaker [office] **So: 767**
　See also Speaker of the House *in this index*
　Canada, Government of (The Senate) **C: 130**
　Parliament (How the House of Commons works) **P: 173**
Speaker, Tris [American baseball player] **So: 768**
　Baseball (table: Hall of Fame) **B: 134b**
Speaker of the House [office]
　Congress of the United States (The House of Representatives) **Ci: 943**
　House of Representatives (The speaker and other leaders) **H: 387**
　Speaker (In the United States) **So: 768**
Speakerphone
　Telephone (Types of telephones) **T: 94-95**
Speakers' Corner [London]
　London (Parks) **L: 435**
Speaking *See* Speech *in this index*
Speaking in tongues [religion]
　Assemblies of God **A: 817**
　Evangelicalism **E: 422**
　Pentecostal churches (Beliefs and practices) **P: 275**
　Religion (Religion today) **R: 223**
Speaking skills
　Public speaking **P: 864**
Spear [weapon] **So: 768** *with pictures*
　Folsom point **F: 326** *with picture*
　Indian, American *pictures on* **I: 140, I: 151**
　Spearfishing **So: 768** *with pictures*
Spear gun
　Spearfishing **So: 768** *with pictures*
Spear thrower [weapon]
　Indian, American *picture on* **I: 144,** *picture on* **I: 172;** (Early days) **I: 151**
Speare, Elizabeth George [American author] **So: 768**

Laura Ingalls Wilder Award (table) **L: 121**
　Newbery Medal (table) **N: 359**
Spearfish [South Dakota]
　Passion play *picture on* **P: 191**
Spearfishing So: 768 *with pictures*
　Indian, American *picture on* **I: 155**
Spearing Fish by Torchlight [painting by Kane]
　Indian, American *picture on* **I: 155**
Spearman, Charles E. [British psychologist]
　Intelligence (Theories of intelligence) **I: 319**
Spearmint [plant] **So: 769** *with picture*
Spears, Britney [American singer] **So: 769**
　Rock music (Teen pop) **R: 380d-381** *with picture*
SPEBSQSA [organization]
　Barbershop quartet singing **B: 107**
Spec, Working on
　Motion picture (Developing the story) **M: 848-849**
Spec car
　Automobile racing (Indy and Champ car racing) **A: 977-978**
Special administrative region
　Hong Kong (The return to Chinese rule) **H: 320**
Special agent
　Federal Bureau of Investigation **F: 62**
Special City
　Korea, North (Local government) **K: 368**
Special committee
　House of Representatives (Committees) **H: 387**
　Parliamentary procedure (Committees) **P: 176**
　United States, Government of the (Committee system) **U: 138**
Special contour milling machine
　Machine tool (Milling) **M: 18**
Special counsel [law] *See* Independent counsel *in this index*
Special court-martial
　Court-martial **Ci: 1104**
Special district [government]
　Local government (Units of local government) **L: 407**
　Metropolitan area (Special districts) **M: 443**
Special Drawing Rights [economics] **So: 770**
Special education So: 770
　Blindness (Education and training) **B: 403**
　Careers (Teaching) **C: 231**
　Disability (Education) **D: 220** *with picture*
　Education (Kinds of education) **E: 87-88** *with picture*
　Gifted children **G: 188**
　Intellectual disability (Treatment) **I: 318**
　Learning disabilities *picture on* **L: 165;** (Diagnosis and treatment) **L: 166**
　School (Other kinds of schools) **S: 182**
Special effects
　Computer graphics (In entertainment and the arts) **Ci: 924g** *with picture*
　Motion picture *pictures on* **M: 854;** (The computer revolution) **M: 872** *with pictures*
　Television (Adding special effects) **T: 112**
　Theater (Lighting methods) **T: 240-241**
Special election
　Recall **R: 174**
Special endorsement
　Negotiable instrument (Endorsement) **N: 119**
Special forces [military]
　Army (Attack) **A: 725**
Special Forces [U.S. Army]
　Army, United States (Special units) **A: 735**
　Commando **Ci: 871**
　Guerrilla warfare (Guerrilla warfare techniqes) **G: 419**
Special handling [service]
　Postal Service, United States (Special handling) **P: 700**
Special-interest group
　City government (Influencing city government) **Ci: 597**
Special jurisdiction [law]
　Court (Types of courts) **Ci: 1101;** (State courts) **Ci: 1102**
Special Libraries Association So: 771
　Library (Special libraries) **L: 250**
Special library
　Library (Special libraries) **L: 250** *with pictures*
Special mission ship
　Navy, United States (Auxiliary ships) **N: 84**
Special Olympics So: 771 *with picture*
Special Operations [military]
　Commando **Ci: 871**
Special Operations Command
　Army, United States (Army service component commands) **A: 736-737**
Special Operations Executive
　World War II (Spies and saboteurs) **W: 494**
Special Political Committee
　United Nations (Committees) **U: 81**

Special prosecutor *See* Independent counsel *in this index*
Special session
　Congress of the United States (When Congress meets) **Ci: 943**
Special student
　Universities and colleges (The student body) **U: 208**
Special Supreme Tribunal [court]
　Greece (Courts) **G: 353**
Special theory of relativity
　Einstein, Albert **E: 146**
　Energy (Energy and matter) **E: 274**
　Motion (Einstein's theories of relativity) **M: 845**
　Relativity **R: 209;** (Special relativity) **R: 210**
Special weapons unit
　Police (Other activities) **P: 621-622** *with picture*
Specialist [role]
　Medicine (Specialty care physicians) **M: 365;** (Primary care physicians) **M: 366**
Specialization [economics]
　Farm and farming (Specialized farms) **F: 30** *with pictures*
　Outsourcing **O: 880**
Specialized farm
　Farm and farming (Specialized farms) **F: 30-32** *with pictures*
Specialized household
　China (Rural life) **C: 482-483**
Specialized magazine
　Magazine (Specialized business magazines) **M: 42**
Specialty camp
　Camping (Organized camping) **C: 96**
Specialty school
　Alternative school **A: 388**
Specialty store
　Retailing (Specialty stores) **R: 265**
Speciation [biology]
　Evolution (Main ideas of evolutionary theory) **E: 426;** (Evolution of new species) **E: 429-430**
Specie [coin]
　Hayes, Rutherford Birchard (Money problems) **H: 121**
Specie Circular [U.S. history]
　Jackson, Andrew (The money surplus) **J: 12-13**
　Van Buren, Martin (The Panic of 1837) **V: 272**
　Wildcat bank **W: 301**
Species [biology]
　Animal (The scientific classification of animals) **A: 472-473;** (How new species are formed) **A: 503**
　Classification, Scientific (Groups in classification) **Ci: 655**
　Creationism (Creationist beliefs) **Ci: 1123**
　Ecology (The role of a species) **E: 54**
　Evolution (Main ideas of evolutionary theory) **E: 426;** (Evolution of new species) **E: 429**
　Extinction **E: 456**
Species diversity
　Biodiversity (Kinds of biodiversity) **B: 310**
Species Plantarum [book by Linnaeus]
　Linnaeus, Carolus **L: 337**
Species rose
　Rose (Types of roses) **R: 474**
Species Survival Plan
　Zoo (Wildlife conservation) **Z: 600**
Specific allergen immunotherapy [medicine]
　Allergy (Treatment) **A: 374**
Specific epiteth [name]
　Flower (Scientific names) **F: 298**
Specific gravity [physics] *See* Gravity, Specific *in this index*
Specific heat capacity [physics]
　Heat (Changes in temperature) **H: 152** *with picture*
Specific illumination [lighting]
　Theater (Lighting methods) **T: 240-241**
Specific immunity [physiology] *See* Acquired immunity *in this index*
Specific learning disability
　Learning disabilities (Types) **L: 165-166**
Specific lien [law]
　Lien **L: 273**
Specific rate
　Vital statistics (Using vital statistics) **V: 429**
Specific rationing
　Rationing **R: 148**
Specific tariff [economics]
　Tariff (Main kinds of tariffs) **T: 43**
Specific weight
　Manometer **M: 166**
Specifications
　Encyclopedia (Preparing specifications) **E: 267**
　Mechanical drawing (Information in the drawing) **M: 353**
Specimen Days [book by Whitman]

Whitman, Walt (His work) **W: 294**
Specimen Ridge [formation]
Yellowstone National Park (The Upper Loop)
Y: 559 *with map*
Specimens of English Dramatic Poets [book by Lamb]
Lamb, Charles (His essays) **L: 50**
Speckled alder [tree]
Alder **A: 339**
Spectacle
Circus (At the circus) **Ci: 562** *with picture*
Drama (Other parts of drama) **D: 325**
Spectacled bear
Bear (Spectacled bears) **B: 186** *with picture*
Spectacled cobra
Cobra **Ci: 742**
Spectacled porpoise
Porpoise **P: 679**
Spectacles *See* Glasses *in this index*
Spectator, The [essays by Addison and Steele]
Addison, Joseph **A: 47**
Magazine (History) **M: 44**
Steele, Sir Richard **So: 882**
Spector, Phil [American record producer]
Rock music (Independent producers) **R: 379**
Spectral class [astronomy]
Star *diagram on* **So: 849**; (Spectral classes)
So: 846
Spectral lines
Astronomy (Spectroscopy) **A: 840**
Planet (Planets in other solar systems) **P: 512-513**
Telescope (Analyzing spectra) **T: 105**
Zeeman effect **Z: 588**
Spectral type [astronomy]
Star (The Hertzsprung-Russell diagram) **So: 845-846**
Spectrograph [instrument]
Hubble Space Telescope (How the telescope works) **H: 403**
Spectrometer **So: 772**
Sun (Analyzing electromagnetic radiation)
So: 983
Telescope (Gathering light for spectrographs)
T: 103
Spectroheliograph [instrument]
Hale, George Ellery **H: 18**
Sun (History of modern solar study) **So: 986**
Spectrometer [instrument] **So: 771** *with diagram*
Atom (How scientists study atoms) **A: 874**
Light (The spectrum of light sources) **L: 284**
Mars Exploration Rover Mission **M: 227**
Spectrophotometer [instrument]
Color (The CIE System of Color Specification)
Ci: 824
Spectrometer **So: 772**
Spectroscope [instrument]
Spectrometer **So: 772**
Spectroscopy [science] **So: 772**
Astronomy (Spectroscopy) **A: 840** *with pictures*
Magnetic resonance imaging **M: 57**
Planet (Planets in other solar systems) **P: 512-513**
Spectrum [optics] **So: 772** *with diagram*
See also Electromagnetic spectrum *in this index*
Astronomy (Spectroscopy) **A: 840**
Color (The relation between color and light)
Ci: 817-818 *with diagram*
Cosmology (The movement of galaxies) **Ci: 1078**
Herzberg, Gerhard **H: 217**
Infrared rays **I: 270**
Light (The spectrum of light sources) **L: 284** *with diagram*
Newton, Sir Isaac (Light and color) **N: 389** *with picture*
Physics (The beginning of modern physics)
P: 440-441
Prism **P: 805** *with picture*
Rainbow (How rainbows appear) **R: 128** *with picture*
Redshift (The Doppler redshift) **R: 192** *with diagram*
Spectrometer **So: 771**
Spectroscopy **So: 772**
Star (Color and temperature) **So: 843-844**
Sun (Analyzing electromagnetic radiation)
So: 983
Telescope (Gathering light for spectrographs)
T: 103; (Analyzing spectra) **T: 105**
Spectrum 7 Energy Corporation
Bush, George Walker (Business career) **B: 722e**
Speculation [economics]
Commodity exchange (Forward and futures contracts) **Ci: 873**
Housing (Private housing) **H: 390**
Merrill, Charles **M: 418**
United States, History of the (The stock market crash of 1929) **U: 191**
Speculations About Jakob [book by Johnson]

German literature (Postwar German literature [1945-1990]) **G: 142**
Speculative mason [person]
Masonry (History) **M: 267**
Speculative risk
Insurance **I: 309**
Speculum [reference]
Encyclopedia (From the 1200's to the 1600's)
E: 268a
Speculum maius [book by Vincent de Beauvais]
Encyclopedia (From the 1200's to the 1600's)
E: 268a
Speech So: 773
Artificial intelligence (Speech and natural language processing) **A: 760**
Communication (Prehistoric times) **Ci: 879**
Dialect **D: 180**
Kinesics **K: 319**
Language **L: 62**
Phonetics **P: 399**
Phonics **P: 400**
Prehistoric people (The development of speech)
P: 752
Pronunciation **P: 820**
Public speaking **P: 864**
A Guide to Speaking Skills **Research Guide: 20**
Speech, Freedom of *See* Freedom of speech *in this index*
Speech clinician [occupation]
Speech therapy **So: 773**
Speech communication [science]
Acoustics **A: 29**
Speech defect
Aphasia **A: 565**
Cleft palate **Ci: 661**
Disability (Speech and language disabilities)
D: 219
Lisping **L: 349**
Speech therapy **So: 773**
Stuttering **S: 934**
Speech-language pathology *See* Speech therapy *in this index*
Speech-language therapy *See* Speech therapy *in this index*
Speech therapy So: 773
Stuttering **S: 934**
Speechreading *See* Lip reading *in this index*
Speed [drug] *See* Methamphetamine *in this index*
Speed [photography] *See* Film speed; Shutter speed *in this index*
Speed [physics]
Animal (Comparative speeds of animals) **A: 489**
Automobile (The transmission) **A: 948-949**
Governor **G: 293**
Mach, Ernst **M: 12b**
Motion (Describing motion) **M: 844**
Transmission **T: 375**
Velocity **V: 297**
Speed governor [mechanics]
Governor **G: 293** *with diagram*
Speed, James [American government official]
Johnson, Andrew (table: Johnson's Cabinet)
J: 140
Justice, Department of (table) **J: 203**
Lincoln, Abraham (table) **L: 323**
Speed of light *See* Light, Speed of *in this index*
Speed of sound *See* Sound, Speed of *in this index*
Speed reading So: 774
Speed record
Aviation (table: Aviation speed records) **A: 990**
Speed skating
Ice skating **I: 10** *with picture*; (Speed skating) **I: 13** *with pictures*
Olympic Games (Winter Olympic Games)
O: 746d-746e
Roller skating (Competitive roller skating) **R: 402a**
Speedcup [mechanics]
Speedometer **So: 775** *with diagram*
Speeding
Radar (In controlling automobile speed and traffic) **R: 67** *with pictures*
Speedometer [instrument] **So: 775** *with diagram*
Speedway race
Kart racing **K: 247**
Speedwell [plant]
Figwort family **F: 97**
Speedwell [ship]
Plymouth Colony (The founding of Plymouth Colony) **P: 582**
Speer, Albert [Nazi leader] **So: 775**
Nuremberg Trials (The trials) **N: 613**
Speke, John Hanning [British explorer]
Exploration (The exploration of Africa) **E: 448** *with map*
Lake Tanganyika **L: 46**
Lake Victoria **L: 48**
Spektr [spacecraft]

Mir **M: 613** *with picture*
Space exploration (Mir) **So: 722**
Spektr-R [radio telescope]
Telescope (Types of radio telescopes) **T: 106-108**
Speleology [geology] **So: 775**
Cave **C: 319**
Speleothem [geology]
Cave **C: 319**
Climate (Speleothems) **Ci: 679**
Spelin [language]
Universal language **U: 205**
Spell
Magic (Magical words) **M: 49**
Witchcraft **W: 371**
Spelling So: 775
English language (Pronunciation and spelling)
E: 312
Phonetics (Phonetics and spelling) **P: 400**
Spelling bee [contest]
Pioneer life in America (Education) **P: 484**
Spelling demon [word]
Spelling (Spelling demons) **So: 777**
Spellings, Margaret [American government official]
Bush, George Walker (table) **B: 722h**
Education, Department of (table) **E: 110**
Spellman, Francis Joseph [American religious leader] **So: 777**
Spellman, John D. [American political leader]
Washington (table) **W: 65**
Spelunker [person]
Cave (Caving) **C: 321**
Speleology **So: 775**
Spemann, Hans [German biologist]
Nobel Prizes (Physiology or medicine: 1935)
N: 445
Spence, Andrew Michael [American economist]
Nobel Prizes (Economics: 2001) **N: 449**
Spence, Catherine Helen [Australian author]
Australia (Literature) **A: 904-905**
Woman suffrage (Australia) **W: 381**
Spencer, Anna Garlin [American social reformer]
So: 777
Spencer, C. M. [American inventor]
Machine tool (History) **M: 20**
Spencer, Lady Diana [British princess] *See* Diana, Princess of Wales *in this index*
Spencer, Herbert [British philosopher] **So: 777**
Social Darwinism **So: 552**
Sociology (Early sociological thought) **So: 566**
Spencer, John C. [American government official]
Tyler, John (table) **T: 534**
Van Buren, Martin (U.S. senator) **V: 271**
Spencer, Octavia [American actress]
Motion picture (Best performance by an actress in a supporting role: 2011) **M: 862b**
Spencer, Platt Rogers [American educator]
Handwriting (Later writing styles) **H: 50**
Spencerian writing
Handwriting (Later writing styles) **H: 50**
Spender, Stephen [British poet] **So: 778**
English literature (Poetry between the wars)
E: 322
Spengler, Oswald [German philosopher] **So: 778**
Civilization (Rise and fall) **Ci: 636**
Spenser [literary figure]
Parker, Robert B. **P: 170**
Spenser, Edmund [English poet] **So: 778**
English literature (Elizabethan poetry) **E: 316-317**
July (Quotations) **J: 189**
May (Quotations) **M: 321**
Spenserian stanza
Spenser, Edmund: *(The Faerie Queene)* **So: 778**
Sperm [biology]
Angiosperm **A: 462**
Animal (Sexual reproduction) **A: 496** *with diagram*
Cell (Meiosis) **C: 331**; (Before 1900) **C: 337**
Corn (How the plant reproduces) **Ci: 1058**
Embryo **E: 257**
Evolution (Mutation) **E: 427-428**
Fertilization **F: 78**
Heredity (Chromosomes and genes) **H: 201**
Human body (The reproductive system) **H: 425**
In vitro fertilization **I: 95**
Infertility (Causes) **I: 265**
Plant (Flowers) **P: 531**; (The reproduction of plants) **P: 532** *with diagrams*
Prostate gland **P: 830**
Reproduction (Through sexual reproduction)
R: 242; (How reproduction has evolved) **R: 243** *with picture*
Reproduction, Human (The human reproductive system) **R: 244-245**; (Fertilization) **R: 246**; (Development of the embryo) **R: 246-248** *with picture*
Seed (How seeds develop) **S: 281**

Sexuality (Before birth) S: 338
Testicle T: 182
Vasectomy V: 287
Sperm oil [animal product]
Sperm whale So: 779
Whale (American whaling) W: 262
Sperm web [zoology]
Spider (Courtship and mating) So: 787
Sperm whale [sea animal] So: 778
Ambergris A: 405
Antarctica (Living things) A: 534-535 *with picture*
Spermaceti So: 779
Whale *picture on* W: 257; (Sperm whales) W: 258;
(American whaling) W: 262
Spermaceti [animal product] So: 779
Whale (American whaling) W: 262-263
Spermatophore [biology]
Salamander (The life of a salamander) S: 60
Spermatozoa [biology]
Fertilization F: 78
Spermicide [birth control]
Birth control (Methods of birth control) B: 378-
379
Sperrin Mountains [Northern Ireland]
Northern Ireland (Surface features) N: 523 *with
map*
Sperry, Armstrong [American author]
Newbery Medal (table) N: 359
Sperry, Elmer Ambrose [American inventor]
So: 779
Gyrocompass G: 453
Gyroscope (History) G: 454
Sperry, Lawrence [American inventor]
Automatic flight control system (History) A: 944
Sperry, Roger Wolcott [American physiologist]
Nobel Prizes (Physiology or medicine: 1981)
N: 446
Sperry Gyroscope Company
Automatic flight control (History) A: 944
Sperry Rand Corporation
Ford, Hannibal Choate F: 379
Spessartite [gem]
Garnet G: 45
Speusippus [nephew of]
Plato (Plato's place in Western thought) P: 569
Speyer, Diet of [European history]
Protestantism P: 833
SPF [physiology] *See* Sun protection factor *in this
index*
Sphagnum moss [plant]
Peat moss P: 225
Sphalerite [mineral] So: 779
Zinc Z: 594
Sphenoid bone [anatomy]
Head *diagram on* H: 123
Human body (table) H: 422 *with diagram*
Skull S: 495
Sphenoid sinus [anatomy]
Sinus S: 474 *with diagram*
Sphere [geology]
Earth (Earth's spheres) E: 18 *with pictures*
Sphere [geometry] So: 779 *with diagram*
Diameter D: 180
Geometry *picture on* G: 104; (Non-Euclidean
geometry) G: 105 *with diagram*
Topology (Algebraic topology) T: 332 *with picture*
Spherical aberration [optics]
Aberration (Point aberration) A: 10 *with diagram*
Spherical triangle
Trigonometry T: 442; (Spherical trigonometry)
T: 444 *with diagram*
Spherical trigonometry
Trigonometry (Spherical trigonometry) T: 444
with diagram
Spheroid [geometry] So: 780
Sphincter [anatomy]
Eye (The uveal tract) E: 460-461 *with picture*
Sphincter of Oddi [anatomy]
Gallbladder G: 14
Sphinx [mythological creature] So: 780 *with
pictures*
Oedipus O: 676 *with picture*
Pyramids (The pyramids of Giza) P: 917
"Sphinx, The" [poem by Emerson]
Emerson, Ralph Waldo (His poetry) E: 259
Sphinx cat
Cat (Short-haired breeds) C: 290-292
Sphinx moth *See* Hawk moth *in this index*
Sphygmomanometer [instrument]
Blood pressure B: 416
Manometer M: 166
Spica [star] So: 781
Spice So: 781
Spice Islands [Indonesia]
Exploration (Magellan's globe-circling
expedition) E: 445
Indonesia (The Molucca Islands) I: 234

Magellan, Ferdinand (Planning the expedition)
M: 46
Spicule [sun]
Sun *picture on* So: 985; (Chromosphere) So: 980;
(Solar activity) So: 980-982
Spicule [zoology]
Sponge (Skeleton) So: 799
Spider So: 782 *with pictures*
Animal *pictures on* A: 475, A: 480, A: 491
Arachnid A: 590b
Arthropod A: 752 *with picture*
Black widow B: 391 *with picture*
Brown recluse B: 645 *with picture*
First aid (Injected poisons) F: 137-138
Tarantula T: 42 *with picture*
Trap-door spider T: 402 *with picture*
Spider [computing]
Search engine S: 269
Spider crab [animal]
Animal *picture on* A: 486
Spider fish
Tripod fish T: 447
Spider-Man [fictional character] So: 791 *with
picture*
Spider monkey So: 791
Animal *picture on* A: 480
Monkey *picture on* M: 727
Spider plant
Gardening *picture on* G: 37
Spidering [computing]
Information retrieval (How information retrieval
works) I: 268b
Spiderling [zoology]
Spider *picture on* So: 787; (Spiderlings) So: 788
Spiegel Grove [home of]
Hayes, Rutherford Birchard (Later years) H: 121
Spiegeleisen [metal]
Iron and steel (The birth of modern steelmaking)
I: 450-451
Spiegelman, Art [American cartoonist] So: 791
American literature (Popular genres) A: 425
Comics (The new comics) Ci: 870
Graphic novel G: 323 *with picture*
Spielberg, Steven [American director] So: 791
Animation (The animation revival) A: 514c; (The
computer revolution) A: 514c
Lucas, George L: 513
Motion picture (Best achievement in directing:
1993, 1998) M: 862; (A new generation of
filmmakers) M: 871
Williams, John W: 310
Spier, Peter [American artist]
Caldecott Medal (table: 1978) C: 26
Spike [botany]
Inflorescence I: 268a
Spike [sports]
Volleyball (The game) V: 445 *with picture*
Spike-tooth harrow [agricultural implement]
Harrow H: 77
Spikelet [botany]
Oats (The oat plant) O: 640
Spiker [machine]
Cotton (Cleaning and blending) Ci: 1091
Spikes
Baseball (Equipment) B: 125
Špilberk fortress [Czech Republic]
Brno B: 634
Spillway [passage]
Dam (Dam safety) D: 19 *with picture*
Spin [physics]
Fermion F: 74
Subatomic particle (Kinds of subatomic particles)
So: 937
Spin-casting [manufacturing]
Telescope *picture on* T: 108; (Reflecting
telescopes) T: 104-105
Spin-casting reel
Fishing (Reels) F: 176 *with picture*
Spin cycle
Washing machine W: 45
Spin ice [material]
Magnetism (Magnetic monopoles) M: 61
Spin magnetic field [physics]
Magnetism (In atoms) M: 60b
Spina bifida [birth defect] So: 792
Folic acid F: 315
Reproduction, Human (Development of organs
and organ systems) R: 248
Spinach [plant] So: 792
Vegetable (Leaves) V: 292 *with picture*
Spinach jade [mineral]
Jade (Nephrite) J: 20
Spinal anesthesia
Anesthesia (Local anesthesia) A: 458
Spinal column *See* Spine *in this index*
Spinal cord [anatomy]
Nervous system *diagram on* N: 134; (The central

nervous system) N: 132-133 *with diagram*
Brain B: 550a
Cerebrospinal fluid C: 362
Encephalitis E: 265
Human body (table) H: 422 *with diagram*
Meningitis M: 400
Multiple sclerosis M: 920
Pain (How the body feels pain) P: 21-22
Paralysis (Paralysis of central nervous system
origin) P: 152
Poliomyelitis (Kinds of poliomyelitis) P: 626
Reproduction, Human (Development of organs
and organ systems) R: 248
Shaken baby syndrome S: 343
Spine So: 792
Spinal nerve [anatomy]
See also Spinal cord *in this index*
Amyotrophic lateral sclerosis A: 447
Cerebral palsy (Treatment) C: 361-362
Nervous system (The peripheral nervous system)
N: 133 *with diagram*
Reflex action (How reflex action occurs) R: 195
Spinal reflex [physiology]
Human body (The central nervous system) H: 425
Nervous system (Simple pathways) N: 134
Spinal tap [medicine]
Cerebrospinal fluid C: 362
Meningitis (Symptoms and diagnosis) M: 401
Spindle [biology]
Cell (Mitosis) C: 330 *with pictures*
Spindle [tool]
Spinning So: 794
Spindle picker [machine]
Cotton (Harvesting) Ci: 1090
Spindletop oil field [Texas]
Beaumont B: 191
Texas (The early 1900's) T: 207 *with picture*
Spine [anatomy] So: 792 *with diagram*
Chiropractic C: 514
Human being (Physical characteristics) H: 413-
414
Human body (table) H: 422 *with diagram*
Hunchback H: 437
Mammal (Skeleton) M: 118-119
Physical fitness (Flexibility of the spine) P: 434
Rib R: 320
Sciatica S: 190
Scoliosis S: 209
Skeleton (The axial skeleton) S: 479 *with
diagrams*
Spina bifida So: 792
Spine [botany]
Leaf (Protective leaves) L: 156 *with picture*
Plant (How plants protect themselves) P: 541
Spine [zoology]
Chordate C: 522
Hedgehog H: 164
Tetrapod T: 182b
Vertebrate V: 340
Spinebill [bird]
Bird (Birds of Australia and New Zealand) B: 346
with picture
Spinelli, Jerry [American author] So: 793
Newbery Medal (table) N: 359
Spinet [musical instrument]
Piano (Upright pianos) P: 447
Spingarn, Joel Elias [American author] So: 793
Spingarn Medal [award] So: 793
Spingarn, Joel Elias So: 793
Spinifex [grass]
Australia *picture on* A: 894
Spinnaker [sail]
Sailing (Sails) S: 24; (Trimming and tacking) S: 26
Spinner [lure]
Fishing *picture on* F: 177; (Artificial bait) F: 178
Spinner dolphin [sea animal]
Dolphin (Other species) D: 297
Spinneret [biology]
Butterfly (The larva) B: 741 *with picture*
Moth (The larva) M: 839
Spider *pictures on* So: 784; (How spiders make
silk) So: 786 *with picture*
Spinneret [machine]
Rayon (How rayon is made) R: 153 *with diagram*
Spinning [thread] So: 794 *with picture*
Cotton *picture on* Ci: 1092; (Spinning) Ci: 1091
Crompton, Samuel Ci: 1151
Industrial Revolution (Spinning machines) I: 248
Rhode Island (Industrial expansion) R: 313
Slater, Samuel S: 501
Spinning frame
Cotton *picture on* Ci: 1092
Textile *picture on* T: 216
Spinning jenny [machine] So: 795
Clothing (Factory-made clothing) Ci: 691
Cotton (In England) Ci: 1092
Hargreaves, James H: 60 *with picture*

Industrial Revolution (Spinning machines)
I: 248-249
Spinning (The spinning jenny) **So:** 794
Spinning lure *See* Spinner *in this index*
Spinning mule [machine]
Cotton (In England) **Ci:** 1092
Crompton, Samuel **Ci:** 1151
Industrial Revolution (Spinning machines)
I: 248-249
Spinning (The mule) **So:** 794
Spinning reel
Fishing (Reels) **F:** 176 *with picture*
Spinning wheel
Industrial Revolution (Spinning machines)
I: 248-249
Spinning (Early spinning wheels) **So:** 794 *with
picture*
Spinone Italiano [dog] **So:** 795
Spinoza, Baruch [Dutch philosopher] **So:** 795
Philosophy (Rationalism) **P:** 388
Spiny anteater *See* Echidna *in this index*
Spiny dogfish
Dogfish **D:** 283 *with picture*
Spiny eel
Fish *picture on* **F:** 156
Spiny-finned fish
Fish *pictures on* **F:** 149; (Bony fish) **F:** 147
Spiny-headed worm *See* Acanthocephala *in this
index*
Spiny lobster
Crustacean *picture on* **Ci:** 1163
Lobster **L:** 405
Spiny mouse
Mouse (Unusual mice) **M:** 902
Spiny puffer [fish] *See* Porcupinefish *in this index*
Spiny softshell turtle
Turtle (Softshell turtles) **T:** 523 *with picture*
Spiny-tailed iguana
Iguana **I:** 50
Spiny-tailed lizard
Desert *picture on* **D:** 155
Spiracle [biology]
Animal (Adaptations for breathing) **A:** 491-492
with picture
Ant (Internal organs) **A:** 522 *with diagram*
Beetle (The abdomen) **B:** 216
Butterfly (The respiratory system) **B:** 739 *with
diagram*
Fly (Abdomen) **F:** 309
Grasshopper (The body) **G:** 327-328 *with diagram*
Insect *diagram on* **I:** 286; (Respiratory system)
I: 289 *with diagram*
Mosquito (Abdomen) **M:** 832
Moth (The abdomen) **M:** 838 *with diagram*
Spider (Respiratory system) **So:** 785
Spiraea [botany] *See* Spirea *in this index*
Spiral fracture [injury]
Fracture **F:** 450 *with diagram*
Spiral galaxy [astronomy]
Andromeda Galaxy **A:** 457
Astronomy (Discovering other galaxies) **A:** 848
Galaxy (Types of galaxies) **G:** 8a *with picture*
Local Group **L:** 409
Milky Way (Shape of the galaxy) **M:** 550
Triangulum Galaxy **T:** 439
Spirant [pronunciation]
Consonant **Ci:** 992
Spire [architecture] **So:** 795
Spire [zoology]
Shell *diagram on* **S:** 385
Spirea [shrub]
Flower (Flowering shrubs) **F:** 281 *with picture*
Spirilla [biology]
Bacteria (The structure of bacteria) **B:** 20
Spirit [being]
Angel **A:** 459
Ghost **G:** 182
Ouija board **O:** 878
Spiritualism **So:** 796
Witchcraft (Witchcraft as sorcery) **W:** 371
Spirit [spacecraft]
Mars (Observation by spacecraft) **M:** 226c-226d
Mars Exploration Rover Mission **M:** 227
Space exploration *picture on* **So:** 709; (Probes to
Mars) **So:** 710
"Spirit, The" [comic strip]
Eisner, Will **E:** 155
Spirit baptism [religion]
Pentecostal churches (Beliefs and practices)
P: 275
Spirit Island [Alberta]
Canada *picture on* **C:** 115
Spirit Lake
Iowa (Rivers and lakes) **I:** 386
Spirit of America [automobile]
Breedlove, Craig **B:** 593
Spirit of Christianity, The [book by Chateaubriand]

Chateaubriand, François-René de **C:** 387
Spirit of Saint Louis [airplane]
Airplane (Fliers of the golden age) **A:** 237
Lindbergh, Charles Augustus (His historic flight)
L: 330 *with picture*
Spirit of Saint Louis, The [book by Lindbergh]
Lindbergh, Charles Augustus (After the war)
L: 331
Spirit of '76 [painting by Willard] **So:** 795 *with
picture*
Spirit of Sweetwater, The [book by Garland]
Garland, Hamlin **G:** 43
Spirit of the Laws, The [book by Montesquieu]
Enlightenment (The orderliness of nature)
E: 326a-326b
Freedom (During the Enlightenment) **F:** 503
Montesquieu **M:** 764
Spirit of the Nation, The [poems]
Irish literature (Early works in English) **I:** 431
Spirit power [religion]
Indian, American (Religion) **I:** 146-147; (After
European contact) **I:** 159-160
Religion (Belief in a deity) **R:** 215
Spirit Sands [Manitoba]
Manitoba (Places to visit) **M:** 152
Spirit varnish
Varnish (Types of varnish) **V:** 286
Spirit vinegar *See* Vinegar *in this index*
Spirit worship
Animism **A:** 514d
Spirit wrestlers [religious group]
Doukhobors **D:** 314
Spirited Away [film]
Animation (New diversity) **A:** 514c
Spirits *See* Alcoholic beverage *in this index*
Spirits of camphor
Camphor **C:** 91
Spiritual [music] **So:** 796
Burleigh, Harry Thacker **B:** 707
Folk music (Kinds of folk music) **F:** 321
Gospel music **G:** 277
Popular music (The American Civil War [1861-
1865]) **P:** 669-670
Spiritual Exercises [book by Loyola]
Loyola, Saint Ignatius **L:** 511
"Spiritual Laws" [essay by Emerson]
Emerson, Ralph Waldo (His prose works) **E:** 259
Spiritual Milk for Boston Babes [book by Cotton]
Literature for children (The Puritans) **L:** 362
Spiritualism [belief] **So:** 796
Argentina (Religion) **A:** 651
Psychical research **P:** 846
Religion (Religion today) **R:** 223-224
Spiritualist, The [book by Gautier]
French literature (Gautier and Nerval) **F:** 521
Spiritualists [art]
Abstract art **A:** 18
Spirituals [religion]
Franciscans **F:** 482
Spirochete [microorganism]
Bacteria (The structure of bacteria) **B:** 20-21 *with
picture*
Relapsing fever **R:** 209
Syphilis **So:** 1069
Yaws **Y:** 553
Spirogram
Spirometer **So:** 797
Spirometer [instrument] **So:** 797
Asthma **A:** 825
Chronic obstructive pulmonary disease **C:** 539
Spirula squid
Shell (Octopuses and squids) **S:** 388
Spit [geography]
Beach **B:** 185
Lagoon **L:** 30
Spitfire [airplane]
Aircraft, Military (World War II [1939-1945]) **A:** 205
World War II *picture on* **W:** 485; (The Battle of
Britain) **W:** 476
Spitsbergen [island, Arctic]
Exploration (The search for a northern passage)
E: 446
Svalbard **So:** 1014
Spittelau viaduct [structure]
Hadid, Zaha **H:** 4 *with picture*
Spitteler, Carl [Swiss author]
Nobel Prizes (Literature: 1919) **N:** 447
Spitting cobra [snake]
Cobra **Ci:** 741
Snake *picture on* **S:** 526; (Protection against
predators) **S:** 531
Spitz [dog] **So:** 797
Finnish spitz **F:** 119 *with picture*
Spitz, Mark [American swimmer]
Olympic Games (Terrorism in Munich) **O:** 752
Swimming (History) **So:** 1047
Spitz Incorporated [company]

Planetarium (Modern planetariums)
P: 514b-514c
Spitzer, Eliot [American political leader]
New York (table) **N:** 313; (The early 2000's) **N:** 320
Spitzer, Lyman, Jr. [American astrophysicist]
So: 797
Spitzer Space Telescope
Observatory (Satellite observatories) **O:** 645
Spix's macaw [bird]
Endangered species (Wildlife trade) **E:** 269
SPLA [political group] *See* Sudan People's
Liberation Army *in this index*
Splat [device]
Furniture (China) **F:** 571 *with picture*
Spleen [anatomy] **So:** 797
Blood (Destruction of worn-out blood
components) **B:** 411
Frog *picture on* **F:** 537
Immune system *diagram on* **I:** 88a
Iron (How bodies use iron) **I:** 435
Lymphatic system (Lymphoid tissue) **L:** 534 *with
diagram*
Thymus **T:** 274
Splendid first strike [warfare]
Nuclear weapon (Mutually assured destruction)
N: 600
Splendid isolation [British history]
United Kingdom (Gladstone and Disraeli) **U:** 69
Splenectomy [medicine]
Spleen **So:** 797
Splice [knot]
Knots, hitches, and splices (Useful knots) **K:** 356
with diagram
Splicing
Cable (Cable installation) **C:** 5
Knots, hitches, and splices **K:** 355
Splint [device]
First aid (Fractures and dislocations) **F:** 140
Split [Croatia] **So:** 797
Split [sports]
Bowling *picture on* **B:** 523; (table) **B:** 521
Split [stocks]
Dow Jones averages **D:** 316
Split complementary colors
Color (Producing color harmony) **Ci:** 823-824
with diagram
Split end
Football (The offensive team) **F:** 356 *with
diagrams*
Split herring [food]
Herring (Uses) **H:** 216
Split-image prism [optics]
Photography (Types of lenses) **P:** 411
Split income [taxation]
Income tax (History of U.S. income taxes) **I:** 105
Split infinitive [grammar]
Adverb (Adverbs that split an infinitive) **A:** 71
Infinitive **I:** 265
Split-leaved philodendron [plant]
Gardening *picture on* **G:** 37
Split-letter system
Encyclopedia (Arrangement of content) **E:** 266
Split pattern
Cast and casting (Patterns for casting) **C:** 278
Split pea
Pea (Kinds of peas) **P:** 205
Split Rock Lighthouse [Minnesota]
Lake Superior (Description) **L:** 45 *with map*
Split screen
Television (Adding special effects) **T:** 112
Split ticket
Ballot (In the United States) **B:** 63
Splitter [device]
Lumber *picture on* **L:** 520
Splitting [industrial process]
Leather (Final processing) **L:** 168 *with picture*
Spock, Benjamin McLane [American doctor]
So: 797
Spode, Josiah [British potter]
Porcelain (English porcelain) **P:** 677
Spodosol [soil]
Soil *map on* **So:** 575; (How soils are classified)
So: 576
Spohr, Louis [German musician]
Opera: (*Faust*) **O:** 804
Spoil [mining]
Mining (Area mining) **M:** 575 *with diagram*
Spoilage
Food preservation (How food spoils) **F:** 341
Spoiled hay
Gardening (Analyzing the soil) **G:** 31-32
Spoiler [device]
Airplane (The wing) **A:** 213-214
Glider (Landing) **G:** 230
Spoils [mining]
Coal (Strip mining) **Ci:** 722
Spoils system [politics] **So:** 798

Arthur, Chester Alan (Custom house collector)
A: 755-756
Civil service (History) **Ci:** 613
Cleveland, Grover (Reforms) **Ci:** 670
Foreign Service (Beginnings) **F:** 388-388a
Grant, Ulysses S. (Political corruption) **G:** 315
Jackson, Andrew (The spoils system) **J:** 10
Jefferson, Thomas (New policies) **J:** 83-84
Patronage **P:** 198
Spokane [Washington] **So:** 798 *with picture*
Washington (Average monthly weather) **W:** 61
Spokane Falls [settlement]
Spokane (Government and history) **So:** 798
Spokane House [U.S. history]
Washington (Settlement) **W:** 66
Spoke [weaving]
Basket making (Methods) **B:** 141
Spoleto Festival USA
South Carolina *picture on* **So:** 651
Sponge [bread]
Bread (How yeast bread is made) **B:** 588-589
Sponge [sea animal] **So:** 799 *with pictures*
Animal (A classification of the animal kingdom)
A: 506 *with picture*
Deep sea (Invertebrates) **D:** 82a-82b *with picture*
Larva **L:** 78
Marine biology (What marine biologists do)
M: 204
Reproduction (Through asexual reproduction)
R: 242
Sponge rubber
Rubber (Sponge rubber) **R:** 505
Spongebob Squarepants Movie, The [film]
Animation (New diversity) **A:** 514c-514d
Spongin
Sponge (Skeleton) **So:** 799
Spongy tissue [botany]
Leaf (Photosynthesis) **L:** 155 *with diagram*
Sponson [boat]
Hydroplane **H:** 471
Motorboat racing (Hull designs) **M:** 876 *with picture*
Sponsor [advertising]
Advertising (Sponsorship) **A:** 76
Radio (Stations and networks) **R:** 90
Sponsored magazine
Magazine (Other magazines) **M:** 42-43
Spontaneous abortion *See Miscarriage in this index*
Spontaneous combustion [chemistry]
Combustion **Ci:** 867
Fire (Kinds of fire) **F:** 120
Hay **H:** 115
Spontaneous emission [physics]
Laser (Producing laser light) **L:** 84
Spontaneous generation So: 801
Biogenesis **B:** 312
Leeuwenhoek, Anton van **L:** 181
Life (Spontaneous generation) **L:** 278
Spontaneous nuclear transformation [physics]
Curie **Ci:** 1194
Spoon [fishing]
Fishing *picture on* **F:** 177; (Bait) **F:** 178
Spoon [utensil]
Africa *picture on* **A:** 116
Indian, American *picture on* **I:** 156
Spoon-billed catfish *See Paddlefish in this index*
Spoon gourd [plant]
Gourd *picture on* **G:** 281
Spoon River
Illinois (Rivers and lakes) **I:** 64-66
Spoon River Anthology [poems by Masters]
Masters, Edgar Lee **M:** 297
Spoonbill [bird] **So:** 801 *with picture*
Bird *picture on* **B:** 363
Florida *picture on* **F:** 256
Shoveler **S:** 437
Sporades [islands, Aegean Sea]
Aegean Sea **A:** 83 *with map*
Sporangiophore [fungus]
Fungi (Parts of a fungus) **F:** 558-559 *with diagram*
Sporangium [biology]
Fern (Parts of a fern) **F:** 74-75 *with picture*
Fungi (Parts of a fungus) **F:** 558-559 *with diagram*
Mold **M:** 690
Plant (Sexual reproduction) **P:** 532-533 *with pictures*
Spore (Plant spores) **So:** 801
Spore [biology] **So:** 801 *with pictures*
Alternation of generations **A:** 388
Anthrax **A:** 545
Bacteria (Where bacteria live) **B:** 21
Club moss **Ci:** 715
Fern **F:** 74
Fungi (Parts of a fungus) **F:** 558-559 *with diagram*
Lichen (How lichens grow) **L:** 269
Mold **M:** 690

Moss (How mosses live) **M:** 834-835
Mushroom (Parts of a mushroom) **M:** 942 *with picture*; (How a mushroom grows) **M:** 942 *with pictures*
Plant (Sexual reproduction) **P:** 532-533 *with diagram*
Protozoan (Reproduction) **P:** 837
Pteridophyte **P:** 854
Reproduction (Fungi) **R:** 243
Rust **R:** 567
Seed (How seeds develop) **S:** 281
Sporidium [botany]
Rust **R:** 567
Sporophyte [botany]
Alternation of generations **A:** 388
Bryophyte **B:** 656
Fern (Life cycle of a fern) **F:** 75 *with picture*
Hornwort **H:** 341
Liverwort **L:** 396
Moss (How mosses live) **M:** 834-835
Plant (Sexual reproduction) **P:** 532-533 *with diagram*
Spore (Plant spores) **So:** 801
Sport [genetics]
Fruit (Developing new fruit cultivars) **F:** 548
Sport [recreation] *See Sports in this index*
Sport aikido [sport]
Aikido **A:** 167
Sport balloon
Balloon (Gas balloons) **B:** 58 *with picture*; (Sport ballooning) **B:** 60
Sport climbing
Climbing (Technical climbing) **Ci:** 680
Sport fisherman [boat]
Boating *picture on* **B:** 430
Sport of kings [name for]
Horse racing (History) **H:** 366
Sport of the Gods, The [book by Dunbar]
Dunbar, Paul Laurence **D:** 383
Sport parachuting *See Skydiving in this index*
Sport shoe
Shoe (Kinds of shoes) **S:** 431 *with picture*
Sport utility vehicle So: 802
Automobile *picture on* **A:** 971; (Safety problems) **A:** 961-962; (The 2000's) **A:** 972
Sporting dog
Dog *pictures on* **D:** 268; (Sporting dogs) **D:** 266
Sports So: 802
See also the list of Related articles in the Sports article
Careers (Sports and entertainment) **C:** 230 *with picture*
Doping **D:** 309
Gambling (Sports betting) **G:** 20
Hall of fame *picture on* **H:** 24; (Sports halls of fame) **H:** 23
Handicap **H:** 45
Hobby (Games and sports) **H:** 273
Indian, American (Current issues) **I:** 182-183
Lawn (Types of lawns) **L:** 142
Olympic Games **O:** 746 *with pictures*
Radio (Information) **R:** 86
Safety (Safety at school) **S:** 11-12; (Safety in recreation) **S:** 12
Sports medicine **So:** 803
Television (Professional sports) **T:** 121
Sports acrobatics
Gymnastics (Sports acrobatics) **G:** 450; (Judging) **G:** 450-451
Sports car [automobile] **So:** 803 *with pictures*
Automobile *picture on* **A:** 967
Automobile racing (Sports car racing) **A:** 977 *with pictures*
Tire *picture on* **T:** 296
SPORTS CAR [organization]
Automobile racing (Racing organizations) **A:** 976
Sports Car Club of America
Automobile racing (Racing organizations) **A:** 976
Sports medicine So: 803
Sports Palace [Rome]
Nervi, Pier Luigi **N:** 131
Rome *picture on* **R:** 430
Sportsman's Sketches, A [book by Turgenev]
Russian literature (Early realism) **R:** 562
Sportswear
Clothing (The 1900's and 2000's) **Ci:** 705
Spot [fish] **So:** 804 *with picture*
Spot announcement
Advertising (Television) **A:** 73
Spot-billed pelican [bird]
Pelican (Pelicans and people) **P:** 231
Spot blotch [plant disease]
Barley (Diseases and insect pests) **B:** 113
Spot bowling
Bowling (Aiming) **B:** 522
Spot market [economics]
Commodity exchange (Cash market contracts)

Ci: 873
Cotton (Selling) **Ci:** 1091
Spot removing
Dry cleaning (How clothes are dry cleaned)
D: 368
Spot time
Advertising (Television) **A:** 73
Spotlight
Theater (Lighting methods) **T:** 240-241
Spotswood, Alexander [American colonial official]
So: 804
Spotsylvania Court House, Battle of [1864]
Civil War, American (table) **Ci:** 624; (Battle of Spotsylvania Court House) **Ci:** 631
Grant, Ulysses S. (Grant in command) **G:** 315
Spotted alder [shrub]
Witch hazel **W:** 371
Spotted bass [fish]
Bass (Black bass) **B:** 157 *with picture*
Spotted cucumber beetle
Beetle *picture on* **B:** 218
Spotted eagle ray [fish]
Fish *picture on* **F:** 153
Spotted fever, Rocky Mountain *See Rocky Mountain spotted fever in this index*
Spotted goatfish
Fish *picture on* **F:** 154
Spotted harrier [bird]
Harrier **H:** 67
Spotted hyena [animal]
Hyena **H:** 474 *with picture*
Spotted knapweed [plant] **So:** 804
Spotted owl [bird] **So:** 804
Animal *picture on* **A:** 478
Owl (Important owls) **O:** 884-886
Spotted pardalote [bird]
Bird (Birds of Australia and New Zealand) **B:** 346 *with picture*
Spotted salamander
Salamander *picture on* **S:** 59
Spotted sandpiper
Bird (Birds of inland waters and marshes) **B:** 340 *with picture*
Sandpiper **S:** 109
Spotted seatrout
Drum **D:** 367
Spotted skunk
Skunk **S:** 496
Spotted spurge [plant]
Spurge **So:** 810
Spotted Swine
Hog (Kinds of hogs) **H:** 285 *with picture*; (table)
H: 286
Spotted Tail [American Indian leader] **So:** 804 *with portrait*
Spotted touch-me-not [plant]
Flower *picture on* **F:** 285
Spotted towhee [bird]
Towhee **T:** 351
Spotter [person]
Trampoline **T:** 369 *with picture*
Spousal revenge infanticide [homicide]
Infanticide **I:** 264
Spouse abuse
Marriage (Marriage problems) **M:** 221
Spout [zoology]
Whale (Respiratory system) **W:** 259-260 *with picture*
Sprague, Charles A. [American political leader]
Oregon (table) **O:** 845
Sprague, Frank Julian [American engineer]
Electric railroad (History) **E:** 188-189
Sprague, William [American political leader]
Rhode Island (table) **R:** 311
Sprague's pipit [bird]
Pipit **P:** 492
Sprain [injury] **So:** 805
Joint **J:** 155
Ligament **L:** 281
Sprat [fish] **So:** 805
Spray-drying
Food preservation (Drying) **F:** 342-343
Spray foam insulation
Insulation (In buildings) **I:** 306 *with picture*
Spray gun [tool]
Airbrush **A:** 201
Paint (Applying the paint) **P:** 25 *with picture*
Spray pond
Electric power (Fossil-fueled steam electric power plants) **E:** 183
Spray skirt [device]
Kayaking **K:** 250a *with picture*
Spraying [agriculture]
Airplane (Special-purpose planes) **A:** 212 *with picture*
Insecticide (Using insecticides) **I:** 302 *with picture*
Spread foundation [structure]

Building construction (Foundations) **B:** 682
Spreading center [geology]
   Earth (Earth's crust) **E:** 23
Spreading dogbane [plant]
   Dogbane **D:** 282 *with picture*
Spreadsheet [computer program] **So:** 805 *with picture*
   Computer (Spreadsheet programs) **Ci:** 917
Spreadsheet modeling
   Computer (Spreadsheet programs) **Ci:** 917
Sprechstimme [music]
   Opera: *(Wozzeck)* **O:** 808
Spree River [Germany]
   Berlin (History) **B:** 264
Sprigg, Samuel [American political leader]
   Maryland (table) **M:** 255
Spring [geology] **So:** 806 *with diagram*
Spring [hardware] **So:** 806
   Torsion bar suspension **T:** 343
Spring [season] **So:** 806
   Groundhog Day **G:** 402
   May Day **M:** 322
   Season (The four seasons) **S:** 270 *with diagram*
Spring barley [plant]
   Barley (Cultivation) **B:** 112
Spring-beauty [plant] **So:** 806 *with picture*
Spring blackstem [plant disease]
   Alfalfa (Diseases and pests) **A:** 347
Spring bloom [organisms]
   Atlantic Ocean (Ocean life) **A:** 866
Spring cankerworm [larva]
   Cankerworm **C:** 177
Spring couplet [scroll]
   Chinese New Year **C:** 512
Spring-driven clock
   Clock (Mechanical clocks) **Ci:** 682j
Spring ephemeral [botany]
   Flower (Flowers of woodlands and forests) **F:** 284
Spring Fiesta [custom]
   New Orleans (Annual events) **N:** 282
Spring latch
   Lock (Types of locks) **L:** 410
Spring lizard
   Lizard **L:** 399
Spring Moon [book by Lord]
   Novel (The novel today) **N:** 575
Spring oats
   Oats (Growing oats) **O:** 640
Spring salmon *See* Chinook salmon *in this index*
Spring scale
   Scale, Weighing (Mechanical scales) **S:** 169
Spring tide
   Ocean (Tides) **O:** 659
   Tide *diagram on* **T:** 281; (The actual tide) **T:** 282
Spring-tooth harrow [tool]
   Harrow **H:** 77
Spring wheat
   Wheat (Winter wheats and spring wheats) **W:** 268 *with pictures*
Springboard diving
   Diving (Types of diving) **D:** 242 *with pictures*
Springbok [animal] **So:** 807 *with picture*
Springbuck [animal] *See* Springbok *in this index*
Springer [architecture]
   Arch *diagram on* **A:** 593
Springer spaniel
   Dog *picture on* **D:** 269
   Welsh springer spaniel **W:** 196
Springfield [Illinois] **So:** 807
   City *picture on* **Ci:** 575
   Illinois (table: Average monthly weather) **I:** 66
   Lincoln, Abraham (Assassination) **L:** 326 *with picture*
Springfield [Massachusetts] **So:** 807
Springfield [Missouri] **So:** 808
Springfield, Lake [Illinois]
   Springfield **So:** 807
Springfield Armory National Historic Site [Massachusetts]
   National Park System (table: National historic sites) **N:** 52-53
Springhaas [rodent]
   Springhare **So:** 808
Springhare [rodent] **So:** 808 *with picture*
Spring's Awakening [play by Wedekind]
   Wedekind, Frank **W:** 178
Springsteen, Bruce [American singer] **So:** 808
   Rock music (Rock videos and MTV) **R:** 380c *with picture*
Springtail [insect]
   Insect *picture on* **I:** 280
Springwood [estate]
   Roosevelt, Franklin Delano (Boyhood) **R:** 450e *with picture*
Sprinkler irrigation
   Gardening (Caring for the garden) **G:** 35
   Vegetable (Irrigation) **V:** 293

Sprinkler system
   Bismuth **B:** 383
   Fire department (Public building inspections) **F:** 125
   Irrigation (Sprinkler irrigation) **I:** 458 *with picture*
Sprint [race]
   Bicycle racing (Track races) **B:** 292
   Kart racing **K:** 247
   Track and field (Track events) **T:** 356
Sprint car
   Automobile racing (Other kinds of racing) **A:** 978
Sprint Center
   Kansas City (History) **K:** 242-243
Sprint Cup [race]
   Automobile racing (Stock car racing) **A:** 978; (NASCAR Sprint Cup champions) **A:** 981
   Gordon, Jeff **G:** 273
   NASCAR **N:** 21
Sprite [image]
   Electronic game (Graphics) **E:** 204b
Sprite [meteorology]
   Lightning (Jets, sprites, and elves) **L:** 301
Sprocket [device]
   Bicycle (Power and speed) **B:** 290
Sproul, William Cameron [American political leader]
   Pennsylvania (table) **P:** 263
Sprout inhibitor [chemical]
   Potato (Harvesting) **P:** 713
Sprouting [botany]
   Germination **G:** 172
Spruance [ship]
   Destroyer **D:** 162 *with picture*
Spruance, Raymond Ames [American admiral] **So:** 809
Spruce [tree] **So:** 809 *with picture*
   Plant *pictures on* **P:** 521, **P:** 524
   Tree *pictures on* **T:** 425, **T:** 427
Spruce bark beetle
   Arctic (Climate change) **A:** 640
Spruce budworm [insect] **So:** 810 *with picture*
Spruce Goose [airplane]
   Hughes, Howard Robard **H:** 409
Spruce grouse [bird]
   Grouse (Habits) **G:** 403-404 *with picture*
Spruce Knob [mountain]
   West Virginia (Land regions) **W:** 218
Spruce-moose biome [biology] *See* Boreal forest *in this index*
Spruce partridge [bird]
   Grouse **G:** 403
Spruce Tree House [Colorado]
   Mesa Verde National Park **M:** 421
Spruce Woods Provincial Park [Manitoba]
   Manitoba *picture on* **M:** 153
Sprudel [spring]
   Karlovy Vary **K:** 247
Sprung rhythm [poetry]
   Hopkins, Gerard Manley **H:** 333
Spry, William [American political leader]
   Utah (table) **U:** 245
Spun silk
   Silk (Spun silk) **S:** 460
Spun soy protein
   Soybean (Soy meal) **So:** 690
Spun yarn
   Textile (Making the yarn) **T:** 215
Spur [biology]
   Chicken (The body of a chicken) **C:** 440 *with picture*
Spur [riding equipment]
   Cowboy (His clothing) **Ci:** 1108-1109
   Horse (Spurs) **H:** 351
Spur gear
   Gear **G:** 75
Spurge [plant] **So:** 810
Spurrier, Steve [American football player]
   Football (table) **F:** 363
Spurs, San Antonio
   Basketball (table) **B:** 150
Spurzheim, Johann Kaspar [German anatomist]
   Phrenology **P:** 430
Sputnik [satellite] **So:** 810
   Sputnik 1
      Eisenhower, Dwight David (The space age) **E:** 154
      Exploration (Space exploration) **E:** 451-452
      Korolev, Sergei Pavlovich **K:** 384
      National Defense Education Act **N:** 14
      Rocket (The space age) **R:** 391
      Space exploration *picture on* **So:** 698; (The first artificial satellites) **So:** 707
      Sputnik **So:** 810
   Sputnik 2
      Eisenhower, Dwight David (The space age) **E:** 154
      Space exploration (The space race begins)

      So: 707
Sputum [physiology]
   Tuberculosis (The disease) **T:** 478; (Diagnosis of tuberculosis) **T:** 479
Spy So: 810
   See also Espionage *in this index*
Spy [newspaper]
   Thomas, Isaiah **T:** 261
Spy, The [book by Cooper]
   Cooper, James Fenimore **Ci:** 1035
Spy satellite *See* Military satellite *in this index*
Spy Who Came in from the Cold, The [book by Le Carré]
   Le Carré, John **L:** 174
Spykman, Nicholas [American scholar]
   Geopolitics **G:** 106b
Spyri, Johanna [Swiss author] **So:** 810
Spyware [computing]
   Internet (Identity and privacy) **I:** 350f
Squab [bird]
   Pigeon (The life of a pigeon) **P:** 459-460
Squad [military]
   Army, United States (table) **A:** 737
Squadron [military unit]
   Air force (The organization of air forces) **A:** 183
   Air Force, United States (Combat commands) **A:** 193
   Navy (The organization of navies) **N:** 77
Squall [weather] **So:** 810
Squall line thunderstorm
   Thunderstorm **T:** 272
Squaloraja [extinct fish]
   Anning, Mary **A:** 517
Squamous cell [physiology]
   Epithelium **E:** 345
Squamous cell cancer [disease]
   Skin cancer (Nonmelanoma skin cancer) **S:** 492
Squanto [American Indian interpreter] **So:** 811
   Plymouth Colony (The first year) **P:** 583
   Thanksgiving Day (Plymouth Colony) **PT:** 230
Square [arithmetic]
   Algebra (Quadratic equations in one unknown) **A:** 358
   Fibonacci, Leonardo **F:** 89
   Multiplication (Multiplication facts) **M:** 921-922
   Power **P:** 728
Square [botany]
   Cotton (Development) **Ci:** 1087
Square [geometry] **So:** 811 *with diagram*
   Series (Working with odd numbers) **S:** 317
Square [tool]
   Woodworking (Planning and design) **W:** 396 *with picture*
Square [unit of measure]
   Weights and measures (table: Miscellaneous weights and measures) **W:** 184
Square centimeter [measurement]
   Metric system (The metric system at a glance) **M:** 438 *with picture*
Square dancing So: 811 *with picture*
   Dance *picture on* **D:** 23
   Folk dancing **F:** 321
Square deal [U.S. history]
   Roosevelt, Theodore (Friend of labor) **R:** 464-465
   United States, History of the (Theodore Roosevelt) **U:** 187
Square division [military]
   Brigade **B:** 618
Square foot [unit of measure]
   Foot **F:** 352
Square kilometer [measurement]
   Metric system (The metric system at a glance) *diagram on* **M:** 438
Square knot
   Knots, hitches, and splices (Useful knots) **K:** 356 *with diagram*
Square measure [unit of measure] **So:** 811
   See also Area *in this index*
   Metric system (Space and time) **M:** 437; (Metric conversion table) **M:** 439 *with pictures*
Square meter [unit of measure]
   Metric system (Space and time) **M:** 437; (The metric system at a glance) **M:** 438 *with picture*
Square-rigger [ship]
   Ship (The full-rigged ship) **S:** 418-419
Square root [mathematics] **So:** 812
   Algebra (Quadratic equations in one unknown) **A:** 358
Square sail
   Ship (Egyptian ships) **S:** 415
   Warship (Early warships) **W:** 41
Squaring [mathematics]
   Square root **So:** 812
Squash [drink]
   England (Food and drink) **E:** 295-296
Squash [microbiology]
   Microtomy **M:** 520

Squash [plant] **So: 812** with pictures
Zucchini **Z: 608** with picture
Squash [sport] **So: 813** with pictures
Squash racquets [sport] See Squash in this index
Squat [weightlifting]
Weightlifting **W: 183**
Squatter [Australian history]
Australia (Expansion) **A: 922**
Squatter [U.S. history] **So: 814**
Kansas (The struggle over slavery) **K: 235**
Pioneer life in America (How the pioneers obtained land) **P: 479**
Pre-emption **P: 734a**
Squatter community [housing]
Colombia (Way of life) **Ci: 779-781**
Peru (Housing) **P: 309**
Squatter sovereignty See Popular sovereignty in this index
Squatter's rights [U.S. history] **So: 814**
Pre-emption **P: 734a**
Squawfeather [plant]
Plant picture on **P: 524**
Squawfish
Minnow **M: 607**
Squeegee [device]
Screen printing **S: 225** with picture
Squeeze [disorder]
Diving, Underwater (Dangers of underwater diving) **D: 246**
Squeeze play
Baseball (Baseball terms) **B: 124**
Squeteague See Weakfish in this index
Squid [animal] **So: 814** with pictures
Animal (Fins, tails, and flippers) **A: 490**
Deep sea (Invertebrates) **D: 82a-82b**
Giant squid **G: 184** with picture
Marine biology (What marine biologists do) **M: 204-205**
Mollusk (Octopuses and squids) **M: 695**
Ocean picture on **O: 656**; (The nekton) **O: 655**
Shell (Octopuses and squids) **S: 388**
SQUID magnetometer [physics]
Magnetometer **M: 62**
Squill [plant] **So: 814a**
Squire [European history]
Knights and knighthood (The squire) **K: 348** with pictures
Squirrel So: 814b with pictures and map
Animal picture on **A: 478**; (Animals of the polar regions) **A: 484**
Fur (table) **F: 561**
Squirrel monkey So: 816 with picture
Squirreltail barley [plant] See Foxtail barley in this index
Sr [symbol]
Strontium **So: 930**
SR-71A [airplane]
Airplane (Military planes) **A: 212**
SRAM [electronics]
Computer chip (Memory chips) **Ci: 924f**
SRBM [missile] See Short-range ballistic missile in this index
Srebrenica massacre [European history] **So: 816**
War crime (The United Nations and war crimes) **W: 27**
SRI International [research organization] **So: 817**
Sri Jayewardenepura Kotte [Sri Lanka] **So: 817**
Sri Lanka **So: 817**
Sri Lanka So: 817 with pictures and map
Asia picture on **A: 802**
Flag picture on **F: 204**
Sri Jayewardenepura Kotte **So: 817**
Sri Lanka Freedom Party [political party]
Sri Lanka (Government) **So: 817**
Srivijaya [former kingdom, Indonesia]
Indonesia (Hindu and Buddhist kingdoms) **I: 236**
SS [German history]
Himmler, Heinrich **H: 234**
Hitler, Adolf (Rise of the Nazis) **H: 266**
Nuremberg Trials (The trials) **N: 613**
SSA [agency] See Social Security Administration in this index
SSB [agency]
New Deal (table) **N: 201**
SSI [program]
Welfare **W: 190**
Ssireum [martial arts]
Martial arts (Korean martial arts) **M: 234a**
SSM [weapon]
Guided missile (Surface-to-surface missiles) **G: 425**
SSN system
Radar (In the military) **R: 65**
SSP [plan] See Species Survival Plan in this index
SSRI [drug] See Selective serotonin reuptake inhibitor in this index
SSS [agency] See Selective Service System in this index

SST [airplane] See Supersonic transport plane in this index
St. ...
Individual saints appear under their names, as in Peter, Saint. Other entries, such as Saint Louis [Missouri], appear under Saint ...
Stabilator [device]
Airplane picture on **A: 214**; (The tail) **A: 214-216**
Stabile [sculpture]
Calder, Alexander **C: 27**
Stabilizer [food]
Food additive (Kinds of additives) **F: 339**
Stabilizer [instrument]
Airplane (The tail) **A: 214** with picture
Glider (The tail) **G: 229**
Stabilizing selection [biology]
Evolution (Natural selection) **E: 428**
Stable [barn]
Horse (The stall) **H: 355**
Stable equilibrium
Gravity, Center of **G: 334**
Staccato [music]
Music (Indicating expression) **M: 955** with diagram
Stacking chair
Eames, Charles **E: 6**
Stacy, Mahlon [American pioneer]
Trenton **T: 434**
Stadacona [Canadian history]
Quebec (Early days) **Q: 36**
Stadholder [title]
Netherlands (Wars with England and France) **N: 149**
Stadhuis [building]
Antwerp (Chief buildings) **A: 561**
Stadion [race]
Olympic Games (The ancient games) **O: 750**
Stadium So: 820
Artificial turf **A: 761**
Staedtler, Frederick [German businessman]
Pencil (History) **P: 236**
Staël, Madame de [French author] **So: 820**
French literature (The Preromantics) **F: 521**
Staël-Holstein, Baron [Swedish diplomat]
Staël, Madame de **So: 820**
Staff [music]
Music (Indicating pitch) **M: 952** with pictures
Staff of life [name for]
Bread **B: 588**
Staff officer
Navy, United States (Training an officer) **N: 83**
Staff ornament
Flag pictures on **F: 194**
Staff sergeant
Rank, Military (table) **R: 140**
Staff writing
Writing **W: 511**
Stafford, James F. [American cardinal]
Cardinal (table: American cardinals) **C: 211**
Stafford, Jean [American author] **So: 820**
Stafford, Robert T. [American political leader]
Vermont (History) **V: 333**
Stafford, Thomas Patten [American astronaut]
Lovell, James Arthur, Jr. **L: 509**
Space exploration (Voskhod and Gemini: The first multiperson space flights) **So: 714**; (The Apollo-Soyuz Test Project) **So: 721** with picture
Staffordshire bull terrier [dog] **So: 820** with picture
Dogfighting **D: 282**
Pit bull **P: 498**
Staffordshire terrier
American Staffordshire terrier **A: 430**
Dog picture on **D: 273**
Stag [animal]
Deer **D: 82d**
Stag at Sharkey's [painting by Bellows]
Bellows, George Wesley **B: 244**
Stag beetle So: 821
Beetle picture on **B: 215**
Insect picture on **I: 283**
Shell picture on **S: 384**
Stage [engine]
Turbine (How turbines work) **T: 495-496**
Stage [microscope]
Microscope (Basic optical microscopes) **M: 517** with pictures
Stage [rocket]
Rocket (Multistage rockets) **R: 386** with diagram
Space exploration (Getting into space and back) **So: 698**
Stage [theater]
Drama (Greek drama) **D: 326** with picture; (Roman drama) **D: 328** with picture; (The Italian stage) **D: 330** with picture; (Elizabethan theaters) **D: 331**; (Religious plays) **D: 333** with picture;

(England) **D: 334** with picture
Shakespeare, William (The stage) **S: 351** with picture
Theater (The stage) **T: 233** with picture
Stage designer
Opera pictures on **O: 799**; (The designers) **O: 794** with picture
Theater (The scene designer) **T: 239**
Stage director
Opera (The stage director) **O: 794**; (Rehearsing a production) **O: 796**
Stage manager
Opera picture on **O: 795**; (The stage manager) **O: 796**
Theater (The director's assistants) **T: 237**
Stage name
Name (Pseudonyms) **N: 7**
Pseudonym **P: 844**
Stage picture
Theater (Rehearsing) **T: 236**
Stagecoach [film]
Westerns **W: 242** with picture
Stagecoach [vehicle] **So: 821** with picture
Colonial life in America (Transportation) **Ci: 805-806**
Postal services (The creation of the Penny Post) **P: 706** with picture
Transportation (Development of inland transport) **T: 388-389** with picture
Stagehand
Opera (The technical staff) **O: 795-796** with picture
Stagflation [economics]
Keynes, John Maynard **K: 308a**
Recession (Recession and inflation) **R: 175**
Stagg, Amos Alonzo [American football coach] **So: 821**
Connecticut (Interesting facts) **Ci: 953**
Staggers Rail Act [1980]
Railroad (Railroads today) **R: 118**
Staghorn sumac [plant]
Sumac **So: 971**
Staging [medicine]
Cancer (Staging) **C: 172**
Staging flock [zoology]
Duck (Habits) **D: 376**
Stagnant anoxia
Anoxia **A: 519**
Stahl, Franklin [American geneticist]
Heredity (The chemistry of genes) **H: 208-209**
Stahl, Georg [German chemist]
Acetic acid **A: 25**
Chemistry (The phlogiston theory) **C: 401**
Ståhlberg, Kaarlo Juho [Finnish political leader]
Finland (The new republic) **F: 117**
Stain [dye] **So: 821**
Cell picture on **C: 326**
Paint (Industrial paints) **P: 24**
Varnish **V: 286**
Stain piece
Wool (Types of wool) **W: 399**
Stained glass [art] **So: 821** with pictures
Glass picture on **G: 222**
Tracery **T: 355**
Window **W: 334**
Stainless steel So: 823
Alloy (Alloys of iron) **A: 377-378**
Chromium **C: 538**
Iron and steel (Kinds of iron and steel) **I: 436-437**
Manganese (Industrial uses) **M: 139**
Stairway
See also Escalator in this index
Safety (Safety at school) **S: 11** with pictures
Stake [diocese]
Mormons (Church organization) **M: 807**
Stakes race
Horse racing (Types of horse races) **H: 364**
Staking [industrial process]
Leather (Final processing) **L: 168**
Stalactite [geology] **So: 824** with picture
Cave (Speleothems) **C: 319** with diagram
Stalagmite **So: 824**
Stalagmite [geology] **So: 824** with picture
Cave (Speleothems) **C: 319** with diagram
Ice age (Evidence from modern galciers and from caves) **I: 7**
Stalactite **So: 824**
Stalemate [chess]
Chess (How chess is played) **C: 413**
Stalemate [warfare]
War (Stalemates) **W: 24**
Stalin, Joseph [Soviet dictator] **So: 824** with pictures
Armenia (History) **A: 718b**
Churchill, Sir Winston Leonard Spencer (Meetings with Roosevelt) **C: 548** with picture
Cold War (The alliance breaks up) **Ci: 763**; (To the

brink and back) **Ci:** 765
Collective farm **Ci:** 775
Communism (Restrictions on personal freedom)
Ci: 891-892; (Under Stalin) **Ci:** 892 *with picture*
Dictatorship **D:** 191
Khrushchev, Nikita Sergeyevich **K:** 308b
Lenin, V. I. (Death) **L:** 195
Malenkov, Georgi Maximilianovich **M:** 105
Roosevelt, Franklin Delano (The Big Three) **R:** 457;
(Yalta Conference) **R:** 458 *with picture*
Russia (Stalin) **R:** 553
Russian Revolution of 1917 (Aftermath) **R:** 566a
Serbia (Communist rule) **S:** 316
Tehran Conference **T:** 88
Tito, Josip Broz (Yugoslav leader) **T:** 302
Trotsky, Leon **T:** 452
Union of Soviet Socialist Republics (History)
U: 35-36 *with picture*
World War II *picture on* **W:** 479; (The rise of
dictatorships) **W:** 469; (The invasion of Poland)
W: 472-473; (The invasion of the Soviet Union)
W: 477; (The war in Europe and North Africa)
W: 480
Yalta Conference **Y:** 549
Yugoslavia (Communist rule) **Y:** 576
Stalinabad [former name]
Dushanbe **D:** 390
Stalingrad [U.S.S.R.] *See* Volgograd *in this index*
Stalingrad, Battle of [1942-1943] **So:** 828 *with
picture*
Russia (World War II) **R:** 554
Union of Soviet Socialist Republics (World War II)
U: 37 *with picture*
World War II (The Battle of Stalingrad) **W:** 481
Stalinism
Stalin, Joseph **So:** 824; (Stalinism) **So:** 828
Stalk [botany]
Corn (How the plant develops) **Ci:** 1057-1058
with picture
Stalk [zoology]
Lobster (Body) **L:** 405
Stalk-cutting [agriculture]
Tobacco (Harvesting) **T:** 306
Stalked sea lily [animal]
Deep sea (Invertebrates) **D:** 82a-82b
Stalking [crime]
Domestic violence **D:** 301
Stalky and Co. [book by Kipling]
Kipling, Rudyard (Childhood) **K:** 334
Stall [aerodynamics]
Aerodynamics (Angle of attack) **A:** 86
Stall [barn]
Barn **B:** 113
Horse (The stall) **H:** 355
Stall-feeding
Dairying (History of dairying) **D:** 8
Stalling [aviation]
Airplane (Stalling) **A:** 225; (Measuring flying
speed) **A:** 225-226
Stallings, Laurence [American author]
Anderson, Maxwell **A:** 452
Stallion
Horse (table: Horse terms) **H:** 343
Stalwarts [U.S. history]
Cannon, Joseph Gurney **C:** 179
Garfield, James Abram (Congressman) **G:** 41-42
Hayes, Rutherford Birchard (Campaign of 1876)
H: 120
Republican Party (The Radical Republicans and
Reconstruction) **R:** 254
Stamen [botany]
Angiosperm **A:** 462
Flower (The parts of a flower) **F:** 293 *with picture*
Plant (Flowers) **P:** 531 *with picture;* (Sexual
reproduction) **P:** 532-533
Pollen **P:** 644 *with diagram*
Seed (Seed development in angiosperms) **S:** 281
Stamford [Connecticut] **So:** 828
Stamford Bridge, Battle of [1066]
Harald III **H:** 55
Staminate flower
Flower (Variations in flower structure) **F:** 294
Stammering *See* Stuttering *in this index*
Stamp **So:** 829
See also Postage stamp *in this index*
Engraving and Printing, Bureau of **E:** 326a
Stamp, Edward [British sea captain]
Vancouver (History) **V:** 277
Stamp Act [1765] **So:** 829 *with picture*
Adams, John (In New England) **A:** 35
Boston (Resistance and revolution) **B:** 503
Franklin, Benjamin (A delegate in London) **F:** 490
Henry, Patrick (Early life) **H:** 189-190
Journalism (Early American journalism) **J:** 174
Massachusetts (Pre-Revolutionary days) **M:** 291
Revolution, American (The Quartering and
Stamp acts) **R:** 272

United States, History of the *pictures on* **U:** 157;
(Policy changes) **U:** 158
Stamp Act Congress [U.S. history]
Federal Hall **F:** 64
Revolution, American (The Quartering and
Stamp acts) **R:** 272-273
Stamp Act **So:** 829
Stamp collecting So: 829 *with pictures*
Liechtenstein (Economy) **L:** 272
Stamp weed [plant] *See* Velvetleaf *in this index*
Stamped envelope
Postal Service, United States (Stamps and other
mailing materials) **P:** 699
Stampede
Western frontier life in America (The cattle drive)
W: 237
Stampeders, Calgary [team]
Football (Canadian Football League) **F:** 364
Stamper [recording]
Phonograph (How phonograph records are
made) **P:** 401
Stamping [industrial process]
Die and diemaking **D:** 195
Stan the Man [nickname]
Musial, Stan **M:** 945
Stanbery, Henry [American government official]
Johnson, Andrew (table: Johnson's Cabinet)
J: 140
Justice, Department of (table) **J:** 203
Stanchion housing [agriculture]
Dairying (Housing) **D:** 7
Stand Up and Cheer [film]
Temple, Shirley **T:** 131
Stand-up pouch
Packaging **P:** 18
Stand-Up Tragedy [play]
Theater *picture on* **T:** 245
Standard [device]
Camera (View cameras) **C:** 83 *with picture*
Standard [ethics]
Television (Regulating U.S. television) **T:** 115
Standard [flag]
Flag (table) **F:** 193; (Flags of individuals) **F:** 195
with pictures
Standard [weapon]
Guided missile *picture on* **G:** 425
Standard & Poor's Corporation
Standard and Poor's indexes **So:** 833
Standard & Poor's Indexes [stock market] **So:** 833
Standard book number
International standard book number **I:** 347
Standard Catalog of World Coins
Coin collecting (Collecting coins of other
countries) **Ci:** 758
Standard deviation
Statistics (Probability) **So:** 868-869
Standard English
Grammar (Grammar and usage) **G:** 304
Standard fire test
Building construction (Classification of buildings)
B: 683
Standard gauge
Railroad (The crossties and rails) **R:** 109
Standard German [language]
Germany (Language) **G:** 150
Standard grade
Beef (Grades of beef) **B:** 209
Standard hive
Bee (As an industry) **B:** 206-207 *with picture*
Standard housing
Housing **H:** 389
Standard lens
Photography (Types of lenses) **P:** 411 *with picture*
Standard mail
Postal Service, United States (Classes of mail)
P: 699
Postal services (Technological advancements)
P: 707
Standard Model [physics] **So:** 833
Higgs, Peter Ware **H:** 227
Subatomic particle (The Standard Model) **So:** 938
Sun (Analyzing neutrinos) **So:** 984
Standard observers
Color (The CIE System of Color Specification)
Ci: 824
Standard of behavior
Child (The preschool years) **C:** 449
Standard of living So: 833
Conservation (To meet demands for resources)
Ci: 975
Economics (Economics and society) **E:** 62 *with
picture*
Food (Economic reasons) **F:** 331-332
Food supply (Increased demand for food) **F:** 348
Income (Income inequality) **I:** 101
Infant mortality **I:** 264
Standard Oil Company So: 834

Exxon Mobil Corporation **E:** 459
Flagler, Henry Morrison **F:** 224
Monopoly and competition (History) **M:** 732
Rockefeller, John Davison (The Standard Oil
Company) **R:** 382
Standard Oil Company, History of the [book by
Tarbell]
Muckrakers **M:** 908
Standard Oil Trust [U.S. history]
Rockefeller, John Davison (The Standard Oil
Company) **R:** 382
Standard Oil Company **So:** 834
Standard poodle [dog]
Poodle **P:** 658 *with picture*
Standard schnauzer [dog] **So:** 835 *with picture*
Standard time So: 835
Time (Local and standard time) **T:** 292 *with map*
Standardbred [horse]
Harness racing (Harness horses) **H:** 63
Horse (table: Some types and breeds of horses)
H: 343; (Light harness horses) **H:** 345 *with
picture*
Standardization [process]
Milk (Separation or standardization) **M:** 548 *with
diagram*
Standardized test
Education (How can student performance be
improved?) **E:** 105
Psychology (Systematic assessment) **P:** 848
Testing **T:** 182
Standards [botany]
Iris **I:** 429 *with picture*
Standards, National Institute of *See* National
Institute of Standards and Technology *in this
index*
Standby Reserve
Air Force, United States (Air Force reserves)
A: 194
Marine Corps, United States (Reserves) **M:** 208
Navy, United States (The active-duty Navy and
reserves) **N:** 85
Standing Committee [China]
China (The Communist Party) **C:** 477
Standing committee [U.S. government]
Congress of the United States (Working in
committees) **Ci:** 944; (table) **Ci:** 944
House of Representatives (Committees) **H:** 387;
(Considering legislation) **H:** 387
Parliamentary procedure (Committees) **P:** 175
Senate (Senate committees) **S:** 295
State government (Organization) **So:** 863-864
United States, Government of the (Committee
system) **U:** 138
Standing Peachtree [settlement]
Atlanta (Early days) **A:** 861
Standing rigging
Sailing (Rigging) **S:** 24
Standing start [movement]
Diving **D:** 243
Standing wave [physics]
Particle accelerator (How accelerators work)
P: 184-185
Sound (Resonance) **So:** 603-604 *with diagram*
Waves *diagram on* **W:** 150; (How waves move)
W: 152
Standing-wave linear accelerator [machine]
Particle accelerator (How accelerators work)
P: 184-185 *with diagram*
Standish, Miles [American colonial leader] **So:** 835
Longfellow, Henry Wadsworth (Narrative poems)
L: 450
Standpipe [water system]
Reservoir **R:** 259
Stanfield, Robert Lorne [Canadian political leader]
So: 836
Clark, Joe (Political worker and student) **Ci:** 640-
641
Nova Scotia (table) **N:** 567
Stanford, Jane Lathrop [American philanthropist]
Stanford University (History) **So:** 836
Stanford, Leland [American political leader]
So: 836
California (table) **C:** 59; (Early statehood) **C:** 62
Stanford University (History) **So:** 836
Stanford, Rawghlie C. [American political leader]
Arizona (table) **A:** 687
Stanford Linear Accelerator Center
Particle accelerator (How accelerators work)
P: 184-185
Stanford Research Institute
SRI International **So:** 817
Stanford University So: 836
California (Libraries) **C:** 40-41
Stanhope, Earl of [British inventor]
Printing (New presses and typecasting machines)
P: 803
Stanhope, Philip [son of]

Chesterfield, Earl of C: 415
Stanhope, Philip Dormer [British author]
Chesterfield, Earl of C: 415
Stanishev, Sergei [Bulgarian political leader]
Bulgaria (Recent developments) B: 693
Stanislas I [king of Poland]
Louis XV L: 476
Stanislas, Saint [Polish religious leader] So: 836
Stanislavski, Konstantin [Russian director] So: 837
Method acting M: 434
Moscow Art Theater M: 828
Theater (Systems of acting) T: 238
Stanislavski method [drama]
Stanislavski, Konstantin So: 837
Theater (Systems of acting) T: 238
Stanley [Falkland Islands]
Falkland Islands F: 15
Stanley, Edward [British nobleman]
Derby D: 152
Stanley, Francis E. [American inventor]
Automobile (The steam car) A: 965 *with picture*
Stanley brothers So: 838
Stanley, Frederick Arthur [British political leader]
See Stanley of Preston, Baron *in this index*
Stanley, Freelan O. [American inventor]
Automobile (The steam car) A: 965 *with picture*
Stanley brothers So: 838
Stanley, Sir Henry Morton [British explorer]
Congo, Democratic Republic of the (The coming
of the Europeans) Ci: 940b
Emin Pasha E: 260
Exploration (The exploration of Africa) E: 448-449
with picture and map
Lake Edward L: 37
Stanley and Livingstone So: 837 *with picture
and map*
Stanley, Thomas B. [American political leader]
Virginia (table) V: 417
Stanley, Wendell Meredith [American biochemist]
Nobel Prizes (Chemistry: 1946) N: 443
Virus (Discovery) V: 427
Stanley, William Eugene [American political
leader]
Kansas (table) K: 234
Stanley and Livingstone [British explorers]
So: 837 *with pictures and map*
See also Livingstone, David; Stanley, Sir Henry
Morton *in this index*
Exploration (The exploration of Africa) E: 448-449
with picture
Stanley brothers [American inventors] So: 838
Automobile (The steam car) A: 965 *with picture*
Stanley Cup So: 838 *with picture*
Hockey (Professional leagues) H: 278-279; (table)
H: 280
Stanley of Preston, Baron So: 838
Stanley of Preston, Baron [British political leader]
So: 838
Hockey (Beginnings) H: 280-281
Stanley Cup So: 838
Stanley Park [Vancouver]
British Columbia (Interesting facts about British
Columbia) B: 613; (Places to visit) B: 620
Vancouver (The city) V: 274 *with map*; (Parks)
V: 276 *with picture*
Stanley steamer [automobile]
Automobile (The steam car) A: 965 *with picture*
Stanley brothers So: 838
Stannous fluoride [chemical]
Tin (Uses) T: 293
Stans, Maurice H. [American government official]
Commerce, Department of (table) Ci: 871
Nixon, Richard Milhous (table) N: 433
Watergate W: 144
Stansbury, Joseph [Canadian author]
Canadian literature (Early English-Canadian
literature) C: 157
Stanton, Charles E. [American military officer]
Pershing, John Joseph (World War I) P: 296
Stanton, Edwin McMasters [American political
leader] So: 838
Emancipation Proclamation *picture on* E: 254
Grant, Ulysses S. (National hero) G: 315
Lincoln, Abraham (table) L: 323
Stanton, Elizabeth Cady [American social
reformer] So: 839 *with portrait*
Anthony, Susan Brownell A: 544
Blatch, Harriot Eaton Stanton B: 398
Mott, Lucretia Coffin M: 880
Woman suffrage (Beginnings of the movement)
W: 380
Women's movement (The beginnings of women's
movements) W: 384-385
Stanton, Frank [American sociologist]
Communication (The effects of media) Ci: 887
Stanton, Henry B. [American reformer]
Blatch, Harriot Eaton Stanton B: 398

Stanza [poetry]
Poetry (table) P: 594
Stanza della Segnatura [Vatican]
Raphael (His works) R: 143
Stanzaic syllabic [poetry]
Poetry (Rhythm and meter) P: 591-592
Stanzas [poems by Malherbe]
Malherbe, François de M: 106
"Stanzas from the Grande Chartreuse" [poem
by Arnold]
Arnold, Matthew A: 742
Stapes [anatomy]
Deafness (Diseases) D: 57
Ear *diagram on* E: 10; (The middle ear) E: 7-8 *with
diagram*; (Diseases) E: 12
Staphylococcus [bacteria] So: 839 *with picture*
Antibiotic (Resistance to antibiotics) A: 551
Boil B: 438
Food poisoning F: 340
Toxic shock syndrome T: 353
Staphylococcus aureus [bacteria]
Osteomyelitis O: 866
Penicillin (Resistance) P: 241
Pneumonia (How pneumonia develops) P: 586
Staphylococcus So: 839
Staple [textiles]
Cotton (Classing) Ci: 1091
Cotton gin Ci: 1094
Textile (Sources of textile fibers) T: 212; (Making
the yarn) T: 215
Staple crop
Agriculture (Cereal grains) A: 147
Staple fiber
Fiber F: 87
Stapledon, Olaf [British author] So: 839
Stapleton, Maureen [American actress]
Motion picture (Best performance by an actress
in a supporting role: 1981) M: 862b
Star [astronomy] So: 840 *with pictures*
See also the list of Related articles in the Star *article*
Astronomy (Observing the sky) A: 835 *with map*;
(Modern astronomy) A: 836-837
Astrophysics A: 850
Binary star B: 308
Black hole (Formation of black holes) B: 388
Brown dwarf B: 644 *with picture*
Constellation Ci: 993
Cosmology Ci: 1077
Fusion F: 589
Galaxy (E: 8 *with pictures*
Herschel, Sir William H: 216
Hydrogen (Occurrence) H: 469
Interstellar medium I: 352
Life (In other solar systems) L: 280
Light (Sources of light) L: 283
Local Group L: 409
Magnetism (Other astronomical bodies) M: 60d
Magnitude M: 62
Milky Way M: 550
Nebula (Diffuse nebulae) N: 116
Nova N: 553 *with pictures*
Planet (Observing the planets) P: 507-508;
(Planets in other solar systems) P: 512
Planetarium P: 514a
Radiation (The sun and other stars) R: 77
Shock wave S: 430
Space exploration (Space between the stars)
So: 696
Star cluster So: 853
Storm (Extraterrestrial storms) So: 913
Supernova So: 994
Time (Astronomical cycles) T: 288
Triangulum Galaxy T: 439
White dwarf W: 285
X rays (In outer space) X: 542-543
Star [award]
Knighthood, Orders of (Honorary orders) K: 347
with pictures
Star [boat]
Sailing (Catboats and sloops) S: 24
Star [entertainer]
Motion picture (Movies become big business)
M: 865
Star [marking]
Horse (Coat and skin) H: 348-349
Star ball [device]
Planetarium (Modern planetariums) P: 514b
Star Chamber [English history] So: 853
Long Parliament L: 448
Star cluster [astronomy] So: 853 *with picture*
Brown dwarf B: 644
"Star Dust" [song]
Carmichael, Hoagy C: 241
Star Maker [book by Stapledon]
Stapledon, Olaf So: 839
Star Man's Son, 2250 A.D. [book by Norton]
Norton, Andre N: 535

Star-nosed mole [animal]
Mammal *picture on* M: 116
Mole (Kinds of moles) M: 690b
Star note [money]
Money (Printing paper money) M: 715
Star of Africa [gem]
Coronation (The British coronation) Ci: 1068
Gem (Some famous gems) G: 79
Star-of-Bethlehem [plant] So: 853 *with picture*
Star of David So: 854 *with picture*
Judaism *picture on* J: 180
Star of India [gem]
Sapphire S: 122
Star of India, Order of [organization]
Knighthood, Orders of *picture on* K: 347
Star of Kazan, The [book by Ibbotson]
Literature for children *picture on* L: 375
Star of the West [ship]
Buchanan, James *picture on* B: 662; (Prelude to
war) B: 661
Star orchid [plant]
Orchid *picture on* O: 824
Star plate [device]
Planetarium (Modern planetariums) P: 514b
Star route service [mail]
Arthur, Chester Alan (The star route frauds)
A: 756
Star ruby cabochon [gem]
Ruby R: 508
Star sapphire [gem]
Sapphire S: 122
Star Scout [rank]
Boy Scouts (Star Scouts, Life Scouts, and Eagle
Scouts) B: 537
Star shell [ammunition]
Ammunition (Artillery ammunition) A: 435-436
Fireworks (Other uses of fireworks) F: 135
"Star-Spangled Banner" [song] So: 854 *with
picture*
Anacreon A: 447
Baltimore B: 66
Flag (Flags of the United States and Canada)
F: 208
Key, Francis Scott K: 307
Maryland (Museums) M: 244; (The War of 1812
and industrial development) M: 258
National anthem N: 29
Star-Spangled Banner Flag House [Baltimore]
Baltimore (Other interesting places to visit) B: 69
Star thistle [plant]
Flower (Flowers of summer-dry regions) F: 288
with picture
Star tracker [device]
Navigation (Modern use) N: 72
Star Wars [film] So: 855
Ford, Harrison H: 379
Jones, James Earl J: 158
Lucas, George L: 513
Motion picture (A new generation of filmmakers)
M: 871
Star Wars: Episode I—The Phantom Menace [film]
Star Wars So: 855
Star Wars: Episode II—Attack of the Clones [film]
Star Wars So: 855
Star Wars: Episode III—Revenge of the Sith [film]
Motion picture *pictures on* M: 854
Star Wars So: 855
Star Wars: Episode V—The Empire Strikes Back
[film]
Star Wars So: 855
Star Wars: Episode VI—Return of the Jedi [film]
Motion picture *picture on* M: 848
Star Wars So: 855
Star Wars defense *See* Strategic Defense Initiative
in this index
Star Wars **series** [films]
Lucas, George L: 513
Star Wars So: 855
Starboard
Boating (Boating regulations) B: 429
Ship (Basic structure) S: 403
Starburst galaxy [astronomy]
Galaxy (Other types of galaxies) G: 8b
Starch So: 855
Carbohydrate (Kinds of carbohydrates) C: 203
with diagram
Dextrin D: 178
Grain (Other uses) G: 301
Nutrition (Carbohydrates) N: 625
Sago S: 19
Sugar (Cornstarch and other starches) So: 960
Stardust [spacecraft]
Aerogel A: 89
Astronomy (Direct sampling) A: 846
Comet (Studying comets) Ci: 868-869
Space exploration (Probes to comets) So: 711
Stare decisis [law]

Supreme Court of the United States (Effects of decisions) **So: 999**
Starevitch, Ladislas [Polish-born artist]
　Animation (Animation in Europe) **A: 514b**
Starfish [sea animal] **So: 856** *with pictures*
　Animal *pictures on* **A: 486, A: 507**
　Coral (Stony corals) **Ci: 1048a**
　Deep sea (Invertebrates) **D: 82a-82b**
　Great Barrier Reef **G: 336**
　Ocean *picture on* **O: 656**
Starflight [program]
　Camp Fire USA (Small group programs) **C: 88** *with picture*
Stargazer
　Fish *picture on* **F: 167**
Stargell, Willie [American baseball player]
　Baseball (table: Hall of Fame) **B: 134b**
Stark [ship]
　Reagan, Ronald Wilson (Persian Gulf conflicts) **R: 170**
Stark, John [American general] **So: 857**
　Manchester **M: 133**
Stark, Lloyd C. [American political leader]
　Missouri (table) **M: 668**
Starkey, Richard [birth name of Ringo Starr]
　Beatles **B: 189**
Starley, J. K. [British inventor]
　Bicycle (Early bicycles) **B: 291**
Starling [bird] **So: 857** *with picture*
　Bird *picture on* **B: 358**; (In nature) **B: 330**
　Migration (How migrating animals find their way) **M: 539**
Starr, Belle [American bandit] **So: 857** *with portrait*
Starr, Ellen Gates [American social reformer]
　Hull House **H: 412**
　Settlement house **S: 324**
Starr, Kenneth Winston [American attorney] **So: 857**
　Clinton, Bill (National affairs) **Ci: 682d-682e**; (Domestic events) **Ci: 682f**
Starr, Ringo [British musician]
　Beatles **B: 189**
　Rock music *picture on* **R: 380**; (The Beatles) **R: 379**
Starry flounder [fish]
　Flounder *picture on* **F: 267**
Starry Night, The [painting by Van Gogh]
　Expressionism **E: 455**
　Painting (Texture) **P: 35** *with picture*; (Postimpressionism) **P: 75**
Stars, Dallas [hockey team] *See* Dallas Stars *in this index*
Stars and Bars [flag]
　Flag *picture on* **F: 210**
Stars & Stripes [boat]
　America's Cup **A: 431**
Stars and Stripes [flag] *See* United States flag *in this index*
Stars and Stripes [newspaper] **So: 858**
　Mauldin, Bill **M: 313**
Stars Look Down, The [book by Cronin]
　Cronin, A. J. **Ci: 1152**
START [treaties] *See* Strategic Arms Reduction Treaty *in this index*
Starter [electricity]
　Fluorescent lamp *diagram on* **F: 305**
Starter [engine] **So: 858** *with diagrams*
　Automobile (Technological advances) **A: 968**
　Invention (The early and middle 1900's) **I: 363**
　Kettering, Charles Franklin **K: 307**
Starter culture [food]
　Cheese (Separating the curd) **C: 392**
Startle reflex
　Baby (The first month) **B: 6**
Starvation So: 859
　Famine **F: 26**
　Somalia (History) **So: 589**
Starved Rock State Park [Illinois]
　La Salle, René-Robert Cavelier, Sieur de (Expeditions to the Gulf of Mexico) **L: 80**
Starving time [U.S. history]
　Colonial life in America (Jamestown) **Ci: 789**
Stasis [biology]
　Evolution (Main ideas of evolutionary theory) **E: 426-427**
Stassen, Harold Edward [American political leader] **So: 859**
　Minnesota (table) **M: 602**
State [physics] *See* Phase, of matter *in this index*
State [political unit]
　Address, Forms of (Officials of the United States) **A: 53**
　Constitution of the United States (Article IV) **Ci: 1010**
　Country **Ci: 1097**
　Indian, American (Empires and states) **I: 144**
　Nationalism (The rise of nationalism) **N: 62**
　Postal Service, United States (table) **P: 700**

State government **So: 862**
Territory (Territories in the United States) **T: 174**
State, Department of [U.S.] **So: 859** *with pictures*
　Foreign policy (The executive) **F: 387**
　Foreign Service **F: 388**
　International relations (Diplomacy) **I: 344**
　Library (United States government libraries) **L: 248**
　Washington, D.C. *map on* **W: 76**
State, Secretary of [U.S.]
　Flag *picture on* **F: 211**
　State, Department of (Secretary of state) **So: 860**
　State government (Other officers) **So: 863**
State, The [book by Wilson]
　Wilson, Woodrow (Teacher) **W: 320**
State Administrative Council
　Korea, North (National government) **K: 368**
State and church *See* Church and state *in this index*
State and Revolution, The [book by Lenin]
　Lenin, V. I. (Return from exile) **L: 193**
State bed
　Bed (History) **B: 198**
　Furniture (The early 1600's) **F: 574-575** *with picture*
State bird
　Bird (table) **B: 332**
　United States (table) **U: 104-105**
State capital
　United States (table) **U: 104**
State Capitol Building [Des Moines]
　Iowa (Places to visit) **I: 384**
State Capitol Building [Nebraska]
　Lincoln *picture on* **L: 309**
State Central Museum of Contemporary History of Russia [Moscow]
　Moscow (Museums and libraries) **M: 825**
　Russia (Museums and libraries) **R: 536**
State church
　Freedom of religion (In other countries) **F: 505-506**
State colleges *See the Education section of specific state articles, such as* Illinois (Education)
State constitution
　State government (State constitutions) **So: 863**
State Council
　China (National government) **C: 477**
State, County, and Municipal Employees, American Federation of *See* American Federation of State, County, and Municipal Employees *in this index*
State court
　Court *picture on* **Ci: 1103**; (State courts) **Ci: 1102**
State Dining Room
　White House *picture on* **W: 288**; (Public rooms) **W: 286** *with picture*
State Duma [Russian legislature]
　Duma **D: 382**
　Russia (National government) **R: 531** *with picture*
State fair
　Dallas (Museums and libraries) **D: 14**
　Fair (Agricultural fairs) **F: 7** *with picture*
　Iowa *picture on* **I: 385**; (Visitor's guide) **I: 384**
　Kansas *picture on* **K: 226**
State farm [agriculture]
　See also Collective farm *in this index*
　Cuba (Agriculture) **Ci: 1174**
　Korea (Agriculture and fishing) **K: 373**
　Russia (Agriculture) **R: 544**
　Slovakia (Communist rule) **S: 509**
　Ukraine (Agriculture) **U: 11**
　Union of Soviet Socialist Republics (Agriculture) **U: 34** *with picture*
State Farmers Union
　National Farmers Union **N: 34**
State FFA degree
　FFA (Degrees) **F: 85**
State flag
　Flag (Civil and state flags) **F: 195**; (Flags of the U.S. states, territories, and District of Columbia) *pictures on* **F: 212**
State flower
　Flower (table) **F: 275**
　United States (table) **U: 104-105**
State government So: 862 *with picture*
　See also the list of Related articles in the State Government *article*
　Civil service (State and local civil service) **Ci: 612**
　Governor **G: 294**
　Library (State libraries) **L: 249**
　Public health (Functions of public health agencies) **P: 855-856**
　United States, Government of the (Federalism) **U: 137**
State Great Hural [legislature]
　Mongolia (Government) **M: 721-722**
State High School Associations, National Federation of

Football (High school competition) **F: 364**
State Historical Museum [Des Moines]
　Iowa (Places to visit) **I: 384**
State Historical Museum [Moscow]
　Moscow (Museums and libraries) **M: 825**
　Russia (Museums and libraries) **R: 536**
State House [Boston]
　Architecture *picture on* **A: 624**
State income tax
　Income tax (State and local income taxes) **I: 105**
State Law and Order Restoration Council [Myanmar]
　Myanmar (National government) **M: 970**; (Military rule) **M: 970e**
State library
　Library (State libraries) **L: 249**
State motto *See the Facts in brief section in the state articles, such as* Kentucky (Facts in brief)
State of Alaska, The [book by Gruening]
　Gruening, Ernest **G: 406**
State of Deseret [U.S. history] *See* Deseret *in this index*
State of Franklin [U.S. history] *See* Franklin, State of *in this index*
State of Illinois Center [Chicago] *See* James R. Thompson Center *in this index*
State of Jefferson [U.S. history] *See* Jefferson, State of *in this index*
State of the Prisons in England and Wales, The [book by Howard]
　Howard, John **H: 399**
　Prison (Early prison reform) **P: 807**
State of the Union [play by Crouse and Lindsay]
　Lindsay, Howard **L: 333**
State of the Union message
　Constitution of the United States (Article II, Section 3) **Ci: 1009**
　President of the United States (Legislative leader) **P: 765**
State park
　See also the Places to visit section in the state articles, such as California (Places to visit)
　Park (State, provincial, and national parks) **P: 168**
State Peace and Development Council [Myanmar]
　Myanmar (Government) **M: 970**; (Recent developments) **M: 970e**
State police
　Police (State police) **P: 622** *with picture*
State popular names
　United States (table) **U: 104**
State press [journalism] **So: 866**
State religion
　Religion (How the major religions are organized) **R: 218**
State seals *See the Government section in the state articles, such as* Arizona (Government)
State second pension
　Pension (Pensions in other countries) **P: 273**
State Shinto [religion]
　Religion (Shinto) **R: 221-222**
　Shinto **S: 401**
State song
　United States (table) **U: 104-105**
State Street [Chicago]
　Chicago (Downtown Chicago) **C: 420-421**
State terrorism
　Terrorism (Other forms of terrorism) **T: 176**
State tree
　Tree (table) **T: 414**
State trooper
　Clothing *picture on* **Ci: 688**
　Police (State police) **P: 622** *with picture*
State university *See the Education section of specific state articles, such as* Illinois (Education)
State University of New York *See* New York, State University of *in this index*
Statelessness
　Citizenship (Statelessness) **Ci: 571**
Statement [banking]
　Bill (In commerce) **B: 300**
　Check (How the checking system works) **C: 390-391**
Statement [mathematics]
　Algebra (Statements and equations) **A: 351**
Statement of cash flows *See* Cash flows, Statement of *in this index*
Staten Island [New York City] **So: 866**
　New York City (The city) **N: 323**; (Staten Island) **N: 330** *with picture*; (Settlement) **N: 341**
　Richmond Town **R: 333**
Staten Island Ferry
　New York City (Staten Island) **N: 330**
Stater [money]
　Money *picture on* **M: 706**
States and Empires of the Moon, The [book by Cyrano de Bergerac]

Cyrano de Bergerac, Savinien de **Ci: 1208**
States and Empires of the Sun, The [book by Cyrano de Bergerac]
Cyrano de Bergerac, Savinien de **Ci: 1208**
States-General [French history] *See* Estates-General *in this index*
States-General [Netherlands]
Netherlands (National government) **N: 139**
States of the Church *See* Papal States *in this index*
States' rights [U.S. history] **So: 866**
Calhoun, John Caldwell **C: 35**
Confederate States of America **Ci: 931**
Constitution of the United States (Amendment 10) **Ci: 1013**
Hayne, Robert Young **H: 122**
McCulloch v. Maryland **M: 332g**
Nullification **N: 603**
Whiskey rebellion **W: 282**
States' Rights Democratic Party *See* Dixiecrat Party *in this index*
Statesman So: 867
Static [electronics] **So: 867**
Static electricity
Electricity (Static electricity) **E: 192**
Thunderstorm **T: 272**
Statice [plant] **So: 867** *with picture*
Statics [physics] **So: 867**
Fluid mechanics (Fluid statics) **F: 304**
Mechanics **M: 354**
Physics (Mechanics) **P: 437**
Statin [drug] **So: 867**
C-reactive protein **C: 2**
Heart (Treatment) **H: 138**
Stroke (Prevention) **So: 930**
Station [fort] *See* Stockade *in this index*
Station [ranch]
Australia (Country life) **A: 902**
Outback **O: 879**
Ranching **R: 134**
Station allowance [income]
Army, United States (Careers in the Army) **A: 734**
Station keeping
Communications satellite (Types of satellites) **Ci: 888a-888b**
Stationary front [weather]
Weather (Synoptic-scale systems) **W: 159-161**
Statistical Abstract of the United States [publication]
Census Bureau, United States **C: 350**
Statistics So: 867 *with diagrams*
Careers (Technical and mathematical occupations) **C: 232**
Criminology (Statistical studies) **Ci: 1145**
Extrasensory perception (Modern ESP research) **E: 457**
Mathematics (Branches of mathematics) **M: 303**
Pearson, Karl **P: 219**
Probability **P: 809**
Statistics, Vital *See* Vital statistics *in this index*
Statistics Canada
Census (Modern censuses) **C: 350**
Unemployment (Measuring unemployment) **U: 22-23**
Statius [Roman poet]
Latin literature (The Imperial Period) **L: 116-117**
Statler, Ellsworth Milton [American businessman]
Hotel (History) **H: 376-377**
Statoil [company]
Manufacturing (table) **M: 170**
Stator [electrical device]
Automobile (Electric motors) **A: 954**
Electric generator (Parts of a generator) **E: 170-171**
Electric motor (AC motors) **E: 181** *with picture*
Electric power (Sources of electric power) **E: 182** *with diagram*
Linear electric motor **L: 334** *with diagram*
Statuary Hall [Washington, D.C.] **So: 870** *with picture*
Statue *See* Sculpture *in this index*
"Statue and the Bust, The" [poem by Browning]
Browning, Robert (Browning's poems) **B: 646-647**
Statue of a seated boxer [sculpture]
Sculpture (Hellenistic sculpture) **S: 246** *with picture*
Statue of Liberty So: 872 *with pictures and map*
Bartholdi, Frédéric Auguste **B: 120**
Hunt, Richard Morris **H: 450**
Liberty Island **L: 233**
New York City (A visitor's guide) **N: 338-339** *with picture*
United States *picture on* **U: 99**
Statue of Liberty National Monument [New York-New Jersey] **So: 879**
See also Statue of Liberty *in this index*
National Park System (table: National monuments) **N: 51**

New York (Places to visit) **N: 302**
Statuette of a dancer [art]
Sculpture (Indus Valley) **S: 235-236** *with picture*
Status [sociology]
Careers (Social status) **C: 216**
Clothing (Identity) **Ci: 687**
Linton, Ralph **L: 339**
Women's movement (Women's status through the ages) **W: 383**
Status Indian [Canadian history]
Indian, American (In Canada) **I: 178**
Status light
Keyboard **K: 309**
Status of Women, Commission on
Women's movement (Women's organizations) **W: 386**
Statute [law]
Code **Ci: 748**
Law (Civil law systems) **L: 132**
Statute league [unit of measure]
League **L: 159**
Statute mile [unit of measure]
Mile **M: 542**
Statute of Charitable Uses [1601]
Philanthropy **P: 368**
Statute of limitations [law] **So: 879**
Debt (Time limits on collection of debts) **D: 66**
Statute of Religious Freedom [1786]
Jefferson, Thomas (Virginia lawmaker) **J: 80**
Madison, James (Virginia assemblyman) **M: 33**
Statute of Rhuddlan [English history]
Wales (Revolts against England) **W: 12**
Statute of Westminster [1931]
Canada, History of (Independence) **C: 147-148**
Commonwealth of Nations (History) **Ci: 876-877**
Statutory law
Code **Ci: 748**
Lien **L: 273**
Statutory rape [crime]
Rape [crime] **R: 141**
Statutory referendum
Initiative and referendum (The referendum) **I: 272**
Staubach, Roger [American football player]
Football (table) **F: 363**
Staudinger, Hermann [German chemist]
Nobel Prizes (Chemistry: 1953) **N: 443**
Stave [device]
Barrel **B: 118** *with picture*
Stax [record label]
Rock music (Soul music) **R: 380a**
Stay [boat]
Sailing (Rigging) **S: 24**
Stay of execution
Reprieve **R: 242**
Stayman [apple]
Apple (table) **A: 571** *with picture*
STD [disease] *See* Sexually transmitted disease *in this index*
Ste. ... *See* Sainte ... *in this index*
Stead, Christina [Australian author]
Australia (Literature) **A: 904-905**
Stead, Erin E. [artist]
Caldecott Medal (table: 2011) **C: 26**
Stead, Rebecca [American author]
Newbery Medal (table) **N: 359**
Stead, Robert [Canadian author]
Canadian literature (Literature between the world wars) **C: 158-159**
Steady state theory [cosmology]
Cosmology (Other theories) **Ci: 1078**
Hoyle, Fred **H: 402**
Universe (Changing views of the universe) **U: 205-206**
Steagall, Henry B. [U.S. political leader]
Bank (The crisis of 1933) **B: 93-94**
Steak
Beef **B: 209**
Steak and kidney pie
England (Food and drink) **E: 295-296**
Steal [baseball] *See* Stolen base *in this index*
Stealing
Kleptomania **K: 344**
Stealth bomber [airplane]
Air Force, United States *picture on* **A: 192**; (Planes and weapons of the Air Force) **A: 190-191**; (The Persian Gulf War of 1991) **A: 196**
Aircraft, Military (Bombers) **A: 202** *with picture*
Bomber (History) **B: 453-454**
Steam So: 880
Boiler **B: 439**
Condensation **Ci: 929**
Energy supply (Geothermal power) **E: 279**
Water (The properties of water) **W: 129-130**
Steam bath
Bath (Bathing for cleanliness) **B: 163**
Steam carriage

Automobile *pictures on* **A: 962**; (The steam car) **A: 965** *with picture*
Evans, Oliver **E: 422**
Steam clock
British Columbia *picture on* **B: 621**
Steam cracking [industrial process]
Petrochemicals (How petrochemicals are made) **P: 329**
Steam distillation [industrial process]
Perfume (Plant substances) **P: 286**
Steam drill
Henry, John **H: 189**
Steam drop hammer
Steam hammer **So: 882**
Steam engine So: 880 *with diagrams*
Coal (Developments in England) **Ci: 731**
Energy supply (The Industrial Revolution) **E: 280**
Evans, Oliver **E: 422**
Fire department (The 1800's) **F: 128** *with picture*
Industrial Revolution (The steam engine) **I: 249**
Invention *picture on* **I: 359**; (The Industrial Revolution) **I: 361**
Locomotive *pictures on* **L: 415**; (Steam locomotives) **L: 416-417** *with picture*; (History) **L: 417**
Newcomen, Thomas **N: 359**
Transportation (The steam age) **T: 389** *with picture*
Turbine (Steam turbines) **T: 497**
Watt, James **W: 148** *with picture*
Steam fitter [career]
Building trade (Career opportunities) **B: 686**
Steam fog
Fog **F: 314**
Steam generator
Nuclear energy (Steam production) **N: 587** *with diagram*
Steam hammer So: 882
Steam heating
Heating (Steam and hot-water heating systems) **H: 159** *with diagram*
Steam-jet refrigeration
Refrigeration (Steam-jet refrigeration) **R: 202**
Steam locomotive *See* Locomotive *in this index*
Steam turbine [device]
Turbine (Steam turbines) **T: 497** *with diagrams*
Coal (Electric power production) **Ci: 718-719**
Electric power (Fossil-fueled steam electric power plants) **E: 183** *with diagram*
Energy (Energy conversion) **E: 274**
Heat (Changing heat into motion) **H: 154** *with diagram*
Invention (The Industrial Revolution) **I: 361-362**
Ship (Engine-driven ships) **S: 406**
Steam engine (Steam turbines) **So: 880**
Steam whistle
Whistle **W: 282**
Steamboat So: 882 *with picture*
Fitch, John **F: 189** *with picture*
Fulton, Robert **F: 555** *with picture*
Ship *picture on* **S: 423**; (The first steamboats) **S: 424**
Transportation *picture on* **T: 389**
United States, History of the (Advances in transportation and communications) **U: 168** *with pictures*
Steamboat Willie [film]
Animation (Walt Disney) **A: 514b**
Disney, Walt *picture on* **D: 236**
Motion picture (The movies talk) **M: 867**
Steamer duck [bird]
Duck (Steamer ducks) **D: 376**
Steaming
Cooking (Steaming) **Ci: 1029**
Steamship
Industrial Revolution *picture on* **I: 254**
Navy (Engineering advances) **N: 79**
Ship (Oceangoing steamships) **S: 424** *with pictures*; (Stronger, faster ships) **S: 425**
Steamboat **So: 882**
Warship (Warships of the 1800's) **W: 41**
Steamtown National Historic Site [Scranton]
National Park System (table: National historic sites) **N: 52-53**
Pennsylvania (Places to visit) **P: 254**
Stearic acid [chemical] **So: 882**
Lard **L: 75**
Life *diagram on* **L: 277**
Stearnes, Turkey [American baseball player]
Baseball (table: Hall of Fame) **B: 134b**
Stearns, Marcellus L. [American political leader]
Florida (table) **F: 260**
Stearns, Onslow [American political leader]
New Hampshire (table) **N: 223**
Steatite [rock] *See* Soapstone *in this index*
Steel *See* Iron and steel *in this index*
Steel City [nickname]

Gary **G:** 47
Pittsburgh **P:** 500a
Steel-cut oats [food]
Oatmeal **O:** 640
Steel guitar
Hawaii (Dancing and music) **H:** 94
Steel mill
Canada picture on **C:** 122
Iron and steel **I:** 436 with picture, picture on **I:** 452
Technology picture on **T:** 74
Steel tape [tool]
Surveying (Surveying tools) **So:** 1011
Steel Wire Gauge
Wire (Sizes of wire) **W:** 344
Steel Workers Organizing Committee
United Steelworkers **U:** 204
Steele, George W. [American political leader]
Oklahoma (Great land rushes) **O:** 732
Steele, John H. [American political leader]
New Hampshire (table) **N:** 223
Steele, Sir Richard [English author] **So:** 882
Addison, Joseph **A:** 47
English literature (Addison and Steele) **E:** 318
Essay (Personal essays) **E:** 359
Steele, Robert W. [American political leader]
Jefferson Territory **J:** 88
Steelers, Pittsburgh [team] See Pittsburgh Steelers
in this index
Steelhead [fish]
Fish picture on **F:** 159
Trout (True trout) **T:** 453
Steelie [marble]
Marbles **M:** 193
Steelworkers, United [union] See United
Steelworkers in this index
Steelyard [instrument]
Scale, Weighing (Balances) **S:** 169
Steen, Jan [Dutch painter] **So:** 883 with picture
Steenbok [antelope] **So:** 883
Antelope (Habits and appearance) **A:** 542
Steenburgen, Mary [American actress]
Motion picture (Best performance by an actress
in a supporting role: 1980) **M:** 862b
Steeping
Tea (Brewing tea) **T:** 63
Steeplechasing [sport] **So:** 883
Grand National **G:** 308
Track and field (Track events) **T:** 356 with picture
Steer
Cattle **C:** 306
Steer roping
Rodeo (Steer roping) **R:** 397
Steer undecorating
Rodeo (All-women's rodeos) **R:** 398
Steer wrestling
Rodeo (Steer wrestling) **R:** 397
Steerage, The [photograph by Stieglitz]
Stieglitz, Alfred picture on **So:** 900
Steering [driving]
Automobile diagram on **A:** 950; (The steering
system) **A:** 949 with diagram
Steering [real estate]
Segregation (De facto segregation) **S:** 285
Steering line
Parachute (How parachutes work) **P:** 143
Steering shaft [device]
Automobile (The steering system) **A:** 949
Steeves, William Henry [Canadian political leader]
Confederation of Canada (Fathers of
Confederation) **Ci:** 935 with picture
Stefan-Boltzmann law [physics]
Boltzmann, Ludwig **B:** 449
Steffe, William [American composer]
Battle Hymn of the Republic **B:** 172
Steffens, Lincoln [American author] **So:** 883
Muckrakers **M:** 908
Steger, Will [American explorer]
Exploration (The exploration of Antarctica) **E:** 450
Stegner, Wallace [American author] **So:** 883
Stegosaur [dinosaur]
Dinosaur (True dinosaurs) **D:** 205b-206c
Stegosaurus [dinosaur] **So:** 884
Dinosaur picture on **D:** 206d; (True dinosaurs)
D: 206b-206c
Steichen, Eduard Jean See Steichen, Edward in
this index
Steichen, Edward [American photographer]
So: 884 with picture
Photography (Artistic advances) **P:** 424-425
Steig, William [American author]
Caldecott Medal (table: 1970) **C:** 26
Cartoon (Single panel cartoons) **C:** 265-266
Steiger, Rod [American actor]
Motion picture (Best performance by an actor:
1967) **M:** 862a
Stein, Gertrude [American author] **So:** 884
American literature (The Lost Generation) **A:** 421

Fiction (History) **F:** 90-91
Lost Generation **L:** 472
Picasso, Pablo (The Rose Period) **P:** 448a; (Early
sculptures) **P:** 448a-448b
Thomson, Virgil **T:** 265
Stein, William Howard [American chemist]
Nobel Prizes (Chemistry: 1972) **N:** 444
Steinbeck, John [American author] **So:** 884
American literature picture on **A:** 416; (Realist
fiction) **A:** 422
Dust Bowl **D:** 391
Grapes of Wrath, The **G:** 321
Novel (New directions in the novel) **N:** 573-574
Steinberg, Saul [American artist] **So:** 885 with
picture
Cartoon (Single panel cartoons) **C:** 265-266
Steinberger, Jack [American physicist]
Neutrino **N:** 154
Nobel Prizes (Physics: 1988) **N:** 442
Steinbok [animal] See Steenbok in this index
Steinem, Gloria [American social critic] **So:** 885
Feminism **F:** 70
Steiner, Rudolf [Austrian-born philosopher]
So: 886
Steiner House [Vienna]
Architecture (Early modern architecture in
Europe) **A:** 627-629 with picture
Steinitz, William [Austrian chess player]
Chess (World chess champions) **C:** 414
Steinman, Ralph M. [Canadian physiologist]
Nobel Prizes (Physiology or medicine: 2011)
N: 447
Steinmetz, Charles Proteus [German-American
physicist] **So:** 886
Steinway, Henry Engelhard [American
businessman] **So:** 886
Piano (History) **P:** 447-448
Steinway & Sons
Steinway, Henry Engelhard **So:** 886
Steinweg, Heinrich Engelhard See Steinway,
Henry Engelhard in this index
Steitz, Thomas A. [American chemist]
Nobel Prizes (Chemistry: 2009) **N:** 444
Stelco Inc.
Iron and steel (In other countries) **I:** 449
Stele [botany]
Root (The core) **R:** 471
Stele [monument]
Maya (Communication and learning) **M:** 324
with picture
Stele of Hammurabi [archaeology]
Hammurabi picture on **H:** 36
Stella [literary figure]
Swift, Jonathan (His life) **So:** 1039
Stella, Frank [American painter] **So:** 886 with
picture
Art and the arts (The aesthetic experience)
A: 745-746 with picture
Stella, Joseph [American painter]
Roaring Twenties (Cultural trends) **R:** 364
Stellar association [astronomy]
Star cluster (Kinds of clusters) **So:** 853
Stellar astronomy
Herschel, Sir William **H:** 216
Stellar wind [astronomy]
Solar wind **So:** 582
Star (Intermediate-mass stars) **So:** 848-849
Stelle, John H. [American political leader]
Illinois (table) **I:** 71
Steller's jay [bird]
Jay **J:** 66
Steller's sea cow [animal]
Sea cow **S:** 262
Steller's sea-eagle [bird]
Eagle (Other kinds of eagles) **E:** 5
Stellite [metal]
Alloy (Other alloys) **A:** 378
Haynes, Elwood **H:** 122
Stelmach, Edward M. [Canadian political leader]
Alberta (table) **A:** 328
Stem [botany] **So:** 887 with diagrams
Fern (Parts of a fern) **F:** 74
Plant diagrams on **P:** 536; (Stems) **P:** 529 with
pictures
Vegetable (Stems) **V:** 292 with picture
Stem [music]
Music (Indicating time values) **M:** 953
Stem [plumbing]
Plumbing (How faucets work) **P:** 579 with
diagram
Stem [ship]
Ship (Nautical terms) **S:** 405 with diagram
Stem cell [biology] **So:** 889
See also Embryonic stem cell in this index
Blood (Formation of new blood components)
B: 411
Bone marrow transplant **B:** 458

Cloning (Ethical concerns) **Ci:** 683
Diabetes (Research) **D:** 180
Medical ethics **M:** 361
Sickle cell anemia **S:** 448
Stem rust [plant disease]
Barley (Diseases and insect pests) **B:** 113
Stenberg v. Carhart [U.S. history]
Abortion (Abortion in the United States) **A:** 15-16
Stencil
Printing (Screen printing) **P:** 801
Screen printing **S:** 225
Stendhal [French author] **So:** 889
French literature (Romantic fiction) **F:** 521
Novel (France) **N:** 573
Stengel, Casey [American baseball manager]
So: 889
Baseball (table: Hall of Fame) **B:** 134b; (Postwar
baseball) **B:** 136
Stenmark, Ingemar [Swedish skier]
Skiing (The middle and late 1900's) **S:** 487-488
Steno, Nicolaus [Danish doctor]
Geology (The rock dispute) **G:** 98
Mineral (The scientific study of mineral crystals)
M: 571
Stenography
Shorthand **S:** 435
Stenosis [disorder]
Heart (Other heart disorders) **H:** 141
Stent [medicine]
Angioplasty **A:** 461
Stentor [animal]
Protozoan (Ciliates) **P:** 838
Step cut
Gem (Types of gem cuts) pictures on **G:** 79
Step-down transformer [device]
Electric generator (Uses of AC generators) **E:** 173
Transformer **T:** 372
Step Pyramid
Egypt, Ancient (The Old Kingdom) **E:** 142 with
picture
Pyramids (The first pyramids) **P:** 916
Step-up transformer [device]
Electric generator (Uses of AC generators) **E:** 173
Electric power (Transmission) **E:** 184-185 with
diagram
Transformer **T:** 372
Stepashin, Sergei Vadimovich [Russian political
leader] **So:** 890
Stepbrother
Family (Family relationships) **F:** 21
Stepfamily
Divorce **D:** 253
Stepfather
Family (Family relationships) **F:** 21
Stephanie Marie Elisabeth [princess of Monaco]
Rainier III **R:** 129
Stephen [king of England] **So:** 890
England (Struggles for power) **E:** 305
Stephen I, Saint [pope]
Pope (table) **P:** 666
Stephen I [king of Hungary]
Hungary (The Kingdom of Hungary) **H:** 445
Stephen II [pope]
Papal States **P:** 132
Pepin the Short **P:** 277
Pope (table) **P:** 666
Stephen III [pope]
Pope (table) **P:** 666
Stephen IV [pope]
Pope (table) **P:** 666
Stephen V [pope]
Pope (table) **P:** 666
Stephen VI [pope]
Pope (table) **P:** 666
Stephen VII [pope]
Pope (table) **P:** 666
Stephen VIII [pope]
Pope (table) **P:** 666
Stephen IX [pope]
Pope (table) **P:** 666
Stephen, Adeline Virginia [birth name of]
Woolf, Virginia **W:** 401
Stephen, Saint [early Christian] **So:** 890
Stephen Foster Folk Culture Center State Park
[Florida]
Florida (Places to visit) **F:** 252
Stephens, Alexander Hamilton [Confederate
political leader] **So:** 890
Civil War, American (Secession) **Ci:** 617
Georgia (table) **G:** 130; (The Civil War) **G:** 132
Stephens, Charles H. [American painter]
Indian, American picture on **I:** 164
Stephens, James [Irish author] **So:** 890
Stephens, John Lloyd [American explorer] **So:** 890
Stephens, Lon V. [American political leader]
Missouri (table) **M:** 668
Stephens, Robert L. (Fox) [American aviator]

Aviation (table: Aviation speed records) **A: 990**
Stephens, Stan [American political leader]
Montana (table) **M: 757**
Stephens, Uriah S. [American labor leader]
Knights of Labor **K: 352**
Stephens, William D. [American political leader]
California (table) **C: 59**
Stephenson, Benjamin F. [American soldier]
Grand Army of the Republic **G: 305**
Stephenson, George [British engineer] **So: 890**
Railroad (Invention of the locomotive) **R: 115**
Rocket **R: 391**
Stephenson, Robert [British engineer] **So: 891**
Locomotive *picture on* **L: 414**; (History) **L: 417**
Rocket **R: 391**
Stepinac, Alojzije [Croatian religious leader]
Yugoslavia (Communist rule) **Y: 576**
Stepmother
Family (Family relationships) **F: 21**
Stepmother's flower [plant] *See* Pansy *in this index*
Steppe [geography] **So: 891**
Climate (Semiarid and desert climates) **Ci: 676b**
Flower (Flowers of prairies and dry plains) **F: 286**
Gobi **G: 242** *with picture*
Grassland **G: 329**
Kazakhstan (Land and climate) **K: 250b** *with
picture*
Plant (Grasslands) **P: 527**
Prairie (Climate and soil) **P: 731**
Russia (Land regions) **R: 539**
Steppe eagle
Eagle (Other kinds of eagles) **E: 5**
Steppe polecat [mammal]
Polecat **P: 619**
Stepped leader [lightning]
Lightning (Lightning strokes) **L: 300**
Steppenwolf Theatre
Theater *picture on* **T: 245**
Steppes rat snake
Snake *picture on* **S: 527**
Stepping motor
Watch (Quartz watches) **W: 114**
Stepsister
Family (Family relationships) **F: 21**
Steradian [measurement]
Candela **C: 175**
Light (Energy and brightness) **L: 290**
Sterbini, Cesare [Italian librettist]
Opera: (*Barber of Seville, The*) **O: 801**
Stereo [electronics] *See* Stereophonic sound
system *in this index*
Stereo camera
Camera (Stereo cameras) **C: 84**
Stereo system *See* Stereophonic sound system *in
this index*
Stereochemistry
Chemistry (Development of physical chemistry)
C: 404
Stereophonic sound system So: 891 *with picture*
Phonograph (How phonographs work) **P: 400**
with diagram; (History) **P: 401-402**
Radio (Stereophonic receivers) **R: 89**; (Radio since
the 1950's) **R: 94**
Tape recorder (Erasing and recording) **T: 38**
Stereoplotter [device]
Photogrammetry **P: 405** *with picture*
Stereoscope [instrument] **So: 893**
Camera (Stereo cameras) **C: 84**
Stereoscopic range finder [instrument]
Rangefinder **R: 139**
Stereoscopic vision
Eye (Depth perception) **E: 463-464**
Human being (Physical characteristics) **H: 413**
Stereotactic radiosurgery [medicine]
Brain (Tumors) **B: 558**
Cancer (Radiation therapy) **C: 172**
Stereotyping [printing] **So: 893**
Stereotyping [behavior] **So: 893**
Advertising (Recent developments) **A: 80**
Ageism **A: 140**
Asian Americans (Asian Americans today) **A: 813**
Hispanic Americans (Entertainment and arts)
H: 249-250
Indian, American (Current issues) **I: 182-183**
Personality (Ratings and self-reports) **P: 301**
Races, Human (Race and discrimination) **R: 59-60**
Segregation (Causes and effects of segregation)
S: 285
Sexuality (Gender roles) **S: 338a**
Women's movement (Women's status through
the ages) **W: 383**
Sterility [biology] **So: 893**
See also Infertility *in this index*
Birth control (Methods of birth control) **B: 378**
Insect (Insect control) **I: 284-285**
Sterilization [hygiene] **So: 893**
Ultraviolet rays (Uses of ultraviolet rays) **U: 17**

Sterilization [surgery]
Birth control (Methods of birth control) **B: 378**
Disability (The 1900's) **D: 221**
Sterilization **So: 894**
Vasectomy **V: 287**
Sterilized milk
Milk (Pasteurization) **M: 548**
Sterling, Pound [money] *See* Pound sterling *in
this index*
Sterling, Ross [American political leader]
Texas (table) **T: 203**
Sterling silver
Silver **S: 463**
Solution (Solid solutions) **So: 587**
Stern [ship]
Sailing (Hull) **S: 23** *with diagram*
Ship *diagram on* **S: 405**; (Basic structure) **S: 403**
Stern, Howard [American radio broadcaster]
Radio (Radio since the 1950's) **R: 94**
Stern, Isaac [American violinist] **So: 894**
Stern, Otto [American physicist]
Nobel Prizes (Physics: 1943) **N: 440**
Stern trawler [boat]
Fishing industry *picture on* **F: 180**; (Nets) **F: 183**
with diagram
Sternberg, Jonas [birth name of]
Von Sternberg, Josef **V: 448**
Sternberg, Robert J. [American psychologist]
Intelligence (Theories of intelligence) **I: 319**
Sternberk Madonna, The
Sculpture (Later medieval sculpture) **S: 250-251**
with diagram
Sterncastle [ship]
Ship (The cog) **S: 417**
Sterne, Laurence [British author] **So: 894**
English literature (The rise of the novel) **E: 318-
319**
Novel (The first English novelists) **N: 572**
Sternocleidomastoid [anatomy]
Head *diagram on* **H: 123**
Throat **T: 270**
Sternpost rudder
Invention (The Middle Ages) **I: 359-360**
Sternum [anatomy]
Bird (Skeleton and muscles) **B: 364** *with diagram*
Collarbone **Ci: 773** *with diagram*
Human body (table) **H: 422** *with diagram*
Rib **R: 320**
Skeleton (The human skeleton) **S: 479-480** *with
diagram*
Steroid [biochemistry] **So: 894**
See also Anabolic steroid *in this index*
Allergy (Treatment) **A: 374**
Hormone (How hormones work) **H: 337**
Life (Lipids) **L: 278**
Lipid (Kinds of lipids) **L: 345**
Sterol [biochemistry]
Vitamin (Vitamin D) **V: 432**
Steropes [legendary figure]
Cyclops **Ci: 1204**
Stesichorus [Greek poet]
Helen of Troy **H: 168**
Stet [publishing]
Proofreading (Proofreaders' marks) **P: 822**
Stethoscope [instrument] **So: 895** *with picture*
Blood pressure **B: 416**
Heart (Invention of new medical instruments)
H: 144
Laënnec, René Théophile Hyacinthe **L: 26**
Stetson, John Batterson [American businessman]
So: 895
Stettin [Poland] *See* Szczecin *in this index*
Stettinius, Edward Riley, Jr. [American
government official] **So: 895**
Truman, Harry S. (table) **T: 469**
United Nations *picture on* **U: 95**
Steuben, Baron von [German-American general]
So: 895
Revolution, American (Valley Forge) **R: 283**
Valley Forge (Conditions at Valley Forge) **V: 266**
Steuben glass
Glass (Types of art glass) **G: 220-221** *with picture*
Steunenberg, Frank [American political leader]
Idaho (table) **I: 42**; (Early statehood) **I: 44**
Steven F. Udvar-Hazy Center
National Air and Space Museum **N: 28**
Stevens, George [American director]
Motion picture (Best achievement in directing:
1951, 1956) **M: 862**
Stevens, H. H. [Canadian political leader]
Bennett, Richard Bedford (Economic reforms)
B: 253
Stevens, Hazard [American mountain climber]
Mount Rainier **M: 887**
Stevens, Isaac Ingalls [American political leader]
Washington (Territorial days) **W: 66**
Stevens, James [American author]

Bunyan, Paul **B: 701**
Stevens, John [American engineer] **So: 895**
Railroad (Developments in the United States)
R: 115
Stevens, John Paul [American jurist] **So: 896**
Stevens, Robert Livingston [American engineer]
So: 896
Stevens, Samuel, Jr. [American political leader]
Maryland (table) **M: 255**
Stevens, Siaka [Sierra Leone political leader]
Sierra Leone (History) **S: 452**
Stevens, Thaddeus [American political leader]
So: 896
Johnson, Andrew (Plans for Reconstruction)
J: 139
Reconstruction (The Radicals and the Moderates)
R: 178
Stevens, Wallace [American poet] **So: 896**
American literature (Modernist poetry) **A: 421**
Stevenson, Adlai Ewing [1835-1914, American
political leader] **So: 896** *with portrait*
Vice president of the United States **V: 348** *with
portrait*
Stevenson, Adlai Ewing [1900-1965, American
statesman] **So: 897** *with portrait*
Eisenhower, Dwight David (Election of 1956)
E: 153
Illinois (table) **I: 71**
Kennedy, John Fitzgerald (Bid for the vice
presidency) **K: 263**
Political convention (The changing role of
conventions) **P: 630**
United Nations (table) **U: 86**
Stevenson, Charles C. [American political leader]
Nevada (table) **N: 173**
Stevenson, Coke R. [American political leader]
Johnson, Lyndon Baines (Election to the Senate)
J: 147
Texas (table) **T: 203**
Stevenson, Edward C. [American physicist]
Muon **M: 929**
Stevenson, Elizabeth Cleghorn [British author]
Gaskell, Elizabeth **G: 61**
Stevenson, Robert [Scottish engineer] **So: 897**
Stevenson, Robert Louis [Scottish author] **So: 897**
with pictures
Apia **A: 566**
Literature for children (Masterpieces of fiction)
L: 363
Stevenson, William E. [American political leader]
West Virginia (table) **W: 225**
Stew [bath]
Bath (History) **B: 164**
Stew [food]
Cooking (Simmering) **Ci: 1028**
Steward [horse racing]
Horse racing ("They're off!") **H: 365**
Steward [office]
Labor movement (Local unions) **L: 8**
Steward Observatory
Telescope (Reflecting telescopes) **T: 104-105**
Stewardess, Airline *See* Flight attendant *in this
index*
Stewart, Charles [Canadian political leader]
Alberta (table) **A: 328**
Stewart, Henry, Earl of Darnley [Scottish
nobleman] *See* Darnley, Lord *in this index*
Stewart, Jackie [British race driver]
Automobile racing (table: Formula One World
Drivers' Championship) **A: 980**
Stewart, James [American actor] **So: 899** *with
portrait*
Motion picture (Best performance by an actor:
1940) **M: 862a**
Stewart, James [Canadian political leader]
Prince Edward Island (table) **P: 791**
Stewart, John W. [American political leader]
Vermont (table) **V: 333**
Stewart, Potter [American jurist] **So: 899**
Stewart, Robert [British statesman]
Castlereagh, Viscount **C: 282**
Stewart, Robert M. [American political leader]
Missouri (table) **M: 668**
Stewart, Sam V. [American political leader]
Montana (table) **M: 757**
Stewart, Tony [American race driver]
Automobile racing (table: NASCAR Sprint Cup
champions) **A: 981**
Stewart Island [New Zealand]
New Zealand (Other islands) **N: 352**
Stewart plaid [pattern]
Tartan *pictures on* **T: 47**
Stewing [cooking]
Meat (How meat is cooked) **M: 350**
Stheno [Greek mythology]
Gorgons **G: 274**
Stibium [element]

Antimony A: 557
Stibnite [mineral]
Antimony A: 557
Mineral *picture on* M: 568
Stick check [sports]
Lacrosse (Men's lacrosse) L: 23
Stick insect *See* Walkingstick *in this index*
Stick lac [substance]
Lac L: 19
Stick welding
Welding (Arc welding) W: 189
Stickball [game]
Indian, American (Recreation) I: 142
Stickleback [fish] So: 899
Sticknet [device]
Tornado (The VORTEX projects) T: 337
Stickney, William W. [American political leader]
Vermont (table) V: 333
Stickpin [fastener]
Pin P: 466 *with picture*
Sticky polemonium
Flower *picture on* F: 289
Stiegel, Henry William [American businessman]
So: 900
Glass (Types of art glass) G: 220-221; (Early American glass) G: 222
Stiegel glass
Antique *picture on* A: 558
Glass (Types of art glass) G: 220-221
Stiegel, Henry William So: 900
Stieglitz, Alfred [American photographer] So: 900 *with picture*
Dove, Arthur Garfield D: 315
Marin, John M: 203
O'Keeffe, Georgia O: 709
Painting (Steiglitz and "291") P: 82
Photography (Artistic advances) P: 424-425; (Dramatic changes) P: 425-426
Stiff-mud process
Brick (Forming bricks) B: 597
Stiff-tailed duck
Duck *picture on* D: 375; (Stiff-tailed ducks) D: 376
Stiffness
Materials (Properties of materials) M: 300b
Stifter, Adalbert [German author]
German literature (Realism) G: 141
Stigler, George Joseph [American economist]
Nobel Prizes (Economics: 1982) N: 449
Stiglitz, Joseph Eugene [American economist]
Nobel Prizes (Economics: 2001) N: 449
Stigma [botany]
Flower *picture on* F: 293; (The carpels) F: 294
Plant *picture on* P: 534; (Flowers) P: 531 *with picture*
Pollen (Fertilization) P: 645 *with picture*
Seed (Seed development in angiosperms) S: 281
Stigma [zoology]
Egg (Development of the bird's egg) E: 117
Stigmata [religion]
Francis of Assisi, Saint F: 482
Stijl, De [art]
Minimalism M: 573
Mondrian, Piet M: 703
Painting (De Stijl) P: 80 *with picture*
Stikine River
British Columbia (Rivers, waterfalls, and lakes) B: 624
Still [device]
Distillation D: 238
Distilling D: 239
Still, Andrew Taylor [American doctor]
Osteopathic medicine (History) O: 867
Still, Clyfford [American painter] So: 900
Painting (Abstract Expressionism) P: 84-85
Still, William [American social reformer] So: 900 *with portrait*
Underground railroad U: 21
Still, William Grant [American composer] So: 901
Still fishing
Fishing F: 175, *diagram on* F: 179
Still life [art]
Harnett, William Michael H: 64
Painting (Still-life paintings) P: 33
Picasso, Pablo (Cubism) P: 448b *with picture*
Still Life with Chair Caning [painting by Picasso]
Picasso, Pablo (Cubism) P: 448b *with picture*
Still Life with Commode [painting by Cézanne]
Painting (Postimpressionism) P: 75 *with picture*
Still rings [event]
Gymnastics (Men's events) G: 448 *with picture*
Still Stands the House [book by Ringwood]
Canadian literature (Literature between the world wars) C: 158-159
Stillness at Appomattox, A [book by Catton]
Catton, Bruce C: 316
Stillwater [Minnesota] So: 901
Stillwater [Oklahoma]

Oklahoma *picture on* O: 717
Stilt [bird] So: 901 *with picture*
Stilt house
Shelter *picture on* S: 394; (Prehistoric times) S: 393
Stilton [cheese]
Cheese (Semisoft cheese) C: 392
Stilwell, Joseph Warren [American general]
So: 901
Burma Road B: 708
World War II (China) W: 492
Stilwell, Mary [wife of]
Edison, Thomas Alva (Family and friends) E: 81
Stilwell and the American Experience in China [book by Tuchman]
Tuchman, Barbara Wertheim T: 480
Stilwell Road [Myanmar-China]
Burma Road B: 708
Stimson, Henry Lewis [American government official]
Roosevelt, Franklin Delano (table) R: 454; (The road to war) R: 455
Truman, Harry S. (table) T: 469
Stimulant [physiology] So: 901
Caffeine C: 14
Cocaine (Physical and psychological effects) Ci: 742
Doping D: 309
Drug (Drugs that affect the nervous system) D: 352
Drug abuse (table: Some commonly abused drugs) D: 363
Methamphetamine M: 433
Ritalin R: 350
Stimulated emission
Laser (Producing laser light) L: 84 *with diagrams*
Stimulus [biology]
Animal (Adaptations for sensing the environment) A: 492-493
Life (Responsiveness) L: 275
Stimulus [psychology]
Habit (How we learn habits) H: 2
Instinct (How instinctive behavior works) I: 304
Learning (Classical conditioning) L: 163
Mind (Parts of the mind) M: 562-563
Stimulus-response [psychology]
Education (How people learn) E: 89
Learning (Classical conditioning) L: 163
Psychology (Behaviorism) P: 849-850; (Modern psychology) P: 850
Reflex action R: 194
Stine, R. L. [American author] So: 902
Sting [British singer]
Rock music (New wave and mainstream rock) R: 380c
Sting [injury]
Ant *picture on* A: 523; (Protection against enemies) A: 524-525
Bee (Sting) B: 202 *with pictures*
First aid (Injected poisons) F: 137; (Animal bites or stings) F: 138
Hornet H: 340
Scorpion S: 210
Wasp W: 111
Sting, The [film]
Motion picture (Best picture: 1973) M: 861
Stingaree [fish] *See* Stingray *in this index*
Stinger [weapon]
Guided missile (Surface-to-air missiles) G: 426
Stinging nettle [plant]
Nettle N: 151
Stingless bee
Bee *picture on* B: 206; (Social bees) B: 205
Stingray [fish] So: 901 *with picture*
Animal *picture on* A: 487
Stink bug So: 902 *with picture*
Insect *picture on* I: 281
Stinkdamp [gas]
Damp D: 22
Stinkhorn [fungus]
Mushroom (Mushroomlike fungi) M: 945
Stinking smut [plant disease]
Smut S: 522
Wheat (Care during growth) W: 271
Stipe [botany]
Fern (Parts of a fern) F: 74-75
Stipule [botany]
Leaf *picture on* L: 153; (The stipules) L: 155
Plant (Leaves) P: 529-531 *with picture*
Stir-frying
Cooking (Sautéing) Ci: 1028
Stirling, James [British admiral]
Perth P: 305
Western Australia (History) W: 231
Stirling, James [British architect]
Architecture (Architecture today) A: 632-633
Stirling, Robert [Scottish inventor]

Stirling engine So: 902
Stirling engine So: 902 *with diagrams*
Stirrer [component]
Microwave oven M: 520 *with diagram*
Stirrup [anatomy]
Ear (The middle ear) E: 7-8 *with diagram*
Stirrup [riding equipment]
Saddle S: 7 *with pictures*
Stitch
Crochet Ci: 1148c *with diagrams*
Embroidery (Embroidery stitches) E: 257 *with picture*
Knitting K: 353 *with diagrams*
Needlepoint N: 118 *with picture*
Petit point P: 326
Sewing (Kinds of stitches) S: 332
Sewing machine *diagrams on* S: 334
Stitchers [stapler]
Printing (Offset presses) P: 798-799
Stitching [industrial process]
Tire (Assembling a tire) T: 296
STM [device] *See* Scanning tunneling microscope *in this index*
Stoat [animal] *See* Ermine *in this index*
Stock [clothing]
Colonial life in America (Clothing) Ci: 799
Necktie N: 117
Stock [gun]
Rifle (The parts of a rifle) R: 338 *with diagram*
Stock [horticulture]
Grafting G: 298 *with pictures*
Stock [plant] So: 903 *with picture*
Stock [securities] So: 903
Corporation (Business corporations) Ci: 1069
Dow Jones averages D: 315
Income tax (Effects of inflation) I: 103
Industry (Capital) I: 258
Initial public offering I: 271
Insider trading I: 303
Investment (Stocks) I: 368
Investment banking I: 369
Property P: 827
Roaring Twenties (Rising prosperity) R: 363
Stock exchange So: 903
Stock anchor
Anchor *picture on* A: 449
Stock Car Auto Racing, National Association for *See* NASCAR *in this index*
Stock car racing
Automobile racing *picture on* A: 975; (Stock car racing) A: 978
NASCAR N: 21
Stock certificate [economics]
Stock So: 903
Stock dividend [economics]
Stock (Stockholders) So: 903
Stock dyeing [process]
Dye (Dyeing textiles) D: 396
Stock exchange [economics] So: 903
See also the list of Related articles in the Stock exchange *article*
Bears and bulls B: 189
Computer *picture on* Ci: 908
Cornering the market Ci: 1065
Dow Jones averages D: 315
Europe *picture on* E: 405
Initial public offering I: 271
Insider trading I: 303
Investment (table) I: 366
New York Stock Exchange N: 345
Standard & Poor's indexes So: 833
Stock (Stockholders) So: 903
Telegraph (Uses for the telegraph) T: 91
Stock Exchange, Amsterdam [building]
Architecture (Early modern architecture in Europe) A: 627-628 *with picture*
Stock index [economics]
See also Dow Jones averages; Standard & Poor's indexes *in this index*
Stock exchange (Stock prices and indexes) So: 904
Stock index fund
Mutual fund M: 969
Stock index futures [economics]
Commodity exchange (Financial futures) Ci: 874
Stock insurance company
Insurance (Types of insurance companies) I: 315
Stock market [economics] *See* Stock exchange *in this index*
Stock market crash [1929]
Great Depression (The stock market crash) G: 340
United States, History of the (The stock market crash of 1929) U: 191 *with picture*
Stock market panic [1907]
Roosevelt, Theodore (Domestic problems) R: 466-467
Stock raising [agriculture]

Livestock **L:** 396 *with pictures*
Stock savings bank [savings institution]
Savings bank **S:** 166
Stock ticker [machine] **So:** 904
Edison, Thomas Alva (Inventor and businessman)
E: 78 *with picture*
Stock exchange (Trading) **So:** 904
Telegraph (Uses for the telegraph) **T:** 91
Stockade [fortification]
Pioneer life in America (Defending a settlement)
P: 485
Stockbroker
Sales (Other types of selling) **S:** 62
Stock exchange **So:** 903
Stockdale, James B. [American naval officer]
Perot, Ross **P:** 292
Stockhausen, Karlheinz [German composer]
So: 905
Stockholder
Business (Stockholders) **B:** 726
Stock (Stockholders) **So:** 903
Stockholm [Sweden] **So:** 905 *with picture*
Sweden *pictures on* **So:** 1020, **So:** 1024; (table:
Average monthly weather) **So:** 1030
Stockings [clothing] **So:** 906
Stockless anchor
Anchor *picture on* **A:** 449
Stockley, Charles C. [American political leader]
Delaware (table) **D:** 109
Stocks [economics] *See* Stock *in this index*
Stocks [punishment] **So:** 906
Colonial life in America (Crime and punishment)
Ci: 796 *with picture*
Stockton, Frank Richard [American author]
So: 906
Stockton, John [American basketball player]
So: 906
Stockton, Richard [American patriot] **So:** 906
Princeton University **P:** 794
Stockton, Robert F. [American military leader]
Frémont, John Charles **F:** 511
Mexican War (The occupation of New Mexico and
California) **M:** 446
Stockton, Thomas [American political leader]
Delaware (table) **D:** 109
Stockton and Darlington Railroad
Railroad (Invention of the locomotive) **R:** 115
Stockyards
Meat packing (Marketing livestock and meat)
M: 350
Ranching (Life on a cattle ranch) **R:** 134
Stoddard, Joshua C. [American inventor]
Calliope **C:** 68
Stoddard, Solomon [grandfather of]
Edwards, Jonathan **E:** 114
Stoddert, Benjamin [American government
official] **So:** 906
Stoic philosophy So: 906
Epictetus **E:** 342
Greek literature (The Greco-Roman Age) **G:** 378
Hellenistic Age **H:** 177
Marcus Aurelius **M:** 197
Mythology (Allegorical approaches) **M:** 988
Philosophy (Stoic philosophy and Epicureanism)
P: 387
Zeno of Citium **Z:** 589
Stojic, Manya [Yugoslavian-born author]
Literature for children *picture on* **L:** 367
Stoke, Battle of [1487]
England (The Wars of the Roses) **E:** 306-307
Stoke-on-Trent [England] **So:** 907
Stoker, Bram [Irish author] **So:** 906
Dracula **D:** 317
Vampire **V:** 268
Stokes, Carl Burton [American political leader]
So: 907
Cleveland (History) **Ci:** 666-667
Stokes, Edward C. [American political leader]
New Jersey (table) **N:** 249
Stokes, George G. [British physicist]
Fluorescence **F:** 305
Stokes, Montfort [American political leader]
North Carolina (table) **N:** 490
Stokowski, Leopold [American conductor] **So:** 907
Ormandy, Eugene **O:** 857
STOL [aircraft]
V/STOL **V:** 452
Stola [clothing]
Clothing (Rome) **Ci:** 697
Rome, Ancient (Clothing) **R:** 440
Stolby National Park [Russia]
National park (table) **N:** 42f
Stolen base [baseball]
Baseball (Base runners—advancing and outs)
B: 129-130; (Recent developments) **B:** 137;
(table: Modern major league records) **B:** 138
Stolen Generation [Australian history] **So:** 907

Aborigines, Australian (Aboriginal life today)
A: 14
Australia (The Stolen Generation) **A:** 924
Stoll, Arthur [Swiss chemist]
LSD **L:** 512
Stollen [food]
Christmas (Christmas feasting) **C:** 534-535
Stolon [botany]
Fungi (Parts of a fungus) **F:** 558-559 *with diagram*
Grass (The grass plant) **G:** 324
Mold **M:** 690
Vegetable (Tubers) **V:** 293
Stomach [anatomy] **So:** 907 *with diagram*
Acid reflux **A:** 27
Alimentary canal **A:** 368 *with diagram*
Bariatric surgery **B:** 109 *with diagram*
Frog *picture on* **F:** 537
Gastritis **G:** 66
Gland (table) **G:** 209
Human body (The digestive system) **H:** 419;
(table) **H:** 422 *with diagram*
Hunger **H:** 449
Insect (Digestive system) **I:** 289 *with diagram*
Prostaglandin **P:** 829
Reptile (Internal organs) **R:** 251
Ruminant **R:** 519 *with diagram*
Spider (Digestive system) **So:** 785 *with diagram*
Vomiting **V:** 447
Weight control (Surgery) **W:** 183
Stomach poison
Insecticide **I:** 301
Stomacher [ornament]
Clothing (The 1700's) **Ci:** 703
Stomata [botany]
Botany *picture on* **B:** 508
Desert (Desert plants) **D:** 156
Leaf (Obtaining the raw materials) **L:** 155 *with
diagram*
Plant (Leaves) **P:** 529-531
Respiration (Respiration in plants) **R:** 261
Stomiatoid fish
Fish *picture on* **F:** 156
Stone [botany]
Fruit (Simple fruits) **F:** 544 *with pictures*
Stone [glassmaking]
Glass (Glass terms) **G:** 222
Stone [rock]
House (Building materials) **H:** 380
Materials (Stone) **M:** 300c
Plastics (To replace wood and stone) **P:** 555
Quarrying **Q:** 7
Stone [sports]
Curling **Ci:** 1195 *with picture*; (The rink) **Ci:** 1196
with diagram
Stone [unit of measure]
Weights and measures (Miscellaneous weights
and measures) **W:** 184
Stone, Barton W. [American religious leader]
Disciples of Christ **D:** 223
Stone, Dan [American political leader]
Lincoln, Abraham (Success in politics) **L:** 314
Stone, David [American political leader]
North Carolina (table) **N:** 490
Stone, Edward Durell [American architect] **So:** 908
Stone, Harlan Fiske [American jurist] **So:** 909
Stone, John H. [American political leader]
Maryland (table) **M:** 255
Stone, John M. [American political leader]
Mississippi (table) **M:** 640
Stone, Lucy [American social reformer] **So:** 909
with portrait
Woman suffrage (Growth of the movement)
W: 380
Women's movement (The right to vote) **W:** 385
Stone, Oliver [American film director] **So:** 909
Motion picture (Best achievement in directing:
1986, 1989) **M:** 862
Stone, Precious *See* Gem *in this index*
Stone, Sir Richard [British economist]
Nobel Prizes (Economics: 1984) **N:** 449
Stone, Thomas [American patriot] **So:** 909
Stone, William Alexis [American political leader]
Pennsylvania (table) **P:** 263
Stone, William Joel [American political leader]
Missouri (table) **M:** 668
Stone, William M. [American political leader]
Iowa (table) **I:** 391
Stone Age [anthropology] **So:** 909
Arrowhead *picture on* **A:** 744
Lake dwelling **L:** 37
Prehistoric people (The Stone Age) **P:** 751
Surgery (History) **So:** 1007
Tool (History of tools) **T:** 330
Stone Angel, The [book by Laurence]
Canadian literature (Modern English-Canadian
fiction) **C:** 160
Stone carving

Petrified Forest National Park *picture on* **P:** 329
Sculpture (Archaic sculpture) **S:** 245
Stone fly *See* Stonefly *in this index*
Stone Mountain [Georgia] **So:** 910 *with picture*
Borglum, Gutzon **B:** 488
Georgia (Visitor's guide) **G:** 122 *with picture*
Stone of Destiny *See* Scone, Stone of *in this index*
Stone of Scone *See* Scone, Stone of *in this index*
Stone plant
Flower *picture on* **F:** 272
Plant *picture on* **P:** 541
Stone Soup [magazine]
Literature for children (New children's magazines)
L: 365-366
Stonebreakers, The [painting by Courbet]
Courbet, Gustave **Ci:** 1100
Painting (Realism) **P:** 70 *with picture*
Stonechat [bird] **So:** 910 *with picture*
Stonecrop [botany]
Leaf *picture on* **L:** 157
Sedum **S:** 280
Stonecutters Bridge [China]
Bridge (table: Cable-stayed) **B:** 603
Stonecutters Island
Hong Kong (British control) **H:** 319
Stonefish So: 910 *with picture*
Fish *picture on* **F:** 167
Stonefly [insect] **So:** 911 *with picture*
Stonehenge [monument, England] **So:** 910 *with
pictures*
Astronomy (History) **A:** 846-847
England (History) **E:** 303
Observatory **O:** 644
Stoneman, Ernest "Pop" [American musician]
Country music *picture on* **Ci:** 1098
Stoneman, George [American political leader]
California (table) **C:** 59
Stones River, Battle of [1863]
Civil War, American (table) **Ci:** 624; (Battle of
Stones River) **Ci:** 629
Stones River National Battlefield [Tennessee]
National Park System (table: National battlefields)
N: 55
Stone's sheep [animal]
Bighorn **B:** 299
Stonewall Inn [New York City]
Gay rights movement (History of gay rights) **G:** 73
Homosexuality (Attitudes toward homosexuality)
H: 307
Stoneware So: 912
Porcelain **P:** 675
Pottery (Stoneware) **P:** 716 *with picture*
Stoney, G. Johnstone [Irish physicist]
Electricity (The electronic age) **E:** 198
Stonies [name for]
Assiniboine Indians **A:** 819
Stony coral
Coral (Stony corals) **Ci:** 1048a *with pictures*
Coral reef (How coral reefs form) **Ci:** 1048b
Stony-iron meteorite
Meteor (Meteorites) **M:** 432
Stony meteorite
Meteor (Meteorites) **M:** 432
Stony Point, Battle of [1779]
Wayne, Anthony **W:** 154
Stookey, S. D. [American inventor]
Glass (table) **G:** 218
Stool [physiology]
Colon cancer **Ci:** 786
Fiber, Dietary **F:** 88
Stoop [flying]
Falcon **F:** 12
Peregrine falcon **P:** 284
Stop [key]
Harmonium **H:** 62
Organ (Pipe organs) **O:** 851-852
Stop bath [chemical]
Photography (Black-and-white negative film)
P: 419
Stop-motion [technique]
Advertising (Production) **A:** 76b
Animation (Stop-motion animation) **A:** 514a
with picture; (New diversity) **A:** 514c-514d *with
picture*
Stop price [investment]
Auction **A:** 881
Stope [mining]
Mining (Self-supported mining) **M:** 576
Stope-and-pillar mining
Mining (Self-supported mining) **M:** 576
Stopes, Marie Carmichael [British social reformer]
Feminism **F:** 70
Stoplight parrotfish
Fish *picture on* **F:** 154
Stoppage [sports]
Rugby football **R:** 510
Stoppard, Tom [British dramatist] **So:** 912

English literature (Recent English drama) **E: 323**
Stopped consonant
Consonant **Ci: 992**
Stopper ball
Plumbing (How toilets work) **P: 579**
"Stopping by Woods on a Snowy Evening"
[poem by Frost]
Frost, Robert (His poems) **F: 543**
Stora Sjofallet National Park [Sweden]
National park (table) **N: 42g**
Storage battery
Edison, Thomas Alva (Batteries) **E: 80**
Lead (Uses) **L: 149** *with picture*
Storage device
Computer (Storage devices) **Ci: 915**
Storage heater
Heating (Electric power) **H: 159**
Storage unit
Furniture (The 1900's to the present) **F: 582**
Storax [tree product]
Sweet gum **So: 1037**
Store
Department store **D: 148**
Interior design *picture on* **I: 327**
Retailing **R: 264**
Shopping center **S: 434**
Store of value
Money **M: 704**
Storebaelt Bridge [Denmark]
Bridge (table: Suspension) **B: 603**
Stored energy [physics] *See* Potential energy *in this index*
Storefront school
Alternative school (Features of alternative schools) **A: 388-389**
Storer College
Harpers Ferry **H: 66b**
Storied Province [name for]
Quebec **Q: 11**
Stories of the Life of St. Francis [painting by Gozzoli]
Roman Catholic Church *picture on* **R: 406**
Storis [ship]
Northwest Passage **N: 529**
Stork **So: 912** *with pictures*
Adjutant **A: 58** *with picture*
Animal (Animal travelers) **A: 502** *with picture*
Bird (Birds of Europe) **B: 344c** *with picture*
Europe *picture on* **E: 401**
Marabou **M: 190** *with picture*
Storksbill [plant]
Flower *picture on* **F: 288**
Geranium **G: 136**
Storm [weather] **So: 913** *with picture*
See also the list of Related articles in the Storm *article*
Cloud (Clouds and the weather) **Ci: 711**
Derecho **D: 152**
Flash flood **F: 227**
Thunderstorm **T: 272**
Weather *pictures on* **W: 167**
Wind (table) **W: 330**
Storm, The [play by Ostrovsky]
Drama (Russian drama and Chekhov) **D: 338**
Russian literature (Early realism) **R: 562**
Storm, Tropical *See* Tropical storm *in this index*
Storm and Stress [literature] *See* Sturm und Drang *in this index*
Storm chaser [meteorology]
Tornado (Studying tornadoes) **T: 336** *with picture*
Storm flag [U.S. Army]
Flag (table) **F: 193**
Storm Lake
Iowa (Rivers and lakes) **I: 386**
Storm-petrel [bird]
Bird (Birds of the ocean and the Antarctic) **B: 344** *with picture*
Petrel **P: 328**
Storm Prediction Center [Norman, Oklahoma]
Weather Service, National **W: 172**
Storm surge [oceanography]
Asia (Natural disasters) **A: 812**
Bangladesh (Climate) **B: 83-84**
Flood (Seacoast floods) **F: 237**
Hurricane (Hurricane damage) **H: 455**; (table) **H: 456** *with picture*
Hurricane Katrina (The storm) **H: 456**
Typhoon **T: 540** *with picture*
Storm troopers [German history]
Hitler, Adolf (Birth of the Nazi Party) **H: 265**
Nazism (The rise to power) **N: 92**
Storm warning
Boating (Buoys and other safety aids) **B: 430** *with picture*
Flag *picture on* **F: 197**; (Flags that talk) **F: 208**
Storm-water drainage
Road (Storm-water drainage) **R: 359**

Störmer, Horst Ludwig [German-born American physicist]
Nobel Prizes (Physics: 1998) **N: 442**
Storni, Alfonsina [Argentine poet]
Latin American literature (The early 1900's) **L: 113**
Storting [government]
Nobel Prizes **N: 439**
Norway (National government) **N: 537-539**
Stortorget [area]
Sweden *picture on* **So: 1024**
Story *See* Storytelling *in this index*
Story, Joseph [American jurist] **So: 914**
Story, Nelson [American settler]
Montana (The cattle industry) **M: 758**
Story of a Novel, The [book by Wolfe]
Wolfe, Thomas **W: 378**
Story of Doctor Dolittle, The [book by Lofting]
Lofting, Hugh **L: 420** *with picture*
Story of Ferdinand, The [book by Leaf]
Lawson, Robert **L: 147**
Story of Lucy Gault, The [book by Trevor]
Irish literature (Fiction) **I: 432**
Story of Mankind, The [book by Van Loon]
Literature for children (Children's nonfiction) **L: 365**
Story of My Life, The [book by Keller]
American literature (Nonfiction writers) **A: 420**
Story of the Malakand Field Force, The [book by Churchill]
Churchill, Sir Winston Leonard Spencer (Soldier and reporter) **C: 546**
Storyboard
Advertising (Creative work) **A: 76b**
Animation (Preliminary steps in animation) **A: 511**
Television (The director) **T: 110d**
Storytelling **So: 914** *with picture*
See also the list of Related articles in the Storytelling *article*
Homer (The Homeric question today) **H: 304**
Humor **H: 435**
Library (Active community service) **L: 236-237** *with picture*
Religion (The use of sacred stories) **R: 217**
Stoss, Veit [German sculptor] **So: 916** *with picture*
Stoss and lee [geology]
Glacier (How glaciers shape the land) **G: 203**
Stothart, Herbert [American composer]
Wizard of Oz, The **W: 374**
Stotz, Carl [American sports figure]
Little League Baseball **L: 392**
Stourbridge Lion [locomotive]
Locomotive *picture on* **L: 414**; (History) **L: 417**
Railroad (Developments in the United States) **R: 115**
Stout [drink]
Beer **B: 211**
England (Food and drink) **E: 295-296**
Ireland (Food and drink) on **I: 424**
Stout, Elihu [American printer]
Indiana (Communication) **I: 213**
Stout, Jacob [American political leader]
Delaware (table) **D: 109**
Stout, Rex [American author] **So: 916**
Detective story (The pattern) **D: 162**
Stout, William B. [American engineer]
Airplane (The golden age) **A: 235**
Stout infantfish [fish]
Fish **F: 144**
Stove *See* Range *in this index*
Stove bolt [hardware]
Bolt **B: 449**
Stove naphtha [fuel]
Gasoline (History) **G: 62**
Stowe [Vermont]
Vermont (Visitor's guide) **V: 326** *with picture*
Stowe, Calvin [American educator]
Stowe, Harriet Beecher (Her life) **So: 916**
Stowe, Harriet Beecher [American author] **So: 916** *with portrait*
American literature (The sentimental novel) **A: 415**
Novel (The United States) **N: 573**
Uncle Tom's Cabin **U: 19**
United States, History of the (The Compromise of 1850) **U: 175**
Stoyanov, Petar [Bulgarian political leader]
Bulgaria (Recent developments) **B: 693**
Strabismic amblyopia [disorder]
Eye (Strabismus) **E: 466**
Strabismus [disorder] **So: 916**
Eye (Strabismus) **E: 466**
Glasses (Prescription glasses) **G: 224-225**
Strabo [Greek geographer] **So: 917**
Geography (Early study) **G: 95**
Geology (The ancient Greeks) **G: 97**
Science (Ancient Rome) **S: 197**

Strachey, Giles Lytton *See* Strachey, Lytton *in this index*
Strachey, Lytton [British author] **So: 917**
Biography (Modern biography) **B: 314**
Strada, La [film]
Fellini, Federico **F: 68**
Motion picture (The art film revival) **M: 870**
Straddle [track and field]
High jump **H: 227**
Stradivari, Antonio [Italian violinmaker] **So: 917** *with picture*
Violin (History) **V: 390**
Stradivarius violin
Stradivari, Antonio **So: 917** *with picture*
Strafford, Earl of [English political leader] **So: 917**
Long Parliament **L: 448**
Straight [poker]
Poker **P: 603**
Straight [sexuality] *See* Heterosexuality *in this index*
Straight, Beatrice [American actress]
Motion picture (Best performance by an actress in a supporting role: 1976) **M: 862b**
Straight-4 engine
Automobile (The engine block) **A: 951-953**
Straight ahead jazz
Jazz (Recent developments) **J: 73-74**
Straight angle
Angle **A: 462** *with diagram*
Straight ball [bowling]
Bowling (How to bowl) **B: 521-522** *with diagram*
Straight-edged razor
Razor (Straight-edged razors) **R: 154**
Straight flush [poker]
Poker **P: 603**
Straight goods fertilizer
Fertilizer (Production and sale) **F: 80**
Straight life insurance
Insurance (Cash value life insurance) **I: 310**
Straight-line inlay machine
Linoleum **L: 338**
Straight photography
Adams, Ansel **A: 32**
Photography (Dramatic changes) **P: 425-426**
Weston, Edward **W: 243**
Straight pin [fastener]
Pin **P: 466**
Straight position
Diving *pictures on* **D: 244**; (Kinds of dives) **D: 243**
Straight-rail billiards [game]
Billiards (Carom billiards) **B: 306**
Straight right
Boxing *picture on* **B: 528**
Straight-stitch sewing machine
Sewing machine (Kinds of sewing machines) **S: 333**
Straight ticket
Ballot (In the United States) **B: 63**
Straight truck [vehicle]
Truck (Kinds of trucks) **T: 457**
Strain [medicine]
Repetitive strain injury **R: 242**
Strain [physics]
Elasticity **E: 156**
Strain-gauge load cell
Scale, Weighing (Electronic scales) **S: 169**
Strait [geography] **So: 917**
Strait cloth
Broadcloth **B: 635**
Strait Is the Gate [book by Gide]
Gide, André **G: 188**
Straits, The [waterway, Turkey]
Turkey **T: 502** *with picture*
Straits Convention [1841]
Bosporus **B: 494**
Straits Settlements [Malaysian history] **So: 918**
Malaysia (Coming of the Europeans) **M: 101**
Stramonine [drug]
Jimson weed **J: 127**
Strand [street]
London (Central London) **L: 429-430** *with map*
Strand, Mark [American poet]
Poet laureate (table: Poets laureate of the United States) **P: 590**
Strand, Paul [American photographer] **So: 918** *with picture*
Photography (Dramatic changes) **P: 425-426** *with picture*
Strand casting [industrial process]
Iron and steel (Continuous casting) **I: 445** *with diagrams*
Strange Bird [sculpture by Noguchi]
Noguchi, Isamu *picture on* **N: 451**
Strange Holiness [poems by Coffin]
Coffin, Robert Peter Tristram **Ci: 756**
Strange Interlude [play by O'Neill]
O'Neill, Eugene **O: 762**
Strange quark [physics]

Quark Q: 7
Subatomic particle (Elementary particles)
So: 937; (Theoretical research) So: 938
Stranger, The [book by Camus]
Camus, Albert C: 97
Stranger in a Strange Land [book by Heinlein]
Heinlein, Robert A. H: 167
Science fiction (The Golden Age) S: 205
Stranger Is Watching, A [book by Clark]
Clark, Mary Higgins Ci: 642
Strangers and Brothers [books by Snow]
Snow, C. P. S: 539
Strangers on a Train [book by Highsmith]
Highsmith, Patricia H: 229
Strangler fig [plant]
Plant *picture on* P: 527
Strangles [disease]
Distemper D: 238
Strangulated hernia
Hernia H: 212
Strank, Michael [American soldier]
Iwo Jima, Battle of *picture on* I: 523
Strap-down system [navigation]
Inertial guidance (Strap-down systems) I: 263
Strapwork [decoration]
Furniture (France) F: 572-573
Strasberg, Lee [American actor-director]
Method acting M: 434
Strasbourg [France] So: 918 *with picture*
Strasbourg, Oaths of [842]
French language (Old French) F: 517
Strasbourg Cathedral [France]
Strasbourg So: 918 *with picture*
Strasbourg University [France]
Strasbourg So: 918
Strasser, Valentine [Sierra Leone political leader]
Sierra Leone (History) S: 452
Strassmann, Fritz [German chemist] So: 918
Fermi, Enrico F: 74
Meitner, Lise M: 387
Nuclear energy (Artificial fission) N: 590
Physics (Uncovering the secrets of the atom)
P: 442
Uranium (History of the use of uranium) U: 216
Strata [geology]
Fossil (Tracing the development of life) F: 423
with pictures
Geology (The rock dispute) G: 98
Rock (Sedimentary rock) R: 372
Sedimentary rock S: 280
STRATCOM [organization] *See* Strategic Command
in this index
Strategic air attack [warfare]
Air Force, United States (Offense) A: 190
Strategic Air Command [U.S.] So: 919
Air Force, United States (Combat commands)
A: 193
LeMay, Curtis Emerson L: 187
Nebraska (The mid-1900's) N: 114 *with picture*
Strategic Arms Limitation Talks So: 919
Arms control (Arms control in the mid-1900's)
A: 721-722
Bush, George Walker (Arms control) B: 722h
Carter, Jimmy (Foreign affairs) C: 257-258
Cold War (Soviet-American relations) Ci: 769;
(The Cold War in the 1970's) Ci: 770
Nuclear weapon (Arms control) N: 600
Union of Soviet Socialist Republics (Détente)
U: 39
Strategic Arms Reduction Treaty So: 919
START I
Strategic Arms Reduction Treaty So: 919
Arms control (Arms control in the late 1900's
and early 2000's) A: 722
Bush, George Herbert Walker (International
affairs) B: 721-722
Communism (The Soviet Union under
Gorbachev) Ci: 895-896
Gorbachev, Mikhail Sergeyevich (International
policies) G: 272
Nuclear weapon (Arms control) N: 600
START II
Strategic Arms Reduction Treaty So: 919
Strategic bomber [aircraft]
Aircraft, Military (Bombers) A: 202 *with picture*
Bomber (Kinds of bombers) B: 453 *with picture*
Strategic Command [U.S.]
Air Force, United States (Combat commands)
A: 193
Nebraska *picture on* N: 114; (Service industries)
N: 107
Offutt Air Force Base O: 678
Strategic Defense Initiative [plan] So: 919
Reagan, Ronald Wilson (Domestic affairs) R: 169
Strategic missile
Guided missile (The warhead) G: 423
Strategic mission [military]

Air force (Combat missions) A: 182
Strategic mobility [warfare]
Army (Armies in the nuclear age) A: 728-729
Strategic nuclear weapon
Nuclear weapon (Strategic nuclear weapons)
N: 598
Strategic Petroleum Reserve [U.S.] So: 920
Strategic Services, Office of [U.S. history]
Espionage (History) E: 358
Propaganda (During World War II) P: 825
World War II (Spies and saboteurs) W: 494
Strategic target [warfare]
Army (Armies in the nuclear age) A: 728
Stratemeyer, Edward [American author] So: 920
Keene, Carolyn K: 254
Stratemeyer Syndicate
Stratemeyer, Edward So: 920
Stratford grammar school [England]
Shakespeare, William (Early years) S: 346 *with
picture*
Stratford Hall [estate]
Archaeology *pictures on* A: 598
Lee, Robert E. L: 177
Virginia (Places to visit) V: 408
Stratford Shakespeare Festival [Ontario] So: 920
Canada (Theater) C: 110 *with picture*
Guthrie, Tyrone G: 444
Ontario (Visitor's guide) O: 774-775
Stratford-upon-Avon [England] So: 920
Shakespeare, William (His life in Stratford) S: 345
with pictures
Theater (Britain) T: 247-248
Strath [geography]
Scotland (Land regions) S: 217
Strathcona [former city]
Edmonton (History) E: 85
Strathcona and Mount Royal, Baron of [Canadian
businessman] So: 920
Stratigraphic trap [geology]
Petroleum *diagram on* P: 337; (Migration)
P: 333-334
Stratigraphy [science]
Archaeology (What archaeologists study)
A: 594-595
Geology (Job opportunities) G: 100-101
Stratocumulus
Cloud *picture on* Ci: 709; (Low clouds) Ci: 707
Stratopause [atmosphere]
Air (The stratosphere) A: 173 *with diagram*
Stratosphere So: 921
Stratosphere [atmosphere] So: 921
Air (Structure of the atmosphere) A: 172 *with
diagram*
Balloon (Balloon explorations) B: 62
Earth (The atmosphere) E: 18-19
Fallout (How fallout is distributed) F: 18-19
Jet stream J: 115
Stratovolcano [geology]
Volcano (Stratovolcanoes) V: 442 *with pictures*
Stratton, Charles C. [American political leader]
New Jersey (table) N: 249; (The 1800's) N: 251
Stratton, Charles Sherwood [American
entertainer] So: 921 *with picture*
Stratton, William G. [American political leader]
Illinois (table) I: 71
Stratum [geology]
Earth (History of Earth) E: 25 *with picture*
Stratus cloud
Cloud *picture on* Ci: 709; (Kinds of clouds) Ci: 707
with picture
Straub, Robert W. [American political leader]
Oregon (table) O: 845
Straus, Oscar [Austrian composer] So: 921
Straus, Oscar S. [American government official]
Commerce, Department of (table) C: 871
Roosevelt, Theodore (table) R: 466
Strauss, Eduard [Austrian conductor]
Strauss, Johann, Jr. So: 921
Strauss, Johann, Sr. [Austrian composer] So: 921
Strauss, Johann, Jr. [Austrian composer] So: 921
Operetta O: 809
Strauss, Joseph B. [American engineer]
Golden Gate Bridge G: 255
Strauss, Levi [American businessman] So: 922
Denim D: 131
Jeans J: 75
Strauss, Lewis L. [American government official]
Commerce, Department of (table) C: 871
Eisenhower, Dwight David (table) E: 152
Strauss, Richard [German composer] So: 922 *with
portrait*
Opera (Richard Strauss) O: 799; (*Rosenkavalier,
Der*) O: 807 *with picture*; (*Salome*) O: 807 *with
picture*
Strauss, William [American author]
Generation Y G: 84
Stravinsky, Igor [Russian-born composer] So: 922

with portrait
Classical music (Igor Stravinsky) Ci: 649;
(Neoclassicism) Ci: 649
Russia (Music) R: 536-537
Straw So: 923
Rye (Uses) R: 573
Straw, Drinking
Air (Weight and pressure) A: 171 *with diagrams*
Straw, Ezekiel A. [American political leader]
New Hampshire (table) N: 223
Straw hat
Straw So: 923
Strawberry [plant] So: 923 *with picture*
Fruit (Types of fruits in botany) F: 544-546 *with
picture*
Plant (Asexual reproduction) P: 535
Strawberry clover
Clover (Strawberry clover) Ci: 713 *with picture*
Strawberry comb [biology]
Chicken (Kinds of chickens) C: 441 *with picture*
Strawberry hedgehog [plant]
Plant *picture on* P: 526
Strawberry mark
Birthmark B: 380
Strawberry tongue [disorder]
Scarlet fever (Symptoms) S: 173
Strawbery Banke [Portsmouth]
New Hampshire (Places to visit) N: 216 *with
picture*
Portsmouth [New Hampshire] P: 685
Strawboard
Cardboard C: 209
Strawflower [plant] So: 924 *with picture*
Strayhorn, Billy [American composer]
Ellington, Duke E: 243
Streak lightning
Lightning (Appearance) L: 300
Streak plate [tool]
Rock (Tools) R: 374
Streak test
Mineral (Other identification tests) M: 567 *with
picture*
Rock (Identifying rocks) R: 373-375
Streaker bee [insect]
Bee (Swarming) B: 204
Stream
River *diagram on* R: 353; (River systems) R: 351
Stream of consciousness [literature]
American literature (Nonfiction writers) A: 420
Irish literature (Fiction) I: 432
Novel (New directions in the novel) N: 573-574;
(After World War II) N: 574
Streamer [meteorology]
Lightning (Lightning strokes) L: 300
Streaming [electronics]
Internet (The evolving Internet) I: 350g-350h
Streamliner [railroad]
Locomotive *picture on* L: 416
Streamlining So: 924 *with diagrams*
Aerodynamics (Drag) A: 86
Streep, Meryl [American actress] So: 924 *with
portrait*
Motion picture (Best performance by an actress:
1982, 2011) M: 862; (Best performance by an
actress in a supporting role: 1979) M: 862b
Street
Road R: 357
Traffic T: 365
Street, Dresden [painting by Kirchner]
Painting (Expressionism) P: 78-79 *with picture*
Street, Jabez C. [American physicist]
Muon M: 929
Street, Kenneth, Jr. [American scientist]
Californium C: 66
Street, Picabo [American skier]
Skiing (The middle and late 1900's) S: 487-488
Street academy [education]
Alternative school (Features of alternative
schools) A: 388-389
Street bike
Motorcycle (Kinds of motorcycles) M: 878
Street Fighter II [electronic game]
Electronic game (Fighting games) E: 204e
Street in Bronzeville, A [poems by Brooks]
Brooks, Gwendolyn B: 641
Street map
Map (Navigation maps) M: 178
Street race
Automobile racing A: 975
Street rod [car]
Hot rod H: 374a
Street Scene [play by Rice]
Rice, Elmer R: 328
Streetcar [vehicle] So: 925
New Orleans *picture on* N: 281
Transportation *pictures on* T: 389, T: 390; (Urban
public transportation) T: 393

Streetcar Named Desire, A [film]
  Brando, Marlon **B: 563**
Streetcar Named Desire, A [play by Williams]
  Brando, Marlon **B: 563**
  Drama (Later United States drama) **D: 340**
  Williams, Tennessee **W: 312**
Strega Nona books
  DePaola, Tomie **D: 148**
Streisand, Barbra [American entertainer] **So: 925**
  with portrait
  Motion picture (Best performance by an actress:
    1968) **M: 862**
Strength
  Materials (Properties of materials) **M: 300b**
  Physical fitness (Performance-related fitness)
    P: 433
Strength position [gymnastics]
  Gymnastics (The still rings) **G: 448** *with picture*
Strep throat [disease] **So: 925**
  Rheumatic fever **R: 291**
Strepsiptera [entomology]
  Insect (table) **I: 300**
Streptococcal pharyngitis [disease] *See* Strep
  throat *in this index*
Streptococcus [bacteria] **So: 926** *with picture*
  Disease *picture on* **D: 229**
  Erysipelas **E: 355**
  Nephritis **N: 127**
  Rheumatic fever **R: 291**
  Scarlet fever (Causes) **S: 173**
  Strep throat **So: 925**
Streptococcus pneumoniae [bacteria]
  Penicillin (Resistance) **P: 241**
  Pneumonia (How pneumonia develops) **P: 586**
  Streptococcus **So: 926**
Streptococcus thermophilus [bacteria]
  Yogurt **Y: 567**
Streptomyces griseus [bacteria]
  Streptomycin **So: 926**
Streptomycin [medication] **So: 926**
  Antibiotic (Damage to organs and tissues) **A: 551**;
    (table) **A: 551**; (History) **A: 552**
  Waksman, Selman Abraham **W: 6**
Stresemann, Gustav [German statesman]
  Germany (The Weimar Republic) **G: 167**
  Nobel Prizes (Peace: 1926) **N: 448a**
Stress [health] **So: 926**
  Aerospace medicine (Aviation medicine) **A: 89**
  Balance of nature (Behavior) **B: 35**
  Child abuse **C: 454**
  Disease (Inherited diseases) **D: 228-229**
  Epinephrine **E: 343**
  Health (Handling stress) **H: 126**
  Mental illness (Social and psychological factors)
    M: 407
Stress [language] *See* Accent *in this index*
Stress [physics]
  Earthquake (Why a quake begins) **E: 36**
  Elasticity **E: 156**
Stress electrocardiogram [medicine] *See* Stress
  test *in this index*
Stress meter [poetry]
  Poetry (Rhythm and meter) **P: 591-592**
Stress test [medicine] **So: 927** *with picture*
  Heart *picture on* **H: 141**; (Symptoms and
    diagnosis) **H: 137**
Stressor [health]
  Stress **So: 926**
Stretto [music]
  Fugue **F: 553**
Streymoy [island, Atlantic]
  Faroe Islands **F: 47**
Striated muscle
  Heart (Outer lining and muscle) **H: 133**
  Human body (Skeletal muscles) **H: 419**
  Muscle (Skeletal muscles) **M: 933** *with diagram*
Striatum [anatomy]
  Brain (The cerebrum) **B: 550a-550b**; (Making
    decisions) **B: 555**
Strickland, Ted [American political leader]
  Ohio (table) **O: 699**
Strickland, William [British architect]
  Architecture (The Greek Revival) **A: 625-626**
Strict creationism [belief]
  Evolution (Acceptance of evolution) **E: 433-434**
Strict liability [law]
  Product liability suit **P: 810**
Stride piano
  Jazz (The 1920's) **J: 70**
Stridulation [entomology]
  Ant (Sense organs) **A: 522**
  Insect (Hearing) **I: 290**
Strife [philosophy]
  Empedocles **E: 261**
  Heraclitus **H: 194**
Strife [play by Galsworthy]
  Galsworthy, John **G: 17**

Strike [labor] **So: 928** *with picture*
  Automobile *picture on* **A: 967**
  Baseball (Recent developments) **B: 137-138**
  Gay Nineties (Industrial growth) **G: 72**
  Hockey (The late 1900's and early 2000's) **H: 282**
  Labor movement (Handling labor disputes) **L: 6**
    with picture
  Labor union **L: 16**
  Lockout **L: 413**
  Massachusetts (The early 1900's) **M: 293**
  New York City (Problems) **N: 342**
  Quebec (The late 1900's) **Q: 32**
  Roosevelt, Theodore (Friend of labor) **R: 464**
  Taft-Hartley Act **T: 12**
  Teaching (Current issues in U.S. teaching) **T: 69**
  West Virginia (History) **W: 226-229** *with picture*
Strike [lock]
  Lock (Types of locks) **L: 410**
Strike [sports]
  Baseball (Outs by batters) **B: 128**; (Rule changes)
    B: 133
  Bowling (Scoring) **B: 521**
Strike-slip fault [geology]
  Earthquake *diagram on* **E: 37**; (Tsunamis) **E: 34**;
    (Transform boundaries) **E: 38**
  Mountain (Fault-block mountains) **M: 893-894**
Strike Up the Band [musical]
  Gershwin, George **G: 174**
Strike zone
  Baseball (Outs by batters) **B: 128**
Strikebreaker
  Labor movement (Handling labor disputes) **L: 6-7**
Strikeout [baseball]
  Baseball (Outs by batters) **B: 128**; (table: Modern
    major league records) **B: 138**
Striker [sports]
  Cricket **Ci: 1131**
Striker mechanism *See* Firing pin *in this index*
Striking circle [hockey]
  Field hockey (The field and equipment) **F: 92**
    with diagram
Striking the flag
  Flag (Raising and lowering the flag) **F: 219**
Strindberg, August [Swedish dramatist] **So: 929**
  Drama (Expressionism) **D: 339**
  Expressionism (Expressionist writing) **E: 455**
  Naturalism (Naturalism in drama) **N: 66**
  Scandinavian literature (The Golden Age) **S: 171**
  Sweden (Arts) **So: 1026-1027**
String [material]
  Catgut **C: 301**
  Macramé **M: 26** *with picture*
  Piano (The strings) **P: 446** *with picture*
  Violin (Parts of the violin) **V: 389** *with pictures*
String [physics]
  Subatomic particle (Theoretical research) **So: 938**
String band
  Country music (Old-time music) **Ci: 1098** *with
    picture*
String galvanometer [instrument]
  Einthoven, Willem **E: 147**
  Electrocardiograph **E: 199**
String level [tool]
  Level **L: 217**
String orchestra
  Orchestra **O: 820**
String quartet [ensemble]
  Chamber music **C: 371**
  Classical music (Chamber music) **Ci: 644** *with
    picture*
  Music *picture on* **M: 946**
String Quartet No. 1 [music by Penderecki]
  Penderecki, Krzysztof **P: 236**
String section [music]
  Orchestra (The musicians) **O: 820**
String theory [physics] **So: 929**
Stringed instrument
  Classical music (Instrumental music) **Ci: 643**
  Music (Stringed instruments) **M: 948** *with pictures*
  Orchestra **O: 820** *with pictures*
Stringer [fishing]
  Fishing (Bait) **F: 178-179**
Stringer [journalism]
  Newspaper (Gathering information) **N: 382**
Stringfellow, John [British engineer]
  Airplane (Powered flight) **A: 230**
Stringless bean
  Bean (Kinds of beans) **B: 181**
Strip, The [district]
  Hollywood **H: 293**
  Los Angeles (Central Los Angeles) **L: 460**
Strip cropping
  Conservation (Soil conservation) **Ci: 979-980**
  Erosion (Controlling erosion) **E: 355**
  Farm and farming (Planting) **F: 35-36**
Strip mall [business]
  Shopping center **S: 434**

Strip mine
  Coal (Strip mining) **Ci: 722** *with picture*;
    (Developments in North America) **Ci: 731-732**
    with pictures
  Kentucky (The late 1900's) **K: 294**
  Mining (Surface mining methods) **M: 575** *with
    diagram*
  Tennessee Valley Authority (Electric power)
    T: 159
Strip steel
  Iron and steel (Rolling) **I: 445**
Stripe smut fungus
  Lawn *picture on* **L: 143**
Striped bass [fish]
  Bass (Temperate bass) **B: 157** *with picture*
Striped bonito [fish]
  Bonito **B: 460**
Striped cucumber beetle
  Insect *picture on* **I: 283**
Striped dolphin [sea animal]
  Dolphin (Other species) **D: 297**
Striped hyena [animal]
  Hyena **H: 474**
Striped marlin [fish]
  Fish *picture on* **F: 152**
  Marlin **M: 215**
Striped mullet [fish]
  Mullet **M: 915**
Striped pear gourd
  Gourd *picture on* **G: 281**
Striped skunk
  Skunk **S: 496** *with picture*
Striplight
  Theater (Lighting methods) **T: 240-241**
Stripling, Robert [American government official]
  Nixon, Richard Milhous *picture on* **N: 430**
Strippable wallpaper
  Wallpaper **W: 19**
Stripper [technician]
  Printing (Platemaking) **P: 798**
Stripper machine
  Cotton (Harvesting) **Ci: 1090**
Stripping [printing]
  Printing (Platemaking) **P: 798**
Stritch, Samuel Alphonsus [American religious
  leader]
  Cardinal (table: American cardinals) **C: 211**
Striving for superiority [psychology]
  Adler, Alfred **A: 58**
Stroboscope [instrument]
  Edgerton, Harold Eugene **E: 76**
Stroessner, Alfredo [Paraguayan political leader]
  Paraguay (Political unrest) **P: 149**; (Stroessner's
    rule and overthrow) **P: 149**
Strøget [mall]
  Copenhagen (The city) **Ci: 1038**
  Denmark *picture on* **D: 135**
Strohfiedel [musical instrument]
  Xylophone **X: 546**
Stroke [disorder] **So: 929**
  Aneurysm **A: 460**
  Aphasia **A: 565**
  Aspirin (Health benefits) **A: 816**
  Brain (Stroke) **B: 558**
  C-reactive protein **C: 2**
  Cerebral hemorrhage **C: 361**
  Circulatory system (Disorders of the circulatory
    system) **Ci: 561**
  Disability **D: 218**
  Disease (Diseases associated with aging) **D: 230**
  Headache (Secondary headache) **H: 124-125**
  Hypertension **H: 476**
  Nervous system (Disorders of the nervous
    system) **N: 136**
Stroke [movement]
  Gasoline engine (Cycle) **G: 63**
Stroke, Lightning
  Lightning **L: 299**; (Lightning strokes) **L: 300** *with
    pictures*
Stroke play
  Golf (Stroke play) **G: 264**
Stroking
  Massage **M: 295**
Stroll in the Air, A [play by Ionesco]
  Ionesco, Eugène **I: 372**
Strom, Erling [American mountain climber]
  Mount McKinley **M: 886**
Strom, Harry E. [Canadian political leader]
  Alberta (table) **A: 328**
Strom Thurmond Dam [Savannah River]
  Savannah River **S: 165**
Stromboli [island, Italy] **So: 930**
  Volcano (table) **V: 442b**
Strombolian eruption [geology]
  Volcano (Describing eruptions) **V: 442b**
Strombosia pustulata [tree]
  Plant *picture on* **P: 527**

Stromeyer, Friedrich [German scientist]
Cadmium **C:** 12
Strong, Caleb [American political leader]
Massachusetts (table) **M:** 288
Strong, John [English explorer]
Falkland Islands **F:** 15
Strong, William [American jurist]
Supreme Court of the United States (table)
So: 1000
Strong electrolyte [chemistry]
Electrolyte **E:** 201
Strong force [physics] See Strong interaction in this index
Strong interaction [physics]
Atom (Forces in the nucleus) **A:** 873
Baryon **B:** 122
Force (The strong force) **F:** 371
Gluon **G:** 237
Neutron **N:** 155
Physics (Physics today) **P:** 442-443
Quantum field theory **Q:** 5
Standard Model **So:** 833
String theory **So:** 929
Subatomic particle (Fundamental forces) **So:** 936;
(Theories of forces) **So:** 937-938
Strong-mayor government
City government (The mayor-council form)
Ci: 595 with diagram
Mayor **M:** 330
Strong motion accelerograph
Seismograph (Detecting earthquakes) **S:** 288
Strong nuclear force [physics] See Strong
interaction in this index
Strong trademark
Trademark **T:** 364
Strongbow [Irish king]
Ireland (The Norman invaders) **I:** 425-426
Strontianite [mineral]
Strontium **So:** 930
Strontium [element] **So:** 930
Strontium 90 [isotope]
Fallout (The fallout hazard) **F:** 19
Strontium **So:** 930
Strophe [poetry]
Ode **O:** 673
Poetry (Lyric poetry) **P:** 591
Strophic song
Classical music (Songs) **Ci:** 644
Strowger, Almon B. [American inventor]
Telephone (Early telephones) **T:** 99-100
Structural analysis [linguistics]
Reading (Comprehending what is perceived)
R: 157
Structural assimilation [sociology]
Minority group (Assimilation) **M:** 609
Structural beam
Iron and steel (Rolling) **I:** 445-447 with diagram
Structural-functionalism [sociology]
Parsons, Talcott **P:** 183
Sociology (Development of social research)
So: 566
Structural glass
Glass (Specialty glasses) **G:** 212
Structural grammar
Grammar **G:** 303
Structural lighting
Lighting (Lighting devices) **L:** 298
Structural linguistics
Lévi-Strauss, Claude **L:** 218
Linguistics (Structuralism) **L:** 337
Structural lumber
Lumber (Softwood lumber) **L:** 517
Structural proteins
Metabolism (Anabolism) **M:** 424
Structural unemployment
Unemployment (Types of unemployment) **U:** 22
Structuralism
Gestalt psychology **G:** 175
Lévi-Strauss, Claude **L:** 218
Mythology (Structuralism approaches) **M:** 991
Psychology (Structuralism) **P:** 849
Sociology (Development of social research)
So: 566
Structure class [grammar]
English language (Grammar) **E:** 312
Strudel [food]
Hungary (Food and drink) **H:** 441
Strugatsky, Arkady [Russian author]
Science fiction (Growing popularity) **S:** 205-206
Strugatsky, Boris [Russian author]
Science fiction (Growing popularity) **S:** 205-206
Strumigenys [ant]
Ant picture on **A:** 520
Strychnine [poison]
Poison (Kinds of poisons) **P:** 600
Stimulant **So:** 901
Strychnos plant

Curare **Ci:** 1193
Stryker Infantry Carrier Vehicle
Army, United States picture on **A:** 736
Stryn [Norway]
Norway picture on **N:** 536
Strzelecki, Sir Paul Edmund de [Polish-born
explorer]
Mount Kosciuszko **M:** 885
Stuart, Alexander H. H. [American government
official]
Fillmore, Millard (table) **F:** 102
Interior, Department of the (table) **I:** 325
Stuart, Charles Edward [Scottish pretender]
Scotland (Union with England) **S:** 220
Stuart, Edwin Sydney [American political leader]
Pennsylvania (table) **P:** 263
Stuart, Gilbert Charles [American artist] **So:** 930
Madison, James picture on **M:** 32
Monroe, James picture on **M:** 734
Rhode Island (Places to visit) **R:** 304
Washington, George picture on **W:** 90
Stuart, Henry Carter [American political leader]
Virginia (table) **V:** 417
Stuart, House of [British history] **So:** 931
England (table) **E:** 308
Scotland (The House of Stuart) **S:** 219
Tartan pictures on **T:** 47
Stuart, James Ewell Brown [Confederate general]
See Stuart, Jeb in this index
Stuart, James Francis Edward [Scottish
nobleman]
Scotland (Union with England) **S:** 220
Stuart, Jeb [Confederate general] **So:** 931
Civil War, American (The peninsular campaign)
Ci: 626; (Cavalry maneuvers) **Ci:** 631
Stuart, Jesse Hilton [American author] **So:** 931
Stuart, John McDouall [British explorer]
Australia map on **A:** 921; (Mapping the continent)
A: 922
Exploration (Exploring Australia's interior) **E:** 448
with map
Northern Territory (History) **N:** 528
Stuart, John Todd [American lawyer]
Lincoln, Abraham (Study) **L:** 314
Stuart, Mary [queen of Scotland] See Mary, Queen
of Scots in this index
Stuart, Robert [American frontiersman]
Nebraska (American exploration and settlement)
N: 111
Oregon Trail **O:** 850
Wyoming (Exploration) **W:** 533
Stuart Little [book by White]
White, E. B. **W:** 284
Stubble-mulch tillage [farming]
Dryland farming **D:** 369
Stubbs, Walter Roscoe [American political leader]
Kansas (table) **K:** 234
Stubbs, William [English historian]
History (History in the universities) **H:** 262-263
Stucco [casting]
(Other types of casting) **C:** 278-279
Stucco [construction]
Plaster **P:** 552
Stuck, Hudson [British religious leader]
Mount McKinley **M:** 886
Stud [construction]
House (The frame) **H:** 382 with diagram
Stud [hardware]
Tire (Tire tread patterns) **T:** 297
Stud fee
Horse (Breeding horses) **H:** 358
Stud poker
Poker **P:** 603
Studbook
American Kennel Club **A:** 412
Dog (table: Dog terms) **D:** 263
Studebaker [automobile]
Automobile picture on **A:** 968
Studebaker, Clement [American businessman]
So: 931
Studebaker, John Mohler [American
businessman] **So:** 932
Studebaker Brothers Manufacturing Company
Studebaker, John Mohler **So:** 932
Studebaker Corporation
Indiana (The mid-1900's) **I:** 216-218
Studebaker, Clement **So:** 931
Studebaker, John Mohler **So:** 932
Student Bill of Rights
Academic freedom (The 2000's) **A:** 20
Student body
Universities and colleges (The student body)
U: 208
Student council
Student government **So:** 932
Student from Salamanca, The [poem by
Espronceda]

Spanish literature (The 1800's) **So:** 761
Student government So: 932
Student National Coordinating Committee See
Student Nonviolent Coordinating Committee in
this index
Student Nonviolent Coordinating Committee
So: 932
African Americans (The growing movement)
A: 136o; (Black militancy) **A:** 136q-136r
Bond, Julian **B:** 455
King, Martin Luther, Jr. (Later years) **K:** 322
Student nurse
Nursing (Professional nursing education) **N:** 618
Student protest
Riot (During the 1900's) **R:** 349
Student teaching
Teaching (Teacher-training programs) **T:** 67-68
Students for a Democratic Society [organization]
So: 932
New Left **N:** 255
Studhorse Man, The [book by Kroetsch]
Canadian literature (Modern English-Canadian
fiction) **C:** 160
Studies in a Dying Colonialism [book by Fanon]
Fanon, Frantz Omar **F:** 27
Studies in the History of the Renaissance [book
by Pater]
Pater, Walter **P:** 195
Studies in the Psychology of Sex [book by Ellis]
Ellis, Havelock **E:** 243
Studio
Ballet (The ballet studio) **B:** 46 with picture
Radio picture on **R:** 83; (Radio stations) **R:** 86
Recording industry (In a recording studio) **R:** 181
with picture
Studio, The [painting by Lawrence]
Lawrence, Jacob picture on **L:** 146
Studio 2b program
Girl Scouts (Girl Scout Cadettes) **G:** 197
Studio piano
Piano (Upright pianos) **P:** 447
Studs Lonigan [books by Farrell]
Farrell, James T. **F:** 48
Study [education] **So:** 932
See also Learning in this index
Reading (Study-type reading) **R:** 156
Study for Swing Landscape [painting by Davis]
Corcoran Gallery of Art picture on **Ci:** 1051
Study group
Parent education (Methods of parent education)
P: 157
Study in Scarlet, A [book by Doyle]
Detective story (History) **D:** 162-163
Study of History, A [book by Toynbee]
Civilization (Rise and fall) **Ci:** 636
Toynbee, Arnold Joseph **T:** 354
Stuffer [yarn]
Rugs and carpets (Weaving) **R:** 515 with pictures
Stuffing [industrial process]
Leather (Tanning) **L:** 167
Stuhr Museum of the Prairie Pioneer [Grand
Island]
Nebraska (Places to visit) **N:** 102
Stull, Oscar M. [American public figure]
Virginia Polytechnic Institute and State University
V: 425
Stump Speaking [painting by Bingham]
United States, History of the picture on **U:** 174
Stumping [sports]
Cricket (Outs) **Ci:** 1132-1133 with picture
Stunning [meat packing]
Meat packing (Inspection and stunning) **M:** 351
Stunt kite
Kite (Types of kites) **K:** 339-340 with picture
Stupa [building]
Architecture (Indian architecture) **A:** 613
India (Architecture and sculpture) **I:** 119
Sculpture (India) **S:** 236-237
Stupor Mundi [name for]
Frederick II **F:** 497
Sturbridge [Massachusetts]
Massachusetts picture on **M:** 270; (Places to visit)
M: 280
Museum picture on **M:** 938
Sturgeon [fish] **So:** 933 with picture
Caviar **C:** 322
Egg (Other kinds of eggs) **E:** 116
Fish picture on **F:** 158; (Bony fish) **F:** 147-148
Russia (Fishing industry) **R:** 546
Sturgeon, Theodore [American author] **So:** 934
Sturgeon, William [British electrician]
Electric motor (History) **E:** 181
Electromagnet **E:** 201
Sturges, Preston [American director] **So:** 934
Sturluson, Snorri [Icelandic author] See Snorri
Sturluson in this index
Sturm und Drang [literature]

German literature (German Preromanticism) G: 139
Herder, Johann Gottfried von H: 199
Sturt, Charles [British explorer]
Australia *map on* A: 921; (Mapping the continent) A: 922
Exploration (Exploring Australia's interior) E: 448 *with map*
Sturtevant, Alfred H. [American biologist]
Heredity (The birth of genetics) H: 208
Stuttering So: 934
Speech therapy (Types of disorders) So: 773
Stuttgart [Germany] So: 934 *with picture*
Germany *picture on* G: 151
Stuttgart pitch [sound]
Pitch P: 498
Stuyvesant, Peter [Dutch colonial official] So: 935 *with portrait*
Delaware (Exploration and early settlement) D: 110
Fire department (Early fire services) F: 128
New Netherland N: 277
New York City (English rule) N: 341
Pennsylvania (Exploration and settlement) P: 264
Sty [disorder]
Eye *picture on* E: 468; (Diseases of the outer parts) E: 468
Style [art]
Fashion F: 50 *with pictures*
Interior design (Elements of design) I: 327
Literature (Style) L: 353
A Guide to Writing Skills **Research Guide: 8**
Style [botany]
Flower *picture on* F: 293; (The carpels) F: 294
Plant *picture on* P: 534; (Flowers) P: 531 *with picture*
Seed (Seed development in angiosperms) S: 281
Style of life [psychology]
Adler, Alfred A: 58
Stylebranch [botany]
Iris I: 429
Stylet [biology]
Insect (Mouthparts) I: 286 *with diagram*
Mosquito (How a mosquito "bites") M: 831 *with diagram*
Ribbon worm R: 321
Stylus [computing]
Computer (A digitizing tablet) Ci: 914
Stylus [recording]
Phonograph (How phonographs work) P: 400; (Parts of a phonograph) P: 400-401 *with diagram*; (How phonograph records are made) P: 401 *with diagram*
Stylus [tool]
Printing (Gravure cylinders) P: 800
Styracosaurus [dinosaur] So: 935
Dinosaur *picture on* D: 206a; (True dinosaurs) D: 206b-208
Styrene [plastic]
Plastics (Making synthetic resins) P: 556
Rubber (Development of synthetic rubbers) R: 501; (General-purpose synthetic rubbers) R: 504
Styrene-butadiene rubber
Rubber (General-purpose synthetic rubbers) R: 504
Styrofoam [plastic]
Polystyrene P: 652
Styron, William [American author] So: 936 *with portrait*
American literature (Experimental styles) A: 425 *with portrait*
Styx [Greek mythology] So: 936
Hades H: 4
Su-chou [China] *See* Suzhou *in this index*
Suanpan [calculator]
Abacus A: 3
Suárez, Francisco [Spanish philosopher] So: 936
Suarez, Xavier L. [American political leader]
Miami (History) M: 480
Subalpine fir [tree]
Fir F: 120
Subalpine forest
Forest (Mountain evergreen forests) F: 395
Subalpine larch [tree]
Larch L: 75
Subanesthetic dose [medicine]
Nitrous oxide N: 427
Subansiri River [Asia]
Brahmaputra River B: 548
Subantarctic Intermediate Water
Atlantic Ocean (Subsurface currents) A: 866
Subarachnoid hemmorrhage [disorder]
Stroke (Causes) So: 930
Subarctic [region]
Arctic (Land regions) A: 636
Climate (Subarctic climates) Ci: 676d

Indian, American (Indians of the Subarctic) I: 153 *with picture and map*
Subarctic woodland
Forest (Subarctic woodlands) F: 396 *with map*
Subatomic particle [physics] So: 936
See also the list of subatomic particles in the Related articles of the Atom *article*
Atom (The nucleus) A: 871 *with diagrams*
Cosmic rays C: 1075
Force (Kinds of force) F: 370
Heisenberg, Werner H: 167
Higgs boson H: 227
Motion M: 843; (The motion of subatomic particles) M: 845
Muon M: 928
Particle accelerator P: 184
Particle detector P: 186
Physics (Advances in the mid-1900's) P: 442; (Physics today) P: 442; (Uncovering the secrets of the atom) P: 442
Quantum mechanics (Quanta of energy) Q: 6
Quark Q: 7
Radiation R: 74
Supersymmetry So: 995
Subbituminous coal
Coal (Coal rank) Ci: 718; (The uses of coal) Ci: 718-719; (How coal was formed) Ci: 720-721; (Where coal is found) Ci: 721
Sub-canopy [botany]
Rain forest (Structure and growth) R: 126a
Subclavian artery
Artery (Principal arteries) A: 751
Human body (table) H: 422 *with diagram*
Subclavian vein
Human body (table) H: 422 *with diagram*
Subconjunctival hemorrhage [disorder]
Eye *picture on* E: 466
Subconscious *See* Unconscious *in this index*
Subcontractor
Building construction (Constructing a skyscraper) B: 683
Building trade (The contracting system) B: 685
Subcritical mass [physics]
Nuclear weapon (Fission weapons) N: 596-597
Subculture [anthropology]
Clothing (Identity) Ci: 687-688
Culture (The boundaries of cultures) Ci: 1186-1187
Subcutaneous injection
Hypodermic injection H: 480
Subcutaneous mastectomy [surgery]
Mastectomy M: 297
Subcutaneous tissue [anatomy]
Human body (Subcutaneous tissues) H: 418
Skin (Structure of the skin) S: 488 *with picture*
Subdeacon
Eastern Orthodox Churches (Clergy) E: 46
Subdirectory [computing]
Computer file Ci: 924g
Subdominant [music]
Music (Tone) M: 950; (Harmony) M: 951 *with diagram*
Subduction [geology]
Earthquake (How an earthquake begins) E: 35-36 *with diagrams*
Plate tectonics (Convergent plate boundaries) P: 562
Subduction accretion [geology]
Plate tectonics (Convergent plate boundaries) P: 562
Subduction erosion [geology]
Plate tectonics (Convergent plate boundaries) P: 562
Subduction zone [geology]
Earth (Subduction) E: 24
Earthquake (How an earthquake begins) E: 35-36; (Convergent boundaries) E: 38
Mountain (Volcanic mountains) M: 892
Plate tectonics (Convergent plate boundaries) P: 562
Ring of Fire R: 343
Volcano (Where volcanoes form) V: 441
Subentry [mining]
Coal (The room-and-pillar system) Ci: 723-724 *with diagram*
Subercaseaux, Pedro [Chilean painter]
Argentina *picture on* A: 657
Suberin [botany]
Bark (Outer bark) B: 110-111
Subfloor [construction]
House (Interior construction) H: 382 *with diagram*
Subhadra [Hindu deity]
Juggernaut J: 186
Subhead [publishing]
Newspaper (table) N: 383
Subhedral crystal
Crystal (Crystallization) Ci: 1166

Subic Bay Naval Station
Philippines (Independence) P: 380; (Recovering democracy) P: 381
Subimago [insect]
Mayfly M: 328
Subinfeudation [European history]
Feudalism (Knighthood under feudalism) F: 82
Subirrigation [agriculture]
Irrigation (Subirrigation) I: 459
Subject [grammar]
Sentence (Subject and predicate) S: 303
Subject [music]
Classical music (Fugue) Ci: 645
Fugue F: 553
Subject card [reference]
A Guide to Research Skills **Research Guide: 28**
Subject-verb-complement
Grammar (The actor-action-goal relationship) G: 303
Subjection of Women, The [book by Mill]
Mill, Harriet Taylor M: 552
Mill, John Stuart M: 552
Philosophy (Philosophy in the 1800's) P: 390
Subjectivism [philosophy]
Philosophy (Ethics and political philosophy) P: 385
Subjunctive mood [grammar]
Conjugation C: 951
Mood M: 780
Sublette, William Lewis [American businessman] So: 938
Wyoming (Exploration) W: 533
Sublevel caving [mining]
Mining (Caving) M: 576
Sublimation [physics] So: 938
Carbon dioxide C: 207
Evaporation E: 422
Melting point M: 390
Refrigeration (Dry ice) R: 201
Vapor V: 285
Sublimation [psychology]
Nietzsche, Friedrich (Psychological ideas) N: 407
Subliminal [psychology] So: 938
Sublingual gland
Saliva S: 68 *with diagram*
Subluxation [disorder]
Chiropractic C: 514
Dislocation D: 235
Submandibular gland
Saliva S: 68 *with diagram*
Submarine So: 939 *with pictures*
See also U-boat *in this index*
Connecticut (The mid-1900's) Ci: 971 *with picture*
Depth charge D: 151
Fulton, Robert (The inventor) F: 555
Holland, John Philip H: 292
Navy (Submarines) N: 78
Navy, United States (Combat ships) N: 84
Periscope P: 288
Sonar So: 590
Warship (Submarines) W: 41; (Warships in the nuclear age) W: 42 *with pictures*
World War I *picture on* W: 457
Submarine canyon [geography]
Atlantic Ocean (The Atlantic seafloor) A: 864
Valley (Kinds of valleys) V: 265
Submarine-launched ballistic missile
Guided missile (Surface-to-surface missiles) G: 425-426
Nuclear weapon (Strategic nuclear weapons) N: 598
Submarine warfare
Submarine (History) So: 942 *with pictures*
Wilson, Woodrow (Declaration of war) W: 324-325
World War I (The war at sea) W: 460 *with picture*; (The United States enters the war) W: 462
Submersible [diving vessel]
Ballard, Robert Duane B: 43
Deep sea (Deep-sea exploration) D: 82c
Diving, Underwater (Diving in vehicles) D: 246
Earle, Sylvia Alice E: 14
Exploration (Deep-sea exploration) E: 450-451
Marine biology (Biological oceanographers) M: 205
Ocean (Submersibles) O: 663 *with picture*
Submission hold [sports]
Mixed martial arts M: 680
Submultiple [measurement]
Metric system (Kinds of metric units) M: 436
Submunition [bomb]
Bomb (Kinds of bombs) B: 450
Suborbital mission
Space exploration (Vostok and Mercury: the first human beings in space) So: 712-713
Subordinate [zoology]
Dominance D: 301

Subordinate clause
Clause Ci: 657
Sentence (Sentence classifications) S: 303
Subordinate group [sociology]
Minority group M: 608
Segregation (Causes and effects of segregation)
S: 285
Subordinating conjunction
Conjunction (Subordinating conjunctions)
Ci: 951
Subordination [grammar]
Grammar (Grammatical relationships) G: 303-304
Subornation of perjury [law]
Clinton, Bill (Domestic events) Ci: 682f
Perjury P: 288
Subpoena [law] So: 943
Witness W: 374
Subpolar region [geography]
Calms, Regions of (Subpolar regions) C: 69
Subprime loan
Bank (Crisis in finance) B: 95
Bush, George Walker (Economy) B: 722j
Mortgage M: 821
Obama, Barack (The 2008 election) O: 640f
Open housing O: 789
United States, History of the (Financial troubles)
U: 196f
Sub-Saharan Africa
Africa A: 99
Subscapularis [muscle]
Rotator cuff R: 486
Subscription
Magazine (Sales) M: 44
Subscription library
Franklin, Benjamin (Civic leader) F: 487-488 *with
picture*
Library (Libraries in the United States) L: 261
Subscription season
Theater (Theater in the United States) T: 244-246
Subset [set theory]
Set theory (Kinds of sets) S: 321 *with diagram*
Subsidence [geology]
Geodesy G: 91
Subsidiary company
Holding company H: 290
Subsidy [economics] So: 943
Economics (The world economy) E: 61
Exports and imports (Export promotion) E: 454
Foreign policy (Domestic policy) F: 387
Nationalization (Advantages and disadvantages)
N: 63
Subsistence agriculture
Agriculture (Agricultural practices) A: 148-149
Subsistence economy
Liberia (Economy) L: 230
Subsistence hunting
Hunting (History) H: 450
Subsonic speed
Aerodynamics (Supersonic aerodynamics) A: 87
Streamlining So: 924
Subspecies [biology]
Classification, Scientific (Groups in classification)
Ci: 655-656
Races, Human R: 53
Substance [philosophy]
Hume, David (Hume's thought) H: 432
Substance abuse *See* Alcoholism; Drug abuse *in
this index*
**Substance Abuse and Mental Health Services
Administration** [U.S.]
Health and Human Services, Department of
(Organization) H: 128
Substance use disorder
Drug abuse D: 361
Substandard housing
City (Physical problems) Ci: 590 *with picture*
Housing H: 389 *with picture*
Substantive due process
Due process of law D: 378
Substitute player
Baseball (Players) B: 125
Substitution [mathematics]
Algebra (Solving linear equations in two
variables) A: 357
Substitution [technique]
Codes and ciphers (Communications security)
Ci: 749
Substrate [electronics]
Transistor (Metal oxide semiconductor field effect
transistors [MOSFET's]) T: 374 *with diagram*
Substrate [material]
Ink I: 272
Printing (Methods of printing) P: 798
Substructure [construction]
Building construction (Parts of a building) B: 681
Subsurface drainage [agriculture]
Drainage (Subsurface drainage) D: 320 *with*

diagram
Subsystem [component]
Satellite, Artificial (Building a satellite) S: 150g
Subterranean clover
Clover (Subterranean clover) Ci: 713
Subterranean stem
Plant (Stems) P: 529
Subterranean termite
Insect I: 281
Subtitle
Closed captioning Ci: 685
Subtle Knife, The [book by Pullman]
Pullman, Philip P: 900
Subtotal hysterectomy [surgery]
Hysterectomy H: 482
Subtraction [mathematics] So: 944 *with pictures*
Addition (Checking addition) A: 51
Algebra (Subtraction) A: 355
Arithmetic (Subtraction) A: 666 *with picture;*
(Arithmetic of negative numbers) A: 668-669
Decimal system (Addition and subtraction) D: 71
with diagrams
Fraction (Calculations using fractions) F: 446
Subtractive color mixture
Color (Mixing colorants) Ci: 819-820 *with
diagrams*
Subtrahend [mathematics]
Subtraction (Subtraction terms) So: 944
Subtransmission substation
Electric power (Distribution) E: 185 *with diagram*
Subtropical dry summer climate
Climate (Subtropical dry summer climates)
Ci: 676c
Subtropical forest
Flower (Flowers of the tropics and subtropics)
F: 292 *with pictures*
Forest (Forests of the United States and Canada)
F: 394 *with map*
Subtropical fruit
Fruit (Types of fruits in horticulture) F: 546 *with
pictures*
Subtropical high [weather]
Calms, Regions of (The horse latitudes) C: 69
Subtropical jet [wind]
Jet stream J: 115 *with map*
Subtropical maritime anticyclone [weather]
Calms, Regions of (The horse latitudes) C: 69
Subtropics [geography]
Flower (Flowers of the tropics and subtropics)
F: 292 *with pictures*
Subunit vaccine [medicine]
Virus (Vaccines) V: 428a
Suburb So: 949
City (Metropolitan cities) Ci: 588
Housing (Suburban developments) H: 390
Metropolitan area M: 442
Transportation (The beginnings of modern
transportation) T: 390-392
United States (Urban life) U: 110 *with picture*
United States, History of the (Suburban growth)
U: 195 *with picture*
Suburbanization [demography]
Local government (Population changes) L: 407
Metropolitan area (Problems of metropolitan
areas) M: 442
Subversion [law]
Un-American Activities Committee U: 18
Subway [railroad] So: 949 *with picture*
Subwoofer [electronics]
Stereophonic sound system (Speakers) So: 892
Success
Learning (Motivation) L: 164
"Success Is Counted Sweetest" [poem by
Dickinson]
Dickinson, Emily (Her poems) D: 190
Successful Peasant, The [book by Marivaux]
Marivaux, Pierre M: 213
Succession [biology] *See* Ecological succession *in
this index*
Succession, Act of [1534]
More, Sir Thomas (His life) M: 801-802
Succession, Presidential *See* Presidential
succession *in this index*
Succession law
Law (Private law) L: 130
Succession planting
Gardening (table) G: 32; (Planning a kitchen
garden) G: 35
Succession wars [European history] So: 950
The War of the Austrian Succession [1740-1748]
Succession wars (The War of the Austrian
Succession) So: 950
Austria (Wars in the 1700's and 1800's) A: 937-
938
French and Indian wars (King George's War)
F: 512
Germany (The rise of Prussia) G: 164

Maria Theresa M: 199
Pragmatic sanction P: 729
The War of the Bavarian Succession [1778-1779]
Succession wars (The War of the Bavarian
Succession) So: 950
The War of the Polish Succession [1733-1738]
Succession wars (The War of the Polish
Succession) So: 950
Louis XV L: 476
The War of the Spanish Succession [1701-1714]
Succession wars (The War of the Spanish
Succession) So: 950
Austria (Wars in the 1700's and 1800's) A: 937-
938
Blenheim, Battle of B: 400
French and Indian wars (Queen Anne's War)
F: 512
Grand Alliance G: 305
Philip V P: 370
Sicilies, Kingdom of the Two S: 447
Spain (The Spanish decline) So: 747
Utrecht, Peace of U: 252
Successive contrast [vision]
Color (Surprising color-vision effects) Ci: 819
Successive hermaphroditism
Hermaphrodite H: 211
Succory [plant] *See* Chicory *in this index*
Succot [custom] *See* Sukkot *in this index*
Succulent [botany] So: 950 *with picture*
Sucker [botany]
Banana (How bananas grow) B: 73
Dodder D: 260
Raspberry (Growing raspberries) R: 145
Sucker [fish] So: 950 *with picture*
Sucker [zoology]
Octopus (The body of an octopus) O: 672 *with
pictures*
Sucking louse [insect]
Louse L: 507
Sucking stomach
Spider (Digestive system) So: 785 *with diagram*
Suckling, Sir John [English poet] So: 951
Cribbage Ci: 1129
Suckling, Maurice [English navigator]
Nelson, Horatio (Early life) N: 121
Sucralose [sweetener]
Artificial sweetener A: 761
Sucre [Bolivia] So: 951
Bolivia B: 442
Sucre, Antonio José de [Bolivian political leader]
So: 951
Bolivia (Independence) B: 447
Ecuador (Spanish rule) E: 73 *with picture*
Peru (The war of independence) P: 315
Sucrose [sugar] So: 951
Candy (Types of candies) C: 175-176
Carbohydrate (Kinds of carbohydrates) C: 203
Fat substitute F: 54
Hydrolysis H: 471
Maple M: 186
Nutrition (Carbohydrates) N: 625
Sugar So: 959
Suction [physics]
Vacuum cleaner V: 257
Suction curettage [surgery]
Abortion (Abortion methods) A: 14
Suction spot [meteorology]
Tornado (The life of a tornado) T: 335
Suction vortice [meteorology] *See* Suction spot
in this index
Sudan So: 951*with pictures and map*
Darfur D: 35
Dinka D: 205
Flag *picture on* F: 200
Middle East M: 530
Nuer N: 603
Sudan, South So: 954
Sudan, South So: 954 *with pictures and map*
Flag *picture on* F: 200
Juba J: 178
Sudan grass So: 956
Grass *picture on* G: 325
Sorghum (Grassy sorghums) So: 596
Sudan People's Liberation Army [political group]
Dinka D: 205
Nuer N: 603
Sudanese Socialist Union [political party]
Sudan (Independence) So: 953
Sudbury [Ontario]
Greater Sudbury G: 350
Sudbury Basin [region]
Ontario (Natural resources) O: 779
Sudbury Neutrino Observatory
Astronomy (Neutrino astronomy) A: 845
Neutrino N: 154 *with picture*
Observatory (Neutrino observatories) O: 645
Sun (Analyzing neutrinos) So: 984-985

Sudden infant death syndrome So: 956
  Baby (Health care and safety) B: 10
Suddhodhana [father of]
  Buddha (Early life) B: 667
Sudeten Germans
  Czech Republic (The creation of Czechoslovakia)
    Ci: 1213
Sudeten Mountains [Czech Republic-Poland]
  Czech Republic (Land and climate) Ci: 1211 with
    picture and map
  Poland (The Sudeten Mountains) P: 609
  Silesia S: 457
Sudetenland [historic region] So: 957
  Czech Republic (The creation of Czechoslovakia)
    Ci: 1213
  Minority group (Minority groups in other
    countries) M: 610
  Munich Agreement (Background) M: 928
  World War II (The failure of appeasement) W: 472
Sudhuroy [island]
  Faroe Islands F: 47
Sudoku [puzzle] So: 957 with picture
Sudra [caste] See Shudra in this index
Sue [fossil]
  Field Museum (Exhibits) F: 94
  Fossil picture on F: 422
Suede [leather]
  Leather (Kinds of leather) L: 167 with picture
Suet So: 957
  Bird (Bird watching) B: 367
Suetonius [Roman author] So: 957
  Biography (Early biographies) B: 312-313
  Latin literature (The Imperial Period) L: 116-117
Suez [Egypt] So: 957
Suez Canal [waterway, Egypt] So: 958 with map
  See also Suez crisis in this index
  Canal (table) C: 164; (The Panama and Suez
    canals) C: 164
  De Lesseps, Ferdinand Marie D: 114
  Egypt (Muhammad Ali and modernization)
    E: 131; (Republic) E: 132 with picture
  Mediterranean Sea (History of the
    Mediterranean) M: 382
  Suez So: 957
Suez Canal Company
  Egypt (British control) E: 131-132
  Suez Canal (History) So: 958
  Suez crisis So: 959
Suez crisis [Egyptian history] So: 958
  Arab-Israeli conflict (The Suez crisis of 1956)
    A: 582
  Cold War (The Suez crisis) Ci: 766
  Egypt (Republic) E: 132
  Middle East (Cold War alliances) M: 534
  United Kingdom (European unity) U: 71-72
  United Nations (Peacekeeping operations)
    U: 90-91
Suffix
  Spelling (Spelling rules) So: 776
Suffocation
  Drowning D: 349
Suffolk [breed]
  Sheep picture on S: 381
Suffolk County [New York]
  New York City (Metropolitan area) N: 330
Suffolk horse
  Horse (table: Some types and breeds of horses)
    H: 343; (Heavy horses) H: 346-347 with picture
Suffolk sheep
  Sheep (Medium-wooled sheep) S: 382
Suffrage See Voting in this index
Suffrage, Woman See Woman suffrage in this index
Suffragette [British history]
  Pankhurst, Emmeline Goulden P: 131
  Woman suffrage (United Kingdom) W: 381
Suffragist
  Woman suffrage W: 380 with picture
  Women's movement (The right to vote) W: 385
Sufism [religion] So: 959
  God (Personal Gods) G: 243
  Muslims (The Abbāsids) M: 964c
  Religion (Islam) R: 223
Sugar So: 959 with pictures
  See also Blood sugar in this index
  Agriculture (Sugar-bearing crops) A: 148
  Artificial sweetener A: 761
  Beet B: 212
  Candy (Types of candies) C: 175-176
  Diabetes D: 179
  Dominican Republic (Economy) D: 304 with
    picture
  Food (Producing energy) F: 330
  Food preservation (Curing) F: 341
  Honey H: 314
  Life diagram on L: 277
  Maple syrup M: 187
  Nutrition (Carbohydrates) N: 625; (Nutrition

  guidelines) N: 626
  Rillieux, Norbert R: 341
  Slavery (The Middle Ages) S: 501; (Modern times)
    S: 502
  Starch So: 855
  Sucrose So: 951
  Sugar beet So: 962
  Sugar cane So: 963
  Teeth (A good diet) T: 81
Sugar Act [1764]
  Revolution, American (The Sugar Act) R: 272
  United States, History of the (Policy changes)
    U: 158
Sugar beet [plant] So: 962 with picture
  Beet B: 212 with picture
  Sugar (The sources of sugar) So: 960; (Sugar from
    sugar beets) So: 962
Sugar bowl [container]
  Colonial life in America picture on Ci: 808
Sugar cane [plant] So: 963 with picture
  Cuba Ci: 1168; (Economy) Ci: 1173 with picture;
    (History) Ci: 1175
  Grass (Sugar cane) G: 326
  Haiti picture on H: 16
  Hawaii (Agriculture) H: 104
  Molasses M: 689
  Puerto Rico (Agriculture) P: 882 with map
  Sugar (The sources of sugar) So: 960; (Sugar from
    sugar cane) So: 961
Sugar Hill Gang [pop group]
  Rap music R: 141
  Rock music (Rap) R: 380d
Sugar Loaf Mountain [Rio de Janeiro]
  Rio de Janeiro R: 345 with picture
Sugar maple [tree]
  Maple (Sugar maple) M: 186 with pictures
  Maple syrup M: 187
  Tree pictures on T: 422
Sugar pine [tree]
  Pine (Western pines) P: 469
  Tree pictures on T: 425
Sugar Street [book by Mahfouz]
  Mahfouz, Naguib M: 65
Sugarberry [tree]
  Hackberry H: 3
Sugarbush [plant]
  Plant picture on P: 525
Sugarcane cycle [books by Rego]
  Latin American literature (The early 1900's) L: 113
Sugarfree gum
  Chewing gum (Ingredients) C: 416; (History)
    C: 416-417
Sugarhouse
  Maple syrup (Production) M: 187-188 with picture
Sugaring season
  Maple syrup (Production) M: 187
Suggestion [psychology]
  Hypnosis (The nature of hypnosis) H: 478
Suharto [Indonesian political leader] So: 963
  Indonesia (Indonesia under Suharto) I: 238 with
    picture; (The fall of Sukarno) I: 238; (The fall of
    Suharto) I: 239
Sui dynasty [Chinese history] So: 964
  China (The period of division) Ci: 501
  Tang dynasty (The rise of the dynasty) T: 25
Suicidal gesture
  Suicide So: 964
Suicidal ideation
  Suicide So: 964
Suicide So: 964
  See also Physician-assisted suicide in this index
  Adolescent (Suicide) A: 64
  Bipolar disorder B: 327
  Borderline personality disorder B: 487
  Death (The right to die) D: 61
  Hara-kiri H: 55
  Mental illness (Mood disorders) M: 405
Suicide [book by Durkheim]
  Durkheim, Émile D: 389
Suicide bombing
  Israel (The early 2000's) I: 489-490
  Nuclear weapon (Post-Cold War strategy) N: 600
  Suicide (Types) So: 964
  Terrorism (Bombings) T: 175; (Terrorist groups
    and movements) T: 178-179; (Recent
    developments) T: 180
Suicide pact
  Suicide (Types) So: 964
Suicide squeeze
  Baseball (Baseball terms) B: 124
Suidas [book]
  Library (Medieval collections) L: 259
Suint [animal product]
  Wool (Types of wool) W: 399
Suit [cards]
  Bridge diagram on B: 604
  Card game (History) C: 209

Suit [clothing]
  Clothing (The 1900's and 2000's) Ci: 705
Suit [law]
  Affidavit A: 91
  Appeal A: 568
  Class action Ci: 642
  Court (How civil courts work) Ci: 1102
  Law (Private law) L: 130
  Law enforcement L: 141
  Receiver R: 174
Suit, Diving
  Diving, Underwater (Ambient diving) D: 245-246
    with picture; (History) D: 247
  Helium picture on H: 176
Suit, Hal [American political leader]
  Carter, Jimmy (Steps to the governorship) C: 254
Suit of Nettles, A [book by Reaney]
  Reaney, James R: 173
Suite [computing]
  Computer (Software suites) Ci: 920
Suite [music] So: 964
  Classical music (Orchestral music) Ci: 644
Suite bergamasque [music by Debussy]
  Debussy, Claude D: 66
Suite du Merlin [book]
  Excalibur E: 435
Suite Provençale [music by Milhaud]
  Milhaud, Darius M: 543
Sukarno [Indonesian political leader] So: 965
  Indonesia (Government) I: 226; (The rise of
    nationalism) I: 237; (Independence) I: 237;
    (The fall of Sukarno) I: 238; (Indonesia under
    Sukarno) I: 238
Sukarno-Hatta International Airport
  Airport (table) A: 245
Sukhona River [Russia]
  Dvina River D: 393
Sukkah [hut]
  Sukkot So: 965 with picture
Sukkot [custom] So: 965 with picture
  Judaism (The pilgrimage festivals) J: 181
Sukothai [ancient country]
  Thailand (Early kingdoms) T: 226
Sukuma [people]
  Tanzania (Population and ancestry) T: 31
Sula [book by Morrison]
  Morrison, Toni M: 817
Sulawesi [island, Indonesia]
  Indonesia picture on I: 229; (The Greater Sunda
    Islands) I: 233 with map
Sule Pagoda
  Yangon picture on Y: 551
Suleiman, Michel [Lebanese political leader]
  Lebanon (After the civil war) L: 174
Süleyman I [sultan of the Ottoman Empire] So: 965
  Muslims (The Ottoman Empire) M: 964d
  Ottoman Empire (Expansion and decline) O: 878
  Turkey picture on T: 503; (The rise of the Ottoman
    Empire) T: 510
Süleyman I, Mosque of
  Istanbul (The city) I: 490-491
  Turkey (The arts) T: 507
Sulfa drug [medicine] So: 965
  Drug (Drugs that fight infection) D: 351; (The
    drug revolution) D: 359
  Medicine (The medical revolution) M: 376
Sulfate [chemical] So: 966
  Baking powder B: 33
  Sulfuric acid (Uses and properties) So: 968
Sulfate process [industrial process]
  Paper (Pulping processes) P: 134-135
Sulfate rosin [by-product]
  Rosin R: 480
Sulfate turpentine [tree product]
  Turpentine T: 519
Sulfide [chemical] So: 966
  Galena G: 10
  Gold (Types of deposits) G: 252
  Ore O: 825
  Silver (Sources of silver) S: 464
Sulfinpyrazone [drug]
  Gout G: 281
Sulfite chemical process [industrial process]
  Paper (Pulping processes) P: 134-135
Sulfonamide [drug] See Sulfa drug in this index
Sulfonate
  Sulfuric acid (Uses and properties) So: 968
Sulfur [element] So: 966 with pictures
  Bleach B: 399
  Climate (Volcanic eruptions) Ci: 676d
  Fungicide F: 560
  Mineral picture on M: 569
  Mining diagram on M: 578; (Pumping methods)
    M: 577
  Rubber (Compounding and mixing) R: 505;
    (Vulcanization) R: 505
Sulfur-bellied flycatcher [bird]

Flycatcher F: 311
Sulfur-crested cockatoo
Parrot *picture on* P: 180
Sulfur dioxide [gas] So: 967
Acid rain A: 27
Coal (Coal research) Ci: 730
Sulfur (Properties) So: 966-967
Sulfuric acid (How sulfuric acid is made) So: 968
Sulfur dye
Dye (Synthetic dyes) D: 395-396
Sulfur sponge [sea animal]
Sponge *picture on* So: 799
Sulfur trioxide [chemical]
Sulfuric acid (How sulfuric acid is made) So: 968;
(Uses and properties) So: 968
Sulfuric acid [chemical] So: 968
Acid (Inorganic acids) A: 27
Acid rain A: 27
Hydrogen (Compounds) H: 469
Sulfur (Uses) So: 966
Sulfurless gunpowder
Gunpowder (Kinds of gunpowder) G: 441
Sulfurous acid [chemical]
Sulfur dioxide So: 968
Sulgrave Manor [England] So: 968
Sulky [vehicle]
Harness racing H: 63
Sulky plow
Plow (The sulky plow) P: 575
Sulla, Lucius Cornelius [Roman general] So: 968
Caesar, Julius (Early life) C: 13
Mithridates VI M: 678
Pompey the Great P: 655
Rome, Ancient (The later years of the republic)
R: 445
Sullivan, Anne Mansfield [American educator]
So: 968
Keller, Helen K: 255 *with picture*
Sullivan, Sir Arthur Seymour [British composer]
So: 969
Gilbert, Sir William Schwenck G: 189
Gilbert and Sullivan G: 190
Sullivan, Danny [American race driver]
Automobile racing (table: Indianapolis 500
winners) A: 980
Sullivan, Eugene C. [American chemist]
Glass (table) G: 218
Sullivan, Harry Stack [American psychiatrist]
So: 969
Sullivan, James [American political leader]
Massachusetts (table) M: 288
Sullivan, John [American general]
New Hampshire (table) N: 223
New York (Statehood) N: 315
Revolution, American (Invasion of the Iroquois
country) R: 284
Trenton, Battle of T: 435
Sullivan, John L. [American boxer] So: 969
Boxing *picture on* B: 532b; (Bare knuckles to
gloves) B: 532
Mississippi *picture on* M: 623
Sullivan, Kathryn D. [American astronaut]
Astronaut (A look at the astronauts) A: 831
Sullivan, Leon Howard [American social reformer]
So: 969
Philadelphia (Urban renewal) P: 367
Sullivan, Louis Henri [American architect] So: 970
with pictures
Adler, Dankmar A: 58
Architecture *picture on* A: 630; (Early modern
architecture in America) A: 629
Wright, Frank Lloyd (Early career) W: 507
Sullivan, Louis Wade [American government
official] So: 970
Sullivan, Mike [American political leader]
Wyoming (table) W: 532
Sullivan, Pat [American cartoonist]
Animation (Pioneers of American animation)
A: 514a-514b
Sullivan, Pat [American football player]
Football (table) F: 363
Sullivan, Thomas [American businessman]
Tea (History) T: 63-64
Sullivan, William E. [American businessman]
Ferris wheel F: 77
Sullivan, William W. [Canadian political leader]
Prince Edward Island (table) P: 791
Sullivan Center [Chicago]
Architecture *picture on* A: 630; (Early modern
architecture in America) A: 629
Sullivan Principles
Sullivan, Leon Howard So: 969
Sullivan's Island [South Carolina]
Fort Moultrie F: 415
Sullivan's Island, Battle of [1776]
South Carolina (The Revolutionary War) So: 659
Sully, Duke of [French nobleman]

France (The age of absolutism) F: 473
Sully, Thomas [American painter] So: 970 *with
picture*
Adams, John Quincy *picture on* A: 40
Sully Prudhomme [French poet]
Nobel Prizes (Literature: 1901) N: 447
Sulphur [butterfly]
Butterfly (Sulphurs and whites) B: 738
Sulphur [element] *See* Sulfur *in this index*
Sulpicius Severus [early Christian author]
Martin of Tours, Saint M: 235
Sulston, John Edward [British biologist]
Nobel Prizes (Physiology or medicine: 2002)
N: 447
Sulta [food]
Yemen (Food, clothing, and customs) Y: 562
Sultan [title] So: 971
Ottoman Empire (Government) O: 877
Sultan Ahmet Mosque
Istanbul (The city) I: 490-491
Sultan Hassan Mosque
Cairo (The city) C: 16 *with picture*
Sultana [grape variety]
Raisin (Varieties) R: 129
Sultana [ship]
Shipwreck (table: Major shipwrecks) S: 428
Sulu [clothing]
Fiji (People) F: 98
Pacific Islands (Clothing) P: 7
Sulu Archipelago
Philippines (The main islands) P: 376 *with map*
Sulzberger, Arthur Hays [American publisher]
So: 971
Sulzer, William [American political leader]
New York (table) N: 313
Sum [mathematics]
Addition (Writing addition) A: 49
Series (Working with infinite series) S: 317
Sumac [tree] So: 971 *with picture*
Sumanguru [king of the Ghana Empire]
Sundiata Keita So: 990
Sumarokov, Alexander [Russian author]
Russian literature (The classical movement)
R: 559-560
Sumatera [island, Indonesia] *See* Sumatra *in this
index*
Sumatra [island, Indonesia] So: 971
Indonesia (The Greater Sunda Islands) I: 233 *with
map;* (Climate) I: 234
Tsunami of 2004 T: 476
Sumatran rhinoceros
Rhinoceros (Kinds of rhinoceroses) R: 294
Sumatriptan [drug]
Migraine M: 538
Sumer [ancient country] So: 972 *with picture*
Architecture (Mesopotamian architecture) A: 611
Army (Ancient armies) A: 726
Asia (The Tigris-Euphrates Valley) A: 804
Babylonia B: 13; (Religion) B: 14; (The Akkadian
and Neo-Sumerian periods) B: 14
Clothing *picture on* Ci: 696
Cuneiform Ci: 1192
Drug (Drugs in ancient times) D: 358 *with picture*
Education (The beginning of formal education)
E: 97
Fertile Crescent F: 78
Iraq (Early days) I: 413
Mesopotamia M: 421
Middle East (Early civilizations) M: 533
Mythology (Middle Eastern mythology) M: 976
with picture
Park (History) P: 168
Sculpture (Middle Eastern) S: 233 *with picture*
Water (Water and civilization) W: 132
Woolley, Sir Leonard W: 402
World, History of the (The Tigris-Euphrates Valley)
W: 422
Writing system (Logograms) W: 512-513;
(Phonetization) W: 513
Sumerians [ancient people] *See* Sumer *in this index*
Summa contra Gentiles [book by Aquinas]
Aquinas, Saint Thomas (His life) A: 580
Summa cum laude
Degree, College (The bachelor's degree) D: 92
*Summa de Arithmetica, Geometria, Proportioni et
Proportionalita* [book by Pacioli]
Accounting (The history of accounting) A: 23
Bookkeeping (History) B: 473
Summa Doctrinae Christianae [book by Canisius]
Canisius, Saint Peter C: 177
Summa Theologica [book by Aquinas]
Aquinas, Saint Thomas (His life) A: 580
Political science (Scholasticism) P: 639
Summary court-martial
Court-martial Ci: 1105
Summary View of the Rights of British America, A
[pamphlet by Jefferson]

Jefferson, Thomas (Revolutionary leader) J: 79
Summer [season] So: 973
Season (The four seasons) S: 270 *with diagram*
Weather (Air temperature) W: 157
Summer-and-autumn rose
Rose (Types of roses) R: 474
Summer Before the Dark, The [book by Lessing]
Lessing, Doris L: 208
Summer camp
Camping (Organized camping) C: 96
Summer Days [painting by O'Keeffe]
O'Keeffe, Georgia *picture on* O: 709
Summer flounder [fish]
Flounder F: 267
Summer of the Swans, The [book by Byars]
Byars, Betsy B: 746
Summer resident [biology]
Bird (The distribution of birds) B: 331-332
Summer solstice [astronomy]
Olympiad O: 746
Season (The four seasons) S: 270-271
Summer squash [plant]
Squash (Summer squashes) So: 813 *with pictures*
Summer tanager
Tanager T: 24 *with picture*
Summer Time
Daylight saving time D: 54
Summer to Die, A [book by Lowry]
Lowry, Lois L: 511
Summer Triangle [astronomy]
Vega V: 291
Summerfield, Arthur E. [American government
official]
Eisenhower, Dwight David (table) E: 152
Summerlin, George [American government
official]
Pearson, Lester Bowles *picture on* P: 222
Summers, Lawrence Henry [American
government official]
Clinton, Bill (table) Ci: 682d
Treasury, Department of the (table) T: 407
Summit conference [international relations]
Cold War (The spirit of Camp David) Ci: 767
Diplomacy (History) D: 217
Eisenhower, Dwight David (Foreign affairs)
E: 152-153
International relations (International conferences
and organizations) I: 344
Summit Lake
Colorado (Rivers and lakes) Ci: 840
Summoned by Bells [poems by Betjeman]
Betjeman, John B: 275
Summons [law] So: 973
Clerk of court Ci: 662b
Sumner, Charles [American political leader]
So: 973
Civil War, American (The Kansas-Nebraska Act)
Ci: 616
Free Soil Party F: 499
Grant, Ulysses S. (Foreign relations) G: 316
Johnson, Andrew (Plans for Reconstruction)
J: 139
Reconstruction (The Radicals and the Moderates)
R: 178
Sumner, Increase [American political leader]
Massachusetts (table) M: 288
Sumner, James Batcheller [American biochemist]
Enzyme E: 340
Nobel Prizes (Chemistry: 1946) N: 443
Sumner, William Graham [American sociologist]
So: 973
Ethnocentrism E: 373
Mores M: 802
Social Darwinism So: 552
Sumner Elementary School
Topeka T: 332
Sumo [sport] So: 973
Japan (Recreation) J: 40 *with picture*
Wrestling W: 504 *with picture*
Sump [reservoir]
Gasoline engine (The lubrication system) G: 66
Mining (Mining terms) M: 577
Sumprun, Jorge [French author]
French literature (Recent French literature) F: 523
Sumptuary law So: 973
Clothing (Political influences) Ci: 690
Fashion (The origins of fashion) F: 50
Sumter, Fort *See* Fort Sumter *in this index*
Sumter, Thomas [American general]
Revolution, American (Savannah and Charleston)
R: 284-285
South Carolina (The Revolutionary War) So: 659-
660
Sumu-abum [king of Babylonia]
Babylon (The Old Babylonian period) B: 11
Sun So: 974 *with pictures*
See also Sunlight *in this index*

Astronomy *picture on* **A: 838**; (How the stars move) **A: 835**
Baily's beads **B: 31**
Calendar **C: 29**
Cassini, Giovanni Domenico **C: 277**
Climate (The role of latitude) **Ci: 676**; (Activity on the sun's surface) **Ci: 676d**
Cosmic rays (Solar cosmic rays) **Ci: 1076**
Eclipse **E: 51**
Heat (Sources of heat) **H: 149**
Heliosphere **H: 174**
Light (Sources of light) **L: 283** *with picture*
Magnetism (The sun) **M: 60d** *with picture*
Milky Way **M: 550**
Mythology (Comparative approaches) **M: 989**
Ocean (Tides) **O: 659**
Planet **P: 507** *with diagrams*
Planetarium **P: 514a**
Radiation **R: 74** *with picture*; (The sun and other stars) **R: 77**
Satellite (Formation) **S: 150**
Season (The four seasons) **S: 270** *with diagram*
Skin cancer **S: 491**
Solar energy **So: 576**
Solar system (The sun) **So: 580** *with diagram*
Space exploration (Solar probes) **So: 710**
Star **So: 840**
Stonehenge **So: 912**
Tide **T: 280** *with diagrams*
Time (Astronomical cycles) **T: 288** *with picture*
Transit **T: 374** *with picture*
Twilight **T: 531**
Weather (Air temperature) **W: 157**
Sun [era]
Mythology (Aztec mythology) **M: 987**
Sun, Temple of the
Pyramids (American pyramids) **P: 917**
Sun Also Rises, The [book by Hemingway]
American literature (The Lost Generation) **A: 421**
Hemingway, Ernest (Rise to fame) **H: 180**
Lost Generation **L: 472**
Novel (New directions in the novel) **N: 573-574**
Sun bath
Sun lamp **So: 988**
Sun bear
Bear **B: 182**, *picture on* **B: 186**; (Sun bears) **B: 185** *with picture*
Zoo *picture on* **Z: 599**
Sun Belt [region]
United States (Urban life) **U: 110-112**
Sun clock [device]
Time (Solar time) **T: 288**
Sun curing
Tobacco (Kinds of tobacco) **T: 305**; (Sun curing) **T: 307**
Sun dance [ceremony] **So: 987**
Indian, American *picture on* **I: 161**; (Ceremonies) **I: 148**
Sun-drying
Food preservation (Drying) **F: 342-343**
Sun gear [mechanics]
Gear **G: 75**
Transmission (Planetary gears) **T: 377** *with diagrams*
Sun god *See* Sun worship *in this index*
Sun King, The [name for]
Louis XIV **L: 474**
Sun lamp So: 987
Sun Microsystems Incorporated
Computer (Manufacturing) **Ci: 924**
Sun protection factor
Sunburn **So: 989**
Sun Records [company]
Presley, Elvis **P: 772**
Rock music (Beginnings of rock music) **R: 376**
Sun Valley [Idaho] **So: 988**
Idaho (Visitor's guide) **I: 34**
Sun worship [religion] **So: 988** *with picture*
Phoenix **P: 399**
Sun dance **So: 987**
Sun Yat-sen [Chinese statesman] **So: 988**
Chiang Kai-shek **C: 418**
China (History) **C: 499-503**
Nanjing (The city) **N: 9-10**
Sunapee Mountain
New Hampshire (Mountains) **N: 220**
Sunbird
Bird (Birds of Asia) **B: 344f** *with picture*
Sunbittern [bird]
Bird (Birds of Central and South America) **B: 344a** *with picture*
Sunburn [injury] **So: 989**
First aid (Burns) **F: 138-139**
Races, Human (Climatic adaptations) **R: 58**
Skin (Burns) **S: 490-491**
Ultraviolet rays (Harmful effects) **U: 17**
Suncor Energy Centre

Calgary (The city) **C: 33**
Sunda clouded leopard
Clouded leopard **Ci: 712**
Sunda Islands
Indonesia (The islands) **I: 233** *with map*
Sundance Film Festival [Park City]
Utah *picture on* **U: 239**
Sundance Institute
Redford, Robert **R: 191**
Sundanese [people]
Indonesia (People) **I: 227**
Java **J: 65**
Sundarbans [swamp, Asia]
Swamp **So: 1015**
Sunday [day] **So: 989**
Colonial life in America (Religion) **Ci: 804-805**
Easter (Easter symbols) **E: 43**
Sabbath **S: 2**
Sunday, Billy [American religious leader] **So: 989**
United States, History of the (Looking backward) **U: 191** *with picture*
Sunday Afternoon on the Island of La Grande Jatte [painting by Seurat]
Painting (What do painters paint?) **P: 28**; (Postimpressionism) **P: 75-76**
Seurat, Georges **S: 324**
"Sunday Bloody Sunday" [song]
Bono **B: 462**
Sunday in the Park with George [musical by Sondheim]
Sondheim, Stephen **So: 591**
Sunday school
Raikes, Robert **R: 103**
Religious education (Private education) **R: 225**
Sundback, Gideon [American inventor]
Zipper **Z: 596**
Sundew [plant] **So: 989**
Carnivorous plant **C: 243**
Plant (Environmental factors) **P: 538-539**
Sundial [clock] **So: 990** *with picture*
Clock (History) **Ci: 682k** *with picture*
Time (Solar time) **T: 288**
Sundiata Keita [king of the Mali Empire] **So: 990**
Mali Empire **M: 109**
Sundlun, Bruce [American political leader]
Rhode Island (table) **R: 311**
Sundquist, Don [American political leader]
Tennessee (table) **T: 152**
Sunfish So: 990
Fish *picture on* **F: 153**
Sunflower So: 990
Evolution (Direct observation of evolution) **E: 431-432** *with picture*
Flower (Garden annuals) **F: 276** *with picture*; (Flowers of prairies and dry plains) **F: 286** *with picture*
Spain *picture on* **So: 743**
Sunflower [book by West]
West, Rebecca **W: 199**
Sunflower oil
Sunflower **So: 990**
Vegetable oil **V: 294**
Sunflower seed
Sunflower **So: 990**
Sunflower starfish [animal]
Starfish (The life of a starfish) **So: 856-857**
Sunflower State [nickname]
Kansas **K: 216**
Sunflowers [painting by Van Gogh]
Art and the arts (The aesthetic experience) **A: 745**
Sung dynasty [Chinese history] *See* Song dynasty *in this index*
Sunglasses
Glasses (Nonprescription glasses) **G: 225**
Polarized light (Polarizing filters) **P: 618**
Sunlight
Dust (Influence on climate) **D: 390**
Greenhouse effect (The natural greenhouse effect) **G: 382**
Leaf (Obtaining the raw materials) **L: 155** *with diagram*
Plant (In ecosystems) **P: 518**; (Photosynthesis) **P: 537**; (Environmental factors) **P: 538** *with pictures*
Races, Human (Climatic adaptations) **R: 58**
Seasonal affective disorder **S: 272**
Solar energy **So: 576**
Sun (Energy output) **So: 976**; (Color) **So: 977**; (Photosphere) **So: 980**
Ultraviolet rays **U: 17**
Sunnah [religion]
Government (Asia and the Middle East) **G: 289-290**
Islam **I: 463**
Muslims (Muhammad) **M: 964a**
Shari`ah **S: 373**

Sunnis **So: 991**
Sunni Ali [king of the Songhai Empire] **So: 991**
Songhai Empire **So: 593**
Sunni Islam [religion] *See* Sunnis *in this index*
Sunnis [religious group] **So: 991**
Arabs (Religion) **A: 586**
Black Muslims **B: 390**
Egypt (Religion) **E: 124**; (Muslim rule) **E: 130**
Iran (Religion) **I: 401**
Iraq (Religion) **I: 411**; (History) **I: 413-414**
Iraq War (Resistance to the coalition) **I: 414e**
Islam (Divisions of Islam) **I: 466**
Lebanon (Ethnic groups and religion) **L: 171**
Libya (Religion) **L: 266** *with picture*
Middle East (Religion) **M: 531**
Muslims (Abū Bakr) **M: 964a**
Saudi Arabia (Religion) **S: 158**
Sunrise
Twilight **T: 531**
Sunrise tellin [sea animal]
Shell *picture on* **S: 387**
Suns, Phoenix
Basketball (table) **B: 150**
Sunset
Mars *picture on* **M: 226b**
Twilight **T: 531**
Sunset Boulevard
Hollywood **H: 293**
Los Angeles (Central Los Angeles) **L: 460**
Sunset Crater Volcano National Monument [Arizona]
National Park System (table: National monuments) **N: 51**
Sunset Strip
Los Angeles (Central Los Angeles) **L: 460**
Sunshade
Umbrella **U: 18**
Sunshine laws So: 991
Sunshine Mine
Idaho (The late 1900's) **I: 45**
Sunshine Sketches of a Little Town [book by Leacock]
Canadian literature (Other literature) **C: 158**
Leacock, Stephen Butler **L: 148**
Sunshine State [nickname]
Florida **F: 242**
Sunshine vitamin
Vitamin (Vitamin D) **V: 430**
Sunsphere
Knoxville *picture on* **K: 359**
Sunspot [astronomy] **So: 991**
Aurora **A: 892**
Climate (Activity on the sun's surface) **Ci: 676d**
Corona **I: 1067**
Magnetism (The sun) **M: 60d**
Sun *pictures on* **So: 982-983**; (Magnetic field) **So: 978**; (Solar activity) **So: 980**
Sunspot cycle
Magnetic storm **M: 57**
Sun (Magnetic field) **So: 977-978** *with diagram*
"Sunstone" [poem by Paz]
Paz, Octavio **P: 205**
Sunstroke [disorder]
Hyperthermia (Forms of hyperthermia) **H: 477**
Sununu, John H. [American political leader]
New Hampshire (table) **N: 223**
SUNY [university] *See* New York, State University of *in this index*
Super [beekeeping]
Bee (As an industry) **B: 206-207**
Super Bowl [game]
Brady, Tom **B: 547**
Football (Professional competition) **F: 364**; (table: U.S. professional football champions) **F: 365**
National Football League **N: 35**
Super-calender [machine]
Paper (Special kinds of paper) **P: 136**
Super Chief [train]
Railroad (The 1920's and the Great Depression) **R: 118**
"Super Diaper Baby" series [books by Pilkey]
Pilkey, Dav **P: 464**
Super G [competition]
Skiing (Alpine competitions) **S: 486-487**
Super giant slalom [competition]
Skiing (Alpine competitions) **S: 486-487**
Super heavyweight
Boxing (table) **B: 527**
Super-Kamiokande neutrino detector [machine]
Astronomy (Neutrino astronomy) **A: 845**
Neutrino **N: 154**
Super Mario Bros. [electronic game]
Electronic game (The Nintendo revolution) **E: 204d**
Super Mario 64 [electronic game]
Electronic game (Renewed interest in consoles) **E: 204e**

Super middleweight [boxing]
Boxing (table) **B: 527**
Super Nintendo Entertainment System
Electronic game (The Nintendo revolution)
E: 204d-204e
Super PAC [organization]
Political action committee **P: 627**
Super Photon Ring-8 GeV [machine]
X rays (Synchrotron radiation) **X: 542**
Super-proton synchrotron [machine]
CERN **C: 363**
Super yacht [boat]
Boating (Motorboats) **B: 428**
Superalloy [material]
Alloy (Other alloys) **A: 378**
Superaspirin [drug]
Aspirin (How aspirin works) **A: 816**
Superb fairywren [bird]
Bird (Birds of Australia and New Zealand) **B: 346**
with picture
Superb lyrebird [bird]
Bird (Birds of Australia and New Zealand) **B: 346**
with picture
Supercarrier [ship]
Aircraft carrier (History) **A: 207**
Supercavitating propeller
Propeller (Ship propellers) **P: 826**
Supercell [meteorology]
Thunderstorm **T: 272**
Tornado (How a tornado forms) **T: 334**
Weather picture on **W: 162**
Supercharger [engine]
Gasoline engine (Air and fuel) **G: 64**
Supercluster [astronomy]
Galaxy (Interactions between galaxies) **G: 8b-9**
Supercomputer
Aerodynamics picture on **A: 87**; (Computational
fluid dynamics) **A: 88**
Computer (Mainframes and supercomputers)
Ci: 910
Superconducting alloy [metal]
Alloy (Characteristics of alloys) **A: 377**
Superconducting cable [electronics]
Cable (Recent developments) **C: 6-7**
Superconducting quantum interference device
Magnetometer **M: 62**
Superconducting Super Collider
Particle accelerator (How accelerators work)
P: 184-186
Superconductivity [physics] So: **992**
Absolute zero **A: 17**
Argonne National Laboratory **A: 660**
Bardeen, John **B: 109**
Carbon (Fullerenes) **C: 205**
Cryogenics **Ci: 1165**
Electric generator (Losses and efficiency of
generators) **E: 171**
Electricity (Conductors and insulators) **E: 193**
Magnetic levitation train (Electrodynamic
maglev) **M: 55**
Magnetism (Superconductivity) **M: 61** with
picture
Materials (Ceramics) **M: 300d**
Matter (Superconductors) **M: 311**
Physics (Solid-state physics) **P: 438**
Solid-state physics So: **583**
Supercontinent [geology]
Earth (The shaping of the continents) **E: 24**
Pangaea **P: 130**
Supercooled water
Cloud seeding (Cloud-seeding methods) **C: 711**
Hail **H: 8**
Rain (The ice-crystal process) **R: 124**
Snow (How snow forms) **S: 539**
Weather (How people affect the weather) **W: 170**
Supercritical mass [physics]
Nuclear energy (Hazards and safeguards) **N: 587**
Nuclear weapon (Fission weapons) **N: 596-597**
Supercritical wing
Aircraft, Military (Recent developments) **A: 205**
Superdome [New Orleans] See Louisiana
Superdome in this index
Superego [psychology]
Ego **E: 119**
Freud, Sigmund (On the mind) **F: 530**
Mythology (Psychological approaches) **M: 990**
Personality (Freud's psychoanalytic theory) **P: 302**
Psychoanalysis (Psychoanalytic theory) **P: 846**
Superfluid [physics] So: **993** with diagram
Absolute zero **A: 17**
Matter (States of matter) **M: 311**
Superfortress [airplane]
Bomber (History) **B: 453**
Superfudge [book by Blume]
Blume, Judy **B: 425**
Superfund See Comprehensive Environmental
Response, Compensation, and Liability Act in
this index

Supergiant star
Star (High-mass stars) So: **849-850**
Superheated steam
Steam So: **880**
Steam engine (Modern steam engines) So: **881**
Superheater
Electric power (Fossil-fueled steam electric power
plants) **E: 183**
Superhero [fictional character]
Comics (Comic books) **Ci: 869** with picture
Lee, Stan **L: 180**
Spider-Man So: **791**
Superman So: **993**
Superheterodyne circuit [electronics]
Armstrong, Edwin Howard **A: 722**
Radio (The tuner) **R: 88**; (Early development)
R: 91
Superhighway
Automobile picture on **A: 946**
Road (Primary highways) **R: 358**
Superinfection [medicine]
Antibiotic (Destruction of helpful microbes)
A: 551
Superintendent [office]
Prison (The prison staff) **P: 806**
Superintendent of public instruction [office]
State government (Other officers) So: **863**
Superintendent of schools [office]
School (Public schools) **S: 182**
Superior, Lake [Canada-U.S.] See Lake Superior in
this index
Superior Court of the Virgin Islands
Virgin Islands, United States (Government)
V: 393-394
Superior National Forest [Minnesota]
Minnesota (Places to visit) **M: 594**
Superior Upland [region, U.S.]
Michigan (Land regions) **M: 500** with map
Superior vena cava [anatomy]
Heart (Blood vessels) **H: 135** with pictures
Human body (The blood vessels) **H: 421**; (table)
H: 422 with diagram
Vein **V: 295**
Superlative [grammar]
Adjective (Comparison of adjectives) **A: 57**
Comparison (The three degrees of comparison)
Ci: 902b
Superman [fictional character] So: **993** with picture
Comics (Comic books) **Ci: 869** with picture
Superman [philosophy]
Nietzsche, Friedrich (Psychological ideas) **N: 407**
Philosophy (Philosophy in the 1800's) **P: 390**
Supermarket
Food (Marketing) **F: 335**
Retailing (Supermarkets) **R: 265** with picture
Supermassive black hole [astronomy]
Andromeda Galaxy **A: 457**
Black hole (Supermassive black holes) **B: 388**
Galaxy (Galaxy evolution) **G: 9**
Supermaximum security prison
Prison (Maximum security prisons) **P: 805**;
(Current problems) **P: 808**
Supermini computer
Computer (Mainframes and supercomputers)
Ci: 910
Supernatural [belief]
Magic **M: 48**
Supernaturalism [philosophy]
Mythology **M: 973**
Supernova [astronomy] So: **994** with picture
Betelgeuse **B: 274**
Brahe, Tycho **B: 548**
Cosmology **Ci: 1077**
Galaxy (Galaxy evolution) **G: 9**
Neutron star **N: 155**
Nova **N: 553**
Quasar **Q: 8**
Shock wave **S: 430**
Star (Supernovae) So: **850**
Sun (Comparison with other stars) So: **978-979**
Supernova remnant [astronomy]
Interstellar medium **I: 352**
Superoxide dismutase [enzyme]
Manganese **M: 139**
Superpartner [physics]
Supersymmetry So: **995**
Superpatriot
Patriotism (Abuses of patriotism) **P: 198**
Superphénix [nuclear reactor]
Nuclear energy (Advanced fission reactors)
N: 594
Superphosphate [chemical]
Phosphate **P: 402**
Superplastic alloy [metal]
Alloy (Characteristics of alloys) **A: 377**
Superposition, Law of

Geology (The rock dispute) **G: 98**
Superpower [international relations]
Nuclear weapon (Nuclear strategy) **N: 600**
Superpressure balloon
Balloon (Superpressure balloons) **B: 59** with
picture
Superregeneration [radio]
Armstrong, Edwin Howard **A: 722**
Supersaurus [dinosaur] So: **994**
Dinosaur (True dinosaurs) **D: 206b-209**
Supersonic combination ramjet [engine]
Jet propulsion (Ramjet) **J: 114**
Supersonic flight
Aerodynamics (Supersonic aerodynamics) **A: 87**
Airplane (Supersonic airplanes) **A: 238**
Jet propulsion (Turbojet) **J: 111**; (Ramjet) **J: 114**
Rocket (Rocket-powered airplanes) **R: 391**
Sound (Supersonic speed) So: **602**
Streamlining So: **924**
Wind tunnel **W: 333**
Supersonic transport plane
Airplane **A: 208**, picture on **A: 237**; (Supersonic
airplanes) **A: 238**
SuperSonics, Seattle [team]
Basketball (table) **B: 150**
Superspeedway
Automobile racing (Stock car racing) **A: 978**
SuperSport Series [award]
Cricket (History) **Ci: 1134-1135**
Superstition So: **995**
See also the list of Related articles in the
Superstition article
Fetish **F: 81**
Folk dancing **F: 320**
Folklore (Superstitions and customs) **F: 324**
Friday **F: 532**
Frog **F: 536**
Superstring theories [physics]
Shadow matter **S: 342**
String theory So: **929**
Subatomic particle (Theoretical research) So: **938**
Superstructure [construction]
Aircraft carrier **A: 206** with pictures
Building construction (Parts of a building) **B: 681**
Ship (Building a ship) **S: 413**
Skyscraper (Building skyscrapers) **S: 497**
Supersymmetry [physics] So: **995**
Supertanker [ship]
Ship (Tankers) **S: 408**
Tanker (Kinds of tankers) **T: 28**
Transportation picture in **T: 391**
Supervised Agricultural Experience program
FFA (What FFA members do) **F: 84**
Supervised assisted living facility
Nursing home (Supervised assisted living
facilities) **N: 620**
Supervisors, Board of
County (Forms of county governments) **Ci: 1099**
Suppé, Franz von [Austrian composer]
Operetta **O: 809**
Supper at Emmaus [painting by Pontormo]
Mannerism picture on **M: 165**
Painting (Space) **P: 35**
Supplemental Nutrition Assistance Program
So: **996**
Agriculture, Department of **A: 161**
Welfare (The Supplemental Nutrition Assistance
Program) **W: 190**
Supplemental Security Income
Welfare (Welfare in the United States) **W: 190**
Supplementary angle [geometry]
Angle **A: 462**
Trigonometry (A special case) **T: 444**
Supplementary medical insurance
Insurance (Medicare) **I: 314**
Supply and demand [economics] So: **996** with
diagram
Agriculture (Economic controls) **A: 152**
Capitalism (Markets) **C: 194**
Economics (The free market) **E: 59**
Inflation **I: 266**
Interest (Events that cause interest rates to vary)
I: 321
Keynes, John Maynard **K: 308a**
Market research **M: 214**
Marketing **M: 214**
Price (How price is determined) **P: 774**
Wheat (Controlling wheat production) **W: 274-
275**
Supply reel
Tape recorder (How tape recorders work) **T: 37**
with picture
Supply sergeant
Army, United States (A typical day) **A: 734**
Supply-side economics
Reagan, Ronald Wilson (The 1980 election) **R: 167**
Support [painting]

Painting (Materials and techniques) **P: 36**
Support command
Air Force, United States (Support commands) **A: 193**
Support price [economics] *See* Price support *in this index*
Support system
Automobile *diagram on* **A: 948**; (Supporting the car) **A: 950**
Support trench [warfare]
World War I (The deadlock on the Western Front) **W: 457**
Supported mining
Mining (Underground mining methods) **M: 576**
Supporter [emblem]
Heraldry (Elements of a coat of arms) **H: 196** *with picture*
Supportive medicine
Palliative care **P: 109**
Supportive psychotherapy
Mental illness (Psychotherapy) **M: 407-408**
Supposes [play by Gascoigne]
Gascoigne, George **G: 60**
Suppositi, I [play by Ariosto]
Drama (Italian Renaissance drama) **D: 330**
Suppression [psychology]
Memory (Motivated forgetting) **M: 393**
Suppressor gene [biology]
Cancer (How damaged genes cause cancer) **C: 169**
Suprarenal gland *See* Adrenal gland *in this index*
Suprasegmentals [grammar]
Grammar (Principles of English grammar) **G: 303**
Supraspinatus [muscle]
Rotator cuff **R: 486**
Supremacy, Acts of [1534, 1559]
Elizabeth I (Problems at home and abroad) **E: 238**
Henry VIII [of England] **H: 188**
Protestantism (The conservative reform movements) **P: 834-835**
Reformation (In England) **R: 198**
Supremacy clause
Constitution of the United States (Article VI) **Ci: 1011**
Suprematism [art]
Hadid, Zaha **H: 4**
Malevich, Kasimir **M: 105**
Painting (Nonobjective painting in Russia) **P: 79**
Russia (Painting and sculpture) **R: 537**
Suprematist Composition: White on White [painting by Malevich]
Malevich, Kasimir **M: 105** *with picture*
Supreme Assembly, International Order of the Rainbow for Girls
Rainbow for Girls **R: 128**
Supreme court
State government (Judicial branch) **So: 864**
Supreme Court Building [Washington, D.C.]
United States, Government of the *picture on* **U: 137**
Supreme Court of Appeal
South Africa (National government) **So: 608**
Supreme Court of Canada So: 996 *with pictures*
Canada, Government of (The courts) **C: 136**
Famous Five **F: 26b**
Supreme Court of Florida
Bush v. Gore **B: 724**
Supreme Court of the United Kingdom
House of Lords **H: 385**
Supreme Court of the United States So: 998 *with pictures*
See also the table, Landmark decisions of the Supreme Court, in the Supreme Court of the United States *article*
Abortion (Abortion in the United States) **A: 15**
Address, Forms of (Officials of the United States) **A: 53**
Affirmative action **A: 91**
Amistad Rebellion **A: 433**
Boy Scouts (Organization) **B: 538**
Capital punishment (History of capital punishment) **C: 193**
Census (Controversy over census results) **C: 349**
Chief justice **C: 447**
Constitution of the United States (Article III) **Ci: 1009**
Court (Federal courts) **Ci: 1102**
Court of appeals **Ci: 1105**
Creationism (The 1900's) **Ci: 1123**
Election of 2000 **E: 161**
Evolution (Acceptance of evolution) **E: 433**
Freedom of assembly (In the United States) **F: 504**
Freedom riders **F: 508**
Gun control (Opposition to gun control) **G: 441**
Holmes, Oliver Wendell, Jr. (Supreme Court justice) **H: 295**

Homosexuality (Attitudes toward homosexuality) **H: 307**
Hypnosis (Enhancing memory) **H: 479**
Insurance (Greater regulation) **I: 316**
Judicial review **J: 184**
Law (Beginnings of U.S. law) **L: 136**
Marshall, John **M: 229**
New Deal (The Hundred Days) **N: 200-201**; (The final measures) **N: 202**
Obscenity and pornography (Legal history for obscenity) **O: 643**
Roosevelt, Franklin Delano (The Supreme Court) **R: 454**
Same-sex marriage **S: 78**
School prayer **S: 185**
Scottsboro case **S: 223**
Second Amendment **S: 278**
Segregation (The beginning of change) **S: 285**
Sentence **S: 304**
Sex discrimination (Sex-based laws) **S: 335**; (Changes in laws) **S: 335**
Sexual harassment (Sexual harassment law) **S: 337**
Taft, William Howard (Chief justice) **T: 12**
United States, Government of the (The Supreme Court) **U: 145**
United States, History of the (The power of the federal government) **U: 164**; (Party splits) **U: 176**
Washington, D.C. *picture on* **W: 72**, *map on* **W: 76**; (Supreme Court Building) **W: 71**
Supreme People's Assembly
Korea, North (National government) **K: 368**
Supreme People's Court
China (Courts) **C: 477-481**
Supreme reality
God **G: 243**
Supreme Soviet [government]
Union of Soviet Socialist Republics (National government) **U: 29**
Supreme War Council
World War I (American troops in Europe) **W: 463**
Supremes [singing group]
Rock music (Independent producers) **R: 379** *with picture*
Ross, Diana **R: 481**
Suq [market]
Asia (City life) **A: 780**
Cairo (The city) **C: 16**
Egypt *picture on* **E: 121**; (Recreation) **E: 124**
Morocco (Way of life) **M: 811**
Sura [river, Russia]
Volga River **V: 444**
Surabaya [Indonesia] **So: 1003**
Suramin [drug]
Sleeping sickness (Treatment and prevention) **S: 507**
Surazo [wind]
Bolivia (Climate) **B: 446**
Surcharged stamp
Stamp collecting (Surcharged stamps) **So: 830**
Surcote [clothing]
Clothing (The Middle Ages) **Ci: 700-701** *with picture*
Knights and knighthood (Clothing) **K: 350**
Sûreté Nationale, La
Police (In other countries) **P: 623**
Surety bond
Bonding **B: 481**
Insurance (Surety bonds) **I: 314**
Will (Administration) **W: 307**
Surface active agent [chemical]
Detergent and soap **D: 163**
Surface area [mathematics]
Area **A: 644**
Surface chemistry
Chemistry (Current research) **C: 405**
Surface drainage [agriculture]
Drainage (Surface drainage) **D: 320** *with diagram*
Surface effect ship [machine]
Air cushion vehicle (How an ACV works) **A: 181**
Surface grinding
Grinding and polishing (Grinding methods) **G: 395**
Machine tool (Abrasive processes) **M: 19**
Surface irrigation
Irrigation (Surface irrigation) **I: 457** *with pictures*
Surface-launched missile
Air Force, United States (Missiles) **A: 191**
Surface measure *See* Area; Square measure *in this index*
Surface mining
Coal (Surface mining) **Ci: 721** *with picture*
Mining (Kinds of mining) **M: 574** *with pictures*
Surface-painted enamel
Enamel (Techniques) **E: 264-**
Surface-piercing hydrofoil [boat]

Hydrofoil (Kinds of hydrofoils) **H: 466-467** *with diagram*
Surface station [weather]
Weather (Land-based observation stations) **W: 162**
Surface-supplied diving
Diving, Underwater (Ambient diving) **D: 245** *with picture*
Surface tension [physics] **So: 1003**
Capillarity **C: 192**
Detergent and soap (Wetting the material) **D: 164**
Water (The properties of water) **W: 129-130** *with diagram*
Surface-to-air guided missile
Guided missile (Surface-to-air missiles) **G: 426**
Surface-to-surface guided missile
Guided missile (Surface-to-surface missiles) **G: 425**
Surface Transportation Board
Interstate Commerce Commission **I: 352**
Railroad (The role of the federal government) **R: 113**
Surface water
Hot springs **H: 374b**
Irrigation (Surface water) **I: 456**
Surface wave [physics]
Earthquake (Surface waves) **E: 38**
Surfaced hardwood dimension
Lumber (Hardwood lumber) **L: 517**
Surfacing [book by Atwood]
Atwood, Margaret **A: 880**
Surfacing [construction]
Road (Paving) **R: 359** *with picture*
Surfactant [chemical]
Detergent and soap **D: 163**
Lung (Other jobs of the lungs) **L: 524**
Surfboard
Surfing **So: 1003** *with picture*
Surfing [sport] **So: 1003** *with picture*
See also Windsurfing *in this index*
Australia *picture on* **A: 904**
Surgeon
Surgery **So: 1004** *with pictures*
Surgeon Dentist, The [book by Fauchard]
Dentistry (Early dentistry) **D: 144-145**
Surgeon general of the United States So: 1004
Surgeonfish
Doctorfish **D: 259** *with picture*
Surgery [medicine] **So: 1004** *with pictures*
See also the list of Related articles in the Surgery *article*
Acupuncture **A: 31**
Amputation **A: 443**
Barber **B: 106**
Brain *picture on* **B: 555**; (Sensing the environment) **B: 552-553**; (Tumors) **B: 558**
Cancer (Surgery) **C: 172**
Dentistry (Oral surgery) **D: 144**
Disease (Medical treatment) **D: 232-233**
Endoscope **E: 273**
Erectile dysfunction **E: 349**
Heart (Treatment) **H: 138** *with pictures*; (Valve disease) **H: 141-142** *with picture*; (Heart failure) **H: 143** *with picture*; (Development of heart surgery) **H: 144**
Hypnosis (Uses of hypnotism) **H: 479**; (Scientific studies) **H: 480**
Hypothermia **H: 481**
Laser *picture on* **L: 81**; (Heating) **L: 82-83**
Light (Light in technology and industry) **L: 291** *with picture*
Lister, Sir Joseph **L: 349**
McDowell, Ephraim **M: 332h** *with picture*
Medicine (Antiseptic surgery) **M: 375** *with pictures*; (The medical revolution) **M: 376-377**
Needle *picture on* **N: 118**
Paré, Ambroise **P: 156**
Placebo **P: 505**
Plastic surgery **P: 553**
Testicular cancer **T: 182**
Transplant **T: 379** *with pictures*
Trephining **T: 435**
Weight control (Surgery) **W: 183**
Surgery [office]
Medicine (The United Kingdom) **M: 366-367**
Surgical expense benefit
Insurance (Surgical expense benefits) **I: 312**
Surgical intensive care unit [medicine]
Intensive care unit **I: 321**
Surgical microscope
Eye *picture on* **E: 467**
Surgical sterilization
Birth control (Methods of birth control) **B: 378**
Surgical unit
Hospital (Hospital units) **H: 372**
Suribachi, Mount [Japan]

World War II (Closing in on Japan) W: 492-493
Suricate [animal]
  Meerkat M: 383 *with picture*
Surimi [fish]
  Fishing industry (Methods of processing)
    F: 186-187
  Ocean (The importance of the ocean) O: 654
  Pollock P: 646
  Seafood S: 265
Surinam *See* Suriname *in this index*
Surinam toad [animal] So: 1008 *with picture*
Suriname So: 1008 *with picture and map*
  Flag *picture on* F: 201
  Indian, American (Indians of the Tropical Forest)
    I: 175
  Netherlands (History) N: 148-150
Surmullet [fish]
  Mullet M: 915
Surname
  Name N: 5
Surplus [economics]
  Balance of payments (How the balance of
    payments is determined) B: 36
  Food supply (Conditions that affect the food
    supply) F: 348
  National budget (Deficits and surpluses) N: 31
Surprise ending [literature]
  Short story S: 434
Surprised by Joy [book by Lewis]
  Lewis, C. S. L: 220
Surratt, Mary E. [American public figure]
  Lincoln, Abraham (The trial of the conspirators)
    L: 326
Surrealism [art] So: 1010 *with picture*
  Breton, André B: 594
  Chagall, Marc C: 368
  Dadaism D: 3
  Dalí, Salvador D: 10 *with picture*
  Ernst, Max E: 354
  French literature (Surrealism) F: 522
  Freud, Sigmund (His influence) F: 531
  Giacometti, Alberto G: 183 *with picture*
  Masson, André M: 296
  Miró, Joan M: 616
  Painting (Surrealism) P: 81 *with picture*
  Picasso, Pablo (The 1920's and 1930's) P: 448b-
    449
Surrealist Manifesto [document]
  Painting (Surrealism) P: 81
Surrender of Breda, The [painting by Velázquez]
  Velázquez, Diego V: 296
Surrender of General Burgoyne at Saratoga
  [painting by Trumbull]
  Burgoyne, John *picture on* B: 704
Surrender of Lord Cornwallis at Yorktown, The
  [painting by Trumbull]
  Revolution, American *picture on* R: 286
Surrender of Seville, The [painting by Zurbarán]
  Moors *picture on* M: 797
Surrey, Earl of [English poet] So: 1010
  Blank verse B: 398
  English literature (Elizabethan poetry) E: 316-317
  Poetry (Renaissance poetry) P: 596
Surrogate birth [medicine] So: 1010
Surrogate mother
  Surrogate birth So: 1010
Surrounded Islands [sculpture by Christo and
  Jeanne-Claude]
  Sculpture (From the mid-1900's to the early
    2000's) S: 259-260 *with picture*
Surrounded Islands [sculpture by Christo]
  Christo C: 537
Surtees, John [British race driver]
  Automobile racing (table: Formula One World
    Drivers' Championship) A: 980
Surtsey [island, Iceland]
  Iceland (The inland plateau) I: 22
  Volcano (table) V: 442b
Survey
  Magazine (Advertising) M: 44
  Psychology (Systematic assessment) P: 848
  Public opinion poll P: 861
  Sociology (Surveys) So: 565
  A Guide to Research Skills **Research Guide:** 34
Survey Act [1824]
  Monroe, James ("The American System") M: 736-
    737
Survey foot [measurement]
  Mile M: 542
Survey mile [measurement]
  Mile M: 542
Survey of the Coast [U.S.]
  Map (Mapping the Americas) M: 184-185
Survey reading
  Reading (Kinds of reading) R: 156
Surveying [measurement] So: 1011
  Egypt, Ancient (Sciences) E: 139

Laser (Measuring) L: 83
Map (Observation and measurement) M: 180;
  (Mapping the Americas) M: 184-185
Parallax P: 151
Radar *picture on* R: 72
Surveyor [occupation]
  Careers (Technical and mathematical
    occupations) C: 232 *with picture*
  Surveying (Careers in surveying) So: 1012
Surveyor [space probes]
  Space exploration (Lunar probes) So: 708-709
Surveyor 3 [spacecraft]
  Conrad, Charles, Jr. Ci: 973
Surveyor's compass
  Surveying (Early tools) So: 1011
Survival bobbing
  Swimming (Water safety) So: 1042-1043
Survival of the fittest
  See also Natural selection; Social Darwinism *in
    this index*
  London, Jack L: 444
Survival story
  Literature for children (Adventure and survival
    stories) L: 359
Survival Through Design [book by Neutra]
  Neutra, Richard Joseph N: 153
Survival training
  Astronaut (Survival training) A: 832
"Survivor" [television program]
  Television *picture on* T: 119
Survivor benefits
  Insurance (Life insurance) I: 309; (Old-age,
    survivors, and disability benefits) I: 314
  Social security (Social Security in the United
    States) So: 553
**Survivors of the Shoah Visual History
  Foundation** [organization]
  Spielberg, Steven So: 791
Susa [ancient city] So: 1012
Susan Constant [ship]
  Jamestown J: 28
Susceptor materials
  Packaging P: 18
Sushi [food] So: 1012
  Asian Americans (Asian influences on American
    culture) A: 812c
Sushruta [Indian physician]
  Leprosy (History) L: 205
Susitna-Cook Inlet
  Alaska (Land regions) A: 292-294
Suspended animation [physiology]
  Cryobiology Ci: 1165
Suspension [chemistry] So: 1012
Suspension bridge
  Bridge *picture on* B: 600; (Suspension bridges)
    B: 601-602 *with diagram*
  George Washington Bridge G: 109
  Golden Gate Bridge G: 255
Suspension feeder [zoology]
  Starfish (The life of a starfish) So: 856-857
Suspension line
  Parachute (Parts of a parachute) P: 142-143
Suspension-of-rules procedure [government]
  Congress of the United States (Passing a bill)
    Ci: 945
Suspension polymerization [industrial process]
  Polyvinyl chloride P: 652
Suspension system
  Automobile (Supporting the car) A: 950
  Torsion bar suspension T: 343 *with diagrams*
  Truck (Common features of trucks) T: 458
Susquehanna Indians
  Virginia (Early days) V: 418
Susquehanna River [U.S.] So: 1012
  Maryland (Rivers and lakes) M: 252
Sussex breed
  Chicken (table) C: 443
Sussex spaniel So: 1012
  Dog *picture on* D: 269
Sustainability [conservation]
  Agriculture (Reforming agricultural practices)
    A: 151; (Adopting sustainable practices) A: 160
  Clothing (The clothing industry) C: 705
  Geography (Environmental conservation) G: 94
  Housing (Sustainable housing) H: 392
  Tree farming T: 432
Sustained yield [conservation]
  Conservation (Forest conservation) Ci: 981
  Forestry (Managing timber resources) F: 404
Susu [people]
  Guinea (People) G: 430
Sutherland, Earl Wilbur, Jr. [American
  physiologist]
  Nobel Prizes (Physiology or medicine: 1971)
    N: 446
Sutherland, Edwin H. [American criminologist]
  Criminology (History) Ci: 1145-1146

Sutherland, George [American jurist]
  Supreme Court of the United States (table)
    So: 1000
Sutherland, Ivan [American computer scientist]
  Virtual reality V: 427
Sutherland, Joan [Australian singer] So: 1013
  Opera *picture on* O: 792
Sutherland Falls [New Zealand] So: 1013
  Waterfall (table: Famous waterfalls of the world)
    W: 143 *with picture*
Sutong Bridge [China]
  Bridge (table: Cable-stayed) B: 603
Suttee [custom] So: 1013
Sutter, Bruce [American baseball player]
  Baseball (table: Hall of Fame) B: 134b
Sutter, John Augustus [American settler]
  California (The gold rush) C: 62
  Marshall, James Wilson M: 229
  Sacramento (History) S: 6
Sutter, John Augustus, Jr. [American settler]
  Sacramento S: 5; (History) S: 6
Sutter's Mill [Coloma]
  California (The gold rush) C: 62
  Gold rush (Gold rushes in the United States)
    G: 254
Suttles, Mule [American baseball player]
  Baseball (table: Hall of Fame) B: 134b
Suttner, Baroness Bertha von [Austrian social
  reformer]
  Nobel Prizes (Peace: 1905) N: 448
Sutton, Don [American baseball player]
  Baseball (table: Hall of Fame) B: 134b
Sutton, Sir Thomas [English businessman]
  Charterhouse C: 386
Sutton, Walter S. [American geneticist]
  Cell (The 1900's) C: 337-338
Suture [anatomy]
  Skull S: 495
Suture [medicine]
  Surgery (Sutures) So: 1005
Suu Kyi, Aung San [Burmese political leader] *See*
  Aung San Suu Kyi *in this index*
SUV [vehicle] *See* Sport utility vehicle *in this index*
Suva [Fiji Islands] So: 1013
  Fiji *picture on* F: 98
  Pacific Islands *picture on* P: 6
Suvarnabhumi International Airport
  Airport (table) A: 245
Suwa, Gen [Japanese anthropologist]
  Prehistoric people (table) P: 754
Suwannee bass [fish]
  Bass (Black bass) B: 156
Suwannee River [Georgia-Florida] So: 1013
Suzhou [China] So: 1013
Suzong [emperor of China]
  Tang dynasty (The middle years) T: 26
Suzuki, Akira [Japanese chemist]
  Nobel Prizes (Chemistry: 2010) N: 444
Suzuki, Ichiro [Japanese baseball player] So: 1013
  Baseball (table: Modern major league records)
    B: 138
Suzuki, Shinichi [Japanese violinist]
  Suzuki method So: 1014
Suzuki method [education] So: 1013
Svalbard [islands, Arctic] So: 1014
Svalbard Global Seed Vault
  Plant *pictures on* P: 543
Svear [ancient people]
  Sweden (Early times) So: 1032
Svedberg, Theodor [Swedish chemist]
  Nobel Prizes (Chemistry: 1926) N: 443
Svengali [literary figure]
  Du Maurier, George D: 382
Sverdlovsk [Russia] *See* Yekaterinburg *in this index*
Svevo, Italo [Italian author]
  Italian literature (The 1900's) I: 495
Svir River [Russia]
  Lake Onega L: 43
Svoboda, Ludvík [Czechoslovak political leader]
  Czechoslovakia (The 1960's) Ci: 1216
Swab [recruit]
  Coast Guard, United States (Training an officer)
    Ci: 736
Swabia [former state, Germany]
  Germany (The breakup of Charlemagne's empire)
    G: 162
Swahili [language]
  Africa (Languages) A: 105
  Kenya (Languages) K: 298
  Swahili So: 1014
  Tanzania (Languages) T: 31
Swahili [people] So: 1014
  Bantu B: 99
Swain, D. L. [American political leader]
  North Carolina (table) N: 490
Swain, William [American miner]
  Western frontier life in America (A typical mining

camp) W: 235
Swains Island [American Samoa]
American Samoa A: 429
Swainson, John B. [American political leader]
Michigan (table) M: 507
Swainson's hawk
Hawk (Migration) H: 111; (Kinds of hawks)
H: 111-112
Swallow [bird] So: 1014 with pictures
Bird picture on B: 344d; (Birds of Europe) B: 344c;
(Building a nest) B: 356-357 with picture
San Juan Capistrano S: 103
Swallowing
Alimentary canal A: 368
Palate P: 101
Speech therapy (Types of disorders) So: 773;
(Diagnosis and referral) So: 773-774
Swallows and Amazons [book by Ransome]
Ransome, Arthur R: 141
Swallowtail [butterfly]
Butterfly pictures on B: 736, B: 737; (Swallowtails)
B: 738; (The thorax) B: 738-739
Insect picture on I: 282
Swallowtail [flag]
Flag picture on F: 194
Swammerdam, Jan [Dutch anatomist] So: 1015
Swamp [geography] So: 1015 with picture
Carboniferous Period C: 208
Everglades E: 424
River (Flood plains) R: 353 with diagram
Wetland W: 252a; (Swamps) W: 252b
Swamp buttercup [plant]
Buttercup B: 731
Swamp chestnut oak
Oak (White oaks) O: 635
Swamp Fox [nickname]
Marion, Francis M: 211
South Carolina (The Revolutionary War) So: 659-
660
Swamp hickory See Bitternut hickory in this index
Swamp partridge [bird]
Grouse G: 403
Swamp rose mallow [plant]
Hibiscus H: 223
Swamp wallaby [animal]
Wallaby (Kinds of wallabies) W: 15
Swamp white oak [tree]
Oak (White oaks) O: 635
Swan [bird] So: 1015 with pictures
Swan, Joseph [English scientist]
Light bulb L: 293
Swan goose
Goose G: 270; (Kinds of geese) G: 270
Swan Islands [islands, Caribbean]
Honduras (The Northeastern Plain) H: 310
Swan Lake [ballet]
Classical music picture on Ci: 650
Swan Mountains
Montana (Land regions) M: 752
Swan Service [tableware by Kändler]
Dresden china D: 347 with picture
Swan Song [book by Galsworthy]
Galsworthy, John G: 17
"Swanee" [song]
Gershwin, George G: 174
Swanee River See Suwannee River in this index
Swank, Hilary [American actress]
Motion picture (Best performance by an actress:
1999, 2004) M: 862a
Swann, Thomas [American political leader]
Maryland (table) M: 255
Swann v. Charlotte-Mecklenburg Board of
Education [1971]
Education (Education for whom?) E: 107
Swann's Way [book by Proust]
Proust, Marcel P: 838
Swansea [Wales] So: 1017
Swanson, Claude A. [American political leader]
Roosevelt, Franklin Delano (table) R: 454
Virginia (table) V: 417
SWAPO [organization] See South West Africa
People's Organization in this index
Swarm
Bee (Swarming) B: 204 with picture
Locust L: 419 with picture
Wasp (Group life) W: 112
Swarte Piet
Christmas (In The Netherlands, Belgium, and
Luxembourg) C: 531 with picture
Swastika [symbol] So: 1017 with pictures
Hitler, Adolf (Birth of the Nazi Party) H: 265-266
World War II picture on W: 470
S.W.A.T. team
Police (Other activities) P: 621-622 with picture
Swayback [disorder]
Spine So: 792
Swayne, Charles [American jurist]

Impeachment (History) I: 91-92
Swayne, Noah H. [American jurist]
Supreme Court of the United States (table)
So: 1000
Swazi [people]
Swaziland (People) So: 1017
Swaziland So: 1017 with picture and map
Flag picture on F: 200
Sweat See Perspiration in this index
Sweat box [container]
Raisin (Preparation for market) R: 129
Sweat gland [anatomy]
Gland (Exocrine glands) G: 207; (table) G: 209
Perspiration P: 305
Skin (Hair, nails, and glands) S: 489
Sweat lodge ceremony
Indian, American (Ceremonies) I: 148
Sweatshop [industry] So: 1019 with picture
King, William Lyon Mackenzie (Education) K: 325
Triangle Shirtwaist Factory Fire T: 438
Sweden So: 1020 with pictures and maps
See also the list of Related articles in the Sweden
article
Army (The rise of modern armies) A: 727
Christmas (In Denmark, Norway, and Sweden)
C: 531 with picture
Clothing picture on Ci: 694
Cooperative (In other countries) Ci: 1036
Denmark (Wars with Sweden) D: 140
Finland F: 108; (Swedish rule) F: 116
Lapland L: 74
Norway (Union with Sweden) N: 545;
(Independence) N: 546
Peter I, the Great (Foreign policy) P: 324
Sami S: 78
Scandinavia S: 170 with map
Sweden (People) So: 1023; (Agriculture) So: 1031
Vikings (The Swedish Vikings) V: 383
Welfare state W: 192
Swedenborg, Emanuel [Swedish religious leader]
Swedenborgians So: 1035
Swedenborgians [religious group] So: 1035
Swedes [plant]
Rape [plant] R: 142
Swedish cress
Cress Ci: 1127
Swedish Match Company
Match (The first safety matches) M: 300a
Swedish Nightingale [nickname]
Lind, Jenny L: 329
Swedish turnip
Rutabaga R: 567
Sweelinck, Jan Pieterszoon [Dutch composer]
Netherlands (Arts) N: 142-144
Sweeney, John Joseph [American labor leader]
So: 1036
Sweep [football]
Football (table) F: 356
Sweep oar rowing
Rowing (Types of rowing) R: 493-494
Sweeping [sports]
Curling picture on Ci: 1195; (The rink) Ci: 1196
Sweet, William E. [American political leader]
Colorado (table) Ci: 844
Sweet Adelines International [organization]
Barbershop quartet singing B: 107
Sweet alyssum So: 1036 with picture
Sweet basil
Basil B: 140
Sweet birch
Birch (Sweet birch) B: 327
Sweet cassava
Cassava C: 276 with picture
Sweet Charity [musical comedy]
Dance picture on D: 30
Sweet Cheat Gone, The [book by Proust]
Proust, Marcel P: 838
Sweet cherry [tree]
Cherry C: 410 with picture
Sweet chestnut [tree]
Tree picture on T: 426
Sweet chocolate
Chocolate (Chocolate products) C: 518-519
Sweet cicely [herb] So: 1036
Sweet cider
Cider Ci: 552
Sweet corn
Corn (Kinds of corn) Ci: 1058-1059
Sweet cream butter
Butter (Churning) B: 730
Sweet flag [plant] So: 1036 with picture
Sweet gum [tree] So: 1036 with picture
Leaf picture on L: 153
Tree pictures on T: 423
Sweet Lavender [play by Pinero]
Pinero, Arthur Wing P: 473
Sweet marjoram [plant]

Marjoram M: 213
Sweet natural buttermilk
Buttermilk B: 744
Sweet orange
Orange (Sweet oranges) O: 815
Sweet pea So: 1037 with picture
Flower (Garden annuals) F: 276 with picture
Leaf (Tendrils) L: 156
Sweet potato So: 1037 with picture
Morning-glory M: 809
Pacific Islands (Food) P: 6
Sweet potato [musical instrument]
Ocarina O: 646
Sweet violet [plant]
Flower picture on F: 278
Sweet William [plant] So: 1038 with picture
Flower picture on F: 277
Phlox P: 391
Sweetbay [plant]
Laurel L: 121 with picture
Magnolia M: 63
Sweetbread [food] So: 1038
Cattle (Beef cattle) C: 308
Sweetbrier [plant]
Eglantine E: 119
Sweetener
Food additive (Kinds of additives) F: 339
Sweetener, Artificial See Artificial sweetener in
this index
Sweetest Dream, The [book by Lessing]
Lessing, Doris L: 208
Sweetheart of the Rodeo [recording]
Rock music (Fresh directions) R: 380
Sweets festival [Islam] See `Id al-Fitr in this index
Sweikert, Bob [American race driver]
Automobile racing (table: Indianapolis 500
winners) A: 980
Swelling [disorder]
Inflammation I: 266
Swept-back wing
Aircraft, Military (Fighters) A: 203
Sweyn Forkbeard [king of Denmark]
Vikings (The Danish Vikings) V: 383
Swietenia mahogani [tree]
Mahogany M: 66
Swift [bird] So: 1038 with pictures
Animal picture on A: 475
Bird picture on B: 353; (Feeding methods) B: 350
with picture; (Building a nest) B: 356
Bird's-nest soup B: 375
Swift [book by Van Doren]
Van Doren, Carl V: 281
Swift [reptile] So: 1039 with picture
Swift, Graham [British author]
Novel (The novel today) N: 575
Swift, Gustavus Franklin [American businessman]
So: 1039
Swift, Henry A. [American political leader]
Minnesota (table) M: 602
Swift, Jane M. [American political leader]
Massachusetts (table) M: 288
Swift, Jonathan [English author] So: 1039 with
pictures
Black humor B: 389
English literature (Swift and Pope) E: 318
Gulliver's Travels G: 440
Irish literature (Early works in English) I: 431
Literature for children (The 1700's) L: 362
Swift, Tom [literary figure]
Stratemeyer, Edward So: 920
Swift & Company
Swift, Gustavus Franklin So: 1039
Swift fox
Fox (Kinds of foxes) F: 440
Swift Gamma Ray Burst Mission [satellite]
Astronomy (Gamma-ray astronomy) A: 845
Telescope (Gamma-ray telescopes) T: 109
Swift-Tuttle, Comet [astronomy]
Comet (table) Ci: 868
Swiftcurrent Lake [Montana]
Glacier National Park (Lakes) G: 205
Swiftly Tilting Planet, A [book by L'Engle]
L'Engle, Madeleine L: 191
Swigert, John Leonard, Jr. [American astronaut]
So: 1041
Lovell, James Arthur Jr. L: 509
Space exploration (The flight of Apollo 13)
So: 718
Swilling, Jack [American prospector]
Phoenix P: 395; (History) P: 398-399
Swim bladder [zoology]
Fish (Special organs) F: 163 with diagram
Isinglass I: 462
Lungfish L: 525
Roughy R: 490
Swim fins
Skin diving (Kinds of skin diving) S: 493 with

pictures
Swimmeret [zoology]
  Lobster (The American lobster) **L: 405-406** *with picture*
  Shrimp (The body of a shrimp) **S: 439-440**
Swimming So: 1042 *with pictures*
  Dolphin (Swimming and diving) **D: 299**
  Drowning (Methods of rescue) **D: 349**
  English Channel **E: 311**
  Fish (How fish swim) **F: 165** *with diagram*
  Olympic Games (Summer Olympic Games)
    O: 746e-747
  Safety (In water sports) **S: 13** *with picture*
  Weight control (table) **W: 182**
Swimming cat *See* Turkish van cat *in this index*
Swimming meet
  Swimming (Swim meets) **So: 1046** *with picture*
Swimming pool So: 1047 *with picture*
  Swimming (The pool) **So: 1044** *with diagram*
Swinburne, Algernon Charles [British poet]
  So: 1048 *with portrait*
Swine *See* Hog *in this index*
Swine flu [disease] **So: 1048**
Swineshead, Richard [English mathematician]
  Physics (The Renaissance) **P: 438-439**
Swing [music]
  Band (Dance bands) **B: 75**
  Jazz (The swing era) **J: 71**
  Popular music (Other new styles of popular
    music) **P: 671**
Swing bridge
  Bridge (Moveable bridges) **B: 602**
Swing-needle sewing machine
  Sewing machine (Kinds of sewing machines)
    S: 333
Swing Time [film]
  Astaire, Fred *picture on* **A: 823**
Swinton, Tilda [British actress]
  Motion picture (Best performance by an actress
    in a supporting role: 2007) **M: 862b**
Swiss [fabric] **So: 1048**
Swiss Alps [mountains]
  Switzerland (The Swiss Alps) **So: 1055** *with map*
Swiss Army knife
  Knife (Types of knives) **K: 345-346**
Swiss bank
  Switzerland (Banking) **So: 1058**
Swiss Brethren [religious group]
  Mennonites **M: 401**
Swiss chard [plant] **So: 1049** *with picture*
Swiss cheese
  Cheese (Kinds of cheese) **C: 392** *with picture*
Swiss cheese plant
  Monstera **So: 741**
Swiss Confederation [Swiss history]
  Switzerland (The struggle for freedom) **So: 1059**
Swiss Family Robinson [book by Wyss]
  Wyss, Johann David **W: 538**
Swiss German
  Switzerland (Language) **So: 1053**
Swiss Guard [European history] **So: 1049**
  Louis XVI **L: 476**
  Vatican City (Armed forces) **V: 288**
Swiss National Park [Switzerland]
  National park (table) **N: 42g**
Swiss People's Party [political party]
  Switzerland (Recent developments) **So: 1061**
Switch [railroad]
  Railroad (What makes up a railroad) **R: 106-107**
Switch, Electric *See* Electric switch *in this index*
Switch engine [train]
  Railroad (Rolling stock) **R: 107**
Switchboard [communications]
  Telephone (Early telephones) **T: 99** *with picture*
Switcher [machine]
  Television (The control room) **T: 112-113**
Switchgrass [plant] **So: 1049** *with picture*
  Plant *picture on* **P: 526**
Switching [electronics]
  Electronics (Transistors) **E: 212**
  Telephone (How a telephone call travels) **T: 95**
  Transistor (What transistors do) **T: 372**
Switching and terminal railroad
  Railroad (Railroad systems) **R: 112**
Switching cost [economics]
  Industry (Search and switching costs) **I: 260**
Switching locomotive
  Locomotive (Kinds of locomotives) **L: 414**
Switchmen's Union of North America
  Railway brotherhoods **R: 122**
Switzerland So: 1050 *with pictures and maps*
  See also the list of Related articles in the
    Switzerland article
  Alps **A: 384** *with pictures*
  Bank (Europe) **B: 92**
  Clothing *picture on* **Ci: 694**
  Europe *picture on* **E: 381**

German literature **G: 138**
  Helvetians **H: 180**
  Lake dwelling **L: 37**
  Militia **M: 544**
Switzerland of America [region]
  Iowa (Land regions) **I: 386**
Switzers [European history]
  Swiss Guard **So: 1049**
Swivel chair
  Jefferson, Thomas *picture on* **J: 78**
Swivel knife
  Leathercraft *picture on* **L: 170**
SWOC [committee]
  United Steelworkers **U: 204**
Sword [weapon] **So: 1061** *with pictures*
  Armor *pictures on* **A: 720**
  Duel **D: 378**
  Fencing **F: 70** *with pictures*
  Indian, American *picture on* **I: 140**
  Vikings *picture on* **V: 380**; (Weapons and armor)
    V: 382 *with picture*
Sword Blades and Poppy Seed [book by Lowell]
  Lowell, Amy **L: 509**
Sword dance
  Folk dancing **F: 320**
Sword fern [plant]
  Evolution (Evolution of new species) **E: 429-430**
  Fern (Kinds of ferns) **F: 75**
  Plant *picture on* **P: 524**
Sword lily [plant]
  Gladiolus **G: 206**
Sword of Damocles
  Damocles **D: 21**
Swordfish So: 1062
  Fish *picture on* **F: 152**
Swordgrass brown [butterfly]
  Butterfly *picture on* **B: 735**
Swordtail [fish]
  Fish *picture on* **F: 157**
Swynford, Katherine [wife of]
  John of Gaunt **J: 134**
Sycamore [tree] **So: 1062**
  Tree *pictures on* **T: 423**
  Wood *picture on* **W: 389**
Sycamore maple [tree]
  Maple (Other maples) **M: 187**
Sycon [sea animal]
  Sponge (Kinds of sponges) **So: 800**
Sydenham, Baron [British political leader]
  So: 1062
Sydenham, Thomas [English doctor] **So: 1063**
Sydney [Australia] **So: 1063** *with picture and map*
  Australia **A: 894** *with picture*
  Exploration (Exploring Australia's interior) **E: 448**
  Olympic Games (The recent games) **O: 753-754**
Sydney [Nova Scotia]
  Canada *picture on* **C: 122**
  Nova Scotia (table: Average monthly weather)
    N: 564
Sydney, University of [Australia]
  New South Wales (People) **N: 286**
Sydney Harbour [Australia]
  Australia *picture on* **A: 895**
  Sydney **So: 1063**
Sydney Harbour Bridge [Australia]
  Bridge (table: Steel arch) **B: 603**
  Sydney *picture on* **So: 1063**
Sydney Opera House [Australia]
  Australia *picture on* **A: 895**; (Architecture) **A: 906**
  Sydney (Cultural life) **So: 1064** *with picture*
Sydney Steel Corporation
  Nova Scotia (The early to middle 1900's) **N: 570**
Sydneysiders [people]
  Sydney (The people) **So: 1063**
Sydow, Max von [Swedish actor]
  Motion picture *picture on* **M: 870**
Sykes, James [American political leader]
  Delaware (table) **D: 109**
Sykes, Lynn R. [American geologist]
  Plate tectonics (History of tectonic theory)
    P: 564-565
Sykes-Picot Agreement [1916]
  Palestine (World War I and the Balfour
    Declaration) **P: 105**
Syllabary [language]
  Indian, American (Writing) **I: 150-151**
  Writing system (Phonetization) **W: 513**
Syllabic meter
  Poetry (Rhythm and meter) **P: 591-592**
Syllable
  Pronunciation (Learning pronunciation) **P: 821**
Syllabogram [symbol]
  Writing system (Phonetization) **W: 513**
Syllabus of Errors [document]
  Pius IX **P: 503**
  Pope (The 1700's and 1800's) **P: 665**
Syllogism [logic]

Aristotle (Logic) **A: 663-664**
  Logic (The categorical syllogism) **L: 425**
Sylphide, La [ballet]
  Ballet (Romantic ballet) **B: 51**
Sylphides, Les [ballet]
  Ballet (Ballet in Russia) **B: 52**
Sylvan Lake [South Dakota]
  Black Hills **B: 387**
Sylverius, Saint [pope]
  Pope (table) **P: 666**
Sylvester I, Saint [pope] **So: 1065**
  Pope (table) **P: 666**
Sylvester II [pope] **So: 1065**
  Pope (table) **P: 666**
Sylvester III [pope]
  Pope (table) **P: 666**
Sylvester IV [antipope]
  Pope (table) **P: 666**
Sylvester, Edmund [American settler]
  Olympia **O: 746**
Sylvester, Francis [American lawyer]
  Van Buren, Martin (Childhood and education)
    V: 270
Sylvia [ballet]
  Delibes, Léo **D: 116**
"**Sylvie**" [poem by Nerval]
  Nerval, Gérard de **N: 131**
Sylvie and Bruno [book by Carroll]
  Carroll, Lewis (Other works) **C: 249**
Sylvis, William H. [American labor leader]
  Labor movement (The first nationwide labor
    organizations) **L: 9**
Sylvite [mineral]
  Potash **P: 710**
Sym, Jane [wife of]
  Mackenzie, Alexander (Emigration to Canada)
    M: 21
Symbionese Liberation Army [terror group]
  Hearst, William Randolph **H: 131**
Symbiosis [biology] **So: 1065**
  Coral reef (Life on coral reefs) **Ci: 1049**
  Deep sea (Invertebrates) **D: 82a-82b**
Symbol So: 1065 *with pictures*
  See also the list of Related articles in the Symbol
    article
  Algebra (Symbols in algebra) **A: 354**
  Bird **B: 328**
  Culture (Using symbols) **Ci: 1187**
  Flag **F: 193** *with picture*
  Mythology (Symbols) **M: 975**
  Propaganda (The use of symbols) **P: 824**
Symbolic logic
  Mathematics (Branches of mathematics) **M: 303**
  Philosophy (Rationalism) **P: 389**
  Set theory (History) **S: 322**
Symbolism [arts] **So: 1066**
  Baudelaire, Charles **B: 173**
  Drama (Symbolism) **D: 339**
  French literature (Symbolism) **F: 522**
  George, Stefan **G: 108**
  German literature (Impressionism,
    Neoromanticism, and Symbolism) **G: 141**
  Mallarmé, Stéphane **M: 110**
  Painting (Symbolism) **P: 76** *with picture*
  Poetry (Beginnings of modern poetry) **P: 597**
  Russian literature (Symbolism) **R: 563**
  Spanish literature (Modernism) **So: 762**
  Verlaine, Paul **V: 317**
Symington, J. Fife [American political leader]
  Arizona (table) **A: 687**; (The late 1900's) **A: 691-**
    692
Symington, Stuart [American political leader]
  So: 1066
Symington, William [British engineer]
  Ship (The first steamboats) **S: 424**
Symmachus, Saint [pope]
  Pope (table) **P: 666**
Symmes, Anna [wife of William Henry Harrison]
  See Harrison, Anna Symmes *in this index*
Symmes, John C. [American businessman]
  Harrison, William Henry (Harrison's family) **H: 74**
Symmetrical system [cryptology] *See* Secret-key
  system *in this index*
Symmetry [geometry] **So: 1066** *with diagrams*
  Gem (Crystal shape) **G: 77**
  Quasicrystal **Q: 9**
Symmetry [physics]
  Higgs boson **H: 227**
  Supersymmetry **So: 995**
Sympathetic nervous system [physiology]
  Beta-blocker **B: 274**
  Nervous system (The autonomic nervous system)
    N: 133 *with diagram*
  Pain (How the body feels pain) **P: 21-22**
Sympathetic ophthalmia [disease]
  Blindness (Diseases) **B: 401-402**
  Ophthalmia **O: 810**

Sympathy strike
Labor movement (Handling labor disputes) **L: 6-7**
Strike (Kinds of strikes) **So: 928**
Taft-Hartley Act **T: 13**
Symphonic ballet
Massine, Léonide **M: 296**
Symphonic band [music]
Band (Concert bands) **B: 74**
Symphonic concerto [music]
Concerto **Ci: 928**
Symphonic drama
Green, Paul Eliot **G: 379**
Symphonic poem [music] **So: 1067**
Classical music (Orchestral music) **Ci: 644**
Overture **O: 882**
Symphonium [musical instrument]
Harmonica **H: 62**
Symphony [music] **So: 1067**
Classical music (Orchestral music) **Ci: 644**; (The Romantic era) **Ci: 648-649**
Orchestra (History) **O: 822**
"Symphony, The" [poem by Lanier]
Lanier, Sidney **L: 68**
Symphony in C [music by Bizet]
Bizet, Georges **B: 385**
Symphony No. 1 [music by Zwilich]
Zwilich, Ellen Taaffe **Z: 610**
Symphony No. 3 [music by Beethoven] See Eroica in this index
Symphony No. 9 [music by Beethoven]
Beethoven, Ludwig van (Beethoven's place in music history) **B: 214**
Symphony orchestra
Orchestra **O: 820** with picture
Symphony society
Orchestra (Orchestra management) **O: 821**
Symphysis, Pubic [anatomy]
Pelvis **P: 233** with diagram
Symposium
Greece, Ancient (Recreation) **G: 367**
Symposium, The [book by Plato]
Plato (The dialogues) **P: 567**
Sympto-thermal method
Birth control (Methods of birth control) **B: 378-379**
Syms Free School [U.S. history]
Virginia (Schools) **V: 402**
Synagogue [religion] **So: 1067**
Judaism (The synagogue) **J: 181**; (Worship) **J: 181**
Synanon [cult]
Cult (Modern cults) **Ci: 1185**
Synapse [anatomy]
Brain **B: 550a**; (Action potentials) **B: 557** with diagram
Fat (Biological and nutritional importance) **F: 52-53**
Memory **M: 392**
Nervous system (The dendrites) **N: 134** with diagram; (Transmission across synapses) **N: 135**
Synapsid [extinct animal]
Dimetrodon **D: 204**
Evolution (pictures on **E: 429**; (The fossil record) **E: 430**
Mammal (The ancestors of mammals) **M: 126**
Permian Period **P: 289**
Prehistoric animal (The Age of Reptiles) **P: 737**
Synaptic cleft See Synaptic gap in this index
Synaptic gap [anatomy]
Brain (Synapses) **B: 557** with diagram
Nervous system (The dendrites) **N: 134**
Synchronic linguistics
Linguistics (Descriptive linguistics) **L: 335**
Synchronicity [recording]
Rock music (New wave and mainstream rock) **R: 380c**
Synchronization [filmmaking]
Motion picture (Preliminary steps) **M: 854**
Synchronized skating
Ice skating (Synchronized skating) **I: 13**
Synchronized swimming
Swimming (Synchronized swimming) **So: 1047** with picture
Synchronized trampoline [sport]
Gymnastics (Trampoline and tumbling) **G: 449**
Synchronizing signal [electronics]
Television (Encoding the color signals) **T: 123**
Synchronous communication
Internet (Communication without limits) **I: 350e**
Synchronous generator
Electric generator (How AC generators work) **E: 171**
Synchronous motor
Electric motor (AC motors) **E: 181**
Synchrotron [machine] **So: 1067**
CERN **C: 363**
Fermi National Accelerator Laboratory **F: 74**
Particle accelerator (How accelerators work)

P: 184-185 with diagram
X rays (In X-ray tubes) **X: 542**
Synchrotron radiation [physics]
Jupiter (Radio emissions) **J: 199**
X rays (Synchrotron radiation) **X: 542**
Syncom 2 [satellite]
Communications satellite (History) **Ci: 888b-889**
Syncopation [music]
Jazz **J: 68**
Music (Rhythm) **M: 951**
Popular music (Ragtime, jazz, and blues) **P: 670**
Syncretic African church [religion]
Africa (Religions) **A: 106-107**
Syncytium inducing protein [biology]
Evolution (Direct observation of evolution) **E: 431**
Syndicalism [labor] **So: 1067**
Collectivism **Ci: 775**
Syndicate [crime]
Crime (Organized crime) **Ci: 1136**
Syndicate, Newspaper See Newspaper syndicate in this index
Syndicated programming
Television (Commercial stations) **T: 114**
Synergetics [book by Fuller]
Fuller, Buckminster **F: 554**
Synesius of Cyrene [Greek scholar]
Hypatia **H: 475**
Synfuel See Synthetic fuel in this index
Synge, John Millington [Irish dramatist] **So: 1067**
Irish literature (The Irish literary revival) **I: 431**
Realism (In drama) **R: 172**
Synge, Richard Laurence Millington [British biochemist]
Nobel Prizes (Chemistry: 1952) **N: 443**
Synod [religion]
Lutherans **L: 529**
Presbyterian Church (U.S.A.) **P: 756**
Presbyterians **P: 756a**
Reformed Church in America **R: 199**
Synodic month [time]
Month **M: 767**
Moon (Rotation and orbit) **M: 783**
Synonym [language] **So: 1068**
Dictionary (What a dictionary tells you) **D: 193**
Synopsis [grammar]
Conjugation **C: 950**
Synoptic Gospels
Bible (The Gospels) **B: 283**
Gospels **G: 278**
New Testament (Critical studies) **N: 288**
Synoptic meteorologist
Weather (Careers in weather) **W: 170**
Synoptic-scale systems
Weather (Weather systems) **W: 158**
Synovial fluid [physiology]
Elbow **E: 157**
Joint **J: 155**
Knee **K: 345**
Synovial membrane [anatomy]
Carpal tunnel syndrome **C: 245** with diagram
Membrane (Serous membranes) **M: 391**
Syntactic clue
Reading (Comprehending what is perceived) **R: 157**
Syntagma Square
Athens (Landmarks) **A: 854** with map
Syntan [chemical]
Leather (Tanning) **L: 167-168**
Syntax [grammar]
Language (Syntax) **L: 63**
Linguistics (The components of a grammar) **L: 336**
Semantics **S: 291**
Synthesis [philosophy]
Hegel, G. W. F. (Hegel's dialectic) **H: 165**
Synthesis gas
Petrochemicals **P: 329**
Synthesizer [machine] **So: 1068**
Classical music (Electronic music) **Ci: 650**
Electronic music **E: 205**
Jazz (Fusion) **J: 74**
Music (Electronic instruments) **M: 950**
Organ (Electronic organs) **O: 852**
Synthetic chemistry
Chemistry (The broad range of study) **C: 399**; (Current research) **C: 405**
Synthetic Cubism [art]
Cubism **Ci: 1181** with picture
Gris, Juan **G: 395**
Painting (Cubism) **P: 77-78**
Picasso, Pablo (Cubism) **P: 448b**
Synthetic diamond
Diamond (Synthetic diamonds) **D: 183** with pictures
Synthetic drug
Drug (Chemical laboratories) **D: 354**
Synthetic dye

Dye (Synthetic dyes) **D: 395**
Synthetic environment [electronics] See Virtual reality in this index
Synthetic fiber
Clothing (Clothing materials) **Ci: 695**
Cotton (Synthetic fibers) **Ci: 1093**
Fiber (Synthetic fibers) **F: 87**
Fur (Artificial fur) **F: 561**
Rope (Synthetic-fiber rope) **R: 473**
Synthetic fuel So: 1068
Conservation (Renewed interest in conservation) **Ci: 986-987**
Fuel (Synthetic liquid fuels) **F: 550**
Synthetic gem
Gem (Imitation and synthetic gems) **G: 79**
Synthetic geometry
Geometry (Types of geometry) **G: 103-104**
Synthetic hormone
Hormone (Synthetic hormones) **H: 337**
Synthetic phonics
Reading (Phonics instruction) **R: 159**
Synthetic polymer [chemistry]
Polyethylene **P: 650**
Synthetic resin
Plastics (How plastics are made) **P: 556**
Resin **R: 259**
Synthetic rubber
Rubber (Development of synthetic rubbers) **R: 501**; (Synthetic rubber) **R: 504**
Synthetic theory [biology]
Evolution (The synthetic theory) **E: 432**
Synthetics So: 1068
See also the list of Related articles in the Synthetics article
Fiber (Synthetic fibers) **F: 87**
Polyester **P: 649**
Synthetism [art]
Gauguin, Paul (Early career) **G: 69** with picture
Syon House [London]
Architecture picture on **A: 624**
Syphilis [disease] **So: 1069**
Disease (table) **D: 226**
Sexually transmitted disease **S: 338b**
Tabes **T: 2**
Syr Darya [river, Asia]
Uzbekistan (Land and climate) **U: 254**
Syracuse [ancient city] **So: 1069**
Oratory (Beginnings) **O: 818**
Syracuse [New York] **So: 1069**
Syracuse, Battle of [415-413 B.C.]
Syracuse (ancient city) **So: 1069**
Syria So: 1070 with pictures and maps
See also the list of Related articles in the Syria article
Arab Americans (Who Arab Americans are) **A: 580a**
Arabs (The search for unity) **A: 590-590a**
Clothing picture on **Ci: 692**
Egypt (The United Arab Republic) **E: 132-133**
Lebanon (War and terrorism) **L: 173**; (After the civil war) **L: 174**
Middle East **M: 530**
Muslim Brotherhood **M: 964**
Obama, Barack (Syria and Iran) **O: 642**
United Arab Republic **U: 46**
Syrian Desert [region, Arabia] **So: 1076**
Iraq (The land) **I: 411-412** with map
Syrian hamster
Hamster **H: 37** with picture
Syringa [plant] **So: 1077**
Mock orange **M: 684**
Syringe So: 1077
Hypodermic injection **H: 480**
Syrinx [Greek mythology]
Pan **P: 113**
Syrinx [zoology]
Bird (Calls and songs) **B: 354**
Syro-Malabar Church [religious group]
Eastern Catholic Church **E: 45**
Syrphid fly
Insect picture on **I: 297**
Syrup
Corn syrup **Ci: 1064**
Maple syrup **M: 187**
Soft drink (How soft drinks are made) **So: 571**
System, Organ [biology] See Organ system in this index
System of Transcendental Idealism [book by Schelling]
Schelling, Friedrich Wilhelm Joseph von **S: 174**
Systema Naturae [book by Linnaeus]
Linnaeus, Carolus **L: 337**
Systematic assessment
Psychology (Systematic assessment) **P: 848**
Systematics [biology]
Biology **B: 316**
Botany (Plant classification and form) **B: 508**

Classification, Scientific **Ci:** 654
Système International d'Unités [measurement] *See* Metric system *in this index*
Systemic
Insecticide **I:** 301
Systemic autoimmune disease
Immune system (Autoimmune disorders) **I:** 88c
Systemic circulation
Circulatory system (In respiration) **Ci:** 559
Heart (Birds and mammals) **H:** 146
Systemic disease
Fungal disease (In people) **F:** 558
Systemic lupus erythematosus [disease]
Immune system (Systemic autoimmune diseases) **I:** 88c
Lupus **L:** 526
Systemic poison
Poison (Kinds of poisons) **P:** 600
Systems analysis **So:** 1077
Systems analyst
Careers (Technical and mathematical occupations) **C:** 232
Computer (Careers) **Ci:** 924a
Systems analysis **So:** 1077
Systems ecologist
Ecology (Ecosystems) **E:** 54
Systems flow chart
Computer (Preparing a program) **Ci:** 923
Systems physiology
Biomedical engineering (Specialty areas of biomedical engineering) **B:** 324
Systems software [electronics]
Software (Kinds of software) **So:** 572
Systole [physiology]
Heart (Regulating the heart rate) **H:** 135 *with diagram*
Systolic pressure
Blood pressure **B:** 416
Heart (Regulating blood pressure) **H:** 136-137
Szczecin [Poland] **So:** 1077
Széchenyi, Stephen [Hungarian political leader]
Hungary (Habsburg rule) **H:** 445
Széchenyi Baths [Budapest]
Hungary *picture on* **H:** 442
Szechwan Basin [region, China] *See* Sichuan Basin *in this index*
Szell, George [Hungarian-American conductor] **So:** 1077
Szent-Györgyi, Albert [American biochemist] **So:** 1077
Nobel Prizes (Physiology or medicine: 1937) **N:** 445
Szentendre [Hungary]
Hungary *picture on* **H:** 441
Szilard, Leo [American physicist] **So:** 1077 *with picture*
Szoka, Edmund Casimir [American religious leader] **So:** 1078
Szold, Henrietta [American social worker] **So:** 1078 *with picture*
Szostak, Jack W. [American biologist]
Nobel Prizes (Physiology or medicine: 2009) **N:** 447
Szymborska, Wisława [Polish poet] **So:** 1078

T

T [letter] **T:** 1 *with pictures*
T-bill *See* Treasury bill *in this index*
T cell [physiology]
Blood (Protecting against disease) **B:** 410; (Formation of new blood components) **B:** 411
Disease (Immune responses) **D:** 231-232
Doherty, Peter Charles **D:** 284
Immune system *diagram on* **I:** 88b; (Parts of the immune system) **I:** 87; (The cell-mediated immune response) **I:** 88
Interleukin **I:** 335
Thymus **T:** 274
Tuberculosis (Primary infection) **T:** 477-478
Virus (Immune response) **V:** 428a
T cell receptor protein [physiology]
Immune system (The cell-mediated immune response) **I:** 88; (Recent advances) **I:** 88d
T. Eaton & Company
Eaton, Timothy **E:** 48
T-formation
Football (The offensive team) **F:** 356 *with diagram*
T-helper cell [physiology]
AIDS (How HIV affects the body) **A:** 164
Cyclosporine **I:** 1204
Disease (Immune responses) **D:** 231-232
Immune system (The cell-mediated immune response) **I:** 88-88a
`T Hooft, Gerardus [Dutch physicist]
Nobel Prizes (Physics: 1999) **N:** 442
T lymphocyte [physiology] *See* T cell *in this index*
T maze

Mouse *picture on* **M:** 902
T quark [physics] *See* Top quark *in this index*
T-Tauri star
Star (Intermediate-mass stars) **So:** 848
Ta [symbol]
Tantalum **T:** 29
Ta Nea [newspaper, Greece]
Greece (Communication) **G:** 361
Tab [aviation]
Airplane (The wing) **A:** 213-214 *with picture*
Taback, Simms [American artist]
Caldecott Medal (table: 2000) **C:** 26
Tabacón Hot Springs [Costa Rica]
Costa Rica *picture on* **Ci:** 1080
Tabard Inn
Canterbury Tales **C:** 184 *with picture*
Tabaré [poem by Zorrilla de San Martín]
Latin American literature (Romanticism) **L:** 112-113
Tabasco [state, Mexico] **T:** 2
Tabassah Mountains
Tunisia (Land) **T:** 488 *with map*
Tabby [cat]
Cat *picture on* **C:** 284; (Coat) **C:** 287 *with picture*
Tabby weave *See* Plain weave *in this index*
Tabei, Junko [Japanese mountain climber]
Mount Everest **M:** 884
Tabernacle [Bible] **T:** 2 *with picture*
Ark of the Covenant **A:** 693
Exodus **E:** 438
Moses (The covenant with God) **M:** 829
Tabernacle, Mormon [Salt Lake City]
Mormons *picture on* **M:** 808
Tabernacles, Feast of [custom]
Sukkot **So:** 965
Tabes [disorder] **T:** 2
Tabes dorsalis [disease]
Tabes **T:** 2
Table [furniture]
Colonial life in America *picture on* **Ci:** 808; (Furnishings) **Ci:** 797
Furniture **F:** 568 *with pictures*
Table, The [painting by Bonnard]
France *picture on* **F:** 463
Table Alphabeticall of Hard Wordes, A [book by Cawdrey]
Dictionary (Early English dictionaries) **D:** 194
Table beet [plant]
Beet **B:** 212 *with picture*
Table game
Game (Table games) **G:** 22
Table loom
Weaving (Kinds of looms) **W:** 174 *with picture*
Table Mountain [South Africa]
Cape Town **C:** 189 *with picture*
Table mushroom
Mushroom (Nonpoisonous mushrooms) **M:** 943 *with picture*
Table of contents [reference]
Book (Inside a book) **B:** 464-465
Table Talk [essays by Hazlitt]
Hazlitt, William **H:** 123
Table tennis [game] **T:** 3 *with pictures*
Olympic Games (Summer Olympic Games) **O:** 746e-748
Table wine
Grape (European grapes) **G:** 318
Wine (Types of wine) **W:** 336
Tableau Économique [economics]
Quesnay, François **Q:** 40
Tableau of French Poetry [book by Sainte-Beuve]
Sainte-Beuve, Charles Augustin **S:** 58
Tablet [medication]
Drug *pictures on* **D:** 353, **D:** 360
Tablet [writing]
Book (Early books) **B:** 465
Communication *picture on* **Ci:** 880
Tablet computer
Bible *picture on* **B:** 286
Computer (Personal computers) **Ci:** 909-910
Handheld computer **H:** 45
Tableware [utensils]
Silver *pictures on* **S:** 464
Tablion [ornament]
Clothing (The Middle Ages) **Ci:** 700
Tabloid [newspaper]
Newspaper (Kinds of newspapers) **N:** 380
Taboo [custom] **T:** 4
Magic (Homeopathic magic) **M:** 49-50
Mythology (Mana and taboo) **M:** 984
Tabor, Horace A. W. [American political leader]
Colorado (Statehood) **Ci:** 845-847
Tabor, Mount [Israel]
Deborah **D:** 65
Taborites [religious group]
Hussites **H:** 458
Tabriz [Iran] **T:** 4

Tabu *See* Taboo *in this index*
Tabular iceberg
Antarctica (Ocean) **A:** 532-534
Iceberg (Antarctic icebergs) **I:** 17
Tabularium [ruins, Rome]
Forum, Roman **F:** 421 *with picture*
Tabulating machine
Computer *picture on* **Ci:** 924a; (Foundations of data processing) **Ci:** 924b
TAC [architecture]
Gropius, Walter **G:** 397
Tacamahac [tree]
Poplar **P:** 668
TACAN [radio]
Airplane (Electronic navigation) **A:** 227
Navigation (Omnirange) **N:** 73
Taché, Sir Étienne-Paschal [Canadian political leader] **T:** 4
Confederation of Canada (Fathers of Confederation) **Ci:** 935
Macdonald, Sir John Alexander (Associate provincial prime minister) **M:** 7
Tachometer [instrument] **T:** 4
Log (A tachometer) **L:** 421
Tachycardia [disorder] **T:** 4
Defibrillator **D:** 88
Drug (Antiarrhythmics) **D:** 351
Heart (Abnormal heart rhythms) **H:** 142
Tachyon [atomic particle] **T:** 4
Tacitus [Roman emperor]
Rome, Ancient (table) **R:** 447
Tacitus, Cornelius [Roman historian] **T:** 4
Agricola, Gnaeus Julius **A:** 144
Biography (Early biographies) **B:** 312-313
History (The ancient Greeks and Romans) **H:** 261-262
Latin literature (The Imperial Period) **L:** 116-117
Lithuania (History) **L:** 389
Sweden (Early times) **So:** 1032
Tack [riding equipment]
Horse (table: Riding equipment) **H:** 351 *with pictures*
Tack hammer
Hammer **H:** 34 *with picture*
Tacke, Ida [German chemist]
Rhenium **R:** 290
Tacking [sailing]
Sailing (Basic sailing maneuvers) **S:** 26; (Trimming and tacking) **S:** 26 *with pictures*
Tackle [hardware]
Block and tackle **B:** 404 *with diagrams*
Tackle [sports]
Football *picture on* **F:** 360; (The offensive team) **F:** 356 *with diagrams*; (The defensive team) **F:** 357 *with diagrams*
Soccer (table) **So:** 546 *with picture*; (Tackling) **So:** 548
Tackle, Fishing
Fishing (Fishing equipment) **F:** 175 *with pictures*
Tackling dummy
Connecticut (Interesting facts) **Ci:** 953
Taco [food]
Hispanic Americans (Food) **H:** 248
Mexico (Food and drink) **M:** 456
Tacoma [Washington] **T:** 5 *with picture*
Tacoma Narrows Bridge [Washington]
Tacoma **T:** 5
Taconic Mountains [Massachusetts-Vermont]
Massachusetts (Land regions) **M:** 282
New York (Mountains) **N:** 306
Vermont (Land regions) **V:** 328 *with map*
Taconite [rock] **T:** 5 *with picture*
Iron and steel (Kinds of iron ore) **I:** 438; (Processing) **I:** 439 *with picture*
Minnesota (The mid-1900's) **M:** 606
Tactical air attack [warfare]
Air Force, United States (Offense) **A:** 190
Tactical Air Command [U.S.]
Air Force, United States (Combat commands) **A:** 193
Langley Air Force Base **L:** 61
Tactical missile
Guided missile (The warhead) **G:** 423-424
Tactical mission
Air force (Combat missions) **A:** 182
Tactical nuclear weapon
Army (Prevention of war) **A:** 725
Nuclear weapon (Tactical nuclear weapons) **N:** 598
Tactical Tomahawk [missile]
Guided missile (Preset guidance) **G:** 426
Tactile corpuscle
Touch **T:** 348
Tactile hair
Cat (Senses) **C:** 287-290
Hair **H:** 9

Mammal (Skin and hair) M: 118
Tactile sense *See* Touch *in this index*
Tactual map
Map (Production and reproduction) M: 1181
TACV
Air cushion vehicle (History) A: 181
Tadić, Boris [Serbian political leader]
Serbia (Recent developments) S: 316a
Tadpole [zoology] T: 6 *with pictures*
Bullfrog B: 697
Frog (Mating) F: 538 *with picture*; (Eggs) F: 538-539 *with pictures*; (Tadpoles) F: 539 *with pictures*
Larva L: 79 *with picture*
Metamorphosis (Other examples) M: 428 *with picture*
Toad (The life of a toad) T: 304
Tadzhikistan *See* Tajikistan *in this index*
Tadzhiks [people] *See* Tajiks *in this index*
Tae kwon do [martial art] T: 6
Asian Americans (Asian influences on American culture) A: 812c
Karate K: 245
Martial arts (Korean martial arts) M: 234a
Olympic Games O: 746e-748
Taegu [Korea] T: 7
Taehan-min'guk [South Korea]
Korea, History of (The Choson dynasty) K: 366-367
Tafari, Ras *See* Haile Selassie I *in this index*
Taffrail log [measuring device]
Log (Logs used in the past) L: 421
Taft, Alphonso [American government official]
Grant, Ulysses S. (table) G: 316
Justice, Department of (table) J: 203
Taft, William Howard (Early life) T: 8
Taft, Bob [American political leader]
Ohio (table) O: 699
Taft, Charles Phelps, II [son of]
Taft, William Howard (Taft's family) T: 9
Taft, Helen Herron [wife of William Howard Taft]
First ladies of the United States (table) F: 142
Taft, William Howard (Taft's family) T: 9; (Life in the White House) T: 11 *with picture*
Taft, Lorado [American sculptor] T: 7 *with picture*
Black Hawk B: 387 *with picture*
Illinois (Places to visit) I: 62
Taft, Louise Maria Torrey [mother of]
Taft, William Howard (Early life) T: 8
Taft, Robert Alphonso [American political leader] T: 7
Eisenhower, Dwight David (Presidential candidate) E: 151
Taft, William Howard (Taft's family) T: 9
Taft, Royal C. [American political leader]
Rhode Island (table) R: 311
Taft, William Howard [U.S. president] T: 8 *with pictures*
Baguio City B: 27
Dollar diplomacy D: 295
Harding, Warren Gamaliel (Entry into politics) H: 57
Republican Party *picture on* R: 256; (The party splits) R: 255
Roosevelt, Theodore (A party split) R: 467
United States, History of the (The Taft and Wilson) U: 187
Taft-Hartley Act [1947] T: 12
Boycott B: 539
Labor movement (The Taft-Hartley Act) L: 13
National Labor Relations Act N: 39
President of the United States (Chief executive) P: 764
Taft Museum [Cincinnati]
Ohio (Museums) O: 685
Tag [baseball]
Baseball (Base runners—advancing and outs) B: 129 *with picture*
Tag [computing]
Computer (The World Wide Web) Ci: 921
HyperText Markup Language H: 477
Tag [symbol]
Graffiti G: 298
Hip-hop H: 238
Tag lock
Wool (Types of wool) W: 399
Tag up [baseball]
Baseball (Base runners—advancing and outs) B: 129
Tagalog [language]
Philippines (Languages) P: 374
Taganrog, Gulf of
Azov, Sea of A: 998
Tagging, Electronic [law enforcement] *See* Electronic tagging *in this index*
Taglioni, Filippo [Italian choreographer]
Ballet (Romantic ballet) B: 51

Taglioni, Marie [Swedish-born dancer]
Ballet (Romantic ballet) B: 51 *with picture*
Tagore, Rabindranath [Indian author] T: 13
Bangladesh (The arts) B: 82
India (Literature: 1913) I: 120
Tagsatzung [government]
Switzerland (Independence and expansion) So: 1059-1060
Tagua [animal]
Peccary P: 226 *with picture*
Tagus River [Portugal-Spain] T: 13
Lisbon L: 348
Portugal (Rivers) P: 690
Spain (The Meseta) So: 739-740 *with map*
Tahat, Mount [mountain, Algeria]
Algeria (The Sahara) A: 363
Tahgahjute [American Indian chief]
Logan L: 423
Tahiti [island, Pacific] T: 13 *with picture*
Clothing *picture on* Ci: 693
Exploration (Exploring the Pacific) E: 447-448
Gauguin, Paul (Gauguin in Tahiti) G: 69
Mythology (Pacific Islands divinities) M: 984
Tahkemoni [book by Alharizi]
Hebrew literature (Medieval works) H: 162
Tahmasb [king of Persia]
Safavid dynasty S: 8
Tahoe, Lake [California-Nevada] *See* Lake Tahoe *in this index*
Tahoe Regional Planning Compact
Nevada (The late 1990's) N: 176-177
Tahquamenon Falls
Michigan *picture on* M: 502; (Places to visit) M: 498
Tahrir Square
Cairo C: 18
Tai [language]
Laos (People) L: 70
Tai [people]
Indochina (The Viets) I: 224-225
Vietnam (People) V: 365
T'ai chi ch'uan [martial art] T: 14
Asian Americans (Asian influences on American culture) A: 812c *with picture*
China *picture on* C: 485
Martial arts (Chinese martial arts) M: 234
Tai Ping Shan [mountain, Hong Kong]
Hong Kong (The metropolis) H: 316-317; (The land) H: 318 *with map*
Taiga [region] T: 14
Arctic A: 635
Biome B: 322; (table) B: 323 *with map*
Forest *picture on* F: 391; (Kinds of forests) F: 392 *with map*; (Boreal forests) F: 396 *with map*
Plant (The taiga) P: 523 *with map*
Russia (Land regions) R: 539
Taijiquan [martial art] *See* T'ai chi ch'uan *in this index*
Taika Reform [Japanese history]
Japan (Chinese influence) J: 53
Taikonaut [astronaut]
Astronaut A: 828
Tail [aviation]
Airplane *picture on* A: 218; (The tail) A: 214 *with pictures*
Glider (The tail) G: 229
Tail [zoology] T: 14
Animal (Fins, tails, and flippers) A: 490 *with picture*
Cat (Body size and structure) C: 286
Dog (Body structure) D: 263; (Why dogs do the things they do) D: 263 *with picture*
Lizard (Defenses) L: 400
Tail coat
Clothing *picture on* Ci: 705
Tail fin [airplane]
Airplane (The tail) A: 214 *with pictures*, A: 214 *with diagrams*
Tail hook [device]
Navy (Aircraft carriers) N: 78
Tail wind [weather]
Wind shear W: 332
Tailed frog
Frog (Other frogs) F: 540
Tailings [by-product]
Copper (Milling) Ci: 1042-1043
Iron and steel (Processing) I: 439
Lead (Production) L: 149
Taillon, L.-Olivier [Canadian political leader]
Quebec (table) Q: 29
Tailorbird [bird] T: 14 *with picture*
Bird *picture on* B: 357
Táin Bó Cuailnge [poem] *See* Cattle Raid of Cooley, The *in this index*
Taíno Indians
Arawak Indians A: 592
Columbus, Christopher (The first landing) Ci: 860;

(Trouble, settlement, and exploration) Ci: 862
Cuba (Early years) Ci: 1175
Puerto Rico (People) P: 874-875
United States, History of the (European discoveries) U: 150
Tainting [English law]
Attainder A: 878
Tainui [people]
New Zealand (Maori-Pakeha relations) N: 356
Taiohae [Marquesas Islands]
Marquesas Islands M: 217
Taipa [island, Pacific Ocean]
Macau M: 4
Taipan [snake]
Snake *picture on* S: 534
Taipei [Taiwan] T: 15 *with picture*
Taipei 101 [skyscraper]
Skyscraper (table) S: 498 *with picture*
Taipei T: 15 *with picture*
Taiping Rebellion [1850-1864]
China (The Taiping Rebellion) C: 502
Nanjing (History) N: 10
Taira [Japanese clan]
Japan (Rise of the shogun) J: 54 *with picture*
Japanese literature (The medieval period) J: 62
World, History of the *picture on* W: 436
Taiwan [island] T: 15 *with pictures and map*
Asia (Way of life in East Asia) A: 785; (Korea and Taiwan) A: 789
Chiang Kai-shek (Communist triumph) C: 419
China C: 475
Eisenhower, Dwight David (Crises in the Middle East and Asia) E: 154
Flag *picture on* F: 204
Mao Zedong (His life) M: 174-175
Taiwan (History)
Taiwan (History) T: 17-18
Taiwan Relations Act [1979]
Taiwan (History) T: 17-18
Taj Mahal [Agra, India] T: 18
Agra A: 143
Architecture (Indian architecture) A: 613
Asia *picture on* A: 772
Building construction B: 681
India *picture on* I: 109; (Architecture and sculpture) I: 119
Ramadan *picture on* R: 132
Tomb T: 326
Tajikistan T: 18 *with picture and map*
Flag *picture on* F: 205
Ruble R: 508
Tajiks [people]
Afghanistan (Ethnic groups and languages) A: 92a
Tajikistan (People) T: 18a
Union of Soviet Socialist Republics (People) U: 31
Tajo River *See* Tagus River *in this index*
Tajumulco [mountain, Guatemala]
Guatemala (The Highlands) G: 414 *with map*
Takaki, Kanehiro [Japanese doctor]
Vitamin (History) V: 432
Takakkaw Falls [British Columbia] T: 18b
British Columbia (Rivers, waterfalls, and lakes) B: 624
Waterfall (table: Famous waterfalls of North America) W: 142
Take [cinematography]
Motion picture (Preparing to shoot) M: 852
Television (Editing) T: 111
Take down [wrestling]
Wrestling *picture on* W: 506
Take-home pay
Income (Gross and net income) I: 100
Wages and hours (Wages) W: 2-3
"Take My Hand, Precious Lord" [song]
Gospel music G: 277
Take-off [aviation]
Aircraft carrier (Flight operations) A: 206
Airplane *diagram on* A: 224; (Gravity and lift) A: 220 *with diagram*
Take-up reel
Tape recorder (How tape recorders work) T: 37 *with picture*
Takekurabe [book by Higuchi Ichiyo]
Higuchi Ichiyo H: 229
Takin [mammal] T: 18b *with picture*
Takin' Off [recording]
Hancock, Herbie H: 38
Taking Steps [play by Ayckbourn]
Ayckbourn, Alan A: 995
Taklimakan Desert [China]
China (The Xinjiang-Mongolian Uplands) C: 491; (Climate) C: 494
Taksin [Thai military leader]
Thailand (The Bangkok era) T: 227
Tal, Mikhail [Russian chess player]
Chess (World chess champions) C: 414
Talabani, Jalal [Iraqi political leader]
Iraq (A new government) I: 414a

Kurds K: 393
Talal I [king of Jordan]
Jordan (The Palestinian conflict) J: 164-165
Talbot, Matthew [American political leader]
Georgia (table) G: 130
Talbot, Ray H. [American political leader]
Colorado (table) Ci: 844
Talbot, Thomas [American political leader]
Massachusetts (table) M: 288
Talbot, William Henry Fox [British scientist] *See*
Fox Talbot, William Henry *in this index*
Talbotype [photography] T: 19
Communication (The 1800's) Ci: 881-882
Photography (The invention of photography)
P: 422-423
Talc [mineral] T: 19
Mineral *picture on* M: 569
Soapstone So: 543
Talcott Family, The [painting by Goldsmith]
Folk art *picture on* F: 317
Talcum powder
Talc T: 19
Tale of a Tub, A [book by Swift]
Swift, Jonathan (Swift's other works) So: 1040-
1041
Tale of Despereaux, The [book by DiCamillo]
DiCamillo, Kate D: 186
Tale of Genji, The [book by Murasaki]
Japan (Literature) J: 43
Japanese literature (The Heian period) J: 61-62
Murasaki Shikibu M: 929
Painting (Japanese painting) P: 47 *with picture*
Tale of Peter Rabbit, The [book by Potter]
Literature for children *picture on* L: 362; (Picture
books) L: 365
Tale of the Bamboo Cutter, The [book]
Japanese literature (The Heian period) J: 61
Tale of the Heiji War Scroll [painting]
World, History of the *picture on* W: 436
Tale of the Heike, The [book]
Japanese literature (The medieval period) J: 62
Tale of Tsar Sultan, The [opera by Rimsky-
Korsakov]
Rimsky-Korsakov, Nikolai R: 341
Tale of Two Cities, A [book by Dickens]
Dickens, Charles (The second phase) D: 188-189
Talent [ability]
Talent T: 19
Talent [entertainment]
Television (Planning and preparation)
T: 110c-110d
Talent [money] T: 19
Talent Education
Suzuki method So: 1014
Talented Mr. Ripley, The [book by Highsmith]
Highsmith, Patricia H: 229
Tales from Shakespeare [book by Lamb]
Lamb, Mary Ann L: 51
Tales from Silver Lands [book by Finger]
Finger, Charles Joseph F: 104
Tales of a Fourth Grade Nothing [book by Blume]
Blume, Judy B: 425
Tales of a Traveller [book by Irving]
Irving, Washington (Years in Europe) I: 460
Tales of a Wayside Inn [poems by Longfellow]
Longfellow, Henry Wadsworth (Narrative poems)
L: 450-451
Tales of an Empty Cabin [book by Grey Owl]
Grey Owl G: 392
Tales of Belkin [stories by Pushkin]
Pushkin, Alexander (His works) P: 911-912
Tales of Hoffmann [opera by Offenbach]
Hoffmann, Ernst Theodor Amadeus H: 284
Offenbach, Jacques O: 676
Tales of Mother Goose [book by Perrault]
Fairy (Fairy tales) F: 11
Perrault, Charles P: 293
Tales of Soldiers and Civilians [book by Bierce]
Bierce, Ambrose B: 295
Tales of the Countryside [music by Cowell]
Cowell, Henry Ci: 1112
Tales of the Folio Club [book by Poe]
Poe, Edgar Allan (Fiction and theory of fiction)
P: 590
Tales of the Grotesque and Arabesque [book by
Poe]
Poe, Edgar Allan (Poe's life) P: 589
Tales of the South Pacific [book by Michener]
Michener, James A. M: 487
Talfourd, Field [British painter]
Browning, Elizabeth Barrett *picture on* B: 646
Taliban [political group] T: 19
Afghanistan A: 92; (Government) A: 92; (Women)
A: 93; (Agriculture) A: 94; (Afghanistan under
the Taliban) A: 96
Afghanistan War A: 97
Air Force, United States (The war in Afghanistan)

A: 196
Bin Laden, Osama B: 307
Guerrilla warfare (History) G: 420-421
Karzai, Hamid K: 247
Pakistan (Struggle for democracy) P: 100;
(Musharraf) P: 100; (Recent developments)
P: 100
Pashtuns P: 190
Qa`ida, Al- Q: 2
September 11 terrorist attacks S: 310
Terrorism (The September 11 terrorist attacks)
T: 179
Taliesin [Welsh poet]
Wales (The arts) W: 9
Taliesin [Wisconsin]
Wisconsin (Places to visit) W: 356
Wright, Frank Lloyd (Later career) W: 508
Taliesin West [Arizona]
Wright, Frank Lloyd (Later career) W: 508
Talipes [birth defect]
Clubfoot Ci: 715
Talipot palm [tree]
Palm (The leaves) P: 109
Talisman [magic]
Magic (Magical objects) M: 49
Talisman, The [book by Scott]
Scott, Sir Walter (The Waverley novels) S: 222
Talk show
Radio (Information) R: 86; (Radio since the 1950's)
R: 94
Television (Commercial television) T: 110a-110b
Talk to Her [film]
Almodóvar, Pedro A: 380
Talkeetna Mountains [Alaska]
Alaska (Land regions) A: 292
Talking Book
Audiobook A: 882
Blindness (Aids for blind people) B: 402
Publishing (Books) B: 468
Talking Heads [musical group]
Rock music (New wave and mainstream rock)
R: 380c
Talking myna [bird]
Myna M: 971 *with picture*
Tall bearded iris [plant]
Flower *picture on* F: 278
Tall oil [by-product]
Rosin R: 480
Tall sunflower [plant]
Flower *picture on* F: 286
Tallahassee [Florida] T: 20
Florida (table: Average monthly weather) F: 256
Tallchief, Maria [American dancer] T: 20 *with
picture*
Talleyrand [French statesman] T: 20
Adams, John (Difficulties with France) A: 38;
(Adams and peace) A: 39
Jefferson, Thomas (The Louisiana Purchase) J: 85
Pinckney, Charles Cotesworth P: 467
XYZ Affair X: 546
Talley's Folly [play by Wilson]
Wilson, Lanford W: 317
Tallgrass Prairie National Preserve
Kansas (Places to visit) K: 226
National Park System (table: National preserves)
N: 58
Tallinn [Estonia] T: 21
Estonia E: 361 *with picture*
Tallis, Thomas [English composer] T: 21
Byrd, William B: 747
Tallmadge, James [American political leader]
Missouri Compromise M: 674
Tallmadge Amendment [U.S. history]
Missouri Compromise M: 674
Tallow [animal product] T: 21
Candle C: 175
Detergent and soap (How detergents are made)
D: 165
Fat F: 52
Talmadge, Eugene [American political leader]
Georgia (table) G: 130
Talmadge, Herman Eugene [American political
leader]
Georgia (table) G: 130
Talmud [religious book] T: 21
Hebrew literature (Early works) H: 162
Jews (The Talmudic period) J: 122
Judaism (The Talmud) J: 180
Rashi R: 144
Talon [zoology]
Animal *picture on* A: 494
Bird of prey (Physical appearance) B: 374a *with
picture*
Eagle E: 3 *with picture*; (Feet and legs) E: 4
Hawk H: 111
Talon, Jean Baptiste [French colonial official] T: 21
Census (Early censuses) C: 349

Talos [Greek mythology]
Daedalus D: 3
Talus bone [anatomy]
Ankle A: 515 *with diagram*
Tama New Town [housing project]
Tokyo (Housing) T: 314
Tamales [food]
Mexico (Food and drink) M: 456
Taman Negara National Park [Malaysia]
National park (table) N: 42f
Tamandua [animal]
Anteater A: 541
Tamar [Georgian queen]
Georgia (History) G: 111
Tamarack [tree]
Larch L: 75
Tree *pictures on* T: 425
Tamarau [animal]
Buffalo B: 674
Tamarin [animal] T: 21 *with picture*
Mammal *picture on* M: 117
Primate (New World monkeys) P: 778-778a
Tamarind [tree] T: 22 *with picture*
Tamaulipas [state, Mexico] T: 22
Tamayo, Rufino [Mexican painter] T: 22
**Tamayo Museum of Contemporary International
Art**
Mexico City (Cultural life and recreation)
M: 476b-477
Tamayo y Baus, Manuel [Spanish author]
Spanish literature (The 1800's) So: 761
Tamazight language
Berbers B: 256
Tambaqui [fish]
Pacu P: 19 *with picture*
Tambon [unit of government]
Thailand (Local government) T: 221
Tambora, Mount [Indonesia]
Volcano (table) V: 442b
Tambour lace
Lace L: 20
Tambourine [musical instrument] T: 22 *with picture*
Tambura [musical instrument]
India (Music and dance) I: 120
Tamburlaine [Mongol conqueror] *See* Timur *in
this index*
Tamburlaine [plays by Marlowe]
Marlowe, Christopher M: 216
Tamenend [American Indian chief]
Pennsylvania (Colonial days) P: 264
Tamerlane [Mongol conqueror] *See* Timur *in this
index*
Tamerlane and Other Poems [book by Poe]
Poe, Edgar Allan (Poe's life) P: 589
Tamiflu [drug]
Virus (Antiviral drugs) V: 428a
Tamil [language]
Dravidians D: 342
India (Languages) I: 114
Malaysia (People) M: 98b-98c
Sri Lanka (People) So: 817; (History) So: 819
Tamil Nadu [state, India]
Chennai C: 408
India (Christianity) I: 117
Tamils [people]
Sri Lanka (People) So: 817; (History) So: 819
Taming of the Shrew, The [play by Shakespeare]
Fairbanks, Douglas, Sr. *picture on* F: 9
Gascoigne, George G: 60
Shakespeare, William *picture on* S: 344; (The
Taming of the Shrew) S: 356
Taming the Star Runner [book by Hinton]
Hinton, S. E. H: 238
Tamino [opera character]
Opera (Magic Flute, The) O: 805
Tamla Records
Gordy, Berry G: 273
Tamm, Igor Yevgenevich [Russian physicist]
Nobel Prizes (Physics: 1958) N: 441
Tammany, Mount [New Jersey]
Delaware Water Gap D: 114
Tammany, Society of [U.S. history] T: 22
Bucktails B: 664
Cleveland, Grover (Governor of New York) Ci: 670
Nast, Thomas N: 24 *with picture*
New York City (The growing city) N: 341-342 *with
picture*; (Formation of Greater New York) N: 342
Roosevelt, Franklin Delano (Entry into politics)
R: 450f
Tweed, William Marcy T: 531
Tammany Hall *See* Tammany, Society of *in this
index*
Tammany Tiger [cartoon]
Nast, Thomas N: 24 *with picture*
Tammen, Harry H. [American editor]
Bonfils, Frederick Gilmer B: 458
Tammuz [month]

Calendar (The Hebrew calendar) **C:** 29
Tamora [literary figure]
  Shakespeare, William: (*Titus Andronicus*) **S:** 356
Tamoxifen [drug] **T:** 23
  Breast cancer **B:** 591
Tampa [Florida] **T:** 23
Tampa [ship]
  Coast Guard, United States (World War I) **Ci:** 737
Tampa Bay [Florida]
  Saint Petersburg [Florida] **S:** 55
Tampa Bay Buccaneers [team]
  Football (National Football League) **F:** 364
Tampa Bay Lightning [team]
  Hockey (table: National Hockey League) **H:** 281
Tampa Bay Rays [team]
  Baseball (table) **B:** 130
Tamper-resistant packaging
  Packaging (Packaging regulations) **P:** 18
Tampere [Finland] **T:** 24
Tampico [Mexico] **T:** 24
  Mexico (The Gulf Coastal Plain) **M:** 462
Tampomas II [ship]
  Shipwreck (table: Major shipwrecks) **S:** 428
Tampon
  Menstruation (Effects of menstruation) **M:** 404
  Toxic shock syndrome **T:** 353
Tan, Amy [American author]
  Novel (The novel today) **N:** 575
Tana, Lake [Ethiopia]
  Lake Tana **L:** 46
Tana River [Africa]
  Kenya (Rivers and lakes) **K:** 301 *with map*
Tanager [bird] **T:** 24 *with picture*
  Bird *pictures on* **B:** 344b, **B:** 358; (Birds of forests and woodlands) **B:** 334 *with picture*; (Birds of Central and South America) **B:** 344a
Tanak [book]
  Bible (The Hebrew Bible) **B:** 279
  Old Testament **O:** 740
Tanaka, Koichi [Japanese engineer]
  Nobel Prizes (Chemistry: 2002) **N:** 442-444
Tanana River [Alaska]
  Yukon River (Upper Yukon) **Y:** 582 *with map*
Tananarive [Madagascar] *See* Antananarivo *in this index*
Tancred of Hauteville [Norman conqueror]
  Normans **N:** 456
Tandem axles [mechanism]
  Truck (Common features of trucks) **T:** 458
Tandem bicycle
  Bicycle (Specialty bicycles) **B:** 290 *with picture*
Tandem-rotor helicopter
  Helicopter (Types of helicopters) **H:** 170-171 *with diagram*
Tandem Van de Graaff generator [machine]
  Particle accelerator (How accelerators work) **P:** 184
Tandja, Mamadou [Nigerien political leader]
  Niger (History) **N:** 409
Tandy, Jessica [American actress]
  Motion picture (Best performance by an actress: 1989) **M:** 862a
Taney, Roger Brooke [American jurist] **T:** 24
  Dred Scott Decision (The Supreme Court ruling) **D:** 345
  Jackson, Andrew (Jackson's second Administration) **J:** 12
  Lincoln, Abraham (Fort Sumter and war) **L:** 321
Taneycomo, Lake [Missouri] *See* Lake Taneycomo *in this index*
TANF [U. S. program] *See* Temporary Assistance to Needy Families *in this index*
Tang dynasty [Chinese history] **T:** 25 *with picture and map*
  Asia (Nomadic invasions) **A:** 805
  China *picture on* **C:** 489; (The Tang dynasty) **C:** 501
  Chinese literature (Poetry) **C:** 511
  Li Yuan **L:** 225
  Painting (Chinese painting) **P:** 44-45
  Sculpture (China) **S:** 238
  World, History of the (China) **W:** 435 *with picture*
Tang Gaozong [emperor of China]
  Tang dynasty (The rise of the dynasty) **T:** 25
Tang Taizong [emperor of China]
  Tang dynasty (The rise of the dynasty) **T:** 25
Tang Wu [empress of China]
  Tang dynasty (The rise of the dynasty) **T:** 25
Tang Xianzu [Chinese dramatist]
  Chinese literature (Drama and fiction) **C:** 511
Tanganyika [region, Africa]
  Tanzania **T:** 30
Tanganyika, Lake *See* Lake Tanganyika *in this index*
Tanganyika African National Union [political party]
  Tanzania (Independence) **T:** 35
Tangaroa [Polynesian god]

Mythology (Pacific Islands divinities) **M:** 984
Tange, Kenzo [Japanese architect]
  Architecture *picture on* **A:** 606; (Architecture today) **A:** 632-633
  Japan *picture on* **J:** 44
  Tokyo (Government buildings) **T:** 316
Tangelo [fruit] **T:** 26
  Mandarin **M:** 136
Tangent [mathematics]
  Circle (Parts of a circle) **Ci:** 558
  Trigonometry (Right triangles) **T:** 443
Tanger [Morocco] *See* Tangier *in this index*
Tangerine [fruit] **T:** 26 *with picture*
  Mandarin **M:** 136
  Orange (Mandarins) **O:** 815
  Tangelo **T:** 26
  Tangor **T:** 27
Tangier [city, Morocco] **T:** 27
Tangier [region, Morocco]
  Tangier **T:** 27
Tangled-web weaver [spider]
  Spider (Web-building spiders) **So:** 789
Tanglewood Music Festival
  Massachusetts (Visitor's guide) **M:** 280 *with picture*
Tanglewood Tales [book by Hawthorne]
  Hawthorne, Nathaniel (His stories and sketches) **H:** 115
Tango [dance] **T:** 27
  Argentina (The arts) **A:** 651 *with picture*
  Ballroom dancing **B:** 63
  Latin America (Dance) **L:** 101
Tango nuevo [dance]
  Argentina (The arts) **A:** 651
Tango Player, The [book by Hein]
  German literature (Recent German literature) **G:** 142
Tangor [fruit] **T:** 27
  Mandarin **M:** 136
Tanguy, Yves [French-born artist]
  Painting (Europeans in America) **P:** 84
Tanimbar Islands
  Indonesia (The Molucca Islands) **I:** 234
Tanis, James [Papuan political leader]
  Papua New Guinea (History) **P:** 141
Tanjung Priok [harbor, Indonesia]
  Jakarta (Economy) **J:** 22
Tank [military vehicle] **T:** 27 *with diagram*
  Ammunition (Armored-vehicle ammunition) **A:** 436
  Army (Armies in the two world wars) **A:** 728
  Army, United States (Armor) **A:** 734
  Automobile (An automobile) **A:** 968
  Michigan (The mid-1900's) **M:** 511 *with picture*
  Periscope **P:** 288
  World War I *picture on* **W:** 457
  World War II *picture on* **W:** 485
Tank, Toilet
  Plumbing (How toilets work) **P:** 579 *with diagrams*
Tank car [railroad]
  Railroad *picture on* **R:** 108
Tank division
  Infantry (Divisions) **I:** 264-265
Tank truck [vehicle]
  Truck *picture on* **T:** 459; (On-highway trucks) **T:** 457
Tanka [poetry]
  Japanese literature (Beginnings) **J:** 61
Tankage [feed]
  Hog (Feeding) **H:** 287
Tankard [cup]
  Antique (Metalwork) **A:** 558
  Colonial life in America *picture on* **Ci:** 808
Tanker [aircraft]
  Air force (Aircraft and missiles) **A:** 183
  Air Force, United States (Other aircraft) **A:** 191 *with picture*
  Aircraft, Military (Tankers) **A:** 203 *with picture*
Tanker [ship] **T:** 28 *with picture*
  Petroleum (Transporting petroleum) **P:** 342 *with diagram*
  Ship (Tankers) **S:** 408 *with picture*; (Pollution) **S:** 413-414
Tanna [island, Vanuatu]
  Vanuatu **V:** 284
Tannenberg, Battle of [1914]
  World War I (The Eastern Front) **W:** 456
Tanner, Beatrice Steller [birth name of]
  Campbell, Mrs. Patrick **C:** 91
Tanner, Henry Ossawa [American painter] **T:** 28 *with picture*
  Painting (Painting outside France) **P:** 72-73 *with picture*
Tanner, John R. [American political leader]
  Illinois (table) **I:** 71
Tannhäuser [German poet] **T:** 29

Tannhäuser [opera by Wagner]
  Liszt, Franz (His life) **L:** 349-350
  Tannhäuser **T:** 29
  Wagner, Richard (Later career) **W:** 4
Tannic acid [chemical] **T:** 29
  Invisible ink **I:** 369
Tannin *See* Tannic acid *in this index*
Tanning [industrial process]
  Lactic acid **L:** 25
  Leather (Tanning) **L:** 167-168 *with picture*
  Tannic acid **T:** 29
Tansy [plant] **T:** 29
Tantalum [element] **T:** 29
Tantalum oxide [mineral]
  Tantalum **T:** 29
Tantalus [Greek mythology] **T:** 29
  Niobe **N:** 424
Tantric Buddhism [religion]
  Buddhism (The Vajrayana) **B:** 669
Tantrism [religion]
  Lamaism **L:** 49
Tanunda [community]
  Australia *picture on* **A:** 902
Tanzania [country] **T:** 30 *with pictures and map*
  See also the list of Related articles in the Tanzania article
  Africa *picture on* **A:** 199
  Clinton, Bill (International affairs) **Ci:** 682f
  Flag *picture on* **F:** 200
  Olympic Games (Boycotts) **O:** 753
  Zanzibar **Z:** 586
Tanzanite [gem] **T:** 36
  Gem *picture on* **G:** 78
Tao [philosophy]
  Taoism **T:** 36
Tao Te Ching [book] *See* Classic of the Way and the Virtue, The *in this index*
Tao Yuanming [Chinese horticulturalist]
  Chrysanthemum **C:** 540
Taoiseach [title]
  Ireland (The prime minister and Cabinet) **I:** 417
Taoism [religion] **T:** 36 *with picture*
  China (Religion) **C:** 485
  Chinese literature (Beginnings) **C:** 511
  Confucianism (Later Confucianism) **Ci:** 937
  Laozi **L:** 72
  Religion **R:** 215, *picture on* **R:** 222; (Taoism) **R:** 221
  Zhuangzi **Z:** 591
Taormina [Sicily]
  Sicily *picture on* **S:** 446
Taos [New Mexico] **T:** 36
Taos Pueblo [New Mexico]
  New Mexico *picture on* **N:** 257
Tap [bowling]
  Bowling (table) **B:** 521
Tap [faucet]
  Plumbing (How faucets work) **P:** 579 *with diagram*
Tap dancing
  Dance (Other forms of theatrical dance) **D:** 32
Tapa cloth
  Pacific Islands (Clothing) **P:** 7
Tapajós River [Brazil]
  Amazon River (The course of the Amazon) **A:** 403
Tape [tool]
  Woodworking (Planning and design) **W:** 396 *with picture*
Tape, Magnetic *See* Magnetic tape *in this index*
Tape deck [electronics] *See* Cassette tape recorder; Tape recorder *in this index*
Tape drive [electronic device]
  Computer (Tape drives) **Ci:** 916
Tape grass [plant]
  Eelgrass **E:** 115
Tape recorder **T:** 36 *with pictures*
  Audio-visual materials (Audio materials) **A:** 883
  Communication *picture on* **Ci:** 886
  Electronic music **E:** 205
  Stereophonic sound system (History) **So:** 892
Taper [candle]
  Colonial life in America *picture on* **Ci:** 808
Taper Forum [theater] *See* Mark Taper forum *in this index*
Tapestry [art] **T:** 39 *with pictures*
  England *picture on* **E:** 305
  Indian, American *picture on* **I:** 175
  Needlepoint **N:** 118
  Unicorn *picture on* **U:** 26
Tapetum lucidum [zoology]
  Cat (Head) **C:** 286-287 *with picture*
  Dog (Senses) **D:** 265
  Eye (Eyes of animals) **E:** 469
  Mammal (Senses) **M:** 120-121
Tapeworm [animal] **T:** 40 *with picture*
  Cat (Veterinary care) **C:** 295
  Flatworm **F:** 229
  Parasite (An endoparasite) **P:** 154 *with picture*

Worm (Flatworms) W: 500 *with picture*
Tapioca [food] T: 41
    Cassava C: 276
Tapiola [Finland] T: 41
Tapir [animal] T: 41 *with picture*
    Animal *pictures on* A: 481
Tapotement [movement]
    Massage M: 295
Tappan, Arthur [American social reformer]
    Abolition movement A: 13
Tappan, Lewis [American social reformer]
    African Americans (The antislavery movement)
        A: 136h
Tapping [industrial process]
    Machine tool (Metal removal) M: 17-18
    Rubber (Tapping the tree) R: 502
Tapping Reeve Law School [Litchfield]
    Connecticut (Schools) Ci: 956
Taproot [botany]
    Plant (Roots) P: 528 *with picture*
    Root (Kinds of roots) R: 469-470 *with diagram*;
        (The importance of roots) R: 471
    Tree (Roots) T: 417
    Vegetable (Roots) V: 292 *with picture*
Tar [building material] T: 41
Tar [tobacco]
    Cigarette Ci: 553
    Smoking (Why smoking is dangerous) S: 520
Tar Baby [book by Morrison]
    American literature (Works by minority writers)
        A: 425
    Morrison, Toni M: 817
Tar Heel State [name for]
    North Carolina N: 473
Tar River
    North Carolina (Rivers, waterfalls, and lakes)
        N: 484 *with map*
Tar sands *See* Bituminous sands *in this index*
Tara [monument]
    Archaeology *picture on* A: 596
Tarabulus [Lebanon]
    Tripoli T: 447
Tarabulus [Libya]
    Tripoli T: 448
Tarai [region]
    Nepal (People) N: 125; (Land and climate) N: 126
Tarantella [dance] T: 41
    Folk dancing F: 320
    Tarantula T: 42
Tarantino, Quentin [American film director]
    Motion picture (A new generation of filmmakers)
        M: 871-872
Tarantism [disease]
    Tarantula T: 42
Tarantula [spider] T: 42 *with picture*
    Animal *picture on* A: 480
    Insect *pictures on* I: 298
    Spider *pictures on* So: 783, So: 788; (Chelicerae)
        So: 784-785 *with picture*; (Hunting spiders)
        So: 790
    Trap-door spider T: 402
Tarantula hawk [insect]
    Insect *pictures on* I: 298
Taras Bulba [book by Gogol]
    Russian literature (Late Romanticism) R: 561-562
Tarascan Indians T: 42
Tarawa [city, Kiribati] T: 42
Tarawa [island, Pacific]
    Kiribati K: 335
    World War II (Island hopping in the South Pacific)
        W: 489 *with picture*
Tarawa [ship]
    Amphibious ship *picture on* A: 442
Tarbela Dam [Indus River, Pakistan] T: 42
Tarbell, Ida Minerva [American author] T: 42 *with portrait*
    Muckrakers M: 908
Tarboosh [clothing]
    Fez F: 84
Target [electronics]
    Image orthicon I: 79
Target [sports]
    Archery (Target archery) A: 602
Target [warfare]
    Rangefinder R: 138
Target archery
    Archery *picture on* A: 604; (Target archery) A: 602
Target cell [anatomy]
    Insulin (How insulin acts in the body) I: 308
Target designator [guidance device]
    Laser (Guiding) L: 83
Target displacement
    Terrorism (Security measures) T: 177
Target game
    Game (Target games) G: 22
Target market
    Advertising (Creating advertisements) A: 76a

Target material
    Nuclear energy (Nuclear fission) N: 582
Target pistol
    Handgun (Single-shot pistols) H: 44
Targioni-Tozzetti, Giovanni [Italian librettist]
    Opera: (Cavalleria Rusticana) O: 803
Targum [translation]
    Bible (The first translations) B: 284
Tariff [tax] T: 43
    Agriculture (Economic controls) A: 152
    Calhoun, John Caldwell (Southern leader) C: 35
    Cleveland, Grover (The currency and the tariff)
        Ci: 671
    Economics (The world economy) E: 61
    Exports and imports (Import restrictions) E: 454
    Foreign trade zone F: 388a
    Free trade F: 499
    Gay Nineties (Industrial growth) G: 72
    General Agreement on Tariffs and Trade G: 83
    Great Depression (Economic breakdown) G: 340
    International trade (Government trade policies)
        I: 348
    McKinley, William (Congressman) M: 339
    North American Free Trade Agreement N: 470
    Reciprocal trade agreement R: 175
    Taxation (Taxes on transactions) T: 53
    United States, History of the (Financial problems)
        U: 162-163; (Jackson as president) U: 171
    World Trade Organization W: 451
Tariff Act [1842]
    Obscenity and pornography (Legal history for
        obscenity) O: 644
Tariff Board [U.S. history]
    Taft, William Howard (Legislative achievements)
        T: 11
Tariff Commission, United States [U.S.]
    International Trade Commission, United States
        I: 349
"Tariff of abominations" [U.S. history]
    Adams, John Quincy (The "tariff of
        abominations") A: 42
    Tariff (United States tariffs) T: 44
    United States, History of the (Jackson as
        president) U: 171
Tarkenton, Fran [American football player] T: 45
Tarkington, Booth [American author] T: 45
Tarleton, Banastre [British general]
    Henry, Patrick (Career as governor) H: 190
    Jefferson, Thomas (Governor) J: 80
    Marion, Francis M: 211
Tarleton State University
    Texas A&M University T: 210
Tarmac [area]
    Airport (Loading aprons and taxiways) A: 245
Tarnish [chemistry] T: 45
    Silver (Properties of silver) S: 463-464
Taro [plant] T: 46
    See also Elephant's-ear *in this index*
    Hawaii (Food) H: 94
    Pacific Islands (Food) P: 6 *with picture*
    Palau (Food) P: 102
Taronga Zoo [Australia]
    Zoo *picture on* Z: 603
Tarpan [animal]
    Horse (Wild horses) H: 348
Tarpaulin
    Camping (Sleeping bags) C: 93-94
Tarpon [fish] T: 46
    Fish *picture on* F: 153
Tarquin the Proud [Roman king] *See* Tarquinius
    Superbus, Lucius *in this index*
Tarquinius Priscus, Lucius [legendary figure]
    Rome, Ancient (The regal period) R: 444
Tarr, Peter [American businessman]
    West Virginia (Early industries) W: 226
Tarragon [plant] T: 46
Tárrega, Francisco [Spanish musician]
    Guitar G: 436
Tarsal bones [anatomy]
    Foot (The bones) F: 352 *with diagram*
    Frog *picture on* F: 537
Tarsier [animal] T: 46 *with picture*
    Eye *picture on* E: 468
    Primate P: 777 *with picture, diagram on* P: 778b;
        (Tarsiers) P: 778
Tarsus [Turkey] T: 46
Tartan [fabric] T: 46 *with pictures*
Tartar [physiology]
    Teeth (Dental checkups) T: 82
Tartar, Cream of [chemical]
    Tartaric acid T: 48
Tartaric acid [chemical] T: 47
Tartarin [literary figure]
    Daudet, Alphonse D: 43
Tartars [people] *See* Tatars *in this index*
Tartarus [Greek mythology] T: 48
    Hades H: 4

Tartini, Giuseppe [Italian violinist] T: 48
Tartu University
    Estonia (People) E: 361
Tartuffe [play by Molière]
    Drama *picture on* D: 324
    Molière M: 694
Tarzan [literary figure]
    Burroughs, Edgar Rice B: 711
Tarzan of the Apes [book by Burroughs]
    Burroughs, Edgar Rice B: 711
Tasajo [food]
    Pemmican P: 233
Taschereau, Elzéar A. [Canadian religious leader]
    Cardinal (table: Canadian cardinals) C: 211
Taschereau, L.-Alexandre [Canadian political
    leader]
    Quebec (table) Q: 29
Tashkent [Uzbekistan] T: 48
Task, The [poem by Cowper]
    Cowper, William Ci: 1113
Task force [military]
    Navy (The organization of navies) N: 77 *with
        picture*
Task lighting
    Lighting (In offices, stores, and factories) L: 296-
        297
Tasman, Abel Janszoon [Dutch explorer] T: 48
    Australia (European explorations) A: 920 *with
        map*
    Exploration (Exploring the Pacific) E: 447 *with
        map*
    New Zealand *picture on* N: 356; (Early European
        contact) N: 354
    Tasman Sea T: 48
    Tasmania (History) T: 49
    Tonga (History) T: 328
Tasman Sea [Australia] T: 48
Tasmania [state, Australia] T: 48 *with picture and
    map*
    Australia (The land) A: 907 *with map*
    Exploration (Exploring the Pacific) E: 447
    Tasman, Abel Janszoon T: 48
Tasmanian devil [animal] T: 49 *with picture*
    Mammal (table) *picture on* M: 128
    Marsupial *picture on* M: 232
Tasmanian tiger [animal] T: 49 *with picture*
Tasmanian wolf *See* Tasmanian tiger *in this index*
Tasses [armor]
    Armor *picture on* A: 720
Tassili-n-Ajjer [region, Africa]
    Sahara (Land and climate) S: 20
Tasso, Torquato [Italian poet] T: 50
    Italian literature (Humanism and the
        Renaissance) I: 494
Taste [sense] T: 50 *with diagrams*
    Animal (Adaptations for sensing the
        environment) A: 492-493 *with picture*
    Fish (Smell and taste) F: 164
    Insect (Taste) I: 291
    Mammal (Senses) M: 120
    Nose N: 549
    Senses S: 301
    Smell (Taste and smell) S: 514
    Tongue T: 329
Taste bud [anatomy]
    Taste T: 50 *with diagrams*
Tatami [mat]
    Tokyo (Visitor's guide) T: 316
Tatra Bridge
    Bridge (table: Cable-stayed) B: 603
Tatara steel
    Iron and steel (The first steel) I: 450
Tatarian honeysuckle [plant]
    Flower *picture on* F: 281
Tatars [people] T: 51
    Crimea Ci: 1142
    Kazan K: 252
    Moscow (History) M: 826
    Russia (The state of Kievan Rus) R: 547-548
    Russian literature (Nonreligious literature) R: 559;
        (The literature of Tatar captivity) R: 559
    Siberia (History) S: 446
    Ukraine (Kievan Rus) U: 12
Tate, Allen [American author] T: 51
    American literature (Modernist poetry) A: 421
Tate, Nahum [English poet]
    Poet laureate (table: Poets laureate of the United
        Kingdom) P: 590
Tate House
    Maine (Places to visit) M: 78
Tatiana [grand duchess of Russia]
    Nicholas II [czar] *picture on* N: 403
Tatler, The [essays by Addison and Steele]
    Addison, Joseph A: 47
    Magazine (History) M: 44
    Steele, Sir Richard So: 882
Tatra National Park [Poland]

National park (table) **N: 42g**
Tatransky National Park [Slovakia/Poland]
National park (table) **N: 42g**
Tatting [lacemaking]
Lace **L: 20** *with picture*
Tattler [bird] *See Willet in this index*
Tattnall, Josiah, Jr. [American political leader]
Georgia (table) **G: 130**
Tattooing [decoration] **T: 51**
Body art **B: 434** *with picture*
Pacific Islands *picture on* **P: 5**
Tatum, Art [American pianist] **T: 51**
Tatum, Edward Lawrie [American biochemist]
Beadle, George Wells **B: 179**
Cell (The 1900's) **C: 337-338**
Nobel Prizes (Physiology or medicine: 1958)
N: 446
Tau [letter]
T **T: 1** *with picture*
Tau [protein]
Alzheimer's disease (Causes) **A: 399**
Tau [subatomic particle]
Lepton **L: 205**
Subatomic particle (Kinds of subatomic particles)
So: 937
Tau-neutrino [subatomic particle]
Astronomy (Neutrino astronomy) **A: 845-846**
Lepton **L: 206**
Neutrino **N: 154**
Physics (Physics today) **P: 442-443**
Taube, Henry [American chemist]
Nobel Prizes (Chemistry: 1983) **N: 444**
Tauchnitz [publisher]
Book (The 1800's) **B: 467-468**
Taufa'ahau [king of Tonga]
Tonga (History) **T: 328**
Taufa'ahau Tupou IV [king of Tonga]
Tonga (History) **T: 328**
Taughannock Falls [falls, New York]
Finger Lakes **F: 104**
Taunton Flag [U.S. history]
Flag *picture on* **F: 210**
Taupin, Bernie [British songwriter]
John, Elton **J: 133**
Tauriskos of Tralles [Greek sculptor]
Farnese Bull **F: 46**
Taurog, Norman [American director]
Motion picture (Best achievement in directing:
1930-31) **M: 862**
Taurus [astrology] **T: 51** *with picture*
Zodiac (The zodiac in astrology) **Z: 597** *with
picture*
Taurus Mountains
Turkey (The land) **T: 507** *with map*
Taussig, Helen Brooke [American doctor] **T: 52**
Tautog [fish]
Blackfish **B: 393**
Tautology [logic]
Enlightenment (Criticism of the Enlightenment)
E: 326b
Tavern
Colonial life in America (Recreation) **Ci: 802-803**
Taw [letter]
T **T: 1** *with picture*
Tawes, J. Millard [American political leader]
Maryland (table) **M: 255**
Tawhid [religion]
Islam (Teachings and practices) **I: 463**
Tawny-orange day lily [plant]
Flower *picture on* **F: 279**
Tax *See Taxation in this index*
Tax accounting
Accounting (Fields of accounting) **A: 23**
Tax Appeals, Board of [U.S. history]
Tax Court, United States **T: 52**
Tax avoidance
Tax evasion **T: 52**
Tax bracket [economics]
Income tax (Effects of inflation) **I: 103**; (Federal
income taxes in the United States) **I: 104**;
(History of U.S. income taxes) **I: 105**
Tax Court, United States T: 52
Internal Revenue Service **I: 337**
Tax Court of Canada
Canada, Government of (Tax and martial courts)
C: 136
Tax credit [economics]
Income tax (Figuring the individual income tax)
I: 104
Poverty (Measures to improve job opportunities)
P: 724-725
Tax evasion [crime] **T: 52**
Tax haven
Channel Islands **C: 375**
Tax incentive
Exports and imports (Export promotion) **E: 454**
Tax liability

Tax evasion **T: 52**
Tax on transactions
Government (Taxation) **G: 283**
Tax Reform Act [1969]
Income tax (History of U.S. income taxes) **I: 105**
Tax Reform Act [1986]
Income tax (History of U.S. income taxes) **I: 105**
Social security (Unemployment insurance)
So: 555-556
Tax return
Income tax (Paying the individual income tax)
I: 104; (Processing income tax returns) **I: 105**
Internal Revenue Service **I: 337**
Tax sharing
Metropolitan area (Tax sharing) **M: 443**
Tax stamp [U.S. history]
Revolution, American (The Quartering and
Stamp acts) **R: 272** *with picture*
Taxable income
Income tax (Types of income taxes) **I: 102**;
(Defining taxable income) **I: 102**
Taxation T: 52 *with diagrams*
See also Income tax in this index
Alcoholic beverage **A: 336**
Assessment **A: 818**
Capital gains tax **C: 192**
City (Solving city problems) **Ci: 592**
Education (How should education be financed?)
E: 108
Environmental pollution (Government action)
E: 335
Global warming (Types of policies) **G: 232c-232d**
Government (Taxation) **G: 283**
Inca (Trade and transportation) **I: 97**
Inland revenue **I: 273**
Internal revenue **I: 336**
Local government (Financial difficulties) **L: 408**
Medicine (Providing medical care) **M: 366**
Metropolitan area (Finances and taxation) **M: 443**
National budget (Government revenue) **N: 30**
Percentage (Taxes) **P: 282**
Road (How roads and highways are paid for)
R: 360
School (Public schools) **S: 182**
Social security (Financing Social Security) **So: 555**
State government (State finances) **So: 865**
Tax evasion **T: 52**
Teaching (Current issues in U.S. teaching) **T: 69**
United States, History of the (The movement for
independence [1754-1783]) **U: 158**; (Financial
problems) **U: 162-163**
Taxation without representation
Franklin, Benjamin (A delegate in London) **F: 490**
Revolution, American (The Townshend Acts)
R: 273
United States, History of the (Colonial reaction)
U: 158
Taxco [Mexico] **T: 55**
Taxi [transportation]
Transportation *picture on* **T: 394**
Taxi Driver [film]
Foster, Jodie **F: 428**
Scorsese, Martin **S: 210**
Taxicab army [World War I]
Paris (Paris in wartime) **P: 166**
Taxidermy T: 55 *with pictures*
Taxiing
Airport (Loading aprons and taxiways) **A: 245**
Taxiway
Airport (Loading aprons and taxiways) **A: 245**
Taxodium [botany]
Tree (Needleleaf trees) **T: 414-415**
Taxoid [drug]
Taxol **T: 56**
Taxol [drug] **T: 56**
Taxonomy [biology]
Biology **B: 316**
Botany (Plant classification and form) **B: 508**
Classification, Scientific **Ci: 654**
Zoology (What zoologists study) **Z: 606-607**
Taxpayer Relief Act [1997]
Income tax (History of U.S. income taxes) **I: 105**
Tay [people]
Vietnam (People) **V: 365**
Tay [river, Scotland]
Scotland (Rivers and lakes) **S: 217** *with map*
Viaduct **V: 347**
Tay, Waren [British physician]
Tay-Sachs disease **T: 56**
Tay-Sachs disease T: 56 *with diagram*
Genetic counseling (Reasons for seeking genetic
counseling) **G: 84a**
Heredity (table) **H: 204**
Races, Human (The founder effect) **R: 59**
Tay Son [dynasty]
Vietnam (Independence) **V: 370**
Tay Son Rebellion [Vietnamese history]

Vietnam (Independence) **V: 370**
Taya, Maawiya Ould Sid Ahmed [Mauritanian
political leader]
Mauritania (History) **M: 315**
Tayler, John [American political leader]
New York (table) **N: 313**
Tayler, Alfred A. [American political leader]
Tennessee **T: 135**; (table) **T: 152**
Taylor, Ann [British author]
Literature for children (Masterpieces of poetry)
L: 364
Taylor, Bayard [American author]
May (Quotations) **M: 321**
Taylor, Ben [American baseball player/manager]
Baseball (table: Hall of Fame) **B: 134b**
Taylor, Charles [Liberian political leader]
Johnson-Sirleaf, Ellen **J: 154**
Liberia (Civil war) **L: 232**; (Recent developments)
L: 232
Taylor, Claudia Alta "Lady Bird" [wife of Lyndon
Baines Johnson] *See Johnson, Lady Bird in this
index*
Taylor, Edward [American poet] **T: 56**
American literature (New England) **A: 414**
Taylor, Elizabeth [American actress] **T: 57** *with
picture*
Motion picture (Best performance by an actress:
1960, 1966) **M: 862**
Taylor, Frederick Winslow [American engineer]
T: 57
Taylor, George [American patriot] **T: 57**
Taylor, Harriet *See Mill, Harriet Taylor in this index*
Taylor, Jane [British author]
Literature for children (Masterpieces of poetry)
L: 364
Taylor, Jeremy [English religious leader]
English literature (Prose writings) **E: 317**
Taylor, John [English artist]
Shakespeare, William *picture on* **S: 345**
Taylor, Joseph Hooton, Jr. [American physicist]
Gravitational wave **G: 333**
Nobel Prizes (Physics: 1993) **N: 442**
Taylor, Kenneth N. [American author]
Bible (Modern English translations) **B: 286**
Taylor, Leon R. [American political leader]
New Jersey (table) **N: 249**
Taylor, Lucy Beaman Hobbs [American dentist]
Dentistry (Early dentistry) **D: 144-145**
Taylor, Margaret Smith [wife of Zachary Taylor]
First ladies of the United States (table) **F: 142**
Taylor, Zachary (Taylor's family) **T: 58**; (Life in the
White House) **T: 60**
Taylor, Maxwell Davenport [American general]
T: 57
Taylor, Mick [British musician]
Rolling Stones **R: 402a**
Taylor, Mildred D. [American author] **T: 57**
Newbery Medal (table) **N: 359**
Taylor, Paul [American choreographer] **T: 57**
Taylor, Richard [Confederate general]
Taylor, Zachary (Taylor's family) **T: 58**
Taylor, Richard [father of]
Taylor, Zachary (Childhood) **T: 58**
Taylor, Richard Edward [Canadian physicist]
Kendall, Henry Way **K: 258**
Nobel Prizes (Physics: 1990) **N: 442**
Taylor, Robert Love [American political leader]
Tennessee **T: 135**; (table) **T: 152**
Taylor, Sarah [daughter of]
Taylor, Zachary (Taylor's family) **T: 58**
Taylor, Sarah Strother [mother of]
Taylor, Zachary (Childhood) **T: 58**
Taylor, William C. [American chemist]
Glass (Design) **G: 218**
Taylor, William R. [American political leader]
Wisconsin (table) **W: 365**
Taylor, William S. [American political leader]
Kentucky (The early 1900's) **K: 293**
Taylor, Zachary [U.S. president] **T: 58** *with pictures*
Barnburners **B: 115**
Fillmore, Millard **F: 100**
Mexican War (Events leading up to the war)
M: 446; (Taylor's campaign) **M: 446**
Mexico (Difficulties of the early republic) **M: 471**
United States, History of the (The Mexican War)
U: 169
Van Buren, Martin (Later years) **V: 273**
Whig Party (Decline of the Whigs) **W: 280**
Taylor Cub [airplane]
Airplane *picture on* **A: 234**
Taylor series [mathematics]
Series **S: 316b**
Taylorism [industry]
Taylor, Frederick Winslow **T: 57**
Tayra [animal] **T: 61** *with picture*
Tazewell, Littleton Waller [American political
leader]

Virginia (table) V: 417
TB [disease] *See* Tuberculosis *in this index*
Tb [symbol]
  Terbium T: 169
Tbilisi [Georgia] T: 61
  Georgia G: 109 *with picture*
TBX [weapon]
  Bomb (Thermobaric explosives [TBX's]) B: 451
Tc [symbol]
  Technetium T: 73
TCA [drug] *See* Tricyclic antidepressant *in this index*
TCDD [chemical]
  Dioxin D: 215
Tchaikovsky, Peter Ilich [Russian composer] T: 61
  with portrait
  Art and the arts *picture on* A: 748
  Ballet (Music) B: 50
  Classical music *picture on* Ci: 650
  Nutcracker, The N: 622
Tchambuli [people]
  Sexuality (Cultural influences) S: 338a
TCP/IP [electronics] *See* Transmission Control
  Protocol/Internet Protocol *in this index*
TDD [machine]
  Deafness (Assistive technology) D: 58-59
Te [symbol]
  Tellurium T: 129
Te Kanawa, Kiri [New Zealand singer] T: 62 *with
  portrait*
Te katei ni Kiribati [customs]
  Pacific Islands (Ways of life) P: 6
Tea [drink] T: 62 *with pictures*
  Africa *picture on* A: 109
  Asia *picture on* A: 771
  England (Food and drink) E: 296
  Food (Customs) F: 332-333
  Indian, American (Food) I: 136d
  Scotland (Food and drink) S: 214
  Sri Lanka *picture on* So: 817
  Taiwan *picture on* T: 17
Tea Act [1773]
  Boston Tea Party B: 506
  Declaration of Independence (Events leading to
    the Declaration) D: 74
  Revolution, American (The Tea Act) R: 273
  United States, History of the (Renewed conflict)
    U: 158
Tea bag
  Tea (History) T: 63-64
Tea Party, Boston *See* Boston Tea Party *in this index*
Tea party movement [U.S. history]
  Obama, Barack (Conservative criticism) O: 640g
Tea plant
  Camellia C: 79
Tea rose
  Flower *picture on* F: 281
  Rose (Types of roses) R: 474 *with picture*
Tea tax *See* Tea Act *in this index*
Teach, Edward [birth name of]
  Blackbeard B: 392
Teacher *See* Teaching *in this index*
Teacher aide
  Careers (Teaching) C: 231-232
  Preschool (Preschools in the United States) P: 757
  Teaching (Certification of teachers) T: 68
Teacher bird
  Ovenbird O: 881 *with picture*
Teacher Educators, Association of [organization]
  Teaching (Teachers organizations) T: 69
Teacher in America [book by Barzun]
  Barzun, Jacques B: 123
Teacher training
  Education (Who should teach?) E: 106-107
  Pestalozzi, Johann Heinrich P: 318
  Teaching (Teacher-training programs) T: 67; (The
    effectiveness of teacher training) T: 70
Teachers, American Federation of *See* American
  Federation of Teachers *in this index*
Teachers College, Columbia University T: 64 *with
  picture*
  Columbia University (Affiliated institutions)
    Ci: 853
Teachers' institute
  Adult education (History of adult education in
    the United States) A: 69
Teachers Insurance and Annuity Association
  Carnegie Foundation for the Advancement of
    Teaching C: 243
Teacher's Word Book [book by Thorndike]
  Thorndike, Edward Lee T: 267
Teaching [career] T: 65 *with pictures*
  See also Education *in this index; and the list of
    Related articles in the* Teaching *article*
  Academic freedom A: 20
  Careers (Teaching) C: 231 *with picture*
  Differentiated instruction D: 200
  Education (How teachers guide learning) E: 90;

(Who should teach?) E: 106
  Educational psychology E: 111
  Elementary school (Elementary school
    instruction) E: 224
  High school H: 228
  Kindergarten (The kindergarten teacher) K: 318
  Pioneer life in America (Education) P: 484 *with
    picture*
  Preschool (The preschool teacher) P: 756b
  Reading (The teaching of reading) R: 157;
    (Working with the school) R: 160
  Universities and colleges (Faculty) U: 208
Teaching certificate
  Teaching (Certification of teachers) T: 68
Teaching fellow
  Universities and colleges (Faculty) U: 208
Teaching hospital
  Hospital (How hospitals are classified) H: 371
  Medicine (Financing advanced medical care)
    M: 377-378
Teagarden, Jack [American musician] T: 70
Teak [tree] T: 71 *with pictures*
Teal [bird] T: 71 *with picture*
  Bird (Birds of inland waters and marshes) B: 340
    with picture
Team handball T: 71
Team roping
  Rodeo (Team roping) R: 397
Team sales
  Sales (Current trends in sales) S: 65
Team teaching
  Education (Elementary education) E: 91
  Elementary school (Elementary school
    instruction) E: 224-225
  Middle school M: 535
Teamsters, International Brotherhood of *See*
  Teamsters Union *in this index*
Teamsters Union T: 72
  American Federation of Labor and Congress of
    Industrial Organizations (History) A: 410
  Hoffa, James Phillip H: 283
  Hoffa, James Riddle H: 283
  Labor movement (table) L: 8
Teapot Dome [U.S. history] T: 72
  Coolidge, Calvin (Corruption in government)
    Ci: 1032
  Fall, Albert Bacon F: 15
  Harding, Warren Gamaliel H: 56
  Roaring Twenties (Changing attitudes) R: 363-
    364
Tear gas [weapon]
  Chemical-biological-radiological warfare
    (Chemical) C: 396
  Mace M: 11
Tear-of-the-Clouds [lake, New York]
  New York (Rivers) N: 306
Tears [physiology] T: 72 *with picture*
  Disease (Natural barriers) D: 231 *with diagram*
  Eye (The outer parts) E: 460 *with picture*
Tears, Trail of [U.S. history] *See* Trail of Tears *in this
  index*
"Tears in Heaven" [song]
  Clapton, Eric Ci: 638
Teasdale, Joseph P. [American political leader]
  Missouri (table) M: 668
Teasdale, Sara [American poet] T: 72
Teasel [plant] T: 73
Teaser [job]
  Glass (Glass terms) G: 222
Teasing
  Hairdressing (The 1900's) H: 12
Teat [zoology]
  Cattle (Udder) C: 308
Teatree [tree]
  Tree T: 426 *with picture*
Teatro Farnese [Parma, Italy]
  Drama (The Italian stage) D: 330-331
Teatro Olimpico [Vicenza, Italy]
  Drama (The Italian stage) D: 330
Teatro San Carlo [Naples, Italy]
  Naples (Way of life) N: 12
Teatro San Cassiano [Venice, Italy]
  Opera (Early Baroque opera) O: 797
Tebaldi, Renata [Italian singer] T: 73
Tebenna [garment]
  Clothing (Rome) Ci: 697
Teberdinskly National Park [Russia]
  National park (table) N: 42g
Tebet [month]
  Calendar (The Hebrew calendar) C: 29
Tebow, Tim [American football player]
  Football (table) F: 363
Technetium [element] T: 73
Technical and career education
  Vocational education (The 1900's and early
    2000's) V: 435
Technical assistance [international relations] T: 73

  Foreign aid (Technical assistance and relief)
    F: 385
  United Nations (Economic and technical aid)
    U: 87
Technical director [career]
  Television (The control room) T: 112-113
Technical fall [wrestling]
  Wrestling (High school and intercollegiate
    wrestling) W: 505
Technical foul [sports]
  Basketball (Fouls) B: 147 *with diagram*, B: 147-
    150
  Lacrosse (Men's lacrosse) L: 23
Technical institute [school]
  Careers (Technical institutes) C: 217
Technical knockout
  Boxing (Scoring a fight) B: 527
  Mixed martial arts M: 680
  Pacquiao, Manny P: 19
Technical library
  Library (Special libraries) L: 250
Technical pen
  Pen (Specialty pens) P: 234 *with picture*
Technical rehearsal
  Theater *picture on* T: 240
Technical rock climbing [sport]
  Climbing Ci: 680 *with picture*
Technical school
  Community college Ci: 898
  England (Education) E: 297
  Vocational education (Public high schools) V: 434
Technical sergeant
  Rank, Military (table) R: 140
Technical writing
  Writing W: 511
Technician
  Careers (Technical institutes) C: 217;
    (Construction, maintenance, and repair)
    C: 221-222
  Radio (Careers) R: 90
Technicolor [photography] T: 73
  Disney, Walt (The first Disney cartoons) D: 235-
    236
Technological intelligence
  Intelligence service I: 320
Technological unemployment
  Unemployment (Structural unemployment) U: 22
Technology T: 74 *with pictures*
  See also Invention *in this index; and the list of
    Related articles in the* Technology *article*
  Careers (Technical and mathematical
    occupations) C: 232 *with picture*
  City (Advances in technology) Ci: 577;
    (Metropolitan cities) Ci: 588-589; (Economy)
    Ci: 590
  Culture (How cultures change) Ci: 1189
  Education (The Enlightenment) E: 101
  Engineering E: 284
  Environmental pollution (Scientific efforts) E: 336
  Exports and imports (Reasons for change) E: 454
  Foundation (Science and technology) F: 431
  Human being H: 413
  Industrial Revolution I: 246
  Industry (Technology) I: 258 *with diagram*
  Mathematics (The importance of mathematics)
    M: 302
  Physics (Physics today) P: 442-443
  Poverty (Economic factors) P: 724
  Science (The importance of science) S: 191
  United States, History of the (The economy--
    boom and bust) U: 191; (Economic changes)
    U: 196b
Technology assessment
  Technology (Using technology safely) T: 77-78
Technology Assessment, Office of [U.S.] T: 78
Technology education
  Industrial arts I: 242; (Recent trends) I: 243-244
Technology museum
  Museum (Science museums) M: 938
Technothriller [fiction]
  Science fiction (The New Wave) S: 206
Tectonic mountain
  Mountain (How different types of mountains
    form) M: 892
Tectonic plate [geology] *See* Plate tectonics *in
  this index*
Tectorial membrane [anatomy]
  Ear *diagram on* E: 10; (The inner ear) E: 8-9 *with
    diagram*
Tecumseh [American Indian chief] T: 78 *with
  picture*
  Creek Indians Ci: 1126
  Harrison, William Henry (Entry into politics)
    H: 74-75
  Indian wars (The Shawnee Prophet) I: 192
  Pioneer life in America (Pioneers and Indians)
    P: 485

Shawnee Indians S: 379
War of 1812 (Thames River) W: 33
Westward movement in America (Indian
conflicts) W: 247
Tecumseh [book by Mair]
Mair, Charles M: 93
Ted Williams Tunnel
Boston (Building boom) B: 504
Tedder, Arthur William [British general] T: 78
Teddy bear [toy]
Roosevelt, Theodore R: 460
Teddy bear cholla [plant]
Cactus (Kinds of cactuses) C: 11
Flower *picture on* F: 291
Tee [sports]
Curling *diagram on* Ci: 1196
Golf (The course) G: 260; (The tee) G: 260
Tee Ball [program]
Little League Baseball L: 392
Teen pop
Rock music (The 1990's) R: 380d
Teenager
See also Adolescent *in this index*
Gang G: 26
High school H: 228
Juvenile delinquency J: 205
Library (Services for young adults) L: 240
Suicide So: 964
Teens in Action [program]
Camp Fire USA (Teens in Action) C: 89
Teepee [dwelling] *See* Tipi *in this index*
Teeth [anatomy] T: 79 *with pictures*
See also Mastication *in this index*
Animal (Teeth and jaws) A: 491 *with picture*
Baby (From 6 to 12 months) B: 7
Dentistry D: 143 *with pictures*
Dog (Body structure) D: 263-265
Human body (table) H: 422 *with diagram*
Lion (The body of a lion) L: 340-341 *with picture*
Mammal (What mammals eat) M: 121 *with
diagrams*
Mouth M: 903 *with diagram*
Orthodontics O: 859
Periodontitis P: 287
Prehistoric animal (Interpreting fossil evidence)
P: 741
Prehistoric people (Studying fossils) P: 754a
Rodent R: 397 *with picture*
Ruminant R: 519
Shell *diagram on* S: 385
Whale (Kinds of toothed whales) W: 258
Teeth [botany]
Leaf (The blade) L: 153 *with picture*
Teeth [mechanical device]
Gear G: 75
Teething
Teeth (Deciduous teeth) T: 79
Teflon [material] T: 87
Tefnut [Egyptian goddess]
Mythology *picture on* M: 977; (The Great Ennead)
M: 979
Tegucigalpa [Honduras] T: 87
Honduras H: 308 *with picture*
Teheran [Iran] *See* Tehran *in this index*
Tehran [Iran] T: 87 *with picture*
Iran (Climate) I: 403
Tehran Conference [1943] T: 88
Roosevelt, Franklin Delano (The Big Three) R: 457
United Nations (The Atlantic Charter) U: 94
World War II (The strategy) W: 480-481
Tehri Dam [India]
Dam (table) D: 18
Tehuantepec, Isthmus of [region, Mexico]
Mexico (The Gulf Coastal Plain) M: 462
Tehuelche Indians
Indian, American *picture on* I: 140; (Indians of the
Marginal Regions) I: 176-177
Teian bard [nickname]
Anacreon A: 447
Teide, Pico de [mountain]
Canary Islands C: 166 *with map*
Teilhard de Chardin, Pierre [French philosopher]
T: 88
Teiresias [legendary figure]
Odyssey: (Odysseus describes his wanderings)
O: 675
Tejano [music]
Selena S: 289
Tejas Indians
Texas T: 184
Tektite [geology] T: 88
Tel Aviv [Israel] T: 88 *with picture*
Israel *picture on* I: 480
Middle East *picture on* M: 534a
Telecine [machine]
Motion picture (Editing the film) M: 855
Telecommunication device for the deaf

Deafness (Assistive technology) D: 58-59
Telecommunication Union, International [UN]
See International Telecommunication Union *in
this index*
Telecommunications T: 89
AT&T Inc. A: 851
Audio-visual materials (Other computerized
tools) A: 883
Modem M: 685
Technology (The use of electricity) T: 75
Telecommunications Act [1996]
Closed captioning Ci: 685
Telephone (Competition in the U.S. telephone
industry) T: 101
Television (Regulating U.S. television) T: 115
Telecommuting
Computer (Personal computers) Ci: 909
Telegraaf, De [newspaper]
Netherlands (Communication) N: 148
Telegram
Telegraph T: 90
Western Union W: 241
Telegraph [communications] T: 90 *with pictures*
Cable (Telegraph cables) C: 5
Communication (The 1800's) Ci: 881-882 *with
picture*
Edison, Thomas Alva (Inventor and businessman)
E: 78
Marconi, Guglielmo M: 196
Morse, Samuel Finley Breese M: 817
Morse code M: 819
Radio (Early development) R: 91
Western frontier life in America (New forms of
communication) W: 233
Western Union W: 241
Telegraph Hill
San Francisco (Downtown San Francisco) S: 92-93
Telegraph plant T: 93
Telegraph Union, International
International Telecommunication Union I: 347
Telegraphone [machine]
Tape recorder (History) T: 38-39
Teleki, Samuel [Hungarian explorer]
Lake Turkana L: 47
Telemachus [legendary figure]
Mentor M: 410
Odyssey: (The *Odyssey* begins) O: 675; (The
Odyssey as literature) O: 676
Ulysses (The Trojan War) U: 17-18
Telemachus
Fénelon, François de Salignac de la Mothe- F: 71
Telemann, Georg Philipp [German composer]
T: 93
Telemarketing [sales] T: 93
Careers (Sales) C: 229-230
Telemetry [measurement] T: 93
Telemundo [network]
Television (The national networks) T: 113
Telenovela [television program]
Television (In Latin America) T: 117
Teleoceras
Prehistoric animal *picture on* P: 740
Teleology [philosophy]
Ethics (Modern ethics) E: 366
God (Ideas about God) G: 244
Mechanist philosophy M: 355
Philosophy (Metaphysics) P: 383-384
Teleost [fish]
Fish (Bony fish) F: 147; (The first modern fish)
F: 171
Teleosteans [fish]
Prehistoric animal (Fish) P: 738
Telepathy T: 93
Extrasensory perception (What
parapsychologists study) E: 457
Telephone T: 94 *with pictures*
See also Cellular telephone *in this index*
AT&T Inc. A: 851
Bank (Electronic banking) B: 89-90
Bell, Alexander Graham (The telephone) B: 241
Berliner, Emile B: 267
Broadband communication B: 634
Cable (Types and functions of cables) C: 4-5;
(Telephone cables) C: 6
Careers (Administrative support) C: 219 *with
picture*
Communication (The telephone) Ci: 882 *with
picture*; (The digital age) Ci: 885
Communications satellite Ci: 888a
Deafness (Assistive technology) D: 58-59
Edison, Thomas Alva *picture on* E: 80; (The Wizard
of Menlo Park) E: 78
Etiquette (Telephone etiquette) E: 374
Fax machine F: 57
Fiber optics (Uses of optical fibers) F: 88-89
Gray, Elisha G: 334
Invention (Research laboratories) I: 357

Modem M: 685
Pager P: 20
Public utility (History) P: 865-866
Rural Electrification Administration (Telephone
program) R: 522
Technology (Technology and society) T: 76
Telecommunications T: 89
Telemarketing T: 93
United States, History of the (New products)
U: 180
Videophone V: 360
Western Union W: 241
Wiretapping W: 345
Telephone answering machine
Telephone *picture on* T: 94
Telephone exchange
Connecticut (Interesting facts) Ci: 953 *with
picture*
Telephone pole design prison
Prison (Prison buildings) P: 806
Telephoto [machine]
Fax machine (History) F: 58
Telephoto lens
Camera (Single-lens reflex [SLR] cameras)
C: 82-83
Photography (Types of lenses) P: 411 *with picture*
Teleprompter [machine]
Television (Talent) T: 110d *with picture*
Telescope T: 102 *with pictures*
Antarctica (Scientific research) A: 539-540 *with
picture*
Arecibo Observatory A: 645
Astronomy (Modern astronomy) A: 836 *with
pictures*
Binoculars B: 309
Galileo G: 12 *with picture*
Green Bank Telescope G: 380
Keck Observatory K: 254
Mauna Kea M: 313
Moon (Early observations with telescopes)
M: 792
Mount Wilson Observatory M: 890
Newton, Sir Isaac (Light and color) N: 389 *with
picture*
Observatory (Observatories with telescopes)
O: 644
Palomar Observatory P: 112
Science *picture on* S: 191
Survey (Surveying tools) So: 1011
World, History of the *picture on* W: 442
Telescope Peak [mountain, California]
Death Valley D: 62
Telescopic sight
Rifle (The parts of a rifle) R: 338 *with diagram*
Telesphorus, Saint [pope]
Pope (table) P: 666
Telesto [satellite]
Saturn (Satellites) S: 151-152
Televisa [network]
Television (In Latin America) T: 117
Television T: 110 *with pictures*
See also Cable television *in this index; and the list
of Related articles in the* Television *article*
Advertising (Television) A: 73 *with picture*; (The
rise of radio and television) A: 79
Animation (New diversity) A: 514c
Audio-visual materials (Multisensory materials)
A: 883
Baird, John Logie B: 31
Boxing (Boxing in the United States) B: 530; (The
1950's) B: 532a; (Boxing today) B: 533
Camcorder (The development of camcorders)
C: 75
Closed captioning Ci: 685
Color (Mixing colored lights) Ci: 821-822
Communication (The development of television)
Ci: 885 *with picture*
Communications satellite Ci: 888a
De Forest, Lee D: 89
Deafness (Assistive technology) D: 58-59
Debate (Political debate) D: 63
Doll (Modern dolls) D: 292
Electronic game (History) E: 204d
Electronics (The vacuum tube era) E: 215
Farnsworth, Philo Taylor F: 46
Federal Communications Commission F: 63
Football (The rise of professional football) F: 366
Image orthicon I: 79
Journalism (Fields of journalism) J: 170 *with
picture*; (Television journalism) J: 175
McLuhan, Marshall M: 343
Motion picture (The movies) M: 847; (Distribution) M: 860;
(Postwar American movies) M: 869
Political convention (Attracting publicity) P: 630
Projector (Projection TV's) P: 817
Public opinion (Radio and television) P: 860
Reading (The importance of reading) R: 155-156

Recreation (Kinds of recreation) **R: 183**
Remote control (Applications of remote control) **R: 230-231**
Remote sensing **R: 231**
Sexuality (The mass media) **S: 338a**
Soap opera **So: 543**
United States, History of the (Postwar prosperity) **U: 194**
Video art **V: 359**
Videotape recorder **V: 360**
Western frontier life in America (Entertainment) **W: 240**
World, History of the *picture on* **W: 448a**
Wrestling, Professional **W: 507**
Writing (Scriptwriting) **W: 512**
Zworykin, Vladimir Kosma **Z: 610**
Television and Radio Artists, American Federation
Labor movement (table) **L: 8**
Television camera
See also Camcorder *in this index*
Television *diagram on* **T: 124**; (Production) **T: 111**; (Creating television signals) **T: 121**
Video art **V: 359**
Television station
Television (The U.S. television industry) **T: 113**
Telex [communications]
Telegraph (Decline) **T: 92**
Telfair, Edward [American political leader]
Georgia (table) **G: 130**
Telford, Thomas [Scottish engineer] **T: 129**
Industrial Revolution (Roads) **I: 251**
Tell, The [region, Algeria]
Algeria (The Tell) **A: 363**
Tell, William [legendary figure] **T: 129** *with picture*
See also William Tell [opera] *in this index*
Lake of Lucerne **L: 42**
Tell el-Amarna [Egypt]
Egypt, Ancient (The New Kingdom) **E: 143**
Tell Mardikh [ruin]
Ebla **E: 48**
Tell Me How Long the Train's Been Gone [book by Baldwin]
Baldwin, James **B: 39**
Teller [religion]
Pope (Present procedures) **P: 662**
Teller, Edward [American physicist] **T: 129**
Teller, Henry Moore [American government official]
Interior, Department of the (table) **I: 325**
Téllez, Gabriel *See* Tirso de Molina *in this index*
Tellico Dam [Little Tennessee River]
Conservation (Water conservation) **Ci: 977-978**
Darter **D: 38**
"Telling the Bees" [poem by Whittier]
Whittier, John Greenleaf **W: 296**
Telltale board [sports]
Squash **So: 813** *with diagram*
Tellurium [element] **T: 129**
Metalloid **M: 426**
Telnaes, Inge [Norwegian programmer]
Slot machine **S: 508a**
Telogen [anatomy]
Hair (Cycles of hair growth) **H: 10**
Telophase [biology]
Cell (Mitosis) **C: 330-331**
Telson [biology]
Crustacean (The body of a crustacean) **Ci: 1162** *with diagram*
Telstar 1 [communications satellite]
Communication *picture on* **Ci: 886**
Communications satellite (History) **Ci: 888b-889**
New Jersey (Communication) **N: 248**
Telugu [language]
Dravidians **D: 342**
India (Languages) **I: 114**; (India in the 1950's and early 1960's) **I: 133**
Temajeq language
Berbers **B: 256**
Temasek [former name]
Singapore (History) **S: 471**
Temin, Howard Martin [American physiologist]
Nobel Prizes (Physiology or medicine: 1975) **N: 446**
Temne [people]
Sierra Leone (People) **S: 451**
Tempel 1 [comet]
Comet (Studying comets) **Ci: 868-869**
Space exploration (Probes to comets) **So: 711**
Tempel-Tuttle, Comet [astronomy]
Comet (table) **Ci: 868**
Meteor (Meteor showers) **M: 431**
Tempera [paint]
Painting (Tempera) **P: 38** *with picture*
Temperament [psychology]
Child (Psychological differences) **C: 450**
Temperance movement [social reform]

Nation, Carry Amelia Moore **N: 26**
Prohibition (Prohibition in the United States) **P: 815**
Women's movement (The beginnings of women's movements) **W: 384-385**
Temperance Union, Woman's Christian *See* Woman's Christian Temperance Union *in this index*
Temperate bass [fish]
Bass (True bass) **B: 156**
Temperate coniferous forest
Biome **B: 322**; (table) **B: 323** *with map*
Plant (Temperate deciduous forests) **P: 523** *with map*; (Plants of the temperate coniferous forest) **P: 524** *with picture*
Temperate deciduous forest
Animal (Animals of the temperate forests) **A: 478** *with pictures*
Biome **B: 324**; (table) **B: 323** *with map*
Forest *picture on* **F: 391**; (Kinds of forests) **F: 392** *with map*
Plant (Temperate deciduous forests) **P: 523** *with map*; (Plants of the temperate deciduous forest) **P: 525** *with picture*
Temperate evergreen forest
Animal (Animals of the temperate forests) **A: 478** *with pictures*
Forest *picture on* **F: 391**; (Kinds of forests) **F: 392z** *with map*
Temperate forest
Forest (Kinds of forests) **F: 392-393**
Temperate fruit
Fruit (Types of fruits in horticulture) **F: 546** *with pictures*
Temperate glacier [geology]
Glacier (Kinds of glaciers) **G: 202**
Temperate savanna
Forest (Temperate savannas) **F: 395** *with map*
Temperate zone [geography]
Bird (The distribution of birds) **B: 331-332**
Gardening (Choosing the site) **G: 31**
Rain (The ice-crystal process) **R: 124**
Temperature **T: 130**
Air *diagram on* **A: 171**
Automation (How automation works) **A: 945** *with diagram*
Celsius scale **C: 342**
Climate **Ci: 675**
Extremophile **E: 458**
Fahrenheit scale **F: 6**
Global warming **G: 232**
Greenhouse effect (Increases in greenhouse gases) **G: 383**
Heat (Temperature and heat) **H: 150**; (Changes in temperature) **H: 152**
Heating **H: 157**
Metric system (Structure of the metric system) **M: 437**; (The metric system at a glance) **M: 438-439** *with picture*; (Heat) **M: 440**
Ocean (Temperature) **O: 653**
Sun **So: 975**
Thermography **T: 254**
Thermometer **T: 254**
Weather (Air temperature) **W: 157**; (table: Weather terms) **W: 157**
Temperature, Body [physiology] **T: 130**
Animal (Some common ways of grouping animals) **A: 472**
Bee (Regulating body temperature) **B: 202**
Cold-blooded animal **Ci: 761**
Dinosaur (How dinosaurs lived) **D: 211**
Fever **F: 83**
First aid (Heatstroke and heat exhaustion) **F: 141**
Fish (How fish adjust to change) **F: 168**
Homeostasis **H: 303**
Hyperthermia **H: 477**
Hypothermia **H: 481**
Perspiration **P: 305**
Races, Human (Climatic adaptations) **R: 58**
Warm-blooded animal **W: 36**
Temperature and pressure relief valve
Plumbing (The water supply system) **P: 577-578**
Temperature-humidity index
Heat index **H: 156**
Temperature inversion [meteorology]
Air (The troposphere) **A: 172-173**
Air pollution (Chief sources of air pollution) **A: 198**; (Health) **A: 199**
Smog **S: 519**
Weather (How people affect the weather) **W: 170**
Tempered glass
Glass (Specialty glasses) **G: 212**
Tempered safety glass
Glass (Specialty glasses) **G: 212**
Tempering [industrial process] **T: 130**
Glass (Tempering) **G: 217**
Tempest, The [painting by Giorgione]

Painting (The Renaissance in Venice) **P: 55-56** *with picture*
Tempest, The [painting by Kokoschka]
Painting (People) **P: 31** *with picture*
Tempest, The [play by Shakespeare]
Shakespeare, William (His last years) **S: 348**; (The Tempest) **S: 365**
Tempietto [Rome]
Bramante, Donato **B: 562** *with picture*
Templars, Knights *See* Knights Templars *in this index*
Temple [fruit]
Tangor **T: 27**
Temple [religion] **T: 131** *with picture*
See also Church *in this index*
Architecture (Mesopotamian architecture) **A: 611** *with picture*; (Classical Greek architecture) **A: 615** *with pictures*
Egypt, Ancient *picture on* **E: 141**; (Arts and sciences) **E: 139**
Greece, Ancient *picture on* **G: 370**; (The arts) **G: 369**
Hinduism (Worship in temples) **H: 237**
India (The arts) **I: 119** *with pictures*
Indonesia (Architecture) **I: 237**
Judaism (The synagogue) **J: 181**
World, History of the *pictures on* **W: 426, W: 430**
Temple, Henry John [British political leader]
Palmerston, Viscount **P: 111**
Temple, Shirley [American actress] **T: 131** *with picture*
Robinson, Bill **R: 367**
Temple, William [American political leader]
Delaware (table) **D: 109**
Temple in Jerusalem
Jerusalem (Jewish sites) **J: 95**; (Ancient times) **J: 100**
Jews (The kingdom of Israel) **J: 121**
Palestine (Invasions and conquests) **P: 104**
Solomon **So: 584**
Tishah be-Av **T: 298**
Temple mound
Mound builders (Mississippian Period) **M: 883** *with picture*
Temple Mount [area]
Israel (The early 2000's) **I: 489**
Sharon, Ariel **S: 377**
Temple of ...
Temples appear under their key words, as in Artemis, Temple of
Temple School [Boston]
Alcott, Bronson **A: 338**
Temple Scroll
Dead Sea Scrolls **D: 56**
Temple Square [Salt Lake City]
Salt Lake City (The city) **S: 76**
Utah (Visitor's guide) **U: 238** *with picture*
Temples of Abu Simbel [Egypt] *See* Abu Simbel, Temples of *in this index*
Templeton, Charles A. [American political leader]
Connecticut (table) **Ci: 967**
Tempo [music]
Music (Indicating time values) **M: 953-955**
Tempo, Il [newspaper]
Rome (Economy) **R: 431**
Temporal artery [anatomy]
Human body (table) **H: 422** *with diagram*
Temporal bone [anatomy]
Ear *diagram on* **E: 8**; (The outer ear) **E: 7**
Head *diagram on* **H: 123**
Human body (table) **H: 422** *with diagram*
Skull **S: 495**
Temporal gland [zoology]
Elephant (Musth) **E: 231**
Temporal lobe [anatomy]
Brain (The cerebrum) **B: 550a-550b** *with diagram*
Temporal muscle [anatomy]
Head *diagram on* **H: 123**
Temporal type [classification]
Archaeology (Classification) **A: 597**
Temporary Assistance to Needy Families [U. S. program]
Aid to Families with Dependent Children **A: 163**
Welfare (Cash aid programs) **W: 190**; (Welfare reform in the United States) **W: 191-192**
Temporary injunction [law]
Injunction **I: 272**
Restraining order **R: 263**
Temporary insider [business]
Insider trading **I: 303**
Temporary magnet
Magnetism (Kinds of magnets) **M: 60**
Temporary visitor [law]
Alien **A: 367**
Temptation of Saint Anthony, The [book by Flaubert]
Flaubert, Gustave **F: 230**

Temptation of Saint Anthony, The [painting by Bosch]
Bosch, Hieronymus **B: 491**
Temptations of Big Bear, The [book by Wiebe]
Canadian literature (Modern English-Canadian fiction) **C: 160**
Temüjin [birth name of]
Genghis Khan (Rise to power) **G: 88**
Ten Commandments [religion] **T: 131**
Ark of the Covenant **A: 693**
Bible (The Law) **B: 280**
Exodus **E: 438**
Law (Early developments in the East) **L: 133**
Moses **M: 828**
Religion *picture on* **R: 220**
Shavuot **S: 377**
Ten Commandments, The [film]
DeMille, Cecil B. **D: 119**
Heston, Charlton **H: 220**
Ten Days That Shook the World [book by Reed]
Reed, John **R: 194**
Ten Days That Shook the World [film]
Eisenstein, Sergei Mikhailovich **E: 155**
Ten-gallon hat
Stetson, John Batterson **So: 895**
Ten-lined June beetle [insect]
Beetle *picture on* **B: 218**
Ten lost tribes [ancient Israel]
Jews (Foreign domination) **J: 121**
Ten Plagues
Moses (The Exodus) **M: 828-829**
10-point must system
Boxing (Scoring a fight) **B: 528**
Ten-second rule
Basketball (Changes in the game) **B: 151-152**
Ten-spot dragonfly
Insect *picture on* **I: 280**
Ten Thousand Smokes, Valley of the
Katmai National Park **K: 249**
Ten Wings [text]
I Ching **I: 2**
Ten Years' War [1868-1878]
Cuba (Struggle against Spain) **Ci: 1176**
Tenancy at will [law]
Tenant **T: 132**
Tenancy for years [law]
Tenant **T: 132**
Tenant [law] **T: 132**
Fixture **F: 191**
Lease **L: 166**
Tenant farming **T: 132**
Tenant farming [agriculture] **T: 132**
Asia (Farm organization) **A: 800**
Farm and farming (Farm owners and farm operators) **F: 41**
United States, History of the (The South and white supremacy) **U: 183-185**
Tenant of Wildfell Hall, The [book by Brontë]
Brontë sisters (Their works) **B: 637**
Tenant's Relief Bill [1886]
Parnell, Charles Stewart **P: 177**
Tenasserim Coast
Myanmar (Climate) **M: 970c**
Tenaya [American Indian chief]
Yosemite National Park (Yosemite Valley) **Y: 570**
Tenaya Lake [California]
Yosemite National Park (Hetch Hetchy Valley) **Y: 570**
Tender [law] *See* Legal tender *in this index*
Tender Is the Night [book by Fitzgerald]
American literature (The Lost Generation) **A: 421**
Fitzgerald, F. Scott **F: 190**
Tender point [anatomy]
Fibromyalgia **F: 90**
Tenderfoot [rank]
Boy Scouts (Boy Scouting) **B: 535**
Tendinitis [disorder]
Rotator cuff **R: 486**
Tendon [anatomy] **T: 132** *with diagrams*
Human body (Skeletal muscles) **H: 419** *with picture*
Muscle (Skeletal muscles) **M: 933**
Rotator cuff **R: 486**
Tendril [botany]
Leaf (Tendrils) **L: 156** *with picture*
Melon **M: 389**
Tendu [movement]
Ballet (table) **B: 45**; (A ballet class) **B: 46**
Tenebrism [art]
Painting (Baroque) **P: 58**
Tenement [housing] **T: 133**
Housing (The Industrial Revolution) **H: 391**
New York City (Manhattan) **N: 323-324**
United States, History of the (The rich and the poor) **U: 182** *with picture*
Urban renewal (History) **U: 220**
Tenement house system

Cottage industry **Ci: 1085**
Tener, John Kinley [American political leader]
Pennsylvania (table) **P: 263**
Tenerife [island]
Canary Islands **C: 165** *with map*
Teng Hsiao-p'ing *See* Deng Xiaoping *in this index*
Teniente, El [mine, Chile]
Chile (Mining) **C: 466**
Teniers, David, the Elder [Flemish artist]
Teniers, David, the Younger **T: 133**
Teniers, David, the Younger [Flemish artist] **T: 133** *with picture*
Tenn-Tom Waterway
Tombigbee River **T: 326**
Tennant, Smithson [British chemist]
Iridium **I: 429**
Osmium **O: 865**
Tennent, Gilbert [American religious leader] **T: 133**
Great Awakening **G: 335**
Tennent, William [American religious leader] **T: 133**
Tennessee **T: 134** *with pictures and maps*
See also the list of Related articles in the Tennessee *article*
Creationism (The 1900's) **Ci: 1123**
Reconstruction (The 14th Amendment) **R: 178**
Westward movement in America (Crossing the Appalachians) **W: 246**
Tennessee, University of **T: 158**
Knoxville (Description) **K: 359**
Tennessee *picture on* **T: 139**
Tennessee Aquarium [Chattanooga]
Tennessee (Places to visit) **T: 144**
Tennessee Banking Association
Tennessee (Reconstruction) **T: 154**
Tennessee Plowboy, The [nickname]
Arnold, Eddy **A: 742**
Tennessee River [U.S.] **T: 158**
Tennessee Valley Authority **T: 158** *with map*
Tennessee Titans [football team]
Football (National Football League) **F: 364**
Tennessee-Tombigbee Waterway
Canal (table) **C: 164**
Tombigbee River **T: 326**
Tennessee Valley [region, U.S.]
Tennessee Valley Authority (The valley) **T: 158**
Tennessee Valley Authority [U.S.] **T: 158** *with picture and map*
Alabama (World War I and the Great Depression) **A: 276-278**
Conservation (The rise of the conservation movement) **Ci: 985-986**
Lilienthal, David Eli **L: 303**
Muscle Shoals **M: 936**
Norris, George William **N: 457**
Tennessee *picture on* **T: 155**; (Rivers and lakes) **T: 148**; (Electric power and utilities) **T: 151**; (The mid-1900's) **T: 156**
Willkie, Wendell Lewis (His life) **W: 314**
Tennessee walking horse
Horse *picture on* **H: 344**; (Saddle horses) **H: 343**; (table) Some types and breeds of horses) **H: 343**
Tennessee *picture on* **T: 138**
Tennessee whiskey
Whiskey **W: 282**
"Tennessee's Partner" [story by Harte]
Harte, Bret **H: 78**
Tenniel, Sir John [British artist] **T: 160** *with pictures*
John Bull **J: 133**
Literature for children *picture on* **L: 376**; (The rise of illustration) **L: 364**
Tennis [sport] **T: 161** *with pictures*
See also the list of Related articles in the Tennis *article*
Davis Cup **D: 50**
Olympic Games (Summer Olympic Games) **O: 746e-748**
Russia *picture on* **R: 535**
Tennis, Platform [sport]
Platform tennis **P: 565** *with picture*
Tennis Association, United States
Tennis (The spread of tennis) **T: 165**
Tennis cabinet [U.S. history]
Roosevelt, Theodore (Life in the White House) **R: 465-466**
Tennis court
Tennis *diagram on* **T: 162**
Tennis Court Oath [French history]
Estates-General **E: 360**
French Revolution (The revolution begins) **F: 525**
Tennis elbow [disorder]
Elbow **E: 157**
Tennis Federation, International
Tennis (Amateur tennis) **T: 165**
Tennis for Two [electronic game]
Electronic game (History) **E: 204d**

Tennis shoes
Shoe (Kinds of shoes) **S: 431** *with picture*
Tennis (Tennis clothes) **T: 162**
Tennyson, Lord [British poet] **T: 166f** *with portrait*
Balaklava, Battle of **B: 34**
English literature (Later Victorian literature) **E: 321**
Galahad, Sir **G: 7**
January (Quotations) **J: 31**
Poetry **P: 591**
Tenochca [people]
Aztec **A: 999**
Tenochtitlan [ancient city, Mexico] **T: 167**
Aztec **A: 999** *with picture and map*
Cortés, Hernán (Arrival in Mexico) **Ci: 1072-1073** *with map*
Exploration (Spain's conquests in the New World) **E: 445**
Hispanic Americans (In Mexico) **H: 248**
Indian, American *picture on* **I: 136**; (Indians of Middle America) **I: 169-171** *with picture*
Mexico (The Mesa Central) **M: 462**; (The Toltec and the Aztec) **M: 468**; (The Spanish conquest) **M: 469**
Mexico City (City of the Aztec) **M: 478**
Montezuma II **M: 764b**
Tenor [voice]
Opera (The singers) **O: 792**
Singing (Voice classification) **S: 472**
Tenor tuba [musical instrument]
Tuba **T: 477**
Tenrec [animal] **T: 167** *with picture*
Mammal *picture on* **M: 128**
Tense [grammar] **T: 167**
Tensile strength [physical property]
Cohesion **Ci: 756**
Tension [sewing]
Sewing (Seams) **S: 332**
Tension-type headache
Headache (Primary headache) **H: 124**
Tenskwatawa *See* Shawnee Prophet *in this index*
Tent [dwelling] **T: 168**
See also Tipi *in this index*
Asia *picture on* **A: 790**
Camping *pictures on* **C: 95**; (Tents) **C: 93**; (Selecting a location) **C: 94**
Circus (The circus grows) **Ci: 562b**
Mongol Empire **M: 719**, *picture on* **M: 721**
Mongolia (The people) **M: 722** *with picture*
Recreational vehicle (Folding camping trailers) **R: 184**
Tent caterpillar [insect] **T: 168** *with picture*
Tent Chautauqua [entertainment]
Chautauqua (Tent Chautauquas) **C: 389**
Tent of Meeting *See* Tabernacle *in this index*
Tent of Miracles [book by Amado]
Amado, Jorge **A: 400**
Tent olive shell
Shell *picture on* **S: 386**
Tent school
Niger (People) **N: 407-408**
Tent stitch
Petit point **P: 326**
Tentacle [zoology] **T: 169**
Jellyfish **J: 90** *with picture*
Mollusk (Gastropods) **M: 695**; (Octopuses and squids) **M: 695**
Octopus (The body of an octopus) **O: 672** *with pictures*
Oyster (Body organs) **O: 890**
Scallop **S: 170** *with picture*
Sea anemone **S: 262**
Snail **S: 522** *with diagram*
Squid (The body of a squid) **So: 814** *with picture*
Tenth Amendment [U.S. Constitution]
Constitution of the United States **Ci: 1013**
Tenth Month, The [book by Hobson]
Hobson, Laura Z. **H: 273**
Tenth Muse Lately Sprung Up in America, The [poems by Bradstreet]
American literature (New England) **A: 414**
Bradstreet, Anne **B: 546**
Tenure [employment]
Teaching (Employment practices) **T: 68**
Tenure [ownership]
Feudalism (The beginnings of feudalism) **F: 81-82**
Tenure of Kings and Magistrates, The [pamphlet by Milton]
Milton, John (Middle years) **M: 557**
Tenure of Office Act [1867]
Johnson, Andrew (Increased tension) **J: 140**
Reconstruction (The impeachment of Johnson) **R: 178**
Tenzin Gyatso [Tibetan religious leader] *See* Dalai Lama *in this index*
Tenzing Norgay [Nepalese mountain climber] **T: 169**

Hillary, Sir Edmund Percival **H: 231** *with picture*
Mount Everest **M: 884**
Teocalli [religion]
Aztec (Religion) **A: 1000**
Teodoro, Rio [river, Brazil]
Madeira River **M: 30**
Teosinte [plant]
Corn (History) **Ci: 1062**
Plant (How crops differ from wild plants) **P: 542** *with picture*
Teotihuacán [ancient city, Mexico] **T: 169**
Indian, American (Before European contact) **I: 169**
Maya (The Classic Period) **M: 325**
Mexico (The Classic Period) **M: 468**
Pyramids (American pyramids) **P: 917** *with picture*
Tepal [botany]
Flower (The calyx) **F: 293**
Tepee [dwelling] *See* Tipi *in this index*
Tepehuan Indians
Durango **D: 387**
Tepes, Vlad [Transylvanian prince]
Dracula **D: 317**
Transylvania **T: 402**
Tequila [drink]
Alcoholic beverage (Other distilled drinks) **A: 337**
Maguey **M: 63**
Ter-Petrosyan, Levon [Armenian political leader]
Armenia (History) **A: 718b-719**
Tera [prefix]
Metric system (Metric prefixes) **M: 439**
Terabyte [unit of measure]
Computer (Computer code) **Ci: 911**
Teratogen [harmful substance]
Reproduction, Human (Development of organs and organ systems) **R: 248**
Terbium [element] **T: 169**
Terbutaline [drug]
Bronchodilator **B: 637**
TERCOM [electronics] *See* Terrain contour mapping *in this index*
Terence [Roman dramatist] **T: 169**
Drama (Comedy) **D: 328**; (Medieval drama) **D: 328**
Latin literature (Early Latin literature) **L: 115-116**
Teres minor [muscle]
Rotator cuff **R: 486**
Teresa, Mother [Indian religious leader] **T: 169** *with portrait*
Teresa, Saint [Spanish religious leader] **T: 170**
Religious life (Religious life in the 1500's and 1600's) **R: 227**
Spanish literature (The 1500's) **So: 759**
Tereshkova, Valentina Vladimirovna [Soviet cosmonaut] **T: 170**
Astronaut *picture on* **A: 833**; (Achievements in space) **A: 829**; (table) **A: 830**
Space exploration (Vostok and Mercury: The first human beings in space) **So: 712-714** *with picture*
Terfel, Bryn [Welsh singer] **T: 170** *with portrait*
Term [mathematics]
Algebra (Statements and equations) **A: 351**
Fraction (In symbols) **F: 444**
Geometry (Axiomatic system) **G: 102**
Progression **P: 812**
Term life insurance
Insurance (Major types of life insurance) **I: 309**
Term limits [government] **T: 170**
Term paper
A Guide to Writing Skills **Research Guide: 14**
Terminal [electricity]
Battery *diagrams on* **B: 170**; (Battery structure) **B: 168**
Electronics (Diodes) **E: 210** *with diagram*
Transistor (How transistors work) **T: 372-373**
Terminal ballistics [engineering]
Ballistics (Terminal ballistics) **B: 56** *with picture*
Terminal bud [botany]
Bud **B: 665** *with diagram*
Plant (Stems) **P: 529** *with pictures*
Terminal building
Airport (The passenger terminal) **A: 244** *with diagrams*; (Terminal designs) **A: 248** *with diagram*
Terminal elevator
Grain elevator (Kinds of grain elevators) **G: 301**
Terminal emulation program [software]
Computer (Internet software) **Ci: 922**
Terminal guidance system
Guided missile (Preset guidance) **G: 426**
Terminal market
Food (Marketing) **F: 335**
Livestock (Marketing livestock) **L: 398**
Meat packing (Marketing livestock and meat) **M: 350**
Terminal moraine [geology]

Glacier (How glaciers shape the land) **G: 203** *with diagram*
Moraine **M: 799**
Terminal side [geometry]
Angle **A: 462**
Terminal Tower Building [Cleveland]
Cleveland *picture on* **Ci: 667**; (Downtown Cleveland) **Ci: 663-664** *with picture and map*
Terminating decimal [mathematics]
Decimal system (Decimals and fractions) **D: 72** *with diagram*
Rational number **R: 148**
Termination policy [U.S. history]
Indian, American (In the United States) **I: 179**
Termination shock [astronomy]
Cosmic rays (Anomalous component cosmic rays) **Ci: 1076**
Heliosphere (Shock waves) **H: 175**
Voyager **V: 452**
Terminator [astronomy]
Moon (Rotation and orbit) **M: 783**
Terminus [Roman mythology]
Mythology (Roman divinities) **M: 982-983**
Terminus [town]
Atlanta (Early days) **A: 861**
Termite [insect] **T: 171** *with pictures*
Insect *pictures on* **I: 279, I: 281**; (Harmful insects) **I: 284**; (Abdomen) **I: 288**; (Reproduction) **I: 292**; (The life cycle of insects) **I: 292**; (Family life) **I: 294-295**
Isoptera **I: 475**
Terms of Endearment [book by McMurtry]
McMurtry, Larry **M: 343**
Terms of Endearment [film]
Motion picture (Best picture: 1983) **M: 861**
Nicholson, Jack **N: 404**
Tern [bird] **T: 172**
Animal *picture on* **A: 468**; (Animal travelers) **A: 502**
Arctic tern **A: 644** *with picture*
Bird *pictures on* **B: 329, B: 344e**; (Birds of the seacoasts) **B: 342** *with picture*; (Birds of the Arctic) **B: 343** *with picture*; (Birds of Europe) **B: 344c**; (Bird migration) **B: 360**
Ternary form [music]
Classical music (Sectional form) **Ci: 644**
Terneplate [metal]
Tin (Uses) **T: 293**
Terpene [chemical]
Lipid (Kinds of lipids) **L: 345**
Terpsichore [Greek mythology]
Muses **M: 937**
Mythology *picture on* **M: 981**
Terra [artificial satellite]
Air (The study of air) **A: 175**
Terra [highland]
Moon **M: 783**
Terra [Roman mythology]
Mythology (table) **M: 981**
Terra Australis Incognita [legendary place]
Antarctica (Exploration) **A: 535**
Exploration (Exploring the Pacific) **E: 447**
Torres, Luis Vaez de **T: 342** *with map*
Terra cotta [pottery] **T: 172**
Della Robbia, Luca **D: 116**
Pottery *pictures on* **P: 717**; (Decorating and glazing) **P: 718**
Sculpture (The sculptor at work) **S: 232**
Terra-cotta army of Xi'an [statues, China] **T: 172** *with picture*
Terra Nostra [book by Fuentes]
Fuentes, Carlos **F: 553**
Terra Nova [ship]
Scott, Robert Falcon **S: 222**
Terra Nova National Park [Newfoundland and Labrador] **T: 173**
Canada (table: National parks and national park reserves) **C: 113**
Newfoundland and Labrador (Places to visit) **N: 368**
Terrace Hill [mansion]
Iowa *picture on* **I: 375**
Terracing [construction]
Agriculture *picture on* **A: 146**
Conservation (Soil conservation) **Ci: 979-980** *with picture*
Erosion (Controlling erosion) **E: 355**
Peru *picture on* **P: 313**
Philippines *picture on* **P: 372**
Terrain contour mapping
Guided missile (Preset guidance) **G: 426**
Terral, Thomas J. [American political leader]
Arkansas (table) **A: 712**
Terramycin [medication]
Drug (Creating a new drug) **D: 355**
Terrane [geology]
Earth (Terrane collisions) **E: 24**

Terrapin [turtle] **T: 173** *with picture*
Turtle (Pond, box, and water turtles) **T: 522**
Terrarium [biology] **T: 173**
Gardening (Kinds of indoor gardens) **G: 36**
Terrazzo [flooring]
Flooring **F: 239**
Terre, La [book by Choquette]
Canadian literature (Fiction: 1850-1918) **C: 157**
Terrell, Joseph M. [American political leader]
Georgia (table) **G: 130**
Terrell, Mary Church [American social reformer] **T: 173**
Terrestrial animal
Animal (Kinds of animals) **A: 472**
Mammal (On land) **M: 121**
Terrestrial gamma-ray flash
Lightning (Emissions) **L: 301**
Terrestrial globe
Globe **G: 233**
Terrestrial photogrammetry [cartography]
Photogrammetry **P: 405**
Terrestrial planet
Planet **P: 507**
Satellite (Satellites of the terrestrial planets) **S: 150** *with picture*
Solar system (Planets) **So: 580**
Terribilità [art]
Painting (The High Renaissance) **P: 54-55**
"Terrible People, The" [poem by Nash]
Nash, Ogden **N: 22**
Terrier [dog] **T: 173**
Dog *pictures on* **D: 274, D: 275**; (Terriers) **D: 266**
Kerry blue terrier **K: 307**
Parson Russell terrier **P: 182** *with picture*
Silky terrier **S: 462**
Toy fox terrier **T: 354**
Territorial asylum
Asylum **A: 851**
Territorial Enterprise [newspaper]
Nevada (Communication) **N: 172**
Twain, Mark (Newspaper work in the West) **T: 529**
Territorial sea [law]
Ocean (Who owns the ocean?) **O: 665**
Territorial waters [international law] **T: 173**
International law (Consent of nations) **I: 341**
Right of search **R: 340**
Territoriality [zoology] **T: 174**
Animal (Home ranges) **A: 501**
Balance of nature (Behavior) **B: 35**
Bird (Calls and songs) **B: 354**; (Selecting a territory) **B: 356**
Dog (Behavior) **D: 277**
Dominance **D: 301**
Hawk (Breeding) **H: 111**
Lion (Habits) **L: 341**
Mammal (Territoriality) **M: 125**
Prairie dog (Habits) **P: 732**
Seal (Seal rookeries) **S: 266**
Tiger (The life of a tiger) **T: 284**
Wolf (Habits) **W: 375-376**
Territory [animal] *See* Territoriality *in this index*
Territory [political unit] **T: 174**
Annexation **A: 517**
Canada, Government of (The three territories) **C: 136**
Commonwealth of Nations (Dependencies) **Ci: 876**
Trust territory **T: 474**
Terror [ship]
Exploration (The exploration of Antarctica) **E: 450**
Terror, Mount [volcano, Antarctica] *See* Mount Terror *in this index*
Terrorism [political] **T: 175** *with pictures*
See also September 11 terrorist attacks *in this index*
Anarchism **A: 448**
Arabs (Relations with Europe and the United States) **A: 590a**
Australia (Iraq War and counterterrorism) **A: 925**
Aviation (Airline safety concerns) **A: 991**; (Recent developments) **A: 991**
Bin Laden, Osama **B: 307**
Central Intelligence Agency (History) **C: 357**
Civil defense **Ci: 605**
Civil rights (The war on terrorism) **Ci: 610**
Clinton, Bill (International affairs) **Ci: 682f**
Crime (Political crime) **Ci: 1137**
Egypt (Recent developments) **E: 133-134**
Federal Bureau of Investigation **F: 62**
Fire department (Recent developments) **F: 129**
Geneva Conventions **G: 88**
Guerrilla warfare **G: 419**
Hamas **H: 28**
Hezbollah **H: 221**
Hijacking **H: 230**
Homeland Security, Department of **H: 301**
Hostage **H: 374a**

Immigration and Naturalization Service I: 86
Improvised explosive device I: 95
India (Recent developments) I: 134-135
Indonesia (Recent developments) I: 239
International relations (The war against
 terrorism) I: 346
Iran (Recent developments) I: 406b
Ireland (The Republic of Ireland) I: 427-428
Irish Republican Army I: 433
Italy (Social problems) I: 518
Jordan (Recent developments) J: 165-166
Ku Klux Klan (Birth of the Klan) K: 390
Lebanon (War and terrorism) L: 173
Libya (Strained relations with the United States)
 L: 268; (United Nations sanctions) L: 268
London (Recent developments) L: 443
Madrid (History) M: 40
Moscow (Recent developments) M: 827
Mumbai (History) M: 925
New York City (Problems) N: 342-343
Northern Ireland (The Troubles) N: 525
Norway (Recent developments) N: 547
Nuclear weapon (Post-Cold War strategy) N: 600
Oklahoma (Recent developments) O: 734
Oklahoma City bombing O: 737 with picture
Olympic Games (Terrorism in Munich) O: 752
Pakistan (Musharraf) P: 100
Patriot Act P: 197
Pentagon Building P: 274
Petroleum (Petroleum and security) P: 346-347
Qa`ida, Al- Q: 2
Reign of Terror R: 207
Ridge, Tom R: 336
Russia (Recent developments) R: 555
September 11 terrorist attacks S: 310
Spain (Growth and discontent) So: 751; (The
 early 2000's) So: 752 with picture
State, Department of (Since World War II) So: 862
Transportation (Transportation security) T: 398
Troubles T: 453
United Kingdom (Recent developments) U: 74
United Nations (Fighting terrorism) U: 93
United States, Government of the (Responding to
 world events) U: 146
United States, History of the (September 11
 terrorist attacks) U: 196d with picture
War (The war against terrorism) W: 26
World, History of the (The war on terrorism)
 W: 448b
World Trade Center W: 451
Yemen (Unification) Y: 564
Terry, Alfred H. [American general]
 Custer, George Armstrong (The 1876 campaign)
 Ci: 1200
Terry, Alice [American actress]
 Valentino, Rudolph V: 264
Terry, Bill [American baseball player]
 Baseball (table: Hall of Fame) B: 134b
Terry, Charles L., Jr. [American political leader]
 Delaware (table) D: 109
Terry, Eli [American inventor]
 Connecticut (The 1800's) Ci: 970
Terry, Ellen [British actress] T: 181
Terry, Lucy [American poet]
 African American literature (Early works) A: 136-
 136a
Terry cloth
 Textile (table: Textile terms) T: 213
Tertiary color
 Color (Producing color harmony) Ci: 823-824
 with diagram
Tertiary consumer [ecology]
 Forest (The flow of energy) F: 396
Tertiary industry
 Industry (By stage of production) I: 256-257
Tertiary recovery [industrial process]
 Petroleum diagram on P: 341; (Secondary and
 tertiary recovery) P: 342
Tertiary sewage treatment
 Sewage (Urban sewerage systems) S: 329
 Water pollution (Sewage treatment) W: 138
Tertz, Abram [Soviet author]
 Russian literature (Modern Soviet literature)
 R: 564
Terza rima [poetry]
 Divine Comedy D: 242
 Poetry (Renaissance poetry) P: 596
Teschen, Treaty of [1779]
 Succession wars (The War of the Bavarian
 Succession) So: 950
Teskey, Laureen [wife of]
 Harper, Stephen Joseph (Reform Party pioneer)
 H: 66a with picture
Tesla [measurement]
 Magnetism (Strength of a magnetic field) M: 60
 Tesla, Nikola (Other inventions) T: 181
 Weber W: 175

Tesla, Nikola [American inventor] T: 181
 Edison, Thomas Alva (Personal life) E: 81
 Electric generator (Uses of AC generators) E: 173
 Electric motor (History) E: 181
 Marconi, Guglielmo (Marconi and Tesla) M: 197
 Radio (Early development) R: 91
 Westinghouse Electric Corporation W: 242
Tesla coil [electronics]
 Radio (Early development) R: 91
 Tesla, Nikola (Other inventions) T: 181
Tesla Electric Company
 Tesla, Nikola (The alternating-current system)
 T: 181
Tesla Roadster [car]
 Automobile picture on A: 947
 Battery picture on B: 168
Teslon [biololgy]
 Horseshoe crab H: 368
Tess of the d'Urbervilles [book by Hardy]
 Hardy, Thomas H: 59
Tessellae
 Mosaic M: 822
Tesserae [art]
 Mosaic M: 822
Tesserae [astronomy]
 Venus (Surface and atmosphere) V: 311-312
Test See Testing in this index
Test [shell]
 Sea urchin S: 263 with picture
Test Acts [English history] T: 181
Test ban [international relations]
 Cold War (Easing Cold War tensions) Ci: 769
 Nuclear weapon (Arms control) N: 600
Test Ban Treaty [1963]
 Fallout (History) F: 19
 Kennedy, John Fitzgerald (Arms control) K: 266
Test match [sports]
 Cricket (History) Ci: 1134-1135
Test pilot [aviation] T: 182
Test-tube baby
 Fertilization F: 78
 In vitro fertilization I: 95
Test tube skin
 Skin grafting S: 494
Testamentary trust [economics]
 Trust fund (Kinds of trusts) T: 474
Testator [law]
 Will W: 306
Testatrix [law]
 Will W: 306
Testaverde, Vinnie [American football player]
 Football (table) F: 363
Testes [anatomy] See Testicle in this index
Testicle [anatomy] T: 182
 Frog picture on F: 537
 Gland G: 209
 Human body (table) H: 422 with diagram; (The
 reproductive system) H: 425
 Reproduction, Human (The human reproductive
 system) R: 244-245 with diagram
 Sexuality (Biological factors) S: 337
 Testicular cancer T: 182
 Testosterone T: 182a
 Vasectomy V: 287
Testicular cancer [disease] T: 182
Testimonial
 Advertising (Testimonials) A: 76 with picture
 Sales (Presentation) S: 63
Testimonial evidence See Direct evidence in this
 index
Testimony [law]
 Deposition D: 149
 Witness W: 374
Testing [evaluation] T: 182
 Clinical psychology (Testing and diagnosis)
 Ci: 681
 College entrance examination Ci: 775
 Differentiated instruction D: 200
 Education (How can student performance be
 improved?) E: 105
 Educational psychology (What educational
 psychologists study) E: 111
 Grading G: 296
 Intelligence quotient (Calculating IQ) I: 320;
 (Problems of intelligence testing) I: 320
 Personality (Ratings and self-reports) P: 301;
 (Projective tests) P: 301
 Psychology (Systematic assessment) P: 848
 Races, Human (Race and discrimination) R: 59-60
 Teaching (Checking student progress) T: 67
Testis See Testicle in this index
Testosterone [hormone] T: 182a
 Adolescent (Physical development) A: 60-61
 Elephant (Musth) E: 231
 Erectile dysfunction E: 349
 Marijuana (Effects) M: 201
 Reproduction, Human (The human reproductive

system) R: 244-245
 Steroid (The sex steroids) So: 894
 Testicle T: 182
TET [reproduction] See Tubal embryo transfer in
 this index
Tet Offensive [1968] T: 182a
 Vietnam War (The Tet Offensive) V: 375
Tetanus [disease] T: 182b
Tetany [disorder] T: 182b
Tête-bêche error
 Stamp collecting picture on So: 831
Tethyan Mountain System
 Mountain (The Tethyan Mountain System) M: 895
Tethys [satellite]
 Satellite (The middle-sized icy satellites of Saturn
 and Uranus) S: 150c
 Saturn (Satellites) S: 151-152
Tethys Sea [geology]
 Mediterranean Sea (Formation) M: 382
Tetley, Glen [American choreographer]
 Ballet (Ballet in Europe) B: 54
Teton, Grand See Grand Teton National Park in
 this index
Teton Dam [Teton River, Idaho]
 Idaho (The late 1900's) I: 45
Teton Range [mountains, Wyoming] T: 182b
 Grand Teton National Park G: 309 with picture
 Mountain picture on M: 895
Teton Sioux Indians
 Crazy Horse Ci: 1123
 Sioux Indians S: 475
Tetra [fish] T: 182b
 Aquarium, Home picture on A: 578a
 Fish picture on F: 157
Tetracycline [medication] T: 182b
 Acne A: 28
 Typhus (Treatment) T: 541
Tetradrachm [coin]
 Coin collecting picture on Ci: 758
Tetragonal system
 Crystal (Classifying crystals) Ci: 1166 with picture
Tetrahedron [geometry]
 Geometry (Solid geometry) G: 104-105
 Polyhedron P: 651 with diagram
Tetrahydrocannabinol [chemical]
 Drug abuse (Marijuana) D: 362
 Hashish H: 82
Tetrahydrofuran [chemical]
 Furfural F: 566
Tetraiodothyronine [hormone] See Thyroxine in
 this index
Tetralogy of Fallot [disorder]
 Heart (Blockage of blood flow) H: 141
Tetrameter [poetry]
 Poetry (table) P: 594
Tetrapod [animal] T: 182b with diagram
 Amphibian (The history of amphibians) A: 441
 Fish (The first fish) F: 171
 Fossil (Tracing the development of life) F: 423
 Prehistoric animal (The move onto land) P: 737
 Tiktaalik T: 287
Tetrode [electronics]
 Vacuum tube (History) V: 259
Tetrodotoxin [chemical]
 Zombie Z: 598
Tetrohydrobiopterin [vitamin]
 Phenylketonuria P: 357
Tetum [language]
 East Timor (People) E: 41
Tetzel, Johann [German religious leader] T: 183
 Luther, Martin (The Ninety-Five Theses) L: 527
Teufelsberg [hill]
 Berlin (Recreation) B: 262
Teutoburg Forest, Battle of [A.D. 9]
 Augustus (Expansion of the empire) A: 889
Teutonic Knights [European history] T: 183
 Estonia (History) E: 362
 Latvia (History) L: 119
 Lithuania (History) L: 389
Teutonic languages
 Teutons T: 183
Teutonic names
 Name (Teutonic names) N: 5
Teutons [ancient people] T: 183
 Mythology picture on M: 975; (Teutonic
 mythology) M: 985 with pictures
TeV [measurement unit]
 Particle accelerator (How accelerators work)
 P: 184
Tevatron [machine]
 Fermi National Accelerator Laboratory F: 74
Tew, Thomas [British pirate]
 Pirate picture on P: 495
Tewkesbury, Battle of [1471]
 Henry VI [of England] H: 187
Tex [book by Hinton]
 Hinton, S. E. H: 237

Texans, Houston [team] *See* Houston Texans *in this index*
Texarkana [Arkansas, Texas]
  Arkansas (Interesting facts about Arkansas) A: 695 *with picture*
Texas [state] T: 184 *with pictures and maps*
  See also the list of Related articles in the Texas *article*
  Austin, Stephen Fuller A: 893
  Bowie, James B: 520
  Buchanan, James (Secretary of state) B: 660
  Bush, George Walker (Governor of Texas) B: 722e
  Flag *pictures on* F: 210
  Hispanic Americans (In the Southwest) H: 251
  Houston, Sam H: 399
  Jackson, Andrew (Slavery and Texas) J: 14
  Jefferson, State of J: 75
  Mexican War (Background of the war) M: 445
  Mexico (Difficulties of the early republic) M: 471
  Mission life in America (Western missions) M: 618-619
  Polk, James Knox (The Mexican War) P: 643
  Public lands (Acquisition of public lands) P: 858
  Santa Anna, Antonio López de (War with Texas) S: 113
  Texas Rangers T: 210
  Tyler, John (The annexation of Texas) T: 534
  United States, History of the *map on* U: 184; (Manifest destiny) U: 167
  Westward movement in America (Texas) W: 249
Texas [locomotive]
  Civil War, American (Raids) Ci: 629
Texas, Republic of [Texas history]
  Texas (The Republic of Texas) T: 206
Texas, University of T: 210
  Texas *picture on* T: 189
Texas A&M International University [Laredo]
  Texas A&M University T: 210
Texas A&M University T: 210
Texas Centennial Exposition [1936]
  Texas (The early 1900's) T: 207-208
Texas Christian University T: 210
Texas City [Texas]
  Texas (The mid-1900's) T: 208
Texas fever [disease]
  Cattle tick C: 316
Texas fever tick [animal]
  Cattle tick C: 316 *with picture*
Texas Governor's Mansion [Austin]
  Texas (Recent developments) T: 209
Texas Instruments [company]
  Dallas *picture on* D: 14
  Kilby, Jack K: 315
Texas longhorn [animal]
  Cattle (American cattle) C: 315
  Cowboy (On the ranch) Ci: 1110; (The trail drive) Ci: 1111
Texas Memorial Museum
  Austin (Description) A: 892-893
  Texas (Places to visit) T: 194
Texas Navy Flag [U.S. history]
  Flag *picture on* F: 210
Texas Rangers [baseball team]
  Baseball (table) B: 130
  Bush, George Walker (Baseball ownership) B: 722e
  Dallas (Recreation) D: 14
  Rodriguez, Alex R: 399
Texas Rangers [law enforcement] T: 210 *with picture*
  Police (Law and order in America) P: 624
  Texas (Conquering the frontier) T: 207 *with picture*
Texas School Book Depository [Dallas]
  Dallas (Landmarks) D: 11
  Kennedy, John Fitzgerald (The death of Oswald) K: 267 *with picture*
Texas snakeroot [plant]
  Snakeroot S: 536
Texas State Library [Austin]
  Texas (Libraries) T: 188
Texas Tech University
  Lubbock (Description) L: 512
Texas tortoise [animal]
  Tortoise T: 344
Texas v. Johnson [U.S. history]
  Supreme Court of the United States (table) So: 1002
Texcoco, Lake [Mexico] *See* Lake Texcoco *in this index*
Texeira Pinto, Bento [Latin-American author]
  Latin American literature (Colonial literature) L: 112
Texoma, Lake [Oklahoma-Texas]
  Lake Texoma L: 46 *with map*
Text
  Book (Inside a book) B: 464-465

Text ad
  Advertising (The Internet) A: 74
Text-based adventure game
  Electronic game (Early computer games) E: 204d
Text-editing typewriter
  Typewriter (Kinds of typewriters) T: 538
Text file [electronics]
  Computer (Storage devices) Ci: 915
  Data compression D: 41
  Newspaper (Making up the pages) N: 383
Text messaging [communication] T: 211
  Instant messaging I: 304
Text-only file [computing]
  Computer file Ci: 924g
Text type [Bible]
  Bible (Literary contexts) B: 287
Textbook
  Reading (The teaching of reading) R: 157
  Teaching (Guiding and assisting student learning) T: 66
Textile [fabric] T: 212 *with pictures*
  See also the list of Related articles in the Textile *article*
  Acetate A: 25
  Bangladesh (Economy) B: 84 *with picture*
  China *picture on* C: 496
  Fiber F: 86
  Industrial Revolution (The textile industry) I: 248
  Interior design (Choosing patterns and textures) I: 332
  Invention (Economic needs) I: 355; (Prehistoric times) I: 358
  Islamic art (Textiles) I: 469 *with picture*
  Knitting K: 353
  Massachusetts (Progress as a state) M: 292; (The early 1900's) M: 293
  Painting (Supports) P: 36
  Polyester P: 649
  Rhode Island (Industrial expansion) R: 313
  Sewing (Choosing the equipment, fabric, and pattern) S: 332
  Spandex So: 753
  Technology (The Industrial Revolution) T: 75
  United Kingdom (Manufacturing) U: 63-64
Textile cone [shell]
  Shell *picture on* S: 386
Textile engineering
  Engineering (Other specialized fields) E: 287-288
Textile Fiber Products Identification Act [1958]
  Textile (In the United States and Canada) T: 218
Textile Labeling Act [Canada]
  Textile (In the United States and Canada) T: 218
Textile Museum [Washington, D.C.]
  Washington, D.C. (Other Washington museums) W: 75
Textile printing
  Batik B: 165
Texting [communication] *See* Text messaging *in this index*
Texture
  Interior design (Pattern and texture) I: 328 *with picture*; (Choosing patterns and textures) I: 332
  Painting (The elements of painting) P: 34-35
Textured vegetable protein
  Soybean (Soy meal) So: 690
Tezcatlipoca [Aztec god]
  Mythology (Aztec mythology) M: 987
TFM [chemical]
  Lamprey (Destructiveness) L: 55
TGV [train]
  Electric railroad (History) E: 188-189 *with picture*
  France (Transportation) F: 470 *with picture*
  Railroad *picture on* R: 104
  Transportation (Intercity public transportation) T: 393-394
Th [symbol]
  Thorium T: 266
Thaba Ntlenyana [mountain]
  Drakensberg D: 323
Thackeray, Isabella Shawe [wife of]
  Thackeray, William Makepeace (Early career) T: 220
Thackeray, William Makepeace [British author] T: 220
  English literature (Early Victorian literature) E: 321
  Novel (Britain) N: 573
Thaddeus [apostle] *See* Jude, Saint *in this index*
Thaddeus Kosciuszko National Memorial [Pennsylvania]
  National Park System (table: National memorials) N: 54
Thai [language]
  Thailand (Languages) T: 224
Thai [people]
  Thailand T: 221
Thai Rak Thai [political party]
  Thailand (Recent developments) T: 228

Thailand T: 221 *with pictures and maps*
  See also the list of Related articles in the Thailand *article*
  Clothing *pictures on* Ci: 691, Ci: 693
  Cold War (The Vietnam War) Ci: 769
  Developing country D: 173
  Flag *picture on* F: 205
  Mongkut M: 718
  Vientiane V: 363
  Vietnam War *map on* V: 374
Thailand, Gulf of
  China Sea C: 508 *with map*
Thaïs [book by France]
  France, Anatole F: 480
Thakins [political movement]
  Myanmar (British conquest and rule) M: 970d
Thaksin Shinawatra [Thai political leader]
  Thailand (Recent developments) T: 228
Thalamotomy [medicine]
  Parkinson disease (Other treatments) P: 171
Thalamus [anatomy]
  Brain *diagram on* B: 551; (The cerebrum) B: 550a-550b; (The brain stem) B: 550c
  Persistent vegetative state P: 300f
Thalassemia [disorder] T: 228
  Anemia (Excessive destruction of red blood cells) A: 458
Thaler [money]
  Dollar D: 295
Thales [Greek philosopher] T: 228
  Geometry (Greek geometry) G: 106
  Mathematics (The Greeks) M: 306
  Pre-Socratic philosophy P: 772
Thalia [Greek mythology]
  Drama *picture on* D: 327
  Graces G: 296 *with picture*
  Muses M: 937
Thalidomide [drug] T: 29
  Drug (Testing with people) D: 356
Thallium [element] T: 229
Thallium bromide [chemical]
  Thallium T: 229
Thallium iodide [chemical]
  Thallium T: 229
Thallium sulfate [poison]
  Thallium T: 229
Thallium sulfide [chemical]
  Thallium T: 229
Thallus [botany]
  Hornwort H: 341
  Liverwort L: 395
Thames, River [England] T: 229
  England (Rivers and lakes) E: 300-301
  Europe *picture on* E: 380
  London *picture on* L: 431; (Greater London) L: 428; (Other places of interest) L: 437
  River (table) R: 352
  United Kingdom (The English Lowlands) U: 59-61 *with map*
Thames Barrier [gates]
  London *picture on* L: 436; (Other places of interest) L: 437
Thames River [Canada]
  London L: 444
Thames River, Battle of [1813]
  Harrison, William Henry (Army commander) H: 75
  Indiana (Territorial days) I: 215-216
  War of 1812 (Thames River) W: 33
Thana [political unit]
  Bangladesh (Local government) B: 79
"Thanatopsis" [poem by Bryant]
  Bryant, William Cullen (His early works) B: 655
Thanatos [Greek mythology]
  Hypnos H: 477
  Sisyphus S: 477
Thane [English history] T: 229
Thang Long [former name]
  Hanoi H: 53
Thank-you note [correspondence]
  Letter writing (Thank-you notes) L: 213
Thankful Poor, The [painting by Tanner]
  Painting (Painting outside France) P: 72-73 *with picture*
Thanksgiving Day [holiday] T: 230 *with picture*
  Colonial life in America (Plymouth colony) Ci: 789-790
  Hale, Sarah Josepha H: 19
  Holiday (In Canada) H: 291
  Massachusetts (The Pilgrims and Plymouth Colony) M: 289
  New York *picture on* N: 303
  November (Activities) N: 576
  Plymouth Colony (The first year) P: 583 *with picture*
Thanksgiving Dinner [painting by Lee]
  Thanksgiving Day *picture on* T: 230
Thant, U [Burmese diplomat] T: 231

United Nations (The secretary-general) U: 83 *with portrait*

Thar Desert [region, India-Pakistan] T: 231
India (The Northern Plains) I: 121-122; (The rainy season) I: 124 *with map*
Pakistan (Land and climate) P: 96 *with picture and map*

Tharp, Twyla [American dancer] T: 231 *with picture*
Dance (Modern dance) D: 30-31 *with picture*

Tharp, William [American political leader]
Delaware (table) D: 109

That Summer in Paris [book by Callaghan]
Callaghan, Morley C: 67

That Was Then, This Is Now [book by Hinton]
Hinton, S. E. H: 237

Thatch roof
Peru (Housing) P: 309 *with picture*
Rye (Uses) R: 573

Thatcher, Margaret [British political leader] T: 231 *with portrait*
Heseltine, Michael Ray Dibdin H: 218
United Kingdom (Thatcher) U: 73

Thatcher, W. Ross [Canadian political leader]
Saskatchewan (table) S: 144

Thatcher Ferry Bridge *See* Bridge of the Americas

Thaw [Russian history]
Russian literature (Modern Soviet literature) R: 564

Thaw lake [geology]
Tundra T: 485

Thawb [clothing]
Saudi Arabia (Clothing) S: 157

Thayendanegea *See* Brant, Joseph *in this index*

Thayer, Ernest Lawrence [American author]
Literature for children (Masterpieces of poetry) L: 364

Thayer, John M. [American political leader]
Nebraska (table) N: 110

Thayer, Sylvanus [American military leader] T: 231
United States Military Academy (History) U: 202

Thayer, W. W. [American political leader]
Oregon (table) O: 845

Thayer School of Engineering
Dartmouth College D: 39

THC [chemical]
Hashish H: 82
Marijuana (Effects) M: 201

Theaetetus [book by Plato]
Plato (The dialogues) P: 567; (The later dialogues) P: 568; (The theory of forms) P: 568

Theater T: 232 *with pictures*
See also Drama *in this index; and the list of Related articles in the* Theater *article*
Ballet B: 44 *with pictures*
Broadway B: 635
Drama *pictures on* D: 326; (Elizabethan theaters) D: 331; (England) D: 334
Europe *picture on* E: 391
Mask (Theatrical masks) M: 265
New York City (Manhattan) N: 323-325
Shakespeare, William (The Elizabethan theater) S: 351 *with pictures*
United Kingdom (The arts) U: 58
United States *pictures on* U: 119
Vaudeville V: 290

Theater arts
Theater T: 232; (Colleges and universities) T: 249

Theater District [New York City]
Broadway B: 635
New York City *pictures on* N: 335, N: 343; (The arts) N: 336

Theater-in-the-round
Theater (The stage) T: 233-234 *with picture*

Theater missile defense
Guided missile (Surface-to-air missiles) G: 426

Theater nuclear weapon *See* Tactical nuclear weapon *in this index*

Theater of Dionysus [Greece]
Athens (Other buildings) A: 856
Drama (Greek drama) D: 326 *with pictures*

Theater of the Absurd
Albee, Edward A: 310
American literature (Drama) A: 426
Black humor B: 389
Drama (Theater of the Absurd) D: 340 *with picture*
French literature (Developments in drama) F: 523
Irish literature (Drama) I: 432

Theater operations
Army, United States (table) A: 737

Theatine order [religious group]
Paul IV P: 200

Theatre, The [London]
English literature (Elizabethan drama) E: 317
Shakespeare, William (The Globe Theatre) S: 348; (Theater buildings) S: 351

Théâtre du Nouveau Monde, Le [theater group]

Canada (Theater) C: 110

Théâtre Libre [theater group]
Drama (Early realism) D: 338

Theatre Passe Muraille [theater group]
Canadian literature (Modern Canadian drama) C: 161

Theatrical dance
Dance (Dances to watch) D: 28 *with pictures*

Thébaïde, La [play by Racine]
Racine, Jean R: 61

Thebaine [chemical]
Oxycodone O: 889

Theban triad [Egyptian mythology]
Amun A: 445

Thebe [satellite]
Jupiter (Inner satellites) J: 200a *with picture*
Planetary table P: 514d

Thebes [ancient Egyptian city] T: 250
Cleopatra's Needles Ci: 662b
Egypt, Ancient (The land) E: 135-136 *with map*

Thebes [ancient Greek city] T: 251
Alexander the Great (His youth) A: 342
Cadmus C: 12
Sparta (History) So: 766
Sphinx (The Greek sphinx) So: 781

Thegn [title] *See* Thane *in this index*

Theiler, Max [South African bacteriologist]
Nobel Prizes (Physiology or medicine: 1951) N: 445
Yellow fever (Prevention) Y: 556

Thein Sein [Burmese political leader]
Myanmar (Recent developments) M: 970e

Their Eyes Were Watching God [book by Hurston]
American literature (The Harlem Renaissance) A: 422
Hurston, Zora Neale H: 457

"Their finest hour" [quotation]
Churchill, Sir Winston Leonard Spencer (The Battle of Britain) C: 548

Their Satanic Majesties Request [recording]
Rock music (Fresh directions) R: 380

Theism T: 251
God (Ideas about God) G: 244
Pantheism P: 131
Religion (Belief in a deity) R: 215

Them [book by Oates]
Oates, Joyce Carol O: 639

Thema [music by Berio]
Berio, Luciano B: 259

Thematic Apperception Test
Personality (Projective tests) P: 301-302

Thematic map
Map (Types of maps) M: 177-178 *with picture*; (Development of thematic and inventory mapping) M: 185

Theme
Classical music (Variation) Ci: 644
Composition Ci: 905
Drama (Thought) D: 325
Literature (Theme) L: 353
Music (Melody) M: 951

Theme and variation *See* Variation *in this index*

Theme park [recreation]
See also Amusement park *in this index*
Amusement park A: 446
Disney, Walt (TV and theme park ventures) D: 237 *with picture*
Walt Disney Company W: 20

Themistocles [Greek political leader] T: 251
Aristides A: 662

Then Again, Maybe I Won't [book by Blume]
Blume, Judy B: 425

Thenard, Louis Jacques [French chemist]
Boron B: 490

Theobald, Lewis [British author]
Pope, Alexander P: 667
Shakespeare, William (Editions of the 1700's and 1800's) S: 369

Theocracy [political science] T: 251
Government (Theocracy) G: 288

Theocritus [Greek poet] T: 251
Greek literature (The Hellenistic Age) G: 378
Idyl I: 47

Theodemir [king of the Ostrogoths]
Theodoric T: 252

Theodolite [instrument]
Surveying (Early tools) So: 1011

Theodor Seuss Geisel Award
Literature for children (Awards) L: 367

Theodora [wife of Justinian I] T: 252
Byzantine Empire *picture on* B: 754; (Society) B: 752-753
Justinian I J: 204

Theodore [antipope]
Pope (table) P: 666

Theodore I [pope]
Pope (table) P: 666

Theodore II [pope]
Pope (table) P: 666

Theodore M. Hesburgh Library
Notre Dame, University of (The campus) N: 551 *with picture*

Theodore Roosevelt [aircraft carrier]
Aircraft carrier (The United States carrier fleet) A: 206

Theodore Roosevelt [ship]
Bartlett, Robert Abram B: 121
Peary, Robert Edwin (Arctic expeditions) P: 224

Theodore Roosevelt Birthplace National Historic Site [New York]
National Park System (table: National historic sites) N: 52-53

Theodore Roosevelt Dam [Salt River, Arizona] *See* Roosevelt Dam *in this index*

Theodore Roosevelt Inaugural National Historic Site [New York]
National Park System (table: National historic sites) N: 52-53

Theodore Roosevelt Island [Washington, D.C.]
Roosevelt, Theodore *picture on* R: 468

Theodore Roosevelt Island National Memorial [Washington, D.C.]
National Park System (table: National memorials) N: 54

Theodore Roosevelt National Park [North Dakota] T: 252
National Park System (table: National parks) N: 48
North Dakota (Places to visit) N: 504 *with picture*
Roosevelt, Theodore (Death) R: 468

Theodoric [antipope]
Pope (table) P: 666

Theodoric [king of the Ostrogoths] T: 252
Goths G: 280
Italy (The Middle Ages) I: 513

Theodosius I [Roman emperor] T: 252
Inquisition I: 277
Olympic Games (The ancient games) O: 750
Rome, Ancient (The decline of the empire) R: 447-448

Theogony [poem by Hesiod]
Greek literature (Epic poetry) G: 377
Hesiod H: 218
Mythology (Interweaving relationships) M: 976; (Greek mythology) M: 980

Theological-Political Treatise [book by Spinoza]
Spinoza, Baruch So: 795

Theological school *See* Seminary *in this index*

Theology [religion] T: 252
See also Religion *in this index*
Philosophy (Medieval philosophy) P: 388

Theology of Liberation, A [book by Gutiérrez]
Latin America (The rise of military regimes) L: 110
Liberation theology L: 228

Theon [Greek mathematician]
Hypatia H: 475

Theophrastus [Greek philosopher]
Geology (The ancient Greeks) G: 97

Theophyline [drug]
Bronchodilator B: 637

Theorell, Hugo [Swedish biochemist]
Nobel Prizes (Physiology or medicine: 1955) N: 446

Theorem [mathematics]
Binomial theorem B: 309
Geometry (Axiomatic system) G: 102
Pythagorean theorem P: 921

Theoretical Physics, Institute for [Copenhagen]
Bohr, Niels B: 438

Theory [science]
Evolution (Main ideas of evolutionary theory) E: 426-427

Theory of ...
Theories appear under their key words, as in Forms, Theory of. *Titles beginning* Theory of... *appear below*

Theory of Business Enterprise, The [book by Veblen]
Veblen, Thorstein Bunde V: 291

Theory of Economic Development, The [book by Schumpeter]
Schumpeter, Joseph Alois S: 188

Theory of Economic Growth [book by Lewis]
Lewis, Sir Arthur L: 220

Theory of Games and Economic Behavior, The [book by Von Neumann and Morgenstern]
Game theory G: 23
Von Neumann, John V: 448

Theory of the Earth [book by Hutton]
Geology (The rock dispute) G: 98-99
Hutton, James H: 459

Theory of the Gene, The [book by Morgan]
Morgan, Thomas Hunt M: 804

Theory of the Leisure Class, The [book by Veblen]
Chicago, University of (Research program) C: 438

Veblen, Thorstein Bunde V: 291
Theosophical Society
　Besant, Annie Wood B: 273
　Theosophy T: 252
Theosophy [philosophy] T: 252
　Besant, Annie Wood B: 273
　Steiner, Rudolf So: 886
Theotokopoulos, Domenikos [birth name of]
　Greco, El G: 351
Thera [Mediterranean Sea]
　Volcano (table) V: 442b
Therapeutic cloning
　Cloning (Ethical concerns) Ci: 683
　Stem cell So: 889
Therapsid [extinct animal]
　Mammal (The ancestors of mammals) M: 126
Therapy [medicine] *See* Chemotherapy;
　Occupational therapy; Physical therapy;
　Psychotherapy *in this index*
Theravada [religion]
　Buddhism (Buddhist schools) B: 669
　Religion (Buddhism) R: 220
There Shall Be No Night [play by Sherwood]
　Sherwood, Robert Emmet S: 398
Theremin [musical instrument] T: 253
Theremin, Leon [Soviet engineer]
　Electronic music E: 205
　Theremin T: 253
Theresa, Saint *See* Teresa, Saint *in this index*
Therese [princess of Saxony-Hildburghausen]
　Oktoberfest O: 738
Thériault, Camille H. [Canadian political leader]
　New Brunswick (table) N: 195
Theriomorphic divinity
　Mythology (Mythical beings) M: 975
Therma [ancient city]
　Thessaloniki T: 258
Thermal [air current]
　Glider (Soaring) G: 229
Thermal bonding [process]
　Textile (Nonwovens) T: 215
Thermal-control system
　Space exploration (Protection against the
　　dangers of space) So: 701
Thermal cracking [industry]
　Petroleum (Conversion) P: 344
Thermal degradation
　Combustion Ci: 867
Thermal efficiency [mechanics]
　Diesel engine (How a diesel engine works) D: 199
Thermal energy [physics] *See* Internal energy *in
this index*
Thermal expansion tank
　Plumbing (The water supply system) P: 577-578
Thermal imaging
　Night vision systems N: 419
Thermal insulator *See* Insulation *in this index*
Thermal inversion *See* Temperature inversion *in
this index*
Thermal pollution T: 253
　Electric power (Fossil-fueled steam electric power
　　plants) E: 183
　Energy supply (Nuclear energy) E: 278;
　　(Environmental effects) E: 281
　Environmental pollution (Water pollution) E: 334
　Fish (How fish adjust to change) F: 168
　Nuclear energy (Steam production) N: 587
　Water pollution (Industrial wastes) W: 136
Thermal power
　Nuclear energy (The role of nuclear energy in
　　power production) N: 580; (Steam production)
　　N: 587
　Water power W: 139
Thermal properties
　Materials (Thermal properties) M: 300c
Thermal radiation
　Big bang B: 297
　Dew D: 176
　Heat (Chemical reactions) H: 149
　Infrared rays I: 269
　Nuclear weapon (Thermal radiation) N: 599
Thermal reactor [nuclear reactor]
　Nuclear energy (Nuclear fission) N: 582-583
Thermal springs [geology] *See* Hot springs *in this
index*
Thermal unit *See* British thermal unit; Calorie *in
this index*
Thermic effect of food [measurement]
　Weight control (Energy expenditure) W: 181
Thermidorian Reaction [French history]
　French Revolution (The revolution ends) F: 526-
　527
Thermistor [electronics]
　Thermometer (Resistance thermometers) T: 255
Thermite [chemical]
　Bomb (Incendiary bombs) B: 451
Thermobaric explosive [weapon]

Bomb (Thermobaric explosives [TBX's]) B: 451
Thermochemical calorie [measurement] *See*
　Calorie *in this index*
Thermocline [oceanography]
　Ocean (Temperature) O: 653
Thermocouple [measuring device] T: 253
　Thermometer (Thermocouple thermometers)
　　T: 254 *with diagram*
Thermodynamics [physics] T: 253
　Absolute zero A: 17
　Clausius, Rudolf Julius Emmanuel Ci: 657
　Entropy E: 328
　Heat (Thermodynamics) H: 155
　Maxwell, James Clerk M: 319
　Perpetual motion machine P: 293
　Physics (Heat) P: 437
Thermodynamics, First law of *See* Conservation of
energy *in this index*
Thermodynamics, Second law of
　Heat (Thermodynamics) H: 155
　Thermodynamics T: 253
　Time (Arrows of time) T: 292b-292c
Thermodynamics, Third law of
　Heat (Thermodynamics) H: 155
Thermoelectricity
　Thermocouple T: 253
Thermoforming [industrial process]
　Plastics (Thermoforming) P: 558 *with picture*
　Polypropylene P: 651
　Polystyrene P: 652
Thermogram [record]
　Energy supply *picture on* E: 281
　Thermography T: 253 *with picture*
Thermograph [instrument]
　Thermography T: 253
Thermography [imaging] T: 253 *with picture*
Thermohaline circulation [oceanography]
　Ocean (How the ocean moves) O: 658 *with
　　picture and map*
Thermoluminescence dating
　Prehistoric people (Placing prehistoric people in
　　time) P: 754a-754b
Thermometer T: 254 *with pictures*
　Bolometer B: 448
　Hygrometer (The psychrometer) H: 474
　Liquid air (Properties) L: 346
　Thermocouple T: 253
　Weather (Land-based observation stations)
　　W: 162
Thermonuclear reaction *See* Fusion *in this index*
Thermonuclear supernova [astronomy]
　Supernova So: 994
Thermonuclear weapon
　Nuclear weapon N: 596, *diagram on* N: 598;
　　(Thermonuclear weapons) N: 597; (The Cold
　　War) N: 601
　Sakharov, Andrei Dmitriyevich S: 59
Thermopane [glass]
　Glass (table) G: 218
Thermophile [biology]
　Extremophile E: 458
Thermoplastics
　Asphalt A: 815
　Fiber (Synthetic fibers) F: 87
　Materials (Plastics) M: 300d
　Plastics (Types of plastics) P: 555; (Making plastic
　　products) P: 557; (Growth of the plastics
　　industry) P: 560; (Recent developments) P: 560
　Polypropylene P: 651
　Polystyrene P: 651
Thermopylae [ancient Greece] T: 255
Thermopylae, Battle of [480 B.C.]
　Aristides A: 662
　Leonidas I L: 202
　Navy (Ancient navies) N: 79
　Salamis S: 60
　Themistocles T: 251
　Thermopylae T: 255
　Xerxes I X: 544
Thermopylae of America [name for]
　Alamo A: 280
Thermos bottle [container] *See* Vacuum bottle *in
this index*
Thermoset *See* Thermosetting plastics *in this index*
Thermosetting plastics
　Adhesive A: 56
　Materials (Plastics) M: 300d
　Phenolic P: 356
　Plastics (Types of plastics) P: 555; (Making plastic
　　products) P: 557; (Growth of the plastics
　　industry) P: 560
　Polyester P: 650
Thermosphere [atmosphere] T: 256
　Air (Structure of the atmosphere) A: 172 *with
　　diagram*
　Mesosphere M: 422
Thermostat [instrument] T: 256

Heating (Central heating systems) H: 157
　Plumbing (The water supply system) P: 577-578
Theron, Charlize [South African/American actress]
　Motion picture (Best performance by an actress:
　　2003) M: 862a
Theropod [dinosaur]
　Dinosaur (True dinosaurs) D: 206b-208; (How
　　dinosaurs lived) D: 211
　Ornitholestes O: 857
Theroux, Paul [American author] T: 256
Thesaurus [reference]
　Dictionary (Specialized dictionaries) D: 192
　Roget, Peter Mark R: 401
Theseus [book by Gide]
　Gide, André G: 188
Theseus [Greek mythology] T: 257
　Helen of Troy H: 168
　Minotaur M: 611 *with picture*
Theseus and the Minotaur [sculpture by Barye]
　Minotaur *picture on* M: 611
Thesis [essay]
　Degree, College (The master's degree) D: 92
Thesis [philosophy]
　Hegel, G. W. F. (Hegel's dialectic) H: 165
Thesis [writing]
　Composition (Organizing your thinking) Ci: 905
　A Guide to Writing Skills **Research Guide: 15,**
　　Research Guide: 16
Thesis play [drama]
　French literature (Realism) F: 522
Thespian [actor]
　Thespis T: 257
Thespis [Greek actor] T: 257
　Drama (Greek drama) D: 326
Thessalonians, Epistles to the [New Testament]
　T: 257
　Bible (The Letters) B: 284
Thessaloniki [Greece] T: 257 *with picture*
　Greece *picture on* G: 355; (Population) G: 353
Thessaly [region, Greece] T: 258 *with maps*
　Greece (Thessaly) G: 357 *with map*
Theta wave [physiology]
　Electroencephalograph E: 200
Thetis [Greek mythology]
　Achilles A: 26
They Knew What They Wanted [play by Howard]
　Howard, Sidney H: 400
They Were Strong and Good [book by Lawson]
　Lawson, Robert L: 147
THF [chemical]
　Furfural F: 566
Thiamine [vitamin]
　Beriberi B: 258
　Nutrition (Vitamins) N: 626
　Vitamin (Thiamine) V: 431; (table) V: 431
Thibault, Jacques A. F. [real name of]
　France, Anatole F: 480
Thibault, Jean [Canadian religious leader]
　Alberta (Missionary activity) A: 329
Thibodaux, Henry S. [American political leader]
　Louisiana (table) L: 496
Thick-billed parrot
　Parrot (Kinds of parrots) P: 179
Thickener [additive]
　Food additive (Kinds of additives) F: 339
Thickness gauge [instrument]
　Gauge (Other types of gauges) G: 69
Thief ant
　Ant (The importance of ants) A: 528
　Insect (Family life) I: 294-295
Thiende, De [pamphlet]
　Decimal system (Use of decimals smaller than
　　one) D: 73
Thierry-Primot, Catherine [wife of]
　Le Moyne, Charles, Sieur de Longueil et de
　　Châteauguay L: 189
Thiers, Louis Adolphe [French political leader]
　T: 258
Thieves' Carnival [play by Anouilh]
　Anouilh, Jean A: 519
Thigh [anatomy]
　Human body (table) H: 422 *with diagram*
　Leg (The thigh) L: 181 *with diagram*
Thigmotropism [biology]
　Tropism T: 451
Thimble Summer [book by Enright]
　Enright, Elizabeth E: 327
Thimbles, The [island, Connecticut]
　Connecticut (Coastline) Ci: 962
Thimonnier, Barthélemy [French inventor]
　Sewing machine (History) S: 333
Thimphu [Bhutan] T: 258
Thin client [machine]
　Computer (Local area networks [LAN's]) Ci: 922
Thin layer chromatography
　Chromatography (Thin layer chromatography)
　　C: 537

Thin Man, The [book by Hammett]
Hammett, Dashiell H: 35
Thin tin [metal]
Tin can T: 294
Thing [government]
Vikings (Ancestry and population) V: 378-379
Things Fall Apart [book by Achebe]
Achebe, Chinua A: 25
Things of This World [poems by Wilbur]
Wilbur, Richard W: 300
Thingvallavatn [lake, Iceland]
Iceland (The inland plateau) I: 22
Thingy Things [books by Raschka]
Raschka, Chris R: 144
Thinhorn [animal] *See* Dall's sheep *in this index*
Thinker, The [painting by Eakins]
Eakins, Thomas E: 6
Thinker, The [sculpture by Rodin]
France *picture on* F: 463
Thinking
Adolescent (Intellectual development) A: 61
Reason R: 173
Thinking Machine [literary figure]
Detective story (History) D: 162-163
"Thinking Things Over with Calvin Coolidge" [column]
Coolidge, Calvin (Later years) Ci: 1033-1034
Thinner [chemical]
Paint P: 23
Painting (Materials and techniques) P: 36 *with picture*
Thinning [farming]
Fruit (Caring for the crop) F: 546-547
Thiopental [drug] T: 258
Thiopental sodium [drug]
Halothane H: 27
Thira [island, Mediterranean]
Atlantis A: 868
Painting (Aegean painting) P: 41 *with picture*
Third [play by Wasserstein]
Wasserstein, Wendy W: 112
Third Amendment
Constitution of the United States Ci: 1012
Third-angle projection [drawing]
Mechanical drawing (Information in the drawing) M: 353-354 *with diagram*
Third baseman [baseball]
Baseball (Player positions) B: 127
Third-class lever
Lever *picture on* L: 218; (Classes of levers) L: 217
Machine (Lever) M: 14
Third-degree burn
Burn (Classification of burns) B: 708
First aid (Burns) F: 138
Skin (Burns) S: 490
Third estate [French history]
Estates-General E: 360
French Revolution (Background) F: 524-525; (The revolution begins) F: 525
Mirabeau, Comte de M: 615
Third gear
Transmission (How a manual transmission works) T: 377-378
Third law of motion [physics]
Motion (Newton's laws of motion) M: 844
Third Man, The [book by Greene]
Greene, Graham G: 381
Third Navigation Act [1672]
Navigation Acts N: 75
Third New Deal [U.S. history]
New Deal (The final measures) N: 202
Third party
Political party (Third parties) P: 636
Third person [literature]
Literature (Style) L: 353
Third-person game
Electronic game (Gameplay) E: 204b-204c
Third Punic War [149-146 B.C.] *See* Punic Wars *in this index*
Third rail [railroad]
Electric railroad (Kinds of electric railroads) E: 188 *with picture*
Elevated railroad E: 233
Third Reich [German history]
Germany (Nazi Germany) G: 167-168
Hitler, Adolf (Dictator of Germany) H: 266
Reich R: 207
Third Republic [French history]
France (The Third Republic) F: 474
Third Residence [poems by Neruda]
Neruda, Pablo N: 131
Third-stream music
Classical music (Third-stream music) Ci: 650
Lewis, John Aaron L: 221
Third World T: 258
See also Developing country; Neutral nation *in this index*

World, History of the (The birth of new nations) W: 448
Thirst T: 259
Thirteen Colonies [U.S. history] *See* Colonial life in America *in this index*
Thirteen-lined ground squirrel [animal]
Ground squirrel G: 401 *with picture*
Thirteen-Month Calendar
Calendar (Calendar reform) C: 32
Thirteenth Amendment
Civil War, American (The Emancipation Proclamation) C: 621
Constitution of the United States Ci: 1013
Dred Scott Decision D: 345
Emancipation Proclamation (Effects of the proclamation) E: 254
Freedom Day, National F: 503
Reconstruction (Early congressional reaction) R: 177
Slavery (The decline of slavery) S: 504
Thirty, The [Greek history] *See* Thirty Tyrants *in this index*
35-millimeter film
Motion picture (The film) M: 857; (The projector) M: 858-859 *with picture*
35-millimeter slide projector
Audio-visual materials (Projection devices) A: 882
Thirty-Nine Articles [religion] T: 259
Church of England (Doctrines) C: 542
Ridley, Nicholas R: 336
Thirty-Nine Steps, The [film by Hitchcock]
Motion picture (Movies in the 1930's) M: 867-868 *with picture*
Thirty Tyrants [ancient Greece] T: 259
Lysander L: 538
Lysias L: 538
Thirty Years' War [1618-1648] T: 259
Army (The rise of modern armies) A: 727
Austria (The Habsburgs) A: 937
Berlin (Early days) B: 264
Christianity (The 1600's and 1700's) C: 525
Counter Reformation (Counteracting Protestantism) Ci: 1096
Czech Republic (Habsburg rule) Ci: 1213
Germany (The Thirty Years' War) G: 164
Guerrilla warfare (History) G: 420
Mazarin, Jules M: 331
Prague (History) P: 730
Richelieu, Cardinal (Thirty Years' War) R: 331
Roman Catholic Church (The Counter Reformation) R: 408
Sweden (The age of expansion) So: 1034
This Country of Ours [book by Harrison]
Harrison, Benjamin (Later years) H: 73
This Gun for Hire [book by Greene]
Greene, Graham G: 381
This Side of Paradise [book by Fitzgerald]
Fitzgerald, F. Scott F: 190
Thisbe [legendary figure]
Pyramus and Thisbe P: 919
Thistle [plant] T: 260
Canada thistle C: 154
Composite family Ci: 904
Flower (Flowers of summer-dry regions) F: 288 *with picture*
Thistle, Order of the [award]
Knighthood, Orders of (Honorary orders) K: 347
Thivai [Greece] *See* Thebes *in this index*
Thjórsa River
Iceland (The inland plateau) I: 22
Thobe [clothing] *See* Thawb *in this index*
Thoc-me-tony [American social reformer]
Winnemucca, Sarah W: 339
Thomas, Andrew S. W. [Australian astronaut]
Astronaut (table) A: 830
Thomas, Bigger [literary figure]
Wright, Richard W: 508
Thomas, Carey [American educator] *See* Thomas, Martha Carey *in this index*
Thomas, Charles [American political leader]
Delaware (table) D: 109
Thomas, Charles S. [American political leader]
Colorado (table) Ci: 844
Thomas, Clarence [American jurist] T: 261
African Americans (Affirmative action) A: 136r
Moseley Braun, Carol M: 828
Supreme Court of the United States *picture on* So: 999
Thomas, Dylan [Welsh poet] T: 261
English literature (Poetry between the wars) E: 322
Thomas, E. Donnall [American physiologist]
Nobel Prizes (Physiology or medicine: 1990) N: 446
Thomas, Francis [American political leader]
Maryland (table) M: 255
Thomas, George Henry [Union general]

Civil War, American (Battle of Chickamauga) Ci: 629-630; (Battle of Chattanooga) Ci: 630
Thomas, Gospel of [document]
Gospels G: 278
Jesus Christ (Other gospels) J: 105
Thomas, Herb [American race driver]
Automobile racing (table: NASCAR Sprint Cup champions) A: 981
Thomas, Isaiah [American publisher] T: 261
Mother Goose (The history of Mother Goose literature) M: 842
Thomas, Isiah [American basketball player]
Basketball *picture on* B: 154a
Thomas, James [American political leader]
Maryland (table) M: 255
Thomas, Lorenzo [American general]
Johnson, Andrew (Increased tension) J: 140
Thomas, Martha Carey [American educator] T: 261
Thomas, Norman Mattoon [American political leader] T: 261
Socialism (World Wars I and II) So: 561
Thomas, Philip Francis [American government official]
Buchanan, James (table) B: 661
Maryland (table) M: 255
Thomas, Rene [American race driver]
Automobile racing (table: Indianapolis 500 winners) A: 980
Thomas, Saint [apostle] T: 262
Thomas à Becket *See* Becket, Saint Thomas *in this index*
Thomas à Kempis [German author] T: 262
Thomas and Beulah [book by Dove]
Dove, Rita D: 315
Thomas Aquinas, Saint *See* Aquinas, Saint Thomas *in this index*
Thomas Carlyle [book by Froude]
Biography (The 1800's) B: 314
Thomas Cup [sports]
Badminton B: 24
Thomas Edison National Historical Park [New Jersey]
National Park System (table: National historical parks) N: 56-57
Thomas Jefferson Building
Library of Congress L: 264
Washington, D.C. *map on* W: 76; (Library of Congress) W: 71
Thomas Jefferson Foundation
Jefferson, Thomas (Jefferson and Sally Hemings) J: 79
Thomas Jefferson Memorial *See* Jefferson Memorial *in this index*
Thomas More College [former name]
Fordham University F: 383
Thomas Stone National Historic Site [Maryland]
National Park System (table: National historic sites) N: 52-53
Thomasin von Zerclaere [German author]
Etiquette (Books on etiquette) E: 375
Thomism [philosophy]
Maritain, Jacques M: 212
Thompson [Manitoba] T: 262
Manitoba M: 144
Thompson, Benjamin [American-British physicist] T: 262
Heat (The study of heat) H: 154-155
Range (History) R: 138
Thompson, Bill [American political leader] *See* Thompson, William Hale *in this index*
Thompson, Charlotte Pottinger [mother of]
Thompson, Sir John Sparrow David (Early life) T: 263
Thompson, David [Barbadian political leader]
Barbados (History) B: 104
Thompson, David [Canadian explorer] T: 262
British Columbia (The overland fur traders) B: 628-630
Idaho (Exploration and early settlement) I: 42
Washington (Discovery and exploration) W: 66
Thompson, Dorothy [American journalist]
Lewis, Sinclair L: 221
Thompson, Elizabeth [British artist]
Painting (Women artists) P: 73-74 *with picture*
Thompson, Emma [British actress]
Motion picture (Best performance by an actress: 1992) M: 862a
Thompson, Ernest Seton [Canadian naturalist] *See* Seton, Ernest Thompson *in this index*
Thompson, Francis [British poet] T: 262
July (Quotations) J: 189
Thompson, Frank [Union soldier]
Edmonds, Sarah Emma Evelyn E: 83
Thompson, J. Edgar [American public figure]
Atlanta (Early days) A: 861
Thompson, Jacob [American government official]
Buchanan, James (table) B: 661

Interior, Department of the (table) **I:** 325
Thompson, James R. [American political leader]
Illinois (table) **I:** 71
Thompson, John Sparrow [father of]
Thompson, Sir John Sparrow David (Early life)
T: 263
Thompson, Sir John Sparrow David [Canadian political leader] **T:** 263 *with portrait*
Abbott, Sir John Joseph Caldwell (Prime minister) **A:** 6
Nova Scotia (table) **N:** 567
Thompson, Melvin E. [American political leader]
Georgia (table) **G:** 130
Thompson, Richard W. [American government official]
Hayes, Rutherford Birchard (table) **H:** 121
Thompson, Sam [American baseball player]
Baseball (table: Hall of Fame) **B:** 134b
Thompson, Smith [American jurist]
Supreme Court of the United States (table) **So:** 1000
Thompson, Stanley G. [American chemist]
Californium **C:** 66
Thompson, Tommy G. [American political leader]
Bush, George Walker (table) **B:** 722h
Health and Human Services, Department of (table) **H:** 128
Wisconsin (table) **W:** 365; (School developments) **W:** 368
Thompson, William Hale [American political leader] **T:** 264
Thompson grapefruit
Grapefruit **G:** 320
Thompson Seedless [grape]
Raisin (Varieties) **R:** 129
Thomson [news agency]
Thomson Reuters **T:** 265
Thomson, Bobby [American baseball player]
Baseball *picture on* **B:** 138
Thomson, Charles [American patriot] **T:** 264
Great Seal of the United States **S:** 348
Washington, George *picture on* **W:** 102
Thomson, Charles Edward Poulett [British political leader]
Sydenham, Baron **So:** 1062
Thomson, Charles Wyville [British naturalist]
Exploration (Deep-sea exploration) **E:** 450-451
Thomson, David [English settler]
New Hampshire (Settlement) **N:** 224
Thomson, Sir George Paget [British physicist]
Nobel Prizes (Physics: 1937) **N:** 440
Thomson, Sir Joseph John **T:** 264
Thomson, James [British poet] **T:** 264
Thomson, Sir Joseph John [British physicist] **T:** 264
Atom (The first descriptions of atomic structure) **A:** 875 *with diagram*
Electricity (The electronic age) **E:** 198
Electronics (Early experiments) **E:** 215 *with picture*
Physics (The beginning of modern physics) **P:** 440-441
Proton **P:** 836
Thomson, Mary Agnes [American public figure]
Keller, Helen **K:** 255
Thomson, Meldrim, Jr. [American political leader]
New Hampshire (table) **N:** 223
Thomson, Robert W. [Scottish engineer]
Tire (History) **T:** 297
Thomson, Tom [Canadian painter] **T:** 265 *with picture*
Canada *picture on* **C:** 110
Group of Seven **G:** 402
Thomson, Vernon W. [American political leader]
Wisconsin (table) **W:** 365
Thomson, Virgil [American composer] **T:** 265
Thomson Reuters [news agency] **T:** 265
Thomson's gazelle
Gazelle **G:** 74 *with picture*
Thone, Charles [American political leader]
Nebraska (table) **N:** 110
Thor [Norse mythology] **T:** 265
Thursday **T:** 273
Vikings (Religion) **V:** 380
Thoracic basket [biology]
Mammal (Skeleton) **M:** 118-119
Thoracic duct [anatomy]
Human body (The lymphatic system) **H:** 424
Lymphatic system (Lymphatic vessels) **L:** 534 *with diagram*
Thoracic surgery
Medicine (table) **M:** 369
Thoracic vertebra [biology]
Mammal (Skeleton) **M:** 118-119 *with diagram*
Spine **So:** 792 *with diagram*
Thorax [zoology]
See also Chest *in this index*
Beetle (The thorax) **B:** 216 *with diagram*

Butterfly (The thorax) **B:** 738 *with diagrams*
Insect (Thorax) **I:** 287 *with diagram*
Moth (The thorax) **M:** 838 *with diagrams*
Thorazine [medication]
Chlorpromazine **C:** 518
Thoreau, Henry David [American philosopher] **T:** 266 *with picture*
American literature (Nonfiction prose) **A:** 418
Civil disobedience (History of civil disobedience) **Ci:** 607
Conservation (Early conservation problems) **Ci:** 985
Massachusetts (Places to visit) **M:** 280
National park (The early national parks) **N:** 42j
Thorium [element] **T:** 266
Actinide **A:** 30
Radiation *diagram on* **R:** 79; (Naturally radioactive substances) **R:** 77
Thorn [botany] **T:** 266
Plant (How plants protect themselves) **P:** 540
Thorn [letter]
Y **Y:** 547
Thorn apple [plant] *See* Datura; Hawthorn; Jimson weed *in this index*
Thorn Birds, The [book by McCullough]
McCullough, Colleen **M:** 332g
Thornburgh, Richard L. [American government official]
Justice, Department of (table) **J:** 203
Pennsylvania (table) **P:** 263
Thorndike, Edward Lee [American psychologist] **T:** 267
Learning (Instrumental conditioning) **L:** 163
Thorndike-Barnhart Dictionary
Thorndike, Edward Lee **T:** 267
Thorndike-Century Dictionary
Thorndike, Edward Lee **T:** 267
Thorne, George R. [American businessman]
Ward, Aaron Montgomery **W:** 35
Thorne, Julia S. [wife of]
Kerry, John Forbes **K:** 306
Thorning-Schmidt, Helle [Danish political leader]
Denmark (Recent developments) **D:** 141
Thornton, Dan [American political leader]
Colorado (table) **Ci:** 844
Thornton, Matthew [American patriot] **T:** 267
Thornton, William [American architect]
Capitol, United States **C:** 197
Thorny-headed worm
Parasite (Effects) **P:** 153-154
Thóroddsen, Jón [Icelandic author]
Scandinavian literature (The Golden Age) **S:** 171
Thoroughbred [horse]
Horse (Kinds of horses) **H:** 343; (table: Some types and breeds of horses) **H:** 343; (Saddle horses) **H:** 343-345 *with picture*
Horse racing (Thoroughbred horses) **H:** 363
Kentucky **K:** 272 *with picture*
Lexington (Description) **L:** 224
Thoroughwort [plant]
Boneset **B:** 458
Thorpe, Jim [American athlete] **T:** 267 *with picture*
Olympic Games (The modern games) **O:** 751 *with picture*
Thorpe, Thomas [English publisher]
Shakespeare, William (The sonnets) **S:** 348; (Composition and publication) **S:** 367
Thorunn Johannsdottir [Icelandic pianist]
Ashkenazy, Vladimir **A:** 769
Thorvaldsen, Bertel [Danish sculptor] **T:** 267
Denmark (Arts) **D:** 136
Sculpture (European sculpture) **S:** 253-254 *with picture*
Thorvaldson, Eric [Viking explorer] *See* Erik the Red *in this index*
Thorwald Erikkson [Norse explorer]
Leif Erikkson **L:** 186
Thorwaldsen, Bertel [Danish sculptor] *See* Thorvaldsen, Bertel *in this index*
Thoth [Egyptian god] **T:** 267
Egypt, Ancient (Religion) **E:** 137
Mythology *picture on* **M:** 977; (Other Egyptian divinities) **M:** 980
Thought *See* Thinking *in this index*
Thought, Freedom of
Academic freedom **A:** 20
Thought-rhythm [poetry]
Whitman, Walt (His work) **W:** 294
Thought transference
Telepathy **T:** 93
Thoughts on Death and Immortality [book by Feuerbach]
Feuerbach, Ludwig Andreas **F:** 83
Thoughts on the Education of Daughters [book by Wollstonecraft]
Wollstonecraft, Mary **W:** 379
Thoughts on the Interpretation of Nature [book

by Diderot]
Diderot, Denis **D:** 195
Thousand and One Nights, The *See* Arabian Nights *in this index*
Thousand Days: John F. Kennedy in the White House, A [book by Schlesinger]
Schlesinger, Arthur Meier, Jr. **S:** 177
Thousand Islands [Saint Lawrence River] **T:** 268 *with picture*
Ontario (Visitor's guide) **O:** 774 *with picture*
Saint Lawrence River (The course of the St. Lawrence) **S:** 41
Thousand Islands International Bridge [Canada-U.S.]
Thousand Islands **T:** 268
Thousands of cubic feet [measurement]
Petroleum (How prices are set) **P:** 346
Thrace [region, Europe] **T:** 268
Bulgaria (Early history) **B:** 692
Greece (Thrace) **G:** 357 *with map*
Thrasher [bird] **T:** 268 *with picture*
Bird *pictures on* **B:** 338, **B:** 358
Brown thrasher **B:** 645
Thread [fiber] **T:** 269 *with diagrams*
Sewing (Choosing the equipment, fabric, and pattern) **S:** 332
Spinning **So:** 794
Thread [hardware]
Screw **S:** 225 *with diagrams*
Thread snake
Snake **S:** 524; (Slender blind snakes) **S:** 535
Threadworm
Pinworm **P:** 475
Threat display [zoology]
Snake (Protection against predators) **S:** 531
Threatened species
See also Endangered species *in this index*
Animal (How human beings protect animals) **A:** 505
Hunting (Laws and conservation) **H:** 450
Plant (Conservation of plants) **P:** 543
Wildlife conservation (Classifications of scarce wildlife) **W:** 304
Zoo (Wildlife conservation) **Z:** 600
Three Affiliated Tribes
Arikara Indians **A:** 661
Mandan Indians **M:** 135
Three-banded armadillo [animal]
Armadillo **A:** 717
Three Cities, The [books by Zola]
Zola, Émile **Z:** 598
Three Comrades [book by Remarque]
Remarque, Erich Maria **R:** 228
Three-Cornered Hat, The [ballet]
Falla, Manuel de **F:** 16
Massine, Léonide **M:** 296
Three-Cornered Hat, The [book by Alarcón]
Alarcón, Pedro Antonio de **A:** 281
Three-cottage problem [puzzle]
Topology (Geometric puzzles) **T:** 333
Three-cushion billiards
Billiards (Carom billiards) **B:** 306
3-D archery
Archery (Indoor archery) **A:** 603
Three-Day Event
Horse (Eventing) **H:** 358
Three-dimensional conformal radiation therapy [medicine]
Cancer (Radiation therapy) **C:** 172
Three-dimensional graphics
Electronic game (Graphics) **E:** 204b; (The growth of computer gaming) **E:** 204e
Three-dimensional model [drawing]
Mechanical drawing (Creating a drawing) **M:** 354
Three-dimensional picture
Holography **H:** 298
Stereoscope **So:** 893
Virtual reality **V:** 426
Three-dimensional vision
Eye (Depth perception) **E:** 463-464
Three Emperors' League
World War I (The Triple Alliance) **W:** 455
Three estates [European history]
Canterbury Tales **C:** 184
French Revolution (Background) **F:** 524-525
Three Fires, The [American Indians]
Potawatomi Indians **P:** 714
Three Flags [painting by Johns]
Painting (The revival of subject matter) **P:** 86 *with picture*
3G [communications]
Cellular telephone (History) **C:** 341
Three Gorges Dam [China] **T:** 270
China *picture on* **C:** 493; (Recent developments) **C:** 506
Dam (History) **D:** 19-20
Yangtze River **Y:** 551

Three-gun RGB projector [device]
Projector (Digital data projectors) **P: 817**
Three Henrys, War of the [1585-1589]
Henry III [of France] **H: 186**
365 Plays/365 Days [project]
Parks, Suzan-Lori **P: 172**
332nd Fighter Group [military]
Tuskegee Airmen **T: 525**
Three Jewish Poems [music by Bloch]
Bloch, Ernest **B: 404**
Three Kingdoms [Korean history]
Korea, History of (Early years) **K: 366** *with map*
Three Lower Counties [U.S. history]
Delaware (English rule) **D: 110**
Three Mile Island [nuclear power plant]
Fallout (History) **F: 19**
Nuclear energy (Safety concerns) **N: 591-592**
Pennsylvania (Economic decline) **P: 268** *with picture*
Three Musketeers, The [book by Dumas]
Buckingham, Duke of **B: 663**
Dumas, Alexandre, père **D: 382**
French literature (Romantic fiction) **F: 521**
Three-of-a-kind [poker]
Poker **P: 603**
Three People's Principles [book by Sun Yat-sen]
Sun Yat-sen **So: 988**
Three-phase current
Electric current (Direct and alternating current) **E: 168**
Three-phase generator
Electric generator (Kinds of AC generators) **E: 173**
Three Philosophical Poets [book by Santayana]
Santayana, George **S: 115**
Three-race theory [anthropology]
Races, Human (The three-race theory) **R: 53-54** *with pictures*
Three Rivers Art Festival
Pittsburgh (The arts) **P: 500c**
Three R's [principles]
Animal experimentation (The "three R's") **A: 510**
Three Sisters [mountain, Oregon]
Oregon *picture on* **O: 840**; (Land regions) **O: 838** *with map*
Three Sisters, The [play by Chekhov]
Chekhov, Anton **C: 395**
Russian literature *picture on* **R: 558**; (Late realism) **R: 562-563**
Three Soldiers [book by Dos Passos]
Dos Passos, John **D: 311**
Three states, Law of the [philosophy]
Comte, Auguste **Ci: 926**
Three-striped night monkey
Monkey *picture on* **M: 728**
Three Tales [stories by Flaubert]
Flaubert, Gustave **F: 230**
Three Tall Women [play by Albee]
Albee, Edward **A: 310**
American literature (Drama) **A: 426**
Three Teachings [religion]
Vietnam (Religion) **V: 366**
Three Tenors, The [singers]
Pavarotti, Luciano **P: 202**
Three Trapped Tigers [book by Infante]
Latin American literature (The post-Boom) **L: 114**
Three-way bulb
Electric light *picture on* **E: 176**
Three-way catalyst [chemistry]
Catalytic converter **C: 298**
Three Wise Men [Biblical figures] *See* Magi *in this index*
Three Women at the Spring [painting by Picasso]
Picasso, Pablo (The 1920's and 1930's) **P: 448b-449**
Threefold Law of Karma
Witchcraft (Role of magic) **W: 372**
Threepenny Opera, The [musical]
Blitzstein, Marc **B: 403**
Brecht, Bertolt **B: 592**
Weill, Kurt **W: 188**
"Threnody" [poem by Emerson]
Emerson, Ralph Waldo (His life) **E: 258**
Threnody for the Victims of Hiroshima [music by Penderecki]
Penderecki, Krzysztof **P: 236**
Thresher [ship]
Shipwreck (table: Major shipwrecks) **S: 428**
Thresher shark [fish]
Shark (Thresher sharks) **S: 376** *with picture*
Threshing [agriculture]
Combine **Ci: 866**
Rice (Harvesting) **R: 326**
Threshing machine **T: 270**
Threshing machine **T: 270** *with picture*
Wheat (The mechanization of wheat farming) **W: 276** *with picture*
Threshold [architecture]

House (Interior construction) **H: 382**
Threshold of audibility [sound]
Sound (Intensity and loudness) **So: 600-601**
Thrift [plant]
Statice **So: 867**
Thrift institution
Bank (Kinds of banks) **B: 90**
Credit union **Ci: 1125**
Savings and loan association **S: 165**
Savings bank **S: 165**
Thrift plan
Pension **P: 272**; (Private pension plans) **P: 273**
Thriller [recording]
Jackson, Michael **J: 15**
Rock music (Madonna and Michael Jackson) **R: 380c**
Thrips [insects] **T: 270**
Gladiolus **G: 206**
Throat [anatomy] **T: 270**
Strep throat **So: 925**
Throckmorton, James W. [American political leader]
Texas (table) **T: 203**
Thrombin [enzyme]
Anticoagulant **A: 553**
Thrombocyte [blood] *See* Platelet *in this index*
Thrombocythemia [disorder]
Blood (Bleeding disorders) **B: 414**
Thrombocytopenia [disorder]
Blood (Bleeding disorders) **B: 414**
Thrombophlebitis [disorder]
Anticoagulant **A: 553**
Thrombosis [disorder]
Blood (Controlling bleeding) **B: 411**
Coronary thrombosis **Ci: 1068**
Stroke (Causes) **So: 930**
Thrombus [physiology]
Arteriosclerosis (Causes) **A: 750**
Blood (Controlling bleeding) **B: 411**
Heart *diagram on* **H: 140**; (Causes) **H: 137**
Throne
Furniture *picture on* **F: 570**; (India) **F: 572**
Tutankhamun *picture on* **T: 526**
Throop, Enos T. [American political leader]
New York (table) **N: 313**
Throstle [machine]
Industrial Revolution (Spinning machines) **I: 248-249**
Throttle [device]
Airplane (Basic movements and controls) **A: 222-223** *with picture*
Carburetor **C: 282**
Gasoline engine *picture on* **G: 63**
Throttle body fuel injection *See* Single point fuel injection *in this index*
Through a Glass Darkly [film]
Bergman, Ingmar **B: 257**
Through the Looking-Glass and What Alice Found There [book by Carroll]
Alice in Wonderland **A: 367**
Carroll, Lewis **C: 248**
Literature for children *picture on* **L: 376**
Tenniel, Sir John **T: 160**
Throw-in [soccer]
Soccer (Restarts) **So: 546**
"Throw of the Dice, A" [poem by Mallarmé]
French literature (Symbolism) **F: 522**
Throwing [process]
Silk (Throwing) **S: 460**
Throwing down the gauntlet [expression]
Gauntlet **G: 70**
Throwing stick *See* Boomerang *in this index*
Thrush [bird] **T: 271** *with picture*
Bird *picture on* **B: 358**; (Birds of inland waters and marshes) **B: 340** *with picture*
Thrush [disease]
Fungal disease (In people) **F: 558**
Horse (Medical care) **H: 356**
Thrust [painting by Gottlieb]
Gottlieb, Adolph *picture on* **G: 280**
Thrust [physics]
Airplane (Principles of flight) **A: 220** *with diagram*
Airship (Thrust) **A: 250**
Guided missile (The engine) **G: 424**
Jet propulsion **J: 110**; (Power in a jet engine) **J: 111** *with picture*
Rocket **R: 384** *with picture*; (How rockets work) **R: 385**
Space exploration (Getting into space and back) **So: 698**
Thrust fault [geology]
Earthquake (Convergent boundaries) **E: 38**
Mountain (Fold-thrust mountains) **M: 893** *with diagram*
Thrust vectoring [engineering]
Guided missile **G: 423**
Thuban [star]

North Star **N: 518**
Thucydides [Greek historian] **T: 271**
Greek literature (Historical literature) **G: 377**
History (The ancient Greeks and Romans) **H: 261**
Oratory (Classical orators) **O: 819**
War (Struggles over power) **W: 23-24**
Thug [history of India] **T: 271**
Thuggee [crime]
Thug **T: 271**
Thule [ancient land] **T: 271**
Exploration (The Greeks) **E: 441**
Thule [people]
Inuit (Inuit origins) **I: 354g**
Nunavut (Early history) **N: 611-612**
Thulium [element] **T: 271**
Thumb [anatomy]
Hand **H: 39**; (Parts of the hand) **H: 40** *with diagram*
Monkey (Hands and feet) **M: 726**
Thumb, Tom [American entertainer] *See* Stratton, Charles Sherwood *in this index*
"Thumbelina" [story by Andersen]
Fairy (Fairy tales) **F: 11**
Thumper truck
Gas [fuel] *picture on* **G: 54**; (Exploring for gas) **G: 53**
Petroleum **P: 338** *with diagram*; (Geophysical studies) **P: 336-337**
Thun, Lake of [Switzerland]
Lake of Thun **L: 43**
Thunder [weather] **T: 272** *with diagram*
Lightning **L: 299**
Shock wave **S: 430**
Thunderstorm **T: 272**
Thunder Bay [Ontario] **T: 272**
Ontario (Shoreline and coastline) **O: 778**
Thunderbird [automobile]
Sports car (History) **So: 803**
Thunderbird Park [Victoria]
British Columbia (Places to visit) **B: 620**
Thunderbirds [United States Air Force]
Air Force, United States *picture on* **A: 188**
Thundercloud *See* Cumulonimbus cloud *in this index*
Thunderhead [weather]
Cloud (Clouds that grow vertically) **Ci: 708**
Thunderstorm [weather] **T: 272**
Derecho **D: 152**
Flash flood **F: 227**
Hail **H: 8**
Storm (Extratropical cyclones) **So: 913** *with picture*
Tornado (How a tornado forms) **T: 333**
Weather *picture on* **W: 167**; (Synoptic-scale systems) **W: 159-161** *with picture*
Thurber, James [American author] **T: 273** *with picture*
Cartoon (Single panel cartoons) **C: 265-266**
Fable **F: 3**
Thurible [device] *See* Censer *in this index*
Thurman, Allen Granberry [American political leader] **T: 273**
Harrison, Benjamin (Election of 1888) **H: 71-72**
Thurmond, Strom [American political leader] **T: 273**
Filibustering **F: 99**
South Carolina (The mid-1900's) **So: 662**
Thurmond Dam [Savannah River]
Savannah River **S: 165**
Thurn and Taxis family
Postal services (The growth of public mail systems) **P: 703**
Thursday **T: 273**
Thursday Island
Torres Strait Islands **T: 343**
Thurston, Howard [American magician]
Magician (Illusions) **M: 51-52**
Thurston Lava Tube
Cave *picture on* **C: 321**
Thurstone, Louis Leon [American psychologist] **T: 273**
Intelligence (Theories of intelligence) **I: 319**
Thus Spake Zarathustra [book by Nietzsche]
Nietzsche, Friedrich (Nietzsche and religion) **N: 406**
Philosophy (Philosophy in the 1800's) **P: 390**
Thutmose II [king of ancient Egypt]
Hatshepsut **H: 86**
Thutmose III **T: 273**
Thutmose III [king of ancient Egypt] **T: 273**
Egypt, Ancient (The New Kingdom) **E: 143** *with picture*
Hatshepsut **H: 86**
Thutmose IV [king of ancient Egypt]
Sphinx (Egyptian sphinxes) **So: 780**
Thyborøn Canal
Denmark (Land regions) **D: 137-138**

Thye, Edward J. [American political leader]
Minnesota (table) **M:** 602
Thylacine [name for]
Tasmanian tiger **T:** 50
Thylakoid [botany]
Chlorophyll **C:** 517
Thyme [plant] **T:** 274
Thymine [biochemistry]
Cell (DNA—the wondrous molecule) **C:** 334-335 *with diagram*
DNA **D:** 258
Heredity (The structure of DNA) **H:** 205
Thymol [medication]
Thyme **T:** 274
Thymosin [physiology]
Gland (Glandlike structures) **G:** 208
Thymus **T:** 274
Thymus [anatomy] **T:** 274 *with diagram*
Blood (Formation of new blood components) **B:** 411
Gland (Glandlike structures) **G:** 208
Immune system *diagram on* **I:** 88a; (Parts of the immune system) **I:** 87
Lymphatic system (Lymphoid tissue) **L:** 534
Thyroid artery [anatomy]
Human body (table) **H:** 422 *with diagram*
Thyroid cartilage [anatomy]
Larynx **L:** 79 *with diagram*
Thyroid gland [anatomy] **T:** 274 *with diagram*
Cancer (table) **C:** 170
Cretinism **Ci:** 1128
Drug (Animals) **D:** 355
Gland (table) **G:** 209
Goiter **G:** 248
Graves' disease **G:** 331
Hormone (Metabolic hormones) **H:** 335
Human body (table) **H:** 422 *with diagram*
Immune system (Autoimmune disorders) **I:** 88c
Parathyroid gland **P:** 155
Thyroid-stimulating hormone
Goiter **G:** 248
Hormone (Endocrine control hormones) **H:** 336
Thyrotopin releasing hormone
Thyroid gland **T:** 274
Thyroxine [hormone]
Drug (Animals) **D:** 355
Goiter **G:** 248
Hormone (Metabolic hormones) **H:** 335
Metabolism (Control of metabolism) **M:** 424
Thyroid gland **T:** 274
Thyrse [botany]
Inflorescence **I:** 268b
Thysanoptera [entomology]
Insect (table) **I:** 300
Thysanura [entomology]
Insect *picture on* **I:** 280; (table) **I:** 299
ThyssenKrupp [company]
Krupp **K:** 389
Manufacturing (table) **M:** 170
Ti [symbol]
Titanium **T:** 300
Ti-pao [newspaper] *See* Dibao *in this index*
TIA [medicine] *See* Transient ischemic attack *in this index*
Tiahuanaco Indians
Bolivia (The arts) **B:** 444; (History) **B:** 446 *with picture*
Indian, American (Indians of the Andes) **I:** 173-174
Tiamat [legendary creature]
Mythology (Babylonian mythology) **M:** 978
Tian Shan [mountains, Asia] **T:** 275
China (The Xinjiang-Mongolian Uplands) **C:** 491
Kazakhstan (Land and climate) **K:** 250b *with map*
Uzbekistan (Land and climate) **U:** 254
Tiananmen Square [Beijing]
Beijing (The city) **B:** 222; (History) **B:** 223-224
China (Protests) **C:** 506 *with picture*
Communism (China after Mao) **Ci:** 896
Tianjin [China] **T:** 275
Tiber River [Italy] **T:** 275
Romulus and Remus **R:** 450a
Tiberias, Sea of [name for]
Galilee, Sea of **G:** 11
Tiberinus [Roman mythology]
Mythology (Roman divinities) **M:** 982-983
Tiberius [Roman emperor] **T:** 275
Caligula **C:** 66
November **N:** 576
Rome, Ancient (The Roman Empire) **R:** 446
Tiberius Claudius Nero [10 B.C. - A.D. 54, Roman emperor] *See* Claudius *in this index*
Tiberius Claudius Nero [42 B.C.- A.D. 37, Roman emperor] *See* Tiberius *in this index*
Tibesti Mountains [Chad]
Sahara (Land and climate) **S:** 20
Tibet T: 276 *with pictures and map*

Asia (Way of life in Central Asia) **A:** 790
China (Nationalities) **C:** 481 *with map*; (The Tibetan Highlands) **C:** 491
Dalai Lama **D:** 9
Tang dynasty (The middle years) **T:** 26
Tibetan Buddhism [religion]
Lamaism **L:** 49
Tibetan spaniel [dog] **T:** 278 *with picture*
Tibetan terrier [dog] **T:** 278 *with picture*
Dog *picture on* **D:** 275
Tibia [anatomy]
Human body (table) **H:** 422 *with diagram*
Knee **K:** 345
Leg (The leg) **L:** 182 *with diagram*
Tibullus [Roman author]
Latin literature (The Augustan Age) **L:** 116
Tic [disorder] **T:** 279
Neuralgia **N:** 152
Tic douloureux [disorder]
Neuralgia **N:** 152
Ticarcillin [drug]
Penicillin (Forms of penicillin) **P:** 240
Tichenor, Isaac [American political leader]
Vermont (table) **V:** 333
Ticino [canton, Switzerland]
Switzerland (Political divisions) *on* **So:** 1056
Ticino River [Italy-Switzerland]
Switzerland (Rivers) **So:** 1056
Tick [animal] **T:** 279 *with pictures*
See also Mite *in this index*
Deer tick **D:** 86 *with picture*
Dog (Grooming) **D:** 278
First aid (Injected poisons) **F:** 137-138
Lyme disease **L:** 533
Relapsing fever **R:** 209
Rocky Mountain spotted fever **R:** 394
Tick fever [disease] **T:** 280
Ticker *See* Stock ticker *in this index*
Ticker tape
Stock ticker **So:** 904
Ticket agent [career]
Airport (Airline passenger services) **A:** 246
Tickseed [plant]
Coreopsis **Ci:** 1052 *with picture*
Flower (Flowers of prairies and dry plains) **F:** 286 *with picture*
Ticonderoga, Battle of [1775]
Allen, Ethan **A:** 371
Arnold, Benedict (A courageous soldier) **A:** 741
Fort Ticonderoga **F:** 416
Ticonderoga class [ship]
Cruiser **Ci:** 1159
Tidal Basin [Washington, D.C.]
Washington, D.C. *map on* **W:** 76, *picture on* **W:** 82; (The Tidal Basin) **W:** 73 *with picture*
Tidal bore [geology]
Tide (The actual tide) **T:** 282
Tidal current [geology]
Tide **T:** 280
Tidal disruption [physics]
Satellite (Satellites of the gas giants) **S:** 150-150a
Tidal forces [physics] **T:** 280
Andromeda Galaxy **A:** 457
Galaxy (Galaxy mergers) **G:** 9
Local Group **L:** 409
Planetary ring **P:** 514d
Satellite (Physical characteristics) **S:** 149-150
Tidal heating [geology]
Enceladus **E:** 265
Europa **E:** 379
Satellite (Major satellites) **S:** 150a
Tidal forces **T:** 280
Tidal locking [physics]
Satellite (Physical characteristics) **S:** 149
Tidal forces **T:** 280
Tidal power plant
Ocean (Sources of energy) **O:** 654
Tidal range [geology]
Tide (The actual tide) **T:** 282
Tidal stream [astronomy]
Andromeda Galaxy **A:** 457
Tidal tail [astronomy]
Andromeda Galaxy **A:** 457
Tidal wave *See* Tsunami *in this index*
Tide [water] **T:** 280 *with diagrams*
Arctic Ocean (Tides) **A:** 644
Atlantic Ocean (Moving ocean waters) **A:** 866
Earth (Ocean currents) **E:** 22
Energy supply (Tidal energy) **E:** 279
Estuary **E:** 364
Pacific Ocean (Tides) **P:** 15
Seashore **S:** 269
Tidal forces **T:** 280
Tide flat [geography]
Seattle (The city) **S:** 273
Tidelands [region, U.S.]
Texas (The mid-1900's) **T:** 208

Tidewater
Virginia (Land regions) **V:** 410
Tidewater aristocracy
Jefferson, Thomas (Revolutionary leader) **J:** 79
Virginia (Royal governors and Cromwell) **V:** 418
Tidewater glacier
Iceberg (Northern Hemisphere icebergs) **I:** 17-18
Tie [music]
Music (Indicating time values) **M:** 953
Tie [railroad]
Railroad (The crossties and rails) **R:** 109 *with picture*
Tie-down roping
Rodeo (All-women's rodeos) **R:** 398
Tie dyeing [handicraft] **T:** 282
Tie plate [construction]
Railroad (The crossties and rails) **R:** 109 *with picture*
Tie stall barn
Dairying (Housing) **D:** 7
Tie-tack microphone *See* Lavalier microphone *in this index*
Tie wig
Hairdressing (The 1700's) **H:** 12
Tieck, Friedrich [German author]
German literature (Romanticism) **G:** 140
Tied arch bridge
Bridge (Arch bridges) **B:** 601
Tiemann, Norbert T. [American political leader]
Nebraska (table) **N:** 110
Tiempo, El [newspaper]
Colombia (Transportation and communication) **Ci:** 783
T'ien-chin [China] *See* Tianjin *in this index*
Tien Shan [mountains, Asia] *See* Tian Shan *in this index*
Tientsin [China] *See* Tianjin *in this index*
Tiepolo, Giambattista [Italian painter] *See* Tiepolo, Giovanni Battista *in this index*
Tiepolo, Giovanni Battista [Italian painter] **T:** 282
Rococo **R:** 396
Tiepolo, Giovanni Domenico [Italian painter]
Mythology *picture on* **M:** 980
Tiergarten [park, Berlin]
Berlin (Recreation) **B:** 262
Tierra del Fuego [islands, Argentina-Chile] **T:** 283 *with maps*
Argentina (Patagonia) **A:** 653
Chile (The Archipelago) **C:** 465
Tietê River [Brazil]
São Paulo (The city) **S:** 117
Tiffany, Charles Lewis [American businessman] **T:** 283
Tiffany, Louis Comfort [American artist] **T:** 283
Art Nouveau **A:** 750
Glass *picture on* **G:** 222; (Types of art glass) **G:** 220-221
Stained glass (Decline and revival) **So:** 823
Tiffany diamond
Diamond *picture on* **D:** 181
Tiffany Favrile glass
Glass (Types of art glass) **G:** 220-221
Tiffany, Louis Comfort **T:** 283
Tiffin, Edward [American political leader]
Ohio (table) **O:** 699
Tiflis [Georgia] *See* Tbilisi *in this index*
Tiger [animal] **T:** 283 *with pictures and map*
Animal *pictures on* **A:** 472, **A:** 481
Endangered species *picture on* **E:** 271; (table) **E:** 270
Mammal *picture on* **M:** 127
Zoo *pictures on* **Z:** 600, **Z:** 605
Tiger at the Gates [play by Fry]
Fry, Christopher **F:** 549
Tiger beetle
Beetle *pictures on* **B:** 218
Insect *picture on* **I:** 283; (Protection from enemies) **I:** 297
Tiger cat [wild cat] *See* Ocelot *in this index*
Tiger-Cats, Hamilton [team]
Football (Canadian Football League) **F:** 364
Tiger cowrie [shell]
Shell *pictures on* **S:** 386
Tiger Cub program
Boy Scouts (Cub Scouting) **B:** 537
Tiger Eyes [book by Blume]
Blume, Judy **B:** 425
Tiger-Lilies [book by Lanier]
Lanier, Sidney **L:** 68
Tiger lily [plant] **T:** 285 *with picture*
Tiger mimic-queen [butterfly]
Butterfly *picture on* **B:** 735
Tiger moth
Cocoon **C:** 747
Moth (Kinds of moths) **M:** 840 *with pictures*
Woollybear **W:** 402
Tiger of France [nickname]

Clemenceau, Georges Ci: 662
Tiger quoll [animal]
    Quoll Q: 44
Tiger Rising, The [book by DiCamillo]
    DiCamillo, Kate D: 186
Tiger shark [fish] T: 285
Tiger snake T: 285
Tiger swallowtail [butterfly]
    Butterfly *picture on* B: 736
Tigers, Detroit [team] *See* Detroit Tigers *in this
    index*
Tight end [football]
    Football (The offensive team) F: 356 *with
    diagrams*
Tight monetary policy
    Inflation (Monetary policy) I: 268
    Recession (Causes of recession) R: 175
Tight packing [slavery]
    African Americans (Beginning of the slave trade)
    A: 136c-136d *with picture*
Tiglath-pileser III [king of Assyria] T: 286
    Assyria (History) A: 822
Tiglon [wild cat]
    Lion (Cubs) L: 341
Tigon [animal]
    Lion (Cubs) L: 341
    Tiger (The body of a tiger) T: 283-284
Tigran II [king of Armenia]
    Armenia (History) A: 718b
Tigrane, II [opera by Scarlatti]
    Scarlatti, Alessandro S: 173
Tigray [region]
    Eritrea (History) E: 353-354
    Ethiopia (The late 1900's) E: 372
Tigrayans [people]
    Ethiopia (People) E: 368
Tigress [wild cat]
    Tiger (The life of a tiger) T: 284
Tigrinya [language]
    Eritrea (People) E: 352
    Ethiopia (People) E: 368
Tigris-Euphrates Valley [region, Iraq]
    Asia (History) A: 804
    City (Ancient cities) Ci: 578
    World, History of the (The Tigris-Euphrates Valley)
    W: 422 *with map*
Tigris River [Iraq-Turkey] T: 286
    Euphrates River E: 378 *with map*
    Fertile Crescent F: 78 *with map*
    Iraq (The southern plain) I: 411 *with map*
Tihama [region]
    Saudi Arabia (The Western Highlands) S: 158
    with map
    Yemen (Land) Y: 562
Tijuana [Mexico] T: 286
Tikal [ancient city, Central America] T: 286
    Architecture *picture on* A: 614
    Guatemala (The Northern Plain) G: 414
    Maya *picture on* M: 326
Tikal National Park [Guatemala]
    National park *picture on* N: 42e; (table) N: 42g;
    (Other interesting national parks) N: 42h
Tikrit [Iraq]
    Hussein, Saddam H: 458
Tiktaalik [fish] T: 286 *with picture*
Tilbury Town [fictional place]
    Robinson, Edwin Arlington R: 368
Tilden, Bill [American tennis player] T: 287
Tilden, Samuel Jones [American political leader]
    T: 287
    Electoral Commission E: 164
    Hayes, Rutherford Birchard (Campaign of 1876)
    H: 120
    New York (table) N: 313
    Reconstruction (The 1876 presidential election)
    R: 179
Tile T: 287
    Interior design (Choosing patterns and textures)
    I: 332-333
    Islamic art (Pottery) I: 470
Tile game
    Game (Tile games) G: 22 *with picture*
Tilefish [fish] T: 287
Tilghman, Benjamin Chew [American inventor]
    Paper (History) P: 136-137
Tilghman Island [Chesapeake Bay]
    Maryland *picture on* M: 240
Till [geology]
    Glacier (How glaciers shape the land) G: 203
    Minnesota (Land regions) M: 596-598
Till, Emmett [American public figure] *See* Emmett
    Till case *in this index*
Till, Mamie [American public figure]
    Emmett Till case E: 260
Till Plains [region]
    Illinois (Land regions) I: 64
    Indiana (Land regions) I: 208

Ohio (Land regions) O: 692
Tillage [agriculture]
    Conservation (Soil conservation) Ci: 979-980
    Cotton (Preparing the soil) Ci: 1090
    Erosion (Controlling erosion) E: 355
    Farm and farming (Preparing the soil) F: 35 *with
    picture*
    Plow P: 575
Tillamook Burn [forest fire]
    Portland [Oregon] (History) P: 684
Tiller [botany]
    Rice (Growth and reproduction) R: 323
    Sugar cane So: 963
Tiller [ship]
    Sailing (Hull) S: 23 *with picture*
Tilley, Leonard P. de W. [Canadian political leader]
    New Brunswick (table) N: 195
Tilley, Sir Samuel Leonard [Canadian patriot]
    Confederation of Canada (Fathers of
    Confederation) Ci: 935 *with picture*
Tillich, Paul [German-American theologian]
    Agnosticism A: 143
Tillie's Punctured Romance [film]
    Sennett, Mack *picture on* S: 301
Tillman, Benjamin Ryan [American political
    leader]
    South Carolina (Industrial growth) So: 660-662
Tillmanites [political group]
    South Carolina (Industrial growth) So: 660-662
Tilly, Count of [Belgian general]
    Thirty Years' War (The Swedish period) T: 260
Tilsit, Treaty of [1807]
    Napoleonic Wars (The alliance of Prussia and
    Russia) N: 18
Tilt-engine aircraft
    V/STOL V: 452
Tilt-up construction
    Building construction (Types of construction)
    B: 683 *with picture*
Tilt-wing aircraft
    V/STOL V: 452
Tilted Arc [sculpture by Serra]
    Serra, Richard S: 318
Tilting [sport]
    Knights and knighthood (Tournaments) K: 350-
    351
Tiltrotor [aircraft]
    Helicopter (Recent developments) H: 174
Timaeus [book by Plato]
    Atlantis A: 868
    Plato (The dialogues) P: 567
Timbales [drums]
    Hispanic Americans *picture on* H: 247
Timber
    Forest F: 390 *with pictures*
    Forest products (Wood products) F: 400 *with
    picture*
    Forestry F: 404 *with pictures*
    Lumber L: 517
Timber dam
    Dam (Other types of dams) D: 19
Timber hitch
    Knots, hitches, and splices (Two half hitches)
    K: 357 *with diagram*
Timber line
    Forest (Mountain evergreen forests) F: 395
    Mountain (As a home for plants and animals)
    M: 892
Timber rattlesnake
    Rattlesnake R: 149 *with picture*
Timber wolf
    Wolf W: 375 *with picture*
Timberlake, John B. [husband of]
    O'Neale, Peggy O: 761
Timberwolves, Minnesota [basketball team]
    Basketball (table) B: 150
Timbre [sound]
    Harmonics H: 62
    Music (Tone color) M: 952
    Sound (Sound quality) So: 601
Timbuktu [Mali] T: 287
    Africa (The empires of west Africa) A: 131
    Exploration (The exploration of Africa) E: 448-
    Mali (History) M: 108-109 *with map*
    Mali Empire M: 109
    World, History of the (African civilizations) W: 437
    with picture
Time T: 288 *with pictures and maps*
    Atomic clock A: 877
    Biological clock B: 314
    Calendar C: 28
    Chronometer C: 539
    Clock Ci: 682i
    Day and night D: 52
    Daylight saving time D: 54
    Fourth dimension F: 438
    Hour H: 379

    Longitude (Longitude and time) L: 452
    Metaphysics (Space and time) M: 429
    Metric system (Structure of the metric system)
    M: 437; (Space and time) M: 437
    Navigation (Keeping time) N: 71
    Relativity (Lorentz transformations) R: 211; (Time
    dilation) R: 211
    Sidereal time S: 448
    Standard time So: 835
    Sundial So: 990 *with picture*
Time [magazine]
    Journalism (The age of sensationalism) J: 175
    Luce, Henry Robinson L: 513
    Magazine (Magazines in the 1900's) M: 45
Time, Forward! [book by Kataev]
    Russian literature (The period of industrial
    literature) R: 564
Time and Free Will [book by Bergson]
    Bergson, Henri B: 258
Time and motion study
    Gilbreth, Frank and Lillian G: 190
    Taylor, Frederick Winslow T: 57
Time and the Conways [play by Priestley]
    Priestley, John Boynton P: 776
Time capsule T: 292c
Time-delay fuse
    Fuse F: 589
Time deposit
    Money (The money supply) M: 715
    Savings bank S: 166
Time dilation [physics]
    Relativity (Time dilation) R: 211
    Time (Time in relativity theory) T: 292b
"Time Fantasy" [books by L'Engle]
    L'Engle, Madeleine L: 191
Time lock
    Lock (Electric locks) L: 412
Time Machine, The [book by Wells]
    Wells, H. G. W: 195
Time of Angels, A [book by Hesse]
    Hesse, Karen K: 219
Time of the Hero, The [book by Vargas Llosa]
    Vargas Llosa, Mario V: 285
Time of Troubles [Russian history]
    Russia (The Time of Troubles) R: 549
Time of Wonder [book by McCloskey]
    McCloskey, Robert M: 332d
Time of Your Life, The [play by Saroyan]
    Saroyan, William S: 127
Time-sharing [computer]
    Computer (Mainframes and supercomputers)
    Ci: 910-911
Time signature [music]
    Music (Indicating time values) M: 953-954 *with
    pictures*
Time to Heal, A [book by Ford]
    Ford, Gerald Rudolph (Later years) F: 379
Time to Kill, A [book by Grisham]
    Grisham, John G: 396
Time travel
    Time (Time travel) T: 292b
Time trial
    Bicycle racing (Track races) B: 292
Time Warner Inc. T: 292d
    Turner, Ted T: 518
Time zone
    Greenwich meridian G: 386
    Standard time So: 835
    Time *maps on* T: 289-291; (Time in today's world)
    T: 292 *with diagram*
Timecode [film]
    Motion picture (The computer revolution) M: 872
Timed-pulse transducer [device]
    Governor G: 294
Timed-release medicine
    Microencapsulation M: 514
Timekeeper [person]
    Basketball (The officials) B: 145
    Boxing (Officials) B: 527
    Hockey (The officials) H: 278
Timer
    Radar (The timer) R: 71 *with diagram*
Times, The [newspaper]
    Communication (The 1800's) Ci: 881
    London (Communication) L: 438
    Murdoch, Rupert M: 930
    Newspaper (In Europe) N: 386
    Sudoku So: 957
Time's arrow
    Entropy E: 328
Times Beach [Missouri]
    Missouri (The late 1900's) M: 672
Times Square [New York City]
    New York City *pictures on* N: 343; (Manhattan)
    N: 323-325; (The arts) N: 336
"Times They Are A-Changin,' The" [song]
    Dylan, Bob D: 397

Times Three [poems by McGinley]
McGinley, Phyllis **M: 334**
Timetable, Geologic *See* Geological time scale *in
this index*
Timgad [ancient city]
City *pictures on* **Ci: 581**
Timimoun [Algeria]
Algeria *picture on* **A: 363**
Timişoara [Romania]
Romania (Protests and political change) **R: 425**
Timms Hill
Wisconsin (Land regions) **W: 358** *with map*
Timofeyevich, Yermak [Russian military leader]
Exploration (The Russians in Siberia) **E: 447**
Timon of Athens [play by Shakespeare]
Shakespeare, William: *(Timon of Athens)* **S: 364**
Timor [island, Southeast Asia] **T: 292d**
See also East Timor *in this index*
Timotheus [Greek sculptor]
Seven Wonders of the Ancient World (The
Mausoleum at Halicarnassus) **S: 325**
Timothy [Biblical figure] **T: 292d**
Timothy [plant] **T: 292d**
Grass *picture on* **G: 325**
Timothy, Epistles to
Bible (The Letters) **B: 284**
Timothy **T: 292d**
Timpani [musical instrument]
Drum **D: 367**
Music *picture on* **M: 949**; (Percussion instruments)
M: 950
Timpanogos Cave National Monument [Utah]
T: 292c
National Park System (table: National
monuments) **N: 51**
Timucua Indians
Jacksonville (Cultural life and recreation) **J: 18**;
(History) **J: 19**
**Timucuan Ecological and Historic National
Preserve** [Florida]
National Park System (table: National preserves)
N: 58
Timur [Mongol conqueror] **T: 292d** *with map*
Delhi Sultanate **D: 116**
India (Period of invasions) **I: 129**
Mongol Empire (Breakup) **M: 721**
Timur Shah [king of Afghanistan]
Afghanistan (United Afghanistan) **A: 95**
Tin [element] **T: 293** *with pictures*
Aluminum (Properties of aluminum alloys)
A: 391-392
Bolivia (Mining) **B: 445**
Cassiterite **C: 277**
Pewter **P: 352**
T'in [people]
Rain forest (Asia) **R: 126b**
Tin [sports]
Squash **So: 813** *with diagram*
Tin can T: 294
Iron and steel (Finishing) **I: 447**
Tin can [ship]
Destroyer **D: 162**
Tin Drum, The [book by Grass]
German literature (Postwar German literature
[1945-1990]) **G: 142**
Grass, Günter **G: 326**
Novel (The novel today) **N: 575**
Tin Flute, The [book by Roy]
Roy, Gabrielle **R: 494**
Tin Lizzie [automobile]
Ford Motor Company **F: 382**
Tin oxide
Majolica **M: 93**
Tin Pan Alley [music]
Popular music (Vaudeville and musical comedy)
P: 670
Song **So: 592**
Tin plate [metal]
Tin **T: 293**
Tina [drug] *See* Methamphetamine *in this index*
Tinbergen, Jan [Dutch economist] **T: 294**
Econometrics **E: 57**
Tinbergen, Nikolaas [Dutch zoologist] **T: 294**
Tincture [heraldry]
Heraldry (Expansion) **H: 194** *with pictures*
Tincture of squill [medication]
Squill **So: 814b**
Tinder
Camping (Building a campfire) **C: 94-96**
Fire (Methods of starting fires) **F: 121**
Tinderbox
Fire (Methods of starting fires) **F: 121**
Tine [zoology]
Deer (Antlers) **D: 83-84**
Ting, Samuel Chao Chung [American physicist]
Asian Americans (Notable Asian American "firsts")
A: 812f

Nobel Prizes (Physics: 1976) **N: 441**
Physics (Advances in the mid-1900's) **P: 442** *with
picture*
Tingley, Clyde [American political leader]
New Mexico (table) **N: 272**
Tinguely, Jean [French sculptor]
Sculpture (Form and treatment) **S: 230-231**
Tinh [government]
Vietnam (Local level) **V: 365**
Tinicum Island [U.S. history]
Pennsylvania (Exploration and settlement) **P: 264**
Tinker, Joe [American baseball player]
Baseball (table: Hall of Fame) **B: 134b**
Tinker Air Force Base [Oklahoma]
Oklahoma City (Economy) **O: 736**
Tinker Bell [literary figure]
Peter Pan **P: 325**
Tinnitus [disorder] **T: 294**
Deafness (Environmental factors) **D: 57**
Ear (Diseases) **E: 12**
Tinoco, Federico [Costa Rican political leader]
Costa Rica (Revolutions and reforms) **Ci: 1084**
Tinstone [mineral]
Cassiterite **C: 277**
Tint
Color *diagram on* **Ci: 822**
Tintoretto [Italian painter] **T: 294** *with picture*
Painting (Mannerism) **P: 56-57** *with picture*
Tiny sparrowhawk [bird]
Hawk (Kinds of hawks) **H: 111**
Tipi [dwelling] **T: 294**
Indian, American *pictures on* **I: 138, I: 154, I: 161**;
(Shelter) **I: 136d**; (Indians of the Plains) **I: 158-
159** *with picture*
New Brunswick *picture on* **N: 196**
Tipitapa River [Nicaragua]
Lake Nicaragua **L: 42**
Tippecanoe, Battle of [1811]
Indian wars (The Shawnee Prophet) **I: 192**
Indiana (Territorial days) **I: 215-216** *with picture*
Tecumseh **T: 78**
Westward movement in America (Indian
conflicts) **W: 247**
"Tippecanoe and Tyler too"
Harrison, William Henry **H: 74**
Van Buren, Martin (Election of 1840) **V: 273**
Tipperary [Ireland] **T: 295**
Tipping [process]
Fur (Dyeing) **F: 563**
Tipping machine
Bookbinding (Forming a book) **B: 470**
Tippit, J. D. [American police officer]
Kennedy, John Fitzgerald (The death of Oswald)
K: 267
Oswald, Lee Harvey **O: 869**
Tirana [Albania] *See* Tiranë *in this index*
Tiranë [Albania] **T: 295**
Albania **A: 306** *with picture*
Tire T: 295 *with pictures*
Automobile (Supporting the car) **A: 950**
Firestone, Harvey Samuel **F: 135**
Materials *picture on* **M: 300c**
Tirich Mir [mountain, Asia]
Hindu Kush **H: 235**
Pakistan *picture on* **P: 92**
Tiro, Marcus Tullius [Roman secretary]
Shorthand **S: 435**
Tirol [Austria] *See* Tyrol *in this index*
Tirso de Molina [Spanish dramatist] **T: 298**
Don Juan **D: 306**
Tirthankara [religion]
Mahavira **M: 65**
Religion (Belief in a deity) **R: 215**
'Tis Pity She's a Whore [play by Ford]
Ford, John **F: 381**
Tisch, Laurence [American businessman]
CBS **C: 323**
Tiselius, Arne W. K. [Swedish chemist]
Immune system (Further breakthroughs) **I: 88d**
Nobel Prizes (Chemistry: 1948) **N: 443**
Tishah be-Av [religion] **T: 298**
Judaism (Other holidays) **J: 182**
Tishri [month]
Calendar (The Hebrew calendar) **C: 29**
Judaism (The High Holidays) **J: 181**
Tisias [Greek orator]
Oratory (Beginnings) **O: 818**
Tisiphone [Greek mythology]
Furies **F: 566**
Tiso, Jozef [Slovak political leader]
Slovakia (World War II) **S: 509**
Tisquantum [American Indian interpreter] *See*
Squanto *in this index*
Tissaphernes [Persian military leader]
Alcibiades **A: 334**
Tississat Falls [Ethiopia]
Ethiopia *picture on* **E: 371**

Tissot, James [French artist]
Painting (Painting outside France) **P: 72**
Tissue [physiology] **T: 298**
Food (Building and repairing tissues) **F: 331**
Histology **H: 260**
Inflammation **I: 266**
Life (Tissues, organs, and organ systems) **L: 277**
with diagram
Plant (Parts of plants) **P: 528**
Transplant **T: 379**
Tree (The parts of a tree) **T: 416** *with picture*
Tissue bank [medicine]
Transplant **T: 379**
Tissue engineering
Biomedical engineering (Developing) **B: 325**
Tissue plasminogen activator [drug]
Heredity (The era of genetic engineering) **H: 209**
Stroke (Treatment) **So: 930**
Tissue transplant [medicine] *See* Transplant *in
this index*
Tisza River [Europe]
Hungary (Rivers and lakes) **H: 443** *with map*
Tit [bird]
Bird *picture on* **B: 344d**; (Birds of Europe) **B: 344c**
Titan [satellite] **T: 299** *with picture*
Cassini **C: 276**
Mountain (On Titan) **M: 895**
Satellite (Major satellites) **S: 150a**
Saturn (Satellites) **S: 151** *with picture*
Voyager **V: 451**
Titan arum [plant]
Flower *picture on* **F: 272**
Titania [gem]
Titanium **T: 300**
Titania [legendary figure]
Fairy (Fairies in literature) **F: 11** *with picture*
Shakespeare, William: *(A Midsummer Night's
Dream)* **S: 357**
Titania [satellite]
Satellite (The middle-sized icy satellites of Saturn
and Uranus) **S: 150b**
Uranus *picture on* **U: 219**
Titanic [film]
Cameron, James **C: 84**
DiCaprio, Leonardo **D: 187**
Motion picture (Best picture: 1997) **M: 861**
Titanic [ship] **T: 299** *with picture*
Ballard, Robert Duane **B: 43**
Sarnoff, David **S: 127**
Titaniferous magnetite [mineral]
Vanadium **V: 269**
Titanium [element] **T: 300**
Alloy (Alloys for strength and lightness) **A: 378**
Titanium dioxide [chemical]
Titanium **T: 300**
Titanium tetrachloride [chemical]
Titanium **T: 300**
Titano, Mount [San Marino]
San Marino [city] **S: 104**
San Marino [country] (Land) **S: 103** *with picture*
Titanomachy [Greek mythology]
Mythology (The Greek creation myth) **M: 980-
981**
Rhea **R: 290**
Titans [Greek mythology] **T: 300**
Atlas **A: 868**
Cronus **Ci: 1152**
Hecate **H: 164**
Mythology (The Greek creation myth) **M: 980**;
(Greek divinities) **M: 982**
Uranus **U: 217**
Titans, Tennessee *See* Tennessee Titans *in this index*
Tithe [tax] **T: 301**
Mormons (Church organization) **M: 807-808**
Tithing [English history]
Police (Early law enforcement in England) **P: 624**
Tithonus [mythology]
Aurora **A: 891**
Titi [monkey] **T: 301** *with picture*
Titian [Italian artist] **T: 301** *with picture*
Drawing *picture on* **D: 344**
Painting (The Renaissance in Venice) **P: 55-56**
with picture
Titicaca, Lake *See* Lake Titicaca *in this index*
Titius, Johann D. [German mathematician]
Bode's law **B: 434**
Title [law] **T: 302**
Occupancy **O: 647**
Tenant **T: 132**
Torrens system **T: 342**
Title [motion picture]
Motion picture (Early motion pictures) **M: 863**
Title [name] *See* Address, Forms of *in this index*
Title, Abstract of [law]
Deed **D: 81**
Title card [reference]
A Guide to Research Skills **Research Guide: 28**

Title insurance
Deed D: 81
Torrens system T: 342
Title of honor
Nobility N: 450
Title page
Book (Inside a book) B: 464-465
Titmarsh, Michael Angelo [pen name]
Thackeray, William Makepeace (Early career) T: 220
Titmouse [bird] T: 302 *with picture*
Bird (Birds of forests and woodlands) B: 334 *with picture*
Tito, Dennis [American businessman]
International Space Station (History) I: 346b-347
Tito, Josip Broz [Yugoslav political leader] T: 302
Cold War (The containment policy) Ci: 764
Croatia (Communist rule) Ci: 1148a-1148b
Podgorica P: 588
Serbia (History) S: 314-316
Slovenia (History) S: 512
Yugoslavia (Communist rule) Y: 576; (World War II) Y: 576
Titograd [former name] *See* Podgorica *in this index*
Titov, Gherman [Russian cosmonaut]
Space exploration (Vostok and Mercury: The first human beings in space) So: 711-713
Tituba [American colonist]
Salem (History) S: 61
Titus [Biblical figure] T: 303
Timothy T: 292d
Titus [Roman emperor] T: 303
Domitian D: 306
Rome, Ancient (The Roman Empire) R: 446
Titus, Epistle to [New Testament]
Bible (The Letters) B: 284
Titus T: 303
Titus Andronicus [play by Shakespeare]
Shakespeare, William: (*Titus Andronicus*) S: 356
Tiv [people]
Tribe T: 440
Tivoli Gardens [park, Copenhagen]
Denmark (Recreation) D: 136-137 *with picture*
Tiw [Norse god]
Tuesday T: 481
Tiwanaku Indians *See* Tiahuanaco Indians *in this index*
TKO [sports]
Boxing (Scoring a fight) B: 527
Tl [symbol]
Thallium T: 229
Tláloc [Aztec god]
Mythology (Aztec mythology) M: 987
Tlatchli [court]
Aztec (Way of life) A: 1000
Tlatelolco [former city]
Aztec *picture on* A: 1004; (The Aztec empire) A: 999 *with map*; (Trade and transportation) A: 1002
Tlatelolco, Treaty of [1967]
Arms control (Arms control in the mid-1900's) A: 721-722
Tlaxcala [city, Mexico]
Tlaxcala T: 303
Tlaxcala [state, Mexico] T: 303
Tlaxcalli [food]
Aztec (Food) A: 1001
Tlaxcalteca Indians
Tlaxcala T: 303
Tlazoltéotl [Aztec goddess]
Mythology (Aztec mythology) M: 987
Tlicho Land Claims and Self-government Act [2005]
Northwest Territories (Recent developments) N: 534
Tlingit Indians T: 303
Alaska (Population) A: 286
Indian, American *pictures on* I: 139
Tm [symbol]
Thulium T: 272
TMR method [agriculture]
Dairying (Feeding) D: 7
TNM system [medicine]
Cancer (Staging) C: 172
TNT [explosive] T: 303
Bomb (The explosive material) B: 450
Nitric acid N: 425
"To a Nightingale" [poem by Keats]
Poetry (Imagery) P: 575
"To a Water Lily" [music by MacDowell]
MacDowell, Edward Alexander M: 11
"To a Waterfowl" [poem by Bryant]
Bryant, William Cullen (His early works) B: 655-656
"To a Wild Rose" [music by MacDowell]
MacDowell, Edward Alexander M: 11
"To Althea from Prison" [poem by Lovelace]

Lovelace, Richard L: 509
"To Anacreon in Heaven" [song]
Key, Francis Scott K: 308
National anthem N: 29
"Star-Spangled Banner" So: 854
To Be a Pilgrim [book by Cary]
Cary, Joyce C: 270
To Be Young, Gifted and Black [book by Hansberry]
Hansberry, Lorraine H: 53
To Bedlam and Part Way Back [poems by Sexton]
Sexton, Anne S: 337
To Every Thing There Is a Season [book by Dillon]
Literature for children *picture on* L: 382
"To Helen" [poem by Poe]
Poe, Edgar Allan (Poe's life) P: 589; (Poetry and poetic theory) P: 589-590
"To His Coy Mistress" [poem by Marvell]
Marvell, Andrew M: 236
"To Juan at the Winter Solstice" [poem by Graves]
Graves, Robert G: 331
To Kill a Mockingbird [book by Lee]
Lee, Harper L: 176
To Let [book by Galsworthy]
Galsworthy, John G: 16
"To Lucasta, Going to the Wars" [poem by Lovelace]
Lovelace, Richard L: 509
To the Christian Nobility of the German Nation [book by Luther]
Luther, Martin (The break with the Roman Catholic Church) L: 528
To the Lighthouse [book by Woolf]
Novel (New directions in the novel) N: 573-574
Woolf, Virginia W: 401
"To the Virgins, to Make Much of Time" [poem by Herrick]
Herrick, Robert H: 215
Toad [animal] T: 303 *with picture*
Amphibian (Kinds of amphibians) A: 440
Frog (Kinds of frogs) F: 539
Tadpole T: 6
Toadfish [fish] T: 304 *with picture*
Toadflax [plant] T: 305 *with picture*
Toadstool
Mushroom M: 942
Toadstool Geological Park
Nebraska N: 102-103 *with picture*
Toana Range [mountains, Nevada]
Nevada (Land regions) N: 166
Toasting [performance]
Rock music (Rap) R: 380d
Tobacco T: 305 *with picture*
See also Smoking *in this index*
Cigar Ci: 552
Cigarette Ci: 552
Colonial life in America (Farming) Ci: 809-810 *with picture*
Drug abuse (Abuse of legal drugs) D: 361
Indian, American (Shamans) I: 147
Jamestown J: 29
Kentucky (Agriculture) K: 289 *with picture*
Lexington L: 224
Nicotine N: 405
North Carolina (Agriculture) N: 488; (Manufacturing) N: 488
Poisonous plant (Some poisonous plants) P: 602
Pure food and drug laws (History) P: 909
Rolfe, John R: 402
Snuff S: 542
South Carolina (Agriculture) So: 655 *with picture*
United States, History of the *picture on* U: 155
Virginia (Manufacturing) V: 413 *with picture*
Tobacco certificate
Colonial life in America (Money) Ci: 811
Tobacco juice [entomology]
Grasshopper G: 327
Tobacco mosaic virus
Mosaic disease M: 822
Virus (Discovery) V: 427; (Structure) V: 427-428 *with picture*
Tobacco Road [book by Caldwell]
Caldwell, Erskine C: 28
Tobacco root *See* Bitter root *in this index*
Tobacco Root Mountains
Montana (Land regions) M: 752
Tobacco Wars [1904-1909]
Kentucky (The early 1900's) K: 293-294
Tobaccowood [shrub]
Witch hazel W: 371
Tobago *See* Trinidad and Tobago *in this index*
Tobey, Charles W. [American political leader]
New Hampshire (table) N: 223
Tobin, James [American economist]
Nobel Prizes (Economics: 1981) N: 449
Tobin, Maurice J. [American government official]
Labor, Department of (table) L: 2
Massachusetts (table) M: 288

Truman, Harry S. (table) T: 469
Tobit [Bible]
Galilee G: 11
Tobogganing [sport] T: 308 *with picture*
Indian, American *picture on* I: 138
Toborochi [tree]
South America *picture on* So: 626
Tochmarc Étaín [story]
Irish literature (Heroic tales, romances, and sagas) I: 430
Toco toucan [bird]
Toucan T: 347 *with picture*
Tocopherol *See* Vitamin E *in this index*
Tocqueville, Alexis de [French philosopher] T: 308
Westward movement in America (The frontier influence) W: 252
"Today and Tomorrow" [newspaper column]
Lippmann, Walter L: 346
Todd, Alexander [British chemist]
Nobel Prizes (Chemistry: 1957) N: 443
Todd, David [American government official]
Ohio (table) O: 699
Todd, Mary [wife of Abraham Lincoln] *See* Lincoln, Mary Todd *in this index*
Todd, Robert S. [father of]
Lincoln, Mary Todd L: 327
Todd, Thomas [American jurist]
Supreme Court of the United States (table) So: 1000
Toddler
Child (The toddler stage) C: 449 *with picture*
Toddy [drink]
Coconut palm Ci: 746
Toe [anatomy]
Bird (Legs and feet) B: 364
Toe dancing
Ballet (Point work) B: 47
Toe pick
Ice skating (Figure skating) I: 11
Toe ring
Ring R: 342
Toe shoe
Ballet *picture on* B: 47
Toenail
Nail N: 4
Toffee
Candy (Chewy candies) C: 176
Tofu [food] T: 308
Asian Americans (Asian influences on American culture) A: 812c
Soybean So: 689
Toga [clothing] T: 309 *with picture*
Clothing (Rome) Ci: 697 *with picture*
Rome, Ancient (Clothing) R: 440
Tunic T: 487
Toggenburg goat
Goat *picture on* G: 241; (Domestic goats) G: 239
Toggle switch
Electric switch E: 189 *with diagram*
Toggling
Leather (Final processing) L: 168
Togo T: 309 *with pictures and map*
Flag *picture on* F: 200
Togo, Heihachiro [Japanese admiral]
Russo-Japanese War (Attack on Lüshun) R: 566b
Togo Mountains
Togo (Land) T: 310 *with map*
Tohono O'odham Indians
Indian, American (Indians of the Southwest) I: 166-167
Rain dance R: 125
Tóibin, Colm [Irish author]
Irish literature (Fiction) I: 432-433
Toilet
Plumbing (How toilets work) P: 579 *with diagrams*; (History) P: 580
Toilet, The [play by Baraka]
Baraka, Amiri B: 103
Toilet soap
Detergent and soap (Bar soaps) D: 164
Toilet training
Baby (From 12 to 18 months) B: 7-8
Child (The preschool years) C: 449
Toilet water
Perfume P: 286
Toiyabe Range [mountains, Nevada]
Nevada (Land regions) N: 166 *with map*
Tojo, Hideki [Japanese military leader] T: 311
Japan (Allied military occupation) J: 58; (World War II) J: 58
Pearl Harbor (Background) P: 218
World War II (The rise of dictatorships) W: 469-470; (Japan attacks) W: 479
Tok Pisin [language]
New Guinea (People) N: 206
Papua New Guinea (People) P: 140
Tokamak [nuclear reactor]

Nuclear energy (Experimental fusion devices)
    N: 592-593 *with pictures*
Tokara Islands [Pacific]
    Ryukyu Islands R: 574
Tokelau [islands, Pacific]
    New Zealand (Overseas territories) N: 348
Tokelau [island, Pacific]
    Pacific Islands (table) P: 9
Tokugawa [Japanese clan]
    Japan (Tokugawa period) J: 55
    Japanese literature (The Tokugawa period) J: 62
    Painting (Japanese painting) P: 47
    Shogun S: 433
    Tokugawa Ieyasu T: 311
Tokugawa Ieyasu [Japanese political leader] T: 311
    Japan (Tokugawa period) J: 55
    Tokyo (Early development) T: 318
Tokyo [Japan] T: 312 *with pictures and maps*
    Advertising *picture on* A: 72
    Architecture *picture on* A: 606
    Japan *pictures on* J: 33, J: 44; (People) J: 35;
        (Climate) J: 48
    Olympic Games (The postwar games) O: 751-752
    Terrorism (Terrorist movements and groups)
        T: 179
Tokyo Bay
    Tokyo (The city) T: 313
Tokyo Cathedral
    Architecture *picture on* A: 606
Tokyo Central Wholesale Market
    Tokyo (Other places of interest) T: 317
Tokyo Disney Resort [amusement park]
    Tokyo (Other places of interest) T: 317
    Walt Disney Company W: 21
Tokyo Dome [sports]
    Tokyo (Recreation) T: 316
Tokyo International Airport
    Airport (table) A: 245
    Tokyo (Transportation) T: 318
Tokyo International Trade Center
    Tokyo (Trade) T: 317-318
Tokyo Metropolitan Prefecture [province, Japan]
    Tokyo (Tokyo Metropolitan Prefecture) T: 313;
        (Government) T: 318
Tokyo Rose [Japanese propagandist] T: 320
    World War II (Propaganda) W: 494-495
Tokyo Stock Exchange [economics]
    Tokyo (Finance) T: 317 *with picture*
Tokyo Tower
    Tokyo (Tokyo Tower) T: 316
Tokyo Trade Center
    Tokyo (Trade) T: 317
Tokyo trials [World War II]
    International law (Punishment) I: 341
    War crime (World War II) W: 27
Toland, Gregg [American cameraman]
    Motion picture (Movies in the 1930's) M: 867-869
Toland, John [English philosopher]
    Freethinker F: 509
Tolbert, William R., Jr. [Liberian political leader]
    Liberia (The 1970's and 1980's) L: 232
Toledo [Spain] T: 320
Toledo [Ohio] T: 321
Toledo, Alejandro [Peruvian political leader]
    Peru (Recent developments) P: 316
Toledo, Fernando Alvarez de [Spanish general]
    See Alba, Duke of *in this index*
Toledo, José Álvarez de [Mexican journalist]
    Texas (Communication) T: 203
Toledo, José Rey [American painter]
    Indian, American *picture on* I: 147
Toledo Bend [lake, Louisiana-Texas]
    Texas (Rivers and lakes) T: 198
Toledo Botanical Garden
    Ohio *picture on* O: 684
Toledo Strip [U.S. history]
    Michigan (Territorial period) M: 509
Toleration Act [1649]
    Toleration Act T: 321
Toleration Act [1689] T: 321
Toleware
    Antique (Metalwork) A: 558
Tolima [volcano, Colombia]
    Andes Mountains (Physical features) A: 452
Tolkien, Christopher [son of]
    Tolkien, J. R. R. T: 322
Tolkien, J. R. R. [British author] T: 321
    Fairy (Fairies in literature) F: 11
    Jackson, Peter J: 15
Toll [tax]
    Road (How roads and highways are paid for)
        R: 360
Toll road
    Transportation (Challenges of modern
        transportation) T: 397
    Turnpike T: 519
Tollán [ancient city]

Toltec Indians T: 323
    Tula T: 482
Toller [dog] *See* Nova Scotia duck tolling retriever
    in this index
Tolmie, Simon F. [Canadian political leader]
    British Columbia (table) B: 628
Tolmie's saxifrage [flower]
    Flower *picture on* F: 289
Tolstoy, Alexei [Russian author] T: 322
    Russian literature (The period of rebirth) R: 564
Tolstoy, Leo [Russian author] T: 322 *with portrait*
    Doukhobors D: 314
    Novel (Russia) N: 573
    Russian literature (The 1860's and 1870's) R: 562
Toltec Indians T: 323
    Architecture (Pre-Columbian architecture) A: 614
    Hidalgo H: 224
    Indian, American *picture on* I: 146; (Before
        European contact) I: 169-170
    Latin America (Early inhabitants) L: 102
    Maya (The Postclassic Period) M: 326
    Mexico (The Toltec and the Aztec) M: 468
    Pyramids (American pyramids) P: 917-919
    Tula T: 482
Toluca [Mexico]
    México M: 475
Toluene [chemical] T: 323
    Saccharin S: 4
Tolypocladium inflatum [fungus]
    Cyclosporine Ci: 1204
Tom [cat]
    Cat (Reproduction) C: 293
Tom Brown's School Days [book by Hughes]
    Hughes, Thomas H: 409
    Rugby School R: 513
Tom Jones [book by Fielding]
    English literature (The rise of the novel) E: 318-
        319
    Fielding, Henry (His novels) F: 94
    Novel (The first English novelists) N: 572
Tom Jones [film]
    Motion picture (Best picture: 1963) M: 861
Tom Sawyer [book by Twain]
    American literature *picture on* A: 416; (Mark
        Twain and Henry James) A: 420
    Twain, Mark (Productive years in Hartford) T: 529
Tom Sawyer Fence Painting Contest [Hannibal]
    Missouri *picture on* M: 654
Tom Shows [U.S. history]
    Stowe, Harriet Beecher So: 916
Tom Thumb [American entertainer] *See* Stratton,
    Charles Sherwood *in this index*
Tom Thumb [locomotive]
    Baltimore (The 1800's) B: 69-70
    Cooper, Peter Ci: 1035 *with picture*
    Maryland (The War of 1812 and industrial
        development) M: 258
    Railroad (Developments in the United States)
        R: 115
Tom-tom [drum] T: 323 *with picture*
    Indian, American (Weapons) I: 144
Tomahawk [weapon] T: 324 *with pictures*
    Indian, American (Weapons) I: 144
Tomahawk cruise missile [weapon]
    Guided missile *picture on* G: 423; (Preset
        guidance) G: 426
Tomahawk Park [Cut Knife]
    Saskatchewan (Interesting facts) S: 129 *with
        picture*
Tomarctus [extinct animal]
    Dog (History) D: 281
Tomato [plant] T: 324 *with pictures*
    Genetically modified food (Development) G: 86
        with picture
    Nightshade N: 421 *with picture*
    Plant *picture on* P: 521
Tomb [structure] T: 325
    China *picture on* C: 487; (Sculpture and pottery)
        C: 488
    Egypt, Ancient *pictures on* E: 140
    Painting (Egyptian painting) P: 40-41
    Sculpture (Later medieval sculpture) S: 250 *with
        picture*
Tomb of Giuliano de' Medici [sculpture by
    Michelangelo]
    Sculpture (Michelangelo) S: 252-253 *with picture*
Tomb of Pope Alexander VII [sculpture by Bernini]
    Sculpture (European sculpture) S: 253 *with
        picture*
Tomb of the Unknowns
    Arlington National Cemetery A: 716 *with picture*
    Unknown soldier U: 212
    Washington, D.C. (Arlington National Cemetery)
        W: 78
Tomb of the Virgin, Church of the
    Gethsemane G: 175
Tomba, Alberto [Italian skier]
    Skiing (The middle and late 1900's) S: 487-488

Tombalbaye, François [Chadian political leader]
    Chad (History) C: 367
Tombaugh, Clyde William [American astronomer]
    Astronomy (Finding new objects) A: 848
    Pluto P: 581
Tombigbee River [Alabama-Mississippi] T: 326
    West Virginia (table) W: 225
Tomblin, Earl Ray [American political leader]
    West Virginia (table) W: 225
Tombouctou [Mali] *See* Timbuktu *in this index*
Tombs of the Kings, Valley of the *See* Valley of the
    Kings *in this index*
Tombstone [Arizona] T: 326
    Arizona *picture on* A: 690; (Places to visit) A: 678
    Earp, Wyatt E: 15
Tomcat *See* Tom *in this index*
Tomei, Marisa [actress]
    Motion picture (Best performance by an actress
        in a supporting role: 1992) M: 862b
Tomie dePaola's Mother Goose [book by dePaola]
    DePaola, Tomi D: 148
Tomiki aikido [sport]
    Aikido A: 167
Tomlin, Bradley Walker [American painter] T: 326
    with picture
Tomlinson, Gideon [American political leader]
    Connecticut (table) Ci: 967
Tomlinson, LaDainian [American football player]
    T: 326
Tommy [rock opera by Townshend]
    Rock music (The Who) R: 380
    Who, The W: 296
Tomographic scan [medicine]
    Positron emission tomography P: 698 *with
        pictures*
    X rays (Uses of X rays) X: 540
Tomonaga, Sin-Itiro [Japanese physicist]
    Feynman, Richard Phillips F: 84
    Nobel Prizes (Physics: 1965) N: 441
Tompkins, Daniel D. [American political leader]
    T: 327
    New York (table) N: 313
Tompkins, William [American businessman]
    West Virginia (Early industries) W: 226
Toms, David [American golfer]
    Golf (U.S. Open) G: 265
Ton [unit of measure] T: 327
    Air conditioning (Capacity of air conditioners)
        A: 179-180
Tonatiuhichan [legendary place]
    Mythology (Aztec mythology) M: 987
Tonawanda Band of Seneca [political group]
    Seneca Indians S: 297
Tone [color]
    Color *diagram on* Ci: 822
    Photography (Tone) P: 410
Tone [language]
    Chinese language (Spoken Chinese) C: 510
Tone [music] T: 327
    Harmonics H: 62
    Music (Musical instruments) M: 948; (Tone)
        M: 950
    Noise N: 451
Tone arm
    Phonograph (Parts of a phonograph) P: 400-401
        with diagram
Tone cluster [music]
    Cowell, Henry Ci: 1112
Tone color *See* Timbre *in this index*
Tone control [electronics]
    Stereophonic sound system (Amplifiers) So: 892
Tone dialing
    Telephone (The dialing mechanism) T: 95
Tone poem [music] *See* Symphonic poem *in this
    index*
Tonegawa, Susumu [Japanese molecular
    biologist]
    Nobel Prizes (Physiology or medicine: 1987)
        N: 446
Toner [chemical]
    Computer (Printers) Ci: 916-917
    Copying machine (Electrostatic copying) Ci: 1045
    Ink (Printing inks) I: 273, I: 273
    Printer (Laser printers) P: 795
Tonga T: 327 *with picture and map*
    Flag *picture on* F: 205
    Pacific Islands (Pacific alliances and
        independence movements) P: 12
Tongariro National Park [New Zealand]
    National park (New Zealand) N: 42d; (table)
        N: 42f
Tongass National Forest [Alaska]
    Alaska (Places to visit) A: 290
Tongatapu [islands]
    Tonga (Land) T: 328 *with map*
Tongue [anatomy] T: 329 *with pictures*
    Chameleon (The life of a chameleon) C: 372 *with
        picture*

Frog (The body of a frog) **F: 536**
Hummingbird (Habits) **H: 435** *with pictures*
Language (The sounds of language) **L: 62** *with diagram*
Mouth **M: 903**
Taste **T: 50** *with diagrams*
Tongue [food]
Meat *pictures on* **M: 349**
Tongue and groove board [building material]
House (Interior construction) **H: 382**
Tongue twister
Nursery rhyme (Tongue twisters) **N: 615**
Tongues [religion] *See* Speaking in tongues *in this index*
Tonic [music]
Key **K: 307**
Music (Tone) **M: 950**; (Harmony) **M: 951**
Tonight at 8:30 [plays by Coward]
Coward, Noël **Ci: 1107**
"Tonight Show Starring Johnny Carson, The" [television program]
Carson, Johnny **C: 250**
Tonio [opera character]
Opera: (*Pagliacci*) **O: 806**
Tonio Kröger [book by Mann]
Mann, Thomas **M: 164**
Tonkin [region, Vietnam]
Indochina (French influence) **I: 225**
Vietnam (French rule) **V: 370**
Tonkin, Gulf of
China Sea **C: 508** *with map*
Tonkin Gulf Resolution [1964]
Vietnam War (The Gulf of Tonkin incident) **V: 375**
Tonkinese cat
Cat (Short-haired breeds) **C: 290-292**
Tonkoro Station [ranch]
Queensland *picture on* **Q: 39**
Tonle Sap Lake [Cambodia]
Flood (Other floods) **F: 237**
Tonle Sap River
Cambodia (Land) **C: 72**
Tono-Bungay [book by Wells]
Wells, H. G. **W: 195**
Tonquin [ship]
McKay, Alexander **M: 336**
Tonsil [anatomy] **T: 329** *with diagram*
Diphtheria (Cause, symptoms, and complications) **D: 216**
Lymphatic system (Lymphoid tissue) **L: 534**
Tonsillitis **T: 329**
Tonsillectomy [surgery]
Tonsillitis **T: 330**
Tonsillitis [disease] **T: 329**
Strep throat **So: 925**
Tonsure [religion]
Hairdressing (The Middle Ages) **H: 11**
Tonti, Henri de [French explorer] *See* Tonty, Henri de *in this index*
Tonto National Monument [Arizona]
National Park System (table: National monuments) **N: 51**
Tontons Macoutes [Haitian history]
Duvalier, François **D: 393**
Haiti (History) **H: 15-16**
Tonty, Henri de [French explorer] **T: 330**
Arkansas (Exploration and settlement) **A: 712**
Too Late the Phalarope [book by Paton]
Paton, Alan **P: 196**
Tool T: 330
See also the list of Related articles in the Tool *article*
Chimpanzee (The life of a chimpanzee) **C: 472-473**
Colonial life in America (Furnishings) **Ci: 797**; (Farming) **Ci: 809**
Pioneer life in America (Tools) **P: 483**
Prehistoric people **P: 743** *with picture*; (How the first people lived) **P: 746**; (How the Neandertals lived) **P: 751**; (The Stone Age) **P: 751** *with pictures*
Stone Age **So: 909**
Technology (Primitive technology) **T: 74**
Woodworking **W: 396** *with pictures*
Tool-and-die maker [occupation]
Die and diemaking **D: 195**
Toolmaking **T: 330**
Tool steel
Alloy (Alloys of iron) **A: 377-378**
Iron and steel (Kinds of iron and steel) **I: 436-437**
Toole, Joseph Kemp [American political leader]
Montana (table) **M: 757**; (Statehood) **M: 760**
Tooled leather
Embossing **E: 256**
Leathercraft (Cutting and assembling) **L: 169** *with picture*
Toolmaking [industry] **T: 330**
Tools, Robert [American patient]
Artificial heart **A: 760**

Toombs, Robert Augustus [Confederate political leader] **T: 330**
Toomer, Jean [American author] **T: 330**
American literature (The Harlem Renaissance) **A: 422**
Harlem Renaissance **H: 61**
Tooth *See* Teeth *in this index*
Tooth decay
Fluoridation **F: 305**
Teeth (Dental decay) **T: 82** *with pictures*
Tooth shell [zoology]
Indian, American (Money) **I: 149** *with picture*
Mollusk (Tooth shells) **M: 695** *with picture*
Shell *picture on* **S: 387**; (Kinds of mollusk shells) **S: 385-388** *with picture*
Toothache
Teeth (Dental decay) **T: 82**
Toothache tree
Prickly-ash **P: 775**
Toothbrush
Teeth (Cleaning the teeth) **T: 81** *with picture*
Toothed whale
Porpoise **P: 679**
Whale **W: 255** *with pictures*; (Kinds of toothed whales) **W: 258** *with picture*
Toothpaste
Teeth (Cleaning the teeth) **T: 81**
Top [toy] **T: 331** *with pictures*
Top dyeing
Wool (Making fabric) **W: 401**
Top Fuel car
Automobile racing (Drag racing) **A: 978**
Top Girls [play by Churchill]
Churchill, Caryl **C: 543**
Top grain
Leather (Final processing) **L: 168**
Top hat
Hat *picture on* **H: 84**
Top hat furnace
Furnace (Heating the charge) **F: 567**
Top-level domain [electronics]
Internet (HTTP) **I: 350d**
Top lighting
Photography (Direction) **P: 415-416** *with picture*
Top quark [physics]
Physics (Physics today) **P: 442-443**
Quark **Q: 7**
Subatomic particle (Elementary particles) **So: 937**; (Theoretical research) **So: 938**
Top speed [aviation]
Airplane (Measuring flying speed) **A: 225-226**
Topa Inca Yupanqui [Inca emperor]
Inca (The empire) **I: 98**
Topalov, Veselin [Bulgarian chess player]
Chess (World chess champions) **C: 414**
Topaz [gem] **T: 331**
Gem *picture on* **G: 78**
Topaz Reservoir
Nevada (Natural resources) **N: 169**
Topdog/Underdog [play by Parks]
American literature (Drama) **A: 426**
Parks, Suzan-Lori **P: 172**
Topeka [Kansas] **T: 331** *with picture*
Kansas *pictures on* **K: 221, K: 234**; (table: Average monthly weather) **K: 230**
Topi, Bamir [Albanian political leader]
Albania (Recent developments) **A: 309**
Topic
Debate (Types of resolutions) **D: 64**
Topic outline
Outline **O: 880**
Topic sentence
A Guide to Writing Skills **Research Guide: 8**
Topical arrangement
Encyclopedia (Arrangement of content) **E: 266**
Topical geography
Geography (Topical geography) **G: 94**
Topkapi Palace
Istanbul (The city) **I: 490-491**
Topographic map
Archaeology (Surveying sites) **A: 596**
Map (General reference maps) **M: 177**; (How maps are made) **M: 180**
Topographic survey
Surveying (Types of surveys) **So: 1011**
Topography [geology]
Soil (Influence of land surface features) **So: 574**
Topolánek, Mirek [Czech political leader]
Czech Republic (Recent developments) **Ci: 1214**
Topology [mathematics] **T: 332** *with pictures*
Geometry (Rise of non-Euclidean geometry) **G: 106**
Mathematics (In the 1800's) **M: 307**
Topped crude [oil]
Asphalt (Asphalt production) **A: 815**
Topper [film]
Grant, Cary **G: 311**

Topping out ceremony
Building construction (Constructing a skyscraper) **B: 683-684**
Topsoil [earth] **T: 333**
Agriculture (Ecosystem destruction) **A: 153**
Loess **L: 420**
Soil (Characteristics of soils) **So: 574-575** *with diagram*; (Soil conservation) **So: 576**
Topspin [tennis]
Tennis (The ball in play) **T: 163-164**
Topsy [literary figure]
Uncle Tom's Cabin **U: 20**
Toquima Range [mountains, Nevada]
Nevada (Land regions) **N: 166** *with map*
Torah [book] **T: 333**
See also Pentateuch *in this index*
Torah Umesorah [organization]
Parochial school **P: 178**
Toraja [people]
Indonesia (Rural life) **I: 229**
Torch [light]
Fire (Light) **F: 122**
Statue of Liberty **So: 872** *with picture, pictures on* **So: 874**; (Repairs and changes) **So: 878** *with pictures*
Torch ginger [flower]
Flower *picture on* **F: 292**
Torchbearers, The [book by Noyes]
Noyes, Alfred **N: 578**
Tordesillas, Treaty of [1494]
Brazil (Portuguese rule) **B: 583**
Latin America (European discovery and exploration) **L: 103**
Line of Demarcation **L: 333** *with map*
"Toreador Song" [aria]
Opera: (*Carmen*) **O: 802-803**
Torii [architecture]
Shinto *picture on* **S: 401**
Torino [Italy] *See* Turin *in this index*
Toril [bullfighting]
Bullfighting (The bullring) **B: 695**
Torn cartilage [anatomy]
Cartilage **C: 263**
Torn Hat, The [painting by Sully]
Sully, Thomas *picture on* **So: 971**
Tornado [weather] **T: 333** *with pictures and map*
Alabama (The 2000's) **A: 279**
Cyclone **Ci: 1203**
Derecho **D: 152**
Insurance (Insurance today) **I: 316-317**
Kansas (The early 2000's) **K: 239**
Missouri (The early 2000's) **M: 672**
Radar (In weather observation and forecasting) **R: 67** *with picture*
Safety (During a tornado) **S: 15**
Waterspout **W: 147** *with picture*
Weather *picture on* **W: 167**; (Synoptic-scale systems) **W: 159-161**
Tornado Alley [region]
Tornado **T: 333**
Tornado Pod [device]
Tornado (The VORTEX projects) **T: 337**
Tornado vortex signature [meteorology]
Tornado (Forecasting tornadoes) **T: 335-336**
Tornado warning
Tornado (Forecasting tornadoes) **T: 335-336**
Tornado watch
Tornado (Forecasting tornadoes) **T: 335-336**
Torne River [Finland-Sweden] **T: 337**
Torngat Mountains
Newfoundland and Labrador (Mountains) **N: 370** *with map*
Torngat Mountains National Park
Canada (table: National parks and national park reserves) **C: 113**
Tornio River
Torne River **T: 337**
Toronto [Ontario] **T: 338** *with pictures and map*
Canada *picture on* **C: 107**
Ontario **O: 764**, *picture on* **O: 765**; (Population) **O: 768**; (table: Average monthly weather) **O: 778**
Toronto, University of T: 340d
Ontario (Schools) **O: 769** *with picture*
Toronto Argonauts [team]
Football (Canadian Football League) **F: 364**
Toronto (Sports) **T: 340a**
Toronto Blue Jays [team]
Baseball (table) **B: 130**
Toronto (Sports) **T: 340a**
Toronto Eaton Centre [Toronto]
Canada *picture on* **C: 107**
Toronto (Landmarks) **T: 338**; (Urban renewal) **T: 340c**
Toronto International Film Festival
Toronto (The arts) **T: 340a**
Toronto Maple Leafs [team]

Hockey (Famous players and All-Star teams) H: 281; (table: National Hockey League) H: 281
Toronto (Sports) T: 340a
Toronto Pearson International Airport
  Ontario (Transportation) O: 782
  Toronto (Transportation and communication) T: 340b
Toronto Raptors [team]
  Basketball (table) B: 150
Toronto Stock Exchange
  Toronto (Finance) T: 340a-340b
Torosaurus [dinosaur]
  Triceratops T: 441
Torpedo [firecracker]
  Fireworks (Other uses of fireworks) F: 135
Torpedo [fish] *See Electric ray in this index*
Torpedo [weapon] T: 340d *with pictures*
  Mine warfare (History) M: 565
Torpedo boat [ship]
  PT boat P: 853
Torpor [zoology]
  Mammal (Hibernation) M: 125
Torquato Tasso [book by Goethe]
  Goethe, Johann Wolfgang von (Middle years) G: 247
Torque [mechanics] T: 341
  Automobile (The transmission) A: 948-949
  Helicopter (Piloting a helicopter) H: 171-173 *with picture*
  Lever (Law of equilibrium) L: 217-218
  Transmission T: 375
Torque converter
  Locomotive (Diesel locomotives) L: 414-416
  Transmission (A torque converter) T: 376 *with diagram*
Torqued Ellipses [sculptures by Serra]
  Serra, Richard S: 318 *with picture*
Torqued Torus Inversion [sculpture by Serra]
  Serra, Richard *picture on* S: 318
Torquemada, Tomás de [Spanish religious leader] T: 341 *with portrait*
Torr [unit of measure]
  Atmosphere A: 869
  Vacuum V: 256
Torre, Joe [American baseball player/manager] T: 341
Torrens, Lake [Australia] *See Lake Torrens in this index*
Torrens, Sir Robert [Australian government official]
  Torrens system T: 342
Torrens Act [1897]
  Torrens system (In the United States) T: 342
Torrens River [Australia] T: 342
Torrens system [law] T: 342
Torrent duck [bird]
  Duck (Torrent ducks) D: 377
Torres, Luis Vaez de [Spanish explorer] T: 342 *with picture and map*
  Australia (European explorations) A: 920
Torres, Trinidad [Spanish anthropologist]
  Prehistoric people (table) P: 754
Torres Bodet, Jaime [Mexican author/statesman] T: 343
Torres de Serranos [gate]
  Valencia V: 260
Torres del Paine National Park [Chile]
  National park (table) N: 42g
Torres Jurado, Antonio de [Spanish guitar maker]
  Guitar G: 436
Torres Naharro, Bartolomé de [Spanish author]
  Spanish literature (The 1500's) So: 758-759
Torres Strait
  Torres, Luis Vaez de T: 342
Torres Strait Islanders [people]
  Aborigines, Australian A: 13
Torres Strait Islands [Australia] T: 343
Torresian crow [bird]
  Crow (Kinds of crows) Ci: 1157
Torretta, Gino [American football player]
  Football (table) F: 363
Torricelli, Evangelista [Italian physicist] T: 343
  Air (The study of air) A: 175
  Barometer B: 115
  Hydraulics (Laws of hydrodynamics) H: 464
Torricelli's law [physics]
  Hydraulics (Laws of hydrodynamics) H: 464
Torriente, Cristóbal [Cuban baseball player]
  Baseball (table: Hall of Fame) B: 134b
Torrijos Espino, Martín [Panamanian political leader]
  Panama (Recent developments) P: 121
Torrijos Herrera, Omar [Panamanian political leader] T: 343
  Carter, Jimmy *picture on* C: 258
  Panama (Relations with the United States) P: 120
Torrone [candy]

Christmas (Christmas feasting) C: 534-535
Torsion balance [instrument] T: 343
Torsion bar suspension [automobile] T: 343 *with diagrams*
Torsion catapult [machine]
  Catapult C: 298
Torsion pendulum
  Pendulum (Other pendulums) P: 238
Tort [law] T: 344
  Law (Private law) L: 130; (Law since 1900) L: 136-137
  Privacy, Right of P: 808a
Tortilla [food]
  Aztec (Food) A: 1001
  Bread (Kinds of bread) B: 588 *with picture*
  Food (Customs) F: 332-333
  Hispanic Americans *picture on* H: 247; (Food) H: 248
  Latin America (Food and drink) L: 97-98
  Mexico (Food and drink) M: 456
Tortoise [animal] T: 344 *with picture*
  Animal *picture on* A: 469
  Ecuador *picture on* E: 70
  Reptile *picture on* R: 250
  Turtle *pictures on* T: 520, T: 523; (Tortoises) T: 524
"Tortoise and the Hare, The" [story]
  Aesop's fables A: 90
  Folklore (Folk tales) F: 323
  La Fontaine, Jean de *picture on* L: 29
Tortoise shell
  Turtle (Turtles and human beings) T: 524
Tortoise-shell cat
  Cat (Coat) C: 287
Tortola [island]
  Virgin Islands V: 392 *with map*
  Virgin Islands, British V: 393
Tortue Island [island, Haiti]
  Haiti (Land) H: 15; (History) H: 15-16
Tortuga Island [island, Haiti] *See Tortue Island in this index*
Tortugas [islands, Florida]
  Dry Tortugas National Park D: 369
Tortuguero National Park [Costa Rica]
  National park (table) N: 42g
Torture T: 345
Torvalds, Linus [Finnish computer programmer] T: 345
Tory [U.S. history]
  Revolution, American (Progress of the war) R: 278
  Tory Party T: 345
Tory, Geofroy [French printer]
  Book (The spread of printed books) B: 467
Tory Island [Ireland] T: 345
Tory Party [British history] T: 345
  Conservative Party Ci: 991
  United Kingdom (Politics) U: 54; (Political confusion) U: 69
Tosa school [Japanese history]
  Painting (Japanese painting) P: 47
Tosafist [scholar]
  Rashi R: 144
Tosca [opera by Puccini]
  Opera: *(Tosca)* O: 807
  Puccini, Giacomo P: 869
Tosca, La [play by Sardou]
  Opera: *(Tosca)* O: 807
Toscana *See Tuscany in this index*
Toscanelli, Paolo [Italian scholar]
  Columbus, Christopher (The plan to sail westward) Ci: 858
Toscanini, Arturo [Italian conductor] T: 345 *with picture*
  Peerce, Jan P: 229
Toshiba Corporation
  Manufacturing (table) M: 170
Toshkent [Uzbekistan] *See Tashkent in this index*
Tosks [people]
  Albania (People) A: 306
Tostada [food]
  Mexico (Food and drink) M: 456
Total [company]
  Manufacturing (table) M: 170
Total aerodynamic force [physics]
  Aerodynamics (Principles of aerodynamics) A: 85
Total blindness
  Blindness B: 401
Total body irradiation [medicine]
  Radiation (Refining the uses of radiation) R: 81
Total communication
  Deafness (Education) D: 59
Total data station [machine]
  Archaeology (Surveying sites) A: 596-597
Total eclipse
  Eclipse (Lunar eclipses) E: 51; (Solar eclipses) E: 51 *with picture*
Total hysterectomy [surgery]
  Hysterectomy H: 482

Total internal reflection [optics]
  Light (Refraction) L: 288
Total mixed ration
  Dairying (Feeding) D: 7
Total serialism [music]
  Classical music (Atonal music) Ci: 649-650
Total station [instrument]
  Surveying (Surveying tools) So: 1011
Total warfare
  Civil War, American (The beginning of modern warfare) Ci: 634
  Neutrality (Neutrality today) N: 154
Totalitarianism [political science] T: 346
  Arendt, Hannah A: 645
  Communism Ci: 889
  Government (Totalitarianism) G: 286; (Totalitarianism and Communism) G: 291
  Nazism (The rise to power) N: 92
Totara [tree]
  Tree *picture on* T: 427
Tote board
  Horse racing (At the races) H: 365
Totem T: 346 *with picture*
  Africa (Marriage and the family) A: 113
  Alaska *pictures on* A: 291, A: 300; (Places to visit) A: 290 *with picture*
  Animal worship A: 510
  British Columbia *picture on* B: 621; (Interesting facts about British Columbia) B: 613 *with picture*
  Clan Ci: 638
  Indian, American (After European contact) I: 163 *with picture*
Tottel's Miscellany [book by Surrey and Wyatt]
  English literature (Elizabethan poetry) E: 316-317
  Surrey, Earl of So: 1010
  Wyatt, Sir Thomas W: 514
Totuava [fish]
  Drum D: 367
Toubou [people]
  Chad (People) C: 366
Toucan [bird] T: 347 *with pictures*
  Bird (Birds of Central and South America) B: 344a *with picture*; (Bills) B: 362
  Rain forest *picture on* R: 126c
Toucanet [bird]
  Toucan T: 347 *with picture*
Toucey, Isaac [American political leader]
  Buchanan, James (table) B: 661
  Connecticut (table) Ci: 967
  Justice, Department of (table) J: 203
  Polk, James Knox (table) P: 643
Touch [fencing]
  Fencing (The foil) F: 70 *with picture*
Touch [sense] T: 348
  Animal (Adaptations for sensing the environment) A: 492-493 *with picture*
  Fish (Touch and the lateral line system) F: 164
  Hand H: 39
  Insect (Touch) I: 291
  Mammal (Senses) M: 120-121
  Senses S: 301
Touch football
  Football F: 354
Touch judge
  Rugby football (Rugby Union) R: 510; (Rugby League) R: 512
Touch line [sports]
  Rugby football (How to play Rugby Union) R: 510-511
  Soccer (The field) So: 544
Touch-me-not [plant]
  Flower (Flowers of woodlands and forests) F: 284 *with picture*
  Impatiens I: 90
  Plant (Seeds) P: 531 *with picture*
Touch of the Poet, A [play by O'Neill]
  O'Neill, Eugene (His plays) O: 762
Touch pad [device] *See Touchpad in this index*
Touch screen [computing]
  Computer (A touch screen) Ci: 914
  Handheld computer H: 45
Touchback
  Football (The kickoff) F: 359-360
Touchdown [sports]
  Football (Scoring) F: 362
Touchhole [gun]
  Harquebus H: 67
Touchpad [electronics]
  Computer (Input devices) Ci: 912 *with picture*
  Keyboard K: 308
  Laptop computer L: 74
Touchstone Pictures [company]
  Walt Disney Company W: 21
Toucouleur [people]
  Fulani F: 553
  Mali (People) M: 106

Mauritania (People) **M: 314**
Toughness
Materials (Mechanical properties) **M: 300b**
Toulon [France] **T: 348**
Toulon, Siege of [1793]
Napoleon I (Early military career) **N: 14**
Toulouse [bird]
Goose (Kinds of geese) **G: 270** *with picture*
Toulouse [France] **T: 348**
Toulouse, Battle of [1814]
Wellington, Duke of (Peninsular War) **W: 194**
Toulouse-Lautrec, Henri de [French artist] **T: 348**
with picture
Art Nouveau **A: 750**
Lithography (History) **L: 387** *with picture*
Painting (Postimpressionism) **P: 75**
Poster **P: 708**
Toungoo [ancient city]
Myanmar (Early days) **M: 970d**
Tour bus
Bus (Special buses) **B: 715**
Tour de France [race] **T: 348**
Armstrong, Lance **A: 722**
Bicycle racing (Road races) **B: 292-293** *with
picture*
France (Recreation) **F: 460** *with picture*
Tour du Crédit Lyonnais [Lyon]
Lyon *picture on* **L: 536**
Tour guide [occupation]
Careers (Tourism and hospitality) **C: 233** *with
picture*
Touraco [bird] *See Turaco in this index*
Tourane [Vietnam] *See Da Nang in this index*
Touré, Amadou Toumani [Malian political leader]
Mali (History) **M: 108-109**
Touré, Sékou [Guinean political leader] **T: 349**
Guinea (History) **G: 432**
Tourette, Georges Gilles de la [French physician]
Tourette syndrome **T: 349**
Tourette syndrome [disorder] **T: 349**
Touring bike
Bicycle (Road bikes) **B: 289**
Motorcycle (Kinds of motorcycles) **M: 878**
Tourism [industry]
*See also the Places to visit section in specific state
and province articles, such as* California (Places
to visit)
Careers (Tourism and hospitality) **C: 233** *with
picture*
National park (Overcrowding) **N: 42i**
Virgin Islands, United States (Economy) **V: 395**
Tourist cabin
Motel **M: 836**
Tourmaline [gem] **T: 349**
Gem *picture on* **G: 78**
Tournachon, Gaspard Félix [French
photographer]
Photography (Artistic advances) **P: 424**
Tournament [sports]
Knights and knighthood (Tournaments) **K: 350**
with picture
Wrestling **W: 505**
Tournament of Roses
California (Visitor's guide) **C: 46** *with picture*
Flower (As a decoration) **F: 272**
Tourneur, Maurice [French film director]
New Jersey *picture on* **N: 253**
Tournier, Michel [French author]
French literature (Recent French literature) **F: 523**
Tourniquet [first aid] **T: 350**
Touro Synagogue [Newport, Rhode Island]
Colonial life in America (Places to visit) **Ci: 801**
Newport **N: 379**
Rhode Island (Interesting facts) **R: 297**
Tours [France] **T: 350**
Tours, Battle of [A.D. 732]
Charles Martel **C: 383**
Tourte, François [French businessman]
Violin (History) **V: 390**
Toussaint, François Dominique *See* Toussaint
Louverture *in this index*
Toussaint Louverture [Haitian patriot] **T: 350** *with
portrait*
Haiti (History) **H: 15-16**
Latin America (The movement toward
independence) **L: 106-107**
Toussaint L'Ouverture [paintings by Lawrence]
Lawrence, Jacob **L: 145**
Tow [fiber]
Linen (Preparing the fibers) **L: 334-335**
TOW missile
Guided missile *picture on* **G: 425;** (Command
guidance) **G: 426**
Tow truck
Truck *picture on* **T: 459**
Towards a New Architecture [book by Le
Corbusier]

Le Corbusier **L: 175**
Tower [architecture] **T: 350**
Tower, Joan [American composer]
Classical music (Classical music today) **Ci: 651**
Tower Bridge [London]
England *picture on* **E: 292**
Tower crane [machine]
Building construction (Constructing a skyscraper)
B: 683-684
Crane **Ci: 1120** *with picture*
Tower of Babel [Babylon] **T: 351** *with picture*
Architecture (Mesopotamian architecture) **A: 611**
Tower of Belém
Lisbon (The city) **L: 348**
Tower of Hercules [lighthouse]
Lighthouse (Notable lighthouses) **L: 295**
Tower of London **T: 351**
England (The Norman Conquest) **E: 305**
London (The Tower of London) **L: 436** *with
picture;* (Ceremonies) **L: 437;** (The Middle Ages)
L: 439-440
Raleigh, Sir Walter (His fall) **R: 131**
Tower of Nesle, The [play by Dumas]
Dumas, Alexandre, père **D: 382**
Tower of silence [custom]
Funeral customs (Burial) **F: 557-558**
Tower of the Americas
San Antonio (The city) **S: 84**
Towhee [bird] **T: 351** *with picture*
Bird *picture on* **B: 358**
Towing point
Kite (How kites fly) **K: 339**
Town [political unit] **T: 352**
See also Township *in this index*
City government **Ci: 594**
Colonial life in America (Economic reasons)
Ci: 788
County (Importance) **Ci: 1099**
Local government **L: 406**
Metropolitan area **M: 442**
Middle Ages (Medieval towns) **M: 527**
Town [zoology]
Prairie dog (Habits) **P: 732**
Town, The [book by Faulkner]
Faulkner, William **F: 55**
Town, The [book by Richter]
Richter, Conrad **R: 334**
Town ball [game]
Baseball (From rounders to baseball) **B: 132**
Town crier **T: 352**
Advertising (History) **A: 79**
Colonial life in America (Communication) **Ci: 806**
Town Hall Square
Copenhagen (The city) **Ci: 1038**
Town house
Housing (Kinds of housing) **H: 389-390**
Town meeting [government] **T: 352**
Democracy **D: 119**
Maine (Local government) **M: 88**
Vermont *picture on* **V: 319**
Town planning *See* City planning *in this index*
Towneley, Richard [English chemist]
Gas [physics] (Gas laws) **G: 48**
Townes, Charles Hard [American physicist]
Betelgeuse **B: 274**
Laser (History) **L: 86**
Nobel Prizes (Physics: 1964) **N: 441**
Towns, George W. [American political leader]
Georgia (table) **G: 130**
Townsend, Francis E. [American political leader]
Townsend Plan **T: 352**
Townsend, John G., Jr. [American political leader]
Delaware (table) **D: 109**
Townsend, Kathleen Kennedy [daughter of
Robert F. Kennedy]
Kennedy, Joseph Patrick (His family) **K: 269-270**
Townsend, M. Clifford [American political leader]
Indiana (table) **I: 214**
Townsend, Willard Saxby [American labor leader]
T: 352
Townsend Plan [U.S. history] **T: 352**
Townsendia
Flower (Flowers of prairies and dry plains) **F: 286**
with picture
Townshend, Charles [British political leader]
Revolution, American (The Townshend Acts)
R: 273
Townshend, Charles [English agricultural
reformer] *See* Townshend, Viscount *in this index*
Townshend, George [British general]
Quebec, Battle of (The attack on Quebec) **Q: 37**
Townshend, Pete [British musician] **T: 352**
Rock music (The Who) **R: 380**
Who, The **W: 296**
Townshend, Viscount [English agricultural
reformer] **T: 352**
Townshend Acts [1767]

Declaration of Independence (Events leading to
the Declaration) **D: 74**
Revolution, American (The Townshend Acts)
R: 273
United States, History of the (Renewed conflict)
U: 158
Township [political unit] **T: 353**
County (Importance) **Ci: 1099**
Local government (Units of local government)
L: 407
Maine (Local government) **M: 88**
Metropolitan area **M: 442**
Town meeting **T: 352**
Township [unit of measure]
Public lands (Management of public lands) **P: 858**
Towton, Battle of [1461]
Edward IV **E: 112**
Toxemia of pregnancy [disorder] *See* Preeclampsia
in this index
Toxic hepatitis [disease]
Liver (Hepatitis) **L: 395**
Toxic phase
Yellow fever (Symptoms) **Y: 556**
Toxic psychosis
Psychosis **P: 851**
Toxic shock syndrome [disorder] **T: 353**
Toxic waste
Hazardous wastes **H: 122**
Incinerator **I: 100**
Toxicology [medicine]
Drug (Effect on the body) **D: 354**
Forensic science (Poisons) **F: 389**
Occupational medicine **O: 647**
Pharmacology **P: 354**
Poison **P: 600**
Toxin [poison] **T: 353**
Allergy (Allergic reactions) **A: 373**
Antitoxin **A: 559**
Bacteria (Protection against harmful bacteria)
B: 20
Bacteriology (Controlling bacterial diseases) **B: 22**
Biological Weapons Convention **B: 315**
Disease (Bacterial diseases) **D: 227**
Mushroom (Poisonous mushrooms) **M: 945**
Pfiesteria **P: 353**
Plant (Diseases) **P: 539;** (How plants protect
themselves) **P: 540**
Poison (Fungi, plant, and animal poisoning)
P: 600
Tetanus **T: 182b**
Toxoid [medication]
Antitoxin **A: 559**
Diphtheria (Prevention) **D: 216**
Immunization (Active immunization) **I: 89**
Tetanus **T: 182b**
Toxophilus [book by Ascham]
Archery (History) **A: 603-604**
Toxoplasma gondii [organism]
Toxoplasmosis **T: 353**
Toxoplasmosis [disease] **T: 353**
Pregnancy (Lifestyle during pregnancy) **P: 735**
Toy T: 353
Doll **D: 286** *with pictures*
Toy books [books by Crane]
Crane, Walter **Ci: 1120**
Toy dog [dog] **T: 354**
Dog *pictures on* **D: 274;** (Toy dogs) **D: 266**
Pug **P: 886**
Toy fox terrier [dog] **T: 354**
Toy Manchester terrier [dog]
Manchester terrier **M: 134**
Toy poodle [dog]
Poodle **P: 658**
Toy Story [film]
Animation (The computer revolution) **A: 514c**
with picture
Pixar Animation Studios **P: 503**
Toy train *See* Railroad, Model *in this index*
Toya Maru [ship]
Shipwreck (table: Major shipwrecks) **S: 428**
Toynbee, Arnold [British social reformer] **T: 354**
Toynbee, Arnold Joseph [British historian] **T: 354**
Civilization (Rise and fall) **Ci: 636**
Toynbee Hall [London]
Settlement house **S: 324**
Toynbee, Arnold **T: 354**
Toyokuni, Utagawa [Japanese artist]
Drama *picture on* **D: 337**
Toyota Motor Corporation **T: 354**
Automobile (The 2000's) **A: 972-973** *with picture*
Manufacturing (table) **M: 170**
Sports car (History) **So: 803**
Toyotomi Hideyoshi [Japanese political leader]
See Hideyoshi *in this index*
Toys in the Attic [play by Hellman]
Hellman, Lillian **H: 178**
TPR valve

Plumbing (The water supply system) P: 577-578
TR-1 [aircraft]
Aircraft, Military (Reconnaissance aircraft) A: 203
Trabea [clothing]
Augur A: 885
Trabecular bone [anatomy]
Bone (Structure of the bones) B: 456
Trace [equipment]
Harness H: 63 *with diagram*
Trace [meteorology]
Rain (Characteristics of rain) R: 122-123
TRACE [satellite] *See* Transition Region and Coronal Explorer *in this index*
Trace elements [biochemistry] T: 355
Enzyme (Structure) E: 341
Trace elements [mining]
Nutrition (Minerals) N: 625-626
Prospecting P: 829
Trace evidence
Crime scene investigation (Collecting evidence) Ci: 1140-1141
Forensic science (What a forensic scientist analyzes) F: 389
Trace fossil
Fossil (Understanding ancient plants and animals) F: 423
Tracer [painting by Rauschenberg]
Rauschenberg, Robert *picture on* R: 150
Tracer [radioisotope]
Isotope *diagram on* I: 477
Radiocarbon (Radiocarbon in biology) R: 98
Radiochemistry R: 98
Tracer bullet
Bullet B: 695
Tracery [architecture] T: 355 *with picture*
Trachea [anatomy] T: 355
Croup Ci: 1157
Human body (Lung) H: 422 *with diagram*
Lung *diagram on* L: 524; (Parts of the lungs) L: 523
Mouth M: 903 *with diagram*
Respiration (Structures of breathing) R: 260
Throat T: 270
Voice (The human voice) V: 436 *with diagram*
Trachea [entomology]
Animal (Adaptations for breathing) A: 491-492 *with picture*
Insect (Respiratory system) I: 289 *with diagram*
Respiration (Breathing in animals without lungs) R: 261
Spider (Respiratory system) So: 785 *with diagram*
Tracheophyte [plant] *See* Vascular plant *in this index*
Tracheotomy [surgery]
Croup Ci: 1157
Surgery (Some common surgical operations) So: 1006
Tetanus T: 182b
Trachoma [disease] T: 355
Blindness (Diseases) B: 401-402
Chlamydia C: 516
Eye (Diseases of the outer parts) E: 468-469
Track [education]
Curriculum (Curriculum planning) Ci: 1197
Track [electronics]
Compact disc (Playback) Ci: 901
Videotape recorder (Recording) V: 361 *with diagram*
Track [railroad]
Railroad (What makes up a railroad) R: 106; (Tracks) R: 108 *with picture*; (Leading countries in railroad transportation) R: 114
Railroad, Model (Track) R: 120 *with picture*
Track and field [sports] T: 356 *with pictures*
See also the list of *Related articles in the* Track and field *article*
Marathon M: 191
Olympic Games (Summer Olympic Games) O: 746e-748
Zaharias, Babe Didrikson Z: 584
Track circuit [device]
Railroad (Automatic block signal systems) R: 111
Track light
Lighting (Lighting devices) L: 298
Track pad [device] *See* Touchpad *in this index*
Track race
Automobile racing A: 975 *with pictures*
Bicycle race (Track races) B: 292
Track tractor [vehicle]
Tractor (Crawler tractors) T: 361 *with picture*
Trackball [computing]
Computer (A trackball) Ci: 914
Keyboard K: 308
Tracked air cushion vehicle
Air cushion vehicle (History) A: 181
Tracking and Data Relay Satellite
Satellite, Artificial *picture on* S: 150d

Tracking chamber [machine]
Particle detector (Tracking chambers) P: 187
Tracking poll
Public opinion poll (History) P: 863
Tractarians [religious group]
Oxford Movement O: 888
Traction control
Brake (Hydraulic brakes) B: 560-562
Traction engine
Tractor (History) T: 361
Traction motor
Electric railroad *picture on* E: 187; (Kinds of electric railroads) E: 188
Elevated railroad E: 233
Tractor T: 360 *with pictures*
Agriculture (Powered machines) A: 158 *with picture*
Iowa *picture on* I: 389
Tractor plow
Plow (The tractor plow) P: 575 *with picture*
Tractor-semitrailer
Truck T: 456, *picture on* T: 459; (Kinds of trucks) T: 457
"Tracts for the Times" [essays]
Oxford Movement O: 889
Tracy, Benjamin F. [American government official]
Harrison, Benjamin (table) H: 72
Tracy, Spencer [American actor] T: 362 *with picture*
Hepburn, Katharine H: 193
Motion picture (Best performance by an actor: 1937, 1938) M: 862a
Tracy, Susan E. [American nurse]
Occupational therapy (History) O: 649
Tradable emmission credit
Environmental pollution (Government action) E: 335-336
Trade [economics] T: 362
See also International trade *in this index; the list of Related articles in the* Trade *article; and the* Economy *section of the various country articles, such as* Argentina (Economy)
Barter B: 120
City (Economy) Ci: 580-581, Ci: 584
Colonial life in America (Colonists and Indians) Ci: 792; (Trade) Ci: 811
Commodity exchange C: 873
Crusades (Results of the Crusades) Ci: 1162
Endangered species (Wildlife trade) E: 269
Fur trade F: 564
Government (Commerce) G: 283
Greece, Ancient (Trade) G: 368
Indian, American (Trade) I: 148 *with pictures*
Latin America (Early years of independence) L: 107-108
Mercantilism M: 411
Middle Ages (The High Middle Ages) M: 526
Rome, Ancient (Trade) R: 443
Sales (The rise of sales) S: 64
Technology (Technological advances) T: 75
World, History of (The age of exploration) W: 440-441
Trade [job]
For a list of articles on career opportunities, see the Related articles in the Careers *article*
Apprentice A: 575
Careers C: 214 *with pictures*
Trade, Balance of [economics] *See* Balance of trade *in this index*
Trade, Board of [economics] *See* Commodity exchange *in this index*
Trade and Development, Conference on *See* United Nations Conference on Trade and Development *in this index*
Trade Commission, Federal *See* Federal Trade Commission *in this index*
Trade deficit [economics] *See* Deficit *in this index*
Trade Expansion Act [1962]
Kennedy, John Fitzgerald (The New Frontier) K: 264
Trade fair [economics]
City *picture on* Ci: 584
Fair (Trade fairs) F: 7
Trade language
Indian, American (Language groups) I: 149-150
Trade magazine
Magazine (Specialized business magazines) M: 42
Trade name *See* Trademark *in this index*
Trade publication [magazine] T: 363
Advertising (Magazines) A: 74-75
Trade rat *See* Woodrat *in this index*
Trade-Related Aspects of Intellectual Property Rights Agreement [1994]
Copyright (International agreements) Ci: 1048
Trade Representative, Office of the United States
President of the United States (The executive

branch) P: 764
Trade route T: 363
Lake (Travel and trade routes) L: 34
Trade school *See* Technical school *in this index*
Trade secret [business] T: 364
Trade union *See* Labor union *in this index*
Trade wind T: 364 *with map*
Air (Air movement) A: 171-172
Atlantic Ocean (Winds) A: 866
Climate (Atmospheric circulation) Ci: 676a
Pacific Ocean (Winds) P: 14
Weather (Planetary-scale systems) W: 158-159
Wind (General circulation) W: 329 *with diagram*
Trademark [law] T: 364
Copyright Ci: 1046
Drug (Drug names) D: 356
Intellectual property I: 318
Piracy P: 493
Public domain P: 855
Trading bank
Bank (Australia and New Zealand) B: 92
Trading Ceremony at York Factory [painting by Scott]
Canada, History of *picture on* C: 138
Trading exchange [business]
E-commerce (Business-to-business transactions) E: 2
Trading post T: 365 *with picture*
Trade (The expansion of trade) T: 363
Tradition *See* Custom *in this index*
Tradition [religion]
Roman Catholic Church R: 402b
Trent, Council of T: 434
Traditional doll
Doll (Traditional dolls) D: 287 *with picture*
Traditional grammar
Grammar G: 303
Traditional interior
Interior design (Style) I: 327
Traditional leaders
South Africa (National government) So: 608
Traditional literature
Literature for children (Traditional literature) L: 357
Traditional monarchy
Government (Monarchy) G: 286
Traditionalists [Chinese history]
Painting (Chinese painting) P: 44-46
Trafalgar, Battle of [1805] T: 365
Napoleonic Wars (Renewed hostilities) N: 18 *with map*
Nelson, Horatio *picture on* N: 121; (Victory at Trafalgar) N: 122
United Kingdom (The Napoleonic Wars) U: 68
Trafalgar Square
London *picture on* L: 428; (Central London) L: 429-430 *with map*; (Squares) L: 435
Nelson, Horatio (Nelson monument) N: 122
Traffic T: 365
Automobile *picture on* A: 963; (table) A: 962
Traffic control
See also Air traffic control *in this index*
Radar (In controlling automobile speed and traffic) R: 67 *with picture*
Railroad (Traffic control) R: 110 *with pictures*
Traffic (Traffic control) T: 366
Traffic engineering
Traffic (Traffic problems) T: 365-366
Traffic jam
City (Description) Ci: 589; (Physical problems) Ci: 590-591
Traffic (Traffic problems) T: 365
Transportation T: 397 *with picture*
Traffic light
Automation (Uses of automation) A: 944
Light (Light and energy efficiency) L: 291
Light-emitting diode *picture on* L: 293
Morgan, Garrett Augustus M: 802
Ohio (Interesting facts) O: 681 *with picture*
Traffic (Signals, signs, and markings) T: 366
Traffic pattern
Airport (Air traffic control) A: 246
Interior design (Planning on paper) I: 330-331
Traffic police
Police (Traffic operations) P: 621
Traffic sign
Automobile (Rules of the road) A: 954 *with pictures*
Traffic (Signals, signs, and markings) T: 366
Trafficking, Drug *See* Drug trafficking *in this index*
Traficant, James A. [American political leader]
Congress of the United States (Congressional ethics) C: 948
Tragedy [drama] T: 366
Dionysus D: 215
Drama (Forms of drama) D: 325; (Tragedy) D: 326; (Roman drama) D: 328; (Italian

Renaissance drama) **D:** 330; (England) **D:** 334-335
English literature (Restoration drama) **E:** 318
Greek literature (Drama) **G:** 377
Racine, Jean **R:** 61
Shakespeare, William (Shakespeare's plays) **S:** 354-355
Tragedy of Pudd'nhead Wilson, The [book by Twain]
Twain, Mark (Later works) **T:** 530
Tragedy of Tragedies, The [book by Fielding]
Fielding, Henry (His life) **F:** 94
Tragic Exodus [musical]
Holm, Hanya **H:** 294
Tragic Overture [music by Brahms]
Brahms, Johannes (His music) **B:** 549
Tragic Sense of Life, The [book by Unamuno]
Unamuno, Miguel de **U:** 19
Tragic Ten Days, The [Mexican Revolution]
Mexico City (Revolution and growth) **M:** 478
Tragical History of Doctor Faustus, The [play by Marlowe]
Faust **F:** 56
Marlowe, Christopher **M:** 216
Tragicomedia de Calisto y Melibea [play]
Spanish literature (The 1400's) **So:** 758
Tragicomedy
Drama (Jacobean and Caroline drama) **D:** 332
Tragopan [bird] **T:** 367 *with picture*
Traianus, Marcus Ulpius [Roman emperor] *See* Trajan *in this index*
Trail
National Trails System **N:** 61
Trail bike
Motorcycle (Kinds of motorcycles) **M:** 878
Trail Blazers, Portland [team]
Basketball (table) **B:** 150
Trail blazing
Road (The first roads) **R:** 361
Trail boss
Cowboy (The trail drive) **Ci:** 1111
Trail drive [ranching]
Chuck wagon **C:** 540
Cowboy *picture on* **Ci:** 1108; (The trail drive) **Ci:** 1111 *with picture*
Trail Herd to Wyoming [painting by Koerner]
Cowboy *picture on* **Ci:** 1108
Trail of Tears [play]
Oklahoma (Visitor's guide) **O:** 722 *with picture*
Trail of Tears [U.S. history] **T:** 367 *with map*
Cherokee Indians **C:** 409 *with picture*
Five Civilized Tribes **F:** 191
Indian, American *picture on* **I:** 178b; (After European contact) **I:** 158
Oklahoma (The Indian nations) **O:** 731
Pioneer life in America (Pioneers and Indians) **P:** 485
United States, History of the (Indian removal) **U:** 172-173 *with picture*
Western frontier life in America (Settlers and Native Americans) **W:** 239
Trail of Tears, The [painting by Lindneux]
Indian, American *on* **I:** 178b
Trailer [vehicle] **T:** 367
See also Mobile home *in this index*
Recreational vehicle (Folding camping trailers) **R:** 184; (Park trailers) **R:** 184; (Travel trailers) **R:** 184
Trailing [custom]
Flag (Raising and lowering the flag) **F:** 219
Trailing arbutus [plant] **T:** 368 *with picture*
Flower *picture on* **F:** 285
Train *See* Electric railroad; Locomotive; Railroad *in this index*
Train [watch]
Watch (Mechanical watches) **W:** 114
Train à grande vitesse *See* TGV *in this index*
Train of Powder, A [book by West]
West, Rebecca **W:** 199
Trainer [aircraft]
Air force (Aircraft and missiles) **A:** 183
Trainer [person]
Boxing **B:** 526
Horse racing (Trainers) **H:** 364
Training, Military *See* Military training *in this index*
Training and Doctrine Command
Army, United States (Army commands) **A:** 736
Training Day [film]
Washington, Denzel **W:** 89
Training of an Orator, The [book by Quintilian]
Oratory (Classical orators) **O:** 819
Quintilian **Q:** 43
Training program [organization]
Industrial psychology (Industrial psychologists) **I:** 245
Training school
Prison (Juvenile correctional institutions) **P:** 806

Reformatory **R:** 199
Training yard
Horse racing (Trainers) **H:** 364
Trainsickness
Motion sickness **M:** 874
Trainspotting [film]
Boyle, Danny **B:** 539
Trait [biology]
Heredity **H:** 200
Traitor
Treason **T:** 406
Trajan [Roman Emperor] **T:** 368
Hadrian **H:** 4
Library (Rome) **L:** 258
Romania (Early days) **R:** 423
Trajan, Markets of [ruins]
Rome (Forums) **R:** 433
Trajan's Column [Rome]
Alphabet (Capital letters) **A:** 383
Rome (Forums) **R:** 433 *with picture*
Sculpture (Roman sculpture) **S:** 247-248 *with picture*
Trajan **T:** 368
Trajan's Forum [Rome]
Rome (Forums) **R:** 433
Trajan **T:** 368
Traje de luces
Bullfighting (Types of bullfights) **B:** 695 *with picture*
Trajectory [physics]
Ballistics (Exterior ballistics) **B:** 56
Tram [streetcar]
Transportation (Urban public transportation) **T:** 393
Trammell, Park [American political leader]
Florida (table) **F:** 260
Tramp, The [film role]
Chaplin, Charlie **C:** 376
Tramp Abroad, A [book by Twain]
Black Forest **B:** 387
Twain, Mark (Productive years in Hartford) **T:** 529
Tramp clown
Clown **Ci:** 713
Trampoline **T:** 368 *with picture*
Gymnastics (Trampoline and tumbling) **G:** 449; (Judging) **G:** 450-451
Tran [dynasty]
Vietnam (Independence) **V:** 370
Trance **T:** 369
Dance (Ritual ethnic dances) **D:** 25
Hypnosis **H:** 478
Tranquilizer [medication] **T:** 369
Drug (Antianxiety and hypnotic drugs) **D:** 352
Drug abuse (table: Some commonly abused drugs) **D:** 363
Trans fats [biochemistry] **T:** 369
Nutrition (Limit intake of saturated fats, trans fats, and cholesterol) **N:** 628
Trans fatty acid *See* Trans fats *in this index*
Trans-Alaska Pipeline System
Alaska (The discovery of oil) **A:** 304 *with picture*
Insulation (In industry) **I:** 306-307
Petroleum (Transporting petroleum) **P:** 342
Pipeline (How pipelines work) **P:** 491 *with picture*
Transportation *picture on* **T:** 396
Transalpine Gaul [former region]
Gaul **G:** 70 *with map*
Transamerica Pyramid
San Francisco (Downtown San Francisco) **S:** 92-93
Transantarctic Mountains
Antarctica (Land) **A:** 531-532 *with map*
Trans-Arabia pipeline
Pipeline (In other countries) **P:** 491
Transatlantic cable
Cable (Telegraph cables) **C:** 5-6; (Telephone cables) **C:** 6
Transaxle [mechanical device]
Automobile *diagram on* **A:** 949
Transmission (Transmissions and drives) **T:** 375
Trans-Canada Highway **T:** 369 *with map*
Montreal (Transportation) **M:** 775-776
Ontario (Transportation) **O:** 782
Trans-Canada Pipeline
Pipeline (In Canada) **P:** 491
Transcaucasia [region]
Caucasus **C:** 317
Transcaucasian Soviet Federated Socialist Republic [Soviet history]
Caucasus **C:** 317
Russia (Civil war and the formation of the U.S.S.R.) **R:** 553
Transceiver [communications]
Citizens band radio **Ci:** 568
Radio, Amateur (Equipment) **R:** 95 *with picture*
Transcendental Club [organization]
Emerson, Ralph Waldo (His prose works) **E:** 259
Transcendental meditation

Cult (Modern cults) **Ci:** 1185
Yoga **Y:** 567
Transcendental Model 1G [aircraft]
V/STOL **V:** 453
Transcendental Philosophy
Philosophy (The philosophy of Immanuel Kant) **P:** 389
Transcendentalism [philosophy] **T:** 370
Alcott, Bronson **A:** 338
American literature (Nonfiction prose) **A:** 418
Brook Farm **B:** 639
Emerson, Ralph Waldo (His prose works) **E:** 259
Philosophy (Philosophy in the 1800's) **P:** 390
Thoreau, Henry David (His life) **T:** 266
Unitarians (History) **U:** 42
Transcontinental railroad **T:** 370
Railroad (The first transcontinental rail lines) **R:** 116 *with picture*
United States, History of the (Railroads) **U:** 180 *with picture*
Transcript [education]
Grading **G:** 296
Transcription [genetics]
Heredity (How proteins are made) **H:** 206
Transcurrent boundary [geology] *See* Transform boundary *in this index*
Transcutaneous energy transmission coil [device]
Artificial heart **A:** 760
Transdanubia [region]
Hungary (The land) **H:** 442 *with map*
Transdermal patch [medicine]
Drug *picture on* **D:** 350; (Entrance into the body) **D:** 353
Trans-Dniestr [region]
Moldova (History) **M:** 690a-690b
Transducer [electronics] **T:** 371
Oscilloscope **O:** 862
Ultrasound (Ultrasound devices) **U:** 16 *with picture*
Transept [structure]
Architecture (table) **A:** 608-609 *with picture*; (Medieval architecture) **A:** 617
Cathedral (The plan of a cathedral) **C:** 301 *with diagram*
Transfer [physics]
Vacuum (Producing a vacuum) **V:** 256
Transfer case [device]
Automobile (The drive system) **A:** 949
Transfer of training
Learning (Transfer of training) **L:** 164
Transfer payment
Economics (Distribution of income) **E:** 63
Gross domestic product (Measuring GDP) **G:** 399
Income **I:** 100
Transfer press [machine]
Money (Printing paper money) **M:** 715
Transfer printing [ceramics]
Porcelain (Transfer printing) **P:** 676
Transfer RNA [biochemistry]
Cell (Producing proteins) **C:** 333-334 *with diagram*
Heredity (Translation) **H:** 208
RNA **R:** 357
Transference [psychology]
Freud, Sigmund (On treatment) **F:** 531
Psychoanalysis (Psychoanalytic treatment) **P:** 846
Transferrin [protein]
Iron (How bodies use iron) **I:** 435
Transfiguration [religion] **T:** 371
Peter, Saint (Life as an apostle) **P:** 324
Transform boundary [geology]
Earthquake (Transform boundaries) **E:** 38
Plate tectonics (Transform plate boundaries) **P:** 563
Transform fault [geology]
Earth (Earthquakes) **E:** 24
Earthquake (Transform boundaries) **E:** 38
Plate tectonics (Transform boundaries) **P:** 563
Transformation [process]
Genetic engineering (How genes are reintroduced into cells) **G:** 84b
Transformation geometry
Geometry (Rise of non-Euclidean geometry) **G:** 106
Transformation mask [art]
Sculpture *picture on* **S:** 245; (Form and treatment) **S:** 230-231
Transformation of energy [physics]
Electric power **E:** 182
Transformational appeal
Advertising (Basic appeals) **A:** 76
Transformational grammar *See* Generative grammar *in this index*

Transformer [electricity] T: 371 *with diagram*
Electric current (Direct and alternating current) E: 168
Electric generator (Uses of AC generators) E: 173
Electric power (Transmitting and distributing electric power) E: 184-185 *with diagrams*
Induction coil I: 240
Magnetism (In industry and business) M: 60a
Transfusion, Blood See Blood transfusion *in this index*
Trans-Gambia Highway
Gambia (Economy) G: 19
Transgendered person
Gay rights movement G: 73
Transgenic pig [animal]
Xenotransplant X: 544
Transgenic technology [genetics]
Fruit (Developing new fruit cultivars) F: 548
Transient [biology]
Bird (The distribution of birds) B: 331-332
Killer whale K: 316
"Transient and Permanent in Christianity, The" [sermon by Parker]
Unitarians (History) U: 42
Transient ischemic attack [disorder]
Stroke (Symptoms) So: 929-930
Transistor [electronics] T: 372 *with pictures*
Computer (Computer code) Ci: 911; (Miniaturization) Ci: 924c
Electricity (Controlling electric current) E: 195; (The electronic age) E: 198
Electronics E: 206, *diagram on* E: 211; (Transistors) E: 212; (The solid-state revolution) E: 215
Hearing aid (History) H: 131
Ignition (Parts of an ignition system) I: 49
Invention (Research laboratories) I: 357
Technology (The computer age) T: 75
Transit [astronomy] T: 374 *with picture*
Mercury (Phases) M: 414
Transit [instrument]
Level L: 217
Surveying (Early tools) So: 1011
Transit [service] T: 374
See also Public transportation *in this index*
Transit 1B [satellite]
Navigation (Electronic navigation) N: 74
Transit map
Map (Navigation maps) M: 178
Transit sign
Advertising (Other ways of advertising) A: 75
Transit Union, Amalgamated
Labor movement (table) L: 8
Transition [sociology]
Rite of passage R: 350
Transition, The [Spanish history]
Spanish literature (Spanish literature today) So: 763
Transition metal [chemistry]
Element, Chemical *diagram on* E: 221
Transition region
Sun (Zones of the sun) So: 979-980 *with diagram*
Transition Region and Coronal Explorer [satellite]
Corona Ci: 1067
Transition temperature [physics]
Magnetism (Superconductivity) M: 61
Transitional bilingual education
Bilingual education (Transitional bilingual education) B: 300
Transitional Federal Government
Somalia (History) So: 589-590
Transitional form [biology]
Evolution (Evidence of evolution) E: 430
Transitive verb
Verb (Transitive and intransitive verbs) V: 315
Transjordan See Jordan *in this index*
Translation [genetics]
Heredity (How proteins are made) H: 206
Translation [literature]
Bible (Translations of the Bible) B: 284 *with picture*
United Nations (Breaking the language barrier) U: 86
Translational research [medicine]
Medicine (Medical researchers) M: 369
Translations [play by Friel]
Friel, Brian F: 533
Irish literature (Drama) I: 432
Translator program
Computer (Compiling or assembling a program) Ci: 923
Translocation [genetics]
Heredity (Mutation) H: 203
Translucence [physical property]
Light (Scattering) L: 288
Marble (Uses) M: 192
Transmigration of the soul See Reincarnation *in*

this index
Transmission [mechanics] T: 375 *with diagrams*
Automobile (From power plant to wheels) A: 948 *with diagram*
Transmission [optics]
Light (Reflection and absorption) L: 287-288
Transmission axis [optics]
Polarized light (Polarizing filters) P: 618
Transmission Control Protocol/Internet Protocol [electronics]
Computer (Internet software) Ci: 922
Internet (Software) I: 350c
Transmission electron microscope
Electron microscope (Transmission electron microscopes) E: 204 *with diagram*
Microscope (Electron microscopes) M: 519
Transmission fluid
Transmission (A torque converter) T: 376
Transmission genetics
Genetics (Transmission genetics) G: 87
Transmission line
Electric power (Transmitting and distributing electric power) E: 184
Transmission pipeline
Gas [fuel] (Transmitting and distributing gas) G: 55
Trans-Mississippi and International Exposition [1898]
Omaha (History) O: 756-757
Transmitter [electronics]
Navigation (Radio navigation) N: 72
Radar (The transmitter) R: 71 *with diagram*
Radio (Transmitting radio waves) R: 86; (Broadcasting power and frequency) R: 87-88
Telephone (Parts of a telephone) T: 95
Television *diagram on* T: 124; (Transmitting television signals) T: 123
Wireless communication (How wireless communication works) W: 344
Transmontane Plains
British Columbia (Land regions) B: 622-624
Transmutation of elements T: 378
See also Radioactive decay *in this index*
Alchemy A: 334
Atom (Radioactivity) A: 873
Chemistry (Beginnings) C: 400
Radiation (Naturally radioactive substances) R: 77
Rutherford, Ernest R: 569
Transnational [person]
Anthropology (Modern anthropology) A: 549
Transnational corporation
Multinational corporation M: 919
Trans-Neptunian disk [astronomy] See Kuiper belt *in this index*
Transoceanic flight
Airplane (Transoceanic transports) A: 238
Transonic flight
Aerodynamics (Supersonic aerodynamics) A: 87
Transorbital lobotomy [surgery]
Lobotomy L: 405
Transparency [photography]
Audio-visual materials (Projection devices) A: 882
Photography (Color reversal film) P: 419
Projector (Overhead projectors) P: 817
Transparency [physical property]
Light (Scattering) L: 288
Transparency [trade policy]
General Agreement on Tariffs and Trade G: 83
Transparent sculpture
Lipchitz, Jacques L: 344
Trans-Pecos Region
Texas (Land regions) T: 196
Transpiration [botany]
Air (Moisture in the air) A: 170
Irrigation (Bringing irrigation water to farms) I: 457
Leaf (Transpiration) L: 156
Plant (Movement of water) P: 537
Rain forest (Environmental value) R: 126c
Water (Water in the air) W: 120
Transpired solar collector
Solar energy (Solar heating) So: 579
Transplant [medicine] T: 379 *with pictures*
AIDS (How HIV is transmitted) A: 164b
Bone marrow transplant B: 457 *with picture*
Cloning (Ethical issues) Ci: 683
Cyclosporine Ci: 1204
Death (Defining death) D: 61
Diabetes (Research) D: 180
Eye bank E: 470
Heart (Heart failure) H: 143 *with picture*; (The first heart transplants and artificial hearts) H: 145
Immune system (The cell-mediated immune response) I: 88-88a
Kidney (Kidney diseases) K: 312
Liver L: 393
Lymphatic system (Rejection of transplanted

tissue) L: 535
Organ donation O: 852
Plastic surgery (Reconstructive plastic surgery) P: 553
Red Cross (Biomedical services) R: 185
Surgery (Technique) So: 1005; (History) So: 1007-1008
Xenotransplant X: 544
Transplanting [horticulture] T: 381 *with pictures*
Gardening (Planting and transplanting) G: 34
Pruning P: 841
Vegetable (Planting) V: 293, V: 293
Transpolar Drift [current]
Arctic Ocean (Sea ice) A: 641
Transponder
Airplane (Safety) A: 227-228
Communications satellite (How communications satellites work) Ci: 888b
Transport [airplane]
Air force (Aircraft and missiles) A: 183
Air Force, United States (Other aircraft) A: 191 *with pictures*
Aircraft, Military (Transports) A: 203 *with picture*
Aviation *picture on* A: 985
Transport airports
Airport (General aviation airports) A: 243
Transport Canada [agency]
Aviation (Aviation agencies) A: 985-986
Railroad (In Canada) R: 113
Transport mission [warfare]
Air force (Transport missions) A: 183
Transport Workers Union of America
Labor movement (table) L: 8
Transportation T: 382 *with pictures*
Careers (Transportation) C: 235 *with picture*
City (Metropolitan cities) Ci: 588-589
City planning (Proposals of the plan) Ci: 599-601 *with diagram*
Colonial life in America (Transportation) Ci: 805 *with picture*
Disability (Housing and transportation) D: 221
Electricity (In transportation) E: 191
Food (Transportation) F: 335
Indian, American (Transportation) I: 142
Industrial Revolution (Transportation) I: 250
Industry (Production location) I: 259
Inland waterway I: 273
Ocean (As a vast highway) O: 655
Radio (In industry) R: 84
Safety (Safety in transportation) S: 14
Social change So: 550
Technology (Technology and society) T: 76
Transit T: 374
Transportation Security Administration T: 400
Truck T: 456
United States, History of the (Advances in transportation and communications) U: 170 *with pictures*
Transportation, Department of [U.S.] T: 399 *with picture*
Johnson, Lyndon Baines (The Great Society) J: 150
United States Merchant Marine Academy U: 200
Transportation, Public See Public transportation *in this index*
Transportation, Secretary of [office]
Flag *picture on* F: 211
Transportation, Department of T: 399
Transportation Act [1920]
Railroad (Regulation and control of U.S. railroads) R: 118
Transportation Average [investment]
Dow Jones averages D: 315
Transportation Command, U.S. [military group]
Army, United States (Army service component commands) A: 736-737
Scott Air Force Base S: 223
Transportation Communications International Union
Labor movement (table) L: 8
Transportation engineering
Engineering (Other specialized fields) E: 287-288
Transportation of convicts [Australian history] T: 400
Australia (History) A: 919-920
Transportation Security Administration [agency] T: 400
Airport A: 242
Aviation (Recent developments) A: 991-992
Homeland Security, Department of (Organization) H: 301
Transportation (Transportation security) T: 398-399
Transportation Union, United
Labor movement (table) L: 8
Transposition
Codes and ciphers (Communications security)

Ci: 749
Transsexualism T: 401
 Sexuality (Special cases of gender identity) S: 338
Trans-Siberian Express [train]
 Trans-Siberian Railroad T: 401
Trans-Siberian Railroad T: 401
 Asia *picture on* A: 789
 Mongolia (Economy) M: 723
 Russia *picture on* R: 546
 Russo-Japanese War (Underlying causes) R: 566a
 Siberia (Economy) S: 444-445
 Transcontinental railroad (Around the world) T: 371
Tranströmer, Tomas [Swedish author]
 Nobel Prizes (Literature: 2011) N: 448
Transubstantiation [religion] T: 401
 Trent, Council of T: 434
 Wycliffe, John W: 515
Transuranium element [chemistry] T: 401
Transvaal [region, South Africa] T: 402
 Anglo-Boer Wars A: 463
 Kruger, Paul K: 388
 Rhodes, Cecil John (Conflict with the Boers) R: 317
 South Africa (The Plateau) So: 614 *with map*; (Discovery of diamonds and gold) So: 618
Transversal [region]
 Paricutín P: 159
Transverse arch [anatomy]
 Foot (The arches) F: 352
Transverse colon [anatomy]
 Colon Ci: 786
 Intestine (The large intestine) I: 353 *with diagram*
Transverse engine
 Transmission (Transmissions and drives) T: 375
Transverse Ranges [mountains, California]
 California (The Transverse Ranges) C: 50
Transverse wave [physics]
 Light (The properties of waves) L: 285
 Waves *diagram on* W: 150; (Types of waves) W: 152
Transvestism
 Sexuality (Special cases of gender identity) S: 338-338a
Transylvania [region, Romania] T: 402
 Hungary (History) H: 445
 Romania (Land regions) R: 419 *with map*; (Unification movement) R: 423; (World War I) R: 424
Transylvania Company [U.S. history]
 Boone, Daniel (The Wilderness Road) B: 477
 Tennessee (Early settlement) T: 153
Transylvania University
 Kentucky (Schools) K: 276
 Lexington (Description) L: 224
Transylvanian Alps [mountains, Europe]
 Romania (Surface features) R: 419
Transylvanian Plateau
 Romania (Land regions) R: 419; (Surface features) R: 419
Traoré, Dioncounda [Malian military leader]
 Mali (History) M: 108-109
Traoré, Moussa [Malian military leader]
 Mali (History) M: 108-109
Trap [fishing]
 Fishing industry (Traps) F: 185 *with diagram*
Trap [geology]
 Gas [fuel] (Exploring for gas) G: 53
Trap [plumbing]
 House (Plumbing) H: 382
 Plumbing (The drain-waste-vent system) P: 578 *with diagram*
Trap [sports]
 Basketball (Defensive strategies) B: 147 *with picture*
 Football (table) F: 356
Trap door [theater]
 Shakespeare, William (The stage) S: 351-352 *with picture*
Trap line
 Fur (Trapping) F: 562
Trapeze artist
 Circus (At the circus) Ci: 562 *with picture*
Trapeze-foil hydrofoil [boat]
 Hydrofoil (Surface-piercing hydrofoils) H: 467
Trapezium bone [anatomy]
 Hand (Parts of the hand) H: 40
Trapezius muscle [anatomy]
 Head *diagram on* H: 123
 Shoulder S: 437 *with picture*
Trapezoid bone [anatomy]
 Hand (Parts of the hand) H: 40
Traphouse [machine]
 Trapshooting T: 404
Trapp, Martin E. [American political leader]
 Oklahoma (table) O: 730; (The 1920's) O: 732

Trapping [fishing]
 Fishing industry (Traps) F: 185 *with diagram*
 Inuit (Hunting and fishing) I: 354d-354e; (History) I: 354f-354g
 Lobster (Lobster fishing) L: 406
Trapping [hunting] T: 402 *with pictures*
 Beaver B: 192
 Conservation (Early conservation problems) Ci: 985
 Fur (Trapping) F: 562
Trapping [sports]
 Soccer (table) So: 546
Trappistines [religious group]
 Trappists T: 404
Trappists [religious group] T: 404
 Cistercians Ci: 567
 Merton, Thomas M: 419
 Religious life (table) R: 227
Trapshooting [sport] T: 404
Trapunto-stuffed quilt
 Quilt Q: 41
Trash *See* Waste disposal *in this index*
Trash [agriculture]
 Cotton (Harvesting) Ci: 1090
Trastuzumab [drug]
 Breast cancer B: 591
Trauma [psychology] T: 404
 Post-traumatic stress disorder P: 710
Trauma center T: 405
 Hospital (Recent developments) H: 374
Travel *See the Places to visit section in specific state and province articles, such as* California (Places to visit), *and* Transportation *in this index*
Travel agency T: 405
 Careers (Tourism and hospitality) C: 233 *with picture*
Travel Pictures [book by Heine]
 Heine, Heinrich H: 166
Travel trailer
 Recreational vehicle *pictures on* R: 183; (Travel trailers) T: 184
 Trailer (Recreational trailers) T: 368
Travelers Aid International T: 405
Travelers Among Mountains [painting by Fan Kuan]
 Painting (Landscapes and seascapes) P: 32-33 *with picture*
Travelers Among Mountains and Streams [painting by Fan Kuan]
 Painting (Chinese painting) P: 44-45 *with picture*
Traveler's check [banking]
 Check (Special checking services) C: 391
Travelers Insurance Company
 Connecticut (Interesting facts) Ci: 953
Traveler's-tree [tree] T: 405 *with picture*
 Tree (Interesting facts about trees) T: 411 *with picture*
Traveling-wave linear accelerator [machine]
 Particle accelerator (How accelerators work) P: 184-185
Traveling-wave tube [electronics]
 Vacuum tube (Microwave tubes) V: 259
Traveller [horse]
 Horse (table: Famous horses in history and legend) H: 361
 Lee, Robert E. *picture on* L: 177
Traveller, The [poem by Goldsmith]
 Goldsmith, Oliver G: 259
Travellers [people]
 Roma R: 402a
Travels in the Interior of Africa [book by Park]
 Park, Mungo P: 168
Travels in Two Democracies [book by Wilson]
 Wilson, Edmund W: 316
Travels in West Africa [book by Kingsley]
 Kingsley, Mary Henrietta K: 331
Travels with a Donkey in the Cévennes [book by Stevenson]
 Stevenson, Robert Louis (Early life) So: 897
Travers, Morris William [British chemist]
 Krypton K: 389
 Neon N: 123
 Xenon X: 543
Travers, P. L. [Australian author] T: 405
Traversing [skiing]
 Skiing *diagram on* S: 484; (Alpine skiing) S: 482
Travertine [rock] T: 405
Traviata, La [opera by Verdi] T: 406
 Dumas, Alexandre, fils D: 382
 Opera: (*Traviata, La*) O: 807 *with picture*
Travis, Merle [American guitarist]
 Atkins, Chet A: 858
Travis, Randy [American singer]
 Country music (Modern country music) Ci: 1098c-1098d
Travis, William Barret [Texas patriot] T: 406
 Alamo (Early days) A: 280

Texas (The Texas revolution) T: 206
Travois [transportation] T: 406
 Indian, American (Transportation) I: 142; (Before European contact) I: 158-159
 Transportation *picture on* T: 386
Travolta, John [American actor] T: 406 *with portrait*
Trawl [net]
 Fishing industry *picture on* F: 180; (Nets) F: 183 *with diagram*
 Shrimp (Shrimp and people) S: 440
Trawler [ship]
 Fishing industry *picture on* F: 180; (Nets) F: 183 *with diagram*
 Ship (Specialized vessels) S: 410
Tray drying
 Food preservation (Drying) F: 342-343
Traynor, Pie [American baseball player]
 Baseball (table: Hall of Fame) B: 134b
Tread
 Tire T: 295 *with pictures*; (Tire tread patterns) T: 297
Treadle [loom]
 Weaving (Kinds of looms) W: 174
Treadmill [machine] T: 406
 Stress test So: 927
Treason T: 406
 Constitution of the United States (Article III, Section 3) Ci: 1010
 Crime (Treason) Ci: 1137
Treasure Island [book by Stevenson]
 Stevenson, Robert Louis (Novels) So: 898
Treasure Island [film]
 Disney, Walt (Full-length movies) D: 236
Treasure of the Humble, The [essays by Maeterlinck]
 Maeterlinck, Maurice M: 41
Treasure of the Sierra Madre, The [film]
 Huston, John H: 458
Treasure State [nickname]
 Montana M: 742
Treasurer [office]
 Parliamentary procedure (Officers) P: 175
 State government (Other officers) So: 863
Treasury, Department of the [U.S.] T: 407 *with picture*
 Customs Service, United States Ci: 1201
 Internal Revenue Service I: 337
 Money (How money is manufactured) M: 714
 Washington, D.C. *map on* W: 76
Treasury, Secretary of the [office]
 Flag *picture on* F: 211
 Treasury, Department of the T: 407
Treasury bill
 Investment (Bonds) I: 368
Treasury bond
 Investment (Bonds) I: 368
Treasury Department Lifesaving Medal
 Medals, decorations, and orders (Civilian awards) M: 355
Treasury of Atreus [Mycenae]
 Architecture (Mycenaean architecture) A: 615
Treatise of Harmony [book by Rameau]
 Rameau, Jean-Philippe R: 133
Treatise of Human Nature, A [book by Hume]
 Hume, David (Hume's life) H: 432
Treatise on Courtesy, A [book by Thomasin von Zerclaere]
 Etiquette (Books on etiquette) E: 374
Treatise on the Education of Girls [book by Fénelon]
 Fénelon, François de Salignac de la Mothe- F: 71
Treatise on the Improvement of Canal Navigation, A [book by Fulton]
 Fulton, Robert (The inventor) F: 555
Treatment plant
 Water (Purifying and treating water) W: 126
Treaty [international relations] T: 408 *with picture*
 Congress of the United States (Approving treaties) Ci: 946
 Fishing industry (International commissions and treaties) F: 187
 Human rights (Treaties) H: 428a
 Indian, American (In the United States) I: 178-178a
 International law I: 340
 International relations (Treaties) I: 344
 Nuclear weapon (Treaties) N: 601
Treaty body [committee]
 Human rights (Monitoring) H: 428a
Treaty Oak [landmark]
 Jacksonville (Cultural life and recreation) J: 18
Treaty of ...
 Treaties appear under their key words, as in Brest-Litovsk, Treaty of
Treaty port [Chinese history] T: 409
Trebia River, Battle of the [218 B.C.]
 Hannibal (His military campaigns) H: 52

Treble [music] T: 409
Treble clef
Music (Indicating pitch) M: 952-953 with picture
Treble T: 409
Treblinka [concentration camp] T: 409
Concentration camp (Nazi concentration camps)
Ci: 926-927
Trebuchet [weapon]
Weapon (Siege weapons) W: 154b
Tredegar Iron Works
Civil War, American (Economy) Ci: 623
Tree T: 410 with pictures
See also Forest and Forest products in this index,
and the list of Related articles in the Tree article
Arbor Day A: 592
Bark B: 110 with diagram
Bonsai B: 463
Climate (Growth rings) Ci: 679
Flower F: 270
Pruning P: 841 with pictures
Rain forest R: 126 with pictures
Sap S: 120 with diagram
Windbreak W: 333
Tree cotton
Cotton (Kinds of cotton) Ci: 1087
Tree cricket [insect]
Cricket Ci: 1130 with picture
Insect (Courtship) I: 294
Tree farming T: 432
Tree fern
Fern picture on F: 75
Plant picture on P: 522
Tree pictures on T: 413; (Tree ferns) T: 415
Tree fox
Fox (Kinds of foxes) F: 440
Tree frog T: 432 with picture
Animal picture on A: 480
Frog picture on F: 536; (Tree frogs) F: 540
Tree heath [plant] See Brier in this index
Tree kangaroo [animal]
Kangaroo (Kinds of kangaroos) K: 213; (Tree
kangaroos) K: 215
Tree line [geography]
Arctic map on A: 637
Tree of heaven See Ailanthus in this index
Tree of Man, The [book by White]
Novel (The novel today) N: 575
White, Patrick W: 284
Tree peony [plant]
Peony P: 276 with picture
Tree shear [machine]
Lumber (Cutting down trees) L: 518
Tree shilling [money]
Money picture on M: 707; (Tree shillings) M: 710
Tree shrew [animal] T: 433 with picture
Mammal (table) M: 129 with picture
Tree snake
Invasive species (How invasive species affect
habitats) I: 354j
Snake (Snakes as invasive species) S: 532
Tree squirrel
Squirrel (Types of squirrels) So: 814b with pictures
Tree surgery T: 433
Tree swallow [bird]
Swallow So: 1014 with picture
Treehopper [insect]
Animal picture on A: 495
Treemonisha [opera by Joplin]
Joplin, Scott J: 160
Treemoss [lichen]
Lichen (The importance of lichens) L: 269
Treen, David C. [American political leader]
Louisiana (table) L: 496
"Trees" [poem by Kilmer]
Kilmer, Joyce K: 316
Trefoil [botany] T: 434
Trefoil [emblem]
Girl Scouts G: 196 with picture
Trek, Great [South African history] See Great Trek
in this index
Trekbokken [animal]
Springbok So: 807 with picture
Trellis [structure]
Gardening (Planning a kitchen garden) G: 34
Grape (Planting and cultivating) G: 319-320
Tomato (Growing, harvesting, and processing)
T: 325
Trematode [animal]
Flatworm F: 229
Tremblay, Michel [Canadian dramatist]
Canadian literature (Modern Canadian drama)
C: 161 with portrait
Tremblay, Paul [Canadian diplomat]
United Nations (table) U: 86
Trembler [bird]
Thrasher T: 268
Tremolo [music]

Music (table) M: 954
Tremolo arm [electronics]
Electric guitar E: 173
Tremont House [Boston]
Hotel (History) H: 376-377
Trench [geography]
Atlantic Ocean (The Mid-Atlantic Ridge) A: 864
Deep sea (The deep-sea floor) D: 82a
Ocean (Depth) O: 651-652; (The land at the
bottom of the sea) O: 659-661
Pacific Ocean (The ocean floor) P: 14
Trench foot [disease]
Immersion foot I: 79
Trench mouth [disease] T: 434
Teeth (Periodontal diseases) T: 85-86
Trench warfare
Army (Armies in the two world wars) A: 728
World, History of the picture on W: 421
World War I picture on W: 453; (Trench warfare)
W: 457 with diagram
Trencher [utensil]
Colonial life in America (Furnishings) Ci: 797
Trend [musical]
Holm, Hanya H: 294
Trend forecaster [occupation]
Clothing (The clothing industry) Ci: 705-706
Trent [ship] See Trent Affair in this index
Trent, Council of [1545-1563] T: 434
Christianity (The Counter Reformation) C: 525
Counter Reformation (Counteracting
Protestantism) Ci: 1096 with picture
Paul III P: 199
Pius IV P: 502
Roman Catholic Church (The Counter
Reformation) R: 408 with picture
Vulgate V: 453
Trent, River [England]
England (Rivers and lakes) E: 300-301
Trent, William [American pioneer]
Trenton T: 434
Trent Affair [U.S. history] T: 435
Lincoln, Abraham (Foreign relations) L: 322
Mason, James Murray M: 266
Slidell, James S: 508
Wilkes, Charles W: 306
Trente Arpents [book by Ringuet]
Canadian literature (Literature between the
world wars) C: 158
Trentino-Alto Adige [region, Italy] See Italian Tyrol
in this index
Trenton [New Jersey] T: 434
New Jersey (Places to visit) N: 240 with picture
United States capitals U: 199
Trenton, Battle of [1776] T: 435
New Jersey (The American Revolution) N: 250
Revolution, American (table) R: 276; (Trenton and
Princeton) R: 282
Washington, George (The army) W: 99 with
picture
Trepang [food] T: 435
Trephine [instrument]
Trephining T: 435
Trephining [surgery] T: 435
Inca (Religion) I: 96-97
Indian, American (Shamans) I: 147-148
Medicine (History) M: 371-372 with picture
Surgery (History) So: 1007
Très Riches Heures, Les [book by Limbourg]
Europe picture on E: 409
Jesus Christ picture on J: 109
Limbourg brothers L: 306
Middle Ages picture on M: 522
World, History of the picture on W: 432
Trespass [law] T: 436
Trespassers, The [book by Hobson]
Hobson, Laura Z. H: 273
Tresselt, Alvin [American author]
Duvoisin, Roger Antoine D: 393
Trethewey, Natasha [American poet]
Poet laureate (table: Poets laureate of the United
States) P: 590
Treutlen, John A. [American political leader]
Georgia (table) G: 130
Treveri [ancient people]
Trier T: 441
Trevi Fountain [Rome]
Rome (Churches, palaces, and fountains) R: 429-
430
Treviño, Elizabeth Borton de [American author]
Newbery Medal (table) N: 359
Trevino, Lee [American golfer] T: 436
Golf (U.S. Open) G: 265
Trevithick, Richard [British inventor] T: 436
Automobile (The steam car) A: 965
Railroad (Invention of the locomotive) R: 115
Steam engine (Modern steam engines) So: 881
Trevor, Claire [American actress]

Motion picture (Best performance by an actress
in a supporting role: 1948) M: 862b
Trevor, William [Irish author]
Irish literature (Fiction) I: 432
T.rex Discovery Centre [Eastend]
Saskatchewan (Places to visit) S: 136 with picture
Triad [color]
Color (Producing color harmony) Ci: 823 with
diagram
Triad [music]
Harmony H: 62
Music (Harmony) M: 951 with diagrams
Triage [medicine]
Emergency room E: 258
Trial [law] T: 436
See also Jury in this index
Constitution of the United States (Amendment
5) Ci: 1012
Court (How courts work) Ci: 1101
Criminal justice system (Pretrial procedures)
Ci: 1143; (The trial) Ci: 1143
Judge J: 183
Trial, The [book by Kafka]
German literature (Expressionism) G: 141-142
Kafka, Franz K: 209
Novel (New directions in the novel) N: 573-574
Trial-and-error behavior [psychology]
Learning (Instrumental conditioning) L: 163
Trial balance [record]
Bookkeeping (Bookkeeping and financial
statements) B: 473
Trial Begins, The [book by Sinyavsky]
Russian literature (Modern Soviet literature)
R: 564
Trial by combat [European history]
Feudalism (Justice under feudalism) F: 82
Trial by jury See Jury; Trial in this index
Trial by ordeal [European history]
Divination D: 241
Middle Ages (Barbarian Europe) M: 523
Trial (History) T: 437
Trial court
Court (Types of courts) Ci: 1101
District court D: 240
United States, Government of the (Lower court
system) U: 144
Trial judge
Judge J: 183
Trial period
Sales (Persuasion) S: 63-64
Triangle [business district]
São Paulo (The city) S: 117
Triangle [geometry] T: 437 with diagrams
Geometry (The study of geometry) G: 101 with
diagram; (Properties of geometric figures)
G: 102 with diagrams
Pyramid P: 916
Pythagorean theorem P: 921
Trigonometry T: 442 with diagrams
Triangle [musical instrument] T: 438 with picture
Triangle Shirtwaist Factory Fire [U.S. history]
T: 438
Triangular bandage
Bandage B: 75
Triangular trade [U.S. history]
African Americans (Beginning of the slave trade)
A: 136c-136d
Colonial life in America (Trade) Ci: 811
Triangulum Galaxy T: 439 with picture
Local Group L: 409
Universe U: 205
Trianon, Treaty of [1920] T: 439
Hungary (Between world wars) H: 446
World War I (The peace settlement) W: 465-466
Trias [geology]
Triassic Period T: 439
Triassic Period [geology] T: 439
Dinosaur (Kinds of dinosaurs) D: 206b
Earth (table) E: 30 with map
Extinction (Mass extinction) E: 456
Prehistoric animal (Amphibians) P: 738; (table)
P: 739
Triathlon [sport] T: 440
Olympic Games (Summer Olympic Games)
O: 746e-749
Triatomic molecule [chemistry]
Molecule (Individual molecules) M: 692-693
Triazolam [drug]
Benzodiazepine B: 256
Tribal council [government]
Indian, American (Tribes) I: 143
Tribal Twenties [name for]
Roaring Twenties R: 363
Tribbitt, Sherman W. [American political leader]
Delaware (table) D: 109
Tribe [sociology] T: 440
Arabs (Family life) A: 587

Family (Non-Western families) F: 24
Indian, American (Tribes) I: 143
Nomad N: 452
Tribelet [American Indian unit]
Miwok Indians M: 679
Tribes and Temples [book by La Farge and Blom]
La Farge, Oliver L: 27
Tribhuvan Shah [king of Nepal]
Nepal (History) N: 126-127
Tribhuvan University
Nepal (People) N: 125
Triboluminescence
Sphalerite So: 779
Tribunal of first instance
Egypt (Courts) E: 121
Tribunal of the Roman Rota
Vatican City (Administration) V: 288
Tribune [ancient Rome] T: 440
Legion L: 183
Plebeians P: 572
Rome, Ancient (The Roman Republic) R: 438
Tribune, New York See New York Tribune in this index
Tribune and Farmer, The [magazine]
Magazine (Magazines in the 1800's) M: 45
Tribune of the people [ancient Rome]
Tribune T: 440
Tributary [geography]
Basin B: 141
River *diagram on* R: 353; (Tributaries) R: 351
Tribute [tax]
Colonialism (Colonial economic policies) Ci: 814
Mexico (Spanish rule) M: 469
Tribute Money, The [fresco by Masaccio]
Painting (The 1400's) P: 52-53 *with picture*
Triceps [anatomy]
Arm A: 717 *with diagram*
Human body (table) H: 422 *with diagram*
Muscle (Skeletal muscles) M: 933
Triceratops [dinosaur] T: 441
Dinosaur *picture on* D: 212; (True dinosaurs) D: 206b-208 *with picture*
Trichina [animal] T: 441
Trichinosis [disease]
Hog (Diseases) H: 287
Pork P: 679
Trichina T: 441
Trichlorofluoromethane [chemical]
Chlorofluorocarbon C: 517
Trichoptera [entomology]
Insect (table) I: 300
Trichromatic theory [color]
Color (The three-component theory) Ci: 826
Trichromatic vision
Color blindness Ci: 827
Trichuriasis [disease]
Roundworm R: 492
Trick
Magician M: 51
Pet (Tricks) P: 321
Trick [cards]
Bridge (Scoring) B: 605
Trick-or-treating [custom]
Halloween (Trick-or-treating) H: 24a *with picture*
Trick score [bridge]
Bridge (Scoring) B: 605
Trick to Catch the Old One, A [play by Middleton]
Massinger, Philip M: 296
Trickle irrigation
Irrigation (Trickle irrigation) I: 458 *with picture*
Trickster [legendary figure]
Folklore (Folk tales) F: 323-324 *with picture*
Trickster of Seville, The [play by Tirso de Molina]
Don Juan D: 306
Spanish literature (The 1600's) So: 759
Tirso de Molina T: 298
Triclinic system [mineralogy]
Crystal (Classifying crystals) Ci: 1166-1167 *with picture*
Tricorne [hat]
Hat *picture on* H: 84
Tricorner Knob [mountain, North Carolina-Tennessee]
Great Smoky Mountains G: 348
Tricuspid valve [anatomy]
Heart (Chambers, valves, and inner lining) H: 133-135 *with pictures*; (The work of the heart) H: 135
Tricycle landing gear
Airplane *picture on* A: 215; (The landing gear) A: 216-217
Tricyclic antidepressant [drug]
Antidepressant A: 553
Trident [weapon]
Gladiator G: 206
Neptune N: 128 *with picture*
Poseidon P: 697

Trident submarine
Submarine (Nuclear submarines) So: 943
Trier [Germany] T: 441
Trier of fact [law]
Evidence E: 425
Trieres [ship] See Trireme in this index
Trieste [Italy] T: 441
Trieste [diving vessel]
Diving, Underwater (Diving in vehicles) D: 246
Piccard, Auguste P: 450
Piccard, Jacques P: 450
Trifecta [betting]
Horse racing (Betting) H: 365
Trifles [play by Glaspell]
Glaspell, Susan G: 210
Trifocal [lens]
Glasses (Prescription glasses) G: 224-225 *with diagrams*
Trifonov, Yuri [Soviet author]
Russian literature (Modern Soviet literature) R: 564-565
Trigeminal nerve [anatomy]
Neuralgia N: 152
Trigger [gun]
Handgun (Types of handguns) H: 43 *with picture*
Trigger [horse]
Rogers, Roy R: 401
Trigger [medicine]
Asthma A: 825
Triggerfish T: 442 *with picture*
Fish *picture on* F: 154
Triglyceride [compound] T: 442
Cholesterol C: 520
Fat (Structure) F: 52
Lard L: 75
Trigonometric ratio
Mathematics (Branches of mathematics) M: 303
Trigonometry (Right triangles) T: 443
Trigonometric series
Series S: 316b
Trigonometry T: 442 *with pictures*
Mathematics (Branches of mathematics) M: 303; (The Renaissance) M: 306
Trigram [figure]
I Ching I: 2
Triiodothyronine [hormone]
Hormone (Metabolic hormones) H: 335
Trilateral Commission
Brzezinski, Zbigniew Kazimierz B: 657
Trilby [book by Du Maurier]
Du Maurier, George D: 382
Trillin, Calvin [American author]
American literature (Essays) A: 426
Trilling, Lionel [American author]
American literature (Essays) A: 426
Trillion [number] T: 445
Trillium [plant] T: 445
Flower (Flowers of woodlands and forests) F: 284 *with picture*
Plant *picture on* P: 525
Trilobite [extinct animal] T: 445
Cambrian Period C: 74
Fossil *pictures on* F: 425, F: 427
Prehistoric animal (The earliest animals) P: 736
Trim tab [device]
Airplane (The wing) A: 213-214 *with picture*; (Basic movements and controls) A: 222-225
Trimaran [boat]
Boating (Sailboats) B: 429
Trimble, Allen [American political leader]
Ohio (table) O: 699
Trimble, David [Irish political leader] T: 445
Nobel Prizes (Peace: 1998) N: 448b
Ulster Unionist Party U: 15
Trimble, Robert [American jurist]
Supreme Court of the United States (table) So: 1000
Trimerophyte [plant]
Plant (The evolution of plants) P: 544
Trimester [pregnancy]
Abortion (Abortion in the United States) A: 15
Pregnancy (How pregnancy affects women) P: 734b
Reproduction, Human (Growth of the fetus) R: 248
Roe v. Wade R: 399
Trimester system [education]
Universities and colleges (The academic calendar) U: 209-210
Trimeter [poetry]
Poetry (table) P: 594
Trimmer saw [machine]
Lumber *picture on* L: 520; (Sawing logs) L: 519
Trimming [sailing]
Sailing (Trimming and tacking) S: 26
Trimotor plane
Airplane *picture on* A: 233; (The golden age)

A: 235
Trimurti [Hindu gods]
Brahman B: 548
Trinh [dynasty]
Vietnam (Independence) V: 370
Trinidad [ship]
Magellan, Ferdinand (The voyage begins) M: 47
Trinidad and Tobago T: 445 *with picture and map*
Calypso C: 71
Flag *picture on* F: 202
West Indies *picture on* W: 201
Trinitrotoluene See TNT *in this index*
Trinity [religion] T: 447
Arianism A: 661
Arius A: 669
Christianity (The Trinity) C: 522g
Jesus Christ (The early Christians) J: 108b-109
Mormons (Church doctrines and ordinances) M: 806-807
Protestantism (Protestant beliefs) P: 833-834; (Worship) P: 834
Roman Catholic Church (The Trinity and creation) R: 403
Trinity Church [Boston]
Boston *picture on* B: 495; (Back Bay) B: 497
Richardson, Henry Hobson R: 330
Trinity College [former name]
Duke University D: 380
Trinity College Dublin T: 447
Ireland (Education) I: 420-421 *with picture*
Trinity River [U.S.]
Dallas (The city) D: 11 *with picture*
Trinity River Greenbelt [region]
Dallas (Recreation) D: 14
Trinity Site [region, New Mexico]
New Mexico (World War II) N: 275 *with picture*
Trinkle, Elbert Lee [American political leader]
Virginia (table) V: 417
Trinucleotide repeat expansion disorder [genetics]
Fragile X syndrome F: 450
Trio [music]
March M: 193
Triode [electronics]
Electronics (Early experiments) E: 215
Vacuum tube (Kinds of vacuum tubes) V: 258-259 *with diagram*
Triolet [poetry]
Poetry (table) P: 594
Trip [drugs]
Hallucinogenic drug H: 26
LSD L: 511
Trip balance [instrument]
Balance B: 34 *with picture*
Trip hammer [machine]
Agriculture (China) A: 156
Trip odometer [measuring device]
Speedometer So: 775
Tripe [food]
Cattle (Beef cattle) C: 308
Tripitaka [religious book]
Buddhism (The dharma) B: 668
Triple [baseball]
Baseball (Reaching base) B: 129
Triple Alliance [European history]
Bismarck, Otto von (Bismarck's diplomacy) B: 382
Germany (Foreign policy) G: 166
Italy (The Kingdom of Italy) I: 516
Russia (World War I) R: 552
World War I (The Triple Alliance) W: 455
Triple Alliance [Mexican history]
Cortés, Hernán (Arrival in Mexico) Ci: 1072-1073
Triple Alliance, War of the [1865-1870]
Brazil (The reign of Pedro II) B: 584
Latin America (Early years of independence) L: 107-108
Paraguay (Military ruin) P: 149
Uruguay (Struggles for power) U: 227
Triple-alpha process [physics]
Star (Fusion of other elements) So: 848; (Intermediate-mass stars) So: 848
Triple Crown [U.S.]
Arcaro, Eddie A: 593
Horse racing (Types of horse races) H: 364-365
Kentucky Derby K: 295
Triple Entente [European history]
France (World War I) F: 475
Germany (Foreign policy) G: 166
Russia (World War I) R: 552
United Kingdom (Gladstone and Disraeli) U: 69
World War I (The Triple Entente) W: 455
Triple jump [track and field] T: 447
Track and field (Jumping events) T: 357
Triple play [baseball]
Baseball (Baseball terms) B: 124
Triple point [physics]
Sublimation So: 938

Triple point temperature [physics]
Temperature T: 130
Triple trailer [truck]
Truck T: 456, *picture on* T: 459
Triplet [gem]
Gem (Imitation and synthetic gems) G: 79
Triplet [poetry]
Poetry (table) P: 594
Triplet code [genetics]
Cell (The genetic code) C: 336
Heredity (How proteins are made) H: 206
Triplets [multiple birth]
Multiple birth M: 919 *with picture*
Tripod [device]
Photography (Shutter speed) P: 412
Tripod fish T: 447
Deep sea *picture on* D: 82; (Fish) D: 82b-82c
Fish *picture on* F: 156
Tripoli [Lebanon] T: 447
Tripoli [Libya] T: 448
Barbary States B: 106 *with map*
Libya *picture on* L: 265; (Early days) L: 267;
(Strained relations with the United States)
L: 268
Tripoli [earth]
Grinding and polishing (Polishing) G: 395
Tripoli, War with [1801-1805]
Decatur, Stephen D: 67
Jefferson, Thomas (War with Tripoli) J: 84 *with
picture*
Marine Corps, United States (The 1800's) M: 208
Tripolitania [province]
Libya (Independence) L: 267
Triptych [painting]
Beckmann, Max B: 197
Triquetrum bone
Hand (Parts of the hand) H: 40
Trireme [ship]
Galley G: 15
Ship (Phoenician and Greek ships) S: 415-416
with picture
Trissino, Giangiorgio [Italian poet]
Drama (Italian Renaissance drama) D: 330
Palladio, Andrea P: 108
Trist, Nicholas P. [American government official]
Mexican War (The peace treaty) M: 447
Tristan [book by Mann]
Mann, Thomas M: 164
Tristan [legendary figure] T: 448
Tristan and Isolde [opera by Wagner]
Wagner, Richard (Later career) W: 4
Tristan and Isolde [poem by Gottfried von
Strassburg]
German literature (The romance) G: 138
Tristano, Lennie [American pianist]
Jazz (Cool jazz) J: 72
Tristeza [plant disease]
Orange (Pests and diseases) O: 815
Tristram [legendary figure]
Round Table (The knights of the Round Table)
R: 491
Tristan T: 448
Tristram [poems by Robinson]
Robinson, Edwin Arlington R: 368
Tristram Shandy [book by Sterne]
English literature (The rise of the novel) E: 318-
319
Novel (The first English novelists) N: 572
Sterne, Laurence So: 894
Triticale [plant] T: 448
Tritium [isotope] T: 448
Atom (The atomic mass number) A: 871-872
Deuterium (Uses) D: 172
Energy supply (Nuclear fusion) E: 278
Fusion F: 589
Hydrogen (Isotopes) H: 469; (Preparation) H: 469
Nuclear energy (Nuclear fusion) N: 583 *with
diagram*; (The industry and the environment)
N: 589
Nuclear weapon (Thermonuclear weapons)
N: 597
Trito-Isaiah [texts]
Bible (The Prophets) B: 280-281
Triton [Greek mythology]
Neptune N: 128
Poseidon P: 697
Triton [satellite] T: 448
Neptune (Satellites and rings) N: 129
Planet *picture on* P: 510
Satellite (Physical characteristics) S: 149; (Triton)
S: 150b
Volcano (Volcanoes in the solar system) V: 442b-
443
Voyager V: 451
Triton [submarine]
Submarine (Nuclear submarines) So: 943
Trittico, Il [operas by Puccini]

Puccini, Giacomo P: 869
Trittye [ancient Greece]
Athens (Democracy) A: 857
Triumph, Arch of *See* Arc de Triomphe *in this index*
Triumph ceremony [zoology]
Swan (Habits) So: 1016-1017
Triumph of Death [painting by Bruegel]
Bruegel, Pieter, the Elder B: 649
Triumph of Life, The [poem by Shelley]
Shelley, Percy Bysshe (His writings) S: 391-392
Triumph of the Egg, The [book by Anderson]
Anderson, Sherwood A: 452
"Triumphal March" [music by Verdi]
Opera *picture on* O: 790; (*Aida*) O: 801
Triumvirate [ancient Rome] T: 448
Rome, Ancient (The later years of the republic)
R: 445
First Triumvirate
Caesar, Julius (Alliance with Pompey) C: 13
Crassus, Marcus Licinius Ci: 1121
Pompey the Great P: 655
Second Triumvirate
Antony, Mark A: 561
Augustus (Rise to power) A: 889
Triune God *See* Trinity *in this index*
Trivia [poem by Gay]
Gay, John G: 71
Trivium [European history]
Education (Christian education in the Middle
Ages) E: 99
tRNA [genetics] *See* Transfer RNA *in this index*
TRNC [Cyprus] *See* Turkish Republic of Northern
Cyprus *in this index*
Trobriand Islands [islands, Pacific]
Mythology (Types of myths) M: 973-974
Trochee [poetry]
Poetry (table) P: 594
Trochophore [zoology]
Larva L: 78
Troglobite [animal]
Cave (Life in caves) C: 320-321
Trogon [bird] T: 448
Quetzal Q: 40
Troika [vehicle]
Sled S: 505
Troilus and Cressida [play by Shakespeare]
Shakespeare, William: (*Troilus and Cressida*) S: 362
Troilus and Criseyde [poem by Chaucer]
Chaucer, Geoffrey (Poetry) C: 388
Trojan asteroid
Asteroid (Orbital groups) A: 824a
Trojan horse [mythology]
Cassandra C: 275
Horse (table: Famous horses in history and
legend) H: 361
Mythology *picture on* M: 980
Trojan War (The fall of Troy) T: 449
Troy (The legendary Troy) T: 454 *with picture*
Trojan horse [program]
Computer (Computer security) Ci: 924
Computer virus Ci: 925
Trojan War T: 449
Helen of Troy H: 168
Homer (Homer's poems) H: 303
Iliad I: 51
Mythology *picture on* M: 980, M: 988; (Greek
heroes) M: 982
Priam P: 774
Troy (The legendary Troy) T: 454
Ulysses (The Trojan War) U: 17
Trojans [people] *See* Troy *in this index*
Troller [boat]
Fishing industry (Hooks) F: 185 *with diagram*
Trolley [mechanism]
Alabama (Interesting facts) A: 257 *with picture*
Streetcar So: 925
Trolley park
Amusement park A: 446
Trolling [fishing]
Fishing F: 175, *diagram on* F: 179
Fishing industry (Hooks) F: 185 *with diagram*
Trollope, Anthony [British author] T: 449
Novel (Britain) N: 573
Trollope, Frances [British author]
Trollope, Anthony T: 449
Trombone [musical instrument] T: 449 *with pictures*
Brass *picture on* B: 566
Jazz (The brass) J: 69 *with picture*
Music *picture on* M: 949; (Wind instruments)
M: 949
Sound *picture on* So: 598
Trompe-l'oeil [art]
Painting (Still-life paintings) P: 33
TRON [film]
Animation (The computer revolution) A: 514c
Trona [mineral]
Wyoming (The mid-1900's) W: 536

Trondheim [Norway] T: 450
Norway (Land regions) N: 541-542 *with map*
Troodon [dinosaur] T: 450
Dinosaur (True dinosaurs) D: 206b-211
Troop [organization]
Army (The organization of armies) A: 725
Boy Scouts (Boy Scouting) B: 535
Girl Scouts (Girls Scouts of the USA) G: 196
Trooper
Police (State police) P: 622 *with picture*
Trooping fairy
Fairy (Kinds of fairies) F: 10
Trooping the Colour [ceremony]
London (Ceremonies) L: 437
Trope [language]
Shakespeare, William (Rhetoric) S: 368
Tropic of Cancer [book by Miller]
Miller, Henry M: 554
Tropic of Cancer [geography] T: 450
Climate (The role of latitude) Ci: 676
Tropics T: 451 *with map*
Tropic of Capricorn [book by Miller]
Miller, Henry M: 554
Tropic of Capricorn [geography] T: 450
Climate (The role of latitude) Ci: 676
Tropics T: 451 *with map*
Tropical air mass [meteorology]
Weather (Synoptic-scale systems) W: 159 *with
diagram*
Tropical cyclone
Cyclone Ci: 1204
Hurricane H: 452
Storm (Cyclonic storms) So: 913
Tropical depression [meteorology]
Hurricane (The life of a hurricane) H: 453
Tropical disturbance [meteorology]
Hurricane (The life of a hurricane) H: 453
Tropical dry forest
Biome B: 324; (table) B: 323 *with map*
Forest *picture on* F: 390; (Kinds of forests) F: 392
with map
Plant *map on* P: 523; (Tropical dry forests) P: 528
Tropical fish T: 450
Fish (Fish of coral reefs) F: 154 *with pictures*; (Fish
of tropical fresh waters) F: 157 *with pictures*
Tropical forest
Forest (Kinds of forests) F: 392
Indian, American (Indians of the Tropical Forest)
I: 175 *with pictures*
Tropical fruit
Fruit (Types of fruits in horticulture) F: 546 *with
pictures*
Tropical rain forest *See* Rain forest *in this index*
Tropical seasonal forest *See* Tropical dry forest *in
this index*
Tropical storm
Hurricane (The life of a hurricane) H: 453
Tropical Storm Agnes
Pennsylvania (Economic decline) P: 268
Tropical Storm Irene
Vermont (Recent developments) V: 337
Tropical Storm Jeanne
Haiti (History) H: 15-17
Tropical Storm Washi
Flood (River floods) F: 236-237
Tropical wet and dry climate
Climate (Tropical wet and dry climates) Ci: 676b
Tropical wet climate
Climate (Kinds of climates) Ci: 676a *with picture*
Tropical year
Year Y: 554
Tropicalism [music]
Brazil (The arts) B: 576-577
Tropicana [company]
PepsiCo, Inc. P: 279
Tropicbird [bird]
Bird (Birds of the ocean and the Antarctic) B: 344
with picture
Tropics [geography] T: 451 *with map*
Bird (The distribution of birds) B: 331-332; (Why
birds migrate) B: 360
Cyclone Ci: 1204
Flower (Flowers of the tropics and subtropics)
F: 292 *with pictures*
Rain forest (Rain forests around the world)
R: 126b
Season (Seasons in the tropics) S: 272
Trade wind T: 364 *with map*
Tropism [botany] T: 451
Auxin A: 981
Plant (Environmental factors) P: 538 *with picture*
Tropopause [atmosphere]
Air (The troposphere) A: 172 *with diagram*
Jupiter (Atmosphere) J: 199
Troposphere T: 452
Troposphere [atmosphere] T: 451
Air (Structure of the atmosphere) A: 172 *with*

diagram
Earth (The atmosphere) E: 18
Fallout (How fallout is distributed) F: 18-19
Jet stream J: 115
Weather (What causes weather) W: 157
Tros [legendary figure]
Troy T: 454
Trot [gait]
Horse (Gaits) H: 353-354 *with picture*
Mammal (On land) M: 121-122
Trotaconventos [literary figure]
Spanish literature (Early medieval literature)
So: 757-758
Trotsky, Leon [Soviet political leader] T: 452 *with portrait*
Lenin, V. I. (The October Revolution) L: 193 *with picture*
Russian Revolution of 1917 (The 1905 Revolution) R: 566; (The October Revolution) R: 566
Union of Soviet Socialist Republics (The October Revolution) U: 35; (Stalin gains power) U: 36
Trotting [sport]
Harness racing H: 63
Trotzky, Leon [Soviet political leader] *See* Trotsky, Leon *in this index*
Troubadour [French history] T: 452
Classical music (Secular music) Ci: 646 *with picture*
French literature (Lyric poetry) F: 518
German literature (Minnesingers) G: 138
Knights and knighthood (Knighthood in literature) K: 351
Minstrel M: 611
Mistral, Frédéric M: 676
Poetry (Medieval poetry) P: 596
Storytelling (The Middle Ages) So: 915
Troubadour, The [play by Gutiérrez]
Spanish literature (The 1800's) So: 761
Troubled Asset Relief Program [U.S.]
Bank of America B: 96
Troubles [Irish history] T: 452
Belfast B: 225
Northern Ireland N: 521, *picture on* N: 524
Trough [physics]
Waves *diagram on* W: 150; (Measuring waves) W: 152
Troup, George M. [American political leader]
Georgia (table) G: 130
Troupe
Ballet B: 44
Puppet P: 905
Trousdale, William [American political leader]
Tennessee (table) T: 152
Trousers
Jeans J: 75
Trout [fish] T: 453 *with pictures*
Animal *picture on* A: 507
Fish *pictures on* F: 148, F: 149, F: 165, F: 169
Grayling G: 335
Lake Superior (Recreation and commerce) L: 45-46
Trout lily [plant] *See* Dogtooth violet *in this index*
Trouvère [French history] T: 454
Classical music (Secular music) Ci: 646
French literature (Lyric poetry) F: 518
Poetry (Medieval poetry) P: 596
Trovador, El [play by García Gutiérrez]
Opera: *(Trovatore, Il)* O: 808
Trovatore, Il [opera by Verdi]
Opera: *(Trovatore, Il)* O: 808
Trowbridge, Alexander B. [American government official]
Commerce, Department of (table) Ci: 871
Johnson, Lyndon Baines (table) J: 151
Trowel [tool]
Archaeology (Excavating sites) A: 597
Gardening (Cultivating an outdoor garden) G: 34
Plaster (Plastering) P: 552 *with pictures*
Troy [ancient city] T: 454 *with pictures and map*
See also Trojan horse *and* Trojan War *in this index and the list of Related articles in the* Trojan War *article*
Aegean civilization (Anatolian culture) A: 83
Greece, Ancient (Learning about ancient Greece) G: 375
Painting (Aegean painting) P: 41
Schliemann, Heinrich S: 177
Trojan War T: 449
Troy [Massachusetts]
Fall River F: 16
Troy Female Seminary
Women's movement (The beginnings of women's movements) W: 384-385
Troy pound [unit of measure]
Pound P: 721
Troy VI [ancient city]

Troy (The archaeological Troy) T: 455 *with picture*
Troy weight [measurement] T: 456
Avoirdupois A: 994
Weights and measures (table: Weight and mass) W: 187
Troyes [France]
Troy weight T: 456
Troyes, Treaty of [1420]
Hundred Years' War H: 437
Truce [warfare] T: 456
Truce of God [European history]
Peace (The Middle Ages) P: 206
Trucial States
United Arab Emirates (History) U: 45
Truck [decoration]
Flag (table) F: 193 *with diagram*
Truck [vehicle] T: 456 *with pictures*
See also Fire truck *in this index*
Freight F: 510
Postal services *picture on* P: 705
Recreational vehicle *picture on* R: 183; (Truck campers) R: 184
Transportation (Land transportation) T: 383
Truck crane
Crane Ci: 1119 *with picture*
Truck farming T: 458
Truck gardening
Truck farming T: 458
Truckdriver [occupation]
Careers (Transportation) C: 235 *with picture*
Truckee River [California-Nevada]
Nevada (Rivers and lakes) N: 166-168 *with map*
Trudeau, Edward Livingston [American doctor] T: 460
Trudeau, Garry [American cartoonist] T: 460 *with picture*
Trudeau, Pierre Elliott [Canadian political leader] T: 461 *with pictures*
Canada, History of (The return of the Liberals) C: 149-150; (Canada under Trudeau) C: 150 *with picture*
Chrétien, Jean (Political career) C: 522b *with picture*
Clark, Joe Ci: 639; (The 1979 election) Ci: 641
Harper, Stephen Joseph (Education and entry into politics) H: 61
Liberal Party of Canada L: 227
Montreal (The separatist movement) M: 779
Quebec (The late 1900's) Q: 32
Trudeau Sanitarium [Saranac Lake, New York]
Trudeau, Edward Livingston T: 460
True, Allen Tupper [American painter]
Lincoln, Abraham *picture on* L: 310
True American [newspaper]
Clay, Cassius Marcellus Ci: 658
True bass [fish]
Bass (True bass) B: 156 *with pictures*
True Believer, The [book by Hoffer]
Hoffer, Eric H: 283
True bill [law]
Bill (In law) B: 301
True frog
Frog (Kinds of frogs) F: 539; (True frogs) F: 540
True History of the Conquest of New Spain, The [book by Díaz del Castillo]
Latin American literature (Colonial literature) L: 112
True Path [political party]
Turkey (Political changes) T: 512
True Relation of...Virginia, A [book by Smith]
American literature (Virginia) A: 414
True rib [anatomy]
Rib R: 320
True spider
Spider So: 782
True toad [zoology]
Toad T: 304
True viper [snake]
Snake (Vipers) S: 535
Viper V: 390
Truffaut, François [French director] T: 465
Motion picture (The New Wave in France) M: 870
Truffle [fungus] T: 465
Truitt, George [American political leader]
Delaware (table) D: 109
Trujillo, Chadwick A. [American astronomer]
Eris E: 352
Planet (Haumea) P: 512
Trujillo Molina, Rafael Leonidas [Dominican political leader] T: 465
Dominican Republic (History) D: 304-305
Truk Islands *See* Chuuk Islands *in this index*
Truman, Bess [wife of Harry S. Truman]
First ladies of the United States (table) F: 142
Truman, Harry S. *picture on* T: 468; (Truman's family) T: 467
Truman, Elizabeth Wallace [wife of Harry S.

Truman] *See* Truman, Bess *in this index*
Truman, Harry S. [U.S. president] T: 466 *with pictures*
Churchill, Sir Winston Leonard Spencer *picture on* C: 549
Cold War (The alliance breaks up) Ci: 763; (The West holds the line) Ci: 764
Democratic Party (The New Deal) D: 126
Fair Deal F: 8
Independence I: 106
International relations *picture on* I: 346
Korean War (The "Battle for the Hills") K: 382
MacArthur, Douglas (The Korean War) M: 3
McCarthyism M: 332c
Pendergast, Thomas Joseph P: 236
President of the United States *picture on* P: 769
Public opinion poll (History) P: 863
Republican Party (After the Great Depression) R: 256
United Nations *picture on* U: 95
United States, History of the (World War II) U: 193
V-J Day V: 256
Vietnam War (The Indochina War) V: 373
White House (Rebuilding and redecorating) W: 290
World War II (The atomic bomb) W: 493
Truman, Margaret [daughter of]
Truman, Harry S. (Truman's family) T: 467
Truman Committee [U.S. history]
Truman, Harry S. (The Truman Committee) T: 468
Truman Doctrine [U.S. history]
Cold War (The containment policy) Ci: 764
Truman, Harry S. (The Truman Doctrine) T: 470
Truman Library *See* Harry S. Truman Library and Museum *in this index*
Trumbauer, Frankie [American conductor]
Beiderbecke, Bix B: 222
Trumbull, John [American painter] T: 472
Adams, John A: 34
Burgoyne, John *picture on* B: 704
Declaration of Independence *picture on* D: 77
Hamilton, Alexander *picture on* H: 32
Hessians *picture on* H: 219
Painting (History paintings) P: 33
Revolution, American *pictures on* R: 282, R: 286
Trumbull, John H. [American political leader]
Connecticut (table) Ci: 967
Trumbull, Jonathan [American political leader] T: 473
Brother Jonathan B: 642
Connecticut (table) Ci: 967; (The Revolutionary War) Ci: 970
Trumbull, Jonathan, II [American political leader]
Connecticut (table) Ci: 967
Trumbull, Joseph [American political leader]
Connecticut (table) Ci: 967
Trumbull, Lyman [American political leader] T: 473
Lincoln, Abraham (A turning point) L: 317
Trump suit [bridge]
Bridge (Bidding) B: 604
Trumpet [musical instrument] T: 473 *with pictures*
Indian, American *picture on* I: 172
Jazz (The brass) J: 69 *with picture*
Music *picture on* M: 949; (Wind instruments) M: 949
Trumpet honeysuckle
Honeysuckle H: 316 *with picture*
Trumpet narcissus [plant]
Daffodil D: 3 *with picture*
Trumpet of the Swan, The [book by White]
White, E. B. W: 284
Trumpet style [jazz]
Hines, Earl H: 237
Trumpeter [bird]
Bird *picture on* B: 344b; (Birds of Central and South America) B: 344a
Trumpeter swan [bird]
Swan (Kinds) So: 1016
Trumpetfish
Fish *picture on* F: 154
Trumpeting
Elephant (Protection against enemies) E: 231
Trumpler, Robert [American astronomer]
Lick Observatory L: 270
Truncated cube
Archimedean solid A: 604 *with diagram*
Trundle bed [furniture]
Bed (History) B: 198 *with picture*
Colonial life in America (Furnishings) Ci: 797
Trunk [botany]
Tree T: 411; (Trunk and branches) T: 416 *with diagram*
Trunk [zoology]
Elephant (The body of an elephant) E: 228 *with pictures*
Trunk hose
Clothing (The Renaissance) Ci: 702-703

Trunk pipeline
Pipeline (Liquid pipelines) P: 490
Truss [construction]
Bridge (Truss bridges) B: 601 *with diagram*
Building construction (Beams, girders, and columns) B: 682-683
Truss bridge
Bridge (Truss bridges) B: 601 *with diagram*
Trust [law]
Antitrust laws A: 560
Business (Antitrust laws) B: 727
Foundation F: 429
Harrison, Benjamin (Domestic affairs) H: 72
McKinley, William ("President of the whole people") M: 341
Monopoly and competition (History) M: 732
Roosevelt, Theodore ("Trust buster") R: 464
United States, History of the (The rise of "trusts") U: 181
Trust busting [U.S. history]
Roosevelt, Theodore ("Trust buster") R: 464
Trust company [banking]
Trust fund (How a trust fund works) T: 473
Trust department [banking]
Trust fund (How a trust fund works) T: 473
Trust estate See Trust fund *in this index*
Trust fund T: 473
Bank (Careers in banking) B: 95
Endowment E: 273
Pension (Private pension plans) P: 273
Trust territory [UN] T: 474
Mandated territory M: 136
United Nations (The Trusteeship Council) U: 84
Trust Territory of the Pacific Islands See Pacific Islands, Trust Territory of the *in this index*
Trustee [economics]
Bankruptcy (Features of bankruptcy) B: 97
Foundation F: 429
Receiver R: 174
Trust fund (How a trust fund works) T: 473
Trustees, Board of
Universities and colleges (Governing boards) U: 208
Trusteeship Council
United Nations (The six major UN organs) U: 78 *with diagram*; (Other main organs) U: 84; (Working for self-government) U: 93
Trustor [law]
Trust fund (How a trust fund works) T: 473
Truth [philosophy]
See also Knowledge *in this index*
Enlightenment (The worship of reason) E: 326a
Metaphysics (Possibility and necessity) M: 430
Philosophy (Epistemology) P: 384
Semantics S: 291
Skepticism S: 481
Truth, Sojourner [American social reformer] T: 474 *with portrait*
Truth and Reconciliation Commission [South Africa]
South Africa (Recent developments) So: 621
Truth commission T: 474
Tutu, Desmond T: 527
Truth commission [organization] T: 474
Truth in Lending Act [1968]
Bank (Changes in banking laws) B: 94
Interest (Regulation of interest rates) I: 323
Proxmire, William P: 841
Truth-in-Securities Act [1933]
New Deal (Helping savers and investors) N: 200-201
Truth serum [drug]
Hypnosis (Enhancing memory) H: 479
Thiopental T: 258
Truxtun, Thomas [American military leader]
Constellation Ci: 994
Truyen Kieu [poem by Nguyen Du]
Vietnam (The arts) V: 366-368
Try [sports]
Rugby football (Rugby Union) R: 510; (Rugby League) R: 512
Try-It [award]
Girl Scouts (Girl Scout Brownies) G: 197
Tryon, William [British colonial official]
North Carolina (Revolution and independence) N: 492
Tryon Palace [New Bern]
North Carolina (Places to visit) N: 482
Trypanosome [microorganism] T: 474
Laveran, Charles Louis Alphonse e L: 129
Protozoan (Flagellates) P: 837
Sleeping sickness (Cause) S: 506-507
Tsetse fly T: 474
Trypanosomiasis [disease]
Sleeping sickness S: 507
Trypillians [people]
Ukraine (Early days) U: 11-12

Trypsin [enzyme]
Digestive system (In the small intestine) D: 202
Tryptophan [biochemistry]
Serotonin S: 318
Vitamin (Niacin) V: 431
TSA [agency] *See* Transportation Security Administration *in this index*
Tsa-La-Gi Ancient Village
Oklahoma (Places to visit) O: 722
Tsad [letter]
S S: 1 *with diagram*
Tsana, Lake [Ethiopia]
Lake Tana L: 46
Tsantsa [trophy]
Jívaro Indians J: 128
Tsar *See* Czar *in this index*
Tsaritsyn [former name]
Volgograd V: 444
Tsar's Bride, The [opera by Rimsky-Korsakov]
Rimsky-Korsakov, Nikolai R: 341
Tsavo National Park [Kenya]
National park (Kenya) N: 42d; (table) N: 42f
Tschaikowsky, Peter Ilich *See* Tchaikovsky, Peter Ilich *in this index*
Tschermak, Erich von [Austrian botanist]
Cell (The 1900's) C: 337-338
Heredity (The birth of genetics) H: 208
Tselinograd [former name] *See* Astana *in this index*
Tsenerene [book]
Yiddish literature Y: 566
Tsetse fly [insect] T: 474
Bruce, Sir David B: 647
Fly (table) F: 310
Sleeping sickness (Cause) S: 506-507 *with picture*
TSH [hormone] *See* Thyroid-stimulating hormone *in this index*
Tshiluba [language]
Luba L: 512
Tshisekedi, Etienne [Congolese political leader]
Congo, Democratic Republic of the (The fall of Mobutu) Ci: 940c
Tshombe, Moïse [Congolese political leader]
Congo, Democratic Republic of the (Civil disorder) Ci: 940c
Tshwane [South Africa]
Pretoria P: 773
Tsien, Roger Y. [American chemist]
Nobel Prizes (Chemistry: 2008) N: 444
Tsimshian Indians T: 475
Alaska (Population) A: 286
Indian, American *picture on* I: 136a
Tsing Ma Bridge [China]
Bridge (table: Suspension) B: 603
Tsinghua University [Beijing]
China *picture on* C: 486
Tsiolkovsky, Konstantin E. [Russian educator]
Rocket (Rockets of the early 1900's) R: 390
Space exploration (Early dreams of space flight) So: 706
Tsiranana, Philibert [Madagascar political leader]
Madagascar (History) M: 29
Tsongas, Paul E. [American political leader]
Clinton, Bill (The Democratic nomination) Ci: 682c
Tsongdu [government]
Bhutan (Government) B: 277
Tsou Kan [Chinese forester]
Redwood (The dawn redwood) R: 192
Tsountas, Christos [Greek archaeologist]
Aegean civilization A: 82
TSS [disorder]
Toxic shock syndrome T: 353
Tsubouchi, Shoyo [Japanese author]
Japanese literature (The modern period) J: 62
Tsui, Daniel Chee [Chinese-born American physicist]
Nobel Prizes (Physics: 1998) N: 442
Tsukiji Market
Tokyo (Other places of interest) T: 317
Tsunami [wave] T: 475 *with diagrams*
Chile (The land) C: 463-464
Disaster (table) D: 223
Earthquake (Tsunamis) E: 34 *with diagram*
Flood (Seacoast floods) F: 237
Japan (Recent developments) J: 59
Maldives (History) M: 104-105
Nuclear energy (Safety concerns) N: 591-592
Ocean *picture on* O: 651; (Waves) O: 659
Pacific Ocean P: 14
Volcano (Tsunami) V: 441
Tsunami of 2004 T: 476
Asia *picture on* A: 811; (Natural disasters) A: 812
Bush, George Herbert Walker (Later years) B: 722a
Clinton, Bill (Later years) Ci: 682g
Disaster (table) D: 223
Flood (Seacoast floods) F: 237

India (Recent developments) I: 134-135
Indonesia (Java) I: 233; (Recent developments) I: 239
Java J: 65
Krakatau K: 386
Sumatra So: 972
Thailand (Recent developments) T: 228
United Nations (Disaster relief) U: 89
Tsurumi Tsubasa [Japan]
Bridge (table: Cable-stayed) B: 603
Tsushima, Battle of [1905]
Russo-Japanese War (Final battles) R: 566b
Tsvangirai, Morgan [Zimbabwean political leader]
Zimbabwe (History) Z: 592-594
Tsvetaeva, Marina [Russian poet]
Russian literature (Post-symbolism) R: 563-564
Tswana [language]
Botswana (People) B: 511
Tswana [people]
Botswana (People) B: 511; (History) B: 512
Namibia (People) N: 8
South Africa (People) So: 609
Tu-144 [airplane] *See* Tupolev Tu-144 *in this index*
Tu Yu [Chinese scholar]
Encyclopedia (The first reference works) E: 268a
Tuamotu Islands [Pacific] T: 476
French Polynesia F: 524
Tuan, Pham [Vietnamese astronaut]
Astronaut (table) A: 830
Tuareg [people] T: 476
Berbers B: 256
Mali (People) M: 106
Niger (People) N: 407
Tuareg empire [African history]
Niger (History) N: 409
Tuatara T: 476
Reptile (Tuatara) R: 251 *with picture*
Tuatha De Danann [Irish clan]
Irish literature (Heroic tales, romances, and sagas) I: 430
Mythology (The Irish cycles) M: 985
Tub [car part]
Automobile racing (Formula One racing) A: 976-977
Tuba [drink]
Coconut palm Ci: 746
Philippines (Way of life) P: 374-375
Tuba [musical instrument] T: 477 *with pictures*
Music (Wind instruments) M: 949
Tubac [settlement]
Arizona (Spanish exploration) A: 688
Tubal embryo transfer [reproduction]
Infertility (Treatment) I: 265
Tubal ligation [surgery]
Birth control (Methods of birth control) B: 378
Tubal pregnancy [disorder] *See* Ectopic pregnancy *in this index*
Tube [optics]
Microscope (Tube and lenses) M: 517
Tube [transportation]
London (Transportation) L: 438 *with picture*
Subway So: 949
Tube-building rotifer [animal]
Rotifer *picture on* R: 488
Tube camera
Television *diagram on* T: 124; (The television camera) T: 122
Tube foot [zoology]
Echinoderm E: 50
Sea urchin S: 263
Starfish (The body of a starfish) So: 856 *with picture*
Tubectomy
Birth control (Methods of birth control) B: 378
Tubeless tire
Tire (History) T: 297-298
Tuber [botany] T: 477
Jerusalem artichoke J: 102 *with picture*
Potato (The potato plant) P: 712 *with picture*
Vegetable (Tubers) V: 293 *with picture*
Tubercle [disorder]
Tuberculosis (Primary infection) T: 477-478
Tubercle bacillus [bacteria]
Tuberculosis T: 477; (Diagnosis of tuberculosis) T: 479 *with pictures*
Tuberculoid leprosy [disease]
Leprosy (Symptoms) L: 204 *with picture*
Tuberculosis [disease] T: 477 *with pictures*
AIDS (Opportunistic illness) A: 164a
Bacteriology (History) B: 22-23
Dairying (Dairy farming regulations) D: 8
Disease (table) D: 226
Lupus L: 526
Races, Human (Susceptibility to genetic diseases) R: 58
Scrofula S: 227
Trudeau, Edward Livingston T: 460

Tuberose [plant] T: 479 *with picture*
Tuberous begonia
Flower (Garden perennials grown from bulbs)
F: 280 *with picture*
Tuberous water lily [plant]
Flower *picture on* F: 285
Tubeworm, Giant [animal]
Deep sea (Invertebrates) D: 82a-82b *with picture*
Hydrothermal vent *picture on* H: 473
Tubman, Harriet [American social reformer] T: 480
with portrait
African Americans (The antislavery movement)
A: 136h *with picture*
Underground railroad U: 21
Tubman, William V. S. [Liberian political leader]
T: 480
Liberia (The Republic of Liberia) L: 231
Tubular bells [musical instrument]
Chimes C: 471
Tubular fluid [anatomy]
Kidney (How the kidneys produce urine) K: 311-
312
Tubulidentata [zoology]
Mammal (table) M: 129 *with picture*
Tuchman, Barbara Wertheim [American historian]
T: 480
Tuck, Friar [literary figure]
Robin Hood R: 367
Tuck, William M. [American political leader]
Virginia (table) V: 417
Tuck position
Diving *picture on* D: 244; (Kinds of dives) D: 243
Tuck School of Business Administration
Dartmouth College D: 39
Tucker, Jim Guy [American political leader]
Arkansas (table) A: 712; (The late 1900's) A: 715
Tucker, Richard [American singer] T: 480
Tucker, Tilghman M. [American political leader]
Mississippi (table) M: 640
Tuckman, Bruce [American psychologist]
Group dynamics G: 402
Tucson [Arizona] T: 481 *with picture*
Arizona (Interesting facts about Arizona) A: 671
with picture; (Population) A: 674
Tucumán, Congress of [Argentine history]
Argentina (Road to becoming a nation) A: 656
Tucumcari [boat]
Hydrofoil (Modern hydrofoil developments)
H: 468
Tudor, Antony [British choreographer]
Ballet (Ballet in the United States) B: 53-54
Tudor, Henry *See* Henry VII [king of England] *in
this index*
Tudor, House of [English history] T: 481
England (table) E: 308
Henry VII [of England] H: 187
Renaissance (Political background) R: 237-238
Tudor, Tasha [American author]
Regina Medal (table: 1971) R: 206
Tudor style
House *picture on* H: 381
Tuesday T: 481
Tuesday [book by Wiesner]
Literature for children *picture on* L: 371
Tuesday Island
Torres Strait Islands T: 343
Tufa [rock]
Limestone L: 307
Sculpture (Etruscan sculpture) S: 246-247
Tuff [geology]
Volcano (Pyroclasts) V: 439
Tufted puffin [bird]
Puffin P: 885
Tufted rug
Rugs and carpets (Tufting) R: 515
Textile (Other textiles) T: 215
Tufted titmouse [bird]
Bird (Birds of forests and woodlands) B: 334 *with
picture*
Titmouse T: 302
Tug *See* Tugboat *in this index*
Tugboat T: 481
Atlantic Intracoastal Waterway *picture on* A: 863
Barge B: 109
Ship *picture on* S: 402; (Specialized vessels) S: 410
Transportation (Water transportation) T: 384
Tugela Falls [waterfall, South Africa]
Drakensberg D: 323
Waterfall (table: Famous waterfalls of the world)
W: 143
Tugela River [South Africa]
Drakensberg D: 323
Tugendhat house
Mies van der Rohe, Ludwig M: 537
Tugurio [housing]
Colombia (Way of life) Ci: 779-781
Tui [bird]

Bird *picture on* B: 348
Tu'i Tonga [title]
Tonga (History) T: 328
Tuileries [palace] T: 481
Paris (Gardens, squares, and parks) P: 162 *with
map*
Tuition [fee]
Parochial school P: 178
Universities and colleges (Recent developments)
U: 210-211
Tuke, William [English merchant]
Mental illness (Humane treatment) M: 408
Tuktut Nogait National Park
Canada (table: National parks and national park
reserves) C: 113
Tukul [shelter]
Sudan, South (People): So: 955
Tula [ancient city, Mexico] T: 482
Maya (The Postclassic Period) M: 326
Mexico (The Toltec and the Aztec) M: 468
Toltec Indians T: 323
Tulane, Paul [American businessman]
Tulane University T: 482
Tulane University T: 482
Tularemia [disease] T: 482
Rabbit (Enemies) R: 48
Veterinary medicine V: 345
Tule Lake [California]
Indian wars (The Modoc War [1872-1873]) I: 194
Modoc Indians M: 686
Tule salmon *See* Chinook salmon *in this index*
Tulip [plant] T: 482 *with picture*
Flower (Garden perennials grown from bulbs)
F: 280 *with picture*
Leaf *picture on* L: 157
Netherlands *picture on* N: 147
Nursery *picture on* N: 614
Oregon *picture on* O: 843
Tulip Festival
Holland H: 292
Iowa *picture on* I: 385
Michigan (Visitor's guide) M: 498
Ottawa (Annual events) O: 873
Tulip-poplar [tree] *See* Yellow-poplar *in this index*
Tulip suite
Furniture *picture on* F: 583; (The retro style) F: 584
Tulipomania [European history]
Tulip T: 482
Tuliptree *See* Yellow-poplar *in this index*
Tull, Jethro [English agriculturist] T: 483
Agriculture *picture on* A: 158
Tulle [fabric]
Net N: 137
Tullus Hostilius [legendary figure]
Mythology (The seven kings) M: 983
Tulsa [Oklahoma] T: 483 *with picture*
Oklahoma *picture on* O: 734; (Population) O: 716
with pictures; (table: Average monthly weather)
O: 726
Riot (During the 1900's) R: 349
Tulsey town
Tulsa (History) T: 483
Tulsidas [Indian poet]
Hindi language (Hindi literature) H: 235
Ramayana R: 132
Tumacácori National Historical Park [Arizona]
National Park System (table: National historical
parks) N: 56-57
Tumasik [former name]
Singapore (History) S: 471
Tumbes [Peru]
Peru (Spanish conquest and rule) P: 314
Tumbler [biology]
Mosquito (Pupa) M: 833
Tumbler [machine]
Washing machine (Types) W: 45
Tumbler lock
Lock (Mechanical locks) L: 411 *with picture*
Tumbleweed [plant] T: 484
Thistle T: 261
Tumbling [sport]
Gymnastics (Trampoline and tumbling) G: 449
Trampoline T: 368 *with picture*
Tumblr [website]
Internet (Social networking websites) I: 350b
Tumboa [plant]
Welwitschia W: 196 *with picture*
Tumbrel [cart]
French Revolution (Terror and equality) F: 526-
527
Tumen River [North Korea-China]
Korea, North (The land) K: 371 *with map*
Tumor [disorder] T: 484
See also Cancer *in this index*
Biopsy B: 326
Birthmark B: 380
Brain *picture on* B: 554; (Tumors) B: 558

Ear (Diseases) E: 12
Epithelioma E: 345
Mole M: 691
Monoclonal antibody M: 731
Neurofibromatosis N: 152
Oncology O: 761
Skin (Tumors) S: 491
Tumor necrosis factor alpha [protein]
Thalidomide T: 229
Tumpline [strap]
Indian, American (Transportation) I: 142
Tumultuous petitioning [English history]
Freedom of assembly (History) F: 504-505
Tuna [fish] T: 485 *with pictures*
Dolphin (Dolphin conservation) D: 299
Tuna [fruit]
Prickly pear P: 776
Tunable laser
Lasers (Dye lasers) L: 85
Tundish [steelmaking]
Iron and steel (Shaping and finishing steel) I: 445
Tundra [geography] T: 485 *with picture*
Alaska (The Arctic Coastal Plain) A: 294
Animal (Animals of the polar regions) A: 484
with picture
Arctic A: 635; (Land regions) A: 636
Asia (Deserts and plains) A: 794
Biome B: 322; (table) B: 323 *with map*
Bird (Birds of the Arctic) B: 343
Canada *picture on* C: 118; (The Arctic Islands)
C: 117
Climate (Tundra climates) Ci: 676d
Flower (Flowers of the Arctic tundra) F: 283;
(Flowers of alpine tundras) F: 289 *with pictures*
Inuit (Plants and animals) I: 354a
Plant *map on* P: 523, *picture on* P: 524; (The
tundra) P: 520; (Plants of the high mountain
tundra) P: 524 *with picture*; (Movement of
water) P: 537
Russia (Land regions) R: 539
Tundra pond
Pond (Kinds of ponds) P: 656-657
Tundra swan
Swan (Kinds) So: 1016 *with picture*
Tundra vole [animal]
Vole V: 444
Tundra wolf
Wolf W: 375
Tuner [electronics]
Digital video recorder D: 203
Radio (The tuner) R: 88 *with picture*
Stereophonic sound system (Program sources)
So: 892
Television (Tuner) T: 122 *with diagram*
Tung oil [tree product] T: 486 *with pictures*
Vegetable oil (Uses) V: 294
Tung tree
Tung oil T: 486 *with pictures*
Tungsten [element] T: 486
Ion microscope *picture on* I: 372
Welding (Arc welding) W: 189
Wolframite W: 378
Tungsten bronze [metal]
Tungsten T: 487
Tungsten carbide [alloy]
Tungsten T: 486
Tungsten-halogen lamp
Electric light (The bulb) E: 174
Tungsten steel [metal]
Tungsten T: 486
Tungurahua [volcano, Ecuador]
Andes Mountains (Volcanoes and earthquakes)
A: 453
Tunguska explosion
Asteroid (Impacts on Earth) A: 824b
Meteor (Meteorites) M: 432
Tunic [clothing] T: 487
Clothing (Handmade clothing) Ci: 691; (Rome)
Ci: 697 *with picture*; (Clothing under Islam)
Ci: 697-698; (The Middle Ages) Ci: 700-701
with picture
Knights and knighthood (Clothing) K: 350
Rome, Ancient (Clothing) R: 440
Tunica [clothing] *See* Tunic *in this index*
Tunicle [clothing]
Tunic T: 487
Tuniit [people]
Exploration (The Tuniit) E: 441
Tuning capacitor [electronics]
Capacitor (Parts) C: 186
Tuning fork [music] T: 487
Sound *picture on* So: 598
Watch (Quartz watches) W: 114
Tunis [Tunisia] T: 487
Tunisia (The land) T: 487 *with picture*
Tunisia T: 487 *with pictures and map*
Barbary States B: 105 *with map*

Flag *picture on* **F: 200**
Middle East **M: 530**
World War II (The Tunisia Campaign) **W: 481**
Tunkhannock Viaduct [Pennsylvania]
Viaduct **V: 347**
Tunnel T: 490 *with pictures*
Channel Tunnel **C: 375**
Coal (The room-and-pillar system) **Ci: 723** *with diagram*
Dam (Construction) **D: 19**
Mining (Mining terms) **M: 577**
Subway **So: 949** *with picture*
United Kingdom *picture on* **U: 73**
Tunnel drying
Food preservation (Drying) **F: 342-343**
Tunnel hull
Motorboat racing (Hull designs) **M: 876** *with picture*
Tunnel kiln [industry]
Brick (Firing bricks) **B: 598**
Tunnel vision [disorder]
Eye (Diseases of the retina) **E: 467**
Tunneling current [electric current]
Scanning probe microscope **S: 172**
Tunnell, Ebe W. [American political leader]
Delaware (table) **D: 109**
Tunney, Gene [American boxer] **T: 492**
Boxing (Boxing's Golden Age) **B: 532-532a**
Dempsey, Jack **D: 130** *with picture*
Tunstall, John G. [American settler]
New Mexico (Territorial days) **N: 275**
Tuolumne Meadows [region, California]
Yosemite National Park (Hetch Hetchy Valley) **Y: 570**
Tuolumne River [California]
Yosemite National Park (Hetch Hetchy Valley) **Y: 570**
Tupac Amaru [Inca leader]
Indian, American (After European contact) **I: 175**
Latin America (Colonial discontent) **L: 106**
Peru (Spanish conquest and rule) **P: 314**
Shakur, Tupac **S: 370**
Tupac Amaru Revolutionary Movement [Peruvian political group]
Peru (Return to civilian government) **P: 316;** (Peru under Fujimori) **P: 316**
Tupamaros [terrorist group]
Uruguay (Military government) **U: 228**
Tupelo [Mississippi]
Mississippi (table: Average monthly weather) **M: 636**
Tupelo [tree] **T: 492** *with picture*
Tree *pictures on* **T: 424**
Tupelo National Battlefield [Mississippi]
National Park System (table: National battlefields) **N: 55**
Tupelogum [tree]
Tupelo **T: 492**
Tupi-Guarani Indians T: 492
Brazil (Ancestry) **B: 572**
Tupinamba Indians
Brazil (History) **B: 583**
Indian, American (Why the Indians fought) **I: 144-145;** (Before European contact) **I: 175-176**
Tupolev Tu-144 [airplane]
Airplane (Supersonic airplanes) **A: 238**
Tupou [kings of Tonga]
Tonga (History) **T: 328**
Tupper, Sir Charles [Canadian patriot] **T: 493** *with pictures*
Bowell, Sir Mackenzie (Cabinet crisis and resignation) **B: 519**
Confederation of Canada (Fathers of Confederation) **C: 935** *with picture*
Tupper, Sir Charles Hibbert [Canadian political leader]
Tupper, Sir Charles (Tupper's family) **T: 493**
Tupper, William J. [Canadian government official]
Tupper, Sir Charles (Tupper's family) **T: 493**
Turabi, Hassan al- [Sudanese political leader]
Sudan (Civil war) **So: 953-354**
Turaco [bird] **T: 494** *with picture*
Turandot [opera by Puccini]
Puccini, Giacomo **P: 869**
Turangalila [music by Messiaen]
Messiaen, Olivier **M: 423**
Turban [clothing] **T: 495** *with pictures*
Afghanistan (Way of life) **A: 92a**
Hat *picture on* **H: 84**
Turban snail
Snail (Snails and people) **S: 523**
Turbellarian [flatworm]
Flatworm **F: 229** *with pictures*
Turbinate bone [anatomy] *See* Concha *in this index*
Turbine [machine] **T: 495** *with pictures*
Coal **Ci: 716**
Electric power (Sources of electric power) **E: 182-**

184 *with diagrams*
Hydraulic engine **H: 463**
Hydraulics (Use of hydrodynamic principles) **H: 464**
Jet propulsion (Turbojet) **J: 111-114**
Locomotive (Kinds of locomotives) **L: 414**
Ship (Engine-driven ships) **S: 406**
Starter (Airplane starters) **So: 859**
Steam engine (Steam turbines) **So: 880**
Wind power (Devices that use wind power) **W: 331-332**
Windmill **W: 333**
Turbinia [ship]
Ship (Stronger, faster ships) **S: 425-426**
Turbine (History) **T: 498-499**
Turbocharger [device]
Automobile racing (Sports car racing) **A: 977**
Gasoline engine (Air and fuel) **G: 64**
Turbofan [engine]
Airplane (Jet engines) **A: 220**
Jet propulsion **J: 112** *with diagram;* (Turbofan) **J: 114**
Turbogenerator
Nuclear energy (Steam production) **N: 587**
Turbojet [engine]
Airplane (Jet engines) **A: 220**
Jet propulsion **J: 112** *with diagram;* (Turbojet) **J: 111**
Turboprop [engine]
Airplane (Turboprop engines) **A: 220**
Jet propulsion **J: 112** *with diagram;* (Turboprop) **J: 114**
Turbot [fish] **T: 500** *with picture*
Turbulence [atmosphere]
Aerodynamics (Friction drag) **A: 86**
Air turbulence **A: 200**
Turbulent flow [atmosphere]
Aerodynamics (Friction drag) **A: 86**
Turcos [soldiers]
Zouaves **Z: 607**
Turcotte, Jean-Claude [Canadian religious leader]
Cardinal (table: Canadian cardinals) **C: 211**
Ture, Kwame [American social reformer]
Carmichael, Stokely **C: 241**
Turf [grass]
Horse racing (At the races) **H: 365**
Turf, Artificial
Artificial turf **A: 761**
Lawn (Types of lawns) **L: 142**
Turfgrass
Grass (Turfgrasses) **G: 324**
Turgeis [Norwegian pirate]
Vikings (The Norwegian Vikings) **V: 382**
Turgenev, Ivan [Russian author] **T: 500**
Drama (Russian drama and Chekhov) **D: 338**
Nihilism **N: 421**
Russian literature (Early realism) **R: 562**
Turgot, Robert [French government official]
Louis XVI **L: 476**
Turia River [river, Spain]
Valencia **V: 260**
Turiddu [opera character]
Opera: (Cavalleria Rusticana) **O: 803**
Turin [Italy] **T: 500** *with picture*
Turin, Shroud of *See* Shroud of Turin *in this index*
Turing, Alan Mathison [British mathematician] **T: 501**
Turing machine
Turing, Alan Mathison **T: 501**
Turk *See* Turks *in this index*
Turkana [people]
Africa *picture on* **A: 120**
Turkana, Lake *See* Lake Turkana *in this index*
Turkestan [region, Asia] **T: 501**
Turkey [country] **T: 502** *with pictures and maps*
Armenian Genocide **A: 719**
Atatürk, Kemal **A: 852**
Cold War (The containment policy) **Ci: 764**
Cuban missile crisis **Ci: 1180**
Cyprus **Ci: 1205**
Dardanelles **D: 36**
Ford, Gerald Rudolph (Early problems) **F: 376** *with picture*
Kurds **K: 392**
Middle East **M: 530**
Ottoman Empire **O: 877**
Turks **T: 514b**
World War I (Political consequences) **W: 464-465**
Turkey [bird] **T: 513** *with picture*
Bird (As a source of food and raw materials) **B: 330** *with picture*
Farm and farming *pictures on* **F: 32**
Meat *pictures on* **M: 348**
Poultry **P: 720**
Turkey [sports]
Bowling (table) **B: 521**
Turkey farm

Farm and farming *picture on* **F: 32**
Turkey oak [tree]
Oak (Red oaks) **O: 635-636**
Turkey Red [plant]
Kansas (The nation's breadbasket) **K: 237**
Wheat (The spread of wheat farming) **W: 275-276**
Turkey-red dye
Madder **M: 29**
Mordant **M: 801**
Turkey vulture [bird]
Buzzard **B: 746**
Vulture (New World vultures) **V: 454** *with picture*
Turkic peoples *See* Turks *in this index*
Turkish Angora cat
Cat *picture on* **C: 289;** (Long-haired breeds) **C: 292**
Turkish bath T: 514
Bath (Bathing for cleanliness) **B: 163**
Turkish Federated State of Cyprus
Cyprus (History) **Ci: 1207**
Turkish knot
Rugs and carpets (Oriental rugs) **R: 516** *with diagram*
Turkish language
Middle East (Identity and language) **M: 530**
Turkey (Languages) **T: 505**
Turkish Republic of Northern Cyprus
Cyprus **Ci: 1205;** (History) **Ci: 1207**
Turkish rug
Islamic art (Rugs) **I: 469**
Rugs and carpets (Oriental rugs) **R: 516-517**
"Turkish Tales" [book by Byron]
Byron, Lord (Byron's poetry) **B: 748**
Turkish van cat
Cat (Long-haired breeds) **C: 292**
Turkistan *See* Turkestan *in this index*
Turkmen [people]
Turkmenistan (People) **T: 514**
Union of Soviet Socialist Republics (People) **U: 31**
Turkmen Soviet Socialist Republic [former name]
Turkmenistan **T: 514**
Turkmenia [former name]
Turkmenistan **T: 514**
Turkmenistan T: 514 *with picture and map*
Flag *picture on* **F: 205**
Turko-Italian War [1911-1912]
Rhodes **R: 317**
Turkoman rug
Rugs and carpets (Oriental rugs) **R: 516-517**
Turkomanchai, Treaty of [1828]
Iran (The Qajar dynasty) **I: 406**
Turks [people] **T: 514b**
Armenia (History) **A: 718b**
Azerbaijan (History) **A: 997**
Bulgaria (People) **B: 689**
Crusades (How the Crusades began) **Ci: 1159-1160**
Europe *picture on* **E: 386**
Middle East (The spread of Islam) **M: 533**
Seljuks **S: 290**
Tatars **T: 51**
Turkey (People) **T: 505**
Turkmenistan (History) **T: 514b**
Union of Soviet Socialist Republics (People) **U: 31**
Turks and Caicos Islands [Caribbean Sea] **T: 514b**
Turku [Finland]
Finland *picture on* **F: 111**
Turmeric [plant] **T: 514b** *with picture*
Turn [sports]
Skiing *diagrams on* **S: 484**
Turn 2 Foundation
Jeter, Derek **B: 116**
Turn of the Screw, The [story by James]
James, Henry (His works) **J: 26**
Turn of the Year, The [book by Grove]
Grove, Frederick Philip **G: 404**
Turn signal [device]
Automobile (Operaring a car) **A: 954-955**
Turnbull, William [Scottish educator]
Glasgow, University of **G: 210**
Turner, Claramae [American singer]
Opera *picture on* **O: 800**
Turner, Daniel W. [American political leader]
Iowa (table) **I: 391**
Turner, Frederick Jackson [American historian] **T: 515**
Turner, J. M. W. [British painter] **T: 515** *with picture*
Painting (Romanticism) **P: 68** *with picture*
Ruskin, John **R: 523**
Turner, James [American political leader]
North Carolina (table) **N: 490**
Turner, Joe [American singer]
Rock music (Musical roots) **R: 376**
Turner, John H. [Canadian political leader]
British Columbia (table) **B: 628**
Turner, John Napier [Canadian political leader] **T: 516** *with picture*
Chrétien, Jean (Political career) **C: 522b**

Mulroney, Brian (The 1984 election) **M:** 917
Turner, Nat [American public figure] **T:** 517
African Americans (The growth of slavery)
A: 136f-136g
United States, History of the (The abolition movement) **U:** 173-174
Virginia (The *Mother of Presidents*) **V:** 421
Turner, Roy J. [American political leader]
Oklahoma (table) **O:** 730
Turner, Ted [American businessman] **T:** 518
Cable News Network **C:** 7
Turner, Thomas G. [American political leader]
Rhode Island (table) **R:** 311
Turner, Tina [American musician] **T:** 518 *with portrait*
Turner Broadcasting System [network]
Time Warner Inc. **T:** 292d
Turner Falls [Oklahoma]
Oklahoma *picture on* **O:** 726
Turner Field [Atlanta]
United States *picture on* **U:** 115
Turner Prize [award]
Whiteread, Rachel **W:** 293
Turner Valley oil fields
Calgary (Economy) **C:** 34; (History) **C:** 34
Turney, Peter [American political leader]
Tennessee (table) **T:** 152
Turning [industrial process]
Machine tool (Metal removal) **M:** 17
Turning [sports]
Skiing (Alpine skiing) **S:** 482
Turnip [plant] **T:** 518 *with picture*
Townshend, Viscount **T:** 352
Turnip, Russian [plant]
Rutabaga **R:** 567
Turnip, Swedish [plant]
Rutabaga **R:** 567
Turnout
Ballet **B:** 44
Turnover [sports]
Basketball (Basketball terms) **B:** 145
Football (Advancing the ball) **F:** 360-362
Turnpike [road] **T:** 518
Pennsylvania Turnpike **P:** 271
Road (How roads and highways are paid for)
R: 360
Turnsole [plant]
Heliotrope **H:** 175 *with picture*
Turnstone [bird] **T:** 519 *with picture*
Turntable
Phonograph (Parts of a phonograph) **P:** 400 *with diagram*
Stereophonic sound system (Phonographs)
So: 892
Turnus [Greek mythology]
Aeneid **A:** 84
Turpan Depression
China (The Xinjiang-Mongolian Uplands) **C:** 491
Turpentine [tree product] **T:** 519
Lacquer **L:** 22
Turpin, Dick [English outlaw] **T:** 519
Turquino, Pico [mountain]
Cuba (The land) **Ci:** 1172 *with map*
Turquoise [gem] **T:** 519
Gem *picture on* **G:** 78
Turret [tower]
Architecture (Carolingian architecture) **A:** 618
Turret lathe [machine]
Machine tool (Metal removal) **M:** 17
Turtle [animal] **T:** 520 *with pictures*
See also Sea turtle *in this index*
Animal *pictures on* **A:** 479, **A:** 507; (Animal migration) **A:** 502-503
Ocean *picture on* **O:** 656
Reptile (Turtles) **R:** 251
Terrapin **T:** 173 *with picture*
Tortoise **T:** 344 *with picture*
Wetland *picture on* **W:** 253
Turtle [submarine]
Submarine (Early submarines) **So:** 942 *with diagram*
Turtle dove [bird] **T:** 524 *with picture*
Turtle Island [book by Snyder]
American literature (Poetry) **A:** 423
Turtle Mountains
North Dakota (Land regions) **N:** 506
Tuscaloosa [American Indian leader]
Alabama (European exploration and settlement)
A: 275
De Soto, Hernando (Journey to the Mississippi)
D: 161
Tuscaloosa Trend [region]
Louisiana (Natural resources) **L:** 493
Tuscan column [architecture]
Architecture **A:** 608-609 *with picture*
Column (The Roman orders) **Ci:** 866 *with picture*
Tuscan dialect
Italian language (Development) **I:** 493
Tuscan Sea *See* Tyrrhenian Sea *in this index*
Tuscany [state, Italy] **T:** 525
Italy *picture on* **I:** 512
Tuscarora Indians
Iroquois Indians **I:** 455
North Carolina (Colonial days) **N:** 492
Tuscarora War [1711-1713]
North Carolina (Colonial days) **N:** 492
Tusche [drawing material]
Lithography (How lithography works) **L:** 387
Screen printing *picture on* **S:** 225
Tusculan Disputations [book by Cicero]
Cicero, Marcus Tullius (His works) **Ci:** 552
Tush [zoology]
Elephant (Kinds of elephants) **E:** 227-228
Tusitala [title]
Stevenson, Robert Louis **So:** 897
Tusk [zoology]
Elephant (Tusks and teeth) **E:** 228 *with pictures*
Hog (Teeth) **H:** 286
Narwhal **N:** 21
Walrus **W:** 20 *with picture*
Tusk shell *See* Tooth shell *in this index*
Tuskegee Airmen [American aviators] **T:** 525
Davis, Benjamin Oliver, Jr. **D:** 47
Tuskegee Airmen National Historic Site
[Alabama]
National Park System (table: National historic sites) **N:** 52-53
Tuskegee Institute [former school] *See* Tuskegee University *in this index*
Tuskegee Institute National Historic Site
[Alabama]
Alabama (Museums) **A:** 261 *with picture*
National Park System (table: National historic sites) **N:** 52-53
Tuskegee University T: 525
Carver, George Washington (Tuskegee instructor and researcher) **C:** 268-269
Washington, Booker T. **W:** 88
Tuskfish [fish]
Fish *picture on* **F:** 155
Tussah silk [fiber]
Moth (Giant silkworm moths and royal moths)
M: 841-842
Silk (Wild silk) **S:** 459
Tussaud, Marie Gresholtz [Swiss sculptor] **T:** 525
Tusser, Thomas [English author]
August (Quotations) **A:** 887
Tussock moth [insect] **T:** 526
Insect *pictures on* **I:** 282
Moth (Tussock moths) **M:** 841 *with pictures*
Rain forest *picture on* **R:** 126c
Tut [king of ancient Egypt] *See* Tutankhamun *in this index*
Tutankhamun [king of ancient Egypt] **T:** 526 *with pictures*
Alabaster *picture on* **A:** 280
Archaeology *picture on* **A:** 599
Carter, Howard **C:** 251
Egypt, Ancient *pictures on* **E:** 141; (The New Kingdom) **E:** 143
Furniture *picture on* **F:** 570
Tutankhaton *See* Tutankhamun *in this index*
Tutor [education]
Harvard University (Educational program) **H:** 80
Oxford, University of (Educational program)
O: 887
Tutsi [people] **T:** 527
Burundi **B:** 712; (History) **B:** 713; (People) **B:** 713
Congo, Democratic Republic of the (The fall of Mobutu) **Ci:** 940c
Hutu **H:** 459
Ruanda-Urundi **R:** 499
Rwanda **R:** 570
Tuttle, Hiram A. [American political leader]
New Hampshire (table) **N:** 223
Tuttle, Julia [American public figure]
Miami (History) **M:** 480
Tutu [clothing]
Ballet (Sets and costumes) **B:** 49-50
Tutu, Desmond [South African social reformer]
T: 527 *with portrait*
South Africa (Recent developments) **So:** 621
Tutu, Osei [Ashanti leader]
Ashanti **A:** 767
Tutuila [island, Pacific]
American Samoa **A:** 429 *with map*
Samoa **So:** 80b
Tuvalu T: 527 *with map*
Flag *picture on* **F:** 205
Tuve, Merle A. [American physicist]
Radar (The first uses of radar) **R:** 71
Tuxtla Gutiérrez [Mexico]
Chiapas **C:** 419
Tuzigoot National Monument [Arizona]
National Park System (table: National monuments) **N:** 52
TV *See* Television *in this index*
TVA *See* Tennessee Valley Authority *in this index*
TVP [food]
Soybean (Soy meal) **So:** 690
TW Services, Inc.
Yellowstone National Park (Recreational activities) **Y:** 559
Twa [people]
Africa (Peoples of Africa) **A:** 104
Burundi (People) **B:** 713
Rwanda (People) **R:** 570
Twain, Mark [American author] **T:** 528 *with picture*
American literature *pictures on* **A:** 416, **A:** 419; (Mark Twain and Henry James) **A:** 420
Autograph *picture on* **A:** 943
Connecticut (Places to visit) **Ci:** 960
Hannibal **H:** 53
Howells, William Dean **H:** 401
Huckleberry Finn **H:** 404
Novel (The United States) **N:** 573
United States, History of the (The Gilded Age)
U: 183
Twain, Shania [Canadian singer] **T:** 530
"'Twas the Night Before Christmas" [poem by Moore]
Christmas (Other customs) **C:** 536
Moore, Clement Clarke **M:** 796
Santa Claus (Santa's appearance) **S:** 114
Tweed [fabric]
Ireland *picture on* **I:** 425
Textile (table: Textile terms) **T:** 213
Tweed, William Marcy [American public figure]
T: 531
Tweed Ring [U.S. history]
Tweed, William Marcy **T:** 531
Tweedie, Lemuel J. [Canadian political leader]
New Brunswick (table) **N:** 195
Tweedsmuir, Baron [British statesman]
Buchan, John **B:** 657
Tweedsmuir Park
British Columbia (Places to visit) **B:** 620
Tween decks
Ship (Nautical terms) **S:** 405 *with diagram*
Tweeter [electronics]
Speaker **So:** 767
Twelfth Amendment
Constitution of the United States **Ci:** 1013
Electoral College (History) **E:** 164
Jefferson, Thomas (Election of 1800) **J:** 83
Twelfth Army Group [World War II]
Bradley, Omar Nelson **B:** 545
Twelfth Night [holiday] **T:** 531
Twelfth Night [play by Shakespeare]
Shakespeare, William: (*Twelfth Night*) **S:** 360
Twelve, The [poem by Blok]
Russian literature (Symbolism) **R:** 563
Twelve Apostles, Quorum of the
Mormons (Church organization) **M:** 807
Twelve Apostles, The [rocks, Australia]
Victoria *picture on* **V:** 357
"Twelve Days of Christmas, The" [song]
Folklore (Folk songs) **F:** 324
Twelve labors of Hercules [Greek mythology]
Hercules (The twelve labors) **H:** 198
Twelve Letters to a Small Town [book by Reaney]
Reaney, James **R:** 173
Twelve Tables, Laws of the [ancient Rome] **T:** 531
Law (Ancient Roman law) **L:** 133
Rome, Ancient (The law) **R:** 438
Twelve-tone music
Berg, Alban **B:** 257
Classical music (Atonal music) **Ci:** 649-650
Dallapiccola, Luigi **D:** 10
Music (Tone) **M:** 950-951
Schoenberg, Arnold **S:** 178
Sessions, Roger **S:** 320
Stravinsky, Igor (The 12-tone works) **So:** 923
Webern, Anton **W:** 176
Twelve Tribes of Israel
Jacob **J:** 19
Jews (Beginnings) **J:** 120-121
Joseph (Settling his family in Egypt) **J:** 168
Palestine (Early history and settlement) **P:** 104 *with map*
Religion (Judaism) **R:** 219
Twelvers [sect] *See* Imāmī Shī`ah *in this index*
Twentieth Amendment
Constitution of the United States **Ci:** 1015
Presidential succession **P:** 771
Twenty-Fifth Amendment
Constitution of the United States **Ci:** 1016
Presidential succession **P:** 771
Vice president of the United States (The 25th Amendment) **V:** 350
Twenty-Fifth of April Bridge

Lisbon (The city) **L: 348**
Twenty-First Amendment
  Constitution of the United States **Ci: 1015**
  Prohibition (The decline of the prohibition movement) **P: 816**
Twenty-Four Proprietors [U.S. history]
  New Jersey (English control) **N: 250**
Twenty-Fourth Amendment
  Constitution of the United States **Ci: 1016**
  Poll tax **P: 644**
Twenty-one [game]
  Gambling (Blackjack) **G: 21**
Twenty-Second Amendment
  Constitution of the United States **Ci: 1015**
Twenty-Seventh Amendment
  Constitution of the United States **Ci: 1016**
Twenty-Sixth Amendment
  Constitution of the United States **Ci: 1016**
Twenty-sixth of July Movement [Cuban history]
  Castro, Fidel **C: 283**
  Cuba (The Castro revolution) **Ci: 1177-1178**
Twenty-Third Amendment
  Constitution of the United States **Ci: 1015**
Twenty-Third Psalm [Bible]
  Metaphor **M: 429**
  Psalms, Book of **P: 844**
Twenty Thousand Leagues Under the Sea [book by Verne]
  Science fiction (The first science fiction) **S: 205**
  Verne, Jules **V: 337**
Twenty Years at Hull House [book by Addams]
  American literature (Nonfiction writers) **A: 420**
Twice-Told Tales [book by Hawthorne]
  Hawthorne, Nathaniel (His stories and sketches) **H: 115**
  Poe, Edgar Allan (Fiction and theory of fiction) **P: 590**
Twickenham Stadium
  London (Recreation) **L: 434**
Twig
  Tree (How trees grow taller) **T: 418**
Twilight **T: 531**
Twilight [book by Meyer]
  Meyer, Stephenie **M: 479**
Twilight of the Gods [opera by Wagner] *See* Götterdämmerung, Die *in this index*
"Twilight" series [books by Meyer]
  Meyer, Stephenie **M: 479**
Twill [weaving] **T: 531**
  Basket making (Methods) **B: 141**
  Cashmere **C: 274**
  Textile (Woven fabrics) **T: 214**
  Weaving (The twill weave) **W: 173** *with picture*
Twin Cities [Minnesota]
  Minneapolis **M: 580**
  Minnesota (Population) **M: 588**
  Saint Paul **S: 52**
Twin Falls [falls, Idaho]
  Idaho (Rivers, waterfalls, springs, and lakes) **I: 38**
Twin prime [mathematics]
  Prime number (Special primes) **P: 780**
Twin-rotor helicopter
  Helicopter (Types of helicopters) **H: 170-171** *with diagrams*
Twin-screw ship
  Propeller (Ship propellers) **P: 826**
Twin Territories [U.S. history]
  Oklahoma (Progress toward statehood) **O: 732**
Twin Towers *See* World Trade Center *in this index*
Twin trailer [truck] *See* Double trailer *in this index*
Twine [rope]
  Rope **R: 472**
Twinflower [plant] **T: 531**
Twining [weaving]
  Basket making (Methods) **B: 141** *with pictures*
Twining, Nathan Farragut [American military leader]
  Joint Chiefs of Staff (table) **J: 156**
Twins [biology]
  Cloning (Differences among clones) **Ci: 683**
  Conjoined twins **Ci: 950** *with picture*
  Heredity (Heredity and environment) **H: 205**
  Intelligence (The roles of heredity and environment) **I: 319**
  Multiple birth **M: 919**
  Reproduction, Human (Multiple birth) **R: 246**
Twins, Minnesota [team] *See* Minnesota Twins *in this index*
Twins, The [constellation] *See* Gemini *in this index*
Twins, The [mountains, Alberta]
  Alberta (The Rocky Mountains and Foothills) **A: 322** *with map*
Twirling, Baton *See* Baton twirling *in this index*
Twiss, L. Peter [British aviator]
  Aviation (table: Aviation speed records) **A: 990**
Twister *See* Tornado *in this index*
Twitch [disorder]

Convulsions **Ci: 1025**
Twitter [website]
  Internet (Social networking websites) **I: 350b**; (The evolving Internet) **I: 350g-350h**
  Journalism (Journalism today) **J: 175**
Two bits [money]
  Money *picture on* **M: 708**; (A scarcity of money) **M: 710**
  Piece of eight **P: 452**
2 by 2 determinant [mathematics]
  Determinant (Using 2 by 2 determinants) **D: 166**
Two Cheeseburgers with Everything [sculpture by Oldenburg]
  Oldenburg, Claes *picture on* **O: 741**
Two-cycle engine *See* Two-stroke cycle engine *in this index*
Two Deaths of Quincas Wateryell, The [book by Amado]
  Amado, Jorge **A: 399**
Two-degree-of-freedom gyroscope
  Gyroscope (Mechanical gyroscopes) **G: 454**
Two-dimensional gel electrophoresis [biology]
  Proteomics **P: 833**
Two-dimensional graphics
  Electronic game (Graphics) **E: 204b**
2,4-D [herbicide]
  Agent Orange **A: 140**
  Herbicide **H: 198**
2,4,5-T [herbicide]
  Agent Orange **A: 140**
  Herbicide (Hazards of herbicides) **H: 198**
Two Gentlemen of Verona [play by Shakespeare]
  Shakespeare, William: (The Two Gentlemen of Verona) **S: 356**
Two half hitches
  Knots, hitches, and splices (Two half hitches) **K: 357** *with diagram*
291 [art gallery]
  Painting (Steiglitz and "291") **P: 82**
Two Noble Kinsmen, The [play]
  Fletcher, John **F: 234**
  Shakespeare, William (Shakespeare's plays) **S: 354**; (The Two Noble Kinsmen) **S: 366**
"Two Offers, The" [story by Harper]
  African American literature (The 1800's) **A: 136a**
Two-party system
  Democracy (Political parties) **D: 120-121**
  Political parties (Two-party systems) **P: 634**
  United States, Government of the (Representative democracy) **U: 137-138**
Two-ranked leaf
  Grass (The grass plant) **G: 324**
Two-second rule [driving]
  Automobile (Safe following distances) **A: 955** *with diagram*
Two Sicilies, Kingdom of the *See* Sicilies, Kingdom of the Two *in this index*
Two Sisters [painting by Renoir]
  Impressionism *picture on* **I: 94**
  Painting (Edouard Manet and the impressionists) **P: 71-72**
Two Sisters, The [engraving by Cournault]
  Engraving *picture on* **E: 326**
Two Solitudes [book by MacLennan]
  Canadian literature (Modern English-Canadian fiction) **C: 160**
  MacLennan, Hugh **M: 25**
Two-stroke cycle engine
  Diesel engine (Kinds of diesel engines) **D: 199**
  Gasoline engine *diagrams on* **G: 65**; (Cycle) **G: 63** *with pictures*
2008 TC [asteroid]
  Asteroid (History of study) **A: 824b**
Two Thousand Guineas [race]
  Horse racing (Types of horse races) **H: 364**
2001: A Space Odyssey [film]
  Clarke, Arthur C. **Ci: 642**
  Motion picture (Movies in the 1960's) **M: 870-871**
2003 UB₃₁₃ [astronomy] *See* Eris *in this index*
Two-tiered health care system
  Health insurance, National **H: 129**
Two-toed sloth
  Animal *picture on* **A: 480**
  Sloth **S: 508b**
Two Towers, The [book by Tolkien]
  Tolkien, J. R. R. **T: 321**
Two Trains Running [play by Wilson]
  Wilson, August **W: 316**
Two Treatises of Government [book by Locke]
  Freedom (The Enlightenment) **F: 503**
  Locke, John **L: 413**
Two-way bilingual education
  Bilingual education (Two-way bilingual education programs) **B: 300**
  Hispanic Americans (Education) **H: 256-257**
Two-way communication
  Radio (Two-way communication) **R: 84**

Two Years Before the Mast [book by Dana]
  Dana, Richard Henry, Jr. **D: 22**
Twospotted lady beetle
  Insect *picture on* **I: 283**
Twostriped grasshopper [insect]
  Insect *picture on* **I: 280**
TWX [communications]
  Telegraph (Decline) **T: 92**
Tybalt [literary figure]
  Shakespeare, William: (Romeo and Juliet) **S: 357-358**
Tyche [Greek mythology]
  Fortuna **F: 419**
Tycho Brahe's Comet [astronomy]
  Comet (table) **Ci: 868**
Tydings-McDuffie Act [1934]
  Asian Americans (Asian immigration halted) **A: 812e-812f**
Tyee *See* Chinook salmon *in this index*
Tygacil [medication]
  Antibiotic (History) **A: 552-553**
"Tyger, The" [poem by Blake]
  Blake, William **B: 397**
Tylenol [medication]
  Acetaminophen **A: 24**
  Analgesic **A: 448**
Tyler, Anne [American author] **T: 531**
Tyler, James Hoge [American political leader]
  Virginia (table) **V: 417**
Tyler, John [American political leader]
  Tyler, John (Early life) **T: 532**
Tyler, John [U.S. president] **T: 532** *with pictures*
  Harrison, William Henry **H: 74**
  Vice president of the United States (Tyler takes over) **V: 353**
  Virginia (table) **V: 417**
  Whig Party (In the 1840's) **W: 280**
Tyler, Julia Gardiner [wife of John Tyler]
  First ladies of the United States (table) **F: 142**
  Tyler, John (Life in the White House) **T: 534** *with picture*
Tyler, Letitia Christian [wife of John Tyler]
  First ladies of the United States (table) **F: 142**
  Tyler, John (Tyler's family) **T: 532**
Tyler, Moses Coit [American author] **T: 535**
Tyler, Priscilla Cooper [daughter-in-law of]
  Tyler, John (Life in the White House) **T: 534**
  White House hostesses **W: 291**
Tyler, Royall [American dramatist] **T: 535**
Tyler, Wat [English rebel]
  England (The Hundred Years' War) **E: 306**
  Wat Tyler's Rebellion **W: 113**
Tylor, Sir Edward Burnett [British anthropologist] **T: 535**
  Animism **A: 514d**
  Mythology (Anthropological approaches) **M: 989**
  Religion (The origin of religion) **R: 218**
Tymiński, Stanisław [Polish political leader]
  Poland (Free elections) **P: 614-615**
Tymoshenko, Yulia [Ukrainian political leader]
  Ukraine (Political changes) **U: 14**
Tympani [musical instrument] *See* Timpani *in this index*
Tympanic membrane *See* Eardrum *in this index*
Tympanum [anatomy] *See* Eardrum *in this index*
Tympanum [zoology]
  Moth (Kinds of moths) **M: 840**
Tympanum of the central portal of Vézelay Abbey [France]
  Sculpture (The importance of sculpture) **S: 228** *with picture*
Týn Church
  Prague (The city) **P: 730** *with picture*
Tyndale, William [English religious leader] **T: 535**
  Bible (Early English translations) **B: 285**
  Puritans (History) **P: 910**
Tyndall, John [British physicist] **T: 536**
  Suspension **S: 1012**
  Tyndall, John **T: 536**
  Ultramicroscope **U: 16**
Tyndall effect [physics]
  Suspension **S: 1012**
  Tyndall, John **T: 536**
  Ultramicroscope **U: 16**
Tynwald Court [government]
  Man, Isle of **M: 131**
Type [printing] **T: 536** *with pictures*
  See also the list of Related articles in the Type article
  Linotype **L: 338** *with picture*
  Photocomposition **P: 404** *with picture*
Type 1 diabetes [disorder]
  Diabetes (Causes) **D: 179**; (Treatment) **D: 179**; (Research) **D: 180**
  Insulin (Diabetes) **I: 308**
Type I supernova
  Star (Binary stars) **So: 852**
Type 2 diabetes [disorder]
  C-reactive protein **C: 2**
  Diabetes (Causes) **D: 179**; (Treatment) **D: 179**

Insulin (Diabetes) **I:** 308
Type II supernova
Star (Supernovae) **So:** 850
Type A blood
Blood (The ABO blood groups) **B:** 412
Races, Human (The clinal approach) **R:** 55-56
Type A influenza [virus]
Influenza **I:** 268b
Swine flu **So:** 1048
Type AB blood
Blood (The ABO blood groups) **B:** 412
Type B blood
Blood (The ABO blood groups) **B:** 412
Races, Human (The clinal approach) **R:** 55-56
Type B influenza [virus]
Influenza **I:** 268b
Type C influenza [virus]
Influenza **I:** 268b
Type face [printing]
Type **T:** 537 *with pictures*
Type form [printing]
Printing (Letterpress printing) **P:** 799
Type O blood
Blood (The ABO blood groups) **B:** 412
Races, Human (The clinal approach) **R:** 55-56
Typee [book by Melville]
Melville, Herman (His early life) **M:** 390
Typesetting [printing]
Gutenberg, Johannes **G:** 444
Linotype **L:** 338
Newspaper (Making up the pages) **N:** 383
Photocomposition **P:** 404 *with pictures*
Printing (Typesetting) **P:** 797
Type **T:** 536
Typesetting machine See Linotype *in this index*
Typewriter T: 538 *with pictures*
Communication *picture on* **Ci:** 883
Glidden, Carlos **G:** 227
Keyboard **K:** 308
Sholes, Christopher Latham **S:** 433
Word processing **W:** 403
Typhlopidae [zoology]
Snake (Blind snakes) **S:** 535
Typhoid fever [disease] **T:** 539
Reed, Walter **R:** 194
Typhoid Mary [American domestic] **T:** 539
Typhoon [book by Conrad]
Conrad, Joseph **Ci:** 973
Typhoon [weather] **T:** 540 *with pictures*
Cyclone **Ci:** 1204
Hurricane **H:** 452
Pacific Ocean (Tropical cyclones) **P:** 14
Storm (Tropical cyclones) **So:** 913
Typhus [disease] **T:** 540
DDT **D:** 55
Enders, John Franklin **E:** 272
Relapsing fever **R:** 209
Rickettsia **R:** 335
Typical owl
Bird of prey **B:** 374a
Typing
Typewriter **T:** 538
Typo
Proofreading (Proofreaders' marks) **P:** 822
Typographical error
Proofreading (Proofreaders' marks) **P:** 822
Typology
Archaeology (Classification) **A:** 597
Tyr [Norse god]
Tuesday **T:** 481
Tyrannosaur [dinosaur]
Dinosaur (True dinosaurs) **D:** 206b-211 *with picture*
Tyrannosaurus [dinosaur] **T:** 541 *with picture*
Dinosaur **D:** 206 *with picture, picture on* **D:** 207;
(True dinosaurs) **D:** 206b-211 *with picture*;
(Changing interpretations of dinosaurs) **D:** 212 *with pictures*
Fossil *picture on* **F:** 422
Prehistoric animal *picture on* **P:** 739
Tyranny [ancient Greece]
Greece, Ancient (New forms of government) **G:** 372
Tyranny **T:** 541
Tyranny [political science] **T:** 541
Tyrant flycatcher [bird]
Flycatcher **F:** 311
Tyre [ancient city] **T:** 541
Alexander the Great (Invasion of Asia) **A:** 342-343
Phoenicia (Religion) **P:** 393; (Trade and manufacturing) **P:** 393; (The spread of Phoenician influence) **P:** 394-395
Tyre [automobile] See Tire *in this index*
Tyrian purple [dye]
Dye (Natural dyes) **D:** 396
Tyrol [region, Austria-Italy] **T:** 542 *with maps*
Innsbruck **I:** 275

Tyrone, Earl of [Irish nobleman]
Ireland (The conquest of Ireland) **I:** 426
Tyrone Guthrie Theater See Guthrie Theater *in this index*
Tyrosine [biochemistry]
Dopamine **D:** 309
Tyrothricin [antibiotic]
Dubos, René Jules **D:** 372
Tyrrell, Joseph Burr [Canadian geologist] **T:** 542
Alberta (Interesting facts) **A:** 313
Tyrrhenian Sea [Mediterranean] **T:** 542
Italy *picture on* **I:** 497
Tyson, Cicely [American actress]
Spingarn Medal (table: 2010) **So:** 794
Tyson, Mike [American boxer] **T:** 542 *with portrait*
Boxing (The late 1900's) **B:** 532b
Tyutchev, Fyodor [Russian poet]
Russian literature (Late Romanticism) **R:** 561
Tzara, Tristan [Romanian poet]
Dadaism **D:** 2
Tzintzuntzan [former city]
Tarascan Indians **T:** 42
Tzolk'in [almanac]
Calendar (The Maya) **C:** 31

U

U [letter] **U:** 1 *with pictures*
U [symbol]
Uranium (Uranium isotopes) **U:** 214
U [title]
Thant, U **T:** 231
U-boat
Submarine (World Wars I and II) **So:** 943 *with picture*
Warship (Warships in the two world wars) **W:** 41
World War I (The war at sea) **W:** 460 *with picture*; (The United States enters the war) **W:** 462
World War II *pictures on* **W:** 476; (The Battle of the Atlantic) **W:** 478
U quark [physics] See Up quark *in this index*
U Thant [Burmese diplomat] See Thant, U *in this index*
U Thong [king of Ayutthaya]
Thailand (Early kingdoms) **T:** 226
U2 [Irish musical group] **U:** 2
Bono **B:** 462
Rock music *picture on* **R:** 376; (New wave and mainstream rock) **R:** 380c; (Rock music today) **R:** 381
U-2 incident [U.S. history]
Cold War (The U-2 incident) **Ci:** 767
Eisenhower, Dwight David (U-2 incident) **E:** 154
Union of Soviet Socialist Republics (Relations with the United States) **U:** 39
U-233 [isotope]
Thorium **T:** 266
U-234 [isotope]
Uranium (Uranium isotopes) **U:** 214
U-235 [isotope]
Actinium **A:** 30
Nuclear energy (The full development of nuclear energy) **N:** 580; (Isotopes) **N:** 581; (Nuclear fission) **N:** 582; (Fuel preparation) **N:** 586
Uranium (Uranium isotopes) **U:** 214; (How uranium is mined and processed) **U:** 215
U-238 [isotope]
Nuclear energy (Isotopes) **N:** 581; (Nuclear fission) **N:** 582-583; (Wastes and waste disposal) **N:** 588
Nuclear weapon *diagram on* **N:** 599
Radium (How radium forms and breaks down) **R:** 100
Uranium (Uranium isotopes) **U:** 214; (How uranium is mined and processed) **U:** 215
Ua Pou [island, Pacific]
Marquesas Islands **M:** 217
Uakari [monkey]
Monkey *picture on* **M:** 728; (Kinds of monkeys) **M:** 725-726
U.A.R. See United Arab Republic *in this index*
UAV [aircraft] See Unmanned aerial vehicle *in this index*
UAW [union] See United Automobile Workers *in this index*
UB II [submarine]
World War I *picture on* **W:** 457
Ubangi River [Africa] **U:** 2
Central African Republic (Land) **C:** 352 *with picture*
Congo, Republic of the (Land) **Ci:** 940d-940e
Ubangi-Shari [former region]
Central African Republic (History) **C:** 353
Ubangi River **U:** 2
Ubar [ancient city]
Archaeology *picture on* **A:** 594
Ubehebe Crater [volcano, California]
Death Valley **D:** 62

Uber Cup [sports]
Badminton **B:** 24
Ubico, Jorge [Guatemalan political leader]
Guatemala (The mid-1900's) **G:** 417
Ubii [people]
Bonn (History) **B:** 461
UBS [bank]
Bank **B:** 92
Ucayali River [Peru]
Amazon River (The course of the Amazon) **A:** 403
Uccello, Paolo [Italian painter] **U:** 2 *with picture*
UCLA [school] See California, University of *in this index*
Udall, Stewart Lee [American political leader]
Interior, Department of the (table) **I:** 325
Johnson, Lyndon Baines (table) **J:** 151
Kennedy, John Fitzgerald (table) **K:** 266
Udder [zoology]
Cattle (Udder) **C:** 308
Uelsmann, Jerry [American photographer]
Photography (A diversity of styles) **P:** 426-427
Uemura, Naomi [Japanese explorer]
North Pole **N:** 517
Ueno Park
Tokyo (Parks and gardens) **T:** 316
Ueshiba, Morihei [Japanese educator]
Aikido **A:** 167
UFCW [union] See United Food and Commercial Workers International Union *in this index*
UFO See Unidentified flying object *in this index*
UFW See United Farm Workers of America *in this index*
Uganda U: 3 *with pictures and map*
Clothing *picture on* **Ci:** 689
Tanzania (The united republic and socialism) **T:** 35
West Nile virus **U:** 205
Uganda Protectorate
Uganda **U:** 3
Ugarit [ancient city]
Phoenicia (Way of life) **P:** 392; (Language) **P:** 393
Ugli [fruit]
Tangelo **T:** 26
Ugolino [birth name of]
Gregory IX **G:** 388
UHF band [communications]
Communications satellite (How communications satellites work) **Ci:** 888b
UHF wave See Ultrahigh frequency waves *in this index*
UHT method [pasteurization]
Milk (Pasteurization) **M:** 548
Uhuru Peak
Kilimanjaro **K:** 315 *with picture*
Uighurs [people] See Uyghurs *in this index*
UIM [organization]
Motorboat racing **M:** 876
Uinta Range [mountains, Utah]
Utah (Land regions) **U:** 240 *with picture and map*
Uintaite [mineral]
Asphalt (Asphalt production) **A:** 815
Uitlanders [people]
Anglo-Boer Wars **A:** 463
South Africa (Discovery of diamonds and gold) **So:** 618
Ujamaa village
Tanzania (The united republic and socialism) **T:** 35
Ujung Kulon National Park [Indonesia]
Java **J:** 65
National park (table) **N:** 42f
U.K. [country] See United Kingdom *in this index*
UKC [organization] See United Kennel Club *in this index*
uKhahlamba/Drakensberg Park [South Africa]
Drakensberg **D:** 323
Ukiyo-e [art]
Japanese print **J:** 62
Painting (Japanese painting) **P:** 47-48
Woodcut **W:** 393
Ukkusiksalik National Park [Nunavut]
Canada (table: National parks and national park reserves) **C:** 113
Nunavut (Economy) **N:** 610
Ukraine U: 5 *with pictures and maps*
Bessarabia **B:** 273
Cimmerians **Ci:** 553
Cossacks **Ci:** 1079
Dnieper River **D:** 258
Europe *picture on* **E:** 394
Flag *picture on* **F:** 207
Russia (The new nation) **R:** 555
Ruthenia **R:** 568
Strategic Arms Reduction Treaty **So:** 919
Union of Soviet Socialist Republics (History) **U:** 35
Ukrainian Catholic Church [religious group]
Eastern Catholic Churches **E:** 45

Ukrainian language
Ukraine (Language) U: 8
Ukrainian Orthodox Church [religious group]
Ukraine (Religion) U: 8
Ukrainian People's Republic [former country]
Ukraine (Soviet rule) U: 13
Ukrainian Soviet Socialist Republic [former name]
Ukraine U: 5
Ukrainians [people]
Ukraine (People) U: 6
Union of Soviet Socialist Republics (People) U: 31 *with picture*
Ukulele [musical instrument] U: 14 *with picture*
Hawaii (Dancing and music) H: 94
Ulaanbaatar [Mongolia] U: 14
Mongolia (Government) M: 721-722 *with map*
"Ulalume" [poem by Poe]
Poe, Edgar Allan (Poetry and poetic theory) P: 589-590
Ulama [religious leaders]
Saudi Arabia (National government) S: 155
Ulan Bator [Mongolia] *See* Ulaanbaatar *in this index*
Ulate, Otilio [Costa Rican political leader]
Costa Rica (Revolutions and reforms) Ci: 1084
Ulbricht, Walter [German political leader]
Germany (East Germany) G: 170
Ulcer [disorder] U: 14 *with pictures*
Antacid A: 529
Bedsore B: 199
Herpes, Genital H: 214
Prostaglandin P: 829
Stomach (Peptic ulcers) So: 908
Ulcerative colitis [disease]
Colitis Ci: 773
Colostomy Ci: 850
Inflammatory bowel disease I: 266
Ulisse [opera by Dallapiccola]
Dallapiccola, Luigi D: 10
Ullamaliztli [game]
Aztec (Way of life) A: 1000
Ulloa, Antonio de [Spanish government official]
New Orleans (French and Spanish rule) N: 283
Platinum (History) P: 567
Ulloa Estate, The [book by Bazán]
Spanish literature (The 1800's) So: 761-762
Ullswater [region, England]
England *picture on* E: 298
Ullswater, Lake [lake, England]
National park *picture on* N: 42e
Ulna [anatomy]
Arm A: 717 *with diagram*
Bird (Skeleton and muscles) B: 364 *with diagram*
Elbow E: 157 *with diagrams*
Human body (table) H: 422 *with diagram*
Wrist W: 510 *with diagram*
Ulnar artery [anatomy]
Human body (table) H: 422 *with diagram*
Ulnar nerve [anatomy]
Funny bone F: 560
Human body (table) H: 422 *with diagram*
Ulpian Library [Rome]
Library (Rome) L: 258
Ulster [former region]
Ireland (The conquest of Ireland) I: 426
Northern Ireland N: 521
Ulster Unionist Party U: 15
Ulster, University of
Northern Ireland (Education) N: 522
Ulster Agreement [1998] *See* Good Friday Agreement *in this index*
Ulster cycle [Irish literature]
Irish literature (Heroic tales, romances, and sagas) I: 430
Mythology (The Irish cycles) M: 985
Ulster Unionist Party [political party] U: 15
Trimble, David T: 445
Ultima muñeca [doll]
Doll (Dolls in celebrations) D: 287-288
Ultima Thule [ancient land] *See* Thule *in this index*
Ultimate analysis [chemistry]
Coal (Analyzing coal composition) Ci: 717
Ultime lettere di Jacopo Ortis, Le [book by Foscolo]
Foscolo, Ugo F: 421
Ultisol [soil]
Indiana (Natural resources) I: 211
Soil *map on* So: 575; (How soils are classified) So: 576
Ultra-high-energy cosmic rays
Cosmic rays (Ultra-high-energy cosmic rays) Ci: 1076
Ultra large crude carrier
Tanker (Kinds of tankers) T: 28
Ultra secret
World War II (The Ultra secret) W: 494
Ultracentrifuge [machine]
Centrifuge C: 358

Ultrafast laser [machine]
Light (Lasers) L: 291
Ultrafiche [film]
Microfilm (Types) M: 514
Ultrafiltration [industrial process]
Cheese (History) C: 394-395
Ultrahigh frequency waves [communications]
Television (Broadcasting) T: 123
Ultrahigh-temperature method
Milk (Pasteurization) M: 548
Ultralight airplane
Airplane (General aviation planes) A: 211-212 *with picture*
Hang gliding H: 51
Ultramarine [book by Lowry]
Lowry, Malcolm L: 511
Ultramarine [pigment]
Lapis lazuli L: 73
Ultramicroscope [instrument] U: 15
Ultramicrotome [instrument]
Microtomy M: 520
Ultrapasteurization
Milk (Pasteurization) M: 548
Ultraquists [religious group]
Hussites H: 458
Ultrasonic transducer
Transducer T: 371
Ultrasound (Ultrasound devices) U: 16 *with picture*
Ultrasonic wave *See* Ultrasound *in this index*
Ultrasound [physics] U: 16 *with picture*
Acoustics A: 28
Amniocentesis A: 438
Burglar alarm B: 704
Genetic counseling (Reasons for seeking genetic counseling) G: 84a
Infertility (Treatment) I: 265
Physics (Sound) P: 437
Pregnancy (Medical care) P: 734-735 *with picture*
Prostate cancer P: 829
Radiology R: 98
Remote control (The parts of a remote control system) R: 230
Reproduction, Human (Checking the fetus) R: 248
Sonar (Other uses) So: 591
Sound (Other uses) So: 599
Ultraviolet astronomy
Astronomy (Ultraviolet astronomy) A: 844
Ultraviolet filter
Photography (Filters) P: 416
Ultraviolet lamp
Prospecting P: 829
Ultraviolet rays [physics] U: 17
Astronomy (table: The electromagnetic spectrum) A: 839; (Ultraviolet astronomy) A: 844
Butterfly (The head) B: 738 *with picture*
Cancer (Avoiding carcinogens) C: 171
Color *diagram on* Ci: 818
Electromagnetic waves (The electromagnetic spectrum) E: 202 *with diagram*
Flower (Bees) F: 295 *with pictures*
Hubble Space Telescope (How the telescope works) H: 403
Light (The spectrum of light sources) L: 284 *with diagram*
Ozone O: 894
Radiation (Electromagnetic radiation) R: 75-76 *with picture*
Southern Ocean (Scientific research) So: 688b
Sun (Energy output) So: 976
Sun lamp So: 988
Telescope (Other telescopes) T: 108
Weather (Air temperature) W: 157
Ultraviolet telescope
Telescope (Ultraviolet telescopes) T: 108
Ulu [tool]
Inuit (Food) I: 354b
Ulubemba [people] *See* Bemba *in this index*
Ulufa'alu, Bartholomew [Solomon Islands political leader]
Solomon Islands (History) So: 585-586
Uluru [rock, Australia] U: 17
Australia *picture on* A: 910; (Mountains) A: 908 *with map*
Uluru-Kata Tjuta National Park [Australia]
National park (table) N: 42f
Uluru U: 17
Ulyanov, Alexander [brother of]
Lenin, V. I. (Education) L: 192
Ulyanov, Ilya Nikolayevich [father of]
Lenin, V. I. (Boyhood) L: 191
Ulyanov, Vladimir Ilyich *See* Lenin, V. I. *in this index*
Ulysses [book by Joyce]
Irish literature (Fiction) I: 432
Joyce, James J: 177

Novel (New directions in the novel) N: 573-574
Obscenity and pornography (Legal history for obscenity) O: 643
Ulysses [butterfly]
Butterfly *picture on* B: 737
Ulysses [legendary figure] U: 17
Achilles A: 26
Aeolus A: 84
Circe Ci: 557
Cyclops Ci: 1204
Mentor M: 410
Mythology (Greek heroes) M: 982
Odyssey O: 675
Penelope P: 238
Sirens S: 476
Troy (The legendary Troy) T: 454
Ulysses [space probe]
European Space Agency E: 418
Heliosphere (Probing the heliosphere) H: 175
Jupiter (History of Jupiter study) J: 200b
Space exploration (Solar probes) So: 710
Sun (History of modern solar study) So: 986
Ulysses S. Grant Home [Galena]
Illinois (Places to visit) I: 62
Ulysses S. Grant National Historic Site [Missouri]
National Park System (table: National historic sites) N: 52-53
Umami [taste]
Taste T: 50
Umar ibn al-Khattāb [Muslim ruler]
Muhammad (His religious life) M: 910-911
Muslims (Umar) M: 964b
UMass [university] *See* Massachusetts, University of *in this index*
Umayyad dynasty [Arab history]
Arabs (The rise and spread of Islam) A: 589-590
Damascus (History) D: 21
Islamic Empire I: 470
Middle East (The spread of Islam) M: 533
Muslims (The Muslim Empire) M: 964c
World, History of the (The Islamic world) W: 434
Umbel [botany]
Inflorescence I: 268a
Umberto [Italian nobleman]
Savoy S: 166
Umbilical cord [anatomy] U: 18
Baby (The developing baby) B: 4-5 *with diagram*; (Birth) B: 6; (Bathing the baby) B: 10
Childbirth (The birth process) C: 456
Placenta P: 505
Reproduction, Human (Nourishing the embryo) R: 247
Umbilicus [anatomy]
Umbilical cord U: 18
Umbo [zoology]
Shell *diagram on* S: 385
Umbra [light]
Penumbra P: 276 *with diagram*
Shadow S: 341 *with diagrams*
Sunspot So: 991
Umbrella U: 18
Umbrella ant *See* Parasol ant *in this index*
Umbrella bird *See* Umbrellabird *in this index*
Umbrella tent
Tent (Kinds of tents) T: 168
Umbrella tree [tree]
Magnolia M: 63
Umbrellabird U: 18 *with picture*
Umbriel [satellite]
Uranus *picture on* U: 219
Umeki, Miyoshi [Japanese actress]
Motion picture (Best performance by an actress in a supporting role: 1957) M: 862b
Umezu, Yoshijiro [Japanese military leader]
World War II *picture on* W: 492
Umiak [boat]
Inuit (Transportation) I: 354c *with picture*
Umm al Qaywayn [state]
United Arab Emirates U: 43
Umm Nasan [island, Bahrain]
Bahrain (Land and climate) B: 30 *with map*
UMP [political party] *See* Union for a Popular Movement *in this index*
Umpire [sports]
Baseball (Player positions) B: 127; (Umpires) B: 130
Basketball (The officials) B: 145
Cricket *picture on* Ci: 1135; (Umpires) Ci: 1133
Football (The officials) F: 362
Tennis (Officials) T: 165
Umpqua River [Oregon]
Jetty *picture on* J: 116
Umstead, William B. [American political leader]
North Carolina (table) N: 490
UMW *See* United Mine Workers of America *in this index*
UN *See* United Nations *in this index*

"Un bel dì" [aria]
Opera: (*Madama Butterfly*) O: 804-805
UN Chronicle
United Nations (Publications and information services) U: 86
Una [magazine]
Davis, Paulina Wright D: 49
Unabomber [U.S. history]
Terrorism (Terrorist groups and movements) T: 178-179
UNAIDS [program]
AIDS (AIDS around the world) A: 166
Unalachtigo Indians
Delaware Indians D: 113
Unalaska [island, Alaska]
Aleutian Islands A: 340
Unam Sanctam [religious document]
Church and state (History) C: 542
Pope (The peak of papal power) P: 663-664
Roman Catholic Church (Boniface VIII) R: 407
Un-American Activities Committee [U.S.] U: 18
Academic freedom (The 1900's) A: 20
Hiss, Alger *picture on* H: 259
Nixon, Richard Milhous (U.S. representative) N: 430
Unami Indians
Delaware Indians D: 113
Unamuno, Miguel de [Spanish author] U: 19
Spanish literature (The Generation of 1898) So: 762
Unangan *See* Aleuts *in this index*
Unanimous consent agreement
Congress of the United States (Passing a bill) Ci: 945
Senate (Considering legislation) S: 295
UNASUR [organization] *See* Union of South American Nations *in this index*
Unau [animal]
Sloth S: 508b
Unauthorized immigrant
Hispanic Americans (Immigration restrictions and growing discrimination) H: 252
Unbearable Bassington, The [book by Munro]
Munro, Hector Hugh M: 928
Uncas [American Indian chief] U: 19
Connecticut (Early days) Ci: 968
Mohegan Indians M: 688
Uncas [literary figure]
Uncas U: 19
Uncertainty principle [physics]
Heisenberg, Werner H: 167
Motion (The motion of subatomic particles) M: 845
Quantum mechanics (The uncertainty principle) Q: 6
UNCF [organization]
United Negro College Fund U: 97
Uncial [writing]
Paleography P: 103
Type (Classes of type) T: 537
Uncirculated coin
Coin collecting (Starting a coin collection) Ci: 757
Uncle
Family (Family relationships) F: 21
Uncle Dan [nickname]
Beard, Daniel Carter B: 187
Uncle Remus [literary figure]
Harris, Joel Chandler H: 68
Uncle Sam [U.S. nickname] U: 19 *with picture*
New York (Interesting facts) N: 291 *with picture*
Uncle Tom's Cabin [book by Stowe] U: 19
American literature (The sentimental novel) A: 415
Stowe, Harriet Beecher So: 916
United States, History of the (The Compromise of 1850) U: 175
Uncle Tom's Children [book by Wright]
Wright, Richard W: 508
Uncle Vanya [play by Chekhov]
Chekhov, Anton C: 395
UNCLOS [treaty]
Law of the Sea Convention L: 141
Uncommon Women and Others [play by Wasserstein]
Wasserstein, Wendy W: 112
Unconditional Surrender [book by Waugh]
Waugh, Evelyn W: 149
Unconditional Surrender [U.S. history]
Grant, Ulysses S. ("Unconditional Surrender" Grant) G: 314
Unconditioned reflex *See* Reflex action *in this index*
Unconscious [psychology] U: 20
Jung, Carl Gustav (His theories) J: 195
Mental illness (table) M: 405
Mythology (Psychological approaches) M: 990
Oedipus complex O: 676

Psychoanalysis (Psychoanalytic theory) P: 846
Psychology (Psychoanalysis) P: 850
Unconsciousness [disorder]
Fainting F: 6 *with picture*
Persistent vegetative state P: 300f
Unconstitutionality [law] *See* Judicial review *in this index*
Uncontested divorce
Divorce (Fault divorce) D: 253
UNCTAD [organization] *See* United Nations Conference on Trade and Development *in this index*
Unction *See* Anointing of the sick *in this index*
Undefined term [mathematics]
Geometry (Axiomatic system) G: 102
Under Milk Wood [play by Thomas]
Thomas, Dylan T: 261
Under Our Skin: Kids Talk About Race [book by Birdseye]
Literature for children (Information books) L: 361
Under Pressure [book by Herbert]
Herbert, Frank H: 197
Under the Net [book by Murdoch]
Murdoch, Iris M: 930
Under the Volcano [book by Lowry]
Lowry, Malcolm L: 511
Under the Window [book by Greenaway]
Literature for children (The rise of illustration) L: 364
Undercard [boxing]
Boxing (Boxing in the United States) B: 530
Undercarriage [device] *See* Landing gear *in this index*
Undercoater [paint]
Paint (Household paints) P: 23-24
Undercover agent
Police (Criminal intelligence) P: 621
Undercut [logging]
Lumber (Cutting down trees) L: 518
Underdeveloped country [economics] *See* Developing country *in this index*
Underdogs, The [book by Azuela]
Latin American literature (The early 1900's) L: 113
Underfur [zoology]
Fur F: 561 *with picture*
Underglaze [art]
Porcelain *picture on* P: 675; (Painting) P: 676
Undergraduate
Universities and colleges (The student body) U: 208; (Undergraduate study) U: 209
Underground [transportation]
London (Transportation) L: 438 *with picture*
Underground [warfare] U: 20
Guerrilla warfare (Types of guerrilla movements) G: 420
Underground City
Montreal *picture on* M: 770; (Downtown Montreal) M: 769 *with picture*
Underground mine
Coal (Underground mining) Ci: 723 *with diagrams*
Gold (Mining) G: 252
Iron and steel (Mining and processing iron ore) I: 438
Mining (Underground mining methods) M: 576 *with diagram*
Uranium (Mining uranium) U: 215
Underground newspaper
Los Angeles (Communication) L: 465
Underground orchid [plant]
Orchid O: 823
Underground railroad [U.S. history] U: 20 *with map*
Abolition movement A: 13
Civil War, American (The Compromise of 1850) Ci: 616
Douglass, Frederick D: 314
Massachusetts (Places to visit) M: 280
Museum of African American History M: 940
Ohio *picture on* O: 701
Still, William So: 900
Tubman, Harriet T: 480
Underground Railroad, The [book by Still]
Still, William So: 900
Underground railway *See* Subway *in this index*
Underground sequestration
Global warming (Carbon sequestration) G: 232c
Underhair [zoology]
Mammal (Skin and hair) M: 118
Underhand loop [knot]
Knots, hitches, and splices (The language of knots) K: 356
Underhead engine
Gasoline engine (Valve arrangement) G: 64
Underhill, Evelyn [British scholar]
Religion (Later theories) R: 219
Underinsured motorists coverage

Insurance (Automobile insurance) I: 313
Undernutrition
Food (How the body uses food) F: 330
Undershot wheel
Water wheel W: 141
Underspin [tennis]
Tennis (The ball in play) T: 163
Understory [forest]
Forest (The understory) F: 392 *with picture*
Rain forest (Structure and growth) R: 126a
Undervote
Voting machine (Advantages and disadvantages) V: 450
Underwater acoustics [science]
Acoustics A: 29
Underwater archaeology
Archaeology (Working underwater) A: 597 *with picture*
Underwater diving *See* Diving, Underwater *in this index*
Underwater sequestration
Global warming (Carbon sequestration) G: 232c
Underwater Society of America [organization]
Skin diving (History) S: 494
Underway replenishment ship
Navy (Auxiliary ships) N: 78
Navy, United States (Auxiliary ships) N: 84
Underwing moth
Moth (Kinds of moths) M: 840 *with pictures*
Underwood, Cecil H. [American political leader]
West Virginia (table) W: 225
Underwood Tariff Act [1913]
Income tax (History of U.S. income taxes) I: 105
Wilson, Woodrow (Legislative program) W: 322
Underworld
Crime (Organized crime) Ci: 1136
Styx So: 936
Underwriting [finance]
Underwriting U: 21
Underwriting [insurance] U: 21
Insurance (Careers in the industry) I: 315; (The growth of insurance) I: 315
Undesirable discharge
Military discharge M: 543
Undocumented immigrant
Hispanic Americans (Immigration restrictions and growing discrimination) H: 252; (Stricter immigration laws) H: 255
UNDP [program] *See* United Nations Development Programme *in this index*
Undset, Ingvald [Norwegian archaeologist]
Undset, Sigrid U: 21
Undset, Sigrid [Norwegian author] U: 21
Undulant fever *See* Brucellosis *in this index*
Unearned income
Income (Sources of income) I: 101
Unearned increment [real estate]
Single tax S: 473
UNEF [UN] *See* United Nations Emergency Force *in this index*
Unemployment U: 21
African Americans (Social struggles) A: 136s
Automation (Automation and jobs) A: 945
Depression D: 150
Ford, Gerald Rudolph (The economy) F: 377
Great Depression G: 338 *with picture*
Hispanic Americans (Employment) H: 258
Homelessness (Causes and conditions) H: 302
Indian, American (Social and economic progress) I: 180-181
Indian reservation (Description) I: 188-189
Inflation (Fiscal policy) I: 268
New Deal N: 200
North American Free Trade Agreement N: 470
Poverty (Economic factors) P: 723; (Measures to improve job opportunities) P: 724
Recession R: 175
United States, History of the (The rich and the poor) U: 182; (The United States in the Great Depression) U: 192
Works Progress Administration W: 405
Unemployment insurance U: 24
Insurance (Unemployment insurance) I: 314
Poverty (Social welfare programs) P: 725
Social security (Unemployment insurance) So: 555; (Social security in Canada) So: 556
Unemployment (Programs and policies) U: 23
Unemployment Insurance Act [Canada]
Social security (History) So: 556-557
Unemployment rate
Economic indicator E: 57
Unemployment U: 21
Unequal treaties [Chinese history]
China (Clash with the Western powers) C: 502
Japan (Renewed relations with the West) J: 56
UNESCO [UN] U: 24
Huxley, Sir Julian Sorell H: 459

Library (International library programs) **L: 254**
National park (International concern for national parks) **N: 42j**
Wildlife conservation (International cooperation) **W: 305**
Uneven bars [sports]
Gymnastics *picture on* **G: 450**; (Women's events) **G: 449**
Unfinished Symphony [music by Schubert]
Schubert, Franz Peter (His works) **S: 187**
Unfinished Tales [book by Tolkien]
Tolkien, J. R. R. **T: 322**
Unforgiven [film]
Motion picture (Best picture: 1992) **M: 861**
Unfortunate Traveller, The [book by Nashe]
English literature (Elizabethan fiction) **E: 317**
Nashe, Thomas **N: 22**
Unfunded mandate [program]
Local government (Financial difficulties) **L: 408**
State government (State finances) **So: 865**
Ungaretti, Giuseppe [Italian poet]
Italian literature (The 1900's) **I: 495**
Ungraded school *See* Nongraded school *in this index*
Unguja [island, Tanzania] *See* Zanzibar Island *in this index*
Ungulate [zoology] **U: 25** *with picture*
See also the list of Related articles in the Ungulate *article*
Hoof **H: 324**
Mammal (table) **M: 128** *with pictures*
Unhairing [industrial process]
Leather (Preparing the hides) **L: 167**
Unholy Loves [book by Oates]
Oates, Joyce Carol **O: 639**
Uniate Churches [religion] *See* Eastern Catholic Churches *in this index*
Unicameral legislature [government]
Government (Branches of government) **G: 284**
Legislature **L: 184**
Nebraska (Legislature) **N: 110** *with picture*
UNICEF [agency] **U: 26** *with picture*
Child welfare **C: 456**
Halloween (Trick-or-treating) **H: 24-24a**
Hepburn, Audrey **H: 193**
Nobel Prizes (Peace: 1965) **N: 448b**
United Nations (Aid to children) **U: 88** *with picture*
Unicorn [mythology] **U: 26** *with picture*
Unicorn and Other Poems, The [book by Lindbergh]
Lindbergh, Anne Morrow **L: 330**
Unicorn at the Fountain, The [tapestry]
Tapestry *picture on* **T: 39**
Unicycle **U: 26** *with picture*
Unidentified flying object **U: 27**
Area 51 **A: 645**
Extraterrestrial intelligence **E: 458**
Roswell **R: 484**
Unidirectional microphone
Microphone **M: 516**
UNIDO [organization] *See* United Nations Industrial Development Organization *in this index*
Unification Church
Cult (Modern cults) **Ci: 1185**
Unified atomic mass unit [physics]
Atom (Relative atomic mass) **A: 872**
Unified field theory [physics]
Einstein, Albert (Further scientific work) **E: 146b**
Unified Team
Olympic Games (The recent games) **O: 753**
Uniform [clothing]
Air Force, United States *pictures on* **A: 189**
Army, United States *pictures on* **A: 732**
Clothing (Identity) **Ci: 687-688** *with picture*
Girl Scouts (Uniforms) **G: 198**
Marine Corps, United States *pictures on* **M: 207, M: 209**
Navy, United States *pictures on* **N: 86**
Uniform Code of Military Justice [U.S.] **U: 27**
Articles of War **A: 759**
Court-martial **Ci: 1104**
Uniform Commercial Code [law]
Negotiable instrument **N: 119**
Product liability suit **P: 810**
Uniform corrosion
Corrosion **Ci: 1072**
Uniform Crime Reporting Program
Crime (Crime in the United States) **Ci: 1138**
Uniform Crime Reports for the United States [publication]
Federal Bureau of Investigation (Other services) **F: 62**
Uniform Determination of Death Act [1980]
Death (Defining death) **D: 61**
Uniform Partnership Act [U.S. history]
Partnership (Changing or ending a partnership) **P: 188**

Uniform resource locator [computing]
Berners-Lee, Tim **B: 270**
Computer (The World Wide Web) **Ci: 921**
Internet (HTTP) **I: 350d**
Website **W: 176**
Uniform Small Loan Law [1916]
Loan company **L: 404**
Uniform velocity [physics]
Velocity (Types of velocity) **V: 297**
Uniformed Division of the Secret Service
Secret Service, United States **S: 278**
Uniformed Services Retirement System [U.S.]
Pension (Federal pension plans) **P: 272-273**
Uniformitarianism, Principle of [geology]
Archaeology (The 1800's) **A: 599**
Geology (The rock dispute) **G: 98-99**
Hutton, James **H: 459**
Lyell, Sir Charles **L: 533**
Uniformity, Act of [1549]
Elizabeth I (Problems at home and abroad) **E: 238-239**
Unigov [government]
Indianapolis (Government) **I: 222**
Unimak [island, Alaska]
Aleutian Islands **A: 340**
Unincorporated territory
Territory (Territories in the United States) **T: 174**
Virgin Islands, United States (Government) **V: 393**
Uninsured motorists coverage
Insurance (Automobile insurance) **I: 313**
Union [building]
Universities and colleges (Campus) **U: 208**
Union [design]
Flag (table) **F: 193**
Union [labor] *See* Labor union *in this index*
Union [mathematics]
Set theory (Using set theory) **S: 322** *with diagrams*
Union, Act of [1536]
Wales (Union with England) **W: 12**
Union, Act of [1543]
Wales (Union with England) **W: 12**
Union, Act of [1707]
England (The Augustan Age) **E: 309**
Scotland (Union with England) **S: 220**
United Kingdom (History) **U: 67**
Union, Act of [1801]
George III **G: 107**
Grattan, Henry **G: 329**
Ireland (Union with Britain) **I: 426**
Pitt, William, the Younger **P: 500a**
United Kingdom (Troubles with Ireland) **U: 68**
Union, Act of [1840] **U: 27**
Canada, History of (Lord Durham's report) **C: 143-144**
Confederation of Canada (Lord Durham's Report) **Ci: 933**
Ontario (Political unrest) **O: 786**
Rebellions of 1837 (Results) **R: 174**
Union, Articles of
Constitution **Ci: 994**
Union, Labor *See* Labor union *in this index*
Union Bag Company
Paper bag **P: 138**
Union Carbide Corporation
Bhopal disaster **B: 276**
Union Catalog, National [U.S.]
Library (Research libraries) **L: 247**
Union Catalogue, Canadian
Library (Canadian government libraries) **L: 249**
Union Colony [U.S. history]
Greeley, Horace (His political role) **G: 379**
Union Flag *See* Union Jack *in this index*
Union for a Popular Movement [political party]
Chirac, Jacques René **C: 514**
France (Politics) **F: 455**
Sarkozy, Nicolas **S: 126**
Union for National Progress [political party]
Burundi (History) **B: 713-714**
Union Government [Canadian history]
Meighen, Arthur (Entry into public life) **M: 385-386**
Union Institute [former name]
Duke University **D: 380**
Union Internationale de la Marionettes
Puppet (Organizations for puppeteers) **P: 907**
Union Jack [flag] **U: 27**
See also Union Flag *in this index*
Flag *picture on* **F: 195**
Union label [manufacturing]
Labor movement (The first nationwide labor organizations) **L: 9-10**
Union Nationale Party [political party]
Quebec (Politics) **Q: 30**
Trudeau, Pierre Elliott (Entry into public life) **T: 462**
Union of Banana Exporting Countries

Banana (The banana industry) **B: 73-74**
Union of Concerned Scientists [organization]
Kendall, Henry Way **K: 258**
Union of European Football Associations Champions League
Soccer (International competition) **So: 548**
Union of International Motorboating
Motorboat racing **M: 876**
Union of Myanmar *See* Myanmar *in this index*
Union of Needletrades, Industrial and Textile Employees
UNITE HERE **U: 43**
Union of South Africa
Smuts, Jan Christiaan **S: 522**
South Africa (The Union of South Africa) **So: 618**
Union of South American Nations
Latin America (In the early 2000's) **L: 111**
South America (International trade) **So: 637**
Union of Soviet Socialist Republics **U: 28** *with pictures and maps*
See also Russia *in this index; and the list of Related articles in the* Union of Soviet Socialist Republics *article*
Asia (Way of life in North Asia) **A: 789-790**; (The spread of Communism) **A: 807**
Collective farm **C: 775**
Flag *pictures on* **F: 217, F: 218**
Ruble **R: 508**
Soros, George **So: 597**
Arts
Union of Soviet Socialist Republics (The arts) **U: 33**
Ballet (Ballet in Russia) **B: 52-53**
Motion picture (Filmmaking in Europe) **M: 866**
Russian literature **R: 558**
Defense
Arms control (History of arms control) **A: 721-722**
Guided missile (Postwar developments) **G: 427**
Hot line **H: 374a**
North Atlantic Treaty Organization **N: 470**
Nuclear weapon (Nuclear strategy) **N: 600**; (Controlling nuclear weapons) **N: 600**; (The Cold War) **N: 601**
Strategic Arms Limitation Talks **So: 919**
Strategic Arms Reduction Treaty **So: 919**
Submarine (Nuclear submarines) **So: 943**
War (The United Nations) **W: 25**; (The Cold War era) **W: 26**
Warsaw Pact **W: 39**
Government
Union of Soviet Socialist Republics (Government) **U: 29**
Communism (Restrictions on personal freedom) **Ci: 891-892**; (Communism in the Soviet Union) **Ci: 892**; (The Soviet Union under Gorbachev) **Ci: 895**
Concentration camp (Other concentration camps) **Ci: 927**
Democracy (Constitutional government) **D: 121**
Dictatorship **D: 191**
Economics *picture on* **E: 65**; (The organization of economies) **E: 58-59**
Five-year plan **F: 191**
Freedom of assembly (In other countries) **F: 504**
International relations (The collapse of the Soviet Union) **I: 346**
Marx, Karl (Marx's influence) **M: 238**
Politburo **P: 627**
Privatization **P: 808b**
Technology and science
Astronaut (The cosmonauts) **A: 833**
Mir **M: 613**
Space exploration **So: 694** *with pictures*
World history
Union of Soviet Socialist Republics (History) **U: 35** *with pictures*
Afghanistan (The Soviet invasion) **A: 96**
Air force (Air forces in the nuclear age) **A: 186**
Alaska (The Russian era) **A: 301**
Angola (History) **A: 465-466**
Arab-Israeli conflict (The Suez crisis of 1956) **A: 582**
Armenia **A: 718**
Astana **A: 823**
Azerbaijan **A: 996**
Baltic States **B: 65**
Belarus (History) **B: 224b-224c**
Berlin (History) **B: 264**
Berlin Airlift **B: 266**
Bush, George Herbert Walker (U.S-Soviet relations) **B: 721**
Caucasus **C: 317**
China (Break with the Soviet Union) **C: 505**
Cold War **Ci: 762** *with pictures*

Cossacks Ci: 1079
Cuba (Economy) Ci: 1173; (History) Ci: 1175-1178
Cuban missile crisis Ci: 1180
Czechoslovakia (Communist rule) Ci: 1216
Estonia (History) E: 362
Foreign aid (Other countries' aid programs) F: 384-385
Georgia (History) G: 111
Gorbachev, Mikhail Sergeyevich G: 272
Helsinki Accords H: 179
Hungary (History) H: 445-447
International relations (History) I: 345
Inuit (New ways of life) I: 354g
Jews (The Jews today) J: 124
Katyn Massacre K: 249
Kazakhstan (History) K: 251
Kennedy, John Fitzgerald (Arms control) K: 266
Khrushchev, Nikita Sergeyevich K: 308b
Korea, History of (A divided peninsula) K: 367
Korea, North (History) K: 373
Korean War K: 379
Kyrgyzstan (History) K: 400
Latin America (Political circumstances in the early to middle 1900's) L: 109-110
Latvia L: 118
League of Nations (The League in action) L: 160
Lenin, V. I. L: 191; (Death) L: 195
Leningrad, Siege of L: 195
Lithuania (History) L: 389-390
Manchuria (History) M: 134
Minority group (Minority groups in other countries) M: 610
Moldova (History) M: 690a
Moscow M: 823
Olympic Games (The modern games) O: 750-752
Pashtuns P: 190
Poland (History) P: 611-613
Reagan, Ronald Wilson (Foreign affairs) R: 168
Romania R: 416; (Communist control) R: 424-425
Russia (Civil war and the formation of the U.S.S.R.) R: 553; (The breakup of the U.S.S.R.) R: 554
Russian language R: 557
Russian Revolution of 1917 R: 565
Russo-Finnish wars R: 566a
Russo-Turkish wars R: 566b
Serbia (Communist rule) S: 316
Socialism (The Cold War) So: 561
Spanish Civil War (Foreign assistance) So: 756a
Suez crisis So: 959
Tajikistan T: 18
Trudeau, Pierre Elliott (Foreign affairs) T: 463-464
Turkestan (History) T: 501
Turkmenistan T: 514
Ukraine U: 5; (Soviet rule) U: 13
United Nations (The end of the Cold War) U: 92
United States, History of the (The Cold War) U: 195; (The end of the Cold War) U: 196d
Uzbekistan (People) U: 253
Warsaw (History) W: 38-39
Women's movement (In Eastern Europe and the former Soviet republics) W: 387
World, History of the (The rise of Communism and the Cold War) W: 446; (The end of the Cold War) W: 448-448a
World War II pictures on W: 479; (The rise of dictatorships) W: 469; (The invasion of the Soviet Union) W: 477; (The Battle of Stalingrad) W: 481; (The Soviet advance) W: 486; (Civilian life) W: 496; (New power struggles) W: 497
Yugoslavia (Communist rule) Y: 576
Union of Soviet Writers
Russian literature (The period of socialist realism) R: 564
Union of Spiritual Communities for Christ [religious group]
Doukhobors D: 314
Union of Utrecht [1579]
Netherlands (Eighty Years' War) N: 148
Union of Utrecht [1889]
Old Catholic churches O: 740
Union Pacific Railroad
Cowboy (The growth of the cattle industry) Ci: 1111-1112
Credit Mobilier of America Ci: 1125
Omaha (History) O: 756-757
Railroad (Railroad systems) R: 112; (The first transcontinental rail lines) R: 116 with picture
Transcontinental railroad (The United States) T: 370-371
Western frontier life in America (Improvements in

transportation) W: 233
Wyoming (Territorial progress) W: 534
Union Party [Canada]
Borden, Sir Robert Laird (Conscription crisis) B: 486
Union Party [U.S.]
Johnson, Andrew (Vice-President) J: 139
Republican Party (The American Civil War) R: 254
Union republic
Union of Soviet Socialist Republics U: 28
Union security
Labor movement (Arranging contracts) L: 4
Union shop [labor] U: 42
Closed shop Ci: 685
Taft-Hartley Act T: 13
Union Solidarity and Development Party [Myanmar]
Myanmar (Recent developments) M: 970e
Union song
Folk music (Kinds of folk music) F: 321
Union states [U.S. history]
Reconstruction R: 176
Union Station [Kansas City]
Kansas City (History) K: 242-243
Union Station [Los Angeles]
Los Angeles (Transportation) L: 465
Union Station [Washington, D.C.]
Washington, D.C. map on W: 76; (Union Station) W: 71; (Transportation) W: 85
Union Stock Yards [Chicago]
Chicago (The South Side) C: 424-425; (Industry) C: 431-432; (Growth as a city) C: 435
Unionist Party [Northern Ireland]
Bloody Sunday (In Northern Ireland) B: 418
Northern Ireland (The division of Ireland) N: 524
Troubles T: 452
Unions, Labor See Labor union in this index
Unique Forms of Continuity in Space [sculpture by Boccioni]
Sculpture (Form and treatment) S: 230-231 with picture; (Cubism and futurism) S: 257
Unisex style
Hairdressing (The 1900's) H: 12-13
Unison [music]
Piano (The strings) P: 446
Unit [measurement] U: 42
Weights and measures W: 184
Unit cell
Mineral (Mineral crystals) M: 567-570 with diagram
Pyroxene P: 920
Quasicrystal Q: 9
Unit commander
Army, United States (A typical day) A: 734
Unit fraction [mathematics]
Fraction (History) F: 449-450
Unit-letter system
Encyclopedia (Arrangement of content) E: 266
Unit of account
Money M: 704
Unit pricing
Consumer protection (The right to information) Ci: 1018
Unit production cost
Marketing (Pricing) M: 214
Unit rule [U.S. history] U: 42
Unit shop
Industrial arts (Industrial arts courses) I: 242
Unit train
Coal (Shipping coal) Ci: 727 with picture
Railroad (At interchanges) R: 110 with picture
UNITA [political group] See National Union for the Total Independence of Angola in this index
Unitarian Universalist Association [religious group] U: 42
Unitarians [literature]
Homer (Analysts and unitarians) H: 304
Unitarians [religious group] U: 42
Congregationalists Ci: 941
Unitary system [government]
Federalism F: 66
Government (Levels of government) G: 285
Italy (Local government) I: 499
Local government L: 406; (Unitary systems) L: 408
Political party (Organizing the government) P: 632
State government So: 862
Unitas, Johnny [American football player] U: 43
UNITE [labor union]
UNITE HERE U: 43
Unite [money]
Pound P: 721
UNITE HERE [labor union] U: 43
Labor movement (table) L: 8
Unite the Union [labor union]
United Steelworkers U: 204

United Arab Emirates U: 43 with pictures and map
Flag picture on F: 205
Middle East M: 530, picture on M: 533
Television (In the Middle East) T: 116
United Arab Republic U: 46
Egypt (The United Arab Republic) E: 132
Nasser, Gamal Abdel N: 24
Syria (Independence) So: 1075
United Arab States [former name]
United Arab Republic U: 46
United Artists [studio]
Cruise, Tom Ci: 1159
Motion picture (Movies become big business) M: 865-866
United Association of Journeymen and Apprentices of the Plumbing and Pipe Fitting Industry of the United States and Canada
Labor movement (table) L: 8
United Australia Party [political party]
Menzies, Sir Robert Gordon M: 410
United Automobile, Aerospace and Agricultural Implement Workers of America, International Union of See United Automobile Workers in this index
United Automobile Workers [labor union] U: 46
American Federation of Labor and Congress of Industrial Organizations (History) A: 410
Bieber, Owen Frederick B: 295
Labor movement (table) L: 8
Michigan (Depression and recovery) M: 509-511
United Bowmen of Philadelphia
Archery (History) A: 603-604
United Brotherhood of Carpenters and Joiners of America See Carpenters and Joiners of America, United Brotherhood of in this index
United Church of Canada [religious group] U: 46
United Church of Canada Act [1924]
United Church of Canada (Doctrine and organization) U: 46
United Church of Christ [religious group] U: 47
United Colonies of New England
New England Confederation N: 204 with map
United Daughters of the Confederacy
Daughters of the Confederacy, United D: 43
United Democratic Party
Belize (History) B: 238
United Empire Loyalists [American history] U: 47
Canada, History of (The United Empire Loyalists) C: 142
Ontario (Early settlement) O: 784
United Farm Workers of America [labor union] U: 47
American Federation of Labor and Congress of Industrial Organizations (History) A: 410
Chavez, Cesar Estrada C: 389
Huerta, Dolores Fernandez H: 408
Labor movement (table) L: 8; (New groups become unionized) L: 14
United Farm Workers Organizing Committee
Chavez, Cesar Estrada C: 389
United Farm Workers of America U: 47
United Farmers of Alberta
Alberta (A new province) A: 329
United Food and Commercial Workers International Union U: 47
Labor movement (table) L: 8
United Fruit Company
Guatemala (Independence) G: 417
Latin America (Political circumstances in the early to middle 1900's) L: 109-110
United Iraqi Alliance
Iraq (A new government) I: 414a
United Irishmen
Ireland (Union with Britain) I: 426
United Kennel Club U: 47
United Kingdom U: 48 with pictures and map
See also England; Great Britain; Northern Ireland; Scotland; Wales in this index; and the list of Related articles in the United Kingdom article
Art and architecture
United Kingdom (The arts) U: 58
Theater (Britain) T: 247 with picture
Communications and mass media
United Kingdom (Communication) U: 66
British Broadcasting Corporation B: 611
Newspaper (In Europe) N: 386
Postal services (The creation of the Penny Post) P: 706 with picture
Radio (Government regulation of radio) R: 90-91
Television (In Europe) T: 117
Defense
United Kingdom (Armed forces) U: 54
Air force (The British air force) A: 184
Army picture on A: 724; (The British Army) A: 726
Marine (Marine forces of the world) M: 203-204

Navy (Major navies of the world) **N:** 78-79
Education
  United Kingdom (Education) **U:** 56 *with picture*
  Education (Education in the United Kingdom)
    E: 95; (Development of British education)
    E: 101
  Library (Western Europe) **L:** 252; (Britain) **L:** 260
  School (In the United Kingdom) **S:** 183; (The
    development of British schools) **S:** 185
Finance and banking
  Bank (Europe) **B:** 92
  Bankruptcy (In other countries) **B:** 97-98
  Money (History of the pound) **M:** 709
Government
  United Kingdom (Government) **U:** 49 *with
    picture*
  Bill of rights (English Bill of Rights) **B:** 301
  British-Irish Council **B:** 632
  Civil service (Civil service in other lands) **Ci:** 613
  Constitution **Ci:** 995
  Corn Laws **Ci:** 1064
  Democracy (Constitutional government)
    D: 121
  Devolution **D:** 175
  Freedom of assembly (History) **F:** 504; (In other
    countries) **F:** 504
  Government (Constitutional framework) **G:** 283
  House of Commons **H:** 384
  Labour Party **L:** 16
  Law (Public law) **L:** 130-131
  Order in Council **O:** 825
  Parliament (The Parliament of the United
    Kingdom) **P:** 172 *with pictures*
  Police (In other countries) **P:** 623
  Speaker (In the United Kingdom) **So:** 768
  Taxation (Taxation in other countries) **T:** 55
  Territory (Territories in other countries)
    T: 174-175
  UNESCO **U:** 25
  Welfare state **W:** 192
Health and welfare
  Abortion (In other countries) **A:** 16
  Disability (The 1900's) **D:** 221-222
  Housing (Sustainable housing) **H:** 392 *with
    picture*
  Installment plan **I:** 304
  Managed care plans (In other countries) **M:** 131
  Medicine (The United Kingdom) **M:** 366
  Pension (Pensions in other countries) **P:** 273
  Social security (Social security in other
    countries) **So:** 556
  Unemployment (Unemployment throughout
    the world) **U:** 23
  Welfare (Welfare throughout the world) **W:** 191
History
  United Kingdom (History) **U:** 67
  Abolition movement **A:** 12
  Afghanistan (History) **A:** 95
  Africa (European colonization in Africa)
    A: 133-134
  Arabs (Ottoman and European rule) **A:** 590
  Asia (The Western conquest of Asia) **A:** 806
  Bahrain (History) **B:** 30-31
  Belize (History) **B:** 238
  Berlin Airlift **B:** 266
  Brunei (History) **B:** 651
  Canada, History of **C:** 138
  Colonial life in America **Ci:** 787
  Colonialism (History of colonialism) **Ci:** 813-
    814
  Cyprus (History) **Ci:** 1207
  Egypt (British control) **E:** 131; (Independence)
    E: 132
  Emancipation Proclamation (Effects of the
    proclamation) **E:** 254
  Falkland Islands **F:** 15
  French and Indian wars **F:** 511
  Gandhi, Mohandas Karamchand **G:** 25
  Gibraltar **G:** 186
  Great Irish Famine **G:** 343
  Hong Kong **H:** 316
  India (British India) **I:** 130-131
  Indian, American (In Canada) **I:** 178
  Indian wars (Colonial days) **I:** 190
  Indonesia (Indonesia under Sukarno) **I:** 238
  Industrial Revolution **I:** 246
  International relations (From the 1500's to the
    1900's) **I:** 345
  Iraq (British rule) **I:** 413
  Iraq War **I:** 414c
  Ireland (Union with Britain) **I:** 426
  Irish Republican Army **I:** 433
  Jerusalem (British rule) **J:** 101
  Kenya (British rule) **K:** 303
  Laurier, Sir Wilfrid (Relations with the United
    Kingdom) **L:** 126
  League of Nations (The League in action)

  L: 160
  Malaysia (History) **M:** 101
  Malta (History) **M:** 113-114
  Maori **M:** 175
  Money (History of the pound) **M:** 709 *with
    picture*
  Monroe Doctrine (Origins) **M:** 739
  Myanmar (British conquest and rule) **M:** 970d
  Nepal (History) **N:** 126
  New France (The British conquest) **N:** 205
  Nigeria (Independence) **N:** 417 *with picture*;
    (The coming of the Europeans) **N:** 417
  Pacific Islands (Colonial rule) **P:** 12
  Pakistan (Colonialism) **P:** 99
  Palestine (World War I and the Balfour
    Declaration) **P:** 105; (World War II and the
    division of Palestine) **P:** 105
  Prince Edward Island (History) **P:** 791
  Revolution, American **R:** 270
  School (History of Canadian schools) **S:** 184
  Seven Years' War **S:** 328
  Seychelles (History) **S:** 340
  Sikkim (History) **S:** 456
  Slavery (The decline of slavery) **S:** 504
  South Africa (History) **So:** 617-618
  Spanish Civil War (Foreign assistance) **So:** 756a
  Sudan (Egyptian and British control) **So:** 953
  Suez Canal (History) **So:** 958
  Suez crisis **So:** 958
  Tanzania (Colonial rule) **T:** 35
  Terrorism (Recent developments) **T:** 180 *with
    picture*
  Transportation of convicts **T:** 400
  Trimble, David **T:** 445
  Troubles **T:** 452
  Ulster Unionist Party **U:** 15
  United Arab Emirates (History) **U:** 45
  United Arab Republic **U:** 46
  United States, History of the (The English
    and French) **U:** 151; (The movement
    for independence [1754-1783]) **U:** 158;
    (Jefferson's foreign policy) **U:** 164; (The War
    of 1812) **U:** 165
  War of 1812 **W:** 28
  Webster-Ashburton Treaty **W:** 178
  Woman suffrage (United Kingdom) **W:** 381
  World War I **W:** 452
  World War II *picture on* **W:** 475; (The Western
    Desert Campaign) **W:** 476; (The Battle of
    Britain) **W:** 476
  Yemen (History) **Y:** 563
  Zimbabwe (History) **Z:** 592-593
  Zionism (The Balfour Declaration) **Z:** 595
Language and literature
  See also English language; English literature
    in this index
  United Kingdom (Language) **U:** 55
People
  United Kingdom (People) **U:** 54 *with picture*
  Census (Modern censuses) **C:** 350
Recreation and sports
  Boxing (Boxing in the United Kingdom) **B:** 530
  Cricket (History) **Ci:** 1134
  Fox hunting **F:** 442
  National park *picture on* **N:** 42e
  Soccer **So:** 344
Social and cultural life
  Christmas (In England, Ireland, Scotland, and
    Wales) **C:** 530 *with picture*
  Flag *pictures on* **F:** 195, **F:** 207
  Girl Scouts (United Kingdom) **G:** 199 *with
    picture*
  Halloween (Halloween customs and symbols)
    H: 24a; (Halloween around the world) **H:** 24b
  Knighthood, Orders of (Honorary orders)
    K: 347 *with picture*
  Knights and knighthood **K:** 348
  Nobility (In the United Kingdom) **N:** 450
  Penny **P:** 271
  Prince **P:** 781
  Prince of Wales **P:** 794
  Remembrance Day **R:** 229
  Tea (History) **T:** 63-64
  Valentine's Day (In Europe) **V:** 261
Technology and science
  Automobile (Early automobiles) **A:** 964-965
  Medicine (Financing advanced medical care)
    M: 377
  Metric system (Acceptance of the metric
    system) **M:** 441
  Ship (Ships of iron) **S:** 424-425
  Transcontinental railroad (Around the world)
    T: 371

United Kingdom of Great Britain and Ireland
  [British history]
  Grattan, Henry **G:** 329
  Great Irish Famine **G:** 343

  Ireland (Union with Britain) **I:** 426
  Pitt, William, the Younger **P:** 500a
  United Kingdom (Troubles with Ireland) **U:** 68
**United Kingdom of Great Britain and Northern
  Ireland** *See* United Kingdom *in this index*
United Kingdom Overseas Territory
  Commonwealth of Nations (Dependencies)
    Ci: 876
United Malays National Organization [political
  party]
  Malaysia (Political parties) **M:** 98b
United Methodist Church [religious group] **U:** 75
  Methodists **M:** 434; (Social change and division)
    M: 435
United Mine Workers of America U: 75
  Coal (Mineworkers) **Ci:** 728-729
  Labor movement (table) **L:** 8
  Lewis, John L. **L:** 221
  Roosevelt, Theodore (Friend of labor) **R:** 464
  United States, History of the (Theodore
    Roosevelt) **U:** 187
  West Virginia (Labor developments) **W:** 229 *with
    picture*
United National Party [political party]
  Sri Lanka (Government) **So:** 817
United Nations U: 76 *with pictures*
  See also the List of Related articles in the United
    Nations *article*
  Address, Forms of (Foreign officials in the United
    States) **A:** 54
  Adoption (International adoptions) **A:** 66
  AIDS (AIDS around the world) **A:** 166
  Annan, Kofi Atta **A:** 516
  Arafat, Yasir **A:** 591
  Ban Ki-moon **B:** 72
  Census **C:** 346
  Cyprus (History) **Ci:** 1207
  Environmental pollution (Government action)
    E: 335-336
  Flag *picture on* **F:** 216
  Global warming (How scientists study global
    warming) **G:** 232d
  Globalization (Features of globalization) **G:** 233
  Human rights **H:** 428
  Human Rights, Universal Declaration of **H:** 428b
  International Criminal Court **I:** 339
  International Labour Organization **I:** 340
  International Monetary Fund **I:** 343
  Law (Developments in international law) **L:** 137
  Law of the Sea Convention **L:** 141
  Library *picture on* **L:** 250
  MacArthur, Douglas (The Korean War) **M:** 3
  Money laundering **M:** 718
  Ocean (Who owns the ocean?) **O:** 665
  Petroleum (Persian Gulf wars) **P:** 349
  Switzerland (Recent developments) **So:** 1061
  UNESCO **U:** 24
  UNICEF **U:** 26
  Water (The challenge of today) **W:** 132
  World *picture on* **W:** 412a
  World Bank **W:** 450
  Economic and technical assistance
    Famine (Fighting famine) **F:** 26a
    Food supply (Food supply programs) **F:** 350
    United Nations (Economic and technical aid)
      U: 87
    Women's movement (In developing nations)
      W: 387
  Founding
    United Nations (The founding of the UN) **U:** 94
    Dumbarton Oaks **D:** 383
    International relations (Collective security)
      I: 345 *with picture*
    Lie, Trygve **L:** 270
    Roosevelt, Franklin Delano (The United States
      goes to war) **R:** 457
    World War II (Birth of the United Nations)
      W: 498
  International diplomacy
    Aristide, Jean-Bertrand **A:** 662
    Arms control (History of arms control) **A:** 721
    Bosnia-Herzegovina (History) **B:** 492-493
    Bush, George Walker (International affairs)
      B: 722g-722h
    Cambodia (History) **C:** 72-74
    Cold War (The Suez crisis) **Ci:** 766; (Africa)
      Ci: 768
    Congo, Democratic Republic of the (Civil
      disorder) **Ci:** 940c; (Cease-fires and power
      sharing) **Ci:** 940c-940d
    Darfur **D:** 36
    East Timor **E:** 40; (History) **E:** 41
    El Salvador (The 1900's) **E:** 252
    Haiti (History) **H:** 15-17
    Hussein, Saddam **H:** 457
    Indonesia (Indonesia under Sukarno) **I:** 238
    International Court of Justice **I:** 338

International law (History) I: 342
International relations (International
   conferences and organizations) I: 344;
   (History) I: 345 with picture
Iran (Recent developments) I: 406b
Iraq (The Persian Gulf War of 1991) I: 414; (The
   Iraq War) I: 414a
Iraq War (Background to the war) I: 414c
Jerusalem (British rule) J: 101
Korea, History of (A divided peninsula) K: 367
Korean War K: 379
Kosovo (History) K: 384b
Liberia (Recent developments) L: 232
Libya (United Nations sanctions) L: 268
Neutrality (Neutrality today) N: 154
Nobel Prizes (Peace) N: 448
Palestine (World War II and the division of
   Palestine) P: 105-106
Persian Gulf War of 1991 P: 300a
Qadhâfî, Mu'ammar Muhammad al- Q: 2
Sanctions, Economic S: 106
Somalia (History) So: 589
Srebrenica massacre So: 816
Suez Canal (History) So: 958
Truman, Harry S. (The Korean War) T: 471
War (Preventing war) W: 25
World, History of the (The world wars) W: 446
Zimbabwe (History) Z: 592-593
Organization and administration
   United Nations (The General Assembly) U: 78
      with picture; (The Security Council) U: 82;
      (The Secretariat) U: 83; (Other main organs)
      U: 84; (Specialized agencies) U: 85
   War crime (The United Nations and war crimes)
      W: 27; (World War II) W: 27
United Nations Charter [1945]
   Human rights (The development of human
      rights) H: 428-428a
   United Nations U: 76; (The charter) U: 78; (The
      San Francisco Conference) U: 95
United Nations Children's Fund See UNICEF in
   this index
United Nations Commission on Human Rights
   United Nations Human Rights Council U: 97
**United Nations Conference on Environment and
   Development** [1992]
   Environmental impact statement E: 329
   Environmental pollution (Global efforts) E: 336
   United Nations (Controlling the environment)
      U: 89
**United Nations Conference on Trade and
   Development**
   Foreign aid (Technical assistance and relief)
      F: 385
   United Nations (Economic and technical aid)
      U: 87
**United Nations Convention on the Law of the
   Sea** [treaty] See Law of the Sea Convention *in
   this index*
United Nations Day [UN]
   United Nations (The San Francisco Conference)
      U: 95
United Nations Development Programme
   Foreign aid (Technical assistance and relief)
      F: 385
   United Nations *picture on* U: 90; (Economic and
      technical aid) U: 87; (Fighting hunger) U: 89
United Nations Disarmament Conference
   Myrdal, Alva Reimer M: 971
United Nations Disengagement Observer Force
   United Nations (Peacekeeping operations)
      U: 90-91
**United Nations Educational, Scientific, and
   Cultural Organization** See UNESCO *in this index*
United Nations Emergency Force
   United Nations (Peacekeeping operations)
      U: 90-91
United Nations Environment Programme
   Mediterranean Sea (History of the
      Mediterranean) M: 382
   United Nations (Controlling the environment)
      U: 89; (Important dates in UN history) U: 94
United Nations High Commissioner for Refugees
   Nobel Prizes (Peace: 1954) N: 448b; (Peace: 1981)
      N: 448b
   Refugee (Efforts to help refugees) R: 203
   United Nations (Important dates in UN history)
      U: 94
United Nations Human Rights Council U: 97
   United Nations (Human rights) U: 88-89
**United Nations Industrial Development
   Organization** U: 97
   Foreign aid (Technical assistance and relief)
      F: 385
   United Nations (Economic and technical aid)
      U: 87
United Nations Intergovernmental Panel on

Climate Change
   Nobel Prizes (Peace: 2007) N: 449
United Nations Interim Force in Lebanon
   Lebanon (War and terrorism) L: 173
   United Nations (Peacekeeping operations)
      U: 90-91
**United Nations International Children's
   Emergency Fund** See UNICEF *in this index*
**United Nations Relief and Rehabilitation
   Administration**
   United Nations (Aid to refugees) U: 88
   World War II (Displaced persons) W: 497
**United Nations Relief and Works Agency for
   Palestine Refugees in the Middle East**
   United Nations (Aid to refugees) U: 88
United Nations Security Council
   United Nations (The six major UN organs) U: 78
      with diagram; (The Security Council) U: 82
      with picture; (Peacekeeping operations) U: 90;
      (Military actions) U: 91; (The Dumbarton
      Oaks Conference) U: 94; (The San Francisco
      Conference) U: 95
   Bush, George Walker (Iraq) B: 722i
   Dumbarton Oaks D: 383
   International law (After World War II) I: 342
   International relations (International conferences
      and organizations) I: 344
   Persian Gulf War of 1991 (The world's reaction)
      P: 300b
United Nations Truce Supervision Organization
   United Nations (Peacekeeping operations)
      U: 90-91
United Nations Trusteeship Council
   Trust territory T: 474
United Nations University U: 97
United Nations War Crimes Commission
   War crime (World War II) W: 27
United Negro College Fund U: 97
United Neighborhood Centers of America
   Settlement house S: 324
United Paperworkers International Union
   United Steelworkers U: 204
United Parcel Service, Inc. [company] U: 97
   Postal services (Competition and privatization)
      P: 707
United Political Organization National Front
   Yemen (Formation of South Yemen) Y: 563-564
United Presbyterian Church
   Presbyterian Church (U.S.A.) P: 756
United Press International [news agency] U: 97
   Scripps, Edward Wyllis S: 227
United Productions of America [studio]
   Animation (Animation in the mid-1900's) A: 514b
United Provinces of Central America See Central
   America, United Provinces of *in this index*
United Provinces of La Plata [Argentine history]
   Argentina (Road to becoming a nation) A: 656
      with map
United Republic of Tanzania See Tanzania *in this
   index*
United Russia [political party]
   Russia (Politics) R: 531-532
United Self-Defense Forces of Colombia
   Colombia (Civil war) Ci: 784-785
United Service Organizations U: 97
United Services College
   Kipling, Rudyard (Childhood) K: 334
United Soccer Leagues
   Soccer (In North America) So: 548
**United Society of Believers in Christ's Second
   Appearing** [religious group]
   Shakers S: 343
United Somali Congress [political party]
   Somalia (History) So: 589
United Spanish War Veterans
   Veterans' organizations (In the United States)
      V: 344
United States U: 98 *with pictures and maps*
   *See also the list of Related articles in the United
      States article*
Art and architecture
   Ballet (Ballet in the United States) B: 53
   Painting (The 1900's in North America) P: 82
      with pictures
Defense
   See also Air Force, United States; Army, United
      States; Marine Corps, United States; Navy,
      United States *in this index*
   Nuclear weapon (Controlling nuclear weapons)
      N: 600; (Nuclear strategy) N: 600
Government See United States, Government of
   the; United States foreign policy *in this index*
Health and welfare
   Life expectancy L: 280
   Managed care plans (In the United States)
      M: 131
   Medicine (The United States) M: 367;

   (Financing advanced medical care) M: 377
   Poverty (Poverty standards) P: 723
   Red Cross (In the United States) R: 187
   Welfare (Welfare in the United States) W: 190
History See United States, History of the *in this
   index*
Manufacturing
   Aluminum (In the United States) A: 396
   Automobile (Where cars are made) A: 959;
      (History) A: 964
   Cotton (Leading cotton-producing countries)
      Ci: 1089 with map
   Electronics (Manufacturing and sales) E: 214
   Iron and steel (In the United States) I: 448
      with map
   Rubber (The rubber industry) R: 501-502
Natural resources
   Coal (Where coal is found) Ci: 721;
      (Developments in North America) Ci: 731
   Copper (Leading producers) Ci: 1042 with
      diagram
   Energy supply (The 1900's) E: 280
   Forest (Forests of the United States and
      Canada) F: 394 with map
   Water (World distribution of water) W: 122
      with map
Parks and monuments See National park; National
   Park System *in this index*
People
   Adoption (The adoption process) A: 66
   African Americans A: 136b
   Arab Americans A: 580a
   Asian Americans A: 812b
   Capital punishment (History of capital
      punishment) C: 193
   Census *map on* C: 348; (United States
      censuses) C: 346
   Divorce (Grounds for divorce) D: 253; (The
      divorce rate) D: 254-255
   Freedom of religion (In the United States)
      F: 505
   Hispanic Americans H: 244
   Immigration (Immigration to the United States)
      I: 81 *with pictures*
   Income *diagrams on* I: 101
   Income tax (Federal income taxes in the United
      States) I: 104
   Indian, American (Social and economic
      progress) I: 180-181
   Jews (The Jews today) J: 124
   Marriage (Laws concerning marriage) M: 219
   Metropolitan area M: 442
   National income (table) N: 38
   New Year's Day (Modern customs) N: 289
   Population (United States population) P: 673
   Races, Human (The social significance of race)
      R: 59
   School (School systems) S: 182; (The
      development of U.S. schools) S: 183
   Teaching (Becoming a teacher) T: 67
Technology and science
   International Space Station I: 346a
   Metric system (Acceptance of the metric
      system) M: 441
   Telephone (In the United States) T: 99
United States [frigate]
   Navy, United States (The earliest colonial
      warships) N: 85-88; (Undeclared war with
      France) N: 88
United States [ocean liner]
   Ship *picture on* S: 425; (Passenger vessels)
      S: 426
   Virginia (Interesting facts) V: 399
United States, Center of the
   Geographic center of the United States G: 92
   United States *map on* U: 120
United States, Government of the U: 136 *with
   pictures*
   See also Constitution of the United States *in
      this index, and the list of Related articles in the
      United States, Government of the article*
   Arabs (Relations with Europe and the United
      States) A: 590a
   Cabinet (Cabinet of the United States) C: 3
   Canada, Government of (Relations with the
      United States) C: 137
   Civil service (Federal civil service) Ci: 612
   Election (Elections in the United States) E: 158
   Food (Government regulations) F: 335
   Freedom of the Press (In the United States) F: 507
   Great Depression (New government policies)
      G: 342
   Insurance (U.S. government programs) I: 314
   Money (Money in the new United States) M: 712
   North American Free Trade Agreement N: 470
   Pioneer life in America (Government) P: 484
   Territory T: 174

Washington, D.C. **W:** 70
United States, History of the U: 148 *with pictures and maps*
See also the list of Related articles in the United States, History of the article, and the History sections of individual state articles
Abortion (Abortion in the United States) **A:** 15
Afghanistan War **A:** 97
Automobile (History) **A:** 964
Aviation (History of the aviation industry) **A:** 986
Bank (History of U.S. banking) **B:** 92
Berlin Airlift **B:** 266
Black Seminole **B:** 391
Bloody Sunday **B:** 418
China (History) **C:** 499-503
Christianity (Growth in the United States) **C:** 526
Colonialism (Later colonialism) **Ci:** 813-814
Concentration camp (Other concentration camps) **Ci:** 927
Conservation (Conservation in the United States) **Ci:** 985 *with pictures*
Cuba (History) **Ci:** 1175-1176
Environmental pollution (History) **E:** 338
Evangelicalism **E:** 422
Flag (Flags of the United States and Canada) **F:** 208 *with pictures*
Freedom of speech (In the United States) **F:** 506
Fur trade **F:** 564
Gay Nineties **G:** 71
Great Depression **G:** 338
High school (Development of U.S. high schools) **H:** 228
Homestead Act **H:** 304
Immigration (Immigration to the United States) **I:** 81
Indian, American (Indians of the Northeast) **I:** 154; (Indians of the Southeast) **I:** 157; (Indians of the Plains) **I:** 158; (Indians of the Northwest Coast) **I:** 161-162; (Indians of California) **I:** 163; (Indians of the Great Basin) **I:** 164; (Indians of the Plateau) **I:** 165; (Indians of the Southwest) **I:** 166; (The destruction of Indian America) **I:** 177-178; (Indians in the early and mid-1900's) **I:** 178b-179; (Social and economic progress) **I:** 180-181
Industrial Revolution (The United States) **I:** 254
International relations (History) **I:** 345
Iran-contra affair **I:** 406b
Iraq (The Persian Gulf War of 1991) **I:** 414; (The Iraq War) **I:** 414a
Iraq War **I:** 414c
Jews (Jews in America) **J:** 123
Labor movement (Development of the American labor movement) **L:** 9 *with pictures*
Latin America (United States involvement) **L:** 109
Libya (Strained relations with the United States) **L:** 268
Mass production **M:** 269
Mexico (Difficulties of the early republic) **M:** 471
Middle East (History) **M:** 533-534a
Money (History of United States currency) **M:** 710 *with picture*
National park (The early national parks) **N:** 42j
Nicaragua (History) **N:** 398-400
Nuclear weapon (Nuclear strategy) **N:** 600; (Controlling nuclear weapons) **N:** 600; (History) **N:** 601
Pacific Islands (Colonial rule) **P:** 12
Pearl Harbor **P:** 218
Persian Gulf War of 1991 **P:** 300a
Philippines (History) **P:** 379-380
Progressive Era **P:** 813
Prohibition (Prohibition in the United States) **P:** 815
Radicalism (In the United States) **R:** 82
Roaring Twenties **R:** 363 *with pictures*
Roman Catholic Church (In the United States) **R:** 412
Slavery (Slavery in the United States) **S:** 502 *with picture and map*
Social security (History) **So:** 556-557
Suez crisis **So:** 959
Trail of Tears **T:** 367
Transcontinental railroad **T:** 370
UNESCO (History) **U:** 25
Union of Soviet Socialist Republics (History) **U:** 35-37
Vietnam **V:** 364; (History) **V:** 369-371
Virgin Islands, United States (United States rule) **V:** 397
Webster-Ashburton Treaty **W:** 178
Welfare (History) **W:** 191
Whiskey rebellion **W:** 282
Women's movement (The beginnings of women's movements) **W:** 384-385
World, History of the (Imperialism) **W:** 445; (The rise of Communism and the Cold War)

W: 446-448
World War I **W:** 452; (The United States enters the war) **W:** 462
World War II (The United States enters the war) **W:** 478 *with picture*
United States Adopted Name
Drug (Drug names) **D:** 356
United States Air Force See Air Force, United States *in this index*
United States Air Force Academy U: 197 *with pictures*
Colorado (Places to visit) **Ci:** 836 *with picture*
United States Air Force Museum
Ohio (Places to visit) **O:** 690 *with picture*
United States Air Forces in Europe
Air Force, United States (Combat commands) **A:** 193
United States Anti-Doping Agency
Armstrong, Lance **A:** 722
United States Army See Army, United States *in this index*
United States Army Maneuver Center of Excellence
Fort Benning **F:** 411
United States Army War College U: 198
Root, Elihu **R:** 472
United States Auto Club
Automobile racing (Racing organizations) **A:** 976
United States Bank See Bank of the United States *in this index*
United States Botanic Garden [Washington D. C.] See Botanic Garden, United States *in this index*
United States Bowling Congress' Masters Champions
Bowling (table) **B:** 524a
United States budget
Budget (Government budgets) **B:** 671
National budget **N:** 30
United States capitals U: 198
United States Civil Service Commission
Civil service (History) **Ci:** 613
United States Claims Court [law]
Court (Federal courts) **Ci:** 1102
United States Coast Guard See Coast Guard, United States *in this index*
United States Coast Guard Academy U: 199 *with pictures*
Coast Guard, United States (Careers in the Coast Guard) **Ci:** 736; (Training an officer) **Ci:** 736
Connecticut (The early 1900's) **Ci:** 970
United States Conference of Catholic Bishops See Conference of Catholic Bishops, United States *in this index*
United States Congress See Congress of the United States *in this index*
United States Constitution See Constitution of the United States *in this index*
United States Copyright Office
Library (United States government libraries) **L:** 248
United States Fencing Association
Fencing (Fencing organizations) **F:** 71
United States Field Hockey Association
Field hockey (History) **F:** 93
United States Fire Administration
Fire department (The 1900's) **F:** 129
United States flag U: 200
Astronaut *picture on* **A:** 828
Flag (Flags of the United States) **F:** 208 *with pictures*; (Honoring a national flag) **F:** 218 *with pictures*; (Manufacturing flags) **F:** 222 *with pictures*
Freedom of speech (In the United States) **F:** 506-507
Hopkinson, Francis **H:** 334
Jones, John Paul (Navy commission) **J:** 158
Key, Francis Scott **K:** 308
(Manufacturing flags) **F:** 222-223 *with pictures*
Pledge of Allegiance **P:** 572
Ross, Betsy **R:** 481 *with picture*
Ship (Flags and registration) **S:** 412
"Star-Spangled Banner" (How the song came to be written) **So:** 854 *with picture*
United States Food Administration [U.S. history]
Hoover, Herbert Clark (Food administrator) **H:** 328
United States foreign policy
See also Foreign policy *in this index;* sections in the articles on the presidents, such as Truman, Harry S. (Foreign affairs)
Arms control (History of arms control) **A:** 721
Cold War **Ci:** 762
Franklin, Benjamin (Serving in France) **F:** 491
Gay Nineties (A growing world power) **G:** 72
Iran-contra affair **I:** 406b
Monroe Doctrine **M:** 739
Pan-American conferences **P:** 113

Panama (Colombian rule) **P:** 120; (Relations with the United States) **P:** 120
Peace Corps **P:** 207
President of the United States (Foreign policy director) **P:** 765
State, Department of **So:** 859
Taiwan (History) **T:** 17-18
United States, History of the (Problems in foreign affairs) **U:** 163
United States Forest Service See Forest Service *in this index*
United States Gemini Program
National Optical Astronomy Observatories **N:** 42
United States Geological Survey See Geological Survey, United States *in this index*
United States Golf Association
Golf (Beginnings) **G:** 264-266
United States government See United States, Government of the *in this index*
United States Government Manual, The [reference]
A Guide to Research Skills **Research Guide:** 34
United States Handball Association
Handball **H:** 42
United States Hang Gliding Association
Glider (Gliding today) **G:** 231
Hang gliding **H:** 51
United States history See United States, History of the *in this index*
United States Holocaust Memorial Museum [Washington, D. C.] See Holocaust Memorial Museum, United States *in this index*
United States Housing Authority
Housing and Urban Development, Department of (History) **H:** 393
United States Information Agency
Propaganda (After World War II) **P:** 825
Voice of America **V:** 437
United States Information Service
United States Information Agency **U:** 200
United States International Trade Commission
International Trade Commission, United States **I:** 349
United States Jaycees [organization]
Jaycees **J:** 67
United States Marine Band
Marine Corps, United States **M:** 206
United States Marine Corps See Marine Corps, United States *in this index*
United States Marine Corps War Memorial
Washington, D.C. (Marine Corps War Memorial) **W:** 78 *with picture*
United States merchant marine
Merchant marine (Merchant fleets) **M:** 413
Ship (The United States merchant marine) **S:** 412
United States Merchant Marine Academy U: 200 *with pictures*
United States Military Academy U: 201 *with pictures*
New York *picture on* **N:** 297
Thayer, Sylvanus **T:** 231
West Point **W:** 205
United States Mint [Philadelphia]
Money *pictures on* **M:** 711; (Modern coins) **M:** 707; (How money is manufactured) **M:** 714
Pennsylvania (Places to visit) **P:** 245
United States National Museum
National Museum of American History **N:** 41
United States Naval Academy U: 202 *with pictures*
Maryland *picture on* **M:** 249
United States Naval Observatory
Naval Observatory, United States **N:** 70
United States Navy See Navy, United States *in this index*
United States Note [money]
Money (Money in the American Civil War) **M:** 713; (U.S. paper money) **M:** 714
United States Open [tournament] See U.S. Open *in this index*
United States Pacific Command
Camp H. M. Smith **C:** 90
United States Postal Service See Postal Service, United States *in this index*
United States President See President of the United States *in this index*
United States Range [mountains, Nunavut]
Nunavut (Land and resources) **N:** 609 *with map*
United States Reports [magazine]
Supreme Court of the United States (Written opinions) **So:** 999
United States Seal See Great Seal of the United States *in this index*
United States Secret Service See Secret Service, United States *in this index*
United States Senate See Senate, United States *in this index*
United States Shipping Board

Merchant marine (Merchant fleets) **M:** 413
United States Soccer Federation
Soccer (History) **So:** 549
United States Steel Corporation U: 204
Gary **G:** 47
Gary, Elbert Henry **G:** 47
Indiana (The early 1900's) **I:** 216 *with picture*
Iron and steel (In the United States) **I:** 448; (Growth of the steel industry) **I:** 451
Morgan, J. P. **M:** 803
United States Student Association
Student government **So:** 932
United States Supreme Court *See* Supreme Court of the United States *in this index*
United States Tariff Commission
International Trade Commission, United States **I:** 349
United States Tennis Association
Tennis (The spread of tennis) **T:** 165
United States Trade Representative, Office of the
President of the United States (The executive branch) **P:** 764
United States Trotting Association
Harness racing (Regulation) **H:** 64
United States v. Butler [U.S. history]
New Deal (Helping the farmers) **N:** 201
United States v. Richard M. Nixon [U.S. history]
Impeachment (In the United States) **I:** 90-91
United States Weather Bureau *See* Weather Service, National *in this index*
United States Youth Soccer Association
Soccer (In North America) **So:** 548
United Steel, Paper and Forestry, Rubber, Manufacturing, Energy, Allied Industrial and Service Workers International Union *See* United Steelworkers *in this index*
United Steelworkers [labor union] **U:** 204
Iron and steel (In the United States) **I:** 448-449
Labor movement (table) **L:** 8
United Steelworkers of America [labor union]
United Steelworkers **U:** 204
United Technologies Corporation
Aviation (Aircraft manufacturing) **A:** 984
United Transportation Union
Labor movement (table) **L:** 8
Railway brotherhoods **R:** 122
United Way Worldwide [organization] **U:** 204
Unitel Telegram Services
Telegraph (Telegraph service today) **T:** 92
Uniting Church
Australia (Religion) **A:** 904
Unitized body construction
Automobile *diagram on* **A:** 957
Unity [design]
Design (Unity) **D:** 157 *with picture*
Unity [political party]
Russia (Politics) **R:** 531; (The rise of Putin) **R:** 555
Unity [space module]
International Space Station (History) **I:** 346b
Unity of opposites [philosophy]
Heraclitus **H:** 194
Unity Temple [Oak Park, Illinois]
Architecture (Frank Lloyd Wright) **A:** 629-630
UNIVAC [computer]
Computer (The first electronic computers) **Ci:** 924b-924c
Eckert, J. Presper, Jr. **E:** 50
Mauchly, John William **M:** 312
Univalve [zoology] *See* Gastropod *in this index*
Universal [philosophy]
Metaphysics (Universals and particulars) **M:** 430
Universal Automatic Computer *See* UNIVAC *in this index*
Universal bank
Bank (Europe) **B:** 92
Universal constant [physics]
Science (Using logic) **S:** 194
Universal Copyright Convention [1952]
Copyright (International agreements) **Ci:** 1048
Universal Declaration of Human Rights *See* Human Rights, Universal Declaration of *in this index*
Universal gas constant
Gas [physics] (Gas laws) **G:** 48-49
Universal gas law
Gas [physics] (Gas laws) **G:** 48-49
Universal History [book by Ibn Khaldūn]
Ibn Khaldūn **I:** 3
Universal House of Justice [religion]
Bahá'ís **B:** 27
Universal jurisdiction [religion]
Old Catholic churches **O:** 740
Universal language U: 205
Universal motor
Electric motor (Universal motors) **E:** 181
Universal Orlando [Orlando]
Florida (Places to visit) **F:** 252

Universal Postal Congress
Postal Union, Universal **P:** 708
Universal postal service
Postal services **P:** 702
Universal Postal Union *See* Postal Union, Universal *in this index*
Universal priesthood [religion]
Calvin, John (Calvinism) **C:** 71
Universal Product Code
Bar coding **B:** 102
Universal set [mathematics]
Boolean algebra **B:** 475 *with diagram*
Set theory (Kinds of sets) **S:** 321 *with diagram*
Universal Studios [Los Angeles]
Los Angeles (Visitor's guide) **L:** 468 *with picture*
Universal Theater of Criticism [book by Feijoo]
Spanish literature (The 1700's) **So:** 760
Universal Time Coordinated
Chronometer **C:** 539
Universalist Church of America
Unitarian Universalist Association **U:** 42
Unitarians (Organization) **U:** 43
Universe [astronomy] **U:** 205
Astrobiology **A:** 826
Astronomy **A:** 834
Big bang **B:** 296
Cosmic microwave background (CMB) radiation **Ci:** 1075
Cosmology **Ci:** 1077
Earth **E:** 16
Galaxy **G:** 8
Inflation theory **I:** 268a
Matter (Dark matter) **M:** 311
Universe [mathematics]
Public opinion poll (Defining the goals) **P:** 862
Universe in a Nutshell, The [book by Hawking]
Hawking, Stephen William **H:** 113
Universities and colleges U: 206 *with pictures*
See also the list of Related articles in the Universities and Colleges *article*
Academic freedom **A:** 20
Address, Forms of (Other forms) **A:** 54
Adolescent (Education) **A:** 64
Adult education **A:** 68
Affirmative action **A:** 91
Baby boom generation (Effects of the baby boom) **B:** 11
Careers (Colleges and universities) **C:** 217; (Teaching) **C:** 231
College entrance examination **Ci:** 775
Community college **Ci:** 898
Curriculum (Curriculum content) **Ci:** 1197
Education (Higher education) **E:** 92; (The rise of the universities) **E:** 99
History (History in the universities) **H:** 262
Library (College and university libraries) **L:** 246 *with pictures*; (Medieval collections) **L:** 259
Middle Ages (Learning and the arts) **M:** 527
Physical education (University and college programs) **P:** 432
Scholarship (Private colleges and universities) **S:** 178; (State colleges and universities) **S:** 178
School (High schools) **S:** 181
Teaching (Teacher-training programs) **T:** 67
Universities and colleges **U:** 206
Women's movement (In Western societies) **W:** 386
Universities Research Association, Incorporated
Fermi National Accelerator Laboratory **F:** 74
University City [district, Philadelphia]
Philadelphia (Residential districts) **P:** 360
University College
Oxford, University of (History) **O:** 887
University extension
Adult education (History of adult education in the United States) **A:** 69
Correspondence school **Ci:** 1071
University of ...
Universities appear under their key words, as in Chicago, University of
University Park [community]
Dallas (The city) **D:** 11
University Settlement [New York]
Settlement house **S:** 324
University Wits [literary group]
English literature (Elizabethan drama) **E:** 317
Greene, Robert **G:** 382
Nashe, Thomas **N:** 22
UniverSoul Circus
Circus (The circus today) **Ci:** 564-565 *with picture*
Univision [network]
Television (The national networks) **T:** 113
UNIX [operating system]
Computer (Operating system software) **Ci:** 917
Thorvalds, Linus **T:** 345
Unkei [Japanese sculptor]
Sculpture (Japan) **S:** 239 *with picture*

Unknown number
Algebra **A:** 350
Unknown soldier U: 211
Arlington National Cemetery **A:** 717
Unlimited presidency
Government (Presidential democracy) **G:** 285-286
Unmanned aerial vehicle [aircraft] **U:** 212
Aircraft, Military **A:** 201; (Special-mission aircraft) **A:** 203 *with picture*
Aviation (Recent developments) **A:** 991-992
Guided missile (Postwar developments) **G:** 427-428
Helicopter (Recent developments) **H:** 174
Unmyelinated axon [anatomy]
Nervous system (The axon) **N:** 133-134
Unpolarized light [physics]
Light (Electromagnetic waves) **L:** 286
UNRRA [agency] *See* United Nations Relief and Rehabilitation Administration *in this index*
UNRWA [agency]
United Nations (Aid to refugees) **U:** 88
Unsafe at Any Speed [book by Nader]
Automobile (The growth of government regulation) **A:** 971
Consumer protection (Growth of the movement) **Ci:** 1019
Nader, Ralph **N:** 2
Unsanitary landfill
Landfill **L:** 58
Waste disposal (Land disposal) **W:** 113
Unsaturated compound [chemistry]
Hydrogenation **H:** 470
Unsaturated fat
Fat (Structure) **F:** 52
Trans fats **T:** 369
Unsaturated polyester [plastic]
Plastics (table) **P:** 556; (Growth of the plastics industry) **P:** 560
Polyester **P:** 649
Unser, Al, Jr. [American race driver]
Automobile racing (table: Indianapolis 500 winners) **A:** 980
Unser, Al, Sr. [American race driver] **U:** 212
Automobile race driver (table: Indianapolis 500 winners) **A:** 980
Unser, Bobby [American race driver]
Automobile racing (table: Indianapolis 500 winners) **A:** 980
Unsoeld, William F. [American mountain climber]
Mount Everest **M:** 884
Unstable element [physics]
Nuclear energy (Radioactive decay) **N:** 582
Unstable equilibrium [physics]
Gravity, Center of **G:** 334
Unsupported mining
Mining (Underground mining methods) **M:** 576
Unsweetened chocolate
Chocolate (Chocolate products) **C:** 518
Unter den Linden [street, Berlin]
Berlin (The city) **B:** 260
Unterseeboot [ship] *See* U-boat *in this index*
Until I Find You [book by Irving]
Irving, John **I:** 459
Untitled Film Stills [photographs by Sherman]
Sherman, Cindy **S:** 396 *with picture*
Untitled (House) [sculpture by Whiteread]
Whiteread, Rachel **W:** 293
Untouchable [sociology]
Caste **C:** 279
Hinduism (Caste) **H:** 236
India (Social structure) **I:** 116
Untouchables [U.S. history]
Ness, Eliot **N:** 136
Untouchables, The [film]
Connery, Sean **Ci:** 973
UNTSO [UN] *See* United Nations Truce Supervision Organization *in this index*
Unvanquished, The [book by Faulkner]
Faulkner, William **F:** 55
Unveiling of the Statue of Liberty, The [painting by Moran]
Statue of Liberty *picture on* **So:** 877
Unwanted child infanticide [homicide]
Infanticide **I:** 264
Unwanted sound
Noise **N:** 451
Unwin, Mary [friend of]
Cowper, William **Ci:** 1113
Unwritten constitution [government]
United Kingdom (National government) **U:** 49
Up Country [region]
South Carolina **So:** 640, *picture on* **So:** 641
Up from Slavery [book by Washington]
American literature (Nonfiction writers) **A:** 420
Washington, Booker T. **W:** 88
Up quark [physics]

Quark Q: 7
Subatomic particle (Elementary particles) So: 937; (Theoretical research) So: 938
Up the River [film]
Tracy, Spencer T: 362
Upanishads [religious writings] U: 212
India (The Aryans) I: 128
Sanskrit literature (The Vedic period) S: 112
Vedas V: 291
Upazilas [political unit]
Bangladesh (Local government) B: 79
UPC See Universal Product Code *in this index*
Updike, John [American author] U: 212
American literature (Fiction and other prose) A: 424
Updraft
Cloud seeding (Cloud-seeding methods) C: 711
Glider G: 228
Tornado (Moisture) T: 333
Upham, James B. [American author]
Pledge of Allegiance P: 572
Upham, William H. [American political leader]
Wisconsin (table) W: 365
Upholstery [furniture]
Needle *picture on* N: 118
UPI [organization] See United Press International *in this index*
Upland cotton
Cotton (Kinds of cotton) Ci: 1087 *with pictures*
Upland cress [plant]
Cress Ci: 1127
Upland District [region]
Finland (Land regions) *map on* F: 113
Upland plover [bird] See Upland sandpiper *in this index*
Upland rice
Grass (Rice) G: 326
Upland sandpiper [bird] U: 213 *with picture*
Uplift [geology]
Mountain (Forces that shape mountains) M: 894
Uploading [communication]
Internet (Information and media) I: 350-350a
Publishing (Scheduling, printing, and posting) P: 867
Upolu [island, Pacific]
Samoa S: 80 *with map*
Upper Avon [river, England]
Avon, River A: 994
Upper Canada [Canadian history]
Canada, History of (The United Empire Loyalists) C: 142 *with map*; (The struggle for responsible government [1816-1867]) C: 143
Confederation of Canada (Early colonies of Canada) Ci: 933
Ontario (Upper Canada) O: 784; (Political unrest) O: 786
Quebec (The 1700's) Q: 36-37
Rebellions of 1837 (In Upper Canada) R: 173
Union, Act of U: 27
Upper Canada Gazette, or American Oracle
Ontario (Communication) O: 782
Upper Canada Village
Ontario (Places to visit) O: 774
Upper-case letter
Alphabet (Small letters) A: 383
Upper class [sociology]
City (The people) Ci: 578-580
Gay Nineties (The privileges of wealth) G: 71
Industrial Revolution (The middle and upper classes) I: 252
Social class (Class structure) So: 550
Upper Cliffs, The [book by Pereda]
Spanish literature (The 1800's) So: 762
Upper Delaware Scenic and Recreational River
National Park System (table: National parkways and other national parklands) N: 56
Upper East Side [district]
New York City (Manhattan) N: 323-325
Upper Egypt
Egypt, Ancient *map on* E: 136; (Beginnings) E: 142
World, History of the (The Nile Valley) W: 424
Upper Fort Garry [Manitoba]
Winnipeg (History) W: 341
Upper house [government]
Parliament (The House of Lords) P: 173
Upper Lake [lake, Ireland]
Lakes of Killarney L: 49 *with map*
Upper Loop [road]
Yellowstone National Park (Touring Yellowstone) Y: 558 *with map*
Upper Paleolithic Period
Lascaux Cave L: 80
Prehistoric people *picture on* P: 754a; (The Stone Age) P: 751
Upper Peninsula
Michigan *picture on* M: 488; (Land regions)

M: 500 *with map*
Upper Peru
Bolivia (Colonial rule) B: 447
Upper Volta See Burkina Faso *in this index*
Upper West Side [district]
New York City (Manhattan) N: 323-326
Uppercut
Boxing *picture on* B: 528
Uppers [drugs] See Amphetamine *in this index*
Uppsala University
Sweden (Education) So: 1024-1025
Upright piano
Piano (Upright pianos) P: 447 *with picture*
Upright tuba [musical instrument]
Tuba T: 477
Upright vacuum cleaner
Vacuum cleaner V: 258 *with diagram*
Uprising, The [painting by Daumier]
Painting (People) P: 31 *with picture*
Uprising of 2nd May, The [painting by Goya]
Goya, Francisco G: 295
UPS [company] See United Parcel Service, Inc. *in this index*
Upsetting machine
Money (Minting coins) M: 714-715
Upshur, Abel P. [American government official]
Tyler, John (table) T: 534
Upside-down catfish
Fish (Bony fish) F: 147
Upsilon [letter]
U U: 1 *with picture*
V V: 255 *with picture*
W W: 1 *with picture*
Y Y: 547 *with picture*
Upsilon Andromedae [star]
Planet (The first discoveries) P: 513
Upsilon particle [physics]
Hadron H: 5
Meson M: 421
Upslope fog
Fog F: 314 *with diagram*
Upturn
Business cycle B: 728
UPU [agency] See Postal Union, Universal *in this index*
Upwelling [ocean]
Fishing industry (Ocean fisheries) F: 181
Ocean (Circulation) O: 658 *with diagram*
Pacific Ocean (Ocean life) P: 15
Ur [ancient city] U: 213
Abraham A: 16
City *pictures on* Ci: 579
Sumer (History) So: 972
Woolley, Sir Leonard W: 402
Ur-Nammu [king of Ur]
Law (Early developments in the East) L: 133
Ur U: 213
Uracil [biochemistry]
Heredity (How proteins are made) H: 206
RNA R: 357
Ural Mountains [Russia] U: 213
Russia (The Ural Mountains) R: 540 *with map*
Ural River [Russia-Kazakhstan] U: 214
Uralic languages
Language *map on* L: 65; (Other language families) L: 66
Urania [Greek mythology]
Aphrodite A: 565
Muses M: 937
Mythology *picture on* M: 981
Uraninite [mineral]
Pitchblende P: 498
Uranium [element] U: 214 *with picture and map*
Actinide A: 30
Curie, Marie Skłodowska Ci: 1194
Isotope (Separating isotopes) I: 476
Nuclear energy (Nuclear fission) N: 582; (How nuclear energy is produced) N: 584
Nuclear weapon (Fission weapons) N: 596-597
Radiation *diagram on* R: 79; (Naturally radioactive substances) R: 77; (Discovery of radioactivity) R: 81
Radiogeology R: 98
Radium (How radium forms and breaks down) R: 100
Uranium dioxide [chemical]
Nuclear energy (Power reactors) N: 584-585; (Fuel preparation) N: 586
Uranium (Refining and processing uranium ore) U: 215
Uranium hexafluoride [chemical]
Uranium (Refining and processing uranium ore) U: 215
Uranus [Greek mythology] U: 217
Mythology (The Greek creation myth) M: 980
Titans T: 300
Uranus [planet] U: 217 *with pictures*

Astronomy (Finding new objects) A: 848
Herschel, Sir William H: 216
Planet P: 507 *with pictures*
Planetary ring P: 514d
Satellite S: 149; (Satellites of the gas giants) S: 150; (table: Major satellites of the solar system) S: 150b
Space exploration (Probes to Jupiter and beyond) So: 711
Voyager V: 451
Uranyl salts [chemistry]
Uranium (Properties of uranium) U: 214
Urartu [ancient kingdom]
Armenia (History) A: 718b
Urbain, Georges [French chemist]
Lutetium L: 527
Terbium T: 169
Urban I, Saint [pope]
Pope (table) P: 666
Urban II [pope] U: 219
Byzantine Empire (The middle period) B: 754
Crusades (How the Crusades began) Ci: 1159-1160
Urban VI [pope] U: 219
Clement VII Ci: 662
Urban VIII [pope]
Pope (table) P: 666
Urban agglomeration
Metropolitan area (Defining metropolitan areas) M: 442
Urban blight
Conservation (Urban conservation) Ci: 984
Urban center
City (The 100 largest urban centers in the world) Ci: 576
Urban Coalition [organization]
Ford, Henry, II F: 381
Urban design
City planning (Proposals of the plan) Ci: 599-601
Urban Development Action Grants
Urban renewal (History) U: 220
Urban economics
Economics (Fields of economics) E: 64
Urban geography
Conservation (Careers in conservation) Ci: 990
Geography (Human geography) G: 94
Urban homesteading
Urban renewal (History) U: 220
Urban League [organization] U: 219
Jacob, John Edward J: 19
Johnson, Charles Spurgeon J: 142
Price, Hugh Bernard P: 775
Urban legend
Storytelling (Urban legends) So: 914
Urban life
Air pollution A: 197 *with pictures*
Bus B: 714
City Ci: 574 *with pictures*; (City problems) Ci: 590
City planning Ci: 598 *with pictures*; (Criticism of city planning) Ci: 602
Conservation (Urban conservation) Ci: 984
Ghetto (Ghettos today) G: 181
Segregation (Racial segregation in the United States) S: 285
Sewage (Urban sewerage systems) S: 329
Subway So: 949
Transportation (Urban public transportation) T: 393
United States (Urban life) U: 110 *with picture*
United States, History of the (The civil rights movement) U: 196a
Urban park
Park (Kinds of parks) P: 168 *with picture*
Urban planning See City planning *in this index*
Urban redevelopment See Urban renewal *in this index*
Urban renewal U: 220
Baltimore (The 1900's) B: 70
City (Description) Ci: 589
City planning Ci: 598; (Governmental authority) Ci: 601
Conservation (Urban conservation) Ci: 984
Housing and Urban Development, Department of (Functions) H: 393
Philadelphia (Urban renewal) P: 367
Urban Renewal Administration
Urban renewal (History) U: 220
Urban shopping center
Shopping center S: 434
Urban sprawl
Conservation (Urban conservation) Ci: 984
Urban terrorism
Guerrilla warfare (Guerrilla warfare techniques) G: 419
Urbánek, Karel [Czech political leader]
Czechoslovakia (The Velvet Revolution) Ci: 1216
Urbanization [sociology]

City (Population growth) **Ci: 578**
Local government (Population changes) **L: 407**
Population (Urban and rural population) **P: 673**
Urd [Norse mythology]
Norns **N: 456**
Urdu language U: 220
Hindi language **H: 234**
India (New Constitution) **I: 132**
Urea [physiology] **U: 220**
Elimination **E: 236**
Fertilizer (Inorganic fertilizers) **F: 79**
Uremia [disorder] **U: 221**
Nephritis **N: 128**
Uremic poisoning See Uremia in this index
Ureter [anatomy]
Bladder **B: 395** with diagram
Human body (table) **H: 422** with diagram; (The urinary system) **H: 424**
Kidney (How the kidneys produce urine) **K: 311-312** with diagram
Urethra [anatomy]
Bladder **B: 395**
Gonorrhea **G: 268**
Human body (table) **H: 422** with diagram; (The urinary system) **H: 424**
Incontinence **I: 106**
Kidney (How the kidneys produce urine) **K: 311-312** with diagram
Prostate cancer **P: 829**
Prostate gland **P: 830**
Reproduction, Human (The human reproductive system) **R: 244-246** with picture
Vagina **V: 259**
Urethral sphincter [anatomy]
Bladder **B: 395**
Incontinence **I: 106**
Urey, Harold Clayton [American chemist] **U: 221**
Deuterium (Discovery) **D: 172**
Life (Creating simple organic compounds) **L: 279**
Moon (Describing lunar evolution) **M: 794**
Urga [former name]
Ulaanbaatar **U: 14**
Urgel [diocese, Spain]
Andorra (Government) **A: 454**; (History) **A: 455**
Urgel, Count of [Spanish nobleman]
Andorra (History) **A: 455**
Uri [canton]
Switzerland (The struggle for freedom) **So: 1059**
Uri Party [political party]
Korea, South (Recent developments) **K: 378d**
Uriah [Biblical figure]
Hittites (History) **H: 269-270**
Urial [animal]
Sheep (Wild sheep) **S: 380-381**
Uribe Veléz, Alvaro [Colombian political leader]
Colombia (Recent developments) **Ci: 785**
Uric acid [physiology] **U: 221**
Gout **G: 281**
Urine **U: 221**
"Uriel" [poem by Emerson]
Emerson, Ralph Waldo (His poetry) **E: 259**
Urinary bladder See Bladder in this index
Urinary incontinence See Incontinence in this index
Urinary system [anatomy]
Cancer (table) **C: 170**
Circumcision **Ci: 561**
Human body (table) **H: 422** with diagram; (The urinary system) **H: 424**
Urination [physiology]
Elimination **E: 236**
Gonorrhea **G: 268**
Incontinence **I: 106**
Prostate cancer **P: 829**
Urine [physiology] **U: 221**
Bladder **B: 395**
Diuretic **D: 240**
Drug testing **D: 366**
Elimination **E: 236**
Human body (The urinary system) **H: 424**
Incontinence **I: 106**
Kidney **K: 311**
Urique River
Mexico (The Plateau of Mexico) **M: 461-462** with map
Uris, Leon [American author] **U: 221**
URL [computing] See Uniform resource locator in this index
Urology
Medicine (table) **M: 369**
Uropygial gland
Goose (The body of a goose) **G: 270**
Urquhart, Jane [Canadian author]
Canadian literature (Modern English-Canadian fiction) **C: 160**
Urquiza, Justo José de [Argentine political leader]
Argentina (Early independence) **A: 656**

Ursa Major [constellation]
Big and Little Dippers (The Big Dipper) **B: 296**
Ursa Minor [constellation]
Big and Little Dippers (The Little Dipper) **B: 296**
North Star **N: 518**
Ursinus [antipope]
Pope (table) **P: 666**
Ursula, Saint [English religious leader]
Virgin Islands, United States **V: 393**
Ursuline Convent [Quebec]
Quebec (Churches) **Q: 36**
Ursulines [religious group]
Religious life (Religious life in the 1500's and 1600's) **R: 227**
Urticaria [disorder]
Hives **H: 270**
Urubamba River [Peru]
Peru picture on **P: 306**
Uruguay U: 222 with pictures and maps
Uruguay [poem by Gama]
Latin American literature (Colonial literature) **L: 112**
Uruguay River [South America] **U: 229**
Uruguay Round [trade negotiations]
General Agreement on Tariffs and Trade **G: 83**
Uruk [ancient city]
Architecture (Mesopotamian architecture) **A: 611**
Ürümqi [city, China]
Xinjiang **X: 545**
U.S. See United States in this index
U.S. 30 [highway]
Lincoln Highway **L: 327**
U.S. 101 [highway]
California (Places to visit) **C: 46**
U.S. Business Hall of Fame
Junior Achievement **J: 195**
U.S. Nationals
Automobile racing (Drag racing) **A: 978**
U.S. Open [tournament]
Bowling (table) **B: 524a**
Golf (U.S. Open) **G: 265**
Tennis (table: U.S. Open) **T: 166c**
U.S. Ski and Snowboard Hall of Fame [Ishpeming]
Michigan (Places to visit) **M: 498** with picture
U.S. Soccer [organization]
Soccer (Soccer competition) **S: 548**
U.S. Term Limits v. Thornton [U.S. history]
Supreme Court of the United States (table) **So: 1002**
U.S. Trustee System
Bankruptcy (In the United States) **B: 97**
U.S. v. Southeastern Underwriters Association [1868]
Insurance (Greater regulation) **I: 316**
U.S. Women's Open [tournament]
Golf (U.S. Women's Open) **G: 266**
US-VISIT [program]
Homeland Security, Department of (History) **H: 301-302**
U.S.A. See United States in this index
U.S.A. [trilogy by Dos Passos]
American literature (Realist fiction) **A: 422**
Dos Passos, John **D: 311**
USA Boxing [organization]
Boxing (Boxing in the United States) **B: 530**
USA Dance [organization]
Ballroom dancing **B: 63**
USA Freedom Corps [organization] **U: 229**
USA Hockey [organization]
Hockey (Amateur organization) **H: 279**; (Amateur development) **H: 281**
USA PATRIOT Act [2001] See Patriot Act in this index
USA Table Tennis [organization]
Table tennis **T: 3**
USA Today [newspaper] **U: 229**
USA Wrestling [organization]
Wrestling **W: 505**
USAC [organization]
Automobile racing (Racing organizations) **A: 976**
Usage [language]
Dictionary (What a dictionary tells you) **D: 193**
Grammar (Grammar and usage) **G: 304**
USA.gov [website]
Library (United States government libraries) **L: 248-249**
USAID [agency] See Agency for International Development in this index
USC [political group] See United Somali Congress in this index
USC Shoah Foundation Institute for Visual History and Education [organization]
Spielberg, Steven **So: 791**
USCIS [agency] See Citizenship and Immigration Services, United States in this index
USDA See Agriculture, Department of in this index
Useful arts

Art and the arts **A: 745**, picture on **A: 747**
Usery, W. J., Jr. [American government official]
Ford, Gerald Rudolph (table) **F: 378**
Labor, Department of (table) **L: 2**
USFA [agency]
Fire department (The 1900's) **F: 129**
USGA [organization]
Golf (Beginnings) **G: 264-266**
USGS [agency] See Geological Survey, United States in this index
USHA [agency] See United States Housing Authority in this index
Ushant [book by Aiken]
Aiken, Conrad Potter **A: 167**
Usher, John P. [American government official]
Interior, Department of the (table) **I: 325**
Lincoln, Abraham (table) **L: 323**
Usherwood, Edith Hilda [British chemist]
Ingold, Sir Christopher **I: 270**
Ushuaia [Tierra del Fuego]
Argentina (Patagonia) **A: 653**
Tierra del Fuego **T: 283**
Usman dan Fodio [African religious leader]
Nigeria (Early kingdoms) **N: 417**
USO [organization] See United Service Organizations in this index
USPS eBillPay [service]
Postal Service, United States (Electronic services) **P: 700**
U.S.S. Monitor Center [exhibit]
Monitor and Merrimack **M: 724**
Ussher, James [Irish clergyman]
Creationism (Early theories about the Creation) **Ci: 1123**
U.S.S.R. See Union of Soviet Socialist Republics in this index
Ussuri River [Asia]
Cold War (The great blocs split) **Ci: 769**
USTA [organization]
Harness racing (Regulation) **H: 64**
Ustinov, Peter [British actor] **U: 229**
Motion picture (Best performance by an actor in a supporting role: 1960, 1964) **M: 862b**
Usumbura [former name]
Bujumbura **B: 686**
Usury [law] **U: 229**
Interest (Regulation of interest rates) **I: 322**; (History) **I: 323**
USW [labor union] See United Steelworkers in this index
USWA [labor union]
United Steelworkers **U: 204**
USX Corporation See United States Steel Corporation in this index
Utah [state] **U: 230** with pictures and maps
See also the list of Related articles in the Utah article
Mormons (Mormons in Utah) **M: 808-809**
Westward movement in America (Utah) **W: 249**
Young, Brigham **Y: 571**
Utah, University of U: 250
Utah Jazz [team]
Basketball (table) **B: 150**
Malone, Karl **M: 111**
Stockton, John **So: 906**
Utah Lake
Utah (Rivers and lakes) **U: 242** with map
Utah War [1857-1858]
Mormons (The Mormons in Utah) **M: 809**
Utah (Territorial days and statehood) **U: 246-248** with picture
Young, Brigham (Settles in Utah) **Y: 571**
Utamaro Kitagawa [Japanese printmaker] **U: 250**
Japanese print (The master print artists) **J: 63**
Ute Indians U: 250 with picture
Pueblo **P: 870**
Utensil
Colonial life in America (Furnishings) **Ci: 797**
Folk art (Household objects) **F: 318** with pictures
Pioneer life in America (Furniture and household utensils) **P: 481**
Uterine tube [anatomy] See Fallopian tube in this index
Uterus [anatomy] **U: 251**
Baby (Before birth) **B: 4** with diagrams
Cancer (Classification by primary body site) **C: 167-168**; (table) **C: 170**
Cervical cancer **C: 364**
Childbirth **C: 456**
Endometriosis **E: 272**
Hormone replacement therapy **H: 338**
Human body (table) **H: 422** with diagram; (The reproductive system) **H: 425**
Hysterectomy **H: 482**
In vitro fertilization **I: 95**
Menstruation **M: 404** with pictures
Pelvic inflammatory disease **P: 232**

Placenta P: 505
Pregnancy P: 734a; (Changes in the uterus)
P: 734b
Progesterone P: 811
Reproduction, Human (The human reproductive
system) R: 244-245 *with diagram*
Sexuality (Biological factors) S: 337
Tamoxifen T: 23
Uther Pendragon [legendary figure]
Arthur, King A: 757
Round Table (Origin) R: 491
Uthmān [Ottoman sultan] *See* Osman I *in this index*
Uthmān ibn Affān [Muslim ruler]
Muslims (Muhammad) M: 964a; (Uthmān)
M: 964b
Utica [ancient city] U: 251
Utica [New York] U: 251
Utilitarianism [book by Mill]
Mill, John Stuart M: 552
Utilitarianism [philosophy] U: 251
Bentham, Jeremy B: 254
Ethics (Bentham and Mill) E: 367
Hedonism H: 165
Mill, Harriet Taylor M: 552
Mill, James M: 552
Mill, John Stuart M: 552
Philosophy (Ethics and political philosophy)
P: 385; (Philosophy in the 1800's) P: 390
Utility [economics]
Marshall, Alfred M: 228
Value (Value and utility) V: 267
Utility, Public *See* Public utility *in this index*
Utility airports
Airport (General aviation airports) A: 243
Utility Average [investment]
Dow Jones averages D: 315
Utility grade
Beef (Grades of beef) B: 209
Utility meter
Electric meter (Utility meters) E: 177 *with pictures*
Utility patent [law]
Patent P: 194
Utility trailer [vehicle]
Trailer (Utility trailers) T: 367
Utility vacuum cleaner [machine]
Vacuum cleaner V: 258
Uto-Aztecan [language group]
Aztec (Language) A: 1002
Utopia [book by More]
More, Sir Thomas (Character and writings) M: 802
Renaissance (Desiderius Erasmus and Saint
Thomas More) R: 238
Science fiction (Forerunners of science fiction)
S: 205
Utopia U: 252
Utopia [philosophy] U: 252
Nauvoo N: 69
New Harmony N: 228
Owen, Robert (New Harmony) O: 883
Science fiction S: 205
Utopia [ship]
Shipwreck (table: Major shipwrecks) S: 428
Utopian community
Family (Varieties of families) F: 20-21
Utrecht [Netherlands] U: 252
Utrecht, Peace of [1713] U: 252
Acadia A: 21
French and Indian wars (Queen Anne's War)
F: 512
Gibraltar (History) G: 186
New Brunswick (French rivals) N: 196
Newfoundland and Labrador (War with France)
N: 375
Nova Scotia (The struggle in Acadia) N: 568
Succession wars (The War of the Spanish
Succession) S: 950
Utrecht, Union of *See* Union of Utrecht *in this index*
Utricle [anatomy]
Ear (The inner ear) E: 8 *with diagram*
Utrillo, Maurice [French painter] U: 252 *with
picture*
Uttar Pradesh [state, India]
India (Religious and ethnic unrest) I: 134
Uttarakhand [state, India]
India (Recent developments) I: 134
Uttaranchal [state, India]
India (Recent developments) I: 134
Utter, George H. [American political leader]
Rhode Island (table) R: 311
Utzon, Jørn [Danish architect]
Australia (Architecture) A: 906
Denmark (Arts) D: 136
UUP [organization] *See* Ulster Unionist Party *in
this index*
Uvarovite [gem]
Garnet G: 45
Uveal tract [anatomy]

Eye (The uveal tract) E: 460; (Diseases of the
uveal tract) E: 467
Uveitis [disease]
Eye (Diseases of the uveal tract) E: 467
Uvula [anatomy]
Palate P: 101 *with diagram*
Uyghurs [people]
Asia (The people) A: 791
China (Nationalities) C: 481 *with map*
Turkestan (Chinese Turkestan) T: 501
Xinjiang X: 545
Uzbekistan U: 253 *with picture and map*
Flag *picture on* F: 205
Uzbeks [people]
Union of Soviet Socialist Republics (People) U: 31
Uzbekistan (People) U: 253; (History) U: 254

V

V [letter] V: 255 *with pictures*
U U: 1 *with pictures*
W W: 1
V [symbol]
Vanadium V: 269
Volt V: 446
V. [book by Pynchon]
Pynchon, Thomas P: 915
V-1 [weapon]
Guided missile (The first guided missiles) G: 427
World War II (The air war) W: 482-483
V-2 [weapon]
Exploration (Space exploration) E: 451
Guided missile *picture on* G: 428; (The first
guided missiles) G: 427
Rocket (Rockets of the early 1900's) R: 390
Space exploration (The first space rockets)
So: 706 *with picture*
V-8 [engine]
Automobile (The engine block) A: 951-953
Ford, Henry (Industrial accomplishments) F: 380
V-bottom hull
Motorboat racing (Hull designs) M: 876 *with
picture*
V-chip [electronics]
Television (Regulating U.S. television) T: 115-116
V-E Day [World War II] V: 256
V-foil hydrofoil [boat]
Hydrofoil (Surface-piercing hydrofoils) H: 467
V for Victory
Churchill, Sir Winston Leonard Spencer (The
Battle of Britain) C: 548
V-J Day [World War II] V: 256
"V-J Day—Times Square" [photograph]
Eisenstaedt, Alfred *picture on* E: 155
V-Letter and Other Poems [book by Shapiro]
Shapiro, Karl Jay S: 372
V-shaped comb
Chicken (Kinds of chickens) C: 441 *with picture*
V-type engine
Automobile (The engine block) A: 951-953
Gasoline engine (Cylinder arrangement) G: 64
with diagram
VA [department] *See* Veterans Affairs, Department
of *in this index*
Vaal River [South Africa]
South Africa (Rivers) So: 615 *with map*
Transvaal T: 402
Vaalserberg [mountain]
Netherlands (The Southern Uplands) N: 145
with map
Vaca, Álvar Núñez Cabeza de *See* Cabeza de Vaca,
Álvar Núñez *in this index*
Vacaroiu, Nicolae [Romanian political leader]
Romania (Recent developments) R: 426
Vacation Bible school
Religious education (Private education) R: 225
Vaccine [medicine]
AIDS (Treatment) A: 165
Alzheimer's disease (Treatment) A: 399
Bacteria (Protection against harmful bacteria)
B: 20
Bacteriology (Controlling bacterial diseases) B: 22
Cold, Common (Prevention) Ci: 761
Drug (Vaccines) D: 351
Human papillomavirus H: 427
Immune system I: 87; (Active immunity) I: 88a;
(The study of the immune system) I: 88d *with
picture*
Immunization I: 89
Influenza (Prevention and treatment) I: 268b
Jenner, Edward J: 91
Pasteur, Louis (His work in medicine) P: 193
Pet (Preventing illness) P: 322
Poliomyelitis (Prevention of poliomyelitis) P: 626
Salk, Jonas Edward S: 68 *with picture*
Smallpox S: 513
Typhoid fever (Treatment and prevention) T: 539
Virus (Vaccines) V: 428a

Vachon, Louis-Albert [Canadian religious leader]
Cardinal (table: Canadian cardinals) C: 211
Váci Útca [district]
Budapest (Economy) B: 666
Hungary *picture on* H: 441
Vacuole [biology]
Ameba A: 406
Cell *diagram on* C: 329
Paramecium P: 152
Vacuum V: 256 *with picture*
Falling bodies, Law of F: 17 *with diagram*
Vacuum bottle V: 257
Vacuum cleaner V: 257
Vacuum aspiration [surgery]
Abortion (Abortion methods) A: 14
Vacuum bottle [container] V: 256 *with diagram*
Vacuum braille former [machine]
Braille B: 550
Vacuum chamber [machine]
Vacuum (Producing a vacuum) V: 256 *with picture*
Vacuum cleaner V: 257 *with diagrams*
Vacuum cooking
Cooking (Other cooking methods) Ci: 1028
Vacuum energy [physics]
Vacuum (In particle physics) V: 256-257
Vacuum gauge [instrument]
Gauge (Vacuum gauges) G: 69
Vacuum packing
Meat (Kinds of meat) M: 347
Vacuum pan process [industrial process]
Rillieux, Norbert R: 341
Vacuum pump
Pump (Jet pumps) P: 900b
Vacuum tube V: 258 *with diagram*
Communication (The development of
electronics) Ci: 883-884
De Forest, Lee D: 89
Electricity (The electronic age) E: 198 *with picture*
Electronics (Active components) E: 210; (The
development of electronics) E: 215 *with picture*
Hearing aid (History) H: 55
Invention (The early and middle 1900's) I: 363
Transistor T: 372
Vaduz [city, Liechtenstein] V: 259
Liechtenstein L: 272 *with picture*
Vaduz [former region]
Liechtenstein (History) L: 273
Vagabond
Vagrancy V: 260
Vagabondia series [poems by Carman and Hovey]
Carman, Bliss C: 240
Vágar [island]
Faroe Islands F: 47
Vagina [anatomy] V: 259
Baby (Birth) B: 6
Childbirth C: 456
Human body (table) H: 422 *with diagram*; (The
reproductive system) H: 425
Menstruation M: 404
Reproduction, Human (The human reproductive
system) R: 244-245 *with diagram*; (The stages
of labor) R: 249 *with picture*
Sexuality (Biological factors) S: 337
Vaginitis V: 260
Vaginal sponge
Birth control (Methods of birth control) B: 378-
379
Vaginitis [disorder] V: 260
Vagrancy [law] V: 260
Vai [people]
Liberia (People) L: 229
Vail, Alfred [American inventor]
Morse, Samuel Finley Breese (Morse as inventor)
M: 818-819
Vail, Theodore N. [American businessman]
Junior Achievement J: 196
Vailima [estate]
Stevenson, Robert Louis (The South Seas)
So: 897-898 *with picture*
Vair [fur]
Heraldry *picture on* H: 195
Vaisheska [philosophy]
Hinduism (The six schools of philosophy) H: 236
Vaisya [sociology]
Caste C: 279
Hinduism (Caste) H: 236
Vaitupu [island, Pacific]
Tuvalu *map on* T: 527; (Land and climate) T: 528
Vajont Dam [Italy]
Dam (table) D: 18
Vajpayee, Atal Bihari [Indian political leader]
India (Religious and ethnic unrest) I: 134
Vajrayana [religion]
Buddhism (Buddhist schools) B: 669
Valacyclovir [drug]
Cold sore Ci: 761
Valcin, Gerard [Haitian painter]

Latin America *picture on* L: 100
Valdemar II [king of Denmark]
  Flag F: 194
Valdivia, Pedro de [Spanish explorer]
  Chile (Spanish conquest) C: 468
  Latin America *map on* L: 105
Vale of Kashmir [region]
  Kashmir K: 247
"Valediction: Forbidding Mourning, A" [poem by Donne]
  Donne, John (His poetry) D: 308
  Poetry (Imagery) P: 595
Valedictorian [education]
  Graduation G: 297
Valence [chemistry] V: 260
  Atom (Chemical behavior) A: 872
  Chemistry (Development of organic chemistry) C: 404
  Faraday, Michael F: 27
Valencia [Spain] V: 260
Valencia orange [tree]
  Orange (Sweet oranges) O: 815
Valenciennes lace [fabric]
  Lace *picture on* L: 21
Valens [Roman emperor]
  Rome, Ancient (table) R: 447
Valens, Ritchie [American musician]
  Rock music (Setbacks) R: 379
Valentine [book by Sand]
  Sand, George S: 106
Valentine [literary figure]
  Shakespeare, William: (The Two Gentlemen of Verona) S: 356
Valentine [pope]
  Pope (table) P: 666
Valentine, Saint [Christian martyr] V: 260
  Valentine's Day (Beginnings) V: 261
Valentine Richmond History Center [Richmond]
  Virginia (Libraries and museums) V: 402-403
Valentine's Day [custom] V: 261 *with pictures*
Valentine's Day Massacre [1929] *See* Saint Valentine's Day Massacre *in this index*
Valentinian I [Roman emperor] V: 264
Valentinian II [Roman emperor] V: 264
  Rome, Ancient (table) R: 447
  Theodosius I T: 252
Valentinian III [Roman emperor] V: 264
  Attila A: 879
Valentino, Rudolph [American actor] V: 264 *with picture*
  Hairdressing (The 1900's) H: 12-13
Valenzuela, Luisa [Argentine author]
  Novel (The novel today) N: 575
Valera, Eamon de [Irish political leader] *See* De Valera, Eamon *in this index*
Valera, Juan [Spanish author]
  Spanish literature (The 1800's) So: 761-762
Valerian [Roman emperor]
  Gallienus G: 15
  Rome, Ancient (table) R: 447
Valerian [botany] V: 264
Valerius Babrius [Greek author]
  Aesop's fables A: 90
Valero Energy [company]
  Manufacturing (table) M: 170
Valéry, Paul [French poet] V: 265
  French literature (The early years) F: 522
  Symbolism So: 1066
Valery, Violetta [opera character]
  Opera: (Traviata, La) O: 807-808 *with picture*
Valet [servant]
  Knights and knighthood (The squire) K: 348
Valet service
  Hotel H: 376
Valette, Jean Parisot de la [Maltese religious leader]
  Malta (History) M: 113-114
Valhalla [Norse mythology] V: 265
  Mythology (Mythical places) M: 975; (The construction of the world) M: 986
  Odin O: 674
  Vikings (Religion) V: 380
Validity
  Deductive method D: 81
  Logic L: 425
  Philosophy (Logic) P: 384
Valiente, Doreen [British author]
  Witchcraft (Witchcraft in modern times) W: 373
Valira River
  Andorra (Land) A: 455
VALIS [book by Dick]
  Dick, Philip K. D: 187
Valium [medication]
  Benzodiazepine B: 256
  Drug abuse (table: Some commonly abused drugs) D: 363
  Tranquilizer T: 369

Valjean, Jean [literary figure]
  Hugo, Victor (His works) H: 410
Valkyrie [opera] *See* Walküre, Die *in this index*
Vallandigham, Clement Laird [American political leader] V: 265
  Ohio (The Civil War) O: 702
Valle, José Cecilio Del [Central American patriot] V: 265
Valle del General [region]
  Costa Rica (The Central Highlands) Ci: 1082
Valle-Inclán, Ramón del [Spanish author]
  Spanish literature (The Generation of 1898) So: 762
Valle y Caviedes, Juan del [Peruvian author]
  Latin American literature (Colonial literature) L: 112
Vallejo, Antonio Buero [Spanish dramatist]
  Spanish literature (Spanish literature today) So: 763
Vallejo, César [Peruvian author]
  Latin American literature (The early 1900's) L: 113
Valles [region]
  Bolivia (The Valles) B: 445 *with map*
Valles Marineris [natural feature]
  Mars (Canyons) M: 226 *with picture*
Valletta [Malta] V: 265
  Malta M: 113 *with picture*
Valley [natural feature] V: 265
  Mars (Channels, valleys, and gullies) M: 226 *with picture*
  Ocean (The land at the bottom of the sea) O: 659-661 *with map*
Valley Forge [Pennsylvania] V: 266 *with picture*
  Revolution, American (Valley Forge) R: 283 *with picture*
  Washington, George (Shortage of supplies) W: 99 *with picture*
Valley Forge National Historical Park [Pennsylvania]
  National Park System (table: National historical parks) N: 57
  Valley Forge (Valley Forge National Historical Park) V: 266
Valley glacier
  Glacier (Kinds of glaciers) G: 202
  Ice formation I: 9
Valley Island
  Hawaii (Maui) H: 100
Valley network [natural feature]
  Mars (Channels, valleys, and gullies) M: 226
Valley of Fire State Park
  Nevada (Places to visit) N: 164 *with picture*
Valley of Mexico
  Aztec (The Aztec empire) A: 999
Valley of Ten Thousand Smokes
  Alaska (Land regions) A: 292-294
  Katmai National Park K: 249
Valley of the Fallen [mausoleum]
  Spain (Architecture) So: 738
Valley of the Kings [region, Egypt] V: 266
  Egypt, Ancient (Learning about ancient Egypt) E: 144
  Thebes T: 251
Valley of the Tombs of the Kings *See* Valley of the Kings *in this index*
Valley of the Vine *See* Barossa Valley *in this index*
Valley of Virginia
  Virginia (Land regions) V: 410
Valli, Frankie [American singer] V: 266 *with picture*
Valmiki [Indian poet]
  Ramayana R: 132
Valmy, Battle of [1792]
  French Revolution (The Legislative Assembly) F: 526
Valois [French history] V: 267
  France (A period of wars) F: 473
Valparaíso [Chile] V: 267
  Chile *picture on* C: 462
Valproic acid [drug]
  Anticonvulsant A: 553
Valse, La [music by Ravel]
  Ravel, Maurice R: 151
Value [belief]
  Business (Moral regulations) B: 727
  Careers (Values) C: 215
  Censorship (Moral censorship) C: 345
  Character education C: 377
  Clothing (Cultural beliefs and values) Ci: 691
  Debate (Types of resolutions) D: 64
  Ethics E: 365
  Law (Early developments in the East) L: 133
  Moral education M: 799; (Methods of moral education) M: 799; (Value analysis) M: 800
  Philosophy (Ethics and political philosophy) P: 385
  Religion (A code of conduct) R: 217
Value [color]

Color (The Munsell Color System) Ci: 824 *with diagrams*
Value [economics] V: 267
Value added by manufacture [economics]
  Gross domestic product (Another way to measure GDP) G: 399
  Input-output analysis (Input-output tables) I: 276
Value-added reseller [sales method]
  Computer (Sales) Ci: 924-924a
Value-added tax V: 268
  Sales tax S: 66
  Taxation (Taxes on transactions) T: 53
Value contention
  Debate (Types of resolutions) D: 64
Value fund
  Mutual fund M: 969
Valve [anatomy]
  Heart H: 132; (Chambers, valves, and inner lining) H: 133 *with pictures*; (The work of the heart) H: 135 *with diagram*; (Blockage of blood flow) H: 141; (Valve disease) H: 141
Valve [mechanics]
  Gasoline engine *picture on* G: 63; (The valves) G: 64 *with diagrams*; (Valve arrangement) G: 64
Valve [zoology]
  Clam (The body of a clam) Ci: 637
  Mussel M: 966
  Oyster (Shell) O: 890
Valve-in-head engine [mechanics]
  Buick, David Dunbar B: 681
Valve seat
  Plumbing (How faucets work) P: 579 *with diagram*
Valve set pressure
  Safety valve S: 17
Vampire [legendary being] V: 268
  Dracula D: 317
  Meyer, Stephenie M: 479
  Transylvania T: 402
Vampire bat [animal] V: 268 *with picture*
  Bat (Vampire bats) B: 161
Van [vehicle]
  Recreational vehicle (Van conversions) R: 184
  Truck T: 456, *pictures on* T: 459
Van ...
  Names beginning with Van are alphabetized as single words or under their key word. Van Eyck, Jan appears after Vandal, and Beethoven, Ludwig van appears after Beet yellows
Van conversion
  Recreational vehicle *picture on* R: 183; (Van conversions) R: 184
Vanadium [element] V: 268
Vanadium oxytrichloride [chemical]
  Vanadium V: 268
Vanadium pentoxide [chemical]
  Vanadium V: 268
Van Alen, James I. [American lawyer]
  Van Buren, Martin (Childhood and education) V: 270-271
Van Allen, James Alfred [American physicist] V: 269
Van Allen belts [physics] V: 269
  Magnetic storm M: 57
Van Allsburg, Chris [American author/artist] V: 269
  Literature for children *picture on* L: 364
  Regina Medal (table: 1993) R: 206
Vanbrugh, Sir John [English author] V: 269
  Architecture (Baroque architecture) A: 622
Van Buren, Abigail [American journalist] V: 269 *with portrait*
  Landers, Ann L: 57
Van Buren, Abraham [father of]
  Van Buren, Martin (Childhood and education) V: 270
Van Buren, Abraham [son of]
  Van Buren, Martin (Van Buren's family) V: 271
Van Buren, Angelica Singleton [daughter-in-law of]
  Van Buren, Martin (Life in the White House) V: 272 *with portrait*
  White House hostesses W: 291
Van Buren, Hannah Hoes [wife of]
  Van Buren, Martin (Van Buren's family) V: 271
Van Buren, John [American political leader]
  Van Buren, Martin (Van Buren's family) V: 271
Van Buren, Maria Hoes [mother of]
  Van Buren, Martin (Childhood and education) V: 270
Van Buren, Martin [U.S. president] V: 270 *with pictures*
  Free Soil Party F: 499
  Harrison, William Henry (Elections of 1836 and 1840) H: 75
  Jackson, Andrew (The spoils system) J: 10
  Kitchen Cabinet K: 337

Polk, James Knox (Election of 1844) **P:** 642
United States, History of the (Politics after Jackson) **U:** 171
Vance, Cyrus Roberts [American government official] **V:** 273
Vance, Dazzy [American baseball player]
Baseball (table: Hall of Fame) **B:** 134b
Vance, Joseph [American political leader]
Ohio (table) **O:** 699
Vance, Philo [literary figure]
Detective story (The pattern) **D:** 162
Vance, Zebulon Baird [American political leader] **V:** 273
North Carolina (table) **N:** 490
Vancomycin [medication]
Antibiotic (Antibacterial antibiotics) **A:** 550; (table) **A:** 551
Vancouver [British Columbia] **V:** 274 *with pictures and map*
British Columbia *picture on* **B:** 613; (Population) **B:** 616; (Visitor's guide) **B:** 620 *with pictures*; (table: Average monthly weather) **B:** 624
Canada *pictures on* **C:** 98, **C:** 105
Park *picture on* **P:** 168
Vancouver [Washington] **V:** 277
Vancouver, George [British explorer] **V:** 277 *with portrait*
Puget, Peter **P:** 886
Washington (Discovery and exploration) **W:** 66
Vancouver, Museum of
Vancouver (Museums) **V:** 276
Vancouver Aquarium
Vancouver (Parks) **V:** 276
Vancouver Canucks
Hockey (table: National Hockey League) **H:** 281
Vancouver (Sports) **V:** 276
Vancouver Foundation V: 278
Foundation (table) **F:** 430
Vancouver Foundation Act [1950]
Vancouver Foundation **V:** 278
Vancouver Island [British Columbia] **V:** 278 *with map*
British Columbia (Land regions) **B:** 622 *with map*
Vancouver Range [mountains, British Columbia]
Vancouver Island (Location, size, and features) **V:** 278
Vandalia [colony]
West Virginia (White settlement) **W:** 226
Vandalia [Illinois]
Illinois (Early statehood) **I:** 74
National Road **N:** 60
Vandalism [crime] **V:** 278
Crime (table) **Ci:** 1137
Vandals [people] **V:** 279
Rome, Ancient (The decline of the empire) **R:** 447-448
Van de Graaff, Robert Jemison [American physicist] **V:** 279
Van de Graaff generator [machine]
Particle accelerator (How accelerators work) **P:** 184
Van de Graaff, Robert Jemison **V:** 279
Vandenberg, Hoyt Sanford [American military leader]
Vandenberg Air Force Base **V:** 279
Vandenberg Air Force Base [California] **V:** 279
Vandenberg Center
Grand Rapids **G:** 309
Vanderbilt, Cornelius [American businessman] **V:** 279
Vanderbilt, Cornelius, II [American businessman]
Rhode Island *picture on* **R:** 296; (Places to visit) **R:** 304
Vanderbilt, William Harry [American political leader]
Rhode Island (table) **R:** 311
Vanderbilt Cup races
Automobile racing (Growth of organized automobile racing) **A:** 979
Vanderbilt Mansion National Historic Site [Hyde Park]
National Park System (table: National historic sites) **N:** 52-54
Vanderbilt University V: 279
Tennessee *picture on* **T:** 135
Vanderbilt, Cornelius **V:** 279
Van der Donck, Adriaen [Dutch colonist]
Yonkers **Y:** 568
Van der Goes, Hugo [Flemish painter] **V:** 280 *with picture*
Vanderhaeghe, Guy [Canadian author]
Canadian literature (Modern English-Canadian fiction) **C:** 160
Vanderhoof, John D. [American political leader]
Colorado (table) **Ci:** 844
Van der Meer, Simon [Dutch physicist]
Nobel Prizes (Physics: 1984) **N:** 442

Vandermeersch, Bernard [French anthropologist]
Prehistoric people (table) **P:** 754
Van der Noot, Henri [Belgian lawyer]
Belgium (The Brabant Revolution) **B:** 233
Vanderpool, Clare [American author]
Newbery Medal (table) **N:** 359
Van der Waals forces [physics]
Materials (Physical bonds) **M:** 301
Molecule (Molecules and matter) **M:** 693
Van der Weyden, Rogier [Flemish painter] **V:** 280 *with picture*
Painting (The northern Renaissance) **P:** 57 *with picture*
Vander Zalm, William N. [Canadian political leader]
British Columbia (table) **B:** 628
Campbell, Kim (Provincial legislator) **C:** 90c
Van Devanter, Willis [American jurist]
Supreme Court of the United States (table) **So:** 1000
Van Diemen's Land [Tasmanian history]
Australia (European explorations) **A:** 920
Tasmania (History) **T:** 49
Van Dine, S. S. [American author] **V:** 280
Vandiver, Ernest [American political leader]
Georgia (table) **G:** 130
Vandiver, William Duncan [American political leader]
Missouri **M:** 651
Van Doren, Carl [American author] **V:** 280
Van Doren, Mark [American author] **V:** 281
Van Dorn, Earl [Confederate general]
Civil War, American (The war in the West--1862-1864) **Ci:** 628
Van Drebbel, Cornelius [Dutch scientist]
Submarine (History of submarines) **Su:** 942
Van Druten, John William [British dramatist] **V:** 281
VanDusen, W. J. [Canadian businessman]
Vancouver Foundation **V:** 278
Van Duyn, Mona [American poet]
Poet laureate (table: Poets laureate of the United States) **P:** 590
Van Dyck, Sir Anthony [Flemish-born painter] **V:** 281 *with picture*
Clothing *pictures on* **Ci:** 702, **Ci:** 703
Painting (Baroque) **P:** 58-61 *with picture*
Vandyke
Beard **B:** 186
Van Dyke, Nicholas [American political leader]
Delaware (table) **D:** 109
Vane [feather]
Archery (Arrows) **A:** 602 *with diagram*
Feather (Kinds and parts of feathers) **F:** 59 *with diagram*
Vane, John Robert [British chemist]
Nobel Prizes (Physiology or medicine: 1982) **N:** 446
Vänern, Lake
Sweden (The Swedish Lowland) **So:** 1028 *with map*
Vanessa [opera by Barber]
Barber, Samuel **B:** 106
Van Eyck, Hubert [brother of]
Van Eyck, Jan **V:** 282
Van Eyck, Jan [Flemish painter] **V:** 282 *with picture*
Jerome, Saint *picture on* **J:** 93
Painting (Religious subjects) **P:** 32; (The northern Renaissance) **P:** 57
Renaissance *picture on* **R:** 238
Van Fleet, James Alward [American general]
Korean War (The "Battle for the Hills") **K:** 382
Van Fleet, Jo [American actress]
Motion picture (Best performance by an actress in a supporting role: 1955) **M:** 862b
Vanga [bird]
Bird (Birds of Africa) **B:** 344h *with picture*
Van Gennep, Arnold [French anthropologist]
Rite of passage **R:** 350
Van Gogh, Vincent [Dutch painter] **V:** 282 *with portrait*
Derain, André **D:** 152
Expressionism **E:** 455
Letter writing *picture on* **L:** 209
Painting (Texture) **P:** 35 *with picture*; (Postimpressionism) **P:** 75
Vlaminck, Maurice de **V:** 433
Vanguard 1 [spacecraft]
Space exploration (The space race begins) **So:** 707-708
Vanhanen, Matti [Finnish political leader]
Finland (Recent developments) **F:** 118
Van Hise, Charles [American educator]
Wisconsin, University of (History) **W:** 369
Vanier, Georges-Philias [Canadian statesman] **V:** 283
Diefenbaker, John George **D:** 196

Vanier Cup
Football (Canadian football) **F:** 364
Vanilla [plant] **V:** 283
Vanilla extract
Vanilla **V:** 283
Vanir [Norse mythology]
Frey **F:** 531
Freyja **F:** 531
Vanishing point [art]
Perspective **P:** 304 *with pictures*
Vanity Fair [book by Thackeray]
English literature (Early Victorian literature) **E:** 321
Thackeray, William Makepeace (Later career) **T:** 220
Vanity Fair [magazine]
Magazine (Magazines in the 1900's) **M:** 45
Vanity press [publishing]
Publishing (Self-publishing) **P:** 869
Van Lang [kingdom]
Vietnam (History) **V:** 369
Van Lawick-Goodall, Jane [British zoologist] *See* Goodall, Jane *in this index*
Van Leeuwenhoek, Anton *See* Leeuwenhoek, Anton van *in this index*
Van Leyden, Lucas [Dutch artist] **V:** 283 *with picture*
Van Loon, Hendrik Willem [American author]
Literature for children (Children's nonfiction) **L:** 365
Newbery Medal (table) **N:** 359
Van Ness, Cornelius [American political leader]
Vermont (table) **V:** 333
Vanoise National Park [France]
National park (table) **N:** 42f
Van Rensselaer, Kiliaen [Dutch businessman] **V:** 284
Antirenters **A:** 558
New York (Exploration and settlement) **N:** 314
Van Rijn, Rembrandt Harmenszoon [Dutch artist] *See* Rembrandt *in this index*
Van Roosevelt, Klaes Martensen [American colonist]
Roosevelt, Theodore (Boyhood and education) **R:** 460-461
Van Sant, Samuel R. [American political leader]
Minnesota (table) **M:** 602
Van't Hoff, Jacobus Henricus [Dutch chemist]
Chemistry (Development of physical chemistry) **C:** 404
Nobel Prizes (Chemistry: 1901) **N:** 442
Van Trump, P.B. [American mountain climber]
Mount Rainier **M:** 887
Vanua Levu [island]
Fiji **F:** 97 *with map*
Vanuatu V: 284 *with picture and map*
Flag *picture on* **F:** 205
Van Vleck, John Hasbrouck [American physicist]
Nobel Prizes (Physics: 1977) **N:** 441
Van Wagoner, Murray D. [American political leader]
Michigan (table) **M:** 507
Van Winkle, Rip [literary figure] *See* Rip Van Winkle *in this index*
Van Zandt, Charles C. [American political leader]
Rhode Island (table) **R:** 311
Vanzetti, Bartolomeo [American public figure]
Sacco-Vanzetti case **S:** 4
Vapor [physics] **V:** 285
Boiling point **B:** 439
Combustion **Ci:** 867
Condensation **Ci:** 929
Evaporation **E:** 422
Steam **So:** 880
Water (The properties of water) **W:** 129
Vapor barrier
Insulation (In buildings) **I:** 306
Vapor capacity [meteorology]
Air (Moisture in the air) **A:** 170
Vapor heating
Heating (Heat pumps) **H:** 157
Vapor lock V: 285
Fuel injection **F:** 552
Gasoline (Gasoline blends) **G:** 61
Vapor pressure
Boiling point **B:** 439
Evaporation (How evaporation occurs) **E:** 422-423
Vapor recovery unit
Petroleum (Separation) **P:** 343
Vapor trail
Contrail **Ci:** 1023
Vaporization [physics]
Distillation **D:** 238
Evaporation **E:** 422
Fallout (How fallout is produced) **F:** 18
Vapor **V:** 285
Vapor lock **V:** 285

Vaquero
Cowboy (A cowboy's gear) **Ci: 1108**
Western frontier life in America (Ranching) **W: 236**
Vaquero of the Brush Country, A [book by Dobie]
Dobie, J. Frank **D: 259**
Vaquita [sea animal]
Porpoise **P: 679** *with picture*
Vara [lance]
Bullfighting (The order of the bullfight) **B: 696** *with picture*
Varanasi [India] **V: 285**
Asia *picture on* **A: 782**
India *picture on* **I: 124**
Varangian Russes [people]
Russia (Early days) **R: 547**
Vardaman, James Kimble [American political leader]
Mississippi (table) **M: 640**
Vardar [river, Macedonia]
Macedonia [country] (Land and climate) **M: 12** *with map*
Varennes, Pierre Gaultier de *See* La Vérendrye, Pierre Gaultier de Varrennes, Sieur de *in this index*
Varenyky [food]
Ukraine (Food and drink) **U: 8**
Varèse, Edgard [French-American composer] **V: 285**
Vargas, Getúlio Dornellas [Brazilian political leader]
Brazil (Birth of the republic) **B: 585**; (Return to constitutional government) **B: 585**; (The Vargas dictatorship) **B: 585**
Latin America (Political circumstances in the early to middle 1900's) **L: 109**
São Paulo (History) **S: 119**
Vargas Llosa, Mario [Peruvian author] **V: 285**
Latin American literature (The "Boom") **L: 114**
Peru (The arts) **P: 311**
Vargueno
Furniture (Spain) **F: 573** *with picture*
Variable [mathematics]
Algebra (Sets and variables) **A: 350**
Variable annuity
Insurance (Annuities) **I: 311**
Variable-area sound recording
Motion picture (The sound track) **M: 857-858**
Variable length coding [electronics]
Data compression **D: 41**
Variable-rate mortgage [economics]
Mortgage **M: 821**
Variable resistor [electrical component]
Electricity (Controlling electric current) **E: 195**
Variable star [astronomy]
Hogg, Helen Sawyer **H: 288**
Payne-Gaposchkin, Cecilia Helena **P: 204**
Variable-sweep wing
Aircraft, Military (Fighters) **A: 203**
Variable transformer [electricity]
Transformer **T: 372**
Variable velocity [physics]
Velocity (Types of velocity) **V: 297**
Variance [statistics]
Statistics (Probability) **So: 868-869**
Variation [compass]
Compass (Variation) **Ci: 902b**
Variation [folklore]
Folklore (Characteristics of folklore) **F: 323**
Variation [genetics]
Races, Human (Alternatives to racial classification) **R: 55**
Variation [music] **V: 286**
Classical music (Variation) **Ci: 644**
Varicella [disease] *See* Chickenpox *in this index*
Varicella zoster [virus]
Chickenpox **C: 446**
Varicose vein [disorder] **V: 286**
Vein **V: 295**
Varietal [wine]
Wine (Where wine comes from) **W: 336-337**
Variety [biology]
Classification, Scientific (Groups in classification) **Ci: 655-656**
Variety Lights [film]
Fellini, Federico **F: 68**
Variety meat [food]
Meat (Kinds of meat) **M: 347**
Meat packing (By-products) **M: 352**
Variety show [theater]
Vaudeville **V: 290**
Variola major [virus]
Smallpox **S: 513**
Variometer [instrument]
Glider (Flying a glider) **G: 229**
Variorum edition
Shakespeare, William (Editions of the 1700's and 1800's) **S: 369**

Varley, Frederick H. [Canadian painter]
Group of Seven **G: 402**
Varmus, Harold Eliot [American physiologist]
Nobel Prizes (Physiology or medicine: 1989) **N: 446**
Varna [Hinduism]
Hinduism (Caste) **H: 236**
India (Social structure) **I: 116**
Varnish **V: 286**
Lacquer **L: 22**
Varnish tree *See* Lacquer tree *in this index*
Varro, Marcus Terentius [Roman author]
Encyclopedia (The first reference works) **E: 268a**
Latin literature (The age of Cicero) **L: 116**
Varsity Scout
Boy Scouts (Varsity Scouts) **B: 538**
"Vårt Land" [poem by Runeberg]
Finland (The arts) **F: 112**
Varying hare *See* Snowshoe hare *in this index*
Vas deferens [anatomy]
Human body (table) **H: 422** *with diagram*
Prostate gland **P: 830**
Reproduction, Human (The human reproductive system) **R: 244-245** *with diagram*
Vasectomy **V: 287**
Vasa, House of [Swedish history]
Gustav I Vasa **G: 443**
Vasaloppet [race]
Sweden *picture on* **So: 1026**; (Recreation) **So: 1025**
Vasari, Giorgio [Italian architect]
Biography (The Renaissance) **B: 313**
Vasco Da Gama [Portuguese explorer] *See* Da Gama, Vasco *in this index*
Vasconcelos, José [Mexican scholar]
Latin America (Attitudes toward race) **L: 94**
Vasconelos, José [Mexican scholar]
National Council of La Raza **N: 33**
Vascons [people]
Gascony **G: 60**
Vascular dementia [disorder]
Dementia **D: 118**
Vascular endothelial growth factor [biology]
Angiogenesis **A: 461**
Vascular plant
Plant (Kinds of plants) **P: 518**; (The evolution of plants) **P: 544**; (Classification of plants) **P: 546** *with pictures*
Vascular ring [botany]
Potato (The potato plant) **P: 712** *with picture*
Vascular sap [botany]
Sap (Vascular sap) **S: 121** *with diagram*
Vascular tissue [botany]
Plant (Vascular plants) **P: 528**; (Parts of plants) **P: 528**
Vase **V: 286**
Vase sponge
Animal *picture on* **A: 506**
Ocean *picture on* **O: 656**
Vasectomy [surgery] **V: 287**
Birth control (Methods of birth control) **B: 378**
Surgery (Some common surgical operations) **So: 1006**
Vaseline [medication]
Petrolatum **P: 329**
Vasilyevskiy Island [Russia]
Russia *picture on* **R: 533**
Vasodilator [drug]
Drug (Drugs that affect the heart and blood vessels) **D: 351**
Heart (Heart failure) **H: 143**
Vasopressin [hormone]
Diabetes (Diabetes insipidus) **D: 180**
Hypothalamus **H: 481**
Pituitary gland **P: 502**
Vásquez de Ayllón, Lucas [Spanish settler] *See* Ayllón, Lucas Vásquez de *in this index*
Vásquez de Coronado, Francisco *See* Coronado, Francisco Vásquez de *in this index*
Vassal [European history]
Feudalism **F: 81**
Government (Feudalism) **G: 290**
Middle Ages (Feudalism) **M: 524**; (The Carolingian Empire) **M: 524**
World, History of the (Medieval Europe) **W: 432**
Vassar, Matthew [American businessman] **V: 287**
Vassar College **V: 287**
Coeducation **Ci: 752**
Education *picture on* **E: 104**
Vassar, Matthew **V: 287**
Vasyuganye Bog [Siberia]
Bog **B: 436**
Vat dye
Indigo **I: 223**
Vatican City **V: 287** *with picture*
Flag *picture on* **F: 207**
Italy (Religion) **I: 503**

Papal States **P: 133**
Pope **P: 660**
Rome **R: 429** *with map*; (Italy's capital) **R: 435**
Vatican Council I **V: 289**
Pius IX **P: 503**
Roman Catholic Church (Vatican Council I) **R: 410**
Vatican Council II **V: 289**
Cardinal **C: 211**
Christianity (Vatican Council II) **C: 526**
John XXIII [pope] **J: 132**
Nun **N: 608**
Paul VI **P: 200**
Protestantism (The ecumenical movement) **P: 835**
Religion (Religion today) **R: 223**
Religious life (Religious life in the 1900's) **R: 227**
Roman Catholic Church (Bishop and diocese) **R: 404**; (Vatican Council II) **R: 410** *with picture*
Vatican Library
Library (Western Europe) **L: 252** *with picture*; (Renaissance collections) **L: 259-260**
Vatican Palace
Pope **P: 660**; (The 1700's and 1800's) **P: 665**
Rome (Museums and art galleries) **R: 429**
Vatican City (Vatican Palace) **V: 287** *with picture*
Vatican 20-lire coin [money]
Coin collecting *picture on* **Ci: 758**
Vatnajökull Glacier
Glacier (Famous glaciers) **G: 204**
Icecap **I: 19**
Iceland (The inland plateau) **I: 22**
Vättern, Lake
Sweden (The Swedish Lowland) **So: 1028** *with map*
Vaudeville [theater] **V: 290**
Peoria **P: 277**
Popular music (Vaudeville and musical comedy) **P: 670**
Vaughan, Arky [American baseball player]
Baseball (table: Hall of Fame) **B: 134b**
Vaughan, Sarah [American singer] **V: 290** *with portrait*
Vaughan Williams, Ralph [British composer] **V: 291**
Vault [architecture] **V: 291**
Architecture *picture on* **A: 615**; (table) **A: 608-609** *with picture*; (Roman architecture) **A: 616**
Hagia Sophia **H: 6**
Rome, Ancient (Architecture and engineering) **R: 442**
Vault [gymnastics]
Gymnastics (Men's events) **G: 448** *with picture*; (Women's events) **G: 449**
Vault table [equipment]
Gymnastics (The vault) **G: 448** *with picture*
Vauquelin, Louis Nicolas [French chemist]
Chromium **C: 538**
Vaux, Calvert [American landscaper]
Landscape architecture (History) **L: 59**
Olmsted, Frederick Law **O: 745**
Park (History) **P: 168**
Vaux, William [American educator]
Wyoming (Schools) **W: 520**
Vaux's swift [bird]
Swift **So: 1038**
Vava'u [islands]
Tonga (Land) **T: 328** *with map*
Vaz Teixeira, Tristão [Portuguese explorer]
Henry the Navigator **H: 191**
Vazov, Ivan [Bulgarian writer]
Bulgaria (The arts) **B: 690-691**
Vázquez Mota, Josefina [Mexican political leader]
Mexico (Recent developments) **M: 474-475**
Vázquez Rosas, Tabaré Ramón [Uruguayan political leader]
Uruguay (Recent developments) **U: 228**
vCJD [disease]
Mad cow disease **M: 26**
VCR [machine] *See* Videocassette recorder *in this index*
VCU [university] *See* Virginia Commonwealth University *in this index*
Ve [Norse mythology]
Mythology (The creation of life) **M: 985-986**
Veadar [month]
Calendar (The Hebrew calendar) **C: 29**
Veal [food] **V: 291**
Cattle (Dual-purpose cattle) **C: 311**
Meat packing **M: 350**
Vealer [animal]
Veal **V: 291**
Veazey, Thomas W. [American political leader]
Maryland (table) **M: 255**
Veblen, Thorstein Bunde [American economist] **V: 291**
American literature (Nonfiction writers) **A: 420**
Chicago, University of (Research program) **C: 438**

Vector [biochemistry]
Heredity (The era of genetic engineering) H: 209
Vector [physics]
Force (Characteristics of force) F: 369
Velocity V: 297
Vector magnetometer [device]
Magnetometer M: 62
Vedanta [religious school]
See also Upanishads in this index
Hinduism (The six schools of philosophy) H: 236
Vedas [religious books] V: 291
Hinduism (Sacred writings) H: 236
India (Literature) I: 120; (The Aryans) I: 128
Mithra M: 678
Philosophy (Eastern philosophy) P: 386
Sanskrit literature (The Vedic period) S: 112
Upanishads U: 212
Veddahs [people]
Sri Lanka (People) So: 817; (History) So: 819
Vedic [language]
Sanskrit language S: 111
Vedic period [Hindu history]
Religion (Hinduism) R: 220
Védrines, Jules [French aviator]
Aviation (table: Aviation speed records) A: 990
Veeck, Bill [American baseball executive]
Baseball (table: Hall of Fame) B: 134b
Veep, The [name for]
Barkley, Alben William B: 111
Vega [airplane]
Airplane picture on A: 233; (The golden age)
A: 235-236
Vega [star] V: 291
North Star N: 518
Solar system (Other solar systems) So: 581
Star (table: The 10 brightest stars as seen from
Earth) So: 842
Vega, Garcilaso de la [Latin American author]
Latin American literature (Colonial literature)
L: 112
Spanish literature (The 1500's) So: 758
Vega, Lope de [Spanish dramatist] V: 292
Drama (Secular drama) D: 333
Spanish literature (The 1600's) So: 759
Vega Real [region, Dominican Republic]
Dominican Republic (Land) D: 304
Vegan [nutrition]
Vegetarianism V: 294
Vegetable V: 292 with pictures
See also the list of Related articles in the Vegetable
article
Antioxidant A: 557
Farm and farming (Specialized crop farms) F: 30-
31 with picture
Flavonoid F: 230
Food (Food from plants) F: 329
Food, Frozen (Freezing food at home) F: 338-339
Gardening (table) G: 32 with diagram; (Planning a
kitchen garden) G: 34
Nutrition (Carbohydrates) N: 625; (Nutrition
guidelines) N: 626
Truck farming T: 458
Vegetarianism V: 294
Vegetable culture [agriculture]
Vegetable (Growing vegetables) V: 293
Vegetable ivory [tree product]
Doum palm D: 314
Ivory palm I: 522 with picture
Vegetable oil V: 294
See also the list of Related articles in the Vegetable
oil article
Margarine M: 198
Olive oil O: 744
Soybean (Soy oil) So: 690
Vegetable parchment
Parchment P: 155
Vegetable tanning
Leather (Tanning) L: 167
Vegetable-type soybean [plant]
Soybean (The soybean plant) So: 689
Vegetarianism V: 294
Vegetation See Plant in this index
Vegetative organ [botany]
Grass (The grass plant) G: 324
Vegetative part [botany]
Plant (Parts of plants) P: 528
Vegetative propagation [botany]
Cloning (Clones in nature) Ci: 684
Plant (The reproduction of plants) P: 532;
(Asexual reproduction) P: 535
Reproduction (Through asexual reproduction)
R: 242
Spanish moss So: 764
Tree (How trees reproduce) T: 419
Vegetative state [disorder]
Persistent vegetative state P: 300f
VEGF [biology]

Angiogenesis A: 461
Vehbi Koç Foundation
Foundation (table) F: 430
Vehicle [chemistry]
Ink I: 272
Paint P: 23
Vehicle electronic control unit [computer]
Ignition (The direct-fire ignition system) I: 49
Vehicle license
License L: 268
Vehicular homicide [crime]
Homicide H: 305
VEI [measurement]
Volcano (Describing eruptions) V: 442b
Veil [botany]
Mushroom (Parts of a mushroom) M: 942
Veil [gem]
Emerald E: 257
Vein [anatomy] V: 295
Blood (What blood does in the body) B: 408
Circulatory system (The blood vessels) Ci: 559
with picture
Heart H: 132 with diagram; (Blood vessels) H: 135
with diagram
Hemorrhoids H: 183
Human body (The blood vessels) H: 421; (table)
H: 422 with diagram
Jugular vein J: 186 with diagram
Varicose vein V: 286
Vein [botany]
Leaf (The blade) L: 153-154 with pictures
Plant (Leaves) P: 529-531 with picture
Tree (Leaves) T: 417 with diagrams
Vein [entomology]
Butterfly (The thorax) B: 738 with diagram
Vein [geology]
Gold (Types of deposits) G: 252
Mining (Mining terms) M: 577
Ore O: 825
Veined squid [animal]
Squid (Kinds of squids) So: 814a
Veitchiana [plant]
Gardenia G: 29
Vela Supernova Remnant
Star picture on So: 851
Velasco Alvarado, Juan [Peruvian political leader]
Latin America (The rise of military regimes)
L: 110-111
Peru (Socialist reforms) P: 316
Velasco Ibarra, José María [Ecuadorean political
leader]
Ecuador (The 1900's) E: 73
Velázquez, Diego [Spanish colonial leader]
Cortés, Hernán (Early life) Ci: 1072
Mexico (The Spanish conquest) M: 469
Velázquez, Diego [Spanish painter] V: 295 with
picture
Baroque (Baroque painting) B: 117
Painting (The Spanish masters) P: 64 with picture
Velcro [fastener] V: 296 with picture
Veld [geography]
Prairie P: 731
Zimbabwe (Land and climate) Z: 592
Veliger [zoology]
Clam (The life of a clam) Ci: 637
Larva L: 78
Oyster (Young) O: 891
Velikiy Novgorod [Russia] V: 296
Icon I: 25
Russia (Early days) R: 547
Vellum [parchment]
Manuscript M: 172
Parchment P: 155
Velociraptor [dinosaur] V: 296 with picture
Dinosaur picture on D: 207; (True dinosaurs)
D: 206b-211
Velocity [physics] V: 297
Einstein, Albert (Famous theories) E: 146-146a
Falling bodies, Law of F: 17
Force (Characteristics of force) F: 369
G G: 2
Gravitation G: 331
Mass M: 268
Metric system (Kinds of metric units) M: 436;
(Space and time) M: 437
Motion (Describing motion) M: 844
Relativity (Galilean relativity) R: 209; (Time
dilation) R: 211
Velocity mode [weather]
Weather (Weather radar) W: 162
Velodrome [track]
Bicycle racing picture on B: 294; (Track races)
B: 292
Veloso, Caetano [Brazilian musician]
Brazil (The arts) B: 576-577
Latin America (Music) L: 100
Velour [fabric]

Textile (table: Textile terms) T: 213
Veltman, Martinus J. G. [Dutch physicist]
Nobel Prizes (Physics: 1999) N: 442
Velvet [fabric] V: 297
Velvet [zoology]
Deer (Antlers) D: 83
Velvet ant [insect]
Wasp W: 111
Velvet leaf [plant] See Velvetleaf in this index
Velvet Revolution [Czechoslovak history]
Czech Republic (The Velvet Revolution) Ci: 1214
Czechoslovakia (The Velvet Revolution) Ci: 1216
Havel, Václav H: 87
Slovakia (The Velvet Revolution) S: 509
Velvet rug
Rugs and carpets (Weaving) R: 515
Velvetleaf [plant] V: 297
Vena cava [anatomy]
Abdomen A: 8
Heart (Blood vessels) H: 135 with picture
Human body (The blood vessels) H: 421
Venator [literary figure]
Walton, Izaak W: 21
Vendée [area, France]
Reign of Terror R: 207
Vendetta [sociology]
Mafia M: 41
Vending machine V: 297
Veneer [stone]
House (Building materials) H: 380
Veneer [wood]
Forest products (Plywood) F: 401
Furniture (Louis XIV furniture) F: 575
Lumber (Engineered lumber) L: 518
Plywood P: 585
Veneman, Ann M. [American government official]
Agriculture, Department of (table) A: 161
Bush, George Walker (table) B: 722h
Venera [space probes]
Space exploration (Probes to Venus and Mercury)
So: 710
Venus (Flights to Venus) V: 313
Venerable Bede, The [English historian] See Bede,
Saint in this index
Venereal disease See Sexually transmitted disease
in this index
Venesection [medicine]
Bloodletting B: 417
Venetian glass
Glass (The Middle Ages) G: 218
Italy picture on I: 505
Venetian lace
Lace picture on L: 21
Venetian Life [book by Howells]
Howells, William Dean H: 401
Venetians [people]
Venice (The people) V: 307
Venezia [Italy] See Venice in this index
Venezuela V: 298 with pictures and maps
See also the list of Related articles in the Venezuela
article
Andean Community A: 450
Bolívar, Simón B: 441
Christmas (In Latin America) C: 532
Cleveland, Grover (Foreign affairs) Ci: 673
Columbus, Christopher (Third voyage westward)
Ci: 862
Indian, American (Indians of the Caribbean)
I: 172; (Indians of the Tropical Forest) I: 175
Organization of the Petroleum Exporting
Countries O: 854
Yanomami Indians Y: 552
Venezuela Affair [1902]
Roosevelt, Theodore (Foreign policy) R: 465
"Veni, vidi, vici" [quotation]
Caesar, Julius (Last victories) C: 13
Venice [Italy] V: 306 with pictures and map
City (The people) Ci: 582; (Economy) Ci: 584
Crusades (The Fourth Crusade) Ci: 1161
Doge D: 282
Europe picture on E: 395
Exploration (The age of European exploration)
E: 443
Flag picture on F: 217
Glass (The Middle Ages) G: 218
Gondola G: 268
Italy picture on I: 510
Navy (The beginning of modern navies) N: 79
Painting (The Renaissance in Venice) P: 55 with
pictures
Renaissance (The Italian Renaissance) R: 233
with map
World, History of the picture on W: 438
Veniot, Peter J. [Canadian political leader]
New Brunswick (table) N: 195
Venison [food]
Deer D: 82d

Venizelos, Eleutherios [Greek political leader]
V: 308
　Greece (George I) G: 362
Venn diagram [mathematics]
　Set theory S: 321
Venom [poison] V: 308
　Hornet H: 340
　Reptile (Internal organs) R: 251
　Snake S: 524; (Fangs and venom glands) S: 528;
　　(Protection against predators) S: 531; (Snakes
　　and people) S: 532; (Snakebite) S: 533
　Snakebite S: 536
　Spider (How spiders help people) So: 790
Venous blood [physiology]
　Vein P: 295
Vent [geology]
　See also Hydrothermal vent *in this index*
　Volcano V: 438 *with picture, diagram on* V: 442a
Vent [plumbing]
　House (Plumbing) H: 382
　Plumbing (The drain-waste-vent system) P: 578
　　with diagram
Vent [zoology]
　Bird *diagram on* B: 366
　Snake (Internal organs) S: 527
Ventifact [geology]
　Desert (Desert climate and land) D: 155-156
Ventilation V: 309
　Air conditioning (Circulating the air) A: 179
　Fire department (Firefighting) F: 123-124 *with
　　picture*
Ventral abdominal vein
　Frog *picture on* F: 537
Ventral margin
　Shell *diagram on* S: 385
Ventral scute [zoology]
　Snake (Scales and color) S: 525
Ventral tegmental area [anatomy]
　Brain (Regulating body processes) B: 554
Ventricle [brain]
　Brain *diagram on* B: 553
Ventricle [heart]
　Heart (Chambers, valves, and inner lining) H: 133-
　　135 *with picture*; (The work of the heart) H: 135
　　with diagram; (Abnormal openings in the
　　heart) H: 141; (Blockage of blood flow) H: 141;
　　(Abnormal heart rhythms) H: 142; (Hearts of
　　animals) H: 146
Ventricular fibrillation [disorder]
　Defibrillator D: 88
　Heart (Diagnosis and treatment) H: 139
Ventricular septal defect [disorder]
　Heart (Abnormal openings in the heart) H: 141;
　　(Blockage of blood flow) H: 141
Ventriloquism V: 309 *with picture*
　Puppet (Dummies) P: 907
Ventris, Michael George Francis [British architect]
V: 309
　Greek language (Development of ancient Greek)
　　G: 376
Ventura, Jesse [American political leader]
　Minnesota (table) M: 602; (The early 2000's)
　　M: 602
Venturer Scout [rank]
　Boy Scouts *picture on* B: 537; (Venturing) B: 538
　Scouts Canada (Age groups) S: 224
Venturi, Robert [American architect] V: 310 *with
picture*
　Architecture (Architecture today) A: 632-633
　Furniture *picture on* F: 586; (Postmodern design)
　　F: 585
　Postmodernism P: 709
Venturi meter
　Water meter W: 135
Venturi tube
　Carburetor C: 208
Venule [anatomy]
　Vein P: 295
Venus [goddess] V: 310
　See also Aphrodite *in this index*
　Mythology (table) M: 981
　Painting (The 1400's) P: 52-53 *with picture*
　Vulcan V: 453
Venus [planet] V: 310 *with pictures*
　Astronomy (How the planets move) A: 835
　Earthquake (Quakes elsewhere in the solar
　　system) E: 38b
　Evening star E: 423
　Life (In our solar system) L: 280
　Lucifer L: 514
　Mountain *picture on* M: 896b; (Mountains on
　　other planets) M: 895
　Planet P: 507 *with picture*
　Radar (In scientific research) R: 68 *with picture*
　Satellite (Satellites of the terrestrial planets)
　　S: 150
　Space exploration *picture on* So: 709; (Probes to

Venus and Mercury) So: 710
　Transit T: 374 *with picture*
　Volcano (Volcanoes in the solar system) V: 442b
Venus and Adonis [poem by Shakespeare]
　English literature (Elizabethan poetry) E: 316-317
　Shakespeare, William (His first poems) S: 347;
　　(Shakespeare's poems) S: 366
Venus de Milo [sculpture] V: 314
　Milos M: 556
Venus Express [space probe]
　European Space Agency E: 418
　Space exploration (Probes to Venus and Mercury)
　　So: 710-711
　Venus (Flights to Venus) V: 313
Venus' girdle [animal]
　Animal *picture on* A: 506
Venus' hair
　Hairdressing (The Renaissance) H: 11-12
Venus Observed [play by Fry]
　Fry, Christopher F: 549
"Venus of Ille, The" [story by Mérimée]
　Mérimée, Prosper M: 417
Venus of Willendorf [sculpture]
　Sculpture (Prehistoric sculpture) S: 233 *with
　　picture*
Venus Plus X [book by Sturgeon]
　Sturgeon, Theodore So: 934
Venus With a Mirror [painting by Velázquez]
　Velázquez, Diego V: 296
Venus's-flower-basket [sea animal]
　Sponge (Kinds of sponges) So: 800
Venus's-flytrap [plant] V: 314 *with picture*
　Carnivorous plant C: 243
　Plant (Environmental factors) P: 538-539 *with
　　picture*
Venus's-girdle [sea animal]
　Ctenophore Ci: 1167
Veracruz [Mexico] V: 314
　Mexico (The Spanish conquest) M: 469
Verb [grammar] V: 314
　Adverb (Verb-adverb combinations) A: 71
　Conjugation Ci: 950
　Infinitive I: 265
　Participle P: 184
　Person P: 300f
　Sentence (Subject and predicate) S: 303
　Tense T: 167
Verbal memory
　Reading (Comprehending what is perceived)
　　R: 157
Verbena [plants] V: 315 *with picture*
　Flower (Fflowers of the desert) F: 290 *with picture*
Verchères, Marie Madeleine Jarret de [French-
Canadian public figure] V: 315
Verd antique [stone]
　Serpentine S: 318
Verdandi [Norse mythology]
　Norns N: 456
Verdi, Giuseppe [Italian composer] V: 316
　Opera (Giuseppe Verdi) O: 798; (*Aida*) O: 801;
　　(*Rigoletto*) O: 806; (*Traviata, La*) O: 807-808
　　with picture; (*Trovatore, Il*) O: 808
　Traviata, La T: 406
Verdict [law]
　Jury (Petit juries) J: 202
　Trial (Reaching a verdict) T: 436
Verdin [bird] V: 316 *with picture*
Verdun, Battles of V: 316
　Pétain, Henri Philippe P: 323
　World War I (The Battle of Verdun) W: 458
Verdun, Treaty of [843] V: 316
　Burgundy B: 705
　Charles II [of France] C: 380
　Germany (The breakup of Charlemagne's empire)
　　G: 162
Vereeniging, Treaty of [1902]
　Anglo-Boer Wars A: 464
Vérendrye, Sieur de la [French-Canadian explorer]
　See La Vérendrye, Pierre Gaultier de Varennes,
　　Sieur de *in this index*
Verga, Giovanni [Italian author] V: 317
　Italian literature (Romanticism) I: 495
Verge [device]
　Clock (Mechanical clocks) Ci: 682j
Vergennes, Count de [French government official]
　Adams, John (Diplomat) A: 36
　Revolution, American (Diplomacy) R: 280-281
Vergil [Roman poet] *See* Virgil *in this index*
Vergoose, Elizabeth [American author]
　Mother Goose (Who was Mother Goose?) M: 842
Verhofstadt, Guy [Belgian political leader]
　Belgium (Recent developments) B: 235
Verifiability criterion of meaning [philosophy]
　Philosophy (Philosophy in the 1900's) P: 390
　Positivism (Logical positivism) P: 697
Verigin, Peter [Russian religious leader]
　Doukhobors D: 314

Verismo [literature]
　Italian literature (Romanticism) I: 495
Verismo opera
　Leoncavallo, Ruggiero L: 202
　Mascagni, Pietro M: 262
　Opera (Verismo opera) O: 799
Verity, C. William [American government official]
　Commerce, Department of (table) Ci: 871
Verizon Communications Inc.
　Telephone (In the United States) T: 99;
　　(Improvements in telephone technology)
　　T: 100-101
Verlaine, Paul [French poet] V: 317
　French literature (Symbolism) F: 522
　Rimbaud, Arthur R: 341
Vermeer, Jan [Dutch painter] V: 317 *with picture*
　Painting (The Dutch masters) P: 62-63 *with
　　picture*
Vermicelli [food]
　Pasta P: 192
Vermiculite [mineral] V: 317
　Plaster P: 552
Vermiform appendix [anatomy] *See* Appendix *in
this index*
Vermilion [pigment] V: 317
Vermilion flycatcher [bird]
　Flycatcher F: 311
Vermilion Indian paintbrush [plant]
　Flower *picture on* F: 284, *picture on* F: 284
Vermilion Range [Minnesota]
　Minnesota (Industrial development) M: 604
Vermilion Sea
　Gulf of California G: 436
Vermont V: 318 *with pictures and maps*
　See also the list of Related articles in the Vermont
　　article
　Civil union Ci: 613
Vermont, University of V: 337
Vermont Gazette, The [newspaper]
　Vermont (Communication) V: 332
Vermont History Museum [Montpelier]
　Vermont (Museums) V: 322
Vermont Marble Museum [Proctor]
　Vermont (Places to visit) V: 326
Vermont Piedmont [Vermont]
　Vermont (Land regions) V: 328
Vermouth [beverage]
　Wine (Flavored wines) W: 336
Vernacular [language]
　Italian literature (The Middle Ages) I: 494
　Latin language (Development) L: 115
　Middle Ages (The growth of humanism) M: 528
　Romance languages R: 415
　Vatican Council II (The Constitution on the
　　Liturgy) V: 289
Vernacular Latin
　Spanish literature So: 757
Vernal equinox [astronomy]
　Equinox E: 348 *with diagram*
　March M: 194
　Sidereal time S: 448
Vernal Falls [waterfall, California]
　Waterfall (table: Famous waterfalls of North
　　America) W: 142
　Yosemite National Park (Waterfalls) Y: 570
Vernam, Gilbert S. [American engineer]
　Codes and ciphers (History) Ci: 751
Verne, Jules [French author] V: 337 *with portrait*
　Literature for children (Masterpieces of fiction)
　　L: 363
　Space exploration *picture on* So: 706
Vernier [measuring device] V: 338 *with picture*
Vernier, Pierre [French mathematician]
　Vernier V: 338
Vernon, Edward [British admiral]
　Mount Vernon (The buildings) M: 888
Vernon, Mount *See* Mount Vernon *in this index*
Verny [former name]
　Almaty A: 379
Veronal [drug]
　Barbiturate B: 107
Veronese, Paolo [Italian painter] V: 338
　Painting (The Renaissance in Venice) P: 55-56
　　with picture
Verrazano-Narrows Bridge [New York City]
　Bridge (table: Suspension) B: 603
　Brooklyn B: 640
　New York City (Staten Island) N: 330;
　　(Transportation) N: 334
　Staten Island So: 866
Verrazzano, Giovanni da [Italian navigator] V: 338
　Cartier, Jacques C: 261
　Exploration *map on* E: 443; (The search for a
　　northern passage) E: 464
　New York (Exploration and settlement) N: 314
　New York City (Exploration) N: 340
　North Carolina (Exploration and settlement)

N: 490
Northwest Passage N: 528
Nova Scotia (Exploration and settlement) N: 567
Rhode Island (Exploration) R: 312
Verrocchio, Andrea del [Italian artist] **V: 338** *with picture*
Leonardo da Vinci (Early career) L: 199; (Paintings) L: 200b
Renaissance *picture on* R: 232
Versailles, Palace of [France] **V: 339** *with picture*
Architecture (Baroque architecture) A: 622
Coysevox, Antoine Ci: 1114
Fountain *picture on* F: 432
Furniture (Louis XIV furniture) F: 575
Louis XIV L: 475
Versailles, Treaty of [1919] **V: 339**
Congress of the United States (Approving treaties) Ci: 946
France (Between World Wars) F: 475
Germany (World War I) G: 167
Hitler, Adolf (The road to war) H: 267
Paris, Treaties of (The treaties of 1919) P: 167
Poincaré, Raymond P: 599
United States, History of the (The peace treaty) U: 189
War crime (World War I) W: 27
World War I (The peace settlement) W: 465; (The postwar world) W: 466
World War II (Causes of the war) W: 468
Verse [poetry]
Ballad B: 43
Ballade B: 43
Meter M: 433
Nursery rhyme (Types) N: 615
Poetry (Rhythm and meter) P: 591-593; (Forms) P: 595
Verse epistle [poetry]
Epistle E: 344
Verse paragraph
Blank verse B: 398
Verso [printing]
Book (Inside a book) B: 464-465
Vert [symbol]
Heraldry *picture on* H: 195
Vertebra [anatomy]
Cartilage C: 263
Frog *picture on* F: 537
Human body (table) H: 422 *with diagram*
Mammal (Skeleton) M: 118-119
Spine So: 792 *with picture*
Vertebral body [anatomy]
Bone (Structure of the bones) B: 456
Vertebral column [anatomy] *See* Spine *in this index*
Vertebrate [zoology] **V: 340**
Animal (Kinds of animals) A: 472; (Invertebrates and vertebrates) A: 488 *with diagram*
Bird B: 328
Brain (The brain in other animals) B: 559 *with pictures*
Cartilage C: 263
Chordate C: 522
Circulatory system (Vertebrates) Ci: 561
Fever F: 83
Invertebrate I: 365
Nervous system (In vertebrates) N: 136
Prehistoric animal (The first animals with backbones) P: 736
Rib R: 320
Sleep (Sleep in animals) S: 506
Territoriality T: 174
Tetrapod T: 182b
Vertebrate paleontology
Paleontology P: 103
Vertex [geometry]
Angle A: 462
Geometry (Congruence) G: 102; (Solid geometry) G: 104
Polygon P: 650 *with diagram*
Polyhedron P: 651
Triangle T: 437 *with diagram*
Vertical crater retreat mining
Mining (Self-supported mining) M: 576
Vertical file
A Guide to Research Skills **Research Guide: 30**
Vertical integration [economics]
Motion picture (Movies become big business) M: 865-866; (Postwar American movies) M: 869
Vertical launch system
Guided missile (Launching equipment) G: 424
Vertical lift bridge
Bridge (Moveable bridges) B: 602 *with diagram*
Vertical line [navigation]
Inertial guidance I: 263
Vertical piano
Piano (Upright pianos) P: 447 *with picture*
Vertical/Short Take-Off and Landing [aircraft] *See*

V/STOL *in this index*
Verticality [dance]
Ballet B: 44
Vertigo [disorder]
Dizziness D: 256
Vertisol [soil]
Soil *map on* So: 575; (How soils are classified) So: 576
"Vertue" [poem by Herbert]
Poetry (Stress meters) P: 592
Vervain [plant]
Verbena V: 315
Vervet [animal]
Guenon G: 419 *with picture*
Mammal *picture on* M: 126
Monkey *picture on* M: 729
Verwoerd, Hendrik [South African political leader] **V: 341**
South Africa (Apartheid) So: 619
Very high frequency waves [communications]
Television (Broadcasting) T: 123
Very Large Telescope
Telescope (Reflecting telescopes) T: 104-105
Very Long Baseline Array Telescope
Astronomy (Radio and microwave astronomy) A: 843
National Radio Astronomy Observatory N: 59 *with picture*
Telescope (Types of radio telescopes) T: 106-107
Very Rich Hours, The [book by Limbourg brothers]
See Très Riches Heures, Les *in this index*
Vesalius, Andreas [Flemish anatomist] **V: 341**
Anatomy A: 448b
Biology (The Renaissance) B: 318 *with picture*
Medicine *picture on* M: 373
Science *picture on* S: 199; (The rebirth of science) S: 197
Zoology (History) Z: 606
Vesey, Denmark [American social reformer] **V: 341**
Vesicle [lunar feature]
Moon (Core) M: 791
Vesicular ringworm [disease]
Ringworm R: 344
Vespasian [Roman emperor] **V: 341**
Rome, Ancient (The Roman Empire) R: 446
Vespasianus, Titus Flavius *See* Vespasian *in this index*
Vesper sparrow [bird]
Bird (Birds of grasslands) B: 336 *with picture*
Vespers [music by Monteverdi]
Monteverdi, Claudio M: 764b
Vespucci, Amerigo [Italian explorer] **V: 341** *with map*
America A: 407
Columbus, Christopher (Third journey to the west) Ci: 862
Exploration *map on* E: 443; (Exploring the New World) E: 444-445
Latin America *map on* L: 105 ; (European discovery and exploration) L: 103
United States, History of the (The European discoveries) U: 150-151
Vessel [botany]
Wood (Wood figure) W: 390
Vessels, Billy [American football player]
Football (table) F: 363
Vessey, John W., Jr. [American military leader]
Joint Chiefs of Staff (table) J: 156
Vessey, Robert S. [American political leader]
South Dakota (table) So: 680
Vesta [asteroid]
Asteroid (Sizes and shapes) A: 824; (History of study) A: 824b
Vesta [Roman mythology] **V: 342**
Fire (Fire in legend and religion) F: 122
Vestal Virgin [religion]
Romulus and Remus R: 450a
Vesta V: 342
Vesterålen Islands [Norway]
Norway (Coast and islands) N: 542 *with map*
"Vesti la giubba" [aria]
Opera: (*Pagliacci*) O: 806
Vestibular nerve [anatomy]
Ear (The inner ear) E: 8-9; (The response to movement) E: 11
Vestibular organs [anatomy]
Ear (The inner ear) E: 8
Motion sickness M: 874
Nausea N: 69
Space exploration (Microgravity) So: 701-702
Vestibule
Ear (The inner ear) E: 8 *with diagram*
Vestibulocochlear nerve [anatomy] *See* Auditory nerve *in this index*
Vestigial organ [biology]
Evolution (Vestigial organs) E: 431
Vestmannaeyjar [Iceland]

Iceland (The inland plateau) I: 22
Vestment
Pope (Titles, clothing, and symbols) P: 661-662 *with picture*
Vestryman [office]
Colonial life in America (Local government) Ci: 795
Vesuvius [volcano, Italy] **V: 342** *with picture*
Herculaneum H: 198
Mountain (table) M: 896 *with diagram*
Naples (The city) N: 12 *with picture*
Pompeii P: 653 *with picture*
Rome, Ancient *picture on* R: 439
Volcano (table) V: 442b
Vesuvius Room [cave]
Cave *picture on* C: 319
Vetch [plant] **V: 343**
Veteran
American GI Forum of the United States A: 411
American Legion A: 412
Civil service (Federal civil service) Ci: 612
Red Cross (Services to military personnel) R: 185-186
Scholarship (Grants to veterans) S: 178
Veterans Affairs, Department of V: 343
Vietnam War (Effects in the United States) V: 377
Veterans Affairs, Department of [U.S.] **V: 343** *with picture*
Mortgage M: 821
Washington, D.C. *map on* W: 76
Veterans Affairs, Secretary of [office]
Flag *picture on* F: 211
Veterans' bonus
Hoover, Herbert Clark (The "Bonus Army") H: 330
Veterans Bureau [U.S. history]
Veterans Affairs, Department of (History) V: 344
Veterans Day [holiday] **V: 344**
Veterans of Foreign Wars of the United States **V: 344** *with picture*
Veterans' organizations V: 344
Veterans' Readjustment Act [1966]
Veterans Affairs, Department of (Benefits and other services) V: 343
Veterans' Readjustment Assistance Act [1952]
Veterans Affairs, Department of (Benefits and other services) V: 343
Veterinarian [career]
Veterinary medicine V: 345 *with pictures*
Address, Forms of (Other forms) A: 54
Careers *picture on* C: 223
Pet (Taking care of pets) P: 321-322 *with picture*
Zoo *picture on* Z: 605; (Medical care) Z: 603
Veterinary Medical Association, American
Veterinary medicine (Careers in veterinary medicine) V: 346
Veterinary medicine V: 345 *with pictures*
Vetluga [river, Russia]
Volga River V: 444
Veto [government] **V: 346**
Congress of the United States (From bill to law) Ci: 945-946; (Continued struggle for power) Ci: 948
Constitution of the United States (Article I, Section 7) Ci: 1006
Plebeians P: 572
President of the United States (Legislative leader) P: 765
United Nations (Voting) U: 82
United States, Government of the (The presidency) U: 140; (Action by the President) U: 144
Washington, George (First veto) W: 104
Vettel, Sebastian [German race car driver]
Automobile racing (table: Formula One World Drivers' Championship) A: 980
Vettisfoss [falls, Norway]
Waterfall (table: Famous waterfalls of the world) W: 143 *with picture*
Vexillology [study]
Flag (table) F: 193
Vexilum [Roman Empire]
Flag F: 195, *picture on* F: 216
Vézelay Abbey [France]
Sculpture (The importance of sculpture) S: 228 *with picture*
VFR map
Map (Navigation maps) M: 178
VFW [organization] *See* Veterans of Foreign Wars of the United States *in this index*
VHF band [communications]
Communications satellite (How communications satellites work) Ci: 888b
VHF wave *See* Very high frequency waves *in this index*
VHS [recording system]
Videotape recorder (History) V: 361
Via del Corso [street]

Rome R: 429
Via Dolorosa [road]
Jerusalem *picture on* J: 98; (Christian sites) J: 96 *with map*
VIA Rail Canada
Canada (Transportation) C: 126
Railroad (In Canada) R: 113
Viability of fetus [law]
Abortion (Abortion in the United States) A: 15
Viacom Inc. [company] V: 347
CBS C: 323
MTV M: 908
Viaduct [engineering] V: 347
Viagra [drug]
Erectile dysfunction E: 349
Vibraphone [musical instrument] V: 347
Hampton, Lionel H: 36
Vibration V: 347
Acoustics A: 28
Harmonics H: 62 *with diagrams*
Pitch P: 498
Sound So: 598 *with picture*
Vibrato [music]
Music (table) M: 954
Singing (Training the voice) S: 472
Vibrato arm [electronics]
Electric guitar E: 173
Vibrio [bacteriology]
Bacteria (The structure of bacteria) B: 20-21 *with picture*
Vibrio cholerae [bacteria]
Cholera C: 519
Vibrissa [zoology]
Cat (Senses) C: 287-290
Mammal (Skin and hair) M: 118
Vibroseis truck *See* Thumper truck *in this index*
Vic [horse]
Horse (table: Famous horses in history and legend) H: 361
Vic-Wells Ballet
De Valois, Ninette D: 173
Vicar of Christ [title]
Pope (The peak of papal power) P: 663-664
Vicar of St. Peter [title]
Pope (The peak of papal power) P: 663-664
Vicar of Wakefield, The [book by Goldsmith]
English literature (The Johnson circle) E: 319
Goldsmith, Oliver G: 259
Vice admiral [rank]
Admiral A: 58
Rank, Military (table) R: 140
Vice president [office] V: 347
Address, Forms of (Officials of the United States) A: 53
Parliamentary procedure (Officers) P: 175
Vice president of the United States V: 348 *with pictures*
Congress of the United States (The Senate) Ci: 942; (Handling presidential election results) Ci: 946
Constitution of the United States (Article I, Section 3) Ci: 1005; (Amendment 12) Ci: 1013
Electoral College E: 161
Flag *picture on* F: 211
Political convention P: 628
Polk, James Knox (Election of 1844) P: 642
Presidential succession P: 771
Senate (Organization of the U.S. Senate) S: 294
Tyler, John T: 532
United States, Government of the (The presidency) U: 140
Vice squad
Police (Investigations of crimes) P: 621
Vicentino, Antonio [Italian painter]
Navy *picture on* N: 80
Viceroy [butterfly]
Butterfly (Brush-footed butterflies) B: 736
Viceroy [title] V: 354
India (British India) I: 130
Viceroy of the Indies [title]
Columbus, Christopher *picture on* Ci: 861
Viceroyalty of New Granada [colony]
Colombia (Spanish rule) Ci: 783
Viceroyalty of the Río de la Plata [South American history]
Argentina (Settlement and colonial life) A: 655-656 *with map*
Paraguay (Independence) P: 149
Vichy [France] V: 354
World War II (The fall of France) W: 475
Vichy government [French history]
Foreign Legion (History) F: 386
France (World War II) F: 475 *with map*
Laval, Pierre L: 128
Pétain, Henri Philippe (Collaborator) P: 323
Vichy V: 354
Vichy water

Vichy V: 354
Vickrey, William Spencer [American economist]
Nobel Prizes (Economics: 1996) N: 449
Vicksburg [Mississippi] V: 354
Mississippi *picture on* M: 642
Vicksburg, Battle of [1863]
Civil War, American (table) Ci: 624; (The Vicksburg campaign) Ci: 629
Mississippi (The American Civil War) M: 642 *with picture*
Vicksburg National Military Park [Mississippi]
Mississippi (Places to visit) M: 632 *with picture*
National Park System (table: National military parks) N: 55
Victim, The [book by Bellow]
Bellow, Saul B: 244
Victimless crime
Crime (Crimes against public order) Ci: 1136
Victor I, Saint [pope]
Pope (table) P: 666
Victor II [pope]
Pope (table) P: 666
Victor III [pope]
Pope (table) P: 666
Victor IV [antipope]
Alexander III A: 341
Pope (table) P: 666
Victor Amadeus II [king of Sardinia]
Sardinia, Kingdom of S: 125
Victor Emmanuel II [king of Italy] V: 355
Italy (Italy united) I: 515; (The Kingdom of Italy) I: 516
Papal States P: 132
Rome (Italy's capital) R: 435
Sardinia, Kingdom of S: 125
Sicilies, Kingdom of the Two S: 446
Victor Emmanuel III [king of Italy] V: 355
Italy (Italy under Mussolini) I: 517; (The Italian republic) I: 517
Victor Emmanuel Monument
Rome *picture on* R: 428
Victor Herbert ASCAP Young Composers Award
Music Clubs, National Federation of M: 958
Victor Talking Machine Company
Recording industry (History) R: 182
Victoria [British queen] V: 355 *with portrait*
Albert, Prince A: 311
Anesthesia (History) A: 459
India (British India) I: 130-131
United Kingdom (The Victorian Age) U: 68
Victoria [mother of]
Wilhelm II W: 305
Victoria [British Columbia] V: 357 *with picture*
British Columbia (Population) B: 616; (Visitor's guide) B: 620 *with picture*
Christmas *picture on* C: 529
Victoria [Hong Kong]
Hong Kong (The metropolis) H: 316
Victoria [Seychelles]
Seychelles S: 339 *with picture*
Victoria [state, Australia] V: 356 *with picture and map*
Victoria [ship, 1500's]
Exploration (Magellan's globe-circling expedition) E: 445
Magellan, Ferdinand (The voyage begins) M: 47
Victoria [vehicle]
Carriage C: 248
Victoria, Guadalupe [Mexican political leader] V: 358
Mexico (Independence) M: 470-471
Victoria, Lake *See* Lake Victoria *in this index*
Victoria, Manuel [Mexican government official]
California (Mexican rule) C: 60
Victoria and Albert Museum [London] V: 358
Victoria Crater [Mars]
Mars (Observation by spacecraft) M: 226c-226d
Victoria Cross
Medals, decorations, and orders (Europe) M: 358 *with picture*; (table) M: 359
Victoria crowned-pigeon
Pigeon (The body of a pigeon) P: 458-459 *with picture*; (Wild pigeons) P: 460
Victoria Day [holiday] V: 358
Victoria Desert [region, Australia]
Great Victoria Desert G: 349
Victoria Falls [Zambia-Zimbabwe] V: 358
Africa (Rivers, waterfalls, and deltas) A: 119 *with picture*
Exploration (The exploration of Africa) E: 448-449
National park (Other interesting national parks) N: 42h
Seven natural wonders of the world (Victoria Falls) S: 324 *with picture*
Waterfall (table: Famous waterfalls of the world) W: 143 *with picture*
Victoria Falls National Park [Zambia-Zimbabwe]

National park (table) N: 42f; (Other interesting national parks) N: 42h
Victoria Harbour [Hong Kong]
Hong Kong (The metropolis) H: 316 *with picture*
Victoria Maria Louisa [mother of]
Victoria (Early years) V: 355
Victoria Nyanza *See* Lake Victoria *in this index*
Victoria Park [Regina]
Saskatchewan *picture on* S: 141
Victoria Peak [mountain, Belize]
Belize (Land and climate) B: 237 *with map*
Victoria Peak [mountain, Hong Kong] *See* Tai Ping Shan *in this index*
Victoria Regina [play]
Hayes, Helen H: 117
Victorian Age [British history]
English literature (Victorian literature) E: 320
Poetry (Victorian poetry) P: 597
United Kingdom (The Victorian Age) U: 68
Victoria V: 355
Victorian architecture
Australia (Architecture) A: 906
Victorio [Indian chief]
New Mexico (Territorial days) N: 275
Victory [book by Conrad]
Conrad, Joseph Ci: 973
Victory [ship]
Nelson, Horatio (Victory at Trafalgar) N: 122
Victory Bond [World War II]
Morgenthau, Henry, Jr. M: 805
Victory dance [custom]
Indian, American *picture on* I: 160
Victory in Europe Day
V-E Day V: 256
"Victory of Jewry over Germandom, The" [pamphlet by Marr]
Anti-Semitism A: 559
Victory Over Japan Day
V-J Day V: 256
Victory ship
Ship (Traditional general cargo ships) S: 406-407
Vicuña [animal] V: 358 *with picture*
Alpaca A: 381
Animal *picture on* A: 474
Vida Breve, La [opera by Falla]
Falla, Manuel de F: 16
Vidal, Gore [American author] V: 359
Videla, Jorge [Argentine political leader]
Argentina (The "dirty war") A: 658
Videnov, Zhan [Bulgarian political leader]
Bulgaria (Recent developments) B: 693
Video, Music *See* Music video; Rock video *in this index*
Video art V: 359
Video assist [device]
Motion picture (Shooting the movie) M: 852-853
Video camera
See also Camcorder *in this index*
Camera *picture on* C: 83; (Motion-picture cameras) C: 84
Videophone V: 360
Videotape recorder V: 360
Video cassette recorder *See* Videocassette recorder *in this index*
Video compact disc player [machine]
Compact disc (Other formats) Ci: 902
Video Computer System
Electronic game (The rise and fall of Atari) E: 204d
Video game *See* Electronic game *in this index*
Video game console [machine]
Computer *picture on* Ci: 919
Electronic game E: 204a; (Gameplay) E: 204b-204c; (Gaming platforms) E: 204c; (Renewed interest in consoles) E: 204e
Television (Electronic game systems) T: 110c
Video paint box [machine]
Television (Adding special effects) T: 112
Video phone [machine] *See* Videophone *in this index*
Video poker [game]
Gambling (Slot machines) G: 20-21
Video presentation
Audio-visual materials (Multisensory materials) A: 883
Video-production system
Audio-visual materials (Multisensory materials) A: 883 *with picture*
Video recorder *See* Digital video recorder; Videocassette recorder; Videotape recorder *in this index*
Video thoracoscopy [medicine]
Lung cancer L: 525
Videocassette recorder [machine]
Audio-visual materials (Multisensory materials) A: 883
Television (Home entertainment systems)

T: 110c; (Technological advances) T: 127
Videotape recorder (Types of videotape recorders) V: 360
Videochat [electronics]
Internet (Communication) I: 350b; (Communication without limits) I: 350e
Videoconferencing
Television (Closed-circuit television) T: 110c
Videodisc
DVD D: 393
Videophone [machine] V: 360
Videotape
Audio-visual materials (Multisensory materials) A: 883
Camcorder (The development of camcorders) C: 75
Copyright (Users' rights) Ci: 1047
Journalism (Television journalism) J: 175
Television (Technological advances) T: 127
Videotape recorder V: 360; (How videotape recorders work) V: 360 with diagram
Videotape recorder V: 360 with pictures
Audio-visual materials (Multisensory materials) A: 883 with picture
Communication (The development of television) Ci: 885
Vidicon [electronics]
Television (Creating the video signals) T: 122
Vidigueira, Count of
Da Gama, Vasco (Later life) D: 4
Vieau, Jacques [American settler]
Milwaukee (Early development) M: 561
Vieira, João Bernardo [Guinea-Bissau political leader]
Guinea-Bissau (History) G: 434
Vienna [Austria] V: 361 with pictures
Austria A: 928 with picture; (People) A: 931 with map
Vienna, Battle of [1683]
Poland (The decline of Poland) P: 612
Vienna, Congress of [1814-1815] V: 363
Ambassador A: 404
Austria (Metternich and revolution) A: 938
Europe (Revolution, democracy, and nationalism) E: 412-413
Germany (The Congress of Vienna) G: 165
Italy (The French Revolution and Napoleon) I: 514-515
World, History of the (The rise of democracy and nationalism) W: 443-444
Vienna Basin [region, Austria]
Austria (Land regions) A: 933
Vienna Boys' Choir
Austria picture on A: 933
Vienna Circle [philosophy]
Positivism (Logical positivism) P: 697
Vienna lake [dye]
Lake L: 35
Vienna sausage [food]
Sausage S: 163
Vienna Secession
Architecture (Early modern architecture in Europe) A: 627-628
Viennese waltz [dance]
Ballroom dancing B: 63
Strauss, Johann, Jr. So: 921
Strauss, Johann, Sr. So: 921
Waltz W: 22
Vientiane [Laos] V: 363
Indochina (A new kingdom) I: 225
Laos L: 70 with map
Vieques [island, Puerto Rico]
Puerto Rico (Puerto Rico today) P: 884
Viet Cong [political group] V: 363
Cold War (To the brink and back) Ci: 765; (The Vietnam War) Ci: 769
Tet Offensive T: 182a
Vietnam War V: 373
Viète, François [French mathematician]
Mathematics (The Renaissance) M: 306
Vietminh [Vietnamese history]
Asia (The spread of Communism) A: 807
Dien Bien Phu, Battle of D: 198
Geneva Accords G: 87
Ho Chi Minh H: 270
Indochina (Independence) I: 225
Vietnam V: 364; (The August Revolution of 1945) V: 370
Vietnam War (The Indochina War) V: 373
Vietnam V: 364 with pictures and maps
See also North Vietnam; South Vietnam in this index
Asia (The spread of Communism) A: 807
Asian Americans (Arrivals of the late 1900's) A: 813
Cambodia (History) C: 72
Communism (Expansion in Southeast Asia)

Ci: 894
Dien Bien Phu, Battle of D: 198
Education picture on E: 96
France (The Fourth Republic) F: 475-476
Geneva Accords G: 87
Ho Chi Minh H: 270
Indochina I: 224 with map
Khmer Rouge K: 308b
Vietnam Peace Talks See Paris Peace Talks in this index
Vietnam Veterans Against the War [political group]
Kerry, John Forbes K: 306
Vietnam Veterans Memorial [Washington, D.C.] V: 372
National Park System (table: National memorials) N: 54
Washington, D.C. map on W: 76; (The Vietnam Veterans Memorial) W: 73 with picture
Vietnam War [1957-1975] V: 372 with pictures and map
See also Antiwar movement in this index
Academic freedom (The 1900's) A: 20
Ace A: 24
Agent Orange A: 140
Air force (During the Vietnam War) A: 187
Air Force, United States (The Vietnam War) A: 195
Army (Armies in the nuclear age) A: 728
Army, United States (The Vietnam War [1957-1975]) A: 739
Asia picture on A: 810; (The spread of Communism) A: 807
Asian Americans (Arrivals of the late 1900's) A: 813
Australia (The Vietnam War) A: 925
Bomb B: 452
Cambodia (History) C: 72-73
Carter, Jimmy (Early programs) C: 257
Central Intelligence Agency (History) C: 357
Coast Guard, United States (The Coast Guard since World War II) C: 738
Cold War picture on Ci: 767; (To the brink and back) Ci: 765; (The Vietnam War) Ci: 769
Communism (Expansion in Southeast Asia) Ci: 894 with picture
Congress of the United States (Continued struggle for power) Ci: 948
Democratic Party (Times of trouble) D: 127
Ford, Gerald Rudolph (Foreign affairs) F: 378
Foreign policy (Public opinion) F: 388
Geneva Accords G: 88
Guerrilla warfare (History) G: 420
Hanoi H: 53
Herbicide (Hazards of herbicides) H: 198
Hmong H: 270
Ho Chi Minh H: 271
Ho Chi Minh City H: 271
Indochina (Independence) I: 225; (The Geneva Accords) I: 225
International relations (The Vietnam War) I: 345
Johnson, Lyndon Baines (Foreign affairs) J: 149; (The widening Vietnam War) J: 150-151; (Johnson declines to run) J: 151
Journalism picture on J: 172
Kennedy, John Fitzgerald (Other developments) K: 266
Kerry, John Forbes K: 306
Kissinger, Henry Alfred K: 337
Laos (History) L: 71-72
McCain, John (Early life) M: 332
McCarthy, Eugene Joseph M: 332a
McNamara, Robert Strange M: 344
My Lai Massacre M: 969
Navy, United States (The Vietnam War [1957-1975]) N: 89
New Left N: 255
Nixon, Richard Milhous (Foreign policy) N: 432-433; (Foreign affairs) N: 435
Paris, Treaties of (The treaties of 1973) P: 168
President of the United States (The Vietnam War) P: 769
Prisoner of war P: 808
Red Cross (In the United States) R: 187
Southeast Asia Treaty Organization So: 687
Students for a Democratic Society So: 932
Television (The 1960's) T: 119 with picture
Tet Offensive T: 182a
Thailand (History) T: 226-227
United States, History of the (The Vietnam War) U: 196a
Unknown soldier U: 212
Viet Cong V: 363
Vietnam V: 364; (The Vietnam War) V: 371
Vietnam Veterans Memorial V: 372
War (Popular support) W: 24; (table) W: 25
War correspondent W: 26
War crime (The Vietnam War) W: 27

World, History of the (The rise of Communism and the Cold War) W: 446-448
Vietnamese [people]
Vietnam (People) V: 365 with picture
Vietnamization [U.S. history]
Nixon, Richard Milhous (Foreign policy) N: 432-433
Vietnam War (Vietnamization) V: 376
Viets [people]
Indochina (The Viets) I: 224
Vieux Carré See French Quarter in this index
Vieux-Montréal [district] See Old Montreal in this index
View
Mechanical drawing (Information in the drawing) M: 353
View camera
Camera (View cameras) C: 83 with picture
Photography (Other types of cameras) P: 409
View from Saturday, The [book by Konigsburg]
Konigsburg, Elaine K: 365
View of Bethlehem, A [engraving by Garrison]
Colonial life in America picture on Ci: 792
View of Genoa [painting by Corot]
Corot, Camille picture on Ci: 1069
View of the English Stage, A [book by Hazlitt]
Hazlitt, William H: 123
View of the Thames [painting by Kokoschka]
Kokoschka, Oskar picture on K: 362
View of Toledo [painting by El Greco]
Greco, El G: 351 with picture
Viewfinder [device]
Camcorder (How a camcorder works) C: 76
Camera (Positioning the camera) C: 80
Photography (How a camera works) P: 407-408; (Compact cameras) P: 408
Viewpoint
Public opinion P: 858
Viganò, Salvatore [Italian choreographer]
Ballet (Ballet d'action) B: 51
Vigée, Louis [French painter]
Vigée-Lebrun, Elisabeth V: 378
Vigée-Lebrun, Elisabeth [French painter] V: 378
Painting (Rococo painting) P: 65
Vigeland, Gustav [Norwegian sculptor]
Norway (Arts) N: 541 with picture
Vigil [ritual]
Knights and knighthood picture on K: 351
Vigilance, Central Office of
Vatican City (Armed forces) V: 288
Vigilante [U.S. history] V: 378
Montana M: 742
Western frontier life in America (Law and order) W: 238
Vigile [police]
Fire department (History) F: 127
Police (History) P: 623-624
Vigilius [pope]
Pope (table) P: 666
Vigny, Alfred de [French poet] V: 378
French literature (Romantic poetry) F: 521
Vijaya [Indian prince]
Sri Lanka (History) So: 819
Viking [rocket]
Rocket (High-altitude rockets) R: 390
Viking [space probes]
Earthquake (Quakes elsewhere in the solar system) E: 38b
Life (In our solar system) L: 280
Mars picture on M: 226; (Observation by spacecraft) M: 226c-226d
Space exploration (Probes to Mars) So: 710
Viking Age
Vikings V: 378
Viking long ship [sailing vessel]
Ship, Model picture on S: 428
Vikings [people] V: 378 with pictures and map
Anglo-Saxons A: 464
Arctic (Arctic exploration) A: 638
Atlantic Ocean (Exploration) A: 867
Canada, History of (Early European exploration) C: 138-139
Denmark (Early days) D: 139
England (The Anglo-Saxon period) E: 304-305
English language (Old English) E: 313
Exploration (Viking exploration) E: 442
Flag picture on F: 209
Greenland (History) G: 385
Humberside H: 431
Ireland (The Viking raiders) I: 425
Navy (Navies in the Middle Ages) N: 79
Normans N: 456
Norway (The Viking period) N: 545 with picture
Nunavut (Arrival of the Europeans) N: 612
Russia (Early days) R: 547
Ship pictures on S: 419; (Viking ships) S: 416
Sweden (The Swedish Vikings) So: 1032 with

picture
  United States, History of the (America before
    colonial times) **U:** 149
  Warship *picture on* **W:** 42; (Early warships) **W:** 41
Vikings, Minnesota [team] *See* Minnesota Vikings
  in this index
Vilas, William F. [American government official]
  Cleveland, Grover (table) **Ci:** 671
  Interior, Department of the (table) **I:** 325
Vili [Norse mythology]
  Mythology (The creation of life) **M:** 985-986
Villa [home]
  Pompeii (Early days) **P:** 653-654
Villa, Pancho [Filipino boxer]
  Boxing (Boxing in Asia) **B:** 531
Villa, Pancho [Mexican general] **V:** 384 *with picture*
  Latin America (In Mexico) **L:** 109
  Mexican Revolution of 1910 (The revolution)
    M: 445
  Mexico (The Revolution of 1910) **M:** 472
  Pershing, John Joseph (Mexican campaign)
    P: 296
  Wilson, Woodrow (Crisis in Mexico) **W:** 323
Villa Ada [park, Rome]
  Rome (Parks and gardens) **R:** 429
Villa Borghese [park, Rome]
  Rome (Parks and gardens) **R:** 429
Villa Giulia, National Museum of the [museum,
  Rome]
  Rome (Museums and art galleries) **R:** 429
Villa Glori [park, Rome]
  Rome (Parks and gardens) **R:** 429
Villa Hammerschmidt [Bonn, Germany]
  Bonn (The city) **B:** 460 *with picture*
Villa-Lobos, Heitor [Brazilian composer] **V:** 384
  Brazil (The arts) **B:** 576-577
Villa Rotonda [Vicenza, Italy]
  Architecture (Later Renaissance architecture)
    A: 621 *with picture*
  Monticello **M:** 767
Villa Savoye [Poissy, France]
  Architecture *picture on* **A:** 632
Villa Sciarra [park, Rome]
  Rome (Parks and gardens) **R:** 429
Village [political unit] **V:** 384
  City government **Ci:** 594
  India *picture on* **I:** 116; (Village life) **I:** 114
  Local government **L:** 406
  Metropolitan area **M:** 442
  Nigeria (Way of life) **N:** 413 *with picture*
Village Historique Acadien [New Brunswick]
  New Brunswick (Places to visit) **N:** 188
Village in Berry [painting by Rousseau]
  Barbizon School *picture on* **B:** 108
Village Landscape in the Morning Light [painting
  by Friedrich]
  Painting (Romanticism) **P:** 68 *with picture*
Village weaver [bird]
  Bird *picture on* **B:** 344h
  Weaver **W:** 172
Village woodlot
  Forestry (Community forestry) **F:** 406
Villagers, The [book by Icaza]
  Latin American literature (The early 1900's) **L:** 113
Villancico [music]
  Hispanic Americans (In Mexico) **H:** 248
Villanelle
  Poetry (table) **P:** 594
Villaraigosa, Antonio R. [American political
  leader]
  Los Angeles (Recent developments) **L:** 470-471
Villard, Paul [French scientist]
  Gamma rays **G:** 23
Villasur, Pedro de [French explorer]
  Nebraska (Exploration) **N:** 111
Ville-Marie [former name]
  Montreal (French settlement) **M:** 777
Villeda Morales, Ramón [Honduran political
  leader]
  Honduras (Revolutions and reforms) **H:** 313
Villehardouin, Geoffroy de [French author]
  French literature (Early prose) **F:** 519
Villein [European history] **V:** 384
Villella, Edward Joseph [American dancer] **V:** 385
Villemaire, Yolande [Canadian poet]
  Canadian literature (Modern Canadian poets)
    C: 161
Villeneuve, Jacques [Canadian automobile racer]
  Automobile racing (table: Formula One World
    Drivers' Championship) **A:** 980; (table:
    Indianapolis 500 winners) **A:** 980
Villeneuve, Jean M. [Canadian religious leader]
  Cardinal (table: Canadian cardinals) **C:** 211
**Villeneuve, Pierre Charles Jean Baptiste
  Sylvestre de** [French admiral]
  Trafalgar, Battle of **T:** 365
Villepin, Dominique de [French political leader]

France (Recent developments) **F:** 478
Villeré, Jacques [American political leader]
  Louisiana (table) **L:** 496
Villette [book by Brontë]
  Brontë sisters (Their works) **B:** 637
Villette, La [building complex]
  Paris (Renewal and new construction) **P:** 166-167
Villi [anatomy]
  Alimentary canal **A:** 369
  Blood (Transporting nutrients and wastes) **B:** 408
    with diagram
  Human body *picture on* **H:** 420
  Intestine (The small intestine) **I:** 353
  Placenta **P:** 505
Villi, Le [opera by Puccini]
  Puccini, Giacomo **P:** 870
Villiers, George [English general]
  Buckingham, Duke of **B:** 663
Villiers de l'Isle-Adam, Comte de [French writer]
  V: 385
Villon, François [French poet] **V:** 385
  Ballade **B:** 43
  French literature (Lyric poetry) **F:** 518
Vilnius [Lithuania] **V:** 385
  Lithuania **L:** 388 *with picture and map*
Vilsack, Tom [American political leader]
  Agriculture, Department of (table) **A:** 161
  Iowa (table) **I:** 391
  Obama, Barack (table) **O:** 640h
Vimeiro, Battle of [1808]
  Wellington, Duke of (Peninsular War) **W:** 194
Vimeur, Jean Baptiste Donatien de *See*
  Rochambeau, Comte de *in this index*
Viminal Hill [Rome]
  Rome **R:** 429
Vimy [airplane]
  Alcock and Brown **A:** 335
Vimy Ridge, Battle of [1917] **V:** 385
  Currie, Sir Arthur **Ci:** 1197
Viña del Mar [Chile] **V:** 385
  Chile (Recreation) **C:** 462 *with picture*
Vinaya [religion]
  Monasticism (Non-Christian monasticism) **M:** 701
Vincennes [Indiana] **V:** 385
Vincennes [ship]
  Reagan, Ronald Wilson (Persian Gulf conflicts)
    R: 170
Vincennes, Battles of [1778-1779]
  Revolution, American (The Illinois campaign)
    R: 284
Vincent, George E. [American sociologist]
  Chicago, University of (Research program) **C:** 438
Vincent, John H. [American religious leader]
  Chautauqua (The Chautauqua Institution) **C:** 389
Vincent de Paul, Saint [French religious leader]
  V: 386
  Roman Catholic Church (Catholic revival in
    France) **R:** 408
Vincent of Beauvais [French religious leader]
  Encyclopedia (From the 1200's to the 1600's)
    E: 268a
Vincentians [religious group]
  Vincent de Paul, Saint **V:** 386
Vincent's infection *See* Trench mouth *in this index*
Vinci, Leonardo da *See* Leonardo da Vinci *in this
  index*
Vindication of the Rights of Woman, A [book by
  Wollstonecraft]
  Feminism **F:** 69
  Wollstonecraft, Mary **W:** 379
  Women's movement (Forces of change) **W:** 384
Vindobona [Roman history]
  Vienna (History) **V:** 362
Vine [botany] **V:** 386
  Ivy **I:** 522 *with pictures*
Vine cactus [shrub]
  Ocotillo **O:** 669 *with picture*
Vinegar **V:** 386
  Acetic acid **A:** 25
  Antiseptic (History) **A:** 559
Vinegar eel [animal] **V:** 386
Vinegar fly [insect]
  Fly (Head) **F:** 309
  Fruit fly **F:** 549
Vinegar Joe [nickname]
  Stilwell, Joseph Warren **So:** 901
Vineland [book by Pynchon]
  Pynchon, Thomas **P:** 915
Viner, Charles [British jurist]
  Blackstone, Sir William **B:** 394
Viniculture [horticulture]
  Horticulture (Pomology) **H:** 369
Vinland [North American history] **V:** 386
  Exploration (Viking exploration) **E:** 442
  Leif Erikkson **L:** 186
  Vikings (The Norwegian Vikings) **V:** 382
Vinson [ship] *See* Carl Vinson *in this index*

Vinson, Frederick Moore [American jurist] **V:** 387
  Truman, Harry S. (table) **T:** 469
Vinson Massif [mountain, Antarctica]
  Antarctica (Land) **A:** 531-532 *with map*
Vintage
  Wine (Harvesting the grapes) **W:** 337
Vintage racing
  Automobile racing (Other kinds of racing)
    A: 978-979
Vinton, Will [American animator]
  Animation (Stop-motion animation) **A:** 514a
Vinyl [plastic]
  Interior design (Choosing patterns and textures)
    I: 332-333
  Plastics (Making synthetic resins) **P:** 556-557
Viol [musical instrument] **V:** 387
  Violin (History) **V:** 390
Viola [literary figure]
  Shakespeare, William: *(Twelfth Night)* **S:** 360-361
Viola [musical instrument] **V:** 387 *with picture*
  Music (Stringed instruments) **M:** 948 *with picture*
Violence
  Child (Problems in the home) **C:** 453
  Death (Attitudes about death) **D:** 62
  Domestic violence **D:** 300
  Electronic game (Controversy) **E:** 204f
  Football (Violence issues) **F:** 368
  Gun control (Approaches to gun control) **G:** 440-
    441
  Pacifism **P:** 17
  Television (The 1960's) **T:** 119; (Harmful
    impressions) **T:** 120-121
  Terrorism **T:** 175
Violence Against Women Act [1994]
  Domestic violence **D:** 301
Violencia, La [Colombian history]
  Colombia (The early to middle 1900's) **Ci:** 784
Violent Land, The [book by Amado]
  Amado, Jorge **A:** 399
  Latin American literature (The early 1900's) **L:** 113
Violent rebellion
  War **W:** 23
Violet [color]
  Color (The relation between color and light)
    Ci: 817-818 *with diagram*
Violet [plant] **V:** 388 *with picture*
  Flower *pictures on* **F:** 285, **F:** 292; (Garden
    perennials) **F:** 278 *with picture*; (table) **F:** 301
    with picture
  Gardening *picture on* **G:** 37
Violin [musical instrument] **V:** 388 *with pictures*
  Amati family **A:** 401
  Jazz (Other instruments) **J:** 69
  Music (Stringed instruments) **M:** 948 *with picture*
  Suzuki method **So:** 1013
  Williamsburg *picture on* **W:** 313
Violin and Palette [painting by Braque]
  Painting (Cubism) **P:** 77-78 *with picture*
Viollet-le-Duc, Eugène Emmanuel [French
  architect]
  Notre Dame, Cathedral of **N:** 551
Violoncello [musical instrument] *See* Cello *in this
  index*
Viotti, Giovanni [Italian violinist]
  Violin (History) **V:** 390
Vipassana [religion]
  Buddhism (Meditation) **B:** 669
Viper [snake] **V:** 390 *with picture*
  Adder **A:** 46 *with picture*
  Bushmaster **B:** 723
  Snake (Fangs and venom glands) **S:** 528 *with
    picture*; (Vipers) **S:** 535 *with pictures*
  Snakebite (Types of venomous snakes) **S:** 536
Viperfish [fish]
  Deep sea (Fish) **D:** 82b-82c *with picture*
Viper's bugloss [plant] **V:** 391
Vira [music]
  Portugal (The arts) **P:** 689-690
Viracocha [Inca god]
  Inca (Religion) **I:** 96
Viral genome [biology]
  Virus (Structure) **V:** 427
Viral hepatitis [disease] *See* Hepatitis *in this index*
Viral infection cycle
  Virus *diagram on* **V:** 427; (Infection) **V:** 428
Viral marketing campaign
  Internet (Spreading ideas) **I:** 350e-350f
Viral meningitis [disease]
  Meningitis **M:** 400
Virchow, Rudolf [German pathologist] **V:** 391
  Biology (Materialistic physiology and the cell
    theory) **B:** 319
Vireo [bird] **V:** 391 *with picture*
  Bird (Birds of forests and woodlands) **B:** 334 *with
    picture*
Virgil [Roman poet] **V:** 391
  Aeneid **A:** 84

Classicism (Rome) **Ci: 653**
Divine Comedy **D: 242**
Latin literature (The Augustan Age) **L: 116**
Poetry (Ancient poetry) **P: 595-596**
Rome, Ancient *picture on* **R: 445**
Virgin and Child Enthroned with Angels and Saints [icon]
Painting (Early Christian and Byzantine art) **P: 49** *with picture*
Virgin and Child with Saint Anne, The [painting by Leonardo]
Leonardo da Vinci *picture on* **L: 200**; (Paintings) **L: 200b**
Virgin birth [religion]
Immaculate Conception **I: 79**
Virgin Gorda [island]
Virgin Islands **V: 392** *with map*
Virgin Islands [islands, Caribbean Sea] **V: 392** *with maps*
Virgin Islands, British [British territory] **V: 393**
Virgin Islands **V: 392** *with map*
Virgin Islands, United States [U.S. territory] **V: 393** *with pictures*
Flag *picture on* **F: 213**
Territory (Territories in the United States) **T: 174**
Virgin Islands **V: 392** *with map*
Virgin Islands, University of the
Virgin Islands, United States (Education) **V: 395**
Virgin Islands Coral Reef National Monument [Virgin Islands]
National Park System (table: National monuments) **N: 52**
Virgin Islands National Park V: 397
National Park System (table: National parks) **N: 48**
Virgin Islands, United States *picture on* **V: 396**
Virgin Lands project [Soviet history]
Kazakhstan (History) **K: 251-252**
Virgin Mary [mother of Jesus] *See* Mary *in this index*
Virgin of Guadalupe
Guadalupe Day **G: 408**
Virgin of Quito [statue]
Ecuador *picture on* **E: 67**
Virgin olive oil
Olive oil **O: 744**
Virgin Queen
Virginia **V: 398**
Virgin River
Nevada (Rivers and lakes) **N: 166** *with map*
Virgin Soil Upturned [book by Sholokhov]
Sholokhov, Mikhail **S: 433**
Virgin Spring, The [film]
Bergman, Ingmar **B: 257**
Virgin with Saint Inés and Saint Tecla, The [painting by El Greco]
Madonna and Child (Types of Madonna paintings) **M: 38**
Virgin wool
Wool (Types of wool) **W: 399**
Virginal [musical instrument] **V: 397**
Virginia [state] **V: 398** *with pictures and maps*
See also the list of Related articles in the Virginia *article*
American literature (Colonial literature [1608-1764]) **A: 414**
Colonial life in America (Development of the Thirteen Colonies) **Ci: 790** *with map*
Insurance (Greater regulation) **I: 315**
Jefferson, Thomas (Colonial statesman) **J: 79**
Newport, Christopher **N: 379**
Randolph, Peyton **R: 137**
United States, History of the (Virginia and Maryland) **U: 153**
Virginia [ironclad]
Civil War, American (First battle between ironclads) **Ci: 626** *with picture*; (The peninsular campaign) **Ci: 626b**
Monitor and *Merrimack* **M: 724**
Virginia [ship]
Maine (Exploration and settlements) **M: 89**
Virginia, University of V: 423
Jefferson, Thomas (Later years) **J: 87** *with picture*
Virginia *picture on* **V: 399**
Virginia, Valley of
Virginia (Land regions) **V: 410**
Virginia Agricultural and Mechanical College [former name]
Virginia Polytechnic Institute and State University **V: 425**
Virginia Beach [Virginia] **V: 423** *with picture*
Virginia (Visitor's guide) **V: 408**
Virginia bluebell [plant]
Bluebell **B: 422**
Cowslip **Ci: 1113**
Virginia City [Nevada] **V: 424**
Nevada **N: 156**; (Visitor's guide) **N: 164** *with picture*; (The Comstock Lode) **N: 174**
Western frontier life in America (Mining) **W: 234-235**

Virginia Colony [U.S. history]
Colonial life in America (Geographic divisions) **Ci: 791** *with map*
West Virginia (White exploration) **W: 226**
Virginia Commonwealth University V: 424
Virginia Company [U.S. history]
Bermuda (History) **B: 268**
Colonial life in America (Early English settlements) **Ci: 789**
Jamestown **J: 29**
London Company **L: 445**
Newport, Christopher **N: 379**
United States, History of the (Virginia and Maryland) **U: 153**
Virginia (The Jamestown settlement) **V: 418**
Virginia Company of Plymouth, The
Plymouth Company **P: 584**
Virginia Conventions [U.S. history]
Jefferson, Thomas (Revolutionary leader) **J: 79**
Virginia cowslip [plant]
Bluebell **B: 422**
Cowslip **Ci: 1113**
Virginia creeper [plant] **V: 424** *with picture*
Ivy **I: 522**
Virginia Declaration of Rights [1776]
Constitution of the United States (The Bill of Rights) **Ci: 1001**
Williamsburg **W: 312**
Virginia deer *See* White-tailed deer *in this index*
Virginia Dynasty [U.S. history]
Virginia: (The Mother of Presidents) **V: 421**
Virginia Gazette [newspaper]
Virginia (Communication) **V: 416**
Williamsburg (Early days) **W: 312-313**
Virginia Military Institute V: 425
Virginia Museum of Fine Arts [Richmond]
Virginia (Libraries and museums) **V: 402-403** *with picture*
Virginia opossum [animal]
Opossum **O: 811**
Virginia pine [tree]
Pine (Southeastern pines) **P: 468**
Virginia Plan [U.S. history]
Constitution of the United States (The compromises) **Ci: 1000**
Randolph, Edmund **R: 137**
Virginia Polytechnic Institute and State University V: 425
Virginia rail [bird]
Rail **R: 103** *with picture*
Virginia Resolutions *See* Kentucky and Virginia Resolutions *in this index*
Virginia Resolves [U.S. history]
Virginia (The course toward independence) **V: 420**
Virginia snakeroot
Snakeroot **S: 536**
Virginia Tech [university] *See* Virginia Polytechnic Institute and State University *in this index*
Virginian, The [book by Wister]
Western frontier life in America (Literature) **W: 239-240**
Virginian, The [film]
Cooper, Gary **Ci: 1034**
Virginian stock [plant]
Stock **So: 903**
Virginium [former name, francium]
Francium **F: 482**
Virginius Affair [1873] **V: 425**
Virgin's-bower [plant]
Clematis **Ci: 661**
Virgo [astrology] **V: 425** *with picture*
Zodiac (The zodiac in astrology) **Z: 597** *with picture*
Virgo Cluster [astronomy]
Galaxy (Galaxy groups, clusters, and beyond) **G: 9**
Viridiana [film]
Buñuel, Luis **B: 700**
Virion [biology]
Virus **V: 427** *with diagram*
Viroid [biology] **V: 426**
Virology [science]
Biology (table) **B: 317**
Virus **V: 427**
Virtanen, Artturi Ilmari [Finnish biochemist]
Nobel Prizes (Chemistry: 1945) **N: 443**
Virtual currency
Internet (Commerce) **I: 350b**
Virtual environment [electronics] *See* Virtual reality *in this index*
Virtual image [optics]
Lens (A virtual image) **L: 196b** *with diagram*
Magnifying glass **M: 62**
Mirror (Plane mirrors) **M: 616**
Virtual particle [physics]
Vacuum (In particle physics) **V: 256-257**

Virtual reality [electronics] **V: 426** *with picture*
Computer graphics **Ci: 924g**
Science fiction (Science fiction today) **S: 206**
Virtual reel system
Slot machine **S: 508a**
Virtue [philosophy]
Ethics (Ancient ethics) **E: 366**
Philosophy (Aristotle) **P: 387**
Virtuoso concerto [music]
Concerto **C: 928**
Virunga Mountains
Rwanda (Land) **R: 571** *with map*
Virunga National Park [Democratic Republic of the Congo]
National park (table) **N: 42f**
Virus [biology] **V: 427** *with pictures*
See also the list of Related articles in the Virus *article*
AIDS **A: 164**
Antiviral drug **A: 560**
Avian influenza **A: 982**
Cancer (Viruses) **C: 171**
Canine parvovirus **C: 177**
Cell (Virus diseases) **C: 336**
Cold, Common **Ci: 760**
Disease *picture on* **D: 229**; (Viral diseases) **D: 227**; (Medical treatment) **D: 232-233**
Electron microscope *picture on* **E: 204**
Epstein-Barr virus **E: 345**
Food poisoning **F: 340**
Hantavirus **H: 54**
Hepatitis **H: 192**
Herpes, Genital **H: 214**
Herpesvirus **H: 214**
Immune system **I: 87**
Influenza (How influenza spreads) **I: 268b**
Interferon **I: 324**
Life **L: 274**
Löffler, Friedrich August Johannes **L: 420**
Microbiology **M: 513**
Monkeypox **M: 730**
Parasite **P: 153**
Plant (Diseases) **P: 539**
Pneumonia (How pneumonia develops) **P: 586**
Rabies (Cause) **R: 49**
Rotavirus **R: 486**
Rous, Francis Peyton **R: 492**
SARS **S: 127**
Science *picture on* **S: 191**
Sexually transmitted disease **S: 338b**
Smallpox **S: 513**
Swine flu **So: 1048**
Viroid **V: 426**
Wart **W: 44**
West Nile virus **W: 205**
Xenotransplant **X: 544**
Yellow fever **Y: 556**
Virus, Computer *See* Computer virus *in this index*
Visa [document] **V: 428b**
Immigration (The fourth wave) **I: 83**
Passport **P: 192**
Visayan Islands [Philippines]
Philippines (The main islands) **P: 376** *with map*
Viscacha [rodent] **V: 428b**
Visceral leishmaniasis [disease] *See* Kala-azar in *this index*
Visceral pleura [membrane]
Lungs (Parts of the lungs) **L: 523**
Pleura **P: 573**
Visconti, Tedaldo *See* Gregory X *in this index*
Viscose [material]
Cellophane (How cellophane is made) **C: 340**
Cellulose (Industrial uses) **C: 341**
Viscose process
Rayon (How rayon is made) **R: 153** *with diagram*
Viscosity [physics] **V: 428b** *with picture*
Aerodynamics (Principles of aerodynamics) **A: 85**
Superfluid **So: 993** *with diagram*
Volcano **V: 438**
Viscount [title] **V: 429**
Nobility (In the United Kingdom) **N: 450**
Viscountess [title]
Lady **L: 25**
Nobility (In the United Kingdom) **N: 450**
Viscous flow [physics]
Vacuum (Properties) **V: 256**
Viscous fluid
Fluid **F: 304**
Vishnu [Hindu god] **V: 429** *with picture*
Hinduism (Deities) **H: 236**
Holi **H: 290**
India *picture on* **I: 119**; (Hinduism) **I: 116**
Krishna **K: 388**
Rama **R: 131**
Ramayana **R: 132**
Vishtaspa [king of Persia]
Zoroastrianism (History) **Z: 607**

Visibility, Distance of
  Horizon H: 335 *with diagram*
Visible Human Project [medicine]
  Medicine *picture on* M: 376; (Computers and electronic communication) M: 370
Visible light
  Light L: 282
Visible load [geology]
  River (River systems) R: 351
Visible spectrum [light]
  Color (The relation between color and light) Ci: 817-818 *with diagram*
  Light (The spectrum of light sources) L: 284 *with diagram*
Visible speech [system]
  Bell, Alexander Graham (His early life) B: 240
  Speech therapy (History) So: 774
VisiCalc [spreadsheet program]
  Computer (Spreadsheet programs) Ci: 917
  Spreadsheet So: 805
Visigoths [people]
  Gaul G: 70
  Goths G: 280
  Rome, Ancient (The decline of the empire) R: 447-448
  Spain (Germanic rule) So: 746
  Theodosius I T: 252
Vision
  See also Eye; Vision test *in this index*
  Alhazen A: 366
  Animal (Adaptations for sensing the environment) A: 492-493
  Artificial intelligence (Computer vision) A: 760
  Bird B: 364 *with pictures*
  Blind spot B: 400
  Brain (Sensing the environment) B: 552
  Color (How we *see* color) Ci: 818-819 *with picture*
  Color blindness Ci: 827
  Compound eye Ci: 906 *with diagram*
  Contact lens Ci: 1020
  Dog (Senses) D: 265
  Hawk *picture on* H: 111
  Human being (Physical characteristics) H: 412-413
  Insect (Sight) I: 290 *with pictures*
  Light (Light in medicine) L: 292
  Mammal (Senses) M: 120
  Optical illusion O: 812
  Optometry O: 814
  Perception (Factors affecting perception) P: 283 *with pictures*
  Reading (How we read) R: 156; (Physical disabilities) R: 162
  Senses S: 301
Vision, A [book by Yeats]
  Yeats, William Butler Y: 555
Vision After the Sermon, The [painting by Gauguin]
  Painting (Postimpressionism) P: 75 *with picture*
Vision engineer [career] *See* Technical director *in this index*
Vision mixer [machine] *See* Switcher *in this index*
Vision of Piers Plowman, The [poem]
  English literature (The age of Chaucer) E: 316
  Langland, William L: 61
  Robin Hood R: 367
Vision of Sir Launfal, The [poem by Lowell]
  Launfal, Sir L: 121
  Lowell, James Russell (Literary success) L: 510
Vision of the Cross, The [painting]
  Christianity *picture on* C: 523
Vision quest [religion]
  Indian, American (Religion) I: 146-147; (Before European contact) I: 165-166
Vision test
  Blind spot B: 400
  Color blindness Ci: 827 *with pictures*
  Eye (Receiving regular eye examinations) E: 469
"Visionary Letter" [poem by Rimbaud]
  Rimbaud, Arthur R: 341
Visions [book by Quevedo]
  Quevedo, Francisco de Q: 41
Visit, The [play by Dürrenmatt]
  Dürrenmatt, Friedrich D: 390
"Visit from Saint Nicholas, A" [poem]
  Christmas (Other customs) C: 536
  Moore, Clement Clarke M: 796
  Santa Claus (Santa's appearance) S: 114
Visitation Order [religious group]
  Francis de Sales, Saint F: 481
Visiting nurse
  Nursing (Community health nursing) N: 617
Visor
  Armor *picture on* A: 720
Visscher, Claes Jansz [Dutch engraver]
  Shakespeare, William *picture on* S: 352
"Vissi d'arte" [aria]

  Opera: *(Tosca)* O: 807
Vistula [former city]
  Toledo (History) T: 321
Vistula River [Poland] V: 429
  Oder River O: 674
  Poland (Rivers and canals) P: 609
Visual acuity
  Blindness B: 401
  Eye (Receiving regular eye examinations) E: 469
Visual arts
  Fine arts F: 104
Visual disability
  Disability *picture on* D: 220; (Visual disabilities) D: 219
Visual Flight Rules [navigation]
  Map (Navigation maps) M: 178
Visual illusion *See* Optical illusion *in this index*
Visual materials
  Audio-visual materials (Visual materials) A: 882 *with picture*
Visual mixing
  Color *diagram on* Ci: 820
Visual purple [pigment]
  Eye (The retina) E: 462
Visual rhyme
  Rhyme R: 319
Visual sensory memory
  Memory (Sensory memory) M: 392
Visual telegraph
  Communication (During ancient times) Ci: 879; (The 1700's) Ci: 880-881 *with picture*
Visual vibration
  Color *diagram on* Ci: 820
Visualization [psychology]
  Imagination I: 79
Vita Nuova, La [poems by Dante]
  Dante Alighieri (His works) D: 34
Vital records
  Genealogy G: 82
Vital statistics V: 429
  Population (Census) P: 673
  Public health (Collecting vital statistics) P: 856
Vital Statistics System
  Vital statistics (Collecting and publishing vital statistics) V: 429-430
Vitalian, Saint [pope]
  Pope (History) P: 666
Vitalism [chemistry]
  Chemistry (Development of organic chemistry) C: 404
Vitamin V: 430
  Baby (Vitamins and iron) B: 9
  Cancer (Alternative medicine) C: 173
  Diet (Normal diet) D: 199
  Dietary supplement D: 200
  Food (Regulating body processes) F: 331
  Food additive (Kinds of additives) F: 339
  Health food (Types of health foods) H: 129
  Liver (Digestion and use of food) L: 394
  Medicine (The medical revolution) M: 376
  Milk (Vitamins) M: 546
  Nutrition (Kinds of nutrients) N: 625; (Deficiency diseases) N: 630; (Evaluate claims about foods and dietary supplements carefully) N: 630
Vitamin A
  Vitamin (Vitamin A) V: 430; (table) V: 431
  Baby (Vitamins and iron) B: 9
  Eye (Adaptation to light and dark) E: 464; (Diseases of the retina) E: 467
  Lipid L: 344
  Milk (Fortification) M: 548
  Nutrition (Vitamins) N: 626
  Plant (Breeding and genetics) P: 542
  Wald, George W: 6
Vitamin B complex
  Vitamin (Water-soluble vitamins) V: 430
  Folic acid F: 315
  Meat (Food value of meat) M: 346-347
  Pellagra P: 232
Vitamin B$_1$ *See* Thiamine *in this index*
Vitamin B$_2$ *See* Riboflavin *in this index*
Vitamin B$_6$
  Vitamin (Vitamin B$_6$, pantothenic acid, and biotin) V: 431; (table) V: 431
  Nutrition (Vitamins) N: 626
Vitamin B$_{12}$
  Vitamin (table) V: 431; (Vitamin B$_{12}$, folic acid, and choline) V: 432
  Anemia (Insufficient production of red blood cells) A: 457
  Cobalt (Uses) Ci: 741
  Nutrition (Vitamins) N: 626
  Vegetarianism V: 295
Vitamin C
  Vitamin (table) V: 431; (Vitamin C) V: 432
  Acerola A: 24
  Antioxidant A: 557

  Baby (Vitamins and iron) B: 9
  Nutrition (Vitamins) N: 626; (Deficiency diseases) N: 630-631
  Scurvy S: 261
Vitamin D
  Vitamin (Vitamin D) V: 430; (table) V: 431; (How vitamins work) V: 432
  Baby (Vitamins and iron) B: 9
  Lipid L: 344
  Milk (Fortification) M: 548
  Nutrition (Vitamins) N: 626; (Deficiency diseases) N: 630-631
  Races, Human (Climatic adaptations) R: 58
  Rickets R: 334
  Ultraviolet rays (Uses of ultraviolet rays) U: 17
Vitamin D$_2$
  Vitamin (Vitamin D) V: 430
Vitamin D$_3$
  Vitamin (Vitamin D) V: 430
Vitamin deficiency
  Malnutrition M: 111
  Nutrition (Deficiency diseases) N: 630
  Vitamin V: 430
Vitamin E
  Vitamin (Vitamin E) V: 430; (table) V: 431
  Antioxidant A: 557
  Lipid L: 344
  Nutrition (Vitamins) N: 626
Vitamin K
  Vitamin (Vitamin K) V: 430; (table) V: 431
  Lipid L: 344
  Nutrition (Vitamins) N: 626
Vitamin P [former name]
  Citrin Ci: 573
Vitelline membrane
  Egg (The yolk) E: 117 *with diagram*
Vitellius [Roman emperor]
  Rome, Ancient (table) R: 447
Viti Levu [island]
  Fiji F: 97 *with map*
Vitiligo [disease] V: 432
Vitis vinifera [plant]
  Wine (Where wine comes from) W: 336
Vitrectomy [medicine]
  Eye (Diseases of the retina) E: 467
Vitreous humor [physiology]
  Blindness (Diseases) B: 401
  Eye (Parts of the eye) E: 460 *with picture*; (Diseases of the retina) E: 467
Vitrification [freezing technique]
  Cryobiology Ci: 1165
Vitrinellid [animal]
  Shell S: 384
Vitrinite [geology]
  Coal (Analyzing coal composition) Ci: 717-718
Vitro fertilization [reproduction] *See* In vitro fertilization *in this index*
Vitruvian man [drawing by Leonardo]
  Leonardo da Vinci *picture on* L: 200b; (Drawings and scientific studies) L: 200-200a
Vitruvius [Roman architect]
  Leonardo da Vinci (Drawings and scientific studies) L: 200-200a
Vitry, Philippe de [French composer]
  Classical music (Secular music) Ci: 646
Vittoria, Alessandro [Italian sculptor]
  Sculpture (Michelangelo) S: 252-253
Vittorini, Elio [Italian author]
  Italian literature (The 1900's) I: 495
Vivace [music]
  Music (table) M: 954
Vivaldi, Antonio [Italian composer] V: 433
Vivian, John C. [American political leader]
  Colorado (table) Ci: 844
Vivian Beaumont Theater
  Lincoln Center for the Performing Arts L: 327
Viviani, Emilia [Italian public figure]
  Shelley, Percy Bysshe (His writings) S: 391
Viviparous animal [zoology] V: 433
  Oviparous animal O: 882
  Reptile (Reproduction) R: 252
Viviparous Quadrupeds of North America, The [book by Audubon and Bachman]
  Audubon, John James (His works) A: 885
Vivisection [biology]
  Animal experimentation A: 509
Vixen [animal]
  Fox (The life of a fox) F: 439 *with pictures*
Vizcaino, Sebastián [Spanish explorer]
  California (Spanish and English exploration) C: 60
  Monterey M: 764
Vizier [title] V: 433
  Egypt, Ancient (Government) E: 139
Vizsla [dog] V: 433 *with picture*
  Dog *picture on* D: 269
Vlacq, Adriaen [Dutch mathematician]
  Logarithms (History) L: 424

Vlad Tepes [prince of Walachia]
Dracula D: 317
Vampire V: 268
Vladimir I [Grand Prince of Kiev] V: 433
Russia (Architecture) R: 536; (The state of Kievan Rus) R: 547-548
Ukraine (Kievan Rus) U: 12
Vikings (The Swedish Vikings) V: 383
Vladivostok [Russia] V: 433
Vlaminck, Maurice de [French painter] V: 433
VLBA [telescope] See Very Long Baseline Array Telescope in this index
VLCC [ship]
Tanker (Kinds of tankers) T: 28
VLT [telescope] See Very Large Telescope in this index
VMI [college] See Virginia Military Institute in this index
VOA See Voice of America in this index
Voaden, Herman [Canadian author]
Canadian literature (Literature between the world wars) C: 158-159
Vocabulary V: 434
English language (Vocabulary) E: 312
Shakespeare, William (Vocabulary) S: 367
Vocal cord [anatomy]
Language (The sounds of language) L: 62 with diagram
Larynx L: 79
Music (Musical instruments) M: 948
Singing (How people sing) S: 472
Voice (The human voice) V: 436 with diagrams
Vocal fold [anatomy] See Vocal cord in this index
Vocal music
Classical music (Vocal music) Ci: 644
Vocal sac [zoology]
Frog (Voice) F: 537-538 with picture
Vocal tract [anatomy]
Language (The sounds of language) L: 62 with diagram
Vocalizing
Speed reading So: 774
Vocation
Career education C: 213
Careers C: 214 with pictures
Vocational blindness
Blindness B: 401
Vocational education V: 434 with picture
See also Career education in this index
Careers (Vocational schools) C: 217
Education (Kinds of education) E: 87-88
Germany (Education) G: 151-152
School (High schools) S: 181
Universities and colleges (Vocational study and the liberal arts) U: 211
Vocational Education, Federal Board for [U.S. history]
Veterans Affairs, Department of (History) V: 344
Vocational Education Act [1963]
Vocational education (The 1900's and early 2000's) V: 435
Vocational Education Amendments [1968]
Vocational education (The 1900's and early 2000's) V: 435
Vocational guidance
Career education C: 213
Guidance (Vocational or career guidance) G: 422
Vocational high school
Vocational education (Public high schools) V: 434
Vocational rehabilitation V: 435
Disability (Employment) D: 221
Vocational Rehabilitation of Disabled Persons Act [1961]
Vocational rehabilitation V: 436
Vocative case [grammar]
Case (Cases in Latin) C: 271-272
"Voce poco fa, Una" [aria]
Opera: (Barber of Seville, The) O: 801
Vodka
Alcoholic beverage (Vodka) A: 336
Vodou [religion] V: 448 with picture
Haiti (People) H: 14
Latin America (Religion) L: 98-99
Magic (Contagious magic) M: 50; (Africa and the Americas) M: 50
Zombie Z: 598
Vodouisant [worshipper]
Vodou V: 436 with picture
Vogelweide, Walther von der [Austrian poet] See Walther von der Vogelweide in this index
Vogt, Steven S. [American astronomer]
Planet (The first discoveries) P: 513
Vohu Manah [religion]
Zoroastrianism (History) Z: 607
Voice [sound] V: 436 with diagrams
See also the list of Related articles in the Voice article

Larynx L: 79
Singing S: 472
Speech therapy (Types of disorders) So: 773
Theater (Body and voice) T: 237; (Creating a role) T: 238
A Guide to Speaking Skills **Research Guide: 23**
Voice [grammar] V: 437
Voice box See Larynx in this index
Voice coil [electricity]
Radio (The speaker) R: 89
Speaker So: 767
Telephone (The speaker) T: 95
Voice mail [recording system]
Telephone (Business services) T: 98
Voice of America [communications] V: 437
Radio (The Golden Age of Broadcasting) R: 92-93
Voice of Scotland [religious group]
Scotland (Religion) S: 215
Voice of the City, The [book by O. Henry]
Henry, O. (His works) H: 189
Voice over Internet Protocol [electronics]
Internet (Communication) I: 350b
Telephone (How a telephone call travels) T: 95-96; (VoIP phone calls) T: 97
Voice-recognition software
Computer (A microphone) Ci: 915
Voice vote
Congress of the United States (Passing a bill) Ci: 945
Parliamentary procedure (Voting on motions) P: 177
Voiceprint
Biometrics B: 325
Voices in the Park [book by Browne]
Literature for children picture on L: 354
Voices of the Night [poems by Longfellow]
Longfellow, Henry Wadsworth (Professor and family man) L: 449
Void [astronomy]
Galaxy (Galaxy groups, clusters, and beyond) G: 9
Voight, Jon [American actor]
Motion picture (Best performance by an actor: 1978) M: 862a
Voigt, Cynthia [American author]
Newbery Medal (table) N: 359
Voile [fabric] V: 437
Voinovich, George Victor [American political leader]
Ohio (table) O: 699
Voinovich, Vladimir [Soviet author]
Russian literature (Modern Soviet literature) R: 564-565
VoIP [computing] See Voice over Internet Protocol in this index
Voir dire [law]
Jury (Petit juries) J: 202
Voisin, Charles [French aviator]
Aviation (Beginnings) A: 986
Voisin, Gabriel [French aviator]
Aviation (Beginnings) A: 986
Voivodship [province]
Poland (Local government) P: 605
Vojvodina [province]
Serbia S: 312
Volapük [language]
Universal language U: 205
Volatile oil
Oil (Volatile oils) O: 707
Volatile RAM [memory]
Electronics (Digital circuits) E: 213-214
Volatility [physics]
Evaporation (How evaporation occurs) E: 422-423; (Uses of evaporation) E: 423
Volcán Barú [mountain, Panama]
Panama (The Central Highland) P: 119
Volcán Tajumulco [mountain]
Guatemala (The Highlands) G: 414 with map
Volcanic ash
Volcano diagram on V: 442a; (Pyroclasts) V: 439; (Pyroclastic hazards) V: 440 with picture
Volcanic Axis [region]
Paricutín P: 159
Volcanic bomb
Rock (Extrusive rock) R: 371
Volcano (Pyroclasts) V: 439; (Pyroclastic hazards) V: 440
Volcanic breccia
Rock (Extrusive rock) R: 371
Volcanic dust
Dust (Influence on climate) D: 390
Volcanic Explosivity Index [geology]
Volcano (Describing eruptions) V: 442b
Volcanic gas geochemistry
Geochemistry G: 91
Volcanic island
Island (Kinds of islands) I: 472 with diagram
Seamount S: 269

Volcanic mountain
Mountain (Volcanic mountains) M: 892
Volcanic rock
Basalt B: 123
Earth (Igneous rocks) E: 21
Igneous rock I: 49
Volcano V: 438 with pictures and map
Antarctica (Land) A: 531
Aviation (Recent developments) A: 991-992
Climate (Volcanic eruptions) Ci: 676d
Coral reef (Kinds of coral reefs) Ci: 1048b
Crater Ci: 1121
Dinosaur (Why dinosaurs died out) D: 213
Disaster (table) D: 223
Extinction (Mass extinction) E: 456
Hot spot H: 374a
Io I: 370
Island (Volcanic islands) I: 472
Lake (How lakes are formed) L: 32 with picture
Lava L: 127
Mars (Volcanoes) M: 226; (The Amazonian Period) M: 226c
Moon (Rilles) M: 790; (Mantle) M: 791
Mount Saint Helens M: 888 with picture
Mountain (Volcanic mountains) M: 892
Ocean (The land at the bottom of the sea) O: 559-661
Plate tectonics P: 561; (Evidence of plate movement) P: 563
Ring of Fire R: 342
Satellite S: 149
Seamount S: 268 with picture
Tsunami T: 475
Volcano Lover, The [book by Sontag]
Sontag, Susan So: 594
Volcano rabbit [rabbit]
Rabbit (The body of a rabbit) R: 47
Volcanoes National Park [Rwanda]
National park (table) N: 42f
Volcanologist [scientist]
Volcano V: 438; (Studying volcanoes) V: 442a
Volcker, Paul Adolph [American government official] V: 443
Vole [animal] V: 443 with picture
Volga-Baltic Waterway [Russia]
Canal (table) C: 164
Volga River [Russia] V: 444
Inland waterway I: 274
River (table) R: 352
Russia (Rivers and lakes) R: 541
Volgograd [Russia] V: 444
Volhynia [region, Europe]
Ukraine (Lithuanian and Polish rule) U: 12
Volkov, Vladislav N. [Soviet cosmonaut]
Astronaut (table) A: 830; (Accidents in space) A: 830-831
Space exploration (Salyut and Skylab) So: 721
Volkswagen AG [company] V: 444
Automobile picture on A: 969
Manufacturing (table) M: 170
Porsche AG P: 680
Volley [sports]
Soccer (table) So: 546
Volleyball [sport] V: 444 with pictures
Beach volleyball B: 179 with picture
Massachusetts (Interesting facts) M: 271
Olympic Games (Summer Olympic Games) O: 746e-746f
Vollmer, August [American criminologist]
Police (Law and order in America) P: 624
Volodymyr I [Grand Prince of Kiev] See Vladimir I in this index
Volos [Greece]
Thessaly T: 258
Volpe, John Anthony [American political leader]
Massachusetts (table) M: 288
Transportation, Department of (table) T: 400
Volpone [play by Jonson]
Jonson, Ben J: 160
Volscians [ancient people]
Coriolanus, Gaius Marcius Ci: 1053
Volstead, Andrew J. [American political leader]
Volstead Act V: 446
Volstead Act [1919] V: 445
Prohibition (The movement toward prohibition) P: 815
Volsunga Saga [Icelandic literature]
Brunhild B: 652
Volsungs [legendary family]
Mythology (Teutonic heroes) M: 987
Volt [electricity] V: 446
Decibel D: 70
Electric current (Conductors and insulators) E: 166
Electromotive force E: 203
Metric system (Electricity) M: 440
Volta, Alessandro [Italian inventor] V: 446

Battery (History) **B:** 171
Electricity (Experiments with electric charge)
  E: 196-197
Physics (Developments in the 1800's) **P:** 440
Volta, Lake
  Ghana (Land) **G:** 179 *with map*
  Lake Volta **L:** 48 *with map*
Volta Laboratory [organization]
  Bell, Alexander Graham (His later life) **B:** 241
Voltage [electricity]
  Battery (Types of batteries) **B:** 169
  Electric generator (A simple generator) **E:** 170
  Electricity (Electrical safety) **E:** 195
  Electronics **E:** 206; (Electronic circuits) **E:** 208
  Inductance **I:** 240
  Volt **V:** 446
Voltaic [people]
  Burkina Faso (People) **B:** 706
Voltaire [French author] **V:** 446 *with portrait*
  Black humor **B:** 389
  Châtelet, Marquise Du **C:** 388
  Democracy (French contributions to democracy)
    D: 122
  Enlightenment **E:** 326a
  Freethinker **F:** 509
  French literature (The Enlightenment) **F:** 520
  Peace (From the 1400's to the 1700's) **P:** 206
  Philosophes **P:** 382
  Sculpture (European sculpture) **S:** 253-254 *with
    picture*
Voltmeter [instrument]
  Electric meter **E:** 176
  Thermocouple **T:** 253
  Thermometer (Thermocouple thermometers)
    T: 254
Volume [measurement] **V:** 447
  Archimedes (His discoveries) **A:** 605
  Cube **Ci:** 1180
  Cylinder **Ci:** 1205
  Density **D:** 142
  Metric system (Space and time) **M:** 437; (The
    metric system at a glance) **M:** 438 *with pictures*;
    (Metric conversion table) **M:** 439 *with pictures*
  Weights and measures (table: Volume and
    capacity) **W:** 186
Volume cycled respirator [machine]
  Respirator **R:** 262
Volumetric model
  Computer graphics (In medicine) **Ci:** 924h
Voluntary bankruptcy
  Bankruptcy (Features of bankruptcy) **B:** 97
Voluntary chain
  Chain store **C:** 369
Voluntary manslaughter
  Manslaughter **M:** 167
Voluntary muscle [anatomy]
  Human body (Skeletal muscles) **H:** 419
  Muscle (Skeletal muscles) **M:** 933-934
  Paralysis **P:** 152
Volunteer fire department
  Fire department (Fire protection in North
    America) **F:** 128
Volunteer State [name for]
  Tennessee **T:** 134
Volunteers of America [organization] **V:** 447
Volute [architecture]
  Column (The Greek orders) **Ci:** 865
Volva [botany]
  Mushroom (Parts of a mushroom) **M:** 942 *with
    picture*
Volvox [alga]
  Algae *picture on* **A:** 349
  Protozoan (Flagellates) **P:** 837
Vomer bone [anatomy]
  Face **F:** 3
Vomiting V: 447
  Motion sickness **M:** 874
  Nausea **N:** 68
Von ...
  Names beginning with Von *are alphabetized either
  as single words or under their key words.* Von
  Neumann, John *appears after* Vonnegut, Kurt
  and Papen, Franz von *appears after* Papeete
Von Békésy, Georg [American physicist]
  Nobel Prizes (Physiology or medicine: 1961)
    N: 446
Von Braun, Wernher [German-American engineer]
  V: 447
  Rocket (Rockets of the early 1900's) **R:** 390
  Space exploration (The first space rockets)
    So: 706
Vonck, Jan [Belgian lawyer]
  Belgium (The Brabant Revolution) **B:** 233
Vondel, Joost van den [Dutch author]
  Netherlands (Arts) **N:** 142
Von Hohenheim, Theophrastus Bombastus *See
  Paracelsus, Philippus Aureolus in this index*

Vonnegut, Kurt [American author] **V:** 448
  American literature (Experimental styles) **A:** 425
    with portrait
Von Neumann, John [Hungarian-American
    mathematician] **V:** 448
  Computer (The first electronic computers)
    Ci: 924b
  Computer virus **Ci:** 925
  Economics (Modern economics) **E:** 64-65
  Game theory **G:** 23
Von Recklinghausen's disease
  Neurofibromatosis **N:** 152
Von Sternberg, Josef [American director] **V:** 448
  Dietrich, Marlene **D:** 200
Von Steuben, Friedrich Wilhelm [German-
    American general] *See* Steuben, Baron von *in
    this index*
Von Willebrand's disease V: 448
  Hemophilia (Major types of hemophilia) **H:** 182
Voodoo [religion] *See* Vodou *in this index*
Voorhees, Foster M. [American political leader]
  New Jersey (table) **N:** 249
Voorhis, Jerry [American political leader]
  Nixon, Richard Milhous (Career in Congress)
    N: 430
VOR [radio]
  Airplane (Electronic navigation) **A:** 227 *with
    picture*
  Navigation (Omnirange) **N:** 73
Vorder Rhine [river, Switzerland]
  Rhine River (The course of the Rhine) **R:** 292
Vorster, Balthazar Johannes [South African
    political leader] **V:** 448
VORTAC [radio]
  Airplane (Electronic navigation) **A:** 227
Vortex [physics]
  Glider (The wings) **G:** 228
  Superfluid **So:** 993
  Tornado **T:** 333
Vortex, The [book by Rivera]
  Latin American literature (The early 1900's) **L:** 113
Vortex, The [play by Coward]
  Coward, Noël **Ci:** 1107
Vortex chamber [device]
  Tornado (Studying tornadoes) **T:** 337
VORTEX projects [meteorology]
  Tornado (The VORTEX projects) **T:** 337
Vortice [physics]
  Aerodynamics (Induced drag) **A:** 86
Vorticella [microorganism]
  Protozoan (Ciliates) **P:** 838
Vortigern [English king]
  Anglo-Saxons **A:** 464
Voskhod program [space exploration]
  Astronaut *picture on* **A:** 833; (Achievements in
    space) **A:** 829
  Space exploration (Voskhod and Gemini: The first
    multiperson space flights) **So:** 714 *with picture*
Voss [book by White]
  White, Patrick **W:** 284
Vostok program [space exploration]
  Astronaut (Achievements in space) **A:** 829
  Exploration (Human space travel) **E:** 452
  Gagarin, Yuri Alekseyevich **G:** 5
  Space exploration *picture on* **So:** 698; (Vostok
    and Mercury: The first human beings in space)
    So: 711 *with pictures*
Vote of confidence
  Prime minister **P:** 778c
Vote of no confidence
  Prime minister of Canada (How the prime
    minister is chosen) **P:** 778d
Voter registration
  Voting (Registration) **V:** 449
Voter turnout
  Voting (Voter turnout) **V:** 450
Voting V: 449
  African Americans (During the early 1900's)
    A: 136l; (Political gains) **A:** 136p
  Apportionment **A:** 574
  Ballot **B:** 63
  Canada, Government of **C:** 128
  Citizenship (The duties of citizens) **Ci:** 569
  Colonial life in America (Government and law
    enforcement) **Ci:** 795
  Congress of the United States (Passing a bill)
    Ci: 945
  Constitution of the United States (Amendment
    14) **Ci:** 1014; (Amendment 15) **Ci:** 1014;
    (Amendment 19) **Ci:** 1015; (Amendment 23)
    Ci: 1015-1016; (Amendment 24) **Ci:** 1016;
    (Amendment 26) **Ci:** 1016
  Debate (Adjudication) **D:** 64
  Election **E:** 152
  Election campaign (Getting out the vote) **E:** 160
  Electoral College **E:** 161
  Fifteenth Amendment **F:** 95

Gerrymander **G:** 174
Grandfather clause **G:** 310
Hispanic Americans (Political developments)
  H: 256 *with picture*
Initiative and referendum **I:** 271
League of Women Voters **L:** 161
Nixon, Richard Milhous (The national scene)
  N: 433-434
Parliamentary procedure (Voting on motions)
  P: 177
Political convention **P:** 628
Poll tax **P:** 644
Recall **R:** 174
Reconstruction (The Republicans in the South)
  R: 179; (Effects of Reconstruction) **R:** 179-180
Scalawags **S:** 169
Sex discrimination (Sex-based laws) **S:** 335
Voting machine **V:** 450
Voting Rights Act of 1965 **V:** 451
Woman suffrage **W:** 380
Woodhull, Victoria Claflin **W:** 393
World *picture on* **W:** 412b
Voting machine V: 450 *with picture*
  Edison, Thomas Alva (Inventor and businessman)
    E: 78
  Voting (Methods of voting) **V:** 449
Voting Rights Act of 1965 [U.S. history] **V:** 451
  African Americans (Political gains) **A:** 136p
  Great Society (Legislation) **G:** 349
  King, Martin Luther, Jr. (The growing movement)
    K: 321-322
  National Association for the Advancement of
    Colored People (Activities) **N:** 29
  Selma marches **S:** 290
  Voting (Who may vote) **V:** 449
Votive figures [art]
  Sculpture (Middle Eastern) **S:** 233 *with picture*
Voucher [business]
  Voucher **V:** 452
Voucher [education] **V:** 451
  Education (Who should choose a child's school?)
    E: 106
  Parochial school **P:** 178
  Wisconsin (School developments) **W:** 368
Vouli [parliament]
  Greece (Government) **G:** 352-353
Voussoir [architecture]
  Arch **A:** 593 *with diagram*
Vow of Louis XIII, The [painting by Ingres]
  Ingres, Jean Auguste Dominique **I:** 271
Vowel [language] **V:** 452
  Hebrew language **H:** 162 *with pictures*
Vowel point [diacritical mark]
  Hebrew language **H:** 162 *with picture*
Voyage, The [opera by Glass]
  Glass, Philip **G:** 224
Voyage of Discovery, A [book by Vancouver]
  Vancouver, George **V:** 278
Voyage of Life, The [paintings by Cole]
  Cole, Thomas **Ci:** 771
Voyage of the Vega [book by Nordenskjöld]
  Nordenskjöld, Nils Adolf Erik **N:** 453
Voyager [space probes] **V:** 451
Voyager 1 [space probe]
  Voyager **V:** 451
  Cosmic rays (Cosmic ray research) **Ci:** 1077
  Exploration (Robotic spacecraft) **E:** 452 *with
    picture*
  Heliosphere (Probing the heliosphere) **H:** 175
  Jupiter (History of Jupiter study) **J:** 200b
  Saturn (History of study) **S:** 153
  Space exploration (Probes to Jupiter and beyond)
    So: 711
  Van Allen belts **V:** 269
Voyager 2 [space probe]
  Voyager **V:** 451
  Exploration (Robotic spacecraft) **E:** 452
  Heliosphere (Probing the heliosphere) **H:** 175
  Jupiter (History of Jupiter study) **J:** 200b
  Neptune (Surface and atmosphere) **N:** 128-129
    with picture
  Planet (The planets of our solar system) **P:** 511
  Planetary ring *picture on* **P:** 514d
  Saturn (History of study) **S:** 153
  Space exploration *pictures on* **So:** 708, **So:** 709;
    (Probes to Jupiter and beyond) **So:** 711
  Triton **T:** 448
  Uranus **U:** 217
  Van Allen belts **V:** 269
Voyages of Doctor Dolittle, The [book by Lofting]
  Lofting, Hugh **L:** 420
Voyages of William Baffin, The [book by Markham]
  Baffin, William **B:** 25
Voyages on the River Saint Lawrence [book by
  Mackenzie]
  Mackenzie, Sir Alexander **M:** 23
Voyageur [Canadian history]

Drummond, William Henry **D: 368**
Voyageurs National Park [Minnesota] **V: 452**
National Park System (table: National parks) **N: 49**
Voyaging: Southward from the Strait of Magellan [book by Kent]
Kent, Rockwell **K: 271**
Voysey Inheritance, The [play by Granville-Barker]
Granville-Barker, Harley **G: 318**
Voznesensky, Andrey [Soviet poet]
Russian literature (Modern Soviet literature) **R: 564**
VR [electronics] *See* Virtual reality *in this index*
Vraka [clothing]
Cyprus (People) **Ci: 1205**
Vranitzky, Franz [Austrian political leader]
Austria (After World War II) **A: 939-940**
Vroom, Peter D. [American political leader]
New Jersey (table) **N: 249**
VSD [medicine] *See* Ventricular septal defect *in this index*
V/STOL [aircraft] **V: 452**
Airplane (Special-purpose planes) **A: 212-213** *with picture*
Aviation (Internationalization) **A: 991**
Ducted propeller **D: 377**
Navy *picture on* **N: 76**; (Aircraft carriers) **N: 78**
VTR *See* Videotape recorder *in this index*
Vuia, Trajan [Romanian inventor]
Airplane (Other pioneer planes and fliers) **A: 233**
Vuillard, Édouard [French painter] **V: 453**
Vujanovic, Filip [Montenegran political leader]
Montenegro (History) **M: 763-764**
Vukovich, Bill [American race driver]
Automobile racing (table: Indianapolis 500 winners) **A: 980**
Vulcan [Roman mythology] **V: 453**
Vulcan [sculpture]
Birmingham (Education and cultural life) **B: 375**
Vulcan aircraft cannon
Machine gun (Aircraft weapons) **M: 16**
Vulcanian eruption [geology]
Volcano (Describing eruptions) **V: 442b**
Vulcanization [industrial process]
Connecticut (The 1800's) **Ci: 970**
Goodyear, Charles **G: 269**
Invention (The inventive process) **I: 355-357**
Rubber (Discovery of vulcanization) **R: 501**; (Vulcanization) **R: 505**
Tire (Assembling a tire) **T: 296**
Vulgate [Bible] **V: 453**
Bible (The first translations) **B: 284-285**
Jerome, Saint **J: 93**
Old Testament (Ancient translations) **O: 741**
Vulgate Cycle [books]
Galahad, Sir **G: 7**
Vulnerable species *See* Threatened species *in this index*
Vulpius, Christiane [wife of]
Goethe, Johann Wolfgang von (Late years) **G: 247**
Vulture [bird] **V: 453** *with pictures*
Animal *picture on* **A: 477**
Bird (Birds of Central and South America) **B: 344a**
Bird of prey **B: 374a**
Buzzard **B: 746**
Condor **Ci: 929** *with pictures*
Ear *picture on* **E: 13**
Eye (Eyes of animals) **E: 469**
Vultures, The [play by Becque]
French literature (Naturalism) **F: 522**
Vulva [anatomy]
Reproduction, Human (The human reproductive system) **R: 245** *with diagram*
Vuntut National Park [Yukon Territory]
Canada (table: National parks and national park reserves) **C: 114**
Vyasa [legendary figure]
Mahabharata **M: 64**
Vychegda River [Russia]
Dvina River **D: 393**
Vygotsky, Lev [Russian psychologist]
Developmental psychology (Sociocultural theory) **D: 174**

W

W [letter] **W: 1** *with pictures*
W [symbol]
Tungsten **T: 486**
W boson [physics]
Physics (Physics today) **P: 442-443**
Standard Model **So: 833**
W. K. Kellogg Foundation *See* Kellogg Foundation *in this index*
Waals, Johannes Diderik van der [Dutch physicist]
Nobel Prizes (Physics: 1910) **N: 440**
Wabash and Erie Canal [waterway, Indiana]
Toledo (History) **T: 321**

Wabash River [river, Indiana-Ohio] **W: 2**
Wabokieshiek [American Indian chief]
Winnebago Indians **W: 339**
WAC [U.S.] *See* Women's Army Corps *in this index*
WAC Corporal [rocket]
Rocket (High-altitude rockets) **R: 390**
Space exploration (The first space rockets) **So: 706-707** *with picture*
Wace [Norman poet]
English literature (The development of English romances) **E: 315**
Round Table (Origin) **R: 491**
Wachusett Reservoir
Massachusetts (Rivers and lakes) **M: 284-285**
Waco [Texas] **W: 2** *with picture*
Wacousta [book by Richardson]
Canadian literature *picture on* **C: 159**; (Early English-Canadian literature) **C: 157**
Wacousta [play by Reaney]
Reaney, James **R: 173**
Waddell, Hugh [American military leader]
North Carolina (Colonial days) **N: 492**
Waddell, Rube [American baseball player]
Baseball (table: Hall of Fame) **B: 134b**
Waddington, Mount [mountain, British Columbia]
British Columbia (Land regions) **B: 622** *with map*
Wade, Abdoulaye [Senegalese political leader]
Senegal (History) **S: 299-300**
Wade, Sir Thomas [British linguist]
Chinese language (Development) **C: 510**
Wade-Giles system [linguistics]
Chinese language (Development) **C: 510**
Wadi [geology]
Desert (Desert climate and land) **D: 155-156**
Egypt (The Eastern Desert) **E: 126**
Yemen (Land) **Y: 562-563**
Wadsworth, James J. [American diplomat]
United Nations (table) **U: 86**
Wadsworth-Longfellow House [Portland]
Maine (Places to visit) **M: 78**
WAF [U.S. history]
Air Force, United States (Air Force women) **A: 190**
Wafer-tumbler lock
Lock (Mechanical locks) **L: 411**
Waffen SS [military unit]
Grass, Günter **G: 326**
Wage and Price Stability, Council on [U.S.]
Ford, Gerald Rudolph (The economy) **F: 377**
Wage base
Social security (Financing Social Security) **So: 555**
Wage-index
Social security (How benefits are figured) **So: 554**
Wage laborer
Plantation ("Free"-labor plantations) **P: 550**
Wage-price controls [economics]
Inflation (Wage and price controls) **I: 268**
Nixon, Richard Milhous (Inflation) **N: 434**; (Events at home) **N: 435-436**
Price control **P: 775**
Wage-price spiral [economics]
Inflation (The cost-push theory) **I: 268**
Wager [gambling] **W: 2**
Wages and hours **W: 2**
Capitalism (Capitalism in its ideal form) **C: 194**
Careers (Probable earnings) **C: 216**; (table: Average salaries for selected occupations) **C: 216**
Child labor (Early child labor laws) **C: 455**
Cost of living **Ci: 1079**
Income **I: 100**
Labor movement (Arranging contracts) **L: 4-5**
Minimum wage **M: 573**
President of the United States (Salary and other allowances) **P: 762**
Profit sharing **P: 811**
Sex discrimination (Persistence of sex discrimination) **S: 335**
Wagner, Cosima von Bülow [wife of Wagner]
Wagner, Richard (Later career) **W: 4**
Wagner, Honus [American baseball player] **W: 3**
Baseball (table: Hall of Fame) **B: 134b**; (The early 1900's) **B: 135**
Wagner, Minna Planer [wife of]
Wagner, Richard (Early career) **W: 3**
Wagner, Otto [Austrian architect]
Architecture (Early modern architecture in Europe) **A: 627-628**
Austria (Architecture) **A: 932-933**
Wagner, Richard [German composer] **W: 3** *with portrait*
Bayreuth **B: 177**
Classical music *picture on* **Ci: 650**
Fafnir **F: 6**
Flagstad, Kirsten **F: 224**
Flying Dutchman **F: 311**
Germany *picture on* **G: 154**; (Music) **G: 153**
Liszt, Franz (His life) **L: 349-350**

Ludwig II **L: 515**
Opera (Richard Wagner) **O: 798** *with pictures*; *(Ring of the Nibelung, The)* **O: 806-807**
Overture **O: 882**
Tannhäuser **T: 29**
Wagner, Robert Ferdinand [American political leader] **W: 4**
National Labor Relations Act **N: 39**
Wagner Act *See* National Labor Relations Act *in this index*
Wagner-Jauregg, Julius [Austrian neurologist]
Nobel Prizes (Physiology or medicine: 1927) **N: 445**
Wagon [scenery]
Theater (Changing scenery) **T: 240**
Wagon [vehicle] **W: 4**
Wagon train
Pioneer life in America *picture on* **P: 476**; (Crossing the Plains) **P: 485-486**
Wagoner, Porter [American singer]
Parton, Dolly **P: 188**
Wagtail [bird]
Bird *pictures on* **B: 361**
Wahhāb, Muhammad ibn Abd al- [Arab religious leader]
Wahhābis **W: 5**
Wahhābis [religious group] **W: 5**
Qatar (History) **Q: 3**
Saudi Arabia (Religion) **S: 158**; (The founding of Saudi Arabia) **S: 161**
Wahl, Arthur Charles [American chemist]
Plutonium **P: 581**
Wahlstatt, Prince of *See* Blücher, Gebhard Leberecht von *in this index*
Wahoo [fish] **W: 5** *with picture*
Wahunsonacock *See* Powhatan *in this index*
Waialeale, Mount *See* Mount Waialeale *in this index*
Waianae Range [mountain]
Hawaii (Oahu) **H: 102**
Waiblingen [estate]
Guelphs and Ghibellines **G: 419**
Waihee, John [American political leader]
Hawaii (table) **H: 105**
Waikato Basin
New Zealand (The North Island) **N: 351**
Waikiki [district]
Honolulu (Economy) **H: 321** *with picture*
Wailing Wall [Jerusalem] *See* Western Wall *in this index*
Waimea Canyon
Hawaii (Places to visit) **H: 98** *with picture*; (Kauai) **H: 102**
United States *picture on* **U: 126**
Wainscoting [woods]
Lumber (History) **L: 521-522**
Wainwright, Jonathan Mayhew [American general] **W: 5**
Philippines (Japanese control) **P: 380**
Wainwright Building [Saint Louis]
Adler, Dankmar **A: 58**
Architecture (Early modern architecture in America) **A: 629**
Waist [entomology]
Ant (The abdomen) **A: 522** *with picture*
Waistcoat
Clothing (The 1600's) **Ci: 703** *with picture*
Waitangi, Treaty of [1840]
Maori **M: 175**
New Zealand (European colonization) **N: 355**; (Maori-Pakeha relations) **N: 356**
Waitangi Tribunal [New Zealand history]
New Zealand (Maori-Pakeha relations) **N: 356**
Waite, Davis H. [American political leader]
Colorado (table) **Co: 844**
Waite, Morrison Remick [American jurist] **W: 5**
Waiting for Godot [play by Beckett]
Drama (Theater of the Absurd) **D: 340** *with picture*
Waiting for Lefty [play by Odets]
Odets, Clifford **O: 674**
Waitomo Caves [New Zealand]
Cave (table) **C: 320**
Waiver of premium rider
Insurance (Riders) **I: 311**
Wakamatsu, Don [American baseball manager]
Asian Americans (Notable Asian American "firsts") **A: 812f**
Wake [funeral] **W: 5**
Funeral customs (Preparation of the body) **F: 557**
Wake Island [Pacific] **W: 5**
Wake-robin [plant]
Trillium **T: 445**
"Wakefield" [story by Hawthorne]
Hawthorne, Nathaniel (His stories and sketches) **H: 115**
Wakefield, Battle of [1460]
York **Y: 568**

Wakefield, Edward Gibbon [British businessman]
New Zealand (European colonization) N: 355
Wakeups [drugs] *See* Amphetamine *in this index*
Waking, The [poems by Roethke]
Roethke, Theodore R: 400
Wakonda [religion]
Indian, American (Beliefs) I: 147
Waksman, Selman Abraham [American biologist]
W: 6
Antibiotic (History) A: 552
Streptomycin So: 926
Wakulla Springs
Florida (Rivers, lakes, and springs) F: 256
Wal-Mart Stores, Inc. W: 6
Chain store C: 369
Walton, Sam W: 22
Walachia [region]
Roma (History) R: 402b
Romania (Land regions) R: 419-420 *with picture and map*; (Unification movement) R: 423;
(Ottoman rule) R: 423
Walcott, Derek [West Indian poet] W: 6
Walcott, Jersey Joe [American boxer]
Marciano, Rocky M: 196
Walcott, Louis Eugene [American religious leader]
See Farrakhan, Louis *in this index*
Wald, George [American biochemist] W: 6
Nobel Prizes (Physiology or medicine: 1967)
N: 446
Wald, Lillian D. [American social worker] W: 6 *with portrait*
Kelley, Florence K: 255
Walden [book by Thoreau]
American literature (Nonfiction prose) A: 418
Thoreau, Henry David T: 266
Walden Pond
Massachusetts (Places to visit) M: 280
Thoreau, Henry David (His beliefs and works)
T: 266 *with picture*
Walden Two [book by Skinner]
Psychology (Behaviorism) P: 849-850
Waldenses [religious group] W: 7
Waldheim, Kurt [Austrian statesman] W: 7
Austria (After World War II) A: 939-940
United Nations (The secretary-general) U: 83 *with portrait*
Waldo, Peter [French religious leader]
Waldenses W: 7
Waldo Canyon Fire
Colorado (The early 2000's) Ci: 847-848
Waldpurgis Night [celebration]
April A: 576
Waldseemüller, Martin [German map maker]
Map (Advances in European cartography) M: 184
Vespucci, Amerigo V: 341
Wales W: 7 *with pictures and maps*
See also the list of Related articles in the Wales *article*
Clothing *picture on* Ci: 694
Edward I E: 112
England (The beginnings of Parliament) E: 306;
(The English Reformation) E: 307
Halloween (Costumes) H: 24a; (Halloween around the world) H: 24b
Mythology (Celtic mythology) M: 984
Parliament (The House of Commons) P: 173
United Kingdom U: 48 *with picture*; (Regional government) U: 50; (Wales) U: 59; (Long-standing conflicts) U: 73
Welsh language W: 195
Wales, Prince of *See* Prince of Wales *in this index*
Wales, University of
Wales (Education) W: 9
Wałęsa, Lech [Polish political leader] W: 13 *with portrait*
Poland (History) P: 611-614
Wali [title]
Algeria (Local government) A: 361
Walk [gait]
Horse (Gaits) H: 353-354 *with picture*
Walk [sports]
Baseball (Reaching base) B: 129; (Rule changes)
B: 133
Walk on the Wild Side, A [book by Algren]
Algren, Nelson A: 366
Walkem, George A. [Canadian political leader]
British Columbia (table) B: 628
Walken, Christopher [American actor]
Motion picture (Best performance by an actor in a supporting role: 1978) M: 862b
Walker [American Indian chief]
Utah (Indian relations) U: 246
Walker, Alice [American author] W: 13
African American literature (The 1900's) A: 136a
American literature (Works by minority writers)
A: 425
Walker, Clifford [American political leader]

Georgia (table) G: 130
Walker, Daniel [American political leader]
Illinois (table) I: 71
Walker, David [American social reformer] W: 13
Walker, David S. [American political leader]
Florida (table) F: 260
Walker, Doak [American football player]
Football (table) F: 363
Walker, Frank C. [American government official]
Roosevelt, Franklin Delano (table) R: 454
Truman, Harry S. (table) T: 469
Walker, George [American comedian]
Williams, Bert W: 310
Walker, George F. [Canadian playwright]
Canadian literature (Modern Canadian drama)
C: 161
Walker, George H. [American settler]
Milwaukee (Early development) M: 561
Walker, Gilbert C. [American political leader]
Virginia (table) V: 417
Walker, Herschel [American football player]
Football (table) F: 363
Walker, Sir Hovenden [British admiral]
Quebec (The 1700's) Q: 36
Walker, Izannah [American dollmaker]
Doll (Cloth dolls) D: 289
Walker, James John [American political leader]
W: 13
Walker, Jimmy [American political leader] *See*
Walker, James John *in this index*
Walker, John [British pharmacist]
Fire (Methods of starting fires) F: 121
Match (The first matches) M: 300
Walker, John [English lexicographer]
Dictionary (Early English dictionaries) D: 194
Walker, John Ernest [British chemist]
Nobel Prizes (Chemistry: 1997) N: 444
Walker, Joseph Marshall [American political leader]
Louisiana (table) L: 496
Walker, Joseph Reddeford [American frontiersman]
Nevada (Exploration) N: 173
Walker, Leroy Pope [Confederate political leader]
W: 13
Walker, Madam C. J. [American businesswoman]
W: 13 *with portrait*
Walker, Mary Edwards [American doctor] W: 14
Civil War, American (Hospitals) Ci: 630
Walker, Mickey [American boxer]
Boxing (Boxing's Golden Age) B: 532-532a
Walker, Olene [American political leader]
Utah (table) U: 245; (The early 2000's) U: 249-250
Walker, Peter [American landscape designer]
National September 11 Memorial and Museum
N: 61
September 11 terrorist attacks (Moving forward)
S: 310b-310c
Walker, Robert J. [American government official]
Polk, James Knox (table) P: 643
Walker, Sarah Breedlove [American businesswoman] *See* Walker, Madam C. J. *in this index*
Walker, Scott [American political leader]
Labor movement (Recent developments) L: 14
Wisconsin (table) W: 365; (A battle over collective bargaining) W: 369
Walker, Walton Harris [American general]
Korean War (Outbreak) K: 379-380; (The Pusan Perimeter) K: 381; (The Allies retreat) K: 382
Walker, William [American adventurer] W: 14
Granada G: 304
Mora, Juan Rafael M: 799
Nicaragua (Independence) N: 398-400
Walker Agent
Walker, Madam C. J. W: 14
Walker Art Center [Minneapolis]
Minnesota (Museums) M: 589
Walker Cup [tournament]
Golf (Tournaments) G: 264
Walker Law [1920]
Boxing (Bare knuckles to gloves) B: 532
Walker River [river, California-Nevada]
Nevada (Rivers and lakes) N: 166
Walker Tariff Act [1846]
Polk, James Knox (Tariff reduction) P: 642
Walker War [1853-1854]
Utah (Indian relations) U: 246
Walkie-talkie [radio] W: 14
Radio (In public safety) R: 84 *with picture*
Walking
Hiking H: 26
Insect (Legs) I: 287
Transportation (Land transportation) T: 383
Weight control (Method) W: 182
Walking [sport] W: 14
Track and field (Walking races) T: 357

Walking catfish
Catfish C: 300
Fish *picture on* F: 145
Walking fish *See* Climbing perch *in this index*
Walking leaf
Leaf insect L: 158 *with picture*
Walking plow
Plow (Kinds of plows) P: 575
Walking to Sleep [poems by Wilbur]
Wilbur, Richard W: 300
Walkingstick [insect] W: 14 *with picture*
Animal *picture on* A: 479
Insect *picture on* I: 278, I: 280; (Protection from enemies) I: 297
Leaf insect L: 158
Walkman [device]
Portable media player P: 681
Walkout [labor]
Labor movement (Handling labor disputes) L: 6-7
Strike (Kinds of strikes) So: 928
Walküre, Die [opera by Wagner]
Opera: (Ring of the Nibelung, The) O: 806-807
Wagner, Richard (Later career) W: 4
Wall [architecture]
House (The frame) H: 382 *with diagram*; (Interior construction) H: 382 *with diagram*
Middle Ages *picture on* M: 528
Wall, Brad [Canadian political leader]
Saskatchewan (table) S: 144
Wall, Garret D. [American political leader]
New Jersey (table) N: 249
Wall cloud
Tornado (Moisture) T: 334
Wall coverings
Interior design (Choosing patterns and textures)
I: 332-333
Wall frame
House (The frame) H: 382
Wall of China *See* Great Wall of China *in this index*
Wall of sound [recording]
Rock music (Independent producers) R: 379
Wall painting
Mural M: 928 *with picture*
Wall Street [film]
Stone, Oliver So: 909
Wall Street [New York City] W: 15
New York City (Settlement) N: 341
New York Stock Exchange N: 345
United States, History of the *picture on* U: 191
Wall Street Journal, The [newspaper]
New York City (Communications) N: 335
Wall tent
Tent (Kinds of tents) T: 168
Wall-to-wall carpeting
Interior design (Planning on paper) I: 330-331
Wallaby [animal] W: 15 *with picture*
Animal *picture on* A: 499
Marsupial (Kinds of marsupials) M: 232 *with picture*
Wallace [Idaho]
Idaho (Places to visit) I: 34
Wallace, Alfred Russel [British naturalist] W: 15
Darwin, Charles Robert (The influence of Darwin's ideas) D: 40
Evolution (Darwin's theory) E: 432
Natural selection N: 65
Wallace, Bobby [American baseball player]
Baseball (table: Hall of Fame) B: 134b
Wallace, Cornelia Ellis Snively [wife of]
Wallace, George Corley W: 16
Wallace, David [American political leader]
Indiana (table) I: 214
Wallace, David Foster [American author]
American literature (Experimental styles) A: 425
Wallace, Elizabeth "Bess" [wife of Harry Truman]
See Truman, Bess *in this index*
Wallace, George Corley [American political leader]
W: 16
Alabama (table) A: 274; (The mid-1900's) A: 278
American Party A: 428
Nixon, Richard Milhous (The 1968 election)
N: 432
Wallace, Henry Agard [American political leader]
W: 16 *with portrait*
Truman, Harry S. (table) T: 469
Wallace, Henry C. [American government official]
Agriculture, Department of (table) A: 161
Coolidge, Calvin (table) Ci: 1032
Harding, Warren Gamaliel (table) H: 58; (Return to normalcy) H: 58
Wallace, Henry Agard W: 16
Wallace, Jonathan H. [American lawyer]
McKinley, William (Congressman) M: 339
Wallace, Lew [American author] W: 16
New Mexico (Territorial days) N: 275
Wallace, Lurleen [American political leader]
Alabama (table) A: 274

Wallace, George Corley W: 16
Wallace, Rusty [American race car driver]
Automobile racing (table: NASCAR Sprint Cup champions) A: 981
Wallace, William [American lawyer]
Harrison, Benjamin (Army commander) H: 70-71
Wallace, Sir William [Scottish patriot] W: 17
Edward I E: 112
Scotland (Fight for independence) S: 219
Wallace & Gromit; The Curse of the Were-Rabbit [film]
Animation (New diversity) A: 514c *with picture*
Wallace v. Jaffree [U.S. history]
School prayer S: 185
Wallace's flying frog
Frog (True frogs) F: 540
Wallace's Line [biology]
Wallace, Alfred Russel W: 15
Wallach, Otto [German chemist]
Nobel Prizes (Chemistry: 1910) N: 443
Wallard, Lee [American race driver]
Automobile racing (table: Indianapolis 500 winners) A: 980
Wallboard [building material] W: 17
House (Interior construction) H: 382
Wallcreeper [bird]
Bird (Birds of Europe) B: 344c *with picture*
Walled city
Babylon *picture on* B: 12
Middle Ages (Medieval towns) M: 527
Wallenberg, Raoul [Swedish diplomat] W: 17
Wallenberg Foundation, Knut and Alice
Foundation (table) F: 430
Wallenstein [play by Schiller]
Wallenstein, Albrecht Wenzel Eusebius von W: 17
Wallenstein, Albrecht Wenzel Eusebius von [Bohemian military leader] W: 17
Thirty Years' War (The Danish period) T: 260; (The Swedish period) T: 260
Waller, Fats [American composer] W: 17
Waller, Thomas M. [American political leader]
Connecticut (table) Ci: 967
Waller, William [American political leader]
Mississippi (table) M: 640
Walleye [disorder]
Eye (Strabismus) E: 466
Walleye [fish]
Fish *picture on* F: 158
Perch P: 284
Pike P: 461
Walleye pollock [fish]
Pollock P: 646
Walleyed pike [fish] *See* Walleye *in this index*
Wallflower [plant] W: 18 *with picture*
Flower *picture on* F: 287
Wallgren, Monrad C. [American political leader]
Washington (table) W: 65
Wallhanging [art]
Rugs and carpets *picture on* R: 517
Tapestry T: 39 *with pictures*
Wallis, Samuel [British explorer]
Exploration (Exploring the Pacific) E: 447-448
Tahiti T: 14
Wallis and Futuna Islands [Pacific]
Pacific Islands (table) P: 9
Wallonia [region, Belgium] W: 18 *with maps*
Belgium (Regions and language communities) B: 227
Walloons W: 18
Walloons [people] W: 18
Belgium B: 226; (Population and ancestry) B: 229; (Independence) B: 233-234; (After World War II) B: 235
Flemings F: 233
Wallonia W: 18
Wallow Fire
Arizona (The early 2000's) A: 692
Wallowa Lake [Oregon]
Oregon (Land and climate) O: 838-840 *with map*
Wallpaper W: 19
Interior design (Choosing patterns and textures) I: 332-333
Paperwork (Wallpaper) P: 138
Walnut [tree] W: 19 *with picture*
Tree *pictures on* T: 417, T: 421, T: 424
Wood *picture on* W: 389
Walnut Canyon National Monument [Arizona]
National Park System (table: National monuments) N: 50-52
Walnut comb
Chicken (Kinds of chickens) C: 441 *with picture*
Walnut Street Jail [Philadelphia]
Prison (Early prison reform) P: 807
Walnut Street Theatre
Philadelphia (The arts) P: 363
Walpole, Horace [British author] W: 19
English literature (Romantic prose) E: 320

Gothic novel G: 279
Walpole, Hugh Seymour [British author] W: 19
Walpole, Sir Robert [English political leader] W: 20
Fielding, Henry (His life) F: 94
Government (The Enlightenment) G: 290-291
Pitt, William P: 499
United Kingdom (The beginning of cabinet government) U: 67
Walras, Léon [French economist]
Econometrics E: 57
Economics (Modern economics) E: 64
Walrus [animal] W: 20 *with picture*
Animal *picture on* A: 485
Mammal (In water) M: 122 *with diagram*
Seal S: 265
Walrus Island [Bering Sea]
Pribilof Islands P: 774
Walsh, David I. [American political leader]
Massachusetts (table) M: 288
Walsh, Donald [American military leader]
Exploration (Deep-sea exploration) E: 450-451
Pacific Ocean (Scientific research) P: 15
Piccard, Jacques P: 450
Walsh, Ed [American baseball player]
Baseball (table: Hall of Fame) B: 134b
Walsh, Enda [Irish dramatist]
Irish literature (Drama) I: 432
Walsh, Fran [New Zealand screenwriter]
Jackson, Peter Jr. 16
Walsh, Lawrence E. [American jurist]
Iran-contra affair (Charges and court actions) I: 407
Walsin-Esterhazy, Marie Charles Ferdinand [French soldier]
Dreyfus affair (Efforts to clear Dreyfus's name) D: 347
Walt Disney Company W: 20
ABC A: 7
Animation (The animation revivial) A: 514c
Walt Disney Concert Hall
Los Angeles (The arts) L: 466 *with picture*
Walt Disney Pictures [company]
Pixar Animation Studios P: 503
Walt Disney Company W: 20
Walt Disney World Resort [Florida]
Florida (Places to visit) F: 252 *with picture*
Graves, Michael Ga: 330 *with picture*
Orlando O: 856
Walt Disney Company W: 20
Walt Whitman [painting by Eakins]
Eakins, Thomas E: 6
Walter, Bruno [German-American conductor] W: 21
Walter, Lucy [mother of]
Monmouth, Duke of M: 730
Walter, Thomas Ustick [American architect] W: 21
Walter Reed National Military Medical Center [Bethesda] [Maryland] W: 21
Bone bank B: 457
Walters, David [American political leader]
Oklahoma (table) O: 730
Walters, Vernon A. [American diplomat]
United Nations (table) U: 86
Walther von der Vogelweide [Austrian poet] W: 21
German literature (Minnesingers) G: 138-139
Walton, Bill [American basketball player]
Basketball *picture on* B: 153
Walton, Ernest Thomas Sinton [Irish physicist] W: 21
Particle accelerator (How accelerators work) P: 184
Walton, Frederick [British inventor]
Linoleum L: 338
Walton, George [American patriot] W: 21
Georgia (table) G: 130
Walton, Izaak [English author] W: 21
Biography (The 1600's) B: 313
Walton, James Lawrence [American businessman]
Wal-Mart Stores, Inc. W: 6
Walton, Sam W: 22
Walton, John C. [American political leader]
Oklahoma (table) O: 730; (The 1920's) O: 732
Walton, Sam [American businessman] W: 22
Wal-Mart Stores, Inc. W: 6
Walton, Sir William [British composer] W: 22
Walton-DeFuniak Library
Florida (Libraries) F: 247
Waltrip, Darrell [American race driver]
Automobile racing (table: NASCAR Sprint Cup champions) A: 981
Waltz W: 22
Ballroom dancing B: 63
Dance (Social dances) D: 26-28 *with picture*
Strauss, Johann, Sr. So: 921
Strauss, Johann, Jr. So: 921
Waltz, Christoph [Austrian actor]

Motion picture (Best performance by an actor in a supporting role: 2009) M: 862b
Waltz King [name for]
Strauss, Johann, Jr. So: 921
Waltz of the Toreadors, The [play by Anouilh]
Anouilh, Jean A: 519
"**Waltzing Matilda**" [song]
Australia (Language) A: 900
Walvis Bay [Namibia]
Namibia (History) N: 9
Walz, Carl [American astronaut]
Astronaut (table) A: 830
Wampanoag Indians
Indian wars (The Pequot War) I: 191
Maine (Indian wars) M: 89
Massasoit M: 295
Philip, King P: 370
Plymouth Colony (Later years) P: 584
Thanksgiving Day (Plymouth Colony) T: 230
Wampler, Joseph [American astronomer]
Lick Observatory L: 270
Wampum [money] W: 22
Colonial life in America (Money) Ci: 811
Indian, American *picture on* I: 156; (Money) I: 149
Wamsutta [American Indian chief]
Massasoit M: 296
WAN [computing] *See* Wide area network *in this index*
Wan-Chun Cheng [Chinese botanist]
Redwood (The dawn redwood) R: 192
Wanamaker, John [American businessman]
Philadelphia (A growing city) P: 367
Wananga [school]
New Zealand (Education) N: 349
Wanderers [art history]
Painting (Painting outside France) P: 72
Wandering albatross [bird]
Albatross A: 310 *with picture*
Antarctica *picture on* A: 535
Wandering Jew [legendary figure] W: 22
Wandering-jew [plant] W: 23
Wandering Song [poems by Darío]
Darío, Rubén D: 36
Wanderings of Oisin, The [poem by Yeats]
Irish literature (The Irish literary revival) I: 431-432
Waner, Lloyd [American baseball player]
Baseball (table: Hall of Fame) B: 134b
Waner, Paul [American baseball player]
Baseball (table: Hall of Fame) B: 134b
Wang Kon [Korean ruler]
Korea, History of (Early years) K: 366
Wang Mang [Chinese emperor]
China (The Han dynasty) C: 500-501
Han dynasty H: 38
Wang Meng [Chinese artist]
Painting (Chinese painting) P: 44-46
Wang Shifu [Chinese dramatist]
Chinese literature (Drama and fiction) C: 511
Wang Wei [Chinese painter] W: 23 *with picture*
Chinese literature (Poetry) C: 511
Wang Yangming [Chinese philosopher]
Confucianism (Later Confucianism) Ci: 937
Wang Yinglin [Chinese scholar]
Encyclopedia (From the 1200's to the 1600's) E: 268a
Wangchuk, Ugyen [king of Bhutan]
Bhutan (History) B: 278
Waning moon
Moon (Phases) M: 783-784
Waning of the Middle Ages, The [book by Huizinga]
Huizinga, Johan H: 411
Wankel, Felix [German engineer]
Rotary engine R: 485
Wankel engine *See* Rotary engine *in this index*
Want ad
Careers (Finding job opportunities) C: 217
Newspaper (Preparing advertisements) N: 383
Wantage Community [religious group]
Religious life (table) R: 227
Wanuskewin Heritage Park [Saskatoon]
Saskatchewan (Places to visit) S: 136 *with picture*
Wapiti [animal]
Elk (The American elk) E: 241 *with picture*
Red deer R: 188
Wapshot Chronicle, The [book by Cheever]
Cheever, John C: 395
Wapshot Scandal, The [book by Cheever]
Cheever, John C: 395
Wapsipinicon River
Iowa (Rivers and lakes) I: 386
Wapusk National Park [Manitoba]
Canada (table: National parks and national park reserves) C: 114
Waqf [foundation]
Jerusalem (Culture) J: 99-100

War W: 23
See also the list of Related articles in the War *article*
Army **A:** 724; (Prevention of war) **A:** 725
Aztec (Warfare) **A:** 1002
Balloon (Balloons in war) **B: 61** *with picture*
Battering ram **B:** 167
Catapult **C:** 298
Censorship (Military censorship) **C:** 346
Civil War, American (The beginning of modern warfare) **Ci:** 634
Conscientious objector **Ci: 974**
Contraband **Ci: 1023**
Famine (Causes of famine) **F:** 26
Flag **F:** 193
Guerrilla warfare **G:** 419
Hague Conventions **H:** 7
Indian, American (Warfare) **I:** 144 *with pictures*; (Indians of the Northeast) **I:** 154-155; (Indians of the Southwest) **I:** 166-168
Infantry (History) **I:** 265
Inflation (Theories about the causes of inflation) **I:** 268
International law (The laws of war) **I:** 341
Jihad **J:** 126
Kellogg-Briand Pact **K:** 256
Logistics **L:** 426
Middle Ages (Feudal Europe) **M:** 524
Military training **M:** 544
Napalm **N:** 12
National budget (Deficits and surpluses) **N:** 31
Nuclear winter **N:** 602
Pacifism **P:** 17
Painting (Romanticism) **P:** 68-69
Petroleum (Petroleum and war) **P:** 346
Post-traumatic stress disorder **P:** 710
Rationing **R:** 148
Revolution (Features of revolution) **R:** 269
Right of search **R:** 340
Slavery (Development of slavery) **S:** 501
Vikings (Warfare) **V:** 381 *with picture*
Yanomami Indians **Y:** 552
War, Articles of [U.S. history]
Articles of War **A:** 759
War, Department of [U.S. history]
Defense, Department of (History) **D:** 88
Eckert, J. Presper, Jr. **E:** 50
War, Prisoner of *See* Prisoner of war *in this index*
War Admiral [horse]
Kentucky Derby (table) **K:** 296
War Against Jugurtha [book by Sallust]
History (The ancient Greeks and Romans) **H:** 261-262
War and Ordnance, Board of [U.S. history]
Army, United States (The Continental Army) **A:** 737-738
War and Peace [book by Tolstoy]
Novel (Russia) **N:** 573
Russian literature (The 1860's and 1870's) **R:** 562
Tolstoy, Leo (His masterpieces) **T:** 322
War and Peace [opera by Prokofiev]
Prokofiev, Sergei Sergeyevich **P:** 817
War and Remembrance [book by Wouk]
Wouk, Herman **W:** 502
War Between the States *See* Civil War, American *in this index*
War bonnet [headdress]
Sioux Indians *picture on* **S:** 475
War Brides Act [1945]
Immigration (A temporary decline) **I:** 83
War club [weapon]
Indian, American *picture on* **I:** 139
War correspondent [career] **W:** 26
War Cries [poem by Núñez de Arce]
Spanish literature (The 1800's) **So:** 761
War crime **W:** 27
Civil War, American (Prisons) **Ci:** 630-631
Crime (War crime) **Ci:** 1137
Croatia (Recent developments) **Ci:** 1148c
Eichmann, Adolf **E:** 145
Geneva Conventions **G:** 88
Genocide **G:** 90
Human rights (Criminal trials) **H:** 428a
International Criminal Court **I:** 338
International law (Violations) **I:** 341
Iran-Iraq War **I:** 407
Law (Developments in international law) **L:** 137
Milošević, Slobodan **M:** 556
Nanking Massacre **N:** 10
Nuremberg Trials **N:** 613
Srebrenica massacre **So:** 816
War (Ethical and legal aspects of war) **W:** 24
World War II (Peace with Germany) **W:** 498
War Crimes Commission [UN]
War crime (World War II) **W:** 27
War debt
Virginia (The Civil War and Reconstruction) **V:** 421-422

War Democrats [political party]
Democratic Party (The slavery issue) **D:** 124-125
War eagle [bird] *See* Golden eagle *in this index*
War guilt [political science]
Versailles, Treaty of (Effects of the treaty) **V:** 340
War Hawks [U.S. history]
Clay, Henry (National leader) **Ci:** 658
United States, History of the (The War of 1812) **U:** 165
War of 1812 (The War Hawks) **W:** 30
War in Heaven [play by Barry]
Barry, Philip **B:** 119
War in the Pacific National Historical Park [Guam]
National Park System (table: National historical parks) **N:** 56-57
War Industries Board [U.S. history]
World War I (The United States enters the war) **W:** 462
War Information, Office of
Propaganda (During World War II) **P:** 825
World War II (Propaganda) **W:** 494-495
War Is Kind [poems by Crane]
Crane, Stephen **Ci:** 1120
War Measures Act [Canadian history]
Canada, History of (The separatist threat) **C:** 150
War of 1812 [1812-1814] **W:** 28 *with pictures*
See also the list of Related articles in the War of 1812 *article*
Army, United States (The War of 1812) **A:** 738
Black Hawk **B:** 387
Canada, History of (The War of 1812) **C:** 143
Ghent, Treaty of **G:** 181
Illinois (Early national period) **I:** 72-74
Indian, American (After European contact) **I:** 156-157
Indian wars (The Shawnee Prophet) **I:** 192
Laffite, Jean **L:** 29
Madison, James (Madison's first administration [1809-1813]) **M:** 35; (Madison's second administration [1813-1817]) **M:** 35 *with picture*
Marine Corps, United States *picture on* **M:** 207; (The early Marine Corps) **M:** 208
Maryland (The War of 1812 and industrial development) **M:** 258
Milan Decree **M:** 541
Navy, United States (The War of 1812 [1812-1814]) **N:** 88
New Orleans, Battle of **N:** 285
Ontario (Upper Canada) **O:** 784
Potawatomi Indians **P:** 714
Secord, Laura Ingersoll **S:** 278
Uncle Sam **U:** 19
United States, History of the (The War of 1812) **U:** 165 *with picture*
War (table) **W:** 25
Washington, D.C. (Slow beginnings) **W:** 86
War of opportunity
War (Struggles over power) **W:** 23
War of Secession *See* Civil War, American *in this index*
War of the American Revolution *See* Revolution, American *in this index*
War of the Austrian Succession *See* Succession wars *in this index*
War of the Bavarian Succession *See* Succession wars *in this index*
War of the End of the World, The [book by Vargas Llosa]
Vargas Llosa, Mario **V:** 286
War of the League of Augsburg [1689-1697]
French and Indian wars (King William's War) **F:** 512
War of the Newts, The [book by Čapek]
Čapek, Karel **C:** 191
War of the Pacific [1879-1883]
Latin America (Early years of independence) **L:** 107-108
Peru (The War of the Pacific) **P:** 315
War of the Polish Succession *See* Succession wars *in this index*
War of the Reform [1858-1860]
Juárez, Benito Pablo **J:** 178
Mexico (Reform) **M:** 471
War of the Spanish Succession *See* Succession wars *in this index*
War of the Thousand Days [1899-1902]
Colombia (Political disorder) **Ci:** 784
War of the Three Henrys [1585-1589]
Henry III [of France] **H:** 186
War of the Triple Alliance *See* Triple Alliance, War of the *in this index*
War of the Worlds, The [book by Wells]
Welles, Orson **W:** 194
Wells, H. G. **W:** 195
War of the Worlds, The [radio broadcast]
Radio (The Golden Age of Broadcasting) **R:** 92

War on Drugs [U.S. policy]
African Americans (Social struggles) **A:** 136s-136t
War on Poverty [U.S. history]
Great Society (Legislation) **G:** 349
Head Start **H:** 124
Johnson, Lyndon Baines (The national scene) **J:** 148
United States, History of the (The civil rights movement) **U:** 196a
Welfare (National welfare systems) **W:** 191
War on terrorism [U.S. history]
Bush, George Walker (Terrorist attacks and military action) **B: 722g**
Musharraf, Pervez **M:** 941
September 11 terrorist attacks (Global war on terrorism) **S:** 310a
Terrorism (The September 11 terrorist attacks) **T:** 179
World, History of the (The war on terrorism) **W: 448b**
War Powers Act *See* War Powers Resolution *in this index*
War Powers Resolution [1973] **W:** 33
Congress of the United States (Continued struggle for power) **Ci:** 948
Nixon, Richard Milhous (Events at home) **N:** 435-436
War prisoner *See* Prisoner of war *in this index*
War Relocation Authority
Japanese American internment **J:** 60
War Requiem [music by Britten]
Britten, Benjamin **B:** 634
War Risk Insurance Act [1914]
Veterans Affairs, Department of (History) **V:** 344
War savings stamp
Stamp **So:** 829
War service medal *See* Campaign medal *in this index*
Warbeck, Perkin [English pretender] **W:** 34
Warble [disorder]
Warble fly **W:** 34
Warble fly W: 34 *with picture*
Bot fly **B:** 507
Warbler [bird] **W:** 34 *with pictures*
Bird *picture on* **B:** 358; (Birds of forests and woodlands) **B:** 334 *with picture*; (Bird migration) **B:** 360
Ovenbird **O:** 881 *with picture*
Warburg, Otto Heinrich [German physiologist]
Nobel Prizes (Physiology or medicine: 1931) **N:** 445
Warburton, Alexander B. [Canadian political leader]
Prince Edward Island (table) **P:** 791
Warburton, Peter Egerton [British explorer]
Australia *map on* **A:** 921
Australian Desert **A:** 927
Exploration *map on* **E:** 448
Ward [law] **W:** 35
Feudalism (The principles of feudalism) **F:** 82
Foster care **F:** 429
Guardian **G:** 411
Ward [political division]
Tokyo (The city) **T:** 313
Ward **W:** 35
Ward [religion]
Mormons (Church organization) **M:** 807
Ward [structure]
Castle (Structure) **C:** 280 *with picture*
Ward, Aaron Montgomery [American businessman] **W:** 35
Ward, Artemus [American humorist] **W:** 35
Ward, Barbara [British economist] **W:** 35
Ward, Charlie [American football player]
Football (table) **F:** 363
Ward, Douglas Turner [American author]
African American literature (The 1900's) **A:** 136a
Ward, Ferdinand [American businessman]
Grant, Ulysses S. (Later years) **G:** 317
Ward, John M. [American baseball player]
Baseball (table: Hall of Fame) **B:** 134b
Ward, Joseph [American religious leader] **W:** 35
Ward, Lynd Kendall [American artist] **W:** 36
Regina Medal (table: 1975) **R:** 206
Ward, Marcus L. [American political leader]
New Jersey (table) **N:** 249
Ward, Montgomery [American businessman] *See* Ward, Aaron Montgomery *in this index*
Ward, Rodger [American race driver]
Automobile racing (table: Indianapolis 500 winners) **A:** 980
Ward, Samuel A. [American composer]
America the Beautiful **A:** 407
Ward, Virgil S. [American educator]
Differentiated instruction **D:** 200
Warded lock
Lock (Mechanical locks) **L:** 411

Warden [prison]
Prison (The prison staff) P: 806
Warden, The [book by Trollope]
Trollope, Anthony T: 449
Wards Island [New York]
New York City (Small islands) N: 330
Ware, Andre [American football player]
Football (table) F: 363
Ware, Charles Pickard [American publisher]
Spiritual So: 796
Ware, Chris [American author]
American literature (Popular genres) A: 425-426
Ware, Lance [British scientist]
Mensa International M: 403
Ware the Hawk [poem by Skelton]
Skelton, John S: 481
Warfare *See* War *in this index*
Warfield, Edwin [American political leader]
Maryland (table) M: 255
Warhead [weapon]
Ammunition (Destroying the attackers) A: 436
with diagram
Guided missile (The warhead) G: 423
Nuclear weapon (Strategic nuclear weapons)
N: 598 *with diagram*
Submarine (Ballistic missile submarines) So: 941
Torpedo (How a torpedo works) T: 340d *with
diagram*
Warhol, Andy [American artist] W: 36 *with picture*
Painting (Pop Art) P: 86
Pop Art P: 659
Warlock [person]
Witchcraft W: 371
Warlocks [musical group]
Grateful Dead G: 329
Warlord
Beijing (History) B: 224
China (The war lord period) C: 503
Warm-air furnace
Heating *diagram on* H: 158; (Warm-air heating)
H: 157
Warm-blooded animal W: 36
Animal (Some common ways of grouping
animals) A: 472
Bird B: 329
Dinosaur (How dinosaurs lived) D: 211;
(Reproduction and growth) D: 211
Fish F: 145
Hibernation (Warm-blooded hibernators) H: 222
Mammal M: 117
Prehistoric animal (The Age of Mammals)
P: 740-741
Temperature, Body T: 130
Warm front [weather]
Weather (Synoptic-scale systems) W: 159-160
with diagram
Warm Springs [spring, Idaho]
Idaho (Rivers, waterfalls, springs, and lakes) I: 38
Warm Springs Foundation, Georgia
Roosevelt, Franklin Delano (Battle with polio)
R: 451
Warmerdam, Cornelius [American athlete]
Track and field (The early and middle 1900's)
T: 360
Warmoth, Henry C. [American political leader]
Louisiana (table) L: 496; (Reconstruction) L: 500
Pinchback, P. B. S. P: 466
Warner, Charles Dudley [American author]
Twain, Mark: (*The Gilded Age*) T: 529
Warner, Fred M. [American political leader]
Michigan (table) M: 507
Warner, Glenn Scobey [American football coach]
See Warner, Pop *in this index*
Warner, Mark R. [American political leader]
Virginia (table) V: 417
Warner, Pop [American football coach] W: 36
Warner, Seth [American general] W: 36
Allen, Ethan A: 371
Green Mountain Boys G: 380
Vermont (The Revolutionary War in America)
V: 334
Warner Brothers [company]
Motion picture (Movies become big business)
M: 865-866
Warner Bros. Entertainment [company]
Time Warner Inc. T: 292d
Warning
Civil defense (Civil defense in action) Ci: 605
Warning coloration
Butterfly (How butterflies protect themselves)
B: 742
Protective coloration P: 831
Snake (Protection against predators) S: 531
Warning signal
Boating (Buoys and other safety aids) B: 430 *with*

pictures
Warp [weaving]
Basket making (Methods) B: 141 *with diagrams*
Rugs and carpets (Weaving) R: 515 *with pictures*
Satin S: 150h
Tapestry (How tapestries are made) T: 39
Textile (Woven fabrics) T: 214
Velvet V: 297
Weaving (Types of weaves) W: 173 *with pictures;*
(How a loom works) W: 173-174 *with picture*
Warp beam
Weaving (How a loom works) W: 173-174
Warp knitting
Knitting machine K: 354
Textile (Knitted fabrics) T: 214
Warping [industrial process]
Cotton (Spinning) Ci: 1091
Warrant [law] W: 37
Arrest A: 743
Law enforcement (Arrest) L: 141
Wiretapping (Laws concerning wiretapping)
W: 345
Warrant officer [rank]
Army, United States (Training an officer) A: 733-
734
Navy, United States *pictures on* N: 86; (Training an
officer) N: 83
Rank, Military R: 139; (table) R: 140
Warranty
Guaranty G: 411
Product liability suit P: 810
Warranty deed [real estate]
Deed D: 81
Warrego River [Australia]
Queensland (Land and climate) Q: 39
Warren [animal home]
Rabbit (Homes) R: 48
Warren, Sir Charles [British government official]
Jack the Ripper J: 3
Warren, Earl [American jurist] W: 37 *with portrait*
California (table) C: 59
Kennedy, John Fitzgerald *picture on* K: 264
Warren Report W: 37
Warren, Francis E. [American political leader]
Wyoming (table) W: 532; (Territorial progress)
W: 534-536
Warren, Fuller [American political leader]
Florida (table) F: 260
Warren, J. Robin [American pathologist]
Nobel Prizes (Physiology or medicine: 2005)
N: 447
Warren, John Collins [American physician]
Morton, William Thomas Green M: 821
Warren, Joseph [American colonial leader] W: 37
Revere, Paul (Revere's ride) R: 268
Revolution, American (Lexington and Concord)
R: 274-275
Warren, Mercy Otis [American author] W: 37
Warren, Robert Penn [American author] W: 37
American literature (Modernist poetry) A: 421;
(Poetry) A: 423
Poet laureate (table: Poets laureate of the United
States) P: 590
Warren, William [American businessman]
Ford, Gerald Rudolph (Marriage) F: 374-375
Warren Air Force Base
Cheyenne (History) C: 417
Wyoming (Service industries) W: 531
Warren Report [U.S. history] W: 37
Kennedy, John Fitzgerald (The assassination
controversy) K: 268
Oswald, Lee Harvey O: 869
Warrior
Knights and knighthood K: 348
Warriors, Golden State
Basketball (table) B: 150
Wars of Religion [European history]
Roman Catholic Church (The Counter
Reformation) R: 408
Wars of succession *See* Succession wars *in this
index*
Wars of the Roses [1455-1485] W: 38
Edward IV E: 112
England (The Wars of the Roses) E: 306
Henry VII [king of England] H: 187
Lancaster L: 55
Shakespeare, William (The English ruler) S: 350;
(Shakespeare's plays) S: 354-356
Tudor, House of T: 481
York Y: 568
Warsaw [Poland] W: 38 *with picture*
Poland *picture on* P: 604
Warsaw, Grand Duchy of [Polish history]
Poland (The partitions) P: 612
Warsaw ghetto
Holocaust *picture on* H: 296b
Jews (The Holocaust) J: 124

Warsaw (History) W: 38-39
Warsaw Pact [alliance] W: 39
Cold War (To the brink and back) Ci: 765
Communism (The Cold War) Ci: 895
Europe (The Cold War) E: 415
Germany (East Germany) G: 170
International relations (The Cold War begins)
I: 345
North Atlantic Treaty Organization N: 471
Organization for Security and Co-operation in
Europe O: 854
Warshawski, V. I. [fictional character]
Paretsky, Sara P: 159
Warship W: 39 *with picture*
*See also and the list of Related articles in the
Warship article*
Navy N: 76 *with pictures;* (Engineering advances)
N: 79
Navy, United States (Combat ships) N: 84
Ship *picture on* S: 418; (Phoenician and Greek
ships) S: 414 *with picture;* (Viking ships) S: 416
Vikings (The Vikings as shipbuilders) V: 381
Warszawa [Poland] *See* Warsaw *in this index*
Wart [disorder] W: 44 *with picture*
Skin (Tumors) S: 491
Toad T: 303
Wart hog W: 44 *with picture*
Warta River [river, Poland]
Oder River O: 674
Warted gourd
Gourd *picture on* G: 281
Wartime Prices and Trade Board [Canada]
World War II (Government controls) W: 495-495
Wartime Relocation and Internment of Civilians,
Commission on [U.S. history]
Asian Americans (World War II and Japanese
Americans) A: 812f
Warton, Thomas [British poet]
Poet laureate (table: Poets laureate of the United
Kingdom) P: 590
Warwick [Rhode Island] W: 44
Warwick [Virginia]
Newport News N: 379
Warwick, Earl of [1428-1471, English political
leader] W: 44
Warwick, Guy of [legendary figure]
Guy of Warwick G: 445
Warwick Academy
Bermuda (Education) B: 268
Warwick Castle
England *picture on* E: 293
Warwick Patent [U.S. history]
Plymouth Colony (Life in Plymouth Colony)
P: 583
Wasatch Range [mountains, Idaho-Utah] W: 44
Salt Lake City S: 75 *with picture*
Utah (Land regions) U: 240 *with map*
Wascana Centre
Regina (The city) R: 204-205
Wash [art]
Drawing (Materials and techniques) D: 342-343
Painting (Water-color painting) P: 39
Wash, The [bay, England]
England (The English Lowlands) E: 300-301
United Kingdom (The English Lowlands) U: 59-61
with map
Wash and wear fabric
Clothing (The 1900's and 2000's) Ci: 705
Wash mill [machine]
Rubber (Plasticization) R: 504
Washakie [American Indian chief] W: 45
Wyoming (Indian and settler conflicts) W: 534
Washburn, Cadwallader Colden [American
political leader]
Wisconsin (table) W: 365
Washburn, Cephas [American educator]
Arkansas (Schools) A: 698
Washburn, Emory [American political leader]
Massachusetts (table) M: 288
Washburn, Henry D. [American government
official]
National Park System (History) N: 58
Yellowstone National Park (History) Y: 559-560
Washburn, Israel, Jr. [American political leader]
Maine (table) M: 87
Washburn, Peter T. [American political leader]
Vermont (table) V: 333
Washburn, William B. [American political leader]
Massachusetts (table) M: 288
Washburn and Moen gauge
Wire (Sizes of wire) W: 344
Washburne, Elihu Benjamin [American political
leader]
Grant, Ulysses S. (Return to the Army) G: 314;
(table) G: 316
Washer [hardware]
Plumbing (How faucets work) P: 579 *with*

diagram
Washerless faucet
Plumbing (How faucets work) **P:** 579
Washerwoman, The [painting by Daumier]
Realism *picture on* **R:** 171
Washi [paper]
Origami **O:** 855
Washing machine W: 45 *with diagrams*
Washing soda
Soda **So:** 568
Washington [Missouri]
Missouri (Interesting facts) **M:** 651
Washington [state] **W:** 46 *with pictures and maps*
Washington, D.C. W: 70 *with pictures and maps*
See also the list of Related articles in the
Washington, D.C. *article*
City planning (The Renaissance) **Ci:** 602-603
Constitution of the United States (Amendment
23) **Ci:** 1015
King, Martin Luther, Jr (The growing movement)
K: 321 *with picture*
March on Washington **M:** 196
Maryland (table: Average monthly weather)
M: 252
Subway **So:** 949 *with picture*
United States, History of the (The War of 1812)
U: 165 *with picture*
United States capitals **U:** 198
Van Buren, Martin **V:** 270
Voucher **V:** 451
Washington, Augustine [half brother of George
Washington]
Ohio Company (The first Ohio Company) **O:** 704
Washington, Booker T. [American educator] **W:** 88
with portrait
African Americans *picture on* **A:** 136k; (The rise of
new black leaders) **A:** 136l
American literature (Nonfiction writers) **A:** 420
Du Bois, W. E. B. **D:** 372
Niagara Movement **N:** 394
Tuskegee University **T:** 525
Washington, Bushrod [American jurist]
Supreme Court of the United States (table)
So: 1000
Washington, Denzel [American actor] **W:** 89 *with
portrait*
African Americans *picture on* **A:** 136s
Motion picture (Best performance by an actor:
2001) **M:** 862a; (Best performance by an actor
in a supporting role: 1989) **M:** 862b
Washington, George [U.S. president] **W:** 90 *with
pictures*
See also the list of Related articles in the
Washington, George, *article*
Adams, John (Vice president) **A:** 37
Brother Jonathan **B:** 642
Cornwallis, Charles **Ci:** 1066
Executive order **E:** 436
Franklin, Benjamin (His place in history) **F:** 492
French and Indian wars (The French and Indian
War) **F:** 512-513
General **G:** 82
Genêt, Edmond Charles Édouard **G:** 84a
Government (The Enlightenment) **G:** 290-291
Greenough, Horatio **G:** 386
Houdon, Jean Antoine **H:** 378 *with picture*
Jefferson, Thomas (Secretary of state) **J:** 81 *with
picture*
Lee, Robert E. (The Civil War) **L:** 178
Masonry *picture on* **M:** 267
Mount Rushmore National Memorial **M:** 887
with picture
Mythology (Types of myths) **M:** 973-974
New Jersey *picture on* **N:** 252; (The American
Revolution) **N:** 250-251 *with picture*
Paine, Thomas (American revolutionary) **P:** 22
Pittsburgh (Early days) **P:** 501
President of the United States (The founding of
the presidency) **P:** 767
Presidents' Day **P:** 772
Princeton University (Campus buildings) **P:** 795
Pulaski, Casimir **P:** 886
Revolution, American **R:** 270 *with pictures and
maps*
Ross, Betsy **R:** 481
Sculpture *picture on* **S:** 256
Stuart, Gilbert Charles **So:** 930
Thanksgiving Day (Later thanksgiving days in the
United States) **T:** 230
Trenton, Battle of **T:** 435
United States, History of the (Establishing
a government) **U:** 161-162 *with pictures*;
(Problems in foreign affairs) **U:** 163
Valley Forge **V:** 266 *with picture*
Virginia (Interesting facts) **V:** 399 *with picture*
Washington, D.C. **W:** 70; (History) **W:** 85
Washington, Martha Custis **W:** 109

William and Mary, College of **W:** 309
Yorktown, Siege of **Y:** 569
Washington, Harold [American political leader]
W: 108
Byrne, Jane Margaret **B:** 747
Chicago (Political developments in the late
1900's) **C:** 436
Washington, John Augustine, Jr. [great grand-
nephew of George Washington]
Mount Vernon (A national shrine) **M:** 890
Washington, Lawrence [ancestor of George
Washington]
Sulgrave Manor **So:** 968
Washington, Lawrence [half-brother of George
Washington]
Mount Vernon (The buildings) **M:** 888
Ohio Company (The first Ohio Company) **O:** 704
Washington, George (Development of character)
W: 92; (Only foreign trip) **W:** 93
Washington, Martha Custis [wife of George
Washington] **W:** 109
Mount Vernon (The grounds and the tomb)
M: 890
Washington, George *pictures on* **W:** 104, **W:** 107;
(Marriage) **W:** 95 *with picture*; (Life in the
Executive Mansion) **W:** 102
Washington, Mount See Mount Washington in
this index
Washington, Robert [ancestor of George
Washington]
Sulgrave Manor **So:** 968
Washington, Treaty of [1871] **W:** 109
Fish, Hamilton **F:** 175
Grant, Ulysses S. (Foreign relations) **G:** 316
Macdonald, Sir John Alexander (Completing the
Dominion) **M:** 8-9
Washington, University of W: 109
Washington, Walter E. [American political leader]
Washington, D.C. (Government changes) **W:** 87
Washington and Lee University
Lee, Robert E. (Last years) **L:** 179
Washington Area Metropolitan Transit Authority
Washington, D.C. (Transportation) **W:** 84
Washington Capitals [team]
Hockey (table: National Hockey League) **H:** 281
Washington College [Virginia]
Lee, Robert E. (Last years) **L:** 179
Washington Conference [1921-1922] **W:** 109
Arms control (History of arms control) **A:** 721
Harding, Warren Gamaliel (Return to normalcy)
H: 58
Meighen, Arthur (First term) **M:** 386
Navy, United States (World War I [1914-1918])
N: 88-89
Washington Crossing the Delaware [painting by
Leutze]
Leutze, Emanuel Gottlieb **L:** 216 *with picture*
Washington Crossing the Delaware [painting by
Rivers]
Rivers, Larry *picture on* **R:** 355
Washington District [U.S. history]
Watauga Association **W:** 113
Washington Dulles International Airport
Washington, D.C. (Transportation) **W:** 84-85
Washington Heights [district]
New York City (Manhattan) **N:** 323-326
Washington Library Center
Chicago (New construction) **C:** 437
Washington-Lincoln Day [holiday] See Presidents'
Day *in this index*
Washington Lodge [organization]
Odd Fellows, Independent Order of (The
American order) **O:** 673
Washington Monument [Baltimore]
Baltimore (Other interesting places to visit) **B:** 69
Washington Monument [Washington, D.C.]
W: 109
Mills, Robert **M:** 555
National Park System (table: National memorials)
N: 54
Obelisk **O:** 642
Washington, D.C. *map on* **W:** 76; (Washington
Monument) **W:** 73
Washington National Cathedral [Washington,
D.C.] **W:** 110 *with picture*
Washington, D.C. (Architectural styles) **W:** 78
Washington Nationals [team] See Nationals,
Washington *in this index*
Washington Naval Conference of 1921-1922 See
Washington Conference *in this index*
Washington of South America [nickname]
Bolívar, Simón **B:** 441
Washington-on-the-Brazos [former town]
Texas (The Texas revolution) **T:** 206
Washington Post, The [newspaper]
Graham, Katharine **G:** 300
Washington Public Power Supply System

Washington (The late 1900's) **W:** 68
Washington Redskins [football team]
Football (National Football League) **F:** 364
Washington State University W: 110
Washington *picture on* **W:** 51
Washington Times-Herald [newspaper]
Onassis, Jacqueline Kennedy **O:** 761
Washington University in St. Louis
Missouri *picture on* **M:** 654
Washington Wizards [basketball team]
Basketball (table) **B:** 150
Washington's Birthday [holiday] **W:** 110
Washita Battlefield National Historic Site
[Oklahoma]
National Park System (table: National historic
sites) **N:** 52-54
Washita River [Arkansas-Louisiana] See Ouachita
River *in this index*
Washita River [Texas-Oklahoma]
Indian wars *picture on* **I:** 194; (Washita River)
I: 193
Washkansky, Louis [patient of]
Barnard, Christiaan Neethling **B:** 114
Washo See Washoe Indians *in this index*
Washoe Indians W: 110
Waskey, Frank H. [American political leader]
Alaska (The early 1900's) **A:** 301
Wasp [insect] **W:** 111 *with pictures*
Ant **A:** 520
Fig **F:** 96
Insect *pictures on* **I:** 283, **I:** 290; (Protection from
enemies) **I:** 297 *with picture*; (Why insects
behave as they do) **I:** 298
Orange (Pests and diseases) **O:** 815
Spider (Enemies) **So:** 788
WASP [U.S. history] See Women Airforce Service
Pilots *in this index*
Wasp, U.S.S [ship]
World War II *picture on* **W:** 485
Wassail [drink]
Christmas (In England, Ireland, Scotland, and
Wales) **C:** 530
Wassermann, August von [German bacteriologist]
W: 112
Wasserstein, Wendy [American dramatist] **W:** 112
Drama (Later United States drama) **D:** 340-341
Wassily chair
Furniture (The Bauhaus) **F:** 582-583 *with picture*
Waste [biology] See Elimination *in this index*
Waste, Pretreatment of
Water pollution (Pretreatment and reduction of
wastes) **W:** 138
Waste disposal W: 112
See also Environmental pollution; Sewage *in
this index*
Air pollution (Burning of solid wastes) **A:** 198
Energy supply (Solid and liquid wastes) **E:** 279
Environmental pollution (Types of pollution)
E: 331-334; (Controlling pollution) **E:** 335
Garbage *picture on* **G:** 28
Incinerator **I:** 99
Landfill **L:** 57 *with diagram*
Nuclear energy (Wastes and waste disposal)
N: 588
Ocean (Marine pollution) **O:** 664
Packaging (The packaging industry) **P:** 18
Plastics (Plastics and the environment) **P:** 560
Plumbing (The drain-waste-vent system) **P:** 578
Recycling **R:** 184
Sanitation **S:** 111
Space exploration (Meeting basic needs in space)
So: 703
Technology (Benefits of technology) **T:** 76 *with
picture*
Thermal pollution **T:** 253
Waste Land, The [poem by Eliot]
American literature (Modernist poetry) **A:** 421
Eliot, T. S. (His works) **E:** 237
English literature (Poetry between the wars)
E: 322
Poetry (Poetry of the 1900's) **P:** 597
Wastewater
Sewage **S:** 329
Ship (Pollution) **S:** 413-414
Thermal pollution **T:** 253
Wasting syndrome [disorder]
AIDS (Symptoms) **A:** 164
Wat Phrathat Doi Suthep [temple]
Thailand *picture on* **T:** 222
Wat Tyler's Rebellion [1381] **W:** 113
England (The Hundred Years' War) **E:** 306
Richard II **R:** 329
Watauga Association [U.S. history] **W:** 113
Tennessee (Early settlement) **T:** 153
Watch [military]
Hour **H:** 379
Navy, United States (A typical day) **N:** 83

Submarine (Life aboard a submarine) **So: 941**
Watch [timepiece] **W: 114** *with pictures*
See also Clock *in this index*
Quartz (Uses) **Q: 8**
Switzerland *picture on* **So: 1057**
Time (Clocks that count repeated actions) **T: 289**
Watch on the Rhine [play by Hellman]
Hellman, Lillian **H: 178**
Watch That Ends the Night, The [book by MacLennan]
MacLennan, Hugh **M: 25**
Watch Tower Bible and Tract Society
Jehovah's Witnesses **J: 89**
Watchful waiting [U.S. history]
Wilson, Woodrow (Crisis in Mexico) **W: 323**
Watchtower, The [magazine]
Jehovah's Witnesses **J: 89**
Water W: 116 *with pictures and maps*
See also Water pollution *in this index; and the list of Related articles in the* Water *article*
Alchemy **A: 334**
Camel (Water) **C: 79**
Compound **C: 906**
Disease (Spread of infectious diseases) **D: 228**
Earth *picture on* **E: 22**; (The hydrosphere) **E: 20**
Electrolysis (How electrolysis works) **E: 200**
Empedocles **E: 261**
Fluoridation **F: 305**
Ground water **G: 401**
Human body (Chemical elements and molecules) **H: 417**
Hydrology **H: 470**
Hydrosphere **H: 472**
Hydrotherapy **H: 472**
Irrigation **I: 456** *with pictures*
Leaf (Obtaining the raw materials) **L: 155**
Life (The chemical basis of life) **L: 277**
Mars (Surface features) **M: 225**; (Possibility of life) **M: 226c**; (Observation by spacecraft) **M: 226c–226d**
Moon **M: 783**
Nutrition (Kinds of nutrients) **N: 625**
Ocean **O: 650**
Plant (Aquatic regions) **P: 528**; (Movement of water) **P: 537**
Sanitation (Water treatment) **S: 111**
Satellite **S: 149**
Space exploration (Meeting basic needs in space) **So: 703**; (Probes to Mars) **So: 710**
Technology (Benefits of technology) **T: 76**
Temperature **T: 130**
Thirst **T: 259**
Tree (How a tree grows) **T: 418**
Waves **W: 150**
Wetland **W: 252a**
World (Physical features of the world) **W: 415**
Water aerobics [exercise]
Hydrotherapy *picture on* **H: 473**
Water arum [plant]
Calla **C: 66**
Water Babies, The [book by Kingsley]
Kingsley, Charles **K: 331**
Water ballast
Airship (Control) **A: 251**
Water ballet
Swimming (Synchronized swimming) **So: 1047** *with picture*
Water based paint
Paint (Household paints) **P: 23**
Water basket [container]
Indian, American (Crafts and weapons) *picture on* **I: 139**
Water bed
Bed (Types of beds) **B: 198**
Water beech [tree]
Ironwood **I: 454**
Water beetle W: 133 *with picture*
Beetle *pictures on* **B: 218**; (Predacious diving beetles) **B: 217**
Water bird
Avian influenza **A: 982**
Bird (Birds of inland waters and marshes) **B: 340** *with pictures*; (Birds of the seacoasts) **B: 342** *with pictures*; (In the water) **B: 353**
Lake (The lake habitat) **L: 33**
Water boa [snake]
Anaconda **A: 447** *with picture*
Water boatman [insect]
Insect (Beneficial insects) **I: 284**
Water bug **W: 133**, *picture on* **W: 134**
Water brash [physiology]
Heartburn **H: 147**
Water buffalo [animal] **W: 133** *with picture*
Animal *picture on* **A: 471**
Water bug W: 133 *with picture*
Insect *picture on* **I: 281**
Water caltrop [plant]

Water chestnut **W: 134**
Water chestnut [plant] **W: 134** *with picture*
Water chinquapin [plant]
Lotus **L: 473**
Water clock W: 134
Clock (History) **Ci: 682k** *with picture*
Time (Clocks that measure change) **T: 289**
Water color [art]
Painting (Materials and techniques) **P: 36**; (Water-color painting) **P: 39**
Water conservation See Conservation *in this index*
Water conveyance canal
Canal **C: 162**
Water-cooled engine
Gasoline engine (Cooling) **G: 63–64**
Water cress [plant]
Cress **Ci: 1127**
Water culture [agriculture]
Hydroponics (Methods of hydroponics) **H: 472** *with diagram*
Water cycle
Evaporation (Uses of evaporation) **E: 423**
Hydrology **H: 470**
Water (Nature's water cycle) **W: 120** *with diagram*
Water distillation
Water *diagram on* **W: 128**; (Distillation) **W: 127**
Water erosion [conservation]
Erosion (How erosion occurs) **E: 355**
Water extinguisher
Fire extinguisher (Water extinguishers) **F: 130**
Water flea W: 134
Crustacean **Ci: 1162**
Egg (Other kinds of eggs) **E: 116**
Water frame [machine]
Arkwright, Sir Richard **A: 716**
Industrial Revolution (Spinning machines) **I: 248–249**
Spinning (The water frame) **So: 794**
Water gap [geology]
Appalachian Mountains (Physical features) **A: 568**
Gap **G: 28**
West Virginia (Land regions) **W: 218**
Water garden
Gardening (Specialty gardens) **G: 31**
Water gas
Carbon monoxide **C: 207**
Gas [fuel] (Other manufactured gases) **G: 56**
Water glass [chemical]
Grinding and polishing (Grinding wheels) **G: 395**
Water hazard
Golf (Hazards) **G: 261** *with picture*
Water heater
Plumbing (The water supply system) **P: 577–578** *with diagram*
Water hemisphere [geography]
Hemisphere **H: 181** *with diagram*
Water hemlock [plant]
Poisonous plant (Some poisonous plants) **P: 602**
Water hog
Capybara **C: 201** *with picture*
Water hyacinth W: 134
Invasive species (How invasive species affect habitats) **I: 354j** *with picture*
Water Island [island, Virgin Islands]
Virgin Islands, United States (Islands) **V: 395**
Water jacket [engine]
Automobile (The cooling system) **A: 953**
Water-jet cutting [manufacturing]
Machine tool (Beam cutting) **M: 19**
Water-level gauge
Gauge (Water-level gauges) **G: 69**
Water Lilies [painting by Monet]
Monet, Claude *picture on* **M: 703**
Water lily W: 135 *with picture*
Flower *picture on* **F: 285**
Leaf **L: 151**
Lotus **L: 473** *with picture*
Wetland *picture on* **W: 253**
Water line
Ship (Nautical terms) **S: 405** *with diagram*
Water management
Farm and farming (Water management) **F: 33**
Water Margin [book]
Chinese literature (Drama and fiction) **C: 511**
Water mass
Arctic Ocean (Water masses) **A: 643**
Pacific Ocean (Water masses) **P: 15**
Water-meal [plant]
Wetland (Aquatic beds) **W: 252b**
Water meter W: 135 *with pictures*
Plumbing (The water supply system) **P: 577** *with diagram*
Water-Method Man, The [book by Irving]
Irving, John **I: 459**
Water moccasin [snake] **W: 135** *with picture*
Snake *diagram on* **S: 527**, *picture on* **S: 534**
Viper **V: 391**

Water mold
Mold **M: 689**
Water mouse
Mouse (Unusual mice) **M: 902**
Water Music [music by Handel]
Handel, George Frideric (His work) **H: 42–43**
Water of crystallization [chemistry]
Hydrate **H: 462**
Water of hydration [chemistry]
Hydrate **H: 462**
Water ouzel [bird]
Dipper **D: 217** *with picture*
Water pig
Capybara **C: 201** *with picture*
Water plant W: 136
See also the list of Related articles in the Water plant *article*
Aquarium, Home (Choosing fish and plants) **A: 578–578a** *with picture*
Lake (The lake habitat) **L: 33**
Plant (Aquatic regions) **P: 528**
Water pollution W: 136 *with diagram*
See also Environmental pollution *in this index*
Arctic Ocean (Threats) **A: 644**
Atlantic Ocean (Pollution) **A: 867**
City (Physical problems) **Ci: 590–591**
Conservation (Water conservation) **Ci: 977–978** *with picture*; (Ocean conservation) **Ci: 978** *with picture*
Environmental pollution *picture on* **E: 330**; (Water pollution) **E: 334**
Eutrophication (Eutrophication and water pollution) **E: 421**
Exxon Valdez oil spill **E: 459**
Fertilizer (Problems of the fertilizer industry) **F: 80**
Fishing industry (Government regulation) **F: 187**
Great Lakes (Water quality) **G: 345**
Ground water **G: 402**
Gulf oil spill of 2010 **G: 437**
Lake Erie **L: 38**
Lawn (Lawns and the environment) **L: 144**
Minnesota (The late 1900's) **M: 606**
Missouri (The late 1900's) **M: 672**
National park (Changes in the environment) **N: 42h**
Nitrogen (Nitrogen and pollution) **N: 426**
Ocean (Marine pollution) **O: 664** *with picture*
Oyster (Water quality) **O: 892**
Pacific Ocean (Offshore pollution) **P: 17**
Rain (Characteristics of rain) **R: 122–123**
Seal (Threats to seal populations) **S: 268**
Ship (Pollution) **S: 413–414**
Tanker (Oil spills) **T: 28**
Thermal pollution **T: 253**
Water hyacinth **W: 135**
Water polo W: 139 *with picture*
Water power W: 139
Electric power (Hydroelectric power plants) **E: 184** *with diagram*
Energy supply (Water power) **E: 278**; (Tidal energy) **E: 279**
Grand Coulee Dam **G: 308**
Turbine (Water turbines) **T: 496** *with diagrams*
Water wheel **W: 141** *with picture*
Water pressure
Extremophile **E: 458**
Water (Distributing water) **W: 127** *with diagram*
Water Project [conservation]
Nevada (The mid-1900's) **N: 176**
Water purification
Ice (Ice "cages") **I: 5**
Water (Purifying and treating water) **W: 126**
Water retriever [dog]
Poodle **P: 658**
Water-retting [industrial process]
Flax (Growing and processing fiber flax) **F: 230–231**
Linen (Preparing the fibers) **L: 334**
Water rights
Colorado (Natural resources) **Ci: 841**
Water safety
Boating (Boating safety programs) **B: 429–431** *with pictures*
Swimming (Water safety) **So: 1042** *with picture*
Water scavenger beetle
Water beetle **W: 133** *with picture*
Water scorpion [insect]
Water bug **W: 133**
Water shrew
Shrew **S: 439**
Water-skiing W: 140 *with picture*
Water snake
Snake *picture on* **S: 533**; (Homalopsids) **S: 535**
Water softening [water treatment] **W: 140**
Water-soluble vitamin
Nutrition (Vitamins) **N: 626**
Vitamin (Kinds of vitamins) **V: 430**

Water spaniel [dog]
American water spaniel A: 430
Water spider
Animal *picture on* A: 491
Spider So: 782 *with picture* ; (Respiratory system)
So: 785
Water sports
Safety (In water sports) S: 13 *with picture*
Water strider [insect]
Insect *picture on* I: 294
Water bug W: 133
Water supply
Aqueduct A: 580
Conservation (Water conservation) Ci: 977
Desert D: 155
Food supply (Limited agricultural resources)
F: 348
Forestry (Managing other forest resources) F: 406
Lake (Water supply) L: 34
Reservoir R: 258
Water W: 116
Water supply system
Plumbing P: 577 *with diagram*
Water table [geology]
Cave (How caves are formed) C: 319 *with diagram*
Drainage D: 320
Ground water G: 401
Irrigation (Bringing irrigation water to farms)
I: 457
Water (Sources of supply) W: 124
Well (Water wells) W: 192-193
Water taxi
Transportation *picture on* T: 394
Water Tower [Chicago]
Chicago Fire C: 438
Water Tower Place [shopping center]
Chicago (New construction) C: 437
Water tupelo [tree]
Tupelo T: 492 *with picture*
Water turbine
Electric power (Hydroelectric power plants)
E: 184 *with diagram*
Turbine (Water turbines) T: 496 *with diagrams*
Water turtle
Turtle (Pond, box, and water turtles) T: 522
Water vapor
Air (Moisture in the air) A: 170
Cloud (How clouds form) Ci: 708
Distillation D: 238
Fog F: 314
Greenhouse effect (The natural greenhouse
effect) G: 382-383
Humidity H: 433
Rain R: 122 *with diagrams*; (Formation of rain)
R: 123
Water (The properties of water) W: 129-130
Weather (What causes weather) W: 157
Water-vascular system [zoology]
Echinoderm E: 50
Water vole
Vole V: 444
Water well
Well (Water wells) W: 193 *with diagrams*
Water wheel W: 141 *with picture*
Turbine (History) T: 498
Water power W: 139
Water witch [bird]
Grebe G: 351
Waterbuck
Antelope (Habits and appearance) A: 542; (Kinds
of antelope) A: 542
Mammal *picture on* M: 127
Waterbury [Connecticut] W: 141
Waterfall W: 141 *with pictures*
See also the list of Related articles in the Waterfall
article
Fall line F: 15
Oregon (Rivers, waterfalls, and lakes) O: 840
River (Waterfalls and rapids) R: 352 *with diagram*
Water *picture on* W: 116
Water power (The mechanics of water power)
W: 139
Water wheel W: 141
Waterfall [print by Escher]
Escher, M. C. *picture on* E: 357
Waterfall in a Rocky Landscape, A [painting by
Ruisdael]
Ruisdael, Jacob van *picture on* R: 518
Waterflooding
Petroleum *diagram on* P: 331; (Secondary and
tertiary recovery) P: 342
Waterford [Ireland] W: 144
Waterford glass
Glass (Types of art glass) G: 220-221 *with picture*
Waterfowl *See* Water bird *in this index*
Waterfront Redevelopment project
Buffalo (History) B: 678

Watergate [U.S. history] W: 144
Bush, George Herbert Walker (Republican Party
chairman) B: 718
Congress of the United States (Continued
struggle for power) Ci: 948
Ford, Gerald Rudolph (Vice president [1973-
1974]) F: 375
Journalism (Investigating wrongdoing) J: 173
Mitchell, John Newton M: 677
Nixon, Richard Milhous N: 428; (Events at home)
N: 435-436
President of the United States (The Watergate
scandal) P: 769
Republican Party (The Watergate scandal) R: 257
Richardson, Elliot Lee R: 330
United States, History of the (Political scandals)
U: 196b *with picture*
Watergate Complex [Washington, D.C.]
Washington, D.C. (Watergate) W: 75
Watering
See also Irrigation *in this index*
Gardening (Caring for the garden) G: 35;
(Cultivating an indoor garden) G: 36
Lawn (Lawns and the environment) L: 144
Waterland [book by Swift]
Novel (The novel today) N: 575
Waterloo [Ontario]
Kitchener K: 338
Waterloo, Battle of [1815] W: 145
Blücher, Gebhard Leberecht von B: 419
Napoleon I (The Hundred Days and Waterloo)
N: 16
Napoleonic Wars (The Hundred Days) N: 20 *with
map*
Wellington, Duke of (Victory at Waterloo)
W: 194-195
Waterloo Village [Stanhope]
New Jersey (Places to visit) N: 240 *with picture*
Waterman, Robert W. [American political leader]
California (table) C: 59
Watermark [manufacturing] W: 145
Paper (Special kinds of paper) P: 136
Stamp collecting (Paper) So: 830
Watermelon W: 146 *with picture*
Fruit (Simple fruits) F: 544 *with picture*
Waterproof match
Match (The invention of book matches) M: 300a
Waterproofing W: 146
Lacquer L: 22
Rubber (Uses of rubber) R: 500; (First uses) R: 500
Silicone (Uses) S: 458
Waters, Ethel [American actress] W: 146
Waters, Muddy [American musician] W: 146
Waters of Kronos, The [book by Richter]
Richter, Conrad R: 334
Watershed [geography]
Forestry (Water) F: 406
Watershed management
Conservation (Water conservation) Ci: 977-978
Waterspout [architecture]
Gargoyle G: 43 *with picture*
Waterspout [weather] W: 147 *with picture*
Tornado (The life of a tornado) T: 335
Waterthrush [bird]
Bird (Birds of inland waters and marshes) B: 340
with picture
Waterton-Glacier International Peace Park
[Alberta-Montana] W: 147
Glacier National Park G: 205
Waterton Lakes National Park [Alberta]
Canada (table: National parks and national park
reserves) C: 114
Glacier National Park G: 205
Waterway [transportation]
Canal C: 162 *with pictures*
Industrial Revolution (Waterways) I: 250
Inland waterway I: 273
Waterweed [plant]
Elodea E: 246
Waterwheel Falls
Yosemite National Park (Hetch Hetchy Valley)
Y: 570
Watery Path [painting by Pollock]
United States *picture on* U: 116
Watie, Stand [Confederate general] W: 147
Watkins, David O. [American political leader]
New Jersey (table) N: 249
Watkins, Frances Ellen [American poet]
Harper, Frances Ellen Watkins H: 65 *with portrait*
Watkins, James D. [American political leader]
Energy, Department of (table) E: 276
Watkins Glen [New York]
Finger Lakes F: 104
Watkins Glen State Park
New York (Places to visit) N: 302
Watling Street
England (The Roman conquest) E: 303-304

Watsen, C. S. [American inventor]
Envelope E: 328
Watson [computer]
Artificial intelligence A: 760
Watson, Chris [Australian political leader]
Australia (table) A: 923
Watson, Doctor John [literary figure]
Detective story (History) D: 162-163
Holmes, Sherlock H: 295
Watson, Homer [Canadian painter] W: 147
Watson, James Dewey [American biologist]
W: 147
Biology (The growth of modern biology) B: 319-
320
Cell (The 1900's) C: 337-338
Franklin, Rosalind Elsie F: 492
Heredity (The chemistry of genes) H: 208-209
Science (Achievements of the mid-1900's) S: 202
with picture
Wilkins, Maurice Hugh Frederick W: 306
Watson, John Broadus [American psychologist]
W: 147
Psychology (Behaviorism) P: 849
Watson, Sheila [Canadian author]
Canadian literature (Modern English-Canadian
fiction) C: 160
Watson, Thomas Augustus [American inventor]
Bell, Alexander Graham (The Boston teacher)
B: 240-241
Telephone (History) T: 99
Watson, Thomas Edward [American political
leader] W: 148
Watson, Thomas John [American businessman]
W: 148
Watson, W. Marvin [American government official]
Johnson, Lyndon Baines (table) J: 151
Watson, William T. [American political leader]
Delaware (table) D: 109
Watson-Crick model [genetics]
Cell (The 1900's) C: 337-338 *with picture*
Crick, Francis Harry Compton Ci: 1130
Watson, James Dewey W: 147
Watson-Watt, Sir Robert Alexander [Scottish
engineer] W: 148
Radar (The first uses of radar) R: 71
Watt [measurement] W: 148
Energy (Energy and power) E: 275
Kilowatt K: 317
Light (Energy and brightness) L: 290
Lighting (Quantity of light) L: 297
Metric system (Mechanics) M: 437-440
Power P: 727
Watt, James [Scottish engineer] W: 148 *with picture*
Automation (History of automation) A: 945
Flour F: 269
Horsepower H: 367
Industrial Revolution (The steam engine) I: 249
Invention *picture in* I: 359; (The Industrial
Revolution) I: 361
Ship (The first steamboats) S: 424
Steam engine (Watt's engine) So: 881
Watt, James G. [American government official]
Interior, Department of the (table) I: 325
Reagan, Ronald Wilson (table) R: 169
Watteau, Antoine [French painter] W: 149
Painting (Rococo painting) P: 65 *with picture*
Wattle [plant]
Australia *picture on* A: 915; (Native plants) A: 911
Tree *picture on* T: 427
Wattle [zoology]
Chicken (The body of a chicken) C: 440 *with
pictures*
Turkey (The body of a turkey) T: 513
Umbrellabird U: 18
Wattle-eye [bird]
Bird (Birds of Africa) B: 344h *with picture*
Wattle house
El Salvador (Housing) E: 249
Wattmeter [instrument] W: 149
Electric meter E: 176
Watts [district, Los Angeles]
African Americans (Unrest in the cities) A: 136q
California (The mid-1900's) C: 62-63
Los Angeles (South Los Angeles) L: 460; (Social
problems) L: 464
Riot (During the 1900's) R: 349
Watts, Charlie [British musician]
Rolling Stones R: 402a
Watts, Isaac [English religious leader] W: 149
Hymn (Words and music) H: 475; (History) H: 475
Watts, J. C., Jr. [American political leader] W: 149
Watts, James [American physician]
Lobotomy L: 405
Watts, Julius Caesar, Jr. [American political leader]
See Watts, J. C., Jr. *in this index*
Watts, Thomas Hill [American political leader]
Alabama (table) A: 274

Watusi [people] *See* Tutsi *in this index*
Waud, Alfred R. [American artist]
　Civil War, American *picture on* Ci: 623
Waugh, Evelyn [British author] **W:** 149
　English literature (Fiction between the wars)
　　E: 322
　Novel (After World War II) **N:** 574
Wave *See* Waves *in this index*
Wave front [physics]
　Lens (Creating an image) **L:** 196
　Telescope (Optical telescopes) **T:** 103
　Waves (Diffraction) **W:** 153
Wave lift [aerodynamics]
　Glider (Soaring) **G:** 229
Wave packet [physics]
　Light (The properties of waves) **L:** 285-286
Wave-particle duality [physics]
　Quantum mechanics (Wave-particle duality) **Q:** 6
Wave theory [physics]
　Huygens, Christiaan **H:** 460
　Light (Our understanding of light) **L:** 285
　Physics (Developments in the 1800's) **P:** 440
　Radiation (Electromagnetic radiation) **R:** 75; (The
　　quantum theory) **R:** 81
Waveform [physics]
　Earthquake (The moment magnitude scale)
　　E: 38b
Wavelength [physics]
　Waves *diagram on* **W:** 150; (Measuring waves)
　　W: 152
　Aberration (Chromatic aberration) **A:** 11
　Astronomy (Electromagnetic radiation) **A:** 838
　Electromagnetic waves **E:** 201
　Electron microscope **E:** 204
　Infrared rays **I:** 270
　Laser (Characteristics of laser light) **L:** 84
　Light (The spectrum of light sources) **L:** 284 *with
　　diagram*
　Microscope (Other kinds of micrscopes) **M:** 519
　Radiation (Electromagnetic radiation) **R:** 75
　Radio wave **R:** 97
　Redshift **R:** 191
　Seismograph (Detecting earthquakes) **S:** 288
　Sound (Wavelength) **So:** 600 *with diagram*
　Spectrum **So:** 772
　Telescope (What telescopes do) **T:** 102-103
　Ultraviolet rays **U:** 17
　X rays **X:** 540; (Wavelength) **X:** 541
Wavelet [physics]
　Waves (Diffraction) **W:** 153
Waverley [book by Scott]
　Scott, Sir Walter (The Waverley novels) **S:** 222
Waverley novels [books by Scott]
　Scott, Sir Walter **S:** 222
Waves [physics] **W:** 150 *with diagrams*
　See also Electromagnetic waves; Shock wave *in
　　this index*
　Diffraction **D:** 201
　Hertz **H:** 217
　Interference **I:** 323 *with diagram*
　Light (Our understanding of light) **L:** 285 *with
　　diagram*; (Electromagnetic waves) **L:** 286
　Ocean (Waves) **O:** 659 *with diagram*
　Polarized light **P:** 617
　Quantum mechanics (Wave-particle duality) **Q:** 6
　Redshift **R:** 191
　Reflection **R:** 194
　Seiche **S:** 287
　Sound (The nature of sound) **So:** 599 *with
　　diagram*
　Surfing **So:** 1003 *with picture*
　Tsunami **T:** 475
WAVES [U.S.]
　McAfee, Mildred Helen **M:** 332
　Navy, United States (World War II [1939-1945])
　　N: 89
Waves, Seismic [geology] *See* Seismic wave *in
　this index*
Waw [letter]
　U **U:** 1 *with picture*
　V **V:** 255 *with picture*
　Y **Y:** 547 *with picture*
Wawasee, Lake
　Indiana (Rivers, lakes, and waterfalls) **I:** 208
Wax W: 153
　See also Beeswax *in this index*
　Candle **C:** 175
　Doll (Wax dolls) **D:** 290 *with picture*
　Ester **E:** 360
　Painting (Encaustic painting) **P:** 36
Wax bean
　Bean (Kinds of beans) **B:** 181
Wax begonia [plant]
　Begonia *picture on* **B:** 219
　Flower **B:** 219 *with picture, picture on* **F:** 292
Wax museum
　Museum (Other types of museums) **M:** 938

Wax myrtle [shrub] **W:** 153
Wax tablet
　Manuscript (Wax tablets) **M:** 172
Waxing moon
　Moon (Phases) **M:** 783-784
Waxwing [bird] **W:** 153 *with picture*
　Bird *picture on* **B:** 358; (Birds of forests and
　　woodlands) **B:** 334 *with picture*; (Kinds of food)
　　B: 350 *with picture*
Waxy corn
　Corn (Kinds of corn) **Ci:** 1058-1059
Way of an Indian, The [book by Remington]
　Remington, Frederic **R:** 230
Way of the World, The [play by Congreve]
　Congreve, William **Ci:** 949
"Way to Wealth, The"
　Poor Richard's Almanac **P:** 659
Way West, The [book by Guthrie]
　Guthrie, A. B., Jr. **G:** 444
Wayang [Indonesian shadow drama]
　Indonesia (The arts) **I:** 232
　Puppet (Shadow puppets) **P:** 907 *with picture*
Wayang wong [dance]
　Dance (Asian theatrical dance) **D:** 28-29
Waybill [shipping]
　Bill (In transportation) **B:** 300-301
Waybright, Josephine [American farmer]
　Western frontier life in America (Shelter) **W:** 238
Wayeb [calendar]
　Calendar (The Maya) **C:** 31
Wayles, John [American lawyer]
　Jefferson, Thomas (Jefferson's family) **J:** 78
Waymouth, George [English explorer]
　Maine (Exploration and settlements) **M:** 89
Wayne, Anthony [American general] **W:** 154 *with
　portrait*
　Fort Wayne **F:** 417
　Indian wars (Conflicts in the Midwest) **I:** 191-192
　　with picture
　Little Turtle **L:** 392
　Northwest Territory (Settlement) **N:** 535
Wayne, Bruce [fictional character]
　Batman **B:** 165 *with picture*
Wayne, James M. [American jurist]
　Supreme Court of the United States (table)
　　So: 1000
Wayne, John [American actor] **W:** 154 *with portrait*
　Motion picture (Best performance by an actor:
　　1969) **M:** 862a
Wayne National Forest [Ohio]
　Ohio (Places to visit) **O:** 690
"Wayside School" series [books by Sachar]
　Sachar, Louis **S:** 5
Wb [symbol]
　Weber **W:** 175
WBA [organization] *See* World Boxing Association
　in this index
WBC [competition]
　Baseball (Recent developments) **B:** 137-139
WBC [organization] *See* World Boxing Council *in
　this index*
WBF [organization]
　Bridge (Regulation of tournaments) **B:** 605
W.C.T.U. [organization] *See* Woman's Christian
　Temperance Union *in this index*
We [book by Lindbergh]
　Lindbergh, Charles Augustus (His historic flight)
　　L: 330
We [book by Zamyatin]
　Science fiction (The early 1900's) **S:** 205
We the Living [book by Rand]
　Rand, Ayn **R:** 136
**We the Peoples: The Role of the United Nations in
　the 21st Century** [report]
　Annan, Kofi Atta **A:** 516
Wea Indians
　Miami Indians **M:** 482
Weak boson [physics]
　Boson **B:** 494
Weak electrolyte [chemistry]
　Electrolyte **E:** 201
Weak force [physics] *See* Weak interaction *in this
　index*
Weak interaction [physics]
　Force (The weak force) **F:** 371
　Neutrino **N:** 154
　Physics (Physics today) **P:** 442-443
　Quantum field theory **Q:** 5
　Standard Model **So:** 833
　String theory **So:** 929
　Subatomic particle (Fundamental forces) **So:** 936
　Subtomic particle (Theories of forces) **So:** 937-
　　938
Weak-mayor government
　City government (The mayor-council form)
　　Ci: 595 *with diagram*
　Mayor **M:** 330

Weak trademark
　Trademark **T:** 364
Weakfish W: 154
　Drum **D:** 367
Weakly interacting massive particle [physics]
　Dark matter **D:** 37
"Wealth" [article by Carnegie]
　Carnegie, Andrew (Retirement) **C:** 242
Wealth [economics]
　See also Distribution of wealth *in this index*
　Agriculture (Changes in demand) **A:** 152
Wealth Against Commonwealth [book by Lloyd]
　Lloyd, Henry Demarest **L:** 402
Wealth of Nations, The [book by Smith]
　Capital **C:** 192
　Capitalism (Capitalism in its ideal form) **C:** 194;
　　(The development of capitalism) **C:** 196
　Economics (The free market) **E:** 59
　Smith, Adam **S:** 515
Wealth tax
　Taxation (Other taxes) **T:** 54
Weaning
　Baby (Feeding procedures) **B:** 9
　Mammal (Care of the young) **M:** 124
Weapon W: 154a *with pictures*
　See also the list of Related articles in the Weapon
　　article
　Arms control **A:** 721
　Army **A:** 724 *with pictures*
　Feudalism (The decline of feudalism) **F:** 83
　Indian, American *pictures on* **I:** 138; (Weapons)
　　I: 144 *with pictures*; (The first Americans) **I:** 151
　Infantry (Equipment) **I:** 265
　War (The basic rules of warfare) **W:** 24; (The
　　history of warfare) **W:** 25
Weapon fire control
　Radar (Weapon fire control) **R:** 66
Weapon of mass destruction
　Arms control (The current arms-control debate)
　　A: 721
　Bush, George Walker (Homeland security)
　　B: 722g; (Iraq) **B:** 722i
　Hussein, Saddam **H:** 458
　Iraq (The Persian Gulf War of 1991) **I:** 414-414a;
　　(The Iraq War) **I:** 414a
　Iraq War (Background to the war) **I:** 414c;
　　(Disagreements over the war) **I:** 414f-415
　Libya (Recent developments) **L:** 268
　Middle East (The 1990's) **M:** 534a-534b
　Nuclear weapon (After the terrorist attacks of
　　Sept. 11, 2001) **N:** 602
　Persian Gulf War of 1991 (Consequences of the
　　war) **P:** 300e
　United Nations (Arms control) **U:** 92-93
　United States, History of the (The Iraq War [2003-
　　2010]) **U:** 196e
　World, History of the (The war on terrorism)
　　W: 448b-449
Weare, Meshech [American political leader]
　New Hampshire (table) **N:** 223
Wearing apparel *See* Clothing *in this index*
Weary Blues, The [book by Hughes]
　Hughes, Langston **H:** 409
Weasel [animal] **W:** 155 *with pictures*
　Ermine **E:** 354
　Grison **G:** 396
　Sable **S:** 3
Weather W: 156 *with pictures and maps*
　See also Meteorology *in this index; and the list of
　　Related articles in the* Weather *article*
　Climate **Ci:** 675
　Clothing (Protection) **Ci:** 686
　Cloud (Clouds and the weather) **Ci:** 711
　Environment (Abiotic environment) **E:** 329
　Environmental pollution (Air pollution) **E:** 331
　Global warming (Changing weather patterns)
　　G: 232a
　Jupiter (Weather) **J:** 200
　Kite (History) **K:** 340-341
　Lake (Climate) **L:** 33
　Remote sensing **R:** 231 *with picture*
　Static **So:** 867
　Troposphere **T:** 451
　Weather satellite **W:** 171
Weather advisory [meteorology]
　Weather (Reporting the weather) **W:** 166
Weather balloon
　Telemetry **T:** 93
　Weather (Weather balloons, airplanes, and ships)
　　W: 163 *with picture*
Weather bureau *See* Weather Service, National *in
　this index*
Weather forecasting
　Barometer (Uses) **B:** 116
　Chaos **C:** 376
　Computer *picture on* **Ci:** 918
　Isobar **I:** 474 *with map*

Isotherm I: 475 *with map*
Meteorology M: 432
Ohio (Interesting facts) O: 681
Radar (In weather observation and forecasting)
    R: 67 *with picture*
Tornado (Forecasting tornadoes) T: 335
Weather W: 156, *picture on* W: 156; (Measuring
    the weather) W: 162; (Weather forecasting)
    W: 164; (Careers in weather) W: 170
Weather front *See* Front *in this index*
Weather map
Map (Advances in European cartography) M: 184
Weather (Weather maps) W: 164 *with picture*
Weather observer
Weather (Land-based observation stations)
    W: 162
Weather radar
Radar (In aviation) R: 64-65
Weather (Weather satellites) W: 163-164
Weather satellite W: 171 *with picture*
Satellite, Artificial (Types of artificial satellites)
    S: 150f *with picture*
Weather *picture on* W: 166; (Weather satellites)
    W: 163
Weather Service, National [U.S.] W: 171
Flood (Reducing flood losses) F: 238
Heat index H: 156
Hurricane (Forecasting hurricanes) H: 456
National Oceanic and Atmospheric
    Administration N: 42
Tornado (Forecasting tornadoes) T: 335
Weather (Land-based observation stations)
    W: 162; (Reporting the weather) W: 166 *with
    picture*
Weather vane W: 172
Folk art (Sculpture) F: 317 *with picture*
Weather (Land-based observation stations)
    W: 162
Wind (Wind direction) W: 330
Weather warning [meteorology]
Weather (Reporting the weather) W: 166
Weather watch [meteorology]
Weather (Reporting the weather) W: 166
Weathercock *See* Weather vane *in this index*
Weatherfish [fish]
Loach L: 403
Weatherford, William [American Indian chief]
Alabama (Territorial days) A: 275
Weathering [geology]
Earth *picture on* E: 28; (Sedimentary rocks) E: 21
Erosion (How erosion occurs) E: 355
Fossil (Collecting fossils) F: 426
Geomorphology G: 106a
Oil spill (Effects) O: 707
Rock (Clastic sediments) R: 372
Sand S: 106
Soil (How soil forms) So: 573 *with diagram*
Weatherly, Joe [American race driver]
Automobile racing (table: NASCAR Sprint Cup
    champions) A: 981
Weaver
Basket making (Methods) B: 141
Weaver [bird] W: 172 *with picture*
Bird (Birds of Africa) B: 344h *with picture*;
    (Building a nest) B: 356 *with picture*
Weaver, Arthur J. [American political leader]
Nebraska (table) N: 110
Weaver, Earl [American baseball manager]
Baseball (table: Hall of Fame) B: 134b
Weaver, James B. [American political leader]
Greenback Party G: 381
Harrison, Benjamin (Bid for reelection) H: 73
Populism (The People's Party) P: 675
Weaver, Robert Clifton [American government
official] W: 172
Weaver, Warren [American mathematician]
Molecular biology (The beginning of molecular
    biology) M: 691-692
Weaver ant
Ant *picture on* A: 520; (Nests) A: 523
Weavers, The [etchings by Kollwitz]
Kollwitz, Käthe *picture on* K: 363
Weavers, The [play by Hauptmann]
German literature (Naturalism) G: 141
Hauptmann, Gerhart H: 86
Weaver's knot
Knots, hitches, and splices *diagram on* K: 356
Weaving [industrial process] W: 173 *with pictures*
Basket making (Methods) B: 141 *with pictures*
Beadwork B: 179 *with picture*
Cotton (Spinning) Ci: 1091
Handicraft *picture on* H: 45
Indian, American *picture on* I: 136a; (Weaving)
    I: 146 *with picture*
Industrial Revolution (Weaving machines) I: 249
Ireland *picture on* I: 425
Islamic art (Textiles) I: 469

Jacquard, Joseph Marie J: 20
Rugs and carpets (Weaving) R: 515 *with pictures*;
    (History) R: 517
Silk (Weaving) S: 460
Tapestry (How tapestries are made) T: 39
Textile T: 212 *with pictures*
Web [wool]
Wool (Making yarn) W: 400 *with picture*
Web [zoology]
Spider *picture on* So: 782; (How spiders use silk)
    So: 786 *with picture*; (Web-building spiders)
    So: 789
Web, The [communications] *See* World Wide Web
in this index
Web 2.0 [computing]
Internet (The evolving Internet) I: 350g-350h
Web and the Rock, The [book by Wolfe]
Wolfe, Thomas W: 377
Web browser [electronics] W: 175
Computer (Web browsers) Ci: 919; (The World
    Wide Web) Ci: 921; (Internet software) Ci: 922
Internet (The World Wide Web) I: 350d; (Internet
    crime) I: 350f
Software (Application software) So: 572
Website W: 176
World Wide Web W: 500
Web-building spider
Spider So: 783; (Web-building spiders) So: 789
Web crawling
Information retrieval (How information retrieval
    works) I: 268b
Search engine S: 269
Web-fed press [machine] *See* Web press *in this
index*
Web of life [biology]
Animal (Importance of animals) A: 470 *with
    picture*
Web page [computing]
Computer *picture on* Ci: 922; (The World Wide
    Web) Ci: 921
Internet (HTTP) I: 350d
Website W: 176
World Wide Web W: 500
Web press [machine]
Offset O: 678
Printing (Methods of printing) P: 798 *with picture*
Web site [computing] *See* Website *in this index*
Webb, Sir Aston [English architect]
Victoria and Albert Museum V: 358
Webb, Beatrice Potter [British social reformer]
Webb, Sidney and Beatrice W: 175
Webb, Chick [American musician]
Fitzgerald, Ella F: 190
Webb, Frank J. [American author]
African American literature (The 1800's) A: 136a
Webb, George J. [American educator]
Mason, Lowell M: 266
Webb, Lucy Ware [wife of Rutherford B. Hayes] *See*
Hayes, Lucy Webb *in this index*
Webb, Matthew [British athlete]
English Channel E: 311
Webb, Phyllis [Canadian poet]
Canadian literature (Modern Canadian poets)
    C: 161
Webb, Sidney and Beatrice [British social
reformers] W: 175
Webb, Sidney James [British social reformer]
Webb, Sidney and Beatrice W: 175
Webb-Kenyon Act [1913]
Prohibition (The movement toward prohibition)
    P: 815
Webbed foot [zoology]
Bird (Legs and feet) B: 364
Frog (Legs) F: 536
Webber, Andrew Lloyd *See* Lloyd Webber, Andrew
in this index
Webber, Helen [American artist]
Rugs and carpets *picture on* R: 517
Webber, John [British painter]
Cook, James *pictures on* Ci: 1025
Webcam [device]
Photography (Other types of cameras) P: 409
Webcasting
Radio (Webcasting and podcasting) R: 87
Webelos [rank]
Boy Scouts (Cub Scouting) B: 535 *with picture*
Weber [unit of measure] W: 175
Weber, Carl Maria von [German composer] W: 175
Opera (Romanticism) O: 798
Weber, Joseph [American physicist]
Gravitational wave G: 333
Weber, Max [German sociologist] W: 176
Bureaucracy B: 703
Protestant ethic P: 833
Puritans (Puritan influence) P: 910-911
Sociology (Development of social research)
    So: 566

Weber, Max [American painter] W: 176
Weber, Wilhelm [German physicist]
Weber W: 175
Webern, Anton [Austrian composer] W: 176
Weblog [computing] *See* Blog *in this index*
Website [computing] W: 176
Advertising *picture on* A: 76
Blog B: 406
Computer (The Internet) Ci: 920
Internet I: 350; (HTTP) I: 350d
Newspaper (Online newspapers) N: 381
Publishing (Scheduling, printing, and posting)
    P: 867; (Blogs and websites) P: 869
Web browser W: 175
World Wide Web W: 500
Webster, Daniel [American political leader] W: 177
    with picture
Dartmouth College case D: 39
Harrison, William Henry (The *Caroline* affair) H: 76
Jackson, Andrew (Election of 1824) J: 9
Nullification N: 603
Tyler, John (Tyler's accomplishments) T: 534
Webster-Ashburton Treaty W: 178
Whittier, John Greenleaf W: 295
Webster, Ephraim [American pioneer]
Syracuse [New York] So: 1069
Webster, John [English dramatist] W: 177
English literature (Jacobean drama) E: 317
Webster, Noah [American lexicographer] W: 177
Dictionary (Early English dictionaries) D: 194
Webster, William H. [American government
official]
Federal Bureau of Investigation (History) F: 62
Webster-Ashburton Treaty [1842] W: 178
Harrison, William Henry (The *Caroline* affair) H: 76
Maine (Statehood) M: 89
Webster v. Reproductive Health Services [U.S.
history]
Abortion (Abortion in the United States) A: 15-16
Webster's Third New International Dictionary
Dictionary (Modern dictionaries) D: 194
Webzine [publication]
Magazine M: 42
Weddell, James [British hunter]
Antarctica *map on* A: 538; (Early explorooation)
    A: 536
Weddell Sea [bay]
Antarctica (Ocean) A: 532-534 *with map*
Southern Ocean (Boundaries) So: 688
Weddell seal
Antarctica (Living things) A: 534-535 *with picture*
Wedding
Clothing (Identity) Ci: 687-688
Folklore (Superstitions and customs) F: 324-325
Marriage M: 219 *with pictures*; (Wedding
    ceremonies) M: 220
Pioneer life in America (Social activities) P: 485
Poland P: 607
Wedding, The [ballet] *See* Noces, Les *in this index*
Wedding anniversary W: 178
"Wedding March" [music by Mendelssohn]
Mendelssohn, Felix (His life) M: 399
Wedding of St. George and Princess Sabra, The
[painting by Rossetti]
Rossetti, Dante Gabriel *picture on* R: 483
Wedding of the Gods, The [opera by Coppola]
Opera *picture on* O: 797
Wedding ring
Marriage (Wedding ceremonies) M: 220
Ring R: 342 *with picture*
Wedding veil
Marriage (Wedding ceremonies) M: 220
Wedekind, Frank [German dramatist] W: 178
Wedell, James [American aviator]
Aviation (table: Aviation speed records) A: 990
Wedge [golf club]
Golf (Golf clubs) G: 262 *with picture*
Wedge [tool] W: 178
Machine (Wedge) M: 15 *with picture*
Simple machines S: 467
Wedge-tailed eagle [bird]
Bird (Birds of Australia and New Zealand) B: 346
    with picture
Wedgwood, Josiah [British businessman]
Coleridge, Samuel Taylor (His life) Ci: 771
Wedgwood ware W: 178
Wedgwood ware [porcelain] W: 178 *with picture*
Porcelain (English porcelain) P: 677
Wednesday [day] W: 179
Wednesday Island
Torres Strait Islands T: 343
Wee Willie Winkie [book by Kipling]
Kipling, Rudyard (Early literary success) K: 334
Weed [drug] *See* Marijuana *in this index*
Weed [plant] W: 179
See also the list of Related articles in the Weed
    article

Cotton (Weeds) **Ci: 1090**
Gardening (Weeds) **G: 35**
Lawn *pictures on* **L: 143**; (Maintenance) **L: 144**
Plant (Asexual reproduction) **P: 535**
Potato (Potato pests) **P: 713**
Vegetable (Pest control) **V: 293**
Wheat (Controlling weeds) **W: 271**
Weed, Thurlow [American political leader] **W: 180**
Fillmore, Millard (Political and public career) **F: 101**
Weedkiller *See* Herbicide *in this index*
Weedy seadragon [animal]
Seadragon **S: 264**
Week W: 180
Weekend [film]
Godard, Jean-Luc **G: 244**
Weekend college
Community college (Importance to students) **Ci: 899**
Weekly Arizonian [newspaper]
Arizona (Communication) **A: 686**
Weekly Herald [newspaper]
Edison, Thomas Alva (Early life) **E: 78**
Weekly Oregonian [newspaper]
Oregon (Communication) **O: 844**
Weeks, Frank B. [American political leader]
Connecticut (table) **Ci: 967**
Weeks, John E. [American political leader]
Vermont (table) **V: 333**
Weeks, John W. [American government official]
Coolidge, Calvin (table) **Ci: 1032**
Harding, Warren Gamaliel (table) **H: 58**
Weeks, Sinclair [American government official]
Commerce, Department of (table) **Ci: 871**
Weeks Act [1911]
Conservation (The rise of the conservation movement) **Ci: 985-986**
Weems, Carrie Mae [American photographer]
Photography (A diversity of styles) **P: 426-427**
Weems, Mason Locke [American author] **W: 180**
Adams, John **A: 34**
Biography (The 1800's) **B: 314**
Lincoln, Abraham (Education) **L: 312-313**
Weeping birch
Birch (Paper birch) **B: 327**
Weeping willow
Tree *pictures on* **T: 424**
Willow **W: 315**
Weevil [insect] **W: 180**
Beetle *picture on* **B: 218**; (The bodies of beetles) **B: 215** *with picture*; (Weevils) **B: 217**
Boll weevil **B: 448**
Grain weevil **G: 302** *with picture*
Pea (Diseases and pests) **P: 205**
Weft [weaving]
Basket making (Methods) **B: 141** *with diagrams*
Rugs and carpets (Weaving) **R: 515** *with pictures*
Satin **S: 150h**
Tapestry (How tapestries are made) **T: 39**
Textile (Woven fabrics) **T: 214**
Weaving (Types of weaves) **W: 173** *with pictures*
Weft knitting
Knitting machine **K: 354**
Textile (Knitted fabrics) **T: 214**
Wegener, Alfred Lothar [German meteorologist]
Pangaea **P: 130**
Plate tectonics (History of tectonic theory) **P: 564**
Wegner, Hans [Danish designer]
Furniture *picture on* **F: 583**
Wehnelt, Arthur [German physicist]
Vacuum tube (History) **V: 259**
Weicker, Lowell P., Jr. [American political leader]
Connecticut (table) **Ci: 967**
Weierstrass, Karl Theodor Wilhelm [German mathematician]
Fractal **F: 443**
Mathematics (In the 1800's) **M: 307**
Weighing scale
Scale, Weighing **S: 169**
Weight [measurement] **W: 180**
Density **D: 142**
Energy (Weight and mass) **E: 275**
Gravitation (Newton's theory of gravitation) **G: 331**
Kilogram **K: 316**
Mass (Mass and weight) **M: 268**
Matter **M: 310**
Metric system (Mechanics) **M: 437**; (The metric system at a glance) **M: 438-439** *with pictures*
Scale, Weighing **S: 169**
Weights and measures (table: Weight and mass) **W: 187**
Weight, Atomic *See* Relative atomic mass *in this index*
Weight, Tables of
Growth (Growth rate) **G: 405**
Weight allowance

Horse racing (Allowance races) **H: 365**
Weight class [boxing]
Boxing (Weight classes) **B: 526**; (table) **B: 527**; (Boxing today) **B: 533**
Weight control W: 181
See also Obesity *in this index*
Bariatric surgery **B: 109**
Diet (Diets for losing or gaining weight) **D: 199**
Disease (Metabolic diseases) **D: 229**
Evolutionary psychology **E: 434**
Nutrition (Do not overeat) **N: 630**
Overeaters Anonymous **O: 881**
Pregnancy (Weight gain) **P: 734b**
Weight-driven clock
Clock *diagram on* **Ci: 682i**; (Mechanical clocks) **Ci: 682j** *with picture*
Weight-gaining product
Industry (Production location) **I: 259**
Weight-losing product
Industry (Production location) **I: 259**
Weight-training *See* Bodybuilding *in this index*
Weighted silk
Silk (Boiling off and weighting) **S: 460**
Weightlessness [space exploration]
Aerospace medicine (Space medicine) **A: 89**
Astronaut *picture on* **A: 831**
International Space Station (Missions) **I: 346b**
Relativity (A "thought experiment") **R: 212**
Space exploration (Living in space) **So: 701** *with pictures*
Weightlifting [athletics] **W: 183** *with picture*
Bodybuilding **B: 435**
Olympic Games (Summer Olympic Games) **O: 746e-749**
Physical fitness *picture on* **P: 434**
Weights and measures W: 184
See also Metric system *in this index*
Laser (Measuring) **L: 83**
Weights and Measures, General Conference on
Metric system **M: 436**; (Evolution of the metric system) **M: 441**
Weights and measures (Measurement systems) **W: 184**
Weights and Measures, International Bureau of
International Bureau of Weights and Measures **I: 338**
Weihnachtsmann [legend]
Christmas (In Germany) **C: 530**
Weill, Kurt [German composer] **W: 188**
Weimar [Germany]
Liszt, Franz (His life) **L: 349-350**
Weimar Republic [German history]
Germany (The Weimar Republic) **G: 167**
Weimaraner [dog] **W: 188**
Dog *picture on* **D: 269**
Weinberg, Steven [American physicist]
Nobel Prizes (Physics: 1979) **N: 441**
Subatomic particle (The Standard Model) **So: 938**
Weinberger, Caspar Willard [American government official] **W: 188**
Iran-contra affair (Charges and court actions) **I: 407**
Weinke, Chris [American football player]
Football (table) **F: 363**
Weir [engineering]
Lamprey (Destructiveness) **L: 55**
Weir, Bob [American singer]
Grateful Dead **G: 329**
Weir, Robert Stanley [Canadian judge]
"O Canada" **O: 635**
Weir, Walter [Canadian political leader]
Manitoba (table) **M: 159**
Weir Farm National Historic Site [Connecticut]
National Park System (table: National historic sites) **N: 52-54**
Weirton
West Virginia (Interesting facts) **W: 207**
Weisgard, Leonard [American artist] **W: 188**
Weismann, August [German biologist] **W: 188**
Weiss, Carl A. [American assassin]
Long (Huey Pierce Long): Long, Huey Pierce **L: 445-446**
Weiss, Ehrich [birth name of]
Houdini, Harry **H: 377**
Weiss, George [American businessman]
Baseball (table: Hall of Fame) **B: 134b**
Weiss, Peter [German dramatist]
Drama (Later German-language drama) **D: 340**
Weissmuller, Johnny [American swimmer]
Olympic Games (Between the wars) **O: 751**
Swimming (History) **So: 1047**
Weisz, Rachel [British actress]
Motion picture (Best performance by an actress in a supporting role: 2005) **M: 862b**
Weitz, Paul J. [American astronaut]
Astronaut (Achievements in space) **A: 829-830**; (table) **A: 830**

Weizman, Ezer [Israeli political leader]
Weizmann, Chaim **W: 189**
Weizmann, Chaim [Israeli statesman] **W: 188** *with portrait*
Israel (Independence and conflict) **I: 487**
Welch, James [American author]
Indian, American (Achievements in the arts) **I: 181**
Welch, Laura Lane [wife of George W. Bush] *See* Bush, Laura Welch *in this index*
Welch, Mickey [American baseball player]
Baseball (table: Hall of Fame) **B: 134b**
Welcome Monument [Jakarta]
Indonesia *picture on* **I: 226**
Welcome to Hard Times [book by Doctorow]
Doctorow, E. L. **D: 260**
Weld, Theodore [American social reformer]
Grimké (Angelina Emily Grimké) **G: 394**
Weld, William F. [American political leader]
Massachusetts (table) **M: 288**
Welded rail
Railroad (The crossties and rails) **R: 109**
Welding [industrial process] **W: 189** *with pictures*
Acetylene **A: 25**
Helium (Uses) **H: 176** *with picture*
Riveting **R: 356**
Sculpture (The sculptor at work) **S: 232** *with picture*
Welding torch
Welding (Arc welding) **W: 189**
Welf [German history]
Guelphs and Ghibellines **G: 418**
Welfare W: 190
See also Welfare state *in this index*
Clinton, Bill (National affairs) **Ci: 682d**
Denmark (Social welfare) **D: 137**
Foundation (The work of foundations) **F: 430-431**
Local government (Functions of local government) **L: 407**
New Deal (Helping the needy) **N: 201**
Norway (Social welfare) **N: 541**
Poverty (Social welfare programs) **P: 725**
State government (State services) **So: 864**
Supplemental Nutrition Assistance Program **So: 996**
Sweden (Social welfare) **So: 1026**; (Period of reform) **So: 1034**
Welfare economics
Arrow, Kenneth Joseph **A: 743**
Marshall, Alfred **M: 228**
Welfare organizations
CARE **C: 213**
Welfare Party
Turkey (Political changes) **T: 512**
Welfare state [government] **W: 192**
Norway (Social welfare) **N: 541**
United Kingdom (The welfare state) **U: 71**
Welfare **W: 190**
Welford, Walter [American political leader]
North Dakota (table) **N: 513**
Well W: 192 *with diagrams*
See also Gas well *in this index*
Artesian well **A: 751** *with diagram*
Irrigation (Bringing irrigation water to farms) **I: 457**
Well log [record]
Petroleum (Geological studies) **P: 335-336**
Well-made play
French literature (Realism) **F: 522**
Ibsen, Henrik **I: 4**
Well of the Saints, The [play by Synge]
Synge, John Millington **So: 1067**
Well-Tempered Clavier [music by Bach]
Bach, Johann Sebastian (His works) **B: 16**
Welland Ship Canal [Lake Erie-Lake Ontario] **W: 193** *with map*
Canal (table) **C: 164**
Great Lakes (Water routes to the sea) **G: 344**
Niagara River (Commerce and industry) **N: 395**
Ontario *picture on* **O: 785**
Saint Lawrence Seaway **S: 43** *with map*; (Early canals) **S: 44**
Wellcome, Sir Henry [British businessman]
Wellcome Trust **W: 193**
Wellcome Trust W: 193
Foundation (table) **F: 430**
Weller, John B. [American political leader]
California (table) **C: 59**
Weller, Thomas Huckle [American biologist]
Enders, John Franklin **E: 272**
Nobel Prizes (Physiology or medicine: 1954) **N: 446**
Welles, Gideon [American political leader] **W: 193**
Emancipation Proclamation *picture on* **E: 254**
Lincoln, Abraham (table) **L: 323**
Welles, Orson [American actor] **W: 194** *with portrait*

Citizen Kane Ci: 568
Motion picture (Movies in the 1930's) M: 868
  with picture
Radio (The Golden Age of Broadcasting) R: 92-93
Wellesley, Arthur *See* Wellington, Duke of *in this index*
Wellesley College W: 194
Wellington [New Zealand] W: 194
Wellington, Duke of [British general] W: 194
Aix-la-Chapelle, Congress of A: 253
Napoleon I (The Hundred Days and Waterloo) N: 16
Portugal (A brief revival) P: 694
Waterloo, Battle of (Napoleon returns to France) W: 145
Wellman, William [American director]
Motion picture (Movies in the 1930's) M: 867
Wells, H. G. [British author] W: 195
English literature (Literature before World War I) E: 322
Science fiction (The first science fiction) S: 205
Wells, Heber M. [American political leader]
Utah (table) U: 245
Wells, Henry [American businessman]
Wells, Fargo & Company W: 195
Wells, Henry H. [American political leader]
Virginia (table) V: 417
Wells, Herbert George [British author] *See* Wells, H. G. *in this index*
Wells, Horace [American dentist]
Anesthesia (History) A: 459
Dentistry (Modern dentistry) D: 144-145
Nitrous oxide N: 427
Wells, James M. [American political leader]
Louisiana (table) L: 496
Wells, Samuel [American political leader]
Maine (table) M: 87
Wells, William Charles [British journalist]
Florida (Communication) F: 260
Wells, Willie [American baseball player]
Baseball (Hall of Fame) B: 134b
Wells and Company [U.S. history]
Fargo, William George F: 28
Wells-Barnett, Ida Bell [American social reformer] W: 195
African Americans (The Harlem Renaissance and other achievements) A: 136m-136n
Wells, Fargo & Company [U.S. history] W: 195
Fargo, William George F: 28
Welsbach, Baron von [Austrian chemist]
Neodymium N: 123
Praseodymium P: 733
Welsh [people]
Wales (People) W: 8; (Way of life) W: 9
Welsh, Jane [wife of]
Carlyle, Thomas (Early career) C: 240
Welsh, Matthew E. [American political leader]
Indiana (table) I: 214
Welsh Church Act [1914]
Wales (Religion) W: 9
Welsh corgi [dog]
Cardigan Welsh corgi C: 210 *with picture*
Pembroke Welsh corgi P: 233
Welsh language W: 195
United Kingdom (Language) U: 55
Wales (Language) W: 8; (The arts) W: 9
Welsh Language Society
Welsh language W: 196
Welsh pony
Horse (Ponies) H: 347 *with picture*
Welsh springer spaniel W: 196 *with picture*
Welsh terrier W: 196
Dog *picture on* D: 272
Welterweight
Boxing (table) B: 527
Welty, Eudora [American author] W: 196
American literature (Southern fiction) A: 424-425
Welwitsch, Friedrich [Austrian botanist]
Welwitschia W: 196
Welwitschia [plant] W: 196 *with picture*
Africa *picture on* A: 125
Plant *picture on* P: 547
Wemyss, Jean Margaret *See* Laurence, Margaret *in this index*
Wen [disorder] W: 196
Wen Jiabao [Chinese political leader]
China (Recent developments) C: 506-507
Wenceslas Square
Prague (The city) P: 730
Wendel, Fritz [German aviator]
Aviation (table) A: 990
Wenteche [people]
Mapuche M: 189
Wentorf, Robert H., Jr. [American chemist]
Borazon B: 482
Wentworth, Benning [American colonial official]
Vermont (Land disputes) V: 334

Wentworth, Thomas *See* Strafford, Earl of *in this index*
Wenyan [text]
China (Literature) C: 487
Wereat, John [American political leader]
Georgia (table) G: 130
Werewolf [legendary creature] W: 197
Wergeland, Henrik Arnold [Norwegian author] W: 197
Wergeland, Oscar [Norwegian painter]
Norway *picture on* N: 546
Werner, Abraham Gottlob [German geologist]
Asbestos (History) A: 765
Geology (The rock dispute) G: 98
Graphite G: 323
Werner, Alfred [Swiss chemist]
Nobel Prizes (Chemistry: 1913) N: 443
Wernher the Gardener [German author]
German literature (Popular literature) G: 139
Wernicke, Carl [German neurologist]
Brain (Language) B: 556
Wernicke's area
Brain (Language) B: 556
Wernigerode [Germany]
Germany *picture on* G: 151
Wertheimer, Max [German psychologist]
Gestalt psychology G: 175
Psychology (Gestalt psychology) P: 850
Wertmüller, Ulrich [Swedish painter]
Marie Antoinette *picture on* M: 200
Werts, George T. [American political leader]
New Jersey (table) N: 249
Wesberry v. Sanders [U.S. history]
Gerrymander G: 174
Weser River [river, Germany] W: 197
Pied Piper of Hamelin P: 453
Wesley, Anthony [Australian astronomer]
Jupiter (History of Jupiter study) J: 200b
Wesley, Charles [British religious leader] W: 197
Hymn (Words and music) H: 475
Methodists (Early history) M: 435
Wesley, John [English religious leader] W: 197 *with portrait*
Christianity (The 1600's and 1700's) C: 525-526
Circuit rider Ci: 559
Free Methodist Church F: 498
Methodists M: 434; (Early history) M: 435
Protestantism (Pietism) P: 835
Wesleyan Church W: 198
Whitefield, George W: 292
Wesleyan Church [religious group] W: 198
Wesleyan Methodist Church [religious group]
Wesleyan Church W: 198
Wesleyan Methodist Connection [religious group]
Methodists (Social change and division) M: 435
Wesleyan University
Agricultural experiment station A: 145
Wesselmann, Tom [American artist]
Pop Art P: 659
Wessex [ancient kingdom]
Alfred the Great A: 348
West, American *See* West, The *in this index*
West, Andrew [American educator]
Wilson, Woodrow (University president) W: 321
West, Benjamin [American painter] W: 198
Monroe, James *picture on* M: 736
United States, History of the *picture on* U: 154
Wolfe, James *picture on* W: 377
West, Comet [astronomy]
Comet (table) Ci: 868
West, Dick [American painter]
Indian, American *picture on* I: 142
West, Jerry [American basketball player] W: 198
Basketball *picture on* B: 154
West, Jessamyn [American author] W: 198
West, Kanye [American rapper/singer] W: 198
West, Mae [American actress] W: 199
Fields, W. C. *picture on* F: 95
West, Nathanael [American author] W: 198
West, Oswald [American political leader]
Oregon (table) O: 845
West, Rebecca [British author] W: 199
West, Roy O. [American government official]
Coolidge, Calvin (table) Ci: 1032
Hoover, Herbert Clark (table) H: 330
Interior, Department of the (table) I: 325
West, The [U.S. history] W: 199
See also Pioneer life in America; Western frontier life in America; Westward movement in America *in this index*
Photography (Artistic advances) P: 424-425
Westerns W: 241
West, Thomas *See* De La Warr, Lord *in this index*
West, Togo D., Jr. [American government official]
Clinton, Bill (table) Ci: 682d
Veterans Affairs, Department of (table) V: 343
West African manatee [animal]

Manatee M: 132
West African Studies [book by Kingsley]
Kingsley, Mary Henrietta K: 331
West Antarctica
Antarctica (Ice) A: 532 *with map*
West Bank [region, Middle East] W: 199 *with picture and map*
Abbas, Mahmoud A: 4
Arab-Israeli conflict (The 1948 war) A: 582; (The 1967 war) A: 582a; (The first intifada) A: 582a; (Peacemaking) A: 582a; (The second intifada) A: 582a
Arafat, Yasir A: 590b
Hamas H: 28
Hebron H: 163
Hussein I H: 457
Intifada I: 353
Israel I: 478; (History) I: 486-488
Jericho J: 93
Jordan J: 160 *with map*; (History) J: 164-165
Kadima K: 208
Middle East *picture on* M: 531; (History) M: 533-534
Palestine (The continuing conflict and peace efforts) P: 106
Palestine Liberation Organization P: 106
Palestinian Authority P: 107
Palestinians P: 107
Rabin, Yitzhak R: 50
Sharon, Ariel S: 377
West Bengal [state, India]
Bengal B: 248
West Berlin [Germany] *See* Berlin *in this index*
West Block [building]
Ottawa (The Parliament Buildings) O: 872
West Brant [painting by Kline]
Abstract Expressionism *picture on* A: 18
West Coast natives
Nootka Indians N: 453
West Edmonton Mall
Alberta (Interesting facts) A: 313
West End [district]
London (Central London) L: 429-430
West End Historic District
Dallas (Landmarks) D: 11
West Falkland [island, Atlantic]
Falkland Islands F: 15
West Florida, Republic of [U.S. history]
Louisiana (Territorial days) L: 498
Mississippi (Exploration and early settlement) M: 641
West Germany *See* Germany *in this index*
West Gulf Coastal Plain [region, U.S.]
Louisiana (Land regions) L: 490
West Highland white terrier W: 201 *with picture*
West India Company, Dutch *See* Dutch West India Company *in this index*
West Indian cherry [fruit]
Acerola A: 24 *with picture*
West Indian chiton [sea animal]
Shell *picture on* S: 387
West Indian manatee [animal]
Manatee M: 132
West Indies [islands, Caribbean] W: 201 *with pictures and maps*
See also the list of Related articles in the West Indies *article*
Columbus, Christopher (The first landing) Ci: 860 *with picture*
East Indies E: 40
Latin America (The movement toward independence) L: 106-107
Transportation of convicts T: 400
West Indies, British [islands, Atlantic]
British West Indies B: 633
West Indies Associated States [islands, Caribbean]
West Indies (Abolition and independence movements) W: 205
West Indies Federation [British history]
Barbados (History) B: 104
Jamaica (History) J: 24
West Indies (Abolition and independence movements) W: 205
West Indies tree fern
Tree *pictures on* T: 413
West Irian *See* Papua *in this index*
West Jerusalem
Jerusalem (West Jerusalem) J: 95
West Lake [China]
Hangzhou H: 51
West Nile virus W: 205
Mosquito (Mosquitoes and people) M: 834
West Okoboji Lake
Iowa (Rivers and lakes) I: 386
West Orange [New Jersey]
Edison, Thomas Alva (Edison in West Orange) E: 80; (Honors) E: 82 *with picture*

West Pakistan
  Pakistan P: 92; (History) P: 98-99
West Point [New York] W: 205
  Arnold, Benedict (Turns traitor) A: 742
  New York *picture on* N: 297; (Places to visit) N: 302
  United States Military Academy U: 201 *with picture*
West Quoddy Head [region]
  Maine M: 68
West Quoddy Lighthouse [Maine]
  Lighthouse *picture on* L: 295
West Roman Empire
  Byzantine Empire (The late Roman period) B: 753
  Christianity (The Roman Empire splits) C: 524
  Goths G: 279
  Law (The Middle Ages) L: 134
  Rome, Ancient *map on* R: 447; (The decline of the empire) R: 447-448
  Romulus Augustulus R: 450a
West Roxbury [district, Boston]
  Boston (Hyde Park and West Roxbury) B: 500
West Shawnee Trail [U.S. history]
  Oklahoma (After the Civil War) O: 731-732
West Side Story [film]
  Motion picture (Best picture: 1961) M: 861
West Side Story [musical]
  Bernstein, Leonard B: 271
  Musical comedy (The modern musical emerges) M: 960
  Robbins, Jerome R: 365
  Sondheim, Stephen So: 591
West Slavs [people]
  Slavs (West Slavs) S: 505
West Virginia W: 206 *with pictures and maps*
  See also the list of Related articles in the West Virginia *article*
  Civil War, American (How the states lined up) Ci: 617
  Pierpont, Francis Harrison P: 457
  United States *picture on* U: 120
West Virginia [ship]
  Miller, Dorie M: 553
West Virginia Independence Hall [Wheeling]
  West Virginia (Places to visit) W: 216
West Virginia University W: 230
  West Virginia *picture on* W: 211
West Wind Drift [current]
  Atlantic Ocean (Moving ocean waters) A: 866
Westbrook, Harriet [wife of]
  Shelley, Percy Bysshe (His life) S: 391
Westchester County [New York]
  New York City (Metropolitan area) N: 330
Westcott, Edward Noyes [American author] W: 230
Westergaard, Harald Malcolm [American engineer] W: 230
Westerly wind
  Climate (Atmospheric circulation) Ci: 676a
  Cyclone Ci: 1203
  Prevailing westerly P: 773
  Weather (Planetary-scale systems) W: 158-159
Westermarck, Edward Alexander [Finnish anthropologist] W: 230
Western [fiction] *See* Westerns *in this index*
Western Addition [district]
  San Francisco (Other neighborhoods) S: 93 *with map*
Western Australia [state, Australia] W: 230 *with picture and map*
Western bloc [world history]
  Cold War Ci: 762
Western bluebird
  Bluebird B: 423
Western Carolina University [Cullowhee]
  North Carolina, University of N: 495
Western Chamber, The [play by Wang Shifu]
  Chinese literature (Drama and fiction) C: 511
Western chimpanzee
  Chimpanzee C: 471
Western Church [European history] W: 231
Western Conference
  Hockey (table: National Hockey League) H: 281
  National Basketball Association N: 30
Western Desert [North Africa]
  See also Libyan Desert *in this index*
  Egypt (Recent developments) E: 133-134
  World War II (The Western Desert Campaign) W: 476
Western Development Museum [Saskatchewan]
  Saskatchewan *picture on* S: 137
Western dewberry [plant]
  Loganberry L: 423
Western European Union [alliance] W: 231
  European Union (Relations with other countries) E: 419
Western Federation of Miners [U.S. history]
  Idaho (Early statehood) I: 44

Western fence lizard
  Swift *picture on* So: 1039
Western Front
  World War I W: 452, *map on* W: 464; (The Western Front) W: 455 *with map*
Western frontier life in America [U.S. history]
  W: 232 *with pictures*
  See also Pioneer life in America; Westward movement in America *in this index; and the Related articles in the* Western frontier Life in America *article*
  Bean, Judge Roy B: 182 *with picture*
  Boom town B: 475
  Buffalo *picture on* B: 675
  Chisholm Trail C: 515
  Gold rush (Gold rushes in the United States) G: 254 *with picture*
  Kansas (The great cattle towns) K: 237
  Stagecoach *picture on* So: 821
  United States, History of the (Expansion [1820-1849]) U: 167 *with picture*; (The end of the Western frontier) U: 185
Western gray kangaroo
  Kangaroo (Kinds of kangaroos) K: 213
Western Hemisphere [geography]
  Hemisphere H: 181 *with diagram*
Western Hemisphere Travel Initiative [policy]
  Homeland Security, Department of (History) H: 302
Western hemlock [tree]
  Hemlock H: 182 *with picture*
  Plant *picture on* P: 524
Western Isles [Scotland]
  Hebrides H: 163
Western Kentucky Coal Field
  Kentucky (Land regions) K: 285-286; (Mining) K: 289 *with picture*
Western kingbird [bird]
  Bird (Birds of grasslands) B: 336 *with picture*
Western larch [tree]
  Larch L: 75
Western lowland gorilla
  Gorilla G: 275
Western meadowlark [bird]
  Bird (Birds of grasslands) B: 336 *with picture*
  Meadowlark M: 345
Western music
  Music (Western music) M: 955
Western pipistrelle bat [animal]
  Bat *picture on* B: 159
Western Plateaus, Basins, and Ranges [region, U.S.]
  North America (Land regions) N: 462
  United States *map on* U: 122; (The Western Plateaus, Basins, and Ranges) U: 125 *with picture*
Western poison oak [plant]
  Poison oak P: 602 *with picture*
Western pygmy blue [butterfly]
  Butterfly B: 732 *with picture*
Western redcedar [tree]
  Cedar (Scale-leaved cedars) C: 324
  Plant *picture on* P: 524
Western Reserve [U.S. history] W: 240
  Ohio (Exploration and settlement) O: 700
Western saddle [riding equipment]
  Horse (The saddle) H: 351 *with picture*
  Saddle S: 7 *with picture*
Western Sahara [region, Africa] W: 241
  Hassan II H: 82
  Mauritania (History) M: 315
  Morocco (Dispute over Western Sahara) M: 815
Western Samoa [territory]
  See also Samoa *in this index*
  Pacific Islands (Pacific alliances and independence movements) P: 12
  Samoa (History) S: 80a-80b
Western skink [reptile]
  Skink *picture on* S: 494
Western soapberry [tree]
  Tree *pictures on* T: 423
Western Star [poem by Benét]
  Benét, Stephen Vincent B: 248
Western Sudan [region, Africa]
  African Americans (The cultural heritage) A: 136c *with map*
Western swing [music]
  Country music (Western swing music) Ci: 1098a
  Popular music (Other new styles of popular music) P: 671
Western sword fern [plant]
  Evolution (Evolution of new species) E: 429-430
  Fern (Kinds of ferns) F: 75
  Plant *picture on* P: 524
Western tanager [bird]
  Tanager T: 24
Western Trail [U.S. history]

  Cowboy (The growth of the cattle industry) Ci: 1111-1112
Western Turkestan
  Turkestan (Western Turkestan) T: 501
Western Union [telegraph company] W: 241
  Cornell, Ezra Ci: 1065
  Dolbear, Amos E. D: 284
  Edison, Thomas Alva (The young telegrapher) E: 78
  Telegraph (Western Union) T: 91; (Service expansion and improvement) T: 91; (Telegraph service today) T: 92
  Telephone (The Bell System) T: 100
Western Wall [Jerusalem] W: 241
  Jerusalem (Jewish sites) J: 95-96 *with picture and map*
  Jews *picture on* J: 120
Western wallflower [plant]
  Flower *picture on* F: 287
Western white pine
  Pine (Western pines) P: 469
Western wood-pewee [bird]
  Pewee P: 352
Western yew [tree]
  Yew Y: 565
Westerner, The [film]
  Cooper, Gary Ci: 1034
Westerns [fiction] W: 241 *with picture*
  American literature (Popular forms) A: 422; (Popular genres) A: 425
  Western frontier life in America (Entertainment) W: 240
Westing Game, The [book by Raskin]
  Raskin, Ellen R: 145
Westinghouse, George [American inventor] W: 242
  Railroad (Engineering improvements) R: 117
  Tesla, Nikola (The alternating-current system) T: 181
  Westinghouse Electric Corporation W: 242
Westinghouse Electric Corporation W: 242
Westliche Post [newspaper]
  Schurz, Carl S: 189
"Westmark trilogy" [books by Alexander]
  Alexander, Lloyd A: 342
Westminster [district]
  London *picture on* L: 431; (Residential areas and housing) L: 432
Westminster, City of [British history]
  London (Central London) L: 429-430
Westminster, Palace of [London]
  London (The Houses of Parliament) L: 435; (The Middle Ages) L: 439-440
  Parliament (The Houses of Parliament) P: 174
Westminster, Statute of [1931] *See* Statute of Westminster *in this index*
Westminster Abbey [London] W: 242 *with picture*
  Edward the Confessor E: 113
  London (Churches) L: 435 *with picture*; (The Middle Ages) L: 439-440
  Unknown soldier U: 211
Westminster Assembly [English history]
  Presbyterians (History) P: 756a
Westminster Confession of Faith [religion]
  Baptists (Early history) B: 101
Westminster Kennel Club Show
  Dog (Dog competitions) D: 280
Westminster School [England] W: 243
Westminster Shorter Catechism [religious book]
  Presbyterians (Teaching and worship) P: 756a
Westmoreland, William Childs [American general] W: 243
  Vietnam War (The opposing forces) V: 375
Weston, Edward [American inventor] W: 243
Weston, Edward [American photographer] W: 243
  Photography (Dramatic changes) P: 425-426
Weston, James A. [American political leader]
  New Hampshire (table) N: 223
Westphalen, Jenny von [wife of Karl Marx]
  Marx, Karl (Marriage and move to Paris) M: 236
Westphalia, Peace of [1648]
  Austria (The Habsburgs) A: 937
  Germany (The Thirty Years' War) G: 164
  Peace (From the 1400's to the 1700's) P: 206
  Pope (Renaissance and Reformation) P: 664-665
  Roman Catholic Church (The Counter Reformation) R: 408
  Thirty Years' War (The Peace of Westphalia) T: 260
  War (Ethical and legal aspects of war) W: 24
Westport
  Kansas City [Missouri] (History) K: 242-243
Westward Ho! [book by Kingsley]
  Kingsley, Charles K: 331
Westward movement in America [U.S. history]
  W: 244 *with pictures and map*
  See also Pioneer life in America; Western frontier life in America *in this index; and the list of*

Related articles in Westward movement in America *article*
Homestead Act (Effects of the law) **H:** 304
Lewis and Clark expedition **L:** 222
Louisiana Purchase **L:** 502 *with map*
Map (Mapping the Americas) **M:** 184
Nebraska (Territorial days) **N:** 112 *with picture*
United States, history of the (Expansion [1820-1849]) **U:** 167 *with pictures and map*
Westward the Course of Empire Takes Its Way [painting by Leutze]
Leutze, Emanuel Gottlieb **L:** 216
Westward the Tide [book by L'Amour]
L'Amour, Louis **L:** 52
Westwood [California]
Los Angeles (West Los Angeles) **L:** 461
Westwork [architecture]
Architecture (Carolingian architecture) **A:** 618
Wet-bulb depression [meteorology]
Hygrometer (The psychrometer) **H:** 474
Wet-bulb thermometer
Hygrometer (The psychrometer) **H:** 474
Wet cell [device]
Battery (Battery structure) **B:** 168
Wet chinook [weather]
Chinook **C:** 513
Wet-collodion process [photography]
Photography (Technical improvements) **P:** 423
Wet macular degeneration [disorder]
Macular degeneration **M:** 26
Wet market system
Meat packing (Marketing livestock and meat) **M:** 350-351
Wet meadow
Wetland **W:** 252a; (Marshes and wet meadows) **W:** 252b
Wet milling [agriculture]
Corn *picture on* **Ci:** 1063; (Corn in industry) **Ci:** 1061
Wet-plate process [photography]
Photography (Technical improvements) **P:** 423
Wet snow avalanche
Avalanche **A:** 982
Wet steam
Steam **So:** 880
Wet suit
Skin diving (Kinds of skin diving) **S:** 493 *with pictures*
Wet-sump engine
Gasoline engine (The lubrication system) **G:** 66
Wethered, Joyce [British golfer]
Golf (Women's golf) **G:** 266
Wetland [geography] **W:** 252a *with pictures*
See also Swamp *in this index*
Conservation (Canada) **Ci:** 988
Marsh **M:** 228
Wetland delineation [law]
Wetland (Conservation) **W:** 253
Wetmore, Andrew R. [Canadian political leader]
New Brunswick (table) **N:** 195; (Confederation and progress) **N:** 198
Wetmore, George P. [American political leader]
Rhode Island (table) **R:** 311
WEU [organization]
Western European Union **W:** 231
Wexler, Jerry [American recording executive]
Rock music (Soul music) **R:** 380a
Weyand, Frederick [American general]
Vietnam War (The opposing forces) **V:** 375
Weybosset Hill
Providence (Government and history) **P:** 840
Weyden, Rogier van der [Flemish painter] *See* Van der Weyden, Rogier *in this index*
Weyerhaeuser, Frederick [American businessman] **W:** 253
Weyerhaeuser Company
Tree farming **T:** 432
Weymouth [Massachusetts] **W:** 253
Weyrich, Paul [American political figure]
Heritage Foundation **H:** 211
Whaam! [painting by Lichtenstein]
Painting (Pop Art) **P:** 86 *with picture*
Whale W: 254 *with pictures*
See also the list of Related articles in the Whale *article*
Animal *picture on* **A:** 469; (Animal travelers) **A:** 502
Antarctica (Living things) **A:** 534 *with picture*
Arctic Ocean (Ocean life) **A:** 643
Atlantic Ocean (Ocean life) **A:** 866
Dolphin **D:** 296
Endangered species (table) **E:** 270
Greenpeace **G:** 386
Mammal *pictures on* **M:** 117, **M:** 119
Southern Ocean (Commercial resources) **So:** 688b
Whale-headed stork [bird]

Shoebill **S:** 432 *with picture*
Whale oil
Blubber **B:** 419
Whale **W:** 254
Whale shark [fish] **W:** 265
Animal *picture on* **A:** 487
Ocean (The nekton) **O:** 655
Shark (Kinds of sharks) **S:** 375-376 *with picture*
Whale song [sounds]
Humpback whale **H:** 436
Whalebone *See* Baleen *in this index*
Whalesucker [fish]
Remora **R:** 230
Whaling [industry]
Whale (The early days of whaling) **W:** 262 *with picture*; (Modern whaling) **W:** 263 *with picture*; (The future of whales) **W:** 264
Colonial life in America (Fishing and whaling) **Ci:** 810
Conservation (Ocean conservation) **Ci:** 978-979
Greenpeace **G:** 386
Inuit *picture on* **I:** 354f; (Hunting and fishing) **I:** 354d-354e
Whaling Commission, International
Whale (The future of whales) **W:** 264
Whammy bar [electronics]
Electric guitar **E:** 173
Wharton, Edith [American author] **W:** 265
American literature (Women writers) **A:** 420
Novel (New directions in the novel) **N:** 573-574
Wharton, Thomas, Jr. [American political leader]
Pennsylvania (table) **P:** 263
Wharton School
Pennsylvania, University of **P:** 270
What Every Woman Knows [play by Barrie]
Barrie, J. M. **B:** 118
"What hath God wrought!" [quotation]
Telegraph (Construction and growth) **T:** 91
What Have I Done to Deserve This? [film]
Almodóvar, Pedro **A:** 380
What-if scenario [accounting]
Computer (Spreadsheet programs) **Ci:** 917
"What Is an Emotion?" [paper by James]
Emotion (The constructivist approach) **E:** 261
"What Is Art?" [essay by Tolstoy]
Tolstoy, Leo (His conversion) **T:** 323
What Is Property? [book by Proudhon]
Proudhon, Pierre Joseph **P:** 838
What Is the Third Estate? [book by Sieyès]
Sieyès, Emmanuel Joseph **S:** 453
What Is to Be Done? [pamphlet by Lenin]
Lenin, V. I. (Beginnings of revolution) **L:** 192
What Price Glory? [play by Anderson and Stallings]
Anderson, Maxwell **A:** 452
What We Talk About When We Talk About Love [book by Carver]
Carver, Raymond **C:** 269
What's Bred in the Bone [book by Davies]
Davies, Robertson **D:** 46
Novel (The novel today) **N:** 575
What's Going On [recording]
Gaye, Marvin **G:** 73
What's O'Clock [book by Lowell]
Lowell, Amy **L:** 509
What's Past Is Prologue [book by Massey]
Massey, Vincent **M:** 296
Wheat [plant] **W:** 266 *with pictures and maps*
See also the list of Related articles in the Wheat *article*
Alberta *picture on* **A:** 324
Australia *picture on* **A:** 919
Borlaug, Norman Ernest **B:** 488
Colonial life in America (Farming) **Ci:** 809-810
Flour **F:** 267
Food supply (Making farmland more productive) **F:** 349
Grain **G:** 301
Grass (Cereals) **G:** 326
Kansas (The nation's breadbasket) **K:** 237
North Dakota (Agriculture) **N:** 511 *with picture*
Oregon *picture on* **O:** 827
Plant *picture on* **P:** 540
Russia *picture on* **R:** 526
Rust **R:** 567
Saskatchewan (Agriculture) **S:** 143
Triticale **T:** 448
Wheat, Zack [American baseball player]
Baseball (table: Hall of Fame) **B:** 134b
Wheat beer
Beer **B:** 211
Wheat bran [cereal]
Bran **B:** 562
Wheat germ
Wheat (Food for people) **W:** 266-267
Wheat malt [grain]
Beer **B:** 211
Wheat pool [economics]

Cooperative (In Canada) **Ci:** 1036
Wheat State [nickname]
Kansas **K:** 216
Wheatgrass
Grass *picture on* **G:** 325
Wheatland [estate]
Buchanan, James (Later years) **B:** 661-662
Wheatley, John [American businessman]
Wheatley, Phillis **W:** 278
Wheatley, Phillis [American poet] **W:** 278
Colonial life in America (Literature) **Ci:** 806-807 *with picture*
Columbia **Ci:** 851
Wheatstone, Sir Charles [British inventor] **W:** 278
Concertina **Ci:** 928
Harmonica **H:** 62
Telegraph (Development of the telegraph) **T:** 90
Wheatstone bridge [instrument] **W:** 278 *with diagram*
Ohm **O:** 706
Wheatstone, Sir Charles **W:** 278
Wheel [food]
Cheese (Packaging) **C:** 393
Wheel [symbol]
Buddhism *picture on* **B:** 668
Wheel and axle [mechanism] **W:** 278
Automobile (From power plant to wheels) **A:** 948 *with diagram*; (Supporting the car) **A:** 950
City (Economy) **Ci:** 580-581
Gear **G:** 75
Invention (Prehistoric times) **I:** 358
Machine (Wheel and axle) **M:** 14 *with pictures*
Pulley **P:** 900 *with diagram*
Simple machines **S:** 467
Transmission **T:** 375
Transportation (The first great civilizations) **T:** 385-386
Wheel and axle **W:** 278
Wheel animal *See* Rotifer *in this index*
Wheel lock [gun]
Handgun (Early handguns) **H:** 45 *with picture*
Harquebus **H:** 67
Musket **M:** 962
Weapon (Firearms) **W:** 154b
Wheel method [pottery]
Pottery (Shaping the clay) **P:** 716-717
Wheel mounted crane [machine]
Crane **Ci:** 1119 *with picture*
Wheel tractor
Tractor (Types of tractors) **T:** 361
Wheelbarrow W: 279
Transportation *picture on* **T:** 388
Wheelchair
Disability (Mobility problems and other physical disabilities) **D:** 218-219 *with picture*; (Housing and transportation) **D:** 221
Wheeler, Burton Kendall [American political leader] **W:** 279
Wheeler, Earle Gilmore [American general]
Joint Chiefs of Staff (table) **J:** 156
Wheeler, Edward L. [American author]
Western frontier life in America (The West in American culture) **W:** 239
Wheeler, George H. [American inventor]
Escalator **E:** 356
Wheeler, Joseph [Confederate general] **W:** 279
Wheeler, William Almon [American political leader] **W:** 279
Hayes, Rutherford Birchard (Campaign of 1876) **H:** 120
Vice president of the United States **V:** 348 *with portrait*
Wheeler Adjustment [1874]
Wheeler, William Almon **W:** 279
Wheeler Dam [Tennessee River, Alabama]
Muscle Shoals **M:** 936
Wheeler Peak
New Mexico (Land regions) **N:** 266 *with map*
Rocky Mountains (Chief ranges of the Rockies) **R:** 394 *with map*
Wheeling [West Virginia] **W:** 279
Wheeling Downs [race track]
Wheeling **W:** 279
Wheeling Island [Ohio River]
Wheeling **W:** 279
Wheelock, Eleazar [American educator]
Dartmouth College **D:** 39
Wheelwright, William [American businessman] **W:** 279
Whelan, Edward [Canadian political leader]
Confederation of Canada (Fathers of Confederation) **Ci:** 935
Wheldon, Dan [British-born race driver]
Automobile racing (table: Indianapolis 500 winners) **A:** 980
Whelk [sea animal] **W:** 279
Mollusk (Gastropods) **M:** 695

Shell **S: 386** *with picture*
Whelp [dog]
Dog (table: Dog terms) **D: 263**
When Guns Speak, Death Settles Disputes
[painting by Russell]
Dodge City *picture on* **D: 261**
"When I Consider How My Light Is Spent" [poem
by Milton]
Milton, John (Middle years) **M: 557**
"When Johnny Comes Marching Home" [song]
Gilmore, Patrick Sarsfield **G: 191**
"When Lilacs Last in the Dooryard Bloom'd"
[poem by Whitman]
Whitman, Walt (His work) **W: 294**
When We Dead Awaken [play by Ibsen]
Drama (Ibsen) **D: 338**
Ibsen, Henrik (His plays) **I: 4**
When William Came [book by Munro]
Munro, Hector Hugh **M: 928**
Where Are the Children? [book by Clark]
Clark, Mary Higgins **Ci: 642**
***Where Do We Come From? What Are We? Where
Are We Going?*** [painting by Gauguin]
Gauguin, Paul (Gauguin in Tahiti) **G: 69-70**
"Where Have All the Flowers Gone?" [song by
Seeger]
Seeger, Pete **S: 283**
Where I Was From [book by Didion]
Didion, Joan **D: 195**
Where I'm Calling From [book by Carver]
Carver, Raymond **C: 269**
Where the Air is Clear [book by Fuentes]
Fuentes, Carlos **F: 553**
Latin American literature (The "Boom") **L: 114**
Where the Sidewalk Ends [book by Silverstein]
Silverstein, Shel **S: 465**
Where the Wild Things Are [book by Sendak]
Literature for children *picture on* **L: 356**
Whey [food]
Cheese *picture on* **C: 394**; (Separating the curd)
C: 392; (History) **C: 394**
Which? [organization]
Consumer protection (The right to information)
Ci: 1018
Whidbey Island [island, Washington]
Puget Sound **P: 886**
Whiffletree [harness]
Transportation (The Middle Ages) **T: 387-388**
Whig Party [British history]
United Kingdom (The era of reform) **U: 68**
Whig Party **W: 280**
Whig Party [U.S. history] **W: 280**
Harrison, William Henry (Elections of 1836 and
1840) **H: 75**
National Republican Party **N: 60**
Raccoon (People and raccoons) **R: 51**
Tyler, John **T: 532**
United States, History of the (Politics after
Jackson) **U: 171**
Webster, Daniel (The man) **W: 177**
Whiggamore [British history]
Whig Party **W: 280**
Whimbrel [bird]
Curlew **Ci: 1195**
Whin [shrub]
Furze **F: 588**
Whip [riding equipment]
Horse (The whip) **H: 351**
Whip, Congressional [office]
Congress of the United States (The Senate)
Ci: 942-943
House of Representatives (The speaker and other
leaders) **H: 387**
Political party (Organizing the government)
P: 632
Senate (The leaders of the senate) **S: 294-295**
Whip grafting
Grafting (Kinds of grafting) **G: 298** *with picture*
Whip-poor-will [bird] **W: 280** *with picture*
Bird *picture on* **B: 358**
Whip snake
Snake *picture on* **S: 524**
Whiplash [injury] **W: 281** *with picture*
Whiplash curve [design]
Furniture (Art Nouveau) **F: 582** *with picture*
Whipped butter
Butter **B: 730**
Whipper-in [hunter]
Fox hunting **F: 442**
Whippet [dog] **W: 281**
Dog *picture on* **D: 271**
Whipping [rope]
Knots, hitches, and splices (Preparing rope for
knots) **K: 356**
Whipping post [punishment] **W: 281**
Whipple, George Hoyt [American physician]
Nobel Prizes (Physiology or medicine: 1934)

N: 445
Whipple, William [American patriot] **W: 281**
Whippoorwill [bird] *See* Whip-poor-will *in this
index*
Whiptail [reptile]
Lizard (Defenses) **L: 400**
Whiptail wallaby [animal]
Wallaby *picture on* **W: 15**
Whirlaway [horse]
Arcaro, Eddie **A: 593**
Kentucky Derby (table) **K: 296**
Whirligig [insect]
Beetle *picture on* **B: 218**
Water beetle **W: 133**
Whirling dervishes [religious group]
Dervish **D: 153**
Sufism **So: 959**
Whirlpool [geography] **W: 281**
Whirlpool bath [medicine]
Hydrotherapy **H: 472**
Whirlpool Rapids [New York]
Niagara Falls (Description) **N: 391-392**
Niagara River (Description) **N: 394**
Whirlwind [weather] **W: 282**
Whirlybird
Helicopter **H: 169**
Whisk fern [plant]
Plant (Ferns and related plants) **P: 518-520**;
(Classification of plants) **P: 546-547** *with picture*
Whisker [hair]
See also Barbel *in this index*
Hair **H: 9**
Mammal (Senses) **M: 120-121**
Whiskey [drink] **W: 282**
Alcoholic beverage (Whiskey) **A: 337**; (History)
A: 337
Distilling **D: 239**
Kentucky *picture on* **K: 273**
Pioneer life in America (Food) **P: 481-482**
Whiskey Rebellion [U.S. history] **W: 282**
Internal revenue (History) **I: 337**
United States, History of the (Financial problems)
U: 162-163
Washington, George (Whiskey Rebellion) **W: 106**
Whiskey Ring [U.S. history] **W: 282**
Grant, Ulysses S. (Government frauds) **G: 317**
**Whiskeytown-Shasta-Trinity National
Recreation Area** [California]
National Park System (table: National recreation
areas) **N: 49**
Whist [game]
Bridge (History) **B: 605**
Hoyle, Edmond **H: 402**
Whistle [musical instrument]
Pipe **P: 488**
Whistle [sound] **W: 282**
Whistle-Stop Campaign [U.S. history]
President of the United States *picture on* **P: 769**
Whistler [animal]
Mountain beaver **M: 897**
Whistler, James Abbott McNeill [American artist]
W: 282 *with picture*
Impressionism (American Impressionism) **I: 94**
Whistler's Mother [painting by Whistler]
Whistler, James Abbott McNeill **W: 282** *with
picture*
Whitaker, Forest [American actor]
Motion picture (Best performance by an actor:
2006) **M: 862a**
Whitaker's Almanack [book]
Almanac **A: 379**
Whitcomb, Edgar D. [American political leader]
Indiana (table) **I: 214**
Whitcomb, James [American political leader]
Indiana (table) **I: 214**
White [butterfly]
Butterfly *picture on* **B: 737**; (Sulphurs and whites)
B: 738
White [horse]
Horse (Light harness horses) **H: 345**
White [light]
Color (The relation between color and light)
Ci: 817
Holography **H: 298** *with diagram*
Light (Incandescence) **L: 283**
White, Albert B. [American political leader]
West Virginia (table) **W: 225**
White, Alfred Holmes [American engineer] **W: 283**
White, Bill [American baseball player] **W: 283**
White, Byron Raymond [American jurist] **W: 284**
White, Canvass [American engineer]
Cement and concrete (History) **C: 345**
White, Charles [American football player]
Football (table) **F: 363**
White, Dan [American assassin]
San Francisco (Political leaders murdered) **S: 98**
White, E. B. [American author] **W: 284**

Democracy (Famous quotations about
democracy) **D: 120**
Essay (Personal essays) **E: 359**
Literature for children *picture on* **L: 363**
White, Edward D. [American political leader]
Louisiana (table) **L: 496**
White, Edward Douglass [American jurist] **W: 284**
White, Edward Higgins, II [American astronaut]
W: 284
Astronaut (Achievements in space) **A: 829**;
(Accidents in space) **A: 830-831**
Space exploration (Voskhod and Gemini: The first
multiperson space flights) **So: 714** *with picture*;
(Making ready) **So: 715**
White, Elwyn Brooks *See* White, E. B. *in this index*
White, Frank [American political leader]
North Dakota (table) **N: 513**
White, Frank D. [American political leader]
Arkansas (table) **A: 712**
Clinton, Bill (Reelection defeat) **Ci: 682b**
White, George [American political leader]
Ohio (table) **O: 699**
White, Horace [American political leader]
New York (table) **N: 313**
White, Hugh L. [American political leader]
Mississippi (table) **M: 640**
White, Hugh Lawson [American political leader]
W: 284
White, Israel C. [American geologist]
West Virginia (Industrial growth) **W: 228-229**
White, James [American pioneer]
Knoxville **K: 359**
White, Jason [American football player]
Football (table) **F: 363**
White, John [English colonist]
Colonial life in America (Early English
settlements) **Ci: 789**
Indian, American *picture on* **I: 156**
Lost Colony **L: 472**
White, Margaret Bourke- [American
photographer] *See* Bourke-White, Margaret *in
this index*
White, Mark [American political leader]
Texas (table) **T: 203**
White, Minor [American photographer]
Photography (A diversity of styles) **P: 426**
White, Patrick [Australian author] **W: 284**
Australia (Literature) **A: 904-905**
Novel (The novel today) **N: 575**
White, Peregrine [American colonist] **W: 284**
White, Rex [American race driver]
Automobile racing (table: NASCAR Sprint Cup
champions) **A: 981**
White, Robert H. [American astronaut]
Airplane (Supersonic airplanes) **A: 238**
White, Shaun [American snowboarder]
Olympic Games *picture on* **O: 746e**
White, Sol [American baseball player/manager]
Baseball (table: Hall of Fame) **B: 134b**
White, Stanford [American architect] **W: 284**
Hall of fame (The Hall of Fame for Great
Americans) **H: 22** *with picture*
White, Susanna [American colonist]
White, Peregrine **W: 284**
Winslow, Edward **W: 342**
White, Tim [American anthropologist]
Prehistoric people (table) **P: 754**
White, Walter Francis [American author] **W: 285**
White, William Allen [American editor] **W: 285**
White, William DeKova [American baseball player]
See White, Bill *in this index*
White agate [mineral]
Chalcedony **C: 369**
White Album, The [book by Didion]
Didion, Joan **D: 195**
White and lavender columbine [plant]
Columbine **Ci: 853**
White ash [tree]
Ash **A: 767**
Tree *pictures on* **T: 420**
White Australia policy [immigration]
Australia (Social policies) **A: 924**
White-balance setting [photography]
Photography (Color) **P: 415**
White bellbird
Bellbird **B: 243**
White-bellied brant [bird]
Brant **B: 564**
White-bellied fish-eagle
Eagle (Other kinds of eagles) **E: 5**
White birch *See* Paper birch *in this index*
White Bird Canyon [region, Idaho]
Indian wars (The Nez Perce War [1877]) **I: 194**
White blood cell
Blood (The composition of blood) **B: 407-408**
with picture; (Protecting against disease) **B: 410**
with picture; (How the body maintains its blood

supply) **B: 410-411**; (White-cell abnormalities) **B: 414**
Cell *picture on* **C: 338**; (Death of a cell) **C: 332**
Disease (Immune responses) **D: 231-232** *with picture*
Human body (The blood) **H: 421-424** *with picture*
Immune system (Parts of the immune system) **I: 87**
Interleukin **I: 335**
Leukemia **L: 215**
White Book [standard]
Compact disc (Video CD's) **Ci: 902**
White bread
Bread (The food value of bread) **B: 589**
White-breasted nuthatch [bird]
Bird (Birds of forests and woodlands) **B: 334** *with picture*
Nuthatch **N: 622**
White-breasted thrasher [bird]
Thrasher **T: 268**
White cabbage [plant]
Cabbage (Kinds of cabbage) **C: 2**
White chocolate
Chocolate (White chocolate) **C: 519**
"White Christmas" [song]
Crosby, Bing **Ci: 1154**
White Citizens' Council
Carter, Jimmy (Businessman and civic leader) **C: 254**
White cliffs of Dover
Dover **D: 315**
England (The English Lowlands) **E: 300-301** *with picture*
White clover
Clover (White clover) **Ci: 713** *with picture*
Leaf (The petiole) **L: 154** *with picture*
White-collar crime
Crime (White-collar crime) **Ci: 1136**
Fraud **F: 496**
White-collar worker
Labor force (Changes in the labor force) **L: 3**
White-crested laughing thrush [bird]
Babbler *picture on* **B: 2**
White croaker [fish]
Drum **D: 367**
White damp [gas]
Damp **D: 22**
White Devil, The [play by Webster]
Webster, John **W: 177**
White dwarf [star] **W: 285**
Chandrasekhar, Subrahmanyan **C: 374**
Magnetism (Other astronomical bodies) **M: 60dc**
Nova **N: 553**
Sirius **S: 476**
Star (White dwarf phase) **So: 849**; (Binary stars) **So: 852**
Sun **So: 975**; (Evolution of the sun) **So: 982**
Supernova (Thermonuclear supernovae) **So: 994**
White elm [tree] *See* American elm *in this index*
White Ensign [United Kingdom]
Flag *picture on* **F: 195**
White evening primrose [plant]
Flower *picture on* **F: 286**
White-eye [bird] **W: 285** *with picture*
White-faced heron [bird]
Heron (Kinds of herons) **H: 214**
White Fang [book by London]
London, Jack **L: 444**
White Flemish Giant [rabbit]
Rabbit (The body of a rabbit) **R: 47**
White flight [sociology]
Segregation (The beginning of change) **S: 285**
White flour
Flour (Types of flour) **F: 268**; (How white flour is milled) **F: 269** *with diagram*
Wheat (Food for people) **W: 266-267**
White-footed mouse [animal]
Lyme disease **L: 533**
Mouse (White-footed mice) **M: 901** *with picture*
White Friars [religious group]
Friar **F: 532**
White Globe [onion]
Onion *picture on* **O: 763**
White Goddess, The [book by Graves]
Graves, Robert **G: 330**
Mythology (Literary approaches) **M: 990-991**
White gold
Gold (Jewelry) **G: 251**
Palladium **P: 108**
Platinum **P: 566**
White goshawk [bird]
Hawk (Kinds of hawks) **H: 111**
White Guard [Finnish history]
Finland (The new republic) **F: 117**
White-handed gibbon [animal]
Gibbon **G: 185**
White heart [plant]

Dutchman's-breeches **D: 393**
White Holland turkey
Turkey (Domestic turkeys) **T: 513**
White horehound [plant]
Horehound **H: 334**
White Horse Tavern [Newport, Rhode Island]
Colonial America in America (Places to visit) **Ci: 801**
White House [Moscow]
Russia (The new nation) **R: 555**
White House [Washington, D.C.] **W: 286** *with pictures*
See also the Life in the White House *sections of the articles on specific presidents, such as* Roosevelt, Franklin Delano (Life in the White House)
Adams, Abigail Smith **A: 32**
Adams, John (Life in the White House) **A: 39** *with picture*
National Park System (Areas preserved for historic importance) **N: 46**; (table: National parkways and other national parklands) **N: 56**
President of the United States (The White House) **P: 766** *with pictures*
Roosevelt, Theodore (Life in the White House) **R: 465**
United States, Government of the *picture on* **U: 137**
Washington, D.C. *map on* **W: 76**; (White House) **W: 74** *with picture*
White House conference [U.S. history] **W: 291**
White House Gang
Roosevelt, Theodore (Life in the White House) **R: 465**
White House hostesses **W: 291**
First ladies of the United States **F: 142**
White House of the Confederacy [Montgomery]
Alabama (Places to visit) **A: 266** *with picture*
Montgomery *picture on* **M: 766**
White House of the Confederacy [Richmond]
Richmond (Other interesting places to visit) **R: 332** *with picture*
Virginia (Libraries and museums) **V: 402-403** *with picture*
White House Office
President of the United States (The executive branch) **P: 764**
Presidential assistant **P: 770**
White House tapes
Nixon, Richard Milhous (Events at home) **N: 435-436**
Watergate (The tape controversy) **W: 144**
White indigo [plant]
Flower *picture on* **F: 287**
White-Jacket [book by Melville]
Melville, Herman (His early life) **M: 390**
White-lined sphinx moth
Moth *picture on* **M: 841**
White-lipped peccary [animal]
Peccary **P: 226**
White-marked tussock moth *See* Whitemarked tussock moth *in this index*
White marlin [fish]
Marlin **M: 241**
White Masonry
Masonry (History) **M: 267-268**
White matter [anatomy]
Brain (The cerebrum) **B: 550a-550b**
Myelin **M: 970f**
Nervous system (The axon) **N: 133-134**
White Monkey, The [book by Galsworthy]
Galsworthy, John **G: 17**
White Mountain, Battle of the [1620]
Czech Republic (Habsburg rule) **Ci: 1213**
Thirty Years' War (The Bohemian period) **T: 260**
White mountain avens [plant]
Flower *picture on* **F: 283**
White Mountain National Forest
Maine (Places to visit) **M: 78**
New Hampshire (Places to visit) **N: 216**
White Mountains [mountains, Maine-New Hampshire] **W: 291**
Maine (Land regions) **M: 80**
New Hampshire (Visitor's guide) **N: 216**; (Land regions) **N: 218** *with map*; (Mountains) **N: 220**
White mulberry [plant]
Mulberry **M: 913**
White mustard [plant]
Mustard **M: 968**
White Nile [river, Africa]
Nile River (The course of the Nile) **N: 422** *with map*
Sudan (Way of life) **So: 951**; (Land and climate) **So: 951** *with map*
Sudan, South (Land and climate) **So: 956** *with picture*
White-nose syndrome [disease]
Bat (Bats and people) **B: 162**
White oak

Leaf *picture on* **L: 153**
Maryland **M: 241**
Oak (White oaks) **O: 635** *with pictures*
Plant *picture on* **P: 525**
White Oak Dance Project [dance company]
Ballet (Recent developments) **B: 55** *with picture*
White opal [gem]
Opal **O: 788** *with picture*
White oryx [animal]
Antelope (Antelope and people) **A: 542-543**
White Pekin duck [bird]
Duck (Dabbling ducks) **D: 376** *with picture*
White pepper [spice]
Pepper **P: 277**
White phlox [plant]
Plant *picture on* **P: 524**
White phosphorus [mineral]
Phosphorus **P: 403**
White pine [tree]
Leaf *picture on* **L: 153**
Pine *picture on* **P: 470**; (North American pines) **P: 468**
White pine blister rust fungus
Currant **Ci: 1196**
White-plumed honeyeater [bird]
Bird (Birds of Australia and New Zealand) **B: 346** *with picture*
White poplar [tree]
Poplar **P: 668**
White primary [voting]
African Americans (During the early 1900's) **A: 136l**; (The Great Depression) **A: 136n**
White print process
Blueprint (Making a blueprint) **B: 424**
White rajah [ruler]
Borneo (History) **B: 490**
White rat
Rat (Rats and people) **R: 147**
White Revolution [Iranian history]
Iran (Reforms and growing unrest) **I: 406**
Mohammad Reza Pahlavi **M: 687**
White rhinoceros
Rhinoceros (Kinds of rhinoceroses) **R: 294-295** *with picture*
White River [river, U.S.]
Arkansas *picture on* **A: 698**
South Dakota (Rivers and lakes) **So: 676** *with map*
White Russians [Russian history]
Lenin, V. I. (Civil war) **L: 194**
White sage [plant]
Plant *picture on* **P: 525**
White Sands Missile Range [New Mexico] **W: 291**
White Sands National Monument [New Mexico] **W: 292**
National Park System (table: National monuments) **N: 50-52**
White Sands Proving Ground
White Sands Missile Range **W: 291**
White scallop squash
Squash (Summer squashes) **So: 813** *with picture*
White Sea [Russia] **W: 292**
White Sea-Baltic Canal [waterway, Russia]
Canal (table) **C: 164**
White shark *See* Great white shark *in this index*
White-sided dolphin [sea animal]
Dolphin *picture on* **D: 298**; (Other species) **D: 297**
White-sided jack rabbit
Jack rabbit **J: 3**
White Snow, Bright Snow [book by Tresselt]
Duvoisin, Roger Antoine **D: 393**
White Sox, Chicago [team] *See* Chicago White Sox *in this index*
White Star Line
Ship (Passenger vessels) **S: 426**
White stork
Animal *picture on* **A: 502**
Bird (Birds of Europe) **B: 344c** *with picture*
Stork **So: 912** *with picture*
White sturgeon [fish]
Sturgeon **So: 934**
White Sulphur Springs [West Virginia] **W: 292**
White-tailed deer [animal]
Animal *picture on* **A: 479**
Deer (Legs and hoofs) **D: 83** *with picture*; (North American deer) **D: 85**; (table) **D: 85**
Lyme disease **L: 533**
White-tailed eagle
Eagle (Other kinds of eagles) **E: 5**
White-tailed ptarmigan [bird]
Ptarmigan **P: 853**
White-tailed tropicbird [bird]
Bird *picture on* **B: 344**
White Temple [Uruk]
Architecture (Mesopotamian architecture) **A: 611**
White tiger [animal]
Tiger (The body of a tiger) **T: 283-284**
White Tower

London (The Tower of London) **L:** 436; (The Middle Ages) **L:** 439-440
White trillium [plant]
Flower *picture on* **F:** 285
White Volta [river, Burkina Faso]
Burkina Faso (Land) **B:** 706
White walnut *See* Butternut *in this index*
White water
Rafting **R:** 102 *with picture*
White water racing
Canoeing (White water racing) **C:** 181 *with picture*
West Virginia *picture on* **W:** 217
White whale
Whale (Belugas and narwhals) **W:** 258
White willow
Willow **W:** 315
White wine
Wine (Types of wine) **W:** 336; (How wine is made) **W:** 337-338
White-winged crossbill [bird]
Crossbill **Ci:** 1156
White Woman of the Genesee [name for]
Jemison, Mary **J:** 91
Whiteaker, John [American political leader]
Oregon (table) **O:** 845
Whitebark pine
Pine (Western pines) **P:** 469
Whitecap [wave]
Ocean (Waves) **O:** 659
Whiteface [cattle]
Cattle (Hereford) **C:** 309 *with picture*
Whiteface clown
Clown **C:** 713
Whitefield, George [British religious leader] **W:** 292
Colonial life in America (Religion) **Ci:** 804-805 *with picture*
Great Awakening **G:** 335
Whitefish W: 292
Fish *picture on* **F:** 159
Whitefly [insect] **W:** 292 *with picture*
Cotton (Insect pests) **Ci:** 1090
Whitehall Palace [London]
Jones, Inigo **J:** 158 *with picture*
London (Palaces) **L:** 435
Whitehead [disorder]
Acne **A:** 27
Pimple **P:** 466
Whitehead, Alfred North [British mathematician] **W:** 292
Logic (Modern logic) **L:** 425
Mathematics (Philosophies of mathematics) **M:** 307
Whitehead, Colson [American author]
African American literature (Recent developments) **A:** 136a
Whitehead, Robert [Scottish engineer]
Torpedo (History) **T:** 341
Whitehead, William [British poet]
Poet laureate (table: Poets laureate of the United Kingdom) **P:** 590
Whitehorse [Yukon] **W:** 293 *with picture*
Yukon **Y:** 578; (The people) **Y:** 578 *with picture and map*
Whiteman, Paul [American conductor]
Grofé, Ferde **G:** 397
Whitemarked tussock moth
Moth *picture on* **M:** 840
Tussock moth **T:** 526
Whiteoaks of Jalna [book by de la Roche]
Canadian literature *picture on* **C:** 159
Whiteread, Rachel [British sculptor] **W:** 293
Whites [people]
See also Race relations *in this index*
Race (The three-race theory) **R:** 53
South Africa (People) **So:** 609; (Ways of life) **So:** 611
Whites [Russian history]
Lenin, V. I. (Civil war) **L:** 194
Russian Revolution of 1917 (The October Revolution) **R:** 566
Union of Soviet Socialist Republics (Civil war) **U:** 36
Whiteshell Nuclear Research Establishment
Manitoba (The mid-1900's) **M:** 162-163
Whitetop Mountain [Virginia]
Virginia (Land regions) **V:** 410
Whitewash [liquid mixture] **W:** 293
Whitewater [U.S. history]
Clinton, Bill (National affairs) **Ci:** 682d-682e; (Domestic events) **Ci:** 682f
Reno, Janet **R:** 240
Starr, Kenneth Winston **So:** 857
Whitewater Falls
North Carolina (Rivers, waterfalls, and lakes) **N:** 484
Whitfield, Henry L. [American political leader]
Mississippi (table) **M:** 640

Whitfield, James [American political leader]
Mississippi (table) **M:** 640
Whitfield House [Guilford]
Connecticut (Places to visit) **Ci:** 960
Whiting [chalk]
Chalk **C:** 370
Whiting [Indiana]
Gary **G:** 47
Indiana *picture on* **I:** 197
Whiting, William F. [American government official]
Commerce, Department of (table) **Ci:** 871
Coolidge, Calvin (table) **Ci:** 1032
Hoover, Herbert Clark (table) **H:** 330
Whitlam, Gough [Australian political leader]
Australia (table) **A:** 923; (Political upheavals) **A:** 925
Whitman, Charles S. [American political leader]
New York (table) **N:** 313
Whitman, Christine Todd [American political leader]
New Jersey (table) **N:** 249; (The late 1900's) **N:** 253
Whitman, Marcus [American missionary] **W:** 293
Oregon (Indian treaties and conflicts) **O:** 846
Whitman, Narcissa **W:** 294
Whitman, Narcissa [American missionary] **W:** 293
Whitman, Marcus **W:** 293
Whitman, Walt [American poet] **W:** 294 *with portrait*
American literature (Walt Whitman and Emily Dickinson) **A:** 419 *with portrait*
Free verse **F:** 500
Poetry (Forms) **P:** 595; (Beginnings of modern poetry) **P:** 597
Whitman massacre [1847]
Whitman, Marcus **W:** 293
Whitman Mission National Historic Site [Washington] **W:** 294
National Park System (table: National historic sites) **N:** 52-54
Whitman Museum [New Jersey]
Camden **C:** 76
Whitnall Park
Milwaukee (Parks) **M:** 560
Whitney, Eli [American inventor] **W:** 295 *with portrait*
Agriculture *picture on* **A:** 158; (Agricultural advances) **A:** 157
Connecticut *picture on* **Ci:** 969; (The 1800's) **Ci:** 970
Cotton (American colonists) **Ci:** 1092
Cotton gin **Ci:** 1094
Georgia (Early statehood) **G:** 132
Invention (Economic needs) **I:** 355
Mass production **M:** 269
Spinning (The mule) **So:** 794
United States, History of the (Cotton and slavery) **U:** 166
Whitney, James P. [Canadian political leader]
Ontario (table) **O:** 783
Whitney, Josiah Dwight [American geologist]
Mount Whitney **M:** 890
Whitney, Mount *See* Mount Whitney *in this index*
Whitney, William C. [American government official]
Cleveland, Grover (table) **Ci:** 671
Whitney Museum of American Art [New York City] **W:** 295
New York City (Museums) **N:** 338
Whitson, Peggy [American astronaut]
International Space Station **I:** 346b-347
Whittaker, Charles Evans [American jurist]
Supreme Court of the United States (table) **So:** 1000
Whittaker, James Warren [American mountain climber]
Mount Everest **M:** 884
Whitten Brown, Sir Arthur [British aviator]
Alcock and Brown **A:** 335
Whittier, John Greenleaf [American poet] **W:** 295 *with portrait*
American literature (Poetry) **A:** 418
December (Quotations) **D:** 69
Frietchie, Barbara **F:** 533
Liberty Party **L:** 233
Whittle, Chris [American businessman]
EdisonLearning, Inc. **E:** 83
Whittle, Sir Frank [British inventor]
Jet propulsion (Development of jet propulsion) **J:** 114
Turbine (History) **T:** 498-500
WHO [organization] *See* World Health Organization *in this index*
Who, The [musical group] **W:** 296
Rock music (The Who) **R:** 380
Townshend, Pete **T:** 352
Who Framed Roger Rabbit [film]

Animation (The animation revival) **A:** 514c
Whole Book of Psalmes, Faithfully Translated into English Metre, The *See* Bay Psalm Book *in this index*
Whole corn meal
Corn (The dry-milling industry) **Ci:** 1061-1062
Whole-grain cereal
Cereal **C:** 361
Whole-language philosophy
Reading (The whole-language philosophy) **R:** 158
Whole life insurance
Insurance (Cash value life insurance) **I:** 310
Whole milk
Milk (Nutrients in milk) **M:** 545-546
Whole number [mathematics]
Division (Division of decimal fractions) **D:** 250
Number (Natural and whole numbers) **N:** 605
Whole tone [music]
Tone **T:** 327
Whole wheat
Flour (Types of flour) **F:** 268
Wheat (Food for people) **W:** 266-267
Whole-word identification *See* Look-and-say instruction *in this index*
Wholemount technique
Microtomy **M:** 520
Wholesale nursery [horticulture]
Nursery **N:** 614
Wholesaler
Food (Marketing) **F:** 335 *with picture*
Sales (Wholesaling) **S:** 62
Trade (The use of markets) **T:** 362
Wholistic medicine *See* Holistic medicine *in this index*
Whooper [bird] *See* Whooping crane *in this index*
Whooper swan
Swan (Kinds) **So:** 1016
Whooping cough W: 296
Whooping crane W: 296
Bird (Endangered species) **B:** 370
Crane (Kinds) **Ci:** 1117 *with picture*
Whorl [zoology]
Shell *diagram on* **S:** 385
Who's Afraid of Virginia Woolf? [play by Albee]
Albee, Edward **A:** 310
American literature (Drama) **A:** 426
Taylor, Elizabeth **T:** 57 *with picture*
Theater (The use of) **T:** 246
Why Are We in Vietnam? [book by Mailer]
Mailer, Norman **M:** 67
Why England Slept [book by Kennedy]
Kennedy, John Fitzgerald (Education) **K:** 261-262
Why Mosquitoes Buzz in People's Ears [book by Aardema]
Dillon, Leo and Diane **D:** 204
Literature for children *picture on* **L:** 373
Why Not Use the L? [painting by Marsh]
Realism *picture on* **R:** 172
Why We Fight [films]
Motion picture (Movies and World War II) **M:** 869
Whymper, Edward [British mountain climber]
Matterhorn **M:** 312
Whyte, William Pinkney [American political leader]
Maryland (table) **M:** 255
Wi-Fi [communications]
Computer (A modem or a network interface card) **Ci:** 915
Computer network **Ci:** 925
Internet (The evolving Internet) **I:** 350g
Telephone (VoIP phone calls) **T:** 97-98
Wireless communication (Wireless networking) **W:** 345
Wicca [religion]
Witchcraft **W:** 371 *with picture*
Wiccan Rede [rules]
Witchcraft (Role of magic) **W:** 372
Wichale, Treaty of [1889]
Menelik II **M:** 400
Wichita [Kansas] **W:** 297 *with picture*
Kansas *picture on* **K:** 225; (table: Average monthly weather) **K:** 230
Wichita Art Museum
Kansas *picture on* **K:** 217
Wichita Falls [Texas] **W:** 298
Wichita Mountains
Oklahoma (Land regions) **O:** 724 *with map*
Wick
Candle **C:** 175
Lamp (Fat or oil lamps) **L:** 52
Wickard, Claude R. [American government official]
Agriculture, Department of (table) **A:** 161
Roosevelt, Franklin Delano (table) **R:** 454
Truman, Harry S. (table) **T:** 469
Wicked [musical]
Musical comedy (Musical comedy today) **M:** 961

Wicker [plant product] W: 298
Wickersham, George Woodward [American lawyer]
Justice, Department of (table) J: 203
Taft, William Howard (table) T: 11
Wickersham, James. W. [Alaskan judge]
Alaska (The early 1900's) A: 301
Wicket [sports]
Cricket Ci: 1131; (The game) Ci: 1132 with picture
Croquet Ci: 1154 with diagram
Wicketkeeper [sports]
Cricket (Outs) Ci: 1132-1133 with picture
Wickford Point [book by Marquand]
Marquand, John Phillips M: 217
Wickiup [dwelling]
Indian, American picture on I: 139; (Shelter) I: 136d
Wickliffe, Charles A. [American political leader]
Tyler, John (table) T: 534
Wickliffe, Robert C. [American political leader]
Louisiana (table) L: 496
Wickremasinghe, Ranil [Sri Lankan political leader]
Sri Lanka (History) So: 819-820
Wide-angle lens
Camera (Single-lens reflex [SLR] cameras) C: 82-83
Photography (Types of lenses) P: 411 with picture
Wide area network
Computer (Computer networks) Ci: 920; (Wide area networks [WAN's]) Ci: 922
Computer network Ci: 925
Wide ball
Cricket (Scoring) Ci: 1132
Wide receiver [football]
Football (The offensive team) F: 356 with diagrams
Wide-wale corduroy [fabric]
Corduroy Ci: 1052
Widjaja, Prince [Javanese ruler]
Indonesia (Hindu and Buddhist kingdoms) I: 236
Widow [cards]
Pinochle P: 474
Widow [title]
Address, Forms of (Other forms) A: 54
Widow Capet [name for]
Marie Antoinette (Downfall of the monarchy) M: 200
Widow for One Year, A [book by Irving]
Irving, John I: 459
Widow spider
See also Black widow in this index
Spider (Dangerous spiders) So: 790
Widowers' Houses [play by Shaw]
Realism (In drama) R: 172
Widow's share [law]
Dower D: 316
Wiebe, Rudy [Canadian author]
Canadian literature (Modern English-Canadian fiction) C: 160
Wieck, Clara [German pianist] See Schumann, Clara in this index
Wieland [book by Brown]
Brown, Charles Brockden B: 642
Wieland, Heinrich Otto [German chemist]
Nobel Prizes (Chemistry: 1927) N: 443
Wieman, Carl Edwin [American physicist]
Nobel Prizes (Physics: 2001) N: 442
Wien [Austria] See Vienna in this index
Wien, Wilhelm [German physicist]
Nobel Prizes (Physics: 1911) N: 440
Proton P: 836
Science (Using logic) S: 194
Wiene, Robert [German director]
Motion picture (Filmmaking in Europe) M: 866 with picture
Wiener [food]
Sausage S: 163
Wiener, Alexander S. [American physiologist]
Blood (History of blood research) B: 414
Landsteiner, Karl L: 60
Rh factor R: 289
Wiener, Norbert [American mathematician]
W: 299
Cybernetics Ci: 1203
Wiener schnitzel [food]
Austria (Way of life) A: 931
Wienerwurst [food]
Sausage S: 163
Wies Pilgrimage Church
Architecture (Rococo architecture) A: 623
Germany picture on G: 154
Wiesbaden [Germany] W: 299
Wieschaus, Eric Francis [American physiologist]
Nobel Prizes (Physiology or medicine: 1995) N: 446
Wiesel, Elie [American author] W: 299

Wiesel, Torsten Nils [Swedish physiologist]
Nobel Prizes (Physiology or medicine: 1981) N: 446
Wiesenthal, Simon [Austrian public figure] W: 299
Wiesner, David [American author]
Caldecott Medal (table: 1992, 2002, 2007) C: 26
Literature for children picture on L: 371
Wiest, Dianne [American actress]
Motion picture (Best performance by an actress in a supporting role: 1986, 1994) M: 862b
Wife
See also Divorce; Parent in this index
Marriage M: 219
Wife of Claude, The [play by Dumas]
Dumas, Alexandre fils D: 382
"Wife of Usher's Well, The" [poem]
Ballad (The ballad style) B: 43
Wig W: 299
Clothing (Egypt) Ci: 696
Colonial life in America (Clothing) Ci: 799
Egypt, Ancient (Food, clothing, and shelter) E: 137
Hairdressing (Ancient times) H: 11 with pictures
Williamsburg picture on W: 313
Wigeon [bird] W: 299
Bird (Birds of inland waters and marshes) B: 340 with picture
Wiggin, Kate Douglas [American author] W: 299
Wiggins, James R. [American diplomat]
United Nations (table) U: 86
Wigglesworth, Michael [American poet] W: 299
American literature (Poetry) A: 414
Wight, Isle of [island, England] W: 300
England (Islands) E: 301
Wightman, Hazel Hotchkiss [American tennis player]
Tennis picture on T: 166d
Wigman, Mary [German choreographer]
Dance (Modern dance) D: 30-31
Holm, Hanya H: 294
Wigner, Eugene Paul [American physicist] W: 300
Wigwag flag [communications]
Flag (Flags that talk) F: 208
Wigwam [dwelling] W: 300
Indian, American picture on I: 138; (Shelter) I: 136d
Wii console
Electronic game (Broadening audiences) E: 204f
Wii Sports [electronic game]
Electronic game (Broadening audiences) E: 204f
Wijetunga, Dingiri Banda [Sri Lankan political leader]
Sri Lanka (History) So: 819-820
Wik decision [court case]
Australia (Aboriginal land decisions) A: 925
Wiki [computing]
Encyclopedia (Today's encyclopedias) E: 268b-269
Internet (The evolving Internet) I: 350g-350h
WikiLeaks [organization]
Internet (Ongoing controversies) I: 350h
Wikipedia [encyclopedia]
Encyclopedia (Today's encyclopedias) E: 268b-269
Internet (The evolving Internet) I: 350g-350h
Wilaya [province]
Algeria (Local government) A: 361
Wilberforce, Samuel [British religious leader]
W: 300
Wilberforce, William [British political leader]
W: 300
Wilberforce University W: 300
Wilbur, Curtis D. [American government official]
Coolidge, Calvin (table) Ci: 1032
Hoover, Herbert Clark (table) H: 330
Wilbur, Isaac [American political leader]
Rhode Island (table) R: 311
Wilbur, Ray L. [American government official]
Hoover, Herbert Clark (table) H: 330
Interior, Department of the (table) I: 325
Wilbur, Richard [American poet] W: 300
Poet laureate (table: Poets laureate of the United States) P: 590
Wilcken, Anna Magdalena [wife of]
Bach, Johann Sebastian (His life) B: 15-16
Wilco [rock band]
Rock music (Rock music today) R: 381
Wilcox, Howdy [American race driver]
Automobile racing (table: Indianapolis 500 winners) A: 980
Wilcox Mansion [Buffalo]
Buffalo (Other interesting places to visit) B: 678
Wilczek, Frank A. [American physicist]
Gluon G: 236
Nobel Prizes (Physics: 2004) N: 442
Subatomic particle (The Standard Model) So: 938
Wilczek Land [island, Arctic]

Franz Josef Land F: 494
Wild, Minnesota [team]
Hockey (table: National Hockey League) H: 281
Wild ass
Donkey D: 307
Onager O: 760
Wild barley [plant] See Foxtail barley in this index
Wild boar See Boar, Wild in this index
Wild canary
Canary C: 165 with picture
Goldfinch G: 256
Wild carrot W: 300 with picture
Wild celery
Eelgrass E: 115
Wild cherry [tree]
Tree pictures on T: 421
Wild Duck, The [play by Ibsen]
Ibsen, Henrik (His plays) I: 4
Wild flower See Wildflower in this index
Wild Geese [book by Ostenso]
Canadian literature (Literature between the world wars) C: 158-159
Wild ginger [plant]
Ginger G: 191
Wild goldfish [fish]
Goldfish G: 257 with picture
Wild Goose-Chase, The [play by Fletcher]
Fletcher, John F: 234
Wild hog
Hog (Wild hogs) H: 286
Wild horse
Horse (Wild horses) H: 348 with picture; (Horses and people) H: 360-362
Przewalski's horse P: 844
Wild Horse Dam [Owyhee River, Nevada]
Nevada (Natural resources) N: 169
Wild indigo
Flower (Flowers of prairies and dry plains) F: 286 with picture
Wild Iris, The [book by Glück]
Glück, Louise G: 236
Wild Irish Girl, The [book by Owenson]
Irish literature (Early works in English) I: 431
Wild jalap [plant] See Mayapple in this index
Wild leek [plant]
Ramp R: 133
Wild lemon [plant] See Mayapple in this index
Wild morning-glory
Bindweed B: 308
Wild onion
Ramp R: 133
Wild rice W: 301
Rice R: 322
Wild rose [plant]
Eglantine E: 119
Rose R: 474
Wild rye
Rye R: 573
Wild silk
Silk (Wild silk) S: 459
Wild Strawberries [film]
Motion picture (The art film revival) M: 870
Wild turkey
Turkey (How wild turkeys live) T: 513 with picture
Wild 2, Comet
Astronomy (Direct sampling) A: 846
Comet (Studying comets) Ci: 868-869
Wild West [U.S. history] See West, The in this index
Wild West show [entertainment]
Buffalo Bill B: 679
Wildcat W: 301
Bobcat B: 432 with picture
Wildcat bank [U.S. history] W: 301
Bank (The Wildcat Period) B: 93
Wildcat currency
Wildcat bank W: 301
Wildcat Ridge
Nebraska (Land regions) N: 104-106
Wildcat strike
Labor movement (Handling labor disputes) L: 6-7
Strike (Kinds of strikes) So: 928
Wildcat well
Gas [fuel] (Exploring for gas) G: 53
Petroleum (table) P: 332
Well (Oil and natural gas wells) W: 193
Wildcatting
Gas [fuel] (Exploring for gas) G: 53
Wilde, Oscar [Irish-British author] W: 301 with portrait
English literature (Later Victorian literature) E: 321-322
Irish literature (Drama) I: 432
Old Bailey O: 740
Opera: (Salome) O: 807
Wildebeest [animal] W: 302 with picture
Africa picture on A: 98
Animal picture on A: 476

Kenya picture on **K: 303**
Wilder, Billy [American director] **W: 302**
Motion picture (Best achievement in directing: 1945, 1960) **M: 862**
Wilder, L. Douglas [American political leader] **W: 302** with portrait
Virginia (table) **V: 417**; (Recent developments) **V: 422**
Wilder, Laura Ingalls [American author] **W: 302** with portrait
Laura Ingalls Wilder Award **L: 121**
Wilder, Samuel See Wilder, Billy in this index
Wilder, Thornton [American author] **W: 303**
American literature (Drama) **A: 422-423**
Lost Generation **L: 472**
Wilderness: A Journal of a Quiet Adventure in Alaska [book by Kent]
Kent, Rockwell **K: 271**
Wilderness, Battle of the [1864]
Civil War, American (table) **Ci: 624**; (Battle of the Wilderness) **Ci: 631**
Wilderness of Mirrors [book by Frisch]
Frisch, Max **F: 535**
Wilderness Road [U.S. history] **W: 303**
Boone, Daniel (The Wilderness Road) **B: 477-478**
Kentucky (Transportation) **K: 289**
Pioneer life in America (Crossing the Appalachians) **P: 477-478** with map
Tennessee (Early settlement) **T: 153**
Wildfire
See also Fire in this index
Forestry (Fire and forests) **F: 407**
Wildflower
Flower **F: 270** with picture; (Wildflowers) **F: 282** with pictures; (Studying wildflowers) **F: 296**
Gardening (Flower gardens) **G: 30-31**
Wildlife biologist [scientist]
Conservation (Careers in conservation) **Ci: 990**
Wildlife conservation W: 303
See also Conservation in this index; and the list of Related articles in the Wildlife conservation article
Africa (Native animals) **A: 122-123**
Animal (How human beings protect animals) **A: 505** with picture
Biodiversity (Protecting biodiversity) **B: 310**
Butterfly (Butterfly conservation) **B: 743** with picture
Conservation (Biodiversity conservation) **Ci: 976** with picture
Darling, Ding **D: 38**
Dolphin (Dolphin conservation) **D: 299**
Endangered species **E: 269**
Fishing industry **F: 181**; (Fishery conservation) **F: 187**
Forestry (Wildlife) **F: 406**
Foundation (Environment and animals) **F: 431**
Hunting (Laws and conservation) **H: 450**
Leopold, Aldo **L: 204**
National park **N: 42a**; (Challenges for the parks) **N: 42b**
Plant (Conservation of plants) **P: 543** with pictures
Primate (Conservation) **P: 778c**
Redwood (Redwood conservation) **R: 193**
Salmon (Salmon conservation) **S: 70**
Trapping (Trapping and wildlife conservation) **T: 403**
Wetland (Conservation) **W: 253**
Whale (The future of whales) **W: 264**
Zoo (Wildlife conservation) **Z: 600**
Wildlife management See Wildlife conservation in this index
Wildlife refuge
Bird (Bird refuges) **B: 368**
Hunting (Laws and conservation) **H: 450**
Miner, Jack **M: 565**
National Wildlife Refuge System **N: 61**
Wildsmith, Brian [British artist]
La Fontaine, Jean de picture on **L: 29**
Wiles, Andrew [British mathematician]
Fermat, Pierre de **F: 73**
Wiley, Harvey W. [American chemist]
Pure food and drug laws (History) **P: 909**
Wilhelm [emperors of Germany]
Wilhelm **W: 305**
Wilhelm I [emperor of Germany]
Wilhelm **W: 305**
Bismarck, Otto von (Bismarck's wars) **B: 382**
Franco-Prussian War (Background to the war) **F: 483**
Germany (The unification of Germany) **G: 165**
Prussia (German empire) **P: 843**
Wilhelm II [emperor of Germany]
Wilhelm (Wilhem II) **W: 305**
Bismarck, Otto von (Bismarck's diplomacy) **B: 382**
Germany (Foreign policy) **G: 166**; (The Weimar Republic) **G: 167**

Hohenzollern **H: 289**
World War I (The fighting ends) **W: 463**
Wilhelm, Hoyt [American baseball player]
Baseball (table: Hall of Fame) **B: 134b**
Wilhelm Meister's Apprenticeship [book by Goethe]
German literature (German Classicism) **G: 139**
Goethe, Johann Wolfgang von (Middle years) **G: 247**
Wilhelm Meister's Journeyman Years [book by Goethe]
Goethe, Johann Wolfgang von (Late years) **G: 248**
Wilhelmina [queen of the Netherlands] **W: 306**
Juliana **J: 187**
Luxembourg (History) **L: 531**
Netherlands (Independence) **N: 149**; (Political changes) **N: 150**
"Wilhelmus van Nassouwe" [song]
National anthem **N: 29**
Wilkes, Charles [American admiral] **W: 306**
Antarctica map on **A: 538**; (Early exploration) **A: 536**
Exploration (The exploration of Antarctica) **E: 450** with map
Lincoln, Abraham (Foreign relations) **L: 322**
Trent Affair **T: 435**
Wake Island **W: 6**
Wilkes-Barre [Pennsylvania]
Wyoming Valley Massacre **W: 538**
Wilkes Islet [Pacific Ocean]
Wake Island **W: 5**
Wilkie, Sir David [Scottish artist]
Painting (Art for a new public) **P: 70**
Wilkins, Sir Hubert [Australian explorer] **W: 306**
Eielson, Carl Ben **E: 145**
Exploration (The exploration of Antarctica) **E: 450**
Wilkins, Mary Eleanor [American author]
Freeman, Mary Eleanor Wilkins **F: 509**
Wilkins, Maurice Hugh Frederick [British biophysicist] **W: 306**
Watson, James Dewey **W: 147**
Wilkins, Roy [American social reformer] **W: 306**
Wilkins, William [American government official]
Tyler, John (table) **T: 534**
Wilkinson, Sir Geoffrey [British chemist]
Nobel Prizes (Chemistry: 1973) **N: 444**
Wilkinson, J. L. [American baseball executive]
Baseball (table: Hall of Fame) **B: 134b**
Wilkinson, James [American general]
Burr, Aaron (Tried for treason) **B: 711**
Jefferson, Thomas (The Burr conspiracy) **J: 86**
War of 1812 (Campaigns of 1813) **W: 31**
Wilkinson, Jeremiah [American inventor]
Nail (How nails are made) **N: 4**
Wilkinson, John [British inventor]
Industrial Revolution (The steam engine) **I: 249**
Machine tool (History) **M: 20**
Wilkinson Microwave Anisotropy Probe [satellite]
Astronomy (Radio and microwave astronomy) **A: 843**
Cosmic microwave background (CMB) radiation **Ci: 1075**
Inflation theory **I: 268a**
Will [law] **W: 306**
Death (The right to die) **D: 61**
Executor **E: 436**
Legacy **L: 182**
Living will **L: 399**
Probate **P: 809**
Will [psychology]
Enlightenment (The worship of reason) **E: 326a**; (Criticism of the Enlightenment) **E: 326b**
Free will **F: 500**
Plato (Psychology and politics) **P: 568**
Schopenhauer, Arthur **S: 186**
Will Rogers Memorial
Oklahoma (Places to visit) **O: 722** with picture
"Will to Believe, The" [essay by James]
James, William (His beliefs) **J: 27**
Will to power [philosophy]
Nietzsche, Friedrich (Psychological ideas) **N: 407**
Philosophy (Philosophy in the 1800's) **P: 390**
Will You Please Be Quiet, Please? [book by Carver]
Carver, Raymond **C: 269**
Will You Sign Here, John Hancock? [book by Fritz]
Literature for children picture on **L: 378**
Willamette Lowland [region]
Oregon (Land regions) **O: 838** with map
Willamette River [Oregon] **W: 307**
Oregon (Land and climate) **O: 838-840** with map
Portland [Oregon] (History) **P: 684**
Willamette Valley [Oregon]
Oregon **O: 827**
Willard, Archibald M. [American painter]
Spirit of Seventy-Six **So: 795**
Willard, Ashbel P. [American political leader]
Indiana (table) **I: 214**

Willard, Emma Hart [American educator] **W: 307**
Women's movement (The beginnings of women's movements) **W: 384-385**
Willard, Frances Elizabeth Caroline [American social reformer] **W: 307**
Woman's Christian Temperance Union **W: 382**
Willard, Jess [American boxer]
Dempsey, Jack **D: 130**
Willard, Nancy [author]
Newbery Medal (table) **N: 359**
Willemite [mineral]
Zinc **Z: 594**
Willemstad [Curaçao] **W: 307**
Curaçao **Ci: 1193**
Netherlands Antilles **N: 151**
Willenbrock [book by Hein]
German literature (Recent German literature) **G: 142**
Willet [bird] **W: 307** with picture
Willey, N. B. [American political leader]
Idaho (table) **I: 42**
William [emperors of Germany] See Wilhelm in this index
William I [king of Netherlands] **W: 308**
Netherlands (Independence) **N: 149**
William I, Prince of Orange [German prince] **W: 308**
Netherlands (Eighty Years' War) **N: 148**
William I, the Conqueror [king of England] **W: 308**
Bayeux Tapestry **B: 176** with picture
Curfew **Ci: 1193**
Domesday Book **D: 300**
England (The Norman Conquest) **E: 305**
Harold II **H: 65**
Hastings, Battle of **H: 83**
London (The Middle Ages) **L: 439-440**
Middle Ages (Feudal government) **M: 524**
Norman Conquest **M: 455**
Privy Council **P: 808b**
Wales (Revolts against England) **W: 12**
William II [king of England] **W: 308**
England (Struggles for power) **E: 305**
William II [king of Netherlands]
William I **W: 308**
William III [king of England] **W: 308**
Boyne, Battle of the **B: 539**
England (The Restoration) **E: 309**; (War with France) **E: 309**
Furniture (The French influence spreads) **F: 575**
Glorious Revolution **G: 234**
Ireland (Religious persecution) **I: 426**
James II **J: 25**
Marlborough, Duke of **M: 215**
Mary II **M: 239**
Netherlands (Wars with England and France) **N: 149**
Northern Ireland (Protestant settlement) **N: 524**
Orange Order **O: 817**
Penn, William (Arrested again) **P: 242**
Pennsylvania (Colonial days) **P: 264**
Postal services (Postal service in the United States) **P: 706**
Williamsburg (Early days) **W: 312-313**
William III [king of Netherlands]
Wilhelmina **W: 306**
William IV [British king] **W: 309**
William, Prince [British prince] **W: 309** with portrait
Catherine, Duchess of Cambridge **C: 302**
Charles, Prince **C: 382**
Diana, Princess of Wales **D: 183**
Elizabeth II (The royal family) **E: 240**
William and Mary, College of W: 309
Law (Law education) **L: 138**
Universities and colleges (The oldest U.S. universities and colleges) **U: 210**
Virginia (Interesting facts) **V: 399**; (Schools) **V: 402**
Williamsburg (Early days) **W: 312**
William Frantz Elementary School [New Orleans]
Bridges, Ruby **B: 607**
William Henry Harrison Home [Vincennes]
Indiana (Places to visit) **I: 206**
William Howard Taft National Historic Site [Ohio]
National Park System (table: National historic sites) **N: 52-54**
William J. Clinton Foundation
Clinton, Bill (Later years) **Ci: 682g**
William Jefferson Clinton National Historic Site [Arkansas]
National Park System (table: National historic sites) **N: 52-54**
William Land Park
Sacramento (Education and cultural life) **S: 6**
William M. Jennings Trophy
Hockey (Professional leagues) **H: 278-279**
William of Ockham [English theologian] **W: 309**
William of Orange See William III (king of England) in this index

William of Rubruck [Flemish explorer]
  Exploration (Medieval European exploration)
    E: 442
William of Wied [German prince]
  Albania (Independence) A: 307
William of Wykeham [English religious leader]
  Winchester College W: 329
William Rufus See William II [king of England] *in this index*
William Shakespeare & the Globe [book by Aliki]
  Literature for children *picture on* L: 381
William Tell [opera by Rossini]
  Alphorn A: 384
  Opera (Grand opera) O: 798
  Rossini, Gioacchino Antonio R: 484
  Tell, William T: 129
William Tell [play by Schiller]
  Tell, William T: 129
William the Conqueror See William I, the Conqueror *in this index*
William the Silent See William I, Prince of Orange *in this index*
"William Wilson" [story by Poe]
  Poe, Edgar Allan (Fiction and theory of fiction)
    P: 590
Williams [banana]
  Banana B: 72
Williams, Abraham J. [American political leader]
  Missouri (table) M: 668
Williams, Arnold [American political leader]
  Idaho (table) I: 42
Williams, Benjamin [American political leader]
  North Carolina (table) N: 490
Williams, Benjamin F. [American businessman]
  Fairless, Benjamin Franklin F: 9
Williams, Bert [American comedian] W: 310
Williams, Betty [Irish social reformer]
  Nobel Prizes (Peace: 1976) N: 448b
Williams, Billy [American baseball player]
  Baseball (table: Hall of Fame) B: 134b
Williams, Charles [American businessman]
  Telephone (Early telephones) T: 100
Williams, Charles K. [American political leader]
  Vermont (table) V: 333
Williams, Daniel Hale [American doctor] W: 310
Williams, Danny [Canadian political leader]
  Newfoundland and Labrador (table) N: 375
Williams, Dick [American baseball manager]
  Baseball (table: Hall of Fame) B: 134b
Williams, Emlyn [Welsh dramatist] W: 310
Williams, Eric [Trinidad political leader]
  Trinidad and Tobago (History) T: 446
Williams, Fred [Australian painter]
  Australia (Painting) A: 905-906
Williams, G. Mennen [American government official]
  Michigan (table) M: 507; (The mid-1900's) M: 511
Williams, Garth [American artist]
  Literature for children *picture on* L: 363
Williams, George [British religious leader]
  Young Men's Christian Association (History)
    Y: 573
Williams, George H. [American government official]
  Grant, Ulysses S. (table) G: 316
  Justice, Department of (table) J: 203
Williams, Greville [British chemist]
  Rubber (The chemistry of rubber) R: 501
Williams, Hank [American musician] W: 310
  Country music (Emergence of the country music industry) Ci: 1098b-1098c *with picture*
Williams, James D. [American political leader]
  Indiana (table) I: 214
Williams, Jared W. [American political leader]
  New Hampshire (table) N: 223
Williams, Jesse [American farmer]
  Cheese (History) C: 394
Williams, Jody [American political activist]
  Nobel Prizes (Peace: 1997) N: 448b
Williams, John [American composer] W: 310
Williams, John Bell [American political leader]
  Mississippi (table) M: 640
Williams, John R. [American political leader]
  Arizona (table) A: 687
Williams, Joseph H. [American political leader]
  Maine (table) M: 87
Williams, R. L. [American political leader]
  Oklahoma (table) O: 730
Williams, Ralph Vaughan [British composer] See Vaughan Williams, Ralph *in this index*
Williams, Raymond [British cultural critic]
  Communication (Communication and culture)
    Ci: 888
Williams, Ricky [American football player]
  Football (table) F: 363
Williams, Robin [American actor] W: 310
  Motion picture (Best performance by an actor in

a supporting role: 1997) M: 862b
Williams, Roger [American colonial leader] W: 311
  Baptists (Baptists in America) B: 101
  Cotton, John Ci: 1094
  Providence P: 839; (Government and history)
    P: 840
  Rhode Island *picture on* R: 314; (Settlement)
    R: 312
Williams, Serena [American tennis player] W: 311
  Tennis (Tennis today) T: 166d-166f *with picture*
  Williams, Venus W: 312
Williams, Smokey Joe [American baseball player]
  Baseball (table: Hall of Fame) B: 134b
Williams, Sunita [American astronaut]
  Space exploration (Completing the station)
    So: 726
Williams, Ted [American baseball player] W: 311
  Baseball (table: Hall of Fame) B: 134b;
    (Depression and war) B: 136 *with picture*
Williams, Tennessee [American dramatist] W: 312
  American literature (Drama) A: 426
  Drama (Later United States drama) D: 340
Williams, Thomas Lanier [American dramatist] See Williams, Tennessee *in this index*
Williams, Venus [American tennis player] W: 312
  Tennis (Tennis today) T: 166d-166f *with picture*
  Williams, Serena W: 311
Williams, Vera B. [American author/illustrator]
  Regina Medal (table: 2008) R: 206
Williams, Walter [husband of]
  Evers-Williams, Myrlie E: 425
Williams, William [American patriot] W: 312
Williams, William Carlos [American poet] W: 312
  American literature (Modernist poetry) A: 421
  Poetry (Poetry of the 1900's) P: 597
Williams-Steiger Occupational Safety and Health Act [1970]
  Occupational Safety and Health Administration
    O: 648
Williamsburg [Virginia] W: 312 *with pictures*
  Colonial life in America *picture on* Ci: 811; (Places to visit) Ci: 801
Williamsburg Bridge
  New York City (Brooklyn) N: 326-328
Williamson, David [Australian playwright]
  Australia (Literature) A: 904-905
Williamson, Hugh [American political leader]
  W: 313
Williamson, Isaac H. [American political leader]
  New Jersey (table) N: 249
Williamson, Oliver E. [American economist]
  Nobel Prizes (Economics: 2009) N: 450
Williamson, William D. [American political leader]
  Maine (table) M: 87
Williamson's sapsucker [bird]
  Sapsucker S: 122
Willie-wagtail [bird]
  Bird (Birds of Australia and New Zealand) B: 346
    with picture
Willingdon, Marquess of [British colonial official]
  W: 314
Willis, Frank B. [American political leader]
  Ohio (table) O: 699
Willis, Vic [American baseball player]
  Baseball (table: Hall of Fame) B: 134b
Willis, William [American adventurer]
  Raft R: 102
Willis Tower [Chicago] W: 314
  Chicago (Places to visit) C: 430-431
  Skyscraper (table) S: 498 *with picture*
  United States *picture on* U: 117
Williston [North Dakota]
  North Dakota (table: Average monthly weather)
    N: 509
Williston Lake
  British Columbia (Rivers, waterfalls, and lakes)
    B: 624
Willitts house [Highland Park, Illinois]
  Wright, Frank Lloyd (Early career) W: 507
Willkie, Wendell Lewis [American political leader]
  W: 314 *with portrait*
  Roosevelt, Franklin Delano (Election of 1940)
    R: 456
Willow [tree] W: 314
  Osier O: 863
  Tree *pictures on* T: 424
  Wicker W: 298
Willow herb [plant] See Fireweed *in this index*
Willow ptarmigan [bird]
  Bird *picture on* B: 343
  Ptarmigan P: 853
Wills, Helen Newington [American tennis player]
  See Moody, Helen Wills *in this index*
Wills, William H. [American political leader]
  Vermont (table) V: 333
Wills, William John [British explorer]
  Australia *map on* A: 921; (Mapping the continent)

A: 922
  Exploration (Exploring Australia's interior) E: 448
    with map
Willson, T. L. [American chemist]
  Calcium carbide C: 21
Willstätter, Richard Martin [German chemist]
  Nobel Prizes (Chemistry: 1915) N: 443
Willy Wonka and the Chocolate Factory [film]
  Dahl, Roald D: 5
Willys, John North [American businessman]
  W: 315
Willys-Overland Company
  Willys, John North W: 315
Wilma Unlimited [book by Krull]
  Diaz, David D: 186
Wilmington [Delaware] W: 315
  Delaware D: 96 *with picture*; (Population) D: 100;
    (table: Average monthly weather) D: 104
  New Sweden N: 287
Wilmington, Earl of [British political leader]
  United Kingdom (table: British prime ministers)
    U: 72
Wilmington and Raleigh Railroad
  North Carolina (Transportation) N: 489
Wilmington Oil Field
  Long Beach (Economy) L: 447
Wilmot, David [American political leader]
  Wilmot Proviso W: 315
Wilmot Proviso [U.S. history] W: 315
  Lincoln, Abraham (Congressman) L: 316
Wilm's tumor [disease]
  Cancer (Cancer in children) C: 169
Wilmut, Ian [Scottish scientist]
  Biology (Current research and issues) B: 320-321
  Cloning (Successes) Ci: 683
  Genetic engineering (In agriculture) G: 84c
  Heredity (The era of genetic engineering) H: 209
Wilpattu National Park [Sri Lanka]
  National park (table) N: 42f
Wilshire Boulevard
  Los Angeles (Central Los Angeles) L: 460
Wilson, A. B. [American inventor]
  Sewing machine (History) S: 333-334
Wilson, Angus [British author] W: 315
Wilson, August [American playwright] W: 316
  African American literature (Recent developments) A: 136a
  Drama (Later United States drama) D: 340-341
    with picture
Wilson, Brian [American musician]
  Beach Boys B: 179 *with picture*
  Rock music (Independent producers) R: 379
Wilson, Cairine [Canadian political leader]
  Famous Five F: 26b
Wilson, Carl [American musician]
  Beach Boys B: 179 *with picture*
Wilson, Charles E. [American government official]
  Defense, Department of (table) D: 87
  Eisenhower, Dwight David (table) E: 152
Wilson, Charles Thomson Rees [British physicist]
  Nobel Prizes (Physics: 1927) N: 440
Wilson, David [American settler]
  Wovoka W: 502
Wilson, Dennis [American musician]
  Beach Boys B: 179 *with picture*
Wilson, Edith Bolling [wife of Woodrow Wilson]
  W: 316 *with portrait*
  First ladies of the United States F: 143
  Wilson, Woodrow (Remarriage) W: 324 *with picture*
Wilson, Edmund [American author] W: 316
  American literature (Essays) A: 426
  Uncle Tom's Cabin U: 20
Wilson, Edward Osborne [American biologist]
  W: 316
Wilson, Ellen Axson [wife of Woodrow Wilson]
  First ladies of the United States F: 142
  Wilson, Woodrow (Wilson's family) W: 320 *with picture*
Wilson, Emanuel W. [American political leader]
  West Virginia (table) W: 225
Wilson, Ethel [Canadian author] W: 317
  Canadian literature (Modern English-Canadian fiction) C: 160
Wilson, George A. [American political leader]
  Iowa (table) I: 391
Wilson, Hack [American baseball player]
  Baseball (table: Hall of Fame) B: 134b; (table: Modern major league records) B: 138
Wilson, Harold [British political leader] W: 317
  Labour Party (History) L: 16
  United Kingdom (Economic recovery—and collapse) U: 72-73
Wilson, Harriet E. [American author]
  African American literature (The 1800's) A: 136a
Wilson, Henry [American political leader] W: 317
  Grant, Ulysses S. (Election of 1872) G: 316-317

Vice president of the United States V: 348 *with portrait*
Wilson, Hugh J. [British aviator]
Aviation (table: Aviation speed records) A: 990
Wilson, Jack [American Indian religious leader] *See* Wovoka *in this index*
Wilson, James [American government official]
Agriculture, Department of (table) A: 161
McKinley, William (table) M: 342
Roosevelt, Theodore (table) R: 466
Taft, William Howard (table) T: 11
Wilson, James [American journalist]
Wilson, Woodrow (Childhood) W: 319
Wilson, James [American patriot] W: 317
Wilson, James H. [American general]
Alabama (The Civil War and Reconstruction) A: 276
Wilson, James Harold [British political leader] *See* Wilson, Harold *in this index*
Wilson, John Anthony Burgess [British author] *See* Burgess, Anthony *in this index*
Wilson, John Lyman [American settler]
Saint Cloud S: 32
Wilson, Jud [American baseball player]
Baseball (table: Hall of Fame) B: 134b
Wilson, Kenneth Geddes [American physicist]
Nobel Prizes (Physics: 1982) N: 442
Wilson, Lanford [American dramatist] W: 317
Drama (Later United States drama) D: 340
Wilson, Lord [British political leader] *See* Wilson, Harold *in this index*
Wilson, Malcolm [American political leader]
New York (table) N: 313
Wilson, Margaret [daughter of Woodrow Wilson]
White House hostesses W: 291
Wilson, Pete [American political leader]
California (table) C: 59
Feinstein, Dianne F: 68
Wilson, R. Kenneth [British physician]
Loch Ness monster L: 410
Wilson, Robert [American playwright]
Glass, Philip G: 224
Wilson, Robert Woodrow [American physicist]
Astronomy (Advances in astrophysics) A: 848
Big bang B: 297
Cosmic microwave background (CMB) radiation Ci: 1075
Nobel Prizes (Physics: 1978) N: 441
Telescope (Microwave telescopes) T: 108
Wilson, S. Clay [American cartoonist]
Comics (Comic books) Ci: 869-870
Wilson, Samuel [American businessman]
New York (Interesting facts) N: 291
Uncle Sam U: 19
Wilson, Stanley C. [American political leader]
Vermont (table) V: 333
Wilson, Teddy [American pianist]
Jazz (The swing era) J: 71
Wilson, William Bauchop [American government official]
Labor, Department of (table) L: 2
Wilson, Woodrow (table) W: 323
Wilson, William L. [American government official]
Cleveland, Grover (table) Ci: 672
West Virginia (Interesting facts) W: 207
Wilson, Woodrow [U.S. president] W: 318 *with pictures*
Congress of the United States (Continued struggle for power) Ci: 948
Democracy (Famous quotations about democracy) D: 120
Democratic Party D: 124; (Wilsonian democracy) D: 125
Fourteen Points F: 437
Haiti (History) H: 15-16
Harding, Warren Gamaliel H: 56
Immigration (The third wave) I: 82
League of Nations L: 159
Marshall, Thomas Riley M: 230
Mexico (The Revolution of 1910) M: 472
Monroe Doctrine (The Roosevelt Corollary) M: 739-740
New Jersey (table) N: 249; (The early 1900's) N: 253
President of the United States (The rebirth of presidential leadership) P: 768-769
United States, History of the (Taft and Wilson) U: 187; (The United States in the war) U: 188
Versailles, Treaty of V: 339
Villa, Pancho V: 384
Wilson, Edith Bolling W: 316
World War I (The United States enters the war) W: 462; (The peace settlement) W: 465
Wilson cloud chamber [physics]
Particle detector (Cloud chambers) P: 186
Wilson cycle [geology]
Earth (The shaping of the continents) E: 24

Wilson Dam [Tennessee River, Alabama]
Muscle Shoals M: 936
Tennessee River T: 158
Tennessee Valley Authority (History) T: 160
Wilson-Gorman Bill [1894]
Cleveland, Grover (Tariff defeat) Ci: 673
Wilson's bird-of-paradise
Bird-of-paradise B: 374
Wilson's Creek [Missouri]
Missouri (The American Civil War) M: 671
Wilson's Creek National Battlefield [Missouri]
National Park System (table: National battlefields) N: 55
Wilson's plover [bird]
Bird (Birds of the seacoasts) B: 342 *with picture*
Plover P: 574
Wilson's snipe [bird]
Snipe S: 538
Wilson's storm-petrel [bird]
Bird (Birds of the ocean and the Antarctic) B: 344 *with picture*
Wilt [plant disease] W: 328
Alfalfa (Diseases and pests) A: 347
Cotton (Diseases) Ci: 1090
Pea (Diseases and pests) P: 205
Tomato (Growing, harvesting, and processing) T: 325
Watermelon W: 146
Wilton [rug]
Rugs and carpets (Weaving) R: 515
Wiltz, Louis A. [American political leader]
Louisiana (table) L: 496
WiMAX [communications]
Wireless communication (Wireless networking) W: 345
Wimbledon [England]
London (Recreation) L: 434
Tennis (Tennis tournaments) T: 165; (Beginnings) T: 165; (table) T: 166b
WIMP [physics]
Dark matter D: 37
WIMP annihilation [physics]
Dark matter D: 37
Wimple [garment]
Clothing *picture on* Ci: 701
Wimsey, Lord Peter [literary figure]
Sayers, Dorothy L. S: 168
Winans, Edwin B. [American political leader]
Michigan (table) M: 507
Winant, John Gilbert [American political leader]
New Hampshire (table) N: 223
Winch [machine]
Crane Ci: 1119 *with picture*
Winchell, Walter [American journalist] W: 328
Winchester [England] W: 328
Winchester, James [American general]
Memphis (History) M: 396
Winchester College [British secondary school] W: 328
Winchester manuscript
Malory, Sir Thomas M: 112
Winckelmann, Johann Joachim [German scholar] W: 329
Wind [tile]
Mah-jongg M: 64 *with picture*
Wind [weather] W: 329 *with diagram*
See also the list of Related articles in the Wind *article*
Air *picture on* A: 169; (Air movement) A: 171 *with picture*
Antarctica (Climate) A: 534
Chinook C: 512
Climate (Atmospheric circulation) Ci: 676a
Cyclone Ci: 1203
Derecho D: 152
Energy supply (Wind power) E: 279
Foehn F: 313
Harmattan H: 61
Heat index H: 156
Hurricane H: 452 *with diagram*
Jupiter (Zones and belts) J: 199
Mars (Wind) M: 226b
Nuclear weapon (Blast wave) N: 599
Ocean (How the ocean moves) O: 658
Pacific Ocean (Climate) P: 14
Plant (Sexual reproduction) P: 532-533 *with picture*
Seiche S: 287
Tornado (Winds) T: 334 *with diagram*
Weather (table: Weather terms) W: 157; (Planetary-scale systems) W: 158; (Synoptic-scale systems) W: 159-161
Weather vane W: 172
Wind chill W: 331
Wind power W: 331
Wind shear W: 332
Wind and Current Charts

Maury, Matthew Fontaine M: 318
Wind Cave National Park [South Dakota] W: 331
National Park System (table: National parks) N: 49
Wind chest [musical instrument]
Organ (Pipe organs) O: 851-852
Wind chill [weather] W: 331
Weather (Reporting the weather) W: 166
Wind ensemble [music]
Band (Wind ensembles) B: 75
Wind erosion
Dust storm D: 392
Earth *picture on* E: 23
Wind farm
Environmental pollution (Scientific efforts) E: 336
Spain *picture on* So: 740
Wind gap [geology]
Appalachian Mountains (Physical features) A: 568
Gap G: 28
Wind in the Door, A [book by L'Engle]
L'Engle, Madeleine L: 191
Wind in the Willows, The [book by Grahame]
Grahame, Kenneth G: 301
Wind instrument
Classical music (Instrumental music) Ci: 643
Music (Wind instruments) M: 949 *with pictures*
Wind power W: 331 *with picture*
See also Windmill *in this index*
Wind-profiling radar
Radar (In weather observation and forecasting) R: 67
Wind River Canyon [Thermopolis]
Wyoming (Places to visit) W: 524
Wind River Indian Reservation
Wyoming *picture on* W: 534
Wind River Range [mountains]
Wyoming (Land regions) W: 526
Wind shear [weather] W: 332
Hurricane (How a hurricane forms) H: 453
Tornado (Winds) T: 334
Wind tunnel [machine] W: 333
Aerodynamics (Wind-tunnel testing) A: 88
Airplane *picture on* A: 227; (Design and testing) A: 228
Airplane, Model A: 240
Automobile *picture on* A: 958
Ohio *picture on* O: 701
Streamlining So: 924
Wind turbine [machine]
Electric power (Other sources of electric power) E: 184
Global warming (Alternative energy sources) G: 232b
Turbine (Wind turbines) T: 498 *with picture*
Wind power (Devices that use wind power) W: 331-332
Windmill W: 333
Wind vane *See* Weather vane *in this index*
Windaus, Adolf Otto [German chemist]
Nobel Prizes (Chemistry: 1928) N: 443
Windbreak [structure] W: 333
Indian, American (Shelter) I: 136d-141
Winder, Levin [American political leader]
Maryland (table) M: 255
Windermere [lake, England] W: 333
Windflower *See* Anemone *in this index*
Windhoek [Namibia] W: 333
Namibia N: 7 *with picture*
Windhover [bird]
Kestrel K: 307
Winding
Ignition (Parts of an ignition system) I: 49
Windjammer Days
Maine *picture on* M: 79
Windlass [machine] W: 333
Machine (Wheel and axle) M: 14
Windmill W: 333 *with picture*
Battery *picture on* B: 166
Electric power (Other sources of electric power) E: 184
Netherlands *picture on* N: 147
Turbine (Wind turbines) T: 498 *with picture*; (History) T: 498 *with pictures*
Wind power (Devices that use wind power) W: 331-332
Windmill Island [park]
Holland H: 292
Michigan (Places to visit) M: 498 *with picture*
Windom, William [American government official]
Garfield, James Abram (table) G: 42
Harrison, Benjamin (table) H: 72
Window W: 334
Glass *picture on* G: 211; (Early American glass) G: 222
House (Building materials) H: 380; (Interior construction) H: 382 *with diagram*
Light (Light and energy efficiency) L: 291-292
Pioneer life in America (A pioneer settlement)

P: 479-481
Stained glass So: 821 *with pictures*
Window [computing]
Computer (Input devices) Ci: 912-914
Printing (Page makeup) P: 797-798
Window air conditioner
Air conditioning (Kinds of air conditioners) A: 179
Window display
Advertising (Other ways of advertising) A: 75
Windows [computer software]
Gates, Bill G: 67
Microsoft Corporation M: 520
Windpipe [anatomy] *See* Trachea *in this index*
Windrow [agriculture]
Hay H: 115
Rake R: 130
Winds, Cave of the
Niagara Falls (Description) N: 391-392
Winds of War, The [book by Wouk]
Wouk, Herman W: 502
Windscale plutonium plant [England]
Fallout (History) F: 19
Windsor [British history] W: 334
Windsor [Ontario] W: 334
Windsor, Duchess of [British public figure] *See*
Simpson, Wallis Warfield *in this index*
Windsor, Duke of [British public figure] *See* Edward
VIII *in this index*
Windsor bean [plant] *See* Broad bean *in this index*
Windsor Castle [England] W: 335 *with picture*
Windsurfing [sport] W: 335 *with picture*
Windward Islands [islands, Caribbean] W: 336
Saint George's S: 34
Windward Maroons [people]
Maroons M: 217
Windward side
Climate (The role of topography) Ci: 676a
Windy City [name for]
Chicago (A city reborn) C: 435
Wine W: 336 *with pictures*
Alcoholic beverage (Wine) A: 336; (History)
A: 337
Antiseptic (History) A: 559
Australia (Food and drink) A: 902-903
California *picture on* C: 56
Champagne C: 373
France *picture on* F: 470; (Agriculture) F: 469
Grape G: 318
Invention (Ancient Greece) I: 359
Portugal (Way of life) P: 687
Tartaric acid T: 48
Yeast (How yeast is used) Y: 554-555
Wine thief [tool]
Wine *picture on* W: 337
"Wine, Women, and Song" [music by Strauss]
Strauss, Johann, Jr. So: 922
Wineland *See* Vinland *in this index*
Winesap
Apple (table) A: 571 *with picture*
Winesburg, Ohio [stories by Anderson]
Anderson, Sherwood A: 452
Winfield, Dave [American baseball player]
Baseball (table: Hall of Fame) B: 134b
Winfrey, Oprah [American entertainer] W: 338
with portrait
African Americans *picture on* A: 136p
Winfrid [English-born religious leader] *See*
Boniface, Saint *in this index*
Wing [device]
Aerodynamics (Lift) A: 85 *with diagrams*;
(Applying aerodynamic principles) A: 88
Airplane *picture on* A: 218; (The wing) A: 213
with pictures; (Principles of flight) A: 220 *with
diagrams*
Daedalus D: 3
Glider (The wings) G: 228 *with pictures*
Helicopter (Lift) H: 171 *with diagram*
Wing [military unit]
Air force (The organization of air forces) A: 183
Air Force, United States (Combat commands)
A: 193
Wing [theater]
Theater (The stage) T: 233-234
Wing [zoology]
Animal (Wings) A: 488 *with picture*
Bat B: 158 *with pictures*
Bee (Wings) B: 201 *with pictures*
Bird (In the air) B: 352 *with diagrams*
Butterfly (The thorax) B: 738 *with pictures*
Fly (Thorax) F: 309 *with diagram*
Insect (Wings) I: 288
Wing walker [acrobat]
Airplane (The golden age) A: 235
Wingate, Orde Charles [British general]
Wingate's Raiders W: 339
Wingate's Raiders [World War II commandos]
W: 339

Winged lion [ancient sculpture]
Assyria *picture on* A: 821
Winged Victory [sculpture] W: 339
Hellenistic Age H: 177
Wingfield, Walter Clopton [British sportsman]
Tennis (Beginnings) T: 165
Wings [band]
McCartney, Paul M: 332c
Wings [film]
Motion picture (Best picture: 1927-28) M: 861
Wings of the Dove, The [book by James]
James, Henry (His works) J: 26
Winkel, Dietrich [Dutch inventor]
Metronome M: 441
Winkelried, Arnold von [legendary figure] W: 339
Winkle, Rip van [literary character] *See* Rip Van
Winkle *in this index*
Winkler, Clemens [German chemist]
Germanium G: 143
Winnebago, Lake *See* Lake Winnebago *in this index*
Winnebago Indians W: 339
See also Ho-Chunk Indians *in this index*
Indian, American (Indians of the Northeast)
I: 154-155
Nebraska (Early days) N: 111
Winnemucca, Sarah [American social reformer]
W: 339
Winnie Mae [airplane]
Post, Wiley W: 698
Winnie-the-Pooh [book by Milne]
Literature for children *picture on* L: 363
Milne, A. A. M: 556
Shepard, Ernest Howard S: 395
Winning of the West, The [book by Roosevelt]
Western frontier life in America (Literature)
W: 239
Winnipeg [Manitoba] W: 339 *with picture and map*
Manitoba M: 144 *with picture, pictures on* M: 145,
M: 148; (Visitor's guide) M: 152 *with picture*;
(table: Average monthly weather) M: 156;
(Other developments) M: 163
Winnipeg, Lake *See* Lake Winnipeg *in this index*
Winnipeg Art Gallery
Winnipeg *picture on* W: 340
Winnipeg Blue Bombers [team]
Football (Canadian Football League) F: 364
Winnipeg Commodity Exchange
Winnipeg (Economy) W: 340
Winnipeg Jets [team]
Hockey (table: National Hockey League) H: 281
Winnipeg River [river, Manitoba-Ontario] W: 342
Winnipegosis, Lake [Manitoba]
Lake Winnipegosis L: 48
Manitoba (Rivers and lakes) M: 154
Winnipesaukee, Lake
New Hampshire (Rivers and lakes) N: 220-221
Winnipesaukee River
New Hampshire (Rivers and lakes) N: 220 *with
map*
Winnowing [agriculture]
Threshing machine T: 270
Wheat (The mechanization of wheat farming)
W: 276
Winogrand, Garry [American photographer]
Photography (A diversity of styles) P: 426
Winslet, Kate [British actress]
Motion picture (Best performance by an actress:
2008) M: 862a
Winslow, Edward [American colonial leader]
W: 342
Cattle (American cattle) C: 315
White, Peregrine W: 284
Winslow, Edward [American physicist]
Betelgeuse B: 274
Winslow, Helen Maria [poet]
August A: 887
Winslow, John A. [Union military leader]
Alabama A: 255
Winslow, Warren [American political leader]
North Carolina (table) N: 490
Winsor, Frederick Albert [German businessman]
Gas [fuel] (First uses of manufactured gas) G: 57
Winston [former city]
Winston-Salem W: 342
Winston, John Anthony [American political
leader]
Alabama (table) A: 274
Winston Churchill Memorial and Library [Fulton,
Missouri (Places to visit) M: 660
Winston Cup [race] *See* Sprint Cup *in this index*
Winston-Salem [North Carolina] W: 342
Winston-Salem State University
North Carolina, University of N: 495
Winter [season] W: 342
Season (The four seasons) S: 270 *with diagram*
Winter, Nuclear *See* Nuclear winter *in this index*
Winter, William F. [American political leader]

Mississippi (table) M: 640
Winter barley [plant]
Barley (Cultivation) B: 112
Winter bud
Leaf (A leaf begins its life) L: 152 *with picture*
Winter cress [plant]
Cress Ci: 1127
Winter depression [disorder]
Seasonal affective disorder S: 272
Winter flounder [fish]
Fish *picture on* F: 153
Flounder F: 267
Winter Games of the Cheyenne [painting by West]
Indian, American *picture on* I: 142
Winter melon
Casaba C: 270
Winter oats
Oats (Growing oats) O: 640
Winter Palace
Russia (The October Revolution) R: 553
Russian Revolution of 1917 (The 1905
Revolution) R: 566; (The October Revolution)
R: 566
Saint Petersburg [Russia] (The city) S: 54 *with
picture*
Winter Poems Along the Rio Grande [book by
Baca]
American literature (Diverse voices) A: 424
Winter resident [biology]
Bird (The distribution of birds) B: 331-332
Winter sleep *See* Hibernation *in this index*
Winter solstice [astronomy]
Season (The four seasons) S: 270-271
Winter sports
Biathlon B: 278
Bobsledding B: 433 *with picture*
Curling Ci: 1195 *with picture*
Hockey H: 274
Ice skating I: 10 *with pictures*
Iceboating I: 18 *with pictures*
Safety (Safety in recreation) S: 12 *with picture*
Skiing S: 482 *with pictures*
Snowboarding S: 541 *with picture*
Snowmobiling S: 541 *with picture*
Tobogganing T: 308
Winter War [1939-1940]
Finland (World War II) F: 117 *with picture*
Russo-Finnish wars (The Winter War) R: 566a
World War II (The invasion of the Soviet Union)
W: 477
Winter wheat [plant]
Wheat (Winter wheats and spring wheats) W: 268
with pictures; (Climate conditions) W: 270
Winter wren [bird]
Wren *picture on* W: 503; W: 504
Winterbloom *See* Witch hazel *in this index*
Wintergreen [plant] W: 342
Winterhoff, Hermann [American inventor]
Vibraphone V: 347
Winterlude [festival]
Ottawa (Annual events) O: 873
Winternationals [race]
Automobile racing (Drag racing) A: 978
Winters, Shelley [American actress]
Motion picture (Best performance by an actress
in a supporting role: 1959, 1965) M: 862b
Winter's Tale, The [play by Shakespeare]
Shakespeare, William: (*The Winter's Tale*) S: 365
Theater *pictures on* T: 236-241
Winterset [play by Anderson]
Anderson, Maxwell A: 452
Winterson, Jeanette [British author]
Novel (The novel today) N: 575
Winterthur Museum & Country Estate [Delaware]
Colonial life in America (Places to visit) Ci: 801
Delaware (Places to visit) D: 102 *with picture*
Winthrop, John [American colonial leader] W: 342
Boston (Early settlement) B: 503
Dudley, Thomas D: 377
Endecott, John E: 271
Massachusetts (Massachusetts Bay Colony)
M: 289
Massachusetts Bay Colony M: 295
Winthrop, John, Jr. [American colonial leader]
W: 343
Connecticut (Expanding the colony) Ci: 968
Wintun Indians W: 343
Wipe [television]
Television (Adding special effects) T: 112
Wire [communications] *See* Telegram *in this index*
Wire [hardware] W: 343 *with diagrams*
Aluminum (Drawing) A: 396
Cable C: 4
Copper Ci: 1041; (Copper wire) Ci: 1043-1044
Diamond (Industrial uses) D: 182-183
Electricity (Conductors and insulators) E: 193
House (Electrical wiring) H: 382

Wire-command system
Guided missile *picture on* G: 425; (Command guidance) G: 426
Wire-EDM [manufacturing]
Machine tool (Electrical discharge machining [EDM]) M: 19
Wire fox terrier [dog] W: 344 *with picture*
Dog *picture on* D: 272
Wire gauge
Wire (Sizes of wire) W: 344
Wire rope
Rope (Wire rope) R: 473 *with picture*
Wire service
Journalism (News services) J: 171
Wire welding
Welding (Arc welding) W: 189
Wiregrass area
Alabama (Land regions) A: 268
Wirehair cat
Cat (Short-haired breeds) C: 290
Wirehaired pointing griffon [dog] W: 344 *with picture*
Wireless
Radio (Early development) R: 91-92
Wireless communication W: 344
Internet (Hardware) I: 350c
Wireless fidelity [communications] *See* Wi-Fi *in this index*
Wireless network interface card [device]
Computer (A modem or a network interface card) Ci: 915
Wireless telegraph
Communication (The development of electronics) Ci: 883 *with picture*
Marconi, Guglielmo M: 196
Wireless Telegraph and Signal Company
Marconi, Guglielmo (Early life) M: 197
Wirephoto [machine]
Fax machine (History) F: 58
Wiretapping W: 345
Patriot Act P: 197
Terrorism (Intelligence efforts) T: 177
Wireworm
Beetle (Click beetles) B: 217
Click beetle Ci: 674
Wiring *See* Wire *in this index*
Wirt, William [American political leader]
Adams, John Quincy (table) A: 43
Anti-Masonic Party A: 556
Justice, Department of J: 203
Wirt, William Albert [American educator]
Indiana (Schools) I: 200-201
Wirtz, William Willard [American government official]
Johnson, Lyndon Baines (table) J: 151
Kennedy, John Fitzgerald (table) K: 266
Labor, Department of (table) L: 2
Wirz, Henry [Confederate officer]
Civil War, American (Prisons) Ci: 630-631
Wisconsin W: 346 *with pictures and maps*
See also the list of Related articles in the Wisconsin *article*
Wisconsin [ship]
Battleship (The modern battleship) B: 172
Wisconsin, University of W: 369 *with picture*
Wisconsin *picture on* W: 350; (University expansion) W: 368
Wisconsin Dells [region]
Dalles *picture on* D: 16
Wisconsin (Places to visit) W: 356 *with picture*
Wisconsin ice age [geology]
Ice age (Evidence of ice ages and their climates) I: 6-7
Wisconsin Idea [U.S. history]
Wisconsin (The Progressive Era) W: 366
Wisconsin, University of (History) W: 369
Wisconsin River [river, Wisconsin] W: 370
Wisconsin State Universities
Wisconsin, University of (History) W: 369
Wisconsin Territory [U.S. history]
Wisconsin (Territorial days) W: 366
Wisdom [philosophy]
Ethics (Plato) E: 366
Philosophy P: 383
Wisdom books [Bible]
Bible (table) B: 281; (The Writings) B: 281-282
Old Testament (Contents) O: 741
Wisdom of Jesus the Son of Sirach [book] *See* Ecclesiasticus *in this index*
Wisdom of Solomon [Bible]
Bible (Development of the Christian Old Testament) B: 282
Wisdom tooth
Dentistry (Oral surgery) D: 144
Teeth (Permanent teeth) T: 79-80 *with picture*
Wise, Bob [American political leader]
West Virginia (table) W: 225

Wise, Henry A. [American political leader]
Virginia (table) V: 417
Wise, Isaac Mayer [American religious leader] W: 370
Wise, John [American religious leader] W: 370
Congregationalists Ci: 941
Wise, Robert [American director]
Motion picture (Best achievement in directing: 1961, 1965) M: 862
Wise, Stephen Samuel [American religious leader] W: 370
Wise Blood [book by O'Connor]
American literature (Southern fiction) A: 424-425
O'Connor, Flannery O: 668
Wise Men *See* Magi *in this index*
Wisecraft [religion]
Witchcraft W: 371
Wisent [animal]
Belarus (Land) B: 224b *with picture*
Buffalo (Protection of bison) B: 675
Wishart, George [Scottish religious leader]
Knox, John (Early years) K: 358
Wisner, Moses [American political leader]
Michigan (table) M: 507
Wisniewski, David [American author]
Caldecott Medal (table: 1997) C: 26
Wistar, Caspar [American businessman]
Glass (Types of art glass) G: 220-221; (Early American glass) G: 222
Wistar glass
Glass (Types of art glass) G: 220-221 *with picture*
Wister, Owen [American author]
American literature (Popular forms) A: 422
Western frontier life in America (Literature) W: 239
Wisteria [botany] W: 370 *with picture*
Plant *picture on* P: 530
Wit
Humor (The types of humor) H: 435
Witch *See* Witchcraft *in this index*
Witch Diggers, The [book by West]
West, Jessamyn W: 198
Witch doctor
Magic (The magician) M: 49
Witch hazel [shrub] W: 371 *with picture*
Witch House [Salem, Massachusetts]
Colonial life in America (Places to visit) Ci: 801
Witch hunt [religious history]
Salem witchcraft trials S: 61
Witchcraft (History) W: 372
"Witch of Coos, The" [poem by Frost]
Frost, Robert (His poems) F: 543
Witchcraft W: 371 *with pictures*
Colonial life in America (Religion) Ci: 804-805
Halloween (Halloween symbols) H: 24b
Salem (History) S: 61
Salem witchcraft trials S: 61
Shakespeare, William *picture on* S: 351
Superstition (Kinds of superstitions) So: 995
Witchcraft Today [book by Gardner]
Witchcraft (Witchcraft in modern times) W: 373
Witches' Sabbath [folklore]
Witchcraft *picture on* W: 373
With Fire and Sword [book by Sienkiewicz]
Sienkiewicz, Henryk S: 450
Withdrawal [birth control]
Birth control (Methods of birth control) B: 378-379
Withdrawal [physiology]
Alcoholism A: 337
Delirium tremens D: 116
Methamphetamine M: 434
Opium O: 811
Withdrawal illness
Benzodiazepine B: 255
Drug abuse D: 361
Mental illness (Substance use disorders) M: 406
Withering, William [British doctor]
Digitalis D: 203
Withering rack
Tea (Processing tea) T: 62
Witherite [mineral]
Barium B: 110
Withers [zoology]
Horse (Size) H: 348
Witherspoon, John [American patriot] W: 373
Witherspoon, Reese [American actress]
Motion picture (Best performance by an actress: 2005) M: 862a
Withholding tax
Income tax (Paying the individual income tax) I: 104
Internal Revenue Service I: 337
Within a Budding Grove [book by Proust]
Proust, Marcel P: 838
Withycombe, James [American political leader]
Oregon (table) O: 845

Witless Bay [Newfoundland and Labrador]
Newfoundland and Labrador (Places to visit) N: 368 *with picture*
Witness [law] W: 374
Deposition D: 149
Witness for the Prosecution [play by Christie]
Christie, Dame Agatha C: 527
Witoto Indians
Indian, American (Why the Indians fought) I: 144-145; (Before European contact) I: 175-176
Witt, Gustav [German astronomer]
Eros E: 355
Witt, Katarina [German skater]
Olympic Games (Charges of steroid use) O: 753
Wittaker, Robert [American ecologist]
Botany (Later developments) B: 509
Wittelsbach [German history]
Munich (History) M: 927
Wittenmyer, Annie [American social reformer]
Woman's Christian Temperance Union W: 382
Wittgenstein, Carolyne von Sayn [German princess]
Liszt, Franz (His life) L: 349-350
Wittgenstein, Ludwig [Austrian philosopher] W: 374
Philosophy (Philosophy in the 1900's) P: 390
Wittig, Georg [German chemist]
Nobel Prizes (Chemistry: 1979) N: 444
Wittig, Monique [French author]
French literature (The middle and late 1900's) F: 523
Witwatersrand [region, South Africa]
Gold (World gold production) G: 253
South Africa (The Plateau) So: 614 *with map*
Transvaal T: 402
Wizard
Witchcraft W: 371
Wizard Island [island, Oregon]
Crater Lake Ci: 1122
Wizard of Menlo Park
Edison, Thomas Alva (The Wizard of Menlo Park) E: 78
Wizard of Oz, The [book by Baum] *See* Wonderful Wizard of Oz, The *in this index*
Wizard of Oz, The [film] W: 374
Garland, Judy G: 43 *with picture*
Motion picture *picture on* M: 846
Wizards, Washington [team]
Basketball (table) B: 150
WLS [radio station]
Country music (Early commercial success) Ci: 1098b
WMO [UN] *See* World Meteorological Organization *in this index*
Wobblies *See* Industrial Workers of the World *in this index*
WOCE [experiment] *See* World Ocean Circulation Experiment *in this index*
Wodehouse, P. G. [British author] W: 374
Kern, Jerome K: 305
Woden [Norse god] *See* Odin *in this index*
Woe from Wit [play by Griboyedov]
Russian literature (Early Romanticism) R: 560-561
Woese, Carl R. [American biologist]
Domain D: 300
Woetzel, Kathrin [German pilot]
Glider (table) G: 230
Wohelo Award
Camp Fire USA (Small group programs) C: 88-89
Wöhler, Friedrich [German chemist] W: 374
Aluminum (The first aluminum) A: 397
Beryllium B: 273
Chemistry *picture on* C: 402; (Development of organic chemistry) C: 404
Urea U: 221
Wojciechowska, Maia [American author]
Newbery Medal (table) N: 359
Wojtyła, Karol Jozef [Polish clergyman] *See* John Paul II *in this index*
Wok [utensil]
Cooking (Sautéing) Ci: 1028
Wolastoqiyik Indians *See* Maliseet Indians *in this index*
Wolcott, Oliver [American patriot] W: 375
Connecticut (table) Ci: 967
Wolcott, Oliver, Jr. [American political leader]
Adams, John (table) A: 38
Connecticut (table) Ci: 967
Wolcott, Roger [American political leader]
Massachusetts (table) M: 288
Wolesi Jirga [assembly]
Afghanistan (Government) A: 92-92a
Wolf [animal] W: 375 *with pictures*
Dominance *picture on* D: 301
Ecology (Ecosystems) E: 54-55
Endangered species (table) E: 270
Moose (The life of a moose) M: 798

Mowat, Farley **M:** 903
National park (Management of fire and wildlife) *picture on* **N:** 42j
Skull **S:** 495 *with picture*
Wolf [rank]
Boy Scouts (Cub Scouting) **B:** 535
Wolf, Christa [German author]
Novel (The novel today) **N:** 575
Wolf, Friedrich August [German scholar]
Homer (Analysts and unitarians) **H:** 304
Wolf, George [American political leader]
Pennsylvania (table) **P:** 263
Wolf, Max [German astronomer]
Asteroid (History of study) **A:** 824b
Wolf, Tasmanian *See* Tasmanian tiger *in this index*
Wolf fish *See* Wolffish *in this index*
Wolf in Sheep's clothing [expression]
Aesop's fables **A:** 90
Wolf pack
Wolf *picture on* **W:** 376; (The life of a wolf) **W:** 375
Wolf spider
Animal *picture on* **A:** 475
Spider *pictures on* **So:** 783, **So:** 789; (Eggs) **So:** 787 *with picture*; (Wolf spiders) **So:** 790
Wolf teeth
Horse (Teeth) **H:** 350
Wolf Trap Farm Park [Virginia]
National Park System (Areas preserved for recreational use) **N:** 46; (table: National parkways and other national parklands) **N:** 56
Wolfe, James [British general] **W:** 377 *with picture*
French and Indian wars (The French and Indian War) **F:** 512-513
Quebec (The 1700's) **Q:** 36
Quebec, Battle of **Q:** 37
Wolfe, Nero [literary figure]
Detective story (The pattern) **D:** 162
Stout, Rex **So:** 916
Wolfe, Reginald [London printer]
Holinshed's Chronicles **H:** 292
Wolfe, Thomas [American author] **W:** 377
American literature (Realist fiction) **A:** 422
Asheville **A:** 768
Wolfe, Tom [American writer] **W:** 378
American literature (Essays) **A:** 426
Wolff, Alfred R. [American engineer]
Air conditioning (History) **A:** 180
Wolff, Caspar Friedrich [German biologist]
Heredity (Early ideas about heredity) **H:** 208
Wolffish [fish] **W:** 378 *with picture*
Fish *picture on* **F:** 153
Wolfgang, Lake [Austria]
Austria *picture on* **A:** 932
Wolfhound [dog] **W:** 378
Dog *pictures on* **D:** 265, **W:** 270
Wolfmonth
January **J:** 30
Wolfram [element] *See* Tungsten *in this index*
Wolfram von Eschenbach [German poet] **W:** 378
German literature (The romance) **G:** 138
Holy Grail **H:** 299
Wolframite [mineral] **W:** 378
Tungsten **T:** 487
Wolfskill, William [American explorer]
Nevada (Exploration) **N:** 173
Wolfson, Louis E. [American financier]
Fortas, Abe **F:** 419
Wolfson Family Foundation
Fortas, Abe **F:** 419
Wollaston, William H. [British chemist]
Palladium **P:** 108
Rhodium **R:** 318
Wolle, Francis [American inventor]
Paper bag **P:** 138
Wollman, Harvey L. [American political leader]
South Dakota (table) **So:** 680
Wollongong [Australia] **W:** 378
Wollstonecraft, Mary [British author] **W:** 379 *with portrait*
Feminism **F:** 69
Godwin, William **G:** 246
Women's movement (Forces of change) **W:** 384
Wolof [people]
Gambia (People) **G:** 18
Senegal (People) **S:** 297
Wologizi Mountains
Liberia (Land and climate) **L:** 230
Wolong National Nature Reserve [China]
National park *picture on* **N:** 42g; (table) **N:** 42f; (Other interesting national parks) **N:** 42h
Wolseley, Garnet Joseph [British general]
Lee, Robert E. (Last years) **L:** 179
Red River Rebellion (End of the conflict) **R:** 189
Wolsey, Thomas [English statesman] **W:** 379 *with portrait*
Cromwell, Thomas **Ci:** 1152
England (The English Reformation) **E:** 307

Henry VIII [of England] **H:** 188
Wolszczan, Alexander [American astronomer]
Planet (The first discoveries) **P:** 513
Pulsar **P:** 900a
Wolverine [animal] **W:** 379 *with picture*
Wolverine State [name for]
Michigan **M:** 489
Wolverstone, Charles [English colonist]
Bridgetown **B:** 607
Woman *See* Female; Human being; Women *in this index*
Woman, I [painting by De Kooning]
De Kooning, Willem **D:** 95
Painting (Abstract Expressionism) **P:** 84 *with picture*
Woman in Me, The [recording]
Twain, Shania **T:** 530
Woman in Mind [play by Ayckbourn]
Ayckbourn, Alan **A:** 995
Woman in the Nineteenth Century [book by Fuller]
Fuller, Margaret **F:** 554
Woman in White, The [book by Collins]
Collins, Wilkie **Ci:** 776
Woman Is a Woman, A [film]
Godard, Jean-Luc **G:** 244
Woman Killed With Kindness, A [play by Heywood]
Heywood, Thomas **H:** 221
Woman of Andros, The [book by Wilder]
Wilder, Thornton **W:** 303
Woman of No Importance, A [play by Wilde]
Wilde, Oscar **W:** 301
Woman of the Year [film]
Tracy, Spencer **T:** 362 *with picture*
Woman suffrage [voting] **W:** 380 *with picture and map*
Anthony, Susan Brownell **A:** 544
Constitution of the United States (Amendment 19) **Ci:** 1015
Davis, Paulina Wright **D:** 49
Feminism *picture on* **F:** 69; **F:** 70
League of Women Voters **L:** 161
Stanton, Elizabeth Cady **So:** 839
United States, History of the (Women's rights) **U:** 173; (The drive for woman suffrage) **U:** 186 *with picture*; (The Roaring Twenties) **U:** 189
Women's movement (The right to vote) **W:** 385
Woman Suffrage Association, National American
Anthony, Susan Brownell **A:** 545
Woman suffrage (Growth of the movement) **W:** 380
Woman Warrior, The [book by Kingston]
American literature (Works by minority writers) **A:** 425
Woman with Suitcases [sculpture by Hanson]
Sculpture (From the mid-1900's to the early 2000's) **S:** 259 *with picture*
Woman Without a Shadow, The [opera by Strauss]
Strauss, Richard **So:** 922
Womanism [movement]
Walker, Alice **W:** 13
Woman's Christian Temperance Union [organization] **W:** 382
Prohibition (The movement toward prohibition) **P:** 815
Willard, Frances Elizabeth Caroline **W:** 307
Woman's Life, A [book by De Maupassant]
De Maupassant, Guy **D:** 118
Woman's Medical College
Philadelphia (Education) **P:** 362
Woman's Relief Corps, National W: 382
Grand Army of the Republic **G:** 305
Woman's State Temperance Society of New York
Anthony, Susan Brownell **A:** 544
Woman's Way Through Unknown Labrador, A [book by Hubbard]
Canadian literature (Other literature) **C:** 158
Woman's Work [painting by Sloan]
Ashcan School *picture on* **A:** 768
Womb *See* Uterus *in this index*
Wombat [animal] **W:** 382 *with picture*
Marsupial (Kinds of marsupials) **M:** 232
Wombeyan Caves [Australia] **W:** 382
Women
See also Women's movement *in this index*
Abortion **A:** 14
Afghanistan (Way of life) **A:** 92a-93 *with picture*
Arabs (Family life) **A:** 587; (Clothing) **A:** 588
Asia (Country life) **A:** 779
Boxing (Women's boxing) **B:** 532b *with picture*
Byzantine Empire (Society) **B:** 752
Chicago, Judy **C:** 437
Clothing (Cultural beliefs and values) **Ci:** 691; (Clothing under Islam) **Ci:** 697-698 *with picture*; (The Renaissance) **Ci:** 702 *with pictures*
Culture (Forming patterns) **Ci:** 1187
Domestic violence **D:** 301

Egypt, Ancient (Family life) **E:** 136; (Government) **E:** 139
Electronic game (Controversy) **E:** 204f-205
Episcopal Church **E:** 344
France (Politics) **F:** 455
Great Depression (Human suffering) **G:** 340-341
Greece, Ancient (Family life) **G:** 367
Japan (Gender roles) **J:** 41
Labor force (Changes in the labor force) **L:** 3
Libya (Way of life) **L:** 265
Marriage **M:** 219
Middle East (Ways of life) **M:** 530
Muslims (The Muslim world today) **M:** 965
Navy, United States (World War I [1914-1918]) **N:** 88; (World War II [1939-1945]) **N:** 89
Obscenity and pornography (Regulating pornography) **O:** 643
Painting (Women artists) **P:** 73; (Symbolism) **P:** 76; (Nonobjective painting in Russia) **P:** 79
Parent (Changes in parenthood) **P:** 156
Physical education (During the 1900's) **P:** 433
Police (In the United States since the mid-1900's) **P:** 624-625
Poverty (Social factors) **P:** 724
Radio (The Golden Age of Broadcasting) **R:** 92-94
Saudi Arabia (Way of life) **S:** 156
Soap opera **So:** 543
Supreme Court of the United States (Civil rights) **So:** 1001; (table) **So:** 1002
Syria (People) **So:** 1071
Teaching (Job opportunities) **T:** 68
Turkey (Ways of life) **T:** 505
Vikings (Daily life) **V:** 379
Voting (Voter turnout) **V:** 450
World War II (Producing for the war) **W:** 495 *with picture*
Wyoming (Territorial progress) **W:** 534
Women, The [play by Luce]
Luce, Clare Boothe **L:** 513
Women Airforce Service Pilots
Air Force, United States (Air Force women) **A:** 190
Cochran, Jacqueline **Ci:** 743
Women and Birds in the Night [painting by Miró]
Miró, Joan *picture on* **M:** 616
Women and Economics [book by Gilman]
Gilman, Charlotte Perkins **G:** 191
Women in Love [book by Lawrence]
Lawrence, D. H. L. **:** 145
Women of Algiers, The [painting by Delacroix]
Delacroix, Eugène **D:** 95
Painting (Romanticism) **P:** 68-70 *with picture*
Women on the Verge of a Nervous Breakdown [film]
Almodóvar, Pedro **A:** 380
Women Professional Bowlers Association
Bowling (Professional bowling) **B:** 524
Women Strike for Peace [organization]
Abzug, Bella Savitzky **A:** 19
Women's Action Alliance
Steinem, Gloria **So:** 886
Women's Army Auxiliary Corps
Army, United States (World War II) **A:** 739
Women's Army Corps [U.S.]
Air Force, United States (Air Force women) **A:** 190
Army, United States (World War II) **A:** 739
Hobby, Oveta Culp **H:** 273
Women's Bible *See* Tsenerene *in this index*
Women's British Open [tournament]
Golf (Tournaments) **G:** 264
Women's Bureau [U.S.] **W:** 382
Women's Equity Action League
Women's movement (Women's organizations) **W:** 386
Women's Franchise League
Pankhurst, Emmeline Goulden **P:** 131
Women's International Bowling Congress
Bowling (The 1900's) **B:** 524b
Women's International League for Peace and Freedom
Addams, Jane **A:** 46
Women's liberation movement
See also Feminism; Women's movement *in this index*
Feminism **F:** 70
Steinem, Gloria **So:** 885
Women's movement (Contemporary women's movements) **W:** 386
Women's magazine
Magazine (Consumer magazines) **M:** 42
Women's movement W: 383 *with pictures*
See also the list of Related articles in the Women's movement article
Abortion (Abortion in the United States) **A:** 15
Army, United States (World War II [1939-1945]) **A:** 739
Australia (The struggle for women's rights) **A:** 923
Civil rights (The struggle for women's rights)

Ci: 609
Coeducation Ci: 752
Colonial life in America (Voting and other rights) Ci: 795
Davis, Paulina Wright D: 49
Dickinson, Anna Elizabeth D: 190
Equal Rights Amendment E: 345
Famous Five F: 26b
Feminism F: 69
Gay Nineties (Social developments) G: 72
Greer, Germaine G: 387
History (Approaches to history) H: 261
Lockwood, Belva Ann Bennett L: 413
Muslims (Reform and renewal) M: 964d-965
National Organization for Women N: 42
Pankhurst, Emmeline Goulden P: 131
Religion (Religion today) R: 223
Revolution, American (The home front) R: 280
Rich, Adrienne R: 328
Rose, Ernestine Potowski R: 476
Stanton, Elizabeth Cady So: 839
Stone, Lucy So: 909
United States, History of the (Women's rights) U: 173; (The Roaring Twenties) U: 189; (World War II) U: 193 with picture; (The civil rights movement) U: 196a
Woman suffrage W: 380
Woodhull, Victoria Claflin W: 393

Women's NBA
Basketball (Professional competition) B: 151

Women's Political Caucus, National
Friedan, Betty F: 533
Steinem, Gloria So: 886

Women's Relief Society
Mormons (Church organization) M: 807-808

Women's rights See Women's movement in this index

Women's Rights Convention [1848]
Mott, Lucretia Coffin M: 880
Stanton, Elizabeth Cady So: 839
Woman suffrage (Beginnings of the movement) W: 380

Women's Rights National Historical Park [New York]
National Park System (table: National historical parks) N: 56-57

Women's Social and Political Union
Pankhurst, Emmeline Goulden P: 131

Women's Strike for Equality
Friedan, Betty F: 533

Women's studies
Education (Nonsexist education) E: 107-108
Feminism F: 70

Women's Temperance Crusade [1873]
Woman's Christian Temperance Union W: 382

Women's Trade Union League of America, National [labor history]
O'Reilly, Leonora O: 851

Wonder, Stevie [American musician] W: 389 with portrait
Gordy, Berry, Jr. G: 273

Wonder Book for Boys and Girls, A [book by Hawthorne]
Hawthorne, Nathaniel (His stories and sketches) H: 115

Wonder drug See Antibiotic in this index
Wonderful Adventures of Nils, The [book by Lagerlöf]
Lagerlöf, Selma L: 30

Wonderful Town [musical]
Bernstein, Leonard B: 271

Wonderful Wizard of Oz, The [book by Baum]
Baum, L. Frank B: 174
Literature for children (Fiction) L: 359 with picture
Wizard of Oz, The W: 374

Wonders, Palace of [Zanzibar]
Tanzania picture on T: 35

Wonders of the World See Seven natural wonders of the world; Seven Wonders of the Ancient World in this index

Wong, Anna May [American actress]
Asian Americans (Notable Asian American "firsts") A: 812f

Wonsan [Korea]
Korean War (Naval warfare) K: 382

Wood W: 389 with pictures
See also Lumber in this index
Doll (Wooden dolls) D: 289 with picture; (Before World War I) D: 291
Energy supply (Wood) E: 278
Forest (Economic value) F: 391
Forest products (Wood products) F: 400 with pictures; (Fuel products) F: 402
Lignin L: 302
Lignum-vitae L: 302
Materials (Biological materials) M: 300d with picture

Painting (Supports) P: 36
Plastics (To replace wood and stone) P: 555
Plywood P: 585 with picture
Stain So: 821
Termite T: 171
Tree (Wood products) T: 412 with picture
Woodworking W: 396

Wood [club]
Golf (Golf clubs) G: 262 with pictures

Wood, Annie [British social reformer] See Besant, Annie Wood in this index

Wood, George T. [American political leader]
Texas (table) T: 203

Wood, Grant [American painter] W: 390
Painting (Regionalism) P: 83 with picture

Wood, Harry O. [American seismologist]
Earthquake (The Modified Mercalli Intensity [MMI] scale) E: 38b

Wood, James [American political leader]
Virginia (table) V: 417

Wood, John [American political leader]
Illinois (table) I: 71

Wood, Leonard [American general] W: 390
Fort Leonard Wood F: 414
Harding, Warren Gamaliel (The smoke-filled room) H: 57
Rough Riders R: 490

Wood, Reuben [American political leader]
Ohio (table) O: 699

Wood, Ron [British guitarist]
Rock music picture on R: 380d
Rolling Stones R: 402a

Wood alcohol See Methanol in this index

Wood anemone [plant]
Anemone A: 458
Plant picture on P: 521

Wood-block print See Woodcut in this index

Wood Buffalo National Park [Alberta-Northwest Territories]
Canada (table: National parks and national park reserves) C: 114
Lake Athabasca L: 35 with map
National park (Canada) N: 42c; (table) N: 42g
Northwest Territories (National parklands) N: 531

Wood-burning stove
Heating (Wood-burning stoves) H: 160

Wood carving [art] See Woodcarving in this index

Wood chips
Lumber L: 517

Wood drill
Drill (Wood drills) D: 348

Wood duck [bird] W: 391
Duck picture on D: 374; (Food) D: 375

Wood engraving [art] See Woodcut in this index

Wood frog
Animal picture on A: 478

Wood girder bridge
Bridge (Girder bridges) B: 600-601

Wood lily [plant]
Lily L: 304 with picture

Wood lizard [reptile]
Lizard L: 399

Wood louse [animal] W: 391 with picture

Wood nymph [butterfly]
Butterfly (Satyrs and wood nymphs) B: 736

Wood oil [tree product]
Tung oil T: 486

Wood pewee [bird]
Pewee P: 352 with picture

Wood pulp [tree product]
Lumber L: 517
Paper (Raw materials) P: 134
Textile (Manufactured fibers) T: 213
Tree (Wood products) T: 412

Wood rat See Woodrat in this index

Wood rosin [by-product]
Rosin R: 480

Wood screw
Screw (Uses) S: 225 with pictures

Wood smoke
Food preservation (Curing) F: 341

Wood sorrel [plant]
Plant pictures on P: 524, P: 538
Shamrock S: 371

Wood stain
Paint (Industrial paints) P: 24

Wood stork [bird]
Stork So: 913

Wood tar
Tar T: 41

Wood thrush [bird]
Thrush T: 271 with picture

Wood tick [animal]
Rocky Mountain spotted fever R: 394

Wood turpentine [tree product]
Turpentine T: 519

Wood-warbler [bird]

Ovenbird O: 881 with picture
Warbler W: 34 with pictures

Wood, Wire, and Metal Lathers' International Union
Carpenters and Joiners of America, United Brotherhood of C: 246

Woodbine [plant]
Honeysuckle H: 316
Virginia creeper V: 424 with picture

Woodbridge, William [American political leader]
Michigan (table) M: 507

Woodbury, Levi [American jurist]
Jackson, Andrew (table) J: 11
New Hampshire (table) N: 223
Supreme Court of the United States (table) So: 1000
Van Buren, Martin (table) V: 273

Woodbury, Urban A. [American political leader]
Vermont (table) V: 333

Woodcarving W: 391 with diagrams
Canada picture on C: 105
Indian, American picture on I: 136a
New Zealand picture on N: 348

Woodchuck [animal] W: 392 with picture
Groundhog Day G: 402
Marmot M: 216

Woodcock [bird] W: 392 with picture
Animal picture on A: 492
Bird (Sight) B: 364-365 with picture

Woodcock, Katherine [wife of]
Milton, John (Middle years) M: 557

Woodcock, Leonard [American labor leader] W: 392

Woodcut [art] W: 392 with pictures
Block printing B: 406
Hokusai H: 289 with picture
Japan (Painting) J: 44 with picture
Japanese print J: 62 with picture
Tokyo picture on T: 319

Wooden, John [American basketball coach] W: 393
Basketball picture on B: 154

Wooden doll
Doll (The history of dolls) D: 288 with picture

Wooden shoe
Netherlands (Rural life) N: 141

Woodhull, Victoria Claflin [American social reformer] W: 393 with portrait

Woodin, William H. [American government official]
Roosevelt, Franklin Delano (table) R: 454

Woodland caribou
Caribou C: 238

Woodland Period
Mound builders (Woodland Period) M: 882

Woodlands Cree Indians
Cree Indians Ci: 1125
Manitoba (Precontact era) M: 160

Woodlands Indians
Iowa (Indian days) I: 393

Woodlawn [Ellsworth]
Maine (Places to visit) M: 78

"Woodnotes" [poem by Emerson]
Emerson, Ralph Waldo (His poetry) E: 259

Woodpecker [bird] W: 393 with pictures
Animal picture on A: 479
Bird pictures on B: 344d, B: 363; (Birds of the desert) B: 339 with picture; (Birds of Europe) B: 344c; (Other means of communication) B: 354; (Building a nest) B: 356 with picture
Sapsucker S: 122
Yellowhammer Y: 557

Woodrat [animal] W: 395

Woodring, Harry H. [American political leader]
Kansas (table) K: 234
Roosevelt, Franklin Delano (table) R: 454

Woodrow Wilson House [Washington, D.C.]
Washington, D.C. (Other Washington museums) W: 75

Woodrow Wilson International Center for Scholars
Smithsonian Institution (Affiliated institutions) S: 519

Woodruff, Rollin S. [American political leader]
Connecticut (table) Ci: 967

Woodruff, Wilford [American religious leader]
Illinois (Places to visit) I: 62
Utah (Territorial days and statehood) U: 246-248

Woodruff, William [American librarian]
Arkansas (Libraries) A: 699

Woodruff Arts Center [Atlanta]
Atlanta (Cultural life) A: 860a

Woods, Eldrick [American golfer] See Woods, Tiger in this index

Woods, George L. [American political leader]
Oregon (table) O: 845

Woods, Granville T. [American inventor] W: 395
Railroad (Engineering improvements) R: 117

Woods, Lake of the [Canada-U.S.]
Lake of the Woods **L:** 42 *with map*
Woods, Rex [Canadian artist]
Canada, History of *pictures on* **C:** 138, **C:** 139
Woods, Tiger [American golfer] **W:** 395
African Americans *picture on* **A:** 136r
Golf (Golf today) **G:** 267 *with picture*
Woods, William B. [American jurist]
Supreme Court of the United States (table)
So: 1000
Woods Cree Indians *See* Woodlands Cree Indians *in this index*
Woods Hole Oceanographic Institution [Massachusetts] **W:** 395
Wood's metal
Alloy (Other alloys) **A:** 378
Woodsia scopulina [plant]
Arkansas (Plant and animal life) **A:** 708
Woodside National Historic Site [Ontario]
Canada (table: National historic sites) **C:** 115
Woodson, Carter Godwin [American historian] **W:** 395
Association for the Study of African American Life and History **A:** 820
Black History Month **B:** 388
Woodson, Charles [American football player]
Football (table) **F:** 363
Woodson, Silas [American political leader]
Missouri (table) **M:** 668
Woodstock [film]
Woodstock festival **W:** 395
Woodstock festival [1969] **W:** 395 *with picture*
Rock music (Outdoor rock festivals) **R:** 380b
Woodstock Nation
Woodstock festival **W:** 395
Woodsworth, James Shaver [Canadian social reformer] **W:** 396
Woodward, Artemus [American manufacturer]
Brush **B:** 652
Woodward, Bob [American journalist]
Watergate (The break-in and cover-up) **W:** 144
Woodward, Calvin M. [American educator]
Industrial arts (Beginnings) **I:** 243
Vocational education (Early vocational education in schools) **V:** 435
Woodward, Joanne [American actress]
Motion picture (Best performance by an actress: 1957) **M:** 862
Newman, Paul **N:** 379
Woodward, William H. [American educator]
Dartmouth College case **D:** 39
Woodwind instrument [music]
Music (Wind instruments) **M:** 949 *with pictures*
Orchestra **O:** 820 *with pictures*
Woodwind section [music]
Orchestra (The musicians) **O:** 820
Woodworkers of America, International [labor union]
Carpenters and Joiners of America, United Brotherhood of **C:** 246
Woodworking [handicraft] **W:** 396 *with pictures*
Careers (Production) **C:** 229
Industrial arts (Industrial arts courses) **I:** 242-243
Tool (Woodworking tools) **T:** 330
United States *picture on* **U:** 113
Woody nightshade [plant]
Bittersweet **B:** 384
Woody perennial [botany]
Flower (Garden flowers) **F:** 274
Woody stem
Leaf (A leaf begins its life) **L:** 152
Plant (Stems) **P:** 529 *with picture*
Stem *pictures on* **So:** 888; (Woody stems) **So:** 887
Woof [weaving]
Weaving (Types of weaves) **W:** 173 *with pictures*
Woofer [electronics]
Speaker **So:** 767
Wool W: 399 *with pictures*
See also the list of Related articles in the Wool *article*
Fiber (Animal fibers) **F:** 87 *with picture*
Goat (Products) **G:** 239-240
Interior design (Choosing patterns and textures) **I:** 332
Rugs and carpets (Materials used in rugs and carpets) **R:** 514
Sheep (Raising sheep) **S:** 383
Textile (Natural fibers) **T:** 212-213
Wool, John E. [American military leader]
Lee, Robert E. (The Mexican War) **L:** 177
Wool Products Labeling Act [1939]
Textile (In the United States and Canada) **T:** 218
Woolaroc Museum & Wildlife Preserve
Oklahoma (Places to visit) **O:** 722
Woolen [yarn]
Wool (Making yarn) **W:** 400
Woolf, Leonard [British author]

Woolf, Virginia W: 401
Woolf, Virginia [British author] **W:** 401
Bloomsbury Group **B:** 419
English literature (Literature before World War I) **E:** 322
Novel (New directions in the novel) **N:** 573-574
Woollaston, Toss [New Zealand painter]
New Zealand (The arts) **N:** 349
Woolley, Sir Leonard [British archaeologist] **W:** 402
Woolley, Mary Emma [American educator] **W:** 402
Woolly bear [insect] *See* Woollybear *in this index*
Woolly daisy
Flower *picture on* **F:** 290
Woolly loco [plant]
Locoweed **L:** 418
Woolly lousewort [plant]
Flower *picture on* **F:** 283
Woolly mammoth [extinct animal]
Fossil (Other processes) **F:** 425 *with picture*
Mammoth **M:** 130
Woolly monkey W: 402
Animal *picture on* **A:** 481
Monkey *pictures on* **M:** 727, **M:** 728
Woolly spider monkey *See* Muriqui *in this index*
Woollybear [insect] **W:** 402 *with picture*
Insect *picture on* **I:** 282
Moth (Tiger moths) **M:** 840-841 *with picture*
Woolman, John [American religious leader] **W:** 402
Woolrich, Cornell [American author] **W:** 402
Woolworth, Charles S. [American businessman] **W:** 403
Woolworth, Frank Winfield [American businessman] **W:** 403
Woolworth Company, F. W.
Woolworth, Charles S. **W:** 403
Woolworth, Frank Winfield **W:** 403
Wootz steel
Iron and steel (The first steel) **I:** 450
Worcester [Massachusetts] **W:** 403
Massachusetts (table: Average monthly weather) **M:** 284
Worcester Art Museum
Massachusetts (Museums) **M:** 275 *with picture*
Worcester porcelain
Porcelain (English porcelain) **P:** 677
Worcester v. Georgia [U.S. history]
Jackson, Andrew (The Indian issue) **J:** 13
Word [electronics]
Computer chip (Word length) **Ci:** 924f
Word [language]
Dictionary **D:** 192
Etymology **E:** 376
Language **L:** 62
Parts of speech **P:** 189
Pronunciation **P:** 820
Semantics **S:** 291
Slang **S:** 499
Spelling **S:** 775
Vocabulary **V:** 434
Word order [grammar]
Adjective (The position of adjectives) **A:** 57
Grammar **G:** 303; (Principles of English grammar) **G:** 303
Word processing W: 403
Computer (Applications software) **Ci:** 917
Teaching (Guiding and assisting student learning) **T:** 66
Word processor [machine]
Word processing **W:** 403
Word-recognition strategy
Reading (Comprehending what is perceived) **R:** 157
Worden, Alfred Merrill [American astronaut] **W:** 404
Wordsworth, William [British poet] **W:** 404
Coleridge, Samuel Taylor (His life) **Ci:** 771
English literature (Romantic poetry) **E:** 320
Lake Poets **L:** 44
Poetry (Rhythm and meter) **P:** 591-594; (Romantic poetry) **P:** 597
Romanticism (Romanticism in literature) **R:** 427
Work [employment] *See* Careers; Employment *in this index*
Work [physics] **W:** 404
Calculus (Integral calculus) **C:** 23
Energy **E:** 273; (Units of work and energy) **E:** 274
Foot-pound **F:** 353
Machine **M:** 13
Metric system (Mechanics) **M:** 437-440
Power **P:** 726
Thermodynamics **T:** 253
Work, Hubert [American government official]
Coolidge, Calvin (table) **Ci:** 1032
Interior, Department of the (table) **I:** 325
Work credit
Social security (Old-age, survivors, and disability insurance) **So:** 553

Work force
Labor force **L:** 3
Work of cohesion [physics]
Cohesion **Ci:** 756
Work Projects Administration [U.S. history] *See* Works Progress Administration *in this index*
Work-release program
Criminal justice system (Problems in the correctional system) **Ci:** 1144
Prison (Special facilities and services) **P:** 806-807
Work rule [labor relations]
Railroad (Rail unions) **R:** 113
Work school [education]
Alternative school (Features of alternative schools) **A:** 388-389
Work shoe
Shoe (Kinds of shoes) **S:** 431 *with picture*
Work song
Folk music (Kinds of folk music) **F:** 321
Work-study
Cooperative education **Ci:** 1037
Work support [program]
Welfare (Other public assistance programs) **W:** 190
Workbook [computer file]
Spreadsheet **So:** 805
Workday
Serf **S:** 316b
Worked lumber
Lumber (Kinds of lumber) **L:** 517
Worker [entomology]
Ant **A:** 520 *with pictures*
Bee (The honey bee colony) **B:** 201 *with pictures*; (Division of labor) **B:** 205 *with pictures*
Bumble bee (Life of the bumble bee) **B:** 698-699 *with picture*
Insect (Family life) **I:** 294-295 *with picture*
Termite (The termite colony) **T:** 171 *with picture*
Wasp (Group life) **W:** 112
Workers' college
China (Education) **C:** 486-487
Workers' compensation W: 405
Insurance *diagram on* **I:** 310; (Wokers' compensation) **I:** 314
Social security (Workers' compensation) **So:** 556
Workers' Party [Brazil]
Brazil (Politics) **B:** 569
Workers' Party [North Korea]
Kim Jong-il **K:** 317
Workers Uniting [labor union]
United Steelworkers **U:** 204
Workforce Investment Act [1998]
Labor force (The government and the labor force) **L:** 3
Vocational education (Other sources) **V:** 434
Workhouse [English history]
Welfare (History) **W:** 191
Working beam [mechanical device]
Watt, James **W:** 148
Working capital [economics]
Industry (Capital) **I:** 259
Working class
Industrial Revolution (The working class) **I:** 251
Marx, Karl (Marx's ideas) **M:** 237
Social class (Class structure) **So:** 550
World, History of the (The Industrial Revolution) **W:** 444-445
Working conditions
Careers (Working conditions) **C:** 215
Workers' compensation **W:** 405
Working dog
Dog (Working dogs) **D:** 266 *with pictures*
Working memory
Memory (Long-term memory) **M:** 392
Workingmen's Association, International [European history] *See* International Workingmen's Association *in this index*
Workmen's Compensation Act [1915]
Indiana (The early 1900's) **I:** 216
Workpiece
Machine tool **M:** 17 *with pictures*
Workplace *See* Employment *in this index*
Workplace literacy
Reading (The importance of reading) **R:** 155-156
Works
Clock (Kinds of clocks) **Ci:** 682i *with diagrams*
Works and Days [poem by Hesiod]
Greek literature (Epic poetry) **G:** 377
Hesiod **H:** 218
Works made for hire [law]
Copyright (Owners' rights) **Ci:** 1047
Works Progress Administration [U.S. history] **W:** 405
Great Depression (The New Deal) **G:** 341
New Deal (Works Progress Administration) **N:** 202
Preschool (History) **P:** 756b-757
Roosevelt, Franklin Delano *picture on* **R:** 454;

(Second New Deal) R: 453
South Dakota (Boom-and-bust economy) So: 684
Worksheet [spreadsheet]
Spreadsheet So: 805
Workstation [electronics]
Computer (Personal computers) Ci: 909
Workweek
Fair Labor Standards Act F: 8
World W: 406 with pictures and maps
See also Earth in this index; and the list of Related articles in the World article
Economics (The world economy) E: 61
Gas [fuel] map on G: 56
Income (International income comparisons) I: 101
Literacy (Literacy in other countries) L: 352
Population (World population) P: 672
Time (World time zones) map on T: 290-291
World, History of the W: 420 with pictures and maps
See also Civilization in this index, and the list of Related articles in the World, History of the article
Races, Human (The three-race theory) R: 53
Writing system W: 512
World, The [newspaper] See New York World, The in this index
World According to Garp, The [book by Irving]
Irving, John I: 459
World AIDS Day
AIDS (Public awareness) A: 165-166
World Alliance of Reformed Churches
Presbyterians P: 756a
World Almanac, The [book]
Almanac A: 379
World Anti-Doping Agency
Doping D: 309
World as Will and Representation, The [work by Schopenhauer]
Schopenhauer, Arthur S: 186
World Association of Girl Guides and Girl Scouts
Girl Scouts G: 196; (In other countries) G: 199
World Bank [UN] W: 450
Africa (Foreign aid, debt, and investment) A: 129
Bank (Multilateral development banks) B: 91
Bretton Woods B: 594
Food supply (Food supply programs) F: 350
Foreign aid (Worldwide lending programs) F: 385
International Development Association I: 339
International Finance Corporation I: 340
International Monetary Fund I: 343
New Hampshire (The mid-1900's) N: 226-227
Poverty (Poverty standards) P: 723
World Baseball Classic [competition]
Baseball (Recent developments) B: 137-139
World Book Advanced [encyclopedia]
Encyclopedia (Today's encyclopedias) E: 268b-269
World Book Dictionary, The
Dictionary (Modern dictionaries) D: 194
World Book Discover [encyclopedia]
Encyclopedia (Today's encyclopedias) E: 268b-269
World Book Encyclopedia, The
Encyclopedia (How a World Book article is prepared) E: 267 with pictures; (Today's encyclopedias) E: 268b-269
Yeti Y: 565
World Book Information Finder, The [encyclopedia]
Encyclopedia (Today's encyclopedias) E: 268b-269
World Book Kids [encyclopedia]
Encyclopedia (Today's encyclopedias) E: 268b-269
World Book Multimedia Encyclopedia, The
Encyclopedia (Today's encyclopedias) E: 268b-269
World Book New Illustrated Information Finder, The [encyclopedia]
Encyclopedia (Today's encyclopedias) E: 268b-269
World Book Online Reference Center
Encyclopedia (Today's encyclopedias) E: 268b-269
World Book Student [encyclopedia]
Encyclopedia (Today's encyclopedias) E: 268b-269
World Book Student Discovery Encyclopedia, The
Encyclopedia (Today's encyclopedias) E: 268b-269
World Book Student Discovery Science Encyclopedia, The
Encyclopedia (Today's encyclopedias) E: 268b-269
World Book Web [publications]
Encyclopedia (Today's encyclopedias) E: 268b-

269
World Boxing Association
Boxing (Boxing today) B: 533
World Boxing Council
Boxing (Boxing today) B: 533
World Boxing Organization
Boxing (Boxing today) B: 533
World Bridge Federation
Bridge (Regulation of tournaments) B: 605
World Calendar, The
Calendar (Calendar reform) C: 32
World Chess Federation See Fédération Internationale des Échecs in this index
World Commission on Protected Areas
National park (International concern for national parks) N: 42j
World Community of Al-Islam in the West See Black Muslims in this index
World Conference on National Parks
National park (International concern for national parks) N: 42j
World Council of Churches W: 450
Missionary (Organization) M: 621
Protestantism (The ecumenical movement) P: 835
World Court [UN] See International Court of Justice in this index
World Crisis [book by Churchill]
Churchill, Sir Winston Leonard Spencer (Between wars) C: 547
World Cup [skiing]
New Hampshire picture on N: 209
Skiing (Skiing as a sport) S: 486
World Cup [soccer] W: 450
Soccer So: 544; (International competition) So: 548; (table: World Cup championship games) So: 549; (History) So: 549
World Day for Water
Water (The challenge of today) W: 132
World Drivers' Championship
Automobile racing (Formula One racing) A: 976-977; (Growth of organized automobile racing) A: 979
World Enough and Time [book by Warren]
Warren, Robert Penn W: 37
World Federation of Occupational Therapists
Occupational therapy (History) O: 649
World Federation of Trade Unions
Labor movement (International organizations) L: 15
World Festival of the Circus of Tomorrow
Circus (Places to visit and annual events) Ci: 566
World Food Conference [UN]
United Nations (Fighting hunger) U: 89
World Food Programme
Food and Agriculture Organization F: 340
Food supply (Food aid programs) F: 351
World Football League
Football (New professional leagues) F: 368
World for Julius, A [book by Echenique]
Latin American literature (The post-Boom) L: 114
World Golf Championships
Golf (Golf today) G: 267
World Health Organization [UN] W: 450
AIDS (AIDS around the world) A: 166
Disease D: 226
Flood (Reducing flood losses) F: 238
Foreign aid (Technical assistance and relief) F: 384
Globalization (Features of globalization) G: 233
Health H: 125
Malaria (Treatment and prevention) M: 96
Medicine (The medical revolution) M: 366-377; (Medical organizations) M: 370
Quarantine Q: 7
Smallpox S: 513
World Heritage List
National park (International concern for national parks) N: 42j
World Hockey Association
Hockey (The late 1900's and early 2000's) H: 282
World Ice Hockey Championships
Hockey (The World Ice Hockey Championships) H: 281
World Intellectual Property Organization [UN]
Copyright (International agreements) Ci: 1048
World Island
Geopolitics G: 106b
World Jamboree
Boy Scouts (Scouting throughout the world) B: 538-539
World Jewish Congress [organization] W: 450
World League of American Football
Football (New professional leagues) F: 368
World map
See also Globe in this index
World map on W: 408

World Medical Association W: 451
Medicine (Medical organizations) M: 370
World Meteorological Organization [UN] W: 451
Hurricane (Tropical storm) H: 453-454
Ultraviolet rays U: 17
Weather (Measuring the weather) W: 162
World Methodist Council
Methodists M: 434
World music
Rock music (World music) R: 380d
World ocean
Ocean (The world ocean) O: 651
World Ocean Circulation Experiment
Atlantic Ocean (New techniques) A: 867
Pacific Ocean (Scientific research) P: 15
World of Apu, The [film]
Ray, Satyajit R: 152
World of Dreams, The [book by Ellis]
Ellis, Havelock E: 243
World of Warcraft [electronic game]
Electronic game picture on E: 204a
World of Wonders [book by Davies]
Davies, Robertson D: 46
World of Yesterday, The [book by Zweig]
Zweig, Stefan Z: 610
World renewal ceremony
Indian, American (Before European contact) I: 163-164
World Scout Conference
Boy Scouts (Scouting throughout the world) B: 538
World Series
Baseball (Major leagues) B: 130; (table) B: 131; (Recent developments) B: 137-138
Massachusetts (Interesting facts) M: 271
World Ski Championships
Skiing (Skiing as a sport) S: 486
World Society for the Protection of Animals
Animal rights movement A: 510
World Summit on Sustainable Development [2002]
Environmental pollution (Global efforts) E: 336
World Swimming Championships
Phelps, Michael P: 356
World Thinking Day
Girl Scouts (Annual events) G: 198
World Tomorrow [journal]
Thomas, Norman Mattoon T: 261
World trade See International trade in this index
World Trade Center [New York City] W: 451 with picture
See also September 11 terrorist attacks in this index
Bush, George Walker (Terrorist attacks and military action) B: 722g
Hijacking H: 230
Hudson River tunnels (The PATH tunnels) H: 406-407
National September 11 Memorial and Museum N: 61
New York (The early 2000's) N: 320
New York City (Manhattan) N: 323-324; (Problems) N: 342-343 with picture
September 11 terrorist attacks S: 310 with pictures
Terrorism picture on T: 175; (The changing face of terrorism) T: 178; (The September 11 terrorist attacks) T: 179
United States, History of the (September 11 terrorist attacks) U: 196d with picture
World Trade Center Building [New Orleans]
New Orleans (Downtown New Orleans) N: 278-279
World Trade Organization W: 451
China (Recent developments) C: 506
Foreign policy (Economic factors) F: 387
General Agreement on Tariffs and Trade G: 83
Globalization (Features of globalization) G: 233
International trade (Government trade policies) I: 348-349
World War I [1914-1918] W: 452 with pictures and maps
See also the list of Related articles in the World War I article
Ace A: 24
African Americans (The black migration to the North) A: 136m
Air force (World War I) A: 185
Aircraft, Military (World War I) A: 204 with pictures
Airplane (World War I [1914-1918]) A: 234 with picture
Airship (World War I) A: 252
American literature (The world wars and depression [1914-1945]) A: 420
Army (Armies in the two world wars) A: 728
Artillery (History) A: 763
Automobile picture on A: 966; (World War I)

A: 968
Aviation (World War I [1914-1918]) A: 987
Balloon (Balloons in war) B: 61
Bomb (History) B: 452
Bosnia-Herzegovina (History) B: 492-493
Camouflage C: 87
Caroline Islands C: 244
Chemical-biological-radiological-warfare
   (History) C: 396
Coast Guard, United States (World War I) Ci: 737
Code talkers Ci: 749
Codes and ciphers (History) Ci: 751
Communism (Before 1917) Ci: 892
Currie, Sir Arthur Ci: 1197
Depth charge D: 151
Draft, Military (Military drafts throughout history)
   D: 318
Europe (World War I) E: 413
Flynn, Elizabeth Gurley F: 313
Foch, Ferdinand F: 313
Franz Ferdinand F: 494
Guerrilla warfare (History) G: 420
Hitler, Adolf (Corporal Hitler) H: 265
Homing pigeon (History) H: 305
Imperialism (History) I: 93
International relations (Collective security) I: 345
Krupp K: 389
Lenin, V. I. (Outcast) L: 193
Logistics L: 426
Mercier, Désiré Joseph M: 413
Mine warfare (History) M: 565
Nationalism (The effects of nationalism) N: 63
Navy (World War I) N: 80
Nazism (The birth of Nazism) N: 92
Neutrality (World War I) N: 153
Nicholas II [czar] N: 402
Novel (The modern novel) N: 573
Pacifism P: 17
Palestine (World War I and the Balfour
   Declaration) P: 105
Paris, Treaties of (The treaties of 1919) P: 167
Pershing, John Joseph (World War I) P: 296
Peter I P: 323
Petroleum (World War I [1914-1918]) P: 348
Propaganda (During World War I) P: 825
Quebec (World War I) Q: 32
Red Cross (In the United States) R: 187
Refugee (Efforts to help refugees) R: 203
Roaring Twenties R: 363
Russian Revolution of 1917 (World War I [1914-
   1918]) R: 566; (The October Revolution) R: 566
Socialism (World Wars I and II) So: 561
Statue of Liberty (Growth as a symbol) So: 877
Unknown soldier U: 211
Versailles, Treaty of (Background of the treaty)
   V: 340
War (table) W: 25; (The building and collapse of
   nations) W: 25; (The world wars) W: 26
War correspondent W: 26
War crime (World War I) W: 27
Warship picture on W: 43; (Warships in the two
   world wars) W: 41
Weapon (World War I) W: 154b
World, History of the picture on W: 421; (The
   world wars) W: 446
World War II (Causes of the war) W: 468
Aftermath
   Arms control (History of arms control) A: 721
   Fascism (History) F: 49
   Fourteen Points F: 437
   Great Depression (The beginning of the Great
      Depression) G: 339
Allies
   A.E.F. A: 81
   Air Force, United States (World War I) A: 194
   Army, United States (World War I) A: 738
   Australia (World War I [1914-1918]) A: 924
   Belgium (The world wars) B: 234
   Canada, History of (World War I and
      independence [1914-1931]) C: 146
   Foreign Legion (History) F: 386
   Italy (World War I) I: 516
   Marine Corps, United States picture on M: 207;
      (The 1900's) M: 209
   Navy, United States (World War I [1914-1918])
      N: 88-89
   North Sea N: 518
   Russia (World War I) R: 552
   Syria (World War I to independence) So: 1075
   United Kingdom (World War I) U: 70
   United States, History of the (World War I and
      postwar growth [1917-1929]) U: 188 with
      picture
Battles
   Alsace-Lorraine A: 387
   Balkans (World War I [1914-1918]) B: 42
   Flanders Field F: 227

Helgoland H: 168
Jutland, Battle of J: 204
Paris (Paris in wartime) P: 166
Reims R: 207
Saarland S: 2
Siegfried Line S: 449
Verdun, Battles of V: 316
Vimy Ridge, Battle of V: 385
Central Powers
   Austria (Austria-Hungary) A: 939
   Austria-Hungary A: 941
   Bulgaria (The world wars) B: 693
   Germany (World War I) G: 166 with picture
      and map

World War II [1939-1945] W: 468 with pictures and
maps
See also the list of Related articles in the World War
   II article
Ace A: 24
African Americans picture on A: 136m; (World
   War II [1939-1945]) A: 136n
Air force (World War II) A: 185
Aircraft, Military (World War II [1939-1945]) A: 205
   with pictures
Airplane (During World War II [1939-1945]) A: 238
Airship (World War II to the present) A: 252
Alsace-Lorraine A: 387
Amphibious warfare A: 442
Army (Armies in the two world wars) A: 728
Army, United States (World War II [1939-1945])
   A: 739
Artillery (History) A: 763
Asian Americans picture on A: 812e; (World War II
   and Japanese Americans) A: 812f
Automobile picture on A: 968; (World War II)
   A: 970
Aviation (World War II [1939-1945]) A: 989
Babi Yar B: 3
Baby boom generation (Causes of the baby
   boom) B: 11
Balkans (World War II [1939-1945]) B: 42
Balloon (Balloons in war) B: 61-62 with picture
Bielski partisans B: 295
Bomb (History) B: 452
Camouflage C: 87
Coast Guard, United States (World War II) Ci: 73
Code talkers Ci: 749
Codes and ciphers (Later developments) Ci: 751
Colonialism (Decolonization) Ci: 814
Concentration camp Ci: 926
D-Day D: 2
Draft, Military (Military drafts throughout history)
   D: 318
Europe picture on E: 413; (World War II) E: 414
Family (Changes) F: 23-24
Flying Tigers F: 312
Foreign aid (United States aid programs) F: 383
Great Depression G: 339
Guerrilla warfare (History) G: 420
Guided missile (The first guided missiles) G: 427
Heisenberg, Werner H: 167
Hiroshima H: 243
Hispanic Americans (Effects of World War II)
   H: 253
Holocaust H: 296
Human rights (The development of human
   rights) H: 428-428a
Indochina (World War II) I: 225
International relations (Collective security) I: 345
Invention (Military needs) I: 355
Japanese American internment J: 60
Katyn Massacre K: 249
Krupp K: 389
Latin America (Political circumstances in the early
   to middle 1900's) L: 109-110
Lidice L: 270
Logistics L: 426
London (The Blitz) L: 442 with picture
Maginot Line M: 52
Mauldin, Bill M: 313
Moscow (Revolution and Soviet rule) M: 827
National World War II Memorial N: 62
Navy (World War II) N: 80
Nazism (Expansion, war, and collapse) N: 92
Neutrality (World War II) N: 154
Nuclear weapon (World War II) N: 601
Pacific Islands (World War II [1939-1945]) P: 12
Paris, Treaties of (The Paris treaties of 1947) P: 168
Petroleum (Petroleum and war) P: 346; (World
   War II [1939-1945]) P: 348
Philippines (Japanese control) P: 380
Poland (World War II) P: 613
Prisoner of war P: 808
Propaganda (During World War II) P: 825
Prussia (Decline of Prussia) P: 843
Quebec (World War II) Q: 32; (The early 1900's)
   Q: 37

Radar (Advances during World War II) R: 72
Radio (The Golden Age of Broadcasting) R: 92-93
Rationing R: 148
Red Cross (In the United States) R: 187
Ridgway, Matthew Bunker R: 336
Saint Petersburg [Russia] (History) S: 55
Salazar, António de Oliveira S: 60
Schindler, Oskar S: 175
Socialism (World Wars I and II) So: 561
Switzerland (Neutrality in the world wars)
   So: 1060
Thailand (In World War II [1939-1945]) T: 227
Tokyo (World War II) T: 319
Tokyo Rose T: 320
Underground U: 20
Union of Soviet Socialist Republics (World War II)
   U: 37 with picture
United States, History of the (World War II) U: 193
   with pictures
War (Information and intelligence) W: 24; (table)
   W: 25; (The world wars) W: 26
War correspondent W: 26
Warship (Warships in the two world wars) W: 41-
   42 with pictures
Weapon (World War II) W: 154b
World, History of the (The world wars) W: 446
Yugoslavia (World War II) Y: 576
Aftermath
   Arms control (Arms control in the mid-1900's)
      A: 721
   Cold War (The coming of the Cold War) Ci: 763
   Communism (The spread of Communism)
      Ci: 893
   Disability (The 1900's) D: 221
   Helsinki Accords H: 179
   Nuremberg Trials N: 613
   Palestine (World War II and the division of
      Palestine) P: 105
   Refugee (Efforts to help refugees) R: 203
   United Nations (The founding of the UN) U: 94
   Unknown soldier U: 212
   War crime (World War II) W: 27
   Women's movement (Decline after 1920)
      W: 385
Allies
   Air Force, United States (World War II) A: 195
   Army, United States (World War II) A: 739
   Australia (World War II [1939-1945]) A: 924
   Belgium (The world wars) B: 234
   Canada, History of (World War II) C: 148 with
      picture
   China (War with Japan) C: 504
   Churchill, Sir Winston Leonard Spencer
      (Wartime prime minister) C: 547 with pictures
   De Gaulle, Charles André Joseph Marie (Leader
      of the Free French) D: 91
   Foreign Legion (History) F: 386
   France (World War II) F: 475 with picture and
      map
   India (World War II [1939-1945]) I: 132
   Indian, American (In the United States) I: 179
   Luxembourg (History) L: 531
   Marine Corps, United States (The 1900's)
      M: 209
   Navy, United States (World War II [1939-1945])
      N: 89
   Netherlands (World War II) N: 149 with picture
   New Zealand (World War II) N: 355
   North Sea N: 518
   Roosevelt, Franklin Delano (The road to war)
      R: 455; (The United States goes to war)
      R: 457 with pictures
   Russia (World War II) R: 554
   Stalin, Joseph (World War II) So: 827
   Tehran Conference T: 88
   United Kingdom (World War II) U: 70
Axis
   Austria (After World War I) A: 939
   Axis A: 994
   Berlin (World War II) B: 264 with picture
   Bulgaria (The world wars) B: 693
   Finland (World War II) F: 117 with picture
   Germany (World War II) G: 168 with picture
      and map
   Hitler, Adolf (World War II) H: 268
   Hungary (World War II) H: 446
   Italy (World War II) I: 517 with picture
   Japan (World War II) J: 58
   Kamikaze K: 212
   Mussolini, Benito (World War II) M: 967
Battles
   Bataan Death March B: 162
   Bulge, Battle of the B: 694
   Caroline Islands C: 244
   Corregidor Ci: 1071
   Dunkerque D: 385
   Gdańsk G: 74

Guam (History and government) **G: 409**
Helgoland **H: 168**
Iwo Jima, Battle of **I: 523** *with picture*
Leningrad, Siege of **L: 195**
Malta (History) **M: 113-114**
Manila Bay **M: 143**
Midway, Battle of **M: 536**
Okinawa **O: 710**
Paris (Paris in wartime) **P: 166**
Pearl Harbor **P: 218**
Reims **R: 208**
Russo-Finnish wars **R: 566a**
Saipan **S: 58**
Sino-Japanese War of 1937-1945 **S: 474**
Stalingrad, Battle of **So: 828**
Wake Island **W: 6**
World War II Valor in the Pacific [historic sites]
National Park System (table: National
monuments) **N: 52**
World Wide Fund for Nature [organization] *See*
WWF *in this index*
World Wide Web [computer network] **W: 499**
See also Internet *in this index*
Advertising (Recent developments) **A: 80**
Audio-visual materials (Other computerized
tools) **A: 883**
Berners-Lee, Tim **B: 270**
Communication (The development of the
Internet) **Ci: 886**
Computer (The World Wide Web) **Ci: 921**
Distance learning **D: 238**
E-commerce (Business-to-consumer
transactions) **E: 2**
Google Inc. **G: 270**
Internet **I: 350**; (How the Internet works) **I: 350b**;
(The World Wide Web) **I: 350d**; (The Web forms)
I: 350g
Web browser **W: 175**
World Wildlife Fund *See* WWF *in this index*
World Zionist Organization
Weizmann, Chaim **W: 188**
WorldCom Inc.
Accounting (The history of accounting) **A: 23**
Business (Recent developments) **B: 727**
United States, History of the (Financial troubles)
U: 196f
World's Columbian Exposition [Chicago]
Chicago (A city reborn) **C: 435** *with picture*
Chicago, University of **C: 438**
City planning (The Industrial Revolution) **Ci: 603**
Ferris wheel **F: 77** *with picture*
Painting (Women artists) **P: 73**
Westinghouse Electric Corporation **W: 242**
"Worlds" debate
Debate (Academic debate) **D: 64**
World's fair **W: 500**
World's Wife, The [book by Duffy]
Duffy, Carol Ann **D: 378**
World's Woman's Christian Temperance Union
Woman's Christian Temperance Union **W: 382**
Worm [animal] **W: 500** *with pictures*
Deep sea (Invertebrates) **D: 82a** *with picture*
Flatworm **F: 229** *with diagram*
Schistosomiasis **S: 176**
Worm [computer]
Computer (Computer security) **Ci: 924**
Computer virus **Ci: 925**
Internet (Internet crime) **I: 350f**
Worm gear
Gear **G: 75**
Worm lizard [reptile] *See* Amphisbaenian *in this
index*
Worm snake *See* Slender blind snake *in this index*
Worms [Germany] **W: 501**
Worms [disorder]
Cat (Veterinary care) **C: 295**
Disease (Other infectious diseases) **D: 227**
Dog (Medical care) **D: 279**
Worms, Concordat of [1122]
Church and state (History) **C: 542**
Worms, Diet of [1521]
Luther, Martin (The Diet of Worms) **L: 528**
Worms **W: 501**
Worms, Edict of **W: 502**
Worms, Edict of [European history] **W: 501**
Luther, Martin (The Diet of Worms) **L: 528**
Reformation (Martin Luther) **R: 197**
Worms Cathedral [Germany]
Architecture *picture on* **A: 619**
Wormwood [plant] **W: 502**
Worship [religion]
Bible (The Bible in worship) **B: 286**
Christianity (Forms of worship) **C: 522h**
Colonial life in America (Religious and political
reasons) **C: 788**
Dance (Why people dance) **D: 24**
Idolatry **I: 47**

Judaism (Worship) **J: 181**
Prayer **P: 734**
Protestantism (Worship) **P: 834**
Religion (Religious rituals) **R: 217**
Sun worship **So: 988**
Worsted [yarn]
Wool (Making yarn) **W: 400**
Wort [liquid]
Brewing (Mashing) **B: 595**
Worth, Jonathan [American political leader]
North Carolina (table) **N: 490**
Worth, William Jenkins [American general]
Fort Worth **F: 417**
Worthington, Thomas [American political leader]
Ohio (table) **O: 699**
Wortis, Edward Irving [American author] *See* Avi
in this index
Wotan [mythology] *See* Odin *in this index*
Wotan [opera character]
Opera: *(Ring of the Nibelung, The)* **O: 806-807**
Wouk, Herman [American author] **W: 502**
Wound [injury]
First aid (First aid for bleeding) **F: 136**
Tetanus **T: 182b**
Wound and the Bow, The [book by Wilson]
Wilson, Edmund **W: 316**
Wound capacitor [electricity]
Capacitor **C: 186**
Wound diphtheria [disease]
Diphtheria (Cause, symptoms, and
complications) **D: 216**
Wounded Knee [South Dakota] **W: 502**
American Indian Movement **A: 411**
Sioux Indians **S: 475**
South Dakota (The mid-1900's) **So: 684**
Wounded Knee, Battle of [1890]
Ghost Dance **G: 182**
Indian, American (After European contact)
I: 159-160
Indian wars (Wounded Knee) **I: 194**
South Dakota (Territorial days) **So: 681-683**
Wounded Knee (The 1890 massacre) **W: 502**
Wovoka **W: 502**
Wounding [industrial process]
Turpentine **T: 519**
Wovoka [American Indian religious leader] **W: 502**
Indian, American (Prophets) **I: 148**
Indian wars (Wovoka) **I: 194**
South Dakota (Territorial days) **So: 681-683**
Western frontier life in America (Settlers and
Native Americans) **W: 239**
Woyzeck [play by Büchner]
Büchner, Georg **B: 663**
German literature (Other writers) **G: 140**
Opera: *(Wozzeck)* **O: 808**
Wozniak, Stephen G. [American engineer]
Apple Inc. **A: 573**
Computer (The personal computer) **Ci: 924c**
with picture
Jobs, Steve **J: 130**
Wozzeck [opera by Berg]
Berg, Alban **B: 257**
Classical music *picture on* **C: 651**
Opera (The search for new forms) **O: 799-800**;
(Wozzeck) **O: 808**
WPA [U.S. history] *See* Works Progress
Administration *in this index*
WPP Group [company]
Advertising (The advertising industry) **A: 77**
Wrangell Mountains [Alaska]
Alaska (Land regions) **A: 292** *with map*
Wrangell-St. Elias National Park [Alaska] **W: 502**
National Park System **N: 43**; (table: National
parks) **N: 49** *with picture*
Wrangell-St. Elias National Preserve [Alaska]
National Park System (table: National preserves)
N: 58
Wrangler
Cowboy (The trail drive) **Ci: 1111**
Wrapped art
Christo **C: 537**
Wrapping paper
Paperwork (Wrapping paper) **P: 138**
Wrasse [fish] **W: 503**
Fish *pictures on* **F: 144, F: 155, F: 168**
Wreath [decoration]
Christmas (Christmas decorations) **C: 535**
Holly **H: 292**
Wren [bird] **W: 503** *with pictures*
Animal *picture on* **A: 483**
Bird *picture on* **B: 358**; (Birds of urban areas)
B: 333 *with picture*; (Birds of brushy areas)
B: 338 *with picture*; (Birds of the desert) **B: 339**
with picture; (Birds of Australia and New
Zealand) **B: 346** *with picture*
Wren, Sir Christopher [English architect] **W: 504**
with picture

Architecture (Baroque architecture) **A: 622** *with
picture*
England (The arts) **E: 298-299**
London (Churches) **L: 435**; (Other places of
interest) **L: 437**; (Rebuilding the City) **L: 441**
Urban renewal (History) **U: 220**
Wrentit [bird]
Babbler **B: 2**
Wrestling [sport] **W: 504** *with pictures*
See also Sumo *in this index*
Mixed martial arts **M: 680**
Olympic Games (Summer Olympic Games)
O: 746e-749
Wrestling, Professional [sport] **W: 506** *with picture*
Lucha libre **L: 513**
Wretched of the Earth, The [book by Fanon]
Fanon, Frantz Omar **F: 27**
Wriggler [insect]
Fly (Larva) **F: 310** *with picture*
Insect (Complete metamorphosis) **I: 293**
Mosquito (Larva) **M: 833**
Wright, Charles H. [American physician]
Museum of African American History **M: 940**
Wright, Fielding L. [American political leader]
Dixiecrat Party **D: 256**
Mississippi (table) **M: 640**
Wright, Frances [American social reformer] **W: 507**
Owen, Robert Dale **O: 883**
Wright, Frank Lloyd [American architect] **W: 507**
with pictures
Architecture *picture on* **A: 631**; (Frank Lloyd
Wright) **A: 629**
Chicago (Architecture) **C: 428**
Florida *picture on* **F: 246**
Furniture (Organic design) **F: 583** *with picture*
Guggenheim Museum **G: 421**
Pennsylvania (Places to visit) **P: 254**
United States *picture on* **U: 117**
Wisconsin (Places to visit) **W: 356**
Wright, George [American baseball player]
Baseball (table: Hall of Fame) **B: 134b**
Wright, Harold Bell [American author]
Branson **B: 564**
Wright, Harry [American sportsman]
Baseball (table: Hall of Fame) **B: 134b**
Wright, James Claude, Jr. [American political
leader]
Congress of the United States (Congressional
ethics) **Ci: 948**
Wright, Jeremiah A., Jr. [American religious
leader]
Obama, Barack (A second autobiography)
O: 640d-640e; (Controversies) **O: 640e**
Wright, John Joseph Patrick [American religious
leader]
Cardinal (table: American cardinals) **C: 211**
Wright, Joseph A. [American political leader]
Indiana (table) **I: 214**
Wright, Luke E. [American government official]
Roosevelt, Theodore (table) **R: 466**
Wright, Orville [American inventor] *See* Wright
brothers *in this index*
Wright, Philemon [American businessman]
Ottawa (Early days) **O: 874**
Wright, Richard [American author] **W: 508**
African American literature (The 1900's) **A: 136a**
American literature (Realist fiction) **A: 422**
Wright, Robert [American political leader]
Maryland (table) **M: 255**
Wright, Sewall [American biologist]
Evolution (The synthetic theory) **E: 432**
Wright, Silas [American political leader]
New York (table) **N: 313**
Polk, James Knox (Election of 1844) **P: 642**
Vice president of the United States (Nomination)
V: 350
Wright, Teresa [American actress]
Motion picture (Best performance by an actress
in a supporting role: 1942) **M: 862b**
Wright, Wilbur [American inventor] *See* Wright
brothers *in this index*
Wright, Will [American game designer]
Electronic game (The growth of computer
gaming) **E: 204e**; (Social gaming) **E: 204e**
Wright, Willard H. [American author] *See* Van Dine,
S. S. *in this index*
Wright A flyer [airplane]
Aircraft, Military *picture on* **A: 204**
Wright brothers [American inventors] **W: 508** *with
pictures*
Air Force, United States (Early years) **A: 194** *with
picture*
Airplane (The Wright brothers) **A: 231** *with
pictures*; (Other pioneer planes and fliers)
A: 233-234
Aviation **A: 984**; (History of the aviation industry)
A: 986; (table: Aviation speed records) **A: 990**

Curtiss, Glenn Hammond Ci: 1199
Glider (Early days) G: 230 *with picture*
Invention (The inventive process) I: 355-357
Kite (History) K: 340-341
Transportation (The beginnings of modern transportation) T: 390
Wright Brothers National Memorial [North Carolina]
National Park System (table: National memorials) N: 54
Wright brothers (Larer life and legacy) W: 510
Wright Company
Aviation (History of the aviation industry) A: 986-987
Wright brothers (Wright Company) W: 510
Wright-Patterson Air Force Base [Ohio]
Ohio (Places to visit) O: 690 *with picture*
Wrinkle-faced bat [animal]
Bat (Face) B: 160 *with picture*
Wrinkle in Time, A [book by L'Engle]
L'Engle, Madeleine L: 191
Wrinkle ridge [astronomy]
Moon (Wrinkle ridges) M: 790
Wrist W: 510 *with diagram*
Carpal tunnel syndrome C: 245 *with diagram*
Hand (Parts of the hand) H: 40
Wrist shot
Hockey (Shooting) H: 277
Wrist watch
Watch (History) W: 115 *with pictures*
Writ of assistance [law] W: 510
Otis, James O: 870
Writ of attachment [law]
Attachment A: 878
Writ of certiorari *See* Certiorari, Writ of *in this index*
Writ of habeas corpus [law]
Habeas corpus H: 2
Writ of mandamus [law]
Mandamus M: 135
Writ of summons
Nobility (The creation of peerages) N: 450
Writer *See* Writing *in this index*
Writer, The [magazine]
Writing (Free-lance markets) W: 511
Writer's Digest [magazine]
Writing (Free-lance markets) W: 511
Writer's Market [book]
Writing (Free-lance markets) W: 511
Writing [career] W: 511
See also the list of Related articles in the Writing article
History (The writing) H: 261
Literature L: 352
Newspaper (The editorial department) N: 381
Television (Planning and preparation) T: 110c-110d
Writing [skill]
See also Composition; Writing system *in this index*
Literacy L: 350
Newspaper (Writing and editing stories) N: 383
Reading (The whole-language philosophy) R: 158
Spelling So: 775
A Guide to Writing Skills **Research Guide: 6**
Writing paper
Paper (Special kinds of paper) P: 136
Writing system W: 512
Alphabet A: 381
Communication (Early writing systems) Ci: 879 *with pictures*
Education (The beginning of formal education) E: 97
Handwriting H: 46 *with pictures*
Hieroglyphics H: 225
Indian, American (Writing) I: 150 *with picture*
Invention (The first civilizations) I: 358
Library (History) L: 256
Manuscript M: 172
Maya (Communication and learning) M: 324 *with picture*
Prehistoric people P: 743; (The end of prehistoric times) P: 753-754a
Scribe S: 226
Sumer So: 972 *with picture*
Writings, The [religious book]
Bible (The Hebrew Bible) B: 279
Wrocław [Poland] W: 513
Poland *picture on* P: 609
Silesia S: 457
Wrong font [printing]
Proofreading (Proofreaders' marks) P: 822
Wroth, Lady Mary [British author]
English literature (Prose writings) E: 317
Wrought iron
Iron and steel (Kinds of iron and steel) I: 436-437; (Making iron products) I: 441
Ironwork, Decorative *pictures on* I: 454

Wryneck [bird] W: 513
WSM [radio station]
Country music (Early commercial success) Ci: 1098b
"Grand Ole Opry" G: 308
"WSM Barn Dance" [radio program]
"Grand Ole Opry" G: 308
WTO [organization] *See* World Trade Organization *in this index*
Wu [dialect]
Chinese language (Spoken Chinese) C: 510
Wu, Chien-shiung [American physicist] W: 513
Wu Bangguo [Chinese political leader]
China (Recent developments) C: 506-507
Wu Chen [Chinese artist]
Painting (Chinese painting) P: 44-46
Wu Cheng'en [Chinese author]
Chinese literature (Drama and fiction) C: 511-512
Wu Daozi [Chinese painter] W: 514
Wu Tao-tzu [Chinese painter] *See* Wu Daozi *in this index*
Wu-Ti [Chinese emperor] *See* Wudi *in this index*
Wu Xinzhi [Chinese anthropologist]
Prehistoric people (table) P: 754
Wuchang [China]
Wuhan W: 514
Wuchereria bancrofti [animal]
Filaria F: 99
Wudi [Chinese emperor]
Exploration (The Chinese) E: 441
Han dynasty H: 38
Wuerffel, Danny [American football player]
Football (table) F: 363
Wuhan [China] W: 514
Wundt, Wilhelm [German psychologist] W: 514
Psychology (Psychology becomes a science) P: 849
Wupatki National Monument [Arizona] W: 514
National Park System (table: National monuments) N: 50-52
Würm ice age [geology]
Ice age (Evidence of ice ages and their climates) I: 6-7
Wuthering Heights [book by Brontë]
Brontë sisters (Their works) B: 637
Wuthrich, Kurt [Swiss chemist]
Nobel Prizes (Chemistry: 2002) N: 444
WWF [organization] W: 514
Wildlife conservation (International cooperation) W: 305
WWJ [radio station, Detroit]
Radio (The start of broadcasting) R: 92
Wyandot City [former city]
Kansas City [Kansas] (Government and history) K: 240
Wyandot Indians
Kansas City [Kansas] (Government and history) K: 240
Wyandotte [breed]
Chicken (table) C: 443
Wyandotte Cave [Indiana]
Indiana (Places to visit) I: 206 *with picture*
Wyatt, Hattie [birth name of]
Caraway, Hattie Ophelia Wyatt C: 202
Wyatt, John [British inventor]
Industrial Revolution (Spinning machines) I: 248-249
Wyatt, Sir Thomas [English poet] W: 514
English literature (Elizabethan poetry) E: 316-317
Poetry (Renaissance poetry) P: 596
Wyatt's Rebellion [English history]
Elizabeth I (Early years) E: 238
Wycherley, William [English dramatist] W: 514
Wycliffe, John [English religious leader] W: 514
Hus, John H: 457
John of Gaunt J: 134
Lollards L: 426
Puritans (Puritan beliefs) P: 910
Wye [river, Great Britain]
Wales (Rivers and coastline) W: 11 *with map*
Wye Oak [tree]
Maryland (Interesting facts) M: 241
Wye River Memorandum [peace agreement]
Israel (The 1990's) I: 489
Wyeth, Andrew [American painter] W: 515 *with picture*
Painting (Space) P: 35; (Tempera) P: 38-39
Wyeth, N. C. [American artist]
Coronado, Francisco Vásquez de *picture on* Ci: 1067
Knights and knighthood *picture on* K: 350
Pyle, Howard P: 915
Robin Hood *picture on* R: 367
Wyeth, Andrew W: 515
Wyeth, Nathaniel J. [American pioneer]
Lee, Jason L: 176
Oregon Trail O: 850

Wyler, William [American director] W: 515
Motion picture (Best achievement in directing: 1942, 1946, 1959) M: 862
Wylie, Elinor [American poet] W: 515
Wyman, Bill [British musician]
Rolling Stones R: 402a
Wyman, Jane [American actress]
Motion picture (Best performance by an actress: 1948) M: 862
Reagan, Ronald Wilson (Family life) R: 166
Wynette, Tammy [American singer]
Country music (Modern country music) Ci: 1098c
"Wynken, Blynken, and Nod" [poem by Field]
Field, Eugene F: 91
Wynn, Early [American baseball player]
Baseball (table: Hall of Fame) B: 134b
Wynne, Arthur [American journalist]
Crossword puzzle Ci: 1156
Wynne, Emanuel [French pirate]
Pirate *picture on* P: 495
Wynne, Robert J. [American government official]
Roosevelt, Theodore (table) R: 466
Wyoming W: 516 *with pictures and maps*
See also the list of Related articles in the Wyoming article
Wyoming [city, Michigan]
Grand Rapids G: 309
Wyoming, University of W: 538
Wyoming (Libraries and museums) W: 520-521 *with picture*
Wyoming State Library [Wyoming]
Wyoming (Libraries and museums) W: 520-521
Wyoming Stock Growers Association
Wyoming (Territorial progress) W: 534-536; (The Johnson County War) W: 536
Wyoming Territorial Library [Cheyenne, Wyoming]
Wyoming (Libraries and museums) W: 520-521
Wyoming Valley [region, Pennsylvania] W: 538
Wyoming Valley Massacre [1778] W: 538
Pennsylvania (The Revolutionary War) P: 265-267
Wyse, Lucien Napoleon Bonaparte [French businessman]
Panama Canal (The French failure) P: 125
Wyspiański, Stanisław [Polish dramatist]
Poland (The arts) P: 607
Wyss, Johann David [Swiss author]
Wyss family W: 538
Wyss, Johann Emmanuel [Swiss author]
Wyss family W: 538
Wyss, Johann Rudolph [Swiss author]
Wyss family W: 538
Wyss family [Swiss authors] W: 538
Wyszyński, Stefan [Polish religious leader] W: 538 *with portrait*
Poland (Communist rule) P: 613-614
Wythe, George [American patriot] W: 538
Jefferson, Thomas (Education) J: 77; (Lawyer) J: 78

X

X [letter] X: 539 *with pictures*
X, Malcolm [American social reformer] *See* Malcolm X *in this index*
X-1 [aircraft]
Jet propulsion (Development of jet propulsion) J: 114-115
Rocket (Atmospheric research) R: 386; (Rocket-powered airplanes) R: 391
X-15 [aircraft]
Airplane (Supersonic airplanes) A: 238
Rocket (Atmospheric research) R: 386; (Rocket-powered airplanes) R: 391
X-axis *See* X-coordinate *in this index*
X chromosome [genetics]
Fragile X syndrome F: 450
Hemophilia (How hemophilia is inherited) H: 182 *with diagram*
Heredity (Chromosomes and sexual determination) H: 202; (Sex-linked genes) H: 202
Rett syndrome (Cause) R: 266
X-coordinate [mathematics]
Algebra (Working with equations) A: 356 *with pictures*
X-linked gene [genetics]
Heredity (Sex-linked genes) H: 202
X-linked recessive disorder
Genetic testing (Genes associated with disease) G: 84d
X-ray astronomy
Astronomy (X-ray astronomy) A: 845
X-ray binary [astronomy]
Star (Binary stars) So: 852
X rays (In outer space) X: 543
X-ray crystallography [physics]
See also X-ray diffraction *in this index*

Bragg, Sir William Henry **B:** 547
Bragg, Sir William Lawrence **B:** 548
Proteomics **P:** 833
X-ray diffraction [physics]
Biophysics **B:** 326
Coal (Analyzing coal composition) **Ci:** 717-718
Diffraction (Uses of diffraction) **D:** 201
Franklin, Rosalind Elsie **F:** 492
Molecule (Studying molecules) **M:** 694
X-ray laser [physics]
Laser (Other kinds of lasers) **L:** 85
X-ray pulsar [star]
Binary star **B:** 308
X-ray spectroscopy
Siegbahn, Karl Manne Georg **S:** 449
X-ray telescope [astronomy]
Telescope (X-ray telescopes) **T:** 109
X rays (Penetrating power) **X:** 541
X-ray tube
X rays *diagram on* **X:** 541; (How X rays are produced) **X:** 542
X rays [radiation] **X:** 540 *with pictures*
Astronomy (table: The electromagnetic spectrum) **A:** 839; (X-ray astronomy) **A:** 845
Atom (How scientists study atoms) **A:** 874
Beryllium **B:** 273
Black hole (Galactic black holes) **B:** 388
Bragg, Sir William Henry **B:** 547
Bragg, Sir William Lawrence **B:** 547
Cancer (Radiation) **C:** 170; (Cancer checkups) **C:** 171 *with picture*; (Radiation therapy) **C:** 172
Computed tomography **Ci:** 907
Electromagnetic waves (The electromagnetic spectrum) **E:** 202 *with diagram*
Electronics (Medicine and research) **E:** 207; (Early experiments) **E:** 215
Fluoroscopy **F:** 306 *with picture*
Invention (The late 1800's) **I:** 362
Light (The spectrum of light sources) **L:** 284 *with diagram*
Mammography **M:** 129
Medicine *picture on* **M:** 364, *picture on* **M:** 376
Metallography **M:** 426
Mineral (Determining the structure of crystals) **M:** 571
Moseley, Henry Gwyn-Jeffreys **M:** 828
Particle accelerator (Uses of accelerators) **P:** 184
Radiation (In medicine) **R:** 74; (Electromagnetic radiation) **R:** 75-76 *with picture*; (Causes of radiation) **R:** 78-79; (Dose) **R:** 79
Radiology **R:** 98 *with picture*
Roentgen, Wilhelm Conrad **R:** 400
Siegbahn, Karl Manne Georg **S:** 450
Sun (Energy output) **So:** 976
Surgery (Instruments) **So:** 1005
Technology (Emerging technologies) **T:** 76
Teeth (Dental checkups) **T:** 82 *with picture*
Telescope (Other telescopes) **T:** 108
Thulium **T:** 272
Xanax [drug]
Benzodiazepine **B:** 256
Drug abuse (table: Some commonly abused drugs) **D:** 363
Xanthippus [Spartan general]
Regulus, Marcus Atilius **R:** 206
Xanthophyll [pigment]
Leaf (The leaf changes color) **L:** 152
Xanthus [legendary animal]
Horse (table: Famous horses in history and legend) **H:** 361
Xavier, Saint Francis [Spanish missionary] **X:** 543
Japan (Warring states period) **J:** 54
Xbox 360 [machine]
Electronic game (Bigger games) **E:** 204f
Xe [symbol]
Xenon **X:** 543
Xena [astronomy] *See* Eris *in this index*
Xenacanthus [fish]
Prehistoric animal *picture on* **P:** 738
Xenon [element] **X:** 543
Xenon rocket
Rocket (Ion rockets) **R:** 389
Xenophobia [psychology]
Phobia **P:** 392
Xenophon [Greek historian] **X:** 543
Economics (Early theories) **E:** 63
Xenotime [mineral]
Ytterbium **Y:** 574
Xenotransplant [surgery] **X:** 544
Transplant (Sources of donor organs) **T:** 380
Xeriscaping [gardening]
Gardening *picture on* **G:** 36; (Specialty gardens) **G:** 31
Xerography [copying]
Copying machine (Electrostatic copying) **Ci:** 1045
Xerox Corporation **X:** 544
Xerophile [biology]

Extremophile **E:** 458
Xerophthalmia [disorder]
Vitamin (Vitamin A) **V:** 430
Xerophyte [plant]
Plant (Deserts) **P:** 523-527
Xerox Corporation X: 544
Xerxes I [king of Persia] **X:** 544
Greece, Ancient (The Persian wars) **G:** 373
Leonidas **L:** 202
Persia, Ancient (The Achaemenid Empire) **P:** 298
Thermopylae **T:** 255
XFY-1 [aircraft]
Airplane *picture on* **A:** 236
V/STOL **V:** 452
Xhosa [people] **X:** 544 *with picture*
Clothing *picture on* **Ci:** 687
South Africa (History) **So:** 617-618
Zulu **Z:** 608
Xi Jiang [river, China] **X:** 545
Asia (Rivers) **A:** 794
China (The Southern Uplands) **C:** 493 *with map*
Xi Lake [China]
Hangzhou **H:** 51
Xi Xia [kingdom]
Genghis Khan (Conquests) **G:** 88-89 *with map*
Xia [people]
China (The first dynasties) **C:** 499
Xia Gui [Chinese painter]
Ma Yuan **M:** 2
Xiamen [China] **X:** 545
Xi'an [China] **X:** 545
Han dynasty **H:** 38
Tang dynasty **T:** 25
Terra-cotta army of Xi'an **T:** 172
Xilhoumen Bridge [China]
Bridge (table: Suspension) **B:** 603
Xilingshi [wife of Huangdi]
Silk (Discovery of silk) **S:** 460
Ximénes de Cisneros, Francisco [Spanish religious leader]
Counter Reformation (Catholic reform) **Ci:** 1096
Xin dynasty [Chinese history]
Han dynasty **H:** 38
Xingu River [river, Brazil]
Amazon River (The course of the Amazon) **A:** 403
Xinjiang [region, China] **X:** 545
Asia (Way of life in Central Asia) **A:** 790
China (The Xinjiang-Mongolian Uplands) **C:** 491 *with picture*
Turkestan (Chinese Turkestan) **T:** 501
Xipe Tótec [Aztec god]
Aztec *picture on* **A:** 1002
Mythology *picture on* **M:** 973
Xiuhtecuhtli [Aztec god]
Aztec *picture on* **A:** 1001
XM Satellite Radio Holdings Inc.
Radio (Radio since the 1950's) **R:** 94
Xmas
Christmas **C:** 529
XMM-Newton [spacecraft]
Astronomy (X-ray astronomy) **A:** 845
Xochimilco [lake, Mexico]
Lake Xochimilco **L:** 48
Xuanzang [Chinese explorer]
Exploration (Chinese exploration) **E:** 442
Xunzi [Chinese philosopher] **X:** 546
Confucianism (Early Confucianism) **Ci:** 936
XY Company
North West Company **N:** 519
Xylem [botany]
Plant (Parts of plants) **P:** 528
Root (The core) **R:** 471 *with diagrams*
Sap (Vascular sap) **S:** 121 *with diagram*
Stem (Herbaceous stems) **So:** 887
Tree (Trunk and branches) **T:** 416 *with diagram*
Xylophone [musical instrument] **X:** 546 *with picture*
Music (Percussion instruments) **M:** 950
XYZ Affair [U.S. history] **X:** 546
Adams, John (Difficulties with France) **A:** 38
Marshall, John (Political career) **M:** 230
Pinckney, Charles Cotesworth **P:** 467
Talleyrand (Joins Napoleon) **T:** 20
United States, History of the (Problems in foreign affairs) **U:** 163

Y

Y [letter] **Y:** 547 *with pictures*
Y [organization] *See* Young Men's Christian Association *in this index*
Y [symbol]
Yttrium **Y:** 575
Y-axis *See* Y-coordinate *in this index*
Y chromosome [genetics]
Fragile X syndrome **F:** 450
Heredity (Chromosomes and sexual determination) **H:** 202
Y-coordinate

Algebra (Working with equations) **A:** 356 *with pictures*
Y-gun [weapon]
Depth charge **D:** 151
Yablonovyy Mountains [mountains, Siberia]
Y: 548
Yacht
America's Cup **A:** 431
Boating *picture on* **B:** 430; (Types of boats) **B:** 428
Radar *picture on* **R:** 65
Yacht club
Boating (Boating safety programs) **B:** 431; (The development of pleasure boating) **B:** 431
Yachting *See* Yacht *in this index*
Yad Vashem [museum]
Jerusalem *picture on* **J:** 100; (West Jerusalem) **J:** 95 *with map*
Yadav, Ram Baran [Nepalese political leader]
Nepal (History) **N:** 126-127
Yadin, Yigael [Israeli archaeologist]
Masada **M:** 262
Yaeyama Islands [islands, Pacific]
Ryukyu Islands **R:** 574
Yafo [Israel]
Tel Aviv **T:** 88
YAG crystal [electronics]
Laser (Solid-state lasers) **L:** 85
Yagua Indians
Indian, American *pictures on* **I:** 140
Yahgan Indians
Indian, American *picture on* **I:** 140
Yahola, Archie [American Indian leader]
Tulsa (History) **T:** 483
Yahoo! Inc. [company] **Y:** 548
Internet (The Web forms) **I:** 350g
Yahoos [fictional people]
Swift, Jonathan: (*Gulliver's Travels*) **So:** 1040
Yahrzeit [custom]
Judaism (Special occasions) **J:** 182
Yahweh [name for God]
God **G:** 243
Jehovah **J:** 89
Yahya Khan, Agha Muhammad [Pakistani political leader]
Bangladesh (East Pakistan) **B:** 85-86
Pakistan (Civil war) **P:** 99-100
Yajurveda [religious book]
Hinduism (The Vedas) **H:** 235
Vedas **V:** 291
Yak [animal] **Y:** 548 *with picture*
Animal *picture on* **A:** 475
Nepal (Land and climate) **N:** 126
Tibet (The people and their work) **T:** 276-277
Yak-38 Forger [aircraft]
V/STOL **V:** 453
Yakima Indians
Indian, American (In the United States) **I:** 179
Yaksa [people]
Sri Lanka (History) **So:** 819
Yakub-al-Mansur [Berber leader]
Rabat **R:** 46
Yakub Beg [king of Turkestan]
Turkestan (History) **T:** 501
Yakuts [people]
Lena River **L:** 190
Yala, Kumba [Guinea-Bissauan political leader]
Guinea-Bissau (History) **G:** 434
Yala National Park [Sri Lanka]
National park (table) **N:** 42f
Yale, Elihu [English philanthropist] **Y:** 548
Yale University (History) **Y:** 549
Yale, Linus, Jr. [American inventor] **Y:** 548
Lock (The development of the lock) **L:** 412
Yale Center for British Art
Yale University (The Yale campus) **Y:** 548-549
Yale University Y: 548
Bush, George Walker (College and military service) **B:** 722d
Connecticut (Cultural life) **Ci:** 953; (Schools) **Ci:** 956
New Haven (Cultural life and recreation) **N:** 229 *with picture*
Rowing (History) **R:** 494
Rudolph, Paul **R:** 509 *with picture*
Universities and colleges (The oldest U.S. universities and colleges) **U:** 210
Yale University Art Gallery [New Haven]
Yale University (The Yale campus) **Y:** 548-549
Yale University Library [New Haven]
See also Beinecke Rare Book and Manuscript Library *in this index*
Connecticut (Libraries) **Ci:** 956
Yale University (The Yale campus) **Y:** 548
Yalow, Rosalyn Sussman [American physiologist]
Nobel Prizes (Physiology or medicine: 1977) **N:** 446
Yalta [Ukraine] **Y:** 549
Crimea *picture on* **Ci:** 1142

Ukraine picture on U: 11
Yalta Conference [1945] Y: 549
  Cold War (The coming of the Cold War) Ci: 763
  Roosevelt, Franklin Delano (Yalta Conference)
    R: 458 with picture
  United Nations (The Dumbarton Oaks
    Conference) U: 94-95
  World War II (The strategy) W: 480-481
Yalu River [Korea-China] Y: 549
  Korea, North (The land) K: 371 with map
Yam [plant] Y: 549 with picture
Yam bean See Jicama in this index
Yama [religion]
  Yoga Y: 567
Yamaguchi, Kristi [American skater]
  Asian Americans (Notable Asian American "firsts")
    A: 812f
Yamamadi Indians
  Indian, American picture on I: 140
Yamamoto, Isoroku [Japanese admiral] Y: 550
  World War II (Rabaul) W: 489
Yamasaki, Minoru [American architect]
  World Trade Center W: 451
Yamashita, Tomoyuki [Japanese general] Y: 550
Yamato [ship]
  Battleship (The modern battleship) B: 172
Yamato-e [style]
  Painting (Japanese painting) P: 47
Yamato period [Japanese history] See Kofun era
  in this index
Yaméogo, Maurice [African political leader]
  Burkina Faso (History) B: 706-707
Yamoussoukro [Côte d'Ivoire] Y: 550 with picture
  Côte d'Ivoire Ci: 1084a, picture on Ci: 1084b
Yamuna River [India] Y: 550
Yana [school]
  Buddhism (Buddhist schools) B: 669
Yancey, William Lowndes [Confederate political
  leader] Y: 550
  Alabama (Early statehood) A: 275-276
Yáñez, Augustín [Mexican author]
  Latin American literature (The mid-1900's) L: 114
Yang [force]
  Acupuncture A: 31
  Medicine (China and India) M: 372
  Taoism picture on T: 36
Yang, Chen Ning [American physicist] Y: 551
Yang, Jerry [American businessman]
  Yahoo! Inc. Y: 548
Yang Chien [Chinese emperor] See Yang Jian in
  this index
Yang di-pertuan agong [office]
  Malaysia (Government) M: 98a
Yang Jian [Chinese emperor]
  Sui dynasty So: 964
Yang Liwei [Chinese astronaut]
  Astronaut (Achievements in space) A: 829-830
Yang-na [former village]
  Los Angeles (Exploration) L: 469
Yangcheng [China] See Guangzhou in this index
Yangdi, Sui [Chinese emperor]
  Sui dynasty So: 964
Yangon [Myanmar] Y: 551 with picture
  Myanmar M: 970 with picture
  Naypyidaw N: 91
Yangshao culture [Chinese culture]
  China (Beginnings of Chinese civilization) C: 499
Yangtze Kiang See Yangtze River in this index
Yangtze River [China] Y: 551
  Asia (Rivers) A: 794
  China picture on C: 493; (The land) C: 490-491
    with map; (Recent developments) C: 506
  Inland waterway I: 274
  River (table) R: 352
  Three Gorges Dam T: 270
Yangtze River dolphin
  River dolphin R: 354
Yangtze Valley [region, China]
  Asia (The Huang He and Yangtze valleys) A: 805
    with map
Yankee [U.S. history] Y: 552
Yankee Division of Massachusetts [U.S. Army]
  Massachusetts (The early 1900's) M: 293
"Yankee Doodle" [song] Y: 552
Yankee Doodle Dandy [film]
  Cagney, James C: 14 with picture
Yankee peddler [U.S. history]
  Connecticut (Colonial life) Ci: 968-970
Yankee Stadium [New York City]
  New York City (Sports) N: 338
  Ruth, Babe R: 568
Yankee terrier [dog] See American Staffordshire
  terrier in this index
Yankees, New York [team] See New York Yankees
  in this index
Yankton Indians
  Sioux Indians S: 475

Yankton Press and Dakotan [newspaper]
  South Dakota (Communication) So: 679
Yankton Sioux, Treaty of
  South Dakota (Agricultural settlement) So: 681
Yanoama See Yanomami Indians in this index
Yanomama See Yanomami Indians in this index
Yanomami Indians Y: 552
  Indian, American (Current issues) I: 182-183
  Rain forest (The Americas) R: 126b
Yanomamö See Yanomami Indians in this index
Yanukovych, Viktor [Ukrainian political leader]
  Ukraine (Political changes) U: 14
Yao [people]
  Laos (People) L: 70
  Tanzania (The development of trade) T: 34-35
Yao Ming [Chinese basketball player]
  Basketball (Basketball today) B: 155
Yaoundé [Cameroon] Y: 552
  Cameroon (People) C: 85 with picture
Yap Islands [Pacific] Y: 552
  Caroline Islands C: 244
  Micronesia, Federated States of (Government)
    M: 515
  Pacific Islands, Trust Territory of the P: 13
Yapok [animal]
  Opossum O: 811
Yaqui Indians Y: 553
Yar'Adua, Umaru [Nigerian political leader]
  Nigeria (Internal conflict) N: 418
Yarborough, Cale [American race driver]
  Automobile racing (table: NASCAR Sprint Cup
    champions) A: 981
Yard [architecture]
  Drama (Elizabethan theaters) D: 331
Yard [unit of measure] Y: 553 with picture
  Foot F: 352
Yard line
  Football (The field) F: 354-355 with diagram
Yard-long bean [plant]
  Cowpea Ci: 1113
Yardang [geology]
  Desert (Desert climate and land) D: 155-156
Yardbirds [rock group]
  Led Zeppelin L: 175
"Yardley Oak" [poem by Cowper]
  Cowper, William Ci: 1113
Yarlung Zangbo [river, Tibet]
  Brahmaputra River B: 548
Yarmouth bloater [food]
  Herring (Uses) H: 216
Yarmulka [clothing]
  Judaism (Orthodox Judaism) J: 180
Yarn [thread]
  Cotton (Spinning) Ci: 1091
  Dye (Dyeing textiles) D: 396 with picture
  Textile T: 212, pictures on T: 216; (Making the
    yarn) T: 215 with picture
  Thread T: 269 with picture
  Wool (Making yarn) W: 400 with picture
Yarn dyeing
  Wool (Making fabric) W: 401
Yarra [river, Australia]
  Melbourne (The city) M: 388 with picture
Yasa [Mongol history]
  Genghis Khan G: 88
Yasak [Mongol history]
  Genghis Khan G: 88
Yasgur, Max [American farmer]
  Woodstock festival W: 395
Yasnaya Polyana [estate]
  Tolstoy, Leo (Early life and works) T: 322
Yasodhara [wife of]
  Buddha (Early life) B: 667
Yassin, Sheik Ahmad [Palestinian political leader]
  Hamas H: 28
Yastrzemski, Carl [American baseball player]
  Baseball (Hall of Fame) B: 134b
Yasukuni Shrine
  Tokyo (Shrines and temples) T: 316
Yates, Elizabeth [American author] Y: 553
  Newbery Medal (table) N: 359
Yates, Joseph C. [American political leader]
  New York (table) N: 313
Yates, Richard [1815-1873, American political
  leader]
  Grant, Ulysses S. (Return to the Army) G: 314
  Illinois (table) I: 71
Yaw [aviation]
  Airplane (Basic movements and controls) A: 222
    with diagrams
Yawar Fiesta [book by Arguedas]
  Latin American literature (The early 1900's) L: 113
Yawkey, Tom [American sportsman]
  Baseball (Hall of Fame) B: 134b
Yawl [sailing]
  Boating (Sailboats) B: 429
  Sailing (Yawls, ketches, and schooners) S: 24

  with picture
Yawning Y: 553
Yaws [disease] Y: 553
Yayoi [Japanese history]
  Japan (Ancestry) J: 35; (Early days) J: 52-53
Yazid [Muslim ruler]
  Muslims (The Muslim Empire) M: 964c
Yazidis [religious group]
  Devil worship D: 175
Yazoo Fraud [U.S. history] Y: 554
Yazoo River [river, Mississippi]
  Mississippi (Rivers and lakes) M: 634 with picture
Yb [symbol]
  Ytterbium Y: 574
Ybor, Vincente Martinez [American businessman]
  Tampa (History) T: 23-24
Ybor City [district]
  Tampa (Description) T: 23
Yding Skovhoj [hill]
  Denmark (The land) D: 137
Yeager, Charles Elwood [American aviator] Y: 554
  Rocket (Rocket-powered airplanes) R: 391
Year [time] Y: 554
  Earth (How Earth moves) E: 17 with diagram
  Hipparchus H: 239
  Leap year L: 162
Year day
  Calendar (Calendar reform) C: 32
Year Down Yonder, A [book by Peck]
  Peck, Richard P: 226
Year of confusion [46 B.C.]
  Calendar (The Julian calendar) C: 31-32
Yeardley, Sir George [American colonial leader]
  House of Burgesses H: 384
Yearling [horse]
  Horse (table: Horse terms) H: 343
  Horse racing (Thoroughbred horses) H: 363-364
Yearling, The [book by Rawlings]
  Rawlings, Marjorie Kinnan R: 152
Years with Laura Díaz, The [book by Fuentes]
  Fuentes, Carlos F: 553
Yeast [book by Kingsley]
  Kingsley, Charles K: 331
Yeast [fungus] Y: 554 with pictures
  Baking (Baking ingredients) F: 73
  Bread (How yeast bread is made) B: 588
  Fermentation F: 73
  Food preservation (How food spoils) F: 341
  Fungi (The importance of fungi) F: 559
  Wine (How wine is made) W: 337-338
Yeast bread [food]
  Bread (Kinds of bread) B: 588 with pictures
Yeats, William Butler [Irish author] Y: 555 with
  portrait
  Irish literature (The Irish literary revival) I: 431
  Pound, Ezra P: 721
  Rhyme R: 319
Yegorov, Boris B. [Soviet cosmonaut]
  Space exploration (Voskhod and Gemini: The first
    multiperson space flights) So: 714
Yehoshua, A. B. [Israeli author]
  Hebrew literature (A new generation of Hebrew
    writers) H: 163
Yekaterinburg [Russia] Y: 556
Yekuno Amlak [king of Ethiopia]
  Ethiopia (The Zagwé dynasty) E: 371
Yell, Archibald [American political leader]
  Arkansas (table) A: 712
Yellow [color]
  Color diagrams on Ci: 821
  Printing (Process color printing) P: 802 with
    picture
Yellow-and-white monkey flower [shrub]
  Flower picture on F: 288
Yellow arc speed [aviation]
  Airplane (Measuring flying speed) A: 225-226
Yellow-bellied sapsucker [bird]
  Bird picture on B: 351
  Sapsucker S: 122
Yellow-bellied wattle-eye [bird]
  Bird (Birds of Africa) B: 344h with picture
Yellow-billed cuckoo [bird]
  Bird (Birds of forests and woodlands) B: 334 with
    picture
  Cuckoo Ci: 1182
Yellow birch [tree]
  Birch (Yellow birch) B: 327
Yellow Book [recording standard]
  Compact disc (CD-ROM's) Ci: 901
Yellow bullhead [fish]
  Bullhead B: 696 with picture
Yellow Christ, The [painting by Gauguin]
  Gauguin, Paul (Early career) G: 69 with picture
Yellow crookneck squash [plant]
  Squash (Summer squashes) So: 813 with picture
Yellow daisy [plant]
  Black-eyed Susan B: 386 with picture

Yellow-dog contracts [labor history]
Labor movement (Organizing workers) **L:** 4; (The Great Depression) **L:** 12
Norris-La Guardia Act **N:** 457
Yellow dogtooth violet [plant]
Flower *picture on* **F:** 285
Yellow fever [disease] **Y:** 556
Finlay, Carlos Juan **F:** 118
Immune system (Active immunity) **I:** 88a
Lazear, Jesse William **L:** 148
New Orleans (The *Paris of America*) **N:** 284
Panama Canal (Victory over disease) **P:** 126
Reed, Walter **R:** 194
Tennessee (Reconstruction) **T:** 154 *with picture*
Yellow Globe Onion
Onion (Cultivation) **O:** 763 *with picture*
Yellow gold
Alloy (Costly and ornamental alloys) **A:** 378
Gold (Jewelry) **G:** 251
Yellow Hat [religious sect]
Dalai Lama **D:** 9
Yellow-headed blackbird
Blackbird **B:** 392
Yellow-headed parrot
Parrot *picture on* **P:** 180
Yellow-headed vulture
Vulture (New World vultures) **V:** 453
Yellow Jack [play by Howard]
Howard, Sidney **H:** 400
Yellow jacket [insect] **Y:** 556
Wasp **W:** 111 *with picture*
Yellow jessamine [plant] **Y:** 556
Yellow journalism
Hearst, William Randolph **H:** 131
Journalism (The age of sensationalism) **J:** 175
Outcault, Richard Felton **O:** 879
Pulitzer, Joseph (His career) **P:** 886a
Spanish-American War **So:** 753
Yellow Kid [cartoon character]
Comics (Comic strips) **Ci:** 869 *with picture*
Outcault, Richard Felton **O:** 879
Yellow lady's-slipper [plant]
Lady's-slipper **L:** 26
Yellow map lichen [plant]
Lichen *picture on* **L:** 269
Yellow perch [fish]
Perch **P:** 284
Yellow pine [tree]
Pine (North American pines) **P:** 468
Yellow-poplar [tree] **Y:** 556 *with picture*
Plant *picture on* **P:** 525
Tree *pictures on* **T:** 424
Yellow race [theory]
Races, Human (The three-race theory) **R:** 53
Yellow River *See* Huang He *in this index*
Yellow-rumped warbler
Warbler **W:** 35 *with picture*
Yellow Sea Y: 557
Huang He **H:** 403
Yellow-shafted flicker [bird]
Bird *picture on* **B:** 334
Flicker **F:** 234
Yellow star thistle [plant]
Flower *picture on* **F:** 288
Yellow Submarine [film]
Beatles **B:** 190
Yellow-tailed woolly monkey
Woolly monkey **W:** 402
Yellow Tavern, Battle of [1864]
Civil War, American (Cavalry maneuvers) **Ci:** 631
Yellow-throated vireo [bird]
Vireo **V:** 391 *with picture*
Yellow wagtail [bird]
Bird *pictures on* **B:** 361
"Yellow Wallpaper, The" [story by Gilman]
Gilman, Charlotte Perkins **G:** 191
Yellow warbler [bird]
Bird *picture on* **B:** 358
Cowbird **Ci:** 1107
Warbler **W:** 35 *with picture*
Yellow water buttercup [plant]
Buttercup **B:** 731
Yellow water lily [plant]
Lotus **L:** 473
Yellowcake [refining]
Uranium (Refining and processing uranium ore) **U:** 215
Yellowfin [fish]
Tuna **T:** 485 *with picture*
Yellowhammer [bird] **Y:** 557
Flicker **F:** 235
Yellowhammer State [name for]
Alabama **A:** 257
Yellowknife [Northwest Territories] **Y:** 557
Northwest Territories *picture on* **N:** 532; (People) **N:** 530; (The early and middle 1900's) **N:** 533-534

Nunavut (Establishment of Nunavut) **N:** 612
Yellowlegs [bird] **Y:** 557 *with picture*
Yellows [disease]
Jaundice **J:** 65
Yellowstone [steamboat]
South Dakota (Exploration and fur trade) **So:** 681
United States, History of the *picture on* **U:** 170
Yellowstone Lake [Wyoming]
Yellowstone National Park (The Lower Loop) **Y:** 558-559 *with picture and map*
Yellowstone River **Y:** 560
Yellowstone Lower Falls [Wyoming]
Waterfall (table: Famous waterfalls of North America) **W:** 142 *with picture*
Wyoming (Rivers and lakes) **W:** 528 *with picture*
Yellowstone National Park [U.S.] **Y:** 557 *with pictures and maps*
Colter, John **Ci:** 850
Montana (Places to visit) **M:** 750 *with picture*
National park *picture on* **N:** 42i; (Management of fire and wildlife) **N:** 42j
National Park System (Areas preserved for natural features) **N:** 43; (table: National parks) **N:** 49
Rocky Mountains (Chief ranges of the Rockies) **R:** 394-395
United States *picture on* **U:** 99
Volcano (Silicic caldera complexes) **V:** 442
Wyoming (Places to visit) **W:** 516; (Territorial progress) **W:** 534
Yellowstone River [Montana-Wyoming] **Y:** 560
Lewis and Clark expedition (The homeward journey) **L:** 222d-223
Montana *picture on* **M:** 754
Yellowtail [fish]
Amberjack **A:** 405
Yellowtail Dam [Bighorn River, Montana]
Montana (Rivers and lakes) **M:** 752-754; (The mid-1900's) **M:** 760
Yellowthroat [bird] **Y:** 560 *with picture*
Yeltsin, Boris Nikolayevich [Russian political leader] **Y:** 560 *with portrait*
Cold War *picture on* **Ci:** 768; (The Cold War after 1980) **Ci:** 770
Putin, Vladimir Vladimirovich **P:** 913
Russia (National government) **R:** 531; (The breakup of the U.S.S.R.) **R:** 554 *with picture*; (The new nation) **R:** 555 *with picture*; (The rise of Putin) **R:** 555
Union of Soviet Socialist Republics (Threats to unity) **U:** 40-41
Yemen Y: 561 *with pictures and map*
Egypt (The United Arab Republic) **E:** 132-133
Flag *picture on* **F:** 205
Middle East **M:** 530
Saudi Arabia (The new kingdom) **S:** 161
United Arab Republic **U:** 46
Yemen Arab Republic *See* North Yemen *in this index*
Yemeni Socialist Party
Yemen (Formation of South Yemen) **Y:** 563-564
Yen [money] **Y:** 564
Yenjing [China] *See* Beijing *in this index*
Yeoman [English history] **Y:** 564
Yeoman [U.S.]
Yeoman **Y:** 564
Yeoman Warder [soldier]
Yeoman **Y:** 564
Yeomen of the Guard [English history]
Yeoman **Y:** 564
Yeomen of the Guard, The [operetta by Gilbert and Sullivan]
Gilbert and Sullivan **G:** 190
Yep, Laurence [American author]
Laura Ingalls Wilder Award (table) **L:** 121
Yerba maté [drink]
Maté **M:** 300a
Yerevan [Armenia] **Y:** 564
Armenia **A:** 718 *with picture*
Yerkes, Charles T. [American businessman]
Yerkes Observatory **Y:** 565
Yerkes, Robert Mearns [American psychologist] **Y:** 564
Yerkes Observatory [Williams Bay, Wisconsin] **Y:** 565
Yerkes Primate Research Center [Atlanta]
Chimpanzee (Chimpanzees and people) **C:** 473
Yermak [Cossack adventurer]
Siberia (History) **S:** 446
Yerovi Indaburu, Clemente [Ecuadorean political leader]
Ecuador (The 1900's) **E:** 73
Yersinia pestis [bacteria]
Black Death **B:** 386
Plague **P:** 505
Yeshiva [school]
Jerusalem (Culture) **J:** 99-100
Jews (The Talmudic period) **J:** 122

Rabbi **R:** 46
Yeşilköy Airport
Istanbul (Economy) **I:** 491
Yeti [legendary creature] **Y:** 565
See also Bigfoot *in this index*
Folklore (Legends) **F:** 324
Mount Everest **M:** 884
Nepal (Land and climate) **N:** 126
Yeutter, Clayton K. [American government official]
Agriculture, Department of (table) **A:** 161
Yevtushenko, Yevgeny [Russian poet] **Y:** 565
Babi Yar **B:** 3
Russian literature (Modern Soviet literature) **R:** 564
Yew [tree] **Y:** 565 *with picture*
Plant *picture on* **P:** 521
Poisonous plant (Some poisonous plants) **P:** 602
Taxol **T:** 56
Tree *picture on* **T:** 417; (Needleleaf trees) **T:** 414-415
Yggdrasil [Norse mythology]
Mythology (The construction of the world) **M:** 986
Yi dynasty [Korean history] *See* Choson dynasty *in this index*
Yi Song-gye [Korean ruler]
Korea, History of (History) **K:** 366
Seoul (History) **S:** 306
Yiddish language Y: 565
Hebrew language **H:** 162
Yiddish literature Y: 566
Yield [physics]
Bomb (The explosive material) **B:** 450
Nuclear weapon (Thermonuclear weapons) **N:** 597
Yield grade
Beef (Grades of beef) **B:** 209
Meat packing (Yield grading) **M:** 351
Yield stress
Materials (Properties of materials) **M:** 300b
Yihequan [Chinese history]
Boxer Rebellion **B:** 525
Yin [force]
Acupuncture **A:** 31
Medicine (China and India) **M:** 372
Taoism *picture on* **T:** 36
Yingluck Shinawatra [Thai political leader]
Thailand (Recent developments) **T:** 228
Yiri [dwellings]
Burkina Faso (People) **B:** 706
Yitzhaqi, Shlomo [birth name of]
Rashi **R:** 144
YMCA *See* Young Men's Christian Association *in this index*
YMHA *See* Young Men's Hebrew Association *in this index*
Ymir [Norse mythology]
Mythology *picture on* **M:** 975; (Teutonic mythology) **M:** 985-986
Odin **O:** 674
Yo! Yes? [book by Raschka]
Raschka, Chris **R:** 144
Yo-yo [toy] **Y:** 566
Yocto [measurement]
Metric system (Metric prefixes) **M:** 439
Yod [letter]
I **I:** 1 *with picture*
J **J:** 1 *with picture*
Y **Y:** 547 *with picture*
Yoga [philosophy] **Y:** 566
Asian Americans (Asian influences on American culture) **A:** 812c-812d
Hinduism (The six schools of philosophy) **H:** 236
India (Hinduism) **I:** 116
Upanishads **U:** 212
Yogh [letter]
Y **Y:** 547
Yoghurt [food] *See* Yogurt *in this index*
Yogi [religion]
Hinduism (Veneration of holy people) **H:** 237
Yoga **Y:** 567
Yogin [religion]
Yoga **Y:** 567
Yogurt [food] **Y:** 567
Ice cream (The composition of ice cream) **I:** 8
Yohkoh [satellite]
Corona **Ci:** 1067
Yoho National Park
Canada (table: National parks and national park reserves) **C:** 114
Yoke [instrument]
Airplane (The controls and instruments) **A:** 217 *with picture*; (Basic movements and controls) **A:** 222-223 *with picture*
Yoknapatawpha County [fictional place]
Faulkner, William **F:** 55
Yokohama [Japan] **Y:** 567

Yokuts Indians Y: 567
Yolen, Jane [American author]
  Regina Medal (table: 1992) R: 206
Yolk [egg]
  Egg (The yolk) E: 117 *with diagram*; (Uses of eggs)
    E: 118
Yolk [wool]
  Wool (Types of wool) W: 399
Yolk sac [anatomy]
  Reproduction, Human *diagram on* R: 247
Yom Kippur [religion] Y: 568
  Fast F: 52
  Feasts and festivals (In Judaism) F: 58
  Judaism (The High Holidays) J: 181
  Rosh Ha-Shanah R: 480
Yomiuri Giants [team]
  Oh, Sadaharu O: 679
  Tokyo (Recreation) T: 316
Yomiuri Shimbun [newspaper]
  Newspaper (In Asia) N: 386
Yonath, Ada E. [Israeli chemist]
  Nobel Prizes (Chemistry: 2009) N: 444
Yonge Library of Florida History [Gainesville]
  Florida (Libraries) F: 247
Yonker Ramp and His Sweetheart [painting by Hals]
  Hals, Frans *picture on* H: 27
Yonkers [New York] Y: 568
Yorick [literary figure]
  Jester J: 103
Yoritomo [Japanese government official] *See*
  Minamoto Yoritomo *in this index*
York [American explorer]
  Lewis and Clark expedition (Interesting facts
    about the Lewis and Clark expedition) L: 222c
York [England] Y: 568
York [English history] Y: 568
  England (The Wars of the Roses) E: 306; (table)
    E: 308
  Henry VI [of England] H: 187
  Plantagenet P: 550
  Wars of the Roses W: 38
York [former name]
  Toronto (Early settlement) T: 340b-340c
York [Pennsylvania]
  United States capitals U: 199
York, Alvin Cullum [American soldier] Y: 568 *with
  portrait*
York, Cape [region, Greenland]
  Cape York C: 191
York, Sergeant [name for]
  York, Alvin Cullum Y: 568 *with portrait*
York Imperial [apple]
  Apple (table) A: 571 *with picture*
York Redoubt National Historic Site [Nova Scotia]
  Canada (table: National historic sites) C: 115
York Rite
  Masonry (The lodges and degrees of Masonry)
    M: 267; (Organization) M: 267
York Tea Party [U.S. history]
  Maine (The Revolutionary War) M: 89
Yorkshire hog
  Hog (American breeds) H: 285 *with picture*;
    (table) H: 286
Yorkshire pudding
  England (Food and drink) E: 295-296
Yorkshire terrier Y: 569
  Dog *picture on* D: 274
Yorktown [ship]
  Midway, Battle of M: 536
Yorktown [Virginia] Y: 569
Yorktown, Siege of [1781] Y: 569
  Cornwallis, Charles Ci: 1066
  Lafayette, Marquis de (Service to the United
    States) L: 28
  Revolution, American (table) R: 276; (Surrender
    at Yorktown) R: 286 *with picture*
  Washington, George (Winning the war) W: 99
Yorkville [Toronto]
  Ontario *picture on* O: 768
Yoruba [people] Y: 569
  Africa *picture on* A: 116; (Peoples of Africa) A: 104
    with picture
  Benin B: 251
  God (Gods of nature) G: 243-244
  Ife I: 47
  Nigeria (The arts) N: 414
  Tribe T: 440
Yosemite Creek [river, California]
  Yosemite National Park (Waterfalls) Y: 570
Yosemite Falls [falls, California] Y: 569
  Waterfall (table: Famous waterfalls of North
    America) W: 142 *with pictures*
  Yosemite National Park (Waterfalls) Y: 570 *with
    picture*
Yosemite Indians
  Yosemite National Park (Yosemite Valley) Y: 570

Yosemite National Park [California] Y: 569 *with
  picture*
  California *picture on* C: 36; (Rivers, waterfalls, and
    lakes) C: 50-51
  Conservation *picture on* Ci: 986
  National Park System *picture on* N: 43; (Crowds)
    N: 47; (table: National parks) N: 49
  Ribbon Falls R: 321
Yosemite National Park Bill [1890]
  Muir, John M: 912
Yosemite Valley [region, California]
  Yosemite National Park (Yosemite Valley) Y: 570
Yoshida Kenko [Japanese author]
  Japanese literature (The medieval period) J: 62
Yoshihito [emperor of Japan]
  Hirohito (Before World War II) H: 242
Yosippon [literature]
  Hebrew literature (Medieval works) H: 162
Yost, Charles W. [American diplomat]
  United Nations (table) U: 86
Yotta [measurement]
  Metric system (Metric prefixes) M: 439
You and I [play by Barry]
  Barry, Philip B: 119
"You Bet Your Life" [television show]
  Marx Brothers M: 238
You Can't Go Home Again [book by Wolfe]
  Wolfe, Thomas W: 377
You Can't Take It with You [film]
  Motion picture (Best picture: 1938) M: 861
You Can't Take It With You [play by Kaufman and
  Hart]
  Hart, Moss H: 77
You Know Me, Al [book by Lardner]
  Lardner, Ring L: 76
Young, Andrew Jackson, Jr. [American
  government official] Y: 570 *with portrait*
  United Nations (table) U: 86
Young, Arthur [English author]
  Industrial Revolution (The working class) I: 251
Young, Brigham [American religious leader] Y: 571
  with portrait
  Illinois (Places to visit) I: 62
  Mormons (The Mormons in Utah) M: 809
  Nevada (Early settlement) N: 174
  Salt Lake City S: 76; (History) S: 76a
  Utah (The Mormons) U: 246
Young, Clement C. [American political leader]
  California (table) C: 59
Young, Coleman Alexander [American political
  leader] Y: 572
  Detroit (The late 1900's) D: 171
Young, Cy [American baseball player] Y: 572
  Baseball (Hall of Fame) B: 134b; (The early
    1900's) B: 135; (table: Modern major league
    records) B: 138
Young, Ed [American author]
  Caldecott Medal (table: 1990) C: 26
  Literature for children *picture on* L: 357
Young, Edward [English poet] Y: 572
Young, Gig [American actor]
  Motion picture (Best performance by an actor in
    a supporting role: 1969) M: 862b
Young, John [American businessman]
  Youngstown Y: 574
Young, John [American political leader]
  New York (table) N: 313
Young, John [Canadian statesman]
  Lisgar, Baron L: 349
Young, John Watts [American astronaut] Y: 572
  Astronaut (Achievements in space) A: 829-830;
    (table) A: 830
  Space exploration *picture on* So: 694
Young, Kevin [American author]
  African American literature (Recent
    developments) A: 136a
Young, Lester Willis [American saxophonist] Y: 572
  Basie, Count B: 140
  Jazz (Cool jazz) J: 72
Young, Loretta [American actress]
  Motion picture (Best performance by an actress:
    1947) M: 862
Young, Samuel B. M. [American general]
  Army, United States (The early 1900's) A: 738
Young, Thomas [British physicist]
  Color (The three-component theory) Ci: 826
  Light (Modern study) L: 285
  Physics (Developments in the 1800's) P: 440
  Radiation (Electromagnetic waves) R: 80
Young, Thomas [British scholar]
  Hieroglyphics (Deciphering hieroglyphic writing)
    H: 226-227
Young, Thomas L. [American political leader]
  Ohio (table) O: 699
Young, Whitney Moore, Jr. [American social
  reformer] Y: 572
Young adult *See* Adolescent; Teenager *in this index*

Young Adult Canadian Book Award
  Literature for children (Awards) L: 367
Young American Medal for Bravery
  Medals, decorations, and orders (Civilian awards)
    M: 355; (table) M: 357 *with picture*
Young American Medal for Service
  Medals, decorations, and orders (Civilian awards)
    M: 355; (table) M: 357
Young and the Damned, The [film]
  Buñuel, Luis B: 700
Young Artist Award
  Music Clubs, National Federation of M: 958
Young Belgium [literary group]
  Belgium (The arts) B: 230
Young British Artists [art group]
  Hirst, Damien H: 243
**Young Democrats-Hungarian Civic Party,
  Federation of** [political party]
  Hungary (Multiparty elections) H: 448
Young Farmers' Club
  Agricultural education (In other countries) A: 145
Young Germany [literary movement]
  German literature (The Young Germany) G: 140
  Heine, Heinrich H: 166
Young Girl of Perth, The [opera by Bizet]
  Bizet, Georges B: 385
"Young Goodman Brown" [story by Hawthorne]
  Hawthorne, Nathaniel (His stories and sketches)
    H: 115
Young-Helmholtz theory
  Color (The three-component theory) Ci: 826
Young Italy [Italian history]
  Mazzini, Giuseppe M: 331
Young Landlords, The [book by Myers]
  Myers, Walter Dean M: 970f
Young Lions, The [book by Shaw]
  Shaw, Irwin S: 378
Young Lonigan [book by Farrell]
  Farrell, James T. F: 48
Young Manhood of Studs Lonigan, The [book by
  Farrell]
  Farrell, James T. F: 48
Young Men's Christian Association Y: 572
Young Men's Hebrew Association
  Jewish community centers J: 119
Young Offenders Act [1984]
  Juvenile court (In Canada) J: 205
Young Person's Guide to the Orchestra, The [music
  by Britten]
  Britten, Benjamin B: 634
Young Plan [German history]
  Dawes Plan D: 51
  Hitler, Adolf (Rise of the Nazis) H: 266
Young Pretender [Scottish history] *See* Stuart,
  Charles Edward *in this index*
Young Turks [Turkish history]
  Turkey (The Young Turks) T: 510
Young Woman Reading a Letter [painting by
  Vermeer]
  Painting (The Dutch masters) P: 62-63 *with
    picture*
Young Women's Christian Association Y: 573
Young Women's Hebrew Association
  Jewish community centers J: 119
Youngdahl, Luther W. [American political leader]
  Minnesota (table) M: 602
Younger Edda [book by Snorri]
  Edda E: 74
Youngs, Ross [American baseball player]
  Baseball (table: Hall of Fame) B: 134b
Youngstown [Ohio] Y: 574
Youngstown steel strike [1916]
  Riot *picture on* R: 348
Yount, Robin [American baseball player]
  Baseball (table: Hall of Fame) B: 134b
"You're the Top" [song by Porter]
  Porter, Cole P: 682
Youth *See* Adolescent; Teenager *in this index*
"Youth" [story by Conrad]
  Conrad, Joseph Ci: 973
Youth Aliyah [organization]
  Szold, Henrietta So: 1078 *with picture*
Youth culture [U.S. history]
  Baby boom generation (Effects of the baby
    boom) B: 11
Youth for Christ International [organization]
  Y: 574
Youth hostel [accommodation] Y: 574
Youth Olympics
  Olympic Games (The recent games) O: 753-754
YouTube [website]
  Internet (The evolving Internet) I: 350g-350h
Youville, Saint Marguerite d' [Canadian religious
  leader] Y: 574
Ypres [Belgium] Y: 574
Ypres, First Battle of [1914]
  World War I (The Western Front) W: 455-456

Ypres, Second Battle of [1915]
World War I (Trench warfare) **W: 457-458**
Ypres, Third Battle of [1917]
World War I (Allied failures) **W: 461**
Yr Wyddfa [mountain] *See* Snowdon *in this index*
Yrigoyen, Hipólito [Argentine political leader]
Argentina (Reform movements) **A: 657**
Ysleta [Texas]
El Paso (History) **E: 247**
Ytterbium [element] **Y: 574**
Lutetium **L: 527**
Yttrium [element] **Y: 575**
Yü Shan [mountain, Taiwan]
Taiwan (Land and climate) **T: 16** *with map*
Yü Shan National Park [Taiwan]
National park (table) **N: 42f**
Yuan [government]
Taiwan (Government) **T: 15**
Yuan [money] **Y: 575**
Yuan dynasty [Chinese history]
China (Mongol rule) **C: 501** *with map*
Kublai Khan **K: 391**
Mongol Empire (Kublai Khan) **M: 720**
Painting (Chinese painting) **P: 44-46**
World, History of the (China) **W: 435**
Yuan Shikai [Chinese political leader]
China (The early republic) **C: 503**
Sun Yat-sen (The Kuomintang Party) **So: 988-989**
Yuca [shrub] *See* Cassava *in this index*
Yucatán Channel
Gulf of Mexico **G: 436**
Yucatán Peninsula [region, Mexico] **Y: 575** *with maps*
Asteroid (Impacts on Earth) **A: 824b** *with map*
Chichén Itzá **C: 439**
Cortés, Hernán (Early life) **Ci: 1072**
Exploration (Spain's conquests in the New World) **E: 445**
Mexico (The Yucatán Peninsula) **M: 463** *with picture;* (The Spanish conquest) **M: 469**
Yucatecos [people]
Yucatán Peninsula **Y: 575**
Yucca [tree] **Y: 575**
Flower *picture on* **F: 272**
Yucca House National Monument [Colorado]
National Park System (table: National monuments) **N: 50-52**
Yucca Mountain [Nevada]
Nevada (The early 2000's) **N: 177**
Nuclear energy (Waste and waste disposal) **N: 588**
Yudhoyono, Susilo Bambang [Indonesian political leader]
Indonesia (Recent developments) **I: 239**
Yue [dialect]
Chinese language (Spoken Chinese) **C: 510**
Yugoslavia Y: 576 *with map*
See also Montenegro; Serbia *in this index*
Albania (Communist control) **A: 308**
Balkans (Recent developments) **B: 42**
Bosnia-Herzegovina (History) **B: 492-493**
Clinton, Bill (International affairs) **Ci: 682f**
Cold War (The Iron Curtain descends) **Ci: 763-764;** (The containment policy) **Ci: 764;** (The great blocs split) **Ci: 769**
Europe (The new nationalism) **E: 416**
Homer (The Homeric question today) **H: 304**
International relations (The Balkan conflicts) **I: 346**
Kosovo (History) **K: 384b**
Montenegro **M: 763**
North Atlantic Treaty Organization (History) **N: 471**
Sarajevo **S: 123**
Serbia **S: 312**
Slovenia **S: 510**
United Nations (Membership questions) **U: 95**
War crime (The United Nations and war cimes) **W: 27**
World War II (Fighting in the Balkans) **W: 477**
Yuit [people]
Arctic (Arctic peoples) **A: 638**
Indian, American (Peoples of the Arctic) **I: 152** *with picture*
Inuit **I: 354**
Yukawa, Hideki [Japanese physicist] **Y: 578**
Meson **M: 421**
Physics (Uncovering the secrets of the atom) **P: 442**
Yukon [Canada] **Y: 578** *with pictures and map*
Yukon-Charley Rivers National Preserve [Alaska]
National Park System (table: National preserves) **N: 58**
Yukon Delta National Wildlife Refuge
Alaska (Federally protected lands) **A: 294**
National Wildlife Refuge System **N: 61**
Yukon First Nations, Council for

Yukon (History) **Y: 581**
Yukon Gold [potato]
Potato *picture on* **P: 711**
Yukon River [Alaska-Yukon] **Y: 581** *with map*
Alaska (Rivers and lakes) **A: 295**
Canada (The Pacific Basin) **C: 120**
Yukon (The land and its resources) **Y: 578**
Yukos Oil Company
Russia (Recent developments) **R: 555-556**
Yule Y: 582
Yule log [custom]
Christmas (Other customs) **C: 536**
Yule **Y: 582**
Yulia Tymoshenko Bloc [political group]
Ukraine (Politics) **U: 6**
Yuma [Arizona] **Y: 582**
Arizona (table: Average monthly weather) **A: 682**
Yuma Indians *See* Quechan Indians *in this index*
Yungas [region, Bolivia]
Bolivia (The Yungas) **B: 445** *with map;* (Climate) **B: 446**
Yungas Road [Bolivia]
Andes Mountains (Transportation) **A: 453**
Yunus, Muhammad [Bangladeshi banker]
Nobel Prizes (Peace: 2006) **N: 449**
Yupik [language]
Inuit **I: 354**
Yuri [Russian nobleman]
Russia (The rise of Moscow) **R: 548**
Yuri Gagarin Russian State Scientific-Research Test Center of Cosmonaut Training
Astronaut **A: 828**
Yurok Indians Y: 582
Yurt [tent]
Asia *picture on* **A: 790**
Kazakhstan (People) **K: 250b**
Mongol Empire **M: 719,** *picture on* **M: 721**
Mongolia (The people) **M: 722** *with picture*
Yushchenko, Viktor [Ukrainian political leader]
Ukraine (Political changes) **U: 14**
Yusuf Ahmed, Abdullahi [Somali political leader]
Somalia (History) **So: 589-590**
Yuzhno-Sakhalinsk [Sakhalin]
Sakhalin **S: 58**
Yvain [poem by Chrétien de Troyes]
Hartmann von Aue **H: 79**
YWCA *See* Young Women's Christian Association *in this index*
YWHA *See* Young Women's Hebrew Association *in this index*

Z

Z [letter] **Z: 583** *with pictures*
Z boson [physics]
Physics (Physics today) **P: 442-443**
Standard Model **So: 833**
Subatomic particle (Elementary particles) **So: 937**
Z Camelopardalis [star system]
Nova *pictures on* **N: 553**
Zabara, Ibn [Hebrew author]
Hebrew literature (Medieval works) **H: 162**
Zacatecas [city, Mexico]
Mexico *picture on* **M: 455**
Zaccaro, John A. [American businessman]
Ferraro, Geraldine Anne **F: 76**
Zachary, Saint [pope]
Pope (table) **P: 666**
"Zadonshchina" [poem]
Russian literature (The literature of Tatar captivity) **R: 559**
Zafy, Albert [Madagascar political leader]
Madagascar (History) **M: 29**
Zagreb [Croatia] **Z: 584**
Croatia **Ci: 1148** *with picture*
Zagros Mountains
Iran (The Mountains) **I: 402**
Iraq (The land) **I: 411-412** *with map*
Zagwé dynasty
Ethiopia (The Zagwé dynasty) **E: 371**
Zaharias, Babe Didrikson [American athlete] **Z: 584** *with portrait*
Golf (Women's golf) **G: 266**
Olympic Games *picture on* **O: 752;** (Between the wars) **O: 751**
Zahir Shah, Muhammad [king of Afghanistan]
Afghanistan (Independence) **A: 95;** (Recent developments) **A: 96** *with picture*
Zaibatsu [Japanese history]
Japan (Meiji era) **J: 56**
Zaire [former country] *See* Congo, Democratic Republic of the *in this index*
Zaïre [play by Voltaire]
Voltaire (Exile and return to France) **V: 446**
Zakat [religion]
Islam (The Five Pillars of Islam) **I: 463-464**
Zakouma National Park
Chad (Land and climate) **C: 366-367** *with map*

Zale, Tony [American boxer]
Boxing (Boxing's Golden Age) **B: 532-532a**
Zama, Battle of [202 B.C.]
Hannibal (The turning point) **H: 52**
Punic Wars (The Second Punic War) **P: 903**
Scipio Africanus, Publius Cornelius **S: 208**
Zambezi River [Mozambique-Zambia] **Z: 584**
Africa (Rivers, waterfalls, and deltas) **A: 119** *with picture*
River (table) **R: 352**
Stanley and Livingstone (Livingstone's discoveries) **So: 837** *with map*
Victoria Falls **V: 358**
Zambia Z: 584 *with picture and map*
Bemba **B: 246**
Flag *picture on* **F: 200**
Zambia, University of
Zambia (People) **Z: 584-585**
Zamenhof, Ludovic L. [Polish linguist]
Esperanto **E: 358**
Zamia [plant]
Cycad **Ci: 1203**
Zamyatin, Yevgeny [Russian author]
Science fiction (The early 1900's) **S: 205**
Zamzam [well]
Islam (The Five Pillars of Islam) **I: 463-464**
Muslims (Before Muhammad) **M: 964**
Zanamivir [drug]
Antiviral drug **A: 560**
Zand dynasty [Iranian history]
Iran (The Qajar dynasty) **I: 406**
Zane, Ebenezer [American settler]
Wheeling **W: 279**
Zane's Trace [road]
Ohio (Transportation) **O: 698**
Zangara, Giuseppe [American assassin]
Roosevelt, Franklin Delano (An uneasy transition) **R: 452**
Zanjón, Pact of [1878]
Cuba (Struggle against Spain) **Ci: 1176**
Zante [island, Greece]
Ionian Islands **I: 373** *with map*
Zante currant [raisin]
Raisin (Varieties) **R: 129**
ZANU-PF [political party]
Mugabe, Robert Gabriel **M: 909**
Zimbabwe (History) **Z: 592-593**
Zanzibar [city, Tanzania] **Z: 586**
Tanzania *picture on* **T: 34**
Zanzibar [islands, Tanzania] **Z: 586**
Tanzania **T: 30**
Zanzibar Island [Tanzania]
Tanzania (The coastal lowlands and islands) **T: 32-33** *with map*
Zanzibar **Z: 586**
Zapata, Emiliano [Mexican patriot] **Z: 586**
Indian, American (In Latin America) **I: 178b**
Latin America (In Mexico) **L: 109**
Mexican Revolution of 1910 (The revolution) **M: 445**
Mexico *picture on* **M: 459;** (The Constitution of 1917) **M: 472** *with picture*
Zapatista Army of National Liberation **Z: 586**
Zapata Off-Shore Company
Bush, George Herbert Walker (Independent oilman) **B: 718**
Zapatero, José Luiz Rodríguez [Spanish political leader]
Spain (The early 2000's) **So: 751**
Zapatista Army of National Liberation [Mexican political group] **Z: 587**
Chiapas **C: 419**
Indian, American (Current issues) **I: 182-183**
Latin America (Neoliberalism) **L: 111**
Mexico (Opposition to the PRI) **M: 474** *with picture*
Zapatistas [political group] *See* Zapatista Army of National Liberation *in this index*
Zapotec Indians Z: 587
Indian, American (Before European contact) **I: 169**
Mexico (The Classic Period) **M: 468**
Mixtec Indians **M: 680**
Monte Albán **M: 762**
Oaxaca **O: 640a**
Rivera, Diego *picture on* **R: 355**
Zápotocký, Antonín [Czechoslovak political leader]
Czechoslovakia (Communist rule) **Ci: 1215-1216**
ZAPU *See* Zimbabwe African People's Union *in this index*
ZAR [former name, Transvaal] *See* South African Republic *in this index*
Zaragoza [Spain] *See* Saragossa *in this index*
Zaragoza, Puebla de [Mexico]
Puebla **P: 870**
Zarathustra [Persian prophet] *See* Zoroaster *in*

this index
Zardari, Asif Ali [Pakistani political leader]
  Pakistan (Musharraf) **P:** 100
Zarqawi, Abu Mussab al- [Jordanian paramilitary
  leader]
  Iraq War (Resistance to the coalition) **I:** 414e
  Qa`ida, Al- **Q:** 2
Zarya [newspaper]
  Lenin, V. I. (Beginnings of revolution) **L:** 192
Zarya [space module]
  International Space Station (History) **I:** 346b
  Space exploration (The International Space
  Station) **So:** 722
Zarzuela [music]
  Spain (Music) **So:** 739
Zátopek, Emil [Czechoslovak runner]
  Olympic Games (The postwar games) **O:** 751-752
  Track and field (The early and middle 1900's)
  T: 360
Zauberflöte, Die [opera] *See* Magic Flute, The *in
  this index*
Zawahiri, Ayman al- [Egyptian paramilitary leader]
  Qa`ida, Al- **Q:** 2
Zawditu [empress of Ethiopia]
  Ethiopia (Menelik II) **E:** 371
Zaydis [Muslim sect]
  Yemen (People) **Y:** 562; (History) **Y:** 563
Zayid bin Sultan al-Nahyan, Sheik [United Arab
  Emirates political leader]
  (History) **U:** 45
Zayn [letter]
  Z **Z:** 583 *with picture*
Zdákov Bridge [Czech Republic]
  Bridge (table: Steel arch) **B:** 603
Zealots [Jewish history]
  Barabbas **B:** 102
  Jerusalem (Roman rule) **J:** 101
  Jews (Roman rule) **J:** 122
  Masada **M:** 262
Zeami Motokiyo [Japanese dramatist]
  Japanese literature (The medieval period) **J:** 62
Zebra Z: 587 *with picture*
  Animal *picture on* **A:** 476
  Lion *pictures on* **L:** 343
Zebra mussel [sea animal] **Z:** 587
  Animal (Introduction of new species) **A:** 505
  Invasive species (How species become invasive)
  I: 354j
  Ship (Invasive species) **S:** 414
Zebu [cattle]
  Cattle (Other beef cattle) **C:** 309
Zebulun [Bible] **Z:** 588
Zechariah [Biblical figure]
  Elizabeth, Saint **E:** 241
  Zechariah, Book of **Z:** 588
Zechariah, Book of [Bible] **Z:** 588
Zed [letter]
  Z **Z:** 583
Zedillo Ponce de León, Ernesto [Mexican political
  leader] **Z:** 588
  Mexico (Opposition to the PRI) **M:** 474
Zeeman, Pieter [Dutch physicist] **Z:** 588
  Lorentz, Hendrik Antoon **L:** 454
  Zeeman effect **Z:** 588
Zeeman effect [physics] **Z:** 588
  Lorentz, Hendrik Antoon **L:** 454
Zeidler, Frank P. [American political leader]
  Milwaukee (The 1900's) **M:** 561
Zeisberger, David [American settler]
  Ohio (Schools) **O:** 684; (Exploration and
  settlement) **O:** 700
Zelaya, José Santos [Nicaraguan political leader]
  Nicaragua (The United States and Nicaragua)
  N: 400
Zelaya, Manuel [Honduran political leader]
  Honduras (Recent developments) **H:** 313
Zelinsky, Paul O. [American author]
  Caldecott Medal (table: 1998) **C:** 26
Zelle, Margaretha Gertrud [German spy]
  Mata Hari **M:** 299
Zellweger, Renee [American actress]
  Motion picture (Best performance by an actress
  in a supporting role: 2003) **M:** 862b
Zelotes [Jewish history] *See* Simon, Saint *in this
  index*
Zelter, Carl Friedrich [German musician]
  Mendelssohn, Felix (His life) **M:** 399
Zemach, Margot [American artist]
  Caldecott Medal (table: 1974) **C:** 26
Zemeckis, Robert [American director]
  Motion picture (Best achievement in directing:
  1994) **M:** 862
Zemi [religion]
  Indian, American (Before European contact)
  I: 172-173
Zemskii Sobor [Russian history]
  Russia (The Time of Troubles) **R:** 549

Zen [religion] **Z:** 588
  Asia (Life in Japan) **A:** 788
  Buddhism (Meditation) **B:** 669
  New Age movement **N:** 178
  Painting (Chinese painting) **P:** 44-46
Zenawi, Meles [Ethiopian political leader]
  Ethiopia (The late 1900's) **E:** 372; (Recent
  developments) **E:** 372
Zener, Karl E. [American psychologist]
  Extrasensory perception (Early ESP research)
  E: 457
Zener card
  Extrasensory perception (Early ESP research)
  E: 457
Zenger, John Peter [American journalist] **Z:** 589
  Freedom of the press (In the United States)
  F: 507-508
  Mount Vernon **M:** 890
  New York (Under British rule) **N:** 314-315
Zenith [astronomy] **Z:** 589
Zeno [East Roman emperor]
  Odoacer **O:** 674
  Theodoric **T:** 252
Zeno of Citium [Greek philosopher] **Z:** 589
  Cynic philosophy **Ci:** 1205
  Philosophy (Stoic philosophy and Epicureanism)
  P: 387
Zeno of Elea [Greek philosopher] **Z:** 589
Zeno of Sidon [Phoenician philosopher]
  Phoenicia (Decline) **P:** 395
Zenobia [Palmyrene ruler]
  Palmyra **P:** 112
Zeolite [mineral] **Z:** 589
  Petroleum (Cracking processes) **P:** 344
  Water softening **W:** 140
Zephaniah, Book of [Bible] **Z:** 589
Zephyr [train]
  Locomotive (History) **L:** 417 *with picture*
  Railroad (The 1920's and the Great Depression)
  R: 118
Zephyrinus, Saint [pope]
  Pope (table) **P:** 666
Zeppelin
  Airship (Rigid airships) **A:** 250; (The zeppelins)
  A: 252; (World War I) **A:** 252
  Transportation *picture on* **T:** 390
  World War I (The war in the air) **W:** 460-461
  Zeppelin, Ferdinand von **Z:** 590
Zeppelin, Ferdinand von [German engineer]
  Z: 590
  Airship (Rigid airships) **A:** 250; (The zeppelins)
  A: 252
Zepto [measurement]
  Metric system (Metric prefixes) **M:** 439
Zerbo, Saye [African political leader]
  Burkina Faso (History) **B:** 707
Zernike, Frits [Dutch physicist]
  Nobel Prizes (Physics: 1953) **N:** 441
  Optics (History) **O:** 813
Zero [number] **Z:** 590
  Arabic numerals **A:** 584
  Decimal system (Invention of the decimal
  system) **D:** 73
  Multiplication (Multiplying by zero) **M:** 923
  Number (The decimal system) **N:** 605; (The
  Hindu-Arabic numeral system) **N:** 607
Zero, Absolute *See* Absolute zero *in this index*
Zero, Mr. [literary figure]
  Rice, Elmer **R:** 328
Zero carbon housing
  Housing (Sustainable housing) **H:** 392-393 *with
  picture*
Zero gravity *See* Microgravity *in this index*
"Zero Hour" [broadcasts]
  Tokyo Rose **T:** 320
Zero population growth [demography]
  Birth and death rates **B:** 377
  Ehrlich, Paul Ralph **E:** 145
  Population (Population control) **P:** 674
Zero-pressure balloon
  Balloon (Zero-pressure balloons) **B:** 59 *with
  picture*
Zero-sum game
  Game theory **G:** 23
Zero-tillage [agriculture]
  Conservation (Soil conservation) **Ci:** 979-980
Zeroual, Liamine [Algerian political leader]
  Algeria (Recent developments) **A:** 365
Zeta [letter]
  Z **Z:** 583 *with picture*
Zeta-Jones, Catherine [Welsh-born actress]
  Motion picture (Best performance by an actress
  in a supporting role: 2002) **M:** 862b
Zetland Islands *See* Shetland Islands *in this index*
Zetta [measurement]
  Metric system (Metric prefixes) **M:** 439
Zeus [Greek mythology] **Z:** 590

See also Jupiter [Roman mythology] *in this index*
  Apollo **A:** 566
  Athena **A:** 853
  Atlas **A:** 868
  Big and Little Dippers (The Little Dipper) **B:** 296
  Cornucopia **Ci:** 1066
  Cronus **C:** 1152
  Dionysus **D:** 215
  Endymion **E:** 273
  Europa **E:** 379
  Ganymede **G:** 27
  God (Cosmic Gods) **G:** 243
  Hades **H:** 4
  Helen of Troy **H:** 168
  Hera **H:** 194
  Hercules (Early life) **H:** 198
  Hesperides **H:** 218
  Io **I:** 369 *with picture*
  Mount Olympus **M:** 886
  Mythology *picture on* **M:** 979; (Genetic
  relationships) **M:** 976; (Greek mythology)
  M: 980; (table) **M:** 981
  Prometheus **P:** 817
  Rhea **R:** 290
  Titans **T:** 300
Zeus, Statue of [ancient Greece]
  Seven Wonders of the Ancient World *picture on*
  S: 326; (The statue of Zeus) **S:** 325
Zewail, Ahmed Hassan [American chemist]
  Nobel Prizes (Chemistry: 1999) **N:** 444
Zhang Heng [Chinese astronomer]
  Map (Ancient maps) **M:** 182-183
Zhang Qian [Chinese explorer]
  Exploration (The Chinese) **E:** 441 *with map*
Zhao Tuo [Vietnamese ruler]
  Vietnam (Nam Viet) **V:** 369
Zhao Ziyang [Chinese government official] **Z:** 590
  China (Deng Xiaoping) **C:** 506
Zhelev, Zhelyu [Bulgarian political leader]
  Bulgaria (Political changes) **B:** 693
Zheng Chenggong [Chinese military leader]
  Taiwan (History) **T:** 17-18
Zheng He [Chinese explorer] **Z:** 590
  Exploration *picture on* **E:** 441; (Chinese
  exploration) **E:** 442
  Ship (Chinese ships) **S:** 419
Zhengyi Tao [religion]
  Taoism **T:** 36
Zhivkov, Todor [Bulgarian political leader]
  Bulgaria (Communist rule) **B:** 693
Zhongguo [name for]
  China **C:** 474
Zhongnanshan Tunnel [China]
  Tunnel (table) **T:** 491
Zhou dynasty [Chinese history] **Z:** 591
  Asia (The Huang He and Yangtze valleys) **A:** 805
  China (The arts) **C:** 487; (The first dynasties)
  C: 499
  Clothing (China) **Ci:** 699
  World, History of the (The unification of China)
  W: 431
  Xi'an **X:** 545
Zhou Enlai [Chinese statesman] **Z:** 591
  China (The beginning of Communist rule) **C:** 505;
  (Improved relations with the West) **C:** 505
  Trudeau, Pierre Elliott *picture on* **T:** 463
Zhu Jiang [river, China]
  Guangzhou **G:** 410
Zhu Rongji [Chinese political leader]
  China (Recent developments) **C:** 506
Zhu Xi [Chinese philosopher]
  China (The Song dynasty) **C:** 501
  Confucianism (Later Confucianism) **Ci:** 937
  Song dynasty **So:** 592
Zhuang [people]
  China (Nationalities) **C:** 481
Zhuangzi [Chinese philosopher] **Z:** 591
  Chinese literature (Beginnings) **C:** 511
Zhuangzi [book by Zhuangzi]
  Taoism **T:** 36
  Zhuangzi **Z:** 591
Zhukov, Georgi Konstantinovich [Soviet general]
  Z: 591
Zhukovsky, Vasili [Russian poet]
  Russian literature (Preromanticism) **R:** 560
Zia, Khaleda [Bangladeshi political leader]
  Bangladesh (The new nation) **B:** 86; (Recent
  developments) **B:** 86
Zia-ul-Haq, Mohammed [Pakistani political leader]
  Bhutto, Benazir **B:** 278
  Pakistan (Struggle for democracy) **P:** 100
Ziaur Rahman [Bangladeshi political leader]
  Bangladesh (The new nation) **B:** 86
Zidovudine [drug] *See* AZT *in this index*
Ziegfeld, Florenz [American producer] **Z:** 591
Ziegfeld Follies [musical]
  Ziegfeld, Florenz **Z:** 591

Ziegler, Karl [German chemist]
Nobel Prizes (Chemistry: 1963) N: 443
Zifeng Center [Nanjing, China]
Skyscraper (table) S: 498
ZIFT [reproduction] See Zygote intrafallopian transfer in this index
Ziggurat [architecture]
Architecture (Mesopotamian architecture) A: 611 with picture
Babylon (The Neo-Babylonian Empire) B: 12
Babylonia (Way of life) B: 13
City picture on Ci: 579
Tower of Babel T: 351 with picture
World, History of the (The Tigris-Euphrates Valley) W: 422-424
Zijin Mountain [China]
Nanjing (The city) N: 9-10
Ziklag [ancient city]
Amalekites A: 400
Zila [political unit]
Bangladesh (Local government) B: 79
Zildjian Company
Cymbal Ci: 1205
Zimbabwe Z: 591 with picture and map
See also the list of Related articles in the Zimbabwe article
Flag picture on F: 200
Great Zimbabwe G: 350
Mozambique (History) M: 905-906
Mugabe, Robert Gabriel M: 909
United Kingdom (Decline of the empire) U: 71
Zambia (History) Z: 585-586
Zimbabwe [former city]
World, History of the (African civilizations) W: 437
Zimbabwe (History) Z: 592
Zimbabwe African National Union [political party]
Zimbabwe (History) Z: 592-593
Zimbabwe African National Union-Patriotic Front See ZANU-PF in this index
Zimbabwe African People's Union [political party]
Zimbabwe (History) Z: 592-593
Zimmer, Fred R. [American political leader]
Wisconsin (table) W: 365
Zimmerman, Robert Allen [birth name of]
Dylan, Bob D: 397
Zimmermann, Arthur [German diplomat]
Codes and ciphers (History) Ci: 751
Zimmermann, Dominikus [German architect]
Architecture (Rococo architecture) A: 623
Zimmermann, Ethel Agnes [birth name of]
Merman, Ethel M: 418
Zimmermann note [1917]
World War I (The United States enters the war) W: 462
Zinc [element] Z: 594
Alaska picture on A: 298
Aluminum (Properties of aluminum alloys) A: 391-392
Brass B: 565
Cadmium C: 12
Cold, Common (Treatment) Ci: 760
Galvanizing G: 17
Sphalerite So: 779
Trace elements T: 355
Zinc blende [mineral]
Sphalerite So: 779
Zinc Z: 594
Zinc chloride [chemical]
Zinc Z: 594
Zinc oxide [chemical]
Zinc Z: 594
Zinc sulfide [chemical]
Zinc Z: 594
Zincite [mineral]
Zinc Z: 594
Zinjanthropus [anthropology] See Australopithecus boisei in this index
Zinkernagel, Rolf Martin [Swiss physiologist]
Nobel Prizes (Physiology or medicine: 1996) N: 446
Zinnemann, Fred [American director] Z: 595
Motion picture (Best achievement in directing: 1953, 1966) M: 862
Zinnia [plant] Z: 595 with pictures
Flower picture on F: 276
Gardening picture on G: 33
Zinoviev, Grigori [Soviet political leader]
Union of Soviet Socialist Republics (Stalin gains power) U: 36
Zinzendorf, Count Nicholas von [German religious leader]
Moravian Church M: 801
Ziolkowski, Korczak [American sculptor]
South Dakota (Places to visit) So: 672
Zion [religion] Z: 595
Zion Canyon [region, Utah]

Zion National Park Z: 595
Zion Investment Associates
Sullivan, Leon Howard So: 969
Zion National Park [Utah] Z: 595
National Park System (table: National parks) N: 49
Zionism [Jewish history] Z: 595
Anti-Semitism A: 559
Arab-Israeli conflict (Historical background) A: 582
Arabs (The Arab-Israeli conflict) A: 590a
Begin, Menachem B: 219
Dreyfus affair (The result of the Dreyfus affair) D: 348
Haskalah H: 82
Hebrew literature (Modern Hebrew literature) H: 162-163
Herzl, Theodor H: 217
Holocaust (After the Holocaust) H: 296b
Israel I: 478
Jerusalem (British rule) J: 101
Jews (The Zionist movement) J: 123
Middle East (The Palestine conflict) M: 534
Minority group (Effects of subordinate status) M: 609
Palestine (The Zionist movement) P: 105
Palestinians P: 107
ZIP Code Z: 596
Postal Service, United States (Classes of mail) P: 699
Zipper Z: 596 with picture
Sewing (Fastenings) S: 332
Zipporah [Biblical figure]
Moses (Early life) M: 828-829
Zircaloy [metal]
Zirconium Z: 596
Zircon [gem] Z: 596
Diamond (Imitation diamonds) D: 183
Earth (Earth's early development) E: 26 with picture
Gem picture on G: 78
Zirconium [element] Z: 596
Zither [musical instrument] Z: 597 with picture
Ziusudra [Sumerian king]
Mythology (The influence of Sumerian mythology) M: 977-978
Zn [symbol]
Zinc Z: 594
Zoar Village [New Philadelphia, Ohio]
Ohio (Places to visit) O: 690
Zócalo [Mexico City]
Mexico City (Downtown) M: 476
Zodiac [astrology] Z: 597 with picture
Astrology (The zodiac) A: 827
Horoscope (Parts of a horoscope) H: 341
Planet (Observing the planets) P: 507-508
Zog I [king of Albania]
Albania (Independence) A: 307
Zohar [religious book]
Hebrew literature (Medieval works) H: 162
Kabbalah K: 208
Zoisite [mineral]
Tanzanite T: 36
Zola, Émile [French author] Z: 598
Dreyfus, Alfred (Efforts to clear Dreyfus's name) D: 347
French literature (Naturalism) F: 522
Naturalism (Naturalism in fiction) N: 65
Novel (France) N: 573
Zöllner, Heinrich [German composer]
Opera: (Faust) O: 804
Zollverein [organization]
Customs union Ci: 1201
Zolotow, Charlotte [American author]
Regina Medal (table: 2002) R: 206
Zombie [folklore] Z: 598
Zona pellucida [anatomy]
Reproduction, Human (Fertilization) R: 246
Zond program
Space exploration (Soviet attempts to reach the moon) So: 720-721
Zone [astronomy]
Jupiter (Zones and belts) J: 199
Saturn (Atmosphere) S: 150j
Zone [military]
Rank, Military (Promotion) R: 140
Zone defense
Basketball (Defensive strategies) B: 147
Football (The defensive team) F: 357-358
Zonians [people]
Panama (Way of life) P: 116
Panama Canal Zone P: 127
Zoning [air conditioning]
Air conditioning (Kinds of air conditioners) A: 179
Zoning [law] Z: 598
Building permit B: 684
City planning (Governmental authority) Ci: 601
Zoning Improvement Plan See ZIP Code in this

index
Zoo Z: 599 with pictures
Zoo Miami
Florida (Places to visit) F: 252
Zoogeography
Geography (Physical geography) G: 94
Zooid [biology]
Bryozoan B: 657
Zoological garden See Zoo in this index
Zoological Society of London
Aquarium, Public (History) A: 579
Zoologist [occupation]
Animal (The scientific classification of animals) A: 472
Careers (Life, physical, and social sciences) C: 225
Zoo (Scientific studies) Z: 600
Zoology (Careers in zoology) Z: 607
Zoology Z: 605
See also Animal in this index; and the list of Related articles in the Zoology article
Biology (table) B: 317
Careers (Life, physical, and social sciences) C: 225
Reproduction R: 242
Zoom lens
Camera (Point-and-shoot cameras) C: 82 with picture
Television (Production) T: 111
Zoonosis [disease]
Cat (Veterinary care) C: 295
Pet (Preventing illness) P: 322
Veterinary medicine V: 345
Virus (Origin) V: 428b
Zooplankton [biology]
Arctic Ocean (Ocean life) A: 643
Environmental pollution (Water pollution) E: 334
Ocean (The plankton) O: 655; (The food cycle) O: 655 with pictures
Pacific Ocean (Ocean life) P: 15
Plankton P: 515
Zoopraxiscope [device]
Muybridge, Eadweard M: 969
Zooxanthella [alga]
Coral (Stony corals) Ci: 1048a
Coral reef (Life on coral reefs) Ci: 1049
Great Barrier Reef G: 336
Zorba the Greek [book by Kazantzakis]
Kazantzakis, Nikos K: 252
Zorn, Anders [Swedish painter]
Sweden (Fine arts) So: 1027 with picture
Zoroaster [Persian prophet]
Persia, Ancient (Religion) P: 297
Zoroastrianism Z: 607
Zoroastrianism [religion] Z: 607 with picture
Fast F: 52
Fire worship F: 132
India (Other religions) I: 117
Magi M: 48
Mithra M: 678
Persia, Ancient (Religion) P: 297
Zorrilla, José [Spanish dramatist]
Don Juan D: 306
Spanish literature (The 1800's) So: 761
Zorrilla de San Martín, Juan [Uruguayan author]
Latin American literature (Romanticism) L: 112-113
Zoser [king of ancient Egypt]
Egypt, Ancient (The Old Kingdom) E: 142 with picture
Imhotep I: 79
Pyramids (The first pyramids) P: 916
Zoshchenko, Mikhail [Russian author]
Russian literature (World War II) R: 564
Zosimus, Saint [pope]
Pope (table) P: 666
Zosterophyll [plant]
Plant (The evolution of plants) P: 544
Zosterophyllophyte [plant]
Plant (The evolution of plants) P: 544
Zouaoua [people]
Zouaves Z: 607
Zouaves [soldiers] Z: 607
Zoysia grass
Lawn (Types of lawns) L: 142
ZPG [demography] See Zero population growth in this index
ZPG-3W [airship]
Airship (Nonrigid airships) A: 250; (World War II to the present) A: 252
Zr [symbol]
Zirconium Z: 596
Zsigmondy, Richard [Austrian chemist]
Nobel Prizes (Chemistry: 1925) N: 443
Zucchini [plant] Z: 608 with picture
Squash (Summer squashes) So: 813 with picture
Zuccone, Lo [sculpture by Donatello]
Donatello D: 307
Zuckerberg, Mark [American businessman] Z: 608

Facebook (History) **F:** 4
Zuckerman Unbound [book by Roth]
    Roth, Philip **R:** 487
Zugspitze [mountain]
    Germany (The Bavarian Alps) **G:** 157
Zuider Zee [bay]
    Netherlands **N:** 138
Zukerman, Pinchas [Israeli violinist] **Z:** 608
Zuleika Dobson [book by Beerbohm]
    Beerbohm, Max **B:** 212
Zulkadah [month]
    Calendar (The Islamic calendar) **C:** 29
Zulu [people] **Z:** 608
    Africa *picture on* **A:** 116b; (Peoples of Africa)
        A: 104; (African societies in the 1800's) **A:** 133
    Bantu **B:** 99
    Inkatha Freedom Party **I:** 273
    Shaka **S:** 343
    South Africa (People) **So:** 609; (History) **So:** 617-618
    Xhosa **X:** 544
Zululand [region, South Africa]
    Natal **N:** 25
Zuma [rock]
    Abuja **A:** 19
Zuma, Jacob [South African political leader]
    African National Congress **A:** 137
    South Africa (Recent developments) **So:** 621
Zuni Indians Z: 609
    Cíbola, Seven Cities of **Ci:** 551
    Coronado, Francisco Vásquez de **Ci:** 1067
    Indian, American *picture on* **I:** 167
    Sculpture (As a record of history) **S:** 228; (The European impact) **S:** 244
    Tribe **T:** 440

Zunz, Leopold [German scholar] **Z:** 609
Zurbarán, Francisco de [Spanish painter] **Z:** 609
    Moors *picture on* **M:** 797
    Painting (The Spanish masters) **P:** 64 *with picture*
Zurich [Switzerland] **Z:** 609 *with picture*
    Lake dwelling **L:** 37
Zurich-London Agreements [1959]
    Cyprus (History) **Ci:** 1207
Zurkhaneh [athletic club]
    Iran (Recreation) **I:** 402 *with picture*
Zuse, Konrad [German inventor]
    Computer (The first electronic computers)
        Ci: 924b
Zvai Leumi [political group]
    Terrorism (Terrorist groups and movements)
        T: 178
Zvezda [spacecraft]
    International Space Station (History) **I:** 346b *with picture*
Zwaanendael [former name]
    Delaware (Exploration and early settlement)
        D: 110
Zwaanendael Museum [Lewes]
    Delaware (Places to visit) **D:** 102
Zwecker, Johann [American artist]
    Indian, American *picture on* **I:** 177
Zweig, George [American physicist]
    Atom (Recent discoveries) **A:** 876
    Physics (Advances in the mid-1900's) **P:** 442
    Quark **Q:** 7
Zweig, Stefan [Austrian author] **Z:** 610
Zwicky, Fritz [Swiss astrophysicist]
    Dark matter **D:** 37
Zwilich, Ellen Taaffe [American composer] **Z:** 610
    Classical music (Classical music today) **Ci:** 651

Zwinger [museum]
    Dresden **D:** 346
Zwingli, Huldreich [Swiss religious leader] **Z:** 610
    Christianity (The Reformed tradition) **C:** 525
    Protestantism (The conservative reform movements) **P:** 834-835
    Reformation (Zwingli and the Anabaptists) **R:** 197
    Switzerland (Religious civil wars) **So:** 1060
Zworykin, Vladimir Kosma [Russian-American physicist] **Z:** 610
    Electronics *picture on* **E:** 216; (The vacuum tube era) **E:** 215
    Iconoscope **I:** 25
    Television (Early development) **T:** 127
Zygomatic bone
    Face **F:** 3
    Head *diagram on* **H:** 123
Zygote [reproduction]
    Alternation of generations **A:** 388
    Bird (The reproductive system) **B:** 366
    Embryo **E:** 257
    Fern (Life cycle of a fern) **F:** 75
    Fertilization **F:** 78
    Moss (How mosses live) **M:** 834-835
    Multiple birth (How multiple births occur) **M:** 919
    Reproduction, Human (How sex is determined) **R:** 246
Zygote intrafallopian transfer [reproduction]
    Infertility (Treatment) **I:** 265
Zytgloggeturm [clock tower]
    Bern (The city) **B:** 269 *with picture*
Zyvox [medication]
    Antibiotic (History) **A:** 552-553